THE RIVERSIDE
CHAUCER

GEOFFREY CHAUCER

From an early painting on wood (artist unknown), by permission
of the Houghton Library, Harvard University

CONTRIBUTORS

ADVISORY TEXT EDITOR

Robert A. Pratt
*University of Pennsylvania
(Emeritus)*

Stephen A. Barney
University of California, Irvine

C. David Benson
University of Connecticut

J. A. Burrow
University of Bristol

Susan H. Cavanaugh
London, England

Martin M. Crow
*University of Texas, Austin
(Emeritus)*

Alfred David
Indiana University

Norman Davis
Oxford University (Emeritus)

Sharon Hiltz DeLong
Fairmont State College

Vincent J. DiMarco
*University of Massachusetts,
Amherst*

Patricia J. Eberle
University of Toronto

A. S. G. Edwards
University of Victoria

John M. Fyler
Tufts University

Warren S. Ginsberg
*State University of New York,
Albany*

Douglas Gray
*Lady Margaret Hall
Oxford University*

Laila Zamuelis Gross
Fairleigh Dickinson University

Ralph Hanna III
*University of California,
Riverside*

Christine Ryan Hilary
Leeds, Massachusetts

Margaret Jennings
St. Joseph's College, Brooklyn

Traugott Lawler
Yale University

Virginia Everett Leland
*Bowling Green State University
(Emerita)*

R. T. Lenaghan
University of Michigan

Ardath McKee
Utica, Michigan

Charles Muscatine
*University of California,
Berkeley*

John Reidy
*Middle English Dictionary
University of Michigan*

Joanne A. Rice
Butler University

Janette Richardson
University of California, Berkeley

Florence H. Ridley
*University of California,
Los Angeles*

V. J. Scattergood
Trinity College, Dublin

M. C. E. Shaner
*University of Massachusetts,
Boston*

M. Teresa Tavormina
Michigan State University

Siegfried Wenzel
University of Pennsylvania

Colin Wilcockson
*Pembroke College
University of Cambridge*

HOUGHTON MIFFLIN COMPANY

BOSTON

Dallas   Geneva, Illinois   Lawrenceville, New Jersey   Palo Alto

THE RIVERSIDE CHAUCER

THIRD EDITION

GENERAL EDITOR

Larry D. Benson, *Harvard University*

BASED ON

The Works of Geoffrey Chaucer

Edited by

F. N. Robinson

The cover shows representatives of the three estates of medieval society—the priest, the knight, and the laborer—from an illuminated letter in Sloane MS 2435, f. 85, The British Library.

Authentic tile motifs from the eleventh through the fourteenth centuries reproduced from *Old English Tile Designs,* ed. Carol Belanger Grafton, with the permission of Dover Publications, Inc., 180 Varick Street, New York, NY 10014.

Printed in the United States of America.

Library of Congress Catalog Card Number: 86-81304

ISBN: 0-395-29031-7

ABCDEFGHIJ–RM–8987

PREFACE

THIS VOLUME, begun under the general editorship of Robert A. Pratt, was originally intended to be a revision of F. N. Robinson's Second Edition of *The Works of Geoffrey Chaucer.* It was first announced as such, and the editors have continued to refer to it informally as "Robinson Three." But it soon became clear that the study of Chaucer had so greatly developed since Robinson completed his work that in fairness both to Robinson's memory and to Chaucer's readers a completely new edition was required. Texts had to be re-edited, the introductory materials completely rewritten, glosses added, and the Bibliography, Explanatory Notes, Textual Notes, Glossary, and Index of Proper Names all greatly expanded. Robinson's Second Edition remained the model. The texts generally retain his spellings, some of his notes are reprinted (marked "R."), and our consistent aim has been to preserve as much as possible the character and quality of Robinson's work.

The Explanatory Notes, like those in Robinson's Second Edition, are highly selective. The First Edition, published in 1933, had provided magisterial surveys of scholarship and criticism, including almost everything worthy of note that had been written on each subject. By 1957, when the Second Edition appeared, the study of Chaucer had begun its great expansion, and such comprehensive treatments were no longer possible; Robinson had to restrict his new citations to only the most notable contributions that had appeared since the First Edition. The volume of scholarship and criticism has increased even more rapidly in the thirty years since the Second Edition. Our notes therefore do not and cannot provide full bibliographies or complete histories of opinion and scholarship on the problems of the particular works; they are intended rather to supply the reader with the information needed to begin the study of the work and to provide references for further investigation. The emphasis has been on the factual rather than the speculative, although important critical interpretations and problems are not ignored. Every effort has been made to represent impartially the diversity of viewpoints.

The texts have been completely re-edited, as explained in the section "The Texts" below and in the introductions to each set of textual notes. The textual notes are much fuller than those in Robinson's Second Edition, but they are nevertheless selective. Only significant variants are recorded. The notes present the manuscript evidence on which the texts were based and often list the readings adopted by other editors. Like the Explanatory Notes, the Textual Notes aim to represent fairly the range of opinion on disputed matters and, by listing manuscript and editorial variants, to present the alternatives that must be considered in choosing between disputed readings.

The production of this book has been a cooperative undertaking. Robert A. Pratt, in addition to his services as Advisory Text Editor, has offered valuable assistance with and advice on many other aspects of the volume. The title page and individual texts and sections of notes show each contributor's direct responsibilities, but the contributors have generously provided help to one another and to the General Editor in a great variety of ways. The most notable product of this cooperation are the glosses and the Glossary. Larry D. Benson and Patricia J. Eberle have primary responsibility for those, but all of the writers of the Explanatory Notes provided glosses for their parts of the texts, often with suggestions for other parts as well, and much of the Glossary thus embodies the work of all of the contributors. Some of the contributors took the time to review the work of others and to offer valuable suggestions: C. David Benson read the explanatory notes to the tales of the Pardoner, the Prioress, the Shipman, and Sir Thopas, as well as the text of *Troilus and Criseyde* and its textual notes; Alfred David reviewed the text and textual notes for the Short Poems and *Anelida and Arcite;* and A. S. G. Edwards reviewed the texts, textual notes, and explanatory notes for *The Book of the Duchess, The House of Fame,* and *The Parliament of Fowls.* John Fyler reviewed the explanatory notes for the tales of the Miller, Reeve, Cook, Squire, Franklin, and Physician. John W. Reidy, an editor of the *Middle English Dictionary* as well as a contributor, generously answered the General Editor's queries on matters of vocabulary.

We have benefited from the help of many others who read our work and made suggestions that improved the finished text. James Dean reviewed the explanatory notes to *Troilus and Criseyde;* Caroline D. Eckhardt read the explanatory notes to the General Prologue; Sigmund Eisner reviewed the text, textual notes, and explanatory notes for *A Treatise on the Astrolabe;* Thomas Hahn reviewed the explanatory notes to the tales of the Wife of Bath, Friar, Summoner, Clerk, and Merchant. Tim William Machan reviewed the text and textual notes for the *Boece.* Monica McAlpine reviewed explanatory notes to The Knight's Tale. Derek Pearsall reviewed the explanatory notes to the Melibee and the tales of the Monk and Nun's Priest. Russell A. Peck reviewed the explanatory notes to the *Boece,* Short Poems, *Anelida and Arcite,* and *Romaunt of the Rose.* Helen Phillips reviewed the text of *The Romaunt of the Rose.* Robert Yeager reviewed the explanatory notes for the tales of the Second Nun, Canon's Yeoman, Manciple, and Parson. None of these scholars is to be blamed for faults that remain in the works they reviewed; we owe thanks to them that the faults are not more numerous.

Sherman Kuhn, of the *Middle English Dictionary,* and David Jost, formerly of the MED and now an editor of *The American Heritage Dictionary,* were generous in responding to the General Editor's inquiries. John F. Leyerle made a number of valuable suggestions for the Bibliography. We owe special thanks to Derek Pearsall, who, in addition to his review of selected explanatory notes, read the entire manuscript and greatly improved the edition with many valuable suggestions for additions, deletions, and corrections.

The General Editor also thanks Kevin T. Cope, who helped check the bibliographical references in the early stages of this work; Gillian Kendall, who worked long hours assembling materials for the Glossary; Kathleen Holden, who cheerfully typed from handwritten cards the entire set of glosses and the Glossary; and Stephen B. Partridge, who provided valuable assistance on the final stages of work on the Glossary. All of the contributors have benefited from the patience and expertise of the editors and staff at Houghton Mifflin Company.

All who worked on this volume are saddened that one of our number, Laila T. Gross, did not live to see her work in print. Her work for this volume will stand as a testimony to her perceptive and thorough scholarship.

L. D. B.

INTRODUCTORY NOTE

THIS EDITION provides the general information on Chaucer's life, language, and works that one needs for a first reading of Chaucer, and difficult words and constructions are glossed on the pages. The Appendix contains the materials, including the extensive notes and glossary, for a more thorough understanding of Chaucer's works.

The page glosses provide only brief explanations of words and allusions unfamiliar to modern readers. These usually suffice for a first reading, though some matters necessary to even an initial understanding of the texts require more explanation than footnotes allow. Such matters are ordinarily indicated in the glosses by "see n.," directing the reader to the discussion in the Explanatory Notes in the Appendix. Even when there is no such indication, the beginning reader as well as the more advanced student should consult the Explanatory Notes. They provide information on sources, problematic passages, and critical interpretations; they offer occasional illustrative materials and include selective bibliographies for further study.

The Textual Notes include information on the establishment of the texts and provide the evidence for the readings adopted. They are thus essential to the student of Chaucer's style and metrics as well as to those interested in the problems of establishing Chaucer's texts.

L. D. B.

CONTENTS

INTRODUCTION

CHAUCER'S LIFE

IN COMPARISON with other major English writers of his time, Chaucer left abundant records of his life. We have no official documents for the life of the author of *Piers Plowman* or for the *Gawain*-poet; records of Gower's life are few and confused. But Chaucer, because he was a public servant, can be traced in the records of his offices. Publication of *Chaucer Life-Records* in 1966 brought together the 493 known items, 150 of them never before assembled, and provided a substantial basis for a Chaucer biography. These records of official acts rarely touch on his personal affairs and never mention his poetry; they do not give the year of his birth or the exact date of his marriage or death. But they do document a useful and eventful life.

Chaucer was a soldier, an esquire of the king's household, a member of diplomatic missions, a controller of customs, a justice of the peace, a member of Parliament, the clerk of the king's works in charge of building and repair at ten royal residences, and a forest official. As a soldier, Chaucer was captured by the French; as a customs controller, he monitored a chief source of the royal revenue; as a member of the 1386 Parliament, he saw the first attacks on Richard II, which led eventually to the deposition of the king in 1399. On the king's business he traveled over much of southeast England, to France a number of times, to Spain, and at least twice to Italy. His responsibilities brought him in contact with many kinds of people, among them: king, chief justice, bishop, and countess; merchant, money-lender, and friar; minstrel, soldier, gardener, and highway robber. Inspired and perhaps influenced, but certainly not distracted, by the world around him, Chaucer yet found time to write thousands of lines, among them some of the best poetry in English.

The Chaucer Family

Chaucer came from a well-to-do merchant family that had lived for several generations in Ipswich, some seventy miles northeast of London. The city exported wool to Flanders and imported wine from France. The family were vintners, wholesale dealers in wine, and also held positions in the customs service. As often happened in medieval families, they did not always use the same surname. Geoffrey Chaucer's paternal great-grandfather was called Andrew de Dinnington; Andrew's son, Robert Malyn le Chaucer; Robert's son, John Chaucer. The name Chaucer, from the French, meant maker of shoes or hose; but none of Chaucer's ancestors were, so far as is known, shoemakers or hosiers.

By the late thirteenth century Robert Chaucer, the grandfather, and his wife Mary had settled in London. Prosperous people, they continued to hold property in Ipswich. In 1324, John, son of Robert and Mary, was kidnapped by an aunt, who intended to marry him to her daughter in order to keep the Ipswich holdings in the family. Instead, the twelve-year-old boy was freed; the aunt and her accomplices went to prison and paid a heavy fine, £250, proof that they were wealthy.

John later married Agnes, daughter of one John Copton and niece of Hamo de Copton, "moneyer" at the mint in the Tower of London. The couple continued to accumulate property. After Hamo's death in 1349, a plague year, Agnes inherited, with Hamo's other London property, twenty-four shops and two gardens. In the same year, John Chaucer inherited property from his half brother, Thomas Heyron. John and Agnes were, then, owners of substantial London property. John Chaucer was a vintner, as his father, stepfather, and half brother had been; like his father, stepfather, and cousins, he also held positions in the customs service.

Geoffrey Chaucer's parentage is clearly established; he described himself in a deed of 19 June 1381 as "son of John Chaucer, vintner, of London." But the date and place of his birth are not precisely known. For the date, the clearest evidence comes from his deposition of 15 October 1386 in the famous Scrope-Grosvenor trial (discussed below). There he testified that he was forty years old "et plus" (and more), making the date of his birth no later than 1345. Some witnesses in that case guessed inaccurately at their ages; but Chaucer added a verifiable statement that supports his testimony. He said that he had borne arms twenty-seven years; he had in fact served in France in the campaign of 1359. It is usual, then, to accept a birth date in the early 1340s.

Fourteenth- and fifteenth-century records tell something of Chaucer's descendants. A London lawsuit of Michaelmas term, 1396, identified "Thomas Chaucer, esquire, son of Geoffrey Chaucer, esquire." Additional evidence that Thomas was the son of Geoffrey rests upon a statement by Dr. Gascoigne, chancellor of Oxford and a neighbor of Thomas, and on the use by Thomas of a seal with Geoffrey Chaucer's coat of arms and name. A retinue roll compiled at Carmarthen Castle in 1403 lists Thomas Chaucer with Lewis Chaucer. Lewis seems to have been the *lyte Lowys my sone* of the *tendir age of ten year* for whom in 1391 the poet composed *A Treatise on the Astrolabe.* Two presumed daughters of Geoffrey Chaucer are also sometimes mentioned, Elizabeth Chaucy, a nun at Barking in 1381, and Agnes, an attendant at the coronation of Henry IV; but the records do not clearly identify them as daughters of the poet.

Nothing more is known of Lewis, Agnes, or Elizabeth, but many records attest to the distinguished career of Thomas Chaucer, as he became one of the most wealthy and influential men in England. Enriched by marriage to a great heiress and by annuities from John of Gaunt, Richard II, and Henry IV, he served as chief butler to four kings, envoy to France, and, often, speaker of the House of Commons. His daughter Alice married as her third husband William de la Pole, Duke of Suffolk; their grandson John, Earl of Lincoln, was designated heir to the throne of his uncle, Richard III. Richard's defeat and death at Bosworth Field in 1485 effectively ended the possibility that a nephew of his could gain the crown. But John de la Pole and, after him, three of his brothers continued to assert the claim until the last of them died in about 1539, a prisoner in the Tower of London, thus ending the line of Chaucer's male descendants.

Chaucer's Early Home and Youth

Though Chaucer's birthplace is unknown, it is known that his parents, Agnes and John Chaucer, held property in Vintry Ward, one of the two wealthiest wards in medieval London, and in what the sixteenth-century antiquary John Stow called "the middes and hart of the city." One Chaucer "tenement" (property holding, not tenement in the modern sense) lay on Thames Street, which ran parallel to the river and a block north. It was largely inhabited by vintners, since wine landed at the quays on the Thames could easily be brought to their cellars for storage. Some of London's leading merchants, among the richest men in the city, lived in the ward as well. Two of them, John Stodeye and Henry Picard, served as mayors and lent thousands of pounds to the king. John Chaucer's name is associated with theirs in such records as wills and deeds. Nobles as well as merchants lived in Vintry Ward. Queen Philippa owned a dwelling there called Tower Royal; after her death it passed to her daughter-in-law, mother of Richard II, Joan of Kent, who took refuge there in 1381. Among the people living nearby were Gascon wine merchants, an Italian family, and Flemings—London in Chaucer's boyhood was a cosmopolitan city.

Wills of neighbors, deeds, and inventories give some idea of the probable plan and furnishings of the Chaucer home. Above the cellars were the hall (not a passageway, but the principal room), the kitchen, a latrine, and upper rooms called "solars." They were furnished comfortably with hangings for the walls and cushions for the benches, and such luxuries as heavy silver pitchers and cups engraved with the owners' coats of arms.

No school records for Chaucer have survived, but it is possible to account for some of the knowledge of Latin classics shown in his works. London merchants' sons in his time could receive a good education. Near the Chaucer home on Thames Street were three schools, among them the almonry school of St. Paul's Cathedral, which has preserved the inventory of books left in 1358 by a schoolmaster, William de Ravenstone, for the use of the pupils. As well as Latin grammars, treatises on theology, and a few music textbooks, there were classics—Virgil's *Georgics;* Claudian's *Rape of Proserpina,* cited three times in Chaucer's poems; ten books of Lucan; the *Thebaid* of Statius, quoted at the beginning of The Knight's Tale and partly summarized in *Troilus and Criseyde;* and the *Metamorphoses* of Ovid, Chaucer's favorite classical Latin source. Chaucer paid tribute, near the end of *Troilus and Criseyde* (5.1792) to five of the great poets of antiquity, *Virgile, Ovide, Omer, Lucan, and Stace.* Chaucer probably did not know Homer directly, but, as Ravenstone's bequest makes clear, works of the four others were available at St. Paul's school.

The earliest known document actually naming Geoffrey Chaucer is a fragmentary household account book, June 1356 to April 1359, kept for Elizabeth de Burgh, Countess of Ulster and wife of Lionel, a son of Edward III. It records purchases in April 1357 for Geoffrey Chaucer—a short jacket, a pair of red and black hose (?), and a pair of shoes; and, "for necessaries at Christmas," there was recorded a gift to him of 2*s.* 6*d.* The relative modesty of the gifts suggests that Chaucer was among the youngest and least important of the retainers of the countess, perhaps in his early teens, and perhaps a page.

Life in the countess's household would offer a young attendant a rich variety of experiences if he accompanied her on her almost constant travels. During the time covered by the accounts, she spent Christmas at Hatfield for a royal hunting party, along with her young brother-in-law John of Gaunt, who later became the richest and most powerful man in England; she purchased mourning in London for the funeral of the dowager queen, Isabella; she visited a royal relative at the convent of Stratford-atte-Bowe (where the Prioress learned her French; General Prologue I.125); and she was a guest at King Edward's Great Feast of St. George at Windsor, the king's favorite castle.

Journeys and the Royal Court

From the household of the countess Chaucer seems to have followed her husband, Prince Lionel, into the king's army. In September 1359 King Edward and his sons, with a large expeditionary force, were invading France. The king, who held King John of France prisoner, hoped to take the city of Reims and to be crowned king of France in Reims Cathedral, traditional site of the coronation of French kings. Chaucer, according to his testimony in the Scrope-Grosvenor case (see below), was at the town of "Retters" (Réthel), near Reims, which Edward was besieging in December and early January 1359–60. Chaucer testified that he was captured, but the captivity was short. By 1 March 1360 the king had contributed £16 to help pay Chaucer's ransom, and he was free. Edward's forces were at that date in the village of Brétigny, in the vicinity of Chartres. The campaign had brought Chaucer within sight of the great cathedrals of Reims and probably Chartres.

The last record of Chaucer in the service of Prince Lionel dates from the peace negotiations at Calais in October 1360, when the prince paid Chaucer for carrying letters from Calais to England.

The expedition and messenger service of 1359–60 were the first of many journeys and commissions for Chaucer. No records have yet been found for him, however, for the years between 1360 and 1366. After the gap in the records the first document concerning Chaucer is a safe-conduct for the period of 22 February to 24 May 1366, granted to Chaucer by Charles II (Charles the Bad) of Navarre; it permitted "Geffroy de Chauserre" with three companions, their servants, horses, and luggage, to travel through Navarre. Perhaps Chaucer was on a pilgrimage, like many others (and like the Wife of Bath; General Prologue I.466), to the popular shrine of Compostela *in Galice at Seint-Jame;* the customary pilgrimage route crossed Navarre. Or Chaucer may have been sent by the Black Prince to recall English mercenaries from the forces of Henry of Trastamara, against whom the prince was mounting an expedition. Another possible explanation for Chaucer's journey is that it was connected with arrangements for the later passage of English troops through Navarre into Castile, where in April of 1367 the prince was to win the battle of Nájera and restore to his throne Pedro the Cruel, called in The Monk's Tale (VII.2375) *O noble, O worthy Petro, glorie of Spayne.*

Other events of 1366 may have been more important to Chaucer than the Navarrese journey: the evidence indicates that Chaucer's father died in that year and that Chaucer married. The last record of John Chaucer is dated 16 January 1366, when he and his wife Agnes signed a deed; on 13 July 1366 Agnes was referred to as the wife of Bartholomew atte Chapel. Chaucer's marriage is implied by the record of a grant, on 12 September 1366, of an exchequer annuity of 10 marks to one Philippa Chaucer, damoiselle of the queen. This annuity was often collected for her "by the hands of" Geoffrey Chaucer. Philippa may have been a member of the Ulster household during Chaucer's service there; the accounts note in 1356 and 1358 clothing bought for one "Philippa Pan." Chaucer's wife seems to have been the daughter of Sir Gilles, called "Paon," de Roet, a knight of Hainault and one of Queen Philippa's countrymen who had accompanied her to England, and who became Guienne King of Arms, that is, chief herald of Aquitaine, when that region was ruled by the Black Prince. Another of the Roet daughters, Katherine Swynford, was for more than twenty years the mistress of John of Gaunt; he married her in 1396. Philippa Chaucer was in attendance on three members of the royal family: King Edward's daughter-in-law, Elizabeth; the queen, Philippa; and, after the queen's death, another daughter-in-law, Constance of Castile, the second wife of John of Gaunt. As Philippa Chaucer had received a royal annuity in 1366, so she also received in 1372 an annuity from the revenues of John of Gaunt.

Geoffrey Chaucer is first recorded as a member of the royal household on 20 June 1367, when he received a royal annuity. One record of that date described him as *valettus;* another of the same date called him *esquier.* At any rate, he was one of a group of some forty young men in the king's service, not personal servants, but expected to make themselves useful around the court. Like Chaucer, other esquires of Edward III did not come from the great noble families. They were often sent about England on the king's business, sometimes performed military service, and occasionally journeyed overseas on the king's behalf. In return, they received rewards such as were given to Chaucer: summer and winter robes, daily wages, annuities, and appointments to office. Geoffrey and Philippa Chaucer, among others, received liveries of mourning for Queen Philippa in 1369.

During the years when Chaucer was in the king's service, he may also have been studying among the lawyers of the Inner Temple, one of the Inns of Court. The tradition that he had received such training arose from a statement by Thomas Speght in his Chaucer edition of 1598 that "Master Buckley" had seen an Inner Temple record "where Geffrye Chaucer was fined two shillings for beatinge a Franciscane Fryer in fletestreate." It is now known that Master Buckley was at that time the keeper of the Inner Temple records, and that the fine was a customary amount. His testimony is accepted as very probably true. Mention of the Manciple (General Prologue I.567) and of the career of the Man of Law (General Prologue I.309–30) seems to show familiarity with the Inns of Court and the lawyers there. In addition, Chaucer's later official positions, as controller of the customs and clerk of the king's works, demanded that he keep records in Chancery hand, and use French and Latin legal formulas, skills taught in the Inns of Court.

During this time Chaucer may have been experimenting with various popular verse forms, in French as well as in English. By their nature, most of them were likely ephemeral, but recent publication of fifteen French lyrics, with the siglum "Ch," from a fourteenth-century French manuscript (Wimsatt, Chaucer and the Poems of "Ch") raises the intriguing possibility that these poems might be by Chaucer. Even if they are not, they represent the kind of French verse Chaucer may well have written during his early years at court.

While he was the king's esquire and, presumably, studying among the lawyers, Chaucer also made a number of journeys overseas. Two years after the Navarre safe-conduct of 1366, he "passed at Dover" on 17 July 1368 and was absent from England for at most 106 days; in that length of time the king's envoys had been able to make the journey to Rome and return. It has, accordingly, been suggested that Chaucer was sent as a messenger to Prince Lionel in Milan. There, in May 1368, the prince had married a daughter of the immensely powerful Visconti family, despots of Milan. Chaucer may, however, have gone no farther than to France or Flanders on this journey.

The Book of the Duchess, Chaucer's first major poem, belongs to this period. It is an elegy for Blanche, Duchess of Lancaster, John of Gaunt's first wife, who died, it is now believed, on 12 September 1368. The duke remarried in 1371; but he continued to remember Blanche, paying £30 on 12 September 1379 for memorial masses on the anniversary of her death and ten silver marks in 1382 to each of the chaplains chanting masses at her tomb in St. Paul's. In his will of 1398 he directed that he be buried beside his "very dear late consort, Blanche." It seems significant, then, that on 13 June 1374 John of Gaunt granted a life annuity of £10 to Chaucer "in consideration of the services rendered by Chaucer to the grantor" and "by the grantee's wife Philippa to the grantor's late mother and to his consort." A few days later, on 18 June 1374, the duke ordered alabaster from which the master mason, Henry Yevele, was to erect a tomb for Blanche. It is clear that in 1374 John of Gaunt was remembering Blanche; by his grant to Chaucer he may have been rewarding the author of *The Book of the Duchess.*

Another Lancaster connection was recorded in 1369, when Chaucer received £10 as one of the members of the king's household who were to accompany John of Gaunt on a military expedition to Picardy (where the Squire of the General Prologue [I.86] served part of his military apprenticeship). There is no record of Chaucer's part in the 1369 campaign. Nor is it known what was the king's business that took Chaucer to "parts beyond the seas" in 1370.

Having made four journeys abroad in four years, 1366–70, Chaucer undertook in 1372–73 a commission that gave him his first recorded contact with Italy. He accompanied two Italian merchants, Giovanni di Mari and Sir Jacopo di Provano, then residents of London, to negotiate on the king's behalf with the doge and people of Genoa, who wanted the use of an English port. The business discussed may have been partly military; Giovanni di Mari, Chaucer's associate, was in the same year hiring Genoese mercenaries for King Edward.

The commission given Chaucer before his departure did not name Florence; yet the expense account submitted on his return, 23 May 1373, recorded treating of the affairs of the king "in Genoa and Florence." The visit to Florence has seemed significant to Chaucer scholars because Petrarch and Boccaccio, still living, were in that region. Chaucer, if he did not meet them, could hardly have avoided hearing a great deal about them and about Dante, who, though he had died in exile fifty years earlier, was now revered in Florence. Quite possibly Chaucer obtained manuscripts of some of these authors' works on this visit. It is customary in this connection to mention the reference to Petrarch in The Clerk's Prologue (IV.31–33), but with the warning that it is the Clerk, and not Chaucer, who claims to have heard the story in The Clerk's Tale from Petrarch.

The journey of 1372–73, it was once thought, gave Chaucer his first acquaintance with the language and literature of Italy; but it is now agreed that Chaucer might well have been chosen for that mission because he already knew some Italian. The hundred days allowed by the 1372–73 journey would hardly have given Chaucer time to learn a language. London in Chaucer's youth provided better opportunities; many Italian families lived in London, some near the Chaucer house in the Vintry; Chaucer's father and grandfather had business dealings with Italians. In any event, Italy had become, by 1373, a part of Chaucer's firsthand experience.

A few months after his return from Florence, he had occasion to deal with Italians again. He was sent by the king to deliver a Genoese ship, detained at Dartmouth, to her master, a merchant of Genoa and an associate of Chaucer's fellow envoy, Giovanni di Mari. This commission has been taken as additional proof of Chaucer's knowledge of Italian. (It is also of interest because the piratical Shipman of the General Prologue [I.389] was *of Dertemouthe.*)

Other Journeys and the Customhouse

Chaucer seems to have had good fortune during the year after his return from Italy. On 23 April 1374, St. George's Day, while the king was celebrating the feast at Windsor, he made an unusual grant to Chaucer. Almost no other business was done on that holiday, but King Edward granted the poet a gallon pitcher of wine daily for life. The wine, it is sometimes suggested, may have been the reward for a poem presented to the king during the festivities. Chaucer collected the wine until the death of Edward III in 1377; Richard II, on his accession, immediately confirmed the gift and, on 18 April 1378, permitted Chaucer to commute it for an annuity of twenty marks, a respectable income.

In 1374, also, Chaucer obtained a home in London. On 10 May, Adam de Bury, mayor of London, and the aldermen leased to Chaucer, rent-free for life, the dwelling over Aldgate, one of the six gates in the city wall. Chaucer was to keep the apartment in good repair, to allow entry for purposes of defense in time of war, and he was not to sublet. Such a lease was not unusual; the city owned dwellings over other gates and sometimes leased them to city officials. Ralph Strode, Chaucer's friend, had a similar apartment over Aldersgate. Adam de Bury, whose name appears on Chaucer's lease, had been an associate of Chaucer's father, had been sent abroad on a mission by the king, and had held a customs office himself. It was once suggested that Chaucer owed the lease to the influence of King Edward's mistress, Alice Perrers, who owned property near Aldgate; but it is more likely that Adam de Bury, because of his contact with the Chaucer family, did, as the lease states, make the arrangement.

The dwelling over Aldgate became, as it turned out, very convenient, just a few minutes walk from the customhouse, where Chaucer was to be employed for the next twelve years. On 8 June 1374 Edward III appointed Chaucer controller of the export tax, or customs, on wool, sheepskins, and leather, in the port of London, and of the subsidy, a heavier tax on the same merchandise. He was to receive an annual salary of £10. Chaucer, the son and grandson of men who had held minor offices in the customs service, was taking up a family occupation.

His task was essential. Because wool was England's principal export, much depended on the wool customs and subsidy. These taxes had helped to finance King Edward's wars in the 1340s and 1350s and were paying for the smaller military expeditions of the 1370s and 1380s. Wool taxes paid the daily costs of government, including, often, royal grants and annuities, and supported the costly court of King Edward and, later, of his grandson, Richard II.

As controller, Chaucer worked with the collectors, the nominal heads of the customs organization for the port of London. The collectors were merchants and were making the king large loans on the security of the revenue from the customs. Among these collector-creditors while Chaucer was in office were the immensely rich Nicholas Brembre, John Philipot, and William Walworth, neighbors of the Chaucer family in Vintry Ward. These three men were leaders of the politically powerful victualers' guilds, *riche and selleres of vitaille,* like the friends of the Friar (General Prologue I.248). At the customhouse the collectors were expected to record each day's shipments and the amount of customs or subsidy collected. The controller, Chaucer, kept the "counter-rolls," independent lists against which theirs were checked. The controller had to monitor the honesty and efficiency of the collectors. Under these conditions, Chaucer's position at the customhouse demanded tact and astuteness.

He had a heavy responsibility because customs receipts while he was in office were large, averaging over a ten-year period £24,600 a year. Dealing with such sums, the controller was, reasonably enough, expected to keep the rolls "with his own hand" and to exercise the office "in his own person." At the end of the fiscal year, at Michaelmas, controller and collectors were summoned to the "view," or audit, a complex and arduous process.

An incident connected with the customs gave Chaucer a sizable reward. He was granted, on 12 July 1376, the value, £71 *4s. 6d.,* of wool forfeited by one John Kent, who had exported it without paying customs. The sum was important, more than seven times Chaucer's annual salary.

Chaucer seems to have been successful as controller. He was appointed on 20 April 1382 to the additional controllership of the petty customs, import and export duties on wine and other merchandise not assessed under the wool customs. He managed to collect his annual salary regularly, a considerable feat in itself. He remained in office twelve years, longer than any other controller of his time; and he received in most years an additional reward for his "unremitting labor and diligence."

One detail from his experience at the customhouse explains the background of the line from the General Prologue (I.277) in which we learn that the Merchant wants the sea protected from pirates *bitwixe Middelburgh and Orewelle:* customed merchandise was, after 1384, shipped to a central "staple" at Middelburg across the sea from Orwell, the seaport for the Chaucers' home city of Ipswich.

While he held the office as controller, Chaucer was pursuing his literary interests. According to the Eagle in *The House of Fame* (653–57), *Geffrey,* when he had made his *rekenynges,* went to his house to sit *at another book.* Presumably the reckonings were at the customhouse, and Chaucer went home to Aldgate to read and write. It is generally believed that during the years when he lived over Aldgate Chaucer was writing major poems: *The Parliament of Fowls, The House of Fame,* and *Troilus and Criseyde.* In addition he was translating the *Consolation of Philosophy* of Boethius from the Latin. It has been observed that Chaucer was most prolific as a writer when he was apparently most busy with other affairs.

But he was too experienced an envoy to be allowed to devote himself entirely to his books and to the customhouse. In 1376, the year when Edward III and his heir, the Black Prince, were both dying, Sir John Burley, knight, and Chaucer, esquire of the king, received payment for journeys "on secret business of the king." The records do not show where they went or what matters they discussed. During 1377 Chaucer was sent overseas several times on royal business. In February he and Sir Thomas Percy were advanced sums for a mission to Flanders, also described as "the king's secret business." But the expense accounts submitted on their return do not mention Flanders. Instead, they note payment to Chaucer for travel to Paris and Montreuil, 17 February to 25 March, and to "parts of France," 30 April to 26 June 1377. The French poet Eustache Deschamps, who in 1386 was to send Chaucer a well-known ballade in his praise, may have been in Paris at that time.

According to Froissart, Chaucer was a member of a mission attempting to negotiate a marriage between Richard and a French princess; but Froissart is frequently inaccurate, and no known English record names Chaucer as a member of such a mission until after the death of Edward III, 21 June 1377. In fact, the only official note concerning the purpose of Chaucer's series of journeys to France is dated 6 March 1381. It speaks of Chaucer as having been in France "to treat of peace in time of Edward III and in time of Richard II to discuss a marriage between the king and a daughter [not named] of his adversary of France." A French marriage did not take place, and war with France was renewed.

Chaucer's next mission gave him another opportunity to visit Italy. He and Sir Edward Berkeley received funds on 28 May 1378 from "the king's treasurers for war," William Walworth and John Philipot, collectors of the London customs, for a journey to Lombardy to discuss "certain business concerning the king's war" with Bernabò Visconti, lord of Milan, and Sir John Hawkwood, the Englishman who was Bernabò's son-in-law and commander of mercenaries. Official records do not give the result of these secret negotiations, but they do indicate that Lombardy maintained relations with England. Exchequer accounts of December 1378 show King Richard's rich gifts to messengers from Bernabò and Hawkwood.

For Chaucer the journey meant a renewal of his acquaintance with Italian literature. The Visconti owned famous libraries and had been patrons of Petrarch. The strong impression they made on Chaucer was recorded in his poems. Bernabò himself, *God of delit, and scourge of Lumbardye,* appears in The Monk's Tale (VII.2399–2400). Observation of Bernabò and his brother, notorious tyrants, may have suggested to Chaucer the phrase *tirauntz of Lumbardye* (LGWPro F 374).

By 19 September 1378 Chaucer had returned to London. He did not go overseas again until his work at the customhouse had ended.

While he was still controller, his name appeared in a record which is not yet fully understood. One Cecilia Chaumpaigne, daughter of a London baker, William Chaumpaigne, and his wife Agnes, acknowledged, on 4 May 1380, a release to Geoffrey Chaucer of all kinds of actions (i.e., legal procedures seeking redress) in respect of her *raptus* as well as of any other matter. The definition of the word *raptus* in the context of this 1380 incident has been discussed repeatedly. It could have meant physical rape; or it could have meant abduction, as it did in the account of John Chaucer's kidnapping and in the case Chaucer was appointed to investigate in 1387, the abduction of a young heiress, Isabella atte Halle. The record, however, is clear; it means that Cecilia Chaumpaigne clears Chaucer of all responsibility. Additional facts, equally ambiguous, further complicate interpretation of these events. On 30 June 1380 Robert Goodchild, cutler, and John Grove, armorer, citizens of London, acknowledged a general release to Chaucer of all actions of law. On the same day

Cecilia Chaumpaigne acknowledged a similar release to Goodchild and Grove. Then, in a recognizance dated 2 July 1380 Grove agreed to pay Cecilia at Michaelmas £10, a sum equivalent to Chaucer's annual salary at the customhouse. It has been suggested that Grove served as an intermediary to bring about a settlement between Chaucer and Cecilia. It has also been suggested that Grove, because of his financial involvement, was the principal in the case and Chaucer only an accessory.

Students of medieval English law disagree on the interpretation of the records. What is undeniable is the high social standing of the witnesses to Chaucer's release: Sir William Beauchamp, chamberlain of the king's household; Sir William Neville, admiral of the king's fleet; Neville's friend, Sir John Clanvowe, author of a religious treatise; John Philipot, collector of customs; and Richard Morel, a merchant and member of Parliament who lived near Chaucer in Aldgate Ward.

The next year was marked by an event of much wider significance than the Chaumpaigne case: the Rising of 1381, the Peasants' Revolt. No record tells us whether Chaucer was at Aldgate when thousands of rebels entered London through that gate or whether he saw them burn John of Gaunt's palace, the Savoy, or whether he saw them behead Simon Sudbury, archbishop of Canterbury and chancellor of the kingdom. A number of the victims came from Vintry Ward, where Chaucer still owned his father's house; they included Richard Lyons, merchant, who had profited by lending thousands of pounds to the king; and scores of Flemings, whose headless bodies were, according to the chroniclers, left piled in the streets near the river. When the Nun's Priest speaks casually of the noise made by the mob *whan that they wolden any Flemyng kille* (NPT VII.3396), Chaucer was talking of events that may once have been of a good deal more than casual importance to him.

The mob was brought under control with the help of John Philipot, Nicholas Brembre, and William Walworth, with all of whom Chaucer had worked at the customhouse. These "gode and worthi men of the city of London," as they were called in a popular account of the revolt, were immediately knighted by the king. Chaucer, on 19 June 1381, four days after the suppression of the revolt, quit-claimed his fa-

ther's holdings on Thames Street to Henry Herbury, a merchant and a man of means.

Chaucer may have been gradually ending his connections with London. He was beginning to entrust the work of the customs to deputies. The terms of his appointment as controller of the petty customs on 20 April 1382 allowed him to name a deputy. During his earlier absences, in France, 1377, and in Italy, 1378, his work had been carried on by deputies. He was permitted to employ a deputy at the wool customs from 23 June to 1 November 1383, and again for a month beginning 25 November 1384. Finally, on 17 February 1385 he was given leave to appoint a permanent deputy.

Chaucer and Kent

The changes at the customhouse have been taken to suggest that Chaucer had already left London for nearby Kent, a county with which he had had earlier associations. In 1375 King Edward had granted him the wardship of two Kentish heirs, William Soles and Edmund Staplegate. Such wardships, often granted to the king's retainers, could be lucrative. Staplegate's father had left large holdings in Canterbury, and Chaucer's profit from the estate was £104.

By 1388, records described Chaucer as "of Kent." He may have been living in Greenwich. The Host's reference in the Reeve's Prologue (I.3907) to *Grenewych, ther many a shrewe* [rascal] *is inne* has often been taken to mean that Chaucer himself was living in Greenwich and making one of his customary self-deprecating jokes.

Knowledge of two official positions Chaucer held in the 1380s strengthens the theory that he was then living in Kent. He was added on 12 October 1385 to a sixteen-member commission of peace for Kent. Other members were Sir Simon Burley, the Black Prince's friend, sometimes called the most influential man in the kingdom of the prince's son, King Richard II; representatives of leading Kentish families, Cobham, Culpepper, and Devereux; and six sergeants-at-law, men of the same high legal rank as Chaucer's Man of Law (General Prologue I.309). Membership on a Kentish peace commission in 1385–86 entailed a special responsibility because the French were at that time threatening to invade the south coast of England. In 1386 Cobham and Devereux were also appointed members of a "great and continual council given comprehensive powers over all matters of state'' in the kingdom. Chaucer remained a member of the peace commission, with one brief and apparently accidental break, until 15 July 1389, a few days after he had been given another position.

Even more important than Chaucer's appointment as a justice of the peace was his election to Parliament in 1386 as one of the two "knights of the shire" (members of the House of Commons) to represent Kent. The Parliament to which he was sent was a turning point in King Richard's reign and in the history of medieval England. When it convened in October, troops had been called up to defend London against the threatened French invasion. But there were no funds to pay them; they were wandering the London streets searching for food and loot. In the sessions of Parliament, powerful noblemen, led by the king's youngest uncle, Thomas of Gloucester, attacked the chancellor and the treasurer of the realm and compelled Richard to dismiss them. Gloucester and his allies may have threatened to depose Richard if he did not comply. Though knights of the shire took a prominent part in the attack, there is no record that Chaucer was more than a quiet observer. He had ties with both sides.

While he was at Westminster attending Parliament, Chaucer, on 15 October 1386, gave his often-cited deposition in the Scrope-Grosvenor case. He was testifying that his friends, the Scrope family, had long borne the coat of arms that the Grosvenors were attempting to make theirs. Chaucer had, he said, seen the device on Scrope armor at the time of the siege of Reims in 1359–60.

Personal Matters

One of the first tributes to Chaucer as poet came from France in 1385–86. Though France at that time was preparing to invade England, Chaucer's friend, Sir Lewis Clifford, returned from France bringing Chaucer a poem of generous praise, written by the leading French poet of the time, Eustache Deschamps. Deschamps's ballade, with the refrain "great translator, noble Geoffrey Chaucer," stressed Chaucer's role as a cultural intermediary who had made Le roman de la rose accessible to English readers. The poem praised Chaucer extravagantly for his brevity of speech, his wisdom, his practical learning. Des-

champs himself, he wrote, would be only a nettle in Chaucer's garden of poetry.

At about the same time, two English writers were commenting on Chaucer's poetry. In late 1385, Thomas Usk, a London clerk, in his prose Testament of Love called Chaucer "the noble philosophical poete." He declared that Chaucer surpassed all other poets in "goodnes of manliche speche" and in sound sense. John Gower's praise in his Confessio amantis (1390), in which he remarked that Chaucer had filled the land with "ditees" and "songes glade," was less emphatic. The remark disappears in the course of Gower's later revision of the Confessio, but for structural reasons, it is now thought, not because of a quarrel between the poets.

On 19 February 1386, Philippa Chaucer was admitted to the fraternity of Lincoln Cathedral. In the same company were the future Henry IV, Henry of Derby, the oldest son of John of Gaunt, and Thomas Swynford and John Beaufort, sons of Philippa's sister, Katherine Swynford. Both John of Gaunt and the Swynford family had been long associated with the cathedral.

Membership in the fraternity was something of a custom with the royal family. King Richard and Queen Anne themselves were enrolled on 26 March 1387 when they visited the cathedral, site of the shrine of the boy martyr, St. Hugh of Lincoln, who is mentioned in The Prioress's Tale (VII.684). It has been argued that this tale was first read on that occasion.

In the late 1380s an important period of Chaucer's life came to an end. On 5 October 1386 he gave up the lease of the Aldgate dwelling, where he had lived for twelve years. New controllers took his positions at the customhouse. Philippa Chaucer, to whom he had been married for at least twenty-one years, disappeared from the records after 18 June 1387 and is presumed to have died. When Chaucer was given a safe-conduct on 5 July 1387 to accompany his friend, Sir William Beauchamp, to Calais, he was making the last of a series of journeys overseas that he had begun in 1359, almost thirty years before. He had apparently reached a low point in his career.

Chaucer lived safely through 1388 when the king's enemies, the Appellants, who dominated Parliament, caused the execution of three men with whom Chaucer had worked, Sir Nicholas Brembre of the customhouse, and two members of the Kent peace commission, Sir Simon Burley and Chief Justice Robert Tresilian. Whether or not Chaucer saw them moving through the London streets to their deaths, he described such a scene memorably in The Man of Law's Tale (II.645–50):

Have ye nat seyn somtyme a pale face,
Among a prees, of hym that hath be lad
Toward his deeth, wher as hym gat no grace,
And swich a colour in his face hath had
Men myghte knowe his face that was bistad
Amonges alle the faces in that route?

Chaucer himself seems to have been harmed during this time only by suits for debt. Twice, 16 and 25 April 1388, he was sued by John Churchman, collector of the customs at London. It is, therefore, sometimes believed that when he made over his annuities to a certain John Scalby on 1 May 1388, he was exchanging future income for cash with which to settle present debts.

Chaucer was not entirely free from official duties; he was still a member of the Kent peace commission. But between 1386 and 1389 he had leisure in which he could work on the General Prologue of The Canterbury Tales and a number of the tales themselves.

Clerk of the Works and Forester

New official tasks, however, soon demanded his attention. King Richard, who had regained power in May 1389, appointed Chaucer on 12 July 1389 to what was possibly his most arduous position: he became clerk of the king's works. He had responsibility for construction and repair at ten royal residences and other holdings of the king. One was the Tower of London, serving at that time as palace, fortress, prison, armory, mint, and place of safekeeping for records. Among other "works" he oversaw were Westminster Palace, center of government as well as occasional dwelling for the royal family; the castle of Berkhamsted; and seven of Richard's favorite manors, including Eltham and Sheen, mentioned in The Legend of Good Women (Pro F 497). He was also overseer of hunting lodges in royal forests, the mews at Charing Cross for the king's falcons, parks (hunting preserves), gardens, mills, pools, and fences. He had purveyors who assisted him at most of these places and a controller who checked his accounts as he had checked those of the customs collectors.

Chaucer's clerkship represented a heavier and more direct responsibility than did the control-

lership. He was not dealing with such large sums of money as he had checked at the customhouse, but he supervised a great number of craftsmen and arranged for the purchase, transportation, and storage of large quantities of supplies. He had to find and pay the men, pursue them if they ran away, and, if necessary, imprison them; he had to choose, purchase, and store building materials, and to see that they were not stolen. Chaucer's wages, at two shillings a day, amounted to more than three and one-half times his base salary at the customhouse.

The importance of Chaucer's position is suggested by the achievements of the king's craftsmen on his payroll. One of them, master mason Henry Yeveley, planned the rebuilding of the naves of Westminster Abbey and Canterbury Cathedral, designed the tombs of Richard II and Queen Anne in the Abbey, and devised the rebuilding of Westminster Hall, sometimes called "the handsomest building in Europe."

Special occasions made special demands. After a storm that caused great damage along the Thames, Chaucer was appointed on 12 March 1390 to a royal commission "of walls and ditches" for the extensive marshes between Woolwich and Greenwich; he may then have been living in the latter town. In May and October of 1390, when King Richard invited knights from overseas to take part in his tournaments, Chaucer was in charge of putting up "scaffolds," seating for the royal and noble spectators, and lists for the combats at Smithfield. Construction of lists in The Knight's Tale (I.1882–84, 1908, 2087–88) has sometimes been compared to Chaucer's task at Smithfield. One of the October guests was to be installed as a Knight of the Garter in St. George's Chapel at Windsor Castle, where the order had been founded; accordingly, on 12 July 1390, Chaucer was commissioned to repair the chapel, described as "ruinous and like to fall to the ground."

No large building projects were under way during Chaucer's clerkship. Average spending by his successors was two and one-half times as great as his. But one useful project, undertaken before Chaucer took office, continued throughout his term and beyond. It was the rebuilding and enlarging of the wharf beside the Tower of London, where wool was brought for customs levy. The wharf repairs and other works near the Tower cost more than half of all the money spent by Chaucer in the works office; and, appropriately, they were paid for by the revenue from wool customs. Chaucer's previous work as controller of customs had brought him daily to the wharf, and he knew well what improvements were needed.

At least once during his clerkship he encountered danger. In early September 1390, probably while traveling from one royal manor to another with money for payrolls, he was attacked by a gang of highwaymen and robbed. The robbers were caught, tried, and convicted. But the legal records differ so widely that it is not possible to determine whether there was one robbery or three; whether the loss was £10 or £20 6s. 8d. or £9 43d.; whether the place was Westminster or Hatcham or the "Foule Oke," a place name or a tree, in Surrey or in Kent. It is certain, however, that Chaucer was not required to repay the king's money.

Chaucer's clerkship of the works ended on 17 June 1391. The robbery, in which he was said to have been wounded, may have caused him to give up the office. Or he may have found the financial situation unsatisfactory; when Chaucer left office, the audit of his account showed more than £87 still owing to him. This was a large sum; it exceeded by £17 the total amount of his wages during the entire term of his appointment.

When Chaucer left the clerkship, another place was waiting for him: at some time before 22 June 1391 he was appointed deputy forester of the royal forest at North Petherton in Somerset. Other royal servants received similar appointments.

The forestership, like Chaucer's earlier positions, was a responsible one, demanding skill in handling money and men, because forests in late medieval England were sources of revenue. Royal forests comprised entire regions that could, and at North Petherton did, include moor, marsh, pastureland, cultivated fields, and villages and their churches, as well as wooded areas. Royal forests yielded many kinds of income, such as fees for pasturing cattle and for allowing swine to feed on acorns and beech mast, and tolls for traveling forest roads.

According to tradition, Chaucer as deputy forester lived at Park House in the forest, though it is not clear whether his duties required that he live there. Wherever he lived, he did not lose touch with the court. In 1393 Chaucer received from King Richard a gift of £10 "for good serv-

ice." The next year Richard granted him an annuity of £20. Henry of Derby gave Chaucer fur to trim a gown of scarlet (a fine cloth) during the year 1395–96. In the same year, Chaucer delivered £10 to Henry from the royal exchequer. King Richard, reminded of an earlier grant, certified to Chaucer in 1398 the yearly gift of a tun of wine.

Last Years

The mood of the court changed in 1397. After several years of peace and moderation Richard moved suddenly to take revenge on the Appellants, who had in 1388 caused the exile or death of a group of his friends. The king arrested his enemies, charged them with treason, and caused them to be imprisoned, exiled, or put to death. Henry, John of Gaunt's son, had been one of the Appellants; he was exiled in 1398. When John of Gaunt died in 1399, Richard seized his estates; Henry returned to claim them and took advantage of the opportunity to depose Richard and have himself crowned as Henry IV.

Of Chaucer in these years we know little. We know that his Petherton appointment was renewed, and that he may have taken his last recorded journey. A royal protection was issued on 4 May 1398 to "Geoffrey Chaucer, our beloved esquire going about divers parts of England on the king's arduous and pressing business."

Henry's accession seems at first glance to have made little difference in Chaucer's life. The poet and his wife had received annuities from Henry's father; Chaucer had written *The Book of the Duchess* as a memorial to Henry's mother; and during the last decade Chaucer had received a gift from Henry himself. As king, Henry renewed the grants Chaucer had received from Richard II and granted an additional forty marks yearly for life. The envoy of a late poem, The Complaint of Chaucer to His Purse, hailed Henry as true king by right of conquest, birth, and *free eleccion* (line 23), though the Complaint itself suggests that the grants approved by the new king had not yet been paid.

Chaucer now provided himself with a home near the court. On 24 December 1399 he took a fifty-three-year lease of a house near the Lady Chapel of Westminster Abbey, on a site now occupied by the Chapel of King Henry VII. For a few months he collected, or others collected for him, his royal grants: on 21 February and 5 June 1400 he received partial payments of the arrears due on his exchequer annuities. No life records of later date have been found.

The inscription on Chaucer's tomb in Westminster Abbey gives the date of his death as 25 October 1400. The tomb may, however, have been erected as late as 1555, and there is no other evidence as to the exact date of his death. He was buried in the Abbey for several reasons, none of them, so far as we know, related to his being a poet. He had a right to burial there because he was a tenant of the Abbey and a member of the parish. Moreover, commoners who had been royal servants were beginning to be buried near the tombs of the kings they had served. No one in England in 1400 could foresee that Chaucer's tomb would be the beginning of Poets' Corner and that Chaucer would become the "stremes hede" of poetry in English.

MARTIN M. CROW AND
VIRGINIA E. LELAND

THE CANON AND CHRONOLOGY OF CHAUCER'S WORKS

The manuscripts and early printed editions attribute to Chaucer a great many works that were demonstrably written not by Chaucer but by his contemporaries or by fifteenth-century "Chaucerians" who emulated his style and poetic forms. These "apocryphal" works (most of which are printed in the supplementary volume 7 of Skeat's edition) were included in collected editions of Chaucer's works until the publication of Skeat's Oxford Chaucer (1894) and the Globe Chaucer (1898). Hence, many of the ideas about Chaucer held by eighteenth- and nineteenth-century poets and critics were shaped by these false attributions.

The problems of the authenticity of the works are discussed in the notes to each. In general, the most important evidence is supplied by Chaucer himself—the lists of his works in the Prologue to *The Legend of Good Women,* the Introduction to The Man of Law's Tale, and the Retraction at the end of *The Canterbury Tales*—and by the testimony of those who knew or could have known him: Henry Scogan, to whom Lenvoy de Chaucer a Scogan was probably addressed and who vouches for the authenticity of Gentilesse; John Lydgate, who began his own poetic career in

Chaucer's lifetime, and who provides a list of Chaucer's works in the Prologue to his *Fall of Princes*; and the copyist John Shirley (c. 1366 – 1454), who, though he retails a good deal of gossip, is usually reliable in his attributions. Such testimony accounts for the authenticity of all but a handful of lyrics, which are accepted as Chaucer's on the basis of their attribution by the scribes and their conformity in style and subject matter to the works authenticated by the testimony of Chaucer and his contemporaries.

Some works in this volume are clearly not by Chaucer, including most of the Supplementary Propositions of the *Astrolabe.* They are printed here because some may indeed be Chaucer's and because they illustrate certain passages in the authentic works. The "B" Fragment of *The Romaunt of the Rose* is also clearly not Chaucer's; neither are all scholars convinced that either the "A" or the "C" Fragments of *The Romaunt of the Rose* are authentic (though most believe that the "A" Fragment is Chaucer's). All three parts of *The Romaunt of the Rose* are printed, because some may be genuine and because the *Romaunt* provides the student with a contemporary translation of a work that had an enormous influence on fourteenth-century literature in general and on Chaucer's works in particular. Among the lyrics, the Complaynt D'Amours and A Balade of Complaint are probably not by Chaucer; they are included because the case on neither is completely closed, and convincing proof for or against their authenticity is still lacking. Against Women Unconstant, Proverbs, and Womanly Noblesse have been accepted by some editors and rejected by others.

Robinson provided a subsection of the lyrics that he labeled "doubtful," and included in that section Merciles Beaute, which almost all scholars now accept as genuine. We have chosen to place that poem, along with the others in Robinson's "doubtful" section, a group labeled "Poems Not Ascribed to Chaucer in the Manuscripts." Robinson doubted the authenticity of Proverbs, but the present editors believe that the work may indeed be Chaucer's; the question, however, remains open. Aside from Proverbs, the canon as Robinson defined it, and thus as represented in this edition, is almost universally accepted.

Apparently, there are a number of lost works. In the Prologue to *The Legend of Good Women* Chaucer lists two works that have since been lost, *Origenes upon the Maudeleyne* (ProLGW F 428) and *Of the Wreched Engendrynge of Mankynde* (ProLGW G 414), a translation of a work by Pope Innocent III, and he implies that he also had written many love lyrics and *many an ympne* for Love's holidays (ProLGW F 422). In the Retraction to the *Tales* he lists a work called *the book of the Leoun* and *othere bookes of legendes of seintes, and omelies, and moralitee, and devocioun* (X.1087–88).

Attempts have been made to identify these lost works, and a number of poems have been proposed for inclusion in the canon: Carleton Brown (PMLA 50, 1935, 997–1011) argued that "An Holy Medytacioun" (in Lydgate's Minor Poems 1.43–48) is Chaucer's lost "Of the Wreched Engendrynge of Mankynde." Eleanor P. Hammond (MLN 19, 1904, 32–34) printed "The Balade of a Plow" and "The Balade of a Reeve" and argued that the former was Chaucer's; Brusendorff (Chaucer Tradition, 278–48) argued for the authenticity of the latter. Rossell H. Robbins (in Comp to Ch, 387) accepts Chaucer's authorship of the "Complaint to My Mortal Foe" and "Complaint to My Lodesterre" (printed in Skeat 4.xxv–xxxi). None of these attributions has gained wide acceptance.

The most important work to be proposed for inclusion in the canon in recent years is the *Equatorie of the Planetis,* a Middle English translation of a Latin work based ultimately on an Arabic source. It describes the construction and use of an equatorium, an instrument for calculating the positions of the planets. In 1952 Derek J. Price discovered this work along with a number of astronomical tables in MS Peterhouse 75.1. (It is now in Cambridge University Library.) In this manuscript, written in the same hand as parts of the text of the *Equatorie,* is the inscription "radix Chaucer" alongside a calculation of the number of days elapsed between the birth of Christ and December 1392, the date (radix) used for calculations in the *Equatorie* and some of the accompanying tables. Price compared the word "Chaucer" with what may have been Chaucer's signature in a record in the 1378 rolls of the controller; he concluded that the hand was the same and consequently that the *Equatorie* was Chaucer's composition, written in his own hand. R. M. Wilson's careful study of the language (printed in Price's edition) showed that the phonology, morphology, and syntax of the *Equatorie* were consistent with Chaucer's own usage. Chaucer, in the preface to the *Astrolabe,* had promised to compose third and fourth parts with materials similar to those in the *Equatorie* manuscript (though not in the *Equatorie* itself). Given this promise, the evidence of the handwriting, and the consistency of the language with Chaucer's usage, the case for the authenticity of the *Equatorie of the Planetis* seemed very strong indeed.

Robinson was not convinced. The argument from the marginal notation, potentially the most persuasive evidence, seemed to him very weak: *The entry "radix Chaucer" hardly constitutes an ascription of the treatise to the poet and might even seem more natural if written by a person other than the author. The argument from the handwriting, which is based on a comparison of the Peterhouse entry with a Record Office note made fourteen years earlier and not proved to be in Chaucer's hand, also rests on slender evidence.*

Robinson therefore rendered a "Scotch verdict" —not proven—on the claim for Chaucer's authorship of the *Equatorie.* Because the work is of purely scientific interest, and because of the availability of Price's edition (1955)—complete with facsimile, transcription, translation, detailed explanatory notes, and full introductory and illustrative materials—Robinson decided not to add the *Equatorie* to his second edition.

Very little has changed since then. No one has offered convincing further evidence of Chaucer's authorship and no one has made a persuasive case against it. We are inclined to share Robinson's skepticism. J. D. North (RES 20, 1969, 132–33) has noted a few possibly significant differences in the technical vocabularies of the *Astrolabe* and the *Equatorie* (though in the absence of the Latin text from which the latter was translated, one cannot make too much of this), and he notes that none of Chaucer's works show any evidence of the use of an equatorium. Most Chaucerians are inclined to believe that the *Equatorie* was written by a contemporary Londoner, perhaps one in Chaucer's own circle of acquaintances, though the question remains open.

We have decided to omit the *Equatorie of the Planetis* from this edition for the same reasons Robinson adduced. The work, while possibly by Chaucer, adds little to our understanding of his undoubtedly genuine works. Though it is of great importance to the student intent on the study of fourteenth-century science as part of

Chaucer's intellectual milieu, such a student is still best served by Price's admirable edition; the *Equatorie* is a scientifically and mathematically much more sophisticated work than the *Treatise on the Astrolabe,* and it requires for its understanding the exhaustive commentary that Price supplies.

There is little concrete evidence for determining exactly when Chaucer's works were written. There are, of course, no records of the "publication" of any of his works, and contemporary references to Chaucer's works are rare. The mention of *Troilus and Criseyde* in Thomas Usk's *Testament of Love* is of some help in establishing the date of *Troilus,* though exactly dating Usk's *Testament* is difficult. Likewise, the reference to *Boece* and *The Romaunt of the Rose* in the ballade that Eustache Deschamps addressed to Chaucer (usually dated 1385–86) is of little help in determining the exact dates of those works.

As might be expected, the works themselves contain little specific information about when they were written. Only the *Treatise on the Astrolabe* contains an actual date, 12 March 1391 (Astr 2.1.7), but there are indications in the text that Chaucer returned to the work after some interval, in the spring of 1393 or even later. (Supplementary Propositions 2.44 and 45 are dated 1397, but they are spurious.) He may therefore have begun writing the *Astrolabe* earlier than 1391; there is no way of knowing when he stopped and left the work unfinished. Likewise, though many of Chaucer's poems may have been "occasional," intended to celebrate or commemorate some important court event, only *The Book of the Duchess* can be positively linked to a specific historical event, the death of Blanche of Lancaster in September 1368. Even this is of limited help, since scholars have differed considerably on the question of how long after Blanche's death the poem was written. Other allusions to historical events are rare in Chaucer's works, rarer than many scholars have been willing to believe; even when they do appear (for example, the unusual conjunction of the stars described in *Troilus* 3.624–30, which actually occurred in 1385), the exact implications of such allusions for dating a poem is a matter of dispute. Moreover, Chaucer sometimes revised his works (as in the case of the Prologue to *The Legend of Good Women*); adapted existing works to new purposes (as in some of *The Canterbury Tales*); or kept by him works to which he turned sporadically over a long period of time (as may have been the case with the *Astrolabe*). It is no wonder that the dates assigned to Chaucer's works are at best approximations.

Chaucer does, however, provide us with some basis for determining the approximate order in which his works were written: for instance, he lists some of his works in the Prologue to *The Legend of Good Women.* The Introduction to The Man of Law's Tale lists some of the lives told in *The Legend of Good Women,* and this shows that at least parts of the *Legend* were written before that Introduction. Likewise, Chaucer's allusions to his own works, such as the mention of the Wife of Bath in The Merchant's Tale and in the Envoy to Bukton, supply evidence for the relative order of composition of those works.

Though clearly less reliable than direct allusions, the internal analysis of Chaucer's works can also provide some evidence for their order of composition. Chaucer sometimes "borrowed" from his own works, and at various stages of his career he concentrated his attention on particular problems of form and subject, producing clusters of works characterized by a striking number of identical lines and shared stylistic devices. Where the date of one work in a group related by form or subject is known, however roughly, the relative dates of the other works can often be inferred.

Chaucer's works also tend to reflect his reading and intellectual interests, and identification of sources common to a group of works can be used in the same way as form and subject to infer relative dates. In the late 1370s Chaucer's reading of Italian poetry, mainly that of Boccaccio, is apparent in almost everything he wrote. In the early 1380s he undertook the translation of Boethius's *Consolation of Philosophy* and this affected almost all that he wrote at that time. In the middle of the 1380s Chaucer developed an interest in the technical aspects of astronomy that led to his *Astrolabe* and a concern with judicial astronomy (astrology) that is apparent in many works probably written in the late 1380s and early 1390s. About this time Chaucer apparently came upon the works included in Jankyn's "Book of Wicked Wives" (mentioned in the Wife of Bath's Prologue) and their influence is apparent throughout the "Marriage Group" of

The Canterbury Tales (the tales from the Wife of Bath's Prologue to The Clerk's Tale).

The tendency of Chaucer's works to reflect his current reading and interests is the basis of the old, not altogether mistaken, division of Chaucer's career into the so-called French, Italian, and English periods. His early works reflect his reading of and admiration for French courtly verse; his discovery of Italian poetry significantly affected the form and subject matter of his poetry; and his last period, the time of *The Canterbury Tales,* is characterized by a profound shift in his ideas about poetry and the representation of English life. These divisions are not mutually exclusive; Chaucer was an English poet from the beginning, and as his career developed he added to rather than rejected his earlier enthusiasms. Yet his interests and his ideas about poetry did change, and tracing such changes can be useful in determining the chronology of his works.

Finally, the scholar intent upon establishing the relative dates of Chaucer's work must consider matters of style and his increasing mastery of his craft. This is a difficult matter, since Chaucer's literary accomplishments are so varied that it may be said that he never "developed" in the manner of many writers. He was the most restlessly experimental of poets, constantly trying and mastering, then abandoning but sometimes later returning to genres, metrical forms, styles, and subject matter. Stylistic comparison for the purpose of determining chronology is thus rendered very difficult indeed. Yet, applied with care, stylistic analysis can help to determine the relative dates of composition.

By such means scholars have developed a chronology of Chaucer's work about which there is, given the nature of the problem, a surprisingly broad consensus. Opinion is not unanimous, however, and the chronology given below represents only a general agreement. In many cases, there is reason to doubt the chronology, and the Explanatory Notes should be consulted for particular details about each work.

BEFORE 1372: Fragment "A" of *The Romaunt of the Rose* (if Chaucer's); possibly the ABC; *The Book of the Duchess* (1368–72).

1372–80: Lyrics such as The Complaint unto Pity and Complaint to His Lady; *Saint Cecelia* (The Second Nun's Tale, possibly later); some of the tragedies later used in The Monk's Tale; *The House of Fame* (1378–80); *Anelida and Arcite.*

1380–87: *The Parliament of Fowls* (1380–82); *Boece; Troilus and Criseyde* (1382–86); Adam Scriveyn; The Complaint of Mars (probably around 1385); The Complaint of Venus; *Palamoun and Arcite* (The Knight's Tale); possibly the "Boethian ballades" (The Former Age, Fortune, Truth, Gentilesse, Lak of Stedfastnesse); *The Legend of Good Women* (though some of the legends may be earlier, and the Prologue was later revised).

1388–92: The General Prologue and the earlier of *The Canterbury Tales; A Treatise on the Astrolabe* (1391–92, with additions in 1393 or later).

1392–95: Most of *The Canterbury Tales,* including probably the "Marriage Group."

1396–1400: The latest of the *Tales,* including probably The Nun's Priest's Tale, The Canon's Yeoman's Tale (though part of the latter is probably earlier), and The Parson's Tale; and several short poems, including Scogan, Bukton, and the Complaint to His Purse.

LARRY D. BENSON

LANGUAGE AND VERSIFICATION

The English language had been used in poetry and prose for at least six centuries before Chaucer began to write. The earliest records show considerable regional variation, but by the end of the tenth century the type that is now called Late West Saxon, though it was not completely homogeneous, had come to serve as a generally accepted written language over most of England. The tradition was destroyed by the great political and cultural upheaval of the Norman Conquest, and for several generations writing in English was not much cultivated. When it revived, in the late twelfth century and after, writers used their own regional forms of the language, and no particular type could claim superiority over the others. Soon after the Conquest, commerce became increasingly centered in London, and government administration and courts of law at Westminster nearby. The London area attracted a varied population from many parts of the country, especially the east and central midlands, and this inflow led eventually to a blend of linguistic elements recognizable as characteristic of the capital. Considerable variation in particular features was evidently accepted until long after Chaucer's time. Thus the frequent assertion that his usage corresponds in all essentials to that of contemporary administrative documents from the city of London is true only if we admit a good many alternatives in pronunciation and inflection, for the usage of neither Chaucerian manuscripts nor the London documents is invariable.

The increasing use of English in every sphere of life in the course of the fourteenth century made it natural that Chaucer should choose to write in it, even though some contemporary writers, notably his friend Gower, used French and Latin as well. Inevitably, too, Chaucer wrote in the English familiar to him from business as well as from court circles in London and Westminster. In some respects, especially in the technique of verse, he was a great innovator, and a substantial number of words and phrases, many of French origin, are first recorded in his work. But the influence he had on the English language seems to have been more a matter of style than substance. He showed that English could be written with an elegance and power that earlier authors had not attained. Once his literary eminence was recognized, as happened during his own lifetime, the type of language in which he wrote gained prestige. Yet, this would concern the cultivation of literature more than the practical affairs of merchants or officials, and Chaucer's example cannot have had much effect in determining what kind of English would later develop into the generally accepted written standard.

Pronunciation

An author as interested in form as Chaucer obviously was cannot be appreciated without attention to the effect of reading aloud. The study of the pronunciation of ancient languages is a complex matter relying on comparison among related languages, observation of known history, and phonetic probability, by which a reasonably convincing view of the relation of writing to pronunciation can be built up. The manuscripts in which Chaucer's works have been preserved are all later than the date of his death, though some are not much later; and it is uncertain how closely they reproduce his original spelling. A fully coherent and uniform system of spelling had not yet been developed—the pre-Conquest system, itself not completely consistent, had been much modified by French conventions.

Some of the variants were evidently matters of writing only, implying no instability of pronunciation. For example, two characters now completely obsolete were still often used as alternatives by the scribes who copied Chaucer's works: the ancient þ (called "thorn") alternated with *th* as a way of representing what must have been the interdental fricative sounds that are now always spelled *th,* as in *thin* and *then;* and ʒ (called "yogh") had a number of possible values, being usually equivalent to *y* in words like ʒ*it* (yet) or to *gh* in *nyʒt* (night). These characters are replaced in most editions, as they are in this one, by their modern equivalents; but other alternative spellings are often, though not always, left unaltered by editors, notably the largely free variation between *i* and *y* representing vowels, as *lif* or *lyf* (life), or between *ou* and *ow* as in *you* or *yow.*

Though individual European languages have developed their own peculiarities in representing pronunciation by means of the Roman alphabet, there is much common ground in the use of the majority of letters. The striking differences between modern English and the continental languages in the way in which letters are associated with sounds, especially the long vowels and diphthongs, did not arise until after Chaucer's time, so that the pronunciation of his English can, however partially and approximately, be recovered by giving the spellings of the manuscripts the values they would have in, say, French or Spanish or Italian. Much information also comes from the rhymes and rhythms of verse. In addition to the articulation of individual sounds, it is necessary to attend to the weight and incidence of stress in words of more than one syllable. Though the main stress very often falls on the same syllable as in modern English (this of course can vary to some extent) there are many differences and alternatives. In words of native English descent, the stress tends to fall on the first syllable, unless it is a prefix; but in those from French often later syllables are stressed.

Many words which in modern English have initial stress are still accented in the French way by Chaucer. So, for example, *licour* (Tales I.3) has the stress on the second syllable, which consequently contains the fully articulated long vowel $\bar{u}$, to rhyme with *flour, ou* being an established French way of writing this sound; and similarly *servyse* (I.250) takes the stress on the second syllable, as modern French *service* still does, and rhymes with *arise,* which had not yet developed the modern English diphthong. Some words of French origin are stressed in more than one way, sometimes—especially at the end of a verse line—on the French pattern, but sometimes with the initial stress characteristic of native English words: *córoune* and *coróune* vary, as in Tales I.2290 and 2875; *requeste* (Tr 3.148) is stressed on the second syllable as in the later language, but in Tales I.1204 and in some other places where the word appears within, rather than at the end of, the line, the first syllable is stressed; and similarly *revers* (VII.2977) has the stress on the prefix (as in the frequent alternative stressing of *research* today). Both the stress and the number of syllables vary with the position in the line of *máner,* as in Tales I.71, but *manére,* rhyming with *cheere,* in lines 139–40, or with *heere,* in lines 875–76. The number of syllables may often differ from that in later pronunciation, notably in words with the frequent suffix *-cio(u)n,* which regularly forms two syllables, so that, for instance, *nacioun* (II.268) has three syllables and *congregacioun* (VII.2988) has five. Such words often rhyme with others having a long *ū* in the final or only syllable, such as *toun,* which implies at least some degree of stress on that syllable. Another type of stress pattern is seen in *remembraunce* (Tr 5.562), which is accented on the first and third syllables and so can rhyme with such words as *chaunce.* This kind of movement appears mostly in words of French origin, but it may also occur in native compounds ending in *-nesse* and even verbal forms ending in *-inge* (a traditional rhyming practice dating back at least to the early thirteenth century). Thus *bisynesse* (Tales I.3643) rhymes with *gesse; dawenynge* (VII.2882) with *synge.*

Though a few particular points remain in doubt, there is good reason to believe that the London English of Chaucer's time used the following vowel sounds in stressed syllables:

short	a e i o u as in *man, men, his, folk, ful*
long	$\bar{a}$ $\bar{e}$ $\bar{e}$ $\bar{i}$ $\bar{o}$ $\bar{o}$ $\bar{u}$ and probably $\bar{\bar{u}}$ as in *name, sweete, breeth, riden, good, foo, flour, muwe*
diphthongs	ai au iu eu ou oi as in *day, cause, newe, fewe, soule, joie*

Both the short and the long *i* were often written *y,* as in *nyght* and *nyne,* respectively, and the short *u* was written *o* (a French convention) especially next to letters consisting of short vertical strokes like *m* and *n,* as in *comen, sonne.*

Long vowels were distinguished by the scribes inconsistently: $\bar{e}$ and $\bar{o},$ whatever their quality, were often shown by the doubled letters *ee* and *oo,* and $\bar{a}$ less frequently by *aa;* $\bar{u}$ was usually written *ou* or *ow.* A single vowel symbol followed by a single consonant and another vowel, as *smale, seke, riden, cote,* normally represented a long vowel, but there are exceptions, especially with *i.* Before certain consonant groups, especially *ld, mb, nd,* vowels were generally long, as in *old, climben, finden.*

Of the short vowels, *a* was evidently a low front sound like that of French *patte,* not the more fronted sound now general in words like English *bat; o* was a rounded vowel more like that of the British *hot* or the first sound in *auction* than the unrounded sound now general in American speech; *u* was always rounded as in *put,* not unrounded as in *putt.*

Of the long vowels, $\bar{a}$ was probably further to the front than the usual articulation of the *a* of "father"; $\bar{e}$ was like the French close *e* in *café,* but longer; $\bar{e}$ like the French open *e* in *fête,* not far from the beginning of the sound of *e* in *there;* $\bar{i}$ was like the *i* in *machine;* $\bar{o}$ was like the French close *o* in *rôle,* not far from the beginning of the sound of *o* in *note;* $\bar{o}$ was like the sound of *oa* in *broad;* $\bar{u}$ like the *u* in *rule.* The distinction between close and open $\bar{e}$ and $\bar{o}$ was not expressed in spelling at the date of most Chaucerian manuscripts. The appropriate sound of *o* or *oo* can usually be deduced from the modern forms of the words concerned, for the sounds have remained distinct and the descendant of close $\bar{o}$ came to be spelled usually *oo,* that of open $\bar{o}$ often *oa.* Close $\bar{o}$ mostly developed to $\bar{u}$ as in *food* (sometimes shortened as in *good*), open $\bar{o}$ mostly to the diphthong now heard in *road* but in *broad* changed little. However, the vowels that were formerly close and open *e* are not generally distinguished in modern English, and the pronunciation has to be learned primarily from etymology, though spellings introduced mainly in the sixteenth century, and often surviving, are also of great help. The close sound was represented by many scribes and printers by *ee,* the open sound by *ea,* and modern forms are usually a good indication of the earlier difference in such pairs as *meet* and

Sound	Pronunciation	Spelling	ME Examples
ā	/a:/	*a in* father *(but fronted)*	a, aa	name, caas
ă	/a/	*a in Fr.* patte *or Ger.* Mann	a	can, that
ē *(close)*	/e:/	*e in Fr.* café *or in* fate *(but a pure vowel)*	e, ee	grene, sweete
ẹ *(open)*	/ɛ:/	*e in Fr.* fête *or in* there *(but a pure vowel)*	e, ee	teche, heeth
ĕ	/e/	*e in* set	e	tendre
e *(in unstressed syllables)*	/ə/	*e in* horses	e	sonne
ī	/i:/	*i in* machine	i, y	shires, ryden
ĭ	/i/	*i in* sit	i, y	this, thyng
ō *(close)*	/o:/	*o in* note *(but a pure vowel)*	o, oo	bote, good
ǭ *(open)*	/ɔ:/	*oa in* broad	o, oo	holy, goon
ŏ	/o/	*o in* hot *(but not unrounded)*	o	oft, folk
ū	/u:/	*oo in* boot *(but a pure vowel)*	ou, ow, ogh	flour, fowles, droghte
ŭ	/u/	*u in* put	u, o	but, yong
ü	/y:/	*u in Fr.* lune *or Ger.* grün	u, eu, ew, uw	vertu, seur, salewe, muwe
au	/au/	*ou in* house	au, aw	cause, lawe
ệi	/ai/ or /æi/	*e + i or a + i*	ay, ai, ey, ei	sayle, day, wey, heir
ēu	/iu/	*i + u*	eu, ew	knew, newe
ẹu	/ɛu/	*e + u*	eu, ew	lewed, fewe
oi	/ɔi/	*oy in* boy	oi, oy	coy
ōu	/ɔu/	*o + u*	ou, ow	growen, soule
ŏu	/ɔu/	*o + u*	o, ou *(before* -gh)	thoght, foughte

meat. (*Break* and *great* exceptionally preserve a different sound relation lost in most other words.) Even in some fifteenth-century manuscripts the beginning of the spelling distinction can be seen—words like *ease, peace* are usually written *ese, pes,* but occasionally *ease, peas.*

The sources of close *ē* were the Old English long *ē* and *ēo,* as in *seke* (seek), *depe* (deep), and short *e* lengthened before consonant groups, as in *feeld* (field) and Old French and Anglo-Norman close *ē,* as in *contree* (country). The main sources of open *ẹ* were Old English *æ* and *ēa,* as in *teche* (teach), *grete* (great), and short *e*

lengthened in an open syllable (i.e., before a single consonant and another vowel), as *ete* (eat), and Old French and Anglo-Norman open *e,* as in *ese* (ease) and *trete* (treat). The existence of *ü,* a vowel like that of French *lune* or German *grün,* is inferred from the fact that words adopted from French containing this sound almost always rhyme with other French words, e.g., *muwe* with *stuwe* (Tales I.349–50), not with native words containing the diphthong *iu,* like *newe.* The sole exception appears to be the rhyme in Tr 4.1310–12, where *muwe* from French *mue* rhymes with *trewe* from Old English *trēowe*. The diphthong in such words was evidently still a "falling" one, that is, with the stress on its first element, not the second, as in modern *few*. Words containing *ēow* or *īw* do not rhyme with those containing the Old English *ēaw* or *ǣw* (a small number), which are also written *ew* in Middle English; thus *newe* does not rhyme with *fewe*. The latter diphthong must still have had a lower vowel, some kind of *e*, as its first element. No such distinction between close and open first elements can be observed in diphthongs containing *o: growen*, which etymologically should contain a close *ō̧*, rhymes with *knowen*, which should have an open *ō̧* — the sounds have evidently coalesced. The diphthong written either *ai/ay* or *ei/ey* somewhat similarly arose from two earlier diphthongs with first elements of distinct quality, as in *day* from Old English *dæg*, and *May* from Old French *mai*, against *wey* from Old English *weg*.

By the early fourteenth century, these sounds had merged, so as to rhyme together, but the quality of the resulting diphthong cannot be confidently determined. Descriptions given much later by grammarians indicate that in the sixteenth century there was much variation in the pronunciation of such words. It is probable that in Chaucer's time the first element of the diphthong was articulated further back, nearer to *a* than to *e*. The diphthong written *oi/oy* seems also to have developed from two earlier sounds, *oi* and *ui*, the former historically expected in *joie, Troie*, and other words, the latter in *destroye, anoye*. These groups are usually, but not invariably, kept apart in rhyme.

The spelling *ou/ow* could represent, in addition to *ū* as already noticed, the diphthong *ou* composed of *o* and *u*, as in *grow*. Scribes varied in writing words in which *o* precedes the back fricative consonant usually written *gh*. The commonest spelling is probably *ou*, but simple *o* is favored by some, so that modern *thought* may be written *thought(e), thowght(e)*, or *thoght(e)*. Scribes did not always match spellings exactly to pronunciation as evidenced by rhyme. In particular, some words descended from forms containing the diphthong *ei* before the consonant *y* were sometimes written with the historical spelling *ei/ey* though the diphthong had developed to the simple vowel *ī*. Thus *eye* might be so spelled though rhyming with such a word as *crye*, as in the *Tales*, VIII.964–65.

Fully unstressed syllables may occur before or after the main stress in a word. Those before the stress are usually in prefixes, most of them presumably containing the same neutral or "central" vowel as in the first syllables of modern *about* and *away*. Those after the stress are the more numerous and important because they include the major grammatical inflections of nouns, adjectives, verbs, and adverbs. Many of these inflections contain a vowel usually written *e*, whether final or before one of the consonants *-s, -n, -d, -st, -th*. When the vowel was final, it was no doubt also the neutral vowel. Such vowels were often elided before a vowel or *h-* beginning a following word. When a consonant closed the unstressed syllable, the vowel could evidently be higher, since it is sometimes written *i* or *y* and may form part of a rhyme with a syllable containing a short *i* as the plural noun *clerkis* rhymes with the singular *clerk is* in Tales VII.3235–36 and the past participle *woundid* with the group *wounde hid* in II.102–3. Unstressed syllables also often contain the vowel *i* in the common adjectival ending usually written *y*, as in *hooly*, and the verbal ending *-ing(e)*. Before the stress *i* occurs in prefixes, especially in past participles like *ybake, yronne* and some adverbs like *yno(u)gh, iwis*, but also in *bi-* as in *biginne;* and in the prefixes *dis-* and *in-* (derived from romance languages) as in *disport, inspired*.

The consonants of Chaucer's English were mostly the same as those used in the modern language and were represented by the same letters. A number of consonants since lost in pronunciation were still sounded: initial *g, k*, and *w* were sounded, as in *gnawen, knowen, wlatsom, writen; l* before consonants, as in *half, folk; r* in all positions, and it was probably trilled, at least between vowels, as in *faren. Wh-* was still always distinct from *w-*, and in *-ng* the *g* was probably sounded as in *finger*. But in French words initial *h* was not pronounced, nor was *g* in the combination *gn* (representing a French palatal consonant): *resygne* (ABC 80) rhymes with *medicyne* (78). The letter *c*, as a spelling, was usually distributed as it still is, representing *s* before a front vowel but *k* before a back one or *l;* however, *k* was sometimes used before a back vowel, as in *kan, kaughte*. The suffix so common in modern English as *-tion* usually had the form *-cio(u)n*, and *cc* was the normal spelling in words like *accioun* (action). *Ch* represented the sound that it still has in *church,* and not the sound that developed in French, as in *machine.* The group now written *tch* was normally spelled *cch,* as *wrecche.* The letter *g* represented, as it does today, the back stop before back vowels, as in *good,* and some others, like *biginne;* before *e* and sometimes *i,* it had the affricate sound heard in modern English *age,* and not its French sound. Initially this sound could be represented by either *g* or *j* (often written *i,* of which *j* is merely a variant shape): *jet* (Tales VIII.1277) is written *get* in some manuscripts. When doubled, *g* could mean either of these sounds: the stop in *bigge* (big) or the affricate in *brigge* (bridge). (The spelling *dg* was not yet in use.) Chaucer's English still used a group of consonantal sounds which the later language has lost —the spelling *gh* represented a fricative consonant, front or back in articulation according to preceding vowels, like that written *ch* in German *ich* and *Bach* and in Scottish *loch.* The nearest sound in modern English is perhaps a strongly articulated initial consonant in *hue.* The fricative sounds represented by *f, s,* and *th* were evidently voiceless, except between vowels or in positions without stress, so that *is,* for example, often rhymes with words such as *this* or *blis,* and *was* with *bras, allas;* but in the fully unstressed syllables of many noun plurals, the *-s* may well have been voiced and pronounced as *-z.* Between vowels and following the stress, all the fricatives were presumably voiced. This can be seen in nouns ending in *-f* in the singular, which are written with *-v-* in the plural (*wif, wives*), or conversely in the relation of the consonants in paradigms such as *yeven* (give), with past singular *yaf;* and the same no doubt held for the other fricatives, though the distinction could not be shown in the spelling; e.g., the *s* in *risen* was pronounced *z.*

In Chaucer's rhymes a distinction is maintained between long and short consonants, though opportunities for it are not very numerous. For instance, *sone* (son) rhymes only with *wone,* noun or verb, which historically had a single *-n-,* whereas *sonne* (sun) rhymes with *yronne, wonne, conne, bigonne,* all with etymologically double *n.*

Inflections

Many words in Chaucer's English retained from an earlier period unstressed final syllables that have since been lost, in pronunciation though not always in writing. Some of these syllables, usually consisting of the neutral vowel written *-e,* were an integral part of the word deriving from a previous form, whether in Old English, Old French, or occasionally some other language. Others were inflections carrying a grammatical significance. They also often consisted of the neutral vowel alone, but often it was followed by a consonant; and some inflections consisted of a consonant alone.

NOUNS   Most nouns modify their forms to indicate plural number and to mark the genitive, or possessive, case. The uninflected form of the singular may end in a consonant, such as *folk* or *flour,* or an unstressed *-e,* as *ende* or *space,* or a stressed vowel or diphthong, as *see* or *array.* A small number of nouns have alternative forms with and without *-e,* the commonest probably being *blis* or *blisse.* The inflections of the plural and the possessive are usually the same, marked by *-s,* or by *-es* if the singular ends in a consonant. Monosyllabic nouns ending in the singular in either a consonant or a diphthong acquire a second syllable in the plural, as *bokes, dayes.* Words ending in *-e* add only *-s* and so remain of the same syllabic structure. Most nouns of more than one syllable and ending in a consonant, especially those of French origin, form the plural with simple *-s,* as *cover-chiefs, parisshens,* and those ending in *-t* often adopt the French spelling *-z,* as *servantz;* but some assume the fuller English ending, as *laxatyves* (sg. *laxatyf*). A small group of nouns form their plurals with *-(e)n* instead of, or as an alternative to, *-(e)s;* a few are still current. Those which always have *-(e)n* are *brethren, children, (e)yen; oxen, keen* (cows), *pesen* (peas) occur once each. Alternatives to forms in *-s* are *asshen, been, doghtren, foon, hosen, shoon, sustren, toon.* Nouns forming the plural by change of vowel, as in modern English, are *men, wommen, feet, gees, teeth, mys.* Some nouns are unchanged in the plural. These may be (a) words derived from Old English nouns whose plural form was the same as the singular, e.g., *deer, hors, neet, sheep,* sometimes *thing;* (b) words denoting measure of time or space, qualified by numerals (which would often have been followed by a genitive plural), such as *foot, myle, pound, night, winter, yeer;* (c) words of French origin ending in *-s,* notably *ca(a)s* and *pa(a)s;* and (d) the word *maner(e)* with numerals and in phrases like *many manere.*

Case in the singular is mostly shown in the genitive, or possessive, by adding -*s* or -*es*. A few possessives take no ending, being descended from Old English nouns that were unchanged in the genitive. These are mainly nouns of relation ending in -*r*, such as *fader, brother, suster;* alternative forms with -*s* are also found. A few others, such as *lady* or *herte,* descend from Old English genitives in -*an.* Proper names ending in -*s* add no suffix in the possessive, as *Priamus, Venus.* In the plural, the possessive is usually identical in form with the nominative, as *hir freendes soules* (Tales III.1725), *senatoures wyves* (VII.3371); but nouns forming the plural by change of vowel also add -*es* in the possessive, as *mennes wittes* (II.202), *wommennes conseils* (VII.3256). In some prepositional phrases a singular noun may add the ending -*e* (and double a final consonant after a short vowel): *to bedde, to shippe, on fire, with childe,* and especially *on live* (alive). *Live* also functions adverbially in a few phrases, such as *al hir lyve* (I.459).

ADJECTIVES   Like nouns, adjectives may end their basic form in -*e,* whether of Old English origin, as *grene, sweete,* or French, as *amiable, debonaire, rude.* Monosyllabic adjectives ending in a consonant do not normally inflect for case, but they regularly add -*e* when qualifying a plural noun and also in the so-called weak declension. The weak form is found in two principal uses: (a) when the adjective is preceded by a defining word, such as the definite article, a demonstrative, or a noun or adjective in the possessive case, as, for instance, *the yonge sonne* (Tales I.7), *this olde man* (VI.714), *Epicurus owene sone* (I.336), *his owene good* (I.611); and (b) in vocative phrases such as *O stronge god* (I.2373), *leve brother* (I.3151). An inflectional -*e* is also sometimes used after prepositions, as *with harde grace* (III.2228). Adjectives in predicative positions are not always inflected in the plural, as *they weren as fayn* (I.2707), *thise ladyes were nat right glad* (IV.375), but many are, as *they were seeke* (I.18), *the bowes weren so brode* (I.2917). Definite uses are rare in this position: uninflected forms appear in *this is the short and playn* (I.1091). An inflectional -*e* is rare in adjectives whose basic form has two syllables, where it would often not fit the rhythm of the verse, but in trisyllabic words the additional weak syllable it provides is often preserved: *The hooly blisful martir* (I.17), but *the semelieste man* (IX.119). The adjective *alle*

inflected as if weak or plural occasionally qualifies a singular noun, as in *As alle trouthe and alle gentilesse* (Tr 2.160) and *alle thyng* with singular verb in *alle thyng hath tyme* (Tales IV.1972). A few plural adjectives, of French origin, have the French ending -*s:* two are in verse, *places delitables* (V.899), *romances that been roiales* (VII.848), and a number in prose, such as *houres inequales* (Astr 2.8.2). A rare survival of a genitive plural ending is -*er* in *aller* (of all; Old English *(e)alra*) in phrases such as *oure aller cost* (Tales I.799); it also functions as an intensive of the superlative in the form *alder-* as in *alderbest* (I.710), and in *bother* (of both; Tr 4.168).

The regular suffixes for the comparison of adjectives are the same as in modern English, -*er* and -*est,* sometimes in the weak forms -*re* and -*este.* Monosyllables ending in a consonant double it before the comparative ending, and a long vowel in the stem syllable is then shortened, as *gretter* from *greet.* The short vowel is extended to the superlative *grettest. Oold, long,* and *strong* change *o* to *e* in the comparative and superlative, *elder, lenger, strenger.* The adjectives *good, yvel* or *badde, muchel,* and *litel* have irregular comparison as in modern English: *bettre* and *bet, werse* (*badder* once), *moore, lasse* or *lesse,* with superlatives *beste, werste* or *worste, mooste,* and *leeste; neigh* has the comparative *neer* and the superlative *nexte.* Comparison may also be expressed by the adverbs *moore* and *mooste,* as *the moore mury* (Tales I.802), *the moore noble* (I.2888), *the mooste stedefast* (IV.1551).

ADVERBS   Many adverbs of manner are derived from adjectives, often by means of the suffix -*e,* as *faire, faste, hoote, lowe.* Such forms may be compared in the same way as adjectives, with suffixes -*er(e)* and -*est(e),* as *The fastere shette they* (Tales VII.2532), *the faireste hewed* (VII.2869). These suffixes are applied similarly to other adverbs, such as *soone,* which doubles the -*n*- (and shortens the vowel) in *sonner* (VII.1450). Adverbs are also formed with -*ly* or -*liche,* which is added to words of French, as well as native, origin, for instance, *myrily, playnly, rudeliche.* Such forms are mostly compared by means of *moore* and *moost,* as *the moore lightly* (X.1041), *moost felyngly* (I.2203). *Murierly* (I.714) is the only example of the addition of the comparative suffix before the ending. Irregular comparison appears in the same group of words as with adjectives: *wel, yvele* or *baddely, muchel* or *muche, litel* or *lite* have, respectively, *bet* or *bettre, wers* or *werre, moo* or *moore, lasse* or *lesse.* In addition, *fer* has *ferre, ny* has *neer,* with *next* as the superlative.

PRONOUNS *Personal* Most forms are like those of modern English. In the first person singular nominative, the normal form is *I* but *ich* appears occasionally, with some variation among manuscripts. It is suffixed to the verb and confirmed by rhyme in two occurrences of *theech* (Tales VI.947 and VIII.929). *Ik* occurs twice and *theek* once in passages spoken by the Reeve from Norfolk (Tales I.3864, 3867, 3888). The second person nominative *thow* is often suffixed to a verb, with assimilation of the consonant, especially when linked to common verbs, as in *artow, wiltow,* but also occasionally when joined to others, as *thynkestow* (Tr 4.849). The possessive adjectives *myn* and *thyn* take the normal plural *-e* when qualifying plural nouns. If they precede a word beginning with a consonant other than *h-,* they lose the *-n,* as *myn hertes queene* but *my wyf* (Tales I.2775). In the third person singular, the possessive of the neuter is the same as the masculine, *his* (not *its*): *the lylie upon his stalke grene* (I.1036). When qualifying a plural noun, the masculine and neuter possessive is often written *hise,* as if inflected like an adjective, but the *-e* does not seem to have been pronounced as a syllable. The neuter nominative (and accusative) singular is usually *it,* but *hit / hyt* appears sometimes in a minority of manuscripts (not of *The Canterbury Tales*). The feminine nominative is always *she,* the objective and possessive usually written *hir* or *hire* within the line but *here* at the end, rhyming with such words as *bere, spere* (I.1421–22, II.459–60). In the plural, the second person nominative *ye* and the objective *you / yow* are distinguished. *Ye(e)* occurs twice (IV.508, Tr 1.5) as a weakened form of the objective. In the third person, the nominative is always *they,* the possessive and objective, *hire / here* and *hem,* respectively. Specifically disjunctive forms of possessive pronouns are *hires, oures, youres.* Reflexive functions of the personal pronouns are usually performed by the ordinary objective case forms, as *I putte me in thy proteccioun* (Tales I.2363), *to dyner they hem sette* (II.1118); but compounds with *self, selve(n),* also occur—*I shrewe myself* (VII.3427), *to hemself* (VIII.510). *Man / men,* an unstressed form of the noun, functions as an indefinite pronoun "one," as in Tales I.2777.

Demonstrative *This* has the plural written *thise* or *these,* in which the *-e* appears not to have been pronounced as a syllable. *That* has the plural *tho.* *Thilke* (from *the* and *ilke* "same," but generally with a less precise sense) has the same form in the singular and plural.

Relative The relatives *that, which, which that,* and *the which (that)* are all used for both persons and things. *Who* is not used in the nominative as a relative; it is the usual interrogative with reference to persons. But the possessive *whos* and objective *whom* are often relative, as *bifore whos child* (Tales II.642), *whom that we diden wo* (III.1491).

Of other pronouns, *oother* has the possessive in *-es,* as *ootheres brother* (I.2734), plural *othere* (I.2885).

VERBS The characteristic ending of the infinitive of nearly all verbs is *-en* or *-e,* but a few monosyllabic words with a long vowel or diphthong in the stem eliminate the *-e-,* as *go(o)n* or *go(o), seyn.* Verbal forms ending in *-n* (infinitive, present tense plural indicative and subjunctive, past tense plural indicative and subjunctive, and past participle) may always have alternatives without *-n.* A few verbs preserve an inflected infinitive in special functions, as *to doone* (Tales VII.1000), *fairer was to sene* (Tr 1.454).

The only simple tenses formally distinguished are the present and the past. In the present all regular verbs are conjugated alike, with distinctive endings for each person of the singular but only one for all persons of the plural. The endings are normally *-e* (1), *-est* (2), *-eth,* (3) *-e(n)* pl. There are a few exceptions: one 2 sg. in *-es* in *brynges* (HF 1908), three 3 sg. in *-es / -is* (confirmed by rhyme) in BD 73 and 257 and HF 426. There is also a group in The Reeve's Tale in which the *-es* is a mark of the students' northern dialect (e.g., *boes, wagges, falles* [Tales I.4027–42]; and in addition *-es* in the plural, e.g., *werkes* [I.4030]). An alternative form of the 3 sg. is sometimes used for metrical convenience in verbs with stems ending in a dental consonant: the ending *-eth* loses its vowel and the consonant is assimilated to that of the stem, giving a monosyllabic form ending in *-t* or *-th,* as *bit* instead of *biddeth* (Tales I.187), *rit* for *rideth* (I.974), *rist* for *riseth* (I.3688), *fynt* for *fyndeth* (I.4071), *worth* for *wortheth* (VII.751). The vowel *o* in the stems of *holden* and *stonden* is also replaced by *a* in the short form, as *halt* (V.61) but *holdeth* (IV.1189), *stant* (V.171), but *stondeth* (V.190). An exceptional contracted form of 2 sg. is *lixt* for *liest* (III.1618, 1761).

The present subjunctive has the same stem as the infinitive, with the ending *-e* in all persons of the singular and *-e(n)* in the plural. The present participle and the verbal noun (gerund) both end in *-ing* or *-inge*.

In the past tense, strong and weak verbs differ completely. Strong verbs, many of which are still current in modern English, make their past tense and past participle by changing the stem vowel, but weak verbs add to the infinitive stem endings containing *d* or *t* mostly according to the preceding consonant, though some of them in addition change the form of the stem. Strong verbs often have different stem vowels in the singular and plural numbers of the past tense and in the past participle, and historically the vowel of the second person singular should be the same as that of the plural; but the pattern has been modified by the influence of related parts on one another, and some verbs have alternative forms. Strong verbs have the same form in the first and third person, with no ending, but the ending *-e* in the second. All verbs have *-e(n)* in the plural, except that singular forms are occasionally used in plural function. Characteristic past inflection of strong verbs is as follows:

	singen	*beren*
1 and 3 sg.	sang, soong	bar, ber, beer
2 sg.	songe	bare, bere
Pl.	songen	baren, beren

In *songe* and *songen,* the *o* represents the vowel *u.* An exceptional range of variants appears in the past of *seen*—in the singular, *say, saugh, saw, seigh, sy,* and in the plural, the same forms, as well as *sawe, seyen, syen.* Some of these are no doubt attributable to copyists, but they cannot always be confidently identified and most of the major variants are confirmed by rhyme. Examples of the use of a singular form in plural function are *yaf* (Tales I.302; it is singular in I.177) and *sat* (VI.664), beside *seten* (VII.2544). Similarly, *drank,* correctly the first and third person form, is used as the second person form in VII.2226.

The past subjunctive normally has the stem vowel of the plural indicative, with endings *-e*

and *-en* in the singular and plural respectively— for instance, *songe* (BD 929).

To form the past participle, all strong verbs may take the full ending *-en,* as *founden, comen, wonnen,* but the *-n* is often dropped.

In weak verbs the past tense and participle are marked by *-d(e)* or *-t(e).* After a long syllable the ending may be *-de,* as *herde, wende* (from *wenen* [think]), *cryde,* or it may be *-ed,* as *cleped, demed, payned, semed.* After a voiceless consonant it is normally *-te,* as *kepte, mette,* but this also occurs in other environments, such as *felte, mente, sente, wente* (from *wenden*). The participle normally has the same form as the past tense but without the final *-e,* though there are a few exceptions, such as *cryed.* Some weak verbs change the vowel of the stem in the past tense and participle. Most are like the forms in modern English, as *solde* from *sellen* and *taughte* from *techen,* but some have not survived, as *dreynte* from *drenchen, queynte* from *quenchen, straughte* from *strecchen, thoughte* from *thinken* (seem), as well as *thenken* (think). Personal endings of weak verbs in the past singular are *-e* in first and third person, and *-est* (like the present) in the second.

The past participle of both strong and weak verbs may optionally take the prefix *i- / y-.*

A verb exceptionally irregular, having features of both strong and weak conjugations, is *hoten,* past *highte,* which has both the active sense "promise" and the passive "be called," and abnormal forms such as *hatte* in 3 sg. present, *heet* in past sg.

Imperatives of both strong and weak verbs for the most part lack an ending in the singular, as *com, help, hoold, set, sey, tel.* Some imperatives of short-stemmed weak verbs are written with *-e,* but meter seldom shows it to have been pronounced: e.g., *make* (Tales I.3720, VIII.300, Tr 3.703, 5.913). Verbs having consonant clusters at the end of the stem need *-e,* as *herkne.* The plural imperative often has the ending *-eth* but may also take the same form as the singular; so we find *herkneth* but also *taak* in the same speech (Tales I.788–89).

A few verbs, surviving in modern English mostly as "modal" auxiliaries, such as *shall, will, can, may,* have past forms like weak verbs, but those of the present tense are patterned on the strong conjugations, except that the second person singular ends in *-st* as *canst, mayst, woost;* or *-t* in *shalt, wilt.* First and third persons are identical, as *can, may, shal, woot;* the plural has a different vowel, as *connen, mowen, shullen, witen,* but the singular forms are often used with plural subjects. The past tenses of these verbs are *coude* or *couthe, mighte, sholde, wiste.*

Other irregular verb forms are:

doon	pr. 2, 3 sg. *doost, dooth,* past *dide*
goon	pr. 2, 3 sg. *goost, gooth,* past supplied by *yede* or *wente*
been	pr. 1, 2, 3 sg. *am, art, is,* pl. *bee(n),* occasionally *are(n)*
	past 1, 3 sg. *was,* 2 sg. *were,* pl. *were(n);* subj. *were, were(n);* imper. *be, beeth;* past part. *(y)been*
wil or *wol*	pr. 1, 3 sg., 2 sg. *wilt, wolt,* pl. *wolle(n), wil,* past *wolde*
haven or *han*	pr. 1 sg. *have,* 2 *hast,* 3 *hath,* pl. *have(n), han,* past *had(de)*

Negative forms occur for parts of *been: nam, nart, nis, nas, nere(n);* of *haven: nath, nad(de);* of *wil: nil, nilt, nolde;* of *woot: noot, nost, niste.*

Some Features of Syntax and Idiom

NOUNS *Number* A noun denoting a material object or an attribute possessed separately by each individual of a group may have a singular form, where the later language would use the plural: *the colour in hir face* (their faces; Tales I.1637), *Thus shal mankynde drenche, and lese hir lyf* (I.3521); but the plural may also be used, as *han lost hir lyves* (III.1997). Some collective nouns are treated variously as singular or plural: *folk* usually has a plural verb, as in *Thanne longen folk* (Tales I.12), but occasionally has a singular, as *While folk is blent* (Tr 2.1743); *mankynde* is referred to by a plural pronoun in the passage just quoted, but usually has a singular verb, as in *Mankynde was lorn* (II.843).

Case Some genitive forms in *-es* are used as adjectives, notably *lyves* (living), in *lyves creature* (Tales I.2395, IV.903, Tr 3.13), *shames* (shameful), as *shames deeth* (Tales II.819, IV.2377). The same ending often appears in adverbial function, as in *algates* (at any rate), *nedes* (necessarily), *ones* (once), and in phrases comprising *thankes* and a

possessive pronoun, meaning "willingly," as *hir thankes* (Tales I.2114).

A noun that is the indirect object of a verb may be preceded by *to,* but may also be simply in the common form: *Men moote yeve silver* to *the povre freres* (Tales I.232), but *pynnes, for to yeven faire wyves* (I.234), and *swich lawe as a man yeveth another wight* (II.43).

When a noun in the genitive is qualified by a phrase, whether with *of* or in apposition, the word on which the genitive depends follows it immediately and the phrase comes after, as *the kyng Priamus sone of Troye* "King Priam of Troy's son" (Tr 1.2), *the Seintes Legende of Cupide* (the legend of the saints of Cupid; Tales II.61), *Seys body the kyng* (BD 142).

ADJECTIVES Most attributive adjectives normally precede the nouns they qualify but in verse they often follow: *his shoures soote* (Tales I.1), *hir fyngres smale* (IV.380), *deere maister soverayn* (VII.3347). Certain set phrases regularly have this order—*(the) blood roial* (Tales I.1018, 1546, II.657, VII.2151, etc.)—and so, even in prose, do some phrases containing more or less technical words of French origin: *the lyf perdurable* (Tales X.184), *the day vulgar* (Astr 2.9 rubric).

In predicative use, superlatives are sometimes reinforced by *oon: she was oon the faireste* (Tales V.734), *oon the beste knyght* (Tr 1.1081). The sense is "the very fairest," etc., differing from the later common partitive use "one of the fairest"—which has, however, intruded into a few places where the noun remains illogically singular, as in *oon of the gretteste auctour* (Tales VII.2984).

An adjective may function as a noun, not only in the plural, such as *the poor* in modern English, or *thise olde wyse* (VIII.1067), but also in the singular, as *the wyse it demeth* (Tr 1.644), *an impossible* (V.1009).

The demonstrative *this* is used idiomatically to draw attention to a character in a narrative, as *This gentil duc* (Tales I.952), sometimes by name, as *This Troilus* (Tr 1.268). It may more generally imply familiarity with, or understanding of, persons or things referred to: *Thise noble wyves and thise loveris* (Tales II.59).

ARTICLES The definite article is sometimes used with nouns of abstract reference, as *Th'experience so preveth* (Tales IV.2238), and with other words that seldom have it in the later language, e.g., *the deeth* (I.1716).

The indefinite article may be prefixed to a numeral to indicate an approximate figure: *Wel ny an eighte busshels* (VI.771).

PRONOUNS   In addressing a single person, the forms historically appropriate to the second person singular, *thow, thee, thy(n),* are often replaced by the plural *ye, yow, youre(s)* (and *ye* as subject takes a plural verb). This is a matter of social usage of some complexity, and a brief statement that would cover all occasions is hardly possible. It is approximately true that the plural forms imply greater formality and politeness; yet they can be used even in intimate conversation, or within a family, in cultivated society—in Book 3 of *Troilus and Criseyde,* they are the prevailing forms used by the lovers to each other: *And that ye me wolde han as faste in mynde / As I have yow* (3.1506–7), though Criseyde momentarily changes to *I am thyn* at the end of the stanza.

A personal pronoun in the object form is often used reflexively with verbs that in the later language are not reflexive: *She gan to rewe, and dredde hire wonder soore* (Tr 2.455), *softely yow pleye* (2.1729). It may also appear with an intransitive verb of motion: *he rideth hym ful right* (Tales I.1691), *She rist hire up* (Tr 2.812). A personal pronoun is occasionally used together with a proper name: *he Jakke Straw and his meynee* (Tales VII.3394), *Of hire Philologie and hym Mercurie* (IV.1734).

When *it* has an identifying function before the verb *be,* the form of the verb is determined by the complement: *it am I* (Tr 1.588), *it were gentilmen* (LGW 1506).

The pronouns *who* and *what,* which are mainly interrogative, also function as indefinites: *Bityde what bityde* (whatever may happen; Tales VII.874). They may imply an antecedent: *Who hath no wyf* (Tales I.3152), *who nede hath* (Tr 3.49). Especially when reinforced by *so,* the indefinite often suggests condition: *whoso wel the stories soghte* "if anyone were to investigate . . ." (Tales VI.488).

ADVERBS AND CONJUNCTIONS   *As* is used in a number of ways that were later largely or wholly lost. *As* may introduce an imperative: *As lene it me* (Tales I.3777). It begins many expressions of time: *as now* (I.2264), *As in his tyme* (VII.2498), *as for a certein tyme* (VII.977). It may intensify an adverb: *as swithe* (as quickly as possible; II.637). It may form a conjunction: *ther as I yow devyse* (I.34).

Ther often introduces a wish, blessing, or the like: *ther Mars his soule gye* (I.2815), *ther God his bones corse* (IV.1308).

Many conjunctions incorporate a redundant *that; Whan that* (I.1), *though that* (I.68), *if that* (I.144).

PREPOSITIONS   Some prepositions have, in addition to senses still current, others which are now obsolete. So for example:

After in *after hir degree* (according to their rank; Tales I.2573), *after oon* (alike; I.341).

At in *at ye* (plainly; I.3016), *at o word* (briefly; II.428), *at regard of* (in comparison with; PF 58).

By in *by the morwe* (in the morning; Tales I.334), *by wyves that been wyse* (about wives . . . ; III.229).

For, besides its common expression of cause or aim, may signify intention or purpose to avoid a certain result, as *For lesynge of richesse* (for fear of losing wealth; Tales VII.2560), *For faylyng* (so as not to fail; Tr 1.928), *For taryinge here* (so as not to delay here; PF 468). When followed by an adjective or past participle, *for* expresses reason, as if constructed with the corresponding noun: *for old* (with age; Tales I.2142), *For wery* (because of weariness; PF 93). This is shown to be the correct analysis of such phrases by the insertion of a qualifying word in *for pure ashamed* (out of very shame; Tr 2.656). *For* is often prefixed to an infinitive, as will be discussed in the section on mood below.

Of often signifies an agent: *I wolde nat of hym corrected be* (Tales III.661), *he was slayn . . . of Achilles* (VII.3148). It appears in numerous phrases, such as *of kynde* (by nature), *of newe* (newly), *of youre curteisye* (I.725), and is equivalent to *over* in *To have victorie of hem* (I.2246). It sometimes expresses a partitive of indefinite amount: *Of smale houndes* (some little dogs; I.146), *of youre wolle* (some of your wool; VI.910).

Out of is equivalent to *without* in *out of doute* (Tales I.487), *out of drede* in the same sense (Tr 1.775).

To indicates role or function in *to borwe* (as a pledge; Tales I.1622), *to wedde* in the same sense (I.1218).

Toward is sometimes divided, with the object between the parts: *To Rome-ward* (II.968), *To scoleward* (VII.549).

Up is equivalent to *upon* in *up peyne of* (on pain of; I.1707), *up peril of* (VII.2944).

Prepositions may follow the nouns or pronouns they govern: *al the fyr aboute* (Tales I.2952), *Rood hym agayns* (II.999), *take oure flessh us fro* (VII.2451), *seyde his maister to* (VIII.1449).

In a relative clause, a preposition governing the relative (whether expressed or not) is usually placed near to the verb rather than at the end of the clause: *That men of yelpe* (that men boast of; Tr 3.307), *Ther is another thing I take of hede* (there is another thing [that] I take heed of; I.577); but the preposition may also be put at the end, and in this position *in* has the form *inne: in what array that they were inne* (Tales I.41). In an infinitive phrase of purpose, a preposition defining the relation of an object to the infinitive is normally placed before the object: *to shorte with oure weye* (to shorten our journey with; I.791), *To saffron with my predicacioun* (to season my preaching with; VI.345); but it is placed finally in *it es to ben wondrid uppon* (Bo 4.pr1.23). An infinitive adjunct to an adjective or noun may be preceded by a preposition: *moore blisful on to see* (more delightful to look at; Tales I.3247), *a myrour in to prye* (Tr 2.404).

VERBS Many important functions are performed by "modal" auxiliaries (see pp. xxxvii–xxxviii above), which are often the same as in modern English but with some additions. Certain verbs that in the later language are only auxiliaries may be used as full verbs. *Conne,* for instance, is the infinitive of a verb meaning principally "to know," as in *his lessoun, that he wende konne* (his lesson which he thought he knew; Tr 3.83); its past tense is *coude,* as in *she koude of that art the olde daunce* (Tales I.476). It is also used in some idiomatic phrases such as *konne thank* (feel gratitude; Tr 2.1466). As an auxiliary, it is frequent in uses mostly resembling those still current, but is especially common in collocation with *may,* as in *as I kan and may* (VII.354). *Shal* has its ancient sense of "owe" in *by that feith I shal Priam of Troie* (Tr 3.791). In auxiliary use it often retains the sense of obligation, necessity, or destiny, as *He moot be deed, the kyng as shal a*

page (Tales I.3030), but also may indicate simple futurity in any person, as *I am agast ye shul it nat susteene* (IV.1760). The past *sholde* has a wide range of modal uses, many of which survive, but some are unfamiliar; e.g., *The time . . . Approcheth, that this weddyng sholde be* (the time . . . approaches when this wedding should take place; IV.260–61), *whan that I my lyf sholde forlete* (when I was about to lose my life; VII.658); *As though a storm sholde bresten every bough* (as though a storm were to break . . . ; I.1980). A comparatively rare usage is that of "uncertified report," in which a statement made by another person is repeated without commitment to its accuracy: *hym told is of a frend of his / How that ye sholden love oon hatte Horaste* (he has been told by a friend of his that you are said to be in love with a certain Horaste; Tr 3.796–97). An important concessive function is a special case of the construction (noted below in discussing the subjunctive) using the introductory adverb *al* and inversion of the verb and subject, as *al sholde I therfore sterve* (though I should die for it; Tr 1.17), *Al sholde hir children sterve* (Tales VI.451). *Wil / wol* and the past *wolde* are generally less complex in implication than *shal / sholde.* The sense of wish or desire is very often present to some degree, as *Whoso wol preye* (III.1879), *I wol nat do no labour* (VI.444), but sometimes no more than simple futurity, in any person, seems to be implied: *My tale I wol bigynne* (VI.462), *right as thou wolt desire* (III.1402). The notion of regular or customary action is added in *Mordre wol out, certeyn, it wol nat faille* (VII.576).

A frequent auxiliary that later fell out of use is *ginne,* especially its past *gan* (plural *gonne*). These form periphrastic tenses of present and past, respectively, in a way comparable to the mainly later use of parts of *do: myn herte gynneth blede* (my heart bleeds; Tr 4.12), *upon hir knes she gan to falle* (she fell on her knees; Tales IV.292). Chaucer rarely uses *do / did* as an auxiliary, as in *why do ye wepe,* and *Is ther no morsel breed that ye do kepe?* (VII.2432, 2434), and probably *Nicholas . . . dooth ful softe unto his chambre carie* (I.3409–10). In other functions *do* is very frequent, both in uses which still survive, and in some now obsolete, notably as a causative followed by an infinitive: *If that ye don us bothe dyen* (Tr 2.327), *he dide doon sleen hem* (he had them killed; Tales III.2042). An auxiliary now obsolete in the present is *mo(o)t,* which has the two almost contrary senses "may" and "must": *Also moote I thee* (as I may prosper; VII.817), *A man moot nedes love* (a man must of necessity love; I.1169). The past tense *moste* expresses past time as in *it moste ben* (it had to be done; Tr 4.216), but is also used modally with reference to present time, like its descendant, modern *must: We moste endure it* (Tales I.1091). Another obsolete auxiliary is *thar* (need), a third person form usually constructed with a pronoun in the objective case, as *what thar thee recche* (why need you care; III.329). Its past subjunctive appears in *Yow thurste nevere han the more fere* (you would not need to feel any greater fear; Tr 3.572).

Such so-called impersonal constructions are found with some other modal verbs, as *Us moste* (we must; Tales VIII.946), *as hire oughte* (as was right for her; Tr 3.581). They are frequent also with a number of other verbs, sometimes with the subject pronoun *it*, as *Me thynketh it* (it seems to me; Tales I.37), *it reweth me* (I regret it; VII.3097), and sometimes without, as *if yow liketh* (if it pleases you; I.777), *hire liste nat* (she had no wish; II.1048), *Hym deigned nat* (he did not deign; VII.3181), *if that yow remembre* (Tr 4.73).

Tense "Expanded" or "progressive" forms of present and past tenses (those made up of a part of the verb *be* and a present participle) are infrequent in comparison with the later language: *My newe wyf is comynge* (Tales IV.805), *As Canacee was pleyyng in hir walk* (V.410), *We han ben waitynge* (I.929). Simple forms are used in such places as *Ye goon to Caunterbury* (you are going . . . ; I.769), *I dye* (Tr 1.420), *Wher as this lady romed to and fro* (Tales I.1113), *Jankyn . . . Redde on his book, as he sat by the fire* (III.713–14). A simple past, rather than a construction with *have*, is used in expressions like *A fairer saugh I nevere* (I have never seen anyone more beautiful; IV.1033). The perfect and pluperfect of intransitive verbs are commonly formed with the verb *be* rather than *have: The constable . . . doun is fare* (II.512), *been they kist* (II.1074), *be they went* (IV.1701), *At nyght was come* (I.23).

A characteristic feature of Chaucer's narrative style is the use of present forms to refer to past time, often with parallel past forms closely following: *She walketh up and doun . . . And as an aungel hevenysshly she soong* (I.1052–55), *He taketh his leve, and she astoned stood* (V.1339).

Future time is expressed mainly by the auxiliaries *shal* and *wil*, the use of which in particular persons is not strictly defined, as has already been pointed out above.

Mood Infinitives may be used in their "plain" form or with a preceding particle *to* or the group *for to*. *To* and *for to* are often simple alternatives without distinction of meaning, even in adjacent phrases, as *Thanne longen folk to goon on pilgrimages, / And palmeres for to seken straunge strondes* (I.12–13). The plain infinitive occurs principally after auxiliary verbs such as *can, may, shal, wil*, as in modern English. (It sometimes occurs also after *oghte*, as in I.660.) The plain infinitive often serves as a complement to verbs of motion, especially with some sense of purpose: *Come soupen in his hous* (Tr 3.560), *go we dyne* (Tales VII.223). It also often follows certain verbs used without personal subject, as *if yow liketh knowen* (Tr 5.1366), *hym liste ride so* (Tales I.102). It is frequent (as it is later) with a noun or pronoun object of verbs of perception and of volition: *Bidde hym descende* (V.321), *they herde a belle clynke* (VI.664). Occasionally, it may depend on an adjective, as *wont art oft upbreyde* (Tr 5.1710), and it may be the subject of an impersonal expression where modern English would use *for: it is good a man been at his large* (Tales I.2288). It is regular after *leten* with an object, both in the primary sense "allow," as *lat my body go* (III.1061), and as a means of forming the equivalent of an imperative of the first or third person—*lat us turne agayn* (II.170), *Lat no man truste* (VII.1997). With *do(o)n* and *leten* in causative function the infinitive often has a passive sense, as if a noun denoting an agent were to be understood: *To pieces do me drawe* (cause [someone] to pull me to pieces, so, have me pulled . . . ; Tr 1.833). *Lat see* is especially frequent as a set phrase "let it be seen, let us see." *Leten* is sometimes followed by the infinitive *doon*, as well as another infinitive, in a phrase of this kind: *Lat do hym calle* (have him summoned; Tales VI.173).

The infinitive with *(for) to* has a wider range of use, largely in the same functions as the modern infinitive with *to*. Thus for example, it may express purpose as in *for to seke* (Tales I.17), *for to tellen* (I.73), *for to doon* (I.78), *To make his Englissh sweete* (I.265), *sooth to seyn* (I.284). It may depend on an adjective, as in *an esy man to yeve penaunce* (I.223), *so worldly for to have office* (I.292). It may function as the subject of an impersonal expression: *Now were it tyme a lady to gon henne* (Tr 3.630). In some phrases the infinitive has a passive sense: *to blame* (Tales I.3710), *to preyse* (VI.42), *to drede* (VII.3063), *for to chese* (Tr 2.470). This is related to the use of the inherited "inflected infinitive" in *ye woot what is to doone* (what is to be done; Tales III.2194). A concessive use of the *for to* infinitive appears in places like *for to dyen in the peyne* (though we were to die under torture; I.1133), *For to be deed* (even if I were to die; IV.364). In sentences expressing the terms of an agreement the infinitive often accompanies a nominative pronoun: *And ye, my lord, to doon right as yow leste* (IV.105).

The subjunctive in main clauses may express wish, as *God yelde yow* (may God reward you; Tales III.2177), an imperative of the first person plural, as *go we se* (Tr 2.615), and concession, as *Bityde what bityde* (Tales VII.874), *Be as be may* (VII.2129). It is used in the apodosis (main clause) of a hypothetical conditional sentence: *A clerk hadde litherly biset his whyle* (a scholar would have wasted his time; I.3299). In dependent clauses it is largely concerned with condition or hypothesis, as *if gold ruste* (I.500), *if thou telle it* (I.3505), and especially in the frequent tag *if so be / were,* with a subordinate clause also using a subjunctive: *if so be that thou my lady wynne* (I.1617). It extends naturally to the negative condition in clauses introduced by *but if* (unless)—*Who may been a fool but if he love?* (I.1799), and the unfulfilled condition expressed by the past subjunctive *nere* (were [it] not), as *Nere myn extorcioun* (if it were not for my extortion; III.1439). Inversion of verb and subject, as in this example, often expresses condition: *Had thou nat toold* (VII.2053), *konne he letterure or konne he noon* (VIII.846). The subjunctive is further used in hypothetical comparison, for instance, *As though he stongen were* (as though he had been stabbed; I.1079); it may express purpose, as *Lest thee repente* (III.2088); and anticipation of a future event, as *er that thou go henne* (I.2356), *til that it dye* (III.1145). It implies the uncertainty of information in *Where that he be I kan nat soothly seyn* (I.3670), and the unwillingness of a speaker to vouch for a report in *I trowe that he be went* (I.3665), though it is likely that in such dependent clauses the use of the subjunctive was at least to some extent conventional. Another principal function of the subjunctive is to mark concession, which may be expressed by the conjunction *though* (that), as *Thogh thou heere walke* (II.784), or by the introductory adverb *al*

with inversion of verb and subject, as *Al speke he never so rudeliche* (I.734), *Al were he short* (III.624), or in other ways such as *hou soore that me smerte* (I.1394), *wher-so she wepe or synge* (II.294). In all these the verb is usually subjunctive, but not invariably: e.g., *Though in this toun is noon apothecarie* (VII.2948), *what so any womman seith* (VII.2912).

Negation   The primary negative adverb is *ne,* placed before the verb (or incorporated in it in those contracted forms noted above in the description of verb forms, p. xxxviii), which is sufficient to mark a sentence as negative: *she ne wiste what it signyfied* (I.2343), *I noot how men hym calle* (I.284). It is very often reinforced by another negative, most frequently *nat* or *nought: he ne lefte nat* (I.492), *Ne studieth noght* (I.841). *Nat* or *nought* alone, following the verb, may also suffice, as in *His arwes drouped noght* (I.107), *It is nat honest; it may nat avaunce* (I.246); exceptionally, it precedes the finite verb, as in *Nat greveth us youre glorie* (I.917), *Ye felen wel youreself that I nought lye* (Tr 2.1283). Sometimes a series of words in a passage, pronouns as well as adverbs, may all be given negative forms: *He nevere yet no vileynye ne sayde / . . . unto no maner wight* (Tales I.70–71).

Interrogation   A positive sentence is normally converted into a question by inversion of verb and subject: *Wostow that wel?* (Tr 1.775), *se ye nought?* (2.1465). When the question concerns two alternatives, the interrogative may be intensified by beginning the sentence with the pronoun *whether,* as *Wheither seistow this in ernest or in pley?* (Tales I.1125). After interrogative words such as *why,* or *what* as object, inversion is also normal: *Why cridestow?* (I.1083), *What do ye?* (I.3437), *how thynke ye?* (III.2204).

Versification

Verse in English in the fourteenth century was composed in two different traditions, which were usually kept distinct, though some authors combined them in the same work. One system, which evolved from Old English and the general Germanic tradition, depended on the pattern of stressed syllables in each line of verse, linked by alliteration of initial sounds; normally lines did not rhyme together. The other, which in England began in the twelfth century and was imitated from French and Latin models, depended partly on the number of syllables in each line and partly on the linking of lines in couplets or groups by rhyming final sounds. Before the fourteenth century, by far the most frequently used of the second type was a line that in principle contained eight syllables, but might in practice vary between seven and ten, arranged in rhyming couplets. This form as used by French writers regularly had eight or nine syllables, and the syllable count determined the line. Syllable stress is more prominent in English than in French, and when this form was imitated in English syllables bearing stress usually alternated with syllables of less weight, so that the line was characterized by four stresses, or beats. The number of unstressed syllables was less restricted than in French, probably owing to the influence of the native type of line. This form was used in many English poems, some long and important, from the early thirteenth century onward, so it was obviously well known long before Chaucer began to write.

In spite of a good deal of irregularity of rhythm in the texts as preserved in the manuscripts, there is no reason to doubt that this familiar type of verse was what Chaucer intended to write in his early poems *The Book of the Duchess* and *The House of Fame.* (Four-stress lines also form part of the "tail-rhyme" stanzas of the Tale of Sir Thopas.) It has, of course, remained popular to this day. In his other poetry, however, Chaucer used a longer line, containing five stresses, or beats, which before his time had appeared only rarely, in a few anonymous poems. It is likely that this form was suggested by the decasyllabic line often used in French, especially arranged in groups to form stanzas, but in part also by the eleven-syllable line used in Italian verse, which is of similar length but freer in rhythm. Chaucer took up the five-stress line early in his writing career, in the eight-line stanza of the ABC (a French form), and used it again in The Monk's Tale. He used the same kind of line in seven-line stanzas (later called "rime royal") in *The Parliament of Fowls, Troilus and Criseyde,* and the tales told by the Man of Law, the Clerk, the Prioress, and the Second Nun, as well as in much of *Anelida and Arcite* and some minor poems. His greatest contribution to the technique of English verse was the arrangement of this five-stress line in rhyming couplets, which he adopted in *The Legend of*

Good Women and most of *The Canterbury Tales.* No earlier model for this has been found; it may well have been his own extension to the five-stress form of the pattern so familiar with the shorter line.

Chaucer wrote rhymed verse in all his poetical works. He clearly knew the alliterative form (see the Parson's comment in Tales X.42–44), and exploited features of it in a few passages (such as I.2605–16), but the alliterative form is never essential to the structure of his verse. His rhymes are in general careful, matching sounds that must have corresponded exactly in the type of English he wrote. In some words, or groups of words, he took advantage of the existence of alternative pronunciations (much as a modern versifier may rhyme *again* either with *main* or with *men*). Thus the verb *die* often appears as *dye,* rhyming with such words as *folye* (e.g., I.1797–98), but sometimes as *deye,* rhyming with words like *weye* (e.g., I.3033–34); the verb *liste* (please) often rhymes with such words as *wiste* (e.g., Tr 1.678–79), but its variant *leste,* a pronunciation characteristic of the southeast of England, rhymes with such words as *beste* (e.g., Tr 1.1028–29). Choice among optional variants such as these is one aspect of the flexibility of Chaucer's use of language.

The most significant difference between Chaucer's verse and that of later centuries lies in the greater number of light syllables required or permitted by the inflectional system of his language, described above. Some of these inflected forms are comparatively familiar because related forms survive in particular circumstances in the modern language; for instance, participial forms such as *aged* and *learned,* when used as adjectives, are pronounced as two syllables. In the fourteenth century the ending *-ed* was pronounced as a separate syllable in other participial functions as well, for example, in *perced* and *bathed* (Tales I.2, 3). Other instances are unfamiliar to a modern reader because the sound is no longer pronounced. These are final unstressed syllables consisting of the neutral vowel written *e* (see p. xxxiii above). This vowel may function as a grammatical inflection (indicating, for example, case, number, mood, or tense) or it may be an integral part of a word—thus in *the yonge sonne* (Tales I.7) the *e* of *yonge* is the mark of the definite form of the adjective, but that of *sonne* had been part of the word already in its Old English form *sunne.* Pronunciation of these endings is, for the most part, necessary to the rhythm of the lines, and Chaucer, in addition, nearly always avoids rhyming words ending in *e* with others in which it would not be etymologically or grammatically in place. A telling example is found in Tr 5.260–64: since the structure of the seven-line stanza requires that the rhyme of the first and third lines should contrast with that of the second, fourth, and fifth, Chaucer uses the rhyme of *-ly* in the adverbs *pitously* and *myghtyly* against *-ie* in the French-derived nouns *fantasie* and *folie* and the (English) infinitive *drye* to achieve the necessary effect. Another indication that these final vowels were sounded appears in such rhymes as *Rome: to me* (Tales I.671–72), where the *to* must be stressed and *Rome* must have two syllables. But though the final vowel was evidently generally pronounced, there are many exceptions within the line. In particular, when a final *-e* is followed by a word beginning with a vowel or with an *h-* that is either silent (as in French words like *honour*) or in weak stress (as often in such words as *he, his, hem, hire*), it is normally elided. Thus in *So hoote he lovede* (Tales I.97), the *-e* of the adverb *hoote*, grammatically correct, is not pronounced before *he*. The *-e* is also silent in many short unstressed words such as *hadde, hire, oure,* and it is sometimes slurred in polysyllables such as *mesurable* (I.435), *benefice* (I.507). Unstressed vowels next to certain consonants within words may also be slurred, so that *hevene* (I.519) has two syllables, *never* (I.734) has one.

A regular line of the longer form contains five stresses, which may vary a good deal in strength according to the sense, and indeed often be potential rather than essential to a natural reading. Usually a light syllable precedes each of the stressed syllables. In

Bifíl that ín that séson ón a dáy,
In Sóuthwerk át the Tábard ás I láy (I.19–20)

a normal reading gives a regular rhythm. But the order of stressed and light syllables is often reversed, as in the next line,

Rédy to wénden ón my pílgrymáge (I.21)

and, more notably, there is sometimes no initial light syllable at all, and the line may be called "headless."

Twénty bóokes, clád in blák or réed (I.294)

A small number of lines lack a light syllable after the second stressed syllable, giving a "broken-backed" effect which some fifteenth-century poets, especially Lydgate, much favored, so that

the line may be called "Lydgatian":

Hire grétteste óoth wás but bý Seinte Lóy (I.120)

On the other hand, there are sometimes more light syllables (mostly only one) than regular rhythm requires. A light syllable may precede a natural pause.

For hé was láte ycóme from hís viáge (I.77)

That nó drópe ne fílle upón hire brést (I.131)

And fórth we ríden a lítel móore than páas (I.825)

But in numerous lines it clearly does not do so:

Of cóurt, and to béen estátlich óf manére (I.140)

Men móote yeve sílver tó the póvre fréres (I.232)

With a thrédbare cópe, as ís a póvre scolér (I.260)

Pékke hem up ríght as they grówe and éte hem ýn
(VII.2967)

(Chaucer did not divide his lines by a regular caesura after a set number of syllables.)

The same features appear in the poems in the four-stress line, and through them and other means Chaucer gave his verse great freedom and variety of movement. To illustrate using a characteristic passage, the following extract from the General Prologue (I.285–308) is marked to show metrical stresses and the probable treatment of unstressed syllables. Stressed syllables are marked by accents, but the degree of stress must, of course, have varied with individual readers. Unstressed *-e* pronounced in final syllables has a dieresis (¨); when it is elided or slurred, it is underdotted (ẹ).

A Clérk ther wás of Óxenfórd alsó,
That únto lógyk háddë lónge ygó.
As léene wás his hórs as ís a ráke,
And hé nas nát right fát, I úndertáke,
But lóoked hólwe, and thérto sóbrelý.
Ful thrédbare wás his óvereste cóurtepý,
For hé hadde géten hym yét no bénefíce,
Ne wás so wórldly fór to háve offíce.
For hým was lévere háve at his béddes héed
Twénty bóokes, clád in blák or réed,
Of Áristótle and hís philósophíe,
Than róbes riche, or fíthele, or gáy sautríe.
But ál be thát he wás a phílosóphre,
Yet hádde hé but lítel góld in cófre;
But ál that hé mýght of his fréendes hénte,
On bóokes ánd on lérnynge hé it spénte,
And bísily gán for the sóules préye
Of hém that yáf hym whérwith tó scoléye.
Of stúdie tóok he móost cúre and móost héede.
Noght ó word spák he móore thán was néede,

And thát was séyd in fórmę and réverénce,
And shórt and qúyk and fúl of hý senténce.
Sównynge in móral vértu wás his spéchë,
And gládly wóldę he lérne and gládly téchë.

NORMAN DAVIS

THE TEXTS

The texts in this volume, with the exception of *The Canterbury Tales,* have been reedited on the basis of a fresh examination of the textual evidence by direct consultation of the authorities, including both manuscripts and early prints, though most often by means of facsimiles and microfilms. These texts are thus at once revisions of Robinson's texts and new editions in their own right. Robinson's text was used as the base; that is, in most cases the editors use the same base manuscripts as Robinson chose and adopt his spellings, but each of his editorial decisions was reconsidered in the light of the evidence. His textual judgments were treated with respect, but there are a good many changes; ideas about editing Middle English have developed considerably since Robinson's first edition appeared in 1933, and the work of scholars and editors in the intervening years has greatly advanced our knowledge of Chaucer's texts. Most important, Robinson did not have direct access to many of the authorities; for the poetic works he was largely dependent on the Chaucer Society's transcriptions, and for the *Boece* and *Astrolabe* he was not able to take account of all the authorities. That his texts emerge from revision with relatively few changes is a tribute to his sound editorial judgment.

The degree of change from Robinson's edition naturally varies from text to text. The text of *The Canterbury Tales* shows relatively few changes, and it must be noted that this is not a new edition in the same sense as are the other texts in this volume. Only a few authorities were consulted directly and those few only on occasion. The editors, initially Robert A. Pratt and later Ralph Hanna III, in consultation with the General Editor, depended instead on work for Pratt's edition, *The Tales of Canterbury,* and on the materials contained in Manly and Rickert's *Text of the Canterbury Tales* (1941). The text presented here is in effect, therefore, a revision of Robinson's work, with errors corrected and relatively few new readings introduced. The appearance of Manly and Rickert's edition, which provided the full collations that he had lacked in editing the text for the 1933 edition, induced Robinson to reconsider his text of the *Tales;* his 1957 edition contained over 160 changed readings. That there were not more shows that Robinson was not convinced by Manly and Rickert's theory that the Ellesmere is an "edited" manuscript whose scribe (or "editor") frequently "corrected" the meter. That theory has now been refuted by George Kane in his essay on the Manly-Rickert edition, which appears in *Editing Chaucer* (ed. Paul G. Ruggiers, 1985). The text printed here represents about the same degree of revision; when Ellesmere stands alone, its readings have been considered with somewhat more skepticism than Robinson showed in 1957, and even more skepticism entered the consideration of those cases where Robinson chose a metrically smoother line from later manuscripts against the testimony of both Ellesmere and Hengwrt. But in those cases where it seemed to the editors that the choice between alternate readings was doubtful, Robinson's decisions were usually accepted. The text of the *Tales* therefore contains no radical departures from Robinson's 1957 edition, though it has been thoroughly revised.

For *The Book of the Duchess, The House of Fame, Anelida and Arcite,* and many of the minor poems, Robinson (like most editors) used the Fairfax manuscript as his base text, and the present editors do the same. This is a late manuscript, compared with Ellesmere or Hengwrt, and it is one of but four authorities for *The Book of the Duchess* and five for *The House of Fame,* all of which are late and, as Robinson noted, "agree in readings unsatisfactory in sense and meter." Earlier editors had therefore freely emended these texts. Robinson was more conservative than his predecessors, and his emendations were for the most part carefully considered. Larry Benson's edition of *The Book of the Duchess* and John Fyler's edition of *The House of Fame* do not greatly differ from Robinson's texts. Many of his emendations have been allowed to stand, though in many other cases the editors have replaced the emendation with the reading attested by the manuscripts, with the result that in a few places the text reads less smoothly than Robinson's. Most of these involve "grammatical forms apocopated in the manuscripts"—final *-e* and *-n*— which Robinson often silently restored.

In those cases where the meter is affected, these restorations have been reconsidered with special care, and where allowed to stand, notice is taken and the manuscript forms are listed in the Textual Notes.

Much of what has been said in the preceding paragraph applies to Vincent DiMarco's edition of *Anelida and Arcite* and to R. T. Lenaghan's edition of the Short Poems, though the textual situation is much more complex in many of these works. Robinson chose the Fairfax manuscript as the basis for the *Anelida,* as does DiMarco, but Robinson frequently rejected the readings of Fairfax in favor of those attested by the other authorities. DiMarco has done the same, and a number of new readings are the result. The Fairfax manuscript is likewise chosen as the base for a number of the short poems, while for the rest the base manuscripts were equally late. Robinson therefore frequently adjusted the language to the norm established in his edition of the *Tales.* Lenaghan has reassessed the textual evidence and in some cases restored the manuscript readings and spellings, though, as in the *Anelida,* changes are relatively few.

For *The Parliament of Fowls* and *The Legend of Good Women,* Robinson used as his base Cambridge MS Gg.4.27, which he recognized was heavily emended by its scribe. (M. B. Parkes and Richard Beadle provide an excellent discussion of this scribe's practices in their commentary accompanying the facsimile edition of Gg.) Gg, for all its peculiarities, is the earliest manuscript, and it contains the only complete version of the roundel in lines 680–92 (though added in another hand). All editors since Skeat (who based his text on Fairfax) have therefore chosen it as their base. Robert A. Pratt, who supplied the editor, Vincent DiMarco, with much of the materials for this edition of the *Parliament,* was even more suspicious of Gg than Robinson was, and in effect he rejected it as the base manuscript. Since Robinson was used as the copy text, however, Gg remains technically the base, though its unique readings were considered with more skepticism than Robinson displayed. Some of these readings—a dozen or so—are undoubtedly genuine, and they have been retained, though fewer appear here than in Robinson's text. A. S. G. Edwards and M. C. E. Shaner, editors of *The Legend of Good Women,* likewise treated Gg with skepticism, though here again its witness is of mixed value; it is the

earliest of the manuscripts, it contains the only copy of the revised version of the Prologue to *The Legend of Good Women,* and some of its unique readings are undoubtedly genuine. A number of unique readings that Robinson accepted are here rejected, and these account for most of the differences between this edition of the *Legend* and Robinson's. Yet changes in the text are relatively few.

The edition of *Boece* by Ralph Hanna III and Traugott Lawler differs from Robinson's for a different reason. As noted above, Robinson—like all editors before these recent years of easy travel and freely available microfilms, photographic reproductions, and good facsimiles—was often not able to consult the authorities directly. He was largely dependent on the evidence provided by transcriptions, textual studies, and previous editions. In the case of *Boece,* he had access to the Chaucer Society transcriptions of Cambridge University Library Ii.iii.21 (C^2), British Library Add. 10340 (A^1), and Cambridge University Library Ii.i.38 (C^1), his base, as well as to the editions of Thynne (in photographic facsimile) and Caxton, if only in the collations in Kellner's edition, and to the variants in Liddell's Globe edition. Hanna and Lawler's edition is the first to be based on a collation of all known authorities.

Stephen A. Barney's edition of *Troilus and Criseyde* also contains more changes than many of the other texts, since again Robinson did not have direct access to all the authorities. He depended on the variants recorded in Root's edition and on the transcriptions published by the Chaucer Society, including that of his base manuscript, Corpus Christi College, Cambridge, MS 61, which contains occasional errors that influenced his text. Fresh transcriptions of all the manuscripts were made by Sister Margaret Jennings and Dr. Ardath McKee, and Robert A. Pratt began the work of editing. The task was handed over to Barney, who had access to photographic and microfilm reproductions of all the authorities as well as the new transcriptions. As Barney explains in the introduction to the textual notes to *Troilus,* one of the main problems here was the question of whether Root, following McCormick, was right in his theory that the surviving manuscripts represent two or three stages of composition and revision; recent studies have confirmed Robinson's belief that the extensive changes Root regarded as authorial revisions are "rather scribal than authoritative." The text therefore does not contain the extensive changes an acceptance of the McCormick-Root theory would have entailed, but the fresh collation of all authorities has led to a good many minor changes, and this is, though based on Robinson, a new edition of the poem.

The case of *A Treatise on the Astrolabe* is similar to that of *Boece*. Robinson did not have access to all the manuscripts, and John Reidy's edition is the first to take account of the evidence of all known authorities. Reidy's collation of the manuscripts confirmed Robinson's choice of Bodleian Library MS Bodley 619 as the basis of the edition, and the text printed here therefore is in appearance very close to Robinson's, though it incorporates a number of important changes and therefore differs from Robinson's text more greatly than many of the other texts in this volume.

The text of *The Romaunt of the Rose* differs more radically from Robinson's than any of the others. The *Romaunt* survives in only one manuscript—Hunterian Museum, Glasgow, MS V.3.7—and in Thynne's printed edition of 1532. Robinson, like all previous editors, regarded Thynne's edition as an authority equal to the one surviving manuscript. Since Thynne supplies a number of lines missing in the manuscript, its version has seemed to some superior to the manuscript, and the most recent editor of the *Romaunt* used Thynne's edition as his base. Robinson used the manuscript as his, but he freely drew on Thynne's readings. It is now known that Thynne used that one manuscript as the copy-text for his edition and that many of the changes he introduced were editorial rather than evidence for another manuscript authority. Alfred David's edition of the *Romaunt* is the first ever to take account of this fact, and it therefore differs significantly from that of Robinson and those of all previous editors.

Robinson's spellings have been retained throughout, with occasional corrections, but with no attempt to make them completely consistent. In the *Tales, Troilus, Boece,* and the *Astrolabe,* Robinson used the spelling of his base manuscripts (with some changes). In the other works, where his manuscripts were late (such as those based on Fairfax) or contained many unusual spellings (such as Gg), he often changed the spellings to conform to what he regarded as the norm established by the early manuscripts. When such changes affect the meter or sense, they are regarded as emendations and are discussed in the Textual Notes.

Since the spelling of the texts printed here is largely the same as that in Robinson, the most obvious and pervasive difference between these texts and Robinson's is in the punctuation. The punctuation of the manuscripts, though sometimes of great interest, is not authorial and is finally of little help to the editor of an edition such as this, intended to be accessible to students and general readers. In punctuating his texts, Robinson employed a set of conventions that no longer obtain: his punctuation was very heavy, combining dashes with commas or semicolons, using exclamation points within sentences, and employing semicolons where modern usage calls for commas and commas where writers today would ordinarily omit them. For many readers such punctuation detracts rather than helps, and the texts have therefore been repunctuated in a style more nearly in accord with modern usage. Middle English differs from Modern English in ways that make it impossible to use a completely modern style of punctuation—independent clauses, for example, do not always require an express subject—and works intended for oral recitation naturally differ from those intended solely for reading. The editors have endeavored to provide a punctuation that is as close as possible to contemporary usage but that takes account of the nature of the texts.

The foregoing is intended only as a general description of the differences between the texts in this edition and those in Robinson. The Textual Notes in the Appendix contain full discussions of the problems of establishing the texts.

LARRY D. BENSON

THE RIVERSIDE
CHAUCER

THE
CANTERBURY
TALES

THE CANTERBURY TALES contains a wide variety of subjects and literary genres, from racy fabliaux to sober tales of Christian suffering, in accents that range from the elegant opening sentence of the General Prologue to the thumping doggerel of Sir Thopas and the solemn prose of the Parson. The whole is lent coherence and verisimilitude by a framing narrative: a pilgrimage provides the occasion for gathering a broadly diverse group of characters to tell a series of tales intercalated with narrative links, in which the pilgrims argue, interrupt one another, or comment on the tales that have been told as they move through the fourteenth-century countryside to their common goal.

It is not known exactly when Chaucer began the *Tales.* The pilgrimage is traditionally dated 1387, but that date is based on a number of doubtful assumptions—that The Man of Law's Tale is told on the second day, that the pilgrimage could not have taken place in Holy Week, and, most important, that Chaucer must have had some specific year in mind. The composition of the *Tales* extended over a considerable length of time, and perhaps the idea of the *Tales* evolved rather than originated at a specific moment. Some of the tales—certainly the Knight's, the Second Nun's, probably the Monk's, and perhaps others—were in existence in some form before Chaucer conceived the idea of *The Canterbury Tales.* They show that he had been interested in short narrative for some time, and The Monk's Tale and *The Legend of Good Women* show a further interest in composing a collection of short narratives. Sometime in the late 1380s he hit upon the idea of a pilgrimage to Canterbury as a framework for his collection.

The use of a narrative framework for a collection of tales was as ancient as *The Thousand and One Nights* and as contemporary as the *Confessio amantis,* on which Chaucer's friend John Gower

was still working (it was completed, in its first form, in 1390). Chaucer doubtless knew Gower's work, as well as other collections such as *The Seven Sages of Rome,* but by far the most suggestive analogue to *The Canterbury Tales* is Boccaccio's *Decameron.*

There is no proof that Chaucer knew the *Decameron.* He never quotes it, and though he and Boccaccio narrate a number of similar tales, in no case has it been clearly demonstrated that Chaucer drew directly on Boccaccio's version. Yet Chaucer must have at least heard of the most famous prose work of his favorite Italian poet, even if he did not have a chance to read it or to acquire a copy of his own, and he most likely did receive from the *Decameron,* however indirectly, some suggestion that helped shape his own narrative framework.

If so, it was only a suggestion, for Chaucer's work differs greatly from Boccaccio's. In the *Decameron,* ten elegant young ladies and gentlemen, accompanied by their servants, journey from villa to villa through the countryside around Florence to avoid the plague then raging in the city. They amuse themselves by telling tales. Each in turn serves as leader for a day and sets the subject for that day's tales. After two weeks' sojourn and ten days of storytelling (Fridays and Saturdays being devoted to preparations for religious observance and other activities), exactly one hundred tales (ten *decades,* hence the title) have been told, and the party returns to Florence.

The resemblances between the *Tales* and the *Decameron* are obvious. Boccaccio, like Chaucer, uses a journey as the occasion for a collection of tales ostensibly told by the travelers (though the tales are told at the villas in which they stay, rather than on the road). The tales vary in tone and attitude, but the device of the leader's setting a common subject provides for their unity and lends each day's tales something of the nature of a debate, like those that develop in Chaucer's work. Boccaccio's tellers, however, are all young aristocrats of the same age and social status, and though they are to some extent individualized, they form a homogeneous group of equals. Their servants provide comic interludes in the framing narrative, but none tells a tale; in the *Decameron,* telling tales is an elegant and well-ordered aristocratic pastime.

That may have been what Harry Bailly, the Host of the Tabard Inn, had in mind when he proposed the storytelling competition and appointed himself leader. Chaucer's pilgrims, however, represent a wide range of social levels, ages, and occupations, and they are apparently gathered not by prior agreement but by mere chance. They have little in common except the goal of their pilgrimage, and the comic disputes that Boccaccio had restricted to the servants in Chaucer break out among the tellers themselves. Despite the Host's attempts to control the situation, the storytelling seems often to develop of its own volition as the pilgrims squabble, interrupt one another, and tell tales that the author would prefer not to relate but that must be told, he helplessly protests, if he is to give a true report of what was actually said and done.

The Canterbury Tales has the air of actuality because it is based on actuality. A pilgrimage was one of the few occasions in medieval life when so diverse a group of people might have gathered on a basis of temporary equality and might have told tales to pass the time on their journey. Chaucer had no literary precedent for this (Sercambi's *Novelle,* once regarded as a possible model, was probably not written until after Chaucer's death), and the journey to Canterbury gains much of its realistic tone from the fact that it was modeled on life.

This is not to say that Chaucer attempts to represent an actual Canterbury pilgrimage. Since the pilgrims are on their way to give thanks for help "whan that they were seeke," we expect some of the jollity that the Wife of Bath associates with religious festivals and relatively little of those penitential aspects of pilgrimage of which the Parson later reminds us. Yet most of these characters seem pure holiday merrymakers. None goes "naked in pilgrimages, or barefoot" (ParsT X.105), and even the Parson rides, lean though his nag may be. We are never told that the pilgrims attend Mass, even on the morning of their departure (in contrast to Boccaccio's characters, who scrupulously attend to their reli-

gious duties, though they are not on a pilgrimage), nor that they take any notice of the famous shrines and relics along the way—the miraculous cross at Rochester or St. Thomas's shoe at Boughton under Blee, which pilgrims customarily stopped to kiss. And they are an unlikely set of pilgrims, including not only those, like the Monk, who probably should not have been on a pilgrimage, but a good many rascals who probably would not have wanted to be on such a journey. Chaucer, in short, does not describe a real pilgrimage; rather, he uses the idea of the journey as a likely occasion and as a metaphor for the world, in which "we been pilgrymes, passynge to and fro" (KnT I.2848). In the manner of the best late medieval art, he presents his metaphor with such a palpably concrete representation of actuality that it seems to come alive.

Much of this lifelike quality is due to Chaucer's eye for authenticating detail and his ear for the rhythms of colloquial speech, but, even more, it is the product of his dramatic method. Chaucer pretends merely to report what he sees and hears; he is content to let his characters speak for themselves, and when he does tell a tale in his own person, he does so as their equal, merely another teller.

Moreover, in many cases the tales are so suited to their tellers that they seem like dramatic soliloquies, further revelations of the characters we first encounter in the General Prologue, though the tales are sometimes unexpected and never completely predictable. The portrait in the General Prologue, the speeches and actions of the character in the links, and the tale he or she tells are, in many cases, all of a piece and cannot be fully understood in isolation from one another.

This celebrated dramatic principle extends to the larger structure of the work, in the creation of a dramatic interplay between the tales. Some, such as the tales of the Friar and the Summoner, function as parts of arguments that develop between the pilgrims. Others, such as those of the Wife of Bath, the Clerk, the Merchant, and the Franklin, are parts of continuing debates between the pilgrims, with each using his or her tale to express his or her viewpoint on a common theme or problem. Still others, such as those of the Second Nun and Canon's Yeoman, are related in more subtle ways, and the recurrence of common themes and subjects throughout the *Tales*—love, justice, the relations between men and women, the proper conduct of life—add reverberations of meaning and reference that extend beyond the limits of the individual tales and groups of tales and provide a sense of coherence and fulness for the whole work, despite the absence of a completed narrative framework.

For reasons unknown, Chaucer left *The Canterbury Tales* incomplete and without final revision. The work survives in ten fragments, labeled with Roman numerals in this edition (the alphabetical designations added in parentheses are those of the Chaucer Society, adopted by Skeat in his edition). These fragments are editorial units determined by the existence of internal signs of linkage—bits of conversation or narrative that explicitly refer to a tale just told or to one that immediately follows. There are no explicit connections between the fragments (save for IX–X and, in the tradition of the Ellesmere manuscript, IV–V) and, consequently, no explicit indication of the order in which Chaucer intended the fragments to be read. (Indeed, there is no explicit indication that he had made a final decision in this matter.) Consequently, modern editions differ in the order in which the tales are presented. Skeat's edition has them in the order followed by the Chaucer Society, with the "Bradshaw shift," whereby Fragment VII (B²) is printed following Fragment II (B), and with Fragment VI following next, so that the complete arrangement is as follows: I (A), II (B), VII (B²), VI (C), III (D), IV (E), V (F), VIII (G), IX (H), X (I). Baugh and Pratt follow this order except for the position of Fragment VI, which they print following Fragment V. Donaldson and Fisher print the tales in the order followed here. Robinson chose that order even though he believed it probable that the "Bradshaw shift" was indeed what Chaucer intended; nevertheless, he wrote, "in the present edition the inconsistent arrangement of the best manuscripts" (by which he meant the Ellesmere and related manuscripts) "is followed and no attempt is made to correct discrepancies left standing by the author."

FRAGMENT I
General Prologue

The General Prologue was presumably written early in the Canterbury period, though it was not necessarily the first part of the *Tales* to be composed and was probably revised from time to time. Some revisions remained to be made; neither the Second Nun nor the Nun's Priest is described, and it seems likely that Chaucer intended to add their portraits in a later revision.

For the General Prologue, as for the Canterbury pilgrimage itself, Chaucer had no exact literary model. The Prologue begins as if it were to be another of his dream visions, cast in the high style evoked by the learned allusions and elaborate syntax of the opening lines. The celebration of the return of spring recalls the opening of *The Romaunt of the Rose*. There the description of spring, with its suggestions of fertility and rebirth, leads to "Than yonge folk entenden ay/ Forto ben gay and amorous" (Rom 82–83). Here it leads to another kind of love: "Thanne longen folk to goon on pilgrimages" (I.12). The narrator encounters not a Temple of Venus or a Garden of Love but a real tavern, the Tabard in Southwark, containing not a series of allegorical portraits but what seems a lively assembly of real people, gathered for an actual pilgrimage to Canterbury.

The portraits of Chaucer's pilgrims nevertheless owe a great deal to medieval traditions of literary portraiture, including the series of allegorical descriptions in *The Romaunt of the Rose*. The hypocritical friar, the hunting monk, the thieving miller and others are familiar types in medieval *estates satire,* in which representatives of various classes and occupations are portrayed with a satiric emphasis on the vices peculiar to their stations in life. Each of Chaucer's fully described characters represents a different occupation, and each is a paragon of his or her craft: "wel koude" and "verray parfit" echo throughout the General Prologue, as we are shown that each character well knows how to realize the potentialities of his or her occupation, whether for good or—far more often—for mischief. Much of this satire still strikes the mark, since Chaucer's characters represent more general types as well as their particular occupations. What John Dryden wrote in his *Preface to the Fables* (1700) remains true today:

We have our Fore-fathers and Great Grand-dames all before us, as they were in Chaucer's days: their general Characters are still remaining in Mankind, and even in England, though they are called by other names than those of Moncks, and Fryars, and Chanons and Lady Abbesses, and Nuns: For Mankind is ever the same, and nothing lost out of Nature, though everything is alter'd.

Nevertheless, each of Chaucer's characters is vividly individualized. The Friar is a representative type of the unctuous hypocrisy one may still encounter in daily life and a clear example of the type of the *hypocritical friar* well known in medieval satire, but he is also a particular individual, with a specific name, Friar Huberd, with his peculiar habits, his lisp, and his own personal history. We even seem to hear the tone of his own voice in his indirectly quoted self-justifications (lines 227–34, 243–48). Likewise, the Knight is an idealized representative of chivalry, but one who has participated in real campaigns, most of them well known to Chaucer's audience, and the Miller is not only the traditional thieving miller, but Robin, with a wart on the end of his nose and the habit of breaking down doors with his head. We glimpse the Prioress weeping when her little dogs are beaten; we are told of the real places from which the pilgrims come; and in such touches as the Wife of Bath's deafness we see the present effects of what seem real past experiences.

It is therefore not disturbing to find among these literary creations real people: Geoffrey Chaucer himself, the tavern-keeper Harry Bailly, the cook Roger de Ware, and possibly Thomas Pinchbeck, a prominent London lawyer whose name may be punningly revealed in the portrait of the Man of Law. Perhaps other portraits were also drawn from life, though clearly some of the pilgrims, such as the Parson and his brother the Plowman, are pure idealizations. Chaucer's artistic triumph is the easy intermingling of the actual and the ideal, with each lending its qualities to the other, so that the real Harry Bailly becomes a literary creation and the idealized Parson gains a measure of actuality.

The most fascinating of the pilgrims is Geoffrey Chaucer himself. He is never described, and we come to know him only indirectly, from the tone of his voice, his words and actions, and the comments of others. We know him thus only as a literary character—the pilgrim-narrator of the *Tales,* a cheerful and self-effacing fellow, filled with admiration for the others in the company. This is not necessarily a faithful self-portrait, and critics, disturbed by the apparent naïveté of a narrator who ignores the most obvious faults of most of the pilgrims, customarily distinguish between Chaucer the pilgrim and Chaucer the man. The pilgrim accepts the Prioress on her own terms and even admires her; the man could not have ignored her serious violations of reli-

gious rules. The pilgrim seems amused by the Shipman's villainies; the man would have condemned them as crimes.

The distinction is useful, though Chaucer the man may have been more complex than this formulation makes him seem. Chaucer the man, the successful courtier and busy government official, could not have been naïve; George Lyman Kittredge long ago observed that a naïve Controller of Customs would be "monstrous." But a rigidly moralizing Controller of Customs, who had to deal every day with cunning merchants and thieving shipmen, would have been impossible, and a courtier unable to wink at others' faults and make the best of people as he found them would not have lasted long even in a court less embroiled in intrigues and jealousies than that that Chaucer knew. Perhaps Chaucer the pilgrim —cheerful, tolerant, but no fool—is closer than has been thought to Chaucer the man, who may even have relished an occasional rascal.

Chaucer, however, eludes even such simple critical formulations as that. As both pilgrim and writer he remains discreetly in the background, allowing his characters to speak for themselves. In the foreground, directing the action, is not Chaucer but Harry Bailly; he proposes the game of storytelling, appoints himself leader, and arranges the draw that "by adventure, or sort, or cas" falls to the Knight.

The Knight's Tale

The Knight's Tale, though written before *The Canterbury Tales* was begun, has been adapted to the *Tales* (lines 875–92) and is well suited to its teller. It is a free adaptation of Boccaccio's *Teseida.* Chaucer greatly compresses his source, omitting all actions not necessary to the main story. Nevertheless, the elaborate descriptions and long speeches lend the narrative an air of stately and unhurried dignity, and the long Boethian passages that Chaucer adds to the tale—on destiny, on love, and most notably Theseus's great speech on the "First Moevere"—sound a meditative, philosophical tone quite foreign to Boccaccio's original. Most important, Chaucer casts the story of the *Teseida,* a classicized, epic narrative, into the form of a *romance*.

This was the dominant genre of long, serious fiction from the twelfth to at least the seventeenth century, and its influence on the *Tales* is apparent not only in Chaucer's chivalric romances (the Knight's and the Squire's tales) but also in the tales of the Wife of Bath, the Franklin, the Man of Law, and the Clerk, as well as Chaucer's own Tale of Sir Thopas. Romance is in many ways the exact opposite of its successor, the realistic novel of the eighteenth and nineteenth centuries (and just as impossible to define precisely): a romance purports to tell not something new, novel, but an old "storie," a true history of events remote in time and often in place, which the romancer has learned from some reliable "auctor" or ancient tradition. The story itself is composed of traditional motifs and usually turns upon wonders, chance happenings, and sudden reversals of fortune. The romancer is consequently little concerned with providing realistic motivations for the actions; these are controlled by thematic necessity rather than a lifelike chain of causes and effects; they usually have less narrative importance than the emotions to which they give rise, and often add less to the advancement of the plot than to the creation of the balanced, symmetrical structures that inform the more sophisticated romances. There is little attempt at creating lifelike characters: the invariably noble heroes and heroines are more types than individuals, and their actions, manners, emotions, and speech represent an ideal of aristocratic conduct. The style is appropriately elaborate, often elevated and slow-moving. Some of the individual parts of romance may be realistic, direct representations of the actualities of chivalric life, but the effect at which the romancer aims is not that of a convincing representation of life but rather of an ideal image of what life might be if all behaved as nobly as the heroes and heroines of the romance.

As a chivalric romance, The Knight's Tale is mainly concerned with love and arms. Chaucer, however, transformed every genre he used. The chance encounters and sudden reversals of fortune characteristic of romance are here used as occasions for philosophical reflections on human destiny, the inevitable alternation of joy and sorrow, and the divine order of the universe. The Knight's Tale is thus a uniquely philosophical romance. It is also a romance with a sharply contemporary flavor. Love and war are here potential sources of disorder held in check by elaborate ceremonials—state funerals, great tournaments, royal weddings—of the sort that were becoming ever more important in late fourteenth-century life, as the new courtly society was coming into existence and bringing an increasing formality and ceremonialism to aristocratic life. The Knight's philosophical romance is to some extent a meditation upon the relation of these noble rites to the divine order and to aristocratic life as it appeared to Chaucer and his contemporaries.

It nevertheless remains a romance, with the happy ending characteristic of that genre. The Knight, as we later learn from his interruption of the Monk, prefers happy endings, and his tale suitably concludes with joy after sorrow in the blissful marriage of Palamoun and Emelye, to the delight of his hearers, "namely the gentils everichon."

The Miller's Prologue

Despite Harry Bailly's best efforts, Robin the Miller, so drunk he can hardly sit on his horse, insists that he be allowed to "quite" the Knight's tale, and the narrator elaborately apologizes for what he must now repeat. If you are easily shocked, he urges the reader, turn the page and choose another tale (advice, one suspects, that has seldom been taken); the Miller, the Reeve, and others are churls, and their tales are of "harlotrie."

Such tales are known to modern scholarship as *fabliaux*, a genre that flourished in thirteenth-century France and was, in the fourteenth century, replaced by the prose novella both in France and elsewhere in Europe. But it found vigorous new life in *The Canterbury Tales*, where the tales of the Miller, the Reeve, the Cook, the Friar, the Summoner, the Merchant, the Shipman, and the Manciple, as well as The Wife of Bath's Prologue, all in varying degrees reflect its influence. A fabliau is a brief comic tale in verse, usually scurrilous and often scatological or obscene. The style is simple, vigorous, and straightforward; the time is the present, and the settings real, familiar places; the characters are ordinary sorts—tradesmen, peasants, priests, students, restless wives; the plots are realistically motivated tricks and ruses. The fabliaux thus present a lively image of everyday life among the middle and lower classes. Yet that representation only seems real; life did not run that high in actual fourteenth-century towns and villages—it never does—and the plots, convincing though they seem, frequently involve incredible degrees of gullibility in the victims and of ingenuity and sexual appetite in the trickster-heroes and -heroines.

The cuckoldings, beatings, and elaborate practical jokes that are the main concern of the fabliaux are distributed in accord with a code of "fabliau justice," which does not always coincide with conventional morality: greed, hypocrisy, and pride are invariably punished, but so too are old age, mere slow-wittedness, and, most frequently, the presumption of a husband, especially an old one, who attempts to guard his wife's chastity. The heroes and heroines, invariably witty and usually young, are those whom society ordinarily scorns—dispossessed intellectuals (lecherous priests, wayward monks, penniless students), clever peasants, and enthusiastically unchaste wives. Their victims are usually those whom society respects—prosperous merchants, hard-working tradesmen, women foolish enough to try to remain chaste. The fabliau, in short, is delightfully subversive—a light-hearted thumbing of the nose at the dictates of religion, the solid virtues of the citizenry, and the idealistic pretensions of the aristocracy and its courtly literature, which the fabliaux frequently parody, though just as frequently they parody lower-class attempts to adopt courtly behavior.

The Miller's Tale

Here Chaucer raises the fabliau to the level of high art; without sacrificing any of the characteristics of the genre, he expands the form, allowing for leisurely descriptions, elaborate dialogue, and the development of character far beyond that customary in his French antecedents. Chaucer also elaborates the plot. The French fabliau is characteristically simple in plot, with a single line of action. Chaucer combines two lines of action—that involving the motif of the "misdirected kiss" and that of the "second flood." The two converge at the moment when Nicholas is burned on the "toute" and shouts for water; old John awakens, cuts the rope, and crashes to the floor, and the whole neighborhood hears the uproar and comes rushing in. It is, wrote E. M. W. Tillyard, sublime in its inevitability, "as if the heavens opened up and the gods looked down and laughed at these foolish mortals."

The heavens actually did open at the climax of The Knight's Tale, when Saturn intervened in the tournament. Neither Nicholas nor Theseus can fully control the chain of events each puts in motion. The Miller's Tale is carefully constructed not only to fit the vigorous nature of its teller but also to "quite" The Knight's Tale. Chaucer fully exploits the parodic tendencies of the genre, and the careful reader will find a surprising number of parallels between the Knight's noble story and this churlish tale of "harlotrie," in which the world as the Knight views it is turned delightfully upside down. The animal impulses that are restrained and controlled by the noble ceremonialism of The Knight's Tale are here given their full play in a celebration of indecorous energy, physical pleasure, and riotous good humor. The Miller thus offers not merely a change in tone but what seems a positive alternative to the Knight's idealism, which fails to take account of a great deal in life, including a sense of fun.

The Reeve's Tale

The Reeve's Tale was probably based directly on a French fabliau, since two surviving fabliaux, both differing versions of the same story, offer a number of close parallels to Chaucer's work. The tale, however, has been carefully adapted to its teller and to the dramatic situation. None of the analogues offers any close parallels to "deynous Symkyn," who bears a considerable resemblance to the Miller on the pilgrimage, nor to his proud wife and ugly daughter, who are a far cry from the village beauties in the analogues. Chaucer's masterful use of dialect—the first extensive literary representation of a dialect in English—is likewise without precedent.

Oswald the Reeve clearly "quites" Robin the Miller in this tale of a thieving miller who is beaten and cuckolded, has his daughter woefully "disparaged," and is deprived not only of his ill-gotten gains but even of the fee that was rightfully his for grinding the grain. He also "quites" The Miller's Tale itself. That rollicking celebration of animal high spirits had seemed to offer an alternative to the Knight's idealism. The Reeve's tale reminds us that the Miller's tale is as idealized as the Knight's. Country girls more often resemble Malyne than Alison, and illicit sex is seldom a matter of uncomplicated fun: it can be, as it is here, a tool to maintain the upper hand in a world populated not by complaisant dupes with beautiful wives but by thieving millers with ugly daughters. In this tale, action matters more than talk; one clerk simply moves the crib, mechanically rearranging the physical space, and the other leaps upon the sleeping daughter, without bothering with Nicholas's elaborate schemes or Absolon's bungling court-ship. The Reeve's view of the world is much less joyful than the Miller's, though it may be closer to reality.

The tale, however, transcends the Reeve's vengeful purpose. Symkyn so obviously de-serves his punishment and the two women so clearly enjoy the clerks' means of revenge that we cannot condemn Aleyn and John for what they do. Moreover, the slapstick comedy of the tale more than compensates for its lack of benev-olent jollity; the climax, beginning with Aleyn's mistaken awakening of the sleeping miller, is a masterpiece of controlled confusion and farcical mayhem. Chaucer manages to infuse the tale with a sense of the Reeve's embittered view of life without sacrificing its comedy.

The Cook's Tale

The Cook's Tale has no known source. It prom-ises to be another fabliau, even more scurrilous than those just told, and it seems to carry the downward movement of Fragment I to its fur-thest extreme. The Knight's Tale ended with Palamoun and Emelye united in a marriage that is happy forever after, undisturbed by jealousy or wrath. This was followed by the cheerful adultery of The Miller's Tale, which was fol-lowed by the relatively joyless cuckolding in The Reeve's Tale, and that, in its turn, is followed by this story of a gambler and thief who moves in with another whose wife is a whore "that heeld for contenance/ A shoppe, and swyved for hir sustenance" (I.4421–22). Whether or not Chaucer intended to finish The Cook's Tale, he chose an ideal couplet at which to stop. We have moved from the remoteness of ancient Athens to "oure citee," London, and from the idealized realm of romance to the sleaziest side of contemporary reality.

FRAGMENT II

Introduction to The Man of Law's Tale

The Host's complicated astronomical calculation (which would have required using a set of ta-bles) fixes the time at exactly 10 A.M. on April 18; why Chaucer specifies this date and whether he intends it to be the first or second day of the journey are not known.

The Host, with an equally elaborate display of legal terminology, then asks for a tale from the Man of Law, whose praise of Chaucer as a writer exclusively of tales of "good women" such as the story of Ceys and Alcione (in *The Book of the Duchess*) and those in *The Legend of Good Women* gains piquancy from the fabliaux just told. Chau-cer would never, the Man of Law says, write such "abhomynacions" as the tales of Canacee and of Apollonius of Tyre. Both are tales of incest that appear in John Gower's *Confessio amantis*. The story of Custance, which the Man of Law now tells, is also in the *Confessio amantis*. Perhaps Chaucer is teasingly challenging his friend to a storytelling contest parallel to that in which the pilgrims are engaged; the Man of Law's, the Wife of Bath's, the Physician's, and the Manciple's tales are all based on stories that also appear in the *Confessio amantis*.

However, the reference to Gower is not cer-tain, and the Man of Law's announcement that he will speak in prose shows that this prologue may have been written for some other tale, per-haps the Melibee. The usually accepted theory is that when Fragment VII was formed, late in the composition of the *Tales,* Chaucer reassigned the Melibee to himself and gave a new tale, the story of Custance, to the Man of Law, intending to remove the reference to prose in a later draft.

The Man of Law's Tale

The Man of Law's Tale is based on a story in the Anglo-Norman Chronicle of Nicholas Trivet and on Gower's version of Trivet's tale. The most significant difference between Chaucer's version and those of Trivet and Gower is the highly elaborated style in which the tale is told. Such a style is well suited to the Man of Law, who uses all the devices recommended by the medieval rhetoricians to move our pity for the heroine, almost as if he were pleading her case in a court of law.

Like the later tale of Griselda, the tale of Cus-tance has been called a secular saint's life. But it is also a romance, though not a chivalric ro-mance of the sort told by the Knight. It is a Christian romance based on the theme of exile and return: the protagonist encounters a series of adventures that test her worthiness of the high position in life that she loses with her exile and finally regains with her return to the imperial court and her son's accession to her father's throne. In broad outline this is the theme of many secular romances. As a Christian rather than a chivalric romance, however, this tale emphasizes the passive suffering of the protagonist rather than knightly achievements, and the virtues tested are Christian rather than chivalric—Patience in the acceptance of unmerited misfortunes and Fortitude in the constant Faith that sustains the heroine and allows her finally to triumph.

Many medieval thinkers maintained that wonder, the emotion we feel when confronted with apparently inexplicable events, is an aid to philosophical and religious thought, since the mind is thus incited to seek out causes. In The Knight's Tale, Chaucer used the wonder arising from sudden reversals of fortune as occasions for philosophical meditation; here, Custance's miraculous adventures provide opportunities to offer religious explanations, and the role of Providence in human affairs, notably absent from the immediately preceding churls' tales, is emphatically reasserted. The Man of Law, like the Knight, is concerned with the problem of the alternation of joy and sorrow in human life, though here it is not a remote First Mover but "Jhesu Crist, that of his myght may sende/Joye after wo."

Epilogue to the Man of Law's Tale

In many, though not all, manuscripts, The Man of Law's Tale is joined to what follows by this lively epilogue. The pilgrim who interrupts the Parson is identified in most manuscripts as the Squire or the Summoner, and, in the great majority of manuscripts containing this Epilogue, The Squire's Tale follows. Yet the rudeness of the speaker hardly fits the character of the Squire, and his disclaimer of any knowledge of Latin does not fit the Summoner, who likes to show off his few Latin phrases when he is in his cups. One late manuscript identifies the speaker as the Shipman, and in that manuscript The Shipman's Tale follows.

The Epilogue probably attests to an early draft of the Tales, when the Man of Law told the Melibee—to which the references to Latin and to "philosophie," "phislyas," and "termes queinte of lawe" seem more suitable than to the tale of Custance—and when the next tale following was that of the Wife of Bath, who in this early version apparently told the tale now assigned to the Shipman. The speaker's reference to "My joly body" (II.1185) seems more suitable to a woman such as the Wife than to a man, and The Shipman's Tale as it now stands con-

tains several references that indicate a feminine teller. When the Wife of Bath and the Man of Law were assigned new tales, the Epilogue was either canceled or set aside for a later revision that it never received.

FRAGMENT III

There is no link between Fragments II and III and no certainty that Chaucer meant The Wife of Bath's Prologue to follow The Man of Law's Tale. Yet his presentation of Custance as an ideal of womanhood—piously convinced that "Wommen are born to thraldom and penance,/And to been under mannes governance" (II.286–87)—must have set Alison's teeth on edge and would have been sufficient to account for her bursting out with her version of the "wo that is in mariage."

That subject is taken up again in the Clerk's and the Merchant's tales, which constitute Fragment IV, and in The Franklin's Tale, which concludes Fragment V. Many critics assume that these tales were intended as parts of a single unit, the *Marriage Group.* The subject is proposed by the Wife of Bath; after the interlude provided by the Friar's and the Summoner's tales, the topic is taken up by the Clerk in his tale and envoy, specifically addressed to the Wife, and again by the Merchant, who directly cites the Wife of Bath in his tale. After another interlude, The Squire's Tale, the debate concludes with The Franklin's Tale, which presents his solution to the problem of who should rule in marriage.

This set of tales is not alone in its concern with marriage and the relations between husbands and wives, which are among the subjects repeatedly explored in the *Tales.* Nor is marriage the only unifying theme in the seven tales of Fragments III through V. The Wife of Bath's Tale turns on the problem of *troth,* keeping one's pledged word, which is an essential ingredient of the tales told by the Friar, the Summoner, the Clerk, and the Franklin, and is at least implied in the Squire's tale of the faithless tercel. The Wife of Bath's Tale likewise treats at length the problem of what constitutes *gentilesse,* and this is also a major concern of the Clerk's, the Merchant's, the Squire's, and the Franklin's tales. Yet, though the problem of marriage is not confined to the tales of these three fragments, and though the tales within these fragments are not restricted to that subject, the Merchant's and the

Clerk's specific references to the Wife of Bath and the Franklin's explicit concern with the proper relationship between husband and wife lend credence to the theory that Chaucer did intend these tales to constitute a kind of debate on the problem of marriage.

The Wife of Bath's Prologue

The Wife of Bath's Prologue has the form of a *literary confession*, a dramatic monologue in which the speaker explains, and often defends, his or her sinful way of life. Chaucer probably got the initial suggestion for The Wife of Bath's Prologue from the long monologue of La Vieille in the *Roman de la rose*, which is at once a literary confession and a lecture to a young woman on how to outwit men. The rich tradition of anti-feminine literature of the sort collected in Jankyn's "book of wicked wives" offered much similar material, however, and Alison is one of a long tradition of bawdy older women that extends from classical times to Juliet's nurse and beyond. Chaucer drew on his knowledge of life as well as his reading, and Alison of Bath transcends all her forebears. Her closest analogue, in La Vieille, is a retired prostitute, bitter in her old age; Alison is a defender of marriage, providing she rules, and, far from being bitter, she has an infectious optimism. "Welcome the sixte!" she cries, ready for yet another marriage and, though the "flour" be gone, determined to enjoy the "bren." Moreover, though most of her characteristics can be traced in anti-feminine satire and she herself embodies almost all the faults traditionally imputed to women (there are no volunteers when she announces her readiness for another marriage), her frankness, vigor, and good humor render her a zestful and engaging defender of life itself.

The Wife of Bath's Tale

The Wife of Bath's Tale is a brief romance, set in the days of King Arthur. It is a version of the tale of the loathly lady—the beautiful princess transformed into an ugly creature who can be released from her spell only by the kiss or embrace of the hero (the feminine version of the still popular fairy story "The Frog Prince"). The particular form of the tale used by Chaucer, with the transformation effected not by the hero's embrace but by his yielding sovereignty to the woman, appears in a number of brief romances

of Chaucer's time and in Gower's *Confessio amantis*. Chaucer's version differs from Gower's and most others in a number of important details. Gower's heroine, for example, has been transformed by a wicked stepmother; the Wife of Bath's heroine is mistress of her own destiny, able to effect her own transformation at will. In Gower's and most other versions the hero must choose whether to have his wife fair by day and foul by night or vice versa; the Wife of Bath, characteristically, makes her hero choose between having his wife ugly and faithful or fair and possibly faithless.

The tale obviously exemplifies the main theme of Alison's prologue, that women should be sovereign in marriage. That heretical doctrine is here combined with a completely orthodox doctrine of *gentilesse*, which the loathly lady defends with arguments often identical with those the Parson later uses in his discussion of the subject. From this standpoint, there are two transformations in the tale, that of the loathly lady and that of the hero. He begins proud of his gentle birth, though he has committed a churlish crime, rape. In the end the old hag convinces him that true *gentilesse* is a matter of deeds, and in this version of the tale, unlike the others, he is moved to address her as "My lady and my love, and wyf so deere" and to yield her sovereignty even before she is transformed. He becomes gentle in accord with the courtly dictum that love makes the lover virtuous, and she becomes beautiful in accordance with the doctrine that to the eyes of a true lover his lady is always beautiful.

The Friar's Tale

The Friar's Tale is based on the widespread story of the damnation of an unpopular official—a steward, a lawyer, or, as in this case, an ecclesiastical officer. In form it is an *exemplum*, a brief anecdote used by a preacher to illustrate a moral. Many exempla were collected into anthologies, such as Caesarius of Heisterbach's *Dialogue on Miracles*, which contains one of the closest analogues to The Friar's Tale. Chaucer's version is notable for its witty account of the corruption of the ecclesiastical courts, the deft characterization of the summoner and the devil, and the ironic reverberation of their dialogue.

The tale is admirably suited to the Friar, a preacher who deals in words, the efficacy of which he proves by making the summoner's words the instrument of his own damnation, first by those he does speak, the troth he pledges to the devil, and then by those he does not, his refusal to repent. In the General Prologue even the usually tolerant narrator was shocked by the Summoner's belief that cursing has no effect; the Friar's exemplum shows how wrong he was.

The Summoner's Tale

The Summoner's Tale retaliates for the Friar's account of a summoner with a devastating portrait of an unctuous and hypocritical friar, who shoos away the cat to sit himself softly down, kisses the wife with more than fraternal enthusiasm, protests that his abstinence prevents his eating much and then orders a roasted pig's head for dinner, and preaches at length against the sin of Wrath, only to become so enraged that he can hardly speak when Thomas has finally given him the "gift" for which he begs.

The gift classifies this tale with other medieval jests and fabliaux involving a satiric legacy, but none of the other medieval examples are of this sort. It consists of sound and wind, the constituents of the words that are the preacher's stock in trade, and it is so exactly appropriate to the preaching friar that it seems most likely to have been Chaucer's own invention. Equally original is the problem the gift poses for the friar, who has pledged his troth that he will part it equally with his brethren. It presents, as the lord observes, a difficult scientific problem. The final humiliation for the friar, who takes pride in his advanced degree, is that a mere squire, no admirer of his sermons, solves the problem of "arsmetrike" in a manner worthy of Euclid or Ptolemy.

FRAGMENT IV

The Clerk's Prologue

When Harry Bailly turns to the Clerk, he fears this solemn scholar will be boring; he begs him not to preach and to speak in a simple style rather than the elaborate "heigh style, as whan that men to kynges write." The Clerk agrees, and, though he tells a tale from the learned Petrarch, he maintains a markedly plain and straightforward style.

The subject of style recurs in the Prologue to The Franklin's Tale, in which the Franklin assures his audience that he will eschew the "colours of rethoryk." The Merchant's and the Squire's tales, on the other hand, are among the most elaborately ornamented productions in the *Tales,* and the Franklin's comment on the Squire's performance rightly emphasizes its style rather than its content. This concern with style and its implications is never far below the surface throughout the *Tales,* but it becomes explicit in Fragments IV and V.

The Clerk's Tale

The Clerk's Tale is based on Petrarch's adaptation of the last tale in Boccaccio's *Decameron* and on a French version of Petrarch's work. It is a Christian romance of the same sort as The Man of Law's Tale. It embodies the Cinderella theme, in which the protagonist rises from the lowest to the highest rank by proving her worthiness though a series of tests. In Griselda's case, they are tests of her patience and faithfulness to her pledge, her troth, that she will unquestioningly obey Walter's every command. She undergoes a series of increasingly cruel ordeals until her final triumph, whereupon she is welcomed back to Walter's arms with the assurance that her children live and that her son will succeed Walter as marquis.

Walter's unmotivated cruelty, what Boccaccio called his "mad bestiality," bothered almost every writer who told this tale. Modern scholars have explained this by assuming an ultimate debt to some folk tale of the Cupid and Psyche type (in which the bride of a supernatural creature must observe certain taboos). Petrarch, followed by the Clerk, provided a moral interpretation: the story is an exemplum, teaching patience not just to wives but to all. To reinforce this interpretation, Petrarch added a number of references to the Book of Job, which Chaucer further developed.

The tale of Griselda inevitably recalls that of Custance; both concern the sufferings of helpless women and both are cast in the rime royal stanzas that Chaucer uses for most of his tales of pathos. In The Man of Law's Tale, however, the pathos is produced by a heavily rhetorical manner of telling, with elaborate appeals to the audience to have pity on the "Emperoures doghter." The Clerk obeys Harry Bailly's injunction to avoid such a "heigh style." Griselda is a peasant girl and, in accord with medieval ideas of stylistic decorum (the "heigh style" for nobles, the plain style for rustics), the Clerk tells her story in a manner as simple as her lowly station in life. Only after she has given final proof of her inner nobility does he allow his style to burst forth in an open appeal to the audience's emotions. The sudden release of Griselda's emotion at the climax, now weeping and swooning with joy at her reunion with her children, emphasizes the self-control she has maintained throughout her trials and confirms the recurring hints that her patience is produced by strength of character rather than mere submissiveness.

The Merchant's Tale

The Merchant's Tale was apparently composed as a companion piece to The Clerk's Tale, which it reflects in a number of details—the setting in Lombardy, the determination of the noble hero to marry as he chooses, his choice of a wife of lower birth than his own, and (here The Clerk's Tale is quoted) his belief that she will not once say "nay" when her husband says "ye" (IV.1345; cf. IV.355).

The plot of The Merchant's Tale, the pear tree episode, is common in fabliaux and popular tales, though no exact source for Chaucer's version has been found, and he may have drawn on some orally transmitted version. The opening debate on marriage, which draws on many of the same sources as The Wife of Bath's Prologue and in which she herself is cited as an "auctoritee," is obviously Chaucer's own invention. Though previous literature offers many examples of the senex amans (the aged lover), Chaucer's January is by far the most appalling, while May, who reads her lover's letters in the privy, is equally original, a worthy mate for this quintessentially dirty old man.

The Merchant's Tale is basically a fabliau. It has the obligatory triangle—jealous old husband, restless young wife, lusty squire—and the inevitable act of adultery achieved through trickery. Chaucer, however, breaks all the other rules of the genre. The style is that of a courtly romance, and the description of January's wedding feast is one of the most ornate in The Canterbury Tales, laden with apostrophes, elaborate comparisons, and classical and biblical allusions.

The tale is built on the courtly dictum "Love is blind." Damyan, the young squire, suffers the pangs of love appropriate to a courtly hero. May purportedly decides to commit adultery because of the nobility of her sentiments, and we are told

this in words that echo The Knight's Tale—"Lo, pitee renneth soone in gentil herte" (IV.1986; cf. I.1761). Pluto, like Saturn in The Knight's Tale, intervenes at the climax, though here Proserpina, his wife, also intervenes, apparently proving that women will have their way even among the gods. The elaborate style and courtly allusions cast an ironic reflection on the sordid action. The tale has more than a trace of the bitterness the Merchant apparently feels at his own recent unwise marriage. Yet the total effect is by no means repulsive, and the description of January's wedding night is one of the great comic scenes in Chaucer.

FRAGMENT V

The Introduction to the Squire's Tale

The Introduction to the Squire's Tale and the Epilogue to the Merchant's Tale are presented as one continuous speech in the manuscripts that have the fragments in the order printed here, and, though editors customarily observe the traditional division between IV and V, almost all scholars agree that they constitute a single unit.

The Squire's Tale

The Squire's Tale is a romance that promises fabulous wonder, high sentiment, and chivalric adventure. The fantastical variety of chivalric romance, quite different from the Knight's sober tale, was becoming fashionable, and in the fifteenth century it would flower in the great works of Boiardo and Ariosto. The Squire's taste in romance is as much in accord with the newest fashions as is his elegant dress. No source is known for the story, though Chaucer apparently drew upon contemporary travel literature, such as the book by the fictional Sir John Mandeville, for his account of the wonders in the court of Cambyuskan, Genghis Khan.

The tale is left unfinished, and though later writers, such as Spenser and John Lane, continued and concluded it, Chaucer most likely intended the tale to remain unfinished, at least once it had been assigned to the Squire. The narrative moves at so leisurely a pace that the story has hardly begun when it is broken off. Had the Squire told all that he promises, his tale would have run to at least four or five thousand lines (Lane's continuation has seven thousand), over twice as long as that told by his father and far out of proportion with the other tales. The squire's youthful enthusiasm for his subject is delightful, but had the tale continued it would soon have begun to pall. Many critics believe that the words of the Franklin to the Squire are intended as an interruption of the tale; if so, they come just in time.

The Franklin's Tale

The Franklin's Tale is, as the Franklin explains, a *Breton lay*, a variety of brief romance purportedly descending from the original Celtic inhabitants of Britain and usually dealing with love and the supernatural. Though the Franklin gives his tale an authentically Breton setting, it is an unusual Breton lay: it has no clear Celtic antecedents, the love involves marriage rather than only courtship, and the supernatural is of the explained variety, produced not by demonic powers but by the skill of a "philosopher." The story is a free adaptation of a tale told in Boccaccio's *Filocolo* as well as in his *Decameron,* with details drawn from a variety of other sources, including The Merchant's Tale, which is echoed in the Franklin's description of marriage (V.803–6; cf. IV.1259–60).

The opening section of the tale offers a solution to the problem of sovereignty in marriage, one well suited to the character of the Franklin, who relishes domestic comfort and would probably prefer compromise to strife; it is also based on common sense, welcome after the extremes presented by the Wife of Bath, the Clerk, and the Merchant. Anger, sickness, the stars, wine, woe, or change of complexion, the Franklin warns, often cause one to act or speak amiss; perfection is impossible, and good will and patience are the first requirements in love.

The tale that follows tests this theory of marriage; whether it proves valid depends on what one makes of the climactic scene, in which Averagus, in a manner suitable to a Walter, flatly orders Dorigen to keep her appointment with Aurelius, and she, like a new Griselda, humbly obeys. This tale, like that of the Wife of Bath and most of the others in Fragments III, IV, and V, turns on a problem of troth, the series of pledges that the characters make to one another. The problem is resolved when all generously forgo demanding their payment. This, the Franklin implies, is the way of true gentilesse, and he ends with a question: Which was the most "fre," who

did the most "gentil dede"? The Franklin supplies no answer. Nor are all the problems of the Marriage Group resolved in this tale; they are concerns that reappear throughout *The Canterbury Tales.*

FRAGMENT VI
The Physician's Tale

The Physician's Tale is another of Chaucer's tales of domestic pathos. Chaucer was the first English poet to explore this source of the pathetic and the first for whom the relation of parent and child was a major theme. The tales of the Man of Law, the Clerk, and the Prioress and the Ugolino episode in The Monk's Tale are all characterized by affecting scenes of parents and children. The scene in which Virginia lays her arms about her father's neck, "as she was wont to do" (VI.231–36) is a good example of the way in which Chaucer uses sharply observed detail to render such scenes effective.

Chaucer reshaped the received story to emphasize its pathetic possibilities. It derives ultimately from the Roman history of Titus Livius, though Chaucer knew several other versions, including those in Gower's *Confessio amantis* and the *Roman de la rose.* The main focus in all these versions is the wickedness of the judge, and in none is Virginia characterized in any detail. Chaucer brings the victim to the center of the action. He adds the long description of Virginia; he domesticates the tragedy by moving the final interview between Virginia and her father from the courtroom to their home; and he adds the touching scene in which Virginia weeps, prays, and meekly begs her father to take her life. He also emphasizes the domestic horror of the tale; instead of stabbing his child in court, as in the other versions, the father decapitates Virginia in their home and carries her bleeding head to the judge.

The tale is not a success. The long digression on governesses may allude to some now forgotten scandal that lent it point in Chaucer's time, but it seems merely intrusive. The moral appended to the tale seems likewise inappropriate. The idea that sin is its own punishment, that though the wicked seem to prosper they are secretly punished from within, is sound Augustinian doctrine but hardly applies to Appius, who is publicly punished for his crime. It does provide a useful perspective on the tale that follows, and perhaps that is its function, a reminder that in The Physician's Tale we are shown how sin is publicly punished and in The Pardoner's Prologue and Tale how sin secretly punishes itself.

The Pardoner's Prologue

The Pardoner's Prologue, like the Wife of Bath's, has the form of a literary confession in which the speaker explains—here boasts of—his vices, and it, too, is based ultimately on the *Roman de la rose,* in this case on the confession of Fals-Semblant (see Rom 6082–7292). The Pardoner's tone, however, is much different from that of the jolly Wife. Though his description of the ruses he employs to extract money from his gullible hearers is amusing, the Pardoner, like all con men, feels only contempt for his dupes; he cares not though their souls go a-blackberrying. Hatred, he says, sometimes motivates his preaching—he tells how he stings his enemies with his "tonge smerte" and how he spits out his "venym under hewe/Of hoolynesse" (VI.413, 421–2). But his chief motivation is greed. With a willfulness underscored by the repeated "I wol," he rejects a life of monastic poverty, the "love celestial" that he should serve, and boasts that he will have wine and women in every town, though a poor widow's children should starve for it. He cynically proclaims his own viciousness; but, he boasts, vicious though he be, he can tell a moral tale.

The Pardoner's Tale

The Pardoner's Tale has some of the characteristics of a sermon, and the story of the three rioters is used as an exemplum to illustrate his theme, *Greed is the root of all evil.* The story is widespread in world literature, and Chaucer's version has many analogues, though none remotely approaches its artistry. The Pardoner skillfully combines a preacher's exhortations with sharply realized scenes and dialogues from tavern life. In the smoothly functioning plot of his story, the three rioters, determined to find Death, do indeed find it in the form of gold. The story provides a forceful illustration of the Pardoner's theme as well as of the Physician's moral that sin punishes itself. Over all hovers the presence of the mysterious old man who cannot die but who

can show the way to death. This impressive figure is not explained, and perhaps cannot be. He implies a mystery transcending the rioters' materialistic view of the world and the almost too smoothly functioning mechanism of the plot, in which each action is motivated in rational human terms—pride, revenge, greed—that we can easily understand. The three rioters, the mysterious figure seems to remind us, are engaged in a drama beyond their ken and ours.

It is a moving tale, and even the Pardoner seems moved, as he ends his sermon with the assurance that he will not deceive his fellow pilgrims. But then he apparently tries to do so by offering his admittedly fake relics to the Host, who retaliates brutally. At this point, the Knight must step in to save the situation; and he reconciles the Host and the Pardoner. George Lyman Kittredge famously characterized the Pardoner as the one lost soul on the pilgrimage. But the Host and Pardoner forgive one another; they exchange the Kiss of Peace, and the pilgrims move on to their common goal.

FRAGMENT VII

Fragment VII, the largest and most varied of the groups of tales, was apparently formed when the composition of *The Canterbury Tales* was well advanced, since it contains two tales, The Shipman's Tale and The Tale of Melibee, which were probably once assigned to other pilgrims. It obviously never received a final revision (The Shipman's Tale, as noted previously, still contains indications that its narrator is a woman) and perhaps a later revision would have clarified some theme that would account for the variety of tales and genres in this fragment. Recent critics have tended to regard the tales of Fragment VII as a *literary group;* they represent a wide variety of genres, two are interpreted on specifically literary grounds, and Sir Thopas and The Nun's Priest's Tale involve literary parody. However that may be, this fragment provides a broad sampling of Chaucer's literary interests.

The Shipman's Tale

The Shipman's Tale may be Chaucer's earliest fabliau, since it is, compared with the Miller's and the Reeve's tales, relatively simple in design and execution. It is nevertheless far more artful than any of its many analogues. The story is based on a popular motif, still current in contemporary indecent anecdotes, known as the *lover's gift regained:* a man pays a woman for her sexual favors with money borrowed from her husband and then tells the husband he has given the repayment to the wife; it thus shows how a quick-witted man seduces an avaricious woman and then tricks her out of the promised payment. Chaucer adds an original conclusion: the wife proves herself as tricky as her lover, and, instead of meekly surrendering the money to her husband, she boldly asserts that she has spent it but will repay it in installments, with her body. The husband is both cuckolded and robbed, while the wife emerges unscathed and can now, in effect, force her husband to pay each time he claims his "marriage debt." No doubt the tale would have been suitable to the Wife of Bath as she was first imagined. However, as Chaucer developed her character she became too complicated for this simple equation of sex and money, and he provided her with a new tale and assigned this to the Shipman, a person well acquainted with merchants and their attitude toward money.

The Prioress's Tale

The Prioress's Tale is a *miracle of the Virgin,* a very popular genre of devotional literature, and the story that she tells was widespread in medieval Europe. Chaucer reproduces the outlines of the usual story with few changes. These, however, account for much of the charm of this tale. Chaucer emphasizes the pathos: the word "litel" rings through the opening stanzas, and Chaucer's "litel clergeoun" is only seven years old rather than ten or more as in the analogues. His telling his fellow of his determination to memorize "O Alma Redemptoris," though he be beaten for not learning his lessons, at once establishes his childish innocence and provides an amusing and convincing vignette of life in fourteenth-century schools. The Virgin's tender reassurance—"Be nat agast; I wol thee nat forsake" (VII.669)—has the eloquence of utter simplicity. One can understand why the tale appealed to Wordsworth, who translated it into modern English, and to Matthew Arnold, who used one of its stanzas (VII.649–55) to illustrate Chaucer's finest verse.

Yet this tender tale is also a story of violence; the Prioress seems to dwell on the sickening details of the child's murder and to exult in the savage punishment meted out to his murderers. Though this is not to the modern taste, the late medieval interest in pathos frequently led to the yoking of such extremes, with an emphasis on the ethereal goodness of the victim and a sensational, often gruesome, depiction of the violence inflicted upon him. The religious art of the period offers many examples; The Physician's Tale is but one of many other literary instances.

Even more difficult for the modern reader is the anti-Semitism of the tale. In Chaucer's time there were almost no Jews in England; they had been banished a hundred years before. The tale is therefore set in far-off Asia, and its Jews are the stock boogiemen of the fairy-tale-like miracles of the Virgin. The tale's anti-Semitism is thus somewhat different from modern varieties. It nevertheless inevitably discomfits twentieth-century readers; we are forced to recognize that Chaucer was a man of his time, sharing its faults as well as its virtues.

Prologue to Sir Thopas

To relieve the sober mood in which The Prioress's Tale has left even the most boisterous pilgrims, the Host turns to Chaucer himself. The reticence the Host here attributes to Chaucer seems hardly in keeping with the affability of the narrator of the General Prologue, who bustled about speaking to every one of the nine and twenty pilgrims and became "of hir felaweshipe anon" before the sun had gone to rest. Yet Chaucer's subdued demeanor and the Host's consequent expectation of "som deyntee thyng" is dramatically appropriate. It has been suggested that the tales of Fragment VII should be called the "surprise group," since so many of its tellers defy Harry Bailly's (and the reader's) expectations. That is clearly the case here when the timid "popet" (doll) from whom Harry expects some delicate tale breaks into the crude and thumping meter of the popular minstrel romance.

Sir Thopas

Sir Thopas was probably written to be interrupted, and it is not therefore surprising that the story, such as it is, has no source. Nevertheless, almost every line has its parallel in one or another of the popular *minstrel romances.* Such works are relatively brief narratives, designed for oral delivery, with frequent direct addresses to the audience and calls for attention at the fit divisions. Their verse is rough, their language characterized by a heavy use of formulas, and their emphasis is on adventurous action rather than the refined emotion of the more sophisticated romances of the time. Chaucer is unmerciful in his parody of this old-fashioned genre. Yet the parody seems affectionate, and Sir Thopas shows evidence of Chaucer's long and close acquaintance with these works.

The satire in Sir Thopas may be social as well as literary, since Thopas is something of a would-be gentleman, who works just a bit too hard at observing the proper forms of romance knighthood, apparently in contemporary Flanders. He swears an oath on ale and bread (rather than on a swan or peacock), he sleeps in the fields, as knights errant once did, and, in imitation of Sir Perceval, he drinks water from a well.

The Tale of Melibee

"The Hoost Stynteth Chaucer of his Tale of Thopas" at just this point, and The Tale of Melibee has seemed to some critics Geoffrey's revenge on Harry Bailly for interrupting him. Judging from the Host's reaction to the tale, however, he greatly appreciated it. So did many others of the time; Albertanus of Brescia's *Liber consolationi et consilii,* the ultimate source of this tale, was translated into a half dozen vernacular languages in the later Middle Ages. A French version by Renaud de Louens provided Chaucer with his source.

The prose here and in The Parson's Tale is workmanlike but uninspired, perhaps because in both cases Chaucer was translating. Partly because of its style, but mostly because of its allegory, moralizing, and long catalogues of proverbs, the Melibee is not often admired by modern readers. Nevertheless, Chaucer chose to tell this tale in his own person, and the sympathetic reader will find that the topics discussed by Melibee and Prudence have interest even today. They are problems of war and peace, of the maintenance of national honor and its relation to a policy of pacific disarmament, of how policy is made and of the proper roles of legislatures and advisers in formulating that policy. Because of its allegorical abstraction, the situation that Prudence and Melibee discuss fits our time as well as Chaucer's; the issues still concern us, and though we conduct our political discussions without long lists of "auctoritees" and sententiae, we have our own clichés, equally boring and much less learned.

The Melibee also touches on matters that concern other pilgrims. The debate on the proper use of advisers echoes the situation at the beginning of The Merchant's Tale, with which it shares a number of lines (e.g., IV.1362–74, VII.1098–1101). Likewise, the proper role of women in marriage is debated by Prudence and Melibee, who cites some of the same authorities as appear in The Wife of Bath's Prologue, and the problem of sovereignty in their marriage is resolved in a manner of which Alison would approve, when Melibee agrees to be completely guided by his wife's advice. Finally, the tale concerns the problem of how one reconciles a noble concern for honor with the Christian duty of forgiveness, and it thus takes up another aspect of the proper conduct of the noble life that had been considered in The Knight's Tale. In recent years the reputation of the Melibee has risen, and some critics now consider it an essential structural unit in the *Tales.*

The Monk's Tale

The Monk's Tale was probably written before *The Canterbury Tales* were begun (and the "Modern Instances," the four contemporary tragedies, added when the work was put in the *Tales*). It may thus represent Chaucer's first experiment with a collection of brief narratives. Boccaccio's *De casibus virorum illustrium (Concerning the Falls of Illustrious Men),* cited in the subtitle, supplied the basic idea of the collection and some of the details of the narratives, with Boccaccio's companion volume, *De claris mulieribus (Concerning Famous Women),* providing information on the tragedy of Zenobia. Chaucer drew on Dante for the account of Ugolino of Pisa and on his own knowledge of contemporary events for the accounts of the two Peters and Bernabò of Milan.

The conception of tragedy that appears here is not the Aristotelian idea of tragedy as a product of some tragic flaw in the protagonist's character but the medieval idea that the protagonist is a victim rather than a hero, raised up and then cast down by the workings of Fortune. This medieval idea of tragedy is not restricted to drama and applies to works we would assign to other genres (such as the *Aeneid* and Chaucer's *Troilus and Criseyde*). Tragedy in this view is a universal concomitant of good fortune and prosperity, for all are subject to Fortune save for those who turn aside from this world, scorn its comforts, and place their faith in a higher power.

The world as it appears in The Monk's Tale is a grim and discouraging place in which happiness is to be avoided since it inevitably leads to tragic misery. Such a view fits well with the Monk's profession; it embodies the monastic imperative to flee this miserable world and seek God in the security of the cloister. Chaucer's hearers, and Chaucer himself, were probably more sympathetic to this idea than are many modern readers. Moreover, the brief narratives that compose the tale are vigorous and to the point, and the account of Ugolino of Pisa is worthy of its source in Dante. However, the prospect of hearing many more such tragedies is daunting (the Monk has said he has a hundred of them in his cell); no one objects when the Knight prevents him from continuing.

The Nun's Priest's Tale

The Nun's Priest is not described—is barely mentioned, if at all—in the General Prologue, but the brilliance of his performance is such that it seems to imply a vividly characterized narrator, an accomplished preacher and a man of learning and wit. He accepts with equanimity his humble position, emblemized by the poor horse that the Prioress has provided him, though his tale itself may be a wittily muted protest. His poor state contrasts sharply with that of the handsomely mounted Monk, and his tale of the near-tragic fall of Chauntecleer, with its fireworks of learning and optimistic view of life, is a welcome response to the Monk's grim viewpoint.

This tale belongs to the genre of *beast fable*, handed down from Aesop (the medieval Isopet) and popular throughout the Middle Ages. The story that Chaucer uses is found in brief fables, such as Marie de France's version, and in the beast-epic the *Roman de Renart*, a thirteenth-century French work (with versions in many other languages) that recounts the adventures of Reynard the Fox in a world of talking animals whose words and deeds often provide satirical comment on the world of humans. The version

in the *Roman de Renart* has a touch of the mock-epic that may have inspired Chaucer's treatment.

The source, however, accounts for little in this tale, which builds an elaborate artifice on the simple foundation provided by the story of Chauntecleer's capture by and subsequent escape from the fox. The tale becomes a mock-heroic tragedy that echoes and comments on many of the tales that have preceded. It begins with Chauntecleer in royal splendor, in sharp contrast to his owner, the widow who lives in a state of humble simplicity that guards her from the blows of Fortune. Chauntecleer is touchingly devoted to the lovely Pertelote, whom he serves as a courtly lover, thus realizing the Franklin's ideal of marriage, though in a barnyard rather than a castle. Chaucer delicately maintains the balance between the two, combining the elegance of courtly discourse with occasional sharp reminders that the characters are, after all, only chickens.

Chauntecleer is learned as well as courtly. He quotes authorities and exempla at length in his demonstration to Pertelote that dreams have significance. The problem is whether Chauntecleer, like Melibee, will be guided by the advice of his wife. Melibee was, to his great advantage; so was Chauntecleer, to his sorrow. His fault, like that of the first tragic hero, Adam, is uxoriousness. He mistranslates the Latin of *Mulier est hominis confusio,* as "Womman is mannes joye and al his blis," and he seems to believe his own mistranslation. Though he clearly demonstrates that dreams are significant, he takes no notice whatever of his demonstration and proceeds to ignore the dream.

The tragic event falls on 3 May, a date that also figures prominently in The Knight's Tale, and, as in that tale, the sad event leads to a meditation on the providential order of the universe, the problem of fate and free will, which the Nun's Priest raises but does not resolve. The climax that follows is one of the finest mock-heroic passages in English literature. The apostrophes to destiny, to Venus, and to the rhetorician Geoffrey of Vinsauf and the comparison of the lamentations of the hens to those of the Trojan women when Ilium fell are followed by a marvelously palpable scene of frenzied action, with dogs running, geese flying, and the whole countryside in an uproar. Then suddenly Fortune turns her wheel, and the fox is cast down and Chauntecleer raised up to safety.

The Nun's Priest ends his tale with a whole cluster of morals drawn by Chauntecleer, the fox, and the narrator, and then, for good measure, adds an invitation to his hearers to find yet another moral—"Taketh the moralite, goode men." Perhaps this solemn assurance that the tale is more than just a "folye, / As of a fox, or of a cok and hen" is but one more literary joke in a tale rich in joking allusions to literature, including to *The Canterbury Tales* itself.

FRAGMENT VIII

The Second Nun's Prologue and Tale were apparently written for some other occasion and taken into the *Tales* with little or no adaptation; the reference to "unworthy sone of Eve" seems to indicate a masculine narrator (VIII.62), and the attribution to the Second Nun occurs only in the rubrics. It seems probable, given the aside to "worshipful chanons religious" (VIII.992), that The Canon's Yeoman's Tale was also written, at least in part, for another occasion, though the Prologue was clearly composed for the *Tales.* Yet, as will be noted below, recent criticism has found significant relations between the two tales.

The Prologue of the Second Nun's Tale

The Prologue of the Second Nun's Tale consists of three parts: four stanzas on idleness that introduce the importance of "leveful bisynesse" exemplified in Cecilia's life; the Invocation to Mary, based on Dante; and the "Interpretation of the name Cecilia which Brother Jacob of Genoa put in his legend." This last consists of a series of invented etymologies derived from extremely far-fetched verbal resemblances. It is a good example of a medieval method of interpretation that adds rather than discovers meaning; it aims not for one but for a variety of interpretations, all of which are right and none of which excludes the others, so that the object of interpretation, here the name Cecilia, gains in richness of meaning and range of reference.

The Second Nun's Tale

The Second Nun's Tale is a *saint's life,* a brief biography setting forth the life, miracles, and martyrdom of the saint. It was the most popular genre of medieval devotional literature, and collections of saints' lives were common in the later Middle Ages. The most widely known of these collections was the *Golden Legend (Legenda aurea)* of Jacob of Genoa (Jacobus de Voraigne), whose interpretation of the name of Cecilia Chaucer adopted, though he may have used some other source for the tale itself.

Since martyrdom is involved in this saint's life, one might have expected Chaucer to have emphasized the pathetic aspects of the tale, with Cecilia yet another example of passively suffering womanhood. Instead, Cecilia is a powerfully active character, the only "good woman" in the *Tales,* aside from the allegorical Prudence in the Melibee, who acts to control and shape not only her own life but the lives of those around her.

Though he closely adheres to the received story of "busy" Cecilia, Chaucer adds his own emphases: Cecilia's appearance before Almachius becomes more clearly a confrontation between her simple faith and the ultimately foolish learning of one who styles himself a philosopher yet worships a stone. Chaucer likewise emphasizes the contrasts between Cecilia's successful conversion of her husband and his brother "al in another kynde" and Almachius's inability, despite the "bath of flambes," even to transform Cecilia from life to death; finally, Chaucer's decision to link this tale with that of the Canon's Yeoman subtly shapes our understanding of both tales. In the light of what follows, the imagery of conversion and transformation in the Life of St. Cecilia acquires an alchemical dimension, and the theme of the vanity of worldly learning, exemplified by the "philosopher" Almachius in the saint's life, provides a clear standard by which to judge the vain attempts of the "philosophers" in the Canon's Yeoman's Tale to transform base metals "al in another kynde."

The Canon's Yeoman's Prologue

The sudden appearance of the Canon and his Yeoman and the Canon's subsequent flight change the character of the pilgrimage, heretofore a closed world of its own, and critics are not agreed on what this means nor on whether Chaucer planned from the beginning this introduction of the Canon's Yeoman into the *Tales.* It is, in any case, a suitably lively introduction for one of Chaucer's most lifelike characters. The form of the Prologue is that of the literary confession, of the sort Chaucer used in the prologues of the Pardoner's and the Wife of Bath's tales. It is used here with great dramatic skill: we see the Canon's Yeoman's character develop before our eyes as, guided by Harry Bailly's questions, he moves from serving as the Canon's accomplice, boasting of his master's power, to admitting that the Canon misuses his intellect, to announcing, in the moment when he breaks completely with the Canon, that he will reveal his former master's rascality.

The Canon's Yeoman's Tale

The Canon's Yeoman's Tale consists of two parts, which together present a portrait of professional trickery in somewhat the same way as The Friar's Tale portrays the workings of ecclesiastical courts or The Summoner's Tale shows the malefactions of friars. It is, like those tales, a kind of occupational satire. The first part has the general form of a literary confession but is an account of the workings of an alchemist's laboratory, with unending experiments that prove the same point as Cecilia's interview with Almachius: "He that semeth the wiseste, by Jhesus, is moost fool, whan it cometh to the preef." The second part tells of a dishonest canon (not his master, the Yeoman says) who dupes a greedy priest with a series of sleight-of-hand tricks.

For those earlier occupational satires Chaucer had a rich literary tradition on which to draw. Alchemy was relatively new in Chaucer's time, and alchemists had not previously appeared in literature. Chaucer had to draw on his own reading and knowledge. His tale shows that he was well acquainted with the literature of alchemy, and the first trick played by the alchemist on the priest shows that Chaucer also had some practical knowledge of chemistry: he knew that mercury would vaporize at a high temperature and thus leave no trace when the silver replaced it in the crucible.

It has been theorized that Chaucer's knowledge of alchemy and of the trickery of dishonest alchemists came from personal experience, that he had been victimized by some fake alchemist, but there is no basis for this assumption. Indeed, the tale is most interesting not for its account of how the dishonest alchemist tricks the priest but for its portrayal of how the honest alchemist tricks himself—how, despite repeated failures, he is drawn on by the "slidynge science," vainly seeking the goal that ever eludes him. Chaucer

manages to catch both the demonic aspects of the laboratory—with its fires, vile smells, and sweating practitioners—and the fascination that the craft held for its devotees. The final advice to abjure "multiplying" is offered not because the quest for the philosopher's stone is impossible or absurd but because alchemy is an attempt to pry into God's "privetee." In Fragment VIII, science in this tale and philosophy in The Second Nun's Tale—important concerns to the author of the *Treatise on the Astrolabe* and the translator of Boethius—are rejected in favor of Faith.

FRAGMENT IX

Fragments IX and X are a single unit, linked by the first line in the Parson's Prologue, "By that the Maunciple hadde his tale al ended." In the Hengwrt manuscript, however, "Maunciple" appears as a correction, and earlier editors held that "Maunciple" could not have been Chaucer's intention, since the Manciple's Prologue is set in the morning (IX.16) and the Parson's at four in the afternoon (X.5) and that the brief Manciple's Tale could not have filled so long a space of time. Consequently, editors customarily follow the practice established by these scholars and divide the Manciple's and the Parson's prologues and tales into two distinct fragments.

The Manciple's Prologue

It is not clear why Harry Bailly now calls on the Cook for a second tale. Roger has already told one (incomplete) tale, and though the original plan called for two tales from each pilgrim on the way to Canterbury (and two on the way back), no other pilgrim is asked for a second tale. This may be due to the incomplete state of *The Canterbury Tales,* or perhaps Harry is merely teasing, since the monumentally besotted Cook is incapable of speech.

The Manciple's Tale

The story of the tell-tale bird was current in many versions, a number of which may have been known to Chaucer. However, Chaucer's tale is based primarily on that in Ovid's *Metamorphoses,* possibly as it appears in the *Ovide moralisé,* with perhaps some hints from those (also based on Ovid) in Gower's *Confessio amantis* and Machaut's *Livre de Voir Dit.* To the Ovidian tale Chaucer adds the digression on language, Phoebus's elaborate rhetorical lament, an emphasis on Phoebus's music, and the Manciple's moralization. Moreover, in Chaucer's version the crow sings beautifully as well as talks, and Phoebus is explicitly a master of song and minstrelsy. In his rage Phoebus breaks not only his bows and arrows, as in the other versions, but "his mynstralcie,/Bothe harpe, and lute, and gyterne, and sautrie" (IX.267–68). The music of Phoebus is silent, and the crow is deprived of both words and song.

The Manciple's moral is a warning against telling tales: "Be noon auctour newe of tidynges, wheither they been false or trewe." Chaucer elsewhere uses the word *auctour* only for great poets. He may not have planned The Manciple's Tale to be the last of the fables in the *Tales*, but it provides a fitting introduction to the Parson, who leaves fabling and poetry behind.

FRAGMENT X

The Parson's Prologue

Whether or not Chaucer ever intended to expand his work to the dimensions Harry Bailly's original plan implied—four tales from each pilgrim—by the time he wrote this prologue he had clearly decided he would end his work with the words of the Parson, with the pilgrims at "a thropes ende," still moving toward a destination they never reach. There is a powerful sense of an ending in this final prologue; the Canterbury pilgrimage began in the early morning, and it ends as evening is coming on.

Only now are we reminded that this is a pilgrimage rather than a mere holiday outing. The Parson brushes aside the Host's rude demand for a fable. Instead he offers "a myrie tale in prose"—merry indeed to one for whom the Gospel is good news—"to knytte up al this feeste" and to show the pilgrims the way to that "parfit glorious pilgrymage that highte Jerusalem celestial." Even Harry is sobered by the thought; he addresses the Parson respectfully for the first time in a polite request that he tell his "meditacioun," and he asserts his authority for the last time only in urging haste, for the sun is about to set on the pilgrims forever.

The Parson's Tale

The Parson's Tale is a tract on penance. This was a common form of didactic literature, and Chaucer drew principally on two well-known handbooks, a treatise on penance by Raymond of Pennaforte and a treatise on the Deadly Sins by William Peraldus. He used the anonymous *Summa virtutum et remedie anime* for the "remedies," as well as a number of other minor sources. It is possible that Chaucer translated all of this directly from some lost source, perhaps in French; it is also possible that Chaucer himself compiled and translated the works that form the basis of The Parson's Tale. The composition of such a treatise by a layman was not unusual in the fourteenth century, a time of greatly increased lay piety. Henry of Lancaster, the father of the duchess memorialized in *The Book of the Duchess*, composed such a treatise *(Le livre de saintz medicins),* and Chaucer's contemporary, Sir John Clanvowe, author of *The Boke of Cupide* (an imitation of Chaucer), composed a devotional treatise, *The Two Ways*.

The Parsons's Tale is not actually a tale nor even a sermon. The language is vigorous and thus suited to the Parson, who would "snybben sharply" the wrongdoers of his parish, and the subject and its treatment are appropriate to his character. But beyond that the tale has no dramatic or even fictional qualities, and if (as is possible) it was written for some purpose other than inclusion in the *Tales,* it shows no signs of adaptation to the larger work beyond the opening paragraph.

Yet it does in some ways fit well with what precedes, and it seems likely that the biblical text with which the Parson introduces his treatise is intended to refer to the preceding tales: "Stondeth upon the weyes, and seeth and axeth of olde pathes (that is to seyn, of olde sentences) which is the goode wey, and walketh in that wey, and ye shal fynde refresshynge for youre soules." Chaucer's travelers have been considering a variety of ways ("that is to seyn, of olde sentences") without reaching a conclusion about what is best. The Parson seems now to show them.

His review of the Seven Deadly Sins reminds us of many of the pilgrims, and some of their characteristics that seemed attractive in the General Prologue, such as the Squire's love of fine clothing or the Franklin's devotion to good food, are now re-examined in a colder light. Likewise, many of the problems that have concerned them—such as gentilesse and marriage—are here resolved by orthodox Christian doctrine. To many critics, The Parson's Tale seems a particularly suitable conclusion to *The Canterbury Tales.*

Yet any review of the Seven Deadly Sins is in effect a review of society, as is *The Canterbury Tales;* the apparent echoes in The Parson's Tale of the characters and themes of the preceding tales are perhaps inevitable and may be unintentional. The Parson's Tale is concerned not with literature but with souls, and he ends with an uncompromising call for repentance. One who heeds the call is Geoffrey Chaucer himself.

Chaucer's Retraction

Chaucer's Retraction is in the tradition of the medieval *palinode,* like the conclusion to *Troilus,* though here the author retracts not a single work but a whole lifetime of writing. Many have wished that Chaucer had been more modern than he was, or at least more in accord with their own ideas about literature and the world, and some have even questioned the authenticity or sincerity of the Retraction. Yet Chaucer had ample precedent; he was neither the first nor the last great writer to conclude that literature is finally less important than salvation.

Among the works Chaucer retracts, "the tales of Caunterbury, thilke that sownen into synne," receive no special emphasis; they neither begin nor end the list but stand merely as one of a whole series of works the poet now regrets having written. It has been inferred that the Retraction was not intended for inclusion in the *Tales* but for some other occasion, perhaps the death-bed repentance attributed to Chaucer in the fifteenth century. Yet the textual tradition links the Retraction firmly with The Parson's Tale and The Parson's Tale just as firmly with the rest of the *Tales.*

The Retraction leaves us in no doubt that, unfinished, unpolished, and incomplete as *The Canterbury Tales* may be, Chaucer is finished with it. One wonders if a more finished, more nearly perfect version could have been any more satisfying.

LARRY D. BENSON

The Canterbury Tales

Fragment I (Group A)

GENERAL PROLOGUE

■

Here bygynneth the Book of the Tales of Caunterbury.

Whan that Aprill with his shoures soote
The droghte of March hath perced to the
    roote,
And bathed every veyne in swich licour
Of which vertu engendred is the flour;
Whan Zephirus eek with his sweete breeth   5
Inspired hath in every holt and heeth
The tendre croppes, and the yonge sonne
Hath in the Ram his half cours yronne,
And smale foweles maken melodye,
That slepen al the nyght with open ye   10
(So priketh hem nature in hir corages),
Thanne longen folk to goon on pilgrimages,
And palmeres for to seken straunge strondes,
To ferne halwes, kowthe in sondry londes;
And specially from every shires ende   15
Of Engelond to Caunterbury they wende,

The hooly blisful martir for to seke,
That hem hath holpen whan that they were
    seeke.
  Bifil that in that seson on a day,
In Southwerk at the Tabard as I lay   20
Redy to wenden on my pilgrymage
To Caunterbury with ful devout corage,
At nyght was come into that hostelrye
Wel nyne and twenty in a compaignye
Of sondry folk, by aventure yfalle   25
In felaweshipe, and pilgrimes were they alle,
That toward Caunterbury wolden ryde.
The chambres and the stables weren wyde,
And wel we weren esed atte beste.
And shortly, whan the sonne was to reste,   30
So hadde I spoken with hem everichon
That I was of hir felaweshipe anon,
And made forward erly for to ryse,
To take oure wey ther as I yow devyse.

This text was revised by RALPH HANNA III and LARRY
D. BENSON, with materials provided by ROBERT A.
PRATT.

1 **his:** its   **shoures soote:** sweet, fragrant showers
2 **droghte:** dryness   **perced:** pierced
3 **veyne:** vein (of the plants)   **swich licour:** such liquid
4 **Of which vertu:** by which power
5 **Zephirus:** the west wind (which blows in Spring)
6 **Inspired:** breathed life into   **holt and heeth:** grove and field
7 **croppes:** shoots, new leaves   **yonge:** young, because the solar
year has just begun with the vernal equinox. The sun has passed
through the second half of the zodiacal sign Aries (the Ram); the
time is thus late April. April 18 is specified in IntrMLT (II.5).
10 **ye:** eye
11 **priketh hem:** spurs, incites them   **hir corages:** their spirits,
hearts
13 **palmeres:** professional pilgrims who had been to the Holy
Land and carried a palm frond as their emblem   **straunge
strondes:** foreign shores
14 **ferne halwes:** distant shrines   **kowthe in sondry londes:**
known in various lands (i.e., famous)

17 **blisful martir:** blessed martyr, St. Thomas à Becket
18 **hem hath holpen:** helped them   **seeke:** sick
19 **Bifil:** it happened   **seson:** season
20 **Southwerk:** Southwark, across the Thames from London
Tabard: the Tabard Inn
22 **corage:** spirit, feelings
25 **sondry folk:** various sorts of people
25-26 **by aventure yfalle In felaweshipe:** fallen by chance into
fellowship
27 **wolden:** desired, intended to
28 **chambres:** bedrooms
29 **esed atte beste:** accommodated in the best way
30 **shortly:** in brief
31 **everichon:** every one
32 **anon:** straightway
33 **forward:** agreement
34 **devyse:** tell

But nathelees, whil I have tyme and
    space,   35
Er that I ferther in this tale pace,
Me thynketh it acordaunt to resoun
To telle yow al the condicioun
Of ech of hem, so as it semed me,
And whiche they weren, and of what de-
    gree,   40
And eek in what array that they were inne;
And at a knyght than wol I first bigynne.

A KNYGHT ther was, and that a worthy man,
That fro the tyme that he first bigan
To riden out, he loved chivalrie,   45
Trouthe and honour, fredom and curteisie.
Ful worthy was he in his lordes werre,
And therto hadde he riden, no man ferre,
As wel in cristendom as in hethenesse,
And evere honoured for his worthynesse;   50
At Alisaundre he was whan it was wonne.
Ful ofte tyme he hadde the bord bigonne
Aboven alle nacions in Pruce;
In Lettow hadde he reysed and in Ruce,
No Cristen man so ofte of his degree.   55
In Gernade at the seege eek hadde he be
Of Algezir, and riden in Belmarye.
At Lyeys was he and at Satalye,
Whan they were wonne, and in the Grete See
At many a noble armee hadde he be.   60
At mortal batailles hadde he been fiftene,
And foughten for oure feith at Tramyssene
In lystes thries, and ay slayn his foo.

This ilke worthy knyght hadde been also
Somtyme with the lord of Palatye   65
Agayn another hethen in Turkye;
And everemoore he hadde a sovereyn prys.
And though that he were worthy, he was wys,
And of his port as meeke as is a mayde.
He nevere yet no vileynye ne sayde   70
In al his lyf unto no maner wight.
He was a verray, parfit gentil knyght.
But for to tellen yow of his array,
His hors were goode, but he was nat gay.
Of fustian he wered a gypon   75
Al bismotered with his habergeon,
For he was late ycome from his viage,
And wente for to doon his pilgrymage.

With hym ther was his sone, a yong SQUIER,
A lovyere and a lusty bacheler,   80
With lokkes crulle as they were leyd in presse.
Of twenty yeer of age he was, I gesse.
Of his stature he was of evene lengthe,
And wonderly delyvere, and of greet strengthe.
And he hadde been somtyme in chyvachie   85
In Flaundres, in Artoys, and Pycardie,
And born hym weel, as of so litel space,
In hope to stonden in his lady grace.
Embrouded was he, as it were a meede
Al ful of fresshe floures, whyte and reede.   90
Syngynge he was, or floytynge, al the day;
He was as fressh as is the month of May.

---

64 **ilke:** same
65 **Somtyme:** once, at one time   **Palatye:** Balat (in modern Turkey)
66 **Agayn:** against
67 **sovereyn prys:** outstanding reputation
68 Although he was a distinguished knight (i.e., brave), he was prudent.
69 **port:** bearing, manner
70 **vileynye:** rudeness
71 **no maner wight:** any sort of person
72 **verray:** true   **parfit:** perfect (complete)   **gentil:** noble
73 **array:** equipment
74 **gay:** gaily dressed, richly attired
75 **fustian:** coarse cloth   **gypon:** tunic
76 **bismotered with his habergeon:** stained by (rust from) his coat of mail
77 **viage:** journey, expedition
79 **Squier:** squire, a young knight in the service of another knight
80 **lovyere:** lover   **lusty:** lively   **bacheler:** young knight, not yet a knight banneret
81 **crulle:** curled   **presse:** press (curler)
82 **yeer:** years
83 **evene lengthe:** moderate height
84 **wonderly:** marvelously   **delyvere:** agile
85 **somtyme:** for a time, once   **in chyvachie:** on a cavalry expedition
86 **Flaundres, Artoys, Pycardie:** Flanders and parts of northern France, where English armies fought
87 **born hym weel:** conducted himself well   **space:** time
88 **stonden in his lady grace:** find favor with his lady
89 **Embrouded:** embroidered   **meede:** meadow
90 **reede:** red
91 **floytynge:** piping, playing the flute

35 **nathelees:** nonetheless   **space:** opportunity
36 **pace:** go, proceed
37 **Me thynketh it:** it seems to me, I think it   **acordaunt to resoun:** in accord with proper order
38 **condicioun:** state, circumstances
39 **ech:** each (one)
40 **degree:** social rank
41 **array:** dress
42 **wol:** will
45 **chivalrie:** prowess
46 **Trouthe:** fidelity   **honour:** good reputation   **fredom:** generosity of spirit   **curteisie:** refinement of manners
47 **werre:** war
48 **ferre:** farther
49 **hethenesse:** heathen lands
51 **Alisaundre:** Alexandria. The places named in lines 51–66 were places where English knights had campaigned in the fourteenth century.
52 **bord bigonne:** sat in the place of honor
53 **Aboven alle nacions:** above knights from all nations   **Pruce:** Prussia
54 **Lettow:** Lithuania   **reysed:** ridden on raids   **Ruce:** Russia
56 **Gernade:** Granada   **seege:** siege   **eek:** also   **be:** been
57 **Algezir:** Algeciras, in Spain   **Belmarye:** Morocco (Benmarin)
58 **Lyeys:** Ayash (in modern Turkey)   **Satalye:** Atalia (in modern Turkey)
59 **Grete See:** Mediterranean
60 **armee:** military expedition
62 **Tramyssene:** Tlemcen (near Morocco)
63 **In lystes:** in formal duels   **ay:** always

Short was his gowne, with sleves longe and
    wyde.
Wel koude he sitte on hors and faire ryde.
He koude songes make and wel endite,   95
Juste and eek daunce, and weel purtreye and
    write.
So hoote he lovede that by nyghtertale
He sleep namoore than dooth a nyghtyngale.
Curteis he was, lowely, and servysable,
And carf biforn his fader at the table.   100
  A YEMAN hadde he and servantz namo
At that tyme, for hym liste ride so,
And he was clad in cote and hood of grene.
A sheef of pecok arwes, bright and kene,
Under his belt he bar ful thriftily   105
(Wel koude he dresse his takel yemanly;
His arwes drouped noght with fetheres lowe),
And in his hand he baar a myghty bowe.
A not heed hadde he, with a broun visage.
Of wodecraft wel koude he al the usage.   110
Upon his arm he baar a gay bracer,
And by his syde a swerd and a bokeler,
And on that oother syde a gay daggere
Harneised wel and sharp as point of spere;
A Cristopher on his brest of silver sheene.   115
An horn he bar, the bawdryk was of grene;
A forster was he, soothly, as I gesse.
  Ther was also a Nonne, a PRIORESSE,
That of hir smylyng was ful symple and coy;
Hire gretteste ooth was but by Seinte Loy;   120
And she was cleped madame Eglentyne.
Ful weel she soong the service dyvyne,
Entuned in hir nose ful semely;

And Frenssh she spak ful faire and fetisly,
After the scole of Stratford atte Bowe,   125
For Frenssh of Parys was to hire unknowe.
At mete wel ytaught was she with alle;
She leet no morsel from hir lippes falle,
Ne wette hir fyngres in hir sauce depe;
Wel koude she carie a morsel and wel kepe   130
That no drope ne fille upon hire brest.
In curteisie was set ful muchel hir lest.
Hir over-lippe wyped she so clene
That in hir coppe ther was no ferthyng sene
Of grece, whan she dronken hadde hir draughte.
Ful semely after hir mete she raughte.   136
And sikerly she was of greet desport,
And ful plesaunt, and amyable of port,
And peyned hire to countrefete cheere
Of court, and to been estatlich of manere,   140
And to ben holden digne of reverence.
But for to speken of hire conscience,
She was so charitable and so pitous
She wolde wepe, if that she saugh a mous   144
Kaught in a trappe, if it were deed or bledde.
Of smale houndes hadde she that she fedde
With rosted flessh, or milk and wastel-breed.
But soore wepte she if oon of hem were deed,
Or if men smoot it with a yerde smerte;
And al was conscience and tendre herte.   150
Ful semyly hir wympul pynched was,
Hir nose tretys, hir eyen greye as glas,
Hir mouth ful smal, and therto softe and reed.

---

94 **koude:** knew how to
96 **Juste:** joust **eek:** also **weel:** well **purtreye:** draw
97 **hoote:** passionately **by nyghtertale:** at nighttime
98 **sleep:** slept
99 **lowely:** modest (humble) **servysable:** willing to serve, attentive
100 **carf:** carved
101 **Yeman:** yeoman, freeborn servant **he:** the Knight **namo:** no other
102 **hym liste:** he preferred to
105 **bar ful thriftily:** bore very properly
106 **koude:** knew how to **dresse his takel:** care for his arrows, equipment for archery **yemanly:** skillfully, as a good yeoman should
107 **drouped noght with fetheres lowe:** did not fall short because of poorly adjusted feathers
109 **not heed:** close-cropped head **broun:** very dark
111 **gay:** bright **bracer:** archer's arm guard
112 **bokeler:** buckler, small shield
114 **Harneised:** ornamented
115 **Cristopher:** image of St. Christopher **sheene:** bright
116 **bar:** bore **bawdryk:** baldric, shoulder strap for the horn
117 **forster:** forester, game-keeper
119 **ful:** very **symple and coy:** unaffected and quiet
120 **ooth:** oath **Seinte Loy:** St. Eligius
121 **cleped:** called
122 **soong:** sang **service dyvyne:** liturgy
123 **Entuned:** intoned **ful semely:** in a very seemly manner

124 **fetisly:** elegantly
125 in the manner of (*After the scole of*) Stratford atte Bowe (rather than that of the royal court)
127 **At mete:** at dinner **with alle:** indeed
128 **leet:** allowed
130 **koude:** knew how to **wel kepe:** take good care
131 **no drope ne fille:** no drop fell
132 Her greatest pleasure (*lest*) was in good manners (*curteisie*).
133 **over-lippe:** upper lip
134 **coppe:** cup **ferthyng:** speck (spot the size of a farthing)
135 **grece:** grease
136 **after hir mete she raughte:** she reached for her food
137 **sikerly:** truly **greet desport:** excellent deportment
138 **port:** bearing, manner
139 **peyned hire:** took pains **countrefete:** imitate
139–40 **cheere Of court:** the manners of the court
140 **estatlich of manere:** dignified in behavior
141 **digne of reverence:** worthy of respect
142 **conscience:** moral sense and solicitude
143 **pitous:** compassionate
144 **saugh:** saw
147 **rosted flessh:** roasted meat **wastel-breed:** expensive fine white bread
148 **soore:** sorely, bitterly
149 **smoot:** beat **yerde:** switch **smerte:** smartly, painfully
151 **Ful semyly:** very properly **wympul:** wimple, a head dress that covers all but the face **pynched:** pleated
152 **tretys:** well formed **greye:** gray (?); the exact color intended is uncertain.
153 **smal:** small, elegant **therto:** moreover **reed:** red

But sikerly she hadde a fair forheed;
It was almoost a spanne brood, I trowe;   155
For, hardily, she was nat undergrowe.
Ful fetys was hir cloke, as I was war.
Of smal coral aboute hire arm she bar
A peire of bedes, gauded al with grene,   159
And theron heng a brooch of gold ful sheene,
On which ther was first write a crowned A,
And after *Amor vincit omnia*.

Another NONNE with hire hadde she,
That was hir chapeleyne, and preestes thre.

A MONK ther was, a fair for the maistrie,   165
An outridere, that lovede venerie,
A manly man, to been an abbot able.
Ful many a deyntee hors hadde he in stable,
And whan he rood, men myghte his brydel
        heere
Gynglen in a whistlynge wynd als cleere   170
And eek as loude as dooth the chapel belle
Ther as this lord was kepere of the celle.
The reule of Seint Maure or of Seint Beneit—
By cause that it was old and somdel streit
This ilke Monk leet olde thynges pace,   175
And heeld after the newe world the space.
He yaf nat of that text a pulled hen,
That seith that hunters ben nat hooly men,
Ne that a monk, whan he is recchelees,
Is likned til a fissh that is waterlees—   180
This is to seyn, a monk out of his cloystre.
But thilke text heeld he nat worth an oystre;

And I seyde his opinion was good.
What sholde he studie and make hymselven
        wood,
Upon a book in cloystre alwey to poure,   185
Or swynken with his handes, and laboure,
As Austyn bit? How shal the world be served?
Lat Austyn have his swynk to hym reserved!
Therfore he was a prikasour aright:
Grehoundes he hadde as swift as fowel in flight;
Of prikyng and of huntyng for the hare   191
Was al his lust, for no cost wolde he spare.
I seigh his sleves purfiled at the hond
With grys, and that the fyneste of a lond;
And for to festne his hood under his chyn,   195
He hadde of gold ywroght a ful curious pyn;
A love-knotte in the gretter ende ther was.
His heed was balled, that shoon as any glas,
And eek his face, as he hadde been enoynt.
He was a lord ful fat and in good poynt;   200
His eyen stepe, and rollynge in his heed,
That stemed as a forneys of a leed;
His bootes souple, his hors in greet estaat.
Now certeinly he was a fair prelaat;
He was nat pale as a forpyned goost.   205
A fat swan loved he best of any roost.
His palfrey was as broun as is a berye.

A FRERE ther was, a wantowne and a merye,
A lymytour, a ful solempne man.
In alle the ordres foure is noon that kan   210
So muchel of daliaunce and fair langage.
He hadde maad ful many a mariage
Of yonge wommen at his owene cost.
Unto his ordre he was a noble post.

154 **sikerly**: certainly
155 **spanne brood**: about seven to nine inches wide **trowe**: believe
156 **hardily**: certainly
157 **Ful fetys**: very elegant, well made **war**: aware
159 **peire**: set **gauded**: divided by large beads (*gaudes*) marking the Paternosters
160 **sheene**: bright
161 **crowned A**: an A surmounted by a crown
162 **Amor vincit omnia**: love conquers all; the phrase could apply to either divine or earthly love.
164 **chapeleyne**: a nun serving as a secretary to a prioress **preestes thre**: three priests; see n.
165 **a fair for the maistrie**: an extremely fine or handsome one
166 **outridere**: monk with business outside the monastery **venerie**: hunting
167 **manly**: generous, virile
168 **deyntee**: fine
169 **myghte his brydel heere**: could hear his bridle
170 **Gynglen**: jingle **als cleere**: as clearly
172 **celle**: a subordinate monastery
173 **reule of Seint Maure . . . Seint Beneit**: the Benedictine Rule, established by St. Benedict and introduced into France by his follower St. Maurus
174 **somdel streit**: somewhat narrow, strict
175–76 This same monk let old things pass away (*pace*) and followed the customs of modern times.
177 **yaf**: gave **text**: authoritative written statement **pulled**: plucked
179 **recchelees**: heedless of rules
180 **til**: to **waterlees**: out of water
182 **thilke**: that **nat worth an oystre**: i.e., worth nothing

184 **wood**: crazy, mad
185 **alwey**: always **poure**: pore over
186 **swynken**: work
187 **Austyn**: St. Augustine, supposed author of a monastic rule **bit** = *biddeth*, commands
189 **prikasour**: horseman, hunter on horseback **aright**: certainly
190 **Grehoundes**: greyhounds
191 **prikyng**: tracking
192 **lust**: pleasure
193 **seigh**: saw **purfiled**: lined with fur
194 **grys**: expensive squirrel fur **fyneste of a lond**: best to be had
196 **curious**: skillfully made
197 **love-knotte**: elaborate knot **gretter**: larger
198 **balled**: bald
199 **enoynt**: anointed, rubbed with oil
200 **in good poynt**: in good condition
201 **stepe**: prominent or bright
202 His eyes gleamed like a furnace under a cauldron (R.).
203 **souple**: pliant **greet estaat**: excellent condition
204 **prelaat**: ecclesiastical dignitary
205 **forpyned goost**: tormented spirit
208 **wantowne**: jovial, pleasure-loving **merye**: merry
209 **lymytour**: friar licensed (by his order) to beg in a specific district **solempne**: dignified, important
210 **ordres foure**: the four orders of friars **kan**: knows
211 **muchel**: much **daliaunce**: sociability
214 **post**: supporter (pillar of the Church)

Ful wel biloved and famulier was he   215
With frankeleyns over al in his contree,
And eek with worthy wommen of the toun;
For he hadde power of confessioun,
As seyde hymself, moore than a curat,
For of his ordre he was licenciat.   220
Ful swetely herde he confessioun,
And plesaunt was his absolucioun:
He was an esy man to yeve penaunce,
Ther as he wiste to have a good pitaunce.
For unto a povre ordre for to yive   225
Is signe that a man is wel yshryve;
For if he yaf, he dorste make avaunt,
He wiste that a man was repentaunt;
For many a man so hard is of his herte,   229
He may nat wepe, althogh hym soore smerte.
Therfore in stede of wepynge and preyeres
Men moote yeve silver to the povre freres.
His typet was ay farsed ful of knyves
And pynnes, for to yeven faire wyves.
And certeinly he hadde a murye note: 235
Wel koude he synge and pleyen on a rote;
Of yeddynges he baar outrely the pris.
His nekke whit was as the flour-de-lys;
Therto he strong was as a champioun.
He knew the tavernes wel in every toun   240
And everich hostiler and tappestere
Bet than a lazar or a beggestere,
For unto swich a worthy man as he
Acorded nat, as by his facultee,
To have with sike lazars aqueyntaunce.   245
It is nat honest; it may nat avaunce,
For to deelen with no swich poraille,
But al with riche and selleres of vitaille.

And over al, ther as profit sholde arise,
Curteis he was and lowely of servyse;   250
Ther nas no man nowher so vertuous.
He was the beste beggere in his hous;
[And yaf a certeyn ferme for the graunt;   252ᵃ
Noon of his bretheren cam ther in his
    haunt;]   252ᵇ
For thogh a wydwe hadde noght a sho,
So plesaunt was his *"In principio,"*
Yet wolde he have a ferthyng, er he wente.   255
His purchas was wel bettre than his rente.
And rage he koude, as it were right a whelp.
In love-dayes ther koude he muchel help,
For ther he was nat lyk a cloysterer
With a thredbare cope, as is a povre scoler,   260
But he was lyk a maister or a pope.
Of double worstede was his semycope,
That rounded as a belle out of the presse.
Somwhat he lipsed, for his wantownesse,   264
To make his Englissh sweete upon his tonge;
And in his harpyng, whan that he hadde songe,
His eyen twynkled in his heed aryght
As doon the sterres in the frosty nyght.
This worthy lymytour was cleped Huberd.

A MARCHANT was ther with a forked berd,
In mottelee, and hye on horse he sat;   271
Upon his heed a Flaundryssh bever hat,
His bootes clasped faire and fetisly.
His resons he spak ful solempnely,
Sownynge alwey th'encrees of his wynnyng.
He wolde the see were kept for any thyng   276
Bitwixe Middelburgh and Orewelle.

216 **frankeleyns:** landowners   **over al:** everywhere
217 **eek:** also
220 **licenciat:** licensed to hear confessions
223 **esy:** lenient   **yeve:** give
224 **wiste:** expected   **pitaunce:** gift (literally food allowed to a member of a religious house)
225 **povre:** poor
226 **yshryve:** confessed, penitent
227 For if a man gave, he (the Friar) dared to assert (R.)
228 **wiste:** knew
230 **may nat:** cannot, is not able to   **hym soore smerte:** he sorely, painfully, suffers
232 **moote yeve:** must give
233 **typet:** the dangling tip of the hood   **farsed:** stuffed
234 **yeven:** give
235 **murye:** merry, pleasing   **note:** voice
236 **rote:** stringed instrument
237 For reciting ballads (*yeddynges*), he absolutely (*outrely*) took the prize.
238 **flour-de-lys:** lily
239 **champioun:** champion, representative in a judicial duel
241 **everich:** every   **hostiler:** innkeeper   **tappestere:** barmaid
242 **Bet:** better   **lazar:** leper   **beggestere:** beggar-woman
243 **swich:** such
244 It was not suitable, in view of his official position.
245 **sike:** sick
246 **honest:** honorable, respectable   **may nat avaunce:** cannot be profitable
247 **swich poraille:** such poor people
248 **vitaille:** victuals, provisions

249 **ther as:** where
250 **lowely of servyse:** graciously humble
251 **nas** = *ne was*, was not   **vertuous:** capable
252ᵃ **ferme:** fee, fixed payment   **graunt:** grant (of an exclusive territory for begging)
252ᵇ **haunt:** territory
253 **sho:** shoe
254 **In principio:** in the beginning (the opening words of Gen. 1 and John 1, popular for devotions)
255 **ferthyng:** farthing
256 **purchas:** total income   **rente:** proper income
257 **rage:** romp, sport (or flirt)   **whelp:** pup
258 **love-dayes:** days on which disputes were reconciled
260 **povre scoler:** poor scholar, student
262 **double worstede:** a very wide (hence expensive) cloth   **semycope:** short cloak
263 **rounded:** was round   **presse:** casting mold
264 **lipsed:** lisped   **wantownesse:** affectation
266 **songe:** sung
267 **aryght:** exactly
268 **sterres:** stars
269 **cleped:** called
271 **mottelee:** parti-colored cloth   **hye on horse:** in a high saddle
272 **Flaundryssh:** Flemish
273 **fetisly:** elegantly, neatly
274 **resons:** remarks, opinions   **solempnely:** ceremoniously, solemnly
275 **Sownynge:** concerned with, or, making known   **wynnyng:** profit
276 **see:** sea   **kept for any thyng:** protected at all costs
277 **Middelburgh:** a Dutch port   **Orewelle:** Orwell, on the English coast

Wel koude he in eschaunge sheeldes selle.
This worthy man ful wel his wit bisette:
Ther wiste no wight that he was in dette,   280
So estatly was he of his governaunce
With his bargaynes and with his chevyssaunce.
For sothe he was a worthy man with alle,
But, sooth to seyn, I noot how men hym calle.

A CLERK ther was of Oxenford also,   285
That unto logyk hadde longe ygo.
As leene was his hors as is a rake,
And he nas nat right fat, I undertake,
But looked holwe, and therto sobrely.
Ful thredbare was his overeste courtepy,   290
For he hadde geten hym yet no benefice,
Ne was so worldly for to have office.
For hym was levere have at his beddes heed
Twenty bookes, clad in blak or reed,
Of Aristotle and his philosophie   295
Than robes riche, or fithele, or gay sautrie.
But al be that he was a philosophre,
Yet hadde he but litel gold in cofre;
But al that he myghte of his freendes hente,
On bookes and on lernynge he it spente,   300
And bisily gan for the soules preye
Of hem that yaf hym wherwith to scoleye.
Of studie took he moost cure and moost heede,
Noght o word spak he moore than was neede,
And that was seyd in forme and reverence,   305
And short and quyk and ful of hy sentence;
Sownynge in moral vertu was his speche,
And gladly wolde he lerne and gladly teche.

A SERGEANT OF THE LAWE, war and wys,
That often hadde been at the Parvys,   310
Ther was also, ful riche of excellence.
Discreet he was and of greet reverence—
He semed swich, his wordes weren so wise.
Justice he was ful often in assise,
By patente and by pleyn commissioun.   315
For his science and for his heigh renoun,
Of fees and robes hadde he many oon.
So greet a purchasour was nowher noon:
Al was fee symple to hym in effect;
His purchasyng myghte nat been infect.   320
Nowher so bisy a man as he ther nas,
And yet he semed bisier than he was.
In termes hadde he caas and doomes alle
That from the tyme of kyng William were
  falle.   324
Therto he koude endite and make a thyng,
Ther koude no wight pynche at his writyng;
And every statut koude he pleyn by rote.
He rood but hoomly in a medlee cote,
Girt with a ceint of silk, with barres smale;
Of his array telle I no lenger tale.   330

A FRANKELEYN was in his compaignye.
Whit was his berd as is the dayesye;
Of his complexioun he was sangwyn.
Wel loved he by the morwe a sop in wyn;
To lyven in delit was evere his wone,   335
For he was Epicurus owene sone,

---

278 **sheeldes:** A *sheeld* was a unit of exchange; selling shields was a way of borrowing money, often at a cost to the seller.
279 **his wit bisette:** used his wits
281 **estatly:** dignified **governaunce:** behavior, management
282 **bargaynes:** buying and selling **chevyssaunce:** financial arrangements, borrowing
283 **For sothe:** truly **with alle:** indeed
284 **noot** = *ne woot,* do not know
285 **Clerk:** university student
286 **unto logyk hadde longe ygo:** had taken (studied) logic a long time
288 **right:** very **undertake:** affirm, declare
289 **holwe:** emaciated **sobrely:** grave, serious
290 **overeste:** uppermost **courtepy:** short coat
291 **benefice:** ecclesiastical living
292 **office:** secular employment
293 **hym was levere:** he would rather **his beddes heed:** head of his bed
296 **fithele:** fiddle **gay sautrie:** elegant psaltry (a harp-like instrument)
297 **al be that:** even though **philosophre:** the word can mean either philosopher or alchemist
299 **myghte of his freendes hente:** could get from his friends
301 **gan . . . preye:** did pray, prayed
302 **scoleye:** attend the schools of the university
303 **cure:** care
304 **o:** one **neede:** necessary
305 **in forme and reverence:** with due formality and respect (R.)
306 **quyk:** vivid, lively **hy sentence:** elevated content
307 **Sownynge in:** consonant with

309 **Sergeant of the Lawe:** a lawyer who belonged to the highest order in his profession **war:** prudent
310 **Parvys:** the porch of St. Paul's Cathedral
311 **ful riche of excellence:** well endowed with superior qualities
312 **Discreet . . . and of greet reverence:** judicious and with much dignity
314 **Justice:** judge **assise:** the court of assizes
315 **patente:** letter of appointment from the king **pleyn commissioun:** full jurisdiction
316 **science:** knowledge
317 **fees and robes:** grants of yearly income (a legal formula) **many oon:** many a one
318 **purchasour:** land-buyer
319 **fee symple:** unrestricted possession
320 **been infect:** be invalidated
323–24 He had in Year Books all the cases (*caas*) and judicial decisions (*doomes*) from the time of William I.
325 **endite and make a thyng:** draft and draw up a legal document
326 **pynche at:** find a flaw in
327 And he knew every statute entirely by heart.
328 **hoomly:** simply **medlee:** parti-colored
329 **Girt:** encircled **ceint:** belt **barres:** stripes
330 **array:** dress
331 **Frankeleyn:** landowner
332 **dayesye:** daisy
333 **complexioun:** temperament, balance of the body's fluids, the four "humors"—blood, phlegm, red or yellow bile (choler), black bile (melancholy) **sangwyn:** of the sanguine humor (dominated by blood)
334 **sop in wyn:** piece of bread in wine
335 **delit:** delight, pleasure **wone:** custom, wont
336 **Epicurus owene sone:** an Epicurean

That heeld opinioun that pleyn delit
Was verray felicitee parfit.
An housholdere, and that a greet, was he;
Seint Julian he was in his contree. 340
His breed, his ale, was alweys after oon;
A bettre envyned man was nowher noon.
Withoute bake mete was nevere his hous,
Of fissh and flessh, and that so plentevous
It snewed in his hous of mete and drynke; 345
Of alle deyntees that men koude thynke,
After the sondry sesons of the yeer,
So chaunged he his mete and his soper.
Ful many a fat partrich hadde he in muwe,
And many a breem and many a luce in stuwe. 350
Wo was his cook but if his sauce were
Poynaunt and sharp, and redy al his geere.
His table dormant in his halle alway
Stood redy covered al the longe day.
At sessiouns ther was he lord and sire; 355
Ful ofte tyme he was knyght of the shire.
An anlaas and a gipser al of silk
Heeng at his girdel, whit as morne milk.
A shirreve hadde he been, and a contour.
Was nowher swich a worthy vavasour. 360
  An Haberdasshere and a Carpenter,
A Webbe, a Dyere, and a Tapycer—
And they were clothed alle in o lyveree
Of a solempne and a greet fraternitee.
Ful fressh and newe hir geere apiked was; 365
Hir knyves were chaped noght with bras
But al with silver, wroght ful clene and weel,

Hire girdles and hir pouches everydeel.
Wel semed ech of hem a fair burgeys
To sitten in a yeldehalle on a deys. 370
Everich, for the wisdom that he kan,
Was shaply for to been an alderman.
For catel hadde they ynogh and rente,
And eek hir wyves wolde it wel assente;
And elles certeyn were they to blame. 375
It is ful fair to been ycleped "madame,"
And goon to vigilies al bifore,
And have a mantel roialliche ybore.
  A Cook they hadde with hem for the nones
To boille the chiknes with the marybones, 380
And poudre-marchant tart and galyngale.
Wel koude he knowe a draughte of Londoun ale.
He koude rooste, and sethe, and broille, and
     frye,
Maken mortreux, and wel bake a pye.
But greet harm was it, as it thoughte me, 385
That on his shyne a mormal hadde he.
For blankmanger, that made he with the beste.
  A Shipman was ther, wonynge fer by weste;
For aught I woot, he was of Dertemouthe.
He rood upon a rouncy, as he kouthe, 390
In a gowne of faldyng to the knee.
A daggere hangynge on a laas hadde he
Aboute his nekke, under his arm adoun.
The hoote somer hadde maad his hewe al
     broun;
And certeinly he was a good felawe. 395
Ful many a draughte of wyn had he ydrawe

337 **That:** who **pleyn delit:** pure pleasure
338 **verray felicitee parfit:** true perfect happiness
340 **Seint Julian:** patron saint of hospitality
341 **after oon:** of the same (good) quality
342 **envyned:** stocked with wine
343 **bake mete:** pie of meat, fowl, or fish
344 **plentevous:** plenteous
345 **snewed:** snowed
346 **deyntees:** fine food and drink
347 **After the sondry sesons:** according to the various seasons. Seasonal adjustment of the diet was a health measure.
349 **partrich:** partridge **muwe:** pen for birds
350 **breem:** bream (a freshwater fish) **luce:** pike **stuwe:** fish pond
351 **but if:** unless
352 **Poynaunt:** spicy, piercing **geere:** utensils
353 **table dormant:** table permanently in place (rather than taken down between meals)
355 He presided at court sessions.
356 **knyght of the shire:** member of Parliament
357 **anlaas:** broad, two-edged dagger **gipser:** purse
359 **shirreve:** sheriff **contour:** auditor
360 **vavasour:** feudal landholder
361 **Haberdasshere:** a dealer in hats or small wares
362 **Webbe:** weaver **Tapycer:** weaver of tapestries, rugs, etc.
363 **o lyveree:** one livery, distinctive dress worn by members of a guild
364 **solempne:** dignified, important **fraternitee:** parish guild
365 **geere:** equipment **apiked:** trimmed, adorned
366 **chaped:** mounted

368 **girdles:** belts **pouches:** purses **everydeel:** every bit
369 **ech:** each (one) **burgeys:** citizen of a city (tradesman)
370 **yeldehalle:** guildhall **deys:** dais
371 **kan:** knows
372 **shaply:** suitable, fit **alderman:** city official
373 **catel:** property **rente:** income
375 **elles:** otherwise
376 **ycleped "madame":** called "my lady"
377 **vigilies:** vigils, feasts held on the eve of a holy day **al bifore:** in front of everyone, heading the procession
378 **roialliche ybore:** royally carried
379 **for the nones:** for the occasion; see n.
380 **chiknes:** chickens **marybones:** marrow bones
381 **poudre-marchant tart:** a tart spice **galyngale:** powdered aromatic root used as a sweet spice
383 **sethe:** simmer
384 **mortreux:** stews or hashes
385 **harm:** pity **it thoughte me:** it seemed to me
386 **mormal:** ulcer; see n.
387 **blankmanger:** a thick stew or mousse of chopped chicken or fish boiled with rice **with the beste:** excellently
388 **wonynge:** dwelling **fer by weste:** far in the west
389 **For aught I woot:** for all I know **Dertemouthe:** Dartmouth, in Devon, in the south west
390 **rouncy:** carthorse, nag **as he kouthe:** as best he could
391 **faldyng:** coarse woolen cloth
392 **laas:** cord
393 **under his arm adoun:** down under his arm
395 **good felawe:** good companion; see n.

Fro Burdeux-ward, whil that the chapman
    sleep.
Of nyce conscience took he no keep.
If that he faught and hadde the hyer hond,
By water he sente hem hoom to every lond.
But of his craft to rekene wel his tydes,   401
His stremes, and his daungers hym bisides,
His herberwe, and his moone, his lodemenage,
Ther nas noon swich from Hulle to Cartage.
Hardy he was and wys to undertake;   405
With many a tempest hadde his berd been
    shake.
He knew alle the havenes, as they were,
Fro Gootlond to the cape of Fynystere,
And every cryke in Britaigne and in Spayne.
His barge ycleped was the Maudelayne.   410
    With us ther was a DOCTOUR OF PHISIK;
In al this world ne was ther noon hym lik,
To speke of phisik and of surgerye,
For he was grounded in astronomye.
He kepte his pacient a ful greet deel   415
In houres by his magyk natureel.
Wel koude he fortunen the ascendent
Of his ymages for his pacient.
He knew the cause of everich maladye,   419
Were it of hoot, or coold, or moyste, or drye,
And where they engendred, and of what hu-
    mour.
He was a verray, parfit praktisour:
The cause yknowe, and of his harm the roote,
Anon he yaf the sike man his boote.
Ful redy hadde he his apothecaries   425
To sende hym drogges and his letuaries,
For ech of hem made oother for to wynne—

Hir frendshipe nas nat newe to bigynne.
Wel knew he the olde Esculapius,
And Deyscorides, and eek Rufus,   430
Olde Ypocras, Haly, and Galyen,
Serapion, Razis, and Avycen,
Averrois, Damascien, and Constantyn,
Bernard, and Gatesden, and Gilbertyn.
Of his diete mesurable was he,   435
For it was of no superfluitee,
But of greet norissyng and digestible.
His studie was but litel on the Bible.
In sangwyn and in pers he clad was al,
Lyned with taffata and with sendal.   440
And yet he was but esy of dispence;
He kepte that he wan in pestilence.
For gold in phisik is a cordial,
Therefore he lovede gold in special.
    A good WIF was ther OF biside BATHE,   445
But she was somdel deef, and that was scathe.
Of clooth-makyng she hadde swich an haunt
She passed hem of Ypres and of Gaunt.
In al the parisshe wif ne was ther noon   449
That to the offrynge bifore hire sholde goon;
And if ther dide, certeyn so wrooth was she
That she was out of alle charitee.
Hir coverchiefs ful fyne weren of ground;
I dorste swere they weyeden ten pound
That on a Sonday weren upon hir heed.   455
Hir hosen weren of fyn scarlet reed,
Ful streite yteyd, and shoes ful moyste and
    newe.
Boold was hir face, and fair, and reed of hewe.
She was a worthy womman al hir lyve: 459
Housbondes at chirche dore she hadde fyve,
Withouten oother compaignye in youthe—

397 **Burdeux-ward:** the direction of Bordeaux **chapman:** merchant **sleep:** slept
398 **nyce:** scrupulous **took he no keep:** he took no notice
399 **If that:** if **the hyer hond:** the upper hand
401 **craft to rekene:** skill to reckon
402 **stremes:** currents **daungers hym bisides:** perils near at hand
403 **herberwe:** harbors, anchorages; see n. **moone:** positions of the moon **lodemenage:** skill in navigation
404 **Hulle:** Hull, on the Yorkshire Coast **Cartage:** Carthage, Tunisia, or Cartagena, Spain
405 **wys to undertake:** prudent in his undertakings
408 **Gootlond . . . cape of Fynystere:** Probably Gotland and Cape Finistere
409 **cryke:** inlet **Britaigne:** Brittany
410 **barge:** sailing vessel; see n.
411 **Phisik:** medicine
414 **grounded:** instructed **astronomye:** the science of astrology; see n.
416 **houres:** astronomical hours **magyk natureel:** science
417 **fortunen the ascendent:** calculate the planetary position
418 **ymages:** talismatic figures in astrology
420 **hoot, coold, moyste, drye:** one of the elemental qualities; see n.
421 **humour:** kind of bodily fluid
422 **verray:** true **parfit:** perfect, complete **praktisour:** practitioner
424 **Anon:** at once **boote:** remedy
426 **drogges:** drugs **letuaries:** electuaries, medicinal mixtures
427 **ech:** each (one) **wynne:** profit

428 **newe to bigynne:** recently begun
429–34 The physician knows the standard medical authorities, from the Greeks (Aesculapius) to the contemporary English Gilbertus Anglicus; see n.
435 **mesurable:** moderate
439 **sangwyn:** red **pers:** blue or bluish gray
440 **taffata, sendal:** varieties of silk
441 **but esy of dispence:** moderate in (careful about) spending
442 **wan:** gained
443 **cordial:** medicine for the heart
444 **in special:** in particular
446 **somdel deef:** somewhat deaf **that was scathe:** that was a pity. See WBPro III.668.
447 **haunt:** skill
448 **Ypres, Gaunt:** Ypres, Ghent, cloth-making centers in modern Belgium
450 **offrynge:** offering (when the people go to the altar with their offerings at Mass)
451 **wrooth:** angry
452 **out of alle charitee:** deeply upset
453 **coverchiefs:** linen coverings for the head **fyne weren of ground:** were fine in texture
454 **dorste swere:** dare swear **weyeden:** weighed
456 **hosen:** stockings
457 **streite yteyd:** closely laced **moyste:** supple
460 **chirche dore:** door of the church
461 **Withouten:** not counting; see n.

But thereof nedeth nat to speke as nowthe.
And thries hadde she been at Jerusalem;
She hadde passed many a straunge strem;
At Rome she hadde been, and at Boloigne, 465
In Galice at Seint-Jame, and at Coloigne.
She koude muchel of wandrynge by the weye.
Gat-tothed was she, soothly for to seye.
Upon an amblere esily she sat,
Ywympled wel, and on hir heed an hat 470
As brood as is a bokeler or a targe;
A foot-mantel aboute hir hipes large,
And on hir feet a paire of spores sharpe.
In felaweshipe wel koude she laughe and carpe.
Of remedies of love she knew per chaunce,
For she koude of that art the olde daunce. 476
    A good man was ther of religioun,
And was a povre PERSOUN OF A TOUN,
But riche he was of hooly thoght and werk.
He was also a lerned man, a clerk, 480
That Cristes gospel trewely wolde preche;
His parisshens devoutly wolde he teche.
Benygne he was, and wonder diligent,
And in adversitee ful pacient,
And swich he was ypreved ofte sithes. 485
Ful looth were hym to cursen for his tithes,
But rather wolde he yeven, out of doute,
Unto his povre parisshens aboute
Of his offryng and eek of his substaunce.
He koude in litel thyng have suffisaunce. 490
Wyd was his parisshe, and houses fer asonder,
But he ne lefte nat, for reyn ne thonder,
In siknesse nor in meschief to visite

The ferreste in his parisshe, muche and lite,
Upon his feet, and in his hand a staf. 495
This noble ensample to his sheep he yaf,
That first he wroghte, and afterward he
    taughte.
Out of the gospel he tho wordes caughte,
And this figure he added eek therto,
That if gold ruste, what shal iren do? 500
For if a preest be foul, on whom we truste,
No wonder is a lewed man to ruste;
And shame it is, if a prest take keep,
A shiten shepherde and a clene sheep.
Wel oghte a preest ensample for to yive, 505
By his clennesse, how that his sheep sholde
    lyve.
He sette nat his benefice to hyre
And leet his sheep encombred in the myre
And ran to Londoun unto Seinte Poules
To seken hym a chaunterie for soules, 510
Or with a bretherhed to been withholde;
But dwelte at hoom, and kepte wel his folde,
So that the wolf ne made it nat myscarie;
He was a shepherde and noght a mercenarie.
And though he hooly were and vertuous, 515
He was to synful men nat despitous,
Ne of his speche daungerous ne digne,
But in his techyng discreet and benygne.
To drawen folk to hevene by fairnesse,
By good ensample, this was his bisynesse. 520
But it were any persone obstinat,
What so he were, of heigh or lough estat,
Hym wolde he snybben sharply for the nonys.
A bettre preest I trowe that nowher noon ys.
He waited after no pompe and reverence, 525
Ne maked him a spiced conscience,

462 **as nowthe:** now
463–66 Jerusalem, Rome, *Boloigne* (Boulogne in France), *in Galice at Seint-Jame* (St. James of Compostella in Galicia, Spain), and *Coloigne* (Cologne) were celebrated places of pilgrimage.
464 **straunge strem:** foreign sea
468 **Gat-tothed:** with teeth set wide apart (R.)
469 **amblere:** a pacing horse **esily:** comfortably
470 **Ywympled wel:** wearing a large wimple, a head dress that covers all but the face
471 **brood as is a bokeler or a targe:** broad as a buckler or shield
472 **foot-mantel:** an apron-like overskirt
473 **spores:** spurs
474 **carpe:** chatter
475 **remedies of love:** remedies for love-sickness **per chaunce:** as it happened
476 **olde daunce:** tricks of the trade, game of love
478 **povre Persoun:** poor parson
482 **parisshens:** parishioners
483 **Benygne:** gracious
485 **ypreved:** proven **ofte sithes:** many times
486 He was very reluctant (*Ful looth*) to excommunicate (*cursen*) those who did not pay the tithes (one-tenth of their income) legally due their priest.
489 **offryng:** voluntary offerings of the people at Mass **substaunce:** fixed income (from property of the Church)
491 **asonder:** apart
492 **ne lefte nat:** did not omit
493 **meschief:** trouble

494 **ferreste:** those farthest away **muche and lite:** great and small, everyone
496 **ensample:** model
498 **tho:** those
499 **figure:** metaphor
501 **foul:** evil
502 **lewed man:** uneducated man, layman
503 **take keep:** is concerned
504 **shiten:** defiled, foul
506 **clennesse:** purity
507 **sette nat . . . to hyre:** did not farm out
508 **leet:** left **encombred:** stuck
509 **Seinte Poules:** St. Paul's Cathedral
510 **chaunterie:** appointment as a chantry priest, to serve in a chapel endowed for prayers for the soul of its patron
511 **bretherhed to been withholde:** to be retained, hired, as its chaplain by a guild
513 **myscarie:** go wrong
516 **despitous:** scornful
517 **daungerous:** domineering **digne:** haughty
518 **discreet:** courteous
519 **fairnesse:** graciousness, kindness
522 **heigh or lough estat:** high or low rank
523 **snybben:** rebuke **for the nonys:** then, at that time
524 **trowe:** believe
525 **waited after:** expected **reverence:** ceremony
526 **spiced:** over-fastidious; see n.

But Cristes loore and his apostles twelve
He taughte; but first he folwed it hymselve.
   With hym ther was a PLOWMAN, was his
     brother,
That hadde ylad of dong ful many a fother;
A trewe swynkere and a good was he,   531
Lyvynge in pees and parfit charitee.
God loved he best with al his hoole herte
At alle tymes, thogh him gamed or smerte,
And thanne his neighebor right as hymselve.
He wolde thresshe, and therto dyke and delve,
For Cristes sake, for every povre wight,   537
Withouten hire, if it lay in his myght.
His tithes payde he ful faire and wel,
Bothe of his propre swynk and his catel.   540
In a tabard he rood upon a mere.
   Ther was also a REVE, and a MILLERE,
A SOMNOUR, and a PARDONER also,
A MAUNCIPLE, and myself—ther were namo.
   The MILLERE was a stout carl for the nones;
Ful byg he was of brawn, and eek of bones.   546
That proved wel, for over al ther he cam,
At wrastlynge he wolde have alwey the ram.
He was short-sholdred, brood, a thikke knarre;
Ther was no dore that he nolde heve of harre,
Or breke it at a rennyng with his heed.   551
His berd as any sowe or fox was reed,
And therto brood, as though it were a spade.
Upon the cop right of his nose he hade
A werte, and theron stood a toft of herys,   555
Reed as the brustles of a sowes erys;
His nosethirles blake were and wyde.
A swerd and a bokeler bar he by his syde.

His mouth as greet was as a greet forneys.
He was a janglere and a goliardeys,   560
And that was moost of synne and harlotries.
Wel koude he stelen corn and tollen thries;
And yet he hadde a thombe of gold, pardee.
A whit cote and a blew hood wered he.   564
A baggepipe wel koude he blowe and sowne,
And therwithal he broghte us out of towne.
   A gentil MAUNCIPLE was ther of a temple,
Of which achatours myghte take exemple
For to be wise in byynge of vitaille;
For wheither that he payde or took by taille,
Algate he wayted so in his achaat   571
That he was ay biforn and in good staat.
Now is nat that of God a ful fair grace
That swich a lewed mannes wit shal pace
The wisdom of an heep of lerned men?   575
Of maistres hadde he mo than thries ten,
That weren of lawe expert and curious,
Of which ther were a duszeyne in that hous
Worthy to been stywardes of rente and lond
Of any lord that is in Engelond,   580
To make hym lyve by his propre good
In honour dettelees (but if he were wood),
Or lyve as scarsly as hym list desire;
And able for to helpen al a shire
In any caas that myghte falle or happe.   585
And yet this Manciple sette hir aller cappe.
   The REVE was a sclendre colerik man.
His berd was shave as ny as ever he kan;

530 **Who had hauled** (*ylad*) full many a cartload (*fother*) of dung (*dong*)
531 **swynkere:** worker
532 **pees:** peace
534 **thogh him gamed or smerte:** whether it pleased or pained him
535 **right as:** exactly as
536 **therto:** moreover **dyke and delve:** make ditches and dig
537 **wight:** person
538 **hire:** payment **myght:** power
540 **propre swynk:** own labor **catel:** possessions
541 **tabard:** workman's loose, sleeveless outer garment **mere:** mare
544 **namo:** no others
545 **carl:** fellow **for the nones:** indeed
546 **byg:** strong **brawn:** muscle
547 **over al:** wherever
548 **have alwey the ram:** always win the ram (given as a prize)
549 **short-sholdred:** stoutly built (with a thick neck) **thikke knarre:** stout fellow
550 **nolde** = *ne wolde,* would not **heve of harre:** lift off its hinges
551 **at a rennyng:** by running against it
554 **cop:** top
555 **werte:** wart **toft of herys:** tuft of hairs
556 **brustles:** bristles **sowes erys:** sow's ears
557 **nosethirles:** nostrils

559 **greet forneys:** large cauldron
560 **janglere:** a teller of dirty stories **goliardeys:** buffoon
561 **harlotries:** deeds of harlotry, obscenities
562 **stelen corn:** steal grain **tollen thries:** take toll (payment) three times
563 **thombe of gold:** golden thumb; an ironic reference to a proverb, with the implication that there are no honest millers **pardee:** indeed
564 **blew:** blue
565 **sowne:** play
567 **Maunciple . . . of a temple:** business agent, purchaser of provisions for a *temple,* an Inn of Court (school of law)
568 **achatours:** buyers **myghte:** could
569 **byynge of vitaille:** purchase of victuals, provisions
570 **by taille:** on credit
571 **Algate:** always **wayted so in his achaat:** watched so carefully (for his opportunity) in his purchases
572 **ay biforn:** always ahead
574 **lewed:** uneducated **pace:** surpass
576 **mo:** more
577 **curious:** skillful
578 **duszeyne:** dozen
579 **stywardes:** stewards **rente:** income
581 **propre good:** own wealth
582 **dettelees:** without debts **but if he were wood:** unless he was crazy
583 **as scarsly as hym list desire:** as economically as he pleased
585 **caas:** case, circumstances **happe:** occur by chance
586 **sette hir aller cappe:** deceived them all
587 **Reve:** reeve, manager of an estate or farm **sclendre:** lean **colerik:** dominated by the humor choler
588 **ny:** close **kan:** can

His heer was by his erys ful round yshorn;
His top was dokked lyk a preest biforn. 590
Ful longe were his legges and ful lene,
Ylyk a staf; ther was no calf ysene.
Wel koude he kepe a gerner and a bynne;
Ther was noon auditour koude on him wynne.
Wel wiste he by the droghte and by the reyn
The yeldynge of his seed and of his greyn. 596
His lordes sheep, his neet, his dayerye,
His swyn, his hors, his stoor, and his pultrye
Was hoolly in this Reves governynge,
And by his covenant yaf the rekenynge, 600
Syn that his lord was twenty yeer of age.
Ther koude no man brynge hym in arrerage.
Ther nas baillif, ne hierde, nor oother hyne,
That he ne knew his sleighte and his covyne;
They were adrad of hym as of the deeth. 605
His wonyng was ful faire upon an heeth;
With grene trees yshadwed was his place.
He koude bettre than his lord purchace.
Ful riche he was astored pryvely.
His lord wel koude he plesen subtilly, 610
To yeve and lene hym of his owene good,
And have a thank, and yet a cote and hood.
In youthe he hadde lerned a good myster:
He was a wel good wrighte, a carpenter.
This Reve sat upon a ful good stot 615
That was al pomely grey and highte Scot.
A long surcote of pers upon he hade,
And by his syde he baar a rusty blade.
Of Northfolk was this Reve of which I telle,
Biside a toun men clepen Baldeswelle. 620
Tukked he was as is a frere aboute,

And evere he rood the hyndreste of oure route.
    A SOMONOUR was ther with us in that place,
That hadde a fyr-reed cherubynnes face,
For saucefleem he was, with eyen narwe. 625
As hoot he was and lecherous as a sparwe,
With scalled browes blake and piled berd.
Of his visage children were aferd.
Ther nas quyk-silver, lytarge, ne brymstoon,
Boras, ceruce, ne oille of tartre noon, 630
Ne oynement that wolde clense and byte,
That hym myghte helpen of his whelkes white,
Nor of the knobbes sittynge on his chekes.
Wel loved he garleek, oynons, and eek lekes,
And for to drynken strong wyn, reed as
        blood; 635
Thanne wolde he speke and crie as he were
        wood.
And whan that he wel dronken hadde the wyn,
Thanne wolde he speke no word but Latyn.
A fewe termes hadde he, two or thre,
That he had lerned out of som decree— 640
No wonder is, he herde it al the day;
And eek ye knowen wel how that a jay
Kan clepen "Watte" as wel as kan the pope.
But whoso koude in oother thyng hym grope,
Thanne hadde he spent al his philosophie; 645
Ay *Questio quid iuris* wolde he crie.
He was a gentil harlot and a kynde;
A bettre felawe sholde men noght fynde.
He wolde suffre for a quart of wyn
A good felawe to have his concubyn 650
A twelf month, and excuse hym atte fulle;
Ful prively a fynch eek koude he pulle.

---

589 **erys:** ears **round yshorn:** closely cropped
590 **top:** top of his head **dokked:** cut short **biforn:** in the front
592 **Ylyk a staf:** like a stick
593 **gerner:** granary **bynne:** bin (for storing grain)
594 **on him wynne:** earn anything (by catching him out)
597 **neet:** cattle **dayerye:** herd of dairy cattle
598 **hors:** horses **stoor:** livestock **pultrye:** poultry
600 **covenant:** agreement, contract
601 **Syn that:** since **yeer:** years
602 **arrerage:** arrears
603 **nas** = *ne was*, was not **baillif:** manager of a farm **hierde:** herdsman **hyne:** servant
604 **sleighte:** trickery **covyne:** treachery
605 **adrad:** afraid **the deeth:** the plague (?); see n.
606 **wonyng:** dwelling
608 **purchace:** buy property
609 **riche:** richly **astored:** provided **pryvely:** secretly
610–12 He could please his lord by lending him some of his (the lord's) own possessions (i.e., what he had stolen from him) and thus obtain thanks and a reward besides (R.).
613 **myster:** craft
615 **stot:** horse
616 **pomely:** dapple **highte:** was called
617 **surcote:** outer coat **pers:** dark blue
620 **clepen:** call
621 **Tukked he was as is a frere:** having his long coat hitched up and held by a girdle (R.), like a friar

622 **hyndreste:** last **route:** company
623 **Somonour:** a server of summonses for an ecclesiastical court
624 **fyr-reed:** fire-red **cherubynnes:** cherub's
625 **saucefleem:** pimpled **eyen narwe:** swollen eyelids
627 **scalled:** infected with the scall, a skin disease; cf. Adam 3
piled: with hair fallen out
629–30 Mercury, lead monoxide (*lytarge*), sulphur (*brymstoon*), borax (*boras*), white lead (*ceruce*), and cream of tartar were all used in medicine.
631 **oynement:** ointment **byte:** burn
632 **whelkes:** pimples, pustules
633 **knobbes:** swellings
634 **garleek, oynons, lekes:** garlic, onions, leeks
636 **wood:** crazy
639 **termes:** technical terms
640 **decree:** decretal, text of ecclesiastical law
643 **clepen "Watte":** say "Walter"
644 **grope:** examine
644–45 But anyone who knew how to test him further found that to be the extent of his learning.
646 **Questio quid iuris:** The question is, what point of the law (applies)?
647 **harlot:** buffoon, jester
649 **suffre:** allow
651 **atte fulle:** completely
652 Secretly (discreetly) he also knew how to pluck a finch (trick or swindle someone).

And if he foond owher a good felawe,
He wolde techen him to have noon awe
In swich caas of the ercedekenes curs,   655
But if a mannes soule were in his purs;
For in his purs he sholde ypunysshed be.
"Purs is the ercedekenes helle," seyde he.
But wel I woot he lyed right in dede;   659
Of cursyng oghte ech gilty man him drede,
For curs wol slee right as assoillyng savith,
And also war hym of a *Significavit.*
In daunger hadde he at his owene gise
The yonge girles of the diocise,
And knew hir conseil, and was al hir reed.   665
A gerland hadde he set upon his heed,
As greet as it were for an ale-stake.
A bokeleer hadde he maad hym of a cake.

    With hym ther rood a gentil PARDONER
Of Rouncivale, his freend and his compeer,   670
That streight was comen fro the court of Rome.
Ful loude he soong "Com hider, love, to me!"
This Somonour bar to hym a stif burdoun;
Was nevere trompe of half so greet a soun.
This Pardoner hadde heer as yelow as wex,   675
But smothe it heeng as dooth a strike of flex;
By ounces henge his lokkes that he hadde,
And therwith he his shuldres overspradde;
But thynne it lay, by colpons oon and oon.
But hood, for jolitee, wered he noon,   680
For it was trussed up in his walet.
Hym thoughte he rood al of the newe jet;
Dischevelee, save his cappe, he rood al bare.

Swiche glarynge eyen hadde he as an hare.
A vernycle hadde he sowed upon his cappe.
His walet, biforn hym in his lappe,   686
Bretful of pardoun comen from Rome al hoot.
A voys he hadde as smal as hath a goot.
No berd hadde he, ne nevere sholde have;
As smothe it was as it were late shave.   690
I trowe he were a geldyng or a mare.
But of his craft, fro Berwyk into Ware
Ne was ther swich another pardoner.
For in his male he hadde a pilwe-beer,
Which that he seyde was Oure Lady veyl;   695
He seyde he hadde a gobet of the seyl
That Seint Peter hadde, whan that he wente
Upon the see, til Jhesu Crist hym hente.
He hadde a croys of latoun ful of stones,
And in a glas he hadde pigges bones.   700
But with thise relikes, whan that he fond
A povre person dwellynge upon lond,
Upon a day he gat hym moore moneye
Than that the person gat in monthes tweye;
And thus, with feyned flaterye and japes,   705
He made the person and the peple his apes.
But trewely to tellen atte laste,
He was in chirche a noble ecclesiaste.
Wel koude he rede a lessoun or a storie,
But alderbest he song an offertorie;   710
For wel he wiste, whan that song was songe,
He moste preche and wel affile his tonge
To wynne silver, as he ful wel koude;
Therefore he song the murierly and loude.   714

    Now have I toold you soothly, in a clause,
Th'estaat, th'array, the nombre, and eek the
        cause

653 **owher:** anywhere
655 **caas:** case, circumstances   **ercedekenes curs:** excommunication
656 **But if:** unless
659 **woot:** know
660 **cursyng:** archdeacon's curse, excommunication   **him drede:** be afraid
661 **wol slee:** will slay   **assoillyng:** absolution
662 **war hym:** let him beware   **Significavit:** order for imprisonment
663 **In daunger:** in (his) control   **at his owene gise:** as he pleased
664 **girles:** young women or young people
665 **conseil:** secrets   **al hir reed:** adviser of them all
666 **gerland:** wreath
667 **ale-stake:** sign of an alehouse
668 **cake:** loaf of bread
669 **Pardoner:** a seller of indulgences
670 **Rouncivale:** a hospital at Charing Cross   **compeer:** companion
671 **court of Rome:** papal court
672 **"Com hider . . .":** Probably the refrain of a popular song
673 **stif burdoun:** strong bass
674 **trompe:** trumpet   **soun:** sound
675 **heer:** hair   **wex:** wax
676 **strike:** clump, hank   **flex:** flax
677 **ounces:** small strands
679 **colpons:** strands   **oon and oon:** one by one
680 **for jolitee:** to make an attractive appearance
681 **trussed:** packed   **walet:** pouch, knapsack
682 **Hym thoughte:** it seemed to him, he thought   **al of the newe jet:** in the very latest fashion
683 **Dischevelee:** with hair unbound, hanging loose   **save:** save for, except

684 **glarynge eyen:** staring eyes
685 **vernycle:** Veronica, a reproduction of St. Veronica's cloth, bearing the imprint of Christ's face; a badge of the pilgrimage to Rome   **sowed:** sewn
686 **walet:** pouch, knapsack   **lappe:** large pocket (in a fold of his clothing)
687 **Bretful:** brimful   **pardoun:** papal indulgences
688 **voys:** voice   **smal:** high   **goot:** goat
691 **trowe:** believe   **geldyng or a mare:** a eunuch or a homosexual
692 **fro Berwyk into Ware:** from one end of England to the other
694 **male:** pouch, bag   **pilwe-beer:** pillow-case
695 **Oure Lady veyl:** Our Lady's veil
696 **gobet of the seyl:** piece of the sail
698 **see:** sea   **til:** until   **hente:** took
699 **croys:** cross   **latoun:** a brass-like alloy
702 **person:** parson   **upon lond:** in the countryside
703 **gat hym:** got himself
704 **tweye:** two
705 **japes:** tricks
706 He made fools (*apes*) of the parson and the people.
707 **atte laste:** at the last, finally
709 **lessoun, storie:** liturgical texts, often from the Bible, read during Mass
710 **alderbest:** best of all   **offertorie:** Offertory (said or sung when offerings are made at Mass)
712 **affile his tonge:** smooth his speech
714 **song:** sang   **murierly:** more merrily
715 **in a clause:** briefly

Why that assembled was this compaignye
In Southwerk at this gentil hostelrye
That highte the Tabard, faste by the Belle.
But now is tyme to yow for to telle   720
How that we baren us that ilke nyght,
Whan we were in that hostelrie alyght;
And after wol I telle of our viage
And al the remenaunt of oure pilgrimage.
But first I pray yow, of youre curteisye,   725
That ye n'arette it nat my vileynye,
Thogh that I pleynly speke in this mateere,
To telle yow hir wordes and hir cheere,
Ne thogh I speke hir wordes proprely.
For this ye knowen al so wel as I: 730
Whoso shal telle a tale after a man,
He moot reherce as ny as evere he kan
Everich a word, if it be in his charge,
Al speke he never so rudeliche and large,
Or ellis he moot telle his tale untrewe,   735
Or feyne thyng, or fynde wordes newe.
He may nat spare, althogh he were his brother;
He moot as wel seye o word as another.
Crist spak hymself ful brode in hooly writ,
And wel ye woot no vileynye is it.   740
Eek Plato seith, whoso kan hym rede,
The wordes moote be cosyn to the dede.
Also I prey yow to foryeve it me,
Al have I nat set folk in hir degree   744
Heere in this tale, as that they sholde stonde.
My wit is short, ye may wel understonde.

   Greet chiere made oure Hoost us everichon,
And to the soper sette he us anon.
He served us with vitaille at the beste;   749
Strong was the wyn, and wel to drynke us leste.
A semely man OURE HOOSTE was withalle
For to been a marchal in an halle.

A large man he was with eyen stepe—
A fairer burgeys was ther noon in Chepe—   754
Boold of his speche, and wys, and wel ytaught,
And of manhod hym lakkede right naught.
Eek therto he was right a myrie man;
And after soper pleyen he bigan,
And spak of myrthe amonges othere thynges,
Whan that we hadde maad oure rekenynges,   760
And seyde thus: "Now, lordynges, trewely,
Ye been to me right welcome, hertely;
For by my trouthe, if that I shal nat lye,
I saugh nat this yeer so myrie a compaignye
Atones in this herberwe as is now.   765
Fayn wolde I doon yow myrthe, wiste I how.
And of a myrthe I am right now bythoght,
To doon yow ese, and it shal coste noght.
   "Ye goon to Caunterbury—God yow speede,
The blisful martir quite yow youre meede!   770
And wel I woot, as ye goon by the weye,
Ye shapen yow to talen and to pleye;
For trewely, confort ne myrthe is noon
To ride by the weye doumb as a stoon;
And therfore wol I maken yow disport,   775
As I seyde erst, and doon yow som confort.
And if yow liketh alle by oon assent
For to stonden at my juggement,
And for to werken as I shal yow seye,
Tomorwe, whan ye riden by the weye,   780
Now, by my fader soule that is deed,
But ye be myrie, I wol yeve yow myn heed!
Hoold up youre hondes, withouten moore
    speche."
   Oure conseil was nat longe for to seche. 784
Us thoughte it was noght worth to make it wys,
And graunted hym withouten moore avys,

719 **faste by:** close to **Belle:** a tavern
721 **baren us:** behaved **ilke:** same
722 **alyght:** arrived
723 **wol:** will **viage:** journey
726 **n'arette it nat:** do not attribute it to **vileynye:** rudeness
728 **cheere:** behavior
730 **al so:** as
731 **Whoso:** whoever **shal:** must
732 **moot reherce:** must repeat **ny:** close **kan:** knows how
733 **Everich a:** every **in his charge:** his responsibility
734 **Al speke he:** although he may speak **rudeliche:** ignorantly, crudely **large:** freely
735 **moot:** must **untrewe:** inaccurately
736 **feyne thyng:** make up things
738 **o:** one
739 **brode:** plainly
740 **woot:** know **vileynye:** rudeness
741 **kan hym rede:** knows how to interpret him
742 **cosyn:** cousin, closely related
744 **Al:** although **degree:** social rank
746 **may:** can
747 **Greet chiere:** good cheer **us everichon:** every one of us
749 **vitaille:** victuals, provisions **at the beste:** of the best sort
750 **wel to drynke us leste:** we were well pleased to drink
751 **semely:** seemly, impressive **withalle:** indeed
752 **marchal:** master of ceremonies

753 **eyen stepe:** bright or large eyes; see n.
754 **burgeys:** citizen of a city (tradesman) **Chepe:** Cheapside
756 **manhod:** manliness, qualities proper to a good man **right naught:** nothing at all
758 **pleyen:** to play, provide amusement
760 **maad oure rekenynges:** paid our bills
763 **trouthe:** faith
764 **saugh:** saw
765 **Atones:** at one time **herberwe:** lodging
766 **Fayn:** gladly **doon yow myrthe:** make you happy **wiste I:** if I knew
767 **am . . . bythoght:** have thought
768 **doon yow ese:** give you pleasure
769 **yow speede:** give you success
770 **quite yow youre meede:** give you your reward
772 **shapen yow:** you intend **talen:** tell tales **pleye:** amuse yourselves
776 **erst:** before
777 **yow liketh alle:** it pleases all of you **by oon assent:** unanimously
779 **werken:** do
781 Now by the soul of my father, who is dead
782 **But ye be:** unless you are, if you are not
784 **conseil:** decision **nat longe for to seche:** i.e., ready at hand
785 **worth:** worthwhile **make it wys:** deliberate on it, raise difficulties
786 **avys:** discussion

And bad him seye his voirdit as hym leste.
"Lordynges," quod he, "now herkneth for the
    beste;
But taak it nought, I prey yow, in desdeyn. 789
This is the poynt, to speken short and pleyn,
That ech of yow, to shorte with oure weye,
In this viage shal telle tales tweye
To Caunterbury-ward, I mene it so,
And homward he shal tellen othere two,
Of aventures that whilom han bifalle. 795
And which of yow that bereth hym best of alle—
That is to seyn, that telleth in this caas
Tales of best sentence and moost solaas—
Shal have a soper at oure aller cost
Heere in this place, sittynge by this post, 800
Whan that we come agayn fro Caunterbury.
And for to make yow the moore mury,
I wol myselven goodly with yow ryde,
Right at myn owene cost, and be youre gyde;
And whoso wole my juggement withseye 805
Shal paye al that we spenden by the weye.
And if ye vouche sauf that it be so,
Tel me anon, withouten wordes mo,
And I wol erly shape me therfore."
   This thyng was graunted, and oure othes
    swore 810
With ful glad herte, and preyden hym also
That he wolde vouche sauf for to do so,
And that he wolde been oure governour,
And of oure tales juge and reportour,
And sette a soper at a certeyn pris, 815
And we wol reuled been at his devys
In heigh and lough; and thus by oon assent
We been acorded to his juggement.
And therupon the wyn was fet anon;
We dronken, and to reste wente echon, 820
Withouten any lenger taryynge.

Amorwe, whan that day bigan to sprynge,
Up roos oure Hoost, and was oure aller cok,
And gadrede us togidre alle in a flok,
And forth we riden a litel moore than paas 825
Unto the Wateryng of Seint Thomas;
And there oure Hoost bigan his hors areste
And seyde, "Lordynges, herkneth, if yow leste.
Ye woot youre foreward, and I it yow recorde.
If even-song and morwe-song accorde, 830
Lat se now who shal telle the firste tale.
As evere mote I drynke wyn or ale,
Whoso be rebel to my juggement
Shal paye for al that by the wey is spent. 834
Now draweth cut, er that we ferrer twynne;
He which that hath the shorteste shal bigynne.
Sire Knyght," quod he, "my mayster and my
    lord,
Now draweth cut, for that is myn accord.
Cometh neer," quod he, "my lady Prioresse.
And ye, sire Clerk, lat be youre shamefastnesse,
Ne studieth noght; ley hond to, every man!"
Anon to drawen every wight bigan, 842
And shortly for to tellen as it was,
Were it by aventure, or sort, or cas,
The sothe is this: the cut fil to the Knyght, 845
Of which ful blithe and glad was every wyght,
And telle he moste his tale, as was resoun,
By foreward and by composicioun,
As ye han herd; what nedeth wordes mo?
And whan this goode man saugh that it was so,
As he that wys was and obedient 851
To kepe his foreward by his free assent,
He seyde, "Syn I shal bigynne the game,
What, welcome be the cut, a Goddes name!
Now lat us ryde, and herkneth what I seye." 855
And with that word we ryden forth oure weye,
And he bigan with right a myrie cheere
His tale anon, and seyde as ye may heere.

787 **voirdit:** verdict
788 **quod:** said **for the beste:** the best course of action
790 **short and pleyn:** clearly and briefly
791 **to shorte with:** in order (with which) to shorten
792 **shal:** must **tweye:** two
794 **othere two:** two others
795 **whilom:** once, in former times **han bifalle:** have happened
796 **bereth hym best:** does best
798 **sentence:** meaning, significance **solaas:** pleasure
799 **at oure aller cost:** at the cost of all of us
803 **goodly:** gladly
804 **gyde:** guide
805 **withseye:** gainsay
806 **Shal:** must
807 **vouche sauf:** grant, agree
808 **anon:** straightway **mo:** more
809 **shape me:** get ready
811 **preyden:** The understood subject is "we."
814 **juge:** judge **reportour:** record keeper
815 **pris:** price
816 **at his devys:** as he wishes
817 **In heigh and lough:** in every respect **by oon assent:** unanimously
819 **fet:** fetched
820 **echon:** each one

823 **oure aller cok:** rooster of us all (awakened us all)
825 **paas:** walk, the slowest gait of a horse
826 **the Wateryng of Seint Thomas:** a brook about two miles from London
827 **areste:** stop
828 **if yow leste:** if you please
829 **foreward:** agreement **recorde:** recall, bring to mind
830 *That is,* if you still agree this morning with what you said last night.
832 **mote:** may
835 **draweth cut:** draw lots **ferrer twynne:** depart further (from London)
838 **accord:** decision
839 **neer:** nearer
840 **lat be:** leave off **shamefastnesse:** modesty
844 **aventure, or sort, or cas:** chance, luck, or destiny
845 **sothe:** truth
847 **resoun:** reasonable, just
848 **composicioun:** agreement
853 **Syn:** since **shal:** must
854 **a:** in
857 **cheere:** expression

THE KNIGHT'S TALE

Heere bigynneth the Knyghtes Tale.

Iamque domos patrias, Scithice post aspera gentis
Prelia, laurigero, &c.

Whilom, as olde stories tellen us,
Ther was a duc that highte Theseus;   860
Of Atthenes he was lord and governour,
And in his tyme swich a conquerour
That gretter was ther noon under the sonne.
Ful many a riche contree hadde he wonne;
What with his wysdom and his chivalrie,   865
He conquered al the regne of Femenye,
That whilom was ycleped Scithia,
And weddede the queene Ypolita,
And broghte hire hoom with hym in his contree
With muchel glorie and greet solempnytee,
And eek hir yonge suster Emelye.   871
And thus with victorie and with melodye
Lete I this noble duc to Atthenes ryde,
And al his hoost in armes hym bisyde.

    And certes, if it nere to long to heere,   875
I wolde have toold yow fully the manere
How wonnen was the regne of Femenye
By Theseus and by his chivalrye;
And of the grete bataille for the nones
Bitwixen Atthenes and Amazones;   880
And how asseged was Ypolita,
The faire, hardy queene of Scithia;
And of the feste that was at hir weddynge,
And of the tempest at hir hoom-comynge;
But al that thyng I moot as now forbere.   885
I have, God woot, a large feeld to ere,
And wayke been the oxen in my plough.

The remenant of the tale is long ynough.
I wol nat letten eek noon of this route;
Lat every felawe telle his tale aboute,   890
And lat se now who shal the soper wynne;
And ther I lefte, I wol ayeyn bigynne.

    This duc, of whom I make mencioun,
Whan he was come almoost unto the toun,
In al his wele and in his mooste pride,   895
He was war, as he caste his eye aside,
Where that ther kneled in the heighe weye
A compaignye of ladyes, tweye and tweye,
Ech after oother clad in clothes blake;
But swich a cry and swich a wo they make   900
That in this world nys creature lyvynge
That herde swich another waymentynge;
And of this cry they nolde nevere stenten
Til they the reynes of his brydel henten.
    "What folk been ye, that at myn hom-
            comynge   905
Perturben so my feste with criynge?"
Quod Theseus. "Have ye so greet envye
Of myn honour, that thus compleyne and crye?
Or who hath yow mysboden or offended?
And telleth me if it may been amended,   910
And why that ye been clothed thus in blak."
    The eldeste lady of hem alle spak,
Whan she hadde swowned with a deedly cheere,
That it was routhe for to seen and heere;
She seyde, "Lord, to whom Fortune hath yiven
Victorie, and as a conqueror to lyven,   916

Iamque domos, *etc.*: And now (Theseus, drawing nigh his)
native land in laurelled car after fierce battling with the Scithian
folk, etc. [is heralded by glad applause and the heaven-flung
shout of the populace and the merry trump of warfare ended].
The lines are from Statius's *Thebaid.*
859 **Whilom**: once   **stories**: histories
860 **duc**: duke   **highte**: was called
866 **regne of Femenye**: country of the Amazons, land of women
870 **solempnytee**: splendor, ceremony
871 **suster**: sister
875 **certes**: certainly   **nere** = *ne were*, were not   **heere**: hear
878 **chivalrye**: knights
881 **asseged**: besieged
883 **feste**: festivity
884 **tempest**: storm
885 **moot as now forbere**: must now forgo
886 **ere**: plow
887 **wayke**: weak

889 **letten**: hinder   **route**: company
890 **aboute**: in turn
892 **ther**: where   **ayeyn**: again
895 **wele**: prosperity
896 **war**: aware
898 **tweye and tweye**: two by two
901 **nys** = *ne ys*, is not
902 **waymentynge**: lamentation
903 **nolde** = *ne wolde*, would not   **stenten**: cease
904 **Til**: until   **henten**: siezed
906 **Perturben**: disturb   **feste**: festival
908 **compleyne**: lament
909 **mysboden**: injured
913 **swowned**: swooned, fainted   **deedly cheere**: deathlike look
914 **routhe**: pity, a sorrowful matter
915 **yiven**: given

Nat greveth us youre glorie and youre honour,
But we biseken mercy and socour.
Have mercy on oure wo and oure distresse!
Som drope of pitee, thurgh thy gentillesse,
Upon us wrecched wommen lat thou falle,   921
For, certes, lord, ther is noon of us alle
That she ne hath been a duchesse or a queene.
Now be we caytyves, as it is wel seene,
Thanked be Fortune and hire false wheel,   925
That noon estaat assureth to be weel.
And certes, lord, to abyden youre presence,
Heere in this temple of the goddesse Clemence
We han ben waitynge al this fourtenyght.
Now help us, lord, sith it is in thy myght.   930
    "I, wrecche, which that wepe and wayle thus,
Was whilom wyf to kyng Cappaneus,
That starf at Thebes — cursed be that day! —
And alle we that been in this array
And maken al this lamentacioun,   935
We losten alle oure housbondes at that toun,
Whil that the seege theraboute lay.
And yet now the olde Creon — weylaway! —
That lord is now of Thebes the citee,
Fulfild of ire and of iniquitee,   940
He, for despit and for his tirannye,
To do the dede bodyes vileynye
Of alle oure lordes whiche that been yslawe,
Hath alle the bodyes on an heep ydrawe,
And wol nat suffren hem, by noon assent,   945
Neither to been yburyed nor ybrent,
But maketh houndes ete hem in despit."
    And with that word, withouten moore respit,
They fillen gruf and criden pitously,   949
"Have on us wrecched wommen som mercy,
And lat oure sorwe synken in thyn herte."
    This gentil duc doun from his courser sterte
With herte pitous, whan he herde hem speke.

Hym thoughte that his herte wolde breke,   954
Whan he saugh hem so pitous and so maat,
That whilom weren of so greet estaat;
And in his armes he hem alle up hente,
And hem conforteth in ful good entente,
And swoor his ooth, as he was trewe knyght,
He wolde doon so ferforthly his myght   960
Upon the tiraunt Creon hem to wreke
That al the peple of Grece sholde speke
How Creon was of Theseus yserved
As he that hadde his deeth ful wel deserved.
And right anoon, withouten moore abood,   965
His baner he desplayeth, and forth rood
To Thebes-ward, and al his hoost biside.
No neer Atthenes wolde he go ne ride,
Ne take his ese fully half a day,
But onward on his wey that nyght he lay,   970
And sente anon Ypolita the queene,
And Emelye, hir yonge suster sheene,
Unto the toun of Atthenes to dwelle,
And forth he rit; ther is namoore to telle.
    The rede statue of Mars, with spere and
        targe,   975
So shyneth in his white baner large
That alle the feeldes glyteren up and doun;
And by his baner born is his penoun
Of gold ful riche, in which ther was ybete   979
The Mynotaur, which that he wan in Crete.
Thus rit this duc, thus rit this conquerour,
And in his hoost of chivalrie the flour,
Til that he cam to Thebes and alighte
Faire in a feeld, ther as he thoughte to fighte.
But shortly for to speken of this thyng,   985
With Creon, which that was of Thebes kyng,
He faught, and slough hym manly as a knyght
In pleyn bataille, and putte the folk to flyght;
And by assaut he wan the citee after,

917 **Nat greveth us:** does not grieve us
918 **biseken:** beseech, ask for
920 **thurgh:** through, because of
924 **caytyves:** miserable wretches
926 **weel:** well
927 **abyden:** wait for
929 **han ben:** have been
930 **sith:** since
933 **starf:** died
934 **array:** state
937 **seege:** siege
938 **weylaway:** alas
941 **despit:** spite
942 **vileynye:** shame, dishonor
943 **yslawe:** slain
944 **on an heep ydrawe:** dragged in a heap
945 **suffren hem:** allow them
946 **yburyed nor ybrent:** buried nor burned, cremated
947 **in despit:** in spite
948 **respit:** delay, respite
949 **fillen gruf:** fell face down
951 **sorwe:** sorrow
952 **gentil:** noble   **courser:** charger, war-horse   **sterte:** leapt
953 **pitous:** compassionate

955 **pitous:** pitiful   **maat:** dejected
956 **whilom:** once, formerly   **so greet estaat:** such high rank
957 **hem alle up hente:** picked them all up
958 **in ful good entente:** with a good will, kindly
959 **trewe:** faithful
960 **so ferforthly:** so completely
961 **wreke:** avenge
963 **of Theseus yserved:** served, treated by Theseus
965 **right anoon:** immediately   **abood:** delay
967 **To Thebes-ward:** toward Thebes
968 **neer:** nearer   **go ne ride:** walk nor ride
970 **on his wey that nyght he lay:** he spent the night on the road
972 **sheene:** bright
974 **rit** = *rideth,* rides
975 **targe:** shield
977 **feeldes glyteren up and doun:** fields glitter all about
979 **ybete:** embroidered
980 **Mynotaur:** the monster slain by Theseus; see LGW 1886–2227.   **wan:** conquered
984 **thoughte:** intended
988 **pleyn bataille:** open battle
989 **assaut:** assault

And rente adoun bothe wall and sparre and
    rafter;
And to the ladyes he restored agayn   991
The bones of hir freendes that were slayn,
To doon obsequies, as was tho the gyse.
But it were al to longe for to devyse
The grete clamour and the waymentynge   995
That the ladyes made at the brennynge
Of the bodies, and the grete honour
That Theseus, the noble conquerour,
Dooth to the ladyes, whan they from hym
    wente;
But shortly for to telle is myn entente.   1000
   Whan that this worthy duc, this Theseus,
Hath Creon slayn and wonne Thebes thus,
Stille in that feeld he took al nyght his reste,
And dide with al the contree as hym leste.
   To ransake in the taas of bodyes dede,   1005
Hem for to strepe of harneys and of wede,
The pilours diden bisynesse and cure
After the bataille and disconfiture.
And so bifel that in the taas they founde,   1009
Thurgh-girt with many a grevous blody
    wounde,
Two yonge knyghtes liggynge by and by,
Bothe in oon armes, wroght ful richely,
Of whiche two Arcita highte that oon,
And that oother knyght highte Palamon.
Nat fully quyke, ne fully dede they were,   1015
But by hir cote-armures and by hir gere
The heraudes knewe hem best in special
As they that weren of the blood roial
Of Thebes, and of sustren two yborn.
Out of the taas the pilours han hem torn,   1020
And han hem caried softe unto the tente
Of Theseus; and he ful soone hem sente
To Atthenes, to dwellen in prisoun
Perpetuelly — he nolde no raunsoun.   1024

And whan this worthy duc hath thus ydon,
He took his hoost, and hoom he rit anon
With laurer crowned as a conquerour;
And ther he lyveth in joye and in honour
Terme of his lyf; what nedeth wordes mo?
And in a tour, in angwissh and in wo,   1030
This Palamon and his felawe Arcite
For everemoore; ther may no gold hem quite.
   This passeth yeer by yeer and day by day,
Till it fil ones, in a morwe of May,
That Emelye, that fairer was to sene   1035
Than is the lylie upon his stalke grene,
And fressher than the May with floures newe —
For with the rose colour stroof hire hewe,
I noot which was the fyner of hem two —
Er it were day, as was hir wone to do,   1040
She was arisen and al redy dight,
For May wole have no slogardie anyght.
The sesoun priketh every gentil herte,
And maketh it out of his slep to sterte,
And seith "Arys, and do thyn observaunce."
This maked Emelye have remembraunce   1046
To doon honour to May, and for to ryse.
Yclothed was she fressh, for to devyse:
Hir yelow heer was broyded in a tresse
Bihynde hir bak, a yerde long, I gesse.   1050
And in the gardyn, at the sonne upriste,
She walketh up and doun, and as hire liste
She gadereth floures, party white and rede,
To make a subtil gerland for hire hede;
And as an aungel hevenysshly she soong.   1055
The grete tour, that was so thikke and stroong,
Which of the castel was the chief dongeoun
(Ther as the knyghtes weren in prisoun
Of which I tolde yow and tellen shal),
Was evene joynant to the gardyn wal   1060
Ther as this Emelye hadde hir pleyynge.

990 **rente adoun:** tore down **sparre:** beam
992 **freendes:** husbands
993 **tho the gyse:** then the custom
994 **devyse:** tell
995 **waymentynge:** lamentation
996 **brennynge:** burning
1000 **entente:** intention
1004 **as hym leste:** as he pleased
1005 **ransake:** search **taas:** heap
1006 **strepe:** strip **harneys:** armor **wede:** clothing
1007 **pilours:** scavengers **diden bisynesse and cure:** took great pains, worked hard
1008 **disconfiture:** defeat
1010 **Thurgh-girt:** pierced through
1011 **liggynge by and by:** lying side by side
1012 **in oon armes:** with the same heraldic device
1015 **quyke:** living
1016 **cote-armures:** tunics embroidered with heraldic devices, worn over the armor **gere:** armor
1017 **heraudes:** heralds **in special:** in particular
1019 **sustren:** sisters
1021 **softe:** gently
1024 **nolde no raunsoun:** would not accept any ransom

1026 **rit** = *rideth,* rides
1027 **laurer:** laurel
1029 **Terme:** for the duration
1030 **tour:** tower
1032 **may . . . hem quite:** can ransom them
1034 **fil ones:** once happened
1035 **to sene:** to be seen, to look upon
1038 **stroof hire hewe:** her hue strove (vied with)
1039 **noot** = *ne woot,* do not know
1040 **wone:** custom, wont
1041 **dight:** prepared
1042 **slogardie:** sluggishness, laziness **anyght:** at night
1043 **sesoun:** season **priketh:** spurs, incites
1044 **sterte:** move suddenly, awake
1049 **broyded:** braided
1050 **yerde:** yard
1051 **sonne upriste:** rising of the sun
1052 **hire liste:** it pleased her, she liked
1054 **subtil gerland:** ingenious, skillfully made, wreath
1055 **hevenysshly:** in a heavenly manner
1057 **dongeoun:** keep, main fortification of a castle
1060 **evene joynant:** just next to
1061 **pleyynge:** amusement

Bright was the sonne and cleer that morwen-
    ynge,
And Palamoun, this woful prisoner,
As was his wone, by leve of his gayler,
Was risen and romed in a chambre an heigh,
In which he al the noble citee seigh,   1066
And eek the gardyn, ful of braunches grene,
Ther as this fresshe Emelye the shene
Was in hire walk, and romed up and doun.
This sorweful prisoner, this Palamoun,   1070
Goth in the chambre romynge to and fro
And to hymself compleynynge of his wo.
That he was born, ful ofte he seyde, "allas!"
And so bifel, by aventure or cas,   1074
That thurgh a wyndow, thikke of many a barre
Of iren greet and square as any sparre,
He cast his eye upon Emelya,
And therwithal he bleynte and cride, "A!"
As though he stongen were unto the herte.
And with that cry Arcite anon up sterte   1080
And seyde, "Cosyn myn, what eyleth thee,
That art so pale and deedly on to see?
Why cridestow? Who hath thee doon offence?
For Goddes love, taak al in pacience
Oure prisoun, for it may noon oother be.   1085
Fortune hath yeven us this adversitee.
Som wikke aspect or disposicioun
Of Saturne, by som constellacioun,
Hath yeven us this, although we hadde it
    sworn;
So stood the hevene whan that we were
    born.   1090
We moste endure it; this is the short and
    playn."
    This Palamon answerde and seyde agayn,
"Cosyn, for sothe, of this opinioun
Thow hast a veyn ymaginacioun.
This prison caused me nat for to crye,   1095
But I was hurt right now thurghout myn ye

Into myn herte, that wol my bane be.
The fairnesse of that lady that I see
Yond in the gardyn romen to and fro
Is cause of al my criyng and my wo.   1100
I noot wher she be womman or goddesse,
But Venus is it soothly, as I gesse."
And therwithal on knees doun he fil,
And seyde, "Venus, if it be thy wil
Yow in this gardyn thus to transfigure   1105
Bifore me, sorweful, wrecched creature,
Out of this prisoun help that we may scapen.
And if so be my destynee be shapen
By eterne word to dyen in prisoun,
Of oure lynage have som compassioun,   1110
That is so lowe ybroght by tirannye."
And with that word Arcite gan espye
Wher as this lady romed to and fro,
And with that sighte hir beautee hurte hym so,
That, if that Palamon was wounded sore,   1115
Arcite is hurt as muche as he, or moore.
And with a sigh he seyde pitously,
"The fresshe beautee sleeth me sodeynly
Of hire that rometh in the yonder place;
And but I have hir mercy and hir grace,   1120
That I may seen hire atte leeste weye,
I nam but deed; ther nis namoore to seye."
    This Palamon, whan he tho wordes herde,
Dispitously he looked and answerde,   1124
"Wheither seistow this in ernest or in pley?"
    "Nay," quod Arcite, "in ernest, by my fey!
God helpe me so, me list ful yvele pleye."
    This Palamon gan knytte his browes tweye.
"It nere," quod he, "to thee no greet honour
For to be fals, ne for to be traitour   1130
To me, that am thy cosyn and thy brother
Ysworn ful depe, and ech of us til oother,
That nevere, for to dyen in the peyne,
Til that the deeth departe shal us tweyne,
Neither of us in love to hyndre oother,   1135
Ne in noon oother cas, my leeve brother,

1064 **by leve of his gayler:** with permission of his jailer
1065 **an heigh:** on high
1066 **seigh:** saw
1068 **shene:** bright
1072 **compleynynge of:** lamenting
1074 And so it happened by chance or accident
1075 **thurgh:** through   **thikke of:** thick(ly set) with
1076 **sparre:** wooden beam
1078 **bleynte:** turned pale
1080 **sterte:** leapt up
1081 **Cosyn:** kinsman   **eyleth:** ails
1082 **on to see:** to look upon
1083 **cridestow** = *cridest thow,* did you cry out
1087–89 Some evil aspect or disposition of the planet Saturn, by arrangement of the heavenly bodies (*constellacioun*) has given us this (fate, which we must suffer) although we had sworn the contrary (would befall).
1091 **this is:** pronounced as one syllable
1092 **agayn:** in reply
1094 **veyn ymaginacioun:** idle, foolish conception
1096 **ye:** eye

1097 **bane:** killer
1101 **noot** = *ne woot,* know not   **wher:** whether
1107 **scapen:** escape
1108 **shapen:** ordained
1110 **lynage:** noble birth
1112 **gan espye:** did espy, saw
1118 **sodeynly:** suddenly
1120 **but:** unless
1121 **atte leeste weye:** at least
1122 **I nam but deed:** I am as good as dead
1123 **tho:** those
1124 **Dispitously:** angrily
1125 **Wheither seistow:** tell me whether you say (*seistow* = *seiest thow*) this
1126 **fey:** faith
1127 **me list ful yvele pleye:** I have very little desire to play
1129 **nere** = *ne were,* would not be (subj.)
1131–32 **brother Ysworn:** sworn brother
1132 **ful depe:** very deeply, sincerely   **til:** to
1133 Never, though we had to die by torture (*in the peyne*)
1136 **leeve:** dear

But that thou sholdest trewely forthren me
In every cas, as I shal forthren thee —
This was thyn ooth, and myn also, certeyn;
I woot right wel, thou darst it nat withseyn.
Thus artow of my conseil, out of doute,   1141
And now thow woldest falsly been aboute
To love my lady, whom I love and serve,
And evere shal til that myn herte sterve.
Nay, certes, false Arcite, thow shalt nat so.
I loved hire first, and tolde thee my wo   1146
As to my conseil and my brother sworn
To forthre me, as I have toold biforn.
For which thou art ybounden as a knyght
To helpen me, if it lay in thy myght,   1150
Or elles artow fals, I dar wel seyn.''
      This Arcite ful proudly spak ageyn:
''Thow shalt,'' quod he, ''be rather fals than I;
And thou art fals, I telle thee outrely,
For paramour I loved hire first er thow.   1155
What wiltow seyen? Thou woost nat yet now
Wheither she be a womman or goddesse!
Thyn is affeccioun of hoolynesse,
And myn is love as to a creature;
For which I tolde thee myn aventure   1160
As to my cosyn and my brother sworn.
I pose that thow lovedest hire biforn;
Wostow nat wel the olde clerkes sawe,
That 'who shal yeve a lovere any lawe?'
Love is a gretter lawe, by my pan,   1165
Than may be yeve to any erthely man;
And therfore positif lawe and swich decree
Is broken al day for love in ech degree.
A man moot nedes love, maugree his heed;
He may nat fleen it, thogh he sholde be deed,
Al be she mayde, or wydwe, or elles wyf. 1171
And eek it is nat likly al thy lyf
To stonden in hir grace; namoore shal I;
For wel thou woost thyselven, verraily,

That thou and I be dampned to prisoun   1175
Perpetuelly; us gayneth no raunsoun.
We stryve as dide the houndes for the boon;
They foughte al day, and yet hir part was noon.
Ther cam a kyte, whil that they were so
            wrothe,
And baar awey the boon bitwixe hem bothe.
And therfore, at the kynges court, my brother,
Ech man for hymself, ther is noon oother. 1182
Love, if thee list, for I love and ay shal;
And soothly, leeve brother, this is al.
Heere in this prisoun moote we endure,   1185
And everich of us take his aventure.''
      Greet was the strif and long bitwix hem
            tweye,
If that I hadde leyser for to seye;
But to th'effect. It happed on a day,
To telle it yow as shortly as I may,   1190
A worthy duc that highte Perotheus,
That felawe was unto duc Theseus
Syn thilke day that they were children lite,
Was come to Atthenes his felawe to visite,
And for to pleye as he was wont to do;   1195
For in this world he loved no man so,
And he loved hym als tendrely agayn.
So wel they lovede, as olde bookes sayn,
That whan that oon was deed, soothly to telle,
His felawe wente and soughte hym doun in
            helle —
But of that storie list me nat to write.   1201
Duc Perotheus loved wel Arcite,
And hadde hym knowe at Thebes yeer by yere,
And finally at requeste and preyere
Of Perotheus, withouten any raunsoun,   1205
Duc Theseus hym leet out of prisoun
Frely to goon wher that hym liste over al,
In swich a gyse as I you tellen shal.
      This was the forward, pleynly for t'endite,
Bitwixen Theseus and hym Arcite: 1210
That if so were that Arcite were yfounde
Evere in his lif, by day or nyght, oo stounde
In any contree of this Theseus,
And he were caught, it was acorded thus,
That with a swerd he sholde lese his heed.

1137 **forthren:** help
1140 **darst it nat withseyn:** dare not deny it
1141 Thus you are (*artow = art thow*, you are) in my confidence
without doubt (*out of doute*); i.e., you know of my love.
1144 **sterve:** die
1152 **ageyn:** in return
1154 **outrely:** utterly, flatly
1155 **paramour:** mistress, human love
1156 **woost:** know
1158 **affeccioun of hoolynesse:** religious feeling, love of a deity
1162 **pose:** posit, suppose for the sake of argument
1163 **clerkes:** scholars'   **sawe:** saying
1165 **by my pan:** by my skull
1167 **positif lawe:** man-made, legislated (as opposed to natural)
law
1168 **al day:** daily
1169 **moot nedes:** must necessarily   **maugree his heed:** despite
his care, in spite of all he could do about it
1170 **fleen:** escape
1171 **Al be she:** whether she be
1173 **stonden in hir grace:** be in her good favor
1174 **verraily:** truly

1175 **dampned:** condemned
1176 **us gayneth no raunsoun:** no ransom avails (can help) us
1179 **wrothe:** angry
1182 **noon oother:** no other (way)
1183 **ay:** always
1184 **leeve:** dear
1186 **everich:** each
1189 **th'effect:** the point
1193 **Syn:** since   **thilke:** that   **lite:** little
1203 **yeer by yere:** year after year, for a long time
1208 **gyse:** manner
1209 **forward:** agreement
1210 **hym Arcite:** this Arcite
1212 **oo stounde:** at one (i.e., any) moment
1215 **lese:** lose

Ther nas noon oother remedie ne reed;   1216
But taketh his leve, and homward he him
    spedde.
Lat hym be war! His nekke lith to wedde.
   How greet a sorwe suffreth now Arcite!
The deeth he feeleth thurgh his herte smyte;
He wepeth, wayleth, crieth pitously;   1221
To sleen hymself he waiteth prively.
He seyde, "Allas that day that I was born!
Now is my prisoun worse than biforn;
Now is me shape eternally to dwelle   1225
Noght in purgatorie, but in helle.
Allas, that evere knew I Perotheus!
For elles hadde I dwelled with Theseus,
Yfetered in his prisoun everemo.   1229
Thanne hadde I been in blisse and nat in wo.
Oonly the sighte of hire whom that I serve,
Though that I nevere hir grace may deserve,
Wolde han suffised right ynough for me.
O deere cosyn Palamon," quod he,
"Thyn is the victorie of this aventure.   1235
Ful blisfully in prison maistow dure —
In prison? Certes nay, but in paradys!
Wel hath Fortune yturned thee the dys,
That hast the sighte of hire, and I th'absence.
For possible is, syn thou hast hire presence,
And art a knyght, a worthy and an able,   1241
That by som cas, syn Fortune is chaungeable,
Thow maist to thy desir somtyme atteyne.
But I, that am exiled and bareyne
Of alle grace, and in so greet dispeir   1245
That ther nys erthe, water, fir, ne eir,
Ne creature that of hem maked is,
That may me helpe or doon confort in this,
Wel oughte I sterve in wanhope and distresse.
Farwel my lif, my lust, and my gladnesse!   1250
   "Allas, why pleynen folk so in commune
On purveiaunce of God, or of Fortune,
That yeveth hem ful ofte in many a gyse
Wel bettre than they kan hemself devyse?
Som man desireth for to han richesse,   1255

That cause is of his mordre or greet siknesse;
And som man wolde out of his prisoun fayn,
That in his hous is of his meynee slayn.
Infinite harmes been in this mateere.   1259
We witen nat what thing we preyen heere;
We faren as he that dronke is as a mous.
A dronke man woot wel he hath an hous,
But he noot which the righte wey is thider,
And to a dronke man the wey is slider.
And certes, in this world so faren we;   1265
We seken faste after felicitee,
But we goon wrong ful often, trewely.
Thus may we seyen alle, and namely I,
That wende and hadde a greet opinioun
That if I myghte escapen from prisoun,   1270
Thanne hadde I been in joye and parfit heele,
Ther now I am exiled fro my wele.
Syn that I may nat seen you, Emelye,
I nam but deed; ther nys no remedye."
   Upon that oother syde Palamon,   1275
Whan that he wiste Arcite was agon,
Swich sorwe he maketh that the grete tour
Resouneth of his youlyng and clamour.
The pure fettres on his shynes grete
Weren of his bittre, salte teeres wete.   1280
"Allas," quod he, "Arcita, cosyn myn,
Of al oure strif, God woot, the fruyt is thyn.
Thow walkest now in Thebes at thy large,
And of my wo thow yevest litel charge.   1284
Thou mayst, syn thou hast wisdom and man-
    hede,
Assemblen alle the folk of oure kynrede,
And make a werre so sharp on this citee
That by som aventure or some tretee
Thow mayst have hire to lady and to wyf
For whom that I moste nedes lese my lyf.   1290
For, as by wey of possibilitee,
Sith thou art at thy large, of prisoun free,

1216 **reed**: course of action
1217 **him spedde**: hurried
1218 **lith to wedde**: lies as a pledge
1222 **sleen**: slay, kill   **waiteth**: awaits an occasion   **prively**:
secretly
1225 **is me shape**: I am destined
1236 **maistow dure**: you can live
1237 **Certes nay**: certainly not
1238 **yturned thee the dys**: cast the dice for you
1242 **by som cas, syn**: by some chance, since
1244 **bareyne**: barren
1246 **nys** = *ne ys*, is not   **erthe, water, fir, ne eir**: earth, water,
fire, nor air (the four elements; i.e., all creation)
1249 **sterve**: die   **wanhope**: despair
1250 **lust**: delight
1251 **pleynen**: complain
1252 **purveiaunce**: foresight, providence
1253 **yeveth**: gives
1254 **devyse**: imagine

1256 **mordre**: murder
1257 **wolde . . . fayn**: eagerly desires (to be)
1258 **of his meynee**: by the members of his household
1260 **witen**: know
1261 **faren**: act
1263 **thider**: thither, there
1264 **slider**: slippery
1265 **certes**: certainly
1269 **wende**: supposed
1271 **heele**: well-being
1272 **wele**: prosperity
1274 **I nam but deed**: I am as good as dead   **nys** = *ne ys*, is
not
1278 **Resouneth of**: resounded with   **youlyng**: howling
1279 **pure fettres**: very fetters   **grete**: large (probably to be
construed with *fetters*)
1283 **at thy large**: freely
1284 **yevest litel charge**: give little care
1286 **kynrede**: family
1287 **werre**: war
1289 **to**: as
1290 **moste nedes lese**: must necessarily lose

And art a lord, greet is thyn avauntage
Moore than is myn, that sterve here in a cage.
For I moot wepe and wayle, whil I lyve,   1295
With al the wo that prison may me yive,
And eek with peyne that love me yeveth also,
That doubleth al my torment and my wo."
Therwith the fyr of jalousie up sterte   1299
Withinne his brest, and hente him by the herte
So woodly that he lyk was to biholde
The boxtree or the asshen dede and colde.

    Thanne seyde he, "O crueel goddes that governe
This world with byndyng of youre word eterne,
And writen in the table of atthamaunt   1305
Youre parlement and youre eterne graunt,
What is mankynde moore unto you holde
Than is the sheep that rouketh in the folde?
For slayn is man right as another beest,
And dwelleth eek in prison and arreest,   1310
And hath siknesse and greet adversitee,
And ofte tymes giltelees, pardee.

    "What governance is in this prescience,
That giltelees tormenteth innocence?   1314
And yet encresseth this al my penaunce,
That man is bounden to his observaunce,
For Goddes sake, to letten of his wille,
Ther as a beest may al his lust fulfille.
And whan a beest is deed he hath no peyne;
But man after his deeth moot wepe and pleyne,   1320
Though in this world he have care and wo.
Withouten doute it may stonden so.
The answere of this lete I to dyvynys,
But wel I woot that in this world greet pyne ys.
Allas, I se a serpent or a theef,   1325
That many a trewe man hath doon mescheef,
Goon at his large, and where hym list may turne.

But I moot been in prisoun thurgh Saturne,
And eek thurgh Juno, jalous and eek wood,
That hath destroyed wel ny al the blood   1330
Of Thebes with his waste walles wyde;
And Venus sleeth me on that oother syde
For jalousie and fere of hym Arcite."
    Now wol I stynte of Palamon a lite,
And lete hym in his prisoun stille dwelle,   1335
And of Arcita forth I wol yow telle.

    The somer passeth, and the nyghtes longe
Encressen double wise the peynes stronge
Bothe of the lovere and the prisoner.
I noot which hath the wofuller mester.   1340
For, shortly for to seyn, this Palamoun
Perpetuelly is dampned to prisoun,
In cheynes and in fettres to been deed;
And Arcite is exiled upon his heed
For everemo, as out of that contree,   1345
Ne nevere mo ne shal his lady see.

    Yow loveres axe I now this questioun:
Who hath the worse, Arcite or Palamoun?
That oon may seen his lady day by day,
But in prison he moot dwelle alway;   1350
That oother wher hym list may ride or go,
But seen his lady shal he nevere mo.
Now demeth as yow liste, ye that kan,
For I wol telle forth as I bigan.   1354

Explicit prima pars

Sequitur pars secunda

    Whan that Arcite to Thebes comen was,
Ful ofte a day he swelte and seyde "Allas!"
For seen his lady shal he nevere mo.
And shortly to concluden al his wo,
So muche sorwe hadde nevere creature   1359
That is, or shal, whil that the world may dure.
His slep, his mete, his drynke, is hym biraft,
That lene he wex and drye as is a shaft;
His eyen holwe and grisly to biholde,
His hewe falow and pale as asshen colde,
And solitarie he was and evere allone,   1365

And waillynge al the nyght, makynge his mone;
And if he herde song or instrument,
Thanne wolde he wepe, he myghte nat be stent.
So feble eek were his spiritz, and so lowe,   1369
And chaunged so, that no man koude knowe
His speche nor his voys, though men it herde.
And in his geere for al the world he ferde
Nat oonly lik the loveris maladye
Of Hereos, but rather lyk manye,
Engendred of humour malencolik   1375
Biforen, in his celle fantastik.
And shortly, turned was al up so doun
Bothe habit and eek disposicioun
Of hym, this woful lovere daun Arcite.
    What sholde I al day of his wo endite?   1380
Whan he endured hadde a yeer or two
This crueel torment and this peyne and wo,
At Thebes, in his contree, as I seyde,
Upon a nyght in sleep as he hym leyde,   1384
Hym thoughte how that the wynged god Mer-
        curie
Biforn hym stood and bad hym to be murie.
His slepy yerde in hond he bar uprighte;
An hat he werede upon his heris brighte.
Arrayed was this god, as he took keep,
As he was whan that Argus took his sleep;   1390
And seyde hym thus: "To Atthenes shaltou
        wende,
Ther is thee shapen of thy wo an ende."
And with that word Arcite wook and sterte.
"Now trewely, hou soore that me smerte,"   1394
Quod he, "to Atthenes right now wol I fare,
Ne for the drede of deeth shal I nat spare
To se my lady, that I love and serve.
In hire presence I recche nat to sterve."
    And with that word he caughte a greet
        mirour,   1399

And saugh that chaunged was al his colour,
And saugh his visage al in another kynde.
And right anon it ran hym in his mynde,
That, sith his face was so disfigured
Of maladye the which he hadde endured,
He myghte wel, if that he bar hym lowe,   1405
Lyve in Atthenes everemoore unknowe,
And seen his lady wel ny day by day.
And right anon he chaunged his array,
And cladde hym as a povre laborer,
And al allone, save oonly a squier   1410
That knew his privetee and al his cas,
Which was disgised povrely as he was,
To Atthenes is he goon the nexte way.
And to the court he wente upon a day,
And at the gate he profreth his servyse   1415
To drugge and drawe, what so men wol devyse.
And shortly of this matere for to seyn,
He fil in office with a chamberleyn
The which that dwellynge was with Emelye,
For he was wys and koude soone espye,   1420
Of every servaunt, which that serveth here.
Wel koude he hewen wode, and water bere,
For he was yong and myghty for the nones,
And therto he was long and big of bones
To doon that any wight kan hym devyse.   1425
A yeer or two he was in this servyse,
Page of the chambre of Emelye the brighte,
And Philostrate he seyde that he highte.
But half so wel biloved a man as he
Ne was ther nevere in court of his degree;
He was so gentil of condicioun   1431
That thurghout al the court was his renoun.
They seyden that it were a charitee
That Theseus wolde enhauncen his degree,
And putten hym in worshipful servyse,   1435

1366 makynge his mone: lamenting
1368 stent: stopped
1371 voys: voice
1372 geere: behavior ferde: behaved
1373–74 loveris maladye Of Hereos: love-sickness; see n. to
lines 1355–76.
1374 manye: mania
1375 humour malencolik: melancholy humor
1376 celle fantastik: the part of the brain that controls the
imagination
1377 up so doun: topsy turvy
1378 habit: physical condition
1379 daun: sir
1380 al day: at length endite: write
1385 Mercurie: Mercury
1387 slepy yerde: sleep-inducing staff
1389 he took keep: Arcite took heed, noticed
1390 Argus: mythical guardian of Io, whom Mercury put to
sleep and then killed
1392 shapen: destined
1394 hou soore that me smerte: however sorely it may pain me
1395 fare: go
1398 recche nat to sterve: care not if I die

1401 in another kynde: (changed) into another sort
1403 sith: since
1404 Of maladye: by illness
1405 myghte: could bar hym lowe: conducted himself humbly
1408 right anon: at once
1411 privetee: private affairs cas: situation
1412 povrely: poorly
1413 nexte: nearest
1415 profreth: offers
1416 drugge and drawe: drudge and draw water devyse:
command
1418 fil in office: fell in service, was employed chamberleyn:
household attendant
1420–21 espye, Of: take notice, take the measure of
1422 bere: bear, carry
1424 long: tall big: strong
1425 wight: person
1427 Page of the chambre: personal servant
1428 highte: was called
1431 condicioun: disposition, manner
1432 renoun: fame, renown
1434 enhauncen his degree: advance, enhance his rank
1435 worshipful servyse: honorable, noble employment

Ther as he myghte his vertu excercise.
And thus withinne a while his name is spronge,
Bothe of his dedes and his goode tonge,
That Theseus hath taken hym so neer   1439
That of his chambre he made hym a squier,
And gaf hym gold to mayntene his degree.
And eek men broghte hym out of his contree,
From yeer to yeer, ful pryvely his rente;
But honestly and slyly he it spente,   1444
That no man wondred how that he it hadde.
And thre yeer in this wise his lif he ladde,
And bar hym so, in pees and eek in werre,
Ther was no man that Theseus hath derre.
And in this blisse lete I now Arcite,
And speke I wole of Palamon a lite.   1450

   In derknesse and horrible and strong prisoun
Thise seven yeer hath seten Palamoun
Forpyned, what for wo and for distresse.
Who feeleth double soor and hevynesse
But Palamon, that love destreyneth so   1455
That wood out of his wit he goth for wo?
And eek therto he is a prisoner
Perpetuelly, noght oonly for a yer.

   Who koude ryme in Englyssh proprely
His martirdom? For sothe it am nat I;   1460
Therfore I passe as lightly as I may.

   It fel that in the seventhe yer, of May
The thridde nyght (as olde bookes seyn,
That al this storie tellen moore pleyn),
Were it by aventure or destynee —   1465
As, whan a thyng is shapen, it shal be —
That soone after the mydnyght Palamoun,
By helpyng of a freend, brak his prisoun
And fleeth the citee faste as he may go.
For he hadde yeve his gayler drynke so   1470
Of a clarree maad of a certeyn wyn,
With nercotikes and opie of Thebes fyn,
That al that nyght, thogh that men wolde him
     shake,
The gayler sleep; he myghte nat awake.   1474
And thus he fleeth as faste as evere he may.

The nyght was short and faste by the day
That nedes cost he moot hymselven hyde,
And til a grove faste ther bisyde
With dredeful foot thanne stalketh Palamon.
For, shortly, this was his opinion: 1480
That in that grove he wolde hym hyde al day,
And in the nyght thanne wolde he take his way
To Thebes-ward, his freendes for to preye
On Theseus to helpe him to werreye;
And shortly, outher he wolde lese his lif   1485
Or wynnen Emelye unto his wyf.
This is th'effect and his entente pleyn.

   Now wol I turne to Arcite ageyn,
That litel wiste how ny that was his care,   1489
Til that Fortune had broght him in the snare.

   The bisy larke, messager of day,
Salueth in hir song the morwe gray,
And firy Phebus riseth up so bright
That al the orient laugheth of the light,
And with his stremes dryeth in the greves   1495
The silver dropes hangynge on the leves.
And Arcita, that in the court roial
With Theseus is squier principal,
Is risen and looketh on the myrie day.
And for to doon his observaunce to May,   1500
Remembrynge on the poynt of his desir,
He on a courser, startlynge as the fir,
Is riden into the feeldes hym to pleye,
Out of the court, were it a myle or tweye.
And to the grove of which that I yow tolde
By aventure his wey he gan to holde   1506
To maken hym a gerland of the greves,
Were it of wodebynde or hawethorn leves,
And loude he song ayeyn the sonne shene:
"May, with alle thy floures and thy grene,
Welcome be thou, faire, fresshe May,   1511
In hope that I som grene gete may."
And from his courser, with a lusty herte,
Into the grove ful hastily he sterte,
And in a path he rometh up and doun,   1515
Ther as by aventure this Palamoun
Was in a bussh, that no man myghte hym se,
For soore afered of his deeth was he.

1436 **vertu:** abilities
1437 **name:** reputation
1439 **neer:** near (though this is usually the comparative *nearer*)
1446 **wise:** manner
1447 **pees:** peace
1448 **hath derre:** holds dearer
1449 **lete:** leave
1453 **Forpyned:** wasted by suffering
1454 **soor:** pain **hevynesse:** sadness
1455 **destreyneth:** afflicts
1465 **aventure or destynee:** chance or fate
1470 **gayler:** jailer
1471 **clarree:** a spiced and sweetened wine
1472 **opie:** opium
1474 **sleep:** slept
1475 **fleeth:** flees, hastens

1477 **nedes cost:** necessarily
1478 **faste:** close
1479 **dredeful:** fearful
1484 **werreye:** wage war
1485 **outher:** either
1487 **th'effect:** the purpose
1495 **stremes:** rays **greves:** groves
1502 **courser:** war-horse, charger **startlynge:** leaping about
1506 **gan to holde:** did hold, held (took his way)
1507 **greves:** branches
1509 **ayeyn the sonne:** in the sun
1512 **som grene:** something green
1514 **sterte:** rushed

No thyng ne knew he that it was Arcite;
God woot he wolde have trowed it ful lite.
But sooth is seyd, go sithen many yeres,   1521
That "feeld hath eyen and the wode hath eres."
It is ful fair a man to bere hym evene,
For al day meeteth men at unset stevene.
Ful litel woot Arcite of his felawe,   1525
That was so ny to herknen al his sawe,
For in the bussh he sitteth now ful stille.

Whan that Arcite hadde romed al his fille,
And songen al the roundel lustily,
Into a studie he fil sodeynly,   1530
As doon thise loveres in hir queynte geres,
Now in the crope, now doun in the breres,
Now up, now doun, as boket in a welle.
Right as the Friday, soothly for to telle,
Now it shyneth, now it reyneth faste,   1535
Right so kan geery Venus overcaste
The hertes of hir folk; right as hir day
Is gereful, right so chaungeth she array.
Selde is the Friday al the wowke ylike.   1539

Whan that Arcite had songe, he gan to sike
And sette hym doun withouten any moore.
"Allas," quod he, "that day that I was bore!
How longe, Juno, thurgh thy crueltee,
Woltow werreyen Thebes the citee?
Allas, ybroght is to confusioun   1545
The blood roial of Cadme and Amphioun —
Of Cadmus, which that was the firste man
That Thebes bulte, or first the toun bigan,
And of the citee first was crouned kyng.
Of his lynage am I and his ofspryng   1550
By verray ligne, as of the stok roial,
And now I am so caytyf and so thral,
That he that is my mortal enemy,
I serve hym as his squier povrely."

And yet dooth Juno me wel moore shame,   1555
For I dar noght biknowe myn owene name;
But ther as I was wont to highte Arcite,
Now highte I Philostrate, noght worth a myte.
Allas, thou felle Mars! Allas, Juno!
Thus hath youre ire oure lynage al fordo,   1560
Save oonly me and wrecched Palamoun,
That Theseus martireth in prisoun.
And over al this, to sleen me outrely
Love hath his firy dart so brennyngly
Ystiked thurgh my trewe, careful herte   1565
That shapen was my deeth erst than my sherte.
Ye sleen me with youre eyen, Emelye!
Ye been the cause wherfore that I dye.
Of al the remenant of myn oother care
Ne sette I nat the montance of a tare,   1570
So that I koude doon aught to youre ples-
    aunce."
And with that word he fil doun in a traunce
A longe tyme, and after he up sterte.

This Palamoun, that thoughte that thurgh his
    herte
He felte a coold swerd sodeynliche glyde,   1575
For ire he quook; no lenger wolde he byde.
And whan that he had herd Arcites tale,
As he were wood, with face deed and pale,
He stirte hym up out of the buskes thikke
And seide: "Arcite, false traytour wikke,   1580
Now artow hent, that lovest my lady so,
For whom that I have al this peyne and wo,
And art my blood, and to my conseil sworn,
As I ful ofte have told thee heerbiforn,
And hast byjaped heere duc Theseus,   1585
And falsly chaunged hast thy name thus!
I wol be deed, or elles thou shalt dye.
Thou shalt nat love my lady Emelye,
But I wol love hire oonly and namo;
For I am Palamon, thy mortal foo.   1590

1521 **go sithen many yeres:** since many years ago
1523 **bere hym evene:** act calmly, moderately
1524 **meeteth men:** people meet   **at unset stevene:** with an unexpected (not set) time
1526 **sawe:** speech
1529 **roundel:** a short poetic and musical form; for an example, see PF 680–92.
1530 **sodeynly:** suddenly
1531 **thise loveres:** lovers in general   **queynte geres:** strange manners
1532 **crope:** leaves (top)   **breres:** briars
1533 **boket:** bucket
1536 **geery:** fickle   **overcaste:** sadden
1538 **gereful:** changeable
1539 Friday is seldom like all the rest of the week.
1540 **sike:** sigh
1544 **werreyen:** wage war on
1545 **confusioun:** ruin
1546 **Cadme and Amphioun:** Cadmus and Amphion, founders of Thebes
1548 **or:** ere
1551 **verray ligne:** true lineage   **stok:** stock, family
1552 **caytyf:** wretched captive   **thral:** enslaved
1554 **povrely:** poor

1556 **biknowe:** acknowledge
1557 **highte:** be called
1558 **myte:** a small Flemish coin of little value
1559 **felle:** fierce
1560 **fordo:** destroyed
1562 **martireth:** torments
1563 **sleen:** slay, kill
1564 **brennyngly:** ardently
1565 **Ystiked:** struck, stabbed   **trewe:** faithful   **careful:** sorrowful
1566 My death was destined before my first garment was made for me (before my birth).
1570 **montance:** amount, value   **tare:** weed (i.e., nothing)
1571 **plesaunce:** pleasure
1576 **quook:** trembled
1579 **buskes:** bushes
1580 **wikke:** wicked
1585 **byjaped:** tricked
1589 **namo:** no others

And though that I no wepene have in this
    place,
But out of prison am astert by grace,
I drede noght that outher thow shalt dye,
Or thow ne shalt nat loven Emelye.
Chees which thou wolt, or thou shalt nat
    asterte!''   1595
  This Arcite, with ful despitous herte,
Whan he hym knew, and hadde his tale herd,
As fiers as leon pulled out his swerd,
And seyde thus: ''By God that sit above,
Nere it that thou art sik and wood for love,   1600
And eek that thow no wepne hast in this place,
Thou sholdest nevere out of this grove pace,
That thou ne sholdest dyen of myn hond.
For I defye the seurete and the bond   1604
Which that thou seist that I have maad to thee.
What! Verray fool, thynk wel that love is free,
And I wol love hire maugree al thy myght!
But for as muche thou art a worthy knyght
And wilnest to darreyne hire by bataille,
Have heer my trouthe; tomorwe I wol nat faille,
Withoute wityng of any oother wight,   1611
That heere I wol be founden as a knyght,
And bryngen harneys right ynough for thee;
And ches the beste, and leef the worste for me.
And mete and drynke this nyght wol I
    brynge   1615
Ynough for thee, and clothes for thy beddynge.
And if so be that thou my lady wynne,
And sle me in this wode ther I am inne,
Thow mayst wel have thy lady as for me.''
  This Palamon answerde, ''I graunte it thee.''
And thus they been departed til amorwe,   1621
Whan ech of hem had leyd his feith to borwe.
  O Cupide, out of alle charitee!
O regne, that wolt no felawe have with thee!
Ful sooth is seyd that love ne lordshipe   1625
Wol noght, his thankes, have no felaweshipe.
Wel fynden that Arcite and Palamoun.

Arcite is riden anon unto the toun,
And on the morwe, er it were dayes light,
Ful prively two harneys hath he dight,   1630
Bothe suffisaunt and mete to darreyne
The bataille in the feeld bitwix hem tweyne;
And on his hors, allone as he was born,
He carieth al the harneys hym biforn.
And in the grove, at tyme and place yset,   1635
This Arcite and this Palamon ben met.
To chaungen gan the colour in hir face;
Right as the hunters in the regne of Trace,
That stondeth at the gappe with a spere,
Whan hunted is the leon or the bere,   1640
And hereth hym come russhyng in the greves,
And breketh bothe bowes and the leves,
And thynketh, ''Heere cometh my mortal
    enemy!
Withoute faille, he moot be deed, or I,   1644
For outher I moot sleen hym at the gappe,
Or he moot sleen me, if that me myshappe.''
So ferden they in chaungyng of hir hewe,
As fer as everich of hem oother knewe.
  Ther nas no good day, ne no saluyng,   1649
But streight, withouten word or rehersyng,
Everich of hem heelp for to armen oother
As freendly as he were his owene brother;
And after that, with sharpe speres stronge
They foynen ech at oother wonder longe.
Thou myghtest wene that this Palamon   1655
In his fightyng were a wood leon,
And as a crueel tigre was Arcite;
As wilde bores gonne they to smyte,
That frothen whit as foom for ire wood.
Up to the ancle foghte they in hir blood.   1660
And in this wise I lete hem fightyng dwelle,
And forth I wole of Theseus yow telle.
  The destinee, ministre general,
That executeth in the world over al   1664
The purveiaunce that God hath seyn biforn,
So strong it is that, though the world had
    sworn
The contrarie of a thyng by ye or nay,

1591 **wepene:** weapons
1592 **astert:** escaped
1593 **drede:** doubt **outher:** either
1595 **Chees:** choose
1596 **despitous:** scornful
1599 **sit** = *sitteth,* sits
1600 **sik:** sick
1604 **defye:** repudiate **seurete:** pledge
1606 **What!:** an exclamation
1607 **maugree:** in spite of
1609 **wilnest:** desire **darreyne hire:** decide the right to her
1610 **trouthe:** pledge
1611 **wityng:** knowledge
1613 **harneys:** armor
1614 **leef:** leave
1618 **ther:** where
1620 **graunte it thee:** agree
1622 **to borwe:** as a pledge
1626 **his thankes:** willingly **felaweshipe:** equal partnership

1630 **two harneys:** two suits of armor **dight:** prepared
1631 **mete:** suitable, fitting
1631-32 **darreyne The bataille:** engage in, decide the battle
1638 **regne of Trace:** kingdom of Thrace
1639 **gappe:** gap (toward which the game is driven)
1646 **me myshappe:** I should suffer misfortune
1649 **saluyng:** greeting
1650 **rehersyng:** conversation
1654 **foynen:** thrust **ech at oother:** at each other
1655 **wene:** suppose
1658 **bores:** boars
1659 **frothen:** foam at the mouth
1664 **executeth:** administers
1665 **purveiaunce:** foresight, providence

Yet somtyme it shal fallen on a day
That falleth nat eft withinne a thousand yeer.
For certeinly, oure appetites heer,   1670
Be it of werre, or pees, or hate, or love,
Al is this reuled by the sighte above.
    This mene I now by myghty Theseus,
That for to hunten is so desirus,
And namely at the grete hert in May,   1675
That in his bed ther daweth hym no day
That he nys clad, and redy for to ryde
With hunte and horn and houndes hym bisyde.
For in his huntyng hath he swich delit
That it is al his joye and appetit   1680
To been hymself the grete hertes bane,
For after Mars he serveth now Dyane.
    Cleer was the day, as I have toold er this,
And Theseus with alle joye and blis,
With his Ypolita, the faire queene,   1685
And Emelye, clothed al in grene,
On huntyng be they riden roially.
And to the grove that stood ful faste by,
In which ther was an hert, as men hym tolde,
Duc Theseus the streighte wey hath holde.
And to the launde he rideth hym ful right,   1691
For thider was the hert wont have his flight,
And over a brook, and so forth on his weye.
This duc wol han a cours at hym or tweye
With houndes swiche as that hym list com-
        aunde.   1695
    And whan this duc was come unto the
        launde,
Under the sonne he looketh, and anon
He was war of Arcite and Palamon,
That foughten breme as it were bores two.
The brighte swerdes wenten to and fro   1700
So hidously that with the leeste strook
It semed as it wolde felle an ook.
But what they were, no thyng he ne woot.
This duc his courser with his spores smoot,
And at a stert he was bitwix hem two,   1705
And pulled out a swerd and cride, "Hoo!

Namoore, up peyne of lesynge of youre heed!
By myghty Mars, he shal anon be deed
That smyteth any strook that I may seen.
But telleth me what myster men ye been,   1710
That been so hardy for to fighten heere
Withouten juge or oother officere,
As it were in a lystes roially."
    This Palamon answerde hastily   1714
And seyde, "Sire, what nedeth wordes mo?
We have the deeth disserved bothe two.
Two woful wrecches been we, two caytyves,
That been encombred of oure owene lyves;
And as thou art a rightful lord and juge,
Ne yif us neither mercy ne refuge,   1720
But sle me first, for seinte charitee!
But sle my felawe eek as wel as me;
Or sle hym first, for though thow knowest it
        lite,
This is thy mortal foo, this is Arcite,   1724
That fro thy lond is banysshed on his heed,
For which he hath deserved to be deed.
For this is he that cam unto thy gate
And seyde that he highte Philostrate.
Thus hath he japed thee ful many a yer,
And thou hast maked hym thy chief squier;
And this is he that loveth Emelye.   1731
For sith the day is come that I shal dye,
I make pleynly my confessioun
That I am thilke woful Palamoun
That hath thy prisoun broken wikkedly.   1735
I am thy mortal foo, and it am I
That loveth so hoote Emelye the brighte
That I wol dye present in hir sighte.
Wherfore I axe deeth and my juwise;
But sle my felawe in the same wise,   1740
For bothe han we deserved to be slayn."
    This worthy duc answerde anon agayn,
And seyde, "This is a short conclusioun.
Youre owene mouth, by youre confessioun,
Hath dampned yow, and I wol it recorde;   1745
It nedeth noght to pyne yow with the corde.
Ye shal be deed, by myghty Mars the rede!"

1669 **eft:** again
1672 **sighte:** foresight
1673 **mene:** say **by:** concerning
1675 **grete hert:** large hart, worthy of hunting
1676 **daweth hym:** dawns for him
1678 **hunte:** huntsman
1681 **bane:** killer
1682 **after Mars:** next to Mars, the god of war **Dyane:** Diana, goddess of hunting
1688 **ful faste by:** very close by
1692 **thider:** thither, there
1694 **cours:** run
1696 **launde:** clearing
1697 **Under the sonne:** in the direction of the sun
1699 **breme:** fiercely
1705 **at a stert:** with a sudden movement, instantly
1706 **Hoo!:** stop!

1707 **up peyne of:** on the penalty of
1710 **what myster men:** what sort of men
1712 **juge or oother officere:** judge or some other officer, as in a properly conducted legal duel (*in a lystes roially*)
1717 **caytyves:** wretches
1718 **encombred:** burdened
1721 **for seinte charitee:** by holy charity (*seinte* is pronounced with two syllables)
1729 **japed:** tricked
1734 **thilke:** that
1737 **hoote:** passionately
1739 **axe:** ask **juwise:** judicial sentence
1745 **dampned:** condemned **recorde:** pronounce
1746 **to pyne yow with the corde:** to torture you (to force a confession) with a cord (twisted about your heads)

The queene anon, for verray wommanhede,
Gan for to wepe, and so dide Emelye,
And alle the ladyes in the compaignye.   1750
Greet pitee was it, as it thoughte hem alle,
That evere swich a chaunce sholde falle,
For gentil men they were of greet estaat,
And no thyng but for love was this debaat;
And saugh hir blody woundes wyde and soore,
And alle crieden, bothe lasse and moore,   1756
"Have mercy, Lord, upon us wommen alle!"
And on hir bare knees adoun they falle
And wolde have kist his feet ther as he stood;
Til at the laste aslaked was his mood,   1760
For pitee renneth soone in gentil herte.
And though he first for ire quook and sterte,
He hath considered shortly, in a clause,
The trespas of hem bothe, and eek the cause,
And although that his ire hir gilt accused,   1765
Yet in his resoun he hem bothe excused,
As thus: he thoghte wel that every man
Wol helpe hymself in love, if that he kan,
And eek delivere hymself out of prisoun.
And eek his herte hadde compassioun   1770
Of wommen, for they wepen evere in oon,
And in his gentil herte he thoughte anon,
And softe unto hymself he seyde, "Fy
Upon a lord that wol have no mercy,
But been a leon, bothe in word and dede,   1775
To hem that been in repentaunce and drede,
As wel as to a proud despitous man
That wol mayntene that he first bigan.
That lord hath litel of discrecioun,
That in swich cas kan no divisioun   1780
But weyeth pride and humblesse after oon."
And shortly, whan his ire is thus agoon,
He gan to looken up with eyen lighte
And spak thise same wordes al on highte:

     "The god of love, a benedicite!   1785
How myghty and how greet a lord is he!
Ayeyns his myght ther gayneth none obstacles.
He may be cleped a god for his myracles,

For he kan maken, at his owene gyse,
Of everich herte as that hym list divyse.   1790
Lo heere this Arcite and this Palamoun,
That quitly weren out of my prisoun,
And myghte han lyved in Thebes roially,
And witen I am hir mortal enemy,
And that hir deth lith in my myght also,   1795
And yet hath love, maugree hir eyen two,
Broght hem hyder bothe for to dye.
Now looketh, is nat that an heigh folye?
Who may been a fool but if he love?
Bihoold, for Goddes sake that sit above,   1800
Se how they blede! Be they noght wel arrayed?
Thus hath hir lord, the god of love, ypayed
Hir wages and hir fees for hir servyse!
And yet they wenen for to been ful wyse
That serven love, for aught that may bifalle.
But this is yet the beste game of alle,   1806
That she for whom they han this jolitee
Kan hem therfore as muche thank as me.
She woot namoore of al this hoote fare,
By God, than woot a cokkow or an hare!   1810
But all moot ben assayed, hoot and coold;
A man moot ben a fool, or yong or oold —
I woot it by myself ful yore agon,
For in my tyme a servant was I oon.
And therfore, syn I knowe of loves peyne   1815
And woot hou soore it kan a man distreyne,
As he that hath ben caught ofte in his laas,
I yow foryeve al hoolly this trespaas,
At requeste of the queene, that kneleth heere,
And eek of Emelye, my suster deere.   1820
And ye shul bothe anon unto me swere
That nevere mo ye shal my contree dere,
Ne make werre upon me nyght ne day,
But been my freendes in all that ye may.
I yow foryeve this trespas every deel."   1825

1748 **wommanhede:** womanliness (having the qualities proper to a woman)
1760 **aslaked:** calmed
1761 **renneth:** moves
1762 **quook:** shook **sterte:** trembled
1763 **in a clause:** briefly
1771 **evere in oon:** continually
1773 **softe:** quietly
1778 **mayntene:** persist in
1779 **discrecioun:** sound judgment
1780 **kan no divisioun:** knows no distinctions
1781 **weyeth:** weighs **after oon:** alike
1784 **on highte:** aloud
1785 **benedicite:** (the Lord) bless you
1787 **gayneth:** avail

1789 **at his owene gyse:** after his own fashion
1790 **divyse:** command
1792 **quitly:** freely
1794 **witen:** know
1796 **maugree:** in spite of
1799 Who can be a fool unless (*but if*) he is in love?
1800 **sit** = *sitteth,* sits
1802 **ypayed:** paid
1804 **wenen for to been:** think themselves
1806 **game:** joke
1807 **jolitee:** passion
1808 Owes them as much gratitude for this as she owes me
1809 **hoote fare:** rash conduct
1810 **cokkow:** cuckoo
1811 **assayed:** experienced
1813 **yore agon:** long ago
1814 **servant:** servant of Love, lover
1816 **distreyne:** afflict
1817 **laas:** snare
1821 **shul:** must
1822 **dere:** harm
1825 **every deel:** completely

And they hym sworen his axyng faire and weel,
And hym of lordshipe and of mercy preyde,
And he hem graunteth grace, and thus he
          seyde:
    "To speke of roial lynage and richesse,
Though that she were a queene or a princesse,
Ech of you bothe is worthy, doutelees,   1831
To wedden whan tyme is; but nathelees —
I speke as for my suster Emelye,
For whom ye have this strif and jalousye —
Ye woot yourself she may nat wedden two   1835
Atones, though ye fighten everemo,
That oon of you, al be hym looth or lief,
He moot go pipen in an yvy leef;
This is to seyn, she may nat now han bothe,
Al be ye never so jalouse ne so wrothe.   1840
And forthy I yow putte in this degree,
That ech of yow shal have his destynee
As hym is shape, and herkneth in what wyse;
Lo, heere youre ende of that I shal devyse.
    My wyl is this, for plat conclusioun,   1845
Withouten any repplicacioun —
If that you liketh, take it for the beste:
That everich of you shal goon where hym leste
Frely, withouten raunson or daunger,
And this day fifty wykes, fer ne ner,   1850
Everich of you shal brynge an hundred
          knyghtes
Armed for lystes up at alle rightes,
Al redy to darreyne hire by bataille.
And this bihote I yow withouten faille,
Upon my trouthe, and as I am a knyght,   1855
That wheither of yow bothe that hath
          myght —
This is to seyn, that wheither he or thow
May with his hundred, as I spak of now,
Sleen his contrarie, or out of lystes dryve,
Thanne shal I yeve Emelya to wyve   1860
To whom that Fortune yeveth so fair a grace.
The lystes shal I maken in this place,

And God so wisly on my soule rewe
As I shal evene juge been and trewe.   1864
Ye shul noon oother ende with me maken,
That oon of yow ne shal be deed or taken.
And if yow thynketh this is weel ysayd,
Seyeth youre avys, and holdeth you apayd.
This is youre ende and youre conclusioun."
    Who looketh lightly now but Palamoun?
Who spryngeth up for joye but Arcite?   1871
Who kouthe telle, or who kouthe it endite,
The joye that is maked in the place
Whan Theseus hath doon so fair a grace?   1874
But doun on knees wente every maner wight,
And thonked hym with al hir herte and myght,
And namely the Thebans often sithe.
And thus with good hope and with herte blithe
They taken hir leve, and homward gonne they
          ride
To Thebes with his olde walles wyde.   1880

Explicit secunda pars

Sequitur pars tercia

    I trowe men wolde deme it necligence
If I foryete to tellen the dispence
Of Theseus, that gooth so bisily
To maken up the lystes roially,
That swich a noble theatre as it was   1885
I dar wel seyen in this world ther nas.
The circuit a myle was aboute,
Walled of stoon, and dyched al withoute.
Round was the shap, in manere of compas,
Ful of degrees, the heighte of sixty pas,   1890
That whan a man was set on o degree,
He letted nat his felawe for to see.
    Estward ther stood a gate of marbul whit,
Westward right swich another in the opposit.
And shortly to concluden, swich a place   1895
Was noon in erthe, as in so litel space;
For in the lond ther was no crafty man
That geometrie or ars-metrike kan,
Ne portreyour, ne kervere of ymages,

1827 **of lordshipe**: to be their lord, protector
1829 **richesse**: wealth
1832 **nathelees**: none the less
1836 **Atones**: at once, at the same time
1837 **al be hym looth or lief**: whether he likes it or not
1838 He may as well go whistle (for consolation).
1840 **wrothe**: angry
1841 **forthy**: therefore   **degree**: situation
1843 **wyse**: manner
1845 **plat**: flat, blunt
1846 **repplicacioun**: reply
1849 **daunger**: resistance
1850 **fer ne ner**: more or less; see n.
1852 **for lystes**: for battle in the lists   **at alle rightes**: in all respects
1853 **darreyne hire**: decide the right to her
1854 **bihote**: promise
1856 **wheither**: whichever
1860 **to wyve**: as a wife

1863 **rewe**: have mercy
1864 **evene**: impartial
1865 **shul**: shall
1868 **avys**: opinion   **apayd**: satisfied
1870 **lightly**: cheerfully
1872 **endite**: describe in writing
1874 **doon so fair a grace**: behaved so graciously
Explicit, *etc.*: Here ends the first part.   **Sequitur**, *etc.*: Here follows the third part.
1882 **dispence**: expenditures
1888 **dyched**: surrounded by a ditch
1889 **manere of compas**: the shape of a circle
1890 **degrees**: tiers, rows of seats   **pas**: paces
1892 **letted**: hindered
1896 **space**: time
1897 **crafty**: skillful, ingenious
1898 **ars-metrike**: art of measurement (arithmetic)   **kan**: knows
1899 **portreyour**: painter   **kervere of ymages**: sculptor

That Theseus ne yaf him mete and wages
The theatre for to maken and devyse.   1901
And for to doon his ryte and sacrifise,
He estward hath, upon the gate above,
In worshipe of Venus, goddesse of love,
Doon make an auter and an oratorie;   1905
And on the gate westward, in memorie
Of Mars, he maked hath right swich another,
That coste largely of gold a fother.
And northward, in a touret on the wal,
Of alabastre whit and reed coral,   1910
An oratorie, riche for to see,
In worshipe of Dyane of chastitee,
Hath Theseus doon wroght in noble wyse.
    But yet hadde I foryeten to devyse
The noble kervyng and the portreitures,   1915
The shap, the contenaunce, and the figures
That weren in thise oratories thre.
    First in the temple of Venus maystow se
Wroght on the wal, ful pitous to biholde,
The broken slepes, and the sikes colde,   1920
The sacred teeris, and the waymentynge,
The firy strokes of the desirynge
That loves servantz in this lyf enduren;
The othes that hir covenantz assuren;   1924
Plesaunce and Hope, Desir, Foolhardynesse,
Beautee and Youthe, Bauderie, Richesse,
Charmes and Force, Lesynges, Flaterye,
Despense, Bisynesse, and Jalousye,
That wered of yelewe gooldes a gerland,
And a cokkow sittynge on hir hand;   1930
Festes, instrumentz, caroles, daunces,
Lust and array, and alle the circumstaunces
Of love, which that I rekned and rekne shal,
By ordre weren peynted on the wal,
And mo than I kan make of mencioun.   1935
For soothly al the mount of Citheroun,
Ther Venus hath hir principal dwellynge,
Was shewed on the wal in portreyynge,

With al the gardyn and the lustynesse.
Nat was foryeten the porter, Ydelnesse,   1940
Ne Narcisus the faire of yore agon,
Ne yet the folye of kyng Salomon,
Ne yet the grete strengthe of Ercules —
Th'enchauntementz of Medea and Circes —
Ne of Turnus, with the hardy fiers corage,
The riche Cresus, kaytyf in servage.   1946
Thus may ye seen that wysdom ne richesse,
Beautee ne sleighte, strengthe ne hardynesse,
Ne may with Venus holde champartie,   1949
For as hir list the world than may she gye.
Lo, alle thise folk so caught were in hir las,
Til they for wo ful ofte seyde "allas!"
Suffiseth heere ensamples oon or two,
And though I koude rekene a thousand mo.
    The statue of Venus, glorious for to se,   1955
Was naked, fletynge in the large see,
And fro the navele doun al covered was
With wawes grene, and brighte as any glas.
A citole in hir right hand hadde she,
And on hir heed, ful semely for to se,   1960
A rose gerland, fressh and wel smellynge;
Above hir heed hir dowves flikerynge.
Biforn hire stood hir sone Cupido;
Upon his shuldres wynges hadde he two,
And blynd he was, as it is often seene;   1965
A bowe he bar and arwes brighte and kene.
    Why sholde I noght as wel eek telle yow al
The portreiture that was upon the wal
Withinne the temple of myghty Mars the
          rede?
Al peynted was the wal, in lengthe and brede,
Lyk to the estres of the grisly place   1971
That highte the grete temple of Mars in Trace,
In thilke colde, frosty regioun
Ther as Mars hath his sovereyn mansioun.

1939 **lustynesse:** pleasure
1941 **Narcisus:** Narcissus, for whom the nymph Echo died; for the story, see Rom 1469–1638.
1942 **folye:** lechery   **Salomon:** Solomon, who had many wives
1943 **Ercules:** Hercules, whose beloved killed him; see MkT VII.2095–142.
1944 **Medea and Circes:** famous sorceresses, who tried to hold their loves by magic
1945 **Turnus:** whose love for Lavinia led to his fatal duel with Aeneas; cf. HF 457–58.
1946 **Cresus, kaytyf in servage:** Croesus, wretched in captivity; see MkT VII.2727–66.
1948 **sleighte:** trickery   **hardynesse:** bravery
1949 **champartie:** partnership in power
1950 **gye:** rule
1951 **las:** snare
1956 **fletynge:** floating
1958 **wawes:** waves
1959 **citole:** a stringed instrument, like a zither
1962 **flikerynge:** fluttering
1967 **eek:** also
1970 **brede:** breadth
1971 **estres:** interior apartments
1974 **sovereyn:** best, most excellent

1901 **devyse:** contrive
1905 **auter:** altar   **oratorie:** shrine, chapel
1908 **fother:** cartload
1909 **touret:** turret
1912 **Dyane of chastitee:** the chaste Diana
1913 **doon wroght:** had made
1915 **kervyng:** sculpture   **portreitures:** paintings
1916 **contenaunce:** appearance
1920 **sikes:** sighs
1921 **waymentynge:** lamentation
1924 **covenantz:** agreements
1925 **Plesaunce:** Pleasure, amusement
1926 **Bauderie:** Mirth, jollity
1927 **Lesynges:** Falsehood, deceit
1928 **Despense:** expenditures   **Bisynesse:** attentiveness
1929 **yelewe:** yellow   **gooldes:** marigolds
1930 **cokkow:** cuckoo (a symbol of cuckoldry)
1931 **caroles:** dance-songs
1934 **By ordre:** sequentially
1936 **Citheroun:** Cithaeron, here confused with the island Cytherea

First on the wal was peynted a forest,   1975
In which ther dwelleth neither man ne best,
With knotty, knarry, bareyne trees olde,
Of stubbes sharpe and hidouse to biholde,
In which ther ran a rumbel in a swough,   1979
As though a storm sholde bresten every bough.
And dounward from an hille, under a bente,
Ther stood the temple of Mars armypotente,
Wroght al of burned steel, of which the entree
Was long and streit, and gastly for to see.
And therout came a rage and swich a veze
That it made al the gate for to rese.   1986
The northren lyght in at the dores shoon,
For wyndowe on the wal ne was ther noon,
Thurgh which men myghten any light discerne.
The dore was al of adamant eterne,   1990
Yclenched overthwart and endelong
With iren tough; and for to make it strong,
Every pyler, the temple to sustene,
Was tonne-greet, of iren bright and shene.

    Ther saugh I first the derke ymaginyng
Of Felonye, and al the compassyng;   1996
The crueel Ire, reed as any gleede;
The pykepurs, and eek the pale Drede;
The smylere with the knyf under the cloke;
The shepne brennynge with the blake
        smoke;   2000
The tresoun of the mordrynge in the bedde;
The open werre, with woundes al bibledde;
Contek, with blody knyf and sharp manace.
Al ful of chirkyng was that sory place.   2004
The sleere of hymself yet saugh I ther —
His herte-blood hath bathed al his heer —
The nayl ydryven in the shode anyght;

The colde deeth, with mouth gapyng upright.
Amyddes of the temple sat Meschaunce,
With disconfort and sory contenaunce.   2010
Yet saugh I Woodnesse, laughynge in his rage,
Armed Compleint, Outhees, and fiers Outrage;
The careyne in the busk, with throte ycorve;
A thousand slayn, and nat of qualm ystorve;
The tiraunt, with the pray by force yraft;   2015
The toun destroyed, ther was no thyng laft.
Yet saugh I brent the shippes hoppesteres;
The hunte strangled with the wilde beres;
The sowe freten the child right in the cradel;
The cook yscalded, for al his longe ladel.   2020
Noght was foryeten by the infortune of Marte.
The cartere overryden with his carte —
Under the wheel ful lowe he lay adoun.
Ther were also, of Martes divisioun,   2024
The barbour, and the bocher, and the smyth,
That forgeth sharpe swerdes on his styth.
And al above, depeynted in a tour,
Saugh I Conquest, sittynge in greet honour,
With the sharpe swerd over his heed
Hangynge by a soutil twynes threed.   2030
Depeynted was the slaughtre of Julius,
Of grete Nero, and of Antonius;
Al be that thilke tyme they were unborn,
Yet was hir deth depeynted ther-biforn
By manasynge of Mars, right by figure;   2035
So was it shewed in that portreiture,
As is depeynted in the sterres above
Who shal be slayn or elles deed for love.
Suffiseth oon ensample in stories olde;   2039
I may nat rekene hem alle though I wolde.

    The statue of Mars upon a carte stood
Armed, and looked grym as he were wood;

1977 **knarry:** gnarled **bareyne:** barren
1978 **stubbes:** stumps
1979 **rumbel:** rumbling noise **swough:** sound of wind
1980 **bresten:** burst
1981 **under:** close to **bente:** grassy slope
1982 **armypotente:** powerful in arms
1983 **burned:** burnished
1984 **streit:** narrow, small **gastly:** terrifying
1985 **rage:** rush of wind **veze:** rush, blast
1986 **rese:** shake
1987 **northren lyght:** light from the north
1990 **adamant:** the hardest of stones
1991 **Yclenched:** bound, clinched **overthwart:** crosswise
endelong: lengthwise
1993 **pyler:** pillar **sustene:** sustain, support
1994 **tonne-greet:** big around as a large barrel
1995 **derke ymaginyng:** malicious plotting
1996 **Felonye:** Wickedness **compassyng:** scheming
1997 **gleede:** glowing coal
1998 **pykepurs:** pick-purse, thief **Drede:** Fear
2000 **shepne:** stable
2001 **mordrynge:** murder
2002 **with woundes al bibledde:** all covered with blood from
wounds
2003 **Contek:** strife
2004 **chirkyng:** groaning, creaking **sory:** sorry, wretched
2005 **sleere:** slayer
2007 **shode:** parting of the hair, temple

2008 **upright:** upwards
2009 **Meschaunce:** Misfortune
2011 **Woodnesse:** Madness
2012 **Compleint:** Grievance, discontent **Outhees:** Outcry,
alarm **Outrage:** Violence, excessive cruelty
2013 **careyne:** corpse **busk:** woods **ycorve:** cut
2014 **of qualm ystorve:** killed by the plague
2015 **pray:** prey **yraft:** taken away
2017 **brent:** burned **hoppesteres:** dancing (on a stormy sea)
2018 **hunte:** hunter **strangled with:** killed by
2019 **freten:** devour
2020 **for al his longe ladel:** despite his long-handled spoon
2021 **infortune of Marte:** evil influence of Mars
2022 **overryden with:** run over by
2024 **Martes divisioun:** those influenced by Mars
2025 **bocher:** butcher
2026 **styth:** anvil
2027 **depeynted:** painted
2030 **soutil twynes threed:** thin thread of twine
2031–32 **Julius, Nero, Antonius:** the Roman emperors
2035 **manasynge:** menace, threat **by figure:** according to the
configuration of the planets; "perhaps a technical reference to a
horoscope" (R.)
2036 **portreiture:** painting
2039 **ensample:** illustrative story **stories:** histories
2041 **carte:** chariot

And over his heed ther shynen two figures
Of sterres, that been cleped in scriptures,
That oon Puella, that oother Rubeus —   2045
This god of armes was arrayed thus.
A wolf ther stood biforn hym at his feet
With eyen rede, and of a man he eet;
With soutil pencel was depeynted this storie
In redoutynge of Mars and of his glorie.   2050
    Now to the temple of Dyane the chaste,
As shortly as I kan, I wol me haste,
To telle yow al the descripsioun.
Depeynted been the walles up and doun
Of huntyng and of shamefast chastitee.   2055
Ther saugh I how woful Calistopee,
Whan that Diane agreved was with here,
Was turned from a womman til a bere,
And after was she maad the loode-sterre.   2059
Thus was it peynted; I kan sey yow no ferre.
Hir sone is eek a sterre, as men may see.
Ther saugh I Dane, yturned til a tree —
I mene nat the goddesse Diane,
But Penneus doghter, which that highte Dane.
Ther saugh I Attheon an hert ymaked,   2065
For vengeaunce that he saugh Diane al naked;
I saugh how that his houndes have hym caught
And freeten hym, for that they knewe hym
        naught.
Yet peynted was a litel forther moor
How Atthalante hunted the wilde boor,   2070
And Meleagre, and many another mo,
For which Dyane wroghte hym care and wo.
Ther saugh I many another wonder storie,
The which me list nat drawen to memorie.
    This goddesse on an hert ful hye seet,   2075
With smale houndes al aboute hir feet,
And undernethe hir feet she hadde a moone —
Wexynge it was and sholde wanye soone.
In gaude grene hir statue clothed was,
With bowe in honde and arwes in a cas.   2080
Hir eyen caste she ful lowe adoun

Ther Pluto hath his derke regioun.
A womman travaillynge was hire biforn;
But for hir child so longe was unborn,
Ful pitously Lucyna gan she calle   2085
And seyde, "Help, for thou mayst best of alle!"
Wel koude he peynten lifly that it wroghte;
With many a floryn he the hewes boghte.
    Now been thise lystes maad, and Theseus,
That at his grete cost arrayed thus   2090
The temples and the theatre every deel,
Whan it was doon, hym lyked wonder weel.
But stynte I wole of Theseus a lite,
And speke of Palamon and of Arcite.
    The day approcheth of hir retournynge,   2095
That everich sholde an hundred knyghtes
        brynge
The bataille to darreyne, as I yow tolde.
And til Atthenes, hir covenant for to holde,
Hath everich of hem broght an hundred
        knyghtes,
Wel armed for the werre at alle rightes.   2100
And sikerly ther trowed many a man
That nevere, sithen that the world bigan,
As for to speke of knyghthod of hir hond,
As fer as God hath maked see or lond,
Nas of so fewe so noble a compaignye.   2105
For every wight that lovede chivalrye
And wolde, his thankes, han a passant name,
Hath preyed that he myghte been of that game;
And wel was hym that therto chosen was,
For if ther fille tomorwe swich a cas,   2110
Ye knowen wel that every lusty knyght
That loveth paramours and hath his myght,
Were it in Engelond or elleswhere,
They wolde, hir thankes, wilnen to be there —
To fighte for a lady, benedicitee!   2115
It were a lusty sighte for to see.
    And right so ferden they with Palamon.
With hym ther wenten knyghtes many on;
Som wol ben armed in an haubergeoun,
And in a brestplate and a light gypoun;   2120

2044 **scriptures:** books
2045 **Puella, Rubeus:** figures in geomancy; see n.
2048 **eet:** ate
2055 **shamefast:** modest
2056 **Calistopee:** Callisto, who was metamorphosed into Ursa Major
2057 **agreved:** angered
2059 **loode-sterre:** polestar, North star
2060 **ferre:** further
2062 **Dane:** Daphne, pursued by Apollo and metamorphosed into the laurel tree
2065 **Attheon:** Actaeon, metamorphosed into a hart by Diana
2068 **freeten:** devoured
2070 **Atthalante:** Atalanta, for whom Meleager (*Meleagre*) hunted the Calydonian boar; see Tr 5.1464–84.
2075 **seet:** sat
2078 **Wexynge:** waxing   **wanye:** wane
2079 **gaude:** yellowish

2083 **travaillynge:** in labor
2085 **Lucyna:** Lucina, Diana as goddess of childbirth
2086 **thou mayst best:** you are best able, have most power
2088 **floryn:** florin, a gold coin   **hewes:** pigments
2090 **arrayed:** prepared
2091 **every deel:** in all respects
2097 **darreyne:** decide
2100 **at alle rightes:** in all respects
2101 **sikerly:** truly   **trowed:** believed
2103 **of hir hond:** of the deeds of their hand, their prowess
2107 **his thankes:** willingly   **passant name:** outstanding reputation
2112 **paramours:** passionately
2114 **wilnen:** desire
2116 **lusty:** pleasing
2119 **Som:** a certain one   **haubergeoun:** coat of mail
2120 **gypoun:** tunic

And som wol have a paire plates large;
And som wol have a Pruce sheeld or a targe;
Som wol ben armed on his legges weel,
And have an ax, and som a mace of steel —
Ther is no newe gyse that it nas old. 2125
Armed were they, as I have yow told,
Everych after his opinioun.
 Ther maistow seen, comynge with Palamoun,
Lygurge hymself, the grete kyng of Trace.
Blak was his berd, and manly was his face;
The cercles of his eyen in his heed, 2131
They gloweden bitwixen yelow and reed,
And lik a grifphon looked he aboute,
With kempe heeris on his browes stoute; 2134
His lymes grete, his brawnes harde and stronge,
His shuldres brode, his armes rounde and longe;
And as the gyse was in his contree,
Ful hye upon a chaar of gold stood he,
With foure white boles in the trays.
In stede of cote-armure over his harnays, 2140
With nayles yelewe and brighte as any gold,
He hadde a beres skyn, col-blak for old.
His longe heer was kembd bihynde his bak;
As any ravenes fethere it shoon for blak; 2144
A wrethe of gold, arm-greet, of huge wighte,
Upon his heed, set ful of stones brighte,
Of fyne rubyes and of dyamauntz.
Aboute his chaar ther wenten white alauntz,
Twenty and mo, as grete as any steer,
To hunten at the leoun or the deer, 2150
And folwed hym with mosel faste ybounde,
Colered of gold, and tourettes fyled rounde.
An hundred lordes hadde he in his route,
Armed ful wel, with hertes stierne and stoute.
 With Arcita, in stories as men fynde, 2155
The grete Emetreus, the kyng of Inde,

Upon a steede bay trapped in steel,
Covered in clooth of gold, dyapred weel,
Cam ridynge lyk the god of armes, Mars.
His cote-armure was of clooth of Tars 2160
Couched with perles white and rounde and
  grete;
His sadel was of brend gold newe ybete;
A mantelet upon his shulder hangynge,
Bret-ful of rubyes rede as fyr sparklynge;
His crispe heer lyk rynges was yronne, 2165
And that was yelow, and glytered as the sonne.
His nose was heigh, his eyen bright citryn,
His lippes rounde, his colour was sangwyn;
A fewe frakenes in his face yspreynd,
Bitwixen yelow and somdel blak ymeynd; 2170
And as a leon he his lookyng caste.
Of fyve and twenty yeer his age I caste.
His berd was wel bigonne for to sprynge;
His voys was as a trompe thonderynge.
Upon his heed he wered of laurer grene 2175
A gerland, fressh and lusty for to sene.
Upon his hand he bar for his deduyt
An egle tame, as any lilye whyt.
An hundred lordes hadde he with hym there,
Al armed, save hir heddes, in al hir gere, 2180
Ful richely in alle maner thynges.
For trusteth wel that dukes, erles, kynges
Were gadered in this noble compaignye,
For love and for encrees of chivalrye.
Aboute this kyng ther ran on every part 2185
Ful many a tame leon and leopart.
And in this wise thise lordes, alle and some,
Been on the Sonday to the citee come
Aboute pryme, and in the toun alight. 2189
 This Theseus, this duc, this worthy knyght,
Whan he had broght hem into his citee,
And inned hem, everich at his degree,
He festeth hem, and dooth so greet labour
To esen hem and doon hem al honour

2121 **paire plates:** set of plate armor
2122 **Pruce:** Prussian
2125 There is no new fashion (*gyse*) that has not been old. (R.)
2127 **after:** according to
2129 **Lygurge:** Lycurgus
2133 **grifphon:** griffin (mythical beast with the body of a lion and the head of an eagle)
2134 **kempe:** shaggy
2135 **lymes greet:** large limbs **brawnes:** muscles
2138 **chaar:** chariot
2139 **boles:** bulls **trays:** traces, harness
2140 **cote-armure:** a tunic embroidered with a heraldic device, worn over the armor
2141 **nayles:** rivets **yelewe:** yellow
2142 **col-blak:** coal-black **for old:** because of age
2143 **kembd:** combed
2144 **for blak:** because of blackness
2145 **arm-greet:** thick as an arm **wighte:** weight
2147 **dyamauntz:** diamonds
2148 **alauntz:** wolfhounds
2151 **mosel:** muzzle
2152 **Colered:** wearing collars **tourettes:** rings for leashes
fyled: smoothed
2153 **route:** company
2154 **stierne:** stern, cruel
2156 **Inde:** India

2157 **bay:** reddish-brown **trapped:** equipped with trappings
2158 **dyapred:** decorated with small geometric patterns
2160 **clooth of Tars:** silk from Tarsia in Turkestan
2161 **Couched:** adorned **perles:** pearls
2162 **brend gold:** refined (pure) gold **ybete:** adorned
2163 **mantelet:** short cloak
2164 **Bret-ful:** brimful
2165 **crispe:** curly **yronne:** fashioned (literally, *run*)
2167 **citryn:** lemon-colored
2168 **sangwyn:** ruddy
2169 **frakenes:** freckles **yspreynd:** sprinkled
2170 **ymeynd:** mingled
2171 **lookyng caste:** looked about
2177 **deduyt:** delight
2184 **encrees:** increase
2185 **on every part:** on all sides
2187 **alle and some:** one and all, everyone
2189 **pryme:** around 9 A.M. **alight:** dismounted, arrived
2192 **inned hem:** provided them lodging
2193 **dooth so greet labour:** makes such an effort
2194 **esen:** accommodate, entertain

That yet men wenen that no mannes wit   2195
Of noon estaat ne koude amenden it.
   The mynstralcye, the service at the feeste,
The grete yiftes to the meeste and leeste,
The riche array of Theseus paleys,
Ne who sat first ne last upon the deys,   2200
What ladyes fairest been or best daunsynge,
Or which of hem kan dauncen best and synge,
Ne who moost felyngly speketh of love;
What haukes sitten on the perche above,
What houndes liggen on the floor adoun —
Of al this make I now no mencioun,   2206
But al th'effect; that thynketh me the beste.
Now cometh the point, and herkneth if yow
     leste.
   The Sonday nyght, er day bigan to sprynge,
Whan Palamon the larke herde synge   2210
(Although it nere nat day by houres two,
Yet song the larke) and Palamon right tho
With hooly herte and with an heigh corage,
He roos to wenden on his pilgrymage
Unto the blisful Citherea benigne —   2215
I mene Venus, honurable and digne.
And in hir houre he walketh forth a pas
Unto the lystes ther hire temple was,
And doun he kneleth, and with humble cheere
And herte soor he seyde as ye shal heere: 2220
   "Faireste of faire, O lady myn, Venus,
Doughter to Jove and spouse of Vulcanus,
Thow gladere of the mount of Citheron,
For thilke love thow haddest to Adoon,
Have pitee of my bittre teeris smerte,   2225
And taak myn humble preyere at thyn herte.
Allas! I ne have no langage to telle
Th'effectes ne the tormentz of myn helle;
Myn herte may myne harmes nat biwreye;
I am so confus that I kan noght seye   2230
But 'Mercy, lady bright, that knowest weele
My thought and seest what harmes that I
     feele!'

Considere al this and rewe upon my soore,
As wisly as I shal for everemoore,   2234
Emforth my myght, thy trewe servant be,
And holden werre alwey with chastitee.
That make I myn avow, so ye me helpe!
I kepe noght of armes for to yelpe,
Ne I ne axe nat tomorwe to have victorie,
Ne renoun in this cas, ne veyne glorie   2240
Of pris of armes blowen up and doun;
But I wolde have fully possessioun
Of Emelye, and dye in thy servyse.
Fynd thow the manere hou and in what wyse:
I recche nat but it may bettre be   2245
To have victorie of hem, or they of me,
So that I have my lady in myne armes.
For though so be that Mars is god of armes,
Youre vertu is so greet in hevene above
That if yow list, I shal wel have my love.   2250
Thy temple wol I worshipe everemo,
And on thyn auter, where I ride or go,
I wol doon sacrifice and fires beete.
And if ye wol nat so, my lady sweete,
Thanne preye I thee, tomorwe with a spere
That Arcita me thurgh the herte bere.   2256
Thanne rekke I noght, whan I have lost my lyf,
Though that Arcita wynne hire to his wyf.
This is th'effect and ende of my preyere:
Yif me my love, thow blisful lady deere."   2260
   Whan the orison was doon of Palamon,
His sacrifice he dide, and that anon,
Ful pitously, with alle circumstaunces,
Al telle I noght as now his observaunces;
But atte laste the statue of Venus shook,   2265
And made a signe, wherby that he took
That his preyere accepted was that day.
For thogh the signe shewed a delay,
Yet wiste he wel that graunted was his boone,
And with glad herte he wente hym hoom ful
     soone.   2270
   The thridde houre inequal that Palamon
Bigan to Venus temple for to gon,

2195 **wenen:** suppose
2197 **mynstralcye:** music
2198 **yiftes:** gifts   **to the meeste and leeste:** to everyone
2199 **array:** adornment
2200 **deys:** dais
2203 **moost felyngly:** with the most delicate understanding
2205 **liggen:** lie   **adoun:** below
2207 **th'effect:** the substance
2212 **tho:** then
2215 **Citherea:** a name for Venus, who rose from the sea at the island Cythera   **benigne:** gracious
2216 **digne:** worthy of honor
2217 **houre:** planetary hour; see Astr 2.12.   **a pas:** slowly
2219 **cheere:** expression
2223 **gladere:** one who brings joy
2224 **Adoon:** Adonis
2228 **tormentz:** tortures
2229 **biwreye:** reveal
2232 **harmes:** sorrows

2233 **rewe:** have mercy   **soore:** pain, misery
2234 **As wisly as:** as surely as
2235 **Emforth:** according to
2237 **so ye me helpe:** providing you help me
2238 **kepe noght:** care nothing   **yelpe:** boast
2239 **Ne I:** to be pronounced as one syllable (n'I)
2241 **pris of armes blowen:** praise for deeds of arms proclaimed
2245 **recche nat but:** care not if
2249 **vertu:** power
2252 **where I ride or go:** wherever I ride or walk (whatever I do)
2253 **beete:** kindle
2260 **Yif:** give
2263 **circumstaunces:** ceremony, due propriety
2264 **Al:** although.
2269 **boone:** request
2271 **houre inequal:** planetary hour; see Astr 2.10.

Up roos the sonne, and up roos Emelye
And to the temple of Dyane gan hye.
Hir maydens, that she thider with hire ladde,
Ful redily with hem the fyr they hadde,   2276
Th'encens, the clothes, and the remenant al
That to the sacrifice longen shal;
The hornes fulle of meeth, as was the gyse —
Ther lakked noght to doon hir sacrifise.   2280
Smokynge the temple, ful of clothes faire,
This Emelye, with herte debonaire,
Hir body wessh with water of a welle.
But hou she dide hir ryte I dar nat telle,
But it be any thing in general;   2285
And yet it were a game to heeren al.
To hym that meneth wel it were no charge;
But it is good a man been at his large.
Hir brighte heer was kembd, untressed al;
A coroune of a grene ook cerial   2290
Upon hir heed was set ful fair and meete.
Two fyres on the auter gan she beete,
And dide hir thynges, as men may biholde
In Stace of Thebes and thise bookes olde.
Whan kyndled was the fyr, with pitous cheere
Unto Dyane she spak as ye may heere: 2296
   "O chaste goddesse of the wodes grene,
To whom bothe hevene and erthe and see is
         sene,
Queene of the regne of Pluto derk and lowe,
Goddesse of maydens, that myn herte hast
         knowe   2300
Ful many a yeer, and woost what I desire,
As keepe me fro thy vengeaunce and thyn ire,
That Attheon aboughte cruelly.
Chaste goddesse, wel wostow that I
Desire to ben a mayden al my lyf,   2305
Ne nevere wol I be no love ne wyf.
I am, thow woost, yet of thy compaignye,
A mayde, and love huntynge and venerye,

And for to walken in the wodes wilde,   2309
And noght to ben a wyf and be with childe.
Noght wol I knowe compaignye of man.
Now help me, lady, sith ye may and kan,
For tho thre formes that thou hast in thee.
And Palamon, that hath swich love to me,
And eek Arcite, that loveth me so soore,   2315
This grace I preye thee withoute moore,
As sende love and pees bitwixe hem two,
And fro me turne awey hir hertes so
That al hire hoote love and hir desir,
And al hir bisy torment, and hir fir   2320
Be queynt, or turned in another place.
And if so be thou wolt nat do me grace,
Or if my destynee be shapen so
That I shal nedes have oon of hem two,
As sende me hym that moost desireth me.   2325
Bihoold, goddesse of clene chastitee,
The bittre teeris that on my chekes falle.
Syn thou art mayde and kepere of us alle,
My maydenhede thou kepe and wel conserve,
And whil I lyve, a mayde I wol thee serve."
   The fires brenne upon the auter cleere,   2331
Whil Emelye was thus in hir preyere.
But sodeynly she saugh a sighte queynte,
For right anon oon of the fyres queynte
And quyked agayn, and after that anon   2335
That oother fyr was queynt and al agon;
And as it queynte it made a whistelynge,
As doon thise wete brondes in hir brennynge,
And at the brondes ende out ran anon
As it were blody dropes many oon;   2340
For which so soore agast was Emelye
That she was wel ny mad and gan to crye,
For she ne wiste what it signyfied,
But oonly for the feere thus hath she cried,
And weep that it was pitee for to heere.   2345
And therwithal Dyane gan appeere,
With bowe in honde, right as an hunteresse,
And seyde, "Doghter, stynt thyn hevynesse.
Among the goddes hye it is affermed,   2349
And by eterne word writen and conformed,

2274 **gan hye:** hurried
2278 **longen:** belong
2279 **meeth:** mead
2281 **Smokynge:** censing
2282 **debonaire:** gentle
2283 **wessh:** washed
2287 **charge:** burden
2288 **at his large:** without restriction
2289 **kembd:** combed   **untressed:** loose
2290 **ook cerial:** an evergreen oak of southern Europe (Quercus
Cerris)
2291 **meete:** suitable, fitting
2292 **beete:** kindle, feed
2293 **thynges:** business, duties
2294 **Stace of Thebes:** Statius's *Thebaid* (quoted as an epigraph
to this tale)
2298 **sene:** visible
2299 **Pluto:** god of the underworld
2302 **As keepe:** keep (*as* is not translated)
2303 **Attheon aboughte:** Actaeon paid for
2308 **venerye:** hunting

2311 **compaignye of man:** sexual intercourse
2313 **tho thre formes:** those three forms (as goddess of the
chase, the moon, the underworld — cf. 2297–99 above)
2320 **bisy:** intense
2321 **queynt:** extinguished
2324 **nedes:** of necessity
2333 **queynte:** curious
2334 **queynte:** went out, was extinguished
2335 **quyked:** rekindled
2336 **queynt:** extinguished
2337 **whistelynge:** roaring sound
2341 **agast:** frightened
2345 **weep:** wept
2348 **stynt:** cease

Thou shalt ben wedded unto oon of tho
That han for thee so muchel care and wo,
But unto which of hem I may nat telle.
Farwel, for I ne may no lenger dwelle.
The fires which that on myn auter brenne   2355
Shulle thee declaren, er that thou go henne,
Thyn aventure of love, as in this cas."
And with that word, the arwes in the caas
Of the goddesse clateren faste and rynge,
And forth she wente and made a vanysshynge;
For which this Emelye astoned was,   2361
And seyde, "What amounteth this, allas?
I putte me in thy proteccioun,
Dyane, and in thy disposicioun."
And hoom she goth anon the nexte weye.   2365
This is th'effect; ther is namoore to seye.

    The nexte houre of Mars folwynge this,
Arcite unto the temple walked is
Of fierse Mars to doon his sacrifise,
With alle the rytes of his payen wyse.   2370
With pitous herte and heigh devocioun,
Right thus to Mars he seyde his orisoun:

    "O stronge god, that in the regnes colde
Of Trace honoured art and lord yholde,
And hast in every regne and every lond   2375
Of armes al the brydel in thyn hond,
And hem fortunest as thee lyst devyse,
Accepte of me my pitous sacrifise.
If so be that my youthe may deserve,   2379
And that my myght be worthy for to serve
Thy godhede, that I may been oon of thyne,
Thanne preye I thee to rewe upon my pyne.
For thilke peyne and thilke hoote fir
In which thow whilom brendest for desir,
Whan that thow usedest the beautee   2385
Of faire, yonge, fresshe Venus free,
And haddest hire in armes at thy wille —
Although thee ones on a tyme mysfille,
Whan Vulcanus hadde caught thee in his las
And foond thee liggynge by his wyf, allas! —
For thilke sorwe that was in thyn herte,   2391
Have routhe as wel upon my peynes smerte.
I am yong and unkonnynge, as thow woost,

And, as I trowe, with love offended moost
That evere was any lyves creature,   2395
For she that dooth me al this wo endure
Ne reccheth nevere wher I synke or fleete.
And wel I woot, er she me mercy heete,
I moot with strengthe wynne hire in the place,
And wel I woot, withouten help or grace   2400
Of thee ne may my strengthe noght availle.
Thanne help me, lord, tomorwe in my bataille,
For thilke fyr that whilom brente thee,
As wel as thilke fyr now brenneth me,
And do that I tomorwe have victorie.   2405
Myn be the travaille, and thyn be the glorie!
Thy sovereyn temple wol I moost honouren
Of any place, and alwey moost labouren
In thy plesaunce and in thy craftes stronge,
And in thy temple I wol my baner honge   2410
And alle the armes of my compaignye,
And everemo, unto that day I dye,
Eterne fir I wol bifore thee fynde.
And eek to this avow I wol me bynde:
My beerd, myn heer, that hongeth long adoun,
That nevere yet ne felte offensioun   2416
Of rasour nor of shere, I wol thee yive,
And ben thy trewe servant whil I lyve.
Now, lord, have routhe upon my sorwes soore;
Yif me [victorie]; I aske thee namoore."   2420

    The preyere stynt of Arcita the stronge,
The rynges on the temple dore that honge,
And eek the dores, clatereden ful faste,
Of which Arcita somwhat hym agaste.   2424
The fyres brenden upon the auter brighte
That it gan al the temple for to lighte;
A sweete smel the ground anon up yaf,
And Arcita anon his hand up haf,
And moore encens into the fyr he caste,
With othere rytes mo; and atte laste   2430
The statue of Mars bigan his hauberk rynge,
And with that soun he herde a murmurynge
Ful lowe and dym, and seyde thus, "Victorie!"

2351 **tho:** those
2356 **henne:** hence, away
2361 **astoned:** astonished
2365 **nexte:** nearest
2367 **houre:** planetary hour
2370 **payen wyse:** pagan manner (of worship)
2377 **hem fortunest:** grant them fortune, control their destinies
2382 **pyne:** pain
2388 **mysfille:** things went wrong (for) you
2389 **Vulcanus:** Vulcan
2390 **liggynge:** lying
2393 **unkonnynge:** ignorant, unskillful

2394 **with:** by
2395 **lyves:** living
2396 **dooth:** makes
2397 **wher I synke or fleete:** whether I sink or float
2398 **heete:** promise
2399 **place:** area where the action takes place, i.e., lists
2405 **do:** cause, bring about
2406 **travaille:** labor
2407 **sovereyn:** best, most excellent
2413 **fynde:** provide
2416 **offensioun:** injury
2417 **shere:** scissors
2421 **stynt:** stinted, stopped
2424 **hym agaste:** was afraid
2428 **haf:** raised
2431 **hauberk:** coat of mail
2432 **soun:** sound

For which he yaf to Mars honour and glorie.
And thus with joye and hope wel to fare   2435
Arcite anon unto his in is fare,
As fayn as fowel is of the brighte sonne.

  And right anon swich strif ther is bigonne,
For thilke grauntyng, in the hevene above,
Bitwixe Venus, the goddesse of love,   2440
And Mars, the stierne god armypotente,
That Juppiter was bisy it to stente,
Til that the pale Saturnus the colde,
That knew so manye of aventures olde,
Foond in his olde experience an art   2445
That he ful soone hath plesed every part.
As sooth is seyd, elde hath greet avantage;
In elde is bothe wysdom and usage;
Men may the olde atrenne and noght atrede.
Saturne anon, to stynten strif and drede,   2450
Al be it that it is agayn his kynde,
Of al this strif he gan remedie fynde.

  "My deere doghter Venus," quod Saturne,
"My cours, that hath so wyde for to turne,
Hath moore power than woot any man.   2455
Myn is the drenchyng in the see so wan;
Myn is the prison in the derke cote;
Myn is the stranglyng and hangyng by the
          throte,
The murmure and the cherles rebellyng,
The groynynge, and the pryvee empoysonyng;
I do vengeance and pleyn correccioun,   2461
Whil I dwelle in the signe of the leoun.
Myn is the ruyne of the hye halles,
The fallynge of the toures and of the walles
Upon the mynour or the carpenter.   2465
I slow Sampsoun, shakynge the piler;
And myne be the maladyes colde,
The derke tresons, and the castes olde;
My lookyng is the fader of pestilence.
Now weep namoore; I shal doon diligence   2470

That Palamon, that is thyn owene knyght,
Shal have his lady, as thou hast him hight.
Though Mars shal helpe his knyght, yet nathe-
          lees
Bitwixe yow ther moot be som tyme pees,
Al be ye noght of o compleccioun,   2475
That causeth al day swich divisioun.
I am thyn aiel, redy at thy wille;
Weep now namoore; I wol thy lust fulfille."

  Now wol I stynten of the goddes above,
Of Mars, and of Venus, goddesse of love,   2480
And telle yow as pleynly as I kan
The grete effect, for which that I bygan.

Explicit tercia pars

Sequitur pars quarta

  Greet was the feeste in Atthenes that day,
And eek the lusty seson of that May   2484
Made every wight to been in swich plesaunce
That al that Monday justen they and daunce,
And spenden it in Venus heigh servyse.
But by the cause that they sholde ryse
Eerly, for to seen the grete fight,
Unto hir reste wenten they at nyght.   2490
And on the morwe, whan that day gan sprynge,
Of hors and harneys noyse and claterynge
Ther was in hostelryes al aboute,
And to the paleys rood ther many a route
Of lordes upon steedes and palfreys.   2495
Ther maystow seen devisynge of harneys
So unkouth and so riche, and wroght so weel
Of goldsmythrye, of browdynge, and of steel;
The sheeldes brighte, testeres, and trappures,
Gold-hewen helmes, hauberkes, cote-armures;
Lordes in parementz on hir courseres,   2501
Knyghtes of retenue, and eek squieres
Nailynge the speres, and helmes bokelynge;
Giggynge of sheeldes, with layneres lacynge —
There as nede is they weren no thyng ydel;

2436 **in:** inn, lodgings
2437 **fayn:** glad
2441 **stierne:** stern, cruel   **armypotente:** powerful in arms
2443 **Saturnus the colde:** Saturn the hostile
2445 **art:** plan
2446 **part:** party, side
2447 **elde:** old age
2448 **usage:** experience
2449 One can outrun the old but not outwit them.
2451 **kynde:** nature
2453 **quod:** said
2454 **cours:** orbit
2456 **drenchyng:** drowning   **wan:** dark
2457 **cote:** cell
2459 **murmure:** grumbling   **cherles:** peasants'
2460 **groynynge:** grumbling   **pryvee:** secret   **empoysonyng:** poisoning
2461 **do . . . correccioun:** punish
2462 **leoun:** the zodiacal sign Leo
2465 **mynour:** miner, digging under the walls
2466 **slow:** slew   **Sampsoun:** Sampson, the biblical hero; cf. MkT VII.2015–94.
2468 **derke:** malicious   **castes:** plots
2469 **lookyng is the fader:** (astrological) aspect is the cause

2472 **hight:** promised
2473 **nathelees:** nonetheless
2475 **o compleccioun:** the same temperament (as determined by the humors)
2477 **aiel:** grandfather
2478 **lust:** desire
Explicit, *etc.*: Here ends the third part.   **Sequitur,** *etc.*: Here follows the fourth part.
2485 **plesaunce:** delight
2486 **justen:** joust
2496 **devisynge of harneys:** preparation of armor
2497 **unkouth:** exotic
2498 **browdynge:** embroidery
2499 **testeres:** head-armor for war horses   **trappures:** horse armor
2500 **Gold-hewen:** gold-colored
2501 **parementz:** richly decorated robes
2502 **of retenue:** in his service
2503 **Nailynge the speres:** fastening the heads to the shafts (R.)   **helmes bokelynge:** buckling on helms
2504 **Giggynge of sheeldes:** fitting the shields with straps (OF *guige*, thong) (R.)   **layneres lacynge:** fastening of straps

The fomy steedes on the golden brydel   2506
Gnawynge, and faste the armurers also
With fyle and hamer prikynge to and fro;
Yemen on foote, and communes many oon
With shorte staves, thikke as they may goon;
Pypes, trompes, nakers, clariounes,   2511
That in the bataille blowen blody sounes;
The paleys ful of peple up and doun,
Heere thre, ther ten, holdynge hir questioun,
Dyvynynge of thise Thebane knyghtes
          two.   2515
Somme seyden thus, somme seyde "it shal be
          so";
Somme helden with hym with the blake berd,
Somme with the balled, somme with the thikke
          herd;
Somme seyde he looked grymme, and he wolde
          fighte:
"He hath a sparth of twenty pound of wighte."
Thus was the halle ful of divynynge,   2521
Longe after that the sonne gan to sprynge.

  The grete Theseus, that of his sleep awaked
With mynstralcie and noyse that was maked,
Heeld yet the chambre of his paleys riche
Til that the Thebane knyghtes, bothe yliche
Honured, were into the paleys fet.   2527
Duc Theseus was at a wyndow set,
Arrayed right as he were a god in trone.
The peple preesseth thiderward ful soone   2530
Hym for to seen, and doon heigh reverence,
And eek to herkne his heste and his sentence.
An heraud on a scaffold made an "Oo!"
Til al the noyse of peple was ydo,   2534
And whan he saugh the peple of noyse al stille,
Tho shewed he the myghty dukes wille:

  "The lord hath of his heigh discrecioun
Considered that it were destruccioun
To gentil blood to fighten in the gyse
Of mortal bataille now in this emprise.   2540
Wherfore, to shapen that they shal nat dye,
He wol his firste purpos modifye.

No man therfore, up peyne of los of lyf,
No maner shot, ne polax, ne short knyf
Into the lystes sende or thider brynge;   2545
Ne short swerd, for to stoke with poynt
          bitynge,
No man ne drawe, ne bere it by his syde.
Ne no man shal unto his felawe ryde
But o cours with a sharpe ygrounde spere;
Foyne, if hym list, on foote, hymself to were.
And he that is at meschief shal be take   2551
And noght slayn, but be broght unto the stake
That shal ben ordeyned on either syde;
But thider he shal by force, and there abyde.
And if so falle the chieftayn be take   2555
On outher syde, or elles sleen his make,
No lenger shal the turneiynge laste.
God spede you! Gooth forth and ley on faste!
With long swerd and with mace fighteth youre
          fille.
Gooth now youre wey; this is the lordes
          wille."   2560

  The voys of peple touchede the hevene,
So loude cride they with murie stevene,
"God save swich a lord, that is so good
He wilneth no destruccion of blood!"
Up goon the trompes and the melodye,   2565
And to the lystes rit the compaignye,
By ordinance, thurghout the citee large,
Hanged with clooth of gold, and nat with sarge.

  Ful lik a lord this noble duc gan ryde,
Thise two Thebans upon either syde,   2570
And after rood the queene and Emelye,
And after that another compaignye
Of oon and oother, after hir degree.
And thus they passen thurghout the citee,
And to the lystes come they by tyme.   2575
It nas nat of the day yet fully pryme
Whan set was Theseus ful riche and hye,
Ypolita the queene, and Emelye,
And othere ladys in degrees aboute.
Unto the seetes preesseth al the route.   2580

2509 **communes:** common soldiers
2510 **goon:** walk
2511 **nakers:** kettle drums   **clariounes:** bugles
2512 **blody:** warlike   **sounes:** sounds
2514 **holdynge hir questioun:** debating
2515 **Dyvynynge of:** conjecturing about
2518 **balled:** bald   **thikke herd:** thickly haired (man)
2519 **he:** that fellow
2520 **sparth:** battle-axe   **wighte:** weight
2521 **divynynge:** speculation
2526 **yliche:** alike
2527 **fet:** fetched, brought
2529 **trone:** throne
2530 **preesseth:** push   **thiderward:** thither, toward there
2532 **heste:** command   **sentence:** decision
2537 **discrecioun:** sound judgment
2540 **emprise:** undertaking
2542 **firste:** previous

2543 **up:** on
2544 **shot:** arrow   **polax:** battle axe
2546 **stoke:** stab, jab
2549 **But o:** only one   **cours:** run (in a joust)
2550 **Foyne:** let him thrust   **were:** protect
2551 **at meschief:** in distress, at a disadvantage
2554 **abyde:** remain
2556 **make:** opponent
2557 **turneiynge:** tournament
2558 **spede you:** give you success
2562 **stevene:** voice
2568 **sarge:** serge
2573 **after hir degree:** according to their rank
2576 **pryme:** 9 A.M.
2577 **riche:** splendidly
2579 **degrees:** tiers, rows of seats

And westward, thurgh the gates under Marte,
Arcite, and eek the hondred of his parte,
With baner reed is entred right anon;
And in that selve moment Palamon
Is under Venus, estward in the place,   2585
With baner whyt and hardy chiere and face.
In al the world, to seken up and doun,
So evene, withouten variacioun,
Ther nere swiche compaignyes tweye,
For ther was noon so wys that koude seye   2590
That any hadde of oother avauntage
Of worthynesse, ne of estaat, ne age,
So evene were they chosen, for to gesse.
And in two renges faire they hem dresse.
Whan that hir names rad were everichon,
That in hir nombre gyle were ther noon,   2596
Tho were the gates shet, and cried was loude:
"Do now youre devoir, yonge knyghtes
        proude!"
    The heraudes lefte hir prikyng up and doun;
Now ryngen trompes loude and clarioun.   2600
Ther is namoore to seyn, but west and est
In goon the speres ful sadly in arrest;
In gooth the sharpe spore into the syde.
Ther seen men who kan juste and who kan
        ryde;   2604
Ther shyveren shaftes upon sheeldes thikke;
He feeleth thurgh the herte-spoon the prikke.
Up spryngen speres twenty foot on highte;
Out goon the swerdes as the silver brighte;
The helmes they tohewen and toshrede;   2609
Out brest the blood with stierne stremes rede;
With myghty maces the bones they tobreste.
He thurgh the thikkeste of the throng gan
        threste;
Ther stomblen steedes stronge, and doun
        gooth al,
He rolleth under foot as dooth a bal;   2614
He foyneth on his feet with his tronchoun,
And he hym hurtleth with his hors adoun;

He thurgh the body is hurt and sithen take,
Maugree his heed, and broght unto the stake;
As forward was, right there he moste abyde.
Another lad is on that oother syde.   2620
And some tyme dooth hem Theseus to reste,
Hem to refresshe and drynken, if hem leste.
Ful ofte a day han thise Thebanes two
Togydre ymet, and wroght his felawe wo;
Unhorsed hath ech oother of hem tweye.   2625
Ther nas no tygre in the vale of Galgopheye,
Whan that hir whelp is stole whan it is lite,
So crueel on the hunte as is Arcite
For jelous herte upon this Palamon.
Ne in Belmarye ther nys so fel leon,   2630
That hunted is, or for his hunger wood,
Ne of his praye desireth so the blood,
As Palamon to sleen his foo Arcite.
The jelous strokes on hir helmes byte;   2634
Out renneth blood on bothe hir sydes rede.
    Som tyme an ende ther is of every dede.
For er the sonne unto the reste wente,
The stronge kyng Emetreus gan hente
This Palamon, as he faught with Arcite,
And made his swerd depe in his flessh to byte,
And by the force of twenty is he take   2641
Unyolden, and ydrawen to the stake.
And in the rescus of this Palamoun
The stronge kyng Lygurge is born adoun,
And kyng Emetreus, for al his strengthe,   2645
Is born out of his sadel a swerdes lengthe,
So hitte him Palamoun er he were take.
But al for noght; he was broght to the stake.
His hardy herte myghte hym helpe naught:
He moste abyde, whan that he was caught,
By force and eek by composicioun.   2651
    Who sorweth now but woful Palamoun,
That moot namoore goon agayn to fighte?
And whan that Theseus hadde seyn this sighte,
Unto the folk that foghten thus echon   2655
He cryde, "Hoo! namoore, for it is doon!
I wol be trewe juge, and no partie.

2582 **parte:** party, side
2584 **selve:** same
2593 **evene:** equally   **for to gesse:** as an estimate
2594 **renges:** ranks   **hem dresse:** arrange themselves
2595 **rad:** read
2596 **gyle:** deception
2597 **shet:** shut
2598 **devoir:** duty
2602 **sadly:** firmly   **arrest:** lance rest (on the breast plate)
2603 **spore into the syde:** spur into the flank
2605 **shyveren:** shiver, break
2606 **herte-spoon:** the spoon-shaped hollow at the end of the breastbone
2609 **tohewen and toshrede:** hew to pieces and cut into shreds
2610 **brest:** burst   **stierne:** strong
2611 **tobreste:** break to pieces
2615 **foyneth:** stabs   **tronchoun:** spear shaft
2616 **hurtleth . . . adoun:** knocks down

2618 **Maugree his heed:** despite all he can do
2619 **abyde:** remain
2621 **dooth hem Theseus to reste:** Theseus makes them rest
2626 **Galgopheye:** probably Gargaphia, a valley in Boetia (Greece)
2627 **whelp:** cub
2630 **Belmarye:** Benmarin (Morocco)
2632 **praye:** prey
2634 **jelous:** fervent, vigorous
2635 **renneth:** runs
2642 **Unyolden:** without having surrendered
2643 **rescus:** rescue
2651 **composicioun:** agreement (that he had made)
2652 **sorweth:** grieves
2655 **echon:** each one
2656 **Hoo!:** stop!
2657 **partie:** partisan

Arcite of Thebes shal have Emelie,
That by his fortune hath hire faire ywonne."
Anon ther is a noyse of peple bigonne   2660
For joye of this, so loude and heighe withalle
It semed that the lystes sholde falle.

What kan now faire Venus doon above?
What seith she now? What dooth this queene
    of love,
But wepeth so, for wantynge of hir wille,   2665
Til that hir teeres in the lystes fille?
She seyde, "I am ashamed, doutelees."

Saturnus seyde, "Doghter, hoold thy pees!
Mars hath his wille, his knyght hath al his
        boone,   2669
And, by myn heed, thow shalt been esed soone."

The trompours, with the loude mynstralcie,
The heraudes, that ful loude yelle and crie,
Been in hire wele for joye of daun Arcite.
But herkneth me, and stynteth noyse a lite,
Which a myracle ther bifel anon.   2675

This fierse Arcite hath of his helm ydon,
And on a courser, for to shewe his face,
He priketh endelong the large place
Lokynge upward upon this Emelye;
And she agayn hym caste a freendlich ye   2680
(For wommen, as to speken in comune,
Thei folwen alle the favour of Fortune)
And was al his chiere, as in his herte.

Out of the ground a furie infernal sterte,
From Pluto sent at requeste of Saturne,   2685
For which his hors for fere gan to turne,
And leep aside, and foundred as he leep;
And er that Arcite may taken keep,
He pighte hym on the pomel of his heed,
That in the place he lay as he were deed,   2690
His brest tobrosten with his sadel-bowe.
As blak he lay as any cole or crowe,
So was the blood yronnen in his face.
Anon he was yborn out of the place,

With herte soor, to Theseus paleys.   2695
Tho was he korven out of his harneys
And in a bed ybrought ful faire and blyve,
For he was yet in memorie and alyve,
And alwey criynge after Emelye.

Duc Theseus, with al his compaignye,   2700
Is comen hoom to Atthenes his citee,
With alle blisse and greet solempnitee.
Al be it that this aventure was falle,
He nolde noght disconforten hem alle.
Men seyde eek that Arcite shal nat dye;   2705
He shal been heeled of his maladye.
And of another thyng they weren as fayn,
That of hem alle was ther noon yslayn,
Al were they soore yhurt, and namely oon,
That with a spere was thirled his brest boon.
To othere woundes and to broken armes   2711
Somme hadden salves, and somme hadden
        charmes;
Fermacies of herbes, and eek save
They dronken, for they wolde hir lymes have.
For which this noble duc, as he wel kan,   2715
Conforteth and honoureth every man,
And made revel al the longe nyght
Unto the straunge lordes, as was right.
Ne ther was holden no disconfitynge
But as a justes or a tourneiynge;   2720
For soothly ther was no disconfiture.
For fallyng nys nat but an aventure,
Ne to be lad by force unto the stake
Unyolden, and with twenty knyghtes take,
O persone allone, withouten mo,   2725
And haryed forth by arme, foot, and too,
And eke his steede dryven forth with staves
With footmen, bothe yemen and eek knaves —
It nas arretted hym no vileynye;
Ther may no man clepen it cowardye.   2730
For which anon duc Theseus leet crye,
To stynten alle rancour and envye,

2665 **wantynge:** lack
2666 **teeres in the lystes fille:** i.e., it rained
2667 **ashamed:** disgraced
2669 **boone:** request
2670 **esed:** relieved
2671 **trompours:** trumpeters
2673 **wele:** prosperity
2675 **Which a:** what a
2676 **of his helm ydon:** taken off his helmet
2677 **shewe:** show
2678 **endelong:** from end to end
2680 **agayn:** toward
2681 **in comune:** in general
2683 **chiere:** source of pleasure
2687 **foundred:** stumbled   **leep:** leapt
2688 **taken keep:** take heed
2689 **pighte hym:** struck himself   **pomel:** pommel (knob on a saddle)
2691 **tobrosten:** shattered
2692 **cole:** coal

2696 **Tho:** then   **korven:** cut
2697 **blyve:** quickly
2698 **in memorie:** conscious
2699 **after:** for
2704 **disconforten:** distress
2707 **fayn:** happy
2709 **namely:** especially
2710 whose breastbone was pierced (*thirled*) by a spear
2713 **Fermacies:** medicines   **save:** sage, in a concoction
2718 **straunge:** foreign
2719 **disconfitynge:** defeat, dishonor
2720 **justes or a tourneiynge:** joust or a tournament
2721 **disconfiture:** dishonor
2724 **Unyolden:** without having surrendered
2725 **mo:** others
2726 **haryed:** dragged   **too:** toe
2728 **knaves:** male servants
2729 He incurred no shameful blame for it
2731 **leet crye:** had proclaimed
2732 **envye:** ill-will

The gree as wel of o syde as of oother,
And eyther syde ylik as ootheres brother;
And yaf hem yiftes after hir degree,   2735
And fully heeld a feeste dayes three,
And conveyed the kynges worthily
Out of his toun a journee largely.
And hoom wente every man the righte way.
Ther was namoore but "Fare wel, have good
        day!"
Of this bataille I wol namoore endite,   2741
But speke of Palamon and of Arcite.

    Swelleth the brest of Arcite, and the soore
Encreesseth at his herte moore and moore.
The clothered blood, for any lechecraft,   2745
Corrupteth, and is in his bouk ylaft,
That neither veyne-blood, ne ventusynge,
Ne drynke of herbes may ben his helpynge.
The vertu expulsif, or animal,
Fro thilke vertu cleped natural   2750
Ne may the venym voyden ne expelle.
The pipes of his longes gonne to swelle,
And every lacerte in his brest adoun
Is shent with venym and corrupcioun.
Hym gayneth neither, for to gete his lif,   2755
Vomyt upward, ne dounward laxatif.
Al is tobrosten thilke regioun;
Nature hath now no dominacioun.
And certeinly, ther Nature wol nat wirche,
Fare wel phisik! Go ber the man to chirche!
This al and som, that Arcita moot dye;   2761
For which he sendeth after Emelye,
And Palamon, that was his cosyn deere.
Thanne seyde he thus, as ye shal after heere:
"Naught may the woful spirit in myn herte
Declare o point of alle my sorwes smerte   2766
To yow, my lady, that I love moost,
But I biquethe the servyce of my goost
To yow aboven every creature,

2733 **gree:** victory
2735 **yiftes:** gifts
2738 **journee:** day's journey
2741 **endite:** write
2743–56 The sense is that Arcite's breast swells, increasing the
pain at his heart. The clotted blood left in the trunk of the body,
despite the efforts of medical science in letting blood and
administering herbs, cannot be voided by the expulsive spirit. The
tubes of the lungs begin to swell, and every muscle in the breast
is destroyed by the venom. Neither purgatives to induce vomiting
nor laxatives help.
2745 **clothered:** clotted
2746 **Corrupteth:** decays   **bouk:** trunk
2747 **veyne-blood:** blood-letting at a vein   **ventusynge:** cupping
2749 **expulsif:** expulsive
2751 **venym:** poison   **voyden:** remove
2752 **longes:** lungs
2753 **lacerte:** muscle
2754 **shent:** destroyed   **corrupcioun:** decayed matter
2755 **Hym gayneth:** it avails him   **gete:** preserve
2759 **wirche:** work
2760 **phisik:** medicine
2761 **This** = *this is*

Syn that my lyf may no lenger dure.   2770
Allas, the wo! Allas, the peynes stronge,
That I for yow have suffred, and so longe!
Allas, the deeth! Allas, myn Emelye!
Allas, departynge of oure compaignye!
Allas, myn hertes queene! Allas, my wyf,   2775
Myn hertes lady, endere of my lyf!
What is this world? What asketh men to have?
Now with his love, now in his colde grave
Allone, withouten any compaignye.
Fare wel, my sweete foo, myn Emelye!   2780
And softe taak me in youre armes tweye,
For love of God, and herkneth what I seye.

    "I have heer with my cosyn Palamon
Had strif and rancour many a day agon
For love of yow, and for my jalousye.   2785
And Juppiter so wys my soule gye,
To speken of a servaunt proprely,
With alle circumstances trewely —
That is to seyen, trouthe, honour, knyghthede,
Wysdom, humblesse, estaat, and heigh kyn-
        rede,
Fredom, and al that longeth to that art —   2791
So Juppiter have of my soule part,
As in this world right now ne knowe I non
So worthy to ben loved as Palamon,
That serveth yow, and wol doon al his lyf.
And if that evere ye shul ben a wyf,   2796
Foryet nat Palamon, the gentil man."
And with that word his speche faille gan,
For from his feet up to his brest was come
The coold of deeth, that hadde hym overcome,
And yet mooreover, for in his armes two   2801
The vital strengthe is lost and al ago.
Oonly the intellect, withouten moore,
That dwelled in his herte syk and soore,
Gan faillen whan the herte felte deeth.   2805
Dusked his eyen two, and failled breeth,
But on his lady yet caste he his ye;
His laste word was, "Mercy, Emelye!"
His spirit chaunged hous and wente ther,
As I cam nevere, I kan nat tellen wher.   2810
Therfore I stynte; I nam no divinistre;
Of soules fynde I nat in this registre,
Ne me ne list thilke opinions to telle

2770 **dure:** last
2777 **asketh men:** does one ask
2781 **softe:** gently
2786 **gye:** guide
2790 **heigh kynrede:** noble lineage
2791 **Fredom:** nobility of character
2792 **So:** as   **of my soule part:** interest in, concern for, my soul
2798 **faille gan:** began to fail
2806 **Dusked:** grew dark
2811 **nam** = *ne am,* am not   **divinistre:** theologian

Of hem, though that they writen wher they
　　dwelle.
Arcite is coold, ther Mars his soule gye!　2815
Now wol I speken forth of Emelye.

　Shrighte Emelye, and howleth Palamon,
And Theseus his suster took anon
Swownynge, and baar hire fro the corps away.
What helpeth it to tarien forth the day　2820
To tellen how she weep bothe eve and morwe?
For in swich cas wommen have swich sorwe,
Whan that hir housbondes ben from hem ago,
That for the moore part they sorwen so,
Or ellis fallen in swich maladye　2825
That at the laste certeinly they dye.

　Infinite been the sorwes and the teeres
Of olde folk and folk of tendre yeeres
In al the toun for deeth of this Theban.　2829
For hym ther wepeth bothe child and man;
So greet wepyng was ther noon, certayn,
Whan Ector was ybroght, al fressh yslayn,
To Troye. Allas, the pitee that was ther,
Cracchynge of chekes, rentynge eek of heer.
"Why woldestow be deed," thise wommen
　　crye,　2835
"And haddest gold ynough, and Emelye?"

　No man myghte gladen Theseus,
Savynge his olde fader Egeus,
That knew this worldes transmutacioun,
As he hadde seyn it chaunge bothe up and
　　doun,
Joye after wo, and wo after gladnesse,　2841
And shewed hem ensamples and liknesse.

　"Right as ther dyed nevere man," quod he,
"That he ne lyvede in erthe in some degree,
Right so ther lyvede never man," he seyde,　2845
"In al this world, that som tyme he ne deyde.
This world nys but a thurghfare ful of wo,
And we been pilgrymes, passynge to and fro.
Deeth is an ende of every worldly soore."
And over al this yet seyde he muchel moore
To this effect, ful wisely to enhorte　2851
The peple that they sholde hem reconforte.

　Duc Theseus, with al his bisy cure,
Caste now wher that the sepulture

Of goode Arcite may best ymaked be,　2855
And eek moost honurable in his degree.
And at the laste he took conclusioun
That ther as first Arcite and Palamoun
Hadden for love the bataille hem bitwene,
That in that selve grove, swoote and grene,
Ther as he hadde his amorouse desires,　2861
His compleynte, and for love his hoote fires,
He wolde make a fyr in which the office
Funeral he myghte al accomplice.　2864
And leet comande anon to hakke and hewe
The okes olde, and leye hem on a rewe
In colpons wel arrayed for to brenne.
His officers with swifte feet they renne
And ryde anon at his comandement.
And after this, Theseus hath ysent　2870
After a beere, and it al overspradde
With clooth of gold, the richeste that he hadde.
And of the same suyte he cladde Arcite;
Upon his hondes hadde he gloves white,　2874
Eek on his heed a coroune of laurer grene,
And in his hond a swerd ful bright and kene.
He leyde hym, bare the visage, on the beere;
Therwith he weep that pitee was to heere.
And for the peple sholde seen hym alle,
Whan it was day, he broghte hym to the halle,
That roreth of the criyng and the soun.　2881

　Tho cam this woful Theban Palamoun,
With flotery berd and ruggy, asshy heeres,
In clothes blake, ydropped al with teeres;
And, passynge othere of wepynge, Emelye,
The rewefulleste of al the compaignye.　2886
In as muche as the servyce sholde be
The moore noble and riche in his degree,
Duc Theseus leet forth thre steedes brynge,
That trapped were in steel al gliterynge,　2890
And covered with the armes of daun Arcite.
Upon thise steedes, that weren grete and white,
Ther seten folk, of whiche oon baar his sheeld,
Another his spere up on his hondes heeld,
The thridde baar with hym his bowe Tur-
　　keys　2895
(Of brend gold was the caas and eek the
　　harneys);

2815 **ther Mars his soule gye:** may Mars guide his soul
2817 **Shrighte:** shrieked
2821 **weep:** wept
2824 **for the moore part:** mostly
2834 **Cracchynge:** scratching
2837 **gladen:** comfort
2838 **Savynge:** except for
2849 **soore:** pain, misery
2851 **enhorte:** encourage
2852 **hem reconforte:** take heart
2853 **bisy cure:** careful attention
2854 **Caste:** considered

2860 **selve:** same　**swoote:** sweet-smelling
2862 **compleynte:** lament
2865 **leet comande:** ordered
2866 **on a rewe:** in a row
2867 **colpons:** piles　**arrayed:** arranged
2871 **beere:** funeral bier　**overspradde:** overspread
2883 **flotery:** waving　**ruggy:** rough
2886 **rewefulleste:** most pitiful
2889 **leet forth . . . brynge:** had brought forth
2890 **trapped:** equipped with trappings
2891 **armes:** heraldic devices
2895 **bowe Turkeys:** Turkish bow
2896 **brend gold:** refined (pure) gold

And riden forth a paas with sorweful cheere
Toward the grove, as ye shul after heere.
The nobleste of the Grekes that ther were
Upon hir shuldres caryeden the beere,   2900
With slakke paas and eyen rede and wete,
Thurghout the citee by the maister strete,
That sprad was al with blak, and wonder hye
Right of the same is the strete ywrye.
Upon the right hond wente olde Egeus,   2905
And on that oother syde duc Theseus,
With vessels in hir hand of gold ful fyn,
Al ful of hony, milk, and blood, and wyn;
Eek Palamon, with ful greet compaignye;
And after that cam woful Emelye,   2910
With fyr in honde, as was that tyme the gyse,
To do the office of funeral servyse.

    Heigh labour and ful greet apparaillynge
Was at the service and the fyr-makynge,   2914
That with his grene top the hevene raughte;
And twenty fadme of brede the armes
            straughte —
This is to seyn, the bowes weren so brode.
Of stree first ther was leyd ful many a lode.
But how the fyr was maked upon highte,
Ne eek the names that the trees highte,   2920
As ook, firre, birch, aspe, alder, holm, popler,
Wylugh, elm, plane, assh, box, chasteyn, lynde,
            laurer,
Mapul, thorn, bech, hasel, ew, whippeltree —
How they weren feld shal nat be toold for me;
Ne hou the goddes ronnen up and doun,   2925
Disherited of hire habitacioun,
In which they woneden in reste and pees,
Nymphes, fawnes and amadrides;
Ne hou the beestes and the briddes alle   2929
Fledden for fere, whan the wode was falle;
Ne how the ground agast was of the light,
That was nat wont to seen the sonne bright;
Ne how the fyr was couched first with stree,
And thanne with drye stikkes cloven a thre,

And thanne with grene wode and spicerye,
And thanne with clooth of gold and with
            perrye,   2936
And gerlandes, hangynge with ful many a flour;
The mirre, th'encens, with al so greet odour;
Ne how Arcite lay among al this,
Ne what richesse aboute his body is;   2940
Ne how that Emelye, as was the gyse,
Putte in the fyr of funeral servyse;
Ne how she swowned whan men made the fyr,
Ne what she spak, ne what was hir desir;
Ne what jeweles men in the fyre caste,   2945
Whan that the fyr was greet and brente faste;
Ne how somme caste hir sheeld, and somme hir
            spere,
And of hire vestimentz, whiche that they were,
And coppes fulle of wyn, and milk, and blood,
Into the fyr, that brente as it were wood;   2950
Ne how the Grekes, with an huge route,
Thries riden al the fyr aboute
Upon the left hand, with a loud shoutynge,
And thries with hir speres claterynge;
And thries how the ladyes gonne crye;   2955
And how that lad was homward Emelye;
Ne how Arcite is brent to asshen colde;
Ne how that lyche-wake was yholde
Al thilke nyght; ne how the Grekes pleye
The wake-pleyes; ne kepe I nat to seye   2960
Who wrastleth best naked with oille enoynt,
Ne who that baar hym best, in no disjoynt.
I wol nat tellen eek how that they goon
Hoom til Atthenes, whan the pley is doon;
But shortly to the point thanne wol I wende
And maken of my longe tale an ende.   2966

    By processe and by lengthe of certeyn yeres,
Al stynted is the moornynge and the teres
Of Grekes, by oon general assent.
Thanne semed me ther was a parlement   2970
At Atthenes, upon certein pointz and caas;
Among the whiche pointz yspoken was,
To have with certein contrees alliaunce,
And have fully of Thebans obeisaunce.
For which this noble Theseus anon   2975
Leet senden after gentil Palamon,
Unwist of hym what was the cause and why,
But in his blake clothes sorwefully

2897 **a paas:** slowly
2900 **beere:** funeral bier
2901 **slakke:** slow
2902 **maister strete:** main street
2913 **apparaillynge:** preparation
2915 **raughte:** reached to
2916 **fadme of brede:** fathoms broad   **armes straughte:** sides
projected
2918 **stree:** straw   **lode:** load
2921 **holm:** probably the holm oak
2922 **Wylugh:** willow   **chasteyn:** chestnut tree   **laurer:** laurel
2923 **bech:** beech   **ew:** yew   **whippeltree:** cornel-tree,
dogwood
2925 **ronnen:** ran
2927 **woneden:** dwelt
2928 **fawnes:** fauns   **amadrides:** Hamadryads (wood nymphs)
2931 **agast was of:** was frightened by
2933 **couched:** laid   **stree:** straw
2934 **stikkes:** tree trunks

2935 **spicerye:** mixture of spices
2936 **perrye:** precious stones
2938 **mirre:** myrrh
2948 **vestimentz:** costumes, garbs
2958 **lyche-wake:** wake
2960 **wake-pleyes:** funeral games
2962 **disjoynt:** difficulty
2967 **processe:** course of events
2970 **parlement:** parliament
2977 **Unwist of:** unknown by

He cam at his comandement in hye.
Tho sente Theseus for Emelye.   2980
Whan they were set, and hust was al the place,
And Theseus abiden hadde a space
Er any word cam fram his wise brest,
His eyen sette he ther as was his lest.
And with a sad visage he siked stille,   2985
And after that right thus he seyde his wille:

"The Firste Moevere of the cause above,
Whan he first made the faire cheyne of love,
Greet was th'effect, and heigh was his entente.
Wel wiste he why, and what thereof he mente,
For with that faire cheyne of love he bond   2991
The fyr, the eyr, the water, and the lond
In certeyn boundes, that they may nat flee.
That same Prince and that Moevere," quod he,
"Hath stablissed in this wrecched world adoun
Certeyne dayes and duracioun   2996
To al that is engendred in this place,
Over the whiche day they may nat pace,
Al mowe they yet tho dayes wel abregge.   2999
Ther nedeth noght noon auctoritee t'allegge,
For it is preeved by experience,
But that me list declaren my sentence.
Thanne may men by this ordre wel discerne
That thilke Moevere stable is and eterne.
Wel may men knowe, but it be a fool,   3005
That every part dirryveth from his hool,
For nature hath nat taken his bigynnyng
Of no partie or cantel of a thyng,
But of a thyng that parfit is and stable,
Descendynge so til it be corrumpable.   3010
And therfore, of his wise purveiaunce,
He hath so wel biset his ordinaunce
That speces of thynges and progressiouns
Shullen enduren by successiouns,
And nat eterne, withouten any lye.   3015
This maystow understonde and seen at ye.

"Loo the ook, that hath so long a norisshynge
From tyme that it first bigynneth to sprynge,
And hath so long a lif, as we may see,
Yet at the laste wasted is the tree.   3020

"Considereth eek how that the harde stoon
Under oure feet, on which we trede and goon,
Yet wasteth it as it lyth by the weye.
The brode ryver somtyme wexeth dreye;   3024
The grete tounes se we wane and wende.
Thanne may ye se that al this thyng hath ende.

"Of man and womman seen we wel also
That nedes, in oon of thise termes two —
This is to seyn, in youthe or elles age —
He moot be deed, the kyng as shal a page;
Som in his bed, som in the depe see,   3031
Som in the large feeld, as men may see;
Ther helpeth noght; al goth that ilke weye.
Thanne may I seyn that al this thyng moot
          deye.

"What maketh this but Juppiter, the kyng,
That is prince and cause of alle thyng,   3036
Convertynge al unto his propre welle
From which it is dirryved, sooth to telle?
And heer-agayns no creature on lyve,
Of no degree, availleth for to stryve.   3040

"Thanne is it wysdom, as it thynketh me,
To maken vertu of necessitee,
And take it weel that we may nat eschue,
And namely that to us alle is due.
And whoso gruccheth ought, he dooth folye,
And rebel is to hym that al may gye.   3046
And certeinly a man hath moost honour
To dyen in his excellence and flour,
Whan he is siker of his goode name;   3049
Thanne hath he doon his freend, ne hym, no
          shame.
And gladder oghte his freend been of his deeth,
Whan with honour up yolden is his breeth,
Than whan his name apalled is for age,
For al forgeten is his vassellage.
Thanne is it best, as for a worthy fame,   3055
To dyen whan that he is best of name.

"The contrarie of al this is wilfulnesse.
Why grucchen we, why have we hevynesse,
That goode Arcite, of chivalrie flour,

2979 **in hye:** in haste
2981 **hust:** quiet
2982 **abiden:** waited
2984 **lest:** pleasure
2986 **seyde his wille:** pronounced his decision
2989 **entente:** plan
2992 The four elements — fire, air, water, earth
2993 **certeyn:** definite, specific
2995 **adoun:** below
2999 **mowe:** can   **abregge:** abridge, shorten
3000 **noon auctoritee t'allegge:** to cite no written authorities
3001 **preeved:** proven
3002 Unless I wish to make my meaning more clear
3006 **his:** its
3008 **partie:** part   **cantel:** portion
3010 **corrumpable:** corruptible
3011 **of his wise purveiaunce:** by his wise foresight
3012 **biset:** established
3013 **speces:** species (types of being)   **progressiouns:** natural processes
3014 **by successiouns:** one after another
3016 **at ye:** plainly

3024 **wexeth:** becomes
3028 **termes:** periods of time
3030 **page:** servant boy
3033 **ilke:** same
3037 Causing everything to return to its own source (*welle*)
3039 **heer-agayns:** against this
3043 **eschue:** escape
3045 **gruccheth ought:** complains in any way
3049 **siker:** sure
3052 **up yolden:** given up (died)
3053 **apalled:** faded
3054 **vassellage:** prowess

Departed is with duetee and honour 3060
Out of this foule prisoun of this lyf?
Why grucchen heere his cosyn and his wyf
Of his welfare, that loved hem so weel?
Kan he hem thank? Nay, God woot, never a
    deel,
That both his soule and eek hemself offende,
And yet they mowe hir lustes nat amende. 3066
    "What may I conclude of this longe serye,
But after wo I rede us to be merye
And thanken Juppiter of al his grace?
And er that we departen from this place 3070
I rede that we make of sorwes two
O parfit joye, lastynge everemo.
And looketh now, wher moost sorwe is herinne,
Ther wol we first amenden and bigynne.
    "Suster," quod he, "this is my fulle assent,
With al th'avys heere of my parlement, 3076
That gentil Palamon, youre owene knyght,
That serveth yow with wille, herte, and myght,
And ever hath doon syn ye first hym knewe,
That ye shul of youre grace upon hym rewe,
And taken hym for housbonde and for lord. 3081
Lene me youre hond, for this is oure accord.
Lat se now of youre wommanly pitee.

He is a kynges brother sone, pardee;
And though he were a povre bacheler, 3085
Syn he hath served yow so many a yeer,
And had for yow so greet adversitee,
It moste been considered, leeveth me,
For gentil mercy oghte to passen right." 3089
    Thanne seyde he thus to Palamon the knight:
"I trowe ther nedeth litel sermonyng
To make yow assente to this thyng.
Com neer, and taak youre lady by the hond."
    Bitwixen hem was maad anon the bond
That highte matrimoigne or mariage, 3095
By al the conseil and the baronage.
And thus with alle blisse and melodye
Hath Palamon ywedded Emelye.
And God, that al this wyde world hath wroght,
Sende hym his love that hath it deere aboght;
For now is Palamon in alle wele, 3101
Lyvynge in blisse, in richesse, and in heele,
And Emelye hym loveth so tendrely,
And he hire serveth so gentilly,
That nevere was ther no word hem bitwene
Of jalousie or any oother teene. 3106
Thus endeth Palamon and Emelye;
And God save al this faire compaignye! Amen.

Heere is ended the Knyghtes Tale.

THE MILLER'S PROLOGUE

Heere folwen the wordes bitwene the Hoost and the Millere.

Whan that the Knyght had thus his tale
    ytoold,
In al the route nas ther yong ne oold 3110
That he ne seyde it was a noble storie
And worthy for to drawen to memorie,
And namely the gentils everichon.

Oure Hooste lough and swoor, "So moot I gon,
This gooth aright; unbokeled is the male. 3115
Lat se now who shal telle another tale;
For trewely the game is wel bigonne.
Now telleth ye, sir Monk, if that ye konne,
Somwhat to quite with the Knyghtes tale."

3060 **with duetee and honour:** with all proper honor
3064 **Kan he hem thank?:** Can he show them his gratitude?
never a deel: not a bit, not at all
3067 **serye:** process of thought, argument
3068 **rede:** advise
3074 **amenden:** make amends
3075 **assent:** opinion
3076 **parlement:** parliament, assembly

3112 **drawen to memorie:** remember
3113 **gentils:** gentlefolk

3085 **bacheler:** young knight
3089 Noble mercy ought to prevail over justice
3091 **sermonyng:** discourse
3100 **deere aboght:** dearly paid for
3101 **alle wele:** complete happiness
3102 **heele:** health, well-being
3106 **teene:** vexation

3115 **unbokeled is the male:** the pouch is opened; i.e., the game is well begun
3118 **konne:** know
3119 **quite with:** with which to repay, or match

The Millere, that for dronken was al pale,
So that unnethe upon his hors he sat,   3121
He nolde avalen neither hood ne hat,
Ne abyde no man for his curteisie,
But in Pilates voys he gan to crie,
And swoor, "By armes, and by blood and
      bones,
I kan a noble tale for the nones,   3126
With which I wol now quite the Knyghtes
      tale."
Oure Hooste saugh that he was dronke
      of ale,
And seyde, "Abyd, Robyn, my leeve brother;
Som bettre man shal telle us first another.
Abyd, and lat us werken thriftily."   3131
   "By Goddes soule," quod he, "that wol
      nat I;
For I wol speke or elles go my wey."
Oure Hoost answerde, "Tel on, a devel wey!
Thou art a fool; thy wit is overcome."   3135
   "Now herkneth," quod the Millere, "alle and
      some!
But first I make a protestacioun
That I am dronke; I knowe it by my soun.
And therfore if that I mysspeke or seye,
Wyte it the ale of Southwerk, I you preye.
For I wol telle a legende and a lyf   3141
Bothe of a carpenter and of his wyf,
How that a clerk hath set the wrightes cappe."
   The Reve answerde and seyde, "Stynt thy
      clappe!
Lat be thy lewed dronken harlotrye.   3145
It is a synne and eek a greet folye
To apeyren any man, or hym defame,
And eek to bryngen wyves in swich fame.
Thou mayst ynogh of othere thynges seyn."
   This dronke Millere spak ful soone ageyn
And seyde, "Leve brother Osewold,   3151

Who hath no wyf, he is no cokewold.
But I sey nat therfore that thou art oon;
Ther been ful goode wyves many oon,   3154
And evere a thousand goode ayeyns oon
      badde.
That knowestow wel thyself, but if thou
      madde.
Why artow angry with my tale now?
I have a wyf, pardee, as wel as thow;
Yet nolde I, for the oxen in my plogh,
Take upon me moore than ynogh,   3160
As demen of myself that I were oon;
I wol bileve wel that I am noon.
An housbonde shal nat been inquisityf
Of Goddes pryvetee, nor of his wyf.
So he may fynde Goddes foyson there,   3165
Of the remenant nedeth nat enquere."
   What sholde I moore seyn, but this
      Millere
He nolde his wordes for no man forbere,
But tolde his cherles tale in his manere.
M'athynketh that I shal reherce it heere.   3170
And therfore every gentil wight I preye,
For Goddes love, demeth nat that I seye
Of yvel entente, but for I moot reherce
Hir tales alle, be they bettre or werse,
Or elles falsen som of my mateere.   3175
And therfore, whoso list it nat yheere,
Turne over the leef and chese another tale;
For he shal fynde ynowe, grete and smale,
Of storial thyng that toucheth gentillesse,
And eek moralitee and hoolynesse.   3180
Blameth nat me if that ye chese amys.
The Millere is a cherl; ye knowe wel this.
So was the Reve eek and othere mo,
And harlotrie they tolden bothe two.
Avyseth yow, and put me out of blame;   3185
And eek men shal nat maken ernest of game.

3120 **for dronken:** because of being drunk
3121 **unnethe:** hardly
3122 **avalen:** take off
3124 **Pilates voys:** a loud, ranting voice
3125 By the arms, blood, and bones of Christ
3127 **quite:** pay back, requite
3129 **Abyd:** wait **leeve:** dear
3131 **thriftily:** properly
3134 **a devel wey:** in the Devil's name
3136 **alle and some:** one and all
3139 **mysspeke or seye:** The prefix *mys-* applies to both verbs.
3140 **Wyte it:** blame it on
3141 **legende:** saint's life; see n.
3143 **set the wrightes cappe:** deceived, made a fool of the carpenter
3144 **Stynt thy clappe:** stop your noisy talk, hold your tongue
3145 **harlotrye:** ribaldry
3147 **apeyren:** injure
3150 **ageyn:** in reply

3152 **cokewold:** cuckold
3155 **ayeyns:** as opposed to
3156 **madde:** go mad
3161 **demen of:** to judge, believe of **oon:** i.e., a cuckold
3162 **wol bileve:** want to believe
3164 **pryvetee:** secrets
3165 **Goddes foyson:** God's plenty
3169 **cherles:** low-born fellows'
3170 **M'athynketh:** it displeases me, I regret **reherce:** repeat, narrate
3177 **chese:** choose
3178 **grete and smale:** of every sort
3179 **storial:** historical, true **toucheth:** concerns
3184 **harlotrie:** ribaldry, dirty stories
3185 **Avyseth yow:** consider, think about (this)
3186 **maken ernest of game:** take a joke seriously

THE MILLER'S TALE

Heere bigynneth the Millere his tale.

Whilom ther was dwellynge at Oxenford
A riche gnof, that gestes heeld to bord,
And of his craft he was a carpenter.   3189
With hym ther was dwellynge a poure scoler,
Hadde lerned art, but al his fantasye
Was turned for to lerne astrologye,
And koude a certeyn of conclusiouns,
To demen by interrogaciouns,
If that men asked hym, in certein houres   3195
Whan that men sholde have droghte or elles
           shoures,
Or if men asked hym what sholde bifalle
Of every thyng; I may nat rekene hem alle.
    This clerk was cleped hende Nicholas.
Of deerne love he koude and of solas;   3200
And therto he was sleigh and ful privee,
And lyk a mayden meke for to see.
A chambre hadde he in that hostelrye
Allone, withouten any compaignye,
Ful fetisly ydight with herbes swoote;   3205
And he hymself as sweete as is the roote
Of lycorys or any cetewale.
His Almageste, and bookes grete and smale,
His astrelabie, longynge for his art,
His augrym stones layen faire apart,   3210
On shelves couched at his beddes heed;
His presse ycovered with a faldyng reed;

And al above ther lay a gay sautrie,
On which he made a-nyghtes melodie
So swetely that all the chambre rong;   3215
And *Angelus ad virginem* he song;
And after that he song the Kynges Noote.
Ful often blessed was his myrie throte.
And thus this sweete clerk his tyme spente
After his freendes fyndyng and his rente.   3220
    This carpenter hadde wedded newe a wyf,
Which that he lovede moore than his lyf;
Of eighteteene yeer she was of age.
Jalous he was, and heeld hire narwe in cage,
For she was wylde and yong, and he was old
And demed hymself been lik a cokewold.   3226
He knew nat Catoun, for his wit was rude,
That bad man sholde wedde his simylitude.
Men sholde wedden after hire estaat,
For youthe and elde is often at debaat.   3230
But sith that he was fallen in the snare,
He moste endure, as oother folk, his care.
    Fair was this yonge wyf, and therwithal
As any wezele hir body gent and smal.
A ceynt she werede, barred al of silk,   3235
A barmcloth as whit as morne milk
Upon hir lendes, ful of many a goore.
Whit was hir smok, and broyden al bifoore
And eek bihynde, on hir coler aboute,
Of col-blak silk, withinne and eek withoute.
The tapes of hir white voluper   3241
Were of the same suyte of hir coler;

3187 **Oxenford**: Oxford
3188 **gnof**: churl   **gestes**: lodgers   **to bord**: as boarders
3190 **poure scoler**: impoverished student
3191 **art**: the arts curriculum at the university, esp. logic
fantasye: fancy, desire
3193 **koude**: knew   **a certeyn of conclusiouns**: a certain
number of astrological operations
3194 To determine by scientific calculations
3195 **in certein houres**: at specific (astrological) hours
3199 **hende**: courteous
3200 **deerne**: secret   **solas**: pleasure, satisfaction (of sexual
desires)
3201 **sleigh**: sly   **privee**: discreet, secretive
3205 Very elegantly adorned with sweet-smelling herbs
3207 **cetewale**: zedoary (a spice resembling ginger, used as a
condiment and stimulant)
3208 **Almageste**: Ptolemy's treatise on astrology
3209 **astrelabie**: astrolabe   **longynge for**: belonging to,
necessary for (his *art,* astronomy)
3210 **augrym stones**: counters, for use on an abacus
3211 **couched**: arranged
3212 **presse**: cupboard, linen press   **faldyng reed**: coarse red
woolen cloth

3213 **sautrie**: psaltry
3214 **a-nyghtes**: at night
3216 **Angelus ad virginem**: "The angel to the virgin [Mary]"
3217 **the Kynges Noote**: the King's Tune (not identified)
3220 According to what his friends provided (*freendes fyndyng*)
and his income (*rente*)
3224 **narwe**: closely
3226 **lik**: like (?)
3227 **Catoun**: Cato, author of an elementary school text   **rude**:
ignorant, unlearned
3228 **simylitude**: equal, counterpart
3230 **elde**: old age
3231 **snare**: trap
3234 **wezele**: weasel   **gent**: delicate   **smal**: slender
3235 **ceynt**: belt   **barred**: with decorative strips
3236 **barmcloth**: apron   **morne**: morning
3237 **lendes**: loins   **goore**: flounce
3238 **smok**: shift, undergarment (over which aprons and more
elaborate items of clothing are worn)   **broyden**: embroidered
3239 **coler**: collar
3241 **tapes**: ribbons   **voluper**: cap
3242 **same suyte of**: same color as

Hir filet brood of silk, and set ful hye.
And sikerly she hadde a likerous ye;
Ful smale ypulled were hire browes two,   3245
And tho were bent and blake as any sloo.
She was ful moore blisful on to see
Than is the newe pere-jonette tree,
And softer than the wolle is of a wether.
And by hir girdel heeng a purs of lether,   3250
Tasseled with silk and perled with latoun.
In al this world, to seken up and doun,
There nys no man so wys that koude thenche
So gay a popelote or swich a wenche.   3254
Ful brighter was the shynyng of hir hewe
Than in the Tour the noble yforged newe.
But of hir song, it was as loude and yerne
As any swalwe sittynge on a berne.
Therto she koude skippe and make game,
As any kyde or calf folwynge his dame.   3260
Hir mouth was sweete as bragot or the meeth,
Or hoord of apples leyd in hey or heeth.
Wynsynge she was, as is a joly colt,
Long as a mast, and upright as a bolt.
A brooch she baar upon hir lowe coler,   3265
As brood as is the boos of a bokeler.
Hir shoes were laced on hir legges hye.
She was a prymerole, a piggesnye,
For any lord to leggen in his bedde,
Or yet for any good yeman to wedde.   3270

   Now, sire, and eft, sire, so bifel the cas
That on a day this hende Nicholas
Fil with this yonge wyf to rage and pleye,
Whil that hir housbonde was at Oseneye,   3274
As clerkes ben ful subtile and ful queynte;

And prively he caughte hire by the queynte,
And seyde, "Ywis, but if ich have my wille,
For deerne love of thee, lemman, I spille."
And heeld hire harde by the haunchebones,
And seyde, "Lemman, love me al atones,   3280
Or I wol dyen, also God me save!"
And she sproong as a colt dooth in the trave,
And with hir heed she wryed faste awey,
And seyde, "I wol nat kisse thee, by my fey!
Why, lat be!" quod she. "Lat be, Nicholas,"
Or I wol crie 'out, harrow' and 'allas'!   3286
Do wey youre handes, for youre curteisye!"

   This Nicholas gan mercy for to crye,
And spak so faire, and profred him so faste,
That she hir love hym graunted atte laste,
And swoor hir ooth, by Seint Thomas of Kent,
That she wol been at his comandement,   3292
Whan that she may hir leyser wel espie.
"Myn housbonde is so ful of jalousie
That but ye wayte wel and been privee,   3295
I woot right wel I nam but deed," quod she.
"Ye moste been ful deerne, as in this cas."

   "Nay, therof care thee noght," quod Nicholas.
"A clerk hadde litherly biset his whyle,
But if he koude a carpenter bigyle."   3300
And thus they been accorded and ysworn
To wayte a tyme, as I have told biforn.

   Whan Nicholas had doon thus everideel
And thakked hire aboute the lendes weel,
He kiste hire sweete and taketh his sawtrie,
And pleyeth faste, and maketh melodie.   3306

   Thanne fil it thus, that to the paryssh chirche,
Cristes owene werkes for to wirche,
This goode wyf went on an haliday.
Hir forheed shoon as bright as any day,   3310
So was it wasshen whan she leet hir werk.
Now was ther of that chirche a parissh clerk,
The which that was ycleped Absolon.
Crul was his heer, and as the gold it shoon,

3243 **filet:** headband
3244 **sikerly:** truly   **likerous:** flirtatious
3245 **ypulled:** plucked
3246 **sloo:** sloe (a plum-like fruit)
3247 **blisful:** pleasing
3248 **pere-jonette:** early-ripe pear
3249 **wolle:** wool   **wether:** sheep (ram)
3250 **girdel:** belt
3251 **perled:** adorned   **latoun:** a brass-like alloy
3253 **thenche:** imagine
3254 **popelote:** little doll   **wenche:** lower-class woman
3256 **Tour:** Tower of London (the mint)   **noble:** a gold coin
(6 shillings, 8 pence)
3257 **yerne:** eager, lively
3258 **swalwe:** swallow   **berne:** barn
3260 **dame:** mother (dam)
3261 **bragot:** country drink   **meeth:** mead
3263 **Wynsynge:** skittish   **joly:** spirited
3264 **upright:** straight   **bolt:** cross-bow bolt
3266 **boos of a bokeler:** raised center of a shield
3268 **prymerole, piggesnye:** primrose, "pig's eye," names of
flowers
3269 **leggen:** lay
3271 **eft:** again
3273 **rage:** sport (sexually)
3274 **Oseneye:** Osney
3275 **queynte:** ingenious, clever

3276 **queynte:** elegant, pleasing (thing); i.e., pudendum
3277 **Ywis:** truly, indeed
3278 **deerne:** secret   **lemman:** my love, sweetheart   **spille:** die
3279 **haunchebones:** thighs
3280 **al atones:** at once, immediately
3281 **also:** as
3282 **sproong:** sprang   **trave:** frame for holding a horse to be
shod
3283 **wryed faste:** turned rapidly, twisted
3289 **profred him:** pressed his suit
3291 **Seint Thomas of Kent:** Thomas Becket
3293 **leyser:** opportunity
3295 **wayte:** await, watch for (an opportunity)   **privee:** discreet,
secretive
3297 **deerne:** secretive
3299 **litherly biset his whyle:** wasted his time
3304 **thakked:** patted   **lendes:** loins
3309 **haliday:** holy day
3311 **leet:** left
3314 **Crul:** curled

And strouted as a fanne large and brode;
Ful streight and evene lay his joly shode. 3316
His rode was reed, his eyen greye as goos.
With Poules wyndow corven on his shoos,
In hoses rede he wente fetisly.
Yclad he was ful smal and proprely 3320
Al in a kirtel of a lyght waget;
Ful faire and thikke been the poyntes set.
And therupon he hadde a gay surplys
As whit as is the blosme upon the rys.
A myrie child he was, so God me save. 3325
Wel koude he laten blood, and clippe and
      shave,
And maken a chartre of lond or acquitaunce.
In twenty manere koude he trippe and daunce
After the scole of Oxenforde tho,
And with his legges casten to and fro, 3330
And pleyen songes on a smal rubible;
Therto he song som tyme a loud quynyble;
And as wel koude he pleye on a giterne.
In al the toun nas brewhous ne taverne
That he ne visited with his solas, 3335
Ther any gaylard tappestere was.
But sooth to seyn, he was somdeel squaymous
Of fartyng, and of speche daungerous.
    This Absolon, that jolif was and gay,
Gooth with a sencer on the haliday, 3340
Sensynge the wyves of the parisshe faste;
And many a lovely look on hem he caste,
And namely on this carpenteris wyf.
To looke on hire hym thoughte a myrie lyf,
She was so propre and sweete and likerous.
I dar wel seyn, if she hadde been a mous, 3346
And he a cat, he wolde hire hente anon.

This parissh clerk, this joly Absolon,
Hath in his herte swich a love-longynge
That of no wyf took he noon offrynge; 3350
For curteisie, he seyde, he wolde noon.
    The moone, whan it was nyght, ful brighte
      shoon,
And Absolon his gyterne hath ytake;
For paramours he thoghte for to wake.
And forth he gooth, jolif and amorous, 3355
Til he cam to the carpenteres hous
A litel after cokkes hadde ycrowe,
And dressed hym up by a shot-wyndowe
That was upon the carpenteris wal.
He syngeth in his voys gentil and smal, 3360
"Now, deere lady, if thy wille be,
I praye yow that ye wole rewe on me,"
Ful wel acordaunt to his gyternynge.
This carpenter awook, and herde him synge,
And spak unto his wyf, and seyde anon, 3365
"What! Alison! Herestow nat Absolon,
That chaunteth thus under oure boures wal?"
And she answerde hir housbonde therwithal,
"Yis, God woot, John, I heere it every deel."
    This passeth forth; what wol ye bet than
      weel?
Fro day to day this joly Absolon 3371
So woweth hire that hym is wo bigon.
He waketh al the nyght and al the day;
He kembeth his lokkes brode, and made hym
      gay;
He woweth hire by meenes and brocage, 3375
And swoor he wolde been hir owene page;
He syngeth, brokkynge as a nyghtyngale;
He sente hire pyment, meeth, and spiced ale,
And wafres, pipyng hoot out of the gleede;
And, for she was of town, he profred meede;
For som folk wol ben wonnen for richesse, 3381
And somme for strokes, and somme for gen-
      tillesse.

3315 **strouted as a fanne:** stretched out like a fan
3316 **joly:** pretty **shode:** parted hair
3317 **rode:** complexion
3318 **Poules wyndow:** window of St. Paul's **corven:** carved
3319 **fetisly:** elegantly
3320 **smal:** tightly, in close-fitting clothes
3321 **kirtel:** tunic **lyght waget:** light blue
3322 **poyntes:** laces
3323 **surplys:** surplice (ecclesiastical gown)
3324 **rys:** twig
3325 **child:** young man **so:** as
3326 **laten blood:** let blood (as a medical treatment) **clippe:** cut hair
3327 **chartre:** deed **acquitaunce:** quitance (legal release of property)
3328 **twenty manere:** twenty ways
3329 **After the scole:** in the style, fashion **tho:** then
3330 **casten:** move quickly
3331 **rubible:** rebeck, a kind of fiddle
3332 **quynyble:** high treble
3333 **giterne:** cithern, a stringed instrument
3335 **solas:** entertainment
3336 **gaylard tappestere:** merry barmaid
3337 **somdeel squaymous:** somewhat squeamish
3338 **daungerous:** fastidious
3339 **jolif:** pretty, lively
3340 **sencer:** censer
3341 **Sensynge:** censing
3342 **lovely:** loving

3354 **For paramours:** for the sake of love **wake:** remain awake
3358 **dressed hym:** took his place **shot-wyndowe:** hinged window (one that opens and closes)
3360 **smal:** high
3362 **rewe:** have mercy
3363 **acordaunt to:** in harmony with **gyternynge:** playing on the cithern
3367 **chaunteth:** sings **under oure boures:** next to our bed chamber's
3369 **Yis:** yes, indeed **every deel:** every bit
3370 **bet than weel:** better than well (i.e., what more would you have?)
3374 **kembeth:** combs
3375 **meenes:** go-betweens **brocage:** use of an agent
3376 **page:** servant
3377 **brokkynge:** trilling
3378 **pyment:** spiced, sweetened wine **meeth:** mead
3379 **wafres:** cakes **pipyng:** whistling, hissing **gleede:** fire
3380 **profred meede:** offered money
3382 **for strokes:** i.e., by force

Somtyme, to shewe his lightnesse and
    maistrye,
He pleyeth Herodes upon a scaffold hye.
But what availleth hym as in this cas?   3385
She loveth so this hende Nicholas
That Absolon may blowe the bukkes horn;
He ne hadde for his labour but a scorn.
And thus she maketh Absolon hire ape,
And al his ernest turneth til a jape.   3390
Ful sooth is this proverbe, it is no lye,
Men seyn right thus: "Alwey the nye slye
Maketh the ferre leeve to be looth."
For though that Absolon be wood or wrooth,
By cause that he fer was from hire sight,   3395
This nye Nicholas stood in his light.

    Now ber thee wel, thou hende Nicholas,
For Absolon may waille and synge "allas."
And so bifel it on a Saterday,
This carpenter was goon til Osenay;   3400
And hende Nicholas and Alisoun
Acorded been to this conclusioun,
That Nicholas shal shapen hym a wyle
This sely jalous housbonde to bigyle;
And if so be the game wente aright,   3405
She sholde slepen in his arm al nyght,
For this was his desir and hire also.
And right anon, withouten wordes mo,
This Nicholas no lenger wolde tarie,   3409
But dooth ful softe unto his chambre carie
Bothe mete and drynke for a day or tweye,
And to hire housbonde bad hire for to seye,
If that he axed after Nicholas,
She sholde seye she nyste where he was;
Of al that day she saugh hym nat with ye;
She trowed that he was in maladye,   3416
For, for no cry hir mayde koude hym calle,
He nolde answere for thyng that myghte falle.

    This passeth forth al thilke Saterday,
That Nicholas stille in his chambre lay,   3420
And eet and sleep, or dide what hym leste,
Til Sonday, that the sonne gooth to reste.
This sely carpenter hath greet merveyle
Of Nicholas, or what thyng myghte hym eyle,

And seyde, "I am adrad, by Seint Thomas,
It stondeth nat aright with Nicholas.   3426
God shilde that he deyde sodeynly!
This world is now ful tikel, sikerly.
I saugh today a cors yborn to chirche   3429
That now, on Monday last, I saugh hym
    wirche.

    "Go up," quod he unto his knave anoon,
"Clepe at his dore, or knokke with a stoon.
Looke how it is, and tel me boldely."

    This knave gooth hym up ful sturdily,   3434
And at the chambre dore whil that he stood,
He cride and knokked as that he were wood,
"What, how! What do ye, maister Nicholay?
How may ye slepen al the longe day?"

    But al for noght; he herde nat a word.
An hole he foond, ful lowe upon a bord,   3440
Ther as the cat was wont in for to crepe,
And at that hole he looked in ful depe,
And at the laste he hadde of hym a sight.
This Nicholas sat evere capyng upright,
As he had kiked on the newe moone.   3445
Adoun he gooth, and tolde his maister soone
In what array he saugh this ilke man.

    This carpenter to blessen hym bigan,
And seyde, "Help us, Seinte Frydeswyde!
A man woot litel what hym shal bityde.   3450
This man is falle, with his astromye,
In some woodnesse or in som agonye.
I thoghte ay wel how that it sholde be!
Men sholde nat knowe of Goddes pryvetee.
Ye, blessed be alwey a lewed man   3455
That noght but oonly his bileve kan!
So ferde another clerk with astromye;
He walked in the feeldes for to prye
Upon the sterres, what ther sholde bifalle,
Til he was in a marle-pit yfalle;   3460
He saugh nat that. But yet, by Seint Thomas,

3383 **lightnesse:** agility   **maistrye:** skill
3384 **Herodes:** the part of Herod   **scaffold hye:** stage
3387 **blowe the bukkes horn:** go whistle
3389 **ape:** fool, dupe
3390 **jape:** joke
3392 **nye slye:** nigh (at hand) sly one
3393 **ferre leeve to be looth:** distant loved one to be disliked
3396 **in his light:** in his way (i.e., prevented his being seen)
3403 **wyle:** trick
3404 **sely:** innocent, simple, hapless
3416 **trowed:** believed   **in maladye:** ill
3418 **falle:** befall, happen
3421 **eet:** ate   **sleep:** slept
3423–24 **hath greet merveyle Of:** wondered about
3424 **eyle:** ail

3427 God forbid (*shilde*) that he should die suddenly.
3428 **tikel:** unstable, ticklish
3429 **cors:** corpse
3430 **That . . . hym:** whom   **wirche:** work
3431 **knave:** servant
3432 **Clepe:** call out
3434 **sturdily:** boldly
3444 **capyng upright:** gaping straight up
3445 **kiked:** gazed
3446 **soone:** immediately
3447 **array:** condition
3449 **Seinte Frydeswyde:** St. Frideswide, noted for her healing powers
3451 **astromye:** astronomy
3452 **agonye:** fit
3454 **Goddes pryvetee:** God's secrets
3455 **Ye:** yes
3456 Who knows nothing but his creed (*bileve*)
3457 **ferde:** fared
3458 **prye:** gaze
3460 **marle-pit:** clay pit

Me reweth soore of hende Nicholas.
He shal be rated of his studiyng,
If that I may, by Jhesus, hevene kyng!
Get me a staf, that I may underspore,   3465
Whil that thou, Robyn, hevest up the dore.
He shal out of his studiyng, as I gesse."
And to the chambre dore he gan hym dresse.
His knave was a strong carl for the nones,
And by the haspe he haaf it of atones;   3470
Into the floor the dore fil anon.
This Nicholas sat ay as stille as stoon,
And evere caped upward into the eir.
This carpenter wende he were in despeir,
And hente hym by the sholdres myghtily,   3475
And shook hym harde, and cride spitously,
"What! Nicholay! What, how! What, looke
          adoun!
Awak, and thenk on Cristes passioun!
I crouche thee from elves and fro wightes."
Therwith the nyght-spel seyde he anon-rightes
On foure halves of the hous aboute,   3481
And on the thresshfold of the dore withoute:
"Jhesu Crist and Seinte Benedight,
Blesse this hous from every wikked wight,
For nyghtes verye, the white *pater-noster!*   3485
Where wentestow, Seinte Petres soster?"
    And atte laste this hende Nicholas
Gan for to sik soore, and seyde, "Allas!
Shal al the world be lost eftsoones now?"   3489
    This carpenter answerde, "What seystow?
What! Thynk on God, as we doon, men that
          swynke."
    This Nicholas answerde, "Fecche me drynke,
And after wol I speke in pryvetee
Of certeyn thyng that toucheth me and thee.
I wol telle it noon oother man, certeyn."   3495

This carpenter goth doun, and comth ageyn,
And broghte of myghty ale a large quart;
And whan that ech of hem had dronke his part,
This Nicholas his dore faste shette,
And doun the carpenter by hym he sette.   3500
    He seyde "John, myn hooste, lief and deere,
Thou shalt upon thy trouthe swere me heere
That to no wight thou shalt this conseil wreye,
For it is Cristes conseil that I seye,
And if thou telle it man, thou art forlore;   3505
For this vengeaunce thou shalt han therfore,
That if thou wreye me, thou shalt be wood."
"Nay, Crist forbede it, for his hooly blood!"
Quod tho this sely man, "I nam no labbe,   3509
Ne, though I seye, I nam nat lief to gabbe.
Sey what thou wolt, I shal it nevere telle
To child ne wyf, by hym that harwed helle!"
    "Now John," quod Nicholas, "I wol nat lye;
I have yfounde in myn astrologye,
As I have looked in the moone bright,   3515
That now a Monday next, at quarter nyght,
Shal falle a reyn, and that so wilde and wood
That half so greet was nevere Noes flood.
This world," he seyde, "in lasse than an hour
Shal al be dreynt, so hidous is the shour.   3520
Thus shal mankynde drenche, and lese hir lyf."
    This carpenter answerde, "Allas, my wyf!
And shal she drenche? Allas, myn Alisoun!"
For sorwe of this he fil almoost adoun,   3524
And seyde, "Is ther no remedie in this cas?"
    "Why, yis, for Gode," quod hende Nicholas,
"If thou wolt werken after loore and reed.
Thou mayst nat werken after thyn owene heed;
For thus seith Salomon, that was ful trewe:
'Werk al by conseil, and thou shalt nat rewe.'
And if thou werken wolt by good conseil,   3531
I undertake, withouten mast and seyl,
Yet shal I saven hire and thee and me.
Hastow nat herd hou saved was Noe,   3534
Whan that oure Lord hadde warned hym
          biforn

3462 **Me reweth soore of:** I feel sorry for
3463 **rated of:** scolded for
3465 **underspore:** pry up from under
3467 **shal:** shall come (verb of motion is understood)
3469 **carl:** fellow
3470 **haaf it of:** heaved it off   **atones:** at once, immediately
3473 **caped:** gaped
3474 **wende he were:** supposed he was
3476 **spitously:** vigorously, loudly
3479 **crouche:** make the sign of the cross as a blessing over
elves: evil spirits   **wightes:** (evil) creatures
3480 **nyght-spel:** a charm   **anon-rightes:** straightaway
3481 **halves:** sides
3482 **thresshfold:** threshold
3483 **Seinte Benedight:** St. Benedict
3484 **wight:** creature
3485 **For nyghtes verye:** against the evil spirits of the night (?)
white pater-noster: a charm
3486 **wentestow:** did you go   **Seinte Petres soster:** St. Peter's
sister
3488 **sik:** sigh
3489 **eftsoones now:** right now
3491 **swynke:** work
3493 **in pryvetee:** in secret, confidentially
3494 **toucheth:** concerns

3497 **myghty:** strong   **large:** full
3499 **shette:** shut
3501 **lief:** beloved
3503 **wreye:** reveal
3505 **forlore:** lost
3507 **wreye:** betray
3509 **sely:** innocent, ignorant, hapless   **labbe:** blabbermouth
3510 **nam nat lief to gabbe:** do not like to gab
3512 **hym that harwed helle:** Christ, who despoiled Hell of its
captives
3516 **a:** on   **quarter nyght:** a quarter way through the night; in
April, after midnight
3518 **Noes:** Noah's
3520 **dreynt:** drowned
3521 **drenche:** drown   **hir lyf:** their lives
3526 **yis:** yes indeed
3527 **loore:** learning   **reed:** (good) advice
3528 **heed:** head (i.e., ideas)
3530 **rewe:** be sorry
3532 **undertake:** affirm, declare

That al the world with water sholde be lorn?"
  "Yis," quod this Carpenter, "ful yoore ago."
  "Hastou nat herd," quod Nicholas, "also
The sorwe of Noe with his felaweshipe,
Er that he myghte gete his wyf to shipe?   3540
Hym hadde be levere, I dar wel undertake,
At thilke tyme, than alle his wetheres blake
That she hadde had a ship hirself allone.
And therfore, woostou what is best to doone?
This asketh haste, and of an hastif thyng   3545
Men may nat preche or maken tariyng.

  "Anon go gete us faste into this in
A knedyng trogh, or ellis a kymelyn,
For ech of us, but looke that they be large,
In which we mowe swymme as in a barge,
And han therinne vitaille suffisant   3551
But for a day — fy on the remenant!
The water shal aslake and goon away
Aboute pryme upon the nexte day.   3554
But Robyn may nat wite of this, thy knave,
Ne eek thy mayde Gille I may nat save;
Axe nat why, for though thou aske me,
I wol nat tellen Goddes pryvetee.
Suffiseth thee, but if thy wittes madde,
To han as greet a grace as Noe hadde.   3560
Thy wyf shal I wel saven, out of doute.
Go now thy wey, and speed thee heer-aboute.

  "But whan thou hast, for hire and thee and
      me,
Ygeten us thise knedyng tubbes thre,   3564
Thanne shaltow hange hem in the roof ful hye,
That no man of oure purveiaunce espye.
And whan thou thus hast doon as I have seyd,
And hast oure vitaille faire in hem yleyd,
And eek an ax to smyte the corde atwo,   3569
Whan that the water comth, that we may go
And breke an hole an heigh, upon the gable,
Unto the gardyn-ward, over the stable,
That we may frely passen forth oure way,

Whan that the grete shour is goon away.
Thanne shaltou swymme as myrie, I undertake,
As dooth the white doke after hire drake.   3576
Thanne wol I clepe, 'How, Alison! How, John!
Be myrie, for the flood wol passe anon.'
And thou wolt seyn, 'Hayl, maister Nicholay!
Good morwe, I se thee wel, for it is day.'   3580
And thanne shul we be lordes al oure lyf
Of al the world, as Noe and his wyf.

  "But of o thyng I warne thee ful right:
Be wel avysed on that ilke nyght
That we ben entred into shippes bord,   3585
That noon of us ne speke nat a word,
Ne clepe, ne crie, but be in his preyere;
For it is Goddes owene heeste deere.

  "Thy wyf and thou moote hange fer atwynne;
For that bitwixe yow shal be no synne,   3590
Namoore in lookyng than ther shal in deede.
This ordinance is seyd. Go, God thee speede!
Tomorwe at nyght, whan men ben alle aslepe,
Into oure knedyng-tubbes wol we crepe,
And sitten there, abidyng Goddes grace.   3595
Go now thy wey; I have no lenger space
To make of this no lenger sermonyng.
Men seyn thus, 'sende the wise, and sey no
      thyng.'
Thou art so wys, it needeth thee nat teche.
Go, save oure lyf, and that I the biseche."   3600
  This sely carpenter goth forth his wey.
Ful ofte he seide "Allas and weylawey,"
And to his wyf he tolde his pryvetee,   3603
And she was war, and knew it bet than he,
What al this queynte cast was for to seye.
But nathelees she ferde as she wolde deye,
And seyde, "Allas! go forth thy wey anon,
Help us to scape, or we been dede echon!
I am thy trewe, verray wedded wyf;   3609
Go, deere spouse, and help to save oure lyf."

  Lo, which a greet thyng is affeccioun!
Men may dyen of ymaginacioun,
So depe may impressioun be take.
This sely carpenter bigynneth quake;
Hym thynketh verraily that he may see   3615

3536 **lorn:** lost
3537 **yoore ago:** long ago
3539 **Noe:** Noah, here as a character in the popular mystery plays
3541–43 He would have preferred (*Hym hadde be levere*), I dare affirm, that she had a ship all to herself, than have all his black sheep (*wetheres*); i.e., he would have given all his sheep for this.
3547 **in:** house
3548 **knedyng trogh:** large trough for kneading dough
kymelyn: large tub for brewing beer
3550 **swymme:** float   **barge:** sailing vessel
3551 **vitaille suffisant:** enough food
3553 **aslake:** subside
3554 **pryme:** around 9 A.M.
3559 **madde:** go mad
3562 **speed thee:** hurry   **heer-aboute:** about this matter
3566 **purveiaunce:** preparations
3569 **atwo:** in two
3571 **an heigh:** above
3572 **Unto the gardyn-ward:** toward the garden

3584 **wel avysed:** well warned
3587 **but be:** unless it be
3588 **heeste:** commandment
3589 **atwynne:** apart
3592 **ordinance:** command
3595 **abidyng:** awaiting
3596 **space:** time
3597 **sermonyng:** talk
3604 **bet:** better
3605 **queynte cast:** ingenious plot   **seye:** mean
3608 **scape:** escape   **echon:** each one
3611 **which a:** what a   **affeccioun:** emotion
3612 **ymaginacioun:** fantasy
3614 **quake:** tremble

Noees flood come walwynge as the see
To drenchen Alisoun, his hony deere.
He wepeth, weyleth, maketh sory cheere;
He siketh with ful many a sory swogh;   3619
He gooth and geteth hym a knedyng trogh,
And after that a tubbe and a kymelyn,
And pryvely he sente hem to his in,
And heng hem in the roof in pryvetee.
His owene hand he made laddres thre,   3624
To clymben by the ronges and the stalkes
Unto the tubbes hangynge in the balkes,
And hem vitailled, bothe trogh and tubbe,
With breed, and chese, and good ale in a jubbe,
Suffisynge right ynogh as for a day.
But er that he hadde maad al this array,   3630
He sente his knave, and eek his wenche also,
Upon his nede to London for to go.
And on the Monday, whan it drow to nyght,
He shette his dore withoute candel-lyght,
And dressed alle thyng as it sholde be.   3635
And shortly, up they clomben alle thre;
They seten stille wel a furlong way.
     "Now, *Pater-noster,* clom!" seyde Nicholay,
And "Clom!" quod John, and "Clom!" seyde
     Alisoun.
This carpenter seyde his devocioun,   3640
And stille he sit, and biddeth his preyere,
Awaitynge on the reyn, if he it heere.
     The dede sleep, for wery bisynesse,
Fil on this carpenter right, as I gesse,
Aboute corfew-tyme, or litel moore;   3645
For travaille of his goost he groneth soore,
And eft he routeth, for his heed myslay.
Doun of the laddre stalketh Nicholay,
And Alisoun ful softe adoun she spedde;
Withouten wordes mo they goon to bedde,
Ther as the carpenter is wont to lye.   3651
Ther was the revel and the melodye;

And thus lith Alison and Nicholas,
In bisynesse of myrthe and of solas,
Til that the belle of laudes gan to rynge,   3655
And freres in the chauncel gonne synge.
     This parissh clerk, this amorous Absolon,
That is for love alwey so wo bigon,
Upon the Monday was at Oseneye   3659
With compaignye, hym to disporte and pleye,
And axed upon cas a cloisterer
Ful prively after John the carpenter;
And he drough hym apart out of the chirche,
And seyde, "I noot; I saugh hym heere nat
     wirche
Syn Saterday; I trowe that he be went   3665
For tymber, ther oure abbot hath hym sent;
For he is wont for tymber for to go
And dwellen at the grange a day or two;
Or elles he is at his hous, certeyn.
Where that he be, I kan nat soothly seyn."   3670
     This Absolon ful joly was and light,
And thoghte, "Now is tyme to wake al nyght,
For sikirly I saugh hym nat stirynge
Aboute his dore, syn day bigan to sprynge.
     "So moot I thryve, I shal, at cokkes crowe,
Ful pryvely knokken at his wyndowe   3676
That stant ful lowe upon his boures wal.
To Alison now wol I tellen al
My love-longynge, for yet I shal nat mysse
That at the leeste wey I shal hire kisse.   3680
Som maner confort shal I have, parfay.
My mouth hath icched al this longe day;
That is a signe of kissyng atte leeste.
Al nyght me mette eek I was at a feeste.   3684
Therfore I wol go slepe an houre or tweye,
And al the nyght thanne wol I wake and
     pleye."
     Whan that the firste cok hath crowe, anon
Up rist this joly lovere Absolon,
And hym arraieth gay, at poynt-devys.
But first he cheweth greyn and lycorys,   3690
To smellen sweete, er he hadde kembd his heer.

3616 **walwynge:** surging
3618 **maketh sory cheere:** looks sad, wretched
3619 **swogh:** groan
3624 **His owene hand:** by himself
3625 **stalkes:** uprights (of the ladder)
3626 **balkes:** beams
3627 **vitailled:** stocked with provisions
3628 **jubbe:** large container, jug
3630 **array:** preparation
3631 **wenche:** servant girl
3632 **nede:** business
3635 **dressed:** arranged
3637 **furlong way:** a couple of minutes
3638 Now say a Paternoster (Lord's Prayer) and then hush
(*clom*).
3641 **sit** = *sitteth,* sits **biddeth:** prays
3643 **for wery bisynesse:** wearied by this work
3645 **corfew-tyme:** dusk
3646 **travaille of his goost:** suffering of his spirit, mental anguish
3647 **eft:** likewise **routeth:** snores **myslay:** lay wrong
3651 **Ther as:** where **wont:** accustomed

3655 **laudes:** an early morning service, before daybreak
3661 **upon cas:** by chance
3663 **drough:** drew
3668 **grange:** outlying farm
3671 **light:** happy
3672 **wake:** remain awake
3675 **So moot I thryve:** as I may prosper
3677 **stant** = *stondith,* stands
3679 **mysse:** fail
3680 **at the leeste wey:** at least
3681 **parfay:** indeed, by my faith
3682 **icched:** itched
3684 **me mette:** I dreamed
3688 **rist** = *riseth,* rises
3689 **hym arraieth gay:** dresses himself handsomely at
poynt-devys: in every detail, completely
3690 **greyn:** Grain of Paradise, cardamom seed, a
breath-sweetener

Under his tonge a trewe-love he beer,
For therby wende he to ben gracious.
He rometh to the carpenteres hous,　　　3694
And stille he stant under the shot-wyndowe —
Unto his brest it raughte, it was so lowe —
And softe he cougheth with a semy soun:
"What do ye, hony-comb, sweete Alisoun,
My faire bryd, my sweete cynamome?　　　3699
Awaketh, lemman myn, and speketh to me!
Wel litel thynken ye upon my wo,
That for youre love I swete ther I go.
No wonder is thogh that I swelte and swete;
I moorne as dooth a lamb after the tete.　　　3704
Ywis, lemman, I have swich love-longynge
That lik a turtel trewe is my moornynge.
I may nat ete na moore than a mayde."

　　"Go fro the wyndow, Jakke fool," she sayde;
"As help me God, it wol nat be 'com pa me.'
I love another — and elles I were to blame —
Wel bet than thee, by Jhesu, Absolon.　　　3711
Go forth thy wey, or I wol caste a ston,
And lat me slepe, a twenty devel wey!"

　　"Allas," quod Absolon, "and weylawey,
That trewe love was evere so yvel biset!　　　3715
Thanne kysse me, syn it may be no bet,
For Jhesus love, and for the love of me."

　　"Wiltow thanne go thy wey therwith?" quod
　　　she.

　　"Ye, certes, lemman," quod this Absolon.

　　"Thanne make thee redy," quod she, "I come
　　　anon."

And unto Nicholas she seyde stille,　　　3721
"Now hust, and thou shalt laughen al thy fille."

　　This Absolon doun sette hym on his knees
And seyde, "I am a lord at alle degrees;
For after this I hope ther cometh moore.　　　3725
Lemman, thy grace, and sweete bryd, thyn
　　　oore!"

　　The wyndow she undoth, and that in haste.

"Have do," quod she, "com of, and speed the
　　　faste,
Lest that oure neighebores thee espie."　　　3729
　　This Absolon gan wype his mouth ful drie.
Derk was the nyght as pich, or as the cole,
And at the wyndow out she putte hir hole,
And Absolon, hym fil no bet ne wers,
But with his mouth he kiste hir naked ers
Ful savourly, er he were war of this.　　　3735
Abak he stirte, and thoughte it was amys,
For wel he wiste a womman hath no berd.
He felte a thyng al rough and long yherd,
And seyde, "Fy! allas! what have I do?"

　　"Tehee!" quod she, and clapte the wyndow
　　　to,
And Absolon gooth forth a sory pas.　　　3741

　　"A berd! A berd!" quod hende Nicholas,
"By Goddes corpus, this goth faire and weel."

　　This sely Absolon herde every deel,
And on his lippe he gan for anger byte,　　　3745
And to hymself he seyde, "I shal thee quyte."

　　Who rubbeth now, who froteth now his
　　　lippes
With dust, with sond, with straw, with clooth,
　　　with chippes,
But Absolon, that seith ful ofte, "Allas!"
"My soule bitake I unto Sathanas,　　　3750
But me were levere than al this toun," quod he,
"Of this despit awroken for to be.
Allas," quod he, "allas, I ne hadde ybleynt!"
His hoote love was coold and al yqueynt;
For fro that tyme that he hadde kist hir ers,
Of paramours he sette nat a kers,　　　3756
For he was heeled of his maladie.
Ful ofte paramours he gan deffie,
And weep as dooth a child that is ybete.
A softe paas he wente over the strete　　　3760
Until a smyth men cleped daun Gerveys,
That in his forge smythed plough harneys;

3692 **trewe-love:** a four-leafed sprig of herb paris (Paris quadrifolia) in the shape of a fourfold true-love knot
3693 **gracious:** attractive
3695 **stant** = *stondeth,* stands　**under:** next to　**shot-wyndowe:** hinged window
3696 **raughte:** reached
3697 **semy soun:** small, gentle sound
3699 **bryd:** bird (i.e., sweetheart)　**cynamome:** cinnamon
3700 **lemman:** sweetheart
3703 **swelte:** grow faint　**swete:** sweat
3704 **moorne:** yearn
3705 **Ywis:** truly, indeed
3706 **turtel:** turtledove
3708 **Jakke fool:** you idiot
3709 **com pa me:** come kiss me
3713 **a twenty devel wey:** in the name of twenty devils
3715 **so yvel biset:** in such miserable circumstances
3722 **hust:** be quiet
3724 **at alle degrees:** in every way
3726 **bryd:** bird (i.e., sweetheart)　**oore:** mercy, grace
3727 **undoth:** opens

3728 **Have do:** finish up　**com of:** hurry up　**speed the faste:** be quick
3731 **pich:** pitch
3733 **wers:** worse
3735 **savourly:** with relish
3738 **long yherd:** long-haired
3741 **a sory pas:** sadly
3742 **A berd! A berd!:** a beard! a trick!
3743 **corpus:** body
3744 **every deel:** every bit
3746 **quyte:** pay back (revenge)
3747 **froteth:** rubs
3750 **bitake:** give
3751 If I would not rather than (own) all this town
3752 **despit:** insult　**awroken:** avenged
3753 **ybleynt:** turned away
3754 **yqueynt:** quenched
3756 **kers:** cress (i.e., something of no value)
3758 **deffie:** repudiate
3761 **Until:** to　**daun:** sir
3762 **plough harneys:** ploughing equipment

He sharpeth shaar and kultour bisily.
This Absolon knokketh al esily,   3764
And seyde, "Undo, Gerveys, and that anon."
   "What, who artow?" "It am I, Absolon."
"What, Absolon! for Cristes sweete tree,
Why rise ye so rathe? Ey, benedicitee!
What eyleth yow? Som gay gerl, God it woot,
Hath broght yow thus upon the viritoot.   3770
By Seinte Note, ye woot wel what I mene."
   This Absolon ne roghte nat a bene
Of al his pley; no word agayn he yaf;
He hadde moore tow on his distaf   3774
Than Gerveys knew, and seyde, "Freend so deere,
That hoote kultour in the chymenee heere,
As lene it me; I have therwith to doone,
And I wol brynge it thee agayn ful soone."
   Gerveys answerde, "Certes, were it gold,
Or in a poke nobles alle untold,   3780
Thou sholdest have, as I am trewe smyth.
Ey, Cristes foo! What wol ye do therwith?"
   "Therof," quod Absolon, "be as be may.
I shal wel telle it thee to-morwe day" —
And caughte the kultour by the colde stele.
Ful softe out at the dore he gan to stele,   3786
And wente unto the carpenteris wal.
He cogheth first, and knokketh therwithal
Upon the wyndowe, right as he dide er.
   This Alison answerde, "Who is ther   3790
That knokketh so? I warante it a theef."
   "Why, nay," quod he, "God woot, my sweete leef,
I am thyn Absolon, my deerelyng.
Of gold," quod he, "I have thee broght a ryng.
My mooder yaf it me, so God me save;   3795
Ful fyn it is, and therto wel ygrave.
This wol I yeve thee, if thou me kisse."

This Nicholas was risen for to pisse,
And thoughte he wolde amenden al the jape;
He sholde kisse his ers er that he scape.   3800
And up the wyndowe dide he hastily,
And out his ers he putteth pryvely
Over the buttok, to the haunche-bon;
And therwith spak this clerk, this Absolon,
"Spek, sweete bryd, I noot nat where thou art."
   This Nicholas anon leet fle a fart   3806
As greet as it had been a thonder-dent,
That with the strook he was almoost yblent;
And he was redy with his iren hoot,
And Nicholas amydde the ers he smoot.   3810
   Of gooth the skyn an hande-brede aboute,
The hoote kultour brende so his toute,
And for the smert he wende for to dye.
As he were wood, for wo he gan to crye,   3814
"Help! Water! Water! Help, for Goddes herte!"
   This carpenter out of his slomber sterte,
And herde oon crien "water!" as he were wood,
And thoughte, "Allas, now comth Nowelis flood!"
He sit hym up withouten wordes mo,   3819
And with his ax he smoot the corde atwo,
And doun gooth al; he foond neither to selle,
Ne breed ne ale, til he cam to the celle
Upon the floor, and ther aswowne he lay.
   Up stirte hire Alison and Nicholay,   3824
And criden "Out" and "Harrow" in the strete.
The neighebores, bothe smale and grete,
In ronnen for to gauren on this man,
That yet aswowne lay, bothe pale and wan,
For with the fal he brosten hadde his arm.
But stonde he moste unto his owene harm;
For whan he spak, he was anon bore doun   3831
With hende Nicholas and Alisoun.
They tolden every man that he was wood;
He was agast so of Nowelis flood

3763 **sharpeth**: sharpens **shaar**: ploughshare **kultour**: vertical blade at the front of the plough
3764 **esily**: gently
3765 **Undo**: open up
3767 **sweete tree**: dear cross
3768 **rathe**: early
3769 **gay gerl**: good-looking girl
3770 **upon the viritoot**: astir (?)
3771 **Seinte Note**: St. Neot
3772 **roghte nat a bene**: cared not a bean (i.e., nothing)
3774 **tow on his distaf**: flax on his distaff (i.e., more business on hand)
3776 **chymenee**: hearth
3777 **As lene**: lend (*as* is not translated)
3780 **poke**: bag **nobles**: gold coins **untold**: countless
3782 **Ey, Cristes foo!**: Ah, by Christ's foe (i.e., the Devil)
3783 **be as be may**: whatever may be
3785 **stele**: handle
3791 **warante**: swear
3792 **leef**: beloved
3793 **deerelyng**: darling
3796 **ygrave**: engraved

3799 **amenden al the jape**: make the joke even better
3803 **haunche-bon**: thigh
3806 **leet fle**: let fly
3807 **thonder-dent**: thunderstroke
3808 **yblent**: blinded
3811 **Of**: off **hande-brede aboute**: width of a hand all around
3812 **toute**: rump
3813 **smert**: pain **wende for to dye**: thought he would die
3815 **herte**: heart
3818 **Nowelis**: Noah's
3821–22 He did not stop to sell bread or ale on the way (i.e., he wasted no time).
3822 **celle**: floor
3823 **aswowne**: in a faint
3826 **smale and grete**: i.e., everyone
3827 **ronnen**: ran **gauren on**: stare at
3829 **brosten**: broken
3830 But he had to stand up, though it turned out badly for him.
3832 **With**: by
3834 **agast**: frightened

Thurgh fantasie that of his vanytee   3835
He hadde yboght hym knedyng tubbes thre,
And hadde hem hanged in the roof above;
And that he preyed hem, for Goddes love,
To sitten in the roof, *par compaignye.*

    The folk gan laughen at his fantasye;   3840
Into the roof they kiken and they cape,
And turned al his harm unto a jape.
For what so that this carpenter answerde,
It was for noght; no man his reson herde.
With othes grete he was so sworn adoun   3845

That he was holde wood in al the toun;
For every clerk anonright heeld with oother.
They seyde, "The man is wood, my leeve
    brother";
And every wight gan laughen at this stryf.
Thus swyved was this carpenteris wyf,   3850
For al his kepyng and his jalousye,
And Absolon hath kist hir nether ye,
And Nicholas is scalded in the towte.
This tale is doon, and God save al the rowte!

Heere endeth the Millere his tale.

THE REEVE'S PROLOGUE

The prologe of the Reves Tale.

Whan folk hadde laughen at this nyce cas
Of Absolon and hende Nicholas,   3856
Diverse folk diversely they seyde,
But for the moore part they loughe and pleyde.
Ne at this tale I saugh no man hym greve,
But it were oonly Osewold the Reve.   3860
By cause he was of carpenteris craft,
A litel ire is in his herte ylaft;
He gan to grucche, and blamed it a lite.
    "So theek," quod he, "ful wel koude I thee
    quite
With bleryng of a proud milleres ye,   3865
If that me liste speke of ribaudye.
But ik am oold; me list not pley for age;
Gras tyme is doon; my fodder is now forage;
This white top writeth myne olde yeris;
Myn herte is also mowled as myne heris,   3870

But if I fare as dooth an open-ers —
That ilke fruyt is ever lenger the wers,
Til it be roten in mullok or in stree.
We olde men, I drede, so fare we:
Til we be roten, kan we nat be rype;   3875
We hoppen alwey whil that the world wol pype.
For in oure wyl ther stiketh evere a nayl,
To have an hoor heed and a grene tayl,
As hath a leek; for thogh oure myght be goon,
Oure wyl desireth folie evere in oon.   3880
For whan we may nat doon, than wol we speke;
Yet in oure asshen olde is fyr yreke.
    "Foure gleedes han we, which I shal de-
    vyse —
Avauntyng, liyng, anger, coveitise;
Thise foure sparkles longen unto eelde.   3885

3835 **vanytee:** foolishness
3839 **par compaignye:** for fellowship's sake, to keep him company
3841 **kiken:** stare **cape:** gape
3845 **sworn adoun:** overcome by oaths

3855 **nyce cas:** foolish business
3859 **hym greve:** get angry
3863 **grucche:** complain
3864 **So theek:** as I may prosper (I swear)
3865 **bleryng of a proud milleres ye:** deluding, tricking a proud miller
3866 **ribaudye:** ribaldry, coarse jesting
3867 **ik:** I
3868 I have left the pasture for the stable.
3869 My white hairs declare my old age.
3870 **also:** as **mowled:** molded

3847 **anonright:** immediately **heeld:** held, agreed
3850 **swyved:** copulated with
3851 **kepyng:** guarding
3852 **nether ye:** lower eye

3871 **open-ers:** fruit of the medlar
3872 **ever lenger the wers:** increasingly worse
3873 **roten:** rotten **mullok:** mullock (rubbish, refuse) **stree:** straw
3876 **hoppen:** dance
3877 We are always goaded by desire (*nayl* = nail).
3878 **hoor:** white-haired
3880 **evere in oon:** continually
3882 Still in our old ashes, fire is raked over (*yreke;* i.e., covered).
3883 **gleedes:** embers, live coals
3884 **Avauntyng:** boasting **coveitise:** greed, avarice
3885 **eelde:** old age

Oure olde lemes mowe wel been unweelde,
But wyl ne shal nat faillen, that is sooth.
And yet ik have alwey a coltes tooth,
As many a yeer as it is passed henne
Syn that my tappe of lif bigan to renne.   3890
For sikerly, whan I was bore, anon
Deeth drough the tappe of lyf and leet it
                gon,
And ever sithe hath so the tappe yronne
Til that almoost al empty is the tonne.   3894
The streem of lyf now droppeth on the chymbe.
The sely tonge may wel rynge and chymbe
Of wrecchednesse that passed is ful yoore;
With olde folk, save dotage, is namoore!''
    Whan that oure Hoost hadde herd this ser-
                monyng,
He gan to speke as lordly as a kyng.   3900
He seide, ''What amounteth al this wit?
What shul we speke alday of hooly writ?

The devel made a reve for to preche,
Or of a soutere a shipman or a leche.
Sey forth thy tale, and tarie nat the tyme.   3905
Lo Depeford, and it is half-wey pryme!
Lo Grenewych, ther many a shrewe is inne!
It were al tyme thy tale to bigynne.''
    ''Now, sires,'' quod this Osewold the Reve,
''I pray yow alle that ye nat yow greve,   3910
Thogh I answere, and somdeel sette his howve;
For leveful is with force force of-showve.
    ''This dronke Millere hath ytoold us heer
How that bigyled was a carpenteer,
Peraventure in scorn, for I am oon.   3915
And, by youre leve, I shal hym quite anoon;
Right in his cherles termes wol I speke.
I pray to God his nekke mote to-breke;
He kan wel in myn eye seen a stalke,
But in his owene he kan nat seen a balke.''   3920

THE REEVE'S TALE

Heere bigynneth the Reves Tale.

At Trumpyngtoun, nat fer fro Cantebrigge,
Ther gooth a brook, and over that a brigge,
Upon the whiche brook ther stant a melle;
And this is verray sooth that I yow telle:
A millere was ther dwellynge many a day.   3925
As any pecok he was proud and gay.
Pipen he koude and fisshe, and nettes beete,
And turne coppes, and wel wrastle and sheete;
Ay by his belt he baar a long panade,
And of a swerd ful trenchant was the blade.

A joly poppere baar he in his pouche;   3931
Ther was no man, for peril, dorste hym touche.
A Sheffeld thwitel baar he in his hose.
Round was his face, and camus was his nose;
As piled as an ape was his skulle.   3935
He was a market-betere atte fulle.
Ther dorste no wight hand upon hym legge,

3886 **lemes:** limbs **unweelde:** feeble
3887 **wyl:** will, desire
3888 **coltes tooth:** young man's desires
3889 **henne:** hence, away
3892 **drough the tappe:** drew the tap, turned on the spigot
3894 **tonne:** barrel, cask
3895 **chymbe:** rim
3896 **chymbe:** chime
3897 **ful yoore:** long ago
3901 What does all this wisdom amount to? (R.)
3902 **What:** why **alday:** all day

3921 **Trumpyngtoun:** Trumpington **Cantebrigge:** Cambridge
3922 **brigge:** bridge
3923 **stant** = *stondith,* stands **melle:** mill
3927 **Pipen:** play the bagpipes **beete:** mend
3928 **turne coppes:** turn up the cups (?), play a drinking game
sheete: shoot (arrows)
3929 **panade:** cutlass
3930 **trenchant:** sharp

3904 **soutere:** cobbler **leche:** physician
3906 **Depeford:** Deptford, about five miles from London
half-wey pryme: about 7:30 A.M. (?)
3907 **Grenewych:** Greenwich (where Chaucer was probably
living), about a half mile past Deptford **shrewe:** scoundrel
3908 **al tyme:** high time
3911 **somdeel:** somewhat **sette his howve:** tip his hood, make
a fool of him; cf. GP I.586.
3912 For it is permitted (*leveful*) to repel (*of-showve*) force with
force
3914 **bigyled:** tricked
3915 **Peraventure:** perhaps **oon:** one (i.e., a carpenter)
3916 **quite:** pay back, exact vengeance on (him)
3917 **cherles termes:** churlish words, rude expressions
3918 **to-breke:** break in pieces
3919 **stalke:** piece of straw
3920 **balke:** beam

3931 **poppere:** small dagger **pouche:** pocket
3932 **dorste:** dared
3933 **Sheffeld thwitel:** Sheffield knife
3934 **camus was his nose:** he had a pug nose
3935 **piled:** bald
3936 **market-betere:** bully, quarrelsome swaggerer
3937 **legge:** lay

That he ne swoor he sholde anon abegge.
A theef he was for sothe of corn and mele,
And that a sly, and usaunt for to stele.   3940
His name was hoote deynous Symkyn.
A wyf he hadde, ycomen of noble kyn;
The person of the toun hir fader was.
With hire he yaf ful many a panne of bras,
For that Symkyn sholde in his blood allye.
She was yfostred in a nonnerye;   3946
For Symkyn wolde no wyf, as he sayde,
But she were wel ynorissed and a mayde,
To saven his estaat of yomanrye.
And she was proud, and peert as is a pye.   3950
A ful fair sighte was it upon hem two;
On halydayes biforn hire wolde he go
With his typet wounde aboute his heed,
And she cam after in a gyte of reed;
And Symkyn hadde hosen of the same.   3955
Ther dorste no wight clepen hire but "dame";
Was noon so hardy that wente by the weye
That with hire dorste rage or ones pleye,
But if he wolde be slayn of Symkyn
With panade, or with knyf, or boidekyn.   3960
For jalous folk ben perilous everemo —
Algate they wolde hire wyves wenden so.
And eek, for she was somdel smoterlich,
She was as digne as water in a dich,
And ful of hoker and of bisemare.   3965
Hir thoughte that a lady sholde hire spare,
What for hire kynrede and hir nortelrie
That she hadde lerned in the nonnerie.

    A doghter hadde they bitwixe hem two
Of twenty yeer, withouten any mo,   3970
Savynge a child that was of half yeer age;
In cradel it lay and was a propre page.

This wenche thikke and wel ygrowen was,
With kamus nose and eyen greye as glas,
With buttokes brode and brestes rounde and
        hye.
But right fair was hire heer; I wol nat lye.   3976
    This person of the toun, for she was feir,
In purpos was to maken hire his heir,
Bothe of his catel and his mesuage,
And straunge he made it of hir mariage.   3980
His purpos was for to bistowe hire hye
Into som worthy blood of auncetrye;
For hooly chirches good moot been despended
On hooly chirches blood, that is descended.
Therfore he wolde his hooly blood hon-
        oure,   3985
Though that he hooly chirche sholde devoure.
    Greet sokene hath this millere, out of doute,
With whete and malt of al the land aboute;
And nameliche ther was a greet collegge   3989
Men clepen the Soler Halle at Cantebregge;
Ther was hir whete and eek hir malt ygrounde.
And on a day it happed, in a stounde,
Sik lay the maunciple on a maladye;
Men wenden wisly that he sholde dye.   3994
For which this millere stal bothe mele and corn
An hundred tyme moore than biforn;
For therbiforn he stal but curteisly,
But now he was a theef outrageously,
For which the wardeyn chidde and made fare.
But therof sette the millere nat a tare;   4000
He craketh boost, and swoor it was nat so.
    Thanne were ther yonge povre scolers two,
That dwelten in this halle, of which I seye.
Testif they were, and lusty for to pleye,
And, oonly for hire myrthe and revelrye,   4005
Upon the wardeyn bisily they crye
To yeve hem leve, but a litel stounde,
To goon to mille and seen hir corn ygrounde;

3938 **abegge:** pay for (it)
3939 **corn:** grain   **mele:** ground meal
3940 **sly:** sly one   **usaunt for to stele:** accustomed to stealing
3941 **hoote:** called   **deynous:** haughty
3943 **person:** parson, priest
3945 **in his blood allye:** make an alliance with his family
3946 **yfostred:** raised
3948 **But:** unless   **ynorissed:** raised, educated   **mayde:** virgin
3949 **To maintain his state** of free (rather than servile) birth
3950 **peert:** impudent   **pye:** magpie
3953 **typet:** the dangling tip of the hood
3954 **gyte:** gown, mantle
3956 **dame:** lady
3958 **rage:** flirt
3960 **panade:** cutlass   **boidekyn:** dagger
3961 **everemo:** always
3962 At least they would like their wives to think so.
3963 **smoterlich:** besmirched, sullied (in reputation, by her illegitimacy)
3964 **as digne as water in a dich:** literally, as haughty as ditch-water (OED: "stinking with pride")
3965 **hoker:** disdain   **bisemare:** scorn
3966 **hire spare:** be aloof
3967 **kynrede:** lineage   **nortelrie:** nurture, education
3972 **page:** boy

3974 **kamus nose:** pug nose
3978 **In purpos was:** intended
3979 **catel:** property   **mesuage:** house and its contents
3980 And he made difficulties about her marriage.
3981 **hye:** nobly
3982 **auncetrye:** noble lineage
3987 **Greet sokene:** large, profitable monopoly (*sokene* = exclusive right to grind grain in a given area)
3990 **Soler Halle:** a name for King's Hall, a college at Cambridge
3992 **in a stounde:** at a time, once
3994 **wisly:** surely
3995 **stal:** stole
3997 **therbiforn:** previously
3998 **outrageously:** to excess
3999 **wardeyn:** master of the college   **chidde and made fare:** chided and made a fuss
4000 **tare:** weed (i.e., nothing)
4001 **craketh boost:** blustered fiercely
4002 **povre scolers:** impoverished students
4004 **Testif:** testy, headstrong
4005 **revelrye:** pleasure, delight
4007 **stounde:** time, while

And hardily they dorste leye hir nekke 4009
The millere sholde not stele hem half a pekke
Of corn by sleighte, ne by force hem reve;
And at the laste the wardeyn yaf hem leve.
John highte that oon, and Aleyn highte that
    oother;
Of o toun were they born, that highte Strother,
Fer in the north; I kan nat telle where. 4015
    This Aleyn maketh redy al his gere,
And on an hors the sak he caste anon.
Forth goth Aleyn the clerk, and also John,
With good swerd and with bokeler by hir syde.
John knew the wey — hem nedede no gyde —
And at the mille the sak adoun he layth. 4021
Aleyn spak first: "Al hayl, Symond, y-fayth!
Hou fares thy faire doghter and thy wyf?"
    "Aleyn, welcome," quod Symkyn, "by my
    lyf!
And John also, how now, what do ye
    heer?" 4025
    "Symond," quod John, "by God, nede has na
    peer.
Hym boes serve hymself that has na swayn,
Or elles he is a fool, as clerkes sayn.
Oure manciple, I hope he wil be deed,
Swa werkes ay the wanges in his heed; 4030
And forthy is I come, and eek Alayn,
To grynde oure corn and carie it ham agayn;
I pray yow spede us heythen that ye may."
    "It shal be doon," quod Symkyn, "by my
    fay!
What wol ye doon whil that it is in hande?" 4034
    "By God, right by the hopur wil I stande,"
Quod John, "and se howgates the corn gas in.
Yet saugh I nevere, by my fader kyn,
How that the hopur wagges til and fra."
    Aleyn answerde, "John, and wiltow swa?
Thanne wil I be bynethe, by my croun, 4041

And se how that the mele falles doun
Into the trough; that sal be my disport.
For John, y-faith, I may been of youre sort;
I is as ille a millere as ar ye." 4045
    This millere smyled of hir nycetee,
And thoghte, "Al this nys doon but for a wyle.
They wene that no man may hem bigyle,
But by my thrift, yet shal I blere hir ye,
For al the sleighte in hir philosophye. 4050
The moore queynte crekes that they make,
The moore wol I stele whan I take.
In stide of flour yet wol I yeve hem bren.
'The gretteste clerkes been noght wisest men,'
As whilom to the wolf thus spak the mare.
Of al hir art counte I noght a tare." 4056
    Out at the dore he gooth ful pryvely,
Whan that he saugh his tyme, softely.
He looketh up and doun til he hath founde
The clerkes hors, ther as it stood ybounde 4060
Bihynde the mille, under a levesel;
And to the hors he goth hym faire and wel;
He strepeth of the brydel right anon.
And whan the hors was laus, he gynneth gon
Toward the fen, ther wilde mares renne, 4065
And forth with "wehee," thurgh thikke and
    thurgh thenne.
    This millere gooth agayn, no word he seyde,
But dooth his note, and with the clerkes
    pleyde
Til that hir corn was faire and weel ygrounde.
And whan the mele is sakked and ybounde,
This John goth out and fynt his hors away, 4071
And gan to crie "Harrow!" and "Weylaway!
Oure hors is lorn, Alayn, for Goddes banes,
Step on thy feet! Com of, man, al atanes!
Allas, our wardeyn has his palfrey lorn." 4075
This Aleyn al forgat, bothe mele and corn;

4009 **hardily:** certainly   **leye:** wager
4011 **sleighte:** trickery   **reve:** rob
4014 **Strother:** a town in the North of England
4020 **hem nedede:** they needed
4022 The clerks speak a Northern dialect; see n.
4026 **nede has na peer:** need has no equal (i.e., necessity knows no law)
4027 **Hym boes:** he must (Nth)   **swayn:** servant
4029 **hope:** expect
4030 **Swa werkes:** so ache (Nth)   **wanges:** teeth
4032 **ham:** home (Nth)
4033 **heythen:** hence (Nth)   **that ye may:** (as fast) as you can
4035 **in hande:** in process
4036 **hopur:** hopper (of the mill)
4037 **howgates:** how (Nth)   **gas:** goes (Nth)
4038 **by my fader kyn:** (I swear) by my father's kin (i.e., on my family's honor)
4039 **wagges til and fra:** wags to and fro (Nth)
4040 **wiltow swa:** will you (do) so (*swa* Nth)
4041 **by my croun:** by my head

4043 **sal:** shall (Nth)   **disport:** amusement
4045 **ille:** poor
4046 **nycetee:** foolishness
4047 **wyle:** trick
4049 **by my thrift:** by my welfare (I swear)   **blere hir ye:** trick them
4050 **philosophye:** learning
4051 **queynte:** ingenious, clever   **crekes:** tricks
4053 **In stide of:** instead of   **bren:** bran
4056 **noght a tare:** not a weed (i.e., nothing)
4061 **levesel:** arbor
4063 **strepeth of:** strips off
4064 **laus:** loose
4065 **fen:** probably Lingay Fen, south of Trumpington
4068 **note:** task, business
4070 **sakked:** put in a sack
4071 **fynt** = *fyndeth,* finds
4072 **Weylaway:** alas
4073 **banes:** bones (Nth)
4074 **Com of:** hurry   **al atanes:** at once (Nth)

Al was out of his mynde his housbondrie.
"What, whilk way is he geen?" he gan to crie.
   The wyf cam lepynge inward with a ren.
She seyde, "Allas! youre hors goth to the fen
With wilde mares, as faste as he may go.   4081
Unthank come on his hand that boond hym so,
And he that bettre sholde han knyt the reyne!"
   "Allas," quod John, "Aleyn, for Cristes peyne
Lay doun thy swerd, and I wil myn alswa.
I is ful wight, God waat, as is a raa;   4086
By Goddes herte, he sal nat scape us bathe!
Why ne had thow pit the capul in the lathe?
Ilhayl! By God, Alayn, thou is a fonne!"
   Thise sely clerkes han ful faste yronne   4090
Toward the fen, bothe Aleyn and eek John.
   And whan the millere saugh that they were
      gon,
He half a busshel of hir flour hath take,
And bad his wyf go knede it in a cake.
He seyde, "I trowe the clerkes were aferd.
Yet kan a millere make a clerkes berd,   4096
For al his art; now lat hem goon hir weye!
Lo, wher he gooth! Ye, lat the children pleye.
They gete hym nat so lightly, by my croun."
   Thise sely clerkes rennen up and doun   4100
With "Keep! Keep! Stand! Stand! Jossa, war-
      derere,
Ga whistle thou, and I shal kepe hym heere!"
But shortly, til that it was verray nyght,
They koude nat, though they dide al hir myght,
Hir capul cacche, he ran alwey so faste,   4105
Til in a dych they caughte hym atte laste.
   Wery and weet, as beest is in the reyn,
Comth sely John, and with him comth Aleyn.
"Allas," quod John, "the day that I was born!
Now are we dryve til hethyng and til scorn.
Oure corn is stoln; men wil us fooles calle,   4111
Bathe the wardeyn and oure felawes alle,
And namely the millere, weylaway!"
   Thus pleyneth John as he gooth by the way
Toward the mille, and Bayard in his hond.

The millere sittynge by the fyr he fond,   4116
For it was nyght, and forther myghte they
      noght;
But for the love of God they hym bisoght
Of herberwe and of ese, as for hir peny.   4119
   The millere seyde agayn, "If ther be eny,
Swich as it is, yet shal ye have youre part.
Myn hous is streit, but ye han lerned art;
Ye konne by argumentes make a place
A myle brood of twenty foot of space.
Lat se now if this place may suffise,   4125
Or make it rowm with speche, as is youre gise."
   "Now, Symond," seyde John, "by Seint Cut-
      berd,
Ay is thou myrie, and this is faire answerd.
I have herd seyd, 'Man sal taa of twa thynges:
Slyk as he fyndes, or taa slyk as he brynges.'
But specially I pray thee, hooste deere,   4131
Get us som mete and drynke, and make us
      cheere,
And we wil payen trewely atte fulle.
With empty hand men may na haukes tulle;
Loo, heere oure silver, redy for to spende."
   This millere into toun his doghter sende   4136
For ale and breed, and rosted hem a goos,
And boond hire hors, it sholde namoore go loos,
And in his owene chambre hem made a bed,
With sheetes and with chalons faire yspred   4140
Noght from his owene bed ten foot or twelve.
His doghter hadde a bed, al by hirselve,
Right in the same chambre by and by.
It myghte be no bet, and cause why?   4144
Ther was no roumer herberwe in the place.
They soupen and they speke, hem to solace,
And drynken evere strong ale atte beste.
Aboute mydnyght wente they to reste.
   Wel hath this millere vernysshed his heed;
Ful pale he was for dronken, and nat reed.   4150
He yexeth, and he spekceth thurgh the nose
As he were on the quakke, or on the pose.

4078 **whilk:** which (Nth) **geen:** gone (Nth)
4079 **with a ren:** at a run, running
4082 **Unthank:** curses
4083 **knyt:** tied
4085 **alswa:** also (Nth)
4086 **wight:** strong **waat:** knows (Nth) **raa:** roe (Nth)
4087 **sal:** shall (Nth) **bathe:** both (Nth)
4088 **pit:** put **capul:** horse **lathe:** barn (Nth)
4089 **Ilhayl:** bad luck **fonne:** fool
4094 **cake:** loaf of bread
4095 **aferd:** leery
4096 **make a . . . berd:** outwit, fool
4100 **Thise sely clerkes:** these poor, hapless clerks
4101 **Keep:** stay **Jossa:** down here **warderere:** watch out behind
4102 **Ga:** go (Nth)
4110 **til hethyng:** to contempt

4119 **herberwe:** lodging **ese:** refreshment, food
4122 **streit:** narrow, small **art:** the arts curriculum at the university, cap. logic
4123 **konne by argumentes make:** know how by logical disputation to make
4126 **rowm:** large, roomy
4127 **Seint Cutberd:** St. Cuthbert
4129–30 Of two things one must take (*taa*) such (*Slyk*) as he finds or take such as he brings.
4134 **tulle:** lure
4140 **chalons:** blankets **yspred:** spread
4143 **by and by:** side by side
4145 **roumer:** larger **herberwe:** lodging
4147 **atte beste:** of the best sort
4149 **vernysshed his heed:** made his head shine
4151 **yexeth:** belches
4152 **on the quakke:** had hoarseness **on the pose:** had a cold

To bedde he goth, and with hym goth his wyf.
As any jay she light was and jolyf,
So was hir joly whistle wel ywet.   4155
The cradel at hir beddes feet is set,
To rokken, and to yeve the child to sowke.
And whan that dronken al was in the crowke,
To bedde wente the doghter right anon;
To bedde goth Aleyn and also John;   4160
Ther nas na moore — hem nedede no dwale.
This millere hath so wisely bibbed ale
That as an hors he fnorteth in his sleep,
Ne of his tayl bihynde he took no keep.
His wyf bar hym a burdon, a ful strong;   4165
Men myghte hir rowtyng heere two furlong;
The wenche rowteth eek, *par compaignye.*

Aleyn the clerk, that herde this melodye,
He poked John, and seyde, "Slepestow?
Herdestow evere slyk a sang er now?   4170
Lo, swilk a complyn is ymel hem alle;
A wilde fyr upon thair bodyes falle!
Wha herkned evere slyk a ferly thyng?
Ye, they sal have the flour of il endyng.
This lange nyght ther tydes me na reste;   4175
But yet, na fors, al sal be for the beste.
For, John," seyde he, "als evere moot I thryve,
If that I may, yon wenche wil I swyve.
Som esement has lawe yshapen us,
For, John, ther is a lawe that says thus: 4180
That gif a man in a point be agreved,
That in another he sal be releved.
Oure corn is stoln, sothly, it is na nay,
And we han had an il fit al this day;
And syn I sal have neen amendement   4185
Agayn my los, I will have esement.
By Goddes sale, it sal neen other bee!''

This John answerde, "Alayn, avyse thee!
The millere is a perilous man," he seyde,
"And gif that he out of his sleep abreyde,   4190
He myghte doon us bathe a vileynye."

Aleyn answerde, "I counte hym nat a flye."
And up he rist, and by the wenche he crepte.
This wenche lay uprighte and faste slepte,
Til he so ny was, er she myghte espie,   4195
That it had been to late for to crie,
And shortly for to seyn, they were aton.
Now pley, Aleyn, for I wol speke of John.

This John lith stille a furlong wey or two,
And to hymself he maketh routhe and wo.   4200
"Allas!" quod he, "this is a wikked jape;
Now may I seyn that I is but an ape.
Yet has my felawe somwhat for his harm;
He has the milleris doghter in his arm.
He auntred hym, and has his nedes sped,   4205
And I lye as a draf-sak in my bed;
And when this jape is tald another day,
I sal been halde a daf, a cokenay!
I wil arise and auntre it, by my fayth!
'Unhardy is unseely,' thus men sayth."   4210
And up he roos, and softely he wente
Unto the cradel, and in his hand it hente,
And baar it softe unto his beddes feet.

Soone after this the wyf hir rowtyng leet,
And gan awake, and wente hire out to
    pisse,   4215
And cam agayn, and gan hir cradel mysse,
And groped heer and ther, but she foond noon.
"Allas!" quod she, "I hadde almoost mysgoon;
I hadde almoost goon to the clerkes bed.
Ey, benedicite! Thanne hadde I foule ysped!"
And forth she gooth til she the cradel fond.
She gropeth alwey forther with hir hond,   4222
And foond the bed, and thoghte noght but
    good,
By cause that the cradel by it stood,
And nyste wher she was, for it was derk;   4225

4157 **sowke:** suck
4158 **crowke:** crock
4161 **hem nedede:** they needed   **dwale:** sleeping potion
4162 **wisely:** surely   **bibbed:** imbibed
4163 **fnorteth:** snorts
4165 **burdon:** bass accompaniment
4166 **rowtyng:** snoring
4167 **par compaignye:** for fellowship's sake, to keep them company
4170 **slyk a sang:** such a song (Nth)
4171 **swilk a complyn:** such a compline, last service of the day   **ymel:** among (Nth)
4172 **wilde fyr:** erysipelas, an acute inflammation of the skin (?)
4173 **Wha:** who (Nth)   **ferly:** amazing
4174 **flour of il endyng:** the best (i.e., worst) of a bad end
4175 **lange:** long (Nth)   **tydes me na reste:** I get no sleep
4176 **na fors:** no matter
4178 **swyve:** copulate with
4179 **esement:** compensation, redress
4181 **gif:** if   **a point:** one point   **agreved:** injured
4182 **sal be releved:** shall be compensated
4183 **it is na nay:** it cannot be denied
4184 **il fit:** hard time
4185 **neen:** none, no (Nth)
4186 **Agayn:** in return for
4187 **sale:** soul (Nth)

4188 **avyse thee:** think carefully
4190 **abreyde:** start, awake
4191 **vileynye:** injury
4192 **nat a flye:** i.e., not at all
4197 **aton:** at one, together
4199 **a furlong wey or two:** five minutes or so
4200 **maketh routhe:** pities (feels sorry for himself)
4201 **jape:** trick
4202 **ape:** fool
4205 **auntred hym:** took a risk   **his nedes sped:** accomplished his purpose
4206 **draf-sak:** sack of chaff or rubbish
4208 **halde a daf:** considered a fool   **cokenay:** weakling
4210 **Unhardy is unseely:** the timid one is unlucky   **men sayth:** it is said (*men* = one)
4214 **hir rowtyng leet:** stopped her snoring
4218 **mysgoon:** gone astray
4225 **nyste** = *ne wiste,* did not know

But faire and wel she creep in to the clerk,
And lith ful stille, and wolde han caught a
    sleep.
Withinne a while this John the clerk up leep,
And on this goode wyf he leith on soore.
So myrie a fit ne hadde she nat ful yoore;   4230
He priketh harde and depe as he were mad.
This joly lyf han thise two clerkes lad
Til that the thridde cok bigan to synge.

    Aleyn wax wery in the dawenynge,
For he had swonken al the longe nyght,   4235
And seyde, "Fare weel, Malyne, sweete wight!
The day is come; I may no lenger byde;
But everemo, wher so I go or ryde,
I is thyn awen clerk, swa have I seel!"   4239
    "Now, deere lemman," quod she, "go, far
    weel!
But er thow go, o thyng I wol thee telle:
Whan that thou wendest homward by the
    melle,
Right at the entree of the dore bihynde
Thou shalt a cake of half a busshel fynde
That was ymaked of thyn owene mele,   4245
Which that I heelp my sire for to stele.
And, goode lemman, God thee save and kepe!"
And with that word almoost she gan to wepe.

    Aleyn up rist, and thoughte, "Er that it dawe,
I wol go crepen in by my felawe,"   4250
And fond the cradel with his hand anon.
"By God," thoughte he, "al wrang I have
    mysgon.
Myn heed is toty of my swynk to-nyght,
That makes me that I ga nat aright.
I woot wel by the cradel I have mysgo;   4255
Heere lith the millere and his wyf also."
And forth he goth, a twenty devel way,
Unto the bed ther as the millere lay.
He wende have cropen by his felawe John,
And by the millere in he creep anon,   4260
And caughte hym by the nekke, and softe he
    spak.

He seyde, "Thou John, thou swynes-heed,
    awak,
For Cristes saule, and heer a noble game.
For by that lord that called is Seint Jame,
As I have thries in this shorte nyght   4265
Swyved the milleres doghter bolt upright,
Whil thow hast, as a coward, been agast."
    "Ye, false harlot," quod the millere, "hast?
A, false traitour! False clerk!" quod he,
Thow shalt be deed, by Goddes dignitee!   4270
Who dorste be so boold to disparage
My doghter, that is come of swich lynage?"
And by the throte-bolle he caughte Alayn,
And he hente hym despitously agayn,   4274
And on the nose he smoot hym with his fest.
Doun ran the blody streem upon his brest;
And in the floor, with nose and mouth tobroke,
They walwe as doon two pigges in a poke;
And up they goon, and doun agayn anon,
Til that the millere sporned at a stoon,   4280
And doun he fil bakward upon his wyf,
That wiste no thyng of this nyce stryf;
For she was falle aslepe a lite wight
With John the clerk, that waked hadde al
    nyght,
And with the fal out of hir sleep she
    breyde.   4285
"Help! hooly croys of Bromeholm," she seyde,
"*In manus tuas!* Lord, to thee I calle!
Awak, Symond! The feend is on me falle.
Myn herte is broken; help! I nam but deed!
Ther lyth oon upon my wombe and on myn
    heed.   4290
Help, Symkyn, for the false clerkes fighte!"
    This John stirte up as faste as ever he
    myghte,
And graspeth by the walles to and fro,
To fynde a staf; and she stirte up also,
And knew the estres bet than dide this John,
And by the wal a staf she foond anon,   4296
And saugh a litel shymeryng of a light,

4226 **creep:** crept
4228 **leep:** leapt
4230 **So myrie a fit:** such a good time **ful yoore:** for a long time
4231 **priketh:** stabs, pierces
4233 **thridde cok:** third crow of the cock, an hour before dawn
4235 **swonken:** worked
4239 **awen:** own (Nth) **swa have I seel:** as I may prosper (I swear)
4246 **heelp:** helped **sire:** father
4252 **wrang:** wrong (Nth)
4253 **toty:** dizzy, fuddled
4254 **ga nat aright:** lose my way
4257 **a twenty devel way:** in the name of twenty devils
4259 **cropen:** crept

4262 **swynes-heed:** pig's head
4263 **saule:** soul
4264 **Seint Jame:** St. James
4266 **Swyved:** copulated with **bolt upright:** lying flat on her back
4271 **disparage:** degrade one's lineage (by a union with someone of lower birth)
4273 **throte-bolle:** Adam's apple
4274 **hente hym:** fetched him, struck him **despitously:** angrily
4278 **poke:** bag
4280 **sporned at:** stumbled on
4283 **a lite wight:** a short time
4285 **breyde:** started up
4286 **hooly croys of Bromeholm:** a famous shrine in Norfolk
4287 **In manus tuas:** "Into thy hands (I commend my spirit)."
4295 **estres:** arrangement of the interior, the nooks and crannies

For at an hole in shoon the moone bright,
And by that light she saugh hem bothe two,
But sikerly she nyste who was who,   4300
But as she saugh a whit thyng in hir ye.
And whan she gan this white thyng espye,
She wende the clerk hadde wered a volupeer,
And with the staf she drow ay neer and neer,
And wende han hit this Aleyn at the fulle, 4305
And smoot the millere on the pyled skulle,
That doun he gooth, and cride, "Harrow!
        I dye!"
Thise clerkes beete hym weel and lete hym
        lye,
And greythen hem, and tooke hir hors anon,
And eek hire mele, and on hir wey they gon.

And at the mille yet they tooke hir cake   4311
Of half a busshel flour, ful wel ybake.
    Thus is the proude millere wel ybete,
And hath ylost the gryndynge of the whete,
And payed for the soper everideel   4315
Of Aleyn and of John, that bette hym weel.
His wyf is swyved, and his doghter als.
Lo, swich it is a millere to be fals!
And therfore this proverbe is seyd ful sooth,
"Hym thar nat wene wel that yvele dooth."
A gylour shal hymself bigyled be.   4321
And God, that sitteth heighe in magestee,
Save al this compaignye, grete and smale!
Thus have I quyt the Millere in my tale.   4324

Heere is ended the Reves Tale.

THE COOK'S PROLOGUE

The prologe of the Cokes Tale.

The Cook of Londoun, whil the Reve spak,
For joye him thoughte he clawed him on the
        bak.
"Ha! ha!" quod he, "For Cristes passion,
This millere hadde a sharp conclusion
Upon his argument of herbergage!
Wel seyde Salomon in his langage,   4330
'Ne bryng nat every man into thyn hous,'
For herberwynge by nyghte is perilous.
Wel oghte a man avysed for to be
Whom that he broghte into his pryvetee.
I pray to God, so yeve me sorwe and care 4335
If evere, sitthe I highte Hogge of Ware,
Herde I a millere bettre yset a-werk.

He hadde a jape of malice in the derk.
But God forbede that we stynte heere;
And therfore, if ye vouche-sauf to heere 4340
A tale of me, that am a povre man,
I wol yow telle, as wel as evere I kan,
A litel jape that fil in oure citee."
    Oure Hoost answerde and seide, "I graunte
        it thee.
Now telle on, Roger; looke that it be good,
For many a pastee hastow laten blood,   4346
And many a Jakke of Dovere hastow soold
That hath been twies hoot and twies coold.
Of many a pilgrym hastow Cristes curs,
For of thy percely yet they fare the wors, 4350
That they han eten with thy stubbel goos,
For in thy shoppe is many a flye loos.

4303 **volupeer:** nightcap
4305 **at the fulle:** squarely
4306 **pyled:** bald
4307 **Harrow!:** Help!
4309 **greythen hem:** dress

4326 **clawed him on the bak:** scratched his back (he so enjoyed the tale it seemed as if the Reeve were scratching his back)
4328–29 **conclusion Upon his argument:** proposition derived from disputation
4332 **herberwynge:** providing lodging
4333 **avysed for to be:** to take heed
4336 **Hogge of Ware:** Roger of Ware (a town in Hertfordshire, some thirty miles from London)
4337 **yset a-werk:** tricked (cf. III.215)

4311 **cake:** loaf
4316 **bette:** beat
4320 One who does evil should not (literally, need not) expect good.
4321 **gylour:** deceiver
4324 **quyt:** repaid

4340 **vouche-sauf:** grant, agree
4344 **graunte it thee:** agree
4346 **pastee:** meat pie   **laten blood:** let blood (draw off the gravy from unsold pies to make them keep longer)
4347 **Jakke of Dovere:** a kind of pie
4349 **Cristes curs:** damnation
4350 **percely:** parsley
4351 **stubbel goos:** fat goose that had been fed on stubble

Now telle on, gentil Roger by thy name.
But yet I pray thee, be nat wroth for game;
A man may seye ful sooth in game and pley."
   "Thou seist ful sooth," quod Roger, "by my
      fey!   4356
But 'sooth pley, quaad pley,' as the Flemyng
      seith.

And therfore, Herry Bailly, by thy feith,
Be thou nat wrooth, er we departen heer,
Though that my tale be of an hostileer.   4360
But nathelees I wol nat telle it yit;
But er we parte, ywis, thou shalt be quit."
And therwithal he lough and made cheere,
And seyde his tale, as ye shul after heere.

THE COOK'S TALE

Heere bigynneth the Cookes Tale.

A prentys whilom dwelled in oure citee,
And of a craft of vitailliers was hee.   4366
Gaillard he was as goldfynch in the shawe,
Broun as a berye, a propre short felawe,
With lokkes blake, ykembd ful fetisly.
Dauncen he koude so wel and jolily   4370
That he was cleped Perkyn Revelour.
He was as ful of love and paramour
As is the hyve ful of hony sweete;
Wel was the wenche with hym myghte meete.
At every bridale wolde he synge and
      hoppe;   4375
He loved bet the taverne than the shoppe.
For whan ther any ridyng was in Chepe,
Out of the shoppe thider wolde he lepe —
Til that he hadde al the sighte yseyn,
And daunced wel, he wolde nat come ayeyn —
And gadered hym a meynee of his sort   4381
To hoppe and synge and maken swich disport;
And ther they setten stevene for to meete,
To pleyen at the dys in swich a streete.
For in the toune nas ther no prentys   4385
That fairer koude caste a paire of dys
Than Perkyn koude, and therto he was free
Of his dispense, in place of pryvetee.
That fond his maister wel in his chaffare,

For often tyme he foond his box ful bare.
For sikerly a prentys revelour   4391
That haunteth dys, riot, or paramour,
His maister shal it in his shoppe abye,
Al have he no part of the mynstralcye.
For thefte and riot, they been convertible,
Al konne he pleye on gyterne or ribible.   4396
Revel and trouthe, as in a lowe degree,
They been ful wrothe al day, as men may see.
   This joly prentys with his maister bood,
Til he were ny out of his prentishood,   4400
Al were he snybbed bothe erly and late,
And somtyme lad with revel to Newegate.
But atte laste his maister hym bithoghte,
Upon a day, whan he his papir soghte,
Of a proverbe that seith this same word: 4405
"Wel bet is roten appul out of hoord
Than that it rotie al the remenaunt."
So fareth it by a riotous servaunt;

4357 **sooth pley, quaad pley:** A true jest is a bad jest.

4365 **prentys:** apprentice
4366 **vitailliers:** victuallers, sellers of food
4367 **Gaillard:** merry   **shawe:** wood, thicket
4368 **Broun as a berye:** very dark-complexioned
4372 **paramour:** wenching
4375 **bridale:** wedding party   **hoppe:** dance
4377 **ridyng:** procession, equestrian display   **Chepe:** Cheapside
4381 **meynee:** company
4383 **setten stevene:** made an appointment
4388 **place of pryvetee:** a private place
4389 **chaffare:** business

4360 **hostileer:** innkeeper
4363 **lough:** laughed

4390 **box:** strongbox
4391 **revelour:** reveller, profligate
4392 **haunteth:** makes a habit of   **dys:** dicing, gambling   **riot:** debauchery   **paramour:** womanizing
4393 **abye:** pay for
4394 **he:** the master   **mynstralcye:** entertainment (for which he pays)
4395 **convertible:** interchangeable
4396 Even though he knows how to play a cithern (*gyterne*) or fiddle (*ribible*, rebeck)
4397–98 Revelling and honesty, in a man of low rank, are always angry (i.e., incompatible) with each other.
4399 **bood:** remained
4400 **prentishood:** apprenticeship
4401 **snybbed:** rebuked
4402 **Newegate:** Newgate prison
4404 **he:** Perkyn   **papir:** probably his written certificate of release
4407 **rotie:** rot
4408 **by:** with respect to, with   **riotous:** dissolute

It is ful lasse harm to lete hym pace,   4409
Than he shende alle the servantz in the place.
Therfore his maister yaf hym acquitance,
And bad hym go, with sorwe and with mes-
        chance!
And thus this joly prentys hadde his leve.
Now lat hym riote al the nyght or leve.   4414
And for ther is no theef withoute a lowke,

That helpeth hym to wasten and to sowke
Of that he brybe kan or borwe may,
Anon he sente his bed and his array
Unto a compeer of his owene sort,
That lovede dys, and revel, and disport,   4420
And hadde a wyf that heeld for contenance
A shoppe, and swyved for hir sustenance.

4409 **pace:** go away
4410 **shende:** corrupt
4412 **meschance:** bad luck to him
4413 **leve:** permission to leave
4414 **riote:** revel, engage in debauchery
4415 There is no thief without an accomplice (*lowke*).

4416 **sowke:** suck (expend)
4417 **brybe:** steal
4419 **compeer:** companion
4421 **contenance:** the sake of appearances
4422 **swyved for hir sustenance:** copulated for a living

INTRODUCTION TO THE MAN OF LAW'S TALE

The wordes of the Hoost to the compaignye.

Oure Hooste saugh wel that the brighte
    sonne
The ark of his artificial day hath ronne
The ferthe part, and half an houre and moore,
And though he were nat depe ystert in loore,
He wiste it was the eightetethe day   5
Of Aprill, that is messager to May;
And saugh wel that the shadwe of every tree
Was as in lengthe the same quantitee
That was the body erect that caused it.
And therfore by the shadwe he took his wit   10
That Phebus, which that shoon so clere and
    brighte,
Degrees was fyve and fourty clombe on highte,
And for that day, as in that latitude,
It was ten of the clokke, he gan conclude,
And sodeynly he plighte his hors aboute.   15
    "Lordynges," quod he, "I warne yow, al this
    route,
The fourthe party of this day is gon.
Now for the love of God and of Seint John,
Leseth no tyme, as ferforth as ye may.   19
Lordynges, the tyme wasteth nyght and day,
And steleth from us, what pryvely slepynge,
And what thurgh necligence in oure wakynge,
As dooth the streem that turneth nevere agayn,
Descendynge fro the montaigne into playn.
Wel kan Senec and many a philosophre   25
Biwaillen tyme moore than gold in cofre;
For 'Los of catel may recovered be,
But los of tyme shendeth us,' quod he.
It wol nat come agayn, withouten drede,   29
Namoore than wole Malkynes maydenhede,

Whan she hath lost it in hir wantownesse.
Lat us nat mowlen thus in ydelnesse.
    "Sire Man of Lawe," quod he, "so have ye
    blis,
Telle us a tale anon, as forward is.   34
Ye been submytted, thurgh youre free assent,
To stonden in this cas at my juggement.
Acquiteth yow now of youre biheeste;
Thanne have ye do youre devoir atte leeste."
    "Hooste," quod he, "*depardieux,* ich assente;
To breke forward is nat myn entente.   40
Biheste is dette, and I wole holde fayn
Al my biheste, I kan no bettre sayn.
For swich lawe as a man yeveth another wight,
He sholde hymselven usen it, by right;
Thus wole oure text. But nathelees, certeyn,
I kan right now no thrifty tale seyn   46
That Chaucer, thogh he kan but lewedly
On metres and on rymyng craftily,
Hath seyd hem in swich Englissh as he kan
Of olde tyme, as knoweth many a man;   50
And if he have noght seyd hem, leve brother,
In o book, he hath seyd hem in another.
For he hath toold of loveris up and doun
Mo than Ovide made of mencioun
In his Episteles, that been ful olde.   55
What sholde I tellen hem, syn they been tolde?
    "In youthe he made of Ceys and Alcione,
And sitthen hath he spoken of everichone,
Thise noble wyves and thise loveris eke.
Whoso that wole his large volume seke,   60

---

2 **ark of his artificial day:** the time the sun is above the horizon; see n. for the Host's calculation of time.
3 **ferthe:** fourth
4 **depe ystert in loore:** far advanced in learning
5 **eightetethe:** eighteenth; see textual notes
10 **took his wit:** judged
11 **Phebus:** the sun
12 **was . . . clombe:** had climbed
15 **plighte:** pulled
17 **party:** part
19 **as ferforth as:** insofar as
21 **what:** what with
28 **shendeth:** ruins
29 **drede:** doubt
30 **Malkynes maydenhede:** Malkin's virginity

32 **mowlen:** grow moldy
37 **Acquiteth yow . . . of:** acquit yourself of (fulfill) **biheeste:** promise
38 **devoir:** duty
39 **depardieux:** in God's name
41 **Biheste is dette:** A promise is an obligation
45 **wole:** says
46 **thrifty:** suitable
47–8 **kan but lewedly On:** knows little about
49 **Hath** = *nath,* has not; see n.
50 **Of olde tyme:** long ago
54 **made of mencioun:** made mention of
55 **Episteles:** Ovid's *Heroides*
57 **made of Ceys and Alcione:** wrote about Ceyx and Alcion; see BD 62–220.
59 **eke:** also
60 **seke:** examine

Cleped the Seintes Legende of Cupide,
Ther may he seen the large woundes wyde
Of Lucresse, and of Babilan Tesbee;
The swerd of Dido for the false Enee;
The tree of Phillis for hire Demophon;   65
The pleinte of Dianire and of Hermyon,
Of Adriane, and of Isiphilee —
The bareyne yle stondynge in the see —
The dreynte Leandre for his Erro;
The teeris of Eleyne, and eek the wo   70
Of Brixseyde, and of the, Ladomya;
The crueltee of the, queene Medea,
Thy litel children hangynge by the hals,
For thy Jason, that was of love so fals!
O Ypermystra, Penelopee, Alceste,   75
Youre wifhod he comendeth with the beste!
    "But certeinly no word ne writeth he
Of thilke wikke ensample of Canacee,
That loved hir owene brother synfully —
Of swiche cursed stories I sey fy! —   80
Or ellis of Tyro Appollonius,
How that the cursed kyng Antiochus
Birafte his doghter of hir maydenhede,
That is so horrible a tale for to rede,
Whan he hir threw upon the pavement.   85
And therfore he, of ful avysement,
Nolde nevere write in none of his sermons
Of swiche unkynde abhomynacions,
Ne I wol noon reherce, if that I may.
    "But of my tale how shal I doon this day?   90
Me were looth be likned, doutelees,
To Muses that men clepe Pierides —
Methamorphosios woot what I mene;
But nathelees, I recche noght a bene
Though I come after hym with hawebake.   95
I speke in prose, and lat him rymes make."

And with that word he, with a sobre cheere,
Bigan his tale, as ye shal after heere.

The prologe of the Mannes Tale of Lawe.

O hateful harm, condicion of poverte!   99
With thurst, with coold, with hunger so con-
        foundid!
To asken help thee shameth in thyn herte;
If thou noon aske, with nede artow so woundid
That verray nede unwrappeth al thy wounde
        hid!
Maugree thyn heed, thou most for indigence
Or stele, or begge, or borwe thy despence!   105

Thow blamest Crist and seist ful bitterly
He mysdeparteth richesse temporal;
Thy neighebor thou wytest synfully,
And seist thou hast to lite and he hath al.   109
"Parfay," seistow, "somtyme he rekene shal,
Whan that his tayl shal brennen in the gleede,
For he noght helpeth needfulle in hir neede."

    Herkne what is the sentence of the wise:
"Bet is to dyen than have indigence";
"Thy selve neighebor wol thee despise."   115
If thou be povre, farwel thy reverence!
Yet of the wise man take this sentence:
"Alle the dayes of povre men been wikke."
Be war, therfore, er thou come to that prikke!

If thou be povre, thy brother hateth thee,   120
And alle thy freendes fleen from thee, allas!
O riche marchauntz, ful of wele been yee,
O noble, o prudent folk, as in this cas!
Youre bagges been nat fild with ambes as,
But with sys cynk, that renneth for youre
        chaunce;
At Cristemasse myrie may ye daunce!   126

---

61 **the Seintes Legende of Cupide:** the Legend of Good Women
63 **Lucresse, and of Babilan Tesbee:** Lucretia, Thisbe of Babylon; see LGW for the stories of the women listed in lines 63–76, except for *Dianire* (Deianira; see MkT VII.2119–35), *Hermyon* (Hermione, the lover of Orestes), *Erro* (Hero, the lover of *Leandre,* Leander), *Eleyne* (Helen of Troy), *Brixseyde* (Briseyde, the lover of Achilles; see HF 398), *Ladomya* (Laodomia, who killed herself on the death of her husband Protesilaus), and *Penelopee* (Penelope, faithful wife of Ulysses).
66 **pleinte:** complaint, lament
68 **bareyne:** barren
69 **dreynte:** drowned
73 **hals:** neck
76 **wifhod:** fidelity as a wife
78 **Canacee:** heroine of a tale of incest told by Gower; see n.
81 **Tyro Appollonius:** Apollonius of Tyre, hero of a popular story, also involving incest, told in Gower's *Confessio Amantis*
83 **Birafte:** deprived
86 **of ful avysement:** after careful consideration
88 **unkynde:** unnatural
91 **Me were looth:** I would hate
92 **Pierides:** the Muses; see n.
93 **Methamorphosios:** Ovid's *Metamorphoses*
94 **recche noght a bene:** don't care a bean
95 **hawebake:** baked hawthorn berries (a poor dish)

97 **a sobre cheere:** a solemn expression
99 **harm:** misfortune
100 **confoundid:** distressed
103 **unwrappeth:** discloses
104 **Maugree thyn heed:** against your will, despite all you can do
105 **Or . . . or:** either . . . or   **despence:** living expenses
107 **mysdeparteth:** wrongly allots
108 **wytest:** accuse
109 **to lite:** too little
110 **Parfay:** by my faith   **rekene:** take account (of it)
111 **brennen in the gleede:** burn in the live coals
112 **needfulle:** the needy
115 **selve:** very
116 **reverence:** respect (that others show you)
118 **wikke:** miserable
119 **prikke:** point
124 **ambes as:** two ones, a losing throw in dice
125 **sys cynk:** six and five, a winning throw   **renneth for youre chaunce:** runs in favor of your luck (*chaunce* = winning number)

Ye seken lond and see for yowre wynnynges;
As wise folk ye knowen al th'estaat
Of regnes; ye been fadres of tidynges
And tales, bothe of pees and of debaat.   130

I were right now of tales desolaat,
Nere that a marchant, goon is many a yeere,
Me taughte a tale, which that ye shal heere.

THE MAN OF LAW'S TALE

Heere begynneth the Man of Lawe his tale.

In Surrye whilom dwelte a compaignye
Of chapmen riche, and therto sadde and trewe,
That wyde-where senten hir spicerye,   136
Clothes of gold, and satyns riche of hewe.
Hir chaffare was so thrifty and so newe
That every wight hath deyntee to chaffare
With hem, and eek to sellen hem hire ware.

Now fil it that the maistres of that sort   141
Han shapen hem to Rome for to wende;
Were it for chapmanhod or for disport,
Noon oother message wolde they thider sende,
But comen hemself to Rome; this is the ende.
And in swich place as thoughte hem avantage
For hire entente, they take hir herbergage.   147

Sojourned han thise merchantz in that toun
A certein tyme, as fil to hire plesance.
And so bifel that th'excellent renoun   150
Of the Emperoures doghter, dame Custance,
Reported was, with every circumstance,
Unto thise Surryen marchantz in swich wyse,
Fro day to day, as I shal yow devyse.   154

This was the commune voys of every man:
"Oure Emperour of Rome — God hym see! —

A doghter hath that, syn the world bigan,
To rekene as wel hir goodnesse as beautee,
Nas nevere swich another as is shee.
I prey to God in honour hire susteene,   160
And wolde she were of al Europe the queene.

"In hire is heigh beautee, withoute pride,
Yowthe, withoute grenehede or folye;
To alle hire werkes vertu is hir gyde;
Humblesse hath slayn in hire al tirannye.   165
She is mirour of alle curteisye;
Hir herte is verray chambre of hoolynesse,
Hir hand, ministre of fredam for almesse."

And al this voys was sooth, as God is trewe.
But now to purpos lat us turne agayn.   170
Thise marchantz han doon fraught hir shippes
                newe,
And whan they han this blisful mayden sayn,
Hoom to Surrye been they went ful fayn,
And doon hir nedes as they han doon yoore,
And lyven in wele; I kan sey yow namoore.   175

Now fil it that thise marchantz stode in grace
Of hym that was the Sowdan of Surrye;
For whan they cam from any strange place,
He wolde, of his benigne curteisye,
Make hem good chiere, and bisily espye   180

130 **debaat:** conflict

134 **Surrye:** Syria
135 **chapmen:** merchants **sadde:** trustworthy
136 **wyde-where:** far and wide **spicerye:** oriental goods
(spices, cloths, and such)
138 **chaffare:** merchandise **thrifty:** serviceable
139 **hath deyntee to chaffare:** is eager to do business
140 **ware:** wares
142 **shapen hem:** arranged
143 **chapmanhod:** business dealings **disport:** amusement
144 **message:** messenger
146 **avantage:** advantageous
147 **herbergage:** lodging
148 **Sojourned:** remained
149 **fil to hire plesance:** accorded with their desires
152 **circumstance:** detail
155 **voys:** opinion
156 **God hym see:** may God look after him

131 **of tales desolaat:** lacking in tales
132 **Nere** = *ne were,* were (it) not

160 **susteene:** sustain
163 **grenehede:** immaturity
168 **fredam for almesse:** generosity in giving alms
169 **voys:** report
170 **to purpos:** to the point
171 **han doon fraught:** have had loaded **newe:** anew
172 **sayn:** seen
174 **doon hir nedes:** conducted their business **yoore:** formerly
176 **grace:** the good graces
177 **Sowdan:** sultan
178 **strange:** foreign
179 **benigne:** gracious

Tidynges of sondry regnes, for to leere
The wondres that they myghte seen or heere.

Amonges othere thynges, specially,
Thise marchantz han hym toold of dame Cus-
        tance
So greet noblesse in ernest, ceriously,   185
That this Sowdan hath caught so greet plesance
To han hir figure in his remembrance,
That al his lust and al his bisy cure
Was for to love hire while his lyf may dure.

Paraventure in thilke large book   190
Which that men clepe the hevene ywriten was
With sterres, whan that he his birthe took,
That he for love sholde han his deeth, allas!
For in the sterres, clerer than is glas,
Is writen, God woot, whoso koude it rede,   195
The deeth of every man, withouten drede.

In sterres, many a wynter therbiforn,
Was writen the deeth of Ector, Achilles,
Of Pompei, Julius, er they were born;
The strif of Thebes; and of Ercules,   200
Of Sampson, Turnus, and of Socrates
The deeth; but mennes wittes ben so dulle
That no wight kan wel rede it atte fulle.

  This Sowdan for his privee conseil sente,
And, shortly of this matiere for to pace,   205
He hath to hem declared his entente,
And seyde hem, certein, but he myghte have
        grace
To han Custance withinne a litel space,
He nas but deed; and charged hem in hye
To shapen for his lyf som remedye.   210

  Diverse men diverse thynges seyden;
They argumenten, casten up and doun;

Many a subtil resoun forth they leyden;
They speken of magyk and abusioun.
But finally, as in conclusioun,   215
They kan nat seen in that noon avantage,
Ne in noon oother wey, save mariage.

Thanne sawe they therinne swich difficultee
By wey of reson, for to speke al playn,
By cause that ther was swich diversitee   220
Bitwene hir bothe lawes, that they sayn
They trowe that no "Cristen prince wolde fayn
Wedden his child under oure lawe sweete
That us was taught by Mahoun, oure prophete."

  And he answerde, "Rather than I lese   225
Custance, I wol be cristned, doutelees.
I moot been hires; I may noon oother chese.
I prey yow hoold youre argumentz in pees;
Saveth my lyf, and beth noght recchelees
To geten hire that hath my lyf in cure,   230
For in this wo I may nat longe endure."

  What nedeth gretter dilatacioun?
I seye, by tretys and embassadrie,
And by the popes mediacioun,
And al the chirche, and al the chivalrie,   235
That in destruccioun of mawmettrie,
And in encrees of Cristes lawe deere,
They been acorded, so as ye shal heere:

How that the Sowdan and his baronage
And alle his liges sholde ycristned be,   240
And he shal han Custance in mariage,
And certein gold, I noot what quantitee;
And heer-to founden sufficient suretee.
This same accord was sworn on eyther syde;
Now, faire Custance, almyghty God thee gyde!

  Now wolde som men waiten, as I gesse,   246
That I sholde tellen al the purveiance
That th'Emperour, of his grete noblesse,
Hath shapen for his doghter, dame Custance.
Wel may men knowen that so greet ordinance
May no man tellen in a litel clause   251

181 **sondry:** various **leere:** learn
185 **ceriously:** in detail
186 **plesance:** desire
187 **figure:** image
188 **lust:** pleasure **bisy cure:** intent concern
190 **Paraventure:** perhaps
195 **rede:** interpret
198 **Ector, Achilles:** Hector and Achilles, the Greek heroes
199 **Pompei, Julius:** Pompey the Great, Julius Caesar; see MkT
VII.2671–2726.
200 **strif of Thebes:** the siege of Thebes, told in part in Tr
5.1457–1512 **Ercules:** Hercules; see MkT VII.2095–2142.
201 **Sampson:** the biblical hero; see MkT VII.2015–94.
Turnus: opponent of Aeneas; see HF 457–58. **Socrates:** the
philosopher; see Bo 1.pr3.26–28.
204 **privee conseil:** privy council, confidential advisors
205 **pace:** pass over
208 **space:** time
209 **nas but deed:** was as good as dead **charged:** commanded
in hye: in haste
212 **casten up and doun:** consider alternatives

214 **abusioun:** deception
221 **hir bothe lawes:** religions of both parties
222 **trowe:** suppose, judge
224 **Mahoun:** Mohammed
229 **recchelees:** negligent
230 **in cure:** in her keeping
232 **dilatacioun:** increase of words
233 **tretys:** treaty **embassadrie:** negociation
235 **chivalrie:** knights
236 **mawmettrie:** idolatry
243 **heer-to founden:** for this provided
246 **waiten:** expect
247 **purveiance:** preparations
250 **ordinance:** preparations

As was arrayed for so heigh a cause.
Bisshopes been shapen with hire for to wende,
Lordes, ladies, knyghtes of renoun,
And oother folk ynowe; this is th'ende;   255
And notified is thurghout the toun
That every wight, with greet devocioun,
Sholde preyen Crist that he this mariage
Receyve in gree and spede this viage.

The day is comen of hir departynge;   260
I seye, the woful day fatal is come,
That ther may be no lenger tariynge,
But forthward they hem dressen, alle and some.
Custance, that was with sorwe al overcome,
Ful pale arist, and dresseth hire to wende;   265
For wel she seeth ther is noon oother ende.

Allas, what wonder is it thogh she wepte,
That shal be sent to strange nacioun
Fro freendes that so tendrely hire kepte,
And to be bounden under subjeccioun   270
Of oon, she knoweth nat his condicioun?
Housbondes been alle goode, and han ben
        yoore;
That knowen wyves; I dar sey yow na moore.

"Fader," she seyde, "thy wrecched child
        Custance,
Thy yonge doghter fostred up so softe,   275
And ye, my mooder, my soverayn plesance
Over alle thyng, out-taken Crist on-lofte,
Custance youre child hire recomandeth ofte
Unto youre grace, for I shal to Surrye,
Ne shal I nevere seen yow moore with ye.   280

"Allas, unto the Barbre nacioun
I moste anoon, syn that it is youre wille;
But Crist, that starf for our redempcioun
So yeve me grace his heestes to fulfille!   284
I, wrecche womman, no fors though I spille!
Wommen are born to thraldom and penance,
And to been under mannes governance."

I trowe at Troye, whan Pirrus brak the wal
Or Ilion brende, at Thebes the citee,
N'at Rome, for the harm thurgh Hanybal   290
That Romayns hath venquysshed tymes thre,
Nas herd swich tendre wepyng for pitee
As in the chambre was for hire departynge;
But forth she moot, wher-so she wepe or synge.

O firste moevyng! Crueel firmament,   295
With thy diurnal sweigh that crowdest ay
And hurlest al from est til occident
That naturelly wolde holde another way,
Thy crowdyng set the hevene in swich array
At the bigynnyng of this fiers viage,   300
That crueel Mars hath slayn this mariage.

Infortunat ascendent tortuous,
Of which the lord is helplees falle, allas,
Out of his angle into the derkeste hous!
O Mars, o atazir, as in this cas!   305
O fieble moone, unhappy been thy paas!
Thou knyttest thee ther thou art nat receyved;
Ther thou were weel, fro thennes artow
        weyved.

Imprudent Emperour of Rome, allas!
Was ther no philosophre in al thy toun?   310
Is no tyme bet than oother in swich cas?
Of viage is ther noon eleccioun,
Namely to folk of heigh condicioun?
Noght whan a roote is of a burthe yknowe?
Allas, we been to lewed or to slowe!   315

288 **Pirrus:** Pyrrhus, one of the Greek warriors at Troy
289 **Or:** ere   **Ilion:** the citadel of Troy   **Thebes:** destroyed in a siege
290 **Hanybal:** Hannibal, the Carthaginian general who attacked Rome
294 **wher-so:** whether
295 **firste moevyng:** primum mobile, the outermost of the nine heavenly spheres; see n.
296 **diurnal sweigh:** daily motion   **crowdest:** pushes
297 **est til occident:** east to west
298 The stars are naturally inclined to move from west to east (see n. for the astronomical details).
299 **array:** arrangement
300 **fiers:** dangerous
302–8 According to the theory of judicial astronomy, at the time of Custance's departure the position of the heavenly bodies was unfavorable, especially because of the evil influence of Mars. See n. for a detailed analysis of the technical vocabulary.
302 **Infortunat ascendent tortuous:** inauspicious oblique ascending sign; see Astr 2.4 and 2.28.
303 **lord:** the "lord of the ascendent" (see Astr 2.4.44–56)
304 **angle:** a "house" at one of the cardinal compass points
305 **atazir:** the dominant planetary influence
306 **unhappy:** unfortunate   **paas:** steps
307 You move into conjunction (*knyttest thee*) where you are not welcomed (by an auspicious planet).
308 **weyved:** banished
310 **philosophre:** astrologer
312 **eleccioun:** choice of an astrologically favorable time
313 **condicioun:** social position
314 **roote . . . of a burthe:** exact time of birth, which provides a date (*roote*) from which an astrological calculation can be made

256 **notified:** made known
259 **in gree:** favorably
263 **hem dressen:** prepare themselves   **alle and some:** one and all
265 **arist** = *ariseth*, arises
271 **condicioun:** disposition
272 **yoore:** long since
275 **softe:** tenderly
277 **out-taken:** except   **on-lofte:** on high
278 **hire recomandeth:** commends herself
279 **shal:** must go (the verb of motion is understood)
281 **Barbre nacioun:** pagan world
282 **moste:** must go
283 **starf:** died
285 **wrecche:** exiled   **no fors:** no matter   **spille:** die
286 **penance:** suffering
287 **governance:** control

To shippe is brought this woful faire mayde
Solempnely, with every circumstance.
"Now Jhesu Crist be with yow alle!" she sayde;
Ther nys namoore, but "Farewel, faire Cus-
    tance!"
She peyneth hire to make good contenance;
And forth I lete hire saille in this manere,   321
And turne I wole agayn to my matere.

    The mooder of the Sowdan, welle of vices,
Espied hath hir sones pleyn entente,
How he wol lete his olde sacrifices;   325
And right anon she for hir conseil sente,
And they been come to knowe what she mente.
And whan assembled was this folk in-feere,
She sette hire doun, and seyde as ye shal heere.

    "Lordes," quod she, "ye knowen everichon,
How that my sone in point is for to lete   331
The hooly lawes of our Alkaron,
Yeven by Goddes message Makomete.
But oon avow to grete God I heete,
The lyf shal rather out of my body sterte   335
Or Makometes lawe out of myn herte!

    "What sholde us tyden of this newe lawe
But thraldom to oure bodies and penance,
And afterward in helle to be drawe,
For we reneyed Mahoun oure creance?   340
But, lordes, wol ye maken assurance,
As I shal seyn, assentynge to my loore,
And I shal make us sauf for everemoore?"

    They sworen and assenten, every man,
To lyve with hire and dye, and by hire stonde,
And everich, in the beste wise he kan,   346
To strengthen hire shal alle his frendes fonde;
And she hath this emprise ytake on honde,
Which ye shal heren that I shal devyse,   349
And to hem alle she spak right in this wyse:

"We shul first feyne us cristendom to take —
Coold water shal nat greve us but a lite! —
And I shal swich a feeste and revel make
That, as I trowe, I shal the Sowdan quite.   354
For thogh his wyf be cristned never so white,
She shal have nede to wasshe awey the rede,
Thogh she a font-ful water with hire lede."

O Sowdanesse, roote of iniquitee!
Virago, thou Semyrame the secounde!
O serpent under femynynytee,   360
Lik to the serpent depe in helle ybounde!
O feyned womman, al that may confounde
Vertu and innocence, thurgh thy malice,
Is bred in thee, as nest of every vice!

O Sathan, envious syn thilke day   365
That thou were chaced from oure heritage,
Wel knowestow to wommen the olde way!
Thou madest Eva brynge us in servage;
Thou wolt fordoon this Cristen mariage.   369
Thyn instrument so — weylawey the while! —
Makestow of wommen, whan thou wolt bigile.

    This Sowdanesse, whom I thus blame and
        warye,
Leet prively hire conseil goon hire way.
What sholde I in this tale lenger tarye?
She rydeth to the Sowdan on a day,   375
And seyde hym that she wolde reneye hir lay,
And cristendom of preestes handes fonge,
Repentynge hire she hethen was so longe,

Bisechynge hym to doon hire that honour,
That she moste han the Cristen folk to
        feeste —   380
"To plesen hem I wol do my labour."
The Sowdan seith, "I wol doon at youre heeste,"
And knelynge thanketh hire of that requeste.
So glad he was, he nyste what to seye.
She kiste hir sone, and hoom she gooth hir
        weye.   385

Explicit prima pars.

317 **circumstance:** ceremony
320 **peyneth hire:** takes pains
325 **lete:** abandon
328 **in-feere:** together
331 **in point . . . for to lete:** on the point of leaving, forsaking
332 **Alkaron:** the Koran
333 **message:** messenger **Makomete:** Mohammed
334 **heete:** promise
336 **Or:** before
337 **tyden:** happen to
340 **reneyed:** renounced **creance:** belief
341 **maken assurance:** pledge
342 **loore:** teaching, advice
343 **sauf:** safe
346 **wise:** way
347 **fonde:** try (i.e., persuade to support her)
348 **emprise:** enterprise

351 **feyne us:** feign
357 **font-ful:** baptismal font full of **lede:** bring
359 **Virago:** woman usurping man's office; see n. **Semyrame:**
Semiramus, a queen famed for her wickedness
360 **under femynynytee:** in a female form
361 **serpent:** Satan
362 **confounde:** destroy
369 **fordoon:** destroy
372 **warye:** curse
376 **reneye:** renounce **lay:** religion
377 **fonge:** receive
381 **do my labour:** make an effort
382 **doon at youre heeste:** act according to your command
Explicit, *etc.*: Here ends the first part.

Sequitur pars secunda.

Arryved been this Cristen folk to londe
In Surrye, with a greet solempne route,
And hastifliche this Sowdan sente his sonde
First to his mooder, and al the regne aboute,
And seyde his wyf was comen, out of doute,
And preyde hire for to ryde agayn the queene,
The honour of his regne to susteene.   392

Greet was the prees, and riche was th'array
Of Surryens and Romayns met yfeere;
The mooder of the Sowdan, riche and gay, 395
Receyveth hire with also glad a cheere
As any mooder myghte hir doghter deere,
And to the nexte citee ther bisyde
A softe paas solempnely they ryde.

Noght trowe I the triumphe of Julius,   400
Of which that Lucan maketh swich a boost,
Was roialler ne moore curius
Than was th'assemblee of this blisful hoost.
But this scorpioun, this wikked goost,
The Sowdanesse, for al hire flaterynge,   405
Caste under this ful mortally to stynge.

The Sowdan comth hymself soone after this
So roially that wonder is to telle,
And welcometh hire with alle joye and blis.
And thus in murthe and joye I lete hem dwelle;
The fruyt of this matiere is that I telle.   411
Whan tyme cam, men thoughte it for the beste
That revel stynte, and men goon to hir reste.

The tyme cam, this olde Sowdanesse   414
Ordeyned hath this feeste of which I tolde,
And to the feeste Cristen folk hem dresse
In general, ye, bothe yonge and olde.
Heere may men feeste and roialtee biholde,
And deyntees mo than I kan yow devyse;
But al to deere they boghte it er they ryse. 420

O sodeyn wo, that evere art successour
To worldly blisse, spreynd with bitternesse,

The ende of the joye of oure worldly labour!
Wo occupieth the fyn of oure gladnesse.
Herke this conseil for thy sikernesse: 425
Upon thy glade day have in thy mynde
The unwar wo or harm that comth bihynde.

For shortly for to tellen, at o word,
The Sowdan and the Cristen everichone
Been al tohewe and stiked at the bord,   430
But it were oonly dame Custance allone.
This olde Sowdanesse, cursed krone,
Hath with hir freendes doon this cursed dede,
For she hirself wolde al the contree lede.

Ne ther was Surryen noon that was converted,
That of the conseil of the Sowdan woot,   436
That he nas al tohewe er he asterted.
And Custance han they take anon, foot-hoot,
And in a ship al steerelees, God woot,
They han hir set, and bidde hire lerne saille
Out of Surrye agaynward to Ytaille.   441

A certein tresor that she thider ladde,
And, sooth to seyn, vitaille greet plentee
They han hire yeven, and clothes eek she
          hadde,
And forth she sailleth in the salte see.   445
O my Custance, ful of benignytee,
O Emperoures yonge doghter deere,
He that is lord of Fortune be thy steere!

She blesseth hire, and with ful pitous voys
Unto the croys of Crist thus seyde she: 450
"O cleere, o welful auter, hooly croys,
Reed of the Lambes blood ful of pitee,
That wessh the world fro the olde iniquitee,
Me fro the feend and fro his clawes kepe,
That day that I shal drenchen in the depe.

Victorious tree, proteccioun of trewe,   456
That oonly worthy were for to bere
The Kyng of Hevene with his woundes newe,
The white Lamb, that hurt was with a spere,

Sequitur, etc.: The second part follows.
388 **sonde**: message
391 **agayn**: toward
393 **prees**: crowd
394 **met yfeere**: met together
399 **A softe paas**: slowly
400 **triumphe**: triumphal procession **Julius**: Julius Caesar
401 **Lucan**: author of the Pharsalia **boost**: boast
402 **curius**: elaborate
404 **goost**: demon
406 **Caste**: planned
411 **fruyt**: essential part
419 **deyntees**: delicacies
420 **al to deere they boghte it**: they paid only too dearly for it
422 **spreynd**: sprinkled

424 **fyn**: end
425 **sikernesse**: safety
427 **unwar**: unexpected
430 **tohewe**: cut to pieces **stiked**: stabbed **bord**: table
431 **But it were**: except for
432 **krone**: hag
437 **asterted**: escaped
438 **foot-hoot**: immediately
439 **steerelees**: without a rudder
441 **agaynward to**: back again to
442 **tresor**: treasure
443 **vitaille**: food
446 **benignytee**: goodness
448 **lord of Fortune**: i.e., God **steere**: rudder, guide
451 **welful auter**: blessed altar
452 **Reed of**: red with
453 **wessh**: washed

Flemere of feendes out of hym and here   460
On which thy lymes feithfully extenden,
Me kepe, and yif me myght my lyf t'amenden.''

Yeres and dayes fleet this creature
Thurghout the See of Grece unto the Strayte
Of Marrok, as it was hire aventure.   465
On many a sory meel now may she bayte;
After hir deeth ful often may she wayte,
Er that the wilde wawes wol hire dryve
Unto the place ther she shal arryve.   469

Men myghten asken why she was nat slayn
Eek at the feeste? Who myghte hir body save?
And I answere to that demande agayn,
Who saved Danyel in the horrible cave
Ther every wight save he, maister and knave,
Was with the leon frete er he asterte?   475
No wight but God that he bar in his herte.

God liste to shewe his wonderful myracle
In hire, for we sholde seen his myghty werkis;
Crist, which that is to every harm triacle,   479
By certeine meenes ofte, as knowen clerkis,
Dooth thyng for certein ende that ful derk is
To mannes wit, that for oure ignorance
Ne konne noght knowe his prudent purveiance.

Now sith she was nat at the feeste yslawe,
Who kepte hire fro the drenchyng in the see?
Who kepte Jonas in the fisshes mawe   486
Til he was spouted up at Nynyvee?
Wel may men knowe it was no wight but he
That kepte peple Ebrayk from hir drenchynge,
With drye feet thurghout the see passynge.

Who bad the foure spirites of tempest   491
That power han t'anoyen lond and see,
Bothe north and south, and also west and est,
''Anoyeth neither see, ne land, ne tree''?
Soothly, the comandour of that was he   495

That fro the tempest ay this womman kepte
As wel whan she wook as whan she slepte.

Where myghte this womman mete and
    drynke have   498
Thre yeer and moore? How lasteth hire vitaille?
Who fedde the Egipcien Marie in the cave,
Or in desert? No wight but Crist, sanz faille.
Fyve thousand folk it was as greet mervaille
With loves fyve and fisshes two to feede.
God sente his foyson at hir grete neede.

She dryveth forth into oure occian   505
Thurghout oure wilde see, til atte laste
Under an hoold that nempnen I ne kan,
Fer in Northhumberlond the wawe hire caste,
And in the sond hir ship stiked so faste
That thennes wolde it noght of al a tyde;   510
The wyl of Crist was that she sholde abyde.

The constable of the castel doun is fare
To seen this wrak, and al the ship he soghte,
And foond this wery womman ful of care;
He foond also the tresor that she broghte.   515
In hir langage mercy she bisoghte,
The lyf out of hir body for to twynne,
Hire to delivere of wo that she was inne.

A maner Latyn corrupt was hir speche,
But algates therby was she understonde.   520
The constable, whan hym lyst no longer seche,
This woful womman broghte he to the londe.
She kneleth doun and thanketh Goddes sonde;
But what she was she wolde no man seye,
For foul ne fair, thogh that she sholde deye.

She seyde she was so mazed in the see   526
That she forgat hir mynde, by hir trouthe.

460–61 Banisher of evil spirits from the man and woman over whom thy limbs faithfully extend (i.e., on whom the sign of the Cross has been made)
463 **fleet** = *fleeteth*, drifts
464 **See of Grece:** the eastern Mediterranean
464–65 **Strayte Of Marrok:** the strait of Gibraltar
466 **bayte:** feed
467 **After:** for
468 **wawes:** waves
472 **demande:** question
475 **frete:** devoured
479 **triacle:** medicine
481 **derk:** mysterious
483 **purveiance:** providence
486 **Jonas:** Jonah
487 **Nynyvee:** Nineveh
489 **peple Ebrayk:** Hebrews
491 **spirites:** angels

500 **Egipcien Marie:** St. Mary the Egyptian
501 **sanz faille:** doubtless
503 **loves:** loaves
504 **foyson:** plenty
505 **occian:** ocean
507 **hoold:** castle   **nempnen:** name
508 **wawe:** wave
509 **stiked:** stuck
510 **of al a tyde:** for the duration of an entire tide
513 **wrak:** wreck   **soghte:** searched
517 **twynne:** separate
519 **Latyn corrupt:** corrupted Latin (?); see n.
520 **algates:** nevertheless
521 **seche:** look about
523 **Goddes sonde:** divine providence (literally, God's sending, what He sends)
525 **For foul ne fair:** under any circumstances
526 **mazed:** bewildered
527 **forgat hir mynde:** lost her memory

The constable hath of hire so greet pitee,
And eek his wyf, that they wepen for routhe.
She was so diligent, withouten slouthe,　　530
To serve and plesen everich in that place
That alle hir loven that looken in hir face.

This constable and dame Hermengyld, his
　　wyf,
Were payens, and that contree everywhere;
But Hermengyld loved hire right as hir lyf,
And Custance hath so longe sojourned there,
In orisons, with many a bitter teere,　　537
Til Jhesu hath converted thurgh his grace
Dame Hermengyld, constablesse of that place.

In al that lond no Cristen dorste route;　　540
Alle Cristen folk been fled fro that contree
Thurgh payens, that conquereden al aboute
The plages of the north, by land and see.
To Walys fledde the Cristyanytee
Of olde Britons dwellynge in this ile;　　545
Ther was hir refut for the meene while.

But yet nere Cristene Britons so exiled
That ther nere somme that in hir privetee
Honoured Crist and hethen folk bigiled,　　549
And ny the castel swiche ther dwelten three.
That oon of hem was blynd and myghte nat see,
But it were with thilke eyen of his mynde
With whiche men seen, after that they ben
　　blynde.

Bright was the sonne as in that someres day,
For which the constable and his wyf also　　555
And Custance han ytake the righte way
Toward the see a furlong wey or two,
To pleyen and to romen to and fro,
And in hir walk this blynde man they mette,
Croked and oold, with eyen faste yshette.　　560

"In name of Crist," cride this blinde Britoun,
"Dame Hermengyld, yif me my sighte agayn!"
This lady weex affrayed of the soun,
Lest that hir housbonde, shortly for to sayn,
Wolde hire for Jhesu Cristes love han slayn,

Til Custance made hire boold, and bad hire
　　wirche　　566
The wyl of Crist, as doghter of his chirche.

The constable weex abasshed of that sight,
And seyde, "What amounteth al this fare?"
Custance answerde, "Sire, it is Cristes myght,
That helpeth folk out of the feendes snare."
And so ferforth she gan oure lay declare　　572
That she the constable, er that it was eve
Converteth, and on Crist made hym bileve.

This constable was nothyng lord of this place
Of which I speke, ther he Custance fond,　　576
But kepte it strongly many a wyntres space
Under Alla, kyng of al Northhumbrelond,
That was ful wys, and worthy of his hond
Agayn the Scottes, as men may wel heere;　　580
But turne I wole agayn to my mateere.

Sathan, that evere us waiteth to bigile,
Saugh of Custance al hire perfeccioun,
And caste anon how he myghte quite hir while,
And made a yong knyght that dwelte in that
　　toun
Love hire so hoote, of foul affeccioun,　　586
That verraily hym thoughte he sholde spille,
But he of hire myghte ones have his wille.

He woweth hire, but it availleth noght;
She wolde do no synne, by no weye.　　590
And for despit he compassed in his thoght
To maken hire on shameful deeth to deye.
He wayteth whan the constable was aweye,
And pryvely upon a nyght he crepte
In Hermengyldes chambre, whil she slepte.

Wery, forwaked in hire orisouns,　　596
Slepeth Custance, and Hermengyld also.
This knyght, thurgh Sathanas temptaciouns,
Al softely is to the bed ygo,
And kitte the throte of Hermengyld atwo,　　600
And leyde the blody knyf by dame Custance,
And wente his wey, ther God yeve hym
　　meschance!

530 **slouthe**: sloth
534 **payens**: pagans
537 **orisons**: prayers
540 **route**: assemble
543 **plages**: coastal regions
544 **Cristyanytee**: Christian community
546 **refut**: refuge
557 **furlong wey**: about an eighth of a mile
563 **weex**: became　**affrayed**: frightened

568 **abasshed**: troubled
569 **fare**: commotion
572 **so ferforth**: to such an extent
579 **worthy of his hond**: brave in battle
582 **waiteth**: seeks an occasion
584 **caste**: plotted　**quite hir while**: repay her
586 **of . . . affeccioun**: with passion
587 **spille**: die
591 **compassed**: plotted
596 Exhausted from lack of sleep because of praying
600 **kitte**: cut　**atwo**: in two

Soone after cometh this constable hoom
  agayn,
And eek Alla, that kyng was of that lond,
And saugh his wyf despitously yslayn,   605
For which ful ofte he weep and wroong his
  hond,
And in the bed the blody knyf he fond
By Dame Custance. Allas, what myghte she
  seye?
For verray wo hir wit was al aweye.   609

    To kyng Alla was toold al this meschance,
And eek the tyme, and where, and in what wise
That in a ship was founden this Custance,
As heer-biforn that ye han herd devyse.
The kynges herte of pitee gan agryse,
Whan he saugh so benigne a creature   615
Falle in disese and in mysaventure.

For as the lomb toward his deeth is broght,
So stant this innocent bifore the kyng.
This false knyght, that hath this tresoun
  wroght,
Berth hire on hond that she hath doon thys
  thyng.   620
But nathelees, ther was greet moornyng
Among the peple, and seyn they kan nat gesse
That she had doon so greet a wikkednesse,

For they han seyn hire evere so vertuous,
And lovynge Hermengyld right as hir lyf.   625
Of this baar witnesse everich in that hous,
Save he that Hermengyld slow with his knyf.
This gentil kyng hath caught a greet motyf
Of this witnesse, and thoghte he wolde enquere
Depper in this, a trouthe for to lere.   630

    Allas! Custance, thou hast no champioun,
Ne fighte kanstow noght, so weylaway!
But he that starf for our redempcioun,
And boond Sathan (and yet lith ther he lay),
So be thy stronge champion this day!   635

For, but if Crist open myracle kithe,
Withouten gilt thou shalt be slayn as swithe.

She sette hire doun on knees, and thus she
  sayde:
"Immortal God, that savedest Susanne
Fro false blame, and thou, merciful mayde,
Marie I meene, doghter to Seint Anne,   641
Bifore whos child angeles synge Osanne,
If I be giltlees of this felonye,
My socour be, for ellis shal I dye!"

    Have ye nat seyn somtyme a pale face,   645
Among a prees, of hym that hath be lad
Toward his deeth, wher as hym gat no grace,
And swich a colour in his face hath had
Men myghte knowe his face that was bistad
Amonges alle the faces in that route?   650
So stant Custance, and looketh hire aboute.

    O queenes, lyvynge in prosperitee,
Duchesses, and ye ladyes everichone,
Haveth som routhe on hire adversitee!
An Emperoures doghter stant allone;   655
She hath no wight to whom to make hir mone.
O blood roial, that stondest in this drede,
Fer been thy freendes at thy grete nede!

    This Alla kyng hath swich compassioun,
As gentil herte is fulfild of pitee,   660
That from his eyen ran the water doun.
"Now hastily do fecche a book," quod he,
"And if this knyght wol sweren how that she
This womman slow, yet wol we us avyse   664
Whom that we wole that shal been oure
  justise."

A Britoun book, written with Evaungiles,
Was fet, and on this book he swoor anoon
She gilty was, and in the meene whiles
An hand hym smoot upon the nekke-boon,
That doun he fil atones as a stoon,   670

605 **despitously:** cruelly
613 **herd devyse:** heard tell
614 **gan agryse:** trembled
616 **disese:** distress
618 **stant** = *stondith,* stands
620 **Berth hire on hond:** accuses her falsely
622 **seyn:** seen
627 **slow:** slew
628 **caught a greet motyf:** was deeply moved
630 **Depper:** more deeply **lere:** learn
631 **champioun:** champion, representative in a judicial duel
633 **starf:** died

636 **kithe:** reveal
637 **Withouten gilt:** guiltless **as swithe:** immediately
639 **Susanne:** Susannah (falsely accused by the Elders in the apocryphal Book of Susannah)
641 **Seint Anne:** the mother of the Virgin
642 **Osanne:** Hosanna
646 **prees:** crowd
649 **bistad:** in trouble
656 **make hir mone:** lament
658 **Fer:** far away
662 **do fecche a book:** have a book brought
664 **us avyse:** think over carefully
667 **fet:** fetched

And bothe his eyen broste out of his face
In sighte of every body in that place.

A voys was herd in general audience,
And seyde, "Thou hast desclaundred, giltelees,
The doghter of hooly chirche in heigh pres-
          ence;   675
Thus hastou doon, and yet holde I my pees!"
Of this mervaille agast was al the prees;
As mazed folk they stoden everichone,
For drede of wreche, save Custance allone.

Greet was the drede and eek the repentance
Of hem that hadden wrong suspecioun   681
Upon this sely innocent, Custance;
And for this miracle, in conclusioun,
And by Custances mediacioun,   684
The kyng — and many another in that place —
Converted was, thanked be Cristes grace!

This false knyght was slayn for his untrouthe
By juggement of Alla hastifly;
And yet Custance hadde of his deeth greet
          routhe.
And after this Jhesus, of his mercy,   690
Made Alla wedden ful solempnely
This hooly mayden, that is so bright and
          sheene;
And thus hath Crist ymaad Custance a queene.

But who was woful, if I shal nat lye,
Of this weddyng but Donegild, and namo, 695
The kynges mooder, ful of tirannye?
Hir thoughte hir cursed herte brast atwo.
She wolde noght hir sone had do so;
Hir thoughte a despit that he sholde take
So strange a creature unto his make.   700

Me list nat of the chaf, ne of the stree,
Maken so long a tale as of the corn.
What sholde I tellen of the roialtee
At mariage, or which cours goth biforn;
Who bloweth in a trumpe or in an horn?   705
The fruyt of every tale is for to seye:

They ete, and drynke, and daunce, and synge,
          and pleye.

They goon to bedde, as it was skile and right;
For thogh that wyves be ful hooly thynges,
They moste take in pacience at nyght   710
Swiche manere necessaries as been plesynges
To folk that han ywedded hem with rynges,
And leye a lite hir hoolynesse aside,
As for the tyme — it may no bet bitide.

On hire he gat a knave child anon,   715
And to a bisshop, and his constable eke,
He took his wyf to kepe, whan he is gon
To Scotlond-ward, his foomen for to seke.
Now faire Custance, that is so humble and
          meke,
So longe is goon with childe, til that stille 720
She halt hire chambre, abidyng Cristes wille.

The tyme is come a knave child she beer;
Mauricius at the fontstoon they hym calle.
This constable dooth forth come a messageer,
And wroot unto his kyng, that cleped was Alle,
How that this blisful tidyng is bifalle, 726
And othere tidynges spedeful for to seye.
He taketh the lettre, and forth he gooth his
          weye.

This messager, to doon his avantage,
Unto the kynges mooder rideth swithe,   730
And salueth hire ful faire in his langage:
"Madame," quod he, "ye may be glad and
          blithe,
And thanketh God an hundred thousand sithe!
My lady queene hath child, withouten doute,
To joye and blisse to al this regne aboute. 735

"Lo, heere the lettres seled of this thyng,
That I moot bere with al the haste I may.
If ye wol aught unto youre sone the kyng,
I am youre servant, bothe nyght and day."

671 **broste**: burst
673 **in general audience**: in the hearing of all
674 **desclaundred**: slandered
675 **in heigh presence**: in presence of the High One (God)
677 **prees**: crowd
678 **mazed**: bewildered, dazed
679 **wreche**: vengeance
682 **sely**: blessed
687 **untrouthe**: perjury
697 **brast atwo**: broke in two
700 **unto his make**: as his spouse
701 **chaf**: chaff (husks) **stree**: straw
702 **corn**: fruit, essential part, of the story

708 **skile**: reasonable
711 **necessaries**: necessities
715 **gat**: begot **knave child**: boy
717 **took**: gave
718 **to Scotlond-ward**: towards Scotland
721 **halt** = *holdeth*, holds, keeps to
723 **fontstoon**: baptismal font
726 **tidyng**: event
727 **spedeful**: useful
729 **to doon his avantage**: to do himself good
730 **swithe**: quickly
733 **sithe**: times
736 **seled**: marked with his seal
738 **wol aught**: want (to send) anything

Donegild answerde, "As now at this tyme,
     nay;   740
But heere al nyght I wol thou take thy reste.
To-morwe wol I seye thee what me leste."

   This messager drank sadly ale and wyn,
And stolen were his lettres pryvely
Out of his box, whil he sleep as a swyn;   745
And countrefeted was ful subtilly
Another lettre, wroght ful synfully,
Unto the kyng direct of this mateere
Fro his constable, as ye shal after heere.

The lettre spak the queene delivered was   750
Of so horrible a feendly creature
That in the castel noon so hardy was
That any while dorste ther endure.
The mooder was an elf, by aventure
Ycomen, by charmes or by sorcerie,   755
And every wight hateth hir compaignye.

   Wo was this kyng whan he this lettre had
     sayn,
But to no wight he tolde his sorwes soore,
But of his owene hand he wroot agayn,
"Welcome the sonde of Crist for everemoore
To me that am now lerned in his loore!   761
Lord, welcome be thy lust and thy plesaunce;
My lust I putte al in thyn ordinaunce.

"Kepeth this child, al be it foul or feir,
And eek my wyf, unto myn hoom-comynge.
Crist, whan hym list, may sende me an heir   766
Moore agreable than this to my likynge."
This lettre he seleth, pryvely wepynge,
Which to the messager was take soone,
And forth he gooth; ther is na moore to doone.

   O messager, fulfild of dronkenesse,   771
Strong is thy breeth, thy lymes faltren ay,
And thou biwreyest alle secreenesse.
Thy mynde is lorn, thou janglest as a jay,
Thy face is turned in a newe array.   775
Ther dronkenesse regneth in any route,
Ther is no conseil hyd, withouten doute.

   O Donegild, I ne have noon Englissh digne
Unto thy malice and thy tirannye!
And therfore to the feend I thee resigne;   780
Lat hym enditen of thy traitorie!
Fy, mannysh, fy! — o nay, by God, I lye —
Fy, feendlych spirit, for I dar wel telle,
Thogh thou heere walke, thy spirit is in helle!

   This messager comth fro the kyng agayn,
And at the kynges moodres court he lighte,   786
And she was of this messager ful fayn,
And plesed hym in al that ever she myghte.
He drank, and wel his girdel underpighte;
He slepeth, and he fnorteth in his gyse   790
Al nyght, til the sonne gan aryse.

Eft were his lettres stolen everychon,
And countrefeted lettres in this wyse:
"The king comandeth his constable anon,   794
Up peyne of hangyng, and on heigh juyse,
That he ne sholde suffren in no wyse
Custance in-with his reawme for t'abyde
Thre dayes and o quarter of a tyde;

"But in the same ship as he hire fond,
Hire, and hir yonge sone, and al hir geere, 800
He sholde putte, and croude hire fro the lond,
And charge hire that she never eft coome
     theere."
O my Custance, wel may thy goost have feere,
And, slepynge, in thy dreem been in penance,
Whan Donegild cast al this ordinance.   805

   This messager on morwe, whan he wook,
Unto the castel halt the nexte way,
And to the constable he the lettre took;
And whan that he this pitous lettre say,
Ful ofte he seyde, "Allas and weylaway!"   810
"Lord Crist," quod he, "how may this world
     endure,
So ful of synne is many a creature?

743 **sadly**: steadily
748 **direct**: addressed
754 **elf**: evil spirit
757 **sayn**: seen
760 **sonde**: dispensation
763 **in thyn ordinaunce**: in your control
768 **seleth**: marks with his seal
769 **take**: given
772 **faltren**: are unsteady
773 **biwreyest**: betray   **secreenesse**: secret information
774 **lorn**: lost   **janglest**: chatter

778 **digne**: fit
780 **resigne**: consign
781 **enditen**: write   **traitorie**: treachery
786 **lighte**: alighted, dismounted
789 **his girdel underpighte**: stuffed (drink) under his belt
790 **fnorteth**: snores
792 **Eft**: again
795 **Up peyne of**: on the penalty of   **juyse**: judicial sentence
797 **reawme**: realm
798 **tyde**: hour, or duration of a tide (ebb and flow)
801 **croude**: push
802 **charge**: command
807 **halt the nexte way**: takes (*halt* = *holdeth*) the shortest (literally, nearest) way
808 **took**: gave
809 **say**: saw

"O myghty God, if that it be thy wille,
Sith thou art rightful juge, how may it be
That thou wolt suffren innocentz to spille,   815
And wikked folk regne in prosperitee?
O goode Custance, allas, so wo is me
That I moot be thy tormentour, or deye
On shames deeth; ther is noon oother weye."

Wepen bothe yonge and olde in al that
          place   820
Whan that the kyng this cursed lettre sente,
And Custance, with a deedly pale face,
The ferthe day toward hir ship she wente.
But nathelees she taketh in good entente   824
The wyl of Crist, and knelynge on the stronde,
She seyde, "Lord, ay welcome be thy sonde!

"He that me kepte fro the false blame
While I was on the lond amonges yow,
He kan me kepe from harm and eek fro shame
In salte see, althogh I se noght how.   830
As strong as evere he was, he is yet now.
In hym triste I, and in his mooder deere,
That is to me my seyl and eek my steere."

Hir litel child lay wepyng in hir arm,
And knelynge, pitously to hym she seyde,   835
"Pees, litel sone, I wol do thee noon harm."
With that hir coverchief of hir heed she breyde,
And over his litel eyen she it leyde,
And in hir arm she lulleth it ful faste,
And into hevene hire eyen up she caste.   840

"Mooder," quod she, "and mayde bright,
          Marie,
Sooth is that thurgh wommanes eggement
Mankynde was lorn, and damned ay to dye,
For which thy child was on a croys yrent.
Thy blisful eyen sawe al his torment;   845
Thanne is ther no comparison bitwene
Thy wo and any wo man may sustene.

"Thow sawe thy child yslayn bifore thyne yen,
And yet now lyveth my litel child, parfay!   849
Now, lady bright, to whom alle woful cryen,
Thow glorie of wommanhede, thow faire may,

Thow haven of refut, brighte sterre of day,
Rewe on my child, that of thy gentillesse
Rewest on every reweful in distresse.

"O litel child, allas! What is thy gilt,   855
That nevere wroghtest synne as yet, pardee?
Why wil thyn harde fader han thee spilt?
O mercy, deere constable," quod she,
"As lat my litel child dwelle heer with thee;
And if thou darst nat saven hym, for blame,
So kys hym ones in his fadres name!"   861

Therwith she looked bakward to the londe,
And seyde, "Farewel, housbonde routhelees!"
And up she rist, and walketh doun the stronde
Toward the ship — hir folweth al the prees —
And evere she preyeth hire child to holde his
          pees;   866
And taketh hir leve, and with an hooly entente
She blisseth hire, and into ship she wente.

Vitailled was the ship, it is no drede,
Habundantly for hire ful longe space,   870
And othere necessaries that sholde nede
She hadde ynogh — heryed be Goddes grace!
For wynd and weder almyghty God purchace,
And brynge hire hoom! I kan no bettre seye,
But in the see she dryveth forth hir weye.   875

Explicit secunda pars.

Sequitur pars tercia.

Alla the kyng comth hoom soone after this
Unto his castel, of the which I tolde,
And asketh where his wyf and his child is.
The constable gan aboute his herte colde,
And pleynly al the manere he hym tolde   880
As ye han herd — I kan telle it no bettre —
And sheweth the kyng his seel and eek his
          lettre,

And seyde, "Lord, as ye comanded me
Up peyne of deeth, so have I doon, certein."
This messager tormented was til he   885

815 spille: die
820 ferthe: fourth
825 stronde: strand, shore
826 sonde: dispensation
832 triste: trust
833 steere: rudder, guide
837 coverchief: kerchief of . . . breyde: drew off
842 eggement: instigation
844 yrent: stretched (literally, *torn*)
849 parfay: by my faith
851 wommanhede: femininity may: maid
852 refut: refuge sterre: star
853 Rewe: take pity
857 spilt: put to death
869 Vitailled: stocked with provisions
870 space: time
871 necessaries: necessities nede: be needed
872 heryed: praised
873 weder: weather purchace: provide
Explicit, *etc.*: Here ends the second part.
Sequitur, *etc.*: The third part follows.
880 al the manere: the whole affair
884 Up peyne of: on the penalty of
885 tormented: tortured

Moste biknowe and tellen, plat and pleyn,
Fro nyght to nyght, in what place he had leyn;
And thus, by wit and sotil enquerynge,
Ymagined was by whom this harm gan sprynge.

    The hand was knowe that the lettre wroot,
And al the venym of this cursed dede,   891
But in what wise, certeinly, I noot.
Th'effect is this: that Alla, out of drede,
His mooder slow — that may men pleynly
      rede —
For that she traitour was to hire ligeance.   895
Thus endeth olde Donegild, with meschance!

    The sorwe that this Alla nyght and day
Maketh for his wyf, and for his child also,
Ther is no tonge that it telle may.
But now wol I unto Custance go,   900
That fleteth in the see, in peyne and wo,
Fyve yeer and moore, as liked Cristes sonde,
Er that hir ship approched unto londe.

    Under an hethen castel, atte laste,   904
Of which the name in my text noght I fynde,
Custance, and eek hir child, the see up caste.
Almyghty God, that saveth al mankynde,
Have on Custance and on hir child som mynde,
That fallen is in hethen hand eft soone,
In point to spille, as I shal telle yow soone. 910

    Doun fro the castel comth ther many a wight
To gauren on this ship and on Custance.
But shortly, from the castel, on a nyght,
The lordes styward — God yeve hym mes-
      chance! —
A theef, that hadde reneyed oure creance,   915
Cam into ship allone, and seyde he sholde
Hir lemman be, wher-so she wolde or nolde.

    Wo was this wrecched womman tho bigon;
Hir child cride, and she cride pitously.
But blisful Marie heelp hire right anon;   920
For with hir struglyng wel and myghtily

The theef fil over bord al sodeynly,
And in the see he dreynte for vengeance;
And thus hath Crist unwemmed kept Custance.

    O foule lust of luxurie, lo, thyn ende!   925
Nat oonly that thou feyntest mannes mynde,
But verraily thou wolt his body shende.
Th'ende of thy werk, or of thy lustes blynde,
Is compleynyng. Hou many oon may men fynde
That noght for werk somtyme, but for th'en-
      tente   930
To doon this synne, been outher slayn or shente!

    How may this wayke womman han this
      strengthe
Hire to defende agayn this renegat?
O Golias, unmesurable of lengthe,
Hou myghte David make thee so maat,   935
So yong and of armure so desolaat?
Hou dorste he looke upon thy dredful face?
Wel may men seen, it nas but Goddes grace.

    Who yaf Judith corage or hardynesse
To sleen hym Olofernus in his tente,   940
And to deliveren out of wrecchednesse
The peple of God? I seye, for this entente,
That right as God spirit of vigour sente
To hem and saved hem out of meschance,
So sente he myght and vigour to Custance.   945

    Forth gooth hir ship thurghout the narwe
      mouth
Of Jubaltare and Septe, dryvynge ay
Somtyme west, and somtyme north and south,
And somtyme est, ful many a wery day,
Til Cristes mooder — blessed be she ay! —   950
Hath shapen, thurgh hir endelees goodnesse,
To make an ende of al hir hevynesse.

    Now lat us stynte of Custance but a throwe,
And speke we of the Romayn Emperour,

886 **biknowe:** reveal **plat:** bluntly
888 **wit:** knowledge **sotil enquerynge:** subtle, skillful
questioning
889 **Ymagined:** deduced
891 **venym:** poison
893 **out of drede:** doubtless
895 **ligeance:** allegiance
901 **fleteth:** floats
908 **mynde:** thought
909 **eft soone:** again
910 **In point to:** on the point of
912 **gauren on:** stare at
914 **styward:** steward
915 **reneyed:** renounced **creance:** belief
917 **lemman:** lover **wher-so:** whether
918 **Wo . . . bigon:** in a sad plight

924 **unwemmed:** undefiled
925 **luxurie:** lechery
926 **feyntest:** weaken
927 **shende:** destroy
929 **compleynyng:** lamentation
930 **werk:** the deed
932 **wayke:** weak
934 **Golias:** Goliath, the biblical giant slain by David
935 **maat:** defeated
936 **of armure so desolaat:** so lacking in arms and armor
937 **dredful:** frightening
939–40 Judith slew the lecherous Holofernes (*Olofernus*); for the
story see MkT VII.2551–74.
946 **narwe mouth:** the narrow strait between Gibraltar
(*Jubaltare*) and Morocco (*Septe*)
952 **hevynesse:** sadness
953 **throwe:** short while

That out of Surrye hath by lettres knowe   955
The slaughtre of cristen folk, and dishonour
Doon to his doghter by a fals traytour,
I mene the cursed wikked Sowdanesse
That at the feeste leet sleen bothe moore and
    lesse.

For which this Emperour hath sent anon   960
His senatour, with roial ordinance,
And othere lordes, God woot, many oon,
On Surryens to taken heigh vengeance.
They brennen, sleen, and brynge hem to mes-
    chance
Ful many a day; but shortly — this is th'ende —
Homward to Rome they shapen hem to wende.

This senatour repaireth with victorie   967
To Rome-ward, saillynge ful roially,
And mette the ship dryvynge, as seith the
    storie,
In which Custance sit ful pitously.   970
Nothyng ne knew he what she was, ne why
She was in swich array, ne she nyl seye
Of hire estaat, althogh she sholde deye.

He bryngeth hire to Rome, and to his wyf
He yaf hire, and hir yonge sone also;   975
And with the senatour she ladde hir lyf.
Thus kan Oure Lady bryngen out of wo
Woful Custance, and many another mo.
And longe tyme dwelled she in that place,
In hooly werkes evere, as was hir grace.   980

The senatoures wyf hir aunte was,
But for al that she knew hire never the moore.
I wol no lenger tarien in this cas,
But to kyng Alla, which I spak of yoore,
That for his wyf wepeth and siketh soore,   985
I wol retourne, and lete I wol Custance
Under the senatoures governance.

Kyng Alla, which that hadde his mooder
    slayn,
Upon a day fil in swich repentance
That, if I shortly tellen shal and playn,   990
To Rome he comth to receyven his penance;
And putte hym in the Popes ordinance
In heigh and logh, and Jhesu Crist bisoghte
Foryeve his wikked werkes that he wroghte.

The fame anon thurgh Rome toun is born,
How Alla kyng shal comen in pilgrymage,   996
By herbergeours that wenten hym biforn;
For which the senatour, as was usage,
Rood hym agayns, and many of his lynage,
As wel to shewen his heighe magnificence
As to doon any kyng a reverence.   1001

Greet cheere dooth this noble senatour
To kyng Alla, and he to hym also;
Everich of hem dooth oother greet honour.
And so bifel that in a day or two   1005
This senatour is to kyng Alla go
To feste, and shortly, if I shal nat lye,
Custances sone wente in his compaignye.

Som men wolde seyn at requeste of Cus-
    tance
This senatour hath lad this child to feeste;
I may nat tellen every circumstance —   1011
Be as be may, ther was he at the leeste.
But sooth is this, that at his moodres heeste
Biforn Alla, durynge the metes space,   1014
The child stood, lookynge in the kynges face.

This Alla kyng hath of this child greet won-
    der,
And to the senatour he seyde anon,
"Whos is that faire child that stondeth yon-
    der?"
"I noot," quod he, "by God, and by Seint John!
A mooder he hath, but fader hath he noon   1020
That I of woot" — and shortly, in a stounde,
He tolde Alla how that this child was founde.

"But God woot," quod this senatour also,
"So vertuous a lyvere in my lyf
Ne saugh I nevere as she, ne herde of mo,   1025
Of worldly wommen, mayde, ne of wyf.
I dar wel seyn hir hadde levere a knyf
Thurghout hir brest, than ben a womman
    wikke;
There is no man koude brynge hire to that
    prikke."

959 **leet sleen:** had (caused to be) slain
972 **nyl** = *ne wyl,* will not
992 **ordinance:** governance
993 **In heigh and logh:** in all things

997 **herbergeours:** servants who travel ahead to arrange lodging
999 **hym agayns:** toward him
1000 **his heighe magnificence:** his own noble state
1012 **Be as be may:** whatever may be
1014 **metes space:** dinner time
1021 **stounde:** little time
1024 **lyvere:** being
1028 **wikke:** evil
1029 **prikke:** point

Now was this child as lyk unto Custance
As possible is a creature to be.   1031
This Alla hath the face in remembrance
Of dame Custance, and ther on mused he
If that the childes mooder were aught she
That is his wyf, and pryvely he sighte,   1035
And spedde hym fro the table that he myghte.

"Parfay," thoghte he, "fantome is in myn heed!
I oghte deme, of skilful juggement,
That in the salte see my wyf is deed."
And afterward he made his argument: 1040
"What woot I if that Crist have hyder ysent
My wyf by see, as wel as he hire sente
To my contree fro thennes that she wente?"

And after noon, hoom with the senatour
Goth Alla, for to seen this wonder chaunce.
This senatour dooth Alla greet honour,   1046
And hastifly he sente after Custaunce.
But trusteth weel, hire liste nat to daunce
Whan that she wiste wherfore was that sonde;
Unnethe upon hir feet she myghte stonde.   1050

Whan Alla saugh his wyf, faire he hire grette,
And weep that it was routhe for to see;
For at the firste look he on hire sette
He knew wel verraily that it was she.
And she, for sorwe, as doumb stant as a tree,
So was hir herte shet in hir distresse,   1056
Whan she remembred his unkyndenesse.

Twyes she swowned in his owene sighte;
He weep, and hym excuseth pitously.
"Now God," quod he, "and his halwes
         brighte
So wisly on my soule as have mercy,   1061
That of youre harm as giltelees am I
As is Maurice my sone, so lyk youre face;
Elles the feend me fecche out of this place!"

Long was the sobbyng and the bitter peyne,
Er that hir woful hertes myghte cesse;   1066
Greet was the pitee for to heere hem pleyne,

Thurgh whiche pleintes gan hir wo encresse.
I pray yow alle my labour to relesse;
I may nat telle hir wo until to-morwe,   1070
I am so wery for to speke of sorwe.

But finally, whan that the sothe is wist
That Alla giltelees was of hir wo,
I trowe an hundred tymes been they kist,
And swich a blisse is ther bitwix hem two   1075
That, save the joye that lasteth everemo,
Ther is noon lyk that any creature
Hath seyn or shal, whil that the world may
         dure.

Tho preyde she hir housbonde mekely,
In relief of hir longe, pitous pyne,   1080
That he wolde preye hir fader specially
That of his magestee he wolde enclyne
To vouche sauf som day with hym to dyne.
She preyde hym eek he sholde by no weye
Unto hir fader no word of hire seye.   1085

Som men wolde seyn how that the child
         Maurice
Dooth this message unto this Emperour;
But, as I gesse, Alla was nat so nyce
To hym that was of so sovereyn honour
As he that is of Cristen folk the flour,   1090
Sente any child, but it is bet to deeme
He wente hymself, and so it may wel seeme.

This Emperour hath graunted gentilly
To come to dyner, as he hym bisoughte;
And wel rede I he looked bisily   1095
Upon this child, and on his doghter thoghte.
Alla goth to his in, and as hym oghte,
Arrayed for this feste in every wise
As ferforth as his konnyng may suffise.   1099

The morwe cam, and Alla gan hym dresse,
And eek his wyf, this Emperour to meete;
And forth they ryde in joye and in gladnesse.
And whan she saugh hir fader in the strete,
She lighte doun, and falleth hym to feete. 1104
"Fader," quod she, "youre yonge child Cus-
         tance
Is now ful clene out of youre remembrance.

1034 **aught**: in any way
1035 **sighte**: sighed
1036 **that he myghte**: as soon as he could
1037 **fantome**: hallucination
1038 **skilful**: discerning
1048 **hire liste nat to daunce**: she did not want to dance (for joy)
1050 **Unnethe**: hardly
1051 **grette**: greeted
1052 **routhe**: pity
1056 **shet**: shut up, pressed by emotion
1060 **halwes**: saints
1061 **So wisly**: surely
1066 **cesse**: cease

1069 **relesse**: relieve
1074 **been they kist**: they kissed each other
1080 **pyne**: pain
1083 **vouche sauf**: grant
1088 **nyce**: foolish
1091 **Sente**: to have sent
1095 **rede I**: I read (in my source)   **bisily**: intently
1104 **hym to feete**: at his feet
1106 **ful clene**: completely

"I am youre doghter Custance," quod she,
"That whilom ye han sent unto Surrye.
It am I, fader, that in the salte see
Was put allone and dampned for to dye.   1110
Now, goode fader, mercy I yow crye!
Sende me namoore unto noon hethenesse,
But thonketh my lord heere of his kyndenesse."

Who kan the pitous joye tellen al
Bitwixe hem thre, syn they been thus ymette?
But of my tale make an ende I shal;   1116
The day goth faste, I wol no lenger lette.
This glade folk to dyner they hem sette;
In joye and blisse at mete I lete hem dwelle
A thousand foold wel moore than I kan
      telle.   1120

This child Maurice was sithen Emperour
Maad by the Pope, and lyved cristenly;
To Cristes chirche he dide greet honour.
But I lete al his storie passen by;
Of Custance is my tale specially.   1125
In the olde Romayn geestes may men fynde
Maurices lyf; I bere it noght in mynde.

This kyng Alla, whan he his tyme say,
With his Custance, his hooly wyf so sweete,
To Engelond been they come the righte way,
Wher as they lyve in joye and in quiete.   1131
But litel while it lasteth, I yow heete,
Joye of this world, for tyme wol nat abyde;
Fro day to nyght it changeth as the tyde.

Who lyved euere in swich delit o day   1135
That hym ne moeved outher conscience,
Or ire, or talent, or som kynnes affray,
Envye, or pride, or passion, or offence?
I ne seye but for this ende this sentence,
That litel while in joye or in plesance   1140
Lasteth the blisse of Alla with Custance.

For Deeth, that taketh of heigh and logh his
      rente,
Whan passed was a yeer, evene as I gesse,
Out of this world this kyng Alla he hente,
For whom Custance hath ful greet hevynesse.
Now lat us prayen God his soule blesse!   1146
And dame Custance, finally to seye,
Toward the toun of Rome goth hir weye.

To Rome is come this hooly creature,
And fyndeth hire freendes hoole and sounde;
Now is she scaped al hire aventure.   1151
And whan that she hir fader hath yfounde,
Doun on hir knees falleth she to grounde;
Wepynge for tendrenesse in herte blithe,
She heryeth God an hundred thousand sithe.

In vertu and in hooly almus-dede   1156
They lyven alle, and nevere asonder wende;
Til deeth departeth hem, this lyf they lede.
And fareth now weel! my tale is at an ende.
Now Jhesu Crist, that of his myght may sende
Joye after wo, governe us in his grace,   1161
And kepe us alle that been in this place! Amen

Heere endeth the tale of the Man of Lawe.

THE EPILOGUE OF THE MAN OF LAW'S TALE

[Owre Hoost upon his stiropes stood anon,
And seyde, "Goode men, herkeneth everych
      on!
This was a thrifty tale for the nones!   1165
Sir Parisshe Prest," quod he, "for Goddes bones,
Telle us a tale, as was thi forward yore.

I se wel that ye lerned men in lore
Can moche good, by Goddes dignitee!"   1169
The Parson him answerde, "Benedicite!
What eyleth the man, so synfully to swere?"

1117 lette: delay
1126 Romayn geestes: Roman histories
1128 say: saw
1130 righte way: direct route

1165 thrifty: worthwhile

1136 moeved: moved outher: either
1137 som kynnes: some kind of affray: fear
1138 Envye: ill-will
1144 hente: snatched
1155 heryeth: praises sithe: times
1156 almus-dede: charitable works
1157 asonder wende: parted

1169 Can moche good: know what you are about

Oure Host answerde, "O Jankin, be ye there?
I smelle a Lollere in the wynd," quod he.
"Now! goode men," quod oure Hoste, "herken-
          eth me;
Abydeth, for Goddes digne passioun,   1175
For we schal han a predicacioun;
This Lollere heer wil prechen us somwhat."
     "Nay, by my fader soule, that schal he nat!"
Seyde the Shipman, "Heer schal he nat preche;
He schal no gospel glosen here ne teche.   1180

We leven alle in the grete God," quod he;
"He wolde sowen som difficulte,
Or springen cokkel in our clene corn.
And therfore, Hoost, I warne thee biforn,
My joly body schal a tale telle,   1185
And I schal clynken you so mery a belle,
That I schal waken al this compaignie.
But it schal not ben of philosophie,
Ne phislyas, ne termes queinte of lawe.
Ther is but litel Latyn in my mawe!"]   1190

1172 **Jankin:** derisive name for a priest
1173 **Lollere:** Lollard, a heretic
1176 **predicacioun:** sermon
1179 **Shipman:** The identity of the speaker is uncertain; see n.
1180 **glosen:** interpret

1181 **leven:** believe
1183 **springen:** sprinkle **cokkel:** corn cockle (a weed)
1189 **phislyas:** files, cases (?); see n. **queinte:** learned, complex

Fragment III (Group D)

THE WIFE OF BATH'S PROLOGUE

The Prologe of the Wyves Tale of Bathe.

"Experience, though noon auctoritee
Were in this world, is right ynogh for me
To speke of wo that is in mariage;
For, lordynges, sith I twelve yeer was of age,
Thonked be God that is eterne on lyve,   5
Housbondes at chirche dore I have had fyve —
If I so ofte myghte have ywedded bee —
And alle were worthy men in hir degree.
But me was toold, certeyn, nat longe agoon is,
That sith that Crist ne wente nevere but onis
To weddyng, in the Cane of Galilee,   11
That by the same ensample taughte he me
That I ne sholde wedded be but ones.
Herkne eek, lo, which a sharp word for the
    nones,
Biside a welle, Jhesus, God and man,   15
Spak in repreeve of the Samaritan:
'Thou hast yhad fyve housbondes,' quod he,
'And that ilke man that now hath thee
Is noght thyn housbonde,' thus seyde he cer-
    teyn.
What that he mente therby, I kan nat seyn;   20
But that I axe, why that the fifthe man
Was noon housbonde to the Samaritan?
How manye myghte she have in mariage?
Yet herde I nevere tellen in myn age
Upon this nombre diffinicioun.   25
Men may devyne and glosen, up and doun,
But wel I woot, expres, withoute lye,
God bad us for to wexe and multiplye;
That gentil text kan I wel understonde.
Eek wel I woot, he seyde myn housbonde   30
Sholde lete fader and mooder and take to me.
But of no nombre mencion made he,

Of bigamye, or of octogamye;
Why sholde men thanne speke of it vileynye?
   Lo, heere the wise kyng, daun Salomon;   35
I trowe he hadde wyves mo than oon.
As wolde God it leveful were unto me
To be refresshed half so ofte as he!
Which yifte of God hadde he for alle his
    wyvys!
No man hath swich that in this world alyve is.
God woot, this noble kyng, as to my wit,   41
The firste nyght had many a myrie fit
With ech of hem, so wel was hym on lyve.
Yblessed be God that I have wedded fyve!
[Of whiche I have pyked out the beste,   44a
Bothe of here nether purs and of here cheste.
Diverse scoles maken parfyt clerkes,
And diverse practyk in many sondry werkes
Maketh the werkman parfyt sekirly;
Of fyve husbondes scoleiyng am I.]   44f
Welcome the sixte, whan that evere he shal.
For sothe, I wol nat kepe me chaast in al.   46
Whan myn housbonde is fro the world ygon,
Som Cristen man shal wedde me anon,
For thanne th'apostle seith that I am free
To wedde, a Goddes half, where it liketh me.
He seith that to be wedded is no synne;   51
Bet is to be wedded than to brynne.
What rekketh me, thogh folk seye vileynye
Of shrewed Lameth and his bigamye?
I woot wel Abraham was an hooly man,   55
And Jacob eek, as ferforth as I kan;
And ech of hem hadde wyves mo than two,

1 **auctoritee:** written authority
10 **onis:** once
11 **Cane:** the town of Cana
14 **Herkne:** listen
16 **repreeve:** reproof
21 **axe:** ask
26 **devyne:** conjecture **glosen, up and doun:** interpret in every way
27 **expres:** clearly
28 **wexe:** increase (breed)
31 **lete:** leave

33 **octogamye:** marrying eight times
34 **vileynye:** in reproach
35 **daun:** sir **Salomon:** Solomon
37 **leveful:** lawful, permissible
39 **Which yifte:** what a gift
41 **wit:** judgment
44b **nether:** lower
44d **practyk:** practice
44e **sekirly:** certainly
44f **scoleiyng:** schooling
46 **chaast:** chaste
49 **th'apostle:** St. Paul
50 **a Goddes half:** by God's side, by God
52 **brynne:** burn
53 **rekketh me:** do I care
54 **shrewed:** cursed, evil **Lameth:** the biblical Lamech, the first bigamist
55–56 **Abraham, Jacob:** the biblical patriarchs

And many another holy man also.
Wher can ye seye, in any manere age,
That hye God defended mariage   60
By expres word? I pray yow, telleth me.
Or where comanded he virginitee?
I woot as wel as ye, it is no drede,
Th'apostel, whan he speketh of maydenhede,
He seyde that precept therof hadde he noon.
Men may conseille a womman to been oon,   66
But conseillyng is no comandement.
He putte it in oure owene juggement;
For hadde God comanded maydenhede,
Thanne hadde he dampned weddyng with the
        dede.
And certes, if ther were no seed ysowe,   71
Virginitee, thanne wherof sholde it growe?
Poul dorste nat comanden, atte leeste,
A thyng of which his maister yaf noon heeste.
The dart is set up for virginitee;   75
Cacche whoso may, who renneth best lat see.
    But this word is nat taken of every wight,
But ther as God lust gyve it of his myght.
I woot wel that th'apostel was a mayde;   79
But nathelees, thogh that he wroot and sayde
He wolde that every wight were swich as he,
Al nys but conseil to virginitee.
And for to been a wyf he yaf me leve
Of indulgence; so nys it no repreve
To wedde me, if that my make dye,   85
Withouten excepcion of bigamye.
Al were it good no womman for to touche —
He mente as in his bed or in his couche,
For peril is bothe fyr and tow t'assemble;
Ye knowe what this ensample may resemble.
This is al and som: he heeld virginitee   91
Moore parfit than weddyng in freletee.
Freletee clepe I, but if that he and she
Wolde leden al hir lyf in chastitee.

I graunte it wel; I have noon envie,   95
Thogh maydenhede preferre bigamye.
It liketh hem to be clene, body and goost;
Of myn estaat I nyl nat make no boost,
For wel ye knowe, a lord in his houshold,
He nath nat every vessel al of gold;   100
Somme been of tree, and doon hir lord servyse.
God clepeth folk to hym in sondry wyse,
And everich hath of God a propre yifte —
Som this, som that, as hym liketh shifte.
    Virginitee is greet perfeccion,   105
And continence eek with devocion,
But Crist, that of perfeccion is welle,
Bad nat every wight he sholde go selle
Al that he hadde, and gyve it to the poore,
And in swich wise folwe hym and his foore.
He spak to hem that wolde lyve parfitly;   111
And lordynges, by youre leve, that am nat I.
I wol bistowe the flour of al myn age
In the actes and in fruyt of mariage.
    Telle me also, to what conclusion   115
Were membres maad of generacion,
And of so parfit wys a [wright] ywroght?
Trusteth right wel, they were nat maad for
        noght.
Glose whoso wole, and seye bothe up and doun
That they were maked for purgacioun   120
Of uryne, and oure bothe thynges smale
Were eek to knowe a femele from a male,
And for noon oother cause — say ye no?
The experience woot wel it is noght so.
So that the clerkes be nat with me wrothe,   125
I sey this: that they maked ben for bothe;
That is to seye, for office and for ese
Of engendrure, ther we nat God displese.
Why sholde men elles in hir bookes sette
That man shal yelde to his wyf hire dette?   130
Now wherwith sholde he make his paiement,
If he ne used his sely instrument?
Thanne were they maad upon a creature
To purge uryne, and eek for engendrure.   134

61 **expres:** explicit
63 **drede:** doubt
64 **Th'apostel:** St. Paul
73 **Poul:** St. Paul
74 **of which his maister yaf noon heeste:** about which his Master made no commandment
75 **dart:** dart offered as a prize
76 **Cacche whoso may:** catch it whoever can
77 **is nat taken of:** does not apply to
78 **lust:** pleases
79 **mayde:** virgin, without sexual experience
82 **Al nys but:** although it is only
84 **Of indulgence:** by permission **repreve:** shame
85 **make:** mate
86 **excepcion of:** objection on the grounds of
89 **tow:** flax
91 **al and som:** the entire matter
92 **in freletee:** because of weakness
93 **but if that:** unless
94 **chastitee:** abstinence from sexual intercourse

96 **preferre:** may have precedence over **bigamye:** in this instance, marriage by or with a widower or widow
98 **nyl** = *ne wyl*, will not
101 **of tree:** made of wood
103 **propre yifte:** special, individual gift
104 **hym liketh shifte:** it pleases God to provide
110 **foore:** footsteps
111 **parfitly:** perfectly
115 **conclusion:** purpose
117 And made by so perfectly wise a maker
119 **Glose:** interpret scripture **up and doun:** in all respects
125 **So that:** providing that
127 **office:** function (of excretion) **ese:** pleasure
128 **engendrure:** procreation
130 **yelde:** pay **dette:** marital debt (obligation to engage in intercourse; see ParsT X.940)
132 **sely instrument:** blessed, innocent tool

But I seye noght that every wight is holde,
That hath swich harneys as I to yow tolde,
To goon and usen hem in engendrure.
Thanne sholde men take of chastitee no cure.
Crist was a mayde and shapen as a man,
And many a seint, sith that the world bigan;
Yet lyved they evere in parfit chastitee.   141
I nyl envye no virginitee.
Lat hem be breed of pured whete-seed,
And lat us wyves hoten barly-breed;
And yet with barly-breed, Mark telle kan,   145
Oure Lord Jhesu refresshed many a man.
In swich estaat as God hath cleped us
I wol persevere; I nam nat precius.
In wyfhod I wol use myn instrument
As frely as my Makere hath it sent.   150
If I be daungerous, God yeve me sorwe!
Myn housbonde shal it have bothe eve and
     morwe,
Whan that hym list come forth and paye his
     dette.
An housbonde I wol have — I wol nat lette —
Which shal be bothe my dettour and my thral,
And have his tribulacion withal   156
Upon his flessh, whil that I am his wyf.
I have the power durynge al my lyf
Upon his propre body, and noght he.
Right thus the Apostel tolde it unto me,   160
And bad oure housbondes for to love us weel.
Al this sentence me liketh every deel" —
   Up stirte the Pardoner, and that anon;
"Now, dame," quod he, "by God and by Seint
     John!
Ye been a noble prechour in this cas.   165
I was aboute to wedde a wyf; allas!
What sholde I bye it on my flessh so deere?
Yet hadde I levere wedde no wyf to-yeere!"
   "Abyde!" quod she, "my tale is nat bigonne.
Nay, thou shalt drynken of another tonne,   170
Er that I go, shal savoure wors than ale.
And whan that I have toold thee forth my tale
Of tribulacion in mariage,
Of which I am expert in al myn age —   174

This is to seyn, myself have been the whippe —
Than maystow chese wheither thou wolt sippe
Of thilke tonne that I shal abroche.
Be war of it, er thou to ny approche;
For I shal telle ensamples mo than ten.
'Whoso that nyl be war by othere men,   180
By hym shul othere men corrected be.'
The same wordes writeth Ptholomee;
Rede in his Almageste, and take it there."
   "Dame, I wolde praye yow, if youre wyl it
     were,"
Seyde this Pardoner, "as ye bigan,   185
Telle forth youre tale, spareth for no man,
And teche us yonge men of youre praktike."
   "Gladly," quod she, "sith it may yow like;
But yet I praye to al this compaignye,
If that I speke after my fantasye,   190
As taketh not agrief of that I seye,
For myn entente nys but for to pleye.
   Now, sire, now wol I telle forth my tale.
As evere moote I drynken wyn or ale,   194
I shal seye sooth; tho housbondes that I hadde,
As thre of hem were goode, and two were
     badde.
The thre were goode men, and riche, and olde;
Unnethe myghte they the statut holde
In which that they were bounden unto me.
Ye woot wel what I meene of this, pardee!   200
As help me God, I laughe whan I thynke
How pitously a-nyght I made hem swynke!
And, by my fey, I tolde of it no stoor.
They had me yeven hir lond and hir tresoor;
Me neded nat do lenger diligence   205
To wynne hir love, or doon hem reverence.
They loved me so wel, by God above,
That I ne tolde no deyntee of hir love!
A wys womman wol bisye hire evere in oon
To gete hire love, ye, ther as she hath noon.

---

135 **holde:** obligated
143 **pured:** refined
144 **hoten:** be called   **barly-breed:** an inexpensive bread
148 **precius:** fussy, fastidious
151 **daungerous:** grudging, niggardly
154 **lette:** leave off, desist
155 **thral:** servant, slave
156 **withal:** also
165 **prechour:** preacher
167 **What:** why   **bye it on:** pay for it with
168 **to-yeere:** this year
170 **tonne:** barrel
171 **savoure:** taste

177 **abroche:** open
178 **to ny:** too close
180–81 He who will not (*nyl = ne wyll*) be admonished by examples offered by others must himself become an example for the correction of others.
182 **Ptholomee:** Ptolemy, the Greek mathematician and astronomer, author of the *Almageste* (cf. MilT I.3208)
187 **praktike:** practice
190 **after my fantasye:** according to my fancy, desire
191 **As taketh not agrief of:** do not be annoyed with (*as* is not translated)
198 **Unnethe:** hardly   **statut:** the conjugal debt (see 130 above)
202 **a-nyght:** at night   **swynke:** work
203 **fey:** faith   **tolde of it no stoor:** set no store by it, regarded it as useless
204 **tresoor:** treasure
208 **ne tolde no deyntee of:** did not value, reckoned little of
209 **bisye hire evere in oon:** be constantly busy

But sith I hadde hem hoolly in myn hond,   211
And sith they hadde me yeven al hir lond,
What sholde I taken keep hem for to plese,
But it were for my profit and myn ese?
I sette hem so a-werke, by my fey,   215
That many a nyght they songen 'Weilawey!'
The bacon was nat fet for hem, I trowe,
That som men han in Essex at Dunmowe.
I governed hem so wel, after my lawe,
That ech of hem ful blisful was and fawe   220
To brynge me gaye thynges fro the fayre.
They were ful glad whan I spak to hem faire,
For, God it woot, I chidde hem spitously.

Now herkneth hou I baar me proprely,
Ye wise wyves, that kan understonde.   225
Thus shulde ye speke and bere hem wrong
        on honde,
For half so boldely kan ther no man
Swere and lyen, as a womman kan.
I sey nat this by wyves that been wyse,
But if it be whan they hem mysavyse.   230
A wys wyf, if that she kan hir good,
Shal beren hym on honde the cow is wood,
And take witnesse of hir owene mayde
Of hir assent. But herkneth how I sayde:

'Sire olde kaynard, is this thyn array?   235
Why is my neighebores wyf so gay?
She is honoured overal ther she gooth;
I sitte at hoom; I have no thrifty clooth.
What dostow at my neighebores hous?
Is she so fair? Artow so amorous?   240
What rowne ye with oure mayde? Benedicite!
Sire olde lecchour, lat thy japes be!
And if I have a gossib or a freend,
Withouten gilt, thou chidest as a feend,
If that I walke or pleye unto his hous!   245
Thou comest hoom as dronken as a mous,
And prechest on thy bench, with yvel preef!
Thou seist to me it is a greet meschief

To wedde a povre womman, for costage;
And if that she be riche, of heigh parage,   250
Thanne seistow that it is a tormentrie
To soffre hire pride and hire malencolie.
And if that she be fair, thou verray knave,
Thou seyst that every holour wol hire have;
She may no while in chastitee abyde,   255
That is assailled upon ech a syde.

Thou seyst som folk desiren us for richesse,
Somme for oure shap, and somme for oure fair-
        nesse,
And som for she kan outher synge or daunce,
And som for gentillesse and daliaunce;   260
Som for hir handes and hir armes smale;
Thus goth al to the devel, by thy tale.
Thou seyst men may nat kepe a castel wal,
It may so longe assailled been overal.

And if that she be foul, thou seist that she
Coveiteth every man that she may se,   266
For as a spanyel she wol on hym lepe,
Til that she fynde som man hire to chepe.
Ne noon so grey goos gooth ther in the lake
As, sëistow, wol been withoute make.   270
And seyst it is an hard thyng for to welde
A thyng that no man wole, his thankes, helde.
Thus seistow, lorel, whan thow goost to bedde,
And that no wys man nedeth for to wedde,
Ne no man that entendeth unto hevene.   275
With wilde thonder-dynt and firy levene
Moote thy welked nekke be tobroke!

Thow seyst that droppyng houses, and eek
        smoke,
And chidyng wyves maken men to flee
Out of hir owene houses; a, benedicitee!   280
What eyleth swich an old man for to chide?

Thow seyst we wyves wol oure vices hide
Til we be fast, and thanne we wol hem shewe —
Wel may that be a proverbe of a shrewe!

213 **taken keep:** take care
215 **sette hem so a-werke:** worked them so hard (or, tricked them; cf. I.4337)
217–18 **bacon . . . in Essex at Dunmowe:** side of bacon awarded to spouses who lived a year and a day without quarrelling
220 **fawe:** eager
223 **chidde hem spitously:** chided, scolded them cruelly
226 **bere hem wrong on honde:** accuse them wrongfully
229 **by:** concerning, about
231 **kan hir good:** knows what's good for her
232 **beren hym on honde:** deceive him by swearing **cow:** chough, a crow-like bird, which can talk
234 **Of hir assent:** of her agreement (i.e., the maid agrees with what she says)
235 **kaynard:** dotard
237 **overal ther:** wherever
238 **thrifty clooth:** serviceable clothing
241 **rowne:** whisper
243 **gossib:** close friend
244 **chidest as:** scold like
247 **with yvel preef:** bad luck to you

249 **costage:** expense
250 **heigh parage:** high birth
251 **tormentrie:** torture
252 **malencolie:** anger, sullenness (due to an excess of the humor)
254 **holour:** lecher
256 **ech a:** every
260 **daliaunce:** socializing
261 **smale:** slender
262 **by thy tale:** according to what you say
268 **chepe:** buy (i.e., take)
270 **make:** mate
271 **welde:** control
272 **his thankes:** willingly **helde:** holde
273 **lorel:** scoundrel
275 **entendeth unto:** hopes (to go) to
276 **thonder-dynt:** thunderstroke **levene:** lightning
277 **welked:** withered **tobroke:** broken to pieces
278 **droppyng:** dripping, leaky
279 **chidyng:** scolding
283 **fast:** securely tied (in marriage)
284 **shrewe:** scoundrel

Thou seist that oxen, asses, hors, and houndes,
They been assayed at diverse stoundes;   286
Bacyns, lavours, er that men hem bye,
Spoones and stooles, and al swich housbondrye,
And so been pottes, clothes, and array;
But folk of wyves maken noon assay,   290
Til they be wedded — olde dotard shrewe! —
And thanne, seistow, we wol oure vices shewe.
　　Thou seist also that it displeseth me
But if that thou wolt preyse my beautee,
And but thou poure alwey upon my face,   295
And clepe me "faire dame" in every place.
And but thou make a feeste on thilke day
That I was born, and make me fressh and gay;
And but thou do to my norice honour,
And to my chamberere withinne my bour,   300
And to my fadres folk and his allyes —
Thus seistow, olde barel-ful of lyes!
　　And yet of oure apprentice Janekyn,
For his crispe heer, shynynge as gold so fyn,
And for he squiereth me bothe up and doun,
Yet hastow caught a fals suspecioun.   306
I wol hym noght, thogh thou were deed to-
　　morwe!
　　But tel me this: why hydestow, with sorwe,
The keyes of thy cheste awey fro me?
It is my good as wel as thyn, pardee!   310
What, wenestow make an ydiot of oure dame?
Now by that lord that called is Seint Jame,
Thou shalt nat bothe, thogh that thou were
　　wood,
Be maister of my body and of my good;   314
That oon thou shalt forgo, maugree thyne yen.
What helpith it of me to enquere or spyen?
I trowe thou woldest loke me in thy chiste!
Thou sholdest seye, "Wyf, go wher thee liste;
Taak youre disport; I wol nat leve no talys.
I knowe yow for a trewe wyf, dame Alys."
We love no man that taketh kep or charge   321
Wher that we goon; we wol ben at oure large.

Of alle men yblessed moot he be,
The wise astrologien, Daun Ptholome,
That seith this proverbe in his Almageste: 325
"Of alle men his wysdom is the hyeste
That rekketh nevere who hath the world in
　　honde."
By this proverbe thou shalt understonde,
Have thou ynogh, what thar thee recche or
　　care
How myrily that othere folkes fare?   330
For, certeyn, olde dotard, by youre leve,
Ye shul have queynte right ynogh at eve.
He is to greet a nygard that wolde werne
A man to lighte a candle at his lanterne;
He shal have never the lasse light, pardee.   335
Have thou ynogh, thee thar nat pleyne thee.
　　Thou seyst also, that if we make us gay
With clothyng, and with precious array,
That it is peril of oure chastitee;   339
And yet — with sorwe! — thou most enforce
　　thee,
And seye thise wordes in the Apostles name:
"In habit maad with chastitee and shame
Ye wommen shul apparaille yow," quod he,
"And noght in tressed heer and gay perree,
As perles, ne with gold, ne clothes riche."   345
After thy text, ne after thy rubriche,
I wol nat wirche as muchel as a gnat.
　　Thou seydest this, that I was lyk a cat;
For whoso wolde senge a cattes skyn,   349
Thanne wolde the cat wel dwellen in his in;
And if the cattes skyn be slyk and gay,
She wol nat dwelle in house half a day,
But forth she wole, er any day be dawed,
To shewe hir skyn and goon a-caterwawed.
This is to seye, if I be gay, sire shrewe,   355
I wol renne out my borel for to shewe.
　　Sire olde fool, what helpeth thee to spyen?
Thogh thou preye Argus with his hundred yen
To be my warde-cors, as he kan best,

286 **diverse stoundes:** different times
287 **Bacyns:** basins **lavours:** wash bowls **bye:** pay for, buy
288 **housbondrye:** household equipment
290 **assay:** trial
291 **dotard shrewe:** senile scoundrel
295 **poure:** gaze intently
299 **norice:** nurse
300 **chamberere:** chambermaid **bour:** bedchamber
301 **allyes:** kinsmen
302 **lyes:** lees (dregs)
304 **crispe:** curly
305 **squiereth:** formally attends
308 **hydestow:** do you hide **with sorwe:** bad luck to you
311 **wenestow:** do you expect **oure dame:** the lady of our
house (me)
312 **Seint Jame:** St. James of Compostella
317 **loke:** lock **chiste:** strongbox, coffer
319 **leve:** believe
322 **at oure large:** free to act as we wish

327 **in honde:** in his control
331 **dotard:** senile fool
332 **queynte:** my elegant, pleasing thing (sexual favors)
333 **werne:** refuse
336 **thar nat pleyne thee:** need not complain
340 **enforce thee:** make an effort
341 **Apostles:** St. Paul's
342 **habit:** clothing
343 **apparaille yow:** dress yourselves
344 **tressed heer:** carefully arranged hair **perree:** precious
stones
346 **rubriche:** words written in red as a heading to a text
349 **senge:** singe
350 **wolde the cat:** the cat would want **dwellen:** remain **his
in:** his dwelling-place
351 **slyk:** sleek, shining
353 **dawed:** dawned
354 **a-caterwawed:** caterwauling
356 **borel:** coarse, poor cloth (of which my clothes are made)
358 **Argus:** the mythical guardian of Io, one of Zeus's loves
359 **warde-cors:** bodyguard

In feith, he shal nat kepe me but me lest;   360
Yet koude I make his berd, so moot I thee!
   Thou seydest eek that ther been thynges thre,
The whiche thynges troublen al this erthe,
And that no wight may endure the ferthe.
O leeve sire shrewe, Jhesu shorte thy lyf!   365
Yet prechestow and seyst an hateful wyf
Yrekened is for oon of thise meschances.
Been ther none othere maner resemblances
That ye may likne youre parables to,
But if a sely wyf be oon of tho?   370
   Thou liknest eek wommenes love to helle,
To bareyne lond, ther water may nat dwelle.
Thou liknest it also to wilde fyr;
The moore it brenneth, the moore it hath desir
To consume every thyng that brent wole be.
Thou seyest, right as wormes shende a tree,   376
Right so a wyf destroyeth hire housbonde;
This knowe they that been to wyves bonde.'
   Lordynges, right thus, as ye have under-
                                          stonde,
Baar I stifly myne olde housbondes on honde
That thus they seyden in hir dronkenesse;   381
And al was fals, but that I took witnesse
On Janekyn, and on my nece also.
O Lord! The peyne I dide hem and the wo,
Ful giltelees, by Goddes sweete pyne!   385
For as an hors I koude byte and whyne.
I koude pleyne, and yit was in the gilt,
Or elles often tyme hadde I been spilt.
Whoso that first to mille comth, first grynt;
I pleyned first, so was oure werre ystynt.   390
They were ful glade to excuse hem blyve
Of thyng of which they nevere agilte hir lyve.
Of wenches wolde I beren hem on honde,
Whan that for syk unnethes myghte they stonde.
   Yet tikled I his herte, for that he   395
Wende that I hadde of hym so greet chiertee!

I swoor that al my walkynge out by nyghte
Was for t'espye wenches that he dighte;
Under that colour hadde I many a myrthe.   399
For al swich wit is yeven us in oure byrthe;
Deceite, wepyng, spynnyng God hath yive
To wommen kyndely, whil that they may lyve.
And thus of o thyng I avaunte me:
Atte ende I hadde the bettre in ech degree,
By sleighte, or force, or by som maner thyng,
As by continueel murmur or grucchyng.   406
Namely abedde hadden they meschaunce:
Ther wolde I chide and do hem no plesaunce;
I wolde no lenger in the bed abyde,
If that I felte his arm over my syde,   410
Til he had maad his raunson unto me;
Thanne wolde I suffre hym do his nycetee.
And therfore every man this tale I telle,
Wynne whoso may, for al is for to selle;
With empty hand men may none haukes lure.
For wynnyng wolde I al his lust endure,   416
And make me a feyned appetit;
And yet in bacon hadde I nevere delit.
That made me that evere I wolde hem chide,
For thogh the pope hadde seten hem biside,
I wolde nat spare hem at hir owene bord,   421
For, by my trouthe, I quitte hem word for
                                          word.
As helpe me verray God omnipotent,
Though I right now sholde make my testament,
I ne owe hem nat a word that it nys quit.   425
I broghte it so aboute by my wit
That they moste yeve it up, as for the beste,
Or elles hadde we nevere been in reste;
For thogh he looked as a wood leon,
Yet sholde he faille of his conclusion.   430
   Thanne wolde I seye, 'Goode lief, taak keep
How mekely looketh Wilkyn, oure sheep!
Com neer, my spouse, lat me ba thy cheke!
Ye sholde been al pacient and meke,

361 **make his berd:** deceive him   **so moot I thee:** as I may
prosper
373 **wilde fyr:** Greek fire, an inflammable mixture, used in
warfare
376 **shende:** destroy
378 **bonde:** bound
380 **Baar I stifly ... on honde:** I firmly swore
382 **but that:** except that
383 **nece:** kinswoman
385 **pyne:** suffering
386 **whyne:** whinny, whine
387 **in the gilt:** in the wrong
388 **spilt:** ruined
389 **grynt** = *gryndeth,* grinds
391 **blyve:** quickly
392 **agilte hir lyve:** been guilty in their lives
393 **beren hem on honde:** accuse them
394 **syk:** illness   **unnethes:** hardly
395 **tikled:** tickled, pleased
396 **chiertee:** fondness

398 **dighte:** copulated with
399 **colour:** pretense
402 **kyndely:** naturally
403 **avaunte me:** boast
404 **in ech degree:** in all respects
406 **murmur:** grumbling   **grucchyng:** complaining
407 **abedde:** in bed
411 **maad his raunson:** paid his penalty
412 **nycetee:** foolishness, lust
416 **wynnyng:** profit
417 **feyned:** pretended
418 **bacon:** bacon (i.e., preserved old meat)
421 **bord:** table
422 **quitte:** repaid
424 **testament:** will
430 **faille of his conclusion:** fail to attain his goal
431 **Goode lief:** sweetheart
432 **mekely:** meekly   **Wilkyn:** Willie
433 **neer:** nearer   **ba:** kiss

And han a sweete spiced conscience,   435
Sith ye so preche of Jobes pacience.
Suffreth alwey, syn ye so wel kan preche;
And but ye do, certein we shal yow teche
That it is fair to have a wyf in pees.
Oon of us two moste bowen, douteless,   440
And sith a man is moore resonable
Than womman is, ye moste been suffrable.
What eyleth yow to grucche thus and grone?
Is it for ye wolde have my queynte allone?
Wy, taak it al! Lo, have it every deel!   445
Peter! I shrewe yow, but ye love it weel;
For if I wolde selle my *bele chose,*
I koude walke as fressh as is a rose;
But I wol kepe it for youre owene tooth.
Ye be to blame, by God! I sey yow sooth.'   450
  Swiche manere wordes hadde we on honde.
Now wol I speken of my fourthe housbonde.
  My fourthe housbonde was a revelour —
This is to seyn, he hadde a paramour —
And I was yong and ful of ragerye,   455
Stibourn and strong, and joly as a pye.
How koude I daunce to an harpe smale,
And synge, ywis, as any nyghtyngale,
Whan I had dronke a draughte of sweete wyn!
Metellius, the foule cherl, the swyn,   460
That with a staf birafte his wyf hir lyf,
For she drank wyn, thogh I hadde been his wyf,
He sholde nat han daunted me fro drynke!
And after wyn on Venus moste I thynke,
For al so siker as cold engendreth hayl,   465
A likerous mouth moste han a likerous tayl.
In wommen vinolent is no defence —
This knowen lecchours by experience.
  But — Lord Crist! — whan that it remem-
      breth me
Upon my yowthe, and on my jolitee,   470

It tikleth me aboute myn herte roote.
Unto this day it dooth myn herte boote
That I have had my world as in my tyme.
But age, allas, that al wole envenyme,
Hath me biraft my beautee and my pith.   475
Lat go. Farewel! The devel go therwith!
The flour is goon; ther is namoore to telle;
The bren, as I best kan, now moste I selle;
But yet to be right myrie wol I fonde.
Now wol I tellen of my fourthe housbonde.
  I seye, I hadde in herte greet despit   481
That he of any oother had delit.
But he was quit, by God and by Seint Joce!
I made hym of the same wode a croce;
Nat of my body, in no foul manere,   485
But certeinly, I made folk swich cheere
That in his owene grece I made hym frye
For angre, and for verray jalousye.
By God, in erthe I was his purgatorie,
For which I hope his soule be in glorie.   490
For, God it woot, he sat ful ofte and song,
Whan that his shoo ful bitterly hym wrong.
Ther was no wight, save God and he, that
      wiste,
In many wise, how soore I hym twiste.
He deyde whan I cam fro Jerusalem,   495
And lith ygrave under the roode beem,
Al is his tombe noght so curyus
As was the sepulcre of hym Daryus,
Which that Appelles wroghte subtilly;
It nys but wast to burye hym preciously.   500
Lat hym fare wel; God yeve his soule reste!
He is now in his grave and in his cheste.
  Now of my fifthe housbonde wol I telle.
God lete his soule nevere come in helle!
And yet was he to me the mooste shrewe;   505
That feele I on my ribbes al by rewe,

---

435 **spiced:** scrupulous
436 **Jobes:** (the biblical) Job's
442 **suffrable:** able to bear suffering
444 **queynte:** elegant, pleasing thing (sexual favors)
445 **have it every deel:** have every bit of it
446 **Peter!:** by, in the name of, St. Peter   **shrewe yow, but ye:**
curse you unless you (if you do not)
447 **bele chose:** beautiful thing (sexual favors)
449 **tooth:** taste, pleasure
450 **I sey yow sooth:** I am telling you the truth
453 **revelour:** reveller, profligate
454 **paramour:** lady-love, concubine
455 **ragerye:** wantonness
456 **Stibourn:** stubborn   **pye:** magpie
460 **Metellius:** Egnatius Metellius   **cherl:** villain
461 **birafte:** took away from
462 **thogh:** although if
463 **daunted:** frightened
465 **al so siker as:** as surely as
466 **likerous mouth:** a gluttonous mouth   **likerous tayl:**
lecherous tail
467 **vinolent:** drunken
469 **it remembreth me:** I remember

471 **herte roote:** the bottom of my heart
472 **dooth myn herte boote:** does my heart good
474 **envenyme:** poison
475 **biraft:** taken away   **pith:** vigor
478 **bren:** bran
479 **fonde:** try
483 **Seint Joce:** St. Judocus
484 **croce:** cross
487 **grece:** grease
490 **hope:** suppose
492 **wrong:** pinched
493 **wiste:** knew
494 **twiste:** tortured
495 **deyde:** died
496 **ygrave:** buried   **roode beem:** beam supporting the cross at
the entrance to the choir of the church
498 **sepulcre:** sepulcher   **hym Daryus:** that Darius
499 **Appelles:** the Jewish craftsman supposedly responsible for
Darius's tomb
500 **preciously:** expensively
502 **cheste:** coffin
505 **mooste shrewe:** greatest scoundrel
506 **by rewe:** in a row, one after another

And evere shal unto myn endyng day.
But in oure bed he was so fressh and gay,
And therwithal so wel koude he me glose,
Whan that he wolde han my *bele chose;*   510
That thogh he hadde me bete on every bon,
He koude wynne agayn my love anon.
I trowe I loved hym best, for that he
Was of his love daungerous to me.
We wommen han, if that I shal nat lye,   515
In this matere a queynte fantasye:
Wayte what thyng we may nat lightly have,
Therafter wol we crie al day and crave.
Forbede us thyng, and that desiren we;
Preesse on us faste, and thanne wol we fle.   520
With daunger oute we al oure chaffare;
Greet prees at market maketh deere ware,
And to greet cheep is holde at litel prys:
This knoweth every womman that is wys.   524
    My fifthe housbonde — God his soule
        blesse! —
Which that I took for love, and no richesse,
He som tyme was a clerk of Oxenford,
And hadde left scole, and wente at hom to bord
With my gossib, dwellynge in oure toun;
God have hir soule! Hir name was Alisoun.   530
She knew myn herte, and eek my privetee,
Bet than oure parisshe preest, so moot I thee!
To hire biwreyed I my conseil al.
For hadde myn housbonde pissed on a wal,
Or doon a thyng that sholde han cost his lyf,
To hire, and to another worthy wyf,   536
And to my nece, which that I loved weel,
I wolde han toold his conseil every deel.
And so I dide ful often, God it woot,
That made his face often reed and hoot   540
For verray shame, and blamed hymself for he
Had toold to me so greet a pryvetee.
    And so bifel that ones in a Lente —
So often tymes I to my gossyb wente,
For evere yet I loved to be gay,   545
And for to walke in March, Averill, and May,
Fro hous to hous, to heere sondry talys —
That Jankyn clerk, and my gossyb dame Alys,

And I myself, into the feeldes wente.
Myn housbonde was at Londoun al that Lente;
I hadde the bettre leyser for to pleye,   551
And for to se, and eek for to be seye
Of lusty folk. What wiste I wher my grace
Was shapen for to be, or in what place?
Therfore I made my visitaciouns   555
To vigilies and to processiouns,
To prechyng eek, and to thise pilgrimages,
To pleyes of myracles, and to mariages,
And wered upon my gaye scarlet gytes.   559
Thise wormes, ne thise motthes, ne thise mytes,
Upon my peril, frete hem never a deel;
And wostow why? For they were used weel.
    Now wol I tellen forth what happed me.
I seye that in the feeldes walked we,
Til trewely we hadde swich daliance,   565
This clerk and I, that of my purveiance
I spak to hym and seyde hym how that he,
If I were wydwe, sholde wedde me.
For certeinly — I sey for no bobance —
Yet was I nevere withouten purveiance   570
Of mariage, n'of othere thynges eek.
I holde a mouses herte nat worth a leek
That hath but oon hole for to sterte to,
And if that faille, thanne is al ydo.   574
    I bar hym on honde he hadde enchanted
        me —
My dame taughte me that soutiltee —
And eek I seyde I mette of hym al nyght,
He wolde han slayn me as I lay upright,
And al my bed was ful of verray blood;
'But yet I hope that ye shal do me good,   580
For blood bitokeneth gold, as me was taught.'
And al was fals; I dremed of it right naught,
But as I folwed ay my dames loore,
As wel of this as of othere thynges moore.
    But now, sire, lat me se what I shal seyn.
A ha! By God, I have my tale ageyn.   586
    Whan that my fourthe housbonde was on
        beere,

509 **glose:** flatter
510 **bele chose:** beautiful thing (sexual favors)
514 **daungerous:** standoffish, hard to get
516 **queynte fantasye:** curious, strange inclination
517 **Wayte what:** note that whatever   **lightly:** easily
520 **Preesse:** press, entreat
521 With niggardliness (*daunger*) we spread out (*oute*) all our
merchandise (*chaffare*).
522 **prees:** crowd   **deere:** expensive
523 **to greet cheep:** too good a bargain
527 **som tyme:** once, formerly
529 **gossib:** close friend
533 **biwreyed:** revealed
542 **pryvetee:** secret

551 **leyser:** leisure, opportunity
552 **seye:** seen
554 **shapen:** destined
556 **vigilies:** gatherings on the evenings before religious holidays
558 **pleyes of myracles:** popular dramas on religious subjects
559 **gytes:** robes
560 **motthes:** moths   **mytes:** small insects
561 **Upon my peril:** (I swear) on peril (of my soul)   **frete:**
devoured   **never a deel:** not a bit
565 **daliance:** flirtation
566 **purveiance:** foresight, provision
569 **bobance:** boast
576 **dame:** mother   **soutiltee:** subtlety, trick
577 **mette:** dreamed
582 **right naught:** not at all
587 **beere:** bier

I weep algate, and made sory cheere,
As wyves mooten, for it is usage,
And with my coverchief covered my visage,
But for that I was purveyed of a make,   591
I wepte but smal, and that I undertake.
    To chirche was myn housbonde born
        a-morwe
With neighebores, that for hym maden sorwe;
And Jankyn, oure clerk, was oon of tho.   595
As help me God, whan that I saugh hym go
After the beere, me thoughte he hadde a paire
Of legges and of feet so clene and faire
That al myn herte I yaf unto his hoold.
He was, I trowe, twenty wynter oold,   600
And I was fourty, if I shal seye sooth;
But yet I hadde alwey a coltes tooth.
Gat-tothed I was, and that bicam me weel;
I hadde the prente of seinte Venus seel.
As help me God, I was a lusty oon,   605
And faire, and riche, and yong, and wel bigon,
And trewely, as myne housbondes tolde me,
I hadde the beste *quoniam* myghte be.
For certes, I am al Venerien
In feelynge, and myn herte is Marcien.   610
Venus me yaf my lust, my likerousnesse,
And Mars yaf me my sturdy hardynesse;
Myn ascendent was Taur, and Mars therinne.
Allas, allas! That evere love was synne!
I folwed ay myn inclinacioun   615
By vertu of my constellacioun;
That made me I koude noght withdrawe
My chambre of Venus from a good felawe.
Yet have I Martes mark upon my face,
And also in another privee place.   620
For God so wys be my savacioun,

I ne loved nevere by no discrecioun,
But evere folwede myn appetit,
Al were he short, or long, or blak, or whit;
I took no kep, so that he liked me,   625
How poore he was, ne eek of what degree.
    What sholde I seye but, at the monthes
        ende,
This joly clerk, Jankyn, that was so hende,
Hath wedded me with greet solempnytee,
And to hym yaf I al the lond and fee   630
That evere was me yeven therbifoore.
But afterward repented me ful soore;
He nolde suffre nothyng of my list.
By God, he smoot me ones on the lyst,
For that I rente out of his book a leef,   635
That of the strook myn ere wax al deef.
Stibourn I was as is a leonesse,
And of my tonge a verray jangleresse,
And walke I wolde, as I had doon biforn,   639
From hous to hous, although he had it sworn;
For which he often tymes wolde preche,
And me of olde Romayn geestes teche;
How he Symplicius Gallus lefte his wyf,
And hire forsook for terme of al his lyf,
Noght but for open-heveded he hir say   645
Lookynge out at his dore upon a day.
    Another Romayn tolde he me by name,
That, for his wyf was at a someres game
Withouten his wityng, he forsook hire eke.
And thanne wolde he upon his Bible seke   650
That ilke proverbe of Ecclesiaste
Where he comandeth and forbedeth faste
Man shal nat suffre his wyf go roule aboute.
Thanne wolde he seye right thus, withouten
        doute:
    'Whoso that buyldeth his hous al of salwes,
And priketh his blynde hors over the falwes,

588 **algate:** continuously
591 **purveyed of:** provided with beforehand
592 **smal:** little   **undertake:** affirm, declare
593 **a-morwe:** next morning
599 **hoold:** keeping
600 **wynter:** years
602 **coltes tooth:** youthful tastes, desires
603 **Gat-tothed:** with teeth set wide apart
604 **prente:** imprint, mark   **Venus seel:** Venus's mark, a
birthmark
606 **wel bigon:** in a good situation
608 **quoniam:** whatsit (literally, *because* or *whereas*), a euphemism
609 **Venerien:** dominated by the planet Venus
610 **Marcien:** dominated by the planet Mars
612 **hardynesse:** boldness
613 **ascendent was Taur:** ascending sign was Taurus, the bull;
see n. for the astro. details in lines 613–20.
615 **inclinacioun:** astrologically determined inclination
616 **constellacioun:** configuration of the heavenly bodies,
horoscope
617 **withdrawe:** withhold
619 **Martes mark:** mark of Mars, a reddish birthmark
620 **privee:** secret
621 **God so wys be:** as may God surely be   **savacioun:**
salvation

622 **discrecioun:** moderation, prudence
625 **so that:** providing that
628 **hende:** courteous
630 **fee:** property
633 **list:** desires
634 **lyst:** ear
635 **rente:** tore
637 **Stibourn:** stubborn
638 **jangleresse:** chatterbox
640 **it sworn:** sworn the contrary
642 **geestes:** stories
643 **Symplicius Gallus:** His story is told by Valerius Maximus,
as is the incident in 647 below.
645 **open-heveded:** bareheaded   **say:** saw
647 **Another Romayn:** See 643 above.
648 **someres game:** midsummer revels
649 **wityng:** knowledge
651 **Ecclesiaste:** Ecclesiasticus
652 **he:** the author of Ecclesiasticus
653 **roule:** wander
655 **salwes:** willow branches
656 **falwes:** open fields (idle land)

And suffreth his wyf to go seken halwes,   657
Is worthy to been hanged on the galwes!'
But al for noght, I sette noght an hawe
Of his proverbes n'of his olde sawe,   660
Ne I wolde nat of hym corrected be.
I hate hym that my vices telleth me,
And so doo mo, God woot, of us than I.
This made hym with me wood al outrely;
I nolde noght forbere hym in no cas.   665
  Now wol I seye yow sooth, by Seint Thomas,
Why that I rente out of his book a leef,
For which he smoot me so that I was deef.
  He hadde a book that gladly, nyght and day,
For his desport he wolde rede alway;   670
He cleped it Valerie and Theofraste,
At which book he lough alwey ful faste.
And eek ther was somtyme a clerk at Rome,
A cardinal, that highte Seint Jerome,
That made a book agayn Jovinian;   675
In which book eek ther was Tertulan,
Crisippus, Trotula, and Helowys,
That was abbesse nat fer fro Parys,
And eek the Parables of Salomon,
Ovides Art, and bookes many on,   680
And alle thise were bounden in o volume.
And every nyght and day was his custume,
Whan he hadde leyser and vacacioun
From oother worldly occupacioun,
To reden on this book of wikked wyves.   685
He knew of hem mo legendes and lyves
Than been of goode wyves in the Bible.
For trusteth wel, it is an impossible
That any clerk wol speke good of wyves,
But if it be of hooly seintes lyves,   690
Ne of noon oother womman never the mo.
Who peyntede the leon, tel me who?

By God, if wommen hadde writen stories,
As clerkes han withinne hire oratories,
They wolde han writen of men moore wikked-
  nesse
Than al the mark of Adam may redresse.   696
The children of Mercurie and of Venus
Been in hir wirkyng ful contrarius;
Mercurie loveth wysdam and science,
And Venus loveth ryot and dispence.   700
And, for hire diverse disposicioun,
Ech falleth in otheres exaltacioun.
And thus, God woot, Mercurie is desolat
In Pisces, wher Venus is exaltat,
And Venus falleth ther Mercurie is reysed.   705
Therfore no womman of no clerk is preysed.
The clerk, whan he is oold, and may noght do
Of Venus werkes worth his olde sho,
Thanne sit he doun, and writ in his dotage
That wommen kan nat kepe hir mariage!   710
  But now to purpos, why I tolde thee
That I was beten for a book, pardee!
Upon a nyght Jankyn, that was oure sire,
Redde on his book, as he sat by the fire,
Of Eva first, that for hir wikkednesse   715
Was al mankynde broght to wrecchednesse,
For which that Jhesu Crist hymself was slayn,
That boghte us with his herte blood agayn.
Lo, heere expres of womman may ye fynde
That womman was the los of al mankynde.   720
  Tho redde he me how Sampson loste his
    heres:
Slepynge, his lemman kitte it with hir sheres;
Thurgh which treson loste he bothe his yen.
  Tho redde he me, if that I shal nat lyen,
Of Hercules and of his Dianyre,   725
That caused hym to sette hymself afyre.
  No thyng forgat he the care and the wo
That Socrates hadde with his wyves two,

657 **seken halwes:** go on pilgrimages
659 **hawe:** haw, hawthorn berry (i.e., nothing)
664 **al outrely:** entirely
665 **forbere:** put up with
671–80 **Valerie and Theofraste:** Valerius, supposed author of the *Dissuasio* (or *Epistola*) *ad Rufinum,* and Theophrastus, author of the *Golden Book on Marriage,* both works attacking marriage. Jankyn's book of "wicked wives" also contains passages from the book by *Jerome* (a father of the Church) *agayn Jovinian* (an unorthodox monk who denied that virginity was necessarily superior to marriage), *Tertulan* (Tertullian, whose works contain misogynist and anti-marriage passages), *Crisippus* (mentioned by Jerome but otherwise unknown), *Trotula* (probably Trotula di Ruggiero, a female physician and author), *Helowys* (Heloïse, lover of Abelard), the *Parables of Salomon* (Prov. 10.1 to 22.16 in the Vulgate), and *Ovides Art* (Ovid's *Ars amatoria*). For further information see n. 669–75.
673 **clerk:** scholar
683 **vacacioun:** spare time
688 **impossible:** impossibility
689 **clerk:** learned man, clergyman
691 **never the mo:** in any way
692 The lion's question when he saw a picture of a man killing a lion

693 **stories:** histories
694 **oratories:** chapels
696 **mark of Adam:** male sex
697 **children of Mercurie:** those dominated by the planet Mercury (scholars) **of Venus:** those dominated by Venus, lovers
698 **wirkyng ful contrarius:** actions directly contrary
699 **science:** knowledge
700 **ryot:** debauchery **dispence:** extravagant expenditures
702 **exaltacioun:** the zodiacal sign in which a planet is most powerful
703 **desolat:** powerless
704 **Pisces:** the zodiacal sign **exaltat:** exalted (has her exaltation, is most powerful)
711 **now to purpos:** now to the point
713 **oure sire:** master of our house
715 **Eva:** Eve
719 **expres:** clearly
721 **Sampson:** For the story see MkT VII.2015–94.
725 **Hercules and . . . Dianyre:** For the story see MkT VII.2119–35.

How Xantippa caste pisse upon his heed.
This sely man sat stille as he were deed;　730
He wiped his heed, namoore dorste he seyn,
But 'Er that thonder stynte, comth a reyn!'

　Of Phasipha, that was the queene of Crete,
For shrewednesse, hym thoughte the tale
　　swete;
Fy! Spek namoore — it is a grisly thyng —　735
Of hire horrible lust and hir likyng.

　Of Clitermystra, for hire lecherye,
That falsly made hire housbonde for to dye,
He redde it with ful good devocioun.

　He tolde me eek for what occasioun　740
Amphiorax at Thebes loste his lyf.
Myn housbonde hadde a legende of his wyf,
Eriphilem, that for an ouche of gold
Hath prively unto the Grekes told
Wher that hir housbonde hidde hym in a place,
For which he hadde at Thebes sory grace.　746

　Of Lyvia tolde he me, and of Lucye:
They bothe made hir housbondes for to dye,
That oon for love, that oother was for hate.
Lyvia hir housbonde, on an even late,　750
Empoysoned hath, for that she was his fo;
Lucia, likerous, loved hire housbonde so
That, for he sholde alwey upon hire thynke,
She yaf hym swich a manere love-drynke
That he was deed er it were by the morwe;
And thus algates housbondes han sorwe.　756

　Thanne tolde he me how oon Latumyus
Compleyned unto his felawe Arrius
That in his gardyn growed swich a tree
On which he seyde how that his wyves thre
Hanged hemself for herte despitus.　761
'O leeve brother,' quod this Arrius,
'Yif me a plante of thilke blissed tree,
And in my gardyn planted shal it bee.'

　Of latter date, of wyves hath he red　765
That somme han slayn hir housbondes in hir
　　bed,

And lete hir lecchour dighte hire al the nyght,
Whan that the corps lay in the floor upright.
And somme han dryve nayles in hir brayn,
Whil that they slepte, and thus they had hem
　　slayn.　770
Somme han hem yeve poysoun in hire drynke.
He spak moore harm than herte may bithynke,
And therwithal he knew of mo proverbes
Than in this world ther growen gras or herbes.
'Bet is,' quod he, 'thyn habitacioun　775
Be with a leon or a foul dragoun,
Than with a womman usynge for to chyde.
Bet is,' quod he, 'hye in the roof abyde,
Than with an angry wyf doun in the hous;
They been so wikked and contrarious,　780
They haten that hir housbondes loven ay.'
He seyde, 'A womman cast hir shame away,
Whan she cast of hir smok'; and forthermo,
'A fair womman, but she be chaast also,
Is lyk a gold ryng in a sowes nose.'　785
Who wolde wene, or who wolde suppose,
The wo that in myn herte was, and pyne?

　And whan I saugh he wolde nevere fyne
To reden on this cursed book al nyght,
Al sodeynly thre leves have I plyght　790
Out of his book, right as he radde, and eke
I with my fest so took hym on the cheke
That in oure fyr he fil bakward adoun.
And he up stirte as dooth a wood leoun,
And with his fest he smoot me on the heed
That in the floor I lay as I were deed.　796
And whan he saugh how stille that I lay,
He was agast and wolde han fled his way,
Til atte laste out of my swogh I breyde.
'O! hastow slayn me, false theef?' I seyde,　800
'And for my land thus hastow mordred me?
Er I be deed, yet wol I kisse thee.'

　And neer he cam, and kneled faire adoun,
And seyde, 'Deere suster Alisoun,
As help me God, I shal thee nevere smyte!
That I have doon, it is thyself to wyte.　806
Foryeve it me, and that I thee biseke!'
And yet eftsoones I hitte hym on the cheke,

729 Xantippa: Xantippe, shrewish wife of *Socrates,* the Greek
philosopher
733 Phasipha: Pasiphae, mother of the Minotaur, fathered on
her by a bull
734 shrewednesse: malignancy
737 Clitermystra: Clytemnestra murdered her husband
Agamemnon, the Greek king who waged war against Troy.
741 Amphiorax: Amphiaraus died at Thebes because he took the
advice of his wife Eriphyle (*Eriphilem*).
743 ouche: brooch
746 sory grace: misfortune
747 Lyvia: Livia, lover of Sejanus　**Lucye:** Lucia, wife of the
Roman poet Lucretius
751 Empoysoned: poisoned
756 algates: always
757–58 Latumyus, Arrius: see n.

767 dighte: copulate with
772 harm: slander　**bithynke:** imagine
777 usynge for to: used to
783 smok: shift, undergarment
788 fyne: cease
790 plyght: plucked
791 radde: read
792 took hym: gave him (a blow)
799 swogh: swoon　**breyde:** started up, awoke
806 to wyte: to blame
808 eftsoones: immediately

And seyde, 'Theef, thus muchel am I wreke;
Now wol I dye, I may no lenger speke.'   810
But atte laste, with muchel care and wo,
We fille acorded by us selven two.
He yaf me al the bridel in myn hond,
To han the governance of hous and lond,
And of his tonge, and of his hond also;   815
And made hym brenne his book anon right tho.
And whan that I hadde geten unto me,
By maistrie, al the soveraynetee,
And that he seyde, 'Myn owene trewe wyf,
Do as thee lust the terme of al thy lyf;   820
Keep thyn honour, and keep eek myn estaat' —
After that day we hadden never debaat.
God helpe me so, I was to hym as kynde
As any wyf from Denmark unto Ynde,
And also trewe, and so was he to me.   825
I prey to God, that sit in magestee,
So blesse his soule for his mercy deere.
Now wol I seye my tale, if ye wol heere."

*Biholde the wordes bitwene the
Somonour and the Frere.*

The Frere lough, whan he hadde herd al this;
"Now dame," quod he, "so have I joye or blis,
This is a long preamble of a tale!"   831
And whan the Somonour herde the Frere gale,

"Lo," quod the Somonour, "Goddes armes two!
A frere wol entremette hym everemo.
Lo, goode men, a flye and eek a frere   835
Wol falle in every dyssh and eek mateere.
What spekestow of preambulacioun?
What! amble, or trotte, or pees, or go sit doun!
Thou lettest oure disport in this manere."
"Ye, woltow so, sire Somonour?" quod the
    Frere;
"Now, by my feith I shal, er that I go,   841
Telle of a somonour swich a tale or two
That alle the folk shal laughen in this place."
"Now elles, Frere, I bishrewe thy face,"
Quod this Somonour, "and I bishrewe me,   845
But if I telle tales two or thre
Of freres er I come to Sidyngborne
That I shal make thyn herte for to morne,
For wel I woot thy pacience is gon."   849
Oure Hooste cride "Pees! And that anon!"
And seyde, "Lat the womman telle hire tale.
Ye fare as folk that dronken ben of ale.
Do, dame, telle forth youre tale, and that is
    best."
"Al redy, sire," quod she, "right as yow lest,
If I have licence of this worthy Frere."   855
"Yis, dame," quod he, "tel forth, and I wol
    heere."

Heere endeth the Wyf of Bathe hir Prologe.

THE WIFE OF BATH'S TALE

Heere bigynneth the Tale of the Wyf of Bathe.

In th'olde dayes of the Kyng Arthour,
Of which that Britons speken greet honour,
Al was this land fulfild of fayerye.
The elf-queene, with hir joly compaignye,   860
Daunced ful ofte in many a grene mede.
This was the olde opinion, as I rede;
I speke of manye hundred yeres ago.
But now kan no man se none elves mo,

For now the grete charitee and prayeres   865
Of lymytours and othere hooly freres,
That serchen every lond and every streem,

---

809 **wreke:** avenged
818 **soveraynetee:** sovereignty, mastery
824 **Denmark unto Ynde:** throughout the whole world
832 **gale:** cry out

859 The whole country was filled with fairies.
860 **elf-queene:** fairy queen

834 **entremette hym:** interfere
837 **preambulacioun:** making a preamble
838 **amble, or trotte, or pees:** amble (an easy lateral walk on horseback; i.e., go slow), trot (i.e., go fast), or keep still
839 **lettest:** hinder
844 **bishrewe:** curse
847 **Sidyngborne:** Sittingbourne, a town between Rochester and Canterbury, about 40 miles from London
848 **morne:** mourn
852 **fare:** act
856 **Yis:** yes indeed

866 **lymytours:** friars (see GP I.209)
867 **serchen:** haunt

As thikke as motes in the sonne-beem,
Blessynge halles, chambres, kichenes, boures,
Citees, burghes, castels, hye toures, 870
Thropes, bernes, shipnes, dayeryes —
This maketh that ther ben no fayeryes.
For ther as wont to walken was an elf
Ther walketh now the lymytour hymself
In undermeles and in morwenynges, 875
And seyth his matyns and his hooly thynges
As he gooth in his lymytacioun.
Wommen may go saufly up and doun.
In every bussh or under every tree
Ther is noon oother incubus but he, 880
And he ne wol doon hem but dishonour.

    And so bifel that this kyng Arthour
Hadde in his hous a lusty bacheler,
That on a day cam ridynge fro ryver,
And happed that, allone as he was born, 885
He saugh a mayde walkynge hym biforn,
Of which mayde anon, maugree hir heed,
By verray force, he rafte hire maydenhed;
For which oppressioun was swich clamour
And swich pursute unto the kyng Arthour 890
That dampned was this knyght for to be deed,
By cours of lawe, and sholde han lost his
        heed —
Paraventure swich was the statut tho —
But that the queene and other ladyes mo
So longe preyeden the kyng of grace 895
Til he his lyf hym graunted in the place,
And yaf hym to the queene, al at hir wille,
To chese wheither she wolde hym save or
        spille.
    The queene thanketh the kyng with al hir
        myght,
And after this thus spak she to the knyght, 900
Whan that she saugh hir tyme, upon a day:
"Thou standest yet," quod she, "in swich array
That of thy lyf yet hastow no suretee.

I grante thee lyf, if thou kanst tellen me 904
What thyng is it that wommen moost desiren.
Be war, and keep thy nekke-boon from iren!
And if thou kanst nat tellen it anon,
Yet wol I yeve thee leve for to gon
A twelf-month and a day, to seche and leere
An answere suffisant in this mateere; 910
And suretee wol I han, er that thou pace,
Thy body for to yelden in this place."
    Wo was this knyght, and sorwefully he siketh;
But what! He may nat do al as hym liketh.
And at the laste he chees hym for to wende
And come agayn, right at the yeres ende, 916
With swich answere as God wolde hym pur-
        veye;
And taketh his leve, and wendeth forth his
        weye.
    He seketh every hous and every place
Where as he hopeth for to fynde grace 920
To lerne what thyng wommen loven moost,
But he ne koude arryven in no coost
Wher as he myghte fynde in this mateere
Two creatures accordynge in-feere. 924
Somme seyde wommen loven best richesse,
Somme seyde honour, somme seyde jolynesse,
Somme riche array, somme seyden lust abedde,
And oftetyme to be wydwe and wedde.
Somme seyde that oure hertes been moost esed
Whan that we been yflatered and yplesed. 930
He gooth ful ny the sothe, I wol nat lye.
A man shal wynne us best with flaterye,
And with attendance and with bisynesse
Been we ylymed, bothe moore and lesse.
    And somme seyen that we loven best 935
For to be free and do right as us lest,
And that no man repreve us of oure vice,
But seye that we be wise and no thyng nyce.
For trewely ther is noon of us alle,
If any wight wol clawe us on the galle, 940
That we nel kike, for he seith us sooth.
Assay, and he shal fynde it that so dooth;

868 **motes:** specks of dust
869 **boures:** bedrooms
870 **burghes:** boroughs
871 **Thropes:** villages **bernes:** barns **shipnes:** stables
dayeryes: dairies
875 **undermeles:** late mornings (from 9 to 12) **morwenynges:**
mornings
876 **matyns:** matins, morning prayers
877 **lymytacioun:** territory
878 **saufly:** safely
880 **incubus:** evil spirit, said to copulate with women
883 **bacheler:** young knight
884 **ryver:** hawking for waterfowl
887 **maugree hir heed:** against her will, despite all she could do
888 **rafte:** took
889 **oppressioun:** wrong
890 **pursute:** suing for justice
893 **Paraventure:** perhaps
898 **spille:** put to death
903 **suretee:** security

906 **iren:** iron (i.e., the executioner's axe)
909 **seche:** search **leere:** learn
911 **suretee:** pledge
912 **yelden:** surrender
917 **purveye:** provide
922 **coost:** coast (region)
924 **accordynge in-feere:** agreeing together, in agreement
931 **gooth ful ny the sothe:** gets very close to the truth
933 **attendance:** attention
934 **ylymed:** caught (as with bird-lime)
936 **us lest:** we please
937 **repreve:** reprove
940 **clawe us on the galle:** rub a sore spot
941 **nel kike:** will not (*nel = ne wil*) kick back

For, be we never so vicious withinne,
We wol been holden wise and clene of synne.
     And somme seyn that greet delit han we   945
For to been holden stable, and eek secree,
And in o purpos stedefastly to dwelle,
And nat biwreye thyng that men us telle.
But that tale is nat worth a rake-stele.
Pardee, we wommen konne no thyng hele;   950
Witnesse on Myda — wol ye heere the tale?
     Ovyde, amonges othere thynges smale,
Seyde Myda hadde, under his longe heres,
Growynge upon his heed two asses eres,   954
The whiche vice he hydde as he best myghte
Ful subtilly from every mannes sighte,
That, save his wyf, ther wiste of it namo.
He loved hire moost, and trusted hire also;
He preyede hire that to no creature
She sholde tellen of his disfigure.   960
     She swoor him, "Nay"; for al this world to
          wynne,
She nolde do that vileynye or synne,
To make hir housbonde han so foul a name.
She nolde nat telle it for hir owene shame.
But nathelees, hir thoughte that she dyde   965
That she so longe sholde a conseil hyde;
Hir thoughte it swal so soore aboute hir herte
That nedely som word hire moste asterte;
And sith she dorste telle it to no man,
Doun to a mareys faste by she ran —   970
Til she cam there hir herte was afyre —
And as a bitore bombleth in the myre,
She leyde hir mouth unto the water doun:
"Biwreye me nat, thou water, with thy soun,"
Quod she; "to thee I telle it and namo;   975
Myn housbonde hath longe asses erys two!
Now is myn herte al hool; now is it oute.
I myghte no lenger kepe it, out of doute."
Heere may ye se, thogh we a tyme abyde,
Yet out it moot; we kan no conseil hyde.   980
The remenant of the tale if ye wol heere,
Redeth Ovyde, and ther ye may it leere.

     This knyght, of which my tale is specially,
Whan that he saugh he myghte nat come
          therby —
This is to seye, what wommen love moost —   985
Withinne his brest ful sorweful was the goost.
But hoom he gooth; he myghte nat sojourne;
The day was come that homward moste he
          tourne.
And in his wey it happed hym to ryde,
In al this care, under a forest syde,   990
Wher as he saugh upon a daunce go
Of ladyes foure and twenty, and yet mo;
Toward the whiche daunce he drow ful yerne,
In hope that som wysdom sholde he lerne.
But certeinly, er he cam fully there,   995
Vanysshed was this daunce, he nyste where.
No creature saugh he that bar lyf,
Save on the grene he saugh sittynge a wyf —
A fouler wight ther may no man devyse.
Agayn the knyght this olde wyf gan ryse,   1000
And seyde, "Sire knyght, heer forth ne lith no
          wey.
Tel me what that ye seken, by youre fey!
Paraventure it may the bettre be;
Thise olde folk kan muchel thyng," quod she.
     "My leeve mooder," quod this knyght, "cer-
          teyn
I nam but deed but if that I kan seyn   1006
What thyng it is that wommen moost desire.
Koude ye me wisse, I wolde wel quite youre
          hire."
     "Plight me thy trouthe heere in myn hand,"
          quod she,
"The nexte thyng that I requere thee,   1010
Thou shalt it do, if it lye in thy myght,
And I wol telle it yow er it be nyght."
     "Have heer my trouthe," quod the knyght,
          "I grante."
     "Thanne," quod she, "I dar me wel avante
Thy lyf is sauf, for I wol stonde therby;   1015
Upon my lyf, the queene wol seye as I.

---

944 **holden:** considered
946 **secree:** discreet, able to keep a secret
948 **biwreye:** betray, reveal
949 **rake-stele:** rake handle (i.e., nothing)
950 **hele:** keep secret
951 **Witnesse on:** take the evidence of   **Myda:** Midas
952 **Ovyde:** Ovid, the Roman poet
960 **disfigure:** deformity
965 **dyde:** would die
966 **conseil:** secret
967 **swal:** swelled
968 **nedely:** of necessity   **asterte:** escape
970 **mareys:** marsh
972 **bitore bombleth in the myre:** bittern bumbles (booms) in
the mire
974 **Biwreye:** betray   **soun:** sound
982 **leere:** learn

987 **sojourne:** remain
989 **it happed hym:** he chanced
990 **under:** by, near
993 **yerne:** eagerly
998 **wyf:** woman
999 **devyse:** imagine
1000 **Agayn:** toward (to meet)
1008 **wisse:** inform, instruct   **quite youre hire:** reward your
efforts
1009 **Plight:** pledge
1010 **requere:** ask
1013 **grante:** consent
1014 **avante:** boast
1015 **sauf:** safe
1016 **seye as I:** say as I do, agree with me

Lat se which is the proudeste of hem alle
That wereth on a coverchief or a calle
That dar seye nay of that I shal thee teche.
Lat us go forth withouten lenger speche."
Tho rowned she a pistel in his ere, 1021
And bad hym to be glad and have no fere.
　　Whan they be comen to the court, this
　　　　knyght
Seyde he had holde his day, as he hadde hight,
And redy was his answere, as he sayde. 1025
Ful many a noble wyf, and many a mayde,
And many a wydwe, for that they been wise,
The queene hirself sittynge as a justise,
Assembled been, his answere for to heere;
And afterward this knyght was bode appeere.
　　To every wight comanded was silence, 1031
And that the knyght sholde telle in audience
What thyng that worldly wommen loven best.
This knyght ne stood nat stille as doth a best,
But to his questioun anon answerde 1035
With manly voys, that al the court it herde:
　　"My lige lady, generally," quod he,
"Wommen desiren to have sovereynetee
As wel over hir housbond as hir love,
And for to been in maistrie hym above. 1040
This is youre mooste desir, thogh ye me kille.
Dooth as yow list; I am heer at youre wille."
In al the court ne was ther wyf, ne mayde,
Ne wydwe that contraried that he sayde,
But seyden he was worthy han his lyf. 1045
And with that word up stirte the olde wyf,
Which that the knyght saugh sittynge on the
　　　　grene:
"Mercy," quod she, "my sovereyn lady queene!
Er that youre court departe, do me right.
I taughte this answere unto the knyght; 1050
For which he plighte me his trouthe there,
The firste thyng that I wolde hym requere
He wolde it do, if it lay in his myghte.
Bifore the court thanne preye I thee, sir
　　　　knyght,"
Quod she, "that thou me take unto thy wyf,
For wel thou woost that I have kept thy lyf.
If I seye fals, sey nay, upon thy fey!" 1057
　　This knyght answerde, "Allas and weyla-
　　　　wey!

I woot right wel that swich was my biheste.
For Goddes love, as chees a newe requeste!
Taak al my good and lat my body go." 1061
　　"Nay, thanne," quod she, "I shrewe us bothe
　　　　two!
For thogh that I be foul, and oold, and poore
I nolde for al the metal, ne for oore
That under erthe is grave or lith above, 1065
But if thy wyf I were, and eek thy love."
　　"My love?" quod he, "nay, my dampna-
　　　　cioun!
Allas, that any of my nacioun
Sholde evere so foule disparaged be!"
But al for noght; the ende is this, that he 1070
Constreyned was; he nedes moste hire wedde,
And taketh his olde wyf, and gooth to bedde.
　　Now wolden som men seye, paraventure,
That for my necligence I do no cure
To tellen yow the joye and al th'array 1075
That at the feeste was that ilke day.
To which thyng shortly answeren I shal:
I seye ther nas no joye ne feeste at al;
Ther nas but hevynesse and muche sorwe.
For prively he wedded hire on morwe,
And al day after hidde hym as an owle, 1081
So wo was hym, his wyf looked so foule.
　　Greet was the wo the knyght hadde in his
　　　　thoght,
Whan he was with his wyf abedde ybroght;
He walweth and he turneth to and fro. 1085
His olde wyf lay smylynge everemo,
And seyde, "O deere housbonde, benedicitee!
Fareth every knyght thus with his wyf as ye?
Is this the lawe of kyng Arthures hous?
Is every knyght of his so dangerous? 1090
I am youre owene love and youre wyf;
I am she which that saved hath youre lyf,
And, certes, yet ne dide I yow nevere unright;
Why fare ye thus with me this firste nyght?
Ye faren lyk a man had lost his wit. 1095
What is my gilt? For Goddes love, tel it,
And it shal been amended, if I may."
　　"Amended?" quod this knyght, "Allas, nay,
　　　　nay!
It wol nat been amended nevere mo.
Thou art so loothly, and so oold also, 1100

1018 **calle:** hairnet worn as a headdress
1021 **rowned:** whispered **pistel:** message
1024 **hight:** promised
1030 **bode appeere:** commanded to appear
1034 **best:** beast
1044 **contraried:** denied
1051 **plighte:** pledged

1059 **biheste:** promise
1060 **as chees:** choose
1064 **oore:** ore
1068 **nacioun:** family
1069 **disparaged:** degraded by a union with someone of lower birth
1075 **array:** rich display
1085 **walweth:** writhes
1096 **gilt:** offense
1100 **loothly:** loathsome

And therto comen of so lough a kynde,
That litel wonder is thogh I walwe and wynde.
So wolde God myn herte wolde breste!"
        "Is this," quod she, "the cause of youre un-
                reste?"
        "Ye, certeinly," quod he, "no wonder is."
        "Now, sire," quod she, "I koude amende al
                this,   1106
If that me liste, er it were dayes thre,
So wel ye myghte bere yow unto me.
        "But, for ye speken of swich gentillesse
As is descended out of old richesse,   1110
That therfore sholden ye be gentil men,
Swich arrogance is nat worth an hen.
Looke who that is moost vertuous alway,
Pryvee and apert, and moost entendeth ay
To do the gentil dedes that he kan;   1115
Taak hym for the grettest gentil man.
Crist wole we clayme of hym oure gentillesse,
Nat of oure eldres for hire old richesse.
For thogh they yeve us al hir heritage,   1119
For which we clayme to been of heigh parage,
Yet may they nat biquethe for no thyng
To noon of us hir vertuous lyvyng,
That made hem gentil men ycalled be,
And bad us folwen hem in swich degree.
        "Wel kan the wise poete of Florence,   1125
That highte Dant, speken in this sentence.
Lo, in swich maner rym is Dantes tale:
'Ful selde up riseth by his branches smale
Prowesse of man, for God, of his goodnesse,
Wole that of hym we clayme oure gentil-
                lesse';   1130
For of oure eldres may we no thyng clayme
But temporel thyng, that man may hurte and
                mayme.
        "Eek every wight woot this as wel as I,
If gentillesse were planted natureelly
Unto a certeyn lynage doun the lyne,   1135
Pryvee and apert thanne wolde they nevere
                fyne
To doon of gentillesse the faire office;
They myghte do no vileynye or vice.

"Taak fyr and ber it in the derkeste hous
Bitwix this and the mount of Kaukasous,   1140
And lat men shette the dores and go thenne;
Yet wole the fyr as faire lye and brenne
As twenty thousand men myghte it biholde;
His office natureel ay wol it holde,
Up peril of my lyf, til that it dye.   1145
        "Heere may ye se wel how that genterye
Is nat annexed to possessioun,
Sith folk ne doon hir operacioun
Alwey, as dooth the fyr, lo, in his kynde.   1149
For, God it woot, men may wel often fynde
A lordes sone do shame and vileynye;
And he that wole han pris of his gentrye,
For he was boren of a gentil hous
And hadde his eldres noble and vertuous,
And nel hymselven do no gentil dedis   1155
Ne folwen his gentil auncestre that deed is,
He nys nat gentil, be he duc or erl,
For vileyns synful dedes make a cherl.
For gentillesse nys but renomee   1159
Of thyne auncestres, for hire heigh bountee,
Which is a strange thyng to thy persone.
Thy gentillesse cometh fro God allone.
Thanne comth oure verray gentillesse of grace;
It was no thyng biquethe us with oure place.
        "Thenketh hou noble, as seith Valerius,   1165
Was thilke Tullius Hostillius,
That out of poverte roos to heigh noblesse.
Reedeth Senek, and redeth eek Boece;
Ther shul ye seen expres that it no drede is
That he is gentil that dooth gentil dedis.   1170
And therfore, leeve housbonde, I thus con-
                clude:
Al were it that myne auncestres were rude,
Yet may the hye God, and so hope I,
Grante me grace to lyven vertuously.
Thanne am I gentil, whan that I bigynne   1175
To lyven vertuously and weyve synne.
        "And ther as ye of poverte me repreeve,
The hye God, on whom that we bileeve,

1101 **comen of so lough a kynde:** descended from such
base-born lineage
1102 **wynde:** twist about
1104 **unreste:** distress
1108 **so:** so that   **bere yow unto me:** behave towards me
1109 **gentillesse:** nobility
1114 **Pryvee and apert:** in private and public, in all
circumstances   **entendeth:** strives
1120 **heigh parage:** noble lineage
1126 **Dant:** Dante Alighieri
1130 **Wole:** desires
1132 **mayme:** injure
1136 **fyne:** cease
1137 **office:** duties

1140 **Kaukasous:** the Caucasus mountains
1141 **thenne:** thence
1142 **lye:** blaze
1146 **genterye:** gentility
1147 **annexed to:** joined with
1148 **ne doon hir operacioun:** do not behave as they should
1152 **pris of his gentrye:** praise for his noble birth
1155 **nel** = *ne wyl,* will not
1159 **renomee:** renown
1160 **bountee:** goodness
1161 **strange thyng:** a thing foreign to, not naturally part of
1165 **Valerius:** Valerius Maximus, the Roman author
1166 **Tullius Hostillius:** legendary third king of Rome
1168 **Senek:** Seneca, Roman author   **Boece:** Boethius (see, e.g.,
Boece 3.pr4)
1172 **Al were:** even though   **rude:** humble
1176 **weyve:** abandon

In wilful poverte chees to lyve his lyf.
And certes every man, mayden, or wyf   1180
May understonde that Jhesus, hevene kyng,
Ne wolde nat chese a vicious lyvyng.
Glad poverte is an honest thyng, certeyn;
This wole Senec and othere clerkes seyn.
Whoso that halt hym payd of his poverte,   1185
I holde hym riche, al hadde he nat a sherte.
He that coveiteth is a povre wight,
For he wolde han that is nat in his myght;
But he that noght hath, ne coveiteth have,
Is riche, although ye holde hym but a knave.
Verray poverte, it syngeth proprely;   1191
Juvenal seith of poverte myrily:
'The povre man, whan he goth by the weye,
Bifore the theves he may synge and pleye.'
Poverte is hateful good and, as I gesse,   1195
A ful greet bryngere out of bisynesse;
A greet amendere eek of sapience
To hym that taketh it in pacience.
Poverte is this, although it seme alenge:
Possessioun that no wight wol chalenge.   1200
Poverte ful ofte, whan a man is lowe,
Maketh his God and eek hymself to knowe.
Poverte a spectacle is, as thynketh me,
Thurgh which he may his verray freendes see.
And therfore, sire, syn that I noght yow greve,
Of my poverte namoore ye me repreve.   1206
    "Now, sire, of elde ye repreve me;
And certes, sire, thogh noon auctoritee
Were in no book, ye gentils of honour
Seyn that men sholde an oold wight doon
        favour   1210
And clepe hym fader, for youre gentillesse;
And auctours shal I fynden, as I gesse.
    "Now ther ye seye that I am foul and old,
Than drede you noght to been a cokewold;
For filthe and eelde, also moot I thee,   1215
Been grete wardeyns upon chastitee.
But nathelees, syn I knowe youre delit,

I shal fulfille youre worldly appetit.
    "Chese now," quod she, "oon of thise thynges
        tweye:
To han me foul and old til that I deye,   1220
And be to yow a trewe, humble wyf,
And nevere yow displese in al my lyf,
Or elles ye wol han me yong and fair,
And take youre aventure of the repair
That shal be to youre hous by cause of me,
Or in som oother place, may wel be.   1226
Now chese yourselven, wheither that yow
        liketh."
    This knyght avyseth hym and sore siketh,
But atte laste he seyde in this manere:
"My lady and my love, and wyf so deere,   1230
I put me in youre wise governance;
Cheseth youreself which may be moost ples-
        ance
And moost honour to yow and me also.
I do no fors the wheither of the two,
For as yow liketh, it suffiseth me."   1235
    "Thanne have I gete of yow maistrie," quod
        she,
"Syn I may chese and governe as me lest?"
    "Ye, certes, wyf," quod he, "I holde it best."
    "Kys me," quod she, "we be no lenger wrothe,
For, by my trouthe, I wol be to yow bothe —
This is to seyn, ye, bothe fair and good.   1241
I prey to God that I moote sterven wood,
But I to yow be also good and trewe
As evere was wyf, syn that the world was newe.
And but I be to-morn as fair to seene   1245
As any lady, emperice, or queene,
That is bitwixe the est and eke the west,
Dooth with my lyf and deth right as yow lest.
Cast up the curtyn, looke how that it is."
    And whan the knyght saugh verraily al this,
That she so fair was, and so yong therto,   1251
For joye he hente hire in his armes two.
His herte bathed in a bath of blisse.
A thousand tyme a-rewe he gan hire kisse,
And she obeyed hym in every thyng   1255
That myghte doon hym plesance or likyng.
    And thus they lyve unto hir lyves ende
In parfit joye; and Jhesu Crist us sende
Housbondes meeke, yonge, and fressh abedde,

1179 **wilful:** willing, voluntary
1185 **halt hym payd:** is satisfied
1189 **have:** to have (anything)
1190 **knave:** peasant
1192 **Juvenal:** the Roman poet
1196 **bryngere out of bisynesse:** one that brings out,
encourages, industry
1197 **amendere:** improver   **sapience:** wisdom
1199 **alenge:** miserable
1200 **chalenge:** claim
1203 **spectacle:** eyeglass
1209 **gentils:** nobles
1212 **auctours:** authoritative writers   **fynden:** find (to support
this)
1214 **cokewold:** cuckold
1215 **thee:** prosper
1216 **wardeyns:** guardians
1217 **delit:** desire

1224 **aventure:** chances   **repair:** resort, visitors
1227 **wheither:** which
1234 **I do no fors:** I don't care
1235 **suffiseth me:** is sufficient for me
1242 **sterven wood:** die insane
1245 **to-morn:** in the morning
1253 **bathed:** basked
1254 **a-rewe:** in succession

And grace t'overbyde hem that we wedde;
And eek I praye Jhesu shorte hir lyves   1261
That noght wol be governed by hir wyves;

And olde and angry nygardes of dispence,
God sende hem soone verray pestilence!

Heere endeth the Wyves Tale of Bathe.

THE FRIAR'S PROLOGUE

The Prologe of the Freres Tale.

This worthy lymytour, this noble Frere,   1265
He made alwey a maner louryng chiere
Upon the Somonour, but for honestee
No vileyns word as yet to hym spak he.
But atte laste he seyde unto the wyf,
"Dame," quod he, "God yeve yow right good
        lyf!   1270
Ye han heer touched, also moot I thee,
In scole-matere greet difficultee.
Ye han seyd muche thyng right wel, I seye;
But, dame, heere as we ryde by the weye,
Us nedeth nat to speken but of game,   1275
And lete auctoritees, on Goddes name,
To prechyng and to scoles of clergye.
But if it lyke to this compaignye,
I wol yow of a somonour telle a game.
Pardee, ye may wel knowe by the name   1280
That of a somonour may no good be sayd;
I praye that noon of you be yvele apayd.
A somonour is a rennere up and doun

With mandementz for fornicacioun,
And is ybet at every townes ende."   1285
    Oure Hoost tho spak, "A, sire, ye sholde be
        hende
And curteys, as a man of youre estaat;
In compaignye we wol have no debaat.
Telleth youre tale, and lat the Somonour be."
    "Nay," quod the Somonour, "lat hym seye to
        me   1290
What so hym list; whan it comth to my lot,
By God, I shal hym quiten every grot.
I shal hym tellen which a greet honour
It is to be a flaterynge lymytour,
And of many another manere cryme   1295
Which nedeth nat rehercen at this tyme;
And his office I shal hym telle, ywis."
    Oure Hoost answerde, "Pees, namoore of
        this!"
And after this he seyde unto the Frere,   1299
"Tel forth youre tale, leeve maister deere."

1260 **t'overbyde:** to outlive

1266 **a maner louryng chiere:** a kind of scowling face
1267 **honestee:** propriety
1268 **vileyns:** rude, churlish
1271 **also moot I thee:** as I may prosper (I swear)
1272 **scole-matere:** subject for debate at the universities
1276 **auctoritees:** quoting from authoritative texts
1278 **lyke:** is pleasing
1282 **yvele apayd:** displeased
1283 **rennere:** runner

1263 **nygardes of dispence:** misers in spending

1284 **mandementz:** summonses
1285 **ybet:** beaten
1292 **grot:** groat, silver coin worth four pence
1297 **office:** i.e., how he performs his duties

THE FRIAR'S TALE

Heere bigynneth the Freres Tale.

Whilom ther was dwellynge in my contree
An erchedeken, a man of heigh degree,
That boldely dide execucioun
In punysshynge of fornicacioun,
Of wicchecraft, and eek of bawderye,   1305
Of diffamacioun, and avowtrye,
Of chirche reves, and of testamentz,
Of contractes and of lakke of sacramentz,
Of usure, and of symonye also.
But certes, lecchours dide he grettest wo;   1310
They sholde syngen if that they were hent;
And smale tytheres weren foule yshent,
If any persoun wolde upon hem pleyne.
Ther myghte asterte hym no pecunyal peyne.
For smale tithes and for smal offrynge   1315
He made the peple pitously to synge,
For er the bisshop caughte hem with his hook,
They weren in the erchedeknes book.
Thanne hadde he, thurgh his jurisdiccioun,
Power to doon on hem correccioun.   1320
He hadde a somonour redy to his hond;
A slyer boye nas noon in Engelond;
For subtilly he hadde his espiaille,
That taughte hym wel wher that hym myghte
          availle.
He koude spare of lecchours oon or two,   1325
To techen hym to foure and twenty mo.
For thogh this Somonour wood were as an hare,
To telle his harlotrye I wol nat spare;

For we been out of his correccioun.
They han of us no jurisdiccioun,   1330
Ne nevere shullen, terme of alle hir lyves.
    "Peter! so been wommen of the styves,"
Quod the Somonour, "yput out of oure cure!"
    "Pees! with myschance and with mysaven-
          ture!"
Thus seyde oure Hoost, "and lat hym telle his
          tale.   1335
Now telleth forth, thogh that the Somonour gale;
Ne spareth nat, myn owene maister deere."
    This false theef, this somonour, quod the
          Frere,
Hadde alwey bawdes redy to his hond,
As any hauk to lure in Engelond,   1340
That tolde hym al the secree that they knewe,
For hire acqueyntance was nat come of newe.
They weren his approwours prively.
He took hymself a greet profit therby;
His maister knew nat alwey what he wan.   1345
Withouten mandement a lewed man
He koude somne, on peyne of Cristes curs,
And they were glade for to fille his purs
And make hym grete feestes atte nale.
And right as Judas hadde purses smale,   1350
And was a theef, right swich a theef was he;
His maister hadde but half his duetee.
He was, if I shal yeven hym his laude,
A theef, and eek a somnour, and a baude.
He hadde eek wenches at his retenue,   1355
That, wheither that sir Robert or sir Huwe,

1302 **erchedeken:** archdeacon
1303 **dide execucioun:** carried out the law
1305 **wicchecraft:** witchcraft **bawderye:** pandering
1306 **diffamacioun:** slander **avowtrye:** adultery
1307 **chirche reves:** robbing of churches
1307–8 **testamentz, contractes:** violations relating to wills and marriage contracts **lakke of sacramentz:** failure to observe any of the sacraments, here probably confession and communion
1309 **usure:** taking interest on loans **symonye:** buying or selling church positions
1312 **smale tytheres:** those who did not pay their full tithes **yshent:** punished
1013 **persoun:** parson
1314 **asterte:** escape **pecunyal peyne:** monetary punishment, fine
1317 **hook:** bishop's staff
1320 **doon . . . correccioun:** punish them
1322 **boye:** knave
1323 **espiaille:** network of spies
1326 **techen:** direct, lead
1328 **harlotrye:** wickedness

1329 **out of his correccioun:** exempt from his authority
1332 **Peter!:** by St. Peter **styves:** brothels, licensed by the archbishop and thus exempt from ecclesiastical intervention
1333 **cure:** jurisdiction
1334 **with myschance and with mysaventure:** bad luck to you
1336 **gale:** complain loudly
1339 **bawdes:** pimps
1340 **lure:** a device to reclaim (call back) hawks
1341 **secree:** secret information
1342 **of newe:** recently
1343 **approwours:** agents
1346 **mandement:** summons
1347 **somne:** summon **Cristes curs:** excommunication
1349 **atte nale:** an ale-house
1350 **purses smale:** small amount of money belonging to the Apostles, entrusted to *Judas*
1352 **duetee:** amount due to him
1353 **laude:** due praise
1355 **at his retenue:** in his service

Or Jakke, or Rauf, or whoso that it were
That lay by hem, they tolde it in his ere.
Thus was the wenche and he of oon assent,
And he wolde fecche a feyned mandement,
And somne hem to chapitre bothe two,   1361
And pile the man, and lete the wenche go.
Thanne wolde he seye, "Freend, I shal for thy
        sake
Do striken hire out of oure lettres blake;
Thee thar namoore as in this cas travaille. 1365
I am thy freend, ther I thee may availle."
Certeyn he knew of briberyes mo
Than possible is to telle in yeres two.
For in this world nys dogge for the bowe 1369
That kan an hurt deer from an hool yknowe
Bet than this somnour knew a sly lecchour,
Or an avowtier, or a paramour.
And for that was the fruyt of al his rente,
Therfore on it he sette al his entente.

        And so bifel that ones on a day   1375
This somnour, evere waityng on his pray,
Rood for to somne an old wydwe, a ribibe,
Feynynge a cause, for he wolde brybe.
And happed that he saugh bifore hym ryde
A gay yeman, under a forest syde.   1380
A bowe he bar, and arwes brighte and kene;
He hadde upon a courtepy of grene,
An hat upon his heed with frenges blake.
        "Sire," quod this somnour, "hayl, and wel
            atake!"   1384
        "Welcome," quod he, "and every good
            felawe!
Wher rydestow, under this grene-wode
        shawe?"
Seyde this yeman, "Wiltow fer to day?"
        This somnour hym answerde and seyde,
            "Nay;
Heere faste by," quod he, "is myn entente
To ryden, for to reysen up a rente   1390
That longeth to my lordes duetee."

"Artow thanne a bailly?" "Ye," quod he.
He dorste nat, for verray filthe and shame
Seye that he was a somonour, for the name.
        "Depardieux," quod this yeman, "deere
            broother,   1395
Thou art a bailly, and I am another.
I am unknowen as in this contree;
Of thyn aqueyntance I wolde praye thee,
And eek of bretherhede, if that yow leste.
I have gold and silver in my cheste;   1400
If that thee happe to comen in oure shire,
Al shal be thyn, right as thou wolt desire."
        "Grant mercy," quod this somonour, "by my
            feith!"
Everych in ootheres hand his trouthe leith,
For to be sworne bretheren til they deye. 1405
In daliance they ryden forth and pleye.
        This somonour, which that was as ful of
            jangles
As ful of venym been thise waryangles
And evere enqueryng upon every thyng,
"Brother," quod he, "where is now youre
            dwellyng
Another day if that I sholde yow seche?" 1411
This yeman hym answerde in softe speche,
        "Brother," quod he, "fer in the north con-
            tree,
Whereas I hope som tyme I shal thee see.
Er we departe, I shal thee so wel wisse   1415
That of myn hous ne shaltow nevere mysse."
        "Now, brother," quod this somonour, "I yow
            preye,
Teche me, whil that we ryden by the weye,
Syn that ye been a baillif as am I,
Som subtiltee, and tel me feithfully   1420
In myn office how that I may moost wynne;
And spareth nat for conscience ne synne,
But as my brother tel me, how do ye."
        "Now, by my trouthe, brother deere," seyde
            he,
"As I shal tellen thee a feithful tale,   1425
My wages been ful streite and ful smale.
My lord is hard to me and daungerous,
And myn office is ful laborous,

1359 **of oon assent:** agreed, in league together
1361 **chapitre:** a session of the archdeacon's court
1362 **pile:** rob
1364 **Do striken hire out:** cause her to be struck out
1365 **thar:** need   **travaille:** trouble yourself
1367 **briberyes:** ways of stealing
1369 **dogge for the bowe:** dog trained to hunt with an archer
1370 **hool:** whole, unhurt
1373 **fruyt of al his rente:** the best portion of his income
1376 **pray:** prey
1377 **Rood:** rode   **ribibe:** fiddle, old woman
1378 **cause:** charge   **brybe:** extort money
1380 **yeman:** yeoman
1382 **courtepy:** jacket
1383 **frenges:** ornamental fringes
1384 **wel atake:** well met
1386 **shawe:** wood, thicket
1391 **duetee:** what is due (to my lord)

1392 **bailly:** bailiff, an agent for a lord's estate who collected
revenues and administered justice
1394 **for the name:** because the name itself was so odious
1395 **Depardieux:** by God
1399 **bretherhede:** sworn brotherhood
1403 **Grant mercy:** thank you
1404 **trouthe:** pledge (i.e., they shook hands on it)
1407 **jangles:** gossip
1408 **waryangles:** shrikes, butcher-birds
1415 **wisse:** inform, instruct
1427 **daungerous:** demanding
1428 **laborous:** laborious

And therfore by extorcions I lyve.
For sothe, I take al that men wol me yive.   1430
Algate, by sleyghte or by violence,
Fro yeer to yeer I wynne al my dispence.
I kan no bettre telle, feithfully."
　　"Now certes," quod this Somonour, "so fare
　　　　I.
I spare nat to taken, God it woot,   1435
But if it be to hevy or to hoot.
What I may gete in conseil prively,
No maner conscience of that have I.
Nere myn extorcioun, I myghte nat lyven,
Ne of swiche japes wol I nat be shryven.   1440
Stomak ne conscience ne knowe I noon;
I shrewe thise shrifte-fadres everychoon.
Wel be we met, by God and by Seint Jame!
But, leeve brother, tel me thanne thy name,"
Quod this somonour. In this meene while
This yeman gan a litel for to smyle.   1446
　　"Brother," quod he, "wiltow that I thee telle?
I am a feend; my dwellyng is in helle,
And heere I ryde aboute my purchasyng,
To wite wher men wol yeve me any thyng.
My purchas is th'effect of al my rente.   1451
Looke how thou rydest for the same entente,
To wynne good, thou rekkest nevere how;
Right so fare I, for ryde wolde I now
Unto the worldes ende for a preye."   1455
　　"A!" quod this somonour, "benedicite! What
　　　　sey ye?
I wende ye were a yeman trewely.
Ye han a mannes shap as wel as I;
Han ye a figure thanne determinat
In helle, ther ye been in youre estat?"   1460
　　"Nay, certeinly," quod he, "ther have we
　　　　noon;
But whan us liketh we kan take us oon,
Or elles make yow seme we been shape;
Somtyme lyk a man, or lyk an ape,
Or lyk an angel kan I ryde or go.   1465
It is no wonder thyng thogh it be so;
A lowsy jogelour kan deceyve thee,
And pardee, yet kan I moore craft than he."

"Why," quod this somonour, "ryde ye thanne
　　or goon
In sondry shap, and nat alwey in oon?"   1470
　　"For we," quod he, "wol us swiche formes
　　　　make
As moost able is oure preyes for to take."
　　"What maketh yow to han al this labour?"
　　"Ful many a cause, leeve sire somonour,"
Seyde this feend, "but alle thyng hath tyme.
The day is short, and it is passed pryme,   1476
And yet ne wan I nothyng in this day.
I wol entende to wynnyng, if I may,
And nat entende oure wittes to declare.
For, brother myn, thy wit is al to bare   1480
To understonde, althogh I tolde hem thee.
But, for thou axest why labouren we —
For somtyme we been Goddes instrumentz
And meenes to doon his comandementz,
Whan that hym list, upon his creatures,   1485
In divers art and in diverse figures.
Withouten hym we have no myght, certayn,
If that hym list to stonden ther-agayn.
And somtyme, at oure prayere, han we leve
Oonly the body and nat the soule greve;   1490
Witnesse on Job, whom that we diden wo.
And somtyme han we myght of bothe two —
This is to seyn, of soule and body eke.
And somtyme be we suffred for to seke
Upon a man and doon his soule unreste   1495
And nat his body, and al is for the beste.
Whan he withstandeth oure temptacioun,
It is a cause of his savacioun,
Al be it that it was nat oure entente
He sholde be sauf, but that we wolde hym
　　hente.   1500
And somtyme be we servant unto man,
As to the erchebisshop Seint Dunstan,
And to the apostles servant eek was I."
　　"Yet tel me," quod the somonour, "feithfully,
Make ye yow newe bodies thus alway   1505
Of elementz?" The feend answerde, "Nay.
Somtyme we feyne, and somtyme we aryse
With dede bodyes, in ful sondry wyse,
And speke as renably and faire and wel
As to the Phitonissa dide Samuel.   1510

1431 **Algate:** anyhow
1432 **dispence:** living expenses
1440 **shryven:** confessed
1441 **Stomak:** stomach (compassion)
1442 **shrifte-fadres:** confessors
1449 **purchasyng:** acquisition of profits
1451 **purchas:** what is acquired (in this way)   **th'effect:** the sum
and substance   **rente:** income
1459 **figure . . . determinat:** definite shape (as opposed to the
shapes devils assume on earth)
1467 **jogelour:** conjurer

1472 **able:** suitable
1480 **al to bare:** entirely inadequate
1486 **art:** methods
1491 **Witnesse on Job:** take the evidence of the Biblical Job
1494–95 **seke Upon:** harass
1495 **unreste:** distress
1502 **Seint Dunstan:** St. Dunstan was said to control devils
1509 **renably:** readily
1510 **Phitonissa:** the Biblical Witch of Endor

(And yet wol som men seye it was nat he;
I do no fors of youre dyvynytee.)
But o thyng warne I thee, I wol nat jape:
Thou wolt algates wite how we been shape;
Thou shalt herafterward, my brother deere,
Come there thee nedeth nat of me to
    leere, 1516
For thou shalt, by thyn owene experience,
Konne in a chayer rede of this sentence
Bet than Virgile, while he was on lyve,
Or Dant also. Now lat us ryde blyve, 1520
For I wole holde compaignye with thee
Til it be so that thou forsake me."
    "Nay," quod this somonour, "that shal nat
      bityde!
I am a yeman, knowen is ful wyde;
My trouthe wol I holde, as in this cas. 1525
For though thou were the devel Sathanas,
My trouthe wol I holde to my brother,
As I am sworn, and ech of us til oother,
For to be trewe brother in this cas; 1529
And bothe we goon abouten oure purchas.
Taak thou thy part, what that men wol thee
    yive,
And I shal myn; thus may we bothe lyve.
And if that any of us have moore than oother,
Lat hym be trewe and parte it with his
    brother."
    "I graunte," quod the devel, "by my
      fey." 1535
And with that word they ryden forth hir wey.
And right at the entryng of the townes ende,
To which this somonour shoop hym for to
    wende,
They saugh a cart that charged was with hey,
Which that a cartere droof forth in his
    wey. 1540
Deep was the wey, for which the carte stood.
The cartere smoot and cryde as he were wood,
"Hayt, Brok! Hayt, Scot! What spare ye for the
    stones?
The feend," quod he, "yow fecche, body and
    bones,

As ferforthly as evere were ye foled, 1545
So muche wo as I have with yow tholed!
The devel have al, bothe hors and cart and
    hey!"
    This somonour seyde, "Heere shal we have a
      pley."
And neer the feend he drough, as noght ne
    were,
Ful prively, and rowned in his ere: 1550
"Herkne, my brother, herkne, by thy feith!
Herestow nat how that the cartere seith?
Hent it anon, for he hath yeve it thee,
Bothe hey and cart, and eek his caples thre."
    "Nay," quod the devel, "God woot, never a
      deel! 1555
It is nat his entente, trust me weel.
Axe hym thyself, if thou nat trowest me;
Or elles stynt a while, and thou shalt see."
    This cartere thakketh his hors upon the
      croupe,
And they bigonne to drawen and to stoupe.
"Heyt! Now," quod he, "ther Jhesu Crist yow
      blesse, 1561
And al his handwerk, bothe moore and lesse!
That was wel twight, myn owene lyard boy.
I pray God save thee, and Seinte Loy!
Now is my cart out of the slow, pardee!" 1565
    "Lo, brother," quod the feend, "what tolde
      I thee?
Heere may ye se, myn owene deere brother,
The carl spak oo thing, but he thoghte another.
Lat us go forth abouten oure viage;
Heere wynne I nothyng upon cariage." 1570
    Whan that they coomen somwhat out of
      towne,
This somonour to his brother gan to rowne:
"Brother," quod he, "heere woneth an old
      rebekke
That hadde almoost as lief to lese hire nekke

1512 **do no fors of:** care nothing for   **dyvynytee:** theology
1513 **jape:** deceive (you)
1514 **algates:** surely
1518 **in a chayer rede of:** in a (professorial) chair lecture on
1519–20 **Virgile, Dant:** Virgil, Dante, poets who described Hell
1520 **blyve:** quickly
1530 **purchas:** acquisition
1534 **parte:** share
1538 **shoop hym:** prepared himself
1539 **charged:** loaded
1541 **Deep was the wey:** the road was deep in mud (cf. 1565)
1543 **Hayt:** giddap   **spare ye:** spare yourselves, stop pulling

1545 **As ferforthly as:** as sure as   **foled:** foaled (i.e., born)
1546 **tholed:** suffered
1549 **as noght ne were:** as if it were nothing (i.e., as if he had no particular purpose)
1550 **rowned:** whispered
1554 **caples:** horses
1559 **thakketh:** pats   **croupe:** hindquarters
1561 **Heyt!:** giddap   **ther Jhesu Crist yow blesse:** may Jesus Christ bless you
1563 **twight:** pulled   **lyard:** dappled
1564 **Seinte Loy:** St. Eligius
1565 **slow:** mud, mire
1568 **carl:** fellow
1569 **viage:** undertaking
1570 **cariage:** a feudal lord's right to the use of a tenant's horses and cart, waived for a money payment
1572 **rowne:** whisper
1573 **woneth:** dwells   **rebekke:** fiddle, old woman
1574 **That hadde almoost as lief:** who would be almost as willing

As for to yeve a peny of hir good.   1575
I wole han twelf pens, though that she be wood,
Or I wol sompne hire unto oure office;
And yet, God woot, of hire knowe I no vice.
But for thou kanst nat, as in this contree,   1579
Wynne thy cost, taak heer ensample of me."
     This somonour clappeth at the wydwes gate.
"Com out," quod he, "thou olde virytrate!
I trowe thou hast som frere or preest with
          thee."
       "Who clappeth?" seyde this wyf, "bene-
          dicitee!
God save you, sire, what is youre sweete
          wille?"   1585
       "I have," quod he, "of somonce here a bille;
Up peyne of cursyng, looke that thou be
Tomorn bifore the erchedeknes knee
T'answere to the court of certeyn thynges."
       "Now, Lord," quod she, "Crist Jhesu, kyng
          of kynges,   1590
So wisly helpe me, as I ne may.
I have been syk, and that ful many a day.
I may nat go so fer," quod she, "ne ryde,
But I be deed, so priketh it in my syde.
May I nat axe a libel, sire somonour,   1595
And answere there by my procuratour
To swich thyng as men wole opposen me?"
       "Yis," quod this somonour, "pay anon —
          lat se —
Twelf pens to me, and I wol thee acquite.
I shal no profit han therby but lite;   1600
My maister hath the profit and nat I.
Com of, and lat me ryden hastily;
Yif me twelf pens, I may no lenger tarye."
       "Twelf pens!" quod she, "Now, lady Seinte
          Marie
So wisly help me out of care and synne,   1605
This wyde world thogh that I sholde wynne,
Ne have I nat twelf pens withinne myn hoold.
Ye knowen wel that I am povre and oold;
Kithe youre almesse on me, povre wrecche."
       "Nay thanne," quod he, "the foule feend me
          fecche   1610

If I th'excuse, though thou shul be spilt!"
       "Allas!" quod she, "God woot, I have no gilt."
       "Pay me," quod he, "or by the sweete Seinte
          Anne,
As I wol bere awey thy newe panne
For dette which thou owest me of old.   1615
Whan that thou madest thyn housbonde coke-
          wold,
I payde at hoom for thy correccioun."
       "Thou lixt!" quod she, "by my savacioun,
Ne was I nevere er now, wydwe ne wyf,
Somoned unto youre court in al my lyf;   1620
Ne nevere I nas but of my body trewe!
Unto the devel blak and rough of hewe
Yeve I thy body and my panne also!"
       And whan the devel herde hire cursen so
Upon hir knees, he seyde in this manere,   1625
"Now, Mabely, myn owene mooder deere,
Is this youre wyl in ernest that ye seye?"
       "The devel," quod she, "so fecche hym er he
          deye,
And panne and al, but he wol hym repente!"
       "Nay, olde stot, that is nat myn entente,"
Quod this somonour, "for to repente me   1631
For any thyng that I have had of thee.
I wolde I hadde thy smok and every clooth!"
       "Now, brother," quod the devel, "be nat
          wrooth;
Thy body and this panne been myne by right.
Thou shalt with me to helle yet tonyght,   1636
Where thou shalt knowen of oure privetee
Moore than a maister of dyvynytee."
And with that word this foule feend hym hente;
Body and soule he with the devel wente   1640
Where as that somonours han hir heritage.
And God, that maked after his ymage
Mankynde, save and gyde us, alle and some,
And leve thise somonours goode men bicome!
       Lordynges, I koude han toold yow, quod this
          Frere,   1645
Hadde I had leyser for this Somnour heere,
After the text of Crist, Poul, and John,
And of oure othere doctours many oon,
Swiche peynes that youre hertes myghte agryse,
Al be it so no tonge may it devyse,   1650
Thogh that I myghte a thousand wynter telle

1579 **But for:** since
1580 **cost:** expenses
1581 **clappeth:** knocks
1582 **virytrate:** hag
1586 **of somonce . . . a bille:** a writ of summons to court
1587 **cursyng:** excommunication
1588 **Tomorn:** in the morning
1591 **So wisly:** surely
1595 **axe a libel:** ask for a written copy of the indictment
1596 **procuratour:** representative
1597 **opposen:** bring against
1602 **Com of:** come on, hurry up
1607 **hoold:** possession
1609 **Kithe:** show   **almesse:** charity

1613 **Seinte Anne:** St. Anne, mother of Mary
1617 **correccioun:** fine
1618 **lixt:** lie
1622 **hewe:** appearance
1630 **stot:** cow, old woman
1644 **leve:** allow
1648 **doctours:** authorities on church doctrine
1649 **agryse:** cause to tremble
1651 **wynter:** years

The peynes of thilke cursed hous of helle.
But for to kepe us fro that cursed place,
Waketh and preyeth Jhesu for his grace
So kepe us fro the temptour Sathanas.   1655
Herketh this word! Beth war, as in this cas:
"The leoun sit in his awayt alway
To sle the innocent, if that he may."

Disposeth ay youre hertes to withstonde
The feend, that yow wolde make thral and
        bonde.   1660
He may nat tempte yow over youre myght,
For Crist wol be youre champion and knyght.
And prayeth that thise somonours hem repente
Of hir mysdedes, er that the feend hem hente!

Heere endeth the Freres Tale.

THE SUMMONER'S PROLOGUE

The Prologe of the Somonours Tale.

This Somonour in his styropes hye stood;
Upon this Frere his herte was so wood   1666
That lyk an aspen leef he quook for ire.
    "Lordynges," quod he, "but o thyng I desire;
I yow biseke that, of youre curteisye,
Syn ye han herd this false Frere lye,   1670
As suffreth me I may my tale telle.
This Frere bosteth that he knoweth helle,
And God it woot, that it is litel wonder;
Freres and feendes been but lyte asonder.
For, pardee, ye han ofte tyme herd telle 1675
How that a frere ravysshed was to helle
In spirit ones by a visioun;
And as an angel ladde hym up and doun,
To shewen hym the peynes that ther were,
In al the place saugh he nat a frere;   1680
Of oother folk he saugh ynowe in wo.
Unto this angel spak the frere tho:
    'Now, sire,' quod he, 'han freres swich a grace
That noon of hem shal come to this place?'
    'Yis,' quod this angel, 'many a millioun!'
And unto Sathanas he ladde hym doun.   1686

'And now hath Sathanas,' seith he, 'a tayl
Brodder than of a carryk is the sayl.
Hold up thy tayl, thou Sathanas!' quod he;
'Shewe forth thyn ers, and lat the frere se
Where is the nest of freres in this place!' 1691
And er that half a furlong wey of space,
Right so as bees out swarmen from an hyve,
Out of the develes ers ther gonne dryve
Twenty thousand freres on a route,   1695
And thurghout helle swarmed al aboute,
And comen agayn as faste as they may gon,
And in his ers they crepten everychon.
He clapte his tayl agayn and lay ful stille.
This frere, whan he looked hadde his fille 1700
Upon the tormentz of this sory place,
His spirit God restored, of his grace,
Unto his body agayn, and he awook.
But natheles, for fere yet he quook,
So was the develes ers ay in his mynde,   1705
That is his heritage of verray kynde.
God save yow alle, save this cursed Frere!
My prologe wol I ende in this manere."

1657 **in . . . awayt:** in ambush

1667 **quook:** trembled
1685 **Yis:** yes indeed

1660 **bonde:** enslaved
1662 **champion:** champion, representative in a judicial duel
1664 **mysdedes:** sins

1688 **carryk:** large sailing ship
1692 **half a furlong wey of space:** in a couple of minutes

THE SUMMONER'S TALE

Heere bigynneth the Somonour his Tale.

Lordynges, ther is in Yorkshire, as I gesse,
A mersshy contree called Holdernesse, 1710
In which ther wente a lymytour aboute
To preche, and eek to begge, it is no doute.
And so bifel that on a day this frere
Hadde preched at a chirche in his manere,
And specially, aboven every thyng, 1715
Excited he the peple in his prechyng
To trentals, and to yeve, for Goddes sake,
Wherwith men myghte hooly houses make,
Ther as divine servyce is honoured,
Nat ther as it is wasted and devoured, 1720
Ne ther it nedeth nat for to be yive,
As to possessioners, that mowen lyve,
Thanked be God, in wele and habundaunce.
"Trentals," seyde he, "deliveren fro penaunce
Hir freendes soules, as wel olde as yonge —
Ye, whan that they been hastily ysonge, 1726
Nat for to holde a preest joly and gay —
He syngeth nat but o masse in a day.
Delivereth out," quod he, "anon the soules!
Ful hard it is with flesshhook or with oules
To been yclawed, or to brenne or bake. 1731
Now spede yow hastily, for Cristes sake!"
And whan this frere had seyd al his entente,
With *qui cum patre* forth his wey he wente.
Whan folk in chirche had yeve him what
    hem leste, 1735
He wente his wey; no lenger wolde he reste.
With scrippe and tipped staf, ytukked hye,
In every hous he gan to poure and prye,
And beggeth mele and chese, or elles corn.
His felawe hadde a staf tipped with horn, 1740

A peyre of tables al of yvory,
And a poyntel polysshed fetisly,
And wroot the names alwey, as he stood,
Of alle folk that yaf hym any good,
Ascaunces that he wolde for hem preye. 1745
"Yif us a busshel whete, malt, or reye,
A Goddes kechyl, or a trype of chese,
Or elles what yow lyst, we may nat cheese;
A Goddes halfpeny, or a masse peny,
Or yif us of youre brawn, if ye have eny; 1750
A dagon of youre blanket, leeve dame,
Oure suster deere — lo! Heere I write youre
    name —
Bacon or beef, or swich thyng as ye fynde."
A sturdy harlot wente ay hem bihynde,
That was hir hostes man, and bar a sak, 1755
And what men yaf hem, leyde it on his bak.
And whan that he was out at dore, anon
He planed awey the names everichon
That he biforn had writen in his tables; 1759
He served hem with nyfles and with fables.
"Nay, ther thou lixt, thou Somonour!" quod
    the Frere.
"Pees," quod oure Hoost, "for Cristes
    mooder deere!
Tel forth thy tale, and spare it nat at al."
"So thryve I," quod this Somonour, "so I
    shal!"
So longe he wente, hous by hous, til he 1765
Cam til an hous ther he was wont to be
Refresshed moore than in an hundred placis.
Syk lay the goode man whos that the place is;
Bedrede upon a couche lowe he lay.

1710 **mersshy:** marshy **Holdernesse:** a town in Yorkshire
1711 **lymytour:** friar
1717 **trentals:** office of thirty requiem Masses sung for a soul in Purgatory
1722 **possessioners:** secular and monastic clergy living on endowments **mowen:** are able
1730 **flesshhook:** meat-hook **oules:** awls
1731 **yclawed:** torn, lacerated **brenne:** burn
1734 **qui cum patre:** "Who with the Father" (beginning of a closing formula for a prayer or sermon)
1737 **scrippe:** bag, satchel **tipped staf:** staff tipped with metal, a symbol of his authority **ytukked hye:** with the skirts of his coat tucked up under his belt
1738 **poure and prye:** pore (look intently) and peer

1741 **peyre of tables:** folding set of writing tablets
1742 **poyntel:** stylus (for writing on wax)
1745 **Ascaunces:** as if
1746 **reye:** rye
1747 **A Goddes kechyl:** a little cake given as alms **trype:** bit
1749 **Goddes halfpeny:** a halfpenny given as alms **masse peny:** money offered for the singing of a Mass
1750 **brawn:** meat
1751 **dagon:** piece **blanket:** undyed woolen cloth
1754 **harlot:** servant
1755 **hostes man:** servant of the host at their inn
1760 **nyfles:** trifles, silly stories **fables:** falsehoods
1761 **lixt:** lie
1768 **goode man:** goodman, head of the household
1769 **Bedrede:** bedridden

"Deus hic!" quod he, "O Thomas, freend, good
    day!"   1770
Seyde this frere, curteisly and softe.
"Thomas," quod he, "God yelde yow! Ful ofte
Have I upon this bench faren ful weel;
Heere have I eten many a myrie meel."
And fro the bench he droof awey the cat,   1775
And leyde adoun his potente and his hat,
And eek his scrippe, and sette hym softe adoun.
His felawe was go walked into toun
Forth with his knave, into that hostelrye
Where as he shoop hym thilke nyght to lye.

    "O deere maister," quod this sike man,   1781
"How han ye fare sith that March bigan?
I saugh yow noght this fourtenyght or moore."
"God woot," quod he, "laboured I have ful
    soore,
And specially for thy savacion   1785
Have I seyd many a precious orison,
And for oure othere freendes, God hem blesse!
I have to day been at youre chirche at messe,
And seyd a sermon after my symple wit —
Nat al after the text of hooly writ,   1790
For it is hard to yow, as I suppose,
And therfore wol I teche yow al the glose.
Glosynge is a glorious thyng, certeyn,
For lettre sleeth, so as we clerkes seyn —
There have I taught hem to be charitable,   1795
And spende hir good ther it is resonable;
And there I saugh oure dame — A! Where is
    she?"

    "Yond in the yerd I trowe that she be,"
Seyde this man, "and she wol come anon."

    "Ey, maister, welcome be ye, by Seint John!"
Seyde this wyf, "How fare ye, hertely?"   1801
    The frere ariseth up ful curteisly,
And hire embraceth in his armes narwe,
And kiste hire sweete, and chirketh as a sparwe
With his lyppes: "Dame," quod he, "right weel,
As he that is youre servant every deel,   1806
Thanked be God, that yow yaf soule and lyf!
Yet saugh I nat this day so fair a wyf
In al the chirche, God so save me!"

    "Ye, God amende defautes, sire," quod she.
"Algates, welcome be ye, by my fey!"   1811
    "Graunt mercy, dame, this have I founde al-
    wey.
But of youre grete goodnesse, by youre leve,
I wolde prey yow that ye nat yow greve,
I wole with Thomas speke a litel throwe.   1815
Thise curatz been ful necligent and slowe
To grope tendrely a conscience
In shrift; in prechyng is my diligence,
And studie in Petres wordes and in Poules.
I walke and fisshe Cristen mennes soules   1820
To yelden Jhesu Crist his propre rente;
To sprede his word is set al myn entente."

    "Now, by youre leve, o deere sire," quod
    she,
"Chideth him weel, for seinte Trinitee!
He is as angry as a pissemyre,   1825
Though that he have al that he kan desire;
Though I hym wrye a-nyght and make hym
    warm,
And over hym leye my leg outher myn arm,
He groneth lyk oure boor, lith in oure sty.
Oother desport right noon of hym have I;   1830
I may nat plese hym in no maner cas."

    "O Thomas, *je vous dy,* Thomas! Thomas!
This maketh the feend; this moste ben
    amended.
Ire is a thyng that hye God defended,
And therof wol I speke a word or two."   1835
    "Now, maister," quod the wyf, "er that I go,
What wol ye dyne? I wol go theraboute."

    "Now, dame," quod he, "now *je vous dy sanz
    doute,*
Have I nat of a capon but the lyvere,
And of youre softe breed nat but a shyvere,
And after that a rosted pigges heed —   1841
But that I nolde no beest for me were deed —
Thanne hadde I with yow hoomly suffisaunce.

1770 **Deus hic!:** God be here
1772 **yelde:** reward
1776 **potente:** walking stick
1778 **was go walked:** was gone
1780 **shoop hym:** intended
1792 **glose:** interpretation
1798 **yerd:** enclosed garden
1801 **hertely:** cordially (I ask it)
1803 **narwe:** closely, tightly
1804 **chirketh:** makes a chirping sound
1806 **every deel:** every bit, completely

1810 **amende defautes:** correct my faults (a self-deprecating
response)
1814 **yow greve:** get angry
1815 **throwe:** while
1817 **grope:** examine (a penitent's conscience)
1818 **shrift:** confession
1821 **yelden:** pay
1825 **pissemyre:** ant
1827 **wrye:** cover
1829 **boor:** boar, pig **lith:** that lies
1832 **je vous dy:** I tell you
1834 **Ire:** the deadly sin of wrath (see ParsT X.533–676)
defended: forbad
1837 **theraboute:** (see) about it
1838 **je vous dy sanz doute:** I say to you indeed
1839 **lyvere:** liver
1840 **shyvere:** sliver
1843 **hoomly suffisaunce:** enough plain food, family fare

I am a man of litel sustenaunce;
My spirit hath his fostryng in the Bible.   1845
The body is ay so redy and penyble
To wake, that my stomak is destroyed.
I prey yow, dame, ye be nat anoyed,
Though I so freendly yow my conseil shewe.
By God! I wolde nat telle it but a fewe."   1850
    "Now, sire," quod she, "but o word er I go.
My child is deed withinne thise wykes two,
Soone after that ye wente out of this toun."
    "His deeth saugh I by revelacioun,"
Seide this frere, "at hoom in oure dortour.   1855
I dar wel seyn that, er that half an hour
After his deeth, I saugh hym born to blisse
In myn avision, so God me wisse!
So dide oure sexteyn and oure fermerer,
That han been trewe freres fifty yeer;   1860
They may now — God be thanked of his
            loone! —
Maken hir jubilee and walke allone.
And up I roos, and al oure covent eke,
With many a teere trillyng on my cheke,
Withouten noyse or claterynge of belles;   1865
Te Deum was oure song, and nothyng elles,
Save that to Crist I seyde an orison,
Thankynge hym of his revelacion.
For, sire and dame, trusteth me right weel,
Oure orisons been moore effectueel,   1870
And moore we seen of Cristes secree thynges,
Than burel folk, although they weren kynges.
We lyve in poverte and in abstinence,
And burell folk in richesse and despence
Of mete and drynke, and in hir foul delit.
We han this worldes lust al in despit.   1876
Lazar and Dives lyveden diversly,
And divers gerdon hadden they therby.
Whoso wol preye, he moot faste and be clene,
And fatte his soule, and make his body
            lene.   1880
We fare as seith th'apostle; clooth and foode

Suffisen us, though they be nat ful goode.
The clennesse and the fastynge of us freres
Maketh that Crist accepteth oure preyeres.
    "Lo, Moyses fourty dayes and fourty nyght
Fasted, er that the heighe God of myght   1886
Spak with hym in the mountayne of Synay.
With empty wombe, fastynge many a day,
Receyved he the lawe that was writen
With Goddes fynger; and Elye, wel ye witen,
In mount Oreb, er he hadde any speche   1891
With hye God, that is oure lyves leche,
He fasted longe and was in contemplaunce.
    "Aaron, that hadde the temple in gover-
            naunce,
And eek the othere preestes everichon,   1895
Into the temple whan they sholde gon
To preye for the peple and do servyse,
They nolden drynken in no maner wyse
No drynke which that myghte hem dronke
            make,
But there in abstinence preye and wake,   1900
Lest that they deyden. Taak heede what I
            seye!
But they be sobre that for the peple preye,
War that — I seye namoore, for it suffiseth.
    "Oure Lord Jhesu, as hooly writ devyseth,
Yaf us ensample of fastynge and preyeres.   1905
Therfore we mendynantz, we sely freres,
Been wedded to poverte and continence,
To charite, humblesse, and abstinence,
To persecucioun for rightwisnesse,
To wepynge, misericorde, and clennesse.   1910
And therfore may ye se that oure preyeres —
I speke of us, we mendynantz, we freres —
Been to the hye God moore acceptable
Than youres, with youre feestes at the table.
Fro Paradys first, if I shal nat lye,   1915
Was man out chaced for his glotonye;
And chaast was man in Paradys, certeyn.
    "But herkne now, Thomas, what I shal seyn.
I ne have no text of it, as I suppose,
But I shal fynde it in a maner glose,   1920
That specially oure sweete Lord Jhesus
Spak this by freres, whan he seyde thus:
'Blessed be they that povere in spirit been.'

1844 a man of litel sustenaunce: one who eats little
1845 fostryng: nourishment
1846 penyble: accustomed to suffering
1847 wake: spend the night in prayer and meditation
1855 dortour: dormitory (in the convent)
1857 born to blisse: carried to heaven
1858 wisse: guide
1859 sexteyn: sacristan, friar in charge of the liturgical vestments
and vessels fermerer: friar in charge of the infirmary
1861 loone: grace
1862 jubilee: fiftieth anniversary
1864 trillyng: trickling
1866 Te Deum: "To You O God" (a hymn of praise)
1872 burel: lay, secular
1877 Lazar and Dives: the poor man and rich man of the New
Testament
1878 gerdon: reward

1883 clennesse: purity
1885 Moyses: Moses
1890 Elye: the biblical Elijah
1891 Oreb: Horeb
1892 leche: healer
1906 mendynantz: mendicants sely: good, blessed
1909 rightwisnesse: righteousness
1910 misericorde: charity, mercy
1919 text: biblical text
1920 in a maner glose: in some interpretation

And so forth al the gospel may ye seen,
Wher it be likker oure professioun,   1925
Or hirs that swymmen in possessioun.
Fy on hire pompe and on hire glotonye!
And for hir lewednesse I hem diffye.
    "Me thynketh they been lyk Jovinyan,
Fat as a whale, and walkynge as a swan,   1930
Al vinolent as botel in the spence.
Hir preyere is of ful greet reverence,
Whan they for soules seye the psalm of Davit:
Lo, 'buf!' they seye, 'cor meum eructavit!'
Who folweth Cristes gospel and his foore,   1935
But we that humble been, and chaast, and
                poore,
Werkeris of Goddes word, nat auditours?
Therfore, right as an hauk up at a sours
Up springeth into th'eir, right so prayeres
Of charitable and chaste bisy freres   1940
Maken hir sours to Goddes eres two.
Thomas, Thomas! So moote I ryde or go,
And by that lord that clepid is Seint Yve,
Nere thou oure brother, sholdestou nat thryve.
In our chapitre praye we day and nyght   1945
To Crist, that he thee sende heele and myght
Thy body for to weelden hastily."
    "God woot," quod he, "no thyng therof
                feele I!
As help me Crist, as I in fewe yeres,
Have spent upon diverse manere freres   1950
Ful many a pound; yet fare I never the bet.
Certeyn, my good have I almoost biset.
Farwel, my gold, for it is al ago!"
    The frere answerde, "O Thomas, dostow so?
What nedeth yow diverse freres seche?   1955
What nedeth hym that hath a parfit leche
To sechen othere leches in the toun?
Youre inconstance is youre confusioun.
Holde ye thanne me, or elles oure covent,
To praye for yow been insufficient?   1960
Thomas, that jape nys nat worth a myte.

Youre maladye is for we han to lyte.
A, yif that covent half a quarter otes!
A, yif that covent foure and twenty grotes!
A, yif that frere a peny, and lat hym go!   1965
Nay, nay, Thomas, it may no thyng be so!
What is a ferthyng worth parted in twelve?
Lo, ech thyng that is oned in himselve
Is moore strong than whan it is toscatered.
Thomas, of me thou shalt nat been yflatered;
Thou woldest han oure labour al for
                noght.   1971
The hye God, that al this world hath wroght,
Seith that the werkman worthy is his hyre.
Thomas, noght of youre tresor I desire
As for myself, but that al oure covent   1975
To preye for yow is ay so diligent,
And for to buylden Cristes owene chirche.
Thomas, if ye wol lernen for to wirche,
Of buyldynge up of chirches may ye fynde
If it be good in Thomas lyf of Inde.   1980
Ye lye heere ful of anger and of ire,
With which the devel set youre herte afyre,
And chiden heere the sely innocent,
Youre wyf, that is so meke and pacient.   1984
And therfore, Thomas, trowe me if thee leste,
Ne stryve nat with thy wyf, as for thy beste;
And ber this word awey now, by thy feith;
Touchynge swich thyng, lo, what the wise seith:
'Withinne thyn hous ne be thou no leon;
To thy subgitz do noon oppression,   1990
Ne make thyne aqueyntances nat to flee.'
And, Thomas, yet eft-soones I charge thee,
Be war from Ire that in thy bosom slepeth;
War fro the serpent that so slily crepeth
Under the gras and styngeth subtilly.   1995
Be war, my sone, and herkne paciently
That twenty thousand men han lost hir lyves
For stryvyng with hir lemmans and hir wyves.
Now sith ye han so hooly meke a wyf,
What nedeth yow, Thomas, to maken stryf?
Ther nys, ywys, no serpent so cruel,   2001
Whan man tret on his tayl, ne half so fel,

1925 **it be likker:** it (the Gospel) more closely resembles
professioun: religious order
1928 **lewednesse:** ignorance **diffye:** repudiate
1929 **Jovinyan:** Jovinianus, who provoked St. Jerome's *Adversus Jovinianum*
1930 **walkynge as:** waddling like
1931 Full of wine as a bottle in the pantry
1934 **buf!:** the sound of a belch **cor meum eructavit:** "My heart has uttered (a good word)," the opening of Psalm 45
1935 **foore:** tracks, path (i.e., example)
1937 **auditours:** hearers (who merely listen)
1938 **sours:** upward flight
1944 **brother:** lay member of our order (see 2126–28)
1945 **chapitre:** assembly of the members of the convent
1946 **heele:** health
1947 **weelden:** move with ease
1952 **biset:** disposed of
1958 **confusioun:** ruin
1961 **myte:** a small Flemish coin of little value

1962 **to lyte:** too little
1963 **otes:** oats
1964 **grotes:** groats, silver coins worth four pence
1967 **ferthyng:** farthing
1968 **oned:** united
1969 **toscatered:** scattered, dispersed
1978 **for to wirche:** i.e., to do good works
1980 **Thomas lyf of Inde:** the life of St. Thomas of India
1988 **Touchynge:** concerning **the wise:** the wise man (i.e., Jesus, son of Sirach, author of the Vulgate Ecclesiasticus)
1992 **eft-soones:** again **charge:** command
1998 **lemmans:** sweethearts
2000 **maken stryf:** cause trouble
2002 **tret** = *tredeth*, steps

As womman is, whan she hath caught an ire;
Vengeance is thanne al that they desire.
Ire is a synne, oon of the grete of sevene, 2005
Abhomynable unto the God of hevene;
And to hymself it is destruccion.
This every lewed viker or person
Kan seye, how ire engendreth homycide.
Ire is, in sooth, executour of pryde. 2010
I koude of ire seye so muche sorwe,
My tale sholde laste til to-morwe.
And therfore preye I God bothe day and nyght
An irous man, God sende hym litel myght!
It is greet harm and certes greet pitee 2015
To sette an irous man in heigh degree.
    "Whilom ther was an irous potestat,
As seith Senek, that, durynge his estaat,
Upon a day out ryden knyghtes two,
And as Fortune wolde that it were so, 2020
That oon of hem cam hoom, that oother noght.
Anon the knyght bifore the juge is broght,
That seyde thus, 'Thou hast thy felawe slayn,
For which I deme thee to the deeth, certayn.'
And to another knyght comanded he, 2025
'Go lede hym to the deeth, I charge thee.'
And happed, as they wente by the weye,
Toward the place ther he sholde deye,
The knyght cam which men wenden had be
       deed.
Thanne thoughte they it were the beste reed 2030
To lede hem bothe to the juge agayn.
They seiden, 'Lord, the knyght ne hath nat slayn
His felawe; heere he standeth hool alyve.'
'Ye shul be deed,' quod he, 'so moot I thryve!
That is to seyn, bothe oon, and two, and
       thre!' 2035
And to the firste knyght right thus spak he,
'I dampned thee; thou most algate be deed.
And thou also most nedes lese thyn heed,
For thou art cause why thy felawe deyth.' 2039
And to the thridde knyght right thus he seith,
'Thou hast nat doon that I comanded thee.'
And thus he dide doon sleen hem alle thre.
    "Irous Cambises was eek dronkelewe,
And ay delited hym to been a shrewe.
And so bifel, a lord of his meynee 2045

That loved vertuous moralitee
Seyde on a day bitwix hem two right thus:
   "'A lord is lost, if he be vicius;
And dronkenesse is eek a foul record
Of any man, and namely in a lord. 2050
Ther is ful many an eye and many an ere
Awaityng on a lord, and he noot where.
For Goddes love, drynk moore attemprely!
Wyn maketh man to lesen wrecchedly
His mynde and eek his lymes everichon.' 2055
   "'The revers shaltou se,' quod he, 'anon,
And preve it by thyn owene experience,
That wyn ne dooth to folk no swich offence.
Ther is no wyn bireveth me my myght
Of hand ne foot, ne of myne eyen sight.' 2060
And for despit he drank ful muchel moore,
An hondred part, than he hadde don bifoore;
And right anon this irous, cursed wrecche
Leet this knyghtes sone bifore hym fecche,
Comandynge hym he sholde bifore hym stonde.
And sodeynly he took his bowe in honde, 2066
And up the streng he pulled to his ere,
And with an arwe he slow the child right there.
'Now wheither have I a siker hand or noon?'
Quod he; 'Is al my myght and mynde agon?
Hath wyn bireved me myn eyen sight?' 2071
What sholde I telle th'answere of the knyght?
His sone was slayn; ther is namoore to seye.
Beth war, therfore, with lordes how ye pleye.
Syngeth *Placebo* and 'I shal, if I kan,' 2075
But if it be unto a povre man.
To a povre man men sholde his vices telle,
But nat to a lord, thogh he sholde go to helle.
    "Lo irous Cirus, thilke Percien,
How he destroyed the ryver of Gysen, 2080
For that an hors of his was dreynt therinne,
Whan that he wente Babiloigne to wynne.
He made that the ryver was so smal
That wommen myghte wade it over al.
Lo, what seyde he that so wel teche kan?' 2085
'Ne be no felawe to an irous man,
Ne with no wood man walke by the weye,
Lest thee repente;' I wol no ferther seye.

2003 **caught an ire:** become angry
2008 **lewed:** ignorant, uneducated   **viker:** vicar
2010 **executour of pryde:** one who carries out Pride's orders
2016 **irous:** angry
2017 **potestat:** potentate
2018 **Senek:** Seneca   **estaat:** term of office
2030 **reed:** plan
2042 **dide doon sleen:** had (caused to be) slain
2043 **Cambises:** king of Persia, son of Cyrus the Elder
(line 2079)   **dronkelewe:** addicted to drink
2045 **meynee:** household

2049 **record:** reputation
2052 **Awaityng on:** observing
2053 **attemprely:** moderately
2054 **lesen:** lose
2064 **Leet . . . fecche:** had fetched
2068 **slow:** slew
2069 **wheither:** tell me whether
2075 **Placebo:** "I shall please" (Psalm 114:9)
2079 **Cirus:** Cyrus the Elder (the Great)   **Percien:** Persian
2080 **Gysen:** the river Gyndes
2081 **dreynt:** drowned
2082 **Babiloigne:** Babylon
2085 **he:** Solomon

"Now, Thomas, leeve brother, lef thyn ire;
Thou shalt me fynde as just as is a squyre.   2090
Hoold nat the develes knyf ay at thyn herte —
Thyn angre dooth thee al to soore smerte —
But shewe to me al thy confessioun."
     "Nay," quod the sike man, "by Seint Sy-
          moun!
I have be shryven this day at my curat.   2095
I have hym toold hoolly al myn estat;
Nedeth namoore to speken of it," seith he,
"But if me list, of myn humylitee."
     "Yif me thanne of thy gold, to make oure
          cloystre,"
Quod he, "for many a muscle and many an
          oystre,   2100
Whan othere men han ben ful wel at eyse,
Hath been oure foode, our cloystre for to reyse.
And yet, God woot, unnethe the fundement
Parfourned is, ne of our pavement
Nys nat a tyle yet withinne oure wones.   2105
By God, we owen fourty pound for stones.
     "Now help, Thomas, for hym that harwed
          helle!
For elles moste we oure bookes selle.
And if yow lakke oure predicacioun,   2109
Thanne goth the world al to destruccioun.
For whoso wolde us fro this world bireve,
So God me save, Thomas, by youre leve,
He wolde bireve out of this world the sonne.
For who kan teche and werchen as we konne?
And that is nat of litel tyme," quod he,   2115
"But syn Elye was, or Elise,
Han freres been — that fynde I of record —
In charitee, ythanked be oure Lord!
Now Thomas, help, for seinte charitee!"   2119
And doun anon he sette hym on his knee.
     This sike man wax wel ny wood for ire;
He wolde that the frere had been on-fire
With his false dissymulacioun.
"Swich thyng as is in my possessioun,"   2124
Quod he, "that may I yeve, and noon oother.

Ye sey me thus, how that I am youre brother?"
     "Ye, certes," quod the frere, "trusteth weel.
I took oure dame oure lettre with oure seel."
     "Now wel," quod he, "and somwhat shal I
          yive
Unto youre hooly covent whil I lyve;   2130
And in thyn hand thou shalt it have anon,
On this condicion, and oother noon,
That thou departe it so, my deere brother,
That every frere have also muche as oother.
This shaltou swere on thy professioun,   2135
Withouten fraude or cavillacioun."
     "I swere it," quod this frere, "by my feith!"
And therwithal his hand in his he leith,
"Lo, heer my feith; in me shal be no lak."   2139
     "Now thanne, put in thyn hand doun by my
          bak,"
Seyde this man, "and grope wel bihynde.
Bynethe my buttok there shaltow fynde
A thyng that I have hyd in pryvetee."
     "A!" thoghte this frere, "That shal go with
          me!"
And doun his hand he launcheth to the clifte
In hope for to fynde there a yifte.   2146
And whan this sike man felte this frere
Aboute his tuwel grope there and heere,
Amydde his hand he leet the frere a fart;
Ther nys no capul, drawynge in a cart,   2150
That myghte have lete a fart of swich a soun.
     The frere up stirte as dooth a wood leoun —
"A, false cherl," quod he, "for Goddes bones!
This hastow for despit doon for the nones.
Thou shalt abye this fart, if that I may!"   2155
     His meynee, whiche that herden this affray,
Cam lepynge in and chaced out the frere;
And forth he gooth, with a ful angry cheere,
And fette his felawe, ther as lay his stoor.
He looked as it were a wilde boor;   2160
He grynte with his teeth, so was he wrooth.
A sturdy paas doun to the court he gooth,
Wher as ther woned a man of greet honour,
To whom that he was alwey confessour.

2090 **just:** true, exact   **squyre:** carpenter's square
2094 **Seint Symoun:** unidentified; possibly Simon Magus, the
false apostle; see n.
2095 **shryven:** confessed
2100 **muscle:** mussel
2102 **reyse:** build
2103 **fundement:** foundation
2104 **Parfourned:** completed
2105 **wones:** dwelling place
2107 **hym that harwed helle:** Christ, who despoiled Hell of its
captives
2109 **predicacioun:** preaching
2111 **bireve:** take away
2113 **sonne:** sun
2116 **Elye, Elise:** Elijah, Elisha; see n.

2126 **youre brother:** lay member of your order
2133 **departe:** share, divide
2134 **also:** as
2135 **professioun:** religious vows
2136 **cavillacioun:** quibbling
2139 **lak:** flaw
2145 **launcheth:** thrusts   **clifte:** cleft of the buttocks
2148 **tuwel:** anus
2150 **capul:** horse
2155 **abye:** pay for
2156 **affray:** disturbance
2159 **fette:** fetched   **stoor:** store (what he had collected)
2161 **grynte with:** ground
2162 **sturdy paas:** quick pace   **court:** manor house
2163 **woned:** dwelt

This worthy man was lord of that village. 2165
This frere cam as he were in a rage,
Where as this lord sat etyng at his bord;
Unnethes myghte the frere speke a word,
Til atte laste he seyde, "God yow see!"   2169
    This lord gan looke, and seide, "Benedicitee!
What, frere John, what maner world is this?
I se wel that som thyng ther is amys;
Ye looken as the wode were ful of thevys.
Sit doun anon, and tel me what youre grief is,
And it shal been amended, if I may."   2175
    "I have," quod he, "had a despit this day,
God yelde yow, adoun in youre village,
That in this world is noon so povre a page
That he nolde have abhomynacioun
Of that I have receyved in youre toun.   2180
And yet ne greveth me nothyng so soore,
As that this olde cherl with lokkes hoore
Blasphemed hath oure hooly covent eke."
    "Now, maister," quod this lord, "I yow
        biseke — "
    "No maister, sire," quod he, "but servitour,
Thogh I have had in scole that honour.   2186
God liketh nat that 'Raby' men us calle,
Neither in market ne in youre large halle."
    "No fors," quod he, "but tel me al youre
        grief."
    "Sire," quod this frere, "an odious meschief
This day bityd is to myn ordre and me,   2191
And so, *per consequens,* to ech degree
Of hooly chirche — God amende it soone!"
    "Sire," quod the lord, "ye woot what is to
        doone.
Distempre yow noght; ye be my confes-
        sour;   2195
Ye been the salt of the erthe and the savour.
For Goddes love, youre pacience ye holde!
Tel me youre grief." And he anon hym tolde,
As ye han herd biforn — ye woot wel what.
    The lady of the hous ay stille sat   2200
Til she had herd what the frere sayde.
"Ey, Goddes mooder," quod she, "Blisful
        mayde!
Is ther oght elles? Telle me feithfully."

    "Madame," quod he, "how thynke ye
        herby?"
    "How that me thynketh?" quod she. "So God
        me speede,   2205
I seye a cherl hath doon a cherles dede.
What shold I seye? God lat hym nevere thee!
His sike heed is ful of vanytee;
I holde hym in a manere frenesye."
    "Madame," quod he, "by God, I shal nat lye,
But I on oother wyse may be wreke,   2211
I shal disclaundre hym over al ther I speke,
This false blasphemour that charged me
To parte that wol nat departed be
To every man yliche, with meschaunce!"   2215
    The lord sat stille as he were in a traunce,
And in his herte he rolled up and doun,
"How hadde this cherl ymaginacioun
To shewe swich a probleme to the frere?   2219
Nevere erst er now herde I of swich mateere.
I trowe the devel putte it in his mynde.
In ars-metrike shal ther no man fynde,
Biforn this day, of swich a question.
Who sholde make a demonstracion
That every man sholde have yliche his part
As of the soun or savour of a fart?   2226
O nyce, proude cherl, I shrewe his face!
Lo, sires," quod the lord, "with harde grace!
Who evere herde of swich a thyng er now?
To every man ylike? Tel me how.   2230
It is an inpossible; it may nat be.
Ey, nyce cherl, God lete him nevere thee!
The rumblynge of a fart, and every soun,
Nis but of eir reverberacioun,
And evere it wasteth litel and litel awey.   2235
Ther is no man kan deemen, by my fey,
If that it were departed equally.
What, lo, my cherl, lo, yet how shrewedly
Unto my confessour to-day he spak!
I holde hym certeyn a demonyak!   2240
Now ete youre mete, and lat the cherl go pleye;

2168 **Unnethes:** hardly
2169 **God yow see!:** may God look after you
2171 **what maner world:** what sort of carrying on
2182 **hoore:** white
2185 **servitour:** servant
2186 **that honour:** Master of Arts degree
2187 **Raby:** rabbi
2189 **No fors:** no matter
2192 **per consequens:** consequently
2195 **Distempre yow noght:** do not be angry
2196 **savour:** delight

2204 **herby:** about this
2207 **lat hym nevere thee:** never allow him to prosper
2209 **frenesye:** madness
2211 **wreke:** avenged
2212 **disclaundre:** defame
2214 **parte:** share, divide
2215 **yliche:** equally
2217 **rolled up and doun:** pondered
2218 **ymaginacioun:** the ingenuity
2219 **probleme:** logical problem
2222 **ars-metrike:** art of measurement (arithmetic)
2223 **question:** logical problem
2224 **make a demonstracion:** prove
2226 **savour:** odor
2228 **with harde grace:** bad luck to him
2231 **inpossible:** impossibilium, a logical exercise; see n.
2240 **demonyak:** possessed by a demon

Lat hym go honge hymself a devel weye!"

The wordes of the lordes squier and
his kervere for departynge of the
fart on twelve.

Now stood the lordes squier at the bord,
That karf his mete, and herde word by word
Of alle thynges whiche I have yow sayd.   2245
"My lord," quod he, "be ye nat yvele apayd,
I koude telle, for a gowne-clooth,
To yow, sire frere, so ye be nat wrooth,
How that this fart sholde evene deled be
Among youre covent, if it lyked me."   2250
    "Tel," quod the lord, "and thou shalt have
            anon
A gowne-clooth, by God and by Seint John!"
    "My lord," quod he, "whan that the weder
            is fair,
Withouten wynd or perturbynge of air,   2254
Lat brynge a cartwheel heere into this halle;
But looke that it have his spokes alle —
Twelve spokes hath a cartwheel comunly.
And bryng me thanne twelve freres. Woot ye
            why?
For thrittene is a covent, as I gesse.   2259
Youre confessour heere, for his worthynesse,
Shal parfourne up the nombre of his covent.
Thanne shal they knele doun, by oon assent,
And to every spokes ende, in this manere,
Ful sadly leye his nose shal a frere.   2264
Youre noble confessour — there God hym
            save! —

Shal holde his nose upright under the nave.
Thanne shal this cherl, with bely stif and toght
As any tabour, hyder been ybroght;
And sette hym on the wheel right of this cart,
Upon the nave, and make hym lete a fart.   2270
And ye shul seen, up peril of my lyf,
By preeve which that is demonstratif,
That equally the soun of it wol wende,
And eke the stynk, unto the spokes ende,
Save that this worthy man, youre confessour,
By cause he is a man of greet honour,   2276
Shal have the firste fruyt, as resoun is.
The noble usage of freres yet is this,
The worthy men of hem shul first be served;
And certeinly he hath it weel disserved.   2280
He hath to-day taught us so muche good
With prechyng in the pulpit ther he stood,
That I may vouche sauf, I sey for me,
He hadde the firste smel of fartes thre;
And so wolde al his covent hardily,   2285
He bereth hym so faire and hoolily."
    The lord, the lady, and ech man, save the
            frere,
Seyde that Jankyn spak, in this matere,
As wel as Euclide [dide] or Ptholomee.   2289
Touchynge the cherl, they seyde, subtiltee
And heigh wit made hym speken as he spak;
He nys no fool, ne no demonyak.
And Jankyn hath ywonne a newe gowne —
My tale is doon; we been almoost at towne.

Heere endeth the Somonours Tale.

2242 **a devel weye:** in the name of the Devil
2246 **yvele apayd:** displeased
2249 **evene deled:** evenly divided out
2253 **weder:** weather
2254 **perturbynge:** disturbance
2255 **Lat brynge:** have brought
2261 **parfourne up:** complete
2264 **sadly:** firmly

2267 **toght:** taut
2268 **tabour:** drum
2270 **nave:** hub
2272 **demonstratif:** demonstrable, logical
2289 **Euclide:** Euclid, the Greek mathematician   **Ptholomee:**
Ptolemy, the astronomer
2291 **wit:** intelligence

Fragment IV (Group E)

THE CLERK'S PROLOGUE

Heere folweth the Prologe of the Clerkes Tale of Oxenford.

"Sire Clerk of Oxenford," oure Hooste sayde,
"Ye ryde as coy and stille as dooth a mayde
Were newe spoused, sittynge at the bord;
This day ne herde I of youre tonge a word.
I trowe ye studie aboute som sophyme;   5
But Salomon seith 'every thyng hath tyme.'

"For Goddes sake, as beth of bettre cheere!
It is no tyme for to studien heere.
Telle us som myrie tale, by youre fey!
For what man that is entred in a pley,   10
He nedes moot unto the pley assente.
But precheth nat, as freres doon in Lente,
To make us for oure olde synnes wepe,
Ne that thy tale make us nat to slepe.

"Telle us som murie thyng of aventures.   15
Youre termes, youre colours, and youre figures,
Keepe hem in stoor til so be ye endite
Heigh style, as whan that men to kynges write.
Speketh so pleyn at this tyme, we yow preye,
That we may understonde what ye seye."   20
This worthy clerk benignely answerde:
"Hooste," quod he, "I am under youre yerde;
Ye han of us as now the governance,
And therfore wol I do yow obeisance,
As fer as resoun axeth, hardily.   25
I wol yow telle a tale which that I
Lerned at Padowe of a worthy clerk,
As preved by his wordes and his werk.

He is now deed and nayled in his cheste;
I prey to God so yeve his soule reste!   30
"Fraunceys Petrak, the lauriat poete,
Highte this clerk, whos rethorike sweete
Enlumyned al Ytaille of poetrie,
As Lynyan dide of philosophie,
Or lawe, or oother art particuler;   35
But Deeth, that wol nat suffre us dwellen heer,
But as it were a twynklyng of an ye,
Hem bothe hath slayn, and alle shul we dye.

"But forth to tellen of this worthy man
That taughte me this tale, as I bigan,   40
I seye that first with heigh stile he enditeth,
Er he the body of his tale writeth,
A prohemye, in the which discryveth he
Pemond and of Saluces the contree,
And speketh of Apennyn, the hilles hye,   45
That been the boundes of West Lumbardye,
And of Mount Vesulus in special,
Where as the Poo out of a welle smal
Taketh his firste spryngyng and his sours,
That estward ay encresseth in his cours   50
To Emele-ward, to Ferrare, and Venyse,
The which a long thyng were to devyse.
And trewely, as to my juggement,
Me thynketh it a thyng impertinent,
Save that he wole conveyen his mateere;   55
But this his tale, which that ye may heere."

---

29 **cheste:** coffin
31 **Fraunceys Petrak:** Petrarch, who was crowned with laurel in 1341
33 **Enlumyned:** made illustrious
34 **Lynyan:** Giovanni da Lignano, professor of canon law at Padua
35 **art particuler:** specialized area of study
43 **prohemye:** proem, introduction   **discryveth:** describes
44 **Pemond:** Piedmont, an area in northern Italy west of Lombardy   **Saluces:** Saluzzo, a region and town in Piedmont
45 **Apennyn:** the Apennines
46 **Lumbardye:** Lombardy, east of the Apennines
47 **Vesulus:** Monte Viso or Monviso, highest of the Italian Alps
48 **Poo:** the river Po   **welle:** spring
49 **sours:** source
51 **To Emele-ward:** toward Emilia, the area of eastern Italy south of Lombardy   **Ferrare:** Ferrara, a town and area in Emilia   **Venyse:** Venice, where the Po empties into the Adriatic Sea
54 **impertinent:** irrelevant
55 **conveyen:** introduce

2 **coy:** quiet, demure
3 **bord:** dinner table
5 **sophyme:** sophism, plausible but fallacious argument
7 **as beth:** be (*as* is not translated)
11 **pley:** rules of the game
16 **termes:** technical terms   **colours:** figures of speech   **figures:** rhetorical devices
17 **in stoor:** in stock, in reserve
18 **Heigh style:** elaborate, ornamented style
22 **under youre yerde:** under your authority
24 **do obeisance:** obey
27 **Padowe:** Padua

THE CLERK'S TALE

Heere bigynneth the Tale of the Clerk of Oxenford.

Ther is, at the west syde of Ytaille,
Doun at the roote of Vesulus the colde,
A lusty playn, habundant of vitaille,   59
Where many a tour and toun thou mayst biholde,
That founded were in tyme of fadres olde,
And many another delitable sighte,
And Saluces this noble contree highte.

A markys whilom lord was of that lond,
As were his worthy eldres hym bifore;   65
And obeisant, ay redy to his hond,
Were alle his liges, bothe lasse and moore.
Thus in delit he lyveth, and hath doon yoore,
Biloved and drad, thurgh favour of Fortune,
Bothe of his lordes and of his commune.   70

Therwith he was, to speke as of lynage,
The gentilleste yborn of Lumbardye,
A fair persone, and strong, and yong of age,
And ful of honour and of curteisye;
Discreet ynogh his contree for to gye,   75
Save in somme thynges that he was to blame;
And Walter was this yonge lordes name.

I blame hym thus: that he considered noght
In tyme comynge what myghte hym bityde,
But on his lust present was al his thoght,   80
As for to hauke and hunte on every syde.
Wel ny alle othere cures leet he slyde,
And eek he nolde — and that was worst of alle —
Wedde no wyf, for noght that may bifalle.

Oonly that point his peple bar so soore   85
That flokmeele on a day they to hym wente,
And oon of hem, that wisest was of loore —
Or elles that the lord best wolde assente
That he sholde telle hym what his peple mente,

Or elles koude he shewe wel swich mateere —
He to the markys seyde as ye shul heere: 91

"O noble markys, youre humanitee
Asseureth us and yeveth us hardinesse,
As ofte as tyme is of necessitee,   94
That we to yow mowe telle oure hevynesse.
Accepteth, lord, now of youre gentillesse
That we with pitous herte unto yow pleyne,
And lat youre eres nat my voys desdeyne.

"Al have I noght to doone in this mateere
Moore than another man hath in this place,
Yet for as muche as ye, my lord so deere,   101
Han alwey shewed me favour and grace
I dar the bettre aske of yow a space
Of audience to shewen oure requeste,
And ye, my lord, to doon right as yow leste.

"For certes, lord, so wel us liketh yow   106
And al youre werk, and evere han doon, that we
Ne koude nat us self devysen how
We myghte lyven in moore felicitee,
Save o thyng, lord, if it youre wille be,   110
That for to been a wedded man yow leste;
Thanne were youre peple in sovereyn hertes
    reste.

"Boweth youre nekke under that blisful yok
Of soveraynetee, noght of servyse,   114
Which that men clepe spousaille or wedlok;
And thenketh, lord, among youre thoghtes wyse
How that oure dayes passe in sondry wyse,
For thogh we slepe, or wake, or rome, or ryde,
Ay fleeth the tyme; it nyl no man abyde.   119

"And thogh youre grene youthe floure as yit,
In crepeth age alwey, as stille as stoon,

58 **roote of Vesulus:** foot of Monte Viso
59 **habundant of vitaille:** rich in agricultural produce
64 **markys:** marquis
69 **drad:** feared, respected
75 **gye:** govern
80 **lust present:** immediate pleasure
82 **slyde:** slip away
85 **bar so soore:** took so badly
86 **flokmeele:** in groups
88–90 **Or elles that . . . Or elles:** either because . . . or

92 **humanitee:** graciousness
93 **Asseureth us:** makes us confident **hardinesse:** boldness
104 **audience:** hearing
105 **yow leste:** it may please you
106–7 **so wel us liketh yow . . . han doon:** you and your work
so well please us and ever have done so
108 **us self:** ourselves
115 **spousaille:** marriage

And deeth manaceth every age, and smyt
In ech estaat, for ther escapeth noon;
And al so certein as we knowe echoon
That we shul deye, as uncerteyn we alle   125
Been of that day whan deeth shal on us falle.

"Accepteth thanne of us the trewe entente,
That nevere yet refuseden youre heeste,
And we wol, lord, if that ye wole assente,
Chese yow a wyf, in short tyme atte leeste,
Born of the gentilleste and of the meeste   131
Of al this land, so that it oghte seme
Honour to God and yow, as we kan deeme.

"Delivere us out of al this bisy drede,
And taak a wyf, for hye Goddes sake!   135
For if it so bifelle, as God forbede,
That thurgh youre deeth youre lyne sholde
    slake,
And that a straunge successour sholde take
Youre heritage, O wo were us alyve!
Wherfore we pray you hastily to wyve."   140

Hir meeke preyere and hir pitous cheere
Made the markys herte han pitee.
"Ye wol," quod he, "myn owene peple deere,
To that I nevere erst thoughte streyne me.
I me rejoysed of my liberte,   145
That seelde tyme is founde in mariage;
Ther I was free, I moot been in servage.

"But nathelees I se youre trewe entente,
And truste upon youre wit, and have doon ay;
Wherfore of my free wyl I wole assente   150
To wedde me, as soone as evere I may.
But ther as ye han profred me to-day
To chese me a wyf, I yow relesse
That choys and prey yow of that profre cesse.

"For God it woot, that children ofte been
Unlyk hir worthy eldres hem bifore;   156
Bountee comth al of God, nat of the streen
Of which they been engendred and ybore.

I truste in Goddes bountee, and therfore
My mariage and myn estaat and reste   160
I hym bitake; he may doon as hym leste.

"Lat me allone in chesynge of my wyf —
That charge upon my bak I wole endure.
But I yow preye, and charge upon youre lyf,
What wyf that I take, ye me assure   165
To worshipe hire, whil that hir lyf may dure,
In word and werk, bothe heere and every-
    wheere,
As she an emperoures doghter weere.

"And forthermoore, this shal ye swere: that ye
Agayn my choys shul neither grucche ne stryve;
For sith I shal forgoon my libertee   171
At youre requeste, as evere moot I thryve,
Ther as myn herte is set, ther wol I wyve;
And but ye wole assente in swich manere,   174
I prey yow, speketh namoore of this matere."

With hertely wyl they sworen and assenten
To al this thyng — ther seyde no wight nay —
Bisekynge hym of grace, er that they wenten,
That he wolde graunten hem a certein day
Of his spousaille, as soone as evere he may;
For yet alwey the peple somwhat dredde,   181
Lest that the markys no wyf wolde wedde.

He graunted hem a day, swich as hym leste,
On which he wolde be wedded sikerly,
And seyde he dide al this at hir requeste.   185
And they, with humble entente, buxomly,
Knelynge upon hir knees ful reverently,
Hym thonken alle; and thus they han an ende
Of hire entente, and hoom agayn they wende.

And heerupon he to his officeres   190
Comaundeth for the feste to purveye,
And to his privee knyghtes and squieres
Swich charge yaf as hym liste on hem leye;
And they to his comandement obeye,
And ech of hem dooth al his diligence   195
To doon unto the feeste reverence.

Explicit prima pars.

Incipit secunda pars.

Noght fer fro thilke paleys honurable,
Wher as this markys shoop his mariage,
There stood a throop, of site delitable,
In which that povre folk of that village   200
Hadden hir beestes and hir herbergage,
And of hire labour tooke hir sustenance,
After that the erthe yaf hem habundance.

Amonges thise povre folk ther dwelte a man
Which that was holden povrest of hem alle;
But hye God somtyme senden kan   206
His grace into a litel oxes stalle;
Janicula men of that throop hym calle.
A doghter hadde he, fair ynogh to sighte,
And Grisildis this yonge mayden highte.   210

But for to speke of vertuous beautee,
Thanne was she oon the faireste under sonne;
For povreliche yfostred up was she,
No likerous lust was thurgh hire herte yronne.
Wel ofter of the welle than of the tonne   215
She drank, and for she wolde vertu plese,
She knew wel labour but noon ydel ese.

But thogh this mayde tendre were of age,
Yet in the brest of hire virginitee
Ther was enclosed rype and sad corage;   220
And in greet reverence and charitee
Hir olde povre fader fostred shee.
A fewe sheep, spynnynge, on feeld she kepte;
She wolde noght been ydel til she slepte.

And whan she homward cam, she wolde
     brynge   225
Wortes or othere herbes tymes ofte,
The whiche she shredde and seeth for hir lyv-
     ynge,
And made hir bed ful hard and nothyng softe;
And ay she kepte hir fadres lyf on-lofte
With everich obeisaunce and diligence   230
That child may doon to fadres reverence.

Upon Grisilde, this povre creature,
Ful ofte sithe this markys sette his ye
As he on huntyng rood paraventure;
And whan it fil that he myghte hire espye,   235
He noght with wantown lookyng of folye
His eyen caste on hire, but in sad wyse
Upon hir chiere he wolde hym ofte avyse,

Commendynge in his herte hir womman-
     hede,
And eek hir vertu, passynge any wight   240
Of so yong age, as wel in chiere as dede.
For thogh the peple have no greet insight
In vertu, he considered ful right
Hir bountee, and disposed that he wolde   244
Wedde hire oonly, if evere he wedde sholde.

The day of weddyng cam, but no wight kan
Telle what womman that it sholde be;
For which merveille wondred many a man,
And seyden, whan they were in privetee,
"Wol nat oure lord yet leve his vanytee?   250
Wol he nat wedde? Allas! Allas, the while!
Why wole he thus hymself and us bigile?"

But nathelees this markys hath doon make
Of gemmes, set in gold and in asure,
Brooches and rynges, for Grisildis sake;   255
And of hir clothyng took he the mesure
By a mayde lyk to hire stature,
And eek of othere aornementes alle
That unto swich a weddyng sholde falle.

The time of undren of the same day   260
Approcheth, that this weddyng sholde be,
And al the paleys put was in array,
Bothe halle and chambres, ech in his degree;
Houses of office stuffed with plentee
Ther maystow seen, of deyntevous vitaille
That may be founde as fer as last Ytaille.   266

This roial markys, richely arrayed,
Lordes and ladyes in his compaignye,
The whiche that to the feeste weren yprayed,
And of his retenue the bachelrye,   270

Incipit, etc.: Here begins the second part.
199 **throop**: village
201 **herbergage**: lodging
209 **to sighte**: in appearance
212 **oon the faireste**: the fairest of all
213 **povreliche**: in poverty
214 **likerous lust**: sensual desire
215 **tonne**: wine barrel
216 **vertu plese**: satisfy the demands of virtue
220 **rype and sad**: mature and steadfast
222 **fostred**: supported
223 **spynnynge**: while spinning
226 **Wortes**: cabbages
227 **shredde**: cut up   **seeth**: boiled
229 **kepte . . . on-lofte**: sustained

234 **paraventure**: by chance
236 **wantown**: lecherous
237 **sad**: serious
239 **wommanhede**: femininity, womanly qualities
244 **disposed**: decided
258 **aornementes**: ornaments
260 **undren**: midmorning, about 9 A.M.
264 **Houses of office**: outbuildings
265 **deyntevous**: delicious
266 **last Ytaille**: farthest Italy, as far as Italy extends
269 **yprayed**: invited
270 And the knights in his service

With many a soun of sondry melodye,
Unto the village of the which I tolde
In this array the righte wey han holde.

Grisilde of this, God woot, ful innocent,
That for hire shapen was al this array,   275
To fecchen water at a welle is went,
And cometh hoom as soone as ever she may;
For wel she hadde herd seyd that thilke day
The markys sholde wedde, and if she myghte,
She wolde fayn han seyn som of that sighte.   280

She thoghte, "I wole with othere maydens
      stonde,
That been my felawes, in oure dore and se
The markysesse, and therfore wol I fonde
To doon at hoom, as soone as it may be,
The labour which that longeth unto me,   285
And thanne I may at leyser hire biholde,
If she this wey unto the castel holde."

And as she wolde over hir thresshfold gon,
The markys cam and gan hire for to calle;
And she set doun hir water pot anon,   290
Biside the thresshfold, in an oxes stalle,
And doun upon hir knes she gan to falle,
And with sad contenance kneleth stille,
Til she had herd what was the lordes wille.

This thoghtful markys spak unto this mayde
Ful sobrely, and seyde in this manere: 296
"Where is youre fader, O Grisildis?" he sayde.
And she with reverence, in humble cheere,
Answerde, "Lord, he is al redy heere."
And in she gooth withouten lenger lette,   300
And to the markys she hir fader fette.

He by the hand thanne took this olde man,
And seyde thus, whan he hym hadde asyde:
"Janicula, I neither may ne kan
Lenger the plesance of myn herte hyde.   305
If that thou vouche sauf, what so bityde,
Thy doghter wol I take, er that I wende,
As for my wyf, unto hir lyves ende.

"Thou lovest me, I woot it wel certeyn,
And art my feithful lige man ybore,   310
And al that liketh me, I dar wel seyn

It liketh thee, and specially therfore
Tel me that poynt that I have seyd bifore,
If that thou wolt unto that purpos drawe,
To take me as for thy sone-in-lawe."   315

This sodeyn cas this man astonyed so
That reed he wax; abayst and al quakynge
He stood; unnethes seyde he wordes mo,
But oonly thus: "Lord," quod he, "my willynge
Is as ye wole, ne ayeynes youre likynge   320
I wol no thyng, ye be my lord so deere;
Right as yow lust, governeth this mateere."

"Yet wol I," quod this markys softely,
"That in thy chambre I and thou and she
Have a collacioun, and wostow why?   325
For I wol axe if it hire wille be
To be my wyf and reule hire after me.
And al this shal be doon in thy presence;
I wol noght speke out of thyn audience."

And in the chambre, whil they were aboute
Hir tretys, which as ye shal after heere,   331
The peple cam unto the hous withoute,
And wondred hem in how honest manere
And tentifly she kepte hir fader deere.
But outrely Grisildis wondre myghte,   335
For nevere erst ne saugh she swich a sighte.

No wonder is thogh that she were astoned
To seen so greet a gest come in that place;
She nevere was to swiche gestes woned,
For which she looked with ful pale face.   340
But shortly forth this matere for to chace,
Thise arn the wordes that the markys sayde
To this benigne, verray, feithful mayde:

"Grisilde," he seyde, "ye shal wel under-
      stonde
It liketh to youre fader and to me   345
That I yow wedde, and eek it may so stonde,
As I suppose, ye wol that it so be.
But thise demandes axe I first," quod he,

273 **righte:** direct
283 **markysesse:** marchioness **fonde:** try
288 **thresshfold:** threshold
299 **al redy:** right
300 **lette:** delay
306 **If that thou vouche sauf:** if you agree
310 **ybore:** born

314 **unto that purpos drawe:** agree with that proposal
317 **abayst:** embarrassed
319 **willynge:** desire
325 **collacioun:** discussion, colloquy
327 **reule hire after me:** conduct herself as I decide
329 **audience:** hearing
331 **tretys:** negotiation
333 **how honest:** what a virtuous
334 **tentifly:** attentively
339 **woned:** accustomed
341 **chace:** pursue
342 **arn:** are
348 **demandes:** questions

"That, sith it shal be doon in hastif wyse,
Wol ye assente, or elles yow avyse?   350

"I seye this: be ye redy with good herte
To al my lust, and that I frely may,
As me best thynketh, do yow laughe or smerte,
And nevere ye to grucche it, nyght ne day?
And eek whan I sey 'ye,' ne sey nat 'nay,'   355
Neither by word ne frownyng contenance?
Swere this, and heere I swere oure alliance."

Wondrynge upon this word, quakynge for
     drede,
She seyde, "Lord, undigne and unworthy
Am I to thilke honour that ye me beede,   360
But as ye wole yourself, right so wol I.
And heere I swere that nevere willyngly,
In werk ne thoght, I nyl yow disobeye,
For to be deed, though me were looth to deye."

"This is ynogh, Grisilde myn," quod he.   365
And forth he gooth with a ful sobre cheere
Out at the dore, and after that cam she,
And to the peple he seyde in this manere:
"This is my wyf," quod he, "that standeth
     heere.
Honoureth hire and loveth hire, I preye,   370
Whoso me loveth; ther is namoore to seye."

And for that no thyng of hir olde geere
She sholde brynge into his hous, he bad
That wommen sholde dispoillen hire right
     theere;
Of which thise ladyes were nat right glad   375
To handle hir clothes, wherinne she was clad.
But nathelees, this mayde bright of hewe
Fro foot to heed they clothed han al newe.

Hir heris han they kembd, that lay untressed
Ful rudely, and with hir fyngres smale   380
A corone on hire heed they han ydressed,
And sette hire ful of nowches grete and smale.
Of hire array what sholde I make a tale?
Unnethe the peple hir knew for hire fairnesse
Whan she translated was in swich richesse.   385

This markys hath hire spoused with a ryng
Broght for the same cause, and thanne hire sette
Upon an hors, snow-whit and wel amblyng,
And to his paleys, er he lenger lette,   389
With joyful peple that hire ladde and mette,
Conveyed hire; and thus the day they spende
In revel, til the sonne gan descende.

And shortly forth this tale for to chace,
I seye that to this newe markysesse
God hath swich favour sent hire of his grace
That it ne semed nat by liklynesse   396
That she was born and fed in rudenesse,
As in a cote or in an oxe-stalle,
But norissed in an emperoures halle.

To every wight she woxen is so deere   400
And worshipful that folk ther she was bore,
And from hire birthe knewe hire yeer by yeere,
Unnethe trowed they — but dorste han swore —
That to Janicle, of which I spak bifore,
She doghter were, for, as by conjecture,   405
Hem thoughte she was another creature.

For though that evere vertuous was she,
She was encressed in swich excellence
Of thewes goode, yset in heigh bountee,
And so discreet and fair of eloquence,   410
So benigne and so digne of reverence,
And koude so the peples herte embrace,
That ech hire lovede that looked on hir face.

Noght oonly of Saluces in the toun
Publiced was the bountee of hir name,   415
But eek biside in many a regioun,
If oon seide wel, another seyde the same;
So spradde of hire heighe bountee the fame
That men and wommen, as wel yonge as olde,
Goon to Saluce upon hire to biholde.   420

Thus Walter lowely — nay, but roially —
Wedded with fortunat honestetee,
In Goddes pees lyveth ful esily
At hoom, and outward grace ynogh had he;
And for he saugh that under low degree   425
Was ofte vertu hid, the peple hym heelde
A prudent man, and that is seyn ful seelde.

---

350 **yow avyse:** consider the matter further (with the implication
of refusal)
359 **undigne:** unsuitable
360 **beede:** offer
374 **dispoillen:** undress
379 **untressed:** unkempt
380 **rudely:** roughly   **hir fyngres smale:** their elegant fingers
381 **corone:** crown, nuptial garland
382 **nowches:** brooches, jewelled ornaments   **grete and smale:**
of every sort
385 **translated:** transformed

388 **wel amblyng:** with a gentle pace
394 **markysesse:** marchioness
397 **rudenesse:** humble, unsophisticated conditions
398 **cote:** peasant's hut
400 **woxen is:** has grown, has become
409 **thewes:** morals, personal qualities
422 **honestetee:** honor, virtue
427 **seelde:** seldom

Nat oonly this Grisildis thurgh hir wit
Koude al the feet of wyfly hoomlinesse,
But eek, whan that the cas required it,   430
The commune profit koude she redresse.
Ther nas discord, rancour, ne hevynesse
In al that land that she ne koude apese,
And wisely brynge hem alle in reste and ese.

Though that hire housbonde absent were
     anon,   435
If gentil men or othere of hire contree
Were wrothe, she wolde bryngen hem aton;
So wise and rype wordes hadde she,
And juggementz of so greet equitee,
That she from hevene sent was, as men wende,
Peple to save and every wrong t'amende.   441

Nat longe tyme after that this Grisild
Was wedded, she a doghter hath ybore,
Al had hire levere have born a knave child;
Glad was this markys and the folk therfore,
For though a mayde child coome al bifore,   446
She may unto a knave child atteyne
By liklihede, syn she nys nat bareyne.

Explicit secunda pars.

Incipit tercia pars.

Ther fil, as it bifalleth tymes mo,
Whan that this child had souked but a throwe,
This markys in his herte longeth so   451
To tempte his wyf, hir sadnesse for to knowe,
That he ne myghte out of his herte throwe
This merveillous desir his wyf t'assaye;
Nedelees, God woot, he thoghte hire for
     t'affraye.   455

He hadde assayed hire ynogh bifore,
And foond hire evere good; what neded it
Hire for to tempte, and alwey moore and
     moore,
Though som men preise it for a subtil wit?
But as for me, I seye that yvele it sit   460

To assaye a wyf whan that it is no nede,
And putten hire in angwyssh and in drede.

For which this markys wroghte in this man-
     ere:
He cam allone a-nyght, ther as she lay,   464
With stierne face and with ful trouble cheere,
And seyde thus: "Grisilde," quod he, "that day
That I yow took out of youre povere array,
And putte yow in estaat of heigh noblesse —
Ye have nat that forgeten, as I gesse?

"I seye, Grisilde, this present dignitee,   470
In which that I have put yow, as I trowe,
Maketh yow nat foryetful for to be
That I yow took in povre estaat ful lowe,
For any wele ye moot youreselven knowe.   474
Taak heede of every word that y yow seye;
Ther is no wight that hereth it but we tweye.

"Ye woot yourself wel how that ye cam heere
Into this hous, it is nat longe ago;
And though to me that ye be lief and deere,
Unto my gentils ye be no thyng so.   480
They seyn, to hem it is greet shame and wo
For to be subgetz and been in servage
To thee, that born art of a smal village.

"And namely sith thy doghter was ybore
Thise wordes han they spoken, doutelees.   485
But I desire, as I have doon bifore,
To lyve my lyf with hem in reste and pees.
I may nat in this caas be recchelees;
I moot doon with thy doghter for the beste,
Nat as I wolde, but as my peple leste.   490

"And yet, God woot, this is ful looth to me;
But nathelees withoute youre wityng
I wol nat doon; but this wol I," quod he,
"That ye to me assente as in this thyng.   494
Shewe now youre pacience in youre werkyng,
That ye me highte and swore in youre village
That day that maked was oure mariage."

Whan she had herd al this, she noght ameved
Neither in word, or chiere, or contenaunce,
For, as it semed, she was nat agreved.   500
She seyde, "Lord, al lyth in youre plesaunce.

---

429 **feet of wyfly hoomlinesse:** feats, skills of a housewife's duties
431 **commune profit:** common good, welfare of the state
redresse: amend, promote
433 **apese:** pacify
437 **aton:** to agreement
444 **levere:** rather   **knave child:** baby boy
Explicit, *etc.:* Here ends the second part.
Incipit, *etc.:* Here begins the third part.
449 **tymes mo:** often
450 **souked:** sucked, fed on the breast   **throwe:** short while
452 **tempte:** test   **sadnesse:** constancy
454 **t'assaye:** to test
455 **t'affraye:** to frighten
460 **yvele it sit:** it ill befits one (**sit** = *sitteth*)

465 **trouble:** troubled
470 **dignitee:** high social position
480 **gentils:** nobles
483 **smal:** humble
488 **recchelees:** careless
492 **wityng:** knowledge
498 **ameved:** changed

My child and I, with hertely obeisaunce,
Been youres al, and ye mowe save or spille
Youre owene thyng; werketh after youre wille.

"Ther may no thyng, God so my soule save,
Liken to yow that may displese me;   506
Ne I desire no thyng for to have,
Ne drede for to leese, save oonly yee.
This wyl is in myn herte, and ay shal be;
No lengthe of tyme or deeth may this deface,
Ne chaunge my corage to another place."   511

Glad was this markys of hire answeryng,
But yet he feyned as he were nat so;
Al drery was his cheere and his lookyng,
Whan that he sholde out of the chambre go.
Soone after this, a furlong wey or two,   516
He prively hath toold al his entente
Unto a man, and to his wyf hym sente.

A maner sergeant was this privee man,   519
The which that feithful ofte he founden hadde
In thynges grete, and eek swich folk wel kan
Doon execucioun in thynges badde.
The lord knew wel that he hym loved and
        dradde;
And whan this sergeant wiste his lordes wille,
Into the chambre he stalked hym ful stille. 525

"Madame," he seyde, "ye moote foryeve it
        me,
Though I do thyng to which I am constreyned.
Ye been so wys that ful wel knowe ye
That lordes heestes mowe nat been yfeyned;
They mowe wel been biwailled or compleyned,
But men moote nede unto hire lust obeye,   531
And so wol I; ther is namoore to seye.

"This child I am comanded for to take" —
And spak namoore, but out the child he hente
Despitously, and gan a cheere make   535
As though he wolde han slayn it er he wente.
Grisildis moot al suffre and al consente,
And as a lamb she sitteth meke and stille,
And leet this crueel sergeant doon his wille.

Suspecious was the diffame of this man,   540
Suspect his face, suspect his word also;
Suspect the tyme in which he this bigan.
Allas! Hir doghter that she loved so,

She wende he wolde han slawen it right tho.
But nathelees she neither weep ne syked,   545
Conformynge hire to that the markys lyked.

But atte laste to speken she bigan,
And mekely she to the sergeant preyde,
So as he was a worthy gentil man,
That she moste kisse hire child er that it deyde.
And in hir barm this litel child she leyde   551
With ful sad face, and gan the child to blisse,
And lulled it, and after gan it kisse.

And thus she seyde in hire benigne voys,
"Fareweel my child! I shal thee nevere see.
But sith I thee have marked with the croys   556
Of thilke Fader — blessed moote he be! —
That for us deyde upon a croys of tree,
Thy soule, litel child, I hym bitake,
For this nyght shaltow dyen for my sake."   560

I trowe that to a norice in this cas
It had been hard this reuthe for to se;
Wel myghte a mooder thanne han cryd "allas!"
But nathelees so sad stidefast was she
That she endured al adversitee,   565
And to the sergeant mekely she sayde,
"Have heer agayn youre litel yonge mayde.

"Gooth now," quod she, "and dooth my
        lordes heeste;
But o thyng wol I prey yow of youre grace,
That, but my lord forbad yow, atte leeste   570
Burieth this litel body in som place
That beestes ne no briddes it torace."
But he no word wol to that purpos seye,
But took the child and wente upon his weye.

This sergeant cam unto his lord ageyn,   575
And of Grisildis wordes and hire cheere
He tolde hym point for point, in short and
        pleyn,
And hym presenteth with his doghter deere.
Somwhat this lord hadde routhe in his manere,
But nathelees his purpos heeld he stille,   580
As lordes doon, whan they wol han hir wille;

And bad this sergeant that he pryvely
Sholde this child softe wynde and wrappe,

---

519 **sergeant:** servant whose duty is to enforce the law   **privee
man:** confidential servant
529 **yfeyned:** evaded (by dissembling)
540 **diffame:** bad reputation

544 **slawen:** slain
551 **barm:** lap
552 **blisse:** bless
558 **tree:** wood
561 **norice:** nurse
562 **reuthe:** pitiful situation
564 **sad stidefast:** firmly steadfast
572 **briddes:** birds   **torace:** tear to pieces

With alle circumstances tendrely,
And carie it in a cofre or in a lappe;   585
But, upon peyne his heed of for to swappe,
That no man sholde knowe of his entente,
Ne whenne he cam, ne whider that he wente;

But at Boloigne to his suster deere,
That thilke tyme of Panik was countesse,   590
He sholde it take and shewe hire this mateere,
Bisekynge hire to doon hire bisynesse
This child to fostre in alle gentillesse;
And whos child that it was he bad hire hyde
From every wight, for oght that may bityde.

The sergeant gooth, and hath fulfild this
    thyng;   596
But to this markys now retourne we.
For now gooth he ful faste ymaginyng
If by his wyves cheere he myghte se,
Or by hire word aperceyve, that she   600
Were chaunged; but he nevere hire koude
    fynde
But evere in oon ylike sad and kynde.

As glad, as humble, as bisy in servyse,
And eek in love, as she was wont to be,
Was she to hym in every maner wyse;   605
Ne of hir doghter noght a word spak she.
Noon accident, for noon adversitee,
Was seyn in hire, ne nevere hir doghter name
Ne nempned she, in ernest nor in game.   609

Explicit tercia pars.

Sequitur pars quarta.

In this estaat ther passed been foure yeer
Er she with childe was, but, as God wolde,
A knave child she bar by this Walter,
Ful gracious and fair for to biholde.
And whan that folk it to his fader tolde,
Nat oonly he but al his contree merye   615
Was for this child, and God they thanke and
    herye.

Whan it was two yeer old, and fro the brest
Departed of his norice, on a day

This markys caughte yet another lest
To tempte his wyf yet ofter, if he may.   620
O nedelees was she tempted in assay!
But wedded men ne knowe no mesure,
Whan that they fynde a pacient creature.

"Wyf," quod this markys, "ye han herd er
    this
My peple sikly berth oure mariage;   625
And namely sith my sone yboren is,
Now is it worse than evere in al oure age.
The murmur sleeth myn herte and my corage,
For to myne eres comth the voys so smerte
That it wel ny destroyed hath myn herte.   630

"Now sey they thus: 'Whan Walter is agon,
Thanne shal the blood of Janicle succede
And been oure lord, for oother have we noon.'
Swiche wordes seith my peple, out of drede.
Wel oughte I of swich murmur taken heede,
For certeinly I drede swich sentence,   636
Though they nat pleyn speke in myn audience.

"I wolde lyve in pees, if that I myghte;
Wherfore I am disposed outrely,
As I his suster servede by nyghte,   640
Right so thenke I to serve hym pryvely.
This warne I yow, that ye nat sodeynly
Out of youreself for no wo sholde outreye;
Beth pacient, and therof I yow preye."

"I have," quod she, "seyd thus, and evere
    shal: 645
I wol no thyng, ne nyl no thyng, certayn,
But as yow list. Naught greveth me at al,
Though that my doughter and my sone be
    slayn —
At youre comandement, this is to sayn.   649
I have noght had no part of children tweyne
But first siknesse, and after, wo and peyne.

"Ye been oure lord; dooth with youre owene
    thyng
Right as yow list; axeth no reed at me.
For as I lefte at hoom al my clothyng,
Whan I first cam to yow, right so," quod she,
"Lefte I my wyl and al my libertee,   656

---

584 **alle circumstances**: every care
585 **lappe**: large pocket (made by a fold in the clothing)
586 **swappe**: strike
588 **whenne**: whence **whider**: whither
590 **Panik**: Panico, near Bologna
598 **ymaginyng**: considering
607 **accident**: accidental (external) sign (of change)
609 **nempned**: named
Explicit, *etc.*: Here ends the third part.
Sequitur, *etc.*: Here follows the fourth part.
616 **herye**: praise

619 **lest**: desire
622 **mesure**: moderation
625 **sikly berth**: dislike, take ill
627 **al oure age**: present times
628 **murmur**: grumbling
629 **smerte**: sharply
636 **sentence**: opinion
639 **disposed**: decided
643 **outreye**: break out in a passion

And took youre clothyng; wherfore I yow
        preye,
Dooth youre plesaunce; I wol youre lust obeye.

    "And certes, if I hadde prescience   659
Youre wyl to knowe, er ye youre lust me tolde,
I wolde it doon withouten necligence;
But now I woot youre lust, and what ye wolde,
Al youre plesance ferme and stable I holde;
For wiste I that my deeth wolde do yow ese,
Right gladly wolde I dyen, yow to plese.   665

    "Deth may noght make no comparisoun
Unto youre love." And whan this markys say
The constance of his wyf, he caste adoun
His eyen two, and wondreth that she may
In pacience suffre al this array;   670
And forth he goth with drery contenance,
But to his herte it was ful greet plesance.

    This ugly sergeant, in the same wyse
That he hire doghter caughte, right so he —
Or worse, if men worse kan devyse —   675
Hath hent hire sone, that ful was of beautee.
And evere in oon so pacient was she
That she no chiere maade of hevynesse,
But kiste hir sone, and after gan it blesse;

    Save this, she preyede hym that, if he
        myghte,   680
Hir litel sone he wolde in erthe grave
His tendre lymes, delicaat to sighte,
Fro foweles and fro beestes for to save.
But she noon answere of hym myghte have.
He wente his wey, as hym no thyng ne roghte,
But to Boloigne he tendrely it broghte.   686

    This markys wondred, evere lenger the
        moore,
Upon hir pacience, and if that he
Ne hadde soothly knowen therbifoore
That parfitly hir children loved she,   690
He wolde have wend that of som subtiltee,
And of malice, or for crueel corage,
That she hadde suffred this with sad visage.

But wel he knew that next hymself, certayn,
She loved hir children best in every wyse.   695
But now of wommen wolde I axen fayn
If thise assayes myghte nat suffise?
What koude a sturdy housbonde moore devyse
To preeve hir wyfhod and hir stedefastnesse,
And he continuynge evere in sturdinesse?   700

    But ther been folk of swich condicion
That whan they have a certein purpos take,
They kan nat stynte of hire entencion,
But, right as they were bounden to that stake,
They wol nat of that firste purpos slake.   705
Right so this markys fulliche hath purposed
To tempte his wyf as he was first disposed.

    He waiteth if by word or contenance
That she to hym was changed of corage,
But nevere koude he fynde variance.   710
She was ay oon in herte and in visage,
And ay the forther that she was in age,
The moore trewe, if that it were possible,
She was to hym in love, and moore penyble.

    For which it semed thus: that of hem two
Ther nas but o wyl, for as Walter leste,   716
The same lust was hire plesance also.
And, God be thanked, al fil for the beste.
She shewed wel, for no worldly unreste
A wyf, as of hirself, nothing ne sholde   720
Wille in effect, but as hir housbonde wolde.

    The sclaundre of Walter ofte and wyde
        spradde,
That of a crueel herte he wikkedly,
For he a povre womman wedded hadde,
Hath mordred bothe his children prively.   725
Swich murmur was among hem comunly.
No wonder is, for to the peples ere
Ther cam no word but that they mordred were.

    For which, where as his peple therbifore
Hadde loved hym wel, the sclaundre of his
        diffame   730
Made hem that they hym hatede therfore.

659 **prescience**: foreknowledge
663 **ferme and stable I holde**: I obey unswervingly
667 **say**: saw
681 **grave**: bury
682 **delicaat to sighte**: pleasing in appearance
685 **roghte**: cared
690 **parfitly**: perfectly, completely
691 **subtiltee**: treachery

698 **sturdy**: harsh, cruel
700 **sturdinesse**: harshness, cruelty
705 **slake**: desist
706 **purposed**: decided
714 **penyble**: painstaking, attentive
719 **for no worldly unreste**: on account of no earthly discomfort
721 **Wille in effect**: desire in fact **but**: except
722 **sclaundre**: ill fame
730 **diffame**: bad reputation

To been a mordrere is an hateful name;
But nathelees, for ernest ne for game,
He of his crueel purpos nolde stente;
To tempte his wyf was set al his entente. 735

Whan that his doghter twelve yeer was of
 age,
He to the court of Rome, in subtil wyse
Enformed of his wyl, sente his message,
Comaundynge hem swiche bulles to devyse
As to his crueel purpos may suffyse — 740
How that the pope, as for his peples reste,
Bad hym to wedde another, if hym leste.

I seye, he bad they sholde countrefete
The popes bulles, makynge mencion
That he hath leve his firste wyf to lete, 745
As by the popes dispensacion,
To stynte rancour and dissencion
Bitwixe his peple and hym; thus seyde the
 bulle,
The which they han publiced atte fulle.

The rude peple, as it no wonder is, 750
Wenden ful wel that it hadde be right so;
But whan thise tidynges came to Grisildis,
I deeme that hire herte was ful wo.
But she, ylike sad for everemo,
Disposed was, this humble creature, 755
The adversitee of Fortune al t'endure,

Abidynge evere his lust and his plesance,
To whom that she was yeven herte and al,
As to hire verray worldly suffisance.
But shortly if this storie I tellen shal, 760
This markys writen hath in special
A lettre, in which he sheweth his entente,
And secreely he to Boloigne it sente.

To the Erl of Panyk, which that hadde tho
Wedded his suster, preyde he specially 765
To bryngen hoom agayn his children two
In honurable estaat al openly.
But o thyng he hym preyede outrely,
That he to no wight, though men wolde en-
 quere, 769
Sholde nat telle whos children that they were,

But seye the mayden sholde ywedded be
Unto the Markys of Saluce anon.
And as this erl was preyed, so dide he;
For at day set he on his wey is goon
Toward Saluce, and lordes many oon 775
In riche array, this mayden for to gyde,
Hir yonge brother ridynge hire bisyde.

Arrayed was toward hir mariage
This fresshe mayde, ful of gemmes cleere;
Hir brother, which that seven yeer was of age,
Arrayed eek ful fressh in his manere. 781
And thus in greet noblesse and with glad
 cheere,
Toward Saluces shapynge hir journey,
Fro day to day they ryden in hir wey.

Explicit quarta pars.

Sequitur pars quinta.

Among al this, after his wikke usage, 785
This markys, yet his wyf to tempte moore
To the outtreste preeve of hir corage,
Fully to han experience and loore
If that she were as stidefast as bifoore,
He on a day in open audience 790
Ful boistously hath seyd hire this sentence:

"Certes, Grisilde, I hadde ynogh plesance
To han yow to my wyf for youre goodnesse,
As for youre trouthe and for youre obeisance,
Noght for youre lynage, ne for youre richesse;
But now knowe I in verray soothfastnesse 796
That in greet lordshipe, if I wel avyse,
Ther is greet servitute in sondry wyse.

"I may nat doon as every plowman may.
My peple me constreyneth for to take 800
Another wyf, and crien day by day;
And eek the pope, rancour for to slake,
Consenteth it — that dar I undertake —
And trewely thus muche I wol yow seye:
My newe wyf is comynge by the weye. 805

"Be strong of herte, and voyde anon hir
 place;
And thilke dowere that ye broghten me,

Explicit, *etc.*: Here ends the fourth part.
Sequitur, *etc.*: Here follows the fifth part.
785 **Among al this**: meanwhile
788 **loore**: knowledge
792 **ynogh**: great
797 **wel avyse**: judge rightly
803 **undertake**: assert
806 **voyde**: vacate

738 **message**: messenger
739 **bulles**: papal edicts
745 **lete**: desert
750 **rude**: ignorant, unlearned
763 **secreely**: secretly

Taak it agayn; I graunte it of my grace.
Retourneth to youre fadres hous," quod he;
"No man may alwey han prosperitee.   810
With evene herte I rede yow t'endure
The strook of Fortune or of aventure."

    And she agayn answerde in pacience:
"My lord," quod she, "I woot, and wiste alway,
How that bitwixen youre magnificence   815
And my poverte no wight kan ne may
Maken comparison; it is no nay.
I ne heeld me nevere digne in no manere
To be youre wyf, no, ne youre chamberere.

    "And in this hous, ther ye me lady maade —
The heighe God take I for my witnesse,   821
And also wysly he my soule glaade —
I nevere heeld me lady ne mistresse,
But humble servant to youre worthynesse,
And evere shal, whil that my lyf may dure,   825
Aboven every worldly creature.

    "That ye so longe of youre benignitee
Han holden me in honour and nobleye,
Where as I was noght worthy for to bee,
That thonke I God and yow, to whom I preye
Foryelde it yow; ther is namoore to seye.   831
Unto my fader gladly wol I wende,
And with hym dwelle unto my lyves ende.

    "Ther I was fostred of a child ful smal,
Til I be deed my lyf ther wol I lede,   835
A wydwe clene in body, herte, and al.
For sith I yaf to yow my maydenhede,
And am youre trewe wyf, it is no drede,
God shilde swich a lordes wyf to take
Another man to housbonde or to make!   840

    "And of youre newe wyf God of his grace
So graunte yow wele and prosperitee!
For I wol gladly yelden hire my place,
In which that I was blisful wont to bee.
For sith it liketh yow, my lord," quod shee, 845
"That whilom weren al myn hertes reste,
That I shal goon, I wol goon whan yow leste.

    "But ther as ye me profre swich dowaire
As I first broghte, it is wel in my mynde   849
It were my wrecched clothes, nothyng faire,
The whiche to me were hard now for to fynde.
O goode God! How gentil and how kynde
Ye semed by youre speche and youre visage
The day that maked was oure mariage!

    "But sooth is seyd — algate I fynde it trewe,
For in effect it preeved is on me —   856
Love is noght oold as whan that it is newe.
But certes, lord, for noon adversitee,
To dyen in the cas, it shal nat bee
That evere in word or werk I shal repente   860
That I yow yaf myn herte in hool entente.

    "My lord, ye woot that in my fadres place
Ye dide me streepe out of my povre weede,
And richely me cladden, of youre grace.
To yow broghte I noght elles, out of drede,   865
But feith, and nakednesse, and maydenhede;
And heere agayn your clothyng I restoore,
And eek your weddyng ryng, for everemore.

    "The remenant of youre jueles redy be
Inwith youre chambre, dar I saufly sayn.   870
Naked out of my fadres hous," quod she,
"I cam, and naked moot I turne agayn.
Al youre plesance wol I folwen fayn;
But yet I hope it be nat youre entente   874
That I smoklees out of youre paleys wente.

    "Ye koude nat doon so dishonest a thyng,
That thilke wombe in which youre children
        leye
Sholde biforn the peple, in my walkyng,
Be seyn al bare; wherfore I yow preye,
Lat me nat lyk a worm go by the weye.   880
Remembre yow, myn owene lord so deere,
I was youre wyf, though I unworthy weere.

    "Wherfore, in gerdon of my maydenhede,
Which that I broghte, and noght agayn I bere,
As voucheth sauf to yeve me, to my meede,
But swich a smok as I was wont to were,   886

811 **evene:** tranquil   **rede:** advise
817 **is no nay:** cannot be denied
818 **in no manere:** in no way
819 **chamberere:** chambermaid
822 **also wysly:** as surely as   **glaade:** may gladden
828 **nobleye:** noble state
831 **Foryelde:** may he repay
839 **shilde:** forbid

848 **dowaire:** dowry
857 When love is old it is not the same as when it was new.
859 **To dyen:** even if I were to die
863 **dide me streepe:** had me stripped   **weede:** clothing
870 **Inwith:** within   **saufly:** confidently
875 **smoklees:** without a smock (i.e., naked)
876 **dishonest:** shameful
883 **gerdon:** requital
885 **to my meede:** as my reward
886 **smok:** simple garment

That I therwith may wrye the wombe of here
That was youre wyf. And heer take I my leeve
Of yow, myn owene lord, lest I yow greve.''

"The smok," quod he, "that thou hast on thy
   bak,   890
Lat it be stille, and bere it forth with thee.''
But wel unnethes thilke word he spak,
But wente his wey, for routhe and for pitee.
Biforn the folk hirselven strepeth she,
And in hir smok, with heed and foot al bare,
Toward hir fadre hous forth is she fare.   896

The folk hire folwe, wepynge in hir weye,
And Fortune ay they cursen as they goon;
But she fro wepyng kepte hire eyen dreye,
Ne in this tyme word ne spak she noon.   900
Hir fader, that this tidynge herde anoon,
Curseth the day and tyme that Nature
Shoop hym to been a lyves creature.

For out of doute this olde poure man
Was evere in suspect of hir mariage;   905
For evere he demed, sith that it bigan,
That whan the lord fulfild hadde his corage,
Hym wolde thynke it were a disparage
To his estaat so lowe for t'alighte,
And voyden hire as soone as ever he myghte.

Agayns his doghter hastily goth he,   911
For he by noyse of folk knew hire comynge,
And with hire olde coote, as it myghte be
He covered hire, ful sorwefully wepynge.
But on hire body myghte he it nat brynge,   915
For rude was the clooth, and moore of age
By dayes fele than at hire mariage.

Thus with hire fader for a certeyn space
Dwelleth this flour of wyfly pacience,
That neither by hire wordes ne hire face,   920
Biforn the folk, ne eek in hire absence,
Ne shewed she that hire was doon offence;
Ne of hire heighe estaat no remembraunce
Ne hadde she, as by hire contenaunce.

No wonder is, for in hire grete estaat   925
Hire goost was evere in pleyn humylitee;
No tendre mouth, noon herte delicaat,

No pompe, no semblant of roialtee,
But ful of pacient benyngnytee,
Discreet and pridelees, ay honurable,   930
And to hire housbonde evere meke and stable.

Men speke of Job, and moost for his hum-
   blesse,
As clerkes, whan hem list, konne wel endite,
Namely of men, but as in soothfastnesse,
Though clerkes preise wommen but a lite,   935
Ther kan no man in humblesse hym acquite
As womman kan, ne kan been half so trewe
As wommen been, but it be falle of newe.

[PART VI.]

Fro Boloigne is this Erl of Panyk come,
Of which the fame up sprang to moore and
   lesse,   940
And to the peples eres, alle and some,
Was kouth eek that a newe markysesse
He with hym broghte, in swich pompe and
   richesse
That nevere was ther seyn with mannes ye
So noble array in al West Lumbardye.   945

The markys, which that shoop and knew al
   this,
Er that this erl was come, sente his message
For thilke sely povre Grisildis;
And she with humble herte and glad visage,
Nat with no swollen thoght in hire corage,   950
Cam at his heste, and on hire knees hire sette,
And reverently and wisely she hym grette.

"Grisilde," quod he, "my wyl is outrely
This mayden, that shal wedded been to me,
Received be to-morwe as roially   955
As it possible is in myn hous to be,
And eek that every wight in his degree
Have his estaat, in sittyng and servyse
And heigh plesaunce, as I kan best devyse.

"I have no wommen suffisaunt, certayn,   960
The chambres for t'arraye in ordinaunce
After my lust, and therfore wolde I fayn
That thyn were al swich manere governaunce.
Thou knowest eek of old al my plesaunce;

---

887 **wrye**: cover
908 **disparage**: degradation
910 **voyden**: get rid of
917 **fele**: many
927 **delicaat**: self-indulgent

928 **semblant**: outward appearance
930 **pridelees**: humble, without pride
938 **of newe**: recently
940 **moore and lesse**: great and humble, everyone
941 **alle and some**: one and all
958 **sittyng**: seating arrangement at the table

Thogh thyn array be badde and yvel biseye,
Do thou thy devoir at the leeste weye.''   966

    "Nat oonly, lord, that I am glad,'' quod she,
"To doon youre lust, but I desire also
Yow for to serve and plese in my degree
Withouten feyntyng, and shal everemo;   970
Ne nevere, for no wele ne no wo,
Ne shal the goost withinne myn herte stente
To love yow best with al my trewe entente.''

    And with that word she gan the hous to
        dighte,
And tables for to sette, and beddes make;   975
And peyned hire to doon al that she myghte,
Preyynge the chambereres, for Goddes sake,
To hasten hem, and faste swepe and shake;
And she, the mooste servysable of alle,
Hath every chambre arrayed and his halle.   980

    Abouten undren gan this erl alighte,
That with hym broghte thise noble children
        tweye,
For which the peple ran to seen the sighte
Of hire array, so richely biseye;
And thanne at erst amonges hem they seye   985
That Walter was no fool, thogh that hym leste
To chaunge his wyf, for it was for the beste.

    For she is fairer, as they deemen alle,
Than is Grisilde, and moore tendre of age,
And fairer fruyt bitwene hem sholde falle,   990
And moore plesant, for hire heigh lynage.
Hir brother eek so fair was of visage
That hem to seen the peple hath caught ples-
        aunce,
Commendynge now the markys governaunce.

    "O stormy peple! Unsad and evere untrewe!
Ay undiscreet and chaungynge as a fane!   996
Delitynge evere in rumbul that is newe,
For lyk the moone ay wexe ye and wane!

Ay ful of clappyng, deere ynogh a jane!
Youre doom is fals, youre constance yvele
        preeveth;   1000
A ful greet fool is he that on yow leeveth.''

    Thus seyden sadde folk in that citee,
Whan that the peple gazed up and doun,
For they were glad, right for the noveltee,
To han a newe lady of hir toun.   1005
Namoore of this make I now mencioun,
But to Grisilde agayn wol I me dresse,
And telle hir constance and hir bisynesse.

    Ful bisy was Grisilde in every thyng
That to the feeste was apertinent.   1010
Right noght was she abayst of hire clothyng,
Thogh it were rude and somdeel eek torent;
But with glad cheere to the yate is went
With oother folk to greete the markysesse,
And after that dooth forth hire bisynesse.   1015

    With so glad chiere his gestes she receyveth,
And so konnyngly, everich in his degree,
That no defaute no man aperceyveth,
But ay they wondren what she myghte bee
That in so povre array was for to see,   1020
And koude swich honour and reverence,
And worthily they preisen hire prudence.

    In al this meene while she ne stente
This mayde and eek hir brother to commende
With al hir herte, in ful benyngne entente,   1025
So wel that no man koude hir pris amende.
But atte laste, whan that thise lordes wende
To sitten doun to mete, he gan to calle
Grisilde, as she was bisy in his halle.   1029

    "Grisilde,'' quod he, as it were in his pley,
"How liketh thee my wyf and hire beautee?''
"Right wel,'' quod she, "my lord; for, in good
        fey,
A fairer saugh I nevere noon than she.
I prey to God yeve hire prosperitee;
And so hope I that he wol to yow sende   1035
Plesance ynogh unto youre lyves ende.

965 **yvel biseye:** ill-looking
966 **devoir:** duty
970 **feyntyng:** flagging, weakening
974 **dighte:** prepare
976 **peyned hire:** took pains
977 **chambereres:** chambermaids
979 **servysable:** willing to serve, attentive
981 **undren:** the third hour, about 9 A.M.
984 **richely biseye:** rich in appearance, splendid
985 **at erst:** for the first time
995 **Unsad:** inconstant
996 **undiscreet:** undiscerning   **fane:** weathervane
997 **rumbul:** rumor
998 **wexe:** wax

999 **clappyng:** chattering   **deere ynogh a jane:** expensive
enough at a halfpenny (i.e., worthless)
1000 **doom:** judgment   **preeveth:** proves
1001 **leeveth:** believes, trusts
1010 **apertinent:** suitable
1012 **torent:** ragged
1017 **konnyngly:** skillfully
1018 **defaute:** fault
1026 **pris amende:** improve her praise, praise her more highly

"O thyng biseke I yow, and warne also,
That ye ne prikke with no tormentynge
This tendre mayden, as ye han doon mo;
For she is fostred in hire norissynge   1040
Moore tendrely, and, to my supposynge,
She koude nat adversitee endure
As koude a povre fostred creature."

And whan this Walter saugh hire pacience,
Hir glade chiere, and no malice at al,   1045
And he so ofte had doon to hire offence,
And she ay sad and constant as a wal,
Continuynge evere hire innocence overal,
This sturdy markys gan his herte dresse
To rewen upon hire wyfly stedfastnesse.   1050

"This is ynogh, Grisilde myn," quod he;
"Be now namoore agast ne yvele apayed.
I have thy feith and thy benyngnytee,
As wel as evere womman was, assayed,
In greet estaat and povreliche arrayed.   1055
Now knowe I, dere wyf, thy stedfastnesse" —
And hire in armes took and gan hire kesse.

And she for wonder took of it no keep;
She herde nat what thyng he to hire seyde;
She ferde as she had stert out of a sleep,   1060
Til she out of hire mazednesse abreyde.
"Grisilde," quod he, "by God, that for us deyde,
Thou art my wyf, ne noon oother I have,
Ne nevere hadde, as God my soule save!

"This is thy doghter, which thou hast sup-
     posed
     1065
To be my wyf; that oother feithfully
Shal be myn heir, as I have ay disposed;
Thou bare hym in thy body trewely.
At Boloigne have I kept hem prively;   1069
Taak hem agayn, for now maystow nat seye
That thou hast lorn noon of thy children tweye.

"And folk that ootherweys han seyd of me,
I warne hem wel that I have doon this deede
For no malice, ne for no crueltee,   1074
But for t'assaye in thee thy wommanheede,

And nat to sleen my children — God for-
     beede! —
But for to kepe hem pryvely and stille,
Til I thy purpos knewe and al thy wille."

Whan she this herde, aswowne doun she
     falleth
For pitous joye, and after hire swownynge
She bothe hire yonge children to hire calleth,
And in hire armes, pitously wepynge,   1082
Embraceth hem, and tendrely kissynge
Ful lyk a mooder, with hire salte teeres
She bathed bothe hire visage and hire heeres.

O which a pitous thyng it was to se   1086
Hir swownyng, and hire humble voys to heere!
"Grauntmercy, lord, God thanke it yow," quod
     she,
"That ye han saved me my children deere!   1089
Now rekke I nevere to been deed right heere;
Sith I stonde in youre love and in youre grace,
No fors of deeth, ne whan my spirit pace!

"O tendre, o deere, o yonge children myne!
Youre woful mooder wende stedfastly
That crueel houndes or som foul vermyne   1095
Hadde eten yow; but God of his mercy
And youre benyngne fader tendrely
Hath doon yow kept" — and in that same
     stounde
Al sodeynly she swapte adoun to grounde.

And in hire swough so sadly holdeth she   1100
Hire children two, whan she gan hem t'em-
     brace,
That with greet sleighte and greet difficultee
The children from hire arm they gonne arace.
O many a teere on many a pitous face   1104
Doun ran of hem that stooden hire bisyde;
Unnethe abouten hire myghte they abyde.

Walter hire gladeth and hire sorwe slaketh;
She riseth up, abaysed, from hire traunce,
And every wight hire joye and feeste maketh
Til she hath caught agayn hire contenaunce.
Walter hire dooth so feithfully plesaunce   1111

1040 norissynge: nurture
1041 to my supposynge: as I believe
1047 sad: firm, steadfast
1048 overal: in every way
1049 sturdy: harsh, cruel dresse: prepare
1052 yvele apayed: displeased
1055 povreliche: poorly
1057 kesse: kiss
1061 mazednesse: bewilderment abreyde: awakened quickly

1095 vermyne: animal pests
1098 Hath doon yow kept: has had you protected stounde: moment
1099 swapte: dropped suddenly
1100 swough: swoon sadly: tightly
1103 arace: tear away
1108 abaysed: disconcerted
1110 caught . . . hire contenaunce: composed herself

That it was deyntee for to seen the cheere
Bitwixe hem two, now they been met yfeere.

Thise ladyes, whan that they hir tyme say,
Han taken hire and into chambre gon,   1115
And strepen hire out of hire rude array,
And in a clooth of gold that brighte shoon,
With a coroune of many a riche stoon
Upon hire heed, they into halle hire broghte,
And ther she was honured as hire oghte.   1120

Thus hath this pitous day a blisful ende,
For every man and womman dooth his myght
This day in murthe and revel to dispende
Til on the welkne shoon the sterres lyght.   1124
For moore solempne in every mannes syght
This feste was, and gretter of costage,
Than was the revel of hire mariage.

Ful many a yeer in heigh prosperitee
Lyven thise two in concord and in reste,
And richely his doghter maryed he   1130
Unto a lord, oon of the worthieste
Of al Ytaille; and thanne in pees and reste
His wyves fader in his court he kepeth,
Til that the soule out of his body crepeth.

His sone succedeth in his heritage   1135
In reste and pees, after his fader day,
And fortunat was eek in mariage,
Al putte he nat his wyf in greet assay.
This world is nat so strong, it is no nay,
As it hath been in olde tymes yoore,   1140
And herkneth what this auctour seith therfoore.

This storie is seyd nat for that wyves sholde
Folwen Grisilde as in humylitee,
For it were inportable, though they wolde,
But for that every wight, in his degree,   1145
Sholde be constant in adversitee
As was Grisilde; therfore Petrak writeth
This storie, which with heigh stile he enditeth.

For sith a womman was so pacient
Unto a mortal man, wel moore us oghte   1150
Receyven al in gree that God us sent;
For greet skile is he preeve that he wroghte.

But he ne tempteth no man that he boghte
As seith Seint Jame, if ye his pistel rede;
He preeveth folk al day, it is no drede,   1155

And suffreth us, as for oure excercise,
With sharpe scourges of adversitee
Ful ofte to be bete in sondry wise;
Nat for to knowe oure wyl, for certes he,
Er we were born, knew al oure freletee;   1160
And for oure beste is al his governaunce.
Lat us thanne lyve in vertuous suffraunce.

But o word, lordynges, herkneth er I go:
It were ful hard to fynde now-a-dayes
In al a toun Grisildis thre or two;   1165
For if that they were put to swiche assayes,
The gold of hem hath now so badde alayes
With bras, that thogh the coyne be fair at ye,
It wolde rather breste a-two than plye.

For which heere, for the Wyves love of
    Bathe —   1170
Whos lyf and al hire secte God mayntene
In heigh maistrie, and elles were it scathe —
I wol with lusty herte, fressh and grene,
Seyn yow a song to glade yow, I wene;
And lat us stynte of ernestful matere.   1175
Herkneth my song that seith in this manere:

Lenvoy de Chaucer.

Grisilde is deed, and eek hire pacience,
And bothe atones buryed in Ytaille;
For which I crie in open audience
No wedded man so hardy be t'assaille   1180
His wyves pacience in trust to fynde
Grisildis, for in certein he shal faille.

O noble wyves, ful of heigh prudence,
Lat noon humylitee youre tonge naille,
Ne lat no clerk have cause or diligence   1185
To write of yow a storie of swich mervaille
As of Grisildis pacient and kynde,
Lest Chichevache yow swelwe in hire entraille!

1113 **met yfeere:** met together
1124 **welkne:** sky
1126 **costage:** cost, expense
1136 **fader:** father's
1141 **therfoore:** concerning this (tale)
1144 **inportable:** intolerable
1151 **in gree:** graciously   **sent** = *sendeth,* sends
1152 **For greet skile is:** it is very reasonable that

1154 **pistel:** epistle
1157 **scourges:** whips
1160 **freletee:** weakness
1162 **suffraunce:** patience, forbearance
1167 **alayes:** alloys
1168 **at ye:** to look at
1169 **plye:** bend
1170 **the Wyves love of Bathe:** the love of the Wife of Bath
1171 **secte:** sex, or school, those of her persuasion (?)
1172 **scathe:** pity
1188 **Chichevache:** a legendary lean cow who feeds on patient wives, and so has little to eat   **swelwe:** swallow

Folweth Ekko, that holdeth no silence,
But evere answereth at the countretaille.   1190
Beth nat bidaffed for youre innocence,
But sharply taak on yow the governaille.
Emprenteth wel this lessoun in youre mynde,
For commune profit sith it may availle.

Ye archewyves, stondeth at defense,   1195
Syn ye be strong as is a greet camaille;
Ne suffreth nat that men yow doon offense.
And sklendre wyves, fieble as in bataille,
Beth egre as is a tygre yond in Ynde;
Ay clappeth as a mille, I yow consaille.   1200

Ne dreed hem nat; doth hem no reverence,
For though thyn housbonde armed be in maille,
The arwes of thy crabbed eloquence
Shal perce his brest and eek his aventaille.
In jalousie I rede eek thou hym bynde,   1205
And thou shalt make hym couche as doth a
    quaille.

If thou be fair, ther folk been in presence,
Shewe thou thy visage and thyn apparaille;
If thou be foul, be fre of thy dispence;
To gete thee freendes ay do thy travaille;
Be ay of chiere as light as leef on lynde,   1211
And lat hym care, and wepe, and wrynge, and
    waille!

[The following stanza appears after the Envoy in
most of the manuscripts that preserve it.

*Bihoold the murye words of the
Hoost.*

This worthy Clerk, whan ended was his
    tale,   1212a
Oure Hooste seyde, and swoor, "By Goddes
    bones,
Me were levere than a barel ale
My wyf at hoom had herd this legende ones!
This is a gentil tale for the nones,
As to my purpos, wiste ye my wille;
But thyng that wol nat be, lat it be stille."]   1212g

Heere endeth the Tale of the Clerk of Oxenford.

THE MERCHANT'S PROLOGUE

The Prologe of the Marchantes Tale.

"Wepyng and waylyng, care and oother sorwe
I knowe ynogh, on even and a-morwe,"   1214
Quod the Marchant, "and so doon other mo
That wedded been. I trowe that it be so,
For wel I woot it fareth so with me.
I have a wyf, the worste that may be;
For thogh the feend to hire ycoupled were,

She wolde hym overmacche, I dar wel swere.
What sholde I yow reherce in special   1221
Hir hye malice? She is a shrewe at al.
Ther is a long and large difference
Bitwix Grisildis grete pacience
And of my wyf the passyng crueltee.   1225
Were I unbounden, also moot I thee,
I wolde nevere eft comen in the snare.
We wedded men lyven in sorwe and care.
Assaye whoso wole, and he shal fynde
That I seye sooth, by Seint Thomas of Ynde,

1189 **Ekko:** Echo
1190 **at the countretaille:** in reply (countertally)
1191 **bidaffed:** fooled, cowed, deafened (?)
1192 **governaille:** control
1194 **commune profit:** common good, welfare of all
1195 **archewyves:** quintessential women **at defense:** ready for battle
1196 **camaille:** camel; see n.
1198 **sklendre:** slender
1199 **egre:** fierce
1200 **clappeth:** wag your tongue
1202 **maille:** mail, armor
1203 **crabbed:** spiteful, angry
1204 **perce:** pierce **aventaille:** a piece of chain mail forming the neck-guard of the helmet

1209 **be fre of thy dispence:** spend freely
1211 **leef on lynde:** leaf on a linden tree
1212 **care:** grieve **wrynge:** wring his hands
1212c **barel ale:** barrel of ale

1220 **overmacche:** outmatch, defeat
1222 **at al:** in every way
1226 **unbounden:** free (of marriage)
1230 **Seint Thomas of Ynde:** St. Thomas of India (the Apostle)

As for the moore part — I sey nat alle.   1231
God shilde that it sholde so bifalle!
　　"A, goode sire Hoost, I have ywedded bee
Thise monthes two, and moore nat, pardee;
And yet, I trowe, he that al his lyve   1235
Wyflees hath been, though that men wolde him
　　　　ryve
Unto the herte, ne koude in no manere

Tellen so muchel sorwe as I now heere
Koude tellen of my wyves cursednesse!"
　　"Now," quod oure Hoost, "Marchaunt, so
　　　　God yow blesse,   1240
Syn ye so muchel knowen of that art
Ful hertely I pray yow telle us part."
　　"Gladly," quod he, "but of myn owene soore,
For soory herte, I telle may namoore."

THE MERCHANT'S TALE

Heere bigynneth the Marchantes Tale.

Whilom ther was dwellynge in Lumbardye
A worthy knyght, that born was of Pavye,   1246
In which he lyved in greet prosperitee;
And sixty yeer a wyflees man was hee,
And folwed ay his bodily delyt
On wommen, ther as was his appetyt,   1250
As doon thise fooles that been seculeer.
And whan that he was passed sixty yeer,
Were it for hoolynesse or for dotage
I kan nat seye, but swich a greet corage   1254
Hadde this knyght to been a wedded man
That day and nyght he dooth al that he kan
T'espien where he myghte wedded be,
Preyinge oure Lord to graunten him that he
Mighte ones knowe of thilke blisful lyf
That is bitwixe an housbonde and his wyf,
And for to lyve under that hooly boond   1261
With which that first God man and womman
　　　　bond.
"Noon oother lyf," seyde he, "is worth a bene,
For wedlok is so esy and so clene,
That in this world it is a paradys."   1265
Thus seyde this olde knyght, that was so wys.
　　And certeinly, as sooth as God is kyng,
To take a wyf it is a glorious thyng,
And namely whan a man is oold and hoor;

Thanne is a wyf the fruyt of his tresor.   1270
Thanne sholde he take a yong wyf and a feir,
On which he myghte engendren hym an heir,
And lede his lyf in joye and in solas,
Where as thise bacheleris synge "allas,"
Whan that they fynden any adversitee   1275
In love, which nys but childyssh vanytee.
And trewely it sit wel to be so,
That bacheleris have often peyne and wo;
On brotel ground they buylde, and brotelnesse
They fynde whan they wene sikernesse.   1280
They lyve but as a bryd or as a beest,
In libertee and under noon arreest,
Ther as a wedded man in his estaat
Lyveth a lyf blisful and ordinaat
Under this yok of mariage ybounde.   1285
Wel may his herte in joy and blisse habounde,
For who kan be so buxom as a wyf?
Who is so trewe, and eek so ententyf
To kepe hym, syk and hool, as is his make?
For wele or wo she wole hym nat forsake;   1290
She nys nat wery hym to love and serve,
Though that he lye bedrede til he sterve.
And yet somme clerkes seyn it nys nat so,
Of whiche he Theofraste is oon of tho.

1231 **moore part:** greater part, majority
1236 **ryve:** stab, pierce
1237 **in no manere:** in no way

1245 **Lumbardye:** Lombardy
1246 **Pavye:** Pavia
1249 **delyt:** pleasure, desire
1251 **seculeer:** of the laity (?)
1262 **bond:** bound
1269 **hoor:** white-haired

1270 **fruyt:** the best part
1277 **sit wel:** is fitting, well suits
1279 **brotel:** brittle, insecure
1280 **wene sikernesse:** expect safety, security
1282 **arreest:** restraint
1284 **ordinaat:** orderly
1287 **buxom:** obedient
1288 **ententyf:** eager, diligent
1289 **make:** mate
1292 **bedrede:** bedridden
1294 **Theofraste:** Theophrastus, author of the *Golden Book on Marriage,* a tract attacking marriage

What force though Theofraste liste lye? 1295
"Ne take no wyf," quod he, "for housbondrye,
As for to spare in houshold thy dispence.
A trewe servant dooth moore diligence
Thy good to kepe than thyn owene wyf,
For she wol clayme half part al hir lyf. 1300
And if thou be syk, so God me save,
Thy verray freendes, or a trewe knave,
Wol kepe thee bet than she that waiteth ay
After thy good and hath doon many a day.
And if thou take a wyf unto thyn hoold 1305
Ful lightly maystow been a cokewold."
This sentence, and an hundred thynges worse,
Writeth this man, ther God his bones corse!
But take no kep of al swich vanytee;
Deffie Theofraste, and herke me. 1310
   A wyf is Goddes yifte verraily;
Alle othere manere yiftes hardily,
As londes, rentes, pasture, or commune,
Or moebles — alle been yiftes of Fortune
That passen as a shadwe upon a wal. 1315
But drede nat, if pleynly speke I shal:
A wyf wol laste, and in thyn hous endure,
Wel lenger than thee list, paraventure.
   Mariage is a ful greet sacrement.
He which that hath no wyf, I holde hym shent;
He lyveth helplees and al desolat — 1321
I speke of folk in seculer estaat.
And herke why — I sey nat this for noght —
That womman is for mannes helpe ywroght.
The hye God, whan he hadde Adam maked,
And saugh him al allone, bely-naked, 1326
God of his grete goodnesse seyde than,
"Lat us now make an helpe unto this man
Lyk to hymself"; and thanne he made him Eve.
Heere may ye se, and heerby may ye preve,
That wyf is mannes helpe and his confort, 1331
His paradys terrestre, and his disport.
So buxom and so vertuous is she,
They moste nedes lyve in unitee. 1334
O flessh they been, and o fleesh, as I gesse,
Hath but oon herte, in wele and in distresse.

A wyf! a, Seinte Marie, benedicite!
How myghte a man han any adversitee
That hath a wyf? Certes, I kan nat seye.
The blisse which that is bitwixe hem tweye
Ther may no tonge telle, or herte thynke. 1341
If he be povre, she helpeth hym to swynke;
She kepeth his good, and wasteth never a deel;
Al that hire housbonde lust, hire liketh weel;
She seith nat ones "nay," whan he seith
      "ye." 1345
"Do this," seith he; "Al redy, sire," seith she.
O blisful ordre of wedlok precious,
Thou art so murye, and eek so vertuous,
And so commended and appreved eek
That every man that halt hym worth a leek
Upon his bare knees oughte al his lyf 1351
Thanken his God that hym hath sent a wyf,
Or elles preye to God hym for to sende
A wyf to laste unto his lyves ende.
For thanne his lyf is set in sikernesse; 1355
He may nat be deceyved, as I gesse,
So that he werke after his wyves reed.
Thanne may he boldely beren up his heed,
They been so trewe and therwithal so wyse;
For which, if thou wolt werken as the wyse,
Do alwey so as wommen wol thee rede. 1361
   Lo, how that Jacob, as thise clerkes rede,
By good conseil of his mooder Rebekke,
Boond the kydes skyn aboute his nekke,
For which his fadres benyson he wan. 1365
   Lo Judith, as the storie eek telle kan,
By wys conseil she Goddes peple kepte,
And slow hym Olofernus, whil he slepte.
   Lo Abigayl, by good conseil how she
Saved hir housbonde Nabal whan that he 1370
Sholde han be slayn; and looke, Ester also
By good conseil delyvered out of wo
The peple of God, and made hym Mardochee
Of Assuere enhaunced for to be.
   Ther nys no thyng in gree superlatyf, 1375
As seith Senek, above an humble wyf.

1295 **What force:** what does it matter
1296 **housbondrye:** domestic economy
1297 **spare:** be sparing **dispence:** expenditures
1302 **knave:** male servant
1306 **cokewold:** cuckold
1308 **ther:** i.e., may (*ther* is not translated; it is used to introduce the subjunctive)
1312 **hardily:** certainly
1313 **commune:** right to use land held in common
1314 **moebles:** personal property
1316 **drede:** doubt
1320 **shent:** ruined
1326 **bely-naked:** stark naked
1332 **paradys terrestre:** earthly paradise
1333 **buxom:** obedient

1343 **never a deel:** not a bit, not at all
1349 **appreved:** tested, proven
1361 **rede:** advise
1362 **rede:** tell, advise
1363 **Rebekke:** Rebecca, who counselled Jacob to trick his father, Isaac, into blessing him
1365 **benyson:** blessing
1368 **Olofernus:** Holofernes, slain by Judith; for the story see MkT VII.2551–74.
1369 **Abigayl:** Abigail saved Nabal from the wrath of King David (cf. VII.1100).
1371 **Ester:** Esther, who saved her uncle Mordecai (*Mardochee*) and her people by an appeal to her husband Ahasuerus (*Assuere*)
1374 **enhaunced:** exalted, advanced
1375 **in gree superlatyf:** superior (in degree of virtue)
1376 **Senek:** Seneca

Suffre thy wyves tonge, as Catoun bit;
She shal comande, and thou shalt suffren it,
And yet she wole obeye of curteisye.
A wyf is kepere of thyn housbondrye;   1380
Wel may the sike man biwaille and wepe,
Ther as ther nys no wyf the hous to kepe.
I warne thee, if wisely thou wolt wirche,
Love wel thy wyf, as Crist loved his chirche.
If thou lovest thyself, thou lovest thy wyf;
No man hateth his flessh, but in his lyf   1386
He fostreth it, and therfore bidde I thee
Cherisse thy wyf, or thou shalt nevere thee.
Housbonde and wyf, what so men jape or
          pleye,
Of worldly folk holden the siker weye;   1390
They been so knyt ther may noon harm bityde,
And namely upon the wyves syde.
For which this Januarie, of whom I tolde,
Considered hath, inwith his dayes olde,
The lusty lyf, the vertuous quyete,   1395
That is in mariage hony-sweete,
And for his freendes on a day he sente,
To tellen hem th'effect of his entente.

With face sad his tale he hath hem toold.
He seyde, "Freendes, I am hoor and oold,   1400
And almoost, God woot, on my pittes brynke;
Upon my soule somwhat moste I thynke.
I have my body folily despended;
Blessed be God that it shal been amended!
For I wol be, certeyn, a wedded man,   1405
And that anoon in al the haste I kan.
Unto som mayde fair and tendre of age,
I prey yow, shapeth for my mariage
Al sodeynly, for I wol nat abyde;
And I wol fonde t'espien, on my syde,   1410
To whom I may be wedded hastily.
But forasmuche as ye been mo than I,
Ye shullen rather swich a thyng espyen
Than I, and where me best were to allyen.

"But o thyng warne I yow, my freendes deere,
I wol noon oold wyf han in no manere.   1416
She shal nat passe twenty yeer, certayn;
Oold fissh and yong flessh wolde I have fayn.

Bet is," quod he, "a pyk than a pykerel,
And bet than old boef is the tendre veel.   1420
I wol no womman thritty yeer of age;
It is but bene-straw and greet forage.
And eek thise olde wydwes, God it woot,
They konne so muchel craft on Wades boot,
So muchel broken harm, whan that hem
          leste,   1425
That with hem sholde I nevere lyve in reste.
For sondry scoles maken sotile clerkis;
Womman of manye scoles half a clerk is.
But certeynly, a yong thyng may men gye,
Right as men may warm wex with handes plye.
Wherfore I sey yow pleynly, in a clause,   1431
I wol noon oold wyf han right for this cause.
For if so were I hadde swich myschaunce
That I in hire ne koude han no plesaunce,
Thanne sholde I lede my lyf in avoutrye   1435
And go streight to the devel whan I dye.
Ne children sholde I none upon hire geten;
Yet were me levere houndes had me eten
Than that myn heritage sholde falle
In straunge hand, and this I telle yow alle.
I dote nat; I woot the cause why   1441
Men sholde wedde, and forthermoore woot I
Ther speketh many a man of mariage
That woot namoore of it than woot my page
For whiche causes man sholde take a wyf.   1445
If he ne may nat lyven chaast his lyf,
Take hym a wyf with greet devocioun,
By cause of leveful procreacioun
Of children to th'onour of God above,
And nat oonly for paramour or love;   1450
And for they sholde leccherye eschue,
And yelde hir dette whan that it is due;
Or for that ech of hem sholde helpen oother
In meschief, as a suster shal the brother,
And lyve in chastitee ful holily.   1455
But sires, by youre leve, that am nat I.
For — God be thanked! — I dar make avaunt
I feele my lymes stark and suffisaunt
To do al that a man bilongeth to;

1419 **pykerel:** young pike
1420 **boef:** beef **veel:** veal
1422 **bene-straw:** dried beanstalks **greet forage:** coarse fodder
1424 **Wades boot:** boat of Wade, an obscure legendary figure, perhaps associated with deception
1425 **So muchel broken harm:** do so much harm, make such mischief
1427 **sotile:** subtle, clever
1429 **gye:** guide
1430 **wex:** wax **plye:** bend, mold
1435 **avoutrye:** adultery
1437 **geten:** beget
1448 **leveful:** lawful
1452 **dette:** the marital debt, obligation to engage in intercourse; see ParsT X.940.
1455 **in chastitee:** under a vow to abstain from sex
1458 **stark:** strong

1377 **Suffre:** endure, forbear **Catoun:** Cato **bit** = *biddeth,* commands
1389 **what so:** however much
1390 **worldly:** lay, secular **siker:** sure, safe
1391 **knyt:** united
1392 **syde:** behalf
1394 **inwith:** in
1398 **th'effect:** the substance
1401 **pittes brynke:** brink of the pit (of death)
1403 **folily despended:** foolishly wasted
1410 **fonde t'espien:** try to discover
1414 **allyen:** ally myself, marry

I woot myselven best what I may do.   1460
Though I be hoor, I fare as dooth a tree
That blosmeth er that fruyt ywoxen bee;
And blosmy tree nys neither drye ne deed.
I feele me nowhere hoor but on myn heed;
Myn herte and alle my lymes been as grene
As laurer thurgh the yeer is for to sene.   1466
And syn that ye han herd al myn entente,
I prey yow to my wyl ye wole assente.''

    Diverse men diversely hym tolde
Of mariage manye ensamples olde.   1470
Somme blamed it, somme preysed it, certeyn,
But atte laste, shortly for to seyn,
As al day falleth altercacioun
Bitwixen freendes in disputisoun,
Ther fil a stryf bitwixe his bretheren two,   1475
Of whiche that oon was cleped Placebo;
Justinus soothly called was that oother.

    Placebo seyde, "O Januarie, brother,
Ful litel nede hadde ye, my lord so deere,
Conseil to axe of any that is heere,   1480
But that ye been so ful of sapience
That yow ne liketh, for youre heighe prudence,
To weyven fro the word of Salomon.
This word seyde he unto us everychon:
'Wirk alle thyng by conseil,' thus seyde he,
'And thanne shaltow nat repente thee.'   1486
But though that Salomon spak swich a word,
Myn owene deere brother and my lord,
So wysly God my soule brynge at reste,
I holde youre owene conseil is the beste.   1490
For, brother myn, of me taak this motyf:
I have now been a court-man al my lyf,
And God it woot, though I unworthy be,
I have stonden in ful greet degree
Abouten lordes of ful heigh estaat;   1495
Yet hadde I nevere with noon of hem debaat.
I nevere hem contraried, trewely;
I woot wel that my lord kan moore than I.
With that he seith, I holde it ferme and stable;
I seye the same, or elles thyng semblable.   1500
A ful greet fool is any conseillour
That serveth any lord of heigh honour,
That dar presume, or elles thenken it,
That his conseil sholde passe his lordes wit.
Nay, lordes been no fooles, by my fay!   1505

Ye han youreselven shewed heer to-day
So heigh sentence, so holily and weel,
That I consente and conferme everydeel
Youre wordes alle and youre opinioun.
By God, ther nys no man in al this toun,   1510
Ne in Ytaille, that koude bet han sayd!
Crist halt hym of this conseil ful wel apayd.
And trewely, it is an heigh corage
Of any man that stapen is in age
To take a yong wyf; by my fader kyn,   1515
Youre herte hangeth on a joly pyn!
Dooth now in this matiere right as yow leste,
For finally I holde it for the beste.''

    Justinus, that ay stille sat and herde,   1519
Right in this wise he to Placebo answerde:
"Now, brother myn, be pacient, I preye,
Syn ye han seyd, and herkneth what I seye.
Senek, amonges othere wordes wyse,
Seith that a man oghte hym right wel avyse
To whom he yeveth his lond or his catel.   1525
And syn I oghte avyse me right wel
To whom I yeve my good awey fro me,
Wel muchel moore I oghte avysed be
To whom I yeve my body for alwey.
I warne yow wel, it is no childes pley   1530
To take a wyf withouten avysement.
Men moste enquere — this is myn assent —
Wher she be wys, or sobre, or dronkelewe,
Or proud, or elles ootherweys a shrewe,
A chidestere, or wastour of thy good,   1535
Or riche, or poore, or elles mannyssh wood.
Al be it so that no man fynden shal
Noon in this world that trotteth hool in al,
Ne man, ne beest, swich as men koude devyse;
But nathelees it oghte ynough suffise   1540
With any wyf, if so were that she hadde
Mo goode thewes than hire vices badde;
And al this axeth leyser for t'enquere.
For, God it woot, I have wept many a teere
Ful pryvely, syn I have had a wyf.   1545
Preyse whoso wole a wedded mannes lyf,
Certein I fynde in it but cost and care
And observances, of alle blisses bare.

1462 **ywoxen:** grown
1466 **laurer:** laurel, an evergreen **for to sene:** to be seen
1476 **Placebo:** "I shall please" (Psalm 114:9)
1477 **Justinus:** "the just one"
1483 **weyven fro:** depart from
1491 **motyf:** idea, advice
1492 **court-man:** courtier
1499 **I holde it ferme and stable:** I view it as unshakably true
1500 **semblable:** similar

1507 **heigh sentence:** good judgment
1512 **halt hym** = *holdeth hym,* considers himself **ful wel apayd:** very well satisfied
1513 **an heigh corage:** a bold act
1514 **stapen is in age:** is advanced (literally *stepped*) in years
1516 **hangeth on a joly pyn:** is lively, merry
1531 **avysement:** deliberation
1532 **assent:** opinion
1533 **dronkelewe:** addicted to drink, habitually drunk
1535 **chidestere:** scolding woman **wastour:** waster
1536 **mannyssh wood:** fierce as a man, man-crazy (?)
1538 **trotteth hool in al:** trots perfectly, is perfect in everything
1542 **thewes:** personal traits
1548 **observances:** duties

And yet, God woot, my neighebores aboute,
And namely of wommen many a route,   1550
Seyn that I have the mooste stedefast wyf,
And eek the mekeste oon that bereth lyf;
But I woot best where wryngeth me my sho.
Ye mowe, for me, right as yow liketh do;
Avyseth yow — ye been a man of age —   1555
How that ye entren into mariage,
And namely with a yong wyf and a fair.
By hym that made water, erthe, and air,
The yongeste man that is in al this route
Is bisy ynough to bryngen it aboute   1560
To han his wyf allone. Trusteth me,
Ye shul nat plesen hire fully yeres thre —
This is to seyn, to doon hire ful plesaunce.
A wyf axeth ful many an observaunce.
I prey yow that ye be nat yvele apayd."   1565
     "Wel," quod this Januarie, "and hastow
          ysayd?
Straw for thy Senek, and for thy proverbes!
I counte nat a panyer ful of herbes
Of scole-termes. Wyser men than thow,
As thou hast herd, assenteden right now   1570
To my purpos. Placebo, what sey ye?"
     "I seye it is a cursed man," quod he,
"That letteth matrimoigne, sikerly."
And with that word they rysen sodeynly,
And been assented fully that he sholde   1575
Be wedded whanne hym liste and where he
          wolde.
     Heigh fantasye and curious bisynesse
Fro day to day gan in the soule impresse
Of Januarie aboute his mariage.
Many fair shap and many a fair visage   1580
Ther passeth thurgh his herte nyght by nyght,
As whoso tooke a mirour, polisshed bryght,
And sette it in a commune market-place,
Thanne sholde he se ful many a figure pace
By his mirour; and in the same wyse   1585
Gan Januarie inwith his thoght devyse
Of maydens whiche that dwelten hym bisyde.
He wiste nat wher that he myghte abyde.
For if that oon have beaute in hir face,
Another stant so in the peples grace   1590
For hire sadnesse and hire benyngnytee

That of the peple grettest voys hath she;
And somme were riche and hadden badde
          name.
But nathelees, bitwixe ernest and game,
He atte laste apoynted hym on oon,   1595
And leet alle othere from his herte goon,
And chees hire of his owene auctoritee;
For love is blynd alday, and may nat see.
And whan that he was in his bed ybroght,
He purtreyed in his herte and in his thoght
Hir fresshe beautee and hir age tendre,   1601
Hir myddel smal, hire armes longe and sklen-
          dre,
Hir wise governaunce, hir gentillesse,
Hir wommanly berynge, and hire sadnesse.
And whan that he on hire was conde-
          scended,   1605
Hym thoughte his choys myghte nat ben
          amended.
For whan that he hymself concluded hadde,
Hym thoughte ech oother mannes wit so badde
That inpossible it were to repplye
Agayn his choys; this was his fantasye.   1610
His freendes sente he to, at his instaunce,
And preyed hem to doon hym that plesaunce,
That hastily they wolden to hym come;
He wolde abregge hir labour, alle and some.
Nedeth namoore for hym to go ne ryde;   1615
He was apoynted ther he wolde abyde.
     Placebo cam, and eek his freendes soone,
And alderfirst he bad hem alle a boone,
That noon of hem none argumentes make   1619
Agayn the purpos which that he hath take,
Which purpos was plesant to God, seyde he,
And verray ground of his prosperitee.
     He seyde ther was a mayden in the toun,
Which that of beautee hadde greet renoun,
Al were it so she were of smal degree;   1625
Suffiseth hym hir yowthe and hir beautee.
Which mayde, he seyde, he wolde han to his
          wyf,
To lede in ese and hoolynesse his lyf;
And thanked God that he myghte han hire al,
That no wight his blisse parten shal.   1630

1553 **wryngeth:** pinches
1561 **han his wyf allone:** have his wife to himself
1565 **yvele apayd:** displeased
1568 **panyer:** bread basket
1569 **scole-termes:** scholastic (philosophical) terms
1573 **letteth:** hinders
1577 **Heigh fantasye:** exaggerated fancy, imagination **curious bisynesse:** painstaking attention, constant thought (of this)
1578 **gan . . . impresse:** made a mark, became fixed
1591 **sadnesse:** seriousness

1592 **voys:** praise
1595 **apoynted hym on:** decided on
1596 **othere:** others
1598 **alday:** always
1602 **sklendre:** slender
1605 **was condescended:** had decided, settled
1611 **instaunce:** request
1614 **abregge:** abridge, shorten
1616 **was apoynted:** had decided
1618 **alderfirst:** first of all **bad . . . a boone:** asked a favor
1621 **plesant:** pleasing
1625 **Al were it so:** although **smal degree:** low rank
1630 **parten:** share

And preyed hem to laboure in this nede,
And shapen that he faille nat to spede;
For thanne, he seyde, his spirit was at ese.
"Thanne is," quod he, "no thyng may me dis-
    plese,
Save o thyng priketh in my conscience,   1635
The which I wol reherce in youre presence.
   "I have," quod he, "herd seyd, ful yoore ago,
Ther may no man han parfite blisses two —
This is to seye, in erthe and eek in hevene.
For though he kepe hym fro the synnes sevene,
And eek from every branche of thilke tree,   1641
Yet is ther so parfit felicitee
And so greet ese and lust in mariage
That evere I am agast now in myn age
That I shal lede now so myrie a lyf,   1645
So delicat, withouten wo and stryf,
That I shal have myn hevene in erthe heere.
For sith that verray hevene is boght so deere
With tribulacion and greet penaunce,
How sholde I thanne, that lyve in swich ples-
    aunce   1650
As alle wedded men doon with hire wyvys,
Come to the blisse ther Crist eterne on lyve ys?
This is my drede, and ye, my bretheren tweye,
Assoilleth me this question, I preye."
   Justinus, which that hated his folye,   1655
Answerde anon right in his japerye;
And for he wolde his longe tale abregge,
He wolde noon auctoritee allegge,
But seyde, "Sire, so ther be noon obstacle
Oother than this, God of his hygh myracle
And of his mercy may so for yow wirche   1661
That, er ye have youre right of hooly chirche,
Ye may repente of wedded mannes lyf,
In which ye seyn ther is no wo ne stryf.
And elles, God forbede but he sente   1665
A wedded man hym grace to repente
Wel ofte rather than a sengle man!
And therfore, sire — the beste reed I kan —
Dispeire yow noght, but have in youre mem-
    orie,
Paraunter she may be youre purgatorie!   1670
She may be Goddes meene and Goddes whippe;

Thanne shal youre soule up to hevene skippe
Swifter than dooth an arwe out of a bowe.
I hope to God, herafter shul ye knowe
That ther nys no so greet felicitee   1675
In mariage, ne nevere mo shal bee,
That yow shal lette of youre savacion,
So that ye use, as skile is and reson,
The lustes of youre wyf attemprely,
And that ye plese hire nat to amorously,   1680
And that ye kepe yow eek from oother synne.
My tale is doon, for my wit is thynne.
Beth nat agast herof, my brother deere,
But lat us waden out of this mateere.
The Wyf of Bathe, if ye han understonde, 1685
Of mariage, which we have on honde,
Declared hath ful wel in litel space.
Fareth now wel. God have yow in his grace."
   And with this word this Justyn and his
    brother   1689
Han take hir leve, and ech of hem of oother.
For whan they saughe that it moste nedes be,
They wroghten so, by sly and wys tretee,
That she, this mayden which that Mayus
    highte,
As hastily as evere that she myghte
Shal wedded be unto this Januarie.   1695
I trowe it were to longe yow to tarie,
If I yow tolde of every scrit and bond
By which that she was feffed in his lond,
Or for to herknen of hir riche array.
But finally ycomen is the day   1700
That to the chirche bothe be they went
For to receyve the hooly sacrement.
Forth comth the preest, with stole aboute his
    nekke,
And bad hire be lyk Sarra and Rebekke
In wysdom and in trouthe of mariage;   1705
And seyde his orisons, as is usage,
And croucheth hem, and bad God sholde hem
    blesse,
And made al siker ynogh with hoolynesse.
   Thus been they wedded with solempnitee,
And at the feeste sitteth he and she   1710
With othere worthy folk upon the deys.

1632 **shapen:** arrange
1641 **thilke tree:** the tree of the seven deadly sins (see ParsT X.387–90).
1646 **delicat:** pleasing
1654 **Assoilleth me this question:** resolve this problem
1656 **japerye:** mockery
1657 **abregge:** abridge, shorten
1658 **allegge:** cite, adduce
1662 **right of hooly chirche:** service (rite) of the Church
1665 **God forbede but he sente:** God forbid that he should not send
1667 **sengle:** single
1671 **meene:** means, instrument

1677 **lette of:** keep from
1678 **skile:** reasonable, proper
1679 **attemprely:** moderately
1684 **waden:** wade, go
1692 **tretee:** negotiation
1697 **scrit:** writ, legal document
1698 **feffed in:** enfeoffed, endowed with
1702 **the hooly sacrement:** i.e., marriage
1704 **Sarra and Rebekke:** Sarah and Rebecca, biblical exemplars of faithfulness and wisdom
1707 **croucheth:** makes the sign of the cross over
1711 **deys:** dais

Al ful of joye and blisse is the paleys,
And ful of instrumentz and of vitaille,
The mooste deyntevous of al Ytaille.
Biforn hem stoode instrumentz of swich soun
That Orpheus, ne of Thebes Amphioun,   1716
Ne maden nevere swich a melodye.
At every cours thanne cam loud mynstralcye
That nevere tromped Joab for to heere,
Nor he Theodomas, yet half so cleere   1720
At Thebes whan the citee was in doute.
Bacus the wyn hem shynketh al aboute,
And Venus laugheth upon every wight,
For Januarie was bicome hir knyght
And wolde bothe assayen his corage   1725
In libertee, and eek in mariage;
And with hire fyrbrond in hire hand aboute
Daunceth biforn the bryde and al the route.
And certeinly, I dar right wel seyn this,
Ymeneus, that god of weddyng is,   1730
Saugh nevere his lyf so myrie a wedded man.
Hoold thou thy pees, thou poete Marcian,
That writest us that ilke weddyng murie
Of hire Philologie and hym Mercurie,
And of the songes that the Muses songe!   1735
To smal is bothe thy penne, and eek thy tonge,
For to descryven of this mariage.
Whan tendre youthe hath wedded stoupyng
        age,
Ther is swich myrthe that it may nat be writen.
Assayeth it youreself; thanne may ye witen
If that I lye or noon in this matiere.   1741

    Mayus, that sit with so benyngne a chiere,
Hire to biholde it semed fayerye.
Queene Ester looked nevere with swich an ye
On Assuer, so meke a look hath she.   1745
I may yow nat devyse al hir beautee.
But thus muche of hire beautee telle I may,
That she was lyk the brighte morwe of May,
Fulfild of alle beautee and plesaunce.

    This Januarie is ravysshed in a traunce   1750
At every tyme he looked on hir face;

But in his herte he gan hire to manace
That he that nyght in armes wolde hire streyne
Harder than evere Parys dide Eleyne.
But nathelees yet hadde he greet pitee   1755
That thilke nyght offenden hire moste he,
And thoughte, "Allas! O tendre creature,
Now wolde God ye myghte wel endure
Al my corage, it is so sharp and keene!
I am agast ye shul it nat susteene.   1760
But God forbede that I dide al my myght!
Now wolde God that it were woxen nyght,
And that the nyght wolde lasten everemo.
I wolde that al this peple were ago."
And finally he dooth al his labour,   1765
As he best myghte, savynge his honour,
To haste hem fro the mete in subtil wyse.

    The tyme cam that resoun was to ryse;
And after that men daunce and drynken faste,
And spices al aboute the hous they caste,   1770
And ful of joye and blisse is every man —
Al but a squyer, highte Damyan,
Which carf biforn the knyght ful many a day.
He was so ravysshed on his lady May   1774
That for the verray peyne he was ny wood.
Almoost he swelte and swowned ther he stood,
So soore hath Venus hurt hym with hire brond,
As that she bar it daunsynge in hire hond;
And to his bed he wente hym hastily.
Namoore of hym at this tyme speke I,   1780
But there I lete hym wepe ynogh and pleyne
Til fresshe May wol rewen on his peyne.

    O perilous fyr, that in the bedstraw bredeth!
O famulier foo, that his servyce bedeth!
O servant traytour, false hoomly hewe,   1785
Lyk to the naddre in bosom sly untrewe,
God shilde us alle from youre aqueyntaunce!
O Januarie, dronken in plesaunce
In mariage, se how thy Damyan,
Thyn owene squier and thy borne man,   1790
Entendeth for to do thee vileynye.
God graunte thee thyn hoomly fo t'espye!
For in this world nys worse pestilence
Than hoomly foo al day in thy presence.   1794

1714 **deyntevous**: delicious
1716 **Orpheus**: the legendary musician **Amphioun**: king of Thebes and a famous harper
1719 **tromped**: trumpeted **Joab**: one of David's generals, who sounded trumpets to direct his army
1720 **Theodomas**: the augur of the army at Thebes
1721 **doute**: danger
1722 **Bacus**: Bacchus, god of wine **shynketh**: pours out
1723 **Venus**: goddess of love
1727 **fyrbrond**: torch
1730 **Ymeneus**: Hymen
1731 **his lyf**: in his life
1732 **Marcian**: Martianus Capella, author of the *Marriage of Philology and Mercury*
1743 **fayerye**: something enchanting
1744 **Ester**: Esther, whose meekness and beauty won the love of King Ahasuerus (*Assuer*)

1752 **manace**: menace, threaten
1753 **streyne**: press
1754 **Eleyne**: Helen of Troy, whose ravishment by Paris (*Parys*) caused the Trojan War (see Tr I.57–63)
1759 **corage**: ardor, sexual desire **keene**: eager
1765 **dooth al his labour**: takes all possible pains
1776 **swelte**: fainted
1777 **brond**: torch
1784 **famulier foo**: enemy in one's own household **bedeth**: offers
1785 **hoomly hewe**: domestic servant
1786 **naddre**: adder, serpent
1792 **hoomly fo**: foe in the household

Parfourned hath the sonne his ark diurne;
No lenger may the body of hym sojurne
On th'orisonte, as in that latitude.
Night with his mantel, that is derk and rude,
Gan oversprede the hemysperie aboute;
For which departed is this lusty route   1800
Fro Januarie, with thank on every syde.
Hoom to hir houses lustily they ryde,
Where as they doon hir thynges as hem leste,
And whan they sye hir tyme, goon to reste.
Soone after that, this hastif Januarie   1805
Wolde go to bedde; he wolde no lenger tarye.
He drynketh ypocras, clarree, and vernage
Of spices hoote t'encreessen his corage;
And many a letuarie hath he ful fyn,
Swiche as the cursed monk, daun Constantyn,
Hath writen in his book *De Coitu;*   1811
To eten hem alle he nas no thyng eschu.
And to his privee freendes thus seyde he:
"For Goddes love, as soone as it may be,
Lat voyden al this hous in curteys wyse."   1815
And they han doon right as he wol devyse.
Men drynken and the travers drawe anon.
The bryde was broght abedde as stille as stoon;
And whan the bed was with the preest yblessed,
Out of the chambre hath every wight hym
      dressed,   1820
And Januarie hath faste in armes take
His fresshe May, his paradys, his make.
He lulleth hire; he kisseth hire ful ofte;
With thikke brustles of his berd unsofte,
Lyk to the skyn of houndfyssh, sharp as brere —
For he was shave al newe in his manere —   1826
He rubbeth hire aboute hir tendre face,
And seyde thus, "Allas! I moot trespace
To yow, my spouse, and yow greetly offende
Er tyme come that I wil doun descende.   1830
But nathelees, considereth this," quod he,
"Ther nys no werkman, whatsoevere he be,
That may bothe werke wel and hastily;
This wol be doon at leyser parfitly.

It is no fors how longe that we pleye;   1835
In trewe wedlok coupled be we tweye,
And blessed be the yok that we been inne,
For in oure actes we mowe do no synne.
A man may do no synne with his wyf,
Ne hurte hymselven with his owene knyf,   1840
For we han leve to pleye us by the lawe."
Thus laboureth he til that the day gan dawe;
And thanne he taketh a sop in fyn clarree,
And upright in his bed thanne sitteth he,   1844
And after that he sang ful loude and cleere,
And kiste his wyf, and made wantown cheere.
He was al coltissh, ful of ragerye,
And ful of jargon as a flekked pye.
The slakke skyn aboute his nekke shaketh   1849
Whil that he sang, so chaunteth he and craketh.
But God woot what that May thoughte in hir
      herte,
Whan she hym saugh up sittynge in his sherte,
In his nyght-cappe, and with his nekke lene;
She preyseth nat his pleyyng worth a bene.
Thanne seide he thus, "My reste wol I take;
Now day is come, I may no lenger wake."   1856
And doun he leyde his heed and sleep til
      pryme.
And afterward, whan that he saugh his tyme,
Up ryseth Januarie; but fresshe May   1859
Heeld hire chambre unto the fourthe day,
As usage is of wyves for the beste.
For every labour somtyme moot han reste,
Or elles longe may he nat endure;
This is to seyn, no lyves creature,
Be it of fyssh, or bryd, or beest, or man.   1865
    Now wol I speke of woful Damyan,
That langwissheth for love, as ye shul heere;
Therfore I speke to hym in this manere:
I seye, "O sely Damyan, allas!
Andswere to my demaunde, as in this cas.   1870
How shaltow to thy lady, fresshe May,
Telle thy wo? She wole alwey seye nay.
Eek if thou speke, she wol thy wo biwreye.
God be thyn helpe! I kan no bettre seye."
    This sike Damyan in Venus fyr   1875
So brenneth that he dyeth for desyr,
For which he putte his lyf in aventure.

1795 **Parfourned:** completed   **ark diurne:** daily transit from horizon to horizon
1796 **sojurne:** remain
1797 **th'orisonte:** the horizon
1799 **hemysperie:** hemisphere (the half of the heavens above the earth)
1801 **on every syde:** from all sides
1804 **sye:** saw
1807 **ypocras, clarree:** strong spiced and sweetened wines; **vernage:** sweet Italian white wine, Vernaccia
1809 **letuarie:** electuary, medical mixture
1810 **Constantyn:** Constantinus Africanus (Afer), author of a work on sexual intercourse containing recipes for aphrodisiacs
1812 **eschu:** averse
1815 **Lat voyden:** clear out
1817 **travers:** curtain (dividing the room)
1825 **houndfyssh:** dogfish, a small shark   **brere:** briar

1835 **It is no fors:** it doesn't matter
1843 **sop in fyn clarree:** a bit of bread soaked in wine
1846 **wantown:** lecherous
1847 **coltissh:** frisky as a colt   **ragerye:** wantonness
1848 **jargon:** chatter   **flekked pye:** spotted magpie
1849 **slakke:** slack, loose
1850 **chaunteth:** sings   **craketh:** croaks
1857 **pryme:** the first canonical hour (part) of the day (from about 6 to 9 A.M.)
1870 **demaunde:** question
1873 **biwreye:** reveal
1877 **in aventure:** at risk

No lenger myghte he in this wise endure,
But prively a penner gan he borwe,
And in a lettre wroot he al his sorwe,   1880
In manere of a compleynt or a lay,
Unto his faire, fresshe lady May;
And in a purs of sylk heng on his sherte
He hath it put, and leyde it at his herte.   1884
    The moone, that at noon was thilke day
That Januarie hath wedded fresshe May
In two of Tawr, was into Cancre glyden;
So longe hath Mayus in hir chambre abyden,
As custume is unto thise nobles alle.
A bryde shal nat eten in the halle   1890
Til dayes foure, or thre dayes atte leeste,
Ypassed been; thanne lat hire go to feeste.
The fourthe day compleet fro noon to noon,
Whan that the heighe masse was ydoon,
In halle sit this Januarie and May,   1895
As fressh as is the brighte someres day.
And so bifel how that this goode man
Remembred hym upon this Damyan,
And seyde, "Seynte Marie! how may this be,
That Damyan entendeth nat to me?   1900
Is he ay syk, or how may this bityde?"
His squieres, whiche that stooden ther bisyde,
Excused hym by cause of his siknesse,
Which letted hym to doon his bisynesse;   1904
Noon oother cause myghte make hym tarye.
    "That me forthynketh," quod this Januarie,
    "He is a gentil squier, by my trouthe!
If that he deyde, it were harm and routhe.
He is as wys, discreet, and as secree
As any man I woot of his degree,   1910
And therto manly, and eek servysable,
And for to been a thrifty man right able.
But after mete, as soone as evere I may,
I wol myself visite hym, and eek May,
To doon hym al the confort that I kan."   1915
And for that word hym blessed every man,
That of his bountee and his gentillesse
He wolde so conforten in siknesse
His squier, for it was a gentil dede.   1919
"Dame," quod this Januarie, "taak good hede,

At after-mete ye with youre wommen alle,
Whan ye han been in chambre out of this halle,
That alle ye go se this Damyan.
Dooth hym disport — he is a gentil man;
And telleth hym that I wol hym visite,   1925
Have I no thyng but rested me a lite;
And spede yow faste, for I wole abyde
Til that ye slepe faste by my syde."
And with that word he gan to hym to calle
A squier, that was marchal of his halle,   1930
And tolde hym certeyn thynges, what he wolde.
    This fresshe May hath streight hir wey
        yholde
With alle hir wommen unto Damyan.
Doun by his beddes syde sit she than,
Confortynge hym as goodly as she may.   1935
This Damyan, whan that his tyme he say,
In secree wise his purs and eek his bille,
In which that he ywriten hadde his wille,
Hath put into hire hand, withouten moore,
Save that he siketh wonder depe and soore,
And softely to hire right thus seyde he: 1941
"Mercy! And that ye nat discovere me,
For I am deed if that this thyng be kyd."
This purs hath she inwith hir bosom hyd
And wente hire wey; ye gete namoore of me.
But unto Januarie ycomen is she,   1946
That on his beddes syde sit ful softe.
He taketh hire, and kisseth hire ful ofte,
And leyde hym doun to slepe, and that anon.
She feyned hire as that she moste gon   1950
Ther as ye woot that every wight moot neede;
And whan she of this bille hath taken heede,
She rente it al to cloutes atte laste,
And in the pryvee softely it caste.
    Who studieth now but faire fresshe May?
Adoun by olde Januarie she lay,   1956
That sleep til that the coughe hath hym
        awaked.
Anon he preyde hire strepen hire al naked;
He wolde of hire, he seyde, han som plesaunce;
He seyde hir clothes dide hym encombraunce,
And she obeyeth, be hire lief or looth.   1961
But lest that precious folk be with me wrooth,
How that he wroghte, I dar nat to yow telle,

1879 **penner:** writing case, with pen and ink
1881 **compleynt:** poetic lament (for examples see the Short Poems) **lay:** song
1883 **heng:** which hung
1885–87 The moon was in the second degree of the zodiacal sign of Taurus and has now moved into the sign of Cancer.
1893 **compleet:** completed
1900 **entendeth nat to:** does not attend, wait on
1906 **That me forthynketh:** that grieves me, I am sorry
1909 **secree:** discreet
1911 **servysable:** willing to serve, attentive
1912 **thrifty:** proper, successful
1917 **bountee:** goodness

1921 **after-mete:** the time after dinner
1926 **Have I no thyng but:** when I have merely
1930 **marchal:** master of ceremonies (cf. I.751–52)
1936 **say:** saw
1937 **bille:** letter
1943 **kyd:** known
1953 **cloutes:** tatters
1960 **dide hym encombraunce:** got in his way
1962 **precious:** fastidious, prudish

Or wheither hire thoughte it paradys or helle.
But heere I lete hem werken in hir wyse   1965
Til evensong rong and that they moste aryse.
    Were it by destynee or by aventure,
Were it by influence or by nature,
Or constellacion, that in swich estaat
The hevene stood that tyme fortunaat   1970
Was for to putte a bille of Venus werkes —
For alle thyng hath tyme, as seyn thise
                    clerkes —
To any womman for to gete hire love,
I kan nat seye; but grete God above,
That knoweth that noon act is causelees,   1975
He deme of al, for I wole holde my pees.
But sooth is this, how that this fresshe May
Hath take swich impression that day
Of pitee of this sike Damyan
That from hire herte she ne dryve kan   1980
The remembrance for to doon hym ese.
"Certeyn," thoghte she, "whom that this thyng
                    displese
I rekke noght, for heere I hym assure
To love hym best of any creature,   1984
Though he namoore hadde than his sherte."
Lo, pitee renneth soone in gentil herte!
    Heere may ye se how excellent franchise
In wommen is, whan they hem narwe avyse.
Som tyrant is, as ther be many oon
That hath an herte as hard as any stoon,   1990
Which wolde han lat hym sterven in the place
Wel rather than han graunted hym hire grace,
And hem rejoysen in hire crueel pryde,
And rekke nat to been an homycide.
    This gentil May, fulfilled of pitee,   1995
Right of hire hand a lettre made she,
In which she graunteth hym hire verray grace.
Ther lakketh noght oonly but day and place
Wher that she myghte unto his lust suffise,
For it shal be right as he wole devyse.   2000
And whan she saugh hir tyme, upon a day
To visite this Damyan gooth May,
And sotilly this lettre doun she threste
Under his pilwe; rede it if hym leste.
She taketh hym by the hand and harde hym
                    twiste   2005

So secrely that no wight of it wiste,
And bad hym been al hool, and forth she wente
To Januarie, whan that he for hire sente.
    Up riseth Damyan the nexte morwe;
Al passed was his siknesse and his sorwe.   2010
He kembeth hym, he preyneth hym and pyketh,
He dooth al that his lady lust and lyketh,
And eek to Januarie he gooth as lowe
As evere dide a dogge for the bowe.
He is so plesant unto every man   2015
(For craft is al, whoso that do it kan)
That every wight is fayn to speke hym good,
And fully in his lady grace he stood.
Thus lete I Damyan aboute his nede,
And in my tale forth I wol procede.   2020
    Somme clerkes holden that felicitee
Stant in delit, and therfore certeyn he,
This noble Januarie, with al his myght,
In honest wyse, as longeth to a knyght,
Shoop hym to lyve ful deliciously.   2025
His housynge, his array, as honestly
To his degree was maked as a kynges.
Amonges othere of his honeste thynges,
He made a gardyn, walled al with stoon;
So fair a gardyn woot I nowher noon.   2030
For, out of doute, I verraily suppose
That he that wroot the Romance of the Rose
Ne koude of it the beautee wel devyse;
Ne Priapus ne myghte nat suffise,
Though he be god of gardyns, for to telle   2035
The beautee of the gardyn and the welle
That stood under a laurer alwey grene.
Ful ofte tyme he Pluto and his queene,
Proserpina, and al hire fayerye,
Disporten hem and maken melodye   2040
Aboute that welle, and daunced, as men tolde.
    This noble knyght, this Januarie the olde,
Swich deyntee hath in it to walke and pleye,
That he wol no wight suffren bere the keye
Save he hymself; for of the smale wyket   2045
He baar alwey of silver a clyket,
With which, whan that hym leste, he it un-
                    shette.

1968 **influence:** power (transmitted by rays from heavenly bodies)
1969 **constellacion:** configuration of the heavenly bodies
1971 **putte a bille:** present a petition
1976 **He deme:** may he judge
1987 **franchise:** generosity of spirit
1988 **hem narwe avyse:** consider carefully
1999 **unto his lust suffise:** satisfy his desires
2003 **sotilly:** craftily   **threste:** thrust
2004 **pilwe:** pillow

2011 **kembeth:** combs   **preyneth hym:** preens himself, makes himself neat   **pyketh:** cleans, adorns
2013 **lowe:** humbly
2014 **dogge for the bowe:** dog trained to hunt with an archer
2024 **honest:** honorable, respectable
2025 **deliciously:** voluptuously
2032 **he:** Guillaume de Lorris (cf. Rom 49–728)
2034 **Priapus:** a phallic god (cf. PF 253–59)
2038–39 **Pluto, Proserpina:** king and queen of the underworld
2043 **deyntee hath:** takes pleasure
2045 **wyket:** wicket gate
2046 **clyket:** latchkey
2047 **unshette:** unlocked

And whan he wolde paye his wyf hir dette
In somer seson, thider wolde he go,   2049
And May his wyf, and no wight but they two;
And thynges whiche that were nat doon
          abedde,
He in the gardyn parfourned hem and spedde.
And in this wyse, many a murye day,
Lyved this Januarie and fresshe May.
But worldly joye may nat alwey dure   2055
To Januarie, ne to no creature.
     O sodeyn hap! O thou Fortune unstable!
Lyk to the scorpion so deceyvable,
That flaterest with thyn heed whan thou wolt
          stynge;
Thy tayl is deeth, thurgh thyn envenymynge.
O brotil joye! O sweete venym queynte!   2061
O monstre, that so subtilly kanst peynte
Thy yiftes under hewe of stidefastnesse,
That thou deceyvest bothe moore and lesse!
Why hastow Januarie thus deceyved,   2065
That haddest hym for thy fulle freend re-
          ceyved?
And now thou hast biraft hym bothe his yen,
For sorwe of which desireth he to dyen.
     Allas, this noble Januarie free,
Amydde his lust and his prosperitee,   2070
Is woxen blynd, and that al sodeynly.
He wepeth and he wayleth pitously;
And therwithal the fyr of jalousie,
Lest that his wyf sholde falle in som folye,
So brente his herte that he wolde fayn   2075
That som man bothe hire and hym had slayn.
For neither after his deeth nor in his lyf
Ne wolde he that she were love ne wyf,
But evere lyve as wydwe in clothes blake,
Soul as the turtle that lost hath hire make. 2080
But atte laste, after a month or tweye,
His sorwe gan aswage, sooth to seye;
For whan he wiste it may noon oother be,
He paciently took his adversitee,
Save, out of doute, he may nat forgoon   2085
That he nas jalous everemoore in oon;
Which jalousye it was so outrageous
That neither in halle, n'yn noon oother hous,
Ne in noon oother place, neverthemo,
He nolde suffre hire for to ryde or go,   2090

But if that he had hond on hire alway;
For which ful ofte wepeth fresshe May,
That loveth Damyan so benyngnely
That she moot outher dyen sodeynly
Or elles she moot han hym as hir leste.   2095
She wayteth whan hir herte wolde breste.
     Upon that oother syde Damyan
Bicomen is the sorwefulleste man
That evere was, for neither nyght ne day
Ne myghte he speke a word to fresshe May,
As to his purpos, of no swich mateere,   2101
But if that Januarie moste it heere,
That hadde an hand upon hire everemo.
But nathelees, by writyng to and fro
And privee signes wiste he what she mente,
And she knew eek the fyn of his entente.   2106
     O Januarie, what myghte it thee availle,
Thogh thou myghtest se as fer as shippes saille?
For as good is blynd deceyved be
As to be deceyved whan a man may se.   2110
     Lo, Argus, which that hadde an hondred yen,
For al that evere he koude poure or pryen,
Yet was he blent, and, God woot, so been mo
That wenen wisly that it be nat so.
Passe over is an ese, I sey namoore.   2115
     This fresshe May, that I spak of so yoore,
In warm wex hath emprented the clyket
That Januarie bar of the smale wyket,
By which into his gardyn ofte he wente;
And Damyan, that knew al hire entente,   2120
The cliket countrefeted pryvely.
Ther nys namoore to seye, but hastily
Som wonder by this clyket shal bityde,
Which ye shul heeren, if ye wole abyde.   2124
     O noble Ovyde, ful sooth seystou, God woot,
What sleighte is it, thogh it be long and hoot,
That Love nyl fynde it out in som manere?
By Piramus and Tesbee may men leere;
Thogh they were kept ful longe streite overal,
They been accorded, rownynge thurgh a wal,
Ther no wight koude han founde out swich a
          sleighte.   2131

2048 **dette:** marital debt (obligation to engage in intercourse)
2057 **hap:** chance
2061 **brotil:** uncertain
2062 **peynte:** disguise
2063 **hewe:** pretense
2080 **Soul:** solitary **turtle:** turtledove
2085 **Save:** except that
2085–86 **forgoon That he nas:** i.e., refrain from being
2087 **outrageous:** excessive
2089 **neverthemo:** no longer

2096 **wayteth:** expects (the time)
2111 **Argus:** mythical guardian of Io
2112 **poure:** look intently, pore **pryen:** gaze, see
2113 **blent:** blinded, deceived
2114 **wenen wisly:** confidently suppose, believe
2115 **Passe over is an ese:** to overlook is an advantage (what
you don't know won't hurt you)
2117 **emprented the clyket:** made an impression of the key
2118 **wyket:** wicket gate
2125 **Ovyde:** Ovid
2126 **sleighte:** trick
2128 **Piramus and Tesbee:** Pyramus and Thisbe; see LGW
706–923.
2129 **streite:** strictly
2130 **rownynge:** whispering

But now to purpos: er that dayes eighte
Were passed [of] the month of [Juyn], bifil
That Januarie hath caught so greet a wil,   2134
Thurgh eggyng of his wyf, hym for to pleye
In his gardyn, and no wight but they tweye,
That in a morwe unto his May seith he:
"Rys up, my wyf, my love, my lady free!
The turtles voys is herd, my dowve sweete;
The wynter is goon with alle his reynes
                    weete.   2140
Com forth now, with thyne eyen columbyn!
How fairer been thy brestes than is wyn!
The gardyn is enclosed al aboute;
Com forth, my white spouse! Out of doute
Thou hast me wounded in myn herte, O wyf!
No spot of thee ne knew I al my lyf.   2146
Com forth, and lat us taken oure disport;
I chees thee for my wyf and my confort."
    Swiche olde lewed wordes used he.
On Damyan a signe made she,   2150
That he sholde go biforn with his cliket.
This Damyan thanne hath opened the wyket,
And in he stirte, and that in swich manere
That no wight myghte it se neither yheere,
And stille he sit under a bussh anon.   2155
    This Januarie, as blynd as is a stoon,
With Mayus in his hand, and no wight mo,
Into his fresshe gardyn is ago,
And clapte to the wyket sodeynly.
    "Now wyf," quod he, "heere nys but thou
                    and I,   2160
That art the creature that I best love.
For by that Lord that sit in hevene above,
Levere ich hadde to dyen on a knyf
Than thee offende, trewe deere wyf!
For Goddes sake, thenk how I thee chees,   2165
Noght for no coveitise, doutelees,
But oonly for the love I had to thee.
And though that I be oold and may nat see,
Beth to me trewe, and I wol telle yow why.
Thre thynges, certes, shal ye wynne therby:
First, love of Crist, and to youreself honour,
And al myn heritage, toun and tour;   2172
I yeve it yow, maketh chartres as yow leste;
This shal be doon to-morwe er sonne reste,
So wisly God my soule brynge in blisse.   2175
I prey yow first, in covenant ye me kisse;

And though that I be jalous, wyte me noght.
Ye been so depe enprented in my thoght
That, whan that I considere youre beautee
And therwithal the unlikly elde of me,   2180
I may nat, certes, though I sholde dye,
Forbere to been out of youre compaignye
For verray love; this is withouten doute.
Now kys me, wyf, and lat us rome aboute."
    This fresshe May, whan she thise wordes
                    herde,   2185
Benyngnely to Januarie answerde,
But first and forward she bigan to wepe.
"I have," quod she, "a soule for to kepe
As wel as ye, and also myn honour,
And of my wyfhod thilke tendre flour,   2190
Which that I have assured in youre hond,
Whan that the preest to yow my body bond;
Wherfore I wole answere in this manere,
By the leve of yow, my lord so deere:
I prey to God that nevere dawe the day   2195
That I ne sterve, as foule as womman may,
If evere I do unto my kyn that shame,
Or elles I empeyre so my name,
That I be fals; and if I do that lak,
Do strepe me and put me in a sak,   2200
And in the nexte ryver do me drenche.
I am a gentil womman and no wenche.
Why speke ye thus? But men been evere un-
                    trewe,
And wommen have repreve of yow ay newe.
Ye han noon oother contenance, I leeve,   2205
But speke to us of untrust and repreeve."
    And with that word she saugh wher Damyan
Sat in the bussh, and coughen she bigan,
And with hir fynger signes made she
That Damyan sholde clymbe upon a tree   2210
That charged was with fruyt, and up he wente.
For verraily he knew al hire entente,
And every signe that she koude make,
Wel bet than Januarie, hir owene make,
For in a lettre she hadde toold hym al   2215
Of this matere, how he werchen shal.
And thus I lete hym sitte upon the pyrie,
And Januarie and May romynge myrie.
    Bright was the day, and blew the firmament;
Phebus hath of gold his stremes doun ysent

2132–33 On or shortly before June 8
2135 **eggyng:** incitement
2141 **columbyn:** dovelike
2150 **On:** to
2166 **coveitise:** greed
2173 **chartres:** contracts, deeds
2176 **in covenant:** to seal the contract

2177 **wyte:** blame
2180 **unlikly:** unsuitable
2187 **first and forward:** first of all
2191 **assured:** entrusted
2198 **empeyre:** damage
2199 **do that lak:** commit that offence
2201 **do me drenche:** have me drowned
2204 **ay newe:** always
2205 **contenance:** manner of behavior
2206 **But:** except   **untrust:** distrust   **repreeve:** reproof
2217 **pyrie:** pear tree

To gladen every flour with his warmnesse.   2221
He was that tyme in Geminis, as I gesse,
But litel fro his declynacion
Of Cancer, Jovis exaltacion.
And so bifel, that brighte morwe-tyde   2225
That in that gardyn, in the ferther syde,
Pluto, that is kyng of Fayerye,
And many a lady in his compaignye,
Folwynge his wyf, the queene Proserpyna,
Which that he ravysshed out of [Ethna]   2230
Whil that she gadered floures in the mede —
In Claudyan ye may the stories rede,
How in his grisely carte he hire fette —
This kyng of Fairye thanne adoun hym sette
Upon a bench of turves, fressh and grene,   2235
And right anon thus seyde he to his queene:
    "My wyf," quod he, "ther may no wight seye
        nay;
Th'experience so preveth every day
The tresons whiche that wommen doon to man.
Ten hondred thousand [tales] tellen I kan
Notable of youre untrouthe and brotilnesse.
O Salomon, wys, and richest of richesse,   2242
Fulfild of sapience and of worldly glorie,
Ful worthy been thy wordes to memorie
To every wight that wit and reson kan.   2245
Thus preiseth he yet the bountee of man:
'Amonges a thousand men yet foond I oon,
But of wommen alle foond I noon.'
    "Thus seith the kyng that knoweth youre
        wikkednesse.
And Jhesus, *filius Syrak,* as I gesse,   2250
Ne speketh of yow but seelde reverence.
A wylde fyr and corrupt pestilence
So falle upon youre bodyes yet to-nyght!
Ne se ye nat this honurable knyght,   2254
By cause, allas, that he is blynd and old,
His owene man shal make hym cokewold.
Lo, where he sit, the lechour, in the tree!
Now wol I graunten, of my magestee,
Unto this olde, blynde, worthy knyght
That he shal have ayen his eyen syght,   2260
Whan that his wyf wold doon hym vileynye.

Thanne shal he knowen al hire harlotrye,
Bothe in repreve of hire and othere mo."
    "Ye shal?" quod Proserpyne, "wol ye so?
Now by my moodres sires soule I swere   2265
That I shal yeven hire suffisant answere,
And alle wommen after, for hir sake,
That, though they be in any gilt ytake,
With face boold they shulle hemself excuse,
And bere hem doun that wolden hem accuse.
For lak of answere noon of hem shal dyen.   2271
Al hadde man seyn a thyng with bothe his yen,
Yit shul we wommen visage it hardily,
And wepe, and swere, and chyde subtilly,
So that ye men shul been as lewed as gees.   2275
    "What rekketh me of youre auctoritees?
I woot wel that this Jew, this Salomon,
Foond of us wommen fooles many oon.
But though that he ne foond no good womman,
Yet hath ther founde many another man   2280
Wommen ful trewe, ful goode, and vertuous.
Witnesse on hem that dwelle in Cristes hous;
With martirdom they preved hire constance.
The Romayn geestes eek make remembrance
Of many a verray, trewe wyf also.   2285
But, sire, ne be nat wrooth, al be it so,
Though that he seyde he foond no good
        womman,
I prey yow take the sentence of the man;
He mente thus, that in sovereyn bontee
Nis noon but God, but neither he ne she.   2290
    "Ey! for verray God that nys but oon,
What make ye so muche of Salomon?
What though he made a temple, Goddes hous?
What though he were riche and glorious?
So made he eek a temple of false goddis.   2295
How myghte he do a thyng that moore for-
        bode is?
Pardee, as faire as ye his name emplastre,
He was a lecchour and an ydolastre,
And in his elde he verray God forsook;
And if God ne hadde, as seith the book,   2300
Yspared him for his fadres sake, he sholde
Have lost his regne rather than he wolde.
I sette right noght, of al the vileynye
That ye of wommen write, a boterflye!

2222–24 The sun was in the sign of Gemini (*Geminis*), not far
from the summer solstice, after which the sun begins to decline in
its apparent altitude (*his declynacion*); this is at the beginning of
Cancer, the sign in which Jupiter exerts its greatest influence
(*Jovis exaltacion*).
2230 **Ethna:** Mt. Etna
2232 **Claudyan:** Claudian, author of the *Rape of Proserpina*
2235 **turves:** pieces of turf
2241 **brotilnesse:** frailty, fickleness
2242 **Salomon:** Solomon
2250 **Jhesus, filius Syrak:** author of *Ecclesiasticus*
2251 **seelde:** seldom
2252 **wylde fyr:** erysipelas, an acute inflammation of the skin
corrupt: infectious

2262 **harlotrye:** wickedness
2265 **my moodres sires soule:** the soul of Saturn, father of
Ceres
2273 **visage it hardily:** face it out boldly
2284 **Romayn geestes:** Roman history   **make remembrance:**
remind
2289 **sovereyn bontee:** perfect goodness
2290 **he ne she:** man nor woman
2297 **emplastre:** apply a medicinal plaster (i.e., gloss over)
2298 **ydolastre:** idolater
2302 **rather:** sooner

I am a womman, nedes moot I speke,   2305
Or elles swelle til myn herte breke.
For sithen he seyde that we been jangleresses,
As evere hool I moote brouke my tresses,
I shal nat spare, for no curteisye,   2309
To speke hym harm that wolde us vileynye."
        "Dame," quod this Pluto, "be no lenger
            wrooth;
I yeve it up! But sith I swoor myn ooth
That I wolde graunten hym his sighte ageyn,
My word shal stonde, I warne yow certeyn.
I am a kyng; it sit me noght to lye."   2315
        "And I," quod she, "a queene of Fayerye!
Hir answere shal she have, I undertake.
Lat us namoore wordes heerof make;
For sothe, I wol no lenger yow contrarie."
        Now lat us turne agayn to Januarie,   2320
That in the gardyn with his faire May
Syngeth ful murier than the papejay,
"Yow love I best, and shal, and oother noon."
So longe aboute the aleyes is he goon,
Til he was come agaynes thilke pyrie   2325
Where as this Damyan sitteth ful myrie
An heigh among the fresshe leves grene.
        This fresshe May, that is so bright and
            sheene,
Gan for to syke, and seyde, "Allas, my syde!
Now sire," quod she, "for aught that may
            bityde,   2330
I moste han of the peres that I see,
Or I moot dye, so soore longeth me
To eten of the smale peres grene.
Help, for hir love that is of hevene queene!
I telle yow wel, a womman in my plit   2335
May han to fruyt so greet an appetit
That she may dyen but she of it have."
        "Allas," quod he, "that I ne had heer a knave
That koude clymbe! Allas, allas," quod he,
"For I am blynd!" "Ye, sire, no fors," quod
            she;   2340
"But wolde ye vouche sauf, for Goddes sake,
The pyrie inwith youre armes for to take,
For wel I woot that ye mystruste me,
Thanne sholde I clymbe wel ynogh," quod she,
"So I my foot myghte sette upon youre
            bak."   2345

"Certes," quod he, "theron shal be no lak,
Mighte I yow helpen with myn herte blood."
He stoupeth doun, and on his bak she stood,
And caughte hire by a twiste, and up she gooth —
Ladyes, I prey yow that ye be nat wrooth;
I kan nat glose, I am a rude man —   2351
And sodeynly anon this Damyan
Gan pullen up the smok, and in he throng.
        And whan that Pluto saugh this grete wrong,
To Januarie he gaf agayn his sighte,   2355
And made hym se as wel as evere he myghte.
And whan that he hadde caught his sighte
            agayn,
Ne was ther nevere man of thyng so fayn,
But on his wyf his thoght was everemo.
Up to the tree he caste his eyen two,   2360
And saugh that Damyan his wyf had dressed
In swich manere it may nat been expressed,
But if I wolde speke uncurteisly;
And up he yaf a roryng and a cry,   2364
As dooth the mooder whan the child shal dye:
"Out! Help! Allas! Harrow!" he gan to crye,
"O stronge lady stoore, what dostow?"
        And she answerde, "Sire, what eyleth yow?
Have pacience and resoun in youre mynde.
I have yow holpe on bothe youre eyen blynde.
Up peril of my soule, I shal nat lyen,   2371
As me was taught, to heele with youre eyen,
Was no thyng bet, to make yow to see,
Than strugle with a man upon a tree.
God woot, I dide it in ful good entente."   2375
        "Strugle?" quod he, "Ye, algate in it wente!
God yeve yow bothe on shames deth to dyen!
He swyved thee; I saugh it with myne yen,
And elles be I hanged by the hals!"
        "Thanne is," quod she, "my medicyne fals;
For certeinly, if that ye myghte se,   2381
Ye wolde nat seyn thise wordes unto me.
Ye han som glymsyng, and no parfit sighte."
        "I se," quod he, "as wel as evere I myghte,
Thonked be God! With bothe myne eyen two,
And by my trouthe, me thoughte he dide thee
            so."   2386
        "Ye maze, maze, goode sire," quod she;
"This thank have I for I have maad yow see.

2307 **jangleresses:** chattering women
2308 **brouke my tresses:** remain alive (literally, *enjoy my hair*)
2315 **sit** = *sitteth,* suits, befits
2319 **contrarie:** contradict
2322 **papejay:** parrot
2324 **aleyes:** alleys, garden paths
2325 **agaynes:** in front of   **pyrie:** pear tree
2331 **peres:** pears
2335 **plit:** condition

2349 **twiste:** branch
2351 **glose:** use circumlocutions
2353 **throng:** thrust
2361 **dressed:** treated
2363 **uncurteisly:** crudely
2366 **Harrow!:** help!
2367 **stronge lady stoore:** bold, crude woman
2370 **holpe:** helped
2378 **swyved:** copulated with
2379 **hals:** neck
2383 **glymsyng:** glimpse
2387 **maze:** are bewildered, dazed

Allas," quod she, "that evere I was so kynde!"
    "Now, dame," quod he, "lat al passe out of
            mynde.   2390
Com doun, my lief, and if I have myssayd,
God helpe me so, as I am yvele apayd.
But, by my fader soule, I wende han seyn
How that this Damyan hadde by thee leyn,
And that thy smok hadde leyn upon his
            brest."   2395
    "Ye, sire," quod she, "ye may wene as yow
            lest.
But, sire, a man that waketh out of his sleep,
He may nat sodeynly wel taken keep
Upon a thyng, ne seen it parfitly,
Til that he be adawed verraily.   2400
Right so a man that longe hath blynd ybe,
Ne may nat sodeynly so wel yse,

First whan his sighte is newe come ageyn,
As he that hath a day or two yseyn.
Til that youre sighte ysatled be a while   2405
Ther may ful many a sighte yow bigile.
Beth war, I prey yow, for by hevene kyng,
Ful many a man weneth to seen a thyng,
And it is al another than it semeth.
He that mysconceyveth, he mysdemeth."   2410
And with that word she leep doun fro the tree.
    This Januarie, who is glad but he?
He kisseth hire and clippeth hire ful ofte,
And on hire wombe he strooketh hire ful softe,
And to his palays hoom he hath hire lad.   2415
Now, goode men, I pray yow to be glad.
Thus endeth heere my tale of Januarie;
God blesse us, and his mooder Seinte Marie!

Heere is ended the Marchantes Tale of Januarie.

EPILOGUE TO THE MERCHANT'S TALE

    "Ey! Goddes mercy!" seyde oure Hooste tho,
"Now swich a wyf I pray God kepe me fro!
Lo, whiche sleightes and subtilitees   2421
In wommen been! For ay as bisy as bees
Been they, us sely men for to deceyve,
And from the soothe evere wol they weyve;
By this Marchauntes tale it preveth weel.   2425
But douteles, as trewe as any steel
I have a wyf, though that she povre be,
But of hir tonge, a labbyng shrewe is she,
And yet she hath an heep of vices mo;

Therof no fors! Lat alle swiche thynges go.   2430
But wyte ye what? In conseil be it seyd,
Me reweth soore I am unto hire teyd.
For and I sholde rekenen every vice
Which that she hath, ywis I were to nyce.
And cause why? It sholde reported be   2435
And toold to hire of somme of this meynee —
Of whom, it nedeth nat for to declare,
Syn wommen konnen outen swich chaffare;
And eek my wit suffiseth nat therto
To tellen al; wherfore my tale is do."   2440

2393 **wende han seyn:** thought to have seen, thought I saw
2400 **adawed verraily:** fully awakened
2402 **yse:** see

2424 **weyve:** deviate
2428 **labbyng:** blabbing

2405 **ysatled:** settled
2409 **al another:** completely otherwise
2410 **mysconceyveth:** misapprehends, misunderstands
mysdemeth: misjudges
2413 **clippeth:** embraces

2431 **In conseil:** confidentially
2432 **Me reweth:** I repent   **teyd:** tied
2433 **and:** if
2436 **meynee:** company
2438 **outen:** display   **chaffare:** wares

Fragment V (Group F)

INTRODUCTION TO THE SQUIRE'S TALE

"Squier, com neer, if it youre wille be,
And sey somwhat of love, for certes ye
Konnen theron as muche as any man."
  "Nay, sire," quod he, "but I wol seye as I kan

With hertly wyl, for I wol nat rebelle   5
Agayn youre lust; a tale wol I telle.
Have me excused if I speke amys;
My wyl is good, and lo, my tale is this."

THE SQUIRE'S TALE

Heere bigynneth the Squieres Tale.

At Sarray, in the land of Tartarye,
Ther dwelte a kyng that werreyed Russye,   10
Thurgh which ther dyde many a doughty man.
This noble kyng was cleped Cambyuskan,
Which in his tyme was of so greet renoun
That ther was nowher in no regioun
So excellent a lord in alle thyng: 15
Hym lakked noght that longeth to a kyng.
As of the secte of which that he was born
He kepte his lay, to which that he was sworn;
And therto he was hardy, wys, and riche,
And pitous and just, alwey yliche;   20
Sooth of his word, benigne, and honurable;
Of his corage as any centre stable;
Yong, fressh, and strong, in armes desirous
As any bacheler of al his hous.
A fair persone he was and fortunat,   25
And kept alwey so wel roial estat
That ther was nowher swich another man.
  This noble kyng, this Tartre Cambyuskan,
Hadde two sones on Elpheta his wyf,
Of whiche the eldeste highte Algarsyf;   30
That oother sone was cleped Cambalo.
A doghter hadde this worthy kyng also,
That yongest was, and highte Canacee.
But for to telle yow al hir beautee,

It lyth nat in my tonge, n'yn my konnyng;
I dar nat undertake so heigh a thyng.   36
Myn Englissh eek is insufficient.
It moste been a rethor excellent
That koude his colours longynge for that art,
If he sholde hire discryven every part.   40
I am noon swich, I moot speke as I kan.
  And so bifel that whan this Cambyuskan
Hath twenty wynter born his diademe,
As he was wont fro yeer to yeer, I deme,
He leet the feeste of his nativitee   45
Doon cryen thurghout Sarray his citee,
The laste Idus of March, after the yeer.
Phebus the sonne ful joly was and cleer,
For he was neigh his exaltacioun
In Martes face and in his mansioun   50
In Aries, the colerik hoote signe.
Ful lusty was the weder and benigne,
For which the foweles, agayn the sonne sheene,
What for the sesoun and the yonge grene,
Ful loude songen hire affecciouns.   55
Hem semed han geten hem protecciouns
Agayn the swerd of wynter, keene and coold.

9 **Sarray:** Tsarev   **Tartarye:** the Mongol Empire
10 **werreyed:** waged war on
12 **Cambyuskan:** Genghis (Chengiz) Khan
17 **As of the secte:** in accord with the religion
18 **lay:** religious laws
24 **bacheler:** young knight

38 **rethor:** rhetorician, master of eloquence
39 **colours longynge for:** rhetorical devices belonging to
45–46 **leet . . . Doon cryen:** had proclaimed
47 Exactly 15 March, in the ordinary course of the year
48–51 The sun is near the position where it has its strongest
influence (*his exaltacioun*), in the first ten degrees of Aries
(*Martes face*); Aries is a hot and dry sign, like the *colerik* humor.
53 **agayn:** facing toward, in response to
54 **What for:** what with

This Cambyuskan, of which I have yow toold,
In roial vestiment sit on his deys,
With diademe, ful heighe in his paleys,   60
And halt his feeste so solempne and so ryche
That in this world ne was ther noon it lyche;
Of which if I shal tellen al th'array,
Thanne wolde it occupie a someres day,
And eek it nedeth nat for to devyse   65
At every cours the ordre of hire servyse.
I wol nat tellen of hir strange sewes,
Ne of hir swannes, ne of hire heronsewes.
Eek in that lond, as tellen knyghtes olde,
Ther is som mete that is ful deynte holde   70
That in this lond men recche of it but smal;
Ther nys no man that may reporten al.
I wol nat taryen yow, for it is pryme
And for it is no fruyt but los of tyme;
Unto my firste I wole have my recours.   75

    And so bifel that after the thridde cours,
Whil that this kyng sit thus in his nobleye,
Herknynge his mynstralles hir thynges pleye
Biforn hym at the bord deliciously,
In at the halle dore al sodeynly   80
Ther cam a knyght upon a steede of bras,
And in his hand a brood mirour of glas.
Upon his thombe he hadde of gold a ryng,
And by his syde a naked swerd hangyng;
And up he rideth to the heighe bord.   85
In al the halle ne was ther spoken a word
For merveille of this knyght; hym to biholde
Ful bisily they wayten, yonge and olde.

    This strange knyght, that cam thus sodeynly,
Al armed, save his heed, ful richely,   90
Saleweth kyng and queene and lordes alle,
By ordre, as they seten in the halle,
With so heigh reverence and obeisaunce,
As wel in speche as in contenaunce,
That Gawayn, with his olde curteisye,   95
Though he were comen ayeyn out of Fairye,
Ne koude hym nat amende with a word.
And after this, biforn the heighe bord,
He with a manly voys seide his message,
After the forme used in his langage,   100
Withouten vice of silable or of lettre;
And for his tale sholde seme the bettre,

Accordant to his wordes was his cheere,
As techeth art of speche hem that it leere.
Al be that I kan nat sowne his stile,   105
Ne kan nat clymben over so heigh a style,
Yet seye I this, as to commune entente:
Thus muche amounteth al that evere he mente,
If it so be that I have it in mynde.

    He seyde, "The kyng of Arabe and of Inde,
My lige lord, on this solempne day   111
Saleweth yow, as he best kan and may,
And sendeth yow, in honour of youre feeste,
By me, that am al redy at youre heeste,
This steede of bras, that esily and weel   115
Kan in the space of o day natureel —
This is to seyn, in foure and twenty houres —
Wher-so yow lyst, in droghte or elles shoures,
Beren youre body into every place
To which youre herte wilneth for to pace,
Withouten wem of yow, thurgh foul or fair;
Or, if yow lyst to fleen as hye in the air   122
As dooth an egle whan hym list to soore,
This same steede shal bere yow evere moore,
Withouten harm, til ye be ther yow leste,   125
Though that ye slepen on his bak or reste,
And turne ayeyn with writhyng of a pyn.
He that it wroghte koude ful many a gyn.
He wayted many a constellacion
Er he had doon this operacion,   130
And knew ful many a seel and many a bond.

    This mirour eek, that I have in myn hond,
Hath swich a myght that men may in it see
Whan ther shal fallen any adversitee
Unto youre regne or to youreself also,   135
And openly who is youre freend or foo.

    And over al this, if any lady bright
Hath set hire herte on any maner wight,
If he be fals, she shal his tresoun see,
His newe love, and al his subtiltee,   140
So openly that ther shal no thyng hyde.
Wherfore, ageyn this lusty someres tyde,
This mirour and this ryng, that ye may see,
He hath sent to my lady Canacee,
Youre excellente doghter that is heere.   145
    The vertu of the ryng, if ye wol heere,
Is this: that if hire lust it for to were

---

68 **heronsewes:** young herons
71 **smal:** little
73 **pryme:** the first hour of the day, from about 6 to 9 A.M.
74 **no fruyt:** not an essential part of the tale
75 **have my recours:** return
77 **nobleye:** noble state
79 **deliciously:** delightfully
85 **heighe bord:** high table
91 **Saleweth:** greets
92 **By ordre:** sequentially **seten:** sat

105 **sowne:** repeat, imitate
110 **of Arabe and of Inde:** of Arabia and India
112 **kan and may:** knows how and can
116 **day natureel:** twenty-four hours; see Astr 2.7.
121 **wem:** harm
123 **soore:** soar
127 **writhyng:** turning
128 **gyn:** ingenious contrivance
129 **constellacion:** configuration of the heavenly bodies
131 **seel:** seal **bond:** knowledge of the practitioner
142 **ageyn:** in anticipation of

Upon hir thombe or in hir purs it bere,
Ther is no fowel that fleeth under the hevene
That she ne shal wel understonde his stevene,
And knowe his menyng openly and pleyn,　151
And answere hym in his langage ageyn;
And every gras that groweth upon roote
She shal eek knowe, and whom it wol do boote,
Al be his woundes never so depe and
　　　wyde.　155
　This naked swerd, that hangeth by my syde,
Swich vertu hath that what man so ye smyte
Thurghout his armure it wole kerve and byte,
Were it as thikke as is a branched ook;　159
And what man that is wounded with the strook
Shal never be hool til that yow list, of grace,
To stroke hym with the plat in thilke place
Ther he is hurt; this is as muche to seyn,
Ye moote with the platte swerd ageyn　164
Stroke hym in the wounde, and it wol close.
This is a verray sooth, withouten glose;
It failleth nat whils it is in youre hoold."
　And whan this knyght hath thus his tale
　　　toold,
He rideth out of halle and doun he lighte.
His steede, which that shoon as sonne brighte,
Stant in the court, stille as any stoon.　171
This knyght is to his chambre lad anoon,
And is unarmed, and to mete yset.
　The presentes been ful roially yfet —
This is to seyn, the swerd and the mirour —　175
And born anon into the heighe tour
With certeine officers ordeyned therfore;
And unto Canacee this ryng is bore
Solempnely, ther she sit at the table.
But sikerly, withouten any fable,　180
The hors of bras, that may nat be remewed,
It stant as it were to the ground yglewed.
Ther may no man out of the place it dryve
For noon engyn of wyndas or polyve;
And cause why? For they kan nat the craft.　185
And therfore in the place they han it laft
Til that the knyght hath taught hem the man-
　ere
To voyden hym, as ye shal after heere.
　Greet was the prees that swarmeth to and
　　　fro

To gauren on this hors that stondeth so,　190
For it so heigh was, and so brood and long,
So wel proporcioned for to been strong,
Right as it were a steede of Lumbardye;
Therwith so horsly, and so quyk of ye,
As it a gentil Poilleys courser were.　195
For certes, fro his tayl unto his ere
Nature ne art ne koude hym nat amende
In no degree, as al the people wende.
But everemoore hir mooste wonder was
How that it koude gon, and was of bras;　200
It was a fairye, as the peple semed.
Diverse folk diversely they demed;
As many heddes, as manye wittes ther been.
They murmureden as dooth a swarm of been,
And maden skiles after hir fantasies,　205
Rehersynge of thise olde poetries,
And seyden it was lyk the Pegasee,
The hors that hadde wynges for to flee;
Or elles it was the Grekes hors Synon,
That broghte Troie to destruccion,　210
As men in thise olde geestes rede.
"Myn herte," quod oon, "is everemoore in
　　　drede;
I trowe som men of armes been therinne,
That shapen hem this citee for to wynne.
It were right good that al swich thyng were
　　　knowe."
Another rowned to his felawe lowe,　216
And seyde, "He lyeth, for it is rather lyk
An apparence ymaad by som magyk,
As jogelours pleyen at thise feestes grete."
Of sondry doutes thus they jangle and trete,
As lewed peple demeth comunly　221
Of thynges that been maad moore subtilly
Than they kan in hir lewednesse comprehende;
They demen gladly to the badder ende.
　And somme of hem wondred on the mirour,
That born was up into the maister-tour,　226
Hou men myghte in it swiche thynges se.
　Another answerde and seyde it myghte wel
　　　be

150 **stevene:** voice, speech
154 **do boote:** cure
162 **plat:** blunt side
166 **withouten glose:** without deception
171 **court:** courtyard
173 **mete:** meal
180 **fable:** falsehood
181 **remewed:** moved
182 **yglewed:** glued
184 **wyndas:** windlass　**polyve:** pulley
188 **voyden:** move

190 **gauren:** stare
194 **horsly:** with the best qualities of a horse　**quyk:** lively
195 **Poilleys:** Apulian
201 **a fairye:** a marvel
204 **been:** bees
205 **skiles:** reasons, arguments
206 **poetries:** poems
207 **Pegasee:** Pegasus
209 **the Grekes hors Synon:** the horse of Synon the Greek; i.e.,
the Trojan horse
218 **apparence:** illusion
219 **jogelours:** conjurers
220 **doutes:** doubts (conjectures)　**jangle:** chatter　**trete:**
discuss, debate
224 **gladly:** habitually
226 **maister-tour:** chief, principal tower

Naturelly, by composiciouns
Of anglis and of slye reflexiouns,   230
And seyde that in Rome was swich oon.
They speken of Alocen, and Vitulon,
And Aristotle, that writen in hir lyves
Of queynte mirours and of perspectives,
As knowen they that han hir bookes herd.   235

    And oother folk han wondred on the swerd
That wolde percen thurghout every thyng,
And fille in speche of Thelophus the kyng,
And of Achilles with his queynte spere,
For he koude with it bothe heele and dere,   240
Right in swich wise as men may with the swerd
Of which right now ye han youreselven herd.
They speken of sondry hardyng of metal,
And speke of medicynes therwithal,
And how and whanne it sholde yharded be,
Which is unknowe, algates unto me.   246

    Tho speeke they of Canacees ryng,
And seyden alle that swich a wonder thyng
Of craft of rynges herde they nevere noon,
Save that he Moyses and kyng Salomon   250
Hadde a name of konnyng in swich art.
Thus seyn the peple and drawen hem apart.
But nathelees somme seiden that it was
Wonder to maken of fern-asshen glas,
And yet nys glas nat lyk asshen of fern;   255
But, for they han yknowen it so fern,
Therfore cesseth hir janglyng and hir wonder.
As soore wondren somme on cause of thonder,
On ebbe, on flood, on gossomer, and on myst,
And alle thyng, til that the cause is wyst.   260
Thus jangle they, and demen, and devyse
Til that the kyng gan fro the bord aryse.

    Phebus hath laft the angle meridional,
And yet ascendynge was the beest roial,
The gentil Leon, with his Aldiran,   265
Whan that this Tartre kyng, Cambyuskan,
Roos fro his bord, ther as he sat ful hye.

Toforn hym gooth the loude mynstralcye
Til he cam to his chambre of parementz,
Ther as they sownen diverse instrumentz   270
That it is lyk an hevene for to heere.
Now dauncen lusty Venus children deere,
For in the Fyssh hir lady sat ful hye,
And looketh on hem with a freendly ye.

    This noble kyng is set upon his trone.   275
This strange knyght is fet to hym ful soone,
And on the daunce he gooth with Canacee.
Heere is the revel and the jolitee
That is nat able a dul man to devyse.   279
He moste han knowen love and his servyse
And been a feestlych man as fressh as May,
That sholde yow devysen swich array.

    Who koude telle yow the forme of daunces
So unkouthe, and swiche fresshe contenaunces,
Swich subtil lookyng and dissymulynges   285
For drede of jalouse mennes aperceyvynges?
No man but Launcelot, and he is deed.
Therfore I passe of al this lustiheed;
I sey namoore, but in this jolynesse
I lete hem til men to the soper dresse.   290

    The styward bit the spices for to hye,
And eek the wyn, in al this melodye.
The usshers and the squiers been ygoon,
The spices and the wyn is come anoon.   294
They ete and drynke, and whan this hadde an
         ende,
Unto the temple, as reson was, they wende.
The service doon, they soupen al by day.
What nedeth yow rehercen hire array?
Ech man woot wel that a kynges feeste   299
Hath plentee to the meeste and to the leeste,
And deyntees mo than been in my knowyng.
At after-soper gooth this noble kyng
To seen this hors of bras, with al a route
Of lordes and of ladyes hym aboute.   304

    Swich wondryng was ther on this hors of bras
That syn the grete sege of Troie was,
Theras men wondreden on an hors also,

229 **composiciouns**: arrangements
231 **swich oon**: such a one (magic mirror)
232 **Alocen**: Alhazen, an authority on optics **Vitulon**: Vitello,
an authority on perspective
233 **Aristotle**: probably mentioned because of his explanation of
rainbows **writen in hir lyves**: wrote during their lifetimes
234 **perspectives**: optical lenses
237 **percen**: pierce
238 **Thelophus**: Telephus, wounded by Achilles's spear
240 **dere**: harm
243 **hardyng**: hardening, tempering
244 **medicynes**: chemicals
250 **he Moyses**: that (famous) Moses, noted, like Solomon, for
his skill in magic
254 **fern-asshen**: ashes of fern
256 **fern**: long ago
257 **cesseth**: stops
259 **gossomer**: spider web
263–65 The sun (*Phebus*) has left the *angle meridional,* through
which it passes from 10 to 12 A.M., and the *beest roial* (the
constellation Leo, *Leon*) and the star *Aldiran* are rising above the
horizon (*ascendynge*); see n.

269 **chambre of parementz**: the Presence Chamber, hung with
tapestries (*parementz*), where a sovereign receives official visitors
272 **Venus children**: those under the influence of the planet
Venus; i.e., lovers
273 **Fyssh**: the zodiacal sign Pisces, in which Venus (*hir lady*) has
her exaltation and is especially powerful
281 **feestlych**: convivial
284 **contenaunces**: expressions
285 **dissymulynges**: dissimulations
287 **Launcelot**: Lancelot, lover of Guinevere in the Arthurian
romances
288 **lustiheed**: pleasure
290 **dresse**: go
291 **styward**: steward **spices**: spiced cakes **hye**: hurry, be
quickly brought
297 **by day**: in daylight
300 **Hath plentee to**: there is plenty for
306 **sege**: siege

Ne was ther swich a wondryng as was tho.
But fynally the kyng axeth this knyght
The vertu of this courser and the myght, 310
And preyde hym to telle his governaunce.

This hors anoon bigan to trippe and daunce,
Whan that this knyght leyde hand upon his
 reyne,
And seyde, "Sire, ther is namoore to seyne,
But, whan yow list to ryden anywhere, 315
Ye mooten trille a pyn, stant in his ere,
Which I shal yow telle bitwix us two.
Ye moote nempne hym to what place also,
Or to what contree, that yow list to ryde.
And whan ye come ther as yow list abyde, 320
Bidde hym descende, and trille another pyn,
For therin lith th'effect of al the gyn,
And he wol doun descende and doon youre
 wille,
And in that place he wol abyde stille.
Though al the world the contrarie hadde
 yswore, 325
He shal nat thennes been ydrawe ne ybore.
Or, if yow liste bidde hym thennes goon,
Trille this pyn, and he wol vanysshe anoon
Out of the sighte of every maner wight,
And come agayn, be it by day or nyght, 330
Whan that yow list to clepen hym ageyn
In swich a gyse as I shal to yow seyn
Bitwixe yow and me, and that ful soone.
Ride whan yow list; ther is namoore to doone."

Enformed whan the kyng was of that knyght,
And hath conceyved in his wit aright 336
The manere and the forme of al this thyng,
Ful glad and blithe, this noble doughty kyng
Repeireth to his revel as biforn.
The brydel is unto the tour yborn 340
And kept among his jueles leeve and deere.
The hors vanysshed, I noot in what manere,
Out of hir sighte; ye gete namoore of me.
But thus I lete in lust and jolitee
This Cambyuskan his lordes festeiynge 345
Til wel ny the day bigan to sprynge.

Explicit prima pars.

Sequitur pars secunda.

The norice of digestioun, the sleep,
Gan on hem wynke and bad hem taken keep

That muchel drynke and labour wolde han
 reste;
And with a galpyng mouth hem alle he
 keste, 350
And seyde that it was tyme to lye adoun,
For blood was in his domynacioun.
"Cherisseth blood, natures freend," quod he.
They thanken hym galpynge, by two, by thre,
And every wight gan drawe hym to his
 reste, 355
As sleep hem bad; they tooke it for the beste.

Hire dremes shul nat now been toold for me;
Ful were hire heddes of fumositee,
That causeth dreem of which ther nys no
 charge.
They slepen til that it was pryme large, 360
The mooste part, but it were Canacee.
She was ful mesurable, as wommen be;
For of hir fader hadde she take leve
To goon to reste soone after it was eve.
Hir liste nat appalled for to be, 365
Ne on the morwe unfeestlich for to se,
And slepte hire firste sleep, and thanne awook.
For swich a joye she in hir herte took
Bothe of hir queynte ryng and hire mirour,
That twenty tyme she changed hir colour; 370
And in hire sleep, right for impressioun
Of hire mirour, she hadde a visioun.
Wherfore, er that the sonne gan up glyde,
She cleped on hir maistresse hire bisyde,
And seyde that hire liste for to ryse. 375

Thise olde wommen that been gladly wyse,
As is hire maistresse, answerde hire anon,
And seyde, "Madame, whider wil ye goon
Thus erly, for the folk been alle on reste?"

"I wol," quod she, "arise, for me leste 380
Ne lenger for to slepe, and walke aboute."
Hire maistresse clepeth wommen a greet
 route,
And up they rysen, wel a ten or twelve;
Up riseth fresshe Canacee hireselve, 384
As rody and bright as dooth the yonge sonne,
That in the Ram is foure degrees up ronne —
Noon hyer was he whan she redy was —
And forth she walketh esily a pas,

311 **his governaunce:** how to make it work
316 **trille:** turn
318 **nempne:** name, tell
322 **gyn:** device
331 **clepen hym ageyn:** call him back
332 **gyse:** manner
Explicit, *etc.*: Here ends the first part.
Sequitur, *etc.*: Here follows the second part.

350 **galpyng:** yawning **keste:** kissed
352 **blood:** the humor blood; see n.
358 **fumositee:** fumes deriving from wine drinking
359 **charge:** weight, significance
360 **pryme large:** fully prime, 9 A.M.
362 **mesurable:** moderate
365 **appalled:** faded, pale-looking
366 **unfeestlich:** unfestive **for to se:** to be seen, in appearance
377 **maistresse:** governess
378 **whider:** whither
385 **rody:** ruddy, fresh-looking **yonge:** young because the solar
year has just begun; cf. 49–51 above and I.7–8.
386 **Ram:** the zodiacal sign Aries

Arrayed after the lusty seson soote
Lightly, for to pleye and walke on foote,   390
Nat but with fyve or sixe of hir meynee;
And in a trench forth in the park gooth she.
    The vapour which that fro the erthe glood
Made the sonne to seme rody and brood;
But nathelees it was so fair a sighte   395
That it made alle hire hertes for to lighte,
What for the seson and the morwenynge,
And for the foweles that she herde synge.
For right anon she wiste what they mente
Right by hir song, and knew al hire entente.
    The knotte why that every tale is toold,   401
If it be taried til that lust be coold
Of hem that han it after herkned yoore,
The savour passeth ever lenger the moore,
For fulsomnesse of his prolixitee;   405
And by the same resoun, thynketh me,
I sholde to the knotte condescende,
And maken of hir walkyng soone an ende.
    Amydde a tree, for drye as whit as chalk,
As Canacee was pleyyng in hir walk,   410
Ther sat a faucon over hire heed ful hye,
That with a pitous voys so gan to crye
That all the wode resouned of hire cry.
Ybeten hadde she hirself so pitously
With bothe hir wynges til the rede blood   415
Ran endelong the tree ther-as she stood.
And evere in oon she cryde alwey and shrighte,
And with hir beek hirselven so she prighte
That ther nys tygre, ne noon so crueel beest
That dwelleth outher in wode or in forest,   420
That nolde han wept, if that he wepe koude,
For sorwe of hire, she shrighte alwey so loude.
For ther nas nevere yet no man on lyve,
If that I koude a faucon wel discryve,
That herde of swich another of fairnesse,   425
As wel of plumage as of gentillesse
Of shap, of al that myghte yrekened be.
A faucon peregryn thanne semed she
Of fremde land; and everemoore, as she stood,
She swowneth now and now for lak of blood,
Til wel neigh is she fallen fro the tree.   431

389 **soote:** sweet-smelling, fragrant
392 **trench:** path
393 **glood:** rose
394 **rody:** red
401 **knotte:** gist, main point
404 **savour:** taste
409 **for drye:** very dry (or because of dryness)
413 **resouned of:** resounded with
416 **endelong:** down the length of
417 **shrighte:** shrieked
418 **prighte:** stabbed
428 **faucon peregryn:** peregrine falcon
429 **fremde:** foreign
430 **now and now:** every now and then

    This faire kynges doghter, Canacee,
That on hir fynger baar the queynte ryng,
Thurgh which she understood wel every thyng
That any fowel may in his leden seyn,   435
And koude answeren hym in his ledene ageyn,
Hath understonde what this faucon seyde,
And wel neigh for the routhe almoost she
        deyde.
And to the tree she gooth ful hastily,
And on this faukon looketh pitously,   440
And heeld hir lappe abroad, for wel she wiste
The faukon moste fallen fro the twiste,
Whan that it swowned next, for lak of blood.
A longe whil to wayten hire she stood
Til atte laste she spak in this manere   445
Unto the hauk, as ye shal after heere:
    "What is the cause, if it be for to telle,
That ye be in this furial pyne of helle?"
Quod Canacee unto this hauk above.
"Is this for sorwe of deeth or los of love?   450
For, as I trowe, thise been causes two
That causen moost a gentil herte wo;
Of oother harm it nedeth nat to speke.
For ye youreself upon yourself yow wreke,
Which proveth wel that outher ire or drede   455
Moot been enchesoun of youre cruel dede,
Syn that I see noon oother wight yow chace.
For love of God, as dooth youreselven grace,
Or what may been youre help? For west nor est
Ne saugh I nevere er now no bryd ne beest
That ferde with hymself so pitously.   461
Ye sle me with youre sorwe verraily,
I have of yow so greet compassioun.
For Goddes love, com fro the tree adoun;
And as I am a kynges doghter trewe,   465
If that I verraily the cause knewe
Of youre disese, if it lay in my myght,
I wolde amenden it er that it were nyght,
As wisly helpe me grete God of kynde!
And herbes shal I right ynowe yfynde   470
To heel with youre hurtes hastily."
    Tho shrighte this faucon yet moore pitously
Than ever she dide, and fil to grounde anon,
And lith aswowne, deed and lyk a stoon,
Til Canacee hath in hire lappe hire take   475
Unto the tyme she gan of swough awake.

435 **leden:** language
441 **heeld hir lappe abroad:** spread wide the skirt of her dress
442 **twiste:** branch
448 **furial pyne:** pain such as the Furies suffer
454 **wreke:** avenge
456 **enchesoun:** reason
458 **dooth youreselven grace:** spare yourself
467 **disese:** distress

And after that she of hir swough gan breyde,
Right in hir haukes ledene thus she seyde:
"That pitee renneth soone in gentil herte,
Feelynge his similitude in peynes smerte,   480
Is preved alday, as men may it see,
As wel by werk as by auctoritee;
For gentil herte kitheth gentillesse.
I se wel that ye han of my distresse
Compassion, my faire Canacee,   485
Of verray wommanly benignytee
That Nature in youre principles hath set.
But for noon hope for to fare the bet,
But for to obeye unto youre herte free,
And for to maken othere be war by me,   490
As by the whelp chasted is the leon,
Right for that cause and that conclusion,
Whil that I have a leyser and a space,
Myn harm I wol confessen er I pace."

And evere, whil that oon hir sorwe tolde,   495
That oother weep as she to water wolde,
Til that the faucon bad hire to be stille,
And, with a syk, right thus she seyde hir wille:

"Ther I was bred — allas, that ilke day! —
And fostred in a roche of marbul gray   500
So tendrely that no thyng eyled me,
I nyste nat what was adversitee,
Til I koude flee ful hye under the sky.
Tho dwelte a tercelet me faste by,
That semed welle of alle gentillesse;   505
Al were he ful of treson and falsnesse,
It was so wrapped under humble cheere,
And under hewe of trouthe in swich manere,
Under plesance, and under bisy peyne,
That no wight koude han wend he koude feyne,
So depe in greyn he dyed his coloures.   511
Right as a serpent hit hym under floures
Til he may seen his tyme for to byte,
Right so this god of loves ypocryte
Dooth so his cerymonyes and obeisaunces,   515
And kepeth in semblaunt alle his observaunces
That sownen into gentillesse of love.

As in a toumbe is al the faire above,
And under is the corps, swich as ye woot,
Swich was this ypocrite, bothe coold and hoot,
And in this wise he served his entente   521
That, save the feend, noon wiste what he
         mente,
Til he so longe hadde wopen and compleyned,
And many a yeer his service to me feyned,
Til that myn herte, to pitous and to nyce,   525
Al innocent of his crouned malice,
Forfered of his deeth, as thoughte me,
Upon his othes and his seuretee,
Graunted hym love, upon this condicioun,
That everemoore myn honour and renoun   530
Were saved, bothe privee and apert;
This is to seyn, that after his desert,
I yaf hym al myn herte and al my thoght —
God woot and he, that ootherwise noght —   534
And took his herte in chaunge of myn for ay.
But sooth is seyd, goon sithen many a day,
'A trewe wight and a theef thenken nat oon.'
And whan he saugh the thyng so fer ygoon
That I hadde graunted hym fully my love
In swich a gyse as I have seyd above,   540
And yeven hym my trewe herte as free
As he swoor he yaf his herte to me,
Anon this tigre, ful of doublenesse,
Fil on his knees with so devout humblesse,
With so heigh reverence, and, as by his cheere,
So lyk a gentil lovere of manere,   546
So ravysshed, as it semed, for the joye
That nevere Jason ne Parys of Troye —
Jason? certes, ne noon oother man
Syn Lameth was, that alderfirst bigan   550
To loven two, as writen folk biforn —
Ne nevere, syn the firste man was born,
Ne koude man, by twenty thousand part,
Countrefete the sophymes of his art,
Ne were worthy unbokelen his galoche,   555
Ther doublenesse or feynyng sholde approche,

---

477 **gan breyde:** started up
480 **similitude:** counterpart
482 **werk:** experience
483 **kitheth:** makes known
487 **principles:** natural disposition
491 **chasted:** chastised
493 **leyser:** leisure, time **space:** opportunity
500 **roche:** rock
501 **eyled:** troubled
503 **flee:** fly
504 **tercelet:** male falcon
511 So deeply in a fast dye (*in greyn*) he disguised (*dyed his coloures*) his true feelings
512 **hit hym** = *hideth hym*, hides himself
514 **ypocryte:** hypocrite
516 **semblaunt:** outward appearance

523 **wopen:** wept
525 **nyce:** foolish
526 **crouned:** sovereign, consummate
527 **Forfered of his deeth:** very frightened that he might die (for love)
531 **privee and apert:** in private and in public, in all circumstances
534 **ootherwise noght:** on any other terms (I would) not at all (have agreed)
543 **doublenesse:** duplicity
548 **Jason:** Jason deserted Medea (see LGW 1580–1679) **Parys:** Paris deserted the nymph Oënone for Helen (see Tr I.652–56)
550 **Lameth:** the biblical Lamech, the first bigamist **alderfirst:** first of all
554 **sophymes:** sophisms, deceitful arguments
555 **unbokelen his galoche:** unbuckle his sandal
556 **approche:** be concerned

Ne so koude thonke a wight as he dide me!
His manere was an hevene for to see
Til any womman, were she never so wys,
So peynted he and kembde at point-devys   560
As wel his wordes as his contenaunce.
And I so loved hym for his obeisaunce,
And for the trouthe I demed in his herte,
That if so were that any thyng hym smerte,
Al were it never so lite, and I it wiste,   565
Me thoughte I felte deeth myn herte twiste.
And shortly, so ferforth this thyng is went
That my wyl was his willes instrument;
This is to seyn, my wyl obeyed his wyl
In alle thyng, as fer as reson fil,   570
Kepynge the boundes of my worshipe evere.
Ne nevere hadde I thyng so lief, ne levere,
As hym, God woot, ne nevere shal namo.

   "This laste lenger than a yeer or two,
That I supposed of hym noght but good.   575
But finally, thus atte laste it stood,
That Fortune wolde that he moste twynne
Out of that place which that I was inne.
Wher me was wo, that is no questioun;
I kan nat make of it discripsioun.   580
For o thyng dar I tellen boldely:
I knowe what is the peyne of deeth therby;
Swich harm I felte for he ne myghte bileve.
So on a day of me he took his leve,
So sorwefully eek that I wende verraily   585
That he had felt as muche harm as I,
Whan that I herde hym speke and saugh his
     hewe.
But nathelees, I thoughte he was so trewe,
And eek that he repaire sholde ageyn
Withinne a litel while, sooth to seyn;   590
And resoun wolde eek that he moste go
For his honour, as ofte it happeth so,
That I made vertu of necessitee,
And took it wel, syn that it moste be.   594
As I best myghte, I hidde fro hym my sorwe,
And took hym by the hond, Seint John to
     borwe,
And seyde hym thus: 'Lo, I am youres al;
Beth swich as I to yow have been and shal.'
What he answerde, it nedeth noght reherce;

Who kan sey bet than he, who kan do
     werse?   600
Whan he hath al wel seyd, thanne hath he doon.
'Therfore bihoveth hire a ful long spoon
That shal ete with a feend,' thus herde I seye.
So atte laste he moste forth his weye,   604
And forth he fleeth til he cam ther hym leste.
Whan it cam hym to purpos for to reste,
I trowe he hadde thilke text in mynde,
That 'alle thyng, repeirynge to his kynde,
Gladeth hymself;' thus seyn men, as I gesse.
Men loven of propre kynde newefangelnesse,
As briddes doon that men in cages fede.   611
For though thou nyght and day take of hem
     hede,
And strawe hir cage faire and softe as silk,
And yeve hem sugre, hony, breed and milk,
Yet right anon as that his dore is uppe   615
He with his feet wol spurne adoun his cuppe,
And to the wode he wole and wormes ete;
So newefangel been they of hire mete,
And loven novelries of propre kynde,
No gentillesse of blood ne may hem bynde.

   "So ferde this tercelet, allas the day!   621
Though he were gentil born, and fressh and
     gay,
And goodlich for to seen, and humble and free,
He saugh upon a tyme a kyte flee,
And sodeynly he loved this kyte so   625
That al his love is clene fro me ago,
And hath his trouthe falsed in this wyse.
Thus hath the kyte my love in hire servyse,
And I am lorn withouten remedie!"
And with that word this faucon gan to crie
And swowned eft in Canacees barm.   631

   Greet was the sorwe for the haukes harm
That Canacee and alle hir wommen made;
They nyste hou they myghte the faucon glade.
But Canacee hom bereth hire in hir lappe,   635
And softely in plastres gan hire wrappe,
Ther as she with hire beek hadde hurt hirselve.
Now kan nat Canacee but herbes delve
Out of the ground, and make salves newe
Of herbes preciouse and fyne of hewe   640
To heelen with this hauk. Fro day to nyght

---

560 **peynted:** painted, disguised **kembde:** arranged (literally
combed) **at point-devys:** in every detail, perfectly
566 **twiste:** twist, wring
571 **worshipe:** honor
572 I never loved anything more, or even as much
573 **namo:** no more, never again
574 **laste:** lasted
577 **twynne:** depart
579 **Wher:** whether
583 **bileve:** remain
589 **repaire:** return
596 **Seint John to borwe:** with St. John as my guarantor

602 **bihoveth hire:** it behooves her, she needs
605 **fleeth:** flies
607 **thilke text:** Boece 3 m2.39–42.
610 **of propre kynde:** by nature **newefangelnesse:** novelty
615 **right anon as:** as soon as **uppe:** up, open
616 **spurne:** kick
618 **newefangel:** fond of novelty
619 **novelries:** novelties
624 **kyte:** kite, a scavenger bird
631 **eft:** immediately **barm:** lap
636 **plastres:** bandages

She dooth hire bisynesse and al hire myght,
And by hire beddes heed she made a mewe
And covered it with veluettes blewe,　　644
In signe of trouthe that is in wommen sene.
And al withoute, the mewe is peynted grene,
In which were peynted alle thise false fowles,
As ben thise tidyves, tercelettes, and owles;
Right for despit were peynted hem bisyde,
Pyes, on hem for to crie and chyde.　　650

　　Thus lete I Canacee hir hauk kepyng;
I wol namoore as now speke of hir ryng
Til it come eft to purpos for to seyn
How that this faucon gat hire love ageyn
Repentant, as the storie telleth us,　　655
By mediacion of Cambalus,
The kynges sone, of which I yow tolde.
But hennesforth I wol my proces holde
To speken of aventures and of batailles
That nevere yet was herd so grete mervailles.

　　First wol I telle yow of Cambyuskan,　　661
That in his tyme many a citee wan;
And after wol I speke of Algarsif,
How that he wan Theodora to his wif,
For whom ful ofte in greet peril he was,　　665
Ne hadde he ben holpen by the steede of bras;
And after wol I speke of Cambalo,
That faught in lystes with the bretheren two
For Canacee er that he myghte hire wynne.
And ther I lefte I wol ayeyn bigynne.　　670

　　　　Explicit secunda pars.

　　　　Incipit pars tercia.

Appollo whirleth up his chaar so hye
Til that the god Mercurius hous, the slye —

　　　　　·　　·　　·

　　*Heere folwen the wordes of the
　　Frankeleyn to the Squier, and the
　　wordes of the Hoost to the
　　Frankeleyn.*

"In feith, Squier, thow hast thee wel yquit
And gentilly. I preise wel thy wit,"　　674
Quod the Frankeleyn, "considerynge thy
　　　　yowthe,
So feelyngly thou spekest, sire, I allow the!
As to my doom, ther is noon that is heere
Of eloquence that shal be thy peere,
If that thou lyve; God yeve thee good chaunce,
And in vertu sende thee continuaunce,　　680
For of thy speche I have greet deyntee.
I have a sone, and by the Trinitee,
I hadde levere than twenty pound worth lond,
Though it right now were fallen in myn hond,
He were a man of swich discrecioun　　685
As that ye been! Fy on possessioun,
But if a man be vertuous withal!
I have my sone snybbed, and yet shal,
For he to vertu listeth nat entende;
But for to pleye at dees, and to despende　　690
And lese al that he hath is his usage.
And he hath levere talken with a page
Than to comune with any gentil wight
Where he myghte lerne gentillesse aright."
　　"Straw for youre gentillesse!" quod oure
　　　　Hoost.　　695
"What, Frankeleyn! Pardee, sire, wel thou
　　　　woost
That ech of yow moot tellen atte leste
A tale or two, or breken his biheste."
　　"That knowe I wel, sire," quod the Frank-
　　　　eleyn.
"I prey yow, haveth me nat in desdeyn,　　700
Though to this man I speke a word or two."
　　"Telle on thy tale withouten wordes mo."
　　"Gladly, sire Hoost," quod he, "I wole obeye
Unto your wyl; now herkneth what I seye.
I wol yow nat contrarien in no wyse　　705
As fer as that my wittes wol suffyse.
I prey to God that it may plesen yow;
Thanne woot I wel that it is good ynow."

---

643 **mewe:** pen
644 **veluettes:** velvet cloths
648 **tidyves:** small birds (cf. LGW 154)　**tercelettes:** male falcons
650 **Pyes:** magpies, chatterers
Explicit, *etc.*: Here ends the second part.
Incipit, *etc.*: Here begins the third part.
671 **chaar:** chariot

673 **thee wel yquit:** conducted yourself well
676 **So feelyngly:** with such delicate understanding　**allow:** praise
677 **As to my doom:** in my judgment
680 **continuaunce:** perseverance
681 **have greet deyntee:** take great pleasure
683 **twenty pound worth lond:** land yielding an annual income of twenty pounds
687 **vertuous:** accomplished, able　**withal:** also
688 **snybbed:** rebuked
692 **page:** servant boy
693 **comune:** have conversation with
698 **breken his biheste:** break his promise

THE FRANKLIN'S PROLOGUE

The Prologe of the Frankeleyns Tale.

Thise olde gentil Britouns in hir dayes
Of diverse aventures maden layes, 710
Rymeyed in hir firste Briton tonge,
Whiche layes with hir instrumentz they
  songe
Or elles redden hem for hir plesaunce;
And oon of hem have I in remembraunce,
Which I shal seyn with good wyl as I kan. 715
  But, sires, by cause I am a burel man,
At my bigynnyng first I yow biseche,
Have me excused of my rude speche.

I lerned nevere rethorik, certeyn;
Thyng that I speke, it moot be bare and
  pleyn. 720
I sleep nevere on the Mount of Pernaso,
Ne lerned Marcus Tullius Scithero.
Colours ne knowe I none, withouten drede,
But swiche colours as growen in the mede,
Or elles swiche as men dye or peynte. 725
Colours of rethoryk been to me queynte;
My spirit feeleth noght of swich mateere.
But if yow list, my tale shul ye heere.

THE FRANKLIN'S TALE

Here bigynneth the Frankeleyns Tale.

In Armorik, that called is Britayne,
Ther was a knyght that loved and dide his
  payne 730
To serve a lady in his beste wise;
And many a labour, many a greet emprise,
He for his lady wroghte er she were wonne.
For she was oon the faireste under sonne,
And eek therto comen of so heigh kynrede 735
That wel unnethes dorste this knyght, for
  drede,
Telle hire his wo, his peyne, and his distresse.
But atte laste she, for his worthynesse,
And namely for his meke obeysaunce,
Hath swich a pitee caught of his penaunce
That pryvely she fil of his accord 741
To take hym for hir housbonde and hir lord,

Of swich lordshipe as men han over hir wyves.
And for to lede the moore in blisse hir lyves,
Of his free wyl he swoor hire as a knyght 745
That nevere in al his lyf he, day ne nyght,
Ne sholde upon hym take no maistrie
Agayn hir wyl, ne kithe hire jalousie,
But hire obeye, and folwe hir wyl in al,
As any lovere to his lady shal, 750
Save that the name of soveraynetee,
That wolde he have for shame of his degree.
  She thanked hym, and with ful greet hum-
  blesse
She seyde, "Sire, sith of youre gentillesse
Ye profre me to have so large a reyne, 755
Ne wolde nevere God bitwixe us tweyne,

---

709 **Britouns:** Bretons
710 **layes:** Breton lays, brief romances; see n.
711 **Rymeyed:** rhymed, versified
716 **burel man:** unlearned man, layman

---

729 **Armorik:** Armorica, ancient name of coastal Brittany
732 **emprise:** chivalric exploit
734 **oon the faireste:** the fairest of all
740 **penaunce:** distress, suffering

---

721 **Pernaso:** Mt. Parnassus, sacred to the muses
722 **Marcus Tullius Scithero:** Cicero, author of authoritative works on rhetoric
723 **Colours:** rhetorical ornaments

---

748 **kithe:** show
752 **for shame of his degree:** in order not to bring shame on his status
755 **so large a reyne:** so loose a rein, such freedom from restraint

As in my gilt, were outher werre or stryf.
Sire, I wol be youre humble trewe wyf —
Have heer my trouthe — til that myn herte
        breste."
Thus been they bothe in quiete and in reste.

    For o thyng, sires, saufly dar I seye,   761
That freendes everych oother moot obeye,
If they wol longe holden compaignye.
Love wol nat been constreyned by maistrye.
Whan maistrie comth, the God of Love anon
Beteth his wynges, and farewel, he is gon!   766
Love is a thyng as any spirit free.
Wommen, of kynde, desiren libertee,
And nat to been constreyned as a thral;
And so doon men, if I sooth seyen shal.   770
Looke who that is moost pacient in love,
He is at his avantage al above.
Pacience is an heigh vertu, certeyn,
For it venquysseth, as thise clerkes seyn,
Thynges that rigour sholde nevere atteyne.   775
For every word men may nat chide or pleyne.
Lerneth to suffre, or elles, so moot I goon,
Ye shul it lerne, wher so ye wole or noon;
For in this world, certein, ther no wight is
That he ne dooth or seith somtyme amys.   780
Ire, siknesse, or constellacioun,
Wyn, wo, or chaungynge of complexioun
Causeth ful ofte to doon amys or speken.
On every wrong a man may nat be wreken.
After the tyme moste be temperaunce   785
To every wight that kan on governaunce.
And therfore hath this wise, worthy knyght,
To lyve in ese, suffrance hire bihight,
And she to hym ful wisly gan to swere   789
That nevere sholde ther be defaute in here.

    Heere may men seen an humble, wys accord;
Thus hath she take hir servant and hir lord —
Servant in love, and lord in mariage.
Thanne was he bothe in lordshipe and servage.
Servage? Nay, but in lordshipe above,   795
Sith he hath bothe his lady and his love;
His lady, certes, and his wyf also,
The which that lawe of love acordeth to.
And whan he was in this prosperitee,   799
Hoom with his wyf he gooth to his contree,

757 **As in my gilt:** through my fault
761 **saufly:** confidently
769 **thral:** servant, slave
772 **at his avantage:** in the best position   **above:** superior
782 **complexioun:** temperament, balance of the humors in one's
body
785 **After the tyme:** according to the time, occasion
786 **kan on:** knows about
788 **suffrance:** patience, forbearance   **bihight:** promised
790 **defaute:** flaw
795 **above:** superior

Nat fer fro Pedmark, ther his dwellyng was,
Where as he lyveth in blisse and in solas.

    Who koude telle, but he hadde wedded be,
The joye, the ese, and the prosperitee
That is bitwixe an housbonde and his wyf?
A yeer and moore lasted this blisful lyf,   806
Til that the knyght of which I speke of thus,
That of Kayrrud was cleped Arveragus,
Shoop hym to goon and dwelle a yeer or tweyne
In Engelond, that cleped was eek Briteyne,
To seke in armes worshipe and honour —   811
For al his lust he sette in swich labour —
And dwelled there two yeer; the book seith
        thus.
    Now wol I stynten of this Arveragus,
And speken I wole of Dorigen his wyf,   815
That loveth hire housbonde as hire hertes lyf.
For his absence wepeth she and siketh,
As doon thise noble wyves whan hem liketh.
She moorneth, waketh, wayleth, fasteth,
        pleyneth;
Desir of his presence hire so destreyneth   820
That al this wyde world she sette at noght.
Hire freendes, whiche that knewe hir hevy
        thoght,
Conforten hire in al that ever they may.
They prechen hire, they telle hire nyght and
        day
That causelees she sleeth hirself, allas!   825
And every confort possible in this cas
They doon to hire with al hire bisynesse,
Al for to make hire leve hire hevynesse.

    By proces, as ye knowen everichoon,
Men may so longe graven in a stoon   830
Til som figure therinne emprented be.
So longe han they conforted hire til she
Receyved hath, by hope and by resoun,
The emprentyng of hire consolacioun,
Thurgh which hir grete sorwe gan aswage;   835
She may nat alwey duren in swich rage.

    And eek Arveragus, in al this care,
Hath sent hire lettres hoom of his welfare,
And that he wol come hastily agayn;
Or elles hadde this sorwe hir herte slayn.   840
    Hire freendes sawe hir sorwe gan to slake
And preyde hire on knees, for Goddes sake,
To come and romen hire in compaignye,

811 **worshipe:** good reputation
820 **destreyneth:** afflicts, presses upon
821 **sette at noght:** reckoned as worth nothing
822 **hevy:** gloomy
834 **emprentyng:** impression
836 **duren:** continue   **rage:** passionate grief

Awey to dryve hire derke fantasye.
And finally she graunted that requeste,   845
For wel she saugh that it was for the beste.

Now stood hire castel faste by the see,
And often with hire freendes walketh shee
Hire to disporte upon the bank an heigh,
Where as she many a ship and barge seigh
Seillynge hir cours, where as hem liste go.   851
But thanne was that a parcel of hire wo,
For to hirself ful ofte, "Allas!" seith she,
"Is ther no ship, of so manye as I se,
Wol bryngen hom my lord? Thanne were myn
     herte   855
Al warisshed of his bittre peynes smerte."
     Another tyme ther wolde she sitte and
          thynke,
And caste hir eyen dounward fro the brynke.
But whan she saugh the grisly rokkes blake,
For verray feere so wolde hir herte quake   860
That on hire feet she myghte hire noght sus-
     tene.
Thanne wolde she sitte adoun upon the grene,
And pitously into the see biholde,
And seyn right thus, with sorweful sikes colde:
     "Eterne God, that thurgh thy purveiaunce
Ledest the world by certein governaunce,   866
In ydel, as men seyn, ye no thyng make.
But, Lord, thise grisly feendly rokkes blake,
That semen rather a foul confusion
Of werk than any fair creacion   870
Of swich a parfit wys God and a stable,
Why han ye wroght this werk unresonable?
For by this werk, south, north, ne west, ne eest,
Ther nys yfostred man, ne bryd, ne beest;
It dooth no good, to my wit, but anoyeth.   875
Se ye nat, Lord, how mankynde it destroyeth?
An hundred thousand bodyes of mankynde
Han rokkes slayn, al be they nat in mynde,
Which mankynde is so fair part of thy werk
That thou it madest lyk to thyn owene merk.
Thanne semed it ye hadde a greet chiertee   881
Toward mankynde; but how thanne may it bee
That ye swiche meenes make it to destroyen,
Whiche meenes do no good, but evere anoyen?

I woot wel clerkes wol seyn as hem leste,   885
By argumentz, that al is for the beste,
Though I ne kan the causes nat yknowe.
But thilke God that made wynd to blowe
As kepe my lord! This my conclusion.
To clerkes lete I al disputison.   890
But wolde God that alle thise rokkes blake
Were sonken into helle for his sake!
Thise rokkes sleen myn herte for the feere."
Thus wolde she seyn, with many a pitous teere.

     Hire freendes sawe that it was no disport
To romen by the see, but disconfort,   896
And shopen for to pleyen somwher elles.
They leden hire by ryveres and by welles,
And eek in othere places delitables;
They dauncen and they pleyen at ches and
     tables.   900
     So on a day, right in the morwe-tyde,
Unto a gardyn that was ther bisyde,
In which that they hadde maad hir ordinaunce
Of vitaille and of oother purveiaunce,
They goon and pleye hem al the longe day.
And this was on the sixte morwe of May,   906
Which May hadde peynted with his softe
     shoures
This gardyn ful of leves and of floures;
And craft of mannes hand so curiously
Arrayed hadde this gardyn, trewely,   910
That nevere was ther gardyn of swich prys
But if it were the verray paradys.
The odour of floures and the fresshe sighte
Wolde han maked any herte lighte
That evere was born, but if to greet siknesse
Or to greet sorwe helde it in distresse,   916
So ful it was of beautee with plesaunce.
At after-dyner gonne they to daunce,
And synge also, save Dorigen allone,
Which made alwey hir compleint and hir
     moone,   920
For she ne saugh hym on the daunce go
That was hir housbonde and hir love also.
But nathelees she moste a tyme abyde
And with good hope lete hir sorwe slyde.
     Upon this daunce, amonges othere men,   925
Daunced a squier biforn Dorigen,

---

844 **fantasye:** imaginings
850 **barge:** sailing vessel
852 **parcel:** portion
856 **warisshed:** cured
865 **purveiaunce:** providence
867 **In ydel:** in vain
869 **confusion:** chaos
874 **nys yfostred:** is not supported (i.e., benefited)
880 **merk:** image
881 **chiertee:** love
884 **anoyen:** cause trouble

886 **argumentz:** logical reasoning
889 **conclusion:** conclusion, inference derived from logical argumentation
890 **disputison:** logical disputation
892 **sonken:** sunk
899 **delitables:** delightful
900 **tables:** backgammon
909 **curiously:** skillfully
924 **slyde:** slip away
926 **squier:** young knight

That fressher was and jolyer of array,
As to my doom, than is the month of May.
He syngeth, daunceth, passynge any man
That is, or was, sith that the world bigan.   930
Therwith he was, if men sholde hym discryve,
Oon of the beste farynge man on lyve;
Yong, strong, right vertuous, and riche, and
    wys,
And wel biloved, and holden in greet prys.
And shortly, if the sothe I tellen shal,   935
Unwityng of this Dorigen at al,
This lusty squier, servant to Venus,
Which that ycleped was Aurelius,
Hadde loved hire best of any creature
Two yeer and moore, as was his aventure,   940
But nevere dorste he tellen hire his grevaunce.
Withouten coppe he drank al his penaunce.
He was despeyred; no thyng dorste he seye,
Save in his songes somwhat wolde he wreye
His wo, as in a general compleynyng;   945
He seyde he lovede and was biloved no thyng.
Of swich matere made he manye layes,
Songes, compleintes, roundels, virelayes,
How that he dorste nat his sorwe telle,   949
But langwissheth as a furye dooth in helle;
And dye he moste, he seyde, as dide Ekko
For Narcisus, that dorste nat telle hir wo.
In oother manere than ye heere me seye,
Ne dorste he nat to hire his wo biwreye,   954
Save that, paraventure, somtyme at daunces,
Ther yonge folk kepen hir observaunces,
It may wel be he looked on hir face
In swich a wise as man that asketh grace;
But nothyng wiste she of his entente.
Nathelees it happed, er they thennes wente,
By cause that he was hire neighebour,   961
And was a man of worshipe and honour,
And hadde yknowen hym of tyme yoore,
They fille in speche; and forth, moore and
    moore,
Unto his purpos drough Aurelius,   965
And whan he saugh his tyme, he seyde thus:
   "Madame," quod he, "by God that this world
    made,

So that I wiste it myghte youre herte glade,
I wolde that day that youre Arveragus
Wente over the see, that I, Aurelius,   970
Hadde went ther nevere I sholde have come
    agayn.
For wel I woot my servyce is in vayn;
My gerdon is but brestyng of myn herte.
Madame, reweth upon my peynes smerte;
For with a word ye may me sleen or save.   975
Heere at youre feet God wolde that I were
    grave!
I ne have as now no leyser moore to seye;
Have mercy, sweete, or ye wol do me deye!"
   She gan to looke upon Aurelius;   979
"Is this youre wyl," quod she, "and sey ye thus?
Nevere erst," quod she, "ne wiste I what ye
    mente.
But now, Aurelie, I knowe youre entente,
By thilke God that yaf me soule and lyf,
Ne shal I nevere been untrewe wyf
In word ne werk, as fer as I have wit;   985
I wol been his to whom that I am knyt.
Taak this for fynal answere as of me."
But after that in pley thus seyde she:
   "Aurelie," quod she, "by heighe God above,
Yet wolde I graunte yow to been youre love,
Syn I yow se so pitously complayne.   991
Looke what day that endelong Britayne
Ye remoeve alle the rokkes, stoon by stoon,
That they ne lette ship ne boot to goon —
I seye, whan ye han maad the coost so clene
Of rokkes that ther nys no stoon ysene,   996
Thanne wol I love yow best of any man;
Have heer my trouthe, in al that evere I kan."
   "Is ther noon oother grace in yow?" quod he.
   "No, by that Lord," quod she, "that maked
    me!   1000
For wel I woot that it shal never bityde.
Lat swiche folies out of youre herte slyde.
What deyntee sholde a man han in his lyf
For to go love another mannes wyf,
That hath hir body whan so that hym liketh?"
   Aurelius ful ofte soore siketh;   1006
Wo was Aurelie whan that he this herde,
And with a sorweful herte he thus answerde:
   "Madame," quod he, "this were an inpos-
    sible!
Thanne moot I dye of sodeyn deth horrible."
And with that word he turned hym anon.   1011

932 **beste farynge**: most handsome
936 **Unwityng of**: unknown to
942 He suffered intensely; see n.
944 **wreye**: reveal
947 **layes**: songs, brief poems
948 **compleintes**: poems lamenting misfortune in love; see the
Short Poems for examples. **roundels**: brief poems or songs with
refrains; see PF 680–92 for an example **virelayes**: a form of the
roundel
951 **Ekko**: Echo, the nymph who loved Narcissus (*Narcisus*); see
Rom 1469–1538.
956 **observaunces**: customs (of courtship)
962 **worshipe**: good reputation

973 **gerdon**: reward, requital
991 **complayne**: lament
994 **lette**: prevent
1009 **an inpossible**: an impossibility

Tho coome hir othere freendes many oon,
And in the aleyes romeden up and doun,
And nothyng wiste of this conclusioun,
But sodeynly bigonne revel newe   1015
Til that the brighte sonne loste his hewe;
For th'orisonte hath reft the sonne his lyght —
This is as muche to seye as it was nyght —
And hoom they goon in joye and in solas,
Save oonly wrecche Aurelius, allas!   1020
He to his hous is goon with sorweful herte.
He seeth he may nat fro his deeth asterte;
Hym semed that he felte his herte colde.
Up to the hevene his handes he gan holde,
And on his knowes bare he sette hym doun,
And in his ravyng seyde his orisoun.   1026
For verray wo out of his wit he breyde.
He nyste what he spak, but thus he seyde;
With pitous herte his pleynt hath he bigonne
Unto the goddes, and first unto the sonne: 1030

  He seyde, "Appollo, god and governour
Of every plaunte, herbe, tree, and flour,
That yevest, after thy declinacion,
To ech of hem his tyme and his seson,
As thyn herberwe chaungeth lowe or heighe,
Lord Phebus, cast thy merciable eighe   1036
On wrecche Aurelie, which that am but lorn.
Lo, lord! My lady hath my deeth ysworn
Withoute gilt, but thy benignytee
Upon my dedly herte have som pitee.   1040
For wel I woot, lord Phebus, if yow lest,
Ye may me helpen, save my lady, best.
Now voucheth sauf that I may yow devyse
How that I may been holpen and in what wyse.

  "Youre blisful suster, Lucina the sheene,   1045
That of the see is chief goddesse and queene
(Though Neptunus have deitee in the see,
Yet emperisse aboven hym is she),
Ye knowen wel, lord, that right as hir desir
Is to be quyked and lighted of youre fir,   1050
For which she folweth yow ful bisily,
Right so the see desireth naturelly
To folwen hire, as she that is goddesse
Bothe in the see and ryveres moore and lesse.
Wherfore, lord Phebus, this is my requeste —

Do this miracle, or do myn herte breste —   1056
That now next at this opposicion
Which in the signe shal be of the Leon,
As preieth hire so greet a flood to brynge   1059
That fyve fadme at the leeste it oversprynge
The hyeste rokke in Armorik Briteyne;
And lat this flood endure yeres tweyne.
Thanne certes to my lady may I seye,
'Holdeth youre heste, the rokkes been aweye.'

  "Lord Phebus, dooth this miracle for me.   1065
Preye hire she go no faster cours than ye;
I seye, preyeth your suster that she go
No faster cours than ye thise yeres two.
Thanne shal she been evene atte fulle alway,
And spryng flood laste bothe nyght and day.
And but she vouche sauf in swich manere   1071
To graunte me my sovereyn lady deere,
Prey hire to synken every rok adoun
Into hir owene dirke regioun
Under the ground, ther Pluto dwelleth inne,
Or nevere mo shal I my lady wynne.   1076
Thy temple in Delphos wol I barefoot seke.
Lord Phebus, se the teeris on my cheke,
And of my peyne have som compassioun."
And with that word in swowne he fil adoun,
And longe tyme he lay forth in a traunce.   1081

  His brother, which that knew of his pen-
       aunce,
Up caughte hym and to bedde he hath hym
       broght.
Dispeyred in this torment and this thoght
Lete I this woful creature lye;   1085
Chese he, for me, wheither he wol lyve or dye.

  Arveragus, with heele and greet honour,
As he that was of chivalrie the flour,
Is comen hoom, and othere worthy men.
O blisful artow now, thou Dorigen,   1090
That hast thy lusty housbonde in thyne armes,
The fresshe knyght, the worthy man of armes,
That loveth thee as his owene hertes lyf.
No thyng list hym to been ymaginatyf,
If any wight hadde spoke, whil he was oute,
To hire of love; he hadde of it no doute.   1096
He noght entendeth to no swich mateere,

1013 **aleyes:** garden paths
1017 **reft:** taken away
1025 **knowes:** knees
1033 **after thy declinacion:** according to your angular distance from the celestial equator (i.e., the height of the sun in each season); see n.
1035 **herberwe:** (astrological) house, position in the zodiac
1036 **Phebus:** Phoebus Apollo, the sun
1040 **dedly:** dying
1045 **Lucina:** goddess of the moon
1047 **Neptunus:** Neptune **deitee:** divine power
1050 **quyked:** kindled

1057 **opposicion:** the position of the sun and moon when they are directly opposite one another, a time of the highest tides; see n.
1058 **Leon:** the zodiacal sign Leo
1060 **fadme:** fathoms **oversprynge:** rise above
1064 **Holdeth youre heste:** keep your promise
1066 **go no faster cours:** go at the same speed
1069 **evene atte fulle:** fully even (with you), in exact opposition
1075 **Pluto:** god of the underworld
1077 **Delphos:** Delphi, in Greece
1080 **swowne:** faint
1087 **heele:** well-being
1094 **ymaginatyf:** suspicious

But daunceth, justeth, maketh hire good
    cheere;
And thus in joye and blisse I lete hem dwelle,
And of the sike Aurelius wol I telle.   1100
  In langour and in torment furyus
Two yeer and moore lay wrecche Aurelyus,
Er any foot he myghte on erthe gon;
Ne confort in this tyme hadde he noon,
Save of his brother, which that was a clerk.
He knew of al this wo and al this werk,   1106
For to noon oother creature, certeyn,
Of this matere he dorste no word seyn.
Under his brest he baar it moore secree
Than evere dide Pamphilus for Galathee.   1110
His brest was hool, withoute for to sene,
But in his herte ay was the arwe kene.
And wel ye knowe that of a sursanure
In surgerye is perilous the cure,
But men myghte touche the arwe or come
    therby.   1115
His brother weep and wayled pryvely,
Til atte laste hym fil in remembraunce,
That whiles he was at Orliens in Fraunce —
As yonge clerkes that been lykerous
To reden artes that been curious   1120
Seken in every halke and every herne
Particuler sciences for to lerne —
He hym remembred that, upon a day,
At Orliens in studie a book he say
Of magyk natureel, which his felawe,   1125
That was that tyme a bacheler of lawe,
Al were he ther to lerne another craft,
Hadde prively upon his desk ylaft;
Which book spak muchel of the operaciouns
Touchynge the eighte and twenty mansiouns
That longen to the moone, and swich folye
As in oure dayes is nat worth a flye —   1132
For hooly chirches feith in oure bileve
Ne suffreth noon illusioun us to greve.
And whan this book was in his remembraunce,
Anon for joye his herte gan to daunce,   1136
And to hymself he seyde pryvely:
"My brother shal be warisshed hastily;
For I am siker that ther be sciences   1139

By whiche men make diverse apparences,
Swiche as thise subtile tregetoures pleye.
For ofte at feestes have I wel herd seye
That tregetours withinne an halle large
Have maad come in a water and a barge,
And in the halle rowen up and doun.   1145
Somtyme hath semed come a grym leoun;
And somtyme floures sprynge as in a mede;
Somtyme a vyne, and grapes white and rede;
Somtyme a castel, al of lym and stoon;
And whan hem lyked, voyded it anon.   1150
Thus semed it to every mannes sighte.
  Now thanne conclude I thus: that if I myghte
At Orliens som oold felawe yfynde
That hadde thise moones mansions in mynde,
Or oother magyk natureel above,   1155
He sholde wel make my brother han his love.
For with an apparence a clerk may make,
To mannes sighte, that alle the rokkes blake
Of Britaigne weren yvoyded everichon,   1159
And shippes by the brynke comen and gon,
And in swich forme enduren a wowke or two.
Thanne were my brother warisshed of his wo;
Thanne moste she nedes holden hire biheste,
Or elles he shal shame hire atte leeste."
  What sholde I make a lenger tale of this?
Unto his brotheres bed he comen is,   1166
And swich confort he yaf hym for to gon
To Orliens that he up stirte anon,
And on his wey forthward thanne is he fare
In hope for to been lissed of his care.   1170
  Whan they were come almoost to that citee,
But if it were a two furlong or thre,
A yong clerk romynge by hymself they mette,
Which that in Latyn thriftily hem grette,
And after that he seyde a wonder thyng: 1175
"I knowe," quod he, "the cause of youre com-
    yng."
And er they ferther any foote wente,
He tolde hem al that was in hire entente.
  This Briton clerk hym asked of felawes   1179
The whiche that he had knowe in olde dawes,
And he answerde hym that they dede were,
For which he weep ful ofte many a teere.
  Doun of his hors Aurelius lighte anon,
And with this magicien forth is he gon   1184

1101 **langour:** suffering **furyus:** like that of the furies in Hell
1110 **Pamphilus, Galathee:** lovers in the thirteenth-century poem *Pamphilus de Amore*
1113 **sursanure:** wound healed only on the surface
1118 **Orliens:** Orleans
1119 **lykerous:** eager
1120 **curious:** arcane
1121 **every halke and every herne:** every nook and cranny
1122 **Particuler sciences:** specialized branches of learning
1124 **in studie:** in a study hall **say:** saw
1125 **magyk natureel:** natural science
1130 **mansiouns:** stations of the moon; see n.

1140 **apparences:** illusions
1141 **tregetoures:** illusionists, magicians
1149 **lym:** lime (mortar)
1150 **voyded:** caused it to disappear
1155 **above:** in addition to
1161 **wowke:** week
1162 **warisshed:** cured
1170 **lissed:** relieved
1174 **thriftily:** suitably, politely

Hoom to his hous, and maden hem wel at ese.
Hem lakked no vitaille that myghte hem plese.
So wel arrayed hous as ther was oon
Aurelius in his lyf saugh nevere noon.

He shewed hym, er he wente to sopeer,
Forestes, parkes ful of wilde deer;   1190
Ther saugh he hertes with hir hornes hye,
The gretteste that evere were seyn with ye.
He saugh of hem an hondred slayn with
          houndes,
And somme with arwes blede of bittre
          woundes.
He saugh, whan voyded were thise wilde deer,
Thise fauconers upon a fair ryver,   1196
That with hir haukes han the heron slayn.

Tho saugh he knyghtes justyng in a playn;
And after this he dide hym swich plesaunce
That he hym shewed his lady on a daunce,
On which hymself he daunced, as hym
          thoughte.   1201
And whan this maister that this magyk
          wroughte
Saugh it was tyme, he clapte his handes two,
And farewel! Al oure revel was ago.   1204
And yet remoeved they nevere out of the hous,
Whil they saugh al this sighte merveillous,
But in his studie, ther as his bookes be,
They seten stille, and no wight but they thre.

To hym this maister called his squier,
And seyde hym thus: "Is redy oure soper?
Almoost an houre it is, I undertake,   1211
Sith I yow bad oure soper for to make,
Whan that thise worthy men wenten with me
Into my studie, ther as my bookes be."

"Sire," quod this squier, "whan it liketh yow,
It is al redy, though ye wol right now."   1216
"Go we thanne soupe," quod he, "as for the
          beste.
Thise amorous folk somtyme moote han hir
          reste."

At after-soper fille they in tretee
What somme sholde this maistres gerdon be
To remoeven alle the rokkes of Britayne,   1221
And eek from Gerounde to the mouth of Sayne.

He made it straunge, and swoor, so God hym
          save,
Lasse than a thousand pound he wolde nat
          have,
Ne gladly for that somme he wolde nat goon.

Aurelius, with blisful herte anoon,   1226
Answerde thus: "Fy on a thousand pound!
This wyde world, which that men seye is
          round,
I wolde it yeve, if I were lord of it.
This bargayn is ful dryve, for we been knyt.
Ye shal be payed trewely, by my trouthe!   1231
But looketh now, for no necligence or slouthe
Ye tarie us heere no lenger than to-morwe."
"Nay," quod this clerk, "have heer my feith
          to borwe."   1234
To bedde is goon Aurelius whan hym leste,
And wel ny al that nyght he hadde his reste.
What for his labour and his hope of blisse,
His woful herte of penaunce hadde a lisse.

Upon the morwe, whan that it was day,
To Britaigne tooke they the righte way,   1240
Aurelius and this magicien bisyde,
And been descended ther they wolde abyde.
And this was, as thise bookes me remembre,
The colde, frosty seson of Decembre.

Phebus wax old, and hewed lyk laton,   1245
That in his hoote declynacion
Shoon as the burned gold with stremes brighte;
But now in Capricorn adoun he lighte,
Where as he shoon ful pale, I dar wel seyn.
The bittre frostes, with the sleet and reyn,   1250
Destroyed hath the grene in every yerd.
Janus sit by the fyr, with double berd,
And drynketh of his bugle horn the wyn;
Biforn hym stant brawen of the tusked swyn,
And "Nowel" crieth every lusty man.   1255

Aurelius in al that evere he kan
Dooth to this maister chiere and reverence,
And preyeth hym to doon his diligence
To bryngen hym out of his peynes smerte,
Or with a swerd that he wolde slitte his
          herte.   1260
This subtil clerk swich routhe had of this man
That nyght and day he spedde hym that he kan

1196 **fauconers:** hunters with falcons **ryver:** hawking ground
1219 **tretee:** negotiation
1222 **Gerounde, Sayne:** the rivers Geronde and Seine
1223 **made it straunge:** raised difficulties

1232 **slouthe:** sloth, laziness
1234 **to borwe:** as a pledge
1238 **lisse:** respite
1240 **righte:** direct
1245 **Phebus wax old:** the sun grew old (reached the end of the solar year) **laton:** a brass-like alloy grayish-silver in color
1246 **hoote declynacion:** the sign of Cancer, when the sun's northern declination is greatest (in summer)
1248 **Capricorn:** the sign of the winter solstice (December 13; see Astr 2.1.18 –19, 23), the lowest altitude of the sun
1251 **yerd:** enclosed garden
1252 **Janus:** god of entries and of the month of January **double berd:** i.e., two faces (one looking forward, the other backward)
1253 **bugle horn:** drinking vessel made from the horn of the bugle, buffalo
1254 **brawen:** meat **tusked swyn:** boar
1255 **Nowel:** Noel

To wayten a tyme of his conclusioun;
This is to seye, to maken illusioun,
By swich an apparence or jogelrye —   1265
I ne kan no termes of astrologye —
That she and every wight sholde wene and seye
That of Britaigne the rokkes were aweye,
Or ellis they were sonken under grounde.
So atte laste he hath his tyme yfounde   1270
To maken his japes and his wrecchednesse
Of swich a supersticious cursednesse.
His tables Tolletanes forth he brought,
Ful wel corrected, ne ther lakked nought,
Neither his collect ne his expans yeeris,   1275
Ne his rootes, ne his othere geeris,
As been his centris and his argumentz
And his proporcioneles convenientz
For his equacions in every thyng.
And by his eighte speere in his wirkyng   1280
He knew ful wel how fer Alnath was shove
Fro the heed of thilke fixe Aries above,
That in the ninthe speere considered is;
Ful subtilly he kalkuled al this.   1284
    Whan he hadde founde his firste mansioun,
He knew the remenaunt by proporcioun,
And knew the arisyng of his moone weel,
And in whos face, and terme, and everydeel;
And knew ful weel the moones mansioun
Acordaunt to his operacioun,   1290
And knew also his othere observaunces
For swiche illusiouns and swiche meschaunces
As hethen folk useden in thilke dayes.
For which no lenger maked he delayes,   1294
But thurgh his magik, for a wyke or tweye,
It semed that alle the rokkes were aweye.
    Aurelius, which that yet despeired is
Wher he shal han his love or fare amys,

1263 **conclusioun:** astronomical operation
1265 **jogelrye:** conjurer's trick
1273 **tables Tolletanes:** astrological tables corrected for a given
latitude, with tables of a planet's positions in single years (*expans
yeeris*) and in twenty-year periods (*collect*); see the Expl. Notes
for the technical vocabulary in lines 1263–84.
1276 **rootes:** dates from which astronomical calculations are made
geeris: apparatus
1277 **centris:** table of distances between certain parts of an
equator **argumentz:** angles used in caluulating astronomical
positions
1278 **proporcioneles convenientz:** tables for computing
planetary motions
1279 **equacions:** divisions of the sphere into astronomical houses
1280 **eighte speere:** sphere of the fixed stars
1281 **Alnath:** a star in the constellation Aries (*fixed Aries*); see
1280n.
1283 **considered:** observed
1285 **mansioun:** position of the moon
1286 He could calculate the positions of the other mansions by
astronomical tables (*by proporcioun;* cf. 1278 above).
1288 **face, terme:** divisions of the zodiacal signs, each of which
was assigned to a planet; see n.
1290 **Acordaunt to:** consonant with
1292 **meschaunces:** evil practices
1295 **wyke:** week
1298 **amys:** badly

Awaiteth nyght and day on this myracle;   1299
And whan he knew that ther was noon obstacle,
That voyded were thise rokkes everychon,
Doun to his maistres feet he fil anon,
And seyde, "I woful wrecche, Aurelius,
Thanke yow, lord, and lady myn Venus,
That me han holpen fro my cares colde."   1305
And to the temple his wey forth hath he holde,
Where as he knew he sholde his lady see.
And whan he saugh his tyme, anon-right hee,
With dredful herte and with ful humble cheere,
Salewed hath his sovereyn lady deere: 1310
    "My righte lady," quod this woful man,
"Whom I moost drede and love as I best kan,
And lothest were of al this world displese,
Nere it that I for yow have swich disese   1314
That I moste dyen heere at youre foot anon,
Noght wolde I telle how me is wo bigon.
But certes outher moste I dye or pleyne;
Ye sle me giltelees for verray peyne.
But of my deeth thogh that ye have no routhe,
Avyseth yow er that ye breke youre trouthe.
Repenteth yow, for thilke God above,   1321
Er ye me sleen by cause that I yow love.
For, madame, wel ye woot what ye han hight —
Nat that I chalange any thyng of right
Of yow, my sovereyn lady, but youre grace —
But in a gardyn yond, at swich a place,   1326
Ye woot right wel what ye bihighten me;
And in myn hand youre trouthe plighten ye
To love me best — God woot, ye seyde so,
Al be that I unworthy am therto.   1330
Madame, I speke it for the honour of yow
Moore than to save myn hertes lyf right now —
I have do so as ye comanded me;
And if ye vouche sauf, ye may go see.   1334
Dooth as yow list; have youre biheste in mynde,
For, quyk or deed, right there ye shal me fynde.
In yow lith al to do me lyve or deye —
But wel I woot the rokkes been aweye."
    He taketh his leve, and she astoned stood;
In al hir face nas a drope of blood.   1340
She wende nevere han come in swich a trappe.
"Allas," quod she, "that evere this sholde
                    happe!
For wende I nevere by possibilitee
That swich a monstre or merveille myghte be!
It is agayns the proces of nature."   1345

1309 **dredful:** fearful
1314 **disese:** distress
1323 **hight:** promised
1324 **chalange:** claim **of right:** as a legal right
1325 **but youre grace:** (I ask) only your favor
1327 **bihighten:** promised
1336 **quyk:** living

And hoom she goth a sorweful creature;
For verray feere unnethe may she go.
She wepeth, wailleth, al a day or two,
And swowneth, that it routhe was to see.
But why it was to no wight tolde shee,   1350
For out of towne was goon Arveragus.
But to hirself she spak, and seyde thus,
With face pale and with ful sorweful cheere,
In hire compleynt, as ye shal after heere:
    "Allas," quod she, "on thee, Fortune, I
        pleyne,   1355
That unwar wrapped hast me in thy cheyne,
Fro which t'escape woot I no socour,
Save oonly deeth or elles dishonour;
Oon of thise two bihoveth me to chese.
But nathelees, yet have I levere to lese   1360
My lif than of my body to have a shame,
Or knowe myselven fals, or lese my name;
And with my deth I may be quyt, ywis.
Hath ther nat many a noble wyf er this,
And many a mayde, yslayn hirself, allas,   1365
Rather than with hir body doon trespas?
    "Yis, certes, lo, thise stories beren witnesse:
Whan thritty tirauntz, ful of cursednesse,
Hadde slayn Phidon in Atthenes atte feste,
They comanded his doghtres for t'areste   1370
And bryngen hem biforn hem in despit,
Al naked, to fulfille hir foul delit,
And in hir fadres blood they made hem daunce
Upon the pavement, God yeve hem mes-
        chaunce!
For which thise woful maydens, ful of drede,
Rather than they wolde lese hir maydenhede,
They prively been stirt into a welle   1377
And dreynte hemselven, as the bookes telle.
    "They of Mecene leete enquere and seke
Of Lacedomye fifty maydens eke,   1380
On whiche they wolden doon hir lecherye.
But was ther noon of al that compaignye
That she nas slayn, and with a good entente
Chees rather for to dye than assente
To been oppressed of hir maydenhede.   1385
Why sholde I thanne to dye been in drede?
Lo, eek, the tiraunt Aristoclides,
That loved a mayden, heet Stymphalides,
Whan that hir fader slayn was on a nyght,
Unto Dianes temple goth she right,   1390
And hente the ymage in hir handes two,
Fro which ymage wolde she nevere go.

No wight ne myghte hir handes of it arace
Til she was slayn, right in the selve place.
    "Now sith that maydens hadden swich despit
To been defouled with mannes foul delit,   1396
Wel oghte a wyf rather hirselven slee
Than be defouled, as it thynketh me.
What shal I seyn of Hasdrubales wyf,
That at Cartage birafte hirself hir lyf?   1400
For whan she saugh that Romayns wan the
        toun,
She took hir children alle, and skipte adoun
Into the fyr, and chees rather to dye
Than any Romayn dide hire vileynye.
Hath nat Lucresse yslayn hirself, allas,   1405
At Rome, whan that she oppressed was
Of Tarquyn, for hire thoughte it was a shame
To lyven whan she hadde lost hir name?
The sevene maydens of Milesie also   1409
Han slayn hemself, for verrey drede and wo,
Rather than folk of Gawle hem sholde oppresse.
Mo than a thousand stories, as I gesse,
Koude I now telle as touchynge this mateere.
Whan Habradate was slayn, his wyf so deere
Hirselven slow, and leet hir blood to glyde
In Habradates woundes depe and wyde,   1416
And seyde, 'My body, at the leeste way,
Ther shal no wight defoulen, if I may.'
    "What sholde I mo ensamples heerof sayn,
Sith that so manye han hemselven slayn   1420
Wel rather than they wolde defouled be?
I wol conclude that it is bet for me
To sleen myself than been defouled thus.
I wol be trewe unto Arveragus,
Or rather sleen myself in som manere,   1425
As dide Demociones doghter deere
By cause that she wolde nat defouled be.
O Cedasus, it is ful greet pitee
To reden how thy doghtren deyde, allas,
That slowe hemself for swich manere cas.
As greet a pitee was it, or wel moore,   1431
The Theban mayden that for Nichanore
Hirselven slow, right for swich manere wo.
Another Theban mayden dide right so;   1434
For oon of Macidonye hadde hire oppressed,
She with hire deeth hir maydenhede redressed.
What shal I seye of Nicerates wyf,
That for swich cas birafte hirself hir lyf?
How trewe eek was to Alcebiades

1356 **unwar:** unexpectedly
1379 **Mecene:** Messene
1380 **Lacedomye:** Lacedaemon (Sparta)

1405 **Lucresse:** Lucretia; see LGW 1680–1885
1409 **Milesie:** Miletus
1411 **Gawle:** Galatia
1428 **Cedasus:** Scedasus
1430 **cas:** cause
1435 **Macidonye:** Macedonia

His love, that rather for to dyen chees   1440
Than for to suffre his body unburyed be.
Lo, which a wyf was Alceste,'' quod she.
"What seith Omer of goode Penalopee?
Al Grece knoweth of hire chastitee.
Pardee, of Laodomya is writen thus,   1445
That whan at Troie was slayn Protheselaus,
Ne lenger wolde she lyve after his day.
The same of noble Porcia telle I may;
Withoute Brutus koude she nat lyve,
To whom she hadde al hool hir herte yive.   1450
The parfit wyfhod of Arthemesie
Honured is thurgh al the Barbarie.
O Teuta, queene, thy wyfly chastitee
To alle wyves may a mirour bee.
The same thyng I seye of Bilyea,   1455
Of Rodogone, and eek Valeria.''

    Thus pleyned Dorigen a day or tweye,
Purposynge evere that she wolde deye.
But nathelees, upon the thridde nyght,   1459
Hoom cam Arveragus, this worthy knyght,
And asked hire why that she weep so soore;
And she gan wepen ever lenger the moore.
"Allas,'' quod she, "that evere was I born!
Thus have I seyd,'' quod she, "thus have I
         sworn'' —
And toold hym al as ye han herd bifore;   1465
It nedeth nat reherce it yow namoore.
This housbonde, with glad chiere, in freendly
         wyse
Answerde and seyde as I shal yow devyse:
"Is ther oght elles, Dorigen, but this?''
    "Nay, nay,'' quod she, "God helpe me so as
         wys!   1470
This is to muche, and it were Goddes wille.''
    "Ye, wyf,'' quod he, "lat slepen that is stille.
It may be wel, paraventure, yet to day.
Ye shul youre trouthe holden, by my fay!
For God so wisly have mercy upon me,   1475
I hadde wel levere ystiked for to be
For verray love which that I to yow have,
But if ye sholde youre trouthe kepe and save.
Trouthe is the hyeste thyng that man may
         kepe'' —   1479

But with that word he brast anon to wepe,
And seyde, "I yow forbede, up peyne of deeth,
That nevere, whil thee lasteth lyf ne breeth,
To no wight telle thou of this aventure —
As I may best, I wol my wo endure —
Ne make no contenance of hevynesse,   1485
That folk of yow may demen harm or gesse.''
    And forth he cleped a squier and a mayde:
"Gooth forth anon with Dorigen,'' he sayde,
"And bryngeth hire to swich a place anon.''
They take hir leve, and on hir wey they gon,
But they ne wiste why she thider wente.   1491
He nolde no wight tellen his entente.
    Paraventure an heep of yow, ywis,
Wol holden hym a lewed man in this
That he wol putte his wyf in jupartie.   1495
Herkneth the tale er ye upon hire crie.
She may have bettre fortune than yow semeth;
And whan that ye han herd the tale, demeth.
    This squier, which that highte Aurelius,
On Dorigen that was so amorus,   1500
Of aventure happed hire to meete
Amydde the toun, right in the quykkest strete,
As she was bown to goon the wey forth right
Toward the gardyn ther as she had hight.
And he was to the gardyn-ward also;   1505
For wel he spyed whan she wolde go
Out of hir hous to any maner place.
But thus they mette, of aventure or grace,
And he saleweth hire with glad entente,
And asked of hire whiderward she wente;   1510
And she answerde, half as she were mad,
"Unto the gardyn, as myn housbonde bad,
My trouthe for to holde — allas, allas!''
    Aurelius gan wondren on this cas,
And in his herte hadde greet compassioun   1515
Of hire and of hire lamentacioun,
And of Arveragus, the worthy knyght,
That bad hire holden al that she had hight,
So looth hym was his wyf sholde breke hir
         trouthe;
And in his herte he caughte of this greet routhe,
Considerynge the beste on every syde,   1521
That fro his lust yet were hym levere abyde

1442 which a: what a Alceste: Alcestis, heroine of the Prologue of LGW, where the story is told briefly (LGW F 511–16)
1443 Omer: Homer Penalopee: faithful wife of Ulysses
1448 Porcia: Portia committed suicide rather than survive her
husband, Brutus.
1451 Arthemesie: Famed for her chastity, she built a magnificent
tomb for her husband.
1452 Barbaric: heathendom
1453 Teuta: queen of Ilyrica and famous for chastity
1455 Bilyea: Bilia, famed for innocent chastity
1456 Rodogone, Valeria: Rhodogune and Valeria refused to
remarry after the deaths of their husbands.
1458 Purposynge: intending

1480 brast . . . to wepe: burst into tears
1486 of yow: concerning you
1495 jupartie: jeopardy
1502 quykkest strete: busiest street
1503 bown: ready, prepared
1505 to the gardyn-ward: (going) toward the garden
1510 whiderward: whither
1522 He would prefer to desist from attaining his desire

Than doon so heigh a cherlyssh wrecchednesse
Agayns franchise and alle gentillesse;
For which in fewe wordes seyde he thus: 1525
    "Madame, seyth to youre lord Arveragus
That sith I se his grete gentillesse
To yow, and eek I se wel youre distresse,
That him were levere han shame (and that
        were routhe)
Than ye to me sholde breke thus youre trouthe,
I have wel levere evere to suffre wo   1531
Than I departe the love bitwix yow two.
I yow relesse, madame, into youre hond
Quyt every serement and every bond
That ye han maad to me as heerbiforn,   1535
Sith thilke tyme which that ye were born.
My trouthe I plighte, I shal yow never repreve
Of no biheste, and heere I take my leve,
As of the treweste and the beste wyf
That evere yet I knew in al my lyf.   1540
But every wyf be war of hire biheeste!
On Dorigen remembreth, atte leeste.
Thus kan a squier doon a gentil dede
As wel as kan a knyght, withouten drede."   1544
    She thonketh hym upon hir knees al bare,
And hoom unto hir housbonde is she fare,
And tolde hym al, as ye han herd me sayd;
And be ye siker, he was so weel apayd
That it were impossible me to wryte.
What sholde I lenger of this cas endyte?   1550
    Arveragus and Dorigen his wyf
In sovereyn blisse leden forth hir lyf.
Nevere eft ne was ther angre hem bitwene.
He cherisseth hire as though she were a queene,
And she was to hym trewe for everemoore.
Of thise two folk ye gete of me namoore.   1556
    Aurelius, that his cost hath al forlorn,
Curseth the tyme that evere he was born:
"Allas!" quod he. "Allas, that I bihighte
Of pured gold a thousand pound of wighte
Unto this philosophre! How shal I do?   1561
I se namoore but that I am fordo.
Myn heritage moot I nedes selle,
And been a beggere; heere may I nat dwelle
And shamen al my kynrede in this place,   1565
But I of hym may gete bettre grace.

But nathelees, I wole of hym assaye,
At certeyn dayes, yeer by yeer, to paye,
And thanke hym of his grete curteisye.
My trouthe wol I kepe, I wol nat lye."   1570
    With herte soor he gooth unto his cofre,
And broghte gold unto this philosophre,
The value of fyve hundred pound, I gesse,
And hym bisecheth, of his gentillesse,
To graunte hym dayes of the remenaunt;   1575
And seyde, "Maister, I dar wel make avaunt,
I failled nevere of my trouthe as yit.
For sikerly my dette shal be quyt
Towardes yow, howevere that I fare
To goon a-begged in my kirtle bare.   1580
But wolde ye vouche sauf, upon seuretee,
Two yeer or thre for to respiten me,
Thanne were I wel; for elles moot I selle
Myn heritage; ther is namoore to telle."
    This philosophre sobrely answerde,   1585
And seyde thus, whan he thise wordes herde:
"Have I nat holden covenant unto thee?"
    "Yes, certes, wel and trewely," quod he.
    "Hastow nat had thy lady as thee liketh?"
    "No, no," quod he, and sorwefully he siketh.
    "What was the cause? Tel me if thou kan."
    Aurelius his tale anon bigan,   1592
And tolde hym al, as ye han herd bifoore;
It nedeth nat to yow reherce it moore.
    He seide, "Arveragus, of gentillesse,   1595
Hadde levere dye in sorwe and in distresse
Than that his wyf were of hir trouthe fals."
The sorwe of Dorigen he tolde hym als;
How looth hire was to been a wikked wyf,   1599
And that she levere had lost that day hir lyf,
And that hir trouthe she swoor thurgh inno-
        cence,
She nevere erst hadde herde speke of apparence.
"That made me han of hire so greet pitee;
And right as frely as he sente hire me,
As frely sente I hire to hym ageyn.   1605
This al and som; ther is namoore to seyn."
    This philosophre answerde, "Leeve brother,
Everich of yow dide gentilly til oother.
Thou art a squier, and he is a knyght;
But God forbede, for his blisful myght,   1610
But if a clerk koude doon a gentil dede
As wel as any of yow, it is no drede!

1524 **franchise:** nobility of character
1529 **him were levere:** he would rather
1533 **relesse:** release, set free
1534 **serement:** oath, pledge
1537 **plighte:** pledge
1544 **withouten drede:** doubtless
1547 **sayd:** say
1548 **apayd:** satisfied
1557 **forlorn:** forfeited
1560 **pured:** refined   **wighte:** weight

1575 **dayes of the remenaunt:** additional time to pay the balance
1580 **a-begged:** a-begging   **kirtle:** tunic
1582 **respiten me:** grant me a respite, additional time
1602 **apparence:** illusion
1606 **al and som:** the entire matter

Sire, I releesse thee thy thousand pound,
As thou right now were cropen out of the
　　ground,
Ne nevere er now ne haddest knowen me.　1615
For, sire, I wol nat taken a peny of thee
For al my craft, ne noght for my travaille.
Thou hast ypayed wel for my vitaille.

It is ynogh, and farewel, have good day!"　1619
And took his hors, and forth he goth his way.
Lordynges, this question, thanne, wol I aske
　　now,
Which was the mooste fre, as thynketh yow?
Now telleth me, er that ye ferther wende.
I kan namoore; my tale is at an ende.

Heere is ended the Frankeleyns Tale.

1613 **releesse thee:** set you free from
1614 **cropen:** crept

THE PHYSICIAN'S TALE

Heere folweth the Phisiciens Tale.

Ther was, as telleth Titus Livius,
A knyght that called was Virginius,
Fulfild of honour and of worthynesse,
And strong of freendes, and of greet richesse.
  This knyght a doghter hadde by his wyf; 5
No children hadde he mo in al his lyf.
Fair was this mayde in excellent beautee
Aboven every wight that man may see;
For Nature hath with sovereyn diligence
Yformed hire in so greet excellence, 10
As though she wolde seyn, "Lo! I, Nature,
Thus kan I forme and peynte a creature,
Whan that me list; who kan me countrefete?
Pigmalion noght, though he ay forge and bete,
Or grave, or peynte; for I dar wel seyn 15
Apelles, Zanzis, sholde werche in veyn
Outher to grave, or peynte, or forge, or bete,
If they presumed me to countrefete.
For He that is the formere principal
Hath maked me his vicaire general, 20
To forme and peynten erthely creaturis
Right as me list, and ech thyng in my cure is
Under the moone, that may wane and waxe,
And for my werk right no thyng wol I axe;
My lord and I been ful of oon accord. 25
I made hire to the worshipe of my lord;
So do I alle myne othere creatures,
What colour that they han or what figures."
Thus semeth me that Nature wolde seye.
  This mayde of age twelve yeer was and
      tweye,
In which that Nature hadde swich delit. 31
For right as she kan peynte a lilie whit,
And reed a rose, right with swich peynture
She peynted hath this noble creature,
Er she were born, upon hir lymes fre, 35
Where as by right swiche colours sholde be;

And Phebus dyed hath hire tresses grete
Lyk to the stremes of his burned heete.
And if that excellent was hire beautee,
A thousand foold moore vertuous was she. 40
In hire ne lakked no condicioun
That is to preyse, as by discrecioun.
As wel in goost as body chast was she,
For which she floured in virginitee
With alle humylitee and abstinence, 45
With alle attemperaunce and pacience,
With mesure eek of beryng and array.
Discreet she was in answeryng alway;
Though she were wis as Pallas, dar I seyn,
Hir facound eek ful wommanly and pleyn, 50
No countrefeted termes hadde she
To seme wys, but after hir degree
She spak, and alle hire wordes, moore and
      lesse,
Sownynge in vertu and in gentillesse. 54
Shamefast she was in maydens shamefastnesse,
Constant in herte, and evere in bisynesse
To dryve hire out of ydel slogardye.
Bacus hadde of hir mouth right no maistrie;
For wyn and youthe dooth Venus encresse,
As men in fyr wol casten oille or greesse. 60
And of hir owene vertu, unconstreyned,
She hath ful ofte tyme syk hire feyned,
For that she wolde fleen the compaignye
Where likly was to treten of folye,
As is at feestes, revels, and at daunces, 65
That been occasions of daliaunces.
Swich thynges maken children for to be
To soone rype and boold, as men may se,

---

1 **Titus Livius:** Livy, the Roman historian
14 **Pigmalion:** the famous Greek sculptor
15 **grave:** carve
16 **Apelles:** legendary sculptor of the tomb of Darius the Great
Zanzis: Zeuxis, an Athenian artist
20 **vicaire general:** chief deputy
25 **ful of oon accord:** completely in accord
33 **peynture:** painting, coloration

37 **Phebus:** Phoebus Apollo, the sun
38 **burned heete:** burnished heat (rays of the sun)
42 **as by discrecioun:** concerning moral discernment
43 **goost:** spirit
46 **attemperaunce:** temperance, moderation
47 **mesure:** moderation **beryng:** bearing, demeanor
49 **Pallas:** Pallas Athena, goddess of wisdom
50 **facound:** way of speaking
54 **Sownynge in:** conducing to
55 **Shamefast:** modest
57 **slogardye:** sluggishness, laziness
58 **Bacus:** Bacchus, god of wine
59 **Venus:** i.e., sexual desire
64 **treten of:** speak about

Which is ful perilous and hath been yoore.
For al to soone may she lerne loore   70
Of booldnesse, whan she woxen is a wyf.
  And ye maistresses, in youre olde lyf,
That lordes doghtres han in governaunce,
Ne taketh of my wordes no displesaunce.
Thenketh that ye been set in governynges   75
Of lordes doghtres oonly for two thynges:
Outher for ye han kept youre honestee,
Or elles ye han falle in freletee,
And knowen wel ynough the olde daunce,
And han forsaken fully swich meschaunce   80
For everemo; therfore, for Cristes sake,
To teche hem vertu looke that ye ne slake.
  A theef of venysoun, that hath forlaft
His likerousnesse and al his olde craft,
Kan kepe a forest best of any man.   85
Now kepeth wel, for if ye wole, ye kan.
Looke wel that ye unto no vice assente,
Lest ye be dampned for youre wikke entente;
For whoso dooth, a traitour is, certeyn.
And taketh kep of that that I shal seyn: 90
Of alle tresons sovereyn pestilence
Is whan a wight bitrayseth innocence.
  Ye fadres and ye moodres eek also,
Though ye han children, be it oon or mo,
Youre is the charge of al hir surveiaunce,   95
Whil that they been under youre governaunce.
Beth war, if by ensample of youre lyvynge,
Or by youre necligence in chastisynge,
That they ne perisse; for I dar wel seye
If that they doon, ye shul it deere abeye.   100
Under a shepherde softe and necligent
The wolf hath many a sheep and lamb torent.
Suffiseth oon ensample now as heere,
For I moot turne agayn to my matere.
  This mayde, of which I wol this tale expresse,
So kepte hirself hir neded no maistresse,   106
For in hir lyvyng maydens myghten rede,
As in a book, every good word or dede

That longeth to a mayden vertuous,
She was so prudent and so bountevous.   110
For which the fame out sprong on every syde,
Bothe of hir beautee and hir bountee wyde,
That thurgh that land they preised hire echone
That loved vertu, save Envye allone,
That sory is of oother mennes wele   115
And glad is of his sorwe and his unheele.
(The Doctour maketh this descripcioun.)
  This mayde upon a day wente in the toun
Toward a temple, with hire mooder deere,
As is of yonge maydens the manere.   120
Now was ther thanne a justice in that toun,
That governour was of that regioun.
And so bifel this juge his eyen caste
Upon this mayde, avysynge hym ful faste,
As she cam forby ther as this juge stood.   125
Anon his herte chaunged and his mood,
So was he caught with beautee of this mayde,
And to hymself ful pryvely he sayde,
"This mayde shal be myn, for any man!"
  Anon the feend into his herte ran,   130
And taughte hym sodeynly that he by slyghte
The mayden to his purpos wynne myghte.
For certes, by no force ne by no meede,   133
Hym thoughte, he was nat able for to speede;
For she was strong of freendes, and eek she
Confermed was in swich soverayn bountee
That wel he wiste he myghte hire nevere wynne
As for to make hire with hir body synne.
For which, by greet deliberacioun,
He sente after a cherl, was in the toun,   140
Which that he knew for subtil and for boold.
This juge unto this cherl his tale hath toold
In secree wise, and made hym to ensure
He sholde telle it to no creature,
And if he dide, he sholde lese his heed.   145
Whan that assented was this cursed reed,
Glad was this juge, and maked him greet
          cheere,
And yaf hym yiftes preciouse and deere.
  Whan shapen was al hire conspiracie
Fro point to point, how that his lecherie   150
Parfourned sholde been ful subtilly,

---

71 **woxen:** became
72 **maistresses:** governesses
77 **honestee:** chastity
78 **freletee:** frailty
79 **olde daunce:** tricks of the trade, game of love
80 **meschaunce:** misconduct
82 **slake:** be slack, desist
83 **venysoun:** game, venison   **forlaft:** abandoned
84 **likerousnesse:** greedy appetite
86 **kepeth wel:** take good care
91 **sovereyn pestilence:** the supreme wickedness
92 **bitrayseth:** betrays
95 **surveiaunce:** surveillance (protection)
99 **perisse:** perish
100 **it deere abeye:** pay dearly for it
102 **torent:** torn to pieces

110 **bountevous:** full of goodness
116 **unheele:** misery
117 **The Doctour:** St. Augustine
125 **forby ther as:** past where
129 **for:** despite
131 **slyghte:** trickery
143 **ensure:** assure, give assurance
147 **maked him greet cheere:** was very friendly to him
151 **Parfourned:** performed, accomplished

As ye shul heere it after openly,
Hoom gooth the cherl, that highte Claudius.
This false juge, that highte Apius,
(So was his name, for this is no fable,   155
But knowen for historial thyng notable;
The sentence of it sooth is, out of doute),
This false juge gooth now faste aboute
To hasten his delit al that he may.
And so bifel soone after, on a day,   160
This false juge, as telleth us the storie,
As he was wont, sat in his consistorie,
And yaf his doomes upon sondry cas.
This false cherl cam forth a ful greet pas,
And seyde, "Lord, if that it be youre wille,   165
As dooth me right upon this pitous bille,
In which I pleyne upon Virginius;
And if that he wol seyn it is nat thus,
I wol it preeve, and fynde good witnesse,
That sooth is that my bille wol expresse."   170
    The juge answerde, "Of this, in his absence,
I may nat yeve diffynytyf sentence.
Lat do hym calle, and I wol gladly heere;
Thou shalt have al right, and no wrong heere."
    Virginius cam to wite the juges wille,   175
And right anon was rad this cursed bille;
The sentence of it was as ye shul heere:
    "To yow, my lord, sire Apius so deere,
Sheweth youre povre servant Claudius
How that a knyght, called Virginius,   180
Agayns the lawe, agayn al equitee,
Holdeth, expres agayn the wyl of me,
My servant, which that is my thral by right,
Which fro myn hous was stole upon a nyght,
Whil that she was ful yong; this wol I preeve   185
By witnesse, lord, so that it nat yow greeve.
She nys his doghter nat, what so he seye.
Wherfore to yow, my lord the juge, I preye,
Yeld me my thral, if that it be youre wille."
Lo, this was al the sentence of his bille.   190
    Virginius gan upon the cherl biholde,
But hastily, er he his tale tolde,
And wolde have preeved it as sholde a knyght,
And eek by witnessyng of many a wight,

That al was fals that seyde his adversarie,   195
This cursed juge wolde no thyng tarie,
Ne heere a word moore of Virginius,
But yaf his juggement, and seyde thus:
    "I deeme anon this cherl his servant have;
Thou shalt no lenger in thyn hous hir save.   200
Go bryng hire forth, and put hire in oure
        warde.
The cherl shal have his thral, this I awarde."
    And whan this worthy knyght Virginius
Thurgh sentence of this justice Apius
Moste by force his deere doghter yiven   205
Unto the juge, in lecherie to lyven,
He gooth hym hoom, and sette him in his halle,
And leet anon his deere doghter calle,
And with a face deed as asshen colde
Upon hir humble face he gan biholde,   210
With fadres pitee stikynge thurgh his herte,
Al wolde he from his purpos nat converte.
    "Doghter," quod he, "Virginia, by thy name,
Ther been two weyes, outher deeth or shame,
That thou most suffre; allas, that I was bore!
For nevere thou deservedest wherfore   216
To dyen with a swerd or with a knyf.
O deere doghter, endere of my lyf,
Which I have fostred up with swich plesaunce
That thou were nevere out of my remem-
        braunce!   220
O doghter, which that art my laste wo,
And in my lyf my laste joye also,
O gemme of chastitee, in pacience
Take thou thy deeth, for this is my sentence.
For love, and nat for hate, thou most be
        deed;   225
My pitous hand moot smyten of thyn heed.
Allas, that evere Apius the say!
Thus hath he falsly jugged the to-day" —
And tolde hire al the cas, as ye bifore
Han herd; nat nedeth for to telle it moore.   230
    "O mercy, deere fader!" quod this mayde,
And with that word she bothe hir armes layde
Aboute his nekke, as she was wont to do.
The teeris bruste out of hir eyen two,
And seyde, "Goode fader, shal I dye?   235
Is ther no grace, is ther no remedye?"
    "No, certes, deere doghter myn," quod he.
    "Thanne yif me leyser, fader myn," quod she,
"My deeth for to compleyne a litel space;

155 **fable:** fiction
156 **historial:** historical
162 **consistorie:** court
163 **doomes:** judgments, decisions
164 **ful greet pas:** at a rapid pace, hurriedly
166 **As dooth me right:** do justice for me   **bille:** formal charge
167 **pleyne upon:** make complaint against
173 **Lat do hym calle:** have him called
176 **rad:** read
182 **expres agayn:** clearly against
183 **thral:** servant, slave
189 **Yeld:** give back
193 **as sholde a knyght:** i.e., in a trial by battle
194 **witnessyng:** testimony

200 **save:** keep
201 **warde:** custody
208 **leet . . . calle:** had . . . called
221 **laste:** greatest
227 **the say:** saw you

For, pardee, Jepte yaf his doghter grace 240
For to compleyne, er he hir slow, allas!
And, God it woot, no thyng was hir trespas,
But for she ran hir fader first to see,
To welcome hym with greet solempnitee."
And with that word she fil aswowne anon, 245
And after, whan hir swownyng is agon,
She riseth up, and to hir fader sayde,
"Blissed be God that I shal dye a mayde!
Yif me my deeth, er that I have a shame;
Dooth with youre child youre wyl, a Goddes
　　name!" 250
　　And with that word she preyed hym ful ofte
That with his swerd he wolde smyte softe;
And with that word aswowne doun she fil.
Hir fader, with ful sorweful herte and wil,
Hir heed of smoot, and by the top it hente, 255
And to the juge he gan it to presente,
As he sat yet in doom in consistorie.
And whan the juge it saugh, as seith the storie,
He bad to take hym and anhange hym faste;
But right anon a thousand peple in thraste, 260
To save the knyght, for routhe and for pitee,
For knowen was the false iniquitee.
The peple anon had suspect in this thyng,

By manere of the cherles chalangyng,
That it was by the assent of Apius; 265
They wisten wel that he was lecherus.
For which unto this Apius they gon
And caste hym in a prisoun right anon,
Ther as he slow hymself; and Claudius,
That servant was unto this Apius, 270
Was demed for to hange upon a tree,
But that Virginius, of his pitee,
So preyde for hym that he was exiled;
And elles, certes, he had been bigyled. 274
The remenant were anhanged, moore and lesse,
That were consentant of this cursednesse.
　　Heere may men seen how synne hath his
　　merite.
Beth war, for no man woot whom God wol
　　smyte
In no degree, ne in which manere wyse;
The worm of conscience may agryse 280
Of wikked lyf, though it so pryvee be
That no man woot therof but God and he.
For be he lewed man, or ellis lered,
He noot how soone that he shal been afered.
Therfore I rede yow this conseil take: 285
Forsaketh synne, er synne yow forsake.

Heere endeth the Phisiciens Tale.

THE INTRODUCTION TO
THE PARDONER'S TALE

The wordes of the Hoost to the Phisicien and the Pardoner.

Oure Hooste gan to swere as he were wood;
"Harrow!" quod he, "by nayles and by blood!
This was a fals cherl and a fals justise.
As shameful deeth as herte may devyse 290
Come to thise juges and hire advocatz!
Algate this sely mayde is slayn, allas!
Allas, to deere boughte she beautee!

Wherfore I seye al day that men may see
That yiftes of Fortune and of Nature 295
Been cause of deeth to many a creature.
Hire beautee was hire deth, I dar wel sayn.
Allas, so pitously as she was slayn!
Of bothe yiftes that I speke of now
Men han ful ofte moore for harm than prow.
But trewely, myn owene maister deere, 301

---

240 **Jepte:** the biblical Jeptha; see n.
257 **in doom in consistorie:** giving judgment in court
259 **anhange:** hang
260 **in thraste:** thrust, pushed in
263 **suspect:** suspicious

---

287 **wood:** mad
288 "Alas," said he, "by the nails and blood of Christ!"
292 **Algate:** at any rate

---

264 **By manere of:** by reason of **chalangyng:** claim
274 **bigyled:** betrayed (i.e., killed)
277 **merite:** reward
280 **agryse:** tremble for fear
285 **rede:** advise

---

300 **prow:** profit, benefit

This is a pitous tale for to heere.
But nathelees, passe over; is no fors.
I pray to God so save thy gentil cors,
And eek thyne urynals and thy jurdones,   305
Thyn ypocras, and eek thy galiones,
And every boyste ful of thy letuarie;
God blesse hem, and oure lady Seinte Marie!
So moot I theen, thou art a propre man,
And lyk a prelat, by Seint Ronyan!   310
Seyde I nat wel? I kan nat speke in terme;
But wel I woot thou doost myn herte to erme,
That I almoost have caught a cardynacle.
By corpus bones! but I have triacle,
Or elles a draughte of moyste and corny ale,
Or but I heere anon a myrie tale,   316

Myn herte is lost for pitee of this mayde.
Thou beel amy, thou Pardoner," he sayde,
"Telle us som myrthe or japes right anon."
    "It shal be doon," quod he, "by Seint Ron-
        yon!   320
But first," quod he, "heere at this alestake
I wol bothe drynke and eten of a cake."
    But right anon thise gentils gonne to crye,
"Nay, lat hym telle us of no ribaudye!   324
Telle us som moral thyng, that we may leere
Som wit, and thanne wol we gladly heere."
    "I graunte, ywis," quod he, "but I moot
        thynke
Upon som honest thyng while that I drynke."

THE PARDONER'S PROLOGUE

Heere folweth the Prologe of the Pardoners Tale.

*Radix malorum est Cupiditas. Ad
Thimotheum, 6°.*

"Lordynges," quod he, "in chirches whan I
        preche,
I peyne me to han an hauteyn speche,   330
And rynge it out as round as gooth a belle,
For I kan al by rote that I telle.
My theme is alwey oon, and evere was —
Radix malorum est Cupiditas.

    "First I pronounce whennes that I come,   335
And thanne my bulles shewe I, alle and some.
Oure lige lordes seel on my patente,

That shewe I first, my body to warente,
That no man be so boold, ne preest ne clerk,
Me to destourbe of Cristes hooly werk.   340
And after that thanne telle I forth my tales;
Bulles of popes and of cardynales,
Of patriarkes and bishopes I shewe,
And in Latyn I speke a wordes fewe,
To saffron with my predicacioun,   345
And for to stire hem to devocioun.
Thanne shewe I forth my longe cristal stones,
Ycrammed ful of cloutes and of bones —
Relikes been they, as wenen they echoon.
Thanne have I in latoun a sholder-boon   350
Which that was of an hooly Jewes sheep.
'Goode men,' I seye, 'taak of my wordes keep;
If that this boon be wasshe in any welle,
If cow, or calf, or sheep, or oxe swelle
That any worm hath ete, or worm ystonge,   355

---

303 **passe over:** let it be   **is no fors:** it does not matter
305 **urynals:** vessels for analyzing urine   **jurdones:** glass vessels
used by physicians
306 **ypocras, galiones:** medicinal drinks named after Hippocrates
and Galen, ancient medical authorities
307 **boyste:** container   **letuarie:** medicine
309 **theen:** prosper
310 **Seint Ronyan:** probably St. Ronan, a Scottish saint
311 **in terme:** in technical language
312 **erme:** grieve
313 **cardynacle:** probably the Host's error for *cardiacle,* heart
attack
314 **By corpus bones!:** by God's bones!   **triacle:** medicine
315 **moyste:** fresh, new   **corny:** malty, strong

Radix malorum, *etc.:* Greed is the root of [all] evils, 1 Timothy
6.10
330 **hauteyn:** impressive, loud
332 **by rote:** by heart
333 **theme:** biblical text for a sermon
336 **bulles:** papal bulls (here indulgences)
337 **lige lordes seel:** seal of our liege lord (the bishop)
patente: letter patent (authorizing his sale of pardons)

318 **beel amy:** fair friend (perhaps used derisively)
321 **alestake:** pole hung with a garland, the sign of an alehouse
322 **cake:** loaf of bread
324 **ribaudye:** ribaldry, coarse jesting

338 **warente:** protect
345 **saffron:** flavor with saffron, season   **predicacioun:** sermon
347 **cristal stones:** glass cases; cf. GP I.700.
348 **cloutes:** rags
350 **in latoun:** mounted in latten, a brass-like alloy
355 **worm:** snake

Taak water of that welle and wassh his tonge,
And it is hool anon; and forthermoore,
Of pokkes and of scabbe, and every soore
Shal every sheep be hool that of this welle   359
Drynketh a draughte. Taak kep eek what I telle:
If that the good-man that the beestes oweth
Wol every wyke, er that the cok hym croweth,
Fastynge, drynken of this welle a draughte,
As thilke hooly Jew oure eldres taughte,
His beestes and his stoor shal multiplie.   365

  'And, sires, also it heeleth jalousie;
For though a man be falle in jalous rage,
Lat maken with this water his potage,
And nevere shal he moore his wyf mystriste,
Though he the soothe of hir defaute wiste,   370
Al had she taken prestes two or thre.

  'Heere is a miteyn eek, that ye may se.
He that his hand wol putte in this mitayn,
He shal have multipliyng of his grayn,
Whan he hath sowen, be it whete or otes,   375
So that he offre pens, or elles grotes.

  'Goode men and wommen, o thyng warne I
        yow:
If any wight be in this chirche now
That hath doon synne horrible, that he
Dar nat, for shame, of it yshryven be,   380
Or any womman, be she yong or old,
That hath ymaked hir housbonde cokewold,
Swich folk shal have no power ne no grace
To offren to my relikes in this place.   384
And whoso fyndeth hym out of swich blame,
He wol come up and offre a Goddes name,
And I assoille him by the auctoritee
Which that by bulle ygraunted was to me.'

  "By this gaude have I wonne, yeer by yeer,
An hundred mark sith I was pardoner.   390
I stonde lyk a clerk in my pulpet,
And whan the lewed peple is doun yset,
I preche so as ye han herd bifoore
And telle an hundred false japes moore.   394
Thanne peyne I me to strecche forth the nekke,
And est and west upon the peple I bekke,
As dooth a dowve sittynge on a berne.

Mync handes and my tonge goon so yerne
That it is joye to se my bisynesse.
Of avarice and of swich cursednesse   400
Is al my prechyng, for to make hem free
To yeven hir pens, and namely unto me.
For myn entente is nat but for to wynne,
And nothyng for correccioun of synne.   404
I rekke nevere, whan that they been beryed,
Though that hir soules goon a-blakeberyed!
For certes, many a predicacioun
Comth ofte tyme of yvel entencioun;
Som for plesance of folk and flaterye,
To been avaunced by ypocrisye,   410
And som for veyne glorie, and som for hate.
For whan I dar noon oother weyes debate,
Thanne wol I stynge hym with my tonge smerte
In prechyng, so that he shal nat asterte
To been defamed falsly, if that he   415
Hath trespased to my bretheren or to me.
For though I telle noght his propre name,
Men shal wel knowe that it is the same,
By signes, and by othere circumstances.   419
Thus quyte I folk that doon us displesances;
Thus spitte I out my venym under hewe
Of hoolynesse, to semen hooly and trewe.

  "But shortly myn entente I wol devyse:
I preche of no thyng but for coveityse.
Therfore my theme is yet, and evere was,   425
Radix malorum est Cupiditas.
Thus kan I preche agayn that same vice
Which that I use, and that is avarice.
But though myself be gilty in that synne,
Yet kan I maken oother folk to twynne   430
From avarice and soore to repente.
But that is nat my principal entente;
I preche nothyng but for coveitise.
Of this mateere it oghte ynogh suffise.

  "Thanne telle I hem ensamples many oon   435
Of olde stories longe tyme agoon.
For lewed peple loven tales olde;
Swiche thynges kan they wel reporte and holde.
What, trowe ye, that whiles I may preche,
And wynne gold and silver for I teche,   440
That I wol lyve in poverte wilfully?

---

358 **pokkes:** pocks, pustules
361 **good-man:** goodman, head of the household   **oweth:** owns
365 **stoor:** stock, possessions
368 **potage:** soup
370 **defaute:** misdeed
372 **miteyn:** mitten
375 **otes:** oats
376 **pens:** pence, pennies   **grotes:** groats, silver coins worth four pence
380 **yshryven:** confessed and forgiven
387 **assoille:** absolve
389 **gaude:** trick
390 **hundred mark:** about sixty-six pounds
396 **bekke:** nod
397 **berne:** barn

398 **yerne:** quickly
405 **beryed:** buried
406 **goon a-blakeberyed:** go blackberry picking
414 **asterte:** escape
420 **quyte:** pay back (revenge)   **doon us displesances:** make trouble for us (pardoners)
421 **hewe:** pretense
424 **coveityse:** greed
427 **agayn:** against
430 **twynne:** depart, turn away from
435 **ensamples:** exempla, illustrative anecdotes
437 **lewed:** ignorant, unlearned
441 **in poverte wilfully:** in voluntary poverty (like a monk)

Nay, nay, I thoghte it nevere, trewely!
For I wol preche and begge in sondry landes;
I wol nat do no labour with myne handes,
Ne make baskettes and lyve therby,   445
By cause I wol nat beggen ydelly.
I wol noon of the apostles countrefete;
I wol have moneie, wolle, chese, and whete,
Al were it yeven of the povereste page,
Or of the povereste wydwe in a village,   450
Al sholde hir children sterve for famyne.
Nay, I wol drynke licour of the vyne

And have a joly wenche in every toun.
But herkneth, lordynges, in conclusioun:
Youre likyng is that I shal telle a tale.   455
Now have I dronke a draughte of corny ale,
By God, I hope I shal yow telle a thyng
That shal by reson been at youre likyng.
For though myself be a ful vicious man,
A moral tale yet I yow telle kan,   460
Which I am wont to preche for to wynne.
Now hoold youre pees! My tale I wol bigynne."

THE PARDONER'S TALE

Heere bigynneth the Pardoners Tale.

In Flaundres whilom was a compaignye
Of yonge folk that haunteden folye,
As riot, hasard, stywes, and tavernes,   465
Where as with harpes, lutes, and gyternes,
They daunce and pleyen at dees bothe day and
      nyght,
And eten also and drynken over hir myght,
Thurgh which they doon the devel sacrifise
Withinne that develes temple in cursed wise
By superfluytee abhomynable.   471
Hir othes been so grete and so dampnable
That it is grisly for to heere hem swere.
Oure blissed Lordes body they totere —
Hem thoughte that Jewes rente hym noght
      ynough —   475
And ech of hem at otheres synne lough.
And right anon thanne comen tombesteres
Fetys and smale, and yonge frutesteres,
Syngeres with harpes, baudes, wafereres,
Whiche been the verray develes officeres   480
To kyndle and blowe the fyr of lecherye,
That is annexed unto glotonye.

The hooly writ take I to my witnesse
That luxurie is in wyn and dronkenesse.
Lo, how that dronken Looth, unkyndely,   485
Lay by his doghtres two, unwityngly;
So dronke he was, he nyste what he wroghte.
Herodes, whoso wel the stories soghte,
Whan he of wyn was repleet at his feeste,
Right at his owene table he yaf his heeste   490
To sleen the Baptist John, ful giltelees.
Senec seith a good word doutelees;
He seith he kan no difference fynde
Bitwix a man that is out of his mynde
And a man which that is dronkelewe,   495
But that woodnesse, yfallen in a shrewe,
Persevereth lenger than doth dronkenesse.
O glotonye, ful of cursednesse!
O cause first of oure confusioun!
O original of oure dampnacioun,   500
Til Crist hadde boght us with his blood agayn!
Lo, how deere, shortly for to sayn,
Aboght was thilke cursed vileynye!
Corrupt was al this world for glotonye.

446 **ydelly:** in vain
448 **wolle:** wool
449 **povereste:** poorest

---

464 **haunteden:** made a habit of
465 **riot:** debauchery **hasard:** dicing **stywes:** brothels
466 **gyternes:** citterns (guitar-like instruments)
467 **dees:** dice
474 **totere:** tear in pieces
476 **lough:** laughed
477 **tombesteres:** dancing girls
478 **Fetys:** elegantly shaped **smale:** slim **frutesteres:** girls who
sell fruit
479 **wafereres:** sellers of wafers

456 **corny:** malty, strong

---

483 **hooly writ:** the Bible
484 **luxurie:** lechery
485 **Looth:** Lot **unkyndely:** unnaturally
486 **unwityngly:** unknowingly
487 **nyste** = *ne wiste,* did not know
488 **Herodes:** Herod **stories:** histories (or possibly the gospel
narratives in Matthew 14 and Mark 6)
489 **repleet:** filled
492 **Senec:** Seneca
495 **dronkelewe:** addicted to drink
497 **Persevereth:** lasts
499 **confusioun:** ruin

Adam oure fader, and his wyf also,   505
Fro Paradys to labour and to wo
Were dryven for that vice, it is no drede.
For whil that Adam fasted, as I rede,
He was in Paradys; and whan that he
Eet of the fruyt deffended on the tree,   510
Anon he was out cast to wo and peyne.
O glotonye, on thee wel oghte us pleyne!
O, wiste a man how manye maladyes
Folwen of excesse and of glotonyes,
He wolde been the moore mesurable   515
Of his diete, sittynge at his table.
Allas, the shorte throte, the tendre mouth,
Maketh that est and west and north and south,
In erthe, in eir, in water, men to swynke   519
To gete a glotoun deyntee mete and drynke!
Of this matiere, O Paul, wel kanstow trete:
"Mete unto wombe, and wombe eek unto mete,
Shal God destroyen bothe," as Paulus seith.
Allas, a foul thyng is it, by my feith,
To seye this word, and fouler is the dede,   525
Whan man so drynketh of the white and rede
That of his throte he maketh his pryvee
Thurgh thilke cursed superfluitee.
    The apostel wepyng seith ful pitously,
"Ther walken manye of whiche yow toold
       have I —   530
I seye it now wepyng, with pitous voys —
They been enemys of Cristes croys,
Of whiche the ende is deeth; wombe is hir
       god!"
O wombe! O bely! O stynkyng cod,
Fulfilled of dong and of corrupcioun!   535
At either ende of thee foul is the soun.
How greet labour and cost is thee to fynde!
Thise cookes, how they stampe, and streyne,
       and grynde,
And turnen substaunce into accident
To fulfille al thy likerous talent!   540
Out of the harde bones knokke they
The mary, for they caste noght awey
That may go thurgh the golet softe and swoote.

Of spicerie of leef, and bark, and roote
Shal been his sauce ymaked by delit,   545
To make hym yet a newer appetit.
But, certes, he that haunteth swiche delices
Is deed, whil that he lyveth in tho vices.
    A lecherous thyng is wyn, and dronkenesse
Is ful of stryvyng and of wrecchednesse.   550
O dronke man, disfigured is thy face,
Sour is thy breeth, foul artow to embrace,
And thurgh thy dronke nose semeth the soun
As though thou seydest ay "Sampsoun, Samp-
       soun!"
And yet, God woot, Sampsoun drank nevere no
       wyn.   555
Thou fallest as it were a styked swyn;
Thy tonge is lost, and al thyn honeste cure,
For dronkenesse is verray sepulture
Of mannes wit and his discrecioun.
In whom that drynke hath dominacioun   560
He kan no conseil kepe; it is no drede.
Now kepe yow fro the white and fro the rede,
And namely fro the white wyn of Lepe
That is to selle in Fysshstrete or in Chepe.
This wyn of Spaigne crepeth subtilly   565
In othere wynes, growynge faste by,
Of which ther ryseth swich fumositee
That whan a man hath dronken draughtes thre,
And weneth that he be at hoom in Chepe,
He is in Spaigne, right at the toune of Lepe —
Nat at the Rochele, ne at Burdeux toun —   571
And thanne wol he seye "Sampsoun, Samp-
       soun!"
    But herkneth, lordynges, o word, I yow
       preye,
That alle the sovereyn actes, dar I seye,
Of victories in the Olde Testament,   575
Thurgh verray God, that is omnipotent,
Were doon in abstinence and in preyere.
Looketh the Bible, and ther ye may it leere.
    Looke, Attilla, the grete conquerour,   579
Deyde in his sleep, with shame and dishonour,
Bledynge ay at his nose in dronkenesse.
A capitayn sholde lyve in sobrenesse.
And over al this, avyseth yow right wel

---

510 **deffended:** forbidden
515 **mesurable:** temperate
519 **swynke:** labor
521 **Paul:** St. Paul the apostle   **trete:** treat, discuss
522 **wombe:** belly
526 **white and rede:** wines
529 **The apostel:** St. Paul
534 **cod:** bag, belly
535 **corrupcioun:** decayed matter
537 **thee to fynde:** to provide food for you
538 **stampe:** pound
539 **substaunce into accident:** the inner reality into the
outward appearance
540 **likerous:** greedy   **talent:** desire, inclination
542 **mary:** marrow
543 **golet:** gullet   **swoote:** sweet

545 **by:** for
547 **delices:** delicacies
550 **stryvyng:** strife, quarrelling
554 **Sampsoun:** Samson (cf. VII.2055)
556 **styked swyn:** stuck pig
557 **honeste cure:** care for decency, self-respect
563 **Lepe:** wine-growing district in Spain
564 **Fysshstrete, Chepe:** streets in London
567 **fumositee:** vapors (rising from the stomach to the head)
571 **Rochele, Burdeux toun:** La Rochelle, Bordeaux,
wine-growing districts in France
579 **Attilla:** king of the Huns
582 **sobrenesse:** sobriety

What was comaunded unto Lamuel —
Nat Samuel, but Lamuel, seye I;   585
Redeth the Bible, and fynde it expresly
Of wyn-yevyng to hem that han justise.
Namoore of this, for it may wel suffise.

    And now that I have spoken of glotonye,
Now wol I yow deffenden hasardrye.   590
Hasard is verray mooder of lesynges,
And of deceite, and cursed forswerynges,
Blaspheme of Crist, manslaughtre, and wast
        also
Of catel and of tyme; and forthermo,
It is repreeve and contrarie of honour   595
For to ben holde a commune hasardour.
And ever the hyer he is of estaat,
The moore is he yholden desolaat.
If that a prynce useth hasardrye,
In alle governaunce and policye   600
He is, as by commune opinioun,
Yholde the lasse in reputacioun.

    Stilboun, that was a wys embassadour,
Was sent to Corynthe in ful greet honour
Fro Lacidomye to make hire alliaunce.   605
And whan he cam, hym happede, par chaunce,
That alle the gretteste that were of that lond,
Pleyynge atte hasard he hem fond.
For which, as soone as it myghte be,
He stal hym hoom agayn to his contree,   610
And seyde, "Ther wol I nat lese my name,
Ne I wol nat take on me so greet defame,
Yow for to allie unto none hasardours.
Sendeth othere wise embassadours;
For, by my trouthe, me were levere dye   615
Than I yow sholde to hasardours allye.
For ye, that been so glorious in honours,
Shul nat allyen yow with hasardours
As by my wyl, ne as by my tretee."
This wise philosophre, thus seyde hee.   620

    Looke eek that to the kyng Demetrius
The kyng of Parthes, as the book seith us,
Sente him a paire of dees of gold in scorn,
For he hadde used hasard ther-biforn;
For which he heeld his glorie or his renoun   625
At no value or reputacioun.

Lordes may fynden oother maner pley
Honest ynough to dryve the day awey.

    Now wol I speke of othes false and grete
A word or two, as olde bookes trete.   630
Gret sweryng is a thyng abhominable,
And fals sweryng is yet moore reprevable.
The heighe God forbad sweryng at al,
Witnesse on Mathew; but in special
Of sweryng seith the hooly Jeremye,   635
"Thou shalt swere sooth thyne othes, and nat
        lye,
And swere in doom and eek in rightwisnesse";
But ydel sweryng is a cursednesse.
Bihoold and se that in the firste table
Of heighe Goddes heestes honurable,   640
Hou that the seconde heeste of hym is this:
"Take nat my name in ydel or amys."
Lo, rather he forbedeth swich sweryng
Than homycide or many a cursed thyng;
I seye that, as by ordre, thus it stondeth;   645
This knoweth, that his heestes understondeth,
How that the seconde heeste of God is that.
And forther over, I wol thee telle al plat
That vengeance shal nat parten from his hous
That of his othes is to outrageous.   650
"By Goddes precious herte," and "By his
        nayles,"
And "By the blood of Crist that is in Hayles,
Sevene is my chaunce, and thyn is cynk and
        treye!"
"By Goddes armes, if thou falsly pleye,   654
This daggere shal thurghout thyn herte go!" —
This fruyt cometh of the bicched bones two,
Forsweryng, ire, falsnesse, homycide.
Now, for the love of Crist, that for us dyde,
Lete youre othes, bothe grete and smale.
But, sires, now wol I telle forth my tale.   660

    Thise riotoures thre of whiche I telle,
Longe erst er prime rong of any belle,

584 **Lamuel:** Lemuel, biblical king of Massa
587 **wyn-yevyng:** giving wine   **justise:** the duty of rendering justice
590 **deffenden:** forbid   **hasardrye:** gambling
591 **Hasard:** dicing   **lesynges:** lies
592 **forswerynges:** perjuries
594 **catel:** property
603 **Stilboun:** possibly the Greek philosopher Stilbo
604 **Corynthe:** Corinth, a Peloponnesian city noted for luxury
605 **Lacidomye:** Lacedaemon, Sparta
622 **Parthes:** Parthia, northern Persia

631 **Gret sweryng:** frequent swearing
632 **reprevable:** blameworthy
634 **Mathew:** St. Matthew
635 **Jeremye:** Jeremiah the prophet
637 **rightwisnesse:** justice
638 **ydel sweryng:** profanity
639 **firste table:** the first three commandments
641 **seconde heeste:** second commandment
643 **rather:** earlier (in the ten commandments)
646 **that:** he who
648 **forther over:** furthermore   **al plat:** flatly
650 **outrageous:** excessive
651 **nayles:** nails
652 **Hayles:** Hales Abbey in Gloucestershire
653 **chaunce:** a call in dicing (the number the shooter is trying to roll)   **cynk:** five   **treye:** three
656 **bicched bones:** cursed dice
661 **riotoures:** debauchers, profligates
662 **erst er:** before   **prime:** first hour of the day, beginning about 6 A.M.

Were set hem in a taverne to drynke,
And as they sat, they herde a belle clynke
Biforn a cors, was caried to his grave.   665
That oon of hem gan callen to his knave:
"Go bet," quod he, "and axe redily
What cors is this that passeth heer forby;
And looke that thou reporte his name weel."
        "Sire," quod this boy, "it nedeth never-a-
                deel;   670
It was me toold er ye cam heer two houres.
He was, pardee, an old felawe of youres,
And sodeynly he was yslayn to-nyght,
Fordronke, as he sat on his bench upright.
Ther cam a privee theef men clepeth Deeth,
That in this contree al the peple sleeth,   676
And with his spere he smoot his herte atwo,
And wente his wey withouten wordes mo.
He hath a thousand slayn this pestilence.
And, maister, er ye come in his presence,   680
Me thynketh that it were necessarie
For to be war of swich an adversarie.
Beth redy for to meete hym everemoore;
Thus taughte me my dame; I sey namoore."
"By Seinte Marie!" seyde this taverner,   685
"The child seith sooth, for he hath slayn this
                yeer,
Henne over a mile, withinne a greet village,
Bothe man and womman, child, and hyne, and
                page;
I trowe his habitacioun be there.
To been avysed greet wysdom it were,   690
Er that he dide a man a dishonour."
        "Ye, Goddes armes!" quod this riotour,
"Is it swich peril with hym for to meete?
I shal hym seke by wey and eek by strete,
I make avow to Goddes digne bones!   695
Herkneth, felawes, we thre been al ones;
Lat ech of us holde up his hand til oother,
And ech of us bicomen otheres brother,
And we wol sleen this false traytour Deeth.
He shal be slayn, he that so manye sleeth,   700
By Goddes dignitee, er it be nyght!"
        Togidres han thise thre hir trouthes plight
To lyve and dyen ech of hem for oother,

As though he were his owene ybore brother.
And up they stirte, al dronken in this rage,   705
And forth they goon towardes that village
Of which the taverner hadde spoke biforn.
And many a grisly ooth thanne han they sworn,
And Cristes blessed body they torente —   709
Deeth shal be deed, if that they may hym hente!
        Whan they han goon nat fully half a mile,
Right as they wolde han troden over a stile,
An oold man and a povre with hem mette.
This olde man ful mekely hem grette,
And seyde thus, "Now, lordes, God yow see!"
        The proudeste of thise riotoures three   716
Answerde agayn, "What, carl, with sory grace!
Why artow al forwrapped save thy face?
Why lyvestow so longe in so greet age?"
        This olde man gan looke in his visage,   720
And seyde thus: "For I ne kan nat fynde
A man, though that I walked into Ynde,
Neither in citee ne in no village,
That wolde chaunge his youthe for myn age;
And therfore moot I han myn age stille,   725
As longe tyme as it is Goddes wille.
Ne Deeth, allas, ne wol nat han my lyf.
Thus walke I, lyk a restelees kaityf,
And on the ground, which is my moodres gate,
I knokke with my staf, bothe erly and late,   730
And seye 'Leeve mooder, leet me in!
Lo how I vanysshe, flessh, and blood, and skyn!
Allas, whan shul my bones been at reste?
Mooder, with yow wolde I chaunge my cheste
That in my chambre longe tyme hath be,   735
Ye, for an heyre clowt to wrappe me!'
But yet to me she wol nat do that grace,
For which ful pale and welked is my face.
        "But, sires, to yow it is no curteisye
To speken to an old man vileynye,   740
But he trespasse in word or elles in dede.
In Hooly Writ ye may yourself wel rede:
'Agayns an oold man, hoor upon his heed,
Ye sholde arise;' wherfore I yeve yow reed,
Ne dooth unto an oold man noon harm
                now,   745
Namoore than that ye wolde men did to yow

---

665 **cors:** corpse
667 **Go bet:** go quickly
670 **boy:** servant   **it nedeth never-a-deel:** it is not at all
necessary
674 **Fordronke:** very drunk
675 **men clepeth:** one calls, is called
679 **this pestilence:** during this plague
684 **dame:** mother
687 **Henne:** hence, from here
688 **hyne:** hind, farm worker   **page:** serving boy
690 **avysed:** forewarned
698 **brother:** sworn brother
702 **plight:** pledged

709 **torente:** tore to pieces
715 **God yow see:** may God look after you
717 **carl:** fellow   **with sory grace:** bad luck to you
718 **forwrapped:** completely wrapped up
722 **Ynde:** India; i.e., the most remote place on earth
728 **kaityf:** wretch
731 **Leeve:** dear
732 **vanysshe:** waste away
734 **cheste:** strongbox for valuables
736 **heyre clowt:** haircloth
738 **welked:** withered

In age, if that ye so longe abyde.
And God be with yow, where ye go or ryde!
I moot go thider as I have to go.''
     ''Nay, olde cherl, by God, thou shalt nat so,''
Seyde this oother hasardour anon;   751
''Thou partest nat so lightly, by Seint John!
Thou spak right now of thilke traytour Deeth.
That in this contree alle oure freendes sleeth.
Have heer my trouthe, as thou art his espye,
Telle where he is or thou shalt it abye,   756
By God and by the hooly sacrement!
For soothly thou art oon of his assent
To sleen us yonge folk, thou false theef!'' 759
     ''Now, sires,'' quod he, ''if that yow be so leef
To fynde Deeth, turne up this croked wey,
For in that grove I lafte hym, by my fey,
Under a tree, and there he wole abyde;
Noght for youre boost he wole him no thyng
          hyde.
Se ye that ook? Right there ye shal hym
          fynde.   765
God save yow, that boghte agayn mankynde,
And yow amende!'' Thus seyde this olde man;
And everich of thise riotoures ran
Til he cam to that tree, and ther they founde
Of floryns fyne of gold ycoyned rounde   770
Wel ny an eighte busshels, as hem thoughte.
No lenger thanne after Deeth they soughte,
But ech of hem so glad was of that sighte,
For that the floryns been so faire and brighte,
That doun they sette hem by this precious
          hoord.   775
The worste of hem, he spak the firste word.
     ''Bretheren,'' quod he, ''taak kep what that I
          seye;
My wit is greet, though that I bourde and
          pleye.
This tresor hath Fortune unto us yiven
In myrthe and jolitee oure lyf to lyven,   780
And lightly as it comth, so wol we spende.
Ey, Goddes precious dignitee! Who wende
To-day that we sholde han so fair a grace?
But myghte this gold be caried fro this place
Hoom to myn hous, or elles unto youres —   785
For wel ye woot that al this gold is oures —
Thanne were we in heigh felicitee.
But trewely, by daye it may nat bee.

Men wolde seyn that we were theves stronge,
And for oure owene tresor doon us honge.   790
This tresor moste ycaried be by nyghte
As wisely and as slyly as it myghte.
Wherfore I rede that cut among us alle
Be drawe, and lat se wher the cut wol falle;
And he that hath the cut with herte blithe   795
Shal renne to the town, and that ful swithe,
And brynge us breed and wyn ful prively.
And two of us shul kepen subtilly
This tresor wel; and if he wol nat tarie,
Whan it is nyght, we wol this tresor carie,   800
By oon assent, where as us thynketh best.''
That oon of hem the cut broghte in his fest,
And bad hem drawe and looke where it wol
          falle;
And it fil on the yongeste of hem alle,
And forth toward the toun he wente anon.   805
And also soone as that he was gon,
That oon of hem spak thus unto that oother:
''Thow knowest wel thou art my sworen
          brother;
Thy profit wol I telle thee anon.
Thou woost wel that oure felawe is agon.   810
And heere is gold, and that ful greet plentee,
That shal departed been among us thre.
But nathelees, if I kan shape it so
That it departed were among us two,
Hadde I nat doon a freendes torn to thee?''   815
     That oother answerde, ''I noot hou that may
          be.
He woot that the gold is with us tweye;
What shal we doon? What shal we to hym
          seye?''
     ''Shal it be conseil?'' seyde the firste shrewe,
''And I shal tellen in a wordes fewe   820
What we shal doon, and brynge it wel aboute.''
     ''I graunte,'' quod that oother, ''out of doute,
That, by my trouthe, I wol thee nat biwreye.''
     ''Now,'' quod the firste, ''thou woost wel we
          be tweye,
And two of us shul strenger be than oon.   825
Looke whan that he is set, that right anoon
Arys as though thou woldest with hym pleye,
And I shal ryve hym thurgh the sydes tweye
Whil that thou strogelest with hym as in game,
And with thy daggere looke thou do the same;

---

747 **abyde:** remain (alive)
758 **oon of his assent:** in league with him
765 **ook:** oak
766 **boghte agayn:** redeemed
770 **floryns:** gold coins
778 **bourde:** jest
779 **tresor:** treasure

789 **theves stronge:** arrant thieves
790 **doon us honge:** have us hanged
793–94 **cut . . . Be drawe:** lots be drawn
796 **ful swithe:** very quickly
815 **freendes torn:** friend's turn, friendly act
823 **biwreye:** betray
828 **ryve:** stab

And thanne shal al this gold departed be,   831
My deere freend, bitwixen me and thee.
Thanne may we bothe oure lustes all fulfille,
And pleye at dees right at oure owene wille."
And thus acorded been thise shrewes tweye
To sleen the thridde, as ye han herd me seye.   836

   This yongeste, which that wente to the toun,
Ful ofte in herte he rolleth up and doun
The beautee of thise floryns newe and brighte.
"O Lord!" quod he, "if so were that I myghte
Have al this tresor to myself allone,   841
Ther is no man that lyveth under the trone
Of God that sholde lyve so murye as I!"
And atte laste the feend, oure enemy,   844
Putte in his thought that he sholde poyson beye,
With which he myghte sleen his felawes tweye;
For-why the feend foond hym in swich lyvynge
That he hadde leve him to sorwe brynge.
For this was outrely his fulle entente,
To sleen hem bothe and nevere to repente.   850
And forth he gooth, no lenger wolde he tarie,
Into the toun, unto a pothecarie,
And preyde hym that he hym wolde selle
Som poyson, that he myghte his rattes quelle;
And eek ther was a polcat in his hawe,   855
That, as he seyde, his capouns hadde yslawe,
And fayn he wolde wreke hym, if he myghte,
On vermyn that destroyed hym by nyghte.

   The pothecarie answerde, "And thou shalt
     have
A thyng that, also God my soule save,   860
In al this world ther is no creature
That eten or dronken hath of this confiture
Noght but the montance of a corn of whete,
That he ne shal his lif anon forlete;
Ye, sterve he shal, and that in lasse while   865
Than thou wolt goon a paas nat but a mile,
This poysoun is so strong and violent."

   This cursed man hath in his hond yhent
This poysoun in a box, and sith he ran
Into the nexte strete unto a man,   870
And borwed [of] hym large botelles thre,
And in the two his poyson poured he;

The thridde he kepte clene for his drynke.
For al the nyght he shoop hym for to swynke
In cariynge of the gold out of that place.   875
And whan this riotour, with sory grace,
Hadde filled with wyn his grete botels thre,
To his felawes agayn repaireth he.

   What nedeth it to sermone of it moore?   879
For right as they hadde cast his deeth bifoore,
Right so they han hym slayn, and that anon.
And whan that this was doon, thus spak that
     oon:
"Now lat us sitte and drynke, and make us
     merie,
And afterward we wol his body berie."   884
And with that word it happed hym, par cas,
To take the botel ther the poyson was,
And drank, and yaf his felawe drynke also,
For which anon they storven bothe two.

   But certes, I suppose that Avycen
Wroot nevere in no canon, ne in no fen,   890
Mo wonder signes of empoisonyng
Than hadde thise wrecches two, er hir endyng.
Thus ended been thise homycides two,
And eek the false empoysonere also.

   O cursed synne of alle cursednesse!   895
O traytours homycide, O wikkednesse!
O glotonye, luxurie, and hasardrye!
Thou blasphemour of Crist with vileynye
And othes grete, of usage and of pride!
Allas, mankynde, how may it bitide   900
That to thy creatour, which that the wroghte
And with his precious herte-blood thee boghte,
Thou art so fals and so unkynde, allas?

   Now, goode men, God foryeve yow youre
     trespas,
And ware yow fro the synne of avarice!   905
Myn hooly pardoun may yow alle warice,
So that ye offre nobles or sterlynges,
Or elles silver broches, spoones, rynges.
Boweth youre heed under this hooly bulle!   909
Cometh up, ye wyves, offreth of youre wolle!
Youre names I entre heer in my rolle anon;
Into the blisse of hevene shul ye gon.

---

838 **rolleth up and doun:** meditates on
842 **trone:** throne
848 **leve:** permission
852 **pothecarie:** apothecary
854 **quelle:** kill
855 **polcat:** weasel **hawe:** yard
857 **wreke hym:** revenge himself
858 **vermyn:** animal pests **destroyed:** were ruining
862 **confiture:** concoction
863 **montance:** amount, size **corn:** grain
864 **forlete:** lose
865 **sterve:** die **while:** time
866 **a paas:** at a walk

874 **shoop hym:** intended
885 **par cas:** by chance
889 **Avycen:** Avicenna, Arabic author of a medical treatise
890 **canon:** set of rules **fen:** a division of Avicenna's book
891 **empoisonyng:** poisoning
894 **empoysonere:** poisoner
897 **luxurie:** lechery
899 **usage:** habit
903 **unkynde:** unnatural
906 **warice:** cure, save
907 **nobles:** gold coins **sterlynges:** silver pennies
910 **wolle:** wool

I yow assoille, by myn heigh power,
Yow that wol offre, as clene and eek as cleer
As ye were born. — And lo, sires, thus I preche.
And Jhesu Crist, that is oure soules leche,   916
So graunte yow his pardoun to receyve,
For that is best; I wol yow nat deceyve.

But, sires, o word forgat I in my tale:
I have relikes and pardoun in my male,   920
As faire as any man in Engelond,
Whiche were me yeven by the popes hond.
If any of yow wole, of devocion,
Offren and han myn absolucion,
Com forth anon, and kneleth heere adoun,   925
And mekely receyveth my pardoun;
Or elles taketh pardoun as ye wende,
Al newe and fressh at every miles ende,
So that ye offren, alwey newe and newe,
Nobles or pens, whiche that be goode and
          trewe.   930
It is an honour to everich that is heer
That ye mowe have a suffisant pardoneer
T'assoille yow in contree as ye ryde,
For aventures whiche that may bityde.
Paraventure ther may fallen oon or two   935
Doun of his hors and breke his nekke atwo.
Looke which a seuretee is it to yow alle
That I am in youre felaweshipe yfalle,
That may assoille yow, bothe moore and lasse,
Whan that the soule shal fro the body passe.
I rede that oure Hoost heere shal bigynne,   941

For he is moost envoluped in synne.
Com forth, sire Hoost, and offre first anon,
And thou shalt kisse the relikes everychon,
Ye, for a grote! Unbokele anon thy purs."   945
     "Nay, nay!" quod he, "thanne have I Cristes
          curs!
Lat be," quod he, "it shal nat be, so theech!
Thou woldest make me kisse thyn olde breech,
And swere it were a relyk of a seint,   949
Though it were with thy fundement depeint!
But, by the croys which that Seint Eleyne fond,
I wolde I hadde thy coillons in myn hond
In stide of relikes or of seintuarie.
Lat kutte hem of, I wol thee helpe hem carie;
They shul be shryned in an hogges toord!"   955
     This Pardoner answerde nat a word;
So wrooth he was, no word ne wolde he seye.
     "Now," quod oure Hoost, "I wol no lenger
          pleye
With thee, ne with noon oother angry man."
But right anon the worthy Knyght bigan,   960
Whan that he saugh that al the peple lough,
"Namoore of this, for it is right ynough!
Sire Pardoner, be glad and myrie of cheere;
And ye, sire Hoost, that been to me so deere,
I prey yow that ye kisse the Pardoner.   965
And Pardoner, I prey thee, drawe thee neer,
And, as we diden, lat us laughe and pleye."
Anon they kiste, and ryden forth hir weye.

Heere is ended the Pardoners Tale.

913 **assoille:** absolve
916 **leche:** physician
917 **graunte:** allow
920 **pardoun:** pardons, papal indulgences   **male:** pouch, bag
937 **which a:** what a   **seuretee:** safeguard

942 **envoluped:** enveloped
945 **grote:** groat, a silver coin worth four pence
946 **Cristes curs:** damnation
947 **so theech** = *so thee ich,* as I may prosper (I swear)
948 **breech:** underpants
950 **fundement:** anus   **depeint:** stained
951 **croys:** cross   **Seint Eleyne:** St. Helen, discoverer of the true
cross
952 **coillons:** testicles
953 **seintuarie:** sanctuary, box for relics
955 **shryned:** enshrined   **toord:** turd
968 **ryden:** rode

THE SHIPMAN'S TALE

Heere bigynneth the Shipmannes Tale.

A marchant whilom dwelled at Seint-Denys,
That riche was, for which men helde hym wys.
A wyf he hadde of excellent beautee;
And compaignable and revelous was she,   4
Which is a thyng that causeth more dispence
Than worth is al the chiere and reverence
That men hem doon at festes and at daunces.
Swiche salutaciouns and contenaunces
Passen as dooth a shadwe upon the wal;
But wo is hym that payen moot for al!   *1200
The sely housbonde, algate he moot paye,
He moot us clothe, and he moot us arraye,
Al for his owene worshipe richely,
In which array we daunce jolily.
And if that he noght may, par aventure,   15
Or ellis list no swich dispence endure,
But thynketh it is wasted and ylost,
Thanne moot another payen for oure cost,
Or lene us gold, and that is perilous.
    This noble marchaunt heeld a worthy
        hous,   *1210
For which he hadde alday so greet repair
For his largesse, and for his wyf was fair,
That wonder is; but herkneth to my tale.
Amonges alle his gestes, grete and smale,
Ther was a monk, a fair man and a boold —   25
I trowe a thritty wynter he was oold —
That evere in oon was drawynge to that place.
This yonge monk, that was so fair of face,
Aqueynted was so with the goode man,
Sith that hir firste knoweliche bigan,   *1220

That in his hous as famulier was he
As it is possible any freend to be.
    And for as muchel as this goode man,
And eek this monk of which that I bigan,
Were bothe two yborn in o village,   35
The monk hym claymeth as for cosynage,
And he agayn; he seith nat ones nay,
But was as glad therof as fowel of day,
For to his herte it was a greet plesaunce.
Thus been they knyt with eterne alliaunce,
And ech of hem gan oother for t'assure   *1231
Of bretherhede whil that hir lyf may dure.
    Free was daun John, and manly of dispence,
As in that hous, and ful of diligence
To doon plesaunce, and also greet costage.   45
He noght forgat to yeve the leeste page
In al that hous; but after hir degree,
He yaf the lord, and sitthe al his meynee,   *1238
Whan that he cam, som manere honest thyng,
For which they were as glad of his comyng
As fowel is fayn whan that the sonne up riseth.
Na moore of this as now, for it suffiseth.
    But so bifel, this marchant on a day
Shoop hym to make redy his array
Toward the toun of Brugges for to fare,   55
To byen there a porcioun of ware;
For which he hath to Parys sent anon
A messager, and preyed hath daun John
That he sholde come to Seint-Denys to pleye
With hym and with his wyf a day or tweye,
Er he to Brugges wente, in alle wise.   *1251
    This noble monk, of which I yow devyse,
Hath of his abbot, as hym list, licence,
By cause he was a man of heigh prudence

---

*For the convenience of the reader in finding references, the
traditional numbering of Group B², marked with asterisks, is
carried alternately with that of Fragment VII.

1 **Seint-Denys:** a town north of Paris
4 **compaignable:** sociable   **revelous:** convivial, fond of revelry
5 **dispence:** expense
6 **chiere:** attention
8 **contenaunces:** courtesies
11 **sely:** poor
13 **worshipe:** honor
20 **heeld a worthy hous:** maintained his household generously
21 **alday:** daily   **so greet repair:** so many visitors
22 **largesse:** generosity
26 **a thritty wynter:** about thirty years
27 **evere in oon:** always
29 **goode man:** the goodman, or head of the household
30 **knoweliche:** acquaintance

36 **cosynage:** kinship
42 **bretherhede:** sworn brotherhood
43 **manly:** generous
45 **doon . . . greet costage:** spend much money
54 **Shoop hym:** prepared
55 **Brugges:** Bruges, now in Belgium
56 **porcioun:** quantity   **ware:** goods

And eek an officer, out for to ryde,   65
To seen hir graunges and hire bernes wyde,
And unto Seint-Denys he comth anon.
Who was so welcome as my lord daun John,
Oure deere cosyn, ful of curteisye?
With hym broghte he a jubbe of malvesye,
And eek another ful of fyn vernage,   *1261
And volatyl, as ay was his usage.
And thus I lete hem ete and drynke and pleye,
This marchant and this monk, a day or tweye.

The thridde day, this marchant up ariseth,
And on his nedes sadly hym avyseth,   76
And up into his countour-hous gooth he
To rekene with hymself, wel may be,
Of thilke yeer how that it with hym stood,
And how that he despended hadde his good,
And if that he encressed were or noon.   *1271
His bookes and his bagges many oon
He leith biforn hym on his countyng-bord.
Ful riche was his tresor and his hord,   84
For which ful faste his countour-dore he shette;
And eek he nolde that no man sholde hym lette
Of his acountes, for the meene tyme;
And thus he sit til it was passed pryme.

Daun John was rysen in the morwe also,
And in the gardyn walketh to and fro,   *1280
And hath his thynges seyd ful curteisly.

This goode wyf cam walkynge pryvely
Into the gardyn, there he walketh softe,
And hym saleweth, as she hath doon ofte.
A mayde child cam in hire compaignye,   95
Which as hir list she may governe and gye,
For yet under the yerde was the mayde.
"O deere cosyn myn, daun John," she sayde,
"What eyleth yow so rathe for to ryse?"

"Nece," quod he, "it oghte ynough suffise
Fyve houres for to slepe upon a nyght,   *1291
But it were for an old appalled wight,
As been thise wedded men, that lye and dare

As in a fourme sit a wery hare,
Were al forstraught with houndes grete and
     smale.
But deere nece, why be ye so pale?   106
I trowe, certes, that oure goode man
Hath yow laboured sith the nyght bigan
That yow were nede to resten hastily."
And with that word he lough ful murily,   *1300
And of his owene thought he wax al reed.

This faire wyf gan for to shake hir heed
And seyde thus, "Ye, God woot al," quod she.
"Nay, cosyn myn, it stant nat so with me;
For, by that God that yaf me soule and lyf,
In al the reawme of France is ther no wyf   116
That lasse lust hath to that sory pley.
For I may synge 'allas and weylawey
That I was born,' but to no wight," quod she,
"Dar I nat telle how that it stant with me.
Wherfore I thynke out of this land to wende,
Or elles of myself to make an ende,   *1312
So ful am I of drede and eek of care."

This monk bigan upon this wyf to stare,
And seyde, "Allas, my nece, God forbede   125
That ye, for any sorwe or any drede,
Fordo youreself; but telleth me youre grief.
Paraventure I may, in youre meschief,
Conseille or helpe; and therfore telleth me
Al youre anoy, for it shal been secree.   *1320
For on my portehors I make an ooth
That nevere in my lyf, for lief ne looth,
Ne shal I of no conseil yow biwreye."

"The same agayn to yow," quod she, "I seye.
By God and by this portehors I swere,   135
Though men me wolde al into pieces tere,
Ne shal I nevere, for to goon to helle,
Biwreye a word of thyng that ye me telle,
Nat for no cosynage ne alliance,
But verraily for love and affiance."   *1330
Thus been they sworn, and heerupon they kiste,
And ech of hem tolde oother what hem liste.

"Cosyn," quod she, "if that I hadde a space,
As I have noon, and namely in this place,
Thanne wolde I telle a legende of my lyf,   145

---

65 **officer:** probably cellarer
66 **graunges:** outlying farms
69 **cosyn:** kinsman
70 **jubbe:** a large container, jug **malvesye:** malmsey
71 **vernage:** white Italian wine (vernaccia)
72 **volatyl:** game fowl
76 **nedes:** business duties
86 **lette:** disturb
88 **pryme:** 9 A.M.
91 **thynges:** devotions
97 **under the yerde:** subject to (adult) authority
99 **rathe:** early
100 **Nece:** kinswoman
102 **appalled:** pallid, feeble
103 **dare:** lie motionless or dozing

104 **fourme:** form (a grassy, often sheltered, hollow)
105 **forstraught:** distraught
108 **laboured:** put to work
116 **reawme:** realm
117 **lust:** pleasure
130 **anoy:** trouble
131 **portehors:** breviary
133 **biwreye:** expose, betray
140 **affiance:** trust
143 **space:** time, space of time
145 **legende:** saint's life

What I have suffred sith I was a wyf
With myn housbonde, al be he youre cosyn."
  "Nay," quod this monk, "by God and Seint
      Martyn,
He is na moore cosyn unto me   *1339
Than is this leef that hangeth on the tree!
I clepe hym so, by Seint Denys of Fraunce,
To have the moore cause of aqueyntaunce
Of yow, which I have loved specially
Aboven alle wommen, sikerly.
This swere I yow on my professioun.   155
Telleth youre grief, lest that he come adoun;
And hasteth yow, and gooth youre wey anon."
  "My deere love," quod she, "O my daun
      John,
Ful lief were me this conseil for to hyde,
But out it moot; I may namoore abyde.
Myn housbonde is to me the worste man   *1351
That evere was sith that the world bigan.
But sith I am a wyf, it sit nat me
To tellen no wight of oure privetee,
Neither abedde ne in noon oother place;   165
God shilde I sholde it tellen, for his grace!
A wyf ne shal nat seyn of hir housbonde
But al honour, as I kan understonde;
Save unto yow thus muche I tellen shal:
As helpe me God, he is noght worth at al   *1360
In no degree the value of a flye.
But yet me greveth moost his nygardye.
And wel ye woot that wommen naturelly
Desiren thynges sixe as wel as I:
They wolde that hir housbondes sholde be   175
Hardy and wise, and riche, and therto free,
And buxom unto his wyf and fressh abedde.
But by that ilke Lord that for us bledde,
For his honour, myself for to arraye,
A Sonday next I moste nedes paye   *1370
An hundred frankes, or ellis I am lorn.
Yet were me levere that I were unborn
Than me were doon a sclaundre or vileynye;
And if myn housbonde eek it myghte espye,
I nere but lost; and therfore I yow preye,   185
Lene me this somme, or ellis moot I deye.

---

148 **seint Martyn:** St. Martin of Tours
151 **Seint Denys:** St. Denis, patron saint of France
155 **professioun:** monastic vows
159 **Ful lief were me:** I would very much like
163 **sit nat me:** is not suitable for me
166 **shilde:** forbid
172 **nygardye:** miserliness
176 **Hardy:** vigorous **free:** generous
177 **buxom:** obedient
181 **An hundred frankes:** about fifteen pounds sterling
183 **sclaundre:** disgrace
185 **nere but:** would be (nothing else) but, would surely be

Daun John, I seye, lene me thise hundred
      frankes.
Pardee, I wol nat faille yow my thankes,
If that yow list to doon that I yow praye.
For at a certeyn day I wol yow paye,   *1380
And doon to yow what plesance and service
That I may doon, right as yow list devise.
And but I do, God take on me vengeance
As foul as evere hadde Genylon of France."
  This gentil monk answerde in this manere:
"Now trewely, myn owene lady deere,   196
I have," quod he, "on yow so greet a routhe
That I yow swere, and plighte yow my trouthe,
That whan youre housbonde is to Flaundres
      fare,
I wol delyvere yow out of this care;   *1390
For I wol brynge yow an hundred frankes."
And with that word he caughte hire by the
      flankes,
And hire embraceth harde, and kiste hire ofte.
"Gooth now youre wey," quod he, "al stille and
      softe,
And lat us dyne as soone as that ye may;   205
For by my chilyndre it is pryme of day.
Gooth now, and beeth as trewe as I shal be."
  "Now elles God forbede, sire," quod she;
And forth she gooth as jolif as a pye,
And bad the cookes that they sholde hem
      hye,   *1400
So that men myghte dyne, and that anon.
Up to hir housbonde is this wyf ygon,
And knokketh at his countour boldely.
  "Quy la?" quod he. "Peter! it am I,"
Quod she; "What, sire, how longe wol ye faste?
How longe tyme wol ye rekene and caste   216
Youre sommes, and youre bookes, and youre
      thynges?
The devel have part on alle swiche rekenynges!
Ye have ynough, pardee, of Goddes sonde;
Com doun to-day, and lat youre bagges
      stonde.   *1410
Ne be ye nat ashamed that daun John
Shal fasting al this day alenge goon?
What, lat us heere a messe, and go we dyne."
  "Wyf," quod this man, "litel kanstow devyne
The curious bisynesse that we have.   225

---

194 **Genylon:** Ganelon, who betrayed Roland; see n.
206 **chilyndre:** portable sundial
209 **pye:** magpie
213 **countour:** counting house
214 *Quy la?*: Who's there? **Peter!:** by St. Peter!
216 **caste:** calculate
219 **Goddes sonde:** what God has sent
222 **alenge:** miserable
225 **curious bisynesse:** worrisome preoccupations

For of us chapmen, also God me save,
And by that lord that clepid is Seint Yve,
Scarsly amonges twelve tweye shul thryve
Continuelly, lastynge unto oure age.
We may wel make chiere and good
   visage,   *1420
And dryve forth the world as it may be,
And kepen oure estaat in pryvetee,
Til we be deed, or elles that we pleye
A pilgrymage, or goon out of the weye.
And therfore have I greet necessitee   235
Upon this queynte world t'avyse me,
For everemoore we moote stonde in drede
Of hap and fortune in oure chapmanhede.

 "To Flaundres wol I go to-morwe at day,
And come agayn, as soone as evere I
   may.   *1430
For which, my deere wyf, I thee biseke,
As be to every wight buxom and meke,
And for to kepe oure good be curious,
And honestly governe wel oure hous.
Thou hast ynough, in every maner wise,   245
That to a thrifty houshold may suffise.
Thee lakketh noon array ne no vitaille;
Of silver in thy purs shaltow nat faille."
And with that word his countour-dore he shette,
And doun he gooth, no lenger wolde he
   lette.   *1440
But hastily a messe was ther seyd,
And spedily the tables were yleyd,
And to the dyner faste they hem spedde,
And richely this monk the chapman fedde.

 At after-dyner daun John sobrely   255
This chapman took apart, and prively
He seyde hym thus: "Cosyn, it standeth so,
That wel I se to Brugges wol ye go.
God and Seint Austyn spede yow and gyde!
I prey yow, cosyn, wisely that ye ryde.   *1450
Governeth yow also of youre diete
Atemprely, and namely in this hete.
Bitwix us two nedeth no strange fare;
Farewel, cosyn; God shilde yow fro care!

And if that any thyng by day or nyght,   265
If it lye in my power and my myght,
That ye me wol comande in any wyse,
It shal be doon right as ye wol devyse.

 "O thyng, er that ye goon, if it may be,
I wolde prey yow: for to lene me   *1460
An hundred frankes, for a wyke or tweye,
For certein beestes that I moste beye,
To stoore with a place that is oures.
God helpe me so, I wolde it were youres!
I shal nat faille surely of my day,   275
Nat for a thousand frankes, a mile way.
But lat this thyng be secree, I yow preye,
For yet to-nyght thise beestes moot I beye.
And fare now wel, myn owene cosyn deere;
Graunt mercy of youre cost and of youre
   cheere."   *1470
This noble marchant gentilly anon
Answerde and seyde, "O cosyn myn, daun John,
Now sikerly this is a smal requeste.
My gold is youres, whan that it yow leste,
And nat oonly my gold, but my chaffare.   285
Take what yow list; God shilde that ye spare.

 "But o thyng is, ye knowe it wel ynogh
Of chapmen, that hir moneie is hir plogh.
We may creaunce whil we have a name,
But goldlees for to be, it is no game.   *1480
Paye it agayn whan it lith in youre ese;
After my myght ful fayn wolde I yow plese."

 Thise hundred frankes he fette forth anon,
And prively he took hem to daun John.   294
No wight in al this world wiste of this loone
Savynge this marchant and daun John allone.
They drynke, and speke, and rome a while and
   pleye,
Til that daun John rideth to his abbeye.

 The morwe cam, and forth this marchant
   rideth
To Flaundres-ward; his prentys wel hym
   gydeth   *1490
Til he came into Brugges murily.
Now gooth this marchant faste and bisily
Aboute his nede, and byeth and creaunceth.
He neither pleyeth at the dees ne daunceth,

---

227 **Seint Yve:** St. Ivo (?); see n.
231 **dryve forth:** endure
233 **pleye:** play or go; see n.
234 **goon out of the weye:** disappear
236 **queynte:** tricky
238 **hap:** risk (chance happening) **chapmanhede:** business dealings
243 **curious:** diligent
246 **thrifty:** prosperous, thriving
248 **faille:** lack
259 **Seint Austyn:** St. Augustine of Hippo
262 **Atemprely:** moderately
263 **strange fare:** elaborate courtesies
264 **shilde:** protect

273 **To stoore with:** with which to stock
276 **a mile way:** by (so much as) twenty minutes
280 **Graunt mercy:** thank you
284 **whan that it yow leste:** when ever you please
285 **chaffare:** goods, merchandise
289 **creaunce:** borrow money, obtain credit
290 **no game:** no laughing matter
294 **took:** gave
295 **loone:** loan
303 **creaunceth:** obtains credit

But as a marchaunt, shortly for to telle,   305
He let his lyf, and there I lete hym dwelle.
   The Sonday next the marchant was agon,
To Seint-Denys ycomen is daun John,
With crowne and berd al fressh and newe
     yshave.   *1499
In al the hous ther nas so litel a knave,
Ne no wight elles, that he nas ful fayn
That my lord daun John was come agayn.
And shortly to the point right for to gon,
This faire wyf acorded with daun John
That for thise hundred frankes he sholde al
     nyght   315
Have hire in his armes bolt upright;
And this acord parfourned was in dede.
In myrthe al nyght a bisy lyf they lede
Til it was day, that daun John wente his way,
And bad the meynee "Farewel, have good
     day!"   *1510
For noon of hem, ne no wight in the toun,
Hath of daun John right no suspecioun.
And forth he rydeth hoom to his abbeye,
Or where hym list; namoore of hym I seye.
   This marchant, whan that ended was the
     faire,
To Seint-Denys he gan for to repaire,   326
And with his wyf he maketh feeste and cheere,
And telleth hire that chaffare is so deere
That nedes moste he make a chevyssaunce,
For he was bounden in a reconyssaunce   *1520
To paye twenty thousand sheeld anon.
For which this marchant is to Parys gon
To borwe of certeine freendes that he hadde
A certeyn frankes; and somme with him he
     ladde.
And whan that he was come into the toun,   335
For greet chiertee and greet affeccioun,
Unto daun John he first gooth hym to pleye;
Nat for to axe or borwe of hym moneye,
But for to wite and seen of his welfare,
And for to tellen hym of his chaffare,
As freendes doon whan they been met
     yfeere.   *1531

Daun John hym maketh feeste and murye
     cheere,
And he hym tolde agayn, ful specially,
How he hadde wel yboght and graciously,
Thanked be God, al hool his marchandise,   345
Save that he moste, in alle maner wise,
Maken a chevyssaunce, as for his beste,
And thanne he sholde been in joye and reste.
   Daun John answerde, "Certes, I am fayn
That ye in heele ar comen hom agayn.   *1540
And if that I were riche, as have I blisse,
Of twenty thousand sheeld sholde ye nat mysse,
For ye so kyndely this oother day
Lente me gold; and as I kan and may,
I thanke yow, by God and by Seint Jame!   355
But nathelees, I took unto oure dame,
Youre wyf, at hom, the same gold ageyn
Upon youre bench; she woot it wel, certeyn,
By certeyn tokenes that I kan hire telle.
Now, by youre leve, I may no lenger
     dwelle;   *1550
Oure abbot wole out of this toun anon,
And in his compaignye moot I goon.
Grete wel oure dame, myn owene nece sweete,
And fare wel, deere cosyn, til we meete!"
   This marchant, which that was ful war and
     wys,
Creanced hath, and payd eek in Parys   366
To certeyn Lumbardes, redy in hir hond,
The somme of gold, and gat of hem his bond;
And hoom he gooth, murie as a papejay,
For wel he knew he stood in swich array   *1560
That nedes moste he wynne in that viage
A thousand frankes aboven al his costage.
   His wyf ful redy mette hym atte gate,
As she was wont of oold usage algate,
And al that nyght in myrthe they bisette;   375
For he was riche and cleerly out of dette.
Whan it was day, this marchant gan embrace
His wyf al newe, and kiste hire on hir face,
And up he gooth and maketh it ful tough.

---

306 **let his lyf:** leads (*let = ledeth*) his life, conducts himself
309 **crowne:** head
316 **bolt upright:** flat on her back
326 **repaire:** return
328 **chaffare:** merchandise
329 **chevyssaunce:** loan; see Expl. Notes on the business transaction described in lines 328–34.
330 **reconyssaunce:** formal pledge
331 **sheeld:** units of exchange
334 **A certeyn:** a certain number of
336 **chiertee:** fondness
341 **yfeere:** together

343 **ful specially:** in great detail
344 **graciously:** successfully
350 **heele:** good health
354 **kan and may:** know how and can
355 **Seint Jame:** St. James of Compostella
356 **took:** gave
359 **tokenes:** confirmatory details, proofs
367 **Lumbardes:** Lombard bankers **redy in hir hond:** promptly and in cash
369 **papejay:** parrot
371 **viage:** undertaking
372 **aboven:** in addition to **costage:** expense
379 **maketh it ful tough:** is unrelenting in his demands

"Namoore," quod she, "by God, ye have
    ynough!"   *1570
And wantownly agayn with hym she pleyde
Til atte laste thus this marchant seyde:
"By God," quod he, "I am a litel wrooth
With yow, my wyf, although it be me looth.
And woot ye why? By God, as that I gesse 385
That ye han maad a manere straungenesse
Bitwixen me and my cosyn daun John.
Ye sholde han warned me, er I had gon,
That he yow hadde an hundred frankes payed
By redy token; and heeld hym yvele apayed,
For that I to hym spak of chevyssaunce;   *1581
Me semed so, as by his contenaunce.
But nathelees, by God, oure hevene kyng,
I thoughte nat to axen hym no thyng.
I prey thee, wyf, ne do namoore so;   395
Telle me alwey, er that I fro thee go,
If any dettour hath in myn absence
Ypayed thee, lest thurgh thy necligence
I myghte hym axe a thing that he hath payed."
  This wyf was nat afered nor affrayed,
But boldely she seyde, and that anon,   *1591
"Marie, I deffie the false monk, daun John!
I kepe nat of his tokenes never a deel;
He took me certeyn gold, that woot I weel —
What! Yvel thedam on his monkes snowte! 405
For, God it woot, I wende, withouten doute,

That he hadde yeve it me bycause of yow
To doon therwith myn honour and my prow,
For cosynage, and eek for beele cheere
That he hath had ful ofte tymes heere.   *1600
But sith I se I stonde in this disjoynt,
I wol answere yow shortly to the poynt.
Ye han mo slakkere dettours than am I!
For I wol paye yow wel and redily
Fro day to day, and if so be I faille,   415
I am youre wyf; score it upon my taille,
And I shal paye as soone as ever I may.
For by my trouthe, I have on myn array,
And nat on wast, bistowed every deel;
And for I have bistowed it so weel   *1610
For youre honour, for Goddes sake, I seye,
As be nat wrooth, but lat us laughe and pleye.
Ye shal my joly body have to wedde;
By God, I wol nat paye yow but abedde!
Forgyve it me, myn owene spouse deere;   425
Turne hiderward, and maketh bettre cheere."
  This marchant saugh ther was no remedie,
And for to chide it nere but folie,
Sith that the thyng may nat amended be.
"Now wyf," he seyde, "and I foryeve it thee;
But, by thy lyf, ne be namoore so large.   *1621
Keep bet thy good, this yeve I thee in charge."
Thus endeth my tale, and God us sende
Taillynge ynough unto oure lyves ende. Amen

Heere endeth the Shipmannes Tale.

*Bihoold the murie wordes of the Hoost to the Shipman and to the
lady Prioresse.*

"Wel seyd, by *corpus dominus,*" quod oure
    Hoost,
"Now longe moote thou saille by the cost, 436
Sire gentil maister, gentil maryneer!
God yeve the monk a thousand last quade yeer!
A ha! Felawes, beth ware of swich a jape!
The monk putte in the mannes hood an ape,
And in his wyves eek, by Seint Austyn!   *1631
Draweth no monkes moore unto youre in.

"But now passe over, and lat us seke aboute,
Who shal now telle first of al this route
Another tale;" and with that word he sayde,
As curteisly as it had been a mayde,   446
"My lady Prioresse, by youre leve,
So that I wiste I sholde yow nat greve,
I wolde demen that ye tellen sholde
A tale next, if so were that ye wolde.   *1640
Now wol ye vouche sauf, my lady deere?"
  "Gladly," quod she, and seyde as ye shal
    heere.

---

381 **wantownly agayn:** wantonly in return
386 **straungenesse:** estrangement
390 **By redy token:** in cash (by clear evidence) **heeld hym
yvele apayed:** he considered himself ill-used
404 **took:** gave
405 **Yvel thedam:** bad luck

---

435 *corpus dominus:* corpus Domini, the body of the Lord
438 **last quade yeer:** cartloads of bad years
440 The monk made a monkey of the man

408 **prow:** profit, benefit
409 **cosynage:** kinship **beele cheere:** good cheer, hospitality
411 **disjoynt:** difficulty
413 **slakkere:** slower (to repay) **dettours:** debtors
416 **score it upon my taille:** mark it on my tally, charge it to
my account; see n.
423 **to wedde:** as a pledge
431 **large:** free-spending
434 **Taillynge:** credit

PROLOGUE OF THE PRIORESS'S TALE

The Prologe of the Prioresses Tale.

Domine dominus noster.

O Lord, oure Lord, thy name how merveil-
    lous
Is in this large world ysprad — quod she —
For noght oonly thy laude precious   455
Parfourned is by men of dignitee,
But by the mouth of children thy bountee
Parfourned is, for on the brest soukynge
Somtyme shewen they thyn heriynge.

Wherfore in laude, as I best kan or may, *1650
Of thee and of the white lylye flour
Which that the bar, and is a mayde alway,
To telle a storie I wol do my labour;
Nat that I may encressen hir honour,
For she hirself is honour and the roote   465
Of bountee, next hir Sone, and soules boote.

O mooder Mayde, O mayde Mooder free!
O bussh unbrent, brennynge in Moyses
    sighte,
That ravyshedest doun fro the Deitee,

Thurgh thyn humblesse, the Goost that in
    th'alighte,   *1660
Of whos vertu, whan he thyn herte lighte,
Conceyved was the Fadres sapience,
Help me to telle it in thy reverence!

Lady, thy bountee, thy magnificence,
Thy vertu and thy grete humylitee   475
Ther may no tonge expresse in no science;
For somtyme, Lady, er men praye to thee,
Thou goost biforn of thy benyngnytee,
And getest us the lyght, of thy preyere,
To gyden us unto thy Sone so deere.   *1670

My konnyng is so wayk, O blisful Queene,
For to declare thy grete worthynesse
That I ne may the weighte nat susteene;
But as a child of twelf month oold, or lesse,
That kan unnethes any word expresse,   485
Right so fare I, and therfore I yow preye,
Gydeth my song that I shal of yow seye.

Explicit.

THE PRIORESS'S TALE

Heere bigynneth the Prioresses Tale.

Ther was in Asye, in a greet citee,
Amonges Cristene folk a Jewerye,
Sustened by a lord of that contree   *1680
For foule usure and lucre of vileynye,

Hateful to Crist and to his compaignye;
And thurgh the strete men myghte ride or
    wende,
For it was free and open at eyther ende.

A litel scole of Cristen folk ther stood   495
Doun at the ferther ende, in which ther were

455 **laude:** praise
458 **soukynge:** suckling
459 **heriynge:** praise
466 **soules boote:** remedy for the soul
468 **unbrent:** unburned   **Moyses:** Moses'

489 **Jewerye:** ghetto
491 **usure:** usury   **lucre of vileynye:** shameful (excessive)
profits

470 **Goost:** Holy Spirit
476 **in no science:** not by the means of, or in the language of,
any human learning

495 **scole:** school

Children an heep, ycomen of Cristen blood,
That lerned in that scole yeer by yere
Swich manere doctrine as men used there,
This is to seyn, to syngen and to rede,   *1690
As smale children doon in hire childhede.

Among thise children was a wydwes sone,
A litel clergeon, seven yeer of age,
That day by day to scole was his wone,
And eek also, where as he saugh th'ymage
Of Cristes mooder, hadde he in usage,   506
As hym was taught, to knele adoun and seye
His *Ave Marie,* as he goth by the weye.

Thus hath this wydwe hir litel sone ytaught *1699
Oure blisful Lady, Cristes mooder deere,
To worshipe ay, and he forgat it naught,
For sely child wol alday soone leere.
But ay, whan I remembre on this mateere,
Seint Nicholas stant evere in my presence,
For he so yong to Crist dide reverence.   515

This litel child, his litel book lernynge,
As he sat in the scole at his prymer,
He *Alma redemptoris* herde synge,
As children lerned hire antiphoner;
And as he dorste, he drough hym ner and
          ner,   *1710
And herkned ay the wordes and the noote,
Til he the firste vers koude al by rote.

Noght wiste he what this Latyn was to seye,
For he so yong and tendre was of age.
But on a day his felawe gan he preye   525
T'expounden hym this song in his langage,
Or telle hym why this song was in usage;
This preyde he hym to construe and declare
Ful often tyme upon his knowes bare.

His felawe, which that elder was than he, *1720
Answerde hym thus: "This song, I have herd
          seye,
Was maked of our blisful Lady free,
Hire to salue, and eek hire for to preye   533

To been oure help and socour whan we deye.
I kan namoore expounde in this mateere.
I lerne song; I kan but smal grammeere."

"And is this song maked in reverence
Of Cristes mooder?" seyde this innocent.
"Now, certes, I wol do my diligence
To konne it al er Cristemasse be went.   *1730
Though that I for my prymer shal be shent
And shal be beten thries in an houre,
I wol it konne Oure Lady for to honoure!"

His felawe taughte hym homward prively,
Fro day to day, til he koude it by rote,   545
And thanne he song it wel and boldely,
Fro word to word, acordynge with the note.
Twies a day it passed thurgh his throte,
To scoleward and homward whan he wente;
On Cristes mooder set was his entente.   *1740

    As I have seyd, thurghout the Juerie
This litel child, as he cam to and fro,
Ful murily than wolde he synge and crie
O Alma redemptoris everemo.
The swetnesse his herte perced so   555
Of Cristes mooder that, to hire to preye,
He kan nat stynte of syngyng by the weye.

    Oure firste foo, the serpent Sathanas,
That hath in Jues herte his waspes nest,
Up swal, and seide, "O Hebrayk peple, allas!
Is this to yow a thyng that is honest,   *1751
That swich a boy shal walken as hym lest
In youre despit, and synge of swich sentence,
Which is agayn youre lawes reverence?"

Fro thennes forth the Jues han conspired   565
This innocent out of this world to chace.
An homycide therto han they hyred,
That in an aleye hadde a privee place;
And as the child gan forby for to pace,
This cursed Jew hym hente, and heeld hym
          faste,   *1760
And kitte his throte, and in a pit hym caste.

---

503 **clergeon**: schoolboy
504 **wone**: custom
508 *Ave Marie*: Hail Mary
514 **Seint Nicholas**: patron of clerks
517 **prymer**: elementary school book
518 *Alma redemptoris*: "Gracious [mother] of the Redeemer"
519 **antiphoner**: book of antiphonal hymns
523 **seye**: mean
526 **T' expounden**: to interpret
529 **knowes**: knees
533 **salue**: greet

536 **kan**: know   **smal grammeere**: little grammar
540 **konne**: learn
541 **for my prymer**: for not learning my lessons   **shent**: scolded
544 **homward**: (as they went) towards home
560 **swal**: swelled
562 **boy**: brat   **hym lest**: he pleases
563 **sentence**: subject, meaning
567 **homycide**: murderer
570 **hym hente**: siezed him

I seye that in a wardrobe they hym threwe
Where as thise Jewes purgen hire entraille.
O cursed folk of Herodes al newe,
What may youre yvel entente yow availle?   575
Mordre wol out, certeyn, it wol nat faille,
And namely ther th'onour of God shal sprede;
The blood out crieth on youre cursed dede.

O martir, sowded to virginitee,
Now maystow syngen, folwynge evere in oon
The white Lamb celestial — quod she —   *1771
Of which the grete evaungelist, Seint John,
In Pathmos wroot, which seith that they that
       goon   583
Biforn this Lamb and synge a song al newe,
That nevere, flesshly, wommen they ne knewe.

This poure wydwe awaiteth al that nyght
After hir litel child, but he cam noght;
For which, as soone as it was dayes lyght,
With face pale of drede and bisy thoght,
She hath at scole and elleswhere hym soght,
Til finally she gan so fer espie   *1781
That he last seyn was in the Juerie.

With moodres pitee in hir brest enclosed,
She gooth, as she were half out of hir mynde,
To every place where she hath supposed   595
By liklihede hir litel child to fynde;
And evere on Cristes mooder meeke and kynde
She cride, and atte laste thus she wroghte:
Among the cursed Jues she hym soghte.

She frayneth and she preyeth pitously   *1790
To every Jew that dwelte in thilke place,
To telle hire if hir child wente oght forby.
They seyde "nay"; but Jhesu of his grace
Yaf in hir thoght inwith a litel space
That in that place after hir sone she cryde,   605
Where he was casten in a pit bisyde.

O grete God, that parfournest thy laude
By mouth of innocentz, lo, heere thy myght!
This gemme of chastite, this emeraude,

And eek of martirdom the ruby bright,
Ther he with throte ykorven lay upright,   *1801
He *Alma redemptoris* gan to synge
So loude that al the place gan to rynge.

The Cristene folk that thurgh the strete wente
In coomen for to wondre upon this thyng,   615
And hastily they for the provost sente;
He cam anon withouten tariyng,
And herieth Crist that is of hevene kyng,
And eek his mooder, honour of mankynde,
And after that the Jewes leet he bynde.   *1810

This child with pitous lamentacioun
Up taken was, syngynge his song alway,
And with honour of greet processioun
They carien hym unto the nexte abbay.
His mooder swownynge by his beere lay;   625
Unnethe myghte the peple that was theere
This newe Rachel brynge fro his beere.

With torment and with shameful deeth echon,
This provost dooth thise Jewes for to sterve
That of this mordre wiste, and that anon.   *1820
He nolde no swich cursednesse observe.
"Yvele shal have that yvele wol deserve";
Therfore with wilde hors he dide hem drawe,
And after that he heng hem by the lawe.

Upon this beere ay lith this innocent   635
Biforn the chief auter, whil the masse laste;
And after that, the abbot with his covent
Han sped hem for to burien hym ful faste;
And whan they hooly water on hym caste,
Yet spak this child, whan spreynd was hooly
       water,   *1830
And song O *Alma redemptoris mater!*

This abbot, which that was an hooly man,
As monkes been — or elles oghte be —
This yonge child to conjure he bigan,

572 **wardrobe:** privy
574 **Herodes al newe:** new Herods
579 **sowded:** firmly united
580 **evere in oon:** always, continually
583 **Pathmos:** Patmos
585 **flesshly:** carnally
600 **frayneth:** asks
602 **oght:** at all
609 **emeraude:** emerald

611 **ykorven:** cut through
616 **provost:** magistrate
618 **herieth:** praises
620 **leet he bynde:** he had bound
626 **Unnethe:** hardly
627 **Rachel:** the biblical mother, who was inconsolable over the loss of her child
628 **torment:** torture **echon:** each one (i.e., both)
629 **sterve:** die
631 **observe:** respect, observe (a practice)
634 **by:** in accordance with
636 **auter:** altar
637 **covent:** convent, the monks in the abbey
640 **spreynd:** sprinkled
644 **conjure:** ask, entreat

And seyde, "O deere child, I halse thee,   645
In vertu of the hooly Trinitee,
Tel me what is thy cause for to synge,
Sith that thy throte is kut to my semynge?"

"My throte is kut unto my nekke boon,"
Seyde this child, "and as by wey of kynde
I sholde have dyed, ye, longe tyme agon.
But Jesu Crist, as ye in bookes fynde,   1842
Wil that his glorie laste and be in mynde,
And for the worship of his Mooder deere
Yet may I synge *O Alma* loude and cleere.   655

"This welle of mercy, Cristes mooder sweete,
I loved alwey, as after my konnynge;
And whan that I my lyf sholde forlete,
To me she cam, and bad me for to synge
This anthem verraily in my deyynge,   *1850
As ye han herd, and whan that I hadde songe,
Me thoughte she leyde a greyn upon my tonge.

"Wherfore I synge, and synge moot certeyn,
In honour of that blisful Mayden free
Til fro my tonge of taken is the greyn;   665
And after that thus seyde she to me:
'My litel child, now wol I fecche thee,
Whan that the greyn is fro thy tonge ytake.
Be nat agast; I wol thee nat forsake.' "

This hooly monk, this abbot, hym meene I,
His tonge out caughte, and took awey the greyn,
And he yaf up the goost ful softely.   *1862
And whan this abbot hadde this wonder seyn,
His salte teeris trikled doun as reyn,
And gruf he fil al plat upon the grounde,   675
And stille he lay as he had ben ybounde.

The covent eek lay on the pavement
Wepynge, and herying Cristes mooder deere,
And after that they ryse, and forth been went,
And tooken awey this martir from his beere;
And in a tombe of marbul stones cleere   *1871
Enclosen they his litel body sweete.
Ther he is now, God leve us for to meete!

O yonge Hugh of Lyncoln, slayn also
With cursed Jewes, as it is notable,   685
For it is but a litel while ago,
Preye eek for us, we synful folk unstable,
That of his mercy God so merciable
On us his grete mercy multiplie,   *1879
For reverence of his mooder Marie. Amen

Heere is ended the Prioresses Tale.

PROLOGUE TO SIR THOPAS

Bihoold the murye wordes of the Hoost to Chaucer.

Whan seyd was al this miracle, every man
As sobre was that wonder was to se,
Til that oure Hooste japen tho bigan,
And thanne at erst he looked upon me,   694
And seyde thus: "What man artow?" quod he;

"Thou lookest as thou woldest fynde an hare,
For evere upon the ground I se thee stare.

"Approche neer, and looke up murily.
Now war yow, sires, and lat this man have
     place!
He in the waast is shape as wel as I;   *1890

645 **halse:** beseech
648 **to my semynge:** as it seems to me
650 **by wey of kynde:** in the natural course of things
656 **welle:** source
658 **forlete:** lose
662 **greyn:** seed

691 **miracle:** tale of a miracle
694 **at erst:** for the first time

675 **gruf:** face down **plat:** flat
683 **leve:** allow
684 **Hugh of Lyncoln:** a child martyr; see n.
685 **With:** by

700 **waast:** waist

This were a popet in an arm t'enbrace
For any womman, smal and fair of face.
He semeth elvyssh by his contenaunce,
For unto no wight dooth he daliaunce.

"Sey now somwhat, syn oother folk han sayd;
Telle us a tale of myrthe, and that anon."   706

"Hooste," quod I, "ne beth nat yvele apayd,
For oother tale certes kan I noon,
But of a rym I lerned longe agoon."
"Ye, that is good," quod he; "now shul we
     heere   *1900
Som deyntee thyng, me thynketh by his
     cheere."

SIR THOPAS

Heere bigynneth Chaucers Tale of Thopas.

The First Fit

Listeth, lordes, in good entent,
And I wol telle verrayment
  Of myrthe and of solas,
Al of a knyght was fair and gent   715
In bataille and in tourneyment;
  His name was sire Thopas.

Yborn he was in fer contree,
In Flaundres, al biyonde the see,
  At Poperyng, in the place.   *1910
His fader was a man ful free,
And lord he was of that contree,
  As it was Goddes grace.

Sire Thopas wax a doghty swayn;
Whit was his face as payndemayn,   725
  His lippes rede as rose;
His rode is lyk scarlet in grayn,
And I yow telle in good certayn
  He hadde a semely nose.

His heer, his berd was lyk saffroun,   *1920
That to his girdel raughte adoun;

His shoon of cordewane.
Of Brugges were his hosen broun,
His robe was of syklatoun,
  That coste many a jane.   735

He koude hunte at wilde deer,
And ride an haukyng for river
  With grey goshauk on honde;
Therto he was a good archeer;
Of wrastlyng was ther noon his peer,   *1930
  Ther any ram shal stonde.

Ful many a mayde, bright in bour,
They moorne for hym paramour,
  Whan hem were bet to slepe;
But he was chaast and no lechour,   745
And sweete as is the brembul flour
  That bereth the rede hepe.

And so bifel upon a day,
For sothe, as I yow telle may,
  Sire Thopas wolde out ride.   *1940
He worth upon his steede gray,

---

701 **popet:** little doll
702 **smal:** slender
703 **elvyssh:** abstracted (literally, mysterious, not of this world)
704 **dooth he daliaunce:** is he sociable

712 **Listeth:** listen
713 **verrayment:** truly
715 **gent:** elegant (?); see n.
719 **Flaundres:** Flanders
720 **Poperyng:** a town in Flanders   **in the place:** right there(?);
see n.
724 **swayn:** young gentleman; see n.
725 **payndemayn:** fine white bread
727 **rode:** complexion   **scarlet in grayn:** deep-dyed scarlet cloth
730 **saffroun:** saffron (deep yellow in color)
731 **raughte:** reached

707 **yvele apayd:** displeased
711 **deyntee:** excellent

732 **shoon:** shoes   **cordewane:** Cordovan leather
733 **Brugges:** Bruges   **hosen:** stockings
734 **syklatoun:** costly silken material
735 **jane:** a Genoese coin worth about half a penny
736 **deer:** either deer or animals
737 **for river:** to hawk for waterfowl
738 **goshauk:** a kind of hawk; see n.
741 **stonde:** stand as a prize
742 **bright in bour:** beautiful in (the ladies') chamber
743 **moorne:** yearn
746 **brembul flour:** dog-rose
747 **hepe:** (rose-)hip
751 **worth upon:** climbs on

And in his hand a launcegay,
A long swerd by his side.

He priketh thurgh a fair forest,
Therinne is many a wilde best,   755
Ye, bothe bukke and hare;
And as he priketh north and est,
I telle it yow, hym hadde almost
Bitid a sory care.

Ther spryngen herbes grete and smale,
The lycorys and the cetewale,   *1951
And many a clowe-gylofre;
And notemuge to putte in ale,
Wheither it be moyste or stale,
Or for to leye in cofre.   765

The briddes synge, it is no nay,
The sparhauk and the papejay,
That joye it was to heere;
The thrustelcok made eek hir lay,
The wodedowve upon the spray   *1960
She sang ful loude and cleere.

Sire Thopas fil in love-longynge,
Al whan he herde the thrustel synge,
And pryked as he were wood.
His faire steede in his prikynge   775
So swatte that men myghte him wrynge;
His sydes were al blood.

Sire Thopas eek so wery was
For prikyng on the softe gras,
So fiers was his corage,   *1970
That doun he leyde him in that plas
To make his steede som solas,
And yaf hym good forage.

"O Seinte Marie, benedicite!
What eyleth this love at me   785
To bynde me so soore?

Me dremed al this nyght, pardee,
An elf-queene shal my lemman be
And slepe under my goore.

"An elf-queene wol I love, ywis,   *1980
For in this world no womman is
Worthy to be my make
In towne;
Alle othere wommen I forsake,
And to an elf-queene I me take   795
By dale and eek by downe!"

Into his sadel he clamb anon,
And priketh over stile and stoon
An elf-queene for t'espye,
Til he so longe hath riden and goon   *1990
That he foond, in a pryve woon,
The contree of Fairye
So wilde;
For in that contree was ther noon
That to him durste ride or goon,   805
Neither wyf ne childe;

Til that ther cam a greet geaunt,
His name was sire Olifaunt,
A perilous man of dede.
He seyde, "Child, by Termagaunt,   *2000
But if thou prike out of myn haunt,
Anon I sle thy steede
With mace.
Heere is the queene of Fayerye,
With harpe and pipe and symphonye,   815
Dwellynge in this place."

The child seyde, "Also moote I thee,
Tomorwe wol I meete with thee,
Whan I have myn armoure;
And yet I hope, *par ma fay,*   *2010
That thou shalt with this launcegay
Abyen it ful sowre.
Thy mawe
Shal I percen, if I may,
Er it be fully pryme of day,   825
For heere thow shalt be slawe."

752 **launcegay:** a light lance
761 **lycorys:** licorice **cetewale:** zedoary (a ginger-like spice used as a condiment and stimulant)
762 **clowe-gylofre:** clove
763 **notemuge:** nutmeg
764 **moyste:** fresh, new **stale:** old
765 **cofre:** chest (to scent clothes?)
766 **it is no nay:** it cannot be denied
767 **sparhauk:** sparrow hawk **papejay:** parrot
769 **thrustelcok:** male thrush
770 **wodedowve:** wood pigeon **spray:** branch
773 **thrustel:** thrush
776 **swatte:** sweated
781 **plas:** place
783 **forage:** grazing (?); see n.
785 What does this passion of love have against me

788 **elf-queene:** fairy queen **lemman:** mistress
789 **goore:** cloak
796 **downe:** hill
797 **clamb:** climbed
801 **woon:** place
808 **sire Olifaunt:** Sir Elephant
810 **Child:** noble youth **Termagaunt:** a supposed Saracen god
811 **haunt:** territory
815 **symphonye:** hurdy-gurdy; see n.
817 **Also moote I thee:** as I may prosper (I swear)
820 *par ma fay:* by my faith
822 Bitterly pay for it

Sire Thopas drow abak ful faste;
This geant at hym stones caste
   Out of a fel staf-slynge.
But faire escapeth child Thopas,   *2020
And al it was thurgh Goddes gras,
   And thurgh his fair berynge.

[*The Second Fit*]

  Yet listeth, lordes, to my tale
Murier than the nightyngale,
   For now I wol yow rowne   835
How sir Thopas, with sydes smale,
Prikyng over hill and dale,
   Is comen agayn to towne.

  His myrie men comanded he
To make hym bothe game and glee,   *2030
   For nedes moste he fighte
With a geaunt with hevedes three,
For paramour and jolitee
   Of oon that shoon ful brighte.

  "Do come," he seyde, "my mynstrales,   845
And geestours for to tellen tales,
   Anon in myn armynge,
Of romances that been roiales,
Of popes and of cardinales,
   And eek of love-likynge."   *2040

  They fette hym first the sweete wyn,
And mede eek in a mazelyn,
   And roial spicerye
Of gyngebreed that was ful fyn,
And lycorys, and eek comyn,   855
   With sugre that is trye.

  He dide next his white leere
Of cloth of lake fyn and cleere,
   A breech and eek a sherte;

And next his sherte an aketoun,   *2050
And over that an haubergeoun
   For percynge of his herte;

  And over that a fyn hawberk,
Was al ywroght of Jewes werk,
   Ful strong it was of plate;   865
And over that his cote-armour
As whit as is a lilye flour,
   In which he wol debate.

  His sheeld was al of gold so reed,
And therinne was a bores heed,   *2060
   A charbocle bisyde;
And there he swoor on ale and breed
How that the geaunt shal be deed,
   Bityde what bityde!

  His jambeux were of quyrboilly,   875
His swerdes shethe of yvory,
   His helm of latoun bright;
His sadel was of rewel boon,
His brydel as the sonne shoon,
   Or as the moone light.   *2070

  His spere was of fyn ciprees,
That bodeth werre, and nothyng pees,
   The heed ful sharpe ygrounde;
His steede was al dappull gray,
It gooth an ambil in the way   885
   Ful softely and rounde
              In londe.
Loo, lordes myne, heere is a fit!
If ye wol any moore of it,
   To telle it wol I fonde.   *2080

The [*Third*] *Fit*

  Now holde youre mouth, *par charitee,*
Bothe knyght and lady free,

---

829 **fel:** terrible   **staf-slynge:** sling on the end of a stick
831 **gras:** grace
835 **rowne:** tell
836 **sydes smale:** slender waist
839 **myrie men:** companions in arms
840 **game and glee:** entertainment
843 **jolitee:** pleasure
845 **Do come:** cause to come, summon   **mynstrales:** musicians
846 **geestours:** tellers of *gestes*, tales
848 **roiales:** royal
850 **love-likynge:** the joys of love
852 **mede:** mead   **mazelyn:** mazer, wooden bowl
853 **spicerye:** delicacies, titbits
854 **gyngebreed:** preserved ginger
855 **lycorys:** licorice   **comyn:** cumin
856 **sugre:** sugar   **trye:** excellent
857 **leere:** flesh
858 **cloth of lake:** fine linen
859 **breech:** pair of trousers; see Expl. Notes for the technical vocabulary in lines 859–66.

860 **aketoun:** quilted jacket worn under the armor
861 **haubergeoun:** chain-mail shirt
862 **For:** to prevent
863 **hawberk:** plate armor
866 **cote-armour:** coat of arms, worn over the armor
868 **debate:** fight, dispute
870 **bores:** boar's
871 **charbocle:** carbuncle, red gemstone; see n.
874 Come what may!
875 **jambeux:** greaves, leg-armor   **quyrboilly:** hardened leather
877 **latoun:** latten, a brass-like alloy
878 **rewel boon:** ivory
881 **ciprees:** cypress
882 **bodeth:** forebodes
885 **ambil:** slow walk
886 **rounde:** easily
888 **fit:** canto
890 **fonde:** try, attempt
891 *par charitee:* for charity's sake, please

And herkneth to my spelle;
Of bataille and of chivalry,
And of ladyes love-drury   895
  Anon I wol yow telle.

Men speken of romances of prys,
Of Horn child and of Ypotys,
  Of Beves and sir Gy,
Of sir Lybeux and Pleyndamour —   *2090
But sir Thopas, he bereth the flour
  Of roial chivalry!

His goode steede al he bistrood,
And forth upon his wey he glood
  As sparcle out of the bronde;   905

Upon his creest he bar a tour,
And therinne stiked a lilie flour —
  God shilde his cors fro shonde!

And for he was a knyght auntrous,
He nolde slepen in noon hous,   *2100
  But liggen in his hoode;
His brighte helm was his wonger,
And by hym baiteth his dextrer
  Of herbes fyne and goode.

Hymself drank water of the well,   915
As dide the knyght sire Percyvell
  So worly under wede,
Til on a day —

Heere the Hoost stynteth Chaucer of his Tale of Thopas.

"Namoore of this, for Goddes dignitee,"
Quod oure Hooste, "for thou makest me *2110
So wery of thy verray lewednesse
That, also wisly God my soule blesse,
Myne eres aken of thy drasty speche.
Now swich a rym the devel I biteche!
This may wel be rym dogerel," quod he.   925
  "Why so?" quod I, "why wiltow lette me
Moore of my tale than another man,
Syn that it is the beste rym I kan?"
  "By God," quod he, "for pleynly, at a word,
Thy drasty rymyng is nat worth a toord! *2120
Thou doost noght elles but despendest tyme.
Sire, at o word, thou shalt no lenger ryme.
Lat se wher thou kanst tellen aught in geeste,
Or telle in prose somwhat, at the leeste,
In which ther be som murthe or som doc-
    tryne."   935
  "Gladly," quod I, "by Goddes sweete pyne!
I wol yow telle a litel thyng in prose
That oghte liken yow, as I suppose,

Or elles, certes, ye been to daungerous.
It is a moral tale vertuous,   *2130
Al be it told somtyme in sondry wyse
Of sondry folk, as I shal yow devyse.
  "As thus: ye woot that every Evaungelist
That telleth us the peyne of Jhesu Crist
Ne seith nat alle thyng as his felawe dooth;
But nathelees hir sentence is al sooth,   946
And alle acorden as in hire sentence,
Al be ther in hir tellyng difference.
For somme of hem seyn moore, and somme
    seyn lesse,
Whan they his pitous passioun expresse —
I meene of Mark, Mathew, Luc, and John —
But doutelees hir sentence is al oon.   *2142
Therfore, lordynges alle, I yow biseche,
If that yow thynke I varie as in my speche,
As thus, though that I telle somwhat moore
Of proverbes than ye han herd bifoore   956
Comprehended in this litel tretys heere,
To enforce with th'effect of my mateere;
And though I nat the same wordes seye
As ye han herd, yet to yow alle I preye   *2150
Blameth me nat; for, as in my sentence,

---

893 **spelle:** tale
895 **love-drury:** passionate love
897 **prys:** excellence
898 **Horn child:** a hero of English romance **Ypotys:** child hero of a pious legend
899 **Beves:** Bevis of Hampton **Gy:** Guy of Warwick
900 **Lybeux:** Lybeaus Desconus ("The Fair Unknown")
Pleyndamour: "Full-of-Love," not identified; see n.
903 **bistrood:** bestrode
904 **glood:** glided
905 **bronde:** burning log

923 **drasty:** crappy, worthless
924 **biteche:** commit
930 **toord:** turd
931 **despendest:** waste
933 **geeste:** alliterating verse (?)

906 **creest:** top of the helmet **tour:** tower
908 **shonde:** harm, shame
909 **knyght auntrous:** knight errant
911 **liggen:** lie
912 **wonger:** pillow
913 **baiteth:** feeds **dextrer:** war-horse
915 **well:** spring
916 **Percyvell:** the chaste hero of the romance of the Holy Grail
917 So worthy in his armor

939 **daungerous:** difficult, hard to please
947 **sentence:** substance, essential meaning

Shul ye nowher fynden difference
Fro the sentence of this tretys lyte
After the which this murye tale I write.

And therfore herkneth what that I shal seye,
And lat me tellen al my tale, I preye."   966

Explicit

THE TALE OF MELIBEE

Heere bigynneth Chaucers Tale of Melibee.

A yong man called Melibeus, myghty and riche, bigat upon his wyf, that called was Prudence, a doghter which that called was Sophie./

Upon a day bifel that he for his desport is went into the feeldes hym to pleye./ His wyf and eek his doghter hath he left inwith his hous, of which the dores weren faste yshette./ Thre of his olde foes han it espyed, and setten laddres to the walles of his hous, and by wyndowes been entred,/ and betten his wyf,   *2160 and wounded his doghter with fyve mortal woundes in fyve sondry places — / this is to seyn, in hir feet, in hire handes, in hir erys, in hir nose, and in hire mouth — and leften hire for deed, and wenten awey./

Whan Melibeus retourned was into his hous, and saugh al this meschief, he, lyk a mad man rentynge his clothes, gan to wepe and crie./

Prudence, his wyf, as ferforth as she dorste, bisoghte hym of his wepyng for to stynte,/ but nat forthy he gan to crie and wepen evere lenger the moore./   975

This noble wyf Prudence remembred hire upon the sentence of Ovide, in his book that cleped is the Remedie of Love, where as he seith,/ "He is a fool that destourbeth the mooder to wepen in the deeth of hire child til she have wept hir fille as for a certein tyme,/ and thanne shal man doon his diligence with amyable wordes hire to reconforte, and preyen hire of hir wepyng for to stynte."/ For which resoun this noble wyf Prudence suffred hir housbonde for to wepe and crie as for a certein space,/ and whan she saugh hir tyme, she seyde hym in this wise: "Allas, my lord," quod

she, "why make ye youreself for to be lyk a fool?/ For sothe it aperteneth nat   *2170 to a wys man to maken swich a sorwe./ Youre doghter, with the grace of God, shal warisshe and escape./ And, al were it so that she right now were deed, ye ne oughte nat, as for hir deeth, youreself to destroye./ Senek seith: 'The wise man shal nat take to greet disconfort for the deeth of his children,/ but, certes, he sholde suffren it in pacience as wel as he abideth the deeth of his owene propre persone.'"/   985

This Melibeus answerde anon and seyde, "What man," quod he, "sholde of his wepyng stente that hath so greet a cause for to wepe?/ Jhesu Crist, oure Lord, hymself wepte for the deeth of Lazarus hys freend."/

Prudence answerde: "Certes, wel I woot attempree wepyng is no thyng deffended to hym that sorweful is, amonges folk in sorwe, but it is rather graunted hym to wepe./ The Apostle Paul unto the Romayns writeth, 'Man shal rejoyse with hem that maken joye and wepen with swich folk as wepen.'/ But though attempree wepyng be ygraunted, outrageous wepyng certes is deffended./   *2180 Mesure of wepyng sholde be considered after the loore that techeth us Senek:/ 'Whan that thy frend is deed,' quod he, 'lat nat thyne eyen to moyste been of teeris, ne to muche drye; although the teeris come to thyne eyen, lat hem nat falle;/ and whan thou hast forgoon thy freend, do diligence to gete

978 **reconforte**: comfort

982 **warisshe**: recover
985 **propre persone**: own self
987 **Lazarus**: see John 11.35.
988 **attempree**: moderate

another freend; and this is moore wysdom than for to wepe for thy freend which that thou hast lorn, for therinne is no boote.'/ And therfore, if ye governe yow by sapience, put awey sorwe out of youre herte./ Remembre yow that Jhesus Syrak seith, 'A man that is joyous and glad in herte, it hym conserveth florissynge in his age; but soothly sorweful herte maketh his bones drye.'/ He seith eek   995 thus, that sorwe in herte sleeth ful many a man./ Salomon seith that right as motthes in the shepes flees anoyeth to the clothes, and the smale wormes to the tree, right so anoyeth sorwe to the herte./ Wherfore us oghte, as wel in the deeth of oure children as in the los of oure othere goodes temporels, have pacience./ Remembre yow upon the pacient Job. Whan he hadde lost his children and his temporeel substance, and in his body endured and receyved ful many a grevous tribulacion, yet seyde he thus:/ 'Oure Lord hath yeve it me; oure Lord hath biraft it me; right as oure Lord hath wold, right so it is doon; blessed be the name of oure Lord!' "/   *2190

To thise forseide thynges answerde Melibeus unto his wyf Prudence: "Alle thy wordes," quod he, "been sothe and therto profitable, but trewely myn herte is troubled with this sorwe so grevously that I noot what to doone."/

"Lat calle," quod Prudence, "thy trewe freendes alle and thy lynage whiche that been wise. Telleth youre cas, and herkneth what they seye in conseillyng, and yow governe after hire sentence./ Salomon seith, 'Werk alle thy thynges by conseil, and thou shalt never repente.' "/

Thanne, by the conseil of his wyf Prudence, this Melibeus leet callen a greet congregacion of folk,/ as surgiens, phisiciens, olde folk and yonge, and somme of his olde enemys reconsiled as by hir semblaunt to his love and into his grace;/ and therwithal ther   1005 coomen somme of his neighebores that diden hym reverence moore for drede than for love, as it happeth ofte./ Ther coomen also ful many subtille flatereres and wise advocatz lerned in the lawe./

And whan this folk togidre assembled weren, this Melibeus in sorweful wise shewed hem his cas./ And by the manere of his speche it semed that in herte he baar a crueel ire, redy to doon vengeaunce upon his foes, and sodeynly desired that the werre sholde bigynne;/ but nathelees, yet axed he hire conseil upon this matiere./ A surgien, by li-   *2200 cence and assent of swiche as weren wise, up roos and to Melibeus seyde as ye may heere:/

"Sire," quod he, "as to us surgiens aperteneth that we do to every wight the beste that we kan, where as we been withholde, and to oure pacientz that we do no damage,/ wherfore it happeth many tyme and ofte that whan twey men han everich wounded oother, oon same surgien heeleth hem bothe;/ wherfore unto oure art it is nat pertinent to norice werre ne parties to supporte./ But certes, as to the warisshynge of youre doghter, al be it so that she perilously be wounded, we shullen do so ententif bisynesse fro day to nyght that with the grace of God she shal be hool and sound as soone as is possible."/   1015

Almoost right in the same wise the phisiciens answerden, save that they seyden a fewe woordes moore:/ that right as maladies been cured by hir contraries, right so shul men warisshe werre by vengeaunce./

His neighebores ful of envye, his feyned freendes that semeden reconsiled, and his flatereres/ maden semblant of wepyng, and empeireden and agreggeden muchel of this matiere in preisynge greetly Melibee of myght, of power, of richesse, and of freendes, despisynge the power of his adversaries,/ and seiden outrely that he anon sholde wreken hym on his foes and bigynne werre./   *2210

Up roos thanne an advocat that was wys, by leve and by conseil of othere that were wise, and seide:/ "Lordynges, the nede for which we been assembled in this place is a ful hevy thyng and an heigh matiere,/ by cause of the wrong and of the wikkednesse that hath be doon, and eek by resoun of the grete damages that in tyme comynge been possible to fallen for this same cause,/ and eek by resoun of the grete richesse and power of the parties bothe,/ for the whiche resouns it were a

---

995 **Jhesus Syrak:** the author of Ecclesiasticus
997 **motthes:** moths **anoyeth:** do injury

1014 **norice:** nourish
1015 **warisshynge:** cure
1019 **maden semblant:** feigned, pretended **empeireden:** made (matters) worse **agreggeden:** aggravated
1023 **by resoun of:** because of

ful greet peril to erren in this matiere./ 1025
Wherfore, Melibeus, this is oure sentence: we conseille yow aboven alle thyng
that right anon thou do thy diligence in
kepynge of thy propre persone in swich
a wise that thou ne wante noon espie ne
wacche thy persone for to save./ And after
that, we conseille that in thyn hous thou sette
sufficeant garnisoun so that they may as wel
thy body as thyn hous defende./ But certes,
for to moeve werre, ne sodeynly for to doon
vengeaunce, we may nat demen in so litel
tyme that it were profitable./ Wherfore we
axen leyser and espace to have deliberacion in
this cas to deme./ For the commune proverbe
seith thus: 'He that soone deemeth,
soone shal repente.'/ And eek men seyn *2220
that thilke juge is wys that soone understondeth a matiere and juggeth by leyser;/ for
al be it so that alle tariyng be anoyful, algates it
is nat to repreve in yevynge of juggement ne
in vengeance takyng, whan it is sufficeant
and resonable./ And that shewed oure Lord
Jhesu Crist by ensample, for whan that the
womman that was taken in avowtrie was broght
in his presence to knowen what sholde be doon
with hire persone, al be it so that he wiste wel
hymself what that he wolde answere, yet ne
wolde he nat answere sodeynly, but he wolde
have deliberacion, and in the ground he wroot
twies./ And by thise causes we axen deliberacioun, and we shal thanne, by the grace of
God, conseille thee thyng that shal be profitable."/

Up stirten thanne the yonge folk atones, and
the mooste partie of that compaignye han
scorned this olde wise man, and bigonnen to make noyse, and seyden that/ 1035
right so as whil that iren is hoot men
sholden smyte, right so men sholde wreken hir
wronges whil that they been fresshe and newe;
and with loud voys they criden "Werre!
Werre!"/

Up roos tho oon of thise olde wise, and with
his hand made contenaunce that men sholde
holden hem stille and yeven hym audience./
"Lordynges," quod he, "ther is ful many a man
that crieth 'Werre, werre!' that woot ful litel
what werre amounteth./ Werre at his bigynnyng hath so greet an entryng and so large that
every wight may entre whan hym liketh and
lightly fynde werre;/ but certes what ende
that shal therof bifalle, it is nat light to
knowe./ For soothly, whan that werre is *2230
ones bigonne, ther is ful many a child
unborn of his mooder that shal sterve yong by
cause of thilke werre, or elles lyve in sorwe and
dye in wrecchednesse./ And therfore, er that
any werre bigynne, men moste have greet conseil and greet deliberacion."/ And whan this
olde man wende to enforcen his tale by resons,
wel ny alle atones bigonne they to rise for to
breken his tale, and beden hym ful ofte his
wordes for to abregge./ For soothly, he that
precheth to hem that listen nat heeren his
wordes, his sermon hem anoieth./ For Jhesus
Syrak seith that "musik in wepynge is a noyous
thyng"; this is to seyn: as muche availleth to
speken bifore folk to which his speche anoieth as it is to synge biforn hym that
wepeth./ And whan this wise man 1045
saugh that hym wanted audience, al
shamefast he sette hym doun agayn./ For
Salomon seith: "Ther as thou ne mayst have
noon audience, enforce thee nat to speke."/
"I see wel," quod this wise man, "that the commune proverbe is sooth, that 'good conseil
wanteth whan it is moost nede.'"/

Yet hadde this Melibeus in his conseil many
folk that prively in his eere conseilled hym
certeyn thyng, and conseilled hym the contrarie in general audience./

Whan Melibeus hadde herd that the gretteste partie of his conseil weren accorded that
he sholde maken werre, anoon he consented to
hir conseillyng and fully affermed hire
sentence./ Thanne dame Prudence, *2240
whan that she saugh how that hir
housbonde shoop hym for to wreken hym on
his foes and to bigynne werre, she in ful humble wise, whan she saugh hir tyme, seide to
hym thise wordes:/ "My lord," quod she, "I
yow biseche, as hertely as I dar and kan, ne
haste yow nat to faste and, for alle gerdons, as
yeveth me audience./ For Piers Alfonce seith,

1026 **propre persone:** own self **wacche:** watchman
1027 **garnisoun:** body of armed men
1028 **moeve werre:** begin or provoke war
1029 **espace:** space, opportunity
1033 **avowtrie:** adultery
1037 **made contenaunce:** signaled

1043 **breken his tale:** interrupt his speech **beden:** prayed
1045 **noyous:** annoying, bothersome
1046 **hym wanted:** he lacked
1053 **Piers Alfonce:** Petrus Alphonsus, author of the popular *Disciplina clericalis*

'Whoso that dooth to thee oother good or harm, haste thee nat to quiten it, for in this wise thy freend wole abyde and thyn enemy shal the lenger lyve in drede.'/ The proverbe seith, 'He hasteth wel that wisely kan abyde,' and 'in wikked haste is no profit.''/

This Melibee answerde unto his wyf Prudence: "I purpose nat," quod he, "to werke by thy conseil, for many causes and resouns. For certes, every wight wolde holde me thanne a fool;/ this is to seyn, if I, for   1055 thy conseillyng, wolde chaungen thynges that been ordeyned and affermed by so manye wyse./ Secoundely, I seye that alle wommen been wikke, and noon good of hem alle. For 'of a thousand men,' seith Salomon, 'I foond o good man, but certes, of alle wommen, good womman foond I nevere.'/ And also, certes, if I governed me by thy conseil, it sholde seme that I hadde yeve to thee over me the maistrie, and God forbede that it so weere!/ For Jhesus Syrak seith that 'if the wyf have maistrie, she is contrarious to hir housbonde.'/ And Salomon seith: 'Nevere in thy lyf to thy wyf, ne to thy child, ne to thy freend ne yeve no power over thyself, for bettre it were that thy children aske of thy persone thynges that hem nedeth than thou see thyself in the handes of thy children.'/ And also if I wolde werke   *2250 by thy conseillyng, certes, my conseil moste som tyme be secree, til it were tyme that it moste be knowe, and this ne may noght be./ [*Car il est escript, la genglerie des femmes ne puet riens celler fors ce qu'elle ne scet./ Apres, le philosophre dit, en mauvais conseil les femmes vainquent les hommes; et par ces raisons je ne dois point user de ton conseil.*]"/

Whanne dame Prudence, ful debonairly and with greet pacience, hadde herd al that hir housbonde liked for to seye, thanne axed she of hym licence for to speke, and seyde in this wise:/ "My lord," quod she, "as to youre firste resoun, certes it may lightly been answered. For I seye that it is no folie to chaunge conseil whan the thyng is chaunged, or elles whan the thyng semeth ootherweyes than it

was biforn./ And mooreover, I seye   1065 that though ye han sworn and bihight to perfourne youre emprise, and nathelees ye weyve to perfourne thilke same emprise by juste cause, men sholde nat seyn therfore that ye were a liere ne forsworn./ For the book seith that 'the wise man maketh no lesyng whan he turneth his corage to the bettre.'/ And al be it so that youre emprise be establissed and ordeyned by greet multitude of folk, yet thar ye nat accomplice thilke ordinaunce but yow like./ For the trouthe of thynges and the profit been rather founden in fewe folk that been wise and ful of resoun than by greet multitude of folk ther every man crieth and clatereth what that hym liketh. Soothly swich multitude is nat honest./ And as to the seconde resoun, where as ye seyn that alle wommen been wikke; save youre grace, certes ye despisen alle wommen in this wyse, and 'he that al despiseth, al displeseth,' as seith the book./ And Senec seith that 'whoso   *2260 wole have sapience shal no man dispreyse, but he shal gladly techen the science that he kan withouten presumpcion or pride;/ and swiche thynges as he noght ne kan, he shal nat been ashamed to lerne hem, and enquere of lasse folk than hymself.'/ And, sire, that ther hath been many a good womman may lightly be preved./ For certes, sire, oure Lord Jhesu Crist wolde nevere have descended to be born of a womman, if alle wommen hadden been wikke./ And after that, for the grete bountee that is in wommen, oure Lord Jhesu Crist, whan he was risen fro deeth to lyve, appeered rather to a womman than to his Apostles./ And though that Salo-   1075 mon seith that he ne foond nevere womman good, it folweth nat therfore that alle wommen ben wikke./ For though that he ne foond no good womman, certes, many another man hath founden many a womman ful good and trewe./ Or elles, per aventure, the entente of Salomon was this: that, as in sovereyn bountee, he foond no womman — /this is to seyn, that ther is no wight that hath sovereyn bountee save God allone, as he hymself recordeth in hys Evaungelie./ For ther nys no creature so good

---

1062–63 **Car il est,** *etc.:* For it is written that the chattering of women can hide nothing except what she does not know. Moreover, the philosopher (i.e., Aristotle) says, in evil counsel women conquer men; and for these reasons I must not use any of your counsel.

1066 **perfourne:** perform, carry out   **emprise:** enterprise
weyve: abandon, leave off
1069 **clatereth:** babbles foolishly
1078 **per aventure:** by chance

that hym ne wanteth somwhat of the
perfeccioun of God, that is his makere./   *2270
Youre thridde reson is this: ye seyn that
if ye governe yow by my conseil, it sholde
seme that ye hadde yeve me the maistrie and
the lordshipe over youre persone./ Sire, save
youre grace, it is nat so. For if it so were that
no man sholde be conseilled but oonly of hem
that hadden lordshipe and maistrie of his persone, men wolden nat be conseilled so ofte./
For soothly thilke man that asketh conseil of
a purpos, yet hath he free choys wheither he
wole werke by that conseil or noon./ And as
to youre fourthe resoun, ther ye seyn that the
janglerie of wommen kan hyde thynges that
they wot noght, as who seith that a womman
kan nat hyde that she woot;/ sire, thise wordes
been understonde of wommen that been
jangleresses and wikked;/ of whiche   1085
wommen men seyn that thre thynges
dryven a man out of his hous — that is to seyn,
smoke, droppyng of reyn, and wikked wyves;/
and of swiche wommen seith Salomon that 'it
were bettre dwelle in desert than with a womman that is riotous.'/ And sire, by youre leve,
that am nat I,/ for ye han ful ofte assayed my
grete silence and my grete pacience, and eek
how wel that I kan hyde and hele thynges that
men oghte secreely to hyde./ And soothly, as
to youre fifthe resoun, where as ye seyn that
in wikked conseil wommen venquisshe men,
God woot, thilke resoun stant heere in
no stede./ For understoond now, ye   *2280
asken conseil to do wikkednesse;/ and if
ye wole werken wikkednesse, and youre wif
restreyneth thilke wikked purpos, and overcometh yow by reson and by good conseil,/
certes youre wyf oghte rather to be preised
than yblamed./ Thus sholde ye understonde
the philosophre that seith, 'In wikked conseil
wommen venquisshen hir housbondes.'/ And
ther as ye blamen alle wommen and hir resouns, I shal shewe yow by manye ensamples
that many a womman hath ben ful good, and
yet been, and hir conseils ful hoolsome
and profitable./ Eek som men han seyd   1095
that the conseillynge of wommen is
outher to deere or elles to litel of pris./ But al

be it so that ful many a womman is badde and
hir conseil vile and noght worth, yet han men
founde ful many a good womman, and ful discret and wis in conseillynge./ Loo, Jacob by
good conseil of his mooder Rebekka wan the
benysoun of Ysaak his fader and the lordshipe
over alle his bretheren./ Judith by hire good
conseil delivered the citee of Bethulie, in
which she dwelled, out of the handes of Olofernus, that hadde it biseged and wolde have al
destroyed it./ Abygail delivered Nabal hir
housbonde fro David the kyng, that wolde
have slayn hym, and apaysed the ire of the
kyng by hir wit and by hir good conseillyng./ Hester by hir good conseil   *2290
enhaunced greetly the peple of God in
the regne of Assuerus the kyng./ And the
same bountee in good conseillyng of many a
good womman may men telle./ And mooreover, whan oure Lord hadde creat Adam, oure
forme fader, he seyde in this wise:/ 'It is nat
good to been a man alloone; make we to
hym an helpe semblable to hymself.'/ Heere
may ye se that if that wommen were nat
goode, and hir conseils goode and profitable,/ oure Lord God of hevene wolde   1105
nevere han wroght hem, ne called hem
help of man, but rather confusioun of man./
And ther seyde oones a clerk in two vers,
'What is bettre than gold? Jaspre. What is
bettre than jaspre? Wisedoom./ And what is
better than wisedoom? Womman. And what is
bettre than a good womman? Nothyng.'/ And,
sire, by manye of othre resons may ye seen
that manye wommen been goode, and hir
conseils goode and profitable./ And therfore, sire, if ye wol triste to my conseil, I shal
restoore yow youre doghter hool and
sound./ And eek I wol do to yow so   *2300
muche that ye shul have honour in this
cause.''/

Whan Melibee hadde herd the wordes of his
wyf Prudence, he seyde thus:/ "I se wel that
the word of Salomon is sooth. He seith that
'wordes that been spoken discreetly by ordinaunce been honycombes, for they yeven swetnesse to the soule and hoolsomnesse to the
body.'/ And, wyf, by cause of thy sweete
wordes, and eek for I have assayed and preved

1080 **wanteth:** lacks
1084 **janglerie:** chatter
1087 **riotous:** dissolute
1089 **hele:** conceal
1090 **stant . . . in no stede:** has no value, is useless

1098 **benysoun:** blessing
1103 **forme fader:** forefather
1104 **semblable:** similar
1113 **hoolsomnesse:** healthfulness

thy grete sapience and thy grete trouthe, I wol governe me by thy conseil in alle thyng."/

"Now, sire," quod dame Prudence, "and syn ye vouche sauf to been governed by my conseil, I wol enforme yow how ye shul governe yourself in chesynge of youre conseillours./ Ye shul first in alle youre werkes   1115 mekely biseken to the heighe God that he wol be youre conseillour;/ and shapeth yow to swich entente that he yeve yow conseil and confort, as taughte Thobie his sone:/ 'At alle tymes thou shalt blesse God, and praye hym to dresse thy weyes, and looke that alle thy conseils been in hym for everemoore.'/ Seint Jame eek seith: 'If any of yow have nede of sapience, axe it of God.'/ And afterward thanne shul ye taken conseil in youreself, and examyne wel youre thoghtes of swich thyng as yow thynketh that is best for youre profit./ And thanne shul ye dryve fro   *2310 youre herte thre thynges that been contrariouse to good conseil;/ that is to seyn, ire, coveitise, and hastifnesse./

"First, he that axeth conseil of hymself, certes he moste been withouten ire, for manye causes./ The firste is this: he that hath greet ire and wratthe in hymself, he weneth alwey that he may do thyng that he may nat do./ And secoundely, he that is irous and wrooth, he ne may nat wel deme;/ and   1125 he that may nat wel deme, may nat wel conseille./ The thridde is this, that he that is irous and wrooth, as seith Senec, ne may nat speke but blameful thynges,/ and with his viciouse wordes he stireth oother folk to angre and to ire./ And eek, sire, ye moste dryve coveitise out of youre herte./ For the Apostle seith that coveitise is roote of alle harmes./ And trust wel that a coveitous   *2320 man ne kan noght deme ne thynke, but oonly to fulfille the ende of his coveitise;/ and certes, that ne may nevere been accompliced, for evere the moore habundaunce that he hath of richesse, the moore he desireth./ And, sire, ye moste also dryve out of youre herte hastifnesse; for certes,/ ye ne may nat deeme for the beste by a sodeyn thought that falleth in youre herte, but ye moste avyse yow on it ful ofte./ For, as ye herde her biforn, the

commune proverbe is this, that 'he that soone deemeth, soone repenteth.'/ Sire,   1135 ye ne be nat alwey in lyk disposicioun;/ for certes, somthyng that somtyme semeth to yow that it is good for to do, another tyme it semeth to yow the contrarie./

"Whan ye han taken conseil in youreself and han deemed by good deliberacion swich thyng as you semeth best,/ thanne rede I yow that ye kepe it secree./ Biwrey nat youre conseil to no persone, but if so be that ye wenen sikerly that thurgh youre biwreyyng youre condicioun shal be to yow the moore profitable./ For Jhesus Syrak seith, 'Nei-   *2330 ther to thy foo ne to thy frend discovere nat thy secree ne thy folie,/ for they wol yeve yow audience and lookynge and supportacioun in thy presence and scorne thee in thyn absence.'/ Another clerk seith that 'scarsly shaltou fynden any persone that may kepe conseil secrely.'/ The book seith, 'Whil that thou kepest thy conseil in thyn herte, thou kepest it in thy prisoun,/ and whan thou biwreyest thy conseil to any wight, he holdeth thee in his snare.'/ And therfore yow   1145 is bettre to hyde youre conseil in youre herte than praye him to whom ye han biwreyed youre conseil that he wole kepen it cloos and stille./ For Seneca seith: 'If so be that thou ne mayst nat thyn owene conseil hyde, how darstou prayen any oother wight thy conseil secrely to kepe?'/ But nathelees, if thou wene sikerly that the biwreiyng of thy conseil to a persone wol make thy condicion to stonden in the bettre plyt, thanne shaltou tellen hym thy conseil in this wise./ First thou shalt make no semblant wheither thee were levere pees or werre, or this or that, ne shewe hym nat thy wille and thyn entente./ For trust wel that comunli thise conseillours been flat-ereres,/ namely the conseillours of grete   *2340 lordes,/ for they enforcen hem alwey rather to speken plesante wordes, enclynynge to the lordes lust, than wordes that been trewe or profitable./ And therfore men seyn that the riche man hath seeld good conseil, but if he have it of hymself./

And after that thou shalt considere thy freendes and thyne enemys./ And as touch-ynge thy freendes, thou shalt considere which of hem been moost feithful and moost wise

---

1117 **Thobie:** Tobias (Tobias 4.10)
1118 **dresse:** direct
1119 **Seint Jame:** James 1.5
1127 **blameful:** blameworthy

1142 **supportacioun:** support

and eldest and most approved in conseillyng;/ and of hem shalt thou aske   1155
thy conseil, as the caas requireth./ I
seye that first ye shul clepe to youre conseil
youre freendes that been trewe./ For Salomon
seith that 'right as the herte of a man deliteth in
savour that is soote, right so the conseil of trewe
freendes yeveth swetnesse to the soule.'/ He
seith also, 'Ther may no thyng be likned to the
trewe freend,/ for certes gold ne silver ben nat
so muche worth as the goode wyl of a
trewe freend.'/ And eek he seith that   *2350
'a trewe freend is a strong deffense;
who so that it fyndeth, certes he fyndeth a
greet tresour.'/ Thanne shul ye eek considere
if that youre trewe freendes been discrete and
wise. For the book seith, 'Axe alwey thy conseil of hem that been wise.'/ And by this same
resoun shul ye clepen to youre conseil of youre
freendes that been of age, swiche as han seyn
and been expert in manye thynges and been
approved in conseillynges./ For the book seith
that 'in olde men is the sapience, and in longe
tyme the prudence.'/ And Tullius seith that
'grete thynges ne been nat ay accompliced by
strengthe, ne by delivernesse of body, but by
good conseil, by auctoritee of persones, and by
science; the whiche thre thynges ne been nat
fieble by age, but certes they enforcen
and encreescen day by day.'/And   1165
thanne shul ye kepe this for a general
reule: First shul ye clepen to youre conseil a
fewe of youre freendes that been especiale;/
for Salomon seith, 'Manye freendes have thou,
but among a thousand chese thee oon to be
thy conseillour.'/ For al be it so that thou first
ne telle thy conseil but to a fewe, thou mayst
afterward telle it to mo folk if it be nede./ But
looke alwey that thy conseillours have thilke
thre condiciouns that I have seyd bifore — that
is to seyn, that they be trewe, wise, and of
oold experience./ And werke nat alwey in
every nede by oon counseillour allone; for somtyme bihooveth it to been conseilled by
manye./ For Salomon seith, 'Salvacion   *2360
of thynges is where as ther been manye
conseillours.'/

"Now, sith that I have toold yow of which
folk ye sholde been counseilled, now wol I
teche yow which conseil ye oghte to eschewe./
First, ye shul eschue the conseillyng of fooles;

for Salomon seith, 'Taak no conseil of a fool,
for he ne kan noght conseille but after his
owene lust and his affeccioun.'/ The book
seith that 'the propretee of a fool is this: he
troweth lightly harm of every wight, and lightly
troweth alle bountee in hymself.'/ Thou shalt
eek eschue the conseillyng of alle flatereres,
swiche as enforcen hem rather to preise youre
persone by flaterye than for to telle yow
the soothfastnesse of thynges./ Wher-   1175
fore Tullius seith, 'Amonges alle the
pestilences that been in freendshipe the gretteste is flaterie.' And therfore is it moore nede
that thou eschue and drede flatereres than any
oother peple./ The book seith, 'Thou shalt
rather drede and flee fro the sweete wordes of
flaterynge preiseres than fro the egre wordes
of thy freend that seith thee thy sothes.'/ Salomon seith that 'the wordes of a flaterere is a
snare to cacche with innocentz.'/ He seith also
that 'he that speketh to his freend wordes of
swetnesse and of plesaunce setteth a net biforn his feet to cacche hym.'/ And therfore
seith Tullius, 'Enclyne nat thyne eres to flatereres, ne taak no conseil of the wordes
of flaterye.'/ And Caton seith, 'Avyse   *2370
thee wel, and eschue the wordes of swetnesse and of plesaunce.'/ And eek thou shalt
eschue the conseillyng of thyne olde enemys
that been reconsiled./ The book seith that 'no
wight retourneth saufly into the grace of his
olde enemy.'/ And Isope seith, 'Ne trust nat
to hem to whiche thou hast had som tyme
werre or enemytee, ne telle hem nat thy
conseil.'/ And Seneca telleth the cause why:
'It may nat be,' seith he, 'that where greet
fyr hath longe tyme endured, that ther
ne dwelleth som vapour of warm-
nesse.'/ And therfore seith Salomon, 'In   1185
thyn olde foo trust nevere.'/ For sikerly,
though thyn enemy be reconsiled, and maketh thee chiere of humylitee, and lowteth to
thee with his heed, ne trust hym nevere./ For
certes he maketh thilke feyned humilitee moore
for his profit than for any love of thy persone,
by cause that he deemeth to have victorie over
thy persone by swich feyned contenance, the
which victorie he myghte nat have by strif or
werre./ And Peter Alfonce seith, 'Make no
felawshipe with thyne olde enemys, for if thou

1165 **Tullius:** Cicero   **delivernesse:** agility

1177 **egre:** sharp
1184 **Isope:** Ysopus, the Latin version of Aesop's *Fables*
1189 **Peter Alfonce:** Petrus Alphonsus

do hem bountee, they wol perverten it into
wikkednesse.'/ And eek thou most eschue
the conseillyng of hem that been thy servantz and beren thee greet reverence, for
peraventure they seyn it moore for drede
than for love./ And therfore seith a phi-   *2380
losophre in this wise: 'Ther is no wight
parfitly trewe to hym that he to soore dredeth.'/ And Tullius seith, 'Ther nys no myght
so greet of any emperour that longe may endure, but if he have moore love of the peple
than drede.'/ Thou shalt also eschue the con-
seiling of folk that been dronkelewe, for they
ne kan no conseil hyde./ For Salomon seith,
'Ther is no privetee ther as regneth dronkenesse.'/ Ye shul also han in suspect the conseillyng of swich folk as conseille yow o thyng
prively and conseille yow the contrarie
openly./ For Cassidorie seith that 'it   1195
is a manere sleighte to hyndre, whan he
sheweth to doon o thyng openly and werketh
prively the contrarie.'/ Thou shalt also have
in suspect the conseillyng of wikked folk. For
the book seith, 'The conseillyng of wikked folk
is alwey ful of fraude.'/ And David seith, 'Blisful is that man that hath nat folwed the con-
seilyng of shrewes.'/ Thou shalt also eschue
the conseillyng of yong folk, for hir conseil is
nat rype./

"Now, sire, sith I have shewed yow of
which folk ye shul take youre conseil and of
which folk ye shul folwe the con-
seil,/ now wol I teche yow how ye shal   *2390
examyne youre conseil, after the doctrine of Tullius./ In the examynynge thanne
of youre conseillour ye shul considere manye
thynges./ Alderfirst thou shalt considere that
in thilke thyng that thou purposest, and upon
what thyng thou wolt have conseil, that verray
trouthe be seyd and conserved; this is to seyn,
telle trewely thy tale./ For he that seith fals
may nat wel be conseilled in that cas of which
he lieth./ And after this thou shalt considere the
thynges that acorden to that thou purposest for
to do by thy conseillours, if resoun accorde therto,/ and eek if thy myght may   1205
atteine therto, and if the moore part and
the bettre part of thy conseillours acorde therto,
or noon./ Thanne shaltou considere what
thyng shal folwe of that conseillyng, as hate,

pees, werre, grace, profit, or damage, and
manye othere thynges./ And in alle thise
thynges thou shalt chese the beste and weyve
alle othere thynges./ Thanne shaltow considere of what roote is engendred the matiere of
thy conseil and what fruyt it may conceyve
and engendre./ Thou shalt eek considere
alle thise causes, fro whennes they been
sprongen./ And whan ye han exam-   *2400
yned youre conseil, as I have seyd, and
which partie is the bettre and moore profitable, and han approved it by manye wise folk
and olde,/ thanne shaltou considere if thou
mayst parfourne it and maken of it a good
ende./ For certes resoun wol nat that any
man sholde bigynne a thyng but if he myghte
parfourne it as hym oghte;/ ne no wight sholde
take upon hym so hevy a charge that he
myghte nat bere it./ For the proverbe seith,
'He that to muche embraceth, distreyneth litel.'/ And Catoun seith, 'Assay   1215
to do swich thyng as thou hast power to
doon, lest that the charge oppresse thee so
soore that thee bihoveth to weyve thyng that
thou hast bigonne.'/ And if so be that thou
be in doute wheither thou mayst parfourne a
thing or noon, chese rather to suffre than bigynne./ And Piers Alphonce seith, 'If thou hast
myght to doon a thyng of which thou most
repente, it is bettre "nay" than "ye." '/ This is
to seyn, that thee is bettre holde thy tonge
stille than for to speke./ Thanne may ye understonde by strenger resons that if thou hast
power to parfourne a werk of which thou shalt
repente, thanne is it bettre that thou suffre than bigynne./ Wel seyn they that   *2410
defenden every wight to assaye a thyng
of which he is in doute wheither he may parfourne it or noon./ And after, whan ye han
examyned youre conseil, as I have seyd biforn,
and knowen wel that ye may parfourne youre
emprise, conferme it thanne sadly til it be at
an ende./

"Now is it resoun and tyme that I shewe yow
whanne and wherfore that ye may chaunge
youre counseil withouten youre repreve./
Soothly, a man may chaungen his purpos and
his conseil if the cause cesseth, or whan a newe
caas bitydeth./ For the lawe seith that 'upon

1196 **Cassidorie:** Cassiodorus
1198 **David:** Psalms 1.1

1208 **weyve:** abandon, waive
1212 **parfourne:** perform, carry out
1215 **distreyneth:** holds, keeps
1222 **conferme:** prosecute, pursue

thynges that newely bityden bihoveth
newe conseil.'/ And Senec seith, 'If thy 1225
conseil is comen to the eeris of thyn enemy, chaunge thy conseil.'/ Thou mayst also
chaunge thy conseil if so be that thou fynde
that by errour, or by oother cause, harm or
damage may bityde./ Also if thy conseil be
dishonest, or ellis cometh of dishonest cause,
chaunge thy conseil./ For the lawes seyn that
'alle bihestes that been dishoneste been of no
value';/ and eek if so be that it be inpossible, or may nat goodly be parfourned
or kept./ *2420

"And take this for a general reule, that
every conseil that is affermed so strongly that
it may nat be chaunged for no condicioun that
may bityde, I seye that thilke conseil is wikked."/

This Melibeus, whanne he hadde herd the
doctrine of his wyf dame Prudence, answerde
in this wyse:/ "Dame," quod he, "as yet into
this tyme ye han wel and covenably taught me
as in general how I shal governe me in the
chesynge and in the withholdynge of my conseillours./ But now wolde I fayn that ye wolde
condescende in especial/ and telle me how liketh yow, or what semeth yow, by oure conseillours that we han chosen in oure present nede."/ 1235

"My lord," quod she, "I biseke yow in al
humblesse that ye wol nat wilfully replie agayn
my resouns, ne distempre youre herte, thogh I
speke thyng that yow displese./ For God woot
that, as in myn entente, I speke it for youre
beste, for youre honour, and for youre profite
eke./ And soothly, I hope that youre benyngnytee wol taken it in pacience./ Trusteth me
wel," quod she, "that youre conseil as in this
caas ne sholde nat, as to speke properly, be
called a conseillyng, but a mocioun or a moevyng of folye,/ in which conseil ye han
erred in many a sondry wise./ *2430

"First and forward, ye han erred in
th'assemblynge of youre conseillours./ For ye
sholde first have cleped a fewe folk to youre
conseil, and after ye myghte han shewed it
to mo folk, if it hadde been nede./ But certes,
ye han sodeynly cleped to youre conseil a greet

multitude of peple, ful chargeant and ful anoyous for to heere./ Also ye han erred, for theras
ye sholden oonly have cleped to youre conseil
youre trewe frendes olde and wise,/ ye han
ycleped straunge folk, yonge folk, false flatereres,
and enemys reconsiled, and folk that
doon yow reverence withouten love./ 1245
And eek also ye have erred, for ye han
broght with yow to youre conseil ire, coveitise,
and hastifnesse,/ the whiche thre thinges been
contrariouse to every conseil honest and profitable;/ the whiche thre thinges ye han nat
anientissed or destroyed hem, neither in youreself, ne in youre conseillours, as yow oghte./
Ye han erred also, for ye han shewed to youre
conseillours youre talent and youre affeccioun
to make werre anon and for to do vengeance./
They han espied by youre wordes to
what thyng ye been enclyned;/ and *2440
therfore han they rather conseilled
yow to youre talent than to youre profit./
Ye han erred also, for it semeth that yow
suffiseth to han been conseilled by thise
conseillours oonly, and with litel avys,/
whereas in so greet and so heigh a nede
it hadde been necessarie mo conseillours
and moore deliberacion to parfourne youre emprise./ Ye han erred also, for ye ne han nat
examyned youre conseil in the forseyde manere, ne in due manere, as the caas requireth./
Ye han erred also, for ye han maked no division bitwixe youre conseillours — this is to
seyn, bitwixen youre trewe freendes and
youre feyned conseillours — / ne ye han 1255
nat knowe the wil of youre trewe
freendes olde and wise,/ but ye han cast alle
hire wordes in an hochepot, and enclyncd
youre herte to the moore part and to the gretter
nombre, and there been ye condescended./
And sith ye woot wel that men shal alwey
fynde a gretter nombre of fooles than of wise
men,/ and therfore the conseils that been at
congregaciouns and multitudes of folk, there as
men take moore reward to the nombre than to
the sapience of persones,/ ye se wel that in
swiche conseillynges fooles han the maistrie."/ *2450

Melibeus answerde agayn, and seyde,
"I graunte wel that I have erred;/ but there

1228 **dishonest:** unjust
1233 **covenably:** fittingly **withholdynge:** retention
1234 **condescende in especial:** get down to particulars
1236 **distempre:** upset
1241 **First and forward:** first of all

1243 **chargeant:** burdensome
1248 **anientissed:** annihilated
1249 **talent:** desire, inclination
1257 **hochepot:** mixture **there been ye condescended:** to that
you have yielded (R.)

as thou hast toold me heerbiforn that he nys nat to blame that chaungeth his conseillours in certein caas and for certeine juste causes,/ I am al redy to chaunge my conseillours right as thow wolt devyse./ The proverbe seith that 'for to do synne is mannyssh, but certes for to persevere longe in synne is werk of the devel.' "/

To this sentence answered anon dame Prudence, and seyde,/ "Examineth," 1265 quod she, "youre conseil, and lat us see the whiche of hem han spoken most resonably and taught yow best conseil./ And for as muche as that the examynacion is necessarie, lat us bigynne at the surgiens and at the phisiciens, that first speeken in this matiere./ I sey yow that the surgiens and phisiciens han seyd yow in youre conseil discreetly, as hem oughte,/ and in hir speche seyden ful wisely that to the office of hem aperteneth to doon to every wight honour and profit, and no wight for to anoye,/ and after hir craft to doon greet diligence unto the cure of hem which that they han in hir governaunce./ *2460 And, sire, right as they han answered wisely and discreetly,/ right so rede I that they been heighly and sovereynly gerdoned for hir noble speche,/ and eek for they sholde do the moore ententif bisynesse in the curacion of youre doghter deere./ For al be it so that they been youre freendes, therfore shal ye nat suffren that they serve yow for noght,/ but ye oghte the rather gerdone hem and shewe hem youre largesse./ And as touchynge 1275 the proposicioun which that the phisiciens encreesceden in this caas — this is to seyn,/ that in maladies that oon contrarie is warissshed by another contrarie — / I wolde fayn knowe hou ye understonde thilke text, and what is youre sentence."/

"Certes," quod Melibeus, "I understonde it in this wise:/ that right as they han doon me a contrarie, right so sholde I doon hem another./ For right as they *2470 han venged hem on me and doon me wrong, right so shal I venge me upon hem and doon hem wrong;/ and thanne have I cured oon contrarie by another."/

"Lo, lo," quod dame Prudence, "how lightly is every man enclined to his owene desir and to his owene plesaunce!/ Certes," quod she, "the wordes of the phisiciens ne sholde nat han been understonden in thys wise./ For certes, wikkednesse is nat contrarie to wikkednesse, ne vengeance to vengeaunce, ne wrong to wrong, but they been semblable./ And therfore o vengeaunce is *2485 nat warissshed by another vengeaunce, ne o wroong by another wroong,/ but everich of hem encreesceth and aggreggeth oother./ But certes, the wordes of the phisiciens sholde been understonden in this wise:/ for good and wikkednesse been two contraries, and pees and werre, vengeaunce and suffraunce, discord and accord, and manye othere thynges;/ but certes, wikkednesse shal be warissshed by goodnesse, discord by accord, werre by pees, and so forth of othere thynges./ And heerto *2480 accordeth Seint Paul the Apostle in manye places./ He seith, 'Ne yeldeth nat harm for harm, ne wikked speche for wikked speche,/ but do wel to hym that dooth thee harm and blesse hym that seith to thee harm.'/ And in manye othere places he amonesteth pees and accord./ But now wol I speke to yow of the conseil which that was yeven to yow by the men of lawe and the wise folk,/ that seyden alle by oon accord, 1295 as ye han herd bifore,/ that over alle thynges ye shal doon youre diligence to kepen youre persone and to warnestoore youre hous;/ and seyden also that in this caas yow oghten for to werken ful avysely and with greet deliberacioun./ And, sire, as to the firste point, that toucheth to the kepyng of youre persone,/ ye shul understonde that he that hath werre shal everemoore mekely and devoutly preyen, biforn alle thynges,/ that Jhesus *2490 Crist of his mercy wol han hym in his proteccion and been his sovereyn helpyng at his nede./ For certes, in this world ther is no wight that may be conseilled ne kept sufficeantly withouten the kepyng of oure Lord Jhesu Crist./ To this sentence accordeth the prophete David, that seith,/ 'If God ne kepe the citee, in ydel waketh he that it kepeth.'/ Now, sire, thanne shul ye committe the kepyng of youre persone to youre trewe freendes that been approved and yknowe,/ 1305

1269 **anoye**: cause trouble
1272 **sovereynly**: chiefly
1273 **curacion**: cure
1275 **gerdone**: to reward

1287 **aggreggeth**: aggravates
1294 **amonesteth**: recommends
1297 **warnestoore**: garrison
1304 **waketh**: keeps watch

and of hem shul ye axen help youre persone
for to kepe. For Catoun seith, 'If thou hast
nede of help, axe it of thy freendes,/ for ther
nys noon so good a phisicien as thy trewe
freend.'/ And after this thanne shul ye kepe
yow fro alle straunge folk, and fro lyeres, and
have alwey in suspect hire compaignye./ For
Piers Alfonce seith, 'Ne taak no compaignye by
the weye of a straunge man, but if so be that
thou have knowe hym of a lenger tyme./ And
if so be that he falle into thy compaignye
paraventure, withouten thyn assent,/ en-   *2500
quere thanne as subtilly as thou mayst of
his conversacion, and of his lyf bifore, and feyne
thy wey; seye that thou [wolt] thider as thou
wolt nat go;/ and if he bereth a spere, hoold
thee on the right syde, and if he bere a swerd,
hoold thee on the lift syde.'/ And after this
thanne shul ye kepe yow wisely from all swich
manere peple as I have seyd bifore, and hem
and hir conseil eschewe./ And after this
thanne shul ye kepe yow in swich manere/
that, for any presumpcion of youre strengthe,
that ye ne dispise nat, ne accompte nat the
myght of youre adversarie so litel that ye lete
the kepyng of youre persone for youre
presumpcioun,/ for every wys man   1315
dredeth   his   enemy./ And   Salomon
seith, 'Weleful is he that of alle hath drede,/
for certes, he that thurgh the hardynesse of
his herte and thurgh the hardynesse of
hymself hath to greet presumpcioun, hym shal
yvel bityde.'/ Thanne shul ye everemoore contrewayte embusshementz and alle espiaille./
For Senec seith that 'the wise man that
dredeth harmes, eschueth harmes,/ ne   *2510
he ne falleth into perils that perils eschueth.'/ And al be it so that it seme that
thou art in siker place, yet shaltow alwey do
thy diligence in kepynge of thy persone;/ this
is to seyn, ne be nat necligent to kepe thy persone nat oonly fro thy gretteste enemys but
fro thy leeste enemy./ Senek seith, 'A man
that is well avysed, he dredeth his leste enemy.'/ Ovyde seith that 'the litel wesele
wol slee the grete bole and the wilde
hert.'/ And the book seith, 'A litel   1325
thorn may prikke a kyng ful soore, and

an hound wol holde the wilde boor.'/ But
nathelees, I sey nat thou shalt be so coward
that thou doute ther wher as is no drede./ The
book seith that 'somme folk han greet lust to
deceyve, but yet they dreden hem to be deceyved.'/ Yet shaltou drede to been empoi-
soned and kepe the from the compaignye of
scorneres./ For the book seith, 'With scorneres make no compaignye, but flee hire
wordes as venym.'/   *2520
   "Now, as to the seconde point, where
as youre wise conseillours conseilled yow to
warnestoore youre hous with gret diligence,/
I wolde fayn knowe how that ye understonde
thilke wordes and what is youre sentence."/
   Melibeus answerde and seyde, "Certes, I understande it in this wise: That I shal warnestoore myn hous with toures, swiche as han
castelles and othere manere edifices, and armure, and artelries,/ by whiche thynges I may
my persone and myn hous so kepen and deffenden that myne enemys shul been in drede
myn hous for to approche."/
   To this sentence answerde anon Prudence:
"Warnestooryng," quod she, "of heighe toures
and of grete edifices apperteyneth somtyme to pryde./ And eek men make   1335
heighe toures, [and grete edifices] with
grete costages and with greet travaille, and
whan that they been accompliced, yet be they
nat worth a stree, but if they be defended by
trewe freendes that been olde and wise./ And
understoond wel that the gretteste and strong-
este garnysoun that a riche man may have, as
wel to kepen his persone as his goodes, is/
that he be biloved with hys subgetz and with
his neighebores./ For thus seith Tullius, that
'ther is a manere garnysoun that no man may
venquysse ne disconfite, and that is/ a lord to
be biloved of his citezeins and of his
peple.'/   *2530
   Now, sire, as to the thridde point,
where as youre olde and wise conseillours
seyden that yow ne oghte nat sodeynly ne
hastily proceden in this nede,/ but that yow
oghte purveyen and apparaillen yow in this caas
with greet diligence and greet deliberacioun;/
trewely, I trowe that they seyden right wisely
and right sooth./ For Tullius seith, 'In every

1311 conversacion: way of life
1315 lete the kepyng: neglect the protection (R.)
1317 Weleful: happy, prosperous
1319 contrewayte: watch out for   embusshementz: ambushes
espiaille: spies
1325 wesele: weasel

1327 doute: fear
1333 artelries: artillery (catapults and cannons)
1336 costages: expenditures
1337 garnysoun: protection

nede, er thou bigynne it, apparaille thee with greet diligence.'/ Thanne seye I that in vengeance-takyng, in werre, in bataille, and in warnestooryng,/ er thow bigynne, I   1345 rede that thou apparaille thee therto, and do it with greet deliberacion./ For Tullius seith that 'longe apparaillyng biforn the bataille maketh short victorie.'/ And Cassidorus seith, 'The garnysoun is stronger whan it is longe tyme avysed.'/

But now lat us speken of the conseil that was accorded by youre neighebores, swiche as doon yow reverence withouten love,/ youre olde enemys reconsiled, youre flatereres,/ that conseilled yow certeyne   *2540 thynges prively, and openly conseilleden yow the contrarie;/ the yonge folk also, that conseilleden yow to venge yow and make werre anon./ And certes, sire, as I have seyd biforn, ye han greetly erred to han cleped swich manere folk to youre conseil,/ which conseillours been ynogh repreved by the resouns aforeseyd./ But nathelees, lat us now descende to the special. Ye shuln first procede after the doctrine of Tullius./   1355 Certes, the trouthe of this matiere, or of this conseil, nedeth nat diligently enquere,/ for it is wel wist whiche they been that han doon to yow this trespas and vileynye,/ and how manye trespassours, and in what manere they han to yow doon al this wrong and al this vileynye./ And after this, thanne shul ye examyne the seconde condicion which that the same Tullius addeth in this matiere./ For Tullius put a thyng which that he clepeth 'consentynge'; this is to seyn,/ who been   *2550 they, and whiche been they and how manye that consenten to thy conseil in thy wilfulnesse to doon hastif vengeance./ And lat us considere also who been they, and how manye been they, and whiche been they that consenteden to youre adversaries./ And certes, as to the firste poynt, it is wel knowen whiche folk been they that consenteden to youre hastif wilfulnesse,/ for trewely, alle tho that conseilleden yow to maken sodeyn werre ne been nat youre freendes./ Lat us now considere whiche been they that ye holde so greetly youre freendes as to youre persone./ For al   1365 be it so that ye be myghty and riche, certes ye ne been but allone,/ for certes ye ne

han no child but a doghter,/ ne ye ne han bretheren, ne cosyns germayns, ne noon oother neigh kynrede,/ wherfore that youre enemys for drede sholde stinte to plede with yow or to destroye youre persone./ Ye knowen also that youre richesses mooten been dispended in diverse parties,/ and whan   *2560 that every wight hath his part, they ne wollen taken but litel reward to venge thy deeth./ But thyne enemys been thre, and they han manie children, bretheren, cosyns, and oother ny kynrede./ And though so were that thou haddest slayn of hem two or three, yet dwellen ther ynowe to wreken hir deeth and to sle thy persone./ And though so be that youre kynrede be moore siker and stedefast than the kyn of youre adversarie,/ yet nathelees youre kynrede nys but a fer kynrede; they been but litel syb to yow,/   1375 and the kyn of youre enemys been ny syb to hem. And certes, as in that, hir condicioun is bet than youres./ Thanne lat us considere also if the conseillyng of hem that conseilleden yow to taken sodeyn vengeaunce, wheither it accorde to resoun./ And certes, ye knowe wel 'nay.'/ For, as by right and resoun, ther may no man taken vengeance on no wight but the juge that hath the jurisdiccioun of it,/ whan it is graunted hym to take thilke vengeance hastily or attemprely, as the lawe requireth./ And yet mooreover of thilke   *2570 word that Tullius clepeth 'consentynge,'/ thou shalt considere if thy myght and thy power may consenten and suffise to thy wilfulnesse and to thy conseillours./ And certes thou mayst wel seyn that 'nay.'/ For sikerly, as for to speke proprely, we may do no thyng but oonly swich thyng as we may doon rightfully./ And certes rightfully ne mowe ye take no vengeance, as of youre propre auctoritee./ Thanne mowe ye   1385 seen that youre power ne consenteth nat, ne accordeth nat, with youre wilfulnesse./

"Lat us now examyne the thridde point, that Tullius clepeth 'consequent.'/ Thou shalt understonde that the vengeance that thou purposest for to take is the consequent;/ and therof folweth another vengeaunce, peril, and werre, and othere damages withoute nombre, of whiche we be nat war, as at this tyme./

1355 **special:** particular

1368 **cosyns germayns:** first cousins
1375 **syb:** related, kin
1386 **ne consenteth:** is not consistent with

And as touchynge the fourthe point,
that Tullius clepeth 'engendrynge,'/   *2580
thou shalt considere that this wrong
which that is doon to thee is engendred of the
hate of thyne enemys,/ and of the vengeance-
takynge upon that wolde engendre another
vengeance, and muchel sorwe and wastynge
of richesses, as I seyde./

"Now, sire, as to the point that Tullius clepeth 'causes,' which that is the laste point,/ thou
shalt understonde that the wrong that thou hast
receyved hath certeine causes,/ whiche that
clerkes clepen *Oriens* and *Efficiens,* and *Causa
longinqua* and *Causa propinqua;* this is
to seyn, the fer cause and the ny cause./   1395
The fer cause is almyghty God, that is
cause of alle thynges./ The neer cause is thy
thre enemys./ The cause accidental was hate./
The cause material been the fyve woundes of
thy doghter./ The cause formal is the manere
of hir werkynge that broghten laddres
and cloumben in at thy wyndowes./   *2590
The cause final was for to sle thy doghter. It letted nat in as muche as in hem was./
But for to speken of the fer cause, as to what
ende they shul come, or what shal finally bityde
of hem in this caas, ne kan I nat deeme but
by conjectynge and by supposynge./ For we
shul suppose that they shul come to a wikked
ende,/ by cause that the Book of Decrees seith,
'Seelden, or with greet peyne, been causes
ybroght to good ende whanne they been baddely bigonne.'/

"Now, sire, if men wolde axe me why that
God suffred men to do yow this vileynye, certes,
I kan nat wel answere, as for no soothfastnesse./ For th'apostle seith that 'the   1405
sciences and the juggementz of oure
Lord God almyghty been ful depe;/ ther may
no man comprehende ne serchen hem suffisantly.'/ Nathelees, by certeyne presumpciouns and conjectynges, I holde and bileeve/
that God, which that is ful of justice and of
rightwisnesse, hath suffred this bityde by juste
cause resonable./

"Thy name is Melibee; this is to seyn,
'a man that drynketh hony.'/ Thou hast   *2600
ydronke so muchel hony of sweete tem-

poreel richesses, and delices and honours of
this world/ that thou art dronken and hast
forgeten Jhesu Crist thy creatour./ Thou ne
hast nat doon to hym swich honour and reverence as thee oughte,/ ne thou ne hast nat
wel ytaken kep to the wordes of Ovide, that
seith,/ 'Under the hony of the goodes of
the body is hyd the venym that sleeth
the soule.'/ And Salomon seith, 'If thou   1415
hast founden hony, ete of it that suffiseth,/ for if thou ete of it out of mesure, thou
shalt spewe' and be nedy and povre./ And
peraventure Crist hath thee in despit, and hath
turned awey fro thee his face and his eeris of
misericorde,/ and also he hath suffred that thou
hast been punysshed in the manere that thow
hast ytrespassed./ Thou hast doon synne
agayn oure Lord Crist,/ for certes, the   *2610
three enemys of mankynde — that is to
seyn, the flessh, the feend, and the world — /
thou hast suffred hem entre in to thyn herte
wilfully by the wyndowes of thy body,/ and
hast nat defended thyself suffisantly agayns
hire assautes and hire temptaciouns, so that they
han wounded thy soule in fyve places;/ this is
to seyn, the deedly synnes that been entred into
thyn herte by thy fyve wittes./ And in the
same manere oure Lord Crist hath woold and
suffred that thy three enemys been entred into thyn house by the wyndowes/   1425
and han ywounded thy doghter in the
forseyde manere."/

"Certes," quod Melibee, "I se wel that ye
enforce yow muchel by wordes to overcome
me in swich manere that I shal nat venge me
of myne enemys,/ shewynge me the perils and
the yveles that myghten falle of this vengeance./ But whoso wolde considere in alle
vengeances the perils and yveles that myghte
sewe of vengeance-takynge,/ a man wolde
nevere take vengeance, and that were
harm;/ for by the vengeance-takynge   *2620
been the wikked men dissevered fro the
goode men,/ and they that han wyl to do wikkednesse restreyne hir wikked purpos, whan
they seen the punyssynge and chastisynge of
the trespassours."/

1401 **letted nat:** did not delay
1402 **conjectynge:** conjecture
1404 **Book of Decrees:** the decrees of Gratian (*Decretum Gratiani*)
1408 **presumpciouns:** assumptions

1411 **delices:** pleasures
1417 **spewe:** vomit
1418 **misericorde:** mercy
1424 **fyve wittes:** five senses
1425 **woold:** willed

*[Et a ce respont dame Prudence, "Certes,"
dist elle, "je t'ottroye que de vengence vient
molt de maulx et de biens;/ Mais vengence
n'appartient pas a un chascun fors seulement
aux juges et a ceulx qui ont la juridicion sur
les malfaitteurs.]/* And yet seye I moore, that
right as a singuler persone synneth in
takynge vengeance of another man,/   1435
right so synneth the juge if he do no
vengeance of hem that it han disserved./ For
Senec seith thus: 'That maister,' he seith, 'is
good that proveth shrewes.'/ And as Cassidore seith, 'A man dredeth to do outrages
whan he woot and knoweth that it displeseth
to the juges and the sovereyns.'/ And another
seith, 'The juge that dredeth to do right maketh men shrewes.'/ And Seint Paul the Apostle seith in his Epistle, whan he writeth unto
the Romayns, that 'the juges beren nat
the spere withouten cause,/ but they   *2630
beren it to punysse the shrewes and mys-
doers and for to defende the goode men.'/ If ye
wol thanne take vengeance of youre enemys, ye
shul retourne or have youre recours to the juge
that hath the jurisdiccion upon hem,/ and he
shal punysse hem as the lawe axeth and requireth."/

"A," quod Melibee, "this vengeance liketh
me no thyng./ I bithenke me now and take
heede how Fortune hath norissed me fro my
childhede and hath holpen me to passe
many a stroong paas./ Now wol I as-   1445
sayen hire, trowynge, with Goddes help,
that she shal helpe me my shame for to
venge."/

"Certes," quod Prudence, "if ye wol werke
by my conseil, ye shul nat assaye Fortune by
no wey,/ ne ye shul nat lene or bowe unto
hire, after the word of Senec,/ for 'thynges that
been folily doon, and that been in hope of
Fortune, shullen nevere come to good ende.'/
And, as the same Senec seith, 'The moore cleer
and the moore shynyng that Fortune is, the
moore brotil and the sonner broken she
is.'/ Trusteth nat in hire, for she nys   *2640
nat stidefast ne stable,/ for whan thow

trowest to be moost seur or siker of hire help,
she wol faille thee and deceyve thee./ And
where as ye seyn that Fortune hath norissed
yow fro youre childhede,/ I seye that in so
muchel shul ye the lasse truste in hire and in
hir wit./ For Senec seith, 'What man that is
norissed by Fortune, she maketh hym
a greet fool.'/ Now thanne, syn ye de-   1455
sire and axe vengeance, and the vengeance that is doon after the lawe and bifore
the juge ne liketh yow nat,/ and the vengeance
that is doon in hope of Fortune is perilous and
uncertein,/ thanne have ye noon oother remedie but for to have youre recours unto the sovereyn Juge that vengeth alle vileynyes and
wronges./ And he shal venge yow after that
hymself witnesseth, where as he seith,/ 'Leveth the vengeance to me, and I shal
do it.'"/   *2650

Melibee answerde, "If I ne venge me
nat of the vileynye that men han doon to me,/
I sompne or warne hem that han doon to me
that vileynye, and alle othere, to do me another
vileynye./ For it is writen, 'If thou take no
vengeance of an oold vileynye, thou sompnest
thyne adversaries to do thee a newe vileynye.'/
And also for my suffrance men wolden do
me so muchel vileynye that I myghte neither
bere it ne susteene,/ and so sholde I
been put and holden overlowe./ For   1465
men seyn, 'In muchel suffrynge shul
manye thynges falle unto thee whiche thou
shalt nat mowe suffre.'"/

"Certes," quod Prudence, "I graunte yow
that over-muchel suffraunce is nat good./ But
yet ne folweth it nat therof that every persone
to whom men doon vileynye take of it vengeance,/ for that aperteneth and longeth al
oonly to the juges, for they shul venge the
vileynyes and injuries./ And therfore tho two
auctoritees that ye han seyd above been
oonly understonden in the juges,/ for   *2660
whan they suffren over-muchel the
wronges and the vileynyes to be doon withouten punysshynge,/ they sompne nat a man
al oonly for to do newe wronges, but they
comanden it./ Also a wys man seith that 'the
juge that correcteth nat the synnere comandeth and biddeth hym do synne.'/ And the juges
and sovereyns myghten in hir land so muchel
suffre of the shrewes and mysdoeres/ that they

1433–34 *Et a ce, etc.:* And to this dame Prudence answered,
"Certainly," she said, "I grant you that from vengeance come
many evils and many goods; but (taking) vengeance does not
appertain to an individual person but solely to judges and to
those who have jurisdiction over evil-doers."
1435 **singuler:** private
1437 **proveth:** reproves
1445 **bithenke me:** consider   **paas:** passage, difficult situation

1462 **sompne:** invite, summon   **warne:** announce

sholden, by swich suffrance, by proces of
tyme wexen of swich power and myght that
they sholden putte out the juges and the
sovereyns from hir places,/ and atte laste   1475
maken hem lesen hire lordshipes./

"But lat us now putte that ye have leve to
venge yow./ I seye ye been nat of myght and
power as now to venge yow,/ for if ye wole
maken comparisoun unto the myght of youre
adversaries, ye shul fynde in manye thynges
that I have shewed yow er this that hire condicion is bettre than youres./ And therfore
seye I that it is good as now that ye suffre and be pacient./   *2670

"Forthermoore, ye knowen wel that
after the comune sawe, 'it is a woodnesse a
man to stryve with a strenger or a moore
myghty man than he is hymself,/ and for to
stryve with a man of evene strengthe — that is
to seyn, with as strong a man as he is — it is
peril,/ and for to stryve with a weyker man, it
is folie.'/ And therfore sholde a man flee stryvynge as muchel as he myghte./ For Salomon
seith, 'It is a greet worshipe to a man to
kepen hym fro noyse and stryf.'/ And   1485
if it so bifalle or happe that a man of
gretter myght and strengthe than thou art do
thee grevaunce,/ studie and bisye thee rather
to stille the same grevaunce than for to venge
thee./ For Senec seith that 'he putteth hym in
greet peril that stryveth with a gretter man
than he is hymself.'/ And Catoun seith, 'If a
man of hyer estaat or degree, or moore myghty
than thou, do thee anoy or grevaunce, suffre
hym,/ for he that oones hath greved thee,
may another tyme releeve thee and
helpe.'/ Yet sette I caas ye have bothe   *2680
myght and licence for to venge yow,/ I
seye that ther be ful manye thynges that shul
restreyne yow of vengeance-takynge/ and
make yow for to enclyne to suffre, and for to
han pacience in the wronges that han been
doon to yow./ First and foreward, if ye wole
considere the defautes that been in youre
owene persone,/ for whiche defautes God hath
suffred yow have this tribulacioun, as I
have seyd yow heer-biforn./ For the   1495
poete seith that 'we oghte paciently
taken the tribulacions that comen to us, whan
we thynken and consideren that we han disserved to have hem.'/ And Seint Gregorie

seith that 'whan a man considereth wel the
nombre of his defautes and of his synnes,/ the
peynes and the tribulaciouns that he suffreth
semen the lesse unto hym;/ and in as muche
as hym thynketh his synnes moore hevy and
grevous,/ in so muche semeth his peyne
the lighter and the esier unto hym.'/   *2690
Also ye owen to enclyne and bowe youre
herte to take the pacience of oure Lord Jhesu
Crist, as seith Seint Peter in his Epistles./
'Jhesu Crist,' he seith, 'hath suffred for us and
yeven ensample to every man to folwe and
sewe hym,/ for he dide nevere synne, ne nevere cam ther a vileyns word out of his mouth./
Whan men cursed hym, he cursed hem noght,
and whan men betten hym, he manaced hem
noght.'/ Also the grete pacience which the
seintes that been in Paradys han had in tribulaciouns that they han ysuffred, withouten
hir desert or gilt,/ oghte muchel stiren   1505
yow to pacience./ Forthermoore ye
sholde enforce yow to have pacience,/ considerynge that the tribulaciouns of this world but
litel while endure and soone passed been and
goon,/ and the joye that a man seketh to have
by pacience in tribulaciouns is perdurable,
after that the Apostle seith in his epistle./ 'The
joye of God,' he seith, 'is perdurable' —
that is to seyn, everelastynge./ Also   *2700
troweth and bileveth stedefastly that he
nys nat wel ynorissed, ne wel ytaught, that kan
nat have pacience or wol nat receyve pacience./ For Salomon seith that 'the doctrine
and the wit of a man is knowen by pacience.'/
And in another place he seith that 'he that is
pacient governeth hym by greet prudence.'/
And the same Salomon seith, 'The angry and
wrathful man maketh noyses, and the pacient
man atempreth hem and stilleth.'/ He seith
also, 'It is moore worth to be pacient
than for to be right strong;/ and he   1515
that may have the lordshipe of his
owene herte is moore to preyse than he that
by his force or strengthe taketh grete citees.'/
And therfore seith Seint Jame in his Epistle that
'pacience is a greet vertu of perfeccioun.' "/

"Certes," quod Melibee, "I graunte yow,
dame Prudence, that pacience is a greet vertu
of perfeccioun;/ but every man may nat have
the perfeccioun that ye seken;/ ne I nam

1477 **putte:** suppose

1510 perdurable: eternal
1514 **atempreth:** moderates
1515 **worth:** worthy

nat of the nombre of right parfite men,/   *2710
for myn herte may nevere been in pees
unto the tyme it be venged./ And al be it so
that it was greet peril to myne enemys to do
me a vileynye in takynge vengeance upon me,/
yet tooken they noon heede of the peril, but
fulfilleden hir wikked wyl and hir corage./
And therfore me thynketh men oghten nat
repreve me, though I putte me in a litel peril
for to venge me,/ and though I do a greet
excesse; that is to seyn, that I venge
oon outrage by another."/   1525

"A," quod dame Prudence, "ye seyn
youre wyl and as yow liketh,/ but in no caas
of the world a man sholde nat doon outrage
ne excesse for to vengen hym./ For Cassidore
seith that 'as yvele dooth he that vengeth hym
by outrage as he that dooth the outrage.'/ And
therfore ye shul venge yow after the ordre of
right; that is to seyn, by the lawe and noght
by excesse ne by outrage./ And also, if ye
wol venge yow of the outrage of youre adversaries in oother manere than right comandeth, ye synnen./ And therfore seith Senec   *2720
that 'a man shal nevere vengen shrewednesse by shrewednesse.'/ And if ye seye that
right axeth a man to defenden violence by violence and fightyng by fightyng,/ certes ye seye
sooth, whan the defense is doon anon withouten intervalle or withouten tariyng or delay,/ for to deffenden hym and nat for to
vengen hym./ And it bihoveth that a man
putte swich attemperance in his def-
fense/ that men have no cause ne mat-   1535
iere to repreven hym that deffendeth
hym of excesse and outrage, for ellis were it
agayn resoun./ Pardee, ye knowen wel that
ye maken no deffense as now for to deffende
yow, but for to venge yow;/ and so seweth
it that ye han no wyl to do youre dede attemprely./ And therfore me thynketh that pacience is good. For Salomon seith that 'he that
is nat pacient shal have greet harm.' "/

"Certes," quod Melibee, "I graunte yow that
whan a man is inpacient and wrooth of that
that toucheth hym noght and that aperteneth
nat unto hym, though it harme hym, it
is no wonder./ For the lawe seith that   *2730
'he is coupable that entremetteth hym or
medleth with swych thyng as aperteneth nat

unto hym.'/ And Salomon seith that 'he that
entremetteth hym of the noyse or strif of another man is lyk to hym that taketh an hound
by the eris.'/ For right as he that taketh a
straunge hound by the eris is outherwhile biten
with the hound,/ right in the same wise is it
resoun that he have harm that by his inpacience medleth hym of the noyse of another
man, wheras it aperteneth nat unto hym./ But
ye knowen wel that this dede — that is to seyn,
my grief and my disese — toucheth me
right ny./ And therfore, though I be   1545
wrooth and inpacient, it is no merveille./
And, savynge youre grace, I kan nat seen that it
myghte greetly harme me though I tooke vengeaunce./ For I am richer and moore myghty
than myne enemys been;/ and wel knowen ye
that by moneye and by havynge grete possessions been alle the thynges of this world governed./ And Salomon seith that 'alle
thynges obeyen to moneye.' "/   *2740

Whan Prudence hadde herd hir housbonde avanten hym of his richesse and of his
moneye, dispreisynge the power of his adversaries, she spak and seyde in this wise:/
"Certes, deere sire, I graunte yow that ye been
riche and myghty/ and that the richesses been
goode to hem that han wel ygeten hem and wel
konne usen hem./ For right as the body of a
man may nat lyven withoute the soule, namoore
may it lyve withouten temporeel goodes./ And
by richesses may a man gete hym grete
freendes./ And therfore seith Pam-   1555
philles: 'If a net-herdes doghter,' seith
he, 'be riche, she may chesen of a thousand
men which she wol take to hir housbonde,/
for, of a thousand men, oon wol nat forsaken
hire ne refusen hire.'/ And this Pamphilles
seith also, 'If thow be right happy — that is to
seyn, if thou be right riche — thou shalt fynde
a greet nombre of felawes and freendes./ And
if thy fortune change that thou wexe povre,
farewel freendshipe and felaweshipe,/ for thou
shalt be alloone withouten any compaignye,
but if it be the compaignye of povre
folk.'/ And yet seith this Pamphilles   *2750
moreover that 'they that been thralle and
bonde of lynage shullen been maad worthy and
noble by the richesses.'/ And right so as by
richesses ther comen manye goodes, right so

1531 **shrewednesse:** wickedness
1532 **defenden:** defend from, fight off
1541 **entremetteth:** interferes, meddles with

1556 **Pamphilles:** hero of the thirteenth-century Latin poem
Pamphilus de Amore   **net-herdes:** cowherd's

by poverte come ther manye harmes and yveles,/ for greet poverte constreyneth a man to do manye yveles./ And therfore clepeth Cassidore poverte the mooder of ruyne;/ that is to seyn, the mooder of overthrowynge or fallynge doun./ And therfore seith   1565 Piers Alfonce, 'Oon of the gretteste adversitees of this world is/ whan a free man by kynde or of burthe is constreyned by poverte to eten the almesse of his enemy,'/ and the same seith Innocent in oon of his bookes. He seith that 'sorweful and myshappy is the condicioun of a povre beggere;/ for if he axe nat his mete, he dyeth for hunger;/ and if he axe, he dyeth for shame; and algates necessitee constreyneth hym to axe.'/ And   *2760 seith Salomon that 'bet it is to dye than for to have swich poverte.'/ And as the same Salomon seith, 'Bettre it is to dye of bitter deeth than for to lyven in swich wise.'/ By thise resons that I have seid unto yow and by manye othere resons that I koude seye,/ I graunte yow that richesses been goode to hem that geten hem wel and to hem that wel usen tho richesses./ And therfore wol I shewe yow hou ye shul have yow, and how ye shul bere yow in gaderynge of richesses, and in what manere ye shul usen hem./   1575

"First, ye shul geten hem withouten greet desir, by good leyser, sokyngly and nat over-hastily./ For a man that is to desirynge to gete richesses abaundoneth hym first to thefte, and to alle othere yveles;/ and therfore seith Salomon, 'He that hasteth hym to bisily to wexe riche shal be noon innocent.'/ He seith also that 'the richesse that hastily cometh to a man soone and lightly gooth and passeth fro a man,/ but that richesse that cometh litel and litel wexeth alwey and multiplieth.'/ And, sire, ye shul geten   *2770 richesses by youre wit and by youre travaille unto youre profit,/ and that withouten wrong or harm doynge to any oother persone./ For the lawe seith that 'ther maketh no man himselven riche, if he do harm to another wight.'/ This is to seyn, that nature deffendeth and forbedeth by right that no man make hymself riche unto the harm of another per-

sone./ And Tullius seith that 'no sorwe, ne no drede of deeth, ne no thyng that may falle unto a man,/ is so muchel agayns   1585 nature as a man to encressen his owene profit to the harm of another man./ And though the grete men and the myghty men geten richesses moore lightly than thou,/ yet shaltou nat been ydel ne slow to do thy profit, for thou shalt in alle wise flee ydelnesse.'/ For Salomon seith that 'ydelnesse techeth a man to do manye yveles.'/ And the same Salomon seith that 'he that travailleth and bisieth hym to tilien his land shal eten breed,/   *2780 but he that is ydel and casteth hym to no bisynesse ne occupacioun shal falle into poverte and dye for hunger.'/ And he that is ydel and slow kan nevere fynde covenable tyme for to doon his profit./ For ther is a versifiour seith that 'the ydel man excuseth hym in wynter by cause of the grete coold, and in somer by enchesoun of the greete heete.'/ For thise causes seith Caton, 'Waketh and enclyneth nat yow over-muchel for to slepe, for over-muchel reste norisseth and causeth manye vices.'/ And therfore seith Seint Jerome, 'Dooth somme goode dedes that the devel, which is oure enemy, ne fynde yow nat unocupied.'/ For the devel ne taketh   1595 nat lightly unto his werkynge swiche as he fyndeth occupied in goode werkes./

"Thanne thus in getynge richesses ye mosten flee ydelnesse./ And afterward, ye shul use the richesses which ye have geten by youre wit and by youre travaille/ in swich a manere that men holde yow nat to scars, ne to sparynge, ne to fool-large — that is to seyen, over-large a spendere./ For right as men blamen an avaricious man by cause of his scarsetee and chyncherie,/ in the same wise is he to   *2790 blame that spendeth over-largely./ And therfore seith Caton: 'Use,' he seith, 'thy richesses that thou hast geten/ in swich a manere that men have no matiere ne cause to calle thee neither wrecche ne chynche,/ for it is a greet shame to a man to have a povere herte and a riche purs.'/ He seith also, 'The goodes that thou hast ygeten, use hem by mesure;' that is to seyn, spende hem mesurably,/

1568 **myshappy:** unfortunate
1575 **hou ye shul have yow:** how you should behave
1576 **sokyngly:** slowly, gradually
1577 **abaundoneth hym:** devotes himself
1584 **no man:** any man

1590 **tilien:** till
1592 **covenable:** suitable
1599 **scars:** niggardly
1600 **scarsetee:** niggardliness   **chyncherie:** miserliness
1603 **chynche:** miser
1605 **mesurably:** moderately

for they that folily wasten and   1606
despenden the goodes that they han,/
whan they han namoore propre of hir owene,
they shapen hem to take the goodes of another
man./ I seye thanne that ye shul fleen avarice,/ usynge youre richesses in swich manere
that men seye nat that youre richesses been
yburyed/ but that ye have hem in
youre myght and in youre weeldynge./   *2800
For a wys man repreveth the avaricious
man, and seith thus in two vers:/ 'Wherto and
why burieth a man his goodes by his grete
avarice, and knoweth wel that nedes moste
he dye?/ For deeth is the ende of every man
as in this present lyf.'/ And for what cause or
enchesoun joyneth he hym or knytteth he hym
so faste unto his goodes/ that alle hise wittes
mowen nat disseveren hym or departen
hym from his goodes,/ and knoweth   1615
wel, or oghte knowe, that whan he is
deed he shal no thyng bere with hym out of
this world?/ And therfore seith Seint Austyn
that 'the avaricious man is likned unto helle,/
that the moore it swelweth the moore desir it
hath to swelwe and devoure.'/ And as wel as
ye wolde eschewe to be called an avaricious
man or chynche,/ as wel sholde ye kepe yow
and governe yow in swich a wise that
men calle yow nat fool-large./ Ther-   *2810
fore seith Tullius: 'The goodes,' he seith,
'of thyn hous ne sholde nat been hyd ne kept
so cloos, but that they myghte been opened
by pitee and debonairetee'/ (that is to seyn, to
yeven part to hem that han greet nede),/ 'ne
thy goodes shullen nat been so opene to been
every mannes goodes.'/ Afterward, in getynge
of youre richesses and in usynge hem ye shul
alwey have thre thynges in youre herte/ (that
is to seyn, oure Lord God, conscience,
and good name)./ First, ye shul have   1625
God in youre herte,/ and for no richesse
ye shullen do no thyng which may in any
manere displese God, that is youre creatour
and makere./ For after the word of Salomon,
'It is bettre to have a litel good with the love
of God/ than to have muchel good and tresour and lese the love of his Lord God.'/ And
the prophete seith that 'bettre it is to been
a good man and have litel good and
tresour/ than to been holden a shrewe   *2820
and have grete richesses.'/ And yet seye

I ferthermoore, that ye sholde alwey doon youre
bisynesse to gete yow richesses,/ so that ye
gete hem with good conscience./ And th'Apostle seith that 'ther nys thyng in this world
of which we sholden have so greet joye as
whan oure conscience bereth us good witnesse.'/ And the wise man seith, 'The substance of a man is ful good, whan synne
is nat in mannes conscience.'/ After-   1635
ward, in getynge of youre richesses and
in usynge of hem,/ yow moste have greet bisynesse and greet diligence that youre goode
name be alwey kept and conserved./ For Salomon seith that 'bettre it is and moore it availleth a man to have a good name than for
to have grete richesses.'/ And therfore he
seith in another place, 'Do greet diligence,'
seith Salomon, 'in kepyng of thy freend and
of thy goode name;/ for it shal lenger abide
with thee than any tresour, be it never
so precious.'/ And certes he sholde nat   *2830
be called a gentil man that after God
and good conscience, alle thynges left, ne
dooth his diligence and bisynesse to kepen his
goode name./ And Cassidore seith that 'it is
signe of a gentil herte whan a man loveth and
desireth to han a good name.'/ And therfore
seith Seint Austyn that 'ther been two thynges
that arn necessarie and nedefulle,/ and that
is good conscience and good loos;/ that is to
seyn, good conscience to thyn owene persone
inward and good loos for thy neighebor
outward.'/ And he that trusteth hym so   1645
muchel in his goode conscience/ that he
displeseth, and setteth at noght his goode
name or loos, and rekketh noght though he
kepe nat his goode name, nys but a crueel
cherl./

     "Sire, now have I shewed yow how ye shul
do in getynge richesses, and how ye shullen
usen hem,/ and I se wel that for the trust
that ye han in youre richesses ye wole moeve
werre and bataille./ I conseille yow that ye
bigynne no werre in trust of youre richesses,
for they ne suffisen noght werres to
mayntene./ And therfore seith a phi-   *2840
losophre, 'That man that desireth and
wole algates han werre, shal nevere have suffisaunce,/ for the richer that he is, the gretter
despenses moste he make, if he wole have wor-

shipe and victorie.'/ And Salomon seith that 'the gretter richesses that a man hath, the mo despendours he hath.'/ And, deere sire, al be it so that for youre richesses ye mowe have muchel folk,/ yet bihoveth it nat, ne it is nat good, to bigynne werre whereas ye mowe in oother manere have pees unto youre worshipe and profit./ For the victorie 1655 of batailles that been in this world lyth nat in greet nombre or multitude of the peple, ne in the vertu of man,/ but it lith in the wyl and in the hand of oure Lord God Almyghty./ And therfore Judas Machabeus, which was Goddes knyght,/ whan he sholde fighte agayn his adversarie that hadde a gretter nombre and a gretter multitude of folk and strenger than was this peple of Machabee,/ yet he reconforted his litel compaignye, and seyde right in this wise:/ 'Als lightly,' quod   *2850 he, 'may oure Lord God Almyghty yeve victorie to a fewe folk as to many folk,/ for the victorie of a bataile comth nat by the grete nombre of peple,/ but it cometh from oure Lord God of hevene.'/ And, deere sire, for as muchel as ther is no man certein if he be worthy that God yeve hym victorie [*ne plus que il est certain se il est digne de l'amour de Dieu*] or naught, after that Salomon seith,/ therfore every man sholde greetly drede werres to bigynne./ And by cause that   1665 in batailles fallen manye perils,/ and happeth outher while that as soone is the grete man slayn as the litel man;/ and as it is writen in the seconde Book of Kynges, 'The dedes of batailles been aventurouse and nothyng certeyne,/ for as lightly is oon hurt with a spere as another';/ and for ther is gret peril in werre, therfore sholde a man flee and eschue werre, in as muchel as a man may goodly./ For Salomon seith, 'He that   *2860 loveth peril shal falle in peril.' "/

After that Dame Prudence hadde spoken in this manere, Melibee answerde and seyde,/ "I see wel, dame Prudence, that by youre faire wordes and by youre resouns that ye han shewed me, that the werre liketh yow no thyng;/ but I have nat yet herd youre conseil, how I shal do in this nede."/

"Certes," quod she, "I conseille yow that ye accorde with youre adversaries and that ye have pees with hem./ For Seint Jame   1675 seith in his Epistles that 'by concord and pees the smale richesses wexen grete,/ and by debaat and discord the grete richesses fallen doun.'/ And ye knowen wel that oon of the gretteste and moost sovereyn thyng that is in this world is unytee and pees./ And therfore seyde oure Lord Jhesu Crist to his apostles in this wise:/ 'Wel happy and blessed been they that loven and purchacen pees, for they been called children of God.' "/   *2870

"A," quod Melibee, "now se I wel that ye loven nat myn honour ne my worshipe./ Ye knowen wel that myne adversaries han bigonnen this debaat and bryge by hire outrage,/ and ye se wel that they ne requeren ne preyen me nat of pees, ne they asken nat to be reconsiled./ Wol ye thanne that I go and meke me, and obeye me to hem, and crie hem mercy?/ For sothe, that were nat my worshipe./ For right as men seyn that   1685 'over-greet hoomlynesse engendreth dispreisynge,' so fareth it by to greet humylitee or mekenesse."/

Thanne bigan dame Prudence to maken semblant of wratthe and seyde:/ "Certes, sire, sauf youre grace, I love youre honour and youre profit as I do myn owene, and evere have doon;/ ne ye, ne noon oother, seyn nevere the contrarie./ And yit if I hadde seyd that ye sholde han purchaced the pees and the reconsiliacioun, I ne hadde nat muchel mystaken me ne seyd amys./ For the   *2880 wise man seith, 'The dissensioun bigynneth by another man, and the reconsilyng bygynneth by thyself.'/ And the prophete seith, 'Flee shrewednesse and do goodnesse;/ seke pees and folwe it, as muchel as in thee is.'/ Yet seye I nat that ye shul rather pursue to youre adversaries for pees than they shuln to yow./ For I knowe wel that ye been so hardherted that ye wol do no thyng for me./ And Salomon seith, 'He that hath   1695 over-hard an herte, atte laste he shal myshappe and mystyde.' "/

1653 **despendours:** officials who disburse money
1664 *ne plus que . . . de Dieu:* no more than it is certain that he is worthy of the love of God
1668 **seconde Book of Kynges:** AV 2 Samuel 11.25.
aventurouse: subject to chance

1676 **Seint Jame:** a misattribution; actually from Seneca
1682 **bryge:** strife
1684 **meke me:** humble myself
1686 **hoomlynesse:** familiarity
1690 **purchaced:** brought about
1694 **shuln** = *shullen,* should (offer peace)
1696 **mystyde:** misbetide, be unlucky

Whanne Melibee hadde herd dame Prudence maken semblant of wratthe, he seyde in this wise:/ "Dame, I prey yow that ye be nat displesed of thynges that I seye,/ for ye knowe wel that I am angry and wrooth, and that is no wonder;/ and they that been wrothe witen nat wel what they don ne what they seyn./ Therfore the prophete seith that   *2890 'troubled eyen han no cleer sighte.'/ But seyeth and conseileth me as yow liketh, for I am redy to do right as ye wol desire;/ and if ye repreve me of my folye, I am the moore holden to love yow and to preyse yow./ For Salomon seith that 'he that repreveth hym that dooth folye,/ he shal fynde gretter grace than he that deceyveth hym by sweete wordes.'"/   1705

Thanne seide dame Prudence, "I make no semblant of wratthe ne anger, but for youre grete profit./ For Salomon seith, 'He is moore worth that repreveth or chideth a fool for his folye, shewynge hym semblant of wratthe,/ than he that supporteth hym and preyseth hym in his mysdoynge and laugheth at his folye.'/ And this same Salomon seith afterward that 'by the sorweful visage of a man' (that is to seyn by the sory and hevy contenaunce of a man)/ 'the fool correcteth and amendeth hymself.'"/   *2900

Thanne seyde Melibee, "I shal nat konne answere to so manye faire resouns as ye putten to me and shewen./ Seyeth shortly youre wyl and youre conseil, and I am al redy to fulfille and parfourne it."/

Thanne dame Prudence discovered al hir wyl to hym and seyde,/ "I conseille yow," quod she, "aboven alle thynges, that ye make pees bitwene God and yow,/ and beth reconsiled unto hym and to his grace./   1715 For, as I have seyd yow heer biforn, God hath suffred yow to have this tribulacioun and disese for youre synnes./ And if ye do as I sey yow, God wol sende youre adversaries unto yow/ and maken hem fallen at youre feet, redy to do youre wyl and youre comandementz./ For Salomon seith, 'Whan the condicioun of man is plesaunt and likynge to God,/ he chaungeth the hertes of the mannes adversaries and constreyneth hem to biseken hym of pees and of grace.'/ And   *2910 I prey yow lat me speke with youre ad-

versaries in privee place,/ for they shul nat knowe that it be of youre wyl or of youre assent./ And thanne, whan I knowe hir wil and hire entente, I may conseille yow the moore seurely."/

"Dame," quod Melibee, "dooth youre wil and youre likynge;/ for I putte me hoolly in youre disposicioun and ordinaunce."/   1725

Thanne dame Prudence, whan she saugh the goode wyl of hir housbonde, delibered and took avys in hirself,/ thinkinge how she myghte brynge this nede unto a good conclusioun and to a good ende./ And whan she saugh hir tyme, she sente for thise adversaries to come unto hire into a pryvee place/ and shewed wisely unto hem the grete goodes that comen of pees/ and the grete harmes and perils that been in werre,/ and   *2920 seyde to hem in a goodly manere hou that hem oughten have greet repentaunce/ of the injurie and wrong that they hadden doon to Melibee hir lord, and unto hire, and to hire doghter./

And whan they herden the goodliche wordes of dame Prudence,/ they weren so supprised and ravysshed and hadden so greet joye of hire that wonder was to telle./ "A, lady," quod they, "ye han shewed unto us the blessynge of swetnesse, after the sawe of David the prophete,/ for the reconsilynge which   1735 we been nat worthy to have in no manere,/ but we oghte requeren it with greet contricioun and humylitee,/ ye of youre grete goodnesse have presented unto us./ Now se we wel that the science and the konnynge of Salomon is ful trewe./ For he seith that 'sweete wordes multiplien and encreescen freendes and maken shrewes to be debonaire and meeke.'/   *2930

"Certes," quod they, "we putten oure dede and al oure matere and cause al hoolly in youre goode wyl/ and been redy to obeye to the speche and comandement of my lord Melibee./ And therfore, deere and benygne lady, we preien yow and biseke yow as mekely as we konne and mowen/ that it lyke unto youre grete goodnesse to fulfillen in dede youre goodliche wordes,/ for we consideren and knowelichen that we han offended and greved my lord Melibee out of mesure,/ so fer-   1745

1707 **worth:** worthy
1711 **konne:** be able to
1723 **seurely:** surely
1726 **delibered:** considered
1734 **supprised:** taken (by it)
1739 **science:** knowledge

forth that we be nat of power to maken
his amendes./ And therfore we oblige and
bynden us and oure freendes for to doon al
his wyl and his comandementz./ But peraventure he hath swich hevynesse and swich wratthe
to us-ward by cause of oure offense/ that he
wole enjoyne us swich a peyne as we mowe
nat bere ne susteene./ And therfore, noble
lady, we biseke to youre wommanly
pitee/ to taken swich avysement in this   *2940
nede that we ne oure freendes be nat
desherited ne destroyed thurgh oure folye."/

"Certes," quod Prudence, "it is an hard
thyng and right perilous/ that a man putte
hym al outrely in the arbitracioun and juggement, and in the myght and power of his enemys./ For Salomon seith, 'Leeveth me, and
yeveth credence to that I shal seyn: I seye,'
quod he, 'ye peple, folk and governours of
hooly chirche,/ to thy sone, to thy wyf,
to thy freend, ne to thy broother/ ne   1755
yeve thou nevere myght ne maistrie of
thy body whil thou lyvest.'/ Now sithen he
deffendeth that man sholde nat yeven to his
broother ne to his freend the myght of his
body,/ by a strenger resoun he deffendeth and
forbedeth a man to yeven hymself to his enemy./ And nathelees I conseille you that ye
mystruste nat my lord,/ for I woot wel and
knowe verraily that he is debonaire and
meeke, large, curteys,/ and nothyng de-   *2950
sirous ne coveitous of good ne richesse./
For ther nys nothyng in this world that he
desireth, save oonly worshipe and honour./
Forthermoore I knowe wel and am right seur
that he shal nothyng doon in this nede withouten my conseil,/ and I shal so werken in this
cause that by the grace of oure Lord God ye
shul been reconsiled unto us."/

Thanne seyden they with o voys, "Worshipful lady, we putten us and oure goodes
al fully in youre wil and disposicioun,/   1765
and been redy to comen, what day that
it like unto youre noblesse to lymyte us or assigne us,/ for to maken oure obligacioun and
boond as strong as it liketh unto youre goodnesse,/ that we mowe fulfille the wille of yow
and of my lord Melibee."/

When dame Prudence hadde herd the answeres of thise men, she bad hem goon agayn

1747 **oblige:** pledge
1757 **nat yeven:** i.e., give
1767 **obligacioun:** surety, pledge

prively;/ and she retourned to hir lord Melibee, and tolde hym how she foond his
adversaries ful repentant,/ knowelech-   *2960
ynge ful lowely hir synnes and trespas,
and how they were redy to suffren all peyne,/
requirynge and preiynge hym of mercy and
pitee./

Thanne seyde Melibee: "He is wel worthy
to have pardoun and foryifnesse of his synne,
that excuseth nat his synne/ but knowelecheth
it and repenteth hym, axinge indulgence./ For
Senec seith, 'Ther is the remissioun and
foryifnesse, where as the confessioun is,'/   1775
for confessioun is neighebor to inno-
cence./ And he seith in another place that 'he
that hath shame of his synne and knowlecheth
[it is worthy remissioun].' And therfore I assente and conferme me to have pees;/ but it
is good that we do it nat withouten the assent
and wyl of oure freendes."/

Thanne was Prudence right glad and joyeful and seyde:/ "Certes, sire," quod
she, "ye han wel and goodly answered,/   *2970
for right as by the conseil, assent, and
help of youre freendes ye han been stired to
venge yow and maken werre,/ right so withouten hire conseil shul ye nat accorden yow
ne have pees with youre adversaries./ For the
lawe seith, 'Ther nys no thyng so good by wey
of kynde as a thyng to be unbounde by hym
that it was ybounde.' "/

And thanne dame Prudence withouten delay or tariynge sente anon hire messages for
hire kyn and for hire olde freendes which
that were trewe and wyse,/ and tolde hem
by ordre in the presence of Melibee al this mateere as it is aboven expressed and declared,/ and preyden hem that they   1785
wolde yeven hire avys and conseil what
best were to doon in this nede./ And whan
Melibees freendes hadde taken hire avys and
deliberacioun of the forseide mateere,/ and
hadden examyned it by greet bisynesse and
greet diligence,/ they yave ful conseil for to
have pees and reste,/ and that Melibee sholde
receyve with good herte his adversaries
to foryifnesse and mercy./   *2980

And whan dame Prudence hadde herd
the assent of hir lord Melibee, and the conseil of his freendes/ accorde with hire wille
and hire entencioun,/ she was wonderly glad
in hire herte and seyde:/ "Ther is an old
proverbe," quod she, "seith that 'the goodnesse that thou mayst do this day, do it,/

and abide nat ne delaye it nat til to-
morwe.'/ And therfore I conseille that   1795
ye sende youre messages, swiche as been
discrete and wise,/ unto youre adversaries,
tellynge hem on youre bihalve/ that if they
wole trete of pees and of accord,/ that they
shape hem withouten delay or tariyng to comen
unto us."/ Which thyng parfourned was
in dede./ And whanne thise trespas-   *2990
sours and repentynge folk of hire folies —
that is to seyn, the adversaries of Melibee — /
hadden herd what thise messengers seyden unto
hem,/ they weren right glad and joyeful, and
answereden ful mekely and benignely,/ yeldynge graces and thankynges to hir lord Melibee and to al his compaignye,/ and shopen
hem withouten delay to go with the messengers
and obeye to the comandement of hir
lord Melibee./   1805

And right anon they tooken hire wey
to the court of Melibee,/ and tooken with hem
somme of hire trewe freendes to maken feith
for hem and for to been hire borwes./ And
whan they were comen to the presence of
Melibee, he seyde hem thise wordes:/ "It standeth thus," quod Melibee, "and sooth it is, that
ye,/ causelees and withouten skile and
resoun,/ han doon grete injuries and   *3000
wronges to me and to my wyf Prudence
and to my doghter also./ For ye han entred
into myn hous by violence,/ and have doon
swich outrage that alle men knowen wel that
ye have disserved the deeth./ And therfore
wol I knowe and wite of yow/ wheither ye
wol putte the punyssement and the chastisynge
and the vengeance of this outrage in the wyl
of me and of my wyf Prudence, or ye
wol nat?"/   1815

Thanne the wiseste of hem thre answerde for hem alle and seyde,/ "Sire," quod
he, "we knowen wel that we been unworthy
to comen unto the court of so greet a lord and
so worthy as ye been./ For we han so greetly
mystaken us, and han offended and agilt in
swich a wise agayn youre heigh lordshipe/
that trewely we han disserved the deeth./ But
yet, for the grete goodnesse and debonairetee
that al the world witnesseth of youre
persone,/ we submytten us to the excel-   *3010
lence and benignitee of youre gracious

lordshipe,/ and been redy to obeie to alle youre
comandementz,/ bisekynge yow that of youre
merciable pitee ye wol considere oure grete
repentaunce   and   lowe   submyssioun/ and
graunten us foryevenesse of oure outrageous
trespas and offense./ For wel we knowe that
youre liberal grace and mercy strecchen hem
ferther into goodnesse than doon oure outra-
geouse giltes and trespas into wikked-
nesse,/ al be it that cursedly and   1825
dampnablely we han agilt agayn youre
heigh lordshipe."/

Thanne Melibee took hem up fro the ground
ful benignely,/ and receyved hire obligaciouns
and hir boondes by hire othes upon hire pledges
and borwes,/ and assigned hem a certeyn day
to retourne unto his court/ for to accepte and
receyve the sentence and juggement that
Melibee wolde comande to be doon on
hem by the causes aforeseyd./ Whiche   *3020
thynges ordeyned, every man retourned
to his hous./

And whan that dame Prudence saugh hir
tyme, she freyned and axed hir lord Melibee/
what vengeance he thoughte to taken of his
adversaries./

To which Melibee answerde and seyde,
"Certes," quod he, "I thynke and purpose me
fully/ to desherite hem of al that evere they
han and for to putte hem in exil for
evere."/   1835

"Certes," quod dame Prudence, "this
were a crueel sentence and muchel agayn resoun./ For ye been riche ynough and han
no nede of oother mennes good,/ and ye
myghte lightly in this wise gete yow a coveitous name,/ which is a vicious thyng, and
oghte been eschued of every good man./ For
after the sawe of the word of the Apos-
tle, 'Coveitise is roote of alle harmes.'/   *3030
And therfore it were bettre for yow to
lese so muchel good of youre owene than for
to taken of hir good in this manere,/ for bettre it is to lesen good with worshipe than it
is to wynne good with vileynye and shame./
And everi man oghte to doon his diligence and
his bisynesse to geten hym a good name./
And yet shal he nat oonly bisie hym in kepynge of his good name,/ but he shal also enforcen hym alwey to do somthyng by

---

1807 **maken feith:** stand surety   **borwes:** guarantors
1815 **punyssement:** punishment

1828 **pledges:** pledges
1832 **freyned:** asked

which he may renovelle his good name./ 1845
For it is writen that 'the olde good loos
or good name of a man is soone goon and
passed, whan it is nat newed ne renovelled.'/
And as touchynge that ye seyn ye wole exile
youre adversaries,/ that thynketh me muchel
agayn resoun and out of mesure,/ considered
the power that they han yeve yow upon hemself./ And it is writen that 'he is worthy
to lesen his privilege that mysuseth the
myght and the power that is yeven
hym.'/ And I sette cas ye myghte en- *3040
joyne hem that peyne by right and by
lawe,/ which I trowe ye mowe nat do;/ I seye
ye mighte nat putten it to execucioun peraventure,/ and thanne were it likly to retourne
to the werre as it was biforn./ And therfore,
if ye wole that men do yow obeisance,
ye moste deemen moore curteisly;/ this 1855
is to seyn, ye moste yeven moore esy sentences and juggementz./ For it is writen that
'he that moost curteisly comandeth, to hym
men moost obeyen.'/ And therfore I prey yow
that in this necessitee and in this nede ye caste
yow to overcome youre herte./ For Senec seith
that 'he that overcometh his herte overcometh
twies.'/ And Tullius seith, 'Ther is no
thyng so comendable in a greet lord/ as *3050
whan he is debonaire and meeke, and
appeseth him lightly.'/ And I prey yow that ye
wole forbere now to do vengeance,/ in swich
a manere that youre goode name may be kept
and conserved,/ and that men mowe have
cause and mateere to preyse yow of pitee and
of mercy,/ and that ye have no cause to
repente yow of thyng that ye doon./ 1865
For Senec seith, 'He overcometh in an
yvel manere that repenteth hym of his victorie.'/ Wherfore I pray yow, lat mercy been in
youre herte,/ to th'effect and entente that
God Almighty have mercy on yow in his laste
juggement./ For Seint Jame seith in his Epistle: 'Juggement withouten mercy shal be doon
to hym that hath no mercy of another wight.' "/

Whanne Melibee hadde herd the grete skiles
and resouns of dame Prudence, and hire
wise informaciouns and techynges,/ his *3060
herte gan enclyne to the wil of his wif,
considerynge hir trewe entente,/ and conformed hym anon and assented fully to werken
after hir conseil,/ and thonked God, of whom
procedeth al vertu and alle goodnesse, that
hym sente a wyf of so greet discrecioun./ And
whan the day cam that his adversaries sholde
appieren in his presence,/ he spak unto
hem ful goodly, and seyde in this wyse:/ 1875
"Al be it so that of youre pride and heigh
presumpcioun and folie, and of youre necligence and unkonnynge,/ ye have mysborn yow
and trespassed unto me,/ yet for as muche as
I see and biholde youre grete humylitee/ and
that ye been sory and repentant of youre
giltes,/ it constreyneth me to doon yow
grace and mercy./ Wherfore I receyve *3070
yow to my grace/ and foryeve yow outrely alle the offenses, injuries, and wronges that
ye have doon agayn me and myne,/ to this
effect and to this ende, that God of his endelees mercy/ wole at the tyme of oure diynge
foryeven us oure giltes that we han trespassed
to hym in this wrecched world./ For doutelees, if we be sory and repentant of the synnes
and giltes which we han trespassed in
the sighte of oure Lord God,/ he is so 1885
free and so merciable/ that he wole foryeven us oure giltes/ and bryngen us to the
blisse that nevere hath ende." Amen.

Heere is ended Chaucers Tale of Melibee and of Dame Prudence.

1845 **renovelle:** renew
1858 **caste yow:** endeavor
1861 **appeseth him:** calms himself

1870 **informaciouns:** counsels
1877 **mysborn yow:** misbehaved yourselves

THE PROLOGUE OF THE MONK'S TALE

The murye wordes of the Hoost to the Monk.

Whan ended was my tale of Melibee,
And of Prudence and hire benignytee,   *3080
Oure Hooste seyde, "As I am feithful man,
And by that precious corpus Madrian,
I hadde levere than a barel ale
That Goodelief, my wyf, hadde herd this tale!
For she nys no thyng of swich pacience   1895
As was this Melibeus wyf Prudence.
By Goddes bones, whan I bete my knaves,
She bryngeth me forth the grete clobbed
          staves,
And crieth, 'Slee the dogges everichoon,
And brek hem, bothe bak and every
          boon!'   *3090
     "And if that any neighebor of myne
Wol nat in chirche to my wyf enclyne,
Or be so hardy to hire to trespace,
Whan she comth hoom she rampeth in my
          face,
And crieth, 'False coward, wrek thy wyf!   1905
By corpus bones, I wol have thy knyf,
And thou shalt have my distaf and go spynne!'
Fro day to nyght right thus she wol bigynne.
'Allas,' she seith, 'that evere I was shape   *3099
To wedden a milksop, or a coward ape,
That wol been overlad with every wight!
Thou darst nat stonden by thy wyves right!'
     "This is my lif, but if that I wol fighte;
And out at dore anon I moot me dighte,
Or elles I am but lost, but if that I   1915
Be lik a wilde leoun, fool-hardy.
I woot wel she wol do me slee som day
Som neighebor, and thanne go my way;
For I am perilous with knyf in honde,
Al be it that I dar nat hire withstonde,
For she is byg in armes, by my feith: *3111

That shal he fynde that hire mysdooth or seith —
But lat us passe awey fro this mateere.
     "My lord, the Monk," quod he, "be myrie of
          cheere,
For ye shul telle a tale trewely.   1925
Loo, Rouchestre stant heer faste by!
Ryde forth, myn owene lord, brek nat oure
          game.
But, by my trouthe, I knowe nat youre name.
Wher shal I calle yow my lord daun John,
Or daun Thomas, or elles daun Albon?   *3120
Of what hous be ye, by youre fader kyn?
I vowe to God, thou hast a ful fair skyn;
It is a gentil pasture ther thow goost.
Thou art nat lyk a penant or a goost:
Upon my feith, thou art som officer,   1935
Som worthy sexteyn, or som celerer,
For by my fader soule, as to my doom,
Thou art a maister whan thou art at hoom;
No povre cloysterer, ne no novys,
But a governour, wily and wys,   *3130
And therwithal of brawnes and of bones
A wel farynge persone for the nones.
I pray to God, yeve hym confusioun
That first thee broghte unto religioun!
Thou woldest han been a tredefowel aright.
Haddestow as greet a leeve as thou hast
          myght   1946
To parfourne al thy lust in engendrure,
Thou haddest bigeten ful many a creature.
Allas, why werestow so wyd a cope?
God yeve me sorwe, but, and I were a pope,
Nat oonly thou, but every myghty man,   *3141

1891 **As I am feithful man:** on my faith as a Christian
1892 **corpus Madrian:** the body of Madrian; see n.
1893 **barel ale:** barrel of ale
1898 **clobbed:** club-shaped
1904 **rampeth:** shakes her fist
1905 **wrek:** avenge
1906 **corpus bones:** God's bones
1907 **distaf:** a small staff used for spinning thread
1911 **overlad:** overborne, browbeaten
1914 **me dighte:** hasten
1917 **do me slee:** cause me to slay
1921 **byg:** strong

1922 **mysdooth or seith:** the prefix *mys-* goes with both words
1926 **Rouchestre:** Rochester, about thirty miles from London; see n.
1927 **brek nat oure game:** do not interrupt our game
1929 **daun John:** sir John
1934 **penant:** penitent
1936 **sexteyn:** the officer in charge of the sacred vessels, vestments, and relics   **celerer:** the officer in charge of kitchen and cellar and of the provision of food and drink
1939 **novys:** novice
1942 **wel farynge:** handsome
1944 **unto religioun:** into a religious order
1945 **tredefowel aright:** excellent copulator of fowls, good breeding stock; cf. EpiNPT VII.3451.
1950 **but:** unless   **and:** if

Though he were shorn ful hye upon his pan,
Sholde have a wyf; for al the world is lorn!
Religioun hath take up al the corn   1954
Of tredyng, and we borel men been shrympes.
Of fieble trees ther comen wrecched ympes.
This maketh that oure heires been so sklendre
And feble that they may nat wel engendre.
This maketh that oure wyves wole assaye
Religious folk, for ye mowe bettre paye
Of Venus paiementz than mowe we;   *3151
God woot, no lussheburghes payen ye!
But be nat wrooth, my lord, though that I
     pleye.
Ful ofte in game a sooth I have herd seye!"

   This worthy Monk took al in pacience,   1965
And seyde, "I wol doon al my diligence,
As fer as sowneth into honestee,
To telle yow a tale, or two, or three.
And if yow list to herkne hyderward,
I wol yow seyn the lyf of Seint Edward;

Or ellis, first, tragedies wol I telle,   *3161
Of whiche I have an hundred in my celle.
Tragedie is to seyn a certeyn storie,
As olde bookes maken us memorie,
Of hym that stood in greet prosperitee,   1975
And is yfallen out of heigh degree
Into myserie, and endeth wrecchedly.
And they ben versified communely
Of six feet, which men clepen *exametron*.
In prose eek been endited many oon,   *3170
And eek in meetre in many a sondry wyse.
Lo, this declaryng oghte ynogh suffise.
     "Now herkneth, if yow liketh for to heere.
But first I yow biseeke in this mateere,
Though I by ordre telle nat thise thynges,   1985
Be it of popes, emperours, or kynges,
After hir ages, as men writen fynde,
But tellen hem som bifore and som bihynde,
As it now comth unto my remembraunce,
Have me excused of myn ignoraunce."   *3180

Explicit

THE MONK'S TALE

Heere bigynneth the Monkes Tale
De Casibus Virorum Illustrium.

I wol biwaille in manere of tragedie
The harm of hem that stoode in heigh degree,
And fillen so that ther nas no remedie
To brynge hem out of hir adversitee.
For certein, whan that Fortune list to flee, 1995
Ther may no man the cours of hire withholde.
Lat no man truste on blynd prosperitee;
Be war by thise ensamples trewe and olde.

Lucifer

At Lucifer, though he an angel were
And nat a man, at hym wol I bigynne.   *3190

For though Fortune may noon angel dere,
From heigh degree yet fel he for his synne
Doun into helle, where he yet is inne.
O Lucifer, brightest of angels alle,   2004
Now artow Sathanas, that mayst nat twynne
Out of miserie, in which that thou art falle.

Adam

Loo Adam, in the feeld of Damyssene
With Goddes owene fynger wroght was he,
And nat bigeten of mannes sperme unclene,
And welte al paradys savynge o tree.   *3200
Hadde nevere worldly man so heigh degree

1952 **pan:** skull
1955 **borel men:** laymen   **shrympes:** shrimps, puny creatures
1956 **wrecched ympes:** weak offshoots
1959 **wol assaye:** want to try out
1962 **lussheburghes:** inferior coins; see n.
1967 **sowneth into honestee:** is conducive to propriety or decency
1970 **Seint Edward:** St. Edward the Confessor

1999 **Lucifer:** Satan

1979 *exametron:* hexameters, the meter of Latin heroic poetry

2001 **dere:** harm
2005 **twynne:** escape
2007 **Damyssene:** of Dammyssene
2010 **welte:** ruled   **o:** one, a single

As Adam, til he for mysgovernaunce
Was dryven out of hys hye prosperitee
To labour, and to helle, and to meschaunce.

Sampson

Loo Sampsoun, which that was annunciat
By th' angel longe er his nativitee,   2016
And was to God Almyghty consecrat,
And stood in noblesse whil he myghte see.
Was nevere swich another as was hee,
To speke of strengthe, and therwith hardynesse;
But to his wyves toolde he his secree,   *3211
Thurgh which he slow hymself for wrecched-
        nesse.

Sampsoun, this noble almyghty champioun,
Withouten wepen save his handes tweye,
He slow and al torente the leoun,   2025
Toward his weddyng walkynge by the weye.
His false wyf koude hym so plese and preye
Til she his conseil knew; and she, untrewe,
Unto his foos his conseil gan biwreye,
And hym forsook, and took another newe.

Thre hundred foxes took Sampson for ire,
And alle hir tayles he togydre bond,   *3222
And sette the foxes tayles alle on fire,
For he on every tayl had knyt a brond;
And they brende alle the cornes in that lond,
And alle hire olyveres, and vynes eke.
A thousand men he slow eek with his hond,
And hadde no wepen but an asses cheke.   2038

Whan they were slayn, so thursted hym that he
Was wel ny lorn, for which he gan to preye
That God wolde on his peyne han some pitee
And sende hym drynke, or elles moste he deye;
And of this asses cheke, that was dreye,   *3233
Out of a wang-tooth sprang anon a welle,
Of which he drank ynogh, shortly to seye;
Thus heelp hym God, as *Judicum* can telle.

By verray force at Gazan on a nyght,   2047
Maugree Philistiens of that citee,
The gates of the toun he hath up plyght,
And on his bak ycaryed hem hath hee   *3240
Hye on an hill whereas men myghte hem see.
O noble, almyghty Sampsoun, lief and deere,
Had thou nat toold to wommen thy secree,
In al this world ne hadde been thy peere!

This Sampson nevere ciser drank ne wyn,   2055
Ne on his heed cam rasour noon ne sheere,
By precept of the messager divyn,
For alle his strengthes in his heeres weere.
And fully twenty wynter, yeer by yeere,
He hadde of Israel the governaunce.   *3250
But soone shal he wepe many a teere,
For wommen shal hym bryngen to meschaunce!

Unto his lemman Dalida he tolde
That in his heeris al his strengthe lay,
And falsly to his foomen she hym solde.   2065
And slepynge in hir barm upon a day,
She made to clippe or shere his heres away,
And made his foomen al his craft espyen;
And whan that they hym foond in this array,
They bounde hym faste and putten out his
        yen.   *3260

But er his heer were clipped or yshave,
Ther was no boond with which men myghte
        him bynde;
But now is he in prison in a cave,   2073
Where-as they made hym at the queerne grynde.
O noble Sampsoun, strongest of mankynde,
O whilom juge, in glorie and in richesse!
Now maystow wepen with thyne eyen blynde,
Sith thou fro wele art falle in wrecchednesse.

The ende of this caytyf was as I shal seye.
His foomen made a feeste upon a day,   *3270
And made hym as hire fool biforn hem pleye;
And this was in a temple of greet array.
But atte laste he made a foul affray,   2083
For he two pilers shook and made hem falle,
And doun fil temple and al, and ther it lay —
And slow hymself, and eek his foomen alle.

2012 **mysgovernaunce:** misconduct
2015 **which that was annunciat:** who (i.e., whose birth) was
foretold
2018 **whil he myghte see:** as long as he preserved his eyesight
(see line 2070)
2025 **torente:** tore to pieces
2026 while he was walking toward his wedding
2034 **brond:** burning piece of wood
2035 **cornes:** grain crops
2036 **olyveres:** olive trees
2038 **cheke:** jawbone
2044 **wang-tooth:** molar
2046 *Judicum:* the Book of Judges

2047 **Gazan:** Gaza
2048 **Philistiens:** Philistines
2055 **ciser:** strong drink
2056 **sheere:** scissors
2063 **Dalida:** Delilah
2066 **barm:** lap
2074 **queerne:** mill
2083 **foul affray:** terrifying assault

This is to seyn, the prynces everichoon,
And eek thre thousand bodyes, were ther slayn
With fallynge of the grete temple of stoon.
Of Sampson now wol I namoore sayn.   *3280
Beth war by this ensample oold and playn
That no men telle hir conseil til hir wyves
Of swich thyng as they wolde han secree fayn,
If that it touche hir lymes or hir lyves.

Hercules

Of Hercules, the sovereyn conquerour,   2095
Syngen his werkes laude and heigh renoun;
For in his tyme of strengthe he was the flour.
He slow and rafte the skyn of the leoun;
He of Centauros leyde the boost adoun;
He Arpies slow, the crueel bryddes felle;
He golden apples rafte of the dragoun;   *3291
He drow out Cerberus, the hound of helle;

He slow the crueel tyrant Busirus
And made his hors to frete hym, flessh and
          boon;
He slow the firy serpent venymus;   2105
Of Acheloys two hornes he brak oon;
And he slow Cacus in a cave of stoon;
He slow the geant Antheus the stronge;
He slow the grisly boor, and that anon;
And bar the hevene on his nekke longe.

Was nevere wight, sith that this world bigan,
That slow so manye monstres as dide he. *3302
Thurghout this wyde world his name ran,
What for his strengthe and for his heigh
          bountee,
And every reawme wente he for to see.   2115
He was so stroong that no man myghte hym
          lette.
At bothe the worldes endes, seith Trophee,
In stide of boundes he a pileer sette.

A lemman hadde this noble champioun,
That highte Dianira, fressh as May;   *3310
And as thise clerkes maken mencioun,

She hath hym sent a sherte, fressh and gay.
Allas, this sherte — allas and weylaway! —
Envenymed was so subtilly withalle
That er that he had wered it half a day   2125
It made his flessh al from his bones falle.

But nathelees somme clerkes hire excusen
By oon that highte Nessus, that it maked.
Be as be may, I wol hire noght accusen; *3319
But on his bak this sherte he wered al naked
Til that his flessh was for the venym blaked.
And whan he saugh noon oother remedye,
In hoote coles he hath hymselven raked,
For with no venym deigned hym to dye.

Thus starf this worthy, myghty Hercules. 2135
Lo, who may truste on Fortune any throwe?
For hym that folweth al this world of prees
Er he be war is ofte yleyd ful lowe.
Ful wys is he that kan hymselven knowe! *3329
Beth war, for whan that Fortune list to glose,
Thanne wayteth she her man to overthrowe
By swich a wey as he wolde leest suppose.

Nabugodonosor

The myghty trone, the precious tresor,
The glorious ceptre, and roial magestee
That hadde the kyng Nabugodonosor   2145
With tonge unnethe may discryved bee.
He twyes wan Jerusalem the citee;
The vessel of the temple he with hym ladde.
At Babiloigne was his sovereyn see,
In which his glorie and his delit he hadde.

The faireste children of the blood roial
Of Israel he leet do gelde anoon,   *3342
And maked ech of hem to been his thral.
Amonges othere Daniel was oon,
That was the wiseste child of everychon, 2155
For he the dremes of the kyng expowned,
Whereas in Chaldeye clerk ne was ther noon
That wiste to what fyn his dremes sowned.

2098 **rafte:** despoiled, took away
2099 **Centauros:** centaurs; for another account of the labors enumerated here see Bo 4.m7.28–62.
2100 **Arpies:** Harpies
2103 **Busirus:** a king of Egypt
2104 **frete:** devour
2106 **Acheloys:** Achelous, a river god, who took the form of a bull in his fight with Hercules
2107 **Cacus:** a monster
2108 **Antheus:** a giant whom Hercules wrestled
2117 **bothe the worldes endes:** the eastern and western ends of the world   **Trophee:** unidentified; see n.
2118 **boundes:** boundary markers   **pileer:** pillar

2129 **Be as be may:** however it may be
2131 **blaked:** blackened
2133 **raked:** covered by raking
2135 **starf:** died
2136 **any throwe:** for any time
2137 **this world of prees:** this dangerous, difficult world
2140 **glose:** beguile, deceive
2145 **Nabugodonosor:** Nebuchadnezzar
2148 **vessel:** plate, vessels
2149 **see:** throne
2152 **leet do gelde:** had castrated
2157 **Chaldeye:** Chaldea, Babylonia
2158 **fyn:** end

This proude kyng leet maken a statue of gold,
Sixty cubites long and sevene in brede,   *3350
To which ymage bothe yong and oold
Comanded he to loute, and have in drede,
Or in a fourneys, ful of flambes rede,
He shal be brent that wolde noght obeye.
But nevere wolde assente to that dede   2165
Daniel ne his yonge felawes tweye.

This kyng of kynges proud was and elaat;
He wende that God, that sit in magestee,
Ne myghte hym nat bireve of his estaat.
But sodeynly he loste his dignytee,   *3360
And lyk a beest hym semed for to bee,
And eet hey as an oxe, and lay theroute
In reyn; with wilde beestes walked hee
Til certein tyme was ycome aboute.

And lik an egles fetheres wax his heres;   2175
His nayles lyk a briddes clawes weere;
Til God relessed hym a certeyn yeres,
And yaf hym wit, and thanne with many a teere
He thanked God, and evere his lyf in feere
Was he to doon amys or moore trespace;
And til that tyme he leyd was on his beere
He knew that God was ful of myght and
     grace.   *3372

Balthasar

His sone, which that highte Balthasar,
That heeld the regne after his fader day,
He by his fader koude noght be war,   2185
For proud he was of herte and of array,
And eek an ydolastre was he ay.
His hye estaat assured hym in pryde;
But Fortune caste hym doun, and ther he lay,
And sodeynly his regne gan divide.   *3380

A feeste he made unto his lordes alle
Upon a tyme and bad hem blithe bee;
And thanne his officeres gan he calle:
"Gooth, bryngeth forth the vesseles," quod he,
"Whiche that my fader in his prosperitee
Out of the temple of Jerusalem birafte;   2196
And to oure hye goddes thanke we
Of honour that oure eldres with us lafte."

Hys wyf, his lordes, and his concubynes
Ay dronken, whil hire appetites laste,   *3390
Out of thise noble vessels sondry wynes.
And on a wal this kyng his eyen caste
And saugh an hand, armlees, that wroot ful
     faste,
For feere of which he quook and siked soore.
This hand that Balthasar so soore agaste
Wroot *Mane, techel, phares,* and namoore.

In all that land magicien was noon   2207
That koude expoune what this lettre mente;
But Daniel expowned it anoon,
And seyde, "Kyng, God to thy fader lente
Glorie and honour, regne, tresour, rente;
And he was proud and nothyng God ne
     dradde,   *3402
And therfore God greet wreche upon hym
     sente,
And hym birafte the regne that he hadde.

"He was out cast of mannes compaignye;   2215
With asses was his habitacioun,
And eet hey as a beest in weet and drye
Til that he knew, by grace and by resoun,
That God of hevene hath domynacioun
Over every regne and every creature;   *3410
And thanne hadde God of hym compassioun,
And hym restored his regne and his figure.

"Eek thou, that art his sone, art proud also,
And knowest alle thise thynges verraily,
And art rebel to God, and art his foo.   2225
Thou drank eek of his vessels boldely;
Thy wyf eek, and thy wenches, synfully
Dronke of the same vessels sondry wynys;
And heryest false goddes cursedly;   *3419
Therefore to thee yshapen ful greet pyne ys.

"This hand was sent from God that on the wal
Wroot *Mane, techel, phares,* truste me;
Thy regne is doon; thou weyest noght at al.
Dyvyded is thy regne, and it shal be
To Medes and to Perses yeven," quod he.   2235
And thilke same nyght this kyng was slawe,
And Darius occupieth his degree,
Thogh he therto hadde neither right ne lawe.

2162 **loute:** bow down **have in drede:** venerate
2166 **tweye:** two (an error for three); see n.
2167 **elaat:** arrogant
2169 **bireve:** deprive
2170 **dignytee:** high office
2177 **a certeyn yeres:** a certain (number of) years
2183 **Balthasar:** Belshazzar
2187 **ydolastre:** idolator
2188 **assured hym:** made him confident

2208 **expoune:** explain
2212 **nothyng God ne dradde:** feared God not at all
2213 **wreche:** vengeance
2229 **heryest:** worship
2233 **weyest noght:** are of no account
2235 **Perses:** Persians
2237 **Darius:** Darius the Mede (Dan. 5.30)

Lordynges, ensample heerby may ye take
How that in lordshipe is no sikernesse,   *3430
For whan Fortune wole a man forsake,
She bereth awey his regne and his richesse,
And eek his freendes, bothe moore and lesse.
For what man that hath freendes thurgh For-
    tune,
Mishap wol maken hem enemys, I gesse;   2245
This proverbe is ful sooth and ful commune.

Cenobia

Cenobia, of Palymerie queene,
As writen Persiens of hir noblesse,
So worthy was in armes and so keene
That no wight passed hire in hardynesse,
Ne in lynage, ne in oother gentillesse.   *3441
Of kynges blood of Perce is she descended.
I seye nat that she hadde moost fairnesse,
But of hir shap she myghte nat been amended.

From hire childhede I fynde that she fledde   2255
Office of wommen, and to wode she wente,
And many a wilde hertes blood she shedde
With arwes brode that she to hem sente.
She was so swift that she anon hem hente;
And whan that she was elder, she wolde kille
Leouns, leopardes, and beres al torente,   *3451
And in hir armes weelde hem at hir wille.

She dorste wilde beestes dennes seke,
And rennen in the montaignes al the nyght,
And slepen under a bussh, and she koude
    eke   2265
Wrastlen, by verray force and verray myght,
With any yong man, were he never so wight.
Ther myghte no thyng in hir armes stonde.
She kepte hir maydenhod from every wight;
To no man deigned hire for to be bonde.   *3460

But atte laste hir freendes han hire maried
To Odenake, a prynce of that contree,
Al were it so that she hem longe taried.
And ye shul understonde how that he
Hadde swiche fantasies as hadde she.   2275
But natheless, whan they were knyt in-feere,
They lyved in joye and in felicitee,
For ech of hem hadde oother lief and deere,

Save o thyng: that she wolde nevere assente,
By no wey, that he sholde by hire lye   *3470
But ones, for it was hir pleyn entente
To have a child, the world to multiplye;
And also soone as that she myghte espye
That she was nat with childe with that dede,
Thanne wolde she suffre hym doon his fan-
    tasye   2285
Eft-soone, and nat but oones, out of drede.

And if she were with childe at thilke cast,
Namoore sholde he pleyen thilke game
Til fully fourty [wikes] weren past;
Thanne wolde she ones suffre hym do the
    same.   *3480
Al were this Odenake wilde or tame,
He gat namoore of hire, for thus she seyde:
It was to wyves lecherie and shame,
In oother caas, if that men with hem pleyde.

Two sones by this Odenake hadde she,   2295
The whiche she kepte in vertu and lettrure.
But now unto oure tale turne we.
I seye, so worshipful a creature,
And wys therwith, and large with mesure,
So penyble in the werre, and curteis eke,   *3490
Ne moore labour myghte in werre endure,
Was noon, though al this world men sholde
    seke.

Hir riche array ne myghte nat be told,
As wel in vessel as in hire clothyng.
She was al clad in perree and in gold,   2305
And eek she lafte noght, for noon huntyng,
To have of sondry tonges ful knowyng,
Whan that she leyser hadde; and for to en-
    tende
To lerne bookes was al hire likyng,   *3499
How she in vertu myghte hir lyf dispende.

And shortly of this storie for to trete,
So doghty was hir housbonde and eek she,
That they conquered manye regnes grete
In the orient, with many a fair citee
Apertenaunt unto the magestee   2315
Of Rome, and with strong hond held hem ful
    faste,

2245 **Mishap:** misfortune
2247 **Cenobia:** Zenobia **Palymerie:** Palmyra, a city in Syria
2252 **Perce:** Persia
2256 **Office:** function, duty
2261 **torente:** tear to pieces
2262 **weelde:** wield, handle
2267 **wight:** active, agile
2272 **Odenake:** Odenathus, ruler of Palmyra

2286 **Eft-soone:** again   **nat but:** only   **out of drede:** without doubt
2287 **cast:** time
2296 **lettrure:** learning
2300 **penyble:** indefatigable
2305 **perree:** precious stones
2306 **lafte:** neglected
2308 **entende:** strive, endeavor
2315 **Apertenaunt:** appertaining, belonging to

Ne nevere myghte hir foomen doon hem flee,
Ay whil that Odenakes dayes laste.

Hir batailles, whoso list hem for to rede,
Agayn Sapor the kyng and othere mo,   *3510
And how that al this proces fil in dede,
Why she conquered and what title had therto,
And after, of hir meschief and hire wo,
How that she was biseged and ytake —
Lat hym unto my maister Petrak go,   2325
That writ ynough of this, I undertake.

Whan Odenake was deed, she myghtily
The regnes heeld, and with hire propre hond
Agayn hir foos she faught so cruelly
That ther nas kyng ne prynce in al that lond
That he nas glad, if he that grace fond,   *3521
That she ne wolde upon his lond werreye.
With hire they maden alliance by bond
To been in pees, and lete hire ride and pleye.

The Emperour of Rome, Claudius   2335
Ne hym bifore, the Romayn Galien,
Ne dorste nevere been so corageus,
Ne noon Ermyn, ne noon Egipcien,
Ne Surrien, ne noon Arabyen,   *3529
Withinne the feeld that dorste with hire fighte,
Lest that she wolde hem with hir handes slen,
Or with hir meignee putten hem to flighte.

In kynges habit wente hir sones two,
As heires of hir fadres regnes alle,
And Hermanno and Thymalao   2345
Hir names were, as Persiens hem calle.
But ay Fortune hath in hire hony galle;
This myghty queene may no while endure.
Fortune out of hir regne made hire falle
To wrecchednesse and to mysaventure.   *3540

Aurelian, whan that the governaunce
Of Rome cam into his handes tweye,
He shoop upon this queene to doon ven-
     geaunce.
And with his legions he took his weye   2354
Toward Cenobie, and shortly for to seye,

He made hire flee, and atte laste hire hente,
And fettred hire, and eek hire children tweye,
And wan the land, and hoom to Rome he
     wente.

Amonges othere thynges that he wan,
Hir chaar, that was with gold wroght and
     perree,   *3550
This grete Romayn, this Aurelian,
Hath with hym lad, for that men sholde it see.
Biforen his triumphe walketh shee,
With gilte cheynes on hire nekke hangynge.
Coroned was she, as after hir degree,   2365
And ful of perree charged hire clothynge.

Allas, Fortune! She that whilom was
Dredeful to kynges and to emperoures,
Now gaureth al the peple on hire, allas!
And she that helmed was in starke
     stoures   *3560
And wan by force townes stronge and toures,
Shal on hir heed now were a vitremyte;
And she that bar the ceptre ful of floures
Shal bere a distaf, hire cost for to quyte.

De Petro Rege Ispannie

O noble, O worthy Petro, glorie of Spayne,
Whom Fortune heeld so hye in magestee,   2376
Wel oghten men thy pitous deeth complayne!
Out of thy land thy brother made thee flee,
And after, at a seege, by subtiltee,
Thou were bitraysed and lad unto his
     tente,   *3570
Where as he with his owene hand slow thee,
Succedynge in thy regne and in thy rente.

The feeld of snow, with th'egle of blak therinne,
Caught with the lymrod coloured as the gleede,
He brew this cursednesse and al this synne.
The wikked nest was werker of this nede.   2386
Noght Charles Olyver, that took ay heede

2320 **Sapor:** Shapur I, king of Persia c. 240–72 A.D.
2325 **Petrak:** Petrarch; see n.
2335–36 **Claudius, Galien:** the emperors Claudius Gothicus
(268–70 A.D.), Gallienus (253–68 A.D.)
2338 **Ermyn:** Armenian
2339 **Surrien:** Syrian
2351 **Aurelian:** the emperor Aurelianus

2360 **chaar:** chariot
2363 **triumphe:** triumphal procession
2369 **gaureth al the peple:** everyone stares
2370 **helmed was:** wore a helmet (i.e., fought)   **starke:** violent
stoures: battles
2372 **vitremyte:** probably a particular kind of woman's
headdress; see n.
2374 **hire cost for to quyte:** to pay for her keep
2375 **Petro:** Pedro of Castile; see n.
2380 **bitraysed:** betrayed
2384 **lymrod:** lime-rod   **gleede:** burning coal; see n.
2385 **He:** Bertrand du Guesclin   **brew:** brewed, contrived
2386 **wikked nest:** a play on the name of Oliver Mauny (see n.)
nede: violence, crisis
2387 **Charles Olyver:** Charlemagne's Oliver, faithful friend of
Roland

Of trouthe and honour, but of Armorike
Genylon-Olyver, corrupt for meede,
Broghte this worthy kyng in swich a brike.

De Petro Rege de Cipro

O worthy Petro, kyng of Cipre, also,   *3581
That Alisandre wan by heigh maistrie,
Ful many an hethen wroghtestow ful wo,
Of which thyne owene liges hadde envie,
And for no thyng but for thy chivalrie   2395
They in thy bed han slayn thee by the morwe.
Thus kan Fortune hir wheel governe and gye,
And out of joye brynge men to sorwe.

De Barnabo de Lumbardia

Off Melan grete Barnabo Viscounte,   *3589
God of delit and scourge of Lumbardye,
Why sholde I nat thyn infortune acounte,
Sith in estaat thow cloumbe were so hye?
Thy brother sone, that was thy double allye,
For he thy nevew was and sone-in-lawe,
Withinne his prisoun made thee to dye —   2405
But why ne how noot I that thou were slawe.

De Hugelino Comite de Pize

Off the Erl Hugelyn of Pyze the langour
Ther may no tonge telle for pitee.
But litel out of Pize stant a tour,
In which tour in prisoun put was he,   *3600
And with hym been his litel children thre;
The eldest scarsly fyf yeer was of age.
Allas, Fortune, it was greet crueltee
Swiche briddes for to putte in swich a cage!

Dampned was he to dyen in that prisoun,   2415
For Roger, which that bisshop was of Pize,
Hadde on hym maad a fals suggestioun,
Thurgh which the peple gan upon hym rise
And putten hym to prisoun in swich wise
As ye han herd, and mete and drynke he
        hadde
                                                *3610

So smal that wel unnethe it may suffise,
And therwithal it was ful povre and badde.

And on a day bifil that in that hour
Whan that his mete wont was to be broght,
The gayler shette the dores of the tour.   2425
He herde it wel, but he spak right noght,
And in his herte anon ther fil a thoght
That they for hunger wolde doon hym dyen.
"Allas!" quod he, "Allas, that I was wroght!"
Therwith the teeris fillen from his yen.   *3620

His yonge sone, that thre yeer was of age,
Unto hym seyde, "Fader, why do ye wepe?
Whanne wol the gayler bryngen oure potage?
Is ther no morsel breed that ye do kepe?
I am so hungry that I may nat slepe.   2435
Now wolde God that I myghte slepen evere!
Thanne sholde nat hunger in my wombe crepe;
Ther is no thyng, but breed, that me were
        levere."

Thus day by day this child bigan to crye,
Til in his fadres barm adoun it lay,   *3630
And seyde, "Farewel, fader, I moot dye!"
And kiste his fader, and dyde the same day.
And whan the woful fader deed it say,
For wo his armes two he gan to byte,   2444
And seyde, "Allas, Fortune, and weylaway!
Thy false wheel my wo al may I wyte."

His children wende that it for hunger was
That he his armes gnow, and nat for wo,
And seyde, "Fader, do nat so, allas!
But rather ete the flessh upon us two.   *3640
Oure flessh thou yaf us, take oure flessh us fro,
And ete ynogh" — right thus they to hym
        seyde,
And after that, withinne a day or two,
They leyde hem in his lappe adoun and deyde.

Hymself, despeired, eek for hunger starf;   2455
Thus ended is this myghty Erl of Pize.
From heigh estaat Fortune awey hym carf.
Of this tragedie it oghte ynough suffise;
Whoso wol here it in a lenger wise,

2388 **Armorike:** Armorica (ancient name of coastal Brittany and Normandy)
2389 **Genylon-Olyver:** i.e., a traitor like Ganelon, who betrayed Roland
2390 **brike:** plight
2391 **Petro:** Pierre de Lusignan; see n. **Cipre:** Cyprus
2392 **Alisandre:** Alexandria
2399 **Melan:** Milan **Barnabo Viscounte:** Bernabò Visconti; see n.
2401 **acounte:** recount (?); see n.
2403 **brother:** brother's **allye:** kinsman
2407 **Hugelyn of Pyze:** Ugolino of Pisa; see n. **langour:** suffering
2416 **Roger:** Ruggieri degli Ubaldini

2421 **unnethe:** scarcely
2425 **gayler:** jailer
2433 **potage:** soup
2443 **deed:** dead **say:** saw
2446 **wyte:** blame
2448 **gnow:** gnawed
2455 **starf:** died; see n.
2457 **carf:** cut

Redeth the grete poete of Ytaille   *3650
That highte Dant, for he kan al devyse
Fro point to point; nat o word wol he faille.

Nero

Although that Nero were as vicius
As any feend that lith ful lowe adoun,
Yet he, as telleth us Swetonius,   2465
This wyde world hadde in subjeccioun,
Bothe est and west, [south], and septemtrioun.
Of rubies, saphires, and of peerles white
Were alle his clothes brouded up and doun,
For he in gemmes greetly gan delite.   *3660

Moore delicaat, moore pompous of array,
Moore proud was nevere emperour than he;
That ilke clooth that he hadde wered o day,
After that tyme he nolde it nevere see.   2474
Nettes of gold threed hadde he greet plentee
To fisshe in Tybre, whan hym liste pleye.
His lustes were al lawe in his decree,
For Fortune as his freend hym wolde obeye.

He Rome brende for his delicasie;
The senatours he slow upon a day   *3670
To heere how that men wolde wepe and crie;
And slow his brother, and by his suster lay.
His mooder made he in pitous array,
For he hire wombe slitte to biholde
Where he conceyved was — so weilaway   2485
That he so litel of his mooder tolde!

No teere out of his eyen for that sighte
Ne cam, but seyde, "A fair womman was she!"
Greet wonder is how that he koude or myghte
Be domesman of hire dede beautee.   *3680
The wyn to bryngen hym comanded he,
And drank anon — noon oother wo he made.
Whan myght is joyned unto crueltee,
Allas, to depe wol the venym wade!

In yowthe a maister hadde this emperour   2495
To teche hym letterure and curteisye,
For of moralitee he was the flour,
As in his tyme, but if bookes lye;

2461 **Dant**: Dante Alighieri
2465 **Swetonius**: Suetonius, author of *The Lives of the Caesars*
2467 **septemtrioun**: north
2469 **brouded**: embroidered
2473 **ilke clooth**: same robe
2479 **delicasie**: pleasure
2486 **of . . . tolde**: esteemed
2490 **domesman**: judge
2494 **wade**: penetrate, go in
2495 **maister**: teacher (Seneca)
2496 **letterure**: literature

And whil this maister hadde of hym mais-
        trye,   *3689
He maked hym so konnyng and so sowple
That longe tyme it was er tirannye
Or any vice dorste on hym uncowple.

This Seneca, of which that I devyse,
By cause Nero hadde of hym swich drede,
For he fro vices wolde hym ay chastise   2505
Discreetly, as by word and nat by dede —
"Sire," wolde he seyn, "an emperour moot nede
Be vertuous and hate tirannye — "
For which he in a bath made hym to blede
On bothe his armes, til he moste dye.   *3700

This Nero hadde eek of acustumaunce
In youthe agayns his maister for to ryse,
Which afterward hym thoughte a greet grev-
        aunce;
Therefore he made hym dyen in this wise.
But natheless this Seneca the wise   2515
Chees in a bath to dye in this manere
Rather than han another tormentise;
And thus hath Nero slayn his maister deere.

Now fil it so that Fortune liste no lenger
The hye pryde of Nero to cherice,   *3710
For though that he were strong, yet was she
        strenger.
She thoughte thus: "By God! I am to nyce
To sette a man that is fulfild of vice
In heigh degree, and emperour hym calle.
By God, out of his sete I wol hym trice;   2525
Whan he leest weneth, sonnest shal he falle."

The peple roos upon hym on a nyght
For his defaute, and whan he it espied,
Out of his dores anon he hath hym dight   *3719
Allone, and ther he wende han been allied
He knokked faste, and ay the moore he cried
The fastere shette they the dores alle.
Tho wiste he wel, he hadde himself mysgyed,
And wente his wey; no lenger dorste he calle.

The peple cried and rombled up and doun,

2500 **sowple**: compliant
2502 **on hym uncowple**: attack (unleash themselves on) him
2507 **nede**: necessarily
2511 **of acustumaunce**: the custom of
2517 **tormentise**: form of torment
2525 **sete**: throne   **trice**: snatch
2528 **defaute**: wickedness
2533 **mysgyed**: misguided, deluded

That with his erys herde he how they seyde,
"Where is this false tiraunt, this Neroun?" 2537
For fere almoost out of his wit he breyde,
And to his goddes pitously he preyde
For socour, but it myghte nat bityde.   *3730
For drede of this hym thoughte that he deyde,
And ran into a gardyn hym to hyde.

And in this gardyn foond he cherles tweye
That seten by a fyr, greet and reed.
And to thise cherles two he gan to preye 2545
To sleen hym and to girden of his heed,
That to his body, whan that he were deed,
Were no despit ydoon for his defame.
Hymself he slow, he koude no bettre reed,
Of which Fortune lough, and hadde a game.

De Oloferno

Was nevere capitayn under a kyng   *3741
That regnes mo putte in subjeccioun,
Ne strenger was in feeld of alle thyng,
As in his tyme, ne gretter of renoun,   2554
Ne moore pompous in heigh presumpcioun
Than Oloferne, which Fortune ay kiste
So likerously, and ladde hym up and doun
Til that his heed was of, er that he wiste.

Nat oonly that this world hadde hym in awe
For lesynge of richesse or libertee,   *3750
But he made every man reneyen his lawe.
"Nabugodonosor was god," seyde hee;
"Noon oother god sholde adoured bee."
Agayns his heeste no wight dorst trespace,
Save in Bethulia, a strong citee,   2565
Where Eliachim a preest was of that place.

But taak kep of the deth of Oloferne:
Amydde his hoost he dronke lay a-nyght,
Withinne his tente, large as is a berne,
And yet, for al his pompe and al his myght,
Judith, a womman, as he lay upright   *3761
Slepynge, his heed of smoot, and from his tente
Ful pryvely she stal from every wight,
And with his heed unto hir toun she wente.

De Rege Antiocho illustri

What nedeth it of kyng Anthiochus   2575
To telle his hye roial magestee,
His hye pride, his werkes venymus?
For swich another was ther noon as he.
Rede which that he was in Machabee,
And rede the proude wordes that he seyde,
And why he fil fro heigh prosperitee,   *3771
And in an hill how wrecchedly he deyde.

Fortune hym hadde enhaunced so in pride
That verraily he wende he myghte attayne
Unto the sterres upon every syde,   2585
And in balance weyen ech montayne,
And alle the floodes of the see restrayne.
And Goddes peple hadde he moost in hate;
Hem wolde he sleen in torment and in payne,
Wenynge that God ne myghte his pride
          abate.   *3780

And for that Nichanore and Thymothee
Of Jewes weren venquysshed myghtily,
Unto the Jewes swich an hate hadde he
That he bad greithen his chaar ful hastily,
And swoor, and seyde ful despitously   2595
Unto Jerusalem he wolde eftsoone
To wreken his ire on it ful cruelly;
But of his purpos he was let ful soone.

God for his manace hym so soore smoot
With invisible wounde, ay incurable,   *3790
That in his guttes carf it so and boot
That his peynes weren importable.
And certeinly the wreche was resonable,
For many a mannes guttes dide he peyne. 2604
But from his purpos cursed and dampnable,
For al his smert, he wolde hym nat restreyne,

But bad anon apparaillen his hoost;
And sodeynly, er he was of it war,
God daunted al his pride and al his boost.

2579 **Machabee:** Book of Maccabees (apocryphal in the
Authorized Version)
2586 **weyen:** weigh
2590 **abate:** reduce
2591 **Nichanore and Thymothee:** Nicanor and Timotheus,
generals defeated by Judas Maccabeus
2594 **greithen:** prepare
2598 **let:** prevented
2601 **boot:** bit
2602 **importable:** intolerable
2603 **wreche:** vengeance
2607 **apparaillen:** prepare
2609 **daunted:** conquered

2538 **breyde:** started, went
2546 **girden of:** cut off
2556 **Oloferne:** Holofernes
2557 **likerously:** wantonly
2560 **For lesynge:** for fear of losing
2561 **reneyen:** renounce
2566 **Eliachim:** Joachim in the Authorized Version

For he so soore fil out of his char   *3800
That it his limes and his skyn totar,
So that he neyther myghte go ne ryde,
But in a chayer men aboute hym bar,
Al forbrused, bothe bak and syde.

The wreche of God hym smoot so cruelly   2615
That thurgh his body wikked wormes crepte,
And therwithal he stank so horribly
That noon of al his meynee that hym kepte,
Wheither so he wook or ellis slepte,
Ne myghte noght the stynk of hym endure.
In this meschief he wayled and eek wepte,
And knew God lord of every creature.   *3812

To al his hoost and to hymself also
Ful wlatsom was the stynk of his careyne;
No man ne myghte hym bere to ne fro.   2625
And in this stynk and this horrible peyne,
He starf ful wrecchedly in a monteyne.
Thus hath this robbour and this homycide,
That many a man made to wepe and pleyne,
Swich gerdoun as bilongeth unto pryde.   *3820

De Alexandro

The storie of Alisaundre is so commune
That every wight that hath discrecioun
Hath herd somwhat or al of his fortune.
This wyde world, as in conclusioun,   2634
He wan by strengthe, or for his hye renoun
They weren glad for pees unto hym sende.
The pride of man and beest he leyde adoun,
Wherso he cam, unto the worldes ende.

Comparisoun myghte nevere yet been maked
Bitwixe hym and another conquerour;   *3830
For al this world for drede of hym hath quaked.
He was of knyghthod and of fredom flour;
Fortune hym made the heir of hire honour.
Save wyn and wommen, no thing myghte
      aswage
His hye entente in armes and labour,   2645
So was he ful of leonyn corage.

What pris were it to hym, though I yow tolde
Of Darius, and an hundred thousand mo
Of kynges, princes, dukes, erles bolde
Whiche he conquered, and broghte hem into
      wo?   *3840
I seye, as fer as man may ryde or go,
The world was his — what sholde I moore de-
      vyse?
For though I write or tolde yow everemo
Of his knyghthod, it myghte nat suffise.

Twelf yeer he regned, as seith Machabee.   2655
Philippes sone of Macidoyne he was,
That first was kyng in Grece the contree.
O worthy, gentil Alisandre, allas,
That evere sholde fallen swich a cas!
Empoysoned of thyn owene folk thou weere;
Thy sys Fortune hath turned into aas,   *3851
And for thee ne weep she never a teere.

Who shal me yeven teeris to compleyne
The deeth of gentillesse and of franchise,
That al the world weelded in his demeyne,
And yet hym thoughte it myghte nat suffise?
So ful was his corage of heigh emprise.   2667
Allas, who shal me helpe to endite
False Fortune, and poyson to despise,
The whiche two of al this wo I wyte?   *3860

De Julio Cesare

By wisedom, manhede, and by greet labour,
From humble bed to roial magestee
Up roos he Julius, the conquerour,
That wan al th'occident by land and see,
By strengthe of hand, or elles by tretee,
And unto Rome made hem tributarie;   2676
And sitthe of Rome the emperour was he
Til that Fortune weex his adversarie.

O myghty Cesar, that in Thessalie
Agayn Pompeus, fader thyn in lawe,   *3870
That of the orient hadde al the chivalrie
As fer as that the day bigynneth dawe,
Thou thurgh thy knyghthod hast hem take and
      slawe,

2611 **totar:** tore apart
2614 **forbrused:** badly bruised
2615 **wreche:** vengeance
2622 **knew:** acknowledged
2624 **wlatsom:** loathsome   **careyne:** body
2631 **Alisaundre:** Alexander the Great   **commune:** widespread
2636 **for pees unto hym sende:** to send envoys to him to sue for peace
2641 **quaked:** trembled

2647 **pris:** praise
2648 **Darius:** king of the Medes
2653 **write:** should write (pret. subjunctive)
2656 **Macidoyne:** Macedonia
2661 Fortune has turned your six (the highest throw of a die) into an ace (the lowest)
2665 **demeyne:** control
2667 **emprise:** knightly courage
2673 **he Julius:** this Julius (Caesar)
2677 **sitthe:** afterwards
2680 **Pompeus:** Pompey the Great

Save fewe folk that with Pompeus fledde,
Thurgh which thou puttest al th'orient in awe.
Thanke Fortune, that so wel thee spedde! 2686

But now a litel while I wol biwaille
This Pompeus, this noble governour
Of Rome, which that fleigh at this bataille.
I seye, oon of his men, a fals traitour, *3880
His heed of smoot, to wynnen hym favour
Of Julius, and hym the heed he broghte.
Allas, Pompeye, of th'orient conquerour,
That Fortune unto swich a fyn thee broghte!

To Rome agayn repaireth Julius 2695
With his triumphe, lauriat ful hye;
But on a tyme Brutus Cassius,
That evere hadde of his hye estaat envye,
Ful prively hath maad conspiracye
Agayns this Julius in subtil wise, *3890
And caste the place in which he sholde dye
With boydekyns, as I shal yow devyse.

This Julius to the Capitolie wente
Upon a day, as he was wont to goon,
And in the Capitolie anon hym hente 2705
This false Brutus and his othere foon,
And stiked hym with boydekyns anoon
With many a wounde, and thus they lete hym
       lye;
But nevere gronte he at no strook but oon,
Or elles at two, but if his storie lye. *3900

So manly was this Julius of herte,
And so wel lovede estaatly honestee,
That though his deedly woundes soore smerte,
His mantel over his hypes caste he,
For no man sholde seen his privetee; 2715
And as he lay of diyng in a traunce,
And wiste verraily that deed was hee,
Of honestee yet hadde he remembraunce.

Lucan, to thee this storie I recomende,
And to Swetoun, and to Valerius also, *3910

That of this storie writen word and ende,
How that to thise grete conqueroures two
Fortune was first freend, and sitthe foo.
No man ne truste upon hire favour longe,
But have hire in awayt for everemoo; 2725
Witnesse on alle thise conqueroures stronge.

Cresus

This riche Cresus, whilom kyng of Lyde,
Of which Cresus Cirus soore hym dradde,
Yet was he caught amyddes al his pryde, *3919
And to be brent men to the fyr hym ladde.
But swich a reyn doun fro the welkne shadde
That slow the fyr, and made hym to escape;
But to be war no grace yet he hadde,
Til Fortune on the galwes made hym gape.

Whanne he escaped was, he kan nat stente
For to bigynne a newe werre agayn. 2736
He wende wel, for that Fortune hym sente
Swich hap that he escaped thurgh the rayn,
That of his foos he myghte nat be slayn; *3929
And eek a sweven upon a nyght he mette,
Of which he was so proud and eek so fayn
That in vengeance he al his herte sette.

Upon a tree he was, as that hym thoughte,
Ther Juppiter hym wessh, bothe bak and
       syde, 2744
And Phebus eek a fair towaille hym broghte
To dryen hym with; and therfore wax his pryde,
And to his doghter, that stood hym bisyde,
Which that he knew in heigh sentence ha-
       bounde,
He bad hire telle hym what it signyfyde,
And she his dreem bigan right thus ex-
       pounde: *3940

"The tree," quod she, "the galwes is to meene,
And Juppiter bitokneth snow and reyn,
And Phebus, with his towaille so clene,
Tho been the sonne stremes for to seyn.

2689 **fleigh:** fled
2697 **Brutus Cassius:** Brutus and Cassius are here considered one person; see n.
2702 **boydekyns:** daggers
2703 **Capitolie:** capitol
2706 **foon:** enemies
2709 **gronte:** groaned
2712 **estaatly honestee:** dignified decorum
2716 **of diyng:** a-dying
2719 **Lucan:** author of the *Pharsalia,* which narrates the wars between Caesar and Pompey
2720 **Swetoun:** Suetonius **Valerius:** Valerius Maximus, whose *Facta et dicta memorabilia* contains stories about the Caesars

2721 **word and ende:** beginning and end
2725 **in awayt:** under observation (i.e., keep an eye on her)
2727 **Cresus:** Croesus, last king of Lydia
2728 **Cirus:** Cyrus the Great
2731 **welkne:** sky
2734 **galwes:** gallows
2740 **sweven:** dream **mette:** dreamed
2745 **towaille:** towel
2748 **in heigh sentence habounde:** to abound in good judgment, wisdom
2751 **is to meene:** is to be interpreted, signifies

Thou shalt anhanged be, fader, certeyn;   2755
Reyn shal thee wasshe, and sonne shal thee
    drye.''
Thus warned hym ful plat and ek ful pleyn
His doghter, which that called was Phanye.

Anhanged was Cresus, the proude kyng;
His roial trone myghte hym nat availe.

Tragediës noon oother maner thyng   *3951
Ne kan in syngyng crie ne biwaille
But that Fortune alwey wole assaille
With unwar strook the regnes that been proude;
For whan men trusteth hire, thanne wol she
    faille,   2765
And covere hire brighte face with a clowde.

Explicit Tragedia.

Heere stynteth the Knyght the Monk of his tale.

THE PROLOGUE OF THE NUN'S PRIEST'S TALE

The prologe of the Nonnes Preestes Tale.

''Hoo!'' quod the Knyght, ''good sire, na-
    moore of this!
That ye han seyd is right ynough, ywis,
And muchel moore; for litel hevynesse
Is right ynough to muche folk, I gesse.   *3960
I seye for me, it is a greet disese,
Whereas men han been in greet welthe and ese,
To heeren of hire sodeyn fal, allas!
And the contrarie is joye and greet solas,
As whan a man hath been in povre estaat,   2775
And clymbeth up and wexeth fortunat,
And there abideth in prosperitee.
Swich thyng is gladsom, as it thynketh me,
And of swich thyng were goodly for to telle.''
    ''Ye,'' quod oure Hooste, ''by Seint Poules
        belle!   *3970
Ye seye right sooth; this Monk he clappeth
    lowde.
He spak how Fortune covered with a clowde
I noot nevere what; and als of a tragedie
Right now ye herde, and pardee, no remedie
It is for to biwaille ne compleyne   2785
That that is doon, and als it is a peyne,
As ye han seyd, to heere of hevynesse.

''Sire Monk, namoore of this, so God yow
    blesse!
Youre tale anoyeth al this compaignye.
Swich talkyng is nat worth a boterflye,   *3980
For therinne is ther no desport ne game.
Wherfore, sire Monk, daun Piers by youre
    name,
I pray yow hertely telle us somwhat elles;
For sikerly, nere clynkyng of youre belles
That on youre bridel hange on every syde,
By hevene kyng that for us alle dyde,   2796
I sholde er this han fallen doun for sleep,
Althogh the slough had never been so deep;
Thanne hadde your tale al be toold in veyn.
For certeinly, as that thise clerkes seyn,
Whereas a man may have noon audi-
    ence,   *3991
Noght helpeth it to tellen his sentence.
    ''And wel I woot the substance is in me,
If any thyng shal wel reported be.   2804
Sir, sey somwhat of huntyng, I yow preye.''
    ''Nay,'' quod this Monk, ''I have no lust to
        pleye.
Now lat another telle, as I have toold.''

2778 **gladsom:** pleasing
2780 **Seint Poules belle:** the bell of St. Paul's Cathedral, London
2781 **clappeth lowde:** talks noisily
2783 **noot** = *ne woot,* do not know

2764 **unwar strook:** unexpected stroke

2794 **nere** = *ne were,* were it not for
2798 **slough:** mud, mire
2803 **the substance is in me:** the meaning is in (i.e., reaches) me

Thanne spak oure Hoost with rude speche
and boold,
And seyde unto the Nonnes Preest anon,
"Com neer, thou preest, com hyder, thou sir
John!   *4000
Telle us swich thyng as may oure hertes glade.
Be blithe, though thou ryde upon a jade.
What thogh thyn hors be bothe foul and lene?

If he wol serve thee, rekke nat a bene.
Looke that thyn herte be murie everemo."   2815
    "Yis, sir," quod he, "yis, Hoost, so moot I go,
But I be myrie, ywis I wol be blamed."
And right anon his tale he hath attamed,
And thus he seyde unto us everichon,
This sweete preest, this goodly man sir
John.   *4010

Explicit.

THE NUN'S PRIEST'S TALE

*Heere bigynneth the Nonnes Preestes Tale of the Cok and Hen,
Chauntecleer and Pertelote.*

A povre wydwe, somdeel stape in age,
Was whilom dwellyng in a narwe cotage,
Biside a grove, stondynge in a dale.
This wydwe, of which I telle yow my tale,
Syn thilke day that she was last a wyf   2825
In pacience ladde a ful symple lyf,
For litel was hir catel and hir rente.
By housbondrie of swich as God hire sente
She foond hirself and eek hir doghtren two.
Thre large sowes hadde she, and namo,   *4020
Three keen, and eek a sheep that highte Malle.
Ful sooty was hire bour and eek hir halle,
In which she eet ful many a sklendre meel.
Of poynaunt sauce hir neded never a deel.
No deyntee morsel passed thurgh hir throte;
Hir diete was accordant to hir cote.   2836
Repleccioun ne made hire nevere sik;
Attempree diete was al hir phisik,
And exercise, and hertes suffisaunce.
The goute lette hire nothyng for to daunce,

N'apoplexie shente nat hir heed.   *4031
No wyn ne drank she, neither whit ne reed;
Hir bord was served moost with whit and
blak —
Milk and broun breed, in which she foond no
lak,
Seynd bacoun, and somtyme an ey or tweye,
For she was, as it were, a maner deye.   2846
    A yeerd she hadde, enclosed al aboute
With stikkes, and a drye dych withoute,
In which she hadde a cok, hight Chaunte-
cleer.   *4039
In al the land, of crowyng nas his peer.
His voys was murier than the murie orgon
On messe-dayes that in the chirche gon.
Wel sikerer was his crowyng in his logge
Than is a clokke or an abbey orlogge.
By nature he knew ech ascencioun   2855
Of the equynoxial in thilke toun;
For whan degrees fiftene weren ascended,

Thanne crew he that it myghte nat been
     amended.
His coomb was redder than the fyn coral,
And batailled as it were a castel wal;   *4050
His byle was blak, and as the jeet it shoon;
Lyk asure were his legges and his toon;
His nayles whitter than the lylye flour,
And lyk the burned gold was his colour.
This gentil cok hadde in his governaunce 2865
Sevene hennes for to doon al his plesaunce,
Whiche were his sustres and his paramours,
And wonder lyk to hym, as of colours;
Of whiche the faireste hewed on hir throte
Was cleped faire damoysele Pertelote.   *4060
Curteys she was, discreet, and debonaire,
And compaignable, and bar hyrself so faire
Syn thilke day that she was seven nyght oold
That trewely she hath the herte in hoold
Of Chauntecleer, loken in every lith; 2875
He loved hire so that wel was hym therwith.
But swich a joye was it to here hem synge,
Whan that the brighte sonne gan to sprynge,
In sweete accord, "My lief is faren in londe!" —
For thilke tyme, as I have understonde,   *4070
Beestes and briddes koude speke and synge.

    And so bifel that in a dawenynge,
As Chauntecleer among his wyves alle
Sat on his perche, that was in the halle,
And next hym sat this faire Pertelote, 2885
This Chauntecleer gan gronen in his throte,
As man that in his dreem is drecched soore.
And whan that Pertelote thus herde hym roore,
She was agast and seyde, "Herte deere,
What eyleth yow, to grone in this manere?
Ye been a verray sleper; fy, for shame!" *4081

    And he answerde, and seyde thus: "Madame,
I pray yow that ye take it nat agrief.
By God, me mette I was in swich meschief
Right now that yet myn herte is soore
     afright.

Now God," quod he, "my swevene recche
     aright, 2896
And kepe my body out of foul prisoun!
Me mette how that I romed up and doun
Withinne our yeerd, wheer as I saugh a beest
Was lyk an hound, and wolde han maad
     areest   *4090
Upon my body, and wolde han had me deed.
His colour was bitwixe yelow and reed,
And tipped was his tayl and bothe his eeris
With blak, unlyk the remenant of his heeris;
His snowte smal, with glowynge eyen tweye.
Yet of his look for feere almoost I deye; 2906
This caused me my gronyng, doutelees."

    "Avoy!" quod she, "fy on yow, hertelees!
Allas," quod she, "for, by that God above,
Now han ye lost myn herte and al my love!
I kan nat love a coward, by my feith!   *4101
For certes, what so any womman seith,
We alle desiren, if it myghte bee,
To han housbondes hardy, wise, and free,
And secree — and no nygard, ne no fool, 2915
Ne hym that is agast of every tool,
Ne noon avauntour, by that God above!
How dorste ye seyn, for shame, unto youre love
That any thyng myghte make yow aferd? *4109
Have ye no mannes herte, and han a berd?
Allas! And konne ye been agast of swevenys?
Nothyng, God woot, but vanitee in sweven is.
Swevenes engendren of replecciouns,
And ofte of fume and of complecciouns, 2924
Whan humours been to habundant in a wight.
Certes this dreem, which ye han met to-nyght,
Cometh of the greete superfluytee
Of youre rede colera, pardee,
Which causeth folk to dreden in hir dremes
Of arwes, and of fyr with rede lemes,   *4120
Of rede beestes, that they wol hem byte,
Of contek, and of whelpes, grete and lyte;

2860 **batailled:** notched with crenelations
2861 **byle:** beak **jeet:** jet, a gemlike coal
2862 **asure:** azure **toon:** toes
2867 **paramours:** concubines
2871 **debonaire:** gracious
2872 **compaignable:** sociable
2874 **hoold:** possession, keeping
2875 **loken in every lith:** locked in every limb (i.e., completely)
2879 **My lief is faren in londe:** "My love has departed to the country," a popular song; see n.
2887 **drecched:** troubled
2888 **roore:** roar
2893 **agrief:** amiss

2896 **swevene:** dream **recche aright:** interpret correctly or favorably (in an auspicious manner)
2900–01 **maad areest Upon:** siezed
2908 **Avoy!:** shame! **hertelees:** coward
2915 **secree:** discreet **nygard:** miser
2916 **tool:** weapon
2917 **avauntour:** boaster
2919 **aferd:** afraid
2920 **berd:** beard; see n.
2923 **replecciouns:** overeating
2924 **fume:** vapor rising from the stomach **complecciouns:** balance of the bodily fluids (*humours*), blood, phlegm, red or yellow bile, and black bile, which produce the sanguinary, phlegmatic, choleric, and melancholy complexions, respectively
2928 **rede colera:** red choleric humor
2930 **lemes:** flames
2932 **contek:** strife **whelpes:** dogs

Right as the humour of malencolie
Causeth ful many a man in sleep to crie
For feere of blake beres, or boles blake,   2935
Or elles blake develes wole hem take.
Of othere humours koude I telle also
That werken many a man sleep ful wo;
But I wol passe as lightly as I kan.   *4129
    "Lo Catoun, which that was so wys a man,
Seyde he nat thus, 'Ne do no fors of dremes'?
    "Now sire," quod she, "whan we flee fro the
        bemes,
For Goddes love, as taak som laxatyf.
Up peril of my soule and of my lyf,
I conseille yow the beste — I wol nat lye —   2945
That bothe of colere and of malencolye
Ye purge yow; and for ye shal nat tarie,
Though in this toun is noon apothecarie,
I shal myself to herbes techen yow
That shul been for youre hele and for youre
        prow;   *4140
And in oure yeerd tho herbes shal I fynde
The whiche han of hire propretee by kynde
To purge yow bynethe and eek above.
Foryet nat this, for Goddes owene love!
Ye been ful coleryk of compleccioun;   2955
Ware the sonne in his ascencioun
Ne fynde yow nat repleet of humours hoote.
And if it do, I dar wel leye a grote,
That ye shul have a fevere terciane,
Or an agu that may be youre bane.   *4150
A day or two ye shul have digestyves
Of wormes, er ye take youre laxatyves
Of lawriol, centaure, and fumetere,
Or elles of ellebor, that groweth there,
Of katapuce, or of gaitrys beryis,   2965
Of herbe yve, growyng in oure yeerd, ther
        mery is;

Pekke hem up right as they growe and ete
        hem yn.
Be myrie, housbonde, for youre fader kyn!
Dredeth no dreem; I kan sey yow namoore."
    "Madame," quod he, "graunt mercy of youre
        loore.   *4160
But nathelees, as touchyng daun Catoun,
That hath of wysdom swich a greet renoun,
Though that he bad no dremes for to drede,
By God, men may in olde bookes rede
Of many a man moore of auctorite   2975
Than evere Caton was, so moot I thee,
That al the revers seyn of this sentence,
And han wel founden by experience
That dremes been significaciouns
As wel of joye as of tribulaciouns   *4170
That folk enduren in this lif present.
Ther nedeth make of this noon argument;
The verray preeve sheweth it in dede.
    "Oon of the gretteste auctour that men rede
Seith thus: that whilom two felawes wente   2985
On pilgrimage, in a ful good entente,
And happed so, they coomen in a toun
Wher as ther was swich congregacioun   *4179
Of peple, and eek so streit of herbergage,
That they ne founde as muche as o cotage
In which they bothe myghte ylogged bee.
Wherfore they mosten of necessitee,
As for that nyght, departen compaignye;
And ech of hem gooth to his hostelrye,
And took his loggyng as it wolde falle.   2995
That oon of hem was logged in a stalle,
Fer in a yeerd, with oxen of the plough;
That oother man was logged wel ynough,
As was his aventure or his fortune,
That us governeth alle as in commune.   *4190
    "And so bifel that, longe er it were day,
This man mette in his bed, ther as he lay,
How that his felawe gan upon hym calle,
And seyde, 'Allas, for in an oxes stalle
This nyght I shal be mordred ther I lye!   3005
Now help me, deere brother, or I dye.
In alle haste com to me!' he sayde.
This man out of his sleep for feere abrayde;
But whan that he was wakened of his sleep,

2933 **humour of malencolie:** melancholy humor
2941 **Ne do no fors of dremes:** Attach no importance to
dreams.
2950 **hele:** good health   **prow:** profit, benefit
2955 **coleryk:** dominated by the choleric humor
2956 **in his ascencioun:** when it is high in the sky
2957 **repleet of:** filled with
2958 **leye a grote:** bet a groat (a silver coin worth four pence)
2959 **fevere terciane:** a fever that recurs every third day; see
Expl. Notes to lines 2942-67.
2960 **agu:** acute fever   **bane:** killer
2961 **digestyves:** medicines to aid the digestion
2963 **lawriol:** spurge laurel; the herbs named in these lines are
nearly all hot, dry, and foul tasting; see n.   **centaure:** centaury
fumetere: fumaria, fumitory
2964 **ellebor:** hellebore
2965 **katapuce:** caper-spurge, euphorbia   **gaitrys beryis:** rhamus
2966 **herbe yve:** ground ivy   **ther mery is:** where it is pleasant
(i.e., in the garden)

2976 **so moot I thee:** as I may prosper (I swear)
2983 **preeve:** proof
2984 **Oon of the gretteste auctour:** one of the greatest authors;
see n.
2989 **streit of:** scanty, short of   **herbergage:** lodging
2991 **ylogged:** lodged
3008 **abrayde:** awakened suddenly

He turned hym and took of this no keep.
Hym thoughte his dreem nas but a vanitee.
Thus twies in his slepyng dremed hee;   *4202
And atte thridde tyme yet his felawe
Cam, as hym thoughte, and seide, 'I am now
          slawe.
Bihoold my bloody woundes depe and wyde!
Arys up erly in the morwe tyde,   3016
And at the west gate of the toun,' quod he,
'A carte ful of dong ther shaltow se,
In which my body is hid ful prively;
Do thilke carte arresten boldely.   *4210
My gold caused my mordre, sooth to sayn,'
And tolde hym every point how he was slayn,
With a ful pitous face, pale of hewe.
And truste wel, his dreem he foond ful trewe,
For on the morwe, as soone as it was day,   3025
To his felawes in he took the way;
And whan that he cam to this oxes stalle,
After his felawe he bigan to calle.
    "The hostiler answerede hym anon,
And seyde, 'Sire, your felawe is agon.   *4220
As soone as day he wente out of the toun.'
    "This man gan fallen in suspecioun,
Remembrynge on his dremes that he mette,
And forth he gooth — no lenger wolde he
          lette —
Unto the west gate of the toun, and fond   3035
A dong-carte, wente as it were to donge lond,
That was arrayed in that same wise
As ye han herd the dede man devyse.
And with an hardy herte he gan to crye
Vengeance and justice of this felonye: *4230
'My felawe mordred is this same nyght,
And in this carte he lith gapyng upright.
I crye out on the ministres,' quod he,
'That sholden kepe and reulen this citee.   3044
Harrow! Allas! Heere lith my felawe slayn!'
What sholde I moore unto this tale sayn?
The peple out sterte and caste the cart to
          grounde,
And in the myddel of the dong they founde
The dede man, that mordred was al newe.
    "O blisful God, that art so just and
          trewe,   *4240
Lo, how that thou biwreyest mordre alway!

Mordre wol out; that se we day by day.
Mordre is so wlatsom and abhomynable
To God, that is so just and resonable,
That he ne wol nat suffre it heled be,   3055
Though it abyde a yeer, or two, or thre.
Mordre wol out, this my conclusioun.
And right anon, ministres of that toun
Han hent the carter and so soore hym pyned,
And eek the hostiler so soore engyned,   *4250
That they biknewe hire wikkednesse anon,
And were anhanged by the nekke-bon.
    "Heere may men seen that dremes been to
          drede.
And certes in the same book I rede,
Right in the nexte chapitre after this —   3065
I gabbe nat, so have I joye or blis —
Two men that wolde han passed over see,
For certeyn cause, into a fer contree,
If that the wynd ne hadde been contrarie,
That made hem in a citee for to tarie   *4260
That stood ful myrie upon an haven-syde;
But on a day, agayn the even-tyde,
The wynd gan chaunge, and blew right as hem
          leste.
Jolif and glad they wente unto hir reste,
And casten hem ful erly for to saille.   3075
But herkneth! To that o man fil a greet mervaille:
That oon of hem, in slepyng as he lay,
Hym mette a wonder dreem agayn the day.
Hym thoughte a man stood by his beddes syde,
And hym comanded that he sholde abyde,
And seyde hym thus: 'If thou tomorwe wende,
Thow shalt be dreynt; my tale is at an ende.'
He wook, and tolde his felawe what he mette,
And preyde hym his viage for to lette;
As for that day, he preyde hym to byde.   3085
His felawe, that lay by his beddes syde,
Gan for to laughe, and scorned him ful faste.
'No dreem,' quod he, 'may so myn herte agaste
That I wol lette for to do my thynges.
I sette nat a straw by thy dremynges,   *4280
For swevenes been but vanytees and japes.
Men dreme alday of owles and of apes,
And of many a maze therwithal;

3020 **Do . . . arresten:** have (it) seized
3029 **hostiler:** innkeeper
3034 **lette:** delay
3036 **donge:** spread dung, fertilize
3042 **upright:** face up
3043 **crye out on:** complain to   **ministres:** magistrates
3049 **al newe:** very recently, just now

3053 **wlatsom:** disgusting, nauseating
3055 **heled:** concealed
3057 **this** = *this is*
3059 **pyned:** tortured
3060 **engyned:** tortured
3061 **biknewe:** acknowledged, confessed
3066 **gabbe:** lie
3072 **agayn:** shortly before
3078 **agayn the day:** shortly before dawn
3084 **viage:** journey   **lette:** give up
3093 **maze:** source of amazement, bewilderment

Men dreme of thyng that nevere was ne shal.
But sith I see that thou wolt heere abyde, 3095
And thus forslewthen wilfully thy tyde,
God woot, it reweth me; and have good day!'
And thus he took his leve, and wente his way.
But er that he hadde half his cours yseyled,
Noot I nat why, ne what myschaunce it eyled, *4290
But casuelly the shippes botme rente,
And ship and man under the water wente
In sighte of othere shippes it bisyde,
That with hem seyled at the same tyde.
And therfore, faire Pertelote so deere, 3105
By swiche ensamples olde maistow leere
That no man sholde been to recchelees
Of dremes; for I seye thee, doutelees,
That many a dreem ful soore is for to drede.

"Lo, in the lyf of Seint Kenelm I rede,
That was Kenulphus sone, the noble kyng
Of Mercenrike, how Kenelm mette a thyng.
A lite er he was mordred, on a day, *4303
His mordre in his avysioun he say.
His norice hym expowned every deel 3115
His sweven, and bad hym for to kepe hym weel
For traisoun; but he nas but seven yeer oold,
And therfore litel tale hath he toold
Of any dreem, so hooly was his herte.
By God! I hadde levere than my sherte *4310
That ye hadde rad his legende, as have I.

"Dame Pertelote, I sey yow trewely,
Macrobeus, that writ the avisioun
In Affrike of the worthy Cipioun, 3124
Affermeth dremes, and seith that they been
Warnynge of thynges that men after seen.
And forthermoore, I pray yow, looketh wel
In the olde testament, of Daniel,
If he heeld dremes any vanitee.
Reed eek of Joseph, and ther shul ye see *4320
Wher dremes be somtyme — I sey nat alle —
Warnynge of thynges that shul after falle.
Looke of Egipte the kyng, daun Pharao,

His bakere and his butiller also,
Wher they ne felte noon effect in dremes. 3135
Whoso wol seken actes of sondry remes
May rede of dremes many a wonder thyng.
Lo Cresus, which that was of Lyde kyng,
Mette he nat that he sat upon a tree,
Which signified he sholde anhanged bee?
Lo heere Andromacha, Ectores wyf, *4331
That day that Ector sholde lese his lyf,
She dremed on the same nyght biforn
How that the lyf of Ector sholde be lorn,
If thilke day he wente into bataille. 3145
She warned hym, but it myghte nat availle;
He wente for to fighte natheles,
But he was slayn anon of Achilles.
But thilke tale is al to longe to telle,
And eek it is ny day; I may nat dwelle. *4340
Shortly I seye, as for conclusioun,
That I shal han of this avisioun
Adversitee; and I seye forthermoor
That I ne telle of laxatyves no stoor,
For they been venymes, I woot it weel; 3155
I hem diffye, I love hem never a deel!

"Now let us speke of myrthe, and stynte al this.
Madame Pertelote, so have I blis,
Of o thyng God hath sent me large grace;
For whan I se the beautee of youre face,
Ye been so scarlet reed aboute youre yen,
It maketh al my drede for to dyen; *4352
For al so siker as *In principio,*
Mulier est hominis confusio —
Madame, the sentence of this Latyn is, 3165
'Womman is mannes joye and al his blis.'
For whan I feele a-nyght your softe syde —
Al be it that I may nat on yow ryde,
For that oure perche is maad so narwe, allas —
I am so ful of joye and of solas, *4360
That I diffye bothe sweven and dreem."

And with that word he fley doun fro the beem,
For it was day, and eke his hennes alle,
And with a chuk he gan hem for to calle,

3096 **forslewthen:** slothfully waste
3101 **casuelly:** by chance
3110 **Seint Kenelm:** See n.
3111 **Kenulphus:** Cenwulf's
3112 **Mercenrike:** Mercia
3114 **avysioun:** a prophetic dream, sent as a warning (MED)
3117 **For:** to prevent, against
3118–19 **litel tale hath he toold Of:** he had little regard for
3123 **Macrobeus:** Macrobius (fl. c. 400 A.D.), author of a commentary on the *Dream of Scipio*
3124 **Cipioun:** Scipio; for his dream see PF 29–84.
3128 **Daniel:** The book of Daniel describes Daniel's prophetic visions.
3130 **Joseph:** famous as the interpreter of Pharoah's dreams
3133 **Pharao:** Pharoah

3134 **butiller:** steward
3135 **effect:** significance
3136 **seken:** examine **actes:** histories **remes:** realms
3138 **Cresus:** Croesus; for his dream see MkT VII.2727–60.
3141 **Ectores:** Hector's
3150 **dwelle:** delay
3154 **telle of . . . no stoor:** regard as worthless
3156 **diffye:** renounce
3163 *In principio:* In the beginning (the opening words of Genesis 1 and John 1); see n.
3164 *Mulier est hominis confusio:* woman is man's ruin
3172 **fley:** flew **beem:** beam, roost
3174 **chuk:** cluck

For he hadde founde a corn, lay in the yerd.
Real he was, he was namoore aferd.   3176
He fethered Pertelote twenty tyme,
And trad hire eke as ofte, er it was pryme.
He looketh as it were a grym leoun,
And on his toos he rometh up and doun;   *4370
Hym deigned nat to sette his foot to grounde.
He chukketh whan he hath a corn yfounde,
And to hym rennen thanne his wyves alle.
Thus roial, as a prince is in his halle,
Leve I this Chauntecleer in his pasture,   3185
And after wol I telle his aventure.
   Whan that the month in which the world
        bigan,
That highte March, whan God first maked man,
Was compleet, and passed were also,
Syn March [was gon], thritty dayes and two,   *4380
Bifel that Chauntecleer in al his pryde,
His sevene wyves walkynge by his syde,
Caste up his eyen to the brighte sonne,
That in the signe of Taurus hadde yronne   3194
Twenty degrees and oon, and somwhat moore,
And knew by kynde, and by noon oother loore,
That it was pryme, and crew with blisful
        stevene.
"The sonne," he seyde, "is clomben up on
        hevene
Fourty degrees and oon, and moore ywis.
Madame Pertelote, my worldes blis,   *4390
Herkneth thise blisful briddes how they synge,
And se the fresshe floures how they sprynge;
Ful is myn herte of revel and solas!"
But sodeynly hym fil a sorweful cas,
For evere the latter ende of joye is wo.   3205
God woot that worldly joye is soone ago;
And if a rethor koude faire endite,
He in a cronycle saufly myghte it write
As for a sovereyn notabilitee.
Now every wys man, lat him herkne me;   *4400
This storie is also trewe, I undertake,
As is the book of Launcelot de Lake,

That wommen holde in ful greet reverence.
Now wol I torne agayn to my sentence.
   A col-fox, ful of sly iniquitee,   3215
That in the grove hadde woned yeres three,
By heigh ymaginacioun forncast,
The same nyght thurghout the hegges brast
Into the yerd ther Chauntecleer the faire
Was wont, and eek his wyves, to repaire;
And in a bed of wortes stille he lay   *4411
Til it was passed undren of the day,
Waitynge his tyme on Chauntecleer to falle,
As gladly doon thise homycides alle
That in await liggen to mordre men.   3225
O false mordrour, lurkynge in thy den!
O newe Scariot, newe Genylon,
False dissymulour, o Greek Synon,
That broghtest Troye al outrely to sorwe!
O Chauntecleer, acursed be that morwe   *4420
That thou into that yerd flaugh fro the bemes!
Thou were ful wel ywarned by thy dremes
That thilke day was perilous to thee;
But what that God forwoot moot nedes bee,
After the opinioun of certein clerkis.   3235
Witnesse on hym that any parfit clerk is,
That in scole is greet altercacioun
In this mateere, and greet disputisoun,
And hath been of an hundred thousand men.
But I ne kan nat bulte it to the bren   *4430
As kan the hooly doctour Augustyn,
Or Boece, or the Bisshop Bradwardyn,
Wheither that Goddes worthy forwityng
Streyneth me nedely for to doon a thyng —
"Nedely" clepe I symple necessitee —   3245
Or elles, if free choys be graunted me
To do that same thyng, or do it noght,
Though God forwoot it er that I was wroght;

3175 **corn:** grain
3176 **Real:** royal
3177 **fethered:** clasped with his wings
3178 **trad:** copulated with
3179 **leoun:** lion
3182 **chukketh:** clucks
3185 **pasture:** feeding place
3189 **compleet:** completed; the action takes place on May 3; see n.
3194 **Taurus:** the Bull, second sign of the zodiac
3196 **kynde:** instinct
3197 **stevene:** voice
3206 **ago:** gone
3207 **rethor:** rhetorician, master of eloquence
3209 **sovereyn notabilitee:** notable fact
3212 **book of Launcelot de Lake:** the romance of Lancelot and Guinevere

3215 **col-fox:** fox with black-tipped feet, ears, and tail
3216 **woned:** dwelt
3217 Foreseen by the exalted imagination or planned ahead with skillful forethought (?); see n.
3218 **hegges:** hedges (serving as a fence)   **brast:** broke
3221 **wortes:** cabbages
3222 **undren:** the third hour, about 9 A.M.
3224 **gladly:** habitually
3227 **Scariot:** Judas Iscariot, who betrayed Christ   **Genylon:** Ganelon, who betrayed Roland
3228 **dissymulour:** deceiver   **Synon:** The story is briefly told in HF 152–56.
3231 **flaugh:** flew
3234 **forwoot:** foreknows
3240 **bulte it to the bren:** bolt (sift) it to the husks (separate completely the valid from the invalid arguments)
3241–42 **doctour:** teacher (doctor of the church)   **Augustyn, Boece, Bradwardyn:** St. Augustine, Boethius, Thomas Bradwardyne; see n.
3243 **forwityng:** foreknowledge
3244 **Streyneth:** constrains   **nedely:** of necessity
3245 **symple necessitee:** plain or ordinary necessity; see n.
3248 **forwoot:** foreknew

Or if his wityng streyneth never a deel
But by necessitee condicioneel.   *4440
I wol nat han to do of swich mateere;
My tale is of a cok, as ye may heere,
That tok his conseil of his wyf, with sorwe,
To walken in the yerd upon that morwe   3254
That he hadde met that dreem that I yow tolde.
Wommennes conseils been ful ofte colde;
Wommannes conseil broghte us first to wo
And made Adam fro Paradys to go,
Ther as he was ful myrie and wel at ese.
But for I noot to whom it myght displese,
If I conseil of wommen wolde blame,   *4451
Passe over, for I seyde it in my game.
Rede auctours, where they trete of swich ma-
        teere,
And what they seyn of wommen ye may heere.
Thise been the cokkes wordes, and nat myne;
I kan noon harm of no womman divyne.   3266

    Faire in the soond, to bathe hire myrily,
Lith Pertelote, and alle hire sustres by,
Agayn the sonne, and Chauntecleer so free
Soong murier than the mermayde in the see
(For Phisiologus seith sikerly   *4461
How that they syngen wel and myrily).
And so bifel that, as he caste his ye
Among the wortes on a boterflye,
He was war of this fox, that lay ful lowe.   3275
Nothyng ne liste hym thanne for to crowe,
But cride anon, "Cok! cok!" and up he sterte
As man that was affrayed in his herte.
For natureelly a beest desireth flee
Fro his contrarie, if he may it see,   *4470
Though he never erst hadde seyn it with his ye.

    This Chauntecleer, whan he gan hym espye,
He wolde han fled, but that the fox anon
Seyde, "Gentil sire, allas, wher wol ye gon?
Be ye affrayed of me that am youre freend?
Now, certes, I were worse than a feend,   3286
If I to yow wolde harm or vileynye!
I am nat come youre conseil for t'espye,
But trewely, the cause of my comynge

Was oonly for to herkne how that ye synge.
For trewely, ye have as myrie a stevene   *4481
As any aungel hath that is in hevene.
Therwith ye han in musyk moore feelynge
Than hadde Boece, or any that kan synge.
My lord youre fader — God his soule blesse! —
And eek youre mooder, of hire gentillesse,   3296
Han in myn hous ybeen to my greet ese;
And certes, sire, ful fayn wolde I yow plese.
But, for men speke of syngyng, I wol seye —
So moote I brouke wel myne eyen tweye —
Save yow, I herde nevere man so synge   *4491
As dide youre fader in the morwenynge.
Certes, it was of herte, al that he song.
And for to make his voys the moore strong,
He wolde so peyne hym that with bothe his
        yen   3305
He moste wynke, so loude he wolde cryen,
And stonden on his tiptoon therwithal,
And strecche forth his nekke long and smal.
And eek he was of swich discrecioun
That ther nas no man in no regioun   *4500
That hym in song or wisedom myghte passe.
I have wel rad in 'Daun Burnel the Asse,'
Among his vers, how that ther was a cok,
For that a preestes sone yaf hym a knok
Upon his leg whil he was yong and nyce,   3315
He made hym for to lese his benefice.
But certeyn, ther nys no comparisoun
Bitwixe the wisedom and discrecioun
Of youre fader and of his subtiltee.
Now syngeth, sire, for seinte charitee;   *4510
Lat se; konne ye youre fader countrefete?"

    This Chauntecleer his wynges gan to bete,
As man that koude his traysoun nat espie,
So was he ravysshed with his flaterie.

    Allas, ye lordes, many a fals flatour   3325
Is in youre courtes, and many a losengeour,
That plesen yow wel moore, by my feith,
Than he that soothfastnesse unto yow seith.
Redeth Ecclesiaste of flaterye;
Beth war, ye lordes, of hir trecherye.   *4520

    This Chauntecleer stood hye upon his toos,
Strecchynge his nekke, and heeld his eyen cloos,

3250 **necessitee condicioneel**: inferential necessity; see n.
3253 **with sorwe**: to his sorrow
3256 **colde**: fatal
3260 **noot** = *ne woot*, know not
3262 **Passe over**: let it be
3266 **kan noon**: am not able or do not know; see n.
3267 **soond**: sand
3269 **Agayn**: facing toward
3271 **Phisiologus**: the bestiary; see n.
3274 **wortes**: cabbages
3278 **affrayed**: frightened

3291 **stevene**: voice
3294 **Boece**: Boethius wrote a textbook on music.
3300 **brouke**: use
3303 **of**: from the
3306 **wynke**: close both eyes
3312 **Daun Burnel the Asse**: *Burnellus*, or the *Speculum Stultorum* (a satiric work of the late twelfth century by Nigel Wireker)
3320 **for seinte charitee**: by holy charity, for the love of God
3326 **losengeour**: flatterer
3329 **Ecclesiaste**: the book of Ecclesiasticus, Ecclesiastes, or possibly even Proverbs; see n.

And gan to crowe loude for the nones.
And daun Russell the fox stirte up atones,
And by the gargat hente Chauntecleer,   3335
And on his bak toward the wode hym beer,
For yet ne was ther no man that hym sewed.

O destinee, that mayst nat been eschewed!
Allas, that Chauntecleer fleigh fro the bemes!
Allas, his wyf ne roghte nat of dremes!   *4530
And on a Friday fil al this meschaunce.

O Venus, that art goddesse of plesaunce,
Syn that thy servant was this Chauntecleer,
And in thy servyce dide al his poweer,
Moore for delit than world to multiplye,   3345
Why woldestow suffre hym on thy day to dye?

O Gaufred, deere maister soverayn,
That whan thy worthy kyng Richard was slayn
With shot, compleynedest his deeth so soore,
Why ne hadde I now thy sentence and thy
     loore,   *4540
The Friday for to chide, as diden ye?
For on a Friday, soothly, slayn was he.
Thanne wolde I shewe yow how that I koude
     pleyne
For Chauntecleres drede and for his peyne.

Certes, swich cry ne lamentacion   3355
Was nevere of ladyes maad whan Ylion
Was wonne, and Pirrus with his streite swerd,
Whan he hadde hent kyng Priam by the berd,
And slayn hym, as seith us *Eneydos,*
As maden alle the hennes in the clos,   *4550
Whan they had seyn of Chauntecleer the sighte.
But sovereynly dame Pertelote shrighte
Ful louder than dide Hasdrubales wyf,
Whan that hir housbonde hadde lost his lyf
And that the Romayns hadde brend Cartage.
She was so ful of torment and of rage   3366
That wilfully into the fyr she sterte
And brende hirselven with a stedefast herte.

O woful hennes, right so criden ye
As whan that Nero brende the citee   *4560
Of Rome cryden senatoures wyves
For that hir husbondes losten alle hir lyves —

Withouten gilt this Nero hath hem slayn.
Now wole I turne to my tale agayn.   3374

This sely wydwe and eek hir doghtres two
Herden thise hennes crie and maken wo,
And out at dores stirten they anon,
And syen the fox toward the grove gon,
And bar upon his bak the cok away,   *4569
And cryden, "Out! Harrow and weylaway!
Ha, ha! The fox!" and after hym they ran,
And eek with staves many another man.
Ran Colle oure dogge, and Talbot and Gerland,
And Malkyn, with a dystaf in hir hand;
Ran cow and calf, and eek the verray hogges,
So fered for the berkyng of the dogges   3386
And shoutyng of the men and wommen eeke
They ronne so hem thoughte hir herte breeke.
They yolleden as feendes doon in helle;
The dokes cryden as men wolde hem quelle;
The gees for feere flowen over the trees;   *4581
Out of the hyve cam the swarm of bees.
So hydous was the noyse — a, benedicitee! —
Certes, he Jakke Straw and his meynee
Ne made nevere shoutes half so shrille   3395
Whan that they wolden any Flemyng kille,
As thilke day was maad upon the fox.
Of bras they broghten bemes, and of box,
Of horn, of boon, in whiche they blewe and
     powped,
And therwithal they skriked and they howped.
It semed as that hevene sholde falle.   *4591

Now, goode men, I prey yow herkneth alle:
Lo, how Fortune turneth sodeynly
The hope and pryde eek of hir enemy!
This cok, that lay upon the foxes bak,   3405
In al his drede unto the fox he spak,
And seyde, "Sire, if that I were as ye,
Yet sholde I seyn, as wys God helpe me,
'Turneth agayn, ye proude cherles alle!
A verray pestilence upon yow falle!   *4600
Now I am come unto the wodes syde;
Maugree youre heed, the cok shal heere abyde.
I wol hym ete, in feith, and that anon!' "

3335 **gargat:** throat
3337 **sewed:** pursued
3347 **Gaufred:** Geoffrey of Vinsauf, author of a standard textbook on rhetoric containing a lament on the death of King Richard I (*kyng Richard*); see n.
3349 **With shot:** by the shot of an arrow
3356 **Ylion:** Ilium, the citadel at Troy
3357 **Pirrus:** Pyrrhus; see n.   **streite swerd:** drawn sword
3359 *Eneydos:* the *Aeneid*
3360 **clos:** enclosure, yard
3362 **sovereynly:** supremely
3363 **Hasdrubales wyf:** Her story is briefly told in FranT V.1399–1404.
3370 **Nero:** For his story see MkT VII.2463–2550.

3386 **fered for:** frightened by   **berkyng:** barking
3388 **breeke:** would break
3389 **yolleden:** yelled
3390 **quelle:** kill
3394 **Jakke Straw:** a supposed leader in the Peasants' Revolt of 1381
3398 **bemes:** trumpets   **box:** boxwood
3399 **powped:** puffed
3400 **skriked:** shrieked   **howped:** whooped
3412 **Maugree youre heed:** in spite of all you can do

The fox answerde, "In feith, it shal be don."
And as he spak that word, al sodeynly   3415
This cok brak from his mouth delyverly,
And heighe upon a tree he fleigh anon.
And whan the fox saugh that the cok was gon,
"Allas!" quod he, "O Chauntecleer, allas!
I have to yow," quod he, "ydoon trespas,   *4611
In as muche as I maked yow aferd
Whan I yow hente and broghte out of the yerd.
But, sire, I dide it in no wikke entente.
Com doun, and I shal telle yow what I mente;
I shal seye sooth to yow, God help me so!"   3425
    "Nay thanne," quod he, "I shrewe us bothe
        two.
And first I shrewe myself, bothe blood and
        bones,
If thou bigyle me ofter than ones.
Thou shalt namoore thurgh thy flaterye   *4619

Do me to synge and wynke with myn ye;
For he that wynketh, whan he sholde see,
Al wilfully, God lat him nevere thee!"
    "Nay," quod the fox, "but God yeve hym
        meschaunce,
That is so undiscreet of governaunce
That jangleth whan he sholde holde his pees."
    Lo, swich it is for to be recchelees   3436
And necligent, and truste on flaterye.
    But ye that holden this tale a folye,
As of a fox, or of a cok and hen,
Taketh the moralite, goode men.   *4630
For Seint Paul seith that al that writen is,
To oure doctrine it is ywrite, ywis;
Taketh the fruyt, and lat the chaf be stille.
Now, goode God, if that it be thy wille,   3444
As seith my lord, so make us alle goode men,
And brynge us to his heighe blisse! Amen.

Heere is ended the Nonnes Preestes Tale.

[EPILOGUE TO THE NUN'S PRIEST'S TALE

"Sire Nonnes Preest," oure Hooste seide anoon,
"I-blessed be thy breche, and every stoon!
This was a murie tale of Chauntecleer.
But by my trouthe, if thou were seculer,
Thou woldest ben a trede-foul aright.   *4641
For if thou have corage as thou hast myght,
Thee were nede of hennes, as I wene,
Ya, moo than seven tymes seventene.   3454

See, whiche braunes hath this gentil preest,
So gret a nekke, and swich a large breest!
He loketh as a sperhauk with his yen;
Him nedeth nat his colour for to dyen
With brasile ne with greyn of Portyngale.
Now, sire, faire falle yow for youre tale!"   *4650
    And after that he, with ful merie chere,
Seide unto another, as ye shuln heere.]

3416 **delyverly:** nimbly
3426 **shrewe:** beshrew, curse

3448 **breche:** buttocks **stoon:** testicle
3451 **trede-foul:** treader (copulator) of fowls, rooster **aright:** excellent

3432 **thee:** prosper
3435 **jangleth:** chatters
3443 **chaf:** husk, chaff

3457 **sperhauk:** sparrow hawk
3459 **brasile:** a red dye **greyn of Portyngale:** a red dyestuff imported from Portugal

THE SECOND NUN'S PROLOGUE

The Prologe of the Seconde Nonnes Tale.

The ministre and the norice unto vices,
Which that men clepe in Englissh Ydelnesse,
That porter of the gate is of delices,
To eschue, and by hire contrarie hire op-
    presse —
That is to seyn, by leveful bisynesse —   5
Wel oghten we to doon al oure entente,
Lest that the feend thurgh ydelnesse us hente.

For he that with his thousand cordes slye
Continuelly us waiteth to biclappe,
Whan he may man in ydelnesse espye,   10
He kan so lightly cache hym in his trappe,
Til that a man be hent right by the lappe,
He nys nat war the feend hath hym in honde.
Wel oghte us werche and ydelnesse withstonde.

And though men dradden nevere for to dye,
Yet seen men wel by resoun, doutelees,   16
That ydelnesse is roten slogardye,
Of which ther nevere comth no good n'encrees;
And syn that slouthe hire holdeth in a lees
Oonly to slepe, and for to ete and drynke,   20
And to devouren al that othere swynke,

And for to putte us fro swich ydelnesse,
That cause is of so greet confusioun,
I have heer doon my feithful bisynesse
After the legende in translacioun   25
Right of thy glorious lif and passioun,
Thou with thy gerland wroght with rose and
    lilie —
Thee meene I, mayde and martyr, Seint Cecile.

Invocacio ad Mariam

And thow that flour of virgines art alle,
Of whom that Bernard list so wel to write,   30
To thee at my bigynnyng first I calle;
Thou confort of us wrecches, do me endite
Thy maydens deeth, that wan thurgh hire
    merite
The eterneel lyf and of the feend victorie,
As man may after reden in hire storie.   35

Thow Mayde and Mooder, doghter of thy Sone,
Thow welle of mercy, synful soules cure,
In whom that God for bountee chees to wone,
Thow humble, and heigh over every creature,
Thow nobledest so ferforth oure nature,   40
That no desdeyn the Makere hadde of kynde
His Sone in blood and flessh to clothe and
    wynde.

Withinne the cloistre blisful of thy sydis
Took mannes shap the eterneel love and pees,
That of the tryne compas lord and gyde is,   45
Whom erthe and see and hevene out of relees
Ay heryen; and thou, Virgine wemmelees,
Baar of thy body — and dweltest mayden
    pure —
The Creatour of every creature.

Assembled is in thee magnificence   50
With mercy, goodnesse, and with swich pitee
That thou, that art the sonne of excellence
Nat oonly helpest hem that preyen thee,
But often tyme of thy benygnytee
Ful frely, er that men thyn help biseche,   55
Thou goost biforn and art hir lyves leche.

---

3 **delices:** pleasures
9 **biclappe:** trap suddenly
12 **lappe:** hem (of a garment)
14 **werche:** work
15 **dradden nevere:** were never to dread
17 **slogardye:** sluggishness, laziness
19 **in a lees:** on a leash
21 **swynke:** earn by working
26 **passioun:** suffering (of a saint)

Invocacio ad Mariam: Invocation to Mary
35 **after:** hereafter
38 **wone:** dwell
40 **nobledest:** ennobled
41 **kynde:** nature (humankind)
45 **That:** he who   **tryne compas:** the threefold universe (earth, heaven, sea)
46 **out of relees:** unceasing
47 **heryen:** praise   **wemmelees:** without blemish
56 **leche:** physician

Now help, thow meeke and blisful faire mayde,
Me, flemed wrecche, in this desert of galle;
Thynk on the womman Cananee, that sayde
That whelpes eten somme of the crommes alle
That from hir lordes table been yfalle;   61
And though that I, unworthy sone of Eve,
Be synful, yet accepte my bileve.

And, for that feith is deed withouten werkis,
So for to werken yif me wit and space,   65
That I be quit fro thennes that most derk is!
O thou, that art so fair and ful of grace,
Be myn advocat in that heighe place
Theras withouten ende is songe "Osanne,"
Thow Cristes mooder, doghter deere of Anne!

And of thy light my soule in prison lighte,   71
That troubled is by the contagioun
Of my body, and also by the wighte
Of erthely lust and fals affeccioun;
O havene of refut, O salvacioun   75
Of hem that been in sorwe and in distresse,
Now help, for to my werk I wol me dresse.

Yet preye I yow that reden that I write,
Foryeve me that I do no diligence
This ilke storie subtilly to endite,   80
For bothe have I the wordes and sentence
Of hym that at the seintes reverence
The storie wroot, and folwen hire legende,
And pray yow that ye wole my werk amende.

Interpretacio nominis Cecilie quam
ponit Frater Jacobus Januensis in
Legenda

First wolde I yow the name of Seint Cecilie
Expowne, as men may in hir storie see.   86
It is to seye in Englissh "hevenes lilie,"
For pure chaastnesse of virginitee;

Or, for she whitnesse hadde of honestee,
And grene of conscience, and of good fame   90
The soote savour, "lilie" was hir name.

Or Cecilie is to seye "the wey to blynde,"
For she ensample was by good techynge;
Or elles Cecile, as I writen fynde,
Is joyned, by a manere conjoynynge   95
Of "hevene" and "Lia"; and heere, in figurynge,
The "hevene" is set for thoght of hoolynesse,
And "Lia" for hire lastynge bisynesse.

Cecile may eek be seyd in this manere,
"Wantynge of blyndnesse," for hir grete light
Of sapience and for hire thewes cleere;   101
Or elles, loo, this maydens name bright
Of "hevene" and "leos" comth, for which by
   right
Men myghte hire wel "the hevene of peple"
   calle,
Ensample of goode and wise werkes alle.   105

For "leos" "peple" in Englissh is to seye,
And right as men may in the hevene see
The sonne and moone and sterres every weye,
Right so men goostly in this mayden free
Seyen of feith the magnanymytee,   110
And eek the cleernesse hool of sapience,
And sondry werkes, brighte of excellence.

And right so as thise philosophres write
That hevene is swift and round and eek
   brennynge,
Right so was faire Cecilie the white   115
Ful swift and bisy evere in good werkynge,
And round and hool in good perseverynge,
And brennynge evere in charite ful brighte.
Now have I yow declared what she highte.

Explicit

---

58 **flemed wrecche:** banished exile **galle:** bitterness
59 **womman Cananee:** Canaanite woman in the New Testament
story (cf. Matt. 15.22)
60 **crommes:** crumbs
65 **space:** time, space of time
66 **quit:** free
73 **wighte:** weight
75 **refut:** refuge
82 **at:** from, out of (reverence for)
Interpretacio, etc.: The interpretation of the name Cecilia that
Brother Jacob of Genoa put in the Legend
86 **Expowne:** expound, explain

89 **honestee:** chastity
96 **in figurynge:** symbolically
100 **Wantynge:** lack
101 **thewes:** morals
109 **goostly:** spiritually
110 **Seyen:** saw
117 **perseverynge:** constancy
119 **highte:** was called

THE SECOND NUN'S TALE

Here bigynneth the Seconde Nonnes Tale
of the lyf of Seinte Cecile.

This mayden bright Cecilie, as hir lif
    seith,   120
Was comen of Romayns and of noble kynde,
And from hir cradel up fostred in the feith
Of Crist, and bar his gospel in hir mynde.
She nevere cessed, as I writen fynde,
Of hir preyere and God to love and drede, 125
Bisekynge hym to kepe hir maydenhede.

And whan this mayden sholde unto a man
Ywedded be, that was ful yong of age,
Which that ycleped was Valerian,
And day was comen of hir marriage, 130
She, ful devout and humble in hir corage,
Under hir robe of gold, that sat ful faire,
Hadde next hire flessh yclad hire in an haire.

And whil the organs maden melodie,
To God allone in herte thus sang she: 135
"O Lord, my soule and eek my body gye
Unwemmed, lest that I confounded be."
And for his love that dyde upon a tree
Every seconde and thridde day she faste,
Ay biddynge in hire orisons ful faste. 140

The nyght cam, and to bedde moste she gon
With hire housbonde, as ofte is the manere,
And pryvely to hym she seyde anon,
"O sweete and wel biloved spouse deere,
Ther is a conseil, and ye wolde it heere, 145
Which that right fayn I wolde unto yow seye,
So that ye swere ye shul it nat biwreye."

Valerian gan faste unto hire swere
That for no cas ne thyng that myghte be,
He sholde nevere mo biwreyen here; 150
And thanne at erst to hym thus seyde she:
"I have an aungel which that loveth me,

That with greet love, wher so I wake or sleepe,
Is redy ay my body for to kepe.

"And if that he may feelen, out of drede, 155
That ye me touche, or love in vileynye,
He right anon wol sle yow with the dede,
And in youre yowthe thus ye shullen dye;
And if that ye in clene love me gye, 159
He wol yow loven as me, for youre clennesse,
And shewen yow his joye and his brightnesse."

Valerian, corrected as God wolde,
Answerde agayn, "If I shal trusten thee,
Lat me that aungel se and hym biholde;
And if that it a verray angel bee, 165
Thanne wol I doon as thou hast prayed me;
And if thou love another man, for sothe
Right with this swerd thanne wol I sle yow
    bothe."

Cecile answerde anon-right in this wise:
"If that yow list, the angel shul ye see, 170
So that ye trowe on Crist and yow baptize.
Gooth forth to Via Apia," quod shee,
"That fro this toun ne stant but miles three,
And to the povre folkes that ther dwelle,
Sey hem right thus, as that I shal yow telle. 175

"Telle hem that I, Cecile, yow to hem sente
To shewen yow the goode Urban the olde,
For secree nedes and for good entente.
And whan that ye Seint Urban han biholde,
Telle hym the wordes whiche I to yow
    tolde;   180
And whan that he hath purged yow fro synne,
Thanne shul ye se that angel, er ye twynne."

Valerian is to the place ygon,
And right as hym was taught by his lernynge,
He foond this hooly olde Urban anon 185

---

133 **haire:** hair shirt
136 **gye:** preserve
137 **Unwemmed:** undefiled **confounded:** destroyed
140 **biddynge:** praying
145 **conseil:** secret
147 **biwreye:** betray

160 **clennesse:** purity
172 **Via Apia:** the Appian Way
181 **purged:** cleansed you (by baptism)
182 **twynne:** depart

Among the seintes buryeles lotynge.
And he anon withouten tariynge
Dide his message; and whan that he it tolde,
Urban for joye his handes gan up holde.

The teeris from his eyen leet he falle.   190
"Almyghty Lord, O Jhesu Crist," quod he,
"Sower of chaast conseil, hierde of us alle,
The fruyt of thilke seed of chastitee
That thou hast sowe in Cecile, taak to thee!
Lo, lyk a bisy bee, withouten gile,   195
Thee serveth ay thyn owene thral Cecile.

"For thilke spouse that she took but now
Ful lyk a fiers leoun, she sendeth heere,
As meke as evere was any lomb, to yow!"
And with that word anon ther gan appeere   200
An oold man, clad in white clothes cleere,
That hadde a book with lettre of gold in honde,
And gan bifore Valerian to stonde.

Valerian as deed fil doun for drede   204
Whan he hym saugh, and he up hente hym tho,
And on his book right thus he gan to rede:
"O Lord, o feith, o God, withouten mo,
O Cristendom, and Fader of alle also,
Aboven alle and over alle everywhere."
Thise wordes al with gold ywriten were.   210

Whan this was rad, thanne seyde this olde man,
"Leevestow this thyng or no? Sey ye or nay."
"I leeve al this thyng," quod Valerian,
"For sother thyng than this, I dar wel say,
Under the hevene no wight thynke may."   215
Tho vanysshed this olde man, he nyste where,
And Pope Urban hym cristned right there.

Valerian gooth hoom and fynt Cecilie
Withinne his chambre with an angel stonde.
This angel hadde of roses and of lilie   220
Corones two, the which he bar in honde;
And first to Cecile, as I understonde,
He yaf that oon, and after gan he take
That oother to Valerian, hir make.   224

"With body clene and with unwemmed thoght
Kepeth ay wel thise corones," quod he;
"Fro paradys to yow have I hem broght,

Ne nevere mo ne shal they roten bee,
Ne lese hir soote savour, trusteth me;
Ne nevere wight shal seen hem with his ye,   230
But he be chaast and hate vileynye.

"And thow, Valerian, for thow so soone
Assentedest to good conseil also,
Sey what thee list, and thou shalt han thy
    boone."
"I have a brother," quod Valerian tho,   235
"That in this world I love no man so.
I pray yow that my brother may han grace
To knowe the trouthe, as I do in this place."

The angel seyde, "God liketh thy requeste,
And bothe with the palm of martirdom   240
Ye shullen come unto his blisful feste."
And with that word Tiburce his brother coom.
And whan that he the savour undernoom,
Which that the roses and the lilies caste,
Withinne his herte he gan to wondre faste,   245

And seyde, "I wondre, this tyme of the yeer,
Whennes that soote savour cometh so
Of rose and lilies that I smelle heer.
For though I hadde hem in myne handes two,
The savour myghte in me no depper go.   250
The sweete smel that in myn herte I fynde
Hath chaunged me al in another kynde."

Valerian seyde: "Two corones han we,
Snow white and rose reed, that shynen cleere,
Whiche that thyne eyen han no myght to
    see;   255
And as thou smellest hem thurgh my preyere,
So shaltow seen hem, leeve brother deere,
If it so be thou wolt, withouten slouthe,
Bileve aright and knowen verray trouthe."

Tiburce answerde, "Seistow this to me   260
In soothnesse, or in dreem I herkne this?"
"In dremes," quod Valerian, "han we be
Unto this tyme, brother myn, ywis.
But now at erst in trouthe oure dwellyng is."
"How woostow this?" quod Tiburce, "and in
    what wyse?"   265
Quod Valerian, "That shal I thee devyse.

"The aungel of God hath me the trouthe
    ytaught

---

186 **buryeles:** burial places (in the catacombs)   **lotynge:** in hiding
192 **hierde:** shepherd
208 **Cristendom:** baptism
214 **sother:** truer

243 **undernoom:** perceived
261 **soothnesse:** truth

Which thou shalt seen, if that thou wolt reneye
The ydoles and be clene, and elles naught."
And of the myracle of thise corones tweye 270
Seint Ambrose in his preface list to seye;
Solempnely this noble doctour deere
Commendeth it, and seith in this manere:

   "The palm of martirdom for to receyve,
Seinte Cecile, fulfild of Goddes yifte, 275
The world and eek hire chambre gan she
        weyve;
Witnesse Tyburces and [Valerians] shrifte,
To whiche God of his bountee wolde shifte
Corones two of floures wel smellynge, 279
And made his angel hem the corones brynge.

The mayde hath broght thise men to blisse
        above;
The world hath wist what it is worth, certeyn,
Devocioun of chastitee to love."
Tho shewed hym Cecile al open and pleyn
That alle ydoles nys but a thyng in veyn, 285
For they been dombe, and therto they been
        deve,
And charged hym his ydoles for to leve.

"Whoso that troweth nat this, a beest he is,"
Quod tho Tiburce, "if that I shal nat lye."
And she gan kisse his brest, that herde this,
And was ful glad he koude trouthe espye. 291
"This day I take thee for myn allye,"
Seyde this blisful faire mayde deere,
And after that she seyde as ye may heere: 294

   "Lo, right so as the love of Crist," quod she,
"Made me thy brotheres wyf, right in that wise
Anon for myn allye heer take I thee,
Syn that thou wolt thyne ydoles despise.
Go with thy brother now, and thee baptise,
And make thee clene, so that thou mowe bi-
        holde 300
The angels face of which thy brother tolde."

   Tiburce answerde and seyde, "Brother deere,
First tel me whider I shal, and to what man?"

"To whom?" quod he, "com forth with right
        good cheere,
I wol thee lede unto the Pope Urban." 305
"Til Urban? Brother myn Valerian,"
Quod tho Tiburce, "woltow me thider lede?
Me thynketh that it were a wonder dede.

"Ne menestow nat Urban," quod he tho,
"That is so ofte dampned to be deed, 310
And woneth in halkes alwey to and fro,
And dar nat ones putte forth his heed?
Men sholde hym brennen in a fyr so reed
If he were founde, or that men myghte hym
        spye,
And we also, to bere hym compaignye; 315

"And whil we seken thilke divinitee
That is yhid in hevene pryvely,
Algate ybrend in this world shul we be!"
To whom Cecile answerde boldely,
"Men myghten dreden wel and skilfully 320
This lyf to lese, myn owene deere brother,
If this were lyvynge oonly and noon oother.

"But ther is bettre lif in oother place,
That nevere shal be lost, ne drede thee noght,
Which Goddes Sone us tolde thurgh his
        grace. 325
That Fadres Sone hath alle thyng ywroght,
And al that wroght is with a skilful thoght;
The Goost, that fro the Fader gan procede,
Hath sowled hem, withouten any drede. 329

"By word and by myracle heigh Goddes Sone,
Whan he was in this world, declared heere
That ther was oother lyf ther men may wone."
To whom answerde Tiburce, "O suster deere,
Ne seydestow right now in this manere, 334
Ther nys but o God, lord in soothfastnesse?
And now of three how maystow bere witnesse?"

   "That shal I telle," quod she, "er I go.
Right as a man hath sapiences three —
Memorie, engyn, and intellect also —
So in o beynge of divinitee, 340
Thre persones may ther right wel bee."

268 **reneye:** deny, renounce
271 **preface:** preface to the canon of the Mass
272 **doctour:** Church father
276 **weyve:** abandon, give up
277 **shrifte:** confession; see n.
278 **shifte:** provide
282 **worth:** worthy
286 **deve:** deaf
288 **a beest:** i.e., lacking human understanding
292 **allye:** kinsman

311 **halkes:** hiding places
315 **we also:** us as well
320 **skilfully:** reasonably
327 **skilful:** discerning
329 **sowled hem:** endowed them with souls
332 **wone:** dwell
338 **sapiences three:** three mental faculties—memory,
imagination (*engyn*), judgment

Tho gan she hym ful bisily to preche
Of Cristes come, and of his peynes teche,

And manye pointes of his passioun;
How Goddes Sone in this world was withholde
To doon mankynde pleyn remissioun,   346
That was ybounde in synne and cares colde;
Al this thyng she unto Tiburce tolde.
And after this Tiburce in good entente
With Valerian to Pope Urban he wente,   350

That thanked God, and with glad herte and
      light
He cristned hym and made hym in that place
Parfit in his lernynge, Goddes knyght.
And after this Tiburce gat swich grace   354
That every day he saugh in tyme and space
The aungel of God; and every maner boone
That he God axed, it was sped ful soone.

   It were ful hard by ordre for to seyn
How manye wondres Jhesus for hem wroghte;
But atte laste, to tellen short and pleyn,   360
The sergeantz of the toun of Rome hem soghte,
And hem biforn Almache, the prefect, broghte,
Which hem apposed, and knew al hire entente,
And to the ymage of Juppiter hem sente,

And seyde, "Whoso wol nat sacrifise,   365
Swape of his heed; this my sentence heer."
Anon thise martirs that I yow devyse,
Oon Maximus, that was an officer
Of the prefectes, and his corniculer,
Hem hente, and whan he forth the seintes
      ladde,   370
Hymself he weep for pitee that he hadde.

Whan Maximus had herd the seintes loore,
He gat hym of the tormentoures leve,
And ladde hem to his hous withoute moore,
And with hir prechyng, er that it were eve,
They gonnen fro the tormentours to reve,   376
And fro Maxime, and fro his folk echone,
The false feith, to trowe in God allone.

Cecile cam, whan it was woxen nyght,   379
With preestes that hem cristned alle yfeere;
And afterward, whan day was woxen light,
Cecile hem seyde with a ful stedefast cheere,
"Now, Cristes owene knyghtes leeve and deere,
Cast alle awey the werkes of derknesse,
And armeth yow in armure of brightnesse.   385

"Ye han for sothe ydoon a greet bataille,
Youre cours is doon, youre feith han ye con-
      served.
Gooth to the corone of lif that may nat faille;
The rightful Juge, which that ye han served,
Shal yeve it yow, as ye han it deserved."   390
And whan this thyng was seyd as I devyse,
Men ledde hem forth to doon the sacrefise.

But whan they weren to the place broght
To tellen shortly the conclusioun,
They nolde encense ne sacrifise right noght,
But on hir knees they setten hem adoun   396
With humble herte and sad devocioun,
And losten bothe hir hevedes in the place.
Hir soules wenten to the Kyng of grace.

This Maximus, that saugh this thyng bityde,
With pitous teeris tolde it anonright,   401
That he hir soules saugh to hevene glyde
With aungels ful of cleernesse and of light,
And with his word converted many a wight;
For which Almachius dide hym so bete   405
With whippe of leed til he his lif gan lete.

   Cecile hym took and buryed hym anon
By Tiburce and Valerian softely
Withinne hire buriyng place, under the stoon;
And after this, Almachius hastily   410
Bad his ministres fecchen openly
Cecile, so that she myghte in his presence
Doon sacrifice and Juppiter encense.

But they, converted at hir wise loore,
Wepten ful soore, and yaven ful credence   415
Unto hire word, and cryden moore and moore,
"Crist, Goddes Sone, withouten difference,
Is verray God — this is al oure sentence —

343 **Cristes come:** Christ's coming
345 **withholde:** compelled to remain
347 **colde:** painful
361 **sergeantz:** officers of the law
363 **apposed:** questioned
366 **Swape:** strike **this** = *this is*
367 **devyse:** tell, narrate
369 **corniculer:** subordinate officer, assistant to a centurion,
prefect, etc.
376 **gonnen fro . . . to reve:** took away from

398 **hevedes:** heads
405 **dide . . . bete:** had him beaten
406 **whippe of leed:** scourge with leaden balls attached **lete:**
gave up
415 **yaven:** gave
417 **withouten difference:** without difference in rank or
authority

That hath so good a servant hym to serve.
This with o voys we trowen, thogh we sterve!"

Almachius, that herde of this doynge,   421
Bad fecchen Cecile, that he myghte hire see,
And alderfirst, lo, this was his axynge.
"What maner womman artow?" tho quod he.
"I am a gentil womman born," quod she.   425
"I axe thee," quod he, "though it thee greeve,
Of thy religioun and of thy bileeve."

"Ye han bigonne youre questioun folily,"
Quod she, "that wolden two answeres conclude
In o demande; ye axed lewedly."   430
Almache answerde unto that similitude,
"Of whennes comth thyn answeryng so rude?"
"Of whennes?" quod she, whan that she was
            freyned,
"Of conscience and of good feith unfeyned."

Almachius seyde, "Ne takestow noon heede
Of my power?" And she answerde hym
            this: 436
"Youre myght," quod she, "ful litel is to dreede,
For every mortal mannes power nys
But lyk a bladdre ful of wynd, ywys.
For with a nedles poynt, whan it is blowe,   440
May al the boost of it be leyd ful lowe."

"Ful wrongfully bigonne thow," quod he,
"And yet in wrong is thy perseveraunce.
Wostow nat how oure myghty princes free
Han thus comanded and maad ordinaunce   445
That every Cristen wight shal han penaunce
But if that he his Cristendom withseye,
And goon al quit, if he wole it reneye?"

"Yowre princes erren, as youre nobleye dooth,"
Quod tho Cecile, "and with a wood sentence
Ye make us gilty, and it is nat sooth.   451
For ye, that knowen wel oure innocence,
For as muche as we doon a reverence
To Crist, and for we bere a Cristen name,
Ye putte on us a cryme and eek a blame.   455

"But we that knowen thilke name so
For vertuous, we may it nat withseye."

Almache answerde, "Chees oon of thise two:
Do sacrifice, or Cristendom reneye,   459
That thou mowe now escapen by that weye."
At which the hooly blisful faire mayde
Gan for to laughe, and to the juge sayde:

"O juge, confus in thy nycetee,
Woltow that I reneye innocence,
To make me a wikked wight?" quod shee.   465
"Lo, he dissymuleth heere in audience;
He stareth, and woodeth in his advertence!"
To whom Almachius, "Unsely wrecche,
Ne woostow nat how fer my myght may
            strecche?

"Han noght oure myghty princes to me yiven,
Ye, bothe power and auctoritee   471
To maken folk to dyen or to lyven?
Why spekestow so proudly thanne to me?"
"I speke noght but stedfastly," quod she;
"Nat proudly, for I seye, as for my syde,   475
We haten deedly thilke vice of pryde.

"And if thou drede nat a sooth to heere,
Thanne wol I shewe al openly, by right,
That thou hast maad a ful gret lesyng heere.
Thou seyst thy princes han thee yeven myght
Bothe for to sleen and for to quyken a wight;
Thou, that ne mayst but oonly lyf bireve,   482
Thou hast noon oother power ne no leve.

"But thou mayst seyn thy princes han thee
            maked
Ministre of deeth; for if thou speke of mo,   485
Thou lyest, for thy power is ful naked."
"Do wey thy booldnesse," seyde Almachius tho,
"And sacrifice to oure goddes er thou go!
I recche nat what wrong that thou me profre,
For I kan suffre it as a philosophre;   490

"But thilke wronges may I nat endure
That thou spekest of oure goddes heere," quod
            he.
Cecile answerde, "O nyce creature!
Thou seydest no word syn thou spak to me
That I ne knew therwith thy nycetee   495
And that thou were in every maner wise
A lewed officer and a veyn justise.

420 **with o voys:** unanimously
423 **alderfirst:** first of all
429 **conclude:** include
431 **similitude:** statement (comparison)
433 **freyned:** asked
447 **withseye:** deny
448 **quit:** free
455 **cryme:** accusation

463 **nycetee:** foolishness
466 **dissymuleth:** dissembles
467 **woodeth:** raves, rages   **advertence:** mind
479 **lesyng:** lying
481 **quyken:** give life to
497 **veyn:** idle, foolish

"Ther lakketh no thyng to thyne outter yen
That thou n'art blynd; for thyng that we seen alle
That it is stoon — that men may wel espyen —
That ilke stoon a god thow wolt it calle.   501
I rede thee, lat thyn hand upon it falle
And taste it wel, and stoon thou shalt it fynde,
Syn that thou seest nat with thyne eyen blynde.

"It is a shame that the peple shal   505
So scorne thee and laughe at thy folye,
For communly men woot it wel overal
That myghty God is in his hevenes hye;
And thise ymages, wel thou mayst espye,
To thee ne to hemself mowen noght profite,
For in effect they been nat worth a myte."   511

    Thise wordes and swiche othere seyde she,
And he weex wroth, and bad men sholde hir lede
Hom til hir hous, and "In hire hous," quod he,
"Brenne hire right in a bath of flambes rede."
And as he bad, right so was doon the dede;   516
For in a bath they gonne hire faste shetten,
And nyght and day greet fyr they under betten.

    The longe nyght, and eek a day also,
For al the fyr and eek the bathes heete   520
She sat al coold and feelede no wo.
It made hire nat a drope for to sweete.
But in that bath hir lyf she moste lete,
For he Almachius, with ful wikke entente,
To sleen hire in the bath his sonde sente.   525

Thre strokes in the nekke he smoot hire tho,
The tormentour, but for no maner chaunce
He myghte noght smyte al hir nekke atwo;
And for ther was that tyme an ordinaunce
That no man sholde doon man swich penaunce
The ferthe strook to smyten, softe or soore,   531
This tormentour ne dorste do namoore,

But half deed, with hir nekke ycorven there,
He lefte hir lye, and on his wey he went.
The Cristen folk, which that aboute hire were,
With sheetes han the blood ful faire yhent.   536
Thre dayes lyved she in this torment,
And nevere cessed hem the feith to teche
That she hadde fostred; hem she gan to preche,

And hem she yaf hir moebles and hir thyng,
And to the Pope Urban bitook hem tho,   541
And seyde, "I axed this of hevene kyng,
To han respit thre dayes and namo
To recomende to yow, er that I go,
Thise soules, lo, and that I myghte do werche
Heere of myn hous perpetuelly a cherche."   546

    Seint Urban with his deknes prively
The body fette and buryed it by nyghte
Among his othere seintes honestly.   549
Hir hous the chirche of Seint Cecilie highte;
Seint Urban halwed it, as he wel myghte;
In which, into this day, in noble wyse,
Men doon to Crist and to his seint servyse.

Heere is ended the Seconde Nonnes Tale.

498–99 **Ther lakketh no thyng . . . blynd:** Your bodily eyes
lack nothing to make you blind (i.e., you are completely blind).
511 **myte:** a small Flemish coin of little value
513 **weex:** grew, became
515 **bath:** cauldron
518 **betten:** fed
522 **sweete:** sweat
525 **sonde:** messenger, servant

527 **for no maner chaunce:** in no way
530 **penaunce:** suffering
540 **moebles:** personal property **thyng:** things
541 **bitook:** entrusted
544 **recomende:** commend
545 **do werche:** have my house made (into a church)
547 **deknes:** deacons
551 **halwed:** consecrated

THE CANON'S YEOMAN'S PROLOGUE

The Prologe of the Chanouns Yemannes Tale.

Whan ended was the lyf of Seinte Cecile,
Er we hadde riden fully fyve mile,   555
At Boghtoun under Blee us gan atake
A man that clothed was in clothes blake,
And undernethe he hadde a whyt surplys.
His hakeney, that was al pomely grys,
So swatte that it wonder was to see;   560
It semed as he had priked miles three.
The hors eek that his yeman rood upon
So swatte that unnethe myghte it gon.
Aboute the peytrel stood the foom ful hye;
He was of foom al flekked as a pye.   565
A male tweyfoold on his croper lay;
It semed that he caried lite array.
Al light for somer rood this worthy man,
And in myn herte wondren I bigan
What that he was til that I understood   570
How that his cloke was sowed to his hood,
For which, whan I hadde longe avysed me,
I demed hym som chanoun for to be.
His hat heeng at his bak doun by a laas,
For he hadde riden moore than trot or paas;
He hadde ay priked lik as he were wood.   576
A clote-leef he hadde under his hood
For swoot and for to keep his heed from heete.
But it was joye for to seen hym swete!
His forheed dropped as a stillatorie   580
Were ful of plantayne and of paritorie.
And whan that he was come, he gan to crye,
"God save," quod he, "this joly compaignye!
Faste have I priked," quod he, "for youre sake,
By cause that I wolde yow atake,   585
To riden in this myrie compaignye."

His yeman eek was ful of curteisye,
And seyde, "Sires, now in the morwe-tyde
Out of youre hostelrie I saugh yow ryde,   589
And warned heer my lord and my soverayn,
Which that to ryden with yow is ful fayn
For his desport; he loveth daliaunce."
    "Freend, for thy warnyng God yeve thee
        good chaunce,"
Thanne seyde oure Hoost, "for certein it wolde
        seme
Thy lord were wys, and so I may wel deme.
He is ful jocunde also, dar I leye!   596
Can he oght telle a myrie tale or tweye,
With which he glade may this compaignye?"
    "Who, sire? My lord? Ye, ye, withouten lye,
He kan of murthe and eek of jolitee   600
Nat but ynough; also, sire, trusteth me,
And ye hym knewe as wel as do I,
Ye wolde wondre how wel and craftily
He koude werke, and that in sondry wise.
He hath take on hym many a greet emprise,
Which were ful hard for any that is heere   606
To brynge aboute, but they of hym it leere.
As hoomly as he rit amonges yow,
If ye hym knewe, it wolde be for youre prow.
Ye wolde nat forgoon his aqueyntaunce   610
For muchel good, I dar leye in balaunce
Al that I have in my possessioun.
He is a man of heigh discrecioun;
I warne yow wel, he is a passyng man."
    "Wel," quod oure Hoost, "I pray thee, tel me
        than,   615
Is he a clerk, or noon? Telle what he is."
    "Nay, he is gretter than a clerk, ywis,"
Seyde this Yeman, "and in wordes fewe,
Hoost, of his craft somwhat I wol yow shewe.
    "I seye, my lord kan swich subtilitee —   620
But al his craft ye may nat wite at me,
And somwhat helpe I yet to his wirkyng —
That al this ground on which we been ridyng,

556 **Boghtoun under Blee:** Boughton under the Blean Forest,
about five miles from Canterbury   **gan atake:** overtook
558 **surplys:** surplice (ecclesiastical gown)
559 **hakeney:** small riding horse   **pomely grys:** dapple grey
560 **swatte:** sweated
564 **peytrel:** horse collar
565 **flekked:** spotted   **pye:** magpie
566 **male tweyfoold:** a double bag
568 **Al light:** lightly clothed
575 **paas:** walk
577 **clote-leef:** burdock leaf
578 **For swoot:** to avoid sweat (running into his eyes)
580 **stillatorie:** still, vessel for distillation
581 **plantayne:** the herb plantain   **paritorie:** pellitory (also a
herb)
585 **atake:** overtake

590 **soverayn:** master
596 **leye:** bet
601 **Nat but ynough:** more than enough
611 **leye in balaunce:** wager
614 **passyng:** outstanding
621 **wite at:** learn from

Til that we come to Caunterbury toun,
He koude al clene turnen up-so-doun,   625
And pave it al of silver and of gold."
    And whan this Yeman hadde this tale ytold
Unto oure Hoost, he seyde, *"Benedicitee!*
This thyng is wonder merveillous to me,
Syn that thy lord is of so heigh prudence,   630
By cause of which men sholde hym reverence,
That of his worshipe rekketh he so lite.
His overslope nys nat worth a myte,
As in effect, to hym, so moot I go,
It is al baudy and totore also.   635
Why is thy lord so sluttissh, I the preye,
And is of power bettre clooth to beye,
If that his dede accorde with thy speche?
Telle me that, and that I thee biseche."
    "Why?" quod this Yeman, "wherto axe ye
       me?   640
God help me so, for he shal nevere thee!
(But I wol nat avowe that I seye,
And therfore keepe it secree, I yow preye.)
He is to wys, in feith, as I bileeve.
That that is overdoon, it wol nat preeve   645
Aright, as clerkes seyn; it is a vice.
Wherfore in that I holde hym lewed and nyce.
For whan a man hath over-greet a wit,
Ful oft hym happeth to mysusen it.   649
So dooth my lord, and that me greveth soore;
God it amende! I kan sey yow namoore."
    "Ther-of no fors, good Yeman," quod oure
       Hoost;
"Syn of the konnyng of thy lord thow woost,
Telle how he dooth, I pray thee hertely,
Syn that he is so crafty and so sly.   655
Where dwelle ye, if it to telle be?"
    "In the suburbes of a toun," quod he,
"Lurkynge in hernes and in lanes blynde,
Whereas thise robbours and thise theves by
       kynde
Holden hir pryvee fereful residence,   660
As they that dar nat shewen hir presence;
So faren we, if I shal seye the sothe."
    "Now," quod oure Hoost, "yit lat me talke to
       the.

Why artow so discoloured of thy face?"
    "Peter!" quod he, "God yeve it harde grace,
I am so used in the fyr to blowe   666
That it hath chaunged my colour, I trowe.
I am nat wont in no mirour to prie,
But swynke soore and lerne multiplie.
We blondren evere and pouren in the fir,   670
And for al that we faille of oure desir,
For evere we lakken oure conclusioun.
To muchel folk we doon illusioun,
And borwe gold, be it a pound or two,
Or ten, or twelve, or manye sommes mo,   675
And make hem wenen, at the leeste weye,
That of a pound we koude make tweye.
Yet is it fals, but ay we han good hope
It for to doon, and after it we grope.
But that science is so fer us biforn,   680
We mowen nat, although we hadden it sworn,
It overtake, it slit away so faste.
It wole us maken beggers atte laste."
    Whil this Yeman was thus in his talkyng,
This Chanoun drough hym neer and herde al
       thyng   685
Which this Yeman spak, for suspecioun
Of mennes speche evere hadde this Chanoun.
For Catoun seith that he that gilty is
Demeth alle thyng be spoke of hym, ywis.
That was the cause he gan so ny hym drawe
To his Yeman, to herknen al his sawe.   691
And thus he seyde unto his Yeman tho:
"Hoold thou thy pees and spek no wordes mo,
For if thou do, thou shalt it deere abye.   694
Thou sclaundrest me heere in this compaignye,
And eek discoverest that thou sholdest hyde."
    "Ye," quod oure Hoost, "telle on, what so
       bityde.
Of al his thretyng rekke nat a myte!"
    "In feith," quod he, "namoore I do but lyte."
And whan this Chanon saugh it wolde nat
       bee,   700
But his Yeman wolde telle his pryvetee,
He fledde awey for verray sorwe and shame.
    "A!" quod the Yeman, "heere shal arise game;
Al that I kan anon now wol I telle.

---

665 **Peter!**: by St. Peter (I swear)! **harde grace**: misfortune
668 **prie**: look, peer
669 **multiplie**: transmute (base metals to gold and silver)
670 **blondren**: blunder **pouren**: stare, pore
681 **although we hadden it sworn**: though we had sworn the contrary
682 **slit** = *slideth*, slips away
688 **Catoun**: Cato
691 **sawe**: speech
696 **discoverest that**: reveal what
698 **thretyng**: threatening

625 **up-so-doun**: topsy turvy
632 **worshipe**: honor
633 **overslope**: outer garment, cassock
634 **As in effect, to hym**: Really, for him; cf. 847.
635 **baudy**: dirty **totore**: tattered
636 **sluttissh**: slovenly
645 **overdoon**: overdone
645–46 **preeve Aright**: turn out right, succeed
648 **over-greet**: excessive
655 **sly**: expert
658 **hernes**: hiding places

Syn he is goon, the foule feend hym quelle! 705
For nevere heerafter wol I with hym meete
For peny ne for pound, I yow biheete.
He that me broghte first unto that game,
Er that he dye, sorwe have he and shame!
For it is ernest to me, by my feith; 710
That feele I wel, what so any man seith.
And yet, for al my smert and al my grief,

For al my sorwe, labour, and meschief,
I koude nevere leve it in no wise.
Now wolde God my wit myghte suffise 715
To tellen al that longeth to that art!
But nathelees yow wol I tellen part.
Syn that my lord is goon, I wol nat spare;
Swich thyng as that I knowe, I wol declare.

Heere endeth the Prologe of the Chanouns Yemannes Tale.

THE CANON'S YEOMAN'S TALE

Heere bigynneth the Chanouns Yeman his Tale.

[Prima Pars]

With this Chanoun I dwelt have seven yeer,
And of his science am I never the neer. 721
Al that I hadde I have lost therby,
And, God woot, so hath many mo than I.
Ther I was wont to be right fressh and gay
Of clothyng and of oother good array, 725
Now may I were an hose upon myn heed;
And wher my colour was bothe fressh and reed,
Now is it wan and of a leden hewe —
Whoso it useth, soore shal he rewe! —
And of my swynk yet blered is myn ye. 730
Lo, which avantage is to multiplie!
That slidynge science hath me maad so bare
That I have no good, wher that evere I fare;
And yet I am endetted so therby
Of gold that I have borwed, trewely, 735
That whil I lyve I shal it quite nevere.
Lat every man be war by me for evere!
What maner man that casteth hym therto,
If he continue, I holde his thrift ydo.
For so helpe me God, therby shal he nat
    wynne, 740
But empte his purs and make his wittes thynne.
And whan he thurgh his madnesse and folye

Hath lost his owene good thurgh jupartye,
Thanne he exciteth oother folk therto,
To lesen hir good as he hymself hath do. 745
For unto shrewes joye it is and ese
To have hir felawes in peyne and disese.
Thus was I ones lerned of a clerk.
Of that no charge; I wol speke of oure werk.
Whan we been there as we shul exercise 750
Oure elvysshe craft, we semen wonder wise,
Oure termes been so clergial and so queynte.
I blowe the fir til that myn herte feynte.
What sholde I tellen ech proporcion
Of thynges whiche that we werche upon — 755
As on fyve or sixe ounces, may wel be,
Of silver, or som oother quantitee —
And bisye me to telle yow the names
Of orpyment, brent bones, iren squames,
That into poudre grounden been ful smal; 760
And in an erthen pot how put is al,
And salt yput in, and also papeer,
Biforn thise poudres that I speke of heer;
And wel ycovered with a lampe of glas;
And of muche oother thyng which that ther
    was; 765
And of the pot and glasses enlutyng

---

705 **quelle:** kill
707 **biheete:** promise

---

721 **never the neer:** no closer to the goal, no better off
728 **leden:** lead-colored
730 **blered is myn ye:** my eye is bleary, I have been deluded
732 **bare:** impoverished
734 **endetted:** in debt
738 **casteth hym:** applies himself
739 **thrift ydo:** prosperity, or welfare, done for

743 **jupartye:** taking risks
749 **no charge:** no matter
751 **elvysshe:** strange, mysterious
752 **clergial:** scholarly, learned **queynte:** complex
753 **feynte:** grows faint
759 **orpyment:** arsenic trisulphide (auripigmentum); the scientific terms in this passage are discussed in the Expl. Notes. **squames:** flakes, scales
762 **papeer:** pepper
764 **lampe:** lamp-shaped vessel
766 **enlutyng:** sealing with "lute," clay

That of the eyr myghte passe out nothyng;
And of the esy fir, and smart also,
Which that was maad, and of the care and wo
That we hadde in oure matires sublymyng,   770
And in amalgamyng and calcenyng
Of quyksilver, yclept mercurie crude?
For alle oure sleightes we kan nat conclude.
Oure orpyment and sublymed mercurie,
Oure grounden litarge eek on the porfurie,   775
Of ech of thise of ounces a certeyn —
Noght helpeth us; oure labour is in veyn.
Ne eek oure spirites ascencioun,
Ne oure materes that lyen al fix adoun,
Mowe in oure werkyng no thyng us availle,   780
For lost is al oure labour and travaille;
And al the cost, a twenty devel waye,
Is lost also, which we upon it laye.

   Ther is also ful many another thyng
That is unto oure craft apertenyng.   785
Though I by ordre hem nat reherce kan,
By cause that I am a lewed man,
Yet wol I telle hem as they come to mynde,
Thogh I ne kan nat sette hem in hir kynde:
As boole armonyak, verdegrees, boras,   790
And sondry vessels maad of erthe and glas,
Oure urynales and oure descensories,
Violes, crosletz, and sublymatories,
Cucurbites and alambikes eek,
And othere swiche, deere ynough a leek —   795
Nat nedeth it for to reherce hem alle —
Watres rubifiyng, and boles galle,
Arsenyk, sal armonyak, and brymstoon;
And herbes koude I telle eek many oon,

As egremoyne, valerian, and lunarie,   800
And othere swiche, if that me liste tarie;
Oure lampes brennyng bothe nyght and day,
To brynge aboute oure purpos, if we may;
Oure fourneys eek of calcinacioun,
And of watres albificacioun;   805
Unslekked lym, chalk, and gleyre of an ey,
Poudres diverse, asshes, donge, pisse, and cley,
Cered pokkets, sal peter, vitriole,
And diverse fires maad of wode and cole;
Sal tartre, alkaly, and sal preparat,   810
And combust materes and coagulat;
Cley maad with hors or mannes heer, and oille
Of tartre, alum glas, berme, wort, and argoille,
Resalgar, and oure materes enbibyng,
And eek of oure materes encorporyng,   815
And of oure silver citrinacioun,
Oure cementyng and fermentacioun,
Oure yngottes, testes, and many mo.

   I wol yow telle, as was me taught also,
The foure spirites and the bodies sevene,   820
By ordre, as ofte I herde my lord hem nevene.

   The firste spirit quyksilver called is,
The seconde orpyment, the thridde, ywis,
Sal armonyak, and the ferthe brymstoon.
The bodyes sevene eek, lo, hem heere anoon:
Sol gold is, and Luna silver we threpe,   826
Mars iren, Mercurie quyksilver we clepe,
Saturnus leed, and Juppiter is tyn,
And Venus coper, by my fader kyn!

768 **smart:** brisk
770 **sublymyng:** sublimation, purifying
771 **amalgamyng:** blending, usually of quicksilver with another metal   **calcenyng:** calcination, reducing a substance to powder by heat
772 **crude:** raw, unrefined
773 **conclude:** succeed
774 **orpyment:** arsenic trisulphide   **sublymed:** purified
775 **litarge:** litharge, lead monoxide   **porfurie:** marble, porphyry (used as a mortar)
776 **a certeyn:** a certain amount of
778 **spirites ascencioun:** vaporization of volatile spirits
779 **fix:** stable, nonvolatile   **adoun:** below, in the bottom of the flask after the vaporization
790 **boole armonyak:** Armenian bole (a styptic)   **verdegrees:** verdigris, copper acetate (a greenish pigment)   **boras:** borax
792 **urynales:** glass flasks   **descensories:** retorts, vessels for distillation
793 **Violes:** vials   **crosletz:** crucibles   **sublymatories:** vessels used for sublimation
794 **Cucurbites:** gourd-shaped vessels (for distillation)   **alambikes:** alembics
795 **deere ynough a leek:** expensive enough at the price of a leek (i.e., worthless)
797 **Watres rubifiyng:** liquids that cause reddening   **boles galle:** bull's gall
798 **Arsenyk:** an arsenic compound (orpiment?)   **sal armonyak:** sal ammoniac, ammonium chloride   **brymstoon:** sulphur

800 **egremoyne:** agrimony, an aromatic herb   **valerian:** valerian, a medicinal herb   **lunarie:** moonwort (Botrychium lunaria)
804 **fourneys:** furnace   **calcinacioun:** calcination (reducing a substance to powder)
805 **watres albificacioun:** whitening by liquids (?); see n.
806 **Unslekked lym:** unslaked lime (a caustic)   **gleyre of an ey:** white of an egg
807 **cley:** clay
808 **Cered pokkets:** waxed (waterproofed) small bags   **sal peter:** saltpeter, potassium nitrate   **vitriole:** sulphate of metal, usually iron or copper
809 **wode and cole:** wood and coal
810 **Sal tartre:** *argoille*, potassium carbonate   **alkaly:** *sal alkaly*, an alkaline from ashes of plants   **sal preparat:** purified salt
811 **combust:** burnt, calcined   **coagulat:** solidified, cohesive
812–13 **oille Of tartre:** cream of tartar
813 **alum glas:** potash alum, crystallized alum   **berme:** barm, brewer's yeast   **wort:** unfermented beer   **argoille:** argol, tartar from fermenting wine, a crude potassium bitartrate
814 **Resalgar:** arsenic disulphide (ratsbane)   **enbibyng:** absorption of fluid, soaking
815 **encorporyng:** forming an amalgam or compound
816 **citrinacioun:** turning to a lemon color
817 **cementyng:** combining, fusing by heat   **fermentacioun:** fermenting, a process causing effervescence
818 **yngottes:** ingots, molds for casting metal   **testes:** cupels, crucibles for trying gold or silver
820 **spirites:** volatile substances, substances easily vaporized by heat   **bodies:** metals
821 **nevene:** name
824 **Sal armonyak:** sal ammoniac
826 **Sol:** the sun   **Luna:** the moon   **threpe:** assert, affirm positively

This cursed craft whoso wole excercise,   830
He shal no good han that hym may suffise,
For al the good he spendeth theraboute
He lese shal; therof have I no doute.
Whoso that listeth outen his folie,
Lat hym come forth and lerne multiplie;   835
And every man that oght hath in his cofre,
Lat hym appiere and wexe a philosophre.
Ascaunce that craft is so light to leere?
Nay, nay, God woot, al be he monk or frere,
Preest or chanoun, or any oother wyght,   840
Though he sitte at his book bothe day and
       nyght
In lernyng of this elvysshe nyce loore,
Al is in veyn, and parde, muchel moore.
To lerne a lewed man this subtiltee —
Fy! Spek nat therof, for it wol nat bee.   845
And konne he letterure or konne he noon,
As in effect, he shal fynde it al oon.
For bothe two, by my savacioun,
Concluden in multiplicacioun
Ylike wel, whan they han al ydo;   850
This is to seyn, they faillen bothe two.

   Yet forgat I to maken rehersaille
Of watres corosif, and of lymaille,
And of bodies mollificacioun,
And also of hire induracioun;   855
Oilles, ablucions, and metal fusible —
To tellen al wolde passen any bible
That owher is; wherfore, as for the beste,
Of alle thise names now wol I me reste,
For, as I trowe, I have yow toold ynowe   860
To reyse a feend, al looke he never so rowe.

   A! Nay! Lat be; the philosophres stoon,
Elixer clept, we sechen faste echoon;
For hadde we hym, thanne were we siker ynow.
But unto God of hevene I make avow,   865
For al oure craft, whan we han al ydo,
And al oure sleighte, he wol nat come us to.
He hath ymaad us spenden muchel good,
For sorwe of which almoost we wexen wood,

But that good hope crepeth in oure herte,   870
Supposynge evere, though we sore smerte,
To be releeved by hym afterward.
Swich supposyng and hope is sharp and hard;
I warne yow wel, it is to seken evere.   874
That futur temps hath maad men to dissevere,
In trust therof, from al that evere they hadde.
Yet of that art they kan nat wexen sadde,
For unto hem it is a bitter sweete —
So semeth it — for nadde they but a sheete
Which that they myghte wrappe hem inne
       a-nyght,   880
And a brat to walken inne by daylyght,
They wolde hem selle and spenden on this craft.
They kan nat stynte til no thyng be laft.
And everemoore, where that evere they goon,
Men may hem knowe by smel of brymstoon.
For al the world they stynken as a goot;   886
Hir savour is so rammyssh and so hoot
That though a man from hem a mile be,
The savour wole infecte hym, trusteth me.
Lo, thus by smellyng and threedbare array,
If that men liste, this folk they knowe may.   891
And if a man wole aske hem pryvely
Why they been clothed so unthriftily,
They right anon wol rownen in his ere,
And seyn that if that they espied were,   895
Men wolde hem slee by cause of hir science.
Lo, thus this folk bitrayen innocence!

   Passe over this; I go my tale unto.
Er that the pot be on the fir ydo,
Of metals with a certeyn quantitee,   900
My lord hem trempreth, and no man but he —
Now he is goon, I dar seyn boldely —
For, as men seyn, he kan doon craftily.
Algate I woot wel he hath swich a name;
And yet ful ofte he renneth in a blame.   905
And wite ye how? Ful ofte it happeth so
The pot tobreketh, and farewel, al is go!
Thise metals been of so greet violence   908
Oure walles mowe nat make hem resistence,
But if they weren wroght of lym and stoon;
They percen so, and thurgh the wal they goon.
And somme of hem synken into the ground —
Thus han we lost by tymes many a pound —

---

834 **outen:** make public
837 **appiere:** appear **wexe:** become **philosophre:** alchemist
838 **Ascaunce:** do you imagine (literally, *as if*) **light to leere:** easy to learn
842 **elvysshe:** strange, mysterious
846 **letterure:** book learning
849 **multiplicacioun:** transmutation
852 **rehersaille:** enumeration
853 **corosif:** acidic **lymaille:** metal filings
854 **mollificacioun:** softening
855 **induracioun:** hardening
856 **ablucions:** cleansings **fusible:** capable of being melted
857 **bible:** book
858 **owher:** anywhere
861 **rowe:** rough, ugly
863 **Elixer:** substance that transmutes base metals to gold or silver, the "philosophers' stone"

874 **to seken evere:** always to be sought; i.e., never to be found
875 **temps:** tense **dissevere:** separate, be separated
877 **wexen sadde:** attain stability, be satisfied
881 **brat:** cloak of rough cloth
887 **rammyssh:** like a ram, strong (in odor)
889 **infecte:** pollute
893 **unthriftily:** poorly
901 **trempreth:** mixes
907 **tobreketh:** shatters
913 **by tymes:** quickly, straightway

And somme are scatered al the floor aboute;
Somme lepe into the roof. Withouten doute,
Though that the feend noght in oure sighte
    hym shewe,   916
I trowe he with us be, that ilke shrewe!
In helle, where that he is lord and sire,
Nis ther moore wo, ne moore rancour ne ire.
Whan that oure pot is broke, as I have
    sayd,   920
Every man chit and halt hym yvele apayd.

  Somme seyde it was long on the fir makyng;
Somme seyde nay, it was on the blowyng —
Thanne was I fered, for that was myn office.
"Straw!" quod the thridde, "ye been lewed and
    nyce.   925
It was nat tempred as it oghte be."
"Nay," quod the fourthe, "stynt and herkne me.
By cause oure fir ne was nat maad of beech,
That is the cause and oother noon, so
    thee'ch!"
I kan nat telle wheron it was long,   930
But wel I woot greet strif is us among.

  "What," quod my lord, "ther is namoore to
    doone;
Of thise perils I wol be war eftsoone.
I am right siker that the pot was crased.
Be as be may, be ye no thyng amased;   935
As usage is, lat swepe the floor as swithe,
Plukke up youre hertes and beeth glad and
    blithe."

  The mullok on an heep ysweped was,
And on the floor ycast a canevas,
And al this mullok in a syve ythrowe,   940
And sifted, and ypiked many a throwe.

  "Pardee," quod oon, "somwhat of oure metal
Yet is ther heere, though that we han nat al.
And though this thyng myshapped have as now,
Another tyme it may be well ynow.   945
Us moste putte oure good in aventure.
A marchant, pardee, may nat ay endure,
Trusteth me wel, in his prosperitee.
Somtyme his good is drowned in the see,   949
And somtyme comth it sauf unto the londe."

"Pees!" quod my lord, "the nexte tyme I wol
    fonde
To bryngen oure craft al in another plite,
And but I do, sires, lat me han the wite.
Ther was defaute in somwhat, wel I woot."
  Another seyde the fir was over-hoot —   955
But, be it hoot or coold, I dar seye this,
That we concluden everemoore amys.
We faille of that which that we wolden have,
And in oure madnesse everemoore we rave.
And whan we been togidres everichoon,   960
Every man semeth a Salomon.
But al thyng which that shineth as the gold
Nis nat gold, as that I have herd told;
Ne every appul that is fair at eye
Ne is nat good, what so men clappe or crye.
Right so, lo, fareth it amonges us: 966
He that semeth the wiseste, by Jhesus,
Is moost fool, whan it cometh to the preef;
And he that semeth trewest is a theef.
That shul ye knowe, er that I fro yow wende,
By that I of my tale have maad an ende.   971

Explicit prima pars.

Et sequitur pars secunda.

  Ther is a chanoun of religioun
Amonges us, wolde infecte al a toun,
Thogh it as greet were as was Nynyvee,
Rome, Alisaundre, Troye, and othere three.
His sleightes and his infinite falsnesse   976
Ther koude no man writen, as I gesse,
Though that he myghte lyve a thousand yeer.
In al this world of falshede nis his peer,
For in his termes he wol hym so wynde,   980
And speke his wordes in so sly a kynde,
Whanne he commune shal with any wight,
That he wol make hym doten anonright,
But it a feend be, as hymselven is.
Ful many a man hath he bigiled er this,   985
And wole, if that he lyve may a while;
And yet men ride and goon ful many a mile
Hym for to seke and have his aqueyntaunce,
Noght knowynge of his false governaunce.

---

921 **chit** = *chideth,* chides **halt hym yvele apayd:** considers himself ill-used (*halt* = *holdeth,* holds)
922 **long on:** owing to
926 **tempred:** mixed
929 **so thee'ch** = *so thee ich,* as I may prosper
930 **wheron it was long:** what caused it
934 **crased:** cracked
935 **amased:** dismayed
938 **mullok:** rubbish **ysweped:** swept
939 **canevas:** canvas
941 **ypiked:** picked through, sorted
944 **myshapped have:** may have turned out badly

952 **plite:** condition
953 **wite:** blame
964 **at eye:** to look at
Explicit, *etc.*: Here ends the first part.
Et sequitur, *etc.*: Here follows the second part.
972 **chanoun of religioun:** a canon regular (not a secular canon of a cathedral or large church)
980 **hym so wynde:** so wrap himself
981 **sly a kynde:** expert a manner
982 **commune:** have conversation with
983 **doten:** behave foolishly
989 **governaunce:** behavior

And if yow list to yeve me audience,   990
I wol it tellen heere in youre presence.
    But worshipful chanons religious,
Ne demeth nat that I sclaundre youre hous,
Although that my tale of a chanoun bee.
Of every ordre som shrewe is, pardee,   995
And God forbede that al a compaignye
Sholde rewe o singuleer mannes folye.
To sclaundre yow is no thyng myn entente,
But to correcten that is mys I mente.
This tale was nat oonly toold for yow,   1000
But eek for othere mo; ye woot wel how
That among Cristes apostelles twelve
Ther nas no traytour but Judas hymselve.
Thanne why sholde al the remenant have a
        blame
That giltlees were? By yow I seye the same,
Save oonly this, if ye wol herkne me: 1006
If any Judas in youre covent be,
Remoeveth hym bitymes, I yow rede,
If shame or los may causen any drede.
And beeth no thyng displesed, I yow preye,
But in this cas herkneth what I shal seye.   1011
    In Londoun was a preest, an annueleer,
That therinne dwelled hadde many a yeer,
Which was so plesaunt and so servysable
Unto the wyf, where as he was at table,   1015
That she wolde suffre hym no thyng for to paye
For bord ne clothyng, wente he never so gaye,
And spendyng silver hadde he right ynow.
Therof no fors; I wol procede as now,
And telle forth my tale of the chanoun   1020
That broghte this preest to confusioun.
    This false chanon cam upon a day
Unto this preestes chambre, wher he lay,
Bisechynge hym to lene hym a certeyn
Of gold, and he wolde quite it hym ageyn.   1025
"Leene me a marc," quod he, "but dayes three,
And at my day I wol it quiten thee.
And if so be that thow me fynde fals,
Another day do hange me by the hals!"
    This preest hym took a marc, and that as
        swithe,   1030
And this chanoun hym thanked ofte sithe,
And took his leve, and wente forth his weye,

And at the thridde day broghte his moneye,
And to the preest he took his gold agayn,
Wherof this preest was wonder glad and
        fayn.   1035
    "Certes," quod he, "no thyng anoyeth me
To lene a man a noble, or two, or thre,
Or what thyng were in my possessioun,
Whan he so trewe is of condicioun
That in no wise he breke wole his day;   1040
To swich a man I kan never seye nay."
    "What!" quod this chanoun, "sholde I be
        untrewe?
Nay, that were thyng yfallen al of newe.
Trouthe is a thyng that I wol evere kepe
Unto that day in which that I shal crepe   1045
Into my grave, and ellis God forbede.
Bileveth this as siker as your Crede.
God thanke I, and in good tyme be it sayd,
That ther was nevere man yet yvele apayd
For gold ne silver that he to me lente,   1050
Ne nevere falshede in myn herte I mente.
And sire," quod he, "now of my pryvetee,
Syn ye so goodlich han been unto me,
And kithed to me so greet gentillesse,
Somwhat to quyte with youre kyndenesse   1055
I wol yow shewe, and if yow list to leere,
I wol yow teche pleynly the manere
How I kan werken in philosophie.
Taketh good heede; ye shul wel seen at ye
That I wol doon a maistrie er I go."   1060
    "Ye," quod the preest, "ye, sire, and wol
        ye so?
Marie, therof I pray yow hertely."
    "At youre comandement, sire, trewely,"
Quod the chanoun, "and ellis God forbeede!"
    Loo, how this theef koude his service beede!
Ful sooth it is that swich profred servyse   1066
Stynketh, as witnessen thise olde wyse,
And that ful soone I wol it verifie
In this chanoun, roote of al trecherie,   1069
That everemoore delit hath and gladnesse —
Swiche feendly thoghtes in his herte impresse —
How Cristes peple he may to meschief brynge.
God kepe us from his false dissymulynge!

---

997 **singuleer:** individual
999 **mys:** amiss
1005 **By:** concerning
1012 **annueleer:** chantry priest, who sings masses for the dead
1014 **plesaunt:** pleasing **servysable:** willing to serve, attentive
1017 **wente he never so gaye:** however well he dressed
1024 **a certeyn:** a certain amount
1026 **marc:** mark, two-thirds of a pound
1029 **hals:** neck
1030 **as swithe:** immediately

1034 **took . . . agayn:** gave back
1040 **breke . . . his day:** fail to pay on the day he promised
1043 **al of newe:** for the first time
1048 **in good tyme be it sayd:** fortunately it may be said
1054 **kithed:** shown
1055 **to quyte with:** with which to requite
1058 **philosophie:** alchemy
1060 **doon a maistrie:** perform a wonderful work requiring great knowledge
1062 **Marie:** by St. Mary
1066 **profred servyse:** favors not asked for

Noght wiste this preest with whom that he
   delte,
Ne of his harm comynge he no thyng felte.
O sely preest! O sely innocent!   1076
With coveitise anon thou shalt be blent!
O gracelees, ful blynd is thy conceite,
No thyng ne artow war of the deceite
Which that this fox yshapen hath to thee!   1080
His wily wrenches thou ne mayst nat flee.
Wherfore, to go to the conclusion,
That refereth to thy confusion,
Unhappy man, anon I wol me hye
To tellen thyn unwit and thy folye,   1085
And eek the falsnesse of that oother wrecche,
As ferforth as that my konnyng wol strecche.

   This chanon was my lord, ye wolden weene?
Sire hoost, in feith, and by the hevenes queene,
It was another chanoun, and nat hee,   1090
That kan an hundred foold moore subtiltee.
He hath bitrayed folkes many tyme;
Of his falsnesse it dulleth me to ryme.
Evere whan that I speke of his falshede,
For shame of hym my chekes wexen rede.   1095
Algates they bigynnen for to glowe,
For reednesse have I noon, right wel I knowe,
In my visage; for fumes diverse
Of metals, whiche ye han herd me reherce,
Consumed and wasted han my reednesse.   1100
Now taak heede of this chanons cursednesse!

   "Sire," quod he to the preest, "lat youre man
   gon
For quyksilver, that we it hadde anon;
And lat hym bryngen ounces two or three;
And whan he comth, as faste shal ye see   1105
A wonder thyng, which ye saugh nevere er
   this."

   "Sire," quod the preest, "it shal be doon,
   ywis."
He bad his servant fecchen hym this thyng,
And he al redy was at his biddyng,
And wente hym forth, and cam anon agayn
With this quyksilver, shortly for to sayn,   1111
And took thise ounces thre to the chanoun;
And he hem leyde faire and wel adoun,
And bad the servant coles for to brynge,
That he anon myghte go to his werkynge.   1115

The coles right anon weren yfet,
And this chanoun took out a crosselet
Of his bosom, and shewed it to the preest.
"This instrument," quod he, "which that thou
   seest,   1119
Taak in thyn hand, and put thyself therinne
Of this quyksilver an ounce, and heer bigynne,
In name of Crist, to wexe a philosofre.
Ther been ful fewe to whiche I wolde profre
To shewen hem thus muche of my science.
For ye shul seen heer, by experience,   1125
That this quyksilver I wol mortifye
Right in youre sighte anon, withouten lye,
And make it as good silver and as fyn
As ther is any in youre purs or myn,
Or elleswhere, and make it malliable;   1130
And elles holdeth me fals and unable
Amonges folk for evere to appeere.
I have a poudre heer, that coste me deere,
Shal make al good, for it is cause of al   1134
My konnyng, which that I yow shewen shal.
Voyde youre man, and lat hym be theroute,
And shette the dore, whils we been aboute
Oure pryvetee, that no man us espie,
Whils that we werke in this philosophie."

   Al as he bad fulfilled was in dede.   1140
This ilke servant anonright out yede,
And his maister shette the dore anon,
And to hire labour spedily they gon.

   This preest, at this cursed chanons biddyng,
Upon the fir anon sette this thyng,   1145
And blew the fir, and bisyed hym ful faste.
And this chanoun into the crosselet caste
A poudre, noot I wherof that it was
Ymaad, outher of chalk, outher of glas,
Or somwhat elles, was nat worth a flye,   1150
To blynde with this preest; and bad hym hye
The coles for to couchen al above
The crosselet. "For in tokenyng I thee love,"
Quod this chanoun, "thyne owene handes two
Shul werche al thyng which that shal heer
   be do."   1155

   "Graunt mercy," quod the preest, and was
   ful glad,
And couched coles as the chanoun bad.
And while he bisy was, this feendly wrecche,

1077 **blent:** blinded, tricked
1078 **gracelees:** lacking (God's) favor, unfortunate   **conceite:**
mind
1081 **wrenches:** tricks
1083 **refereth:** applies
1084 **Unhappy:** unfortunate
1085 **unwit:** lack of prudence
1088 **weene:** suppose (this)
1096 **Algates:** at least

1117 **crosselet:** crucible
1126 **mortifye:** harden, make nonvolatile
1131 **unable:** worthless
1136 **Voyde:** send away
1152 **couchen:** arrange
1153 **in tokenyng:** as a sign that
1156 **Graunt mercy:** many thanks

This false chanoun — the foule feend hym
    fecche! —
Out of his bosom took a bechen cole,   1160
In which ful subtilly was maad an hole,
And therinne put was of silver lemaille
An ounce, and stopped was, withouten faille,
This hole with wex, to kepe the lemaille in.
And understondeth that this false gyn   1165
Was nat maad ther, but it was maad bifore;
And othere thynges I shal tellen moore
Herafterward, whiche that he with hym
    broghte.
Er he cam there, hym to bigile he thoghte,
And so he dide, er that they wente atwynne;
Til he had terved hym, koude he nat blynne.
It dulleth me whan that I of hym speke.   1172
On his falshede fayn wolde I me wreke,
If I wiste how, but he is heere and there;
He is so variaunt, he abit nowhere.   1175

   But taketh heede now, sires, for Goddes love!
He took his cole of which I spak above,
And in his hand he baar it pryvely.
And whiles the preest couched bisily
The coles, as I tolde yow er this,   1180
This chanoun seyde, "Freend, ye doon amys.
This is nat couched as it oghte be;
But soone I shal amenden it," quod he.
"Now lat me medle therwith but a while,
For of yow have I pitee, by Seint Gile!   1185
Ye been right hoot; I se wel how ye swete.
Have heere a clooth, and wipe awey the wete."
And whiles that the preest wiped his face,
This chanoun took his cole — with sory
    grace! —
And leyde it above upon the myddeward   1190
Of the crosselet, and blew wel afterward
Til that the coles gonne faste brenne.
   "Now yeve us drynke," quod the chanoun
    thenne;
"As swithe al shal be wel, I undertake.
Sitte we doun, and lat us myrie make."   1195
And whan that this chanounes bechen cole
Was brent, al the lemaille out of the hole
Into the crosselet fil anon adoun;
And so it moste nedes, by resoun,
Syn it so evene above couched was.   1200

But therof wiste the preest nothyng, alas!
He demed alle the coles yliche good,
For of that sleighte he nothyng understood.
And whan this alkamystre saugh his tyme,
"Ris up," quod he, "sire preest, and stondeth
    by me;   1205
And for I woot wel ingot have ye noon,
Gooth, walketh forth, and bryngeth a chalk
    stoon;
For I wol make it of the same shap
That is an ingot, if I may han hap.
And bryngeth eek with yow a bolle or a panne
Ful of water, and ye shul se wel thanne   1211
How that oure bisynesse shal thryve and
    preeve.
And yet, for ye shul han no mysbileeve
Ne wrong conceite of me in youre absence,
I ne wol nat been out of youre presence,   1215
But go with yow and come with yow ageyn."
The chambre dore, shortly for to seyn,
They opened and shette, and wente hir weye.
And forth with hem they carieden the keye,
And coome agayn withouten any delay.   1220
What sholde I tarien al the longe day?
He took the chalk and shoop it in the wise
Of an ingot, as I shal yow devyse.

   I seye, he took out of his owene sleeve   1224
A teyne of silver — yvele moot he cheeve! —
Which that ne was nat but an ounce of weighte.
And taaketh heede now of his cursed sleighte!

   He shoop his ingot in lengthe and in breede
Of this teyne, withouten any drede,
So slyly that the preest it nat espide,   1230
And in his sleve agayn he gan it hide,
And fro the fir he took up his mateere,
And in th'yngot putte it with myrie cheere,
And in the water-vessel he it caste,
Whan that hym luste, and bad the preest as
    faste,   1235
"Loke what ther is; put in thyn hand and grope.
Thow fynde shalt ther silver, as I hope."
What, devel of helle, sholde it elles be?
Shaving of silver silver is, pardee!
He putte his hand in and took up a teyne   1240
Of silver fyn, and glad in every veyne
Was this preest, whan he saugh it was so.
"Goddes blessyng, and his moodres also,

1160 **bechen cole:** charcoal made of beechwood
1162 **lemaille:** metal filings
1165 **gyn:** contrivance
1170 **atwynne:** apart
1171 **terved:** skinned (robbed him of everything) **blynne:** cease
1175 **variaunt:** changeable **abit** = *abideth,* remains
1179 **couched:** arranged
1189 **with sory grace!:** bad luck to him!
1190 **myddeward:** middle

1204 **alkamystre:** alchemist
1210 **bolle:** bowl
1212 **preeve:** succeed
1213 **mysbileeve:** skepticism
1214 **conceite:** opinion
1225 **teyne:** small metal rod **cheeve:** fare
1228 **breede:** breadth

And alle halwes, have ye, sire chanoun,"
Seyde the preest, "and I hir malisoun,   1245
But, and ye vouche-sauf to techen me
This noble craft and this subtilitee,
I wol be youre in al that evere I may."
  Quod the chanoun, "Yet wol I make assay
The seconde tyme, that ye may taken heede
And been expert of this, and in youre neede
Another day assaye in myn absence   1252
This disciplyne and this crafty science.
Lat take another ounce," quod he tho,
"Of quyksilver, withouten wordes mo,   1255
And do therwith as ye han doon er this
With that oother, which that now silver is."
  This preest hym bisieth in al that he kan
To doon as this chanoun, this cursed man,
Comanded hym, and faste blew the fir,   1260
For to come to th'effect of his desir.
And this chanon, right in the meene while,
Al redy was this preest eft to bigile,
And for a contenaunce in his hand he bar
An holwe stikke — taak kep and be war! —   1265
In the ende of which an ounce, and namoore,
Of silver lemaille put was, as bifore
Was in his cole, and stopped with wex weel
For to kepe in his lemaille every deel.
And whil this preest was in his bisynesse,   1270
This chanoun with his stikke gan hym dresse
To hym anon, and his poudre caste in
As he dide er — the devel out of his skyn
Hym terve, I pray to God, for his falshede!
For he was evere fals in thoght and dede —
And with this stikke, above the crosselet,   1276
That was ordeyned with that false jet,
He stired the coles til relente gan
The wex agayn the fir, as every man,
But it a fool be, woot wel it moot nede,   1280
And al that in the stikke was out yede,
And in the crosselet hastily it fel.
  Now, good sires, what wol ye bet than wel?
Whan that this preest thus was bigiled ageyn,
Supposynge noght but treuthe, sooth to seyn,
He was so glad that I kan nat expresse   1286
In no manere his myrthe and his gladnesse;
And to the chanoun he profred eftsoone
Body and good. "Ye," quod the chanoun soone,

"Though poure I be, crafty thou shalt me fynde.
I warne thee, yet is ther moore bihynde.   1291
Is ther any coper herinne?" seyde he.
  "Ye," quod the preest, "sire, I trowe wel ther
        be."
  "Elles go bye us som, and that as swithe;
Now, goode sire, go forth thy wey and hy
        the."   1295
  He wente his wey, and with the coper cam,
And this chanon it in his handes nam,
And of that coper weyed out but an ounce.
  Al to symple is my tonge to pronounce,
As ministre of my wit, the doublenesse   1300
Of this chanoun, roote of alle cursednesse!
He semed freendly to hem that knewe hym
        noght,
But he was feendly bothe in werk and thoght.
It weerieth me to telle of his falsnesse,
And nathelees yet wol I it expresse,   1305
To th'entente that men may be war therby,
And for noon oother cause, trewely.
  He putte this ounce of coper in the crosselet,
And on the fir as swithe he hath it set,
And caste in poudre, and made the preest to
        blowe,   1310
And in his werkyng for to stoupe lowe,
As he dide er — and al nas but a jape;
Right as hym liste, the preest he made his ape!
And afterward in the ingot he it caste,
And in the panne putte it at the laste   1315
Of water, and in he putte his owene hand,
And in his sleve (as ye biforen-hand
Herde me telle) he hadde a silver teyne.
He slyly took it out, this cursed heyne,
Unwityng this preest of his false craft,   1320
And in the pannes botme he hath it laft;
And in the water rombled to and fro,
And wonder pryvely took up also
The coper teyne, noght knowynge this preest,
And hidde it, and hym hente by the breest,
And to hym spak, and thus seyde in his
        game: 1326
"Stoupeth adoun. By God, ye be to blame!
Helpeth me now, as I dide yow whileer;
Putte in youre hand, and looketh what is theer."

1244 **halwes:** saints'
1245 **malisoun:** curse
1265 **holwe:** hollow
1271 **hym dresse:** address himself, go
1274 **terve:** skin, flay
1277 **ordeyned:** prepared   **jet:** contrivance
1278 **relente:** soften, melt
1281 **yede:** went

1297 **nam:** took
1300 **doublenesse:** duplicity
1304 **weerieth:** wearies, tires
1313 **ape:** dupe
1319 **heyne:** wretch
1320 **Unwityng . . . of:** ignorant of
1322 **rombled:** groped noisily about
1327 **to blame:** blameworthy
1328 **whileer:** just now

This preest took up this silver teyne anon, 1330
And thanne seyde the chanoun, "Lat us gon
With thise thre teynes, whiche that we han wroght,
To som goldsmyth and wite if they been oght,
For, by my feith, I nolde, for myn hood,
But if that they were silver fyn and good, 1335
And that as swithe preeved it shal bee."

Unto the goldsmyth with thise teynes three
They wente and putte thise teynes in assay
To fir and hamer; myghte no man seye nay,
But that they weren as hem oghte be. 1340

This sotted preest, who was gladder than he?
Was nevere brid gladder agayn the day,
Ne nyghtyngale, in the sesoun of May,
Was nevere noon that luste bet to synge;
Ne lady lustier in carolynge, 1345
Or for to speke of love and wommanhede,
Ne knyght in armes to doon an hardy dede,
To stonden in grace of his lady deere,
Than hadde this preest this soory craft to leere.
And to the chanoun thus he spak and seyde:
"For love of God, that for us alle deyde, 1351
And as I may deserve it unto yow,
What shal this receite coste? Telleth now!"

"By oure Lady," quod this chanon, "it is deere,
I warne yow wel; for save I and a frere, 1355
In Engelond ther kan no man it make."

"No fors," quod he, "now, sire, for Goddes sake,
What shal I paye? Telleth me, I preye."

"Ywis," quod he, "it is ful deere, I seye.
Sire, at o word, if that thee list it have, 1360
Ye shul paye fourty pound, so God me save!
And nere the freendshipe that ye dide er this
To me, ye sholde paye moore, ywis."

This preest the somme of fourty pound anon
Of nobles fette, and took hem everichon 1365
To this chanoun for this ilke receite.
Al his werkyng nas but fraude and deceite.

"Sire preest," he seyde, "I kepe han no loos
Of my craft, for I wolde it kept were cloos;
And, as ye love me, kepeth it secree. 1370
For, and men knewen al my soutiltee,
By God, they wolden han so greet envye

To me by cause of my philosophye
I sholde be deed; ther were noon oother weye."

"God it forbeede," quod the preest, "what sey ye? 1375
Yet hadde I levere spenden al the good
Which that I have, and elles wexe I wood,
Than that ye sholden falle in swich mescheef."

"For youre good wyl, sire, have ye right good preef," 1379
Quod the chanoun, "and farwel, grant mercy!"
He wente his wey, and never the preest hym sy
After that day; and whan that this preest shoolde
Maken assay, at swich tyme as he wolde,
Of this receit, farwel! It wolde nat be.
Lo, thus byjaped and bigiled was he! 1385
Thus maketh he his introduccioun,
To brynge folk to hir destruccioun.

Considereth, sires, how that, in ech estaat,
Bitwixe men and gold ther is debaat
So ferforth that unnethes is ther noon. 1390
This multiplying blent so many oon
That in good feith I trowe that it bee
The cause grettest of swich scarsetee.
Philosophres speken so mystily 1394
In this craft that men kan nat come therby,
For any wit that men han now-a-dayes.
They mowe wel chiteren as doon jayes,
And in hir termes sette hir lust and peyne,
But to hir purpos shul they nevere atteyne.
A man may lightly lerne, if he have aught, 1400
To multiplie, and brynge his good to naught!

Lo! swich a lucre is in this lusty game,
A mannes myrthe it wol turne unto grame,
And empten also grete and hevye purses,
And maken folk for to purchacen curses 1405
Of hem that han hir good therto ylent.
O, fy, for shame! They that han been brent,
Allas, kan they nat flee the fires heete?
Ye that it use, I rede ye it leete,
Lest ye lese al; for bet than nevere is late. 1410
Nevere to thryve were to long a date.
Though ye prolle ay, ye shul it nevere fynde.
Ye been as boold as is Bayard the blynde,
That blondreth forth and peril casteth noon.

1333 **oght:** anything, worth anything
1341 **sotted:** besotted, foolish
1342 **agayn the day:** just before dawn
1349 **soory:** wretched
1352 **deserve it unto yow:** repay you
1353 **receite:** recipe, formula
1362 **And nere:** if it were not for
1368–69 **I kepe han no loos Of:** I don't care to have fame for

1384 **receit:** recipe
1385 **byjaped:** tricked
1386 **introduccioun:** introductory gambit
1394 **mystily:** obscurely
1397 **chiteren:** chatter
1402 **lucre:** profit
1403 **grame:** sorrow
1409 **leete:** let (it) alone, abandon (it)
1411 **date:** time
1412 **prolle ay:** search or prowl forever
1414 **blondreth:** blunders **casteth:** considers, reckons

He is as boold to renne agayn a stoon　　　1415
As for to goon bisides in the weye.
So faren ye that multiplie, I seye.
If that youre eyen kan nat seen aright,
Looke that youre mynde lakke noght his sight.
For though ye looken never so brode and stare,
Ye shul nothyng wynne on that chaffare,　　1421
But wasten al that ye may rape and renne.
Withdraweth the fir, lest it to faste brenne;
Medleth namoore with that art, I mene,　　1424
For if ye doon, youre thrift is goon ful clene.
And right as swithe I wol yow tellen heere
What philosophres seyn in this mateere.
　　Lo, thus seith Arnold of the Newe Toun,
As his Rosarie maketh mencioun;
He seith right thus, withouten any lye:　　1430
"Ther may no man mercurie mortifie
But it be with his brother knowlechyng";
How [be] that he which that first seyde this thyng
Of philosophres fader was, Hermes;
He seith how that the dragon, doutelees,　　1435
Ne dyeth nat but if that he be slayn
With his brother; and that is for to sayn,
By the dragon, Mercurie, and noon oother
He understood, and brymstoon by his brother,
That out of Sol and Luna were ydrawe.　　1440
"And therfore," seyde he — taak heede to my
　　　sawe —
"Lat no man bisye hym this art for to seche,
But if that he th'entencioun and speche
Of philosophres understonde kan;
And if he do, he is a lewed man.　　1445
For this science and this konnyng," quod he,
"Is of the secree of the secretes, pardee."
　　Also ther was a disciple of Plato,

That on a tyme seyde his maister to,
As his book Senior wol bere witnesse,　　1450
And this was his demande in soothfastnesse:
"Telle me the name of the privee stoon."
　　And Plato answerde unto hym anoon,
"Take the stoon that Titanos men name."
　　"Which is that?" quod he. "Magnasia is the
　　　same,"　　1455
Seyde Plato. "Ye, sire, and is it thus?
This is *ignotum per ignocius*.
What is Magnasia, good sire, I yow preye?"
　　"It is a water that is maad, I seye,
Of elementes foure," quod Plato.　　1460
　　"Telle me the roote, good sire," quod he tho,
"Of that water, if it be youre wil."
　　"Nay, nay," quod Plato, "certein, that I nyl.
The philosophres sworn were everychoon
That they sholden discovere it unto noon,　　1465
Ne in no book it write in no manere.
For unto Crist it is so lief and deere
That he wol nat that it discovered bee,
But where it liketh to his deitee
Men for t'enspire, and eek for to deffende　　1470
Whom that hym liketh; lo, this is the ende."
　　Thanne conclude I thus, sith that God of
　　　hevene
Ne wil nat that the philosophres nevene
How that a man shal come unto this stoon,
I rede, as for the beste, lete it goon.　　1475
For whoso maketh God his adversarie,
As for to werken any thyng in contrarie
Of his wil, certes, never shal he thryve,
Thogh that he multiplie terme of his lyve.
And there a poynt, for ended is my tale.　　1480
God sende every trewe man boote of his bale!

Heere is ended the Chanouns Yemannes Tale.

1422 **rape and renne:** seize and run; see n.
1424 **mene:** say
1425 **thrift:** prosperity, welfare
1428 **Arnold of the Newe Toun:** Arnaldus of Villanova, author of the *Rosarie,* an alchemical treatise
1432 **his brother knowlechyng:** his brother's (sulphur's) help
1434 **Hermes:** Hermes Trismegistus, legendary founder of alchemy
1440 **Sol:** the sun (gold)　**Luna:** the moon (silver)

1450 **book Senior:** an alchemical treatise attributed to Senior Zadith
1454–55 **Titanos, Magnasia:** probably gypsum and magnesium oxide, but used as "cover names," intended to conceal the identity of the materials
1457 *ignotum per ignocius:* explaining the unknown by the more unknown
1470 **t'enspire:** to enlighten
1473 **nevene:** name
1477 **any thyng:** at all
1481 **boote of his bale:** remedy for his suffering

Fragment IX (Group H)

THE MANCIPLE'S PROLOGUE

Heere folweth the Prologe of the Maunciples Tale.

Woot ye nat where ther stant a litel toun
Which that ycleped is Bobbe-up-and-doun,
Under the Blee, in Caunterbury Weye?
Ther gan oure Hooste for to jape and pleye,
And seyde, "Sires, what! Dun is in the myre!
Is ther no man, for preyere ne for hyre,   6
That wole awake oure felawe al bihynde?
A theef myghte hym ful lightly robbe and
          bynde.
See how he nappeth! See how, for cokkes bones,
That he wol falle fro his hors atones!   10
Is that a cook of Londoun, with meschaunce?
Do hym come forth, he knoweth his penaunce;
For he shal telle a tale, by my fey,
Although it be nat worth a botel hey.
Awake, thou Cook," quod he, "God yeve thee
          sorwe!   15
What eyleth thee to slepe by the morwe?
Hastow had fleen al nyght, or artow dronke?
Or hastow with som quene al nyght yswonke,
So that thow mayst nat holden up thyn heed?"
    This Cook, that was ful pale and no thyng
          reed,   20
Seyde to oure Hoost, "So God my soule blesse,
As ther is falle on me swich hevynesse,
Noot I nat why, that me were levere slepe
Than the beste galon wyn in Chepe."
    "Wel," quod the Maunciple, "if it may doon
          ese   25
To thee, sire Cook, and to no wight displese,
Which that heere rideth in this compaignye,
And that oure Hoost wole, of his curteisye,
I wol as now excuse thee of thy tale.
For, in good feith, thy visage is ful pale,   30
Thyne eyen daswen eek, as that me thynketh,

And, wel I woot, thy breeth ful soure stynketh:
That sheweth wel thou art nat wel disposed.
Of me, certeyn, thou shalt nat been yglosed.
See how he ganeth, lo, this dronken wight,   35
As though he wolde swolwe us anonright.
Hoold cloos thy mouth, man, by thy fader kyn!
The devel of helle sette his foot therin!
Thy cursed breeth infecte wole us alle.
Fy, stynkyng swyn! Fy, foule moote thee falle!
A, taketh heede, sires, of this lusty man.   41
Now, sweete sire, wol ye justen atte fan?
Therto me thynketh ye been wel yshape!
I trowe that ye dronken han wyn ape,   44
And that is whan men pleyen with a straw."
And with this speche the Cook wax wrooth
          and wraw,
And on the Manciple he gan nodde faste
For lakke of speche, and doun the hors hym
          caste,
Where as he lay, til that men hym up took.
This was a fair chyvachee of a cook!   50
Allas, he nadde holde hym by his ladel!
And er that he agayn were in his sadel,
Ther was greet showvyng bothe to and fro
To lifte hym up, and muchel care and wo,
So unweeldy was this sory palled goost.   55
And to the Manciple thanne spak oure Hoost:
    "By cause drynke hath dominacioun
Upon this man, by my savacioun,
I trowe he lewedly wolde telle his tale.
For, were it wyn or oold or moysty ale   60
That he hath dronke, he speketh in his nose,
And fneseth faste, and eek he hath the pose.
    "He hath also to do moore than ynough
To kepen hym and his capul out of the slough;

---

2 **Bobbe-up-and-doun:** Harbledown, two miles from
Canterbury; see n.
3 **the Blee:** Blean Forest
5 **Dun is in the myre:** Things are at a standstill; see n.
8 **lightly:** easily
9 **nappeth:** dozes   **cokkes bones:** cock's bones (euphemism for
God's bones)
14 **botel hey:** small bundle of hay (i.e., worthless)
17 **fleen:** fleas
18 **quene:** trollop, whore
22 **hevynesse:** drowsiness
24 **galon wyn:** gallon of wine
31 **daswen:** are dazed

33 **nat wel disposed:** indisposed, unwell
35 **ganeth:** yawns
42 **justen atte fan:** joust at the quintain; see n.
44 **dronken han wyn ape:** have reached an advanced stage of
drunkenness
46 **wraw:** angry
47 **nodde:** shake his head
50 **chyvachee:** feat of horsemanship
51 **ladel:** long-handled spoon
55 **unweeldy:** feeble   **palled:** grown pale
60 **oold or moysty ale:** old or new ale; see n.
62 **fneseth:** sneezes   **pose:** head cold
64 **slough:** mud, mire

282

And if he falle from his capul eftsoone,　　65
Thanne shal we alle have ynogh to doone
In liftyng up his hevy dronken cors.
Telle on thy tale; of hym make I no fors.
　　"But yet, Manciple, in feith thou art to nyce,
Thus openly repreve hym of his vice.　　70
Another day he wole, peraventure,
Reclayme thee and brynge thee to lure;
I meene, he speke wole of smale thynges,
As for to pynchen at thy rekenynges,
That were nat honest, if it cam to preef."　　75
　　"No," quod the Manciple, "that were a greet
　　　　mescheef!
So myghte he lightly brynge me in the snare.
Yet hadde I levere payen for the mare
Which he rit on, than he sholde with me stryve.
I wol nat wratthen hym, also moot I thryve!　　80
That that I spak, I seyde it in my bourde.
And wite ye what? I have heer in a gourde
A draghte of wyn, ye, of a ripe grape,
And right anon ye shul seen a good jape.
This Cook shal drynke therof, if I may.　　85

Up peyne of deeth, he wol nat seye me nay."
　　And certeynly, to tellen as it was,
Of this vessel the Cook drank faste, allas!
What neded hym? He drank ynough biforn.
And whan he hadde pouped in this horn,　　90
To the Manciple he took the gourde agayn;
And of that drynke the Cook was wonder fayn,
And thanked hym in swich wise as he koude.
　　Thanne gan oure Hoost to laughen wonder
　　　　loude,
And seyde, "I se wel it is necessarie,　　95
Where that we goon, good drynke with us
　　　　carie;
For that wol turne rancour and disese
T'acord and love, and many a wrong apese.
　　"O Bacus, yblessed be thy name,
That so kanst turnen ernest into game!　　100
Worshipe and thank be to thy deitee!
Of that mateere ye gete namoore of me.
Telle on thy tale, Manciple, I thee preye."
　　"Wel, sire," quod he, "now herkneth what I
　　　　seye."

THE MANCIPLE'S TALE

Heere bigynneth the Maunciples Tale of the Crowe.

Whan Phebus dwelled heere in this erthe
　　adoun,　　105
As olde bookes maken mencioun,
He was the mooste lusty bachiler
In al this world, and eek the beste archer.
He slow Phitoun, the serpent, as he lay
Slepynge agayn the sonne upon a day;　　110
And many another noble worthy dede
He with his bowe wroghte, as men may rede.
　　Pleyen he koude on every mynstralcie,
And syngen that it was a melodie

To heeren of his cleere voys the soun.　　115
Certes the kyng of Thebes, Amphioun,
That with his syngyng walled that citee,
Koude nevere syngen half so wel as hee.
Therto he was the semelieste man
That is or was sith that the world bigan.　　120
What nedeth it his fetures to discryve?
For in this world was noon so faire on-lyve.
He was therwith fulfild of gentillesse,
Of honour, and of parfit worthynesse.
　　This Phebus, that was flour of bachilrie,　　125
As wel in fredom as in chivalrie,
For his desport, in signe eek of victorie
Of Phitoun, so as telleth us the storie,
Was wont to beren in his hand a bowe.　　129

---

65 **capul:** horse　**eftsoone:** again
66 **have ynogh to doone:** have our hands full
72 Recall you with a lure (as a hawk)
74 **pynchen at:** find fault with
80 **wratthen:** anger
81 **bourde:** jest
82 **gourde:** gourd-shaped flask

---

105 **Phebus:** Phoebus Apollo
109 **Phitoun:** Python; see n.
110 **agayn the sonne:** in front of or in the sun
113 **mynstralcie:** musical instrument

---

90 **pouped:** blown
91 **took . . . agayn:** gave back
98 **apese:** remedy
99 **Bacus:** Bacchus, god of wine

---

125 **bachilrie:** knighthood

Now hadde this Phebus in his hous a crowe
Which in a cage he fostred many a day,
And taughte it speken, as men teche a jay.
Whit was this crowe as is a snow-whit swan,
And countrefete the speche of every man
He koude, whan he sholde telle a tale.   135
Therwith in al this world no nyghtyngale
Ne koude, by an hondred thousand deel,
Syngen so wonder myrily and weel.
    Now hadde this Phebus in his hous a wyf
Which that he lovede moore than his lyf,   140
And nyght and day dide evere his diligence
Hir for to plese and doon hire reverence,
Save oonly, if the sothe that I shal sayn,
Jalous he was, and wolde have kept hire fayn.
For hym were looth byjaped for to be,   145
And so is every wight in swich degree;
But al in ydel, for it availleth noght.
A good wyf, that is clene of werk and thoght,
Sholde nat been kept in noon awayt, certayn;
And trewely the labour is in vayn   150
To kepe a shrewe, for it wol nat bee.
This holde I for a verray nycetee,
To spille labour for to kepe wyves:
Thus writen olde clerkes in hir lyves.
    But now to purpos, as I first bigan: 155
This worthy Phebus dooth al that he kan
To plesen hire, wenynge for swich plesaunce,
And for his manhede and his governaunce,
That no man sholde han put hym from hir
            grace.
But God it woot, ther may no man embrace
As to destreyne a thyng which that nature   161
Hath natureelly set in a creature.
    Taak any bryd, and put it in a cage,
And do al thyn entente and thy corage
To fostre it tendrely with mete and drynke   165
Of alle deyntees that thou kanst bithynke,
And keep it al so clenly as thou may,
Although his cage of gold be never so gay,
Yet hath this brid, by twenty thousand foold,
Levere in a forest that is rude and coold   170
Goon ete wormes and swich wrecchednesse.
For evere this brid wol doon his bisynesse
To escape out of his cage, yif he may.
His libertee this brid desireth ay.   174

Lat take a cat, and fostre hym wel with milk
And tendre flessh, and make his couche of
            silk,
And lat hym seen a mous go by the wal,
Anon he weyveth milk and flessh and al,
And every deyntee that is in that hous,
Swich appetit hath he to ete a mous.   180
Lo, heere hath lust his dominacioun,
And appetit fleemeth discrecioun.
    A she-wolf hath also a vileyns kynde.
The lewedeste wolf that she may fynde,
Or leest of reputacioun, wol she take,   185
In tyme whan hir lust to han a make.
    Alle thise ensamples speke I by thise men
That been untrewe, and nothyng by wommen.
For men han evere a likerous appetit
On lower thyng to parfourne hire delit   190
Than on hire wyves, be they never so faire,
Ne never so trewe, ne so debonaire.
Flessh is so newefangel, with meschaunce,
That we ne konne in nothyng han plesaunce
That sowneth into vertu any while.   195
    This Phebus, which that thoghte upon no
            gile,
Deceyved was, for al his jolitee.
For under hym another hadde shee,
A man of litel reputacioun,
Nat worth to Phebus in comparisoun.   200
The moore harm is, it happeth ofte so,
Of which ther cometh muchel harm and wo.
    And so bifel, whan Phebus was absent,
His wyf anon hath for hir lemman sent.   204
Hir lemman? Certes, this is a knavyssh speche!
Foryeveth it me, and that I yow biseche.
    The wise Plato seith, as ye may rede,
The word moot nede accorde with the dede.
If men shal telle proprely a thyng,
The word moot cosyn be to the werkyng.   210
I am a boystous man, right thus seye I:
Ther nys no difference, trewely,
Bitwixe a wyf that is of heigh degree,
If of hir body dishonest she bee,
And a povre wenche, oother than this —   215

139 **wyf:** woman
145 **byjaped:** tricked
149 **kept in . . . awayt:** watched suspiciously
158 **manhede:** qualities of a good man   **governaunce:** behavior
161 **destreyne:** restrain
164 And give all your attention, take all pains
166 **bithynke:** imagine
167 **clenly:** carefully
169–170 **hath Levere:** would rather be

175 **Lat take:** assume that one takes
178 **weyveth:** refuses
182 **fleemeth:** drives out
183 **vileyns:** churlish, evil
193 **newefangel:** fond of novelty
195 **sowneth into:** tends toward, is conducive to
197 **jolitee:** attractiveness
198 **under:** in addition to
204 **lemman:** lover
205 **knavyssh:** churlish
211 **boystous:** plain
214 **dishonest:** unchaste
215 **wenche:** low-class woman

If it so be they werke bothe amys —
But that the gentile, in estaat above,
She shal be cleped his lady, as in love;
And for that oother is a povre womman,   219
She shal be cleped his wenche or his lemman.
And, God it woot, myn owene deere brother,
Men leyn that oon as lowe as lith that oother.

    Right so bitwixe a titlelees tiraunt
And an outlawe or a theef erraunt,
The same I seye: ther is no difference.   225
To Alisaundre was toold this sentence,
That, for the tirant is of gretter myght
By force of meynee for to sleen dounright,
And brennen hous and hoom, and make al
        playn,
Lo, therfore is he cleped a capitayn;   230
And for the outlawe hath but smal meynee,
And may nat doon so greet an harm as he,
Ne brynge a contree to so greet mescheef,
Men clepen hym an outlawe or a theef.
But for I am a man noght textueel,   235
I wol noght telle of textes never a deel;
I wol go to my tale, as I bigan.
Whan Phebus wyf had sent for hir lemman,
Anon they wroghten al hire lust volage.   239
    The white crowe, that heeng ay in the cage,
Biheeld hire werk, and seyde never a word.
And whan that hoom was come Phebus, the
        lord,
This crowe sang "Cokkow! Cokkow! Cokkow!"
    "What, bryd?" quod Phebus. "What song
        syngestow?
Ne were thow wont so myrily to synge   245
That to myn herte it was a rejoysynge
To heere thy voys? Allas, what song is this?"
    "By God," quod he, "I synge nat amys.
Phebus," quod he, "for al thy worthynesse,
For al thy beautee and thy gentilesse,   250
For al thy song and al thy mynstralcye,
For al thy waityng, blered is thyn ye
With oon of litel reputacioun,
Noght worth to thee, as in comparisoun,   254
The montance of a gnat, so moote I thryve!
For on thy bed thy wyf I saugh hym swyve."
    What wol ye moore? The crowe anon hym
        tolde,

By sadde tokenes and by wordes bolde,
How that his wyf had doon hire lecherye,
Hym to greet shame and to greet vileynye,   260
And tolde hym ofte he saugh it with his yen.
    This Phebus gan aweyward for to wryen,
And thoughte his sorweful herte brast atwo.
His bowe he bente, and sette therinne a flo,
And in his ire his wyf thanne hath he slayn.
This is th'effect; ther is namoore to sayn;   266
For sorwe of which he brak his mynstralcie,
Bothe harpe, and lute, and gyterne, and sautrie;
And eek he brak his arwes and his bowe,
And after that thus spak he to the crowe: 270
    "Traitour," quod he, "with tonge of scor-
        pioun,
Thou hast me broght to my confusioun;
Allas, that I was wroght! Why nere I deed?
O deere wyf! O gemme of lustiheed!
That were to me so sad and eek so trewe,   275
Now listow deed, with face pale of hewe,
Ful giltelees, that dorste I swere, ywys!
O rakel hand, to doon so foule amys!
O trouble wit, O ire recchelees,
That unavysed smyteth gilteles!   280
O wantrust, ful of fals suspecion,
Where was thy wit and thy discrecion?
O every man, be war of rakelnesse!
Ne trowe no thyng withouten strong witnesse.
Smyt nat to soone, er that ye witen why,   285
And beeth avysed wel and sobrely
Er ye doon any execucion
Upon youre ire for suspecion.
Allas, a thousand folk hath rakel ire
Fully fordoon, and broght hem in the mire.
Allas! For sorwe I wol myselven slee!"   291
    And to the crowe, "O false theef!" seyde he,
"I wol thee quite anon thy false tale.
Thou songe whilom lyk a nyghtyngale;
Now shaltow, false theef, thy song forgon,   295
And eek thy white fetheres everichon,
Ne nevere in al thy lif ne shaltou speke.
Thus shal men on a traytour been awreke;
Thou and thyn ofspryng evere shul be blake,

258 **sadde tokenes:** strong confirmatory details, proofs
262 **wryen:** turn, go
264 **flo:** arrow
268 **gyterne:** cithern   **sautrie:** psaltry, a lute-like instrument
274 **lustiheed:** delight
275 **sad:** stable
278 **rakel:** rash, hasty
280 **unavysed:** recklessly
281 **wantrust:** distrust
283 **rakelnesse:** rashness, haste
290 **fordoon:** undone
295 **forgon:** lose
298 **awreke:** avenged

228 **force of meynee:** power of his retinue, size of his army
235 **textueel:** learned in authoritative texts
239 **volage:** flighty, foolish
243 **Cokkow:** cuckoo (i.e., you are a cuckold)
246 **rejoysynge:** joy
252 **blered is thyn ye:** you have been tricked, deluded
255 **montance:** value
256 **swyve:** copulate with

Ne nevere sweete noyse shul ye make,   300
But evere crie agayn tempest and rayn,
In tokenynge that thurgh thee my wyf is slayn."
And to the crowe he stirte, and that anon,
And pulled his white fetheres everychon,   304
And made hym blak, and refte hym al his song,
And eek his speche, and out at dore hym slong
Unto the devel, which I hym bitake;
And for this caas been alle crowes blake.

Lordynges, by this ensample I yow preye,
Beth war, and taketh kep what that ye seye:
Ne telleth nevere no man in youre lyf   311
How that another man hath dight his wyf;
He wol yow haten mortally, certeyn.
Daun Salomon, as wise clerkes seyn,
Techeth a man to kepen his tonge weel.   315
But, as I seyde, I am noght textueel.
But nathelees, thus taughte me my dame:
"My sone, thenk on the crowe, a Goddes name!
My sone, keep wel thy tonge, and keep thy
        freend.
A wikked tonge is worse than a feend;   320
My sone, from a feend men may hem blesse.
My sone, God of his endelees goodnesse
Walled a tonge with teeth and lippes eke,
For man sholde hym avyse what he speeke.
My sone, ful ofte, for to muche speche   325
Hath many a man been spilt, as clerkes teche,
But for litel speche avysely
Is no man shent, to speke generally.
My sone, thy tonge sholdestow restreyne   329
At alle tymes, but whan thou doost thy peyne
To speke of God, in honour and preyere.
The firste vertu, sone, if thou wolt leere,
Is to restreyne and kepe wel thy tonge;
Thus lerne children whan that they been yonge.
My sone, of muchel spekyng yvele avysed,   335
Ther lasse spekyng hadde ynough suffised,
Comth muchel harm; thus was me toold and
        taught.
In muchel speche synne wanteth naught.
Wostow wherof a rakel tonge serveth?
Right as a swerd forkutteth and forkerveth   340
An arm a-two, my deere sone, right so
A tonge kutteth freendshipe al a-two.
A jangler is to God abhomynable.
Reed Salomon, so wys and honurable;
Reed David in his psalmes; reed Senekke.   345
My sone, spek nat, but with thyn heed thou
        bekke.
Dissimule as thou were deef, if that thou heere
A janglere speke of perilous mateere.
The Flemyng seith, and lerne it if thee leste,
That litel janglyng causeth muchel reste.   350
My sone, if thou no wikked word hast seyd,
Thee thar nat drede for to be biwreyd;
But he that hath mysseyd, I dar wel sayn,
He may by no wey clepe his word agayn.   354
Thyng that is seyd is seyd, and forth it gooth,
Though hym repente, or be hym nevere so
        looth.
He is his thral to whom that he hath sayd
A tale of which he is now yvele apayd.
My sone, be war, and be noon auctour newe
Of tidynges, wheither they been false or trewe.
Whereso thou come, amonges hye or lowe,   361
Kepe wel thy tonge and thenk upon the
        crowe."

Heere is ended the Maunciples Tale of the Crowe.

---

302 **In tokenynge:** as a sign
304 **pulled:** plucked
305 **refte:** took away
306 **slong:** slung, threw
307 **bitake:** commit
312 **dight:** had sexual intercourse with
316 **textueel:** learned in texts
319 **keep wel thy tonge:** hold your tongue
327 **avysely:** discreetly

335 **yvele avysed:** ill-considered
338 **wanteth naught:** is not lacking
339 **rakel:** rash
340 **forkutteth and forkerveth:** cuts and hews to pieces
343 **jangler:** chatterer
345 **Senekke:** Seneca
346 **bekke:** nod
347 **Dissimule as:** pretend
359 **auctour:** author

Fragment X (Group I)

THE PARSON'S PROLOGUE

Heere folweth the Prologe of the Persouns Tale.

By that the Maunciple hadde his tale al
    ended,
The sonne fro the south lyne was descended
So lowe that he nas nat, to my sighte,
Degreës nyne and twenty as in highte.
Foure of the clokke it was tho, as I gesse,   5
For ellevene foot, or litel moore or lesse,
My shadwe was at thilke tyme, as there
Of swiche feet as my lengthe parted were
In sixe feet equal of proporcioun.
Therwith the moones exaltacioun —   10
I meene Libra — alwey gan ascende
As we were entryng at a thropes ende;
For which oure Hoost, as he was wont to gye,
As in this caas, oure joly compaignye,
Seyde in this wise: "Lordynges everichoon,   15
Now lakketh us no tales mo than oon.
Fulfilled is my sentence and my decree;
I trowe that we han herd of ech degree;
Almoost fulfild is al myn ordinaunce.
I pray to God, so yeve hym right good chaunce,
That telleth this tale to us lustily.   21
   "Sire preest," quod he, "artow a vicary?
Or arte a person? Sey sooth, by thy fey!
Be what thou be, ne breke thou nat oure pley;
For every man, save thou, hath toold his
    tale.   25
Unbokele and shewe us what is in thy male;
For trewely, me thynketh by thy cheere
Thou sholdest knytte up wel a greet mateere.
Telle us a fable anon, for cokkes bones!"
   This Persoun answerde, al atones,   30
"Thou getest fable noon ytoold for me,
For Paul, that writeth unto Thymothee,
Repreveth hem that weyven soothfastnesse

And tellen fables and swich wrecchednesse.
Why sholde I sowen draf out of my fest,   35
Whan I may sowen whete, if that me lest?
For which I seye, if that yow list to heere
Moralitee and vertuous mateere,
And thanne that ye wol yeve me audience,
I wol ful fayn, at Cristes reverence,   40
Do yow plesaunce leefful, as I kan.
But trusteth wel, I am a Southren man;
I kan nat geeste 'rum, ram, ruf,' by lettre,
Ne, God woot, rym holde I but litel bettre;
And therfore, if yow list — I wol nat glose —
I wol yow telle a myrie tale in prose   46
To knytte up al this feeste and make an ende.
And Jhesu, for his grace, wit me sende
To shewe yow the wey, in this viage,
Of thilke parfit glorious pilgrymage   50
That highte Jerusalem celestial.
And if ye vouche sauf, anon I shal
Bigynne upon my tale, for which I preye
Telle youre avys; I kan no bettre seye.
   "But nathelees, this meditacioun   55
I putte it ay under correccioun
Of clerkes, for I am nat textueel;
I take but the sentence, trusteth weel.
Therfore I make protestacioun
That I wol stonde to correccioun."   60
   Upon this word we han assented soone,
For, as it seemed, it was for to doone —
To enden in som vertuous sentence,
And for to yeve hym space and audience,
And bade oure Hoost he sholde to hym seye   65
That alle we to telle his tale hym preye.
   Oure Hoost hadde the wordes for us alle;
"Sire preest," quod he, "now faire yow bifalle!

3 **to my sighte:** from my point of view
7 **as there:** in that place
10 **exaltacioun:** zodiacal sign in which a planet has its strongest
influence
12 **thropes ende:** the edge of a village
22 **vicary:** vicar
24 **breke . . . oure pley:** spoil our game
26 **Unbokele:** unbuckle, open up **in thy male:** i.e., what you
have to tell
28 **knytte up:** conclude
29 **cokkes bones:** cock's bones (euphemism for God's bones)
33 **weyven:** turn aside from

35 **draf:** chaff
39 **that:** if
41 **leefful:** lawful, legitimate
42 **Southren:** That is, not from the north, where much
alliterative poetry was written
43 **geeste . . . by lettre:** tell a story in alliterative verse; see n.
57 **textueel:** learned in authoritative texts
58 **sentence:** substance, essential meaning
64 **space:** time
67 **hadde the wordes for us alle:** was our spokesman
68 **faire yow bifalle:** good luck to you

Telleth," quod he, "youre meditacioun.
But hasteth yow; the sonne wole adoun;   70
Beth fructuous, and that in litel space,

And to do wel God sende yow his grace!
Sey what yow list, and we wol gladly heere."
And with that word he seyde in this manere.

Explicit prohemium.

THE PARSON'S TALE

Heere bigynneth the Persouns Tale.

Jer. 6°. State super vias, et videte, et inter-
rogate de viis antiquis que sit via bona, et am-
bulate in ea; et invenietis refrigerium animabus
vestris, etc.

Oure sweete Lord God of hevene, that no
man wole perisse but wole that we comen alle
to the knoweleche of hym and to the blisful lif that is perdurable,/ amonesteth us   75
by the prophete Jeremie, that seith in thys
wyse:/ "Stondeth upon the weyes, and seeth
and axeth of olde pathes (that is to seyn, of olde
sentences) which is the goode wey,/ and walketh in that wey, and ye shal fynde refresshynge
for youre soules, etc."/ Manye been the weyes
espirituels that leden folk to oure Lord Jhesu
Crist and to the regne of glorie./ Of whiche
weyes ther is a ful noble wey and a ful covenable, which may nat fayle to man ne to womman that thurgh synne hath mysgoon fro
the righte wey of Jerusalem celestial;/ and   80
this wey is cleped Penitence, of which man
sholde gladly herknen and enquere with al
his herte/ to wyten what is Penitence, and
whennes it is cleped Penitence, and in how
manye maneres been the acciouns or werkynges of Penitence,/ and how manye speces
ther been of Penitence, and whiche thynges
apertenen and bihoven to Penitence, and
whiche thynges destourben Penitence./

Seint Ambrose seith that Penitence is the
pleynynge of man for the gilt that he hath
doon, and namoore to do any thyng for which

hym oghte to pleyne./ And som doctour seith,
"Penitence is the waymentynge of man that
sorweth for his synne and pyneth hymself for he hath mysdoon."/ Penitence,   85
with certeyne circumstances, is verray repentance of a man that halt hymself in sorwe
and oother peyne for his giltes./ And for he
shal be verray penitent, he shal first biwaylen
the synnes that he hath doon, and stidefastly
purposen in his herte to have shrift of mouthe,
and to doon satisfaccioun,/ and nevere to doon
thyng for which hym oghte moore to biwayle
or to compleyne, and to continue in goode
werkes, or elles his repentance may nat availle./
For, as seith Seint Ysidre, "He is a japere and
a gabbere and no verray repentant that eftsoone dooth thyng for which hym oghte repente."/ Wepynge, and nat for to stynte to
do synne, may nat avayle./ But nathelees,   90
men shal hope that every tyme that man
falleth, be it never so ofte, that he may arise
thurgh Penitence, if he have grace; but certeinly it is greet doute./ For, as seith Seint
Gregorie, "Unnethe ariseth he out of his synne,
that is charged with the charge of yvel usage."/
And therfore repentant folk, that stynte for to
synne and forlete synne er that synne forlete
hem, hooly chirche holdeth hem siker of hire
savacioun./ And he that synneth and verraily
repenteth hym in his laste, hooly chirche yet
hopeth his savacioun, by the grete mercy of
oure Lord Jhesu Crist, for his repentaunce; but
taak the siker wey./

And now, sith I have declared yow what
thyng is Penitence, now shul ye understonde

---

71 **fructuous:** fruitful

State super vias, etc.: translated in lines 77–78
76 **amonesteth:** admonishes
77 **sentences:** teachings, opinions
80 **covenable:** suitable
83 **apertenen:** belong to

85 **som:** a certain **waymentynge:** lamenting **pyneth:** punishes
89 **Ysidre:** Isidore of Seville **gabbere:** foolish talker

that ther been three acciouns of Penitence./ The firste is that if a man be bap-   95
tized after that he hath synned./ Seint Augustyn seith, "But he be penytent for his olde
synful lyf, he may nat bigynne the newe clene
lif."/ For, certes, if he be baptized withouten
penitence of his olde gilt, he receyveth the mark
of baptesme but nat the grace ne the remission
of his synnes, til he have repentance verray./
Another defaute is this: that men doon deedly
synne after that they han receyved baptesme./
The thridde defaute is that men fallen in
venial synnes after hir baptesme fro day
to day./ Therof seith Seint Augustyn that   100
penitence of goode and humble folk is the
penitence of every day./

The speces of Penitence been three. That
oon of hem is solempne, another is commune,
and the thridde is privee./ Thilke penance that
is solempne is in two maneres; as to be put out
of hooly chirche in Lente for slaughtre of children, and swich maner thyng./ Another is,
whan a man hath synned openly, of which
synne the fame is openly spoken in the contree, and thanne hooly chirche by juggement
destreyneth hym for to do open penaunce./
Commune penaunce is that preestes enjoynen
men communly in certeyn caas, as for to goon
peraventure naked in pilgrimages, or barefoot./ Pryvee penaunce is thilke that men   105
doon alday for privee synnes, of whiche we
shryve us prively and receyve privee penaunce./

Now shaltow understande what is bihovely
and necessarie to verray parfit Penitence. And
this stant on three thynges:/ Contricioun of
Herte, Confessioun of Mouth, and Satisfaccioun./ For which seith Seint John Crisostom,
"Penitence destreyneth a man to accepte benygnely every peyne that hym is enjoyned,
with contricioun of herte, and shrift of mouth,
with satisfaccioun, and in werkynge of alle
manere humylitee."/ And this is fruytful penitence agayn three thynges in which we
wratthe oure Lord Jhesu Crist;/ this is to   110
seyn, by delit in thynkynge, by reccheleesnesse in spekynge, and by wikked synful werkynge./ And agayns thise wikkede giltes is Penitence, that may be likned unto a tree./

The roote of this tree is Contricioun, that
hideth hym in the herte of hym that is verray
repentaunt, right as the roote of a tree hydeth
hym in the erthe./ Of the roote of Contricioun
spryngeth a stalke that bereth braunches and
leves of Confessioun, and fruyt of Satisfaccioun./ For which Crist seith in his gospel,
"Dooth digne fruyt of Penitence"; for by this
fruyt may men knowe this tree, and nat by the
roote that is hyd in the herte of man, ne by the
braunches, ne by the leves of Confessioun./ And therfore oure Lord Jhesu   115
Crist seith thus: "By the fruyt of hem shul
ye knowen hem."/ Of this roote eek spryngeth
a seed of grace, the which seed is mooder of
sikernesse, and this seed is egre and hoot./ The
grace of this seed spryngeth of God thurgh remembrance of the day of doom and on the
peynes of helle./ Of this matere seith Salomon that in the drede of God man forleteth his
synne./ The heete of this seed is the love of
God and the desiryng of the joye perdurable./ This heete draweth the herte   120
of a man to God and dooth hym haten his
synne./ For soothly ther is nothyng that savoureth so wel to a child as the milk of his
norice, ne nothyng is to hym moore abhomynable than thilke milk whan it is medled with
oother mete./ Right so the synful man that
loveth his synne, hym semeth that it is to him
moost sweete of any thyng;/ but fro that tyme
that he loveth sadly oure Lord Jhesu Crist, and
desireth the lif perdurable, ther nys to him no
thyng moore abhomynable./ For soothly the
lawe of God is the love of God; for which
David the prophete seith: "I have loved thy
lawe and hated wikkednesse and hate"; he
that loveth God kepeth his lawe and his
word./ This tree saugh the prophete   125
Daniel in spirit, upon the avysioun of the
kyng Nabugodonosor, whan he conseiled hym
to do penitence./ Penaunce is the tree of lyf
to hem that it receyven, and he that holdeth
hym in verray penitence is blessed, after the
sentence of Salomon./

In this Penitence or Contricioun man shal
understonde foure thynges; that is to seyn, what
is Contricioun, and whiche been the causes that
moeven a man to Contricioun, and how he

---

95 **acciouns:** effects
104 **destreyneth:** constrains, compels
107 **bihovely:** necessary
110 **wratthe:** anger

115 **digne:** worthy
117 **egre:** bitter
122 **medled:** mixed
124 **perdurable:** eternal

sholde be contrit, and what Contricioun availleth to the soule./ Thanne is it thus: that Contricioun is the verray sorwe that a man receyveth in his herte for his synnes, with sad purpos to shryve hym, and to do penaunce, and neveremoore to do synne./ And this sorwe shal been in this manere, as seith Seint Bernard: "It shal been hevy and grevous, and ful sharp and poynaunt in herte."/ First, for man 130 hath agilt his Lord and his Creatour; and moore sharp and poynaunt for he hath agilt hys Fader celestial;/ and yet moore sharp and poynaunt for he hath wrathed and agilt hym that boghte hym, that with his precious blood hath delivered us fro the bondes of synne, and fro the crueltee of the devel, and fro the peynes of helle./

The causes that oghte moeve a man to Contricioun been sixe. First a man shal remembre hym of his synnes;/ but looke he that thilke remembraunce ne be to hym no delit by no wey, but greet shame and sorwe for his gilt. For Job seith, "Synful men doon werkes worthy of confusioun."/ And therfore seith Ezechie, "I wol remembre me alle the yeres of my lyf in bitternesse of myn herte."/ And 135 God seith in the Apocalipse, "Remembreth yow fro whennes that ye been falle"; for biforn that tyme that ye synned, ye were the children of God and lymes of the regne of God;/ but for youre synne ye been woxen thral, and foul, and membres of the feend, hate of aungels, sclaundre of hooly chirche, and foode of the false serpent, perpetueel matere of the fir of helle;/ and yet moore foul and abhomynable, for ye trespassen so ofte tyme as dooth the hound that retourneth to eten his spewyng./ And yet be ye fouler for youre longe continuyng in synne and youre synful usage, for which ye be roten in youre synne, as a beest in his dong./ Swiche manere of thoghtes maken a man to have shame of his synne, and no delit, as God seith by the prophete Ezechiel,/ "Ye shal remem- 140 bre yow of youre weyes, and they shuln displese yow." Soothly synnes been the weyes that leden folk to helle./

The seconde cause that oghte make a man to have desdeyn of synne is this: that, as seith Seint Peter, "whoso that dooth synne is thral of synne"; and synne put a man in greet thraldom./ And therfore seith the prophete Ezechiel: "I wente sorweful in desdayn of myself." Certes, wel oghte a man have desdayn of synne and withdrawe hym from that thraldom and vileynye./ And lo, what seith Seneca in this matere? He seith thus: "Though I wiste that neither God ne man ne sholde nevere knowe it, yet wolde I have desdayn for to do synne."/ And the same Seneca also seith, "I am born to gretter thynges than to be thral to my body, or than for to maken of my body a thral."/ 145 Ne a fouler thral may no man ne womman maken of his body than for to yeven his body to synne./ Al were it the fouleste cherl or the fouleste womman that lyveth, and leest of value, yet is he thanne moore foul and moore in servitute./ Evere fro the hyer degree that man falleth, the moore is he thral, and moore to God and to the world vile and abhomynable./ O goode God, wel oghte man have desdayn of synne, sith that thurgh synne ther he was free now is he maked bonde./ And therfore seyth Seint Augustyn: "If thou hast desdayn of thy servant, if he agilte or synne, have thou thanne desdayn that thou thyself sholdest do synne."/ Tak reward of thy 150 value, that thou ne be to foul to thyself./ Allas, wel oghten they thanne have desdayn to been servauntz and thralles to synne, and soore been ashamed of hemself/ that God of his endelees goodnesse hath set hem in heigh estaat, or yeven hem wit, strengthe of body, heele, beautee, prosperitee,/ and boghte hem fro the deeth with his herte-blood, that they so unkyndely, agayns his gentilesse, quiten hym so vileynsly to slaughtre of hir owene soules./ O goode God, ye wommen that been of so greet beautee, remembreth yow of the proverbe of Salomon. He seith,/ "Likneth a fair 155 womman that is a fool of hire body lyk to a ryng of gold that were in the groyn of a soughe."/ For right as a soughe wroteth in everich ordure, so wroteth she hire beautee in the stynkynge ordure of synne./

The thridde cause that oghte moeve a man to Contricioun is drede of the day of doom and of the horrible peynes of helle./ For as Seint

---

130 **poynaunt:** piercing
131 **agilt:** sinned against
133 **causes:** considerations or topics for meditation that will lead one to contrition
135 **Ezechie:** Ezekiel
138 **spewyng:** vomit

149 **bonde:** bondsman, slave
151 **Tak reward of:** have regard for
153 **heele:** health
154 **agayns:** in return for   **vileynsly:** cruelly   **to slaughtre:** to the slaughter
156 **groyn of a soughe:** snout of a sow
157 **wroteth:** roots

Jerome seith, "At every tyme that me remembreth of the day of doom I quake;/ for whan I ete or drynke, or what so that I do, evere semeth me that the trompe sowneth in myn ere:/ 'Riseth up, ye that been dede, 160 and cometh to the juggement.' "/ O goode God, muchel oghte a man to drede swich a juggement, "ther as we shullen been alle," as Seint Poul seith, "biforn the seete of oure Lord Jhesu Crist";/ whereas he shal make a general congregacioun, whereas no man may been absent./ For certes there availleth noon essoyne ne excusacioun./ And nat oonly that oure defautes shullen be jugged, but eek that alle oure werkes shullen openly be knowe./ 165 And, as seith Seint Bernard, "Ther ne shal no pledynge availle, ne no sleighte; we shullen yeven rekenynge of everich ydel word."/ Ther shul we han a juge that may nat been deceyved ne corrupt. And why? For, certes, alle oure thoghtes been discovered as to hym, ne for preyere ne for meede he shal nat been corrupt./ And therfore seith Salomon, "The wratthe of God ne wol nat spare no wight, for preyere ne for yifte"; and therfore, at the day of doom ther nys noon hope to escape./ Wherfore, as seith Seint Anselm, "Ful greet angwyssh shul the synful folk have at that tyme;/ ther shal the stierne and wrothe juge sitte above, and under hym the horrible pit of helle open to destroyen hym that moot biknowen his synnes, whiche synnes openly been shewed biforn God and biforn every creature;/ 170 and in the left syde mo develes than herte may bithynke, for to harye and drawe the synful soules to the peyne of helle;/ and withinne the hertes of folk shal be the bitynge conscience, and withouteforth shal be the world al brennynge./ Whider shal thanne the wrecched synful man flee to hiden hym? Certes, he may nat hyden hym; he moste come forth and shewen hym."/ For certes, as seith Seint Jerome, "the erthe shal casten hym out of hym, and the see also, and the eyr also, that shal be ful of thonder-clappes and lightnynges."/ Now soothly, whoso wel remembreth hym of thise thynges, I gesse that his synne shal nat turne hym into delit, but to greet sorwe for drede of the peyne of helle./ 175 And therfore seith Job to God, "Suffre,

Lord, that I may a while biwaille and wepe, er I go withoute returnyng to the derke lond, covered with the derknesse of deeth,/ to the lond of mysese and of derknesse, whereas is the shadwe of deeth, whereas ther is noon ordre or ordinaunce but grisly drede that evere shal laste."/ Loo, heere may ye seen that Job preyde respit a while to biwepe and waille his trespas, for soothly oo day of respit is bettre than al the tresor of this world./ And forasmuche as a man may acquiten hymself biforn God by penitence in this world, and nat by tresor, therfore sholde he preye to God to yeve hym respit a while to biwepe and biwaillen his trespas./ For certes, al the sorwe that a man myghte make fro the bigynnyng of the world nys but a litel thyng at regard of the sorwe of helle./ The cause why that Job 180 clepeth helle the "lond of derknesse":/ understondeth that he clepeth it "lond" or erthe, for it is stable and nevere shal faille; "derk," for he that is in helle hath defaute of light material./ For certes, the derke light that shal come out of the fyr that evere shal brenne shal turne hym al to peyne that is in helle for it sheweth him to the horrible develes that hym tormenten./ "Covered with the derknesse of deeth" — that is to seyn, that he that is in helle shal have defaute of the sighte of God, for certes the sighte of God is the lyf perdurable./ "The derknesse of deeth" been the synnes that the wrecched man hath doon, whiche that destourben hym to see the face of God, right as dooth a derk clowde bitwixe us and the sonne./ "Lond of misese," by cause that 185 ther been three maneres of defautes, agayn three thynges that folk of this world han in this present lyf; that is to seyn, honours, delices, and richesses./ Agayns honour, have they in helle shame and confusioun./ For wel ye woot that men clepen honour the reverence that man doth to man, but in helle is noon honour ne reverence. For certes, namoore reverence shal be doon there to a kyng than to a knave./ For which God seith by the prophete Jeremye, "Thilke folk that me despisen shul been in despit."/ Honour is eek cleped greet lordshipe; ther shal no wight serven other, but of harm and torment. Honour is eek cleped greet dignytee and heighnesse, but in helle shul they been al fortroden of develes./ And 190

162 seete: throne
164 essoyne: legal excuse for failure to appear at court
171 harye: drag
172 withouteforth: outside

182 light material: physical light
190 fortroden of: trod upon by, trampled by

God seith, "The horrible develes shulle goon and comen upon the hevedes of the dampned folk." And this is for as muche as the hyer that they were in this present lyf, the moore shulle they been abated and defouled in helle./ Agayns the richesse of this world shul they han mysese of poverte, and this poverte shal been in foure thynges:/ In defaute of tresor, of which that David seith, "The riche folk, that embraceden and oneden al hire herte to tresor of this world, shul slepe in the slepynge of deeth; and nothyng ne shal they fynden in hir handes of al hir tresor."/ And mooreover the myseyse of helle shal been in defaute of mete and drinke./ For God seith thus by Moyses: "They shul been wasted with hunger, and the briddes of helle shul devouren hem with bitter deeth, and the galle of the dragon shal been hire drynke, and the venym of the dragon hire morsels."/ And forther 195 over, hire myseyse shal been in defaute of clothyng, for they shulle be naked in body as of clothyng, save the fyr in which they brenne, and othere filthes;/ and naked shul they been of soule, as of alle manere vertues, which that is the clothyng of the soule. Where been thanne the gaye robes, and the softe shetes, and the smale shertes?/ Loo, what seith God of hem by the prophete Ysaye: that "under hem shul been strawed motthes, and hire covertures shulle been of wormes of helle."/ And forther over, hir myseyse shal been in defaute of freendes. For he nys nat povre that hath goode freendes; but there is no frend,/ for neither God ne no creature shal been freend to hem, and everich of hem shal haten oother with deedly hate./ "The sones and the 200 doghtren shullen rebellen agayns fader and mooder, and kynrede agayns kynrede, and chiden and despisen everich of hem oother bothe day and nyght," as God seith by the prophete Michias./ And the lovynge children, that whilom loveden so flesshly everich oother, wolden everich of hem eten oother if they myghte./ For how sholden they love hem togidre in the peyne of helle, whan they hated everich of hem oother in the prosperitee of this lyf?/ For truste wel, hir flesshly love was deedly hate, as seith the prophete David:

193 **oneden:** united
197 **smale:** delicate
198 **strawed:** strewn **motthes:** maggots **covertures:** bedclothes, covers
201 **Michias:** Micah

"Whoso that loveth wikkednesse, he hateth his soule."/ And whoso hateth his owene soule, certes, he may love noon oother wight in no manere./ And therfore, in helle is no 205 solas ne no freendshipe, but evere the moore flesshly kynredes that been in helle, the moore cursynges, the more chidynges, and the moore deedly hate ther is among hem./ And forther over, they shul have defaute of alle manere delices. For certes, delices been after the appetites of the fyve wittes, as sighte, herynge, smellynge, savorynge, and touchynge./ But in helle hir sighte shal be ful of derknesse and of smoke, and therfore ful of teeres; and hir herynge ful of waymentynge and of gryntynge of teeth, as seith Jhesu Crist./ Hir nosethirles shullen be ful of stynkynge stynk; and, as seith Ysaye the prophete, "hir savoryng shal be ful of bitter galle";/ and touchynge of al hir body ycovered with "fir that nevere shal quenche and with wormes that nevere shul dyen," as God seith by the mouth of Ysaye./ And for as muche as they shul 210 nat wene that they may dyen for peyne, and by hir deeth flee fro peyne, that may they understonden by the word of Job, that seith, "ther as is the shadwe of deeth."/ Certes, a shadwe hath the liknesse of the thyng of which it is shadwe, but shadwe is nat the same thyng of which it is shadwe./ Right so fareth the peyne of helle; it is lyk deeth for the horrible angwissh, and why? For it peyneth hem evere, as though they sholde dye anon; but certes, they shal nat dye./ For, as seith Seint Gregorie, "To wrecche caytyves shal be deeth withoute deeth, and ende withouten ende, and defaute withoute failynge./ For hir deeth shal alwey lyven, and hir ende shal everemo bigynne, and hir defaute shal nat faille."/ 215 And therfore seith Seint John the Evaungelist, "They shullen folwe deeth, and they shul nat fynde hym; and they shul desiren to dye, and deeth shal flee fro hem."/ And eek Job seith that in helle is noon ordre of rule./ And al be it so that God hath creat alle thynges in right ordre, and no thyng withouten ordre, but alle thynges been ordeyned and nombred; yet, nathelees, they that been dampned been nothyng in ordre, ne holden noon ordre,/ for the erthe ne shal bere hem no fruyt./ For, as the prophete David seith, "God shal destroie the fruyt of the erthe as fro hem; ne water ne

209 **nose-thirles:** nostrils

shal yeve hem no moisture, ne the eyr no refresshyng, ne fyr no light."/ For, as 220 seith Seint Basilie, "The brennynge of the fyr of this world shal God yeven in helle to hem that been dampned,/ but the light and the cleernesse shal be yeven in hevene to his children," right as the goode man yeveth flessh to his children and bones to his houndes./ And for they shullen have noon hope to escape, seith Seint Job atte laste that "ther shal horrour and grisly drede dwellen withouten ende."/ Horrour is alwey drede of harm that is to come, and this drede shal evere dwelle in the hertes of hem that been dampned. And therfore han they lorn al hire hope, for sevene causes./ First, for God, that is hir juge, shal be withouten mercy to hem; and they may nat plese hym ne noon of his halwes; ne they ne may yeve no thyng for hir raunsoun;/ 225 ne they have no voys to speke to hym; ne they may nat fle fro peyne; ne they have no goodnesse in hem, that they mowe shewe to delivere hem fro peyne./ And therfore seith Salomon: "The wikked man dyeth, and whan he is deed, he shal have noon hope to escape fro peyne."/ Whoso thanne wolde wel understande thise peynes and bithynke hym weel that he hath deserved thilke peynes for his synnes, certes, he sholde have moore talent to siken and to wepe than for to syngen and to pleye./ For, as that seith Salomon, "Whoso that hadde the science to knowe the peynes that been establissed and ordeyned for synne, he wolde make sorwe."/ "Thilke science," as seith Seint Augustyn, "maketh a man to waymenten in his herte."/ 230

The fourthe point that oghte maken a man to have contricion is the sorweful remembraunce of the good that he hath left to doon heere in erthe, and eek the good that he hath lorn./ Soothly, the goode werkes that he hath lost, outher they been the goode werkes that he wroghte er he fel into deedly synne or elles the goode werkes that he wroghte while he lay in synne./ Soothly, the goode werkes that he dide biforn that he fil in synne been al mortefied and astoned and dulled by the ofte synnyng./ The othere goode werkes, that he wroghte whil he lay in deedly synne, thei been outrely dede, as to the lyf perdurable in hev-

ene./ Thanne thilke goode werkes that been mortefied by ofte synnyng, whiche goode werkes he dide whil he was in charitee, ne mowe nevere quyken agayn withouten verray penitence./ And therof seith God by 235 the mouth of Ezechiel, that "if the rightful man returne agayn from his rightwisnesse and werke wikkednesse, shal he lyve?"/ Nay, for alle the goode werkes that he hath wroght ne shul nevere been in remembraunce, for he shal dyen in his synne./ And upon thilke chapitre seith Seint Gregorie thus: that "we shulle understonde this principally;/ that whan we doon deedly synne, it is for noght thanne to rehercen or drawen into memorie the goode werkes that we han wroght biforn."/ For certes, in the werkynge of the deedly synne, ther is no trust to no good werk that we han doon biforn; that is to seyn, as for to have therby the lyf perdurable in hevene./ But nathelees, the 240 goode werkes quyken agayn, and comen agayn, and helpen, and availlen to have the lyf perdurable in hevene, whan we han contricioun./ But soothly, the goode werkes that men doon whil they been in deedly synne, for as muche as they were doon in deedly synne, they may nevere quyke agayn./ For certes, thyng that nevere hadde lyf may nevere quykene; and nathelees, al be it that they ne availle noght to han the lyf perdurable, yet availlen they to abregge of the peyne of helle, or elles to geten temporal richesse,/ or elles that God wole the rather enlumyne and lightne the herte of the synful man to have repentaunce;/ and eek they availlen for to usen a man to doon goode werkes, that the feend have the lasse power of his soule./ And thus the 245 curteis Lord Jhesu Crist ne wole that no good werk be lost, for in somwhat it shal availle./ But, for as muche as the goode werkes that men doon whil they been in good lyf been al mortefied by synne folwynge, and eek sith that alle the goode werkes that men doon whil they been in deedly synne been outrely dede as for to have the lyf perdurable,/ wel may that man that no good werk ne dooth synge thilke newe Frenshe song, *Jay tout perdu mon temps et mon labour.*"/ For certes, synne bireveth a man bothe goodnesse of nature and eek the goodnesse of grace./ For soothly, the grace of

---

221 **Seint Basilie:** St. Basil
228 **talent:** desire
230 **waymenten:** lament
233 **mortefied:** killed   **astoned:** paralyzed, rendered lifeless

235 **quyken:** revive
243 **abregge:** shorten
248 *Jay tout . . . labour:* I have altogether wasted my time and effort.

the Hooly Goost fareth lyk fyr, that may nat been ydel; for fyr fayleth anoon as it forleteth his wirkynge, and right so grace fayleth anoon as it forleteth his werkynge./ Then 250 leseth the synful man the goodnesse of glorie, that oonly is bihight to goode men that labouren and werken./ Wel may he be sory thanne, that oweth al his lif to God as longe as he hath lyved, and eek as longe as he shal lyve, that no goodnesse ne hath to paye with his dette to God to whom he oweth al his lyf./ For trust wel, "He shal yeven acountes," as seith Seint Bernard, "of alle the goodes that han be yeven hym in this present lyf, and how he hath hem despended,/ [in] so muche that ther shal nat perisse an heer of his heed, ne a moment of an houre ne shal nat perisse of his tyme, that he ne shal yeve of it a rekenyng."/

The fifthe thyng that oghte moeve a man to contricioun is remembrance of the passioun that oure Lord Jhesu Crist suffred for oure synnes./ For, as seith Seint Bernard, 255 "Whil that I lyve I shal have remembrance of the travailles that oure Lord Crist suffred in prechyng:/ his werynesse in travaillyng, his temptaciouns whan he fasted, his longe wakynges whan he preyde, hise teeres whan that he weep for pitee of good peple,/ the wo and the shame and the filthe that men seyden to hym, of the foule spittyng that men spitte in his face, of the buffettes that men yaven hym, of the foule mowes, and of the repreves that men to hym seyden,/ of the nayles with whiche he was nayled to the croys, and of al the remenant of his passioun that he suffred for my synnes, and no thyng for his gilt."/ And ye shul understonde that in mannes synne is every manere of ordre or ordinaunce turned up-so-doun./ For it is sooth that 260 God, and resoun, and sensualitee, and the body of man been so ordeyned that everich of thise foure thynges sholde have lordshipe over that oother,/ as thus: God sholde have lordshipe over resoun, and resoun over sensualitee, and sensualitee over the body of man./ But soothly, whan man synneth, al this ordre or ordinaunce is turned up-so-doun./ And therfore thanne, for as muche as the resoun of man ne wol nat be subget ne obeisant to God, that is his lord by right, therfore leseth it the lord-

shipe that it sholde have over sensualitee, and eek over the body of man./ And why? For sensualitee rebelleth thanne agayns resoun, and by that way leseth resoun the lordshipe over sensualitee and over the body./ 265 For right as resoun is rebel to God, right so is bothe sensualitee rebel to resoun and the body also./ And certes this disordinaunce and this rebellioun oure Lord Jhesu Crist aboghte upon his precious body ful deere, and herkneth in which wise./ For as muche thanne as resoun is rebel to God, therfore is man worthy to have sorwe and to be deed./ This suffred oure Lord Jhesu Crist for man, after that he hadde be bitraysed of his disciple, and distreyned and bounde so that his blood brast out at every nayl of his handes, as seith Seint Augustyn./ And forther over, for as muchel as resoun of man ne wol nat daunte sensualitee whan it may, therfore is man worthy to have shame; and this suffred oure Lord Jhesu Crist for man, whan they spetten in his visage./ And forther over, for as muchel 270 thanne as the caytyf body of man is rebel bothe to resoun and to sensualitee, therfore is it worthy the deeth./ And this suffred oure Lord Jhesu Crist for man upon the croys, where as ther was no part of his body free withouten greet peyne and bitter passioun./ And al this suffred Jhesu Crist, that nevere forfeted. And therfore resonably may be seyd of Jhesu in this manere: "To muchel am I peyned for the thynges that I nevere deserved, and to muche defouled for shendshipe that man is worthy to have."/ And therfore may the synful man wel seye, as seith Seint Bernard, "Acursed be the bitternesse of my synne, for which ther moste be suffred so muchel bitternesse."/ For certes, after the diverse [disordinaunces] of oure wikkednesses was the passioun of Jhesu Crist ordeyned in diverse thynges./ As thus: Certes, synful mannes 275 soule is bitraysed of the devel by coveitise of temporeel prosperitee, and scorned by deceite whan he cheseth flesshly delices; and yet is it tormented by inpacience of adversitee and bispet by servage and subjeccioun of synne; and atte laste it is slayn fynally./ For

---

257 **wakynges:** vigils
258 **mowes:** grimaces   **repreves:** insults

267 **disordinaunce:** rebelliousness against order   **aboghte upon:** purchased with
270 **spetten:** spat
273 **forfeted:** sinned   **shendshipe:** shame
276 **bispet:** spat upon

this disordinaunce of synful man was Jhesu Crist first bitraysed, and after that was he bounde, that cam for to unbynden us of synne and peyne./ Thanne was he byscorned, that oonly sholde han been honoured in alle thynges and of alle thynges./ Thanne was his visage, that oghte be desired to be seyn of al man-kynde, in which visage aungels desiren to looke, vileynsly bispet./ Thanne was he scourged, that no thyng hadde agilt; and finally, thanne was he crucified and slayn./ 280 Thanne was acompliced the word of Ysaye, "He was wounded for oure mysdedes and de-fouled for oure felonies."/ Now sith that Jhesu Crist took upon hymself the peyne of alle oure wikkednesses, muchel oghte synful man wepen and biwayle, that for his synnes Goddes sone of hevene sholde al this peyne endure./

The sixte thyng that oghte moeve a man to contricioun is the hope of three thynges; that is to seyn, foryifnesse of synne, and the yifte of grace wel for to do, and the glorie of hevene, with which God shal gerdone man for his goode dedes./ And for as muche as Jhesu Crist yeveth us thise yiftes of his largesse and of his sovereyn bountee, therfore is he cleped *Jhesus Nazarenus rex Judeorum./ Jhesus* is to seyn "saveour" or "salvacioun," on whom men shul hope to have foryifnesse of synnes, which that is proprely salvacioun of synnes./ And therfore seyde the aungel 285 to Joseph, "Thou shalt clepen his name Jhesus, that shal saven his peple of hir synnes."/ And heerof seith Seint Peter: "Ther is noon oother name under hevene that is yeve to any man, by which a man may be saved, but oonly Jhesus."/ *Nazarenus* is as muche for to seye as "florisshynge," in which a man shal hope that he that yeveth hym remissioun of synnes shal yeve hym eek grace wel for to do. For in the flour is hope of fruyt in tyme comynge, and in foryifnesse of synnes hope of grace wel for to do./ "I was atte dore of thyn herte," seith Jhesus, "and cleped for to entre. He that open-eth to me shal have foryifnesse of synne./ I wol entre into hym by my grace and soupe with hym," by the goode werkes that he shal doon, whiche werkes been the foode of God;

"and he shal soupe with me" by the grete joye that I shal yeven hym./ Thus shal 290 man hope, for his werkes of penaunce that God shal yeven hym his regne, as he bi-hooteth hym in the gospel./

Now shal a man understonde in which man-ere shal been his contricioun. I seye that it shal been universal and total. This is to seyn, a man shal be verray repentaunt for alle his synnes that he hath doon in delit of his thoght, for delit is ful perilous./ For ther been two manere of consentynges: that oon of hem is cleped consentynge of affeccioun, whan a man is moeved to do synne, and deliteth hym longe for to thynke on that synne;/ and his reson aperceyveth it wel that it is synne agayns the lawe of God, and yet his resoun refreyneth nat his foul delit or talent, though he se wel apertly that it is agayns the reverence of God. Al-though his resoun ne consente noght to doon that synne in dede,/ yet seyn somme doctours that swich delit that dwelleth longe, it is ful perilous, al be it nevere so lite./ And 295 also a man sholde sorwe namely for al that evere he hath desired agayn the lawe of God with parfit consentynge of his resoun, for therof is no doute, that it is deedly synne in consent-ynge./ For certes, ther is no deedly synne that it nas first in mannes thought and after that in his delit, and so forth into consentynge and into dede./ Wherfore I seye that many men ne repenten hem nevere of swiche thoghtes and delites, ne nevere shryven hem of it, but oonly of the dede of grete synnes outward./ Wher-fore I seye that swiche wikked delites and wik-ked thoghtes been subtile bigileres of hem that shullen be dampned./ Mooreover, man oghte to sorwe for his wikkede wordes as wel as for his wikkede dedes. For certes, the repentaunce of a synguler synne, and nat repente of alle his othere synnes, or elles repenten hym of alle his othere synnes and nat of a synguler synne, may nat availle./ For certes, God al- 300 myghty is al good, and therfore he for-yeveth al or elles right noght./ And heerof seith Seint Augustyn,/ "I wot certeynly that God is enemy to everich synnere." And how thanne? He that observeth o synne, shal he have foryifnesse of the remenaunt of his othere synnes? Nay./ And further over, contricioun

---

278 **byscorned:** scorned
279 **vileynsly:** rudely
280 **scourged:** whipped
281 **Ysaye:** Isaiah　**mysdedes:** sins
284 *Jhesus Nazarenus rex Judeorum:* Jesus the Nazarene, king of the Jews

290 **soupe:** sup
294 **refreyneth:** restrains　**apertly:** clearly
299 **bigileres:** deceivers

sholde be wonder sorweful and angwissous; and therfore yeveth hym God pleynly his mercy; and therfore, whan my soule was angwissous withinne me, I hadde remembrance of God that my preyere myghte come to hym./ Forther over, contricioun moste be continueel, and that man have stedefast purpos to shriven hym, and for to amenden hym of his lyf./ For soothly, whil contricioun lasteth, 305 man may evere have hope of foryifnesse; and of this comth hate of synne, that destroyeth synne, bothe in himself and eek in oother folk at his power./ For which seith David: "Ye that loven God, hateth wikkednesse." For trusteth wel, to love God is for to love that he loveth, and hate that he hateth./

The laste thyng that men shal understonde in contricioun is this: wherof avayleth contricioun. I seye that somtyme contricioun delivereth a man fro synne;/ of which that David seith, "I seye," quod David (that is to seyn, I purposed fermely) "to shryve me, and thow, Lord, relessedest my synne."/ And right so as contricion availleth noght withouten sad purpos of shrifte, if man have oportunitee, right so litel worth is shrifte or satisfaccioun withouten contricioun./ And mooreover 310 contricion destroyeth the prisoun of helle, and maketh wayk and fieble alle the strengthes of the develes, and restoreth the yiftes of the Hooly Goost and of alle goode vertues;/ and it clenseth the soule of synne, and delivereth the soule fro the peyne of helle, and fro the compaignye of the devel, and fro the servage of synne, and restoreth it to alle goodes espirituels, and to the compaignye and communyoun of hooly chirche./ And forther over, it maketh hym that whilom was sone of ire to be sone of grace; and alle thise thynges been preved by hooly writ./ And therfore, he that wolde sette his entente to thise thynges, he were ful wys; for soothly he ne sholde nat thanne in al his lyf have corage to synne, but yeven his body and al his herte to the service of Jhesu Crist, and therof doon hym hommage./ For soothly oure sweete Lord Jhesu Crist hath spared us so debonairly in oure folies that if he ne hadde pitee of mannes soule, a sory song we myghten alle synge./   315

Explicit prima pars Penitentie; Et sequitur secunda pars eiusdem.

The seconde partie of Penitence is Confessioun, that is signe of contricioun./ Now shul ye understonde what is Confessioun, and wheither it oghte nedes be doon or noon, and whiche thynges been covenable to verray Confessioun./

First shaltow understonde that Confessioun is verray shewynge of synnes to the preest./ This is to seyn "verray," for he moste confessen hym of alle the condiciouns that bilongen to his synne, as ferforth as he kan./ Al moot be seyd, and no thyng excused ne hyd ne forwrapped, and noght avaunte thee of thy goode werkes./ And forther over, it is neces- 320 sarie to understonde whennes that synnes spryngen, and how they encreessen, and whiche they been./

Of the spryngynge of synnes seith Seint Paul in this wise: that "Right as by a man synne entred first into this world, and thurgh that synne deeth, right so thilke deeth entred into alle men that synneden."/ And this man was Adam, by whom synne entred into this world, whan he brak the comaundementz of God./ And therfore, he that first was so myghty that he sholde nat have dyed, bicam swich oon that he moste nedes dye, wheither he wolde or noon, and al his progenye in this world, that in thilke man synneden./ Looke that in th'estaat of innocence, whan Adam and Eve naked weren in Paradys, and nothyng ne hadden shame of hir nakednesse,/ how that the serpent, 325 that was moost wily of alle othere beestes that God hadde maked, seyde to the womman, "Why comaunded God to yow ye sholde nat eten of every tree in Paradys?"/ The womman answerde: "Of the fruyt," quod she, "of the trees in Paradys we feden us, but soothly, of the fruyt of the tree that is in the myddel of Paradys, God forbad us for to ete, ne nat touchen it, lest per aventure we sholde dyen."/ The serpent seyde to the womman, "Nay, nay, ye shul nat dyen of deeth; for sothe, God woot that what day that ye eten therof, youre eyen shul opene and ye shul been as goddes, knowynge good and harm."/ The womman thanne

---

304 **angwissous:** anxious
Explicit, *etc.:* Here ends the first part of Penance; and its second part follows.

---

320 **forwrapped:** concealed

saugh that the tree was good to feedyng, and fair to the eyen, and delitable to the sighte. She took of the fruyt of the tree, and eet it, and yaf to hire housbonde, and he eet, and anoon the eyen of hem bothe openeden./ And whan that they knewe that they were naked, they sowed of fige leves a maner of breches to hiden hire membres./ There 330 may ye seen that deedly synne hath, first, suggestion of the feend, as sheweth heere by the naddre; and afterward, the delit of the flessh, as sheweth heere by Eve; and after that, the consentynge of resoun, as sheweth heere by Adam./ For trust wel, though so were that the feend tempted Eve — that is to seyn, the flessh — and the flessh hadde delit in the beautee of the fruyt defended, yet certes, til that resoun — that is to seyn, Adam — consented to the etynge of the fruyt, yet stood he in th' estaat of innocence./ Of thilke Adam tooke we thilke synne original, for of hym flesshly descended be we alle, and engendred of vile and corrupt mateere./ And whan the soule is put in oure body, right anon is contract original synne; and that that was erst but oonly peyne of concupiscence is afterward bothe peyne and synne./ And therfore be we alle born sones of wratthe and of dampnacioun perdurable, if it nere baptesme that we receyven, which bynymeth us the culpe. But for sothe, the peyne dwelleth with us, as to temptacioun, which peyne highte concupiscence./ And this concu- 335 piscence, whan it is wrongfully disposed or ordeyned in man, it maketh hym coveite, by coveitise of flessh, flesshly synne, by sighte of his eyen as to erthely thynges, and eek coveitise of hynesse by pride of herte./

Now, as for to speken of the firste coveitise, that is concupiscence, after the lawe of oure membres that weren lawefulliche ymaked and by rightful juggement of God,/ I seye, forasmuche as man is nat obeisaunt to God, that is his lord, therfore is the flessh to hym disobeisaunt thurgh concupiscence, which yet is cleped norrissynge of synne and occasioun of synne./ Therfore, al the while that a man hath in hym the peyne of concupiscence, it is impossible but he be tempted somtime and moeved in his flessh to synne./ And this thyng may nat faille as longe

as he lyveth; it may wel wexe fieble and faille by vertu of baptesme and by the grace of God thurgh penitence,/ but fully ne shal 340 it nevere quenche, that he ne shal som tyme be moeved in hymself, but if he were al refreyded by siknesse, or by malefice of sorcerie, or colde drynkes./ For lo, what seith Seint Paul: "The flessh coveiteth agayn the spirit, and the spirit agayn the flessh; they been so contrarie and so stryven that a man may nat alway doon as he wolde."/ The same Seint Paul, after his grete penaunce in water and in lond — in water by nyght and by day in greet peril and in greet peyne; in lond, in famyne and thurst, in coold and cloothlees, and ones stoned almoost to the deeth/ — yet seyde he, "Allas, I caytyf man! Who shal delivere me fro the prisoun of my caytyf body?"/ And Seint Jerome, whan he longe tyme hadde woned in desert, where as he hadde no compaignye but of wilde beestes, where as he ne hadde no mete but herbes, and water to his drynke, ne no bed but the naked erthe, for which his flessh was blak as an Ethiopeen for heete, and ny destroyed for coold,/ yet seyde he that "the 345 brennynge of lecherie boyled in al his body."/ Wherfore I woot wel sykerly that they been deceyved that seyn that they ne be nat tempted in hir body./ Witnesse on Seint Jame the Apostel, that seith that "every wight is tempted in his owene concupiscence"; that is to seyn, that everich of us hath matere and occasioun to be tempted of the norissynge of synne that is in his body./ And therfore seith Seint John the Evaungelist, "If that we seyn that we be withoute synne, we deceyve us selve, and trouthe is nat in us."/

Now shal ye understonde in what manere that synne wexeth or encreesseth in man. The firste thyng is thilke norissynge of synne of which I spak biforn, thilke flesshly concupiscence./ And after that comth the 350 subjeccioun of the devel — this is to seyn, the develes bely, with which he bloweth in man the fir of flesshly concupiscence./ And after that, a man bithynketh hym wheither he wol doon or no thilke thing to which he is tempted./ And thanne, if that a man withstonde and weyve the firste entisynge of his flessh and of the feend, thanne is it no synne;

330 **membres:** genitals
335 **bynymeth:** takes away from   **culpe:** guilt

341 **refreyded:** cooled   **malefice:** evildoing
351 **bely:** bellows

and if it so be that he do nat so, thanne feeleth he anoon a flambe of delit./ And thanne is it good to be war and kepen hym wel, or elles he wol falle anon into consentynge of synne; and thanne wol he do it, if he may have tyme and place./ And of this matere seith Moyses by the devel in this manere: "The feend seith, 'I wole chace and pursue the man by wikked suggestioun, and I wole hente hym by moevynge or stirynge of synne. And I wol departe my prise or my praye by deliberacioun, and my lust shal been acompliced in delit. I wol drawe my swerd in consentynge' " — /   355 for certes, right as a swerd departeth a thyng in two peces, right so consentynge departeth God fro man — " 'and thanne wol I sleen hym with myn hand in dede of synne'; thus seith the feend."/ For certes, thanne is a man al deed in soule. And thus is synne acompliced by temptacioun, by delit, and by consentynge; and thanne is the synne cleped actueel./

For sothe, synne is in two maneres; outher it is venial or deedly synne. Soothly, whan man loveth any creature moore than Jhesu Crist oure Creatour, thanne is it deedly synne. And venial synne is it, if man love Jhesu Crist lasse than hym oghte./ For sothe, the dede of this venial synne is ful perilous, for it amenuseth the love that men sholde han to God moore and moore./ And therfore, if a man charge hymself with manye swiche venial synnes, certes, but if so be that he somtyme descharge hym of hem by shrifte, they mowe ful lightly amenuse in hym al the love that he hath to Jhesu Crist;/ and in this wise   360 skippeth venial into deedly synne. For certes, the moore that a man chargeth his soule with venial synnes, the moore is he enclyned to fallen into deedly synne./ And therfore lat us nat be necligent to deschargen us of venial synnes. For the proverbe seith that "Manye smale maken a greet."/ And herkne this ensample. A greet wawe of the see comth som tyme with so greet a violence that it drencheth the ship. And the same harm doon som tyme the smale dropes of water, that entren thurgh a litel crevace into the thurrok, and in the botme of the ship, if men be so necligent that they ne descharge hem nat by

tyme./ And therfore, although ther be a difference bitwixe thise two causes of drenchynge, algates the ship is dreynt./ Right so fareth it somtyme of deedly synne, and of anoyouse veniale synnes, whan they multiplie in a man so greetly that [the love of] thilke worldly thynges that he loveth, thurgh whiche he synneth venyally, is as greet in his herte as the love of God, or moore./ And ther-   365 fore, the love of every thyng that is nat biset in God, ne doon principally for Goddes sake, although that a man love it lasse than God, yet is it venial synne;/ and deedly synne whan the love of any thyng weyeth in the herte of man as muchel as the love of God, or moore./ "Deedly synne," as seith Seint Augustyn, "is whan a man turneth his herte fro God, which that is verray sovereyn bountee, that may nat chaunge, and yeveth his herte to thyng that may chaunge and flitte."/ And certes, that is every thyng save God of hevene. For sooth is that if a man yeve his love, the which that he oweth al to God with al his herte, unto a creature, certes, as muche of his love as he yeveth to thilke creature, so muche he bireveth fro God;/ and therfore dooth he synne. For he that is dettour to God ne yeldeth nat to God al his dette; that is to seyn, al the love of his herte./   370

Now sith man understondeth generally which is venial synne, thanne is it covenable to tellen specially of synnes whiche that many a man peraventure ne demeth hem nat synnes, and ne shryveth him nat of the same thynges, and yet natheless they been synnes / soothly, as thise clerkes writen; this is to seyn, that at every tyme that a man eteth or drynketh moore than suffiseth to the sustenaunce of his body, in certein he dooth synne./ And eek whan he speketh moore than it nedeth, it is synne. Eke whan he herkneth nat benignely the compleint of the povre;/ eke whan he is in heele of body and wol nat faste whan other folk faste, withouten cause resonable; eke whan he slepeth moore than nedeth, or whan he comth by thilke enchesoun to late to chirche, or to othere werkes of charite;/ eke whan he useth his wyf withouten sovereyn desir of engendrure to the honour of God or for the entente to yelde to his wyf the dette of his body;/ eke whan   375 he wol nat visite the sike and the prisoner, if he may; eke if he love wyf or child, or oother

355 **departe:** separate (as a single sheep from a flock) **prise:** prize, what is to be captured
360 **amenuse:** diminish
363 **thurrok:** bilge (of a ship)

368 **flitte:** pass away

worldly thyng, moore than resoun requireth;
eke if he flatere or blandise moore than hym
oghte for any necessitee;/ eke if he amenuse
or withdrawe the almesse of the povre; eke if
he apparailleth his mete moore deliciously than
nede is, or ete it to hastily by likerousnesse;/
eke if he tale vanytees at chirche or at Goddes
service, or that he be a talker of ydel wordes of
folye or of vileynye, for he shal yelden acountes
of it at the day of doom;/ eke whan he biheteth or assureth to do thynges that he may nat
parfourne; eke whan that he by lightnesse or
folie mysseyeth or scorneth his neighebor;/
eke whan he hath any wikked suspecioun
of thyng ther he ne woot of it no soothfastnesse:/ thise thynges, and mo with- 380
oute nombre, been synnes, as seith Seint
Augustyn./

Now shal men understonde that, al be it so
that noon erthely man may eschue alle venial
synnes, yet may he refreyne hym by the brennynge love that he hath to oure Lord Jhesu
Crist, and by preyeres and confessioun and
othere goode werkes, so that it shal but litel
greve./ For, as seith Seint Augustyn, "If a man
love God in swich manere that al that evere he
dooth is in the love of God and for the love of
God verraily, for he brenneth in the love of
God,/ looke how muche that a drope of water that falleth in a fourneys ful of fyr anoyeth
or greveth, so muche anoyeth a venial synne
unto a man that is parfit in the love of Jhesu
Crist."/ Men may also refreyne venial synne
by receyvynge worthily of the precious
body of Jhesu Crist;/ by receyvynge eek 385
of hooly water, by almesdede, by general
confessioun of *Confiteor* at masse and at complyn, and by blessynge of bisshopes and of
preestes, and by oothere goode werkes./

Explicit secunda pars Penitentie.

*Sequitur de septem peccatis mortalibus et eorum dependenciis,
circumstanciis, et speciebus.*

Now is it bihovely thyng to telle whiche
been the sevene deedly synnes, this is to seyn,
chieftaynes of synnes. Alle they renne in o
lees, but in diverse manneres. Now been they
cleped chieftaynes, for as muche as they been
chief and spryng of alle othere synnes./ Of
the roote of thise sevene synnes, thanne, is
Pride the general roote of alle harmes. For of
this roote spryngen certein braunches, as Ire,
Envye, Accidie or Slewthe, Avarice or Coveitise
(to commune understondynge), Glotonye, and
Lecherye./ And everich of thise chief synnes
hath his braunches and his twigges, as shal be
declared in hire chapitres folwynge./

De Superbia.

And thogh so be that no man kan outrely telle the nombre of the twigges 390
and of the harmes that cometh of Pride,
yet wol I shewe a partie of hem, as ye shul
understonde./ Ther is inobedience, avauntynge, ypocrisie, despit, arrogance, inpudence,
swellynge of herte, insolence, elacioun,
inpacience, strif, contumacie, presumpcioun,
irreverence, pertinacie, veyneglorie, and many
another twig that I kan nat declare./ Inobedi-
ent is he that disobeyeth for despit to the comandementz of God, and to his sovereyns, and
to his goostly fader./ Avauntour is he that bosteth of the harm or of the bountee that he hath
doon./ Ypocrite is he that hideth to shewe
hym swich as he is and sheweth hym swich
as he noght is./ Despitous is he that hath
desdeyn of his neighebor — that is to seyn, of
his evene-Cristene — or hath despit to doon
that hym oghte to do./ Arrogant is he 395
that thynketh that he hath thilke bountees
in hym that he hath noght, or weneth that he
sholde have hem by his desertes, or elles he
demeth that he be that he nys nat./ Inpudent
is he that for his pride hath no shame of his

---

376 **blandise:** blandish, fawn upon
378 **tale:** talk

Explicit, *etc.*: Here ends the second part on Penance. Now
follows the section on the seven deadly sins and their
subdivisions, circumstances, and species.
387 **bihovely:** useful, necessary   **Alle they renne in o lees:**
they all run on one leash; see n.   **spryng:** wellspring
De Superbia: Concerning pride.

382 **refreyne:** bridle, restrain
384 **anoyeth:** damages
386 *Confiteor:* I confess, first word of the general confession of
sins   **complyn:** compline, the last service sung before retiring

391 **elacioun:** defined at 400   **contumacie:** defined at 402
pertinacie: defined at 404
395 **evene-Cristene:** fellow Christian

synnes./ Swellynge of herte is whan a man rejoyseth hym of harm that he hath doon./ Insolent is he that despiseth in his juggement alle othere folk, as to regard of his value, and of his konnyng, and of his spekyng, and of his beryng./ Elacioun is whan he ne may neither suffre to have maister ne felawe./ Inpa- 400 cient is he that wol nat been ytaught ne undernome of his vice, and by strif werreieth trouthe wityngly, and deffendeth his folye./ *Contumax* is he that thurgh his indignacioun is agayns everich auctoritee or power of hem that been his sovereyns./ Presumpcioun is whan a man undertaketh an emprise that hym oghte nat do, or elles that he may nat do; and this is called surquidrie. Irreverence is whan men do nat honour there as hem oghte to doon, and waiten to be reverenced./ Pertinacie is whan man deffendeth his folie and trusteth to muchel to his owene wit./ Veyneglorie is for to have pompe and delit in his temporeel hynesse, and glorifie hym in this worldly estaat./ Janglynge is whan a man speketh 405 to muche biforn folk, and clappeth as a mille, and taketh no keep what he seith./

And yet is ther a privee spece of Pride that waiteth first to be salewed er he wole salewe, al be he lasse worth than that oother is, peraventure; and eek he waiteth or desireth to sitte, or elles to goon above hym in the wey, or kisse pax, or been encensed, or goon to offryng biforn his neighebor,/ and swiche semblable thynges, agayns his duetee, peraventure, but that he hath his herte and his entente in swich a proud desir to be magnified and honoured biforn the peple./

Now been ther two maneres of Pride: that oon of hem is withinne the herte of man, and that oother is withoute./ Of whiche, soothly, thise forseyde thynges, and mo than I have seyd, apertenen to Pride that is in the herte of man; and that othere speces of Pride been withoute./ But natheles that oon 410 of thise speces of Pride is signe of that oother, right as the gaye leefsel atte taverne is signe of the wyn that is in the celer./ And this is in manye thynges: as in speche and con-

tenaunce, and in outrageous array of clothyng./ For certes, if ther ne hadde be no synne in clothyng, Crist wolde nat so soone have noted and spoken of the clothyng of thilke riche man in the gospel./ And, as seith Seint Gregorie, that "precious clothyng is cowpable for the derthe of it, and for his softenesse, and for his strangenesse and degisynesse, and for the superfluitee, or for the inordinat scantnesse of it."/ Allas, may man nat seen, as in oure dayes, the synful costlewe array of clothynge, and namely in to muche superfluite, or elles in to desordinat scantnesse?/ 415

As to the first synne, that is in superfluitee of clothynge, which that maketh it so deere, to harm of the peple;/ nat oonly the cost of embrowdynge, the degise endentynge or barrynge, owndynge, palynge, wyndynge or bendynge, and semblable wast of clooth in vanitee,/ but ther is also costlewe furrynge in hir gownes, so muche pownsonynge of chisels to maken holes, so muche daggynge of sheres;/ forthwith the superfluitee in lengthe of the forseide gownes, trailynge in the dong and in the mire, on horse and eek on foote, as wel of man as of womman, that al thilke trailyng is verraily as in effect wasted, consumed, thredbare, and roten with donge, rather than it is yeven to the povre, to greet damage of the forseyde povre folk./ And that in sondry wise; this is to seyn that the moore that clooth is wasted, the moore moot it coste to the peple for the scarsnesse./ And forther over, if so be that 420 they wolde yeven swich pownsoned and dagged clothyng to the povre folk, it is nat convenient to were for hire estaat, ne suffisant to beete hire necessitee, to kepe hem fro the distemperance of the firmament./ Upon that oother side, to speken of the horrible disordinat scantnesse of clothyng, as been thise kutted sloppes, or haynselyns, that thurgh hire shortnesse ne covere nat the shameful mem-

---

399 **konnyng:** understanding
401 **undernome of:** reproved for
403 **surquidrie:** arrogance, presumption
405 **glorifie hym:** exult
407 **pax:** an object made of wood or metal and used during the Mass for the kiss of peace
408 **agayns his duetee:** beyond what is due or owed to him
411 **leefsel:** bush for a tavern sign **celer:** storeroom

414 **derthe:** costliness **strangenesse:** exotic style **degisynesse:** elaborateness
415 **costlewe:** excessively expensive **desordinat:** excessive
417 **embrowdynge:** embroidering **degise endentynge:** ostentatious notching of the borders **barrynge:** ornamenting with decorative strips **owndynge:** undulating stripes **palynge:** vertical stripes **wyndynge:** folding **bendynge:** decorative borders **semblable:** similar
418 **furrynge:** fur trimming **pownsonynge of chisels:** punching designs with blades **daggynge of sheres:** slitting with shears
421 **pownsoned:** punched with ornamental holes **dagged:** ornamented with cutouts **beete:** provide for **distemperance of the firmament:** disturbance of the heavens (bad weather)
422 **disordinat:** excessive **kutted sloppes:** loose outer coats cut short **haynselyns:** short jackets

bres of man, to wikked entente./ Allas, somme of hem shewen the boce of hir shap, and the horrible swollen membres, that semeth lik the maladie of hirnia, in the wrappynge of hir hoses;/ and eek the buttokes of hem faren as it were the hyndre part of a she-ape in the fulle of the moone./ And mooreover, the wrecched swollen membres that they shewe thurgh disgisynge, in departynge of hire hoses in whit and reed, semeth that half hir shameful privee membres weren flayne./ And if so be that   425 they departen hire hoses in othere colours, as is whit and blak, or whit and blew, or blak and reed, and so forth,/ thanne semeth it, as by variaunce of colour, that half the partie of hire privee membres were corrupt by the fir of Seint Antony, or by cancre, or by oother swich meschaunce./ Of the hyndre part of hir buttokes, it is ful horrible for to see. For certes, in that partie of hir body ther as they purgen hir stynkynge ordure,/ that foule partie shewe they to the peple prowdly in despit of honestitee, which honestitee that Jhesu Crist and his freendes observede to shewen in hir lyve./ Now, as of the outrageous array of wommen, God woot that though the visages of somme of hem seme ful chaast and debonaire, yet notifie they in hire array of atyr likerousnesse and pride./ I sey nat that honestitee in cloth-   430 ynge of man or woman is uncovenable, but certes the superfluitee or disordinat scanti-tee of clothynge is reprevable./ Also the synne of aornement or of apparaille is in thynges that apertenen to ridynge, as in to manye delicat horses that been hoolden for delit, that been so faire, fatte, and costlewe;/ and also in many a vicious knave that is sustened by cause of hem; and in to curious harneys, as in sadeles, in crouperes, peytrels, and bridles covered with precious clothyng, and riche barres and plates of gold and of silver./ For which God seith by Zakarie the prophete, "I wol confounde the rideres of swiche horses."/ This folk taken litel reward of the ridynge of Goddes sone of hev-

ene, and of his harneys whan he rood upon the asse, and ne hadde noon oother harneys but the povre clothes of his disciples; ne we ne rede nat that evere he rood on oother beest./ I speke this for the synne of super-   435 fluitee, and nat for resonable honestitee, whan reson it requireth./ And forther over, certes, pride is greetly notified in holdynge of greet meynee, whan they be of litel profit or of right no profit,/ and namely whan that meynee is felonous and damageous to the peple by hardynesse of heigh lordshipe or by wey of offices./ For certes, swiche lordes sellen thanne hir lordshipe to the devel of helle, whanne they sustenen the wikkednesse of hir meynee./ Or elles, whan this folk of lowe degree, as thilke that holden hostelries, sustenen the thefte of hire hostilers, and that is in many manere of deceites./ Thilke manere of folk been   440 the flyes that folwen the hony, or elles the houndes that folwen the careyne. Swich for-seyde folk stranglen spiritually hir lordshipes;/ for which thus seith David the prophete: "Wik-ked deeth moote come upon thilke lordshipes, and God yeve that they moote descenden into helle al doun, for in hire houses been iniquitees and shrewednesses and nat God of hevene."/ And certes, but if they doon amendement, right as God yaf his benysoun to [Laban] by the service of Jacob, and to [Pharao] by the service of Joseph, right so God wol yeve his malisoun to swiche lordshipes as sustenen the wikkednesse of hir servauntz, but they come to amendement./ Pride of the table appeereth eek ful ofte; for certes, riche men been cleped to festes, and povre folk been put awey and re-buked./ Also in excesse of diverse metes and drynkes, and namely swich manere bake-metes and dissh-metes, brennynge of wilde fir and peynted and castelled with papir, and sem-blable wast, so that it is abusioun for to thynke./ And eek in to greet precious-   445 nesse of vessel and curiositee of mynstral-cie, by whiche a man is stired the moore to deli-ces of luxurie,/ if so be that he sette his herte

---

423 **boce:** bulge   **hirnia:** hernia   **hoses:** leggings
424 **hyndre:** back
425 **disgisynge:** style of clothing   **flayne:** stripped of skin
427 **fir of Seint Antony:** erysipelas, an acute inflammation of the skin
430 **notifie:** make known   **array of atyr:** appearance of their dress
431 **uncovenable:** unseemly   **reprevable:** blameworthy
432 **aornement:** adornment   **costlewe:** expensive
433 **to:** too   **crouperes:** covers for the hindquarters of a horse   **peytrels:** horse collars
434 **Zakarie:** Zechariah

437 **notified:** made known
438 **damageous:** injurious
441 **careyne:** carrion
442 **shrewednesses:** wicked deeds
443 **benysoun:** blessing   **malisoun:** curse
444 **cleped:** invited
445 **bake-metes:** pies of meat, fowl, or fish   **dissh-metes:** stews   **castelled with papir:** adorned with battlements of paper   **abusioun:** absurdity
446 **curiositee:** intricate, skillful performances   **luxurie:** lechery

the lasse upon oure Lord Jhesu Crist, certeyn it is a synne; and certeinly the delices myghte been so grete in this caas that man myghte lightly falle by hem into deedly synne./ The especes that sourden of Pride, soothly whan they sourden of malice ymagined, avised, and forncast, or elles of usage, been deedly synnes, it is no doute./ And whan they sourden by freletee unavysed, and sodeynly withdrawen ayeyn, al been they grevouse synnes, I gesse that they ne been nat deedly./

Now myghte men axe wherof that Pride sourdeth and spryngeth, and I seye, somtyme it spryngeth of the goodes of nature, and somtyme of the goodes of fortune, and somtyme of the goodes of grace./ Certes, the goodes 450 of nature stonden outher in goodes of body or in goodes of soule./ Certes, goodes of body been heele of body, strengthe, delivernesse, beautee, gentrice, franchise./ Goodes of nature of the soule been good wit, sharp understondynge, subtil engyn, vertu natureel, good memorie./ Goodes of fortune been richesse, hyghe degrees of lordshipes, preisynges of the peple./ Goodes of grace been science, power to suffre spiritueel travaille, benignitee, vertuous contemplacioun, withstondynge of temptacioun, and semblable thynges./ Of 455 whiche forseyde goodes, certes it is a ful greet folye a man to priden hym in any of hem alle./ Now as for to speken of goodes of nature, God woot that somtyme we han hem in nature as muche to oure damage as to oure profit./ As for to speken of heele of body, certes it passeth ful lightly, and eek it is ful ofte enchesoun of the siknesse of oure soule. For, God woot, the flessh is a ful greet enemy to the soule, and therfore, the moore that the body is hool, the moore be we in peril to falle./ Eke for to pride hym in his strengthe of body, it is an heigh folye. For certes, the flessh coveiteth agayn the spirit, and ay the moore strong that the flessh is, the sorier may the soule be./ And over al this, strengthe of body and worldly hardynesse causeth ful ofte many a man to peril and meschaunce./ Eek for to pride 460 hym of his gentrie is ful greet folie; for ofte tyme the gentrie of the body binymeth the gentrie of the soule; and eek we ben alle of o fader and of o mooder; and alle we been of o nature, roten and corrupt, bothe riche and

povre./ For sothe, o manere gentrie is for to preise, that apparailleth mannes corage with vertues and moralitees, and maketh hym Cristes child./ For truste wel that over what man that synne hath maistrie, he is a verray cherl to synne./

Now been ther generale signes of gentillesse, as eschewynge of vice and ribaudye and servage of synne, in word, in werk, and contenaunce,/ and usynge vertu, curteisye, and clennesse, and to be liberal — that is to seyn, large by mesure, for thilke that passeth mesure is folie and synne./ Another is to remembre hym of 465 bountee that he of oother folk hath receyved./ Another is to be benigne to his goode subgetis; wherfore seith Senek, "Ther is no thing moore covenable to a man of heigh estaat than debonairetee and pitee./ And therfore thise flyes that men clepen bees, whan they maken hir kyng, they chesen oon that hath no prikke wherwith he may stynge."/ Another is, a man to have a noble herte and a diligent to attayne to heighe vertuouse thynges./ Now certes, a man to pride hym in the goodes of grace is eek an outrageous folie, for thilke yifte of grace that sholde have turned hym to goodnesse and to medicine, turneth hym to venym and to confusioun, as seith Seint Gregorie./ Certes also, whoso prid- 470 eth hym in the goodes of fortune, he is a ful greet fool; for somtyme is a man a greet lord by the morwe, that is a caytyf and a wrecche er it be nyght;/ and somtyme the richesse of a man is cause of his deth; somtyme the delices of a man ben cause of the grevous maladye thurgh which he dyeth./ Certes, the commendacioun of the peple is somtyme ful fals and ful brotel for to triste; this day they preyse, tomorwe they blame./ God woot, desir to have commendacioun eek of the peple hath caused deeth to many a bisy man./

Remedium contra peccatum Superbie.

Now sith that so is that ye han understonde what is Pride, and whiche been the speces of it, and whennes Pride sourdeth and spryngeth,/ now shul ye understonde which is 475

---

448 **sourden of:** arise, originate from **ymagined:** plotted
forncast: premeditated
452 **delivernesse:** agility **gentrice:** gentle (aristocratic) birth

464 **eschewynge:** avoidance **ribaudye:** debauchery
465 **large by mesure:** reasonably generous
468 **flyes:** insects
Remedium, *etc.*: The remedy against the sin of Pride.
475 **sourdeth:** arises

the remedie agayns the synne of Pride; and that is humylitee, or mekenesse./ That is a vertu thurgh which a man hath verray knoweleche of hymself, and holdeth of hymself no pris ne deyntee, as in regard of his desertes, considerynge evere his freletee./ Now been ther three maneres of humylitee: as humylitee in herte; another humylitee is in his mouth; the thridde in his werkes./ The humilitee in herte is in foure maneres. That oon is whan a man holdeth hymself as noght worth biforn God of hevene. Another is whan he ne despiseth noon oother man./ The thridde is whan he rekketh nat, though men holde hym noght worth. The ferthe is whan he nys nat sory of his humiliacioun./ Also the   480 humilitee of mouth is in foure thynges: in attempree speche, and in humblesse of speche, and whan he biknoweth with his owene mouth that he is swich as hym thynketh that he is in his herte. Another is whan he preiseth the bountee of another man, and nothyng therof amenuseth./ Humilitee eek in werkes is in foure maneres. The firste is whan he putteth othere men biforn hym. The seconde is to chese the loweste place over al. The thridde is gladly to assente to good conseil./ The ferthe is to stonde gladly to the award of his sovereyns, or of hym that is in hyer degree. Certein, this is a greet werk of humylitee./

Sequitur de Invidia.

After Pride wol I speken of the foule synne of Envye, which that is, as by the word of the Philosophre, "sorwe of oother mannes prosperitee"; and after the word of Seint Augustyn, it is "Sorwe of oother mennes wele, and joye of othere mennes harm."/ This foule synne is platly agayns the Hooly Goost. Al be it so that every synne is agayns the Hooly Goost, yet nathelees, for as muche as bountee aperteneth proprely to the Hooly Goost, and Envye comth proprely of malice, therfore it is proprely agayn the bountee of the Hooly Goost./ Now hath   485 malice two speces; that is to seyn, hardnesse of herte in wikkednesse, or elles the flessh of man is so blynd that he considereth nat that he is in synne or rekketh nat that he is in synne, which is the hardnesse of the devel./ That oother spece of malice is whan a man werreyeth trouthe, whan he woot that it is trouthe; and eek whan he werreyeth the grace that God hath yeve to his neighebor; and al this is by Envye./ Certes, thanne is Envye the worste synne that is. For soothly, alle othere synnes been somtyme oonly agayns o special vertu,/ but certes Envye is agayns alle vertues and agayns alle goodnesses. For it is sory of alle the bountees of his neighebor, and in this manere it is divers from alle othere synnes./ For wel unnethe is ther any synne that it ne hath som delit in itself, save oonly Envye, that evere hath in itself angwissh and sorwe./   490 The speces of Envye been thise. Ther is first, sorwe of oother mannes goodnesse and of his prosperitee; and prosperitee is kyndely matere of joye; thanne is Envye a synne agayns kynde./ The seconde spece of Envye is joye of oother mannes harm, and that is proprely lyk to the devel, that evere rejoyseth hym of mannes harm./ Of thise two speces comth bakbityng; and this synne of bakbityng or detraccion hath certeine speces, as thus: Som man preiseth his neighebor by a wikked entente,/ for he maketh alwey a wikked knotte atte laste ende. Alwey he maketh a "but" atte laste ende, that is digne of moore blame than worth is al the preisynge./ The seconde spece is that if a man be good and dooth or seith a thing to good entente, the bakbitere wol turne al thilke goodnesse up-so-doun to his shrewed entente./ The thridde is to amenuse the   495 bountee of his neighebor./ The fourthe spece of bakbityng is this: that if men speke goodnesse of a man, thanne wol the bakbitere seyn, "Parfey, swich a man is yet bet than he," in dispreisynge of hym that men preise./ The fifte spece is this: for to consente gladly and herkne gladly to the harm that men speke of oother folk. This synne is ful greet and ay encreesseth after the wikked entente of the bakbitere./ After bakbityng cometh gruchchyng or murmuracioun; and somtyme it spryngeth of inpacience agayns God, and somtyme agayns man./ Agayn God it is whan a man gruccheth agayn the peyne of helle, or agayns poverte, or los of catel, or agayn reyn or tempest; or elles gruccheth that shrewes han prosperitee, or elles for that goode men han adversitee./ And alle thise   500 thynges sholde man suffre paciently, for they comen by the rightful juggement and

477 **deyntee:** dignity, worth
481 **amenuseth:** diminishes
483 **award of his sovereyns:** decision of his rulers
Sequitur, *etc.*: Now follows the section on envy.
484 **the Philosophre:** Aristotle
485 **platly:** flatly, directly
499 **murmuracioun:** grumbling

ordinaunce of God./ Somtyme comth grucching of avarice; as Judas grucched agayns the
Magdaleyne whan she enoynted the heved of
oure Lord Jhesu Crist with hir precious oynement./ This manere murmure is swich as whan
man gruccheth of goodnesse that hymself
dooth, or that oother folk doon of hir owene
catel./ Somtyme comth murmure of Pride, as
whan Simon the Pharisee gruchched agayn the
Magdaleyne whan she approched to Jhesu
Crist and weep at his feet for hire synnes./
And somtyme grucchyng sourdeth of Envye,
whan men discovereth a mannes harm that
was pryvee or bereth hym on hond
thyng that is fals./ Murmure eek is ofte   505
amonges servauntz that grucchen whan hir
sovereyns bidden hem doon leveful thynges;/
and forasmuche as they dar nat openly withseye the comaundementz of hir sovereyns, yet
wol they seyn harm, and grucche, and murmure prively for verray despit;/ whiche wordes
men clepen the develes *Pater noster,* though
so be that the devel ne hadde nevere *Pater
noster,* but that lewed folk yeven it swich a
name./ Somtyme it comth of Ire or prive hate
that norisseth rancour in herte, as afterward I
shal declare./ Thanne cometh eek bitternesse
of herte, thurgh which bitternesse every good
dede of his neighebor semeth to hym bitter and unsavory./ Thanne cometh dis-   510
cord that unbyndeth alle manere of
freendshipe. Thanne comth scornynge of his
neighebor, al do he never so weel./ Thanne
comth accusynge, as whan man seketh occasioun to anoyen his neighebor, which that is
lyk the craft of the devel, that waiteth bothe
nyght and day to accusen us alle./ Thanne
comth malignitee, thurgh which a man anoyeth his neighebor prively, if he may;/ and if
he noght may, algate his wikked wil ne shal
nat wante, as for to brennen his hous pryvely,
or empoysone or sleen his beestes, and semblable thynges./

Remedium contra peccatum Invidie.

Now wol I speke of remedie agayns this
foule synne of Envye. First is the love of God
principal and lovyng of his neighebor as hymself, for soothly that oon ne may nat been
withoute that oother./ And truste wel that   515
in the name of thy neighebor thou shalt

understonde the name of thy brother; for certes
alle we have o fader flesshly and o mooder —
that is to seyn, Adam and Eve — and eek o fader
espiritueel, and that is God of hevene./ Thy
neighebor artow holden for to love and wilne
hym alle goodnesse; and therfore seith God,
"Love thy neighebor as thyselve" — that is to
seyn, to salvacioun bothe of lyf and of soule./
And mooreover thou shalt love hym in word,
and in benigne amonestynge and chastisynge,
and conforten hym in his anoyes, and preye for
hym with al thyn herte./ And in dede thou
shalt love hym in swich wise that thou shalt
doon to hym in charitee as thou woldest that
it were doon to thyn owene persone./ And
therfore thou ne shalt doon hym no damage
in wikked word, ne harm in his body, ne in
his catel, ne in his soule, by entissyng of
wikked ensample./ Thou shalt nat desiren   520
his wyf ne none of his thynges. Understoond eek that in the name of neighebor is
comprehended his enemy./ Certes, man shal
loven his enemy, by the comandement of God;
and soothly thy freend shaltow love in God./
I seye, thyn enemy shaltow love for Goddes
sake, by his commandement. For if it were reson
that man sholde haten his enemy, for sothe
God nolde nat receyven us to his love that been
his enemys./ Agayns three manere of wronges
that his enemy dooth to hym, he shal doon
three thynges, as thus:/ Agayns hate and rancour of herte, he shal love hym in herte.
Agayns chidyng and wikkede wordes, he shal
preye for his enemy. Agayns the wikked dede
of his enemy, he shal doon hym boun-
tee./ For Crist seith, "Loveth youre ene-   525
mys, and preyeth for hem that speke yow
harm, and eek for hem that yow chacen and
pursewen, and dooth bountee to hem that yow
haten." Loo, thus comaundeth us oure Lord
Jhesu Crist to do to oure enemys./ For soothly,
nature dryveth us to loven oure freendes, and
parfey, oure enemys han moore nede to love
than oure freendes; and they that moore nede
have, certes to hem shal men doon goodnesse;/
and certes, in thilke dede have we remembraunce of the love of Jhesu Crist that deyde
for his enemys./ And in as muche as thilke
love is the moore grevous to parfourne, so
muche is the moore gret the merite; and ther-

---

514 **wante:** be lacking
Remedium, *etc.*: The remedy against the sin of Envy.

517 **wilne:** wish
518 **amonestynge:** admonishment
526 **pursewen:** persecute

fore the lovynge of oure enemy hath con-founded the venym of the devel./ For right as the devel is disconfited by humylitee, right so is he wounded to the deeth by love of oure enemy./ Certes, thanne is love the 530 medicine that casteth out the venym of Envye fro mannes herte./ The speces of this paas shullen be moore largely declared in hir chapitres folwynge./

Sequitur de Ira.

After Envye wol I discryven the synne of Ire. For soothly, whoso hath envye upon his neighebor, anon he wole comuly fynde hym a matere of wratthe, in word or in dede, agayns hym to whom he hath envye./ And as wel comth Ire of Pride as of Envye, for soothly he that is proud or envyous is lightly wrooth./

This synne of Ire, after the discryvyng of Seint Augustyn, is wikked wil to been avenged by word or by dede./ Ire, after 535 the Philosophre, is the fervent blood of man yquyked in his herte, thurgh which he wole harm to hym that he hateth./ For certes, the herte of man, by eschawfynge and moev-ynge of his blood, wexeth so trouble that he is out of alle juggement of resoun./ But ye shal understonde that Ire is in two maneres; that oon of hem is good, and that oother is wik-ked./ The goode Ire is by jalousie of good-nesse, thurgh which a man is wrooth with wik-kednesse and agayns wikkednesse; and ther-fore seith a wys man that Ire is bet than pley./ This Ire is with debonairetee, and it is wrooth withouten bitternesse; nat wrooth agayns the man, but wrooth with the mysdede of the man, as seith the prophete David, *"Irascimini et nolite peccare."*/ Now understondeth 540 that wikked Ire is in two maneres; that is to seyn, sodeyn Ire or hastif Ire, withouten avisement and consentynge of resoun./ The menyng and the sens of this is that the resoun of a man ne consente nat to thilke sodeyn Ire, and thanne is it venial./ Another Ire is ful wikked, that comth of felonie of herte avysed and cast biforn, with wikked wil to do venge-ance, and therto his resoun consenteth; and

soothly this is deedly synne./ This Ire is so displesant to God that it troubleth his hous and chaceth the Hooly Goost out of mannes soule, and wasteth and destroyeth the liknesse of God — that is to seyn, the vertu that is in mannes soule — / and put in hym the liknesse of the devel, and bynymeth the man fro God, that is his rightful lord./ 545

This Ire is a ful greet plesaunce to the devel, for it is the develes fourneys, that is eschawfed with the fir of helle./ For certes, right so as fir is moore mighty to destroyen erthely thynges than any oother element, right so Ire is myghty to destroyen alle spiritueel thynges./ Looke how that fir of smale gleedes that been almost dede under asshen wollen quike agayn whan they been touched with brymstoon; right so Ire wol everemo quyken agayn whan it is touched by the pride that is covered in mannes herte./ For certes, fir ne may nat comen out of no thyng, but if it were first in the same thyng natureelly, as fir is drawen out of flyntes with steel./ And right so as pride is ofte tyme matere of Ire, right so is rancour norice and kepere of Ire./ Ther is a maner 550 tree, as seith Seint Ysidre, that whan men maken fir of thilke tree and covere the coles of it with asshen, soothly the fir of it wol lasten al a yeer or moore./ And right so fareth it of rancour; whan it is ones conceyved in the hertes of som men, certein, it wol lasten per-aventure from oon Estre day unto another Estre day, and moore./ But certes, thilke man is ful fer fro the mercy of God al thilke while./

In this forseyde develes fourneys ther forgen three shrewes: Pride, that ay bloweth and en-creesseth the fir by chidynge and wikked wordes;/ thanne stant Envye and holdeth the hoote iren upon the herte of man with a peire of longe toonges of long rancour;/ 555 and thanne stant the synne of Contumelie, or strif and cheeste, and batereth and forgeth by vileyns reprevynges./ Certes, this cursed synne anoyeth bothe to the man hymself and eek to his neighebor. For soothly, almoost al the harm that any man dooth to his neighebor comth of wratthe./ For certes, outrageous wratthe dooth al that evere the devel hym comaundeth, for he ne spareth neither Crist ne

532 paas: passage, process (?); see n.
Sequitur, *etc.*: Now follows the section on Anger.
536 **fervent**: hot   **yquyked**: stirred, enlivened
537 **eschawfynge**: heating
539 **jalousie of goodnesse**: zeal for the good
540 **mysdede**: sin   *Irascimini et nolite peccare:* Be angry and do not sin.

546 **eschawfed**: heated
551 **a maner tree**: a kind of tree, the juniper   **Ysidre**: Isidore of Seville
556 **Contumelie**: contentiousness   **cheeste**: quarrelling

his sweete Mooder./ And in his outrageous anger and ire — allas, allas! — ful many oon at that tyme feeleth in his herte ful wikkedly, bothe of Crist and eek of alle his halwes./ Is nat this a cursed vice? Yis, certes. Allas! It bynymeth from man his wit and his resoun, and al his debonaire lif espiritueel that sholde kepen his soule./ Certes, it bynymeth eek Goddes 560 due lordshipe, and that is mannes soule and the love of his neighebores. It stryveth eek alday agayn trouthe. It reveth hym the quiete of his herte and subverteth his soule./

Of Ire comen thise stynkynge engendrures: First, hate, that is oold wratthe; discord, thurgh which a man forsaketh his olde freend that he hath loved ful longe;/ and thanne cometh werre and every manere of wrong that man dooth to his neighebor, in body or in catel./ Of this cursed synne of Ire cometh eek manslaughtre. And understonde wel that homycide, that is manslaughtre, is in diverse wise. Som manere of homycide is spiritueel, and som is bodily./ Spiritueel manslaughtre is in sixe thynges. First by hate, as seith Seint John: "He that hateth his brother is an homycide."/ Homycide is eek by bakbitynge, 565 of whiche bakbiteres seith Salomon that "they han two swerdes with whiche they sleen hire neighebores." For soothly, as wikke is to bynyme his good name as his lyf./ Homycide is eek in yevynge of wikked conseil by fraude, as for to yeven conseil to areysen wrongful custumes and taillages./ Of whiche seith Salomon, "Leon rorynge and bere hongry been like to the cruel lordshipes" in withholdynge or abreggynge of the shepe (or the hyre), or of the wages of servauntz, or elles in usure, or in withdrawynge of the almesse of povre folk./ For which the wise man seith, "Fedeth hym that almoost dyeth for honger"; for soothly, but if thow feede hym, thou sleest hym; and alle thise been deedly synnes./ Bodily manslaughtre is, whan thow sleest him with thy tonge in oother manere, as whan thou comandest to sleen a man or elles yevest hym conseil to sleen a man./ Manslaughtre in dede is in foure 570 maneres. That oon is by lawe, right as a justice dampneth hym that is coupable to the deeth. But lat the justice be war that he do it rightfully, and that he do it nat for delit to

spille blood but for kepynge of rightwisnesse./ Another homycide is that is doon for necessitee, as whan o man sleeth another in his defendaunt and that he ne may noon ootherwise escape from his owene deeth./ But certeinly if he may escape withouten slaughtre of his adversarie, and sleeth hym, he dooth synne and he shal bere penance as for deedly synne./ Eek if a man, by caas or aventure, shete an arwe, or caste a stoon with which he sleeth a man, he is homycide./ Eek if a womman by neclicence overlyeth hire child in hir slepyng, it is homycide and deedly synne./ Eek 575 whan man destourbeth concepcioun of a child, and maketh a womman outher bareyne by drynkynge venenouse herbes thurgh which she may nat conceyve, or sleeth a child by drynkes wilfully, or elles putteth certeine material thynges in hire secree places to slee the child,/ or elles dooth unkyndely synne, by which man or womman shedeth hire nature in manere or in place ther as a child may nat be conceived, or elles if a woman have conceyved, and hurt hirself and sleeth the child, yet is it homycide./ What seye we eek of wommen that mordren hir children for drede of worldly shame? Certes, an horrible homicide./ Homycide is eek if a man approcheth to a womman by desir of lecherie, thurgh which the child is perissed, or elles smyteth a womman wityngly, thurgh which she leseth hir child. Alle thise been homycides and horrible deedly synnes./ Yet comen ther of Ire manye mo synnes, as wel in word as in thoght and in dede; as he that arretteth upon God, or blameth God of thyng of which he is hymself gilty, or despiseth God and alle his halwes, as doon thise cursede hasardours in diverse contrees./ This cursed synne doon they, 580 whan they feelen in hir herte ful wikkedly of God and of his halwes./ Also whan they treten unreverently the sacrement of the auter, thilke synne is so greet that unnethe may it been releessed, but that the mercy of God passeth alle his werkes; it is so greet, and he so benigne./ Thanne comth of Ire attry angre. Whan a man is sharply amonested in his shrifte to forleten his synne,/ thanne wole he be angry, and answeren hokerly and angrily, and

561 **bynymeth:** takes away
567 **areysen:** impose   **custumes:** duties (customary rents, services, or tolls)   **taillages:** taxes
568 **abreggynge:** reduction   **shepe:** payment   **usure:** usury

572 **in his defendaunt:** in defending himself
575 **overlyeth:** lies upon
577 **unkyndely:** unnatural
579 **perissed:** killed
580 **arretteth upon:** blames
583 **attry:** poisonous
584 **hokerly:** disdainfully

deffenden or excusen his synne by unstedefastnesse of his flessh; or elles he dide it for
to holde compaignye with his felawes; or elles,
he seith, the feend enticed hym;/ or elles he
dide it for his youthe; or elles his compleccioun is so corageous that he may nat forbere;
or elles it is his destinee, as he seith, unto a
certein age; or elles, he seith, it cometh hym
of gentillesse of his auncestres; and semblable thynges./ Alle thise manere of folk 585
so wrappen hem in hir synnes that they ne
wol nat delivere hemself. For soothly, no wight
that excuseth hym wilfully of his synne may
nat been delivered of his synne til that he
mekely biknoweth his synne./ After this,
thanne cometh sweryng, that is expres agayn
the comandement of God; and this bifalleth
ofte of anger and of Ire./ God seith, "Thow
shalt nat take the name of thy Lord God in
veyn or in ydel." Also oure Lord Jhesu Crist
seith, by the word of Seint Mathew,/ "Ne wol
ye nat swere in alle manere; neither by hevene, for it is Goddes trone; ne by erthe, for
it is the bench of his feet; ne by Jerusalem,
for it is the citee of a greet kyng; ne by thyn
heed, for thou mayst nat make an heer whit
ne blak./ But seyeth by youre word 'ye, ye,'
and 'nay, nay'; and what that is moore, it
is of yvel"—thus seith Crist./ For Cristes 590
sake, ne swereth nat so synfully in dis-
membrynge of Crist by soule, herte, bones, and
body. For certes, it semeth that ye thynke that
the cursede Jewes ne dismembred nat ynough
the preciouse persone of Crist, but ye dismem-
bre hym moore./ And if so be that the lawe
compelle yow to swere, thanne rule yow after
the lawe of God in youre sweryng, as seith
Jeremye, *quarto capitulo:* Thou shalt kepe
three condicions: thou shalt swere "in trouthe,
in doom, and in rightwisnesse."/ This is to
seyn, thou shalt swere sooth, for every lesynge
is agayns Crist; for Crist is verray trouthe.
And thynk wel this: that "every greet swerere,
nat compelled lawefully to swere, the wounde
shal nat departe from his hous" whil he useth
swich unleveful sweryng./ Thou shalt sweren
eek in doom, whan thou art constreyned by thy
domesman to witnessen the trouthe./ Eek thow
shalt nat swere for envye, ne for favour, ne for
meede, but for rightwisnesse, for declaracioun

of it, to the worshipe of God and helpyng
of thyne evene-Cristene./ And therfore 595
every man that taketh Goddes name in
ydel, or falsly swereth with his mouth, or elles
taketh on hym the name of Crist, to be called
a Cristen man and lyveth agayns Cristes lyvynge and his techynge, alle they taken Goddes
name in ydel./ Looke eek what Seint Peter
seith, *Actuum quarto, Non est aliud nomen
sub celo, etc.,* "Ther nys noon oother name,"
seith Seint Peter, "under hevene yeven to
men, in which they mowe be saved"; that is to
seyn, but the name of Jhesu Crist./ Take kep
eek how precious is the name of Crist, as seith
Seint Paul, *ad Philipenses secundo, In nomine
Jhesu, etc.,* "That in the name of Jhesu every
knee of hevenely creatures, or erthely, or of helle
sholde bowe," for it is so heigh and so worshipful that the cursede feend in helle sholde trem-
blen to heeren it ynempned./ Thanne semeth
it that men that sweren so horribly by his
blessed name, that they despise it moore
booldely than dide the cursede Jewes or elles
the devel, that trembleth whan he heereth his
name./

Now certes, sith that sweryng, but if it
be lawefully doon, is so heighly deffended,
muche worse is forsweryng falsly, and yet
nedelees./ 600

What seye we eek of hem that deliten
hem in sweryng, and holden it a gentrie or a
manly dede to swere grete othes? And what
of hem that of verray usage ne cesse nat to
swere grete othes, al be the cause nat worth
a straw? Certes, this is horrible synne./ Swer-
ynge sodeynly withoute avysement is eek a
synne./ But lat us go now to thilke horrible
sweryng of adjuracioun and conjuracioun, as
doon thise false enchauntours or nigromanciens in bacyns ful of water, or in a bright
swerd, in a cercle, or in a fir, or in a shulder-
boon of a sheep./ I kan nat seye but that they
doon cursedly and dampnably agayns Crist and
al the feith of hooly chirche./

What seye we of hem that bileeven on divynailes, as by flight or by noyse of briddes, or
of beestes, or by sort, by nigromancie, by dremes,
by chirkynge of dores or crakkynge of houses,

585 corageous: ardent
592 Jeremye: Jeremiah *quarto capitulo:* in the fourth chapter
593 unleveful: unlawful
594 doom: a case at law domesman: judge

597 *Actuum quarto:* Acts, chapter four
598 *ad Philipenses secundo:* (Epistle) to the Philippians, second
chapter
600 forsweryng falsly: perjury
603 adjuracioun: exorcism conjuracioun: conjuring up spirits
nigromanciens: necromancers
605 divynailes: divinations sort: divination chirkynge:
squeaking crakkynge: creaking

by gnawynge of rattes, and swich manere wrecchednesse?/ Certes, al this thyng is 605 deffended by God and by hooly chirche. For which they been acursed, til they come to amendement, that on swich filthe setten hire bileeve./ Charmes for woundes or maladie of men or of beestes, if they taken any effect, it may be peraventure that God suffreth it, for folk sholden yeve the moore feith and reverence to his name./

Now wol I speken of lesynges, which generally is fals signyficaunce of word, in entente to deceyven his evene-Cristene./ Som lesynge is of which ther comth noon avantage to no wight; and som lesynge turneth to the ese and profit of o man, and to disese and damage of another man./ Another lesynge is for to saven his lyf or his catel. Another lesynge comth of delit for to lye, in which delit they wol forge a long tale and peynten it with alle circumstaunces, where al the ground of the tale is fals./ Som lesynge comth for he wole 610 sustene his word; and som lesynge comth of reccheleesnesse withouten avisement; and semblable thynges./

Lat us now touche the vice of flaterynge, which ne comth nat gladly but for drede or for coveitise./ Flaterye is generally wrongful preisynge. Flatereres been the develes norices, that norissen his children with milk of losengerie./ For sothe, Salomon seith that "Flaterie is wors than detraccioun." For somtyme detraccion maketh an hauteyn man be the moore humble, for he dredeth detraccion; but certes flaterye, that maketh a man to enhauncen his herte and his contenaunce./ Flatereres been the develes enchauntours; for they make a man to wene of hymself be lyk that he nys nat lyk./ They been lyk to Judas that bi- 615 traysen a man to sellen hym to his enemy; that is to the devel./ Flatereres been the develes chapelleyns, that syngen evere *Placebo./* I rekene flaterie in the vices of Ire, for ofte tyme if o man be wrooth with another, thanne wole he flatere som wight to sustene hym in his querele./

Speke we now of swich cursynge as comth of irous herte. Malisoun generally may be seyd every maner power of harm. Swich cursynge bireveth man fro the regne of God, as seith Seint Paul./ And ofte tyme swich cursynge wrongfully retorneth agayn to hym that curseth, as a bryd that retorneth agayn to his owene nest./ And over alle thyng men 620 oghten eschewe to cursen hire children, and yeven to the devel hire engendrure, as ferforth as in hem is. Certes, it is greet peril and greet synne./

Lat us thanne speken of chidynge and reproche, whiche been ful grete woundes in mannes herte, for they unsowen the semes of freendshipe in mannes herte./ For certes, unnethes may a man pleynly been accorded with hym that hath hym openly revyled and repreved and disclaundred. This is a ful grisly synne, as Crist seith in the gospel./ And taak kep now, that he that repreveth his neighebor, outher he repreveth hym by som harm of peyne that he hath on his body, as "mesel," "croked harlot," or by som synne that he dooth./ Now if he repreve hym by harm of peyne, thanne turneth the repreve to Jhesu Crist, for peyne is sent by the rightwys sonde of God, and by his suffrance, be it meselrie, or maheym, or maladie./ And if he repreve hym 625 uncharitably of synne, as "thou holour," "thou dronkelewe harlot," and so forth, thanne aperteneth that to the rejoysynge of the devel, that evere hath joye that men doon synne./ And certes, chidynge may nat come but out of a vileyns herte. For after the habundance of the herte speketh the mouth ful ofte./ And ye shul understonde that looke, by any wey, whan any man shal chastise another, that he be war from chidynge or reprevynge. For trewely, but he be war, he may ful lightly quyken the fir of angre and of wratthe, which that he sholde quenche, and peraventure sleeth hym which that he myghte chastise with benignitee./ For as seith Salomon, "The amyable tonge is the tree of lyf" — that is to seyn, of lyf espirituieel — and soothly, a deslavee tonge sleeth the spirites of hym that repreveth and eek of hym that is repreved./ Loo, what seith Seint Augustyn: "Ther is nothyng so lyk the develes child as he that ofte chideth." Seint Paul seith eek, "The servant of God bihoveth nat to chide."/ And how that chidynge be a 630 vileyns thyng bitwixe alle manere folk,

---

614 **hauteyn:** haughty
617 *Placebo:* "I shall please"
618 **querele:** dispute

622 **unsowen:** unravel, undo **semes:** seams
624 **mesel:** leper **croked harlot:** crippled rascal
625 **rightwys:** just **sonde:** dispensation **meselrie:** leprosy
maheym: bodily injury
626 **holour:** lecher
629 **deslavee:** unbridled

yet is it certes moost uncovenable bitwixe a man and his wyf, for there is nevere reste. And therfore seith Salomon, "An hous that is uncovered and droppynge and a chidynge wyf been lyke."/ A man that is in a droppynge hous in manye places, though he eschewe the droppynge in o place, it droppeth on hym in another place. So fareth it by a chydynge wyf; but she chide hym in o place, she wol chide hym in another./ And therfore, "Bettre is a morsel of breed with joye than an hous ful of delices with chidynge," seith Salomon./ Seint Paul seith, "O ye wommen, be ye subgetes to youre housbondes as bihoveth in God, and ye men loveth youre wyves." *Ad Colossenses tertio.*/

Afterward speke we of scornynge, which is a wikked synne, and namely whan he scorneth a man for his goode werkes./ 635 For certes, swiche scorneres faren lyk the foule tode, that may nat endure to smelle the soote savour of the vyne whanne it florissheth./ Thise scorneres been partyng felawes with the devel; for they han joye whan the devel wynneth and sorwe whan he leseth./ They been adversaries of Jhesu Crist, for they haten that he loveth — that is to seyn, salvacioun of soule./

Speke we now of wikked conseil, for he that wikked conseil yeveth is a traytour. For he deceyveth hym that trusteth in hym, *ut Achitofel ad Absolonem.* But nathelees, yet is his wikked conseil first agayn hymself./ For, as seith the wise man, "Every fals lyvynge hath this propertee in hymself, that he that wole anoye another man, he anoyeth first hymself."/ 640 And men shul understonde that man shal nat taken his conseil of fals folk, ne of angry folk, or grevous folk, ne of folk that loven specially to muchel hir owene profit, ne to muche worldly folk, namely in conseilynge of soules./

Now comth the synne of hem that sowen and maken discord amonges folk, which is a synne that Crist hateth outrely. And no wonder is, for he deyde for to make concord./ And moore shame do they to Crist than dide they that hym crucifiede, for God loveth bettre that

freendshipe be amonges folk, than he dide his owene body, the which that he yaf for unitee. Therfore been they likned to the devel, that evere is aboute to maken discord./

Now comth the synne of double tonge, swiche as speken faire byforn folk and wikkedly bihynde, or elles they maken semblant as though they speeke of good entencioun, or elles in game and pley, and yet they speke of wikked entente./

Now comth biwreying of conseil, thurgh which a man is defamed; certes, unnethe may he restoore the damage./   645

Now comth manace, that is an open folye, for he that ofte manaceth, he threteth moore than he may parfourne ful ofte tyme./

Now cometh ydel wordes, that is withouten profit of hym that speketh tho wordes, and eek of hym that herkneth tho wordes. Or elles ydel wordes been tho that been nedelees or withouten entente of natureel profit./ And al be it that ydel wordes been somtyme venial synne, yet sholde men douten hem, for we shul yeve rekenynge of hem bifore God./

Now comth janglynge, that may nat been withoute synne. And, as seith Salomon, "It is a sygne of apert folye."/ And therfore a philosophre seyde, whan men axed hym how that men sholde plese the peple, and he answerde, "Do manye goode werkes, and spek fewe jangles."/   650

After this comth the synne of japeres, that been the develes apes, for they maken folk to laughe at hire japerie as folk doon at the gawdes of an ape. Swiche japeres deffendeth Seint Paul./ Looke how that vertuouse wordes and hooly conforten hem that travaillen in the service of Crist, right so conforten the vileyns wordes and knakkes of japeris hem that travaillen in the service of the devel./ Thise been the synnes that comen of the tonge, that comen of Ire and of othere synnes mo./

Sequitur remedium contra
peccatum Ire.

The remedie agayns Ire is a vertu that men clepen mansuetude, that is debonairetee; and

---

631 **uncovenable:** unsuitable   **droppynge:** leaking
634 *Ad Colossenses tertio:* (Epistle) to the Colossians, chapter three
636 **tode:** toad
637 **partyng felawes:** partners
639 *ut Achitofel ad Absolonem:* as Achitophel (did) to Absalom
641 **grevous:** hostile

643 **aboute to:** busied with
644 **maken semblant:** feign, pretend
649 **apert:** clear
650 **jangles:** idle words
651 **japeres:** mockers   **gawdes:** tricks
652 **knakkes:** tricks
Sequitur remedium, *etc.*: Now follows the remedy against the sin of Anger.
654 **mansuetude:** meekness

eek another vertu, that men callen pacience or suffrance./

Debonairetee withdraweth and refreyneth the stirynges and the moevynges of mannes corage in his herte, in swich manere that they ne skippe nat out by angre ne by ire./ Suf- 655 france suffreth swetely alle the anoyaunces and the wronges that men doon to man outward./ Seint Jerome seith thus of debonairetee, that "it dooth noon harm to no wight ne seith; ne for noon harm that men doon or seyn, he ne eschawfeth nat agayns his resoun."/ This vertu somtyme comth of nature, for, as seith the Philosophre, "A man is a quyk thyng, by nature debonaire and tretable to goodnesse; but whan debonairetee is enformed of grace, thanne is it the moore worth."/

Pacience, that is another remedie agayns Ire, is a vertu that suffreth swetely every mannes goodnesse, and is nat wrooth for noon harm that is doon to hym./ The Philosophre seith that pacience is thilke vertu that suffreth debonairely alle the outrages of adversitee and every wikked word./ This vertu mak- 660 eth a man lyk to God, and maketh hym Goddes owene deere child, as seith Crist. This vertu disconfiteth thyn enemy. And therfore seith the wise man, "If thow wolt venquysse thyn enemy, lerne to suffre."/ And thou shalt understonde that man suffreth foure manere of grevances in outward thynges, agayns the whiche foure he moot have foure manere of paciences./

The firste grevance is of wikkede wordes. Thilke suffrede Jhesu Crist withouten grucchyng, ful paciently, whan the Jewes despised and repreved hym ful ofte./ Suffre thou therfore paciently; for the wise man seith, "If thou stryve with a fool, though the fool be wrooth or though he laughe, algate thou shalt have no reste."/ That oother grevance outward is to have damage of thy catel. Theragayns suffred Crist ful paciently, whan he was despoyled of al that he hadde in this lyf, and that nas but his clothes./ The thridde grevance is a 665 man to have harm in his body. That suffred Crist ful paciently in al his passioun./ The fourthe grevance is in outrageous labour in werkes. Wherfore I seye that folk that maken

hir servantz to travaillen to grevously or out of tyme, as on haly dayes, soothly they do greet synne./ Heer-agayns suffred Crist ful paciently and taughte us pacience, whan he baar upon his blissed shulder the croys upon which he sholde suffren despitous deeth./ Heere may men lerne to be pacient, for certes noght oonly Cristen men been pacient for love of Jhesu Crist and for gerdoun of the blisful lyf that is perdurable, but certes, the olde payens that nevere were Cristene commendeden and useden the vertu of pacience./

A philosophre upon a tyme, that wolde have beten his disciple for his grete trespas, for which he was greetly amoeved, and broghte a yerde to scoure with the child;/ and 670 whan this child saugh the yerde, he seyde to his maister, "What thenke ye do?" "I wol bete thee," quod the maister, "for thy correccioun."/ "For sothe," quod the child, "ye oghten first correcte youreself, that han lost al youre pacience for the gilt of a child."/ "For sothe," quod the maister al wepynge, "thow seyst sooth. Have thow the yerde, my deere sone, and correcte me for myn inpacience."/ Of pacience comth obedience, thurgh which a man is obedient to Crist and to alle hem to whiche he oghte to been obedient in Crist./ And understond wel that obedience is parfit whan that a man dooth gladly and hastily, with good herte entierly, al that he sholde do./ Obedience generally is to 675 parfourne the doctrine of God and of his sovereyns, to whiche hym oghte to ben obeisaunt in alle rightwisnesse./

Sequitur de Accidia.

After the synne of Envye and of Ire, now wol I speken of the synne of Accidie. For Envye blyndeth the herte of a man, and Ire troubleth a man, and Accidie maketh hym hevy, thoghtful, and wraw./ Envye and Ire maken bitternesse in herte, which bitternesse is mooder of Accidie, and bynymeth hym the love of alle goodnesse. Thanne is Accidie the angwissh of troubled herte; and Seint Augustyn seith, "It is anoy of goodnesse and joye of harm."/ Certes, this is a dampnable synne, for it dooth wrong to Jhesu Crist, in as muche

655 **refreyneth:** restrains
657 **eschawfeth:** becomes inflamed (with emotion)
658 **the Philosophre:** Aristotle
667 **outrageous labour in werkes:** forced labor, service demanded beyond the customary obligations

670 **yerde:** stick, rod   **scoure:** punish
Sequitur, *etc.*: Now follows the section on Sloth.
677 **wraw:** fretful
678 **anoy:** vexation

as it bynymeth the service that men oghte doon to Crist with alle diligence, as seith Salomon./ But Accidie dooth no swich diligence. He dooth alle thyng with anoy, and with wrawnesse, slaknesse, and excusacioun, and with ydelnesse, and unlust; for which the book seith, "Acursed be he that dooth the service of God necligently."/ Thanne is Accidie en- 680 emy to everich estaat of man, for certes the estaat of man is in three maneres./ Outher it is th'estaat of innocence, as was th'estaat of Adam biforn that he fil into synne, in which estaat he was holden to wirche as in heriynge and adowrynge of God./ Another estaat is the estaat of synful men, in which estaat men been holden to laboure in preiynge to God for amendement of hire synnes, and that he wole graunte hem to arysen out of hir synnes./ Another estaat is th'estaat of grace, in which estaat he is holden to werkes of penitence. And certes, to alle thise thynges is Accidie enemy and contrarie, for he loveth no bisynesse at al./ Now certes this foule synne Accidie is eek a ful greet enemy to the liflode of the body, for it ne hath no purveaunce agayn temporeel necessitee, for it forsleweth and forsluggeth and destroyeth alle goodes temporeles by recch-eleesnesse./   685

The fourthe thyng is that Accidie is lyk hem that been in the peyne of helle, by cause of hir slouthe and of hire hevynesse, for they that been dampned been so bounde that they ne may neither wel do ne wel thynke./ Of Accidie comth first that a man is anoyed and encombred for to doon any goodnesse, and maketh that God hath abhomynacion of swich Accidie, as seith Seint John./

Now comth Slouthe, that wol nat suffre noon hardnesse ne no penaunce. For soothly, Slouthe is so tendre and so delicaat, as seith Salomon, that he wol nat suffre noon hardnesse ne penaunce, and therfore he shendeth al that he dooth./ Agayns this roten-herted synne of Accidie and Slouthe sholde men exercise hemself to doon goode werkes, and manly and vertuously cacchen corage wel to doon, thynkynge that oure Lord Jhesu Crist quiteth every good dede, be it never so lite./ Usage of labour is

a greet thyng, for it maketh, as seith Seint Bernard, the laborer to have stronge armes and harde synwes; and slouthe maketh hem feble and tendre./ Thanne comth drede 690 to bigynne to werke anye goode werkes. For certes, he that is enclyned to synne, hym thynketh it is so greet an emprise for to undertake to doon werkes of goodnesse,/ and casteth in his herte that the circumstaunces of goodnesse been so grevouse and so chargeaunt for to suffre, that he dar nat undertake to do werkes of goodnesse, as seith Seint Gregorie./

Now comth wanhope, that is despeir of the mercy of God, that comth somtyme of to muche outrageous sorwe, and somtyme of to muche drede, ymaginynge that he hath doon so muche synne that it wol nat availlen hym, though he wolde repenten hym and forsake synne,/ thurgh which despeir or drede he abaundoneth al his herte to every maner synne, as seith Seint Augustin./ Which dampnable synne, if that it continue unto his ende, it is cleped synnyng in the Hooly Goost./ This hor- 695 rible synne is so perilous that he that is despeired, ther nys no felonye ne no synne that he douteth for to do, as shewed wel by Judas./ Certes, aboven alle synnes thanne is this synne moost displesant to Crist, and moost adversarie./ Soothly, he that despeireth hym is lyk the coward champioun recreant, that seith "creant" withoute nede. Allas, allas, nedeles is he recreant and nedelees despeired./ Certes, the mercy of God is evere redy to the penitent, and is aboven alle his werkes./ Allas, kan a man nat bithynke hym on the gospel of Seint Luc, 15, where as Crist seith that "as wel shal ther be joye in hevene upon a synful man that dooth penitence, as upon nynty and nyne rightful men that neden no penitence."/ 700 Looke forther, in the same gospel, the joye and the feeste of the goode man that hadde lost his sone, whan his sone with repentaunce was retourned to his fader./ Kan they nat remembren hem eek that, as seith Seint Luc, 23, how that the theef that was hanged bisyde Jhesu Crist seyde, "Lord, remembre of me, whan thow comest into thy regne"?/ "For sothe," seyde Crist, "I seye to thee, to-day shaltow been with me in paradys."/ Certes,

680 **wrawnesse:** fretfulness **slaknesse:** slowness, idleness
excusacioun: making excuses **unlust:** disinclination
685 **liflode:** livelihood, sustenance **forsleweth:** loses by
delaying **forsluggeth:** spoils through sluggishness
689 **quiteth:** rewards

692 **chargeaunt:** burdensome
693 **wanhope:** despair
695 **in:** against
698 **recreant:** cowardly, confessing himself defeated (*creant*)

ther is noon so horrible synne of man that it ne may in his lyf be destroyed by penitence, thurgh vertu of the passion and of the deeth of Crist./ Allas, what nedeth man thanne to been despeired, sith that his mercy so redy is and large? Axe and have./ Thanne com- 705 eth sompnolence, that is sloggy slombrynge, which maketh a man be hevy and dul in body and in soule, and this synne comth of Slouthe./ And certes, the tyme that, by wey of resoun, men sholde nat slepe, that is by the morwe, but if ther were cause resonable./ For soothly, the morwe tyde is moost covenable a man to seye his preyeres, and for to thynken on God, and for to honoure God, and to yeven almesse to the povre that first cometh in the name of Crist./ Lo, what seith Salomon: "Whoso wolde by the morwe awaken and seke me, he shal fynde."/ Thanne cometh necligence, or reccheleesnesse, that rekketh of no thyng. And how that ignoraunce be mooder of alle harm, certes, necligence is the norice./ Necligence ne dooth no 710 fors, whan he shal doon a thyng, wheither he do it weel or baddely./

Of the remedie of thise two synnes, as seith the wise man, that "He that dredeth God, he spareth nat to doon that him oghte doon."/ And he that loveth God, he wol doon diligence to plese God by his werkes and abaundone hymself, with al his myght, wel for to doon./ Thanne comth ydelnesse, that is the yate of alle harmes. An ydel man is lyk to a place that hath no walles; the develes may entre on every syde, or sheten at hym at discovert, by temptacion on every syde./ This ydelnesse is the thurrok of alle wikked and vileyns thoghtes, and of alle jangles, trufles, and of alle ordure./ 715 Certes, the hevene is yeven to hem that wol labouren, and nat to ydel folk. Eek David seith that "they ne been nat in the labour of men, ne they shul nat been whipped with men" — that is to seyn, in purgatorie./ Certes, thanne semeth it they shul be tormented with the devel in helle, but if they doon penitence./

Thanne comth the synne that men clepen *tarditas,* as whan a man is to laterede or tariynge er he wole turne to God, and certes that is a greet folie. He is lyk to hym that falleth in the dych and wol nat arise./ And this vice comth of a fals hope, that he thynketh that he shal lyve longe; but that hope faileth ful ofte./

Thanne comth lachesse; that is he that whan he biginneth any good werk anon he shal forleten it and stynten, as doon they that han any wight to governe and ne taken of hym namoore kep anon as they fynden any contrarie or any anoy./ Thise been 720 the newe sheepherdes that leten hir sheep wityngly go renne to the wolf that is in the breres, or do no fors of hir owene governaunce./ Of this comth poverte and destruccioun, bothe of spiritueel and temporeel thynges. Thanne comth a manere cooldnesse, that freseth al the herte of a man./ Thanne comth undevocioun, thurgh which a man is so blent, as seith Seint Bernard, and hath swich langour in soule that he may neither rede ne singe in hooly chirche, ne heere ne thynke of no devocioun, ne travaille with his handes in no good werk, that it nys hym unsavory and al apalled./ Thanne wexeth he slough and slombry, and soone wol be wrooth, and soone is enclyned to hate and to envye./ Thanne comth the synne of worldly sorwe, swich as is cleped *tristicia,* that sleeth man, as seith Seint Paul./ For 725 certes, swich sorwe werketh to the deeth of the soule and of the body also; for therof comth that a man is anoyed of his owene lif./ Wherfore swich sorwe shorteth ful ofte the lif of man, er that his tyme be come by wey of kynde./

Remedium contra peccatum Accidie.

Agayns this horrible synne of Accidie, and the branches of the same, ther is a vertu that is called *fortitudo* or strengthe, that is an affeccioun thurgh which a man despiseth anoyouse thinges./ This vertu is so myghty and so vigerous that it dar withstonde myghtily and wisely kepen hymself fro perils that been wikked, and wrastle agayn the assautes of the devel./ For it enhaunceth and enforceth the soule, right as Accidie abateth it and maketh it fieble. For this *fortitudo* may endure by long suffraunce the travailles that been covenable./   730

This vertu hath manye speces; and the firste is cleped magnanimitee, that is to seyn,

706 **sloggy:** sluggish **slombrynge:** sleeping
713 **abaundone:** devote
714 **discovert:** an exposed position
715 **thurrok:** bilge, storage place **trufles:** trifles, idle jests
718 **laterede:** tardy, sluggish

720 **lachesse:** laziness
722 **freseth:** freezes
723 **undevocioun:** lack of devotion **apalled:** faded
724 **slough:** slow, sluggish **slombry:** sleepy
Remedium, *etc.*: The remedy against the sin of Sloth.
728 **anoyouse:** noisome, harmful
730 **abateth:** reduces

greet corage. For certes, ther bihoveth greet corage agains Accidie, lest that it ne swolwe the soule by the synne of sorwe, or destroye it by wanhope./ This vertu maketh folk to undertake harde thynges and grevouse thynges, by hir owene wil, wisely and resonably./ And for as muchel as the devel fighteth agayns a man moore by queyntise and by sleighte than by strengthe, therfore men shal withstonden hym by wit and by resoun and by discrecioun./ Thanne arn ther the vertues of feith and hope in God and in his seintes to acheve and acomplice the goode werkes in the whiche he purposeth fermely to continue./ Thanne comth seuretee or sikernesse, and that is whan a man ne douteth no travaille in tyme comynge of the goode werkes that a man hath bigonne./ Thanne comth magnificence; that is to seyn, whan a man dooth and parfourneth grete werkes of goodnesse; and that is the ende why that men sholde do goode werkes, for in the acomplissynge of grete goode werkes lith the grete gerdoun./ Thanne is ther constaunce, that is stablenesse of corage, and this sholde been in herte by stedefast feith, and in mouth, and in berynge, and in chiere, and in dede./ Eke ther been mo speciale remedies against Accidie in diverse werkes, and in consideracioun of the peynes of helle and of the joyes of hevene, and in the trust of the grace of the Holy Goost, that wole yeve hym myght to parfourne his goode entente./

Sequitur de Avaricia.

After Accidie wol I speke of Avarice and of Coveitise, of which synne seith Seint Paul that "the roote of alle harmes is Coveitise." *Ad Thimotheum Sexto./* For soothly, whan the herte of a man is confounded in itself and troubled, and that the soule hath lost the confort of God, thanne seketh he an ydel solas of worldly thynges./   740

Avarice, after the descripcioun of Seint Augustyn, is a likerousnesse in herte to have erthely thynges./ Som oother folk seyn that Avarice is for to purchacen manye erthely thynges and no thyng yeve to hem that han nede./ And understoond that Avarice ne stant nat oonly in lond ne catel, but somtyme in science and in glorie, and in every manere of outrageous thyng is Avarice and Coveitise./

And the difference bitwixe Avarice and Coveitise is this: Coveitise is for to coveite swiche thynges as thou hast nat; and Avarice is for to withholde and kepe swiche thynges as thou hast, withoute rightful nede./ Soothly, this Avarice is a synne that is ful dampnable, for al hooly writ curseth it and speketh agayns that vice, for it dooth wrong to Jhesu Crist./ For it bireveth hym the love that   745 men to hym owen, and turneth it bakward agayns alle resoun,/ and maketh that the avaricious man hath moore hope in his catel than in Jhesu Crist, and dooth moore observance in kepynge of his tresor than he dooth to the service of Jhesu Crist./ And therfore seith Seint Paul *Ad Ephesios quinto,* that an avaricious man is the thraldom of ydolatrie./

What difference is bitwixe an ydolastre and an avaricious man, but that an ydolastre, per aventure, ne hath but o mawmet or two, and the avaricious man hath manye? For certes, every floryn in his cofre is his mawmet./ And certes, the synne of mawmettric is the firste thyng that God deffended in the ten comaundementz, as bereth witnesse in *Exodi capitulo vicesimo:/* "Thou shalt have no false   750 goddes bifore me, ne thou shalt make to thee no grave thyng." Thus is an avaricious man, that loveth his tresor biforn God, an ydolastre,/ thurgh this cursed synne of avarice. Of Coveitise comen thise harde lordshipes, thurgh whiche men been distreyned by taylages, custumes, and cariages, moore than hire duetee or resoun is. And eek taken they of hire bonde-men amercimentz, whiche myghten moore resonably ben cleped extorcions than amercimentz./ Of whiche amercimentz and raunsonynge of boonde-men somme lordes stywardes seyn that it is rightful, for as muche as a cherl hath no temporeel thyng that it ne is his lordes, as they seyn./ But certes, thise lordshipes doon wrong that bireven hire bondefolk thynges that they nevere yave hem. *Augustinus, De Civitate libro nono./* "Sooth is that the condicioun of thraldom and the firste

---

733 **queyntise:** cunning trickery
Sequitur, *etc.*: Now follows the section on Avarice.
739 *Ad Thimotheum Sexto:* (Epistle) to Timothy, chapter six

748 *Ad Ephesios quinto:* (Epistle) to the Ephesians, chapter five
749 **ydolastre:** idolater   **mawmet:** idol
750 **mawmettrie:** idolatry   *Exodi capitulo vicesimo:* twentieth chapter of Exodus
752 **taylages:** taxes   **custumes:** duties (customary rents, services, or tolls)   **cariages:** services of providing transportation for the lord, or payments in lieu of the same   **bonde-men:** serfs   **amercimentz:** fines imposed at the mercy of the court
753 **raunsonynge of:** forcing payment from
754 *Augustinus, De Civitate libro nono:* St. Augustine, *City* (of God), in the ninth book

cause of thraldom is for synne. *Genesis nono.* / Thus may ye seen that the gilt 755 disserveth thraldom, but nat nature."/ Wherfore thise lordes ne sholde nat muche glorifien hem in hir lordshipes, sith that by natureel condicion they been nat lordes over thralles, but that thraldom comth first by the desert of synne./ And forther over, ther as the lawe seith that temporeel goodes of boonde-folk been the goodes of hir lordshipes, ye, that is for to understonde, the goodes of the emperour, to deffenden hem in hir right, but nat for to robben hem ne reven hem./ And therfore seith Seneca, "Thy prudence sholde lyve benignely with thy thralles."/ Thilke that thou clepest thy thralles been Goddes peple, for humble folk been Cristes freendes; they been contubernyal with the Lord./   760

Thynk eek that of swich seed as cherles spryngen, of swich seed spryngen lordes. As wel may the cherl be saved as the lord./ The same deeth that taketh the cherl, swich deeth taketh the lord. Wherfore I rede, do right so with thy cherl, as thou woldest that thy lord dide with thee, if thou were in his plit./ Every synful man is a cherl to synne. I rede thee, certes, that thou, lord, werke in swich wise with thy cherles that they rather love thee than drede./ I woot wel ther is degree above degree, as reson is, and skile is that men do hir devoir ther as it is due, but certes, extorcions and despit of youre underlynges is dampnable./

And forther over, understoond wel that thise conquerours or tirauntz maken ful ofte thralles of hem that been born of as roial blood as been they that hem conqueren./ This 765 name of thraldom was nevere erst kowth til that Noe seyde that his sone Canaan sholde be thral to his bretheren for his synne./ What seye we thanne of hem that pilen and doon extorcions to hooly chirche? Certes, the swerd that men yeven first to a knyght, whan he is newe dubbed, signifieth that he sholde deffenden hooly chirche, and nat robben it ne pilen it; and whoso dooth is traitour to Crist./ And, as seith Seint Augustyn, "They been the develes wolves that stranglen the sheep of Jhesu Crist," and doon worse than wolves./

For soothly, whan the wolf hath ful his wombe, he stynteth to strangle sheep. But soothly, the pilours and destroyours of the godes of hooly chirche ne do nat so, for they ne stynte nevere to pile./

Now as I have seyd, sith so is that synne was first cause of thraldom, thanne is it thus: that thilke tyme that al this world was in synne, thanne was al this world in thraldom and subjeccioun./ But certes, sith the 770 time of grace cam, God ordeyned that som folk sholde be moore heigh in estaat and in degree, and som folk moore lough, and that everich sholde be served in his estaat and in his degree./ And therfore in somme contrees, ther they byen thralles, whan they han turned hem to the feith, they maken hire thralles free out of thraldom. And therfore, certes, the lord oweth to his man that the man oweth to his lord./ The Pope calleth hymself servant of the servantz of God; but for as muche as the estaat of hooly chirche ne myghte nat han be, ne the commune profit myghte nat han be kept, ne pees and rest in erthe, but if God hadde ordeyned that som men hadde hyer degree and som men lower,/ therfore was sovereyntee ordeyned, to kepe and mayntene and deffenden hire underlynges or hire subgetz in resoun, as ferforth as it lith in hire power, and nat to destroyen hem ne confounde./ Wherfore I seye that thilke lordes that been lyk wolves, that devouren the possessiouns or the catel of povre folk wrongfully, withouten mercy or mesure,/ they shul receyven by the same 775 mesure that they han mesured to povre folk the mercy of Jhesu Crist, but if it be amended./ Now comth deceite bitwixe marchaunt and marchant. And thow shalt understonde that marchandise is in manye maneres; that oon is bodily, and that oother is goostly; that oon is honest and leveful, and that oother is deshonest and unleveful./ Of thilke bodily marchandise that is leveful and honest is this: that, there as God hath ordeyned that a regne or a contree is suffisaunt to hymself, thanne is it honest and leveful that of habundaunce of this contree, that men helpe another contree that is moore nedy./ And therfore ther moote been marchantz to bryngen fro that o contree to that oother hire marchandises./ That oother marchandise, that men haunten with fraude and

---

755 *Genesis nono:* Genesis, in the ninth chapter
760 **contubernyal:** on familiar terms
764 **underlynges:** inferiors, thralls
766 **Noe:** Noah **Canaan:** Ham
767 **pilen:** rob

769 **pilours:** thieves

trecherie and deceite, with lesynges and
false othes, is cursed and dampnable./ Es- 780
piritueel marchandise is proprely symonye,
that is ententif desir to byen thyng espiritueel;
that is, thyng that aperteneth to the seintuarie
of God and to cure of the soule./ This desir,
if so be that a man do his diligence to parfournen it, al be it that his desir ne take noon
effect, yet is it to hym a deedly synne; and if
he be ordred, he is irreguleer./ Certes symonye
is cleped of Simon Magus, that wolde han
boght for temporeel catel the yifte that God
hadde yeven by the Hooly Goost to Seint
Peter and to the apostles./ And therfore understoond that bothe he that selleth and he that
beyeth thynges espirituels been cleped symonyals, be it by catel, be it by procurynge, or
by flesshly preyere of his freendes, flesshly
freendes or espiritueel freendes:/ Flesshly in
two maneres; as by kynrede, or othere freendes.
Soothly, if they praye for hym that is nat
worthy and able, it is symonye, if he take the
benefice; and if he be worthy and able,
ther nys noon./ That oother manere is 785
whan men or wommen preyen for folk to
avauncen hem, oonly for wikked flesshly affeccioun that they han unto the persone, and
that is foul symonye./ But certes, in service,
for which men yeven thynges espirituels unto
hir servantz, it moot been understonde that the
service moot been honest and elles nat; and
eek that it be withouten bargaynynge, and that
the persone be able./ For, as seith Seint Damasie, "Alle the synnes of the world, at regard
of this synne, arn as thyng of noght." For it
is the gretteste synne that may be, after the
synne of Lucifer and Antecrist./ For by this
synne God forleseth the chirche and the soule
that he boghte with his precious blood, by hem
that yeven chirches to hem that been nat
digne./ For they putten in theves that stelen
the soules of Jhesu Crist and destroyen his
patrimoyne./ By swiche undigne preestes 790
and curates han lewed men the lasse reverence of the sacramentz of hooly chirche, and

swiche yeveres of chirches putten out the children of Crist and putten into the chirche the
develes owene sone./ They sellen the soules
that lambes sholde kepen to the wolf that strangleth hem. And therfore shul they nevere han
part of the pasture of lambes, that is the blisse
of hevene./ Now comth hasardrie with his
apurtenaunces, as tables and rafles, of which
comth deceite, false othes, chidynges, and alle
ravynes, blasphemynge and reneiynge of God,
and hate of his neighebores, wast of goodes,
mysspendynge of tyme, and somtyme manslaughtre./ Certes, hasardours ne mowe nat
been withouten greet synne whiles they haunte
that craft./ Of Avarice comen eek lesynges,
thefte, fals witnesse, and false othes. And ye
shul understonde that thise been grete synnes
and expres agayn the comaundementz of
God, as I have seyd./ Fals witnesse is in 795
word and eek in dede. In word, as for to
bireve thy neighebores goode name by thy fals
witnessyng, or bireven hym his catel or his
heritage by thy fals witnessyng, whan thou for
ire, or for meede, or for envye, berest fals
witnesse, or accusest hym or excusest hym by
thy fals witnesse, or elles excusest thyself
falsly./ Ware yow, questemongeres and nota-
ries! Certes, for fals witnessyng was Susanna
in ful gret sorwe and peyne, and many another
mo./ The synne of thefte is eek expres agayns
Goddes heeste, and that in two maneres, corporeel or spiritueel./ Corporeel, as for to take
thy neighebores catel agayn his wyl, be it by
force or by sleighte, be it by met or by mesure;/ by stelyng eek of false enditementz upon
hym, and in borwynge of thy neighebores catel,
in entente nevere to payen it agayn, and
semblable thynges./ Espiritueel thefte is 800
sacrilege; that is to seyn, hurtynge of hooly
thynges, or of thynges sacred to Crist, in two
maneres: by reson of the hooly place, as
chirches or chirche-hawes,/ for which every
vileyns synne that men doon in swiche places
may be cleped sacrilege, or every violence in
the semblable places; also, they that withdrawen falsly the rightes that longen to hooly
chirche./ And pleynly and generally, sacrilege

---

782 **ordred:** ordained **irreguleer:** in violation of the rules of
his religious order
784 **symonyals:** simoniacs **procurynge:** procuring a benefice
for someone or soliciting it
785 **able:** suitable
787 **bargaynynge:** fraud
788 **Damasie:** Pope Damasus
789 **forleseth:** loses completely
790 **patrimoyne:** inheritance
791 **undigne:** unworthy **yeveres:** givers

793 **hasardrie:** gambling **tables:** backgammon **rafles:** game
played with three dice **ravynes:** robberies **mysspendynge:**
waste
797 **questemongeres:** conductors of inquests, jurymen
799 **Corporeel:** bodily, natural **met:** measurement
800 **of false:** by means of false
801 **by reson of:** because of **chirche-hawes:** churchyards

is to reven hooly thyng fro hooly place, or unhooly thyng out of hooly place, or hooly thing
out of unhooly place./

Relevacio contra peccatum Avaricie.

Now shul ye understonde that the releevynge
of Avarice is misericorde, and pitee largely
taken. And men myghten axe why that misericorde and pitee is releevynge of Avarice./
Certes, the avricious man sheweth no pitee ne
misericorde to the nedeful man, for he deliteth hym in the kepynge of his tresor, and nat
in the rescowynge ne releevynge of his evene-
Cristen. And therfore speke I first of misericorde./ Thanne is misericorde, as seith   805
the Philosophre, a vertu by which the corage of a man is stired by the mysese of hym
that is mysesed./ Upon which misericorde
folweth pitee in parfournynge of charitable
werkes of misericorde./ And certes, thise
thynges moeven a man to the misericorde of
Jhesu Crist, that he yaf hymself for oure gilt,
and suffred deeth for misericorde, and forgaf
us oure originale synnes,/ and therby relessed
us fro the peynes of helle, and amenused the
peynes of purgatorie by penitence, and yeveth
grace wel to do, and atte laste the blisse of
hevene./ The speces of misericorde been, as
for to lene and for to yeve, and to foryeven
and relesse, and for to han pitee in herte
and compassioun of the meschief of his evene-
Cristene, and eek to chastise, there as nede
is./ Another manere of remedie agayns   810
avarice is resonable largesse; but soothly,
heere bihoveth the consideracioun of the grace
of Jhesu Crist, and of his temporeel goodes,
and eek of the goodes perdurables that Crist
yaf to us;/ and to han remembrance of the
deeth that he shal receyve, he noot whanne,
where, ne how; and eek that he shal forgon al
that he hath, save oonly that he hath despended
in goode werkes./

But for as muche as som folk been unmesurable, men oghten eschue fool-largesse, that
men clepen wast./ Certes, he that is fool-large
ne yeveth nat his catel, but he leseth his catel.
Soothly, what thyng that he yeveth for veyne
glorie, as to mynstrals and to folk for to beren
his renoun in the world, he hath synne therof

and noon almesse./ Certes, he leseth foule his
good that ne seketh with the yifte of his
good nothyng but synne./ He is lyk to an   815
hors that seketh rather to drynken drovy
or trouble water than for to drynken water of
the clere welle./ And for as muchel as they
yeven ther as they sholde nat yeven, to hem
aperteneth thilke malisoun that Crist shal
yeven at the day of doom to hem that shullen
been dampned./

Sequitur de Gulâ.

After Avarice comth Glotonye, which is expres eek agayn the comandement of God. Glotonye is unmesurable appetit to ete or to drynke,
or elles to doon ynogh to the unmesurable appetit and desordeynee coveitise to eten or to
drynke./ This synne corrumped al this world,
as is wel shewed in the synne of Adam and of
Eve. Looke eek what seith Seint Paul of Glotonye:/ "Manye," seith Saint Paul, "goon, of
whiche I have ofte seyd to yow, and now I
seye it wepynge, that been the enemys of the
croys of Crist; of whiche the ende is deeth, and
of whiche hire wombe is hire god, and hire
glorie in confusioun of hem that so savouren erthely thynges."/ He that is   820
usaunt to this synne of glotonye, he ne
may no synne withstonde. He moot been in
servage of alle vices, for it is the develes hoord
ther he hideth hym and resteth./ This synne
hath manye speces. The firste is dronkenesse,
that is the horrible sepulture of mannes resoun;
and therfore, whan a man is dronken, he hath
lost his resoun; and this is deedly synne./ But
soothly, whan that a man is nat wont to strong
drynke, and peraventure ne knoweth nat the
strengthe of the drynke, or hath feblesse in his
heed, or hath travailed, thurgh which he drynketh the moore, al be he sodeynly caught with
drynke, it is no deedly synne, but venyal./ The
seconde spece of glotonye is that the spirit
of a man wexeth al trouble, for dronkenesse
bireveth hym the discrecioun of his wit./ The
thridde spece of glotonye is whan a man de-
voureth his mete and hath no rightful
manere of etynge./ The fourthe is whan,   825
thurgh the grete habundaunce of his mete,

Relevacio, *etc.*: The relief against the sin of Avarice.
804 **misericorde:** mercy
806 **mysese:** distress
813 **unmesurable:** immoderate

816 **drovy:** dirty
Sequitur, *etc.*: Now follows the section on Gluttony.
818 **desordeynee:** excessive
821 **usaunt:** accustomed

the humours in his body been distempred./ The fifthe is foryetelnesse by to muchel drynkynge, for which somtyme a man foryeteth er the morwe what he dide at even, or on the nyght biforn./

In oother manere been distinct the speces of Glotonye, after Seint Gregorie. The firste is for to ete biforn tyme to ete. The seconde is whan a man get hym to delicaat mete or drynke./ The thridde is whan men taken to muche over mesure. The fourthe is curiositee, with greet entente to maken and apparaillen his mete. The fifthe is for to eten to gredily./ Thise been the fyve fyngres of the develes hand, by whiche he draweth folk to synne./   830

Remedium contra peccatum Gule.

Agayns Glotonye is the remedie abstinence, as seith Galien; but that holde I nat meritorie, if he do it oonly for the heele of his body. Seint Augustyn wole that abstinence be doon for vertu and with pacience./ "Abstinence," he seith, "is litel worth but if a man have good wil therto, and but it be enforced by pacience and by charitee, and that men doon it for Godes sake, and in hope to have the blisse of hevene."/

The felawes of abstinence been attemperaunce, that holdeth the meene in alle thynges; eek shame, that eschueth alle deshonestee; suffisance, that seketh no riche metes ne drynkes, ne dooth no fors of to outrageous apparailynge of mete;/ mesure also, that restreyneth by resoun the deslavee appetit of etynge; sobrenesse also, that restreyneth the outrage of drynke;/ sparynge also, that restreyneth the delicaat ese to sitte longe at his mete and softely, wherfore some folk stonden of hir owene wyl to eten at the lasse leyser./   835

Sequitur de Luxuria.

After Glotonye thanne comth Lecherie, for thise two synnes been so ny cosyns that ofte

tyme they wol nat departe./ God woot, this synne is ful displesaunt thyng to God, for he seyde hymself, "Do no lecherie." And therfore he putte grete peynes agayns this synne in the olde lawe./ If womman thral were taken in this synne, she sholde be beten with staves to the deeth; and if she were a gentil womman, she sholde be slayn with stones; and if she were a bisshoppes doghter, she sholde been brent, by Goddes comandement./ Forther over, by the synne of lecherie God dreynte al the world at the diluge. And after that he brente fyve citees with thonder-leyt, and sank hem into helle./

Now lat us speke thanne of thilke stynkynge synne of Lecherie that men clepe avowtrie of wedded folk; that is to seyn, if that oon of hem be wedded, or elles bothe./ Seint John   840 seith that avowtiers shullen been in helle, in a stank brennynge of fyr and of brymston — in fyr for hire lecherye, in brymston for the stynk of hire ordure./ Certes, the brekynge of this sacrement is an horrible thyng. It was maked of God hymself in paradys, and confermed by Jhesu Crist, as witnesseth Seint Mathew in the gospel: "A man shal lete fader and mooder and taken hym to his wif, and they shullen be two in o flessh."/ This sacrement bitokneth the knyttynge togidre of Crist and of hooly chirche./ And nat oonly that God forbad avowtrie in dede, but eek he comanded that thou sholdest nat coveite thy neighebores wyf./ "In this heeste," seith Seint Augustyn, "is forboden alle manere coveitise to doon lecherie." Lo, what seith Seint Mathew in the gospel, that "whoso seeth a womman to coveitise of his lust, he hath doon lecherie with hire in his herte."/ Heere may ye seen that   845 nat oonly the dede of this synne is forboden, but eek the desir to doon that synne./ This cursed synne anoyeth grevousliche hem that it haunten. And first to hire soule, for he obligeth it to synne and to peyne of deeth that is perdurable./ Unto the body anoyeth it grevously also, for it dreyeth hym, and wasteth him, and shent hym, and of his blood he maketh sacrifice to the feend of helle. It wasteth eek his catel and his substaunce./ And certes, if it be a foul thyng a man to waste his catel on wommen, yet is it a fouler thyng whan that, for

---

826 **distempred:** out of balance
827 **foryetelnesse:** forgetfulness
829 **curiositee:** elaborate preparation
Remedium, *etc.*: The remedy against the sin of Gluttony.
831 **Galien:** Galen, the Greek authority on medicine
meritorie: meritorious
833 **deshonestee:** dishonor, shameful acts
834 **deslavee:** uncontrolled **sobrenesse:** sobriety **outrage:** excess
835 **sparynge:** moderation, frugality
Sequitur, *etc.*: Now follows the section on Lechery.

839 **thonder-leyt:** lightning bolts
841 **stank:** pond, pool
848 **dreyeth:** drains (dries)

swich ordure, wommen dispenden upon men hir catel and substaunce./ This synne, as seith the prophete, bireveth man and womman hir goode fame and al hire honour, and it is ful plesaunt to the devel, for therby wynneth he the mooste partie of this world./ And right as a marchant deliteth hym moost in chaffare that he hath moost avantage of, right so deliteth the fend in this ordure./

This is that oother hand of the devel with fyve fyngres to cacche the peple to his vileynye./ The firste fynger is the fool lookynge of the fool womman and of the fool man; that sleeth, right as the basilicok sleeth folk by the venym of his sighte, for the coveitise of eyen folweth the coveitise of the herte./ The seconde fynger is the vileyns touchynge in wikkede manere. And therfore seith Salomon that "whoso toucheth and handleth a womman, he fareth lyk hym that handleth the scorpioun that styngeth and sodeynly sleeth thurgh his envenymynge"; as whoso toucheth warm pych, it shent his fyngres./ The thridde is foule wordes, that fareth lyk fyr, that right anon brenneth the herte./ The fourthe fynger is the kissynge; and trewely he were a greet fool that wolde kisse the mouth of a brennynge oven or of a fourneys./ And moore fooles been they that kissen in vileynye, for that mouth is the mouth of helle; and namely thise olde dotardes holours, yet wol they kisse, though they may nat do, and smatre hem./ Certes, they been lyk to houndes; for an hound, whan he comth by the roser or by othere [bushes], though he may nat pisse, yet wole he heve up his leg and make a contenaunce to pisse./ And for that many man weneth that he may nat synne for no likerousnesse that he dooth with his wyf, certes, that opinion is fals. God woot, a man may sleen hymself with his owene knyf, and make hymselve dronken of his owene tonne./ Certes, be it wyf, be it child, or any worldly thyng that he loveth biforn God, it is his mawmet, and he is an ydolastre./ Man sholde loven hys wyf by discrecioun, paciently and atemprely, and thanne is she as though it were his suster./ The fifthe fynger of the develes hand is the stynk-

850

855

860

ynge dede of Leccherie./ Certes, the fyve fyngres of Glotonie the feend put in the wombe of a man, and with his fyve fingres of Lecherie he gripeth hym by the reynes for to throwen hym into the fourneys of helle,/ ther as they shul han the fyr and the wormes that evere shul lasten, and wepynge and wailynge, sharp hunger and thurst, [and] grymnesse of develes, that shullen al totrede hem withouten respit and withouten ende./ Of Leccherie, as I seyde, sourden diverse speces, as fornicacioun, that is bitwixe man and womman that been nat maried, and this is deedly synne and agayns nature./ Al that is enemy and destruccioun to nature is agayns nature./ Parfay, the resoun of a man telleth eek hym wel that it is deedly synne, for as muche as God forbad leccherie. And Seint Paul yeveth hem the regne that nys dewe to no wight but to hem that doon deedly synne./ Another synne of Leccherie is to bireve a mayden of hir maydenhede, for he that so dooth, certes, he casteth a mayden out of the hyeste degree that is in this present lif/ and bireveth hire thilke precious fruyt that the book clepeth the hundred fruyt. I ne kan seye it noon ootherweyes in Englissh, but in Latyn it highte *Centesimus fructus.*/ Certes, he that so dooth is cause of manye damages and vileynyes, mo than any man kan rekene; right as he somtyme is cause of alle damages that beestes don in the feeld, that breketh the hegge or the closure, thurgh which he destroyeth that may nat been restoored./ For certes, namoore may maydenhede be restoored than an arm that is smyten fro the body may retourne agayn to wexe./ She may have mercy, this woot I wel, if she do penitence; but nevere shal it be that she nas corrupt./ And al be it so that I have spoken somwhat of avowtrie, it is good to shewen mo perils that longen to avowtrie, for to eschue that foule synne./ Avowtrie in Latyn is for to seyn approchynge of oother mannes bed, thurgh which tho that whilom weren o flessh abawndone hir bodyes to othere persones./ Of this synne, as seith the wise man, folwen manye harmes. First, brekynge of feith,

865

870

---

853 **basilicok:** basilisk, a fabulous serpent
854 **pych:** pitch
857 **holours:** lechers **smatre hem:** defile or besmatter themselves
858 **roser:** rosebush
860 **mawmet:** idol **ydolastre:** idolater

863 **reynes:** loins or kidneys (seat of the passions)
864 **grymnesse:** fierceness **totrede:** trample upon
865 **sourden:** arise, originate
869 *Centesimus fructus:* hundredfold fruit; see n.
870 **right as he:** he (i.e., the deflowerer of virgins) is like beasts in the field **closure:** fence
874 **abawndone:** yield, give over

and certes in feith is the keye of Cristendom./ And whan that feith is broken 875 and lorn, soothly Cristendom stant veyn and withouten fruyt./ This synne is eek a thefte, for thefte generally is for to reve a wight his thyng agayns his wille./ Certes, this is the fouleste thefte that may be, whan a womman steleth hir body from hir housbonde and yeveth it to hire holour to defoulen hire, and steleth hir soule fro Crist and yeveth it to the devel./ This is a fouler thefte than for to breke a chirche and stele the chalice, for thise avowtiers breken the temple of God spiritually, and stelen the vessel of grace, that is the body and the soule, for which Crist shal destroyen hem, as seith Seint Paul./ Soothly, of this thefte douted gretly Joseph, whan that his lordes wyf preyed hym of vileynye, whan he seyde, "Lo, my lady, how my lord hath take to me under my warde al that he hath in this world, ne no thyng of his thynges is out of my power, but oonly ye, that been his wyf./ And how sholde I thanne do this 880 wikkednesse, and synne so horribly agayns God and agayns my lord? God it forbeede!" Allas, al to litel is swich trouthe now yfounde./ The thridde harm is the filthe thurgh which they breken the comandement of God, and defoulen the auctour of matrimoyne, that is Crist./ For certes, in so muche as the sacrement of mariage is so noble and so digne, so muche is it gretter synne for to breken it, for God made mariage in paradys, in the estaat of innocence, to multiplye mankynde to the service of God./ And therfore is the brekynge therof the moore grevous; of which brekynge comen false heires ofte tyme, that wrongfully ocupien folkes heritages. And therfore wol Crist putte hem out of the regne of hevene, that is heritage to goode folk./ Of this brekynge comth eek ofte tyme that folk unwar wedden or synnen with hire owene kynrede, and namely thilke harlotes that haunten bordels of thise fool wommen, that mowe be likned to a commune gong, where as men purgen hire ordure./ What seye we eek of pu- 885 tours that lyven by the horrible synne of putrie, and constreyne wommen to yelden hem a certeyn rente of hire bodily puterie, ye,

somtyme of his owene wyf or his child, as doon thise bawdes? Certes, thise been cursede synnes./ Understoond eek that Avowtrie is set gladly in the ten comandementz bitwixe thefte and manslaughtre; for it is the gretteste thefte that may be, for it is thefte of body and of soule./ And it is lyk to homycide, for it kerveth atwo and breketh atwo hem that first were maked o flessh. And therfore, by the olde lawe of God, they sholde be slayn./ But nathelees, by the lawe of Jhesu Crist, that is lawe of pitee, whan he seyde to the womman that was founden in avowtrie, and sholde han been slayn with stones, after the wyl of the Jewes, as was hir lawe, "Go," quod Jhesu Crist, "and have namoore wyl to synne," or, "wille namoore to do synne."/ Soothly the vengeaunce of Avowtrie is awarded to the peynes of helle, but if so be that it be destourbed by penitence./ Yet been ther mo speces of this 890 cursed synne; as whan that oon of hem is religious, or elles bothe; or of folk that been entred into ordre, as subdekne, or dekne, or preest, or hospitaliers. And evere the hyer that he is in ordre, the gretter is the synne./ The thynges that gretly agreggen hire synne is the brekynge of hire avow of chastitee, whan they receyved the ordre./ And forther over, sooth is that hooly ordre is chief of al the tresorie of God and his especial signe and mark of chastitee to shewe that they been joyned to chastitee, which that is the moost precious lyf that is./ And thise ordred folk been specially titled to God, and of the special meignee of God, for which, whan they doon deedly synne, they been the special traytours of God and of his peple; for they lyven of the peple, to preye for the peple, and while they ben suche traitours, here preyer avayleth nat to the peple./ Preestes been aungels, as by the dignitee of hir mysterye; but for sothe, Seint Paul seith that Sathanas transformeth hym in an aungel of light./ Soothly, the preest that haunt- 895 eth deedly synne, he may be likned to the aungel of derknesse transformed in the aungel of light. He semeth aungel of light, but for sothe he is aungel of derknesse./ Swiche preestes been the sones of Helie, as sheweth

879 **breke:** break into
880 **warde:** custody
885 **bordels:** brothels   **gong:** latrine
886 **putours:** pimps   **puterie:** prostitution

887 **gladly:** fittingly
891 **religious:** in a religious order   **subdekne:** subdeacon
hospitaliers: Knights Hospitallers
892 **agreggen:** aggravate, make worse
893 **tresorie:** treasury
894 **ordred:** ordained   **titled:** dedicated

in the Book of Kynges, that they weren the sones of Belial — that is, the devel./ Belial is to seyn, "withouten juge." And so faren they; hem thynketh they been free and han no juge, na-moore than hath a free bole that taketh which cow that hym liketh in the town./ So faren they by wommen. For right as a free bole is ynough for al a toun, right so is a wikked preest corrupcioun ynough for al a parisshe, or for al a contree./ Thise preestes, as seith the book, ne konne nat the mysterie of preesthod to the pe-ple, ne God ne knowe they nat. They ne helde hem nat apayd, as seith the book, of soden flessh that was to hem offred, but they tooke by force the flessh that is rawe./ 900 Certes, so thise shrewes ne holden hem nat apayed of roosted flessh and sode flessh, with which the peple feden hem in greet reverence, but they wole have raw flessh of folkes wyves and hir doghtres./ And certes, thise wommen that consenten to hire harlotrie doon greet wrong to Crist, and to hooly chirche, and alle halwes, and to alle soules; for they bireven alle thise hym that sholde worshipe Crist and hooly chirche and preye for Cristene soules./ And therfore han swiche preestes, and hire lem-manes eek that consenten to hir leccherie, the malisoun of al the court Cristien, til they come to amendement./ The thridde spece of avow-trie is somtyme bitwixe a man and his wyf, and that is whan they take no reward in hire as-semblynge but oonly to hire flesshly delit, as seith Seint Jerome,/ and ne rekken of noth-yng but that they been assembled; by cause that they been maried, al is good ynough, as thynketh to hem./ But in swich folk 905 hath the devel power, as seyde the aungel Raphael to Thobie, for in hire assemblynge they putten Jhesu Crist out of hire herte and yeven hemself to alle ordure./ The fourthe spece is the assemblee of hem that been of hire kynrede, or of hem that been of oon affyn-ytee, or elles with hem with whiche hir fadres or hir kynrede han deled in the synne of lech-erie. This synne maketh hem lyk to houndes,

that taken no kep to kynrede./ And certes, par-entele is in two maneres, outher goostly or flesshly; goostly, as for to deelen with his god-sibbes./ For right so as he that engendreth a child is his flesshly fader, right so is his god-fader his fader espiritueel. For which a wom-man may in no lasse synne assemblen with hire godsib than with hire owene flesshly brother./ The fifthe spece is thilke abhom-ynable synne, of which that no man unnethe oghte speke ne write; nathelees it is openly reherced in holy writ./ This cur-   910 sednesse doon men and wommen in diverse entente and in diverse manere; but though that hooly writ speke of horrible synne, certes hooly writ may nat been defouled, na-moore than the sonne that shyneth on the mixne./ Another synne aperteneth to leccherie, that comth in slepynge, and this synne cometh ofte to hem that been maydenes, and eek to hem that been corrupt; and this synne men clepen polucioun, that comth in foure maneres./ Som-tyme of langwissynge of body, for the humours been to ranke and to habundaunt in the body of man; somtyme of infermetee, for the fieblesse of the vertu retentif, as phisik maketh mencion; somtyme for surfeet of mete and drynke;/ and somtyme of vileyns thoghtes that been enclosed in mannes mynde whan he gooth to slepe, which may nat been withoute synne; for which men moste kepen hem wisely, or elles may men synnen ful grevously./

Remedium contra peccatum
Luxurie.

Now comth the remedie agayns Leccherie, and that is generally chastitee and conti-nence, that restreyneth alle the desordeynee moevynges that comen of flesshly tal-entes./ And evere the gretter merite shal 915 he han that moost restreyneth the wik-kede eschawfynges of the [ardour] of this synne. And this is in two maneres — that is to seyn, chastitee in mariage, and chastitee of widwe-hod./ Now shaltow understonde that matri-moyne is leefful assemblynge of man and of womman that receyven by vertu of the sacre-

---

898 **juge:** yoke; see n. **free bole:** bull allowed to run free with the village herd
900 **mysterie:** office (ministerium) **soden:** boiled, cooked
902 **harlotrie:** lechery
903 **court Cristien:** ecclesiastical court
904 **reward:** regard (of the proper purpose)
906 **Thobie:** Tobias
907 **affynytee:** relationship between persons, other than the spouses themselves, established by marriage, as distinguished from **kynrede,** consanguinity

908 **parentele:** kinship **godsibbes:** children of one's godparents or those for whom one's parents are godparents
911 **mixne:** dunghill
913 **langwissynge:** weakness **vertu retentif:** body's power to retain fluids **phisik:** science of medicine
Remedium, *etc.*: The remedy against the sin of Lechery.
916 **eschawfynges:** inflaming with passion

ment the boond thurgh which they may nat be departed in al hir lyf — that is to seyn, whil that they lyven bothe./ This, as seith the book, is a ful greet sacrement. God maked it, as I have seyd, in paradys, and wolde hymself be born in mariage./ And for to halwen mariage he was at a weddynge, where as he turned water into wyn, which was the firste miracle that he wroghte in erthe biforn his disciples./ Trewe effect of mariage clenseth fornicacioun and replenysseth hooly chirche of good lynage, for that is the ende of mariage; and it chaungeth deedly synne into venial synne bitwixe hem that been ywedded, and maketh the hertes al oon of hem that been ywedded, as wel as the bodies./ This is verray mariage, that ⁹²⁰ was establissed by God, er that synne bigan, whan natureel lawe was in his right poynt in paradys; and it was ordeyned that o man sholde have but o womman, and o womman but o man, as seith Seint Augustyn, by manye resouns./

First, for mariage is figured bitwixe Crist and holy chirche. And that oother is for a man is heved of a womman; algate, by ordinaunce it sholde be so./ For if a womman hadde mo men than oon, thanne sholde she have moo hevedes than oon, and that were an horrible thyng biforn God; and eek a womman ne myghte nat plese to many folk at oones. And also ther ne sholde nevere be pees ne reste amonges hem, for everich wolde axen his owene thyng./ And forther over, no man ne sholde knowe his owene engendrure, ne who sholde have his heritage; and the womman sholde been the lasse biloved fro the tyme that she were conjoynt to many men./

Now comth how that a man sholde bere hym with his wif, and namely in two thynges; that is to seyn, in suffraunce and reverence, as shewed Crist whan he made first womman./ For he ne made hire nat ⁹²⁵ of the heved of Adam, for she sholde nat clayme to greet lordshipe./ For ther as the womman hath the maistrie, she maketh to muche desray. Ther neden none ensamples of this; the experience of day by day oghte suffise./ Also, certes, God ne made nat womman of the foot of Adam, for she ne sholde nat been holden to lowe; for she kan nat paciently suffre. But God made womman of the ryb of Adam, for womman sholde be felawe unto man./ Man sholde bere hym to his wyf in feith, in trouthe, and in love, as seith Seint Paul, that a man sholde loven his wyf as Crist loved hooly chirche, that loved it so wel that he deyde for it. So sholde a man for his wyf, if it were nede./

Now how that a womman sholde be subget to hire housbonde, that telleth Seint Peter. First, in obedience./ And eek, as ⁹³⁰ seith the decree, a womman that is wyf, as longe as she is a wyf, she hath noon auctoritee to swere ne to bere witnesse withoute leve of hir housbonde, that is hire lord; algate, he sholde be so by resoun./ She sholde eek serven hym in alle honestee, and been attempree of hire array. I woot wel that they sholde setten hire entente to plesen hir housbondes, but nat by hire queyntise of array./ Seint Jerome seith that "wyves that been apparailled in silk and in precious purpre ne mowe nat clothen hem in Jhesu Crist." Loke what seith Seint John eek in thys matere?/ Seint Gregorie eek seith that "No wight seketh precious array but oonly for veyne glorie, to been honoured the moore biforn the peple."/ It is a greet folye, a womman to have a fair array outward and in hirself be foul inward./ A wyf ⁹³⁵ sholde eek be mesurable in lookynge and in berynge and in lawghynge, and discreet in alle hire wordes and hire dedes./ And aboven alle worldly thyng she sholde loven hire housbonde with al hire herte, and to hym be trewe of hir body./ So sholde an housbonde eek be to his wyf. For sith that al the body is the housbondes, so sholde hire herte been, or elles ther is bitwixe hem two, as in that, no parfit mariage./ Thanne shal men understonde that for thre thynges a man and his wyf flesshly mowen assemble. The firste is in entente of engendrure of children to the service of God, for certes that is the cause final of matrimoyne./ Another cause is to yelden everich of hem to oother the dette of hire bodies, for neither of hem hath power of his owene body. The thridde is for to eschewe leccherye and vileynye. The ferthe is for sothe deedly synne./ As to the firste, it is ⁹⁴⁰

918 **as I have seyd:** at 842 and 883
920 **replenysseth:** fills
921 **right poynt:** proper condition, true state
922 **figured:** symbolized
927 **desray:** disorder

932 **queyntise of array:** finery
936 **mesurable:** modest

meritorie; the seconde also, for, as seith the decree, that she hath merite of chastitee that yeldeth to hire housbonde the dette of hir body, ye, though it be agayn hir likynge and the lust of hire herte./ The thridde manere is venyal synne; and, trewely, scarsly may ther any of thise be withoute venial synne, for the corrupcion and for the delit./ The fourthe manere is for to understonde, as if they assemble oonly for amorous love and for noon of the foreseyde causes, but for to accomplice thilke brennynge delit, they rekke nevere how ofte. Soothly it is deedly synne; and yet, with sorwe, somme folk wol peynen hem moore to doon than to hire appetit suffiseth./

The seconde manere of chastitee is for to been a clene wydewe, and eschue the embracynges of man, and desiren the embracynge of Jhesu Crist./ Thise been tho that han been wyves and han forgoon hire housbondes, and eek wommen that han doon leccherie and been releeved by penitence./ And certes,   945 if that a wyf koude kepen hire al chaast by licence of hir housbonde, so that she yeve nevere noon occasion that he agilte, it were to hire a greet merite./ Thise manere wommen that observen chastitee moste be clene in herte as wel as in body and in thought, and mesurable in clothynge and in contenaunce, and been abstinent in etynge and drynkynge, in spekynge, and in dede. They been the vessel or the boyste of the blissed Magdelene, that fulfilleth hooly chirche of good odour./ The thridde manere of chastitee is virginitee, and it bihoveth that she be hooly in herte and clene of body. Thanne is she spouse to Jhesu Crist, and she is the lyf of angeles./ She is the preisynge of this world, and she is as thise martirs in egalitee; she hath in hire that tonge may nat telle ne herte thynke./ Virginitee baar oure Lord Jhesu Crist, and virgine was hymselve./   950

Another remedie agayns Leccherie is specially to withdrawen swiche thynges as yeve occasion to thilke vileynye, as ese, etynge, and drynkynge. For certes, whan the pot boyleth strongly, the beste remedie is to withdrawe the fyr./ Slepynge longe in greet quiete is eek a greet norice to Leccherie./

Another remedie agayns Leccherie is that a man or a womman eschue the compaignye of hem by whiche he douteth to be tempted, for al be it so that the dede be withstonden, yet is ther greet temptacioun./ Soothly, a whit wal, although it ne brenne noght fully by stikynge of a candele, yet is the wal blak of the leyt./ Ful ofte tyme I rede that no man truste in his owene perfeccioun, but he be stronger than Sampson, and hoolier than David, and wiser than Salomon./   955

Now after that I have declared yow, as I kan, the sevene deedly synnes, and somme of hire braunches and hire remedies, soothly, if I koude, I wolde telle yow the ten comandementz./ But so heigh a doctrine I lete to divines. Natheless, I hope to God, they been touched in this tretice, everich of hem alle./

Sequitur secunda pars Penitencie.

Now for as muche as the seconde partie of Penitence stant in confessioun of mouth, as I bigan in the firste chapitre, I seye, Seint Augustyn seith,/ "Synne is every word and every dede, and al that men coveiten, agayn the lawe of Jhesu Crist; and this is for to synne in herte, in mouth, and in dede, by thy fyve wittes, that been sighte, herynge, smellynge, tastynge or savourynge, and feelynge."/ Now is it good to understonde the circumstances that agreggen muchel every synne./ Thou   960 shalt considere what thow art that doost the synne, wheither thou be male or femele, yong or oold, gentil or thral, free or servant, hool or syk, wedded or sengle, ordred or unordred, wys or fool, clerk or seculeer;/ if she be of thy kynrede, bodily or goostly, or noon; if any of thy kynrede have synned with hire, or noon; and manye mo thinges./

Another circumstaunce is this: wheither it be doon in fornicacioun or in avowtrie or noon, incest or noon, mayden or noon, in manere of homicide or noon, horrible grete synnes or smale, and how longe thou hast continued in synne./ The thridde circumstaunce is the place ther thou hast do synne, wheither in oother mennes hous or in thyn owene, in feeld or in chirche or in chirchehawe, in chirche

---

941 **meritorie:** meritorious
945 **forgoon:** lost
947 **boyste:** container
949 **as thise martirs in egalitee:** equal to the martyrs

954 **leyt:** flame
957 **divines:** theologians
Sequitur, *etc.*: Now follows the second part of Penance.
960 **agreggen:** aggravate, make more serious
961 **sengle:** single

dedicaat or noon./ For if the chirche be
halwed, and man or womman spille his kynde
inwith that place by wey of synne or by wikked temptacioun, the chirche is entredited
til it be reconsiled by the bysshop./ And   965
the preest sholde be enterdited that dide
swich a vileynye; to terme of al his lif he sholde
namoore synge masse, and if he dide, he sholde
doon deedly synne at every time that he so
songe masse./ The fourthe circumstaunce is
by whiche mediatours, or by whiche messagers, as for enticement, or for consentement to
bere compaignye with felaweshipe; for many
a wrecche, for to bere compaignye, wol go to
the devel of helle./ Wherfore they that eggen
or consenten to the synne been parteners of
the synne, and of the dampnacioun of the synnere./

The fifthe circumstaunce is how manye
tymes that he hath synned, if it be in his mynde,
and how ofte that he hath falle./ For he that
ofte falleth in synne, he despiseth the mercy
of God, and encreesseth hys synne, and is unkynde to Crist; and he wexeth the moore
fieble to withstonde synne, and synneth
the moore lightly,/ and the latter ariseth,   970
and is the moore eschew for to shryven
hym, and namely, to hym that is his confessour./
For which that folk, whan they falle agayn in
hir olde folies, outher they forleten hir olde
confessours al outrely or elles they departen
hir shrift in diverse places; but soothly, swich
departed shrift deserveth no mercy of God of
his synnes./ The sixte circumstaunce is why
that a man synneth, as by which temptacioun,
and if hymself procure thilke temptacioun, or by
the excitynge of oother folk; or if he synne
with a womman by force, or by hire owene
assent;/ or if the womman, maugree hir hed,
hath been afforced, or noon. This shal she
telle: for coveitise, or for poverte, and if it was
hire procurynge, or noon; and swich manere
harneys / The seventhe circumstaunce is in
what manere he hath doon his synne, or how
that she hath suffred that folk han doon
to hire./ And the same shal the man telle   975
pleynly with alle circumstaunces; and

wheither he hath synned with comune bordel
wommen or noon,/ or doon his synne in hooly
tymes or noon, in fastyng tymes or noon, or
biforn his shrifte, or after his latter shrifte,/
and hath peraventure broken therfore his penance enjoyned, by whos help and whos conseil,
by sorcerie or craft; al moste be toold./ Alle
thise thynges, after that they been grete or
smale, engreggen the conscience of man. And
eek the preest, that is thy juge, may the bettre
been avysed of his juggement in yevynge of
thy penaunce, and that is after thy contricioun./ For understond wel that after tyme
that a man hath defouled his baptesme by
synne, if he wole come to salvacioun, ther is
noon other wey but by penitence and
shrifte and satisfaccioun,/ and namely by   980
the two, if ther be a confessour to which
he may shriven hym, and the thridde, if he
have lyf to parfournen it./

Thanne shal man looke and considere that
if he wole maken a trewe and a profitable confessioun, ther moste be foure condiciouns./
First, it moot been in sorweful bitternesse of
herte, as seyde the kyng Ezechias to God, "I
wol remembre me alle the yeres of my lif in
bitternesse of myn herte."/ This condicioun of
bitternesse hath fyve signes. The firste is that
confessioun moste be shamefast, nat for to covere ne hyden his synne, for he hath agilt his
God and defouled his soule./ And herof seith
Seint Augustyn, "The herte travailleth for
shame of his synne"; and for he hath greet
shamefastnesse, he is digne to have greet
mercy of God./ Swich was the confes-   985
sioun of the publican that wolde nat heven
up his eyen to hevene, for he hadde offended
God of hevene; for which shamefastnesse he
hadde anon the mercy of God./ And therof
seith Seint Augustyn that swich shamefast folk
been next foryevenesse and remissioun./ Another signe is humylitee in confessioun, of
which seith Seint Peter, "Humbleth yow under
the myght of God." The hond of God is
myghty in confessioun, for therby God foryeveth thee thy synnes, for he allone hath the
power./ And this humylitee shal been in herte
and in signe outward, for right as he hath humylitee to God in his herte, right so sholde he

---

964 **dedicaat:** consecrated
965 **kynde:** semen   **entredited:** under an interdict, prohibited
from use
968 **eggen:** incite
971 **eschew:** disinclined, reluctant
974 **afforced:** violated   **procurynge:** contrivance   **harneys:**
trappings (circumstances)

976 **bordel wommen:** prostitutes
979 **engreggen:** burden
983 **Ezechias:** Hezekiah
984 **shamefast:** made with a sense of shame

humble his body outward to the preest, that sit in Goddes place./ For which in no manere, sith that Crist is sovereyn, and the preest meene and mediatour bitwixe Crist and the synnere, and the synnere is the laste by wey of resoun,/ thanne sholde nat the 990 synnere sitte as heighe as his confessour, but knele biforn hym or at his feet, but if maladie destourbe it. For he shal nat taken kep who sit there, but in whos place that he sitteth./ A man that hath trespased to a lord, and comth for to axe mercy and maken his accord, and set him doun anon by the lord, men wolde holden hym outrageous, and nat worthy so soone for to have remissioun ne mercy./ The thridde signe is how that thy shrift sholde be ful of teeris, if man may, and if man may nat wepe with his bodily eyen, lat hym wepe in herte./ Swich was the confession of Seint Peter, for after that he hadde forsake Jhesu Crist, he wente out and weep ful bitterly./ The fourthe signe is that he ne lette nat for shame to shewen his confessioun./ 995 Swich was the confessioun of the Magdalene, that ne spared for no shame of hem that weren atte feeste, for to go to oure Lord Jhesu Crist and biknowe to hym hire synne./ The fifthe signe is that a man or a womman be obeisant to receyven the penaunce that hym is enjoyned for his synnes, for certes, Jhesu Crist, for the giltes of o man, was obedient to the deeth./

The seconde condicion of verray confession is that it be hastily doon. For certes, if a man hadde a deedly wounde, evere the lenger that he taried to warisshe hymself, the moore wolde it corrupte and haste hym to his deeth, and eek the wounde wolde be the wors for to heele./ And right so fareth synne that longe tyme is in a man unshewed./ Certes, a man oghte hastily shewen his synnes for manye causes; as for drede of deeth, that cometh ofte sodeynly, and no certeyn what tyme it shal be, ne in what place; and eek the drecchynge of o synne draweth in another;/ and 1000 eek the lenger that he tarieth, the ferther he is fro Crist. And if he abide to his laste day, scarsly may he shryven hym or remembre hym of his synnes or repenten hym, for the grevous maladie of his deeth./ And for as muche as he ne hath nat in his lyf herkned Jhesu Crist whanne he hath spoken, he shal crie to Jhesu Crist at his laste day, and scarsly wol he herkne hym./ And understond that this condicioun moste han foure thynges. Thi shrift moste be purveyed bifore and avysed; for wikked haste dooth no profit; and that a man konne shryve hym of his synnes, be it of pride, or of envye, and so forth with the speces and circumstances;/ and that he have comprehended in hys mynde the nombre and the greetnesse of his synnes, and how longe that he hath leyn in synne;/ and eek that he be contrit of his synnes, and in stidefast purpos, by the grace of God, nevere eft to falle in synne; and eek that he drede and countrewaite hymself, that he fle the occasiouns of synne to whiche he is enclyned./ Also 1005 thou shalt shryve thee of alle thy synnes to o man, and nat a parcel to o man and a parcel to another; that is to understonde, in entente to departe thy confessioun, as for shame or drede, for it nys but stranglynge of thy soule./ For certes Jhesu Crist is entierly al good; in hym nys noon imperfeccioun, and therfore outher he foryeveth al parfitly or elles never a deel./ I seye nat that if thow be assigned to the penitauncer for certein synne, that thow art bounde to shewen hym al the remenaunt of thy synnes, of whiche thow hast be shryven of thy curaat, but if it like to thee of thyn humylitee; this is no departynge of shrifte./ Ne I seye nat, ther as I speke of divisioun of confessioun, that if thou have licence for to shryve thee to a discreet and an honest preest, where thee liketh, and by licence of thy curaat, that thow ne mayst wel shryve thee to him of alle thy synnes./ But lat no blotte be bihynde; lat no synne been untoold, as fer as thow hast remembraunce./ And whan thou shalt be 1010 shryven to thy curaat, telle hym eek alle the synnes that thow hast doon syn thou were last yshryven; this is no wikked entente of divisioun of shrifte./

Also the verray shrifte axeth certeine condiciouns. First, that thow shryve thee by thy free wil, noght constreyned, ne for shame of folk, ne for maladie, ne swiche thynges. For

---

990 **meene:** agent, instrument
999 **unshewed:** unconfessed
1000 **drecchynge:** continuance

1005 **countrewaite:** watch
1006 **parcel:** portion
1008 **penitauncer:** a priest with special powers granted by a pope or bishop to hear confession, give dispensations, or absolve from particular sins
1010 **untoold:** unconfessed

it is resoun that he that trespaseth by his free wyl, that by his free wyl he confesse his trespas,/ and that noon oother man telle his synne but he hymself; ne he shal nat nayte ne denye his synne, ne wratthe hym agayn the preest for his amonestynge to lete synne./ The seconde condicioun is that thy shrift be laweful; that is to seyn, that thow that shryvest thee and eek the preest that hereth thy confessioun been verraily in the feith of hooly chirche,/ and that a man ne be nat despeired of the mercy of Jhesu Crist, as Caym or Judas./ 1015 And eek a man moot accusen hymself of his owene trespas, and nat another; but he shal blame and wyten hymself and his owene malice of his synne, and noon oother./ But nathelees, if that another man be occasioun or enticere of his synne, or the estaat of a persone be swich thurgh which his synne is agregged, or elles that he may nat pleynly shryven hym but he telle the persone with which he hath synned, thanne may he telle it,/ so that his entente ne be nat to bakbite the persone, but oonly to declaren his confessioun./

Thou ne shalt nat eek make no lesynges in thy confessioun, for humylitee, peraventure, to seyn that thow hast doon synnes of whiche thow were nevere gilty./ For Seint Augustyn seith, "If thou, by cause of thyn humylitee, makest lesynges on thyself, though thow ne were nat in synne biforn, yet artow thanne in synne thurgh thy lesynges."/ Thou 1020 most eek shewe thy synne by thyn owene propre mouth, but thow be woxe dowmb, and nat by no lettre; for thow that hast doon the synne, thou shalt have the shame therfore./ Thow shalt nat eek peynte thy confessioun by faire subtile wordes, to covere the moore thy synne; for thanne bigilestow thyself, and nat the preest. Thow most tellen it platly, be it nevere so foul ne so horrible./ Thow shalt eek shryve thee to a preest that is discreet to conseille thee; and eek thou shalt nat shryve thee for veyne glorie, ne for ypocrisye, ne for no cause but oonly for the doute of Jhesu Crist and the heele of thy soule./ Thow shalt nat eek renne to the preest sodeynly to tellen hym lightly thy synne, as whoso telleth a jape or a tale, but avysely and with greet devocioun./ And generally, shryve thee ofte. If thou ofte falle, ofte thou arise by confessioun./ 1025 And though thou shryve thee ofter than ones of synne of which thou hast be shryven, it is the moore merite. And, as seith Seint Augustyn, thow shalt have the moore lightly relessyng and grace of God, bothe of synne and of peyne./ And certes, oones a yeere atte leeste wey it is laweful for to been housled, for certes, oones a yeere alle thynges renovellen./

Now have I toold yow of verray Confessioun, that is the seconde partie of Penitence./

Explicit secunda pars Penitencie, et sequitur tercia pars eiusdem.

The thridde partie of Penitence is Satisfaccioun, and that stant moost generally in almesse and in bodily peyne./ Now been ther thre manere of almesse: contricion of herte, where a man offreth hymself to God; another is to han pitee of defaute of his neighebores; and the thridde is in yevynge of good conseil and comfort, goostly and bodily, where men han nede, and namely in sustenaunce of mannes foode./ And tak kep that a man hath 1030 nede of thise thinges generally: he hath nede of foode, he hath nede of clothyng and herberwe, he hath nede of charitable conseil and visitynge in prisone and in maladie, and sepulture of his dede body./ And if thow mayst nat visite the nedeful with thy persone, visite hym by thy message and by thy yiftes./ Thise been general almesses or werkes of charitee of hem that han temporeel richesses or discrecioun in conseilynge. Of thise werkes shaltow heren at the day of doom./

Thise almesses shaltow doon of thyne owene propre thynges, and hastily and prively, if thow mayst./ But nathelees, if thow mayst nat doon it prively, thow shalt nat forbere to doon almesse though men seen it, so that it be nat doon for thank of the world, but oonly for thank of Jhesu Crist./ For, as 1035 witnesseth Seint Mathew, *capitulo quinto,*

1013 **nayte:** disclaim

Explicit, *etc.*: Here ends the second part of Penance, and its third part follows.

1027 **laweful:** decreed by (Church) law   **housled:** given communion   **renovellen:** renew themselves

1036 *capitulo quinto:* in the fifth chapter

"A citee may nat been hyd that is set on a montayne, ne men lighte nat a lanterne and put it under a busshel, but men sette it on a candle-stikke to yeve light to the men in the hous./ Right so shal youre light lighten bifore men, that they may seen youre goode werkes, and glorifie youre fader that is in hevene."/

Now as to speken of bodily peyne, it stant in preyeres, in wakynges, in fastynges, in vertuouse techynges of orisouns./ And ye shul understonde that orisouns or preyeres is for to seyn a pitous wyl of herte, that redresseth it in God and expresseth it by word outward, to remoeven harmes and to han thynges espiritueel and durable, and somtyme temporele thynges; of whiche orisouns, certes, in the orison of the *Pater noster* hath Jhesu Crist enclosed moost thynges./ Certes, it is privyleged of thre thynges in his dignytee, for which it is moore digne than any oother preyere, for that Jhesu Crist hymself maked it;/ and it is short, for it sholde 1040 be koud the moore lightly, and for to withholden it the moore esily in herte, and helpen hymself the ofter with the orisoun,/ and for a man sholde be the lasse wery to seyen it, and for a man may nat excusen hym to lerne it, it is so short and so esy, and for it comprehendeth in it self alle goode preyeres./ The exposicioun of this hooly preyere, that is so excellent and digne, I bitake to thise maistres of theologie, save thus muchel wol I seyn; that whan thow prayest that God sholde foryeve thee thy giltes as thou foryevest hem that agilten to thee, be ful wel war that thow ne be nat out of charitee./ This hooly orison amenuseth eek venyal synne, and therfore it aperteneth specially to penitence./

This preyere moste be trewely seyd, and in verray feith, and that men preye to God ordinatly and discreetly and devoutly; and alwey a man shal putten his wyl to be subget to the wille of God./ This orisoun moste eek 1045 been seyd with greet humblesse and ful pure, honestly and nat to the anoyaunce of any man or womman. It moste eek been continued with the werkes of charitee./ It avayleth eek agayn the vices of the soule, for, as seith Seint Jerome, "By fastynge been saved the vices of the flessh, and by preyere the vices of the soule."/

After this, thou shalt understonde that bodily peyne stant in wakynge, for Jhesu Crist seith, "Waketh and preyeth, that ye ne entre in wikked temptacioun."/ Ye shul understanden also that fastynge stant in thre thynges: in forberynge of bodily mete and drynke, and in forberynge of worldly jolitee, and in forberynge of deedly synne; this is to seyn, that a man shal kepen hym fro deedly synne with al his myght./

And thou shalt understanden eek that God ordeyned fastynge, and to fastynge appertenen foure thinges:/ largenesse to 1050 povre folk, gladnesse of herte espiritueel, nat to been angry ne anoyed, ne grucche for he fasteth, and also resonable houre for to ete; ete by mesure; that is for to seyn, a man shal nat ete in untyme, ne sitte the lenger at his table to ete for he fasteth./

Thanne shaltow understonde that bodily peyne stant in disciplyne or techynge, by word, or by writynge, or in ensample; also in werynge of heyres, or of stamyn, or of haubergeons on hire naked flessh, for Cristes sake, and swiche manere penances./ But war thee wel that swiche manere penaunces on thy flessh ne make nat thyn herte bitter or angry or anoyed of thyself, for bettre is to caste awey thyn heyre, than for to caste awey the swetenesse of Jhesu Crist./ And therfore seith Seint Paul, "Clothe yow, as they that been chosen of God, in herte of misericorde, debonairetee, suffraunce, and swich manere of clothynge,"/ of whiche Jhesu Crist is moore apayed than of heyres, or haubergeouns, or hauberkes./

Thanne is discipline eek in knokkynge of thy brest, in scourgynge with yerdes, in knelynges, in tribulacions,/ in suffrynge 1055 paciently wronges that been doon to thee, and eek in pacient suffraunce of maladies, or lesynge of worldly catel, or of wyf, or of child, or othere freendes./

Thanne shaltow understonde whiche thynges destourben penaunce; and this is in foure maneres: that is, drede, shame, hope, and wanhope, that is desperacion./ And for to speke first of drede, for which he weneth that he may suffre no penaunce;/ ther-agayns is remedie for to thynke that bodily penaunce is but short and litel at regard of the peyne of helle,

---

1039 **pitous:** pious **redresseth it:** directs itself toward
1040 **privyleged of:** endowed with
1045 **ordinatly:** in an orderly manner

1051 **largenesse:** generosity
1052 **heyres:** hair shirts **stamyn:** coarse woolen cloth
haubergeons: coats of mail
1055 **scourgynge:** whipping
1057 **desperacion:** despair

that is so crueel and so long that it lasteth withouten ende./

Now again the shame that a man hath to shryven hym, and namely thise ypocrites that wolden been holden so parfite that they han no nede to shryven hem;/ agayns that 1060 shame sholde a man thynke that, by wey of resoun, that he that hath nat been shamed to doon foule thinges, certes hym oghte nat been ashamed to do faire thynges, and that is confessiouns./ A man sholde eek thynke that God seeth and woot alle his thoghtes and alle his werkes, to hym may no thyng been hyd ne covered./ Men sholden eek remembren hem of the shame that is to come at the day of doom to hem that been nat penitent and shryven in this present lyf./ For alle the creatures in hevene, in erthe, and in helle shullen seen apertly al that they hyden in this world./

Now for to speken of the hope of hem that been necligent and slowe to shryven hem, that stant in two maneres./ That 1065 oon is that he hopeth for to lyve longe and for to purchacen muche richesse for his delit, and thanne he wol shryven hym; and, as he seith, hym semeth thanne tymely ynough to come to shrifte./ Another is of surquidrie that he hath in Cristes mercy./ Agayns the firste vice, he shal thynke that oure lif is in no sikernesse, and eek that alle the richesses in this world ben in aventure and passen as a shadwe on the wal;/ and, as seith Seint Gregorie, that it aperteneth to the grete rightwisnesse of God that nevere shal the peyne stynte of hem that nevere wolde withdrawen hem fro synne, hir thankes, but ay continue in synne; for thilke perpetueel wil to do synne shul they han perpetueel peyne./

Wanhope is in two maneres: the firste wanhope is in the mercy of Crist; that oother is that they thynken that they ne myghte nat longe persevere in goodnesse./ The 1070 firste wanhope comth of that he demeth that he hath synned so greetly and so ofte, and so longe leyn in synne, that he shal nat be saved./ Certes, agayns that cursed wanhope sholde he thynke that the passion of Jhesu Crist is moore strong for to unbynde than synne is strong for to bynde./ Agayns the seconde wanhope he shal thynke that as ofte as he falleth he may arise agayn by penitence. And though he never so longe have leyn in synne, the mercy of Crist is alwey redy to receiven hym to mercy./ Agayns the wanhope that he demeth that he sholde nat longe persevere in goodnesse, he shal thynke that the feblesse of the devel may nothyng doon, but if men wol suffren hym;/ and eek he shal han strengthe of the help of God, and of al hooly chirche, and of the proteccioun of aungels, if hym list./   1075

Thanne shal men understonde what is the fruyt of penaunce; and, after the word of Jhesu Crist, it is the endelees blisse of hevene,/ ther joye hath no contrarioustee of wo ne grevaunce; ther alle harmes been passed of this present lyf; ther as is the sikernesse fro the peyne of helle; ther as is the blisful compaignye that rejoysen hem everemo, everich of otheres joye;/ ther as the body of man, that whilom was foul and derk, is moore cleer than the sonne; ther as the body, that whilom was syk, freele, and fieble, and mortal, is inmortal, and so strong and so hool that ther may no thyng apeyren it;/ ther as ne is neither hunger, thurst, ne coold, but every soule replenyssed with the sighte of the parfit knowynge of God./ This blisful regne may men purchace by poverte espiritueel, and the glorie by lowenesse, the plentee of joye by hunger and thurst, and the reste by travaille, and the lyf by deeth and mortificacion of synne./ 1080

1067 **surquidrie:** arrogance

1077 **contrarioustee:** opposite
1078 **apeyren:** injure
1079 **replenyssed:** filled

Heere taketh the makere of this book his leve.

Now preye I to hem alle that herkne this litel tretys or rede, that if ther be any thyng in it that liketh hem, that therof they thanken oure Lord Jhesu Crist, of whom procedeth al wit and al goodnesse./ And if ther be any thyng that displese hem, I preye hem also that they arrette it to the defaute of myn unkonnynge and nat to my wyl, that wolde ful fayn have seyd bettre if I hadde had konnynge./ For oure book seith, "Al that is writen is writen for oure doctrine," and that is myn entente./ Wherfore I biseke yow mekely, for the mercy of God, that ye preye for me that Crist have mercy on me and foryeve me my giltes;/ and namely of my translacions and enditynges of worldly vanitees, the whiche I revoke in my retracciouns:/ as is the book of Troi- 1085 lus; the book also of Fame; the book of the XXV. Ladies; the book of the Duchesse; the book of Seint Valentynes day of the Parlement of Briddes; the tales of Caunterbury, thilke that sownen into synne;/ the book of the Leoun; and many another book, if they were in my remembrance, and many a song and many a leccherous lay, that Crist for his grete mercy foryeve me the synne./ But of the translacion of Boece de Consolacione, and othere bookes of legendes of seintes, and omelies, and moralitee, and devocioun,/ that thanke I oure Lord Jhesu Crist and his blisful Mooder, and alle the seintes of hevene,/ bisekynge hem that they from hennes forth unto my lyves ende sende me grace to biwayle my giltes and to studie to the salvacioun of my soule, and graunte me grace of verray penitence, confessioun and satisfaccioun to doon in this present lyf,/ thurgh the benigne grace of 1090 hym that is kyng of kynges and preest over alle preestes, that boghte us with the precious blood of his herte,/ so that I may been oon of hem at the day of doom that shulle be saved. *Qui cum Patre et Spiritu Sancto vivit et regnat Deus per omnia secula. Amen.*

Heere is ended the book of the tales of Caunterbury, compiled by Geffrey Chaucer, of whos soule Jhesu Crist have mercy. Amen.

1081 **this litel tretys:** the preceding tale; see n.
1082 **arrette:** attribute
1086 **book of the XXV. Ladies:** The Legend of Good Women
sownen into synne: tend toward, are conducive to, sin.

1087 **book of the Leoun:** a lost work; see n.
1092 *Qui cum Patre . . . Amen:* He who lives and reigns with the Father and Holy Spirit, God, world without end. Amen.

THE
BOOK OF THE
DUCHESS

THE BOOK OF THE DUCHESS is the earliest of Chaucer's major poems. His translation of the *Roman de la rose* may have preceded it, and his ABC (which tradition holds was written at the request of the Duchess Blanche) was probably also an earlier work; doubtless some of the hymns of love mentioned in the Prologue to *The Legend of Good Women* and some of the many songs and lecherous lays mentioned in the Retraction also preceded the composition of this poem. At any rate, and despite occasional roughness of meter, *The Book of the Duchess* shows Chaucer already in full command of the idiom and conventions of the poetry of love, which was to be one of his major concerns for the next two decades.

There is a good deal of evidence, both external and internal, that Chaucer wrote *The Book of the Duchess* to commemorate the death of Blanche, Duchess of Lancaster and wife of John of Gaunt. In the Prologue to *The Legend of Good Women* Chaucer says that he wrote a poem called "the Deeth of Blaunche the Duchesse" and this is almost certainly what he later calls "the book of the Duchesse" (Retr. X.1086). A note in the Fairfax Manuscript, evidently in the hand of the Elizabethan antiquary John Stowe, says that this poem was written at John of Gaunt's request. In the poem it seems likely that the word *white* is a translation pun in several instances, notably in line 948, "And goode faire White she het." There is also an apparent series of word plays in 1318–19, where *white* appears and John of Gaunt is hinted at in "seynt Johan" and where there are probable references to Richmond and Lancaster (Gaunt was Earl of Richmond and Duke of Lancaster).

While this would seem to settle the date of the composition of the poem, which is usually placed between 1369 and 1372, at the latest,

there are, in fact, two questions that must raise doubts. In the first place, though the generally accepted date of Blanche's death is 12 September 1369, a more recent study suggests that 12 September 1368 is the probable date. In the second place, it has been argued that the poem was not, as hitherto supposed, written within a few months of Blanche's death but for one of the later and highly elaborate annual commemoration services.

At the time of writing the poem Chaucer was strongly influenced by some of the sophisticated French poets, notably Guillaume de Lorris and Jean de Meun (authors of the *Roman de la rose*), Froissart, and Machaut. To the last of these in particular he owes a special debt, not only in the many lines he borrows for *The Book of the Duchess,* but also in the form of his elegy. One of Guillaume de Machaut's *dits,* the *Jugement dou Roy de Behaingne,* recounts how the poet walks in the meadows one morning in late April and overhears a lady and a knight lamenting: she because her truelove has died, he because his beloved has proved faithless. They argue about which has the greater cause for sorrow, and eventually Guillaume takes them to the court of love of the King of Bohemia (Behaingne). The King's verdict is that infidelity, rather than bereavement, merits the greater grief. It has been plausibly suggested that in *The Book of the Duchess* the Dreamer's superficially obtuse questionings of the Black Knight are instrumental in making him declare that he knew perfect and reciprocated love cut off eventually by death, and that it is thus demonstrated to Gaunt out of his "own" mouth that his situation is identical to that of the Lady in the *Behaingne.* The companion poem, the *Jugement dou Roy de Navarre,* gives judgment in favor of a woman, and a number of lines are borrowed by Chaucer from that work. Perhaps a more specific and historical relationship, setting the ideals of *fin'amor* against a backdrop of tragedy, lies in the opening 458 lines of the *Navarre,* in which the horrors of the outbreak of the Black Death (1349) are described. Chaucer's quotations from the *Navarre* may well have reminded his audience of the "horribles merveilles,/Sur toutes autres despareilles, /Dont homme puet avoir memoire," the horrifying wonders, greater than any others that one can recall. (Blanche's only sister had died of that disease and it was the cause of death of her father and of Blanche herself.) It is possible that the recollection of the countless thousands who mourned their dead was intended to provide Gaunt with the consolation of companionship in grief.

Critics have argued about the possibility that Chaucer's depiction of the Narrator in *The Book of the Duchess* may contain autobiographical elements. No doubt there are instances in his works when this is so, as in some details of the self-portrait in *The House of Fame;* but the highly formalized narrator-persona of French courtly poetry, often melancholy and lovesick, is such a common figure that we should be very wary of assuming that the *I* of *The Book of the Duchess* represents Chaucer himself. The comic touches of exaggeration or incompetence that seem so individual can be found in Machaut, whose influence on Chaucer has already been noted.

The distancing effect of the dream motif makes it easier for Chaucer to offer consolation to Gaunt by presenting his patron as a mourning knight recalling the beauty, outward and inward, of his wife. The poem is a marvellous blend of comedy and poignancy, of scenes of birdsong and a winsome puppy, yet with the leitmotif "To lytel while oure blysse lasteth."

The intricate tripartite structure of dying Narrator, grief-stricken Alcione, and mourning Knight gives it, further, a sense of form that is both intellectually and aesthetically satisfying.

COLIN WILCOCKSON

The Book of the Duchess

I have gret wonder, be this lyght,
How that I lyve, for day ne nyght
I may nat slepe wel nygh noght;
I have so many an ydel thoght
Purely for defaute of slep   5
That, by my trouthe, I take no kep
Of nothing, how hyt cometh or gooth,
Ne me nys nothyng leef nor looth.
Al is ylyche good to me —
Joye or sorowe, wherso hyt be —   10
For I have felynge in nothyng,

But as yt were a mased thyng,
Alway in poynt to falle a-doun;
For sorwful ymagynacioun
Ys alway hooly in my mynde.   15
    And wel ye woot, agaynes kynde
Hyt were to lyven in thys wyse,
For nature wolde nat suffyse
To noon erthly creature
Nat longe tyme to endure   20
Withoute slep and be in sorwe.
And I ne may, ne nyght ne morwe,
Slepe; and thus melancolye
And drede I have for to dye.
Defaute of slep and hevynesse   25

This text was edited by LARRY D. BENSON.

3 **may:** can
5 **defaute:** lack
6 **take no kep:** do not notice, care about
8 I don't care about anything.
9 **ylyche:** equally
10 **wherso:** wherever

12 **mased:** dazed, bewildered
14 **ymagynacioun:** imagination; see n.
16 **kynde:** nature
25 **hevynesse:** sadness

Hath sleyn my spirit of quyknesse
That I have lost al lustyhede.
Suche fantasies ben in myn hede
So I not what is best to doo.

    But men myght axe me why soo   30
I may not slepe and what me is.
But natheles, who aske this
Leseth his asking trewely.
Myselven can not telle why
The sothe; but trewly, as I gesse,   35
I holde hit be a sicknesse
That I have suffred this eight yeer;
And yet my boote is never the ner,
For there is phisicien but oon
That may me hele; but that is don.   40
Passe we over untill eft;
That wil not be mot nede be left;
Our first mater is good to kepe.

  So whan I saw I might not slepe
Til now late this other night,   45
Upon my bed I sat upright
And bad oon reche me a book,
A romaunce, and he it me tok
To rede and drive the night away;
For me thoughte it better play   50
Then playe either at ches or tables.
And in this bok were written fables
That clerkes had in olde tyme,
And other poetes, put in rime
To rede and for to be in minde,   55
While men loved the lawe of kinde.
This bok ne spak but of such thinges,
Of quenes lives, and of kinges,
And many other thinges smale.
Amonge al this I fond a tale   60
That me thoughte a wonder thing.

    This was the tale: There was a king
That highte Seys, and had a wif,
The beste that mighte bere lyf,
And this quene highte Alcyone.   65
So it befil thereafter soone

This king wol wenden over see.
To tellen shortly, whan that he
Was in the see thus in this wise,
Such a tempest gan to rise   70
That brak her mast and made it falle,
And clefte her ship, and dreinte hem alle,
That never was founde, as it telles,
Bord ne man, ne nothing elles.
Right thus this king Seys loste his lif.   75

    Now for to speke of Alcyone, his wif:
This lady, that was left at hom,
Hath wonder that the king ne com
Hom, for it was a longe terme.
Anon her herte began to [erme];   80
And for that her thoughte evermo
It was not wele [he dwelte] so,
She longed so after the king
That certes it were a pitous thing
To telle her hertely sorowful lif   85
That she had, this noble wif,
For him, alas, she loved alderbest.
Anon she sent bothe eest and west
To seke him, but they founde nought.
"Alas!" quod she, "that I was wrought!   90
And wher my lord, my love, be deed?
Certes, I nil never ete breed,
I make avow to my god here,
But I mowe of my lord here!"
Such sorowe this lady to her tok   95
That trewly I, that made this book,
Had such pittee and such rowthe
To rede hir sorwe that, by my trowthe,
I ferde the worse al the morwe
Aftir to thenken on hir sorwe.   100

    So whan this lady koude here noo word
That no man myghte fynde hir lord,
Ful ofte she swouned, and sayed "Alas!"
For sorwe ful nygh wood she was,
Ne she koude no reed but oon;   105
But doun on knees she sat anoon
And wepte that pittee was to here.

    "A, mercy, swete lady dere!"
Quod she to Juno, hir goddesse,
"Helpe me out of thys distresse,   110

26 **quyknesse:** liveliness
27 **lustyhede:** vigor
30 **men:** one
31 **what me is:** what is wrong with me
33 **Leseth:** loses, wastes
38 **boote:** remedy   **never the ner:** no nearer
41 **eft:** again, another time
42 **What won't** come about must be done without.
45 **Til now late:** until recently
48 **romaunce:** Ovid's *Metamorphoses*
50 **me thoughte:** it seemed to me
51 **tables:** backgammon
52 **fables:** stories
56 **lawe of kinde:** natural law
64 **that:** who
65 **highte:** was called

70 **gan to rise:** did rise, arose; see n.
71 **her:** their
72 **dreinte:** drowned
80 **erme:** grieve
87 **alderbest:** best of all
90 **quod:** said
91 **wher:** whether (introducing a question)
92 **nil** = *ne wyl,* will not
94 **But:** unless
99 **ferde:** fared
104 **wood:** mad
105 **reed:** plan of action

And yeve me grace my lord to se
Soone or wite wher-so he be,
Or how he fareth, or in what wise,
And I shal make yow sacrifise,
And hooly youres become I shal   115
With good wille, body, herte, and al;
And but thow wolt this, lady swete,
Send me grace to slepe and mete
In my slep som certeyn sweven
Wherthourgh that I may knowen even   120
Whether my lord be quyk or ded."
    With that word she heng doun the hed
And fel a-swowne as cold as ston.
Hyr women kaught hir up anoon
And broghten hir in bed al naked,   125
And she, forweped and forwaked,
Was wery; and thus the dede slep
Fil on hir or she tooke kep,
Throgh Juno, that had herd hir bone,
That made hir to slepe sone.   130
For as she prayede, ryght so was don
In dede; for Juno ryght anon
Called thus hir messager
To doo hir erande, and he com ner.
    Whan he was come, she bad hym thus: 135
"Go bet," quod Juno, "to Morpheus —
Thou knowest hym wel, the god of slep.
Now understond wel and tak kep!
Sey thus on my half: that he
Go faste into the Grete Se,   140
And byd hym that, on alle thyng,
He take up Seys body the kyng,
That lyeth ful pale and nothyng rody.
Bid hym crepe into the body
And doo hit goon to Alcione   145
The quene, ther she lyeth allone,
And shewe hir shortly, hit ys no nay,
How hit was dreynt thys other day;
And do the body speke ryght soo,
Ryght as hyt was woned to doo   150

The whiles that hit was alyve.
Goo now faste, and hye the blyve!"
    This messager tok leve and wente
Upon hys wey, and never ne stente
Til he com to the derke valeye   155
That stant betwixe roches tweye
Ther never yet grew corn ne gras,
Ne tre, ne noght that ought was,
Beste, ne man, ne noght elles,
Save ther were a fewe welles   160
Came rennynge fro the clyves adoun,
That made a dedly slepynge soun,
And ronnen doun ryght by a cave
That was under a rokke ygrave
Amydde the valey, wonder depe.   165
There these goddes lay and slepe,
Morpheus and Eclympasteyr,
That was the god of slepes heyr,
That slep and dide noon other werk.
This cave was also as derk   170
As helle-pit overal aboute.
They had good leyser for to route,
To envye who myghte slepe best.
Somme henge her chyn upon hir brest
And slept upryght, hir hed yhed,   175
And somme lay naked in her bed
And slepe whiles the dayes laste.
    This messager com fleynge faste
And cried, "O, how! Awake anoon!"
Hit was for noght; there herde hym non. 180
"Awake!" quod he, "whoo ys lyth there?"
And blew his horn ryght in here eere,
And cried "Awaketh!" wonder hyë.
This god of slep with hys oon yë
Cast up, and axed, "Who clepeth ther?"   185
    "Hyt am I," quod this messager.
"Juno bad thow shuldest goon" —
And tolde hym what he shulde doon
(As I have told yow here-to-fore;
Hyt ys no nede reherse hyt more)   190
And went hys wey whan he had sayd.
Anoon this god of slep abrayd
Out of hys slep, and gan to goon,
And dyde as he had bede hym doon:

111 **yeve:** give
118 **mete:** dream
119 **sweven:** dream
120 **even:** exactly
121 **quyk:** alive
126 **forweped:** exhausted from weeping   **forwaked:** exhausted
from lack of sleep
128 **or she tooke kep:** before she noticed
129 **bone:** request
130 **sone:** immediately
136 **Go bet:** go quickly
139 **half:** behalf
140 **Grete Se:** Mediterranean
141 **on alle thyng:** above all
142 **Seys body the kyng:** the body of King Ceyx
143 **nothyng rody:** not at all ruddy
145 **doo hit goon:** make it go
147 **hit ys no nay:** there is no denying it
149 **do the body speke:** make the body speak
150 **woned:** accustomed

152 **hye the blyve:** hurry yourself quickly
154 **stente:** stopped
161 **clyves:** cliffs
162 **dedly:** lifeless
164 **ygrave:** cut
168 **heyr:** heir
171 **helle-pit:** the pit of Hell
172 **route:** snore
173 **envye:** contend
175 **yhed:** hidden, covered
182 **here:** their
183 **hyë:** loudly
185 **clepeth:** calls
192 **Anoon:** at once   **abrayd:** started
194 **bede:** bade, asked

Took up the dreynte body sone   195
And bar hyt forth to Alcione,
Hys wif the quene, ther as she lay
Ryght even a quarter before day,
And stood ryght at hyr beddes fet,
And called hir ryght as she het   200
By name, and sayde, "My swete wyf,
Awake! Let be your sorwful lyf,
For in your sorwe there lyth no red;
For, certes, swete, I am but ded.
Ye shul me never on lyve yse.   205
But, goode swete herte, that ye
Bury my body, for such a tyde
Ye mowe hyt fynde the see besyde;
And farewel, swete, my worldes blysse!
I praye God youre sorwe lysse.   210
To lytel while oure blysse lasteth!"
   With that hir eyen up she casteth
And saw noght. "Allas!" quod she for sorwe,
And deyede within the thridde morwe.
But what she sayede more in that swow   215
I may not telle yow as now;
Hyt were to longe for to dwelle.
My first matere I wil yow telle,
Wherfore I have told this thyng
Of Alcione and Seys the kyng,   220
For thus moche dar I saye wel:
I had be dolven everydel
And ded, ryght thurgh defaute of slep,
Yif I ne had red and take kep
Of this tale next before.   225
And I wol telle yow wherfore:
For I ne myghte, for bote ne bale,
Slepe or I had red thys tale
Of this dreynte Seys the kyng
And of the goddes of slepyng.   230
   Whan I had red thys tale wel
And overloked hyt everydel,
Me thoghte wonder yf hit were so,
For I had never herd speke or tho
Of noo goddes that koude make   235
Men to slepe, ne for to wake,
For I ne knew never god but oon,
And in my game I sayde anoon

(And yet me lyst ryght evel to pleye)
Rather then that y shulde deye   240
Thorgh defaute of slepynge thus,
I wolde yive thilke Morpheus,
Or hys goddesse, dame Juno,
Or som wight elles, I ne roghte who —
"To make me slepe and have som reste   245
I wil yive hym the alderbeste
Yifte that ever he abod hys lyve.
And here on warde, ryght now as blyve,
Yif he wol make me slepe a lyte,
Of down of pure dowves white   250
I wil yive hym a fether-bed,
Rayed with gold and ryght wel cled
In fyn blak satyn doutremer,
And many a pilowe, and every ber
Of cloth of Reynes, to slepe softe —   255
Hym thar not nede to turnen ofte —
And I wol yive hym al that falles
To a chambre, and al hys halles
I wol do peynte with pure gold
And tapite hem ful many fold   260
Of oo sute; this shal he have
(Yf I wiste where were hys cave),
Yf he kan make me slepe sone,
As did the goddesse quene Alcione.
And thus this ylke god, Morpheus,   265
May wynne of me moo feës thus
Than ever he wan; and to Juno,
That ys hys goddesse, I shal soo do,
I trow, that she shal holde hir payd."
   I hadde unneth that word ysayd   270
Ryght thus as I have told hyt yow,
That sodeynly, I nyste how,
Such a lust anoon me took
To slepe that ryght upon my book
Y fil aslepe, and therwith even   275
Me mette so ynly swete a sweven,
So wonderful that never yit
Y trowe no man had the wyt
To konne wel my sweven rede;
No, not Joseph, withoute drede,   280

239 **me lyst ryght evel:** I had little desire
246 **alderbeste:** very best, best of all
247 **abod:** hoped to receive, experienced   **hys lyve:** in his life
248 **on warde:** in (his) possession   **as blyve:** immediately
249 **lyte:** little
252 **Rayed:** striped   **cled:** covered
253 **doutremer:** from abroad
254 **ber:** pillowcase
255 **cloth of Reynes:** linen from Rennes (in France)
257 **falles:** belongs
260 **tapite:** cover with tapestry
261 **Of oo sute:** matching
266 **feës:** payments, offerings
269 **shal holde hir payd:** will be pleased
270 **unneth:** hardly
272 **nyste** = *ne wiste,* did not know
278–79 **the wyt To konne wel my sweven rede:** the intelligence to interpret my dream correctly
280 **drede:** doubt

198 **a quarter before day:** three hours before dawn
203 **red:** good advice, remedy
205 **yse:** see
206–7 **that ye Bury:** see that you bury
207 **such a tyde:** at a certain time
215 **swow:** anguish
217 **dwelle:** delay
222 **dolven:** buried   **everydel:** every bit, completely
224 **take kep:** taken heed
225 **next before:** immediately preceding, just now related
227 **bote ne bale:** ease or suffering, good or ill
228 **or:** before
234 **or tho:** before then

Of Egipte, he that redde so
The kynges metynge Pharao,
No more than koude the lest of us;
Ne nat skarsly Macrobeus
(He that wrot al th'avysyoun   285
That he mette, kyng Scipioun,
The noble man, the Affrikan —
Suche marvayles fortuned than),
I trowe, arede my dremes even.
Loo, thus hyt was; thys was my sweven.   290
    Me thoghte thus: that hyt was May,
And in the dawenynge I lay
(Me mette thus) in my bed al naked
And loked forth, for I was waked
With smale foules a gret hep   295
That had affrayed me out of my slep
Thorgh noyse and swetnesse of her song.
And, as me mette, they sate among
Upon my chambre roof wythoute,
Upon the tyles, overal aboute,   300
And songe, everych in hys wyse,
The moste solempne servise
By noote that ever man, y trowe,
Had herd, for som of hem song lowe,
Som high, and al of oon acord.   305
To telle shortly, att oo word,
Was never herd so swete a steven
But hyt had be a thyng of heven —
So mery a soun, so swete entewnes,
That certes, for the toun of Tewnes   310
I nolde but I had herd hem synge;
For al my chambre gan to rynge
Thurgh syngynge of her armonye;
For instrument nor melodye
Was nowhere herd yet half so swete,   315
Nor of acord half so mete;
For ther was noon of hem that feyned
To synge, for ech of hem hym peyned
To fynde out mery crafty notes.
They ne spared not her throtes.   320
And sooth to seyn, my chambre was
Ful wel depeynted, and with glas

Were al the wyndowes wel yglased
Ful clere, and nat an hoole ycrased,
That to beholde hyt was gret joye.   325
For hooly al the story of Troye
Was in the glasynge ywroght thus,
Of Ector and of kyng Priamus,
Of Achilles and of kyng Lamedon,
And eke of Medea and of Jason,   330
Of Paris, Eleyne, and of Lavyne.
And alle the walles with colours fyne
Were peynted, bothe text and glose,
Of al the Romaunce of the Rose.
My wyndowes were shette echon,   335
And throgh the glas the sonne shon
Upon my bed with bryghte bemes,
With many glade gilde stremes;
And eke the welken was so fair —
Blew, bryght, clere was the ayr,   340
And ful attempre for sothe hyt was;
For nother to cold nor hoot yt nas,
Ne in al the welken was a clowde.
    And as I lay thus, wonder lowde
Me thoght I herde an hunte blowe   345
T'assay hys horn and for to knowe
Whether hyt were clere or hors of soun.
And I herde goynge bothe up and doun
Men, hors, houndes, and other thyng;
And al men speken of huntyng,   350
How they wolde slee the hert with strengthe,
And how the hert had upon lengthe
So moche embosed — y not now what.
    Anoon ryght whan I herde that,
How that they wolde on-huntynge goon,   355
I was ryght glad, and up anoon
Took my hors, and forth I wente
Out of my chambre; I never stente
Til I com to the feld withoute.
Ther overtok y a gret route   360
Of huntes and eke of foresteres,
With many relayes and lymeres,

282 The dream (*metynge*) of King Pharaoh (interpreted by Joseph; Gen. 41)
284 **Macrobeus:** Macrobius
286 That King Scipio dreamed (Scipio Africanus; for his dream, see PF 36–84)
288 **fortuned:** happened
289 **arede:** explain **even:** correctly
296 **affrayed:** startled
298 **among:** together
303 **By noote:** in harmony
304 **som:** probably singular
307 **steven:** voice
309 **entewnes:** tunes; see n.
310 **Tewnes:** Tunis
316 **mete:** suitable, fitting
319 **crafty:** skillful, ingenious

324 **ycrased:** broken
326 **hooly:** wholly **story of Troye:** history of Troy; see Troilus and Criseyde for the characters named here, with the exception of Medea and Jason (see LGW 1580–1679) and Lavinia (*Lavyne*), Aeneas's wife (see HF 458)
327 **glasynge:** glasswork
333 **glose:** gloss; see n.
338 **gilde:** golden
339 **welken:** sky
341 **attempre:** moderate
345 **hunte:** hunter
351 **slee the hert with strengthe:** kill the hart (male red deer) in the chase
353 **embosed:** become exhausted from the hunt
358 **stente:** stopped
361 **foresteres:** trackers of game
362 **relayes:** sets of fresh hounds to take up the chase **lymeres:** hounds trained to track by scent

And hyed hem to the forest faste
And I with hem. So at the laste
I asked oon, ladde a lymere: 365
"Say, felowe, who shal hunte here?"
Quod I, and he answered ageyn,
   "Syr, th'emperour Octovyen,"
Quod he, "and ys here faste by."
   "A Goddes half, in good tyme!" quod I,   370
"Go we faste!" and gan to ryde.
Whan we came to the forest syde,
Every man dide ryght anoon
As to huntynge fil to doon.
The mayster-hunte anoon, fot-hot,   375
With a gret horn blew thre mot
At the uncouplynge of hys houndes.
Withynne a while the hert yfounde ys,
Yhalowed, and rechased faste
Longe tyme; and so at the laste   380
This hert rused and staal away
Fro alle the houndes a privy way.
The houndes had overshote hym alle
And were on a defaute yfalle.
Therwyth the hunte wonder faste   385
Blew a forloyn at the laste.
   I was go walked fro my tree,
And as I wente, ther cam by mee
A whelp, that fauned me as I stood,
That hadde yfolowed and koude no good.   390
Hyt com and crepte to me as lowe
Ryght as hyt hadde me yknowe,
Helde doun hys hed and joyned hys eres,
And leyde al smothe doun hys heres.
I wolde have kaught hyt, and anoon   395
Hyt fledde and was fro me goon;
And I hym folwed, and hyt forth wente
Doun by a floury grene wente
Ful thikke of gras, ful softe and swete.
With floures fele, faire under fete,   400
And litel used; hyt semed thus,

For both Flora and Zephirus,
They two that make floures growe,
Had mad her dwellynge ther, I trowe;
For hit was, on to beholde,   405
As thogh the erthe envye wolde
To be gayer than the heven,
To have moo floures, swiche seven,
As in the welken sterres bee.
Hyt had forgete the povertee   410
That wynter, thorgh hys colde morwes,
Had mad hyt suffre, and his sorwes;
All was forgeten, and that was sene,
For al the woode was waxen grene;
Swetnesse of dew had mad hyt waxe.   415
   Hyt ys no nede eke for to axe
Wher there were many grene greves,
Or thikke of trees, so ful of leves;
And every tree stood by hymselve
Fro other wel ten foot or twelve —   420
So grete trees, so huge of strengthe,
Of fourty or fifty fadme lengthe,
Clene withoute bowgh or stikke,
With croppes brode, and eke as thikke —
They were nat an ynche asonder —   425
That hit was shadewe overal under.
And many an hert and many an hynde
Was both before me and behynde.
Of founes, sowres, bukkes, does
Was ful the woode, and many roes,   430
And many sqwirelles that sete
Ful high upon the trees and ete,
And in hir maner made festes.
Shortly, hyt was so ful of bestes
That thogh Argus, the noble countour,   435
Sete to rekene in hys countour,
And rekene with his figures ten —
For by tho figures mowe al ken,
Yf they be crafty, rekene and noumbre,
And telle of every thing the noumbre —   440

---

365 **oon, ladde a lymere:** one who was leading a hound (on a leash)
368 **Octovyen:** Octavian, Augustus Caesar
370 **A Goddes half, in good tyme!:** For God's sake, that is timely!
375 **mayster-hunte:** chief huntsman **fot-hot:** immediately
376 **mot:** notes
379 **Yhalowed:** hallooed after **rechased:** pursued
381 **rused:** backtracked, to confuse the hounds
384 And were stopped by loss of the scent
386 **forloyn:** a hunting call indicating the hounds are far from the game
387 **was go walked:** had walked, had gone **tree:** the tree by which he had been posted, toward which the game was to be driven by the hounds
389 **fauned:** fawned on
390 **koude no good:** did not know what to do
398 **wente:** path
400 **fele:** many

402 **Flora:** the goddess of flowers **Zephirus:** the west wind
406 **envye:** contend
408 **swiche seven:** seven times as many
417 **Wher:** whether **greves:** branches
418 **Or thikke of:** or whether (the branches were) thick on
422 **fadme:** fathom
423 **stikke:** twig (on the trunks)
424 **croppes:** crowns, tree-tops
426 **overal under:** everywhere beneath
427 **hynde:** female deer
429 **founes:** fawns, year-old bucks **sowres:** four-year-old bucks **bukkes:** six-year-old bucks
435 **Argus:** Algus, inventor of Arabic numerals **countour:** mathematician
436 **Sete:** were to sit **countour:** counting house
437 **figures ten:** Arabic numerals
438 **mowe al ken:** all may learn
440 **telle:** count

Yet shoulde he fayle to rekene even
The wondres me mette in my sweven.
    But forth they romed ryght wonder faste
Doun the woode; so at the laste
I was war of a man in blak,   445
That sat and had yturned his bak
To an ook, an huge tree.
"Lord," thoght I, "who may that be?
What ayleth hym to sitten her?"
Anoon-ryght I wente ner;   450
Than found I sitte even upryght
A wonder wel-farynge knyght —
By the maner me thoghte so —
Of good mochel, and ryght yong therto,
Of the age of foure and twenty yer,   455
Upon hys berd but lytel her,
And he was clothed al in blak.
I stalked even unto hys bak,
And there I stood as stille as ought,
That, soth to saye, he saw me nought;   460
For-why he heng hys hed adoun,
And with a dedly sorwful soun
He made of rym ten vers or twelve
Of a compleynte to hymselve —
The moste pitee, the moste rowthe,   465
That ever I herde; for, by my trowthe,
Hit was gret wonder that Nature
Myght suffre any creature
To have such sorwe and be not ded.
Ful pitous pale and nothyng red,   470
He sayd a lay, a maner song,
Withoute noote, withoute song;
And was thys, for ful wel I kan
Reherse hyt; ryght thus hyt began:

    "I have of sorwe so gret won   475
That joye gete I never non,
Now that I see my lady bryght,
Which I have loved with al my myght,
Is fro me ded and ys agoon.
    "Allas, deth, what ayleth the,   481
That thou noldest have taken me,
Whan thou toke my lady swete,
That was so fair, so fresh, so fre,

So good that men may wel se   485
Of al goodnesse she had no mete!"

    Whan he had mad thus his complaynte,
Hys sorwful hert gan faste faynte
And his spirites wexen dede;
The blood was fled for pure drede   490
Doun to hys herte, to make hym warm —
For wel hyt feled the herte had harm —
To wite eke why hyt was adrad
By kynde, and for to make hyt glad,
For hit ys membre principal   495
Of the body; and that made al
Hys hewe chaunge and wexe grene
And pale, for ther noo blood ys sene
In no maner lym of hys.
Anoon therwith whan y sawgh this —   500
He ferde thus evel there he set —
I went and stood ryght at his fet,
And grette hym; but he spak noght,
But argued with his owne thoght,
And in hys wyt disputed faste   505
Why and how hys lyf myght laste;
Hym thoughte hys sorwes were so smerte
And lay so colde upon hys herte.
So, throgh hys sorwe and hevy thoght,
Made hym that he herde me noght;   510
For he had wel nygh lost hys mynde,
Thogh Pan, that men clepeth god of kynde,
Were for hys sorwes never so wroth.
    But at the last, to sayn ryght soth,
He was war of me, how y stood   515
Before hym and did of myn hood,
And had ygret hym as I best koude,
Debonayrly, and nothyng lowde.
He sayde, "I prey the, be not wroth.
I herde the not, to seyn the soth,   520
Ne I sawgh the not, syr, trewely."
    "A, goode sir, no fors," quod y,
"I am ryght sory yif I have ought
Destroubled yow out of your thought.
Foryive me, yif I have mystake."   525

---

441 **even:** correctly
450 **Anoon-ryght:** instantly   **ner:** nearer
451 **even upryght:** erect
452 **wel-farynge:** attractive
454 **Of good mochel:** pleasing in size, well proportioned
therto: moreover
459 **as stille as ought:** as quietly as anything (as possible)
464 **compleynte:** a poem lamenting one's experience in love; see
Short Poems for examples.
471 **maner:** kind of
475 **won:** abundance
479–81 On the numbering of these lines, see textual note.

486 **mete:** equal
490 **pure:** utter
493–94 **To wite eke why hyt was adrad By kynde:** to find out
also why it (the heart), by instinct, was terrified
495 **membre principal:** principal, chief organ
501 He was becoming so ill while he sat there
504 **argued:** debated
509 **hevy:** gloomy
512 **god of kynde:** god of nature
516 **did of:** took off
518 **Debonayrly:** courteously, modestly
522 **no fors:** it does not matter
524 **Destroubled:** disturbed

"Yis, th'amendes is lyght to make,"
Quod he, "for ther lyeth noon therto;
There ys nothyng myssayd nor do."
  Loo, how goodly spak thys knyght,
As hit had be another wyght;   530
He made hyt nouther towgh ne queynte.
And I saw that, and gan me aqueynte
With hym, and fond hym so tretable,
Ryght wonder skylful and resonable,
As me thoghte, for al hys bale.   535
Anoon ryght I gan fynde a tale
To hym, to loke wher I myght ought
Have more knowynge of hys thought.
"Sir," quod I, "this game is doon.
I holde that this hert be goon;   540
These huntes konne hym nowher see."
  "Y do no fors therof," quod he;
"My thought ys theron never a del."
  "By oure Lord," quod I, "y trow yow wel;
Ryght so me thinketh by youre chere.   545
But, sir, oo thyng wol ye here?
Me thynketh in gret sorowe I yow see;
But certes, sire, yif that yee
Wolde ought discure me youre woo,
I wolde, as wys God helpe me soo,   550
Amende hyt, yif I kan or may.
Ye mowe preve hyt be assay;
For, by my trouthe, to make yow hool
I wol do al my power hool.
And telleth me of your sorwes smerte;   555
Paraunter hyt may ese youre herte,
That semeth ful sek under your syde."
  With that he loked on me asyde,
As who sayth, "Nay, that wol not be."
"Graunt mercy, goode frend," quod he,   560
"I thanke the that thow woldest soo,
But hyt may never the rather be doo.
No man may my sorwe glade,
That maketh my hewe to falle and fade,
And hath myn understondynge lorn   565
That me ys wo that I was born!
May noght make my sorwes slyde,
Nought al the remedyes of Ovyde,

Ne Orpheus, god of melodye,
Ne Dedalus with his playes slye;   570
Ne hele me may no phisicien,
Noght Ypocras ne Galyen;
Me ys wo that I lyve houres twelve.
But whooso wol assay hymselve
Whether his hert kan have pitee   575
Of any sorwe, lat hym see me.
Y wrecche, that deth hath mad al naked
Of al the blysse that ever was maked,
Yworthe worste of alle wyghtes,
That hate my dayes and my nyghtes!   580
My lyf, my lustes, be me loothe,
For al welfare and I be wroothe.
The pure deth ys so ful my foo
That I wolde deye, hyt wolde not soo;
For whan I folwe hyt, hit wol flee;   585
I wolde have hym, hyt nyl nat me.
This ys my peyne wythoute red,
Alway deynge and be not ded,
That Cesiphus, that lyeth in helle,
May not of more sorwe telle.   590
And whoso wiste al, by my trouthe,
My sorwe, but he hadde rowthe
And pitee of my sorwes smerte,
That man hath a fendly herte;
For whoso seeth me first on morwe   595
May seyn he hath met with sorwe,
For y am sorwe, and sorwe ys y.
  "Allas! and I wol tel the why:
My song ys turned to pleynynge,
And al my laughtre to wepynge,   600
My glade thoghtes to hevynesse;
In travayle ys myn ydelnesse
And eke my reste; my wele is woo,
My good ys harm, and evermoo
In wrathe ys turned my pleynge   605
And my delyt into sorwynge.
Myn hele ys turned into seknesse,
In drede ys al my sykernesse;
To derke ys turned al my lyght,
My wyt ys foly, my day ys nyght,   610
My love ys hate, my slep wakynge,
My myrthe and meles ys fastynge,

---

527 **ther lyeth noon therto:** nothing of that sort is needed
531 He was neither haughty nor standoffish.
533 **tretable:** tractable, affable
535 **bale:** suffering
536 **Anoon ryght:** straightaway
542 **do no fors:** care not
549 **discure:** reveal
552 **preve hyt be assay:** test it by trying it out
553 **hool:** healthy
554 **hool:** whole
557 **sek:** sick
560 **Graunt mercy:** thank you
565 **lorn:** lost
568 **remedyes of Ovyde:** Ovid's *Remedia Amoris*

569 **Orpheus:** the famous musician
570 **Dedalus:** Daedalus, famed for his mechanical skill
572 **Ypocras, Galyen:** Hippocrates, Galen, ancient authorities on medicine
579 **Yworthe:** become
583 **pure deth:** death itself
586 **hyt nyl nat me:** it does not want me
587 **red:** good advice, remedy
589 **Cesiphus:** Sisiphus; see n.
594 **fendly:** fiendish, evil
607 **hele:** good health **seknesse:** sickness
608 **drede:** dread, doubt **sykernesse:** certainty

My countenaunce ys nycete
And al abaved, where so I be;
My pees in pledynge and in werre.   615
Allas, how myghte I fare werre?
My boldnesse ys turned to shame,
For fals Fortune hath pleyd a game
Atte ches with me, allas the while!
The trayteresse fals and ful of gyle,   620
That al behoteth and nothyng halt,
She goth upryght and yet she halt,
That baggeth foule and loketh faire,
The dispitouse debonaire
That skorneth many a creature!   625
An ydole of fals portrayture
Ys she, for she wol sone wrien;
She is the monstres hed ywrien,
As fylthe over-ystrawed with floures.
Hir moste worshippe and hir flour ys   630
To lyen, for that ys hyr nature;
Withoute feyth, lawe, or mesure
She ys fals, and ever laughynge
With oon eye, and that other wepynge.
That ys broght up she set al doun.   635
I lykne hyr to the scorpioun,
That ys a fals, flaterynge beste,
For with his hed he maketh feste,
But al amydde hys flaterynge
With hys tayle he wol stynge   640
And envenyme; and so wol she.
She ys th'envyouse charite
That ys ay fals and semeth wel;
So turneth she hyr false whel
Aboute, for hyt ys nothyng stable —   645
Now by the fire, now at table;
For many oon hath she thus yblent.
She ys pley of enchauntement,
That semeth oon and ys not soo.
The false thef! What hath she doo,   650
Trowest thou? By oure Lord I wol the seye:
    "At the ches with me she gan to pleye;
With hir false draughtes dyvers
She staal on me and tok my fers.

And whan I sawgh my fers awaye,   655
Allas, I kouthe no lenger playe,
But seyde, 'Farewel, swete, ywys,
And farewel al that ever ther ys!'
    "Therwith Fortune seyde 'Chek her!
And mat in the myd poynt of the chekker,   660
With a poun errant!' Allas,
Ful craftier to pley she was
Than Athalus, that made the game
First of the ches, so was hys name.
But God wolde I had oones or twyes   665
Ykoud and knowe the jeupardyes
That kowde the Grek Pictagores!
I shulde have pleyd the bet at ches
And kept my fers the bet therby.
And thogh wherto? For trewely   670
I holde that wyssh nat worth a stree!
Hyt had be never the bet for me,
For Fortune kan so many a wyle
Ther be but fewe kan hir begile;
And eke she ys the lasse to blame;   675
Myself I wolde have do the same,
Before God, hadde I ben as she;
She oghte the more excused be.
For this I say yet more therto:
Had I be God and myghte have do   680
My wille when she my fers kaughte,
I wolde have drawe the same draughte.
For, also wys God yive me reste,
I dar wel swere she took the beste.
But through that draughte I have lorn   685
My blysse; allas, that I was born!
For evermore, y trowe trewly,
For al my wille, my lust holly
Ys turned; but yet, what to doone?
Be oure Lord, hyt ys to deye soone.   690
For nothyng I leve hyt noght,
But lyve and deye ryght in this thoght;
For there nys planete in firmament,
Ne in ayr ne in erthe noon element,
That they ne yive me a yifte echone   695

Of wepynge whan I am allone.
For whan that I avise me wel
And bethenke me every del
How that ther lyeth in rekenyng,
In my sorwe, for nothyng,   700
And how ther leveth no gladnesse
May glade me of my distresse,
And how I have lost suffisance,
And therto I have no plesance,
Than may I say I have ryght noght.   705
And whan al this falleth in my thoght,
Allas, than am I overcome!
For that ys doon ys not to come.
I have more sorowe than Tantale."
    And whan I herde hym tel thys tale   710
Thus pitously, as I yow telle,
Unnethe myght y lenger dwelle,
Hyt dyde myn herte so moche woo.
"A, goode sir," quod I, "say not soo!
Have som pitee on your nature   715
That formed yow to creature.
Remembre yow of Socrates,
For he ne counted nat thre strees
Of noght that Fortune koude doo."
    "No," quod he, "I kan not soo."   720
    "Why so, good syr? Yis parde!" quod y;
"Ne say noght soo, for trewely,
Thogh ye had lost the ferses twelve,
And ye for sorwe mordred yourselve,
Ye sholde be dampned in this cas   725
By as good ryght as Medea was,
That slough hir children for Jasoun;
And Phyllis also for Demophoun
Heng hirself — so weylaway! —
For he had broke his terme-day   730
To come to hir. Another rage
Had Dydo, the quene eke of Cartage,
That slough hirself for Eneas
Was fals — which a fool she was!

And Ecquo died for Narcisus   735
Nolde nat love hir, and ryght thus
Hath many another foly doon;
And for Dalida died Sampson,
That slough hymself with a piler.
But ther is no man alyve her   740
Wolde for a fers make this woo!"
    "Why so?" quod he, "hyt ys nat soo.
Thou wost ful lytel what thou menest;
I have lost more than thow wenest."
    "Loo, [sey] how that may be?" quod y;   745
"Good sir, telle me al hooly
In what wyse, how, why, and wherfore
That ye have thus youre blysse lore."
    "Blythely," quod he; "com sytte adoun!
I telle the upon a condicioun   750
That thou shalt hooly, with al thy wyt,
Doo thyn entent to herkene hit."
    "Yis, syr." "Swere thy trouthe therto."
    "Gladly." "Do thanne holde hereto!"
    "I shal ryght blythely, so God me save,   755
Hooly, with al the wit I have,
Here yow as wel as I kan."
    "A Goddes half!" quod he, and began:
"Syr," quod he, "sith first I kouthe
Have any maner wyt fro youthe,   760
Or kyndely understondyng
To comprehende in any thyng
What love was, in myn owne wyt,
Dredeles, I have ever yit
Be tributarye and yive rente   765
To Love, hooly with good entente,
And throgh plesaunce become his thral
With good wille, body, hert, and al.
Al this I putte in his servage,
As to my lord, and dide homage;   770
And ful devoutly I prayed hym to
He shulde besette myn herte so
That hyt plesance to hym were
And worship to my lady dere.
    "And this was longe, and many a yer   775
Or that myn herte was set owher,
That I dide thus, and nyste why;
I trowe hit cam me kyndely.

697 avise me wel: consider
699–700 ther lyeth in rekenyng, In my sorwe, for nothyng:
there is nothing owing to me in the way of sorrow
701 leveth: remains
703 suffisance: contentment
709 Tantale: Tantalus, tormented in Hades by having sustenance
just out of reach (cf. Bo 3 m12.38–40)
712 Unnethe: hardly
717 Socrates: celebrated for his indifference to fortune; see For
17–22.
720 kan not soo: cannot (do) so
723 ferses twelve: twelve queens; see n.
726–27 Medea, Jasoun: for their story, see LGW 1580–1679.
728 Phyllis, Demophoun: for the story, see LGW 2394–2561.
729 weylaway: alas
730 terme-day: appointed day
731 rage: violent grief
732–33 Dydo, Eneas: For the story see LGW 924–1367 and HF
221–382.

735 Ecquo, Narcisus: For the story of Echo and Narcissus, see
Rom 1469–1538.
738 Dalida, Sampson: For the story of Delilah and Samson, see
MkT VII.2063–70.
748 lore: lost
761 kyndely: natural
764 Dredeles: doubtless
765 tributarye: a vassal, who pays tribute (rente)
766 hooly: completely
772 besette: employ, use
776 owher: anywhere
777 nyste = ne wiste, did not know
778 kyndely: naturally

Paraunter I was therto most able,
As a whit wal or a table,   780
For hit ys redy to cacche and take
Al that men wil theryn make,
Whethir so men wil portreye or peynte,
Be the werkes never so queynte.
   "And thilke tyme I ferde ryght so,   785
I was able to have lerned tho,
And to have kend as wel or better,
Paraunter, other art or letre;
But for love cam first in my thoght,
Therfore I forgat hyt noght.   790
I ches love to my firste craft;
Therfore hit ys with me laft,
For-why I tok hyt of so yong age
That malyce hadde my corage
Nat that tyme turned to nothyng   795
Thorgh to mochel knowlechyng.
For that tyme Yowthe, my maistresse,
Governed me in ydelnesse;
For hyt was in my firste youthe,
And thoo ful lytel good y couthe,   800
For al my werkes were flyttynge
That tyme, and al my thoght varyinge.
Al were to me ylyche good
That I knew thoo; but thus hit stood:
   "Hit happed that I cam on a day   805
Into a place ther that I say
Trewly the fayrest companye
Of ladyes that evere man with yë
Had seen togedres in oo place.
Shal I clepe hyt hap other grace   810
That broght me there? Nay, but Fortune,
That ys to lyen ful comune,
The false trayteresse pervers!
God wolde I koude clepe hir wers,
For now she worcheth me ful woo,   815
And I wol telle sone why soo.
   "Among these ladyes thus echon,
Soth to seyen, y sawgh oon
That was lyk noon of the route;
For I dar swere, withoute doute,   820
That as the someres sonne bryght
Ys fairer, clerer, and hath more lyght
Than any other planete in heven,

The moone or the sterres seven,
For al the world so hadde she   825
Surmounted hem alle of beaute,
Of maner, and of comlynesse,
Of stature, and of wel set gladnesse,
Of goodlyhede so wel beseye —
Shortly, what shal y more seye?   830
By God and by his halwes twelve,
Hyt was my swete, ryght as hirselve.
She had so stedfast countenaunce,
So noble port and meyntenaunce,
And Love, that had wel herd my boone,   835
Had espyed me thus soone,
That she ful sone in my thoght,
As helpe me God, so was ykaught
So sodenly that I ne tok
No maner counseyl but at hir lok   840
And at myn herte; for-why hir eyen
So gladly, I trow, myn herte seyen
That purely tho myn owne thoght
Seyde hit were beter serve hir for noght
Than with another to be wel.   845
And hyt was soth, for everydel
I wil anoon ryght telle thee why.
   "I sawgh hyr daunce so comlily,
Carole and synge so swetely,
Laughe and pleye so womanly,   850
And loke so debonairly,
So goodly speke and so frendly,
That certes y trowe that evermor
Nas seyn so blysful a tresor.
For every heer on hir hed,   855
Soth to seyne, hyt was not red,
Ne nouther yelowe ne broun hyt nas;
Me thoghte most lyk gold hyt was.
   "And whiche eyen my lady hadde!
Debonaire, goode, glade, and sadde,   860
Symple, of good mochel, noght to wyde.
Therto hir look nas not asyde
Ne overthwert, but beset so wel
Hyt drew and took up everydel
Al that on hir gan beholde.   865
Hir eyen semed anoon she wolde

779 **Paraunter:** perhaps **able:** capable
784 **queynte:** elaborately decorated, contrived
787 **kend:** learned
788 **other . . . or:** either . . . or
789 **for:** because
794 **malyce:** misease, trouble **corage:** heart
801 **flyttynge:** impermanent
806 **say:** saw
812 **comune:** accustomed
819 **route:** company

824 **sterres seven:** the Pleiades (?)
827 **comlynesse:** graciousness
829 **goodlyhede:** excellence **beseye:** provided
831 **halwes:** saints, apostles
834 **meyntenaunce:** bearing, demeanor
835 **boone:** request
842 **seyen:** behold
843 **tho:** then
848 **comlily:** in a becoming way
849 **Carole:** dance
860 **sadde:** serious
861 **Symple:** unaffected **of good mochel:** well proportioned, of pleasing size
863 **overthwert:** askance, sidewise

Have mercy — fooles wenden soo —
But hyt was never the rather doo.
Hyt nas no countrefeted thyng;
Hyt was hir owne pure lokyng   870
That the goddesse, dame Nature,
Had mad hem opene by mesure
And close; for were she never so glad,
Hyr lokynge was not foly sprad,
Ne wildely, thogh that she pleyde;   875
But ever, me thoght, hir eyen seyde,
'Be God, my wrathe ys al foryive!'
    "Therwith hir lyste so wel to lyve,
That dulnesse was of hir adrad.
She nas to sobre ne to glad;   880
In alle thynges more mesure
Had never, I trowe, creature.
But many oon with hire lok she herte,
And that sat hyr ful lyte at herte,
For she knew nothyng of her thoght;   885
But whether she knew or knew it nowght
Algate she ne roughte of hem a stree! —
To gete her love no ner nas he
That woned at hom than he in Ynde;
The formest was alway behynde.   890
But goode folk, over al other,
She loved as man may do hys brother;
Of which love she was wonder large,
In skilful places that bere charge.
    "But which a visage had she thertoo!   895
Allas, myn herte ys wonder woo
That I ne kan discryven hyt!
Me lakketh both Englyssh and wit
For to undo hyt at the fulle;
And eke my spirites be so dulle   900
So gret a thyng for to devyse.
I have no wit that kan suffise
To comprehende hir beaute.
But thus moche dar I sayn, that she
Was whit, rody, fressh, and lyvely hewed,   905
And every day hir beaute newed.
And negh hir face was alderbest,
For certes Nature had swich lost
To make that fair that trewly she

Was hir chef patron of beaute,   910
And chef ensample of al hir werk,
And moustre; for be hyt never so derk,
Me thynketh I se hir ever moo.
And yet moreover, thogh alle thoo
That ever livede were now alyve,   915
Ne sholde have founde to discryve
Yn al hir face a wikked synge,
For hit was sad, symple, and benygne.
    "And which a goodly, softe speche
Had that swete, my lyves leche!   920
So frendly, and so wel ygrounded,
Up al resoun so wel yfounded,
And so tretable to alle goode
That I dar swere wel, by the roode,
Of eloquence was never founde   925
So swete a sownynge facounde,
Ne trewer tonged, ne skorned lasse,
Ne bet koude hele — that, by the masse
I durste swere, thogh the pope hit songe,
That ther was never yet throgh hir tonge   930
Man ne woman gretly harmed;
As for her, was al harm hyd —
Ne lasse flaterynge in hir word,
That purely hir symple record
Was founde as trewe as any bond   935
Or trouthe of any mannes hond;
Ne chyde she koude never a del;
That knoweth al the world ful wel.
    "But swich a fairnesse of a nekke
Had that swete that boon nor brekke   940
Nas ther non sene that myssat.
Hyt was whit, smothe, streght, and pure flat,
Wythouten hole or canel-boon,
As be semynge had she noon.
Hyr throte, as I have now memoyre,   945
Semed a round tour of yvoyre,
Of good gretnesse, and noght to gret.
    "And goode faire White she het;
That was my lady name ryght.
She was bothe fair and bryght;   950

910 **patron:** pattern
912 **moustre:** model, pattern
916 **discryve:** discover
920 **leche:** physician
921 **ygrounded:** instructed
922 **Up:** upon
923 **tretable:** amenable
924 **roode:** cross
926 **sownynge facounde:** eloquent speech
934 **record:** promise
940 **brekke:** blemish
941 **myssat:** was unbecoming
943 **canel-boon:** collarbone
944 **As be semynge:** to all appearances
947 **gretnesse:** size
948 **het:** was called

867 **wenden:** believed
878 **hir lyste:** she desired
881 **mesure:** moderation
883 **herte:** hurt
884 **sat hyr ful lyte:** did not weigh heavily, did not afflict
887 **Algate:** nevertheless   **roughte:** reckoned   **stree:** straw
889 **woned:** dwelt, remained   **Ynde:** India
890 **formest:** very first
893 **large:** generous
894 In reasonable situations that are of some consequence
899 **undo:** explain, unfold

She hadde not hir name wrong.
Ryght faire shuldres and body long
She had, and armes, every lyth
Fattyssh, flesshy, not gret therwith;
Ryght white handes, and nayles rede;   955
Rounde brestes; and of good brede
Hyr hippes were; a streight flat bak.
I knew on hir noon other lak
That al hir lymmes nere pure sewynge
In as fer as I had knowynge.   960
    "Therto she koude so wel pleye,
Whan that hir lyste, that I dar seye
That she was lyk to torche bryght
That every man may take of lyght
Ynogh, and hyt hath never the lesse.   965
Of maner and of comlynesse
Ryght so ferde my lady dere,
For every wight of hir manere
Myght cacche ynogh, yif that he wolde,
Yif he had eyen hir to beholde;   970
For I dar swere wel, yif that she
Had among ten thousand be,
She wolde have be, at the leste,
A chef myrour of al the feste,
Thogh they had stonden in a rowe,   975
To mennes eyen that koude have knowe;
For wher-so men had pleyd or waked,
Me thoghte the felawsshyppe as naked
Withouten hir that sawgh I oones
As a corowne withoute stones.   980
Trewly she was, to myn yë,
The soleyn fenix of Arabye,
For ther livyth never but oon,
Ne swich as she ne knowe I noon.
    "To speke of godnesse, trewly she   985
Had as moche debonairte
As ever had Hester in the Bible,
And more, yif more were possyble.
And soth to seyne, therwythal
She had a wyt so general,   990
So hool enclyned to alle goode,
That al hir wyt was set, by the rode,
Withoute malyce, upon gladnesse;
And therto I saugh never yet a lesse

Harmful than she was in doynge.   995
I sey nat that she ne had knowynge
What harm was, or elles she
Had koud no good, so thinketh me.
    "And trewly for to speke of trouthe,
But she had had, hyt hadde be routhe.   1000
Therof she had so moche hyr del —
And I dar seyn and swere hyt wel —
That Trouthe hymself over al and al
Had chose hys maner principal
In hir that was his restyng place.   1005
Therto she hadde the moste grace
To have stedefast perseveraunce
And esy, atempre governaunce
That ever I knew or wyste yit,
So pure suffraunt was hir wyt;   1010
And reson gladly she understood;
Hyt folowed wel she koude good.
She used gladly to do wel;
These were hir maners everydel.
    "Therwith she loved so wel ryght   1015
She wrong do wolde to no wyght.
No wyght myghte do hir noo shame,
She loved so wel hir owne name.
Hyr lust to holde no wyght in honde,
Ne, be thou siker, she wolde not fonde   1020
To holde no wyght in balaunce
By half word ne by countenaunce —
But if men wolde upon hir lye —
Ne sende men into Walakye,
To Pruyse, and into Tartarye,   1025
To Alysaundre, ne into Turkye,
And byd hym faste anoon that he
Goo hoodles into the Drye Se
And come hom by the Carrenar,
And seye, 'Sir, be now ryght war   1030
That I may of yow here seyn
Worshyp or that ye come ageyn!'
She ne used no suche knakkes smale.

953 **lyth**: limb
954 **Fattyssh**: well rounded   **flesshy**: shapely
956 **brede**: breadth
958 **lak**: flaw
959 **nere pure sewynge**: were not perfectly conformable
(proportioned)
969 **yif that**: if
982 **soleyn fenix**: solitary phoenix (the mythical bird)
986 **debonairte**: graciousness
987 **Hester**: Esther, a biblical model of wifely virtue
990 **general**: liberal, affable to all
992 **rode**: cross

997–98 **or elles she Had koud no good**: otherwise she would
not have known what goodness was
1000 **But she had had**: if she had not had it (*trouthe*)
1003 **al and al**: everything
1004 **maner**: manor, residence
1010 **suffraunt**: tolerant
1019 **to holde no wyght in honde**: to encourage no one with
false hopes
1020 **fonde**: strive
1021 **balaunce**: suspense
1022 **half word**: insinuation
1023 Unless someone wanted to give a false report about her
1024 **Walakye**: Wallachia, in Rumania
1025 **Pruyse**: Prussia   **Tartarye**: Outer Mongolia
1026 **Alysaundre**: Alexandria
1028 **hoodles**: bareheaded   **Drye Se**: the Gobi Desert
1029 **Carrenar**: Kara-Nor, on the east side of the Gobi
1033 **knakkes smale**: petty tricks

"But wherfore that y telle my tale?
Ryght on thys same, as I have seyd,   1035
Was hooly al my love leyd;
For certes she was, that swete wif,
My suffisaunce, my lust, my lyf,
Myn hap, myn hele, and al my blesse,
My worldes welfare, and my goddesse,   1040
And I hooly hires and everydel."

    "By oure Lord," quod I, "y trowe yow wel!
Hardely, your love was wel beset;
I not how ye myghte have do bet."
"Bet? Ne no wyght so wel," quod he.   1045
"Y trowe hyt wel, sir," quod I, "parde!"
"Nay, leve hyt wel!" "Sire, so do I;
I leve yow wel, that trewely
Yow thoghte that she was the beste
And to beholde the alderfayreste,   1050
Whoso had loked hir with your eyen."

    "With myn? Nay, alle that hir seyen
Seyde and sworen hyt was soo.
And thogh they ne hadde, I wolde thoo
Have loved best my lady free,   1055
Thogh I had had al the beaute
That ever had Alcipyades,
And al the strengthe of Ercules,
And therto had the worthynesse
Of Alysaunder, and al the rychesse   1060
That ever was in Babyloyne,
In Cartage, or in Macedoyne,
Or in Rome, or in Nynyve;
And therto also hardy be
As was Ector, so have I joye,   1065
That Achilles slough at Troye —
And therfore was he slayn alsoo
In a temple, for bothe twoo
Were slayne, he and Antylegyus
(And so seyth Dares Frygius),   1070
For love of Polixena —
Or ben as wis as Mynerva,
I wolde ever, withoute drede,
Have loved hir, for I moste nede.
'Nede?' Nay, trewly, I gabbe now,   1075

Noght 'nede,' and I wol tellen how:
For of good wille myn herte hyt wolde,
And eke to love hir I was holde
As for the fairest and the beste.
She was as good, so have I reste,   1080
As ever was Penelopee of Grece,
Or as the noble wif Lucrece,
That was the beste — he telleth thus,
The Romayn, Tytus Lyvyus —
She was as good, and nothyng lyk   1085
(Thogh hir stories be autentyk),
Algate she was as trewe as she.

    "But wherfore that I telle thee
Whan I first my lady say?
I was ryght yong, soth to say,   1090
And ful gret nede I hadde to lerne;
Whan my herte wolde yerne
To love, hyt was a gret empryse.
But as my wyt koude best suffise,
After my yonge childly wyt,   1095
Withoute drede, I besette hyt
To love hir in my beste wyse,
To do hir worship and the servise
That I koude thoo, be my trouthe,
Withoute feynynge outher slouthe,   1100
For wonder feyn I wolde hir se.
So mochel hyt amended me
That whan I saugh hir first a-morwe
I was warished of al my sorwe
Of al day after; til hyt were eve   1105
Me thoghte nothyng myghte me greve,
Were my sorwes never so smerte.
And yet she syt so in myn herte
That, by my trouthe, y nolde noght
For al thys world out of my thoght   1110
Leve my lady; noo, trewely!"

    "Now, by my trouthe, sir," quod I,
"Me thynketh ye have such a chaunce
As shryfte wythoute repentaunce."

    "Repentaunce? Nay, fy!" quod he,   1115
"Shulde y now repente me

1039 **hap:** good fortune
1057 **Alcipyades:** Alcibiades
1058 **Ercules:** Hercules
1060 **Alysaunder:** Alexander the Great
1061 **Babyloyne:** Babylon
1062 **Cartage:** Carthage **Macedoyne:** Macedonia
1063 **Nynyve:** the biblical Nineveh
1065 **Ector:** Hector
1069 **Antylegyus:** Antilochus (i.e., Archilogus; he and Achilles were slain as the latter was about to marry *Polixena*)
1070 **Dares Frygius:** supposed author of a history of the Trojan War
1072 **Mynerva:** the goddess of wisdom
1075 **gabbe:** talk nonsense

1077 **hyt wolde:** wished it
1078 **holde:** obligated
1081 **Penelopee:** faithful wife of Ulysses
1082 **Lucrece:** Lucretia; for her story see LGW 1680–1885.
1084 **Tytus Lyvyus:** Livy, the Roman historian
1085 **nothyng lyk:** not like Lucretia (save in goodness)
1086 **autentyk:** true
1089 **say:** saw
1093 **empryse:** difficult task
1095 **After:** in accordance with
1099 **koude thoo:** knew how at that time
1100 **Withoute feynynge:** wholeheartedly
1103 **a-morwe:** in the morning
1104 **warished:** cured
1114 **shryfte wythoute repentaunce:** forgiveness without contrition; see n.

To love? Nay, certes, than were I wel
Wers than was Achitofel,
Or Anthenor, so have I joye,
The traytor that betraysed Troye,   1120
Or the false Genelloun,
He that purchased the tresoun
Of Rowland and of Olyver.
Nay, while I am alyve her,
I nyl foryete hir never moo."   1125
    "Now, goode syre," quod I thoo,
"Ye han wel told me herebefore;
Hyt ys no nede to reherse it more,
How ye sawe hir first, and where.
But wolde ye tel me the manere   1130
To hire which was your firste speche —
Therof I wolde yow beseche —
And how she knewe first your thoght,
Whether ye loved hir or noght?
And telleth me eke what ye have lore,   1135
I herde yow telle herebefore."
    "Yee!" seyde he, "thow nost what thow
            menest;
I have lost more than thou wenest."
    "What los ys that?" quod I thoo;
"Nyl she not love yow? Ys hyt soo?   1140
Or have ye oght doon amys,
That she hath left yow? Ys hyt this?
For Goddes love, telle me al."
    "Before God," quod he, "and I shal.
I saye ryght as I have seyd,   1145
On hir was al my love leyd,
And yet she nyste hyt nat, never a del
Noght longe tyme, leve hyt wel!
For be ryght siker, I durste noght
For al this world telle hir my thoght,   1150
Ne I wolde have wraththed hir, trewely.
For wostow why? She was lady
Of the body; she had the herte,
And who hath that may not asterte.
But for to kepe me fro ydelnesse,   1155
Trewly I dide my besynesse
To make songes, as I best koude,
And ofte tyme I song hem loude;
And made songes thus a gret del,
Althogh I koude not make so wel   1160
Songes, ne knewe the art al,
As koude Lamekes sone Tubal,

That found out first the art of songe;
For as hys brothres hamers ronge
Upon hys anvelt up and doun,   1165
Therof he took the firste soun —
But Grekes seyn Pictagoras,
That he the firste fynder was
Of the art (Aurora telleth so);
But therof no fors of hem two.   1170
Algates songes thus I made
Of my felynge, myn herte to glade;
And, lo, this was [the] altherferste —
I not wher hyt were the werste.

    'Lord, hyt maketh myn herte lyght   1175
Whan I thenke on that swete wyght
That is so semely on to see;
And wisshe to God hit myghte so bee
That she wolde holde me for hir knyght,
My lady, that is so fair and bryght!'   1180

    "Now have I told thee, soth to say,
My firste song. Upon a day
I bethoghte me what woo
And sorwe that I suffred thoo
For hir, and yet she wyste hyt noght,   1185
Ne telle hir durste I nat my thoght.
'Allas,' thoghte I, 'y kan no red;
And but I telle hir, I nam but ded;
And yif I telle hyr, to seye ryght soth,
I am adred she wol be wroth.   1190
Allas, what shal I thanne do?'
    "In this debat I was so wo
Me thoghte myn herte braste atweyne!
So at the laste, soth to sayne,
I bethoghte me that Nature   1195
Ne formed never in creature
So moche beaute, trewely,
And bounte, wythoute mercy.
In hope of that, my tale I tolde
With sorwe, as that I never sholde,   1200
For nedes, and mawgree my hed,
I most have told hir or be ded.
I not wel how that I began;
Ful evel rehersen hyt I kan;

1118 **Achitofel:** the evil counselor who urged Absalom to rebel
against David
1119 **Anthenor:** Antenor
1121 **Genelloun:** Ganelon, who betrayed *Rowland* and *Olyver,*
heroes of the *Chanson de Roland*
1137 **nost** = *ne wost,* know not **menest:** say
1162 **Lamekes sone Tubal:** Lamech's son Tubal; see n.

1165 **anvelt:** anvil
1167 **Pictagoras:** Pythagoras
1169 **Aurora:** a twelfth-century commentary on parts of the Bible
by Peter of Riga
1171 **Algates:** nevertheless
1173 **altherferste:** first of all
1188 **nam but ded:** am as good as dead
1193 **atweyne:** in two
1200 **With sorwe:** badly (literally, with bad luck) **as that:** in a
way that (i.e., he presented his case poorly)
1201 For of necessity and in spite of all I could do

And eke, as helpe me God withal, 1205
I trowe hyt was in the dismal,
That was the ten woundes of Egipte —
For many a word I over-skipte
In my tale, for pure fere
Lest my wordes mysset were. 1210
With sorweful herte and woundes dede,
Softe and quakynge for pure drede
And shame, and styntynge in my tale
For ferde, and myn hewe al pale —
Ful ofte I wex bothe pale and red — 1215
Bowynge to hir, I heng the hed;
I durste nat ones loke hir on,
For wit, maner, and al was goon.
I seyde 'Mercy!' and no more.
Hyt nas no game; hyt sat me sore. 1220
  "So at the laste, soth to seyn,
Whan that myn hert was come ageyn,
To telle shortly al my speche,
With hool herte I gan hir beseche
That she wolde be my lady swete; 1225
And swor, and gan hir hertely hete
Ever to be stedfast and trewe,
And love hir alwey fresshly newe,
And never other lady have,
And al hir worship for to save 1230
As I best koude. I swor hir this:
'For youres is alle that ever ther ys
For evermore, myn herte swete!
And never to false yow, but I mete,
I nyl, as wys God helpe me soo!' 1235
  "And whan I had my tale y-doo,
God wot, she acounted nat a stree
Of al my tale, so thoghte me.
To telle shortly ryght as hyt ys,
Trewly hir answere hyt was this — 1240
I kan not now wel counterfete
Hir wordes, but this was the grete
Of hir answere: she sayde 'Nay'
Al outerly. Allas, that day
The sorowe I suffred and the woo 1245
That trewly Cassandra, that soo
Bewayled the destruccioun
Of Troye and of Ilyoun,
Had never swich sorwe as I thoo.

I durste no more say thertoo 1250
For pure fere, but stal away;
And thus I lyved ful many a day,
That trewely I hadde no ned
Ferther than my beddes hed
Never a day to seche sorwe; 1255
I fond hyt redy every morwe,
For-why I loved hyr in no gere.
  "So hit befel, another yere
I thoughte ones I wolde fonde
To do hir knowe and understonde 1260
My woo; and she wel understod
That I ne wilned thyng but god,
And worship, and to kepe hir name
Over alle thynges, and drede hir shame,
And was so besy hyr to serve, 1265
And pitee were I shulde sterve,
Syth that I wilned noon harm, ywis.
So whan my lady knew al this,
My lady yaf me al hooly
The noble yifte of hir mercy, 1270
Savynge hir worship by al weyes —
Dredles, I mene noon other weyes.
And therwith she yaf me a ryng;
I trowe hyt was the firste thyng;
But if myn herte was ywaxe 1275
Glad, that is no nede to axe!
As helpe me God, I was as blyve
Reysed as fro deth to lyve —
Of al happes the alderbeste,
The gladdest, and the moste at reste. 1280
For trewely that swete wyght,
Whan I had wrong and she the ryght,
She wolde alway so goodly
Foryeve me so debonairly.
In al my yowthe, in al chaunce, 1285
She took me in hir governaunce.
Therwyth she was alway so trewe
Our joye was ever ylyche newe;
Oure hertes wern so evene a payre
That never nas that oon contrayre 1290
To that other for no woo.
For sothe, ylyche they suffred thoo
Oo blysse and eke oo sorwe bothe;
Ylyche they were bothe glad and wrothe;
Al was us oon, withoute were. 1295
And thus we lyved ful many a yere
So wel I kan nat telle how."

1206 **dismal:** unlucky days; see n.
1208 **over-skipte:** skipped, passed over
1210 **mysset:** misplaced
1214 **For ferde:** out of fear
1220 **sat:** afflicted
1226 **hete:** promise
1234 **mete:** dream
1242 **the grete:** the main point
1244 **outerly:** utterly
1246 **Cassandra:** daughter of King Priam of Troy
1248 **Ilyoun:** Ilium, the citadel of Troy

1257 **in no gere:** in no changeable fashion
1259 **fonde:** try
1266 **sterve:** die
1269 **yaf:** gave
1272 **Dredles:** doubtless
1277 **as blyve:** very quickly
1295 **were:** doubt

"Sir," quod I, "where is she now?"
"Now?" quod he, and stynte anoon.
Therwith he wax as ded as stoon   1300
And seyde, "Allas, that I was bore!
That was the los that here-before
I tolde the that I hadde lorn.
Bethenke how I seyde here-beforn,
'Thow wost ful lytel what thow menest;   1305
I have lost more than thow wenest.'
God wot, allas! Ryght that was she!"
      "Allas, sir, how? What may that be?"
      "She ys ded!" "Nay!" "Yis, be my trouthe!"
      "Is that youre los? Be God, hyt ys routhe!"
And with that word ryght anoon   1311
They gan to strake forth; al was doon,
For that tyme, the hert-huntyng.
      With that me thoghte that this kyng
Gan homwarde for to ryde   1315
Unto a place, was there besyde,

Which was from us but a lyte —
A long castel with walles white,
Be Seynt Johan, on a ryche hil,
As me mette; but thus hyt fil.   1320
Ryght thus me mette, as I yow telle,
That in the castell ther was a belle,
As hyt hadde smyten houres twelve.
Therwyth I awook myselve
And fond me lyinge in my bed;   1325
And the book that I hadde red,
Of Alcione and Seys the kyng,
And of the goddes of slepyng,
I fond hyt in myn hond ful even.
Thoghte I, "Thys ys so queynt a sweven   1330
That I wol, be processe of tyme,
Fonde to put this sweven in ryme
As I kan best, and that anoon."
This was my sweven; now hit ys doon.

Explicit the Bok of the Duchesse.

1304 **Bethenke:** consider
1312 **strake forth:** sound the signal on a hunting horn for going
homeward

1318 **long castel:** a reference to Lancaster; see Expl. Notes to
1314–29.
1330 **queynt:** curious

THE
HOUSE OF FAME

THE HOUSE OF FAME is in the form of octosyllabic couplets, which Chaucer had used in *The Book of the Duchess,* and, like that work, it is a dream vision ultimately based on French models. Yet a considerable interval probably passed between the composition of the one poem and that of the other. Robinson rightly observed: "As compared with *The Book of the Duchess, The House of Fame* shows a marked advance in technical mastery of style and meter. In both works the verse has something of the roughness or irregularity of the traditional English accentual type; but in *The House of Fame* it has become a freer instrument of expression." *The House of Fame,* moreover, shows the beginnings of the Italian influence on Chaucer's poetry, and it draws not only on Dante but on Boccaccio's poetry, which Chaucer is generally believed not to have known until after his journey to Italy in 1378 (see "Chaucer's Life," beginning on page xv). The influence of Boccaccio is slight, however, apparent only in a few ornamental details in the proems to Books II and III, as contrasted to the heavy use of Boccaccio in *Anelida* and the skilled assimilation of the Italian influences in *The Parliament of Fowls.* Such considerations led Robinson to place the work, as it appears here, after *The Book of the Duchess* and before *Anelida* and *The Parliament of Fowls,* "as the first specimen, among the longer works, of Chaucer's Italian period."

Robinson's dating of *The House of Fame* is generally accepted, though the most recent editor of Chaucer's works, John H. Fisher, places the poem after *The Parliament of Fowls.* The usually suggested date is 1379–80, partly in order to conform with the most plausible identifications of the promised tidings of love and of the "man of gret auctorite" who is presumably to deliver them. Although speculations on this matter are often interesting, Robinson's comment remains just: "The tidings which Chaucer was to hear have been taken to refer to the marriage of Richard and Anne, or to the expected betrothal of Philippa, the daughter of John of Gaunt. Such explanations derive a certain support from the mention of the 'man of gret auctorite' at the end of the poem. But no good evidence has been found for the particular applications proposed, and if Chaucer had such an event in mind it seems likely to remain undiscovered."

Whatever one believes of its occasion, *The House of Fame* does reveal some continuities in Chaucer's poetic concerns. It has several features in common with the other dream visions: a dreamer who is not a lover, or at least not a successful one; an abiding interest in dream theory; and a concern with the nature and effects of love. Moreover, Chaucer again makes use of his apparent innovation—the reading of a book as the occasion and provocation for a dream—though here the book, Virgil's *Aeneid,* is inside the dream, in a series of wall paintings. But *The House of Fame* also stands by itself: its most distinctive quality, which gives it—more than the other visions—an experimental character, is its notable speculative energy.

Chaucer seems to have begun with a germinal meditation on the goddess Fama, as she and her dwelling place are described in the *Aeneid* and in Ovid's *Metamorphoses.* The scope and interests of this meditation, however, widen rapidly in several directions. Chaucer exhibits a remarkable range of reading, as he alludes to and adapts Virgil and Ovid, other classical and medieval Latin authors, the Bible, Boethius, and the French love poets. His trip to the heavens in Book II places his vision in comic contrast with the classics of visionary literature, for he implic-

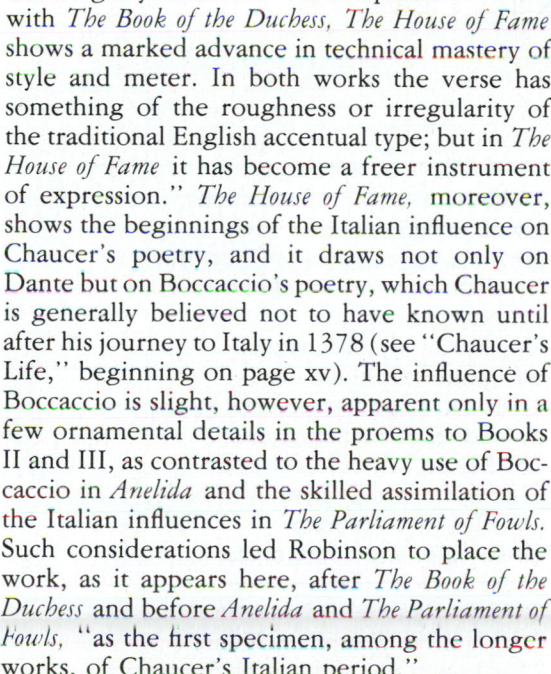

itly compares himself with earlier celestial travelers whose journeys are described by, among others, St. Paul, the author of the book of Revelation, Martianus Capella, Boethius, and Alanus de Insulis. Dante is pre-eminent among these travelers; and, indeed, as Robinson noted, Chaucer "makes so much use of Dante that the poem has been regarded—unjustifiably, to be sure—as an imitation of the Divine Comedy." Even so, it is apparent that *The House of Fame* and *The Divine Comedy* have several interests in common and that Chaucer does sustain an ironic counterpoint to Dante's poem. Though to very different effect, he offers his own version of some of Dante's central concerns. *The House of Fame,* above all, is Chaucer's fullest exploration of the poet's position and responsibilities, the sources of his knowledge, and the limits of his vision.

JOHN M. FYLER

The House of Fame

BOOK I

∎

Proem

 God turne us every drem to goode!
For hyt is wonder, be the roode,
To my wyt, what causeth swevenes
Eyther on morwes or on evenes,
And why th'effect folweth of somme, 5
And of somme hit shal never come;
Why that is an avision
And why this a revelacion,
Why this a drem, why that a sweven,
And noght to every man lyche even; 10
Why this a fantome, why these oracles,
I not; but whoso of these miracles
The causes knoweth bet then I,
Devyne he, for I certeinly
Ne kan hem noght, ne never thinke 15
To besily my wyt to swinke
To knowe of hir signifiaunce
The gendres, neyther the distaunce
Of tymes of hem, ne the causes,
Or why this more then that cause is — 20

As yf folkys complexions
Make hem dreme of reflexions,
Or ellys thus, as other sayn,
For to gret feblenesse of her brayn,
By abstinence or by seknesse, 25
Prison-stewe or gret distresse,
Or ellys by dysordynaunce
Of naturel acustumaunce,
That som man is to curious
In studye, or melancolyous, 30
Or thus so inly ful of drede
That no man may hym bote bede;
Or elles that devocion
Of somme, and contemplacion
Causeth suche dremes ofte; 35
Or that the cruel lyf unsofte
Which these ilke lovers leden
That hopen over-muche or dreden,

This text was edited by JOHN M. FYLER.

2 **roode:** cross
5 **th'effect:** the realization of the prediction
10 **lyche even:** the same
11 **fantome:** hallucination
18 **gendres:** kinds
18–19 **distaunce Of tymes:** interval between dreams (?)

21 **complexions:** balance of bodily humors; cf. NPT VII.2923–39.
22 **reflexions:** reflections (of waking events); see PF 99–105.
25 **seknesse:** sickness
26 **Prison-stewe:** Prison cell; see n.
27 **dysordynaunce:** disordering
28 **acustumaunce:** custom, routine
29 **curious:** diligent
30 **melancolyous:** melancholy
32 **bote bede:** offer a remedy
38 **over-muche:** too much, excessively

That purely her impressions
Causeth hem avisions;   40
Or yf that spirites have the myght
To make folk to dreme a-nyght;
Or yf the soule of propre kynde
Be so parfit, as men fynde,
That yt forwot that ys to come,   45
And that hyt warneth alle and some
Of everych of her aventures
Be avisions or be figures,
But that oure flessh ne hath no myght
To understonde hyt aryght,   50
For hyt is warned to derkly —
But why the cause is, noght wot I.
Wel worthe of this thyng grete clerkys
That trete of this and other werkes,
For I of noon opinion   55
Nyl as now make mensyon,
But oonly that the holy roode
Turne us every drem to goode!
For never sith that I was born,
Ne no man elles me beforn,   60
Mette, I trowe stedfastly,
So wonderful a drem as I
The tenthe day now of Decembre,
The which, as I kan now remembre,
I wol yow tellen everydel.   65

The Invocation

But at my gynnynge, trusteth wel,
I wol make invocacion,
With special devocion,
Unto the god of slep anoon,
That duelleth in a cave of stoon   70
Upon a strem that cometh fro Lete,
That is a flood of helle unswete,
Besyde a folk men clepeth Cymerie —
There slepeth ay this god unmerie
With his slepy thousand sones,   75
That alwey for to slepe hir wone is.
And to this god that I of rede
Prey I that he wol me spede

My sweven for to telle aryght,
Yf every drem stonde in his myght.   80
And he that mover ys of al,
That is and was and ever shal,
So yive hem joye that hyt here
Of alle that they dreme to-yere,
And for to stonden alle in grace   85
Of her loves, or in what place
That hem were levest for to stonde,
And shelde hem fro poverte and shonde,
And from unhap and ech disese,
And sende hem al that may hem plese,   90
That take hit wel and skorne hyt noght,
Ne hyt mysdemen in her thoght
Thorgh malicious entencion.
And whoso thorgh presumpcion,
Or hate, or skorn, or thorgh envye,   95
Dispit, or jape, or vilanye,
Mysdeme hyt, pray I Jesus God
That (dreme he barefot, dreme he shod),
That every harm that any man
Hath had syth the world began   100
Befalle hym therof or he sterve,
And graunte he mote hit ful deserve,
Lo, with such a conclusion
As had of his avision
Cresus, that was kyng of Lyde,   105
That high upon a gebet dyde.
This prayer shal he have of me;
I am no bet in charyte!
Now herkeneth, as I have yow seyd,
What that I mette or I abreyd.   110

Story

Of Decembre the tenthe day,
Whan hit was nyght to slepe I lay
Ryght ther as I was wont to done,
And fil on slepe wonder sone,
As he that wery was forgo   115
On pilgrymage myles two
To the corseynt Leonard,
To make lythe of that was hard.
   But as I slepte, me mette I was
Withyn a temple ymad of glas,   120

39 **impressions**: sensations or emotions fixed in the mind; see Tr
5.372–74.
43 **of propre kynde**: by nature, naturally
45 **forwot**: foreknows
48 **figures**: ambiguous dreams
49 **flessh**: physical senses
53 **Wel worthe**: well be it, good luck (to great clerks who deal
with this matter)
56 **mensyon**: mention
66 **gynnynge**: beginning
71 **Lete**: Lethe, the river of forgetfulness
72 **flood**: river
73 **Cymerie**: Cimmerians
77 **rede**: speak, give an account

87 **hem were levest for to**: they would most like to
88 **shelde**: protect **shonde**: harm, shame
89 **unhap**: misfortune **disese**: source of discomfort, trouble
92 **mysdemen**: misinterpret
96 **Dispit**: malice
98 **barefot . . . shod**: That is, night or day
105 **Cresus**: Croesus, king of Lydia (*Lyde*); see MkT VII.
2727–60.
106 **gebet**: gibbet
115 **wery was forgo**: was all exhausted
117 **corseynt Leonard**: the shrine of St. Leonard; see n.
118 **lythe**: soft, easy

In which ther were moo ymages
Of gold, stondynge in sondry stages,
And moo ryche tabernacles,
And with perre moo pynacles,
And moo curiouse portreytures,   125
And queynte maner of figures
Of olde werk, then I saugh ever.
For certeynly, I nyste never
Wher that I was, but wel wyste I
Hyt was of Venus redely,   130
The temple; for in portreyture
I sawgh anoon-ryght hir figure
Naked fletynge in a see,
And also on hir hed, pardee,
Hir rose garlond whit and red,   135
And hir comb to kembe hyr hed,
Hir dowves, and daun Cupido
Hir blynde sone, and Vulcano,
That in his face was ful broun.

  But as I romed up and doun,   140
I fond that on a wall ther was
Thus writen on a table of bras:
"I wol now synge, yif I kan,
The armes and also the man
That first cam, thurgh his destinee,   145
Fugityf of Troy contree,
In Itayle, with ful moche pyne
Unto the strondes of Lavyne."
And tho began the story anoon,
As I shal telle yow echon.   150

  First sawgh I the destruction
Of Troye thurgh the Grek Synon,
[That] with his false forswerynge,
And his chere and his lesynge,
Made the hors broght into Troye,   155
Thorgh which Troyens loste al her joye.
And aftir this was grave, allas,
How Ilyon assayled was
And wonne, and kyng Priam yslayn
And Polytes his sone, certayn,   160
Dispitously, of daun Pirrus.

And next that sawgh I how Venus,
Whan that she sawgh the castel brende,
Doun fro the heven gan descende,
And bad hir sone Eneas flee;   165
And how he fledde, and how that he
Escaped was from al the pres,
And took his fader Anchises,
And bar hym on hys bak away,
Cryinge, "Allas, and welaway!"   170
The whiche Anchises in hys hond
Bar the goddes of the lond,
Thilke that unbrende were.

  And I saugh next, in al thys fere,
How Creusa, daun Eneas wif,   175
Which that he lovede as hys lyf,
And hir yonge sone Iulo,
And eke Askanius also,
Fledden eke with drery chere,
That hyt was pitee for to here;   180
And in a forest as they wente,
At a turnynge of a wente,
How Creusa was ylost, allas,
That ded, not I how, she was;
How he hir soughte, and how hir gost   185
Bad hym to flee the Grekes host,
And seyde he moste unto Itayle,
As was hys destinee, sauns faille;
That hyt was pitee for to here,
When hir spirit gan appere,   190
The wordes that she to hym seyde,
And for to kepe hir sone hym preyde.
Ther sawgh I graven eke how he,
Hys fader eke, and his meynee,
With hys shippes gan to saylle   195
Towardes the contree of Itaylle
As streight as that they myghte goo.
Ther saugh I thee, cruel Juno,
That art daun Jupiteres wif,
That hast yhated al thy lyf   200
Al the Troianysshe blood,
Renne and crye as thou were wood
On Eolus, the god of wyndes,
To blowen oute, of alle kyndes,
So lowde that he shulde drenche   205
Lord and lady, grom and wenche,

122 **stages:** stands, supports for statues
123 **tabernacles:** elaborately decorated niches for statues
124 **perre:** precious stones **pynacles:** pinnacles (the pointed decorations at the tops of the tabernacles)
130 **Venus:** goddess of love **redely:** truly
133 **fletynge:** floating
137 **daun Cupido:** Cupid
138 **Vulcano:** Vulcan, husband of Venus
139 **ful broun:** blackened (from work at his forge)
142 **bras:** brass
146 **Fugityf of:** fleeing from
148 **Lavyne:** Lavinium, in Italy
153 **forswerynge:** perjury
154 **lesynge:** lying
155 **Made the hors broght:** had the horse brought
158 **Ilyon:** Ilium, the citadel of Troy
160 **Polytes:** a son of Priam killed by Pyrrhus, the son of Achilles
161 **Dispitously:** cruelly **Pirrus:** Pyrrhus

165 **Eneas:** Aeneas
167 **pres:** crowd
173 **unbrende:** unburned
177 **Iulo:** Iulus; see n.
178 **Askanius:** Ascanius
179 **drery:** frightened
182 **wente:** passage
188 **sauns faille:** for certain, without doubt
203 **Eolus:** Aeolus
204 **of alle kyndes:** in every way
205 **drenche:** drown
206 **grom:** young man

Of al the Troian nacion,
Withoute any savacion.
   Ther saugh I such tempeste aryse
That every herte myght agryse   210
To see hyt peynted on the wal.
   Ther saugh I graven eke withal,
Venus, how ye, my lady dere,
Wepynge with ful woful chere,
Prayen Jupiter on hye   215
To save and kepe that navye
Of the Troian Eneas,
Syth that he hir sone was.
   Ther saugh I Joves Venus kysse,
And graunted of the tempest lysse.   220
Ther saugh I how the tempest stente,
And how with alle pyne he wente,
And prively tok arryvage
In the contree of Cartage;
And on the morwe, how that he   225
And a knyght highte Achate
Mette with Venus that day,
Goynge in a queynt array
As she had ben an hunteresse,
With wynd blowynge upon hir tresse;   230
How Eneas gan hym to pleyne,
When that he knew hir, of his peyne;
And how his shippes dreynte were,
Or elles lost, he nyste where;
How she gan hym comforte thoo,   235
And bad hym to Cartage goo,
And ther he shulde his folk fynde,
That in the see were left behynde.
   And, shortly of this thyng to pace,
She made Eneas so in grace   240
Of Dido, quene of that contree,
That, shortly for to tellen, she
Becam hys love and let him doo
Al that weddynge longeth too.
What shulde I speke more queynte,   245
Or peyne me my wordes peynte
To speke of love? Hyt wol not be;
I kan not of that faculte.
And eke to telle the manere
How they aqueynteden in fere,   250
Hyt were a long proces to telle,
And over-long for yow to dwelle.
   Ther sawgh I grave how Eneas
Tolde Dido every caas

That hym was tyd upon the see.   255
   And after grave was how shee
Made of hym shortly at oo word
Hyr lyf, hir love, hir lust, hir lord,
And dide hym al the reverence
And leyde on hym al the dispence   260
That any woman myghte do,
Wenynge hyt had al be so
As he hir swor; and herby demed
That he was good, for he such semed.
Allas! what harm doth apparence,   265
Whan hit is fals in existence!
For he to hir a traytour was;
Wherfore she slow hirself, allas!
Loo, how a woman doth amys
To love hym that unknowen ys!   270
For, be Cryste, lo, thus yt fareth:
"Hyt is not al gold that glareth."
For also browke I wel myn hed,
Ther may be under godlyhed
Kevered many a shrewed vice.   275
Therfore be no wyght so nyce
To take a love oonly for chere,
Or speche, or for frendly manere,
For this shal every woman fynde,
That som man, of his pure kynde,   280
Wol shewen outward the fayreste,
Tyl he have caught that what him leste;
And thanne wol he causes fynde
And swere how that she ys unkynde,
Or fals, or privy, or double was.   285
Al this seye I be Eneas
And Dido, and hir nyce lest,
That loved al to sone a gest;
Therfore I wol seye a proverbe,
That "he that fully knoweth th'erbe   290
May saufly leye hyt to his yë" —
Withoute drede, this ys no lye.
   But let us speke of Eneas,
How he betrayed hir, allas,
And lefte hir ful unkyndely.   295
So when she saw al utterly
That he wolde hir of trouthe fayle,
And wende fro hir to Itayle,
She gan to wringe hir hondes two.
"Allas," quod she, "what me ys woo!   300

210 **agryse:** tremble
222 **he:** Aeneas
223 **tok arryvage:** landed
226 **Achate:** Achates
245 **queynte:** elaborately
246 **my wordes peynte:** use circumlocutions
248 **faculte:** field of learning
250 **in fere:** together.

260 **dispence:** expenditure
272 **glareth:** glitters
273 **also browke I . . . myn hed:** as I hope to keep my head
274 **godlyhed:** righteousness
275 **Kevered:** covered
285 **double:** duplicitous
286 **be Eneas:** by, with reference to, Aeneas
287 **nyce lest:** foolish desire
288 **gest:** guest
290 **th'erbe:** the medicinal herb
296 **al utterly:** entirely

Allas, is every man thus trewe,
That every yer wolde have a newe,
Yf hit so longe tyme dure,
Or elles three, peraventure?
As thus: of oon he wolde have fame   305
In magnyfyinge of hys name;
Another for frendshippe, seyth he;
And yet ther shal the thridde be
That shal be take for delyt,
Loo, or for synguler profit."   310
In suche wordes gan to pleyne
Dydo of hir grete peyne,
As me mette redely —
Non other auctour alegge I.
"Allas!" quod she, "my swete herte,   315
Have pitee on my sorwes smerte,
And slee mee not! Goo noght awey!
O woful Dido, wel-away!"
Quod she to hirselve thoo.
"O Eneas, what wol ye doo?   320
O that your love, ne your bond
That ye have sworn with your ryght hond,
Ne my crewel deth," quod she,
"May holde yow stille here with me!
O haveth of my deth pitee!   325
Iwys, my dere herte, ye
Knowen ful wel that never yit,
As ferforth as I hadde wyt,
Agylte [I] yow in thoght ne dede.
O, have ye men such godlyhede   330
In speche, and never a del of trouthe?
Allas, that ever hadde routhe
Any woman on any man!
Now see I wel, and telle kan,
We wrechched wymmen konne noon art;   335
For certeyn, for the more part,
Thus we be served everychone.
How sore that ye men konne groone,
Anoon as we have yow receyved,
Certaynly we ben deceyvyd!   340
For, though your love laste a seson,
Wayte upon the conclusyon,
And eke how that ye determynen,
And for the more part diffynen.
    "O wel-away that I was born!   345
For thorgh yow is my name lorn,
And alle myn actes red and songe

Over al thys lond, on every tonge.
O wikke Fame! — for ther nys
Nothing so swift, lo, as she is!   350
O, soth ys, every thing ys wyst,
Though hit be kevered with the myst.
Eke, though I myghte duren ever,
That I have don rekever I never,
That I ne shal be seyd, allas,   355
Yshamed be thourgh Eneas,
And that I shal thus juged be:
'Loo, ryght as she hath don, now she
Wol doo eft-sones, hardely' —
Thus seyth the peple prively."   360
But that is don, is not to done;
Al hir compleynt ne al hir moone,
Certeyn, avayleth hir not a stre.
    And when she wiste sothly he
Was forth unto his shippes goon,   365
She into hir chambre wente anoon,
And called on hir suster Anne,
And gan hir to compleyne thanne,
And seyde that she cause was
That she first loved him, allas,   370
And thus counseylled hir thertoo.
But what! When this was seyd and doo,
She rof hirselve to the herte
And deyde thorgh the wounde smerte.
And al the maner how she deyde,   375
And alle the wordes that she seyde,
Whoso to knowe hit hath purpos,
Rede Virgile in Eneydos
Or the Epistle of Ovyde,
What that she wrot or that she dyde;   380
And nere hyt to long to endyte,
Be God, I wolde hyt here write.
    But wel-away, the harm, the routhe,
That hath betyd for such untrouthe,
As men may ofte in bokes rede,   385
And al day sen hyt yet in dede,
That for to thynken hyt, a tene is.
    Loo Demophon, duk of Athenys,
How he forswor hym ful falsly,
And traysed Phillis wikkidly,   390
That kynges doghtre was of Trace,
And falsly gan hys terme pace;
And when she wiste that he was fals,
She heng hirself ryght be the hals,

310 **synguler profit**: personal pleasure
313 **redely**: truly
314 **auctour**: author, authority   **alegge**: cite as proof
329 **Agylte . . . yow**: wronged you
343 **determynen**: end up
344 **diffynen**: conclude, come out in the end
346 **my name**: my good name, reputation

352 **kevered**: covered
354 **rekever**: recover
378 **Eneydos**: *Aeneid*
379 **Epistle of Ovyde**: *Heroides* 7 (Dido to Aeneas)
388–90 **Demophon, Phillis**: Their story is told in LGW 2394–2561.
392 **terme pace**: appointed time (to return) pass by

For he had doon hir such untrouthe.   395
Loo, was not this a woo and routhe?
   Eke lo how fals and reccheles
Was to Breseyda Achilles,
And Paris to Oenone,
And Jason to Isiphile,   400
And eft Jason to Medea,
And Ercules to Dyanira,
For he left hir for Yole,
That made hym cache his deth, parde.
   How fals eke was he Theseus,   405
That, as the story telleth us,
How he betrayed Adriane —
The devel be hys soules bane!
For had he lawghed, had he loured,
He moste have ben al devoured,   410
Yf Adriane ne had ybe.
And for she had of hym pite,
She made hym fro the deth escape,
And he made hir a ful fals jape;
For aftir this, withyn a while,   415
He lefte hir slepynge in an ile
Desert allone, ryght in the se,
And stal away and let hir be,
And took hir suster Phedra thoo
With him, and gan to shippe goo.   420
And yet he had ysswore to here
On al that ever he myghte swere
That, so she saved hym hys lyf,
He wolde have take hir to hys wif;
For she desired nothing ellis,   425
In certeyn, as the book us tellis.
   But to excusen Eneas
Fullyche of al his grete trespas,
The book seyth Mercurie, sauns fayle,
Bad hym goo into Itayle,   430
And leve Auffrikes regioun,
And Dido and hir faire toun.
   Thoo sawgh I grave how to Itayle
Daun Eneas is goo to sayle;
And how the tempest al began,   435
And how he loste hys sterisman,

Which that the stere, or he tok kep,
Smot over bord, loo, as he slep.
   And also sawgh I how Sybile
And Eneas, besyde an yle,   440
To helle wente for to see
His fader, Anchyses the free;
How he ther fond Palinurus,
And Dido, and eke Deiphebus;
And every turment eke in helle   445
Saugh he, which is longe to telle;
Which whoso willeth for to knowe,
He moste rede many a rowe
On Virgile or on Claudian,
Or Daunte, that hit telle kan.   450
   Tho saugh I grave al the aryvayle
That Eneas had in Itayle;
And with kyng Latyne hys tretee
And alle the batayles that hee
Was at hymself, and eke hys knyghtis,   455
Or he had al ywonne his ryghtis;
And how he Turnus reft his lyf,
And wan Lavina to his wif;
And alle the mervelous signals
Of the goddys celestials;   460
How, mawgree Juno, Eneas,
For al hir sleight and hir compas,
Acheved al his aventure,
For Jupiter took of hym cure
At the prayer of Venus —   465
The whiche I preye alwey save us,
And us ay of oure sorwes lyghte!
   When I had seen al this syghte
In this noble temple thus,
"A, Lord," thoughte I, "that madest us,   470
Yet sawgh I never such noblesse
Of ymages, ne such richesse,
As I saugh graven in this chirche;
But not wot I whoo did hem wirche,
Ne where I am, ne in what contree.   475
But now wol I goo out and see,
Ryght at the wiket, yf y kan
See owhere any stiryng man
That may me telle where I am."

398 **Breseyda:** the lover of **Achilles** in the *Iliad* and Ovid
399 **Paris, Oenone:** Paris deserted the nymph Oenone for Helen of Troy; see Tr 1.652–56.
400 **Jason, Isiphile:** for the story of Jason and Hypsipyle see LGW 1396–1579.
401 **Medea:** for the story of Jason and Medea see LGW 1580–1679.
402 **Ercules, Dyanira:** for the story see MkT VII.2095–2142.
403 **Yole:** Iole, a maiden whom Hercules loved
405 **he Theseus:** that (famous) Theseus; for his betrayal of *Adriane* (Ariadne) see LGW 1886–2227.
408 **bane:** destroyer
419 **Phedra:** Phaedra
429 **sauns fayle:** for certain, without doubt
436 **sterisman:** helmsman

439 **Sybile:** Sibyl, priestess of Apollo at Cumae
443 **Palinurus:** Aeneas's helmsman (see 436 above)
444 **Deiphebus:** son of King Priam
449 **Claudian:** author of *De Raptu Proserpinae* (The Rape of Proserpina)
450 **Daunte:** Dante
451 **aryvayle:** landing
453 **Latyne:** Latinus, king of Latium (at the mouth of the Tiber)
457 **Turnus:** king of the Rutuli and a suitor of Lavinia
458 **Lavina:** Lavinia, daughter of King Latinus
461 **Juno:** Juno favored the Greeks and hence was Aeneas's enemy.
462 **compas:** cunning
474 **wirche:** make
477 **wiket:** gate, door

When I out at the dores cam,   480
I faste aboute me beheld.
Then sawgh I but a large feld,
As fer as that I myghte see,
Withouten toun, or hous, or tree,
Or bush, or grass, or eryd lond;   485
For al the feld nas but of sond
As smal as man may se yet lye
In the desert of Lybye.
Ne no maner creature
That ys yformed be Nature   490
Ne sawgh I, me to rede or wisse.
"O Crist," thoughte I, "that art in blysse,
Fro fantome and illusion
Me save!" And with devocion

Myn eyen to the hevene I caste.   495
Thoo was I war, lo, at the laste,
That faste be the sonne, as hye
As kenne myghte I with myn yë,
Me thoughte I sawgh an egle sore,
But that hit semed moche more   500
Then I had any egle seyn.
But this as sooth as deth, certeyn,
Hyt was of gold, and shon so bryghte
That never sawe men such a syghte,
But yf the heven had ywonne   505
Al newe of gold another sonne;
So shone the egles fethers bryghte,
And somwhat dounward gan hyt lyghte.

Explicit liber primus.

BOOK II

Incipit liber secundus.

Proem

Now herkeneth every maner man
That Englissh understonde kan   510
And listeth of my drem to lere,
For now at erste shul ye here
So sely an avisyon,
That Isaye, ne Scipion,
Ne kyng Nabugodonosor,   515
Pharoo, Turnus, ne Elcanor,
Ne mette such a drem as this.
Now faire blisfull, O Cipris,
So be my favour at this tyme!
And ye, me to endite and ryme   520
Helpeth, that on Parnaso duelle,
Be Elicon, the clere welle.

O Thought, that wrot al that I mette,
And in the tresorye hyt shette
Of my brayn, now shal men se   525
Yf any vertu in the be
To tellen al my drem aryght.
Now kythe thyn engyn and myght!

The Dream

This egle, of which I have yow told,
That shon with fethres as of gold,   530
Which that so hye gan to sore,
I gan beholde more and more
To se the beaute and the wonder;
But never was ther dynt of thonder,
Ne that thyng that men calle fouder,   535
That smot somtyme a tour to powder
And in his swifte comynge brende,
That so swithe gan descende
As this foul, when hyt beheld
That I a-roume was in the feld.   540
And with hys grymme pawes stronge,

485 **eryd:** cultivated
488 **Lybye:** Libya
491 **rede or wisse:** advise or direct
493 **fantome:** hallucination

Incipit, *etc.:* Here begins the second book.
514 **Isaye:** Isaiah   **Scipion:** Scipio; for his dream, see PF 29–84.
515 **Nabugodonosor:** Nebuchadnezzar; for the story, see MkT
VII.2143–82.
516 **Pharoo:** Pharaoh, whose dream was interpreted by Joseph
Turnus: king of the Rutuli (see 457 above), warned by Iris of
Aeneas's arrival in Italy   **Elcanor:** unidentified; see n.
518 **Cipris:** Venus
519 **favour:** help, helper
520–21 **ye . . . that on Parnaso duelle:** the Muses, who dwell
on Mt. Parnassus
522 **Elicon:** Helicon

498 **kenne:** perceive
499 **sore:** soar
Explicit, *etc.:* Here ends the first book.

528 **kythe:** make known   **engyn:** skill
535 **fouder:** thunderbolt
540 **a-roume:** at large, in the open

Withyn hys sharpe nayles longe,
Me, fleynge, in a swap he hente,
And with hys sours ayen up wente,
Me caryinge in his clawes starke 545
As lyghtly as I were a larke,
How high, I can not telle yow,
For I cam up, y nyste how.
For so astonyed and asweved
Was every vertu in my heved, 550
What with his sours and with my drede,
That al my felynge gan to dede,
For-whi hit was to gret affray.
    Thus I longe in hys clawes lay,
Til at the laste he to me spak 555
In mannes vois, and seyde, "Awak!
And be not agast so, for shame!"
And called me tho by my name,
And for I shulde the bet abreyde,
Me mette "Awak," to me he seyde 560
Ryght in the same vois and stevene
That useth oon I koude nevene;
And with that vois, soth for to seyn,
My mynde cam to me ageyn,
For hyt was goodly seyd to me, 565
So nas hyt never wont to be.
    And here-withal I gan to stere,
And he me in his fet to bere,
Til that he felte that I had hete,
And felte eke tho myn herte bete. 570
And thoo gan he me to disporte,
And with wordes to comforte,
And sayde twyes, "Seynte Marye,
Thou art noyous for to carye!
And nothyng nedeth it, pardee, 575
For also wis God helpe me,
As thou noon harm shalt have of this,
And this caas that betyd the is,
Is for thy lore and for thy prow.
Let see! Darst thou yet loke now? 580
Be ful assured, boldely,
I am thy frend." And therwith I
Gan for to wondren in my mynde.
"O God," thoughte I, "that madest kynde,
Shal I noon other weyes dye? 585
Wher Joves wol me stellyfye,
Or what thing may this sygnifye?

I neyther am Ennok, ne Elye,
Ne Romulus, ne Ganymede,
That was ybore up, as men rede, 590
To hevene with daun Jupiter,
And mad the goddys botiller."
Loo, this was thoo my fantasye.
But he that bar me gan espye
That I so thoughte, and seyde this: 595
"Thow demest of thyself amys,
For Joves ys not theraboute —
I dar wel putte the out of doute —
To make of the as yet a sterre;
But er I bere the moche ferre, 600
I wol the telle what I am,
And whider thou shalt, and why I cam
To do thys, so that thou take
Good herte, and not for fere quake."
"Gladly," quod I. "Now wel," quod he, 605
"First, I, that in my fet have the,
Of which thou hast a fere and wonder,
Am dwellynge with the god of thonder,
Which that men callen Jupiter,
That dooth me flee ful ofte fer 610
To do al hys comaundement.
And for this cause he hath me sent
To the. Now herke, be thy trouthe:
Certeyn, he hath of the routhe
That thou so longe trewely 615
Hast served so ententyfly
Hys blynde nevew Cupido,
And faire Venus also,
Withoute guerdon ever yit,
And never-the-lesse hast set thy wit — 620
Although that in thy hed ful lyte is —
To make bookys, songes, dytees,
In ryme or elles in cadence,
As thou best canst, in reverence
Of Love and of hys servantes eke, 625
That have hys servyse soght, and seke;
And peynest the to preyse hys art,
Although thou haddest never part.
Wherfore, also God me blesse,
Joves halt hyt gret humblesse 630
And vertu eke, that thou wolt make
A-nyght ful ofte thyn hed to ake

---

543 **swap:** blow, stroke
544 **sours:** upward flight
545 **starke:** strong
549 **asweved:** dazed
552 **felynge:** consciousness **dede:** deaden, die
553 **affray:** fear
561 **vois:** voice **stevene:** sound of the voice
567 **stere:** stir, move
574 **noyous for to carye:** troublesome to carry
581 **assured:** confident
586 **me stellyfye:** make me into a star

588 **Ennok, Elye:** Enoch, Elijah, who, according to the Old
Testament, were taken up to heaven, Elijah in a chariot of fire
589 **Romulus:** Romulus was carried up to heaven by Mars
Ganymede: Ganymede was carried to heaven by Jove (*Jupiter*)
in the form of an eagle
592 **botiller:** cup-bearer
597 **ys not theraboute:** has no intention, is not about to
604 **quake:** tremble
616 **ententyfly:** diligently
617 **nevew:** grandson
622 **dytees:** literary works
623 **cadence:** rhythm of prose in poetry

In thy studye, so thou writest,
And ever mo of love enditest,
In honour of hym and in preysynges,   635
And in his folkes furtherynges,
And in hir matere al devisest,
And noght hym nor his folk dispisest,
Although thou maist goo in the daunce
Of hem that hym lyst not avaunce.   640
    "Wherfore, as I seyde, ywys,
Jupiter considereth this,
And also, beau sir, other thynges:
That is, that thou hast no tydynges
Of Loves folk yf they be glade,   645
Ne of noght elles that God made;
And noght oonly fro fer contree
That ther no tydynge cometh to thee,
But of thy verray neyghebores,
That duellen almost at thy dores,   650
Thou herist neyther that ne this;
For when thy labour doon al ys,
And hast mad alle thy rekenynges,
In stede of reste and newe thynges
Thou goost hom to thy hous anoon,   655
And, also domb as any stoon,
Thou sittest at another book
Tyl fully daswed ys thy look;
And lyvest thus as an heremyte,
Although thyn abstynence ys lyte.   660
    "And therfore Joves, thorgh hys grace,
Wol that I bere the to a place
Which that hight the Hous of Fame,
To do the som disport and game,
In som recompensacion   665
Of labour and devocion
That thou hast had, loo causeles,
To Cupido the rechcheles.
And thus this god, thorgh his merite,
Wol with som maner thing the quyte,   670
So that thou wolt be of good chere.
For truste wel that thou shalt here,
When we be come there I seye,
Mo wonder thynges, dar I leye,
And of Loves folk moo tydynges,   675
Both sothe sawes and lesinges,
And moo loves newe begonne,

And longe yserved loves wonne,
And moo loves casuelly
That ben betyd, no man wot why,   680
But as a blynd man stert an hare;
And more jolytee and fare
While that they fynde love of stel,
As thinketh hem, and over-al wel;
Mo discordes, moo jelousies,   685
Mo murmures and moo novelries,
And moo dissymulacions,
And feyned reparacions,
And moo berdys in two houres
Withoute rasour or sisoures   690
Ymad then greynes be of sondes;
And eke moo holdynge in hondes,
And also moo renovelaunces
Of olde forleten aqueyntaunces;
Mo love-dayes and acordes   695
Then on instrumentes be cordes;
And eke of loves moo eschaunges
Then ever cornes were in graunges —
Unnethe maistow trowen this?"
Quod he. "Noo, helpe me God so wys,"   700
Quod I. "Noo? why?" quod he. "For hyt
Were impossible, to my wit,
Though that Fame had alle the pies
In al a realme, and alle the spies,
How that yet she shulde here al this,   705
Or they espie hyt." "O yis, yis!"
Quod he to me, "that kan I preve
Be reson worthy for to leve,
So that thou yeve thyn advertence
To understonde my sentence.   710
    "First shalt thou here where she duelleth,
And so thyn oune bok hyt tellith:
Hir paleys stant, as I shal seye,
Ryght even in myddes of the weye
Betwixen hevene and erthe and see,   715
That what so ever in al these three
Is spoken, either privy or apert,
The way therto ys so overt,

---

633 **so:** as
636 And in support of his people
639 **daunce:** game of love
643 **beau sir:** good sir
658 **daswed:** dazed
659 **heremyte:** hermit
665 **recompensacion:** recompense
668 **rechcheles:** careless, heedless of rules
670 **quyte:** reward
674 **leye:** wager

679 **casuelly:** (happening) by chance
681 **stert:** flushes
686 **murmures:** grumblings, complaints **novelries:** novelties,
news
689 **berdys:** beards (tricks, delusions)
690 **rasour:** razor **sisoures:** scissors
692 **holdynge in hondes:** cajoling, putting off with false hopes
693 **renovelaunces:** renewals
694 **forleten:** neglected
695 **love-dayes:** days of reconciliation
696 **cordes:** strings
698 **cornes:** seeds of grain **graunges:** granaries
703 **pies:** magpies (chatterboxes)
706 **yis:** yes indeed
709 **advertence:** attention
712 **thyn oune bok:** Ovid's *Metamorphoses*

And stant eke in so juste a place
That every soun mot to hyt pace;   720
Or what so cometh from any tonge,
Be hyt rouned, red, or songe,
Or spoke in suerte or in drede,
Certeyn, hyt moste thider nede.
    "Now herkene wel, for-why I wille   725
Tellen the a propre skille
And a worthy demonstracion
In myn ymagynacion.
    "Geffrey, thou wost ryght wel this,
That every kyndely thyng that is   730
Hath a kyndely stede ther he
May best in hyt conserved be;
Unto which place every thyng
Thorgh his kyndely enclynyng
Moveth for to come to   735
Whan that hyt is awey therfro;
As thus: loo, thou maist alday se
That any thing that hevy be,
As stoon, or led, or thyng of wighte,
And bere hyt never so hye on highte,   740
Lat goo thyn hand, hit falleth doun.
Ryght so seye I be fyr or soun,
Or smoke or other thynges lyghte,
Alwey they seke upward on highte,
While ech of hem is at his large: 745
Lyght thing upward, and dounward charge.
And for this cause mayst thou see
That every ryver to the see
Enclyned ys to goo by kynde,
And by these skilles, as I fynde,   750
Hath fyssh duellynge in flood and see,
And treës eke in erthe bee.
Thus every thing, by thys reson,
Hath his propre mansyon
To which hit seketh to repaire,   755
Ther-as hit shulde not apaire.
Loo, this sentence ys knowen kouth
Of every philosophres mouth,
As Aristotle and daun Platon,
And other clerkys many oon;   760
And to confirme my resoun,
Thou wost wel this, that spech is soun,

719 **juste:** exact
730 **kyndely thyng:** thing in nature
731 **kyndely stede:** natural place
734 **kyndely enclynyng:** natural inclination
744 **seke:** seek, move
745 **at his large:** free, unconstrained by some other force
746 **charge:** heavy thing
751 **flood:** river
754 **mansyon:** dwelling place
756 **apaire:** deteriorate
757 **kouth:** manifestly
759 **Platon:** Plato
762 **soun:** sound

Or elles no man myghte hyt here;
Now herke what y wol the lere.
    "Soun ys noght but eyr ybroken;   765
And every speche that ys spoken,
Lowd or pryvee, foul or fair,
In his substaunce ys but air;
For as flaumbe ys but lyghted smoke,
Ryght soo soun ys air ybroke.   770
But this may be in many wyse,
Of which I wil the twoo devyse,
As soun that cometh of pipe or harpe.
For whan a pipe is blowen sharpe
The air ys twyst with violence   775
And rent — loo, thys ys my sentence.
Eke whan men harpe-strynges smyte,
Whether hyt be moche or lyte,
Loo, with the strok the ayr tobreketh;
And ryght so breketh it when men speketh.   780
Thus wost thou wel what thing is speche.
    "Now hennesforth y wol the teche
How every speche, or noyse, or soun,
Thurgh hys multiplicacioun,
Thogh hyt were piped of a mous,   785
Mot nede come to Fames Hous.
I preve hyt thus — take hede now —
Be experience; for yf that thow
Throwe on water now a stoon,
Wel wost thou hyt wol make anoon   790
A litel roundell as a sercle,
Paraunter brod as a covercle;
And ryght anoon thow shalt see wel
That whel wol cause another whel,
And that the thridde, and so forth, brother,   795
Every sercle causynge other
Wydder than hymselve was;
And thus fro roundel to compas,
Ech aboute other goynge
Causeth of othres sterynge   800
And multiplyinge ever moo,
Til that hyt be so fer ygoo
That hyt at bothe brynkes bee.
Although thou mowe hyt not ysee
Above, hyt gooth yet alway under,   805
Although thou thenke hyt a gret wonder.
And whoso seyth of trouthe I varye,
Bid hym proven the contrarye.
And ryght thus every word, ywys,
That lowd or pryvee spoken ys,   810

791 **roundell:** ring
792 **covercle:** pot lid
798 **fro roundel to compas:** from small circle to full circumference

Moveth first an ayr aboute,
And of thys movynge, out of doute,
Another ayr anoon ys meved;
As I have of the watir preved,
That every cercle causeth other,   815
Ryght so of ayr, my leve brother:
Everych ayr another stereth
More and more, and speche up bereth,
Or voys, or noyse, or word, or soun,
Ay through multiplicacioun,   820
Til hyt be atte Hous of Fame —
Take yt in ernest or in game.
   "Now have I told, yf thou have mynde,
How speche or soun, of pure kynde,
Enclyned ys upward to meve —   825
This mayst thou fele wel I preve —
And that same place, ywys,
That every thyng enclyned to ys
Hath his kyndelyche stede:
That sheweth hyt, withouten drede,   830
That kyndely the mansioun
Of every speche, of every soun,
Be hyt eyther foul or fair,
Hath hys kynde place in ayr.
And syn that every thyng that is   835
Out of hys kynde place, ywys,
Moveth thidder for to goo,
Yif hyt aweye be therfroo —
As I have before preved the —
Hyt seweth, every soun, parde,   840
Moveth kyndely to pace
Al up into his kyndely place.
And this place of which I telle,
Ther as Fame lyst to duelle,
Ys set amyddys of these three,   845
Heven, erthe, and eke the see,
As most conservatyf the soun.
Than ys this the conclusyoun:
That every speche of every man,
As y the telle first began,   850
Moveth up on high to pace
Kyndely to Fames place.
   "Telle me this now feythfully,
Have y not preved thus symply,
Withoute any subtilite   855
Of speche, or gret prolixite

Of termes of philosophie,
Of figures of poetrie,
Or colours of rethorike?
Pardee, hit oughte the to lyke,   860
For hard langage and hard matere
Ys encombrous for to here
Attones; wost thou not wel this?"
And y answered and seyde, "Yis."
   "A ha," quod he, "lo, so I can   865
Lewedly to a lewed man
Speke, and shewe hym swyche skiles
That he may shake hem be the biles,
So palpable they shulden be.
But telle me this, now praye y the,   870
How thinketh the my conclusyon?"
[Quod he]. "A good persuasion,"
Quod I, "hyt is, and lyk to be
Ryght so as thou hast preved me."
"Be God," quod he, "and as I leve,   875
Thou shalt have yet, or hit be eve,
Of every word of thys sentence
A preve by experience,
And with thyne eres heren wel,
Top and tayl and everydel,   880
That every word that spoken ys
Cometh into Fames Hous, ywys,
As I have seyd; what wilt thou more?"
And with this word upper to sore
He gan, and seyde, "Be Seynt Jame,   885
Now wil we speken al of game!"
   "How farest thou?" quod he to me.
"Wel," quod I. "Now see," quod he,
"By thy trouthe, yond adoun,
Wher that thou knowest any toun,   890
Or hous, or any other thing.
And whan thou hast of ought knowyng,
Looke that thou warne me,
And y anoon shal telle the
How fer that thou art now therfro."   895
   And y adoun gan loken thoo,
And beheld feldes and playnes,
And now hilles, and now mountaynes,
Now valeyes, now forestes,
And now unnethes grete bestes,   900
Now ryveres, now citees,
Now tounes, and now grete trees,
Now shippes seyllynge in the see.

811 **an ayr:** a surrounding circle or sphere of air
813 **meved:** moved
824 **of pure kynde:** by its inherent nature
826 **fele:** experience
840 **seweth:** follows
847 **conservatyf the soun:** preserving (conservative of) the sound

859 **colours of rethorike:** figures of speech
862 **encombrous:** troublesome
866 **Lewedly:** simply, without learning
868 **biles:** bills, beaks
872 **persuasion:** argument

But thus sone in a while he
Was flowen fro the ground so hye   905
That al the world, as to myn yë,
No more semed than a prikke;
Or elles was the air so thikke
That y ne myghte not discerne.
With that he spak to me as yerne,   910
And seyde, "Seest thou any toun
Or ought thou knowest yonder doun?"
I sayde, "Nay." "No wonder nys,"
Quod he, "for half so high as this
Nas Alixandre Macedo;   915
Ne the kyng, Daun Scipio,
That saw in drem, at poynt devys,
Helle and erthe and paradys;
Ne eke the wrechche Dedalus,
Ne his child, nyce Ykarus,   920
That fleigh so highe that the hete
Hys wynges malt, and he fel wete
In myd the see, and ther he dreynte,
For whom was maked moch compleynte.
"Now turn upward," quod he, "thy face,   925
And behold this large space,
This eyr, but loke thou ne be
Adrad of hem that thou shalt se,
For in this region, certeyn,
Duelleth many a citezeyn,   930
Of which that speketh Daun Plato;
These ben the eyryssh bestes, lo!"
And so saw y all that meynee
Boothe goon and also flee.
"Now," quod he thoo, "cast up thyn yë.   935
Se yonder, loo, the Galaxie,
Which men clepeth the Milky Wey
For hit ys whit (and somme, parfey,
Kallen hyt Watlynge Strete),
That ones was ybrent with hete,   940
Whan the sonnes sone the rede,
That highte Pheton, wolde lede
Algate hys fader carte, and gye.
The carte-hors gonne wel espye
That he koude no governaunce,   945

And gonne for to lepe and launce,
And beren hym now up, now doun,
Til that he sey the Scorpioun,
Which that in heven a sygne is yit.
And he for ferde loste hys wyt   950
Of that, and let the reynes gon
Of his hors; and they anoon
Gonne up to mounte and doun descende,
Til bothe the eyr and erthe brende,
Til Jupiter, loo, atte laste,   955
Hym slow, and fro the carte caste.
Loo, ys it not a gret myschaunce
To lete a fool han governaunce
Of thing that he can not demeyne?"
And with this word, soth for to seyne,   960
He gan alway upper to sore,
And gladded me ay more and more,
So feythfully to me spak he.
    Tho gan y loken under me
And beheld the ayerissh bestes,   965
Cloudes, mystes, and tempestes,
Snowes, hayles, reynes, wyndes,
And th'engendrynge in hir kyndes,
All the wey thrugh which I cam.
"O God," quod y, "that made Adam,   970
Moche ys thy myght and thy noblesse!"
And thoo thoughte y upon Boece,
That writ, "A thought may flee so hye
Wyth fetheres of Philosophye,
To passen everych element,   975
And whan he hath so fer ywent,
Than may be seen behynde hys bak
Cloude" — and al that y of spak.
    Thoo gan y wexen in a were,
And seyde, "Y wot wel y am here,   980
But wher in body or in gost
I not, ywys, but God, thou wost,"
For more clere entendement
Nas me never yit ysent.
And than thoughte y on Marcian,   985
And eke on Anteclaudian,

---

907 **prikke:** pinpoint, dot
910 **as yerne:** very eagerly
915 **Alixandre Macedo:** Alexander the Macedonian (the Great)
916 **Daun Scipio:** his dream is told in Cicero's *Somnium Scipionis* (see PF 29–84).
919–20 **Dedalus, Ykarus:** Daedalus, Icarus, who attempted flight
922 **malt:** melted
923 **In myd the see:** in the middle of the sea
930–32 **many a citezeyn . . . eyryssh bestes:** demons of the air; see n.
942 **Pheton:** Phaethon, son of Apollo, the god of the sun
943 **Algate:** at any cost

946 **launce:** rear up, spring forward
948 **the Scorpioun:** the zodiacal sign (or the constellation) Scorpio
950 **for ferde:** out of fear
959 **demeyne:** control
963 **feythfully:** convincingly
965 **ayerissh:** aerial
972 **Boece:** Boethius; see Bo 4.m1.
979 **were:** state of doubt, perplexity
981 **gost:** spirit
983 **entendement:** understanding
985 **Marcian:** Martianus Capella, whose work contains an extended discussion of astronomy
986 **Anteclaudian:** the *Anticlaudianus* of Alanus de Insulis

That sooth was her descripsion
Of alle the hevenes region,
As fer as that y sey the preve;
Therfore y kan hem now beleve.   990
    With that this egle gan to crye,
"Lat be," quod he, "thy fantasye!
Wilt thou lere of sterres aught?"
"Nay, certeynly," quod y, "ryght naught."
"And why?" "For y am now to old."   995
"Elles I wolde the have told,"
Quod he, "the sterres names, lo,
And al the hevenes sygnes therto,
And which they ben." "No fors," quod y.
"Yis, pardee," quod he; "wostow why?   1000
For when thou redest poetrie,
How goddes gonne stellifye
Bridd, fissh, best, or him or here,
As the Raven or eyther Bere,
Or Arionis harpe fyn,   1005
Castor, Pollux, or Delphyn,
Or Athalantes doughtres sevene,
How alle these arn set in hevene;
For though thou have hem ofte on honde,
Yet nostow not wher that they stonde."   1010
"No fors," quod y, "hyt is no nede.
I leve as wel, so God me spede,
Hem that write of this matere,
As though I knew her places here;
And eke they shynen here so bryghte,   1015
Hyt shulde shenden al my syghte
To loke on hem." "That may wel be,"
Quod he. And so forth bar he me
A while, and than he gan to crye,
That never herde I thing so hye,   1020
"Now up the hed, for al ys wel;
Seynt Julyan, loo, bon hostel!
Se here the Hous of Fame, lo!
Maistow not heren that I do?"
"What?" quod I. "The grete soun,"   1025
Quod he, "that rumbleth up and doun
In Fames Hous, full of tydynges,
Bothe of feir speche and chidynges,
And of fals and soth compouned.
Herke wel; hyt is not rouned.   1030
Herestow not the grete swogh?"

"Yis, parde," quod y, "wel ynogh."
"And what soun is it lyk?" quod hee.
"Peter, lyk betynge of the see,"
Quod y, "ayen the roches holowe,   1035
Whan tempest doth the shippes swalowe,
And lat a man stonde, out of doute,
A myle thens, and here hyt route;
Or elles lyk the last humblynge
After the clappe of a thundringe,   1040
Whan Joves hath the air ybete.
But yt doth me for fere swete."
"Nay, dred the not therof," quod he;
"Hyt is nothing will byten the;
Thou shalt non harm have trewely."   1045
    And with this word both he and y
As nygh the place arryved were
As men may casten with a spere.
Y nyste how, but in a strete
He sette me fair on my fete,   1050
And seyde, "Walke forth a pas,
And tak thyn aventure or cas
That thou shalt fynde in Fames place."
    "Now," quod I, "while we han space
To speke, or that I goo fro the,   1055
For the love of God, telle me —
In sooth, that wil I of the lere —
Yf thys noyse that I here
Be, as I have herd the tellen,
Of folk that doun in erthe duellen,   1060
And cometh here in the same wyse
As I the herde or this devyse;
And that there lives body nys
In al that hous that yonder ys,
That maketh al this loude fare."   1065
"Noo," quod he, "by Seynte Clare,
And also wis God rede me;
But o thing y will warne the,
Of the whiche thou wolt have wonder.
Loo, to the Hous of Fame yonder,   1070
Thou wost now how, cometh every speche —
Hyt nedeth noght eft the to teche.
But understond now ryght wel this:
Whan any speche ycomen ys
Up to the paleys, anon-ryght   1075
Hyt wexeth lyk the same wight
Which that the word in erthe spak,
Be hyt clothed red or blak;
And hath so verray hys lyknesse

1002 **stellifye:** make into a star
1004 **the Raven:** the constellation Corvus   **eyther Bere:** Ursa
Major and Ursa Minor
1005 **Arionis harpe:** the constellation Lyra
1006 **Castor, Pollux:** the constellation Gemini (Castor and
Pollux)   **Delphyn:** the constellation Delphinus, the Dolphin
1007 **Athalantes doughtres:** daughters of Atlas, the Pleiades
1022 **Seynt Julyan:** patron saint of hospitality   **bon hostel:**
(grant) good lodging
1029 **compouned:** composed
1031 **swogh:** sound of wind

1034 **Peter:** by St. Peter (I swear)
1038 **route:** roar
1039 **humblynge:** rumbling
1063 **lives body:** living body
1066 **Seynte Clare:** a disciple of St. Francis of Assisi

That spak the word, that thou wilt gesse   1080
That it the same body be,
Man or woman, he or she.
And ys not this a wonder thyng?"
"Yis," quod I tho, "by heven kyng!"
And with this word, "Farewel," quod he, 1085

"And here I wol abyden the;
And God of heven sende the grace
Some good to lernen in this place."
And I of him tok leve anon,
And gan forth to the paleys gon.   1090

Explicit liber secundus.

BOOK III

Incipit liber tercius.

Invocation

O God of science and of lyght,
Appollo, thurgh thy grete myght,
This lytel laste bok thou gye!
Nat that I wilne, for maistrye,
Here art poetical be shewed,   1095
But for the rym ys lyght and lewed,
Yit make hyt sumwhat agreable,
Though som vers fayle in a sillable;
And that I do no diligence
To shewe craft, but o sentence.   1100
And yif, devyne vertu, thow
Wilt helpe me to shewe now
That in myn hed ymarked ys —
Loo, that is for to menen this,
The Hous of Fame for to descryve —   1105
Thou shalt se me go as blyve
Unto the nexte laure y see,
And kysse yt, for hyt is thy tree.
Now entre in my brest anoon!

The Dream

Whan I was fro thys egle goon,   1110
I gan beholde upon this place.
And certein, or I ferther pace,
I wol yow al the shap devyse
Of hous and site, and al the wyse
How I gan to thys place aproche,   1115
That stood upon so hygh a roche,

Hier stant ther non in Spayne.
But up I clomb with alle payne,
And though to clymbe it greved me,
Yit I ententyf was to see,   1120
And for to powren wonder lowe,
Yf I koude any weyes knowe
What maner stoon this roche was.
For hyt was lyk alum de glas,
But that hyt shoon ful more clere;   1125
But of what congeled matere
Hyt was, I nyste redely.
But at the laste aspied I,
And found that hit was every del
A roche of yse, and not of stel.   1130
Thoughte I, "By Seynt Thomas of Kent,
This were a feble fundament
To bilden on a place hye.
He ought him lytel glorifye
That hereon bilt, God so me save!"   1135
    Tho sawgh I al the half ygrave
With famous folkes names fele,
That had iben in mochel wele,
And her fames wide yblowe.
But wel unnethes koude I knowe   1140
Any lettres for to rede
Hir names by; for, out of drede,
They were almost ofthowed so
That of the lettres oon or two
Was molte away of every name,   1145

Explicit, *etc.:* Here ends the second book.

Incipit, *etc.:* Here begins the third book.
1096 **lyght:** easy   **lewed:** unsophisticated
1098 **fayle in:** lack
1100 **o sentence:** only the meaning, the meaning alone
1107 **laure:** laurel tree
1116 **roche:** rock

1120 **ententyf:** eager
1124 **alum de glas:** crystallized alum
1130 **yse:** ice
1131 **Seynt Thomas of Kent:** St. Thomas Becket
1134 **He ought to take little pride in (it)**
1143 **ofthowed:** thawed
1145 **molte:** melted

So unfamous was woxe hir fame.
But men seyn, "What may ever laste?"
   Thoo gan I in myn herte caste
That they were molte awey with hete,
And not awey with stormes bete.   1150
For on that other syde I say
Of this hil, that northward lay,
How hit was writen ful of names
Of folkes that hadden grete fames
Of olde tyme, and yet they were   1155
As fressh as men had writen hem here
The selve day ryght, or that houre
That I upon hem gan to poure.
But wel I wiste what yt made;
Hyt was conserved with the shade   1160
Of a castel that stood on high —
Al this writynge that I sigh —
And stood eke on so cold a place
That hete myghte hit not deface.
Thoo gan I up the hil to goon,   1165
And fond upon the cop a woon,
That al the men that ben on lyve
Ne han the kunnynge to descrive
The beaute of that ylke place,
Ne coude casten no compace   1170
Swich another for to make,
That myght of beaute ben hys make,
Ne so wonderlych ywrought;
That hit astonyeth yit my thought,
And maketh al my wyt to swynke,   1175
On this castel to bethynke,
So that the grete craft, beaute,
The cast, the curiosite
Ne kan I not to yow devyse;
My wit ne may me not suffise.   1180
   But natheles al the substance
I have yit in my remembrance;
For whi me thoughte, be Seynt Gyle,
Al was of ston of beryle,
Bothe the castel and the tour,   1185
And eke the halle and every bour,
Wythouten peces or joynynges.
But many subtil compassinges,
Babewynnes and pynacles,
Ymageries and tabernacles   1190
I say; and ful eke of wyndowes

As flakes falle in grete snowes.
And eke in ech of the pynacles
Weren sondry habitacles,
In which stoden, al withoute —   1195
Ful the castel, al aboute —
Of alle maner of mynstralles
And gestiours that tellen tales
Both of wepinge and of game,
Of al that longeth unto Fame.   1200
   Ther herde I pleyen on an harpe,
That sowned bothe wel and sharpe,
Orpheus ful craftely,
And on his syde, faste by,
Sat the harper Orion,   1205
And Eacides Chiron,
And other harpers many oon,
And the Bret Glascurion;
And smale harpers with her gleës
Sate under hem in dyvers seës,   1210
And gunne on hem upward to gape,
And countrefete hem as an ape,
Or as craft countrefeteth kynde.
   Tho saugh I stonden hem behynde,
Afer fro hem, al be hemselve,   1215
Many thousand tymes twelve,
That maden lowde mynstralcies
In cornemuse and shalemyes,
And many other maner pipe,
That craftely begunne to pipe,   1220
Bothe in doucet and in rede,
That ben at festes with the brede;
And many flowte and liltyng horn,
And pipes made of grene corn,
As han thise lytel herde-gromes   1225
That kepen bestis in the bromes.
Ther saugh I than Atiteris,
And of Athenes daun Pseustis,

1166 **cop:** top
1170 **casten no compace:** lay no plan; see n.
1178 **cast:** contrivance **curiosite:** intricate, skillful workmanship
1183 **Seynt Gyle:** St. Aegidius
1188 **compassinges:** devices
1189 **Babewynnes:** gargoyles, grotesques **pynacles:** pinnacles
1190 **Ymageries:** carvings **tabernacles:** elaborately decorated recesses for statues

1194 **habitacles:** niches
1198 **gestiours:** storytellers
1203 **Orpheus:** the famous musician (cf. BD 569)
1205 **Orion:** Arion, a famous poet and harper
1206 **Eacides Chiron:** Chiron the Centaur, skilled in music
1208 **Bret:** Briton, Welsh **Glascurion:** a famous Welsh bard
1209 **gleës:** musical instruments
1210 **seës:** seats
1213 **craft countrefeteth kynde:** art imitates nature
1217 **mynstralcies:** sounds of music
1218 **cornemuse:** bagpipe **shalemyes:** shawms, reed-pipes
1221 **doucet:** wind instrument resembling a flute **rede:** reed (wind instrument)
1222 **brede:** roast meat
1223 **flowte:** flute **liltyng horn:** clarion
1224 **pipes made of grene corn:** i.e., the simple pipes made by shepherds
1225 **herde-gromes:** shepherd boys
1226 **bromes:** broom bushes
1227–28 **Atiteris, Pseustis:** shepherd-poets in Latin eclogues; see n.

And Marcia that loste her skyn,
Bothe in face, body, and chyn,   1230
For that she wolde envien, loo,
To pipen bet than Appolloo.
Ther saugh I famous, olde and yonge,
Pipers of the Duche tonge,
To lerne love-daunces, sprynges,   1235
Reyes, and these straunge thynges.
Tho saugh I in an other place
Stonden in a large space,
Of hem that maken blody soun
In trumpe, beme, and claryoun;   1240
For in fight and blod-shedynge
Ys used gladly clarionynge.
Ther herde I trumpen Messenus,
Of whom that speketh Virgilius.
There herde I trumpe Joab also,   1245
Theodomas, and other mo;
And alle that used clarion
In Cataloigne and Aragon,
That in her tyme famous were
To lerne, saugh I trumpe there.   1250
There saugh I sitte in other seës,
Pleyinge upon sondry gleës,
Whiche that I kan not nevene,
Moo than sterres ben in hevene,
Of whiche I nyl as now not ryme,   1255
For ese of yow and los of tyme.
For tyme ylost, this knowen ye,
Be no way may recovered be.
Ther saugh I pleye jugelours,
Magiciens, and tregetours,   1260
And Phitonesses, charmeresses,
Olde wicches, sorceresses,
That use exorsisacions,
And eke these fumygacions;
And clerkes eke, which konne wel   1265
Al this magik naturel,

That craftely doon her ententes
To make, in certeyn ascendentes,
Ymages, lo, thrugh which magik
To make a man ben hool or syk.   1270
Ther saugh I the, quene Medea,
And Circes eke, and Calipsa;
Ther saugh I Hermes Ballenus,
Limote, and eke Symon Magus.
There saugh I, and knew hem by name,   1275
That by such art don men han fame.
Ther saugh I Colle tregetour
Upon a table of sycamour
Pleye an uncouth thyng to telle —
Y saugh him carien a wynd-melle   1280
Under a walsh-note shale.
    What shuld I make lenger tale
Of alle the pepil y ther say,
Fro hennes into domes day?
Whan I had al this folk beholde,   1285
And fond me lous and nought yholde,
And eft imused longe while
Upon these walles of berile,
That shoone ful lyghter than a glas
And made wel more than hit was   1290
To semen every thing, ywis,
As kynde thyng of Fames is,
I gan forth romen til I fond
The castel-yate on my ryght hond,
Which that so wel corven was   1295
That never such another nas;
And yit it was be aventure
Iwrought, as often as be cure.
Hyt nedeth noght yow more to tellen,
To make yow to longe duellen,   1300
Of this yates florisshinges,
Ne of compasses, ne of kervynges,
Ne how they hatte in masoneries,
As corbetz, ful of ymageries.

1229 **Marcia:** Marsyas, a satyr defeated by Apollo in a singing contest and punished by being flayed
1231 **envien:** contend
1235 **sprynges:** a kind of dance
1236 **Reyes:** a round dance
1239 **blody:** warlike
1240 **beme:** horn
1242 **gladly:** commonly   **clarionynge:** playing clarions, bugles
1243 **Messenus:** Misenus, trumpeter to Hector and Aeneas
1245 **Joab:** the biblical general of David's army, who blew a trumpet to stop a battle
1246 **Theodomas:** Thiodamas, augur of the army at Thebes, whose attack on the city was accompanied by trumpets
1259 **jugelours:** enchanters, wizards
1260 **tregetours:** sleight-of-hand artists
1261 **Phitonesses:** women who call up spirits   **charmeresses:** enchantresses
1262 **wicches:** witches
1263 **exorsisacions:** magical means of calling up spirits
1264 **fumygacions:** ritual incensing in incantations
1266 **magik naturel:** natural science (astrology)

1268 **ascendentes:** ascendants (necessary for casting horoscopes; see Astr 2.4)
1269 **Ymages:** astrological images used in medicine
1271 **Medea:** Medea, a famed sorceress; cf. LGW 1649–50.
1272 **Circes:** Circe, whose magic turned men into beasts
Calipsa: Calypso, the nymph whose magic detained Odysseus on her island (*Odyssey* 1)
1273 **Hermes Ballenus:** a legendary magician; see n.
1274 **Limote:** probably Elymas, in Acts 13.8   **Symon Magus:** a sorcerer, in Acts 8.9
1277 **Colle tregetour:** an English magician
1279 **uncouth:** strange
1280 **wynd-melle:** windmill
1281 **walsh-note: shale:** walnut shell
1284 **domes day:** Judgment Day
1286 **lous:** free
1302 **compasses:** images   **kervynges:** sculptures
1303 **hatte:** are called
1304 **corbetz:** corbels, decorated supports for arches and cornices
ymageries: carvings

But Lord, so fair yt was to shewe,   1305
For hit was al with gold behewe.
But in I wente, and that anoon.
Ther mette I cryinge many oon,
"A larges, larges, hold up wel!
God save the lady of thys pel,   1310
Our oune gentil lady Fame,
And hem that wilnen to have name
Of us!" Thus herde y crien alle,
And faste comen out of halle
And shoken nobles and sterlynges.   1315
And somme corouned were as kynges,
With corounes wroght ful of losenges;
And many ryban and many frenges
Were on her clothes trewely.
     Thoo atte last aspyed y   1320
That pursevantes and heraudes,
That crien ryche folkes laudes,
Hyt weren alle; and every man
Of hem, as y yow tellen can,
Had on him throwen a vesture   1325
Which that men clepe a cote-armure,
Enbrowded wonderliche ryche,
Although they nere nought ylyche.
But noght nyl I, so mote y thryve,
Ben aboute to dyscryve   1330
Alle these armes that ther weren,
That they thus on her cotes beren,
For hyt to me were impossible;
Men myghte make of hem a bible
Twenty foot thykke, as y trowe.   1335
For certeyn, whoso koude iknowe
Myghte ther alle the armes seen
Of famous folk that han ybeen
In Auffrike, Europe, and Asye,
Syth first began the chevalrie.   1340
     Loo, how shulde I now telle al thys?
Ne of the halle eke what nede is
To tellen yow that every wal
Of hit, and flor, and roof, and al
Was plated half a foote thikke   1345
Of gold, and that nas nothyng wikke,
But for to prove in alle wyse,
As fyn as ducat in Venyse,
Of which to lite al in my pouche is?

And they were set as thik of nouchis   1350
Ful of the fynest stones faire
That men rede in the Lapidaire,
As grasses growen in a mede.
But hit were al to longe to rede
The names, and therfore I pace.   1355
     But in this lusty and ryche place
That Fames halle called was,
Ful moche prees of folk ther nas,
Ne crowdyng for to mochil prees.
But al on hye, above a dees,   1360
Sitte in a see imperiall,
That mad was of a rubee all,
Which that a carbuncle ys ycalled,
Y saugh, perpetually ystalled,
A femynyne creature,   1365
That never formed by Nature
Nas such another thing yseye.
For alther-first, soth for to seye,
Me thoughte that she was so lyte
That the lengthe of a cubite   1370
Was lengere than she semed be.
But thus sone in a whyle she
Hir tho so wonderliche streighte
That with hir fet she erthe reighte,
And with hir hed she touched hevene,   1375
Ther as shynen sterres sevene,
And therto eke, as to my wit,
I saugh a gretter wonder yit,
Upon her eyen to beholde;
But certeyn y hem never tolde,   1380
For as feele eyen hadde she
As fetheres upon foules be,
Or weren on the bestes foure
That Goddis trone gunne honoure,
As John writ in th'Apocalips.   1385
Hir heer, that oundy was and crips,
As burned gold hyt shoon to see;
And soth to tellen, also she
Had also fele upstondyng eres
And tonges, as on bestes heres;   1390

1309 **larges**: (give us) a gift
1310 **pel**: peel, small castle
1315 **shoken**: poured out, cast about
1316 **kynges**: kings-of-arms (heralds)
1317 **losenges**: diamond-shaped figures
1318 **ryban**: ribbons **frenges**: fringes
1321 **pursevantes**: pursuivants, heralds' assistants **heraudes**: heralds
1327 **Enbrowded**: embroidered
1334 **bible**: book
1348 **fyn**: pure **ducat**: a gold coin from Venice (*Venyse*)

1350 **nouchis**: jewelled clasps
1352 **Lapidaire**: *De Lapidibus,* a popular treatise on gems and their supposed powers
1354 **rede**: recount, tell
1360 **dees**: dais
1361 **see**: throne
1364 **ystalled**: enthroned
1370 **cubite**: the distance from the elbow to the top of the middle finger
1374 **reighte**: reached
1376 **sterres sevene**: seven planets
1384 **gunne honoure**: honored
1385 **th'Apocalips**: the Apocalypse, book of Revelation
1386 **oundy**: wavy **crips**: curly
1389 **also fele**: as many

And on hir fet woxen saugh Y
Partriches wynges redely.
    But Lord, the perry and the richesse
I saugh sittyng on this godesse!
And Lord, the hevenyssh melodye   1395
Of songes ful of armonye
I herde aboute her trone ysonge,
That al the paleys-walles ronge.
So song the myghty Muse, she
That cleped ys Caliope,   1400
And hir cighte sustren eke,
That in her face semen meke;
And ever mo, eternally,
They songe of Fame, as thoo herd y:
"Heryed be thou and thy name,   1405
Goddesse of Renoun or of Fame!"
    Tho was I war, loo, atte laste,
As I myne eyen gan up caste,
That thys ylke noble quene
On her shuldres gan sustene   1410
Bothe th'armes and the name
Of thoo that hadde large fame:
Alexander and Hercules,
That with a sherte hys lyf les.
And thus fond y syttynge this goddesse   1415
In nobley, honour, and rychesse;
Of which I stynte a while now,
Other thing to tellen yow.
    Tho saugh I stonde on eyther syde,
Streight doun to the dores wide,   1420
Fro the dees, many a peler
Of metal that shoon not ful cler;
But though they nere of no rychesse,
Yet they were mad for gret noblesse,
And in hem hy and gret sentence;   1425
And folk of digne reverence,
Of which I wil yow telle fonde,
Upon the piler saugh I stonde.
    Alderfirst, loo, ther I sigh
Upon a piler stonde on high,   1430
That was of led and yren fyn,
Hym of secte saturnyn,
The Ebrayk Josephus the olde,

That of Jewes gestes tolde;
And he bar on hys shuldres hye   1435
The fame up of the Jewerye.
And by hym stoden other sevene,
Wise and worthy for to nevene,
To helpen him bere up the charge,
Hyt was so hevy and so large.   1440
And for they writen of batayles,
As wel as other olde mervayles,
Therfor was, loo, thys piler
Of which that I yow telle her,
Of led and yren bothe, ywys,   1445
For yren Martes metal ys,
Which that god is of batallye;
And the led, withouten faille,
Ys, loo, the metal of Saturne,
That hath a ful large whel to turne.   1450
    Thoo stoden forth on every rowe
Of hem which that I koude knowe,
Though I hem noght be ordre telle,
To make yow to longe to duelle,
These of whiche I gynne rede.   1455
There saugh I stonden, out of drede,
Upon an yren piler strong
That peynted was al endelong
With tigres blod in every place,
The Tholosan that highte Stace,   1460
That bar of Thebes up the fame
Upon his shuldres, and the name
Also of cruel Achilles.
And by him stood, withouten les,
Ful wonder hy on a piler   1465
Of yren, he, the gret Omer;
And with him Dares and Tytus
Before, and eke he Lollius,
And Guydo eke de Columpnis,
And Englyssh Gaufride eke, ywis;   1470
And ech of these, as have I joye,
Was besy for to bere up Troye.
So hevy therof was the fame
That for to bere hyt was no game.
But yet I gan ful wel espie,   1475

1392 **Partriches wynges**: partridges' wings; see n.
1393 **perry**: jewels
1400 **Caliope**: the Muse of epic poetry
1401 **hir eighte sustren**: the others of the nine Muses
1406 **Renoun**: fame, renown
1413–14 **Hercules . . . hys lyf les**: Hercules . . . lost his life; see
MkT VII.2119–34.
1421 **peler**: pillar
1431 **led and yren**: lead and iron
1432 **secte saturnyn**: sect governed by Saturn (the Jewish
religion); see n.
1433 **Ebrayk Josephus**: Josephus the Hebrew, author of *The
History of the Jews*

1437 **other sevene**: presumably other Jewish historians
1450 **whel**: orbit (Saturn's was the largest orbit of the planets)
1460 **Tholosan**: native of Toulouse   **Stace**: Statius, author of the
Thebaid (which tells of the siege and fall of Thebes) and of the
Achilleid
1464 **withouten les**: truly
1466 **Omer**: Homer
1467 **Dares and Tytus**: Dares Phrygius and Dictys Cretensis,
supposed historians of the Trojan War
1468 **he**: that (famous)   **Lollius**: supposed authority on the
Trojan War
1469 **Guydo . . . de Columpnis**: Guido delle Colonne,
thirteenth-century author of a Latin prose history of Troy
1470 **Gaufride**: Geoffrey of Monmouth, author of the *History of
the Kings of Britain*, the first of whom were Trojans

Betwex hem was a litil envye.
Oon seyde that Omer made lyes,
Feynynge in hys poetries,
And was to Grekes favorable;
Therfor held he hyt but fable.   1480

    Tho saugh I stonde on a piler,
That was of tynned yren cler,
The Latyn poete Virgile,
That bore hath up a longe while
The fame of Pius Eneas.   1485

    And next hym on a piler was,
Of coper, Venus clerk Ovide,
That hath ysowen wonder wide
The grete god of Loves name.
And ther he bar up wel hys fame   1490
Upon this piler, also hye
As I myghte see hyt with myn yë;
For-why this halle, of which I rede,
Was woxen on highte, length, and brede,
Wel more be a thousand del   1495
Than hyt was erst, that saugh I wel.

    Thoo saugh I on a piler by,
Of yren wroght ful sternely,
The grete poete daun Lucan,
And on hys shuldres bar up than,   1500
As high as that y myghte see,
The fame of Julius and Pompe.
And by him stoden alle these clerkes
That writen of Romes myghty werkes,
That yf y wolde her names telle,   1505
Al to longe most I dwelle.

    And next him on a piler stood
Of soulfre, lyk as he were wood,
Daun Claudian, the sothe to telle,
That bar up al the fame of helle,   1510
Of Pluto, and of Proserpyne,
That quene ys of the derke pyne.

    What shulde y more telle of this?
The halle was al ful, ywys,
Of hem that writen olde gestes   1515
As ben on treës rokes nestes;
But hit a ful confus matere
Were alle the gestes for to here
That they of write, or how they highte.

But while that y beheld thys syghte,   1520
I herde a noyse aprochen blyve,
That ferde as been don in an hive
Ayen her tyme of out-fleynge;
Ryght such a maner murmurynge,
For al the world, hyt semed me.   1525
Tho gan I loke aboute and see
That ther come entryng into the halle
A ryght gret companye withalle,
And that of sondry regiouns,
Of alleskynnes condiciouns   1530
That dwelle in erthe under the mone,
Pore and ryche. And also sone
As they were come in to the halle,
They gonne doun on kneës falle
Before this ilke noble quene,   1535
And seyde, "Graunte us, lady shene,
Ech of us of thy grace a bone!"
And somme of hem she graunted sone,
And somme she werned wel and faire,
And some she graunted the contraire   1540
Of her axyng outterly.
But thus I seye yow, trewely,
What her cause was, y nyste.
For of this folk ful wel y wiste
They hadde good fame ech deserved,   1545
Although they were dyversly served;
Ryght as her suster, dame Fortune,
Ys wont to serven in comune.

    Now herke how she gan to paye
That gonne her of her grace praye;   1550
And yit, lo, al this companye
Seyden sooth, and noght a lye.

    "Madame," seyde they, "we be
Folk that here besechen the
That thou graunte us now good fame,   1555
And let our werkes han that name.
In ful recompensacioun
Of good werkes, yive us good renoun."

    "I werne yow hit," quod she anon;
"Ye gete of me good fame non,   1560
Be God, and therfore goo your wey."
"Allas," quod they, "and welaway!
Telle us what may your cause be."
"For me lyst hyt noght," quod she;
"No wyght shal speke of yow, ywis,   1565
Good ne harm, ne that ne this."
And with that word she gan to calle
Her messager, that was in halle,

1478 **poetries:** poems
1480 **held he hyt but fable:** he regarded it as fictitious
1487 **coper:** copper, Venus's metal; see CYT VIII.829.
1488 **ysowen:** spread
1498 **sternely:** grimly
1499 **Lucan:** author of the *Pharsalia,* which narrates the wars between Caesar (*Julius*) and Pompey (*Pompe*)
1508 **soulfre:** brimstone, sulphur
1509 **Claudian:** author of *De Raptu Proserpinae* (see 449 above)
1511 **Pluto:** god of the underworld   **Proserpyne:** Proserpina
1516 **rokes:** rooks

1523 **out-fleynge:** flying out
1530 **alleskynnes:** all kinds of
1539 **werned:** refused
1557 **recompensacioun:** recompense

And bad that he shulde faste goon,
Upon peyne to be blynd anon,   1570
For Eolus the god of wynde —
"In Trace, ther ye shal him fynde,
And bid him bringe his clarioun,
That is ful dyvers of his soun,
And hyt is cleped Clere Laude,   1575
With which he wont is to heraude
Hem that me list ypreised be.
And also bid him how that he
Brynge his other clarioun,
That highte Sklaundre in every toun,   1580
With which he wont is to diffame
Hem that me liste, and do hem shame."
    This messager gan faste goon,
And found where in a cave of ston,
In a contree that highte Trace,   1585
This Eolus, with harde grace,
Held the wyndes in distresse,
And gan hem under him to presse,
That they gonne as beres rore,
He bond and pressed hem so sore.   1590
    This messager gan faste crie,
"Rys up," quod he, "and faste hye,
Til thou at my lady be;
And tak thy clariouns eke with the,
And sped the forth." And he anon   1595
Tok to a man that highte Triton
Hys clarions to bere thoo,
And let a certeyn wynd to goo,
That blew so hydously and hye
That hyt ne lefte not a skye   1600
In alle the welken long and brod.
This Eolus nowhere abod
Til he was come to Fames fet,
And eke the man that Triton het;
And ther he stod, as stille as stoon.   1605
And her-withal ther come anoon
Another huge companye
Of goode folk, and gunne crie,
"Lady, graunte us now good fame,
And lat oure werkes han that name   1610
Now in honour of gentilesse,
And also God your soule blesse!
For we han wel deserved hyt,
Therfore is ryght that we ben quyt."

"As thryve I," quod she, "ye shal faylle!   1615
Good werkes shal yow noght availle
To have of me good fame as now.
But wite ye what? Y graunte yow
That ye shal have a shrewed fame,
And wikkyd loos, and worse name,   1620
Though ye good loos have wel deserved.
Now goo your wey, for ye be served.
And thou, dan Eolus, let see,
Tak forth thy trumpe anon," quod she,
"That is ycleped Sklaundre lyght,   1625
And blow her loos, that every wight
Speke of hem harm and shrewednesse
In stede of good and worthynesse.
For thou shalt trumpe alle the contrayre
Of that they han don wel or fayre."   1630
"Allas," thoughte I, "what aventures
Han these sory creatures!
For they, amonges al the pres,
Shul thus be shamed gilteles.
But what, hyt moste nedes be."   1635
    What dide this Eolus, but he
Tok out hys blake trumpe of bras,
That fouler than the devel was,
And gan this trumpe for to blowe,
As al the world shulde overthrowe,   1640
That throughout every regioun
Wente this foule trumpes soun,
As swifte as pelet out of gonne
Whan fyr is in the poudre ronne.
And such a smoke gan out wende   1645
Out of his foule trumpes ende,
Blak, bloo, grenyssh, swartish red,
As doth where that men melte led,
Loo, al on high fro the tuel.
And therto oo thing saugh I wel,   1650
That the ferther that hit ran,
The gretter wexen hit began,
As dooth the ryver from a welle,
And hyt stank as the pit of helle.
Allas, thus was her shame yronge,   1655
And gilteles, on every tonge!
    Tho come the thridde companye,
And gunne up to the dees to hye,
And doun on knes they fille anon,
And seyde, "We ben everychon   1660
Folk that han ful trewely
Deserved fame ryghtfully,

1571 **Eolus**: Aeolus
1572 **Trace**: Thrace
1575 **Clere Laude**: pure praise
1576 **heraude**: sound the praise of
1580 **Sklaundre**: slander
1586 **harde grace**: ill will
1587 **in distresse**: in control, under restraint
1596 **Triton**: a sea god, who blows on a conch to cause winds
at sea
1600 **skye**: cloud

1620 **wikkyd loos**: bad reputation
1625 **lyght**: quick, nimble
1643 **pelet**: cannonball   **gonne**: cannon
1644 **poudre**: gunpowder
1647 **bloo**: dark blue-gray   **swartish**: dark
1649 **tuel**: chimney-hole

And praye yow, hit mote be knowe
Ryght as hit is, and forth yblowe."
"I graunte," quod she, "for me list   1665
That now your goode werkes be wist,
And yet ye shul han better loos,
Right in dispit of alle your foos,
Than worthy is, and that anoon.
Lat now," quod she, "thy trumpe goon,   1670
Thou Eolus, that is so blak;
And out thyn other trumpe tak
That highte Laude, and blow yt soo
That thrugh the world her fame goo
Al esely, and not to faste,   1675
That hyt be knowen atte laste."
"Ful gladly, lady myn," he seyde;
And out hys trumpe of gold he brayde
Anon, and sette hyt to his mouth,
And blew it est, and west, and south,   1680
And north, as lowde as any thunder,
That every wight hath of hit wonder,
So brode hyt ran or than hit stente.
And, certes, al the breth that wente
Out of his trumpes mouth it smelde   1685
As men a pot of bawme helde
Among a basket ful of roses.
This favour dide he til her loses.
    And ryght with this y gan aspye,
Ther come the ferthe companye —   1690
But certeyn they were wonder fewe —
And gunne stonden in a rewe,
And seyden, "Certes, lady bryght,
We han don wel with al our myght,
But we ne kepen have no fame.   1695
Hyde our werkes and our name,
For Goddys love; for certes we
Han certeyn doon hyt for bounte,
And for no maner other thing."
"I graunte yow alle your askyng,"   1700
Quod she; "let your werkes be ded."
    With that aboute y clew myn hed,
And saugh anoon the fifte route
That to this lady gunne loute,
And doun on knes anoon to falle;   1705
And to hir thoo besoughten alle
To hide her goode werkes ek,
And seyden they yeven noght a lek
For fame ne for such renoun;

For they for contemplacioun   1710
And Goddes love hadde ywrought,
Ne of fame wolde they nought.
"What?" quod she, "and be ye wood?
And wene ye for to doo good,
And for to have of that no fame?   1715
Have ye dispit to have my name?
Nay, ye shul lyven everychon!
Blow thy trumpes, and that anon,"
Quod she, "thou Eolus, y hote,
And ryng this folkes werk be note,   1720
That al the world may of hyt here."
And he gan blowe her loos so clere
In his golden clarioun
That thrugh the world wente the soun
Also kenely and eke so softe;   1725
But atte last hyt was on-lofte.
    Thoo come the sexte companye,
And gunne faste on Fame crie.
Ryght verraily in this manere
They seyden: "Mercy, lady dere!   1730
To tellen certeyn as hyt is,
We han don neither that ne this,
But ydel al oure lyf ybe.
But natheles yet preye we
That we mowe han as good a fame,   1735
And gret renoun and knowen name,
As they that han doon noble gestes,
And acheved alle her lestes,
As wel of love as other thyng.
Al was us never broche ne ryng,   1740
Ne elles noght, from wymmen sent,
Ne ones in her herte yment
To make us oonly frendly chere,
But myghten temen us upon bere;
Yet lat us to the peple seme   1745
Suche as the world may of us deme
That wommen loven us for wod.
Hyt shal doon us as moche good,
And to oure herte as moche avaylle
To countrepese ese and travaylle,   1750
As we had wonne hyt with labour;
For that is dere boght honour
At regard of oure grete ese.
And yet thou most us more plese:
Let us be holden eke therto   1755

1678 **brayde:** snatched up
1685 **smelde:** smelled
1686 **bawme:** aromatic balsam **helde:** poured
1688 **til her loses:** to their reputations
1702 **clew:** scratched
1704 **gunne loute:** bowed down
1708 **noght a lek:** not even a leek (i.e., nothing)

1719 **hote:** command
1722 **loos:** praise
1725 **kenely:** sharply
1744 **temen us upon bere:** bring us upon our biers (i.e., would just as soon see us dead)
1747 **for wod:** madly
1750 **countrepese:** balance
1753 **At regard of:** compared with

Worthy, wise, and goode also,
And riche, and happy unto love.
For Goddes love, that sit above,
Thogh we may not the body have
Of wymmen, yet, so God yow save —   1760
Leet men gliwe on us the name —
Sufficeth that we han the fame."
    "I graunte," quod she, "be my trouthe!
Now, Eolus, withouten slouthe,
Tak out thy trumpe of gold, let se,   1765
And blow as they han axed me,
That every man wene hem at ese,
Though they goon in ful badde lese."
This Eolus gan hit so blowe
That thrugh the world hyt was yknowe.   1770
    Thoo come the seventh route anoon,
And fel on knees everychoon,
And seyde, "Lady, graunte us sone
The same thing, the same bone,
That [ye] this nexte folk han doon."   1775
"Fy on yow," quod she, "everychon!
Ye masty swyn, ye ydel wrechches,
Ful of roten, slowe techches!
What? False theves! Wher ye wolde
Be famous good, and nothing nolde   1780
Deserve why, ne never ye roughte?
Men rather yow to hangen oughte!
For ye be lyke the sweynte cat
That wolde have fissh; but wostow what?
He wolde nothing wete his clowes.   1785
Yvel thrift come to your jowes,
And eke to myn, if I hit graunte,
Or do yow favour, yow to avaunte!
Thou Eolus, thou kyng of Trace,
Goo blowe this folk a sory grace,"   1790
Quod she, "anon; and wostow how?
As I shal telle thee ryght now.
Sey: 'These ben they that wolde honour
Have, and do noskynnes labour,
Ne doo no good, and yet han lawde;   1795
And that men wende that bele Isawde
Ne coude hem noght of love werne,
And yet she that grynt at a querne
Ys al to good to ese her herte.'"

This Eolus anon up sterte,   1800
And with his blake clarioun
He gan to blasen out a soun
As lowde as beloweth wynd in helle;
And eke therwith, soth to telle,
This soun was so ful of japes,   1805
As ever mowes were in apes.
And that wente al the world aboute,
That every wight gan on hem shoute
And for to lawghe as they were wod,
Such game fonde they in her hod.   1810
    Tho come another companye,
That had ydoon the trayterye,
The harm, the grettest wikkednesse
That any herte kouthe gesse;
And prayed her to han good fame,   1815
And that she nolde doon hem no shame,
But yeve hem loos and good renoun,
And do hyt blowe in a clarioun.
"Nay, wis," quod she, "hyt were a vice.
Al be ther in me no justice,   1820
Me lyste not to doo hyt now,
Ne this nyl I not graunte yow."
    Tho come ther lepynge in a route,
And gunne choppen al aboute
Every man upon the crowne,   1825
That al the halle gan to sowne,
And seyden: "Lady, leef and dere,
We ben suche folk as ye mowe here.
To tellen al the tale aryght,
We ben shrewes, every wyght,   1830
And han delyt in wikkednesse,
As goode folk han in godnesse;
And joye to be knowen shrewes,
And ful of vice and wikked thewes;
Wherefore we praye yow, a-rowe,   1835
That oure fame such be knowe
In alle thing ryght as hit ys."
"Y graunte hyt yow," quod she, "ywis.
But what art thow that seyst this tale,
That werest on thy hose a pale,   1840
And on thy tipet such a belle?"
"Madame," quod he, "soth to telle,
I am that ylke shrewe, ywis,
That brende the temple of Ysidis
In Athenes, loo, that citee."   1845
"And wherfor didest thou so?" quod she.

1761 **gliwe**: glue, affix
1768 **in ful badde lese**: in a very bad situation (*lese,* literally, pasture)
1777 **masty**: fat, sluggish
1778 **slowe**: slothful, idle **techches**: qualities
1783 **sweynte**: wearied, lazy
1785 **clowes**: claws
1786 **Yvel thrift**: bad luck **jowes**: jaws
1794 **noskynnes labour**: labor of no kind
1796 **that bele Isawde**: that beautiful Isolde (or Iseult), mistress of Tristan
1797 **werne**: deny, refuse
1798 **grynt** = *gryndeth,* grinds **querne**: hand-mill

1802 **blasen**: blow
1806 **mowes**: grimaces
1810 They found them so ridiculous
1824 **choppen**: strike
1835 **a-rowe**: successively
1840 **pale**: a perpendicular stripe; with the bells, "the garb of a fool" (R.)
1844 **Ysidis**: Isis; see n.

"By my thrift," quod he, "madame,
I wolde fayn han had a fame,
As other folk hadde in the toun,
Although they were of gret renoun   1850
For her vertu and for her thewes.
Thoughte y, as gret a fame han shrewes,
Though hit be for shrewednesse,
As goode folk han for godnesse;
And sith y may not have that oon,   1855
That other nyl y noght forgoon.
And for to gette of Fames hire,
The temple sette y al afire.
Now do our loos be blowen swithe,
As wisly be thou ever blythe!"   1860
"Gladly," quod she; "thow Eolus,
Herestow not what they prayen us?"
"Madame, yis, ful wel," quod he,
And I wil trumpen it, parde!"
And tok his blake trumpe faste,   1865
And gan to puffen and to blaste,
Til hyt was at the worldes ende.
     With that y gan aboute wende,
For oon that stood ryght at my bak,
Me thoughte, goodly to me spak,   1870
And seyde, "Frend, what is thy name?
Artow come hider to han fame?"
"Nay, for sothe, frend," quod y;
"I cam noght hyder, graunt mercy,
For no such cause, by my hed!   1875
Sufficeth me, as I were ded,
That no wight have my name in honde.
I wot myself best how y stonde;
For what I drye, or what I thynke,
I wil myselven al hyt drynke,   1880
Certeyn, for the more part,
As fer forth as I kan myn art."
"But what doost thou here than?" quod he.
Quod y, "That wyl y tellen the,
The cause why y stonde here: 1885
Somme newe tydynges for to lere,
Somme newe thinges, y not what,
Tydynges, other this or that,
Of love or suche thynges glade.
For certeynly, he that me made   1890
To comen hyder, seyde me,
Y shulde bothe here and se
In this place wonder thynges;
But these be no suche tydynges
As I mene of." "Noo?" quod he.   1895
And I answered, "Noo, parde!

For wel y wiste ever yit,
Sith that first y hadde wit,
That somme folk han desired fame
Diversly, and loos, and name.   1900
But certeynly, y nyste how
Ne where that Fame duelled, er now,
And eke of her descripcioun,
Ne also her condicioun,
Ne the ordre of her dom,   1905
Unto the tyme y hidder com."
"Whych than be, loo, these tydynges,
That thou now [thus] hider brynges,
That thou hast herd?" quod he to me;
"But now no fors, for wel y se   1910
What thou desirest for to here.
Com forth and stond no lenger here,
And y wil thee, withouten drede,
In such another place lede
Ther thou shalt here many oon."   1915
     Tho gan I forth with hym to goon
Out of the castel, soth to seye.
Tho saugh y stonde in a valeye,
Under the castel, faste by,
An hous, that Domus Dedaly,   1920
That Laboryntus cleped ys,
Nas mad so wonderlych, ywis,
Ne half so queyntelych ywrought.
And ever mo, as swyft as thought,
This queynte hous aboute wente,   1925
That never mo hyt stille stente.
And therout com so gret a noyse
That, had hyt stonden upon Oyse,
Men myghte hyt han herd esely
To Rome, y trowe sikerly.   1930
And the noyse which that I herde,
For al the world ryght so hyt ferde
As dooth the rowtynge of the ston
That from th'engyn ys leten gon.
And al thys hous of which y rede   1935
Was mad of twigges, falwe, rede,
And grene eke, and somme weren white,
Swiche as men to these cages thwite,
Or maken of these panyers,
Or elles hottes or dossers;   1940

1857 **hire**: reward
1879 **drye**: experience, suffer
1895 **mene**: speak

1920–21 **Domus Dedaly, Laboryntus**: House of Daedalus, Labyrinth (cf. LGW 2012–14)
1923 **queyntelych**: elaborately, elegantly
1925 **aboute wente**: turned
1928 **Oyse**: the river Oise (near Paris)
1933 **rowtynge**: roar
1934 **th'engyn**: the catapult
1936 **falwe**: fallow, yellow
1938 **thwite**: whittle, carve
1939 **panyers**: wicker bread baskets
1940 **hottes**: wicker baskets carried on the back **dossers**: wicker baskets carried on the backs of horses

That, for the swough and for the twygges,
This hous was also ful of gygges,
And also ful eke of chirkynges,
And of many other werkynges;
And eke this hous hath of entrees   1945
As fele as of leves ben in trees
In somer, whan they grene been;
And on the roof men may yet seen
A thousand holes, and wel moo,
To leten wel the soun out goo.   1950
And be day, in every tyde,
Been al the dores opened wide,
And be nyght echon unshette;
Ne porter ther is noon to lette
No maner tydynges in to pace.   1955
Ne never rest is in that place
That hit nys fild ful of tydynges,
Other loude or of whisprynges;
And over alle the houses angles
Ys ful of rounynges and of jangles   1960
Of werres, of pes, of mariages,
Of reste, of labour, of viages,
Of abood, of deeth, of lyf,
Of love, of hate, acord, of stryf,
Of loos, of lore, and of wynnynges,   1965
Of hele, of seknesse, of bildynges,
Of faire wyndes, and of tempestes,
Of qwalm of folk, and eke of bestes;
Of dyvers transmutacions
Of estats, and eke of regions;   1970
Of trust, of drede, of jelousye,
Of wit, of wynnynge, of folye;
Of plente, and of gret famyne,
Of chepe, of derthe, and of ruyne;
Of good or mys governement,   1975
Of fyr, and of dyvers accident.
   And loo, thys hous, of which I write,
Syker be ye, hit nas not lyte,
For hyt was sixty myle of lengthe.
Al was the tymber of no strengthe,   1980
Yet hit is founded to endure
While that hit lyst to Aventure,
That is the moder of tydynges,
As the see of welles and of sprynges;
And hyt was shapen lyk a cage.   1985

"Certys," quod y, "in al myn age,
Ne saugh y such an hous as this."
And as y wondred me, ywys,
Upon this hous, tho war was y
How that myn egle faste by   1990
Was perched hye upon a stoon;
And I gan streghte to hym gon,
And seyde thus: "Y preye the
That thou a while abide me,
For Goddis love, and lete me seen   1995
What wondres in this place been;
For yit, paraunter, y may lere
Som good theron, or sumwhat here
That leef me were, or that y wente."
   "Petre, that is myn entente,"   2000
Quod he to me; "therfore y duelle.
But certeyn, oon thyng I the telle,
That but I bringe the therinne,
Ne shalt thou never kunne gynne
To come into hyt, out of doute,   2005
So faste hit whirleth, lo, aboute.
But sith that Joves, of his grace,
As I have seyd, wol the solace
Fynally with these thinges,
Unkouthe syghtes and tydynges,   2010
To passe with thyn hevynesse,
Such routhe hath he of thy distresse,
That thou suffrest debonairly —
And wost thyselven outtirly
Disesperat of alle blys,   2015
Syth that Fortune hath mad amys
The [fruit] of al thyn hertys reste
Languisshe and eke in poynt to breste —
That he, thrugh hys myghty merite,
Wol do the an ese, al be hyt lyte,   2020
And yaf in expres commaundement,
To which I am obedient,
To further the with al my myght,
And wisse and teche the aryght
Where thou maist most tidynges here.   2025
Shaltow here anoon many oon lere."
With this word he ryght anoon
Hente me up bytweene hys toon,
And at a wyndowe yn me broghte,
That in this hous was, as me thoghte —   2030
And therwithalle, me thoughte hit stente,
And nothing hyt aboute wente —
And me sette in the flor adoun.
But which a congregacioun

1941 swough: sound of wind
1942 gygges: a squeaking sound
1943 chirkynges: creakings
1953 unshette: unlocked
1959 angles: corners
1960 jangles: gossip
1962 viages: journeys
1963 abood: staying
1966 bildynges: comforting
1968 qwalm: plague, death
1974 chepe: good supply   derthe: high costs

2004 kunne gynne: know the trick
2015 Disesperat: without hope
2016–18 Since Fortune has wrongly (amys) made the fruition
(fruit, happy outcome) that would give your heart ease (reste)
languish and even be on the point of coming to naught

Of folk, as I saugh rome aboute,   2035
Some wythin and some wythoute,
Nas never seen, ne shal ben eft;
That, certys, in the world nys left
So many formed be Nature,
Ne ded so many a creature;   2040
That wel unnethe in that place
Hadde y a fote-brede of space.
And every wight that I saugh there
Rouned everych in others ere
A newe tydynge prively,   2045
Or elles tolde al openly
Ryght thus, and seyde: "Nost not thou
That ys betyd, lo, late or now?"
"No," quod he, "telle me what."
And than he tolde hym this and that,   2050
And swor therto that hit was soth —
"Thus hath he sayd," and "Thus he doth,"
"Thus shal hit be," "Thus herde y seye,"
"That shal be founde," "That dar I leye" —
That al the folk that ys alyve   2055
Ne han the kunnynge to discryve
The thinges that I herde there,
What aloude, and what in ere.
But al the wondermost was this:
Whan oon had herd a thing, ywis,   2060
He com forth ryght to another wight,
And gan him tellen anon-ryght
The same that to him was told,
Or hyt a forlong way was old,
But gan somwhat for to eche   2065
To this tydynge in this speche
More than hit ever was.
And nat so sone departed nas
Tho fro him, that he ne mette
With the thridde; and or he lette   2070
Any stounde, he told him als;
Were the tydynge soth or fals,
Yit wolde he telle hyt natheles,
And evermo with more encres
Than yt was erst. Thus north and south   2075
Wente every tydyng fro mouth to mouth,
And that encresing ever moo,
As fyr ys wont to quyke and goo
From a sparke spronge amys,
Til al a citee brent up ys.   2080
And whan that was ful yspronge,
And woxen more on every tonge

Than ever hit was, [hit] wente anoon
Up to a wyndowe out to goon;
Or, but hit myghte out there pace,   2085
Hyt gan out crepe at som crevace,
And flygh forth faste for the nones.
And somtyme saugh I thoo at ones
A lesyng and a sad soth sawe,
That gonne of aventure drawe   2090
Out at a wyndowe for to pace;
And, when they metten in that place,
They were achekked bothe two,
And neyther of hem moste out goo
For other, so they gonne crowde,   2095
Til ech of hem gan crien lowde,
"Lat me go first!" "Nay, but let me!
And here I wol ensuren the,
Wyth the nones that thou wolt do so,
That I shal never fro the go,   2100
But be thyn owne sworen brother!
We wil medle us ech with other,
That no man, be they never so wrothe,
Shal han on [of us] two, but bothe
At ones, al besyde his leve,   2105
Come we a-morwe or on eve,
Be we cried or stille yrouned."
Thus saugh I fals and soth compouned
Togeder fle for oo tydynge.

    Thus out at holes gunne wringe   2110
Every tydynge streght to Fame,
And she gan yeven ech hys name,
After hir disposicioun,
And yaf hem eke duracioun,
Somme to wexe and wane sone,   2115
As doth the faire white mone,
And let hem goon. Ther myghte y seen
Wynged wondres faste fleen,
Twenty thousand in a route,
As Eolus hem blew aboute.   2120
    And, Lord, this hous in alle tymes
Was ful of shipmen and pilgrimes,
With scrippes bret-ful of lesinges,
Entremedled with tydynges,
And eek allone be hemselve.   2125
O, many a thousand tymes twelve
Saugh I eke of these pardoners,
Currours, and eke messagers,

2042 **fote-brede:** foot's breadth
2048 **late or now:** just recently
2053 **Thus shal hit be:** thus it is reported to be (?); see n.
2054 **leye:** wager
2059 **wondermost:** most wonderful
2065 **eche:** increase

2093 **achekked:** stopped
2099 **Wyth the nones:** on the condition
2102 **medle:** mix, intermingle
2105 **al besyde his leve:** entirely without his leave
2108 **compouned:** compounded
2109 **fle:** fly   **for:** as
2123 **scrippes:** bags, satchels   **bret-ful:** brimful
2124 **Entremedled:** mixed
2128 **Currours:** couriers

With boystes crammed ful of lyes
As ever vessel was with lyes.   2130
And as I alther-fastest wente
About, and dide al myn entente
Me for to pleyen and for to lere,
And eke a tydynge for to here,
That I had herd of som contre   2135
That shal not now be told for me —
For hit no nede is, redely;
Folk kan synge hit bet than I;
For al mot out, other late or rathe,
Alle the sheves in the lathe —   2140
I herde a gret noyse withalle
In a corner of the halle,
Ther men of love-tydynges tolde,

And I gan thiderward beholde;
For I saugh rennynge every wight   2145
As faste as that they hadden myght,
And everych cried, "What thing is that?"
And somme sayde, "I not never what."
And whan they were alle on an hepe,
Tho behynde begunne up lepe,   2150
And clamben up on other faste,
And up the nose and yën kaste,
And troden fast on others heles,
And stampen, as men doon aftir eles.
Atte laste y saugh a man,   2155
Which that y [nevene] nat ne kan;
But he semed for to be
A man of gret auctorite. . . .

[*Unfinished.*]

2129 **boystes:** containers
2130 **lyes:** dregs (lees)
2136 **for me:** by me
2140 **sheves:** sheaves   **lathe:** barn

2154 **eles:** eels

ANELIDA AND ARCITE

THE ANELIDA seems clearly an experimental work, and it is usually taken to be Chaucer's first attempt to make use of Boccaccio's *Teseida.* Its form, the combination of narrative and lyric love-complaint, is French, but the epic machinery with which the narrative is introduced is Italian (and Latin), and Chaucer seems not yet able to combine the Italian and French elements in a smoothly coordinated whole.

The poem begins with an elaborate Invocation, drawn mainly from Boccaccio. Mars and Bellona, god and goddess of war, are invoked to help tell the story of Queen Anelida and false Arcite, as if this were to be a poem of epic battles. Then the poet calls for the aid of Polyhymnia and her sister Muses and names his ancient authorities: "Stace" (Statius), the author of the *Thebaid*, and the mysterious "Corynne," perhaps the Theban poetess Corinna, whose works have been lost but who is said to have defeated the great Pindar in a poetry competition.

The next section, the Story, is introduced with the same epigraph from Statius's *Thebaid* that Chaucer was later to use in The Knight's Tale, and it opens with the scene (drawn mainly from the *Teseida*) that also begins the later tale, the account of Theseus's triumphant return to Athens with Hippolyta and her sister Emily. A rather bald transition (45–49) shifts the scene to Thebes, and Chaucer gives a summary of Statius's entire account of the Seven against Thebes (again drawn from Boccaccio). From this point to the end of the Story (71–210) the poem focuses on the romantic relation of the Queen of Armenia, Anelida (whose presence in Thebes is not explained), with the Theban nobleman Arcite, who appears so suddenly (85) that one might almost suspect a stanza is missing. Though the name Arcite is taken from Boc-

caccio, and Chaucer claims he follows ancient Latin sources, the tale of Anelida and the "false" Arcite seems to have been his own invention.

Anelida's Complaint repeats many of the incidents narrated in the Story. It is structurally and metrically Chaucer's most elaborate surviving work, divided into Proem, Strophe (220–80), Antistrophe (281–341), and Conclusion, with the Proem and Strophe exactly matching the Antistrophe and Conclusion in their intricate stanzaic forms, and with the last line of the Complaint almost exactly matching the first. For whatever reason, Chaucer never again wrote in so complex a form.

Then follows a brief stanza that promises a continuation of the story: Anelida vows to sacrifice at the temple of Mars. Perhaps, as critics have often speculated, Chaucer meant next to use that passage in the *Teseida* on which he later drew for the description of the temple of Mars in The Knight's Tale. The poem abruptly ends here, however, apparently unfinished.

"In general," Robinson wrote, "the *Anelida* testifies at once to Chaucer's enlarging literary knowledge and to the immaturity of his art." He was apparently not yet ready to undertake so grand a narrative as the epic introduction and final stanza imply and had not yet found a way to assimilate in his own work those elements he admired in Boccaccio. The work is unsatisfactory in many respects. The introductory story of Anelida and Arcite is thin compared with the epic machinery that introduces it, and the characters, especially Arcite, seem barely realized. Yet the narrative moves with some of the swift assurance of Chaucer's later works; in little more than a hundred lines it establishes the emotional situation that is to be developed in the Complaint. In the narrator's sympathy for his heroine (162–68) and his implied inability to deviate from his source there is even a hint of the narrative stance that Chaucer was to employ so effectively in *Troilus*.

The Complaint is more successful—is indeed one of Chaucer's finest works in this genre—and it has been justly compared to the Middle English *Pearl*. As in *Pearl*, the complexity of the form seems to reinforce rather than impede the emotional intensity. Partly because of its repetition of events in the Story, the Complaint has a concreteness and specificity rarely found in earlier French love-complaints, and Anelida's dramatic monologue is a psychologically impressive analysis of what Clemen calls an "ebb and flow of moods, a movement of unconscious feeling that obeys some inner urge as it moves from one thought to the next." In its intensely dramatic representation of a personality in conflict, the Complaint of Anelida shows Chaucer already a master of a mode he would later bring even closer to perfection.

VINCENT J. DiMARCO

Anelida and Arcite

The Compleynt of feire Anelida and fals Arcite.

■

Invocation.

Thou ferse god of armes, Mars the rede,
That in the frosty contre called Trace,
Within thy grisly temple ful of drede
Honoured art as patroun of that place;
With thy Bellona, Pallas, ful of grace,   5
Be present and my song contynue and guye;
At my begynnyng thus to the I crye.

For hit ful depe is sonken in my mynde,
With pitous hert in Englyssh to endyte
This olde storie, in Latyn which I fynde,   10
Of quene Anelida and fals Arcite,
That elde, which that al can frete and bite,
As hit hath freten mony a noble storie,
Hath nygh devoured out of oure memorie.

Be favorable eke, thou Polymya,   15
On Parnaso that with thy sustres glade,
By Elycon, not fer from Cirrea,

Singest with vois memorial in the shade,
Under the laurer which that may not fade,
And do that I my ship to haven wynne.   20
First folowe I Stace, and after him Corynne.

The Story.

Iamque domos patrias Cithice post aspera gentis
Prelia laurigero subeunte Thesea curru
Letifici plausus missusque ad sidera vulgi

When Theseus with werres longe and grete
The aspre folk of Cithe had overcome,
With laurer corouned, in his char gold-bete,
Hom to his contre-houses is he come,   25
For which the peple, blisful al and somme,
So cryëden that to the sterres hit wente,
And him to honouren dide al her entente.

This text was edited by VINCENT J. DiMARCO.

1 **ferse:** fierce
2 **Trace:** Thrace
4 **patroun:** patron saint
5 **Bellona:** goddess of war   **Pallas:** Pallas Athena
12 **frete and bite:** gnaw upon and consume
15 **Polymya:** Polyhymnia, Muse of sacred song
16–17 **Parnaso, Elycon, Cirrea:** Parnassus, Helicon, Cirra, homes of the Muses

18 **memorial:** inspired by memory
19 **laurer:** laurel tree
21 **Stace, Corynne:** Statius, author of the *Thebaid,* quoted in the epigraph below; the Theban poetess Corinna, to whom Chaucer may have come upon a reference; see introductory note.
Iamque domos, etc.: And now Theseus, after the fierce battle with the Scythians, [was] drawing near his native land in laurelled chariot, to the applause of the happy people resounding to the stars. Cf. the translation in the following stanza.
22 **werres:** wars
23 **aspre:** harsh   **Cithe:** Scythia
25 **contre-houses:** houses of his country

Beforn this duk, in signë of victorie,
The trompes come, and in his baner large   30
The ymage of Mars, and in tokenyng of glorie
Men myghte sen of tresour many a charge,
Many a bright helm, and many a spere and
   targe,
Many a fresh knyght, and many a blysful route,
On hors, on fote, in al the feld aboute.   35

Ipolita his wif, the hardy quene
Of Cithia, that he conquered hadde,
With Emelye her yonge suster shene,
Faire in a char of gold he with him ladde,
That al the ground about her char she spradde
With brightnesse of the beaute in her face,   41
Fulfilled of largesse and of alle grace.

With his tryumphe and laurer-corouned thus,
In al the flour of Fortunes yevynge,
Let I this noble prince Theseus   45
Toward Athenes in his wey rydinge,
And founde I wol in shortly for to bringe
The slye wey of that I gan to write,
Of quene Anelida and fals Arcite.

Mars, which that through his furious cours of
   ire,   50
The olde wrathe of Juno to fulfille,
Hath set the peples hertes bothe on fire
Of Thebes and Grece, everich other to kille
With blody speres, ne rested never stille,
But throng now her, now ther, among hem
   bothe,   55
That everych other slough, so were they
   wrothe.

For when Amphiorax and Tydeus,
Ipomedon, Parthonope also
Were ded, and slayn proude Campaneus,
And when the wrecched Thebans, bretheren
   two,   60
Were slayn, and kyng Adrastus hom ago,
So desolat stod Thebes and so bare
That no wight coude remedie of his fare.

And when the olde Creon gan espye
How that the blood roial was broght a-doun,   65

He held the cite by his tyrannye
And dyde the gentils of that regioun
To ben his frendes and wonnen in the toun.
So, what for love of him and what for awe,
The noble folk were to the toun idrawe.   70

Among al these Anelida, the quene
Of Ermony, was in that toun dwellynge,
That fairer was then is the sonne shene.
Thurghout the world so gan her name springe
That her to seen had every wyght likynge,   75
For, as of trouthe, is ther noon her lyche
Of al the women in this worlde riche.

Yong was this quene, of twenty yer of elde,
Of mydel stature, and of such fairenesse
That Nature had a joye her to behelde;   80
And for to speken of her stidfastnesse,
She passed hath Penelope and Lucresse;
And shortly, yf she shal be comprehended,
In her ne myghte no thing been amended.

This Theban knyght [Arcite] eke, soth to seyn,
Was yong and therwithal a lusty knyght,   86
But he was double in love and no thing pleyn,
And subtil in that craft over any wyght,
And with his kunnyng wan this lady bryght;
For so ferforth he gan her trouthe assure   90
That she him trusted over any creature.

What shuld I seyn? She loved Arcite so
That when that he was absent any throwe,
Anon her thoghte her herte brast a-two;
For in her sight to her he bar hym lowe,   95
So that she wende have al his hert yknowe;
But he was fals; hit nas but feyned chere —
As nedeth not to men such craft to lere.

But nevertheles ful mykel besynesse
Had he er that he myghte his lady wynne,   100
And swor he wolde dyen for distresse
Or from his wit he seyde he wolde twynne.
Alas, the while! For hit was routhe and synne
That she upon his sorowes wolde rewe;   104
But nothing thinketh the fals as doth the trewe.

Her fredom fond Arcite in such manere
That al was his that she hath, moche or lyte;

---

32 **charge**: heavy load
36 **Ipolita**: Hippolyta, queen of the Amazons
47 **founde**: try
48 **slye wey**: sly, deceitful course of action
57–59 **Amphiorax, Tydeus, Ipomedon, Parthonope,
Campaneus**: See Tr 5.1485–1510 for an account of these heroes
of the siege of Thebes.
60 **bretheren two**: Eteocles and Polynices (see Tr 5.1506–08)
61 **Adrastus**: king of Argos, leader of the Seven against Thebes
63 **fare**: plight
64 **Creon**: tyrant of Thebes (cf. KnT I.938–47)

72 **Ermony**: Armenia
78 **elde**: age
82 **Penelope and Lucresse**: exemplars of womanly virtue;
Penelope was the faithful wife of Ulysses; Lucretia's story is told
in LGW 1680–1885.
87 **double**: duplicitous, faithless
99 **mykel**: much

Ne to no creature made she chere
Ferther then that hit lyked to Arcite.
Ther nas no lak with which he myghte her
    wite;   110
She was so ferforth yeven hym to plese
That al that lyked hym hit dyde her ese.

Ther nas to her no maner lettre sent
That touched love, from any maner wyght,   114
That she ne shewed hit him er hit was brent;
So pleyn she was and dide her fulle myght
That she nyl hiden nothing from her knyght,
Lest he of any untrouthe her upbreyde.
Withoute bode his heste she obeyde.

And eke he made him jelous over here,   120
That what that any man had to her seyd
Anoon he wolde preyen her to swere
What was that word or make him evel apaid.
Then wende she out of her wyt have breyd;
But al this nas but sleght and flaterie;   125
Withoute love he feyned jelousye.

And al this tok she so debonerly
That al his wil her thoghte hit skilful thing,
And ever the lenger she loved him tendirly
And dide him honour as he were a kyng.   130
Her herte was to him wedded with a ring;
So ferforth upon trouthe is her entente
That wher he gooth her herte with him wente.

When she shal ete, on him is so her thoght
That wel unnethe of mete tok she kep;   135
And when that she was to her reste broght,
On him she thoghte alwey til that she slep;
When he was absent, prevely she wep:
Thus lyveth feire Anelida the quene
For fals Arcite, that dide her al this tene.   140

This fals Arcite, of his newfanglenesse,
For she to him so lowly was and trewe,
Tok lesse deynte of her stidfastnesse
And saw another lady, proud and newe,   144
And ryght anon he cladde him in her hewe —
Wot I not whethir in white, rede, or grene —
And falsed fair Anelida the quene.

But neverthelesse, gret wonder was hit noon
Thogh he were fals, for hit is kynde of man

110 **wite:** blame
119 **bode:** delay
138 **prevely:** privily

Sith Lamek was, that is so longe agoon,   150
To ben in love as fals as evere he can;
He was the firste fader that began
To loven two, and was in bigamye,
And he found tentes first, but yf men lye.

This fals Arcite, sumwhat moste he feyne, 155
When he wex fals, to covere his traitorie,
Ryght as an hors that can both bite and pleyne,
For he bar her on honde of trecherie,
And swor he coude her doublenesse espie,
And al was falsnes that she to him mente.   160
Thus swor this thef, and forth his way he
    wente.

Alas, what herte myght enduren hit,
For routhe and wo, her sorwe for to telle?
Or what man hath the cunnyng or the wit?
Or what man mighte within the chambre
    dwelle,   165
Yf I to him rehersen sholde the helle
That suffreth fair Anelida the quene
For fals Arcite, that dide her al this tene.

She wepith, waileth, swowneth pitously;
To grounde ded she falleth as a ston;   170
Craumpyssheth her lymes crokedly;
She speketh as her wit were al agon;
Other colour then asshen hath she noon;
Non other word speketh she, moche or lyte,
But "Merci, cruel herte myn, Arcite!"   175

And thus endureth til that she was so mat
That she ne hath foot on which she may
    sustene,
But forth languisshing evere in this estat,
Of which Arcite hath nouther routhe ne tene.
His herte was elleswhere, newe and grene, 180
That on her wo ne deyneth him not to thinke;
Him rekketh never wher she flete or synke.

His newe lady holdeth him so narowe
Up by the bridil, at the staves ende,
That every word he dredeth as an arowe;   185
Her daunger made him bothe bowe and bende,
And as her liste, made him turne or wende,

150 **Lamek:** Lamech, the first bigamist
158 **bar her on honde:** accused her
159 **doublenesse:** duplicity
160 **mente:** said
171 **Craumpyssheth:** cramps, contracts painfully
183 **narowe:** tightly (with the reins)
184 **staves ende:** ends of the shafts (of a horse-cart)

For she ne graunted him in her lyvynge
No grace whi that he hath lust to singe,

But drof hym forth. Unnethe liste her knowe   190
That he was servaunt unto her ladishippe;
But lest that he were proud, she held him lowe.
Thus serveth he withoute fee or shipe;
She sent him now to londe, now to shippe;
And for she yaf him daunger al his fille,   195
Therfor she hadde him at her owne wille.

Ensample of this, ye thrifty wymmen alle,
Take her of Anelida and Arcite,
That for her liste him "dere herte" calle
And was so meke, therfor he loved her lyte.   200
The kynde of mannes herte is to delyte
In thing that straunge is, also God me save!
For what he may not gete, that wolde he have.

Now turne we to Anelida ageyn,
That pyneth day be day in langwisshinge,   205
But when she saw that her ne gat no geyn,
Upon a day, ful sorowfully wepinge,
She caste her for to make a compleynynge,
And of her owne hond she gan hit write,
And sente hit to her Theban knyght, Arcite.   210

        The compleynt of Anelida the
        quene upon fals Arcite.

    Proem.

    So thirleth with the poynt of remembraunce
The swerd of sorowe, ywhet with fals ples-
            aunce,
Myn herte, bare of blis and blak of hewe,
That turned is in quakyng al my daunce,
My surete in awhaped countenaunce,   215
Sith hit availeth not for to ben trewe;
For whoso trewest is, hit shal hir rewe
That serveth love and doth her observaunce
Alwey til oon, and chaungeth for no newe.

    Strophe.

        1.

I wot myself as wel as any wight,   220
For I loved oon with al myn herte and myght,
More then myself an hundred thousand sithe,

And called him myn hertes lif, my knyght,
And was al his, as fer as hit was ryght;
And when that he was glad, then was I blithe,
And his disese was my deth as swithe;   226
And he ayein his trouthe hath me plyght
For evermore, his lady me to kythe.

        2.

Now is he fals, alas, and causeles,
And of my wo he is so routheles   230
That with a word him list not ones deyne
To bringe ayen my sorowful herte in pes,
For he is caught up in another les.
Ryght as him list, he laugheth at my peyne,
And I ne can myn herte not restreyne   235
For to love him alwey nevertheles;
And of al this I not to whom me pleyne.

        3.

And shal I pleyne — alas, the harde stounde! —
Unto my foo that yaf myn herte a wounde
And yet desireth that myn harm be more?   240
Nay, certis, ferther wol I never founde
Non other helpe, my sores for to sounde.
My destinee hath shapen hit so ful yore;
I wil non other medecyne ne lore;
I wil ben ay ther I was ones bounde.   245
That I have seid, be seid for evermore!

        4.

Alas! Wher is become your gentilesse,
Youre wordes ful of plesaunce and humblesse,
Youre observaunces in so low manere,
And your awayting and your besynesse   250
Upon me, that ye calden your maistresse,
Your sovereyne lady in this world here?
Alas! Is ther now nother word ne chere
Ye vouchen sauf upon myn hevynesse?
Alas! Youre love, I bye hit al to dere.   255

        5.

Now, certis, swete, thogh that ye
Thus causeles the cause be
Of my dedly adversyte,
Your manly resoun oghte hit to respite
To slen your frend, and namely me,   260

---

189 **whi that he hath lust to singe:** for which (*grace*) he would
have the desire to sing (for joy)
193 **shipe:** pay
205 **pyneth:** suffers
206 **geyn:** gain
208 **caste her:** decided
211 **thirleth:** pierces
215 **awhaped:** stunned

228 **kythe:** acknowledge
230 **routheles:** without compassion
233 **les:** snare
241 **founde:** seek
242 **sounde:** heal, make sound
250 **awayting:** solicitude
258 **dedly:** grievous
259 **respite:** grant a respite to

That never yet in no degre
Offended yow, as wisly He
That al wot, out of wo my soule quyte!
But for I, Arcite, shewed yow
Al that men wolde to me write,   265
And was so besy yow to delyte —
Myn honor save — meke, kynde, and fre,
Therfor ye put on me this wite,
And of me rekke not a myte,
Thogh that the swerd of sorwe byte   270
My woful herte through your cruelte.

6.

My swete foo, why do ye so, for shame?
And thenke ye that furthered be your name
To love a newe, and ben untrewe? Nay!   274
And putte yow in sclaunder now and blame,
And do to me adversite and grame,
That love yow most — God, wel thou wost —
      alway?
Yet come ayein, and yet be pleyn som day,
And than shal this, that now is mys, be game,
And al foryive, while that I lyve may.   280

Antistrophe.

1.

Lo, herte myn, al this is for to seyne
As whether shal I preve or elles pleyne?
Which is the wey to doon yow to be trewe?
For either mot I have yow in my cheyne   284
Or with the deth ye mote departe us tweyne;
Ther ben non other mene weyes newe.
For God so wisly upon my soule rewe,
As verrayly ye sleen me with the peyne;
That may ye se unfeyned of myn hewe.

2.

For thus ferforth have I my deth [y-]soght?   290
Myself I mordre with my privy thoght;
For sorowe and routhe of your unkyndenesse
I wepe, I wake, I faste; al helpeth noght;
I weyve joye that is to speke of oght,
I voyde companye, I fle gladnesse.   295
Who may avaunte her beter of hevynesse
Then I? And to this plyte have ye me broght,
Withoute gilt — me nedeth no witnesse.

3.

And shal I preye, and weyve womanhede? —
Nay! Rather deth then do so foul a dede! —   300

268 **put on:** impute to **wite:** blame
275 **sclaunder:** ill fame
279 **mys:** amiss
286 **mene:** middle
294 **weyve:** give up, relinquish
295 **voyde:** avoid

And axe merci, gilteles — what nede?
And yf I pleyne what lyf that I lede,
Yow rekketh not; that knowe I, out of drede;
And if that I to yow myne othes bede
For myn excuse, a skorn shal be my mede.   305
Your chere floureth, but it wol not sede;
Ful longe agoon I oghte have taken hede.

4.

For thogh I hadde yow to-morowe ageyn,
I myghte as wel holde Aperill fro reyn
As holde yow, to make yow be stidfast.   310
Almyghty God, of trouthe sovereyn,
Wher is the trouthe of man? Who hath hit
      slayn?
Who that hem loveth, she shal hem fynde as
      fast
As in a tempest is a roten mast.
Is that a tame best that is ay feyn   315
To fleen away when he is lest agast?

5.

Now merci, swete, yf I mysseye!
Have I seyd oght amys, I preye?
I noot; my wit is al aweye.
I fare as doth the song of *Chaunte-pleure*;   320
For now I pleyne, and now I pleye;
I am so mased that I deye;
Arcite hath born awey the keye
Of al my world, and my good aventure.
For in this world nis creature   325
Wakynge in more discomfiture
Then I, ne more sorowe endure.
And yf I slepe a furlong wey or tweye,
Then thynketh me that your figure
Before me stont, clad in asure,   330
To profren eft and newe assure
For to be trewe, and merci me to preye.

6.

The longe nyght this wonder sight I drye,
And on the day for thilke afray I dye,
And of al this ryght noght, iwis, ye reche.   335
Ne nevere mo myn yen two be drie,
And to your routhe, and to your trouthe, I crie.
But welawey! To fer be they to feche;
Thus holdeth me my destinee a wreche.

306 Your expression (*chere*) blooms, but it will not bear fruit
(i.e., you make promises you do not fulfill)
313 **fast:** firm
320 *Chaunte-pleure:* "Now sing, now weep"; see n.
322 **mased:** dazed, bewildered
331 **assure:** pledge
333 **drye:** experience
339 **wreche:** cause of misery, punishment

But me to rede out of this drede, or guye, 340
Ne may my wit, so weyk is hit, not streche.

Conclusion.

Then ende I thus, sith I may do no more.
I yeve hit up for now and evermore,
For I shal never eft putten in balaunce
My sekernes, ne lerne of love the lore. 345
But as the swan, I have herd seyd ful yore,
Ayeins his deth shal singen his penaunce,
So singe I here my destinee or chaunce,

How that Arcite Anelida so sore 349
Hath thirled with the poynt of remembraunce.

The Story continued.

When that Anelida, this woful quene,
Hath of her hand ywriten in this wise,
With face ded, betwixe pale and grene,
She fel a-swowe; and sith she gan to rise,
And unto Mars avoweth sacrifise 355
Withinne the temple, with a sorowful chere,
That shapen was as ye shal after here.

341 **weyk:** weak
345 **sekernes:** security
347 **penaunce:** misery, suffering

354 **a-swowe:** aswoon, in a faint

THE
PARLIAMENT OF
FOWLS

THE PARLIAMENT OF FOWLS is surely the most delightful—and possibly the first—celebration of Saint Valentine's Day ever written. No one knows how 14 February became one of love's "halydayes," for which Chaucer wrote "many an ympne" (ProLGW 422). There is no basis for the old theory that he drew on some folk tradition, no association of love with Saint Valentine's Day in previous literature, and little in the saint's legend to suggest such an association. Perhaps Chaucer himself hit upon the pleasant idea of enlivening the dreariest of winter months with an occasion redolent of spring. The idea first appears in the works of Chaucer (The Complaint of Mars and, if authentic, the Complaynt D'Amours are later examples), and in poems of his friends John Gower (*Cinkante balades*, nos. 34 and 35), John Clanvowe (*The Boke of Cupide*), and Oton de Grandson (two *Complaintes de Saint Valentin*), and it later appears in the works of Chaucer's English and French successors. Yet no other Valentine poem made so happy a use of the idea as *The Parliament of Fowls,* and none approaches it in richness of texture and complexity of theme.

The *Parliament* is another of Chaucer's dream visions, with a slightly comic narrator, like that in *The Book of the Duchess.* This narrator, like the Geoffrey Chaucer in *The House of Fame*, is a student, rather than a practitioner, of the art of love, eagerly reading in the hope of learning a "certeyn thing." The poem begins with his reading of a book (not Ovid but the ascetic *Somnium Scipionis*, Cicero's "Dream of Scipio") and, as in *The House of Fame*, his reading is rewarded with the appearance of a slightly condescending visionary guide, who promises to show him "mater of to wryte." He passes through the idealized landscape that leads to Venus's dark temple, and then to the bright sunlight where Dame Nature presides over the great flock of birds gathered, as is their custom on this day, to choose their mates. There he sees the three tercel eagles, who plead for the hand of the formel at such length that finally the birds of "lowere kynde" raucously object and launch into a comic parliamentary debate, rich in insults and speeches at cross-purposes, which Nature herself must finally bring to an end. As for the three tercels, none wins the formel; with maidenly reserve, she defers her choice until the following year. That decision at least frees the other birds to choose, and the dream ends with their joyful roundel to welcome the coming spring. Yet it leaves the dreamer unsatisfied, and he returns to his books, still hoping to learn something "for to fare the bet."

The conclusion is reminiscent of *The House of Fame.* In that work Chaucer greatly expands the compass of the dream vision as he had used it in *The Book of the Duchess*; he considers problems of poetry and philosophy, as well as love, includes a broad variety of incidents, from Dido's piteous lament to the slapstick comedy of the House of Rumor, and ends with an abruptness that leaves both the narrator and the reader still waiting for the "tydynge" we never learn. The *Parliament* is much the same. Love is considered in its philosophical, social, and poetic, as well as its erotic and progenitive, aspects; the poem moves from the solemnity of Scipio's dream to the comic squabbling of the birds; and it abruptly ends before the reader learns whom the formel will choose and the dreamer learns the "certeyn thing" he seeks. Yet *The Parliament of Fowls,* unlike *The House of Fame,* is both finished and

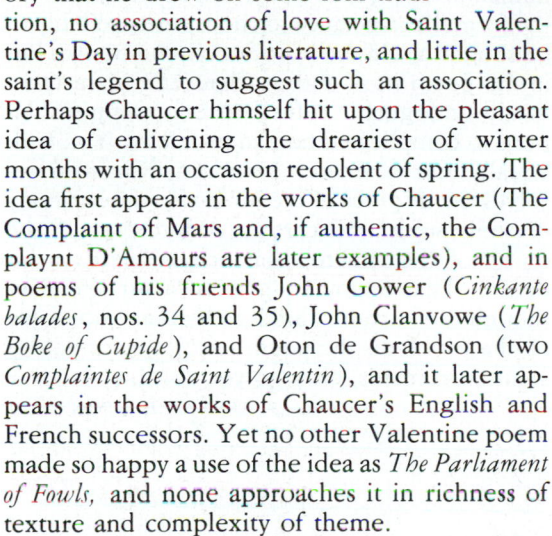

complete, marked by an elegance of structure and an easy confidence of style notably lacking in that earlier work.

This new confidence is perhaps partly due to the rime royal stanza, which Chaucer had tried as a narrative form in *Anelida* and perfects here. Chaucer was deeply affected by the pseudo-classical style that allowed Dante and Boccaccio to raise their vernacular to epic heights. He drew heavily on that style in the invocations in *The House of Fame,* but the four-beat couplet, which he was then still using, seems more suited to parodying than reproducing the classics ("I wol now synge, yif I kan,/The armes and also the man" HF 143–44). Chaucer apparently found the longer line and less obtrusive rhyme scheme of his new stanza better suited to achieving in English some of the elegant effects he admired in Boccaccio. The close similarity of rime royal to *ottava rima* (Boccaccio's stanza) enabled him to transpose smoothly whole passages of the *Teseida* into English (in the description of Venus's temple). At the same time, rime royal was flexible enough to accommodate the colloquial, "palpable" style, which he had perfected in the eagle's speeches in *The House of Fame* and which he uses here to such fine effect in the debate of the birds of "lowere kynde." In the *Parliament,* Chaucer succeeded in assimilating what he had learned from his Italian masters with what he had learned from French dream visions, from English song—the roundel at the end is sung to a tune made in France, but its simple diction echoes the earlier English lyric—and from his own experiments and experience.

The result is the richest and most satisfying poem that Chaucer had yet written.

The date of *The Parliament of Fowls* and the occasion—if any—for which it was composed are matters that have been much disputed. Recently the old theory that it is an "occasional poem" has been revived, and it has been argued that the poem concerns the negotiations in 1380 for the betrothal of Richard II to Anne of Bohemia, with Anne represented by the formel eagle and her three suitors (Richard II, Charles of France, and Friedrich of Meissen) by the three tercels. Yet such theories cannot be proven. Moreover, we know by historical hindsight that Anne did choose the royal tercel, Richard. But when Chaucer wrote this poem (assuming the theory is valid), he could not be sure she would do so. The proposed marriage provided the occasion for a searching consideration of the contradictions, ambivalences, and uncertainties of human love, royal or not. The poetic reasons for the formel's reluctance to choose are probably to be sought not in the historical circumstances but in the poem itself and in Chaucer's characteristically undogmatic refusal to offer simple solutions to complicated human problems. Yet, with equally characteristic optimism, Chaucer resolves the disputes of the birds into the harmony of their song, the earthly counterpart of the music of the spheres that Scipio heard in his dream. That happy song is an assurance that, though the narrator (and reader) may not solve all the problems the poem raises, a harmonious solution remains, elusive, yet possible.

LARRY D. BENSON

The Parliament of Fowls

■

Here begyneth the Parlement of Foules.

The lyf so short, the craft so long to lerne,
Th'assay so hard, so sharp the conquerynge,
The dredful joye alwey that slit so yerne:
Al this mene I by Love, that my felynge
Astonyeth with his wonderful werkynge   5
So sore, iwis, that whan I on hym thynke
Nat wot I wel wher that I flete or synke.

For al be that I knowe nat Love in dede,
Ne wot how that he quiteth folk here hyre,
Yit happeth me ful ofte in bokes reede   10
Of his myrakles and his crewel yre.
There rede I wel he wol be lord and syre;
I dar nat seyn, his strokes been so sore,
But "God save swich a lord!" — I can na
        moore.

Of usage — what for lust and what for lore — 15
On bokes rede I ofte, as I yow tolde.
But wherfore that I speke al this? Nat yoore
Agon it happede me for to beholde
Upon a bok, was write with lettres olde,
And therupon, a certeyn thing to lerne,   20
The longe day ful faste I redde and yerne.

For out of olde feldes, as men seyth,
Cometh al this newe corn from yer to yere,
And out of olde bokes, in good feyth,

Cometh al this newe science that men lere.   25
But now to purpos as of this matere:
To rede forth hit gan me so delite
That al that day me thoughte but a lyte.

This bok of which I make mencioun
Entitled was al ther, as I shal telle: 30
"Tullyus of the Drem of Scipioun."
Chapitres sevene it hadde, of hevene and helle
And erthe, and soules that therinne dwelle,
Of whiche, as shortly as I can it trete,
Of his sentence I wol yow seyn the greete.   35

Fyrst telleth it, whan Scipion was come
In Affrike, how he meteth Massynisse,
That hym for joie in armes hath inome;
Thanne telleth [it] here speche and al the blysse
That was betwix hem til the day gan mysse,   40
And how his auncestre, Affrycan so deere,
Gan in his slep that nyght to hym apere.

Thanne telleth it that, from a sterry place,
How Affrycan hath hym Cartage shewed,
And warnede hym beforn of al his grace,   45
And seyde hym what man, lered other lewed,
That lovede commune profyt, wel ithewed,

This text was edited by VINCENT J. DiMARCO and
LARRY D. BENSON.

2 **assay:** attempt
3 **dredful:** fearful **slit** = *slideth,* slides away
4 **felynge:** consciousness
7 **flete or synke:** sink or swim
9 **quiteth folk here hyre:** rewards people's efforts
13–14 **seyn . . . But:** say anything but
15 **lust:** pleasure **lore:** learning
17–18 **yoore Agon:** long since
21 **redde:** read
22 **men seyth:** one says, it is said

31 **Tullyus:** Tully, Cicero **Scipioun:** Scipio Africanus; the book
is Cicero's *Somnium Scipionis* ("Dream of Scipio"), the final part
of his *De Re Publica* ("Republic"). It was preserved for the
Middle Ages by Macrobius (c. 400) along with a long
commentary. In it the Roman general Scipio the Younger
("Scipioun") dreams that he meets his famous grandfather, Scipio
the Elder ("Affrycan").
32 **Chapitres:** main topics (?)
35 **his:** its **sentence:** meaning **greete:** substance
37 **Massynisse:** Masinissa, king of Numidia (now Libya)
38 **inome:** taken
40 **mysse:** fail
47 **commune profyt:** public good, welfare of the state
wel ithewed: endowed with virtues

He shulde into a blysful place wende
There as joye is that last withouten ende.

Thanne axede he if folk that here been dede 50
Han lyf and dwellynge in another place.
And Affrican seyde, "Ye, withouten drede,"
And that oure present worldes lyves space
Nis but a maner deth, what wey we trace;
And rightful folk shul gon, after they dye, 55
To hevene; and shewede hym the Galaxye.

Thanne shewede he hym the lytel erthe that
    here is,
At regard of the hevenes quantite;
And after shewede he hym the nyne speres;
And after that the melodye herde he 60
That cometh of thilke speres thryes thre,
That welle is of musik and melodye
In this world here, and cause of armonye.

Than bad he hym, syn erthe was so lyte,
And dissevable and ful of harde grace, 65
That he ne shulde hym in the world delyte.
Thanne tolde he hym, in certeyn yeres space
That every sterre shulde come into his place
Ther it was first, and al shulde out of mynde
That in this world is don of al mankynde. 70

Thanne preyede hym Scipion to telle hym al
The wey to come into that hevene blisse.
And he seyde, "Know thyself first immortal,
And loke ay besyly thow werche and wysse
To commune profit, and thow shalt not mysse
To comen swiftly to that place deere 76
That ful of blysse is and of soules cleere.

"But brekers of the lawe, soth to seyne,
And likerous folk, after that they ben dede,
Shul whirle aboute th'erthe alwey in peyne, 80
Tyl many a world be passed, out of drede,
And than, foryeven al hir wikked dede,

Than shul they come into that blysful place,
To which to comen God the sende his grace."

The day gan faylen, and the derke nyght, 85
That reveth bestes from here besynesse,
Berafte me my bok for lak of lyght,
And to my bed I gan me for to dresse,
Fulfyld of thought and busy hevynesse;
For bothe I hadde thyng which that I nolde, 90
And ek I ne hadde that thyng that I wolde.

But fynally my spirit at the laste,
For wery of my labour al the day,
Tok reste, that made me to slepe faste;
And in my slep I mette, as that I lay, 95
How Affrican, ryght in the selve aray
That Scipion hym say byfore that tyde,
Was come and stod right at my beddes syde.

The wery huntere, slepynge in his bed,
To wode ayeyn his mynde goth anon; 100
The juge dremeth how his plees been sped;
The cartere dremeth how his cart is gon;
The riche, of gold; the knyght fyght with his
    fon;
The syke met he drynketh of the tonne;
The lovere met he hath his lady wonne. 105

Can I not seyn if that the cause were
For I hadde red of Affrican byforn
That made me to mete that he stod there;
But thus seyde he: "Thow hast the so wel born
In lokynge of myn olde bok totorn, 110
Of which Macrobye roughte nat a lyte,
That sumdel of thy labour wolde I quyte."

Cytherea, thow blysful lady swete,
That with thy fyrbrond dauntest whom the lest
And madest me this sweven for to mete, 115
Be thow myn helpe in this, for thow mayst best!
As wisly as I sey the north-north-west,

---

53 **present worldes lyves space:** time of life in this present world
56 **Galaxye:** the Milky Way
58 **At regard of:** compared to
59 **speres:** spheres. The ancients imagined the universe to consist of the fixed Earth surrounded by eight or nine concentric spheres. Their movement was supposed to produce a perfectly harmonious music.
64 **bad:** advised, urged
65 **dissevable:** deceptive
67 **certeyn yeres space:** a certain period of time, meaning many thousands of years, when the heavenly bodies return to their starting points
72 **hevene:** heaven's
74 **wysse:** direct (yourself)
77 **cleere:** bright, splendid
81 **many a world:** many ages

87 **Berafte:** deprived
89 **busy:** intense
91 **ne hadde:** pronounced *n'adde.*
93 **For wery of:** exhausted by
101 **plees:** cases
103 **fyght** = *fighteth,* fights **fon:** enemies
104 **syke:** sick person **met** = *meteth,* dreams
111 **roughte:** cared
112 **sumdel:** a part **quyte:** reward
113 **Cytherea:** Venus
114 **dauntest:** conquer **whom the lest:** whom you please
117 **sey the:** saw you **north-north-west:** The meaning has been much debated, since Venus is never seen from London as far to the north as north-northwest. It may mean "not at all," or "in an unconventional, oblique way."

Whan I began my sweven for to write,
So yif me myght to ryme, and endyte!

This forseyde Affrican me hente anon   120
And forth with hym unto a gate broughte,
Ryght of a park walled with grene ston;
And over the gate, with lettres large iwroughte,
There were vers iwriten, as me thoughte,
On eyther half, of ful gret difference,   125
Of which I shal yow seyn the pleyn sentence:

"Thorgh me men gon into that blysful place
Of hertes hele and dedly woundes cure;
Thorgh me men gon unto the welle of grace,   129
There grene and lusty May shal evere endure.
This is the wey to al good aventure.
Be glad, thow redere, and thy sorwe of-caste;
Al open am I — passe in, and sped thee faste!"

"Thorgh me men gon," than spak that other
          side,
"Unto the mortal strokes of the spere   135
Of which Disdayn and Daunger is the gyde,
Ther nevere tre shal fruyt ne leves bere.
This strem yow ledeth to the sorweful were
There as the fish in prysoun is al drye;
Th'eschewing is only the remedye!"   140

These vers of gold and blak iwriten were,
Of whiche I gan astoned to beholde.
For with that oon encresede ay my fere
And with that other gan myn herte bolde;   144
That oon me hette, that other dide me colde;
No wit hadde I, for errour, for to chese
To entre or flen, or me to save or lese.

Right as betwixen adamauntes two
Of evene myght, a pece of yren set
Ne hath no myght to meve to ne fro —   150
For what that oon may hale, that other let —
Ferde I, that nyste whether me was bet
To entre or leve, til Affrycan, my gide,
Me hente and shof in at the gates wide,

And seyde, "It stondeth writen in thy face,   155
Thyn errour, though thow telle it not to me;
But dred the not to come into this place,
For this writyng nys nothyng ment bi the,
Ne by non but he Loves servaunt be:
For thow of love hast lost thy tast, I gesse, 160
As sek man hath of swete and bytternesse.

"But natheles, although that thow be dul,
Yit that thow canst not do, yit mayst thow se.
For many a man that may nat stonde a pul
Yet liketh hym at wrastlyng for to be,   165
And demen yit wher he do bet or he.
And if thow haddest connyng for t'endite,
I shal the shewe mater of to wryte."

With that myn hand in his he tok anon,   169
Of which I confort caughte, and wente in faste.
But, Lord, so I was glad and wel begoon!
For overal where that I myne eyen caste
Were treës clad with leves that ay shal laste,
Ech in his kynde, of colour fresh and greene
As emeraude, that joye was to seene.   175

The byldere ok, and ek the hardy asshe;
The piler elm, the cofre unto carayne;
The boxtre pipere, holm to whippes lashe;
The saylynge fyr; the cipresse, deth to playne;
The shetere ew; the asp for shaftes pleyne;   180
The olyve of pes, and eke the dronke vyne;
The victor palm, the laurer to devyne.

A gardyn saw I ful of blosmy bowes
Upon a ryver, in a grene mede,
There as swetnesse everemore inow is,   185
With floures white, blewe, yelwe, and rede,
And colde welle-stremes, nothyng dede,
That swymmen ful of smale fishes lighte,
With fynnes rede and skales sylver bryghte.

132 **of-caste:** cast off, throw away
136 **Daunger:** (a lady's) tendency to snub a suitor
138 **were:** weir
140 **Th'eschewing:** the avoidance
144 **bolde:** embolden
145 **hette:** heated, inflamed
146 **errour:** confusion
148 **adamauntes:** stones with magnetic powers
151 **hale:** attract   **let** = *letteth,* repels
152 **me was bet:** was better for me, I should
154 **shof:** pushed

159 **Loves servaunt:** Cupid's vassal; i.e., a man in love
161 **sek:** sick
164 **pul:** fall (at wrestling)
167 **connyng:** ability
171 **wel begoon:** in a happy situation
172 **overal where:** wherever
174 **in his kynde:** according to its nature
177 **piler:** pillar, perhaps a support for vines   **cofre unto
carayne:** a coffin for corpses (elm was used for making coffins)
178 **boxtre pipere:** boxwood tree for making pipes, whistles
holm: holly
179 **deth to playne:** for lamenting death
180 **shetere:** shooter (used for making arrows)   **ew:** yew
182 **laurer:** laurel   **devyne:** practice divination
183 **blosmy:** filled with blossoms
184 **ryver:** river bank
186 **yelwe:** yellow
187 **welle-stremes:** springs   **nothyng dede:** not sluggish
188 **swymmen ful of:** abound in   **lighte:** lively

On every bow the bryddes herde I synge, 190
With voys of aungel in here armonye;
Some besyede hem here bryddes forth to
      brynge;
The litel conyes to here pley gonne hye;
And ferther al aboute I gan aspye 194
The dredful ro, the buk, the hert and hynde,
Squyrels, and bestes smale of gentil kynde.

Of instruments of strenges in acord
Herde I so pleye a ravyshyng swetnesse,
That God, that makere is of al and lord,
Ne herde nevere beter, as I gesse. 200
Therwith a wynd, unnethe it myghte be lesse,
Made in the leves grene a noyse softe
Acordaunt to the foules song alofte.

Th'air of that place so attempre was 204
That nevere was grevaunce of hot ne cold.
There wex ek every holsom spice and gras;
No man may there waxe sek ne old;
Yit was there joye more a thousandfold
Than man can telle; ne nevere wolde it nyghte,
But ay cler day to any mannes syghte. 210

Under a tre, besyde a welle, I say
Cupide, oure lord, his arwes forge and file;
And at his fet his bowe al redy lay;
And Wille, his doughter, temprede al this while
The hevedes in the welle, and with hire wile 215
She couchede hem, after they shulde serve
Some for to sle, and some to wounde and kerve.

Tho was I war of Plesaunce anon-ryght,
And of Aray, and Lust, and Curteysie, 219
And of the Craft that can and hath the myght
To don by force a wyght to don folye —
Disfigurat was she, I nyl nat lye;
And by hymself, under an ok, I gesse,
Saw I Delyt, that stod with Gentilesse.

I saw Beute withouten any atyr, 225
And Youthe, ful of game and jolyte;
Foolhardynesse, Flaterye, and Desyr,
Messagerye, and Meede, and other thre —

Here names shul not here be told for me —
And upon pilers greete of jasper longe 230
I saw a temple of bras ifounded stronge.

Aboute the temple daunsedyn alwey
Women inowe, of whiche some ther weere
Fayre of hemself, and some of hem were gay;
In kertels, al dishevele, wente they there: 235
That was here offyce alwey, yer by yeere.
And on the temple, of dowves white and fayre
Saw I syttynge many an hundred peyre.

Byfore the temple-dore ful soberly
Dame Pees sat, with a curtyn in hire hond, 240
And by hire syde, wonder discretly,
Dame Pacience syttynge there I fond,
With face pale, upon an hil of sond;
And aldernext, withinne and ek withoute,
Byheste and Art, and of here folk a route. 245

Withinne the temple, of sykes hoote as fyr
I herde a swogh that gan aboute renne,
Whiche sikes were engendered with desyr,
That maden every auter for to brenne
Of newe flaume; and wel espyed I thenne 250
That al the cause of sorwes that they drye
Cam of the bittere goddesse Jelosye.

The god Priapus saw I, as I wente,
Withinne the temple in sovereyn place stonde,
In swich aray as whan the asse hym shente 255
With cri by nighte, and with hys sceptre in
      honde.
Ful besyly men gonne assaye and fonde
Upon his hed to sette, of sondry hewe,
Garlondes ful of freshe floures newe.

And in a prive corner in disport 260
Fond I Venus and hire porter Richesse,
That was ful noble and hautayn of hyre port —
Derk was that place, but afterward lightnesse
I saw a lyte, unnethe it myghte be lesse —
And on a bed of gold she lay to reste, 265
Til that the hote sonne gan to weste.

193 **conyes:** rabbits
195 **dredful ro:** timid roe **hert:** stag, full-grown red deer
hynde: female deer
196 **gentil kynde:** noble nature
197 **in acord:** in harmony
206 **gras:** herb
209 **nyghte:** become night
215 **wile:** skill
216 **couchede:** placed, arranged
219 **Aray:** clothing **Lust:** desire
225 **atyr:** adornment
228 **Messagerye:** sending of messages **Meede:** reward, bribery

234 **gay:** gaily dressed, richly attired
235 **kertels:** frocks **dishevele:** with hair hanging loose
240 **curtyn:** the significance of the curtain is obscure; see n.
245 **Byheste:** promises **Art:** craft, skill
250 **flaume:** flame
253 **Priapus:** the god of gardens and fertility, here represented as in Ovid's *Fasti* 1.415–40, where he is embarrassingly interrupted as he is about to copulate with a nymph
255 **aray:** state
256 **sceptre:** a phallic metaphor
262 **hautayn:** dignified
266 **weste:** go westward

Hyre gilte heres with a golden thred
Ibounden were, untressed as she lay,
And naked from the brest unto the hed   269
Men myghte hire sen; and, sothly for to say,
The remenaunt was wel kevered to my pay,
Ryght with a subtyl coverchef of Valence —
Ther was no thikkere cloth of no defense.

The place yaf a thousand savours sote,
And Bachus, god of wyn, sat hire besyde,   275
And Ceres next, that doth of hunger boote,
And, as I seyde, amyddes lay Cypride,
To whom on knees two yonge folk ther cryde
To ben here helpe. But thus I let hire lye,
And ferther in the temple I gan espie   280

That, in dispit of Dyane the chaste,
Ful many a bowe ibroke heng on the wal
Of maydenes swiche as gonne here tymes waste
In hyre servyse; and peynted overal
Ful many a story, of which I touche shal   285
A fewe, as of Calyxte and Athalante,
And many a mayde of which the name I wante.

Semyramis, Candace, and Hercules,
Biblis, Dido, Thisbe, and Piramus,
Tristram, Isaude, Paris, and Achilles,   290
Eleyne, Cleopatre, and Troylus,
Silla, and ek the moder of Romulus:
Alle these were peynted on that other syde,
And al here love, and in what plyt they dyde.

Whan I was come ayeyn into the place   295
That I of spak, that was so sote and grene,
Forth welk I tho myselven to solace.
Tho was I war wher that ther sat a queene

That, as of lyght the somer sonne shene
Passeth the sterre, right so over mesure   300
She fayrer was than any creature.

And in a launde, upon an hil of floures,
Was set this noble goddesse Nature.
Of braunches were here halles and here boures
Iwrought after here cast and here mesure;   305
Ne there nas foul that cometh of engendrure
That they ne were prest in here presence
To take hire dom and yeve hire audyence.

For this was on Seynt Valentynes day,
Whan every foul cometh there to chese his
        make,   310
Of every kynde that men thynke may,
And that so huge a noyse gan they make
That erthe, and eyr, and tre, and every lake
So ful was that unethe was there space
For me to stonde, so ful was al the place.   315

And right as Aleyn, in the Pleynt of Kynde,
Devyseth Nature of aray and face,
In swich aray men myghte hire there fynde.
This noble emperesse, ful of grace,
Bad every foul to take his owne place,   320
As they were woned alwey fro yer to yeere,
Seynt Valentynes day, to stonden theere.

That is to seyn, the foules of ravyne
Weere hyest set, and thanne the foules smale
That eten, as hem Nature wolde enclyne,   325
As worm or thyng of which I telle no tale;
And water-foul sat lowest in the dale;
But foul that lyveth by sed sat on the grene,
And that so fele that wonder was to sene.

There myghte men the royal egle fynde,   330
That with his sharpe lok perseth the sonne,
And othere egles of a lowere kynde,
Of whiche that clerkes wel devyse conne.
Ther was the tiraunt with his fetheres donne

268 **untressed:** loose
271 **kevered:** covered **pay:** pleasure, satisfaction
272 **Valence:** a French textile center
273 **of no defense:** I.e., that would be transparent
276 **Ceres:** goddess of agriculture (i.e., of food) **doth . . .
boote:** provides the remedy
277 **Cypride:** Venus
281 **Dyane:** Diana, goddess of chastity
286 **Calyxte:** Callisto, loved by Jupiter **Athalante:** Atalanta,
wife of Hippomenes
288 **Semyramis:** queen of Assyria, celebrated for her lust
Candace: either the queen of India who loved Alexander or the
incestuous Canace (see IntrMLT II.77–80) **Hercules:** slain by
his wife Deianira (see MkT VII.2119–34)
289 **Biblis:** an incestuous lover **Dido:** for her story see LGW
924–1367, HF 239–432 **Thisbe, and Piramus:** Thisbe and
Pyramus; for their story see LGW 706–923.
290 **Tristram, Isaude:** Tristan and Isolde, the famous lovers
Paris: his abduction of Helen (*Eleyne*) caused the Trojan War
Achilles: died for the love of Polyxena (see BD 1067–71)
291 **Cleopatre:** for her story see LGW 580–705 **Troylus:** his
story is told in Troilus and Criseyde.
292 **Silla:** daughter of Nisus; for her story see LGW 1900–1921.
moder of Romulus: Ilia (Rhea Silvia), a priestess of Diana
297 **welk:** walked

302 **launde:** glade
305 **cast:** design
306 **engendrure:** procreation
307 **prest:** ready
308 **audyence:** hearing
316 **Aleyn, Pleynt of Kynde:** Alanus de Insulis, *De planctu
naturae* (The Complaint of Nature), a twelfth-century
philosophical dream-vision in which Nature complains of
mankind's failure to live by her laws. It contains a long
description of Nature, including many birds that form part of the
decoration of her robe.
323 **foules of ravyne:** birds of prey
328 **sed:** seed
331 **perseth:** pierces, looks straight into
333 **conne:** know how to
334 **donne:** dun, greyish brown

And grey — I mene the goshauk that doth pyne
To bryddes for his outrageous ravyne.   336

The gentyl faucoun, that with his feet dis-
        trayneth
The kynges hand; the hardy sperhauk eke,
The quayles foo; the merlioun, that payneth
Hymself ful ofte the larke for to seke;   340
There was the douve with hire yën meke;
The jelous swan, ayens his deth that syngeth;
The oule ek, that of deth the bode bryngeth;

The crane, the geaunt, with his trompes soun;
The thef, the chough; and ek the janglynge
        pye;   345
The skornynge jay; the eles fo, heroun;
The false lapwynge, ful of trecherye;
The stare, that the conseyl can bewrye;
The tame ruddok, and the coward kyte;
The kok, that orloge is of thorpes lyte;   350

The sparwe, Venus sone; the nyghtyngale,
That clepeth forth the grene leves newe;
The swalwe, mortherere of the foules smale
That maken hony of floures freshe of hewe;
The wedded turtil, with hire herte trewe;   355
The pekok, with his aungels fetheres bryghte;
The fesaunt, skornere of the cok by nyghte;

The waker goos; the cukkow ever unkynde;
The popynjay, ful of delicasye;
The drake, stroyere of his owene kynde;   360
The stork, the wrekere of avouterye;
The hote cormeraunt of glotenye;
The raven wys; the crowe with vois of care;
The throstil old; the frosty feldefare.

335 **pyne:** harm
336 **ravyne:** rapine, greed
337 **distrayneth:** grasps
338 **sperhauk:** sparrow hawk
339 **quayles foo:** quail's foe   **merlioun:** merlin (small falcon)
341 **yën meke:** meek eyes
342 **ayens:** in anticipation of
343 **bode:** omen, foreboding
344 **geaunt:** giant
345 **chough:** a bird of the crow family   **pye:** magpie
346 **eles fo:** eel's foe
347 **false:** treacherous; see n.
348 **stare:** starling   **bewrye:** reveal, betray
349 **ruddok:** robin redbreast (English robin)
350 **orloge:** timepiece   **thorpes lyte:** small villages
351 **Venus sone:** son of Venus, reputed to be lecherous
353 **mortherere of the foules smale:** murderer of bees
357 **fesaunt:** pheasant
358 **waker:** watchful   **unkynde:** unnatural (see 613)
359 **popynjay:** parrot
360 **stroyere:** destroyer
361 **wrekere:** punisher   **avouterye:** adultery
362 **cormeraunt:** the cormorant, an aquatic bird notorious for its
appetite
363 **vois of care:** sad voice
364 **throstil:** thrush   **frosty:** with a white chest   **feldefare:**
fieldfare, a kind of thrush

What shulde I seyn? Of foules every kynde   365
That in this world han fetheres and stature
Men myghten in that place assembled fynde
Byfore the noble goddesse Nature,
And ech of hem dide his besy cure
Benygnely to chese or for to take,   370
By hire acord, his formel or his make.

But to the poynt: Nature held on hire hond
A formel egle, of shap the gentilleste
That evere she among hire werkes fond,
The moste benygne and the goodlieste.   375
In hire was everi vertu at his reste,
So ferforth that Nature hireself hadde blysse
To loke on hire, and ofte hire bek to kysse.

Nature, the vicaire of the almyghty Lord,   379
That hot, cold, hevy, lyght, moyst, and dreye
Hath knyt by evene noumbres of acord,
In esy voys began to speke and seye,
"Foules, tak hed of my sentence, I preye,
And for youre ese, in fortheryng of youre nede,
As faste as I may speke, I wol yow speede.   385

"Ye knowe wel how, Seynt Valentynes day,
By my statut and thorgh my governaunce,
Ye come for to cheese — and fle youre wey —
Youre makes, as I prike yow with plesaunce;
But natheles, my ryghtful ordenaunce   390
May I nat lete for al this world to wynne,
That he that most is worthi shal begynne.

"The tersel egle, as that ye knowe wel,
The foul royal, above yow in degre,
The wyse and worthi, secre, trewe as stel,   395
Which I have formed, as ye may wel se,
In every part as it best liketh me —
It nedeth not his shap yow to devyse —
He shal first chese and speken in his gyse.

"And after hym by ordre shul ye chese,   400
After youre kynde, everich as yow lyketh,
And, as youre hap is, shul ye wynne or lese.
But which of yow that love most entriketh,

369 **dide his besy cure:** worked diligently
370 **Benygnely:** graciously
371 **formel:** female (bird)
379 **vicaire:** deputy
380 The elementary qualities (cf. Bo 3. m9.18–24).
381 **evene noumbres of acord:** equal, matching proportions
382 **esy:** gentle
393 **tersel:** tercel (male eagle or hawk)
395 **secre:** discreet
403 **entriketh:** entangles

God sende hym hire that sorest for hym
    syketh!"
And therwithal the tersel gan she calle,   405
And seyde, "My sone, the choys is to the falle.

"But natheles, in this condicioun
Mot be the choys of everich that is heere,
That she agre to his eleccioun,
Whoso he be that shulde be hire feere.   410
This is oure usage alwey, fro yer to yeere,
And whoso may at this tyme have his grace
In blisful tyme he cam into this place!"

With hed enclyned and with humble cheere
This royal tersel spak, and tariede noght: 415
"Unto my soverayn lady, and not my fere,
I chese, and chese with wil, and herte, and
    thought,
The formel on youre hond, so wel iwrought,
Whos I am al, and evere wol hire serve,
Do what hire lest, to do me lyve or sterve;   420

"Besekynge hire of merci and of grace,
As she that is my lady sovereyne;
Or let me deye present in this place.
For certes, longe may I nat lyve in payne,
For in myn herte is korven every veyne.   425
Havynge reward only to my trouthe,
My deere herte, have on my wo som routhe.

"And if that I be founde to hyre untrewe,
Disobeysaunt, or wilful necligent,
Avauntour, or in proces love a newe,   430
I preye to yow this be my jugement:
That with these foules I be al torent,
That ilke day that evere she me fynde
To hir untrewe, or in my gilt unkynde.

"And syn that non loveth hire so wel as I,   435
Al be she nevere of love me behette,
Thanne oughte she be myn thourgh hire mercy,
For other bond can I non on hire knette.
Ne nevere for no wo ne shal I lette
To serven hire, how fer so that she wende;   440
Say what yow list, my tale is at an ende."

Ryght as the freshe, rede rose newe
Ayeyn the somer sonne coloured is,
Ryght so for shame al wexen gan the hewe
Of this formel, whan she herde al this;   445
She neyther answerde wel, ne seyde amys,
So sore abasht was she, tyl that Nature
Seyde, "Doughter, drede yow nought, I yow
    assure."

Another tersel egle spak anon,   449
Of lower kynde, and seyde, "That shal nat be!
I love hire bet than ye don, by Seint John,
Or at the leste I love hire as wel as ye,
And lenger have served hire in my degre;
And if she shulde have loved for long lovynge,
To me allone hadde be the guerdonynge.   455

"I dar ek seyn, if she me fynde fals,
Unkynde, janglere, or rebel any wyse,
Or jelous, do me hangen by the hals!
And, but I bere me in hire servyse
As wel as that my wit can me suffyse,   460
From poynt in poynt, hyre honour for to save,
Take she my lif and al the good I have!"

The thridde tercel egle answerde tho,
"Now, sires, ye seen the lytel leyser heere;
For every foul cryeth out to ben ago   465
Forth with his make, or with his lady deere;
And ek Nature hireself ne wol not heere,
For taryinge here, not half that I wolde seye;
And but I speke, I mot for sorwe deye.

"Of long servyse avaunte I me nothing;   470
But as possible is me to deye to-day
For wo as he that hath ben languysshyng
This twenty wynter, and wel happen may;
A man may serven bet and more to pay
In half a yer, although it were no moore,   475
Than som man doth that hath served ful yoore.

"I seye not this by me, for I ne can
Don no servyse that may my lady plese;
But I dar seyn, I am hire treweste man
As to my dom, and faynest wolde hire ese.   480
At shorte wordes, til that deth me sese
I wol ben heres, whether I wake or wynke,
And trewe in al that herte may bethynke."

---

404 **sorest:** most sorely, intensely   **for hym:** on his own behalf
409 **eleccioun:** choice
410 **feere:** spouse
416 **fere:** equal
426 **reward:** regard
430 **Avauntour:** boaster   **proces:** the course of time
436 **Al be:** even though   **behette:** promised
438 **knette:** fasten
439 **lette:** stop

457 **janglere:** a gossip
461 **poynt in poynt:** beginning to end
468 **For:** to avoid
470 **avaunte I me:** I boast
474 **to pay:** satisfactorily
481 **sese:** seize
482 **wynke:** sleep

Of al my lyf, syn that day I was born,
So gentil ple in love or other thyng   485
Ne herde nevere no man me beforn —
Who that hadde leyser and connyng
For to reherse hire chere and hire spekyng;
And from the morwe gan this speche laste   489
Tyl dounward went the sonne wonder faste.

The noyse of foules for to ben delyvered
So loude rong, "Have don, and lat us wende!"
That wel wende I the wode hadde al to-
        shyvered.
"Com of!" they criede, "allas, ye wol us shende!
Whan shal youre cursede pletynge have an
        ende?   495
How sholde a juge eyther parti leve
For ye or nay withouten any preve?"

The goos, the cokkow, and the doke also
So cryede, "Kek kek! kokkow! quek quek!" hye,
That thourgh myne eres the noyse wente
        tho.   500
The goos seyde, "Al this nys not worth a flye!
But I can shape herof a remedie,
And I wol seye my verdit fayre and swythe
For water-foul, whoso be wroth or blythe!"   504

"And I for worm-foul," seyde the fol kokkow,
"For I wol of myn owene autorite,
For comune spede, take on the charge now,
For to delyvere us is gret charite."
"Ye may abyde a while yit, parde!"
Quod the turtel, "If it be youre wille   510
A wight may speke, hym were as fayr be stylle.

"I am a sed-foul, oon the unworthieste,
That wot I wel, and litel of connynge.
But bet is that a wyghtes tonge reste
Than entermeten hym of such doinge,   515
Of which he neyther rede can ne synge;

And whoso hit doth ful foule hymself acloyeth,
For office uncommytted ofte anoyeth."

Nature, which that alwey hadde an ere
To murmur of the lewednesse behynde,   520
With facound voys seyde, "Hold youre tonges
        there!
And I shal sone, I hope, a conseyl fynde
Yow to delyvere, and fro this noyse unbynde:
I juge, of every folk men shul oon calle
To seyn the verdit for yow foules alle."   525

Assented were to this conclusioun
The briddes alle; and foules of ravyne
Han chosen fyrst, by pleyn eleccioun,
The tercelet of the faucoun to diffyne
Al here sentence, and as him lest, termyne;   530
And to Nature hym gonne to presente,
And she accepteth hym with glad entente.

The terslet seyde thanne in this manere:
"Ful hard were it to preve by resoun
Who loveth best this gentil formel heere;   535
For everych hath swich replicacioun
That non by skilles may be brought adoun.
I can not se that argumentes avayle:
Thanne semeth it there moste be batayle."

"Al redy!" quod these egles tercels tho.   540
"Nay, sires," quod he, "if that I durste it seye,
Ye don me wrong, my tale is not ido!
For, sires — ne taketh not agref I preye —
It may not gon as ye wolde in this weye;   544
Oure is the voys that han the charge in honde,
And to the juges dom ye moten stonde.

"And therfore pes! I seye, as to my wit,
Me wolde thynke how that the worthieste
Of knyghthod, and lengest had used it,
Most of estat, of blod the gentilleste,   550
Were sittyngest for hire, if that hir leste;
And of these thre she wot hireself, I trowe,
Which that he be, for it is light to knowe."

485 **ple:** appeal. Parliamentary language is used here and in the
next two stanzas.
491 **delyvered:** dismissed
492 **Have don:** finish up   **wende:** go
493 **wende:** thought
494 **Com of!:** Come on, hurry up!
495 **pletynge:** argument
496 **leve:** believe
499 **hye:** loudly
503 **verdit:** verdict
505 **fol:** foolish
507 **comune spede:** good of all   **charge:** matter to be discussed
510–11 If a body have your (i.e., the hearers') permission to
speak, (I would say that) it would be a good thing if he (i.e., the
cuckoo) kept his mouth shut.
512 **sed-foul:** bird that feeds on seeds
513 **connynge:** understanding
515 **entermeten hym of:** interfere with

517 **acloyeth:** overburdens
518 **uncommytted:** not entrusted to one, i.e., not asked for
521 **facound:** eloquent
523 **unbynde:** free
525 **verdit:** verdict
529 **tercelet:** young male   **diffyne:** state exactly, sum up
530 **sentence:** opinion   **termyne:** reach a conclusion
536 **replicacioun:** reply
537 **skilles:** reasons, arguments   **brought adoun:** refuted
539 **batayle:** trial by battle, judicial duel
545–46 We who have the responsibility for deciding may speak,
but you must abide by the judge's decision.
551 **sittyngest:** most suitable
553 **light:** easy

The water-foules han here hedes leid
Togedere, and of a short avysement,   555
Whan everych hadde his large golee seyd,
They seyden sothly, al by oon assent,
How that the goos, with here facounde gent,
"That so desyreth to pronounce oure nede,
Shal telle oure tale," and preyede "God hire
    spede!"   560

And for these water-foules tho began
The goos to speke, and in hire kakelynge
She seyde, "Pes! Now tak kep every man,
And herkeneth which a resoun I shal forth
    brynge!
My wit is sharp; I love no taryinge;   565
I seye I rede hym, though he were my brother,
But she wol love hym, lat hym love another!"

"Lo, here a parfit resoun of a goos!"
Quod the sperhauk; "Nevere mot she thee!
Lo, swich it is to have a tonge loos!   570
Now parde, fol, yit were it bet for the
Han holde thy pes than shewed thy nycete.
It lyth nat in his wit, ne in his wille,
But soth is seyd, 'a fol can not be stille.' "

The laughter aros of gentil foules alle,   575
And right anon the sed-foul chosen hadde
The turtle trewe, and gonne hire to hem calle,
And preyeden hire to seyn the sothe sadde
Of this matere, and axede what she radde.
And she answerde that pleynly hire entente   580
She wolde shewe, and sothly what she mente.

"Nay, God forbede a lovere shulde chaunge!"
The turtle seyde, and wex for shame al red,
"Though that his lady everemore be straunge,
Yit lat hym serve hire ever, til he be ded.   585
Forsothe, I preyse nat the goses red;
'For, though she deyede, I wolde non other
    make;
I wol ben hires, til that the deth me take.' "

"Wel bourded," quod the doke, "by myn hat!
That men shulde loven alwey causeles!   590
Who can a resoun fynde or wit in that?

Daunseth he murye that is myrtheles?
Who shulde recche of that is recheles?"
"Ye queke," seyde the goos, "ful wel and fayre!
There been mo sterres, God wot, than a
    payre!"   595

"Now fy, cherl!" quod the gentil tercelet,
"Out of the donghil cam that word ful right!
Thow canst nat seen which thyng is wel beset!
Thow farst by love as oules don by lyght: 599
The day hem blent, ful wel they se by nyght.
Thy kynde is of so low a wrechednesse
That what love is, thow canst nouther seen ne
    gesse."

Tho gan the kokkow putte hym forth in pres
For foul that eteth worm, and seyde blyve: —
"So I," quod he, "may have my make in pes,
I reche nat how longe that ye stryve.   606
Lat ech of hem be soleyn al here lyve!
This is my red, syn they may nat acorde;
This shorte lessoun nedeth nat recorde."

"Ye, have the glotoun fild inow his paunche,
Thanne are we wel!" seyde the merlioun;   611
"Thow mortherere of the heysoge on the
    braunche
That broughte the forth, thow reufullest
    glotoun!
Lyve thow soleyn, wormes corupcioun,
For no fors is of lak of thy nature!   615
Go, lewed be thow whil the world may dure!"

"Now pes," quod Nature, "I comaunde heer!
For I have herd al youre opynyoun,
And in effect yit be we nevere the neer.
But fynally, this is my conclusioun,   620
That she hireself shal han hir eleccioun
Of whom hire lest; whoso be wroth or blythe,
Hym that she cheest, he shal hire han as swithe.

---

555 **short avysement**: brief deliberation
556 **golee**: mouthful
558 **facounde gent**: genteel eloquence
579 **radde**: would advise
586 **red**: advice
589 **Wel bourded**: wittily jested (i.e., you're joking)

593 Who should care about one who does not care?
594 **Ye queke**: you quack (i.e., speak)
598 **wel beset**: proper, well employed
599 **farst by love**: fare, act, concerning love
602 **nouther**: pronounced as one syllable (nor)
607 **soleyn**: single
609 **nedeth nat recorde**: does not need to be repeated over and over (to be learned)
610 **fild**: filled   **paunche**: belly
611 **merlioun**: merlin (small falcon)
612 **heysoge**: hedge sparrow
613 **broughte the forth**: hatched you (the cuckoo was thought to lay its eggs in the nests of other birds)   **reufullest**: most pitiful
619 **nevere the neer**: no closer to our goal, no better off
623 **cheest** = cheeseth, chooses

"For sith it may not here discussed be
Who loveth hire best, as seyde the tercelet, 625
Thanne wol I don hire this favour, that she
Shal han right hym on whom hire herte is set,
And he hire that his herte hath on hire knet:
Thus juge I, Nature, for I may not lye;
To non estat I have non other yë.   630

"But as for counseyl for to chese a make,
If I were Resoun, thanne wolde I
Conseyle yow the royal tercel take,
As seyde the tercelet ful skylfully,
As for the gentilleste and most worthi,   635
Which I have wrought so wel to my plesaunce
That to yow hit oughte to been a suffisaunce."

With dredful vois the formel hire answerde,
"My rightful lady, goddesse of Nature!
Soth is that I am evere under youre yerde,   640
As is everich other creature,
And mot be youres whil my lyf may dure;
And therfore graunteth me my firste bone,
And myn entente I wol yow sey right sone."

"I graunte it yow," quod she; and right anon
This formel egle spak in this degre: 646
"Almyghty queen, unto this yer be don,
I axe respit for to avise me,
And after that to have my choys al fre.
This al and som that I wol speke and seye;   650
Ye gete no more, although ye do me deye!

"I wol nat serve Venus ne Cupide,
Forsothe as yit, by no manere weye."
"Now, syn it may non otherwise betyde,"
Quod Nature, "heere is no more to seye.   655
Thanne wolde I that these foules were aweye,
Ech with his make, for taryinge lengere heere!"
And seyde hem thus, as ye shul after here.

"To yow speke I, ye tercelets," quod Nature,
"Beth of good herte, and serveth alle thre.   660
A yer is nat so longe to endure,

And ech of yow peyne him in his degre
For to do wel, for, God wot, quyt is she
Fro yow this yer; what after so befalle,
This entremes is dressed for yow alle."   665

And whan this werk al brought was to an ende,
To every foul Nature yaf his make
By evene acord, and on here way they wende.
And, Lord, the blisse and joye that they make!
For ech of hem gan other in wynges take,   670
And with here nekkes ech gan other wynde,
Thankynge alwey the noble goddesse of kynde.

But fyrst were chosen foules for to synge,
As yer by yer was alwey hir usaunce
To synge a roundel at here departynge,   675
To don Nature honour and plesaunce.
The note, I trowe, imaked was in Fraunce,
The wordes were swiche as ye may heer fynde,
The nexte vers, as I now have in mynde.

"Now welcome, somer, with thy sonne softe,
That hast thes wintres wedres overshake,   681
And driven away the longe nyghtes blake!

"Saynt Valentyn, that art ful hy on-lofte,
Thus syngen smale foules for thy sake:
[Now welcome, somer, with thy sonne softe,   685
That hast thes wintres wedres overshake.]

"Wel han they cause for to gladen ofte,
Sith ech of hem recovered hath hys make,
Ful blissful mowe they synge when they wake:
[Now welcome, somer, with thy sonne softe,   690
That hast thes wintres wedres overshake,
And driven away the longe nyghtes blake!"]

And with the shoutyng, whan the song was do
That foules maden at here flyght awey,
I wok, and othere bokes tok me to,   695
To reede upon, and yit I rede alwey.
I hope, ywis, to rede so som day
That I shal mete som thyng for to fare
The bet, and thus to rede I nyl nat spare.

Explicit parliamentum Auium in die sancti Valentini tentum,
secundum Galfridum Chaucers. Deo gracias.

624 **discussed:** decided
627 **right:** exactly
628 **on hire knet:** joined to her
632 **Resoun:** Reason; i.e., if (as in a personification allegory) she
were Reason rather than Nature, her advice on choosing a mate
would follow rational judgment rather than natural desire.
634 **skylfully:** reasonably
640 **yerde:** authority
648 **respit:** period of delay
657 **for taryinge:** to prevent tarrying

663 **quyt:** free
665 **This entremes is dressed:** this between-course dish is
prepared
668 **evene acord:** mutual agreement
674 **usaunce:** custom
675 **roundel:** a French lyric form using repeated lines as a refrain
677 **note:** tune **Fraunce:** Some manuscripts give the name of a
French song here.
681 **wedres:** storms **overshake:** shaken off
688 **recovered:** got back, found again

BOECE

THE PHILOSOPHER Anicius Manlius Severinus Boethius was born about 480 A.D. in Rome and was put to death in prison in Pavia in 524. He was a public servant — in 510, consul — under Theodoric, king of the Ostrogoths and after 493 de facto ruler of Rome, who had continuous reason to be grateful for his services, but who eventually imprisoned and executed him as a traitor for defending too strenuously the rights of the Senate. Boethius, conceiving of his service to Rome in the broadest cultural terms, developed an ambitious program to improve the minds and hearts of his countrymen by translating into Latin, commenting on, and reconciling with each other the works of Aristotle and Plato. He finished only the logical works of Aristotle and a comparison of Cicero's and Aristotle's *Topics.* He also left books on arithmetic, geometry, and music and several treatises on major theological issues of his day. Many of his books were standard texts in schools and universities throughout the Middle Ages.

The *Consolation of Philosophy* has proven the most lasting of all. In genre both a Platonic dialogue and an "invitation to the philosophic life," modeled apparently on Aristotle's *Protreptikon* and Cicero's *Hortensius,* two works now lost, it records in the allegorical form of a conversation between Boethius and Lady Philosophy the process of thought that enabled him to reconcile himself to his imprisonment. The wisdom and insistent logic with which it distinguishes between partial, contingent, apparent goods and the "one true good" or God raises it from the realm of prison literature into what E. K. Rand has called "a theodicy of great power and scope," which has given philosophical direction to the everyday life of many. Gibbon's famous remark that it is "a golden volume not unworthy of the leisure of Plato or of Tully" is somewhat misleading. No one's leisure could have produced it; it is the product of suffering, not of leisure; and though it is more personal, less abstract, than Plato's dialogues and the philosophical writings of Cicero, it is great precisely because it brings philosophical thought fruitfully to bear on the problems of an actual life.

The *Consolation* belongs to imaginative literature as well as to philosophy. Though hardly as frank and detailed as Augustine's *Confessions* (397–401), it has a place in the history of autobiography: in it, Boethius is articulate not only about his thoughts but about his emotions and about his response to the events of his life. It had a major influence on the development of allegory, in particular on the figure of the female counselor. Nature in *The Parliament of Fowls,* for example, is a descendant of Lady Philosophy, as is, pre-eminently, Dante's Beatrice. The goddess Fortuna, who dominates the second book of the *Consolation,* became one of the dominant images of medieval culture. And the choice the "hero" Boethius has to make between these two women, the alluring but false Fortune and the plain but true Philosophy, reflects an archetypal plot of great literary importance. Boethius by no means invented it but he surely helped to give it currency.

Philosophy begins her discipline by chasing away the Muses. This implies that Boethius had first sought consolation in literature but failed to find it, and that failure has troubled lovers of literature ever since. Yet presumably what has been chased away is only meretricious poetry that focuses on partial goods, for poetry is embedded deeply in the fabric of the work: verse alternates with prose throughout, enhancing and deepening the argument by giving it an imagistic base. Some of the poems, notably 2.8, 3.9, and 4.6, remain among the loveliest celebrations

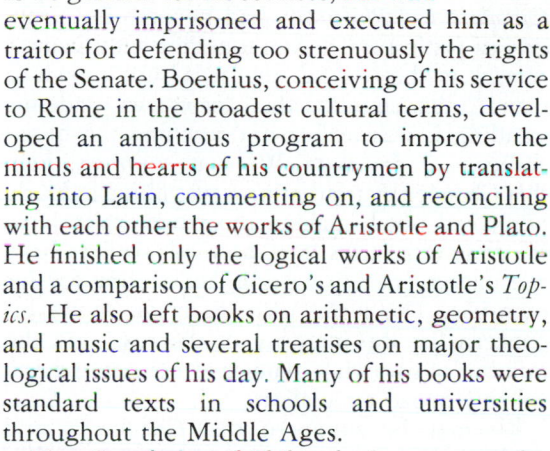

of cosmic harmony we have and were of profound importance to Dante, Spenser, and Milton as well as to Chaucer. The vision of the physical universe in many of the poems is of opposing forces bound and reconciled; and it is precisely such a reconciliation of the oppositions in human experience — success and failure, joy and sorrow, good and evil, stability and change, liberty and bondage, affirmation and skepticism — toward which the play of ideas in the proses progresses. At the same time, the poems have the further effect of belittling earth by placing it in a transcendent cosmos; and side-by-side with the urge to reconciliation is Philosophy's urge to transcend, to make Boethius see the gap between our everyday understanding of the world and the world as it actually is.

Among the partial goods that men and women seek Boethius does not list human love. Yet he makes it clear that one of the major pains of imprisonment is his separation from his family, and, in the memorable poem on Orpheus that ends the third book, Orpheus's grief at Eurydice's death, and the power of his appeal to Pluto to give her back to him, are movingly sung. In what is perhaps the most austere moment in the book, however, Orpheus's turning to look at Eurydice is taken as a turning from the one true good toward a partial good. And this very austerity, this clear focus on permanent values, seems in fact to be what made the *Consolation* appealing to Chaucer as he meditated on the instability of human love. It is granted to Troilus finally to see love from a more sublime point of vantage than that from which Orpheus saw it. Chaucer's understanding, not only of love but of human life itself, seems to have been fundamentally Boethian. He expresses that understanding most directly in the beautiful Boethian lyrics The Former Age, Lak of Stedfastnesse, and Truth, and he gives it supreme fictive embodiment in *Troilus* and The Knight's Tale. It is surely present also, though less conspicuously, in the ethic of "patient suffraunce" that pervades such of *The Canterbury Tales* as The Clerk's Tale, The Franklin's Tale, The Parson's Tale, and The Tale of Melibee, and in the master image of pilgrimage, which reflects, however distantly, the Boethian-Platonic-Christian myth of the soul in exile, seeking to journey home to God. Boethius gave Chaucer a capacity to focus on fundamental general questions, augmenting his sense of character, his human touch, and his tolerance.

It is Boethius who made Chaucer a philosophical poet, and not simply a courtly maker.

Chaucer may have been led to the *Consolation of Philosophy* by Jean de Meun's continuation of the *Roman de la rose.* Jean probably owed to Boethius not only various individual sentiments but his development of the central student-teacher relationship between the dreamer and his three guides: the God of Love, Reason, and Nature. The *Roman de la rose* may even have provided Chaucer with the impetus to translate, for one of Jean's citations of the *Consolation* is introduced thus:

Anyone who thinks that his native land is here is very much a slave and a naive fool. Your native land is not on earth, as you can learn from the clerks who lecture on Boethius's Consolation *and the ideas in it. If someone were to translate it for the laity he would do them a great favor (5033–40).*

What is noteworthy here is not merely the call for a translation (which may slyly pave the way for Jean's own) but the clear implication that the *Consolation of Philosophy* had become the property of professors. Taken together with Dante's remark in the *Convivio* that it is "not known to many," this suggests that despite its academic standing it was in fact not reaching the broad audience it deserved. We may suppose, then, that Chaucer by translating it was filling a clearly perceived need, making the work available to his contemporaries, not, as some readers have speculated, merely writing out a pony for his own use. The lyric Adam Scriveyn shows his concern for the integrity of the text, and the number of surviving manuscripts suggests a reasonably broad circulation.

"It may be supposed that Chaucer would apply more than common attention to an author of so much celebrity," wrote Samuel Johnson in *Idler* 69, but in fact "he has attempted nothing higher than a version strictly literal, and has degraded the poetical parts to prose, that the constraint of versification might not obstruct his zeal for fidelity." This is a just estimate, although Johnson underestimated how uncommon Chaucer's attention, and his zeal for fidelity, in fact were. His version is an attempt not merely to translate Boethius accurately but to fuse with it, in an effort to provide a definitive guide to the work, both Jean de Meun's French translation and the Latin commentary tradition, especially the commentary of Nicholas Trivet. Jean's translation was particularly important to Chaucer. It was probably Jean's example that persuaded him to "degrade" the poetical parts to prose. Furthermore, in setting the *Consolation* into French, Jean had, as it were, parsed it for Chaucer, identifying the antecedents of pronouns, arranging Boethius's artful word order into the analytic syntax of French, clarifying the relationships of clauses in lengthy sentences, resolving absolute phrases. All this Chaucer found of inestimable value. Yet it is evident that he also checked Jean's work rigorously against the Latin. He sought always to render the Latin sense faithfully, and where Jean wavers into paraphrase — as he does frequently in the poems — Chaucer returned directly and aptly to the Latin. The result is still "a version strictly literal," but ambitiously so, a version that makes frequent use of both Jean's French *Consolation* and the commentary tradition to render Boethius for English readers with full clarity. In the process Chaucer also transformed his own sensibility, as his poetry shows.

RALPH HANNA III and
TRAUGOTT LAWLER

Boece

■

Incipit Liber Boecii de Consolacione Philosophie.

CARMINA QUI QUONDAM STUDIO FLORENTE PEREGI. — *Metrum 1*

Allas! I wepynge, am constreyned to bygynnen vers of sorwful matere, that whilom in florysschyng studie made delitable ditees. For lo, rendynge muses of poetes enditen to me thynges to ben writen, and drery vers of wretchidnesse weten my face with verray teres. At the leeste, no drede ne myghte overcomen tho muses, that thei ne were felawes, and folwyden my wey (*that is to seyn, whan I was exiled*). They that weren glorie of my youthe, whilom weleful and grene, conforten nowe the sorwful wyerdes of me, olde man. For eelde is comyn unwarly uppon me, hasted by the harmes that Y have, and sorwe hath comandid his age to ben in me. Heeris hore arn schad overtymeliche upon myn heved, and the slakke skyn trembleth of myn emptid body. Thilke deth of men is weleful that ne comyth noght in yeeris that ben swete, but cometh to wrecches often yclepid. Allas, allas! With how deef an ere deth, cruwel, turneth awey fro wrecches and nayteth to closen wepynge eien. Whil Fortune, unfeithful, favourede me with lyghte goodes, the sorwful houre (*that is to seyn, the deth*) hadde almoost dreynt myn heved. But now, for Fortune cloudy hath chaunged hir deceyvable chere to meward, myn unpietous lif draweth along unagreable duellynges in me. O ye, my frendes, what or wherto avaunted ye

10
20
30

This text was edited by RALPH HANNA III and TRAUGOTT LAWLER.

Incipit, *etc.*: Here begins Boethius's *Book of the Consolation of Philosophy.*
Carmina, *etc.*: The first few words of the Latin are quoted at the beginning of each section.
Metrum **1.3 ditees:** poems
4 **rendynge:** tearing
11 **grene:** green, flourishing
12 **wyerdes:** fates

16 **overtymeliche:** prematurely
17 **emptid:** exhausted
22 **nayteth:** refuses
24 **lyghte:** inconsequential
26 **dreynt:** overcome (drowned)
28 **to meward:** toward me   **unpietous:** pitiless, wretched
28–29 **draweth along:** drags out
29 **duellynges:** lingering

me to be weleful? For he that hath fallen stood
noght in stedefast degre.

HEC DUM MECUM TACITUS. — *Prosa 1*

In the mene while that I, stille, recordede
these thynges with myself and merkid my weply compleynte with office of poyntel, I saw,
stondynge aboven the heghte of myn heved, a
womman of ful greet reverence by semblaunt,
hir eien brennynge and cleer-seynge over the
comune myghte of men; with a lifly colour
and with swich vigour and strengthe that it ne
myghte nat ben emptid, al were it so
that sche was ful of so greet age that men   10
ne wolden nat trowen in no manere that
sche were of our elde. The stature of hire was
of a doutous jugement, for somtyme sche constreyned and schronk hirselven lik to the comune mesure of men, and somtyme it semede
that sche touchede the hevene with the heghte
of here heved. And whan sche hef hir heved
heyere, sche percede the selve hevene so that
the sighte of men lokynge was in ydel.

Hir clothes weren makid of right delye   20
thredes and subtil craft of perdurable matere; the whiche clothes sche hadde woven with
hir owene handes, as I knew wel aftir by hirselve declarynge and schewynge to me. The
beaute [of] the whiche clothes a derknesse of a
forleten and despised elde hadde duskid and
dirked, as it is wont to dirken besmokede
ymages. In the nethereste hem or bordure of
thise clothes, men redden ywoven in a
Grekissch P (that signifieth the lif actif);   30
and aboven that lettre, in the heieste
bordure, a Grekyssh T (that signifieth the lif
contemplatif). And bytwixen thise two lettres
ther were seyn degrees nobly ywrought in
manere of laddres, by whiche degrees men
myghten clymben fro the nethereste lettre to the
uppereste. Natheles handes of some men hadden korve that cloth by violence and by
strengthe, and everich man of hem hadde
boren awey swiche peces as he myghte   40

geten. And forsothe this forseide womman bar
smale bokis in hir right hand, and in hir left hand
sche bar a ceptre.

And whan she saughe thise poetical muses
aprochen aboute my bed and enditynge wordes
to my wepynges, sche was a litil amoeved, and
glowede with cruel eighen. "Who," quat sche,
"hath suffred aprochen to this sike man thise
comune strompettis of swich a place that
men clepen the theatre? The whiche nat   50
oonly ne asswagen noght his sorwes with
none remedies, but thei wolden fedyn and
noryssen hym with sweete venym. Forsothe
thise ben tho that with thornes and prikkynges
of talentz or affeccions, whiche that ne bien
nothyng fructifyenge nor profitable, destroyen
the corn plentyvous of fruytes of resoun. For
thei holden hertes of men in usage, but thei
delyvre noght folk fro maladye. But yif ye
muses hadden withdrawen fro me with   60
youre flateries any unkunnynge and unprofitable man, as men ben wont to fynde
comonly among the peple, I wolde wene suffre
the lasse grevosly; forwhi, in swych an unprofitable man, myne ententes weren nothyng
endamaged. But ye withdrawen me this man,
that hath ben noryssed in the studies or scoles of
Eleaticis and Achademycis in Grece. But goth
now rather awey, ye mermaydenes, whiche
that ben swete til it be at the laste, and   70
suffreth this man to ben cured and heeled
by myne muses (that is to seyn, by noteful
sciences)."

And thus this companye of muses, iblamed,
casten wrothly the chere dounward to the erthe,
and, schewynge by rednesse hir schame, thei
passeden sorwfully the thresschefold. And I, of
whom the sighte, ploungid in teeres, was dirked
so that Y ne myghte noght knowen what
that womman was of so imperial auctorite,   80
I wax al abayssched and astoned, and caste
my syghte doun to the erthe, and bygan stille for
to abide what sche woolde doon aftirward. Tho
com sche ner and sette her doun upon the
uttereste corner of my bed; and sche, byholdynge my chere that was cast to the erthe

---

Prosa 1.1 **recordede:** remembered
2–3 **weply:** tearful   **with office of poyntel:** using a stylus (to
write on wax tablets)
13 **of a doutous jugement:** doubtful, difficult to judge
17 **hef:** raised
20 **delye:** fine
22–24 **sche . . . declarynge:** at 1.pr3.40–41
26 **forleten:** neglected
27 **besmokede:** smoke-stained
28 **nethereste:** lowest
34 **degrees:** steps
37 **uppereste:** highest, uppermost

55 **talentz:** desires
58 **holden hertes of men in usage:** restrain men's hearts by
habit
63 **wolde wene suffre:** would expect to suffer
68 **Eleaticis and Achademycis:** two prominent philosophic
schools, the followers of Zeno of Elea and Plato, respectively
69 **mermaydenes:** sirens
72 **noteful:** useful
75 **wrothly:** sad; see n.
85 **uttereste:** outermost

hevy and grevous of wepynge, compleynede with thise wordis that I schal seyn the perturbacion of my thought.

HEU QUAM PRECIPITI MERSA PROFUNDO.
— *Metrum 2*

"Allas! How the thought of this man, dreynt in overthrowynge depnesse, dulleth and forleteth his propre clernesse, myntynge to gon into foreyne dirknesses as ofte as his anoyos bysynes waxeth withoute mesure, that is dryven with werldly wyndes. This man, that whilom was fre, to whom the hevene was opyn and knowen, and was wont to gon in hevenliche pathes, and saughe the lyght-nesse of the rede sonne, and saughe the   10 sterres of the coolde mone, and whiche sterre in hevene useth wandrynge recourses iflyt by diverse speeris — this man, overcomere, hadde comprehendid al this by nombre (*of acontynge in astronomye*). And, over this, he was wont to seken the causes whennes the sounynge wyndes moeven and bysien the smothe watir of the see; and what spirit turneth the stable hevene; and why the sterre ariseth out of the rede est, to fallen in the westrene   20 wawes; and what attemprith the lusty houres of the firste somer sesoun, that highteth and apparaileth the erthe with rosene floures; and who maketh that plentyvous autumpne in fulle [yere] fletith with hevy grapes. And eek this man was wont to tellen the diverse causes of nature that weren yhidd. Allas! Now lyth he emptid of lyght of his thoght, and his nekke is pressyd with hevy cheynes, and bereth his chere enclyned   30 adoun for the grete weyghte, and is constreyned to loken on the fool erthe!"

SET MEDICINE INQUIT TEMPUS. — *Prosa 2*

"But tyme is now," quod sche, "of medicyne more than of compleynte." Forsothe thanne sche, entendynge to meward with al the lookynge of hir eien, seyde: "Art nat thou he," quod sche, "that whilom, norissched with my

melk and fostred with myne metes, were escaped and comyn to corage of a parfit man? Certes I yaf the swiche armures that, yif thou thiselve ne haddest first cast hem awey, they schulden han defended the in seker-   10 nesse that mai nat ben overcomyn. Knowestow me nat? Why arttow stille? Is it for schame or for astonynge? It were me levere that it were for schame, but it semeth me that astonynge hath oppresside the." And whan sche say me nat oonly stille but withouten office of tunge and al dowmbe, sche leyde hir hand soofly uppon my breest and seide: "Here nys no peril," quod sche; "he is fallen into a litargye, whiche that is a comune seknesse   20 to hertes that been desceyved. He hath a litil foryeten hymselve, but certes he schal lightly remembren hymself yif so be that he hath knowen me or now; and that he may so doon, I will wipe a litil his eien that ben dirked by the cloude of mortel thynges." Thise woordes seide sche, and with the lappe of hir garnement yplited in a frownce sche dryede myn eien, that weren fulle of the wawes of my wepynges.   30

TUNC ME DISCUSSA, *&c.* — *Metrum 3*

Thus, whan that nyght was discussed and chased awey, dirknesses forleten me, and to myn eien repeyred ayen hir firste strengthe. And ryght by ensaumple as the sonne is hydd whan the sterres ben clustred (*that is to seyn, whan sterres ben covered with cloudes*) by a swyft wynd that hyghte Chorus, and that the firmament stant dirked with wete plowngy cloudes; and that the sterres nat apeeren upon hevene, so that the nyght semeth   10 sprad upon erthe: yif thanne the wynde that hyghte Boreas, isent out of the kaves of the cuntre of Trace, betith this nyght (*that is to seyn, chaseth it awey*) and discovereth the closed day, thanne schyneth Phebus ischaken with sodeyn light and smyteth with his beemes in merveylynge eien.

Metrum 2.3 **myntynge:** intending
12–13 **wandrynge . . . speeris:** Ptolemaic astronomers thought the planets, or "wandering stars," were borne on invisible spheres. **recourses:** orbits
13 **iflyt:** moved
15 **acontynge:** calculation
22–23 **highteth:** adorns
25 **fletith with:** abounds in (flows with)
Prosa 2.3 **entendynge:** looking

7 **corage:** spiritual state
13 **astonynge:** astonishment
20 **litargye:** lethargy
28 **yplited:** pleated   **frownce:** fold
Metrum 3.1 **discussed:** driven away
2 **forleten:** left
5 **clustred:** gathered in a mass
7 **Chorus:** the northwest wind
8 **plowngy:** stormy
12 **Boreas:** the north wind
15 **ischaken:** shaken, shimmering

HAUT ALITER TRISTICIE. — *Prosa 3*

Ryght so, and noon other wise, the cloudes of sorwe dissolved and doon awey, I took hevene, and resceyved mynde to knowe the face of my fisycien; so that [whan that] I sette myne eien on hir and fastned my lookynge, I byholde my noryce, Philosophie, in whoos houses I hadde conversed and hauntyd fro my youthe; and I seide thus: "O thou maystresse of alle vertues, descended from the sovereyne sete, whi arttow comen into this solitarie 10 place of myn exil? Artow comen for thou art maad coupable with me of false blames?"

"O," quod sche, "my nory, schulde I forsake the now, and schulde I nat parten with the by comune travaile the charge that thow hast suffred for envye of my name? Certes it nere nat leveful ne syttynge thyng to Philosophie to leten withouten companye the weye of hym that is innocent. Schulde I thanne redowte my blame and agrysen as though ther were 20 byfallen a newe thyng? For trowestow that Philosophie be now alderferst assailed in periles by folk of wykkide maneris? Have I noght stryven with ful greet strif in old tyme, byfor the age of my Plato, ayens the foolhardynesse of folye? And eek, the same Plato lyvynge, his mayster Socrates desserved victorie of unryghtful deth in my presence. The heritage of the whiche Socrates (*the heritage is to seyn the doctryne of the whiche Socrates* 30 *in his opinyoun of felicite, that I clepe welefulnesse*) whan that the peple of Epycuriens and Stoyciens and manye othere enforceden hem to gon ravyssche everyche man for his part (*that is to seyn, that everych of hem wolde drawen to the deffense of his opinyoun the wordes of Socrates*), they as in partye of hir preye todrowen me, cryinge and debatyng ther-ayens, and korven and torente my clothes that I hadde woven with myn 40 handes; and with tho cloutes that thei hadden arased out of my clothes thei wenten awey wenynge that I hadde gon with hem every

del. In whiche Epycuriens and Stoyciens for as myche as ther semede some traces or steppes of myn abyte, the folie of men wenynge tho Epycuryens and Stoyciens my familiers pervertede some thurw the errour of the wikkide or unkunnynge multitude of hem. (*This is to seyn, that for they semeden* 50 *philosophres thei weren pursuyed to the deth and slayn.*)

"So yif thou ne hast noght knowen the exilynge of Anaxogore, ne the empoisonynge of Socrates, ne the turmentz of Zeno, for they weren straungiers, yit myghtestow han knowen the Seneciens and the Canyos and the Soranas, of whiche folk the renoun is neyther over-oold ne unsollempne. The whiche men nothyng elles ne broght hem to the deeth but oonly 60 for thei weren enformyd of myne maneris, and semyde moost unlyk to the studies of wykkid folk. And forthi thou oughtest noght to wondren thoughe that I, in the byttere see of this lif, be fordryven with tempestes blowynge aboute, in the whiche this is my moste purpoos, that is to seyn to displesen to wikkide men. Of whiche schrewes al be the oost nevere so greet, it es to despise; for it nys nat governyd with no ledere (*of resoun*), but it es ravyssched 70 oonly by fleetynge errour folyly and lyghtly; and yif they somtyme, makynge an oost ayens us, assayle us as strengere, our ledere draweth togidre his richesses into his tour, and they ben ententyf aboute sarpleris or sachelis, unprofitable for to taken. But we that ben heghe above, syker fro alle tumolte and wood noyse, warnstoryd and enclosed in swiche a palys whider as that chaterynge or anoyinge folye ne may nat atayne, we scorne swyche 80 ravyneres and henteres of fouleste thynges.

QUISQUIS COMPOSITO. — *Metrum 4*

"Whoso it be that is cleer of vertue, sad and wel ordynat of lyvynge, that hath put under fote the proude wierdes, and loketh upryght

*Prosa 3.*2–3 **took hevene:** saw the sky again
3 **resceyved mynde:** came to my senses
6 **noryce:** nurse
10 **sete:** seat
13 **nory:** pupil (foster child)
14 **parten:** share
19 **redowte:** fear
20 **agrysen:** shudder
33 **Stoyciens:** Stoics
38 **todrowen:** tore apart
42 **arased:** torn

46 **abyte:** habit, garment
51 **pursuyed:** persecuted
54 **Anaxogore:** Anaxagoras, the Greek philosopher
57 **the Seneciens, Canyos, Soranas:** men like Seneca, Canius, and Soranus; see n.
59 **unsollempne:** uncelebrated
67 **displesen:** be displeasing
73 **as strengere:** i.e., supposing themselves stronger than we
75 **sarpleris or sachelis:** canvas bags and satchels, trivial and useless spoils
78 **warnstoryd:** fortified **palys:** palisade
81 **ravyneres:** plunderers **henteres:** takers

upon either fortune, he may holden his chere
undesconfited. The rage ne the manaces of the
see, commoevynge or chasynge upward hete
fro the botme, ne schal nat moeve that man.
Ne the unstable mowntaigne that highte Visevus, that writhith out thurw his brokene
chemeneyes smokynge fieres, ne the wey of   10
thonderleit, that is wont to smyten hye
toures, ne schal nat moeve that man. Wharto
thanne, o wrecches, drede ye tirauntz that ben
wode and felenous withouten ony strengthe?
Hope aftir no thyng, ne drede nat; and so
schaltow desarmen the ire of thilke unmyghty
tiraunt. But whoso that, qwakynge, dredeth
or desireth thyng that nys noght stable of his
ryght, that man that so dooth hath cast
awey his scheeld, and is remoeved from   20
his place, and enlaceth hym in the cheyne
with whiche he mai ben drawen.

SENTISNE, INQUIT. — *Prosa 4*

"Felistow," quod sche, "thise thynges, and
entren thei aughte in thy corage? Artow like
an asse to the harpe? Why wepistow, why
spillestow teeris? Yif thou abidest after helpe
of thi leche, the byhoveth discovere thy
wownde."

Tho I, that hadde gaderyd strengthe in my
corage, answeride and seide: "And nedeth it
yit," quod I, "of rehersynge or of ammonicioun? And scheweth it nat ynoghe by   10
hymselve the sharpnesse of Fortune, that
waxeth wood ayens me? Ne moeveth it nat
the to seen the face or the manere of this place?
Is this the librarye which that thou haddest
chosen for a ryght certein sege to the in myn
hous, there as thow disputedest ofte with me
of the sciences of thynges touchynge dyvin-
yte and mankynde? Was thanne myn habit
swiche as it is now? Was my face or my
chere swyche as now when I soghte with   20
the the secretis of nature, whan thow enformedest my maneris and the resoun of al my
lif to the ensaumple of the ordre of hevene? Is
noght this the gerdouns that I referre to the, to
whom I have ben obeisaunt?

"Certes thou confermedest by the mouth of
Plato this sentence, that is to seyn that comune
thynges or comunalites weren blisful yif they
that hadden studied al fully to wysdom
governeden thilke thynges; or elles yif it so   30
befille that the governours of comunalites
studieden to geten wysdom. Thou seidest eek by
the mouth of the same Plato that it was a
necessarie cause wise men to taken and desire
the governance of comune thynges, for that the
governementz of cites, ilefte in the handes of
felonous turmentours citezeens, ne schulde
noght bryngen in pestilence ande destruccioun
to good folk. And therfore I, folwynge
thilke auctorite, desired to putten forth in   40
execucion and in acte of comune ad-
ministracioun thilk thynges that I hadde lernyd
of the among my secre restyng-whiles.

"Thow and God, that putte the in the
thoughtes of wise folk, ben knowynge with me
that nothyng ne brought me to maistrie or
dignyte but the comune studie of alle goodnesse. And therof cometh it that bytwixen
wikkid folk and me han ben grevous
discordes, that ne myghte nat ben relessed   50
by preyeris; for this liberte hath the fredom
of conscience, that the wraththe of more myghty
folk hath alwey ben despised of me for savacioun
of right. How ofte have I resisted and withstonden thilke man that highte Connigaste, that
made alwey assawtes ayens the propre fortunes
of pore feble folk! How ofte eek have I put of
or cast out hym Trygwille, provoste of the
kyngis hous, bothe of the wronges that he
hadde bygunne to doon, and ek fully   60
performed! How ofte have I covered and
defended by the auctorite of me put ayens perils
(*that is to seyn, put myn auctorite in peril for*)
the wrecche pore folk, that the covetise of
straungiers unpunyschid tormentyde alwey with
myseses and grevances out of nombre! Nevere
man ne drow me yit fro right to wrong. Whan
I say the fortunes and the richesses of the peple
of the provinces ben harmed or amenuced
outher be pryve ravynes or by comune   70
tributz or cariages, as sory was I as they
that suffriden the harm. (*Glosa*. Whan that

Metrum 4.8–9 **Visevus:** Vesuvius, the volcano
11 **thonderleit:** lightning
21 **enlaceth hym:** entangles himself
Prosa 4.2–3 **like an asse to the harpe:** i.e., insensitive
9–10 **ammonicioun:** reminding
15 **sege:** seat
21–22 **enformedest:** formed
23–24 **Is noght:** i.e., is; see n.

37 **turmentours:** violent (a plural adjective)
43 **restyng-whiles:** times of leisure
45 **with me:** with respect to me
51–52 **this liberte hath the fredom of conscience:** (my)
freedom of conscience has given me the further freedom
69 **amenuced:** diminished
70 **ravynes:** robberies
71 **cariages:** feudal taxes imposed in place of service as a carrier

Theodoric, the kyng of Gothes, in a dere yeer, hadde his gerneeris ful of corn, and comaundede that no man schulde byen no coorn til his corn were soold, and that at a grevous dere prys, Boece withstood that ordenaunce and overcome it, knowynge al this the kyng hymselve. Coempcioun is to seyn comune achat or beyinge togidre, *that were es-* 80 *tablissed upon the peple by swich a manere imposicioun, as whoso boughte a busschel corn, he most yyve the kyng the fyfte part.) Textus.* Whan it was in the sowre hungry tyme, ther was establissed or cryed grevous and unplitable coempcioun, that men sayen wel it schulde gretly tormenten and endamagen al the provynce of Campayne, I took stryf ayens the provost of the pretorie for comune profit; and, the kyng knowynge of it, Y overcom 90 it, so that the coempcioun ne was nat axid ne took effect. Paulyn, a conseiller of Rome, the richesses of the whiche Paulyn the howndes of the paleys (*that is to seyn, the officeres*) wolden han devoured by hope and covetyse, yit drowe I hym out of the jowes of hem that gapeden. And for as moche as the peyne of the accusacioun ajugid byforn ne schulde noght sodeynli henten ne punyssche wrongfully Albyn, a conseiller of Rome, I putte me ayens the 100 hates and indignacions of the accusour Cyprian. Is it nat thanne inoghe isene that I have purchaced grete discordes ayens myself? But I oughte be the more asseured ayens alle othere folk, that for the love of rightwisnesse I ne reservede nevere nothyng to myselve to hemward of the kyngis halle, by whiche I were the more syker. But thurw tho same accusours accusynge I am condempned.

"Of the nombre of whiche accusours, 110 oon Basilius, that whilom was chased out of the kyngis servyse, is now compelled in accusynge of my name for nede of foreyne moneye. Also Opilion and Gaudencius han accused me, al be it so that the justise regal hadde whilom demed hem bothe to gon into exil for hir trecheries and frawdes withouten nombre, to whiche juggement they nolden nat obeye, but de-

fendeden hem by the sikernesse of holi houses (*that is to seyn, fledden into* 120 *seyntewarie*); and whan this was aperceyved to the kyng, he comandide that, but they voydide the cite of Ravenne by certeyn day assigned, that men scholde marken hem on the forheved with an hoot iren and chasen hem out of towne. Now what thyng semyth myghte ben likned to this cruelte? For certes thilke same day was resceyved the accusynge of myn name by thilke same accusours. What may ben seyd herto? Hath my studie and my kunnynge 130 disserved thus? Or elles the forseyde dampnacioun of me — made that hem ryghtfulle accusours or no? Was noght Fortune aschamed of this? Certes, al hadde noght Fortune ben aschamed that innocence was accused, yit oughte sche han hadde schame of the fylthe of myn accusours.

"But axestow in somme of what gylt I am accused? Men seyn that I wolde saven the companye of the senatours. And 140 desirestow to heren in what manere? I am accused that I schulde han disturbed the accusour to beren lettres, by whiche he scholde han maked the senatours gylty ayens the kynges real majeste. O Maystresse, what demestow of this? Schal I forsake this blame, that Y ne be no schame to the? Certes I have wolde it (*that is to seyn, the savacioun of the senat*), ne I schal nevere letten to wilne it. And that I confesse and am aknowe; but the entente of 150 the accusour to ben distorbed schal cese. For schal I clepe it thanne a felonye or a synne that I have desired the savacioun of the ordre of the senat? And certes yit hadde thilke same senat don by me thurw hir decretz and hir jugementz as thoughe it were a synne and a felonye (*that is to seyn, to wilne the savacioun of hem*). But folye, that lyeth alwey to hymselve, may noght chaunge the merite of thynges, ne I trowe nat by the jugement of Socrates that it were 160 leveful to me to hide the sothe ne assente to lesynges.

"But certes, how so evere it be of this, I putte it to gessen or prisen to the jugement of the and of wys folk. Of whiche thyng al the ordenaunce and the sothe, for as moche as folk that been to comen aftir our dayes schullen knowen it, I have

---

80 **achat:** purchase
84 **sowre:** bitter
86 **unplitable:** unreasonable
89 **pretorie:** Pretorian guard
96 **jowes:** jaws
105–08 **I . . . syker:** I retained for myself nothing from the courtiers (i.e., made no alliances with members of Theodoric's court) by which I might have been safer.
113 **for nede of foreyne moneye:** i.e., because he is pressed by debts

134 **aschamed of:** disgraced by
142–43 **that . . . beren:** of preventing the accuser from bearing
150 **am aknowe:** acknowledge
164 **prisen:** appraise

put it in scripture and in remembraunce. For
touchynge the lettres falsly maked, by
whiche lettres I am accused to han hoped   170
the fredom of Rome, what aperteneth me
to speken therof? Of whiche lettres the fraude
hadde ben schewed apertely, yif I hadde had
liberte for to han used and ben at the confessioun of myn accusours, the whiche thyng in
alle nedes hath greet strengthe. For what other
fredom mai men hopen? Certes I wolde that som
other fredom myghte ben hoped; I wolde
thanne han answeryd by the wordys of a
man that hyghte Canyus. For whan he was   180
accused by Gaius Cesar, Germaynes sone,
that he was knowynge and consentynge of a
conjuracioun ymaked ayens hym, this Canyus
answeride thus: 'Yif I hadde wyst it, thou
haddest noght wyst it.'

"In whiche thyng sorwe hath noght so dullid
my wyt that I pleyne oonly that schrewed folk
apparailen felonyes ayens vertu; but I wondre
gretly how that thei may performe thynges
that thei han hoped for to doon. Forwhy to   190
wylne schrewydnesse — that cometh peraventure of our defaute; but it is lyk a monstre and a merveyle how that, in the presente sight of God, may ben acheved and performed swiche thynges as every felonous man
hath conceyved in his thoght ayens innocentz. For whiche thynge oon of thy familiers noght unskilfully axed thus: 'Yif God
is, whennes comen wikkide thyngis? And
yif God ne is, whennes comen gode   200
thynges?' But al hadde it ben leveful that
felonous folk, that now desiren the blood and
the deeth of alle gode men and ek of al the senat,
han wilned to gon destroyen me, whom they han
seyn alwey bataylen and defenden gode men
and eek al the senat, yit hadde I nought
disservyd of the faderes (that is to seyn, of
the senatours) that they schulden wilne my
destruccioun.

"Thow remembrest wel, as I gesse, that   210
whan I wolde doon or seyn any thyng,
thow thiselve alwey present reuledest me. [And
wel thow remembrest] at the cite of Verone,
whan that the kyng, gredy of comune slaughtre,
caste hym to transporten upon al the ordre of the
senat the gilt of his real majeste, of the whiche

gilt that Albyn was accused, with how gret
sykernesse of peril to me defended I al the senat! Thow woost wel that I sey sooth, ne
I n'avawntede me nevere in preysynge   220
of myselve. For alwey whan any wyght
resceyveth precious renoun in avauntynge
hymselve of his werkes, he amenuseth the secre
of his conscience. But now thow mayst wel seen
to what eende I am comen for myn innocence;
I resceyve peyne of fals felonye for guerdoun of
verrai vertue. And what opene confessioun of
felonye hadde evere juges so accordaunt in
cruelte (*that is to seyn, as myn accusynge
hath*) that either errour of mannys wit, or   230
elles condicion of fortune, that is uncerteyn
to alle mortel folk, ne submyttede some of hem
(*that is to seyn, that it ne enclynede som juge
to have pite or compassioun*)? For althoughe I
hadde ben accused that I wolde brenne holi
houses and straungle preestis with wykkid
sweerd, or that I hadde greythed deth to alle
gode men, algates the sentence scholde han
punysshed me present, confessed or convict. But now I am remuwed fro the cite of   240
Rome almost fyve hundred thowsand paas,
I am withoute deffense dampnyd to pro-
scripcion and to the deth for the studie and
bountes that I have doon to the senat. But, O,
wel ben thei wurthy of meryte (*as who seith,
nay*), ther myghte nevere yit noon of hem ben
convicte of swiche a blame as myn is! Of whiche
trespas myne accusours sayen ful wel the
dignete; the whiche dignyte, for thei
wolden derken it with medlynge of some   250
felonye, they bare me on hande and lieden
that I hadde pollut and defouled my conscience
with sacrilegie for covetise of dignyte. And
certes thou thiselve, that art plaunted in me,
chacedest out of the sege of my corage alle
covetise of mortel thynges, ne sacrilege ne
hadde no leve to han a place in me byforn
thyne eien. For thow droppiddest every day
in myn eris and in my thought thilke
comaundement of Pictagoras, that is to   260
seyn, men schal serven to God and noght
to goddes. Ne it was noght convenient ne no
nede to taken help of the fouleste spiritz — I,

173 **apertely:** clearly
181 **Germaynes sone:** Caligula
183 **conjuracioun:** conspiracy
188 **apparailen:** prepare, contrive

223 **amenuseth:** diminishes
236 **straungle:** kill
237 **greythed:** plotted
240 **remuwed:** removed
241 **fyve . . . paas:** five hundred miles, a rhetorical exaggeration
244 **bountes:** good deeds
248 **sayen:** see
260 **Pictagoras:** Pythagoras

that thow hast ordeyned and set in swiche excellence, that thou makedest me lyk to God. And over this, the right clene secre chaumbre of myn hous (*that is to seyn, my wif*), and the companye of myne honeste freendes, and my wyves fadir, as wel holi as worthy to ben reverenced thurw his owene dedes, 270 defenden me fro alle suspecioun of swiche blame. But O malice! For they that accusen me taken of the, Philosophie, feith of so greet blame, for they trowen that I have had affinyte to malefice or enchauntement, bycause that I am replenysshid and fulfild with thy techynges, and enformed of thi maneris. And thus it suffiseth nat oonly that thi reverence ne avayle me nat, but yif that thow of thy free wil rather be blemessched with myne offencioun. 280

"But certes, to the harmes that I have, ther bytideth yit this encrees of harm, that the gessynge and the jugement of moche folk ne loken nothyng to the desertes of thynges, but oonly to the aventure of fortune; and jugen that oonly swiche thynges ben purveied of God, whiche that temporel welefulnesse commendeth. (*Glose. As thus: that yif a wyght have prosperite, he is a good man and worthy to han that prosperite; and* 290 *whoso hath adversite, he is a wikkid man, and God hath forsake hym, and he is worthy to han that adversite. This is the opinyoun of some folk.*) *Textus.* And therof cometh that good gessynge, first of alle thynge, forsaketh wrecches. Certes it greveth me to thynke ryght now the diverse sentences that the peple seith of me. And thus moche I seie, that the laste charge of contrarious fortune is this: that whan eny blame is leid upon a 300 caytif, men wenen that he hath desservyd that he suffreth. And I, that am put awey fro gode men, and despoyled of dignytes, and defouled of myn name by gessynge, have suffride torment for my gode dedes. Certes me semyth that I se the felonous covynes of wykkid men habounden in joye and in gladnesse; and I se that every lorel schapeth hym to fynde out newe fraudes for to accuse good folk; and I se that goode men [lien] overthrowen for 310

drede of my peril, and every luxurious turmentour dar doon alle felonye unpunysschyd, and ben excited therto by yiftes; and innocentz ne ben noght oonly despoiled of sikernesse, but of defense; and therfore me lyst to crie to God in this manere:

O STELLIFERI CONDITOR ORBIS. — *Metrum 5*

"O thow makere of the wheel that bereth the sterres, whiche that art festnyd to thi perdurable chayer, and turnest the hevene with a ravysschynge sweighe, and constreynest the sterres to suffren thi lawe; so that the moone somtyme, schynynge with hir fulle hornes metynge with alle the beemes of the sonne hir brothir, hideth the sterres that ben lasse; and somtyme, whan the moone pale with hir derke hornes aprocheth the sonne, leeseth 10 hir lyghtes; and that the eve sterre, Hesperus, whiche that in the first tyme of the nyght bryngeth forth hir colde arysynges, cometh eft ayen hir used cours, and is pale by the morwe at rysynge of the sonne, and is thanne clepid Lucyfer! Thow restreynest the day by schortere duellynge in the tyme of coold wynter that maketh the leeves falle. Thow devydest the swyfte tydes of the nyght, whan the hote somer is comen. Thy myghte attempreth 20 the variauntz sesouns of the yer, so that Zephirus, the debonere wynd, bryngeth ayen in the first somer sesoun the leeves that the wynd that hyghte Boreas hath reft awey in autumpne (*that is to seie, in the laste ende of somer*); and the seedes that the sterre that highte Arcturus saugh ben waxen heye cornes whan the sterre Syrius eschaufeth hem. Ther nys no thyng unbounde from his olde lawe, ne forleteth the werk of his propre estat. 30

"O thou governour, governynge alle thynges by certein ende, whi refusestow oonly to governe the werkes of men by duwe manere? Why suffrestow that slydynge Fortune turneth so grete enterchaungynges of thynges? So that anoyous peyne, that scholde duweliche punysche felons, punysscheth innocentz; and folk of wikkide maneres sitten in heie chayeres; and anoyinge folk treden, and that un-

---

277–80 **And thus . . . offencioun:** i.e., it is not just that my reverence for you does not help me; it is worse. I offend them, and thus you are done positive injury; see n.
295 **gessynge:** opinion
304 **gessynge:** (ill) opinion
306 **covynes:** companies
308 **lorel:** scoundrel

Metrum 5.1–2 **wheel . . . sterres:** the Primum Mobile
4 **ravysschynge sweighe:** powerful motion
13–14 **cometh . . . cours:** comes back again (on) her regular course or comes back against her regular course (?); see n.
21 **variauntz:** changing
27 **Arcturus:** the brightest star in Boötes
28 **Syrius:** Sirius, the Dog Star

rightfully, on the nekkes of holi men; and   40
vertu, cleer and schynynge naturely, is
hidde in derke derknesses; and the rightful man
bereth the blame and the peyne of the feloun; ne
the forswerynge ne the fraude covered and
kembd with a false colour, ne anoieth nat to
schrewes? The whiche schrewes, whan hem list
to usen hir strengthe, they rejoyssen hem to
putten undir hem the sovereyne kynges, whiche
that peple withouten nombre dreden. O
thou, what so evere thou be that knyttest   50
alle boondes of thynges, loke on thise
wrecchide erthes. We men, that ben noght a foul
partie, but a fair partie of so greet a werk, we
ben turmented in this see of fortune. Thow
governour, withdraughe and restreyne the
ravysschynge flodes, and fastne and ferme thise
erthes stable with thilke boond by whiche thou
governest the hevene that is so large."

HEC UBI CONTINUATO DOLORE DELATRAUI.
— *Prosa 5*

When I hadde with a contynuel sorwe
sobbyd or borken out thise thynges, sche, with
hir cheere pesible and nothyng amoeved with
my compleyntes, seide thus: "Whan I saugh
the," quod sche, "sorwful and wepynge, I
wiste anoon that thow were a wrecche and
exiled; but I wyste nevere how fer thyn exil
was yif thy tale ne hadde schewid it me. But
certes, al be thow fer fro thy cuntre, thou
n'art nat put out of it, but thow hast fayled   10
of thi weye and gon amys. And yif thou
hast levere for to wene that thow be put out
of thy cuntre, thanne hastow put out thyself
rather than ony other wyght hath. For no
wyght but thyselve ne myghte nevere han doon
that to the. For yif thow remembre of what
cuntre thow art born, it nys nat governed by
emperoures, ne by governement of multitude,
as weren the cuntrees of hem of Atthenes;
but o lord and o kyng, and that is God, that   20
is lord of thi cuntre, whiche that rejoisseth
hym of the duellynge of his citezeens, and nat
for to putten hem in exil; of the whiche lord
it is a sovereyn fredom to ben governed by the
brydel of hym and obeye to his justice. Hastow
foryeten thilke ryghte oolde lawe of thi citee, in
the whiche cite it es ordeyned and estab-

lysschid that what wyght that hath levere
founden therin his sete or his hous than
elleswhere, he may nat ben exiled by no   30
ryght fro that place? For whoso that is
contened inwith the palys and the clos of
thilke cite, ther nys no drede that he mai deserve to ben exiled; but who that leteth the
wil for to enhabyten there, he forleteth also
to deserve to ben citezen of thilke cite. So that
I seie that the face of this place ne moeveth
me noght so mochel as thyn owene face, ne
I ne axe nat rather the walles of thy librarye, apparayled and wrought with yvory   40
and with glas, than after the sete of thi
thought, in whiche I put noght whilom bookes,
but I putte that that maketh bokes wurthy
of prys or precyous, that is to seyn the sentence
of my bookes.

"And certeynly of thy dessertes bystowed in
comune good thow hast seyd soth, but after the
multitude of thy gode dedes thou hast seyd
fewe. And of the honestete or of the falsnesse of thynges that ben opposed ayens   50
the, thow hast remembred thynges that ben
knowen to alle folk. And of the felonyes and
fraudes of thyn accusours, it semeth the have
touched it for sothe ryghtfully and schortly, al
myghten tho same thynges betere and more
plentevously ben couth in the mouth of the
peple that knoweth al this. Thow hast eek
blamed gretly and compleyned of the wrongdede of the senat, and thow hast sorwyd
for my blame, and thow hast wepen for   60
the damage of thi renoun that is apayred;
and thi laste sorwe eschaufede ayens Fortune,
and compleyndest that guerdouns ne ben nat
eveneliche yolden to the dessertes of folk. And
in the lattre eende of thy wode muse, thow
preydest that thilke pees that governeth the
hevene schulde governe the erthe.

"But for that many [turbacions] of affeccions
han assailed the, and sorwe and ire and
wepynge todrawen the diversely, as thou   70
art now feble of thought, myghtyere remedies ne schullen noght yit touchen the. For
wyche we wol usen somdel lyghtere medicynes,

---

52 **erthes:** lands
57 **thilke boond:** the chain of love described in 2.m8
Prosa 5.2 **borken out:** barked out
3 **pesible:** peaceful

32 **palys:** palisade   **clos:** enclosure
47 **after:** i.e., in comparison to
50 **opposed:** charged
51 **remembred:** recalled
53 **semeth the have:** seems to you (that) you have
61 **apayred:** injured
62 **eschaufede:** grew hot
65 **muse:** musing
70 **todrawen the:** pull you apart

so that thilke passiouns that ben waxen hard in swellynge by perturbacions flowynge into thy thought, mowen waxen esy and softe to resceyven the strengthe of a more myghty and more egre medicyne, by an esyere touchynge.

CUM PHEBI RADIIS GRAVE CANCRI SIDUS INESTUAT. — *Metrum 6*

"Whan that the hevy sterre of the Cancre eschaufeth by the bemes of Phebus (that is to seyn, whan that Phebus the sonne is in the sygne of the Cancre), whoso yeveth thanne largely his seedes to the feeldes that refusen to resceyven hem, lat hym gon, begiled of trust that he hadde to his corn, to accornes of okes. Yif thow wolt gadere vyolettes, ne go thow nat to the purpre wode whan the feeld, chirkynge, agryseth of cold by the felnesse 10 of the wynd that hyghte Aquilon. Yif thou desirest or wolt usen grapes, ne seek thou nat with a glotonos hand to streyne and presse the stalkes of the vyne in the first somer sesoun; for Bachus, the god of wyn, hath rather yyven his yiftes to autumpne (*the lattere ende of somer*). God tokneth and assigneth the tymes, ablynge hem to hir propre offices, ne he ne suffreth nat the stowndes whiche that hymself hath devyded and constreyned to ben   20 imedled togidre. And forthy he that forleteth certein ordenaunce of doynge by overthrowynge wey, he hath no glad issue or ende of his werkes.

PRIMUM IGITUR PATERISNE ME PAUCULIS ROGACIONIBUS. — *Prosa 6*

"First wiltow suffre me to touche and assaye th'estaat of thi thought by a fewe demaundes, so that I may understande what be the manere of thi curacioun?"

"Axe me," quod I, "at thi wille what thou wolt, and I schal answere." Tho seyde sche thus: "Whethir wenestow," quod sche, "that this world be governed by foolyssche happes and fortunows, or elles wenestow that ther be inne it ony governement of resoun?"   10

"Certes," quod I, "I ne trowe nat in no manere that so certeyn thynges schulden be moeved by fortunows [folie]; but I woot wel that God, makere and maister, is governour of his werk, ne nevere nas yit day that myghte putte me out of the sothnesse of that sentence."

"So it is," quod sche, "for the same thyng songe thow a litil herebyforn, and bywayledest and byweptest, that oonly men weren put out of the cure of God; for of alle othere   20 thynges thou ne doutedest the nat that they nere governed by resoun. But owgh! I wondre gretly, certes, whi that thou art sik, syn that thow art put in so holsome a sentence. But lat us seken deppere; I conjecte that ther lakketh Y not what. But sey me this: syn that thow ne doutest noght that this world be governed by God, with whiche governayles takestow heede that it is governed?"

"Unnethes," quod I, "knowe I the sentence of thy questioun, so that I ne may   30 nat yit answeren to thy demandes."

"I nas nat desseyved," quod sche, "that ther ne faileth somwhat, by whiche the maladye of perturbacion is crept into thi thought, so as [by] the strengthe of the palys chynynge [and] open. But sey me this: remembrestow what is the ende of thynges, and whider that the entencion of alle kende tendeth?"

"I have herd tolde it somtyme," quod I,   40 "but drerynesse hath dulled my memorie."

"Certes," quod sche, "thou wost wel whennes that alle thynges bien comen and proceded?"

"I woot wel," quod I, and answerede that God is bygynnynge of al.

"And how may this be," quod sche, "that, syn thow knowest the bygynnynge of thynges, that thow ne knowest nat what is the eende of thynges? But swiche ben the customes of perturbaciouns, and this power they han,   50 that they mai moeve a man from his place (*that is to seyn, fro the stabelnesse and perfeccion of his knowynge*); but certes, thei mai nat al arrace hym, ne aliene hym in al. But I wolde that thou woldest answere to this: Remembrestow that thow art a man?"

Boece. "Whi schulde I nat remembren that?" quod I.

---

78 **egre:** bitter
Metrum 6.1–4 **Whan . . . Cancre:** i.e., in June
6–7 **lat hym gon . . . to accornes:** i.e., will have to eat acorns
10 **chirkynge:** roaring   **agryseth:** shudders
11 **Aquilon:** Aquilo, the north wind
18 **ablynge hem to:** making them fit for
22–23 **overthrowynge:** headstrong
Prosa 6.7 **Whethir wenestow:** do you think
9 **fortunows:** accidental

18 **herebyforn:** at 1.m5.31ff.
22 **owgh:** oh (exclamation)
28 **governayles:** controls
35–37 **so . . . open:** i.e., as if through a gaping (*chynynge*) hole in a fortification
54 **arrace:** uproot

Philosophie. "Maystow noght telle me thanne," quod sche, "what thyng is a man?"   60

"Axestow me nat," quod I, "whethir that I [woot wel that I] be a resonable mortel beste? I woot wel, and I confesse wel that I am it."

"Wystestow nevere yit that thow were ony othir thyng?" quod sche.

"No," quod I.

"Now woot I," quod sche, "other cause of thi maladye, and that ryght greet: thow hast left for to knowen thyselve what thou art.   70 Thurw whiche I have pleynly fownde the cause of thi maladye, or elles the entree of recoverynge of thyn hele. For-why, for thow art confunded with foryetynge of thiself, forthi sorwestow that thow art exiled [and despoyled] of thy propre goodes; and for thow ne woost what is the eende of thynges, forthy demestow that felonus and wikkide men ben myghty and weleful; and for thow hast foryeten by whiche governementz the werld is gov-   80 erned, forthy weenestow that thise muta-cions of fortunes fleten withouten gov-ernour. Thise ben grete causes, noght oonly to maladye, but certes gret causes to deth. But I thanke the auctour and the makere of hele, that nature hath nat al forleten the. I have gret noryssynges of thyn hele, and that is, the sothe sentence of governance of the world, that thou bylevest that the governynge of it nis nat subgit ne underput to the folye of thise   90 happes aventurous, but to the resoun of God. And therfore doute the nothing, for of this litel spark thine heet of liif schal shine.

"But for as moche as it is nat tyme yet of fastere remedies, and the nature of thoughtes desceyved is this, that, as ofte as they casten awey sothe opynyouns, they clothen hem in false opynyouns, of the whiche false opynyouns the derknesse of perturbacion waxeth up, that confowndeth the verray insyghte — [that]   100 derknesse schal I assaie somwhat to maken thynne and wayk by lyghte and meneliche remedies; so that, aftir that the derknesse of desceyvynge desyrynges is doon away, thow mowe knowe the schynynge of verraye light.

NUBIBUS ATRIS CONDITA. — *Metrum 7*

"The sterres, covred with blake cloudes, ne mowen yeten adoun no lyght. Yif the truble wynd that hyghte Auster, turnynge and wal-wynge the see, medleth the heete (*that is to seyn, the boylynge up fro the botme*), the wawes, that whilom weren clere as glas and lyk to the fayre bryghte dayes, withstande anon the syghtes of men by the filthe and ordure that is resolved. And the fleetynge streem, that royleth doun diversely fro heye   10 montaygnes, is areestid and resisted ofte tyme by the encountrynge of a stoon that is departed and fallen fro some roche. And forthy, yif thou wolt loken and demen soth with cleer lyght, and hoolden the weye with a ryght path, weyve thow joie, dryf fro the drede, fleme thow hope, ne lat no sorwe aproche (*that is to seyn, lat non of thise foure passiouns overcomen the or blenden the*). For cloudy and derk is thilke thoght, and bownde with bridelis,   20 where as thise thynges reignen."

Explicit Liber Primus

Incipit Liber Secundus

POSTEA PAULISPER CONTICUIT. — *Prosa 1*

Aftir this sche stynte a lytel; and after that sche hadde ygadrede by atempre stillenesse myn attencioun, she seyde thus (as who so myghte seyn thus: after thise thynges sche stynte a litil, and whan sche aperceyved by atempre stillenesse that I was ententyf to herkne hire, sche bygan to speke in this wyse): "If I," quod sche, "have undirstonden and knowen outrely the causes and the habyt of thy maladye, thow languyssest and art desfeted for desir   10 and talent of thi rather fortune. Sche (that ilke Fortune) oonly, that is chaunged, as thow feynest, to the-ward, hath perverted the cleernesse and the estat of thi corage. I undirstonde the felefolde colours and desceytes of thilke merveylous monstre Fortune and how

Metrum 7.2 **yeten:** pour, shed   **truble:** turbulent
3 **Auster:** the south wind
4 **medleth:** stirs up
10 **royleth:** rolls
16 **fleme:** put to flight
18 **passiouns:** the four Stoic affects, or crippling passions of the mind
Explicit, *etc.:* Here ends the first book. Here begins the second book.
Prosa 1.9 **habyt:** condition, nature
10 **desfeted:** wasted away
11 **rather:** earlier
15 **felefolde:** manifold

71 **pleynly:** fully
82 **fleten:** float
90 **underput:** subjected
91 **happes aventurous:** chance events
95 **fastere:** firmer, stronger
102 **meneliche:** moderate

sche useth ful flaterynge famylarite with hem that sche enforceth to bygyle, so longe, til that sche confounde with unsuffrable sorwe hem that sche hath left in despeer un- 20 purveied. And yif thou remembrest wel the kende, the maneris, and the desserte of thilke Fortune, thou shalt wel knowe that, as in hir, thow nevere ne haddest ne hast ylost any fair thyng. But, as I trowe, I schal nat greetly travailen to don the remembren on thise thynges. For thow were wont to hurtlen and despysen hir with manly woordes whan sche was blaundyssching and present, and pursuydest hir with sentences that weren 30 drawen out of myn entre (*that is to seyn, of myn enformacioun*). But no sodeyn muta- cioun ne bytideth noght withouten a manere chaungynge of corages; and so is it byfallen that thou art a litil departed fro the pees of thi thought.

"But now is tyme that thou drynke and ataste some softe and delitable thynges, so that whanne thei ben entred withynne the, it mowe maken wey to strengere drynkes of med- 40 ycines. Com now forth, therfore, the suasyoun of swetnesse rethorien, whiche that goth oonly the righte wey while sche forsaketh nat myn estatutz. And with Rethorice com forth Musice, a damoysele of our hous, that syng- eth now lightere moedes or prolacions, now hevyere. What eyleth the, man? What is it that hath cast the into moornynge and into wepynge? I trow that thou hast seyn some newe thyng and unkouth. Thou wenest that Fortune be 50 chaunged ayens the; but thow wenest wrong (*yif thou that wene*): alway tho ben hir maneres. Sche hath rather kept, as to the-ward, hir propre stablenesse in the chaungynge of hirself. Ryght swiche was sche whan sche flateryd the and desseyved the with unleful lykynges of false welefulnesse. Thou hast now knowen and ateynt the doutous or double visage of thilke blynde goddesse Fortune. Sche, that yit covereth and wympleth hir to other 60 folk, hath schewyd hir every del to the. Yif thou approvest here (*and thynkest that sche is good*), use hir maneris and pleyne the nat; and

yif thou agriesest hir false trecherie, despise and cast awey hir that pleyeth so harmfully. For sche, that is now cause of so mochel sorwe to the, sholde ben cause to the of pees and of joye. Sche hath forsaken the, forsothe, the whiche that nevere man mai ben siker that sche ne schal forsaken hym. (*Glose. But natheles some* 70 *bookes han the texte thus: forsothe sche hath forsaken the, ne ther nys no man siker that sche ne hath nat forsake.*) Holdestow thanne thilke welefulnesse precious to the, that schal passen? And is present Fortune dereworth to the, whiche that nys nat feithful for to duelle, and whan sche goth awey that sche bryngeth a wyght in sorwe? For syn she may nat ben withholden at a mannys wille, [and] sche maketh hym a wrecche whan sche de- 80 parteth fro hym, what other thyng is flyttynge Fortune but a maner schewynge of wrecchidnesse that is to comen? Ne it suffiseth nat oonly to loken on thyng that is present byforn the eien of a man; but wisdom loketh and mesureth the ende of thynges. And the same chaungynge from oon into another (*that is to seyn, fro adversite into prosperite*) maketh that the manaces of Fortune ne ben nat for to dreden, ne the flaterynges of hir to ben 90 desired. Thus, at the laste, it byhoveth the to suffren wyth evene wil in pacience al that is doon inwith the floor of Fortune (that is to seyn, in this world), syn thou hast oonys put thy nekke undir the yok of hir. For yif thow wilt writen a lawe of wendynge and of duellynge to Fortune, whiche that thow hast chosen frely to ben thi lady, artow nat wrongful in that, and mak- est Fortune wroth and aspre by thyn inpacience? And yit thow mayst nat 100 chaungen hir. Yif thou committest and betakest thi seyles to the wynd, thow schalt ben shoven, nat thider that thow woldest, but whider that the wynd schouveth the. Yif thow castest thi seedes in the feeldes, thou sholdest han in mynde that the yeres ben amonges, outherwhile plentevous and outherwhile bareyne. Thow hast bytaken thiself to the governaunce of Fortune and forthi it byhoveth the to ben obeisaunt to the maneris of thi lady. Enforcestow the 110 to aresten or withholden the swyftnesse

---

18 **enforceth**: endeavors
20–21 **unpurveied**: not provided for
27 **hurtlen**: attack
31 **entre**: entry; see n.
42 **suasyoun**: persuasion **rethorien**: rhetorical
46 **moedes**: rhythms **prolacions**: tunes
60 **wympleth hir**: covers her face with a wimple

64 **agrisest**: dread
93 **floor**: threshing floor
96 **wendynge and . . . duellynge**: going and staying
99 **aspre**: harsh
102 **betakest**: entrust
106 **amonges**: mingled, variable **outherwhile**: sometimes

and the sweighe of hir turnynge wheel? O thow fool of alle mortel foolis! Yif Fortune bygan to duelle stable, she cessede thanne to ben Fortune.

HEC CUM SUPERBA, &c. — *Metrum 1*

"Whan Fortune with a proud ryght hand hath turned hir chaungynge stowndes, sche fareth lyke the maneres of the boylynge Eurippe. (*Glosa. Eurippe is an arm of the see that ebbeth and floweth, and somtyme the streem is on o side, and somtyme on the tothir.) Textus.* She, cruel Fortune, casteth adoun kynges that whilom weren ydradd; and sche, desceyvable, enhaunceth up the humble chere of hym that is discounfited. Ne sche neither heer-   10 eth ne rekketh of wrecchide wepynges; and she is so hard that sche leygheth and scorneth the wepynges of hem, the whiche sche hath maked wepe with hir free wille. Thus sche pleyeth, and thus sche prooveth hir strengthes, and scheweth a greet wonder to alle hir servauntz yif that a wyght is seyn weleful and overthrowe in an houre.

VELLEM AUTEM PAUCA. — *Prosa 2*

"Certes I wolde pleten with the a fewe thynges, usynge the woordes of Fortune. Tak hede now thyselve, yif that sche asketh ryght: 'O thow man, wherfore makestow me gyltyf by thyne every dayes pleynynges? What wrong have I don the? What godes have I byreft the that weren thyne? Stryf or pleet with me by-forn what juge that thow wolt of the posses-sioun of rychesses or of dignytees; and yif thou maist schewen me that ever any mor-   10 tel man hath resceyved ony of tho thynges to ben hise in propre, thanne wil I graunte freely that thilke thynges weren thyne whiche that thow axest.

"Whan that nature brought the foorth out of thi modir wombe, I resceyved the nakid and nedy of alle thynges, and I norisshed the with my richesses, and was redy and ententyf thurwe my favour to sustene the — and that mak-eth the now inpacient ayens me; and I   20 envyrounde the with al the habundaunce and schynynge of alle goodes that ben in my ryght. Now it liketh me to withdrawe myn

hand. Thow hast had grace as he that hath used of foreyne goodes; thow hast no ryght to pleyne the, as though thou haddest outrely forlorn alle thy thynges. Why pleynestow thanne? I have doon the no wrong. Richesses, honours, and swiche othere thinges ben of my right. My servauntz knowen me for   30 hir lady; they comen with me, and departen whan I wende. I dar wel affermen hardely that, yif tho thynges of whiche thow pleyn-est that thou hast forlorn [hem] hadden ben thyne, thow ne haddest nat lorn hem. Schal I thanne, oonly, be defended to usen my ryght?

"Certes it is leveful to the hevene to maken clere dayes, and after that to coveren tho same dayes with dirke nyghtes. The yeer hath eek leve to apparaylen the visage of the   40 erthe, now with floures, and now with fruyt, and to confownden hem somtyme with reynes and with coldes. The see hath eek his ryght to ben somtyme calm and blaundyssch-yng with smothe watir, and somtyme to ben horrible with wawes and with tempestes. But the covetise of men, that mai nat be stawnched — schal it bynde me to ben stedfast, syn that stidfastnesse is uncouth to my maneris? Swiche is my strengthe, and this pley   50 I pleye continuely. I torne the whirlynge wheel with the turnynge sercle; I am glad to chaungen the loweste to the heyeste, and the heyeste to the loweste. Worth up yif thow wolt, so it be by this lawe, that thow ne holde nat that I do the wroong, though thow descende adown whan the resoun of my pley axeth it. Wystestow nat how Cresus, kyng of Lydyens, of whiche kyng Cirus was ful sore agast a lytil byforn — that this rewliche Cresus   60 was caught of Cirus and lad to the fyer to ben brend; but that a rayn descendede down fro hevene that rescowyde hym? And is it out of thy mynde how that Paulus, consul of Rome, whan he had taken the kyng of Percyens, weep pitously for the captivyte of the selve kyng? What other thynge bywaylen the cryinges of tragedyes but oonly the dedes of Fortune, that with an unwar strook overturneth the realmes of greet nobleye? (*Glose. Trage-*   70 *dye is to seyn a dite of a prosperite for a*

Metrum 1.3 **Euruppe:** the strait Euripus, between Euboea and Boeotia, noted for strong and variable currents
Prosa 2.1 **pleten:** dispute
12 **in propre:** as his own
21 **envyrounde:** surrounded
22–23 **in my ryght:** in my jurisdiction

25 **foreyne:** extrinsic, alien to one's self
44–45 **blaundysschyng:** gentle
54 **Worth up:** ascend (on the wheel)
60 **rewliche:** pitiful
71 **dite:** literary work

tyme, that endeth in wrecchidnesse.) Lernedest nat thow in Greek whan thow were yong, that in the entre or in the seler of Juppiter ther ben cowched two tonnes, the toon is ful of good, and the tother is ful of harm? What ryght hastow to pleyne, yif thou hast taken more plentevously of the gode side (*that is to seyn, of my richesses and prosperites*)? And what ek yif Y ne be nat al departed fro the? What eek yif my mutabilite yeveth the ryghtful cause of hope to han yit bettere thynges? Natheles dismaye the nat in thi thought; and thow that art put in the comune realme of alle, desire nat to lyven by thyn oonly propre ryght.

SI QUANTAS RAPIDIS. — Metrum 2

"Though Plente that is goddesse of rychesses hielde adoun with ful horn, and withdraweth nat hir hand, as many richesses as the see torneth upward sandes whan it is moeved with ravysshynge blastes, or elles as manye rychesses as ther schynen bryghte sterres in hevene on the sterry nyghtes; yit, for al that, mankende nolde nat cese to wepe wrecchide pleyntes. And al be it so that God resceyveth gladly hir preiers, and yyveth hem, as fool-large, moche gold, and apparayleth coveytous folk with noble or cleer honours; yit semeth hem haven igeten nothyng, but alwey hir cruel ravyne, devourynge al that they han geten, scheweth othere gapynges (that is to seyn, gapyn and desiren yit after mo rychesses). What brydles myghte withholden to any certeyn ende the disordene covetise of men, whan evere the rather that it fletith in large yiftes, the more ay brenneth in hem the thurst of havynge? Certes he that qwakynge and dredful weneth hymselven nedy, he ne lyveth nevermo ryche.

HIIS IGITUR SI PRO SE, &c. — Prosa 3

"Therfore, yif that Fortune spake with the for hirself in this manere, forsothe thow ne haddest noght what thou myghtest answere. And yif thow hast any thyng wherwith thow mayst rightfully defenden thi compleynte, it behoveth the to schewen it, and I wol yyve the space to tellen it."

"Serteynly," quod I thanne, "thise ben faire thynges and enoynted with hony swetnesse of Rethorik and Musike; and oonly whil thei ben herd thei ben delycious, but to wrecches is a deppere felyng of harm (*this is to seyn, that wrecches felen the harmes that thei suffren more grevously than the remedies or the delites of thise wordes mowen gladen or conforten hem*). So that, whanne thise thynges stynten for to soune in eris, the sorwe that es inset greveth the thought."

"Right so is it," quod sche. "For thise ne ben yit none remedies of thy maladye, but they ben a maner norisschynges of thi sorwe, yit rebel ayen thi curacioun. For whan that tyme is, I schal moeve and ajuste swiche thynges that percen hemselve depe. But natheles that thow schalt noght wilne to leten thiself a wrecche, hastow foryeten the nowmbre and the maner of thi welefulnesse? I holde me stille how that the sovereyn men of the cite token the in cure and in kepynge, whan thow were orphelyn of fadir and of modir, and were chose in affynite of pryncces of the cite; and thow bygonne rather to ben leef and deere than for to been a neyghebour, the whiche thyng is the moste precyous kende of any propinquyte or alliaunce that mai ben. Who is it that ne seide tho that thow neere right weleful, with so gret a nobleye of thi fadres-in-lawe, and with the chastete of thy wyf, and with the oportunyte and noblesse of thyne masculyn children (*that is to seyn, thy sones*)? And over al this me list to passen of comune thynges, how thow haddest in thy youthe dignytees that weren wernd to oolde men; but it deliteth me to comen now to the synguler uphepynge of thi welefulnesse. Yif any fruyt of mortel thynges mai han any weyghte or pris of welefulnesse, myghtestow evere forgeten, for any charge of harm that myghte byfalle the, remembraunce of thilke day that thow seye thi two sones maked conseileris and iladde togidre fro thyn hous under so greet assemble of senatours and under the blithnesse of peple, and whan thow saye hem set in the court in hir chayeres of dignytes? Thow, rethorien or

---

74 **entre:** entry; see Textual Notes.   **seler:** storeroom
86 **propre:** own
Metrum 2.2 **hielde:** pour
10 **yyveth:** gives
19–20 **fletith in:** flows with

Prosa 3.18 **inset:** implanted
22 **rebel:** rebellious (modifying *sorwe*)
30 **orphelyn:** orphaned
31 **chose in affynite of:** allied with (by marriage)
44 **wernd:** denied
45 **uphepynge:** culmination
55 **rethorien:** orator

pronouncere of kynges preysynges, desservedest glorie of wit and of eloquence whan thow, syttynge bytwixen thi two sones conseylers, in the place that highte Circo, fulfildest the abydynge of the multitude of peple that was sprad abouten the with so large preysynge and laude as men syngen in victories. Tho yave thow woordes to Fortune, as I trowe, (*that is to seyn, tho feffedestow Fortune with glosynge wordes and desceyvedest hir*) whan sche accoyede the and norysside the as hir owne delices. Thow bare awey of Fortune a yifte (*that is to seye, swich guerdoun*) that sche nevere yaf to prive man. Wiltow therfore leye a reknynge with Fortune? Sche hath now twynkled first upon the with a wikkid eye. If thow considere the nowmbre and the maner of thy blisses and of thy sorwes, thow mayst noght forsaken that thow nart yit blisful. For yif thou therfore wenest thiself nat weleful, for thynges that tho semeden joyeful ben passed, ther nys nat why thow sholdest wene thiself a wrecche; for thynges that semen now sory passen also. Artow now comen first, a sodeyn gest, into the schadowe or tabernacle of this lif? Or trowestow that any stedfastnesse be in mannes thynges, whan ofte a swyft hour dissolveth the same man (*that is to seyn, whan the soule departeth fro the body*)? For although that zelde is ther any feith that fortunous thynges wollen dwellen, yet natheles the laste day of a mannes lif is a maner deth to Fortune, and also to thilke that hath dwelt. And therfore what wenestow dar rekke, yif thow forleete hir in deyinge, or elles that sche, Fortune, forleete the in fleynge awey?

CUM PRIMO POLO. — *Metrum 3*

"Whan Phebus, the sonne, bygynneth to spreden his clernesse with rosene chariettes, thanne the sterre, ydymmed, paleth hir white cheeres by the flambes of the sonne that overcometh the sterre lyght. (*This to seyn, whan*

the sonne is rysen, the day-sterre waxeth pale, and leeseth hir lyght for the grete bryghtnesse of the sonne.*) Whan the wode waxeth rody of rosene floures in the fyrst somer sesoun thurw the breeth of the wynd Zephirus that waxeth warm, yif the cloudy wynd Auster blowe felliche, than goth awey the fairnesse of thornes. Ofte the see is cleer and calm without moevynge flodes, and ofte the horrible wynd Aquylon moeveth boylynge tempestes, and overwhelveth the see. Yif the forme of this world is so zeeld stable, and yif it torneth by so manye entrechaungynges, wiltow thanne trusten in the tumblenge fortunes of men? Wiltow trowen on flyttynge goodes? It is certeyn and establissched by lawe perdurable, that nothyng that is engendred nys stedfast ne stable."

TUM EGO VERA INQUAM. — *Prosa 4*

Thanne seide I thus: "O norysshe of alle vertues, thou seist ful sooth; ne I mai noght forsake the ryght swyfte cours of my prosperite (that is to seyn, that prosperite ne be comen to me wonder swyftli and sone); but this is a thyng that greetly smerteth me whan it remembreth me. For in alle adversites of fortune the moost unzeely kynde of contrarious fortune is to han ben weleful."

"But that thow," quod sche, "abyest thus the torment of thi false opynioun, that maistow nat ryghtfully blamen ne aretten to thynges. (*As who seith, for thow hast yit manye habundances of thynges.*) *Textus.* For al be it so that the ydel name of aventuros welefulnesse moeveth the now, it is leveful that thow rekne with me of how many grete thynges thow hast yit plente. And therfore yif that thilke thyng that thow haddest for moost precyous in al thy rychesse of fortune be kept to the yit by the grace of God unwemmed and undefouled, maistow thanne pleyne ryghtfully upon the mescheef of Fortune, syn thow hast yit thi beste thynges? Certes yit lyveth in good poynt thilke precyous honour of mankynde, Symacus, thi wyves fader,

---

57 **of:** i.e., for your
59 **Circo:** the Circus
59–60 **fulfildest the abydynge:** satisfied the expectation
64 **feffedestow:** you endowed
66 **accoyede:** soothed
67 **delices:** darling
70 **leye a reknynge with:** present a bill to
71 **twynkled:** winked
74 **forsaken:** deny
85 **zelde:** seldom
88–89 **and . . . dwelt:** i.e., even to such fortune as remains stable
89–90 **what . . . rekke:** why should you care (**dar** = *thar*, need); see n.

*Metrum 3.*8 **rody:** red
11 **Auster:** the south wind
13 **of thornes:** from the hawthorn bushes
15 **Aquylon:** the north wind
16 **overwhelveth:** sets tumbling
Prosa 4.1 **norysshe:** nurse
8 **unzeely:** unhappy
12 **aretten:** impute
15 **aventuros:** accidental

whiche that is a man maked al of sapience and
of vertu, the whiche man thow woldest byen
redyly with the pris of thyn owene lif. He
bywayleth the wronges that men don to   30
the, and nat for hymself; for he lyveth in
sikernesse of anye sentences put ayens hym.
And yit lyveth thi wyf, that is atempre of wyt
and passynge othere wommen in clennesse of
chastete; and, for I wol closen schortly hir
bountes, sche is lyk to hir fadir. I telle the wel
that sche lyveth, loth of this lyf, and kepeth
to the oonly hir goost, and is al maat and overcomen by wepynge and sorwe for desir of
the; in the whiche thyng oonly I moot   40
graunten that thi welefulnesse is amenused.
What schal I seyn eek of thi two sones con-
seylours, of whiche, as of children of hir age,
ther shyneth the liknesse of the wit of hir fadir
or of hir eldefader! And syn the sovereyne
cure of al mortel folk is to saven hir owene
lyves, O how weleful artow, if thow knowe
thy goodes! For yit ben ther thynges dwelled
to the-ward that no man douteth that they
ne be more derworthe to the than thyn   50
owene lif. And forthy drye thi teeris, for
yit nys nat every fortune al hateful to the-
ward, ne overgreet tempest hath nat yit fallen
upon the, whan that thyne ancres clyven faste,
that neither wolen suffren the counfort of this
tyme present ne the hope of tyme comyng to
passen ne to faylen."

"And I preie," quod I, "that faste mote thei
halden; for, whiles that thei halden, how so
evere that thynges been, I shal wel fleetyn   60
forth and escapyn: but thou mayst wel seen
how grete apparailes and array that me lakketh, that ben passed awey fro me."

"I have somwhat avaunced and forthred
the," quod sche, "yif that thow anoye nat, or
forthynke nat of al thy fortune. (*As who seith,
I have somwhat conforted the, so that thou
tempeste the nat thus with al thy fortune, syn
thow hast yit thy beste thynges.*) But I mai
nat suffren thi delices, that pleynest the so   70
wepynge and angwysschous for that ther
lakketh somwhat to thy welefulnesse. For what

man is so sad or of so parfite welefulnesse, that
he ne stryveth and pleyneth on some halfe
ayen the qualite of his estat? Forwhy ful anguysschous thing is the condicioun of mannes
goodes; for eyther it cometh nat altogidre to
a wyght, or elles it ne last nat perpetuel. For
som man hath gret rychesse, but he is
aschamed of his ungentil lynage; and som   80
man is renomyd of noblesse of kynrede, but
he is enclosed in so greet angwyssche of nede
of thynges that hym were levere that he were
unknowe; and som man haboundeth bothe in
rychesse and noblesse, but yit he bewayleth his
chaste lyf, for he ne hath no wyf; and som man
is wel and zelily ymaried, but he hath no children, and norissheth his rychesses to the eyres
of straunge folk; and som man is gladed
with children, but he wepeth ful sory for   90
the trespas of his sone or of his doughter.
And for this ther ne accordeth no wyght lyghtly
to the condicioun of his fortune; for alwey to
every man ther is in somwhat that, unassayed,
he ne woot nat, or elles he dredeth that he hath
assaied. And adde this also, that every weleful
man hath a ful delicaat feelynge; so that, but
yif alle thynges byfalle at his owene wil, for
he is inpacient or is nat used to have noon
adversite, anoon he is throwen adoun for   100
every litil thyng. And ful litel thynges ben
tho that withdrawen the somme or the perfeccioun of blisfulnesse fro hem that been most
fortunat. How manye men trowestow wolde
demen hemself to ben almoste in hevene, yif
thei myghten atayne to the leste partye of the
remenaunt of thi fortune? This same place
that thow clepest exil is contre to hem that
enhabiten here, and forthi nothyng [is]
wrecchide but whan thou wenest it. (*As   110
who seith, thow thiself ne no wyght elles
nis a wrecche but whanne he weneth hymself
a wrechche by reputacion of his corage.*) And
ayenward, alle fortune is blisful to a man by
the aggreablete or by the egalyte of hym that
suffreth it. What man is that that is so weleful
that nolde chaunge his estat whan he hath lost
pacience? The swetnesse of mannes welefulnesse is spraynd with many bitternesses;
the whiche welefulnesse although it seme   120

35–36 **closen schortly hir bountes:** summarize her goodness
45 **eldefader:** grandfather
54 **clyven:** cleave, cling
55–57 **that . . . faylen:** that will allow neither present comfort
nor future hope to pass away or fail
67 **so that:** provided that
70 **delices:** self-indulgence

87 **zelily:** happily
88 **eyres:** heirs
94 **is in:** inheres; see n.   **unassayed:** untried
113 **by reputacion of his corage:** by dwelling on it in his heart
115 **egalyte:** equanimity
119 **spraynd:** sprinkled

swete and joieful to hym that useth it, yit
mai it nat ben withholden that it ne goth awey
whan it wole. Thanne is it wele seene how
wrecchid is the blisfulnesse of mortel thynges,
that neyther it dureth perpetuel with hem that
every fortune resceyven agreablely or egaly, ne
it deliteth nat in al to hem that ben angwyssous.

"O ye mortel folk, what seeke ye thanne blisfulnesse out of yourself whiche that is put
in yowrself? Errour and folie confound-   130
eth yow. I schal schewe the schortly the
poynt of soverayn blisfulnesse. Is there anythyng more precyous to the than thiself? Thow
wolt answere, 'nay.' Thanne, yif it so be that
thow art myghty over thyself (*that is to seyn,
by tranquillite of thi soule*), than hastow thyng
in thi powere that thow noldest nevere leesen,
ne Fortune may nat bynymen it the. And that
thow mayst knowe that blisfulnesse ne mai
nat standen in thynges that ben fortunous   140
and temporel, now undirstond and gadere
it togidre thus: yif blisfulnesse be the soverayn good of nature that lyveth by resoun,
ne thilke thyng nys nat soverayn good that
may ben taken awey in any wise (for more
worthy thyng and more dygne is thilke thyng
that mai nat ben take awey); than scheweth
it wel that the unstablenesse of fortune may
nat atayne to resceyven verray blisfulnesse.
And yit more over, what man that this   150
towmblynge welefulnesse ledeth, eyther
he woot that it is chaungeable, or elles he woot
it nat. And yif he woot it nat, what blisful
fortune may ther ben in the blyndnesse of ignoraunce? And yif he woot that it is chaungeable, he mot alwey ben adrad that he ne lese
that thyng that he ne douteth nat but that he
may leesen it (*as who seith he mot bien alwey
agast lest he lese that he woot wel he may
lese it*); for whiche the contynuel drede that   160
he hath ne suffreth hym nat to ben weleful — or elles yif he lese it he weneth to ben
despised and forleten. Certes eek that is a
ful litel good that is born with evene herte
whan it es lost (*that is to seyn, that men do no
more force of the lost than of the havynge*).
And for as moche as thow thiself art he to
whom it hath be [sewed] and proved by ful

many demonstracyons, as I woot wele that
the soules of men ne mowen nat deyen in   170
no wyse; and ek syn it es cleer and certeyn
that fortunous welefulnesse endeth by the deth
of the body; it mai nat be douted that, yif that
deth may take awey blisfulnesse, that al the
kynde of mortel thyng ne descendeth into
wrecchidnesse by the ende of the deth. And
syn we knowe wel that many a man hath
sought the fruyt of blysfulnesse, nat oonly with
suffrynge of deeth, but eek with suffrynge
of peynes and tormentz, how myghte   180
thanne this present lif make men blisful,
syn that whanne thilke selve lif es ended it
ne maketh folk no wrechches?

QUISQUIS VOLET PERHENNEM CAUTUS, &c.
— *Metrum 4*

"What maner man stable and war, that wol
fownden hym a perdurable seete, and ne wol
noght ben cast doun with the lowde blastes of
the wynd Eurus, and wole despise the see
manasynge with flodes; lat hym eschuwen to
bilde on the cop of the mountaigne, or in the
moyste sandes; for the felle wynd Auster tormenteth the cop of the mountaigne with alle
hise strengthes, and the lause sandes refusen to beren the hevy weyghte. And   10
forthi, yif thow wolt fleen the perilous
aventure (*that is to seyn, of the world*) have
mynde certeynly to fycchen thin hous of a
myrie sete in a low stoon. For although the
wynd troublynge the see thondre with overthrowynges, thou, that art put in quiete and
weleful by strengthe of thi palys, schalt leden
a cler age, scornynge the woodnesses and the
ires of the eyr.

SET CUM RACIONUM IAM IN TE, &c. — *Prosa 5*

"But for as mochel as the norisschynges of
my resouns descenden now into the, I trowe it
were tyme to usen a litel strengere medicynes.
Now undirstand heere; al were it so that the
yiftes of Fortune ne were noght brutel ne transitorie, what is ther in hem that mai be thyn
in any tyme, or elles that it nys fowl, yif that

---

122 **withholden:** kept
138 **bynymen it the:** take it away from you
159–60 **that he woot wel he may lese it:** what he well knows
he can lose
168 **sewed:** planted; see textual note.

Metrum **4.2 fownden hym:** establish for himself
4 **Eurus:** the southeast wind
7 **Auster:** the south wind
9 **lause:** loose
13 **fycchen:** fix firmly
15–16 **overthrowynges:** upsurges
Prosa **5.3 medicynes:** see 1.pr5.68n. and 3.pr1.14ff.
5 **brutel:** brittle

it be considered and lookyd parfitely? Richesses ben they preciouse by the nature of hemself, or elles by the nature of the? What is most worth of rychesses? Is it nat gold or myght of moneye assembled? Certes thilke gold and thilke moneye schyneth and yeveth bettre renoun to hem that dispenden it than to thilke folk that mokeren it; for avaryce maketh alwey mokereres to ben hated, and largesse maketh folk cleer of renoun. For, syn that swiche thyng as is transferred fro o man to an othir ne may nat duellen with no man, certes thanne is thilke moneye precyous whan it is translated into other folk and stynteth to ben had by usage of large yyvynge of hym that hath yeven it. And also yif al the moneye that is overal in the world were gadryd toward o man, it scholde make alle othere men to be nedy as of that. And certes a voys al hool (that is to seyn, withouten amenusynge) fulfilleth togydre the herynge of moche folk. But certes your rychesses ne mowen noght passen unto moche folk withouten amenusynge; and whan they ben apassed, nedes they maken hem pore that forgoon tho rychesses. O streyte and nedy clepe I this richesse, syn that many folk ne mai nat han it al, ne al mai it nat comen to o man withoute povert of alle othere folk. And the schynynge of gemmes (that I clepe precyous stones) draweth it nat the eighen of folk to hem-ward (*that is to seyn, for the beautes*)? But certes, yif ther were beaute or bountee in the schynynge of stones, thilke clernesse is of the stones hemselve, and nat of men; for whiche I wondre gretly that men merveylen on swiche thynges. Forwhi what thyng is it that, yif it wanteth moevynge and joynture of soule and body, that by right myghte semen a fair creature to hym that hath a soule of resoun? For al be it so that gemmes drawen to hemself a litel of the laste beaute of the world thurw the entente of hir creatour and thurw the distinccioun of hemself, yit, for as mochel as thei ben put under yowr excellence, thei ne han nat desserved by no way that ye schulde merveylen on hem. And the beaute of feeldes, deliteth it nat mochel unto yow?"

Boece. "Why schulde it nat deliten us, syn that it is a [fayr] porcioun of the ryght fair werk (that is to seyn, of this worlde)? And right so ben we gladed somtyme of the face of the see whan it es cleer; and also merveylen we on the hevene, and on the sterres, and on the sonne, and on the moone."

Philosophie. "Aperteneth," quod sche, "any of thilke thynges to the? Why darstow glorifye the in the shynynge of any swiche thynges? Artow distyngwed and embelysed by the spryngynge floures of the first somer sesoun, or swelleth thi plente in fruites of somer? Whi artow ravyssched with idel joies? Why enbracest thow straunge goodes as they weren thyne? Fortune ne schal nevere maken that swiche thynges ben thyne that nature of thynges hath maked foreyne fro the. Soth is that, withouten doute, the fruites of the erthe owen to be to the noryssynge of beestis; and yif thow wilt fulfille thyn nede after that it suffiseth to nature, thanne is it no nede that thow seke aftir the superfluyte of fortune. For [with] fewe thynges and with ful litel thynges nature halt hir apayed; and yif thow wolt achoken the fulfillynge of nature with superfluytees, certes thilke thynges that thow wolt thresten or powren into nature schulle ben unjoyeful to the, or elles anoyous. Wenestow eek that it be a fair thyng to schyne with diverse clothynge? Of whiche clothynge yif the beaute be aggreable to loken uppon, I wol merveylen on the nature of the matiere of thilke clothes, or elles on the werkman that wroughte hem. But also a long route of meyne, maketh that a blisful man? The whiche servantz yif thei ben vicyous of condyciouns, it is a gret charge and a destruccioun to the hous, and a gret enemy to the lord hymself; and yif they ben gode men, how schal straunge or foreyne goodnesse ben put in the nowmbre of thi richesse? So that by alle thise forseide thynges it es cleerly schewed, that nevere oon of thilke thynges that thou acountedest for thyne goodes nas nat thi good.

"In the whiche thynges yif ther be no beaute to ben desired, why scholdestow ben sory

---

11 **Is it nat:** i.e., is it
15 **mokeren:** hoard
21 **translated into:** transferred to
22 **yyvynge:** giving
27–28 **fulfilleth togydre:** fills at once
31 **apassed:** passed away
32–33 **that forgoon tho rychesses:** whom riches desert
49 **laste:** most removed (from some source of value), basest

63–64 **Aperteneth . . . to the?:** do any of these things belong to you?
66 **distyngwed:** distinguished
67 **first somer sesoun:** spring; see n.
70 **straunge:** external
73 **foreyne fro:** exterior to
81 **achoken:** overstuff
84 **anoyous:** harmful
90–91 **long route of meyne:** great train of servants
96 **straunge or foreyne goodnesse:** the goodness of others

yif thou leese hem, or whi scholdestow rejoysen
the for to holden hem? For yif thei ben faire
of hir owene kynde, what aperteneth that to
the? For al so wel scholde they han ben fayre
by hemselve, though thei were departed fro
alle thyne rychesses. Forwhy fair ne precyous
were thei nat for that thei comen among
thi rychesses; but for they semeden fair   110
and precyous, therfore thou haddest levere
rekne hem among thi rychesses. But what
desirestow of Fortune with so greet a noyse
and with so greet [affraie]? I trowe thou seeke
to dryve awey nede with habundaunce of
thynges, but certes it turneth to you al in the
contrarie. Forwhy certes it nedeth of ful manye
helpynges to kepyn the diversite of precious
ostelementz; and sooth it es that of many
thynges han they nede, that many thynges   120
han; and ayenward of litel nedeth hem
that mesuren hir fille after the nede of kynde,
and nat after the oultrage of covetyse.

   "Is it thanne so, that ye men ne han no propre
good iset in yow, for whiche ye mooten seke
outward your goodes in foreyne and subgit
thynges? So is thanne the condicion of thynges
turned up-so-doun, that a man, that is a devyne
beest be meryte of his resoun, thynketh
that hymself nys neyther fair ne noble but   130
yif it be thurw possessioun of ostelementz
that ne han no soules. And certes alle othere
thynges ben apayed of hir owene beautes, but ye
men that ben semlable to God by yowr
resonable thought, desiren to apparailen your
excellent kynde of the loweste thynges; ne ye
undirstanden nat how greet a wrong ye don to
your creatour. For he wolde that mankynde
were moost wurthy and noble of any
othere erthly thynges, and ye thresten   140
adoun yowre dignytes bynethen the loweste thynges. For yif that al the good of every
thyng be more precyous than is thilke thyng
whos that the good es, syn ye demen that the
fowleste thynges ben your goodes, thanne
submitten ye and putten yourselven undir the
fouleste thynges by your estimacioun; and certes
this betydeth nat withouten your desert. For
certes swiche is the condicioun of alle mankynde, that oonly when it hath knowynge   150
of itself, thanne passeth it in noblesse alle
othere thynges; and whan it forletith the
knowynge of itself, thanne is it brought

bynethen alle beestes. Forwhi alle othere lyvynge beestes han of kynde to knowe nat hemself; but whan that men leeten the knowynge of hemself, it cometh hem of vice. But
how broode scheweth the errour and the folie of
yow men, that wenen that anythyng mai
ben apparailed with straunge apparaile-   160
mentz! But forsothe that mai nat be done.
For yif a wyght schyneth with thynges that
ben put to hym (*as thus, yif thilke thynges
schynen with whiche a man is aparayled*),
certes thilke thynges ben comended and preysed
with whiche he is apparayled; but natheles, the
thyng that is covered and wrapped under that
duelleth in his felthe.

   "And I denye that thilke thyng be good
that anoyeth hym that hath it. Gabbe I of   170
this? Thow wolt sey 'nay.' Sertes rychesses
han anoyed ful ofte hem that han tho rychesses,
syn that every wikkide schrewe — and for his
wikkidnesse the more gredy aftir othir folkes
rychesses, wher so evere it be in ony place, be
it gold or precyous stones — [weneth] hym
oonly most worthy that hath hem. Thow thanne,
that so bysy dredest now the swerd and the
spere, yif thou haddest entred in the path
of this lif a voyde weyfarynge man, thanne   180
woldestow syngen byfor the theef. (*As
who seith, a pore man that bereth no rychesse
on hym by the weie may boldely synge byforn
theves, for he hath nat whereof to be robbed.*)
O precyous and ryght cleer is the blisfulnesse of
mortel rychesses, that, whan thow hast geten it,
thanne hastow lorn thi sekernesse!

FELIX NIMIUM PRIOR ETAS. — *Metrum 5*

   "Blisful was the firste age of men. They
heelden hem apayed with the metes that the
trewe feeldes broughten forth. They ne destroyeden ne desseyvede nat hemself with outrage. They weren wont lyghtly to slaken hir
hungir at even with accornes of ookes. They
ne coude nat medle the yift of Bachus to the
cleer hony (*that is to seyn, they coude make
no pyement or clarree*), ne they coude nat
medle the bryghte fleezes of the contre of   10
Seryens with the venym of Tyrie (*this

119 **ostelementz:** household goods
123 **oultrage:** excess

160–61 **apparailementz:** adornments
168 **duelleth in his felthe:** is still vile
170 **anoyeth:** harms   **Gabbe:** speak idly, lie
173–74 **and for his wikkidnesse the more gredy:** and insofar
as he is wicked he is the greedier
178 **bysy:** worried
180 **voyde:** i.e., of both money and worries
Metrum 5.9 **pyement, clarree:** spiced, sweetened wines
11 **Seryens:** Syrians; see n.   **venym:** dye (literally, venom)
Tyrie: Tyre

to seyn, thei coude nat deyen white fleezes
of Syrien contre with the blood of a maner
schellefyssche that men fynden in Tirie, with
whiche blood men deyen purpre). They
slepen holsome slepes upon the gras, and
dronken of the rennynge watres, and layen
undir the schadwes of the heye pyn-trees. Ne
no gest ne straunger ne karf yit the heye
see with oores or with schipes; ne thei ne   20
hadden seyn yit none newe stroondes to
leden marchandise into diverse contrees. Tho
weren the cruele claryouns ful hust and ful
stille. Ne blood ischad by egre hate ne hadde
nat deyed yit armures. For wherto or which
woodnesse of enemys wolde first moeven
armes whan thei seyen cruele wowndes, ne
none medes be of blood ischad? I wolde that
our tymes sholde torne ayen to the oolde
maneris! But the anguysschous love of   30
havynge brenneth in folk more cruely than
the fyer of the mountaigne of Ethna that ay
brenneth. Allas! What was he that first dalf
up the gobbettes or the weyghtes of gold covered undir erthe and the precyous stones that
wolden han be hydd? He dalf up precious
periles. (*That is to seyn, that he that hem
firsst up dalf, he dalf up a precious peril;
for-why, for the preciousnesse of swich
thyng hath many man ben in peril.*)   40

QUID AUTEM DE DIGNITATIBUS. — *Prosa 6*

"But what schal I seye of dignytes and of
powers, the whiche ye men, that neither
knowen verray dignyte ne verray powere,
areysen hem as heyghe as the hevene? The
whiche dignytees and poweres yif thei comen
to any wikkid man, thei doon as greet damages and destrucciouns as doothe the flaumbe
of the mountaigne Ethna whan the flaumbe
walweth up, ne no deluge ne doth so cruele
harmes. Certes the remembreth wel, as I   10
trowe, that thilke dignyte that men clepyn
the imperie of consulers, the whiche that
whilom was begynnynge of fredom, yowr eldres
coveyteden to han don away that dignyte for
the pride of the consulers. And ryght for the
same pride yowr eldres byforn that tyme hadden doon away out of the cite of Rome the

kynges name (*that is to seyn, thei nolden han
no lengere no kyng*).

"But now, if so be that dignytees and pow-   20
eris ben yyven to gode men, the whiche
thyng is ful zelde, what aggreable thynges is
ther in tho dignytees or powers but oonly the
goodnesse of folk that usen hem? And therfore it is thus that honour ne cometh nat to
vertu for cause of dygnite, but, ayenward, honour cometh to dignyte for cause of vertu. But
whiche is thilke your derworthe power that is
so cleer and so requerable? O, ye erthliche
bestes, considere ye nat over whiche thyng   30
that it semeth that ye han power? Now yif
thou saye a mows among othere mysz that chalanged to hymself-ward ryght and power over
alle othere mysz, how gret scorn woldestow han
of it! (*Glosa.* So fareth it by men [that the
wikkid men have power over the wikkid men;
that is to seye], the body hath power over the
body.) For yif thou looke wel upon the body of
a wyght, what thyng schaltow fynde more
freele than is mankynde; the whiche men   40
ful ofte ben slayn with bytynge of smale
flyes, or elles with the entrynge of crepynge
wormes into the pryvetees of mannes body?
But wher schal men fynden any man that mai
exercen or haunten any ryght upon another
man, but oonly on his body, or elles upon
thynges that ben lowere than the body, the
whiche I clepe fortunous possessiouns? Maystow
evere have any comaundement over a free
corage? Maystowe remuwen fro the estat   50
of his propre reste a thought that is
clyvynge togidre in hymself by stedfast resoun?
As whilom a tyraunt wende to confownde a fre
man of corage, and wende to constreyne hym by
torment to maken hym discoveren and accusen
folk that wisten of a conjuracioun (*which I clepe
a confederacye*) that was cast ayens this tyraunt;
but this fre man boot of his owene tonge, and
caste it in the visage of thilk wode tyraunt.
So that the tormentz that this tyraunt   60
wende to han maked matere of cruelte, this
wise man maked it matere of vertu. But what
thing is it that a man may doon to an other man,
that he ne may resceyven the same thyng of

---

23 **claryouns**: bugles   **hust**: hushed, quiet
24 **egre**: bitter
28 **none medes be of**: nothing is gained from
33 **dalf**: delved, dug
Prosa 6.12 **imperie of consulers**: rule of the consuls; see n.

28 **thilke . . . power**: this precious power of yours
29 **requerable**: desirable
32 **saye . . . mysz**: saw a mouse among other mice
32–33 **chalanged**: claimed
45 **exercen or haunten**: exercise or practice habitually
50 **remuwen**: remove
52 **clyvynge**: cleaving
58 **boot of**: bit off

other folk in hymself? (*Or thus: what may a man don to folk, that folk ne may don hym the same?*) I have herd told of Busyrides, that was wont to sleen his gestes that herberweden in his hous, and he was slayn hymself of Ercules that was his gest. Regulus hadde 70 taken in bataile manye men of Affryke and cast hem into feteres, but sone after he most yyve hise handes to ben bownde with the cheynes of hem that he hadde whilom overcomen. Wenestow thanne that he be myghty that hath no power to doon a thyng that othere ne mai doon in hym that he doth in othere?

"And yit moreover, yif it so were that thise dygnytes or poweris hadden any 80 propre or naturel goodnesse in hemself, nevere nolde they comen to schrewes. For contrarious thynges ne ben nat wont to ben ifelaschiped togydre. Nature refuseth that contrarious thynges ben ijoygned. And so, as I am in certeyn that ryght wykkyd folk han dignytees ofte tyme, thanne scheweth it wel that dignytees and poweres ne ben nat gode of hir owene kynde, syn that they suffren hemselve to cleven or joynen hem to 90 schrewes. And certes the same thyng mai I most digneliche juggen and seyn of alle the yiftes of Fortune that most plentevously comen to schrewes. Of the whiche yiftes I trowe that it oughte ben considered, that no man douteth that he ne is strong in whom he seeth strengthe; and in whom that swyftnesse is, sooth it is that he is swyft; also musyke maketh mucisyens, and phisyk maketh phisicyeens, and rethoryke, rethoriens. Forwhy the nature of every 100 thyng maketh his proprete, ne it is nat entremedlyd with the effectz of contrarious thynges, and as of wil it chaseth out thynges that to it ben contrarie. But certes rychesse mai nat restreyne avarice unstaunched; ne power ne maketh nat a man myghty over hymselve, whiche that vicyous lustes holden destreyned with cheynes that ne mowen nat ben unbownden. And dignytees that ben yyven to schrewide folk nat oonly ne maketh hem 110 nat digne, but it scheweth rather al opynly that they been unworthy and undigne. And whi is it thus? Certes for ye han joie to clepen thynges with false names, that beren hem al in the contrarie; the whiche names ben ful [ethe] reproved by the effect of the same thynges; so that thise ilke rychesses ne oughten nat by ryghte to ben cleped rychesses, ne swyche power ne aughte nat ben clepyd power, ne swiche dignyte ne aughte nat ben clepyd dignyte. 120 And at the laste, I may conclude the same thyng of alle the yyftes of Fortune, in whiche ther nys nothyng to ben desired, ne that hath in hymselve naturel bownte, as it es ful wel yseene. For neither thei ne joygnen hem nat alwey to gode men, ne maken hem alwey gode to whom they been ijoyned.

NOVIMUS QUANTAS DEDERIT. — *Metrum 6*

"We han wel knowen how many grete harmes and destrucciouns weren idoon by the emperour Nero. He leet brennen the cite of Rome, and made sleen the senatours; and he cruel whilom sloughe his brothir, and he was maked moyst with the blood of his modir (that is to seyn, he leet sleen and slitten the body of his modir to seen wher he was conceyved); and he lookede on every halve uppon hir cold deed body, ne no teer ne wette his face, 10 but he was so hardherted that he myghte ben domesman or juge of hir dede beaute. And natheles yit governed this Nero by septre alle the peples that Phebus, the sonne, may seen, comynge fro his uttreste arysynge til he hide his bemes undir the wawes. (*That is to seyn he governede al the peples by ceptre imperial that the sonne goth aboute from est to west.*) And ek this Nero governyde by ceptre alle the peples that ben undir the colde sterres 20 that highten the septemtryones. (*This is to seyn he governede alle the peples that ben under the partye of the north.*) And eek Nero governede alle the peples that the vyolent wynd Nothus scorklith, and baketh the brennynge sandes by his drye heete (*that is to seyn,*

---

67 **Busyrides:** Busirus; see n.
70 **Regulus:** M. Atilius Regulus; see n.
75–78 Do you then consider him mighty who has power only to do that thing to another which the other may also do to him in return?
100 **rethoriens:** rhetoricians, orators
101 **maketh his proprete:** establishes what is proper to it
102 **entremedlyd:** mixed
105 **unstaunched:** insatiable

111 **digne:** worthy
114 **that:** *thynges* is the antecedent
115 **ethe:** easily
116 **reproved:** proven false
Metrum 6.12 **domesman:** judge
15 **uttreste:** farthest (in the east)
21 **septemtryones:** the seven stars of the Little Dipper; hence, line 23, *the north*
25 **Nothus:** Notus, the south wind   **scorklith:** scorches

al the peples in the south). But yit ne myghte nat al his heie power torne the woodnesse of this wikkid Nero? Allas! It is grevous fortune as ofte as wikkid sweerd is joyned to   30 cruel venym (*that is to seyn, venymows cruelte to lordschipe*)."

TUM EGO SCIS INQUAM. — *Prosa* 7

Thanne seyde I thus: "Thow woost wel thiselve that the covetise of mortel thynges ne hadde nevere lordschipe of me, but I have wel desired matere of thynges to done (as who seith, I desirede to have matiere of governaunce over comunalites), for vertue stille sholde nat elden (*that is to seyn, that list that or he waxe oold, his vertu, that lay now ful stille, ne schulde nat perysshe unexercised in governaunce of comune, for whiche men   10 myghten speken or wryten of his gode governement*)."

Philosophie. "For sothe," quod sche, "and that is [o] thyng that mai drawen to governaunce swiche hertes as ben worthy and noble of hir nature, but natheles it may nat drawen or tollen swiche hertes as ben ibrought to the ful feccioun of vertue; that is to seyn, covetise of glorie and renoun to han wel adminystred the comune thynges, or doon gode desertes   20 to profyt of the comune. For see now and considere how litel and how voyde of alle prys is thylk glorye. Certeyn thyng es, as thou hast leerned by the demonstracioun of astronomye, that al the envyrounynge of the erthe aboute ne halt but the resoun of a prykke at regard of the gretnesse of hevene; that is to seyn that, yif ther were maked comparysoun of the erthe to the gretnesse of hevene, men wolde juggen in al that the erthe ne heelde   30 no space. Of the whiche litel regioun of this world, the ferthe partye is enhabited with lyvynge beestes that we knowen, as thou hast thyselve leerned by Tholome that proveth it. And yif thow haddest withdrawen and abated in thy thought fro thilke ferthe partie as moche space as the see and the mareys contene and overgoon, and as moche space as the regioun of drowghte overstreccheth (*that is to seyn, sandes and desertes*), wel unnethe   40

sholde ther duellen a ryght streyte place to the habitacioun of men. And ye thanne, that ben envyrouned and closed withynne the leeste prykke of thilke prykke, thynken ye to manyfesten or publisschen your renoun and doon yowr name for to be born forth? But yowr glorye that is so narwe and so streyt ithrungen into so litel bowndes, how mochel conteneth it in largesse and in greet doynge? And also set this therto: that manye a nacioun, diverse   50 of tonge and of maneris and ek of resoun of hir lyvynge, ben enhabited in the cloos of thilke lytel habitacle; to the whiche nacyons, what for difficulte of weyes, and what for diversite of langages, and what for defaute of unusage [of] entrecomunynge of marchandise, nat oonly the names of synguler men ne may nat strecchen, but eek the fame of citees ne may nat strecchen. At the laste, certes, in the tyme of Marcus Tulyus, as hymselve   60 writ in his book, that the renoun of the comune of Rome ne hadde nat yit passid ne clomben over the montaigne that highte Caucasus; and yit was thilke tyme Rome wel waxen, and greetly redouted of the Parthes and eek of the othere folk enhabitynge aboute. Seestow nat thanne how streyte and how compressid is thilke glorie that ye travailen aboute to schewe and to multeplye? May thanne the glorie of a synguler Romeyn strecchen thider   70 as the fame of the name of Rome may nat clymben ne passen? And ek seestow nat that the maneris of diverse folk and ek hir lawes ben discordaunt among hemselve, so that thilke thyng that som men juggen worthy of preysynge, other folk juggen that it is worthy of torment? And therof comyth it that, though a man delyte hym in preysynge of his renoun, he ne mai nat in no wyse bryngen forthe ne spreden his name to many manere peples.   80 And therfore every maner man aughte to ben apayed of his glorie that is publysschid among his owene neyghebours; and thilke noble renoun schal ben restreyned withynne the boundes of o manere folk.

41 **streyte:** restricted, narrow
43 **envyrouned:** circumscribed
47 **streyt ithrungen:** tightly compressed
51–52 **resoun of hir lyvynge:** their way of life
52 **cloos:** enclosure
53 **habitacle:** dwelling place
56 **unusage:** disuse **entrecomunynge of marchandise:** commerce
60 **Marcus Tulyus:** Cicero
62 **comune:** republic
65 **redouted of:** feared by

Prosa 7.6 **stille:** silent, inactive
7 **elden:** grow old **that list that:** who desired that
16 **tollen:** attract, lure
26–27 **at regard of:** with respect to
34 **Tholome:** Ptolemy
37 **mareys:** marshes (i.e., watery places)

"But how many a man, that was ful noble in his tyme, hath the wrecchid and nedy foryetynge of writeris put out of mynde and doon awey; al be it so that, certes, thilke wrytynges profiten litel, the whiche writynges long 90 and dirk eelde doth awey, bothe hem and ek hir auctours! But yow men semeth to geten yow a perdurablete, whan ye thynken that in tyme comynge your fame schal lasten. But natheles yif thow wolt maken comparysoun to the endles spaces of eternyte, what thyng hastow by whiche thow mayst rejoisen the of long lastynge of thi name? For yif ther were makyd comparysoun of the abydynge of a moment to ten thowsand wynter, for as mochel as 100 bothe tho spaces ben endyd, [yit] hath the moment som porcioun of it, although it litel be. But natheles thilke selve nowmbre of yeeris, and eek as many yeris as therto mai be multiplyed, ne mai nat certes be comparysoned to the perdurablete that is endlees; for of thinges that han ende may ben maked comparysoun, but of thynges that ben withouten ende to thynges that han ende may be makid no comparysoun. And forthi is it that, although renome, of as 110 longe tyme as evere the list to thynken, were thought to the regard of eternyte, that is unstaunchable and infynyt, it ne sholde nat only semen litel, but pleynliche ryght noght.

"But ye men, certes, ne konne doon no thyng aryght, but yif it be for the audience of peple and for idel rumours; and ye forsaken the grete worthynesse of conscience and of vertu, and ye seeken yowr gerdouns of the smale wordes of straunge folk. Have now here and 120 undirstand, in the lyghtnesse of swiche pryde and veyne glorye, how a man scornede festyvaly and myriely swich vanyte. Whilom ther was a man that hadde [assaillede] with stryvynge wordes another man, the whiche, nat for usage of verray vertu but for proud veyn glorie, had taken upon hym falsly the name of a philosophre. This rather man that I spak of thoughte he wolde assaie where he, thilke, were a philosophre or no; that is to seyn, yif that 130 he wolde han suffride lyghtly in pacience the wronges that weren doon unto hym. This feynede philosophre took pacience a litel while; and when he hadde resceyved wordes of

outrage, he, as in stryvynge ayen and rejoysynge of hymself, seide at the laste ryght thus: 'undirstondistow nat that I am a philosophre?' The tother man answerede ayen ful bytyngely and seyde: 'I hadde wel undirstonden it yif thou haddest holde thi tonge stille.'   140

"But what is it to thise noble worthy men (for, certes, of swych folk speke I) that seken glorie with vertue? What is it?" quod sche. "What atteyneth fame to swiche folk, whan the body is resolved by the deeth at the laste? For if it so be that men dyen in all (that is to seyen, body and soule), the whiche thing our reson defendeth us to byleeven, thanne is ther no glorie in no wyse; for what schulde thilke glorie ben, whan he, of whom thilke glorie 150 is seyd to be, nys ryght naught in no wise? And yif the soule, whiche that hath in itself science of gode werkes, unbownden fro the prysone of the erthe, weendeth frely to the hevene, despiseth it nat thanne al erthly ocupacioun; and [usynge] hevene rejoyseth that it is exempt fro alle erthly thynges? (As who seith, thanne rekketh the soule of no glorye of renoun of this world.)

QUICUMQUE SOLAM MENTE. — *Metrum 7*

"Whoso that with overthrowynge thought oonly seketh glorie of fame, and weneth that it be sovereyn good, lat hym looke upon the brode schewynge contrees of the hevene, and upon the streyte sete of this erthe; and he schal be asschamed of the encres of his name, that mai nat fulfille the litel compas of the erthe. O, what coveyten proude folk to lyften up hir nekkes on idel in the dedly yok of this world? For although that renoun ysprad, 10 passynge to ferne peples, goth by diverse tonges; and although that greet houses or kynredes shynen with cleer titles of honours; yit natheles deth despiseth al heye glorie of fame, and deth wrappeth togidre the heyghe heved and the lowe, and maketh egal and evene the heygheste to the loweste. Where wonen now the bones of trewe Fabricius?

92 **geten**: beget
93 **perdurablete**: immortality
110 **renome**: renown
120 **Have now here**: i.e., listen now

135 **stryvynge ayen**: opposition (to the charge)
145 **resolved**: dissolved
153 **science of gode werkes**: i.e., conscience, the ability to know moral worth
154 **weendeth**: goes
156 **usynge**: enjoying
Metrum 7.1 **overthrowynge**: headlong
4 **brode schewynge**: wide open
6 **encres**: increase, spreading
16 **egal**: equal
18 **Fabricius**: hero of the war with Pyrrhus

What is now Brutus or stierne Catoun? The
thynne fame yit lastynge of here idel names   20
is marked with a fewe lettres. But althoughe that we han knowen the fayre wordes
of the fames of hem, it is nat yyven to knowen
hem that ben dede and consumpt. Liggeth
thanne stille, al outrely unknowable, ne fame
ne maketh yow nat knowe. And yif ye wene to
lyve the lengere for wynd of yowr mortel name
whan o cruel day schal ravyssche yow, than is
the seconde deth duellynge unto yow."
(*Glose. The first deeth he clepeth here de-*   30
partynge of the body and the soule, and
the seconde deth he clepeth as here the stynt-
ynge of the renoun of fame.)

SET NE ME INEXORABILE. — *Prosa 8*

"But for as mochel as thow schalt nat
wenen," quod sche, "that I bere an untretable
batayle ayens Fortune, yit somtyme it byfalleth
that sche desceyvable desserveth to han ryght
good thank of men. And that is whan sche hirself opneth, and whan sche discovereth hir
frownt and scheweth hir maneris. Peraventure
yit undirstandestow nat that I schal seie. It is
a wonder that I desire to telle, and forthi
unnethe may I unplyten my sentence with   10
wordes. For I deme that contrarious Fortune profiteth more to men than Fortune debonayre. For alwey, whan Fortune semeth debonayre, thanne sche lieth, falsly byhetynge the
hope of welefulnesse; but forsothe contraryous
Fortune is alwey sothfast, whan sche scheweth
hirself unstable thurw hir chaungynge. The
amyable Fortune desceyveth folk; the contrarie
Fortune techeth. The amyable Fortune
byndeth with the beaute of false goodes   20
the hertes of folk that usen hem: the contrarye Fortune unbyndeth hem by the knowynge of freel welefulnesse. The amyable Fortune maystow seen alwey wyndy and flowynge,
and evere mysknowynge of hirself; the contrarie Fortune is atempre and restreyned and
wys thurw exercise of hir adversite. At the
laste, amyable Fortune with hir flaterynges

draweth myswandrynge men fro the sovereyne good; the contrarious Fortune ledeth   30
ofte folk ayen to sothfast goodes, and
haleth hem ayen as with an hook. Wenestow
thanne that thow aughtest to leeten this a litel
thyng, that this aspre and horrible Fortune
hath discovered to the the thoughtes of thi
trewe freendes? Forwhy this ilke Fortune hath
departed and uncovered to the bothe the certein visages and eek the doutous visages of thi
felawes. Whan she departed awey fro the,
she took awey hir freendes and lefte the   40
thyne freendes. Now whanne thow were
ryche and weleful, as the semede, with how
mochel woldestow han bought the fulle knowynge of thys (*that is to seyn, the knowynge of*
thyne verray freendes)? Now pleyne the nat
thanne of rychesse ylorn, syn thow hast
fownden the moste precyous kynde of rychesses, that is to seyn, thi verray freendes.

QUOD MUNDUS STABILI FIDE. — *Metrum 8*

"That the world with stable feyth varieth
accordable chaungynges; that the contrarious
qualites of elementz holden among hemself
allyaunce perdurable; that Phebus, the sonne,
with his goldene chariet bryngeth forth the
rosene day; that the moone hath comaundement over the nyghtes, whiche nyghtes Es-
perus, the eve-sterre, hath brought; that the
see, gredy to flowen, constreyneth with a
certein eende his floodes, so that it is nat   10
leveful to strecche his brode termes or
bowndes upon the erthes (that is to seyn, to
coveren al the erthe) — al this accordaunce
[and] ordenaunce of thynges is bounde with
love, that governeth erthe and see, and hath also
comandement to the hevene. And yif this love
slakede the bridelis, alle thynges that now loven
hem togidres wolden make batayle contynuely,
and stryven to fordo the fassoun of this
world, the which they now leden in   20
accordable feith by fayre moevynges. This
love halt togidres peples joyned with an holy
boond, and knytteth sacrement of mariages of
chaste loves; and love enditeth lawes to trewe
felawes. O weleful were mankynde, yif thilke

---

19 **Brutus:** identity uncertain; see n.   **Catoun:** Cato the Censor,
M. Porcius Cato, 234–149 B.C.
24 **consumpt:** consumed
Prosa 8.2–3 **untretable batayle:** uncompromising hostility
6–7 **discovereth hir frownt:** uncovers her face
10 **unplyten:** explain
15 **forsothe:** in fact
24 **wyndy:** variable
25 **mysknowynge:** ignorant

29 **myswandrynge:** erring
32 **haleth:** pulls
33 **leeten:** allow, consider
36 **Forwhy:** for
Metrum 8.2 **accordable:** harmonious
19 **fassoun:** fashion; i.e., fabric, structure

love that governeth hevene governede yowr corages."

Explicit Liber Secundus

Incipit Liber Tertius

IAM CANTUM ILLA, &c. — *Prosa 1*

By this sche hadde ended hir song, whan the swetnesse of here dite hadde thurw-perced me, that was desyrous of herknynge, and I astoned hadde yit streyghte myn eres (*that is to seyn, to herkne the bet what sche wolde seye*). So that a litel herafter I seide thus: "O thow that art sovereyne confort of angwyssous corages, so thow hast remounted and norysshed me with the weyghte of thi sentences and with de- lyt of thy syngynge; so that I trowe nat 10 nowe that I be unparygal to the strokes of Fortune (as who seith, I dar wel now suffren alle the assautes of Fortune and wel defende me fro hir). And tho remedies whiche that thou seydest herbyforn that weren ryght scharpe, nat oonly that I ne am nat agrisen of hem now, but I, desiros of herynge, axe gretly to heren tho remedies."

Thanne seyde sche thus: "That feeled I ful wel," quod sche, "whan that thow en- 20 tentyf and stille ravysschedest my wordes, and I abood til that thou haddest swich habite of thi thought as thou hast now, or elles til that I myself hadde maked to the the same habite, whiche that is a more verray thyng. And certes the remenant of thynges that ben yet to seie ben swiche that first whan men tasten hem they ben bytynge; but whan they ben resceyved withynne a wyght, thanne ben thei swete. But for thou seyst that thow art so desyrous 30 to herkne hem, with how greet brennynge woldestow glowen, yif thow wistest whider I wol leden the!"

"Whider is that?" quod I.

"To thilke verraye welefulnesse," quod sche, "of whiche thyn herte dremeth; but forasmoche as thi syghte is ocupyed and destourbed by imagynacioun of erthly thynges, thow mayst nat yit seen thilke selve welefulnesse."

"Do," quod I, "and schewe me what is 40 thilke verray welefulnesse, I preie the, withoute taryinge."

"That wol I gladly do," quod sche, "for the cause of the. But I wol first marken the by woordes, and I wol enforcen me to enforme the, thilke false cause of blisfulnesse that thou more knowest; so that whanne thow hast fully by- hoolden thilke false goodes and torned thin eighen to the tother syde, thow mowe knowe the cleernesse of verray blisful- 50 nesse.

QUI SERERE INGENUUM. — *Metrum 1*

"Whoso wole sowe a feld plentevous, let hym first delyvren it of thornes, and kerve asondir with his hook the bussches and the feern, so that the corn may comen hevy of erys and of greynes. Hony is the more swete, if mouthes han first tasted savours that ben wykke. The sterres schynen more aggreablely whan the wynd Nothus leteth his plowngy blastes; and aftir that Lucifer, the day-sterre, hath chased awey the dirke nyght, the day the 10 fairere ledeth the rosene hors (*of the sonne*). And ryght so thow, byhooldyng ferst the false goodes, bygyn to withdrawe thy nekke fro the yok (*of erthely affeccions*); and afterward the verray goodes schullen entren into thy corage."

TUM DEFIXO PAULULUM. — *Prosa 2*

Tho fastnede sche a litel the syghte of hir eyen, and withdrowghe hir ryght as it were into the streyte seete of here thought, and bygan to speke ryght thus: "Alle the cures," quod sche, "of mortel folk, whiche that travailen hem in many manere studies, gon certes by diverse weyes; but natheles thei enforcen hem alle to comyn oonly to oon ende of blisfulnesse. And blisfulnesse is swiche a good, that whoso that hath geten it, he ne may over that 10 nothyng more desire. And this thyng for- sothe is the soverayn good that conteneth in hymself alle maner goodes; to the whiche goode if ther fayled any thyng, it myghte nat ben sovereyn good, for thanne wer ther som good

---

Explicit, *etc.:* Here ends the second book. Here begins the third book.
Prosa 1.4 **streyghte:** stretched, strained
8 **remounted:** lifted back up
11 **unparygal:** unequal
15 **herbyforn:** at 1.pr5.70ff. (see n. to 1.pr5.68ff.)
20–21 **ententyf:** attentive
22 **habite:** disposition

44 **marken the:** designate for you (the *cause,* line 46)
Metrum 1.8 **Nothus:** Notus, the south wind   **plowngy:** rainy, stormy
Prosa 2.1 **fastnede:** i.e., narrowed
4 **cures:** pursuits
7 **enforcen hem:** strive

out of thilke sovereyn good, that myghte ben
desired. Now is it cleer and certeyne thanne,
that blisfulnesse is a parfyt estat by the congregacioun of alle goodes; the whiche blisful-
nesse, as I have seyd, alle mortel folk en-   20
forcen hem to geten by diverse weyes.
Forwhy the covetise of verray good is naturely
iplauntyd in the hertes of men, but the myswandrynge errour mysledeth hem into false
goodes. Of the whiche men, some of hem
wenen that sovereyn good be to lyven withoute
nede of any thyng, and travaylen hem to ben
habundaunt of rychesses. And some othere
men demen that sovereyn good be for to be
ryght digne of reverence, and enforcen   30
hem to ben reverenced among hir neygh-
bours by the honours that thei han igeten. And
some folk ther ben that holden that ryght heye
power be sovereyn good, and enforcen hem for
to reignen or elles to joygnen hem to hem that
reignen. And it semeth to some other folk, that
noblesse of renoun be the sovereyn good, and
hasten hem to geten hem gloryouse name by the
artz of werre or of pees. And many folk
mesuren and gessen that the sovereyne   40
good be joye and gladnesse, and wenen
that it be ryght blisful thyng to plowngen hem
in voluptuous delyt. And ther ben folk that
entrechaungen the causes and the endes of
thyse forseyde goodes, as they that desiren
rychesses to han power and delitz, or elles they
desiren power for to have moneye or for cause
of renoun. In thise thynges and in swiche other
thynges is torned al the entencioun of desyrynges and werkes of men; as thus: 50
noblesse and favour of peple, whiche that
yyveth to men, as it semeth hem, a maner
cleernesse of renoun; and wyf and children,
that men desiren for cause of delyt and myry-
nesse. But forsothe freendes ne schulde nat ben
rekned among the goodes of fortune, but of
vertu, for it is a ful hooly maner thyng; alle
thise othere thinges forsothe ben taken for
cause of power or elles for cause of delyt.
Certes now am I redy to referren the   60
goodes of the body to thise forseide thynges
aboven; for it semeth that strengthe and gretnesse of body yyven power and worthynesse,
and that beaute and swyftnesse yyven noblesse

and glorie of renoun; and heele of body semeth
yyven delyt. In alle thise thynges it semeth
oonly that blisfulnesse is desyred; forwhy thilk
thing that every man desireth moost over alle
thynges he demeth that it be the sovereyn
good; but I have diffyned that blisfulnesse   70
is the sovereyn good; for whiche every
wyght demeth that thilke estat that he desireth
over alle thynges, that it be blisfulnesse.
  "Now hastow thanne byforn thyne eien almest al the purposede forme of the welefulnesse of mankynde: that is to seyn rychesses,
honours, power, glorie, and delitz. The whiche
delit oonly considered Epicurus, and juggid
and establissyde that delyt is the soverayn
good, for as moche as alle othere thynges,   80
as hym thoughte, byrefte awey joye and
myrthe from the herte. But I retorne ayen to
the studies of men, of whiche men the corage
alwey reherceth and seketh the sovereyne good,
al be it so that it be with a dyrkyd memorie;
but he not by whiche path, ryght as a dronke
man not nat by whiche path he may retourne
hom to his hous. Semeth it thanne that folk
foleyen and erren, that enforcen hem to
have nede of nothyng? Certes ther nys   90
noon other thyng that mai so wel performe
blisfulnesse, as an estat plentevous of alle godes,
that ne hath nede of noon other thyng, but
that it is suffisant of hymself unto hymself.
And foleyen swiche folk, thanne, that wenen
that thilk thyng that is ryght good, that it be
eek ryght worthy of honour and of reverence?
Certes, nay. For that thyng nis neither foul ne
worthy to ben despysed that wel neyghe al
the entencioun of mortel folk [travayleth]   100
for to geten it. And power, aughte nat that
ek to ben rekned amonge goodes? What elles?
For it nys nat to wene that thilke thyng that is
most worthy of alle thynges be feble and
withoute strengthe. And cleernesse of renoun,
aughte that to ben despysed? Certes ther may no
man forsake, that alle thyng that is right
excellent and noble, that it ne semeth to ben
ryght cleer and renomed. For certes it
nedeth nat to saie that blisfulnesse be   110
[n'angwyssous] ne drery, ne subgit to
grevaunces ne to sorwes; syn that in ryght litele
thynges folk seken to haven and to usen that may

delyten hem. Certes thise ben the thinges that men wolen and desiren to geten, and for this cause desiren they rychesses, dignytes, reignes, glorie, and delices; for therby wenen they to han suffysaunce, honour, power, renoun, and gladnesse. Thanne is it good that men seken thus, by so manye diverse studies; in whiche desir it mai lyghtly be schewyd how greet is the strengthe of nature. For how so that men han diverse sentences and discordynge, algates men accorden alle in lovynge the eende of good.

120

QUANTAS RERUM FLECTAT. — *Metrum 2*

"It liketh me to schewe by subtil soong, with slakke and delytable sown of strenges, how that Nature, myghty, enclyneth and flytteth the governementz of thynges, and by whiche lawes sche, purveiable, kepith the grete world; and how sche, byndynge, restreyneth alle thynges by a boond that may nat be unbownde. Al be it so that the lyouns of the contre of Pene beren the fayre chaynes, and taken metes of the handes of folk that yeven it hem, and dreden hir stourdy [maistre] of whiche thei ben wont to suffre betynges; yif that hir horrible mouthes ben bybled (that is to seyn, of beestes devoured), hir corage of tyme passed, that hath ben idel and rested, repeireth ayen, and thei roren grevously, and remembren on hir nature, and slaken hir nekkes from hir cheynes unbownde; and hir mayster fyrst, totorn with blody tooth, assaieth the wode wratthes of hem (this to seyn, thei freten hir maister). And the janglynge brid that syngeth on the heghe braunches (that is to seyn, in the wode), and after is enclosed in a streyte cage, althoughe that the pleyinge bysynes of men yeveth [hym] honyed drynkes and large metes with swete studye, yit natheles yif thilke bryd skippynge out of hir streyte cage seith the agreables schadwes of the wodes, sche defouleth with hir feet hir metes ischad, and seketh mornynge oonly the wode, and twytereth desyrynge the wode with hir swete voys. The yerde of a tree, that is haled adoun by

10

20

30

myghty strengthe, boweth redily the crop adown; but yif that the hand of hym that it bente leet it goon ageyn, anoon the crop loketh upryght to hevene. The sonne, Phebus, that falleth at even in the westrene wawes, retorneth ayen eftsones his cart, by a pryve path, there as it is wont t'aryse. Alle thynges seken ayen to hir propre cours, and alle thynges rejoysen hem of hir retornynge ayen to hir nature. Ne noon ordenaunce is bytaken to thynges, but that that hath joyned the endynge to the bygynnynge, and hath maked the cours of itself stable (that it chaunge nat from his propre kynde).

40

VOS QUOQUE TERRENA ANIMALIA. — *Prosa 3*

"Certes also ye men, that ben erthliche beestes, dremen alwey your bygynnynge, althoughe it be with a thynne ymaginacioun; and by a maner thought, al be it nat clerly ne parfitely, ye loken from afer to thilke verray fyn of blisfulnesse. And therfore naturel entencioun ledeth yow to thilke verray good, but many maner errours mystorneth yow therfro. Considere now yif that by thilke thynges by whiche a man weneth to geten hym blisfulnesse, yif that he mai comen to thilk ende that he weneth to come by nature. For yif that moneye, or honours, or thise othere forseyde thynges, brynge to men swiche a thyng that no good ne fayle hem ne semeth faile, certes thanne wol I graunte that they ben maked blisful by thilke thynges that thei han geten. But yif so be that thilke thynges ne mowen nat performen that they byheten, and that there be defaute of manye goodis, scheweth it nat thanne clerly that false beute of blysfulnesse is knowen and ataynt in thilke thynges? First and forward thow thiself, that haddest haboundances of rychesses nat longe agoon, I aske the yif that, in the habowndance of alle thilke rychesses, thow were nevere angwysous ne sory in thy corage of any wrong or grevance that bytydde the on any side?"

10

20

"Certes," quod I, "it ne remembreth me nat that evere I was so fre of my thought that I ne was alwey in angwyse of somwhat."

30

"And was nat that," quod sche, "for that the lakkide somwhat that thow noldest nat han

---

122 **how so that:** no matter how
Metrum 2.3 **flytteth:** moves, steers
8 **Pene:** Carthage
11 **stourdy:** harsh, cruel
13 **bybled:** be-bled, bloodied
17 **slaken:** loosen
29 **ischad:** scattered
30 **mornynge:** mourning
32 **yerde:** trunk   **haled:** pulled

33 **crop:** top
42 **bytaken:** entrusted

lakkid, or elles thou haddest that thow noldest nat han had?"

"Ryght so is it," quod I.

"Than desiredest thow the presence of the toon and the absence of the tothir?"

"I graunte wel," quod I.   40

"Forsothe," quod sche, "thanne nedeth ther somwhat that every man desireth?"

"Yee, ther nedeth," quod I.

"Certes," quod sche, "and he that hath lak or nede of aught nys nat in every wey suffisant to hymself?"

"No," quod I.

"And thow," quod sche, "in al the plente of thy richesses haddest thilke lakke of suffi-saunce?"   50

"What elles?" quod I.

"Thanne mai nat richesses maken that a man nys nedy, ne that he be suffisaunt to hymself; and yit that was it that thei byhighten, as it semeth. And eek certes I trow that this be gretly to considere, that moneye ne hath nat in his owene kynde that it ne mai ben bynomen of hem that han it, maugre hem."

"I byknowe it wel," quod I.

"Whi sholdestow nat byknowen it,"   60 quod sche, "whan every day the strengere folk bynymen it fro the feblere maugre hem? For whennes comen elles alle thise [forense] compleyntes or quereles of pledynges but for that men axen ayen hir moneye that hath ben bynomen hem by force or by gyle, and alwey maugre hem?"

"Right so is it," quod I.

"Than," quod sche, "hath a man nede to seken hym foreyne help by whiche he may   70 defenden his moneye?"

"Who mai seie nay?" quod I.

"Certes," quod sche, "and hym nedide noon help yif he ne hadde no moneye that he myghte leese."

"That is douteles," quod I.

"Than is this thyng torned into the con-trarie," quod sche; "for rychesses, that men wenen scholde maken suffisaunce, they maken a man rather have nede of foreyne   80 help. Whiche is the maner or the gyse," quod sche, "that rychesse mai dryve awey

nede? Riche folk, mai they neyther han hungir ne thurst? Thise riche men, may they fele no cold on hir lymes in wynter? But thow wolt answeren that ryche men han inoghe wherwith thei mai staunchen hir hungir, and slaken hir thurst, and don awey cold. In this wise mai nede be conforted by richesses, but certes nede ne mai nat al outrely be doon awey;   90 for thoughe this nede that is alwey gapynge and gredy, be fulfild with richesses, and axe any thyng, yit duelleth thanne a nede that myghte be fulfild. I holde me stille and telle nat how that litel thyng suffiseth to nature; but certes to avarice inowghe ne suffiseth nothyng. For syn that rychesse ne mai nat al doon awey nede, but richesses maken nede, what mai it thanne be that ye wenen that richesses mowen yyven yow suffisaunce?   100

QUAMVIS FLUENTE DIVES. — *Metrum 3*

"Al weere it so that a riche coveytous man hadde a ryver or a goter fletynge al of gold, yit sholde it nevere staunchen his covetise; and thoughe he hadde his nekke charged with pre-cyous stones of the Rede See, and thoughe he do ere his feeldes plentevous with an hundred oxen, nevere ne schal his bytynge bysynesse forleeten hym whil he lyveth, ne the lyghte richesses ne schal nat beren hym companye whan he is deed.   10

SET DIGNITATES. — *Prosa 4*

"But dignytees, to whom thei ben comen, make they hym honourable and reverent? Han thei nat so gret strengthe that thei mai putten vertus in the hertes of folk that usen the lord-schipes of hem, or elles may they don awey the vices? Certes thei ben nat wont to don awey wikkidnesse, but thei ben wont rather to schewen wykkydnesse. And therof cometh it that Y have right gret disdayn that dig-nytes ben yyven ofte to wikkide men. For   10 which thyng Catullus clepid a consul of Rome that hyghte Nonyus 'postum' or 'boch' (*as who seith, he clepid hym a congregacioun of vices in his brest, as a postum is ful of cor-rupcioun*), al were this Nonyus set in chayere of dygnite. Sestow nat thanne how grete

---

Prosa 3.57–58 **bynomen of:** taken from
59 **byknowe:** acknowledge
62 **bynymen:** take
63 **forense:** legal
64 **quereles of pledynges:** suits
70 **foreyne:** outside

Metrum 3.2 **goter:** watercourse
6 **do ere:** have plowed
Prosa 4.2–3 **Han thei nat:** have they
9 **disdayn:** anger
12 **boch:** ulcer

vylenye dignytes don to wikkide men? Certes unworthynesse of wikkide men schulde ben the lesse isene if thei neere renomed of none honours. Certes thou thiself ne myghtest [20] nat ben broght, with as many perils as thow myghtest suffren, that thow woldest beren the magistrat with Decorat (*that is to seyn, that for no peril that myghte byfallen the by offence of the kyng Theodorik, thou noldest nat be felawe in governaunce with Decorat*), whan thow seye that he hadde wikkide corage of a likerous schrewe and of an accusour. Ne I ne mai nat for swiche honours juggen hem worthy of reverence that I deme and holde [30] unworthy to han thilke same honours. Now yif thow seie a man that were fulfild of wysdom, certes thou ne myghtest nat deme that he were unworthy to the honour or elles to the wisdom of whiche he is fulfild?"

"No," quod I.

"Certes dignytees," quod sche, "aperteignen properly to vertu, and vertu transporteth dignyte anoon to thilke man to whiche sche hirself is conjoigned. And for as moche as [40] honours of peple ne mai nat maken folk digne of honour, it is wel seyn cleerly that thei ne han no propre beaute of dignyte. And yet men aughten taken more heede in this. For yif a wykkyd wyght be in so mochel the fowlere and the more outcast that he is despysed of moost folk, so as dignyte ne mai nat maken schrewes worthy of no reverence, the whiche schrewes dignyte scheweth to moche folk; than maketh dignyte schrewes rather so [50] much more despised than preysed, and forsothe nat unpunyssched (that is for to seyn that schrewes revengen hem ayenward uppon dignytes), for thei yelden ayen to dignytees as greet gerdoun, whan they byspotten and defoulen dignytes with hir vylenye. And for as mochel as thou now knowe that thilke verray reverence ne mai nat comen by thise schadwy transitorie dignytes, undirstond now thus: yif that a man hadde used and had manye [60] maner dignytees of consules, and weere comen peraventure among straunge nacions, scholde thilke honour maken hym worschipful and redouted of straunge folk? Certes yif that honour of peple were a natureel yifte to dignytes, it ne myghte nevere cesen nowhere

amonges no maner folk to don his office; right as fyer in every contre ne stynteth nat to eschaufen and to ben hoot. But for as mochel as for to be holden honurable or [70] reverent ne cometh nat to folk of hir propre strengthe of nature, but oonly of the false opynyoun of folk (that is to seyn, that weenen that dignytees maken folk digne of honour), anoon therfore, whan that thei comen there as folk ne knowen nat thilke dignytees, hir honours vanysschen away, and that anoon. But that is amonges straunge folk, maystow seyn. Ne amonges hem ther thei weren born, ne duren nat thilke dignytes alwey? Certes the [80] dignyte of the provostrye of Rome was whilom a greet power; now nys it no thyng but an idel name, and the rente of the senatorie a greet charge; and yif a wyght whilom hadde the office to taken heede to the vitayles of the peple, as of corn and othere thynges, he was holden amonges grete; but what thyng is now more outcast than thilke provostrye? And, as I have seyd a litel herebyforn, that thilke thyng that hath no propre beute of hymself [90] resceyveth somtyme prys and schynynge, and somtyme leeseth it, by the opinyoun of usaunces. Now yif that dignytes thanne ne mowen nat make folk digne of reverence, and if that dignytees waxen foule of hir wil by the filthe of schrewes, and yif dignytees leesen hir schynynge by chaungynge of tymes, and yif thei waxen fowle by estimacion of peple, what is it that they han in hemself of beaute that oughte ben desired? (*As who seith noon;* [100] *thanne ne mowen they yeven no beute of dignyte to noone othere.*)

QUAMVIS SE TIRIO. — *Metrum 4*

"Al be it so that the proude Nero, with al his wode luxure, kembde hym and apparayled hym with faire purpres of Tyrie and with white peerles, algates yit throf he haatful to alle folk (*this is to seyn that, al was he byhated of alle folk, yit this wikkide Nero hadde gret lord-schipe*), and yaf whilom to the reverentz sena-tours the unworschipful seetis of dignytees. (*Unworschipful seetes he clepeth here, for that*

---

81 **provostrye:** a civil office; see n.
83 **rente:** salary; see n.
89 **herebyforn:** at 40–43, 69–77 above
92–93 **by the opinyoun of usaunces:** according to current opinion; see n.
Metrum 4.2 **luxure:** self-indulgence
3 **Tyrie:** Tyre

24–25 **by offence of:** by offending
28 **accusour:** informer

Nero, that was so wikkide, yaf tho dig-   10
nytees.) Who wolde thanne resonably
wenen that blisfulnesse were in swiche honours
as ben yyven by vycious schrewes?

AN VERO REGNA. — *Prosa 5*

"But regnes, and familiarites of kynges, mai
thei maken a man to ben myghti? How elles,
whan hir blisfulnesse dureth perpetuely? But
certes the olde age of tyme passed, and ek the
present tyme now, is ful of ensaumples how
that kynges han chaungyd into wrecchidnesse
out of hir welefulnesse. O, a noble thyng and
a cleer thyng is power, that is nat fownden
myghty to kepe itself! And yif that power
of remes be auctour and makere of blisful-   10
nesse, yif thilke power lakketh on any syde,
amenuseth it nat thilke blisfulnesse and bryngeth in wrecchidnesse? But yit, al be it so that
the remes of mankynde strecchen broode, yit
moot ther nede ben moche folk over whiche
that every kyng ne hath no lordschipe ne
comaundement. And certes uppon thilke syde
that power fayleth, whiche that maketh folk blisful, ryght on that same syde noun-power
entreth undirnethe, that maketh hem   20
wrecches. In this manere thanne moten
kynges han more porcioun of wrecchidnesse
than of welefulnesse. A tyraunt, that was kyng
of Sysile, that hadde assayed the peril of his
estat, schewede by simylitude the dredes of
remes by gastnesse of a swerd that heng over
the heved of his familyer. What thyng is
thanne this power, that mai nat done awey the
bytynges of bysynesse, ne eschewe the
prykkes of drede? And certes yit wolde   30
thei lyven in sykernesse, but thei may nat,
and yit they glorifien hem in hir power. Holdestow thanne that thilke man be mighty, that
thow seest that he wolde doon that he may nat
done? And holdestow thanne hym a myghti
man, that hath envyrowned his sydes with men
of armes or sergeantz, and dredeth more hem
that he maketh agast thanne thei dreden hym,
and that is put in the handes of hise servauntz for he scholde seme myghty? But of   40
familiers or servantz of kynges, what

Prosa 5.1 **familiarites of:** association with
10 **remes:** realms, ruling
19 **noun-power:** lack of power, impotence
23 **A tyraunt:** Dionysius of Syracuse
24 **Sysile:** Sicily
26 **gastnesse:** terror
27 **familyer:** associate

scholde I telle the any thyng, syn that I myself
have schewyd the that rewmes hemself ben
ful of greet feblesse? The whiche famylieres,
certes, the real power of kynges, in hool estat
and in estaat abated, ful ofte throweth adoun.
Nero constreynede Senek, his familyer and his
mayster, to chesen on what deeth he wolde
deye. Antonyus comaundede that knyghtes
slowen with here swerdes Papynian (*his*   50
famylier) [whiche] that had ben long
tyme ful myghty amonges hem of the court.
And yet certes thei wolden bothe han renounced hir power; of whiche two Senek enforcede hym to yeven to Nero his richesses, and
also to han gon into solitarie exil. But whan the
grete weyghte (*that is to seyn, of lordes power*
or of fortune) draweth hem that schullen falle,
neither of hem ne myghte don that he
wolde. What thyng is thanne thilke powere,   60
that though men han it, yit thei ben agast;
and whanne thow woldest han it, thou nart nat
siker; and yif thou woldest forleeten it, thow
mayst nat eschuen it? But whethir swiche men
ben freendes at nede, as ben [consyled] by fortune and nat be vertu? Certes swiche folk as
weleful fortune maketh frendes, contraryous
fortune maketh hem enemys. And what pestilence is more myghty for to anoye a wyght
than a famylier enemy?   70

QUI SE VOLET ESSE POTENTEM. — *Metrum 5*

"Whoso wol ben myghti he moot daunten his
cruel corages, ne putte nat his nekke, overcomen, undir the foule reynes of leccherie. For
al be it so that thi lordschipe strecche so fer
that the contre of Ynde quaketh at thy comaundementz or at thi lawes, and that the laste
ile in the see that highte Tyle be thral to the,
yit yif thou maist nat putten awey thi foule
dirke desires, and dryven out fro the
wrecchide compleyntes, certes it nys no   10
power that thow hast.

GLORIA VERO QUAM FALLAX. — *Prosa 6*

"But glorie, how deceyvable and how foul is
it ofte! For which thyng nat unskilfully a tragedien (*that is to seyn, a makere of dytees that*
highten tragedies) cride and seide: "O glorie,
glorie," quod he, "thow nart nothyng elles to

---

70 **famylier enemy:** enemy in one's own household
Metrum 5.6–7 **the laste ile . . . Tyle:** ultima Thule, an island
thought to be beyond Britain
Prosa 6.2–3 **a tragedien:** Euripides; see n.

thousandes of folk but a greet swellere of eres!"
For manye han had ful greet renoun by the
false opinyoun of the peple, and what thyng
mai ben thought foulere than swiche preysynge? For thilke folk that ben preysed   10
falsly, they mote nedes han schame of hire
preysynges. And yif that folk han geten hem
thonk or preysynge by here dissertes, what
thyng hath thilke pris echid or encresed to the
conscience of wise folk, that mesuren hir good,
nat by the rumour of the peple, but by the
sothfastnesse of conscience? And yif it seme a
fair thyng a man to han encreced and sprad his
name, thanne folweth it that it is demed to
ben a foul thyng yif it ne be yspradde and   20
encreced. But, as I seide a litil herebyforn,
that syn ther moot nedes ben many folk to
whiche folk the renoun of [o] man ne mai nat
comen, it byfalleth that he that thow wenest be
glorious and renomed semeth in the nexte
partie of the erthes to ben withouten glorie and
withouten renoun. And certes amonges thise
thynges I ne trowe nat that the pris and the
grace of the peple nys neyther worthi to
ben remembred, ne cometh of wys juge-   30
ment, ne is ferme perdurably.

"But now of this name of gentilesse, what
man is it that ne may wele seen how veyn and
how flyttynge a thyng it es? For yif the name
of gentilesse be referred to renoun and cleernesse of lynage, thanne is gentil name but a
foreyne thyng (*that is to seyn, to hem that glo-
ryfien hem of hir lynage.*) For it semeth that
gentilesse be a maner preisynge that cometh of the dessertes of auncestres; and yif   40
preisynge make gentilesse, thanne mote
they nedes ben gentil that been preysed. For
whiche thing it folweth that yif thou ne have no
gentilesse of thiself (*that is to seyn, prys that
cometh of thy deserte*), foreyne gentilesse ne
maketh the nat gentil. But certes yif ther be
ony good in gentilesse, I trowe it be al only
this, that it semeth as that a maner necessite
be imposed to gentil men for that thei ne
schulde nat owtrayen or forlynen fro the   50
vertus of hir noble kynrede.

OMNE HOMINUM GENUS IN TERRIS.
— *Metrum 6*

"Alle the lynage of men that ben in erthe ben
of semblable byrthe. On allone is fadir of
thynges; on allone mynystreth alle thynges.
He yaf to the sonne his bemes, he yaf to the
moone hir hornes, he yaf the men to the erthe,
he yaf the sterres to the hevene. He encloseth
with membres the soules that comen from his
heye sete. Thanne comen alle mortel folk of
noble seed. Why noysen ye or bosten of
your eldres? For yif thow loke youre by-   10
gynnyng, and God your auctour and yowr
makere, thanne nis ther none forlyned wyght or
ongentil, but if he noryssche his corage unto
vices and forlete his propre byrthe.

QUID AUTEM DE CORPORIS. — *Prosa 7*

"But what schal I seye of delyces of body, of
whiche delices the desirynges ben ful of anguyssch, and the fulfillynges of hem ben ful of
penance? How grete seknesses and how grete
sorwes unsuffrable, ryght as a maner fruyt
of wykkidnesse, ben thilke delices wont to
bryngen to the bodyes of folk that usen hem!
Of whiche delices I not what joie mai ben had
of here moevynge, but this woot I wel, that
whosoevere wol remembren hym of hise   10
luxures, he schal wel undirstonden that the
issues of delices ben sorweful and sorye. And
yif thilke delices mowen maken folk blisful,
thanne by the same cause moten thise beestis
ben clepid blisful, of whiche beestis al the entencioun hasteth to fulfille here bodily jolyte.
And the gladnesse of wyf and children were an
honest thyng, but it hath ben seyd that it is
overmochel ayens kynde that children han
ben fownden tormentours to here fadris, I   20
not how manye; of whiche children how
bytynge is every condicioun, it nedeth nat to
tellen it the that hast er this tyme assayed it,
and art yit now angwysshous. In this approve
I the sentence of my disciple Euripidis, that
seide that he that hath no children is weleful
by infortune.

HABET HOC VOLUPTAS. — *Metrum 7*

"Every delit hath this, that it angwisscheth
hem with prykkes that usen it. It resembleth

6 **swellere of eres:** sweller of ears (because you make them
eager to hear themselves praised; you give them "rabbit ears")
14 **echid:** increased, added
21 **herebyforn:** at 2.pr7.49ff. (or, less exactly, at 3.pr5.13)
35–36 **cleernesse:** brightness, fame
50 **owtrayen:** stray unnaturally, go to excess **forlynen:**
degenerate

Prosa 7.11 **luxures:** lusts
12 **issues:** results, aftermath
Metrum 7.1 **angwisscheth:** torments

to thise flyenge flyes that we clepen ben; that, aftir that the be hath sched hise agreable honyes, he fleeth awey, and styngeth the hertes of hem that ben ysmyte, with bytynge overlonge holdynge.

"Now is it no doute thanne that thise weyes ne ben a maner mysledynges to blisfulnesse, ne that they ne mowen nat leden folk thider as thei byheeten to leden hem. But with how grete harmes thise forseide weyes ben enlaced, I schal schewe the shortly. Forwhy yif thou enforcest the to assemble moneye, thow must byreven hym his moneye that hath it; and yif thow wolt schynen with dignytees, thow must bysechen and supplyen hem that   10 yyven tho dignytees; and yif thow coveytest be honour to gon byfore othere folk, thow schalt defoule thiself thurw humblesse of axynge. Yif thou desirest power, thow schalt, be awaytes of thy subgetis, anoyously ben cast undir by manye periles. Axestow glorye? Thow schalt so bien distract by aspere thynges that thow schalt forgon sykernesse. And yif thow wolt leden thi lif in delyces, every wyght schal despysen the and forleeten the, as   20 thow that art thral to thyng that is right foul and brutyl (that is to seyn, servaunt to thi body). Now is it thanne wel yseyn how litil and how brotel possessioun thei coveyten that putten the goodes of the body aboven hir owene resoun. For maystow surmounten thise olifauntes in gretnesse or weighte of body? Or maistow ben strengere than the bole? Maystow ben swyftere than the tigre? Byhoold the spaces and the stablenesse and the swyft   30 cours of the hevene, and stynt somtyme to wondren on foule thynges. The whiche hevene certes nys nat rathere for thise thynges to ben wondryd upon, than for the resoun by whiche it is governed. But the schynynge of thi forme (*that is to seyn, the beute of thi body*), how swyftly passynge is it, and how transitorie! "Certes it es more flyttynge than the mutabilite of floures of the somer sesoun. For so as Aristotle telleth, that if that men hadden   40 eyghen of a beeste that highte lynx, so that

the lokynge of folk myghte percen thurw the thynges that withstonden it, whoso lokide thanne in the entrayles of the body of Alcibiades, that was ful fair in the superfice withoute, it schulde seme ryght foul. And forthi yif thow semest fair, thy nature ne maketh nat that, but the deceyvaunce or the feblesse of the eighen that loken. But preise the goodes of the body as mochil as evere the lyst, so that   50 thow knowe algatis that, whatso it be (*that is to seyn, of the godes of the body*) whiche that thou wondrist uppon, mai ben destroied or dissolvid by the heete of a fevere of thre dayes. Of alle whiche forseide thynges Y mai reducen this schortly in a somme: that thise worldly goodes, whiche that ne mowen nat yeven that they byheeten, ne ben nat parfite by the congregacioun of alle goodis, that they ne ben nat weyes ne pathes that bryngen men to   60 blisfulnesse, ne maken men to ben blisful.

"Allas! Whiche folie and whiche ignorance mysledeth wandrynge wrecchis fro the path of verray good! Certes ye ne seke no gold in grene trees, ne ye gadere nat precyous stones in the vynes, ne ye ne hiden nat yowre gynnes in heye mountaignes to kacchen fyssche of whiche ye mai maken riche festes. And if yow liketh to hunte to roos, ye ne gon nat to the foordes of the watir that highte Tyrene. And over this, men knowen wel the krikes and the   10 cavernes of the see yhidde in the flodes, and knowen ek whiche watir is moost plentevous of white peerlis, and knowen whiche watir haboundeth moost of reed purpre (that is to seyn, of a maner schellefyssche with whiche men deien purpre), and knowen whiche strondes habounden most of tendre fysches, or of scharpe fyssches that hyghten echynnys. But folk suffren hemselve to ben so blynde, that hem ne reccheth nat to knowe where thilke   20 goodes ben yhud whiche that thei coveyten, but ploungen hem in erthe, and seken there thilke good that surmounteth the hevene

---

3 **flyes:** insects   **ben:** bees
6–7 **bytynge overlonge holdynge:** too lasting a bite
*Prosa 8.*5 **enlaced:** entangled
10 **supplyen:** supplicate
15 **awaytes:** plots
27 **olifauntes:** elephants

45 **in the superfice:** on the surface
55 **reducen:** sum up
58 **byheeten:** promise
58–59 **congregacioun:** gathering together, amassing
*Metrum 8.*5 **gynnes:** traps
8 **roos:** roes, deer
9 **watir that highte Tyrene:** the Tyrrhenian or Tuscan sea, on the west coast of Italy
10 **krikes:** crevices, nooks
14 **reed:** red
18 **echynnys:** sea urchins

that bereth the sterris. What preyere mai I make, that be digne to the nyce thoughtes of men? But I preie that thei coveyten rychesses and honours, so that, whanne thei han geten tho false goodes with greet travaile, that therby they mowen knowen the verray goodes.

HACTENUS MENDACIS FORMAM. — *Prosa 9*

"It suffiseth that I have schewyd hiderto the forme of fals welefulnesse, so that yif thou loke now cleerly, the ordre of myn entencioun requireth from hennes forth to schewe the verray welefulnesse."

"Forsothe," quod I, "I se wel now that suffisaunce may nat comen by rychesse, ne power by remes, ne reverence by dignites, ne gentilesse by glorie, ne joie be delices."

"And hastow wel knowen the causes," quod sche, "whi it es?" [10]

"Certes me semeth," quod I, "that Y see hem ryght as thoughe it were thurw a litil clyfte, but me were levere knowen hem more opynly of the."

"Certes," quod sche, "the resoun is al redy. For thilke thyng that symply is o thyng withouten ony devysioun, the errour and folie of mankynde departeth and divideth it, and mysledeth it and transporteth from verray [20] and parfit good to godes that ben false and inparfit. But seye me this. Wenestow that he that hath nede of power, that hym ne lakketh nothyng?"

"Nay," quod I.

"Certes," quod sche, "thou seyst aryght; for if so be that ther is a thyng that in ony partie be feblere of power, certes, as in that, it moot nedes be nedy of foreyne help."

"Ryght so is it," quod I. [30]

"Suffisaunce and power ben thanne of o kynde?"

"So semeth it," quod I.

"And demestow," quod sche, "that a thyng that is of this manere (*that is to seyn, suffisaunt and myghty*) oughte ben despised, or ellis that it be right digne of reverence aboven alle thynges?"

"Certes," quod I, "it nys no doute that it nys right worthy to ben reverenced." [40]

"Lat us," quod sche, "adden thanne reverence to suffisaunce and to power, so that we demen that thise thre thynges be al o thyng."

"Certes," quod I, "lat us adden it, yif we wiln graunten the sothe."

"What demestow thanne," quod sche, "is that a dirk thyng and nat noble that is suffisaunt, reverent, and myghty; or elles that it is ryght noble and ryght cleer by celebrete of renoun? Considere thanne," quod sche, "as [50] we han grauntide hirbyfore that he that ne hath nede of no thyng and is moost myghty and moost digne of honour, if hym nedeth ony cleernesse of renoun, whiche clernesse he myght nat graunten of hymself; so that for lak of thilke cleernesse he myghte seme the feblere on any side, or the more outcast." (*Glose. This to seyn, nay; for whoso that is suffisaunt, myghty, and reverent, clernesse of renoun folweth of the forseyde thynges; he hath it [60] al redy of his suffysaunce.*)

Boece. "I mai nat," quod I, "denye it, but I moot granten, as it is, that this thyng be ryght celebrable by clernesse of renoun and noblesse."

"Thanne folweth it," quod sche, "that we adden clernesse of renoun to the thre forseyde thynges, so that there ne be amonges hem no difference."

"This a consequence," quod I.

"This thyng thanne," quod sche, "that ne [70] hath nede of no foreyne thyng, and that may don alle thynges by hise strengthis, and that is noble and honourable, nys nat that a myry thyng and a joyful?"

Boece. "But whennes," quod I, "that any sorwe myghte comen to this thyng that is swiche, certes I mai nat thynke."

Philosophie. "Thanne mote we graunten," quod sche, "that this thing be ful of gladnesse, if the forseide thynges ben sothe; [80] and certes also mote we graunten that suffisaunce, power, noblesse, reverence, and gladnesse be oonly diverse by names, but hir substaunce hath no diversite."

Boece. "It moot nedly ben so," quod I.

Philosophie. "Thilke thyng thanne," quod sche, "that is oon and symple in his nature, the wikkidnesse of men departeth it and divideth it; and whanne thei enforcen hem to gete partie of a thyng that ne hath no part, thei [90] ne geten hem neyther thilke partie that nis noon, ne the thyng al hool that thei ne desire nat."

Boece. "In whiche manere?" quod I.

Prosa 9.13 **clyfte:** chink   64 **celebrable:** famous

Philosophie. "Thilke man," quod sche, "that seketh richesse to fleen poverte, he ne travaileth hym nat for to geten power, for he hath lever ben dirk and vyl; and eek withdraweth from hymself manye naturel delites, for he nolde leese the moneie that he hath as-   100 sembled. But certes in this manere he ne geteth hym nat suffisance, that power forleteth, and that moleste prikketh, and that filthe maketh outcaste, and that dirknesse hideth. And certes he that desireth oonly power, he wasteth and scatereth rychesse, and despyseth delices and eek honour that is withoute power, ne he ne preiseth glorie nothyng. Certes thus seestow wel that manye thynges failen to hym, for he hath som tyme defaute of manye neces-   110 sites, and manye anguysshes byten hym; and whan he ne mai nat do tho defautes awey, he forletith to ben myghty, and that is the thyng that he moost desireth. And ryght thus mai I make semblable resouns of honours, and of glorie, and of delyces; for so as every of thise forseide thinges is the same that thise othere thynges ben (*that is to seyn, al oon thyng*), whoso that evere seketh to geten the toon of thise, and nat the tothir, he ne   120 geteth nat that he desireth."

Boece. "What seystow thanne, yif that a man coveyte to geten alle thise thynges togidre?"

Philosophie. "Certes," quod sche, "I wolde seye that he wolde geten hym sovereyn blisfulnesse; but that schal he nat fynde in tho thynges that I have schewed that ne mowen nat yeven that thei byheeten?"

Boece. "Certes no," quod I.   130

"Thanne," quod sche, "ne sholde men nat by no weye seken blisfulnesse in siche thynges as men wenen that they ne mowen yeven but o thyng sengly of al that men seken."

Boece. "I graunte wel," quod I, "ne no sothere thyng ne may be seyd."

Philosophie. "Now hastow thanne," quod sche, "the forme and the causes of fals welefulnesse. Now torne and flytte the   140 eighen of thi thought, for ther shaltow seen anoon thilke verray blisfulnesse that I have behyght the."

Boece. "Certes," quod I, "it is cler and opene, theyghe it were to a blynd man; and that schewedestow me ful wel a litel herbyforn, whan thow enforcedest the to schewe me the causes of the fals blisfulnesse. For, but if I be begiled, thanne is thilke the verray parfit blisfulnesse that parfitly maketh a man suf-   150 fisaunt, myghty, honourable, noble, and ful of gladnesse. And for thow schalt wel knowe that I have wel undirstonden thise thinges withynne myn herte, I knowe wel that thilke blisfulnesse that may verrayly yeven on of the forseyde thynges, syn thei ben alle oon —I knowe dowtelees that thilke thyng is the ful blysfulnesse."

Philosophie. "O my nory," quod sche, "by this opynyoun I seie that thow art   160 blisful, yif thow putte this therto that I schal seyn."

"What is that?" quod I.

"Trowestow that ther be any thyng in this erthly, mortel, toumblynge thynges that may brynge this estat?"

"Certes," quod I, "Y trowe it nought; and thow hast schewyd me wel that over thilke good ther nys no thyng more to ben desired."

Philosophie. "Thise thynges thanne,"   170 quod sche (*that is to seyn, erthly suffysaunce and power and swiche thynges*), "outher thei semen lyknesses of verray good, or elles it semeth that thei yeve to mortel folk a maner of goodes that ne be nat parfyt. But thilke good that is verray and parfyt, that mai thei nat yeven."

Boece. "I accorde me wel," quod I.

Philosophie. "Thanne," quod sche, "for as moche as thou hast knowen whiche is thilke   180 verray blisfulnesse, and eek whiche thilke thynges ben that lyen falsly blisfulnesse (*that is to seyn, that be deceyte semen verray goodes*), now byhoveth the to knowe, whennes and where thow mowe seke thilke verrai blisfulnesse."

"Certes," quod I, "that desire I gretly and have abyden longe tyme to herkne it."

"But for as moche," quod sche, "as it liketh to my disciple Plato, in his book of   190 *In Thymeo,* that in ryght litel thynges men

---

102 **that:** whom
103 **moleste:** trouble
115 **semblable resouns:** similar arguments
128 **I have schewed:** at 3.pr8.55ff.

146 **herbyforn:** at 10ff. above
159 **nory:** pupil
161 **putte this therto:** add this
165 **toumblynge:** tumbling (i.e., transitory)
182 **lyen falsly:** counterfeit
191 **In Thymeo:** *Timaeus*

schulde byseche the help of God, what juggestow that be now to done, so that we may
desserve to fynde the seete of thilk sovereyn
good?"

Boece. "Certes," quod I, "Y deme that we
schul clepe to the Fadir of alle [thyng], for
withouten hym nis ther no [begynnyng] founded aryght."

"Thow seyst aryght," quod sche, and   200
bygan anoon to syngen right thus:

O QUI PERPETUA. — *Metrum 9*

"O thow Fadir, soowere and creatour of
hevene and of erthes, that governest this world
by perdurable resoun, that comaundest the
tymes to gon from syn that age hadde bygynnynge; thow that duellest thiselve ay stedefast
and stable, and yevest alle othere thynges to
ben meved, ne foreyne causes necesseden the
nevere to compoune werk of floterynge matere,
but oonly the forme of sovereyn good iset
within the withoute envye, that moevede   10
the frely. Thow, that art althir-fayrest,
berynge the faire world in thy thought, formedest this world to the lyknesse semblable of
that faire world in thy thought. Thou drawest
alle thyng of thy sovereyn ensaumpler and
comaundest that this world, parfytely ymakid,
have frely and absolut hise parfyte parties.
Thow byndest the elementis by nombres proporcionables, that the coolde thinges
mowen accorde with the hote thinges, and   20
the drye thinges with the moyste; that the
fuyer, that is purest, ne fle nat over-heye, ne that
the hevynesse ne drawe nat adoun over-lowe the
erthes that ben ploungid in the watris. Thow
knyttest togidere the mene soule of treble
kynde moevynge alle thingis, and divydest it
by membrys accordynge; and whan it es thus
divyded [and] hath assembled a moevynge
into two rowndes, it gooth to torne ayen
to hymself, and envyrouneth a ful deep   30
thought and turneth the hevene by semblable ymage. Thow by evene-lyke causes enhauncest the soules and the lasse lyves; and,

ablynge hem heye by lyghte waynes or cartes,
thow sowest hem into hevene and into erthe.
And whan thei ben convertyd to the by thi
benygne lawe, thow makest hem retourne ayen
to the by ayen-ledynge fyer. O Fadir, yyve
thou to the thought to steyen up into the
streyte seete; and graunte hym to envi-   40
roune the welle of good; and, the lyght
ifounde, graunte hym to fycchen the clere
syghtes of his corage in the; and skatere thou
and tobreke the weyghtes and the cloudes of
erthly hevynesse; and schyn thou by thi bryghtnesse, for thou art cleernesse, thow art pesible
reste to debonayre folk; thow thiself art bygynnynge, berere, ledere, path, and terme; to looke
on the, that is our ende.

QUONIAM IGITUR QUE SIT. — *Prosa 10*

"For as moche thanne as thow hast seyn
whiche is the fourme of good that nys nat parfit,
and whiche is the forme of good that is parfit,
now trowe I that it were good to schewe in
what this perfeccioun of blisfulnesse is set.
And in this thing I trowe that we schulde first
enquere for to witen, yf that any swich maner
good as thilke good that thow hast dyffinysshed
a litel herebyforn (*that is to seyn, sovereyn
good*) may be founde in the nature of   10
thinges, for that veyn ymagynacioun of
thought ne desceyve us nat, and put us out of
the sothfastnesse of thilke thing that is sum-
mytted to us. But it may nat be denyed that
thilke good ne is, and that it nys ryght as a
welle of alle goodes. For alle thing that is
cleped inparfyt is proevid inparfit be the
amenusynge of perfeccioun or of thing that is
parfit. And herof cometh it that in every
thing general, yif that men seen any thing   20
that is inparfit, certes in thilke general ther
moot ben som thing that is parfit. For yif so be
that perfeccioun is don awey, men may nat
thinke ne say fro whennes thilke thing is that
is cleped inparfyt. For the nature of thinges ne
took nat hir begynnynge of thinges amenused
and inparfit, but it procedith of thinges that
ben alle hole and absolut, and descendith so
doun into uttereste thinges and into thinges

Metrum 9.8 **compoune werk of:** make this work from
15 **ensaumpler:** archetype
22 **ne fle nat over-heye:** not fly too high
25–26 **mene soule of treble kynde:** middle soul of three
natures; see n.
28–29 **assembled . . . rowndes:** combined its movements in two
orbits
30 **envyrouneth:** comprehends
32 **by evene-lyke causes:** likewise

34 **ablynge hem heye:** enabling them to rise
39 **steyen:** ascend
40–41 **enviroune:** comprehend
Prosa 10.9 **herebyforn:** see 3.pr9.149ff.
15 **ne is, nys:** is; is; see n.
18 **amenusynge:** diminishment
28 **absolut:** complete
29 **uttereste:** most remote

empty and withouten fruyt. But, as I have   30
schewid a litel herebyforn that yif ther be
a blisfulnesse that be freel and veyn and inparfyt, ther may no man doute that ther nys
som blisfulnesse that is sad, stedefast, and
parfyt."

Boece. "This is concluded," quod I, "feermely
and soothfastly."

Philosophie. "But considere also," quod sche,
"in whom this blissefulnes enhabiteth. The
comune accordaunce and conceyt of the   40
corages of men proveth and graunteth that
God, prince of alle thinges, is good. For, so as
nothyng mai ben thought betere than God, it
mai nat ben douted thanne that he that no
thinge nys betere, that he nys good. Certes resoun scheweth that God is so good that it
proeveth by verray force that parfyt good is in
hym. For yif God nys swyche, he ne mai nat be
prince of alle thinges; for certes somthing
possessyng in itself parfyt good schulde be   50
more worthy than God, and it scholde
semen that thilke thing were first and eldere than
God. For we han schewyd apertely that alle
thinges that ben parfyt ben first er thynges that
ben inparfit; and forthy, for as moche as that
my resoun or my proces ne go nat awey withouten an ende, we owe to graunte that the
sovereyn God is ryght ful of sovereyn parfit
good. And we han establissched that the
sovereyne good is verray blisfulnesse.   60
Thanne moot it nedis be that verray blisfulnesse is set in sovereyn God."

Boece. "This take I wel," quod I, "ne this
ne mai nat be withseid in no manere."

"But I preye the," quod sche, "see now how
thou mayst proeven holily and withoute corrupcioun this that I have seid, that the sovereyn God is ryght ful of sovereyne good."

"In whiche manere?" quod I.

"Wenestow aught," quod sche, "that this   70
prince of alle thynges have itake thilke sovereyne good anywher out of hymself, of whiche
sovereyne good men proeveth that he is ful;
ryght as thou myghtest thenken that God, that
hath blisfulnesse in hymself, and thilke blisfulnesse that is in hym, were divers in substaunce?
For yif thow wene that God have resseyved

thilke good out of hymself, thow mayst wene
that he that yaf thilke good to God be more
worth than is God. But I am beknowe and   80
confesse, and that ryght dignely, that God
is ryght worthy aboven alle thinges. And yif
so be that this good be in hym by nature, but
that it is dyvers from hym by wenynge resoun,
syn we speke of God prynce of alle thynges,
feyne who so feyne mai who was he that
hath conjoyned thise divers thynges togidre.
And eek at the laste se wel that a thing that is
divers from any thing, that thilke thing nys
nat that same thing fro whiche it es undir-   90
stonden to be diverse. Thanne folweth it
that thilke thing that be his nature is divers
from sovereyn good, that that thyng nys nat
sovereyn good; but certes it were a felenous
cursydnesse to thinken that of hym that no
thing nys more worth. For alwey, of alle
thinges, the nature of hem ne may nat ben betere
thanne hir begynnynge. For whiche I mai concluden by ryght verray resoun that thilke
that is begynnynge of alle thinges, thilke   100
same thing is sovereyn good in his substaunce."

Boece. "Thow hast seyd ryghtfully," quod I.
Philosophie. "But we han graunted," quod
sche, "that the sovereyn good is blisfulnesse."

"That is sooth," quod I.

"Thanne," quod sche, "moten we nedes
granten and confessen that thilke same sovereyn good be God."

"Certes," quod I, "Y ne may nat denye   110
ne withstonde the resouns purposed; and
I se wel that it folweth by strengthe of the
premisses."

"Loke now," quod sche, "yif this be proevid
yet more fermely thus, that there ne mowen not
ben two sovereyn goodis that ben divers among
hemself. For certes the goodis that ben divers
among hemself, the toon is nat that that the
tothir is; thanne ne mowen neither of hem
ben parfit, so as eyther of hem lakketh to   120
othir. But that that nys nat parfit, men
mai seen apertely that it nys not sovereyn. The
thinges thanne that ben sovereynly gode ne
mowe by no weie be divers. But I have wel
concluded that blisfulnesse and God ben the
sovereyn good; for whiche it mote nedes be that
sovereyne blisfulnesse is sovereyn devynite."

---

31 **herebyforn:** throughout the preceding parts of Book 3
33 **nys:** is (as in line 15 above)
55–57 **for as moche . . . ende:** i.e., to avoid an infinite
progression
57 **owe:** ought
59 **we han establissched:** in pr9; see lines 149–50.

80 **am beknowe:** acknowledge
84 **by wenynge resoun:** by a supposition
123 **sovereynly:** supremely

"No thing," quod I, "nys more sothfaste than
this, ne more ferme by resoun, ne a more
worthy thing than God mai not ben con-   130
cluded."

Philosophie. "Upon thise thynges thanne," quod
sche, "ryght as thise geometriens whan thei han
schewed her proposicions ben wont to bryngen
yn thinges that thei clepen porismes or declaracions of forseide thinges, right so wol I yeve
the here as a corolarie or a meede of coroune.
Forwhy, for as moche as by the getynge of blisfulnesse men ben makid blisful, and blisfulnesse is dyvinite, than is it manifest and   140
opene that by the getynge of dyvinite men
ben makid blisful. Right as by the getynge of
justise [men ben maked just], and be the getynge of sapience thei ben maked wise, ryght so
nedes by the semblable resoun, whan they han
geten dyvinite thei ben maked goddes. Thanne
is every blisful man God. But certes by nature
ther nys but o God; but by the participacioun
of dyvinite ther ne let ne distourbeth nothyng that ther ne ben many goddis."   150

"This ys," quod I, "a fair thing and a
precious, clepe it as thou wilt, be it corolarie, or
porisme, or mede of coroune, or declarynges."

"Certes," quod sche, "nothing nys fairere
than is the thing that by resoun schulde ben
addide to thise forseide thinges."

"What thing?" quod I.

"So, quod sche, "as it semeth that blisfulnesse conteneth many thinges, it weere for
to witen whether that alle thise thinges   160
maken or conjoynen as a maner body of
blisfulnesse by diversite of parties or membres,
or elles yif ony of alle thilke thinges be swich
that it acomplise by hymself the substaunce of
blisfulnesse, so that alle thise othere thynges
ben referrid and brought to blisfulnesse (*that
is to seyn, as to the cheef of hem*)."

"I wolde," quod I, "that thow madest me
clerly to undirstonde what thou seist, and
that thou recordidest me the forseide   170
thinges."

"Have I not jugged," quod sche, "that blisfulnesse is good?"

"Yys for sothe," quod I, "and that sovereyn
good."

"Adde thanne," quod sche, "thilke good that
is maked blisfulnesse to alle the forseide

thinges. For thilke same blisfulnesse [is]
demed to ben sovereyn suffisaunce, thilke
selve is sovereyn power, sovereyn rev-   180
erence, sovereyn clernesse or noblesse, and
sovereyn delyt. What seistow thanne of alle
thise thinges, that is to seyn, suffisaunce, power,
and thise othere thinges, — ben thei thanne as
membris of blisfulnesse, or ben they reffered
and brought to sovereyne good ryght as alle
thinges [ben] brought to the cheef of hem?"

Boece. "I undirstonde wel," quod I, "what
thou purposest to seke, but I desire for
to herkne that thow schew it me."   190

Philosophie. "Tak now thus the discrecioun of this questioun," quod sche; "yif alle thise
thinges," quod sche, "weren membris to felicite, thanne weren thei dyverse that on fro that
othir. And swich is the nature of parties or of
membres, that diverse membris compounen a
body."

"Certes," quod I, "it hath wel ben schewyd
herebyforn that alle thise thinges ben
al o thyng."   200

"Thanne ben thei none membres," quod
sche, "for elles it schulde seme that blisfulnesse were conjoyned al of o membre allone;
but that is a thing that mai not ben don."

"This thing," quod I, "nys not doutous; but
I abide to herknen the remenaunt of the question."

"This is opene and cler," quod sche, "that
alle othere thinges ben referrid and
brought to good. For therfore is suffi-   210
saunce requerid, for it is demyd to ben
good; and forthy is power requirid, for men
trowen also that it be good; and this same thing
mowen we thinken and conjecten of reverence,
and of noblesse, and of delyt. Thanne is sovereyn good the somme and the cause of al that
oughte ben desired; forwhy thilke thing that
withholdeth no good in itselve, ne semblance of good, it ne mai not wel in no
manere be desired ne requerid. And the   220
contrarie; for thoughe that thinges by here
nature ne ben not gode, algates yif men wene
that thei ben gode, yet ben thei desired as
theigh that thei were verrayliche gode; and
therefore is it that men oughte to wene by ryghte
that bounte be the sovereyn fyn and the cause
of alle the thinges that ben to requiren. But
certes thilke that is cause for whiche men

---

135 **porismes:** corollaries
135–36 **declaracions:** clarifications
137 **meede of coroune:** "gift of a garland"; i.e., a bonus; see n.
149 **distourbeth:** prevents
170 **recordidest me:** would remind me of

191–92 **discrecioun:** solution
196 **compounen:** compose

requiren any thing, it semeth that thilke same thing be moost desired. As thus: yf that a wyght wolde ryden for cause of hele, he ne desireth not so mochel the moevyng to ryden, as the effect of his hele. Now thanne, syn that alle thynges ben required for the grace of good, thei ne ben not desired of alle folk more than the same good. But we han grauntide that blisfulnesse is that thing for whiche that alle thise othere thinges ben desired; thanne is it thus that certes oonly blysfulnesse is requered and desired. By whiche thing it scheweth cleerly that of good and of blisfulnesse is al on and the same substaunce."

"I se nat," quod I, "wherfore that men myghten discorden in this."

"And we han schewed that God and verray blisfulnesse is al o thing."

"That is sooth," quod I.

"Thanne mowen we concluden sykerly, that the substaunce of God is set in thilke same good, and in noon other place.

NUNC OMNES PARITER VENITE CAPTI.
— *Metrum 10*

"Cometh alle to-gidre now, ye that ben ykaught and ybounde with wikkide cheynes by the desceyvable delyt of erthly thynges enhabitynge in yowr thought! Her schal ben the reste of your labours, her is the havene stable in pesible quiete; this allone is the open refut to wreches. (*Glose. This to seyn, that ye that ben combryd and disseyvid with worldly affeccions, cometh now to this sovereyn good, that is God, that is refut to hem that wolen come to hym.) Textus.* Alle the things that the ryver Tagus yyveth yow with his goldene gravelis, or elles alle the things that the ryver Hermus yeveth with his rede brinke, or that Indus yyveth, that is next the hote partie of the world, that medleth the grene stones with the white, ne scholden not cleren the lookynge of your thought, but hiden rather your blynde corages withynne here derknesse. Al that liketh yow here, and exciteth and moeveth your thoughtes, the erthe hath norysschid it in his lowe caves. But

the schynynge by whiche the hevene is governed and whennes that it hath his strengthe, that eschueth the derke overthrowynge of the soule; and whosoevere may knowen thilke light (*of blisfulnesse*), he schal wel seyn that the white beemes of the sonne ne ben nat cleer."

ASSENCIOR INQUAM CUNCTA. — *Prosa 11*

Boece. "I assente me," quod I, "for alle thise things ben strongly bounden with ryght ferme resouns."

"How mychel wiltow preysen it," quod sche, "yif that thow knowe what thilke good is?"

"I wol preyse it," quod I, "be pris withouten ende, yif it schal betyde me to knowe also togidre God that is good."

"Certes," quod sche, "that schal I [undo] the be verray resoun, yif that tho things that I have concluded a litel herebyforn duellen only in hir first grauntynge."

Boece. "Thei dwellen graunted to the," quod I. (*This to seyn as who seith, "I graunte thi forseide conclusyouns."*)

"Have I nat schewed the," quod sche, "that the things that ben required of many folk ne ben not verray goodis ne parfite, for thei ben divers that on fro that othir; and so as iche of hem is lakkynge to othir, thei ne han no power to bryngen a good that is ful and absolut; but thanne at erste ben thei verraye good, whan thei ben gadred togidre [als] into o forme and into oon werkynge, so that thilke thing that is suffisaunce, thilke same be power, and reverence, and noblesse, and myrthe; and for sothe, but yif alle thise things ben alle o same thing, thei ne han not wherby that thei mowen be put in the nombre of things that oughten ben required or desired?"

Boece. "It is schewyd," quod I, "ne herof mai ther no man douten."

Philosophie. "The things thanne," quod sche, "that ne ben none goodis whan thei ben diverse, and whanne thei bygynnen to ben al o thing, thanne ben thei goodes — ne cometh it hem nat thanne be the getynge of unyte that thei ben maked goodes?"

Boece. "So it semeth," quod I.

"But alle thing that is good," quod sche, "grauntestow that it be good by the participacioun of good, or no?"

"I graunte it," quod I.

232–33 **moevyng to ryden:** motion of riding
234 **grace:** sake; see note.
245 **we han schewed:** at lines 107–9 above
Metrum 10.6 **pesible:** peaceful
8 **combryd:** encumbered
12 **Tagus:** the river Tajo in Spain
14 **Hermus:** a river (now Sarabat) in Asia Minor
15 **Indus:** the river Indus, in India

Prosa 11.9–10 **undo:** show; see textual note.
11–12 **herebyforn:** at pr10.114ff.
12 **only:** construe with *yif* (10)

"Thanne mustow graunten," quod sche, "by
semblable resoun that oon and good be o same
thing; for of thinges of whiche that the effect nys
nat naturely divers, nedes the substaunce moot
be oo same thing."

"I ne may nat denye it," quod I.

"Hastow nat knowen wel," quod sche,   50
"that alle thing that is hath so longe his
duellynge and his substaunce as longe as it es
oon, but whanne it forletith to be oon, it moot
nedys deien and corrumpen togidres?"

"In whiche manere?" quod I.

"Ryght as in beestes," quod sche, "whanne
the soule and the body ben conjoyned in oon
and dwellen togidre, it es cleped a beeste; and
whanne her unyte is destroyed be the
disseveraunce the toon fro the tothir,   60
thanne scheweth it wel that it is a deed
thing, and that it nys no lengere no beeste. And
the body of a wyght, while it duelleth in oo
fourme be conjunccion of membris, it is wel
seyn that it is a figure of mankynde; and yif
the parties of the body ben so devyded and
disseverid the ton fro the tother that thei destroyen unite, the body forletith to ben that it was
beforn. And whoso wolde renne in the
same manere be alle thinges, he scholde   70
seen that withouten doute every thing is in
his substaunce as longe as it is oon; and whanne
it forletith to ben oon, it dyeth and peryssheth."

Boece. "Whanne I considere," quod I, "manye
thinges, I se noon other."

"Is ther any thing thanne," quod sche, "that,
in as moche as it lyveth naturely, that forletith
the talent or the appetyt of his beynge and
desireth to come to deth and to corrupcioun?"   80

"Yif I considere," quod I, "the beestes
that han any maner nature of wyllynge and of
nyllynge, I ne fynde no beeste, but if it be
constreyned fro withoute-forth, that forletith or
despiseth the entencion to lyven and to duren;
or that wole, his thankes, hasten hym to dyen.
For every beest travaileth hym to defende and
kepe the savacion of his lif, and eschueth deeth
and destruccioun. But certes I doute me of
herbes and of trees [and] I am in a doute   90
of swiche thinges [as] ne han no felyng
soules (*ne no naturel werkynges servynge to
appetites as beestes han, whether thei han
appetyt to duellen and to duren*).

"Certes," quod sche, "ne therof thar the nat
doute. Now looke upon thise herbes and thise
trees. They wexen first in suche places as ben
covenable to hem, in whiche places thei mowen
nat sone deye ne dryen, as longe as hir
nature mai defenden hem. For some of   100
hem waxen in feeldis, and some in mountaynes, and othere waxen in mareys, and
othre cleven on roches, and some wexen
plentyvous in soondes; and yif any wyght
enforce hym to bere hem into other places, thei
wexen drye. For nature yeveth to every thing
that that is convenient to hym, and travailleth
that they ne deie nat, as longe as thei han power
to duellen and to lyven. What wiltow seyn
of this, that thei drawen alle here   110
norysschynges by here rootes, ryght as thei
hadden here mouthes yplounged withynne the
erthes, and sheden be hir maryes hir wode and
hir bark? And what wyltow seyn of this, that
thilke thing that is ryght softe, as the marie is,
that it is alwey hyd in the seete al withinne, and
that it is defended fro withoute by the
stedfastnesse of wode, and that the outreste bark
is put ayens the distemperaunce of the
hevene as a deffendour myghty to suffren   120
harm? And thus certes maistow wel seen
how greet is the diligence of nature; for alle
thinges renovelen and publysschen hem with
seed ymultiplied, ne ther nys no man that ne
woot wel that they ne ben ryght as a foundement
and edifice for to duren, noght oonly for a tyme,
but ryght as for to dure perdurably by
generacion.

And the thinges eek that men wenen ne
haven none soules, ne desire thei nat, iche   130
of hem, by semblable resoun to kepyn that
that is hirs (*that is to seyn, that is accordynge
to hir nature in conservacioun of hir beynge
and endurynge*)? For wherfore ellis bereth
lightnesse the flaumbes up, and the weyghte
presseth the erthe adoun, but for as moche as
thilke places and thilke moevynges ben covenable to everyche of hem? And forsothe every
thing kepeth thilke that is accordynge
and propre to hym, ryght as thinges that   140
ben contrarious and enemys corrumpen
hem. And yet the harde thinges, as stones,

---

54 **corrumpen:** decay
69–70 **renne in the same manere:** continue in the same way
84 **withoute-forth:** the outside

95 **thar the:** you need
102 **mareys:** marshes
113 **sheden be hir maryes:** build up around their marrows
119 **distemperaunce:** disturbance
123 **renovelen and publysschen hem:** renew and propagate themselves
141 **corrumpen:** destroy

clyven and holden here parties togidere ryght faste and harde, and defenden hem in withstondynge that thei ne departe nat lyghtly atwynne. And the thinges that ben softe and fletynge, as is watir and eyr, thei departen lyghtly and yeven place to hem that breken or divyden hem; but natheles they retorne sone ageyn into the same thinges fro 150 whennes thei ben arraced; but fyer fleeth and refuseth alle dyvisioun.

"Ne I ne trete not here now of willeful moevynges of the soule that is knowyng, but of the naturel entencioun of thinges, as thus: ryght as we swolwen the mete that we resseyven and ne thinke nat on it, and as we drawen our breeth in slepynge that we witen it nat while we slepyn. For certes in the beestis the love of hire lyvynges ne of hire beynges ne cometh 160 not of the wilnynges of the soule, but of the bygynnynges of nature. For certes, thurw constreynynge causes, wil desireth and embraceth ful ofte tyme the deeth that nature dredeth. (*That is to seyn as thus: that a man may be constreyned so, by som cause, that his wille desireth and taketh the deeth whiche that nature hateth and dredeth ful sore.*) And somtyme we seen the contrarye, as thus: that the wil of a wyght distourbeth and 170 constreyneth that that nature desireth and requirith alwey, that is to seyn the werk of generacioun, by whiche generacioun only duelleth and is susteyned the longe durablete of mortel thinges. And thus this charite and this love, that every thing hath to hymself, ne cometh not of the moevynge of the soule, but of the entencioun of nature. For the purveaunce of God hath yeven to thinges that ben creat of hym this, that is a ful grete cause to lyven 180 and to duren, for whiche they desiren naturely here lif as longe as evere thei mowen. For which thou mayst not drede be no manere that alle the thinges that ben anywhere, that thei ne requiren naturely the ferme stablenesse of perdurable duellynge, and eek the eschuynge of destruccioun."

Boece. "Now confesse I wel," quod I, "that Y see wel now certeynly withouten doutes the thinges that whilom semeden uncer- 190 teyn to me."

Philosophie. "But," quod sche, "thilke thing that desireth to be and to duelle perdurably, he

desireth to ben oon. For yif that oon were destroyed, certes, beynge schulde ther noon duellen to no wyght."

"That is sooth," quod I.

"Thanne," quod sche, "desiren alle thinges oon."

"I assente," quod I.   200

"And I have schewed," quod sche, "that thilke same oon is thilke that is good."

Boece. "Ye, forsothe," quod I.

"Alle thinges thanne," quod sche, "requiren good; and thilke good thow mayst descryven ryght thus: good is thilk thing that every wyght desireth."

"Ther ne may be thought," quod I, "no more verraye thing. For eyther alle thinges ben referrid and brought to noght, and floteren 210 withouten governour, despoyled of oon as of hire propre heved; or elles, yif ther be any thing to whiche that alle thinges tenden and hyen to, that thing muste ben the sovereyn good of alle goodes."

Philosophie. Thanne seide sche thus: "O my nory," quod sche, "I have greet gladnesse of the, for thow hast fycched in thyn herte the [marke of the] myddel sothfastnesse, (*that is to seyn, the prykke*). But [in] this thing 220 hath ben discoveryd to the [that] thow seydest that thow wistest not a litel herbyforn."

"What was that?" quod I.

"That thou ne wistest noght," quod sche, "whiche was the ende of thinges. And certes that is the thyng that every wyght desireth; and for as mochel as we han gadrid and comprehendid that good is thilke thing that is desired of alle, thanne mote we nedys confessen that good is the fyn of alle thinges.   230

QUISQUIS PROFUNDA. — *Metrum 11*

"Whoso that seketh sooth by a deep thought, and coveyteth not to ben disseyvid by no mysweyes, lat hym rollen and trenden withynne hymself the lyght of his ynwarde sighte; and let hym gaderyn ayein, enclynynge into a compas, the longe moevynges of his thoughtes; and let hym techyn his corage that he hath enclosid

143 **clyven:** cleave, adhere
147 **fletynge:** fluid
151 **arraced:** torn
190 **whilom:** at lines 89–94 above

201 **I have schewed:** at lines 44–48 above
218 **fycched:** fixed
219 **myddel:** central
220 **prykke:** bull's-eye; see n.
222 **herbyforn:** at 1.pr6.40–41 (see also 3.pr12.6–16)
Metrum 11.2–3 **mysweyes:** sidetracks
3 **trenden:** revolve
5–6 **enclynynge into a compas:** gathering together (as into a circle)
7–8 **he, his, he:** i.e., the soul

and hid in his tresors al that he compasseth or secheth fro withoute. And thanne thilke thing that the blake cloude of errour 10 whilom hadde ycovered schal lighte more clerly than Phebus hymself ne schyneth. (*Glosa. Whoso wol seke the depe ground of soth in his thought, and wil nat ben disseyvid by false proposiciouns that goon amys fro the trouthe, lat hym wel examine and rolle withynne hymself the nature and the propretes of the thing; and let hym yet eftsones examinen and rollen his thoughtes by good delibera- cioun or that he deme, and lat hym techyn 20 his soule that it hath, by naturel principles kyndeliche yhud withynne itself, al the trouthe the whiche he ymagineth to ben in thinges withoute. And thanne al the derknesse of his mysknowynge shall [schewen] more evydently to the sighte of his undirstondynge then the sonne ne semeth to the sighte withoute-forth.*) For certes the body, bryngynge the weighte of foryetynge, ne hath nat chased out of your thought al the cleernesse of your knowyng; 30 for certeynli the seed of soth haldeth and clyveth within yowr corage, and it is awaked and excited by the wynde and by the blastes of doctrine. For wherfore elles demen ye of your owene wil the ryghtes, whan ye ben axid, but if so were that the norysschynges of resoun ne lyvede yplounged in the depe of your herte? (*This to seyn, how schulde men deme the sothe of any thing that were axid, yif ther nere a rote of sothfastnesse that were yploungid 40 and hyd in the naturel principles, the whiche sothfastnesse lyvede within the dep- nesse of the thought?*) And if so be that the Muse and the doctrine of Plato syngeth soth, al that every wyght leerneth, he ne doth no thing elles thanne but recordeth, as men re- corden thinges that ben foryeten."

TUNC EGO PLATONI INQUAM. — *Prosa 12*

Thanne seide I thus: "I accorde me gretly to Plato, for thou recordist and remembrist me thise thinges yet the seconde tyme; that is to seye, first whan I loste my memorie be the con- tagious conjunccioun of the body with the soule, and eftsones aftirward, whan Y lost it confounded by the charge and be the burdene of my sorwe."

And thanne seide sche thus: "Yif thow loke," quod sche, "first the thynges that 10 thou hast graunted, it ne schal nat ben ryght fer that thow ne schalt remembren thilke thing that thou seidest that thou nystist nat."

"What thing?" quod I.

"By whiche governement," quod sche, "that this world is governed."

"Me remembreth it wel," quod I; "and I con- fesse wel that I ne wyste it nat. But al be it so that I see now from afer what thou pur- posist, algates I desire yit to herknen it of 20 the more pleynly."

"Thou ne wendest nat," quod sche, "a litel herebyforn, that men schulde doute that this world nys governed by God."

"Certes," quod I, "ne yet ne doute I it naught, ne I nyl nevere wene that it were to doute" (*as who seith, "but I woot wel that God governeth this world"*); "and I schal schort- ly answeren the be what resouns I am brought to this. This world," quod I, 30 "of so manye diverse and contraryous parties, ne myghte nevere han ben assembled in o forme, but yif ther ne were oon that con- joyned so manye diverse thinges; and the same diversite of here natures, that so discorden the ton fro that other, most departen and unjoynen the thinges that ben conjoynid, yif ther ne were oon that contenyde that he hath conjoynid and ybounden. Ne the certein ordre of nature ne schulde not brynge forth so ordene moev- 40 ynges by places, by tymes, by doynges, by spaces, by qualites, yif ther ne were on, that were ay stedfaste duellynge, that ordeynide and disponyde thise diversites of moevynges. And thilke thing, whatsoevere it be, by whiche that alle things ben ymaked and ilad, Y clepe hym 'God,' that is a word that is used to alle folk."

Thanne seide sche: "Syn thou feelist thus thise thinges," quod sche, "I trowe that I have litel more to done that thou, myghty 50 of welefulnesse, hool and sound, ne see eftsones thi contre. But let us loken the thinges that we han purposed herebyforn. Have I nat nombrid and seid," quod sche, "that suffisaunce is in blisfulnesse, and we han accorded that God is thilke same blisfulnesse?"

"Yis, forsothe," quod I.

---

11 **lighte:** shine
21 **principles:** dispositions
25 **schewen:** be seen, appear
46 **recordeth:** remembers
Prosa 12.4–5 **contagious:** contaminating

13 **thou seidest:** at 1.pr6.30–32.
23 **herebyforn:** cf. 1.pr6.11–16, 84–92.
38 **contenyde:** held together
40 **ordene:** well-ordered
54 **nombrid:** reckoned

"And that to governen this world," quod sche, "ne schal he nevere han nede of noon help fro withoute? For elles, yif he hadde nede of any help, he ne schulde nat have no ful suffisaunce?"   60

"Yys, thus it moot nedes be," quod I.

"Thanne ordeyneth he be hymself alone alle thinges?" quod sche.

"That may noght ben denyed," quod I.

"And I have schewyd that God is the same good?"

"It remembreth me wel," quod I.

"Thanne ordeigneth he alle thinges by thilke good," quod sche, "syn he, whiche that we han accordid to ben good, governeth alle thinges by hymself; and he is as a keye and a styere, by whiche that the edifice of this world is kept stable and withouten corrumpynge."   70

"I accorde me greetly," quod I. "And I aperceyvede a litil herebyforn that thow woldest seyn thus, al be it so that it were by a thynne suspecioun."

"I trowe it wel," quod sche; "for, as I trowe, thou ledist now more ententyfliche thyn eyen to loken the verray goodes. But natheles the thing that I schal telle the yet ne scheweth not lesse to loken."   80

"What is that?" quod I.

"So as men trowen," quod sche, "and that ryghtfully, that God governeth alle thinges by the keye of his goodnesse, and alle thise same thinges, as I have taught the, hasten hem by naturel entencioun to come to good, ther may no man douten that thei ne ben governed voluntariely, and that they ne converten hem of here owene wil to the wil of here ordeynour, as thei that ben accordynge and enclynynge to here governour and here kyng."   90

"It moot nedes be so," quod I, "for the reume ne schulde nat seme blisful yif ther were a yok of mysdrawynges in diverse parties, ne the savynge of obedient thynges ne scholde nat be."   100

"Thanne is ther nothyng," quod sche, "that kepith his nature, that enforceth hym to gon ayen God."

"No," quod I.

"And yif that any thing enforcede hym to withstonde God, myghte it avayle at the laste ayens hym that we han graunted to ben almyghty by the ryght of blisfulnesse?"

"Certes," quod I, "al outrely it ne myghte nat avaylen hym."   110

"Thanne is ther nothing," quod she, "that either mai or wole withstonden to this sovereyn good."

"I trowe nat," quod I.

"Thanne is thilke the sovereyn good," quod sche, "that alle thinges governeth strongly and ordeyneth hem softly?"

Thanne seide I thus: "I delite me," quod I, "nat oonly in the eendes or in the somme of the resouns that thou hast concluded and proved, but thilke woordes that thou usest deliten me moche more. So that, at the laste, foolis that somtyme reenden grete thinges oughten ben asschamid of hemself (*that is to seyn, that we foolis that reprehenden wikkidly the thinges that touchen Godis governaunce, we aughten ben asschamid of ourself*), as I, that seide that God refuseth oonly the werkis of men and ne entremetith nat of it."   120   130

Philosophie. "Thow hast wel herd," quod sche, "the fables of the poetis, how the geauntis assaileden hevene with the goddis, but forsothe the debonayre force of God disposide hem as it was worthy (that is to sey, destroyed the geauntes, as it was worthy). But wiltow that we joynen togidres thilke same resouns, for paraventure of swiche conjunccioun may sterten up som fair sparcle of soth?"   140

"Do," quod I, "as the list."

"Wenestow," quod sche, "that God ne be almyghty? No man is in doute of it."

"Certes," quod I, "no wyght ne douteth it, yif he be in his mynde."

"But he," quod sche, "that is almyghti, ther nys no thyng that he ne may?"

"That is sooth," quod I.

"May God don evel?" quod sche.

"Nay, forsothe," quod I.   150

"Thanne is evel nothing," quod sche, "syn that he ne may not don evel, that mai doon alle thinges."

"Scornestow me," quod I, "or elles, pleyestow or disseyvistow me, that hast so wov-

---

74 **styere:** rudder
75 **corrumpynge:** decay
81 **ententyfliche:** attentively
84 **scheweth not lesse to loken:** is equally clear
99 **mysdrawynges:** conflicting pulls

124 **reenden:** tear down, criticize
134 **with:** against or and; see n.

en me with thi resouns the hous of Didalus,
so entrelaced that it is unable to ben unlaced,
thow that otherwhile entrist ther thow issist,
and other while issist ther thow entrest?
Ne fooldist thou nat togidre by replica-   160
cioun of wordes a manere wondirful sercle or envirounynge of the simplicite devyne?
For certes a litel herebyforne, whanne thou bygunne at blisfulnesse, thou seidest that it is
sovereyn good, and seidest that it is set in sovereyn God; and seidest that God hymself is
sovereyn good, and that God is the ful blisfulnesse; for whiche thou yave me as a covenable yifte, that is to seyn, that no wyght nis
blisful, but yif he be God also therwith.   170
And seidest eke that the forme of good is
the substaunce of God and of blisfulnesse; and
seidest that thilke same oon is thilke same good
that is required and desired of al the kynde of
thinges. And thou provedest in disputynge that
God governeth alle the thinges of the world by
the governementis of bounte, and seidest that
alle thinges wolen obeyen to hym, and seidest
that the nature of yvel nys no thing. And
thise thinges ne schewedest thou naught   180
with noone resouns ytaken fro withouten,
but by proeves in cercles and homliche knowen,
the whiche proeves drawen to hemself heer
feyth and here accord eriche of hem of othir.''

   Thanne seide sche thus: "I ne scorne the nat,
ne pleie, ne disceyve the; but I have schewed
the the thing that is grettest over alle thinges,
by the yifte of God that we whelome prayeden.
For this is the forme of the devyne substaunce, that is swiche that it ne slideth nat   190
into uttreste foreyne thinges, ne ne resceyveth noone straunge thinges in hym; but
ryght as Parmanydes seide in Grees of thilke
devyne substaunce — he seide thus: that thilke
devyne substaunce tornith the world and the
moevable sercle of thinges, while thilke devyne
substaunce kepith itself withouten moevynge
(*that is to seyn, that it ne moeveth nevere mo,
and yet it moeveth alle othere thinges*).
But natheles, yif I have styred resouns   200

that ne ben nat taken from withouten the compas of the thing of whiche we treten, but resouns that ben bystowyd withinne that compas,
ther nys nat why that thou schuldest merveillen, sith thow hast lernyd by the sentence
of Plato that nedes the wordis moot be cosynes
to the thinges of whiche thei speken.

FELIX QUI POTUIT. — *Metrum 12*

   "Blisful is that man that may seen the clere
welle of good! Blisful is he that mai unbynden
hym fro the boondes of the hevy erthe! The
poete of Trace, Orpheus, that whilome hadde
ryght greet sorwe for the deth of his wyf, aftir
that he hadde makid by his weeply songes the
wodes moevable to renne, and hadde makid
the ryveris to stonden stille, and hadde maked
the hertes and the hyndes to joynen dreedles here sydes to cruel lyouns for to herk-   10
nen his song, and hadde maked that the
hare was nat agast of the hound, whiche was
plesed by his song; so, whanne the moste ardaunt love of his wif brende the entrayles of his
breest, ne the songes that hadden overcomen
alle thinges ne mighten nat asswagen hir lord
Orpheus, he pleynid hym of the hevene
goddis that weren cruel to hym.
   He wente hym to the houses of helle,
and ther he tempride his blaundysschinge   20
songes by resounynge strenges, and spak
and song in wepynge al that evere he hadde
resceyved and lavyd out of the noble welles of
his modir Callyope the goddesse. And he sang
with as mochel as he myghte of wepynge, and
with as moche as love that doublide his sorwe
myghte yeve hym and teche hym, and he
commoevde the helle, and requyred and bysoughte by swete preyere the lordes of
soules in helle of relessynge, that is to seyn,   30
to yelden hym his wyf. Cerberus, the porter
of helle, with hise thre hevedes, was caught and
al abasschid of the newe song. And the thre
goddesses, furiis and vengeresses of felonyes,
that tormenten and agasten the soules by anoy,
woxen sorweful and sory, and wepyn teeris for
pite. Tho was nat the heved of Yxion ytormented
by the overthrowynge wheel. And Tantalus, that

---

156 **the hous of Didalus:** the Labyrinth
158 **otherwhile:** sometimes   **issist:** issue, come out
160–61 **by replicacioun of wordes:** i.e., by weaving complicated patterns of words
163 **herebyforne:** at 3.pr10.104ff.
182 **proeves in cercles:** circular arguments   **homliche:** i.e., from within, not from without
188 **whelome:** at 3.m9.38ff.
191 **uttreste:** remote
193 **Parmanydes:** Parmenides, the Greek philosopher

Metrum 12.20 **blaundysschinge:** pleasant
21 **resounynge:** resounding
23 **lavyd:** scooped, drawn up (as water)
25 **with as mochel as he myghte of wepynge:** with all the added power his weeping gave him
35 **anoy:** torture

was destroied by the woodnesse of long
thurst, despyseth the floodes to drynken.   40
The foul that highte voltor, that etith the
stomak or the gyser of Tycius, is so fulfild of
his song that it nil eten ne tiren no more. At the
laste the lord and juge of soules was moevid to
misericordes, and cryede: 'We ben overcomen,'
quod he; 'yyve we to Orpheus his wif to beren
hym compaignye; he hath wel ybought hire by
his faire song and his ditee. But we wolen putten
a lawe in this and covenaunt in the yifte;
that is to seyn that, til he be out of helle, yif   50
he loke byhynde hym, that his wyf schal
comen ageyn unto us.' But what is he that may
yeven a lawe to loverys? Love is a grettere lawe
and a strengere to hymself thanne any lawe that
men mai yyven. Allas! Whanne Orpheus and his
wif weren almost at the termes of the nyght
(*that is to seyn, at the laste boundes of helle*),
Orpheus lokede abakward on Erudyce his wif,
and lost hire, and was deed.

This fable apertenith to yow alle, who-   60
soevere desireth or seketh to lede his
thought into the sovereyn day, that is to seyn, to
cleernesse of sovereyn good. For whoso that
evere be so overcomen that he ficche his eien
into the put of helle, that is to seyn, whoso sette
his thoughtes in erthly thinges, al that evere he
hath drawen of the noble good celestial he lesith
it, whanne he looketh the helles, that is to seyn,
into lowe thinges of the erthe.''

Explicit Liber Tercius

Incipit Liber Quartus

HEC CUM PHILOSOPHIA DIGNITATE VULTUS.
— *Prosa 1*

Whanne Philosophie hadde songen softly
and delitably the forseide thinges, kepynge the
dignyte of hir cheere and the weyghte of hir
wordes, I, thanne, that ne hadde nat al outrely
foryeten the wepynge and the moornynge that
was set in myn herte, forbrak the entencioun of
hir that entendede yit to seyn some othere
thinges. ''O,'' quod I, ''thou that art gyderesse
of verray light, the thinges that thou hast
seid me hidirto ben to me so cleer and so   10

schewynge by the devyne lookynge of hem,
and by thy resouns, that they ne mowen nat
ben overcomen. And thilke thinges that thou
toldest me, al be it so that I hadde whilom foryeten hem for the sorwe of the wrong that hath
ben don to me, yet nathales thei ne weren not
al outrely unknowen to me. But this same is
namely a ryght gret cause of my sorwe: that so
as the governour of thinges is good, yif
that eveles mowen ben by any weyes,   20
or elles yif that evelis passen withouten
punysschynge. The whiche thing oonly, how
worthy it es to ben wondrid uppon, thou considerest it wel thiselve certeynly. But yit to this
thing ther is yit another thing ijoyned more to
ben wondrid uppon: for felonye is emperisse,
and floureth ful of richesses, and vertu nis nat al
oonly withouten meedes, but it is cast undir
and fortroden undir the feet of felenous
folk, and it abyeth the tormentz in stede of   30
wikkide felouns. Of alle whiche thinges
ther nys no wyght that may merveillen ynowghe
ne compleyne that swiche thinges ben don in
the reigne of God, that alle things woot and
alle thinges may and ne wole nat but only
gode thinges.''

Thanne seide sche thus: ''Certes,'' quod sche,
''that were a greet merveille and an abaysschinge
withouten ende, and wel more horrible than
alle monstres, yif it were as thou wenest;   40
that is to seyn, that in the ryght ordene
hous of so mochel a fadir and an ordeynour of
meyne, that the vesselis that ben foule and vyl
schulden ben honoured and heryed, and the
precious vesselis schulden ben defouled and
vyl. But it nys nat so. For yif the thinges that
I have concluded a litel herebyforn ben kept
hoole and unaraced, thou schalt wel knowe by
the auctorite of God, of the whos reigne I
speke, that certes the gode folk ben alwey   50
myghty and schrewes ben alwey outcast
and feble; ne the vices ben neveremo withouten peyne, ne the vertus ne ben nat withouten mede; and that blisfulnesses comen alwey
to good folk, and infortune comith alwey to
wykkide folk. And thou schalt wel knowe
manye thinges of this kynde, that schullen
cesen thi pleyntis and strengthen the with stedfaste sadnesse. And for thou hast seyn the

---

42 **gyser:** gizzard, liver   **Tycius:** Tityus
43 **tiren:** tear
65 **put:** pit
Explicit, *etc.:* Here ends the third book. Here begins the fourth
book.
Prosa 1.6 **forbrak:** interrupted
8 **gyderesse:** guide

---

11 **schewynge:** evident
18–19 **so as:** although; see n.
38 **abaysschinge:** source of amazement
42–43 **ordeynour of meyne:** householder
48 **unaraced:** untorn

forme of the verray blisfulnesse by me that   60
have whilom yschewid it the, and thow
hast knowen in whom blisfulnesse is yset, alle
thingis ytreted that I trowe ben necessarie to
putten forth, I schal schewe the the weye that
schal bryngen the ayen unto thyn hous; and I
schal fycchen fetheris in thi thought, by whiche
it mai arisen in heighte; so that, alle tribulacioun idon awey, thow, by my gyding and by
my path and by my sledys, shalt mowen
retourne hool and sownd into thi contree.   70

SUNT ETENIM PENNE VOLUCRES MICHI.
— Metrum 1

"I have, forthi, swifte fetheris that surmounten the heighte of the hevene. Whanne
the swift thoght hath clothid itself in tho
fetheris, it despiseth the hateful erthes, and surmounteth the rowndenesse of the gret ayr; and
it seth the clowdes byhynde his bak, and passeth the heighte of the regioun of the fir, that
eschaufeth by the swifte moevynge of the firmament, til that he areyseth hym into the
houses that beren the sterres, and joyneth   10
his weies with the sonne, Phebus, and
felawschipeth the weie of the olde colde Saturnus; and he, imaked a knyght of the clere
sterre (that is to seyn, whan the thought is
makid Godis knyght by the sekynge of
trouthe to comen to the verray knowleche of
God) — and thilke soule renneth by the cercle
of the sterres in alle the places there as the
schynynge nyght is ypainted (that is to
sey, the nyght that is cloudeles; for on   20
nyghtes that ben cloudeles it semeth as
the hevene were peynted with diverse ymages
of sterres). And whan [that] he hath gon there
inoghe, he schal forleten the laste point of the
hevene, and he schal pressen and wenden on
the bak of the swifte firmament, and he schal
be makid parfit of the worschipful lyght [or]
dredefulle clerenesse of God. There halt the
lord of kynges the septre of his myght and
atemprith the governementz of the world,   30
and the schynynge juge of thinges, stable in
hymself, governeth the swifte cart or wayn (that
is to seyn, the circuler moevynge of the sonne).
And yif thi wey ledeth the ayein so that thou be
brought thider, thanne wiltow seye now that
that is the contre that thou requerist, of whiche

thow ne haddest no mynde — 'but now it
remembreth me wel, here was I born, her wol
I fastne my degree, here wol I duelle.' But
yif the liketh thanne to looken on the   40
derknesse of the erthe that thou hast
forleten, thanne shaltow seen that these felonus
tirantz, that the wrecchide peple dredeth now,
schullen ben exiled fro thilke faire contre."

TUM EGO PAPE INQUAM UT MAGNA.
— Prosa 2

Thanne seide I thus: "Owh! I wondre me
that thow byhetist me so grete thinges. Ne I
ne doute nat that thou ne maist wel parforme
that thow behetist; but I preie the oonly this,
that thow ne tarie nat to telle me thilke thinges
that thou hast moevid."

"First," quod sche, "thow most nedes knowen
that good folk ben alwey strong and myghti,
and the schrewes ben feble and desert and
naked of alle strengthes. And of thise   10
thinges, certes, everiche of hem is declared
and schewed by other. For so as good and
yvel ben two contraries, yif so be that good be
stedfast, thanne scheweth the feblesse of yvel
al opynly; and yif thow knowe clerly the freel-
nesse of yvel, the stedfastnesse of good is
knowen. But for as moche as the fey of my
sentence schal ben the more ferme and haboundant, I wil gon by the to weye and by the
tothir, and I wil conferme the thinges that   20
ben purposed, now on this side and now on
that side.

"Two thinges ther ben in whiche the effect of
alle the dedes of mankynde standeth (that is to
seyn, wil and power); and yif that oon of thise
two faileth, ther nys nothing that may be doon.
For yif that wille lakketh, ther nys no wyght that
undirtaketh to done that he wol nat doon; and
yif power faileth, the wil nys but in idel and
stant for naught. And therof cometh it that   30
yif thou see a wyght that wolde geten that
he mai not geten, thow maist nat douten that
power ne faileth hym to have that he wolde."

"This is open and cler," quod I, "ne it ne mai
nat be denyed in no manere."

"And yif thou se a wyght," quod sche, "that
hath doon that he wolde doon, thow nilt nat
douten that he ne hath had power to doon it?"

"No," quod I.

---

66 **fetheris:** wings
69 **sledys:** sleds
Metrum 1.8 **eschaufeth:** grows hot
12 **felawschipeth:** accompanies

Prosa 2.6 **that:** whom (the antecedent is *me*, line 5)
17 **fey:** trustworthiness
19 **the to:** the one
23 **effect:** realization

"And in that that every wyght may, in 40
that men may holden hym myghti. (*As
who seith, in so moche as a man is myghty to
doon a thing, in so mochel men halt hym
myghti.*) And in that that he ne mai, in that men
demen hym to ben feble."

"I confesse it wel," quod I.

"Remembreth the," quod sche, "that I have
gaderid and ischewid by forseide resouns that al
the entencioun of the wil of mankynde,
whiche that is lad by diverse studies, 50
hasteth to comen to blisfulnesse."

"It remembreth me wel," quod I, "that it hath
ben schewed."

"And recordeth the nat thanne," quod sche,
"that blisfulnesse is thilke same good that men
requiren, so that whanne that blisfulnesse is
required of alle, that good also is required and
desired of alle?"

"It ne recordeth me noght," quod I, "for
I have it gretly alwey ficched in my mem- 60
orie."

"Alle folk thanne," quod sche, "goode and
eek badde, enforcen hem withoute difference of
entencioun to comen to good."

"This is a verray consequence," quod I.

"And certein is," quod sche, "that by the
getynge of good ben men ymakid gode."

"This is certein," quod I.

"Thanne geten gode men that thei desiren?" 70

"So semeth it," quod I.

"But wikkide folk," quod sche, "yif thei geten
the good that thei desiren, thei ne mowe nat
ben wikkid."

"So is it," quod I.

"Than so as the ton and the tothir," quod
sche, "desiren good, and the gode folk geten
good and not the wikkide folk, than is it no
doute that the gode folk ne ben myghty
and wikkid folk ben feble." 80

"Whoso that evere," quod I, "douteth
of this, he ne mai nat considere the nature of
thinges ne the consequence of resouns."

"And over this," quod sche, "if that ther ben
two thinges that han o same purpos by kynde,
and that oon of hem pursuweth and performeth
thilke same thing by naturel office, and the
tother mai nat doon thilke naturel office, but
folweth, by other manere than is covenable
to nature, hym that acomplisseth his pur- 90

pos kyndely, and yit he ne acomplisseth
nat his owene purpos — whethir of thise two
demestow for more myghti?"

"Yif that I conjecte," quod I, "that thou wilt
seie, algates yit I desire to herkne it more
pleynly of the."

"Thou nilt nat thanne denye," quod sche,
"that the moevement of goynge nys in men by
kynde?"

"No, forsothe," quod I. 100

"Ne thou ne doutest nat," quod sche,
"that thilke naturel office of goinge ne be the
office of feet?"

"I ne doute it nat," quod I.

"Thanne," quod sche, "yif that a wight be
myghti to moeve, and goth uppon hise feet, and
another, to whom thilke naturel office of feet
lakketh, enforceth hym to gone crepinge uppon
his handes, whiche of thise two oughte to
ben holden the more myghty by right?" 110

"Knyt forth the remenaunt," quod I,
"for no wight ne douteth that he that mai gon
by naturel office of feet ne be more myghti than
he that ne may nat."

"But the soverein good," quod sche, "that is
eveneliche purposed to the good folk and to
badde, the gode folk seken it by naturel office of
vertus, and the schrewes enforcen hem to getin
it by diverse coveytise of erthly thinges,
whiche that nys noon naturel office to gete 120
thilke same soverein good. Trowestow that
it be any other wise?"

"Nai," quod I, "for the consequence is opene
and schewynge of thinges that I have graunted,
that nedes good folk moten be myghty, and
schrewes feble and unmyghti."

"Thou rennist aryght byforn me," quod sche,
"and this is the jugement (*that is to sein, I juge
of the*), ryght as thise leches ben wont to
hopin of sike folk, whan thei aperceyven 130
that nature is redressed and withstondeth
to the maladye. But for I se the now al redy to
the undirstondynge, I schal schewe the more
thikke and contynuel resouns. For loke now,
how greetly scheweth the feblesse and infirmite
of wikkid folk, that ne mowen nat comen to that
hir naturel entencioun ledeth hem; and yit
almest thilke naturel entencioun constreyneth
hem. And what were to demen thanne of

---

48 **forseide resouns:** at 3.pr2.4ff. and throughout Book 3

98 **goynge:** walking
111 **Knyt forth the remenaunt:** go on with your argument
130 **hopin of:** hope for
134 **thikke and contynuel:** condensed

schrewes, yif thilk naturel help hadde 140
forleten hem, the whiche naturel help of
entencioun goth alwey byforn hem and is so gret
that unnethe it mai ben overcome? Considere
thanne how gret defaute of power and how gret
feblesse ther is in wikkide felonous folke. (*As
who seith, the grettere thing that is coveyted
and the desir nat acomplissed, of the lasse
myght is he that coveyteth it and mai nat
acomplisse; and forthi Philosophie seith
thus be sovereyn good.*) Ne schrewes ne 150
requeren not lighte meedes ne veyne
games, whiche thei ne mai nat folwen ne holden;
but thei failen of thilke somme and of the
heighte of thinges (*that is to seyn, soverein
good*). Ne these wrecches ne comen nat to the
effect of sovereyn good, the whiche thei enforcen hem oonly to geten by nyghtes and by
dayes. In the getyng of whiche good the
strengthe of good folk is ful wel yseene.
For ryght so as thou myghtest demen hym 160
myghty of goinge that goth on his feet til
he myghte comen to thilke place fro the whiche
place ther ne laye no weie forthere to be gon,
ryght so mostow nedes demen hym for ryght
myghty, that geteth and atteyneth to the ende of
alle thinges that ben to desire, byyonde the
whiche ende ther nys no thing to desire. Of the
whiche power of good folk men mai conclude
that the wikkide men semen to be bareyne
and naked of alle strengthe. 170

"For whi forleten thei vertus and folwen
vices? Nys it nat for that thei ne knowen nat the
godes? But what thing is more feble and more
caytif than is the blyndnesse of ignorance? Or
elles thei knowen ful wel whiche thinges that
thei oughten folwe, but lecherie and covetise
overthroweth hem mystorned. And certes so
doth distempraunce to feble men, that ne
mowen nat wrastlen ayen the vices. Ne
knowen thei nat thanne wel that thei 180
forleten the good wilfully, and turnen hem
wilfully to vices?

"And in this wise thei ne forleten nat oonly to
ben myghti, but thei forleten al outrely in any
wise for to been. For thei that forleten the
comune fyn of alle thinges that ben, thei forleten
also therwithal for to been. And peraventure
it scholde seme to som folk that this were
a merveile to seien, that schrewes, whiche

that contenen the more partie of men, ne 190
ben nat ne han no beynge; but natheles it
is so, and thus stant this thing. For thei that ben
schrewes I denye nat that they ben schrewes, but
I denye and seie simply and pleynly that thei ne
ben nat, ne han no beynge. For right as thou
myghtest seyn of the careyne of a man, that it
were a deed man, but thou ne myghtest nat
symply callen it a man; so graunte I wel forsothe
that vicyous folk ben wikkid, but I ne may
nat graunten absolutly and symply that thei 200
ben. For thilke thing that withholdeth
ordre and kepeth nature, thilke thing es, and
hath beinge; but what thing that faileth of
that (*that is to seyn, he that forleteth naturel
ordre*), he forleteth thilke beinge that is set in his
nature.

But thow wolt seyn that schrewes mowen.
Certes, that ne denye I nat; but certes hir
power ne desscendeth nat of strengthe,
but of feblesse. For thei mowen don 210
wikkydnesses, the whiche thei ne myghten
nat don yif thei myghten duellen in the forme
and in the doynge of good folk. And thilke
power scheweth ful evidently that they ne
mowen ryght nat. For so as I have gadrid
and proevid a litil herebyforn that evel is
nawght, and so as schrewes mowen oonly but
schrewednesses, this conclusion is al cler, that
schrewes ne mowen ryght nat, ne han no
power. 220
And for as moche as thou undirstonde
which is the strengthe of this power of schrewes,
I have diffinysched a litil herbyforn that no thing
is so myghti as sovereyn good."

"That is soth," quod I.

"And thilke same sovereyn good may don
noon yvel?"

"Certes, no," quod I.

"Is ther any wyght thanne," quod sche,
"that weneth that men mowen don alle 230
thinges?"

"No man," quod I, "but yif he be out of his
wyt."

"But certes schrewes mowen don evel?" quod
sche.

"Ye. Wolde God," quod I, "that thei ne
myghten don noon!"

190 **contenen:** comprise
196 **careyne:** corpse
201 **withholdeth:** maintains
207 **mowen:** have power
216 **herebyforn:** at 3.pr12.151–53, 178–79
223 **diffinysched:** defined, explained **herbyforn:** at
3.pr12.112ff.

177 **mystorned:** misdirected
178 **distempraunce:** intemperance

"Thanne," quod sche, "so as he that is myghty to doon oonly but goode thinges mai doon alle thinges, and thei that ben myghti to   240 doon yvele thinges ne mowen nat alle thinges, thanne is it open thing and manyfest that thei that mowen doon yvele ben of lasse power.

"And yit to proeve this conclusioun ther helpeth me this, that I have schewed herebyforn, that alle power is to be noumbred among thinges that men oughten requere; and I have schewed that alle thinges that oughten ben desired ben referred to good, ryght as to a   250 maner heighte of hir nature. But for to mowen don yvel and felonye ne mai nat ben referrid to good; thanne nys nat yvel of the nombre of thinges that oughten ben desired. But alle power aughte ben desired and requerid; thanne is it open and cler that the power ne the mowynge of schrewes nis no power.

"And of alle thise thinges it scheweth wel that the gode folk ben certeinli myghty, and the schrewes doutelees ben unmyghty. And   260 it is cler and opene that thilke sentence of Plato is verray and soth, that seith that oonly wise men may doon that thei desiren, and schrewes mowen haunten that hem liketh, but that thei desiren (that is to seyn, to come to sovereyn good), thei ne han no power to acomplissen that. For schrewes don that hem lyst whan, by tho thinges in whiche thei deliten, thei wenen to ateynen to thilke good that thei desiren; but thei ne geten ne ateyne nat   270 therto, for vices ne comen nat to blis-fulnesse.

QUOS VIDES SEDERE CELSOS. — *Metrum 2*

"Whoso that the coverturis of hir veyn apparailes myghte strepen of thise proude kynges, that thow seest sitten an hye in here chayeres, gliterynge in schynynge purpre, envyrowned with sorwful armures, manasyng with cruel mowth, blowynge by woodnesse of herte, he schulde seen thanne that thilke lordis berin withynne hir corages ful streyte cheynes. For lecherye tormenteth hem on that o side with gredy venymes; and trowblable ire,   10 that areyseth in hem the floodes of trow-blynges, tormenteth upon that othir side hir thought; or sorwe halt hem wery and icawght, or slidynge and desceyvynge hope turmenteth hem. And therfore, syn thow seest on heved (*that is to seyn, o tiraunt*) beren so manye tyranyes, than ne doth thilke tyraunt nat that he desireth, syn he is cast doun with so manye wikkide lordes (*that is to seyn, with so manye vices that han so wikkidly lord-   20 schipes over hym*).

VIDESNE IGITUR QUANTO. — *Prosa 3*

"Seestow nat thanne in how greet filthe thise schrewes been iwrapped, and with which clernesse thise gode folk schynen? In this scheweth it wel that to good folk ne lakketh neveremo hir meedes, ne schrewes ne lakken neveremo turmentes. For of alle thinges that ben idoon, thilke thing for which any thing is doon, it semeth as by ryght that thilke thing be the mede of that; as thus, yif a man renneth in the stadye or in the forlonge for the   10 corone, thanne lith the mede in the coroune for whiche he renneth. And I have schewed that blisfulnesse is thilke same good for whiche that alle thinges ben doon; thanne is thilke same good purposed to the werkes of man-kynde right as a comune mede, which mede ne may nat ben disseveryd fro good folk. For no wight as by ryght, fro thennesforth that hym lakketh goodnesse, ne schal ben cleped good. For whiche thing folk of gode man-   20 eres, hir medes ne forsaken hem neveremo. For al be it so that schrewes waxen as wode as hem lyst ayein good folk, yit natheles the coroune of wise men ne schal nat fallen ne faden; for foreyne schrewednesse ne bynemeth nat fro the corages of good folk hir propre honour. But yif that any wyght rejoysede hym of goodnesse that he hadde taken fro withoute (*as who seith, yif any man hadde his good-nesse of any other man than of hymself*),   30 certes he that yaf hym thilke goodnesse, or elles som other wyght, myghte benymen it hym. But for as moche as to every wyght his owene propre bounte yeveth hym his mede, thanne at erste schal he failen of mede whan he forletith to ben good. And at the laste, so as alle medes ben requerid for men wenen that

---

246 **herebyforn**: at 3.pr9.22–33
257 **mowynge**: ability, power
264 **haunten**: keep doing
Metrum 2.5 **manasyng**: menacing
6 **blowynge**: blustering
11 **areyseth**: arouses

15 **on**: one
Prosa 3.10 **stadye**: stadium   **forlonge**: racetrack
12 **I have schewed**: at 3.pr2.4–8.
25 **foreyne schrewednesse**: the wickedness of others

thei ben gode, who is he that nolde deme that he that is ryght myghti of good were part-lees of the mede? And of what mede schal he ben gerdoned? Certes of ryght fair mede and ryght greet aboven alle medes. Re-membre the of thilke noble corrolarie that I yaf the a litel herebyforn, and gadre it togidre in this manere: so as good [hytself] is blisful-nesse, thanne is it cler and certein that alle gode folk ben imaked blisful for thei ben gode; and thilke folk that ben blisful it accordeth and is covenable to ben goddes. Thanne is the mede of good folk swych that no day ne schal empeiren it, ne no wikkidnesse schal derkne it, ne power of no wyght ne schal nat amenusen it; that is to seyn, to ben maked goddes. And syn it is thus (*that gode men ne failen neveremo of hir mede*), certes no wise man ne may doute of the undepartable peyne of schrewes (*that is to seyn, that the peyne of schrewes ne departeth nat from hemself nevere-mo*). For so as good and yvel, and peyne and medes, ben contrarie, it moot nedes ben that, ryght as we seen betyden in guerdoun of gode, that also moot the peyne of yvel an-swere by the contrarie partie to schrewes. Now thanne, so as bounte and pruesse ben the mede to good folk, also is schrewidnesse itself tor-ment to schrewes. Thanne whoso that evere is entecchid or defouled with peyne, he ne dout-eth nat that he nys entecchid and defouled with yvel. Yif schrewes thanne wol preysen hemself, may it semen to hem that thei ben withouten parti of torment, syn thei ben swiche that the uttreste wikkidnesse (*that is to seyn, wikkide thewes, which that is the utter-este and the worst kynde of schrewednesse*) ne defouleth ne enteccheth nat hem oonly, but enfecteth and envenymeth hem greetly? And also loke on schrewes, that ben the contrarie partie of gode men, how gret peyne felaw-schipith and folweth hem! For thou hast lerned a litil herebyforn that alle thing that is and hath beynge is oon, and thilke same oon is good: than is this the consequence, that it semeth wel that al that is and hath beynge is good. (*This is to seyn, as who seith that*

beinge and unite and goodnesse is al oon.) And in this manere it folweth thanne that alle thing that fayleth to ben good, it stynteth for to be and for to han any beynge. Wherfore it es that schrewes stynten for to ben that thei weeren. But thilke othir forme [of the body] of mankynde (*that is to seyn, the [forme] withowte*) scheweth yit that thise schrewes weren whilom men. Wherfore, whan thei ben perverted and turned into malice, certes, thanne have thei forlorn the nature of mankynde. But so as oonly bownte and prow-esse may enhawnsen every man over othere men, than moot it nedes be that schrewes, whiche that schrewednesse hath cast out of the condicion of mankynde, ben put undir the merit and the dissert of men. Than betidith it that, yif thou seest a wyght that be transformed into vices, thow ne mayst nat wene that he be a man. For if he be ardaunt in avaryce, and that he be a ravynour by violence of foreyne richesse, thou schalt seyn that he is lik to the wolf; and if he be felonows and withoute reste, and exercise his tonge to chidynges, thow schalt likne hym to the hownd; and if he be a pryve awaytour yhid, and rejoiseth hym to ravyssche be wiles, thow schalt seyn hym lik to the fox whelpes; and yif he be distempre, and quakith for ire, men schal wene that he bereth the corage of a lyoun; and yif he be dredful and fleynge, and dredith thinges that ne aughte nat to ben dredd, men schal holden hym lik to the hert; and yf he be slow, and astonyd, and lache, he lyveth as an asse; yif he be lyght and unstedfast of corage and chaungith ay his studies, he is likned to briddes; and if he be ploungid in fowle and unclene luxuris, he is withholden in the foule delices of the fowle sowe. Than folweth it that he that forleteth bounte and prowesse, he forletith to ben a man; syn he ne may nat passe into the condicion of God, he is torned into a beeste.

VELA NARICII DUCIS. — *Metrum 3*

"Eurus, the wynd, aryved the sayles of Ulixes, duc of the cuntre of Narice, and his wan-drynge shippes by the see, into the ile theras

39–40 **partlees**: without a share
44 **herebyforn**: at 3.pr10.137
51 **empeiren**: impair
64 **pruesse**: prowess, excellence
67 **entecchid**: stained
75 **enteccheth**: stains
78–79 **felawschipith**: accompanies
80 **herebyforn**: at 3.pr12.171–75

105 **ravynour**: plunderer
110 **awaytour**: one lying in ambush
112 **distempre**: enraged, distempered
117 **astonyd**: stupid
118 **lache**: lazy
121 **luxuris**: lusts
Metrum 3.1 **Eurus**: the southeast wind **aryved**: drove ashore
2 **cuntre of Narice**: Ithaca, site of mount Neritos

Cerces, the faire goddesse, dowhter of the
sonne, duelleth, that medleth to hir newe
gestes drynkes that ben touchid and makid
with enchauntementz. And aftir that hir hand,
myghti over the erbes, hadde chaunged hir
gestes into diverse maneres, that oon of
hem is coverid his face with forme of a   10
boor; the tother is chaungid into a lyoun
of the contre of Marmoryke, and his nayles and
his teth waxen; that oother of hem is newliche
chaunged into a wolf, and howleth whan he
wolde wepe; that other goth debonayrely in
the hows as a tigre of Inde. But al be it so
that the godhede of Mercurie, that is cleped
the bridde of Arcadye, hath had merci of the
duc Ulixes, bysegid with diverse yveles,
and hath unbownden hym fro the pesti-   20
lence of his oostesse, algates the rowerys
and the maryneres hadden by this idrawen into
hir mouthes and dronken the wikkide drynkes.
Thei that weren woxen swyn hadden by this
ichaunged hir mete of breed for to eten ak-
kornes of ookes. Noon of hir lymes ne duelleth with hem hool, but thei han lost the voys
and the body; oonly hir thought duelleth with
hem stable, that wepeth and bywayleth the
monstruous chaungynge that thei suffren.   30
O overlyght hand! (*As who seith: O
feble and light is the hand of Circes the en-
chaunteresse, that chaungith the bodyes of
folk into beestes, to regard and to comparysoun of mutacioun that is makid by vices!*)
Ne the herbes of Circes ne ben nat myghty.
For al be it so that thei mai chaungen the
lymes of the body, algates yit thei may nat
chaungen the hertes. For withinne is ihidd
the strengthe and the vygour of men, in the   40
secre tour of hir hertes, (that is to seyn, the
strengthe of resoun); but thilke venyms of vices
todrawen a man to hem more myghtely than
the venym of Circes. For vices ben so cruel
that they percen and thurw-passen the corage
withinne; and, thoughe thei ne anoye nat the
body, yit vices woden to destroyen men by
wounde of thought."

Thanne seide I thus: "I confesse and am
aknowe it," quod I, "ne I ne se nat that men
may seyn as by ryght that schrewes ne ben
chaunged into beestes by the qualite of hir
soules, al be it so that thei kepin yit the forme
of the body of mankynde. But I nolde nat of
schrewes, of whiche the thought crwel woodeth alwey into destruccion of gode men, that
it were leveful to hem to don that."

"Certes," quod sche, "ne it is nat leveful   10
to hem, as I schal wel schewen the in covenable place. But natheles, yif so were that
thilke that men wenen ben leveful to schrewes
were bynomyn hem, so that they ne myghte
nat anoyen or doon harm to gode men, certes
a gret partie of the peyne to schrewes scholde
ben alegged and releved. For al be it so that
this ne seme nat credible thing peraventure to
some folk, yit moot it nedes be that
schrewes ben more wrecches and unsely   20
whan thei mai doon and parforme that
thei coveyten, than yif thei ne myghte nat
acomplissen that thei coveiten. For yif so
be that it be wrecchidnesse to wilne to doon
yvel, thanne is it more wrecchidnesse to mowe
don yvel, withoute whiche mowynge the wrecchid wil scholde langwisse withouten effect.
Thanne syn that everiche of thise thinges hath his
wrecchidnesse (that is to seyn, wil to don
ivel and mowynge to don yvel), it moot   30
nedes be that schrewes ben constreyned by
thre unselynesses, that wolen, and mowen, and
parformen felonyes and schrewednesses."

"I acorde me," quod I; "but I desire gretly
that schrewes losten sone thilke unselynesses,
that is to seyn, that schrewes weren despoyled
of mowynge to don yvel."

"So schollen thei," quod sche, "sonnere peraventure than thou woldest, or sonnere
than they hemselve wene. For ther nis   40
nothing so late, in so schorte bowndes of
this lif, that is long to abyde, nameliche to a corage immortel. Of whiche schrewes the grete
hope and the heye compassynges of schrewednesses is ofte destroyed by a sodeyn ende, or

---

4 **Cerces:** Circe
5 **medleth to:** mixes for
12 **Marmoryke:** Marmarica, in eastern Libya
15 **debonayrely:** tamely
18 **bridde of Arcadye:** a reference to Mercury's wings and his
birth on Mt. Cyllene in Arcadia   **merci of:** mercy on
21 **oostesse:** hostess
47 **woden:** rage, desire passionately

Prosa 4.1–2 **am aknowe:** acknowledge
7–8 **woodeth:** rages
11–12 **in covenable place:** at 154ff. below, and 4.pr6.168ff. in
response to the question raised at 4.pr5.20ff.
17 **alegged:** allayed
20 **unsely:** unlucky
26 **mowynge:** power
44 **compassynges:** schemes

thei ben war; and that thing establisseth to schrewes the ende of hir schrewednesse. For yf that schrewednesse makith wrecches, than mot he nedes ben moost wrecchide that lengest is a schrewe. The whiche wikkide 50 schrewes wolde I demen althermost unsely and kaytifs, yif that hir schrewednesse ne were fynissched at the leste weye by the owtreste deth; for yif I have concluded soth of the un-selynesse of schrewednesse, thanne schewith it clerly that thilke wrecchidnesse is withouten ende the whiche is certein to ben perdurable."

"Certes," quod I, "this conclusioun is hard and wondirful to graunte; but I knowe wel that it accordeth moche to the thinges that 60 I have grauntid herebiforn."

"Thou hast," quod sche, "the ryght estima-cion of this. But whosoevere wene that it be an hard thing to accorde hym to a conclu-sioun, it is ryght that he schewe that some of the premysses ben false, or elles he mot schewe that the collacioun of proposicions nis nat spedful to a necessarie conclusioun; and yif it ne be nat so, but that the prem-isses ben ygraunted, ther nys nat why he 70 scholde blame the argument. For this thing that I schal telle the now ne schal nat seme lesse wondirful, but of the thingis that ben taken also it is necessarie." (*As who seith, it folweth of that which that is purposed by-forn.*)

"What is that?" quod I.

"Certes," quod sche, "that is that thise wik-kid schrewes ben more blisful, or elles lasse wrecches, that abyen the tormentz 80 that thei han desservid, than if no peyne of justise ne chastisede hem. Ne this ne seie I nat now for that any man myghte thinke that the maneris of schrewes ben coriged and chas-tised by vengeaunce and that thei ben brought to the ryghte weye by the drede of the torment, ne for that they yeven to other folk ensaumple to fleen fro vices; but I undirstonde yit in an-other manere that schrewes ben more un-sely whan thei ne ben nat punyssched, al 90 be it so that ther ne be hadde no resoun or lawe of correccioun, ne noon ensample of lokynge."

"And what manere schal that be," quod I, "other than hath ben told herbyforn?"

"Have we nat thanne graunted," quod sche, "that good folk ben blisful and schrewes ben wrecches?"

"Yis," quod I.

"Thanne," quod sche, "yif that any good 100 were added to the wrecchidnesse of any wyght, nis he nat more blisful than he that ne hath no medlynge of good in his solitarie wrecchidnesse?"

"So semeth it," quod I.

"And what seistow thanne," quod sche, "of thilke wrecche that lakketh alle goodes so that no good nys medlyd in his wrecchidnesse, and yit over al his wikkidnesse, for which he is a wrecche, that ther be yit another 110 yvel anexed and knyt to hym — schal nat men demen hym more unsely thanne thilke wrecche of whiche the unselynesse is relevid by the participacioun of som good?"

"Why sholde he nat?" quod I.

"Thanne certes," quod sche, "han schrewes, whan thei ben punyschid, somwhat of good anexid to hir wrecchidnesse (that is to seyn, the same peyne that thei suffren, which that is good by the resoun of justice); and whanne 120 thilke same schrewes ascapen withouten torment, than han they somwhat more of yvel yit over the wikkidnesse that thei han don, that is to seyn, defaute of peyne, whiche defaute of peyne thou hast grauntid is yvel for the disserte of felonye?"

"I ne may nat denye it," quod I.

"Moche more thanne," quod sche, "ben schrewes unsely whan thei ben wrong-fully delivred fro peyne, thanne whan thei 130 ben punyschid by ryghtful vengeaunce. But this is opene thing and cleer, that it is ryght that schrewes ben punyschid, and it is wik-kidnesse and wrong that thei escapen unpun-yschid."

"Who myghte denye that?" quod I.

"But," quod sche, "may any man denye that al that is ryght nis good, and also the contra-rie, that al that is wrong is wikke?"

"Certes," quod I, "thise thinges ben 140 clere ynowe, and [folwen that] that we han concluded a lytel herebyforn. But I preye the

67 **collacioun:** comparison
68 **spedful:** conducive
75 **purposed:** supposed, conceded
84 **coriged:** corrected
92–93 **ensample of lokynge:** example for others to behold

125–26 **for the disserte of felonye:** with regard to what crime deserves; see n.
142 **herebyforn:** at 30–33 above; see n. to 116–31

that thow telle me, yif thow accordest to leten
no torment to the soules aftir that the body is
ended by the deeth?" (*This to seyn, "Un-
dirstondestow aught that soules han any
torment aftir the deeth of the body?"*)

"Certes," quod sche, "ye, and that ryght
greet. Of whiche soules," quod sche, "I
trowe that some ben tormented by aspre-   150
nesse of peyne, and some soules I trowe
ben excercised by a purgynge mekenesse; but
my conseil nys nat to determyne of thise peynes.

"But I have travailed and told yit hiderto for
thou scholdest knowe that the mowynge of
schrewes, whiche mowynge the semeth to ben
unworthy, nis no mowynge; and ek of schrewes,
of whiche thou pleynedest that they ne were nat
punysschid, that thow woldest seen that
thei ne were neveremo withouten the   160
tormentz of hir wikkidnesse; and of the
licence of mowynge to don yvel that thou
preyedest that it myghte sone ben ended, and
that thou woldest fayn lernen that it ne sholde
nat longe endure, and that schrewes ben more
unsely yif thei were of lengere durynge, and
most unsely yif thei weren perdurable. And aftir
this I have schewyd the that more unsely ben
schrewes whan thei escapen withouten hir
ryghtful peyne thanne whan thei ben   170
punyschid by ryghtful venjaunce; and of
this sentence folweth it that thanne ben schrewes
constreyned at the laste with most grevous
torment, whan men wene that thei ne ben nat
punyssched."

"Whan I considere thi resouns," quod I, "I ne
trowe nat that men seyn any thing more
verrayly. And yif I turne ayein to the studies of
men, who is he to whom it sholde seme that
he ne scholde nat oonly leven thise thinges,   180
but ek gladly herkne hem?"

"Certes," quod sche, "so it es — but men may
nat. For they have hir eien so wont to the
derknesse of erthly thinges that they ne may nat
lyften hem up to the light of cler sothfastnesse,
but thei ben lyk to briddes of whiche the nyght
lightneth hir lokynge and the day blendith hem.
For whan men loke nat the ordre of thinges, but
hir lustes and talentz, they wene that either
the leve or the mowynge to don wik-   190
kidnesse, or elles the scapynge withouten peyne be weleful.

"But considere the jugement of the perdurable lawe. For yif thou conferme thi corage to the
beste thinges, thow ne hast noon nede of no juge
to yeven the prys or mede; for thow hast joyned
thiself to the most excellent thing. And yif thow
have enclyned thi studies to the wikkide thinges,
ne seek no foreyne wrekere out of thiself;
for thow thiself hast thrist thiself into wikke   200
thinges, ryght as thow myghtest loken by
diverse tymes the fowle erthe and the hevene,
and that alle othere thinges stynten fro withoute,
so that thow nere neyther in [hevene] ne in
erthe, ne saye no thyng more; thanne scholde it
semen to the as by oonly resoun of lokynge that
thow were now in the sterres, and now in the
erthe. But the peple ne loketh nat on these
thinges. What thanne? Schal we thanne
approchen us to hem that I have schewed   210
that thei ben lyke to beestes? And what
wyltow seyn of this: yif that a man hadde al
forlorn his syghte, and hadde foryeten that he
evere sawhe, and wende that no thing ne faylede
hym of perfeccioun of mankynde; now we that
myghten sen the same thinges — wolde we nat
wene that he were blynd? Ne also ne accordeth
nat the peple to that I schal seyn, the whiche
thing is sustenyd by as stronge foundementz of resouns, that is to seyn, that   220
more unsely ben they that doon wrong to
othere folk, than they that the wrong suffren."

"I wolde here thilke same resouns," quod I.

"Denyestow," quod sche, "that alle schrewes
ne ben worthy to han torment?"

"Nay," quod I.

"But," quod sche, "I am certein by many
resouns that schrewes ben unsely."

"It accordeth," quod I.

"Thanne ne dowtestow nat," quod sche,   230
"that thilke folk that ben worthy of
torment, that they ne ben wrecches?"

"It accordeth wel," quod I.

"Yif thou were thanne iset a juge or a
knowere of thinges, whethir trowestow that men
scholden tormenten, hym that hath don the
wrong or elles hym that hath suffred the
wrong?"

"I ne doute nat," quod I, "that I nolde
doon suffisaunt satisfaccioun to hym that   240
hadde suffrid the wrong, by the sorwe of
hym that hadde doon the wrong."

---

143 **leten:** allow for
150–51 **aspresnesse:** bitterness
153 **conseil:** intention
189 **talentz:** desires

196 **the:** thee
199 **wrekere:** avenger
201–2 **loken by diverse tymes:** look in turn at
205 **saye:** saw, were to see
235 **whethir:** which of the two

"Thanne semeth it," quod sche, "that the doere of wrong is more wrecche than he that hath suffride wrong?"

"That folweth wel," quod I.

"Than," quod sche, "by thise causes and by othere causes that ben enforced by the same roote, that filthe [of] synne be the propre nature of it maketh men wrecches, [it]   250 scheweth wel that the wrong that men doon nis nat the wrecchidnesse of hym that resceyveth the wrong, but the wrecchidnesse of hym that dooth the wrong. But certes," quod sche, "thise oratours or advocattes don al the contrarie; for thei enforcen hem to commoeve the juges to han pite of hem that han suffrid and resceyved the thinges that ben grevous and aspre, and yit men scholden more ryghtfully han pite of hem that doon the   260 grevances and the wronges: the whiche schrewes it were a more covenable thing that the accusours or advocattes, nat wrooth but pytous and debonayre, ledden tho schrewes that han don wrong to the jugement ryght as men leden syke folk to the leche, for that thei sholden seken out the maladyes of synne by torment. And by this covenant, eyther the entent of the deffendours or advocatz sholde fayle and cesen in al, or elles, yif the office of   270 advocatz wolde betre profiten to men, it sholde be torned into the habyte of accusacioun. (*That is to seyn, thei scholden accuse schrewes, and nat excusen hem.*) And eek the schrewes hemself, yif it were leveful to hem to seen at any clifte the vertu that thei han forleten, and sawen that they scholden putten adoun the filthes of hir vices by the tormentz of peynes, they ne aughten nat, ryght for the recompensacioun for to geten hem bounte   280 and prowesse whiche that thei han lost, demen ne holden that thilke peynes weren tormentz to hem; and eek thei wolden refuse the attendaunce of hir advocattz, and taken hemself to hir juges and to hir accusours. For whiche it betydeth that, as to the wise folk, ther nis no place yleten to hate (*that is to seyn, that hate ne hath no place among wise men*); for no wyght nil haten gode men, but yif he were overmochel a fool, and for to haten   290

schrewes it nis no resoun. For ryght so as langwissynge is maladye of body, ryght so ben vices and synne maladye of corage; and so as we ne deme nat that they that ben sike of hir body ben worthy to ben hated, but rather worthy of pite; wel more worthy nat to ben hated, but for to ben had in pite, ben thei of whiche the thoughtes ben constreyned by felonous wikkidnesse, that is more crwel than any langwissynge of body.   300

QUID TANTOS IUVAT. — *Metrum 4*

"What deliteth yow to exciten so grete moevynges of hatredes, and to hasten and bysien the fatal disposicioun of your deth with your propre handes (*that is to seyn, by batayles or contek*)? For yif ye axen the deth, it hasteth hym of his owene wil, ne deth ne taryeth nat his swifte hors. And the men that the serpent, and the lyoun, and the tigre, and the bere, and the boor, seken to sleen with hir teeth, yit thilke same men seken to sleen   10 everiche of hem oothir with swerd. Lo, for hir maneres ben diverse and discordaunt, thei moeven unryghtful oostes and cruel batayles, and wilnen to perise by entrechaungynge of dartes! But the resoun of cruelte nis nat inowhe ryghtful. Wiltow thanne yelden a covenable gerdoun to the dissertes of men? Love ryghtfully good folk, and have pite on schrewes."

HINC EGO VIDEO INQUAM. — *Prosa 5*

"Thus se I wel," quod I, "eyther what blisfulnesse or elles what unselynesse is establisshid in the dissertes of gode men and of schrewes. But in this ilke fortune of peple I se somwhat of good and somwhat of yvel. For no wise man hath nat levere ben exiled, pore and nedy and nameles, thanne for to duellen in his cyte, and flouren of rychesses, and be redowtable by honour and strong of power. For in this wise more clerly and more wit-   10 nesfully is the office of wise men ytreted, whanne the blisfulnesse and the pouste of gouvernours is, as it ware, ischadde among peples that ben neyghbors and subgitz; syn that namely prisown, lawe, and thise othere tormentz of laweful peynes ben rather owed to

---

252 **wrecchidnesse of:** i.e., misery for
255 **oratours or advocattes:** i.e., prosecutors
256 **commoeve:** move
263 **accusours or advocattes:** i.e., prosecutors
264 **debonayre:** kindly
269 **deffendours or advocatz:** i.e., defense attorneys
276 **clifte:** chink
284 **attendaunce:** service

Metrum 4.1 **What:** why
5 **contek:** strife
7 **hors:** horses
Prosa 5.10–11 **witnesfully:** evidently
11 **office:** social function   **ytreted:** exercised; see n. to 10–19.
12 **pouste:** power

felonus citezeins, for the whiche felonus citezeens tho peynes ben establisschid than for
good folk.

"Thanne I merveile me gretly," quod I,   20
"why that the thinges ben so mysentrechaunged that tormentz of felonyes pressen and
confounden good folk, and schrewes ravysschen medes of vertu and ben in honours
and in grete estatz; and I desire eek for to
witen of the what semeth the to be the resoun
of this so wrongful a confusioun; for I wolde
wondre wel the lasse, yif I trowede that alle
thise thinges weren medled by fortunows
hap. But now hepith and encreseth myn   30
astonyenge God, governour of thinges,
that, so as God yyveth ofte tymes to gode men
godes and myrthes, and to schrewes yvelis and
aspre thinges, and yeveth ayeinward to good
folk hardnesses, and to schrewes he graunteth
hem hir wil and that they desiren — what difference thanne may ther be bytwixen that that
God doth and the hap of fortune, yif men ne
knowe nat the cause why that it is?"

"Ne it nis no merveile," quod sche,   40
"thowh that men wenen that ther be somwhat foolisshe and confus, whan the resoun of
the ordre is unknowe. But although that thou
ne knowe nat the cause of so gret a disposicioun, natheles for as moche as God, the gode
governour, atempreth and governeth the world,
ne doute the nat that alle thinges ne ben don
aryght.

SI QUIS ARCTURI SIDERA. — *Metrum 5*

"Whoso that ne knowe nat the sterres of
Arctour, ytorned neyghe to the sovereyne centre or poynt (that is to seyn, ytorned neyghe to
the sovereyne pool of the firmament), and wot
nat why the sterre Boetes passeth or gadreth
his waynes and drencheth his late flaumbes in
the see; and whi that Boetes, the sterre, unfooldeth hise overswifte arysynges, thanne schal
he wondryn of the lawe of the heie eyr.
And eek yif that he ne knowe nat why that   10
the hornes of the fulle mone waxen pale

and infect by bowndes of the derk nyght, and
how the mone derk and confus discovereth the
sterres that sche hadde covered by hir clere
vysage. The comune errour moeveth folk, and
[the Coribantes maken hir tabours sounen and
maken] weery hir basyns of bras by thikke
strokes. (*That is to seyn, that ther is a maner
peple that hyghte Coribantes, that wenen
that whan the mone is in the eclips that*   20
*it be enchaunted, and therfore for to
rescowe the mone thei betyn hir basyns with
thikke strokes.*) Ne no man ne wondreth
whanne the blastes of the wynd Chorus beten
the strondes of the see by quakynge floodes; ne
no man ne wondrith whan the weighte of the
snowh, ihardid by the cold, is resolvyd by the
brennynge hete of Phebus, the sonne; for her
seen men redily the causes. But [ther] the
causes yhidd (*that is to seyn, in hevene*)   30
trowblen the brestes of men. The
moevable peple is astoned of alle thinges that
comen seelde and sodeynly in our age; but yif
the trubly errour of our ignoraunce departed fro
us, so that we wisten the causes why that swiche
thinges bytyden, certes thei scholde cesen to
seme wondres."

ITA EST INQUAM. — *Prosa 6*

"Thus is it," quod I. "But so as thou hast
yeven or byhyght me to unwrappen the hidde
causes of thinges, and to discovere me the
resouns covered with derknes, I preie the that
thou devyse and juge me of this matere, and
that thou do me to undirstonden it. For this
miracle or this wonder trowbleth me ryght
gretly."

And thanne sche, a litelwhat smylinge,
seide: "Thou clepist me," quod sche, "to   10
telle thing that is gretteste of alle thingis
that mowen ben axed, and to the whiche questioun unethes is ther aught inowh to laven
it. (As who seith, unnethes is ther suffisauntly
any thing to answeren parfitly to thy questioun.) For the matere of it is swich, that
whan o doute is determined and kut awey, ther
waxen othere doutes withoute nombre, ryght
as the hevedes wexen of Idre, the serpent

21–22 **mysentrechaunged:** topsy-turvy
29–30 **thise . . . hap:** i.e., these confusions were caused by mere
chance
Metrum 5.1 **Whoso that:** i.e., if there is one who
2 **Arctour:** the constellation Arcturus (Boötes)
4 **sovereyne pool:** North Pole
5–6 **passeth or gadreth his waynes:** goes or drives his carts; see
n.
7–8 **unfooldeth hise overswifte arysynges:** i.e., rises so soon
after setting so late

16 **Coribantes:** priests of Cybele; see n. to line 17.
24 **Chorus:** Caurus, the northwest wind
32 **moevable:** impressionable
34 **trubly:** cloudy
Prosa 6.2 **unwrappen:** disclose
13 **laven:** draw up, exhaust
19 **Idre:** Hydra, whose heads, when cut off, grew back as two;
see m7.41–42.

that Hercules slowh. Ne ther ne were no   20
manere ne noon ende, but if that a wyght
constreynede tho doutes by a ryght lifly and
quyk fir of thought (that is to seyn, by vigour and strengthe of wit). For in this matere
men weren wont to maken questiouns of the
symplicite of the purveaunce of God, and of
the ordre of destyne, and of sodeyn hap, and
of the knowynge and predestinacioun devyne,
and of the liberte of fre wil; the whiche
things thou thiself aperceyvest wel of   30
what weighte thei ben. But for as moche
as the knowynge of thise thinges is a maner
porcioun of the medycyne to the, al be it so
that I have litil tyme to doon it, yit natheles
Y wol enforcen me to schewe somwhat of it.
But although the noryssynges of dite of musyk
deliteth the, thou most suffren and forberen a
litel of thilke delit, whil that I weve to the resouns yknyt by ordre.''

"As it liketh to the,'' quod I, ''so do.''   40
Tho spak sche ryght as by another bygynnynge, and seide thus: ''The engendrynge
of alle thinges,'' quod sche, ''and alle the progressiouns of muable nature, and al that moeveth in any manere, taketh hise causes, his ordre,
and his formes, of the stablenesse of the devyne thought. And thilke devyne thought that
is iset and put in the tour (that is to seyn, in
the heighte) of the simplicite of God, stab-
lissith many maner gises to thinges that ben   50
to done; the whiche manere whan that
men looken it in thilke pure clennesse of the
devyne intelligence, it is ycleped purveaunce;
but whanne thilke manere is referred by men
to thinges that it moeveth and disponyth, than
of olde men it was clepyd destyne. The whiche
thinges yif that any wyght loketh wel in his
thought the strengthe of that oon and of that
oothir, he schal lyghtly mowen seen that
thise two thinges ben dyvers. For pur-   60
veaunce is thilke devyne resoun that is establissed in the sovereyn prince of thinges, the
whiche purveaunce disponith alle thinges; but,
certes, destyne is the disposicioun and ordenance clyvynge to moevable thinges, by the
whiche disposicion the purveaunce knytteth
alle thingis in hir ordres; for purveaunce enbraceth alle thinges to-hepe, althoghe that thei

ben diverse and although thei ben infinit.
But destyne, certes, departeth and ordeyn-   70
eth alle thinges singulerly and devyded in
moevynges in places, in formes, in tymes, as
thus: lat the unfoldynge of temporel ordenaunce, assembled and oonyd in the lokynge
of the devyne thought, be cleped purveaunce,
and thilke same assemblynge and oonynge, devyded and unfolden by tymes, lat that ben
called destyne.

"And al be it so that thise thinges ben
diverse, yit natheles hangeth that oon of   80
that oother; forwhi the ordre destynal
procedith of the simplicite of purveaunce. For
ryght as a werkman that aperceyveth in his
thought the forme of the thing that he wol make,
and moeveth the effect of the werk, and ledith
that he hadde lookid byforn in his thought
symplely and presently by temporel ordenaunce; certes, ryght so God disponith in his
purveaunce singulerly and stably the
thinges that ben to doone; but he   90
amynistreth in many maneris and in diverse
tymes by destyne thilke same thinges that he
hath disponyd. Thanne, whethir that destyne be
exercised outhir by some devyne spiritz,
servantz to the devyne purveaunce, or elles by
some soule, or elles by alle nature servynge to
God, or elles by the celestial moevynges of
sterres, or ellis by vertu of aungelis, or elles by
divers subtilite of develis, or elles by any of
hem, or elles by hem alle the destinal   100
ordenaunce is ywoven and acomplissid,
certes, it es opene thing that the purveaunce is
an unmoevable and symple forme of thinges
to doone, and the moevable bond and the
temporel ordenaunce of thinges whiche that the
devyne symplicite of purveaunce hath ordeyned
to doone, that is destyne.

"For whiche it is that alle thinges that ben
put undir destyne ben certes subgitz to
purveaunce, to whiche purveaunce destyne   110
itself is subgit and under. But some thinges
ben put undir purveaunce, that sourmounten
the ordenance of destyne; and tho ben thilke
that stably ben ifycchid neyghe to the first
godhede. They surmounten the ordre of
destynal moevablete. For ryght as of cerklis that

73–74 **temporel ordenaunce:** events in time
74 **oonyd:** united
80 **hangeth . . . of:** i.e., depends on
81 **forwhi:** for
87–88 **symplely . . . ordenaunce:** construe the adverbs with *hadde lookid* and the prepositional phrase with *ledith*
116 **destynal moevablete:** predestined mutability

---

21 **manere:** (easy) way
36 **dite of musyk:** verse
38 **weve to the:** weave for you
43–44 **progressiouns:** natural processes
68 **to-hepe:** in a heap, en masse

tornen aboute a same centre or aboute a poynt,
thilke cerkle that is innerest or most withinne
joyneth to the symplesse of the myddle,
and is, as it were, a centre or a poynt to the   120
tothere cerklis that tornen abouten hym;
and thilke that is utterest, compased by a largere
envyrownynge, is unfolden by largere spaces in
so moche as it is ferthest fro the myddel
symplicite of the poynt; and yif ther be any thing
that knytteth and felawschipeth hymself to thilke
myddel poynt, it is constreyned into simplicite
(*that is to seyn, into unmoevablete*), and it
ceseth to ben schad and to fleten diversely;
ryght so, by semblable reson, thilke thing   130
that departeth ferrest fro the firste thought
of God, it is unfolden and summittid to grettere
bondes of destyne; and in so moche is the thing
more fre and laus fro destyne, as it axeth and
hooldeth hym neer to thilke centre of thinges
(*that is to seyn, to God*); and yif the thing
clyveth to the stedfastnesse of the thought of
God and be withoute moevynge, certes it
surmounteth the necessite of destyne.
Thanne ryght swich comparysoun as is of   140
skillynge to undirstondyng, and of thing
that ys engendrid to thing that is, and of tyme to
eternite, and of the cercle to the centre; ryght so
is the ordre of moevable destyne to the stable
symplicite of purveaunce.
    "Thilke ordenaunce moveth the hevene and
the sterres, and atemprith the elementz togidre
amonges hemself, and transformeth hem by
entrechaungeable mutacioun. And thilke
same ordre neweth ayein alle thinges   150
growynge and fallynge adoun, by semblable progressions of sedes and of sexes (that
is to seyn, male and femele). And this ilke
ordre constreyneth the fortunes and the dedes of
men by a bond of causes nat able to ben
unbownde; the whiche destynal causes, whan
thei passen out fro the bygynnynges of the
unmoevable purveaunce, it moot nedes be that
thei ne be nat mutable. And thus ben the
thinges ful wel igoverned yif that the   160
symplicite duellynge in the devyne thoght
scheweth forth the ordre of causes unable to ben
ibowed. And this ordre constreyneth by his

propre stablete the moevable thingis, or elles
thei scholden fleten folyly.
    "For whiche it es that alle thingis semen to
ben confus and trouble to us men, for we ne
mowen nat considere thilke ordenaunce.
Natheles the propre maner of every thing,
dressynge hem to gode, disponith hem alle,   170
for ther nys no thing doon for cause of yvel,
ne thilk thing that is doon by wikkid folk nys nat
doon for yvel, the whiche schrewes, as I have
schewed ful plentyvously, seken good, but
wikkid errour mystorneth hem; ne the ordre
comynge fro the poynt of sovereyn good ne
declyneth nat fro his bygynnynge.
    "But thou mayst seyn, 'What unreste may ben
a worse confusioun than that gode men
han somtyme adversite and somtyme   180
prosperite, and schrewes also han now
thingis that they desiren and now thinges that
thei haten?' Whethir men lyven now in swich
holnesse of thought (as who seith, ben men now
so wyse) that swiche folk as thei demen to ben
gode folk or schrewes, that it moste nedes ben
that folk ben swiche as thei wenen? But in this
manere the domes of men discorden, that thilke
men that som folk demen worthy of mede,
other folk demen hem worthy of torment.   190
But lat us graunten, I pose, that som man
may wel demen or knowen the good folk and
the badde; may he thanne knowen and seen
thilke innereste atempraunce of corages as it
hath ben wont to ben seyd of bodyes? (*As who
seith, may a man speken and determinen of
atempraunce in corages, as men were wont to
demen or speken of complexions and atempraunces of bodies?*) Ne it ne is nat an
unlike miracle to hem that ne knowen it nat   200
(*as who seith, but it is lik a mervayle or
miracle to hem that ne knowen it nat*) whi
that swete thinges ben covenable to some bodies
that ben hole, and to some bodies byttere
thinges ben covenable; and also why that some
syk folk ben holpen with lyghte medicynes, and
some folk ben holpen with sharpe medicynes.
But natheles the leche, that knoweth the manere
and the atempraunce of hele and of
maladye, ne merveyleth of it nothyng. But   210
what othir thing semeth hele of corages but

---

123 **envyrownynge:** orbit   **unfolden by:** opened out into
128 **unmoevablete:** stability
129 **schad:** scattered
134 **laus:** loose   **axeth:** i.e., seeks
141 **skillynge:** reasoning
149 **entrechaungeable:** reciprocal
152 **progressions:** natural processes
163 **ibowed:** diverted

170 **dressynge hem to:** directing themselves toward
177 **declyneth:** turns aside
178 Philosophy returns to the subject of the preceding prose
(pr5.30ff.).
194 **atempraunce:** temperament

bounte and prowesse? And what othir thing semeth maladye of corages but vices? Who is elles kepere of good or dryvere awey of yvel but God, governour and lechere of thoughtes? The whiche God, whan he hath byholden from the hye tour of his purveaunce, he knoweth what is covenable to every wight, and lenyth hem that he woot that is covenable to hem. Lo, herof comyth and herof is don this noble miracle   220 of the ordre destynal, whan God, that al knoweth, dooth swiche thing, of whiche thing unknowynge folk ben astonyd.

"But for to constreyne (*as who seith, but for to comprehende and to telle*) a fewe thingis of the devyne depnesse the whiche that mannys resoun may undirstonde, thilke man that thow wenest to ben ryght just and ryght kepynge of equite, the contrarie of that semeth to the devyne purveaunce, that al woot. And   230 Lucan, my famylier, telleth that the victorious cause likide to the goddes, and the cause overcomen likide to Catoun. Thanne whatsoevere thou mayst seen that is doon in this world unhopid or unwened, certes it es the ryghte ordre of thinges, but as to thi wikkid opynioun it is a confusioun. But I suppose that som man be so wel ithewed that the devyne jugement and the jugement of mankynde accorden hem togidre of hym; but he is so   240 unstidfast of corage that, yif any adversite come to hym, he wol forleten peraventure to continue innocence by the whiche he ne may nat withholden fortune. Thanne the wise dispensacion of God sparith hym, the whiche man adversite myghte enpeyren; for that God wol nat suffren hym to travaile to whom that travaile nis nat covenable. Anothir man is parfit in alle vertus, and is an holi man and neigh to God, so that the purveaunce of God   250 wolde deme that it were a felonie that he were touched with any adversites; so that he wol nat suffre that swich a man be moeved with any bodily maladye. But so as seyde a philosophre, the more excellent by me — he seyde in Grec that 'vertues han edified the body of the holi man.'

"And ofte tyme it betydeth that the somme of thingis that ben to done is taken to governe to good folk, for that the malice   260 haboundaunt of schrewes scholde ben abated. And God yeveth and departeth to other folk prosperites and adversites imedled to-hepe aftir the qualite of hir corages, and remordith some folk by adversite, for thei ne scholden nat waxen proude by long welefulnesse; and other folk he suffreth to ben travailed with harde thinges for that thei scholden confermen the vertues of corage by the usage and the exercitacioun of pacience. And other folk   270 dreden more than thei oughten the whiche thei myghte wel beren, and thilke folk God ledeth into experience of hemself by aspre and sorweful thingis. And many other folk han bought honourable renoun of this world by the prys of glorious deth; and som men, that ne mowen nat ben overcomen by torment, han yeven ensample to other folk that vertu mai nat ben overcomyn by adversites. And of alle thise thinges ther nis no doute that thei ne   280 ben doon ryghtfully and ordeynly, to the profit of hem to whom we seen thise thingis betyde.

"For certes, that adversite cometh somtyme to schrewes and somtyme that that they desiren, it comith of thise forseyde causes. And of sorweful thinges that betyden to schrewes, certes, no man ne wondreth; for alle men wenen that thei han wel desservid it, and that thei ben of wykkid meryt. Of whiche schrewes the torment   290 somtyme agasteth othere to don felonyes, and somtyme it amendeth hem that suffren the tormentz; and the prosperite that is yeven to schrewes scheweth a gret argument to good folk what thing thei scholde demen of thilke welefulnesse, the whiche prosperite men seen ofte serven to schrewes. In the whiche thing I trowe that God dispenseth. For peraventure the nature of som man is so overthrowynge to yvel, and so uncovenable, that the nedy   300 poverte of his houshold myghte rather egren hym to don felonyes; and to the maladye of hym God putteth remedye to yeven hym

231 **Lucan:** the Roman poet
233 **Catoun:** Cato, the orator
235 **unwened:** unexpected
238 **he so wel ithewed:** conduct himself so well
244 **withholden fortune:** keep his fortune
246 **enpeyren:** make worse
255 **by me:** according to me, in my opinion
256 **edified:** perfected

259 **taken:** given, entrusted
263 **imedled to-hepe:** mixed together
264 **aftir:** according to **remordith:** afflicts
268 **confermen:** strengthen
270 **exercitacioun:** exercise
291 **agasteth . . . to don:** frightens . . . from doing
299 **overthrowynge:** strongly inclined
300 **uncovenable:** perverse
302 **egren:** spur

rychesses. And som othir man byholdeth his conscience defouled with synnes, and makith comparysoun of his fortune and of hymself, and dredith peraventure that his blisfulnesse, of whiche the usage is joyeful to hym, that the lesynge of thilke blisfulnesse ne be nat sorwful to hym; and therfore he wol   310 chaunge his maneris, and, for he dredith to lesen his fortune, he forletith his wikkidnesse. To other folke is welefulnesse iyeven unworthely, the whiche overthroweth hem into destruccioun, that thei han disservid; and to som othir folk is yeven power to punysshen, for that it schal be cause of contynuacioun and exercisynge to good folk, and cause of torment to schrewes. For so as ther nis noon alliaunce bytwixe good folk and schrewes,   320 ne schrewes ne mowen nat acorden among hemself. And whi nat? For schrewes discorden of hemself by hir vices, the whiche vices al toreenden her consciences, and doon ofte time thinges the whiche thingis, whan thei han doon hem, they demen that tho thinges ne scholden nat han ben doon.

"For whiche thing thilke sovereyne purveaunce hath makid ofte tyme fair myracle, so that schrewes han makid   330 schrewes to ben gode men. For whan that some schrewes seen that they suffren wrongfully felonyes of othere schrewes, they wexen eschaufed into hate of hem that anoyed hem, and retornen to the fruyt of vertu, whan thei studien to ben unlyke to hem that thei han hated. Certis oonly this is the devyne myght to the whiche myghte yvelis ben thanne gode whan it useth the yvelis covenably and draweth out the effect of any good. (*As who seith that*   340 *yvel is good only to the myghte of God, for the myght of God ordeyneth thilke yvel to good.*)

"For oon ordre enbraseth alle thinges, so that what wyght that departeth fro the resoun of thilke ordre whiche that is assigned to hym, algatis yit he slideth into an othir ordre; so that no thing nis leveful to folye in the reaume of the devyne purveaunce (*as who seith, no thing nis withouten ordenaunce in the*   350 *reame of the devyne purveaunce*), syn that the ryght strong God governeth alle thinges in this world. For it nis nat leveful to man to comprehenden by wit, ne unfolden by word, alle the subtil ordenaunces and disposiciounis of the devyne entente. For oonly it owghte suffise to han lokid that God hymself, makere of alle natures, ordeineth and dresseth alle thingis to gode; whil that he hasteth to withholden the thingis that he hath makid into his   360 semblaunce (*that is to seyn, for to withholden thingis into gode, for he hymself is good*), he chasith out alle yvel fro the boundes of his comynalite by the ordre of necessite destinable. For whiche it folweth that, yif thou loke the purveaunce ordeynynge the thinges that men wenen ben outraious or haboundaunt in erthis, thou ne schalt nat seen in no place no thing of yvel.

"But I se now that thou art charged with   370 the weyghte of the questioun, and wery with the lengthe of my resoun, and that thou abydest som swetnesse of songe. Tak thanne this drawght, and, whanne thou art wel reffressched and refect, thou schalt be more stedfast to stye into heyere questions or thinges.

SI VIS CELSI IURA. — *Metrum 6*

"Yif thou, wys, wilt demen in thi pure thought the ryghtes or the lawes of the heye thondrere (that is to seyn, of God), loke thou and byhoold the heightes of the sovereyn hevene. Ther kepin the sterres, be ryghtful alliaunce of thinges, hir oolde pees. The sonne, imoevid by his rody fyr, ne distorbeth nat the colde cercle of the mone. Ne the sterre yclepid the Bere, that enclyneth his ravysschynge coursis abowte the sovereyn heighte of the world   10 — ne the same sterre Ursa nis nevere mo wasschen in the depe westrene see, ne coveyteth nat to deeyen his flaumbes in the see of the Occian, although it see othere sterres iplowngid in the see. And Hesperus the sterre bodith and telleth alwey the late nyghtes, and Lucyfer the sterre bryngeth ayein the clere day.

"And thus maketh Love entrechaungeable the perdurable courses; and thus is discordable bataile yput out of the contre of   20 the sterres. This accordaunce atempryth by evenelyke maneres the elementz, that the moiste thingis, stryvynge with the drye thingis, yeven place by stoundes; and that the colde thingis

339 **covenably:** fittingly

359 **withholden:** maintain
370 **charged:** burdened
372–73 **thou abydest:** you await
375 **refect:** restored   **stye:** ascend
Metrum 6.8 **Bere:** Ursa Major
9 **ravysschynge:** violent
13 **deeyen:** dye (i.e., dip)
19–20 **entrechaungeable:** mutual (modifying *Love*)

joynen hem by feyth to the hote thingis; and that the lyghte fyr ariseth into heighte, and the hevy erthes avalen by her weyghtes. By thise same causes the floury yer yeldeth swote smelles in the first somer sesoun 30 warmynge; and the hote somer dryeth the cornes; and autumpne comith ayein hevy of apples; and the fletyng reyn bydeweth the wynter. This atempraunce norysscheth and bryngeth forth alle thinges that brethith lif in this world; and thilke same attempraunce, ravysschynge, hideth and bynymeth, and drencheth undir the laste deth, alle thinges iborn.

"Among thise thinges sitteth the heye 40 makere, kyng and lord, welle and bygyn-nynge, lawe and wys juge to don equite, and governeth and enclyneth the brydles of thinges. And tho thinges that he stireth to gon by moevynge, he withdraweth and aresteth, and affermeth the moevable or wandrynge thinges. For yif that he ne clepide nat ayein the ryght goynge of thinges, and yif that he ne con-streynede hem nat eftsones into round-nesses enclyned, the thinges that ben now 50 contynued by stable ordenaunce, thei schol-den departen from hir welle (that is to seyn, from hir bygynnynge), and failen (that is to seyn, tornen into noght). This is the comune love to alle thingis, and alle thinges axen to ben holden by the fyn of good. For elles ne myghten they nat lasten yif thei ne comen nat eftsones ayein, by love retorned, to the cause that hath yeven hem beinge (that is to seyn, to God).   60

IAMNE IGITUR VIDES. — *Prosa 7*

"Sestow nat thanne what thing folweth alle the thingis that I have seyd?"

"What thing?" quod I.

"Certes," quod sche, "al outrely that alle for-tune is good."

"And how may that be?" quod I.

"Now undirstand," quod sche. "So as al for-tune, whethir so it be joyeful fortune or aspre fortune, is yeven eyther by cause of ger-donynge or elles of exercisynge of good 10 folk or elles by cause to punysschen or elles chastisen schrewes; thanne is alle fortune good, the whiche fortune is certeyn that it be either ryghtful or elles profitable."

"Forsothe this is a ful verray resoun," quod I; "and yif I considere the purveaunce and the destyne that thou taughtest me a litel here-byforn, this sentence is sustenyd by stedfast resouns. But yif it like unto the, lat us nombren [hyt] amonges thilke thingis, of 20 whiche thow seydest a litel herebyforn that thei ne were nat able to ben wened to the peple."

"Why so?" quod sche.

"For that the comune word of men," quod I, "mysuseth this manere speche of fortune, and seyn ofte tymes that the fortune of som wyght is wikkid."

"Woltow thanne," quod sche, "that I ap-proche a litil to the wordis of the peple, 30 so that it seme nat to hem that I be over-moche departed as fro the usage of mankynde?"

"As thou wilt," quod I.

"Demestow nat," quod sche, "that alle thing that profiteth is good?"

"Yis," quod I.

"And certes thilke thing that exerciseth or corrigith profitith?"

"I confesse it wel," quod I.

"Thanne is it good," quod sche.   40

"Why nat?" quod I.

"But this is the fortune," quod sche, "of hem that eyther ben put in vertu and batayllen ayein aspre thingis, or elles of hem that es-chuen and declynen fro vices and taken the weye of vertu."

"This ne mai I nat denye," quod I.

"But what seistow of the merye fortune that is yeven to good folk in gerdoun — dem-eth aught the peple that it is wikkid?"   50

"Nay forsothe," quod I; "but thei demen, as it soth is, that it is ryght good."

"And what seistow of that othir fortune," quod sche, "that, although it be aspre and restreyneth the schrewes by ryghtful torment, weneth aught the peple that it be good?"

"Nay," quod I, "but the peple demeth that it is moost wrecchid of alle thingis that mai ben thought."

"War now and loke wel," quod sche,   60 "lest that we, in folwynge the opynioun of the peple, have confessid and concluded thing that is unable to be wened to the peple."

---

*Prosa 7.*17–18 **herebyforn:** in the preceding prose
18 **sustenyd:** sustained, supported
21 **herebyforn:** at 4.pr4.182ff.
22 **wened to:** understood by
38 **corrigith:** corrects
45 **declynen:** turn aside

28 **avalen:** sink
35 **brethith lif:** i.e., live
49–50 **roundnesses:** orbits

"What is that?" quod I.

"Certis," quod sche, "it folweth or comith of thingis that ben grauntid that alle fortune, what so evere it be, of hem that ben eyther in possessioun of vertu, or in the encres of vertu, or elles in the purchasynge of vertu, that thilke fortune is good; and that alle fortune is ryght wikkid to hem that duellen in schrewidnesse." (*As who seith: "And thus weneth nat the peple."*)

"That is soth," quod I, "al be it so that no man dar confessen it ne byknowen it."

"Whi so?" quod sche; "for ryght as the stronge man ne semeth nat to abaissen or disdaignen as ofte tyme as he herith the noyse of the bataile, ne also it ne semeth nat to the wise man to beren it grevously as ofte as he is lad into the stryf of fortune. For, bothe to the to man and eek to the tothir thilke difficulte is the matere, to the to man of encres of his glorious renoun, and to the tothir man to confermen his sapience (that is to seyn, to the asprenesse of his estat). For therfore it is called 'vertu,' for that it sustenith and enforceth by hise strengthes that it nis nat overcomen by adversites. Ne certes thou, that art put in the encres or in the heyghte of vertu, ne hast nat comen to fleten with delices, and for to welken in bodily lust; thou sowest or plawntest a ful egre bataile in thy corage ayeins every fortune, for that the sorwful fortune ne confownde the nat, ne that the myrie fortune ne corrumpe the nat. Ocupye the mene by stidefast strengthes; for al that evere is undir the mene, or elles al that overpasseth the mene, despyseth welefulnesse (*as who seith, it is vycious*), and ne hath no mede of his travaile. For it is set in your hand (as who seith, it lyth in your power) what fortune yow is levest (*that is to seyn, good or yvel*). For alle fortune that semeth scharp or aspre, yif it ne exercise nat the good folk ne chastiseth the wikkide folk, it punysseth.

BELLA BIS QUINIS. — *Metrum 7*

"The wrekere Attrides (that is to seyn, Agamenon), that wrought and contynued the batailes by ten yer, recovered and purgide in wrekynge, by the destruccioun of Troye, the loste chaumbris of mariage of his brothir. (*That is to seyn, that he, Agamenon, wan ayein Eleyne that was Menelaus wif his brothir.*) In the mene while that thilke Agamenon desirede to yeven sayles to the Grykkyssche naveye, and boughte ayein the wyndes by blood, he unclothide hym of pite of fadir; and the sory preest yeveth in sacrifyenge the wrecchide kuttynge of throte of the doughter. (*That is to seyn that Agamenon leet kutten the throte of his doughter by the preest, to maken alliaunce with his goddes and for to han wynd with whiche he myghte wenden to Troye.*)

"Ytakus (that is to seyn, Ulixes) bywepte his felawes ilorne, the whiche felawes the fyerse Poliphemus, ligginge in his grete cave, had fretyn and dreynt in his empty wombe. But natheles Poliphemus, wood for his blynde visage, yald to Ulixes joye by his sorwful teres. (This to seyn, that Ulixes smoot out the eye of Poliphemus, that stood in his forheed, for whiche Ulixes hadde joye whan he say Poliphemus wepynge and blynd).

"Hercules is celebrable for his harde travailes. He dawntide the proude Centauris (*half hors, half man*), and he byrafte the dispoilynge fro the cruel lyoun (*that is to seyn, he slouhe the lyoun and rafte hym his skyn*); he smot the briddes that hyghten Arpiis with certein arwes; he ravysschide applis fro the wakynge dragoun, and his hand was the more hevy for the goldene metal; he drowh Cerberus, the hound of helle, by his treble cheyne; he, overcomer, as it is seyd, hath put an unmeke lord foddre to his crwel hors (this to seyn, that Hercules slowh Diomedes, and made his hors to freten hym); and he, Hercules, slowh Idra the serpent, and brende the venym; and Acheleous the flod, defowled in his forheed, dreynte his schamefast visage in his strondes (*that is to seyn, that Achaleous coude transfiguren hymself into diverse liknesse, and, as he faughte with Hercules, at the laste he torned hym into a bole, and Hercules brak of oon of his hornes, and he for schame hidde hym in his ryver*); and he, Hercules, caste adoun Antheus the geaunt in the [sondes] of Libye; and Kacus apaysede the wratthes of

---

77 **abaissen**: be afraid
77–78 **disdaignen**: take offense
86 **asprenesse**: bitterness
92 **welken**: waste away
93 **egre**: fierce
Metrum 7.4 **wrekynge**: avenging, vengeance

18 **Ytakus**: the Ithacan
23 **yald**: gave
28 **celebrable**: praiseworthy
33 **Arpiis**: Harpies
38 **unmeke**: proud
39, 41 **hors**: horses
42 **Idra**: Hydra **venym**: the serpent's head or, according to Trivet, the serpent itself

Evander (*this to seyn, that Hercules slouh the monstre Kacus, and apaysed with that deth the wratthe of Evander*); and the bristilede boor markide with scomes the scholdres of Hercules, the whiche scholdres the heye cercle of hevene sholde thriste; and the laste of his labours was that he susteynede the hevene uppon his nekke unbowed; and he disservide eftsones the hevene to ben the pris of his laste travaile.

"Goth now thanne, ye stronge men, ther as the heye wey of the greet ensaumple ledith yow. O nyce men! why nake ye your bakkes? (*As who seith, 'O ye slowe and delicat men! whi flee ye adversites, and ne fyghte nat ayeins hem by vertu, to wynnen the mede of the hevene?'*) For the erthe overcomen yeveth the sterres." (*This to seyn, that whan that erthly lust is overcomyn, a man is makid worthy to the hevene.*)

Explicit Liber Quartus

Incipit Liber Quintus

DIXERAT ORATIONISQUE CURSUM. — *Prosa 1*

Sche hadde seyd, and torned the cours of hir resoun to some othere thingis to ben treted and to ben ispedd. Thanne seide I, "Certes ryghtful is thin amonestynge and ful digne by auctorite. But that thou seydest whilom that the questioun of the devyne purveaunce is enlaced with many othere questiouns, I undirstande wel and prove it by the same thing. But I axe yif that thou wenest that hap be anything in any weys; and yif thou wenest that hap be anything, what is it?"

Thanne quod sche, "I haste me to yelden and assoilen to the the dette of my byheste, and to schewen and openen [the] the wey, by whiche wey thou maist comen ayein to thi contre. But al be it so that the thingis whiche that thou axest ben ryght profitable to knowe, yit ben thei divers somwhat fro the path of my purpos; and

it is to douten that thou ne be makid weery by mysweyes, so that thou ne maist nat suffise to mesuren the ryghte weie."

"Ne doute the therof nothing," quod I; "for for to knowen thilke thingis togidre, in the whiche thinges I delite me gretly — that schal ben to me in stede of reste, syn it nis nat to douten of the thingis folwynge, whan every syde of thi disputesoun schal han ben stedfast to me by undoutous feyth."

"Thanne," seide sche, "that manere wol I don the," and bygan to speken ryght thus: "Certes," quod sche, "yif any wyght diffynisse hap in this manere, that is to seyn that 'hap is bytydynge ibrought forth by foolisshe moevynge and by no knyttynge of causes,' I conferme that hap nis ryght naught in no wise; and I deme al outrely that hap nis [but an idel] voys (*as who seith, but an idel word*), withouten any significacioun of thing summitted to that voys. For what place myght ben left or duellynge to folie and to disordenaunce, syn that God ledeth and constreyneth alle thingis by ordre? For this sentence is verray and soth, that 'no thing hath his beynge of naught,' to the whiche sentence noon of thise oolde folk ne withseide nevere; al be it so that they ne undirstoden ne meneden it nat by God, prince and bygynnere of wirkynge, but thei casten as a maner foundement of subject material (that is to seyn, of the nature of alle resouns). And yif that any thing is woxen or comen of no causes, thanne schal it seme that thilke thing is comen or woxen of nawght; but yif this ne mai nat ben don, thanne is it nat possible that hap be any swich thing as I have diffynysschid a litil herebyforn."

"How schal it thanne be?" quod I. "Nys ther thanne nothing that by right may ben clepid other hap or elles aventure of fortune; or is ther awght, al be it so that it is hidd fro the peple, to whiche thing thilke wordes ben covenable?"

"Myn Aristotle," quod sche, "in the book of his Phisic diffynysseth this thing by schort resoun, and nyghe to the sothe."

"In whiche manere?" quod I.

"As ofte, quod sche, "as men don any thing for grace of any other thing, and another thing

---

55 **bristilede:** bristly
56 **scomes:** scums, foam
58 **thriste:** thrust up, support
61 **eftsones:** in return
65 **nake:** bare (i.e., show in flight)
Explicit, *etc.:* Here ends the fourth book. Here begins the fifth book.
Prosa 1.3 **ispedd:** dispatched
4 **amonestynge:** admonishing, advice
5 **whilom:** at 4.pr6.10ff.
6–7 **enlaced:** entangled
9 **hap:** chance
10 **weys:** wise, manner
13 **assoilen:** release

19 **to douten that:** to be feared lest
28 **undoutous:** undoubting
29 **manere:** behavior (Lat. *morem*); i.e., I will do what you ask.
32 **diffynisse:** define
38–39 **summitted to:** subjected to (designated by)
48 **casten as a maner foundement:** constructed it as a kind of foundation, i.e., posited it as a basic principle; see n.
55 **herebyforn:** at 33–34 above
67 **grace:** sake

than thilke thing that men entenden to don
bytideth by some causes, it is clepid hap.
Ryght as a man dalf the erthe bycause of   70
tylyinge of the feld, and founde ther a
gobet of gold bydolven; thanne wenen folk
that it is byfalle by fortunous bytydynge. But
forsothe it nis nat of naught, for it hath his
propre causes, of whiche causes the cours un-
forseyn and unwar semeth to han makid hap.
For yif the tiliere of the feeld ne dulve nat in the
erthe, and yif the hidere of the gold ne hadde
hyd the gold in thilke place, the gold ne
hadde nat ben founde. Thise ben thanne   80
the causes of the abregginge of fortuit hap,
the whiche abreggynge of fortuit hap cometh of
causes encontrynge and flowynge togidere to
hemself, and nat by the entencioun of the doere.
For neither the hidere of the gold ne the delvere
of the feeld ne undirstoden nat that the gold
sholde han ben founde; but, as I seide, it bytidde
and ran togidre that he dalf thare as that oothir
had hid the gold. Now mai I thus diffinysshen hap: hap is an unwar betydinge   90
of causes assembled in thingis that ben
doon for som oothir thing; but thilke ordre,
procedinge by an uneschuable byndinge togidre, whiche that descendeth fro the welle of
purveaunce that ordeyneth alle thingis in hir
places and in hir tymes, makith that the causes
rennen and assemblen togidre.

RUPIS ACHEMENIE. — *Metrum 1*

"Tigrys and Eufrates resolven and springen
of o welle in the cragges of the roche of the
contre of Achemenye, ther as the fleinge bataile ficcheth hir dartes retorned in the breestis
of hem that folwen hem. And sone aftir the
same ryverys, Tigris and Eufrates, unjoignen
and departen hir watres. And if thei comen togidre and ben assemblid and clepid togidre
into o cours, thanne moten thilke thingis
fleten togidre whiche that the watir of   10
the entrechaungynge flood bryngeth. The
schippes and the stokkes araced with the flood
moten assemblen; and the watris imedled

81 **abregginge:** i.e., "bridging" or short cut; see n.
83 **encontrynge:** encountering (one another)
83–84 **to hemself:** into each other
91 **of:** from
93 **uneschuable:** inevitable
Metrum 1.1 **resolven:** flow out
3 **Achemenye:** Persia; see n.
3–4 **bataile:** troop; see n. to 3.
4 **retorned in:** shot back into
11 **entrechaungynge:** mingling
12 **stokkes araced with:** tree trunks uprooted by

wrappeth or emplieth many fortunel happes
or maneris; the whiche wandrynge happes
natheles thilke enclynynge lowenesse of the
erthe and the flowinge ordre of the slydinge
watir governeth. Right so fortune, that semeth as it fletith with slakid or ungoverned
bridles, it suffreth bridelis (that is to seyn,   20
to ben governed), and passeth by thilke
lawe (that is to seyn, by the devyne ordenaunce)."

ANIMADVERTO INQUAM. — *Prosa 2*

"This undirstonde I wel," quod I, "and I accorde me that it is ryght as thou seist. But I
axe yif ther be any liberte of fre wille in this
ordre of causes that clyven thus togidre in
hemself, or elles I wolde witen yif that the
destinal cheyne constrinith the moevynges of
the corages of men."

"Yis," quod sche, "ther is liberte of fre wil,
ne ther ne was nevere no nature of resoun
that it ne hadde liberte of fre wil. For ev-   10
ery thing that may naturely usen resoun,
it hath doom by whiche it discernith and demeth every thing; thanne knoweth it by itself
thinges that ben to fleen and thinges that ben
to desiren. And thilke thing that any wight
demeth to ben desired, that axeth or desireth
he; and fleeth thilke thing that he troweth be
to fleen. Wherfore in alle thingis that resoun
is, in hem also is liberte of willynge and of
nillynge. But I ne ordeyne nat (as who   20
seith, I ne graunte nat) that this liberte be
evenelyk in alle thinges. Forwhy in the sovereynes devynes substaunces (that is to seyn,
in spiritz) jugement is more cleer, and wil nat
icorrumped, and myght redy to speden thinges
that ben desired. But the soules of men moten
nedes be more fre whan thei loken hem in the
speculacioun or lokynge of the devyne thought;
and lasse fre whan thei slyden into the bodyes; and yit lasse fre whan thei ben gad-   30
rid togidre and comprehended in erthli
membres; but the laste servage is whan that
thei ben yeven to vices and han ifalle fro the
possessioun of hir propre resoun. For aftir that
thei han cast awey hir eyghen fro the lyght
of the sovereyn sothfastnesse to lowe thinges
and derke, anon thei derken by the cloude of
ignoraunce and ben troubled by feionous tal-

14 **emplieth:** involves   **fortunel:** accidental
Prosa 2.27 **loken:** look out for, keep; see textual note.

entz; to the whiche talentz whan thei approchen and assenten, thei [helpen] and   40
encrecen the servage whiche thei han
joyned to hemself; and in this manere thei ben
caytifs fro hir propre liberte. The whiche thingis
natheles the lokynge of the devyne purveaunce
seth, that alle thingis byholdeth and seeth fro
eterne, and ordeyneth hem everiche in here
merites as thei ben predestinat; and it is seid in
Greke that 'alle thinges he seeth and alle thinges
he herith.'

PURO CLARUM LUMINE. — *Metrum 2*

"Homer with the hony mouth (that is to seyn,
Homer with the swete ditees) singeth that the
sonne is cler by pure light; natheles yit ne
mai it nat, by the infirme light of his bemes,
breken or percen the inward entrayles of the
erthe or elles of the see. So ne seth nat God,
makere of the grete werld. To hym, that loketh alle thinges from an hey, ne withstondeth
no thinges by hevynesse of erthe, ne the
nyght ne withstondeth nat to hym by the   10
blake cloudes. Thilke God seeth in o strok
of thought alle thinges that ben, or weren, or
schollen comen; and thilke God, for he loketh
and seeth alle thingis alone, thou maist seyn
that he is the verrai sonne."

TUM EGO EN INQUAM. — *Prosa 3*

Thanne seide I, "Now am I confowndide by
a more hard doute than I was."

"What doute is that?" quod sche, "for certes I
conjecte now by whiche thingis thou art trubled."

"It semeth," quod I, "to repugnen and to
contrarien gretly, that God knoweth byforn alle
thinges and that ther is any fredom of liberte.
For yif so be that God loketh alle thinges
byforn, ne God ne mai nat ben desceyved
in no manere, thanne moot it nedes ben that   10
alle thinges betyden the whiche that the
purveaunce of God hath seyn byforn to comen.
For whiche, yif that God knoweth byforn nat
oonly the werkes of men, but also hir conseilles
and hir willes, thanne ne schal ther be no liberte of arbitrie; ne certes ther ne may be noon
othir dede, ne no wil, but thilke whiche that the
devyne purveaunce, that ne mai nat ben disseyved, hath felid byforn. For yif that thei

myghten writhen awey in othere manere   20
than thei ben purveyed, thanne ne sholde
ther be no stedefast prescience of thing to
comen, but rather an uncerteyn opynioun; the
whiche thing to trowen of God, I deme it felonye and unleveful.

"Ne I ne proeve nat thilke same resoun (as who
seith, I ne allowe nat, or I ne preyse nat, thilke
same resoun) by whiche that som men wenen
that thei mowe assoilen and unknytten the
knotte of this questioun. For certes thei   30
seyn that thing nis nat to comen for that the
purveaunce of God hath seyn byforn that it is to
comen, but rathir the contrarie; and that is this:
that, for that the thing is to comen, that therfore
ne mai it nat ben hidd fro the purveaunce of
God; and in this manere this necessite slideth
ayein into the contrarie partie: ne it ne byhoveth nat nedes that thinges betiden that ben
ipurveied, but it byhoveth nedes that thinges
that ben to comen ben ipurveied — but as   40
it were Y travailed (*as who seith, that
thilke answere procedith ryght as though men
travaileden or weren besy*) to enqueren the
whiche thing is cause of the whiche thing, as
whethir the prescience is cause of the necessite
of thinges to comen, or elles that the necessite of
thinges to comen is cause of the purveaunce. But
I ne enforce me nat now to schewen it, that
the bytidynge of thingis iwyst byforn is
necessarie, how so or in what manere that   50
the ordre of causes hath itself; although
that it ne seme naught that the prescience bringe
in necessite of bytydinge to thinges to comen.

"For certes yif that any wyght sitteth, it byhoveth by necessite that the opynioun be soth of
hym that conjecteth that he sitteth; and
ayeinward also is it of the contrarie: yif the
opinioun be soth of any wyght for that he sitteth,
it byhoveth by necessite that he sitte.
Thanne is here necessite in the toon and in   60
the tothir; for in the toon is necessite of
syttynge, and certes in the tothir is necessite of
soth. But therfore ne sitteth nat a wyght for that
the opynioun of the sittynge is soth, but the
opinioun is rather soth for that a wyght sitteth
byforn. And thus, althoughe that the cause of the
soth cometh of that other side (*as who seith,
that althoughe the cause of soth cometh of the
sittynge, and nat of the trewe opinioun*),

Prosa 3.5 repugnen: be self-contradictory
7 **fredom of liberte:** free will; see n.
16 **arbitrie:** will

20 **writhen awey in:** be diverted to
29 **assoilen:** loosen, solve

algatis yit is ther comune necessite in that   70
oon and in that othir. Thus scheweth it that
Y may make semblable skiles of the purveaunce
of God and of thingis to comen. For althoughe
that for that thingis ben to comen therfore ben
thei purveied, and nat certes for thei be purveied
therfore ne bytide thei nat; yit natheles byhoveth
it by necessite that eyther the thinges to comen
ben ipurveied of God, or elles that the thinges
that ben ipurveyed of God betyden. And
this thing oonly suffiseth inow to destroien   80
the fredom of oure arbitre (that is to seyn,
of our fre wil).

"But certes now schewith it wel how fer fro
the sothe and how up-so-doun is this thing that
we seyn, that the betydynge of temporel thingis
is cause of the eterne prescience. But for to
wenen that God purveieth the thinges to comen
for thei ben to comen — what oothir thing is it
but for to wene that thilke thinges that
bytidden whilom ben cause of thilke   90
soverein purveaunce that is in God? And
herto I adde yit this thing: that ryght as whanne
that I woot that a thing is, it byhoveth by
necessite that thilke selve thing be; and eek
whan I have knowen that any thing schal
betyden; so byhovith it by necessite that thilke
same thing betide; so folweth it thanne that the
betydynge of the thing iwyste byforn ne may nat
ben eschued. And at the laste, yif that any
wyght wene a thing to ben oothir weyes   100
than it is, it nis nat oonly unscience, but it
is desceyvable opynioun ful divers and fer fro
the sothe of science. Wherfore, yif any thing be
so to comen that the betidynge of it ne be nat
certein ne necessarie, who mai witen byforn that
thilke thing is to comen? For ryght as science ne
may nat ben medled with falsnesse (*as who
seith, that yif I woot a thing, it ne mai nat
ben fals that I ne woot it*), ryght so thilke
thing that is conceyved by science ne may   110
nat ben noon other weies than as it is
conceyved. For that is the cause why that science
wanteth lesynge (*as who seith, why that
wytynge ne resceyveth nat lesynge of that it
woot*); for it byhoveth by necessite that every
thing be ryght as science comprehendeth it
to be.

"What schal I thanne seyn? In whiche manere
knoweth God byforn the thinges to comen,
yif thei ne ben nat certein? For yif that he   120
deme that thei ben to comen uneschewably, and so may be that it is possible that thei
ne schollen nat comen, God is disseyved. But
not oonly to trowe that God is disseyved, but for
to speke it with mouthe, it is a felonous synne.
But yif that God woot that ryght so as thinges
ben to comen, so schollen they comen, so that he
wite egaly (*as who seith, indifferently*) that
thingis mowen ben doon or elles nat
idoon, what is thilke prescience that ne   130
comprehendeth no certein thing ne stable?
Or elles what difference is ther bytwixe the
prescience and thilke japeworthi devynynge of
Tyresie the divynour, that seide, 'Al that I seie,'
quod he, 'either it schal be or elles it ne schal nat
be?' Or elles how mochel is worth the devyne
prescience more than the opinioun of mankynde, yif so be that it demeth the thinges
uncertayn, as men doon, of the whiche
domes of men the betydinge nis nat   140
certein? But yif so be that noon uncertein
thing ne mai ben in hym that is right certeyn
welle of alle thingis, than is the betydinge
certein of thilke thingis whiche he hath wist
byforn fermely to comen. For whiche it folweth
that the fredom of the conseiles and of the
werkis of mankynde nis noon, syn that the
thought of God, that seeth alle thinges withouten errour of falsnesse, byndeth and
constreyneth hem to [o] bytidynge by   150
necessite.

"And yif this thing be oonys igrauntid and
resceyved (*that is to seyn, that ther nis no fre
wil*), thanne scheweth it wel how gret destruccioun and how gret damages ther folwen of
thingis of mankynde. For in idel ben ther thanne
purposed and byhyght medes to good folk, and
peynes to badde folk, syn that no moevynge of
fre corage [and] voluntarie ne hath nat
disservid hem (*that is to seyn, neither*   160
mede ne peyne). And it scholde seme
thanne that thilke thing is alther-worst whiche
that is now demed for alther-moost just and
moost ryghtful, that is to seyn that schrewes ben
punysschid or elles that good folk ben
igerdoned, the whiche folk syn that hir propre
wil ne sent hem nat to the toon ne to that othir

---

72 **make semblable skiles:** reason similarly
75–76 **and nat certes . . . bytide thei nat:** i.e., and although it
is certainly not true that things happen because they are foreseen
101 **unscience:** false knowledge, error
104 **so to comen:** so far in the future (Lat. *ita futurum*)
113 **wanteth lesynge:** lacks lying, is free from falsehood

121–22 **uneschewably:** inevitably
134 **Tyresie:** Tiresias

(that is to seyn, neither to good ne to harm), but constreyneth hem certein necessite of thingis to comen. Thanne ne schulle ther 170 nevere be, ne nevere were, vice ne vertu, but it scholde rather ben confusion of alle dissertes medlid withouten discrecioun. And yit ther folweth anothir inconvenient, of the whiche ther ne mai be thought no more felonous ne more wikke, and that is this: that, so as the ordre of thingis is iled and cometh of the purveaunce of God, ne that nothing is leveful to the conseiles of mankynde (as who seith that men han no power to don nothing ne wilne 180 nothing), thanne folweth it that oure vices ben referrid to the makere of alle good (*as who seith, thanne folweth it that God oughte han the blame of our vices*), syn he constreyneth us by necessite to doon vices.

"Than nis ther no resoun to han hope in God, ne for to preien to God. For what scholde any wyght hopen to God, or why scholde he preien to God, syn that the ordenance of destyne whiche that mai nat ben enclyned knytteth 190 and streyneth alle thingis that men mai desiren? Thanne scholde ther be don awey thilke oonly alliaunce bytwixen God and men (that is to seyn, to hopen and to preien). But by the pris of ryghtwisnesse and of verray mekenesse we disserven the gerdon of the devyne grace whiche that is inestimable (that is to seyn, that it is so greet that it ne mai nat ben ful ipreysed). And this is oonly the manere (that is to seyn, hope and preieris) for 200 whiche it semeth that men mowen spekyn with God, and by resoun of supplicacion be conjoyned to thilke cleernesse that nis nat aprochid no rather or that men byseken it and impetren it. And yif men ne wene nat that hope ne preieris ne han no strengthis by the necessite of thingis to comen iresceyved, what thing is ther thanne by whiche we mowen ben conjoyned and clyven to thilke sovereyne prince of thingis? For whiche it byhoveth 210 by necessite that the lynage of mankynde, as thou songe a litil herebyforn, be departed and unjoyned from his welle, and failen of his bygynnynge (that is to seyn, God).

---

190 **enclyned:** bent
199 **oonly the manere:** the only manner
200-01 **for whiche:** by which
204 **no rather or that:** i.e., before
205 **impetren:** ask for
212 **herebyforn:** at 4.m6.51–54

QUENAM DISCORS. — *Metrum 3*

"What discordable cause hath torent and unjoyned the byndynge or the alliaunce of thingis (that is to seyn, the conjunccions of God and of man)? Whiche god hath establisschid so gret bataile bytwixen these two sothfast or verreie thinges (that is to seyn, bytwyxen the purveaunce of God and fre wil) that thei ben singuler and dyvided, ne that they ne wole nat ben medled ne couplid togidre? But ther nis no discord to the verray thinges, 10 but thei clyven alwey certein to hemself; but the thought of man, confownded and overthrowen by the derke membres of the body, ne mai nat be fyr of his derked lookynge (*that is to seyn, by the vigour of his insyghte while the soule is in the body*) knowen the thynne sutile knyttynges of thinges. But wherfore eschaufeth it so by so gret love to fynden thilke notes of soth icovered? (*That is to seyn, wherfore eschaufeth the thought of 20 man by so gret desir to knowen thilke notificaciouns that ben ihid undir the covertures of soth?*) Woot it aught thilke thing that it angwisshous desireth to knowe? (*As who seith, nay; for no man ne travaileth for to witen thingis that he wot. And therfore the texte seith thus:*) But who travaileth to wite thingis iknowe? And yif that he ne knoweth hem nat, what sekith thilke blynde thoght? What is he that desireth any thyng of which he wot 30 right naught? (*As who seith, whoso desireth any thing, nedes somwhat he knoweth of it, or elles he ne coude nat desiren it.*) Or who may folwen thinges that ne ben nat iwist? And thoughe that he seke tho thingis, wher schal he fynde hem? What wyght that is al unkunnynge and ignoraunt may knowe the forme that is ifounde? But whanne the soule byholdeth and seeth the heye thought (that is to seyn, God), thanne knoweth it togidre the 40 somme and the singularites (*that is to seyn, the principles and everyche by hymself*)? But now, while the soule is hidd in the cloude and in the derknesse of the membres of the body, it ne hath nat al foryeten itself, but it withholdeth the somme of thinges and lesith the singularites. Thanne who so that sekith sothnesse, he nis in neyther nother habite, for he

---

Metrum 3.45–46 **withholdeth:** retains
48 **habite:** condition

not nat al, ne he ne hath nat al foryeten;
but yit hym remembreth the somme of   50
thinges that he withholdeth, and axeth conseile, and retretith deepliche thinges iseyn by-
forne (*that is to seyn, the grete somme in his
mynde*) so that he mowe adden the parties
that he hath foryeten to thilke that he hath
withholden.''

TUM ILLA VETUS INQUIT HEC EST. — *Prosa 4*

Than seide sche, ''This is,'' quod sche, ''the
olde questioun of the purveaunce of God. And
Marcus Tullius, whan he devyded the divyna-
ciouns (*that is to seyn, in his book that he wrot
of dyvynaciouns*), he moevede gretly this questioun; and thou thiself hast ysought it mochel
and outrely and longe. But yit ne hath it nat
ben determined ne isped fermely and diligently
of any of yow. And the cause of this dirknesse and of this difficulte is, for that the   10
moevynge of the resoun of mankynde ne
may nat moeven to (*that is to seyn, applien
or joignen to*) the simplicite of the devyne prescience; the whiche symplicite of the devyne
prescience, yif that men myghte thinken it
in any manere (*that is to seyn, that yif
men myghten thinken and comprehenden the
thinges as God seeth hem*), thanne ne scholde
ther duelle outrely no doute. The whiche
resoun and cause of difficulte I schal assaye   20
at the laste to schewe and to speden, whan
I have first ispendid and answerd to the resouns by whiche thou art ymoeved.

''For I axe whi thou wenest that thilke [re-
soun] of hem that assoilen this questioun ne be
nat speedful inow ne sufficient; the whiche solu-
cioun, or the whiche resoun, for that it demeth
that the prescience nis nat cause of necessite
to thinges to comen, than ne weneth it
nat that fredom of wil be distorbed or   30
ylet be prescience. For ne drawestow nat
argumentz fro elleswhere of the necessite of
thingis to comen (*as who seith, any oothir wey
than thus*) but that thilke thinges that the
prescience woot byforn ne mowen nat unbetyde (*that is to seyn, that thei moten betide*)?
But thanne, yif that prescience ne putteth

no necessite to thingis to comen, as thou thiself
hast confessed it and byknowen a litel
herebyforn, what cause or what is it (*as   40
who seith, ther may no cause be*) by
whiche that the endes voluntarie of thinges
myghten be constreyned to certein bytydynge?
For by grace of posicioun, so that thou mowe the
betere undirstonde this that folweth, I pose that
ther ne be no prescience. Thanne axe I,'' quod
sche, ''in as moche as aperteneth to that,
scholden thanne thingis that comen of fre wil
ben constreyned to bytiden by necessite?''

Boecius. ''Nay,'' quod I.   50

''Thanne ayeinward,'' quod sche, ''I
suppose that ther be prescience, but that it ne
putteth no necessite to thingis; thanne trowe I
that thilke selve fredom of wil schal duellen al
hool and absolut and unbounden. But thou wolt
seyn that, al be it so that prescience nis nat cause
of the necessite of bytydynge to thingis to
comen, algatis yit it is a signe that the thingis ben
to bytyden by necessite. By this manere
thanne, althoughe the prescience ne hadde   60
nevere iben, yit algate, or at the leste wey,
it is certein thing that the endes and bytydinges
of thingis to comen scholden ben necessarie. For
every signe scheweth and signifieth oonly what
the thing is, but it ne makith nat the thing that
it signifieth. For whiche it byhoveth first to
schewen that nothing ne bytideth that it ne
betideth by necessite, so that it mai apiere that
the prescience is signe of this necessite; or
elles, yif ther nere no necessite, certes   70
thilke prescience ne myghte nat ben signe
of thing that nis nat. But certes, it is now certein
that the proeve of this, isusteyned by stedfast
resoun, ne schal nat ben lad ne proeved by
signes, ne by argumentz itaken fro withoute, but
by causes covenable and necessarie.

''But thou mayst seyn, 'How may it be that the
thingis ne betyden nat that ben ipurveied to
comen? But certes, ryght as we [troweden]
that tho thingis whiche that the purveaunce   80
woot byforn to comen, ne ben nat to
bytiden!' But that ne scholde we nat demen; but
rathir, althoughe that thei schal betyden, yit ne
have thei no necessite of hir kynde to betyden.
And this maystow lyghtly aperceyven by this
that I schal seyn. For we seen many thingis whan

---

52 **retretith:** reconsiders, treats again
Prosa 4.3 **Marcus Tullius:** Cicero
8 **isped:** dispatched
21 **speden:** dispatch
22 **ispendid:** considered; see n.
25 **assoilen this questioun:** resolve this problem
26 **speedful:** efficacious
35–36 **unbetyde:** fail to happen

40 **herebyforn:** at 5.pr3.37ff.
42 **endes voluntarie:** undetermined outcomes
44 **by grace of posicioun:** for the sake of argument, as a
supposition

thei ben done byforn oure eyen, ryght as men seen the cartere worken in the tornynge and in atemprynge or adressynge of hise cartes or chariottes, and by this manere (as who seith, maistow undirstonden) of alle othere werkmen. Is ther thanne any necessite (as who seith, in our lookynge) that constreynith or compelleth any of thilke thingis to ben don so?''

Boece. ''Nay,'' quod I, ''for in idel and in veyn were al the effect of craft, yif that alle thingis weren moeved by constreynynge (that is to seyn, by constreinynge of our eyen or of our sighte).''

Philosophie. ''The thingis thanne,'' quod she, ''that, whan men doon hem, ne han no necessite that men doon hem, eek tho same thingis, first or thei ben don, thei ben to comen withoute necessite. Forwhy ther ben some thingis to betyden, of whiche the eendes and the bytydynges of hem ben absolut and quit of alle necessite. For certes I ne trowe nat that any man wolde seyn this: that tho thingis that men don now, that thei ne weren to bytiden first or thei weren idoon; and thilke same thinges, althoughe that men hadden iwyst hem byforn, yit thei han fre bytydynges. For ryght as science of thingis present ne bryngith in no necessite to thingis that men doon, right so the prescience of thinges to comen ne bryngith in no necessite to thinges to bytiden.

''But thou maist seyn that of thilke same it is idouted, as whethir that of thilke thingis that ne han noon issues and bytidynges necessaries, yif therof mai ben any prescience. For certes thei semen to discorden, for thou wenest that yif that thingis ben iseyn byfore, that necessite folwith hem; and yif necessite faileth hem, thei ne myghten nat ben wist byforn; and that nothing may be comprehended by science but certein. And yif tho thinges that ne han no certein bytydingis ben ipurveied as certein, it scholde ben dirknesse of opinioun, nat soth-fastnesse of science. And thou wenest that it be dyvers fro the holnesse of science that any man scholde deme a thing to ben other-wyse than it is itself.

''And the cause of this errour is that of alle the thingis that every wyght hath iknowe, thei wenen that tho thingis ben iknowe al only by the strengthe and by the nature of the thinges that

ben iwyst or iknowe. And it is al the contra-rye; for al that evere is iknowe, it is rather comprehendid and knowen, nat aftir his strengthe and his nature, but aftir the faculte (that is to seyn, the power and the nature) of hem that knowen. And, for that this schal mowen schewen by a schort ensaumple, the same rowndnesse of a body, otherweys the sighte of the eighe knoweth it, and otherweys the touchynge. The lookynge, by castynge of his bemys, waiteth and seeth fro afer al the body togidre, withoute moevynge of itself; but the touchynge clyveth and conjoyneth to the rounde body, and moeveth aboute the envyrounynge, and comprehendeth by parties the roundnesse. And the man hymself, ootherweys wit byholdeth hym, and ootherweys ymaginacioun, and otherweyes resoun, and ootherweies intelligence. For the wit comprehendith withoute-forth the figure of the body of the man that is establisschid in the matere subgett; but the ymaginacioun com-prehendith oonly the figure withoute the matere; resoun surmountith ymaginacioun and comprehendith by an universel lok-ynge the comune spece that is in the singuler peces. But the eighe of intelligence is heyere, for it surmountith the envyrounynge of the universite, and loketh over that bi pure subtilte of thought thilke same symple forme of man that is perdurablely in the devyne thought. In whiche this oughte gretly to ben considered, that the heyeste strengthe to comprehenden thinges enbraseth and contienith the lowere strengthe; but the lower strengthe ne ariseth nat in no manere to the heyere strengthe. For wit ne mai no thing comprehende out of matere ne the ymaginacioun ne loketh nat the universel speces, ne resoun ne taketh nat the symple forme so as intelligence takith it; but intelligence, that lookith [as] aboven, whanne it hath comprehended the forme, it knowith and demyth alle the thinges that ben undir that foorme; but sche knoweth hem in thilke manere in the whiche it comprehendith thilke same symple forme that ne may

---

89 **atemprynge:** controlling
111 **han fre bytydynges:** i.e., are not determined
125 **certein:** i.e., something certain

142 **schal mowen schewen:** may appear
144-45 **otherweys . . . otherweys:** in one way . . . in another way
152 **wit:** the senses; see n.
161-62 **spece . . . peces:** species that inheres in particular things
163-64 **envyrounynge of the universite:** boundaries of the universe
164 **over that:** beyond that

nevere ben knowen to noon of that othere (that is to seyn, to none of tho thre forseyde strengthis of the soule). For it knoweth the universite of resoun, and the figure of ymaginacioun, and the sensible material conceyved by wit; ne it ne useth nat nor of resoun ne of ymaginacioun ne of wit withoute-forth; but it byholdeth alle thingis, so as I schal seie, by [o] strook of thought formely (*withoute discours or* 190 *collacioun*). Certes resoun, whan it lok-ith any thing universel, it ne useth nat of ymaginacioun, nor of wit; and algatis yit it comprehendith the thingis ymaginable and sensible. For reson is she that diffynyscheth the universel of here conceyte ryght thus: man is a resonable two-foted beest. And how so that this knowynge is universel, yit nis ther no wyght that ne wot wel that a man is a thing ymaginable and sensible; and this same considereth wel 200 resoun; but that nis nat by ymaginacioun nor by wit, but it lookith it by resonable concepcioun. Also ymaginacioun, albeit so that it takith of wit the bygynnynges to seen and to formen the figures, algates althoughe that wit ne were nat present, yit it envyrowneth and comprehendith alle thingis sensible, nat by resoun sensible of demynge, but by resoun ymaginatyf. Seestow nat thanne that alle the thingis in knowynge usen more of hir 210 faculte or of hir power than thei don of the faculte or power of thingis that ben iknowe? Ne that nis nat wrong; for so as every jugement is the dede or the doyng of hym that demeth, it byhoveth that every wyght performe the werk and his entencioun, nat of foreyne power, but of his propre power.

QUONDAM PORTICUS ATTULIT. — *Metrum 4*

"The porche (that is to seyn, a gate of the toun of Athenis there as philosophris hadden hir congregacioun to desputen) — thilke porche broughte somtyme olde men, ful dirke in hir sentences (*that is to seyn, philosophris that hyghten Stoycienis*), that wenden that ymages and sensibilities (*that is to seyn, sensible ymag-inaciouns or ellis ymaginaciouns of sensible*

thingis) weren enprientid into soules fro bodyes withoute-forth (*as who seith that* 10 *thilke Stoycienis wenden that the sowle had ben nakid of itself, as a mirour or a clene parchemyn, so that alle figures most first comen fro thinges fro withoute into soules, and ben emprientid into soules*); (*Textus*) ryght as we ben wont somtyme by a swift poyntel to fycchen lettres emprientid in the smothnesse or in the pleynesse of the table of wex or in parchemyn that ne hath no figure ne note in it. (*Glose. But now argueth* 20 *Boece ayens that opynioun and seith thus:*) But yif the thryvynge soule ne unpliteth nothing (that is to seyn, ne doth nothing) by his propre moevynges, but suffrith and lith subgit to the figures and to the notes of bodies withoute-forth, and yeldith ymages ydel and vein in the manere of a mirour, whennes thryveth thanne or whennes comith thilke knowynge in our soule, that discernith and byholdith alle thinges? And whennes is 30 thilke strengthe that byholdeth the singuler thinges? Or whennes is the strengthe that devydeth thinges iknowe; and thilke strengthe that gadreth togidre the thingis devyded; and the strengthe that chesith his entrechaunged wey? For somtyme it hevyth up the heved (*that is to seyn, that it hevyth up the entencioun*) to ryght heye thinges, and somtyme it des-cendith into ryght lowe thinges; and whan it retorneth into hymself it reproveth and 40 destroyeth the false thinges by the trewe thinges. Certes this strengthe is cause more efficient, and mochel more myghty to seen and to knowe thinges, than thilke cause that suffrith and resceyveth the notes and the figures empressid in manere of matere. Algatis the passion (that is to seyn, the suffraunce or the wit) in the quyke body goth byforn, excitynge and moevynge the strengthes of the thought, ryght so as whan that cleernesse smyteth 50 the eyen and moeveth hem to seen, or ryght so as voys or soun hurteleth to the eres and commoeveth hem to herkne; than is the strengthe of the thought imoevid and excited, and clepith forth to semblable moevyngis the

---

184 **universite:** universals
190 **formely:** formally, i.e., in terms of pure form; see 162–66 above.
191 **collacioun:** comparison
199–200 **ymaginable and sensible:** endowed with imagination and feelings
208 **demynge:** judging
Metrum 4.1 **The porche:** the Stoa Poikile in Athens
6 **Stoycienis:** Stoics

17 **poyntel:** stylus
18 **pleynesse:** clean surface
22 **thryvynge:** vigorous, active **unpliteth:** unfolds, discovers
25 **notes:** impressions, written marks
35 **entrechaunged:** varying

speces that it halt withynne itself, and addith
tho speces to the notes and to the thinges
withoute-forth, and medleth the ymagis of
thinges withoute-forth to the foormes ihidd
withynne hymself.   60

QUOD SI IN CORPORIBUS SENCIENDIS.
— *Prosa 5*

"But what yif that in bodyes to ben feled
(*that is to seyn, in the takynge of knowlech-*
ynge of bodily thinges), and albeit so that the
qualites of bodies that ben object fro withoute-
forth moeven and entalenten the instrumentz
of the wittes, and albeit so that the passioun
of the body (that is to seyn, the wit or the suffraunce) goth toforn the strengthe of the wirkynge corage, the whiche passioun or
sufraunce clepith forth the dede of the   10
thought in hymself and moeveth and exciteth in this menewhile the formes that resten
within-forth, and yif that in sensible bodies,
as I have seid, our corage nis nat ytaught or
emprientid by passioun to knowe thise thinges,
but demeth and knoweth of his owne strengthe
the passioun or suffrance subject to the body —
moche more than tho thingis that ben absolut
and quit fro alle talentz or affecciouns of
bodyes (as God or his aungelis) ne folwen   20
nat in discernynge thinges object fro withoute-forth, but thei acomplissen and speden
the dede of hir thought. By this resoun,
thanne, ther comen many maner knowynges to
dyverse and differynge substaunces. For the
wit of the body, the whiche wit is naked and
despoiled of alle oothre knowynges — thilke
wit cometh to beestis that ne mowen nat
moeven hemself her and ther, as oistres
and muscles and oothir swich schelle-   30
fyssche of the see that clyven and ben noris-
schid to roches. But the ymaginacioun cometh
to remuable bestis, that semen to han talent to
fleen or to desiren any thing. But resoun is al
oonly to the lynage of mankynde, ryght as
intelligence is oonly the devyne nature. Of
whiche it folweth that thilke knowynge is more
worth than thise oothre, syn it knoweth by his

Prosa 5.4 **object:** presented
5 **entalenten:** stimulate
6, 9, 15, 17 **passioun:** sensation
13 **within-forth:** inside
14 **as I have seid:** cf. m4.1–20.
18 **than:** then
21 **object:** presented
26 **wit:** sensation
33 **remuable:** capable of movement

propre nature nat oonly his subget (as who
seith, it ne knoweth nat al oonly that aperte-   40
nith properly to his knowinge) but it know-
eth the subjectz of alle othre knowynges.

"But how schal it thanne be, yif that wit and
ymaginacioun stryven ayein resonynge and seyn
that, of thilke universel thingis that resoun
weneth to seen, that it nis ryght naught? For wit
and ymaginacioun seyn that that that is sensible
or ymaginable, it ne mai nat ben universel;
thanne is either the jugement of resoun
soth, ne that ther nis no thing sensible; or   50
elles, for that resoun woot wel that many
thinges ben subject to wit and to ymaginacioun,
thanne is the concepcioun of resoun veyn and
fals, whiche that lokith and comprehendith that
that is sensible and singuler as universel. And yif
that resoun wolde answere ayein to thise two
(*that is to seyn, to wit and to ymaginacioun*),
and seyn that sothly sche hirselve (*that is to*
seyn, resoun) lokith and comprehendith,
by resoun of universalite, bothe that that is   60
sensible and that that is ymaginable;
and that thilke two (that is to seyn, wit and
ymaginacioun) ne mowen nat strecchen ne
enhaunsen hemself to knowynge of universalite,
for that the knowynge of hem ne mai exceden ne
surmounten the bodily figures: certes of the
knowynge of thinges, men oughten rather yeven
credence to the more stidfast and to the mor
parfit jugement; in this manere stryvynge,
thanne, we that han strengthe of resonynge   70
and of ymagynynge and of wit (that is to
seyn, by resoun and by imagynacioun and by
wit), we scholde rathir preise the cause of resoun
(*as who seith, than the cause of wit and of*
ymaginacioun).

"Semblable thing is it, that the resoun of
mankynde ne weneth nat that the devyne
intelligence byholdeth or knoweth thingis to
comen, but ryght as the resoun of
mankynde knoweth hem. For thou arguist   80
and seist thus: that if it ne seme nat to men
that some thingis han certeyn and necessarie
bytydynges, thei ne mowen nat ben wist byforn
certeinly to betyden, and thanne nis ther no
prescience of thilke thinges; and yif we trowe
that prescience be in thise thingis, thanne is ther
nothing that it ne bytydeth by necessite. But
certes yif we myghten han the jugement of
the devyne thoght, as we ben parsoners of

89 **parsoners:** partakers

resoun, ryght so as we han demyd that it   90
byhovith that ymaginacioun and wit ben
bynethe resoun, ryght so wolde we demen that
it were ryghtfull thing that mannys resoun
oughte to summytten itself and to ben bynethe
the devyne thought. For whiche yif that we
mowen (*as who seith that, if that we mowen,
I conseile that*) we enhaunse us into the heighte
of thilke soverein intelligence; for ther schal
resoun wel seen that that it ne mai nat
byholden in itself, and certes that is this: 100
in what manere the prescience of God
seeth alle thinges certeins and diffinyssched,
althoughe thei ne han no certein issues or
bytydyngis; ne this nis noon opinioun, but it is
rather the simplicite of the soverein science,
that nis nat enclosed nor ischet withinne none
boundes.

QUAM VARIIS TERRAS. — *Metrum 5*

"The beestes passen by the erthes be ful
diverse figures. For some of hem han hir bodyes straught, and crepyn in the dust, and drawen
aftir hem a traas or a furwe icontynued (that
is to sein, as naddres or snakes); and oothre
beestis by the wandrynge lyghtnesse of hir
wynges beten the wyndes, and overswymmen
the spaces of the longe eir by moyst fleynge;
and oothere beestes gladen hemself to dig-
gen hir traas or hir steppys in the erthe   10
with hir goinges or with hir feet, and to
gon either by the grene feeldes or elles to
walken undir the wodes. And al be it so that
thou seest that thei alle discorden by diverse
foormes, algatis hir faces enclyned hevyeth hir
dulle wittes. Only the lynage of man heveth
heyest his heie heved, and stondith light with
his upryght body, and byholdeth the erthes
undir hym. And, but yif thou, erthly man,
waxest yvel out of thi wit, this figure   20
amonesteth the, that axest the hevene with
thi ryghte visage and hast areised thi forheved,
to beren up an hye thi corage, so that thi thought
ne be nat ihevyed ne put lowe undir fote, syn
that thi body is so heyghe areysed.

QUONIAM IGITUR UTI PAULO ANTE. — *Prosa 6*

"Therfore thanne, as I have schewed a litel
herebyforne that alle thing that is iwist nis nat

knowen by his nature propre, but by the nature of hem that comprehenden it, lat us loke
now, in as mochil as it is leveful to us (as who
seith, lat us loke now as we mowen) whiche that
the estat is of the devyne substaunce; so that
we mowe eek knowen what his science is. The
comune jugement of alle creatures resonables thanne is this: that God is eterne.   10
Lat us considere thanne what is eternite;
for certes that schal schewen us togidre the
devyne nature and the devyne science. Eternite, thanne, is parfit possessioun and al togidre
of lif interminable; and that schewethe more
cleerly by the comparysoun or collacioun of
temporel thinges. For alle thing that lyveth in
tyme, it is present and procedith fro preteritz
into futures (that is to seyn, fro tyme passed
into tyme comynge), ne ther nis nothing   20
establisshed in tyme that mai enbrasen togidre al the space of his lif. For certis yit ne
hath it nat taken the tyme of tomorwe, and it
hath lost that of yusterday, and certes in the
lif of this dai ye ne lyve namore but right
as in this moevable and transitorie moment.
Thanne thilke thing that suffreth temporel condicioun, althoughe that it nevere bygan to
be, ne thoughe it nevere ne cese for to be,
as Aristotile deemed of the world, and   30
althoughe that the lif of it be strecchid with
infinite of tyme; yit algatis nis it no swich thing
that men mighten trowen by ryght that it is
eterne. For althouhe that it comprehende and
embrase the space of lif infinit, yit algatis ne
enbraseth it nat the space of the lif al togidre; for
it ne hath nat the futuris (*that ne ben nat yit*),
ne it ne hath no lengere the preteritz (*that
ben idoon or ipassed*). But thilke thing,
thanne, that hath and comprehendith   40
togidre al the plente of the lif interminable,
to whom ther ne faileth naught of the future, and
to whom ther nis noght of the preteryt escaped
nor ipassed, thilke same is iwitnessed and
iproevid by right to ben eterne; and it byhovith
by necessite that thilke thing be alwey present to
hymself and compotent (as who seith, alwey
present to hymselve and so myghty that al be
right at his plesaunce), and that he have al
present the infinit of the moevable tyme.   50

"Wherfore som men trowen wrongfully
that, whan thei heren that it semede to Plato that
this world ne hadde nevere bygynnynge of
tyme, ne that it nevere schal han failynge, thei

---

104 **bytydyngis**: realizations
Metrum 5.3 **straught**: stretched out
7 **overswymmen**: float over
8 **moyst**: liquid; see n.
15 **enclyned**: bowed down (to the earth)   **hevyeth**: make
heavy
Prosa 6.2 **herebyforne**: at 5.pr4.136ff.

47 **compotent**: utterly powerful
50 **infinit**: infinity

wenen in this manere that this world be makid coeterne with his makere. (*As who seith, thei wene that this world and God ben makid togidre eterne, and that is a wrongful wenynge.*) For other thing is it to ben ilad by lif interminable, as Plato grauntide to　60 the world, and oothir is it to enbrace togidre al the presence of the lif intermynable, the whiche thing it is cleer and manyfest that it is propre to the devyne thought. Ne it ne scholde nat semen to us that God is eldere than things that ben imaked by quantite of tyme, but rathir by the proprete of his simple nature. For this ilke infinit moevyng of temporel things folweth this presentarie estat of the lif inmoevable; and, so as it ne mai nat　70 contrefetin it ne feynen it, ne be evene lik to it, [fro] the immoevablete (that is to sein, that is in the eternite of God) it faileth and fallith into moevynge, [and] fro the simplicite of the presence of [God] disencresith into the infinit quantite of future and of preterit; and so as it ne mai nat han togidre al the plente of the lif, algates yit, for as moche as it ne ceseth nevere for to ben in som manere, it semyth somdel to us that it folwith and resembleth thilke　80 thing that it ne mai nat atayne to ne fulfillen, and byndeth itself to som maner presence of this litle and swift moment, the whiche presence of this litle and swifte moment, for that it bereth a maner ymage or liknesse of the ai duellynge presence of God, it grauntith to swich manere thinges as it betydith to that it semeth hem that thise thinges han iben and ben. And for that the presence of swiche litil moment ne mai nat duelle, therfore it　90 ravysschide and took the infynit wey of tyme (*that is to seyn, by successioun*). And by this manere is it idoon for that it sholde contynue the lif in goinge, of the whiche lif it ne myght nat enbrace the plente in duellinge. And forthi yif we wollen putten worthi names to thinges and folwen Plato, lat us seyen thanne sothly that God is 'eterne,' and that the world is 'perpetuel.'

"Thanne, syn that every jugement knoweth and comprehendith by his owne na-　100 ture thinges that ben subgect unto hym, ther is sothly to God alweys an eterne and presentarie estat; and the science of hym, that overpasseth alle temporel moevement, duelleth in the simplicite of his presence, and embraceth and considereth alle the infynit spaces of tymes preteritz and futures, and lokith in his simple knowynge alle thinges of preterit ryght as thei weren idoon presently ryght now. Yif thou wolt thanne thinken and avise the　110 prescience by whiche it knoweth alle thinges, thou ne schalt naught demen it as prescience of thinges to comen, but thou schalt demen more ryghtfully that it is science of presence or of instaunce that nevere ne faileth. For whiche it nis nat ycleped 'previdence,' but it sholde rathir ben clepid 'purveaunce,' that is establisshed ful fer fro ryght lowe thinges, and byholdeth fro afer alle thingis, right as it were fro the heye heighte of thinges.　120

"Why axestow thanne, or whi desputestow thanne, that thilke thingis ben doon by necessite whiche that ben yseyn and knowen by the devyne sighte, syn that forsothe men ne maken nat thilke thinges necessarie whiche that thei seen ben idoon in hir sighte? For addith thi byholdynge any necessite to thilke thinges that thou byholdest present?"

"Nay," quod I.

Philosophie. "Certes, thanne, yif men　130 myghte maken any digne comparysoun or collacioun of the presence devyne and of the presence of mankynde, ryght so as ye seen some thinges in this temporel present, ryght so seeth God alle thinges by his eterne present.

"Wherfore this devyne prescience ne chaungeth nat the nature ne the proprete of thinges, but byholdeth swiche thingis present to hymward as thei shollen betyde to yow-ward in tyme to comen. Ne it ne confound-　140 eth nat the jugementz of thingis; but by o sight of his thought he knoweth the thinges to comen, as wel necessarie as nat necessarie. Ryght so as whan ye seen togidre a man walke on the erthe and the sonne arisen in the hevene, albeit so that ye seen and byholden the ton and the tothir togidre, yit natheles ye demen and discerne that the toon is voluntarie and the tothir is necessarie. Ryght so thanne the devyne lookynge, byholdynge　150 alle thinges undir hym, ne trowbleth nat the qualite of thinges that ben certeinly present to hym-ward but, as to the condicioun of tyme,

---

69　**presentarie estat:** ever-present quality
70　**so as:** since
71　**evene lik:** the same
75　**disencresith:** is reduced
76　**so as:** although
88　**han iben and ben:** have been and are

110　**avise:** consider
115　**instaunce:** present time
116　**previdence:** prevision, seeing beforehand
117　**purveaunce:** providence

forsothe thei ben futur. For which it folwith that
this nis noon opynioun, but rathir a stidfast
knowynge istrengthid by soothnesse that, whan
that God knoweth any thing to be, he ne unwot
not that thilke thing wantith necessite to be.
(This is to sein that whan that God knoweth
any thing to betide, he wot wel that it ne   160
hath no necessite to betyde.)

"And yif thou seist here that thilke thing that
God seeth to betide, it ne may nat unbytide (*as
who seith, it moot bytide*), and thilke thing that
ne mai nat unbytide, it mot bytiden by necessite,
and that thou streyne me to this name of
necessite, certes I wol wel confessen and
byknowen a thing of ful sad trouthe. But
unnethe schal ther any wight mowe seen it
or come therto, but yif that he be   170
byholdere of the devyne thought. For I wol
answeren the thus: that thilke thing that is futur,
whan it is referred to the devyne knowynge,
than is it necessarie; but certis whan it is
undirstonden in his owene kynde, men seen it
outrely fre and absolut fro alle necessite.

"For certes ther ben two maneris of
necessites: that oon necessite is symple, as thus:
that it byhovith by necessite that alle men
ben mortal or dedly; anothir necessite is   180
condicionel, as thus: yif thow wost that a
man walketh, it byhovith by necessite that he
walke. Thilke thing, thanne, that any wight hath
iknowe to be, it ne mai ben noon oothir weys
thanne he knowith it to be. But this condicion ne
draweth nat with hir thilke necessite simple; for
certes this necessite condicionel — the propre
nature of it ne makith it nat, but the adjeccioun
of the condicioun makith it. For no necessite ne constreyneth a man to gon that   190
goth by his propre wil, al be it so that whan
he goth that it is necessarie that he goth. Ryght
on this same manere thanne, yf that the
purveaunce of God seeth any thyng present,
than moot thilke thing ben by necessite,
althoghe that it ne have no necessite of his owne
nature. But certes the futures that bytiden by
fredom of arbitrie, God seth hem alle togidre
presentz. Thise thinges thanne, yif thei ben
referrid to the devyne sighte, than ben they   200
maked necessarie by the condicioun of the

157 **any thing to be:** that anything will happen
157–58 **he ne unwot not:** he does not fail to know
163 **unbytide:** fail to happen
168 **sad:** solid
188 **adjeccioun:** addition
198 **arbitrie:** will

devyne knowynge. But certes yif thilke thingis
ben considered by hemself, thei ben absolut of
necessite, and ne forleten nat ne cesen nat of
the liberte of hir owne nature. Thanne certes
withoute doute alle the thinges shollen ben
doon whiche that God woot byforn that thei ben
to comen. But some of hem comen and bytiden
of fre arbitrie or of fre wil, that, al be it so
that thei bytiden, yit algates ne lese thei nat   210
hir propre nature in beinge, by the whiche,
first or that thei weren idon, thei hadden power
noght to han bytyd."

Boece. "What is this to seyn thanne," quod I,
"that thinges ne ben nat necessarie by hir propre
nature, so as thei comen in alle maneris in the
liknesse of necessite by the condicioun of the
devyne science?"

Philosophie. "This is the difference,"
quod sche, "that tho thinges that I pur-   220
poside the a litil herbyforn — that is to seyn,
the sonne arysynge and the man walkynge —
that ther-whiles that thilke thinges ben idoon,
they ne myghte nat ben undoon; natheles that
oon of hem, or it was idoon, it byhovide by
necessite that it was idoon, but nat that oothir.
Ryght so is it here, that the thinges that God
hath present, withoute doute thei shollen ben.
But some of hem descendith of the nature
of thinges (as the sonne arysynge); and   230
some descendith of the power of the doeris
(as the man walkynge). Thanne seide I no wrong
that, yif that thise thinges ben referred to the
devyne knowynge, thanne ben thei necessarie;
and yif thei ben considered by hemself, than ben
thei absolut fro the boond of necessite. Right so
as alle thingis that apiereth or scheweth to the
wittes, yif thou referre it to resoun, it is
universel; and yif thou loke it or referre it
to itself, than is it singuler.   240

"But now yif thou seist thus: that, 'If it be
in my power to chaunge my purpos, than schal
I voiden the purveaunce of God, whan paraventure I schal han chaungid the thingis that
he knoweth byforn,' thanne schal I answeren
the thus: 'Certes thou maist wel chaungen thi
purpos; but for as mochil as the present
sothnesse of the devyne purveaunce byholdeth
that thou maist chaunge thi purpos, and
whethir thou wolt chaunge it or no, and   250
whider-ward that thou torne it, thou ne

203 **absolut:** free
216–17 **in alle maneris . . . necessite:** exactly as if they were
necessary

maist nat eschuen the devyne prescience, ryght
as thou ne maist nat fleen the sighte of the
present eye, althoghe that thou torne thiself by
thi fre wil into diverse acciouns.' But thou maist
sein ayein: 'How schal it thanne be — schal nat
the devyne science ben chaunged by my
disposicioun whan that I wol o thing now and
now anothir? And thilke prescience — ne
semeth it nat to entrechaunge stoundis of   260
knowynge?' '' (As who seith, ne schal it nat
seme to us that the devyne prescience entrechaungith hise diverse stoundes of knowynge,
so that it knowe somtyme o thing, and somtyme the contrarie?)

"No, forsothe," quod she, "for the devyne
sighte renneth toforn and seeth alle futures, and
clepith hem ayen and retorneth hem to the
presence of his propre knowynge; ne he ne
entrechaungith nat, so as thou wenest, the   270
stoundes of foreknowynge, as now this,
now that; but he ay duellynge cometh byforn,
and enbraseth at o strook alle thi mutaciouns.
And this presence to comprehenden and to seen
alle thingis — God ne hath nat taken it of the
bytidynge of things to come, but of his propre
symplicite. And herby is assoiled thilke thing
that thou puttest a litel herebyforn; that is to
seyn, that it is unworthy thing to seyn that
our futures yeven cause of the science of   280
God. For certis this strengthe of the devyne
science, whiche that embraseth alle thinges by
his presentarie knowynge, establissheth manere
to alle thinges, and it ne oweth nawht to lattere
thinges.

"And syn that thise thinges ben thus (that is
to seyn, syn that necessite nis nat in thinges by
the devyne prescience), thanne is ther fredom of
arbitrie, that duelleth hool and unwemmed
to mortal men; ne the lawes ne purposen   290
nat wikkidly medes and peynes to the
willynges of men that ben unbownden and quyt
of alle necessite; and God, byholdere and
forwytere of alle thingis, duelleth above, and the
present eternite of his sighte renneth alwey with
the diverse qualite of our dedes, dispensynge
and ordeynynge medes to gode men and
tormentz to wikkide men. Ne in ydel ne in veyn
ne ben ther put in God hope and preyeris
that ne mowen nat ben unspedful ne   300
withouten effect whan they been ryghtful.

"Withstond thanne and eschue thou vices;
worschipe and love thou vertues; areise thi
corage to ryghtful hopes; yilde thou humble
preieres an heyhe. Gret necessite of prowesse
and vertu is encharged and comaunded to yow,
yif ye nil nat dissimulen; syn that ye worken and
don (*that is to seyn, your dedes or your werkes*)
byforn the eyen of the juge that seeth and
demeth alle thinges.''   310

Explicit liber Boecii.

254 **present eye:** eye of someone watching you
278 **herebyforn:** at 5.pr3.83ff.

283 **presentarie:** present   **manere:** due measure (Lat. modum)
294 **forwytere:** foreknower
300 **unspedful:** unsuccessful
304 **yilde:** render, send
Explicit liber Boecii: Here ends Boethius's book.

TROILUS AND CRISEYDE

BEFORE 1388, probably in the early 1380s, Chaucer enlarged his canon with three new works: *Boece*, The Knight's Tale, and the *Troilus*. In a French ballade, Eustache Deschamps addresses Chaucer as "grant translateur," mentioning his Englishing of the *Roman de la rose;* these new works continue his career as a translator, but with substantial variation. Like *The Romaunt of the Rose, Boece* is close and faithful to its Latin original, but there the likeness ends. Like the *Romaunt,* The Knight's Tale and *Troilus,* both long narratives, take "modern" vernacular poems for models, but there again the larger likeness ends.

In the new poems, Chaucer turns from French to Italian for his sources; he turns from an allegorical to a pseudo-historical mode of representation; he freely alters, augmenting and contracting his sources so much that the poems are essentially new. The influence of Boethius pervades both *Troilus* and The Knight's Tale, enriching them with a philosophical gravity and a consciousness of antique thought hitherto unknown in English letters. By making these poems, Chaucer transformed himself from a skilled occasional versifier in the current fashion of the French tradition into a serious contender for the laurel, a learned European poet, the deliberate rival of the great Italians, a seeker after fame.

The source of *Troilus and Criseyde* is an Italian poem, *Il Filostrato,* composed by Giovanni Boccaccio in the late 1330s. Chaucer probably used a French translation of the *Filostrato* along with the Italian, but the French in any case is so close to the original as to serve as a trot rather than an independent source. The historical event underlying Boccaccio's poem, the Trojan War, was a favorite matter for medieval writers, who regularly retold the story of the war, in the manner of chroniclers, from beginning to end. Boccaccio stimulated a new tradition that flourished in the fourteenth century — taking a small episode or group of episodes from the great chronicles and treating them in more elaborate detail, just as the Greeks had elaborated segments of the Homeric cycles as independent works. Like the romances of Chrétien de Troyes and his followers, these new works could explore nuances of human relations, develop moral and philosophical themes, rearrange and give point and conclusiveness to the structure of events, and represent details of settings, conversations, private complaints, public speeches, and the subtlest gestures. The *Filostrato* has the character of a "true," authoritative, received history of Troy and also that of a fiction, a love story that resembles in its vicissitudes, Boccaccio claims, his own troubled love affair. We now name this genre historical romance, a genre frequently and skillfully used by Shakespeare, Stendhal, Dickens, Tolstoy, and Faulkner.

The story of Troilus and Criseyde was first told, in interwoven episodes, in a long French poem of the mid-twelfth century, the *Roman de Troie* of Benoît de Sainte-Maure. Benoît invented that part of the tale that describes the separation of the lovers and Criseyde's infidelity; the earlier events were Boccaccio's invention, based largely on Benoît's account of the love affair of Achilles and Polyxena and on the love affair of Florio and Biancafiore in Boccaccio's own *Filocolo*. Benoît's ultimate sources were classical and pseudo-classical accounts of the Trojan War. Homer's *Iliad* gives the names Chryseis, Pandarus, Calchas, and, of course, the names of the principal figures at Troy — Priam, Troilus, Deiphebus, Hector, Helen, Achilles, and the rest — but none of Benoît's love story appears in Homer. Chryseis in Homer is what her name means, daughter of Chryses, not of Calchas (Chriseide is the accusative form of the patronymic). In Benoît, the woman who loves Troilus is named Briseida, a name derived from Homer's Briseis, "daughter of Brises," who, in Homer, also has nothing to do with Troilus. In the *Iliad,* Chryseis and Briseis were Trojan girls taken captive by Achilles. When Achilles had to give up Briseis to Agamemnon, the leader of the Greeks, he sulked; his wrath is the theme of the poem. Benoît actually tells this Homeric story, giving Briseis and Chryseis the names assigned to them by post-Homeric commentators: in their French form, Ypodamia and Astynome (26837–27037). Benoît was entirely ignorant that his Briseida and Ypodamia were originally the same person. Boccaccio, perhaps taking a hint from the *Florita* (1325) of his fellow Italian Armannino, gives the name Criseida to Benoît's figure Briseida.

Besides widely known details about the war derived from Virgil, Ovid, and other traditional lore, Benoît's main sources for his *Roman de Troie* were two prose accounts in Latin, known to the Middle Ages by the names of their purported authors, Dares and Dictys. Dares Phrygius and Dictys Cretensis claimed to be better "auctoritees" than Homer for the Trojan War, and medieval readers in Western Europe accepted this claim; Homer, in any case, was still untranslated and was largely unknown in the West, except by name, until the Renaissance. Although Dares and Dictys do not tell of a love affair between Troilus and Briseida, some details of their portraits of the two lovers passed into the tradition that came down through Benoît to Chaucer.

In 1287, Guido delle Colonne completed his Latin *Historia destructionis Troiae,* a prose redaction of Benoît's *Roman* that (possibly because writings in Latin seemed more grave and authentic scholarly resources) largely superseded Benoît as the authority on the Trojan War. Guido's work was translated into several languages and was known, along with Benoît, to Boccaccio.

By Chaucer's time, the story of Troy had appeared in a number of full-scale accounts, and details often found their way into chronicles and other historical treatises. Geoffrey of Monmouth's history of Britain had associated the foundation of Britain with the Trojan hero Brut. There was talk in the 1380s of renaming London "Troynovant." Most of the Trojan material was immediately available to French-speaking Englishmen in French and in Anglo-Norman. In Chaucer's lifetime the author of *Sir Gawain and the Green Knight* could casually open and close his poem with allusions to the seige of Troy, allusions that must have been generally comprehensible. Chaucer says "yt is wel wist" that the Greeks beseiged Troy (1.57). It must have been well-known; in a work as early as *The Book of the Duchess,* Chaucer refers to Hector, Achilles, Antenor, Priam, Helen, Paris, and even "Dares Frygius," without explanation. When Chaucer took up his story from Boccaccio, then, he was treating familiar, perhaps even fashionable, matter, and he was conscious of the full tradition of Trojan history. He knew and directly used material from Virgil, Ovid, Benoît, and Guido. He names Dares and Dictys but probably knew the former only through the poetic redaction of Dares by Joseph of Exeter and the latter not at all. Chaucer presents himself in the poem as something of a historiographer, a pedantic scholar, even pretending that one Lollius, a Latin writer, is his authentic source. The evidence of his researches is manifest and suggests that he deliberately made himself an expert in the subject. On occasion, Chaucer apparently took pains to reconcile conflicting details from various sources.

Remarkable, then, is Chaucer's freedom in handling the story, especially the text of his chief source, the *Filostrato.* He radically transforms Boccaccio's poem, redistributing the weight given various parts of the story, adding long scenes, wholly re-imagining the characters of Troilus, Criseyde, and Pandarus, and inserting a number of rich dialogues, apostrophes, epic machinery, soliloquies, proverbs, and the like, which alter, especially under the influence of Boethius, the tone of the poem. Compared with Boccaccio's poem, Chaucer's is at once funnier and graver, more learned and more light-hearted, tighter in organization and broader in implication, less original and less smoothly crafted, yet a fair companion to the works of those poets whom Chaucer names at the end: Virgil, Ovid, Homer, Lucan, and Statius.

STEPHEN A. BARNEY

Troilus and Criseyde

BOOK I

The double sorwe of Troilus to tellen,
That was the kyng Priamus sone of Troye,
In lovynge, how his aventures fellen
Fro wo to wele, and after out of joie,
My purpos is, er that I parte fro ye.   5
Thesiphone, thow help me for t'endite
Thise woful vers, that wepen as I write.

To the clepe I, thow goddesse of torment,
Thow cruwel Furie, sorwynge evere in peyne,
Help me, that am the sorwful instrument,   10
That helpeth loveres, as I kan, to pleyne;
For wel sit it, the sothe for to seyne,
A woful wight to han a drery feere,
And to a sorwful tale, a sory chere.

For I, that God of Loves servantz serve,   15
Ne dar to Love, for myn unliklynesse,
Preyen for speed, al sholde I therfore sterve,
So fer am I from his help in derknesse.
But natheles, if this may don gladnesse
Unto any lovere, and his cause availle,   20
Have he my thonk, and myn be this travaille!

But ye loveres, that bathen in gladnesse,
If any drope of pyte in yow be,
Remembreth yow on passed hevynesse
That ye han felt, and on the adversite   25
Of othere folk, and thynketh how that ye
Han felt that Love dorste yow displese,
Or ye han wonne hym with to gret an ese.

And preieth for hem that ben in the cas
Of Troilus, as ye may after here,   30
That Love hem brynge in hevene to solas;
And ek for me preieth to God so dere
That I have myght to shewe, in som manere,
Swich peyne and wo as Loves folk endure,
In Troilus unsely aventure.   35

And biddeth ek for hem that ben despeired
In love, that nevere nyl recovered be,
And ek for hem that falsly ben apeired
Thorugh wikked tonges, be it he or she;
Thus biddeth God, for his benignite,   40
So graunte hem soone owt of this world to pace,
That ben despeired out of Loves grace.

And biddeth ek for hem that ben at ese,
That God hem graunte ay good perseveraunce,
And sende hem myght hire ladies so to plese   45
That it to Love be worship and plesaunce.
For so hope I my sowle best avaunce,

This text was edited by STEPHEN A. BARNEY, with the assistance of materials provided by ROBERT A. PRATT and collations provided by MARGARET JENNINGS and ARDATH MCKEE.

2 kyng Priamus sone of Troye: the son of King Priam of Troy
5 ye: you (the unstressed form of *yow*)
6 Thesiphone: the Fury Tisiphone
7 vers: verses
12 sit = *sitteth*, suits, befits
13 feere: companion
14 chere: expression
16 unliklynesse: unsuitability
17 speed: success   al: although   sterve: die

22 bathen: bask
27 dorste: dared
28 han: have
35 unsely: unhappy, unfortunate
36 biddeth: pray
37 nyl = *ne wyl*, will not
38 apeired: injured
47 avaunce: cause to prosper

To prey for hem that Loves servauntz be,
And write hire wo, and lyve in charite,

And for to have of hem compassioun,   50
As though I were hire owne brother dere.
Now herkneth with a good entencioun,
For now wil I gon streght to my matere,
In which ye may the double sorwes here
Of Troilus in lovynge of Criseyde,   55
And how that she forsook hym er she deyde.

  Yt is wel wist how that the Grekes stronge
In armes with a thousand shippes wente
To Troiewardes, and the cite longe
Assegeden, neigh ten yer er they stente,   60
And in diverse wise and oon entente,
The ravysshyng to wreken of Eleyne,
By Paris don, they wroughten al hir peyne.

Now fel it so that in the town ther was
Dwellynge a lord of gret auctorite,   65
A gret devyn, that clepid was Calkas,
That in science so expert was that he
Knew wel that Troie sholde destroied be,
By answere of his god, that highte thus:
Daun Phebus or Appollo Delphicus.   70

So whan this Calkas knew by calkulynge,
And ek by answer of this Appollo,
That Grekes sholden swich a peple brynge,
Thorugh which that Troie moste ben fordo,
He caste anon out of the town to go;   75
For wel wiste he by sort that Troye sholde
Destroyed ben, ye, wolde whoso nolde.

For which for to departen softely
Took purpos ful this forknowynge wise,
And to the Grekes oost ful pryvely   80
He stal anon; and they, in curteys wise,
Hym diden bothe worship and servyce,
In trust that he hath konnynge hem to rede
In every peril which that is to drede.

Gret rumour gan, whan it was first aspied   85
Thorugh al the town, and generaly was spoken,
That Calkas traitour fled was and allied
With hem of Grece, and casten to be wroken
On hym that falsly hadde his feith so broken,
And seyden he and al his kyn at-ones   90
Ben worthi for to brennen, fel and bones.

Now hadde Calkas left in this meschaunce,
Al unwist of this false and wikked dede,
His doughter, which that was in gret penaunce,
For of hire lif she was ful sore in drede,   95
As she that nyste what was best to rede;
For bothe a widewe was she and allone
Of any frend to whom she dorste hir mone.

Criseyde was this lady name al right.
As to my doom, in al Troies cite   100
Nas non so fair, forpassynge every wight,
So aungelik was hir natif beaute,
That lik a thing inmortal semed she,
As doth an hevenyssh perfit creature,   104
That down were sent in scornynge of nature.

This lady, which that alday herd at ere
Hire fadres shame, his falsnesse and tresoun,
Wel neigh out of hir wit for sorwe and fere,
In widewes habit large of samyt broun,
On knees she fil biforn Ector adown   110
With pitous vois, and tendrely wepynge,
His mercy bad, hirselven excusynge.

Now was this Ector pitous of nature,
And saugh that she was sorwfully bigon,
And that she was so fair a creature;   115
Of his goodnesse he gladede hire anon,
And seyde, "Lat youre fadres treson gon
Forth with meschaunce, and ye youreself in
          joie
Dwelleth with us, whil yow good list, in Troie.

"And al th'onour that men may don yow have,
As ferforth as youre fader dwelled here,   121

---

60 **stente:** ceased
62 **wreken:** avenge   **Eleyne:** Helen of Troy
63 **peyne:** efforts
64 **fel it:** it happened
66 **devyn:** divine, soothsayer
71 **calkulynge:** astrological computation; see n.
74 **fordo:** ruined
75 **caste:** planned, plotted
76 **sort:** drawing or casting lots
77 **wolde whoso nolde:** whether anyone wished it or not
79 **forknowynge wise:** provident and shrewd man
80 **oost:** host, army
82 **worship:** honor
83 **rede:** advise

88 **casten:** they plotted   **wroken:** avenged
91 **brennen:** burn   **fel:** skin
93 **unwist:** uninformed
96 **nyste** = *ne wyste,* knew not
98 **dorste hir mone:** dared to complain
99 **al right:** exactly
101 **forpassynge:** surpassing
102 **natif:** native, natural
109 **large:** ample   **samyt:** samite (rich silk)
110 **Ector:** Hector, Troilus's eldest brother
112 **bad:** prayed for
114 **sorwfully bigon:** in a sorrowful situation
118 **with meschaunce:** with bad luck
119 **whil yow good list:** as long as you please
121 **As ferforth as:** as much as when

Ye shul have, and youre body shal men save,
As fer as I may ought enquere or here.''
And she hym thonked with ful humble chere,
And ofter wolde, and it hadde ben his wille, 125
And took hire leve, and hom, and held hir stille.

And in hire hous she abood with swich meyne
As til hire honour nede was to holde;
And whil she was dwellynge in that cite,
Kepte hir estat, and both of yonge and olde 130
Ful wel biloved, and wel men of hir tolde.
But wheither that she children hadde or noon,
I rede it naught, therfore I late it goon.

The thynges fellen, as they don of werre,
Bitwixen hem of Troie and Grekes ofte; 135
For som day boughten they of Troie it derre,
And eft the Grekes founden nothing softe
The folk of Troie; and thus Fortune on lofte
And under eft gan hem to whielen bothe 139
Aftir hir course, ay whil that thei were wrothe.

But how this town com to destruccion
Ne falleth naught to purpos me to telle,
For it were a long digression
Fro my matere, and yow to long to dwelle.
But the Troian gestes, as they felle, 145
In Omer, or in Dares, or in Dite,
Whoso that kan may rede hem as they write.

But though that Grekes hem of Troie shetten,
And hir cite biseged al aboute,
Hire olde usage nolde they nat letten, 150
As for to honoure hir goddes ful devoute;
But aldirmost in honour, out of doute,
Thei hadde a relik, heet Palladion,
That was hire trist aboven everichon.

And so bifel, whan comen was the tyme 155
Of Aperil, whan clothed is the mede
With newe grene, of lusty Veer the pryme,
And swote smellen floures white and rede,
In sondry wises shewed, as I rede,

The folk of Troie hire observaunces olde, 160
Palladiones feste for to holde.

And to the temple, in al hir beste wise,
In general ther wente many a wight,
To herknen of Palladions servyce;
And namely, so many a lusty knyght, 165
So many a lady fressh and mayden bright,
Ful wel arayed, both meeste, mene, and leste,
Ye, bothe for the seson and the feste.

Among thise othere folk was Criseyda,
In widewes habit blak; but natheles, 170
Right as oure firste lettre is now an A,
In beaute first so stood she, makeles.
Hire goodly lokyng gladed al the prees.
Nas nevere yet seyn thyng to ben preysed derre,
Nor under cloude blak so bright a sterre 175

As was Criseyde, as folk seyde everichone
That hir behelden in hir blake wede.
And yet she stood ful lowe and stille allone,
Byhynden other folk, in litel brede,
And neigh the dore, ay undre shames drede, 180
Simple of atir and debonaire of chere,
With ful assured lokyng and manere.

This Troilus, as he was wont to gide
His yonge knyghtes, lad hem up and down
In thilke large temple on every side, 185
Byholding ay the ladies of the town,
Now here, now there; for no devocioun
Hadde he to non, to reven hym his reste,
But gan to preise and lakken whom hym leste.

And in his walk ful faste he gan to wayten 190
If knyght or squyer of his compaignie
Gan for to syke, or lete his eighen baiten
On any womman that he koude espye.
He wolde smyle and holden it folye,
And seye hym thus, "God woot, she slepeth softe 195
For love of the, whan thow turnest ful ofte!

123 ought: in any way
125 wolde: would (have thanked him) and: if
126 hom: went home
127 abood: remained meyne: household attendants
133 rede: read (in my source)
136 boughten . . . it derre: bought it at a greater cost (had the worst of it)
137 eft: another time
139 whielen: wheel, cause to turn on Fortune's wheel
145 gestes: deeds, stories
146 Omer, Dares, Dite: Homer, Dares Phrygius, Dictys Cretensis, historians of the Trojan war
148 shetten: shut in
153 heet: called Palladion: Palladium, image of Pallas
157 lusty: delightful Veer: Springtime pryme: first hour, beginning

161 feste: religious festival
164 herknen of: listen to
167 meeste, mene, and leste: highest, middling, and lowest (in rank); i.e., everyone
172 makeles: matchless
173 prees: crowd
174 derre: more highly
177 wede: clothing
178 ful lowe: very humbly
179 in litel brede: in a little space
181 atir: clothing debonaire: gracious
182 assured: confident
188 reven: deprive
189 lakken: disparage
190 wayten: watch
192 baiten: feast
195 woot: knows

"I have herd told, pardieux, of youre lyvynge,
Ye loveres, and youre lewed observaunces,
And which a labour folk han in wynnynge 199
Of love, and in the kepyng which doutaunces;
And whan youre prey is lost, woo and pen-
          aunces.
O veray fooles, nyce and blynde be ye!
Ther nys nat oon kan war by other be."

And with that word he gan caste up the browe,
Ascaunces, "Loo! is this naught wisely spoken?"
At which the God of Love gan loken rowe 206
Right for despit, and shop for to ben wroken.
He kidde anon his bowe nas naught broken;
For sodeynly he hitte hym atte fulle —
And yet as proud a pekok kan he pulle. 210

O blynde world, O blynde entencioun!
How often falleth al the effect contraire
Of surquidrie and foul presumpcioun;
For kaught is proud, and kaught is debonaire.
This Troilus is clomben on the staire, 215
And litel weneth that he moot descenden;
But alday faileth thing that fooles wenden.

As proude Bayard gynneth for to skippe
Out of the weye, so pryketh hym his corn,
Til he a lasshe have of the longe whippe — 220
Than thynketh he, "Though I praunce al byforn
First in the trays, ful fat and newe shorn,
Yet am I but an hors, and horses lawe
I moot endure, and with my feres drawe" —

So ferde it by this fierse and proude knyght:
Though he a worthy kynges sone were, 226
And wende nothing hadde had swich myght
Ayeyns his wille that shuld his herte stere,
Yet with a look his herte wex a-fere,
That he that now was moost in pride above, 230
Wax sodeynly moost subgit unto love.

Forthy ensample taketh of this man,
Ye wise, proude, and worthi folkes alle,
To scornen Love, which that so soone kan
The fredom of youre hertes to hym thralle; 235
For evere it was, and evere it shal byfalle,
That Love is he that alle thing may bynde,
For may no man fordon the lawe of kynde.

That this be soth, hath preved and doth yit.
For this trowe I ye knowen alle or some, 240
Men reden nat that folk han gretter wit
Than they that han be moost with love ynome;
And strengest folk ben therwith overcome,
The worthiest and grettest of degree:
This was, and is, and yet men shall it see. 245

And trewelich it sit wel to be so,
For alderwisest han therwith ben plesed;
And they that han ben aldermost in wo,
With love han ben comforted moost and esed;
And ofte it hath the cruel herte apesed, 250
And worthi folk maad worthier of name,
And causeth moost to dreden vice and shame.

Now sith it may nat goodly ben withstonde,
And is a thing so vertuous in kynde,
Refuseth nat to Love for to ben bonde, 255
Syn, as hymselven liste, he may yow bynde;
The yerde is bet that bowen wole and wynde
Than that that brest, and therfore I yow rede
To folowen hym that so wel kan yow lede.

But for to tellen forth in special 260
Of this kynges sone of which I tolde,
And leten other thing collateral,
Of hym thenke I my tale forth to holde,
Bothe of his joie and of his cares colde;
And al his werk, as touching this matere, 265
For I it gan, I wol therto refere.

Withinne the temple he wente hym forth
          pleyinge,
This Troilus, of every wight aboute,

---

197 **pardieux:** indeed, by God
198 **lewed:** foolish
199 **which:** how much
200 **doutaunces:** uncertainties
202 **veray:** true
205 **Ascaunces:** as if to say
206 **rowe:** roughly, angrily
207 **shop:** intended **wroken:** avenged
208 **kidde:** made known
210 **pulle:** pluck
213 **surquidrie:** arrogance, pride
214 **debonaire:** humble
216 **weneth:** supposes
218 **Bayard:** a common horse's name
222 **First in the trays:** the lead horse in a tandem team
228 **stere:** steer, control (or, stir, disturb)
229 **a-fere:** on fire
230 **above:** superior

234 **To scornen:** with regard to scorning
235 **thralle:** enslave
238 **fordon:** break, violate **kynde:** nature
239 **preved:** proven (true)
240 **alle or some:** one and all, everyone
242 **ynome:** taken
246 **sit** = *sitteth*, sits (suits)
247 **alderwisest:** the wisest of all
256 **as hymselven liste:** as he pleases
257 **yerde:** rod, sapling
260 **in special:** in particular
262 **leten:** leave aside
266 **For I it gan:** because I began (to tell of) it **refere:** return

On this lady, and now on that, lokynge,
Wher so she were of town or of withoute;   270
And upon cas bifel that thorugh a route
His eye percede, and so depe it wente,
Til on Criseyde it smot, and ther it stente.

And sodeynly he wax therwith astoned,
And gan hir bet biholde in thrifty wise.   275
"O mercy, God," thoughte he, "wher hastow
        woned,
That art so feyr and goodly to devise?"
Therwith his herte gan to sprede and rise,
And softe sighed, lest men myghte hym here,
And caught ayeyn his firste pleyinge chere.   280

She nas nat with the leste of hire stature,
But alle hire lymes so wel answerynge
Weren to wommanhod, that creature
Was nevere lasse mannyssh in semynge;
And ek the pure wise of hire mevynge   285
Shewed wel that men myght in hire gesse
Honour, estat, and wommanly noblesse.

To Troilus right wonder wel with alle
Gan for to like hire mevynge and hire chere,
Which somdel deignous was, for she let falle
Hire look a lite aside in swich manere,   291
Ascaunces, "What, may I nat stonden here?"
And after that hir lokynge gan she lighte,
That nevere thoughte hym seen so good a
        syghte.

And of hire look in him ther gan to quyken   295
So gret desir and such affeccioun,
That in his herte botme gan to stiken
Of hir his fixe and depe impressioun.
And though he erst hadde poured up and
        down,
He was tho glad his hornes in to shrinke: 300
Unnethes wiste he how to loke or wynke.

Lo, he that leet hymselven so konnynge,
And scorned hem that Loves peynes dryen,
Was ful unwar that Love hadde his dwellynge
Withinne the subtile stremes of hir yen;   305
That sodeynly hym thoughte he felte dyen,
Right with hire look, the spirit in his herte:
Blissed be Love, that kan thus folk converte!

She, this in blak, likynge to Troilus
Over alle thing, he stood for to biholde;   310
Ne his desir, ne wherfore he stood thus,
He neither chere made, ne word tolde;
But from afer, his manere for to holde,
On other thing his look som tyme he caste,
And eft on hire, whil that servyse laste.   315

And after this, nat fullich al awhaped,
Out of the temple al esilich he wente,
Repentynge hym that he hadde evere ijaped
Of Loves folk, lest fully the descente   319
Of scorn fille on hymself; but what he mente,
Lest it were wist on any manere syde,
His woo he gan dissimilen and hide.

Whan he was fro the temple thus departed,
He streght anon unto his paleys torneth.
Right with hire look thorugh-shoten and
        thorugh-darted,   325
Al feyneth he in lust that he sojorneth,
And al his chere and speche also he borneth,
And ay of Loves servantz every while,
Hymself to wrye, at hem he gan to smyle,

And seyde, "Lord, so ye lyve al in lest,   330
Ye loveres! For the konnyngeste of yow,
That serveth most ententiflich and best,
Hym tit as often harm therof as prow.
Youre hire is quyt ayeyn, ye, God woot how!

270 **Wher so:** whether
271 **upon cas:** by chance **route:** crowd
273 **stente:** stopped
275 **thrifty:** prudent
276 **woned:** dwelt
277 **devise:** look upon
282 **answerynge:** corresponding
284 **semynge:** appearance
285 **pure wise:** very, mere manner **mevynge:** motion, movements
286 **gesse:** infer, perceive
289 **like:** be pleasing
290 **deignous:** haughty
292 **Ascaunces:** as if to say
293 **lighte:** brighten
295 **quyken:** arise
299 **erst:** before **poured:** gazed intently, pored
301 **Unnethes:** hardly **wynke:** close his eyes

302 **leet:** considered
303 **dryen:** suffer
304 **unwar:** unaware
305 **subtile:** delicate **yen:** eyes
307 **spirit:** the vital spirit
309 **likynge:** pleasing
312 **chere made:** revealed by his expression
316 **awhaped:** stunned
317 **esilich:** slowly
318–19 **ijaped Of:** made fun of
320 **fille:** should fall
325 **thorugh-shoten:** shot through **thorugh-darted:** pierced
326 **lust:** pleasure **sojorneth:** continues
327 **borneth:** polishes
329 **wrye:** cover, hide
330 **lest:** delight
332 **ententiflich:** diligently
333 **Hym tit** = *hym tydeth*, befalls him, happens to him **prow:** profit
334 **Youre hire is quyt:** you are repaid **woot:** knows

Nought wel for wel, but scorn for good servyse.
In feith, youre ordre is ruled in good wise! 336

"In nouncerteyn ben alle youre observaunces,
But it a sely fewe pointes be;
Ne no thing asketh so gret attendaunces
As doth youre lay, and that knowe alle ye; 340
But that is nat the worste, as mote I the!
But, tolde I yow the worste point, I leve,
Al seyde I soth, ye wolden at me greve.

"But take this: that ye loveres ofte eschuwe,
Or elles doon, of good entencioun,   345
Ful ofte thi lady wol it mysconstruwe,
And deme it harm in hire oppynyoun;
And yet if she, for other enchesoun,
Be wroth, than shaltow have a groyn anon. 349
Lord, wel is hym that may ben of yow oon!"

But for al this, whan that he say his tyme,
He held his pees — non other boote hym
          gayned —
For love bigan his fetheres so to lyme
That wel unnethe until his folk he fayned
That other besy nedes hym destrayned;   355
For wo was hym, that what to doon he nyste,
But bad his folk to gon wher that hem liste.

And whan that he in chambre was allone,
He doun upon his beddes feet hym sette,
And first he gan to sike, and eft to grone, 360
And thought ay on hire so, withouten lette,
That, as he sat and wook, his spirit mette
That he hire saugh a-temple, and al the wise
Right of hire look, and gan it newe avise.

Thus gan he make a mirour of his mynde 365
In which he saugh al holly hire figure,
And that he wel koude in his herte fynde.
It was to hym a right good aventure

To love swich oon, and if he dede his cure
To serven hir, yet myghte he falle in grace, 370
Or ellis for oon of hire servantz pace.

Imagenynge that travaille nor grame
Ne myghte for so goodly oon be lorn
As she, ne hym for his desir no shame,
Al were it wist, but in pris and up-born   375
Of alle lovers wel more than biforn,
Thus argumented he in his gynnynge,
Ful unavysed of his woo comynge.

Thus took he purpos loves craft to suwe,
And thoughte he wolde werken pryvely,   380
First to hiden his desir in muwe
From every wight yborn, al outrely,
But he myghte ought recovered be therby,
Remembryng hym that love to wide yblowe
Yelt bittre fruyt, though swete seed be sowe. 385

And over al this, yet muchel more he thoughte
What for to speke, and what to holden inne;
And what to arten hire to love he soughte,
And on a song anon-right to bygynne,
And gan loude on his sorwe for to wynne;   390
For with good hope he gan fully assente
Criseyde for to love, and nought repente.

And of his song naught only the sentence,
As writ myn auctour called Lollius,
But pleinly, save oure tonges difference,   395
I dar wel seyn, in al, that Troilus
Seyde in his song, loo, every word right thus
As I shal seyn; and whoso list it here,
Loo, next this vers he may it fynden here.

Canticus Troili.

"If no love is, O God, what fele I so?   400
And if love is, what thing and which is he?
If love be good, from whennes cometh my woo?

336 **ordre:** religious order
337 **nouncerteyn:** uncertainty
338 **sely:** insignificant
339 **attendaunces:** attentions
340 **lay:** religious belief
341 **the:** prosper
343 **Al:** even if   **at me greve:** be angry with me
344 **that:** that which
348 **enchesoun:** reason
349 **groyn:** scolding
351 **say:** saw
352 **boote hym gayned:** remedy was of any help to him
353 **lyme:** smear with birdlime (to capture him)
354 **unnethe:** with difficulty   **until:** to
355 **destrayned:** pressed on, constrained
357 **hem liste:** it pleased them, they pleased
359 **beddes feet:** foot of the bed
361 **lette:** ceasing
362 **mette:** dreamed
364 **avise:** consider

369 **dede his cure:** took pains
372 **grame:** suffering
373 **lorn:** lost, wasted
375 **Al were it wist:** even if it became known   **in pris:** (he would be) esteemed, honored   **up-born:** exalted
377 **gynnynge:** beginning
378 **unavysed:** unaware
379 **suwe:** follow
381 **in muwe:** in secret
382 **outrely:** utterly
383 **But:** unless   **ought recovered:** in any way benefitted
384 **to:** too   **yblowe:** spread abroad
385 **Yelt** = *yeldeth*, yields
388 **arten:** urge
390 **wynne:** overcome (?), complain (?); see n.
394 **writ** = *writeth*, writes   **auctour:** authority   **Lollius:** Chaucer's fictitious source
395 **pleinly:** fully   **save:** save for, except
396 **in al, that:** entirely, that which (?); see n.
398 **list it here:** wishes to hear it
Canticus Troili: Troilus's Song

If it be wikke, a wonder thynketh me,
When every torment and adversite   404
That cometh of hym may to me savory thinke,
For ay thurst I, the more that ich it drynke.

"And if that at myn owen lust I brenne,
From whennes cometh my waillynge and my
          pleynte?
If harm agree me, wherto pleyne I thenne?
I noot, ne whi unwery that I feynte.   410
O quike deth, O swete harm so queynte,
How may of the in me swich quantite,
But if that I consente that it be?

"And if that I consente, I wrongfully
Compleyne, iwis. Thus possed to and fro,   415
Al sterelees withinne a boot am I
Amydde the see, bitwixen wyndes two,
That in contrarie stonden evere mo.
Allas, what is this wondre maladie?
For hote of cold, for cold of hote, I dye."   420

And to the God of Love thus seyde he
With pitous vois, "O lord, now youres is
My spirit, which that oughte youres be.
Yow thanke I, lord, that han me brought to
          this.
But wheither goddesse or womman, iwis,   425
She be, I not, which that ye do me serve;
But as hire man I wol ay lyve and sterve.

"Ye stonden in hir eighen myghtily,
As in a place unto youre vertu digne;
Wherfore, lord, if my service or I   430
May liken yow, so beth to me benigne;
For myn estat roial I here resigne
Into hire hond, and with ful humble chere
Bicome hir man, as to my lady dere."

In hym ne deyned spare blood roial   435
The fyr of love — wherfro God me blesse —
Ne him forbar in no degree, for al
His vertu or his excellent prowesse,

But held hym as his thral lowe in destresse,
And brende hym so in soundry wise ay newe,
That sexti tyme a day he loste his hewe.   441

So muche, day by day, his owene thought,
For lust to hire, gan quiken and encresse,
That every other charge he sette at nought.
Forthi ful ofte, his hote fir to cesse,   445
To sen hire goodly lok he gan to presse;
For therby to ben esed wel he wende,
And ay the ner he was, the more he brende.

For ay the ner the fir, the hotter is —
This, trowe I, knoweth al this compaignye;   450
But were he fer or ner, I dar sey this:
By nyght or day, for wisdom or folye,
His herte, which that is his brestez yë,
Was ay on hire, that fairer was to sene
Than evere werc Eleyne or Polixene.   455

Ek of the day ther passed nought an houre
That to hymself a thousand tyme he seyde,
"Good goodly, to whom serve I and laboure
As I best kan, now wolde God, Criseyde,
Ye wolden on me rewe, er that I deyde!   460
My dere herte, allas, myn hele and hewe
And lif is lost, but ye wol on me rewe!"

Alle other dredes weren from him fledde,
Both of th'assege and his savacioun;
N'yn him desir noon other fownes bredde,   465
But argumentes to his conclusioun:
That she of him wolde han compassioun,
And he to ben hire man while he may dure.
Lo, here his lif, and from the deth his cure!

The sharpe shoures felle of armes preve   470
That Ector or his othere brethren diden
Ne made hym only therfore ones meve;
And yet was he, where so men wente or riden,
Founde oon the beste, and longest tyme abiden

405 **savory:** pleasant   **thinke:** seem
407 **lust:** desire
408 **pleynte:** lament
409 **agree:** be agreeable to
410 **unwery:** without weariness
411 **quike:** living   **queynte:** strange
412 **may:** can there be
415 **Compleyne:** lament   **possed:** tossed
416 **sterelees:** without a rudder
426 **not** = ne wot, know not
428 She esteems you greatly
429 **digne:** worthy
436 **wherfro:** from which
437 **forbar:** spared

440 **ay newe:** always
443 **quiken:** grow lively
444 **sette at nought:** took no account of, considered nothing
445 **cesse:** stop, cause to cease
447 **wende:** supposed
453 **yë:** eye
455 **Eleyne:** Helen of Troy   **Polixene:** Polyxena, Troilus's sister, beloved of Achilles
458 **goodly:** good, pleasing one
460 **rewe:** have pity
461 **hele:** health
464 **th'assege:** the siege   **savacioun:** safety
465 Nor did desire breed any other offspring in him (*fownes*, the young of any animal)
468 **dure:** endure, live
470 **shoures:** storms, assaults   **felle:** terrible   **armes preve:** proof (deeds) of combat
474 **oon the beste:** the very best   **longest tyme abiden:** (to have) remained the longest time

Ther peril was, and dide ek swich travaille 475
In armes, that to thenke it was merveille.

But for non hate he to the Grekes hadde,
Ne also for the rescous of the town,
Ne made hym thus in armes for to madde,
But only, lo, for this conclusioun: 480
To liken hire the bet for his renoun.
Fro day to day in armes so he spedde
That the Grekes as the deth him dredde.

And fro this forth tho refte hym love his slep,
And made his mete his foo, and ek his sorwe
Gan multiplie, that, whoso tok kep,   486
It shewed in his hewe both eve and morwe.
Therfor a title he gan him for to borwe
Of other siknesse, lest men of hym wende
That the hote fir of love hym brende,   490

And seyde he hadde a fevere and ferde amys.
But how it was, certeyn, kan I nat seye,
If that his lady understood nat this,
Or feynede hire she nyste, oon of the tweye;
But wel I rede that, by no manere weye,   495
Ne semed it that she of hym roughte,
Or of his peyne, or whatsoevere he thoughte.

But thanne felte this Troilus swich wo
That he was wel neigh wood; for ay his drede
Was this, that she som wight hadde loved
                    so,   500
That nevere of hym she wolde han taken hede,
For which hym thoughte he felte his herte
                    blede;
Ne of his wo ne dorste he nat bygynne
To tellen hir, for al this world to wynne.

But whan he hadde a space from his care,   505
Thus to hymself ful ofte he gan to pleyne;
He seyde, "O fool, now artow in the snare,
That whilom japedest at loves peyne.
Now artow hent, now gnaw thin owen cheyne!
Thow were ay wont ech lovere reprehende 510
Of thing fro which thou kanst the nat defende.

"What wol now every lovere seyn of the,
If this be wist, but evere in thin absence
Laughen in scorn, and seyn, 'Loo, ther goth he
That is the man of so gret sapience,   515
That held us loveres leest in reverence.
Now, thanked God, he may gon in the
                    daunce
Of hem that Love list febly for to avaunce.'

"But, O thow woful Troilus, God wolde,
Sith thow most loven thorugh thi destine,   520
That thow beset were on swich oon that sholde
Know al thi wo, al lakked hir pitee!
But also cold in love towardes the
Thi lady is as frost in wynter moone,
And thow fordon as snow in fire is soone.   525

"God wold I were aryved in the port
Of deth, to which my sorwe wol me lede!
A, Lord, to me it were a gret comfort;
Than were I quyt of languisshyng in drede;
For, be myn hidde sorwe iblowe on brede, 530
I shal byjaped ben a thousand tyme
More than that fol of whos folie men ryme.

"But now help, God, and ye, swete, for whom
I pleyne, ikaught, ye, nevere wight so faste!
O mercy, dere herte, and help me from   535
The deth, for I, whil that my lyf may laste,
More than myself wol love yow to my laste;
And with som frendly lok gladeth me, swete,
Though nevere more thing ye me byheete."

Thise wordes, and ful many an other to,   540
He spak, and called evere in his compleynte
Hire name, for to tellen hire his wo,
Til neigh that he in salte teres dreynte.
Al was for nought: she herde nat his pleynte;
And whan that he bythought on that folie, 545
A thousand fold his wo gan multiplie.

Bywayling in his chambre thus allone,
A frend of his that called was Pandare
Com oones in unwar, and herde hym groone,

478 **rescous:** rescue
479 **madde:** go mad
481 **liken:** please
482 **spedde:** prospered
484 **fro this forth:** from this time on
485 **mete:** food
486 **tok kep:** noticed
491 **ferde:** fared
496 **roughte:** reckoned, cared
499 **wood:** crazy, mad
505 **space:** respite
508 **That:** you who   **whilom:** formerly
509 **hent:** caught

517 **daunce:** procession
518 **list:** wishes   **avaunce:** cause to prosper
520 **most:** must
521 **beset were on:** were bestowed upon
522 **al lakked hir pitee:** though she lack pity
523 **also:** as
525 **fordon:** ruined
529 **quyt:** free
530 **iblowe on brede:** blown abroad, widely talked about
531 **byjaped:** mocked
532 **fol:** fool
539 **byheete:** should promise
543 **dreynte:** drowned
545 **bythought on:** considered

And say his frend in swich destresse and care:
"Allas," quod he, "who causeth al this fare? 551
O mercy, God! What unhap may this meene?
Han now thus soone Grekes maad yow leene?

"Or hastow som remors of conscience,
And art now falle in som devocioun, 555
And wailest for thi synne and thin offence,
And hast for ferde caught attricioun?
God save hem that biseged han oure town,
That so kan leye oure jolite on presse,
And bringe oure lusty folk to holynesse!" 560

Thise wordes seyde he for the nones alle,
That with swich thing he myght hym angry
    maken,
And with angre don his wo to falle,
As for the tyme, and his corage awaken.
But wel he wist, as fer as tonges spaken, 565
Ther nas a man of gretter hardinesse
Thanne he, ne more desired worthinesse.

"What cas," quod Troilus, "or what aventure
Hath gided the to sen me langwisshinge,
That am refus of every creature? 570
But for the love of God, at my preyinge,
Go hennes awey; for certes my deyinge
Wol the disese, and I mot nedes deye;
Therfore go wey, ther is na more to seye.

"But if thow wene I be thus sik for drede, 575
It is naught so, and therfore scorne nought.
Ther is another thing I take of hede
Wel more than aught the Grekes han yet
    wrought,
Which cause is of my deth, for sorowe and
    thought;
But though that I now telle it the ne leste, 580
Be thow naught wroth; I hide it for the beste."

This Pandare, that neigh malt for wo and
    routhe,
Ful ofte seyde, "Allas, what may this be?
Now frend," quod he, "if evere love or trouthe

Hath ben, or is, bitwixen the and me, 585
Ne do thow nevere swich a crueltee
To hiden fro thi frend so gret a care!
Wostow naught wel that it am I, Pandare?

"I wol parten with the al thi peyne,
If it be so I do the no comfort, 590
As it is frendes right, soth for to seyne,
To entreparten wo as glad desport.
I have, and shal, for trewe or fals report,
In wrong and right iloved the al my lyve:
Hid nat thi wo fro me, but telle it blyve." 595

Than gan this sorwful Troylus to syke,
And seide hym thus: "God leve it be my beste
To telle it the; for sith it may the like,
Yet wol I telle it, though myn herte breste.
And wel woot I thow mayst do me no reste;
But lest thow deme I truste nat to the, 601
Now herke, frend, for thus it stant with me.

"Love, ayeins the which whoso defendeth
Hymselven most, hym alderlest avaylleth,
With disespeyr so sorwfulli me offendeth, 605
That streight unto the deth myn herte sailleth.
Therto desir so brennyngly me assailleth,
That to ben slayn it were a gretter joie
To me than kyng of Grece ben and Troye.

"Suffiseth this, my fulle frend Pandare, 610
That I have seyd, for now wostow my wo;
And for the love of God, my colde care,
So hide it wel — I tolde it nevere to mo,
For harmes myghten folwen mo than two
If it were wist — but be thow in gladnesse, 615
And lat me sterve, unknowe, of my destresse."

"How hastow thus unkyndely and longe
Hid this fro me, thow fol?" quod Pandarus.
"Paraunter thow myghte after swich oon longe,
That myn avys anoon may helpen us." 620
"This were a wonder thing," quod Troilus;
"Thow koudest nevere in love thiselven wisse.
How devel maistow brynge me to blisse?"

---

551 **fare:** commotion
557 **for ferde:** because of fear **attricioun:** attrition (imperfect remorse for sin, something less than contrition)
559 **leye . . . on presse:** lay away, shelve (as in a cupboard for clothing or books)
560 **holynesse:** religious observance, piety
561 **nones:** immediate occasion, nonce
564 **As for the tyme:** temporarily
568 **cas:** chance **aventure:** chance happening
570 **refus of:** rejected by
573 **disese:** distress
577 **take of hede:** take heed of, care about
580 Though I do not wish to tell it to you now
582 **malt:** melted **routhe:** pity

592 **entreparten:** share
595 **blyve:** quickly
596 **syke:** sigh
597 **leve:** grant
599 **breste:** should break
602 **stant** = *stondeth,* stands
603–604 **ayeins . . . avaylleth:** against which he succeeds least (literally, it profits him least) who defends himself most (i.e., fighting against it makes it worse)
607 **brennyngly:** ardently
613 **mo:** others
619 **Paraunter:** perhaps **after swich oon longe:** long for such a one
622 **wisse:** inform, instruct (i.e., help)
623 **How devel:** how the devil (?)

"Ye, Troilus, now herke," quod Pandare;
"Though I be nyce, it happeth often so,   625
That oon that excesse doth ful yvele fare
By good counseil kan kepe his frend therfro.
I have myself ek seyn a blynd man goo
Ther as he fel that couthe loken wide;
A fool may ek a wis-man ofte gide.   630

"A wheston is no kervyng instrument,
But yet it maketh sharppe kervyng tolis;
And there thow woost that I have aught mys-
            went,
Eschuw thow that, for swich thing to the
            scole is;
Thus often wise men ben war by foolys.   635
If thow do so, thi wit is wel bewared;
By his contrarie is every thyng declared.

"For how myghte evere swetnesse han ben
            knowe
To him that nevere tasted bitternesse?
Ne no man may ben inly glad, I trowe,   640
That nevere was in sorwe or som destresse.
Eke whit by blak, by shame ek worthinesse,
Ech set by other, more for other semeth,
As men may se, and so the wyse it demeth.

"Sith thus of two contraries is o lore,   645
I, that have in love so ofte assayed
Grevances, oughte konne, and wel the more,
Counseillen the of that thow art amayed.
Ek the ne aughte nat ben yvel appayed,
Though I desyre with the for to bere   650
Thyn hevy charge; it shal the lasse dere.

"I woot wel that it fareth thus be me
As to thi brother, Paris, an herdesse
Which that icleped was Oënone
Wrot in a compleynte of hir hevynesse.   655

Yee say the lettre that she wrot, I gesse?"
"Nay, nevere yet, ywys," quod Troilus.
"Now," quod Pandare, "herkne, it was thus:

" 'Phebus, that first fond art of medicyne,'
Quod she, 'and couthe in every wightes care   660
Remedye and reed, by herbes he knew fyne,
Yet to hymself his konnyng was ful bare,
For love hadde hym so bounden in a snare,
Al for the doughter of the kyng Amete,
That al his craft ne koude his sorwes bete.'   665

"Right so fare I, unhappyly for me.
I love oon best, and that me smerteth sore;
And yet, peraunter, kan I reden the
And nat myself; repreve me na more.
I have no cause, I woot wel, for to sore   670
As doth an hauk that listeth for to pleye;
But to thin help yet somwhat kan I seye.

"And of o thyng right siker maistow be,
That certein, for to dyen in the peyne,
That I shal nevere mo discoveren the;   675
Ne, by my trouthe, I kepe nat restreyne
The fro thi love, theigh that it were Eleyne
That is thi brother wif, if ich it wiste:
Be what she be, and love hire as the liste!

"Therfore, as frend, fullich in me assure,   680
And tel me plat what is th'enchesoun
And final cause of wo that ye endure;
For douteth nothyng, myn entencioun
Nis nat to yow of reprehencioun,
To speke as now, for no wight may byreve   685
A man to love, tyl that hym list to leve.

"And witteth wel that bothe two ben vices:
Mistrusten alle, or elles alle leve.
But wel I woot, the mene of it no vice is,

625 **nyce:** foolish
626 **excesse doth ful yvele fare:** excess causes to fare badly
630 **ek:** also
631 **wheston:** whetstone
632 **tolis:** tools
633 **there:** where **aught myswent:** went astray in any way
634 **to the scole is:** is a lesson to you
636 **bewared:** employed
637 **declared:** revealed, defined
640 **inly:** entirely
643 **for other:** because of the other
645 **o lore:** one principle that may be learned
646 **assayed:** experienced
647 **oughte konne:** should be able
648 **amayed:** dismayed
649 **yvel appayed:** displeased
651 **dere:** injure, harm
652 **be:** by, concerning
653 **herdesse:** shepherdess
654 **icleped:** called **Oënone:** a nymph deserted by Paris for Helen
655 **compleynte:** Ovid's *Heroides* 5

656 **say:** saw
659 **Phebus:** Phoebus Apollo
661 **reed:** advice (for the patient) **fyne:** fully, well
662 **ful bare:** completely barren, useless
664 **Amete:** Admetus, king of Pherae
665 **bete:** improve, assuage
666 **unhappyly:** unfortunately
668 **reden the:** advise you
670 **sore:** soar
673 **siker:** certain
674 **for to dyen in the peyne:** though I were to die by torture
675 **discoveren:** betray
676 **kepe nat restreyne:** don't care about restraining
681 **plat:** flatly, bluntly **th'enchesoun:** the reason, occasion
684 **reprehencioun:** reproach
685-86 **byreve . . . to love:** stop from loving
686 **tyl that hym list to leve:** until he desires to leave off (loving)
687 **witteth:** know
688 **leve:** believe
689 **mene:** mean (between the two extremes)

For to trusten som wight is a preve   690
Of trouth; and forthi wolde I fayn remeve
Thi wrong conseyte, and do the som wyght triste
Thi wo to telle; and tel me, if the liste.

"The wise seith, 'Wo hym that is allone,   694
For, and he falle, he hath non helpe to ryse';
And sith thow hast a felawe, tel thi mone;
For this nys naught, certein, the nexte wyse
To wynnen love — as techen us the wyse —
To walwe and wepe as Nyobe the queene,
Whos teres yet in marble ben yseene.   700

"Lat be thy wepyng and thi drerynesse,
And lat us lissen wo with oother speche;
So may thy woful tyme seme lesse.
Delyte nat in wo thi wo to seche,
As don thise foles that hire sorwes eche   705
With sorwe, whan thei han mysaventure,
And listen naught to seche hem other cure.

"Men seyn, 'to wrecche is consolacioun
To have another felawe in hys peyne.'
That owghte wel ben oure opynyoun,   710
For bothe thow and I of love we pleyne.
So ful of sorwe am I, soth for to seyne,
That certeinly namore harde grace
May sitte on me, for-why ther is no space.

"If God wol, thow art nat agast of me,   715
Lest I wolde of thi lady the bygyle!
Thow woost thyself whom that I love, parde,
As I best kan, gon sithen longe while.
And sith thow woost I do it for no wyle,   719
And sith I am he that thow trustest moost,
Tel me somwhat, syn al my wo thow woost."

Yet Troilus for al this no word seyde,
But longe he ley as stylle as he ded were;
And after this with sikynge he abreyde,

And to Pandarus vois he lente his ere,   725
And up his eighen caste he, that in feere
Was Pandarus, lest that in frenesie
He sholde falle, or elles soone dye;

And cryde "Awake!" ful wonderlich and sharpe;
"What! Slombrestow as in a litargie?   730
Or artow lik an asse to the harpe,
That hereth sown whan men the strynges plye,
But in his mynde of that no melodie
May sinken hym to gladen, for that he
So dul ys of his bestialite?"   735

And with that, Pandare of his wordes stente;
And Troilus yet hym nothyng answerde,
For-why to tellen nas nat his entente
To nevere no man, for whom that he so ferde;
For it is seyd, "Man maketh ofte a yerde   740
With which the maker is hymself ybeten
In sondry manere," as thise wyse treten,

And namelich in his counseil tellynge
That toucheth love that oughte ben secree;
For of himself it wol ynough out sprynge,   745
But if that it the bet governed be.
Ek som tyme it is a craft to seme fle
Fro thyng whych in effect men hunte faste;
Al this gan Troilus in his herte caste.

But natheles, whan he hadde herd hym crye
"Awake!" he gan to syken wonder soore,   751
And seyde, "Frend, though that I stylle lye,
I am nat deef. Now pees, and crye namore,
For I have herd thi wordes and thi lore;
But suffre me my meschief to bywaille,   755
For thi proverbes may me naught availle.

"Nor other cure kanstow non for me;
Ek I nyl nat ben cured; I wol deye.
What knowe I of the queene Nyobe?   759
Lat be thyne olde ensaumples, I the preye."
"No," quod Pandarus, "therfore I seye,
Swych is delit of foles to bywepe
Hire wo, but seken bote they ne kepe.

---

690 **preve:** proof
691 **fayn:** gladly   **remeve:** remove
692 **conseyte:** opinion   **do the som wyght triste:** cause, make you trust someone
694 **The wise:** Solomon
696 **mone:** moan (i.e., grief)
697 **nexte wyse:** most direct manner
699 **Nyobe:** Niobe turned to stone while grieving.
702 **lissen:** alleviate
704 **seche:** seek
705 **eche:** increase
707 **listen naught:** do not desire
708 **wrecche:** a miserable person
713 **harde grace:** bad fortune
714 **for-why:** because
716 **bygyle:** defraud
718 **gon sithen longe while:** since a long time ago
719 **wyle:** guile
724 **sikynge:** sighing   **abreyde:** started up

727 **frenesie:** frenzy, madness
730 **Slombrestow:** do you sleep   **litargie:** lethargy
732 **plye:** ply, pluck
736 **stente:** ceased
739 **for whom that he so ferde:** on whose account he so behaved
740 **yerde:** rod
742 **treten:** treat, say
743 **namelich:** especially
744 **toucheth:** concerns
746 **But if:** unless
748 **in effect:** in fact, actually
763 **bote:** remedy

"Now knowe I that ther reson in the failleth.
But tel me, if I wiste what she were   765
For whom that the al this mysaunter ailleth,
Dorstestow that I tolde in hire ere
Thi wo, sith thow darst naught thiself for feere,
And hire bysoughte on the to han som routhe?"
"Why, nay," quod he, "by God and by my
          trouthe!"   770

"What, nat as bisyly," quod Pandarus,
"As though myn owene lyf lay on this nede?"
"No, certes, brother," quod this Troilus,
"And whi? For that thow scholdest nevere
          spede."
"Wostow that wel?" — "Ye, that is out of
          drede,"   775
Quod Troilus; "for al that evere ye konne,
She nyl to noon swich wrecche as I ben
          wonne."

Quod Pandarus, "Allas! What may this be,
That thow dispeired art thus causeles?
What! lyveth nat thi lady, bendiste?   780
How wostow so that thow art graceles?
Swich yvel is nat alwey booteles.
Why, put nat impossible thus thi cure,
Syn thyng to come is oft in aventure.

"I graunte wel that thow endurest wo   785
As sharp as doth he Ticius in helle,
Whos stomak foughles tiren evere moo
That hightyn volturis, as bokes telle;
But I may nat endure that thow dwelle
In so unskilful an oppynyoun   790
That of thi wo is no curacioun.

"But oones nyltow, for thy coward herte,
And for thyn ire and folisish wilfulnesse,
For wantrust, tellen of thy sorwes smerte,
Ne to thyn owen help don bysynesse   795
As muche as speke a resoun moore or lesse,

But list as he that lest of nothyng recche.
What womman koude loven swich a wrecche?

"What may she demen oother of thy deeth,
If thow thus deye, and she not why it is,   800
But that for feere is yolden up thy breth,
For Grekes han biseged us, iwys?
Lord, which a thonk than shaltow han of this!
Thus wol she seyn, and al the town attones,   804
'The wrecche is ded, the devel have his bones!'

"Thow mayst allone here wepe and crye and
          knele —
But love a womman that she woot it nought,
And she wol quyte it that thow shalt nat fele;
Unknowe, unkist, and lost that is unsought.
What, many a man hath love ful deere ybought
Twenty wynter that his lady wiste,   811
That nevere yet his lady mouth he kiste.

"What sholde he therfore fallen in dispayr,
Or be recreant for his owne tene,
Or slen hymself, al be his lady fair?   815
Nay, nay, but evere in oon be fressh and grene
To serve and love his deere hertes queene,
And thynk it is a guerdon hire to serve,
A thousand fold moore than he kan deserve."

Of that word took hede Troilus,   820
And thoughte anon what folie he was inne,
And how that soth hym seyde Pandarus,
That for to slen hymself myght he nat wynne,
But bothe don unmanhod and a synne,
And of his deth his lady naught to wite;   825
For of his wo, God woot, she knew ful lite.

And with that thought he gan ful sore syke,
And seyde, "Allas! What is me best to do?"
To whom Pandare answered, "If the like,
The beste is that thow telle me al thi wo;   830
And have my trouthe, but thow it fynde so
I be thi boote, er that it be ful longe,
To pieces do me drawe and sithen honge!"

764 **ther:** there (in this matter)
766 **mysaunter:** misfortune **ailleth:** afflicts
767 **Dorstestow:** would you dare
774 **spede:** succeed
780 **bendiste:** bless you
781 **graceles:** out of favor
782 **booteles:** without remedy
783 **put nat:** do not suppose
786 **Ticius:** Tityus, tortured in Hades (see Bo 3.m12.41–43)
787 **foughles:** fowls **tiren:** tear (with their beaks)
788 **hightyn:** are called
790 **unskilful:** unreasonable
791 **curacioun:** cure
792 **nyltow** = *ne wylt thou,* will you not
794 **wantrust:** distrust **sorwes smerte:** painful sorrows (or, sorrow's pain)

797 **list** = *liest,* you lie there **lest of nothyng recche:** desires to care for nothing
800 **not** = *ne wot,* knows not
801 **yolden:** yielded
803 **which a thonk:** what sort of thanks
808 **quyte it that:** requite it so that
813 **What:** why
814 **recreant:** cowardly, confessing himself defeated **tene:** sorrow, grief
816 **evere in oon:** always
818 **guerdon:** reward
825 **naught to wite:** (would be) not to blame
828 **me:** for me
832 **er that:** before

"Ye, so thow seyst," quod Troilus tho, "allas!
But, God woot, it is naught the rather so.   835
Ful hard were it to helpen in this cas,
For wel fynde I that Fortune is my fo;
Ne al the men that riden konne or go
May of hire cruel whiel the harm withstonde;
For as hire list she pleyeth with free and
     bonde."   840

Quod Pandarus, "Than blamestow Fortune
For thow art wroth; ye, now at erst I see.
Woost thow nat wel that Fortune is comune
To everi manere wight in som degree?
And yet thow hast this comfort, lo, parde,   845
That, as hire joies moten overgon,
So mote hire sorwes passen everechon.

"For if hire whiel stynte any thyng to torne,
Than cessed she Fortune anon to be.
Now, sith hire whiel by no way may sojourne,
What woostow if hire mutabilite   851
Right as thyselven list wol don by the,
Or that she be naught fer fro thyn helpynge?
Paraunter thow hast cause for to synge.

"And therfore wostow what I the biseche?   855
Lat be thy wo and tornyng to the grounde;
For whoso list have helyng of his leche,
To hym byhoveth first unwre his wownde.
To Cerberus yn helle ay be I bounde,
Were it for my suster, al thy sorwe,   860
By my wil she sholde al be thyn to-morwe.

"Look up, I seye, and telle me what she is
Anon, that I may gon about thy nede.
Knowe ich hire aught? For my love, telle me
     this.
Thanne wolde I hopen rather for to spede." 865
Tho gan the veyne of Troilus to blede,
For he was hit, and wax al reed for shame.
"A ha!" quod Pandare; "Here bygynneth game."

And with that word he gan hym for to shake,
And seyde, "Thef, thow shalt hyre name telle."
But tho gan sely Troilus for to quake   871
As though men sholde han led hym into helle,
And seyde, "Allas, of al my wo the welle,
Thanne is my swete fo called Criseyde!"
And wel neigh with the word for feere he
     deide.   875

And whan that Pandare herde hire name
     nevene,
Lord, he was glad, and seyde, "Frend so deere,
Now far aright, for Joves name in hevene.
Love hath byset the wel; be of good cheere!
For of good name and wisdom and manere   880
She hath ynough, and ek of gentilesse.
If she be fayr, thow woost thyself, I gesse,

"Ne nevere saugh a more bountevous
Of hire estat, n'a gladder, ne of speche
A frendlyer, n'a more gracious   885
For to do wel, ne lasse hadde nede to seche
What for to don; and al this bet to eche,
In honour, to as fer as she may strecche,
A kynges herte semeth by hyrs a wrecche.

"And forthi loke of good comfort thow be;   890
For certeinly, the ferste poynt is this
Of noble corage and wel ordeyné,
A man to have pees with hymself, ywis.
So oghtist thow, for noht but good it is
To love wel, and in a worthy place;   895
The oghte not to clepe it hap, but grace.

"And also thynk, and therwith glade the,
That sith thy lady vertuous is al,
So foloweth it that there is some pitee
Amonges alle thise other in general;   900
And forthi se that thow, in special,
Requere naught that is ayeyns hyre name;
For vertu streccheth naught hymself to shame.

835 **rather:** sooner
838 **go:** walk
840 **free and bonde:** freeman and serf (i.e., everyone)
842 **at erst:** for the first time
844 **everi manere wight:** every sort of creature
845 **parde:** indeed
846 **moten overgon:** must pass away
848 **stynte:** were to stop   **any thyng:** at all
849 **cessed she:** she would cease
850 **sojourne:** stop
852 **by the:** concerning you, in your case
857 **leche:** physician
858 **To hym byhoveth:** it behooves him, he must   **unwre:** reveal
859 **Cerberus:** the three-headed watchdog of Hades; see Bo 3.m12.31–33.
865 **rather:** sooner

871 **sely:** hapless, wretched
873 **welle:** source
876 **nevene:** named
878 **far aright:** do well
879 **byset the wel:** put you in a good situation
881 **gentilesse:** nobility
883 **bountevous:** full of goodness, generous
887 **eche:** increase
888 **strecche:** be concerned with
890 **forthi:** therefore
892 **ordeyné:** arranged, regulated
896 **hap:** fortune, chance
897 **glade the:** rejoice
900 **other:** other virtues
902 **Requere:** desire, request   **name:** reputation

"But wel is me that evere that I was born,
That thow biset art in so good a place;   905
For by my trouthe, in love I dorste have sworn
The sholde nevere han tid thus fayr a grace.
And wostow why? For thow were wont to chace
At Love in scorn, and for despit him calle
'Seynt Idiot, lord of thise foles alle.'   910

"How often hastow maad thi nyce japes,
And seyd that Loves servantz everichone
Of nycete ben verray Goddes apes;
And some wolde mucche hire mete allone,   914
Liggyng abedde, and make hem for to grone;
And som, thow seydest, hadde a blaunche fevere,
And preydest God he sholde nevere kevere.

"And som of hem took on hym, for the cold,
More than ynough, so seydestow ful ofte.
And som han feyned ofte tyme, and told   920
How that they waken, whan thei slepen softe;
And thus they wolde han brought hemself alofte,
And natheles were under at the laste.
Thus seydestow, and japedest ful faste.

"Yet seydestow that for the moore part   925
Thise loveres wolden speke in general,
And thoughten that it was a siker art,
For faylyng, for t'assaien overal.
Now may I jape of the, if that I shal;
But natheles, though that I sholde deye,   930
That thow art non of tho, I dorste saye.

"Now bet thi brest, and sey to God of Love,
'Thy grace, lord, for now I me repente,
If I mysspak, for now myself I love.'
Thus sey with al thyn herte in good entente."
Quod Troilus, "A, lord! I me consente,   936
And preye to the my japes thow foryive,
And I shal nevere more whyle I live."

"Thow seist wel," quod Pandare, "and now I hope
That thow the goddes wrathe hast al apesed;
And sithen thow hast wopen many a drope,   941
And seyd swych thyng wherwith thi god is plesed,
Now wolde nevere god but thow were esed!
And thynk wel, she of whom rist al thi wo
Hereafter may thy comfort be also.   945

"For thilke grownd that bereth the wedes wikke
Bereth ek thise holsom herbes, as ful ofte
Next the foule netle, rough and thikke,
The rose waxeth swoote and smothe and softe;
And next the valeye is the hil o-lofte;   950
And next the derke nyght the glade morwe;
And also joie is next the fyn of sorwe.

"Now loke that atempre be thi bridel,
And for the beste ay suffre to the tyde,
Or elles al oure labour is on ydel: 955
He hasteth wel that wisely kan abyde.
Be diligent and trewe, and ay wel hide;
Be lusty, fre; persevere in thy servyse,
And al is wel, if thow werke in this wyse.

"But he that departed is in everi place   960
Is nowher hol, as writen clerkes wyse.
What wonder is, though swich oon have no grace?
Ek wostow how it fareth of som servise,
As plaunte a tree or herbe, in sondry wyse,
And on the morwe pulle it up as blyve!   965
No wonder is, though it may nevere thryve.

"And sith that God of Love hath the bistowed
In place digne unto thi worthinesse,
Stond faste, for to good port hastow rowed;
And of thiself, for any hevynesse,   970
Hope alwey wel; for, but if drerinesse
Or over-haste oure bothe labour shende,
I hope of this to maken a good ende.

907 **tid:** befallen
908–909 **chace At:** harass, hound
913 **nycete:** foolishness   **Goddes apes:** natural-born fools (?); cf. 2.370.
914 **mucche:** munch, eat
916 **blaunche fevere:** white fever (lovesickness, which turns lovers pale)
917 **kevere:** recover
918 **took on hym:** put on clothing (?)
921 **waken:** keep awake
926 **in general:** i.e., about no particular lady
927 **siker art:** safe course
928 **For faylyng:** to avoid failure   **t'assaien overal:** to try everywhere
929 **jape of:** mock   **shal:** would
934 **mysspak:** said something wrong   **myself I:** I myself

941 **wopen:** wept
943 Now may God wish nothing except that you be comforted
944 **rist** = *riseth,* arises
946 **wikke:** wicked
952 **fyn:** end
953 **atempre:** moderate, restrained
954 **suffre to:** submit to, be patient in accordance with
955 **on ydel:** in vain
957 **hide:** conceal (your love)
958 **lusty:** cheerful   **fre:** generous
960 **departed:** divided
962 **though swich oon:** that such a one (so-and-so)
965 **blyve:** quickly
968 **digne:** worthy
972 **shende:** ruin

"And wostow why I am the lasse afered
Of this matere with my nece trete?   975
For this have I herd seyd of wyse lered,
Was nevere man or womman yet bigete
That was unapt to suffren loves hete,
Celestial, or elles love of kynde;
Forthy som grace I hope in hire to fynde.   980

"And for to speke of hire in specyal,
Hire beaute to bithynken and hire youthe,
It sit hire naught to ben celestial
As yet, though that hire liste bothe and kowthe;
But trewely, it sate hire wel right nowthe   985
A worthi knyght to loven and cherice,
And but she do, I holde it for a vice.

"Wherfore I am, and wol ben, ay redy
To peyne me to do yow this servyse;
For bothe yow to plese thus hope I   990
Herafterward; for ye ben bothe wyse,
And konne it counseil kepe in swych a wyse
That no man schal the wiser of it be;
And so we may ben gladed alle thre.

"And, by my trouthe, I have right now of the
A good conceyte in my wit, as I gesse,   996
And what it is, I wol now that thow se.
I thenke, sith that Love, of his goodnesse,
Hath the converted out of wikkednesse,
That thow shalt ben the beste post, I leve,
Of al his lay, and moost his foos to greve.   1001

"Ensample why, se now thise wise clerkes,
That erren aldermost ayeyn a lawe,
And ben converted from hire wikked werkes
Thorugh grace of God that list hem to hym
            drawe,   1005
Thanne arn thise folk that han moost God in
            awe,
And strengest feythed ben, I undirstonde,
And konne an errowr alderbest withstonde."

Whan Troilus hadde herd Pandare assented
To ben his help in lovyng of Cryseyde,   1010
Weex of his wo, as who seith, untormented,
But hotter weex his love, and thus he seyde,
With sobre chere, although his herte pleyde:
"Now blisful Venus helpe, er that I sterve,
Of the, Pandare, I mowe som thank deserve.

"But, deere frend, how shal my wo be lesse   1016
Til this be doon? And good, ek telle me this:
How wiltow seyn of me and my destresse,
Lest she be wroth — this drede I moost, ywys —
Or nyl nat here or trowen how it is?   1020
Al this drede I, and ek for the manere
Of the, hire em, she nyl no swich thyng here."

Quod Pandarus, "Thow hast a ful gret care
Lest that the cherl may falle out of the moone!
Whi, Lord! I hate of the thi nyce fare!   1025
Whi, entremete of that thow hast to doone!
For Goddes love, I bidde the a boone:
So lat m'alone, and it shal be thi beste."
"Whi, frend," quod he, "now do right as the
            leste.

"But herke, Pandare, o word, for I nolde   1030
That thow in me wendest so gret folie,
That to my lady I desiren sholde
That toucheth harm or any vilenye;
For dredeles me were levere dye
Than she of me aught elles understode   1035
But that that myghte sownen into goode."

Tho lough this Pandare, and anon answerde,
"And I thi borugh? Fy! No wight doth but so.
I roughte naught though that she stood and
            herde
How that thow seist! but farewel, I wol go.   1040
Adieu! Be glad! God spede us bothe two!
Yef me this labour and this bisynesse,
And of my spede be thyn al that swetnesse."

---

975 **trete**: to discuss
976 **lered**: learned men
978 **unapt**: not disposed
979 **Celestial**: heavenly (love of God)   **love of kynde**: natural (i.e., procreative) love
982 **bithynken**: consider
983 **sit** = *sitteth*, suits
985 **sate**: would befit   **nowthe**: now
987 **but she do**: unless she does so
989 **peyne me**: take pains
992 **it counseil kepe**: keep it secret
996 **conceyte**: opinion
1000 **post**: pillar (of the church, *his lay*)   **leve**: believe
1001 **greve**: injure
1002 **Ensample why**: for example
1003 **erren**: do wrong
1005 **that list**: whom it pleases
1007 **strengest feythed**: strongest in the faith
1008 **alderbest**: best of all

1011 **Weex**: he waxed, became
1014 **sterve**: die
1015 That I might deserve some thanks from you, Pandarus (for helping you as you now help me)
1017 **good**: good friend
1020 **trowen**: believe
1021 **for the manere**: for the sake of appearance (?); see n.
1022 **em**: uncle
1024 **cherl**: i.e., the man in the moon
1025 **nyce fare**: foolish (or, too scrupulous) behavior
1026 **entremete of**: meddle with, worry about
1028 **thi beste**: best for you
1034 **dredeles**: doubtless   **me were levere**: I would rather
1036 **sownen into**: tend toward, be conducive to
1038 **And I thi borugh**: With me as your guarantor (of honorable behavior)   **no wight doth but so**: no one does anything but this
1039 **I roughte naught**: I would not care
1041 **spede**: grant success to

Tho Troilus gan doun on knees to falle,
And Pandare in his armes hente faste,   1045
And seyde, "Now, fy on the Grekes alle!
Yet, parde, God shal helpe us atte laste.
And dredelees, if that my lyf may laste,
And God toforn, lo, som of hem shal smerte;
And yet m'athenketh that this avant m'asterte!

"Now, Pandare, I kan na more seye,   1051
But, thow wis, thow woost, thow maist, thow
        art al!
My lif, my deth, hol in thyn hond I leye.
Help now!" Quod he, "Yis, by my trowthe, I
        shal."
"God yelde the, frend, and this in special,"   1055
Quod Troilus, "that thow me recomande
To hire that to the deth me may comande."

This Pandarus, tho desirous to serve
His fulle frend, than seyde in this manere: 1059
"Farwell, and thenk I wol thi thank deserve!
Have here my trowthe, and that thow shalt wel
        here."
And went his wey, thenkyng on this matere,
And how he best myghte hire biseche of grace,
And fynde a tyme therto, and a place.

For everi wight that hath an hous to founde   1065
Ne renneth naught the werk for to bygynne

With rakel hond, but he wol bide a stounde,
And sende his hertes line out fro withinne
Aldirfirst his purpos for to wynne.
Al this Pandare in his herte thoughte,   1070
And caste his werk ful wisely or he wroughte.

But Troilus lay tho no lenger down,
But up anon upon his stede bay,
And in the feld he pleyde tho leoun;
Wo was that Grek that with hym mette a-day!
And in the town his manere tho forth ay   1076
Soo goodly was, and gat hym so in grace,
That ecch hym loved that loked on his face.

For he bicom the frendlieste wight,
The gentilest, and ek the mooste fre,   1080
The thriftiest, and oon the beste knyght
That in his tyme was or myghte be;
Dede were his japes and his cruelte,
His heighe port and his manere estraunge,
And ecch of tho gan for a vertu chaunge.   1085

Now lat us stynte of Troilus a stounde,
That fareth lik a man that hurt is soore,
And is somdeel of akyngge of his wownde
Ylissed wel, but heeled no deel moore,
And, as an esy pacyent, the loore   1090
Abit of hym that gooth aboute his cure;
And thus he dryeth forth his aventure.

Explicit liber primus.

1047 **parde:** by God, indeed   **atte:** at the
1049 **God toforn:** before God (I swear)
1050 **m'athenketh:** I regret   **avant m'asterte:** boast escapes from my lips
1052 **wis:** wise one
1054 **Yis:** yes indeed
1055 **yelde:** reward   **this in special:** particularly for this
1056 **recomande:** commend
1058 **tho:** then
1065 **founde:** build

1067 **rakel:** hasty   **stounde:** while
1068 **hertes line:** imaginary line (plan or builders' cord)
1069 **Aldirfirst:** first of all
1071 **caste:** plotted   **or:** before
1073 **bay:** reddish brown
1081 **thriftiest:** most admirable   **oon the beste knyght:** the very best knight
1084 **heighe port:** proud bearing   **estraunge:** distant, standoffish
1085 **tho:** those
1088 **somdeel:** somewhat   **of akyngge of:** in pain, aching from
1089 **Ylissed:** comforted
1090 **esy:** compliant   **loore:** advice
1091 **Abit** = *abideth*, abides
1092 **dryeth forth:** endures, bears up under
Explicit liber primus: Here ends the first book.

BOOK II

Incipit prohemium secundi libri.

Owt of thise blake wawes for to saylle,
O wynd, o wynd, the weder gynneth clere;
For in this see the boot hath swych travaylle,
Of my connyng, that unneth I it steere.
This see clepe I the tempestous matere   5
Of disespeir that Troilus was inne;
But now of hope the kalendes bygynne.

O lady myn, that called art Cleo,
Thow be my speed fro this forth, and my Muse,
To ryme wel this book til I have do;   10
Me nedeth here noon other art to use.
Forwhi to every lovere I me excuse,
That of no sentement I this endite,
But out of Latyn in my tonge it write.

Wherfore I nyl have neither thank ne blame   15
Of al this werk, but prey yow mekely,
Disblameth me if any word be lame,
For as myn auctour seyde, so sey I.
Ek though I speeke of love unfelyngly,
No wondre is, for it nothyng of newe is;   20
A blynd man kan nat juggen wel in hewis.

Ye knowe ek that in forme of speche is
        chaunge
Withinne a thousand yeer, and wordes tho
That hadden pris, now wonder nyce and
        straunge

Us thinketh hem, and yet thei spake hem so,
And spedde as wel in love as men now do;   26
Ek for to wynnen love in sondry ages,
In sondry londes, sondry ben usages.

And forthi if it happe in any wyse,
That here be any lovere in this place   30
That herkneth, as the storie wol devise,
How Troilus com to his lady grace,
And thenketh, "So nold I nat love purchace,"
Or wondreth on his speche or his doynge,
I noot; but it is me no wonderynge.   35

For every wight which that to Rome went
Halt nat o path, or alwey o manere;
Ek in som lond were al the game shent,
If that they ferde in love as men don here,
As thus, in opyn doyng or in chere,   40
In visityng in forme, or seyde hire sawes;
Forthi men seyn, "Ecch contree hath his lawes."

Ek scarsly ben ther in this place thre
That have in love seid lik, and don, in al;
For to thi purpos this may liken the,   45
And the right nought; yet al is seid or schal;
Ek som men grave in tree, some in ston wal,
As it bitit. But syn I have bigonne,
Myn auctour shal I folwen, if I konne.

Explicit prohemium secundi libri.

Incipit, *etc.:* Here begins the prologue of the second book.
2 gynneth clere: begins to clear
3–4 boot . . . Of my connyng: boat of my skill
5 clepe: call
7 kalendes: the first day of the month (i.e., the beginning)
8 Cleo: Clio, the Muse of history
9 speed: help, cause of success
12 Forwhi: therefore, wherefore
13 sentement: emotion, personal feeling
14 Latyn: Chaucer's Lollius supposedly wrote in Latin.
17 Disblameth: excuse
20 of newe: recent, novel
24 pris: value, currency

25 Us thinketh hem: they seem to us
31 devise: tell
36 went = *wendeth*, goes
37 Halt = *holdeth*, holds
38 shent: ruined
40 opyn doyng or in chere: public conduct or appearance
41 in forme: formally   seyde: said (i.e., saying)   sawes:
speeches
47 grave: carve   tree: wood
48 bitit = *bitydith*, happens
Explicit, *etc.:* Here ends the prologue of the second book.

Incipit liber secundus.

In May, that moder is of monthes glade,   50
That fresshe floures, blew and white and rede,
Ben quike agayn, that wynter dede made,
And ful of bawme is fletyng every mede,
Whan Phebus doth his bryghte bemes sprede
Right in the white Bole, it so bitidde,   55
As I shal synge, on Mayes day the thrydde,

That Pandarus, for al his wise speche,
Felt ek his part of loves shotes keene,
That, koude he nevere so wel of lovyng preche,
It made his hewe a-day ful ofte greene.   60
So shop it that hym fil that day a teene
In love, for which in wo to bedde he wente,
And made, er it was day, ful many a wente.

The swalowe Proigne, with a sorowful lay,
Whan morwen com, gan make hire wayment-
            ynge   65
Whi she forshapen was; and ever lay
Pandare abedde, half in a slomberynge,
Til she so neigh hym made hire cheterynge
How Tereus gan forth hire suster take,
That with the noyse of hire he gan awake,   70

And gan to calle, and dresse hym up to ryse,
Remembryng hym his erand was to doone
From Troilus, and ek his grete emprise;
And caste and knew in good plit was the moone
To doon viage, and took his way ful soone   75
Unto his neces palays ther biside.
Now Janus, god of entree, thow hym gyde!

Whan he was come unto his neces place,
"Wher is my lady?" to hire folk quod he;
And they hym tolde, and he forth in gan pace,
And fond two othere ladys sete and she,   81
Withinne a paved parlour, and they thre
Herden a mayden reden hem the geste
Of the siege of Thebes, while hem leste.

Quod Pandarus, "Madame, God yow see,   85
With youre book and all the compaignie!"
"Ey, uncle myn, welcome iwys," quod she;
And up she roos, and by the hond in hye
She took hym faste, and seyde, "This nyght
            thrie,
To goode mot it turne, of yow I mette."   90
And with that word she doun on bench hym
            sette.

"Ye, nece, yee shal faren wel the bet,
If God wol, al this yeer," quod Pandarus;
"But I am sory that I have yow let
To herken of youre book ye preysen thus.   95
For Goddes love, what seith it? telle it us!
Is it of love? O, som good ye me leere!"
"Uncle," quod she, "youre maistresse is nat
            here."

With that thei gonnen laughe, and tho she
            seyde,
"This romaunce is of Thebes that we rede;   100
And we han herd how that kyng Layus deyde
Thorugh Edippus his sone, and al that dede;
And here we stynten at thise lettres rede —
How the bisshop, as the book kan telle,   104
Amphiorax, fil thorugh the ground to helle."

Quod Pandarus, "Al this knowe I myselve,
And al th'assege of Thebes and the care;
For herof ben ther maked bookes twelve.
But lat be this, and telle me how ye fare.
Do wey youre barbe, and shew youre face
            bare;   110
Do wey youre book, rys up, and lat us daunce,
And lat us don to May som observaunce."

"I! God forbede!" quod she. "Be ye mad?
Is that a widewes lif, so God yow save?
By God, ye maken me ryght soore adrad!   115
Ye ben so wylde, it semeth as ye rave.

Incipit, *etc.*: Here begins the second book.
53 **bawme:** aromatic balsam   **fletyng:** overflowing
54 **Phebus:** the sun
55 **Bole:** the zodiacal sign Taurus
61 **shop it:** it was destined   **fil:** befell   **teene:** sorrow, grief
63 **wente:** turning
64 **Proigne:** Procne; *hire suster* (line 69) is Philomela, the
nightingale; for their story see LGW 2228–2393   **lay:** song
65 **waymentynge:** lamentation
66 **forshapen:** transformed
68 **cheterynge:** twittering
71 **dresse hym:** prepare himself
73 **emprise:** task
74 **caste:** forecast with an astrological calculation   **plit:** position
75 **viage:** journey, business
83 **geste:** story

85 **God yow see:** may God look after you (a common greeting)
88 **in hye:** quickly
89 **thrie:** thrice
90 **mette:** dreamed
94 **let:** hindered
97 **leere:** teach
101 **Layus:** king of Thebes, killed by his son Oedipus
(*Edippus*)
102 **dede:** deed
103 **lettres rede:** rubrics (here probably a book or chapter
heading)
105 **Amphiorax:** Amphiaraus, a soothsayer, dies in the action of
the *Seven Against Thebes.*
110 **barbe:** a veil-like headdress (wimple) that covers all but the
face
113 **I!** = *ey,* oh

It satte me wel bet ay in a cave
To bidde and rede on holy seyntes lyves;
Lat maydens gon to daunce, and yonge wyves."

"As evere thrive I," quod this Pandarus, 120
"Yet koude I telle a thyng to doon yow pleye."
"Now, uncle deere," quod she, "telle it us
For Goddes love; is than th'assege aweye?
I am of Grekes so fered that I deye." 124
"Nay, nay," quod he, "as evere mote I thryve,
It is a thing wel bet than swyche fyve."

"Ye, holy God," quod she, "what thyng is that?
What! Bet than swyche fyve? I! Nay, ywys!
For al this world ne kan I reden what 129
It sholde ben; some jape I trowe is this;
And but youreselven telle us what it is,
My wit is for t'arede it al to leene. 132
As help me God, I not nat what ye meene."

"And I youre borugh, ne nevere shal, for me,
This thyng be told to yow, as mote I thryve!"
"And whi so, uncle myn? Whi so?" quod she.
"By God," quod he, "that wol I telle as blyve!
For proudder womman is ther noon on lyve,
And ye it wiste, in al the town of Troye. 139
I jape nought, as evere have I joye!"

Tho gan she wondren moore than biforn
A thousand fold, and down hire eyghen caste;
For nevere, sith the tyme that she was born,
To knowe thyng desired she so faste;
And with a syk she seyde hym atte laste, 145
"Now, uncle myn, I nyl yow nought displese,
Nor axen more that may do yow disese."

So after this, with many wordes glade,
And frendly tales, and with merie chiere,
Of this and that they pleide, and gonnen wade
In many an unkouth, glad, and dep matere, 151
As frendes doon whan thei ben mette yfere,
Tyl she gan axen hym how Ector ferde,
That was the townes wal and Grekes yerde.

"Ful wel, I thonk it God," quod Pandarus, 155
"Save in his arm he hath a litel wownde;
And ek his fresshe brother Troilus,
The wise, worthi Ector the secounde,
In whom that alle vertu list habounde,
As alle trouthe and alle gentilesse, 160
Wisdom, honour, fredom, and worthinesse."

"In good feith, em," quod she, "that liketh me
Thei faren wel; God save hem bothe two!
For trewelich I holde it gret deynte
A kynges sone in armes wel to do, 165
And ben of goode condiciouns therto;
For gret power and moral vertu here
Is selde yseyn in o persone yfeere."

"In good faith, that is soth," quod Pandarus.
"But, by my trouthe, the kyng hath sones
    tweye — 170
That is to mene, Ector and Troilus —
That certeynly, though that I sholde deye,
Thei ben as voide of vices, dar I seye,
As any men that lyven under the sonne:
Hire myght is wyde yknowe, and what they
    konne. 175

"Of Ector nedeth it namore for to telle:
In al this world ther nys a bettre knyght
Than he, that is of worthynesse welle;
And he wel moore vertu hath than myght;
This knoweth many a wis and worthi wight. 180
The same pris of Troilus I seye;
God help me so, I knowe nat swiche tweye."

"By God," quod she, "of Ector that is sooth.
Of Troilus the same thyng trowe I;
For, dredeles, men tellen that he doth 185
In armes day by day so worthily,
And bereth hym here at hom so gently
To everi wight, that alle pris hath he
Of hem that me were levest preysed be."

"Ye sey right sooth, ywys," quod Pandarus; 190
"For yesterday, whoso had with hym ben,
He myghte han wondred upon Troilus;

117 **satte me wel bet**: would befit me much better
118 **bidde**: pray
123 **th'assege**: the siege
126 **swyche fyve**: five such (pieces of news)
129 **reden**: say
132 **t'arede**: to explain **leene**: feeble (her wit)
134 **And I youre borugh**: as I am your guarantor (i.e., I give
you my word)
137 **as blyve**: forthwith
139 **And**: if
147 **disese**: distress
150 **wade**: proceed
151 **unkouth**: unfamiliar
152 **mette yfere**: met one another
154 **yerde**: rod, scourge

160 **gentilesse**: nobility
161 **fredom**: nobility, generosity of character
162 **em**: uncle
164 **gret deynte**: a great honor
168 **yfeere**: together
173 **voide**: devoid
178 **welle**: source
181 **pris**: praise
185 **dredeles**: doubtless
189 Of those by whom I would most like to be praised

For nevere yet so thikke a swarm of been
Ne fleigh, as Grekes for hym gonne fleen,
And thorugh the feld, in everi wightes eere,
Ther nas no cry but 'Troilus is there!'   196

"Now here, now ther, he hunted hem so faste,
Ther nas but Grekes blood — and Troilus.
Now hem he hurte, and hem al down he caste;
Ay wher he wente, it was arayed thus: 200
He was hire deth, and sheld and lif for us,
That, as that day, ther dorste non withstonde
Whil that he held his blody swerd in honde.

"Therto he is the frendlieste man
Of gret estat that evere I saugh my lyve;   205
And wher hym lest, best felawshipe kan
To swich as hym thynketh able for to thryve."
And with that word tho Pandarus, as blyve,
He took his leve, and seyde, "I wol gon henne."
"Nay, blame have I, myn uncle," quod she
          thenne.   210

"What aileth yow to be thus wery soone,
And namelich of wommen? Wol ye so?
Nay, sitteth down; by God, I have to doone
With yow, to speke of wisdom er ye go."
And everi wight that was aboute hem tho,   215
That herde that, gan fer awey to stonde,
Whil they two hadde al that hem liste in honde.

Whan that hire tale al brought was to an ende,
Of hire estat and of hire governaunce,
Quod Pandarus, "Now tyme is that I wende.   220
But yet, I say, ariseth, lat us daunce,
And cast youre widewes habit to mischaunce!
What list yow thus youreself to disfigure,
Sith yow is tid thus fair an aventure?"   224

"A, wel bithought! For love of God," quod she,
"Shal I nat witen what ye meene of this?"
"No, this thing axeth leyser," tho quod he,

"And eke me wolde muche greve, iwys,
If I it tolde and ye it toke amys.
Yet were it bet my tonge for to stille   230
Than seye a soth that were ayeyns youre wille.

"For, nece, by the goddesse Mynerve,
And Jupiter, that maketh the thondre rynge,
And by the blisful Venus that I serve,   234
Ye ben the womman in this world lyvynge —
Withouten paramours, to my wyttynge —
That I best love, and lothest am to greve;
And that ye weten wel youreself, I leve."

"Iwis, myn uncle," quod she, "grant mercy!
Youre frendshipe have I founden evere yit.   240
I am to no man holden, trewely,
So muche as yow, and have so litel quyt;
And with the grace of God, emforth my wit,
As in my gylt I shal yow nevere offende;
And if I have er this, I wol amende.   245

"But for the love of God I yow biseche,
As ye ben he that I love moost and triste,
Lat be to me youre fremde manere speche,
And sey to me, youre nece, what yow liste."
And with that word hire uncle anoon hire
          kiste,   250
And seyde, "Gladly, leve nece dere!
Tak it for good, that I shal sey yow here."

With that she gan hire eighen down to caste,
And Pandarus to coghe gan a lite,
And seyde, "Nece, alwey — lo! — to the laste,
How so it be that som men hem delite   256
With subtyl art hire tales for to endite,
Yet for al that, in hire entencioun
Hire tale is al for som conclusioun.

"And sithe th'ende is every tales strengthe,
And this matere is so bihovely,   261
What sholde I peynte or drawen it on lengthe
To yow, that ben my frend so feythfully?"

193 **been:** bees
194 **fleigh:** flew   **gonne fleen:** fled
199 **hem . . . hem:** these . . . those
200 **arayed:** disposed
202 **as:** as concerns, for
205 **my lyve:** during my life
206 **best felawshipe kan:** knows how (to show) greatest
friendliness
207 **able for to thryve:** worthy of prospering, deserving
209 **henne:** hence
213 **have to doone:** have business
217 While they did whatever business they wished
218 **tale:** conversation
222 **to mischaunce:** to bad luck (i.e., to the devil)
224 **is tid:** has befallen
225 **wel bithought:** nicely put
226 **witen:** know
227 **axeth leyser:** requires time

230 **stille:** silence, hold still
232 **Mynerve:** Minerva, goddess of wisdom
233 **Jupiter:** Jove, who hurls thunderbolts
236 **Withouten paramours:** apart from the question of amorous
relations (Root) or excepting my own mistress(es)   **wyttynge:**
knowledge
237 **lothest:** most loath
243 **emforth my wit:** to the extent of my understanding,
intentionally
244 **As in my gylt:** by my fault
245 **amende:** make amends
248 **Lat be:** give up   **fremde:** distant, strange
255 **to the laste:** in the end, after all
261 **bihovely:** useful
262 **What:** why   **peynte:** adorn (the tale)

And with that word he gan right inwardly
Byholden hire and loken on hire face, 265
And seyde, "On swich a mirour goode grace!"

Than thought he thus: "If I my tale endite
Aught harde, or make a proces any whyle,
She shal no savour have therin but lite,
And trowe I wolde hire in my wil bigyle; 270
For tendre wittes wenen al be wyle
Theras thei kan nought pleynly understonde;
Forthi hire wit to serven wol I fonde" —

And loked on hire in a bysi wyse,
And she was war that he byheld hire so, 275
And seyde, "Lord! so faste ye m'avise!
Sey ye me nevere er now? What sey ye, no?"
"Yis, yys," quod he, "and bet wole er I go!
But be my trouthe, I thoughte now if ye
Be fortunat, for now men shal it se. 280

"For to every wight som goodly aventure
Som tyme is shape, if he it kan receyven;
But if he wol take of it no cure,
Whan that it commeth, but wilfully it weyven,
Lo, neyther cas ne fortune hym deceyven, 285
But ryght his verray slouthe and wrecched-
         nesse;
And swich a wight is for to blame, I gesse.

"Good aventure, O beele nece, have ye
Ful lightly founden, and ye konne it take;
And for the love of God, and ek of me, 290
Cache it anon, lest aventure slake!
What sholde I lenger proces of it make?
Yif me youre hond, for in this world is noon —
If that yow list — a wight so wel bygon.

"And sith I speke of good entencioun, 295
As I to yow have told wel herebyforn,
And love as wel youre honour and renoun
As creature in al this world yborn,

By alle the othes that I have yow sworn,
And ye be wrooth therfore, or wene I lye, 300
Ne shal I nevere sen yow eft with yë.

"Beth naught agast, ne quaketh naught!
         Wherto?
Ne chaungeth naught for fere so youre hewe!
For hardely the werst of this is do; 304
And though my tale as now be to yow newe,
Yet trist alwey ye shal me fynde trewe;
And were it thyng that me thoughte unsit-
         tynge,
To yow wolde I no swiche tales brynge."

"Now, good em, for Goddes love, I preye,"
Quod she, "come of, and telle me what it is!
For both I am agast what ye wol seye, 311
And ek me longeth it to wite, ywys;
For whethir it be wel or be amys,
Say on, lat me nat in this feere dwelle."
"So wol I doon; now herkeneth! I shal telle:

"Now, nece myn, the kynges deere sone, 316
The goode, wise, worthi, fresshe, and free,
Which alwey for to don wel is his wone,
The noble Troilus, so loveth the,
That, but ye helpe, it wol his bane be. 320
Lo, here is al! What sholde I moore seye?
Doth what yow lest to make hym lyve or deye.

"But if ye late hym deyen, I wol sterve —
Have here my trouthe, nece, I nyl nat lyen —
Al sholde I with this knyf my throte kerve."
With that the teris breste out of his yën, 326
And seide, "If that ye don us bothe dyen
Thus gilteles, than have ye fisshed fayre!
What mende ye, though that we booth appaire?

"Allas, he which that is my lord so deere, 330
That trewe man, that noble gentil knyght,
That naught desireth but youre frendly cheere,
I se hym dyen, ther he goth upryght,
And hasteth hym with al his fulle myght
For to ben slayn, if his fortune assente. 335
Allas, that God yow swich a beaute sente!

264 **inwardly:** deeply
267 **my tale:** what I have to say
268 **proces:** elaborate story
269 **savour:** delight
271 **al be wyle:** everything is guile, trickery
273 Therefore I shall try (*fonde*) to adapt my speech to her level
of intelligence
274 **in a bysi wyse:** in an intense manner, intently
276 **m'avise:** stare at me
277 **Sey . . . sey:** saw . . . say
279 **thoughte now if:** was just now thinking whether
284 **weyven:** waive, forgo
288 **beele:** lovely
289 **and:** if
291 **aventure slake:** the opportunity drift away
294 **so wel bygon:** in such a happy situation, so happy
295 **of:** out of, with

304 **hardely:** certainly
307 **unsittynge:** unsuitable, inappropriate
309 **em:** uncle
310 **come of:** come on, hurry up
318 **wone:** custom, wont
320 **bane:** destruction, killer
325 **Al sholde I:** even if I had to
328 **fisshed fayre:** made a fine catch
329 **What mende ye:** how do you improve (what do you gain
by it?) **appaire:** should perish

"If it be so that ye so cruel be
That of his deth yow liste nought to recche,
That is so trewe and worthi, as ye se,
Namoore than of a japer or a wrecche —   340
If ye be swich, youre beaute may nat strecche
To make amendes of so cruel a dede;
Avysement is good byfore the nede.

"Wo worth the faire gemme vertulees!
Wo worth that herbe also that dooth no boote!
Wo worth that beaute that is routheles!   346
Wo worth that wight that tret ech undir foote!
And ye, that ben of beaute crop and roote,
If therwithal in yow ther be no routhe,
Than is it harm ye lyven, by my trouthe!   350

"And also think wel that this is no gaude;
For me were levere thow and I and he
Were hanged, than I sholde ben his baude,
As heigh as men myghte on us alle ysee!
I am thyn em; the shame were to me,   355
As wel as the, if that I sholde assente
Thorugh myn abet that he thyn honour shente.

"Now understonde, for I yow nought requere
To bynde yow to hym thorugh no byheste,
But only that ye make hym bettre chiere   360
Than ye han doon er this, and moore feste,
So that his lif be saved atte leeste;
This al and som, and pleynly, oure entente.
God help me so, I nevere other mente!

"Lo, this requeste is naught but skylle, ywys,
Ne doute of resoun, pardee, is ther noon.   366
I sette the worste, that ye dreden this:
Men wolde wondren sen hym come or goon.
Ther-ayeins answere I thus anoon,
That every wight, but he be fool of kynde,   370
Wol deme it love of frendshipe in his mynde.

"What, who wol demen, though he se a man
To temple go, that he th'ymages eteth?
Thenk ek how wel and wisely that he kan   374
Governe hymself, that he no thyng foryeteth,
That where he cometh he pris and thank hym
        geteth;
And ek therto, he shal come here so selde,
What fors were it though al the town byhelde?

"Swych love of frendes regneth al this town;
And wre yow in that mantel evere moo,   380
And God so wys be my savacioun,
As I have seyd, youre beste is to do soo.
But alwey, goode nece, to stynte his woo,
So lat youre daunger sucred ben a lite,
That of his deth ye be naught for to wite."   385

Criseyde, which that herde hym in this wise,
Thoughte, "I shal felen what he meneth, ywis."
"Now em," quod she, "what wolde ye devise?
What is youre reed I sholde don of this?"
"That is wel seyd," quod he. "Certein, best is
That ye hym love ayeyn for his lovynge,   391
As love for love is skilful guerdonynge.

"Thenk ek how elde wasteth every houre
In ech of yow a partie of beautee;
And therfore er that age the devoure,   395
Go love; for old, ther wol no wight of the.
Lat this proverbe a loore unto yow be:
To late ywar, quod Beaute, whan it paste;
And Elde daunteth Daunger at the laste.

"The kynges fool is wont to crien loude,   400
Whan that hym thinketh a womman berth hire
        hye,
'So longe mote ye lyve, and alle proude,
Til crowes feet be growe under youre yë,
And sende yow than a myrour in to prye,
In which that ye may se youre face a morwe!'
I bidde wisshe yow namore sorwe."   406

338 **nought to recche**: to care nothing
341–42 **strecche To**: extend to, prove capable of
343 **Avysement**: deliberation
344 **Wo worth**: woe be to   **vertulees**: lacking the power that gems were believed to have
346 **routheles**: without compassion
347 **tret** = *tredeth*, treads
348 **crop and roote**: all, top to root (i.e., totality, essence)
351 **gaude**: trick
352 **me were levere**: I would rather that
353 **baude**: pimp
357 **abet**: help, abetting   **shente**: injured
359 **byheste**: promise
361 **feste**: welcoming attention
363 **This** = this is   **pleynly**: fully
365 **skylle**: reasonable
366 **doute of resoun**: reasonable fear
367 **I sette the worste**: I set, pose as a hypothesis, the worst possibility
370 **fool of kynde**: congenital fool
371 **love of frendshipe**: affection between friends (rather than lovers)

377 **selde**: seldom
378 **byhelde**: should see (it)
379 **regneth**: governs, flourishes in
380 **wre**: conceal   **mantel**: cloak (of amity)
382 **youre beste**: your best course
384 **daunger**: disdain, standoffishness   **sucred**: sugared, sweetened
385 **wite**: blame
388 **devise**: advise
392 **skilful**: reasonable   **guerdonynge**: reward, repayment
393 **elde**: aging, passing years
394 **partie**: part
398 **ywar**: aware
399 **daunteth**: subdues
401 **berth hire hye**: acts proud
404 **prye**: peer
406 **bidde**: intend, would

With this he stynte, and caste adown the heed,
And she began to breste a-wepe anoon,
And seyde, "Allas, for wo! Why nere I deed?
For of this world the feyth is al agoon.   410
Allas, what sholden straunge to me doon,
When he that for my beste frend I wende
Ret me to love, and sholde it me defende?

"Allas! I wolde han trusted, douteles,
That if that I, thorugh my dysaventure,   415
Hadde loved outher hym or Achilles,
Ector, or any mannes creature,
Ye nolde han had no mercy ne mesure
On me, but alwey had me in repreve.
This false world — allas! — who may it leve?   420

"What, is this al the joye and al the feste?
Is this youre reed? Is this my blisful cas?
Is this the verray mede of youre byheeste?
Is al this paynted proces seyd — allas! —
Right for this fyn? O lady myn, Pallas!   425
Thow in this dredful cas for me purveye,
For so astoned am I that I deye."

Wyth that she gan ful sorwfully to syke.
"A, may it be no bet?" quod Pandarus;   429
"By God, I shal namore come here this wyke,
And God toforn, that am mystrusted thus!
I se wel that ye sette lite of us,
Or of oure deth! Allas, I woful wrecche!
Might he yet lyve, of me is nought to recche.

"O cruel god, O dispitouse Marte,   435
O Furies thre of helle, on yow I crye!
So lat me nevere out of this hous departe,
If I mente harm or vilenye!
But sith I se my lord mot nedes dye,
And I with hym, here I me shryve, and seye
That wikkedly ye don us bothe deye.   441

"But sith it liketh yow that I be ded,
By Neptunus, that god is of the see,
Fro this forth shal I nevere eten bred

Til I myn owen herte blood may see;   445
For certeyn I wol deye as soone as he."
And up he sterte, and on his wey he raughte,
Til she agayn hym by the lappe kaughte.

Criseyde, which that wel neigh starf for feere,
So as she was the ferfulleste wight   450
That myghte be, and herde ek with hire ere
And saugh the sorwful ernest of the knyght,
And in his preier ek saugh noon unryght,
And for the harm that myghte ek fallen moore,
She gan to rewe and dredde hire wonder
          soore,   455

And thoughte thus: "Unhappes fallen thikke
Alday for love, and in swych manere cas
As men ben cruel in hemself and wikke;
And if this man sle here hymself — allas! —
In my presence, it wol be no solas.   460
What men wolde of hit deme I kan nat seye;
It nedeth me ful sleighly for to pleie."

And with a sorowful sik she sayde thrie,
"A, Lord! What me is tid a sory chaunce!
For myn estat lith in a jupartie,   465
And ek myn emes lif is in balaunce;
But natheles, with Goddes governaunce,
I shal so doon, myn honour shal I kepe,
And ek his lif" — and stynte for to wepe.

"Of harmes two, the lesse is for to chese;   470
Yet have I levere maken hym good chere
In honour, than myn emes lyf to lese.
Ye seyn, ye nothyng elles me requere?"
"No, wis," quod he, "myn owen nece dere."
"Now wel," quod she, "and I wol doon my
          peyne;   475
I shal myn herte ayeins my lust constreyne.

"But that I nyl nat holden hym in honde,
Ne love a man ne kan I naught ne may

408 a-wepe: into weeping
411 straunge: strangers
413 Ret = redeth, advises   defende: forbid
419 repreve: reproach
420 leve: believe
422 reed: advice
423 mede: payoff, fulfillment   byheeste: promise
424 paynted proces: ornate and specious discourse
425 Pallas: Pallas Athene
426 dredful: frightening   purveye: provide
430 wyke: week
431 God toforn: before God (I swear)
432 sette lite of: think little of
435 dispitouse: malicious   Marte: Mars
440 me shryve: make my confession

447 raughte: started out (literally, reached)
448 lappe: fold, hem of (his) clothing
452 ernest: seriousness
456 Unhappes: misfortunes
457 Alday: continually
460 solas: comfort
462 sleighly: adroitly, shrewdly
463 thrie: thrice
464 What me is tid a sory chaunce: what an unhappy fate has
befallen me
465 in a jupartie: in jeopardy
466 emes: uncle's
470 harmes: evils
471 have I levere: I would rather
472 lese: lose
474 wis = ywis, certainly
475 doon my peyne: undergo the hardship
477 holden hym in honde: cajole him with false hopes

Ayeins my wyl, but elles wol I fonde,
Myn honour sauf, plese hym fro day to day.
Therto nolde I nat ones han seyd nay,   481
But that I drede, as in my fantasye;
But cesse cause, ay cesseth maladie.

"And here I make a protestacioun
That in this proces if ye depper go,   485
That certeynly, for no salvacioun
Of yow, though that ye sterven bothe two,
Though al the world on o day be my fo,
Ne shal I nevere of hym han other routhe."
"I graunte wel," quod Pandare, "by my trowthe.

"But may I truste wel to yow," quod he,   491
"That of this thyng that ye han hight me here,
Ye wole it holden trewely unto me?"
"Ye, doutelees," quod she, "myn uncle deere."
"Ne that I shal han cause in this matere,"   495
Quod he, "to pleyne, or ofter yow to preche?"
"Why, no, parde; what nedeth moore speche?"

Tho fellen they in other tales glade,
Tyl at the laste, "O good em," quod she tho,
"For his love, that us bothe made,   500
Tel me how first ye wisten of his wo.
Woot noon of it but ye?" He seyde, "No."
"Kan he wel speke of love?" quod she; "I preye
Tel me, for I the bet me shal purveye."

Tho Pandarus a litel gan to smyle,   505
And seyde, "By my trouthe, I shal yow telle.
This other day, naught gon ful longe while,
In-with the paleis gardyn, by a welle,
Gan he and I wel half a day to dwelle,
Right for to speken of an ordinaunce,   510
How we the Grekes myghten disavaunce.

"Soon after that bigonne we to lepe,
And casten with oure dartes to and fro,
Tyl at the laste he seyde he wolde slepe,
And on the gres adoun he leyde hym tho;   515
And I afer gan romen to and fro,

Til that I herde, as that I welk alone,
How he bigan ful wofully to grone.

"Tho gan I stalke hym softely byhynde,
And sikirly, the soothe for to seyne,   520
As I kan clepe ayein now to my mynde,
Right thus to Love he gan hym for to pleyne:
He seyde, 'Lord, have routhe upon my peyne,
Al have I ben rebell in myn entente;
Now, *mea culpa,* lord, I me repente!   525

" 'O god, that at thi disposicioun
Ledest the fyn by juste purveiaunce
Of every wight, my lowe confessioun
Accepte in gree, and sende me swich penaunce
As liketh the, but from disesperaunce,   530
That may my goost departe awey fro the,
Thow be my sheld, for thi benignite.

" 'For certes, lord, so soore hath she me
          wounded,
That stood in blak, with lokyng of hire eyen,
That to myn hertes botme it is ysounded,   535
Thorugh which I woot that I moot nedes deyen.
This is the werste, I dar me nat bywreyen;
And wel the hotter ben the gledes rede,
That men hem wrien with asshen pale and
          dede.'

"Wyth that he smot his hed adown anon,   540
And gan to motre, I noot what, trewely.
And I with that gan stille awey to goon,
And leet therof as nothing wist had I,
And com ayein anon, and stood hym by,
And seyde, 'Awake, ye slepen al to longe!   545
It semeth nat that love doth yow longe,

" 'That slepen so that no man may yow wake.
Who sey evere or this so dul a man?'
'Ye, frend,' quod he, 'do ye youre hedes ake
For love, and lat me lyven as I kan.'   550
But though that he for wo was pale and wan,

479 **elles:** otherwise, in all else **fonde:** try
480 **Myn honour sauf:** except for what could impair my
honour **plese:** to please
483 **cesse cause:** if the cause should cease
485 **proces:** business **depper:** further
488 **on o:** in one
491 **to yow:** on your part
492 **hight:** promised
504 Tell me, so that I can better prepare myself
507 **gon:** past, ago
510 **ordinaunce:** plan
511 **disavaunce:** repel
513 **dartes:** spears

517 **welk:** walked
521 **clepe ayein:** recall
524 **Al:** although **entente:** mind
525 *mea culpa:* (I confess that) the blame is mine
527 **Ledest the fyn:** direct the end **purveiaunce:** providence
529 **in gree:** graciously
530 **disesperaunce:** despair
535 **ysounded:** plummeted
537 **bywreyen:** reveal
538 **gledes:** glowing coals
539 **wrien:** cover
541 **motre:** mutter
543 And acted as though I knew nothing about it
546 **longe:** to pine with longing (or, pertain to)

Yet made he tho as fresshe a countenaunce
As though he sholde have led the newe daunce.

"This passed forth til now, this other day,
It fel that I com romyng al allone   555
Into his chaumbre, and fond how that he lay
Upon his bed; but man so soore grone
Ne herde I nevere, and what that was his mone
Ne wist I nought; for, as I was comynge,
Al sodeynly he lefte his complaynynge.   560

"Of which I took somwat suspecioun,
And ner I com, and fond he wepte soore;
And God so wys be my savacioun,
As nevere of thyng hadde I no routhe moore;
For neither with engyn, ne with no loore,   565
Unnethes myghte I fro the deth hym kepe,
That yet fele I myn herte for hym wepe.

"And God woot, nevere sith that I was born
Was I so besy no man for to preche,
Ne nevere was to wight so depe isworn,   570
Or he me told who myghte ben his leche.
But now to yow rehercen al his speche,
Or alle his woful wordes for to sowne,
Ne bid me naught, but ye wol se me swowne.

"But for to save his lif, and elles nought,   575
And to noon harm of yow, thus am I dryven;
And for the love of God, that us hath wrought,
Swich cheer hym dooth that he and I may
        lyven!
Now have I plat to yow myn herte shryven,
And sith ye woot that myn entent is cleene,
Take heede therof, for I non yvel meene.   581

"And right good thrift, I prey to God, have ye,
That han swich oon ykaught withouten net!
And be ye wis as ye be fair to see,
Wel in the ryng than is the ruby set.   585
Ther were nevere two so wel ymet,
Whan ye ben his al hool as he is youre;
Ther myghty God graunte us see that houre!"

"Nay, therof spak I nought, ha, ha!" quod she;
"As helpe me God, ye shenden every deel!"   590

"O, mercy, dere nece," anon quod he,
"What so I spak, I mente naught but wel,
By Mars, the god that helmed is of steel!
Now beth naught wroth, my blood, my nece
        dere."
"Now wel," quod she, "foryeven be it
        here!"   595

With this he took his leve, and hom he wente;
And, Lord, he was glad and wel bygon!
Criseyde aros, no lenger she ne stente,
But streght into hire closet wente anon,
And set hire doun as stylle as any ston,   600
And every word gan up and down to wynde
That he had seyd, as it com hire to mynde,

And wex somdel astoned in hire thought
Right for the newe cas; but whan that she
Was ful avysed, tho fond she right nought   605
Of peril why she ought afered be.
For man may love, of possibilite,
A womman so, his herte may tobreste,
And she naught love ayein, but if hire leste.

But as she sat allone and thoughte thus,   610
Ascry aros at scarmuch al withoute,
And men criden in the strete, "Se, Troilus
Hath right now put to flighte the Grekes route!"
With that gan al hire meyne for to shoute,
"A, go we se! Cast up the yates wyde!   615
For thorwgh this strete he moot to paleys ride;

"For other wey is to the yate noon
Of Dardanus, there opyn is the cheyne."
With that com he and al his folk anoon
An esy pas rydyng, in routes tweyne,   620
Right as his happy day was, sooth to seyne,
For which, men seyn, may nought destourbed
        be
That shal bityden of necessitee.

This Troilus sat on his baye steede
Al armed, save his hed, ful richely;   625
And wownded was his hors, and gan to blede,
On which he rood a pas ful softely.

565 **engyn:** trickery
566 **Unnethes:** hardly
569 **no man:** any man
571 **Or:** before   **leche:** physician
574 **but ye wol se:** unless you wish to see
579 **plat:** flatly   **shryven:** confessed
582 **good thrift:** good luck, success
590 **shenden every deel:** spoil everything

593 **helmed is:** wears a helmet
601 **wynde:** turn
602 **com hire to mynde:** came to her mind
608 **tobreste:** break in pieces
611 **Ascry:** outcry   **scarmuch:** skirmish
614 **meyne:** household attendants
615 **yates:** gates
620 **An esy pas:** at a slow gait
621 **happy:** lucky
627 **a pas:** at a walk

But swich a knyghtly sighte trewely
As was on hym, was nought, withouten faille,
To loke on Mars, that god is of bataille.   630

So lik a man of armes and a knyght
He was to seen, fulfilled of heigh prowesse,
For bothe he hadde a body and a myght
To don that thing, as wel as hardynesse;
And ek to seen hym in his gere hym dresse,
So fressh, so yong, so weldy semed he,   636
It was an heven upon hym for to see.

His helm tohewen was in twenty places,
That by a tyssew heng his bak byhynde;
His sheeld todasshed was with swerdes and
          maces,   640
In which men myghte many an arwe fynde
That thirled hadde horn and nerf and rynde;
And ay the peple cryde, "Here cometh oure
          joye,
And, next his brother, holder up of Troye!"

For which he wex a litel reed for shame   645
When he the peple upon hym herde cryen,
That to byholde it was a noble game
How sobrelich he caste down his yën.
Criseÿda gan al his chere aspien,
And leet it so softe in hire herte synke,   650
That to hireself she seyde, "Who yaf me
          drynke?"

For of hire owen thought she wex al reed,
Remembryng hire right thus, "Lo, this is he
Which that myn uncle swerith he moot be
          deed,
But I on hym have mercy and pitee."   655
And with that thought, for pure ashamed, she
Gan in hire hed to pulle, and that as faste,
Whil he and alle the peple forby paste,

And gan to caste and rollen up and down
Withinne hire thought his excellent prowesse,
And his estat, and also his renown,   661
His wit, his shap, and ek his gentilesse;
But moost hire favour was, for his distresse

Was al for hire, and thoughte it was a routhe
To sleen swich oon, if that he mente trouthe.

Now myghte som envious jangle thus: 666
"This was a sodeyn love; how myght it be
That she so lightly loved Troilus
Right for the firste syghte, ye, parde?"
Now whoso seith so, mote he nevere ythe!   670
For every thyng a gynnyng hath it nede
Er al be wrought, withowten any drede.

For I sey nought that she so sodeynly
Yaf hym hire love, but that she gan enclyne
To like hym first, and I have told yow whi;   675
And after that, his manhod and his pyne
Made love withinne hire for to myne,
For which by proces and by good servyse
He gat hire love, and in no sodeyn wyse.

And also blisful Venus, wel arrayed,   680
Sat in hire seventhe hous of hevene tho,
Disposed wel, and with aspectes payed,
To helpe sely Troilus of his woo.
And soth to seyne, she nas not al a foo
To Troilus in his nativitee;   685
God woot that wel the sonner spedde he.

Now lat us stynte of Troilus a throwe,
That rideth forth, and lat us torne faste
Unto Criseyde, that heng hire hed ful lowe
Ther as she sat allone, and gan to caste   690
Where on she wolde apoynte hire atte laste,
If it so were hire em ne wolde cesse
For Troilus upon hire for to presse.

And, Lord! So she gan in hire thought argue
In this matere of which I have yow told,   695
And what to doone best were, and what eschue,
That plited she ful ofte in many fold.

632 **to seen**: to be seen, to look upon
635 **gere**: armor
636 **weldy**: vigorous
638 **tohewen**: chopped in pieces
639 **tyssew**: band, tissue
640 **todasshed**: broken in pieces
642 **thirled**: pierced **horn and nerf and rynde**: horn and
sinew and skin (materials of which shields were made)
656 **for pure ashamed**: for very shame

664 **routhe**: pity
666 **jangle**: chatter idly
668 **lightly**: quickly, easily
670 **ythe**: prosper
671 For everything must have a beginning
676 **pyne**: torment
677 **myne**: undermine (as in a siege)
681 **hous**: division of the celestial sphere; cf. Astr 2.36, 37.
682 **Disposed wel**: favorably inclined **with aspectes payed**:
pleased, made propitious, by the positions of the signs and
heavenly bodies
683 **sely**: wretched, poor
684 **foo**: foe (The planet Venus was not in an entirely
unfavorable position at the time of Troilus's *nativitee*, i.e., birth.)
686 **sonner**: sooner
687 **throwe**: while
691 **apoynte hire**: decide
692 **cesse**: cease
697 **plited**: folded

Now was hire herte warm, now was it cold;
And what she thoughte somwhat shal I write,
As to myn auctour listeth for t'endite.   700

She thoughte wel that Troilus persone
She knew by syghte, and ek his gentilesse,
And thus she seyde, "Al were it nat to doone
To graunte hym love, yet for his worthynesse
It were honour with pley and with gladnesse
In honestee with swich a lord to deele,   706
For myn estat, and also for his heele.

"Ek wel woot I my kynges sone is he,
And sith he hath to se me swich delit,
If I wolde outreliche his sighte flee,   710
Peraunter he myghte have me in dispit,
Thorugh whicch I myghte stonde in worse plit.
Now were I wis, me hate to purchace,
Withouten need, ther I may stonde in grace?

"In every thyng, I woot, ther lith mesure;   715
For though a man forbede dronkenesse,
He naught forbet that every creature
Be drynkeles for alwey, as I gesse.
Ek sith I woot for me is his destresse,
I ne aughte nat for that thing hym despise,   720
Sith it is so he meneth in good wyse.

"And eke I knowe of longe tyme agon
His thewes goode, and that he is nat nyce;
N'avantour, seith men, certein, he is noon;
To wis is he to doon so gret a vice;   725
Ne als I nyl hym nevere so cherice
That he may make avaunt, by juste cause,
He shal me nevere bynde in swich a clause.

"Now sette a caas: the hardest is, ywys,
Men myghten demen that he loveth me.   730
What dishonour were it unto me, this?
May ich hym lette of that? Why, nay, parde!
I knowe also, and alday heere and se,

Men loven wommen al biside hire leve,   734
And whan hem leste namore, lat hem byleve!

"I thenke ek how he able is for to have
Of al this noble town the thriftieste
To ben his love, so she hire honour save.
For out and out he is the worthieste,
Save only Ector, which that is the beste;   740
And yet his lif al lith now in my cure.
But swich is love, and ek myn aventure.

"Ne me to love, a wonder is it nought;
For wel woot I myself, so God me spede —
Al wolde I that noon wiste of this thought —   745
I am oon the faireste, out of drede,
And goodlieste, who that taketh hede,
And so men seyn, in al the town of Troie.
What wonder is though he of me have joye?

"I am myn owene womman, wel at ese —   750
I thank it God — as after myn estat,
Right yong, and stonde unteyd in lusty leese,
Withouten jalousie or swich debat:
Shal noon housbonde seyn to me 'Chek mat!'
For either they ben ful of jalousie,   755
Or maisterfull, or loven novelrie.

"What shal I doon? To what fyn lyve I thus?
Shal I nat love, in cas if that me leste?
What, pardieux! I am naught religious.
And though that I myn herte sette at reste   760
Upon this knyght, that is the worthieste,
And kepe alwey myn honour and my name,
By alle right, it may do me no shame."

But right as when the sonne shyneth brighte
In March, that chaungeth ofte tyme his
          face,   765
And that a cloude is put with wynd to flighte,
Which oversprat the sonne as for a space,
A cloudy thought gan thorugh hire soule pace,
That overspradde hire brighte thoughtes alle,
So that for feere almost she gan to falle.   770

---

706 **In honestee:** honorably
707 **heele:** health, well-being
710 **outreliche:** utterly
712 **plit:** condition
713 **me hate to purchace:** to bring enmity on myself
715 **mesure:** moderation
717 **forbet** = *forbedeth* (i.e., enjoins, requires; see n.)
720 **aughte:** ought
723 **thewes:** morals, personal qualities   **nyce:** foolish
724 **n'avantour:** nor boaster   **seith men:** it is said
726 **als:** as, because (or, also); see n.
728 **clause:** article, stipulation (as in a legal contract)
729 **sette a caas:** assume this situation, hypothesize
732 **lette:** hinder, prevent
733 **alday:** continually

734 **al biside hire leve:** entirely without their leave
735 **byleve:** leave off
737 **thriftieste:** most attractive
741 **cure:** care, responsibility
746 **oon the:** the very
751 **as after myn estat:** as befits my station in life (or, with regard to my wealth)
752 **unteyd in lusty leese:** untethered, free, in a pleasant pasture (i.e., in a happy situation); see n.
756 **maisterfull:** domineering   **novelrie:** novelty (i.e., new loves)
759 **pardieux:** by God   **religious:** a nun
767 **oversprat** = *overspredeth*, covers

That thought was this: "Allas! Syn I am free,
Sholde I now love, and put in jupartie
My sikernesse, and thrallen libertee?
Allas, how dorst I thenken that folie?
May I naught wel in other folk aspie   775
Hire dredfull joye, hire constreinte, and hire
    peyne?
Ther loveth noon, that she nath why to pleyne.

"For love is yet the mooste stormy lyf,
Right of hymself, that evere was bigonne;
For evere som mystrust or nice strif   780
Ther is in love, som cloude is over that sonne.
Therto we wrecched wommen nothing konne,
Whan us is wo, but wepe and sitte and thinke;
Oure wrecche is this, oure owen wo to drynke.

"Also thise wikked tonges ben so prest   785
To speke us harm; ek men ben so untrewe,
That right anon as cessed is hire lest,
So cesseth love, and forth to love a newe.
But harm ydoon is doon, whoso it rewe:
For though thise men for love hem first torende,
Ful sharp bygynnyng breketh ofte at ende.   791

"How ofte tyme hath it yknowen be
The tresoun that to wommen hath ben do!
To what fyn is swich love I kan nat see,
Or wher bycometh it, whan that it is ago.   795
Ther is no wight that woot, I trowe so,
Where it bycometh. Lo, no wight on it sporneth;
That erst was nothing, into nought it torneth.

"How bisy, if I love, ek most I be   799
To plesen hem that jangle of love, and dremen,
And coye hem, that they seye noon harm of me!
For though ther be no cause, yet hem semen
Al be for harm that folk hire frendes quemen;
And who may stoppen every wikked tonge,   804
Or sown of belles whil that thei ben ronge?"

And after that, hire thought gan for to clere,
And seide, "He which that nothing under-
    taketh,
Nothyng n'acheveth, be hym looth or deere."
And with an other thought hire herte quaketh;
Than slepeth hope, and after drede awak-
    eth;   810
Now hoot, now cold; but thus, bitwixen tweye,
She rist hire up, and wente hire for to pleye.

Adown the steyre anonright tho she wente
Into the gardyn with hire neces thre,
And up and down ther made many a wente —
Flexippe, she, Tharbe, and Antigone —   816
To pleyen that it joye was to see;
And other of hire wommen, a gret route,
Hire folowede in the gardyn al aboute.   819

This yerd was large, and rayled alle th'aleyes,
And shadewed wel with blosmy bowes grene,
And benched newe, and sonded alle the weyes,
In which she walketh arm in arm bitwene,
Til at the laste Antigone the shene
Gan on a Troian song to singen cleere,   825
That it an heven was hire vois to here.

She seyde, "O Love, to whom I have and shal
Ben humble subgit, trewe in myn entente,
As I best kan, to yow, lord, yeve ich al
For everemo myn hertes lust to rente;   830
For nevere yet thi grace no wight sente
So blisful cause as me, my lif to lede
In alle joie and seurte out of drede.

"Ye, blisful god, han me so wel byset
In love, iwys, that al that bereth lif   835
Ymagynen ne kouthe how to be bet;
For, lord, withouten jalousie or strif,
I love oon which is moost ententif
To serven wel, unweri or unfeyned,   839
That evere was, and leest with harm desteyned.

"As he that is the welle of worthynesse,
Of trouthe grownd, mirour of goodlihed,

---

773 **thrallen:** enslave
776 **dredfull:** fearful **constreinte:** constraint, distress
777 **why:** reason
784 our misery, wretchedness, is this, that we are obliged to
endure (*drynke*) woes of our own making
785 **prest:** quick
787 **anon as:** as soon as **hire lest:** their desire
790 **hem . . . torende:** torture themselves
791 **Ful sharp:** very (too) eager
795 **wher bycometh it:** what becomes of it
797 **on it sporneth:** trips over it (it is too insubstantial to make
anyone stumble)
800 **jangle:** chatter **dremen:** dream up things
801 **coye:** pacify, cajole
802–803 **hem semen Al be for harm:** it seems to them that all is
for some harmful purpose
803 **quemen:** please

808 **be hym looth or deere:** whether he like it or not
815 **wente:** turn
820 **yerd:** enclosed garden **rayled:** bordered, fenced
822 **benched newe:** furnished with new benches (topped with
turf; see ProLGW G 98)
824 **shene:** bright
830 **to rente:** as tribute
833 **seurte:** security
838 **ententif:** diligent
839 **unweri:** without weariness **unfeyned:** sincere
840 **desteyned:** stained
842 **goodlihed:** excellence

Of wit Apollo, stoon of sikernesse,
Of vertu roote, of lust fynder and hed,
Thorough which is alle sorwe fro me ded —   845
Iwis, I love hym best, so doth he me;
Now good thrift have he, wherso that he be!

"Whom shulde I thanken but yow, god of Love,
Of al this blisse, in which to bathe I gynne?
And thanked be ye, lord, for that I love!   850
This is the righte lif that I am inne,
To flemen alle manere vice and synne:
This dooth me so to vertu for t'entende,
That day by day I in my wille amende.

"And whoso seith that for to love is vice,   855
Or thraldom, though he feele in it destresse,
He outher is envyous, or right nyce,
Or is unmyghty, for his shrewednesse,
To loven; for swich manere folk, I gesse,
Defamen Love, as nothing of hym knowe.   860
Thei speken, but thei benten nevere his bowe!

"What is the sonne wers, of kynde right,
Though that a man, for feeblesse of his yen,
May nought endure on it to see for bright?
Or love the wers, though wrecches on it
          crien?   865
No wele is worth, that may no sorwe dryen.
And forthi, who that hath an hed of verre,
Fro cast of stones war hym in the werre!

"But I with al myn herte and al my myght,
As I have seyd, wol love unto my laste   870
My deere herte and al myn owen knyght,
In which myn herte growen is so faste,
And his in me, that it shal evere laste.
Al dredde I first to love hym to bigynne,
Now woot I wel, ther is no peril inne."   875

And of hir song right with that word she stente,
And therwithal, "Now nece," quod Cryseyde,
"Who made this song now with so good en-
          tente?"
Antygone answerde anoon and seyde,

"Madame, iwys, the goodlieste mayde   880
Of gret estat in al the town of Troye,
And let hire lif in moste honour and joye."

"Forsothe, so it semeth by hire song,"
Quod tho Criseyde, and gan therwith to sike,
And seyde, "Lord, is ther swych blisse among
Thise loveres, as they konne faire endite?"   886
"Ye, wis," quod fresshe Antigone the white,
"For alle the folk that han or ben on lyve
Ne konne wel the blisse of love discryve.

"But wene ye that every wrecche woot   890
The parfit blisse of love? Why, nay, iwys!
They wenen all be love, if oon be hoot.
Do wey, do wey, they woot no thyng of this!
Men moste axe at seyntes if it is
Aught fair in hevene (Why? For they kan telle),
And axen fendes is it foul in helle."   896

Criseyde unto that purpos naught answerde,
But seyde, "Ywys, it wol be nyght as faste."
But every word which that she of hire herde,
She gan to prenten in hire herte faste,   900
And ay gan love hire lasse for t'agaste
Than it dide erst, and synken in hire herte,
That she wex somwhat able to converte.

The dayes honour, and the hevenes yë,   904
The nyghtes foo — al this clepe I the sonne —
Gan westren faste, and downward for to wrye,
As he that hadde his dayes cours yronne,
And white thynges wexen dymme and donne
For lak of lyght, and sterres for t'apere,
That she and alle hire folk in went yfeere.   910

So whan it liked hire to go to reste,
And voided weren thei that voiden oughte,
She seyde that to slepen wel hire leste.
Hire wommen soone til hire bed hire broughte.
Whan al was hust, than lay she stille and
          thoughte   915
Of al this thing; the manere and the wise
Reherce it nedeth nought, for ye ben wise.

843 **Apollo:** god of wisdom
844 **of lust fynder and hed:** originator and head (source) of pleasure
849 **bathe:** bask **gynne:** begin
852 **flemen:** banish
858 **unmyghty:** unable **shrewednesse:** wickedness
861 **benten nevere his bowe:** i.e., never tried it for themselves
862 **What:** in what way, how **of kynde right:** in its proper nature
866 **wele is worth:** prosperity is worthy **dryen:** endure
867 **verre:** glass
874 **Al dredde I:** although I was afraid

882 **let** = *ledeth,* leads
886 **endite:** describe it
887 **wis:** surely
888 **han or ben:** have (been) or are (now)
894 **axe at:** ask of
898 **as faste:** soon
900 **prenten:** imprint
901 **t'agaste:** to frighten
906 **westren:** go westward **wrye:** turn, go
908 **donne:** dun, grey-brown
910 **yfeere:** together
912 **voided:** withdrawn
915 **hust:** quiet

A nyghtyngale, upon a cedre grene,
Under the chambre wal ther as she ley,
Ful loude song ayein the moone shene,   920
Peraunter in his briddes wise a lay
Of love, that made hire herte fressh and gay.
That herkned she so longe in good entente,
Til at the laste the dede slep hire hente.

And as she slep, anonright tho hire mette   925
How that an egle, fethered whit as bon,
Under hire brest his longe clawes sette,
And out hire herte he rente, and that anon,
And dide his herte into hire brest to gon —   929
Of which she nought agroos, ne nothyng
          smerte —
And forth he fleigh, with herte left for herte.

Now lat hire slepe, and we oure tales holde
Of Troilus, that is to paleis riden
Fro the scarmuch of the which I tolde,
And in his chaumbre sit and hath abiden   935
Til two or thre of his messages yeden
For Pandarus, and soughten hym ful faste,
Til they hym founde and broughte hym at the
          laste.

This Pandarus com lepyng in atones,
And seyde thus: "Who hath ben wel ibete   940
To-day with swerdes and with slynge-stones,
But Troilus, that hath caught hym an hete?"
And gan to jape, and seyde, "Lord, so ye swete!
But ris and lat us soupe and go to reste."   944
And he answerde hym, "Do we as the leste."

With al the haste goodly that they myghte
They spedde hem fro the soper unto bedde;
And every wight out at the dore hym dyghte,
And where hym liste upon his wey him spedde.
But Troilus, that thoughte his herte bledde   950
For wo, til that he herde som tydynge,
He seyde, "Frend, shal I now wepe or synge?"

Quod Pandarus, "Ly stylle and lat me slepe,
And don thyn hood; thy nedes spedde be!

And ches if thow wolt synge or daunce or lepe!
At shorte wordes, thow shal trowen me: 956
Sire, my nece wol do wel by the,
And love the best, by God and by my trouthe,
But lak of pursuyt make it in thi slouthe.

"For thus ferforth I have thi werk bigonne
Fro day to day, til this day by the morwe   961
Hire love of frendshipe have I to the wonne,
And therto hath she leyd hire feyth to borwe.
Algate a foot is hameled of thi sorwe!"
What sholde I lenger sermon of it holde?   965
As ye han herd byfore, al he hym tolde.

But right as floures, thorugh the cold of nyght
Iclosed, stoupen on hire stalke lowe,
Redressen hem ayein the sonne bright,
And spreden on hire kynde cours by rowe,   970
Right so gan tho his eighen up to throwe
This Troilus, and seyde, "O Venus deere,
Thi myght, thi grace, yheried be it here!"

And to Pandare he held up bothe his hondes,
And seyde, "Lord, al thyn be that I have!   975
For I am hool, al brosten ben my bondes.
A thousand Troyes whoso that me yave,
Ech after other, God so wys me save,
Ne myghte me so gladen; lo, myn herte,
It spredeth so for joie it wol tosterte!   980

"But, Lord, how shal I doon? How shal I lyven?
Whan shal I next my deere herte see?
How shal this longe tyme awey be dryven
Til that thow be ayein at hire fro me?
Thow maist answer, 'Abid, abid,' but he   985
That hangeth by the nekke, soth to seyne
In gret disese abideth for the peyne."

"Al esily, now, for the love of Marte,"
Quod Pandarus, "for every thing hath tyme.
So longe abid til that the nyght departe,   990
For also siker as thow list here by me,

919 **Under:** next to
920 **shene:** bright
921 **Peraunter:** by chance
924 **dede:** dead, deep   **hente:** seized
925 **mette:** dreamed
930 **agroos:** was frightened   **smerte:** felt pain
934 **scarmuch:** skirmish
935 **sit** = *sitteth,* sits
936 **messages:** messengers   **yeden:** went
943 **swete:** sweat
945 **the leste:** you please
948 **hym dyghte:** departed
954 **don thyn hood:** put on your hood (of uncertain sense;
see n.)   **spedde be:** have come out well

959 Unless due to your sloth a lack of perseverance make it (turn
out otherwise)
960 **ferforth:** far
963 **feyth to borwe:** word as a pledge
964 At any rate one foot of your sorrow is crippled, hambled
(and thus it cannot pursue you so fast).
969 **Redressen hem:** straighten themselves
970 **kynde cours:** natural course   **by rowe:** in a row
973 **yheried:** praised
976 **brosten:** broken
977 **yave:** would give
980 **tosterte:** burst
985 **Abid:** wait
987 **disese:** distress
991 **also siker as:** as surely as   **list** = *liest,* lie down

And God toforn, I wol be ther at pryme;
And forthi, werk somwhat as I shal seye,
Or on som other wight this charge leye.

"For, pardee, God woot I have evere yit   995
Ben redy the to serve, and to this nyght
Have I naught feyned, but emforth my wit
Don al thi lust, and shal with al my myght.
Do now as I shal seyn, and far aright;
And if thow nylt, wite al thiself thi care!   1000
On me is nought along thyn yvel fare.

"I woot wel that thow wiser art than I
A thousand fold, but if I were as thow,
God help me so, as I wolde outrely
Of myn owen hond write hire right now   1005
A lettre, in which I wolde hire tellen how
I ferde amys, and hire biseche of routhe.
Now help thiself, and leve it nought for
        slouthe!

"And I myself wol therwith to hire gon;
And whan thow woost that I am with hire
        there,   1010
Worth thow upon a courser right anon —
Ye, hardily, right in thi beste gere —
And ryd forth by the place, as nought ne were,
And thow shalt fynde us, if I may, sittynge
At som wyndow, into the strete lokynge.   1015

"And if the list, than maystow us salue;
And upon me make thow thi countenaunce;
But by thi lif, be war and faste eschue
To tarien ought — God shilde us fro mes-
        chaunce!
Rid forth thi wey, and hold thi govern-
        aunce;   1020
And we shal speek of the somwhat, I trowe,
Whan thow art gon, to don thyn eris glowe!

"Towchyng thi lettre, thou art wys ynough.
I woot thow nylt it dygneliche endite,
As make it with thise argumentes tough;   1025
Ne scryvenyssh or craftyly thow it write;

Biblotte it with thi teris ek a lite;
And if thow write a goodly word al softe,
Though it be good, reherce it nought to ofte.

"For though the beste harpour upon lyve   1030
Wolde on the beste sowned joly harpe
That evere was, with alle his fyngres fyve
Touche ay o stryng, or ay o werbul harpe,
Were his nayles poynted nevere so sharpe,
It sholde maken every wight to dulle,   1035
To here his glee, and of his strokes fulle.

"Ne jompre ek no discordant thyng yfeere,
As thus, to usen termes of phisik
In loves termes; hold of thi matere
The forme alwey, and do that it be lik;   1040
For if a peyntour wolde peynte a pyk
With asses feet, and hedde it as an ape,
It cordeth naught, so were it but a jape."

This counseil liked wel to Troilus,
But, as a dredful lovere, he seyde this: 1045
"Allas, my deere brother Pandarus,
I am ashamed for to write, ywys,
Lest of myn innocence I seyde amys,
Or that she nolde it for despit receyve;
Than were I ded: ther myght it nothyng
        weyve."   1050

To that Pandare answered, "If the lest,
Do that I seye, and lat me therwith gon;
For by that Lord that formede est and west,
I hope of it to brynge answere anon
Of hire hond; and if that thow nylt noon,   1055
Lat be, and sory mote he ben his lyve
Ayeins thi lust that helpeth the to thryve."

Quod Troilus, "Depardieux, ich assente!
Sith that the list, I wil arise and write;
And blisful God prey ich with good entente,
The viage, and the lettre I shal endite,   1061

992 **pryme:** the first time period of the day, from 6 to 9 A.M.
997 **emforth:** to the extent of
999 **far aright:** do well
1000 **wite:** impute to
1001 **On me . . . along:** due to me, my fault
1011 **Worth:** get, mount   **courser:** war-horse, charger
1013 **nought ne were:** i.e., nothing had been arranged
1020 **hold thi governaunce:** keep your self-control
1024 **dygneliche:** haughtily
1025 **make it . . . tough:** put on airs
1026 **scryvenyssh:** in a formal (scrivener's) way   **craftyly:** artfully

1027 **Biblotte:** blot
1028 **softe:** tender
1033 **o werbul:** one tune
1035 **dulle:** be bored
1036 **glee:** music   **fulle:** sated
1037 **jompre:** jumble
1038 **As thus:** for example   **phisik:** medicine
1039 **hold:** maintain
1040 **lik:** similar; i.e., consistent with the subject
1041 **peyntour:** painter   **pyk:** pike (the fish)
1042 **hedde it as an ape:** give it the head of an ape
1043 **cordeth naught:** is not at all fitting
1050 **weyve:** turn aside
1056 **his lyve:** all his life
1057 **that:** anyone who
1058 **Depardieux:** by God
1061 **viage:** undertaking

So spede it; and thow, Minerva, the white,
Yif thow me wit my lettre to devyse."
And sette hym down, and wrot right in this
        wyse:

First he gan hire his righte lady calle,   1065
His hertes lif, his lust, his sorwes leche,
His blisse, and ek thise other termes alle
That in swich cas thise loveres alle seche;
And in ful humble wise, as in his speche,
He gan hym recomaunde unto hire grace;   1070
To telle al how, it axeth muchel space.

And after this ful lowely he hire preyde
To be nought wroth, thogh he, of his folie,
So hardy was to hire to write, and seyde
That love it made, or elles most he die,   1075
And pitousli gan mercy for to crye;
And after that he seyde — and leigh ful loude —
Hymself was litel worth, and lasse he koude;

And that she sholde han his konnyng excused,
That litel was, and ek he dredde hire soo;   1080
And his unworthynesse he ay acused;
And after that than gan he telle his woo —
But that was endeles, withouten hoo —
And seyde he wolde in trouthe alwey hym
        holde;
And radde it over, and gan the lettre folde.

And with his salte teris gan he bathe   1086
The ruby in his signet, and it sette
Upon the wex deliverliche and rathe.
Therwith a thousand tymes er he lette
He kiste tho the lettre that he shette,   1090
And seyde, "Lettre, a blisful destine
The shapyn is: my lady shal the see!"

This Pandare tok the lettre, and that bytyme
A-morwe, and to his neces paleis sterte,   1094
And faste he swor that it was passed prime,
And gan to jape, and seyde, "Ywys, myn herte,
So fressh it is, although it sore smerte,
I may naught slepe nevere a Mayes morwe;
I have a joly wo, a lusty sorwe."

Criseyde, whan that she hire uncle herde,   1100
With dredful herte, and desirous to here
The cause of his comynge, thus answerde:
"Now, by youre fey, myn uncle," quod she,
        "dere,
What manere wyndes gydeth yow now here?
Tel us youre joly wo and youre penaunce.   1105
How ferforth be ye put in loves daunce?"

"By God," quod he, "I hoppe alwey byhynde!"
And she to laughe, it thoughte hire herte brest.
Quod Pandarus, "Loke alwey that ye fynde
Game in myn hood; but herkneth, if yow
        lest!   1110
Ther is right now come into town a gest,
A Greek espie, and telleth newe thinges,
For which I come to telle yow tydynges.

"Into the gardyn go we, and ye shal here,
Al pryvely, of this a long sermoun."   1115
With that they wenten arm in arm yfeere
Into the gardyn from the chaumbre down;
And whan that he so fer was that the sown
Of that he spak no man heren myghte,   1119
He seyde hire thus, and out the lettre plighte:

"Lo, he that is al holy youres free
Hym recomaundeth lowely to youre grace,
And sente yow this lettre here by me.
Avyseth yow on it, whan ye han space,   1124
And of som goodly answere yow purchace,
Or, helpe me God, so pleynly for to seyne,
He may nat longe lyven for his peyne."

Ful dredfully tho gan she stonden stylle,
And took it naught, but al hire humble chere
Gan for to chaunge, and seyde, "Scrit ne
        bille,   1130
For love of God, that toucheth swich matere,
Ne bryng me noon; and also, uncle deere,
To myn estat have more reward, I preye,
Than to his lust! What sholde I more seye?

"And loketh now if this be resonable,   1135
And letteth nought, for favour ne for slouthe,

1062 **Minerva:** Roman goddess of wisdom
1070 **recomaunde:** commend
1077 **leigh ful loude:** lied quite openly
1078 **lasse he koude:** he could do even less than his small
reputation (*litel worth*) implied
1083 **hoo:** ceasing
1088 **deliverliche:** deftly   **rathe:** quickly
1089 **lette:** left off
1093–94 **bytyme A-morwe:** early the next morning
1095 **prime:** 9 A.M.

1107 **hoppe alwey byhynde:** i.e., always come last in the dance
1108 **to laughe:** laughed; see n.
1109–10 **fynde Game in myn hood:** find me amusing
1111 **gest:** visitor
1120 **plighte:** pulled
1125 **yow purchace:** provide yourself
1130 **Scrit:** script, writing   **bille:** petition, letter
1133 **reward:** regard
1136 **letteth nought:** do not hesitate

To seyn a sooth; now were it covenable
To myn estat, by God and by youre trouthe,
To taken it, or to han of hym routhe,
In harmyng of myself, or in repreve?   1140
Ber it ayein, for hym that ye on leve!"

This Pandarus gan on hire for to stare,
And seyde, "Now is this the grettest wondre
That evere I seigh! Lat be this nyce fare!
To dethe mot I smyten be with thondre,   1145
If for the citee which that stondeth yondre,
Wolde I a lettre unto yow brynge or take
To harm of yow! What list yow thus it make?

"But thus ye faren, wel neigh alle and some,
That he that most desireth yow to serve,   1150
Of hym ye recche leest wher he bycome,
And whethir that he lyve or elles sterve.
But for al that that ever I may deserve,
Refuse it naught," quod he, and hente hire
        faste,
And in hire bosom the lettre down he thraste,

And seyde hire, "Now cast it awey anon,   1156
That folk may seen and gauren on us tweye."
Quod she, "I kan abyde til they be gon";
And gan to smyle, and seyde hym, "Em, I
        preye,
Swich answere as yow list, youreself purveye,
For trewely I nyl no lettre write."   1161
"No? than wol I," quod he, "so ye endite."

Therwith she lough, and seyde, "Go we dyne."
And he gan at hymself to jape faste,
And seyde, "Nece, I have so gret a pyne   1165
For love, that everich other day I faste — "
And gan his beste japes forth to caste,
And made hire so to laughe at his folye,
That she for laughter wende for to dye.

And whan that she was comen into halle,   1170
"Now, em," quod she, "we wol go dyne anon."
And gan some of hire wommen to hire calle,
And streght into hire chambre gan she gon;
But of hire besynesses this was on —

Amonges othere thynges, out of drede —   1175
Ful pryvely this lettre for to rede;

Avysed word by word in every lyne,
And fond no lak, she thoughte he koude good,
And up it putte, and wente hire in to dyne.
But Pandarus, that in a studye stood,   1180
Er he was war, she took hym by the hood,
And seyde, "Ye were caught er that ye wiste."
"I vouche sauf," quod he. "Do what you liste."

Tho wesshen they, and sette hem down, and
        ete;
And after noon ful sleighly Pandarus   1185
Gan drawe hym to the wyndowe next the strete,
And seyde, "Nece, who hath araied thus
The yonder hous, that stant aforyeyn us?"
"Which hous?" quod she, and gan for to by-
        holde,   1189
And knew it wel, and whos it was hym tolde;

And fillen forth in speche of thynges smale,
And seten in the windowe bothe tweye.
Whan Pandarus saugh tyme unto his tale,
And saugh wel that hire folk were alle aweye,
"Now, nece myn, tel on," quod he; "I seye,
How liketh yow the lettre that ye woot?   1196
Kan he theron? For, by my trouthe, I noot."

Therwith al rosy hewed tho wex she,
And gan to homme, and seyde, "So I trowe."
"Aquite hym wel, for Goddes love," quod he;
"Myself to medes wol the lettre sowe."   1201
And held his hondes up, and sat on knowe;
"Now, goode nece, be it nevere so lite,
Yif me the labour it to sowe and plite."

"Ye, for I kan so writen," quod she tho;   1205
"And ek I noot what I sholde to hym seye."
"Nay, nece," quod Pandare, "sey nat so.
Yet at the leeste thonketh hym, I preye,
Of his good wille, and doth hym nat to deye.

1137 **covenable:** suitable
1140 **in repreve:** as a reproach (to me)
1147 **take:** give
1148 **What list you thus it make?:** Why are you pleased to take
it this way?
1149 **alle and some:** one and all, everyone
1151 **wher he bycome:** what becomes of him
1155 **thraste:** thrust
1157 **gauren:** stare
1162 **endite:** compose, dictate it

1177 **Avysed:** having deliberated
1178 **fond:** having found   **he koude good:** he knew how to act
in the circumstances
1183 **vouche sauf:** grant it
1184 **wesshen:** washed
1187 **araied:** decorated
1188 **stant** = *standeth*, stands   **aforyeyn:** opposite
1197 **Kan he theron?:** Does he know about such matters?
1199 **homme:** hum
1200 **Aquite:** repay
1201 **to medes:** in return   **sowe:** sew (the parchment shut)
1202 **knowe:** knee
1204 **plite:** fold

Now, for the love of me, my nece deere,   1210
Refuseth nat at this tid my prayere!"

"Depardieux," quod she, "God leve al be wel!
God help me so, this is the firste lettre
That evere I wroot, ye, al or any del."
And into a closet, for t'avise hire bettre,   1215
She wente allone, and gan hire herte unfettre
Out of desdaynes prison but a lite,
And sette hire down, and gan a lettre write,

Of which to telle in short is myn entente
Th'effect, as fer as I kan understonde.   1220
She thanked hym of al that he wel mente
Towardes hire, but holden hym in honde
She nolde nought, ne make hireselven bonde
In love; but as his suster, hym to plese,
She wolde fayn to doon his herte an ese.   1225

She shette it, and to Pandare in gan goon,
Ther as he sat and loked into the strete,
And down she sette hire by hym on a stoon
Of jaspre, upon a quysshyn gold-ybete,
And seyde, "As wisly help me God the grete,
I nevere dide thing with more peyne   1231
Than writen this, to which ye me constreyne,"

And took it hym. He thonked hire and seyde,
"God woot, of thyng ful often looth bygonne
Comth ende good; and nece myn, Criseyde,
That ye to hym of hard now ben ywonne   1236
Oughte he be glad, by God and yonder sonne;
For-whi men seith, 'Impressiounes lighte
Ful lightly ben ay redy to the flighte.'

"But ye han played tirant neigh to longe,   1240
And hard was it youre herte for to grave.
Now stynte, that ye no lenger on it honge,
Al wolde ye the forme of daunger save,
But hasteth yow to doon hym joye have;
For trusteth wel, to longe ydoon hardnesse
Causeth despit ful often for destresse."   1246

And right as they declamed this matere,
Lo, Troilus, right at the stretes ende,
Com rydyng with his tenthe som yfere,
Al softely, and thiderward gan bende   1250
Ther as they sete, as was his way to wende
To paleis-ward; and Pandare hym aspide,
And seyde, "Nece, ysee who comth here ride!

"O fle naught in (he seeth us, I suppose),   1254
Lest he may thynken that ye hym eschuwe."
"Nay, nay," quod she, and wex as red as rose.
With that he gan hire humbly to saluwe
With dredful chere, and oft his hewes muwe;
And up his look debonairly he caste,
And bekked on Pandare, and forth he paste.

God woot if he sat on his hors aright,   1261
Or goodly was biseyn, that ilke day!
God woot wher he was lik a manly knyght!
What sholde I drecche, or telle of his aray?
Criseyde, which that alle thise thynges say,
To telle in short, hire liked al in-fere,   1266
His persoun, his aray, his look, his chere,

His goodly manere, and his gentilesse,
So wel that nevere, sith that she was born,
Ne hadde she swych routh of his des-
          tresse;   1270
And how so she hath hard ben here-byforn,
To God hope I, she hath now kaught a thorn,
She shal nat pulle it out this nexte wyke.
God sende mo swich thornes on to pike!

Pandare, which that stood hire faste by,   1275
Felte iren hoot, and he bygan to smyte,
And seyde, "Nece, I pray yow hertely,
Telle me that I shal axen yow a lite:
A womman that were of his deth to wite,   1279
Withouten his gilt, but for hire lakked routhe,
Were it wel doon?" Quod she, "Nay, by my
          trouthe!"

"God help me so," quod he, "ye sey me soth.
Ye felen wel youreself that I nought lye.

1211 **tid:** time
1212 **Depardieux:** by God   **leve:** grant
1222 **holden hym in honde:** cajole him with false promises
1229 **quysshyn:** cushion   **gold-ybete:** embroidered with gold
1230 **wisly:** certainly
1233 **took:** gave
1236 **of hard:** with difficulty
1239 **lightly:** quickly
1240 **neigh:** almost
1241 **grave:** engrave (with the impression of Troilus)
1242 Now stop, that you may remain undecided no longer
1243 **forme of daunger:** appearance of disdain, standoffishness
1245 **hardnesse:** resistance

1247 **declamed:** discussed
1249 **with his tenthe som yfere:** with his party of ten (he and nine, or ten, others)
1258 **his hewes muwe:** the colors (in his face) change
1259 **debonairly:** graciously
1260 **bekked on:** nodded at
1262 **ilke:** same
1264 **drecche:** delay
1265 **say:** saw
1266 **al in-fere:** all together
1274 **mo:** more (or, others)   **pike:** pull out
1278 **that:** what

Lo, yond he rit!" Quod she, "Ye, so he doth!"
"Wel," quod Pandare, "as I have told yow
       thrie,   1285
Lat be youre nyce shame and youre folie,
And spek with hym in esyng of his herte,
Lat nycete nat do yow bothe smerte."

But theron was to heven and to doone.
Considered al thing it may nat be;   1290
And whi? For speche; and it were ek to soone
To graunten hym so gret a libertee.
For pleynly hire entente, as seyde she,
Was for to love hym unwist, if she myghte,
And guerdoun hym with nothing but with
       sighte.   1295

But Pandarus thought, "It shal nought be so,
Yif that I may; this nyce opynyoun
Shal nought be holden fully yeres two."
What sholde I make of this a long sermoun?
He moste assente on that conclusioun,   1300
As for the tyme; and whan that it was eve,
And al was wel, he roos and tok his leve.

And on his wey ful faste homward he spedde,
And right for joye he felte his herte daunce;
And Troilus he fond allone abedde,   1305
That lay, as do thise lovers, in a traunce
Bitwixen hope and derk disesperaunce.
But Pandarus, right at his in-comynge,
He song, as who seyth, "Somwhat I brynge,"

And seyde, "Who is in his bed so soone   1310
Iburied thus?" "It am I, frend," quod he.
"Who, Troilus? Nay, help me so the moone,"
Quod Pandarus, "thow shalt arise and see
A charme that was sent right now to the,
The which kan helen the of thyn accesse,
If thow do forthwith al thi bisynesse."   1316

"Ye, thorugh the myght of God," quod Troilus,
And Pandarus gan hym the lettre take,
And seyde, "Parde, God hath holpen us!
Have here a light, and loke on al this blake."

But ofte gan the herte glade and quake   1321
Of Troilus, whil that he gan it rede,
So as the wordes yave hym hope or drede.

But finaly, he took al for the beste   1324
That she hym wroot, for somwhat he byheld
On which hym thoughte he myghte his herte
       reste,
Al covered she tho wordes under sheld.
Thus to the more worthi part he held,
That what for hope and Pandarus byheste,
His grete wo foryede he at the leste.   1330

But as we may alday oureselven see,
Thorugh more wode or col, the more fir,
Right so encreese hope, of what it be,
Therwith ful ofte encresseth ek desir;
Or as an ook comth of a litel spir,   1335
So thorugh this lettre which that she hym
       sente
Encrescen gan desir, of which he brente.

Wherfore I seye alwey, that day and nyght
This Troilus gan to desiren moore
Thanne he did erst, thorugh hope, and did his
       myght   1340
To preessen on, as by Pandarus loore,
And writen to hire of his sorwes soore.
Fro day to day he leet it nought refreyde,
That by Pandare he wroot somwhat or seyde;

And dide also his other observaunces   1345
That til a lovere longeth in this cas;
And after that thise dees torned on chaunces,
So was he outher glad or seyde "Allas!"
And held after his gistes ay his pas;
And after swiche answeres as he hadde,   1350
So were his dayes sory outher gladde.

But to Pandare alwey was his recours,
And pitously gan ay tyl hym to pleyne,
And hym bisoughte of reed and som socours.
And Pandarus, that sey his woode peyne,   1355
Wex wel neigh ded for routhe, sooth to seyne,

1284 rit = rideth, rides
1285 thrie: thrice
1288 nycete: scrupulosity
1289 to heven and to doone: to exert (oneself) and do (work);
i.e., there was much to be done
1291 speche: (fear of) malicious gossip
1295 guerdoun: reward
1315 accesse: fever
1318 gan . . . take: gave
1319 holpen: helped
1320 blake: black ink (writing)

1323 yave: gave
1327 under sheld: i.e., her language was guarded
1330 grete: the greater part of   foryede: forwent, set aside
1333 encreese hope: if hope should increase   what: whatever
1335 spir: sprout
1341 preessen: push
1343 refreyde: grow cold
1347 And according to the luck of the dice (chaunces, winning
throws for one player or the other)
1349 And always conformed his pace to his stopovers (gistes); i.e.,
flowed with the tide
1355 sey: saw   woode: crazed

And bisily with al his herte caste
Som of his wo to slen, and that as faste;

And seyde, "Lord, and frend, and brother
          dere,
God woot that thi disese doth me wo.   1360
But wiltow stynten al this woful cheere,
And, by my trouthe, er it be dayes two,
And God toforn, yet shal I shape it so,
That thow shalt come into a certeyn place,
There as thow mayst thiself hire preye of grace.

"And certeynly — I noot if thow it woost,   1366
But tho that ben expert in love it seye —
It is oon of the thynges forthereth most,
A man to han a layser for to preye,
And siker place his wo for to bywreye;   1370
For in good herte it mot som routhe impresse,
To here and see the giltlees in distresse.

"Peraunter thynkestow: though it be so,
That Kynde wolde don hire to bygynne
To have a manere routhe upon my woo,   1375
Seyth Daunger, 'Nay, thow shalt me nevere
          wynne!'
So reulith hire hir hertes gost withinne,
That though she bende, yeet she stant on roote;
What in effect is this unto my boote?   1379

"Thenk here-ayeins: whan that the stordy ook,
On which men hakketh ofte, for the nones,
Receyved hath the happy fallyng strook,
The greete sweigh doth it come al at ones,
As don thise rokkes or thise milnestones;   1384
For swifter cours comth thyng that is of wighte,
Whan it descendeth, than don thynges lighte.

"And reed that boweth down for every blast,
Ful lightly, cesse wynd, it wol aryse;
But so nyl nought an ook, whan it is cast;
It nedeth me nought the longe to forbise.   1390
Men shal rejoissen of a gret empryse

Acheved wel, and stant withouten doute,
Al han men ben the lenger theraboute.

"But, Troilus, yet telle me, if the lest,
A thing now which that I shal axen the: 1395
Which is thi brother that thow lovest best,
As in thi verray hertes privetee?"
"Iwis, my brother Deiphebus," quod he.
"Now," quod Pandare, "er houres twyes twelve,
He shal the ese, unwist of it hymselve.   1400

"Now lat m'alone, and werken as I may,"
Quod he; and to Deiphebus wente he tho,
Which hadde his lord and grete frend ben ay;
Save Troilus, no man he loved so.
To telle in short, withouten wordes mo,   1405
Quod Pandarus, "I pray yow that ye be
Frend to a cause which that toucheth me."

"Yis, parde," quod Deiphebus, "wel thow
          woost,
In al that evere I may, and God tofore,
Al nere it but for man I love moost,   1410
My brother Troilus; but sey wherfore
It is; for sith that day that I was bore,
I nas, ne nevere mo to ben I thynke,
Ayeins a thing that myghte the forthynke."

Pandare gan hym thanke, and to hym seyde,
"Lo, sire, I have a lady in this town,   1416
That is my nece, and called is Criseyde,
Which some men wolden don oppressioun,
And wrongfully han hire possessioun;
Wherfore I of youre lordship yow biseche   1420
To ben oure frend, withouten more speche."

Deiphebus hym answerde, "O, is nat this,
That thow spekest of to me thus straungely,
Criseda, my frend?" He seyde, "Yis."
"Than nedeth," quod Deiphebus, "hardyly,
Namore to speke, for trusteth wel that I   1426
Wol be hire champioun with spore and yerde;
I roughte nought though alle hire foos it herde.

"But tel me how — thow woost of this matere —
It myghte best avaylen." "Now lat se,"   1430

1358 **slen:** slay
1368 **forthereth:** that advances (one's case)
1369 **layser:** opportunity   **preye:** plead (with his lady)
1370 **bywreye:** reveal
1374 **Kynde:** nature, the lady's natural inclination
1376 **Daunger:** disdain, standoffishness
1378 **on roote:** firmly rooted
1380 **here-ayeins:** on the contrary
1381 **for the nones:** purposefully, indeed
1382 **happy:** fortunate
1383 **sweigh:** swaying, momentum
1384 **milnestones:** millstones (extremely heavy objects)
1385 **wighte:** weight
1390 **forbise:** prove by examples

1392 **stant** = *standeth,* (this) stands; see n.
1393 Although people have taken that much longer about it
1398 **Deiphebus:** Priam and Hecuba's third son
1414 **the forthynke:** displease you
1418 **Which:** to whom
1423 **straungely:** distantly, as if she were a stranger
1427 **spore:** spur   **yerde:** rod (i.e., spear)
1428 **roughte nought:** would not care

Quod Pandarus; "if ye, my lord so dere,
Wolden as now do this honour to me,
To preyen hire to-morwe, lo, that she
Come unto yow, hire pleyntes to devise,
Hire adversaries wolde of it agrise. 1435

"And yif I more dorste preye as now,
And chargen yow to han so gret travaille,
To han som of youre bretheren here with yow,
That myghten to hire cause bet availle,
Than wot I wel she myghte nevere faille 1440
For to ben holpen, what at youre instaunce,
What with hire other frendes governaunce."

Deiphebus, which that comen was of kynde
To alle honour and bounte to consente,
Answerd, "It shal be don; and I kan fynde 1445
Yet grettere help to this in myn entente.
What wiltow seyn if I for Eleyne sente
To speke of this? I trowe it be the beste,
For she may leden Paris as hire leste. 1449

"Of Ector, which that is my lord, my brother,
It nedeth naught to preye hym frend to be;
For I have herd hym, o tyme and ek oother,
Speke of Cryseyde swich honour that he
May seyn no bet, swich hap to hym hath she.
It nedeth naught his helpes for to crave; 1455
He shal be swich, right as we wol hym have.

"Spek thow thiself also to Troilus
On my byhalve, and prey hym with us dyne."
"Syre, al this shal be don," quod Pandarus,
And took his leve, and nevere gan to fyne, 1460
But to his neces hous, as streyght as lyne,
He com; and fond hire fro the mete arise,
And sette hym down, and spak right in this
    wise:

He seide, "O verray God, so have I ronne!
Lo, nece myn, se ye nought how I swete? 1465
I not wheither ye the more thank me konne.
Be ye naught war how false Poliphete
Is now aboute eftsones for to plete,

And brynge on yow advocacies newe?" 1469
"I, no!" quod she, and chaunged al hire hewe.

"What is he more aboute, me to drecche
And don me wrong? What shal I doon, allas?
Yet of hymself nothing ne wolde I recche,
Nere it for Antenor and Eneas,
That ben his frendes in swich manere cas. 1475
But, for the love of God, myn uncle deere,
No fors of that; lat hym han al yfeere,

"Withouten that I have ynough for us."
"Nay," quod Pandare, "it shal nothing be so.
For I have ben right now at Deiphebus, 1480
At Ector, and myn oother lordes moo,
And shortly maked ech of hem his foo,
That, by my thrift, he shal it nevere wynne,
For aught he kan, whan that so he bygynne."

And as thei casten what was best to doone,
Deiphebus, of his owen curteisie, 1486
Com hire to preye, in his propre persone,
To holde hym on the morwe compaignie
At dyner, which she nolde nought denye,
But goodly gan to his preier obeye. 1490
He thonked hire, and went upon his weye.

Whan this was don, this Pandare up anon,
To telle in short, and forth gan for to wende
To Troilus, as stille as any ston;
And al this thyng he tolde hym, word and
    ende, 1495
And how that he Deiphebus gan to blende,
And seyde hym, "Now is tyme, if that thow
    konne,
To bere the wel tomorwe, and al is wonne.

"Now spek, now prey, now pitously compleyne;
Lat nought for nyce shame, or drede, or
    slouthe! 1500
Somtyme a man mot telle his owen peyne.
Bileve it, and she shal han on the routhe:
Thow shalt be saved by thi feyth, in trouthe.
But wel woot I thow art now in drede,
And what it is, I leye, I kan arede. 1505

1434 **devise:** set forth
1435 **agrise:** tremble
1437 **chargen:** request
1441 **what at:** what with **instaunce:** request
1444 **bounte:** goodness
1454 **hap to:** favor (good fortune) with
1460 **gan to fyne:** stopped
1462 **the mete:** dinner **arise:** rising
1466 I do not know whether (because of my exertions) you are the more grateful to me.
1468 **eftsones:** again **plete:** sue at law

1469 **advocacies:** charges
1470 **I:** oh (exclamation)
1471 **What:** why **more aboute:** about to do more **drecche:** trouble
1474 **Antenor, Eneas:** the Trojan warriors who ultimately betrayed the city
1477 **al yfeere:** everything
1478 **Withouten:** except, providing
1487 **propre persone:** own self, personally
1495 **word and ende:** beginning and end
1496 **blende:** blind, deceive
1500 **Lat:** stop, leave off
1505 **leye:** wager **arede:** guess

"Thow thynkest now, 'How sholde I don al this?
For by my cheres mosten folk aspie
That for hire love is that I fare amys;
Yet hadde I levere unwist for sorwe dye.'
Now thynk nat so, for thow dost gret folie;
For I right now have founden o manere   1511
Of sleyghte, for to coveren al thi cheere.

"Thow shalt gon over nyght, and that bylyve,
Unto Deiphebus hous as the to pleye,
Thi maladie awey the bet to dryve —   1515
For-whi thow semest sik, soth for to seye.
Sone after that, down in thi bed the leye,
And sey thow mayst no lenger up endure,
And ly right there, and byd thyn aventure.

"Sey that thi fevre is wont the for to take   1520
The same tyme, and lasten til a-morwe;
And lat se now how wel thow kanst it make,
For, parde, sik is he that is in sorwe.
Go now, farwel! And Venus here to borwe,
I hope, and thow this purpos holde ferme,   1525
Thi grace she shal fully ther conferme."

Quod Troilus, "Iwis, thow nedeles
Conseilest me that siklich I me feyne,
For I am sik in ernest, douteles,
So that wel neigh I sterve for the peyne."   1530
Quod Pandarus, "Thow shalt the bettre pleyne,
And hast the lasse need to countrefete,
For hym men demen hoot that men seen swete.

"Lo, hold the at thi triste cloos, and I
Shal wel the deer unto thi bowe dryve."   1535
Therwith he took his leve al softely,
And Troilus to paleis wente blyve.
So glad ne was he nevere in al his lyve,
And to Pandarus reed gan al assente,   1539
And to Deiphebus hous at nyght he wente.

What nedeth yow to tellen al the cheere
That Deiphebus unto his brother made,
Or his accese, or his sikliche manere,
How men gan hym with clothes for to lade
Whan he was leyd, and how men wolde hym
     glade?   1545

But al for nought; he held forth ay the wyse
That ye han herd Pandare er this devyse.

But certayn is, er Troilus hym leyde,
Deiphebus had hym preied over-nyght
To ben a frend and helpyng to Criseyde.   1550
God woot that he it graunted anon-right,
To ben hire fulle frend with al his myght.
But swich a nede was to preye hym thenne,
As for to bidde a wood man for to renne!

The morwen com, and neighen gan the tyme
Of meeltid, that the faire queene Eleyne   1556
Shoop hire to ben, an houre after the prime,
With Deiphebus, to whom she nolde feyne;
But as his suster, homly, soth to seyne,
She com to dyner in hire pleyne entente.   1560
But God and Pandare wist al what this mente.

Com ek Criseyde, al innocent of this,
Antigone, hire suster Tarbe also.
But fle we now prolixitee best is,
For love of God, and lat us faste go   1565
Right to th'effect, withouten tales mo,
Whi al this folk assembled in this place;
And lat us of hire saluynges pace.

Gret honour did hem Deiphebus, certeyn,   1569
And fedde hem wel with al that myghte like;
But evere mo "Allas!" was his refreyn,
"My goode brother Troilus, the syke,
Lith yet" — and therwithal he gan to sike;
And after that, he peyned hym to glade
Hem as he myghte, and cheere good he made.

Compleyned ek Eleyne of his siknesse   1576
So feythfully that pite was to here,
And every wight gan waxen for accesse
A leche anon, and seyde, "In this manere
Men curen folk." — "This charme I wol yow
     leere."   1580
But ther sat oon, al list hire nought to teche,
That thoughte, "Best koud I yet ben his leche."

1513 **bylyve:** quickly
1519 **byd thyn aventure:** await what happens
1522 **make:** i.e., feign
1524 **Venus here to borwe:** with Venus present as a guarantor
1534 **triste:** the hunters' station in a deer hunt, toward which the game would be driven
1543 **accese:** onset of fever
1544 **clothes:** bedclothes   **lade:** cover (load)

1549 **over-nyght:** the night before (Criseyde came)
1554 **renne:** run (wild)
1555 **neighen gan:** drew nigh
1556 **meeltid:** mealtime
1557 **an houre after the prime:** 10 A.M., the dinner hour
1559 **homly:** familiarly
1560 **in hire pleyne entente:** willingly
1566 **tales:** words, conversation
1568 **saluynges:** greetings
1577 **feythfully:** sincerely
1578 **for accesse:** with regard to fever

After compleynte, hym gonnen they to preyse,
As folk don yet whan som wight hath bygonne
To preise a man, and up with pris hym
      reise   1585
A thousand fold yet heigher than the sonne:
"He is, he kan, that fewe lordes konne."
And Pandarus, of that they wolde afferme,
He naught forgat hire preisynge to conferme.

Herde al this thyng Criseyde wel inough,   1590
And every word gan for to notifie;
For which with sobre cheere hire herte lough.
For who is that ne wolde hire glorifie,
To mowen swich a knyght don lyve or dye?
But al passe I, lest ye to longe dwelle;   1595
For for o fyn is al that evere I telle.

The tyme com fro dyner for to ryse,
And as hem aughte, arisen everichon.
And gonne a while of this and that devise.
But Pandarus brak al that speche anon,   1600
And seide to Deiphebus, "Wol ye gon,
If it youre wille be, as I yow preyde,
To speke here of the nedes of Criseyde?"

Eleyne, which that by the hond hire held,
Took first the tale, and seyde, "Go we blyve";
And goodly on Criseyde she biheld,   1606
And seyde, "Joves lat hym nevere thryve
That doth yow harm, and brynge hym soone
      of lyve,
And yeve me sorwe, but he shal it rewe,
If that I may, and alle folk be trewe!"   1610

"Tel thow thi neces cas," quod Deiphebus
To Pandarus, "for thow kanst best it telle."
"My lordes and my ladys, it stant thus:
What sholde I lenger," quod he, "do yow
      dwelle?"
He rong hem out a proces lik a belle   1615
Upon hire foo that highte Poliphete,
So heynous that men myghten on it spete.

Answerde of this ech werse of hem than other,
And Poliphete they gonnen thus to warien:

"Anhonged be swich oon, were he my brother!
And so he shal, for it ne may nought varien!"
What shold I lenger in this tale tarien?   1622
Pleynliche, alle at ones, they hire highten
To ben hire help in al that evere they
      myghten.

Spak than Eleyne, and seyde, "Pandarus,   1625
Woot ought my lord, my brother, this matere —
I meene Ector — or woot it Troilus?"
He seyde, "Ye, but wole ye now me here?
Me thynketh this, sith that Troilus is here,
It were good, if that ye wolde assente,   1630
She tolde hireself hym al this er she wente.

"For he wol have the more hir grief at herte,
By cause, lo, that she a lady is;
And, by youre leve, I wol but in right sterte
And do yow wyte, and that anon, iwys,   1635
If that he slepe, or wol ought here of this."
And in he lepte, and seyde hym in his ere,
"God have thi soule, ibrought have I thi beere!"

To smylen of this gan tho Troilus,
And Pandarus, withouten rekenynge,   1640
Out wente anon to Eleyne and Deiphebus,
And seyde hem, "So ther be no taryinge,
Ne moore prees, he wol wel that ye brynge
Criseda, my lady, that is here;
And as he may enduren, he wol here.   1645

"But wel ye woot, the chaumbre is but lite,
And fewe folk may lightly make it warm;
Now loketh ye (for I wol have no wite
To brynge in prees that myghte don hym harm,
Or hym disesen, for my bettre arm)   1650
Wher it be bet she bide til eft-sonys;
Now loketh ye that knowen what to doon is.

"I sey for me, best is, as I kan knowe,
That no wight in ne wente but ye tweye,
But it were I, for I kan in a throwe   1655
Reherce hire cas unlik that she kan seye;
And after this she may hym ones preye

1591 **notifie:** record
1593 **hire glorifie:** be proud of herself
1594 To be able (*mowen*) to make (*don*) such a knight live or die
1595 **dwelle:** delay
1605 **Took first the tale:** began to speak
1608 **brynge . . . of lyve:** kill
1615 **rong:** rang out, proclaimed   **proces:** argument, case
1617 **heynous:** hateful   **spete:** spit
1619 **warien:** curse

1621 **varien:** be otherwise
1622 **tale:** talk, discourse
1634 **but in right sterte:** just run in
1635 **do yow wyte:** let you know
1638 **beere:** funeral bier
1640 **withouten rekenynge:** without calculation, immediately
1643 **prees:** crowd
1648 **wite:** blame
1650 **bettre arm:** right arm
1651 **Wher:** whether   **eft-sonys:** later
1655 **throwe:** short time
1656 **unlik that:** i.e., better than

To ben good lord, in short, and take hire leve.
This may nought muchel of his ese hym reve.

"And ek, for she is straunge, he wol for-
    bere   1660
His ese, which that hym thar nought for yow;
Ek oother thing that toucheth nought to here
He wol yow telle — I woot it wel right now —
That secret is, and for the townes prow."   1664
And they, that nothyng knewe of his entente,
Withouten more, to Troilus in they wente.

Eleyne, in al hire goodly softe wyse,
Gan hym salue, and wommanly to pleye,
And seyde, "Iwys, ye moste alweies arise!
Now faire brother, beth al hool, I preye!"   1670
And gan hire arm right over his shulder leye,
And hym with al hire wit to reconforte;
As she best koude, she gan hym to disporte.

So after this quod she, "We yow biseke,
My deere brother Deiphebus and I,   1675
For love of God — and so doth Pandare eke —
To ben good lord and frend, right hertely,
Unto Criseyde, which that certeynly
Receyveth wrong, as woot weel here Pandare,
That kan hire cas wel bet than I declare."   1680

This Pandarus gan newe his tong affile,
And al hire cas reherce, and that anon.
Whan it was seyd, soone after in a while,
Quod Troilus, "As sone as I may gon,   1684
I wol right fayn with al my myght ben oon —
Have God my trouthe — hire cause to sustene."
"Good thrift have ye!" quod Eleyne the queene.

Quod Pandarus, "And it youre wille be
That she may take hire leve, er that she go?"
"O, elles God forbede it," tho quod he,   1690
"If that she vouche sauf for to do so."
And with that word quod Troilus, "Ye two,

Deiphebus and my suster lief and deere,
To yow have I to speke of o matere,   1694

"To ben avysed by youre reed the bettre — "
And fond, as hap was, at his beddes hed
The copie of a tretys and a lettre
That Ector hadde hym sent to axen red
If swych a man was worthi to ben ded,
Woot I nought who; but in a grisly wise   1700
He preyede hem anon on it avyse.

Deiphebus gan this lettre for t'onfolde
In ernest greet; so did Eleyne the queene;
And romyng outward, faste it gonne byholde,
Downward a steire, into an herber greene.   1705
This ilke thing they redden hem bitwene,
And largely, the mountance of an houre,
Thei gonne on it to reden and to poure.

Now lat hem rede, and torne we anon
To Pandarus, that gan ful faste prye   1710
That al was wel, and out he gan to gon
Into the grete chaumbre, and that in hye,
And seyde, "God save al this compaynye!
Com, nece myn; my lady queene Eleyne
Abideth yow, and ek my lordes tweyne.   1715

"Rys, take with yow youre nece Antigone,
Or whom yow list; or no fors; hardyly
The lesse prees, the bet; com forth with me,
And loke that ye thonken humblely
Hem alle thre, and whan ye may goodly   1720
Youre tyme se, taketh of hem youre leeve,
Lest we to longe his restes hym byreeve."

Al innocent of Pandarus entente,
Quod tho Criseyde, "Go we, uncle deere";
And arm in arm inward with hym she wente,
Avysed wel hire wordes and hire cheere;   1726
And Pandarus, in ernestful manere,
Seyde, "Alle folk, for Goddes love, I preye,
Stynteth right here, and softely yow pleye.

1659 ese: comfort   reve: deprive
1660 straunge: not of the family   forbere: forgo
1661 which that hym thar nought: which he need not (forbere)
1662 here: her
1664 prow: profit
1669 alweies: by all means   arise: i.e., get well
1670 beth al hool: get well
1672 reconforte: comfort
1673 disporte: cheer up
1681 affile: file smooth
1684 gon: walk
1685 oon: one of her supporters
1690 elles: otherwise
1691 vouche sauf: agree

1696 as hap was: as it chanced
1700 grisly wise: grim manner
1705 Downward a steire: down a staircase
1706 ilke: same
1707 mountance: extent
1708 poure: pore
1710 prye: spy out
1712 in hye: speedily
1717 no fors: it doesn't matter   hardyly: certainly
1722 restes: times of rest
1726 Avysed: having considered

"Aviseth yow what folk ben hire withinne, 1730
And in what plit oon is, God hym amende!"
And inward thus, "Ful softely bygynne,
Nece, I conjure and heighly yow defende,
On his half which that soule us alle sende,
And in the vertu of corones tweyne, 1735
Sle naught this man, that hath for yow this
      peyne!

"Fy on the devel! Thynk which oon he is,
And in what plit he lith; com of anon!
Thynk al swich taried tyde, but lost it nys.
That wol ye bothe seyn, whan ye ben oon.
Secoundely, ther yet devyneth noon 1741
Upon yow two; come of now, if ye konne!
While folk is blent, lo, al the tyme is wonne.

"In titeryng, and pursuyte, and delayes,
The folk devyne at waggyng of a stree; 1745
And though ye wolde han after mirye dayes,
Than dar ye naught. And whi? For she, and she
Spak swych a word; thus loked he, and he!
Las, tyme ilost! I dar nought with yow dele.
Com of, therfore, and bryngeth hym to hele!"

But now to yow, ye loveres that ben here, 1751
Was Troilus nought in a kankedort,
That lay, and myghte whisprynge of hem here,
And thoughte, "O Lord, right now renneth my
      sort
Fully to deye, or han anon comfort!" 1755
And was the firste tyme he shulde hire preye
Of love; O myghty God, what shal he seye?

Explicit secundus liber.

BOOK III

Incipit prohemium tercii libri.

O blisful light of which the bemes clere
Adorneth al the thridde heven faire!
O sonnes lief, O Joves doughter deere,
Plesance of love, O goodly debonaire,
In gentil hertes ay redy to repaire! 5
O veray cause of heele and of gladnesse,
Iheryed be thy myght and thi goodnesse!

In hevene and helle, in erthe and salte see
Is felt thi myght, if that I wel descerne,

As man, brid, best, fissh, herbe, and grene tree
Thee fele in tymes with vapour eterne. 11
God loveth, and to love wol nought werne,
And in this world no lyves creature
Withouten love is worth, or may endure.

Ye Joves first to thilke effectes glade, 15
Thorugh which that thynges lyven alle and be,
Comeveden, and amorous him made
On mortal thyng, and as yow list, ay ye
Yeve hym in love ese or adversitee,

1732 **inward:** on the way in (or, privately)
1733 **conjure:** implore   **heighly yow defende:** strictly forbid you
1734 **On his half:** on his behalf
1735 And in the power of two crowns (the sense is obscure)
1738 **com of:** come on, hurry up
1739 **taried tyde:** time spent in delaying
1741–42 **devyneth noon Upon yow:** no one suspects anything about you
1743 **blent:** deceived

Incipit, *etc.:* Here begins the prologue of the third book.
2 **thridde heven:** the third planetary sphere, that of Venus (Jove's daughter)
3 **sonnes lief:** beloved of the sun
5 **repaire:** go
7 **Iheryed:** praised

1744 **titeryng:** vacillation, hesitation   **pursuyte:** (prolonged) suing, entreating
1745 People conjecture about, find meaning in, the moving of a straw
1746 **wolde han after:** desire afterwards to have
1749 **Las:** alas
1752 **kankedort:** difficult situation (?); see n.
1754 **sort:** lot, destiny
Explicit, *etc.:* Here ends the second book.

---

11 **in tymes:** at (certain) seasons   **vapour:** influence, emanation
12 **werne:** deny (anything to love)
14 **worth:** worthy, of any value
15 **Joves:** Jove (the object of the verbs in 17)
17 **Comeveden:** moved emotionally, excited

And in a thousand formes down hym sente 20
For love in erthe, and whom yow liste he
    hente.

Ye fierse Mars apaisen of his ire,
And as yow list, ye maken hertes digne;
Algates hem that ye wol sette a-fyre,   24
They dreden shame, and vices they resygne;
Ye do hem corteys be, fresshe and benigne;
And heighe or lowe, after a wight entendeth,
The joies that he hath, youre myght it send-
    eth.

Ye holden regne and hous in unitee;
Ye sothfast cause of frendship ben also;   30
Ye knowe al thilke covered qualitee
Of thynges, which that folk on wondren so,
Whan they kan nought construe how it may jo
She loveth hym, or whi he loveth here,

As whi this fissh, and naught that, comth to
    were.   35

Ye folk a lawe han set in universe,
And this knowe I by hem that lovers be,
That whoso stryveth with yow hath the werse.
Now, lady bryght, for thi benignite,
At reverence of hem that serven the,   40
Whos clerc I am, so techeth me devyse
Som joye of that is felt in thi servyse.

Ye in my naked herte sentement
Inhielde, and do me shewe of thy swetnesse.
Caliope, thi vois be now present,   45
For now is nede: sestow nought my destresse,
How I mot telle anonright the gladnesse
Of Troilus, to Venus heryinge?
To which gladnesse, who nede hath, God hym
    brynge!

Explicit prohemium tercii libri.

Incipit liber tercius.

Lay al this mene while Troilus,   50
Recordyng his lesson in this manere:
"Mafay," thoughte he, "thus wol I sey, and
    thus;
Thus wol I pleyne unto my lady dere;
That word is good, and this shal be my cheere;
This nyl I nought foryeten in no wise."   55
God leve hym werken as he kan devyse!

And, Lord, so that his herte gan to quappe,
Heryng hire come, and shorte for to sike!
And Pandarus, that ledde hire by the lappe,
Com ner, and gan in at the curtyn pike,   60
And seyde, "God do boot on alle syke!
Se who is here yow comen to visite:
Lo, here is she that is youre deth to wite."

Therwith it semed as he wepte almost.
"Ha, a," quod Troilus so reufully,   65
"Wher me be wo, O myghty God, thow woost!
Who is al ther? I se nought trewely."
"Sire," quod Criseyde, "it is Pandare and I."
"Ye, swete herte? Allas, I may nought rise,
To knele and do yow honour in som wyse."   70

And dressed hym upward, and she right tho
Gan bothe hire hondes softe upon hym leye.
"O, for the love of God, do ye nought so
To me," quod she, "I! What is this to seye?
Sire, comen am I to yow for causes tweye: 75
First, yow to thonke, and of youre lordshipe eke
Continuance I wolde yow biseke."

This Troilus, that herde his lady preye
Of lordshipe hym, wax neither quyk ne ded,

---

20 **formes:** the forms (bull, swan, etc.) that Jove adopted to court his loves
24 **Algates:** always, at any rate
25 **resygne:** reject
27 **after a wight entendeth:** as a person wishes
30 **sothfast:** true
31 **covered:** hidden (inner)
33 **jo:** happen (?)

Incipit, *etc.:* Here begins the third book.
52 **Mafay:** by my faith
57 **so that:** how   **quappe:** beat
59 **lappe:** fold or hem of a garment
60 **curtyn:** the curtains of the canopy that encloses the bed
pike: peek
63 **youre deth to wite:** to blame for your death

---

35 **were:** weir, a trap for fish
36 **in universe:** universally
40 **At:** in
43 **sentement:** emotion, feeling
44 **Inhielde:** pour in   **do me shewe of:** make me show forth some of (i.e., inspire my verse with some of)
45 **Caliope:** Calliope, muse of epic poetry
48 **to Venus heryinge:** in praise of Venus
Explicit, *etc.:* Here ends the prologue of the third book.

---

65 **reufully:** pitifully
66 **Wher me be wo:** if I am woeful (ill)
71 **dressed hym:** raised himself
76 **lordshipe:** protection, patronage
77 **Continuance:** continued support

Ne myghte o word for shame to it seye,   80
Although men sholde smyten of his hed.
But Lord, so he wex sodeynliche red,
And sire, his lessoun, that he wende konne
To preyen hire, is thorugh his wit ironne.

Criseyde al this aspied wel ynough,   85
For she was wis, and loved hym nevere the
          lasse,
Al nere he malapert, or made it tough,
Or was to bold, to synge a fool a masse.
But whan his shame gan somwhat to passe,
His resons, as I may my rymes holde,   90
I yow wol telle, as techen bokes olde.

In chaunged vois, right for his verray drede,
Which vois ek quook, and therto his manere
Goodly abaist, and now his hewes rede,
Now pale, unto Criseyde, his lady dere,   95
With look down cast and humble iyolden chere,
Lo, the alderfirste word that hym asterte
Was, twyes, "Mercy, mercy, swete herte!"

And stynte a while, and whan he myghte out
          brynge,
The nexte word was, "God woot, for I have,
As ferforthly as I have had konnynge,   101
Ben youres al, God so my soule save,
And shal til that I, woful wight, be grave!
And though I dar, ne kan, unto yow pleyne,
Iwis, I suffre nought the lasse peyne.   105

"Thus muche as now, O wommanliche wif,
I may out brynge, and if this yow displese,
That shal I wreke upon myn owen lif
Right soone, I trowe, and do youre herte an ese,
If with my deth youre wreththe may apese.   110
But syn that ye han herd me somwhat seye,
Now recche I nevere how soone that I deye."

Therwith his manly sorwe to biholde
It myghte han mad an herte of stoon to rewe;
And Pandare wep as he to water wolde,   115

And poked evere his nece new and newe,
And seyde, "Wo bygon ben hertes trewe!
For love of God, make of this thing an ende,
Or sle us both at ones er ye wende."

"I, what?" quod she, "by God and by my
          trouthe,   120
I not nat what ye wilne that I seye."
"I, what?" quod he, "That ye han on hym
          routhe,
For Goddes love, and doth hym nought to
          deye!"
"Now than thus," quod she, "I wolde hym
          preye
To telle me the fyn of his entente.   125
Yet wist I nevere wel what that he mente."

"What that I mene, O swete herte deere?"
Quod Troilus, "O goodly, fresshe free,
That with the stremes of youre eyen cleere
Ye wolde somtyme frendly on me see,   130
And thanne agreen that I may ben he,
Withouten braunche of vice on any wise,
In trouthe alwey to don yow my servise,

"As to my lady right and chief resort,
With al my wit and al my diligence;   135
And I to han, right as yow list, comfort,
Under yowre yerde, egal to myn offence,
As deth, if that I breke youre defence;
And that ye deigne me so muchel honoure
Me to comanden aught in any houre;   140

"And I to ben youre — verray, humble, trewe,
Secret, and in my paynes pacient,
And evere mo desiren fresshly newe
To serve, and ben ylike diligent,
And with good herte al holly youre talent   145
Receyven wel, how sore that me smerte;
Lo, this mene I, myn owen swete herte."

Quod Pandarus, "Lo, here an hard requeste,
And resonable, a lady for to werne!

83 **wende konne:** thought he knew, had learned
87 Even though he was not presumptuous, nor was he too self assured, arrogant
88 **synge a fool a masse:** flatter deceptively (?); see n.
90 **resons:** speeches
94 **abaist:** abashed
96 **iyolden:** yielded (submissive)
97 **alderfirste:** very first **asterte:** escaped
101 **As ferforthly as:** insofar as
103 **grave:** buried
106 **wommanliche wif:** womanly woman (having the best feminine characteristics)
110 **wreththe:** wrath

116 **new and newe:** again and again
121 **wilne:** wish
125 **fyn of his entente:** end, object of his intentions
131 **agreen:** agree
132 **braunche:** i.e., any sort
134 **resort:** resource
137 **Under yowre yerde:** under your authority, subject to your punishment **egal:** equal, appropriate
138 **breke youre defence:** violate your prohibition
139 **deigne:** grant
141 **youre:** yours
145 **talent:** desire, inclination
146 **how:** however
149 **werne:** refuse

Now, nece myn, by natal Joves feste,   150
Were I a god, ye sholden sterve as yerne,
That heren wel this man wol nothing yerne
But youre honour, and sen hym almost sterve,
And ben so loth to suffren hym yow serve.''

With that she gan hire eyen on hym caste   155
Ful esily and ful debonairly,
Avysyng hire, and hied nought to faste
With nevere a word, but seyde hym softely,
"Myn honour sauf, I wol wel trewely,
And in swich forme as he gan now devyse,   160
Receyven hym fully to my servyse,

"Bysechyng hym, for Goddes love, that he
Wolde, in honour of trouthe and gentilesse,
As I wel mene, ek menen wel to me,
And myn honour with wit and bisynesse   165
Ay kepe; and if I may don hym gladnesse,
From hennesforth, iwys, I nyl nought feyne.
Now beth al hool; no lenger ye ne pleyne.

"But natheles, this warne I yow,'' quod she,
"A kynges sone although ye be, ywys,   170
Ye shal namore han sovereignete
Of me in love, than right in that cas is;
N'y nyl forbere, if that ye don amys,
To wratthe yow; and whil that ye me serve,
Chericen yow right after ye disserve.   175

"And shortly, deere herte and al my knyght,
Beth glad, and draweth yow to lustinesse,
And I shal trewely, with al my myght,
Youre bittre tornen al into swetenesse.
If I be she that may yow do gladnesse,   180
For every wo ye shal recovere a blisse'' —
And hym in armes took, and gan hym kisse.

Fil Pandarus on knees, and up his eyen
To heven threw, and held his hondes highe:
"Immortal god,'' quod he, "that mayst nought
          deyen,   185
Cupide I mene, of this mayst glorifie;
And Venus, thow mayst maken melodie!
Withouten hond, me semeth that in the towne,
For this merveille ich here ech belle sowne.

"But ho! namore as now of this matere;   190
For-whi this folk wol comen up anon,
That han the lettre red; lo, I hem here.
But I conjure the, Criseyde, anon,
And to, thow Troilus, whan thow mayst goon,
That at myn hous ye ben at my warnynge,   195
For I ful well shal shape youre comynge;

"And eseth there youre hertes right ynough;
And lat se which of yow shal bere the belle
To speke of love aright!'' — therwith he
          lough —
"For ther have ye a leiser for to telle.''   200
Quod Troilus, "How longe shal I dwelle,
Er this be don?'' Quod he, "Whan thow mayst
          ryse,
This thyng shal be right as I yow devyse.''

With that Eleyne and also Deiphebus   204
Tho comen upward, right at the steires ende;
And Lord, so thanne gan gronen Troilus,
His brother and his suster for to blende.
Quod Pandarus, "It tyme is that we wende.
Tak, nece myn, youre leve at alle thre,
And lat hem speke, and cometh forth with me.''

She took hire leve at hem ful thriftily,   211
As she wel koude, and they hire reverence
Unto the fulle diden, hardyly,
And wonder wel speken, in hire absence,
Of hire in preysing of hire excellence —   215
Hire governaunce, hire wit, and hire manere
Comendeden, it joie was to here.

Now lat hire wende unto hire owen place,
And torne we to Troilus ayein,
That gan ful lightly of the lettre pace   220
That Deiphebus hadde in the gardyn seyn;
And of Eleyne and hym he wolde feyn
Delivered ben, and seyde that hym leste
To slepe, and after tales have reste.

Eleyne hym kiste, and took hire leve blyve, 225
Deiphebus ek, and hom wente every wight;
And Pandarus, as faste as he may dryve,
To Troilus tho com, as lyne right,

150 **natal Joves feste:** the feast of Jupiter (?); see n.
151 **as yerne:** very quickly
152 **yerne:** yearn for, desire
167 **feyne:** feign, hold back
175 **right after:** just as
181 **recovere:** get in return
186 **glorifie:** glory in, exult

193 **conjure:** ask
194 **to:** i.e., you also
195 **warnynge:** summons
198 **bere the belle:** have first place
207 **blende:** blind, deceive
209 **at:** of
220 **pace:** go over (glance at or treat briefly)
224 **tales:** conversation
227 **dryve:** go, move

And on a paillet al that glade nyght
By Troilus he lay, with mery chere,   230
To tale; and wel was hem they were yfeere.

Whan every wight was voided but they two,
And alle the dores weren faste yshette,
To telle in short, withouten wordes mo,
This Pandarus, withouten any lette,   235
Up roos, and on his beddes syde hym sette,
And gan to speken in a sobre wyse
To Troilus, as I shal yow devyse:

"Myn alderlevest lord, and brother deere,
God woot, and thow, that it sat me so soore,
When I the saugh so langwisshyng to-yere 241
For love, of which thi wo wax alwey moore,
That I, with al my myght and al my loore,
Have evere sithen don my bisynesse
To brynge the to joye out of distresse,   245

"And have it brought to swich plit as thow
          woost,
So that thorugh me thow stondest now in weye
To faren wel; I sey it for no bost,
And wostow whi? For shame it is to seye:
For the have I bigonne a gamen pleye   250
Which that I nevere do shal eft for other,
Although he were a thousand fold my brother.

"That is to seye, for the am I bicomen,
Bitwixen game and ernest, swich a meene
As maken wommen unto men to comen;   255
Al sey I nought, thow wost wel what I meene.
For the have I my nece, of vices cleene,
So fully maad thi gentilesse triste,
That al shal ben right as thiselven liste.

"But God, that al woot, take I to witnesse, 260
That nevere I this for coveitise wroughte,
But oonly for t'abregge that distresse
For which wel neigh thow deidest, as me
          thoughte.
But, goode brother, do now as the oughte,
For Goddes love, and kep hire out of blame,
Syn thow art wys, and save alwey hire
          name.   266

"For wel thow woost, the name as yet of here
Among the peeple, as who seyth, halwed is;
For that man is unbore, I dar wel swere,
That evere wiste that she dide amys.   270
But wo is me, that I, that cause al this,
May thynken that she is my nece deere,
And I hire em, and traitour eke yfeere!

"And were it wist that I, thorugh myn engyn,
Hadde in my nece yput this fantasie,   275
To doon thi lust and holly to ben thyn,
Whi, al the world upon it wolde crie,
And seyn that I the werste trecherie
Dide in this cas, that evere was bigonne,
And she forlost, and thow right nought ywonne. 280

"Wherfore, er I wol ferther gon a pas,   281
The preie ich eft, althogh thow shuldest deye,
That privete go with us in this cas;
That is to seyn, that thow us nevere wreye;
And be nought wroth, though I the ofte preye
To holden secree swich an heigh matere,   286
For skilfull is, thow woost wel, my praiere.

"And thynk what wo ther hath bitid er this,
For makyng of avantes, as men rede;
And what meschaunce in this world yet ther
          is,   290
Fro day to day, right for that wikked dede;
For which thise wise clerkes that ben dede
Han evere yet proverbed to us yonge,
That 'firste vertu is to kepe tonge.'

"And nere it that I wilne as now t'abregge 295
Diffusioun of speche, I koude almoost
A thousand olde stories the allegge
Of wommen lost through fals and foles bost.
Proverbes kanst thiself ynowe and woost
Ayeins that vice, for to ben a labbe,   300
Al seyde men soth as often as thei gabbe.

"O tonge, allas, so often here-byforn
Hath mad ful many a lady bright of hewe
Seyd 'Weilaway, the day that I was born!'

229 **paillet:** pallet
235 **lette:** delay
239 **alderlevest:** most beloved
241 **to-yere:** this year
254 **meene:** means, intermediary
258 **triste:** trust
261 **coveitise:** greed
262 **t'abregge:** to abridge, alleviate

268 **halwed:** revered
274 **engyn:** contrivance
280 **forlost:** ruined, dishonored
281 **pas:** step
283 **privete:** secrecy
284 **wreye:** reveal
287 **skilfull:** reasonable
293 **proverbed:** told in proverbs
294 **to kepe tonge:** to hold (one's) tongue
297 **allegge:** cite
300 **labbe:** blabbermouth
301 **Al:** even if
302 **O:** one

And many a maydes sorwe for to newe;   305
And for the more part, al is untrewe
That men of yelpe, and it were brought to
        preve.
Of kynde non avauntour is to leve.

"Avauntour and a lyere, al is on;
As thus: I pose, a womman graunte me   310
Hire love, and seith that other wol she non,
And I am sworn to holden it secree,
And after I go telle it two or thre —
Iwis, I am avauntour at the leeste,
And lyere, for I breke my biheste.   315

"Now loke thanne, if they be nought to blame,
Swich manere folk — what shal I clepe hem,
        what? —
That hem avaunte of wommen, and by name,
That nevere yet bihyghte hem this ne that,
Ne knewe hem more than myn olde hat!   320
No wonder is, so God me sende hele,
Though wommen dreden with us men to dele.

"I sey nought this for no mistrust of yow,
Ne for no wis-man, but for foles nyce,
And for the harm that in the werld is now,   325
As wel for folie ofte as for malice;
For wel woot I, in wise folk that vice
No womman drat, if she be wel avised;
For wyse ben by foles harm chastised.

"But now to purpos; leve brother deere,   330
Have al this thyng that I have seyd in mynde,
And kep the clos, and be now of good cheere,
For at thi day thow shalt me trewe fynde.
I shal thi proces set in swych a kynde,
And God toforn, that it shal the suffise,   335
For it shal be right as thow wolt devyse.

"For wel I woot, thow menest wel, parde;
Therfore I dar this fully undertake.
Thow woost ek what thi lady graunted the,
And day is set the chartres up to make.   340
Have now good nyght, I may no lenger wake;
And bid for me, syn thow art now in blysse,
That God me sende deth or soone lisse."

Who myghte tellen half the joie or feste
Which that the soule of Troilus tho felte,   345
Heryng th'effect of Pandarus byheste?
His olde wo, that made his herte swelte,
Gan tho for joie wasten and tomelte,
And al the richesse of his sikes sore
At ones fledde; he felte of hem namore.   350

But right so as thise holtes and thise hayis,
That han in wynter dede ben and dreye,
Revesten hem in grene when that May is,
Whan every lusty liketh best to pleye;
Right in that selve wise, soth to seye,   355
Wax sodeynliche his herte ful of joie,
That gladder was ther nevere man in Troie.

And gan his look on Pandarus up caste
Ful sobrely, and frendly for to se,
And seyde, "Frend, in Aperil the laste —   360
As wel thow woost, if it remembre the —
How neigh the deth for wo thow fownde me,
And how thow dedest al thi bisynesse
To knowe of me the cause of my destresse.

"Thow woost how longe ich it forbar to seye
To the, that art the man that I best triste;   366
And peril non was it to the bywreye,
That wist I wel; but telle me, if the liste,
Sith I so loth was that thiself it wiste,
How dorst I mo tellen of this matere,   370
That quake now, and no wight may us here?

"But natheles, by that God I the swere,
That, as hym list, may al this world governe —
And, if I lye, Achilles with his spere
Myn herte cleve, al were my lif eterne,   375
As I am mortal, if I late or yerne
Wolde it bewreye, or dorst, or sholde konne,
For al the good that God made under sonne —

"That rather deye I wolde, and determyne,
As thynketh me, now stokked in prisoun,   380
In wrecchidnesse, in filthe, and in vermyne,
Caytif to cruel kyng Agamenoun;

305 **newe:** renew
307 **yelpe:** boast
310 **pose:** posit, suppose for the sake of argument
328 **drat** = *dredeth*, fears
329 **chastised:** admonished, warned
332 **kep the clos:** keep (it) to yourself
338 **undertake:** assert
340 **the chartres up to make:** draw up the documents, close the deal
342 **bid:** pray **blysse:** in a state of bliss, in heaven (where, like a saint, you can intercede for me)
343 **lisse:** comfort

347 **swelte:** grow faint
348 **tomelte:** melt away
349 **richesse:** abundance
351 **holtes:** groves, woods **hayis:** hedges
355 **selve:** selfsame
367 **bywreye:** reveal
370 **mo:** others
374 **Achilles:** the Greek hero
376 **yerne:** early
379 **determyne:** come to an end
380 **stokked:** put in the stocks, imprisoned
382 **Caytif to:** captive of **Agamenoun:** Agamemnon, Helen's husband and leader of the Greek army

And this in all the temples of this town
Upon the goddes alle, I wol the swere
To-morwe day, if that it liketh here. 385

"And that thow hast so muche ido for me
That I ne may it nevere more disserve,
This know I wel, al myghte I now for the
A thousand tymes on a morwe sterve.
I kan namore, but that I wol the serve 390
Right as thi sclave, whider so thow wende,
For evere more, unto my lyves ende.

"But here, with al myn herte, I the biseche
That nevere in me thow deme swich folie
As I shal seyn: me thoughte by thi speche 395
That this which thow me dost for compaignie,
I sholde wene it were a bauderye.
I am nought wood, al if I lewed be!
It is nought so, that woot I wel, parde!

"But he that gooth for gold or for ricchesse
On swich message, calle hym what the list; 401
And this that thow doost, calle it gentilesse,
Compassioun, and felawship, and trist.
Departe it so, for wyde-wher is wist
How that ther is diversite requered 405
Bytwixen thynges like, as I have lered.

"And that thow knowe I thynke nought ne
      wene
That this servise a shame be or jape,
I have my faire suster Polixene,
Cassandre, Eleyne, or any of the frape — 410
Be she nevere so fair or wel yshape,
Tel me which thow wilt of everychone,
To han for thyn, and lat me thanne allone.

"But, sith thow hast don me this servyse
My lif to save and for non hope of mede, 415
So for the love of God, this grete emprise
Perfourme it out, for now is moste nede;
For heigh and lough, withowten any drede,
I wol alwey thyn hestes alle kepe.
Have now good nyght, and lat us bothe slepe."

Thus held hym ech of other wel apayed, 421
That al the world ne myghte it bet amende;
And on the morwe, whan they were arayed,
Ech to his owen nedes gan entende.
But Troilus, though as the fir he brende 425
For sharp desir of hope and of plesaunce,
He nought forgat his goode governaunce,

But in hymself with manhod gan restreyne
Ech racle dede and ech unbridled cheere,
That alle tho that lyven, soth to seyne, 430
Ne sholde han wist, by word or by manere,
What that he mente, as touchyng this matere.
From every wight as fer as is the cloude
He was, so wel dissimilen he koude.

And al the while which that I yow devyse, 435
This was his lif: with all his fulle myght,
By day, he was in Martes heigh servyse —
This is to seyn, in armes as a knyght;
And for the more part, the longe nyght 439
He lay and thoughte how that he myghte serve
His lady best, hire thonk for to deserve.

Nil I naught swere, although he lay ful softe,
That in his thought he nas somwhat disesed,
Ne that he torned on his pilwes ofte, 444
And wold of that hym missed han ben sesed.
But in swich cas men is nought alwey plesed,
For aught I woot, namore than was he;
That kan I deme of possibilitee.

But certeyn is, to purpos for to go,
That in this while, as writen is in geeste, 450
He say his lady somtyme, and also
She with hym spak, whan that she dorst or
      leste;
And by hire bothe avys, as was the beste,
Apoynteden full warly in this nede,
So as they durste, how they wolde procede. 455

But it was spoken in so short a wise,
In swich await alwey, and in swich feere,
Lest any wight devynen or devyse
Wolde of hem two, or to it laye an ere,
That al this world so leef to hem ne were 460
As that Cupide wolde hem grace sende
To maken of hire speche aright an ende.

---

385 **To-morwe day:** tomorrow morning **here:** her
391 **sclave:** slave **whider so:** wherever
396 **compaignie:** companionship, friendship
397 **bauderye:** pandering
401 **message:** an errand
403 **trist:** trust
404 **Departe it:** make the distinction (i.e., be clear about this)
wyde-wher: far and wide
410 **frape:** company
413 **and lat me thanne allone:** and leave me to arrange it alone
415 **mede:** reward
417 **Perfourme it out:** carry it out
418 **For heigh and lough:** regardless of anything

421 **apayed:** pleased
429 **racle:** hasty
444 **pilwes:** pillows
445 **sesed:** put in possession
450 **while:** time
454 **Apoynteden:** decided, arranged things **warly:** prudently
457 **await:** watchfulness
458 **devyse:** imagine, conjecture

But thilke litel that they spake or wroughte,
His wise goost took ay of al swych heede,
It semed hire he wiste what she thoughte   465
Withouten word, so that it was no nede
To bidde hym ought to doon, or ought for-
        beede;
For which she thought that love, al come it
        late,
Of alle joie hadde opned hire the yate.

And shortly of this proces for to pace,   470
So wel his werk and wordes he bisette,
That he so ful stood in his lady grace,
That twenty thousand tymes, er she lette,
She thonked God that evere she with hym
        mette.
So koude he hym governe in swich servyse,   475
That al the world ne myght it bet devyse.

For whi she fond hym so discret in al,
So secret, and of swich obëisaunce,
That wel she felte he was to hire a wal
Of stiel, and sheld from every displesaunce;
That to ben in his goode governaunce,   481
So wis he was, she was namore afered —
I mene, as fer as oughte ben requered.

And Pandarus, to quike alwey the fir,
Was evere ylike prest and diligent;   485
To ese his frend was set al his desir.
He shof ay on, he to and fro was sent;
He lettres bar whan Troilus was absent;
That nevere man, as in his frendes nede,
Ne bar hym bet than he, withouten drede.   490

But now, paraunter, som man wayten wolde
That every word, or soonde, or look, or cheere
Of Troilus that I rehercen sholde,
In al this while unto his lady deere —
I trowe it were a long thyng for to here —   495
Or of what wight that stant in swich disjoynte,
His wordes alle, or every look, to poynte.

For sothe, I have naught herd it don er this
In story non, ne no man here, I wene;
And though I wolde, I koude nought, ywys;

For ther was som epistel hem bitwene,   501
That wolde, as seyth myn autour, wel contene
Neigh half this book, of which hym liste nought
        write.
How sholde I thanne a lyne of it endite?

But to the grete effect: than sey I thus,   505
That stondyng in concord and in quiete,
Thise ilke two, Criseyde and Troilus,
As I have told, and in this tyme swete —
Save only often myghte they nought mete,
Ne leiser have hire speches to fulfelle —   510
That it bifel right as I shal yow telle:

That Pandarus, that evere dide his myght
Right for the fyn that I shal speke of here,
As for to bryngen to his hows som nyght
His faire nece and Troilus yfere,   515
Wheras at leiser al this heighe matere,
Touchyng here love, were at the fulle up-
        bounde,
Hadde out of doute a tyme to it founde.

For he with gret deliberacioun
Hadde every thyng that herto myght availle
Forncast and put in execucioun,   521
And neither left for cost ne for travaille.
Come if hem list, hem sholde no thyng faille;
And for to ben in ought aspied there,
That, wiste he wel, an impossible were.   525

Dredeles, it cler was in the wynd
Of every pie and every lette-game;
Now al is wel, for al the world is blynd
In this matere, bothe fremde and tame.
This tymbur is al redy up to frame;   530
Us lakketh nought but that we witen wolde
A certeyn houre, in which she comen sholde.

And Troilus, that al this purveiaunce
Knew at the fulle, and waited on it ay,
Hadde hereupon ek mad gret ordinaunce,
And found his cause, and therto his aray,   536
If that he were missed, nyght or day,

464 **goost:** spirit, mind
469 **yate:** gate
471 **bisette:** applied
484 **quike:** quicken
485 **prest:** ready
487 **shof:** pressed
491 **wayten:** expect
496 **what wight:** whatever person, anyone   **disjoynte:** difficulty
497 **poynte:** describe, specify

502 **contene:** fill
510 **fulfelle:** complete
517 **upbounde:** bound up, concluded
521 **Forncast:** planned
522 **left:** left anything undone
525 **an impossible:** an impossibility
526 **cler was in the wynd:** downwind, safe from discovery
527 **pie:** magpie, chatterbox   **lette-game:** spoilsport
529 **fremde and tame:** wild and tame (i.e., every creature)
536 **aray:** preparations

Ther-while he was aboute this servyse,
That he was gon to don his sacrifise,

And moste at swich a temple allone wake,   540
Answered of Apollo for to be;
And first to sen the holy laurer quake,
Er that Apollo spak out of the tree,
To telle hym next whan Grekes sholde flee —
And forthy lette hym no man, God forbede,   545
But prey Apollo helpen in this nede.

Now is ther litel more for to doone,
But Pandare up and, shortly for to seyne,
Right sone upon the chaungynge of the moone,
Whan lightles is the world a nyght or
   tweyne,   550
And that the wolken shop hym for to reyne,
He streght o morwe unto his nece wente —
Ye han wel herd the fyn of his entente.

Whan he was com, he gan anon to pleye
As he was wont, and of hymself to jape;   555
And finaly he swor and gan hire seye,
By this and that, she sholde hym nought es-
   cape,
Ne lenger don hym after hire to cape;
But certeynly she moste, by hire leve,
Come soupen in his hous with hym at eve.   560

At which she lough, and gan hire faste excuse,
And seyde, "It reyneth; lo, how sholde I gon?"
"Lat be," quod he, "ne stant nought thus to
   muse.
This moot be don! Ye shal be ther anon."
So at the laste herof they fille aton,   565
Or elles, softe he swor hire in hire ere,
He nolde nevere comen ther she were.

Soone after this, she to hym gan to rowne,
And axed hym if Troilus were there.
He swor hire nay, for he was out of towne,   570
And seyde, "Nece, I pose that he were;
Yow thurste nevere han the more fere;

For rather than men myghte hym ther aspie,
Me were levere a thousand fold to dye."

Nought list myn auctour fully to declare   575
What that she thoughte whan he seyde so,
That Troilus was out of towne yfare,
As if he seyde therof soth or no;
But that, withowten await, with hym to go,
She graunted hym, sith he hire that bisoughte,
And, as his nece, obeyed as hire oughte.   581

But natheles, yet gan she hym biseche,
Although with hym to gon it was no fere,
For to ben war of goosissh poeples speche,
That dremen thynges whiche as nevere
   were,   585
And wel avyse hym whom he broughte there;
And seyde hym, "Em, syn I moste on yow triste,
Loke al be wel, and do now as yow liste."

He swor hire yis, by stokkes and by stones,
And by the goddes that in hevene dwelle,   590
Or elles were hym levere, soule and bones,
With Pluto kyng as depe ben in helle
As Tantalus — what sholde I more telle?
Whan al was wel, he roos and took his leve,
And she to soper com, whan it was eve,   595

With a certein of hire owen men,
And with hire faire nece Antigone,
And other of hire wommen nyne or ten.
But who was glad now, who, as trowe ye,
But Troilus, that stood and myght it se   600
Thoroughout a litel wyndow in a stewe,
Ther he bishet syn mydnyght was in mewe,

Unwist of every wight but of Pandare?
But to the point: now whan that she was come,
With alle joie and alle frendes fare   605
Hire em anon in armes hath hire nome,
And after to the soper, alle and some,
Whan tyme was, ful softe they hem sette.
God woot, ther was no deynte for to fette!

---

533 **Ther-while:** the while that, while
542 **laurer:** laurel, sacred to Apollo
549 **chaungynge of the moone:** new moon, its invisible phase
(i.e., a dark night)
551 **wolken shop hym:** sky prepared itself
552 **o morwe:** in the morning
558 **after hire to cape:** hunt (gape) after her
563 **ne stant** = ne stondeth, do not stand
565 **aton:** at one, in agreement
568 **rowne:** whisper
571 **pose:** posit, suppose for the sake of argument
572 **thurste:** need

579 **await:** delay
584 **goosissh:** goose-like, silly
587 **moste:** must (?); see n.   **on yow triste:** trust in you
589 **by stokkes and by stones:** by tree stumps and stones (i.e.,
objects of pagan worship)
592 **Pluto:** god of the underworld
593 **Tantalus:** eternally punished in hell; cf. Bo 3. m12.38–40.
596 **a certein:** a certain number of
601 **stewe:** small room, closet (not necessarily heated)
602 Where he had been shut up in hiding since midnight
605 **frendes fare:** friendly ceremonial
606 **nome:** taken
609 **was no deynte for to fette:** no fine food was lacking

And after soper gonnen they to rise,   610
At ese wel, with herte fresshe and glade;
And wel was hym that koude best devyse
To liken hire, or that hire laughen made:
He song; she pleyde; he tolde tale of Wade.
But at the laste, as every thyng hath ende,   615
She took hire leve, and nedes wolde wende.

But O Fortune, executrice of wierdes,
O influences of thise hevenes hye!
Soth is, that under God ye ben oure hierdes,
Though to us bestes ben the causez wrie.   620
This mene I now: for she gan homward hye,
But execut was al bisyde hire leve
The goddes wil, for which she moste bleve.

The bente moone with hire hornes pale,
Saturne, and Jove, in Cancro joyned were,   625
That swych a reyn from heven gan avale
That every maner womman that was there
Hadde of that smoky reyn a verray feere;
At which Pandare tho lough, and seyde thenne,
"Now were it tyme a lady to gon henne!   630

"But goode nece, if I myghte evere plese
Yow any thyng, than prey ich yow," quod he,
"To don myn herte as now so gret an ese
As for to dwelle here al this nyght with me,
For-whi this is youre owen hous, parde.   635
For by my trouthe, I sey it nought a-game,
To wende as now, it were to me a shame."

Criseyde, which that koude as muche good
As half a world, took hede of his preiere;
And syn it ron, and al was on a flod,   640
She thoughte, "As good chep may I dwellen
    here,
And graunte it gladly with a frendes chere,
And have a thonk, as grucche and thanne abide;
For hom to gon, it may nought wel bitide."

"I wol," quod she, "myn uncle lief and deere;
Syn that yow list, it skile is to be so.   646

I am right glad with yow to dwellen here;
I seyde but a-game I wolde go."
"Iwys, graunt mercy, nece," quod he tho,
"Were it a game or no, soth for to telle,   650
Now am I glad, syn that yow list to dwelle."

Thus al is wel; but tho bigan aright
The newe joie and al the feste agayn.
But Pandarus, if goodly hadde he myght,
He wolde han hyed hire to bedde fayn,   655
And seyde, "Lord, this is an huge rayn!
This were a weder for to slepen inne —
And that I rede us soone to bygynne.

"And nece, woot ye wher I wol yow leye,
For that we shul nat liggen far asonder,   660
And for ye neither shullen, dar I seye,
Heren noyse of reynes nor of thonder?
By God, right in my litel closet yonder.
And I wol in that outer hous allone
Be wardein of youre wommen everichone.   665

"And in this myddel chaumbre that ye se
Shal youre wommen slepen, wel and softe;
And there I seyde shal youreselven be;
And if ye liggen wel to-nyght, com ofte,
And careth nought what weder is alofte.   670
The wyn anon, and whan so that yow leste,
So go we slepe: I trowe it be the beste."

Ther nys no more, but hereafter soone,
The voide dronke, and travers drawe anon,   674
Gan every wight that hadde nought to done
More in the place out of the chaumbre gon.
And evere mo so sterneliche it ron,
And blew therwith so wondirliche loude,
That wel neigh no man heren other koude.   679

Tho Pandarus, hire em, right as hym oughte,
With wommen swiche as were hire most aboute,
Ful glad unto hire beddes syde hire broughte,
And took his leve, and gan ful lowe loute,
And seyde, "Here at this closet dore withoute,
Right overthwart, youre wommen liggen alle,
That whom yow list of hem ye may here
    calle."   686

614 **Wade:** a legendary hero; see n.
617 **executrice of wierdes:** she who carries out (the plan of)
the Fates
618 **influences:** astrological influences
619 **hierdes:** shepherds
620 **wrie:** concealed, hidden
621 **hye:** hasten
622 **execut:** done   **bisyde hire leve:** without her leave
623 **bleve:** remain
625 The planets Saturn and Jupiter (*Jove*) were in conjunction
(*joyned*) in the zodiacal sign of Cancer.
626 **avale:** come down
636 **a-game:** in sport, as a joke
640 **ron:** rained
641 **As good chep:** as good a bargain (i.e., I might as well)
643 **grucche:** complain

654 But Pandarus, if he could decently have done so
663 **closet:** bedroom
664 **outer hous:** curtained part of the great hall near the door
665 **wardein:** guardian
674 **voide:** wine taken before retiring   **travers:** a screen or
curtain (dividing the room)
677 **sterneliche:** violently   **ron:** rained
681 **most aboute:** closest (i.e., her personal attendants)
683 **loute:** bow down
685 **Right overthwart:** directly opposite (the door)

So whan that she was in the closet leyd,
And alle hire wommen forth by ordinaunce
Abedde weren, ther as I have seyd,
There was nomore to skippen nor to traunce,
But boden go to bedde, with meschaunce,   691
If any wight was steryng anywhere,
And lat hem slepen that abedde were.

But Pandarus, that wel koude ech a deel
Th'olde daunce, and every point therinne,   695
Whan that he sey that alle thyng was wel,
He thought he wolde upon his werk bigynne,
And gan the stuwe doore al softe unpynne;
And stille as stoon, withouten lenger lette,
By Troilus adown right he hym sette,   700

And shortly to the point right for to gon,
Of al this werk he tolde hym word and ende,
And seyde, "Make the redy right anon,
For thow shalt into hevene blisse wende."
"Now, blisful Venus, thow me grace sende!"
Quod Troilus, "For nevere yet no nede   706
Hadde ich er now, ne halvendel the drede."

Quod Pandarus, "Ne drede the nevere a deel,
For it shal be right as thow wolt desire;
So thryve I, this nyght shal I make it weel,   710
Or casten al the gruwel in the fire."
"Yet, blisful Venus, this nyght thow me en-
        spire,"
Quod Troilus, "As wys as I the serve,
And evere bet and bet shal, til I sterve.

"And if ich hadde, O Venus ful of myrthe,   715
Aspectes badde of Mars or of Saturne,
Or thow combust or let were in my birthe,
Thy fader prey al thilke harm disturne
Of grace, and that I glad ayein may turne,   719

For love of hym thow lovedest in the shawe —
I meene Adoun, that with the boor was slawe.

"O Jove ek, for the love of faire Europe,
The which in forme of bole awey thow fette,
Now help! O Mars, thow with thi blody cope,
For love of Cipris, thow me nought ne lette!   725
O Phebus, thynk whan Dane hireselven shette
Under the bark, and laurer wax for drede;
Yet for hire love, O help now at this nede!

"Mercurie, for the love of Hierse eke,
For which Pallas was with Aglawros wroth,   730
Now help! And ek Diane, I the biseke
That this viage be nought to the looth!
O fatal sustren which, er any cloth
Me shapen was, my destine me sponne,
So helpeth to this werk that is bygonne!"   735

Quod Pandarus, "Thow wrecched mouses herte,
Artow agast so that she wol the bite?
Wy! Don this furred cloke upon thy sherte,
And folwe me, for I wol have the wite.
But bid, and lat me gon biforn a lite."   740
And with that word he gan undon a trappe,
And Troilus he brought in by the lappe.

The sterne wynd so loude gan to route
That no wight oother noise myghte heere;
And they that layen at the dore withoute,   745
Ful sikerly they slepten alle yfere;
And Pandarus, with a ful sobre cheere,
Goth to the dore anon, withouten lette,
There as they laye, and softely it shette.

And as he com ayeynward pryvely,   750
His nece awook, and axed, "Who goth there?"
"My dere nece," quod he, "it am I.
Ne wondreth nought, ne have of it no fere."

And ner he com and seyde hire in hire ere,
"No word, for love of God, I yow biseche!   755
Lat no wight risen and heren of oure speche."

"What, which wey be ye comen, benedicite?"
Quod she; "And how, unwist of hem alle?"
"Here at this secre trappe-dore," quod he.   759
Quod tho Criseyde, "Lat me som wight calle!"
"I! God forbede that it sholde falle,"
Quod Pandarus, "that ye swich folye wroughte!
They myghte demen thyng they nevere er
     thoughte.

"It is nought good a slepyng hound to wake,
Ne yeve a wight a cause to devyne: 765
Youre wommen slepen alle, I undertake,
So that, for hem, the hous men myghte myne,
And slepen wollen til the sonne shyne.
And whan my tale brought is to an ende,
Unwist, right as I com, so wol I wende.   770

"Now, nece myn, ye shul wel understonde,"
Quod he, "so as ye wommen demen alle,
That for to holde in love a man in honde,
And hym hire lief and deere herte calle,
And maken hym an howve above a calle —   775
I meene, as love another in this while —
She doth hireself a shame and hym a gyle.

"Now, wherby that I telle yow al this:
Ye woot yourself, as wel as any wight,
How that youre love al fully graunted is   780
To Troilus, the worthieste knyght,
Oon of this world, and therto trouthe yplight,
That, but it were on hym along, ye nolde
Hym nevere falsen while ye lyven sholde.

"Now stant it thus, that sith I fro yow wente,
This Troilus, right platly for to seyn,   786
Is thorugh a goter, by a pryve wente,
Into my chaumbre come in al this reyn,
Unwist of every manere wight, certeyn,
Save of myself, as wisly have I joye,   790
And by that feith I shal Priam of Troie.

"And he is come in swich peyne and distresse
That, but he be al fully wood by this,
He sodeynly mot falle into wodnesse,
But if God helpe; and cause whi this is: 795
He seith hym told is of a frend of his,
How that ye sholden love oon hatte Horaste;
For sorwe of which this nyght shal ben his
     laste."

Criseyde, which that al this wonder herde,
Gan sodeynly aboute hire herte colde,   800
And with a sik she sorwfully answerde,
"Allas! I wende, whoso tales tolde,
My deere herte wolde me nought holde
So lightly fals! Allas, conceytes wronge,
What harm they don! For now lyve I to longe!

"Horaste! Allas, and falsen Troilus?   806
I knowe hym nought, God helpe me so!" quod
     she.
"Allas, what wikked spirit tolde hym thus?
Now certes, em, tomorwe and I hym se,
I shal therof as ful excusen me,   810
As evere dide womman, if hym like."
And with that word she gan ful soore sike.

"O God," quod she, "so worldly selynesse,
Which clerkes callen fals felicitee,
Imedled is with many a bitternesse!   815
Ful angwissous than is, God woot," quod she,
"Condicioun of veyn prosperitee:
For either joies comen nought yfeere,
Or elles no wight hath hem alwey here.

"O brotel wele of mannes joie unstable!   820
With what wight so thow be, or how thow
     pleye,
Either he woot that thow, joie, art muable,
Or woot it nought; it mot ben oon of tweye.
Now if he woot it nought, how may he seye
That he hath verray joie and selynesse,   825
That is of ignoraunce ay in derknesse?

"Now if he woot that joie is transitorie,
As every joie of worldly thyng mot flee,
Than every tyme he that hath in memorie,

765 **devyne:** make conjectures
767 **myne:** undermine (as in a siege)
773 **holde . . . in honde:** put off, tease with false promises
775 **And make him a hood over a cap** (i.e., deceive him)
777 **gyle:** deception
781–82 **the worthieste knyght, Oon of this world:** the most worthy knight of this world
783 **on hym along:** due to him, his fault
786 **platly:** flatly, bluntly
787 **goter:** eavestrough (?); see n.   **pryve wente:** secret passage
791 **shal:** owe

797 **sholden:** are said to   **hatte:** called
800 **colde:** grow cold
804 **lightly:** easily, without good reason   **conceytes:** ideas
813 **selynesse:** happiness
815 **Imedled:** mixed together
816 **angwissous:** painful
820 **brotel:** fragile
822 **muable:** mutable

The drede of lesyng maketh hym that he   830
May in no perfit selynesse be;
And if to lese his joie he sette a myte,
Than semeth it that joie is worth ful lite.

"Wherfore I wol diffyne in this matere,
That trewely, for aught I kan espie,   835
Ther is no verray weele in this world heere.
But O thow wikked serpent, jalousie,
Thow mysbyleved envyous folie,
Why hastow Troilus mad to me untriste,
That nevere yet agylte hym, that I wiste?"   840

Quod Pandarus, "Thus fallen is this cas —"
"Wy! Uncle myn," quod she, "who tolde hym
          this?
Why doth my deere herte thus, allas?"
"Ye woot, ye, nece myn," quod he, "what is.
I hope al shal be wel that is amys,   845
For ye may quenche al this, if that yow leste —
And doth right so, for I holde it the beste."

"So shal I do to-morwe, ywys," quod she,
"And God toforn, so that it shal suffise."
"To-morwe? Allas, that were a fair!" quod he;
"Nay, nay, it may nat stonden in this wise,   851
For, nece myn, thus writen clerkes wise,
That peril is with drecchyng in ydrawe;
Nay, swiche abodes ben nought worth an hawe.

"Nece, alle thyng hath tyme, I dar avowe;   855
For whan a chaumbre afire is or an halle,
Wel more nede is, it sodeynly rescowe
Than to dispute and axe amonges alle
How this candel in the strawe is falle.
A, benedicite! For al among that fare   860
The harm is don, and fare-wel feldefare!

"And nece myn — ne take it naught agrief —
If that ye suffre hym al nyght in this wo,
God help me so, ye hadde hym nevere lief!
That dar I seyn, now ther is but we two.   865

But wel I woot that ye wol nat do so;
Ye ben to wys to doon so gret folie,
To putte his lif al nyght in jupertie."

"Hadde I hym nevere lief? by God, I weene
Ye hadde nevere thyng so lief!" quod she.   870
"Now by my thrift," quod he, "that shal be
          seene!
For syn ye make this ensaumple of me,
If ich al nyght wolde hym in sorwe se,
For al the tresour in the town of Troie,
I bidde God I nevere mote have joie.   875

"Now loke thanne, if ye that ben his love
Shul putte his lif al night in jupertie
For thyng of nought, now by that God above,
Naught oonly this delay comth of folie,
But of malice, if that I shal naught lie.   880
What! Platly, and ye suffre hym in destresse,
Ye neyther bounte don ne gentilesse."

Quod tho Criseyde, "Wol ye don o thyng
And ye therwith shal stynte al his disese?   884
Have heere, and bereth hym this blewe ryng,
For ther is nothyng myghte hym bettre plese,
Save I myself, ne more hys herte apese;
And sey my deere herte that his sorwe
Is causeles; that shal be sene to-morwe."

"A ryng?" quod he, "Ye haselwodes shaken!
Ye, nece myn, that ryng moste han a stoon   891
That myghte dede men alyve maken;
And swich a ryng trowe I that ye have non.
Discrecioun out of youre hed is gon;
That fele I now," quod he, "and that is routhe.
O tyme ilost, wel maistow corsen slouthe!   896

"Woot ye not wel that noble and heigh corage
Ne sorweth nought, ne stynteth ek, for lite?
But if a fool were in a jalous rage,
I nolde setten at his sorwe a myte,   900
But feffe hym with a fewe wordes white
Anothir day, whan that I myghte hym fynde;
But this thyng stant al in another kynde.

"This is so gentil and so tendre of herte   904
That with his deth he wol his sorwes wreke;

For trusteth wel, how sore that hym smerte,
He wol to yow no jalous wordes speke.
And forthi, nece, er that his herte breke,
So speke youreself to hym of this matere,
For with o word ye may his herte stere.   910

"Now have I told what peril he is inne,
And his comynge unwist is to every wight;
Ne, parde, harm may ther be non, ne synne:
I wol myself be with yow al this nyght.
Ye knowe ek how it is youre owen knyght,   915
And that bi right ye moste upon hym triste,
And I al prest to fecche hym whan yow liste."

This accident so pitous was to here,
And ek so like a sooth at prime face,
And Troilus hire knyght to hir so deere,   920
His prive comyng, and the siker place,
That though that she did hym as thanne a
                                    grace,
Considered alle thynges as they stoode,
No wonder is, syn she did al for goode.

Criseyde answerde, "As wisly God at reste 925
My soule brynge, as me is for hym wo!
And em, iwis, fayn wolde I don the beste,
If that ich hadde grace to do so;
But whether that ye dwelle or for hym go,
I am, til God me bettre mynde sende,   930
At dulcarnoun, right at my wittes ende."

Quod Pandarus, "Yee, nece, wol ye here?
Dulcarnoun called is 'flemyng of wrecches':
It semeth hard, for wrecches wol nought lere,
For verray slouthe or other wilfull tecches; 935
This seyd by hem that ben nought worth two
                                    fecches;
But ye ben wis, and that we han on honde
Nis neither hard, ne skilful to withstonde."

"Than, em," quod she, "doth herof as yow list.
But er he com, I wil up first arise,   940
And for the love of God, syn al my trist
Is on yow two, and ye ben bothe wise,

So werketh now in so discret a wise
That I honour may have, and he plesaunce:
For I am here al in youre governaunce."   945

"That is wel seyd," quod he, "my nece deere.
Ther good thrift on that wise gentil herte!
But liggeth stille, and taketh hym right here —
It nedeth nought no ferther for hym sterte.
And ech of yow ese otheres sorwes smerte,   950
For love of God! And Venus, I the herye;
For soone hope I we shul ben alle merye."

This Troilus ful soone on knees hym sette
Ful sobrely, right be hyre beddes hed,
And in his beste wyse his lady grette.   955
But Lord, so she wex sodeynliche red!
Ne though men sholde smyten of hire hed,
She kouthe nought a word aright out brynge
So sodeynly, for his sodeyn comynge.

But Pandarus, that so wel koude feele   960
In every thyng, to pleye anon bigan,
And seyde, "Nece, se how this lord kan knele!
Now for youre trouthe, se this gentil man!"
And with that word he for a quysshen ran,   964
And seyde, "Kneleth now, while that yow leste;
There God youre hertes brynge soone at reste!"

Kan I naught seyn, for she bad hym nought
                                    rise,
If sorwe it putte out of hire remembraunce,
Or elles that she took it in the wise
Of dewete, as for his observaunce;   970
But wel fynde I she dede hym this plesaunce,
That she hym kiste, although she siked sore,
And bad hym sitte adown withouten more.

Quod Pandarus, "Now wol ye wel bigynne.
Now doth hym sitte, goode nece deere,   975
Upon youre beddes syde al ther withinne,
That ech of yow the bet may other heere."
And with that word he drow hym to the feere,
And took a light, and fond his contenaunce,
As for to looke upon an old romaunce.   980

Criseyde, that was Troilus lady right,
And cler stood on a ground of sikernesse,

910 **stere:** steer (control)
917 **prest:** ready
918 **accident:** occurrence
919 **at prime face:** at first sight, on the surface
931 **At dulcarnoun:** in a state of perplexity (as if confronted
with a difficult theorem in geometry)
933 **flemyng of wrecches:** banishment of wretches, a name for a
difficult Euclidean proposition (which wretched dunces cannot
learn)
tecches: faults, blemishes
936 **This** = *this is* **by:** about **fecches:** vetches (beans)

947 **Ther good thrift on:** good luck to (*ther* is not translated)
951 **herye:** praise
957 **of:** off
964 **quysshen:** cushion
970 **dewete:** an honor due (her)
976 **withinne:** within the curtains of the canopied bed
978 **feere:** fire
979 **fond his contenaunce:** assumed the attitude or appearance

Al thoughte she hire servant and hire knyght
Ne sholde of right non untrouthe in hire gesse,
Yet natheles, considered his distresse,   985
And that love is in cause of swich folie,
Thus to hym spak she of his jalousie:

"Lo, herte myn, as wolde the excellence
Of love, ayeins the which that no man may —
Ne oughte ek — goodly make resistence,   990
And ek bycause I felte wel and say
Youre grete trouthe and servise every day,
And that youre herte al myn was, soth to seyne,
This drof me for to rewe upon youre peyne.

"And youre goodnesse have I founde alwey yit,
Of which, my deere herte and al my knyght, 996
I thonke it yow, as fer as I have wit,
Al kan I nought as muche as it were right;
And I, emforth my connyng and my might,
Have and ay shal, how sore that me smerte,   1000
Ben to yow trewe and hool with al myn herte,

"And dredeles, that shal be founde at preve.
But, herte myn, what al this is to seyne
Shal wel be told, so that ye nought yow greve,
Though I to yow right on youreself compleyne,
For therwith mene I fynaly the peyne   1006
That halt youre herte and myn in hevynesse
Fully to slen, and every wrong redresse.

"My goode myn, noot I for-why ne how
That jalousie, allas, that wikked wyvere,   1010
Thus causeles is cropen into yow,
The harm of which I wolde fayn delyvere.
Allas, that he, al hool or of hym slyvere,
Shuld han his refut in so digne a place;
Ther Jove hym sone out of youre herte arace!

"But O, thow Jove, O auctour of nature,   1016
Is this an honour to thi deyte,
That folk ungiltif suffren hire injure,
And who that giltif is, al quyt goth he?

O, were it leful for to pleyn on the,   1020
That undeserved suffrest jalousie,
Of that I wolde upon the pleyne and crie!

"Ek al my wo is this, that folk now usen
To seyn right thus, 'Ye, jalousie is love!'
And wolde a busshel venym al excusen,   1025
For that o greyn of love is on it shove.
But that woot heighe God that sit above,
If it be likkere love, or hate, or grame;
And after that, it oughte bere his name.

"But certeyn is, som manere jalousie   1030
Is excusable more than som, iwys;
As whan cause is, and som swich fantasie
With piete so wel repressed is
That it unnethe doth or seyth amys,
But goodly drynketh up al his distresse —   1035
And that excuse I, for the gentilesse;

"And som so ful of furie is and despit
That it sourmounteth his repressioun.
But herte myn, ye be nat in that plit,
That thonke I God; for which youre passioun
I wol nought calle it but illusioun   1041
Of habundaunce of love and besy cure,
That doth youre herte this disese endure.

"Of which I am right sory but nought wroth;
But, for my devoir and youre hertes reste, 1045
Wherso yow list, by ordal or by oth,
By sort, or in what wise so yow leste,
For love of God, lat preve it for the beste;
And if that I be giltif, do me deye!
Allas, what myght I more don or seye?"   1050

With that a fewe brighte teris newe
Owt of hire eighen fille, and thus she seyde,
"Now God, thow woost, in thought ne dede
        untrewe
To Troilus was nevere yet Criseyde."   1054
With that here heed down in the bed she leyde,
And with the sheete it wreigh, and sighte soore,
And held hire pees; nought o word spak she
        more.

---

984 **untrouthe:** faithlessness   **gesse:** guess, suspect
986 **in cause of:** the cause of
991 **say:** saw
999 **emforth:** to the extent of
1000 **how:** however
1009 **myn:** mine (used here as a noun), possession
1010 **wyvere:** wyvern, snake
1011 **cropen:** crept
1013 **of hym slyvere:** even a small part of him
1014 **refut:** refuge, dwelling place
1015 **arace:** root (out)
1017 **deyte:** deity
1018 **ungiltif:** innocent

1020 **leful:** permitted
1026 **shove:** i.e., placed
1028 **likkere:** more like   **grame:** anger, hatred
1029 **after:** according to   **his:** its (love's or hate's)
1033 **piete:** piety, a regard for duty
1035 **goodly:** willingly   **drynketh up:** i.e., endures
1042 **besy cure:** anxious care
1045 **devoir:** duty
1046 **ordal:** trial by ordeal   **oth:** oath
1047 **sort:** sortilege, drawing lots
1056 **wreigh:** covered   **sighte:** sighed

But now help God to quenchen al this sorwe!
So hope I that he shal, for he best may.
For I have seyn of a ful misty morwe   1060
Folowen ful ofte a myrie someris day;
And after wynter foloweth grene May;
Men sen alday, and reden ek in stories,
That after sharpe shoures ben victories.

This Troilus, whan he hire wordes herde,   1065
Have ye no care, hym liste nought to slepe;
For it thoughte hym no strokes of a yerde
To heere or seen Criseyde, his lady, wepe;
But wel he felt aboute his herte crepe,
For everi tere which that Criseyde asterte,   1070
The crampe of deth to streyne hym by the
        herte.

And in his mynde he gan the tyme acorse
That he com there, and that, that he was born;
For now is wikke torned into worse,
And al that labour he hath don byforn,   1075
He wende it lost; he thoughte he nas but lorn.
"O Pandarus," thoughte he, "allas, thi wile
Serveth of nought, so weylaway the while!"

And therwithal he heng adown the heed,
And fil on knees, and sorwfully he sighte.   1080
What myghte he seyn? He felte he nas but
        deed,
For wroth was she that sholde his sorwes lighte.
But natheles, whan that he speken myghte,
Than seyde he thus, "God woot that of this
        game,   1084
Whan al is wist, than am I nought to blame."

Therwith the sorwe so his herte shette
That from his eyen fil there nought a tere,
And every spirit his vigour in knette,
So they astoned or oppressed were.
The felyng of his sorwe, or of his fere,   1090
Or of aught elles, fled was out of towne;
And down he fel al sodeynly a-swowne.

This was no litel sorwe for to se;
But al was hust, and Pandare up as faste;
"O nece, pes, or we be lost!" quod he,   1095

"Beth naught agast!" But certeyn, at the laste,
For this or that, he into bed hym caste,
And seyde, "O thef, is this a mannes herte?"
And of he rente al to his bare sherte,

And seyde, "Nece, but ye helpe us now,   1100
Allas, youre owen Troilus is lorn!"
"Iwis, so wolde I, and I wiste how,
Ful fayn," quod she. "Allas, that I was born!"
"Yee, nece, wol ye pullen out the thorn
That stiketh in his herte?" quod Pandare.   1105
"Sey 'Al foryeve,' and stynt is al this fare!"

"Ye, that to me," quod she, "ful levere were
Than al the good the sonne aboute gooth."
And therwithal she swor hym in his ere,
"Iwys, my deere herte, I am nought wroth,   1110
Have here my trouthe!" — and many an
        other oth.
"Now speke to me, for it am I, Criseyde!"
But al for nought; yit myght he nought
        abreyde.

Therwith his pous and paumes of his hondes
They gan to frote, and wete his temples
        tweyne;   1115
And to deliveren hym fro bittre bondes
She ofte hym kiste; and shortly for to seyne,
Hym to revoken she did al hire peyne;
And at the laste, he gan his breth to drawe,
And of his swough sone after that adawe,   1120

And gan bet mynde and reson to hym take,
But wonder soore he was abayst, iwis;
And with a sik, whan he gan bet awake,
He seyde, "O mercy, God, what thyng is this?"
"Why do ye with youreselven thus amys?"   1125
Quod tho Criseyde, "Is this a mannes game?
What, Troilus, wol ye do thus for shame?"

And therwithal hire arm over hym she leyde,
And al foryaf, and ofte tyme hym keste.
He thonked hire, and to hire spak, and seyde
As fil to purpos for his herte reste;   1131
And she to that answerde hym as hire leste,
And with hire goodly wordes hym disporte
She gan, and ofte his sorwes to comforte.

1064 **shoures:** assaults
1067 **no:** i.e., not merely
1073 **that, that:** the fact that (or, the time in which)
1076 **nas but lorn:** was as good as lost
1077 **wile:** guile
1082 **lighte:** lighten
1088 Each vital spirit contracted its force
1094 **hust:** hushed, quiet

1113 **abreyde:** awaken
1114 **pous:** pulse (i.e., wrists) **paumes:** palms
1115 **frote:** rub
1118 **revoken:** recall (to consciousness)
1120 **swough:** swoon **adawe:** awaken
1122 **abayst:** abashed
1133 **hym disporte:** cheer him up

Quod Pandarus, "For aught I kan aspien,   1135
This light, nor I, ne serven here of nought.
Light is nought good for sike folkes yën!
But, for the love of God, syn ye ben brought
In thus good plit, lat now no hevy thought
Ben hangyng in the hertes of yow tweye" —
And bar the candel to the chymeneye.   1141

Soone after this, though it no nede were,
Whan she swiche othes as hire leste devyse
Hadde of hym take, hire thoughte tho no fere,
Ne cause ek non to bidde hym thennes rise.
Yet lasse thyng than othes may suffise   1146
In many a cas, for every wyght, I gesse,
That loveth wel, meneth but gentilesse.

But in effect she wolde wite anon
Of what man, and ek wheer, and also why   1150
He jalous was, syn ther was cause non;
And ek the sygne that he took it by,
She badde hym that to telle hire bisily,
Or elles, certeyn, she bar hym on honde
That this was don of malice, hire to fonde.

Withouten more, shortly for to seyne,   1156
He most obeye unto his lady heste;
And for the lasse harm, he moste feyne.
He seyde hire, whan she was at swich a feste,
She myght on hym han loked at the leste —   1160
Noot I nought what, al deere ynough a rysshe,
As he that nedes most a cause fisshe.

And she answerde, "Swete, al were it so,
What harm was that, syn I non yvel mene?
For, by that God that bought us bothe two,
In alle thyng is myn entente cleene.   1166
Swiche argumentes ne ben naught worth a
        beene.
Wol ye the childissh jalous contrefete?
Now were it worthi that ye were ybete."

Tho Troilus gan sorwfully to sike —   1170
Lest she be wroth, hym thoughte his herte
        deyde —
And seyde, "Allas, upon my sorwes sike
Have mercy, swete herte myn, Criseyde!

And if that in tho wordes that I seyde
Be any wrong, I wol no more trespace.   1175
Doth what yow list; I am al in youre grace."

And she answerde, "Of gilt misericorde!
That is to seyn, that I foryeve al this;
And evere more on this nyght yow recorde,
And beth wel war ye do namore amys.'   1180
"Nay, dere herte myn," quod he, "iwys!"
"And now," quod she, "that I have don yow
        smerte,
Foryeve it me, myn owene swete herte."

This Troilus, with blisse of that supprised,
Putte al in Goddes hand, as he that mente   1185
Nothyng but wel; and sodeynly avysed,
He hire in armes faste to hym hente.
And Pandarus with a ful good entente
Leyde hym to slepe, and seyde, "If ye be wise,
Swouneth nought now, lest more folk arise!"

What myghte or may the sely larke seye,   1191
Whan that the sperhauk hath it in his foot?
I kan namore; but of thise ilke tweye —
To whom this tale sucre be or soot —
Though that I tarie a yer, somtyme I moot,
After myn auctour, tellen hire gladnesse,   1196
As wel as I have told hire hevynesse.

Criseyde, which that felte hire thus itake,
As writen clerkes in hire bokes olde,
Right as an aspes leef she gan to quake,   1200
Whan she hym felte hire in his armes folde.
But Troilus, al hool of cares colde,
Gan thanken tho the bryghte goddes sevene;
Thus sondry peynes bryngen folk in hevene.

This Troilus in armes gan hire streyne,   1205
And seyde, "O swete, as evere mot I gon,
Now be ye kaught; now is ther but we tweyne!
Now yeldeth yow, for other bote is non!"
To that Criseyde answerde thus anon,   1209
"Ne hadde I er now, my swete herte deere,
Ben yolde, ywis, I were now nought heere!"

1139 hevy: gloomy
1141 chymeneye: fireplace
1154 bar hym on honde: accused him
1155 fonde: test
1161 al deere ynough a rysshe: expensive enough at the cost of
a rush (i.e., worthless)
1162 a cause fisshe: invent a reason
1168 contrefete: imitate

1177 misericorde: mercy
1179 recorde: remember
1184 supprised: seized
1192 sperhauk: sparrow hawk
1194 sucre: sugar   soot: soot (i.e., bitter)
1200 aspes: aspen's
1202 al hool of: all recovered from
1203 goddes sevene: the seven planets
1211 yolde: yielded

O, sooth is seyd, that heled for to be
As of a fevre or other gret siknesse,
Men moste drynke, as men may ofte se,   1214
Ful bittre drynke; and for to han gladnesse
Men drynken ofte peyne and gret distresse —
I mene it here, as for this aventure,
That thorugh a peyne hath founden al his cure.

And now swetnesse semeth more swete,
That bitternesse assaied was byforn;   1220
For out of wo in blisse now they flete;
Non swich they felten sithen they were born.
Now is this bet than bothe two be lorn.
For love of God, take every womman heede
To werken thus, if it comth to the neede.   1225

Criseyde, al quyt from every drede and tene,
As she that juste cause hadde hym to triste,
Made hym swych feste it joye was to sene,
Whan she his trouthe and clene entente wiste;
And as aboute a tree, with many a twiste,   1230
Bytrent and writh the swote wodebynde,
Gan ech of hem in armes other wynde.

And as the newe abaysed nyghtyngale,
That stynteth first whan she bygynneth to
          synge,
Whan that she hereth any herde tale,   1235
Or in the hegges any wyght stirynge,
And after siker doth hire vois out rynge,
Right so Criseyde, whan hire drede stente,
Opned hire herte and tolde hym hire entente.

And right as he that seth his deth yshapen,   1240
And dyen mot, in ought that he may gesse,
And sodeynly rescous doth hym escapen,
And from his deth is brought in sykernesse,
For al this world, in swych present gladnesse
Was Troilus, and hath his lady swete.   1245
With worse hap God lat us nevere mete!

Hire armes smale, hire streghte bak and softe,
Hire sydes longe, flesshly, smothe, and white
He gan to stroke, and good thrift bad ful ofte

Hire snowissh throte, hire brestes rounde and
          lite.   1250
Thus in this hevene he gan hym to delite,
And therwithal a thousand tyme hire kiste,
That what to don, for joie unnethe he wiste.

Than seyde he thus: "O Love, O Charite!
Thi moder ek, Citheria the swete,   1255
After thiself next heried be she —
Venus mene I, the wel-willy planete! —
And next that, Imeneus, I the grete,
For nevere man was to yow goddes holde
As I, which ye han brought fro cares colde.   1260

"Benigne Love, thow holy bond of thynges,
Whoso wol grace and list the nought honouren,
Lo, his desir wol fle withouten wynges;
For noldestow of bownte hem socouren
That serven best and most alwey labouren,   1265
Yet were al lost, that dar I wel seyn, certes,
But if thi grace passed oure desertes.

"And for thow me, that koude leest disserve
Of hem that noumbred ben unto thi grace,
Hast holpen, ther I likly was to sterve,   1270
And me bistowed in so heigh a place
That thilke boundes may no blisse pace,
I kan namore; but laude and reverence
Be to thy bounte and thyn excellence!"

And therwithal Criseyde anon he kiste,   1275
Of which certein she felte no disese,
And thus seyde he: "Now wolde God I wiste,
Myn herte swete, how I yow myght plese!
What man," quod he, "was evere thus at ese
As I, on which the faireste and the beste   1280
That evere I say deyneth hire herte reste?

"Here may men seen that mercy passeth right;
Th'experience of that is felt in me,
That am unworthi to so swete a wight.
But herte myn, of youre benignite,   1285
So thynketh, though that I unworthi be,
Yet mot I nede amenden in som wyse,
Right thorugh the vertu of youre heigh servyse.

1220 **That:** to the degree that
1221 **flete:** float
1226 **tene:** trouble
1230 **twiste:** tendril, vine-branch
1231 **Bytrent** = *bitrendeth*, encircles **writh** = *wretheth*, wreathes **wodebynde:** woodbine, honeysuckle
1233 **newe abaysed:** suddenly startled
1235 **herde:** shepherd **tale:** speak
1242 **rescous:** rescue
1248 **flesshly:** shapely

1250 **snowissh:** snowy white
1255 **Citheria:** Venus, mother of the god of love
1257 **wel-willy:** benevolent
1258 **Imeneus:** Hymen, god of marriage
1259 **holde:** beholden
1264 **socouren:** help
1282 **passeth:** surpasses, overcomes **right:** justice
1288 **youre heigh servyse:** nobly serving you

"And for the love of God, my lady deere,
Syn God hath wrought me for I shall yow
      serve — 1290
As thus I mene: he wol ye be my steere,
To do me lyve, if that yow liste, or sterve —
So techeth me how that I may disserve
Youre thonk, so that I thorugh myn ignoraunce
Ne do no thing that yow be displesaunce. 1295

"For certes, fresshe wommanliche wif,
This dar I seye, that trouth and diligence,
That shal ye fynden in me al my lif;
N'y wol nat, certein, breken youre defence;
And if I do, present or in absence, 1300
For love of God, lat sle me with the dede,
If that it like unto youre wommanhede."

"Iwys," quod she, "myn owen hertes list,
My ground of ese, and al myn herte deere,
Gramercy, for on that is al my trist! 1305
But lat us falle awey fro this matere,
For it suffiseth, this that seyd is heere,
And at o word, withouten repentaunce,
Welcome, my knyght, my pees, my suffisaunce!"

Of hire delit or joies oon the leeste 1310
Were impossible to my wit to seye;
But juggeth ye that han ben at the feste
Of swich gladnesse, if that hem liste pleye!
I kan namore, but thus thise ilke tweye
That nyght, bitwixen drede and sikernesse,
Felten in love the grete worthynesse. 1316

O blisful nyght, of hem so longe isought,
How blithe unto hem bothe two thow weere!
Why nad I swich oon with my soule ybought,
Ye, or the leeste joie that was theere? 1320
Awey, thow foule daunger and thow feere,
And lat hem in this hevene blisse dwelle,
That is so heigh that al ne kan I telle!

But sooth is, though I kan nat tellen al,
As kan myn auctour, of his excellence, 1325
Yet have I seyd, and God toforn, and shal
In every thyng, al holly his sentence;
And if that ich, at Loves reverence,
Have any word in eched for the beste,
Doth therwithal right as youreselven leste. 1330

For myne wordes, heere and every part,
I speke hem alle under correccioun
Of yow that felyng han in loves art,
And putte it al in youre discrecioun
To encresse or maken dymynucioun 1335
Of my langage, and that I yow biseche.
But now to purpos of my rather speche.

Thise ilke two, that ben in armes laft,
So loth to hem asonder gon it were,
That ech from other wenden ben biraft, 1340
Or elles — lo, this was hir mooste feere —
That al this thyng but nyce dremes were,
For which ful ofte ech of hem seyde, "O swete,
Clippe ich yow thus, or elles I it meete?"

And Lord! So he gan goodly on hire se 1345
That nevere his look ne bleynte from hire face,
And seyde, "O deere herte, may it be
That it be soth, that ye ben in this place?"
"Yee, herte myn, God thank I of his grace,"
Quod tho Criseyde, and therwithal hym kiste,
That where his spirit was, for joie he nyste. 1351

This Troilus ful ofte hire eyen two
Gan for to kisse, and seyde, "O eyen clere,
It weren ye that wroughte me swich wo,
Ye humble nettes of my lady deere! 1355
Though ther be mercy writen in youre cheere,
God woot, the text ful hard is, soth, to fynde!
How koude ye withouten bond me bynde?"

Therwith he gan hire faste in armes take,
And wel a thousand tymes gan he syke — 1360
Naught swiche sorwfull sikes as men make
For wo, or elles when that folk ben sike,
But esy sykes, swiche as ben to like,
That shewed his affeccioun withinne;
Of swiche sikes koude he nought bilynne. 1365

Soone after this they spake of sondry thynges,
As fel to purpos of this aventure,
And pleyinge entrechaungeden hire rynges,
Of whiche I kan nought tellen no scripture;
But wel I woot, a broche, gold and asure, 1370

1291 **steere:** guide, steersman
1299 **breken youre defence:** violate your prohibition
1303 **hertes list:** heart's desire
1305 **Gramercy:** thank you
1306 **falle awey:** turn aside
1310 **oon the leeste:** the very least
1329 **eched:** added

1333 **felyng:** understanding
1337 **to purpos:** to the point   **rather:** earlier
1340 That each of them thought he (she) was torn away from the other
1344 **Clippe:** embrace   **meete:** dream
1346 **bleynte:** turned away
1355 **humble:** modest
1363 **to like:** pleasing
1365 **bilynne:** cease
1369 **scripture:** the motto or posy on the ring

In which a ruby set was lik an herte,
Criseyde hym yaf, and stak it on his sherte.

Lord, trowe ye a coveytous or a wrecche,
That blameth love and halt of it despit,
That of tho pens that he kan mokre and
        kecche   1375
Was evere yit yyeven hym swich delit
As is in love, in o poynt, in som plit?
Nay, douteles, for also God me save,
So perfit joie may no nygard have.

They wol seyn "Yis," but Lord, so they lye,
Tho besy wrecches, ful of wo and drede!   1381
Thei callen love a woodnesse or folie,
But it shall falle hem as I shal yow rede:
They shal forgon the white and ek the rede,
And lyve in wo, ther God yeve hem mes-
        chaunce,   1385
And every lovere in his trouthe avaunce!

As wolde God tho wrecches that dispise
Servise of love hadde erys also longe
As hadde Mida, ful of coveytise,
And therto dronken hadde as hoot and stronge
As Crassus did for his affectis wronge,   1391
To techen hem that they ben in the vice,
And loveres nought, although they holde hem
        nyce.

Thise ilke two of whom that I yow seye,
Whan that hire hertes wel assured were,   1395
Tho gonne they to speken and to pleye,
And ek rehercen how, and whan, and where
Thei knewe hem first, and every wo and feere
That passed was; but al swich hevynesse —
I thank it God — was torned to gladnesse. 1400

And evere mo, when that hem fel to speke
Of any wo of swich a tyme agoon,
With kissyng al that tale sholde breke
And fallen in a newe joye anoon;
And diden al hire myght, syn they were oon,
For to recoveren blisse and ben at eise,   1406
And passed wo with joie contrepeise.

Resoun wol nought that I speke of slep,
For it acordeth nought to my matere.
God woot, they took of that ful litel kep! 1410
But lest this nyght, that was to hem so deere,
Ne sholde in veyn escape in no manere,
It was byset in joie and bisynesse
Of al that souneth into gentilesse.

But whan the cok, comune astrologer,   1415
Gan on his brest to bete and after crowe,
And Lucyfer, the dayes messager,
Gan for to rise and out hire bemes throwe,
And estward roos — to hym that koude it
        knowe —
Fortuna Major, that anoon Criseyde,   1420
With herte soor, to Troilus thus seyde:

"Myn hertes lif, my trist, al my plesaunce,
That I was born, allas, what me is wo,
That day of us moot make disseveraunce!
For tyme it is to ryse and hennes go,   1425
Or ellis I am lost for evere mo!
O nyght, allas, why nyltow over us hove
As longe as whan Almena lay by Jove?

"O blake nyght, as folk in bokes rede,
That shapen art by God this world to hide   1430
At certeyn tymes wyth thi derke wede,
That under that men myghte in reste abide,
Wel oughten bestes pleyne and folk the chide,
That there as day wyth labour wolde us breste,
That thow thus fleest, and deynest us nought
        reste."   1435

"Thow doost, allas, to shortly thyn office,
Thow rakle nyght! Ther God, maker of kynde,
The, for thyn haste and thyn unkynde vice,
So faste ay to oure hemysperie bynde
That nevere more under the ground thow
        wynde!   1440
For now, for thow so hiest out of Troie,
Have I forgon thus hastili my joie!"

1372 **stak:** stuck, pinned
1375 **pens:** money (pence) **mokre:** rake in, hoard **kecche:**
catch, hunt down
1384 **white . . . rede:** silver and gold (?); see n.
1389 **Mida:** Midas, renowned for his avarice
1391 **Crassus:** avaricious Roman general who had molten gold
poured into his mouth **affectis:** desires
1401 **hem fel:** they happened
1403 **breke:** interrupt
1407 **passed:** past **contrepeise:** to counterbalance

1412 **in no manere:** in any way
1414 **souneth into:** tends toward, is conducive to
1417 **Lucyfer:** the morning star, Venus
1420 *Fortuna Major:* here a constellation or planet, but also a
figure in geomancy; see n.
1423 **what me is wo:** how I regret
1427 **hove:** hover
1428 **Almena:** Alcmena, mother of Hercules, for whom Jove
extended the night
1431 **wede:** garment
1434 **breste:** afflict (literally, break)
1435 **deynest:** grant
1437 **rakle:** hasty **Ther:** to be omitted in translation
1438 **unkynde:** unnatural

This Troilus, that with tho wordes felte,
As thoughte hym tho, for piëtous distresse
The blody teris from his herte melte,   1445
As he that nevere yet swich hevynesse
Assayed hadde, out of so gret gladnesse,
Gan therwithal Criseyde, his lady deere,
In armes streyne, and seyde in this manere:

"O cruel day, accusour of the joie   1450
That nyght and love han stole and faste iwryen,
Acorsed be thi comyng into Troye,
For every bore hath oon of thi bryghte yën!
Envyous day, what list the so to spien?   1454
What hastow lost? Why sekestow this place?
Ther God thi light so quenche, for his grace!

"Allas, what have thise loveris the agylt,
Dispitous day? Thyn be the peyne of helle!
For many a lovere hastow slayn, and wilt;
Thy pourynge in wol nowher lat hem dwelle.
What profrestow thi light here for to selle?   1461
Go selle it hem that smale selys grave;
We wol the nought; us nedeth no day have."

And ek the sonne, Titan, gan he chide,
And seyde, "O fool, wel may men the dispise,
That hast the dawyng al nyght by thi syde,   1466
And suffrest hire so soone up fro the rise
For to disese loveris in this wyse.
What, holde youre bed ther, thow, and ek thi
          Morwe!
I bidde God, so yeve yow bothe sorwe!"   1470

Therwith ful soore he syghte, and thus he
          seyde:
"My lady right, and of my wele or wo
The welle and roote, O goodly myn Criseyde,
And shal I rise, allas, and shal I so?
Now fele I that myn herte moot a-two,   1475
For how sholde I my lif an houre save,
Syn that with yow is al the lyf ich have?

"What shal I don? For, certes, I not how,
Ne whan, allas, I shal the tyme see

That in this plit I may ben eft with yow,   1480
And of my lif, God woot how that shal be,
Syn that desir right now so streyneth me
That I am ded anon, but I retourne.
How sholde I longe, allas, fro yow sojourne?

"But natheles, myn owen lady bright,   1485
Were it so that I wiste outrely
That I, youre humble servant and youre knyght,
Were in youre herte iset so fermely
As ye in myn — the which thyng, trewely,
Me levere were than thise worldes tweyne —
Yet sholde I bet enduren al my peyne."   1491

To that Criseyde answerde right anon,
And with a sik she seyde, "O herte deere,
The game, ywys, so ferforth now is gon
That first shal Phebus fallen fro his spere,   1495
And everich egle ben the dowves feere,
And everich roche out of his place sterte,
Er Troilus oute of Criseydes herte.

"Ye ben so depe in-with myn herte grave,
That, though I wolde it torne out of my
          thought,   1500
As wisly verray God my soule save,
To dyen in the peyne, I koude nought.
And, for the love of God that us hath wrought,
Lat in youre brayn non other fantasie
So crepe that it cause me to dye!   1505

"And that ye me wolde han as faste in mynde
As I have yow, that wolde I yow biseche;
And if I wiste sothly that to fynde,
God myghte nought a poynt my joies eche.
But herte myn, withouten more speche,   1510
Beth to me trewe, or ellis were it routhe,
For I am thyn, by God and by my trouthe!

"Beth glad, forthy, and lyve in sikernesse!
Thus seyde I nevere er this, ne shal to mo;
And if to yow it were a gret gladnesse   1515
To torne ayeyn soone after that ye go,
As fayn wolde I as ye that it were so,
As wisly God myn herte brynge at reste!"
And hym in armes tok, and ofte keste.

1444 **piëtous**: pitiful
1450 **accusour**: revealer, betrayer
1451 **iwryen**: hidden
1453 **bore**: opening, chink
1457 **what**: how   **agylt**: offended
1460 **pourynge**: staring, poring
1461 **profrestow**: do you offer
1462 **smale selys grave**: engrave small seals (requiring good light)
1464 **Titan**: the sun (here merged with Tithonus, the lover of Aurora, the dawn (*dawyng*)
1469 **Morwe**: dawn, Aurora
1475 **a-two**: (break) in two

1482 **streyneth**: grips, presses
1490 **thise worldes tweyne**: the realms of both Greece and Troy (or, than to have two worlds such as this; see n.)
1495 **spere**: sphere (of the sun, *Phebus*)
1497 **roche**: rock
1498 **oute**: go out
1502 **To dyen in the peyne**: even if I were to die by torture
1509 **a**: one   **eche**: increase

Agayns his wil, sith it mot nedes be,   1520
This Troilus up ros, and faste hym cledde,
And in his armes took his lady free
An hondred tyme, and on his wey hym spedde;
And with swich voys as though his herte
          bledde,
He seyde, "Farwel, dere herte swete;   1525
Ther God us graunte sownde and soone to
          mete!"

To which no word for sorwe she answerde,
So soore gan his partyng hire distreyne;
And Troilus unto his paleys ferde,
As wo-bygon as she was, soth to seyne.   1530
So harde hym wrong of sharp desir the peyne
For to ben eft there he was in plesaunce,
That it may nevere out of his remembraunce.

Retorned to his real paleys soone,
He softe into his bed gan for to slynke,   1535
To slepe longe, as he was wont to doone.
But al for nought; he may wel ligge and wynke,
But slep ne may ther in his herte synke,
Thynkyng how she for whom desir hym
          brende
A thousand fold was worth more than he
          wende.   1540

And in his thought gan up and down to wynde
Hire wordes alle, and every countenaunce,
And fermely impressen in his mynde
The leeste point that to him was plesaunce;
And verraylich of thilke remembraunce   1545
Desir al newe hym brende, and lust to brede
Gan more than erst, and yet took he non hede.

Criseyde also, right in the same wyse,
Of Troilus gan in hire herte shette
His worthynesse, his lust, his dedes wise,   1550
His gentilesse, and how she with hym mette,
Thonkyng Love he so wel hire bisette,
Desiryng eft to han hire herte deere
In swich a plit, she dorste make hym cheere.

Pandare, o-morwe, which that comen was   1555
Unto his nece and gan hire faire grete,

Seyde, "Al this nyght so reyned it, allas,
That al my drede is that ye, nece swete,
Han litel laiser had to slepe and mete.
Al nyght," quod he, "hath reyn so do me wake,
That som of us, I trowe, hire hedes ake."   1561

And ner he com, and seyde, "How stant it now
This mury morwe? Nece, how kan ye fare?"
Criseyde answerde, "Nevere the bet for yow,
Fox that ye ben! God yeve youre herte kare!
God help me so, ye caused al this fare,   1566
Trowe I," quod she, "for al youre wordes white.
O, whoso seeth yow knoweth yow ful lite."

With that she gan hire face for to wrye
With the shete, and wax for shame al reed;   1570
And Pandarus gan under for to prie,
And seyde, "Nece, if that I shal be ded,
Have here a swerd and smyteth of myn hed!"
With that his arm al sodeynly he thriste   1574
Under hire nekke, and at the laste hire kyste.

I passe al that which chargeth nought to seye.
What! God foryaf his deth, and she al so
Foryaf, and with here uncle gan to pleye,
For other cause was ther noon than so.
But of this thing right to the effect to go: 1580
Whan tyme was, hom til here hous she wente,
And Pandarus hath fully his entente.

Now torne we ayeyn to Troilus,
That resteles ful longe abedde lay,
And pryvely sente after Pandarus,   1585
To hym to com in al the haste he may.
He com anon — nought ones seyde he nay —
And Troilus ful sobrely he grette,
And down upon his beddes syde hym sette.

This Troilus, with al th'affeccioun   1590
Of frendes love that herte may devyse,
To Pandarus on knowes fil adown,
And er that he wolde of the place arise
He gan hym thonken in his beste wise   1594
An hondred sythe, and gan the tyme blesse
That he was born, to brynge hym fro destresse.

He seyde, "O frend of frendes the alderbeste
That evere was, the sothe for to telle,

1521 **cledde:** dressed
1526 **sownde:** healthy
1528 **distreyne:** press upon, afflict
1531 **wrong:** wrung
1534 **real:** royal
1537 **wynke:** close (both) his eyes
1546 **lust:** desire   **brede:** arise, grow
1550 **lust:** vigor, eagerness
1555 **o-morwe:** in the morning   **which that:** who

1567 **white:** specious, misleading
1571 **prie:** peer
1576 **chargeth nought:** does not matter
1577 **God foryaf his deth:** i.e., Christ forgave his crucifixion
1592 **knowes:** knees
1597 **alderbeste:** best of all

Thow hast in hevene ybrought my soule at
    reste
Fro Flegitoun, the fery flood of helle,   1600
That, though I myght a thousand tymes selle
Upon a day my lif in thi servise,
It myghte naught a moote in that suffise.

"The sonne, which that al the world may se,
Saugh nevere yet my lif, that dar I leye,   1605
So inly fair and goodly as is she
Whos I am al, and shal, tyl that I deye.
And that I thus am hires, dar I seye,
That thanked be the heighe worthynesse
Of Love, and ek thi kynde bysynesse.   1610

"Thus hastow me no litel thing yyive,
For which to the obliged be for ay
My lif. And whi? For thorugh thyn help I lyve,
Or elles ded hadde I ben many a day."
And with that word down in his bed he lay,
And Pandarus ful sobrely hym herde   1616
Til al was seyd, and than he thus answerde:

"My deere frend, if I have don for the
In any cas, God wot, it is me lief,
And am as glad as man may of it be,   1620
God help me so; but tak now nat a-grief
That I shal seyn: be war of this meschief,
That, there as thow now brought art in thy
    blisse,
That thow thiself ne cause it nat to misse.

"For of fortunes sharpe adversitee   1625
The worste kynde of infortune is this,
A man to han ben in prosperitee,
And it remembren whan it passed is.
Th'art wis ynough; forthi do nat amys:
Be naught to rakel, theigh thow sitte warme,
For if thow be, certeyn it wol the harme. 1631

"Thow art at ese, and hold the wel therinne;
For also seur as reed is every fir,
As gret a craft is kepe wel as wynne.
Bridle alwey wel thi speche and thi desir, 1635
For worldly joie halt nought but by a wir.

That preveth wel, it brest al day so ofte;
Forthi nede is to werken with it softe."

Quod Troilus, "I hope, and God toforn,
My deere frend, that I shal so me beere   1640
That in my gylt ther shal nothyng be lorn,
N'y nyl nought rakle as for to greven heere.
It nedeth naught this matere ofte stere;
For wystestow myn herte wel, Pandare,
God woot, of this thow woldest litel care." 1645

Tho gan he telle hym of his glade nyght,
And wherof first his herte dred, and how,
And seyde, "Frend, as I am trewe knyght,
And by that feyth I shal to God and yow,
I hadde it nevere half so hote as now;   1650
And ay the more that desir me biteth
To love hire best, the more it me deliteth.

"I not myself naught wisly what it is,
But now I feele a newe qualitee —
Yee, al another than I dide er this."   1655
Pandare answerd, and seyde thus, that "he
That ones may in hevene blisse be,
He feleth other weyes, dar I leye,
Than thilke tyme he first herde of it seye."

This is o word for al: this Troilus   1660
Was nevere ful to speke of this matere,
And for to preisen unto Pandarus
The bounte of his righte lady deere,
And Pandarus to thanke and maken cheere.
This tale ay was span-newe to bygynne, 1665
Til that the nyght departed hem atwynne.

Soon after this, for that Fortune it wolde,
Icomen was the blisful tyme swete
That Troilus was warned that he sholde,
There he was erst, Criseyde his lady mete, 1670
For which he felte his herte in joie flete
And feithfully gan alle the goddes herie.
And lat se now if that he kan be merie!

And holden was the forme and al the wise
Of hire commyng, and of his also,   1675

1600 **Flegitoun:** Phlegethon, one of the rivers of hell **flood:** river
1603 **moote:** speck of dust
1605 **my lif:** in my lifetime **leye:** wager
1606 **inly:** entirely
1624 **misse:** fail
1630 **rakel:** rash **theigh thow sitte warme:** though you are comfortable now
1633 **seur:** surely
1636 **wir:** wire (i.e., thread)

1642 **rakle:** (be) rash, importunate
1643 **stere:** stir, bring up
1644 **wystestow:** if you knew
1649 **shal:** owe
1660 **for al:** i.e., that will suffice for all
1661 Never had enough of speaking about this matter
1665 **ay was span-newe to bygynne:** always had to be started over brand new
1666 **atwynne:** apart
1671 **flete:** float
1672 **herie:** praise

As it was erst, which nedeth nought devyse.
But pleynly to th'effect right for to go:
In joie and suerte Pandarus hem two
Abedde brought, whan that hem bothe leste,
And thus they ben in quyete and in reste.   1680

Nought nedeth it to yow, syn they ben met,
To axe at me if that they blithe were;
For if it erst was wel, tho was it bet
A thousand fold; this nedeth nought enquere.
Ago was every sorwe and every feere;   1685
And bothe, ywys, they hadde, and so they
        wende,
As muche joie as herte may comprende.

This is no litel thyng of for to seye;
This passeth every wit for to devyse;
For ech of hem gan otheres lust obeye.   1690
Felicite, which that thise clerkes wise
Comenden so, ne may nought here suffise;
This joie may nought writen be with inke;
This passeth al that herte may bythynke.   1694

But cruel day — so wailaway the stounde! —
Gan for t'aproche, as they by sygnes knewe,
For which hem thoughte feelen dethis wownde.
So wo was hem that chaungen gan hire hewe,
And day they gonnen to despise al newe,
Callyng it traitour, envyous, and worse,   1700
And bitterly the dayes light thei corse.

Quod Troilus, "Allas, now am I war
That Piros and tho swifte steedes thre,
Which that drawen forth the sonnes char,
Han gon som bi-path in dispit of me;   1705
That maketh it so soone day to be;
And for the sonne hym hasteth thus to rise,
Ne shal I nevere don hire sacrifise."

But nedes day departe hem moste soone,   1709
And whan hire speche don was and hire cheere,
They twynne anon, as they were wont to doone,
And setten tyme of metyng eft yfeere;
And many a nyght they wroughte in this
        manere,
And thus Fortune a tyme ledde in joie
Criseyde and ek this kynges sone of Troie.   1715

In suffisaunce, in blisse, and in singynges,
This Troilus gan al his lif to lede.
He spendeth, jousteth, maketh festeynges;
He yeveth frely ofte, and chaungeth wede,
And held aboute hym alwey, out of drede,   1720
A world of folk, as com hym wel of kynde,
The fresshest and the beste he koude fynde;

That swich a vois was of hym and a stevene,
Thoroughout the world, of honour and largesse,
That it up rong unto the yate of hevene;   1725
And, as in love, he was in swich gladnesse
That in his herte he demed, as I gesse,
That ther nys lovere in this world at ese
So wel as he; and thus gan love hym plese.

The goodlihede or beaute which that kynde
In any other lady hadde yset   1731
Kan nought the montance of a knotte unbynde
Aboute his herte of al Criseydes net.
He was so narwe ymasked and yknet,
That it undon on any manere syde,   1735
That nyl naught ben, for aught that may bitide.

And by the hond ful ofte he wolde take
This Pandarus, and into gardyn lede,
And swich a feste and swich a proces make
Hym of Criseyde, and of hire womanhede,   1740
And of hire beaute, that withouten drede
It was an hevene his wordes for to here;
And thanne he wolde synge in this manere:

Canticus Troili.

"Love, that of erthe and se hath governaunce,
Love, that his hestes hath in hevene hye,   1745
Love, that with an holsom alliaunce
Halt peples joyned, as hym lest hem gye,
Love, that knetteth lawe of compaignie,
And couples doth in vertu for to dwelle,
Bynd this acord, that I have told and telle.   1750

"That, that the world with feith which that is
        stable
Diverseth so his stowndes concordynge,

1685 **Ago:** gone
1694 **bythynke:** think of, conceive
1695 **stounde:** time
1703 **Piros:** Pyrois, one of the sun's horses
1704 **char:** chariot
1705 **bi-path:** shortcut
1708 **hire sacrifise:** their sacrifice (i.e., to the sun and its chariot-team)
1711 **twynne:** separate

1718 **maketh festeynges:** gives feasts
1721 **as com hym wel of kynde:** as became him by nature
1723 **vois:** i.e., repute   **stevene:** talking, report
1732 **montance:** extent (so much as)   **unbynde:** untie
1734 **ymasked:** enmeshed   **yknet:** tied
1735 **undon:** to untie, release
1739 And make so merry and talk so much
Canticus Troili: Troilus's Song
1745 **hestes:** commands
1747 **hym lest hem gye:** as it pleases him to direct them
1751 **That, that the world:** this, namely that the world (the first *that* anticipates *this* in line 1757)
1752 **stowndes:** times, seasons   **concordynge:** harmonious

That elementz that ben so discordable
Holden a bond perpetuely durynge,   1754
That Phebus mote his rosy day forth brynge,
And that the mone hath lordshipe over the
    nyghtes:
Al this doth Love, ay heried be his myghtes! —

"That, that the se, that gredy is to flowen,
Constreyneth to a certeyn ende so
His flodes that so fiersly they ne growen   1760
To drenchen erthe and al for evere mo;
And if that Love aught lete his bridel go,
Al that now loveth asondre sholde lepe,
And lost were al that Love halt now to-hepe.

"So wolde God, that auctour is of kynde,   1765
That with his bond Love of his vertu liste
To cerclen hertes alle and faste bynde,
That from his bond no wight the wey out wiste;
And hertes colde, hem wolde I that he twiste
To make hem love, and that hem liste ay
    rewe   1770
On hertes sore, and kepe hem that ben
    trewe!"

In alle nedes for the townes werre
He was, and ay, the first in armes dyght,
And certeynly, but if that bokes erre,
Save Ector most ydred of any wight;   1775
And this encrees of hardynesse and myght
Com hym of love, his ladies thank to wynne,
That altered his spirit so withinne.

In tyme of trewe, on haukyng wolde he ride,
Or elles honte boor, beer, or lyoun;   1780
The smale bestes leet he gon biside.
And whan that he com ridyng into town,
Ful ofte his lady from hire wyndow down,
As fressh as faukoun comen out of muwe,
Ful redy was hym goodly to saluwe.   1785

And moost of love and vertu was his speche,
And in despit hadde alle wrecchednesse;
And douteles, no nede was hym biseche
To honouren hem that hadde worthynesse,
And esen hem that weren in destresse;   1790
And glad was he if any wyght wel ferde,
That lovere was, whan he it wiste or herde.

For soth to seyne, he lost held every wyght,
But if he were in Loves heigh servise —
I mene folk that oughte it ben of right.   1795
And over al this, so wel koude he devyse
Of sentement and in so unkouth wise
Al his array, that every lovere thoughte
That al was wel, what so he seyde or wroughte.

And though that he be come of blood roial,   1800
Hym liste of pride at no wight for to chace;
Benigne he was to ech in general,
For which he gat hym thank in every place.
Thus wolde Love — yheried be his grace! —
That Pride, Envye, Ire, and Avarice   1805
He gan to fle, and everich other vice.

Thow lady bryght, the doughter to Dyone,
Thy blynde and wynged sone ek, daun Cupide,
Yee sustren nyne ek, that by Elicone
In hil Pernaso listen for t'abide,   1810
That ye thus fer han deyned me to gyde —
I kan namore, but syn that ye wol wende,
Ye heried ben for ay withouten ende!

Thorough yow have I seyd fully in my song
Th'effect and joie of Troilus servise,   1815
Al be that ther was som disese among,
As to myn auctour listeth to devise.
My thridde bok now ende ich in this wyse,
And Troilus in lust and in quiete
Is with Criseyde, his owen herte swete.   1820

Explicit liber tercius.

1753 **discordable**: inclined to discord
1754 **durynge**: enduring
1759 **Constreyneth to a certeyn ende**: restrains within a fixed limit
1761 **drenchen**: drown
1764 **to-hepe**: together
1768 **wiste**: might know
1769 **twiste**: would wring, force
1773 **dyght**: prepared, ready
1777 **thank**: gratitude
1779 **trewe**: truce
1781 **leet he gon biside**: he ignored
1784 **out of muwe**: out of pen, coop (newly moulted)

1791 **ferde**: fared
1793 **lost held**: considered lost
1795 **of right**: rightfully, appropriately
1796–99 And moreover, he knew so well how to order (*devyse*) all his behavior (*array*) feelingly (*Of sentement*) and in so striking a way (*unkouth wise*) that lovers thought all was well done, whatever he said or did.
1801 **chace**: persecute, harass
1807 **Dyone**: mother of Venus
1809 **sustren nyne**: the Muses   **Elicone**: Helicon
1810 **Pernaso**: Parnassus   **listen**: are pleased
1811–13 Since you will now leave me, I can only say "Praised be ye who have thus far deigned to guide me." (P. F. Baum's trans.; see n.)
1816 **among**: mixed in
1819 **lust**: delight
Explicit, *etc.*: Here ends the third book.

BOOK IV

Incipit prohemium quarti libri

But al to litel, weylaway the whyle,
Lasteth swich joie, ythonked be Fortune,
That semeth trewest whan she wol bygyle
And kan to fooles so hire song entune   4
That she hem hent and blent, traitour comune!
And whan a wight is from hire whiel ythrowe,
Than laugheth she, and maketh hym the mowe.

From Troilus she gan hire brighte face
Awey to writhe, and tok of hym non heede,
But caste hym clene out of his lady grace,   10
And on hire whiel she sette up Diomede;
For which myn herte right now gynneth blede,
And now my penne, allas, with which I write,
Quaketh for drede of that I moste endite.

For how Criseyde Troilus forsook —   15
Or at the leeste, how that she was unkynde —
Moot hennesforth ben matere of my book,
As writen folk thorugh which it is in mynde.
Allas, that they sholde evere cause fynde
To speke hire harm! And if they on hire lye,   20
Iwis, hemself sholde han the vilanye.

O ye Herynes, Nyghtes doughtren thre,
That endeles compleignen evere in pyne,
Megera, Alete, and ek Thesiphone,
Thow cruel Mars ek, fader to Quyryne,   25
This ilke ferthe book me helpeth fyne,
So that the losse of lyf and love yfeere
Of Troilus be fully shewed heere.

Explicit prohemium quarti libri.

Incipit liber quartus.

Liggyng in oost, as I have seyd er this,
The Grekys stronge aboute Troie town,   30
Byfel that, whan that Phebus shynyng is
Upon the brest of Hercules lyoun,
That Ector, with ful many a bold baroun,
Caste on a day with Grekis for to fighte,
As he was wont, to greve hem what he myghte.

Not I how longe or short it was bitwene   36
This purpos and that day they issen mente,
But on a day, wel armed, brighte, and shene,
Ector and many a worthi wight out wente,
With spere in honde and bigge bowes bente;   40
And in the berd, withouten lenger lette,
Hire fomen in the feld hem faste mette.

The longe day, with speres sharpe igrounde,
With arwes, dartes, swerdes, maces felle,
They fighte and bringen hors and man to
          grounde,   45
And with hire axes out the braynes quelle.
But in the laste shour, soth for to telle,
The folk of Troie hemselven so mysledden
That with the worse at nyght homward they
          fledden.

At which day was taken Antenore,   50
Maugre Polydamas or Monesteo,
Santippe, Sarpedoun, Polynestore,
Polite, or ek the Trojan daun Rupheo,
And other lasse folk as Phebuseo;

Incipit, *etc.:* Here begins the prologue of the fourth book.
4 **entune:** sing
5 **blent** = *blendeth,* blinds
7 **mowe:** moue, grimace
9 **writhe:** turn

Incipit, *etc.:* Here begins the fourth book.
29 **Liggyng in oost:** besieging
31 **Phebus:** the sun
32 **brest:** i.e., the first part   **Hercules lyoun:** the zodiacal sign Leo (which the sun enters in July)
37 **issen:** go out (to attack)
40 **bigge:** strong
41 **in the berd:** face to face

18 **thorugh which it is in mynde:** by whom it is made known, recorded
22 **Herynes:** the Erinyes, the three Furies
24 **Alete:** Alecto
25 **Quyryne:** Quirinus, a name of Romulus
26 **fyne:** finish
Explicit, *etc.:* Here ends the prologue of the fourth book.

44 **felle:** cruel, terrible
46 **quelle:** dash
47 **shour:** assault
48 **hemselven so mysledden:** conducted themselves so badly
51 **Maugre:** in spite of (the efforts of)

So that, for harm, that day the folk of Troie 55
Dredden to lese a gret part of hire joie.

Of Priamus was yeve, at Grek requeste,
A tyme of trewe, and tho they gonnen trete
Hire prisoners to chaungen, meste and leste,
And for the surplus yeven sommes grete. 60
This thing anon was couth in every strete,
Bothe in th'assege, in town, and everywhere,
And with the firste it com to Calkas ere.

Whan Calkas knew this tretis sholde holde,
In consistorie among the Grekes soone 65
He gan in thringe forth with lordes olde,
And sette hym there as he was wont to doone;
And with a chaunged face hem bad a boone,
For love of God, to don that reverence,
To stynte noyse and yeve hym audience. 70

Than seyde he thus: "Lo, lordes myn, ich was
Troian, as it is knowen out of drede;
And, if that yow remembre, I am Calkas,
That alderfirst yaf comfort to youre nede,
And tolde wel how that ye shulden spede. 75
For dredeles, thorugh yow shal in a stownde
Ben Troie ybrend and beten down to grownde.

"And in what forme, or in what manere wise,
This town to shende, and al youre lust t'acheve,
Ye han er this wel herd me yow devyse; 80
This knowe ye, my lordes, as I leve.
And for the Grekis weren me so leeve,
I com myself, in my propre persone,
To teche in this how yow was best to doone.

"Havyng unto my tresor ne my rente 85
Right no resport, to respect of youre ese,
Thus al my good I lefte and to yow wente,
Wenyng in this yow lordes for to plese.
But al that los ne doth me no disese.
I vouchesauf, as wisly have I joie, 90
For yow to lese al that I have in Troie,

"Save of a doughter that I lefte, allas,
Slepyng at hom, whanne out of Troie I sterte.
O sterne, O cruel fader that I was!
How myghte I have in that so hard an herte? 95
Allas, I ne hadde ibrought hire in hire sherte!
For sorwe of which I wol nought lyve to-
        morwe,
But if ye lordes rewe upon my sorwe.

"For by that cause I say no tyme er now
Hire to delivere, ich holden have my pees; 100
But now or nevere, if that it like yow,
I may hire have right soone, douteles.
O help and grace amonges al this prees!
Rewe on this olde caytyf in destresse,
Syn I thorugh yow have al this hevynesse. 105

"Ye have now kaught and fetered in prisoun
Troians ynowe, and if youre willes be,
My child with oon may han redempcioun;
Now for the love of God and of bounte,
Oon of so fele, allas, so yive hym me! 110
What nede were it this preiere for to werne,
Syn ye shul bothe han folk and town as yerne?

"On peril of my lif, I shal nat lye;
Appollo hath me told it feithfully;
I have ek founde it be astronomye, 115
By sort, and by augurye ek, trewely,
And dar wel say, the tyme is faste by
That fire and flaumbe on al the town shal
        sprede,
And thus shal Troie torne to asshen dede.

"For certein, Phebus and Neptunus bothe, 120
That makeden the walles of the town,
Ben with the folk of Troie alwey so wrothe
That they wol brynge it to confusioun,
Right in despit of kyng Lameadoun;
Bycause he nolde payen hem here hire, 125
The town of Troie shal ben set on-fire."

Tellyng his tale alwey, this olde greye,
Humble in his speche and in his lokyng eke,
The salte teris from his eyen tweye
Ful faste ronnen down by either cheke. 130

57 **Of:** by **yeve:** granted
58 **trewe:** truce **trete:** negotiate
60 **surplus:** prisoners for whom there was no one to exchange
62 **th'assege:** the besieging force
64 **tretis:** negotiation **holde:** be held
65 **consistorie:** council
66 **thringe:** press
76 **stownde:** while
79 **shende:** destroy
83 **propre:** own
85 **rente:** income
86 **resport:** regard **to respect of:** regarding, with respect to
90 **vouchesauf:** am willing, grant

96 **in hire sherte:** in her nightshirt, without even giving her time
to dress
99 **by that cause:** because **say:** saw
104 **caytyf:** wretched man
108 **with:** i.e., in exchange for
110 **fele:** many
111 **werne:** deny
112 **as yerne:** very quickly
115 **astronomye:** astrological divination
120 **Phebus:** Apollo **Neptunus:** Neptune
124 **Lameadoun:** Laomedon, who refused to pay for the walls

So longe he gan of socour hem biseke
That, for to hele hym of his sorwes soore,
They yave hym Antenor, withouten moore.

But who was glad ynough but Calkas tho?
And of this thyng ful soone his nedes leyde   135
On hem that sholden for the tretis go,
And hem for Antenor ful ofte preyde
To bryngen hom kyng Toas and Criseyde.
And whan Priam his save-garde sente,
Th'embassadours to Troie streight they wente.

The cause itold of hire comyng, the olde   141
Priam, the kyng, ful soone in general
Let her-upon his parlement to holde,
Of which th'effect rehercen yow I shal.
Th'embassadours ben answerd for fynal;   145
Th'eschaunge of prisoners and al this nede
Hem liketh wel, and forth in they procede.

This Troilus was present in the place
Whan axed was for Antenor Criseyde,
For which ful soone chaungen gan his face,   150
As he that with tho wordes wel neigh deyde.
But natheles he no word to it seyde,
Lest men sholde his affeccioun espye;
With mannes herte he gan his sorwes drye,

And ful of angwissh and of grisly drede   155
Abod what lordes wolde unto it seye;
And if they wolde graunte — as God forbede —
Th'eschaunge of hire, than thoughte he thynges
     tweye:
First, how to save hire honour, and what weye
He myghte best th'eschaunge of hire with-
     stonde.   160
Ful faste he caste how al this myghte stonde.

Love hym made al prest to don hire byde,
And rather dyen than she sholde go;
But Resoun seyde hym, on that other syde,
"Withouten assent of hire ne do nat so,   165
Lest for thi werk she wolde be thy fo,
And seyn that thorugh thy medlynge is iblowe
Youre bother love, ther it was erst unknowe."

For which he gan deliberen, for the beste,
That though the lordes wolde that she wente,
He wolde lat hem graunte what hem leste,   171
And telle his lady first what that they mente;
And whan that she hadde seyd hym hire en-
     tente,
Therafter wolde he werken also blyve,
Theigh al the world ayeyn it wolde stryve.   175

Ector, which that wel the Grekis herde,
For Antenor how they wolde han Criseyde,
Gan it withstonde, and sobrely answerde:
"Syres, she nys no prisonere," he seyde;
"I not on yow who that this charge leyde,   180
But, on my part, ye may eftsone hem telle,
We usen here no wommen for to selle."

The noyse of peple up stirte thanne at ones,
As breme as blase of straw iset on-fire;
For infortune it wolde, for the nones,   185
They sholden hire confusioun desire.
"Ector," quod they, "what goost may yow en-
     spyre
This womman thus to shilde and don us leese
Daun Antenor — a wrong wey now ye chese —

"That is so wys and ek so bold baroun?   190
And we han nede to folk, as men may se.
He is ek oon the grettest of this town.
O Ector, lat tho fantasies be!
O kyng Priam," quod they, "thus sygge we,
That al oure vois is to forgon Criseyde."   195
And to deliveren Antenor they preyde.

O Juvenal, lord, trewe is thy sentence,
That litel wyten folk what is to yerne,
That they ne fynde in hire desir offence;
For cloude of errour let hem to discerne   200
What best is. And lo, here ensample as yerne:
This folk desiren now deliveraunce
Of Antenor, that brought hem to meschaunce,

136 **tretis:** negotiation
138 **Toas:** Thoas
139 **save-garde:** safe conduct
145 **for fynal:** finally
154 **drye:** endure
156 **Abod:** waited to see
160 **withstonde:** oppose
167 **iblowe:** blown abroad, made public
168 **Youre bother love:** the love of both of you

169 **gan deliberen:** considered (it)
174 **also blyve:** very swiftly
175 **Theigh:** though
180 **charge:** commission, responsibility
182 **usen here no:** are not accustomed here
184 **breme:** fiercely   **blase:** blaze
185 **infortune:** misfortune
191 **to:** of
192 **oon the grettest:** the very greatest
194 **sygge:** say
195 **vois:** i.e., vote   **forgon:** surrender
197 **Juvenal:** the Roman satiric poet
198 **to yerne:** to be desired
200 **errour:** confusion   **let hem to discerne:** hinders them from
discerning
201 **as yerne:** forthwith

For he was after traitour to the town
Of Troye. Allas, they quytte hym out to rathe!
O nyce world, lo, thy discrecioun! 206
Criseyde, which that nevere dide hem scathe,
Shal now no lenger in hire blisse bathe;
But Antenor, he shal com hom to towne,
And she shal out; thus seyden here and howne.

For which delibered was by parlement 211
For Antenor to yelden out Criseyde,
And it pronounced by the president,
Altheigh that Ector "nay" ful ofte preyde.
And fynaly, what wight that it withseyde, 215
It was for nought; it moste ben and sholde,
For substaunce of the parlement it wolde.

Departed out of parlement echone,
This Troilus, withouten wordes mo,
Unto his chambre spedde hym faste allone, 220
But if it were a man of his or two
The which he bad out faste for to go
Bycause he wolde slepen, as he seyde,
And hastily upon his bed hym leyde.

And as in wynter leves ben biraft, 225
Ech after other, til the tree be bare,
So that ther nys but bark and braunche ilaft,
Lith Troilus, byraft of ech welfare,
Ibounden in the blake bark of care,
Disposed wood out of his wit to breyde, 230
So sore hym sat the chaungynge of Criseyde.

He rist hym up, and every dore he shette,
And wyndow ek, and tho this sorwful man
Upon his beddes syde adown hym sette,
Ful lik a ded ymage, pale and wan; 235
And in his brest the heped wo bygan
Out breste, and he to werken in this wise
In his woodnesse, as I shal yow devyse.

Right as the wylde bole bygynneth sprynge,
Now her, now ther, idarted to the herte, 240

And of his deth roreth in compleynynge,
Right so gan he aboute the chaumbre sterte,
Smytyng his brest ay with his fistes smerte;
His hed to the wal, his body to the grounde
Ful ofte he swapte, hymselven to confounde.

His eyen two, for piete of herte, 246
Out stremeden as swifte welles tweye;
The heighe sobbes of his sorwes smerte
His speche hym refte; unnethes myghte he
        seye,
"O deth, allas, why nyltow do me deye? 250
Acorsed be that day which that Nature
Shop me to ben a lyves creature!"

But after, whan the furie and al the rage,
Which that his herte twiste and faste threste,
By lengthe of tyme somwhat gan aswage, 255
Upon his bed he leyde hym down to reste.
But tho bygonne his teeris more out breste,
That wonder is the body may suffise
To half this wo which that I yow devyse

Than seyde he thus: "Fortune, allas the while!
What have I don? What have I thus agylt? 261
How myghtestow for rowthe me bygile?
Is ther no grace, and shal I thus be spilt?
Shal thus Creiseyde awey, for that thow wilt?
Allas, how maistow in thyn herte fynde 265
To ben to me thus cruwel and unkynde?

"Have I the nought honoured al my lyve,
As thow wel woost, above the goddes alle?
Whi wiltow me fro joie thus deprive?
O Troilus, what may men now the calle 270
But wrecche of wrecches, out of honour falle
Into miserie, in which I wol bewaille
Criseyde — allas! — til that the breth me faille?

"Allas, Fortune, if that my lif in joie
Displesed hadde unto thi foule envye, 275
Why ne haddestow my fader, kyng of Troye,
Byraft the lif, or don my bretheren dye,
Or slayn myself, that thus compleyne and crye —
I, combre-world, that may of nothyng serve,
But evere dye and nevere fulli sterve. 280

204 **after:** afterwards
205 **quytte hym out to rathe:** released him too readily
207 **scathe:** harm
210 **shal out:** must go out **here and howne:** master and
members of his household alike (i.e., one and all)
215 **withseyde:** spoke against
217 **substaunce:** the majority
218 **Departed:** having departed **echone:** each one
228 **welfare:** source of happiness
229 **bark:** i.e., of a tree
230 In a state to go mad out of his mind
236 **heped:** heaped up
239 **bole:** bull
240 **idarted:** pierced

243 **smerte:** smartly, painfully
245 **swapte:** struck **confounde:** destroy
246 **piete:** pity
247 **stremeden:** flowed
252 **lyves:** living
254 **threste:** pressed
263 **spilt:** killed
279 **combre-world:** an encumbrance on the world

"If that Criseyde allone were me laft,
Nought roughte I whiderward thow woldest me
    steere;
And hire, allas, than hastow me biraft.
But everemore, lo, this is thi manere,
To reve a wight that most is to hym deere,   285
To preve in that thi gerful violence.
Thus am I lost; ther helpeth no diffence.

"O verrey lord, O Love! O god, allas!
That knowest best myn herte and al my
    thought,
What shal my sorwful lif don in this cas,   290
If I forgo that I so deere have bought?
Syn ye Criseyde and me han fully brought
Into youre grace, and bothe oure hertes seled,
How may ye suffre, allas, it be repeled?

"What shal I don? I shal, while I may dure   295
On lyve in torment and in cruwel peyne
This infortune or this disaventure,
Allone as I was born, iwys, compleyne;
Ne nevere wol I seen it shyne or reyne,
But ende I wol, as Edippe, in derknesse   300
My sorwful lif, and dyen in distresse.

"O wery goost, that errest to and fro,
Why nyltow fleen out of the wofulleste
Body that evere myghte on grounde go?
O soule, lurkynge in this wo, unneste,   305
Fle forth out of myn herte, and lat it breste,
And folowe alwey Criseyde, thi lady dere.
Thi righte place is now no lenger here.

"O woful eyen two, syn youre disport
Was al to sen Criseydes eyen brighte,   310
What shal ye don but, for my discomfort,
Stonden for naught, and wepen out youre
    sighte,
Syn she is queynt that wont was yow to lighte?
In vayn fro this forth have ich eyen tweye
Ifourmed, syn youre vertu is aweye.   315

"O my Criseyde, O lady sovereigne
Of thilke woful soule that thus crieth,
Who shal now yeven comfort to my peyne?
Allas, no wight. But whan myn herte dieth,
My spirit, which that so unto yow hieth,   320
Receyve in gree, for that shal ay yow serve;
Forthi no fors is, though the body sterve.

"O ye loveris, that heigh upon the whiel
Ben set of Fortune, in good aventure,
God leve that ye fynde ay love of stiel,   325
And longe mote youre lif in joie endure!
But whan ye comen by my sepulture,
Remembreth that youre felawe resteth there;
For I loved ek, though ich unworthi were.

"O oold, unholsom, and myslyved man —   330
Calkas I mene — allas, what eiled the
To ben a Grek, syn thow art born Troian?
O Calkas, which that wolt my bane be,
In corsed tyme was thow born for me!
As wolde blisful Jove, for his joie,   335
That I the hadde wher I wolde, in Troie!"

A thousand sikes, hotter than the gleede,
Out of his brest ech after other wente,
Medled with pleyntes new, his wo to feede,
For which his woful teris nevere stente;   340
And shortly, so his peynes hym torente,
And wex so mat, that joie nor penaunce
He feleth non, but lith forth in a traunce.

Pandare, which that in the parlement
Hadde herd what every lord and burgeys
    seyde,   345
And how ful graunted was by oon assent
For Antenor to yelden so Criseyde,
Gan wel neigh wood out of his wit to breyde,
So that for wo he nyste what he mente,
But in a rees to Troilus he wente.   350

A certeyn knyght that for the tyme kepte
The chambre door undide it hym anon;
And Pandare, that ful tendreliche wepte,

---

284 **everemore:** always
285 **reve:** take from **that:** that which
286 **gerful:** unpredictable
287 **diffence:** remedy
293 **seled:** sealed, legally bound
294 **repeled:** repealed
295 **dure:** live
296 **On lyve:** in life, alive
300 **Edippe:** Oedipus, who died blind
302 **that errest:** you who wander
305 **unneste:** go out of the nest
306 **Fle:** fly
312 **Stonden for naught:** be worth nothing
313 **queynt:** extinguished
315 **Ifourmed:** i.e., been endowed with **vertu:** power
(usefulness)

321 **in gree:** favorably, graciously
322 **no fors is:** it doesn't matter
330 **unholsom:** corrupt **myslyved:** wicked
333 **bane:** killer, destruction
335 **As wolde blisful Jove:** would that blessed Jove (would
grant)
337 **gleede:** glowing coal
339 **Medled:** mingled
341 **hym torente:** tore him to pieces
342 **mat:** defeated, dejected
345 **burgeys:** citizen, serving as a member of the assembly
350 **rees:** rush

Into the derke chambre, as stille as ston,
Toward the bed gan softely to gon,   355
So confus that he nyste what to seye;
For verray wo his wit was neigh aweye.

And with his chiere and lokyng al totorn
For sorwe of this, and with his armes folden,
He stood this woful Troilus byforn,   360
And on his pitous face he gan byholden.
But Lord, so ofte gan his herte colden,
Seyng his frend in wo, whos hevynesse
His herte slough, as thoughte hym, for des-
    tresse.

This woful wight, this Troilus, that felte   365
His frend Pandare ycomen hym to se,
Gan as the snow ayeyn the sonne melte;
For which this sorwful Pandare, of pitee,
Gan for to wepe as tendreliche as he;
And specheles thus ben thise ilke tweye,   370
That neither myghte o word for sorwe seye.

But at the laste this woful Troilus,
Neigh ded for smert, gan bresten out to rore,
And with a sorwful noise he seyde thus,
Among hise sobbes and his sikes sore: 375
"Lo, Pandare, I am ded, withouten more.
Hastow nat herd at parlement," he seyde,
"For Antenor how lost is my Criseyde?"

This Pandarus, ful ded and pale of hewe,
Ful pitously answerde and seyde, "Yis!   380
As wisly were it fals as it is trewe,
That I have herd, and woot al how it is.
O mercy, God, who wolde have trowed this?
Who wolde have wend that in so litel a throwe
Fortune oure joie wold han overthrowe?   385

"For in this world ther is no creature,
As to my dom, that ever saugh ruyne
Straunger than this, thorugh cas or aventure.
But who may al eschue, or al devyne?
Swich is this world! Forthi I thus diffyne: 390
Ne trust no wight to fynden in Fortune
Ay propretee; hire yiftes ben comune.

"But telle me this: whi thow art now so mad
To sorwen thus? Whi listow in this wise,
Syn thi desir al holly hastow had,   395
So that, by right, it oughte ynough suffise?
But I, that nevere felte in my servyse
A frendly cheere or lokyng of an eye,
Lat me thus wepe and wailen til I deye.

"And over al this, as thow wel woost thiselve,
This town is ful of ladys al aboute;   401
And, to my doom, fairer than swiche twelve
As evere she was, shal I fynde in som route —
Yee, on or two, withouten any doute.
Forthi be glad, myn owen deere brother!   405
If she be lost, we shal recovere an other.

"What! God forbede alwey that ech plesaunce
In o thyng were and in non other wight!
If oon kan synge, an other kan wel daunce;
If this be goodly, she is glad and light;   410
And this is fair, and that kan good aright.
Ech for his vertu holden is for deere,
Both heroner and faucoun for ryvere.

"And ek, as writ Zanzis, that was ful wys,
'The newe love out chaceth ofte the olde';   415
And upon newe cas lith newe avys.
Thenk ek, thi lif to saven artow holde.
Swich fir, by proces, shal of kynde colde,
For syn it is but casuel plesaunce,
Som cas shal putte it out of remembraunce;   420

"For also seur as day comth after nyght,
The newe love, labour, or oother wo,
Or elles selde seynge of a wight,
Don olde affecciouns alle over-go.
And, for thi part, thow shalt have oon of tho   425
T'abregge with thi bittre peynes smerte;   426
Absence of hire shal dryve hire out of herte."

Thise wordes seyde he for the nones alle,
To help his frend, lest he for sorwe deyde;
For douteles, to don his wo to falle,   430

367 **ayeyn the sonne:** facing the sun, in the sunshine
374 **noise:** voice
381 **As wisly were it:** would that it were surely as
382 **woot:** I know
384 **litel a throwe:** brief a time
388 **cas:** chance
389 **devyne:** foresee
390 **diffyne:** conclude
392 **propretee:** one's own possessions (i.e., special consideration)   **comune:** common to all

394 **listow:** are you lying down
402 **swiche twelve:** twelve such
410 **light:** light-hearted, merry
413 **heroner:** falcon for hunting herons   **faucon for ryvere:** falcon for hunting waterfowl
414 **Zanzis:** unidentified; see n.
417 **holde:** obliged
419 **casuel:** due to chance
420 **cas:** chance event (with a play on *casuel,* trivial, transitory, in 419)
421 **seur:** surely
424 **over-go:** pass away
425 **tho:** those experiences (or, those women)
426 **T'abregge with:** with which to shorten, alleviate

He roughte nought what unthrift that he seyde.
But Troilus, that neigh for sorwe deyde,
Took litel heede of al that evere he mente —
Oon ere it herde, at tother out it wente —

But at the laste answerde, and seyde,
    "Frend,   435
This lechecraft, or heeled thus to be,
Were wel sittyng, if that I were a fend —
To traysen a wight that trewe is unto me!
I pray God lat this conseil nevere ythe;
But do me rather sterve anon-right here,   440
Er I thus do as thow me woldest leere!

"She that I serve, iwis, what so thow seye,
To whom myn herte enhabit is by right,
Shal han me holly hires til that I deye.
For Pandarus, syn I have trouthe hire hight,
I wol nat ben untrewe for no wight,   446
But as hire man I wol ay lyve and sterve,
And nevere other creature serve.

"And ther thow seist thow shalt as faire fynde
As she, lat be; make no comparisoun   450
To creature yformed here by kynde!
O leve Pandare, in conclusioun,
I wol nat ben of thyn opynyoun
Touchyng al this. For which I the biseche,
So hold thi pees; thow sleest me with thi
    speche!   455

"Thow biddest me I shulde love another
Al fresshly newe, and lat Criseyde go!
It lith nat in my power, leeve brother;
And though I myght, I wolde nat do so.
But kanstow playen raket, to and fro,   460
Nettle in, dok out, now this, now that, Pandare?
Now foule falle hire for thi wo that care!

"Thow farest ek by me, thow Pandarus,
As he that, whan a wight is wo bygon,   464
He cometh to hym a paas and seith right thus:

'Thynk nat on smert, and thow shalt fele non.'
Thow moost me first transmewen in a ston,
And reve me my passiones alle,
Er thow so lightly do my wo to falle.

"The deth may wel out of my brest departe   470
The lif, so longe may this sorwe myne,
But fro my soule shal Criseydes darte
Out nevere mo; but down with Proserpyne,
Whan I am ded, I wol go wone in pyne,
And ther I wol eternaly compleyne   475
My wo, and how that twynned be we tweyne.

"Thow hast here made an argument for fyn,
How that it sholde a lasse peyne be
Criseyde to forgon, for she was myn
And lyved in ese and in felicite.   480
Whi gabbestow, that seydest unto me
That 'hym is wors that is fro wele ythrowe,
Than he hadde erst noon of that wele yknowe'?

"But tel me now, syn that the thynketh so
    light
To changen so in love ay to and fro,   485
Whi hastow nat don bisily thi myght
To chaungen hire that doth the al thi wo?
Why nyltow lete hire fro thyn herte go?
Whi nyltow love an other lady swete,
That may thyn herte setten in quiete?   490

"If thou hast had in love ay yet myschaunce
And kanst it not out of thyn herte dryve,
I, that levede yn lust and in plesaunce
With here, as muche as creature on lyve,
How sholde I that foryete, and that so blyve?
O, where hastow ben hid so longe in muwe,   496
That kanst so wel and formely arguwe?

"Nay, God wot, nought worth is al thi red,
For which, for what that evere may byfalle,
Withouten wordes mo, I wol be ded.   500
O deth, that endere art of sorwes alle,
Com now, syn I so ofte after the calle;
For sely is that deth, soth for to seyne,
That, ofte ycleped, cometh and endeth peyne.

---

431 **unthrift:** nonsense
433 **mente:** said
434 **tother:** the other
436 **lechecraft:** medicine
437 **sittyng:** suitable, fitting
438 **traysen:** betray
439 **ythe:** succeed
443 **enhabit:** settled, devoted
452 **leve:** dear
460 **raket:** rackets, a form of tennis
461 **Nettle in, dok out:** nettle (a thorn) in, dock (an herb) out (i.e., first one thing and then another)
462 Now may evil befall her who may care for (take pity on) your woe.
465 **a paas:** apace, swiftly

467 **transmewen:** transmute, transform
471 **myne:** undermine
472 **darte:** arrow
473 **Out:** go out **Proserpyne:** Proserpina, queen of the underworld
474 **wone:** dwell
476 **twynned:** separated
477 **for fyn:** to (this) conclusion (or, for this purpose)
484 **light:** easy
496 **hid . . . in muwe:** cooped up, in hiding
497 **formely:** correctly
498 **red:** advice
503 **sely:** blessed, happy

"Wel wot I, whil my lyf was in quyete,   505
Er thow me slowe, I wolde have yeven hire;
But now thi comynge is to me so swete
That in this world I nothing so desire.
O deth, syn with this sorwe I am a-fyre,
Thou other do me anoon yn teris drenche,   510
Or with thi colde strok myn hete quenche.

"Syn that thou sleest so fele in sondry wyse
Ayens hire wil, unpreyed, day and nyght,
Do me at my requeste this service:
Delyvere now the world — so dostow right —
Of me, that am the wofulleste wyght   516
That evere was; for tyme is that I sterve,
Syn in this world of right nought may I serve."

This Troylus in teris gan distille,
As licour out of a lambyc ful faste;   520
And Pandarus gan holde his tunge stille,
And to the ground his eyen doun he caste.
But natheles, thus thought he at the laste:
"What! Parde, rather than my felawe deye,
Yet shal I somwhat more unto hym seye."   525

And seyde, "Frend, syn thow hast swych dis-
              tresse,
And syn the list myn argumentz to blame,
Why nylt thiselven helpen don redresse
And with thy manhod letten al this grame?
Go ravysshe here! Ne kanstow nat, for shame?
And other lat here out of towne fare,   531
Or hold here stille, and leve thi nyce fare.

"Artow in Troie, and hast non hardyment
To take a womman which that loveth the
And wolde hireselven ben of thyn assent?   535
Now is nat this a nyce vanitee?
Ris up anon, and lat this wepyng be,
And kith thow art a man; for in this houre
I wol ben ded, or she shal bleven oure."

To this answerde hym Troilus ful softe,   540
And seyde, "Parde, leve brother deere,
Al this have I myself yet thought ful ofte,
And more thyng than thow devysest here.
But whi this thyng is laft, thow shalt wel here;

And whan thow me hast yeve an audience,   545
Therafter maystow telle al thi sentence.

"First, syn thow woost this town hath al this
              werre
For ravysshyng of wommen so by myght,
It sholde nought be suffred me to erre,
As it stant now, ne don so gret unright.   550
I sholde han also blame of every wight,
My fadres graunt if that I so withstoode,
Syn she is chaunged for the townes goode.

"I have ek thought, so it were hire assent,
To axe hire at my fader, of his grace;   555
Than thynke I this were hire accusement,
Syn wel I woot I may hire nought purchace;
For syn my fader, in so heigh a place
As parlement hath hire eschaunge enseled,
He nyl for me his lettre be repeled.   560

"Yet drede I moost hire herte to perturbe
With violence, if I do swich a game;
For if I wolde it openly desturbe,
It mooste be disclaundre to hire name.
And me were levere ded than hire diffame —
As nolde God but if I sholde have   566
Hire honour levere than my lif to save!

"Thus am I lost, for aught that I kan see.
For certeyn is, syn that I am hire knyght,
I moste hire honour levere han than me   570
In every cas, as lovere ought of right.
Thus am I with desir and reson twight:
Desir for to destourben hire me redeth,
And reson nyl nat; so myn herte dredeth."

Thus wepyng that he koude nevere cesse,   575
He seyde, "Allas, how shal I, wrecche, fare?
For wel fele I alwey my love encresse,
And hope is lasse and lasse alway, Pandare.
Encressen ek the causes of my care.
So weilaway, whi nyl myn herte breste?   580
For, as in love, ther is but litel reste."

506 **hire**: ransom
510 **other**: either
512 **fele**: many
513 **unpreyed**: unasked for
520 **lambyc**: alembic, retort used in distilling
529 **letten al this grame**: prevent all this grief
530 **ravysshe**: abduct
533 **hardyment**: daring
538 **kith**: make known
539 **bleven oure**: remain ours

548 **ravysshyng**: abduction
549 **suffred me to erre**: allowed for me to break the law
553 **chaunged**: exchanged
555 **at**: from
556 **this were hire accusement**: this would be an accusation against her
557 **purchace**: obtain
559 **enseled**: ratified
560 **repeled**: repealed, nullified
561 **perturbe**: disturb
564 **disclaundre**: slander
566 **As nolde God but if**: God forbid it, unless
572 **twight**: pulled (one way then the other)

Pandare answerde, "Frend, thow maist, for me,
Don as the list; but hadde ich it so hoote,
And thyn estat, she sholde go with me,
Though al this town cride on this thyng by
    note.   585
I nolde sette at al that noys a grote!
For whan men han wel cryd, than wol they
    rowne;
Ek wonder last but nyne nyght nevere in
    towne.

"Devyne not in resoun ay so depe
Ne preciously, but help thiself anon.   590
Bet is that othere than thiselven wepe,
And namely, syn ye two ben al on,
Ris up, for by myn hed, she shal not goon!
And rather be in blame a lite ifounde
Than sterve here as a gnat, withouten wounde.

"It is no rape, in my dom, ne no vice,   596
Hire to witholden that ye love moost;
Peraunter she myghte holde the for nyce
To late hire go thus unto the Grekis oost.
Thenk ek Fortune, as wel thiselven woost,   600
Helpeth hardy man unto his enprise,
And weyveth wrecches for hire cowardise.

"And though thy lady wolde a lite hire greve,
Thow shalt thiself thi pees hereafter make;
But as for me, certeyn, I kan nat leve   605
That she wolde it as now for yvel take.
Whi sholde thanne of ferd thyn herte quake?
Thenk ek how Paris hath, that is thi brother,
A love; and whi shaltow nat have another?

"And Troilus, o thyng I dar the swere: 610
That if Criseyde, which that is thi lief,
Now loveth the as wel as thow dost here,
God help me so, she nyl nat take a-grief,
Theigh thow do boote anon in this meschief;
And if she wilneth fro the for to passe,   615
Thanne is she fals; so love hire wel the lasse.

"Forthi tak herte, and thynk right as a knyght:
Thorugh love is broken al day every lawe.
Kith now somwhat thi corage and thi myght;

Have mercy on thiself for any awe.   620
Lat nat this wrecched wo thyn herte gnawe,
But manly sette the world on six and sevene;
And if thow deye a martyr, go to hevene!

"I wol myself ben with the at this dede,
Theigh ich and al my kyn upon a stownde   625
Shulle in a strete as dogges liggen dede,
Thorough-girt with many a wid and blody
    wownde;
In every cas I wol a frend be founde.
And if the list here sterven as a wrecche,
Adieu, the devel spede hym that it recche!"   630

This Troilus gan with tho wordes quyken,
And seyde, "Frend, graunt mercy, ich assente.
But certeynly thow maist nat so me priken,
Ne peyne non ne may me so tormente,
That, for no cas, it is nat myn entente,   635
At shorte wordes, though I deyen sholde,
To ravysshe hire, but if hireself it wolde."

"Whi, so mene I," quod Pandare, "al this day.
But telle me thanne, hastow hire wil assayed,
That sorwest thus?" And he answerde hym,
    "Nay."   640
"Wherof artow," quod Pandare, "thanne
    amayed,
That nost nat that she wol ben yvele appayed
To ravysshe hire, syn thow hast nought ben
    there,
But if that Jove told it in thyn ere?

"Forthi ris up, as nought ne were, anon,   645
And wassh thi face, and to the kyng thow
    wende,
Or he may wondren whider thow art goon.
Thow most with wisdom hym and othere
    blende,
Or, upon cas, he may after the sende
Er thow be war; and shortly, brother deere,   650
Be glad, and lat me werke in this matere,

"For I shal shape it so, that sikerly
Thow shalt this nyght som tyme, in som
    manere,
Come speken with thi lady pryvely,
And by hire wordes ek, and by hire cheere,   655

584 **estat:** status, power
585 **by note:** in unison
586 **grote:** groat, a silver coin worth four pence
587 **rowne:** whisper (quiet down)
589 **Devyne:** speculate
590 **preciously:** too scrupulously
602 **weyveth:** denies
606 **it . . . for yvel take:** take it amiss
607 **of ferd:** for fright
608 **Paris:** abductor of Helen
614 **do boote:** provide a remedy
619 **Kith:** make known

620 **for any awe:** despite any fear
622 **sette the world on six and sevene:** bet the world on a throw of the dice
627 **Thorugh-girt:** pierced through
630 **spede hym:** help (i.e., take) him   **recche:** may care
641 **amayed:** amazed
642 **nost** = *ne wost*, know not   **yvele appayed:** displeased
643 **To ravysshe hire:** by your carrying her off

Thow shalt ful sone aperceyve and wel here
Al hire entente, and in this cas the beste.
And far now wel, for in this point I reste."

The swifte Fame, which that false thynges
Egal reporteth lik the thynges trewe,   660
Was thoroughout Troie yfled with preste wynges
Fro man to man, and made this tale al newe,
How Calkas doughter, with hire brighte hewe,
At parlement, withouten wordes more,
Ygraunted was in chaunge of Antenore.   665

The whiche tale anon-right as Criseyde
Hadde herd, she, which that of hire fader
          roughte,
As in this cas, right nought, ne whan he deyde,
Ful bisily to Jupiter bisoughte
Yeve hem meschaunce that this tretis broughte;
But shortly, lest thise tales sothe were,   671
She dorst at no wight asken it, for fere.

As she that hadde hire herte and al hire mynde
On Troilus iset so wonder faste
That al this world ne myghte hire love un-
          bynde,   675
Ne Troilus out of hire herte caste,
She wol ben his, while that hire lif may laste.
And thus she brenneth both in love and drede,
So that she nyste what was best to reede.

But as men seen in towne and al aboute   680
That wommen usen frendes to visite,
So to Criseyde of wommen com a route,
For pitous joie, and wenden hire delite;
And with hire tales, deere ynough a myte,   684
Thise wommen, which that in the cite dwelle,
They sette hem down and seyde as I shall telle.

Quod first that oon, "I am glad, trewely,
Bycause of yow, that shal youre fader see."
Another seyde, "Ywis, so nam nat I,
For al to litel hath she with us be."   690
Quod tho the thridde, "I hope, ywis, that she
Shal bryngen us the pees on every syde,
That, whan she goth, almyghty God hire gide!"

Tho wordes and tho wommanysshe thynges,
She herde hem right as though she thennes
          were;   695

For God it woot, hire herte on othir thyng is.
Although the body sat among hem there,
Hire advertence is alwey elleswhere,
For Troilus ful faste hire soule soughte;   699
Withouten word, on hym alwey she thoughte.

Thise wommen, that thus wenden hire to plese,
Aboute naught gonne alle hire tales spende.
Swich vanyte ne kan don hire non ese,
As she that al this mene while brende
Of other passioun than that they wende,   705
So that she felte almost hire herte dye
For wo and wery of that compaignie.

For which no lenger myghte she restreyne
Hir teeris, so they gonnen up to welle,
That yaven signes of the bittre peyne   710
In which hir spirit was, and moste dwelle,
Remembryng hir, fro heven into which helle
She fallen was, syn she forgoth the syghte
Of Troilus, and sorwfully she sighte.

And thilke fooles sittynge hire aboute   715
Wenden that she wepte and siked sore
Bycause that she sholde out of that route
Departe, and nevere pleye with hem more.
And they that hadde yknowen hire of yore
Seigh hire so wepe and thoughte it kynde-
          nesse,   720
And ech of hem wepte ek for hire destresse.

And bisyly they gonnen hire comforten
Of thyng, God woot, on which she litel
          thoughte;
And with hire tales wenden hire disporten,
And to be glad they often hire bysoughte;   725
But swich an ese therwith they hire wroughte,
Right as a man is esed for to feele
For ache of hed to clawen hym on his heele!

But after al this nyce vanyte
They toke hire leve, and hom they wenten alle.
Criseyde, ful of sorwful piete,   731
Into hire chambre up went out of the halle,
And on hire bed she gan for ded to falle,
In purpos nevere thennes for to rise;   734
And thus she wroughte, as I shal yow devyse.

Hire ownded heer, that sonnyssh was of hewe,
She rente, and ek hire fyngeres longe and smale

---

660 **Egal . . . lik:** equally, as equal to
661 **preste:** swift
665 **chaunge of:** exchange for
679 **to reede:** as advice (i.e., to do)
683 **pitous joie:** compassionate well-wishing
684 **deere ynough a myte:** expensive enough at the cost of a
myte, a small Flemish coin (i.e., worthless)

698 **advertence:** attention
702 **gonne . . . tales spende:** made conversation
707 **For wo and wery:** out of grief and weariness (?); see n.
720 **Seigh:** saw
728 **clawen:** scratch
736 **ownded:** wavy   **sonnyssh:** sunny, golden

She wrong ful ofte, and bad God on hire rewe,
And with the deth to doon boote on hire bale.
Hire hewe, whilom bright, that tho was
      pale,   740
Bar witnesse of hire wo and hire constreynte;
And thus she spak, sobbyng in hire com-
      pleynte:

"Allas," quod she, "out of this regioun
I, woful wrecche and infortuned wight,
And born in corsed constellacioun,   745
Moot goon and thus departen fro my knyght!
Wo worth, allas, that ilke dayes light
On which I saugh hym first with eyen tweyne,
That causeth me, and ich hym, al this peyne!"

Therwith the teris from hire eyen two   750
Down fille, as shour in Aperil ful swithe;
Hire white brest she bet, and for the wo
After the deth she cryed a thousand sithe,
Syn he that wont hire wo was for to lithe
She moot forgon; for which disaventure   755
She held hireself a forlost creature.

She seyde, "How shal he don, and ich also?
How sholde I lyve if that I from hym twynne?
O deere herte eke, that I love so,
Who shal that sorwe slen that ye ben inne?   760
O Calkas, fader, thyn be al this synne!
O moder myn, that cleped were Argyve,
Wo worth that day that thow me bere on lyve!

"To what fyn sholde I lyve and sorwen thus?
How sholde a fissh withouten water dure?   765
What is Criseyde worth, from Troilus?
How sholde a plaunte or lyves creature
Lyve withouten his kynde noriture?
For which ful ofte a by-word here I seye,
That 'rooteles moot grene soone deye.'   770

"I shal doon thus — syn neither swerd ne darte
Dar I noon handle, for the crueltee —
That ilke day that I from yow departe,
If sorwe of that nyl nat my bane be:

Thanne shal no mete or drynke come in me   775
Til I my soule out of my breste unshethe,
And thus myselven wol I don to dethe.

"And, Troilus, my clothes everychon
Shul blake ben in tokenyng, herte swete,
That I am as out of this world agon,   780
That wont was yow to setten in quiete;
And of myn ordre, ay til deth me mete,
The observance evere, in youre absence,
Shal sorwe ben, compleynt, and abstinence.

"Myn herte and ek the woful goost therinne
Byquethe I with youre spirit to compleyne   786
Eternaly, for they shal nevere twynne;
For though in erthe ytwynned be we tweyne,
Yet in the feld of pite, out of peyne,
That highte Elisos, shal we ben yfeere,   790
As Orpheus and Erudice, his fere.

"Thus, herte myn, for Antenor, allas,
I soone shal be chaunged, as I wene.
But how shul ye don in this sorwful cas?
How shal youre tendre herte this sustene?   795
But, herte myn, foryete this sorwe and tene,
And me also; for sothly for to seye,
So ye wel fare, I recche naught to deye."

How myghte it evere yred ben or ysonge,
The pleynte that she made in hire destresse?
I not; but, as for me, my litel tonge,   801
If I discryven wolde hire hevynesse,
It sholde make hire sorwe seme lesse
Than that it was, and childisshly deface
Hire heigh compleynte, and therfore ich it
      pace.   805

Pandare, which that sent from Troilus
Was to Criseyde — as ye han herd devyse
That for the beste it was acorded thus,
And he ful glad to doon hym that servyse —
Unto Criseyde, in a ful secree wise,   810
Ther as she lay in torment and in rage,
Com hire to telle al hoolly his message,

And fond that she hireselven gan to trete
Ful pitously, for with hire salte teris
Hire brest, hire face, ybathed was ful wete; 815

---

739 **doon boote on hire bale:** provide a remedy for her
suffering
741 **constreynte:** distress
744 **infortuned:** ill-fortuned
745 And born when the planets were in an unfavorable
combination (i.e., star-crossed)
753 **sithe:** times
754 **he:** him (object of *forgon*) **lithe:** soothe
756 **forlost:** completely lost
768 **noriture:** nourishment
769 **by-word:** proverb

776 **unshethe:** draw out
779 **in tokenyng:** as a sign
782 **ordre:** religious order
790 **Elisos:** Elysium, the counterpart of heaven in classical lore
791 **Orpheus and Erudice:** For the story, see Bo 3.m12. **fere:**
mate
811 **rage:** passionate grief

The myghty tresses of hire sonnysshe heeris
Unbroiden hangen al aboute hire eeris,
Which yaf hym verray signal of martire
Of deth, which that hire herte gan desire. 819

Whan she hym saugh, she gan for shame anon
Hire tery face atwixe hire armes hide;
For which this Pandare is so wo-bygon
That in the hous he myghte unnethe abyde,
As he that pite felt on every syde; 824
For if Criseyde hadde erst compleyned soore,
Tho gan she pleyne a thousand tymes more.

And in hire aspre pleynte thus she seyde:
"Pandare first of joies mo than two
Was cause causyng unto me, Criseyde,
That now transmewed ben in cruel wo. 830
Wher shal I seye to yow welcom or no,
That alderfirst me broughte unto servyse
Of love — allas! — that endeth in swich wise?

"Endeth than love in wo? Ye, or men lieth,
And alle worldly blisse, as thynketh me. 835
The ende of blisse ay sorwe it occupieth;
And whoso troweth nat that it so be,
Lat hym upon me, woful wrecche, ysee,
That myself hate and ay my burthe acorse,
Felyng alwey fro wikke I go to worse. 840

"Whoso me seeth, he seeth sorwe al atonys —
Peyne, torment, pleynte, wo, distresse!
Out of my woful body harm ther noon is,
As angwissh, langour, cruel bitternesse,
Anoy, smert, drede, fury, and ek siknesse. 845
I trowe, ywys, from hevene teeris reyne
For pite of myn aspre and cruel peyne."

"And thow, my suster, ful of discomfort,"
Quod Pandarus, "what thynkestow to do?
Whi ne hastow to thyselven som resport? 850
Whi wiltow thus thiself, allas, fordo?
Leef al this werk, and tak now heede to
That I shal seyn; and herkne of good entente
This which by me thi Troilus the sente."

816 sonnysshe: sunny, golden
817 Unbroiden: unbraided
818 martire: martyrdom
827 aspre: bitter
829 cause causyng: the primary cause (in logic)
830 transmewed: transmuted, transformed
831 Wher: whether (not translated; used to introduce a question)
838 ysee: look
839 burthe: birth
844 langour: suffering
845 Anoy: trouble
850 resport: regard
852 Leef: leave off   werk: pain

Tornede hire tho Criseyde, a wo makynge 855
So gret that it a deth was for to see.
"Allas," quod she, "what wordes may ye
      brynge?
What wol my deere herte seyn to me,
Which that I drede nevere mo to see?
Wol he han pleynte or teris er I wende? 860
I have ynough, if he therafter sende!"

She was right swich to seen in hire visage
As is that wight that men on beere bynde;
Hire face, lik of Paradys the ymage,
Was al ychaunged in another kynde. 865
The pleye, the laughter, men was wont to
      fynde
On hire, and ek hire joies everichone,
Ben fled; and thus lith now Criseyde allone.

Aboute hire eyen two a purpre ryng
Bytrent, in sothfast tokenyng of hire peyne,
That to biholde it was a dedly thyng; 871
For which Pandare myghte nat restreyne
The teeris from his eighen for to reyne;
But natheles, as he best myghte, he seyde
From Troilus thise wordes to Criseyde: 875

"Lo, nece, I trowe ye han herd al how
The kyng with othere lordes, for the beste,
Hath mad eschaunge of Antenor and yow,
That cause is of this sorwe and this unreste.
But how this cas dooth Troilus moleste, 880
That may non erthly mannes tonge seye —
As he that shortly shapith hym to deye.

"For which we han so sorwed, he and I,
That into litel bothe it hadde us slawe;
But thorugh my conseyl this day finaly 885
He somwhat is fro wepynge now withdrawe,
And semeth me that he desireth fawe
With yow to ben al nyght, for to devyse
Remedie in this, if ther were any wyse.

"This, short and pleyn, th'effect of my message,
As ferforth as my wit kan comprehende, 891
For ye that ben of torment in swich rage
May to no long prologe as now entende.
And hereupon ye may answere hym sende;

863 beere: funeral bier
869 purpre: purple
870 Bytrent: encircles
871 dedly: grievous
880 dooth . . . moleste: causes injury to
884 into litel: nearly (?); see n.   hadde . . . slawe: would have slain
887 fawe: eagerly

And for the love of God, my nece deere,   895
So lef this wo er Troilus be here!''

"Gret is my wo," quod she, and sighte soore
As she that feleth dedly sharp distresse;
"But yit to me his sorwe is muchel more,
That love hym bet than he hymself, I gesse.   900
Allas, for me hath he swich hevynesse?
Kan he for me so pitously compleyne?
Iwis, his sorwe doubleth al my peyne.

"Grevous to me, God woot, is for to twynne,"
Quod she, "but yet it harder is to me   905
To sen that sorwe which that he is inne;
For wel I woot it wol my bane be,
And deye I wol in certeyn," tho quod she;
"But bid hym come, er deth, that thus me
          threteth,
Dryve out that goost which in myn herte
          beteth."   910

Thise wordes seyd, she on hire armes two
Fil gruf, and gan to wepen pitously.
Quod Pandarus, "Allas, whi do ye so,
Syn wel ye woot the tyme is faste by
That he shal come? Aris up hastily,   915
That he yow nat bywopen thus ne fynde,
But ye wole have hym wood out of his mynde.

"For wiste he that ye ferde in this manere,
He wolde hymselven sle; and if I wende
To han this fare, he sholde nat come here   920
For al the good that Priam may dispende.
For to what fyn he wolde anon pretende,
That knowe ich wel; and forthi yet I seye:
So lef this sorwe, or platly he wol deye.

"And shapeth yow his sorwe for t'abregge,   925
And nought encresse, leeve nece swete!
Beth rather to hym cause of flat than egge,
And with som wisdom ye his sorwe bete.
What helpeth it to wepen ful a strete,
Or though ye bothe in salte teeris dreynte?   930
Bet is a tyme of cure ay than of pleynte.

"I mene thus: whan ich hym hider brynge,
Syn ye be wise and bothe of oon assent,

So shapeth how destourbe youre goynge,
Or come ayeyn soon after ye be went.   935
Women ben wise in short avysement;
And lat sen how youre wit shal now availle,
And that that I may helpe, it shal nat faille."

"Go," quod Criseyde, "and uncle, trewely,
I shal don al my myght me to restreyne   940
From wepyng in his sighte, and bisily
Hym for to glade I shal don al my peyne,
And in myn herte seken every veyne.
If to his sore ther may be fonden salve,
It shal nat lakke, certeyn, on my halve."   945

Goth Pandarus, and Troilus he soughte
Til in a temple he fond hym al allone,
As he that of his lif no lenger roughte;
But to the pitouse goddes everichone   949
Ful tendrely he preyde and made his mone,
To doon hym sone out of this world to pace,
For wel he thoughte ther was non other grace.

And shortly, al the sothe for to seye,
He was so fallen in despeir that day,
That outrely he shop hym for to deye.   955
For right thus was his argument alway:
He seyde he nas but lorn, weylaway!
"For al that comth, comth by necessitee:
Thus to ben lorn, it is my destinee.

"For certeynly, this wot I wel," he seyde,   960
"That forsight of divine purveyaunce
Hath seyn alwey me to forgon Criseyde,
Syn God seeth every thyng, out of doutaunce,
And hem disponyth, thorugh his ordinaunce,
In hire merites sothly for to be,   965
As they shul comen by predestyne.

"But natheles, allas, whom shal I leeve?
For ther ben grete clerkes many oon
That destyne thorugh argumentes preve;
And som men seyn that nedely ther is noon,
But that fre chois is yeven us everychon.   971
O, welaway! So sleighe arn clerkes olde
That I not whos opynyoun I may holde.

"For som men seyn, if God seth al biforn —
Ne God may nat deceyved ben, parde —   975

896 So lef: leave off
909 threteth: threatens
912 gruf: face down
916 bywopen: i.e., tear-stained
918 ferde: behaved
920 this fare: this sort of behavior
922 pretende: aim, seek
927 flat: flat of a sword (which heals)   egge: cutting edge
928 bete: assuage
929 ful a strete: a streetful

934 destourbe: hinder, prevent
936 short avysement: short deliberation, quick decisions
944 to: i.e., for
945 on my halve: on my part
961 purveyaunce: providence, foresight
964 disponyth: regulates, disposes
966 predestyne: predestination
972 sleighe: sly, clever

Than moot it fallen, theigh men hadde it sworn,
That purveiance hath seyn before to be.
Wherfore I sey, that from eterne if he
Hath wist byforn oure thought ek as oure dede,
We han no fre chois, as thise clerkes rede.   980

"For other thought, nor other dede also,
Myghte nevere ben, but swich as purveyaunce,
Which may nat ben deceyved nevere mo,
Hath feled byforn, withouten ignoraunce.
For yf ther myghte ben a variaunce   985
To writhen out fro Goddis purveyinge,
Ther nere no prescience of thyng comynge,

"But it were rather an opynyoun
Uncerteyn, and no stedfast forseynge;
And certes, that were an abusioun,   990
That God sholde han no parfit cler wytynge
More than we men that han doutous wenynge.
But swich an errour upon God to gesse
Were fals and foul, and wikked corsednesse.

"Ek this is an opynyoun of some   995
That han hire top ful heighe and smothe
     yshore:
They seyn right thus, that thyng is nat to come
For that the prescience hath seyn byfore
That it shal come; but they seyn that therfore
That it shal come, therfore the purveyaunce
Woot it byforn, withouten ignoraunce;   1001

"And in this manere this necessite
Retorneth in his part contrarie agayn.
For nedfully byhoveth it nat to bee
That thilke thynges fallen in certayn   1005
That ben purveyed; but nedly, as they sayn,
Byhoveth it that thynges whiche that falle,
That they in certayn ben purveyed alle.

"I mene as though I laboured me in this
To enqueren which thyng cause of which thyng
     be: 1010
As wheither that the prescience of God is

The certeyn cause of the necessite
Of thynges that to comen ben, parde,
Or if necessite of thyng comynge
Be cause certeyn of the purveyinge.   1015

"But now n'enforce I me nat in shewynge
How the ordre of causes stant; but wel woot I
That it byhoveth that the byfallynge
Of thynges wist byfore certeynly
Be necessarie, al seme it nat therby   1020
That prescience put fallynge necessaire
To thyng to come, al falle it foule or faire.

"For if ther sitte a man yond on a see,
Than by necessite bihoveth it
That, certes, thyn opynyoun sooth be   1025
That wenest or conjectest that he sit.
And further over now ayeynward yit,
Lo, right so is it of the part contrarie,
As thus — now herkne, for I wol nat tarie:

"I sey that if the opynyoun of the   1030
Be soth, for that he sitte, than sey I this:
That he mot sitten by necessite;
And thus necessite in eyther is.
For in hym, nede of sittynge is, ywys,
And in the, nede of soth; and thus, forsothe,
There mot necessite ben in yow bothe.   1036

"But thow mayst seyn, the man sit nat therfore
That thyn opynyoun of his sittynge soth is,
But rather, for the man sit ther byfore,
Therfore is thyn opynyoun soth, ywis.   1040
And I seye, though the cause of soth of this
Comth of his sittyng, yet necessite
Is entrechaunged, both in hym and the.

"Thus in this same wise, out of doutaunce,
I may wel maken, as it semeth me,   1045
My resonyng of Goddes purveyaunce
And of the thynges that to comen be;
By which resoun men may wel yse
That thilke thynges that in erthe falle,
That by necessite they comen alle.   1050

"For although that for thyng shal come, ywys,
Therfore is it purveyed, certeynly —
Nat that it comth for it purveyed is —

976 it sworn: i.e., sworn it would not happen
977 That: that which
984 feled: perceived
985 variaunce: variation (various possible courses of action)
986 writhen out: twist out, escape   purveyinge: providence
987 nere = ne were, would not be   prescience: foreknowledge
989 forseynge: foresight
990 abusioun: falsehood, absurdity
992 doutous wenynge: doubtful, uncertain understanding
996 smothe yshore: smoothly shaven; learned theologians would
be clergymen and thus tonsured.
1003–8 Turns back upon itself, since it is not necessary that things
happen because they have been foreseen; but it is necessary, as
they (clerks) say, that all things that happen have been foreseen.
1009 I intend, as if I were taking pains about this matter (see n.).

1016 enforce . . . me: trouble myself, insist on
1018 it byhoveth: it is necessary   byfallynge: happening
1021 put fallynge necessaire: makes occurring necessary
1022 al falle it foule or faire: i.e., however it turns out
1023 see: seat
1026 conjectest: conjecture
1027 ayeynward: on the other hand
1043 entrechaunged: mutual

Yet natheles, bihoveth it nedfully
That thing to come be purveyd, trewely,   1055
Or elles, thynges that purveyed be,
That they bitiden by necessite.

"And this suffiseth right ynough, certeyn,
For to destruye oure fre chois every del.
But now is this abusioun, to seyn   1060
That fallyng of the thynges temporel
Is cause of Goddes prescience eternel.
Now trewely, that is a fals sentence,
That thyng to come sholde cause his prescience.

"What myght I wene, and I hadde swich a
       thought,   1065
But that God purveyeth thyng that is to come
For that it is to come, and ellis nought?
So myghte I wene that thynges alle and some
That whilom ben byfalle and overcome
Ben cause of thilke sovereyne purveyaunce
That forwoot al withouten ignoraunce.   1071

"And over al this, yet sey I more herto:
That right as whan I wot ther is a thyng,
Iwys, that thyng moot nedfully be so;
Ek right so, whan I woot a thyng comyng,   1075
So mot it come; and thus the bifallyng
Of thynges that ben wist bifore the tyde,
They mowe nat ben eschued on no syde."

Thanne seyde he thus: "Almyghty Jove in
       trone,
That woost of al thys thyng the sothfastnesse,
Rewe on my sorwe: or do me deyen sone,   1081
Or bryng Criseyde and me fro this destresse!"
And whil he was in al this hevynesse,
Disputyng with hymself in this matere,   1084
Com Pandare in, and seyde as ye may here:

"O myghty God," quod Pandarus, "in trone,
I! Who say evere a wis man faren so?
Whi, Troilus, what thinkestow to doone?
Hastow swich lust to ben thyn owen fo?
What, parde, yet is nat Criseyde ago!   1090
Whi list the so thiself fordoon for drede
That in thyn hed thyne eyen semen dede?

"Hastow nat lyved many a yer byforn
Withouten hire, and ferd ful wel at ese?
Artow for hire and for noon other born?   1095
Hath Kynde the wrought al only hire to plese?
Lat be, and thynk right thus in thi disese:
That, in the dees right as ther fallen chaunces,
Right so in love ther come and gon plesaunces.

"And yet this is a wonder most of alle,   1100
Whi thow thus sorwest, syn thow nost nat yit,
Touchyng hire goyng, how that it shal falle,
Ne yif she kan hireself destourben it.
Thow hast nat yet assayed al hire wit.
A man may al bytyme his nekke beede   1105
Whan it shal of, and sorwen at the nede.

"Forthi tak hede of that that I shal seye:
I have with hire yspoke and longe ybe,
So as acorded was bitwixe us tweye;
And evere mor me thynketh thus, that she   1110
Hath somwhat in hire hertes privete
Wherwith she kan, if I shal right arede,
Destourbe al this of which thow art in drede.

"For which my counseil is, whan it is nyght
Thow to hire go and make of this an ende;   1115
And blisful Juno thorugh hire grete myght
Shal, as I hope, hire grace unto us sende.
Myn herte seyth, 'Certeyn, she shal nat wende.'
And forthi put thyn herte a while in reste,
And hold this purpos, for it is the beste."   1120

This Troilus answerd, and sighte soore:
"Thow seist right wel, and I wol don right so."
And what hym liste, he seyde unto it more.
And whan that it was tyme for to go,
Ful pryvely hymself, withouten mo,   1125
Unto hire com, as he was wont to doone;
And how they wroughte, I shal yow tellen
       soone.

Soth is, that whan they gonnen first to mete,
So gan the peyne hire hertes for to twiste
That neyther of hem other myghte grete,   1130
But hem in armes toke, and after kiste.
The lasse woful of hem bothe nyste
Wher that he was, ne myghte o word out
       brynge,
As I seyde erst, for wo and for sobbynge.

1054 **nedfully**: necessarily
1060 **abusioun**: falsehood, heresy
1066 **purveyeth**: foresees
1071 **forwoot**: foreknows
1077 **tyde**: time (of their happening)
1079 **trone**: throne

1098 **dees**: dice   **chaunces**: winning throws (for one or the
other of the players)
1103 **destourben**: hinder
1105 **al bytyme**: soon enough   **beede**: offer (extend)
1106 **shal of**: must (be cut) off

The woful teeris that they leten falle   1135
As bittre weren, out of teris kynde,
For peyne, as is ligne aloes or galle —
So bittre teeris weep nought, as I fynde,
The woful Mirra thorugh the bark and rynde —
That in this world ther nys so hard an herte   1140
That nolde han rewed on hire peynes smerte.

But whan hire woful weri goostes tweyne
Retourned ben ther as hem oughte dwelle,
And that somwhat to wayken gan the peyne
By lengthe of pleynte, and ebben gan the welle
Of hire teeris, and the herte unswelle,   1146
With broken vois, al hoors forshright, Criseyde
To Troilus thise ilke wordes seyde:

"O Jove, I deye, and mercy I beseche!
Help, Troilus!" And therwithal hire face   1150
Upon his brest she leyde and loste speche —
Hire woful spirit from his propre place,
Right with the word, alwey o poynt to pace.
And thus she lith with hewes pale and grene,
That whilom fressh and fairest was to sene.   1155

This Troilus, that on hire gan biholde,
Clepyng hire name — and she lay as for ded —
Without answere, and felte hire lymes colde,
Hire eyen throwen upward to hire hed,
This sorwful man kan now noon other red,   1160
But ofte tyme hire colde mowth he kiste.
Wher hym was wo, God and hymself it wiste!

He rist hym up, and long streght he hire leyde;
For signe of lif, for aught he kan or may,
Kan he non fynde in nothyng on Criseyde,   1165
For which his song ful ofte is "weylaway!"
But whan he saugh that specheles she lay,
With sorweful vois and herte of blisse al bare,
He seyde how she was fro this world yfare.   1169

So after that he longe hadde hire compleyned,
His hondes wrong, and seyd that was to seye,
And with his teeris salt hire brest byreyned,
He gan tho teeris wypen of ful dreye,

And pitously gan for the soule preye,   1174
And seyde, "O Lord, that set art in thi trone,
Rewe ek on me, for I shal folwe hire sone!"

She cold was, and withouten sentement
For aught he woot, for breth ne felte he non,
And this was hym a pregnant argument
That she was forth out of this world agon.   1180
And whan he say ther was non other woon,
He gan hire lymes dresse in swich manere
As men don hem that shal ben layd on beere.

And after this, with sterne and cruel herte,   1184
His swerd anon out of his shethe he twighte
Hymself to slen, how sore that hym smerte,
So that his soule hire soule folwen myghte
Ther as the doom of Mynos wolde it dighte,
Syn Love and cruel Fortune it ne wolde
That in this world he lenger lyven sholde.   1190

Than seyde he thus, fulfild of heigh desdayn:
"O cruel Jove, and thow, Fortune adverse,
This al and som: that falsly have ye slayn
Criseyde, and syn ye may do me no werse,
Fy on youre myght and werkes so dyverse!   1195
Thus cowardly ye shul me nevere wynne;
Ther shal no deth me fro my lady twynne.

"For I this world, syn ye have slayn hire thus,
Wol lete and folwe hire spirit low or hye;
Shal nevere lovere seyn that Troilus   1200
Dar nat for fere with his lady dye;
For certeyn I wol beere hire compaignie.
But syn ye wol nat suffre us lyven here,
Yet suffreth that oure soules ben yfere.

"And thow, cite, which that I leve in wo,   1205
And thow, Priam, and bretheren alle yfeere,
And thow, my moder, farwel, for I go;
And Atropos, make redy thow my beere;
And thow, Criseyde, o swete herte deere,
Receyve now my spirit!" wolde he seye,   1210
With swerd at herte, al redy for to deye.

1136 **out of teris kynde:** unlike the nature of tears
1137 **ligne aloes:** a bitter medicine
1138 **weep:** wept
1139 **Mirra:** Myrrha, changed into a tree, wept tears of myrrh
1142 **goostes:** souls
1144 **wayken:** weaken
1146 **unswelle:** decrease in fullness
1147 **hoors:** hoarse   **forshright:** exhausted from screaming
1153 **o poynt to:** about to, on the point of
1162 **Wher:** whether, if
1163 **long streght:** stretched out at length
1172 **byreyned:** rained upon
1173 **of:** off   **dreye:** dry

1177 **sentement:** feeling
1179 **pregnant:** urgent, convincing
1181 **woon:** resource, course of action
1182 **dresse:** arrange
1185 **twighte:** pulled
1186 **how sore:** however painfully
1188 **Mynos:** judge of the dead   **dighte:** dispose
1195 **dyverse:** contrary, hostile
1199 **lete:** abandon
1208 **Atropos:** the Fate who cuts the thread of life; see line 1546.

But as God wolde, of swough therwith
    sh'abreyde,
And gan to sike, and "Troilus" she cride;
And he answerde, "Lady myn, Criseyde,
Lyve ye yet?" and leet his swerd down glide.
"Ye, herte myn, that thonked be Cipride!" 1216
Quod she; and therwithal she soore syghte,
And he bigan conforte hire as he myghte,

Took hire in armes two, and kiste hire ofte,
And hire to glade he did al his entente; 1220
For which hire goost, that flikered ay o-lofte,
Into hire woful herte ayeyn it wente.
But at the laste, as that hire eye glente
Asyde, anon she gan his swerd espie,
As it lay bare, and gan for fere crye, 1225

And asked hym, whi he it hadde out drawe.
And Troilus anon the cause hire tolde,
And how hymself therwith he wolde han slawe;
For which Criseyde upon hym gan biholde,
And gan hym in hire armes faste folde, 1230
And seyde, "O mercy, God! Lo, which a dede!
Allas, how neigh we weren bothe dede!

"Than if I nadde spoken, as grace was,
Ye wolde han slayn youreself anon?" quod she.
"Yee, douteles"; and she answerde, "Allas,
For by that ilke Lord that made me, 1236
I nolde a forlong wey on lyve have be
After youre deth, to han ben crowned queene
Of al that lond the sonne on shyneth sheene.

"But with this selve swerd, which that here is,
Myselve I wolde han slawe," quod she tho. 1241
"But hoo, for we han right ynough of this,
And lat us rise, and streght to bedde go,
And there lat us speken of oure wo;
For, by the morter which that I se brenne, 1245
Knowe I ful wel that day is nat far henne."

Whan they were in hire bed, in armes folde,
Naught was it lik tho nyghtes here-byforn.
For pitously ech other gan byholde,
As they that hadden al hire blisse ylorn, 1250
Bywaylinge ay the day that they were born;

Til at the laste this sorwful wight, Criseyde,
To Troilus thise ilke wordes seyde:

"Lo, herte myn, wel woot ye this," quod she,
"That if a wight alwey his wo compleyne 1255
And seketh nought how holpen for to be,
It nys but folie and encrees of peyne;
And syn that here assembled be we tweyne
To fynde boote of wo that we ben inne,
It were al tyme soone to bygynne. 1260

"I am a womman, as ful wel ye woot,
And as I am avysed sodeynly,
So wol I telle yow, whil it is hoot.
Me thynketh thus: that nouther ye nor I
Ought half this wo to maken, skilfully; 1265
For ther is art ynough for to redresse
That yet is mys, and slen this hevynesse.

"Soth is, the wo, the which that we ben inne,
For aught I woot, for nothyng ellis is
But for the cause that we sholden twynne. 1270
Considered al, ther nys namore amys.
But what is thanne a remede unto this,
But that we shape us soone for to meete?
This al and som, my deere herte sweete.

"Now, that I shal wel bryngen it aboute 1275
To come ayeyn, soone after that I go,
Therof am I no manere thyng in doute;
For, dredeles, withinne a wowke or two
I shal ben here; and that it may be so
By alle right and in a wordes fewe, 1280
I shal yow wel an heep of weyes shewe.

"For which I wol nat make long sermoun —
For tyme ylost may nought recovered be —
But I wol gon to my conclusioun,
And to the beste, in aught that I kan see. 1285
And for the love of God, foryeve it me
If I speke aught ayeyns youre hertes reste;
For trewely, I speke it for the beste,

"Makyng alwey a protestacioun
That now thise wordes which that I shal seye
Nis but to shewen yow my mocioun 1291

1216 **Cipride:** Venus, to whom Cyprus was sacred
1217 **syghte:** sighed
1223 **glente:** glanced
1237 **a forlong wey:** a couple of minutes; i.e., even a few moments
1242 **hoo:** stop
1245 **morter:** a candle (or a bowl of wax with a wick) used as a night light

1260 **al tyme:** high time
1262 **avysed sodeynly:** suddenly resolved
1265 **skilfully:** reasonably
1267 **mys:** amiss
1274 **This al and som:** this is the sum and substance of the matter
1278 **wowke:** week
1291 **mocioun:** desire (or, proposal)

To fynde unto oure help the beste weye;
And taketh it non other wise, I preye,
For in effect, what so ye me comaunde,
That wol I don, for that is no demaunde.   1295

"Now herkneth this: ye han wel understonde
My goyng graunted is by parlement
So ferforth that it may nat be withstonde
For al this world, as by my jugement.
And syn ther helpeth non avisement   1300
To letten it, lat it passe out of mynde,
And lat us shape a bettre wey to fynde.

"The soth is this: the twynnyng of us tweyne
Wol us disese and cruelich anoye,
But hym byhoveth somtyme han a peyne   1305
That serveth Love, if that he wol have joye.
And syn I shal no ferther out of Troie
Than I may ride ayeyn on half a morwe,
It oughte lesse causen us to sorwe;

"So as I shal not so ben hid in muwe,   1310
That day by day, myn owne herte deere —
Syn wel ye woot that it is now a trewe —
Ye shal ful wel al myn estat yheere.
And er that trewe is doon, I shal ben heere;
And thanne have ye both Antenore ywonne 1315
And me also. Beth glad now, if ye konne,

"And thenk right thus: 'Criseyde is now agon.
But what, she shal come hastiliche ayeyn!'
And whanne, allas? By God, lo, right anon,
Er dayes ten, this dar I saufly seyn.   1320
And than at erste shal we be so feyn,
So as we shal togideres evere dwelle,
That al this world ne myghte oure blisse telle.

"I se that oft-tyme, there as we ben now,
That for the beste, oure counseyl for to hide,
Ye speke nat with me, nor I with yow   1326
In fourtenyght, ne se yow go ne ride.
May ye naught ten dayes thanne abide,
For myn honour, in swich an aventure?
Iwys, ye mowen ellis lite endure!   1330

"Ye knowe ek how that al my kyn is heere,
But if that onliche it my fader be,
And ek myn othere thynges alle yfeere,
And nameliche, my deere herte, ye,
Whom that I nolde leven for to se   1335
For al this world, as wyd as it hath space,
Or ellis se ich nevere Joves face!

"Whi trowe ye my fader in this wise
Coveyteth so to se me, but for drede
Lest in this town that folkes me despise 1340
Because of hym, for his unhappy dede?
What woot my fader what lif that I lede?
For if he wiste in Troie how wel I fare,
Us neded for my wendyng nought to care.

"Ye sen that every day ek, more and more, 1345
Men trete of pees, and it supposid is
That men the queene Eleyne shal restore,
And Grekis us restoren that is mys;
So, though ther nere comfort non but this,
That men purposen pees on every syde,   1350
Ye may the bettre at ese of herte abyde.

"For if that it be pees, myn herte deere,
The nature of the pees moot nedes dryve
That men moost entrecomunen yfeere,
And to and fro ek ride and gon as blyve 1355
Alday as thikke as been fleen from an hyve,
And every wight han liberte to bleve
Whereas hym liste the bet, withouten leve.

"And though so be that pees ther may be non,
Yet hider, though ther nevere pees ne were,
I moste come; for whider sholde I gon,   1361
Or how, meschaunce, sholde I dwelle there
Among tho men of armes evere in feere?
For which, as wisly God my soule rede,
I kan nat sen wherof ye sholden drede.   1365

"Have here another wey, if it so be
That al this thyng ne may yow nat suffise:
My fader, as ye knowen wel, parde,
Is old, and elde is ful of coveytise,
And I right now have founden al the gise, 1370

1295 for that is no demaunde: there is no question about it; see
line 1694.
1304 anoye: disturb
1307 shal: shall go
1310 in muwe: cooped up, in hiding
1313 myn estat yheere: hear of my condition
1314 trewe: truce
1320 saufly: safely
1324–26 i.e., considering our situation, I think it best that we do
not speak to each other often, in order to conceal our plans.
1327 fourtenyght: a fortnight, two weeks
1330 mowen: can

1332 onliche: only
1337 se ich: may I see
1341 unhappy: unfortunate
1344 Us neded: we would need
1346 trete of: discuss, negotiate
1348 mys: amiss
1350 purposen: intend, propose
1354 entrecomunen yfeere: have dealings with one another
1356 been: bees fleen: fly
1357 bleve: remain
1370 gise: way

Withouten net, wherwith I shal hym hente.
And herkeneth how, if that ye wol assente:

"Lo, Troilus, men seyn that hard it is
The wolf ful and the wether hool to have;
This is to seyn, that men ful ofte, iwys,   1375
Mote spenden part the remenant for to save;
For ay with gold men may the herte grave
Of hym that set is upon coveytise;
And how I mene, I shal it yow devyse:

"The moeble which that I have in this town
Unto my fader shal I take, and seye   1381
That right for trust and for savacioun
It sent is from a frend of his or tweye,
The whiche frendes ferventliche hym preye
To senden after more, and that in hie,   1385
Whil that this town stant thus in jupartie.

"And that shal ben an huge quantite —
Thus shal I seyn — but lest it folk espide,
This may be sent by no wyght but by me.
I shal ek shewen hym, yf pees bytyde,   1390
What frendes that ich have on every syde
Toward the court, to don the wrathe pace
Of Priamus and don hym stonde in grace.

"So what for o thyng and for other, swete,
I shal hym so enchaunten with my sawes   1395
That right in hevene his sowle is, shal he mete;
For al Appollo, or his clerkes lawes,
Or calkullynge, avayleth nought thre hawes;
Desir of gold shal so his soule blende
That, as me lyst, I shal wel make an ende.   1400

"And yf he wolde ought by hys sort it preve
If that I lye, in certayn I shal fonde
Distorben hym and plukke hym by the sleve,
Makynge his sort, and beren hym on honde
He hath not wel the goddes understonde;   1405
For goddes speken in amphibologies,
And for o soth they tellen twenty lyes.

"Ek, 'Drede fond first goddes, I suppose' —
Thus shal I seyn — and that his coward herte
Made hym amys the goddes text to glose,   1410
Whan he for fered out of Delphos sterte.
And but I make hym soone to converte
And don my red withinne a day or tweye,
I wol to yow oblige me to deye."

And treweliche, as writen wel I fynde   1415
That al this thyng was seyd of good entente,
And that hire herte trewe was and kynde
Towardes hym, and spak right as she mente,
And that she starf for wo neigh whan she
        wente,
And was in purpos evere to be trewe: 1420
Thus writen they that of hire werkes knewe.

This Troilus, with herte and erys spradde,
Herde al this thyng devysen to and fro,
And verrayliche him semed that he hadde
The selve wit; but yet to late hire go   1425
His herte mysforyaf hym evere mo;
But fynaly, he gan his herte wreste
To trusten hire, and took it for the beste.

For which the grete furie of his penaunce
Was queynt with hope, and therwith hem bi-
        twene   1430
Bigan for joie th'amorouse daunce;
And as the briddes, whanne the sonne is shene,
Deliten in hire song in leves grene,
Right so the wordes that they spake yfeere
Delited hem, and made hire hertes clere.   1435

But natheles, the wendyng of Criseyde,
For al this world, may nat out of his mynde,
For which ful ofte he pitously hire preyde
That of hire heste he myghte hire trewe fynde,
And seyde hire, "Certes, if ye be unkynde,   1440
And but ye come at day set into Troye,
Ne shal I nevere have hele, honour, ne joye.

"For also soth as sonne uprist o-morwe —
And God so wisly thow me, woful wrecche,

1374 **wether:** sheep
1377 **grave:** make an impression on
1380 **moeble:** personal property
1392 **Toward:** i.e., at
1395 **sawes:** speeches
1396 **mete:** dream, imagine
1397 **clerkes lawes:** learned precepts
1398 **calkullynge:** calculating   **hawes:** hawthorn berries (i.e.,
nothing)
1404 **beren hym on honde:** swear to him, deceive him
1406 **amphibologies:** ambiguities
1407 **o:** one

1408 **fond:** invented
1410 **glose:** interpret
1411 **fered:** fright   **Delphos:** Delphi, the temple of the oracle
1413 **don my red:** execute my plan
1414 **oblige:** pledge
1422 **erys spradde:** ears spread wide (i.e., listening eagerly)
1425 **selve wit:** same idea   **late:** let
1426 **mysforyaf:** had misgivings
1427 **wreste:** constrain, force
1430 **queynt with:** extinguished by
1436 **wendyng:** departure
1443 **uprist** = *upriseth,* rises up

To reste brynge out of this cruel sorwe! —   1445
I wol myselven sle if that ye drecche.
But of my deeth though litel be to recche,
Yet, er that ye me causen so to smerte,
Dwelle rather here, myn owen swete herte.

"For trewely, myn owne lady deere,   1450
Tho sleghtes yet that I have herd yow stere
Ful shaply ben to faylen alle yfeere.
For thus men seyth 'That on thenketh the
          beere,
But al another thenketh his ledere.'
Youre syre is wys; and seyd is, out of drede,   1455
'Men may the wise atrenne, and naught atrede.'

"It is ful hard to halten unespied
Byfore a crepel, for he kan the craft;
Youre fader is in sleght as Argus eyed;
For al be that his moeble is hym biraft,   1460
His olde sleighte is yet so with hym laft
Ye shal nat blende hym for youre womman-
          hede,
Ne feyne aright; and that is al my drede.

"I not if pees shal evere mo bitide;
But pees or no, for ernest ne for game,   1465
I woot, syn Calkas on the Grekis syde
Hath ones ben and lost so foule his name,
He dar nomore come here ayeyn for shame;
For which that wey, for aught I kan espie,
To trusten on nys but a fantasie.   1470

"Ye shal ek sen, youre fader shal yow glose
To ben a wif; and as he kan wel preche,
He shal som Grek so preyse and wel alose
That ravysshen he shal yow with his speche,
Or do yow don by force as he shal teche;   1475
And Troilus, of whom ye nyl han routhe,
Shal causeles so sterven in his trouthe!

"And over al this, youre fader shal despise
Us alle, and seyn this cite nys but lorn,

And that th'assege nevere shal aryse,   1480
For-whi the Grekis han it alle sworn,
Til we be slayn and down oure walles torn.
And thus he shal yow with his wordes fere,
That ay drede I that ye wol bleven there.

"Ye shal ek seen so many a lusty knyght   1485
Among the Grekis, ful of worthynesse,
And ech of hem with herte, wit, and myght
To plesen yow don al his bisynesse,
That ye shul dullen of the rudenesse
Of us sely Troians, but if routhe   1490
Remorde yow, or vertu of youre trouthe.

"And this to me so grevous is to thynke
That fro my brest it wol my soule rende;
Ne dredeles, in me ther may nat synke
A good opynyoun, if that ye wende,   1495
For whi youre fadres sleghte wol us shende.
And if ye gon, as I have told yow yore,
So thenk I n'am but ded, withoute more.

"For which, with humble, trewe, and pitous
          herte,
A thousand tymes mercy I yow preye;   1500
So rueth on myn aspre peynes smerte,
And doth somwhat as that I shal yow seye,
And lat us stele awey bitwixe us tweye;
And thynk that folie is, whan man may chese,
For accident his substaunce ay to lese.   1505

"I mene thus: that syn we mowe er day
Wel stele awey and ben togidere so,
What wit were it to putten in assay,
In cas ye sholden to youre fader go,
If that ye myghten come ayeyn or no?   1510
Thus mene I: that it were a gret folie
To putte that sikernesse in jupertie.

"And vulgarly to speken of substaunce
Of tresour, may we bothe with us lede
Inough to lyve in honour and plesaunce   1515
Til into tyme that we shal ben dede;
And thus we may eschuen al this drede.

1446 **drecche:** delay
1451 **sleghtes:** tricks   **stere:** propose
1452 **Ful shaply:** very likely
1453 **beere:** bear
1455 **syre:** father
1456 **atrenne:** outrun   **atrede:** outwit
1457 **halten:** (pretend to) limp   **unespied:** undetected
1458 **crepel:** cripple
1459 **in sleght as Argus eyed:** in matters of deception with eyes
like Argus (who had a hundred eyes)
1461 **sleighte:** shrewdness, cunning
1471 **glose:** cajole
1473 **alose:** commend, praise
1475 **do yow don:** make you do

1483 **fere:** frighten
1484 **bleven:** remain
1489 **rudenesse:** boorishness
1490 **sely:** ignorant
1491 **Remorde yow:** cause you remorse   **vertu:** power
1495 **opynyoun:** expectation
1496 **For whi:** because
1505 **accident:** inessential attribute   **substaunce:** underlying
reality
1508 **in assay:** to the test
1513 **vulgarly:** common (not philosophical) parlance; see note
to 1505.   **substaunce:** wealth
1517 **eschuen:** eschew, avoid

For everich other wey ye kan recorde,
Myn herte, ywis, may therwith naught acorde.

"And hardily, ne dredeth no poverte,   1520
For I have kyn and frendes elleswhere
That, though we comen in oure bare sherte,
Us sholde neyther lakken gold ne gere,
But ben honured while we dwelten there.
And go we anon; for as in myn entente,   1525
This is the beste, if that ye wole assente."

Criseyde, with a sik, right in this wise
Answerde, "Ywis, my deere herte trewe,
We may wel stele awey, as ye devyse,
And fynden swich unthrifty weyes newe,   1530
But afterward ful soore it wol us rewe.
And helpe me God so at my mooste nede,
As causeles ye suffren al this drede!

"For thilke day that I for cherisynge
Or drede of fader, or for other wight,   1535
Or for estat, delit, or for weddynge,
Be fals to yow, my Troilus, my knyght,
Saturnes doughter, Juno, thorugh hire myght,
As wood as Athamante do me dwelle
Eternalich in Stix, the put of helle!   1540

"And this on every god celestial
I swere it yow, and ek on ech goddesse,
On every nymphe and deite infernal,
On satiry and fawny more and lesse,
That halve goddes ben of wildernesse;   1545
And Attropos my thred of lif tobreste
If I be fals! Now trowe me if yow leste!

"And thow, Symois, that as an arwe clere
Thorugh Troie rennest downward to the se,
Ber witnesse of this word that seyd is here: 1550
That thilke day that ich untrewe be
To Troilus, myn owene herte fre,
That thow retourne bakward to thi welle,
And I with body and soule synke in helle!

"But that ye speke, awey thus for to go   1555
And leten alle youre frendes, God forbede
For any womman that ye sholden so,

And namely syn Troie hath now swich nede
Of help. And ek of o thyng taketh hede:
If this were wist, my lif lay in balaunce,   1560
And youre honour; God shilde us fro mes-
         chaunce!

"And if so be that pees heere-after take,
As alday happeth after anger game,
Whi, Lord, the sorwe and wo ye wolden make,
That ye ne dorste come ayeyn for shame!   1565
And er that ye juparten so youre name,
Beth naught to hastif in this hoote fare,
For hastif man ne wanteth nevere care.

"What trowe ye the peple ek al aboute
Wolde of it seye? It is ful light t'arede.   1570
They wolden seye, and swere it out of doute,
That love ne drof yow naught to don this dede,
But lust voluptuous and coward drede.
Thus were al lost, ywis, myn herte deere,
Youre honour, which that now shyneth so clere.

"And also thynketh on myn honeste,   1576
That floureth yet, how foule I sholde it shende,
And with what filthe it spotted sholde be,
If in this forme I sholde with yow wende.
Ne though I lyved unto the werldes ende,   1580
My name sholde I nevere ayeynward wynne;
Thus were I lost, and that were routhe and
         synne.

"And forthi sle with resoun al this hete!
Men seyn, 'The suffrant overcomith,' parde;
Ek 'Whoso wol han lief, he lief moot lete.'   1585
Thus maketh vertu of necessite
By pacience, and thynk that lord is he
Of Fortune ay that naught wole of hire recche,
And she ne daunteth no wight but a wrecche.

"And trusteth this: that certes, herte swete,   1590
Er Phebus suster, Lucina the sheene,
The Leoun passe out of this Ariete,
I wol ben here, withouten any wene.
I mene, as helpe me Juno, hevenes quene,

1518 **recorde**: call to mind, think of
1523 **gere**: possessions
1530 **unthrifty**: profitless, foolish
1539 **Athamante**: Athamas, driven mad (*wood*) by Juno
1540 **Stix**: usually a river or marsh **put**: pit
1544 **satiry**: satyrs **fawny**: fauns
1545 **halve goddes**: demigods
1548 **Symois**: a river

1562 **take**: take place (?); see n.
1563 **alday**: frequently
1566 **juparten**: endanger
1567 **hoote fare**: rash conduct
1576 **honeste**: reputation for decency
1584 **suffrant**: patient one
1585 Also, 'Whoever will have something he wants must give up
something he wants.'
1591 **Lucina**: the moon
1592 Pass out of this (the present) sign, Aries (*Ariete*), to the sign
Leo (*Leoun*), which would take about ten days
1593 **wene**: doubt

The tenthe day, but if that deth m'assaile,   1595
I wol yow sen withouten any faille."

"And now, so this be soth," quod Troilus,
"I shal wel suffre unto the tenthe day,
Syn that I se that nede it mot be thus.
But for the love of God, if it be may,   1600
So late us stelen priveliche away;
For evere in oon, as for to lyve in reste,
Myn herte seyth that it wol be the beste."

"O mercy, God, what lif is this?" quod she.
"Allas, ye sle me thus for verray tene!   1605
I se wel now that ye mystrusten me,
For by youre wordes it is wel yseene.
Now for the love of Cinthia the sheene,
Mistrust me nought thus causeles, for routhe,
Syn to be trewe I have yow plight my trouthe.

"And thynketh wel that somtyme it is wit   1611
To spende a tyme, a tyme for to wynne;
Ne, parde, lorn am I naught fro yow yit,
Though that we ben a day or two atwynne.
Drif out the fantasies yow withinne,   1615
And trusteth me, and leveth ek youre sorwe,
Or here my trouthe: I wol naught lyve tyl
       morwe.

"For if ye wiste how soore it doth me smerte,
Ye wolde cesse of this; for, God, thow wost,
The pure spirit wepeth in myn herte   1620
To se yow wepen that I love most,
And that I mot gon to the Grekis oost.
Ye, nere it that I wiste remedie
To come ayeyn, right here I wolde dye!

"But certes, I am naught so nyce a wight   1625
That I ne kan ymaginen a wey
To come ayeyn that day that I have hight.
For who may holde a thing that wol awey?
My fader naught, for al his queynte pley!
And by my thrift, my wendyng out of Troie
Another day shal torne us alle to joie.   1631

"Forthi with al myn herte I yow biseke,
If that yow list don ought for my preyere,
And for that love which that I love yow eke,
That er that I departe fro yow here,   1635
That of so good a confort and a cheere

I may yow sen that ye may brynge at reste
Myn herte, which that is o poynt to breste.

"And over al this I prey yow," quod she tho,
"Myn owene hertes sothfast suffisaunce,   1640
Syn I am thyn al hol, withouten mo,
That whil that I am absent, no plesaunce
Of oother do me fro youre remembraunce;
For I am evere agast, forwhy men rede
That love is thyng ay ful of bisy drede.   1645

"For in this world ther lyveth lady non,
If that ye were untrewe — as God defende! —
That so bitraised were or wo-bigon
As I, that alle trouthe in yow entende.
And douteles, if that ich other wende,   1650
I ner but ded; and er ye cause fynde,
For Goddes love, so beth me naught unkynde!"

To this answerde Troilus and seyde,
"Now God, to whom ther nys no cause ywrye,
Me glade, as wys I nevere unto Criseyde,   1655
Syn thilke day I saugh hire first with yë,
Was fals, ne nevere shal til that I dye.
At shorte wordes, wel ye may me leve.
I kan na more; it shal be founde at preve."

"Grant mercy, goode myn, iwys!" quod she,
"And blisful Venus lat me nevere sterve   1661
Er I may stonde of plesaunce in degree
To quyte hym wel that so wel kan deserve;
And while that God my wit wol me conserve,
I shal so don, so trewe I have yow founde,   1665
That ay honour to me-ward shal rebounde.

"For trusteth wel that youre estat roial,
Ne veyn delit, nor only worthinesse
Of yow in werre or torney marcial,
Ne pompe, array, nobleye, or ek richesse   1670
Ne made me to rewe on youre destresse,
But moral vertu, grounded upon trouthe —
That was the cause I first hadde on yow routhe!

"Eke gentil herte and manhod that ye hadde,
And that ye hadde, as me thoughte, in despit
Every thyng that souned into badde,   1676
As rudenesse and poeplissh appetit,

1638 **o poynt to:** about to, on the point of
1648 **bitraised:** betrayed
1650 **wende:** supposed
1654 **ywrye:** hidden
1662 **of plesaunce in degree:** in so happy a situation
1666 **rebounde:** return
1669 **torney marcial:** tournament
1677 **poeplissh appetit:** vulgar, low desire

1602 **evere in oon:** continually
1605 **tene:** sorrow (or, vexation)
1608 **Cinthia:** Cynthia, the moon
1629 **queynte:** ingenious, clever

And that youre resoun bridlede youre delit,
This made, aboven every creature,
That I was youre, and shal while I may
            dure.   1680

"And this may lengthe of yeres naught fordo,
Ne remuable Fortune deface.
But Juppiter, that of his myght may do
The sorwful to be glad, so yeve us grace
Or nyghtes ten to meten in this place,   1685
So that it may youre herte and myn suffise!
And fareth now wel, for tyme is that ye rise."

And after that they longe ypleyned hadde,
And ofte ykist, and streite in armes folde,

The day gan rise, and Troilus hym cladde,   1690
And rewfullich his lady gan byholde,
As he that felte dethes cares colde,
And to hire grace he gan hym recomaunde.
Wher hym was wo, this holde I no demaunde.

For mannes hed ymagynen ne kan,   1695
N'entendement considere, ne tonge telle
The cruele peynes of this sorwful man,
That passen every torment down in helle.
For whan he saugh that she ne myghte dwelle,
Which that his soule out of his herte rente,   1700
Withouten more out of the chaumbre he
            wente.

Explicit liber quartus.

BOOK V

Incipit liber quintus.

Aprochen gan the fatal destyne
That Joves hath in disposicioun,
And to yow, angry Parcas, sustren thre,
Committeth to don execucioun;
For which Criseyde moste out of the town,   5
And Troilus shal dwellen forth in pyne
Til Lachesis his thred no lenger twyne.

The gold-tressed Phebus heighe on-lofte
Thries hadde alle with his bemes cleene
The snowes molte, and Zepherus as ofte   10
Ibrought ayeyn the tendre leves grene,
Syn that the sone of Ecuba the queene
Bigan to love hire first for whom his sorwe
Was al, that she departe sholde a-morwe.

Ful redy was at prime Diomede   15
Criseyde unto the Grekis oost to lede,
For sorwe of which she felt hire herte blede,
As she that nyste what was best to rede.
And trewely, as men in bokes rede,
Men wiste nevere womman han the care,   20
Ne was so loth out of a town to fare.

This Troilus, withouten reed or loore,
As man that hath his joies ek forlore,
Was waytyng on his lady evere more   24
As she that was the sothfast crop and more
Of al his lust or joies heretofore.
But Troilus, now far-wel al thi joie,
For shaltow nevere sen hire eft in Troie!

1678 **bridlede:** controlled
1682 **remuable:** variable
1689 **streite:** tightly

Incipit, *etc.:* Here begins the fifth book.
3 **Parcas:** the Fates
7 **Lachesis:** usually the Fate who measures the thread of life,
while Clotho spins it   **twyne:** twist, spin
9 **cleene:** pure (beams) or completely (melted)
10 **molte:** melted   **Zepherus:** the west wind of spring
12 **Ecuba:** Hecuba (Troilus's mother)

1691 **rewfullich:** ruefully, sadly
1696 **entendement:** intellect
Explicit, *etc.:* Here ends the fourth book.

----

15 **prime:** the first three hours of the day, from about 6 to 9
18 **to rede:** as advice, what to do
20 **the care:** i.e., such care
23 **forlore:** lost
25 **crop and more:** foliage and root (hence, totality)

Soth is that while he bood in this manere,
He gan his wo ful manly for to hide,   30
That wel unnethe it sene was in his chere;
But at the yate ther she sholde out ride,
With certeyn folk he hoved hire t'abide,
So wo-bigon, al wolde he naught hym pleyne,
That on his hors unnethe he sat for peyne.   35

For ire he quook, so gan his herte gnawe,
Whan Diomede on horse gan hym dresse,
And seyde to hymself this ilke sawe:
"Allas," quod he, "thus foul a wrecchednesse,
Whi suffre ich it? Whi nyl ich it redresse?   40
Were it nat bet atones for to dye
Than evere more in langour thus to drye?

"Whi nyl I make atones riche and pore
To have inough to doone er that she go?
Why nyl I brynge al Troie upon a roore?   45
Whi nyl I slen this Diomede also?
Why nyl I rather with a man or two
Stele hire away? Whi wol I this endure?
Whi nyl I helpen to myn owen cure?"

But why he nolde don so fel a dede,   50
That shal I seyn, and whi hym liste it spare:
He hadde in herte alweyes a manere drede
Lest that Criseyde, in rumour of this fare,
Sholde han ben slayn; lo, this was al his care.
And ellis, certeyn, as I seyde yore,   55
He hadde it don, withouten wordes more.

Criseyde, whan she redy was to ride,
Ful sorwfully she sighte, and seyde "Allas!"
But forth she moot, for aught that may bitide;
Ther is non other remedie in this cas.   60
And forth she rit ful sorwfully a pas.
What wonder is, though that hire sore smerte,
Whan she forgoth hire owen swete herte?

This Troilus, in wise of curteysie,   64
With hauk on honde and with an huge route
Of knyghtes, rood and did hire companye,
Passyng al the valeye fer withoute,

And ferther wolde han riden, out of doute,
Ful fayn, and wo was hym to gon so sone;
But torne he moste, and it was ek to done.   70

And right with that was Antenor ycome
Out of the Grekis oost, and every wight
Was of it glad, and seyde he was welcome.
And Troilus, al nere his herte light,
He peyned hym with al his fulle myght   75
Hym to withholde of wepyng atte leeste,
And Antenor he kiste and made feste.

And therwithal he moste his leve take,
And caste his eye upon hire pitously,
And neer he rood, his cause for to make,   80
To take hire by the honde al sobrely.
And Lord, so she gan wepen tendrely!
And he ful softe and sleighly gan hire seye,
"Now holde youre day, and do me nat to deye."

With that his courser torned he aboute   85
With face pale, and unto Diomede
No word he spak, ne non of al his route;
Of which the sone of Tideus took hede,
As he that koude more than the crede
In swich a craft, and by the reyne hire hente;   90
And Troilus to Troie homward he wente.   91

This Diomede, that ledde hire by the bridel,
Whan that he saugh the folk of Troie aweye,
Thoughte, "Al my labour shal nat ben on ydel,
If that I may, for somwhat shal I seye,   95
For at the werste it may yet shorte oure weye.
I have herd seyd ek tymes twyes twelve,
'He is a fool that wol foryete hymselve.'"

But natheles, this thoughte he wel ynough,
That "Certeynlich I am aboute nought,   100
If that I speke of love or make it tough;
For douteles, if she have in hire thought
Hym that I gesse, he may nat ben ybrought
So soon awey; but I shal fynde a meene   104
That she naught wite as yet shal what I mene."

---

29 **bood:** waited
33 **hoved hire t'abide:** lingered to wait for her
37 **gan hym dresse:** mounted
45 **roore:** uproar
50 **fel:** fierce
53 **in rumour of this fare:** in the uproar of this action
61 **rit** = *rideth*, rides **sorwfully a pas:** at a sorrowful (slow) pace
64 **in wise of curteysie:** in a courteous manner (for peace rather than war)

70 **to done:** to be done, had to be done
77 **made feste:** made much of him
80 **make:** i.e., plead
88 **the sone of Tideus:** Diomede
89 Like one who knew more than the bare rudiments (*crede*, creed)
90 **reyne:** reins
94 **on ydel:** wasted, in vain
98 **foryete hymselve:** forget his self-interest
100 **aboute nought:** wasting my time
101 **make it tough:** be too bold
104 **meene:** means, device

This Diomede, as he that koude his good,
Whan tyme was, gan fallen forth in speche
Of this and that, and axed whi she stood
In swich disese, and gan hire ek biseche
That if that he encresse myghte or eche   110
With any thyng hire ese, that she sholde
Comaunde it hym, and seyde he don it wolde.

For treweliche he swor hire as a knyght
That ther nas thyng with which he myghte hire
        plese,
That he nolde don his peyne and al his myght
To don it, for to don hire herte an ese;   116
And preyede hire she wolde hire sorwe apese,
And seyde, "Iwis, we Grekis kan have joie
To honouren yow as wel as folk of Troie."

He seyde ek thus: "I woot yow thynketh
        straunge —   120
Ne wonder is, for it is to yow newe —
Th'aquayntaunce of thise Troianis to chaunge
For folk of Grece, that ye nevere knewe.
But wolde nevere God but if as trewe
A Grek ye sholde among us alle fynde   125
As any Troian is, and ek as kynde.

"And by the cause I swor yow right, lo, now,
To ben youre frend, and helply, to my myght,
And for that more aquayntaunce ek of yow   129
Have ich had than another straunger wight,
So fro this forth, I pray yow, day and nyght
Comaundeth me, how soore that me smerte,
To don al that may like unto youre herte;

"And that ye me wolde as youre brother trete,
And taketh naught my frendshipe in despit;
And though youre sorwes be for thynges
        grete —   136
Not I nat whi — but out of more respit
Myn herte hath for t'amende it gret delit;
And if I may youre harmes nat redresse,
I am right sory for youre hevynesse,   140

"For though ye Troians with us Grekes wrothe
Han many a day ben, alwey yet, parde,
O god of Love in soth we serven bothe.
And for the love of God, my lady fre,

Whomso ye hate, as beth nat wroth with me,
For trewely, ther kan no wyght yow serve   146
That half so loth youre wratthe wold disserve.

"And nere it that we ben so neigh the tente
Of Calcas, which that sen us bothe may,
I wolde of this yow telle al myn entente —   150
But this enseled til anothir day.
Yeve me youre hond; I am, and shal ben ay,
God helpe me so, while that my lyf may dure,
Youre owene aboven every creature.

"Thus seyde I nevere er now to womman born,
For God myn herte as wisly glade so,   156
I loved never womman here-biforn
As paramours, ne nevere shal no mo.
And for the love of God, beth nat my fo,
Al kan I naught to yow, my lady deere,   160
Compleyne aright, for I am yet to leere.

"And wondreth nought, myn owen lady bright,
Though that I speke of love to yow thus blyve;
For I have herd er this of many a wight,
Hath loved thyng he nevere saigh his lyve.   165
Ek I am nat of power for to stryve
Ayeyns the god of Love, but hym obeye
I wole alwey; and mercy I yow preye.

"Ther ben so worthi knyghtes in this place,
And ye so fayr, that everich of hem alle   170
Wol peynen hym to stonden in youre grace.
But myghte me so faire a grace falle,
That ye me for youre servant wolde calle,
So lowely ne so trewely yow serve
Nil non of hem as I shal til I sterve."   175

Criseyde unto that purpos lite answerde,
As she that was with sorwe oppressed so
That, in effect, she naught his tales herde
But here and ther, now here a word or two.
Hire thoughte hire sorwful herte brast a-two,
For whan she gan hire fader fer espie   181
Wel neigh down of hire hors she gan to sye.

But natheles she thonketh Diomede
Of al his travaile and his goode cheere,

106 **koude his good:** knew what was to his own advantage
107 **fallen forth:** engage in
110 **eche:** add to
128 **helply:** helpful
137 **out of more respit:** without more delay
141 **wrothe:** angered
143 **O:** one

145 **Whomso:** whomsoever   **as beth:** be (*as* is not translated)
147 **loth:** reluctantly
151 **this** = *this is*   **enseled:** sealed up
153 **dure:** last
158 **As paramours:** by way of passionate love
165 **saigh:** saw
182 **sye:** sink

And that hym list his frendshipe hire to bede;
And she accepteth it in good manere,   186
And wol do fayn that is hym lief and dere,
And tristen hym she wolde, and wel she
    myghte,
As seyde she; and from hire hors sh'alighte.

Hire fader hath hire in his armes nome,   190
And twenty tyme he kiste his doughter sweete,
And seyde, "O deere doughter myn, welcome!"
She seyde ek she was fayn with hym to mete,
And stood forth muwet, milde, and mansuete.
But here I leve hire with hire fader dwelle,
And forth I wol of Troilus yow telle.   196

To Troie is come this woful Troilus,
In sorwe aboven alle sorwes smerte,
With feloun look and face dispitous.
Tho sodeynly doun from his hors he sterte,   200
And thorugh his paleis, with a swollen herte,
To chaumbre he wente; of nothyng took he
    hede,
Ne non to hym dar speke a word for drede.

And ther his sorwes that he spared hadde
He yaf an issue large, and "Deth!" he criede;
And in his throwes frenetik and madde   206
He corseth Jove, Appollo, and ek Cupide;
He corseth Ceres, Bacus, and Cipride,
His burthe, hymself, his fate, and ek nature,
And, save his lady, every creature.   210

To bedde he goth, and walwith ther and torn-
    eth
In furie, as doth he Ixion in helle,
And in this wise he neigh til day sojorneth.
But tho bigan his herte a lite unswelle
Thorugh teris, which that gonnen up to welle,
And pitously he cryde upon Criseyde,   216
And to hymself right thus he spak, and seyde,

"Wher is myn owene lady, lief and deere?
Wher is hire white brest? Wher is it, where?
Wher ben hire armes and hire eyen cleere   220

That yesternyght this tyme with me were?
Now may I wepe allone many a teere,
And graspe aboute I may, but in this place,
Save a pilowe, I fynde naught t'enbrace.

"How shal I do? Whan shal she come ayeyn?
I not, allas, whi lete ich hire to go;   226
As wolde God ich hadde as tho ben sleyn!
O herte myn, Criseyde, O swete fo!
O lady myn, that I love and na mo,
To whom for evermo myn herte I dowe,   230
Se how I dey, ye nyl me nat rescowe!

"Who seth yow now, my righte lode-sterre?
Who sit right now or stant in youre presence?
Who kan conforten now youre hertes werre?
Now I am gon, whom yeve ye audience?   235
Who speketh for me right now in myn absence?
Allas, no wight; and that is al my care,
For wel woot I, as yvele as I ye fare.

"How sholde I thus ten dayes ful endure,
Whan I the firste nyght have al this tene?   240
How shal she don ek, sorwful creature?
For tendernesse, how shal she sustene
Swich wo for me? O pitous, pale, grene
Shal ben youre fresshe, wommanliche face
For langour, er ye torne unto this place."   245

And whan he fil in any slomberynges,
Anon bygynne he sholde for to grone
And dremen of the dredefulleste thynges
That myghte ben; as mete he were allone
In place horrible makyng ay his mone,   250
Or meten that he was amonges alle
His enemys, and in hire hondes falle.

And therwithal his body sholde sterte,
And with the stert al sodeynliche awake,
And swich a tremour fele aboute his herte   255
That of the fere his body sholde quake;
And therwithal he sholde a noyse make,
And seme as though he sholde falle depe
From heighe o-lofte; and thanne he wolde
    wepe,

185 **bede:** offer
187 **fayn:** gladly
190 **nome:** taken
194 **muwet:** mute   **mansuete:** gentle, meek
199 **feloun:** hostile   **dispitous:** cruel
205 **yaf an issue large:** gave full vent to (his feelings)
206 **throwes:** throes, sufferings   **frenetik:** frantic
208 **Ceres:** goddess of agriculture   **Bacus:** Bacchus, god of
wine   **Cipride:** Venus
212 **Ixion:** Ixion was bound eternally to a turning wheel in hell;
see Bo 3.m12.37–38.

221 **yesternyght:** last night
230 **dowe:** give
231 **ye nyl:** if you will not
232 **lode-sterre:** guiding star
238 **as yvele as I ye fare:** you suffer as much as I
243 **grene:** with a greenish pallor, pale
246 **slomberynges:** slumber
253 **sterte:** move suddenly

And rewen on hymself so pitously   260
That wonder was to here his fantasie.
Another tyme he sholde myghtyly
Conforte hymself, and sein it was folie
So causeles swich drede for to drye;
And eft bygynne his aspre sorwes newe,   265
That every man myght on his sorwes rewe.

Who koude telle aright or ful discryve
His wo, his pleynt, his langour, and his pyne?
Naught alle the men that han or ben on lyve.
Thow, redere, maist thiself ful wel devyne   270
That swich a wo my wit kan nat diffyne;
On ydel for to write it sholde I swynke,
Whan that my wit is wery it to thynke.

On hevene yet the sterres weren seene,
Although ful pale ywoxen was the moone,   275
And whiten gan the orisonte shene
Al estward, as it wont is for to doone;
And Phebus with his rosy carte soone
Gan after that to dresse hym up to fare
Whan Troilus hath sent after Pandare.   280

This Pandare, that of al the day biforn
Ne myghte han comen Troilus to se,
Although he on his hed it hadde sworn —
For with the kyng Priam al day was he,
So that it lay nought in his libertee   285
Nowher to gon — but on the morwe he wente
To Troilus, whan that he for hym sente.

For in his herte he koude wel devyne
That Troilus al nyght for sorwe wook;
And that he wolde telle hym of his pyne,   290
This knew he wel ynough, withoute book.
For which to chaumbre streght the wey he took,
And Troilus tho sobrelich he grette,
And on the bed ful sone he gan hym sette.

"My Pandarus," quod Troilus, "the sorwe   295
Which that I drye I may nat longe endure.
I trowe I shal nat lyven til to-morwe.
For which I wolde alweys, on aventure,
To the devysen of my sepulture

The forme; and of my moeble thow dispone
Right as the semeth best is for to done.   301

"But of the fir and flaumbe funeral
In which my body brennen shal to glede,
And of the feste and pleyes palestral
At my vigile, I prey the, tak good hede   305
That that be wel; and offre Mars my steede,
My swerd, myn helm; and, leve brother deere,
My sheld to Pallas yef, that shyneth cleere.

"The poudre in which myn herte ybrend shal
    torne,
That preye I the thow take and it conserve   310
In a vessell that men clepeth an urne,
Of gold, and to my lady that I serve,
For love of whom thus pitouslich I sterve,
So yeve it hire, and do me this plesaunce,
To preyen hire kepe it for a remembraunce.

"For wele I fele, by my maladie   316
And by my dremes now and yore ago,
Al certeynly that I mot nedes dye.
The owle ek, which that hette Escaphilo,
Hath after me shright al thise nyghtes two.   320
And god Mercurye, of me now, woful wrecche,
The soule gyde, and whan the liste, it fecche!"

Pandare answerde and seyde, "Troilus,
My deere frend, as I have told the yore,
That it is folye for to sorwen thus,   325
And causeles, for which I kan namore.
But whoso wil nought trowen reed ne loore,
I kan nat sen in hym no remedie,
But lat hym worthen with his fantasie.

"But, Troilus, I prey the, tel me now   330
If that thow trowe er this that any wight
Hath loved paramours as wel as thow?
Ye, God woot, and fro many a worthi knyght
Hath his lady gon a fourtenyght,
And he nat yet made halvendel the fare.   335
What nede is the to maken al this care?

---

269 **han or ben:** have (been) or are (now)
270 **devyne:** guess, infer
276 **orisonte:** horizon
278 **carte:** chariot
279 **dresse hym up to fare:** prepare to travel (across the sky)
281 **This Pandare:** This subject has no predicate (the device of anacoluthon, common in colloquial speech).
293 **grette:** greeted
298 **alweys:** in any event   **on aventure:** to provide for that event
299 **the:** thee   **devysen:** describe   **sepulture:** sepulchre

300 **moeble:** personal possessions   **dispone:** dispose
303 **glede:** glowing embers
304 **pleyes palestral:** (funeral) athletic games
305 **vigile:** wake
308 **Pallas:** Pallas Athena, guardian goddess of Troy   **yef:** give
319 **Escaphilo:** Ascalaphus, whom Proserpine changed into an owl
320 **shright:** shrieked
322 **gyde:** guide
329 **lat hym worthen:** leave him be
332 **paramours:** with passion
335 **halvendel the fare:** half the fuss

"Syn day by day thow maist thiselven se
That from his love, or ellis from his wif,
A man mot twynnen of necessite —
Ye, though he love hire as his owene lif — 340
Yet nyl he with hymself thus maken strif.
For wel thou woost, my leve brother deere,
That alwey frendes may nat ben yfeere.

"How don this folk that seen hire loves wedded
By frendes myght, as it bitit ful ofte, 345
And sen hem in hire spouses bed ybedded?
God woot, they take it wisly, faire, and softe,
Forwhi good hope halt up hire herte o-lofte.
And for they kan a tyme of sorwe endure,
As tyme hem hurt, a tyme doth hem cure. 350

"So shuldestow endure, and laten slide
The tyme, and fonde to ben glad and light.
Ten dayes nys so longe nought t'abide.
And syn she the to comen hath bihyght,
She nyl hire heste breken for no wight. 355
For dred the nat that she nyl fynden weye
To come ayein; my lif that dorste I leye.

"Thi swevnes ek and al swich fantasie
Drif out and lat hem faren to meschaunce,
For they procede of thi malencolie 360
That doth the fele in slep al this penaunce.
A straw for alle swevenes signifiaunce!
God helpe me so, I counte hem nought a bene!
Ther woot no man aright what dremes mene.

"For prestes of the temple tellen this, 365
That dremes ben the revelaciouns
Of goddes, and as wel they telle, ywis,
That they ben infernals illusiouns;
And leches seyn that of complexiouns
Proceden they, or fast, or glotonye. 370
Who woot in soth thus what thei signifie?

"Ek oother seyn that thorugh impressiouns,
As if a wight hath faste a thyng in mynde,
That therof cometh swiche avysiouns;
And other seyn, as they in bokes fynde, 375
That after tymes of the yer, by kynde,

Men dreme, and that th'effect goth by the
        moone.
But leve no drem, for it is nought to doone.

"Wel worthe of dremes ay thise olde wives,
And treweliche ek augurye of thise fowles, 380
For fere of which men wenen lese here lyves,
As revenes qualm, or shrichyng of thise owles.
To trowen on it bothe fals and foul is.
Allas, allas, so noble a creature
As is a man shal dreden swich ordure! 385

"For which with al myn herte I the biseche,
Unto thiself that al this thow foryyve;
And ris now up withowten more speche,
And lat us caste how forth may best be dryve
This tyme, and ek how fresshly we may
        lyve 390
Whan that she comth, the which shal be right
        soone.
God helpe me so, the beste is thus to doone.

"Ris, lat us speke of lusty lif in Troie
That we han led, and forth the tyme dryve;
And ek of tyme comyng us rejoie, 395
That bryngen shal oure blisse now so blyve;
And langour of thise twyes dayes fyve
We shal therwith so foryete or oppresse
That wel unneth it don shal us duresse.

"This town is ful of lordes al aboute, 400
And trewes lasten al this mene while.
Go we pleye us in som lusty route
To Sarpedoun, nat hennes but a myle;
And thus thow shalt the tyme wel bygile,
And dryve it forth unto that blisful morwe 405
That thow hire se, that cause is of thi sorwe.

"Now ris, my deere brother Troilus,
For certes it non honour is to the
To wepe and in thi bedde to jouken thus;

345 **By frendes myght:** i.e., in an arranged marriage **bitit =**
bitideth, happens
351 **slide:** slide by, pass
352 **fonde:** try
355 **heste:** promise
356 **dred the nat:** doubt not
358 **swevnes:** dreams
369 **complexiouns:** temperaments, balance of the bodily fluids,
the humors
376 **after tymes of the yer:** according to the time of year

377 **goth by:** is affected by, is dependent upon
379 May it always be well with these old women concerning
dreams (i.e., leave dreams to old women)
381 **lese:** to lose
382 **revenes:** raven's **qualm:** croak **shrichyng:** screeching
385 **ordure:** filth, nonsense
387 **foryyve:** forgive (yourself for believing this nonsense)
389 **dryve:** spent
390 **fresshly:** joyously
395 **us rejoie:** let us rejoice
398 **oppresse:** repress
399 **duresse:** hardship, suffering
401 **mene while:** meanwhile, the ten days
402 **route:** company
403 **Sarpedoun:** Sarpedon, king of Licia and ally of Troy
404 **bygile:** wile away
409 **jouken:** roost (as a falcon), rest

For trewelich, of o thyng trust to me: 410
If thow thus ligge a day, or two, or thre,
The folk wol seyn that thow for cowardise
The feynest sik, and that thow darst nat rise!"

This Troilus answerde, "O brother deere,
This knowen folk that han ysuffred peyne,   415
That though he wepe and make sorwful cheere
That feleth harm and smert in every veyne,
No wonder is; and though ich evere pleyne,
Or alwey wepe, I am no thyng to blame,
Syn I have lost the cause of al my game.   420

"But syn of fyne force I mot arise,
I shal arise as soone as evere I may;
And God, to whom myn herte I sacrifice,
So sende us hastely the tenthe day!
For was ther nevere fowel so fayn of May   425
As I shal ben whan that she comth in Troie
That cause is of my torment and my joie.

"But whider is thi reed," quod Troilus,
"That we may pleye us best in al this town?"
"By God, my conseil is," quod Pandarus,   430
"To ride and pleye us with kyng Sarpedoun."
So longe of this they speken up and down
Til Troilus gan at the laste assente
To rise, and forth to Sarpedoun they wente.

This Sarpedoun, as he that honourable   435
Was evere his lyve, and ful of heigh largesse,
With al that myghte yserved ben on table
That deynte was, al coste it gret richesse,
He fedde hem day by day, that swich noblesse,
As seyden bothe the mooste and ek the leeste,
Was nevere er that day wist at any feste.   441

Nor in this world ther is non instrument
Delicious, thorugh wynd or touche of corde,
As fer as any wight hath evere ywent,
That tonge telle or herte may recorde,   445
That at that feste it nas wel herd acorde;
Ne of ladys ek so fair a compaignie
On daunce, er tho, was nevere iseye with ië.

But what availeth this to Troilus,
That for his sorwe nothyng of it roughte?   450

For evere in oon his herte pietous
Ful bisyly Criseyde, his lady, soughte.
On hire was evere al that his herte thoughte,
Now this, now that, so faste ymagenynge
That glade, iwis, kan hym no festeyinge.   455

Thise ladies ek that at this feste ben,
Syn that he saugh his lady was aweye,
It was his sorwe upon hem for to sen,
Or for to here on instrumentes pleye.
For she that of his herte berth the keye   460
Was absent, lo, this was his fantasie —
That no wight sholde maken melodie.

Nor ther nas houre in al the day or nyght,
Whan he was there as no wight myghte hym
     heere,
That he ne seyde, "O lufsom lady bryght,   465
How have ye faren syn that ye were here?
Welcome, ywis, myn owne lady deere!"
But weylaway, al this nat but a maze.
Fortune his howve entended bet to glaze!

The lettres ek that she of olde tyme   470
Hadde hym ysent, he wolde allone rede
An hondred sithe atwixen noon and prime,
Refiguryng hire shap, hire wommanhede,
Withinne his herte, and every word or dede
That passed was; and thus he drof t'an
     ende   475
The ferthe day, and seyde he wolde wende.

And seyde, "Leve brother Pandarus,
Intendestow that we shal here bleve
Til Sarpedoun wol forth congeyen us?
Yet were it fairer that we toke oure leve.   480
For Goddes love, lat us now soone at eve
Oure leve take, and homward lat us torne,
For treweliche, I nyl nat thus sojourne."

Pandare answerde, "Be we comen hider
To fecchen fir and rennen hom ayein?   485
God help me so, I kan nat tellen whider

420 **game:** happiness
421 **of fyne force:** by sheer compulsion
443 **corde:** string (of an instrument)
444 **ywent:** supposed
446 **acorde:** harmonized, played
448 **ië:** eye

451 **evere in oon:** continually   **pietous:** pitiful
455 **festeyinge:** festivity
465 **lufsom:** loveable
468 **this** = *this is*   **maze:** delusion
469 **his howve . . . bet to glaze:** to delude him even further
(literally, to make him a better hood or helmet of glass)
472 **sithe:** times   **atwixen noon and prime:** between the
periods of noon (12 to 3 P.M.) and prime (6 to 9 A.M.); i.e., all
afternoon and night
475 **drof t'an ende:** passed
478 **bleve:** remain
479 **congeyen:** say farewell to (i.e., dismiss)
485 **fecchen fir:** get a light (for our stove)

We myghte gon, if I shal sothly seyn,
Ther any wight is of us more feyn
Than Sarpedoun; and if we hennes hye
Thus sodeynly, I holde it vilanye.   490

"Syn that we seyden that we wolde bleve
With hym a wowke, and now, thus sodeynly,
The ferthe day to take of hym owre leve —
He wolde wondren on it, trewely!
Lat us holden forth oure purpos fermely;   495
And syn that ye bihighten hym to bide,
Holde forward now, and after lat us ride."

Thus Pandarus, with alle peyne and wo,
Made hym to dwelle; and at the wikes ende
Of Sarpedoun they toke hire leve tho,   500
And on hire wey they spedden hem to wende.
Quod Troilus, "Now Lord me grace sende,
That I may fynden at myn hom-comynge
Criseyde comen!" And therwith gan he synge.

"Ye, haselwode!" thoughte this Pandare,   505
And to hymself ful softeliche he seyde,
"God woot, refreyden may this hote fare,
Er Calkas sende Troilus Criseyde!"
But natheles, he japed thus, and pleyde,   509
And swor, ywys, his herte hym wel bihighte
She wolde come as soone as evere she myghte.

Whan they unto the paleys were ycomen
Of Troilus, they doun of hors alighte,
And to the chambre hire wey than han they
        nomen;
And into tyme that it gan to nyghte   515
They spaken of Criseÿde the brighte;
And after this, whan that hem bothe leste,
They spedde hem fro the soper unto reste.

On morwe, as soone as day bygan to clere,
This Troilus gan of his slep t'abrayde,   520
And to Pandare, his owen brother deere,
"For love of God," ful pitously he sayde,
"As go we sen the palais of Criseyde;
For syn we yet may have namore feste,
So lat us sen hire paleys atte leeste."   525

And therwithal, his meyne for to blende,
A cause he fond in towne for to go,
And to Criseydes hous they gonnen wende.
But Lord, this sely Troilus was wo!   529
Hym thoughte his sorwful herte braste a-two.
For whan he saugh hire dores spered alle,
Wel neigh for sorwe adoun he gan to falle.

Therwith, whan he was war and gan biholde
How shet was every wyndow of the place, 534
As frost, hym thoughte, his herte gan to colde;
For which with chaunged dedlich pale face,
Withouten word, he forthby gan to pace,
And as God wolde, he gan so faste ride
That no wight of his contenance espide.

Than seide he thus: "O paleys desolat,   540
O hous of houses whilom best ihight,
O paleys empty and disconsolat,
O thow lanterne of which queynt is the light,
O paleys, whilom day, that now art nyght,
Wel oughtestow to falle, and I to dye,   545
Syn she is went that wont was us to gye!

"O paleis, whilom crowne of houses alle,
Enlumyned with sonne of alle blisse!
O ryng, fro which the ruby is out falle,   549
O cause of wo, that cause hast ben of lisse!
Yet, syn I may no bet, fayn wolde I kisse
Thy colde dores, dorste I for this route;
And farwel shryne, of which the seynt is oute!"

Therwith he caste on Pandarus his yë,   554
With chaunged face, and pitous to biholde;
And whan he myghte his tyme aright aspie,
Ay as he rood to Pandarus he tolde
His newe sorwe and ek his joies olde,
So pitously and with so ded an hewe
That every wight myghte on his sorwe rewe.

Fro thennesforth he rideth up and down,   561
And every thyng com hym to remembraunce
As he rood forby places of the town

---

496 **bihighten:** promised
497 **Holde forward:** keep your promise
499 **wikes:** week's
505 **Ye, haselwode:** yes indeed, hazelwood (an expression of skeptical incredulity)
507 **refreyden:** grow cold   **hote fare:** passionate affair
510 **bihighte:** assured
514 **nomen:** taken
515 **nyghte:** become night

526 **his meyne for to blende:** to deceive the members of his household
530 **braste:** would burst
531 **spered:** barred
537 **forthby:** past
541 **ihight:** adorned (or, called)
543 **queynt:** quenched, extinguished
546 **gye:** guide
548 **Enlumyned:** illuminated
550 **lisse:** joy
552 **dorste I:** if I dared
556 **his tyme aright aspie:** find an opportunity
563 **forby:** past

In which he whilom hadde al his plesaunce.
"Lo, yonder saugh ich last my lady daunce;
And in that temple, with hire eyen cleere,   566
Me kaughte first my righte lady dere.

"And yonder have I herd ful lustyly
My dere herte laugh; and yonder pleye
Saugh ich hire ones ek ful blisfully;   570
And yonder ones to me gan she seye,
'Now goode swete, love me wel, I preye';
And yond so goodly gan she me biholde
That to the deth myn herte is to hire holde.

"And at that corner, in the yonder hous,   575
Herde I myn alderlevest lady deere
So wommanly, with vois melodious,
Syngen so wel, so goodly, and so cleere
That in my soule yet me thynketh ich here
The blisful sown; and in that yonder place   580
My lady first me took unto hire grace."

Thanne thoughte he thus: "O blisful lord Cu-
        pide,
Whan I the proces have in my memorie
How thow me hast wereyed on every syde,
Men myght a book make of it, lik a storie.   585
What nede is the to seke on me victorie,
Syn I am thyn and holly at thi wille?
What joie hastow thyn owen folk to spille?

"Wel hastow, lord, ywroke on me thyn ire,
Thow myghty god, and dredefull for to greve!
Now mercy, lord! Thow woost wel I desire   591
Thi grace moost of alle lustes leeve,
And lyve and dye I wol in thy byleve;
For which I n'axe in guerdoun but o bone —
That thow Criseyde ayein me sende sone.   595

"Destreyne hire herte as faste to retorne
As thow doost myn to longen hire to see;
Than woot I wel that she nyl naught sojorne.
Now blisful lord, so cruel thow ne be
Unto the blood of Troie, I preye the,   600
As Juno was unto the blood Thebane,
For which the folk of Thebes caughte hire
        bane."

And after this he to the yates wente
Ther as Criseyde out rood a ful good paas,   604
And up and down ther made he many a wente,
And to hymself ful ofte he seyde, "Allas,
Fro hennes rood my blisse and my solas!
As wolde blisful God now, for his joie,
I myghte hire sen ayein come into Troie!

"And to the yonder hille I gan hire gyde,   610
Allas, and ther I took of hire my leve!
And yond I saugh hire to hire fader ride,
For sorwe of which myn herte shal tocleve;
And hider hom I com whan it was eve,
And here I dwelle out cast from alle joie,   615
And shal, til I may sen hire eft in Troie."

And of hymself ymagened he ofte
To ben defet, and pale, and waxen lesse
Than he was wont, and that men seyden softe,
"What may it be? Who kan the sothe gesse
Whi Troilus hath al this hevynesse?"   621
And al this nas but his malencolie,
That he hadde of hymself swich fantasie.

Another tyme ymaginen he wolde
That every wight that wente by the weye   625
Hadde of hym routhe, and that they seyen
        sholde,
"I am right sory Troilus wol deye."
And thus he drof a day yet forth or tweye,
As ye have herd; swich lif right gan he lede
As he that stood bitwixen hope and drede.   630

For which hym likede in his songes shewe
Th'encheson of his wo, as he best myghte;
And made a song of wordes but a fewe,
Somwhat his woful herte for to lighte;
And whan he was from every mannes syghte,
With softe vois he of his lady deere,   636
That absent was, gan synge as ye may heere:

Canticus Troili.

"O sterre, of which I lost have al the light,
With herte soor wel oughte I to biwaille   639
That evere derk in torment, nyght by nyght,
Toward my deth with wynd in steere I saille;
For which the tenthe nyght, if that I faille

574 **holde:** bound, obligated
576 **alderlevest:** most beloved
584 **wereyed:** made war on
588 **spille:** destroy
589 **ywroke:** avenged
593 **in thy byleve:** i.e., believing in you
594 **o bone:** one boon, gift
596 **Destreyne:** compel
602 **bane:** destruction, death

605 **wente:** turn
613 **tocleve:** split, break in two
618 **defet:** disfigured **waxen lesse:** grown smaller
632 **Th'encheson:** the occasion, cause
Canticus Troili: Troilus's Song
641 **in steere:** astern, at my back
642 **faille:** lack

The gydyng of thi bemes bright an houre,
My ship and me Caribdis wol devoure.''

This song whan he thus songen hadde, soone
He fil ayeyn into his sikes olde;   646
And every nyght, as was his wone to doone,
He stood the brighte moone to byholde,
And al his sorwe he to the moone tolde,
And seyde, "Ywis, whan thow art horned newe,
I shal be glad, if al the world be trewe!   651

"I saugh thyn hornes olde ek by the morwe
Whan hennes rood my righte lady dere
That cause is of my torment and my sorwe;
For which, O brighte Latona the clere,   655
For love of God, ren faste aboute thy spere!
For whan thyne hornes newe gynnen sprynge,
Than shal she come that may my blisse brynge.''

The dayes moore and lenger every nyght   659
Than they ben wont to be, hym thoughte tho,
And that the sonne went his cours unright
By lenger weye than it was wont to do;
And seyde, "Ywis, me dredeth evere mo
The sonnes sone, Pheton, be on lyve,
And that his fader carte amys he dryve.''   665

Upon the walles faste ek wolde he walke,
And on the Grekis oost he wolde se;
And to hymself right thus he wolde talke:
"Lo, yonder is myn owene lady free,
Or ellis yonder, ther tho tentes be;   670
And thennes comth this eyr, that is so soote
That in my soule I fele it doth me boote.

"And hardily, this wynd that more and moore
Thus stoundemele encresseth in my face
Is of my ladys depe sikes soore.   675
I preve it thus: for in noon other place
Of al this town, save onliche in this space,
Fele I no wynd that sowneth so lik peyne;
It seyth, 'Allas! Whi twynned be we tweyne?' ''

This longe tyme he dryveth forth right thus
Til fully passed was the nynthe nyght;   681
And ay bisyde hym was this Pandarus,
That bisily did al his fulle myght
Hym to conforte and make his herte light,   684
Yevyng hym hope alwey the tenthe morwe
That she shal come and stynten al his sorwe.

Upon that other syde ek was Criseyde,
With wommen fewe, among the Grekis stronge,
For which ful ofte a day "Allas,'' she seyde,   689
"That I was born! Wel may myn herte longe
After my deth, for now lyve I to longe.
Allas, and I ne may it nat amende,
For now is wors than evere yet I wende!

"My fader nyl for nothyng do me grace
To gon ayeyn, for naught I kan hym queme;
And if so be that I my terme pace,   696
My Troilus shal in his herte deme
That I am fals, and so it may wel seme:
Thus shal ich have unthonk on every side —
That I was born so weilaway the tide!   700

"And if that I me putte in jupartie
To stele awey by nyght, and it bifalle
That I be kaught, I shal be holde a spie;
Or elles — lo, this drede I moost of alle —
If in the hondes of som wrecche I falle,   705
I nam but lost, al be myn herte trewe.
Now, myghty God, thow on my sorwe rewe!''

Ful pale ywoxen was hire brighte face,
Hire lymes lene, as she that al the day   709
Stood, whan she dorste, and loked on the place
Ther she was born, and ther she dwelt hadde
          ay;
And al the nyght wepyng, allas, she lay.
And thus despeired, out of alle cure,
She ladde hire lif, this woful creature.

Ful ofte a day she sighte ek for destresse,   715
And in hireself she wente ay purtraynge
Of Troilus the grete worthynesse,
And al his goodly wordes recordynge
Syn first that day hire love bigan to springe.
And thus she sette hire woful herte afire   720
Thorugh remembraunce of that she gan desire.

644 **Caribdis:** Charybdis, the whirlpool opposite the rock Scylla
between Italy and Sicily
647 **wone:** habit
650 **horned newe:** i.e., the new, crescent moon
652 **hornes olde:** i.e., the moon had waned to its last phase
655 **Latona:** the moon; see n.
656 **spere:** sphere, orbit
659 **moore:** greater (longer)
664 **Pheton:** Phaeton; for his story, see HF 940–56.
665 **fader:** father's
671 **eyr:** breeze
674 **stoundemele:** hour by hour, gradually
678 **sowneth:** makes a sound

694 **do me grace:** allow me
695 **queme:** please
696 **terme pace:** appointed time pass by
699 **unthonk:** blame
700 **tide:** time
713 **out of alle cure:** beyond any help

In al this world ther nys so cruel herte
That hire hadde herd compleynen in hire sorwe
That nolde han wepen for hire peynes smerte,
So tendrely she weep, bothe eve and morwe.
Hire nedede no teris for to borwe!   726
And this was yet the werste of al hire peyne:
Ther was no wight to whom she dorste hire
          pleyne.

Ful rewfully she loked upon Troie,
Biheld the toures heigh and ek the halles;   730
"Allas," quod she, "the plesance and the joie,
The which that now al torned into galle is,
Have ich had ofte withinne yonder walles!
O Troilus, what dostow now?" she seyde.
"Lord, wheyther thow yet thenke upon Cri-
          seyde?   735

"Allas, I ne hadde trowed on youre loore
And went with yow, as ye me redde er this!
Than hadde I now nat siked half so soore.
Who myghte han seyd that I hadde don amys
To stele awey with swich oon as he ys?   740
But al to late comth the letuarie
Whan men the cors unto the grave carie.

"To late is now to speke of that matere.
Prudence, allas, oon of thyne eyen thre
Me lakked alwey, er that I come here!   745
On tyme ypassed wel remembred me,
And present tyme ek koud ich wel ise,
But future tyme, er I was in the snare,
Koude I nat sen; that causeth now my care.

"But natheles, bityde what bityde,   750
I shal to-morwe at nyght, by est or west,
Out of this oost stele in som manere syde,
And gon with Troilus where as hym lest.
This purpos wol ich holde, and this is best.
No fors of wikked tonges janglerie,   755
For evere on love han wrecches had envye.

"For whoso wol of every word take hede,
Or reulen hym by every wightes wit,

Ne shal he nevere thryven, out of drede;
For that that som men blamen evere yit,   760
Lo, other manere folk comenden it.
And as for me, for al swich variaunce,
Felicite clepe I my suffisaunce.

"For which, withouten any wordes mo,
To Troie I wole, as for conclusioun."   765
But God it wot, er fully monthes two,
She was ful fer fro that entencioun!
For bothe Troilus and Troie town
Shal knotteles thoroughout hire herte slide;
For she wol take a purpos for t'abide.   770

This Diomede, of whom yow telle I gan,
Goth now withinne hymself ay arguynge,
With al the sleghte and al that evere he kan,
How he may best, with shortest taryinge,
Into his net Criseydes herte brynge.   775
To this entent he koude nevere fyne;
To fisshen hire he leyde out hook and lyne.

But natheles, wel in his herte he thoughte
That she nas nat withoute a love in Troie,   779
For nevere sythen he hire thennes broughte
Ne koude he sen hire laughe or maken joie.
He nyst how best hire herte for t'acoye;
"But for t'asay," he seyde, "it naught
          n'agreveth,
For he that naught n'asaieth naught
          n'acheveth."

Yet seyde he to hymself upon a nyght,   785
"Now am I nat a fool, that woot wel how
Hire wo for love is of another wight,
And hereupon to gon assaye hire now?
I may wel wite it nyl nat ben my prow,
For wise folk in bookes it expresse,   790
'Men shal nat wowe a wight in hevynesse.'

"But whoso myghte wynnen swich a flour
From hym for whom she morneth nyght and
          day,

735 **wheyther thow:** do you (*wheyther* serves only to introduce a question)
736 **trowed on:** believed in
737 **redde:** advised
741 **to:** too   **letuarie:** medicine
744 **eyen thre:** Prudence has three eyes, looking to past, present, and future.
750 **bityde what bityde:** come what may
752 **in som manere syde:** on one side or the other
755 **janglerie:** gossip
758 **wit:** opinion

759 **out of drede:** beyond doubt
763 I call happiness my sufficiency (i.e., happiness is enough for me)
765 **wole:** mean to go
769 **knotteles:** like a thread or rope that, if without knots, slides freely
773 **sleghte:** ingenuity   **kan:** knows how to do
776 **fyne:** cease, leave off
782 **t'acoye:** to soothe
783 **t'asay:** to make an attempt   **agreveth:** harms
789 **my prow:** to my profit
791 **wowe:** woo
793 **morneth:** longs for

He myghte seyn he were a conquerour."
And right anon, as he that bold was ay,   795
Thoughte in his herte, "Happe how happe may,
Al sholde I dye, I wol hire herte seche!
I shal namore lesen but my speche."

This Diomede, as bokes us declare,
Was in his nedes prest and corageous,   800
With sterne vois and myghty lymes square,
Hardy, testif, strong, and chivalrous
Of dedes, lik his fader Tideus.
And som men seyn he was of tonge large;
And heir he was of Calydoigne and Arge.   805

Criseyde mene was of hire stature;
Therto of shap, of face, and ek of cheere,
Ther myghte ben no fairer creature.
And ofte tymes this was hire manere:
To gon ytressed with hire heres clere   810
Doun by hire coler at hire bak byhynde,
Which with a thred of gold she wolde bynde;

And, save hire browes joyneden yfeere,
Ther nas no lak, in aught I kan espien.
But for to speken of hire eyen cleere,   815
Lo, trewely, they writen that hire syen
That Paradis stood formed in hire yën.
And with hire riche beaute evere more
Strof love in hire ay, which of hem was more.

She sobre was, ek symple, and wys withal,
The best ynorisshed ek that myghte be,   821
And goodly of hire speche in general,
Charitable, estatlich, lusty, fre;
Ne nevere mo ne lakked hire pite;
Tendre-herted, slydynge of corage;   825
But trewely, I kan nat telle hire age.

And Troilus wel woxen was in highte,
And complet formed by proporcioun

So wel that kynde it nought amenden myghte;
Yong, fressh, strong, and hardy as lyoun;   830
Trewe as stiel in ech condicioun;
Oon of the beste entecched creature
That is or shal whil that the world may dure.

And certeynly in storye it is yfounde
That Troilus was nevere unto no wight,   835
As in his tyme, in no degree secounde
In durryng don that longeth to a knyght.
Al myghte a geant passen hym of myght,
His herte ay with the first and with the beste
Stood paregal, to durre don that hym leste.   840

But for to tellen forth of Diomede:
It fel that after, on the tenthe day
Syn that Criseyde out of the citee yede,
This Diomede, as fressh as braunche in May,
Com to the tente ther as Calkas lay,   845
And feyned hym with Calkas han to doone;
But what he mente, I shal yow tellen soone.

Criseyde, at shorte wordes for to telle,
Welcomed hym and down hym by hire sette —
And he was ethe ynough to maken dwelle!
And after this, withouten longe lette,   851
The spices and the wyn men forth hem fette;
And forth they speke of this and that yfeere,
As frendes don, of which som shal ye heere.

He gan first fallen of the werre in speche   855
Bitwixe hem and the folk of Troie town;
And of th'assege he gan hire ek biseche
To telle hym what was hire opynyoun;
Fro that demaunde he so descendeth down
To axen hire if that hire straunge thoughte   860
The Grekis gise and werkes that they wroughte;

And whi hire fader tarieth so longe
To wedden hire unto som worthy wight.
Criseyde, that was in hire peynes stronge
For love of Troilus, hire owen knyght,   865
As ferforth as she konnyng hadde or myght
Answerde hym tho; but as of his entente,
It semed nat she wiste what he mente.

796 **Happe how happe may**: whatever may happen
797 **seche**: seek
800 **prest**: prompt, eager
801 **lymes**: limbs
802 **testif**: testy, impetuous
804 **of tonge large**: lavish of speech
805 **Calydoigne**: Calydon in Aetolia (modern Asia Minor)
Arge: Argos
806 **mene . . . of hire stature**: of moderate size, not too tall
810 **clere**: bright
813 **joyneden yfeere**: were joined together
816 **syen**: saw
819 **Strof**: vied
820 **symple**: unaffected
821 **ynorisshed**: brought up
823 **estatlich**: dignified
825 **slydynge**: wavering, changeable   **corage**: determination, mood
828 **complet**: perfectly

831 **ech condicioun**: every situation (or, every quality)
832 **entecched**: endowed, imbued with (good characteristics)
837 **durryng don that**: daring to do that which
840 **paregal**: fully equal
843 **yede**: went
845 **lay**: stayed
850 **ethe**: easy
852 **spices**: spiced cakes or sweetmeats
861 **gise**: manners

But natheles, this ilke Diomede
Gan in hymself assure, and thus he seyde: 870
"If ich aright have taken of yow hede,
Me thynketh thus, O lady myn, Criseyde,
That syn I first hond on youre bridel leyde,
Whan ye out come of Troie by the morwe,
Ne koude I nevere sen yow but in sorwe.   875

"Kan I nat seyn what may the cause be,
But if for love of som Troian it were,
The which right sore wolde athynken me
That ye for any wight that dwelleth there
Sholden spille a quarter of a tere   880
Or pitously youreselven so bigile —
For dredeles, it is nought worth the while.

"The folk of Troie, as who seyth, alle and some
In prisoun ben, as ye youreselven se;
Nor thennes shal nat oon on-lyve come   885
For al the gold atwixen sonne and se.
Trusteth wel, and understondeth me,
Ther shal nat oon to mercy gon on-lyve,
Al were he lord of worldes twiës fyve!

"Swich wreche on hem for fecchynge of
Eleyne   890
Ther shal ben take, er that we hennes wende,
That Manes, which that goddes ben of peyne,
Shal ben agast that Grekes wol hem shende,
And men shul drede, unto the worldes ende,
From hennesforth to ravysshen any queene,
So cruel shal oure wreche on hem be seene.   896

"And but if Calkas lede us with ambages —
That is to seyn, with double wordes slye,
Swiche as men clepen a word with two visages —
Ye shal wel knowen that I naught ne lie,   900
And al this thyng right sen it with youre yë,
And that anon, ye nyl nat trowe how sone;
Now taketh hede, for it is for to doone.

"What! Wene ye youre wise fader wolde
Han yeven Antenor for yow anon,   905
If he ne wiste that the cite sholde
Destroied ben? Whi, nay, so mote I gon!
He knew ful wel ther shal nat scapen oon
That Troian is; and for the grete feere
He dorste nat ye dwelte lenger there.   910

"What wol ye more, lufsom lady deere?
Lat Troie and Troian fro youre herte pace!
Drif out that bittre hope, and make good
cheere,
And clepe ayeyn the beaute of youre face
That ye with salte teris so deface,   915
For Troie is brought in swich a jupartie
That it to save is now no remedie.

"And thenketh wel, ye shal in Grekis fynde
A moore parfit love, er it be nyght,
Than any Troian is, and more kynde,   920
And bet to serven yow wol don his myght.
And if ye vouchesauf, my lady bright,
I wol ben he to serven yow myselve,
Yee, levere than be kyng of Greces twelve!"

And with that word he gan to waxen red,   925
And in his speche a litel wight he quok,
And caste asyde a litel wight his hed,
And stynte a while; and afterward he wok,
And sobreliche on hire he threw his lok,
And seyde, "I am, al be it yow no joie,   930
As gentil man as any wight in Troie.

"For if my fader Tideus," he seyde,
"Ilyved hadde, ich hadde ben er this
Of Calydoyne and Arge a kyng, Criseyde!
And so hope I that I shal yet, iwis.   935
But he was slayn — allas, the more harm is! —
Unhappily at Thebes al to rathe,
Polymyte and many a man to scathe.

"But herte myn, syn that I am youre man —
And ben the first of whom I seche grace —
To serve yow as hertely as I kan,   941
And evere shal whil I to lyve have space,
So, er that I departe out of this place,
Ye wol me graunte that I may to-morwe,
At bettre leyser, telle yow my sorwe."   945

What sholde I telle his wordes that he seyde?
He spak inough for o day at the meeste.
It preveth wel; he spak so that Criseyde

878 **athynken:** displease
881 **bigile:** delude
890 **wreche:** vengeance
892 **Manes:** gods of the lower world
897 **ambages:** ambiguities
903 **is for to doone:** must be done

911 **lufsom:** loveable
914 **clepe ayeyn:** summon back, recall
916 **jupartie:** danger
917 **is:** there is
926 **a litel wight:** a little bit
932 **Tideus:** Tydeus fought on the side of Polynices (*Polymyte*) in the struggle of the *Seven Against Thebes.*
937 **Unhappily:** unfortunately   **al to rathe:** all too soon
938 **to scathe:** as a harm to
940 **ben:** you are
943 **So:** as long as, if (?); see textual note to 944.
945 **At bettre leyser:** at greater length

Graunted on the morwe, at his requeste,
For to speken with hym at the leeste —   950
So that he nolde speke of swich matere.
And thus to hym she seyde, as ye may here,

As she that hadde hire herte on Troilus
So faste that ther may it non arace;
And strangely she spak, and seyde thus: 955
"O Diomede, I love that ilke place
Ther I was born; and Joves, for his grace,
Delyvere it soone of al that doth it care!
God, for thy myght, so leve it wel to fare!

"That Grekis wolde hire wrath on Troie wreke,
If that they myght, I knowe it wel, iwis;   961
But it shal naught byfallen as ye speke,
And God toforn! And forther over this,
I woot my fader wys and redy is,
And that he me hath bought, as ye me tolde,
So deere, I am the more unto hym holde.   966

"That Grekis ben of heigh condicioun
I woot ek wel; but certeyn, men shal fynde
As worthi folk withinne Troie town,
As konnyng, and as parfit, and as kynde,   970
As ben bitwixen Orkades and Inde;
And that ye koude wel yowre lady serve,
I trowe ek wel, hire thank for to deserve.

"But as to speke of love, ywis," she seyde,
"I hadde a lord, to whom I wedded was,   975
The whos myn herte al was, til that he deyde;
And other love, as help me now Pallas,
Ther in myn herte nys, ne nevere was.
And that ye ben of noble and heigh kynrede,
I have wel herd it tellen, out of drede.   980

"And that doth me to han so gret a wonder
That ye wol scornen any womman so.
Ek, God woot, love and I ben fer ysonder!
I am disposed bet, so mot I go,
Unto my deth, to pleyne and maken wo.   985
What I shal after don I kan nat seye;
But trewelich, as yet me list nat pleye.

"Myn herte is now in tribulacioun,
And ye in armes bisy day by day.

Herafter, whan ye wonnen han the town,   990
Peraventure so it happen may
That whan I se that nevere yit I say
Than wol I werke that I nevere wroughte!
This word to yow ynough suffisen oughte.   994

"To-morwe ek wol I speken with yow fayn,
So that ye touchen naught of this matere.
And whan yow list, ye may come here ayayn;
And er ye gon, thus muche I sey yow here:
As help me Pallas with hire heres clere,
If that I sholde of any Grek han routhe,   1000
It sholde be youreselven, by my trouthe!

"I say nat therfore that I wol yow love,
N'y say nat nay; but in conclusioun,
I mene wel, by God that sit above!"
And therwithal she caste hire eyen down,   1005
And gan to sike, and seyde, "O Troie town,
Yet bidde I God in quiete and in reste
I may yow sen, or do myn herte breste."

But in effect, and shortly for to seye,
This Diomede al fresshly newe ayeyn   1010
Gan pressen on, and faste hire mercy preye;
And after this, the sothe for to seyn,
Hire glove he took, of which he was ful feyn;
And finaly, whan it was woxen eve
And al was wel, he roos and tok his leve.   1015

The brighte Venus folwede and ay taughte
The wey ther brode Phebus down alighte;
And Cynthea hire char-hors overraughte
To whirle out of the Leoun, if she myghte;
And Signifer his candels sheweth brighte   1020
Whan that Criseyde unto hire bedde wente
Inwith hire fadres faire brighte tente,

Retornyng in hire soule ay up and down
The wordes of this sodeyn Diomede,
His grete estat, and perel of the town,   1025
And that she was allone and hadde nede
Of frendes help; and thus bygan to brede
The cause whi, the sothe for to telle,
That she took fully purpos for to dwelle.

951 **So that:** as long as (see 996)
954 **arace:** uproot
955 **strangely:** distantly, coldly
959 **leve:** allow
964 **redy:** quick-witted, resourceful
971 **Orkades and Inde:** the Orkneys and India, the western and eastern limits of the world
982 **scornen:** i.e., treat disrespectfully

991 **Peraventure:** perhaps
992 **say:** saw (i.e., have seen)
1007 **bidde:** pray
1015–20 *Venus,* the evening star, followed the sun (*Phebus*), which appears broad (*brode*) as it sets; the moon (*Cynthea*) whirls out of the zodiacal sign of Leo (*Leoun*); and the sign-bearer, the Zodiac (*Signifer*), shows its bright stars (*candels*).
1018 **char-hors:** chariot horses   **overraughte:** reached over (to urge on)
1023 **Retornyng:** turning over
1024 **sodeyn:** sudden, impetuous

The morwen com, and gostly for to speke,   1030
This Diomede is come unto Criseyde;
And shortly, lest that ye my tale breke,
So wel he for hymselven spak and seyde
That alle hire sikes soore adown he leyde;
And finaly, the sothe for to seyne,   1035
He refte hire of the grete of al hire peyne.

And after this the storie telleth us
That she hym yaf the faire baye stede
The which he ones wan of Troilus;   1039
And ek a broche — and that was litel nede —
That Troilus was, she yaf this Diomede.
And ek, the bet from sorwe hym to releve,
She made hym were a pencel of hire sleve.

I fynde ek in stories elleswhere,   1044
Whan thorugh the body hurt was Diomede
Of Troilus, tho wep she many a teere
Whan that she saugh his wyde wowndes blede,
And that she took, to kepen hym, good hede;
And for to helen hym of his sorwes smerte,
Men seyn — I not — that she yaf hym hire
          herte.   1050

But trewely, the storie telleth us,
Ther made nevere womman moore wo
Than she, whan that she falsed Troilus.
She seyde, "Allas, for now is clene ago
My name of trouthe in love, for everemo!   1055
For I have falsed oon the gentileste
That evere was, and oon the worthieste!

"Allas, of me, unto the worldes ende,
Shal neyther ben ywriten nor ysonge
No good word, for thise bokes wol me shende.
O, rolled shal I ben on many a tonge!   1061
Thoroughout the world my belle shal be ronge!
And wommen moost wol haten me of alle.
Allas, that swich a cas me sholde falle!

"Thei wol seyn, in as muche as in me is,   1065
I have hem don dishonour, weylaway!
Al be I nat the first that dide amys,
What helpeth that to don my blame awey?

But syn I se ther is no bettre way,
And that to late is now for me to rewe,   1070
To Diomede algate I wol be trewe.

"But, Troilus, syn I no bettre may,
And syn that thus departen ye and I,
Yet prey I God, so yeve yow right good day,
As for the gentileste, trewely,   1075
That evere I say, to serven feythfully,
And best kan ay his lady honour kepe."
And with that word she brast anon to wepe.

"And certes yow ne haten shal I nevere;
And frendes love, that shal ye han of me,   1080
And my good word, al sholde I lyven evere.
And trewely I wolde sory be
For to seen yow in adversitee;
And gilteles, I woot wel, I yow leve.   1084
But al shal passe; and thus take I my leve."

But trewely, how longe it was bytwene
That she forsok hym for this Diomede,
Ther is non auctour telleth it, I wene.
Take every man now to his bokes heede,
He shal no terme fynden, out of drede.   1090
For though that he bigan to wowe hire soone,
Er he hire wan, yet was ther more to doone.

Ne me ne list this sely womman chyde
Forther than the storye wol devyse.
Hire name, allas, is publysshed so wide   1095
That for hire gilt it oughte ynough suffise.
And if I myghte excuse hire any wise,
For she so sory was for hire untrouthe,
Iwis, I wolde excuse hire yet for routhe.

This Troilus, as I byfore have told,   1100
Thus driveth forth, as wel as he hath myght;
But often was his herte hoot and cold,
And namely that ilke nynthe nyght,
Which on the morwe she hadde hym bihight
To com ayeyn. God woot, ful litel reste   1105
Hadde he that nyght — nothyng to slepe hym
          leste.

The laurer-crowned Phebus with his heete
Gan, in his cours ay upward as he wente,
To warmen of the est se the wawes weete,

1030 **gostly for to speke**: to speak devoutly (truly), or,
figuratively; see n.
1032 **breke**: interrupt (with impatience)
1036 **grete**: main part
1039 **wan of**: won from (in battle)
1043 **pencel of hire sleve**: her sleeve as a pennon
1060 **shende**: ruin, disgrace
1062 **my belle shal be ronge**: i.e., my story shall be told
1065 **in as muche as in me is**: i.e., inasmuch as it is my doing,
to the extent that the fault is mine

1071 **algate**: at any rate, at least
1076 **say**: saw (i.e., have seen)
1090 **terme**: specified period of time
1091 **wowe**: woo
1101 **driveth forth**: endures
1109 **wawes**: waves

And Nysus doughter song with fressh entente,
Whan Troilus his Pandare after sente;   1111
And on the walles of the town they pleyde,
To loke if they kan sen aught of Criseyde.

Tyl it was noon they stoden for to se
Who that ther come, and every maner wight
That com fro fer, they seyden it was she —   1116
Til that thei koude knowen hym aright.
Now was his herte dul, now was it light.
And thus byjaped stonden for to stare
Aboute naught this Troilus and Pandare.   1120

To Pandarus this Troilus tho seyde,
"For aught I woot, byfor noon, sikirly,
Into this town ne comth nat here Criseyde.
She hath ynough to doone, hardyly,
To wynnen from hire fader, so trowe I.   1125
Hire olde fader wol yet make hire dyne
Er that she go — God yeve hys herte pyne!"

Pandare answerede, "It may wel be, certeyn.
And forthi lat us dyne, I the byseche,   1129
And after noon than maystow come ayeyn."
And hom they go, withoute more speche,
And comen ayeyn — but longe may they seche
Er that they fynde that they after cape.
Fortune hem bothe thenketh for to jape!

Quod Troilus, "I se wel now that she   1135
Is taried with hire olde fader so,
That er she come, it wol neigh even be.
Com forth; I wol unto the yate go.
Thise porters ben unkonnyng evere mo,
And I wol don hem holden up the yate   1140
As naught ne were, although she come late."

The day goth faste, and after that com eve,
And yet com nought to Troilus Criseyde.
He loketh forth by hegge, by tre, by greve,
And fer his hed over the wal he leyde;   1145
And at the laste he torned hym and seyde,
"By God, I woot hire menyng now, Pandare!
Almoost, ywys, al newe was my care.

"Now douteles, this lady kan hire good;
I woot she meneth riden pryvely.   1150
I comende hire wisdom, by myn hood!
She wol nat maken peple nycely
Gaure on hire whan she comth, but softely
By nyghte into the town she thenketh ride.
And, deere brother, thynk nat longe t'abide.

"We han naught elles for to don, ywis,   1156
And Pandarus, now woltow trowen me?
Have here my trouthe, I se hire! Yond she is!
Heve up thyn eyen, man! Maistow nat se?"
Pandare answerede, "Nay, so mote I the!   1160
Al wrong, by God! What saistow, man? Where
          arte?
That I se yond nys but a fare-carte."

"Allas, thow seyst right soth," quod Troilus.
"But, hardily, it is naught al for nought
That in myn herte I now rejoysse thus;   1165
It is ayeyns som good I have a thought.
Not I nat how, but syn that I was wrought
Ne felte I swich a comfort, dar I seye;
She comth to-nyght, my lif that dorste I
          leye!"   1169

Pandare answerde, "It may be, wel ynough,"
And held with hym of al that evere he seyde.
But in his herte he thoughte, and softe lough,
And to hymself ful sobreliche he seyde,
"From haselwode, there joly Robyn pleyde,
Shal come al that that thow abidest heere.
Ye, fare wel al the snow of ferne yere!'   1176

The warden of the yates gan to calle
The folk which that withoute the yates were,
And bad hem dryven in hire bestes alle,
Or all the nyght they moste bleven there.   1180
And fer withinne the nyght, with many a teere,
This Troilus gan homward for to ride,
For wel he seth it helpeth naught t'abide.

But natheles, he gladed hym in this:
He thought he misacounted hadde his day,

1110 **Nysus doughter:** Scylla, who was changed into a bird; for
part of her story, see LGW 1900–1921.
1119 **byjaped:** deceived
1125 **wynnen from:** get away from
1133 **cape:** gape
1139 **porters:** gate-keepers   **unkonnyng:** ignorant, unskillful
1140 **holden up:** keep open
1141 **As naught ne were:** as if it were nothing, without making
a fuss
1144 **greve:** grove

1152 **nycely:** foolishly
1153 **Gaure:** stare, gape
1160 **the:** prosper
1161 **arte** = *art thou*, are you
1162 **fare-carte:** wagon for hauling goods
1166 **ayeyns:** in anticipation of
1171 **held with hym:** agreed with him
1174 **haselwode:** hazelwood   **Robyn:** a common name for a
rustic
1175 **abidest:** await
1176 **ferne yere:** yesteryear
1177 **warden:** guard
1185 **misacounted:** miscounted

And seyde, "I understonde have al amys.   1186
For thilke nyght I last Criseyde say,
She seyde, 'I shal ben here, if that I may,
Er that the moone, O deere herte swete,
The Leoun passe, out of this Ariete.'   1190

"For which she may yet holde al hire byheste."
And on the morwe unto the yate he wente,
And up and down, by west and ek by este,
Upon the walles made he many a wente.   1194
But al for nought; his hope alwey hym blente.
For which at nyght, in sorwe and sikes sore,
He wente hym hom, withouten any more.

His hope al clene out of his herte fledde;
He nath wheron now lenger for to honge;
But for the peyne hym thoughte his herte
          bledde,   1200
So were his throwes sharpe and wonder stronge;
For whan he saugh that she abood so longe,
He nyste what he juggen of it myghte,
Syn she hath broken that she hym bihighte.

The thridde, ferthe, fifte, sexte day   1205
After tho dayes ten of which I tolde,
Bitwixen hope and drede his herte lay,
Yet somwhat trustyng on hire hestes olde.
But whan he saugh she nolde hire terme holde,
He kan now sen non other remedie   1210
But for to shape hym soone for to dye.

Therwith the wikked spirit, God us blesse,
Which that men clepeth woode jalousie,
Gan in hym crepe, in al this hevynesse;
For which, by cause he wolde soone dye,   1215
He ne et ne drank, for his malencolye,
And ek from every compaignye he fledde:
This was the lif that al the tyme he ledde.

He so defet was, that no manere man
Unneth hym myghte knowen ther he wente;
So was he lene, and therto pale and wan,   1221
And feble, that he walketh by potente;
And with his ire he thus hymselve shente.
But whoso axed hym wherof hym smerte,   1224
He seyde his harm was al aboute his herte.

Priam ful ofte, and ek his moder deere,
His bretheren and his sustren gonne hym freyne

Whi he so sorwful was in al his cheere,
And what thyng was the cause of al his peyne;
But al for naught. He nolde his cause pleyne,
But seyde he felte a grevous maladie   1231
Aboute his herte, and fayn he wolde dye.

So on a day he leyde hym doun to slepe,
And so byfel that yn his slep hym thoughte
That in a forest faste he welk to wepe   1235
For love of here that hym these peynes
          wroughte;
And up and doun as he the forest soughte,
He mette he saugh a bor with tuskes grete,
That slepte ayeyn the bryghte sonnes hete.

And by this bor, faste in his armes folde,   1240
Lay, kyssyng ay, his lady bryght, Criseyde.
For sorwe of which, whan he it gan byholde,
And for despit, out of his slep he breyde,
And loude he cride on Pandarus, and seyde:
"O Pandarus, now know I crop and roote.   1245
I n'am but ded; ther nys noon other bote.

"My lady bryght, Criseyde, hath me bytrayed,
In whom I trusted most of ony wight.
She elliswhere hath now here herte apayed.
The blysful goddes thorugh here grete myght
Han in my drem yshewed it ful right.   1251
Thus yn my drem Criseyde have I
          byholde" —
And al this thing to Pandarus he tolde.

"O my Criseyde, allas, what subtilte,   1254
What newe lust, what beaute, what science,
What wratthe of juste cause have ye to me?
What gilt of me, what fel experience
Hath fro me raft, allas, thyn advertence?
O trust, O feyth, O depe asseuraunce!   1259
Who hath me reft Criseyde, al my plesaunce?

"Allas, whi leet I you from hennes go,
For which wel neigh out of my wit I breyde?
Who shal now trowe on any othes mo?
God wot, I wende, O lady bright, Criseyde,
That every word was gospel that ye seyde!

1199 **honge:** hang on to
1201 **throwes:** throes, sufferings
1209 **terme:** appointed time
1219 **defet:** disfigured
1222 **by potente:** with a crutch
1227 **gonne hym freyne:** asked him

1230 **cause:** case   **pleyne:** lament (reveal)
1235 **faste:** thick   **welk:** walked
1237 **soughte:** explored
1238 **mette:** dreamed
1243 **despit:** anger
1245 **crop and roote:** everything
1249 **apayed:** pleased
1254 **subtilte:** guile
1255 **science:** knowledge
1257 **gilt of me:** guilt of mine   **fel:** dreadful
1258 **raft:** taken away   **advertence:** attention (i.e., concern)
1265 **gospel:** absolute truth

But who may bet bigile, yf hym lyste,   1266
Than he on whom men weneth best to triste?

"What shal I don, my Pandarus, allas?
I fele now so sharp a newe peyne,
Syn that ther lith no remedye in this cas,   1270
That bet were it I with myn hondes tweyne
Myselven slowh alwey than thus to pleyne;
For thorugh the deth my wo sholde han an ende,
Ther every day with lyf myself I shende."

Pandare answerde and seyde, "Allas the while
That I was born! Have I nat seyd er this,   1276
That dremes many a maner man bigile?
And whi? For folk expounden hem amys.
How darstow seyn that fals thy lady ys   1279
For any drem, right for thyn owene drede?
Lat be this thought; thow kanst no dremes rede.

"Peraunter, ther thow dremest of this boor,
It may so be that it may signifie
Hire fader, which that old is and ek hoor,
Ayeyn the sonne lith o poynt to dye,   1285
And she for sorwe gynneth wepe and crie,
And kisseth hym, ther he lith on the grounde:
Thus sholdestow thi drem aright expounde!"

"How myghte I than don," quod Troilus,   1289
"To knowe of this, yee, were it nevere so lite?"
"Now seystow wisly," quod this Pandarus;
"My red is this: syn thow kanst wel endite,
That hastily a lettre thow hire write,
Thorugh which thow shalt wel bryngyn it
          aboute
To know a soth of that thow art in doute.   1295

"And se now whi: for this I dar wel seyn,
That if so is that she untrewe be,
I kan nat trowen that she wol write ayeyn.
And if she write, thow shalt ful sone yse
As wheither she hath any liberte   1300
To come ayeyn; or ellis in som clause,
If she be let, she wol assigne a cause.

"Thow hast nat writen hire syn that she wente,
Nor she to the; and this I dorste laye,
Ther may swich cause ben in hire entente

That hardily thow wolt thiselven saye   1306
That hire abod the best is for yow twaye.
Now writ hire thanne, and thow shalt feele
          sone
A soth of al. Ther is namore to done."

Acorded ben to this conclusioun,   1310
And that anon, thise ilke lordes two;
And hastily sit Troilus adown,
And rolleth in his herte to and fro
How he may best discryven hire his wo.
And to Criseyde, his owen lady deere,   1315
He wrot right thus, and seyde as ye may here:

Litera Troili.

"Right fresshe flour, whos I ben have and shal,
Withouten part of elleswhere servyse,
With herte, body, lif, lust, thought, and al,
I, woful wyght, in everich humble wise   1320
That tonge telle or herte may devyse,
As ofte as matere occupieth place,
Me recomaunde unto youre noble grace.

"Liketh yow to witen, swete herte,
As ye wel knowe, how longe tyme agon   1325
That ye me lefte in aspre peynes smerte,
Whan that ye wente, of which yet boote non
Have I non had, but evere wors bigon
Fro day to day am I, and so mot dwelle,   1329
While it yow list, of wele and wo my welle.

"For which to yow, with dredful herte trewe,
I write, as he that sorwe drifth to write,
My wo, that everich houre encresseth newe,
Compleynyng, as I dar or kan endite.
And that defaced is, that may ye wite   1335
The teris which that fro myn eyen reyne,
That wolden speke, if that they koude, and
          pleyne.

"Yow first biseche I, that youre eyen dere
To loke on this defouled ye nat holde;
And over al this, that ye, my lady deere,   1340
Wol vouchesauf this lettre to byholde;

1270 **lith**: lies, is
1272 **slowh**: should slay
1278 **expounden**: interpret
1281 **rede**: interpret
1290 I.e., to know the correct interpretation, even if it were a trifling matter
1302 **let**: prevented (from coming)
1304 **laye**: wager

1307 **abod**: delay **twaye**: two
1310 **Acorded**: agreed
1312 **sit** = *sitteth*, sits
Litera Troili: Troilus's Letter
1318 Without any share of my service given elsewhere
1322 **As ofte as**: i.e., as long as
1324 **Liketh yow to witen**: (may it) please you to recall
1328 **wors bigon**: in worse condition
1332 **drifth**: drives, compels
1335 **that defaced is**: that (my letter) which is defaced **wite**: blame on
1339 You do not consider (your eyes) defiled by looking on this letter
1340 **over al this**: moreover

And by the cause ek of my cares colde
That sleth my wit, if aught amys m'asterte,
Foryeve it me, myn owen swete herte!

"If any servant dorste or oughte of right   1345
Upon his lady pitously compleyne,
Thanne wene I that ich oughte be that wight,
Considered this, that ye thise monthes tweyne
Han taried, ther ye seyden, soth to seyne,
But dayes ten ye nolde in oost sojourne —
But in two monthes yet ye nat retourne.   1351

"But for as muche as me moot nedes like
Al that yow liste, I dar nat pleyne moore,
But humblely, with sorwful sikes sike,
Yow write ich myn unresty sorwes soore,   1355
Fro day to day desiryng evere moore
To knowen fully, if youre wille it weere,
How ye han ferd and don whil ye be theere;

"The whos welfare and hele ek God encresse
In honour swich that upward in degree   1360
It growe alwey, so that it nevere cesse.
Right as youre herte ay kan, my lady free,
Devyse, I prey to God so moot it be,
And graunte it that ye soone upon me rewe,
As wisly as in al I am yow trewe.   1365

"And if yow liketh knowen of the fare
Of me, whos wo ther may no wit discryve,
I kan namore but, chiste of every care,
At wrytyng of this lettre I was on-lyve,
Al redy out my woful gost to dryve,   1370
Which I delaye, and holde hym yet in honde,
Upon the sighte of matere of youre sonde.

"Myn eyen two, in veyn with which I se,
Of sorwful teris salte arn waxen welles;
My song, in pleynte of myn adversitee;   1375
My good, in harm; myn ese ek woxen helle is;
My joie, in wo; I kan sey yow naught ellis,
But torned is — for which my lif I warie —
Everich joie or ese in his contrarie;   1379

"Which with youre comyng hom ayeyn to Troie
Ye may redresse, and more a thousand sithe
Than evere ich hadde encressen in me joie.
For was ther nevere herte yet so blithe
To han his lif as I shal ben as swithe   1384
As I yow se; and though no manere routhe
Commeve yow, yet thynketh on youre trouthe.

"And if so be my gilt hath deth deserved,
Or if yow list namore upon me se,
In guerdoun yet of that I have yow served,
Byseche I yow, myn owen lady free,   1390
That hereupon ye wolden write me,
For love of God, my righte lode-sterre,
That deth may make an ende of al my werre;

"If other cause aught doth yow for to dwelle,
That with youre lettre ye me recomforte;   1395
For though to me youre absence is an helle,
With pacience I wol my wo comporte,
And with youre lettre of hope I wol desporte.
Now writeth, swete, and lat me thus nat pleyne;
With hope, or deth, delivereth me fro peyne.

"Iwis, myne owene deere herte trewe,   1401
I woot that whan ye next upon me se,
So lost have I myn hele and ek myn hewe,
Criseyde shal nought konne knowen me.
Iwys, myn hertes day, my lady free,   1405
So thursteth ay myn herte to byholde
Youre beute, that my lif unnethe I holde.

"I say namore, al have I for to seye
To yow wel more than I telle may;
But wheither that ye do me lyve or deye,   1410
Yet praye I God, so yeve yow right good day!
And fareth wel, goodly, faire, fresshe may,
As she that lif or deth may me comande!
And to youre trouthe ay I me recomande,

"With hele swich that, but ye yeven me   1415
The same hele, I shal non hele have.
In yow lith, whan yow liste that it so be,
The day in which me clothen shal my grave;
In yow my lif, in yow myght for to save

1343 **m'asterte:** escape from me
1349 **ther:** whereas
1350 **oost:** the besieging army
1355 **unresty:** distressing
1357 **if youre wille it weere:** i.e., if it would please you
1359 **The whos:** i.e., Criseyde's   **hele:** well-being
1366–67 **fare Of me:** how I am doing
1368 **chiste of every care:** receptacle of every sorrow
1371 **holde hym yet in honde:** put him off with promises
1372 Until I see the content (*matere*) of your message (*sonde*)
1378 **warie:** curse

1384 **as swithe:** as soon
1386 **Commeve:** move emotionally   **trouthe:** pledge
1392 **lode-sterre:** guiding star
1395 **That:** i.e., I beseech you that   **recomforte:** comfort
1397 **comporte:** endure
1398 **desporte:** cheer up
1412 **may:** maid, young woman
1415 **hele:** health (the closing salutation of the letter)

Me fro disese of alle peynes smerte;   1420
And far now wel, myn owen swete herte!
            Le vostre T."

This lettre forth was sent unto Criseyde,
Of which hire answere in effect was this:
Ful pitously she wroot ayeyn, and seyde,
That also sone as that she myghte, ywys,   1425
She wolde come, and mende al that was mys.
And fynaly she wroot and seyde hym thenne,
She wolde come, ye, but she nyste whenne.

But in hire lettre made she swich festes
That wonder was, and swerth she loveth hym
      best,   1430
Of which he fond but botmeles bihestes.
But Troilus, thow maist now, est or west,
Pipe in an ivy lef, if that the lest!
Thus goth the world. God shilde us fro mes-
      chaunce,
And every wight that meneth trouthe avaunce!

Encressen gan the wo fro day to nyght   1436
Of Troilus, for tarying of Criseyde;
And lessen gan his hope and ek his myght,
For which al down he in his bed hym leyde.
He ne eet, ne dronk, ne slep, ne word seyde,
Ymagynyng ay that she was unkynde,   1441
For which wel neigh he wex out of his mynde.

This drem, of which I told have ek byforn,
May nevere outen of his remembraunce.
He thought ay wel he hadde his lady lorn,
And that Joves of his purveyaunce   1446
Hym shewed hadde in slep the signifiaunce
Of hire untrouthe and his disaventure,
And that the boor was shewed hym in figure.

For which he for Sibille his suster sente,   1450
That called was Cassandre ek al aboute,
And al his drem he tolde hire er he stente,
And hire bisoughte assoilen hym the doute
Of the stronge boor with tuskes stoute;

And fynaly, withinne a litel stounde,   1455
Cassandre hym gan right thus his drem ex-
      pounde:

She gan first smyle, and seyde, "O brother
      deere,
If thow a soth of this desirest knowe,
Thow most a fewe of olde stories heere,
To purpos how that Fortune overthrowe   1460
Hath lordes olde, thorugh which, withinne a
      throwe,
Thow wel this boor shalt knowe, and of what
      kynde
He comen is, as men in bokes fynde.

"Diane, which that wroth was and in ire
For Grekis nolde don hire sacrifice,   1465
Ne encens upon hire auter sette afire,
She, for that Grekis gonne hire so despise,
Wrak hire in a wonder cruel wise;
For with a boor as gret as ox in stalle   1469
She made up frete hire corn and vynes alle.

"To sle this boor was al the contre raysed,
Amonges which ther com, this boor to se,
A mayde, oon of this world the beste ypreysed;
And Meleagre, lord of that contree,
He loved so this fresshe mayden free   1475
That with his manhod, er he wolde stente,
This boor he slough, and hire the hed he sente;

"Of which, as olde bokes tellen us,
Ther ros a contek and a gret envye;
And of this lord descended Tideus   1480
By ligne, or ellis olde bookes lye.
But how this Meleagre gan to dye
Thorugh his moder, wol I yow naught telle,
For al to longe it were for to dwelle."

She tolde ek how Tideus, er she stente,   1485
Unto the stronge citee of Thebes,
To cleymen kyngdom of the citee, wente,
For his felawe, daun Polymytes,

1421 **Le vostre T.**: your T.
1429 **made she swich festes**: made such a fuss over him, treated him with such endearments
1431 **botmeles bihestes**: promises with no foundation
1433 **Pipe in an ivy lef**: go whistle (in vain)
1435 **avaunce**: to further
1444 **outen**: come out
1446 **purveyaunce**: foreknowledge
1449 **in figure**: symbolically or as a prefiguration
1450 **Sibille**: prophetess, apparently taken as a second name for Cassandra (*Cassandre*)
1453 **assoilen hym the doute**: resolve his doubt

1461 **throwe**: short time
1464 **Diane**: Diana, the goddess
1468 **Wrak**: avenged
1470 **made up frete**: caused to be devoured
1473 **A mayde**: Atalanta
1474 **Meleagre**: Meleager, son of the king of Calydon
1479 **contek**: strife
1483 **Thorugh**: by the agency of
1488 **Polymytes**: Polynices, son of Oedipus; he and his brother Eteocles (*Ethiocles*) were to alternate as rulers. Eteocles would not give up the kingship, and Polynices summoned six champions to gain the city.

Of which the brother, daun Ethiocles,
Ful wrongfully of Thebes held the strengthe;
This tolde she by proces, al by lengthe.   1491

She tolde ek how Hemonydes asterte,
Whan Tideus slough fifty knyghtes stoute.
She tolde ek alle the prophecyes by herte,
And how that seven kynges with hire route
Bysegeden the citee al aboute;   1496
And of the holy serpent, and the welle,
And of the furies, al she gan hym telle;*

Of Archymoris brennynge and the pleyes,
And how Amphiorax fil thorugh the grounde,
How Tideus was sleyn, lord of Argeyes,   1501
And how Ypomedoun in litel stounde
Was dreynt, and ded Parthonope of wownde;
And also how Capaneus the proude   1504
With thonder-dynt was slayn, that cride loude.

She gan ek telle hym how that eyther brother,
Ethiocles and Polymyte also,
At a scarmuche ech of hem slough other,
And of Argyves wepynge and hire wo;   1509

*Almost all MSS have the following Latin argument of
Statius's *Thebaid* immediately following line 1498:
Associat profugum Tideo primus Polymytem;   1498a
Tidea legatum docet insidiasque secundus;
Tercius Hemoniden canit et vates latitantes;
Quartus habet reges ineuntes prelia septem;   1498d
Mox furie Lenne quinto narratur et anguis;
Archymory bustum sexto ludique leguntur;
Dat Grayos Thebes et vatem septimus umbris;
Octavo cecidit Tideus, spes, vita Pelasgis;   1498h
Ypomedon nono moritur cum Parthonopea;
Fulmine percussus decimo Capaneus superatur;
Undecimo sese perimunt per vulnera fratres;   1498k
Argiva flentem narrat duodenus et ignem.

[*The first (book) associates the exiled Polynices with Tydeus; the second
tells of the embassy of Tydeus and of the ambush (by Eteocles); the third
sings of Hemonides (Maeon, son of Haemon) and of the secretive seers; the
fourth has the seven kings going to battle; then in the fifth the Furies
of Lemnos and the serpent are told of; in the sixth the cremation of Archemorus
and the games are read about; the seventh brings the Greeks to Thebes and
the seer (Amphiaraus) to the shades; in the eighth fell Tydeus, hope, life
of the Pelasgians; in the ninth Hippomedon dies along with Parthenopaeus;
struck by lightning, Capaneus is overcome in the tenth; in the eleventh the
brothers (Eteocles and Polynices) kill one another with wounds; the twelfth
tells about weeping Argia about the fire.*]

1492 **Hemonydes:** Maeon, son of Haemon **asterte:** escaped
1495 **seven kynges:** the "Seven Against Thebes," whose fates are
summarized below
1497 **holy serpent:** a serpent sent by Jove to kill Archemorus
(*Archymoris*), infant son of King Lycurgus
1499 **pleyes:** the Nemean games, instituted at Archemorus's
funeral by the army on its way to Thebes
1500 **Amphiorax:** Amphiaraus, swallowed by the earth
1501 **Argeyes:** Argives, people of Argos
1502 **Ypomedoun:** Hippomedon
1503 **dreynt:** drowned **Parthonope:** Parthenopaeus
1505 **thonder-dynt:** thunderbolt; Capaneus boasted (*cride loude*)
that even Zeus could not stop him, whereupon he was struck
with a thunderbolt.
1508 **scarmuche:** skirmish
1509 **Argyves wepynge:** the weeping of Argia, wife of Polynices

And how the town was brent, she tolde ek tho;
And so descendeth down from gestes olde
To Diomede, and thus she spak and tolde:

"This ilke boor bitokneth Diomede,
Tideus sone, that down descended is
Fro Meleagre, that made the boor to blede;
And thy lady, wherso she be, ywis,   1516
This Diomede hire herte hath, and she his.
Wep if thow wolt, or lef, for out of doute,
This Diomede is inne, and thow art oute."

"Thow seyst nat soth," quod he, "thow sor-
          ceresse,   1520
With al thy false goost of prophecye!
Thow wenest ben a gret devyneresse!
Now sestow nat this fool of fantasie
Peyneth hire on ladys for to lye?   1524
Awey!" quod he. "Ther Joves yeve the sorwe!
Thow shalt be fals, peraunter, yet tomorwe!

"As wel thow myghtest lien on Alceste,
That was of creatures, but men lye,
That evere weren, kyndest and the beste!
For whan hire housbonde was in jupertye   1530
To dye hymself but if she wolde dye,
She ches for hym to dye and gon to helle,
And starf anon, as us the bokes telle."

Cassandre goth, and he with cruel herte
Foryat his wo, for angre of hire speche;   1535
And from his bed al sodeynly he sterte,
As though al hool hym hadde ymad a leche.
And day by day he gan enquere and seche
A sooth of this with al his fulle cure;
And thus he drieth forth his aventure.   1540

Fortune, which that permutacioun
Of thynges hath, as it is hire comitted
Thorugh purveyaunce and disposicioun
Of heighe Jove, as regnes shal be flitted   1544
Fro folk in folk, or when they shal be smytted,
Gan pulle awey the fetheres brighte of Troie
Fro day to day, til they ben bare of joie.

1518 **lef:** leave it
1521 **goost:** spirit
1522 **devyneresse:** prophetess
1523 **fool of fantasie:** victim of delusions (Cassandra)
1524 **Peyneth hire:** takes pains
1527 **Alceste:** Alcestis, heroine of the Prologue of LGW
1538 **seche:** seek
1539 **fulle cure:** entire attention
1540 **drieth forth:** bears up under
1544 **flitted:** transferred
1545 **in:** i.e., to **smytted:** sullied, disgraced (or, struck down;
see n.)

Among al this, the fyn of the parodie
Of Ector gan aprochen wonder blyve.   1549
The fate wolde his soule sholde unbodye,
And shapen hadde a mene it out to dryve,
Ayeyns which fate hym helpeth nat to stryve;
But on a day to fighten gan he wende,
At which — allas! — he caughte his lyves ende.

For which me thynketh every manere wight
That haunteth armes oughte to biwaille   1556
The deth of hym that was so noble a knyght;
For as he drough a kyng by th'aventaille,
Unwar of this, Achilles thorugh the maille   1559
And thorugh the body gan hym for to ryve;
And thus this worthi knyght was brought of
          lyve.

For whom, as olde bokes tellen us,
Was mad swich wo that tonge it may nat telle,
And namely, the sorwe of Troilus,
That next hym was of worthynesse welle;   1565
And in this wo gan Troilus to dwelle
That, what for sorwe, and love, and for unreste,
Ful ofte a day he bad his herte breste.

But natheles, though he gan hym dispaire,
And dradde ay that his lady was untrewe,
Yet ay on hire his herte gan repaire.   1571
And as thise lovers don, he soughte ay newe
To gete ayeyn Criseyde, brighte of hewe;
And in his herte he wente hire excusynge,
That Calkas caused al hire tariynge.   1575

And ofte tyme he was in purpos grete
Hymselven lik a pilgrym to desgise
To seen hire; but he may nat contrefete
To ben unknowen of folk that weren wise,
Ne fynde excuse aright that may suffise   1580
If he among the Grekis knowen were;
For which he wep ful ofte and many a tere.

To hire he wroot yet ofte tyme al newe
Ful pitously — he lefte it nought for slouthe —

Bisechyng hire that sithen he was trewe,   1585
That she wol come ayeyn and holde hire
          trouthe.
For which Criseyde upon a day, for routhe —
I take it so — touchyng al this matere,
Wrot hym ayeyn, and seyde as ye may here:

Litera Criseydis.

"Cupides sone, ensample of goodlyheede,   1590
O swerd of knyghthod, sours of gentilesse,
How myght a wight in torment and in drede
And heleles, yow sende as yet gladnesse?
I herteles, I sik, I in destresse!   1594
Syn ye with me, nor I with yow, may dele,
Yow neyther sende ich herte may nor hele.

"Youre lettres ful, the papir al ypleynted,
Conceyved hath myn hertes pietee.
I have ek seyn with teris al depeynted   1599
Youre lettre, and how that ye requeren me
To come ayeyn, which yet ne may nat be;
But whi, lest that this lettre founden were,
No mencioun ne make I now, for feere.

"Grevous to me, God woot, is youre unreste,
Youre haste, and that the goddes ordinaunce
It semeth nat ye take it for the beste.   1606
Nor other thyng nys in youre remembraunce,
As thynketh me, but only youre plesaunce.
But beth nat wroth, and that I yow biseche;
For that I tarie is al for wikked speche.   1610

"For I have herd wel moore than I wende,
Touchyng us two, how thynges han ystonde,
Which I shal with dissymelyng amende.
And beth nat wroth, I have ek understonde
How ye ne do but holden me in honde.   1615
But now no force. I kan nat in yow gesse
But alle trouthe and alle gentilesse.

"Come I wole; but yet in swich disjoynte
I stonde as now that what yer or what day
That this shal be, that kan I naught apoynte.
But in effect I pray yow, as I may,   1621
Of youre good word and of youre frendship ay;

1548 **Among al this:** meanwhile   **parodie:** period, lifetime
1550 **unbodye:** leave the body
1551 **mene:** means
1556 **haunteth:** uses
1558 **th'aventaille:** the piece of chain mail forming the neck-guard of the helmet
1559 **Unwar of this:** unaware of it
1560 **ryve:** stab
1561 **brought of lyve:** killed
1571 **gan repaire:** returned, resorted
1572 **ay newe:** always
1576 **in purpos grete:** filled with intention

Litera Criseydis: Criseyde's Letter
1593 **heleles:** ill (healthless)
1594 **herteles:** disheartened   **sik:** sick
1597 **ypleynted:** filled with laments
1598 **Conceyved:** engendered, aroused
1599 **depeynted:** stained
1615 How you are only leading me on, deceiving me
1616 **gesse:** suppose, imagine
1618 **disjoynte:** predicament
1620 **apoynte:** decide, specify

For trewely, while that my lif may dure,
As for a frend ye may in me assure.

"Yet preye ich yow, on yvel ye ne take   1625
That it is short which that I to yow write;
I dar nat, ther I am, wel lettres make,
Ne nevere yet ne koude I wel endite.
Ek gret effect men write in place lite;
Th'entente is al, and nat the lettres space.   1630
And fareth now wel. God have yow in his grace!
                              La vostre C."

This Troilus this lettre thoughte al straunge
Whan he it saugh, and sorwfullich he sighte;
Hym thoughte it lik a kalendes of chaunge.
But fynaly, he ful ne trowen myghte   1635
That she ne wolde hym holden that she hyghte;
For with ful yvel wille list hym to leve
That loveth wel, in swich cas, though hym
                              greve.

But natheles men seyen that at the laste,
For any thyng, men shal the soothe se;   1640
And swich a cas bitidde, and that as faste,
That Troilus wel understod that she
Nas nought so kynde as that hire oughte be.
And fynaly, he woot now out of doute
That al is lost that he hath ben aboute.   1645

Stood on a day in his malencolie
This Troilus, and in suspecioun
Of hire for whom he wende for to dye.
And so bifel that thoroughout Troye town,
As was the gise, iborn was up and down   1650
A manere cote-armure, as seith the storie,
Byforn Deiphebe, in signe of his victorie;

The whiche cote, as telleth Lollius,
Deiphebe it hadde rent fro Diomede
The same day. And whan this Troilus   1655
It saugh, he gan to taken of it hede,
Avysyng of the lengthe and of the brede,
And al the werk; but as he gan byholde,
Ful sodeynly his herte gan to colde,

As he that on the coler fond withinne   1660
A broch that he Criseyde yaf that morwe
That she from Troie moste nedes twynne,
In remembraunce of hym and of his sorwe.
And she hym leyde ayeyn hire feith to borwe
To kepe it ay! But now ful wel he wiste,   1665
His lady nas no lenger on to triste.

He goth hym hom and gan ful soone sende
For Pandarus, and al this newe chaunce,
And of this broche, he tolde hym word and
                              ende,
Compleynyng of hire hertes variaunce,   1670
His longe love, his trouthe, and his penaunce.
And after deth, withouten wordes moore,
Ful faste he cride, his reste hym to restore.

Than spak he thus, "O lady myn, Criseyde,
Where is youre feith, and where is youre bi-
                              heste?   1675
Where is youre love? Where is youre trouthe?"
                              he seyde.
"Of Diomede have ye now al this feeste!
Allas, I wolde han trowed atte leeste
That syn ye nolde in trouthe to me stonde,
That ye thus nolde han holden me in honde!

"Who shal now trowe on any othes mo?   1681
Allas, I nevere wolde han wend, er this,
That ye, Criseyde, koude han chaunged so;
Ne, but I hadde agilt and don amys,   1684
So cruel wende I nought youre herte, ywis,
To sle me thus! Allas, youre name of trouthe
Is now fordon, and that is al my routhe.

"Was ther non other broch yow liste lete
To feffe with youre newe love," quod he,
"But thilke broch that I, with teris wete,   1690
Yow yaf as for a remembraunce of me?
Non other cause, allas, ne hadde ye
But for despit, and ek for that ye mente
Al outrely to shewen youre entente.

"Thorugh which I se that clene out of youre
                              mynde   1695
Ye han me cast — and I ne kan nor may,
For al this world, withinne myn herte fynde

1625 **on yvel ye ne take:** that you take it not amiss
1631 **La vostre C.:** your C.
1634 **kalendes:** beginning, harbinger
1637 For he is very reluctant to believe
1638 **That:** he who   **hym greve:** it may trouble him
1640 **For:** despite
1650 **gise:** custom
1651 **cote-armure:** a tunic embroidered with a heraldic device, worn over the armor
1654 **rent:** torn

1660 **coler:** collar
1664 **to borwe:** as a pledge
1666 **on to triste:** to put trust in
1669 **word and ende:** beginning and end, everything
1675 **feith:** pledged word
1688 **yow liste lete:** it pleased you to let go
1689 **To feffe with:** with which to enfeoff, endow

To unloven yow a quarter of a day!
In corsed tyme I born was, weilaway,
That yow, that doon me al this wo endure,
Yet love I best of any creature!   1701

"Now God," quod he, "me sende yet the grace
That I may meten with this Diomede!
And trewely, if I have myght and space,
Yet shal I make, I hope, his sydes blede.   1705
O God," quod he, "that oughtest taken heede
To fortheren trouthe, and wronges to punyce,
Whi nyltow don a vengeaunce of this vice?

"O Pandarus, that in dremes for to triste
Me blamed hast, and wont art oft upbreyde,
Now maistow sen thiself, if that the liste,   1711
How trewe is now thi nece, bright Criseyde!
In sondry formes, God it woot," he seyde,
"The goddes shewen bothe joie and tene
In slep, and by my drem it is now sene.   1715

"And certeynly, withouten moore speche,
From hennesforth, as ferforth as I may,
Myn owen deth in armes wol I seche;
I recche nat how soone be the day!
But trewely, Criseyde, swete may,   1720
Whom I have ay with al my myght yserved,
That ye thus doon, I have it nat deserved."

This Pandarus, that al thise thynges herde,
And wiste wel he seyde a soth of this,
He nought a word ayeyn to hym answerde;
For sory of his frendes sorwe he is,   1726
And shamed for his nece hath don amys,
And stant, astoned of thise causes tweye,
As stille as ston; a word ne kowde he seye.

But at the laste thus he spak, and seyde: 1730
"My brother deer, I may do the namore.
What sholde I seyen? I hate, ywys, Cryseyde;
And, God woot, I wol hate hire evermore!
And that thow me bisoughtest don of yoore,
Havyng unto myn honour ne my reste   1735
Right no reward, I dide al that the leste.

"If I dide aught that myghte liken the,
It is me lief; and of this tresoun now,
God woot that it a sorwe is unto me!
And dredeles, for hertes ese of yow,   1740
Right fayn I wolde amende it, wiste I how.

And fro this world, almyghty God I preye
Delivere hire soon! I kan namore seye."

Gret was the sorwe and pleynte of Troilus,
But forth hire cours Fortune ay gan to holde.
Criseyde loveth the sone of Tideüs,   1746
And Troilus moot wepe in cares colde.
Swich is this world, whoso it kan byholde;
In ech estat is litel hertes reste.
God leve us for to take it for the beste!   1750

In many cruel bataille, out of drede,
Of Troilus, this ilke noble knyght,
As men may in thise olde bokes rede,
Was seen his knyghthod and his grete myght;
And dredeles, his ire, day and nyght,   1755
Ful cruwely the Grekis ay aboughte;
And alwey moost this Diomede he soughte.

And ofte tyme, I fynde that they mette
With blody strokes and with wordes grete,
Assayinge how hire speres weren whette;   1760
And, God it woot, with many a cruel hete
Gan Troilus upon his helm to bete!
But natheles, Fortune it naught ne wolde
Of oothers hond that eyther deyen sholde.

And if I hadde ytaken for to write   1765
The armes of this ilke worthi man,
Than wolde ich of his batailles endite;
But for that I to writen first bigan
Of his love, I have seyd as I kan —
His worthi dedes, whoso list hem heere,   1770
Rede Dares, he kan telle hem alle ifeere —

Bysechyng every lady bright of hewe,
And every gentil womman, what she be,
That al be that Criseyde was untrewe,
That for that gilt she be nat wroth with me.
Ye may hire gilt in other bokes se;   1776
And gladlier I wol write, yif yow leste,
Penolopeës trouthe and good Alceste.

N'y sey nat this al oonly for thise men,
But moost for wommen that bitraised be   1780

1750 **leve:** grant
1756 **aboughte:** paid for, suffered
1760 **whette:** sharpened
1761 **hete:** passion, rage
1771 **Dares:** Dares Phrygius, supposed ancient author of a history
of the Trojan War
1777 **gladlier:** more willingly
1778 **Penolopeës trouthe:** the faithfulness of Penelope, wife of
Ulysses
1780 **bitraised:** betrayed

Thorough false folk — God yeve hem sorwe,
    amen! —
That with hire grete wit and subtilte
Bytraise yow. And this commeveth me
To speke, and in effect yow alle I preye,
Beth war of men, and herkneth what I seye!

Go, litel bok, go, litel myn tragedye,   1786
Ther God thi makere yet, er that he dye,
So sende myght to make in som comedye!
But litel book, no makyng thow n'envie,
But subgit be to alle poesye;   1790
And kis the steppes where as thow seest pace
Virgile, Ovide, Omer, Lucan, and Stace.

And for ther is so gret diversite
In Englissh and in writyng of oure tonge,
So prey I God that non myswrite the,   1795
Ne the mysmetre for defaute of tonge;
And red wherso thow be, or elles songe,
That thow be understonde, God I biseche!
But yet to purpos of my rather speche:

The wrath, as I bigan yow for to seye,   1800
Of Troilus the Grekis boughten deere,
For thousandes his hondes maden deye,
As he that was withouten any peere,
Save Ector, in his tyme, as I kan heere.
But — weilawey, save only Goddes wille,   1805
Despitously hym slough the fierse Achille.

And whan that he was slayn in this manere,
His lighte goost ful blisfully is went
Up to the holughnesse of the eighthe spere,
In convers letyng everich element;   1810
And ther he saugh with ful avysement
The erratik sterres, herkenyng armonye
With sownes ful of hevenyssh melodie.

And down from thennes faste he gan avyse
This litel spot of erthe that with the se   1815
Embraced is, and fully gan despise
This wrecched world, and held al vanite
To respect of the pleyn felicite
That is in hevene above; and at the laste,   1819
Ther he was slayn his lokyng down he caste,

And in hymself he lough right at the wo
Of hem that wepten for his deth so faste,
And dampned al oure werk that foloweth so
The blynde lust, the which that may nat laste,
And sholden al oure herte on heven caste;   1825
And forth he wente, shortly for to telle,
Ther as Mercurye sorted hym to dwelle.

Swich fyn hath, lo, this Troilus for love!
Swich fyn hath al his grete worthynesse!
Swich fyn hath his estat real above!   1830
Swich fyn his lust, swich fyn hath his noblesse!
Swych fyn hath false worldes brotelnesse!
And thus bigan his lovyng of Criseyde,
As I have told, and in this wise he deyde.

O yonge, fresshe folkes, he or she,   1835
In which that love up groweth with youre age,
Repeyreth hom fro worldly vanyte,
And of youre herte up casteth the visage
To thilke God that after his ymage   1839
Yow made, and thynketh al nys but a faire,
This world that passeth soone as floures faire.

And loveth hym the which that right for love
Upon a crois, oure soules for to beye,
First starf, and roos, and sit in hevene above;
For he nyl falsen no wight, dar I seye,   1845
That wol his herte al holly on hym leye.
And syn he best to love is, and most meke,
What nedeth feynede loves for to seke?

Lo here, of payens corsed olde rites!   1849
Lo here, what alle hire goddes may availle!
Lo here, thise wrecched worldes appetites!
Lo here, the fyn and guerdoun for travaille
Of Jove, Appollo, of Mars, of swich rascaille!

1783 **commeveth:** moves emotionally
1787 **Ther God:** i.e., may God
1788 **make in:** compose
1789 **envien':** do notvie with, contend with
1792 **Omer, Lucan, and Stace:** Homer, Lucan (author of the *Pharsalia*), and Statius (author of the *Thebaid*)
1796 **mysmetre:** ruin the meter **defaute of tonge:** deficiency of his (the scribe's) language (because of the diversity of dialects)
1799 **rather:** earlier
1803 **peere:** equal
1805 But alas—except that it was God's will
1808 **is went:** has gone
1809 Up to the concavity (inner surface) of the eighth sphere
1810 Leaving every element (the planetary spheres or the four elements) on the other side (*In convers*)
1812 **erratik sterres:** wandering stars (i.e. the seven planets)
armonye: the music of the spheres

1818 Regarding, with respect to, the full or perfect felicity
1825 **caste:** bestow
1827 **sorted:** allotted, assigned
1830 **real:** royal
1832 **brotelnesse:** undependability
1837 **Repeyreth hom:** return to (your real) home (heaven)
1840 **faire:** fair (i.e., a temporary amusement)
1843 **beye:** buy, redeem
1849 **payens:** pagans'
1853 **rascaille:** worthless mob, rabble

Lo here, the forme of olde clerkis speche
In poetrie, if ye hire bokes seche.   1855

O moral Gower, this book I directe
To the and to the, philosophical Strode,
To vouchen sauf, ther nede is, to correcte,
Of youre benignites and zeles goode.   1859
And to that sothfast Crist, that starf on rode,
With al myn herte of mercy evere I preye,
And to the Lord right thus I speke and seye:

Thow oon, and two, and thre, eterne on lyve,
That regnest ay in thre, and two, and oon,
Uncircumscript, and al maist circumscrive,
Us from visible and invisible foon   1866
Defende, and to thy mercy, everichon,
So make us, Jesus, for thi mercy, digne,
For love of mayde and moder thyn benigne.
        Amen.

Explicit liber Troili et Criseydis.

1854 **forme:** essential principle (or, style; see n.)
1856 **Gower:** John Gower
1857 **Strode:** Radulphus Strode (?); see n.
1860 **rode:** cross

1863 **eterne on lyve:** eternally living
1865 **Uncircumscript:** boundless **circumscrive:** circumscribe,
limit
Explicit, *etc.:* Here ends the book of Troilus and Criseyde.

THE
LEGEND OF GOOD
WOMEN

THE LEGEND OF GOOD WOMEN is a product of Chaucer's artistic maturity, written not long after (and purportedly as an atonement for) *Troilus and Criseyde* and before or during the composition of *The Canterbury Tales.* It is an ambitious work, the third longest of his poems (only *Troilus* and the *Tales* are longer). Chaucer apparently regarded the *Legend* as important (the Man of Law discusses this "large volume" at length in the introduction to his tale, II.60–76), and he liked it well enough to revise it (at least the Prologue) after a number of years.

The *Legend* is an important work in the development of Chaucer's art. The Prologue is the last, and one of the best, of his dream visions, and with the legends it forms the first of his narratives (perhaps the first in English) in the decasyllabic couplet that he was to use for most of his *Canterbury Tales.* In content, the *Legend* presents Chaucer's most detailed treatment of several stories that he had long admired and that he had alluded to or briefly told in his earlier poems: those of Medea (BD 715–27, HF 401), Phyllis (BD 728–31, HF 388–96), Hypsipyle (HF 400), Ariadne (HF 405–26), and, most notably, Dido (BD 731–34; HF 151–382, 427–67). In form, the *Legend* is an attempt to write a collection of tales more ambitious in scope than that in The Monk's Tale, most of which probably antedates this work, and obviously an important preparation for *The Canterbury Tales.*

Yet *The Legend of Good Women* is usually regarded as a critical paradox — a work of Chaucer's prime, on which he obviously expended much care, and yet a failure. For many years critics (for example, Lounsbury, Tatlock, and others) explained this paradox on the assumption that the scene in the Prologue in which Queen Alceste sets Chaucer the task of writing

the *Legend* was based on fact: that Chaucer was writing in reluctant response to a royal command — an unwilling poet writing on an assigned topic. Chaucer, this theory held, grew increasingly bored with the work and finally abandoned it. Yet, while there is some evidence (the dedication to the queen in the F Prologue) that Chaucer did write at the queen's request, there can be no certainty that the request was as restrictive or specific as Alceste's command in the Prologue. The dialogue of the poet, the God of Love, and Alceste probably owes more to literary convention (compare Machaut's *Jugement dou Roy de Navarre*) than to any actual event. Even if Chaucer was given some specific assignment, there is no reason to assume that he therefore wrote reluctantly. The lines usually cited as evidence that Chaucer was bored with his task (994–97, 1002–3, 1564–65, 1678–79, 1692–93, 2452–64, 2469–71, 2490–93) are merely examples of the rhetorical devices *abbreviatio* and *occupatio,* and each has its proper artistic function (note the comparable use in The Knight's Tale; for example, I.1187–9 and I.1201). The unfinished condition of the poem as it has come down to us is no more an indication that Chaucer abandoned it in distaste than is the unfinished state of *The House of Fame* or, for that matter, of *The Canterbury Tales.*

Despite the low critical reputation of this work, many passages (in the F Prologue in particular) are justly noted for their beauty, and the ballade (F 249–69, G 203–23) is a striking example of Chaucer's skill in meeting the demands of a relatively rigid, non-narrative form. Nor is the action of the legends boring. The battle scene in The Legend of Cleopatra (635–53) is a rare and exciting instance of Chaucer's talent for vivid description applied to military (in this case naval) action. The gathering of the hunt in The Legend of Dido (1194–1209) is vibrant with color and movement. Each separate legend has beauties of detail, and some of the legends, such as Hypsipyle's and Lucretia's, achieve genuine pathos. The work was much admired in Chaucer's time, and there is ample evidence that it continued to be admired in the fifteenth century. (See Spurgeon, *Five Hundred Years of Chaucer Criticism and Allusion: 1357–1900.*)

Nevertheless, the *Legend* does have features that are displeasing to the modern taste. Inherent in the assignment that Alceste gives the narrator is a repetition of subject matter and narrative treatment, and the legends offer little variety in plot and character. The tone varies considerably, sometimes within the same legend, fluctuating between the serious (sometimes bordering on the tragic) and the comic (sometimes approaching the ludicrous). Although this variation can be a source of genuine pleasure to the reader, it can also be a source of confusion and uncertainty. (See, especially, R. W. Frank, Jr., *Chaucer and* The Legend of Good Women, 1972, 114–33, on tone in Ariadne.)

The Legend of Good Women is one of Chaucer's more problematical works but not one of his least fascinating. In recent years it has attracted more serious and sympathetic study than heretofore (such as Frank's book, cited above), and future study and criticism may eventually provide both more appropriate ways of reading and interpreting it and a clearer sense of its value in the canon of Chaucer's work.

M. C. E. SHANER

The Legend of Good Women

The Seintes Legende of Cupide

■

TEXT F

A thousand tymes have I herd men telle
That ther ys joy in hevene and peyne in helle,
And I acorde wel that it ys so;
But, natheles, yet wot I wel also
That ther nis noon dwellyng in this contree   5
That eyther hath in hevene or helle ybe,
Ne may of hit noon other weyes witen
But as he hath herd seyd or founde it writen;
For by assay ther may no man it preve.
But God forbede but men shulde leve   10
Wel more thing then men han seen with ye!
Men shal not wenen every thing a lye
But yf himself yt seeth or elles dooth;
For, God wot, thing is never the lasse sooth,

This text was edited by A. S. G. EDWARDS and M. C. E. SHANER.

9 **assay**: experiment
10 **but men**: that men

TEXT G

A thousand sythes have I herd men telle
That there is joye in hevene and peyne in helle,
And I acorde wel that it be so;
But natheles, this wot I wel also,
That there ne is non that dwelleth in this con-
    tre   5
That eyther hath in helle or hevene ybe,
Ne may of it non other weyes witen
But as he hath herd seyd or founde it writen;
For by assay there may no man it preve.
But Goddes forbode but men shulde leve   10
Wel more thyng than men han seyn with ye!
Men shal nat wenen every thyng a lye
For that he say it nat of yore ago.
God wot a thyng is nevere the lesse so

G 10 **Goddes forbode**: (by) God's prohibition (?)

Thogh every wight ne may it nat ysee.   15
Bernard the monk ne saugh nat all, pardee!
   Than mote we to bokes that we fynde,
Thurgh whiche that olde thinges ben in mynde,
And to the doctrine of these olde wyse,
Yeve credence, in every skylful wise,   20
That tellen of these olde appreved stories
Of holynesse, of regnes, of victories,
Of love, of hate, of other sondry thynges,
Of whiche I may not maken rehersynges.
And yf that olde bokes were aweye,   25
Yloren were of remembraunce the keye.
Wel ought us thanne honouren and beleve
These bokes, there we han noon other preve.
   And as for me, though that I konne but lyte,
On bokes for to rede I me delyte,   30
And to hem yive I feyth and ful credence,
And in myn herte have hem in reverence
So hertely, that ther is game noon
That fro my bokes maketh me to goon,
But yt be seldom on the holyday,   35
Save, certeynly, whan that the month of May
Is comen, and that I here the foules synge,
And that the floures gynnen for to sprynge,
Farewel my bok and my devocioun!
   Now have I thanne eek this condicioun,   40
That, of al the floures in the mede,
Thanne love I most thise floures white and
        rede,
Swiche as men callen daysyes in our toun.
To hem have I so gret affeccioun,
As I seyde erst, whanne comen is the May,   45
That in my bed ther daweth me no day
That I nam up and walkyng in the mede
To seen this flour ayein the sonne sprede,
Whan it upryseth erly by the morwe.
That blisful sighte softneth al my sorwe,   50
So glad am I, whan that I have presence
Of it, to doon it alle reverence,
As she that is of alle floures flour,
Fulfilled of al vertu and honour,
And evere ilyke faire and fressh of hewe;   55
And I love it, and ever ylike newe,
And evere shal, til that myn herte dye.
Al swere I nat, of this I wol nat lye;
Ther loved no wight hotter in his lyve.
And whan that hit ys eve, I renne blyve,   60
As sone as evere the sonne gynneth weste,

Thow every wyght ne may it nat yse.   15
Bernard the monk ne say nat al, parde!
   Thanne mote we to bokes that we fynde,
Thourgh whiche that olde thynges ben in
        mynde,
And to the doctryne of these olde wyse
Yeven credence, in every skylful wyse,   20
And trowen on these olde aproved storyes
Of holynesse, of regnes, of victoryes,
Of love, of hate, of othere sondry thynges,
Of which I may nat make rehersynges.
And if that olde bokes weren aweye,   25
Yloren were of remembrance the keye.
Wel oughte us thanne on olde bokes leve,
There as there is non other assay by preve.
   And as for me, though that my wit be lite,
On bokes for to rede I me delyte,   30
And in myn herte have hem in reverence,
And to hem yeve swich lust and swich credence
That there is wel unethe game non
That fro my bokes make me to gon,
But it be other upon the halyday,   35
Or ellis in the joly tyme of May,
Whan that I here the smale foules synge,
And that the floures gynne for to sprynge.
Farwel my stodye, as lastynge that sesoun!
   Now have I therto this condicioun,   40
That, of alle the floures in the mede,
Thanne love I most these floures white and
        rede,
Swyche as men calle dayesyes in oure toun.
To hem have I so gret affeccioun,
As I seyde erst, whan comen is the May,   45
That in my bed there daweth me no day
That I n'am up and walkynge in the mede
To sen these floures agen the sonne sprede
Whan it up ryseth by the morwe shene,
The longe day thus walkynge in the grene.   50

And whan the sonne gynneth for to weste,

16 **Bernard the monk**: probably St. Bernard of Clairvaux
19 **wyse**: wise writers
21 **appreved**: proven true
26 **Yloren**: lost
55 **ilyke**: equally
61 **weste**: go westward

G 39 **as lastynge that sesoun**: as long as that season lasts

To seen this flour, how it wol go to reste,
For fere of nyght, so hateth she derknesse.

Hire chere is pleynly sprad in the brightnesse
Of the sonne, for ther yt wol unclose. 65
Allas, that I ne had Englyssh, ryme or prose,
Suffisant this flour to preyse aryght!
But helpeth, ye that han konnyng and myght,
Ye lovers that kan make of sentement;
In this cas oghte ye be diligent 70
To forthren me somwhat in my labour,
Whethir ye ben with the leef or with the flour.
For wel I wot that ye han her-biforn
Of makyng ropen, and lad awey the corn,
And I come after, glenyng here and there, 75
And am ful glad yf I may fynde an ere
Of any goodly word that ye han left.
And thogh it happen me rehercen eft
That ye han in your fresshe songes sayd,
Forbereth me, and beth nat evele apayd, 80
Syn that ye see I do yt in the honour
Of love, and eke in service of the flour
Whom that I serve as I have wit or myght.

[CF. LL. 188 –96, BELOW]

She is the clernesse and the verray lyght 84
That in this derke world me wynt and ledeth.
The hert in-with my sorwfull brest yow dredeth
And loveth so sore that ye ben verrayly
The maistresse of my wit, and nothing I.
My word, my werk ys knyt so in youre bond
That, as an harpe obeieth to the hond 90
And maketh it soune after his fyngerynge,
Ryght so mowe ye oute of myn herte bringe
Swich vois, ryght as yow lyst, to laughe or
    pleyne.
Be ye my gide and lady sovereyne!
As to myn erthly god to yow I calle, 95
Bothe in this werk and in my sorwes alle.
    But wherfore that I spak, to yive credence
To olde stories and doon hem reverence,

Thanne closeth it, and draweth it to reste,
So sore it is afered of the nyght,
Til on the morwe that it is dayes lyght.
This dayesye, of alle floures flour, 55
Fulfyld of vertu and of alle honour,
And evere ylike fayr and fresh of hewe,
As wel in wynter as in somer newe,
Fayn wolde I preysen, if I coude aryght;
But wo is me, it lyth nat in my myght. 60

For wel I wot that folk han here-beforn
Of makyng ropen, and lad awey the corn;
[And] I come after, glenynge here and there,
And am ful glad if I may fynde an ere
Of any goodly word that they han left. 65
And if it happe me rehersen eft
That they han in here freshe songes said,
I hope that they wole nat ben evele apayd,
Sith it is seyd in fortheryng and honour
Of hem that eyther serven lef or flour. 70
For trusteth wel, I ne have nat undertake
As of the lef agayn the flour to make,
Ne of the flour to make ageyn the lef,
No more than of the corn agen the shef;
For, as to me, is lefer non, ne lother. 75
I am witholde yit with never nother;
I not who serveth lef ne who the flour.
That nys nothyng the entent of my labour.
For this werk is al of another tonne,
Of olde story, er swich strif was begonne. 80

But wherfore that I spak, to yeve credence
To bokes olde and don hem reverence,

69 **make of**: write about
74 **Of makyng ropen**: reaped (the fruit) of writing
75 **glenyng**: gleaning
76 **ere**: ear (of grain)
80 **Forbereth me**: bear with me
85 **wynt** = *wyndeth*, turns, directs

And that men mosten more thyng beleve　99
Then men may seen at eye, or elles preve —
That shal I seyn, whanne that I see my tyme;
I may not al at-ones speke in ryme.
My besy gost, that thursteth alwey newe
To seen this flour so yong, so fressh of hewe,
Constreyned me with so gledy desir　105
That in myn herte I feele yet the fir
That made me to ryse er yt were day —
And this was now the firste morwe of May —
With dredful hert and glad devocioun,
For to ben at the resureccioun　110
Of this flour, whan that yt shulde unclose
Agayn the sonne, that roos as red as rose,
That in the brest was of the beste, that day,
That Agenores doghtre ladde away.

[CF. LL. 197–210, BELOW]

And doun on knes anoon-ryght I me sette,　115
And, as I koude, this fresshe flour I grette,
Knelyng alwey, til it unclosed was,
Upon the smale, softe, swote gras,
That was with floures swote enbrouded al,
Of swich swetnesse and swich odour overal,　120
That, for to speke of gomme, or herbe, or tree,
Comparisoun may noon ymaked bee;
For yt surmounteth pleynly alle odoures,
And of riche beaute alle floures.
Forgeten hadde the erthe his pore estat　125
Of wynter, that hym naked made and mat,
And with his swerd of cold so sore greved;
Now hath th'atempre sonne all that releved,
That naked was, and clad him new agayn.
The smale foules, of the sesoun fayn,　130
That from the panter and the net ben scaped,
Upon the foweler, that hem made awhaped
In wynter, and distroyed hadde hire brood,
In his dispit hem thoghte yt did hem good
To synge of hym, and in hir song despise　135
The foule cherl that, for his coveytise,

Is for men shulde autoritees beleve,
There as there lyth non other assay by preve.
For myn entent is, or I fro yow fare,　85
The naked text in English to declare
Of many a story, or elles of many a geste,
As autours seyn; leveth hem if yow leste.

Whan passed was almost the month of May,
And I hadde romed, al the someres day,　90
The grene medewe, of which that I yow tolde,
Upon the freshe dayseie to beholde,
And that the sonne out of the south gan weste,
And closed was the flour and gon to reste,
For derknesse of the nyght, of which she
　　　　dredde,　95
Hom to myn hous ful swiftly I me spedde,
And in a lytel herber that I have,
Ybenched newe with turves fresshe ygrave,
I bad men shulde me my couche make;
For deynte of the newe someres sake,　100
I bad hem strowe floures on my bed.
Whan I was layd, and hadde myn eyen hed,
I fel aslepe withinne an hour or two.
Me mette how I was in the medewe tho,
And that I romede in that same gyse,　105
To sen that flour, as ye han herd devyse.
Fayr was this medewe, as thoughte me, overal;
With floures sote enbrouded was it al.
As for to speke of gomme, or herbe, or tre,
Comparisoun may non ymaked be;　110
For it surmountede pleynly alle odoures,
And of ryche beaute alle floures.
Forgeten hadde the erthe his pore estat
Of wynter, that hym naked made and mat,
And with his swerd of cold so sore hadde
　　　　greved.　115
Now hadde th'atempre sonne al that releved,
And clothed hym in grene al newe ageyn.
The smale foules, of the seson fayn,
That from the panter and the net ben skaped,
Upon the foulere, that hem made awhaped　120
In wynter, and distroyed hadde hire brod,
In his dispit hem thoughte it dide hem good
To synge of hym, and in here song despise
The foule cherl that for his coveytyse

103 **besy gost**: eager spirit
105 **gledy**: burning
113 **in the brest was of the beste**: in the middle part of the
zodiacal sign Taurus (the Bull); see **n**.
114 **Agenores doghtre**: Europa, loved by Jupiter in the form of
a bull
119 **enbrouded**: adorned (literally, embroidered)
121 **gomme**: gum
131 **panter**: bird snare
132 **awhaped**: stunned, bewildered

G 101 **strowe**: strew
G 116 **th'atempre sonne**: the temperate sun

Had hem betrayed with his sophistrye.
This was hire song: "The foweler we deffye,
And al his craft." And somme songen clere
Layes of love, that joye it was to here,   140
In worship and in preysinge of hir make;
And for the newe blisful somers sake,
Upon the braunches ful of blosmes softe,
In hire delyt they turned hem ful ofte,
And songen, "Blessed be Seynt Valentyn,   145
For on his day I chees yow to be myn,
Withouten repentyng, myn herte swete!"
And therwithalle hire bekes gonnen meete,
Yeldyng honour and humble obeysaunces
To love, and diden hire other observaunces   150
That longeth onto love and to nature;
Construeth that as yow lyst, I do no cure.
And thoo that hadde doon unkyndenesse —
As dooth the tydif, for newfangelnesse —
Besoghte mercy of hir trespassynge,   155
And humblely songen hire repentynge,
And sworen on the blosmes to be trewe
So that hire makes wolde upon hem rewe,
And at the laste maden hire acord.
Al founde they Daunger for a tyme a lord,   160
Yet Pitee, thurgh his stronge gentil myght,
Forgaf, and made Mercy passen Ryght,
Thurgh innocence and ruled Curtesye.
But I ne clepe nat innocence folye,
Ne fals pitee, for vertu is the mene,   165
As Etik seith; in swich maner I mene.
And thus thise foweles, voide of al malice,
Acordeden to love, and laften vice
Of hate, and songen alle of oon acord,
"Welcome, somer, oure governour and lord!"
    And Zepherus and Flora gentilly   171
Yaf to the floures, softe and tenderly,
Hire swoote breth, and made hem for to
        sprede,
As god and goddesse of the floury mede;
In which me thoghte I myghte, day by day,
Duellen alwey, the joly month of May,   176
Withouten slep, withouten mete or drynke.
Adoun ful softely I gan to synke,
And, lenynge on myn elbowe and my syde,
The longe day I shoop me for t'abide   180
For nothing elles, and I shal nat lye,

Hadde hem betrayed with his sophistrye.   125
This was here song, "The foulere we defye,
[And al his craft." And some songen clere
Layes] of love that joye it was to here,
In worshipe and in preysyng of hire make;
And [for] the newe blysful somers sake,   130

[They] sungen, "Blyssed be Seynt Valentyn!
[For on] his day I ches yow to be myn,
Withoute repentynge, myn herte swete!"
And therwithal here bekes gonne mete,
[Yelding] honour and humble obeysaunces;
And after diden othere observaunces   136
Ryht [longing] onto love and to nature;
So ech of hem [doth wel] to creature.
This song to herkenen I dide al myn entente,
For-why I mette I wiste what they mente,   140

---

137 **sophistrye:** sophistry, trickery
154 **tydif:** a small bird, known for inconstancy (cf. FranT V.648)
160 **Daunger:** (a lady's) resistance to a lover
162 **passen Ryght:** surpass, overcome Justice
163 **ruled:** decorous, self-controlled
165 **mene:** middle between two extremes (the golden mean)
166 **Etik:** Horace (?); see n.
167 **voide:** devoid
171 **Zepherus:** the West Wind   **Flora:** the goddess of flowers

But for to loke upon the dayesie,
That wel by reson men it calle may
The "dayesye," or elles the "ye of day,"
The emperice and flour of floures alle. 185
I pray to God that faire mote she falle,
And alle that loven floures, for hire sake!
But natheles, ne wene nat that I make
In preysing of the flour agayn the leef,
No more than of the corn agayn the sheef; 190
For, as to me, nys lever noon ne lother.
I nam withholden yit with never nother;
Ne I not who serveth leef ne who the flour.
Wel browken they her service or labour;
For this thing is al of another tonne, 195
Of olde storye, er swich stryf was begonne.
    Whan that the sonne out of the south gan
          weste,
And that this flour gan close and goon to reste
For derknesse of the nyght, the which she
          dredde,
Hom to myn hous ful swiftly I me spedde 200
To goon to reste, and erly for to ryse,
To seen this flour to sprede, as I devyse.
And in a litel herber that I have,
That benched was on turves fressh ygrave,
I bad men sholde me my couche make; 205
For deyntee of the newe someres sake,
I bad hem strawen floures on my bed.
Whan I was leyd and had myn eyen hed,
I fel on slepe within an houre or twoo.
Me mette how I lay in the medewe thoo, 210
To seen this flour that I so love and drede;
And from afer com walkyng in the mede
The god of Love, and in his hand a quene,
And she was clad in real habit grene.
A fret of gold she hadde next her heer, 215
And upon that a whit corowne she beer
With flourouns smale, and I shal nat lye;
For al the world, ryght as a dayesye
Ycorouned ys with white leves lyte, 219
So were the flowrouns of hire coroune white.
For of o perle fyn, oriental,
Hire white coroune was ymaked al;
For which the white coroune above the grene
Made hire lyk a daysie for to sene,
Considered eke hir fret of gold above. 225

[CF. LL. 71– 80, ABOVE]

[CF. LL. 93–106, ABOVE]

Tyl at the laste a larke song above:
"I se," quod she, "the myghty god of Love.
Lo! yond he cometh! I se his wynges sprede."
Tho gan I loken endelong the mede 144
And saw hym come, and in his hond a quene
Clothed in real habyt al of grene.
A fret of goold she hadde next hyre her
And upon that a whit corone she ber
With many floures, and I shal nat lye;
For al the world, ryght as the dayesye 150
Ycorouned is with white leves lite,
Swiche were the floures of hire coroune white.
For of o perle fyn and oryental
Hyre white coroun was ymaked al;
For which the white coroun above the grene
Made hire lyk a dayesye for to sene, 156
Considered ek the fret of gold above.

192 **withholden:** retained **with never nother:** by neither party
194 **browken:** may they profit from
195 **al of another tonne:** entirely from another barrel, a
different matter altogether
204 That was furnished with benches of newly dug turf
207 **strawen:** strew
208 **was leyd:** had lain down
215 **fret:** ornamental hairnet
217 **flourouns:** flowers
221 **o perle:** a single pearl **oriental:** of finest quality

G 147 **hyre her:** her hair

Yclothed was this myghty god of Love
In silk, enbrouded ful of grene greves,
In-with a fret of rede rose-leves,
The fresshest syn the world was first bygonne.
His gilte heer was corowned with a sonne   230
Instede of gold, for hevynesse and wyghte.
Therwith me thoghte his face shoon so bryghte
That wel unnethes myghte I him beholde;
And in his hand me thoghte I saugh him holde
Twoo firy dartes as the gledes rede,   235
And aungelyke hys wynges saugh I sprede.
And al be that men seyn that blynd ys he,
Algate me thoghte that he myghte se;
For sternely on me he gan byholde,
So that his loking dooth myn herte colde.   240
And by the hand he held this noble quene
Corowned with whit and clothed al in grene,
So womanly, so benigne, and so meke,
That in this world, thogh that men wolde seke,
Half hire beaute shulde men nat fynde   245
In creature that formed ys by kynde.

[CF. LL. 276–96, BELOW]

And therfore may I seyn, as thynketh me,
This song in preysyng of this lady fre:

Yclothed was this myghty god of Love
Of silk, ybrouded ful of grene greves,
A garlond on his hed of rose-leves   160
Stiked al with lylye floures newe.
But of his face I can not seyn the hewe,
For sikerly his face shon so bryghte
That with the glem astoned was the syghte;
A furlong-wey I myhte hym not beholde.   165
But at the laste in hande I saw hym holde
Two firy dartes as the gleedes rede,
And aungellych hys winges gan he sprede.
And al be that men seyn that blynd is he,
Algate me thoughte he myghte wel yse;   170
For sternely on me he gan beholde,
So that his lokynge doth myn herte colde.
And by the hond he held the noble quene
Corouned with whit and clothed al in grene,
So womanly, so benygne, and so meke,   175
That in this world, thogh that men wolde
    seke,
Half hire beaute shulde men nat fynde
In creature that formed is by kynde.
Hire name was Alceste the debonayre.
I preye to God that evere falle she fayre,   180
For ne hadde confort been of hire presence,
I hadde be ded, withouten any defence,
For dred of Loves wordes and his chere,
As, whan tyme is, hereafter ye shal here.
    Byhynde this god of Love, upon this grene,
I saw comynge of ladyes nyntene   186
In real habyt, a ful esy pas,
And after hem come of wemen swich a tras
That, syn that God Adam [had] mad of erthe,
The thridde part of wemen, ne the ferthe,   190
Ne wende I not by possibilite
Hadden evere in this [wyde] world ybe;
And trewe of love these wemen were echon.
    Now whether was that a wonder thyng or
        non,
That ryght anon as that they gonne espye   195
This flour, which that I clepe the dayesye,
Ful sodeynly they stynten alle atones,
And knelede adoun, as it were for the nones.
And after that they wenten in compas,
Daunsynge aboute this flour an esy pas,   200
And songen, as it were in carole-wyse,
This balade, which that I shal yow devyse.

---

227 **greves:** branches, sprays
231 **for hevynesse:** to avoid heaviness
235 **gledes:** glowing embers
239 **sternely:** grimly

G 159 **ybrouded:** embroidered
G 161 **Stiked:** stuck, adorned
G 164 **glem:** radiance
G 201 **carole-wyse:** in the manner of a dance

Balade

Hyd, Absolon, thy gilte tresses clere;
Ester, ley thou thy meknesse al adown;　　　250
Hyd, Jonathas, al thy frendly manere;
Penalopee and Marcia Catoun,
Make of youre wifhod no comparysoun;
Hyde ye youre beautes, Ysoude and Eleyne:
My lady cometh, that al this may disteyne.　255

Thy faire body, lat yt nat appere,
Lavyne; and thou, Lucresse of Rome toun,
And Polixene, that boghten love so dere,
And Cleopatre, with al thy passyoun,
Hyde ye your trouthe of love and your re-
　　　noun;　　　260
And thou, Tisbe, that hast for love swich peyne:
My lady cometh, that al this may disteyne.

Herro, Dido, Laudomia, alle yfere,
And Phillis, hangyng for thy Demophoun,
And Canace, espied by thy chere,　　　265
Ysiphile, betrayed with Jasoun,
Maketh of your trouthe neythir boost ne soun;
Nor Ypermystre or Adriane, ye tweyne:
My lady cometh, that al this may dysteyne.

This balade may ful wel ysongen be,　　　270
As I have seyd erst, by my lady free;
For certeynly al thise mowe nat suffise
To apperen wyth my lady in no wyse.
For as the sonne wole the fyr disteyne,
So passeth al my lady sovereyne,　　　275
That ys so good, so faire, so debonayre,
I prey to God that ever falle hire faire!
For, nadde comfort ben of hire presence,
I hadde ben ded, withouten any defence,
For drede of Loves wordes and his chere,　280
As, when tyme ys, herafter ye shal here.
　Behynde this god of Love, upon the grene,
I saugh comyng of ladyes nyntene,

Balade

Hyd, Absalon, thy gilte tresses clere;
Ester, ley thow thy meknesse al adoun;
Hyd, Jonathas, al thyn frendly manere;　205
Penelope and Marcia Catoun,
Mak of youre wyfhod no comparisoun;
Hyde ye youre beautes, Ysoude and Eleyne:
Alceste is here, that al that may desteyne.

Thy fayre body, lat it nat apeere,　　　210
Laveyne; and thow, Lucresse of Rome toun,
And Polixene, that boughte love so dere,
Ek Cleopatre, with al thy passioun,
Hide ye youre trouth in love and youre renoun;
And thow, Tysbe, that hast for love swich
　　　peyne:　　　215
Alceste is here, that al that may desteyne.

Herro, Dido, Laodomya, alle in-fere,
Ek Phillis, hangynge for thy Demophoun,
And Canace, espied by thy chere,
Ysiphile, betrayed with Jasoun,　　　220
Mak of youre trouthe in love no bost ne soun;
Nor Ypermystre or Adriane, ne pleyne:
Alceste is here, that al that may disteyne.

Whan that this balade al ysongen was,

[CF. LL. 179–98, ABOVE]

249 **Absolon:** Absalom, son of David, noted for his beauty
250 **Ester:** Esther, a biblical model of meekness
252 **Penalopee:** Penelope, faithful wife of Ulysses   **Marcia
Catoun:** a faithful Roman wife
254 **Ysoude:** Iseult, the celebrated lover of Tristan   **Eleyne:**
Helen of Troy
255 **disteyne:** make pale (by comparison)
257 **Lavyne:** Lavinia, wife of Aeneas   **Lucresse:** Lucretia (whose
legend is told below)
258 **Polixene:** Polyxena, faithful lover of Achilles
259 **Cleopatre:** Cleopatra's legend, and those of *Tisbe, Dido,
Phillis, Ysiphile, Ypermystre,* and *Adriane,* are told below.
263 **Herro:** Hero, beloved of Leander   **Laudomia:** Laodamia,
faithful wife of Protesilaus
265 **Canace:** Canacee, the incestous lover of her brother (cf.
IntrMLT II.78–9)   **espied by thy chere:** disclosed by your
demeanor
273 **apperen:** be equal to

In real habit, a ful esy paas,   284
And after hem coome of wymen swich a traas
That, syn that God Adam hadde mad of erthe,
The thridde part, of mankynde, or the ferthe,
Ne wende I not by possibilitee
Had ever in this wide world ybee;   289
And trewe of love thise women were echon.
   Now wheither was that a wonder thing or
      non,
That ryght anoon as that they gonne espye
Thys flour which that I clepe the dayesie,
Ful sodeynly they stynten al attones,
And kneled doun, as it were for the nones,   295
And songen with o vois, "Heel and honour
To trouthe of womanhede, and to this flour
That bereth our alder pris in figurynge!
Hire white corowne bereth the witnessynge."
And with that word, a-compas enviroun,   300
They setten hem ful softely adoun.
First sat the god of Love, and syth his
      quene
With the white corowne, clad in grene,
And sithen al the remenaunt by and by,
As they were of estaat, ful curteysly;   305
Ne nat a word was spoken in the place
The mountaunce of a furlong wey of space.
   I, knelying by this flour, in good entente,
Abood to knowen what this peple mente,
As stille as any ston; til at the laste   310
This god of Love on me hys eyen caste,
And seyde, "Who kneleth there?" And I an-
      swerde
Unto his askynge, whan that I it herde,
And seyde, "Sir, it am I," and com him ner,
And salwed him. Quod he, "What dostow
      her
So nygh myn oune floure, so boldely?   316
Yt were better worthy, trewely,
A worm to neghen ner my flour than thow."
"And why, sire," quod I, "and yt lyke yow?"
"For thow," quod he, "art therto nothing able.
Yt is my relyke, digne and delytable,   321
And thow my foo, and al my folk werreyest,
And of myn olde servauntes thow mysseyest,
And hynderest hem with thy translacioun,
And lettest folk from hire devocioun   325
To serve me, and holdest it folye

Upon the softe and sote grene gras   225
They setten hem ful softely adoun,
By order alle in compas, enveroun.
Fyrst sat the god of Love, and thanne this
      queene
With the white corone, clad in grene,
And sithen al the remenant by and by,   230
As they were of degre, ful curteysly;
Ne nat a word was spoken in that place
The mountaunce of a furlong-wey of space.
   I, lenynge faste by under a bente,
Abod to knowe what this peple mente,   235
As stille as any ston, til at the laste
The god of Love on me his eye caste
And seyde, "Who restith there?" And I an-
      swerde
Unto his axynge, whan that I hym herde,
And seyde, "Sire, it am I," and cam hym ner,
And salewede hym. Quod he, "What dost thow
      her   241
In my presence, and that so boldely?
For it were better worthi, trewely,
A worm to comen in my syght than thow."
"And why, sire," quod I, "and it lyke yow?" 245
"For thow," quod he, "art therto nothyng able.
My servaunts ben alle wyse and honourable.
Thow art my mortal fo and me werreyest,
And of myne olde servauntes thow mysseyest,
And hynderest hem with thy translacyoun,   250
And lettest folk to han devocyoun
To serven me, and holdest it folye

---

285 **traas:** procession
298 **our alder pris in figurynge:** the prize of us all in
symbolizing (i.e., best exemplifies the faithfulness of women)
304 **by and by:** side by side
305 **As they were of estaat:** according to their rank
309 **Abood to knowen:** waited to see
318 **neghen:** draw nigh
320 **therto nothing able:** not at all worthy of it
321 **relyke:** relic, treasure
323 **mysseyest:** slander

To serve Love. Thou maist yt nat denye,
For in pleyn text, withouten nede of glose,
Thou hast translated the Romaunce of the Rose,
That is an heresye ayeins my lawe,   330
And makest wise folk fro me withdrawe;

And of Creseyde thou hast seyd as the lyste,
That maketh men to wommen lasse triste,
That ben as trewe as ever was any steel.
Of thyn answere avise the ryght weel;   335

To truste on me. Thow mayst it nat denye,
For in pleyn text, it nedeth nat to glose,
Thow hast translated the Romauns of the Rose,
That is an heresye ageyns my lawe,   256
And makest wise folk fro me withdrawe;
And thynkest in thy wit, that is ful col,
That he nys but a verray propre fol
That loveth paramours to harde and hote.   260
Wel wot I therby thow begynnyst dote,
As olde foles whan here spiryt fayleth;
Thanne blame they folk, and wite nat what hem
        ayleth.
Hast thow nat mad in Englysh ek the bok
How that Crisseyde Troylus forsok,   265
In shewynge how that wemen han don mis?
But natheles, answere me now to this;
Why noldest thow as wel [han] seyd goodnesse
Of wemen, as thow hast seyd wikednesse?
Was there no good matere in thy mynde,   270
Ne in alle thy bokes ne coudest thow nat fynde
Som story of wemen that were goode and
        trewe?
Yis, God wot, sixty bokes olde and newe
Hast thow thyself, alle ful of storyes grete,
That bothe Romayns and ek Grekes trete   275
Of sundry wemen, which lyf that they ladde,
And evere an hundred goode ageyn oon badde.
This knoweth God, and alle clerkes eke
That usen swiche materes for to seke.
What seith Valerye, Titus, or Claudyan?   280
What seith Jerome agayns Jovynyan?
How clene maydenes and how trewe wyves,
How stedefaste widewes durynge alle here
        lyves,
Telleth Jerome, and that nat of a fewe,
But, I dar seyn, an hundred on a rewe,   285
That it is pite for to rede, and routhe,
The wo that they endure for here trouthe.
For to hyre love were they so trewe
That, rathere than they wolde take a newe,
They chose to be ded in sondry wyse,   290
And deiden, as the story wol devyse;
And some were brend, and some were cut the
        hals,
And some dreynt for they wolden not be fals;
For alle keped they here maydenhede,
Or elles wedlok, or here widewehede.   295

G 258 **col**: cool, dull
G 260 **paramours**: by way of romantic love
G 266 **wemen**: women   **mis**: wrong
G 280 **Valerye**: probably the author of the *Epistola Valerii ad Rufinum*   **Titus**: Titus Livius, the Roman historian   **Claudyan**: the author of *De Raptu Proserpina;* see n.
G 295 **wedlok**: wedlock   **widewehede**: widowhood

And this thing was nat kept for holynesse,
But al for verray vertu and clennesse,
And for men schulde sette on hem no lak;
And yit they were hethene, al the pak,
That were so sore adrad of alle shame.   300
These olde wemen kepte so here name
That in this world I trowe men shal nat fynde
A man that coude be so trewe and kynde
As was the leste woman in that tyde.
What seyth also the epistel of Ovyde   305
Of trewe wyves and of here labour?
What Vincent in his Estoryal Myrour?
Ek al the world of autours maystow here,
Cristene and hethene, trete of swich matere;
It nedeth nat al day thus for to endite.   310
But yit, I seye, what eyleth the to wryte
The draf of storyes, and forgete the corn?
By Seynt Venus, of whom that I was born,
Althogh thow reneyed hast my lay,
As othere olde foles many a day,   315

Thow shalt repente it, so that it shal be sene!"
Thanne spak Alceste, the worthyeste queene,
And seyde, "God, ryght of youre curteysye,
Ye moten herkenen if he can replye
Ageyns these poynts that ye han to hym meved.
A god ne sholde not thus been agreved,   321
But of his deite he shal be stable,
And therto ryghtful, and ek mercyable.
He shal nat ryghtfully his yre wreke
Or he have herd the tother partye speke.   325
Al ne is nat gospel that is to yow pleyned;
The god of Love hereth many a tale yfeyned.
For in youre court is many a losengeour,
And many a queynte totelere accusour,
That tabouren in youre eres many a thyng   330
For hate, or for jelous ymagynyng,
And for to han with you som dalyaunce.
Envye — I preye to God yeve hire mys-
                    chaunce! —
Is lavender in the grete court alway,
For she ne parteth, neyther nyght ne day,   335
Out of the hous of Cesar; thus seyth Dante;
Whoso that goth, alwey she mot [nat] wante.
This man to yow may wrongly ben acused,
There as by ryght hym oughte ben excusid.
Or elles, sire, for that this man is nyce,   340
He may translate a thyng in no malyce,
But for he useth bokes for to make,
And taketh non hed of what matere he take,

For thogh thou reneyed hast my lay,
As other wrecches han doon many a day,
By Seynt Venus that my moder ys,
If that thou lyve, thou shalt repenten this
So cruelly that it shal wel be sene!"   340
Thoo spak this lady, clothed al in grene,
And seyde, "God, ryght of youre curtesye,
Ye moten herken yf he can replye
Agayns al this that ye have to him meved.
A god ne sholde nat thus be agreved,   345
But of hys deitee he shal be stable,
And therto gracious and merciable.
And yf ye nere a god, that knowen al,
Thanne myght yt be as I yow tellen shal:
This man to yow may falsly ben accused   350
That as by right him oughte ben excused.
For in youre court ys many a losengeour,
And many a queynte totelere accusour,
That tabouren in youre eres many a sown,
Ryght after hire ymagynacioun,   355
To have youre daliance, and for envie.
Thise ben the causes, and I shal not lye.
Envie ys lavendere of the court alway,
For she ne parteth, neither nyght ne day,   359
Out of the hous of Cesar; thus seith Dante;
Whoso that gooth, algate she wol nat wante.

[CF. LL. 350–51, ABOVE]

And eke, peraunter, for this man ys nyce,
He myghte doon yt, gessyng no malice,
But for he useth thynges for to make;
Hym rekketh noght of what matere he take.

344 to him meved: accused him of
352 losengeour: flatterer
353 queynte totelere accusour: crafty tatling slanderer
354 tabouren: drum
358 lavendere: laundress (who knows the dirty linens)

G 298 lak: blame
G 305 epistel of Ovyde: Ovid's *Heroides*
G 307 Estoryal Myrour: the *Speculum Historiale* of Vincent of Beauvais
G 312 draf: chaff (husks)

Or him was boden maken thilke tweye   366
Of som persone, and durste yt nat withseye;
Or him repenteth outrely of this.
He ne hath nat doon so grevously amys
To translaten that olde clerkes writen,   370
As thogh that he of malice wolde enditen
Despit of love, and had himself yt wroght.
This shoolde a ryghtwis lord have in his thoght,
And nat be lyk tirauntz of Lumbardye,
That han no reward but at tyrannye.   375
For he that kynge or lord ys naturel,
Hym oghte nat be tiraunt ne crewel
As is a fermour, to doon the harm he kan.
He moste thinke yt is his lige man,

And is his tresour and his gold in cofre.   380
This is the sentence of the Philosophre,
A kyng to kepe his liges in justice;
Withouten doute, that is his office.

Al wol he kepe his lordes hire degree,
As it ys ryght and skilful that they bee   385
Enhaunced and honoured, and most dere —
For they ben half-goddes in this world here —
Yit mot he doon bothe ryght, to poore and
        ryche,
Al be that hire estaat be nat yliche,
And han of poore folk compassyoun.   390
For loo, the gentil kynde of the lyoun:
For whan a flye offendeth him or biteth,
He with his tayl awey the flye smyteth
Al esely; for, of hys genterye,
Hym deyneth not to wreke hym on a flye,   395
As dooth a curre, or elles another best.
In noble corage ought ben arest,
And weyen every thing by equytee,
And ever have reward to his owen degree.
For, syr, yt is no maistrye for a lord   400
To dampne a man without answere of word,
And for a lord that is ful foul to use.
And if so be he may hym nat excuse,
But asketh mercy with a dredeful herte,

Therfore he wrot the Rose and ek Crisseyde
Of innocence, and nyste what he seyde.   345
Or hym was boden make thilke tweye
Of som persone, and durste it not withseye;
For he hath write many a bok er this.
He ne hath not don so grevously amys
To translate that olde clerkes wryte,   350
As thogh that he of maleys wolde endyte
Despit of love, and hadde hymself ywrought.
This shulde a ryghtwys lord han in his thought,
And not ben lyk tyraunts of Lumbardye,
That usen wilfulhed and tyrannye.   355
For he that kyng or lord is naturel,
Hym oughte nat be tyraunt and crewel
As is a fermour, to don the harm he can.
He moste thynke it is his lige man,
And that hym oweth, of verray duetee,   360
Shewen his peple pleyn benygnete,
And wel to heren here excusacyouns,
And here compleyntes and petyciouns,
In duewe tyme, whan they shal it profre.
This is the sentence of the Philosophre,   365
A kyng to kepe his lyges in justice;
Withouten doute, that is his office.
And therto is a kyng ful depe ysworn
Ful many an hundred wynter herebeforn,
And for to kepe his lordes hir degre,   370
As it is ryght and skylful that they be
Enhaunsed and honoured, [and] most dere —
For they ben half-goddes in this world here —
This shal he don bothe to pore [and] ryche,
Al be that her estat be nat alyche,   375
And han of pore folk compassioun.
For lo, the gentyl kynde of the lyoun:
For whan a flye offendeth hym or byteth,
He with his tayl awey the flye smyteth
Al esyly; for, of his genterye,   380
Hym deyneth nat to wreke hym on a flye,
As doth a curre, or elles another best.
In noble corage oughte ben arest,
And weyen every thing by equite,
And evere han reward to his owen degre.   385
For, sire, it is no maystrye for a lord
To dampne a man withoute answere or word,
And, for a lord, that is ful foul to use.
And if so be he may hym nat excuse,
[But] axeth mercy with a sorweful herte,   390

366 **boden maken thilke tweye:** commanded to compose those
two works
373 **ryghtwis:** just
378 **fermour:** tax collector
381 **the Philosophre:** Aristotle
394 **of hys genterye:** because of his gentle lineage
396 **curre:** cur, mongrel
397 **arest:** restraint

G 355 **wilfulhed:** willfulness, arrogance
G 360 **hym oweth:** he ought

And profereth him, ryght in his bare sherte,
To ben ryght at your owen jugement,   406
Than oght a god by short avysement
Consydre his owne honour and hys trespas.
For, syth no cause of deth lyeth in this caas,
Yow oghte to ben the lyghter merciable;   410
Leteth youre ire, and beth sumwhat tretable.
The man hath served yow of his kunnynge,
And furthred wel youre lawe in his makynge.

Al be hit that he kan nat wel endite,
Yet hath he maked lewed folk delyte   415
To serve yow, in preysinge of your name.
He made the book that hight the Hous of
        Fame,
And eke the Deeth of Blaunche the Duchesse,
And the Parlement of Foules, as I gesse,
And al the love of Palamon and Arcite   420
Of Thebes, thogh the storye ys knowen lyte;
And many an ympne for your halydayes,
That highten balades, roundels, virelayes;
And, for to speke of other holynesse,
He hath in prose translated Boece,   425

And maad the lyf also of Seynt Cecile.
He made also, goon ys a gret while,
Origenes upon the Maudeleyne.
Hym oughte now to have the lesse peyne;
He hath maad many a lay and many a thing.
    Now as ye be a god and eke a kyng,   431
I, your Alceste, whilom quene of Trace,
Y aske yow this man, ryght of your grace,
That ye him never hurte in al his lyve;
And he shal swere to yow, and that as blyve,
He shal no more agilten in this wyse,   436
But he shal maken, as ye wol devyse,
Of wommen trewe in lovyng al hire lyve,
Wherso ye wol, of mayden or of wyve,
And forthren yow as muche as he mysseyde
Or in the Rose or elles in Creseyde."   441
    The god of Love answerede hire thus anoon:
"Madame," quod he, "it is so long agoon

And profereth hym, ryght in his bare sherte,
To been ryght at youre owene jugement,
Than ought a god, by short avisement,
Considere his owene honour and his trespas.
For syth no cause of deth lyth in this cas, 395
Yow oughte to ben the lyghter merciable;
Leteth youre yre, and beth somwhat tretable.
The man hath served yow of his konnynge,
And forthered [wel] youre lawe with his mak-
        ynge.
Whil he was yong, he kepte youre estat;   400
I not wher he be now a renegat.
But wel I wot, with that he can endyte
He hath maked lewed folk to delyte
To serven yow, in preysynge of youre name.
He made the bok that highte the Hous of
        Fame,   405
And ek the Deth of Blaunche the Duchesse,
And the Parlement of Foules, as I gesse,
And al the love of Palamon and Arcite
Of Thebes, thogh the storye is knowen lite;
And many an ympne for your halydayes,   410
That highten balades, roundeles, vyrelayes;
And, for to speke of other besynesse,
He hath in prose translated Boece,
And Of the Wreched Engendrynge of Man-
        kynde,
As man may in Pope Innocent yfynde;   415
And mad the lyf also of Seynt Cecile.
He made also, gon is a gret while,
Orygenes upon the Maudeleyne.
Hym oughte now to have the lesse peyne;
He hath mad many a lay and many a thyng.
    Now as ye ben a god and ek a kyng,   421
I, youre Alceste, whilom quene of Trace,
I axe yow this man, ryght of youre grace,
That ye hym nevere hurte in al his lyve;
And he shal swere to yow, and that as blyve,
He shal no more agilten in this wyse,   426
But he shal maken, as ye wol devyse,
Of women trewe in lovynge al here lyve,
Wherso ye wol, of mayden or of wyve,
And fortheren yow as muche as he mysseyde
Or in the Rose or elles in Crisseyde."   431
    The god of Love answerede hire thus anon:
"Madame," quod he, "it is so longe agon

420 **Palamon and Arcite:** an early version of the Knight's Tale
422 **ympne:** hymn
423 **roundels:** short lyrics (see PF 680–92 for an example)
virelayes: poems in a variant form of the roundel
424 **other holynesse:** apparently "another religion." The works
that follow are Christian (R.).
426 **lyf . . . of Seynt Cecile:** an early version of the Second
Nun's Tale
428 **Origenes upon the Maudeleyne:** a lost work; see n.
439 **Wherso:** whichever (of the two)

G 401 **renegat:** apostate, renegade

That I yow knew so charitable and trewe,
That never yit syn that the world was newe
To me ne fond y better noon than yee.   446
If that I wol save my degree,
I may, ne wol, nat werne your requeste.
Al lyeth in yow, dooth wyth hym what yow
        leste.
I al foryeve, withouten lenger space;   450
For whoso yeveth a yifte or dooth a grace,
Do it by tyme, his thank ys wel the more.
And demeth ye what he shal doo therfore.
Goo thanke now my lady here," quod he.
    I roos, and doun I sette me on my knee, 455
And seyde thus: "Madame, the God above
Foryelde yow that ye the god of Love
Han maked me his wrathe to foryive,
And yeve me grace so longe for to lyve
That I may knowe soothly what ye bee   460
That han me holpe and put in this degree.
But trewly I wende, as in this cas,
Naught have agilt, ne doon to love trespas.
For-why a trewe man, withouten drede,
Hath nat to parten with a theves dede;   465
Ne a trewe lover oght me not to blame
Thogh that I speke a fals lovere som shame.
They oghte rather with me for to holde
For that I of Creseyde wroot or tolde,
Or of the Rose; what so myn auctour mente,
Algate, God woot, yt was myn entente   471
To forthren trouthe in love and yt cheryce,
And to ben war fro falsnesse and fro vice
By swich ensample; this was my menynge."
    And she answerde, "Lat be thyn arguynge, 475
For Love ne wol nat countrepleted be
In ryght ne wrong; and lerne that at me!
Thow hast thy grace, and hold the ryght therto.
Now wol I seyn what penance thou shalt do
For thy trespas. Understonde yt here: 480
Thow shalt, while that thou lyvest, yer by yere,
The moste partye of thy tyme spende
In makyng of a glorious legende
Of goode wymmen, maydenes and wyves,
That weren trewe in lovyng al hire lyves;   485
And telle of false men that hem bytraien,
That al hir lyf ne don nat but assayen
How many women they may doon a shame;
For in youre world that is now holde a game.
And thogh the lyke nat a lovere bee,   490
Speke wel of love; this penance yive I thee.
And to the god of Love I shal so preye

That I yow knew so charytable and trewe,
That nevere yit sith that the world was newe
To me ne fond I betere non than ye;   436
That, if that I wol save my degre,
I may, ne wol, not warne youre requeste.
Al lyth in yow, doth with hym what yow
        leste;
And al foryeve, withoute lenger space.   440
For whoso yeveth a yifte or doth a grace,
Do it by tyme, his thank is wel the more.
And demeth ye what he shal do therfore.
Go thanke now my lady here," quod he.
    I ros, and doun I sette me on my kne,   445
And seyde thus, "Madame, the God above
Foryelde yow that ye the god of Love
Han maked me his wrathe to foryive,
And yeve me grace so longe for to live
That I may knowe sothly what ye be   450
That han me holpen and put in swich degre.
But trewely I wende, as in this cas,
Naught have agilt, ne don to love trespas.
For-why a trewe man, withoute drede,
Hath nat to parte with a theves dede;   455
Ne a trewe lovere oghte me nat to blame
Thogh that I speke a fals lovere som shame.
They oughte rathere with me for to holde
For that I of Criseyde wrot or tolde,
Or of the Rose; what so myn auctour mente,
Algate, God wot, it was myn entente   461
To forthere trouthe in love and it cheryce,
And to be war fro falsnesse and fro vice
By swich ensaumple; this was my menynge."
    And she answerde, "Lat be thyn arguynge,
For Love ne wol nat counterpletyd be   466
In ryght ne wrong; and lerne this at me!
Thow hast thy grace, and hold the ryght therto.
Now wol I seyn what penaunce thow shalt do
For thy trespas, and understond it here: 470
Thow shalt, whil that thow livest, yer by yere,
The moste partye of thy tyme spende
In makynge of a gloryous legende
Of goode women, maydenes and wyves,
That were trewe in lovynge al here lyves;   475
And telle of false men that hem betrayen,
That al here lyf ne don nat but assayen
How manye wemen they may don a shame;
For in youre world that is now holden game.
And thogh the lesteth nat a lovere be,   480
Spek wel of love; this penaunce yeve I thee.
And to the god of Love I shal so preye

457 **Foryelde:** repay
461 **degree:** situation
476 **countrepleted:** argued against
490 **the lyke nat:** you are unlikely

That he shal charge his servantz by any weye
To forthren thee, and wel thy labour quyte.
Goo now thy wey, this penaunce ys but
    lyte.   495
And whan this book ys maad, yive it the quene,
On my byhalf, at Eltham or at Sheene."
  The god of Love gan smyle, and than he
    sayde:
"Wostow," quod he, "wher this be wyf or
    mayde,
Or queene, or countesse, or of what degre,   500
That hath so lytel penance yiven thee,
That hast deserved sorer for to smerte?
But pite renneth soone in gentil herte;
That maistow seen; she kytheth what she ys."
And I answered, "Nay, sire, so have I blys,   505
No moore but that I see wel she is good."
"That is a trewe tale, by myn hood!"
Quod Love; "And that thou knowest wel, par-
    dee,
If yt be so that thou avise the.
Hastow nat in a book, lyth in thy cheste,   510
The grete goodnesse of the quene Alceste,
That turned was into a dayesye;
She that for hire housbonde chees to dye,
And eke to goon to helle, rather than he,
And Ercules rescowed hire, parde,   515
And broght hir out of helle agayn to blys?"
And I answerd ageyn, and sayde, "Yis,
Now knowe I hire. And is this good Alceste,
The dayesie, and myn owene hertes reste?
Now fele I weel the goodnesse of this wyf,   520
That both aftir hir deth and in hir lyf
Hir grete bounte doubleth hire renoun.
Wel hath she quyt me myn affeccioun
That I have to hire flour, the dayesye.
No wonder ys thogh Jove hire stellyfye,   525
As telleth Agaton, for hire goodnesse!
Hire white corowne berith of hyt witnesse;
For also many vertues hadde shee
As smale florouns in hire corowne bee.
In remembraunce of hire and in honour   530
Cibella maade the daysye and the flour
Ycrowned al with whit, as men may see;
And Mars yaf to hire corowne reed, pardee,
In stede of rubyes, sette among the white."
  Therwith this queene wex reed for shame a
    lyte   535
Whan she was preysed so in hire presence.

That he shal charge his servaunts by any weye
To fortheren the, and wel thy labour quite.
Go now thy wey, thy penaunce is but
    lyte."   485

  The god of Love gan smyle, and thanne he
    seyde:
"Wostow," quod he, "wher this be wif or
    mayde,
Or queen, or countesse, or of what degre,
That hath so lytel penaunce yiven the,
That hast deserved sorer for to smerte?   490
But pite renneth sone in gentil herte;
That mayst thow sen; she kytheth what she is."
And I answerde, "Nay, sire, so have I blys,
No more but that I se wel she is good."
"That is a trewe tale, by myn hood!"   495
Quod Love, "and that thow knowest wel,
    parde,
Yif it be so that thow avise the.
Hast thow nat in a bok, lyth in thy cheste,
The grete goodnesse of the queene Alceste,
That turned was into a dayesye;   500
She that for hire husbonde ches to dye,
And ek to gon to helle rather than he,
And Ercules rescued hire, parde,
And broughte hyre out of helle ageyn to blys?"
And I answerde ayen, and seyde, "Yis,   505
Now knowe I hire. And is this goode Alceste,
The dayesye, and myn owene hertes reste?
Now fele I wel the goodnesse of this wif,
That bothe after hire deth and in hire lyf
Hire grete bounte doubleth hire renoun.   510
Wel hath she quit me myn affeccioun
That I have to hire flour, the dayesye.
No wonder is thogh Jove hire stellifye,
As telleth Agaton, for hyre goodnesse!
Hire white coroun bereth of it witnesse;   515
For also manye vertues hadde she
As smale flourys in hyre coroun be.
In remembraunce of hire and in honour
Cibella made the dayesye and the flour
Ycoroned al with whit, as men may se;   520
And Mars yaf to hire corone red, parde,
In stede of rubies, set among the white."
  Therwith this queene wex red for shame a
    lyte
Whan she was preysed so in hire presence.   524

497 **Eltham, Sheene:** royal residences near London
502 **sorer:** more sorely
511 **Alceste:** Alcestis, faithful wife of Admetus
525 **stellyfye:** make into a star
526 **Agaton:** probably Plato's *Symposium;* see n.
529 **florouns:** petals
531 **Cibella:** Cybele, a goddess of fertility

Thanne seyde Love, "A ful gret necligence
Was yt to the, that ylke tyme thou made
'Hyd, Absolon, thy tresses,' in balade,
That thou forgate hire in thi song to sette,   540
Syn that thou art so gretly in hire dette,
And wost so wel that kalender ys shee
To any woman that wol lover bee.
For she taught al the craft of fyn lovynge,
And namely of wyfhod the lyvynge,   545
And al the boundes that she oghte kepe.
Thy litel wit was thilke tyme aslepe.
But now I charge the upon thy lyf
That in thy legende thou make of thys wyf
Whan thou hast other smale ymaad before;   550
And far now wel, I charge the namore.
But er I goo, thus muche I wol the telle:
Ne shal no trewe lover come in helle.
Thise other ladies sittynge here arowe   554
Ben in thy balade, yf thou kanst hem knowe,
And in thy bookes alle thou shalt hem fynde.
Have hem now in thy legende al in mynde;
I mene of hem that ben in thy knowynge.
For here ben twenty thousand moo sittynge
Than thou knowest, goode wommen alle,   560
And trewe of love for oght that may byfalle.
Make the metres of hem as the lest —
I mot goon hom (the sonne draweth west)
To paradys, with al this companye —
And serve alwey the fresshe dayesye.   565
At Cleopatre I wol that thou begynne,
And so forth, and my love so shal thou wynne.
For lat see now what man that lover be,
Wol doon so strong a peyne for love as she.
I wot wel that thou maist nat al yt ryme   570
That swiche lovers diden in hire tyme;
It were to long to reden and to here.
Suffiseth me thou make in this manere:
That thou reherce of al hir lyf the grete,
After thise olde auctours lysten for to trete. 575
For whoso shal so many a storye telle,
Sey shortly, or he shal to longe dwelle."
And with that word my bokes gan I take,
And ryght thus on my Legende gan I make.

Thanne seyde Love, "A ful gret neglygence
Was it to the, to write unstedefastnesse
Of women, sith thow knowest here goodnesse
By pref, and ek by storyes herebyforn.
Let be the chaf, and writ wel of the corn.
Why noldest thow han writen of Alceste,   530
And laten Criseide ben aslepe and reste?
For of Alceste shulde thy wrytynge be,
Syn that thow wost that calandier is she
Of goodnesse, for she taughte of fyn lovynge,
And namely of wifhod the lyvynge,   535
And alle the boundes that she oughte kepe.
Thy litel wit was thilke tyme aslepe.
But now I charge the upon thy lyf
That in thy legende thow make of this wif
Whan thow hast othere smale mad byfore; 540
And far now wel, I charge the no more.

At Cleopatre I wol that thow begynne,
And so forth, and my love so shalt thow
        wynne."

And with that word, of slep I gan awake,
And ryght thus on my Legende gan I make. 545

Explicit prohemium.

---

542 **kalender:** almanac; hence, guide, model
544 **fyn lovynge:** refined courtship
550 **smale:** less important legends
574 **grete:** essential matter
Explicit prohemium: Here ends the Prologue.

G 528 **pref:** proof
G 529 **chaf:** chaff (husks)

I

THE LEGEND OF CLEOPATRA

Incipit Legenda Cleopatrie, martiris, Egipti regine.

After the deth of Tholome the kyng, 580
That al Egipt hadde in his governyng,
Regned his queene Cleopataras;
Tyl on a tyme befel there swich a cas
That out of Rome was sent a senatour
For to conqueren regnes and honour 585
Unto the toun of Rome, as was usaunce,
To han the world at hire obesaunce,
And soth to seyne, Antonius was his name.
So fil it, as Fortune hym oughte a shame,
Whan he was fallen in prosperite 590
Rebel unto the toun of Rome is he.
And over al this, the suster of Cesar,
He lafte hire falsly, or that she was war,
And wolde algates han another wyf,
For which he tok with Rome and Cesar stryf.
Natheles, for sothe, this ilke senatour 596
Was a ful worthy gentil werreyour,
And of his deth it was ful gret damage.
But love hadde brought this man in swich a
        rage
And hym so narwe bounden in his las, 600
Al for the love of Cleopataras,
That al the world he sette at no value.
Hym thoughte there nas nothyng to hym so
        due
As Cleopatras for to love and serve;
Hym roughte nat in armes for to sterve 605
In the defence of hyre and of hire ryght.
This noble queene ek lovede so this knyght,
Thourgh his desert, and for his chyvalrye;
As certeynly, but if that bokes lye,
He was, of persone and of gentillesse, 610
And of discrecioun and hardynesse,
Worthi to any wyght that liven may;
And she was fayr as is the rose in May.
And, for to make shortly is the beste,
She wax his wif, and hadde hym as hire leste.

The weddynge and the feste to devyse, 616
To me, that have ytake swich empryse
Of so many a story for to make,
It were to longe, lest that I shulde slake
Of thyng that bereth more effect and charge;
For men may overlade a ship or barge. 621
And forthy to th'effect thanne wol I skyppe,
And al the remenaunt, I wol lete it slippe.

Octovyan, that wod was of this dede,
Shop hym an ost on Antony to lede 625
Al uterly for his destruccioun,
With stoute Romeyns, crewel as lyoun;
To ship they wente, and thus I lat hem sayle.
Antonius was war, and wol nat fayle
To meten with these Romeyns, if he may; 630
Tok ek his red, and bothe, upon a day,
His wif and he, and al his ost, forth wente
To shipe anon, no lengere they ne stente;
And in the se it happede hem to mete.
Up goth the trompe, and for to shoute and
        shete, 635
And peynen hem to sette on with the sunne.
With grysely soun out goth the grete gonne,
And heterly they hurtelen al atones,
And from the top doun come the grete stones.
In goth the grapenel, so ful of crokes; 640
Among the ropes renne the sherynge-hokes.
In with the polax preseth he and he;
Byhynde the mast begynnyth he to fle,
And out ageyn, and dryveth hym overbord;
He styngeth hym upon his speres ord; 645
He rent the seyl with hokes lyke a sithe;

Incipit, *etc.:* Here begins the Legend of Cleopatra, martyr, Queen of Egypt.
583 **on a tyme:** soon after the battle of Philippi (42 B.C.)
586 **usaunce:** custom
597 **werreyour:** warrior
599 **rage:** passionate desire

621 **overlade:** overload
624 **Octovyan:** Octavius, later the emperor Augustus
634 **se:** sea (the Gulf of Arta)
635 **shete:** shoot
636 **sette on with the sunne:** attack with the sun at their backs
637 **out goth the grete gonne:** the large cannon goes off, shoots
638 **heterly:** fiercely
640 **grapenel:** a clawlike device at the end of a rope, hurled at another vessel to lay hold of it and draw it alongside   **crokes:** hooks
641 **sherynge-hokes:** shearing hooks (used to cut ships' rigging)
642 **polax:** battle axe   **he and he:** this one and that one
645 **speres ord:** spear's point
646 **rent** = *rendeth*, tears   **sithe:** scythe

He bryngeth the cuppe and biddeth hem be
    blythe;
He poureth pesen upon the haches slidere;
With pottes ful of lyme they gon togidere;
And thus the longe day in fyght they spende,
Tyl at the laste, as every thyng hath ende,   651
Antony is schent and put hym to the flyghte,
And al his folk to-go that best go myghte.

   Fleth ek the queen, with al hire purpre sayl,
For strokes, whiche that wente as thikke as
    hayl;   655
No wonder was she myghte it nat endure.
And whan that Antony saw that aventure,
"Allas," quod he, "the day that I was born!
My worshipe in this day thus have I lorn."
And for dispeyr out of his wit he sterte   660
And rof hymself anon thourghout the herte
Or that he ferther wente out of the place.
His wif, that coude of Cesar have no grace,
To Egipt is fled for drede and for destresse.
But herkeneth, ye that speken of kyndenesse,
Ye men that falsly sweren many an oth   666
That ye wol deye if that youre love be wroth,
Here may ye sen of wemen which a trouthe!
This woful Cleopatre hath mad swich routhe
That ther is tonge non that may it telle.   670
But on the morwe she wolde no lengere dwelle,
But made hire subtyl werkmen make a shryne
Of alle the rubyes and the stones fyne
In al Egypte that she coude espie,
And putte ful the shryne of spicerye,   675
And let the cors enbaume, and forth she fette

This dede cors, and in the shryne it shette.
And next the shryne a pit thanne doth she
    grave,
And alle the serpentes that she myghte have,
She putte hem in that grave, and thus she
    seyde: 680
"Now, love, to whom my sorweful herte obeyde
So ferforthly that from that blisful houre
That I yow swor to ben al frely youre —
I mene yow, Antonius, my knyght —
That nevere wakynge, in the day or nyght,   685
Ye nere out of myn hertes remembraunce,
For wel or wo, for carole or for daunce,
And in myself this covenaunt made I tho,
That ryght swich as ye felten, wel or wo,
As fer forth as it in my power lay,   690
Unreprovable unto my wyfhod ay,
The same wolde I fele, lyf or deth —
And thilke covenant whil me lasteth breth
I wol fulfille; and that shal ben wel sene,   694
Was nevere unto hire love a trewer quene."
And with that word, naked, with ful good herte,
Among the serpents in the pit she sterte,
And there she ches to have hire buryinge.
Anon the nadderes gonne hire for to stynge,
And she hire deth receyveth with good cheere
For love of Antony that was hire so dere.   701
And this is storyal soth, it is no fable.
Now, or I fynde a man thus trewe and stable,
And wol for love his deth so frely take,
I preye God let oure hedes nevere ake!
    Amen.   705

Explicit Legenda Cleopatre, martiris.

---

647 **cuppe**: cup of woe (?)
648 **pesen**: peas, to make the decks slippery   **haches**: planks
forming a ship's deck   **slidere**: slippery
649 **lyme**: quicklime (for throwing in the enemies' eyes)
654 **purpre**: purple
655 **For strokes**: because of the blows of missiles
661 **rof**: stabbed
669 **routhe**: sorrow, lament

682 **So ferforthly**: so completely
691 **Unreprovable**: irreproachable
699 **nadderes**: adders, serpents
702 **storyal**: historical, factual
Explicit, *etc.*: Here ends the Legend of Cleopatra, martyr.

II
THE LEGEND OF THISBE

Incipit Legenda Tesbe Babilonie, martiris.

At Babiloyne whylom fil it thus,
The whyche toun the queen Semyramus
Let dychen al aboute and walles make
Ful hye, of hard tiles wel ybake:
There were dwellyng in this noble toun   710
Two lordes, whiche that were of gret renoun,
And woneden so nygh, upon a grene,
That there nas but a ston-wal hem betweene,
As ofte in grete tounes is the wone.
And soth to seyne, that o man hadde a sone,
Of al that lond oon of the lustyeste.   716
That other hadde a doughter, the fayreste
That estward in the world was tho dwellynge.
The name of everych gan to other sprynge
By women that were neighebores aboute.   720
For in that contre yit, withouten doute,
Maydenes been ykept, for jelosye,
Ful streyte, lest they diden som folye.
This yonge man was called Piramus,   724
Tysbe hight the maide, Naso seyth thus;
And thus by report was hire name yshove
That, as they wex in age, wex here love.
And certeyn, as by resoun of hire age,
There myghte have ben bytwixe hem maryage,
But that here fadres nolde it nat assente;   730
And bothe in love ylyke sore they brente,
That non of alle hyre frendes myght it lette,
But pryvyly som tyme yit they mette
By sleyghte, and spoken som of here desyr;
As wry the glede and hotter is the fyr,   735
Forbede a love, and it is ten so wod.

This wal, which that bitwixe hem bothe stod,
Was clove a-two, ryght from the cop adoun,
Of olde tyme of his fundacioun;
But yit this clyfte was so narw and lyte   740
It nas nat sene, deere ynogh a myte.
But what is that that love can nat espye?

Ye loveres two, if that I shal nat lye,
Ye founden first this litel narwe clifte;
And with a soun as softe as any shryfte,   745
They lete here wordes thourgh the clifte pace,
And tolden, whil that they stode in the place,
Al here compleynt of love and al here wo,
At every tyme whan they durste so.
Upon that o syde of the wal stod he,   750
And on that other side stod Thesbe,
The swote soun of other to receyve.
And thus here wardeyns wolde they deceyve,
And every day this wal they wolde threte,   754
And wisshe to God that it were doun ybete.
Thus wolde they seyn: "Alas, thow wikkede
     wal!
Thorgh thyn envye thow us lettest al.
Why nylt thow cleve or fallen al a-two?
Or at the leste, but thou woldist so,
Yit woldest thow but ones lat us mete,   760
Or ones that we myghte kyssen swete,
Thanne were we covered of oure cares colde.
But, natheles, yit be we to thee holde,
In as muche as thow sufferest for to gon   764
Oure wordes thourgh thy lym and ek thy ston.
Yit oughte we with the been wel apayd."
And whan these ydele wordes weren sayd,
The colde wal they wolden kysse of ston,
And take here leve and forth they wolden gon.
And this was gladly in the eve-tyde,   770
Or wonder erly, lest men it espyde.
And longe tyme they wroughte in this manere,
Tyl on a day, whan Phebus gan to cleere —
Aurora with the stremes of hire hete   774
Hadde dreyed up the dew of herbes wete —
Unto this clyft, as it was wont to be,
Com Piramus, and after com Thysbe,
And plyghten trouthe fully in here fey
That ilke same nyght to stele awey,
And to begile here wardeyns everichon,   780

Incipit, *etc.*: Here begins the Legend of Thisbe of Babylon, martyr.
707 **Semyramus:** Semiramis
725 **Naso:** Ovid (Publius Ovidius Naso)
726 **yshove:** driven about, widely known
735 **wry:** cover
736 **ten so wod:** ten times as mad (frenzied)
740 **clyfte:** chink
741 **deere ynogh a myte:** to the slightest extent

745 **softe as any shryfte:** quietly as any words in a confessional
762 **covered of:** recovered from   **colde:** painful
763 **holde:** obligated
770 **gladly:** usually   **eve-tyde:** evening
773 **Phebus:** the sun
774 **Aurora:** the dawn

And forth out of the cite for to goon;
And, for the feldes ben so brode and wide,
For to mete in o place at o tyde,
They sette mark here metynge sholde be
There kyng Nynus was grave under a tre —
For olde payens that idoles heryed   786
Useden tho in feldes to ben beryed —
And faste by this grave was a welle.
And shortly of this tale for to telle,   789
This covenaunt was affermed wonder faste;
And longe hem thoughte that the sonne laste,
That it nere gon under the se adoun.

This Tisbe hath so gret affeccioun
And so gret lykinge Piramus to se,
That whan she say hire tyme myghte be,   795
At nyght she stal awey ful pryvyly,
With hire face ywympled subtyly;
For alle hire frendes — for to save hire
        trouthe —
She hath forsake; allas, and that is routhe
That evere woman wolde ben so trewe   800
To truste man, but she the bet hym knewe.
And to the tre she goth a ful good pas,
For love made hire so hardy in this cas,
And by the welle adoun she gan hyre dresse.
Allas! Than cometh a wilde lyonesse   805
Out of the wode, withoute more arest,
With blody mouth, of strangelynge of a best,
To drynken of the welle there as she sat.
And whan that Tisbe hadde espyed that,
She rist hire up, with a ful drery herte,   810
And in a cave with dredful fot she sterte,
For by the mone she say it wel withalle.
And as she ran hire wympel let she falle
And tok non hed, so sore she was awhaped,
And ek so glad that that she was escaped;   815
And thus she sit and darketh wonder stylle.
Whan that this lyonesse hath dronke hire fille,
Aboute the welle gan she for to wynde,
And ryght anon the wympel gan she fynde,
And with hire blody mouth it al torente.   820
Whan this was don, no lengere she ne stente,
But to the wode hire weye thanne hath she
        nome.
And at the laste this Piramus is come;
But al to longe, allas, at hom was he!

The mone shon, and he myghte wel yse,   825
And in his wey, as that he com ful faste.
His eyen to the ground adoun he caste,
And in the sond, as he byheld adoun,
He sey the steppes brode of a lyoun,
And in his herte he sodeynly agros,   830
And pale he wex; therwith his heer aros,
And ner he com, and fond the wimpel torn.
"Allas," quod he, "the day that I was born!
This o nyght wol us lovers bothe sle!
How shulde I axe mercy of Tisbe,   835
Whan I am he that have yow slayn, allas!
My biddyng hath yow slayn, as in this cas.
Allas, to bidde a woman gon by nyghte
In place there as peril falle myghte!
And I so slow! Allas, I ne hadde be   840
Here in this place a furlong wey or ye!
Now what lyoun that be in this forest,
My body mote he renten, or what best
That wilde is, gnawe mote he now myn herte!"
And with that word he to the wympel sterte,
And kiste it ofte, and wep on it ful sore,   846
And seyde, "Wympel, allas! There is no more
But thow shalt feele as wel the blod of me
As thow hast felt the bledyng of Thisbe!"   849
And with that word he smot hym to the herte.
The blod out of the wounde as brode sterte
As water whan the condit broken is.

Now Tisbe, which that wiste nat of this,
But sittynge in hire drede, she thoughte thus:
"If it so falle that my Piramus   855
Be comen hider, and may me not yfynde,
He may me holde fals and ek unkynde."
And out she cometh and after hym gan espien,
Bothe with hire herte and with hire yen,
And thoughte, "I wol hym tellen of my drede,
Bothe of the lyonesse and al my deede."   861
And at the laste hire love thanne hath she
        founde,
Betynge with his heles on the grounde,
Al blody, and therwithal a-bak she sterte,
And lik the wawes quappe gan hire herte,   865
And pale as box she was, and in a throwe
Avisede hire, and gan hym wel to knowe,
That it was Piramus, hire herte deere.
Who coude wryte which a dedly cheere   869
Hath Thisbe now, and how hire heer she rente,
And how she gan hireselve to turmente,
And how she lyth and swouneth on the
        grounde,

784 sette mark: agreed on a place (where)   here: their
785 Nynus: Ninus, husband of Semiramis and founder of
Nineveh
793 affeccioun: desire
795 say: saw
797 ywympled: wearing a covering like the wimple of a nun
over her neck and about her face
802 a ful good pas: rapidly
806 arest: delay
810 drery: frightened
811 dredful: fearful
816 darketh: hides in the dark

830 agros: trembled
837 biddyng: prayer
852 condit: conduit, water pipe
865 quappe gan: beat

And how she wep of teres ful his wounde;
How medeleth she his blod with hire com-
    pleynte;
How with his blod hireselve gan she peynte;
How clyppeth she the deede cors, allas!   876
How doth this woful Tisbe in this cas!
How kysseth she his frosty mouth so cold!
"Who hath don this, and who hath been so
    bold
To sle my leef? O spek, my Piramus!   880
I am thy Tisbe, that the calleth thus."
And therwithal she lifteth up his hed.

    This woful man, that was nat fully ded,
Whan that he herde the name of Tisbe cryen,
On hire he caste his hevy, dedly yen,   885
And doun agayn, and yeldeth up the gost.
Tysbe ryst up withouten noyse or bost,
And saw hire wympel and his empty shethe,
And ek his swerd that hym hath don to dethe.
Thanne spak she thus: "My woful hand," quod
    she,   890
"Is strong ynogh in swich a werk to me;
For love shal yeve me strengthe and hardy-
    nesse
To make my wounde large ynogh, I gesse.
I wol thee folwe ded, and I wol be
Felawe and cause ek of thy deth," quod
    she.   895
"And thogh that nothing, save the deth only,

Mighte thee fro me departe trewely,
Thow shalt no more departe now fro me
Than fro the deth, for I wol go with thee.
And now, ye wrechede jelos fadres oure,   900
We that whilom were children youre,
We preyen yow, withouten more envye,
That in o grave yfere we moten lye,
Sith love hath brought us to this pitous ende.
And ryghtwis God to every lovere sende,   905
That loveth trewely, more prosperite
Than evere yit had Piramus and Tisbe!
And lat no gentil woman hyre assure
To putten hire in swich an aventure.
But God forbede but a woman can   910
Ben as trewe in lovynge as a man!
And for my part, I shal anon it kythe."
And with that word his swerd she tok as
    swythe,
That warm was of hire loves blod, and hot,
And to the herte she hireselven smot.   915
And thus are Tisbe and Piramus ygo.
Of trewe men I fynde but fewe mo
In alle my bokes, save this Piramus,
And therfore have I spoken of hym thus.
For it is deynte to us men to fynde   920
A man that can in love been trewe and kynde.
Here may ye se, what lovere so he be,
A woman dar and can as wel as he.

Explicit Legenda Tesbe.

III

THE LEGEND OF DIDO

Incipit Legenda Didonis martiris, Cartaginis Regine.

    Glorye and honour, Virgil Mantoan,
Be to thy name! and I shal, as I can,   925
Folwe thy lanterne, as thow gost byforn,
How Eneas to Dido was forsworn.
In thyn Eneyde and Naso wol I take
The tenor, and the grete effectes make.

Whan Troye brought was to destruccioun   930
By Grekes sleyghte, and namely by Synoun,
Feynynge the hors offered unto Mynerve,
Thourgh which that many a Troyan moste
    sterve;

887 **bost:** talk

Incipit, *etc.*: Here begins the Legend of Dido, martyr, Queen of
Carthage.
924 **Virgil Mantoan:** Virgil, born in Mantua
928 **Naso:** Ovid

905 **ryghtwis:** just
908 **hyre assure:** be overconfident, take the chance
920 **deynte:** pleasing
Explicit, *etc.*: Here ends the Legend of Thisbe.

931 **sleyghte:** trickery **Synoun:** Sinon
932 **Mynerve:** Minerva

And Ector hadde, after his deth, apeered;
And fyr so wod it myghte nat been steered
In al the noble tour of Ylioun,   936
That of the cite was the chef dongeoun;
And al the contre was so lowe ybrought,
And Priamus the kyng fordon and nought;
And Enyas was charged by Venus   940
To fleen awey, he tok Ascanius,
That was his sone, in his ryght hand and
          fledde;
And on his bak he bar and with hym ledde
His olde fader cleped Anchises,
And by the weye his wif Creusa he les.   945
And moche sorwe hadde he in his mynde,
Or that he coude his felaweshipe fynde.
But at the laste, whan he hadde hem founde,
He made hym redy in a certeyn stounde,
And to the se ful faste he gan him hye,   950
And sayleth forth with al his companye
Toward Ytayle, as wolde his destinee.
But of his aventures in the se
Nis nat to purpos for to speke of here,
For it acordeth nat to my matere.   955
But, as I seyde, of hym and of Dido
Shal be my tale, til that I have do.
   So longe he saylede in the salte se
Tyl in Libie unnethe aryvede he
With shipes sevene and with no more navye;
And glad was he to londe for to hye,   961
So was he with the tempest al toshake.
And whan that he the haven hadde ytake,
He hadde a knyght, was called Achates,
And hym of al his felawshipe he ches   965
To gon with hym, the cuntre for t'espie.
He tok with hym no more companye,
But forth they gon, and lafte his shipes ryde,
His fere and he, withouten any gyde.
So longe he walketh in this wildernesse,   970
Til at the laste he mette an hunteresse.
A bowe in hande and arwes hadde she;
Hire clothes cutted were unto the kne.
But she was yit the fayreste creature
That evere was yformed by Nature;   975
And Eneas and Achates she grette,
And thus she to hem spak whan she hem
          mette:
"Saw ye," quod she, "as ye han walked wyde,
Any of my sustren walke yow besyde
With any wilde bor or other best,   980
That they han hunted to, in this forest,

Ytukked up, with arwes in hire cas?"
"Nay, sothly, lady," quod this Eneas;
"But by thy beaute, as it thynketh me,
Thow myghtest nevere erthly woman be,   985
But Phebus syster art thow, as I gesse.
And if so be that thow be a goddesse,
Have mercy on oure labour and oure wo."
"I n'am no goddesse, sothly," quod she tho;
"For maydens walken in this contre here,   990
With arwes and with bowe, in this manere.
This is the reyne of Libie there ye ben,
Of which that Dido lady is and queen" —
And shortly tolde hym al the occasyoun
Why Dido cam into that regioun,   995
Of which as now me lesteth nat to ryme;
It nedeth nat, it were but los of tyme.
For this is al and som, it was Venus,
His owene moder, that spak with him thus,
And to Cartage she bad he sholde hym dighte,
And vanyshed anon out of his syghte.   1001
I coude folwe, word for word, Virgile,
But it wolde lasten al to longe while.
   This noble queen that cleped was Dido,
That whilom was the wif of Sytheo,   1005
That fayrer was than is the bryghte sonne,
This noble toun of Cartage hath bigonne;
In which she regneth in so gret honour
That she was holden of alle queenes flour
Of gentillesse, of fredom, of beaute,   1010
That wel was hym that myghte hire ones se;
Of kynges and of lordes so desyred
That al the world hire beaute hadde yfyred,
She stod so wel in every wightes grace.
   Whan Eneas was come unto that place,   1015
Unto the mayster temple of al the toun
Ther Dido was in hire devocyoun,
Ful pryvyly his weye than hath he nome.
Whan he was in the large temple come,
I can nat seyn if that it be possible,   1020
But Venus hadde hym maked invysible —
Thus seyth the bok, withouten any les.
And whan this Eneas and Achates
Hadden in this temple ben overal,
Thanne founde they, depeynted on a wal,   1025
How Troye and al the lond destroyed was.
"Allas, that I was born!" quod Eneas;
"Thourghout the world oure shame is kid so
          wyde,
Now it is peynted upon every syde.
We, that weren in prosperite,   1030

---

936 **Ylioun:** Ilium
937 **dongeoun:** keep, the main fortification of a castle
945 **les:** lost
959 **Libie:** Libya

982 **Ytukked up:** with skirt tucked up
986 **Phebus syster:** Diana, goddess of the chase
1005 **Sytheo:** Sichaeus
1022 **withouten any les:** without any lie, truly

Been now desclandred, and in swich degre,
No lenger for to lyven I ne kepe."
And with that word he brast out for to wepe
So tenderly that routhe it was to sene.
This fresshe lady, of the cite queene,   1035
Stod in the temple in hire estat real,
So rychely and ek so fayr withal,
So yong, so lusty, with hire eyen glade,
That, if that God, that hevene and erthe made,
Wolde han a love, for beaute and good-
                  nesse,   1040
And womanhod, and trouthe, and semelynesse,
Whom shulde he loven but this lady swete?
Ther nys no woman to hym half so mete.
Fortune, that hath the world in governaunce,
Hath sodeynly brought in so newe a chaunce
That nevere was ther yit so fremde a cas.   1046
For al the companye of Eneas,
Which that he wende han loren in the se,
Aryved is nat fer from that cite;
For which the gretteste of his lordes some   1050
By aventure ben to the cite come,
Unto that same temple, for to seke
The queene, and of hire socour to beseke,
Swich renoun was there sprongen of hire good-
                  nesse.
And whan they hadden told al here distresse,
And al here tempest and here harde cas,   1056
Unto the queen apeered Eneas,
And openly biknew that it was he.
Who hadde joye thanne but his meyne,
That hadde founde here lord, here gover-
                  nour?   1060
The queen saugh that they dide hym swych
                  honour,
And hadde herd ofte of Eneas er tho,
And in hire herte she hadde routhe and wo
That evere swich a noble man as he
Shal ben disherited in swich degre;   1065
And saw the man, that he was lyk a knyght,
And suffisaunt of persone and of myght,
And lyk to been a verray gentil man;
And wel his wordes he besette can,
And hadde a noble visage for the nones,   1070
And formed wel of braunes and of bones.
For after Venus hadde he swich fayrnesse
That no man myghte be half so fayr, I gesse;
And wel a lord he semede for to be.
And, for he was a straunger, somwhat she   1075

Likede hym the bet, as, God do bote,
To som folk ofte newe thyng is sote.
Anon hire herte hath pite of his wo,
And with that pite love com in also;
And thus, for pite and for gentillesse,   1080
Refreshed moste he been of his distresse.
She seyde, certes, that she sory was
That he hath had swych peryl and swich cas;
And, in hire frendly speche, in this manere
She to hym spak, and seyde as ye may here:
"Be ye nat Venus sone and Anchises?   1086
In good feyth, al the worshipe and encres
That I may goodly don yow, ye shal have.
Youre shipes and youre meyne shal I save."
And many a gentil word she spak hym to,   1090
And comaunded hire messageres to go
The same day, withouten any fayle,
His shippes for to seke, and hem vitayle.
Ful many a beste she to the shippes sente,   1094
And with the wyn she gan hem to presente,
And to hire royal paleys she hire spedde,
And Eneas alwey with hire she ledde.
What nedeth yow the feste to descrive?
He nevere beter at ese was in his lyve.   1099
Ful was the feste of deyntees and rychesse,
Of instruments, of song, and of gladnesse,
Of many an amorous lokyng and devys.
This Eneas is come to paradys
Out of the swolow of helle, and thus in joye
Remembreth hym of his estat in Troye.   1105
    To daunsynge chaumberes ful of paramentes,
Of riche beddes, and of ornementes,
This Eneas is led after the mete.
And with the quene, whan that he hadde sete,
And spices parted, and the wyn agon,   1110
Unto his chambres was he led anon
To take his ese and for to have his reste,
With al his folk, to don what so hem leste.
There nas courser wel ybrydeled non,
Ne stede, for the justing wel to gon,   1115
Ne large palfrey, esy for the nones,
Ne jewel, fretted ful of ryche stones,
Ne sakkes ful of gold, of large wyghte,
Ne ruby non, that shynede by nyghte,
Ne gentil hawtein faucoun heroner,   1120

1031 **desclandred:** brought into disgrace
1041 **semelynesse:** comeliness
1046 **fremde:** strange
1048 **wende han loren:** supposed he had lost
1072 **after Venus:** taking after Venus, his mother

1076 **God do bote:** may God help (us), by God
1087 **encres:** assistance
1093 **vitayle:** stock with provisions
1102 **devys:** scheme
1104 **swolow:** mouth (or gulf)
1106 **paramentes:** tapestries
1110 **spices parted:** spiced cakes departed, taken away
1115 **justing:** jousting
1117 **fretted ful of:** thickly set with
1118 **wyghte:** weight
1120 **hawtein:** proud   **faucoun heroner:** falcon for hunting herons

Ne hound for hert or wilde bor or der,
Ne coupe of gold, with floreyns newe ybete,
That in the land of Libie may be gete,
That Dido ne hath it Eneas ysent;
And al is payed, what that he hath spent.   1125
Thus can this quene honurable hire gestes calle,
As she that can in fredom passen alle.
Eneas sothly ek, withouten les,
Hadde sent unto his ship by Achates
After his sone, and after riche thynges,   1130
Bothe sceptre, clothes, broches, and ek rynges,
Some for to were, and some for to presente
To hire that alle thise noble thynges hym
          sente;
And bad his sone how that he shulde make
The presenting, and to the queen it take.   1135
Repeyred is this Achates agayn,
And Eneas ful blysful is and fayn
To sen his yonge sone Ascanyus.
But natheles, oure autour telleth us,
That Cupido, that is the god of love,   1140
At preyere of his moder hye above,
Hadde the liknesse of the child ytake,
This noble queen enamored to make
On Eneas; but, as of that scripture,
Be as be may, I take of it no cure.   1145
But soth is this, the queen hath mad swich
          chere
Unto this child, that wonder is to here;
And of the present that his fader sente
She thanked hym ful ofte, in good entente.

     Thus is this queen in plesaunce and in joye,
With alle these newe lusty folk of Troye.   1151
And of the dedes hath she more enquered
Of Eneas, and al the story lered
Of Troye, and al the longe day they tweye
Entendeden to speken and to pleye;   1155
Of which ther gan to breden swich a fyr
That sely Dido hath now swich desyr
With Eneas, hire newe gest, to dele,
That she hath lost hire hewe and ek hire hele.

     Now to th'effect, now to the fruyt of al,   1160
Whi I have told this story, and telle shal.
Thus I begynne: it fil upon a nyght,
Whan that the mone up reysed hadde his lyght,
This noble queene unto hire reste wente.   1164
She siketh sore, and gan hyreself turmente;
She waketh, walweth, maketh many a breyd,
As don these lovers, as I have herd seyd.

And at the laste, unto hire syster Anne
She made hire mone, and ryght thus spak she
          thanne:
"Now, dere sister myn, what may it be   1170
That me agasteth in my drem?" quod she.
"This newe Troyan is so in my thoght,
For that me thynketh he is so wel ywrought,
And ek so likly for to ben a man,
And therwithal so moche good he can,   1175
That al my love and lyf lyth in his cure.
Have ye nat herd him telle his aventure?
Now certes, Anne, if that ye rede it me,
I wolde fayn to hym ywedded be;
This is th'effect; what sholde I more seye?   1180
In hym lyth al, to do me live or deye."
Hyre syster Anne, as she that coude hire good,
Seyde as hire thoughte, and somdel it withstod.
But herof was so long a sermounynge
It were to long to make rehersynge.   1185
But finaly, it may nat ben withstonde;
Love wol love, for nothing wol it wonde.

     The dawenyng up-rist out of the se.
This amorous queene chargeth hire meyne
The nettes dresse, and speres brode and kene;
An huntyng wol this lusty freshe queene,   1191
So priketh hire this newe joly wo.
To hors is al hir lusty folk ygo;
Into the court the houndes been ybrought;
And upon coursers swift as any thought   1195
Hire yonge knyghtes hoven al aboute,
And of hire women ek an huge route.
Upon a thikke palfrey, paper-whit,
With sadel red, enbrouded with delyt,
Of gold the barres up enbosede hye,   1200
Sit Dido, al in gold and perre wrye;
And she as fair as is the bryghte morwe,
That heleth syke folk of nyghtes sorwe.
Upon a courser stertlynge as the fyr —
Men myghte turne hym with a litel wyr —   1205
Sit Eneas, lik Phebus to devyse,
So was he fressh arayed in his wyse.
The fomy brydel with the bit of gold
Governeth he ryght as hymself hath wold.
And forth this noble queen thus lat I ride   1210
On huntynge, with this Troyan by hyre side.

1182 **coude hire good**: knew what was best
1187 **wonde**: cease, desist
1188 **up-rist** = *up-riseth*, rises
1191 **An huntyng wol**: A-hunting will go
1196 **hoven**: linger
1198 **thikke palfrey**: sturdy riding horse
1199 **enbrouded with delyt**: delightfully adorned
1200 **enbosede**: embossed, in relief
1201 **wrye**: covered
1204 **stertlynge**: leaping about
1206 **lik Phebus to devyse**: (who would be) like the god of the
sun to describe

1122 **coupe**: cup   **with floreyns newe ybete**: with florins (gold
coins) newly minted
1155 **Entendeden**: were intentive
1158 **dele**: have sexual intercourse
1166 **breyd**: start, sudden movement

The herde of hertes founden is anon,
With "Hay! Go bet! Pryke thow! Lat gon, lat
        gon!
Why nyl the leoun comen, or the bere,   1214
That I myghte ones mete hym with this spere?"
Thus seyn these yonge folk, and up they kylle
These bestes wilde, and han hem at here wille.
Among al this to rumbelen gan the hevene;
The thunder rored with a grisely stevene;
Doun cam the reyn with hayl and slet so faste,
With hevenes fyr, that it so sore agaste   1221
This noble queen, and also hire meyne,
That ech of hem was glad awey to fle.
And shortly, from the tempest hire to save,
She fledde hireself into a litel cave,   1225
And with hire wente this Eneas also.
I not, with hem if there wente any mo;
The autour maketh of it no mencioun.
And here began the depe affeccioun   1229
Betwixe hem two; this was the firste morwe
Of hire gladnesse, and gynning of hire sorwe.
For there hath Eneas ykneled so,
And told hire al his herte and al his wo,
And swore so depe to hire to be trewe   1234
For wel or wo and chaunge hire for no newe;
And as a fals lovere so wel can pleyne,
That sely Dido rewede on his peyne,
And tok hym for husbonde and becom his wyf
For everemo, whil that hem laste lyf.   1239
And after this, whan that the tempest stente,
With myrthe out as they comen, hom they
        wente.
    The wikke fame upros, and that anon,
How Eneas hath with the queen ygon
Into the cave; and demede as hem liste.
And whan the kyng that Yarbas highte it
        wiste,   1245
As he that hadde hir loved evere his lyf,
And wowede hyre, to han hire to his wyf,
Swich sorwe as he hath maked, and swich
        cheere,
It is a routhe and pite for to here.
But as in love, alday it happeth so   1250
That oon shal laughen at anothers wo.
Now laugheth Eneas and is in joye
And more richesse than evere he was in Troye.
    O sely wemen, ful of innocence,
Ful of pite, of trouthe and conscience,   1255
What maketh yow to men to truste so?
Have ye swych routhe upon hyre feyned wo,

And han swich olde ensaumples yow beforn?
Se ye nat alle how they ben forsworn?   1259
Where sen ye oon that he ne hath laft his leef,
Or ben unkynde, or don hire som myscheef,
Or piled hire, or bosted of his dede?
Ye may as wel it sen as ye may rede.
Tak hede now of this grete gentil-man,
This Troyan, that so wel hire plesen can,   1265
That feyneth hym so trewe and obeysynge,
So gentil, and so privy of his doinge,
And can so wel don alle his obeysaunces,
And wayten hire at festes and at daunces,
And whan she goth to temple and hom ageyn,
And fasten til he hath his lady seyn,   1271
And beren in his devyses, for hire sake,
Not I not what; and songes wolde he make,
Justen, and don of armes many thynges,   1274
Sende hire lettres, tokens, broches, rynges —
Now herkneth how he shal his lady serve!
There as he was in peril for to sterve
For hunger, and for myschef in the se,
And desolat, and fled from his cuntre,
And al his folk with tempest al todryven,   1280
She hath hire body and ek hire reame yiven
Into his hand, there as she myghte have been
Of othere land than of Cartage a queen,
And lyved in joye ynogh; what wole ye more?
This Eneas, that hath so depe yswore,   1285
Is wery of his craft withinne a throwe;
The hote ernest is al overblowe.
And pryvyly he doth his shipes dyghte,
And shapeth hym to stele awey by nyghte.
    This Dido hath suspecioun of this,   1290
And thoughte wel that it was al amys.
For in hir bed he lyth a-nyght and syketh;
She axeth hym anon what hym myslyketh —
"My dere herte, which that I love most?"
    "Certes," quod he, "this nyght my faderes
        gost   1295
Hath in my slep so sore me tormented,
And ek Mercurye his message hath presented,
That nedes to the conquest of Ytayle
My destine is sone for to sayle;   1299
For which, me thynketh, brosten is myn herte!"
Therwith his false teres out they sterte,
And taketh hire withinne his armes two.
    "Is that in ernest?" quod she; "Wole ye so?
Have ye nat sworn to wyve me to take?
Allas, what woman wole ye of me make?   1305

1262 **piled:** robbed
1266 **obeysynge:** obedient
1272 **devyses:** heraldic devices
1287 **ernest:** sincere passion   **overblowe:** blown over, past
1293 **myslyketh:** displeases

1213 **Go bet!:** Hurry up!   **Pryke thow!:** Use the spurs!   **Lat gon!:** Let (the dogs) go!

I am a gentil woman and a queen.
Ye wole nat from youre wif thus foule fleen?
That I was born, allas! What shal I do?''
To telle in short, this noble quen Dydo,
She seketh halwes and doth sacryfise;   1310
She kneleth, cryeth, that routhe is to devyse;
Conjureth hym, and profereth hym to be
His thral, his servant in the leste degre;
She falleth hym to fote and swouneth ther,
Dischevele, with hire bryghte gilte her,   1315
And seyth, ''Have mercy; let me with yow
          ryde!
These lordes, which that wonen me besyde,
Wole me distroyen only for youre sake.
And, so ye wole me now to wive take,   1319
As ye han sworn, thanne wol I yeve yow leve
To slen me with youre swerd now sone at eve!
For thanne yit shal I deyen as youre wif.
I am with childe, and yeve my child his lyf!
Mercy, lord! Have pite in youre thought!''

    But al this thing avayleth hire ryght nought,
For on a nyght, slepynge he let hire lye,   1326
And stal awey unto his companye,
And as a traytour forth he gan to sayle
Toward the large contre of Ytayle.
Thus he hath laft Dido in wo and pyne,   1330
And wedded ther a lady hyghte Lavyne.

    A cloth he lafte, and ek his swerd stondynge,
Whan he from Dido stal in hire slepynge,
Ryght at hire beddes hed, so gan he hie,
Whan that he stal awey to his navye;   1335
Which cloth, whan sely Dido gan awake,
She hath it kyst ful ofte for his sake,

And seyde, ''O swete cloth, whil Juppiter it
          leste,
Tak now my soule, unbynd me of this unreste!
I have fulfild of fortune al the cours.''   1340
And thus, allas, withouten his socours,
Twenty tyme yswouned hath she thanne.
And whanne that she unto hire syster Anne
Compleyned hadde — of which I may nat
          wryte,
So gret a routhe I have it for t'endite —   1345
And bad hire norice and hire sister gon
To fechen fyr and other thyng anon,
And seyde that she wolde sacryfye —
And whan she myghte hire tyme wel espie,
Upon the fir of sacrifice she sterte,   1350
And with his swerd she rof hyre to the herte.

    But, as myn auctour seith, yit thus she seyde;
Or she was hurt, byforen or she deyde,
She wrot a lettre anon that thus began:
''Ryght so,'' quod she, ''as that the white swan
Ayens his deth begynnyth for to synge,   1356
Right so to yow make I my compleynynge.
Not that I trowe to geten yow ageyn,
For wel I wot that it is al in veyn,
Syn that the goddes been contraire to me.   1360
But syn my name is lost thorugh yow,'' quod
          she,
''I may wel lese on yow a word or letter,
Al be it that I shal ben nevere the better;
For thilke wynd that blew youre ship awey,
The same wynd hath blowe awey youre fey.''
But who wol al this letter have in mynde,   1366
Rede Ovyde, and in hym he shal it fynde.

Explicit Legenda Didonis martiris, Cartaginis Regine.

1310 **halwes:** shrines
1312 **Conjureth:** implores
1315 **Dischevele:** with hair hanging loose
1331 **Lavyne:** Lavinia

1339 **unbynd me of:** free me from
1348 **sacryfye:** sacrifice
1352 **myn auctour:** Ovid
1356 **Ayens:** in anticipation of
Explicit, *etc.:* Here ends the Legend of Dido, martyr, Queen of Carthage.

IV
THE LEGEND OF HYPSIPYLE AND MEDEA

Incipit Legenda Ysiphile et Medee, martirum.

Thow rote of false lovers, Duc Jasoun,
Thow sly devourere and confusioun
Of gentil wemen, tendre creatures,   1370
Thow madest thy recleymyng and thy lures
To ladyes of thy statly aparaunce,
And of thy wordes farced with plesaunce,
And of thy feyned trouthe and thy manere,
With thyn obesaunce and humble cheere,
And with thy contrefeted peyne and wo.   1376
There othere falsen oon, thow falsest two!
O, often swore thow that thow woldest dye
For love, whan thow ne feltest maladye
Save foul delyt, which that thow callest love!
Yif that I live, thy name shal be shove   1381
In English that thy sekte shal be knowe!
Have at thee, Jason! Now thyn horn is blowe!
But certes, it is bothe routhe and wo
That love with false loveres werketh so;   1385
For they shal have wel betere love and chere
Than he that hath abought his love ful dere,
Or hadde in armes many a blody box.
For evere as tendre a capoun et the fox,   1389
Thow he be fals and hath the foul betrayed,
As shal the good-man that therfore hath payed.
Al have he to the capoun skille and ryght,
The false fox wol have his part at nyght.
On Jason this ensaumple is wel ysene
By Isiphile and Medea the queene.   1395

1. *The Legend of Hypsipyle*

In Tessalie, as Guido tellith us,
There was a kyng that highte Pelleus,

That hadde a brother which that highte Eson;
And whan for age he myghte unnethes gon,
He yaf to Pelleus the governyng   1400
Of al his regne and made hym lord and kyng.
Of which Eson this Jason geten was,
That in his tyme in al that land there nas
Nat swich a famous knyght of gentilesse,   1404
Of fredom, and of strengthe and lustynesse.
After his fadres deth he bar hym so
That there nas non that liste ben his fo,
But dide hym al honour and companye.
Of which this Pelleus hadde gret envye,
Imagynynge that Jason myghte be   1410
Enhaunsed so and put in swich degre
With love of lordes of his regioun,
That from his regne he may ben put adoun.
And in his wit a-nyght compassed he
How Jason myghte best distroyed be   1415
Withoute sclaunder of his compassement,
And at the last he tok avysement
To senden hym into som fer contre,
There as this Jason may destroyed be.
This was his wit, al made he to Jasoun   1420
Gret chere of love and of affeccioun,
For drede lest his lordes it espide.
So fyl it, so as fame renneth wide,
There was swich tydyng overal and swich loos,
That in an yle that called was Colcos,   1425
Beyonde Troye, estward in the se,
That therin was a ram that men mighte se
That hadde a fles of gold that shon so bryghte
That nowher was ther swich anothir syghte;
But it was kept alwey with a dragoun,   1430
And many other merveyles, up and doun,
And with two boles maked al of bras,
That spitten fyr, and moche thyng there was.
But this was ek the tale, natheles,
That whoso wolde wynne thylke fles,   1435
He moste bothe, or he it wynne myghte,

Incipit, *etc.*: Here begins the Legend of Hypsipyle and Medea,
martyrs.
1368 **rote:** root, source (i.e., model)
1371 **lures:** devices for calling back (*recleymyng*) hawks
1373 **farced:** filled, stuffed
1381 **shove:** driven about, widely known
1382 **sekte:** sect (i.e., men like you)
1388 **box:** blow
1389 **et** = *eteth*, eats
1391 **good-man:** goodman, head of the household
1396 **Tessalie:** Thessaly   **Guido:** Guido delle Colonne, author of
the *Historia Troiana*
1397 **Pelleus:** Pelias; Chaucer follows Guido's spellings
throughout.

1398 **Eson:** Aeson, the father of Jason
1405 **lustynesse:** vigor
1414 **compassed:** plotted
1416 **sclaunder:** disgrace   **compassement:** plotting
1424 **loos:** rumor, talk
1425 **Colcos:** Colchis, in the Black Sea
1428 **fles:** fleece

With the boles and the dragoun fyghte.
And kyng Oetes lord was of that yle.

This Pelleus bethoughte upon this wile,
That he his neveu Jason wolde enhorte   1440
To saylen to that lond, hym to disporte,
And seyde, "Nevew, if it myghte be
That swich a worshipe myghte fallen the,
That thow this famous tresor myghtest wynne,
And bryngen it my regioun withinne,   1445
It were to me gret plesaunce and honour.
Thanne were I holde to quyte thy labour;
And al the cost I wol myselven make.
And chees what folk that thow wilt with the
     take;
Lat sen now, darst thow take this viage?"   1450
Jason was yong, and lusty of corage,
And undertok to don this ilke empryse.
Anon Argus his shipes gan devyse;
With Jason wente the stronge Ercules,
And many another that he with hym ches.   1455
But whoso axeth who is with hym gon,
Lat hym go rede Argonautycon,
For he wole telle a tale long ynogh.
Philotetes anon the sayl up drogh,
Whan that the wynd was good, and gan hym
     hye   1460
Out of his contre called Thessalye.
So longe he seyled in the salte se,
Til in the yle of Lemnon aryvede he —
Al be this nat rehersed of Guido,
Yit seyth Ovyde in his Epistels so —   1465
And of this ile lady was and quene
The fayre yonge Ysiphele, the shene,
That whylom Thoas doughter was, the kyng.

Isiphile was gon in hire pleying,
And, romynge on the clyves by the se,   1470
Under a banke anon aspied she
Where that the ship of Jason gan aryve.
Of hire goodnesse adoun she sendeth blyve
To witen if that any straunge wight   1474
With tempest thider were yblowe a-nyght,
To don him socour, as was hire usaunce
To fortheren every wight, and don plesaunce
Of verrey bounte and of curteysye.
This messangeer adoun hym gan to hye,

And fond Jason and Ercules also,   1480
That in a cog to londe were ygo,
Hem to refreshen and to take the eyr.
The morwenynge attempre was and fayr,
And in his weye this messanger hem mette.
Ful cunnyngly these lordes two he grette,   1485
And dide his message, axinge hem anon
If they were broken, or ought wo begon,
Or hadden nede of lodman or vitayle;
For of socour they sholde nothyng fayle,
For it was outrely the quenes wille.   1490
Jason answerde mekely and stylle:
"My lady," quod he, "thanke I hertely
Of hire goodnesse; us nedeth, trewely,
Nothyng as now, but that we wery be,
And come for to pleye out of the se   1495
Tyl that the wynd be better in oure weye."
This lady rometh by the clyf to pleye,
With hire meyne, endelong the stronde,
And fynt this Jason and this other stonde
In spekynge of this thyng, as I yow tolde.   1500
This Ercules and Jason gan beholde
How that the queen it was, and fayre hire
     grette
Anon-ryght as they with this lady mette;
And she tok hed, and knew by hyre manere,
By hire aray, by wordes, and by chere,   1505
That it were gentil-men of gret degre,
And to the castel with hire ledeth she
These straunge folk and doth hem gret honour,
And axeth hem of travayle and labour
That they han suffered in the salte se;   1510
So that, withinne a day, or two, or thre,
She knew, by folk that in his shipes be,
That it was Jason, ful of renone,
And Ercules, that hadde the grete los,
That soughten the aventures of Colcos;   1515
And dide hem honour more than before,
And with hem deled evere lenger the more,
For they ben worthy folk, withouten les.
And namely, most she spak with Ercules;
To hym hire herte bar, he shulde be   1520
Sad, wys, and trewe, of wordes avyse,
Withouten any other affeccioun
Of love, or evyl ymagynacyoun.
This Ercules hath so this Jason preysed   1524
That to the sonne he hath hym up areysed,

1438 **Oetes:** Aeëtes, king of Colchis and father of Medea
1440 **neveu:** nephew   **enhorte:** encourage
1448 And I will pay all the expenses
1453 **Argus:** the builder of the ship *Argo*
1457 **Argonautycon:** the *Argonautica* of Valerius Flaccus (a
first-century account of the adventure)
1459 **Philotetes:** Philoctetes
1463 **Lemnon:** Lemnos
1465 **Epistels:** Ovid's *Heroides*
1467 **Ysiphele:** Hypsipyle
1476 **usaunce:** custom

1480 **Ercules:** Hercules
1481 **cog:** small boat
1485 **cunnyngly:** skillfully
1488 **lodman:** pilot
1498 **stronde:** strand, shore
1513 **renone:** renown
1514 **los:** fame, reputation
1521 **avyse:** discreet

That half so trewe a man there nas of love
Under the cope of heven that is above;
And he was wis, hardy, secre, and ryche.
Of these thre poyntes there nas non hym liche:
Of fredom passede he, and lustyhede,   1530
Alle tho that lyven or been dede;
Therto so gret a gentilman was he,
And of Thessalye likly kyng to be.
There nas no lak, but that he was agast
To love, and for to speke shamefast.   1535
He hadde lever hymself to morder, and dye,
Than that men shulde a lovere hym espye.
"As wolde God that I hadde yive
My blod and flesh, so that I myghte live,
With the nones that he hadde owher a wif
For hys estat; for swich a lusty lyf   1541
She shulde lede with this lusty knyght!"
    And al this was compassed on the nyght
Bytwixe hym Jason and this Ercules.
Of these two here was a shrewed lees,   1545
To come to hous upon an innocent!
For to bedote this queen was here assent.
And Jason is as coy as is a mayde;
He loketh pitously, but nought he sayde,
But frely yaf he to hire conseyleres   1550
Yiftes grete, and to hire officeres.
As wolde God I leyser hadde and tyme
By proces al his wowyng for to ryme!
But in this hous if any fals lovere be,   1554
Ryght as hymself now doth, ryght so dide he,
With feynynge, and with every subtil dede.
Ye gete namore of me, but ye wole rede
Th'origynal, that telleth al the cas.
    The somme is this: that Jason wedded was
Unto this queen and tok of hir substaunce   1560
What so hym leste unto his purveyaunce;
And upon hire begat he children two,
And drogh his sayl and saw hir nevere mo.
A letter sente she to hym, certeyn,
Which were to longe to wryten and to sen,   1565
And hym reprevith of his grete untrouthe,
And preyeth him on hire to have som routhe.
And of his children two she seyde hym this:
That they ben lyk of alle thyng, ywis,

To Jason, save they coude nat begile;   1570
And preyede God, or it were longe while,
That she that hadde his herte yraft hire fro
Moste fynden hym untrewe to hir also,
And that she moste bothe hire chyldren spylle,
And alle tho that sufferede hym his wille.   1575
And trewe to Jason was she al hire lyf,
And evere kepte hire chast, as for his wif;
Ne nevere hadde she joye at hire herte,
But deyede for his love, of sorwes smerte.

2. *The Legend of Medea*

    To Colcos comen is this duc Jasoun,   1580
That is of love devourer and dragoun.
As mater apetiteth forme alwey
And from forme into forme it passen may,
Or as a welle that were botomles,
Ryght so can false Jason have no pes.   1585
For to desyren thourgh his apetit
To don with gentil women his delyt,
This is his lust and his felicite.
    Jason is romed forth to the cyte
That whilom cleped was Jaconitos,   1590
That was the mayster-toun of al Colcos,
And hath ytold the cause of his comyng
Unto Oetes, of that contre kyng,
Preyinge hym that he moste don his assay
To gete the fles of gold if that he may;   1595
Of which the kyng assenteth to his bone,
And doth hym honour, as it was to done,
So fer forth that his doughter and his eyr,
Medea, which that was so wis and fayr
That fayrer say there nevere man with ye,   1600
He made hire don to Jason companye
At mete, and sitte by hym in the halle.
    Now was Jason a semely man withalle,
And lyk a lord, and hadde a gret renoun,
And of his lok as real as a leoun,   1605
And goodly of his speche, and famiier,
And coude of love al craft and art pleyner
Withoute bok, with everych observaunce.
And, as Fortune hire oughte a foul myschaunce,
She wex enamoured upon this man.   1610
    "Jason," quod she, "for ought I se or can,
As of this thyng the whiche ye ben aboute,
Ye han youreself yput in moche doute.
For whoso wol this aventure acheve,
He may nat wel asterten, as I leve,   1615
Withouten deth, but I his helpe be.

1530 **lustyhede:** vigor
1534 **but that:** except that
1538–40 "Would God that I had given my blood and flesh, provided I still might live, if only he had a worthy wife [*wif For hys estat*]." This seems to mean "I would gladly give him my flesh and blood, if only I could live to see the outcome." (R.)
1545 **lees:** deception
1546 **To come to hous upon:** to become intimate with
1547 **bedote:** make a fool of
1548 **coy:** demure
1553 **wowyng:** wooing, courtship

1582 **apetiteth:** desires, has a natural tendency toward
1607 **pleyner:** fully, completely
1609 **hire oughte:** owed her
1613 **doute:** danger

But natheles, it is my wylle," quod she,
"To fortheren yow so that ye shal nat die,
But turnen sound hom to youre Tessalye."
    "My ryghte lady," quod this Jason tho,   1620
"That ye han of my deth or of my wo
Any reward, and don me this honour,
I wot wel that my myght ne my labour
May nat disserve it in my lyves day.
God thanke yow there I ne can ne may!   1625
Youre man I am, and lowely yow beseche
To ben my helpe, withoute more speche;
But, certes, for my deth shal I nat spare."
    Tho gan this Medea to hym declare
The peril of this cas from poynt to poynt,   1630
And of his batayle, and in what disjoynt
He mote stonde, of which no creature
Save only she ne myghte his lyf assure.
And shortly to the poynt ryght for to go,
They been acorded ful bytwixe hem two   1635
That Jason shal hire wedde, as trewe knyght;
And terme set to come sone at nyght
Unto hire chamber and make there his oth
Upon the goddes, that he for lef or loth
Ne sholde nevere hire false, nyght ne day,   1640
To ben hire husbonde whil he lyve may,
As she that from his deth hym saved here.
And hereupon at nyght they mette in-feere,
And doth his oth, and goth with hire to bedde;
And on the morwe upward he hym spedde,
For she hath taught hym how he shal nat fayle
The fles to wynne and stynten his batayle;
And saved hym his lyf and his honour;   1648

And gat hym a name ryght as a conquerour,
Ryght thorugh the sleyghte of hire enchaunte-
        ment.   1650
    Now hath Jason the fles, and hom is went
With Medea, and tresor ful gret won;
But unwist of hire fader is she gon
To Tessaly with Duk Jason hire lef,
That afterward hath brought hire to myschef.
For as a traytour he is from hire go,   1656
And with hire lafte his yonge children two,
And falsly hath betraysed hire, allas,
As evere in love a chef traytour he was;
And wedded yit the thridde wif anon,   1660
That was the doughter of the kyng Creon.
    This is the mede of lovynge and guerdoun
That Medea receyved of Jasoun
Ryght for hire trouthe and for hire kyndenesse,
That lovede hym beter than hireself, I gesse,
And lafte hire fader and hire herytage.   1666
And of Jason this is the vassellage,
That in his dayes nas ther non yfounde
So fals a lovere goinge on the grounde.
And therfore in hire letter thus she seyde   1670
Fyrst, whan she of his falsnesse hym upbreyde:
"Whi lykede me thy yelwe her to se
More than the boundes of myn honeste?
Why lykede me thy youthe and thy fayrnesse,
And of thy tonge, the infynyt graciousnesse?
O, haddest thow in thy conquest ded ybe,   1676
Ful mikel untrouthe hadde ther deyd with the!"
Wel can Ovyde hire letter in vers endyte,
Which were as now to long for me to wryte.

Explicit Legenda Ysiphile et Medee, martirum.

1639 **for lef or loth:** for any reason

1652 **won:** abundance
1667 **vassellage:** knightly virtue
1669 **goinge on the grounde:** i.e., alive
1677 **mikel:** much
Explicit, *etc.:* Here ends the Legend of Hypsipyle and Medea, martyrs.

V

THE LEGEND OF LUCRECE

Incipit Legenda Lucrecie Rome, martiris.

Now mot I seyn the exilynge of kynges   1680
Of Rome, for here horible doinges,
And of the laste kyng Tarquinius,
As seyth Ovyde and Titus Lyvius.
But for that cause telle I nat this storye,
But for to preyse and drawe to memorye   1685
The verray wif, the verray trewe Lucresse,
That for hyre wifhod and hire stedefastnesse
Nat only that these payens hire comende,
But he that cleped is in oure legende
The grete Austyn hath gret compassioun   1690
Of this Lucresse, that starf at Rome toun;
And in what wise, I wol but shortly trete,
And of this thyng I touche but the grete.

Whan Ardea beseged was aboute   1694
With Romeyns, that ful sterne were and stoute,
Ful longe lay the sege and lytel wroughten,
So that they were half idel, as hem thoughten;
And in his pley Tarquinius the yonge
Gan for to jape, for he was lyght of tonge,
And seyde that it was an ydel lyf;   1700
No man dide there no more than his wif.
"And lat us speke of wyves, that is best;
Preyse every man his owene as hym lest,
And with oure speche lat us ese oure herte."

A knyght that highte Colatyn up sterte,
And seyde thus: "Nay, sire, it is no nede   1706
To trowen on the word, but on the dede.
I have a wif," quod he, "that, as I trowe,
Is holden good of alle that evere hire knowe.
Go we to-nyght to Rome, and we shal se."   1710
Tarquinius answerde, "That liketh me."
To Rome be they come, and faste hem dyghte
To Colatynes hous and doun they lyghte,
Tarquinius and ek this Colatyn.
The husbonde knew the estris wel and fyn,

And prively into the hous they gon,   1716
Nor at the yate porter nas there non,
And at the chambre-dore they abyde.
This noble wif sat by hire beddes side
Dischevele, for no malyce she ne thoughte;
And softe wolle oure bok seyth that she
        wroughte   1721
To kepen hire from slouthe and idelnesse;
And bad hire servaunts don hire besynesse,
And axeth hem, "What tydyngs heren ye?
How seyth men of the sege, how shal it be?
God wolde the walles were falle adoun!   1726
Myn husbonde is to longe out of this toun,
For which the drede doth me so to smerte
That with a swerd it stingeth to myn herte
Whan I thynke on the sege or on that place.
God save my lord, I preye hym for his grace!"
And therwithal ful tenderly she wep,   1732
And of hire werk she tok no more kep,
And mekely she let hyre eyen falle;
And thilke semblaunt sat hire wel withalle.
And eek hire teres, ful of honeste,   1736
Embelished hire wifly chastite;
Hyre contenaunce is to hire herte dygne,
For they acorde bothe in dede and sygne.
And with that word hire husbonde Colatyn,
Or she of him was war, com stertynge in   1741
And seyde, "Drede the nat, for I am here!"
And she anon up ros with blysful chere
And kiste hym, as of wives is the wone.

Tarquinius, this proude kynges sone,   1745
Conceyved hath hire beaute and hyre cheere,
Hire yelwe her, hire shap, and hire manere,
Hire hew, hire wordes, that she hath com-
        pleyned
(And by no craft hire beaute nas nat feyned),
And caughte to this lady swich desyr   1750
That in his herte brende as any fyr,
So wodly that his wit was al forgeten.

Incipit, *etc.:* Here begins the Legend of Lucretia of Rome, martyr.
1683 **Titus Lyvius:** Livy, the Roman historian
1686 **Lucresse:** Lucretia
1690 **Austyn:** St. Augustine
1694 **Ardea:** capital of the Rutuli, in Latium
1705 **Colatyn:** Collatinus
1715 **estris:** arrangement of the interior apartments   **wel and fyn:** completely

1721 **wolle:** wool   **oure bok:** Ovid's *Fasti*   **wroughte:** worked on, spun
1725 **how shal it be:** how is it said to be
1738 **dygne:** suitable
1752 **wodly:** madly, passionately   **his wit was al forgeten:** he lost his wits

For wel thoghte he she wolde nat ben geten;
And ay the more that he was in dispayr,
The more he coveyteth and thoughte hire fayr.
His blynde lust was al his coveytynge.   1756
 A-morwe, whan the brid began to synge,
Unto the sege he cometh ful privily,
And by hymself he walketh soberly,   1759
Th'ymage of hire recordynge alwey newe:
"Thus lay hire her, and thus fresh was hyre
          hewe;
Thus sat, thus spak, thus span; this was hire
          chere;
Thus fayr she was, and this was hire manere."
Al this conseit hys herte hath newe ytake.
And as the se, with tempest al toshake,   1765
That after, whan the storm is al ago,
Yit wol the water quappe a day or two,
Ryght so, thogh that hire forme were absent,
The plesaunce of hire forme was present;
But natheles, nat plesaunce but delit,   1770
Or an unrightful talent, with dispit —
"For, maugre hyre, she shal my leman be!
Hap helpeth hardy man alday," quod he;
"What ende that I make, it shal be so."   1774
And girte hym with his swerd and gan to go,
And forth he rit til he to Rome is come,
And al alone his wey than hath he nome
Unto the hous of Colatyn ful ryght.
Doun was the sonne and day hath lost his
          lyght;
And in he cometh into a prive halke,   1780
And in the nyght ful thefly gan he stalke,
Whan every wight was to his reste brought,
Ne no wight hadde of tresoun swich a thought.
Were it by wyndow or by other gyn,
With swerd ydrawe shortly he com in   1785
There as she lay, this noble wif Lucresse.
And as she wok, hire bed she felte presse.
"What beste is that," quod she, "that weyeth
          thus?"
"I am the kynges sone, Tarquinius,"
Quod he, "but, and thow crye or noyse make,
Or if there any creature awake,   1791
By thilke God that formed man alyve,
This swerd thourghout thyn herte shal I ryve."
And therwithal unto hire throte he sterte,   1794
And sette the poynt al sharp upon hire herte.
No word she spak, she hath no myght therto.

1762 span: spun
1767 quappe: toss about
1775 girte hym with his swerd: buckled on his sword
1780 halke: corner, nook
1781 stalke: move stealthily

What shal she seyn? Hire wit is al ago.
Ryght as a wolf that fynt a lomb alone,   1798
To whom shal she compleyne or make mone?
What, shal she fyghte with an hardy knyght?
Wel wot men that a woman hath no myght.
What, shal she crye, or how shal she asterte
That hath hire by the throte with swerd at
          herte?
She axeth grace, and seyth al that she can.
"Ne wilt thow nat," quod he, this crewel man,
"As wisly Jupiter my soule save,   1806
As I shal in the stable slen thy knave,
And ley hym in thy bed, and loude crye
That I the fynde in swich avouterye.
And thus thow shalt be ded and also lese   1810
Thy name, for thow shalt non other chese."
 These Romeyns wyves lovede so here name
At thilke tyme, and dredde so the shame,
That, what for fer of sclaunder and drede of
          deth,
She loste bothe at ones wit and breth,   1815
And in a swogh she lay, and wex so ded
Men myghte smyten of hire arm or hed;
She feleth no thyng, neyther foul ne fayr.
 Tarquinius, that art a kynges eyr,
And sholdest, as by lynage and by ryght,   1820
Don as a lord and as a verray knyght,
Whi hastow don dispit to chivalrye?
Whi hastow don this lady vilanye?
Allas, of the this was a vileyns dede!
 But now to purpos; in the story I rede,   1825
Whan he was gon and this myschaunce is falle,
This lady sente after hire frendes alle,
Fader, moder, husbonde, alle yfeere;
And al dischevele, with hire heres cleere,
In habit swich as women used tho   1830
Unto the buryinge of hire frendes go,
She sit in halle with a sorweful sighte.
Hyre frendes axen what hire eylen myghte,
And who was ded; and she sit ay wepynge;
A word, for shame, forth ne myght she brynge,
Ne upon hem she durste nat beholde.   1836
But atte last of Tarquyny she hem tolde
This rewful cas and al thys thing horryble.
The woo to tellen were an impossible,
That she and al hir frendes made attones.   1840
Al hadde folkes hertes ben of stones,
Hyt myght have maked hem upon hir rewe,
Hir herte was so wyfly and so trewe.
She sayde that, for hir gylt ne for hir blame,
Hir husbonde shulde nat have the foule name,
That wolde she nat suffre by no wey.   1846
And they answerden alle, upon hir fey,

That they forgave yt hyr, for yt was ryght;
It was no gilt, it lay not in hir myght;
And seyden hir ensamples many oon.   1850
But al for noght; for thus she seyde anoon:
"Be as be may," quod she, "of forgyvyng,
I wol not have noo forgyft for nothing."
But pryvely she kaughte forth a knyf,
And therwithal she rafte hirself hir lyf;   1855
And as she fel adoun, she kaste hir lok,
And of hir clothes yet she hede tok.
For in hir fallynge yet she had a care,
Lest that hir fet or suche thyng lay bare;
So wel she loved clennesse and eke trouthe.
Of hir had al the toun of Rome routhe,   1861
And Brutus by hir chaste blood hath swore
That Tarquyn shulde ybanysshed be therfore,
And al hys kyn; and let the peple calle,
And openly the tale he tolde hem alle,   1865
And openly let cary her on a bere

Thurgh al the toun, that men may see and here
The horryble dede of hir oppressyoun,
Ne never was ther kyng in Rome toun
Syn thilke day; and she was holden there   1870
A seynt, and ever hir day yhalwed dere
As in hir lawe; and thus endeth Lucresse,
The noble wyf, as Tytus bereth witnesse.
    I telle hyt for she was of love so trewe,
Ne in hir wille she chaunged for no newe;   1875
And for the stable herte, sadde and kynde,
That in these wymmen men may alday fynde.
Ther as they kaste hir herte, there it dwelleth.
For wel I wot that Crist himself telleth
That in Israel, as wyd as is the lond,   1880
That so gret feyth in al that he ne fond
As in a woman; and this is no lye.
And as of men, loke ye which tirannye
They doon alday; assay hem whoso lyste,
The trewest ys ful brotel for to triste.   1885

Explicit Legenda Lucrecie Rome, martiris.

VI
THE LEGEND OF ARIADNE

Incipit Legenda Adriane de Athenes.

Juge infernal, Mynos, of Crete kyng,
Now cometh thy lot, now comestow on the
        ryng.
Nat for thy sake oonly write I this storye,
But for to clepe ageyn unto memorye
Of Theseus the grete untrouthe of love;   1890
For which the goddes of the heven above
Ben wrothe, and wreche han take for thy synne.
Be red for shame! Now I thy lyf begynne.
    Mynos, that was the myghty kyng of Crete,
That hadde an hundred citees stronge and
        grete,   1895
To scole hath sent hys sone Androgeus,
To Athenes; of the which hyt happed thus,

That he was slayn, lernynge philosophie,
Ryght in that citee, nat but for envye.
The grete Mynos, of the which I speke,   1900
Hys sones deth ys come for to wreke.
Alcathoe he besegeth harde and longe;
But natheles, the walles be so stronge,
And Nysus, that was kyng of that citee,
So chevalrous, that lytel dredeth he;   1905
Of Mynos or hys ost tok he no cure,
Til on a day befel an aventure,
That Nysus doughter stod upon the wal,
And of the sege saw the maner al.
So happed it that at a scarmishyng   1910

1853 **forgyft:** forgiveness

Incipit, *etc.*: Here begins the Legend of Ariadne of Athens.
1886 **Juge infernal:** judge in hell; Minos of Crete was thought to
be identical with Minos, judge of the underworld.
1887 **lot:** turn **on the ryng:** into the arena
1892 **wreche:** vengeance

1871 **yhalwed:** worshipped
1879 **Crist himselve telleth:** Matt. 15.28.
Explicit, *etc.*: Here ends the Legend of Lucretia of Rome,
martyr.

1902 **Alcathoe:** the citadel at Megara, near Athens
1908 **Nysus doughter:** Scylla, daughter of Nisus, king of Megara
1909 **the maner al:** the whole affair
1910 **scarmishyng:** skirmish

She caste hire herte upon Mynos the kyng,
For his beaute and for his chyvalrye,
So sore that she wende for to dye.
And, shortly of this proces for to pace,
She made Mynos wynnen thilke place,   1915
So that the cite was al at his wille,
To saven whom hym leste or elles spille.
But wikkedly he quitte hire kyndenesse,
And let hire drenche in sorwe and distresse,
Nere that the goddes hadde of hire pite;   1920
But that tale were to long as now for me.
Athenes wan thys kyng Mynos also,
As Alcathoe, and other tounes mo.
And this th'effect, that Mynos hath so driven
Hem of Athenes that they mote hym yiven
From yer to yer hire owene children dere   1926
For to be slayne right as ye shal here.

   This Mynos hadde a monstre, a wiked best,
That was so crewel that, withoute arest,   1929
Whan that a man was brought in his presence,
He wolde hym ete; ther helpeth no defence.
And every thridde yeer, withouten doute,
They caste lot, and as it com aboute
On riche, on pore, he moste his sone take,
And of his child he moste present make   1935
Unto Minos, to save hym or to spylle,
Or lete his best devoure hym at his wille.
And this hath Mynos don, ryght in dispit;
To wreke his sone was set al his delyt,
And maken hem of Athenes his thral   1940
From yer to yer, whil that he liven shal;
And hom he sayleth whan this toun is wonne.
This wiked custom is so longe yronne,
Til that of Athenes kyng Egeus
Mot senden his owene sone, Theseus,   1945
Sith that the lot is fallen hym upon,
To ben devoured, for grace is there non.
And forth is lad this woful yonge knyght
Unto the court of kyng Mynos ful ryght,
And into a prysoun, fetered, cast is he   1950
Tyl thilke tyme he sholde freten be.

   Wel maystow wepe, O woful Theseus,
That art a kynges sone, and dampned thus.
Me thynketh this, that thow were depe yholde
To whom that savede thee from cares colde!
And if now any woman helpe the,   1956
Wel oughtestow hire servaunt for to be,
And ben hire trewe lovere yer be yere!
But now to come ageyn to my matere.

1928 **monstre**: the Minotaur, half bull and half man
1931 **defence**: means of defense, resistance
1933 **caste lot**: drew lots
1944 **Egeus**: Aegeus
1954 **depe yholde**: deeply obligated

The tour there as this Theseus is throwe   1960
Doun in the botom derk and wonder lowe,
Was joynynge in the wal to a foreyne;
And it was longynge to the doughtren tweyne
Of Mynos, that in hire chaumbers grete
Dwellten above, toward the mayster-strete
Of Athenes, in joye and in solas.   1966
Noot I not how, it happede par cas,
As Theseus compleynede hym by nyghte,
The kynges doughter, Adryane that highte,
And ek hire syster Phedra, herden al   1970
His compleynynge as they stode on the wal
And lokeden upon the bryghte mone.
Hem leste nat to go to bedde so sone;
And of his wo they hadde compassioun.
A kynges sone to ben in swich prysoun,   1975
And ben devoured, thoughte hem gret pite.
This Adryane spak to hire syster fre,
And seyde, "Phedra, leve syster dere,
This woful lordes sone may ye nat here,
How pitously compleyneth he his kyn,   1980
And ek his povre estat that he is in,
And gilteles? Now, certes, it is routhe!
And if ye wol assenten, by my trouthe,
He shal ben holpen, how so that we do."
Phedra answerde, "Ywis, me is as wo   1985
For hym as evere I was for any man;
And, to his help, the beste red I can
Is that we do the gayler prively
To come and speke with us hastily,
And don this woful man with hym to come.
For if he may this monstre overcome,   1991
Thanne were he quyt; ther is non other bote.
Lat us wel taste hym at his herte-rote,
That if so be that he a wepen have,
Wher that he dar, his lyf to kepe and save, 1995
Fyghten with the fend, and hym defende.
For in the prysoun ther he shal descende,
Ye wote wel that the beste is in a place
That nys nat derk, and hath roum eek and
                    space
To welde an ax, or swerd, or staf, or knyf; 2000
So that, me thynketh, he shulde save his lyf.
If that he be a man, he shal do so.
And we shul make hym balles ek also
Of wex and tow, that whan he gapeth faste,
Into the bestes throte he shal hem caste   2005

1962 **joynynge**: adjoining   **foreyne**: privy (chambre foreine)
1967 **par cas**: by chance
1969 **Adryane**: Ariadne
1970 **Phedra**: Phaedra
1993 **taste**: test
1999 **roum**: room, space
2004 **tow**: unspun flax   **he gapeth faste**: he (the Minotaur)
opens his mouth wide

To slake his hunger and encombre his teth;
And right anon, whan that Theseus seth
The beste achoked, he shal on hym lepe
To slen hym or they comen more to-hepe.
This wepen shal the gayler, or that tyde,   2010
Ful prively withinne the prysoun hyde;
And for the hous is krynkeled to and fro,
And hath so queynte weyes for to go —
For it is shapen as the mase is wrought —
Therto have I a remedye in my thought,   2015
That, by a clewe of twyn, as he hath gon,
The same weye he may returne anon,
Folwynge alwey the thred as he hath come.
And whan that he this beste hath overcome,
Thanne may he flen awey out of this drede,
And ek the gayler may he with hym lede,   2021
And hym avaunce at hom in his cuntre,
Syn that so gret a lordes sone is he.
This is my red, if that he dar it take."
What sholde I lenger sarmoun of it make?   2025
This gayler cometh, and with hym Theseus.
Whan these thynges ben acorded thus,
Adoun sit Theseus upon his kne —
"The ryghte lady of my lyf," quod he,
"I, sorweful man, ydampned to the deth,   2030
Fro yow, whil that me lasteth lyf or breth,
I wol nat twynne, after this aventure,
But in youre servise thus I wol endure,
That, as a wreche unknowe, I wol yow serve
For everemo, til that myn herte sterve.   2035
Forsake I wol at hom myn herytage,
And, as I seyde, ben of youre court a page,
If that ye vouche-sauf that in this place
Ye graunte me to han so gret a grace   2039
That I may han nat but my mete and drynke.
And for my sustenaunce yit wol I swynke,
Ryght as yow leste, that Mynos ne no wight —
Syn that he saw me nevere with eyen syght —
Ne no man elles, shal me conne espye;
So slyly and so wel I shal me gye,   2045
And me so wel disfigure and so lowe,
That in this world ther shal no man me knowe,
To han my lyf, and for to han presence
Of yow, that don to me this excellence.
And to my fader shal I sende here   2050
This worthy man that is now youre gaylere,
And hym so gwerdone that he shal wel be

Oon of the gretteste men of my cuntre.
And if I durste seyn, my lady bryght,
I am a kynges sone and ek a knyght.   2055
As wolde God, if that it myghte be
Ye weren in my cuntre, alle thre,
And I with yow to bere yow compaignye,
Thanne shulde ye se if that I therof lye.
And if I profre yow in low manere   2060
To ben youre page and serven yow ryght here,
But I yow serve as lowly in that place,
I preye to Mars to yeve me swich a grace
That shames deth on me ther mote falle,
And deth and poverte to my frendes alle;   2065
And that my spirit by nyghte mote go,
After my deth, and walke to and fro,
That I mote of traytour have a name,
For which my spirit go, to do me shame!
And if I evere cleyme other degre,   2070
But if ye vouche-sauf to yeve it me,
As I have seyd, of shames deth I deye!
And mercy, lady! I can nat elles seye."
   A semely knyght was Theseus to se,
And yong, but of a twenty yer and thre.   2075
But whoso hadde seyn his contenaunce,
He wolde have wept for routhe of his pen-
                                        aunce;
For which this Adryane in this manere
Answerde hym to his profre and to his chere:
"A kynges sone, and ek a knyght," quod she,
"To ben my servaunt in so low degre,   2081
God shilde it, for the shame of wemen alle,
And lene me nevere swich a cas befalle!
But sende yow grace of herte and sleyghte also,
Yow to defende and knyghtly slen youre fo,
And leve hereafter that I may yow fynde   2086
To me and to my syster here so kynde,
That I repente nat to yeve yow lyf!
Yit were it betere that I were youre wyf,
Syn that ye ben as gentil born as I,   2090
And have a reaume, nat but faste by,
Than that I suffered, gilteles, yow sterve,
Or that I let yow as a page serve.
It nys no profre as unto youre kynrede;
But what is that that man nyl don for drede?
And to my syster, syn that it is so   2096
That she mot gon with me, if that I go,
Or elles suffre deth as wel as I,
That ye unto youre sone as trewely

2006 **encombre:** encumber (by sticking to)
2010 **gayler:** jailer
2012 **hous:** the Labyrinth   **krynkeled:** full of winding passages
2014 **mase:** maze
2016 **clewe of twyn:** ball of twine
2025 **sarmoun:** talk, sermon
2046 **disfigure:** disguise
2052 **gwerdone:** reward

2064 **shames deth:** shameful death
2070 **other degre:** higher rank than that of a page
2079 **profre:** offer
2082 **shilde:** forbid
2099 **youre sone:** Hippolytus

Don hire ben wedded at youre hom-comyng.
This is the final ende of al this thyng;   2101
Ye swere it here, upon al that may be sworn."
   "Ye, lady myn," quod he, "or ellis torn
Mote I be with the Mynotaur to-morwe!
And haveth hereof myn herte blod to borwe,
If that ye wole; if I hadde knyf or spere,   2106
I wolde it laten out, and theron swere,
For thanne at erst I wot ye wole me leve.
By Mars, that is the chef of my beleve,
So that I myghte liven and nat fayle   2110
To-morwe for t'acheve my batayle,
I wolde nevere from this place fle,
Til that ye shulde the verray preve se.
For now, if that the sothe I shal yow say,
I have yloved yow ful many a day,   2115
Thogh ye ne wiste it nat, in my cuntre,
And aldermost desired yow to se
Of any erthly livynge creature.
Upon my trouthe I swere and yow assure,
This sevene yer I have youre servaunt be.   2120
Now have I yow, and also have ye me,
My dere herte, of Athenes duchesse!"
   This lady smyleth at his stedefastnesse,
And at his hertely wordes and his chere,
And to hyre sister seyde in this manere,   2125
Al softely: "Now, syster myn," quod she,
"Now be we duchesses, bothe I and ye,
And sekered to the regals of Athenes,
And bothe hereafter likly to ben quenes;
And saved from his deth a kynges sone,   2130
As evere of gentil women is the wone
To save a gentyl man, emforth hire myght,
In honest cause, and namely in his ryght.
Me thynketh no wight oughte us herof blame,
Ne beren us therfore an evil name."   2135
And shortly of this mater for to make,
This Theseus of hire hath leve take,
And every poynt was performed in dede
As ye han in this covenaunt herd me rede.
His wepne, his clewe, his thyng, that I have
   sayd,   2140
Was by the gayler in the hous yleyd,
Ther as the Mynotaur hath his dwellynge,
Ryght faste by the dore, at his entrynge.
And Theseus is lad unto his deth,
And forth unto this Mynotaur he geth,   2145

2124 hertely: sincere, from the heart
2128 sekered: betrothed   regals: royal family
2130 And saved: and (to have) saved. The construction changes
from future to present perfect.
2132 emforth hire myght: insofar as they have power
2140 clewe: ball of twine
2145 geth: goes

And by the techynge of this Adryane
He overcom this beste and was his bane;
And out he cometh by the clewe agayn
Ful prively, whan he this beste hath slayn;
And by the gayler geten hath a barge,   2150
And of his wyves tresor gan it charge,
And tok his wif, and ek hire sister fre,
And ek the gayler, and with hem alle thre
Is stole awey out of the lond by nyghte,
And to the contre of Ennopye hym dyghte   2155
There as he hadde a frend of his knowynge.
There feste they, there daunce they and synge;
And in his armes hath this Adryane,
That of the beste hath kept hym from his bane;
And gat hym there a newe barge anon,   2160
And of his contre-folk a ful gret won,
And taketh his leve, and homward sayleth he.
And in an yle amyd the wilde se,
Ther as there dwelled creature non
Save wilde bestes, and that ful many oon,   2165
He made his ship a-londe for to sette;
And in that yle half a day he lette,
And seyde that on the lond he moste hym reste.
His maryners han don ryght as hym leste;
And, for to tellen shortly in this cas,   2170
Whan Adryane his wif aslepe was,
For that hire syster fayrer was than she,
He taketh hire in his hond and forth goth he
To shipe, and as a traytour stal his wey,
Whil that this Adryane aslepe lay,   2175
And to his contre-ward he sayleth blyve —
A twenty devel-wey the wynd hym dryve! —
And fond his fader drenched in the se.
   Me lest no more to speke of hym, parde.
These false lovers, poysoun be here bane!   2180
But I wol turne ageyn to Adryane,
That is with slep for werynesse atake.
Ful sorwefully hire herte may awake.
Allas, for thee myn herte hath now pite!
Ryght in the dawenyng awaketh she,   2185
And gropeth in the bed, and fond ryght nought.
"Allas," quod she, "that evere I was wrought!
I am betrayed!" and hire her torente,
And to the stronde barefot faste she wente,
And cryed, "Theseus, myn herte swete!   2190
Where be ye, that I may nat with yow mete,
And myghte thus with bestes ben yslayn?"
The holwe rokkes answerde hire agayn.
No man she saw, and yit shyned the mone,

2155 Ennopye: Oenopia (the island of Aegina)
2161 contre-folk: fellow countrymen

And hye upon a rokke she wente sone,   2195
And saw his barge saylynge in the se.
Cold wex hire herte, and ryght thus seyde she:
"Meker than ye fynde I the bestes wilde!"
Hadde he nat synne that hire thus begylde?
She cryed, "O turn ageyn, for routhe and
    synne!   2200
Thy barge hath nat al his meyne inne!"
Hire coverchef on a pole up steked she,
Ascaunce that he shulde it wel yse,
And hym remembre that she was behynde,
And turne ageyn, and on the stronde hire
    fynde.   2205
But al for nought; his wey he is ygon.
Adoun she fyl aswoune upon a ston;
And up she rist, and kyssed, in al hire care,
The steppes of his fet ther he hath fare,   2209
And to hire bed ryght thus she speketh tho:

"Thow bed," quod she, "that hast receyved two,
Thow shalt answere of two, and nat of oon!
Where is thy gretter part awey ygon?
Allas! Where shal I, wreche wight, become?
For thogh so be that ship or boot here come,
Hom to my contre dar I nat for drede.   2216
I can myselven in this cas nat rede."
What shulde I more telle hire compleynyng?
It is so long, it were an hevy thyng.
In hire Epistel Naso telleth al;   2220
But shortly to the ende I telle shal.
The goddes han hire holpen for pite,
And in the signe of Taurus men may se
The stones of hire corone shyne clere.
I wol no more speke of this mateere;   2225
But thus this false lovere can begyle
His trewe love, the devel quyte hym his while!

Explicit Legenda Adriane de Athenes.

VII

THE LEGEND OF PHILOMELA

Incipit Legenda Philomene.

Deus dator formarum.

Thow yevere of the formes, that hast
    wrought
This fayre world and bar it in thy thought
Eternaly er thow thy werk began,   2230
Why madest thow, unto the slaunder of man,
Or, al be that it was nat thy doing,
As for that fyn, to make swich a thyng,
Whi sufferest thow that Tereus was bore,
That is in love so fals and so forswore,   2235
That fro this world up to the firste hevene
Corrumpeth whan that folk his name nevene?
And, as to me, so grisely was his dede
That, whan that I his foule storye rede,
Myne eyen wexe foule and sore also.   2240

Yit last the venym of so longe ago,
That it enfecteth hym that wol beholde
The storye of Tereus, of which I tolde.
   Of Trace was he lord, and kyn to Marte,   2244
The crewel god that stant with blody darte;
And wedded hadde he, with a blysful cheere,
Kyng Pandiones fayre doughter dere,
That highte Progne, flour of hire cuntre,
Thogh Juno lyst nat at the feste to be,
Ne Imeneus that god of wedyng is;   2250

2214 **Where shal I . . . become?:** what shall become of me?
2220 **hire Epistel:** *Heroides* 10
2223 **in the signe of Taurus:** when the sun is in the zodiacal sign of Taurus
2224 **stones of hire corone:** the constellation Corona Borealis, opposite Taurus
2227 **quyte hym his while:** repay him for his time (i.e., wreak revenge on him)
Explicit, *etc.:* Here ends the Legend of Ariadne of Athens.

2203 **Ascaunce:** as if (i.e., in the hope that)

Incipit, *etc.:* Here begins the Legend of Philomela. God is the giver of forms.
2228 **yevere:** giver
2236 **firste hevene:** outermost sphere
2240 **wexe foule:** grow painful

2241 **last** = *lasteth,* lasts
2244 **Trace:** Thrace **Marte:** Mars
2247 **Pandiones . . . doughter:** daughter of Pandion, king of Athens
2248 **Progne:** Procne
2249 **Juno:** wife of Jupiter and protectoress of marriage
2250 **Imeneus:** Hymen

But at the feste redy ben, ywis,
The Furies thre with al here mortal brond.
The oule al nyght aboute the balkes wond,
That prophete is of wo and of myschaunce.
This revel, ful of song and ek of daunce,   2255
Laste a fortenyght, or lytel lasse.
But shortly of this story for to passe,
For I am wery of hym for to telle,
Fyve yer his wif and he togeder dwelle,
Til on a day she gan so sore longe   2260
To sen hire sister that she say nat longe,
That for desyr she nyste what to seye.
But to hire husbonde gan she for to preye,
For Godes love, that she moste ones gon
Hyre syster for to sen, and come anon,   2265
Or elles, but she moste to hire wende,
She preyde hym that he wolde after hire sende;
And this was day by day al hire preyere,
With al humblesse of wifhod, word and chere.

This Tereus let make his shipes yare,   2270
And into Grece hymself is forth yfare.
Unto his fadyr-in-lawe gan he preye
To vouche-sauf that for a month or tweye
That Philomene, his wyves syster, myghte
On Progne his wyf but ones han a syghte —
"And she shal come to yow ageyn anon.   2276
Myself with hyre wol bothe come and gon,
And as myn hertes lyf I wol hire kepe."

This olde Pandion, this kyng, gan wepe
For tendernesse of herte for to leve   2280
His doughter gon, and for to yeve hire leve;
Of al this world he loveth nothyng so;
But at the laste leve hath she to go.
For Philomene with salte teres eke
Gan of hire fader grace to beseke   2285
To sen hire syster that she loveth so,
And hym embraseth with hire armes two.
And therwithal so yong and fayr was she
That, whan that Tereus saw hire beaute,   2289
And of aray that there was non hire lyche,
And yit of beaute was she two so ryche,
He caste his fyry herte upon hyre so
That he wol have hir, how so that it go;
And with his wiles kneled and so preyde,
Tyl at the laste Pandyon thus seyde: 2295
"Now, sone," quod he, "that art to me so dere,
I the betake my yonge doughter here
That bereth the keye of al myn hertes lyf.
And gret me wel my doughter and thy wif,
And yif hire leve somtyme for to pleye,   2300

That she may sen me ones er I deye."
And sothly, he hath mad hym riche feste,
And to his folk, the moste and ek the leste,
That with hym com; and yaf hym yiftes grete,
And hym conveyeth thourgh the mayster-strete
Of Athenes, and to the se hym broughte,   2306
And turneth hom; no malyce he ne thoughte.

The ores pullen forth the vessel faste,
And into Trace aryveth at the laste,
And up into a forest he hire ledde,   2310
And to a cave pryvely hym spedde;
And in this derke cave, yif hir leste,
Or leste nat, he bad hire for to reste;
Of which hire herte agros, and seyde thus:
"Where is my sister, brother Tereus?"   2315
And therwithal she wepte tenderly
And quok for fere, pale and pitously,
Ryght as the lamb that of the wolf is biten;
Or as the culver that of the egle is smiten,
And is out of his clawes forth escaped,   2320
Yit it is afered and awhaped,
Lest it be hent eft-sones; so sat she.
But utterly it may non other be.
By force hath this traytour don a dede,
That he hath reft hire of hire mayden-
    hede,   2325
Maugre hire hed, by strengthe and by his
    myght.
Lo! here a dede of men, and that a ryght!
She cryeth "Syster!" with ful loud a stevene,
And "Fader dere!" and "Help me, God in
    hevene!"
Al helpeth nat; and yit this false thef   2330
Hath don this lady yit a more myschef,
For fere lest she shulde his shame crye
And don hym openly a vilenye,
And with his swerd hire tonge of kerveth he,
And in a castel made hire for to be   2335
Ful pryvely in prisoun everemore,
And kepte hire to his usage and his store,
So that she myghte hym neveremore asterte.
O sely Philomene, wo is thyn herte!
God wreke thee, and sende the thy bone!   2340
Now is it tyme I make an ende sone.

This Tereus is to his wif ycome,
And in his armes hath his wif ynome,
And pitously he wep and shok his hed,
And swor hir that he fond hir sister ded;   2345
For which this sely Progne hath swich wo

2253 **balkes:** beams **wond:** wound about, flew
2261 **say nat longe:** had not seen for a long time
2266 **but she moste:** unless she could
2274 **Philomene:** Philomela

2314 **agros:** trembled
2317 **quok:** trembled
2319 **culver:** dove
2321 **awhaped:** confounded
2337 **to his usage and his store:** for his use and as his
possession

That nygh hire sorweful herte brak a-two.
And thus in terys lete I Progne dwelle,
And of hire sister forth I wol yow telle.
　This woful lady lerned hadde in youthe 2350
So that she werken and enbroude couthe,
And weven in hire stol the radevore
As it of wemen hath be woned yore.
And, sothly for to seyne, she hadde hire fille
Of mete and drynk, and clothyng at hire
　　　wille. 2355
She coude eek rede and wel ynow endyte,
But with a penne coude she nat wryte.
But letters can she weve to and fro,
So that, by that the yer was al ago,
She hadde ywoven in a stamyn large 2360
How she was brought from Athenes in a barge,
And in a cave how that she was brought;
And al the thyng that Tereus hath wrought,
She waf it wel, and wrot the storye above,
How she was served for hire systers love. 2365
And to a knave a ryng she yaf anon,
And preyed hym by signes for to gon
Unto the queen, and beren hir that cloth,
And by signes swor hym many an oth 2369
She wolde hym yeven what she geten myghte.

This knave anon unto the quene hym dyghte,
And tok it hire, and al the maner tolde.
And whan that Progne hath this thing beholde,
No word she spak, for sorwe and ek for rage,
But feynede hire to gon on pilgrymage 2375
To Bacus temple; and in a litel stounde
Hire dombe sister sittynge hath she founde,
Wepynge in the castel, here alone.
Allas! The wo, the compleynt, and the mone
That Progne upon hire doumbe syster mak-
　　　eth! 2380
In armes everych of hem other taketh,
And thus I late hem in here sorwe dwelle.
　The remenaunt is no charge for to telle,
For this is al and som: thus was she served,
That nevere harm agilte ne deserved 2385
Unto this crewel man, that she of wiste.
Ye may be war of men, if that yow liste.
For al be it that he wol nat, for shame,
Don as Tereus, to lese his name,
Ne serve yow as a morderour or a knave, 2390
Ful lytel while shal ye trewe hym have —
That wol I seyn, al were he now my brother —
But it so be that he may have non other.

Explicit Legenda Philomene.

VIII
THE LEGEND OF PHYLLIS

Incipit Legenda Phillis.

　By preve as wel as by autorite,
That wiked fruit cometh of a wiked tre, 2395
That may ye fynde, if that it like yow.
But for this ende I speke this as now,
To tellen yow of false Demophon.
In love a falser herde I nevere non,
But if it were his fader Theseus. 2400
"God, for his grace, fro swich oon kepe us!"

Thus may these women preyen that it here.
Now to the effect turne I of my matere.
　Destroyed is of Troye the cite;
This Demophon com seylynge in the se 2405
Toward Athenes, to his paleys large.
With hym com many a ship and many a barge
Ful of his folk, of whiche ful many oon
Is wounded sore, and sek, and wo begon,
As they han at th'asege longe yleyn. 2410
Byhynde hym com a wynd and ek a reyn
That shof so sore his sayl ne myghte stonde;

2351 **enbroude:** embroider
2352 **stol:** frame (for making tapestry)　**radevore:** tapestry
2360 **stamyn large:** broad woolen tapestry cloth
2364 **waf:** wove

Incipit, *etc.:* Here begins the Legend of Phyllis.
2398 **Demophon:** Demophoön, son of Theseus and Phaedra

2371 **hym dyghte:** hastened
Explicit, *etc.:* Here ends the Legend of Philomela.

Hym were levere than al the world a-londe,
So hunteth hym the tempest to and fro.
So derk it was, he coude nowher go;   2415
And with a wawe brosten was his stere.
His ship was rent so lowe, in swich manere,
That carpenter ne coude it nat amende.
The se, by nyghte, as any torche it brende
For wod, and possith hym now up, now doun,
Til Neptune hath of hym compassioun,   2421
And Thetis, Thorus, Triton, and they alle,
And maden hym upon a lond to falle,
Wherof that Phillis lady was and queene,
Ligurges doughter, fayrer on to sene   2425
Than is the flour ageyn the bryghte sonne.
Unnethe is Demophon to londe ywonne,
Wayk, and ek wery, and his folk forpyned
Of werynesse, and also enfamyned,
That to the deth he almost was ydriven.   2430
His wise folk to conseyl han hym yiven
To seken help and socour of the queen,
And loke what his grace myghte been,
And maken in that lond som chevysaunce,
To kepen hym fro wo and fro myschaunce.
For syk he was, and almost at the deth;   2436
Unnethe myghte he speke or drawe his breth,
And lyth in Rodopeya hym for to reste.
Whan he may walke, hym thoughte it was the
        beste
Unto the court to seken for socour.   2440
Men knewen hym wel and diden hym honour;
For of Athenes duk and lord was he,
As Theseus his fader hadde be,
That in his tyme was of gret renoun,
No man so gret in al the regyoun,   2445
And lyk his fader of face and of stature,
And fals of love; it com hym of nature.
As doth the fox Renard, the foxes sone,
Of kynde he coude his olde faders wone
Withoute lore, as can a drake swimme   2450
Whan it is caught and caryed to the brymme.
This honurable Phillis doth hym chere;
Hire liketh wel his port and his manere.
But, for I am agroted herebyforn

To wryte of hem that ben in love forsworn,
And ek to haste me in my legende,   2456
(Which to performe God me grace sende)
Therfore I passe shortly in this wyse.
Ye han wel herd of Theseus devyse
In the betraysynge of fayre Adryane   2460
That of hire pite kepte him from his bane.
At shorte wordes, ryght so Demophon
The same wey, the same path hath gon,
That dide his false fader Theseus.
For unto Phillis hath he sworen thus,   2465
To wedden hire, and hire his trouthe plyghte,
And piked of hire al the good he myghte,
Whan he was hol and sound, and hadde his
        reste;
And doth with Phillis what so that hym leste,
As wel coude I, if that me leste so,   2470
Tellen al his doynge to and fro.
    He seyde unto his contre moste he sayle,
For there he wolde hire weddynge aparayle,
As fel to hire honour and his also.
And openly he tok his leve tho,   2475
And hath hire sworn he wolde nat sojorne,
But in a month he wolde ageyn retorne;
And in that lond let make his ordenaunce
As verray lord, and tok the obeysaunce
Wel and homly, and let his shipes dighte,   2480
And hom he goth the nexte wey he myghte.
For unto Phillis yit ne com he nought,
And that hath she so harde and sore abought —
Allas! — that, as the storyes us recorde,   2484
She was hire owene deth ryght with a corde,
Whan that she saw that Demophon hire
        trayed.
But to hym first she wrot, and faste him prayed
He wolde come and hire delyvere of peyne,
As I reherce shal a word or tweyne.
Me lyste nat vouche-sauf on hym to swynke,
Ne spende on hym a penne ful of ynke,   2491
For fals in love was he, ryght as his syre.
The devil sette here soules bothe afyre!
But of the letter of Phillis wol I wryte
A word or two, althogh it be but lyte.   2495
"Thyn hostesse," quod she, "O Demophon,
Thy Phillis, which that is so wo begon,
Of Rodopeye, upon yow mot compleyne
Over the terme set bytwixe us tweyne,
That ye ne holde forward, as ye seyde.   2500
Youre anker, which ye in oure haven leyde,

2416 **brosten:** broken
2420 **For wod:** madly, "like mad"   **possith:** tosses
2421 **Neptune:** god of the sea
2422 **Thetis:** a nereid, a sea nymph   **Thorus:** unidentified, but
apparently a sea god; see n.   **Triton:** a sea god
2425 **Ligurges:** Lycurgus's
2428 **forpyned:** tormented
2429 **enfamyned:** famished
2434 **chevysaunce:** purchase of provisions
2438 **Rodopeya:** the country near Rhodope, a mountain range in
Thrace
2451 **brymme:** bank
2454 **agroted:** surfeited, fed up

2486 **trayed:** betrayed
2492 **syre:** father

Hyghte us that ye wolde comen, out of doute,
Or that the mone wente ones aboute.
But tymes foure the mone hath hid hire face,
Syn thilke day ye wente from this place,   2505
And foure tymes lyghte the world ageyn.
But for al that, yif I shal soothly seyn,
Yit hath the strem of Sytho nat ybrought
From Athenes the ship; yit cometh it noght.
And if that ye the terme rekene wolde   2510
As I or as a trewe lovere shulde,
I pleyne nat, God wot, byforn my day."
But al hire letter wryten I ne may
By order, for it were to me a charge;
Hire letter was ryght long and therto large.
But here and ther in rym I have it layd,   2516
There as me thoughte that she wel hath sayd.
She seyde, "Thy sayles come nat agen,
Ne to thy word there is no fey certeyn;
But I wot why ye come nat," quod she,   2520
"For I was of my love to yow to fre.
And of the goddes that ye han forswore,
Yif hire vengeaunce falle on yow therfore,
Ye be nat suffisaunt to bere the peyne.
To moche trusted I, wel may I pleyne,   2525
Upon youre lynage and youre fayre tonge,
And on youre teres falsly out yronge.
How coude ye wepe so by craft?" quod she.
"May there swiche teres feyned be?
Now certes, yif ye wol have in memorye,   2530
It oughte be to yow but lyte glorye
To han a sely mayde thus betrayed!

To God," quod she, "preye I, and ofte have
     prayed,
That it mot be the grettest prys of alle   2534
And most honour that evere the shal befalle!
And whan thyne olde auncestres peynted be,
In which men may here worthynesse se,
Thanne preye I God thow peynted be also
That folk may rede forby as they go,
'Lo! this is he that with his flaterye   2540
Bytraised hath and don hire vilenye
That was his trewe love in thought and dede!'
But sothly, of oo poynt yit may they rede,
That ye ben lyk youre fader as in this,
For he begiled Adriane, ywis,   2545
With swich an art and with swich subtilte
As thow thyselven hast begyled me.
As in that poynt, althogh it be nat fayr,
Thow folwest hym, certayn, and art his ayr.
But syn thus synfully ye me begile,   2550
My body mote ye se withinne a while,
Ryght in the haven of Athenes fletynge,
Withoute sepulture and buryinge,
Thogh ye ben harder than is any ston."
And whan this letter was forth sent anon,   2555
And knew how brotel and how fals he was,
She for dispeyr fordide hyreself, allas.
Swych sorwe hath she, for she besette hire so.
Be war, ye wemen, of youre subtyl fo,
Syn yit this day men may ensaumple se;   2560
And trusteth, as in love, no man but me.

Explicit Legenda Phillis.

IX
THE LEGEND OF HYPERMNESTRA

Incipit Legenda Ypermystre.

In Grece whilom weren brethren two,
Of whiche that oon was called Danao,
That many a sone hath of his body wonne,
As swiche false lovers ofte conne.   2565

Among his sones alle there was oon
That aldermost he lovede of everychoon.
And whan this child was born, this Danao
Shop hym a name and callede hym Lyno.
That other brother called was Egiste,   2570
That was of love as fals as evere hym liste,

2502 **Hyghte:** promised
2506 **lyghte:** lighted
2508 **strem of Sytho:** sea of Thrace

Incipit, *etc.:* Here begins the Legend of Hypermnestra.
2563 **Danao:** Danaus

Explicit, *etc.:* Here ends the Legend of Phyllis.
2567 **aldermost . . . of everychoon:** most of all
2569 **Lyno:** Lynceus
2570 **Egiste:** Aegyptus

And many a doughter gat he in his lyf;
Of whiche he gat upon his ryghte wyf
A doughter dere, and dide hire for to calle
Ypermystra, yongeste of hem alle.　　　2575
The whiche child of hire natyvyte
To alle thewes goode yborn was she,
As likede to the goddes er she was born,
That of the shef she sholde be the corn.
The Wirdes, that we clepen Destine,　　　2580
Hath shapen hire that she mot nedes be
Pyëtous, sad, wis, and trewe as stel,
As to these wemen it acordeth wel.
For thogh that Venus yaf hire gret beaute,
With Jupiter compouned so was she　　　2585
That conscience, trouthe, and drede of shame,
And of hyre wifhod for to kepe hire name,
This, thoughte hire, was felycite as here.
The rede Mars was that tyme of the yeere
So feble that his malyce is hym raft;　　　2590
Repressed hath Venus his crewel craft,
That, what with Venus and other oppressioun
Of houses, Mars his venim is adoun,
That Ypermystra dar nat handle a knyf
In malyce, thogh she shulde lese hire lyf.　　　2595
But natheles, as hevene gan tho turne,
To badde aspectes hath she of Saturne,
That made hire for to deyen in prisoun,
As I shal after make mencioun.

To Danao and Egistes also,　　　2600
Althogh so be that they were brethren two —
For thilke tyme was spared no lynage —
It lykede hem to make a maryage
Bytwixen Ypermystre and hym Lyno,
And casten swich a day it shal be so,　　　2605
And ful acorded was it utterly;
The aray is wrought, the tyme is faste by.
And thus Lyno hath of his faders brother
The doughter wedded, and ech of hem hath
　　　other.
The torches brennen, and the laumpes bryghte;
The sacryfices ben ful redy dighte;　　　2611
Th'encens out of the fyre reketh sote;
The flour, the lef is rent up by the rote
To maken garlondes and crounes hye.
Ful is the place of soun of minstralsye,　　　2615

Of songes amorous of maryage,
As thylke tyme was the pleyne usage.
And this was in the paleys of Egiste,
That in his hous was lord, ryght as hym lyste.
And thus the day they dryve to an ende;　　　2620
The frendes taken leve, and hom they wende;
The nyght is come, the bryd shal go to bedde.
Egistus to his chamber faste hym spedde,
And prively he let his doughter calle.　　　2624
Whan that the hous was voyded of hem alle,
He loketh on his doughter with glad chere
And to hire spak, as ye shal after here:
"My ryghte doughter, tresor of myn herte,
Syn fyrst that day that shapen was my sherte,
Or by the fatal systren had my dom,　　　2630
So nygh myn herte nevere thyng ne com
As thow, myn Ypermystre, doughter dere.
Tak hed what I, thy fader, seye the here,
And werk after thy wiser evere mo.
For alderfirst, doughter, I love the so　　　2635
That al the world to me nis half so lef;
Ne I nolde rede the to thy myschef
For al the good under the colde mone.
And what I mene, it shal be seyd right sone,
With protestacioun, as in this wyse,　　　2640
That, but thow do as I shal the devyse,
Thow shalt be ded, by hym that al hath
　　　wrought!
At shorte wordes, thow ne scapest nought
Out of my paleys or that thow be ded,
But thow consente and werke after my red;
Tak this to thee for ful conclusioun."　　　2646
　This Ypermystre caste hire eyen doun,
And quok as doth the lef of aspe grene.
Ded wex hire hew, and lyk an ash to sene,
And seyde, "Lord and fader, al youre wille,
After my myght, God wot, I shal fulfille,　　　2651
So it to me be no confusioun."
"I nele," quod he, "have non excepcioun";
And out he caught a knyf, as rasour kene.
"Hyd this," quod he, "that it be nat ysene;
And whan thyn husbonde is to bedde go,　　　2656
Whil that he slepeth, kit his throte atwo.
For in my dremes it is warned me
How that my nevew shal my bane be,
But which I noot, wherfore I wol be siker.　　　2660
If thow sey nay, we two shul have a biker,
As I have seyd, by hym that I have sworn!"
　This Ipermystre hath nygh hire wit forlorn;
And, for to passen harmles of that place,

2575 **Ypermystra:** Hypermnestra
2580 **Wirdes:** Fates
2582 **Pyëtous:** compassionate
2585 **With Jupiter compouned:** tempered by the influence of Jupiter
2589 **that tyme:** the time of Hypermnestra's birth, when Venus and Jupiter were in conjunction and repressed the evil influence of Mars; however, she suffers from the evil influence of Saturn.
2592–93 **oppressioun Of houses:** repression (of Mars) by astrological houses (positions of the planets)
2597 **To:** too
2602 **was spared no lynage:** consanguinity was no bar to marriage; see n.
2612 **reketh:** reeks, smokes

2625 **voyded:** emptied
2634 **werk after thy wiser:** do as your superior in wisdom (advises)
2636 **me nis half so lef:** is not half so dear to me
2661 **biker:** quarrel
2664 **harmles:** unharmed

She graunteth hym; ther is non other grace.
And therwithal a costret taketh he,   2666
And seyde, "Herof a draught, or two, or thre,
Yif hym to drynke, whan he goth to reste,
And he shal slepe as longe as evere thee leste,
The narcotyks and opies ben so stronge.   2670
And go thy wey, lest that him thynke longe."
Out cometh the bryd, and with ful sobre cheere,
As is of maydens ofte the manere,
To chaumbre is brought with revel and with
          song.
And shortly, lest this tale be to long,   2675
This Lyno and she ben brought to bedde,
And every wight out at the dore hym spedde.
  The nyght is wasted, and he fyl aslepe.
Ful tenderly begynneth she to wepe;   2679
She rist hire up, and dredfully she quaketh,
As doth the braunche that Zepherus shaketh,
And hust were alle in Argon that cite.
As cold as any frost now waxeth she;
For pite by the herte hire streyneth so,
And drede of deth doth hire so moche wo,   2685
That thryes doun she fyl in swich a were.
She rist yit up, and stakereth her and there,
And on hire hondes faste loketh she.
"Allas! and shal myne hondes blody be?
I am a mayde, and, as by my nature,   2690
And bi my semblaunt and by my vesture,
Myne handes ben nat shapen for a knyf,
As for to reve no man fro his lyf.
What devel have I with the knyf to do?

And shal I have my throte korve a-two?   2695
Thanne shal I blede, allas, and me beshende!
And nedes-cost this thyng moste have an ende;
Or he or I mot nedes lese oure lyf.
Now certes," quod she, "syn I am his wif,
And hath my feyth, yit is it bet for me   2700
For to be ded in wifly honeste
Than ben a traytour lyvynge in my shame.
Be as be may, for ernest or for game,
He shal awake, and ryse, and gon his way,
Out at this goter, or that it be day" —   2705
And wep ful tenderly upon his face,
And in hyre armes gan hym to enbrace,
And hym she roggeth and awaketh softe.
And at a wyndow lep he fro the lofte,
Whan she hath warned hym, and don hym
          bote.   2710
This Lyno swift was, and lyght of fote,
And from his wif he ran a ful good pas.
This sely woman is so weik — Allas! —
And helples, so that or that she fer wente,
Hire crewel fader dide hire for to hente.   2715
Allas, Lyno, whi art thow so unkynde?
Why ne haddest thow remembred in thy mynde
To taken hire, and lad hire forth with the?
For whan she saw that gon awey was he,
And that she myghte nat so faste go,   2720
Ne folwen hym, she sat hire doun ryght tho,
Til she was caught and fetered in prysoun.
This tale is seyd for this conclusioun —

[*Unfinished.*]

2666 **costret:** flask
2670 **opies:** opiates
2671 **thynke longe:** think you have been away too long
2680 **dredfully:** fearfully
2681 **Zepherus:** the West Wind
2682 **Argon:** a city in the Peloponnesus
2686 **were:** distress

2697 **nedes-cost:** necessarily
2705 **goter:** drain
2708 **roggeth:** shakes
2709 **lofte:** upper room

THE
SHORT POEMS

THE POEMS printed here, Robinson explained, "are miscellaneous in character and have little in common except that they are short. They obviously belong to different periods of Chaucer's life." However, these poems are informed by a common tradition, that of French courtly verse, which was the literary tradition best known to the courts in which Chaucer grew up. When Alceste in the Prologue to *The Legend of Good Women* (F 422–23) pleads on Chaucer's behalf that he has made, "many an ympne for [Love's] halydayes / that highten balades, roundels, virelayes," she specifies the fixed forms of French courtly verse and says that Chaucer has written many of them, though only two roundels (that in *The Parliament of Fowls* and Merciles Beaute, if it is Chaucer's) and no virelays have survived. Probably some of Chaucer's early lyrics were written in French and have since been lost or remain unidentified in manuscripts. It is even more likely that a number of his English lyrics have also been lost, especially those of his youth; the writing of love songs and poems was an ordinary part of the amusements of the court and was one of the expected attainments of young courtiers, such as the Squire in the General Prologue, who "koude songes make and wel endite."

Most of these "ditees and songes glade" that John Gower said Chaucer wrote in the flower of his youth (*Confessio amantis,* 8.*2942–*47) must have been brief and simple songs, such as those embodied in *The Book of the Duchess,* rather than the more elaborate forms exemplified in the surviving short poems. Probably, too, some of these early lyrics were composed for actual singing. The specification that the Man in Black's lay, "a maner song," is "withoute noote, withoute song" (*The Book of the Duchess,* 471–72) seems to imply that singing was ordinarily expected, and, though the word *song* is used very loosely in Middle English, at least some of the references in the works to singing clearly imply lyrics that were actually sung. Moreover, Chaucer's favorite lyric form, the ballade, was for his master in this, Guillaume de Machaut, a specific musical form. Nevertheless, aside from the roundel in *The Parliament of Fowls* and, possibly, Merciles Beaute, it is unlikely that many of Chaucer's surviving lyrics were meant to be sung. He seems to have followed the example not of the older Machaut but of his contemporary, Eustache Deschamps, who in his poetic treatise *L'art de dictier et de fere chançons, balades, virelais et rondeaux* (*Oeuvres* 7:266–92) distinguishes between the "artificial" music produced by the singing voice or musical instruments and the more difficult and sophisticated "natural" music, which consists in skillful versification in the fixed forms and which is recited rather than sung. Apparently almost all of Chaucer's surviving lyrics belong to the category of "natural" music.

Until quite recent years, Chaucer's short poems received little critical attention; though many of them are personal, they lack the lyric *cri de coeur* that early critics prized in this genre, and the best of the short poems are often satirical or didactic, qualities not thought suitable to lyrics. Those concerning the pangs of love, as Robinson noted, "sound rather like exercises in a conventional style of composition," as indeed they are, and this too was regarded as a flaw by critics who believed that a lyric should be a direct and sincere expression of personal feeling. In recent years critical attitudes have greatly changed, and these shorter works are now receiving some of the sympathetic attention they deserve.

631

Chaucer was the first to use the form of the French ballade in English, taking the form and often much of his material from his older contemporary Guillaume de Machaut (d. 1377). The classic ballade consists of three eight-line stanzas (*a b a a b b c b C*), each using the same set of rhymes throughout and ending with a refrain (*C*), usually with a brief envoy addressing either a lady, *Madame,* or, more often, a *Prince* (the "prince" of a *puys,* a gathering of amateur poets, or an actual prince). To Rosemounde is a strict ballade, though lacking an envoy (it is probable that some of the envoys in Chaucer's ballades were added later), as is the doubtful Against Women Unconstant. Womanly Noblesse is cast in the classic form, with a slight change in rhyme scheme. Fortune is a triple ballade — three connected ballades with an envoy — as is The Complaint of Venus. Lenvoy de Chaucer a Scogan is a variation on the form, a double ballade in rime royal without the repeated rhymes or the refrain, and Lenvoy de Chaucer a Bukton shows the same variation in the form of a simple ballade. In Truth, Gentilesse, Lak of Stedfastnesse, and The Complaint of Chaucer to His Purse, the form is strictly observed, though in rime royal rather than the eight-line stanza of the standard French form. All of Chaucer's ballades are in his favorite five-accent decasyllabic line rather than the octosyllabic line standard in French ballades.

Such changes in the form of the ballade show Chaucer's concern with poetic technique and his willingness to experiment. What may be the earliest of the shorter poems, An ABC, is in the decasyllabic line, which was rarely used in English before his time. He may have derived it from French (Machaut had used decasyllabic couplets), but his use of it in stanzas was probably inspired by the *endecasillabi* of the Italian poets whom he admired. The Complaint to His Lady contains not only an apparent brief experiment in *terza rima,* the first in English, but what are probably the earliest surviving English examples of rime royal, the seven-line stanza that Chaucer was to use in so many of his poems and was to leave as his principal legacy to the courtly poets of the fifteenth century. There are precedents for Chaucer's rime royal in French lyric poetry that may account for its use in some of the lyrics here, but its close relationship to Boccaccio's narrative stanza, the Italian *ottava rima* (*a b a b b c b c*; rime royal omits the seventh line: *a b a b b c c*), doubtless

influenced Chaucer's use of this stanza in his narrative poems.

Chaucer's favorite lyric genre is the complaint, and he was the first to use the French word *complaint* in this sense. He applies it loosely to a variety of forms, from Ovid's *Heroides* to relatively brief lyrics, and he sometimes uses it even with the sense of a legal bill of petition (as in The Complaint unto Pity). Though Chaucer's usage sometimes implies that it is a distinct poetic form (as in The Franklin's Tale, in which Aurelius makes "layes, songes, compleintes, roundels, virelayes"), the complaint has no fixed form. It may be a ballade, like The Complaint of Venus, a straightforward lyric (A Complaint to His Lady), or a lyric introduced by a narrative (The Complaint unto Pity, The Complaint of Mars) or interpolated into a longer narrative, like the complaints of Troilus, and, as seems to have been the intention, the complaint in *Anelida.* All, however, share a common theme — the pangs of unrequited or disappointed love — and a common use of a first-person speaker and of the conventions of courtly love.

Except for An ABC and The Complaint of Venus, the lyrics have no direct sources. However, almost all show the influence of French courtly verse, especially the poems of Machaut and the *Roman de la rose,* and many are indebted to Boethius's *Consolation of Philosophy* (sometimes as conveyed by Machaut's poems or the *Roman,* which are themselves permeated with Boethian ideas and materials), and the ideas, images, vocabulary, and attitudes are drawn from the commonplaces of the courtly poetry of the time. Though Chaucer's principal subject is love, his poems, like those of his French predecessors and contemporaries, show a considerable range of topics, from the devotional An ABC and the philosophical Boethian lyrics (The Former Age, Fortune, Truth, and Gentilesse) to the light-hearted Chaucers Wordes unto Adam, His Owne Scriveyn and The Complaint of Chaucer to His Purse. Most striking is the wide range of tone and attitude; Chaucer shifts easily from the deeply serious to the bantering or even cynical, sometimes within the same poem. This, too, was part of the courtly tradition that Chaucer inherited, but, as with his handling of the sources for *Troilus* and many of the *Canterbury Tales,* Chaucer makes that tradition distinctly his own; even in the less successful of these short poems it is notable how often he makes the thoroughly traditional and commonplace seem fresh and original.

It seems likely that many of these poems were written for specific occasions, but in the great majority of cases scholarship has failed to identify those occasions. Consequently, the dates of composition are usually impossible to determine with precision. Such matters are discussed in the Explanatory Notes, and the order in which these poems are here printed represents only an approximation of their relative dates.

An ABC

This poem, called in the manuscripts "La priere de Nostre Dame," is a translation, close but skillful, of a prayer in Guillaume de Deguilleville's long allegorical poem, *Pelerinaige de vie humaine.* It consists of a series of stanzas, each addressed to the Virgin and each beginning with a different letter of the alphabet, progressing from A to Z. Each stanza evokes a different symbol or image, though the common image of the crucified Christ and the sorrowful Mary is intentionally omitted (81–82). The poem is notable for its use of legal terminology (though this is a terminology conventionally associated with the Redemption), as the speaker, almost as if in a court of law, begs the Virgin to intercede on his behalf.

The Complaint unto Pity

Even for a complaint, this poem is markedly gloomy. It is permeated by death, with burials, biers, hearses, and the speaker's announcement that Pity is dead and so is he. Yet it is also an intricate work, and its elaborate use of allegory — this is Chaucer's most heavily allegorical poem — lends it a sharply visual quality. It shares with An ABC a frequent use of legal language; indeed, the speaker presents his "Bill of Complaint" in accord with the established legal practices of the time, again as if he were in an actual court of law. This is apparently the earliest of the poems consisting of a third-person narrative introduction to a first-person complaint. The device provides a sense of specificity, even a sort of verisimilitude, to the lyric complaint.

A Complaint to His Lady

This work (called "A Balade of Pity" in some editions) is fragmentary, and it is not certain that its parts were meant to form a single poem. They are unified only in their common theme of unrequited love. The work, whether one poem or several, is unfinished, and it is best read as an experiment in versification: Part I is in rimeroyal stanzas, possibly the earliest to have survived; Parts II and III are apparently in *terza rima,* the first appearance of Dante's rhyme scheme in English; and Part IV is in a ten-line stanza (also apparently here used for the first time in the language) that bears some resemblance to the nine-line stanza of *Anelida* (with which this poem shares a number of verbal resemblances). The possible relation to *Anelida* suggests a later date than is usually assigned to the Complaint to His Lady, which is generally taken to be an early work on the basis of its thoroughly conventional imagery and language.

The Complaint of Mars

This work is composed of three unequal parts: the Proem, sung by a bird on St. Valentine's Day; the Story, told by the narrator "in . . . briddes wise," which concerns the love of the planets Venus and Mars; and the Complaint, spoken by Mars. The parts are not tightly unified, and Chaucer may have composed the Story and Complaint separately and then added the Proem to tie the two together, though critics have not found fault with this aspect of the poem.

The Story is simple in plot, though the astronomical terminology is difficult for the modern reader. It tells the well-known story of the love of Mars and Venus, translated into astronomical terms: the two planets move closer to one another in the skies as they come into conjunction in the zodiacal sign of Taurus. The sun is also moving toward Taurus, thus threatening to discover their assignation; Venus, who moves more rapidly through her orbit than Mars does through his, flees to the next zodiacal sign, leaving behind the slower-moving Mars to be overtaken and rendered "combust" by the sun, now fast approaching. The details of the planetary motions are for the most part quite accurate, and they closely (but not exactly) fit the actual conditions of the skies in the year 1385. Yet Chaucer blends astronomy, mythology, and human emotions without visible effort, as he evokes the familiar visual images of the planet-gods in their chariots, making their stately way through the zodiac, and of the gods of the myth — here

Venus and Mars pursued by the sun (usually Vulcan's role) — in a very human predicament.

The Complaint is the longest of the three parts and has little connection to what precedes it. Only in the last few lines is it clear that the speaker is Mars and his lady Venus, and the preceding sections contain no astrological or mythological allusions. Instead, the frame of reference is pessimistically Christian.

As a whole, the poem is very impressive. Its blend of astronomy, mythology, and human love is unique in medieval literature and results in a work that raises questions, however briefly and lightly, about such matters as freedom of will and the nature of love. These are among the important concerns of Chaucer's longer and better-known works, and one can understand why in recent years critics have seen the poem as a "miniature *Troilus*."

The Complaint of Venus

This poem follows Mars in a number of manuscripts, and they are linked by the colophons in John Shirley's copy, which records the tradition that Mars is to be identified with John Holland and Venus with Isabel of York. The Complaint of Venus is an adaptation of three ballades by the French poet Oton de Grandson, whom Chaucer probably knew personally. Chaucer changes the speaker to a woman, which is unusual (though not unknown) and unnecessary unless the poem is to be taken as Venus's reply to Mars or as somehow connected with some court lady, though there is no way of knowing the identity of that lady nor whether there is any substance to the tradition that Shirley reports.

Despite the title, there are no astrological or mythical allusions in the three ballades to connect the poem with Venus, and the poem has little in common with the ordinary complaint in which a lover begs for mercy. The theme of love binds the three parts together, but each develops a different idea. Skeat entitled them: The Lover's Worthiness, Disquietude Caused by Jealousy, Satisfaction in Constancy.

In the envoy (which may have been written later), Chaucer laments the "skarsete" of rhyme in English and his consequent inability to follow the "curiosite" of Grandson. This is a variation of the "affected modesty" topos, which calls attention to the virtuosity of the performance: Chaucer strictly maintains the same rhymes throughout each ballade and carries one rhyme

(on *-aunce*) through all three ballades and into the envoy itself.

To Rosemounde

This is one of Chaucer's most graceful poems, easily moving from adoration of the lady to lightly humorous mock-seriousness, which was very much a part of the courtly game of love but which is here distinctively Chaucerian. The work is notable for the ease with which Chaucer fulfills the requirements of the ballade form. The inscription "tregentil ——— chaucer" written at the end of the poem in the unique manuscript has been the cause of much speculation but has yet to be explained to everyone's satisfaction.

Womanly Noblesse

Robinson, following Skeat, accepted the authenticity of this poem, as has Fisher. Other editors have rejected it; Heath labeled it "doubtful," Koch omitted it from his edition, and its most recent editors, Pace and David, raise some serious objections. Although it is called a ballade in the manuscript and has an envoy, the poem is very unusual in form, since it lacks a refrain and uses nine lines in each stanza, with all three stanzas having but two rhymes and all using the same two rhymes throughout, one of which also appears in the envoy. Though the rhymes are fairly easy ones, this is a considerable accomplishment; Skeat, who discovered the poem, was especially impressed by what he considered its technical mastery.

Chaucers Wordes unto Adam, His Owne Scriveyn

"The lines to Adam Scriveyn, which read like one of the personal epigrams of the ancients, reveal some of the anxieties which beset an author before the invention of printing. The poem could hardly be more vivid if the record searchers should succeed in discovering Adam's family name" (Robinson). The record searchers have now generally abandoned that task, and the poem remains as vivid as it was for Robinson.

The Former Age

This and the four poems that follow all show the specific and general influence of Boethius.

They are, therefore, commonly grouped together as *Boethian lyrics,* though the degree of Boethian influence differs from one to another and they were probably composed over a period of several years rather than together as part of a projected group of poems. They are moral poems of the sort popular in both French and English poetry of the time, and though attempts have been made to attach some of them to specific occasions, they are too general in application to fit exactly any one of the various occasions scholars have proposed for their composition.

In The Former Age Chaucer takes the well-worn commonplaces of the Golden Age — primarily from Boethius (Bo 2.m5), Ovid, the *Roman de la rose,* and possibly Virgil — and invests them with freshness and vigor. The "blissed folk" of this primeval time live in Spartan simplicity, which Chaucer characterizes mainly by negatives (in the third stanza each line begins with *no* or *ne*), in contrast with modern civilization, which is seen primarily as a source of pain. The direct comment on "oure dayes" in the final lines echoes the *Roman de la rose* but has the ring of conviction.

Fortune

The concept of Fortune in this ballade, technically one of Chaucer's most skillful, is drawn primarily from Boethius's *Consolation of Philosophy,* in which there is also a complaint against Fortune, a defense, and a discussion of her significance. However, Chaucer also draws upon Jean de Meun and Dante (as in Dante, Fortune is here drawn into the Christian system as executrix of God's will) and on the common visual image of Fortune blindly turning her wheel. The envoy, with its unusual address to a group of princes, has been explained as an appeal to the Dukes of Lancaster, York, and Gloucester, who in 1390 controlled gifts given in the name of the king. If so, the poem dates from the early 1390s, though the envoy could easily be a later addition.

Truth

Judging from the number of manuscripts in which it is preserved (twenty-two, plus the early editions of Caxton and Thynne), Truth was Chaucer's most popular lyric; of all his other works, only *The Canterbury Tales* and *A Treatise*

on the Astrolabe are preserved in more manuscripts than Truth. In these manuscripts, Truth is usually called "Balade de Bon Conseyl," and it is exactly that. The good advice is given in a series of strong imperatives, ending with an exhortation to the reader to set forth on a spiritual pilgrimage, with the refrain echoing the familiar words of St. John, "Ye shall know the truth and the truth shall make you free." The ideas are commonplace, but they are expressed here with a power that carries conviction. In one manuscript (MS Add 10340 fol. 41r) Truth appears next to an excerpt from the General Prologue, the portrait of the Parson; clearly the poem has some of the same appeal as that idealized but affecting portrait.

The envoy, addressed to *Vache,* has been the subject of much speculation, but it exists in only one of the many manuscripts and thus seems clearly a later addition.

Gentilesse

The doctrine of *gentilesse* set forth in this rime-royal ballade is that which the Wife of Bath expounds in her tale, where she cites as her source Dante, who, with Boethius and Jean de Meun, is echoed in this poem. Such sentiments, as Robinson wrote, sound very modern, but here, as in the other moral ballades, Chaucer expresses the received opinions of his time, commonplaces of contemporary morality. The poem succeeds not because of the originality of its thought but because of the vigor and polish of its expression.

Lak of Stedfastnesse

The "complaint upon the times" is a familiar theme in medieval poetry, though unusual in Chaucer, who seldom writes direct political comment of the sort in "Lenvoy to King Richard." The assumption that this must have been evoked by some specific occasion and Shirley's report that the poem was written in Chaucer's "laste yeeres" have led some scholars to assign it to the late 1390s, when Richard's "swerd of castigacioun" was sorely needed. Robinson and others argue that the poem would have been equally appropriate in the late 1380s. In genre it belongs with the other moral ballades in the Boethian group, though its relation to Boethius is very general. Its date, like those of most of these poems, cannot be surely fixed.

Lenvoy de Chaucer a Scogan

Envoy here is used in the sense of "message" or "letter," and this free double ballade is a dazzling example (perhaps the first in English) of light epistolary verse. The tone is lively, urbane, mock-serious, as Chaucer plays with the conventions of literature and love. He first makes Scogan (whom he addresses no fewer than seven times) responsible for a natural catastrophe, warns him of the fearful consequences, and protests that he will write no more verse (though that is exactly what he is doing at the moment). In the fourth through sixth stanzas Chaucer slyly allies himself with his friend at court, so that in the Envoy it is Scogan who kneels before the prince at "the stremes hed" (Windsor castle) to beg a favor for both.

The Scogan addressed is probably Henry Scogan, who himself wrote a moral ballade, addressed to the sons of Henry IV (whose tutor he was), in which the whole of Chaucer's *Gentilesse* is quoted.

Lenvoy de Chaucer a Bukton

The identity of this Bukton is unknown; he could be either Sir Robert Bukton of Suffolk or, slightly more likely, Sir Peter Bukton of Holdernesse (the setting of The Summoner's Tale). The date is likewise uncertain (though the reference to capture "in Frise" has been taken as evidence for composition in 1396). But there is no doubt about the occasion: Bukton is about to marry, and Chaucer wittily pretends to dissuade him, beginning with the authority of Christ and holy writ and ending with an assurance that "experience shal the teche" and an appeal to that experienced authority on such matters, the Wife of Bath. Her personality apparently had as strong a hold on her creator's imagination as it has had on modern readers. "It ought not to be necessary to add," Robinson wrote in a warning still germane, "but some remarks of the commentators invite the observation, that the Envoy is not to be taken as evidence that Chaucer either disapproved of his friend's marriage or regretted his own!"

The Complaint of Chaucer to His Purse

Here Chaucer observes the classic ballade form, in rime royal, with the same rhymes throughout and with a refrain that plays upon the broad range of meanings of the words *hevy* (heavy, sad, pregnant, etc.) and *light* (light, cheerful, wanton, etc.). The conventions of the love complaint are playfully employed to turn the mundane need for cash into an appeal for pity from his new lady, his purse. The envoy, clearly addressed to Henry IV, differs in tone, language, and versification from the body of the ballade, and it may be a later addition. However, the poem as we have it, addressed to Henry, must date after his coronation in October of 1399; it is therefore the last work known to have come from Chaucer's hand.

Proverbs

These lines are given their manuscript title, "A Proverbe of Chaucer," by some editors, and are called "Proverbs of Chaucer" in Skeat's edition. They were not ascribed to Chaucer in the copy by John Shirley. For this reason, and because of the suspicious rhyme *compas : embrace,* which Koch and Skeat believed proved they could not be Chaucer's, Robinson placed them in the "doubtful category." The poem's most recent editors, Pace and David, and R. T. Lenaghan, the editor for this edition, regard it as authentic. Certainty is, of course, impossible in so brief a work. The lines may be fragments of some longer poem, though possibly they were intended to stand as they are; critics have noted a similar set of verses in the works of Deschamps, and Middle English offers other examples of brief sententious verse.

POEMS NOT ASCRIBED TO CHAUCER IN THE MANUSCRIPTS

The following poems appear in manuscripts that contain undoubtedly genuine works by Chaucer but are not themselves attributed to Chaucer by the scribes.

Against Women Unconstant

This poem is titled "New Fangelnesse" in some editions. It was first printed among Chaucer's works by Stowe (1561), and Skeat was convinced that it was genuine, mainly because of its Chaucerian manner and the quality of its verse. Robinson believed it was "almost certainly" by Chaucer. Its most recent editors, Pace and

David, are doubtful. Yet if Chaucer did not write it, he need not have been ashamed to have it ascribed to him; it is livelier and has a more natural and personal tone than some of the ballades unquestioningly accepted as genuine, and technically it is as impressive as any ballade that Chaucer wrote, which is saying a good deal, given his high standards.

Complaynt D'Amours

This poem is called by its manuscript title, "An Amorous Complaint," by some editors. It was first proposed for inclusion in the canon by Skeat, who was impressed by its Chaucerian touches and the obvious allusion to *The Parliament of Fowls*. Few critics have shared his opinion. It was perhaps written as a poetic exercise for St. Valentine's Day by one of Chaucer's skilled but uninspired admirers.

Merciles Beaute

Bishop Percy discovered this poem in the Pepys manuscript, which contains a number of genuine works by Chaucer, and it was first published as

Chaucer's in Percy's *Reliques of Ancient English Poetry* (1767). Its authenticity has been questioned, but almost all critics now accept it, and it has been frequently anthologized. It is a technically impressive triple roundel, with a touch of typically Chaucerian humor in the third, and it is heavily influenced by French courtly verse, even in its movement from adoration to witty dismissal. Skeat justly wrote: "If it is not Chaucer's, it is by someone who contrived to surpass his own style."

A Balade of Complaint

Skeat came upon this poem in a manuscript by Shirley, and, though Shirley did not ascribe it to Chaucer, Skeat was so impressed with its "melodious flow" that he printed it in his edition, though in a section (along with Against Women Unconstant and the Complaynt D'Amours) reserved for works for which there was a "lack of external evidence" for their authenticity. There is no persuasive reason for the attribution; it is a good example of pedestrian verse, heavily indebted to Chaucer but far from attaining his standard.

LAILA Z. GROSS

The Short Poems

AN ABC

Incipit carmen secundum ordinem litterarum alphabeti.

Almighty and al merciable queene,
To whom that al this world fleeth for socour,
To have relees of sinne, of sorwe, and teene,
Glorious virgine, of alle floures flour,
To thee I flee, confounded in errour.   5
Help and releeve, thou mighti debonayre,
Have mercy on my perilous langour.
Venquisshed me hath my cruel adversaire.

Bountee so fix hath in thin herte his tente
That wel I wot thou wolt my socour bee;   10
Thou canst not warne him that with good entente
Axeth thin helpe, thin herte is ay so free.
Thou art largesse of pleyn felicitee,
Haven of refut, of quiete, and of reste.
Loo, how that theeves sevene chasen mee.   15
Help, lady bright, er that my ship tobreste.

The texts of the short poems were edited by R. T. LENAGHAN.

Incipit, etc.: Here begins a song following the order of the letters of the alphabet.
3 **relees**: forgiveness **teene**: trouble
6 **debonayre**: gracious (person)
7 **langour**: weakness

11 **warne**: refuse
14 **refut**: refuge
15 **theeves sevene**: the Seven Deadly Sins
16 **tobreste**: burst apart

Comfort is noon but in yow, ladi deere;
For loo, my sinne and my confusioun,
Which oughten not in thi presence appeere,
Han take on me a greevous accioun   20
Of verrey right and desperacioun;
And as bi right thei mighten wel susteene
That I were wurthi my dampnacioun,
Nere merci of you, blisful hevene queene.   24

Dowte is ther noon, thou queen of misericorde,
That thou n'art cause of grace and merci heere;
God vouched sauf thurgh thee with us to ac-
          corde.
For certes, Crystes blisful mooder deere,
Were now the bowe bent in swich maneere
As it was first of justice and of ire,   30
The rightful God nolde of no mercy heere;
But thurgh thee han we grace as we desire.

Evere hath myn hope of refut been in thee,
For heer-biforn ful ofte in many a wyse
Hast thou to misericorde receyved me.   35
But merci, ladi, at the grete assyse
Whan we shule come bifore the hye justyse.
So litel fruit shal thanne in me be founde
That, but thou er that day correcte [vice],
Of verrey right my werk wol me confounde.

Fleeinge, I flee for socour to thi tente   41
Me for to hide from tempeste ful of dreede,
Biseeching yow that ye you not absente
Thouh I be wikke. O, help yit at this neede!
Al have I ben a beste in wil and deede,   45
Yit, ladi, thou me clothe with thi grace.
Thin enemy and myn — ladi, tak heede —
Unto my deth in poynt is me to chace!

Glorious mayde and mooder, which that nevere
Were bitter, neither in erthe nor in see,   50
But ful of swetnesse and of merci evere,
Help that my Fader be not wroth with me.
Spek thou, for I ne dar not him ysee,
So have I doon in erthe, allas the while,
That certes, but if thou my socour bee,   55
To stink eterne he wole my gost exile.

He vouched sauf, tel him, as was his wille,
Bicome a man, to have oure alliaunce,
And with his precious blood he wrot the bille
Upon the crois as general acquitaunce   60
To every penitent in ful creaunce;
And therfore, ladi bright, thou for us praye.
Thanne shalt thou bothe stinte al his grevaunce,
And make oure foo to failen of his praye.

I wot it wel, thou wolt ben oure socour,   65
Thou art so ful of bowntee, in certeyn,
For whan a soule falleth in errour
Thi pitee goth and haleth him ayein.
Thanne makest thou his pees with his sovereyn
And bringest him out of the crooked strete.   70
Whoso thee loveth, he shal not love in veyn,
That shal he fynde as he the lyf shal lete.

Kalenderes enlumyned ben thei
That in this world ben lighted with thi name,
And whoso goth to yow the righte wey,   75
Him thar not drede in soule to be lame.
Now, queen of comfort, sith thou art that same
To whom I seeche for my medicyne,
Lat not my foo no more my wounde entame;
Myn hele into thin hand al I resygne.   80

Ladi, thi sorwe kan I not portreye
Under the cros, ne his greevous penaunce;
But for youre bothes peynes I yow preye,
Lat not oure alder foo make his bobaunce
That he hath in his lystes of mischaunce   85
Convict that ye bothe have bought so deere.
As I seide erst, thou ground of oure substaunce,
Continue on us thi pitous eyen cleere!

Moises, that saugh the bush with flawmes rede
Brenninge, of which ther never a stikke brende,
Was signe of thin unwemmed maidenhede.   91

20 **accioun:** accusation, legal action
23 **wurthi:** deserving
24 **Nere** = *ne were,* were (there) not
26 **n'art:** i.e., are
27 **vouched sauf:** granted
36 **the grete assyse:** the Last Judgment
39 **correcte [vice]:** correct my vices
40 **Of verrey right:** in strict justice, not quite as in line 21
(Skeat)
56 **stink eterne:** i.e., hell

57 **tel him:** to himself
59 **wrot the bille:** drew up the legal document
60 **acquitaunce:** aquittal
61 **in ful creaunce:** in full belief (i.e., who has good faith)
64 **praye:** prey
68 **haleth him ayein:** pulls him back
73 **Kalenderes enlumyned ben:** church calendars mark the high
festivals with red or illuminated letters.
75 **righte:** direct, straight
76 **Him thar:** he need
78 **seeche:** beseech, make request
79 **entame:** open
80 **resygne:** consign, entrust
84 **oure alder foo:** foe of us all (the devil)   **bobaunce:** boast
85 **lystes:** lists, where a judicial combat is fought
86 **Convict that ye bothe:** convicted (overcome) him (the soul)
whom you both (Mary and Christ)
90 **stikke:** twig
91 **unwemmed:** unstained

Thou art the bush on which ther gan descende
The Holi Gost, the which that Moyses wende
Had ben a-fyr, and this was in figure.
Now, ladi, from the fyr thou us defende   95
Which that in helle eternalli shal dure.

Noble princesse, that nevere haddest peere,
Certes if any comfort in us bee,
That cometh of thee, thou Cristes mooder
     deere.
We han noon oother melodye or glee   100
Us to rejoyse in oure adversitee,
Ne advocat noon that wole and dar so preye
For us, and that for litel hire as yee
That helpen for an Ave-Marie or tweye.

O verrey light of eyen that ben blynde,   105
O verrey lust of labour and distresse,
O tresoreere of bountee to mankynde,
Thee whom God ches to mooder for humblesse!
From his ancille he made the maistresse   109
Of hevene and erthe, oure bille up for to beede.
This world awaiteth evere on thi goodnesse
For thou ne failest nevere wight at neede.

Purpos I have sum time for to enquere
Wherfore and whi the Holi Gost thee soughte
Whan Gabrielles vois cam to thin ere.   115
He not to werre us swich a wonder wroughte,
But for to save us that he sithen boughte.
Thanne needeth us no wepen us for to save,
But oonly ther we dide not, as us oughte,
Doo penitence, and merci axe and have.   120

Queen of comfort, yit whan I me bithinke
That I agilt have bothe him and thee,
And that my soule is worthi for to sinke,
Allas, I caityf, whider may I flee?
Who shal unto thi Sone my mene bee?   125
Who, but thiself, that art of pitee welle?
Thou hast more reuthe on oure adversitee
Than in this world might any tonge telle.

Redresse me, mooder, and me chastise,
For certeynly my Faderes chastisinge,   130
That dar I nouht abiden in no wise,

So hidous is his rightful rekenynge.
Mooder, of whom oure merci gan to springe,
Beth ye my juge and eek my soules leche;
For evere in you is pitee haboundinge   135
To ech that wole of pitee you biseeche.

Soth is that God ne granteth no pitee
Withoute thee; for God of his goodnesse
Foryiveth noon, but it like unto thee.
He hath thee maked vicaire and maistresse   140
Of al this world, and eek governouresse
Of hevene, and he represseth his justise
After thi wil; and therfore in witnesse
He hath thee corowned in so rial wise.   144

Temple devout, ther God hath his woninge,
Fro which these misbileeved deprived been,
To you my soule penitent I bringe.
Receyve me — I can no ferther fleen.
With thornes venymous, O hevene queen,
For which the eerthe acursed was ful yore,   150
I am so wounded, as ye may wel seen,
That I am lost almost, it smert so sore.

Virgine, that art so noble of apparaile,
And ledest us into the hye tour
Of Paradys, thou me wisse and counsaile
How I may have thi grace and thi socour,
All have I ben in filthe and in errour.   157
Ladi, unto that court thou me ajourne
That cleped is thi bench, O freshe flour,
Ther as that merci evere shal sojourne.   160

Xristus, thi sone, that in this world alighte
Upon the cros to suffre his passioun,
And eek that Longius his herte pighte
And made his herte blood to renne adoun,
And al was this for my salvacioun;   165
And I to him am fals and eek unkynde,
And yit he wole not my dampnacioun —
This thanke I yow, socour of al mankynde!

Ysaac was figure of his deth, certeyn,
That so fer forth his fader wolde obeye   170
That him ne roughte nothing to be slayn;

94 **in figure:** symbolic
100 **glee:** music
106 **lust of:** joy to (those in)
109 **ancille:** maidservant
110 **bille:** petition   **beede:** offer (pray)
115 **Gabrielles vois:** the voice of Gabriel, the angel of the
Annunciation
116 **to werre:** for war, hostility
117 **sithen:** afterwards
125 **mene:** intermediary

132 **rightful rekenynge:** just account keeping
140 **vicaire:** vicar
144 **rial:** royal
146 **misbileeved:** infidels
153 **apparaile:** behavior, bearing (Fisher)
158 **ajourne:** summon on another day
159 **bench:** court of law
163 **Longius:** Longinus, the blind centurion supposed to have
pierced *(pighte)* Christ's side with his spear
169 **Ysaac:** the sacrifice of Isaac (Gen. 22) was thought to
prefigure the Crucifixion.
171 **roughte:** cared (impersonal)

Right soo thi Sone list as a lamb to deye.
Now, ladi ful of merci, I yow preye,
Sith he his merci mesured so large,
Be ye not skant, for alle we singe and seye 175
That ye ben from vengeaunce ay oure targe.

Zacharie yow clepeth the open welle

To wasshe sinful soule out of his gilt.
Therfore this lessoun oughte I wel to telle,
That, nere thi tender herte, we were spilt. 180
Now, ladi bryghte, sith thou canst and wilt
Ben to the seed of Adam merciable,
Bring us to that palais that is bilt
To penitentes that ben to merci able. Amen.

Explicit carmen.

THE COMPLAINT UNTO PITY

Pite, that I have sought so yore agoo
With herte soore and ful of besy peyne,
That in this world was never wight so woo
Withoute deth — and yf I shal not feyne,
My purpos was to Pite to compleyne   5
Upon the crueltee and tirannye
Of Love, that for my trouthe doth me dye.

And when that I, be lengthe of certeyne yeres,
Had evere in oon a tyme sought to speke,
To Pitee ran I al bespreynt with teres   10
To prayen hir on Cruelte me awreke.
But er I myghte with any word outbreke
Or tellen any of my peynes smerte,
I fond hir ded, and buried in an herte.

Adoun I fel when that I saugh the herse, 15
Ded as a ston while that the swogh me laste;
But up I roos with colour ful dyverse
And pitously on hir myn eyen I caste,
And ner the corps I gan to presen faste,
And for the soule I shop me for to preye. 20
I was but lorn, ther was no more to seye.

Thus am I slayn sith that Pite is ded.
Allas, that day, that ever hyt shulde falle.
What maner man dar now hold up his hed?
To whom shal any sorwful herte calle?   25
Now Cruelte hath cast to slee us alle,

In ydel hope, folk redeless of peyne,
Syth she is ded, to whom shul we compleyne?

But yet encreseth me this wonder newe,
That no wight woot that she is ded, but I — 30
So many men as in her tyme hir knewe —
And yet she dyed not so sodeynly,
For I have sought hir ever ful besely
Sith first I hadde wit or mannes mynde,
But she was ded er that I koude hir fynde. 35

Aboute hir herse there stoden lustely,
Withouten any woo as thoughte me,
Bounte parfyt, wel armed and richely,
And fresshe Beaute, Lust, and Jolyte,
Assured Maner, Youthe, and Honeste,   40
Wisdom, Estaat, Drede, and Governaunce,
Confedred both by bonde and alliaunce.

A compleynt had I, writen in myn hond,
For to have put to Pite as a bille;
But when I al this companye ther fond,   45
That rather wolden al my cause spille
Then do me help, I held my pleynte stille,
For to that folk, withouten any fayle,
Withoute Pitee ther may no bille availe.

Then leve I al these vertues, sauf Pite,   50
Kepynge the corps as ye have herd me seyn,
Confedered alle by bond of Cruelte

177 **Zacharie:** Zechariah, the biblical prophet

9 **evere in oon:** continually
10 **bespreynt:** sprinkled
15 **herse:** a frame for lights at a funeral
16 **swogh:** swoon
19 **presen:** press forward
20 **shop me:** disposed myself, began
21 **was but lorn:** was as good as lost (dead)
26 **cast:** decided, planned

183–84 **bilt To:** built for

27 **redeless of peyne:** with no cure (advice) for pain (cf. BD 587)
36 **lustely:** happily
42 **Confedred:** confederated, joined together
46 **spille:** destroy
50 **sauf:** except for
51 **Kepynge:** watching over

And ben assented when I shal be sleyn.
And I have put my complaynt up ageyn,
For to my foes my bille I dar not shewe,   55
Th'effect of which seith thus, in wordes fewe:

The Bill of Complaint

Humblest of herte, highest of reverence,
Benygne flour, coroune of vertues alle,
Sheweth unto youre rial excellence
Youre servaunt, yf I durste me so calle,   60
Hys mortal harm in which he is yfalle,
And noght al oonly for his evel fare,
But for your renoun, as he shal declare.

Hit stondeth thus: your contraire, Crueltee,
Allyed is ayenst your regalye   65
Under colour of womanly Beaute —
For men shulde not, lo, knowe hir tirannye —
With Bounte, Gentilesse, and Curtesye,
And hath depryved yow now of your place
That hyghte "Beaute apertenant to Grace."   70

For kyndely by youre herytage ryght
Ye ben annexed ever unto Bounte;
And verrayly ye oughte do youre myght
To helpe Trouthe in his adversyte.
Ye be also the corowne of Beaute,   75
And certes yf ye wanten in these tweyne,
The world is lore; ther is no more to seyne.

Eke what availeth Maner and Gentilesse
Withoute yow, benygne creature?
Shal Cruelte be your governeresse?   80
Allas, what herte may hyt longe endure?
Wherfore, but ye the rather take cure
To breke that perilouse alliaunce,
Ye sleen hem that ben in your obeisaunce.

And further over yf ye suffre this,   85
Youre renoun ys fordoo than in a throwe;

Ther shal no man wite well what Pite is.
Allas, that your renoun is falle so lowe!
Ye be than fro youre heritage ythrowe
By Cruelte that occupieth youre place,   90
And we despeyred that seken to your grace.

Have mercy on me, thow Herenus quene,
That yow have sought so tendirly and yore;
Let som strem of youre lyght on me be sene
That love and drede yow ever lenger the
        more;   95
For sothly for to seyne I bere the soore,
And though I be not konnynge for to pleyne,
For Goddis love have mercy on my peyne.

My peyne is this, that what so I desire
That have I not, ne nothing lyk therto;   100
And ever setteth Desir myn hert on fire.
Eke on that other syde where so I goo,
What maner thing that may encrese my woo,
That have I redy, unsoght, everywhere;
Me lakketh but my deth and than my
        bere.   105

What nedeth to shewe parcel of my peyne?
Syth every woo that herte may bethynke
I suffre and yet I dar not to yow pleyne;
For wel I wot although I wake or wynke,
Ye rekke not whether I flete or synke.   110
But natheles yet my trouthe I shal sustene
Unto my deth, and that shal wel be sene.

This is to seyne I wol be youres evere,
Though ye me slee by Crueltee your foo,
Algate my spirit shal never dissevere   115
Fro youre servise for any peyne or woo.
Sith ye be ded — allas that hyt is soo —
Thus for your deth I may wel wepe and pleyne
With herte sore and ful of besy peyne.

Explicit.

59 **rial:** royal
65 **regalye:** royal rule, authority
67 **For:** so that
70 **apertenant:** suitable, properly belonging to
72 **annexed:** joined   **Bounte:** goodness, generosity
76 **wanten in these tweyne:** be lacking to these two (i.e., if Truth and Beauty lack Pity)
82 **cure:** care, pains
86 **in a throwe:** instantly

92 **Herenus quene:** queen of the Furies; see n.
104 **unsoght:** ready at hand
105 **bere:** funeral bier
106 **parcel:** part, small portion

A COMPLAINT TO HIS LADY

I

The longe nightes, whan every creature
Shulde have hir rest in somwhat as by kynde,
Or elles ne may hir lif nat longe endure,
Hit falleth most into my woful mynde
How I so fer have broght myself behynde   5
That, sauf the deeth, ther may nothyng me
        lisse,
So desespaired I am from alle blisse.

This same thoght me lasteth til the morwe
And from the morwe forth til hit be eve;
Ther nedeth me no care for to borwe,   10
For bothe I have good leyser and good leve;
Ther is no wyght that wol me wo bereve
To wepe ynogh and wailen al my fille;
The sore spark of peyne now doth me spille.

II

This Love, that hath me set in such a place
    That my desir [he] nevere wol fulfille,   16
For neither pitee, mercy, neither grace
    Can I nat fynde, and yit my sorwful herte
    For to be deed I can hit nought arace.
The more I love, the more she doth me smerte,
    Thourgh which I see withoute remedye   21
    That from the deeth I may no wyse asterte.

III

Now sothly what she hight I wol reherse:

Hir name is Bountee set in womanhede,   24
Sadnesse in youthe and Beautee prydelees
And Plesaunce under governaunce and drede;
Hir surname is eek Faire Rewthelees
    The Wyse, yknit unto Good Aventure,
    That, for I love hir, she sleeth me giltelees.

Hir love I best, and shal, whyl I may dure,   30
    Bet than myself an hundred thousand deel,
    Than al this worldes richesse or creature.
Now hath not Love me bestowed weel

To love ther I never shal have part?
    Allas, right thus is turned me the wheel,   35
Thus am I slayn with Loves fyry dart!
    I can but love hir best, my swete fo;
    Love hath me taught no more of his art
But serve alwey and stinte for no wo.

IV

In my trewe [and] careful herte ther is   40
So moche wo and [eek] so litel blis
That wo is me that ever I was bore;
For al that thyng which I desyre I mis
And al that ever I wolde not ywis,
That finde I redy to me evermore;   45
And of al this I not to whom me pleyne.
For she that mighte me out of this brynge
Ne reccheth nought whether I wepe or synge,
So litel rewthe hath she upon my peyne.

Allas! Whan slepyng-tyme is than I wake,   50
Whan I shulde daunce, for fere, lo, than I
        quake.
This hevy lif I lede, lo, for your sake
Thogh ye therof in no wyse hede take,
Myn hertes lady and hool my lyves quene.
For trewly durste I seye as that I fele,   55
Me semeth that your swete herte of stele
Is whetted now ageynes me to kene.

My dere herte and best beloved fo,
Why lyketh yow to do me al this wo?
What have I doon that greveth yow or sayd,
But for I serve and love yow and no mo?   61
And while I lyve I wol ever do so,
And therfor, swete, ne beth nat yvel apayd.
For so good and so fair as ye be
Hit were right gret wonder but ye hadde   65
Of alle servantes, bothe of goode and badde;
And leest worthy of alle hem, I am he.

But nevertheles, my righte lady swete,
Thogh that I be unconnyng and unmete

---

6 **lisse:** relieve
7 **desespaired . . . from:** deprived of
10 **to borwe:** as a pledge
12 **bereve:** take away
19 **arace:** uproot, tear away
25 **Sadnesse:** constancy **prydelees:** humble, without pride
26 **Governaunce:** self-control **Drede:** fear (of scandal)
31 **deel:** times

35 **wheel:** Fortune's wheel
40 **careful:** sorrowful
46 **not** = *ne wot*, know not
54 **hool:** entirely
57 **to kene:** too sharply
61 **But for:** except that
69 **unmete:** unsuited

To serve, as I coude best, ay your hynesse,
Yit is ther noon fayner, that wolde I hete,   71
Than I, to do yow ese, or elles bete
What so I wiste that were to youre hevynesse;
And hadde I myght as good as I have wille,
Than shulde ye fele wher it were so or noon;
For in this world livyng than is ther noon
That fayner wolde your hertes wil fulfille.   77

For bothe I love and eek drede yow so sore,
And algates moot, and have doon yow, ful
            yore,
That bettre loved is noon ne never shal;   80
And yit I wolde beseche yow of no more,
But leveth wel and be not wrooth therfore,
And lat me serve yow forth; lo, this is al.
For I am not so hardy ne so wood,
For to desire that ye shulde love me,   85
For wel I wot — allas — that wil nat be;
I am so litel worthy and ye so good.

For ye be oon the worthiest on-lyve
And I the most unlykly for to thryve,
Yit for al this, witeth ye right wele   90
That ye ne shul me from your servyce dryve
That I ne wil ay, with alle my wittes fyve,
Serve yow trewly, what wo so that I fele.
For I am set on yow in such manere
That, thogh ye never wil upon me rewe,   95
I moste yow love and been ever as trewe
As any man can, or may, on-lyve [here].

But the more that I love yow, goodly free,
The lasse fynde I that ye loven me;
Allas, whan shal that harde wit amende?
Wher is now al your wommanly pitee,   101
Your gentilesse and your debonairtee?
Wil ye nothyng therof upon me spende?
And so hool, swete, as I am youres al,
And so gret wil as I have yow to serve,   105
Now certes, and ye lete me thus sterve,
Yit have ye wonne theron but a smal.

For at my knowyng I do nought why,
And this I wol beseche yow hertely,
That ther ever ye fynde, whyles ye lyve,   110
A trewer servant to yow than am I,
Leveth thanne and sleeth me hardely,
And I my deeth to yow wol al foryive.
And if ye fynde no trewer verrayly,
Wil ye suffre than that I thus spille   115
And for no maner gilt but my good wille?
As good were thanne untrewe as trewe to be.

But I, my lyf and deeth, to yow obeye
And with right buxom herte hooly I preye
As is your moste plesure, so doth by me;
Wel lever is me liken yow and deye   121
Than for to anythyng or thynke or seye
That yow myghte offende in any tyme.
And therfor, swete, rewe on my peynes smerte,
And of your grace graunteth me som drope,
For elles may me laste no blis ne hope,   126
Ne dwelle within my trouble careful herte.

THE COMPLAINT OF MARS

[*The Proem*]

  Gladeth, ye foules, of the morowe gray.
Lo, Venus, rysen among yon rowes rede,
And floures fressh, honoureth ye this day;
For when the sunne uprist then wol ye sprede.
But ye lovers, that lye in any drede,   5

Fleeth, lest wikked tonges yow espye.
Lo, yond the sunne, the candel of jelosye!

Wyth teres blewe and with a wounded herte
Taketh your leve, and with Seint John to
            borowe
Apeseth sumwhat of your sorowes smerte.   10

---

71 **fayner:** more eager   **hete:** promise
72 **bete:** make better, alleviate
79 **ful yore:** long since·
89 **unlykly:** unsuitable

1 **Gladeth:** rejoice   **morowe gray:** dim, early morning
2 **Venus:** the planet, as the morning star   **rowes rede:** red
streaks or rays of light
4 **uprist** = *upriseth,* rises up

100 **harde wit:** cruel spirit
102 **debonairtee:** graciousness
108 since to my knowledge I do nothing to cause this (your
attitude)
122 **or . . . or:** either . . . or

8 **blewe:** livid
9 **with Seint John to borowe:** with St. John as my guarantor

Tyme cometh eft that cese shal your sorowe;
The glade nyght ys worth an hevy morowe —
Seynt Valentyne, a foul thus herde I synge
Upon thy day er sonne gan up-sprynge.

Yet sang this foul — I rede yow al awake,   15
And ye that han not chosen in humble wyse,
Without repentynge cheseth yow your make,
And ye that han ful chosen as I devise,
Yet at the leste renoveleth your servyse.
Confermeth hyt perpetuely to dure,   20
And paciently taketh your aventure.

And for the worship of this highe feste,
Yet wol I, in my briddes wise, synge
The sentence of the compleynt, at the leste,
That woful Mars made atte departyng   25
Fro fresshe Venus in a morwenynge,
Whan Phebus with his firy torches rede
Ransaked every lover in hys drede.

[*The Story*]

Whilom the thridde hevenes lord above,
As wel by hevenysh revolucioun   30
As by desert, hath wonne Venus his love,
And she hath take him in subjeccioun,
And as a maistresse taught him his lessoun,
Commaundynge him that nevere, in her servise,
He nere so bold no lover to dispise.   35

For she forbad him jelosye at al,
And cruelte, and bost, and tyrannye.
She made him at her lust so humble and tal,
That when her deyned to cast on hym her ye,
He tok in pacience to lyve or dye.   40
And thus she brydeleth him in her manere,
With nothing but with scourging of her chere.

Who regneth now in blysse but Venus,
That hath thys worthy knyght in governaunce?
Who syngeth now but Mars, that serveth thus
The faire Venus, causer of plesaunce?   46

24 sentence: substance, main point
28 Ransaked: searched out
29 thridde hevenes lord: Mars, the planet of the third celestial
sphere, counting inward
30 hevenysh revolucioun: movement in its orbit, which brings
Mars in conjunction with the planet Venus, which moderates the
usually baneful influences of Mars. In the narrative Mars and
Venus move into conjunction in Taurus; since Venus moves more
swiftly through the heavens than Mars, she must move on and
leave Mars behind as the sun approaches.
38 tal: prompt, ready (to obey her)
41 brydeleth: controls (as with a bridle)
42 scourging: correction, punishment   chere: look (astrological
aspect)

He bynt him to perpetuall obeisaunce,
And she bynt her to loven him for evere,
But so be that his trespas hyt desevere.

Thus be they knyt and regnen as in hevene
Be lokyng moost; til hyt fil on a tyde   51
That by her bothe assent was set a stevene
That Mars shal entre, as fast as he may glyde,
Into hir nexte paleys, and ther abyde,
Walkynge hys cours, til she had him atake,   55
And he preide her to haste her for his sake.

Then seyde he thus, "Myn hertes lady swete,
Ye knowe wel my myschef in that place,
For sikerly, til that I with yow mete,
My lyf stant ther in aventure and grace;   60
But when I se the beaute of your face,
Ther ys no drede of deth may do me smerte,
For al your lust is ese to myn herte."

She hath so gret compassioun of her knyght,
That dwelleth in solitude til she come —   65
For hyt stod so that thilke tyme no wight
Counseyled hym ther, ne seyde to hym wel-
        come —
That nygh her wit for wo was overcome;
Wherfore she sped her as faste in her weye
Almost in oo day as he dyde in tweye.   70

The grete joye that was betwix hem two
When they be mette ther may no tunge telle.
Ther is no more but unto bed thei go,
And thus in joy and blysse I lete hem duelle.
This worthi Mars, that is of knyghthod
        welle,   75
The flour of feyrnesse lappeth in his armes,
And Venus kysseth Mars, the god of armes.

Sojourned hath this Mars of which I rede
In chambre amyd the paleys prively
A certeyn tyme, til him fel a drede   80
Throgh Phebus, that was comen hastely
Within the paleys yates sturdely,

47 bynt = *byndeth,* binds
49 desevere: separate
51 lokyng: (astrological) aspect
52 stevene: appointed time
54 paleys: zodiacal sign (here Taurus)
55 atake: overtaken
60 stant = *stondeth,* stands
76 lappeth: enfolds
78 rede: speak
81 Phebus: the sun
82 sturdely: boldly

With torche in honde, of which the stremes
    bryghte
On Venus chambre knokkeden ful lyghte.

The chambre ther as ley this fresshe quene
Depeynted was with white boles grete,   86
And by the lyght she knew, that shon so shene,
That Phebus cam to brenne hem with his hete.
This sely Venus nygh dreynt in teres wete
Enbraceth Mars and seyde, "Alas, I dye!   90
The torche is come that al this world wol wrie."

Up sterte Mars; hym liste not to slepe
When he his lady herde so compleyne,
But, for his nature was not for to wepe,
In stede of teres, from his eyen tweyne   95
The firi sparkes brosten out for peyne,
And hente his hauberk that ley hym besyde.
Fle wolde he not, ne myghte himselven hide.

He throweth on his helm of huge wyghte,   99
And girt him with his swerd, and in his hond
His myghty spere, as he was wont to fyghte,
He shaketh so that almost hit towond.
Ful hevy was he to walken over lond;
He may not holde with Venus companye
But bad her fleen lest Phebus her espye.   105

O woful Mars — alas — what maist thou seyn,
That in the paleys of thy disturbaunce
Art left byhynde in peril to be sleyn?
And yet therto ys double thy penaunce,
For she that hath thyn herte in governaunce
Is passed half the stremes of thin yën;   111
That thou nere swift, wel maist thou wepe and
    crien.

Now fleeth Venus unto Cilenios tour
With voide cours for fere of Phebus lyght —
Alas — and ther ne hath she no socour,   115
For she ne found ne saugh no maner wyght,
And eke as ther she hath but litil myght,
Wherfor, herselven for to hyde and save,
Within the gate she fledde into a cave.   119

Derk was this cave and smokyng as the helle;
Not but two pas within the yate hit stod.
A naturel day in derk I lete her duelle.
Now wol I speke of Mars, furious and wod.
For sorow he wolde have sen his herte blod;
Sith that he myghte don her no companye,   125
He ne roghte not a myte for to dye.

So feble he wex for hete and for his wo
That nygh he swelte, he myghte unnethe en-
    dure;
He passeth but o steyre in dayes two.
But nathelesse, for al his hevy armure,   130
He foloweth her that is his lyves cure,
For whos departyng he tok gretter ire
Then for al his brennyng in the fire.

After he walketh softely a paas,
Compleynyng, that hyt pite was to here,   135
He seyde, "O lady bryght, Venus, alas,
That evere so wyd a compas ys my spere!
Alas, when shal I mete yow, herte dere?
This twelfte daye of April I endure
Throgh jelous Phebus this mysaventure."   140

Now God helpe sely Venus allone.
But as God wolde, hyt happed for to be
That, while that Venus weping made her mone,
Cilenius, rydinge in his chevache,
Fro Venus valaunse myghte his paleys se,   145
And Venus he salueth and doth chere,
And her receyveth as his frend ful dere.

Mars dwelleth forth in his adversyte,
Compleynyng ever on her departynge,
And what his compleynt was, remembreth me;
And therfore, in this lusty morwenynge   151
As I best can, I wol hit seyn and synge,
And after that I wol my leve take,
And God yève every wyght joy of his make!

The Compleynt of Mars

The ordre of compleynt requireth skylfully 155
That yf a wight shal pleyne pitously,
Ther mot be cause wherfore that men pleyne;

86 **boles:** bulls
91 **wrie:** reveal, betray
99 **wyghte:** weight
100 **girt him with his swerd:** buckled on his sword
102 **towond:** broke in pieces
111 **half the stremes of thin yën:** half the extent of Mars's
influence (the conjunction is ending)
114 **voide:** solitary

121 **two pas:** two degrees
122 **naturel day:** twenty-four hours (cf. Astr 2.7)
129 **o steyre:** one degree
144 **Cilenius:** Mercury **chevache:** course
145 **valaunse:** detrimentum, the zodiacal sign opposite a planet's
domicile (but see n.)
155 **ordre of:** rule for **skylfully:** with reason

Or men may deme he pleyneth folily
And causeles; alas, that am not I.
Wherfore the ground and cause of al my peyne,
So as my troubled wit may hit atteyne,   161
I wol reherse; not for to have redresse,
But to declare my ground of hevynesse.

I

The firste tyme, alas, that I was wroght
And for certeyn effectes hider broght   165
Be him that lordeth ech intelligence,
I yaf my trewe servise and my thoght
For evermore — how dere I have hit boght —
To her that is of so gret excellence
That what wight that first sheweth his pres-
        ence,   170
When she is wroth and taketh of hym no cure,
He may not longe in joye of love endure.

This is no feyned mater that I telle;
My lady is the verrey sours and welle
Of beaute, lust, fredom, and gentilnesse,   175
Of riche aray — how dere men hit selle! —
Of al disport in which men frendly duelle,
Of love and pley, and of benigne humblesse,
Of soun of instrumentes of al swetnesse;
And therto so wel fortuned and thewed   180
That thorogh the world her goodnesse is
        yshewed.

What wonder ys it then, thogh I besette
My servise on such on that may me knette
To wele or wo sith hit lyth in her myght?
Therfore my herte forever I to her hette,   185
Ne truly, for my deth, I shal not lette
To ben her truest servaunt and her knyght.
I flater noght, that may wete every wyght;
For this day in her servise shal I dye.
But grace be, I se her never wyth ye.   190

II

To whom shal I than pleyne of my distresse?
Who may me helpe? Who may my harm re-
        dresse?
Shal I compleyne unto my lady fre?
Nay, certes, for she hath such hevynesse,
For fere and eke for wo that, as I gesse,   195

In lytil tyme hit wol her bane be.
But were she sauf, hit were no fors of me.
Alas, that ever lovers mote endure
For love so many a perilous aventure!

For thogh so be that lovers be as trewe   200
As any metal that is forged newe,
In many a cas hem tydeth ofte sorowe.
Somtyme her lady wil not on hem rewe;
Somtyme yf that jelosie hyt knewe,   204
They myghten lyghtly leye her hed to borowe;
Somtyme envyous folk with tunges horowe
Depraven hem; alas, whom may they plese?
But he be fals, no lover hath non ese.

But what availeth such a long sermoun
Of aventures of love up and doun?   210
I wol returne and speken of my peyne.
The poynt is this of my distruccioun:
My righte lady, my savacyoun,
Is in affray, and not to whom to pleyne.
O herte swete, O lady sovereyne!   215
For your disese wel oughte I swowne and
        swelte,
Though I non other harm ne drede felte.

III

To what fyn made the God, that sit so hye,
Benethen him love other companye
And streyneth folk to love, malgre her hed?
And then her joy, for oght I can espye,   221
Ne lasteth not the twynkelyng of an ye,
And somme han never joy til they be ded.
What meneth this? What is this mystihed?
Wherto constreyneth he his folk so faste   225
Thing to desyre, but hit shulde laste?

And thogh he made a lover love a thing
And maketh hit seme stedfast and during,
Yet putteth he in hyt such mysaventure
That reste nys ther non in his yeving.   230
And that is wonder, that so juste a kyng
Doth such hardnesse to his creature.
Thus, whether love breke or elles dure,
Algates he that hath with love to done
Hath ofter wo then changed ys the mone.   235

166 **lordeth:** governs   **intelligence:** an angel governing a
heavenly sphere
176 **how dere men hit selle:** how very expensive it is
180 **thewed:** endowed with good characteristics
185 **hette:** vowed
188 **flater:** lie, deceive   **wete:** know

196 **bane:** slayer
205 **to borowe:** as a pledge
206 **horowe:** ugly, filthy
207 **Depraven:** slander
214 **in affray:** frightened   **not** = *ne wot,* does not know
218 **fyn:** end, purpose
219 **other companye:** or companionship
220 **malgre her hed:** despite all they could do
224 **mystihed:** mysteriousness

Hit semeth he hath to lovers enmyte,
And lyk a fissher, as men alday may se,
Baiteth hys angle-hok with som plesaunce
Til many a fissh ys wod til that he be
Sesed therwith; and then at erst hath he   240
Al his desir, and therwith al myschaunce;
And thogh the lyne breke, he hath penaunce;
For with the hok he wounded is so sore
That he his wages hath for evermore.

IV

The broche of Thebes was of such a kynde,
So ful of rubies and of stones of Ynde   246
That every wight, that sette on hit an ye,
He wende anon to worthe out of his mynde;
So sore the beaute wolde his herte bynde.
Til he hit had, him thoghte he moste dye;   250
And whan that hit was his, then shulde he
          drye
Such woo for drede, ay while that he hit hadde,
That wel nygh for the fere he shulde madde.

And whan hit was fro his possessioun,
Then had he double wo and passioun   255
For he so feir a tresor had forgo;
But yet this broche as in conclusioun
Was not the cause of his confusioun,
But he that wroghte hit enfortuned hit so
That every wight that had hit shulde have wo;
And therfore in the worcher was the vice,   261
And in the covetour that was so nyce.

So fareth hyt by lovers and by me;
For thogh my lady have so gret beaute
That I was mad til I had gete her grace,   265
She was not cause of myn adversite,
But he that wroghte her, also mot I the,

That putte such a beaute in her face,
That made me coveyten and purchace
Myn oune deth — him wite I that I dye,   270
And myn unwit that ever I clamb so hye.

V

But to yow, hardy knyghtes of renoun,
Syn that ye be of my devisioun,
Al be I not worthy to so gret a name,
Yet, seyn these clerkes, I am your patroun;   275
Therfore ye oghte have som compassioun
Of my disese, and take hit not a-game.
The proudest of yow may be mad ful tame;
Wherfore I prey yow of your gentilesse
That ye compleyne for myn hevynesse.   280

And ye, my ladyes, that ben true and stable,
Be wey of kynde, ye oughten to be able
To have pite of folk that be in peyne.
Now have ye cause to clothe yow in sable,
Sith that youre emperise, the honurable,   285
Is desolat; wel oghte ye to pleyne.
Now shulde your holy teres falle and reyne.
Alas, your honour and your emperise,
Negh ded for drede ne can her not chevise!

Compleyneth eke, ye lovers, al in-fere,   290
For her that with unfeyned humble chere
Was evere redy to do yow socour;
Compleyneth her that evere hath had yow
          dere;
Compleyneth Beaute, Fredom, and Manere;
Compleyneth her that endeth your labour;   295
Compleyneth thilke ensample of al honour,
That never dide but al gentilesse;
Kytheth therfore on her sum kyndenesse.

239–40 To many a fish that is crazed (with desire) until it is in
possession of it (this bait) and then for the first time.
240 Sesed: put in possession of   at erst: for the first time
245 broche of Thebes: a brooch made by Vulcan; the story is
told in Statius's *Thebaid.*
248 worthe: go
251 drye: suffer
253 madde: go mad
259 enfortuned: gave (it) the power (fortune)

271 unwit: foolishness
273 of my devisioun: those ruled by the planetary influence of
Mars
275 patroun: patron saint
277 a-game: in sport, as a jest
284 sable: i.e., black
285 emperise: empress (Venus)
286 desolat: desolate, in an astrologically unfortunate position
289 chevise: attain her goal
298 Kytheth . . . on: show to

THE COMPLAINT OF VENUS

I

Ther nys so high comfort to my pleasaunce,
When that I am in any hevynesse,
As for to have leyser of remembraunce
Upon the manhod and the worthynesse,
Upon the trouthe and on the stidfastnesse   5
Of him whos I am al, while I may dure.
Ther oghte blame me no creature,
For every wight preiseth his gentilesse.

In him is bounte, wysdom, governaunce,
Wel more then any mannes wit can gesse,   10
For grace hath wold so ferforth hym avaunce
That of knyghthod he is parfit richesse.
Honour honoureth him for his noblesse;
Therto so wel hath formed him Nature
That I am his for ever, I him assure,   15
For every wight preyseth his gentilesse.

And notwithstondyng al his suffisaunce,
His gentil herte is of so gret humblesse
To me in word, in werk, in contenaunce,
And me to serve is al his besynesse,   20
That I am set in verrey sikernesse.
Thus oghte I blesse wel myn aventure
Sith that him list me serven and honoure,
For every wight preiseth his gentilesse.

II

Now certis, Love, hit is right covenable   25
That men ful dere bye thy nobil thing,
As wake abedde and fasten at the table,
Wepinge to laughe and singe in compleynyng,
And doun to caste visage and lokyng,
Often to chaunge hewe and contenaunce,   30
Pleyne in slepyng and dremen at the daunce,
Al the revers of any glad felyng.

Jelosie be hanged by a cable!
She wolde al knowe thurgh her espying;
Ther doth no wyght nothing so resonable   35
That al nys harm in her ymagenyng.
Thus dere abought is Love in yevyng,

Which ofte he yiveth withouten ordynaunce,
As sorwe ynogh and litil of plesaunce,
Al the revers of any glad felyng.   40

A lytel tyme his yift ys agreable,
But ful encomberous is the usyng,
For subtil Jelosie, the deceyvable,
Ful often tyme causeth desturbyng.
Thus be we ever in drede and sufferyng;   45
In nouncerteyn we languisshe in penaunce,
And han wele ofte many an hard mischaunce,
Al the revers of any glad felyng.

III

But certes, Love, I sey not in such wise
That for t'escape out of youre las I mente,   50
For I so longe have ben in your servise
That for to lete of wil I never assente;
No fors thogh Jelosye me turmente.
Sufficeth me to sen hym when I may,
And therfore certes, to myn endyng day   55
To love hym best ne shal I never repente.

And certis, Love, when I me wel avise
On any estat that man may represente,
Then have ye made me thurgh your fraun-
          chise
Chese the best that ever on erthe wente.   60
Now love wel, herte, and lok thou never stente,
And let the jelous putte it in assay
That for no peyne wol I not sey nay;
To love him best ne shal I never repente.

Herte, to the hit oughte ynogh suffise   65
That Love so high a grace to the sente
To chese the worthieste in alle wise
And most agreable unto myn entente.
Seche no ferther, neythir wey ne wente,
Sith I have suffisaunce unto my pay.   70
Thus wol I ende this compleynt or this lay;
To love hym best ne shal I never repente.

38 **withouten ordynaunce:** without regulation, freely
42 **encomberous:** troublesome
46 **nouncerteyn:** uncertainty
50 **las:** snare
52 **lete of:** cease
59 **fraunchise:** nobility of character
69 **wente:** path
70 **pay:** pleasure, satisfaction

10 **gesse:** estimate
11 **hath wold:** has willed, desired
12 **parfit richesse:** finest example
25 **covenable:** suitable, fitting
26 **ful dere bye:** pay dearly for

Lenvoy

Princes, receyveth this compleynt in gre,
Unto your excelent benignite
Direct after my litel suffisaunce.   75
For elde, that in my spirit dulleth me,
Hath of endyting al the subtilte

Wel nygh bereft out of my remembraunce,
And eke to me it ys a gret penaunce,
Syth rym in Englissh hath such skarsete,   80
To folowe word by word the curiosite
Of Graunson, flour of hem that make in
    Fraunce.

Here endith the Compleynt of Venus.

TO ROSEMOUNDE

A Balade

Madame, ye ben of al beaute shryne
As fer as cercled is the mapamounde,
For as the cristal glorious ye shyne,
And lyke ruby ben your chekes rounde.
Therwith ye ben so mery and so jocounde   5
That at a revel whan that I see you daunce,
It is an oynement unto my wounde,
Thogh ye to me ne do no daliaunce.

For thogh I wepe of teres ful a tyne,
Yet may that wo myn herte nat confounde;   10
Your semy voys that ye so smal out twyne
Maketh my thoght in joy and blis habounde.
So curtaysly I go with love bounde

That to myself I sey in my penaunce,
"Suffyseth me to love you, Rosemounde,   15
Thogh ye to me ne do no daliaunce."

Nas never pyk walwed in galauntyne
As I in love am walwed and ywounde,
For which ful ofte I of myself devyne
That I am trewe Tristam the secounde.   20
My love may not refreyde nor affounde,
I brenne ay in an amorous plesaunce.
Do what you lyst, I wyl your thral be founde,
Thogh ye to me ne do no daliaunce.

tregentil————————//————————chaucer

WOMANLY NOBLESSE

Balade That Chaucier Made

So hath myn herte caught in remembraunce
Your beaute hoole and stidefast governaunce,
Your vertues al and yowre hie noblesse,
That you to serve is set al my plesaunce.
So wel me liketh your womanly contenaunce,
Your fresshe fetures and your comlynesse,   6
That whiles I live myn hert to his maystresse

You hath ful chose in trewe perséveraunce
Never to chaunge, for no maner distresse.

78 **bereft out**: taken away
81 **curiosite**: intricate and skillful workmanship
82 **Graunson**: Oton de Grandson (d. 1397), author of the
ballades that are the source of the foregoing

17 **pyk walwed in galauntyne**: pike steeped in galantine, a
sauce; see n.
20 **Tristam**: Tristan, the idealized lover of Isolde in medieval
romance
21 **refreyde**: grow cold **affounde**: grow numb, turn cold
tregentil: This, which may be a proper name or an epithet
("very gentle"), has not been explained; it may be merely an
imitation of a similar colophon to *Troilus*, which immediately
precedes this poem in the manuscript. It is printed here as it is in
the manuscript, with a line, or flourish, connecting it with (or
separating it from) the word *chaucer*.

73 **in gre**: favorably
75 **Direct**: dedicated

2 **mapamounde**: map of the world
7 **oynement**: ointment, salve
8 **to me ne do no daliaunce**: are not friendly, encouraging, to
me
9 **tyne**: barrel
11 **semy**: small, high **out twyne**: twist out

And sith I shal do [you] this observaunce,   10
Al my lif withouten displesaunce
You for to serve with al my besynesse,
And have me somwhat in your souvenaunce.
My woful herte suffreth greet duresse,
And [loke] how humbly with al symplesse
My wil I cónforme to your ordynaunce,   16
As you best list, my peynes for to redresse.

Considryng eke how I hange in balaunce
In your service, such, lo, is my chaunce,
Abidyng grace, whan that your gentilnesse   20
Of my grete wo liste do alleggeaunce,
And with your pite me som wise avaunce

In ful rebatyng of myn hevynesse;
And thynketh by resoun that wommanly no-
blesse
Shuld nat desire for to do the outrance   25
Ther as she fyndeth non unbuxumnesse.

Lenvoye

Auctour of norture, lady of plesaunce,
Soveraigne of beautee, floure of wommanhede,
Take ye non hede unto myn ignoraunce,
But this receyveth of your goodlihede,   30
Thynkyng that I have caught in remembraunce,
Your beaute hole, your stidefast governaunce.

CHAUCERS WORDES UNTO ADAM, HIS OWNE SCRIVEYN

Adam scriveyn, if ever it thee bifalle
Boece or Troylus for to wryten newe,
Under thy long lokkes thou most have the
scalle,

But after my makyng thow wryte more trewe;
So ofte adaye I mot thy werk renewe,   5
It to correcte and eke to rubbe and scrape,
And al is thorough thy negligence and rape.

THE FORMER AGE

A blisful lyf, a paisible and a swete,
Ledden the peples in the former age.
They helde hem payed of the fruites that they
ete,
Which that the feldes yave hem by usage;
They ne were nat forpampred with outrage.   5
Unknowen was the quern and ek the melle;
They eten mast, hawes, and swich pounage,
And dronken water of the colde welle.

Yit nas the ground nat wounded with the
plough,
But corn up-sprong, unsowe of mannes hond,
The which they gnodded and eete nat half
ynough.   11
No man yit knew the forwes of his lond,
No man the fyr out of the flint yit fond,
Unkorven and ungrobbed lay the vyne;
No man yit in the morter spyces grond   15
To clarre ne to sause of galantyne.

12–13 Apparently a line, rhyming on *-aunce,* has been lost here.
13 **souvenaunce:** remembrance
14 **duresse:** hardship, distress
15 **symplesse:** simplicity
17 **redresse:** amend, alleviate
21 **alleggeaunce:** alleviation

---

3 **scalle:** a scaly eruption of the scalp

---

1 **paisible:** peaceful
2 **former:** first
4 **by usage:** by custom, naturally (without cultivation)
5 **forpampred:** overindulged   **outrage:** excess
6 **quern:** handmill   **melle:** mill
7 **mast:** nuts (acorns and beechnuts)   **hawes:** hawthorn berries
pounage: food for pigs

---

23 **rebatyng:** abatement
25 **outrance:** excessive harm
26 **unbuxumnesse:** disobedience
Lenvoye: the dedication
27 **norture:** good manners (literally, nourishment)

---

6 **scrape:** erase (by scraping the parchment)
7 **rape:** haste

---

11 **gnodded:** shelled, husked (literally, rubbed)
12 **knew the forwes:** knew the furrows (i.e., fields were
unplowed)
14 **Unkorven:** unpruned   **ungrobbed:** untilled
16 **clarre:** spiced and sweetened wine   **galantyne:** a sauce

No mader, welde, or wood no litestere
Ne knew; the flees was of his former hewe;
No flesh ne wiste offence of egge or spere.   19
No coyn ne knew man which was fals or trewe,
No ship yit karf the wawes grene and blewe,
No marchaunt yit ne fette outlandish ware.
No trompes for the werres folk ne knewe,
Ne toures heye and walles rounde or square.

What sholde it han avayled to werreye?   25
Ther lay no profit, ther was no richesse;
But cursed was the tyme, I dare wel seye,
That men first dide hir swety bysinesse
To grobbe up metal, lurkinge in derknesse,
And in the riveres first gemmes soghte.   30
Allas, than sprong up al the cursednesse
Of coveytyse, that first our sorwe broghte.

Thise tyraunts putte hem gladly nat in pres
No wildnesse ne no busshes for to winne,
Ther poverte is, as seith Diogenes,
Ther as vitaile is ek so skars and thinne   35
That noght but mast or apples is therinne;
But, ther as bagges ben and fat vitaile,
Ther wol they gon, and spare for no sinne
With al hir ost the cite for to asayle.   40

Yit was no paleis-chaumbres ne non halles;
In caves and wodes softe and swete
Slepten this blissed folk withoute walles
On gras or leves in parfit quiete.
Ne doun of fetheres ne no bleched shete   45
Was kid to hem, but in seurtee they slepte.
Hir hertes were al oon withoute galles;
Everich of hem his feith to other kepte.

Unforged was the hauberk and the plate;
The lambish peple, voyd of alle vyce,   50
Hadden no fantasye to debate,
But ech of hem wolde other wel cheryce.
No pryde, non envye, non avaryce,
No lord, no taylage by no tyrannye;   54
Humblesse and pees, good feith the emperice.

Yit was not Jupiter the likerous,
That first was fader of delicacye,
Come in this world; ne Nembrot, desirous
To regne, had nat maad his toures hye.
Allas, allas, now may men wepe and crye!   60
For in oure dayes nis but covetyse,
Doublenesse, and tresoun, and envye,
Poyson, manslawhtre, and mordre in sondry
        wyse.

Finit Etas Prima. Chaucers.

17 **mader, welde, wood:** plants used for making red, yellow, and blue dyes   **litestere:** dyer
18 **flees:** fleece   **former:** first, natural
19 **egge:** edge (of a sword)
20 **fals or trewe:** counterfeit or genuine
22 **outlandish:** foreign   **ware:** wares, merchandise
25 **werreye:** wage war
28 **swety bysinesse:** sweaty efforts
29 **grobbe:** dig
33 **putte hem . . . in pres:** make an effort   **gladly:** ordinarily, usually
35 **Diogenes:** the Greek philosopher
36 **skars:** scarce
38 **bagges:** bags (of goods or money)   **fat vitaile:** fat foodstuffs
39 **spare for no sinne:** desist for no sense of sin

45 **bleched:** whitened
46 **kid:** known   **seurtee:** security
47 **galles:** feelings of envy
49 **plate:** plate armor
50 **lambish:** lamb-like
51 **fantasye:** desire
52 **cheryce:** cherish
54 **taylage:** taxation
55 **emperice:** empress, ruler. A line is missing following 55; see n.
56 **likerous:** lecherous
57 **delicacye:** voluptuousness
58 **Nembrot:** Nimrod, regarded as the founder of cities and builder of the tower of Babel
Finit Etas Prima: Here ends the First Age.

FORTUNE

Balades de Visage sanz Peinture

I. Le Pleintif countre Fortune

This wrecched worldes transmutacioun,
As wele or wo, now povre and now honour,
Withouten ordre or wys discrecioun
Governed is by Fortunes errour.
But natheles, the lak of hir favour   5
Ne may nat don me singen though I dye,
Jay tout perdu mon temps et mon labour;
For fynally, Fortune, I thee defye.

Yit is me left the light of my resoun
To knowen frend fro fo in thy mirour.   10
So muchel hath yit thy whirling up and doun
Ytaught me for to knowen in an hour.
But trewely, no force of thy reddour
To him that over himself hath the maystrye.
My suffisaunce shal be my socour,   15
For fynally Fortune, I thee defye.

O Socrates, thou stidfast champioun,
She never mighte be thy tormentour;
Thou never dreddest hir oppressioun,
Ne in hir chere founde thou no savour.   20
Thou knewe wel the deceit of hir colour,
And that hir moste worshipe is to lye.
I knowe hir eek a fals dissimulour,
For fynally, Fortune, I thee defye!

II. La respounse de Fortune au Pleintif

No man is wrecched but himself it wene,   25
And he that hath himself hath suffisaunce.
Why seystow thanne I am to thee so kene,
That hast thyself out of my governaunce?
Sey thus: "Graunt mercy of thyn habound-
        aunce
That thou hast lent or this." Why wolt thou
        stryve?   30

What wostow yit how I thee wol avaunce?
And eek thou hast thy beste frend alyve.

I have thee taught divisioun bitwene
Frend of effect and frend of countenaunce;
Thee nedeth nat the galle of noon hyene,   35
That cureth eyen derked for penaunce;
Now seestow cleer that were in ignoraunce.
Yit halt thyn ancre and yit thou mayst arryve
Ther bountee berth the keye of my substaunce,
And eek thou hast thy beste frend alyve.   40

How many have I refused to sustene
Sin I thee fostred have in thy plesaunce.
Woltow than make a statut on thy quene
That I shal been ay at thyn ordinaunce?
Thou born art in my regne of variaunce,   45
Aboute the wheel with other most thou dryve.
My lore is bet than wikke is thy grevaunce,
And eek thou hast thy beste frend alyve.

III. La respounse du Pleintif countre Fortune

Thy lore I dampne; it is adversitee.   49
My frend maystow nat reven, blind goddesse;
That I thy frendes knowe, I thanke it thee.
Tak hem agayn, lat hem go lye on presse.
The negardye in keping hir richesse
Prenostik is thou wolt hir tour assayle;
Wikke appetyt comth ay before syknesse.   55
In general, this reule may nat fayle.

La respounse de Fortune countre le Pleintif

Thou pinchest at my mutabilitee
For I thee lente a drope of my richesse,
And now me lyketh to withdrawe me.

Balades de Visage sanz Peinture: ballades on a face without
painting; see n.
Le Pleintif countre Fortune: the plaintiff (as in a court of law
pleads) against Fortune
4 errour: fickleness
7 *Jay tout,* etc.: "I have lost all my time and labor," the opening
line of a "new French song," quoted in ParsT X.248
13 no force of: has no force, does not matter   reddour:
severity, harshness
22 moste worshipe: greatest dignity
La respounse, etc.: Fortune's response to the plaintiff
25 wene: suppose (it to be so)
30 or: ere

34 of effect: in actuality, in deeds   of countenaunce: in
appearance
35 hyene: hyena
38 halt = *holdeth,* holds fast   ancre: anchor
43 statut on: law applying to
47 "My teaching benefits you more than your affliction injures
you" (R.)
La respounse, etc.: The plaintiff's response to Fortune.
50 reven: take away
52 lye on presse: keep to themselves, stay away (as in a closet)
53 negardye: miserliness
54 Prenostik is: is a sign that
56 In general: universally
La respounse, etc.: Fortune's response to the plaintiff
57 pinchest at: find fault with

Why sholdestow my realtee oppresse? 60
The see may ebbe and flowen more or lesse;
The welkne hath might to shyne, reyne, or
        hayle;
Right so mot I kythen my brotelnesse.
In general, this reule may nat fayle.

Lo, th'execucion of the majestee 65
That al purveyeth of his rightwysnesse,
That same thing "Fortune" clepen ye,
Ye blinde bestes ful of lewednesse.
The hevene hath propretee of sikernesse,

This world hath ever resteles travayle; 70
Thy laste day is ende of myn intresse.
In general, this reule may nat fayle.

Lenvoy de Fortune

Princes, I prey you of your gentilesse
Lat nat this man on me thus crye and pleyne,
And I shal quyte you your bisinesse 75
At my requeste, as three of you or tweyne,
And but you list releve him of his peyne,
Preyeth his beste frend of his noblesse
That to som beter estat he may atteyne.

Explicit.

TRUTH

Balade de Bon Conseyl

Flee fro the prees and dwelle with sothfast-
        nesse;
Suffyce unto thy thing, though it be smal,
For hord hath hate, and climbing tikelnesse,
Prees hath envye, and wele blent overal.
Savour no more than thee bihove shal, 5
Reule wel thyself that other folk canst rede,
And trouthe thee shal delivere, it is no drede.

Tempest thee noght al croked to redresse
In trust of hir that turneth as a bal;
Gret reste stant in litel besinesse. 10
Be war therfore to sporne ayeyns an al,
Stryve not, as doth the crokke with the wal.
Daunte thyself, that dauntest otheres dede,
And trouthe thee shal delivere, it is no drede.

That thee is sent, receyve in buxumnesse; 15

The wrastling for this world axeth a fal.
Her is non hoom, her nis but wildernesse:
Forth, pilgrim, forth! Forth, beste, out of thy
        stal!
Know thy contree, look up, thank God of al;
Hold the heye wey and lat thy gost thee
        lede, 20
And trouthe thee shal delivere, it is no drede.

Envoy

Therfore, thou Vache, leve thyn old wrecched-
        nesse;
Unto the world leve now to be thral.
Crye him mercy, that of his hy goodnesse
Made thee of noght, and in especial 25
Draw unto him, and pray in general
For thee, and eek for other, hevenlich mede;
And trouthe thee shal delivere, it is no drede.

Explicit Le bon counseill de G. Chaucer.

---

60 **realtee:** royalty, royal power
65 **th'execucion:** the performance, executor **majestee:** i.e., God
69 **sikernesse:** security, stability

Balade de Bon Conseyl: ballade of good counsel
1 **prees:** crowd (the ambitious crowd at court)
2 **thyng:** possessions (Lat. *res*)
3 **hord:** avarice (literally, hoarding) **tikelnesse:** instability
4 **blent** = *blendeth*, blinds, deceives
7 **delivere:** set free
8 **Tempest thee:** trouble yourself **croked:** crooked, wrong (things)
9 **hir . . . bal:** That is, Fortune and her wheel
11 **sporne:** kick **al:** awl, which wounds the foot of one who kicks it
12 **crokke:** crock, which will break if it strikes a wall
13 **Daunte:** overcome, rule **dede:** deeds
15 **buxumnesse:** obedience

71 **intresse:** interest
Lenvoy de Fortune: The dedication concerning Fortune

---

20 **the heye wey:** the main, sure road
22 **Vache:** Sir Philip de la Vache (?); see n.
23 **leve:** leave off, cease
27 **mede:** reward
Explicit, etc.: Here ends the good counsel of G. Chaucer.

GENTILESSE

Moral Balade of Chaucier

The firste stok, fader of gentilesse —
What man that desireth gentil for to be
Must folowe his trace, and alle his wittes dresse
Vertu to love and vyces for to flee.
For unto vertu longeth dignitee   5
And noght the revers, saufly dar I deme,
Al were he mytre, croune, or diademe.

This firste stok was ful of rightwisnesse,
Trewe of his word, sobre, pitous, and free,
Clene of his gost, and loved besinesse,   10
Ayeinst the vyce of slouthe, in honestee;

And, but his heir love vertu as dide he,
He is noght gentil, thogh he riche seme,
Al were he mytre, croune, or diademe.

Vyce may wel be heir to old richesse,   15
But ther may no man, as men may wel see,
Bequethe his heir his vertuous noblesse
(That is appropred unto no degree
But to the firste fader in magestee,
That maketh hem his heyres that him queme),
Al were he mytre, croune, or diademe.   21

LAK OF STEDFASTNESSE

Balade

Somtyme the world was so stedfast and stable
That mannes word was obligacioun,
And now it is so fals and deceivable
That word and deed, as in conclusioun,
Ben nothing lyk, for turned up-so-doun   5
Is al this world for mede and wilfulnesse,
That al is lost for lak of stedfastnesse.

What maketh this world to be so variable
But lust that folk have in dissensioun?
For among us now a man is holde unable,   10
But if he can by som collusioun
Don his neighbour wrong or oppressioun.
What causeth this but wilful wrecchednesse,
That al is lost for lak of stedfastnesse?

Trouthe is put doun, resoun is holden fable,

Vertu hath now no dominacioun;   16
Pitee exyled, no man is merciable.
Through covetyse is blent discrecioun.
The world hath mad a permutacioun
Fro right to wrong, fro trouthe to fikelnesse,
That al is lost for lak of stedfastnesse.   21

Lenvoy to King Richard

O prince, desyre to be honourable,
Cherish thy folk and hate extorcioun.
Suffre nothing that may be reprevable
To thyn estat don in thy regioun.   25
Shew forth thy swerd of castigacioun,
Dred God, do law, love trouthe and worthi-
    nesse,
And wed thy folk agein to stedfastnesse.

Explicit.

---

1 **stok:** stock, ancestor
3 **trace:** tracks, footsteps
7 **Al:** although   **were he:** he may wear   **mytre, croune, or diademe:** the visual symbols of bishop, king, and emperor

2 **obligacioun:** surety, bond
6 **mede:** payment, bribery
9 **lust:** pleasure
10 **holde unable:** considered ineffectual
15 **fable:** falsehood, deceit

15 **old richesse:** wealth long in a family
18 **appropred unto:** appropriated to, the exclusive possession of
20 **queme:** please

18 **blent:** blinded, deceived
24 **reprevable:** damaging, a reproof

LENVOY DE CHAUCER A SCOGAN

Tobroken been the statutz hye in hevene
That creat were eternally to dure,
Syth that I see the bryghte goddis sevene
Mowe wepe and wayle, and passioun endure,
As may in erthe a mortal creature.   5
Allas, fro whennes may thys thing procede,
Of which errour I deye almost for drede?

By word eterne whilom was it shape
That fro the fyfte sercle, in no manere,
Ne myght a drope of teeres doun escape.   10
But now so wepith Venus in hir spere
That with hir teeres she wol drenche us here.
Allas! Scogan, this is for thyn offence;
Thow causest this diluge of pestilence.   14

Hastow not seyd, in blaspheme of the goddis,
Thurgh pride, or thrugh thy grete rekelnesse,
Swich thing as in the lawe of love forbode is,
That, for thy lady sawgh nat thy distresse,
Therfore thow yave hir up at Michelmesse?
Allas! Scogan, of olde folk ne yonge   20
Was never erst Scogan blamed for his tonge.

Thow drowe in skorn Cupide eke to record
Of thilke rebel word that thow hast spoken,
For which he wol no lenger be thy lord.
And, Scogan, though his bowe be nat broken,

He wol nat with his arwes been ywroken   26
On the, ne me, ne noon of oure figure;
We shul of him have neyther hurt ne cure.

Now certes, frend, I dreed of thyn unhap,   29
Lest for thy gilt the wreche of Love procede
On alle hem that ben hoor and rounde of shap,
That ben so lykly folk in love to spede.
Than shal we for oure labour have no mede;
But wel I wot, thow wolt answere and saye,
"Lo, olde Grisel lyst to ryme and playe!"   35

Nay, Scogan, say not so, for I m'excuse —
God helpe me so! — in no rym, dowteles,
Ne thynke I never of slep to wake my muse,
That rusteth in my shethe stille in pees.
While I was yong, I put hir forth in prees;   40
But al shal passe that men prose or ryme;
Take every man hys turn, as for his tyme.

[Envoy]

Scogan, that knelest at the stremes hed
Of grace, of alle honour and worthynesse,
In th'ende of which strem I am dul as ded,   45
Forgete in solytarie wildernesse —
Yet, Scogan, thenke on Tullius kyndenesse;
Mynne thy frend, there it may fructyfye!
Far-wel, and loke thow never eft Love dyffye.

LENVOY DE CHAUCER A BUKTON

My maister Bukton, whan of Crist our kyng
Was axed what is trouthe or sothfastnesse,
He nat a word answerde to that axing,
As who saith, "No man is al trewe," I gesse.

And therfore, though I highte to expresse   5
The sorwe and wo that is in mariage,
I dar not writen of it no wikkednesse,
Lest I myself falle eft in swich dotage.

---

1 **statutz:** edicts, laws
2 **creat:** created
3 **goddis sevene:** the seven planets
4 **passioun:** suffering
7 **errour:** confusion
9 **fyfte sercle:** fifth sphere, that of Venus, counting from the outside inward
14 **diluge of pestilence:** pestilential deluge
16 **rechelesnesse:** rashness
19 **Michelmesse:** September 29, the beginning of the fall business and court term
21 **erst:** before
22 **to record:** as a witness

27 **of oure figure:** shaped like us
30 **wreche:** vengeance
31 **hoor and rounde of shap:** gray and chubby
32 **so lykly:** such likely (i.e., so unlikely)
35 **olde Grisel:** the old grey horse (?); see n.
40 **in prees:** in public
43 **stremes hed:** the head of the Thames (Windsor castle)
45 **th'ende of which strem:** the mouth of the Thames (London)
48 **Mynne:** remember **there it may fructyfye:** where it (remembrance of your friend) can bear fruit, be of help
49 **dyffye:** defy, repudiate

---

5 **highte:** promised
8 **eft:** again **dotage:** foolishness

I wol nat seyn how that yt is the cheyne
Of Sathanas, on which he gnaweth evere,   10
But I dar seyn, were he out of his peyne,
As by his wille he wolde be bounde nevere.
But thilke doted fool that eft hath levere
Ycheyned be than out of prison crepe,
God lete him never fro his wo dissevere,   15
Ne no man him bewayle, though he wepe.

But yet, lest thow do worse, take a wyf;
Bet ys to wedde than brenne in worse wise.
But thow shal have sorwe on thy flessh, thy lyf,
And ben thy wives thral, as seyn these wise;
And yf that hooly writ may nat suffyse,   21

Experience shal the teche, so may happe,
That the were lever to be take in Frise
Than eft to falle of weddynge in the trappe.

[Envoy]

This lytel writ, proverbes, or figure   25
I sende yow; take kepe of yt, I rede;
Unwys is he that kan no wele endure.
If thow be siker, put the nat in drede.
The Wyf of Bathe I pray yow that ye rede
Of this matere that we have on honde.   30
God graunte yow your lyf frely to lede
In fredam, for ful hard is to be bonde.

Explicit.

THE COMPLAINT OF CHAUCER TO HIS PURSE

To yow, my purse, and to noon other wight
Complayne I, for ye be my lady dere.
I am so sory, now that ye been lyght;
For certes but yf ye make me hevy chere,
Me were as leef be layd upon my bere;   5
For which unto your mercy thus I crye,
Beth hevy ageyn, or elles mot I dye.

Now voucheth sauf this day or hyt be nyght
That I of yow the blisful soun may here
Or see your colour lyk the sonne bryght   10
That of yelownesse hadde never pere.
Ye be my lyf, ye be myn hertes stere.
Quene of comfort and of good companye,
Beth hevy ageyn, or elles moot I dye.

Now purse that ben to me my lyves lyght   15
And saveour as doun in this world here,
Out of this toune helpe me thurgh your myght,
Syn that ye wole nat ben my tresorere;
For I am shave as nye as any frere.
But yet I pray unto your curtesye,   20
Beth hevy agen, or elles moot I dye.

Lenvoy de Chaucer

O conquerour of Brutes Albyon,
Which that by lyne and free eleccion
Been verray kyng, this song to yow I sende,
And ye, that mowen alle oure harmes amende,
Have mynde upon my supplicacion.   26

---

10 **Sathanas:** Satan
12 **As by:** so far as it concerns
15 **dissevere:** part, get away from

3 **lyght:** light in weight, merry, wanton
4 **butyf ye make me hevy chere:** unless you look gravely at me, take me seriously
7 **hevy:** heavy in weight, serious, pregnant
12 **stere:** rudder, guide

23 **take:** taken prisoner   **Frise:** Frisia
25 **writ:** composition   **proverbes:** series of proverbs   **figure:** metaphorical statement
29 **Wyf of Bathe:** The Wife of Bath's Prologue

19 **shave as nye as any frere:** as bare of money as a friar's tonsure is of hair
22 **conquerour:** Henry IV   **Brutes Albyon:** the Albion (Britain) of Brutus
23 **lyne:** lineage, descent
26 **Have mynde upon:** be mindful of

PROVERBS

Proverbe of Chaucer

What shul these clothes thus manyfold,
  Lo this hote somers day?
After grete hete cometh cold;
  No man caste his pilche away.

Of al this world the large compas   5
  Yt wil not in myn armes tweyne;
Who so mochel wol embrace,
  Litel therof he shal distreyne.

Poems Not Ascribed to Chaucer in the Manuscripts

AGAINST WOMEN UNCONSTANT

Balade

Madame, for your newefangelnesse
Many a servaunt have ye put out of grace.
I take my leve of your unstedfastnesse,
For wel I wot, whyl ye have lyves space,
Ye can not love ful half yeer in a place,   5
To newe thing your lust is ay so kene.
In stede of blew, thus may ye were al grene.

Right as a mirour nothing may impresse,
But, lightly as it cometh, so mot it pace,
So fareth your love, your werkes beren wit-
    nesse.   10

Ther is no feith that may your herte enbrace,
But as a wedercok, that turneth his face
With every wind, ye fare, and that is sene;
In stede of blew, thus may ye were al grene.

Ye might be shryned for your brotelnesse   15
Bet than Dalyda, Creseyde or Candace,
For ever in chaunging stant your sikernesse;
That tache may no wight fro your herte arace.
If ye lese oon, ye can wel tweyn purchace;   19
Al light for somer (ye woot wel what I mene),
In stede of blew, thus may ye were al grene.

Explicit.

8 **distreyne:** retain

---

12 **wedercok:** weathercock, wind vane
15 **shryned:** enshrined, like a saint; cf. Ros 1. **brotelnesse:** brittleness, instability
16 **Dalyda:** Delilah, who betrayed Samson (see MkT VII.2063–70) **Creseyde:** the unfaithful lover of Troilus **Candace:** a queen of India, who tricked Alexander to get him in her power
18 **tache:** blemish, defect
20 **Al light for somer:** Apparently with the implication of fickleness or wantonness. The phrase occurs, in a wholly different context, in CYPro VIII.568 (R.).

---

1 **shul:** shall (be done with)
4 **pilche:** fur outer garment

---

1 **newefangelnesse:** instability, desire for novelty
4 **lyves space:** time in your life (i.e., while you live)
5 **a:** one
7 **blew:** blue, the color of fidelity **grene:** green, the color of unfaithfulness
8 **impresse:** engrave, make a permanent mark on

COMPLAYNT D'AMOURS

An Amorous Complaint, Made at Windsor

I, which that am the sorwefulleste man
That in this world was ever yit livinge,
And leest recoverer of himselven can,
Beginne right thus my deedly compleininge
On hir that may to lyf and deeth me bringe,
Which hath on me no mercy ne no rewthe,   6
That love hir best, but sleeth me for my
    trewthe.

Can I noght doon ne seye that may yow lyke?
Ne, certes now; allas, allas the whyle!
Your plesaunce is to laughen whan I syke,   10
And thus ye me from al my blisse exyle.
Ye han me cast in thilke spitous yle
Ther never man on lyve mighte asterte;
This have I, for I love you, swete herte!

Sooth is, that wel I woot, by lyklinesse,   15
If that it were a thing possible to do
For to acompte youre beautee and goodnesse,
I have no wonder thogh ye do me wo;
Sith I, th'unworthiest that may ryde or go,
Durste ever thinken in so hy a place.   20
What wonder is, thogh ye do me no grace?

Allas, thus is my lyf brought to an ende;
My deeth, I see, is my conclusioun.
I may wel singe, "In sory tyme I spende
My lyf." That song may have confusioun.   25
For mercy, pitee, and deep affeccioun,
I sey for me, for al my deedly chere,
Alle thise diden, in that, me love yow dere.

And in this wyse and in dispayr I live
In love — nay, but in dispayr I dye!   30
But shal I thus yow my deeth foryive,
That causeles doth me this sorwe drye?
Ye, certes, I! For she of my folye
Hath nought to done although she do me
    sterve,
Hit is nat with hir wil that I hir serve.   35

Than sithen I am of my sorwe the cause
And sithen I have this withoute hir reed,
Than may I seyn right shortly in a clause,
It is no blame unto hir womanheed
Though swich a wrecche as I be for hir deed.
Yet alwey two thinges doon me dye,   41
That is to seyn, hir beautee and myn yë;

So that, algates, she is verray rote
Of my disese and of my deth also,
For with oon word she mighte be my bote,   45
If that she vouched sauf for to do so.
But than is hir gladnesse at my wo?
It is hir wone plesaunce for to take
To seen hir servaunts dyen for hir sake.

But certes, than is al my wonderinge,   50
Sithen she is the fayrest creature,
As to my doom, that ever was livinge,
The benignest and beste eek that Nature
Hath wrought or shal, whyl that the world may
    dure,
Why that she lefte Pite so behinde?   55
It was, ywis, a greet defaute in Kinde.

Yit is al this no lak to hir, pardee,
But God or Nature sore wolde I blame.
For though she shewe no pite unto me,
Sithen that she doth othere men the same,   60
I ne oughte to despyse my ladyes game;
It is hir pley to laughen whan men syketh,
And I assente al that hir list and lyketh!

Yet wolde I, as I dar, with sorwful herte
Biseche unto your meke womanhede   65
That I now dorste my sharpe sorwes smerte
Shewe by word, that ye wolde ones rede
The compleynte of me, which ful sore I drede
That I have seid here, through myn unkon-
    ninge,
In any word to your displesinge.   70

Lothest of anything that ever was loth
Were me, as wisly God my soule save,

---

3 **recoverer:** remedy   **can:** knows
9 **ne:** a variant of *nay* (i.e., no)
12 **spitous yle:** hateful, inhospitable island; see n.
15 **by lyklinesse:** probably
17 **acompte:** recount
27 **for me:** so far as I am concerned
28 All these made me, in this case, love you dearly.
32 **drye:** suffer, feel

37 **reed:** permission (literally, advice)
43 **rote:** cause (root)
48 **wone:** custom
68 **of me:** concerning myself (or possibly this is possessive)
70 **displesinge:** displeasure

To seyn a thing through which ye might be
    wroth;
And, to that day that I be leyd in grave,
A trewer servaunt shulle ye never have;   75
And, though that I have pleyned unto you
    here,
Foryiveth it me, myn owne lady dere.

Ever have I been, and shal, how-so I wende,
Outher to live or dye, your humble trewe.
Ye been to me my ginning and myn ende,   80
Sonne of the sterre bright and clere of hewe;

Alwey in oon to love yow freshly newe,
By God and by my trouthe, is myn entente;
To live or dye, I wol it never repente!

This compleynte on Seint Valentynes day,   85
Whan every foughel chesen shal his make,
To hir, whos I am hool and shal alwey,
This woful song and this compleynte I make,
That never yit wolde me to mercy take;
And yit wol I evermore her serve   90
And love hir best, although she do me sterve.

Explicit.

MERCILES BEAUTE

A Triple Roundel

I

Your yen two wol slee me sodenly;
I may the beautee of hem not sustene,
So woundeth hit thourghout my herte kene.

And but your word wol helen hastily
My hertes wounde while that hit is grene,   5
    Your yen [two wol slee me sodenly;
    I may the beautee of hem not sustene].

Upon my trouthe I sey you feithfully
That ye ben of my lyf and deeth the quene,
For with my deeth the trouthe shal be sene.   10
    Your yen [two wol slee me sodenly;
    I may the beautee of hem not sustene,
    So woundeth it thourghout my herte kene].

II

So hath your beautee fro your herte chaced
Pitee, that me ne availeth not to pleyne,   15
For Daunger halt your mercy in his cheyne.

Giltles my deeth thus han ye me purchaced;
I sey you sooth, me nedeth not to feyne;
    So hath your beautee [fro your herte chaced

Pitee, that me ne availeth not to pleyne].   20

Allas, that Nature hath in you compassed
So greet beautee, that no man may atteyne
To mercy though he sterve for the peyne.
    So hath your beautee [fro your herte chaced
    Pitee, that me ne availeth not to pleyne,   25
    For Daunger halt your mercy in his cheyne].

III

Sin I fro Love escaped am so fat,
I never thenk to ben in his prison lene;
Sin I am free, I counte him not a bene.

He may answere and seye this and that;   30
I do no fors, I speke right as I mene.
    Sin I fro Love [escaped am so fat,
    I never thenk to ben in his prison lene].

Love hath my name ystrike out of his sclat,
And he is strike out of my bokes clene   35
For evermo; [ther] is non other mene.
    Sin I fro Love [escaped am so fat,
    I never thenk to ben in his prison lene;
    Sin I am free, I counte him not a bene].

Explicit.

---

79 **trewe:** true (servant)
81 **Sonne of the sterre bright:** That is, source of light to Venus, the lovers' star

---

6–7 **two . . . sustene:** See Textual Notes.
15 **Daunger:** disdain, standoffishness **halt** = *holdeth,* holds

---

86 **foughel:** bird

---

31 **do no fors:** pay no attention
34 **sclat:** slate
36 **mene:** means, course of action

A BALADE OF COMPLAINT

Compleyne ne koude, ne might myn herte
    never,
My peynes halve, ne what torment I have,
Though that I sholde in your presence ben ever,
Myn hertes lady, as wisly he me save   4
That Bountee made, and Beautee list to grave
In your persone, and bad hem bothe in-fere
Ever t'awayte, and ay be wher ye were.

As wisly he gye alle my joyes here
As I am youres, and to yow sad and trewe,
And ye, my lyf and cause of my gode chere,

And deeth also, whan ye my peynes newe,   11
My worldes joye, whom I wol serve and sewe,
Myn heven hool, and al my suffisaunce,
Whom for to serve is set al my plesaunce.

Beseching yow in my most humble wyse   15
T'accepte in worth this litel pore dyte,
And for my trouthe my servyce not despyse,
Myn observaunce eke have not in despyte,
Ne yit to longe to suffren in this plyte;
I yow beseche, myn hertes lady, here,   20
Sith I yow serve, and so wil yeer by yere.

6 **in-fere:** together
8 **gye:** guide

11 **newe:** renew
16 **dyte:** poem
20 **here:** hear (my complaint)

A
TREATISE ON THE
ASTROLABE

In writing on the astrolabe Chaucer tells us that he was responding to a request, the "besy praier" of the ten-year-old Lewis. If this is true, and not merely the parent's folly of wishing his own enthusiasms onto his children, then we can well believe that Lewis's interest was stimulated by Chaucer's. For in this treatise we find the same  interest in an intellectual pursuit that Chaucer evinces elsewhere in his knowledge of literature, philosophy, natural philosophy, medicine, and alchemy. As with these subjects, so with astronomy; Chaucer is the well-read, interested layman; he lacks the full knowledge of the professional — being too many-sided a man for such specialization — but he is too serious to be the dilettante. Moreover, he was sufficiently convinced of the importance in education of astronomy, one of the seven liberal arts, to undertake writing an elementary textbook meant for a young child.

In 1929, Robert T. Gunther called this "the oldest work written in English upon an elaborate scientific instrument"; it can still maintain that claim, though narrowly, since it antedates *The Equatorie of the Planetis* by only about a year. For clarity, the style of the latter, though dry, bears comparison with Chaucer's. But compared with the writing in some other medieval textbooks in English, the translations of Guy de Chauliac's *Surgery,* for example, Chaucer's skill as a writer "sticks fiery off indeed"; one need only read the account of square- and cube-roots in *The Earliest Arithmetics in English* (ed. Steele, EETS e.s. 118, 1922) to appreciate the perspicuity of the *Astrolabe.*

The *Astrolabe* is also well planned. The description in Part I is perfectly adequate for one who had his own instrument to hand, and there is a certain progression in the difficulty of the conclusions of Part II. After these practical exercises, Chaucer planned, though never executed, an account of the theory of planetary motions; for a young boy the pedagogical method is sound. Of course, some little theory was needed to understand the practice, but Chaucer had apparently provided this by preliminary demonstration with the *speer solide.* Above all he seems to have tried — probably successfully, at least in part — to retain the interest of his reader through a sustained, delicate rapport achieved by means of a mode of address in which the magistral and the familiar are happily blended.

It must be allowed that, to some extent, the clarity is due to what an astronomer, then or now, would think the simplicity of the material. Chaucer's propositions are for a ten-year-old, and the astrolabe was, as Emmanuel Poulle reminds us, the elementary astronomical instrument of the Middle Ages. However, most of us moderns have had very little experience of even elementary astronomical problems. The use of the globe is no longer part of general education. The difficulty involved and the effort required are considerable in imagining the movements of stars and planets in the celestial sphere from the point of view of a stationary earth, and their risings and settings upon an *embelif orizonte.* For this reason, the text is best used with the Explanatory Notes, which are founded upon experience of the difficulty; they attempt to ease the effort for those who "wondryn of the lawe of the heye eyr." The hope is that the reader may thereby find less obstruction and easier understanding and that his passage through the work may attain, if not to a "ravysshinge sweigh," at least to all deliberate speed.

JOHN REIDY

661

A Treatise on the Astrolabe

Lyte Lowys my sone, I aperceyve wel by certeyne evydences thyn abilite to lerne sciences
touching nombres and proporciouns; and as wel
considre I thy besy praier in special to lerne the
tretys of the Astrelabie. Than for as moche as a
philosofre saith, "he wrappith him in his frend,
that condescendith to the rightfulle praiers of his
frend," therfore have I yeven the a suffisant Astrolabie as for oure orizonte, compowned
after the latitude of Oxenforde; upon   10
which, by mediacioun of this litel tretys, I
purpose to teche the a certein nombre of conclusions aperteynyng to the same instrument. I
seie a certein of conclusions, for thre causes. The
first cause is this: truste wel that alle the conclusions that han be founde, or ellys possibly
might be founde in so noble an instrument as is
an Astrelabie ben unknowe parfitly to eny mortal
man in this regioun, as I suppose. Another
cause is this, that sothly in any tretis of the   20
Astrelabie that I have seyn, there be somme
conclusions that wol not in alle thinges parformen her bihestes; and somme of hem ben to
harde to thy tendir age of ten yeer to conceyve.

This tretis, divided in 5 parties, wol I shewe
the under full light reules and naked wordes in
Englissh, for Latyn canst thou yit but small,
my litel sone. But natheles suffise to the these
trewe conclusions in Englissh as wel as suf-
ficith to these noble clerkes Grekes these   30
same conclusions in Grek; and to Arabiens
in Arabik, and to Jewes in Ebrew, and to
Latyn folk in Latyn; whiche Latyn folk had
hem first out of othere dyverse langages, and

writen hem in her owne tunge, that is to seyn,
in Latyn. And God woot that in alle these
langages and in many moo han these conclusions ben suffisantly lerned and taught, and yit
by diverse reules; right as diverse pathes
leden diverse folk the righte way to Rome.   40
Now wol I preie mekely every discret persone that redith or herith this litel tretys to have
my rude endityng for excusid, and my superfluite of wordes, for two causes. The firste cause
is for that curious endityng and hard sentence
is ful hevy at onys for such a child to lerne.
And the secunde cause is this, that sothly me
semith better to writen unto a child twyes a
god sentence, than he forgete it onys.

And Lowys, yf so be that I shewe the in   50
my lighte Englissh as trewe conclusions
touching this mater, and not oonly as trewe
but as many and as subtile conclusiouns, as
ben shewid in Latyn in eny commune tretys
of the Astrelabie, konne me the more thank.
And preie God save the king, that is lord of
this langage, and alle that him feith berith and
obeieth, everich in his degre, the more and
the lasse. But considre wel that I ne usurpe
not to have founden this werk of my labour   60
or of myn engyn. I n'am but a lewd compila-
tor of the labour of olde astrologiens, and have it
translatid in myn Englissh oonly for thy doctrine. And with this swerd shal I sleen envie.

Prima pars. — The firste partie of this tretys
shal reherse the figures and the membres of
thyn Astrelabie by cause that thou shalt have
the gretter knowing of thyn oune instrument.

This text was edited by JOHN REIDY.

8 **suffisant:** adequate
9 **compowned:** constructed
12–13 **conclusions:** propositions, problems
14 **a certein of:** a certain number of

45 **curious:** abstruse, recondite
55 **konne me the more thank:** owe me greater thanks
59 **usurpe:** falsely claim
66 **figures:** markings, scales, etc.
67 **by cause:** for the purpose

Secunda pars. — The secunde partie shal techen the worken the verrey practik 70 of the forseide conclusiouns, as ferforth and as narwe as may be shewed in so small an instrument portatif aboute. For wel woot every astrologien that smallist fraccions ne wol not be shewid in so small an instrument as in subtile tables calculed for a cause.

Tertia pars. — The thirde partie shal contene diverse tables of longitudes and latitudes of sterres fixe for the Astrelabie, and tables of the declinacions of the sonne, and tables 80 of longitudes of citees and townes; and tables as well for the governaunce of a clokke, as for to fynde the altitude meridian; and many anothir notable conclusioun after the kalenders of the reverent clerkes, Frere J. Somer and Frere N. Lenne.

Quarta pars. — The fourthe partie shal ben a theorike to declare the moevyng of the celestiall bodies with the causes. The whiche fourthe partie in speciall shal shewen a 90 table of the verrey moeving of the mone from houre to houre every day and in every signe after thyn almenak. Upon which table there folewith a canoun suffisant to teche as wel the manere of the worchynge of the same conclusioun as to knowe in oure orizonte with which degre of the zodiak that the mone arisith in any latitude, and the arisyng of any planete after his latitude fro the ecliptik lyne.

Quinta pars. — The fifthe partie shal 100 be an introductorie, after the statutes of oure doctours, in which thou maist lerne a gret part of the generall rewles of theorik in astrologie. In which fifthe partie shalt thou fynden tables of equaciouns of houses after the latitude of Oxenforde; and tables of dignitees of planetes, and othere notefull thinges, yf God wol vouche saaf and his Moder the Maide, moo then I behete.

PART I

Here begynneth the descripcioun of thin Astralabie.

1. Thyn Astrolabie hath a ring to putten on the thombe of thi right hond in taking the height of thinges. And tak kep, for from henes forthward I wol clepen the heighte of any thing that is taken by the rewle "the altitude," withoute moo wordes.

2. This ryng renneth in a maner toret fast to the moder of thyn Astrelabie in so rowme a space that it distourbith not the instrument to hangen after his right centre.

3. The moder of thin Astrelabye is thikkest plate, perced with a large hool, that resceiveth in hir wombe the thynne plates compowned for diverse clymates, and thy reet shapen in manere of a nett or of a web of a loppe.

4. This moder is dividid on the bakhalf with a lyne that cometh descending fro the ring doun to the netherist bordure. The whiche lyne, fro the forseide ring unto the centre of the large hool amidde, is clepid the south lyne, or ellis the lyne meridional. And the remenaunt of this lyne doun to the bordure is

---

72 **narwe:** precisely
73 **portatif aboute:** portable
76 **subtile:** carefully compiled
80 **declinacions:** angular distance of the sun from the equator at the various times of the year
83 **altitude meridian:** altitude of the sun at noon
84 **kalenders:** astronomical tables
85 **Frere J. Somer:** John Somer, a Franciscan friar and astonomer; see n.
86 **Frere N. Lenne:** Nicholas of Lynn; see n.
88 **theorike:** theoretical exposition, theory

1.5 **altitude:** the angle between the celestial object and the observer's horizon
2.1 **toret:** eye (through which the ring passes)
2.2 **moder:** the body of an astrolabe   **rowme:** large, roomy

93 **almenak:** set of astronomical tables
94 **canoun:** set of rules
96 **orizonte:** the observer's horizon, or rather the plane parallel to it through the center of the earth, extended to the celestial sphere
99 **ecliptik lyne:** path of the sun through the zodiac
105 **equaciouns of houses:** divisions of the sphere into houses; see 2.36 below
106 **dignitees:** positions in which a planet exercises its greatest influence
107 **notefull:** useful

3.4 **clymates:** terrestrial latitudes   **reet:** rete (*riet;* see 1.21)
3.5 **loppe:** spider
4.1 **bakhalf:** reverse side

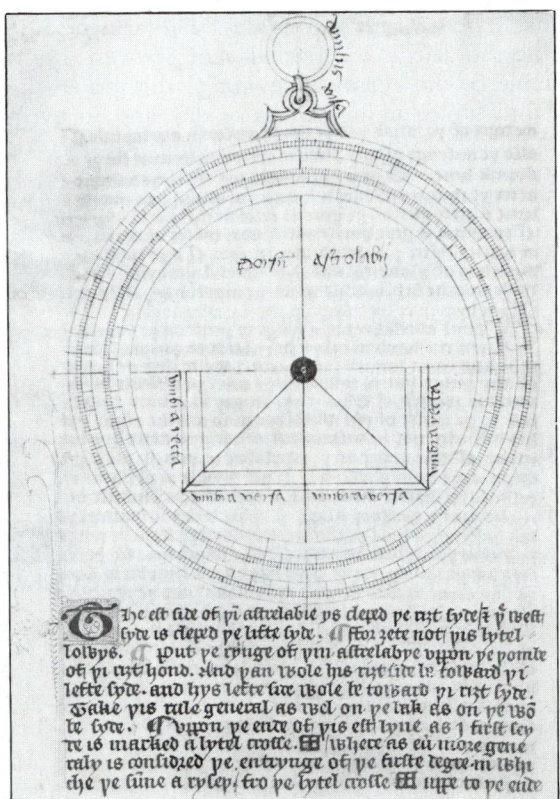

*Figure 1. MS Rawlinson
D.913, folio 24ᵛ.
The back of an astrolabe* (Dorsum
Astrolabii), *showing the various sets of
graduations round the rim* [1.4–1.11],
and the shadow square (skale) *marked*
vmbra recta *and* vmbra versa *the
wrong way round, as in all MSS* [1.12,
7–9 *and textual note*]. *The ring*
(Anulus) *is at the top* [1.1 *and* 2]. *MS.
Rawl. D. 913, fol. 24ᵛ, the Bodleian
Library, Oxford.*

clepid the north lyne, or ellis the lyne of mid-
nyght.

5. Overthwart this forseide longe lyne ther
crossith him another lyne of the same lengthe
from eest to west. Of the whiche lyne, from
a litel cros (+) in the bordure unto the centre of the large hool, is clepid the est lyne, or
ellis the lyne orientale. And the remenaunt of
this lyne, fro the forseide centre unto the bordure, is clepid the west lyne, or ellis the lyne
occidentale. Now hast thou here the foure
quarters of thin Astrolabie divided after the   10

foure principales plages or quarters of the firmament.

6. The est syde of thyn Astrolabie is clepid
the right syde, and the west syde is clepid the
left syde. Forget not thys, litel Lowys. Put
the ryng of thyn Astrolabie upon the thombe
of thi right hond, and than wol his right side
be toward thi lift side, and his left side wol be
toward thy right side. Tak this rewle generall,
as wel on the bak as on the wombe syde. Upon
the ende of this est lyne, as I first seide, is
marked a litel cros (+), where as evere   10
moo generaly is considerid the entring of
the first degre in which the sonne arisith.

7. Fro this litel cros (+) up to the ende
of the lyne meridionall, under the ryng, shalt
thou fynden the bordure divided with 90 degrees; and by that same proporcioun is every
quarter of thin Astrolabie divided. Over the
whiche degrees there ben noumbres of augrym
that dividen thilke same degres fro 5 to 5, as
shewith by longe strikes bitwene. Of whiche
longe strikes the space bitwene contenith
a myle wey, and every degre of the bor-   10
dure conteneth 4 minutes; this is to seien,
mynutes of an houre.

8. Under the compas of thilke degrees ben
writen the names of the 12 Signes: as
Aries, Taurus, Gemini, Cancer, Leo, Virgo,
Libra, Scorpio, Sagittarius, Capricornus, Aquarius, Piscis. And the nombres of the degrees of
thoo signes be writen in augrym above, and
with longe divisiouns fro 5 to 5, dyvidid fro
the tyme that the signe entrith unto the last
ende. But understond wel that these degres of signes ben everich of hem consid-   10
red of 60 mynutes, and every mynute of
60 secundes, and so furth into smale fraccions
infinite, as saith Alkabucius. And therfore
knowe wel that a degre of the bordure contenith 4 minutes, and a degre of a signe conteneth 60 minutes, and have this in mynde.

9. Next this folewith the cercle of the daies,
that ben figured in manere of degres, that contenen in nombre 365, dividid also with longe
strikes fro 5 to 5, and the nombre in augrym
writen under that cercle.

5.11 **plages:** quarters, compass bearings
7.2 **meridionall:** southern
7.6 **noumbres of augrym:** Arabic numerals; cf. MilT I.3210.
7.8 **strikes:** marks, divisions
7.10 **myle wey:** twenty minutes; see 1.16.14–16.
8.13 **Alkabucius:** Alchabitius, tenth-century Arab astronomer
9.2 **figured:** depicted
9.4 **strikes:** strokes, lines

10. Next the cercle of the daies folewith the cercle of the names of the monthes, that is to say, Januarius, Februarius, Marcius, Aprilis, Maius, Junius, Julius, Augustus, September, October, November, December. The names of these monthes were clepid somme for her propirtees and somme by statutes of Arabiens, somme by othre lordes of Rome. Eke of these monthes, as liked to Julius Cesar and to Cesar Augustus, somme were 10 compouned of diverse nombres of daies, as Julie and August. Than hath Januarie 31 daies, Februarie 28, March 31, Aprill 30, May 31, Junius 30, Julius 31, Augustus 31, Septembre 30, Octobre 31, Novembre 30, Decembre 31. Natheles, all though that Julius Cesar toke 2 daies out of Feverer and putte hem in his month of Juyll, and Augustus Cesar clepid the month of August after his name and or- deined it of 31 daies, yit truste wel that the 20 sonne dwellith therfore nevere the more ne lasse in oon signe than in another.

11. Than folewen the names of the holy daies in the Kalender, and next hem the let- tres of the A B C on whiche thei fallen.

12. Next the forseide cercle of the A B C, under the cross lyne, is marked the skale in manere of 2 squyres, or ellis in manere of lad- dres, that serveth by his 12 pointes and his dyvisiouns of ful many a subtil conclusioun. Of this forseide skale fro the cross lyne unto the verrey angle is clepid Umbra Versa, and the nethir partie is clepid Umbra Recta, or ellis Umbra Extensa.

13. Than hast thou a brod reule, that hath on either ende a square plate perced with cer- tein holes, somme more and somme lasse, to resceyve the stremes of the sonne by day, and eke by mediacioun of thin eye to knowe the altitude of sterres by night.

14. Than is there a large pyn in manere of an extre, that goth thorugh the hole that halt the tables of the clymates and the riet in the wombe of the moder; thorugh which pyn ther goth a litel wegge, which that is clepid the hors, that streynith all these parties to-hepe. Thys forseide grete pyn in manere of an extre

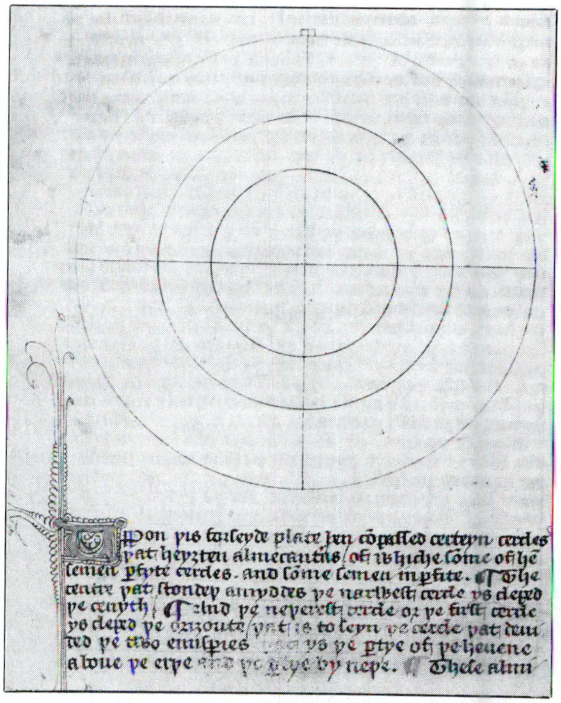

Figure 2.   MS Rawlinson D.913, folio 27v. *The plate, partly inscribed, showing the two cross lines, south (top) to north, and east (left) to west; also showing the three principal circles: Cancer (innermost), the Equinoxial, and Capricorn (outermost)* [1.17]. *The center is the projection of the North Pole* [1.14, 7–9]. MS. Rawl. D. 913, fol. 27t, *the Bodleian Library, Oxford.*

is ymagyned to be the Pool Artik in thyn Astralabie.

15. The wombe syde of thyn Astrelabie is also divided with a longe cros in 4 quarters from est to west, fro southe to northe, fro right syde to left side, as is the bakside.

16. The bordure of which wombe side is divided fro the point of the est lyne unto the point of the south lyne under the ring, in 90 degrees; and by that same proporcioun is every quarter divided, as is the bakside. That amountith 360 degrees. And understand wel that degres of this bordure ben aunswering and consentrike to the degrees of the equinoxiall, that is dividid in the same nombre as every

---

11.2–3 **lettres of the A B C:** the dominical or Sunday letters
12.2 **skale:** measuring scale
12.3 **squyres:** squares, rulers
12.7 **verrey angle:** right angle
13.1 **reule:** alidade, sighting device on an astrolabe
14.2 **extre:** axle tree
14.3 **tables of the clymates:** plates for different latitudes   **riet:** rete of an astrolabe (see 1.21)
14.5 **wegge:** wedge

14.8 **ymagyned:** assumed, taken
16.7 **aunswering:** corresponding
16.8 **equinoxiall:** equinoctial, celestial equator

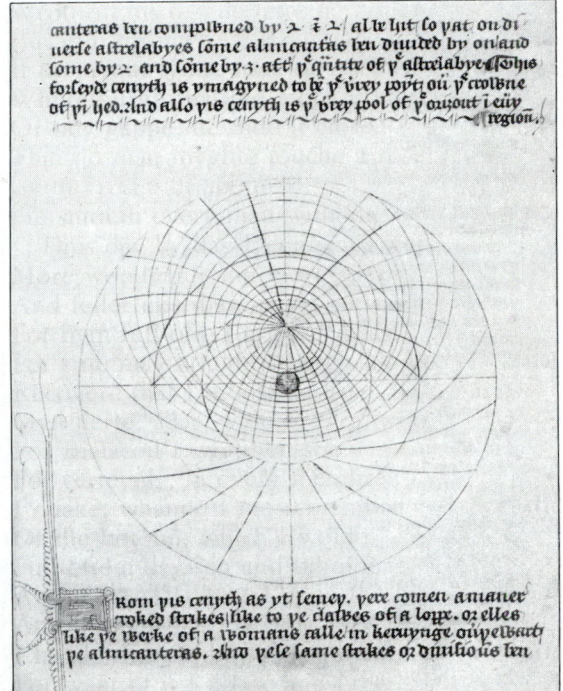

*Figure 3. MS Rawlinson D.913, folio 28ᵣ.
The plate, more fully inscribed, showing the
azimutz [1.19] descending from the zenith
[1.18, 4–6, 15–19], which is a little above
the central pole, to the horizon; also showing
the almycanteras, of which the lowest, zero
degrees, is the horizon [1.18]. Below the
horizon line and running to the edge of the
plate are ten arcs, which together with the
line from center to bottom mark out the hours
of the planets, or unequal hours [1.20,
2.10, 2.12]. MS. Rawl. D. 913, fol. 28ᵣ,
the Bodleian Library, Oxford.*

othir cercle is in the highe hevene. This   10
same bordure is divided also with 23
lettres capitals and a small cross (+) above
the south lyne, that shewith the 24 houres
equals of the clokke. And, as I have seid, 5
of these degres maken a myle wey, and 3 mile-
wei maken an houre. And every degre of thys
bordure contenith 4 minutes, and every minute 60 secundes. Now have I told the twyes.

17. The plate under the riet is discrived
with 3 cercles, of whiche the leest is
clepid the cercle of Cancre by cause that the
heved of Cancre turnith evermo consen-

trik upon the same cercle. In this heved
of Cancer is the grettist declinacioun northward of the sonne, and therfore is he clepid
solsticium of somer; which declinacioun, after
Ptholome, is 23 degrees and 50 minutes as
wel in Cancer as in Capricorn. This signe   10
of Cancer is clepid the tropik of somer, of
tropos, that is to seien "ageynward." For than
beginneth the sonne to passen from us-ward.

The myddel cercle in wydnesse, of these 3,
is clepid the cercle equinoxiall, upon which
turnith evermo the hevedes of Aries and Libra.
And understond wel that evermo thys cercle
equinoxiall turnith justly from verrey est to verrey west as I have shewed the in the speer
solide. This same cercle is clepid also   20
Equator, that is the weyer of the day; for
whan the sonne is in the hevedes of Aries and
Libra, than ben the dayes and the nightes ylike
of lengthe in all the world. And therfore ben
these 2 signes called the equinoxiis. And all
that moeveth withinne the hevedes of these
Aries and Libra, his moevyng is clepid northward; and all that moevith withoute these
hevedes, his moevyng is clepid southward,
as fro the equinoxiall. Tak kep of these   30
latitudes north and south, and forget it nat.
By this cercle equinoxiall ben considred the
24 houres of the clokke; for evermo the arisyng
of 15 degrees of the equinoxiall makith an
houre equal of the clokke. This equinoxiall is
clepid the gurdel of the first moeving, or ellis
of the firste moevable. And note that the firste
moevyng is clepid moevyng of the firste moevable of the 8 speer, which moeving is from
est to west, and eft ageyn into est. Also   40
it is clepid girdel of the firste moeving for it
departith the firste moevable, that is to seyn
the spere, in two like partyes evene distantz
fro the poles of this world.

The widest of these 3 principale cercles is
clepid the cercle of Capricorne, by cause that
the heved of Capricorne turneth evermo consentrik upon the same cercle. In the heved of
this forseide Capricorne is the grettist declinacioun southward of the sonne, and ther-   50
fore it is clepid the solsticium of wynter.
This signe of Capricorne is also clepid the

17.1 **discrived:** inscribed

17.6 **declinacioun:** angular distance from the equinoctial
17.15 **cercle equinoxiall:** the celestial equator
17.19–20 **speer solide:** an astronomical globe; see 2.26.1.
17.21 **weyer:** weigher, equator
17.31 **latitudes:** i.e., declinations; see n.
17.36 **first moeving:** the Primum Mobile
17.37 **firste moevable:** the Primum Mobile

tropic of wynter, for than begynneth the sonne to come ageyn to us-ward.

18. Upon this forseide plate ben compassed certeyn cercles that highten almycanteras, of whiche somme of hem semen parfit cercles and somme semen inparfit. The centre that stondith amyddes the narwest cercle is clepid the cenyth. And the netherist cercle, or the firste cercle, is clepid the orizonte, that is to seyn, the cercle that divideth the two emysperies, that is, the partie of the hevene above the erthe and the partie bynethe. These almy- [10] kanteras ben compowned by 2 and 2, all be it so that on diverse Astrelabies somme almykanteras ben divided by oon, and somme by two, and somme by thre, after the quantite of the Astrelabie. This forseide cenyth is ymagined to ben the verrey point over the crowne of thin heved. And also this cenyth is the verray pool of the orizonte in every regioun.

19. From this cenyth, as it semeth, there comen a maner croked strikes like to the clawes of a loppe, or elles like the werk of a wommans calle, in kervyng overthwart the almykanteras. And these same strikes or divisiouns ben clepid azimutz, and thei dividen the orisounte of thin Astrelabie in 24 divisiouns. And these azymutz serven to knowe the costes of the firmament, and to othre conclusiouns, as for to knowe the cenyth of the sonne and [10] of every sterre.

20. Next these azymutz, under the cercle of Cancer, ben there 12 divisiouns embelif, muche like to the shap of the azemutz, that shewen the spaces of the houres of planetes.

21. The riet of thin Astrelabie with thy zodiak, shapen in manere of a net or of a lopweb after the olde descripcioun, which thou maist turnen up and doun as thiself liketh, contenith certein nombre of sterres fixes, with her longitudes and latitudes determinat, yf so be that the

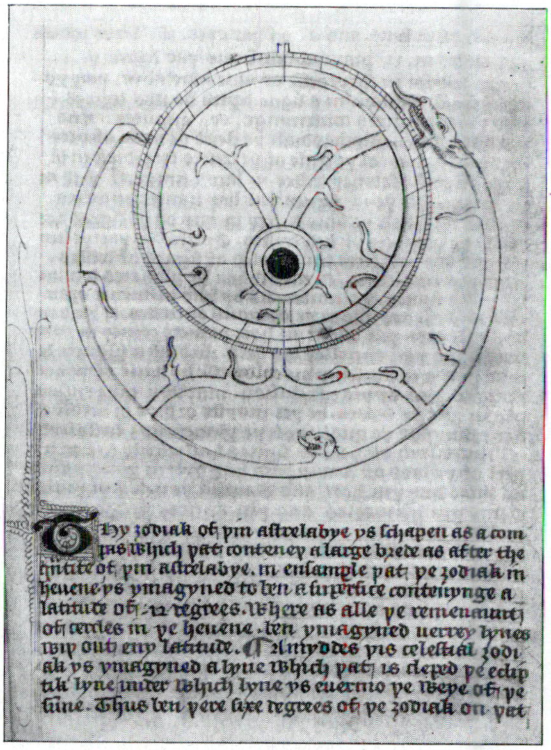

Figure 4. MS Rawlinson D.913, folio 29r.
A simplified drawing of the rete. The outer frame should continue to the top, the denticle of Capricorne [1.21, 90]. The zodiac circle is marked out in graduations of two degrees, but not labeled. The six signs below the east-west line are, from left to right, Aries to Virgo. The small pointers are projections of fixed stars [1.21, 4–10], the lowest being Alhabor, or Sirius the Dog Star [2.3, 43]. MS. Rawl. D. 913, fol. 29r, the Bodleian Library, Oxford.

maker have not errid. The names of the sterres ben writen in the margyn of the riet there as thei sitte, of whiche sterres the smale point is clepid the centre. And understond also that [10] alle the sterres sitting within the zodiak of thin Astrelabie ben clepid sterres of the north, for thei arise by northe the est lyne. And all the remenaunt fixed oute of the zodiak ben clepid sterres of the south. But I seie not that thei arisen alle by southe the est lyne; witnesse on Aldeberan and Algomeysa. Generaly understond this

18.2 **almycanteras**: almucantars, which indicate altitudes
18.6 **cenyth**: zenith
18.7 **orizonte**: the observer's horizon, or rather the plane parallel to it through the center of the earth, extended to the celestial sphere
18.8 **emysperies**: celestial hemispheres
18.18 **pool of the orizonte**: zenith
19.3 **loppe**: spider
19.4 **calle**: hairnet worn as a woman's headdress
19.6 **azimutz**: lines of azimuth, vertical circles from the zenith, cutting the horizon (and of course the almucantars) at right angles
19.8 **costes**: divisions, bearings
19.10 **cenyth of the sonne**: azimuth of the sun
20.2 **embelif**: oblique
21.2 **lopweb**: spider web

21.16–17 **Aldeberan**: Aldebaran
21.17 **Algomeysa**: the star alpha Canis Minoris

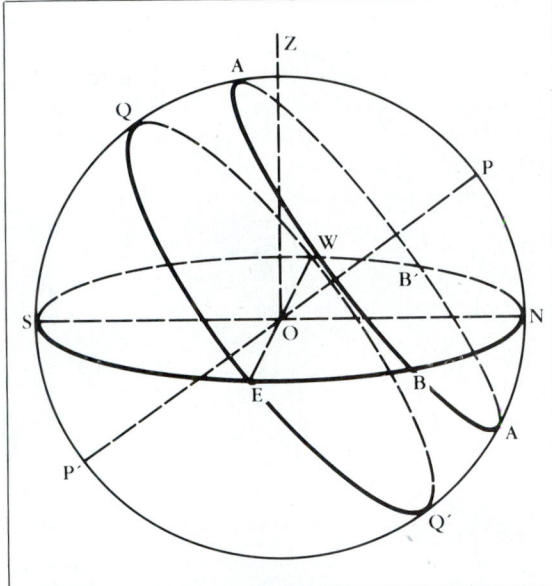

Figure 5.   A view of the Universe.
The outer circle is the sphere of the universe, PP'
the north and south celestial poles,
QEQ'W the celestial equator or equinoxial.
Observer O is at the center, north of the terrestrial
equator (about the latitude of Ann Arbor,
Michigan); his horizon is NESW, N being his
north point. A heavenly body circling the poles in
orbit A'BAB' daily will be above the horizon longer
than one with orbit Q'EQW; clearly the farther
north a star or planet is, the earlier it rises and the
later it sets. This principle applies in 1.21,
17–23; 2.19; and 2.28. Also, angles SOZ, NOZ,
POQ are right angles, hence angles SOQ and POZ
are equal, as are NOP, QOZ [2.22]. Adapted
from Henry Noris Russell, Raymond Smith Dugan,
and John Quincy Stewart, Astronomy: A
Revision of Young's Manual of Astronomy, I,
The Solar System *(Ginn & Company, 1926),*
p. 24, Fig. 9.

rewle, that thilke sterres that ben clepid sterres
of the north arisen rather than the degre of
her longitude, and alle the sterres of the   20
south arisen after the degre of her longitude — this is to seyn, sterres fixed in thyn
Astrelabie. The mesure of this longitude of
sterres is taken in the lyne ecliptik of hevene,

21.19 **rather:** earlier
21.24 **lyne ecliptik:** ecliptic circle

under which lyne, whan that the sonne and the
mone be lyne-right, or ellis in the superficie of
this lyne, than is the eclipse of the sonne or of
the mone, as I shal declare, and eke the cause
why. But sothly the ecliptik lyne of thy
zodiak is the utterist bordure of thy zodiak   30
there the degrees be marked.
    Thy zodiak of thin Astrelabie is shapen as
a compas which that contenith a large brede
as after the quantite of thyn Astrelabie, in ensample that the zodiak in hevene is ymagyned
to ben a superfice contenyng a latitude of 12
degrees, whereas alle the remenaunt of cercles
in the hevene ben ymagyned verrey lynes withoute eny latitude. Amiddes this celestial
zodiak is ymagined a lyne which that is   40
clepid the ecliptik lyne, under which lyne
is evermo the wey of the sonne. Thus ben
there 6 degres of the zodiak on that oo syde
of the lyne and 6 degres on that othir. This
zodiak is dividid in 12 principale divisiouns that
departen the 12 signes, and, for the streitnesse
of thin Astrolabie, than is every smal divisioun
in a signe departed by two degrees and two, I
mene degrees contenyng 60 mynutes. And
this forseide hevenysshe zodiak is clepid   50
the cercle of the signes, or the cercle of the
bestes, for "zodia" in langage of Grek sowneth
"bestes" in Latyn tunge. And in the zodiak
ben the 12 signes that han names of bestes,
or ellis for whan the sonne entrith in eny
of tho signes he takith the propirte of suche
bestes, or ellis for that the sterres that ben
ther fixed ben disposid in signes of bestes or
shape like bestes, or elles whan the planetes
ben under thilke signes thei causen us by   60
her influence operaciouns and effectes like
to the operaciouns of bestes.
    And understond also that whan an hot plan-
ete cometh into an hot signe, than encrescith
his hete; and yf a planete be cold, than amenusith his coldnesse by cause of the hoote sygne.
And by thys conclusioun maist thou take ensample in alle the signes, be thei moist or drie,
or moeble or fixe, reknyng the qualite of the
planete as I first seide. And everich of   70
these 12 signes hath respect to a certeyn

21.26 **lyne-right:** exactly aligned with the earth   **in the**
superficie: on the surface, very close to
21.33 **compas:** circle   **brede:** breadth
21.36 **superfice:** surface
21.52 **sowneth:** means
21.61 **influence:** power
21.65–66 **amenusith:** grows less

parcel of the body of a man, and hath it in governaunce; as Aries hath thin heved, and Taurus thy nekke and thy throte, Gemini thin armholes and thin armes, and so furth, as shall be shewid more pleyn in the 5 partie of this tretis.

This zodiak, which that is part of the 8 speer, over-kervith the equinoxial, and he over-kervith him ageyn in evene parties; and 80 that oo half declineth southward; and that othir northward, as pleinly declarith the Tretys of the Speer.

Than hast thou a label that is shapen like a reule, save that it is streit and hath no plates on either ende with holes. But with the smale point of the forseide label shalt thou calcule thin equaciouns in the bordure of thin Astralabie, as by thin almury.

Thin almury is clepid the denticle of 90 Capricorne, or ellis the calculer. This same almury sitt fix in the heved of Capricorne, and it serveth of many a necessarie conclusioun in equacions of thinges as shal be shewid.

Here endith the descripcioun of the Astrelabie and here begynne the conclusions of the Astrelabie.

PART II

1. *To fynde the degre in which the sonne is day by day, after his cours aboute.*

Rekne and knowe which is the day of thy month, and ley thy rewle upon that same day, and than wol the verrey poynt of thy rewle sitten in the bordure upon the degre of thy sonne.

Ensample as thus: The yeer of oure Lord 1391, the 12 day of March at midday, I wolde knowe the degre of the sonne. I soughte in the bakhalf of myn Astrelabie and fond the cercle of the daies, the whiche I knowe by 10 the names of the monthes writen under the same cercle. Tho leyde I my reule over this foreseide day, and fond the point of my reule in the bordure upon the firste degre of Aries, a litel within the degre. And thus knowe I this conclusioun.

Anothir day I wolde knowen the degre of my sonne, and this was at midday in the 13 day of Decembre. I fond the day of the month in manere as I seide; tho leide I my 20 rewle upon this foreseide 13 day, and fond the point of my rewle in the bordure upon the firste degre of Capricorne a lite within the degre. And than had I of this conclusioun the ful experience.

2. *To knowe the altitude of the sonne or of othre celestial bodies.*

Put the ryng of thyn Astrelabie upon thy right thombe, and turne thi lift syde ageyn the light of the sonne; and remewe thy rewle up and doun til that the stremes of the sonne shine thorugh bothe holes of thi rewle. Loke than how many degrees thy rule is areised fro the litel cros upon thin est lyne, and tak there the altitude of thi sonne. And in this same wise maist thow knowe by night the altitude of the mone or of brighte sterres. 10

This chapitre is so generall evere in oon that there nedith no more declaracioun; but forget it not.

3. *To knowe every tyme of the day by light of the sonne; and every tyme of the nyght by the sterres fixe; and eke to knowe by nyght or by day the degre of eny signe that ascendith on the est orisonte, which that is clepid comounly the ascendent, or ellis horoscopum.*

Tak the altitude of the sonne whan the list, as I have seid, and set the degre of the sonne, in caas that it be beforn the myddel of the day,

---

1.9 **bakhalf:** reverse side

21.84 **label:** brass rule
21.89 **almury:** pointer; the pointer on the rete of an astrolabe at 0° Capricorn

---

2.3 **remewe:** move
2.11 **generall evere in oon:** universally applicable

among thyn almykanteras on the est syde of thin Astrelabie; and if it be after the myddel of the day, set the degre of thy sonne upon the west syde. Tak this manere of settyng for a general rule, ones for evere. And whan thou hast set the degre of thy sonne upon as many almykanteras of height as was the al- 10 titude of the sonne taken by thy rule, ley over thi label upon the degre of the sonne; and than wol the point of thi labell sitte in the bordure upon the verrey tyde of the day.

Ensample as thus: The yeer of oure lord 1391, the 12 day of March, I wolde knowe the tyde of the day. I tok the altitude of my sonne, and fond that it was 25 degrees and 30 min- utes of height in the bordure on the bak side. Tho turned I myn Astrelabye, and by 20 cause that it was before mydday, I turned my riet and sette the degre of the sonne, that is to seyn the firste degre of Aries, on the right side of myn Astrelabye upon 25 degrees and 30 mynutes of height among myn almykanteras. Tho leide I my label upon the degre of my sonne, and fond the point of my label in the bordure upon a capital lettre that is clepid an X. Tho rekned I alle the capitale lettres fro the lyne of mydnight unto this forseide 30 lettre X, and fond that it was 9 of the clokke of the day. Tho loked I doun upon myn est orizonte, and fond there the 20 degre of Geminis ascendyng, which that I tok for myn ascendent. And in this wise had I the expe- rience for evermo in which manere I shulde knowe the tyde of the day and eke myn as- cendent.

Tho wolde I wite the same nyght folew- yng the houre of the nyght, and wroughte 40 in this wise: Among an heep of sterres fixe it liked me for to take the altitude of the faire white sterre that is clepid Alhabor, and fond hir sittyng on the west side of the lyne of midday, 12 degrees of heighte taken by my rewle on the bak side. Tho sette I the centre of this Alhabor upon 12 degrees among myn almykanteras upon the west side, by cause that she was founde on the west side. Tho leyde I my label over the degre of the 50 sonne, that was discendid under the west orisounte, and rekned all the lettres capitals

fro the lyne of midday unto the point of my label in the bordure, and fond that it was passed 9 of the clokke the space of 10 degrees. Tho lokid I doun upon myn est orisounte, and fond there 10 degrees of Scorpius ascendyng, whom I tok for myn ascendent. And thus lerned I to knowe onys for ever in which manere I shuld come to the houre of the 60 nyght, and to myn ascendent, as verrely as may be taken by so smal an instrument.

But natheles this rule in generall wol I warne the for evere: Ne make the nevere bold to have take a just ascendent by thin Astrelabie, or elles to have set justly a clokke, whan eny celestial body by which that thou wenyst gov- erne thilke thinges be nigh the south lyne. For trust wel, whan the sonne is nygh the meridional lyne, the degre of the sonne 70 renneth so longe consentrik upon the al- mykanteras that sothly thou shalt erre fro the just ascendent. The same conclusioun sey I by the centre of eny sterre fix by nyght. And more over, by experience I wot wel that in oure orisounte, from xi of the clokke unto oon of the clokke, in taking of a just ascendent in a portatif Astrelabie it is to hard to knowe — I mene from xi of the clokke before the houre of noon til oon of the clokke next 80 folewyng.

4. *A special declaracioun of the ascendent.*
The ascendent sothly, as wel in alle nativites as in questions and eleccions of tymes, is a thing which that these astrologiens gretly ob- serven. Wherfore me semeth convenyent, syth that I speke of the ascendent, to make of it speciall declaracioun.

The ascendent sothly, to take it at the larg- est, is thilke degre that ascendith at eny of these forseide tymes upon the est orisounte. And therfore, yf that eny planete ascende 10 at thatt same tyme in thilke forseide degre, than hath he no latitude fro the ecliptik lyne, but he is than in the degre of the ecliptik which that is the degre of his longitude. Men sayn that thilke planete is *in horoscopo.*

But sothly the hous of the ascendent, that is to seyn, the first hous or the est angle, is a

---

3.14 **tyde:** hour
3.35 **ascendent:** the degree of the zodiac on the eastern horizon
3.43 **Alhabor:** Sirius, the Dog Star

3.63 **in generall:** without exception
4.2 **eleccions of tymes:** selecting astrologically auspicious times for undertakings
4.16 **hous:** one of twelve astrological divisions of the heavens; see n.

thing more brod and large. For, after the statutes of astrologiens, what celestial body
that is 5 degrees above thilke degre that 20
ascendith, or withinne that nombre, that is
to seyn neer the degree that ascendith, yit
rekne they thilke planete in the ascendent.
And what planete that is under thilke degre
that ascendith the space of 25 degres, yit seyn
thei that thilke planete is "like to him that is
the hous of the ascendent." But sothly, if he
passe the boundes of these forseide spaces,
above or bynethe, thei seyn that the planete is "fallyng fro the ascendent." Yit saien 30
these astrologiens that the ascendent and
eke the lord of the ascendent may be shapen
for to be fortunat or infortunat, as thus: A
"fortunat ascendent" clepen they whan that no
wicked planete, as Saturne or Mars or elles
the Tayl of the Dragoun, is in the hous of the
ascendent, ne that no wicked planete have
noon aspect of enemyte upon the ascendent.
But thei wol caste that thei have a fortunat
planete in hir ascendent, and yit in his fe- 40
licite; and than sey thei that it is wel.
Further over thei seyn that the infortunyng of
an ascendent is the contrarie of these forseide
thinges. The lord of the ascendent, sey thei
that he is fortunat whan he is in god place
fro the ascendent, as in an angle, or in a succident where as he is in hys dignite and com-
fortid with frendly aspectes of planetes and
wel resceyved; and eke that he may seen
the ascendent; and that he be not retro- 50
grad, ne combust, ne joyned with no
shrewe in the same signe; ne that he be not
in his discencioun, ne joyned with no planete
in his descencioun, ne have upon him noon
aspect infortunat; and than sey thei that he is
well.

Natheles these ben observaunces of judicial
matere and rytes of payens, in whiche my

spirit hath no feith, ne knowing of her
horoscopum. For they seyn that every 60
signe is departid in thre evene parties by
10 degrees, and thilke porcioun they clepe a
face. And although that a planete have a latitude fro the ecliptik, yit sey somme folk, so
that the planete arise in that same signe with
eny degre of the forseide face in which his
longitude is rekned, that yit is the planete
in horoscopo, be it in nativyte or in eleccion,
etc.

5. To knowe the verrey equacioun of the
degre of the sonne yf so be that it falle bitwene
thyn almykanteras.

For as muche as the almykanteras in thin
Astrelabie ben compowned by two and two,
where as somme almykanteras in sondry astrelabies be compowned by 1 and 1, or elles by 2
and 2, it is necessarie to thy lernyng to teche
the first to knowe and worke with thin oune
instrument. Wherfore whan that the degre of
thi sonne fallith bytwixe 2 almykanteras, or
ellis yf thin almykanteras ben graven with
over-gret a poynt of a compas (for bothe 10
these thinges may causen errour as wel in
knowing of the tide of the day, as of the verrey ascendent), thou must worken in this
wise:

Set the degre of thy sonne upon the hyer
almykanteras of bothe, and wayte wel where
as thin almury touchith the bordure and set
there a prikke of ynke. Sett doun agayn the
degre of the sunne upon the nether almykanteras of bothe, and sett there an- 20
other pricke. Remeve than thin almury in
the bordure evene amiddes bothe prickes, and
this wol lede justly the degre of thi sonne to
sitte bitwene bothe almykanteras in his right
place. Ley than thy label over the degre of
thi sonne, and fynd in the bordure the verrey
tyde of the day, or of the night. And as verraily shalt thou fynde upon thin est orisonte
thin ascendent.

6. To knowe the spryng of the dawenyng
and the ende of the evenyng, the whiche ben
called the two crepuscules.

Set the nadir of thy sonne upon 18 degrees
of height among thyn almykanteras on the west

4.33 **fortunat:** auspicious **infortunat:** inauspicious
4.36 **Tayl of the Dragoun:** the point at which the moon crosses
the ecliptic moving southward
4.38 **aspect:** angular distance between one planet and another
planet, or celestial position
4.40–41 **in his felicite:** in a favorable aspect, position of influence
4.46 **angle:** one of the first, fourth, seventh, or tenth astrological
houses
4.46–47 **succident:** one of the second, fifth, eighth, or eleventh
houses
4.50–51 **retrograd:** moving from east to west
4.51 **combust:** obscured by the sun (and the planetary influence
thus diminished)
4.53 **discencioun:** descent, passage southward in the zodiac, from
Cancer to Sagittarius
4.57–58 **judicial matere:** judicial astrology, concerning the
influence of heavenly bodies on human actions

4.63 **face:** a division (ten degrees) of a zodiacal sign
5.16 **wayte wel:** watch carefully
6 *Rubric* **crepuscles:** times of twilight
6.1 **nadir:** a point on the celestial sphere diametrically opposite
to another

syde; and ley thy label on the degre of thy sonne, and than shal the point of thy label shewen the spryng of the day. Also set the nader of thy sonne upon 18 degrees of height among thin almykanteras on the est side, and ley over thy label upon the degre of the sonne, and with the point of thy label fynd in the bordure the ende of the evenyng, that is   10 verrey nyght.

The nader of the sonne is thilke degre that is opposyt to the degre of the sonne, in the 7 signe, as thus: every degre of Aries by ordir is nadir to every degre of Libra by ordre, and Taurus to Scorpioun, Gemini to Sagittarie, Cancer to Capricorne, Leo to Aquarie, Virgo to Piscis. And if eny degre in thy zodiak be derk, his nadir shal declare hym.

7. *To knowe the arch of the day, that some folk callen the day artificiall, fro sonne arisyng tyl it go to reste.*

Set the degre of thi sonne upon thin est orisonte, and ley thy label on the degre of the sonne, and at the point of thy label in the bordure set a pricke. Turne than thy riet aboute tyl the degre of the sonne sitte upon the west orisonte, and ley thy label upon the same degre of the sonne, and at the poynt of thy label set another pricke. Rekne than the quantite of tyme in the bordure bitwixe bothe prickes, and tak there thyn arch of   10 the day. The remenaunt of the bordure under the orisonte is the arch of the nyght. Thus maist thou rekne bothe arches, or every porcioun, of whether that the liketh. And by this manere of worching maist thou se how longe that eny sterre fix dwelleth above the erthe, fro tyme that he riseth til he go to reste. But the day naturall, that is to seyn 24 hours, is the revolucioun of the equinoxial with as muche partie of the zodiak as the sonne of   20 his propre moeving passith in the mene while.

8. *To turne the houres inequales in houres equales.*

Know the nombre of the degrees in the houres inequales, and depart hem by 15, and tak there thin houres equales.

9. *To knowe the quantite of the day vulgar, that is to seyn fro spryng of the day unto verrey nyght.*

Know the quantite of thy crepuscles, as I have taught in the 3 chapitre bifore, and adde hem to the arch of thy day artificial, and tak there the space of all the hool day vulgar unto verrey night. The same manere maist thou worche to knowe the quantite of the vulgar nyght.

10. *To knowe the quantite of houres inequales by day.*

Understond wel that these houres inequales ben clepid houres of planetes. And understond wel that som tyme ben thei lenger by day than by night, and som tyme the contrarie. But understond wel that evermo generaly the houre inequal of the day with the houre inequal of the night contenen 30 degrees of the bordure, which bordure is evermo answeryng to the degrees of the equinoxial. Wherfore departe the arch of the day arti-   10 ficial in 12, and tak there the quantite of the houre inequale by day. And if thou abate the quantite of the houre inequale by day out of 30, than shal the remenaunt that levith parforme the houre inequale by night.

11. *To knowe the quantite of houres equales.*

The quantite of houres equales, that is to seyn the houres of the clokke, ben departid by 15 degrees alredy in the bordure of thin Astrelaby, as wel by night as by day, generaly for evere. What nedith more declaracioun?

Wherfore whan the list to knowe hou many houres of the clokke ben passed, or eny part of eny of these houres that ben passed, or ellis how many houres or parties of houres ben to come fro such a tyme to such a tyme by   10 day or by night, know the degre of thy sonne, and ley thy label on it. Turne thy ryet aboute joyntly with thy label, and with the poynt of it rekne in the bordure fro the sonne arise unto that same place there thou desirist, by day as by nyght. This conclusioun wol I declare in the laste chapitre of the 4 partie of this

7 *Rubric* **arch:** arc
7.14 **whether:** whichever
7.18 **day naturall:** from noon to noon

9 *Rubric* **day vulgar:** from daybreak until dark
9.3 **day artificial:** from sunrise to sunset
10 *Rubric* **houres inequales:** Each is one twelfth part of the day artificial.
10.10–11 **departe . . . in 12:** divide by twelve
10.12–14 **abate . . . out of:** subtract from
10.14 **levith:** is left
10.14–15 **parforme:** be equivalent to

tretys so openly that ther shal lakke no word
that nedith to the declaracioun.

12. *Special declaracioun of the houres of
planetes.*

Understond wel that evermo, fro the arisyng of the sonne til it go to reste, the nadir of
the sonne shal shewe the houre of the planete;
and fro that tyme forward al the night til the
sonne arise, than shal the verrey degre of the
sonne shewe the houre of the planete.

Ensample as thus: The xiij day of March
fyl upon a Saturday, peraventure, and atte risyng of the sonne I fond the secunde degre
of Aries sittyng upon myn est orisonte, all   10
be it that it was but litel. Than fond I the
2 degre of Libra, nadir of my sonne, discending
on my west orisonte, upon which west orisonte
every day generaly, atte sonne arist, entrith the
houre of eny planete, after which planete the
day berith his name, and endith in the next
strike of the plate under the forseide west
orisonte. And evere as the sonne clymbith upper and upper, so goth his nadir downer
and downer, teching by suche strikes the   20
houres of planetes by ordir as they sitten
in the hevene. The firste houre inequal of
every Saturday is to Saturne, and the secunde to Jupiter, the thirde to Mars, the fourthe
to the sonne, the fifte to Venus, the sixte to
Mercurius, the seventhe to the mone. And
then ageyn the 8 is to Saturne, the 9 to
Jupiter, the 10 to Mars, the 11 to the sonne,
the 12 to Venus. And now is my sonne gon
to reste as for that Saturday. Than shewith   30
the verrey degre of the sonne the houre
of Mercurie entring under my west orisonte at
eve; and next him succedith the mone, and
so furth by ordir, planete after planete in houre
after houre, all the nyght longe til the sonne
arise. Now risith the sonne that Sonday by
the morwe, and the nadir of the sonne upon
the west orisonte shewith me the entring of the
houre of the forseide sonne. And in this
manere succedith planete under planete fro   40
Saturne unto the mone, and fro the mone up
ageyn to Saturne, houre after houre generaly.
And thus knowe I this conclusyoun.

13. *To knowe the altitude of the sonne in
myddes of the day that is clepid the altitude
meridian.*

12.14 **sonne arist:** sunrise

Set the degre of the sonne upon the lyne
meridional, and rekne how many degres of
almykanteras ben bitwyxe thin est orisonte and
the degre of thy sonne; and tak there thin altitude meridian, this to seyn, the highest of the
sonne as for that day. So maist thou knowe in
the same lyne the heighest cours that eny sterre
fix clymbeth by night. This is to seyn that whan
eny sterre fix is passid the lyne meridional,
than begynneth it to descende; and so doth   10
the sonne.

14. *To knowe the degre of the sonne by thy
ryet, for a maner curiosite.*

Sek besily with thy rule the highest of the
sonne in mydde of the day. Turne than thin
Astrelabie, and with a pricke of ynke marke
the nombre of that same altitude in the lyne
meridional; turne than thy ryet aboute tyl thou
fynde a degre of thy zodiak according with the
pricke, this is to seyn, sitting on the pricke.
And in soth thou shalt finde but 2 degrees in
all the zodiak of that condicioun; and yit
thilke 2 degrees ben in diverse signes.   10
Than maist thou lightly, by the sesoun of
the yere, knowe the signe in which that is the
sonne.

15. *To knowe which day is lik to which
day as of lengthe.*

Loke whiche degrees ben ylike fer fro the
hevedes of Cancer and Capricorne, and loke
when the sonne is in eny of thilke degrees;
than ben the dayes ylike of lengthe. This is
to seyn that as longe is that day in that month,
as was such a day in such a month; there varieth but litel.

Also, yf thou take 2 dayes naturales in the
yere ylike fer fro either point of the equinoxiall in the opposyt parties, than as longe   10
is the day artificiall of that oon day as is the
night of that othir, and the contrarie.

16. *This chapitre is a maner declaracioun
to conclusiouns that folewen.*

Understond wel that thy zodiak is departed
in two halve circles, as fro the heved of Capricorne unto the heved of Cancer, and ageynward fro the heved of Cancer unto the heved
of Capricorne. The heved of Capricorne is
the lowest point where as the sonne goth in
wynter, and the heved of Cancer is the heighist
point in which the sonne goth in somer. And
therfore understond wel that eny two degrees

that ben ylike fer fro eny of these two   10
hevedes, truste wel that thilke two degrees
ben of ilike declinacioun, be it southward or
northward, and the daies of hem ben ilike of
lengthe and the nyghtes also, and the shad-
ewes ilyke, and the altitudes ylike atte midday
for evere.

17. *To knowe the verrey degre of eny maner*
sterre, straunge or unstraunge, after his lon-
gitude; though he be indetermynat in thin
Astralabye, sothly to the trouthe thus he shal
be knowe.

Tak the altitude of this sterre whan he is on
the est syde of the lyne meridionall, as nye
as thou mayst gesse; and tak an ascendent anon
right by som manere sterre fix which that thou
knowist; and forget not the altitude of the firste
sterre ne thyn ascendent. And whan that this
is don, aspye diligently whan this same firste
sterre passith eny thyng the south westward;
and cacche him anon right in the same
nombre of altitude on the west syde of this   10
lyne meridional, as he was kaught on the
est syde; and tak a newe ascendent anon-ryght
by som maner sterre fix which that thou knowist, and forget not this secunde ascendent. And
whan that this is don, rekne than how many
degrees ben bitwixe the firste ascendent and
the secunde ascendent; and rekne wel the myddel degre bitwene bothe ascendentes, and set
thilke myddel degre upon thyn est orizonte;
and wayte than what degre that sitte upon   20
the lyne meridional, and tak there the verrey degre of the ecliptik in which the sterre
stondith for the tyme. For in the ecliptik is the
longitude of a celestiall body rekned, evene
fro the heved of Aries unto the ende of Pisces;
and his latitude is rekned after the quantite of
his declynacioun north or south toward the
polys of this world.

As thus: Yif it be of the sonne or of
eny fix sterre, rekne hys latitude or his   30
declinacioun fro the equinoxiall cercle; and
if it be of a planete, rekne than the quantite
of his latitude fro the ecliptik lyne, all be it
so that fro the equinoxiall may the declinacioun
or the latitude of eny body celestiall be rekned

after the site north or south and after the quantite of his declinacioun. And right so may the
latitude or the declinacioun of eny body celestiall, saaf oonly of the sonne, after hys site
north or south and after the quantite of his   40
declinacioun, be rekned fro the ecliptik
lyne; fro which lyne alle planetes som tyme
declinen north or south saaf oonly the forseide
sonne.

18. *To knowe the degrees of longitudes of*
fixe sterres after that they be determynat in
thin Astrelabye, yf so be that thei be trewly
sette.

Set the centre of the sterre upon the lyne
meridionall, and tak kep of thy zodiak, and
loke what degre of eny signe that sitte upon
the same lyne meridionall at that same tyme,
and tak there the degre in which the sterre
stondith; and with that same degre cometh that
same sterre unto that same lyne fro the orisonte.

19. *To knowe with which degre of the zo-*
diak eny sterre fix in thin Astrelabie arisith
upon the est orisonte, all though his dwellyng
be in another signe.

Set the centre of the sterre upon the est
orisonte, and loke what degre of eny signe that
sitt upon the same orisonte at that same tyme.
And understond wel that with that same degre
arisith that same sterre.

And thys merveylous arisyng with a straunge
degre in another signe is by cause that the
latitude of the sterre fix is either north or south
fro the equinoxiall. But sothly the latitudes
of planetes be comounly rekened fro the   10
ecliptyk, by cause that noon of hem declyneth but fewe degrees out fro the brede of the
zodiak. And tak god kep of this chapitre of
arisyng of celestialle bodies; for truste wel that
neyther mone ne sterre, as in our embelif
orisonte, arisith with that same degre of his
longitude saaf in oo cas, and that is whan they
have no latitude fro the ecliptyk lyne. But
natheles som tyme is everich of these planetes under the same lyne.   20

20. *To knowe the declinacioun of eny degre*
in the zodiak fro the equinoxiall cercle.

Set the degre of eny signe upon the lyne
meridionall, and rekne hys altitude in the

16.12 **declinacioun**: angular distance from the equator
17 *Rubric* **straunge**: not shown on the astrolabe
indetermynat: not marked on the rete
17.8 **passith eny thyng the south westward**: crosses the south
line, however little, moving westward
17.24 **longitude**: angular distance from 0° Aries eastward
around the ecliptic
17.26 **latitude**: angular distance north or south from the
equinoctial; see note 17.23–44.

17.43 **declinen**: diverge
18 *Rubric* **determynat**: placed (on the rete)
18.1 **centre**: tip of the pointer for the star, in the rete
19.6 **straunge**: different
19.9 **equinoxiall**: See 2.17.29–31.

almykanteras fro the est orisonte up to the same degre set in the forseide lyne, and set there a prikke; turne up than thy riet, and set the heved of Aries or Libra in the same meridionall lyne, and set there a nother prikke. And whan that this is don, considre the altitudes of hem bothe; for sothly the difference of thilke altitudes is the declinacioun of thilke degre fro the ⟨10⟩ equinoxiall. And yf it so be that thilke degre be northward fro the equinoxiall, than is his declinacyoun north; yif it be southward, than is it south.

21. *To knowe for what latitude in eny region the almykanteras of eny table ben compowned.*

Rekene how many degrees of almykanteras in the meridionall lyne ben fro the cercle equinoxiall unto the cenyth, or elles from the pool artyk unto the north orisonte; and for so gret a latitude, or for so smal a latitude, is the table compowned.

22. *To knowe in speciall the latitude of oure countre, I mene after the latitude of Oxenford, and the height of oure pool.*

Understond wel that as fer is the heved of Aries or Libra in the equinoxiall fro oure orisonte as is the cenyth fro the pool artik; and as high is the pool artik fro the orisonte as the equinoxiall is fer fro the cenyth. I prove it thus by the latitude of Oxenford: understond wel that the height of oure pool artik fro oure north orisonte is 51 degrees and 50 mynutes; than is the cenyth fro oure pool artik 38 degrees and 10 mynutes; than is the equinoxial from oure cenyth 51 degrees and 50 ⟨10⟩ mynutes; than is oure south orisonte from oure equinoxiall 38 degrees and 10 mynutes. Understond wel this rekenyng. Also forget not that the cenyth is 90 degrees of height from the orisonte, and oure equinoxiall is 90 degres from oure pool artik. Also this shorte rule is soth, that the latitude of eny place in a region is the distaunce fro the cenyth unto the equinoxiall.   ⟨20⟩

23. *To prove evidently the latitude of eny place in a region by the preve of the height of the pool artik in that same place.*

In som wynters nyght whan the firmament is cler and thikke sterred, wayte a tyme til that eny sterre fix sitte lyne-right perpendicu-

ler over the pool artik, and clepe that sterre A; and wayte another sterre that sitte lyne-right under A, and under the pool, and clepe that sterre F. And understond wel that F is not considrid but oonly to declare that A sitte evene over the pool. Tak than anoon-right the altitude of A from the orisonte, and for- ⟨10⟩ get it not; let A and F goo fare wel tyl ageynst the dawenyng a gret while, and com than ageyn, and abid til that A is evene under the pool, and under F; for sothly than wol F sitte over the pool, and A wol sitte under the pool. Tak than eftsonys the altitude of A from the orisonte, and note as wel his secunde altitude as hys firste altitude. And whan that this is doon, rekene how many degrees that the firste altitude of A excedith his secunde alti- ⟨20⟩ tude, and tak half thilke porcioun that is excedid and adde it to his secunde altitude, and tak there the elevacioun of thy pool, and eke the latitude of thy region; for these two ben of oo nombre, this is to seyn, as many degres as thy pool is elevat, so muche is the latitude of the region.

Ensample as thus: Peraventure the altitude of A in the evenyng is 56 degrees of height; than wol his secunde altitude or the dawen- ⟨30⟩ yng be 48 degres, that is 8 degrees lasse than 56, that was his first altitude att even. Tak than the half of 8 and adde it to 48 that was his secunde altitude, and than hast thou 52. Now hast thou the height of thy pool and the latitude of the region. But understond wel that to prove this conclusioun and many another faire conclusioun, thou must have a plomet hongyng on a lyne, heygher than thin heved, on a perche; and thilke lyne ⟨40⟩ must hange evene perpendiculer bytwixe the pool and thin eye; and than shalt thou seen yf A sitte evene over the pool, and over F atte evene; and also yf F sitte evene over the pool and over A or day.

24. *Another conclusioun to prove the height of the pool artik fro the orisonte.*

Tak eny sterre fix that never descendith under the orisonte in thilke region, and considre his heighist altitude and his lowist altitude fro the orisonte, and make a nombre of bothe these altitudes; tak than and abate half

23.4 **pool artik**: north celestial pole
23.39 **plomet**: plummet, weight
23.40 **perche**: rod
24.5 **abate**: subtract

22 *Rubric*   **pool**: the (north) celestial pole

that nombre, and take there the elevacioun of
the pool artik in that same regioun.

25. *Another conclusioun to prove the lati-*
tude of the regioun.

Understond wel that the latitude of eny
place in a regioun is verrely the space bytwixe
the cenyth of hem that dwellen there and the
equinoxiall cercle north or south, takyng the
mesure in the meridional lyne, as shewith in
the almykanteras of thin Astrelabye. And thilke
space is as much as the pool artike is high in
that same place fro the orisonte. And than is
the depressioun of the pool antartik, that
is to seyn, than is the pool antartik, by-   10
nethe the orisonte the same quantite of
space neither more ne lasse.

Than if thou desire to knowe this latitude
of the regioun, tak the altitude of the sonne
in the myddel of the day, whan the sonne is
in the hevedes of Aries or of Libra; for than
moeveth the sonne in the lyne equinoxiall;
and abate the nombre of that same sonnes altitude out of 90 degrees, and than is the
remenaunt of the nombre that leveth   20
the latitude of the regioun. As thus:
I suppose that the sonne is thilke day at
noon 38 degrees of height; abate than 38
degrees oute of 90; so leveth there 52; than is
52 degrees the latitude. I say not this but for
ensample; for wel I wot the latitude of Oxenford is certeyn minutes lasse; thow might
preve the same.

Now yf so be that the semeth to longe a
tarieng to abide til that the sonne be in the   30
hevedes of Aries or of Libra, than wayte
whan the sonne is in eny othir degre of the
zodiak, and considre the degre of his declinacioun fro the equinoxiall lyne; and if it so be
that the sonnes declinacioun be northward fro
the equinoxiall, abate than fro the sonnes altitude at non the nombre of his declinacioun,
and than hast thou the height of the hevedes
of Aries and Libra. As thus: My sonne
is peraventure in the 10 degre of Leoun,   40
almost 56 degrees of height at non,
and his declinacioun is almost 18 degrees
northward fro the equinoxiall; abate than thilke
18 degrees of declinacioun out of the altitude
at non; than leveth there 38 degrees and odde

minutes. Lo there the heved of Aries or Libra
and thin equinoxiall in that regioun. Also if
so be that the sonnes declinacioun be southward fro the equinoxiall, adde than thilke
declinacioun to the altitude of the sonne at   50
noon, and tak there the hevedes of Aries
and Libra and thin equinoxial; abate than the
height of the equinoxial out of 90 degrees;
than leveth there the distance of the pool of
that regioun fro the equinoxiall. Or elles, if
the list, tak the highest altitude fro the equinoxial of eny sterre fix that thou knowist, and
tak his netherest elongacioun (lengthing) fro
the same equinoxial lyne, and work in the
manere forseid.   60

26. *Declaracioun of the ascensioun of*
signes.

The excellence of the spere solide, amonges
othir noble conclusiouns, shewith manyfest the
diverse ascenciouns of signes in diverse places,
as wel in the right cercle as in the embelif
cercle. These auctours writen that thilke signe
is cleped of right ascensioun with which more
part of the cercle equinoxiall and lasse part of
the zodiak ascendith; and thilke signe ascendith embelif with which lasse part of the
equinoxiall and more part of the zodiak   10
ascendith. Ferther-over, they seyn that in
thilke cuntrey where as the senith of hem that
dwellen there is in the equinoxial lyne, and
her orisonte passyng by the two poles of this
world, thilke folk han this right cercle and
the right orisonte; and evermore the arch of
the day and the arch of the night is there ilike
longe; and the sonne twies every yer passing
thorugh the cenith of hir heed, and two
someres and two wynters in a yer han these   20
forseide peple. And the almycanteras in
her Astrelabyes ben streight as a lyne, so as
shewith in the figure.

The utilite to knowe the ascensions of signes
in the right cercle is this: Truste wel that
by mediacioun of thilke ascensions these astrologiens, by her tables and her instrumentes,
knowen verreily the ascensioun of every degre
and minute in all the zodiak in the embelif

24.6 **elevacioun:** altitude
25.9 **depressioun:** angular distance below the horizon **pool**
antartik: south celestial pole
25.20 **leveth:** is left

25.58 **lengthing:** lengthening
26.1 **spere solide:** Cf. 1.17.19–20 above.
26.4 **right cercle:** equator; the daily path of a heavenly body
around the earth on a circle parallel to the equinoctial
26.4–5 **embelif cercle:** a great circle oblique to the plane of the
observer's horizon
26.5 **These auctours:** authorities in general
26.11 **Ferther-over:** furthermore

cercle, as shal be shewed. And *nota* that 30
this forseide right orisonte, that is clepid
Orison Rectum, dividith the equinoxial into
right angles; and the embelif orisonte, where
as the pool is enhaunced upon the orisonte,
overkervith the equinoxiall in embilif angles,
as shewith in the figure.

27. *This is the conclusioun to knowe the ascensions of signes in the right cercle, that is circulus directus.*

Set the heved of what signe the lyst to knowe
his ascendyng in the right cercle upon the lyne
meridionall, and wayte where thyn almury
touchith the bordure, and set there a prikke;
turne than thy riet westward til that the ende
of the forseide signe sitte upon the meridional
lyne and eftsonys wayte where thin almury
touchith the bordure, and set there another
pricke. Rekene than the nombre of degres
in the bordure bitwixe bothe prikkes, and 10
tak the ascensioun of the signe in the right
cercle. And thus maist thou werke with every
porcioun of thy zodiak.

28. *To knowe the ascensions of signes in the embelif cercle in every regioun, I mene, in circulo obliquo.*

Set the heved of the signe which as the list
to knowe his ascensioun upon the est orisonte,
and wayte where thin almury touchith the bordure, and there set a prikke. Turne than thy
riet upward til that the ende of the same signe
sitte upon the est orisonte, and wayte eftsonys
where as thin almury touchith the bordure,
and set there a nother prikke. Rekene than
the nombre of degrees in the bordure bitwyxe bothe prikkes and tak there the as- 10
censioun of the signe in the embelif cercle.
And understond wel that alle the signes in thy
zodiak, fro the heved of Aries unto the ende
of Virgo, ben clepid signes of the north fro
the equinoxiall. And these signes arisen bitwyxe the verrey est and the verrey north in
oure orisonte generaly for evere. And alle the
signes fro the heved of Libra unto the ende
of Pisces ben clepid signes of the south fro
the equinoxial; and these signes arisen 20
evermore bitwixe the verrey est and the
verrey south in oure orisonte. Also every signe
bitwixe the heved of Capricorne unto the ende
of Geminis arisith on oure orisonte in lasse

than 2 houres equales. And these same signes
fro the heved of Capricorne unto the ende of
Geminis ben cleped tortuose signes, or croked
signes, for thei arise embelyf on oure orisonte.
And these croked signes ben obedient to
the signes that ben of right ascensioun. 30
The signes of right ascencioun ben fro the
heved of Cancer unto the ende of Sagittarie;
and these signes arisen more upright, and thei
ben called eke sovereyn signes and everich of
hem arisith in more space than 2 houres. Of
whiche signes Gemini obeieth to Cancer, and
Taurus to Leo, Aries to Virgo, Pisces to Libra,
Aquarius to Scorpioun, and Capricorne to Sagittarie. And thus evermore 2 signes that
ben ilike fer fro the heved of Capricorne 40
obeyen everich of hem to othir.

29. *To knowe justly the 4 quarters of the world, as Est, West, North, and South.*

Tak the altitude of thy sonne whan the list,
and note wel the quarter of the world in which
the sonne is for the tyme by the azymutz.
Turne than thin Astrelabie, and set the degre
of the sonne in the almykanteras of his altitude
on thilke syde that the sonne stant, as is the
manere in takyng of houres, and ley thy label
on the degre of the sonne; and rekene how
many degrees of the bordure ben bitwixe
the lyne meridional and the point of thy 10
label, and note wel that nombre. Turne
than ageyn thin Astrelabie, and set the point
of thy gret rule there thou takist thin altitudes
upon as many degrees in his bordure fro his
meridional as was the point of thy label fro
the lyne meridional on the wombe side. Take
than thin Astrelabie with bothe hondes sadly
and slighly, and let the sonne shyne thorugh
bothe holes of thy rule, and slighly in thilke
shynyng lat thin Astrelabie kouche adoun 20
evene upon a smothe ground, and than wol
the verrey lyne meridional of thin Astrelabie
lye evene south, and the est lyne wol lye est,
and the west lyne west, and the north lyne
north, so that thou worke softly and avysely
in the kouching. And thus hast thou the 4
quarters of the firmament.

30. *To knowe the latitude of planetes fro the wey of the sonne, whethir so they be north or south fro the forseide wey.*

26.34 **enhaunced:** raised

28.30 **right ascensioun:** rising of a zodiacal sign nearly perpendicular to the horizon
29.20 **kouche:** lie down, be set down

Loke whan that a planete is in the lyne meridional, yf that hir altitude be of the same height that is the degre of the sonne for that day, and than is the planete in the verrey wey of the sonne and hath no latitude. And if the altitude of the planete be heigher than the degre of the sonne, than is the planete north fro the wey of the sonne such a quantite of latitude as shewith by thin almykanteras. And if the altitude of the planete be lasse   10 than the degre of the sonne, than is the planete south fro the wey of the sonne such a quantite of latitude as shewith by thin almykanteras. This is to seyn, fro the wey where as the sonne went thilke day, but not fro the wey of the sonne in every place of the zodiak.

31. *To knowe the cenyth of the arising of the sonne, this is to seyn, the partie of the orisonte in which that the sonne arisith.*

Thou must first considere that the sonne arisith not alwey verrey est, but somtyme by northe the est and somtyme by south the est. Sothly the sonne arisith nevere moo verrey est in oure orisonte, but he be in the heved of Aries or Libra. Now is thin orisonte departed in 24 parties by thin azimutes in significacioun of 24 parties of the world; al be it so that shipmen rekene thilke parties in 32. Than is there no more but wayte in which azimut that thy   10 sonne entrith at his arisyng, and take there the cenith of the arisyng of the sonne.

The manere of the divisioun of thin Astrelabie is this, I mene as in this cas: First it is divided in 4 plages principalis with the lyne that goth from est to west; and than with another lyne that goth fro south to north; than is it divided in smale parties of azymutz, as est, and est by south, where as is the first azymut above the est lyne; and so furth fro   20 partie to partie til that thou come ageyn unto the est lyne. Thus maist thou understonde also the cenyth of eny sterre, in which partie he riseth.

32. *To knowe in which partie of the firmament is the conjunccyoun.*

Considere the tyme of the conjunccyoun by the kalender, as thus: Loke hou many houres thilke conjunccioun is fro the midday of the day precedent, as shewith by the canon of thy kalender. Rekene than thilke nombre of houres in the bordure of thin Astrelabie, as thou art wont to do in knowyng of the houres of the day or of the nyght, and ley thy label over the degre of the sonne, and than wol the point of thy label sitte upon the houre   10 of the conjunccioun. Loke than in which azymut the degre of thy sonne sittith, and in that partie of the firmament is the conjunccioun.

33. *To knowe the cenyth of the altitude of the sonne.*

This is no more to seyn but eny tyme of the day tak the altitude of the sonne, and by the azymut in which he stondith maist thou seen in which partie of the firmament he is. And the same wise maist thou seen by night, of eny sterre, wheither the sterre sitte est or west, or north or south, or eny partie bitwene, after the name of the azimut in which is the sterre.

34. *To knowe sothly the degre of the longitude of the mone, or of eny planete that hath no latitude for the tyme fro the ecliptik lyne.*

Tak the altitude of the mone, and rekne thy altitude up among thyn almykanteras on which syde that the mone stondith, and set there a prikke. Tak than anon-right upon the mones syde the altitude of eny sterre fix which that thou knowist, and set his centre upon his altitude among thyn almykanteras there the sterre is founde. Wayte than which degre of the zodiak touchith the prykke of the altitude of the mone, and tak there the degre   10 in which the mone stondith. This conclusioun is verrey soth, yf the sterres in thin Astrelabie stonden after the trouthe. Comoun tretes of the Astrelabie ne maken non excepcioun whether the mone have latitude or noon, ne on wheyther syde of the mone the altitude of the sterre fixe be taken.

And *nota* that yf the mone shewe himself by light of day, than maist thou worche this same conclusioun by the sonne, as wel   20 as by the fixe sterre.

35. *This is the worchinge of the conclusioun to knowe yf that eny planete be direct or retrograd.*

31.15 **plages:** quarters, divisions
32 *Rubric* **conjunccyoun:** proximity of two heavenly bodies, esp. of sun and moon

32.4 **canon:** table
33 *Rubric* **cenyth:** azimuth (as used above)
35 *Rubric* **direct:** from west to east, as the sun through the zodiac

Tak the altitude of eny sterre that is clepid a planete, and note it wel; and tak eke anon the altitude of any sterre fix that thou know- ist, and note it wel also. Com than ageyn the thridde or the fourthe nyght next folewing, for than shalt thou perceyve wel the moeving of a planete, wheither so he moeve forward or bakward. Awayte wel than whan that thy sterre fixe is in the same altitude that she was whan thou toke hir firste altitude.   10 And tak than eft-sones the altitude of the forseide planete and note it wel; for truste wel yf so be that the planete be on the right syde of the meridional lyne, so that his secunde alti- tude be lasse than hys first altitude was, than is the planete direct; and yf he be on the west syde in that condicioun, than is he retrograd. And yf so be that this planete be upon the est side whan his altitude is ytaken, so that his secunde altitude be more than his first alti-   20 tude, than is he retrograd. And if he be on the west syde, than is he direct. But the con- trarie of these parties is of the cours of the mone; for certis the mone moeveth the con- trarie from othre planetes as in hir epicicle, but in noon othir manere.

36. *The conclusioun of equaciouns of houses after the Astrelabie.*

Set the begynnyng of the degre that ascend- ith upon the ende of the 8 houre inequal; than wol the begynnyng of the 2 hous sitte upon the lyne of mydnight. Remeve than the degre that ascendith, and set him on the ende of the 10 houre inequal, and than wol the begynnyng of the 3 hous sitte up on the mydnight lyne. Bring up ageyn the same degre that ascended first, and set him upon the est orisonte, and than wol the begynnyng of the 4 hous sitte   10 upon the lyne of mydnight. Tak than the nader of the degre that first ascendid, and set him on the ende of the 2 houre inequal; and than wol the begynnyng of the 5 hous sitte upon the lyne of mydnight. Set than the nader of the ascendent on the ende of the 4 houre inequal, and than wol the begynnyng of the 6 hous sitte on the mydnight lyne. The be- gynnyng of the 7 hous is nader of the as- cendent, and the begynnyng of the 8 hous   20 is nader of the 2, and the begynnyng of the 9 hous is nader of the 3, and the be- gynnyng of the 10 hous is nader of the 4, and the begynnyng of the 11 hous is nader

of the 5, and the begynnyng of the 12 hous is nader of the 6.

37. *Another maner of equaciouns of houses by the Astrelabye.*

Tak thin ascendent, and than hast thou thy 4 angles; for wel thou wost that the opposit of thin ascendent, that is to seyn, the begyn- nyng of the 7 hous, sitt upon the west orisonte, and the begynnyng of the 10 hous sitt upon the lyne meridional, and his opposyt upon the lyne of mydnight. Than ley thy label over the degre that ascendith, and rekne fro the point of thy label alle the degrees in the bordure tyl thou come to the meridional lyne; and   10 departe alle thilke degrees in 3 evene par- ties, and take there the evene equacions of 3 houses; for ley thy label over everich of these 3 parties, and than maist thou se by thy label, in the zodiak, the begynnyng of everich of these same houses fro the ascendent; that is to seyn, the begynnyng of the 12 hous next above thin ascendent, the begynnyng of the 11 hous, and than the 10 upon the meridi- onal lyne, as I first seide. The same wise   20 worch thou fro the ascendent doun to the lyne of mydnyght, and thus hast thou othre 3 houses; that is to seyn, the begynnyng of the 2, and the 3, and the 4 hous. Than is the nader of these 3 houses the begynnyng of the 3 houses that folewen.

38. *To fynde the lyne meridional to dwelle fix in eny certeyn place.*

Tak a round plate of metal; for werpyng, the brodder the better; and make there upon a just compas a lite within the bordure. And ley this rounde plate upon an evene ground, or on an evene ston, or on an evene stok fix in the ground; and ley it evene by a level. And in the centre of the compas styke an evene pyn, or a wyr, upright, the smaller the better; set thy pyn by a plom-rule evene upright, and let this pyn be no lenger than   10 a quarter of the dyametre of thy compas, fro the centre amiddes. And wayte bisely aboute 10 or 11 of the clokke, whan the sonne shineth, whan the shadewe of the pyn entrith enythyng within the cercle of thy compas an heer-mele; and marke there a pricke with inke. Abid than stille waityng on the sonne til after 1 of the clokke, til that the shadewe of the wyr,

35.25 **epicicle:** the circle made by a planet about its own orbit

38.1 **for werpyng:** to avoid warping
38.16 **heer-mele:** hair's breadth

or of the pyn, passe enything out of the
cercle of the compas, be it nevere so lyte,   20
and set there another pricke of ynke. Tak
than a compas, and mesure evene the myddel
bitwixe bothe prickes, and set there a prikke.
Tak me than a rule and draw a strike evene
a-lyne, fro the pyn unto the middel prikke; and
tak there thi lyne meridional for evermore, as
in that same place. And yif thou drawe a
cross-lyne overthwart the compas justly over
the lyne meridional, than hast thou est and
west and south, and par consequens,   30
the opposit of the south lyne, i.e. the north.

39. *Descripcion of the meridional lyne, of
longitudes and latitudes of citees and townes,
as wel as of climates.*

     Thys lyne meridional is but a maner descrip-
cioun, or lyne ymagined, that passith upon the
poles of this world and by the cenyth of oure
heved. And it is cleped the lyne meridional,
for in what place that eny man is at any tyme
of the yer, whan that the sonne, by mevynge
of the firmament, cometh to his verrey meridian
place, than is it verrey mydday, that we clepen
oure non, as to thilke man. And therfore
is it clepid the lyne of midday. And *nota*   10
that evermore of eny 2 cytes or of 2 townes,
of which that oo town approchith ner toward the est than doth that othir town, trust
wel that thilke townes han diverse meridians.
Nota also that the arch of the equinoxial that
is contened or bownded bitwixe the 2 meridians is clepid the longitude of the toun. And
yf so be that two townes have ilike meridian
or oon meridian, than is the distaunce of
hem bothe ilike fer fro the est, and the con-   20
trarie; and in this manere thei change not
her meridian. But sothly thei chaungen her
almykanteras, for the enhaunsyng of the pool
and the distance of the sonne.

     The longitude of a climat is a lyne ymag-
ined fro est to west ilike distant fro the equinoxiall. And the latitude of a climat may be
cleped the space of the erthe fro the begynnyng of the first clymat unto the verrey
ende of the same clymat evene direct   30
ageyns the pool artyke. Thus sayn somme
auctours; and somme of hem sayn that yf men
clepe the latitude of a cuntrey the arch meridian that is contened or intercept bitwix the

cenyth and the equinoxial, than say they that
the distance fro the equinoxial unto the ende
of a clymat evene ageynst the pool artik is the
latitude of a clymat forsoothe.

40. *To knowe with which degre of the zodiak that eny planete ascendith on the orisonte, wheither so that his latitude be north
or south.*

     Know by thin almenak the degre of the
ecliptik of eny signe in which that the planete
is rekned for to be, and that is clepid the
degre of his longitude. And know also the
degre of his latitude fro the ecliptik north or
south. And by these ensamples folewynge in
speciall maist thou worche in general in every
signe of the zodiak:

     The degree of the longitude peraventure
of Venus or of another planete was 1 of   10
Capricorne, and the latitude of him was
northward 4 degrees fro the ecliptik lyne. Than
tok I a subtil compas, and clepid that oo point
of my compas A, and that other point F. Than
tok I the point of A and sette it in the ecliptik lyne in my zodiak in the degre of the longitude of Venus, that is to seyn, in the 1 degre
of Capricorne; and than sette I the point of
F upward in the same signe by cause that
latitude was north upon the latitude of   20
Venus, that is to seyn, in the 4 degre fro the
heved of Capricorne; and thus have I 4 degrees
bitwixe my two prickes. Than leide I down
softly my compas, and sette the degre of the
longitude upon the orisonte; tho tok I and
waxed my label in manere of a peire tables to
receyve distinctly the prickes of my compas.
Tho tok I thys forseide label, and leyde it fix
over the degre of my longitude; tho tok I
up my compas and sette the point of A in   30
the wax on my label, as evene as I koude
gesse, over the ecliptik lyne in the ende of the
longitude, and sette the point of F endelong
in my label upon the space of the latitude,
inward and over the zodiak, that is to seyn
northward fro the ecliptik. Than leide I doun
my compas, and loked wel in the wey upon
the prickes of A and of F; tho turned I my ryet
til that the pricke of F satt upon the orisonte; than saw I wel that the body of   40
Venus in hir latitude of 4 degrees septem-
trionals ascendid, in the ende of the 8 degre,
fro the heved of Capricorne.

38.24 **rule**: ruler, straight edge
38.30 **par consequens**: consequently
39 *Rubric* **climates**: zones defined by lines of latitude

40.13 **compas**: a compass or dividers

And *nota* that in this manere maist thou worche with any latitude septemtrional in alle signes. But sothly the latitude meridional of a planete in Capricorne ne may not be take by cause of the litel space bitwixe the ecliptyk and the bordure of the Astrelabie; but sothely in all othre signes it may.   50

2 pars hujus conclusio.

Also the degre peraventure of Jupiter, or of another planete, was in the first degre of Piscis in longitude, and his latitude was 2 degrees meridional; tho tok I the point of A and sette it in the first degre of Piscis on the ecliptik; and than sette I the point of F dounward in the same signe by cause that the latitude was south 2 degres, that is to seyn, fro the heved of Piscis; and thus have I 2 degres bitwixe bothe prikkes. Than sette I the degre of   60 the longitude upon the orisonte; tho tok I my label, and leide it fix upon the degre of the longitude; tho sette I the point of A on my label evene over the ecliptik lyne in the ende of the degre of the longitude, and sette the point of F endlong in my label the space of 2 degres of the latitude outward fro the zodiak (this is to seyn southward fro the ecliptik toward the bordure), and turned my riet til that the pricke of F saat upon the ori-   70 sonte. Than say I wel that the body of Jupiter in his latitude of 2 degrees meridional ascendid with 8 degres of Piscis *in horoscopo.* And in this manere maist thou worche with any latitude meridional, as I first seide, save in Capricorne. And yif thou wilt pleye this craft with the arisyng of the mone, loke thou rekne wel hir cours houre by houre, for she ne dwellith not in a degre of hir longitude but litel while, as thow wel knowist. But natheles   80 yf thou rekne hir verrey moevyng by thy tables houre after houre, [thou shalt do wel ynow].

SUPPLEMENTARY PROPOSITIONS

41. *Umbra Recta.*

Yif it so be that thou wilt werke by *umbra recta,* and thou may come to the bas of the tour, in this maner shalt thou werke. Tak the altitude of the tour by bothe holes, so that thy rewle ligge even in a poynt. Ensample as thus: I see him thorw at the poynt of 4; than mete I the space betwixe me and the tour, and I finde it 20 foot; than beholde I how 4 is to 12, right so is the space betwixe thee and the tour to the altitude of the tour.   10 For 4 is the thridde part of 12, so is the space between thee and the tour the thridde part of the altitude of the tour; than thryes 20 foot is the heyghte of the tour, with adding of thyn owne persone to thyn eye. And this rewle is general in *umbra recta,* fro the poynt of oon to 12. And yif thy rewle falle upon 5, than is 5 12-partyes of the heyght the space between thee and the tour; with adding of thyn owne heyghte.   20

42. *Umbra Versa.*

Another maner of the werkinge, by *umbra versa.* Yif so be that thou may nat come to the bas of the tour, I see him thorw at the nombre of 1; I sette ther a prikke at my fot; than go I neer to the tour, and I see him thorw at the poynt of 2, and there I sette another prikke; and I beholde how 1 hath him to 12, and ther finde I that it hath him twelfe sythes; than beholde I how 2 hath him to 12, and thou shalt finde it sexe sythes; than thou shalt   10 finde that 12 passith 6 by the numbre of 6; right so is the space between thy two prikkes the space of 6 tymes thyn altitude. And note, that at the ferste altitude of 1, thou settest a prikke; and afterward, whan thou seest him at 2, ther thou settest another prikke; than thou findest betwyx thes two prikkys 60 foot; than thou shalt finde that 10 is the 6-party of 60. And then is 10 feet the altitude of the tour. For other poyntis, yif it fille in *umbra versa,*   20 as thus: I sette caas it fill upon 2, and at the secunde upon 3; than schalt thou finde that 2 is 6 partyes of 12; and 3 is 4 partyes of 12; than passeth 6 4, by nombre of 2; so is the space between two prikkes twyes the heyghte of the tour. And yif the differens were thryes, than shulde it be three tymes; and thus mayst thou werke fro 1 to 12; and yif it be 4, 4 tymes; or 5, 5 tymes; *et sic de ceteris.*

43. *Umbra Recta.*

Another maner of wyrking, by *umbra recta:* Yif it so be that thou mayst nat come to the baas of the tour, in this maner thou schalt werke. Set thy rewle upon 1 till thou see the altitude, and set at thy foot a prikke. Than set thy rewle upon 2, and behold what is the differense between 1 and 2, and thou shalt finde that it is 1. Than mete the space be-tween two prikkes, and that is the 12 par-tie of the altitude of the tour. And yif ther were 2, it were the 6 partye; and yif ther were 3, the 4 partye; *et sic deinceps.* And note, yif it were 5, it were the 5 party of 12; and 7, 7 party of 12; and note, at the altitude of thy conclusion, adde the stature of thyn heyghte to thyn eye.

*   *   *

44. *Another maner conclusion, to knowe the mene mote and the argumentis of any planete. To know the mene mote and the ar-gumentis of every planete fro yeer to yeer, from day to day, from houre to houre, and from smale fraccionis infinite.*

In this maner shalt thou worche; consider thy rote first, the whiche is made the begin-ning of the tables fro the yer of oure Lord 1397, and enter hit into thy slate for the laste meridie of December; and than consider the yer of oure Lord, what is the date, and behold whether thy date be more or lasse than the yer 1397. And yf hit so be that hit be more, loke how many yeres hit passeth, and with so many enter into thy tables in the first lyne theras is writen *anni collecti et ex-pansi.* And loke where the same planet is writen in the hed of thy table, and than loke what thou findest in direct of the same yer of oure Lord which is passid, be hit 8, or 9, or 10, or what nombre that evere it be, til the tyme that thou come to 20, or 40, or 60. And that thou findest in direct wryt in thy slate un-der thy rote, and adde hit togeder, and that is

thy mene mote, for the laste meridian of the December, for the same yer which that thou hast purposed. And if hit so be that hit passe 20, consider wel that fro 1 to 20 ben *anni expansi,* and fro 20 to 3000 ben *anni col-lecti;* and if thy nomber passe 20, than tak that thou findest in direct of 20, and if hit be more, as 6 or 18, than tak that thou findest in direct thereof, that is to sayen, signes, degrees, min-utes, and secoundes, and adde togedere unto thy rote; and thus to make rotes. And note, that if hit so be that the yer of oure Lord be lasse than the rote, which is the yer of oure Lord 1397, than shalt thou wryte in the same wyse first thy rote in thy slate, and after enter into thy table in the same yer that be lasse, as I taught before; and than consider how many signes, degrees, minutes, and sec-oundes thyn entringe conteyneth. And so be that ther be 2 entrees, than adde hem to-geder, and after withdraw hem from the rote, the yer of oure Lord 1397; and the residue that leveth is thy mene mote for the laste meridie of December, the whiche thou hast purposid; and if hit so be that thou wolt witen thy mene mote for any day, or for any fraccioun of day, in this maner thou shalt worche. Make thy rote fro the laste day of December in the maner as I have taught, and afterward behold how many monethes, dayes, and houres ben passid from the meridie of December, and with that enter with the laste moneth that is ful passed, and take that thou findest in direct of him, and wryt hit in thy slate; and enter with as mony dayes as be more, and wryt that thou findest in direct of the same planete that thou worchest for; and in the same wyse in the table of houres, for houres that ben passed, and adde alle these to thy rote; and the residue is the mene mote for the same day and the same houre.

45. *Another manere to knowe the mene mote.*

Whan thou wolt make the mene mote of eny planete to be by Arsechieles tables, tak thy rote, the which is for the yer of oure Lord 1397; and if so be that thy yer be passid the date, wryt that date, and than wryt the nom-ber of the yeres. Than withdraw the yeres

---

43.3 **baas:** base
44 *Rubric* **mene mote:** mean position of the sun or a planet considered as moving at a constant rate along its orbit
argumentis: measurements of angular movements of a planet around its epicycle
44.2 **rote:** a figure for the position of a planet at a base date, from which positions on other dates can be found from the table

44.20 **meridian:** noon, midday
44.43 **meridie:** noon, midday

out of the yeres that ben passed that rote.
Ensampul as thus: the yer of oure Lord 1400,
I wolde wyten, precise, my rote; than wrot
I first 1400. And under that nomber I
wrot a 1397; than withdrow I the laste
nomber out of that, and than fond I the residue was 3 yer; I wiste that 3 yer was passed
fro the rote, the which was writen in my
tables. Than afterward soghte I in my tables
the *annis collectis et expansis,* and among myn
expanse yeres fond I 3 yeer. Than tok I alle
the signes, degrees, and minutes, that I fond
direct under the same planete that I
wroghte for, and wrot so many signes,
degrees, and minutes in my slate, and afterward added I to signes, degrees, minutes, and
secoundes, the whiche I fond in my rote the
yer of oure Lord 1397; and kepte the residue;
and than had I the mene mote for the laste
day of December. And if thou woldest wete
the mene mote of any planete in March, April,
or May, other in any other tyme or moneth of
the yer, loke how many monethes and
dayes ben passed from the laste day of December, the yer of oure Lord 1400; and so
with monethis and dayes enter into thy table
ther thou findest thy mene mote iwriten in
monethes and dayes, and tak alle the signes,
degrees, minutes, and secoundes that thou findest ywrite in direct of thy monethes, and adde
to signes, degrees, minutes, and secoundes that
thou findest with thy rote the yer of oure
Lord 1400, and the residue that leveth is the
mene mote for that same day. And note,
if hit so be that thou woldest wite the mene
mote in any yer that is lasse than thy rote,
withdraw the nomber of so many yeres as hit
is lasse than the yer of oure Lord a 1397, and
kep the residue; and so many yeres, monethes,
and dayes enter into thy tables of thy mene
mote. And tak alle the signes, degrees, and
minutes, and secoundes, that thou findest in
direct of alle the yeres, monethes, and
dayes, and wryt hem in thy slate; and
above thilke nomber wryt the signes, degrees, minutes, and secoundes, the which thou
findest with thy rote the yer of oure Lord a
1397; and withdraw alle the nethere signes
and degrees fro the signes and degrees, minutes, and secoundes of other signes with thy

rote; and thy residue that leveth is thy mene
mote for that day.

46. *For to knowe at what houre of the day,*
or of the night, shal be flod or ebbe.

First wite thou certeinly, hou that haven
stondeth, that thou list to werke for; that is
to say in which place of the firmament the
mone beyng, makith full see. Than awayte
thou redily in what degree of the zodiak that
the mone at that tyme is ynne. Bring furth
than the label, and set the point therof in
that same cost that the mone makith flod, and
set thou there the degree of the mone according with the egge of the label. Than
afterward awayte where is than the degree
of the sonne, at that tyme. Remeve thou than
the label fro the mone, and bring and set it
justly upon the degree of the sonne. And the
point of the label shal than declare to thee, at
what houre of the day or of the night shal
be flod. And there also maist thou wite by the
same point of the label, whethir it be, at that
same tyme, flod or ebbe, or half flod, or
quarter flod, or ebbe, or half or quarter
ebbe; or ellis at what houre it was last, or
shal be next by night or by day, thou than
shalt esely knowe, &c. Furthermore, if it so
be that thou happe to worke for this matere
aboute the tyme of the conjunccioun, bring
furth the degree of the mone with the label
to that coste as it is before seyd. But than thou
shalt understonde that thou may not bringe
furth the label fro the degree of the mone
as thou dide before; for-why the sonne is
than in the same degree with the mone.
And so thou may at that tyme by the point of
the label unremevid knowe the houre of the
flod or of the ebbe, as it is before seyd, &c.
And evermore as thou findest the mone passe
fro the sonne, so remeve thou the label than
fro the degree of the mone, and bring it to
the degree of the sonne. And work thou than
as thou dide before, &c. Or ellis know
thou what houre it is that thou art inne,
by thyn instrument. Than bring thou furth
fro thennes the label and ley it upon the degree of the mone, and therby may thou wite
also whan it was flod, or whan it wol be next,
be it night or day; &c.

THE
ROMAUNT OF THE
ROSE

THE ROMAUNT OF THE ROSE is a fragmentary translation of the *Roman de la rose,* the most popular and influential secular poem of the later Middle Ages. The *Roman* was begun around 1237 by Guillaume de Lorris, a young poet and lover (by his own account), as a gift to the lady of his heart; his work, he claims, encompasses "al the art of love." Guillaume tells how, in his twentieth year, he dreamed that on a lovely May morning he comes to the Garden of Love, where he encounters Mirth, Gladness, a dazzling group of dancing and singing young people, and the God of Love himself. The dreamer wanders to the well of Narcissus, where he sees a beautiful rosebud. Love's arrow strikes through his eye and into his heart. He swears allegiance to Love and receives instructions on the duties and sufferings of a lover. He then approaches the rose garden, where Bialacoil (Fair Welcome) allows him to enter. But the churlish Daunger (Standoffishness, Disdain), Shame, Dread, and Wicked Tongue oppose him. Though with the help of Venus he is granted a kiss, Jealousy drives him from the garden and imprisons the rosebud in a strong fortress. The lover is left to lament his sad situation. Here Guillaume's poem ends, unfinished.

Much of the pleasure of Guillaume's work arises from the allegory itself, for it provides a fascinating psychological analysis of the experience of love from the lover's and from the lady's points of view. Medieval readers must have also been delighted by Guillaume's style, by the elegance of his elaborate descriptions and of the lover's complaints. Judging from his imitators, Guillaume's most impressive achievement was his use of the love vision, by which he cast the experience of love in the form of an allegorical dream, told in the lyric first person of the dreamer himself and encompassing an idealized world comprehensive enough to accommodate a broad range of emotions and characters, from Idleness and Mirth to the churlish Wicked Tongue and Daunger.

The love vision, as Guillaume used it, became the dominant genre of courtly verse narrative. The dream, the idealized spring landscape, and the allegorical personages became the stock devices of love poetry until at least the sixteenth century, and for countless readers Guillaume defined the elegant craft of aristocratic love. Geoffrey Chaucer was more deeply influenced by the *Roman de la rose* than by any other French or English work. *The Book of the Duchess, The Parliament of Fowls,* the Prologue to *The Legend of Good Women,* and even the famous opening sentence of the General Prologue to *The Canterbury Tales* are all ultimately dependent upon Guillaume's work.

Guillaume left this work unfinished, perhaps because of his death. Some forty years later, Jean de Meun (le Clopinel), undertook the completion of the poem. Jean was an intellectual and a scholar, the translator of Boethius, Vegetius, Giraldus Cambrensis, and Aelred of Rievaulx. His continuation greatly expands the scope and tone of the work; love remains the unifying theme, but love — principally, though not exclusively, a refined aristocratic pastime in Guillaume's work — is now expanded to include everything from sex and friendship to divine love. Reason, appearing but briefly in Guillaume's work, becomes a major character, as does Nature, and these characters allow the introduction of a wide range of topics. Guillaume's brief touches of satire (such as Wicked Tongue's antifeminist tirade) are developed into broad satiric attacks on women, friars, knights, and society in general. And Guillaume's hints of the

685

complexity of love — most notably the well of Narcissus — are developed into a broad consideration of love in relation to nature, reason, and life itself. Guillaume's vision thus became the vehicle for a varied and amusing survey of the intellectual interests of the time that extends the work to almost 22,000 lines, until finally, with a graphic description of the sexual act only thinly disguised as allegory, the lover plucks the rosebud.

Jean's work was as influential as Guillaume's, and Chaucer drew on it throughout his career, from the account of the game of chess in *The Book of the Duchess* to the characterization of the Wife of Bath, which owes a good deal to Jean's La Vieille. Perhaps even Chaucer's characteristic style, with its humor and realism, owes something to Jean's example.

Le Roman de la rose, as expanded by Jean de Meun, evoked strong reactions. In Chaucer's time a great critical debate about the meaning and value of the work raged in Parisian literary circles; Christine de Pisan was unrelenting in her condemnation of the work, which, she believed, was a mere handbook for lechers: "So long a process, so sly a cautele/For to deceive a sely damoisele" (Hoccleve's translation of her *Epistle of Cupid*). On the other hand, the *Gawain*-poet, in *Cleanness,* praises "clene Clopinel" — decent, elegant Jean de Meun. Chaucer's God of Love,

in the Prologue to *The Legend of Good Women,* roundly condemns Chaucer for having translated the *Roman de la rose* with its slander of womanhood.

What Chaucer thought, as usual, cannot be known. However he interpreted the work, it is clear that he read it with pleasure and care, and he thought well enough of it to undertake the translation that earned him the God of Love's displeasure. Whether the Middle English version, printed here, is that translation is a matter of some doubt. This version, first printed as Chaucer's in Thynne's 1532 edition, contains the work of two or possibly three different authors, responsible for Fragments A (1–1705), B (1706–5810), and C (5811–7692). A and B consist of all of Guillaume's work (1 – 4432) and Jean's continuation to line 5810; C takes up the translation some 5,000 lines later in Jean's work, with Love's barons planning an attack on Jealousy's fortress and the confession of Faus-Semblant (False-Seeming). None of the three fragments can with certainty be attributed to Chaucer. Fragment A is Chaucerian in style and language and has been accepted by most scholars as an early work of Chaucer's; B, written in a Northern dialect, is definitely not Chaucer's; C is Chaucerian in language and manner but has been rejected by most scholars.

LARRY D. BENSON

The Romaunt of the Rose

·

Fragment A

Many men sayn that in sweveninges
Ther nys but fables and lesynges;
But men may some sweven[es] sen
Whiche hardely that false ne ben,
But afterward ben apparaunt.   5

This may I drawe to warraunt
An authour that hight Macrobes,
That halt nat dremes false ne lees,
But undoth us the avysioun
That whilom mette kyng Cipioun.   10

This text was edited by ALFRED DAVID.

1 **sweveninges:** dreams
5 **apparaunt:** apparent (i.e., come to pass)

6 **to warraunt:** as a guarantee
7 **Macrobes:** Macrobius
9 **undoth:** explains
10 **Cipioun:** Scipio; for his dream, see PF 36–84.

And whoso saith or weneth it be
A jape, or elles nycete,
To wene that dremes after falle,
Let whoso lyste a fol me calle.
For this trowe I, and say for me, 15
That dremes signifiaunce be
Of good and harm to many wightes
That dremen in her slep a-nyghtes
Ful many thynges covertly
That fallen after al openly. 20
    Within my twenty yer of age,
Whan that Love taketh his cariage
Of yonge folk, I wente soone
To bedde, as I was wont to done,
And faste I slepte; and in slepyng 25
Me mette such a swevenyng
That lyked me wonders wel.
But in that sweven is never a del
That it nys afterward befalle,
Ryght as this drem wol tel us alle. 30
    Now this drem wol I ryme aright
To make your hertes gaye and lyght,
For Love it prayeth, and also
Commaundeth me that it be so.
And if there any aske me, 35
Whether that it be he or she,
How this book, which is here,
Shal hatte, that I rede you here:
It is the Romance of the Rose,
In which al the art of love I close. 40
    The mater fayre is of to make;
God graunt me in gree that she it take
For whom that it begonnen is!
And that is she that hath, ywis,
So mochel pris, and therto she 45
So worthy is biloved to be,
That she wel ought, of pris and ryght,
Be cleped Rose of every wight.
    That it was May me thoughte tho —
It is fyve yer or more ago — 50
That it was May, thus dremed me,
In tyme of love and jolite,
That al thing gynneth waxen gay,
For ther is neither busk nor hay
In May that it nyl shrouded ben 55
And it with newe leves wren.
These wodes eek recoveren grene,
That drie in wynter ben to sene,
And the erthe wexith proud withalle,

For swote dewes that on it falle, 60
And the pore estat forget
In which that wynter had it set.
And than bycometh the ground so proud
That it wole have a newe shroud,
And makith so queynt his robe and faire 65
That it hath hewes an hundred payre
Of gras and flouris, ynde and pers,
And many hewes ful dyvers —
That is the robe I mene, iwys,
Through which the ground to preisen is. 70
    The briddes that haven left her song,
While thei suffride cold so strong,
In wedres gryl and derk to sighte,
Ben in May for the sonne brighte
So glade that they shewe in syngyng 75
That in her hertis is sich lykyng
That they mote syngen and be light.
Than doth the nyghtyngale hir myght
To make noyse and syngen blythe,
Than is blisful many sithe 80
The chelaundre and papyngay,
Than yonge folk entenden ay
Forto ben gay and amorous —
The tyme is than so saverous.
Hard is the hert that loveth nought 85
In May whan al this mirth is wrought,
Whan he may on these braunches here
The smale briddes syngen clere
Her blisful swete song pitous.
And in this sesoun delytous, 90
Whan love affraieth alle thing,
Me thought a-nyght in my sleping,
Right in my bed, ful redily,
That it was by the morowe erly,
And up I roos and gan me clothe. 95
Anoon I wissh myn hondis bothe.
A sylvre nedle forth I drough
Out of an aguler queynt ynough,
And gan this nedle threde anon,
For out of toun me list to gon 100
The song of briddes forto here
That in thise buskes syngen clere.
And in [the] swete seson that leef is,
With a thred bastyng my slevis,
Alone I wente in my plaiyng, 105
The smale foules song harknyng.

19 covertly: secretly
22 cariage: feudal tax
38 hatte: be called   rede you here: advise you to hear
54 hay: hedge
56 wren: cover

65 queynt: elegant
67 ynde: indigo blue   pers: bluish gray
73 gryl: terrible
81 chelaundre: calandra, a variety of lark   papyngay: parrot
84 saverous: pleasing
90 delytous: delightful
96 wissh: washed
98 aguler: needle case
104 bastyng: sewing

They peyned hem, ful many peyre,
To synge on bowes blosmed feyre.
Joly and gay, ful of gladnesse,
Toward a ryver gan I me dresse   110
That I herd renne faste by,
For fairer plaiyng non saugh I
Than playen me by that ryver.
For from an hill that stood ther ner
Cam doun the strem ful stif and bold.   115
Cleer was the water, and as cold
As any welle is, soth to seyne,
And somdel lasse it was than Seyne,
But it was strayghter wel away.
And never saugh I, er that day,   120
The watir that so wel lyked me,
And wondir glad was I to se
That lusty place and that ryver.
And with that watir, that ran so cler,
My face I wyssh. Tho saugh I well   125
The botme paved everydell
With gravel, ful of stones shene.
The medewe softe, swote, and grene,
Beet right on the watir syde.
Ful cler was than the morowtyde,   130
And ful attempre, out of drede.
     Tho gan I walke thorough the mede,
Dounward ay in my pleiyng,
The ryver syde costeiyng.
And whan I had a while goon,   135
I saugh a gardyn right anoon,
Ful long and brood, and everydell
Enclosed was, and walled well
With highe walles enbatailled,
Portraied without and wel entailled   140
With many riche portraitures.
And bothe the ymages and the peyntures
Gan I biholde bysyly,
And I wole telle you redyly
Of thilk ymages the semblaunce,   145
As fer as I have in remembraunce.
     Amydde saugh I Hate stonde,
That for hir wrathe, yre, and onde,
Semede to ben a mynoresse,
An angry wight, a chideresse;   150
And ful of gyle and fel corage,

By semblaunt, was that ilk ymage.
And she was nothyng wel arraied,
But lyk a wod womman afraied.
Frounced foule was hir visage,   155
And grennyng for dispitous rage,
Hir nose snorted up for tene.
Ful hidous was she for to sene,
Ful foul and rusty was she, this.
Hir heed writhen was, ywis,   160
Ful grymly with a greet towayle.
     An ymage of another entayle
A lyft half was hir faste by.
Hir name above hir heed saugh I,
And she was called Felonye.   165
     Another ymage that Vilanye
Clepid was saugh I and fond
Upon the wal on hir right hond.
Vilany was lyk somdell
That other ymage, and, trustith wel,   170
She semede a wikked creature.
By countenaunce in portrayture
She semed be ful dispitous,
And eek ful proud and outragious.
Wel coude he peynte, I undirtake,   175
That sich ymage coude make.
Ful foul and cherlyssh semed she,
And eek vylayneus for to be,
And litel coude of norture
To worshipe any creature.   180
     And next was peynted Coveitise,
That eggith folk in many gise
To take and yeve right nought ageyn,
And gret tresouris up to leyn.
And that is she that for usure   185
Leneth to many a creature
The lasse for the more wynnyng,
So coveitous is her brennyng.
And that is she that penyes fele
Techith for to robbe and stele   190
These theves and these smale harlotes;
And that is routh, for by her throtes
Ful many oon hangith at the laste.
She makith folk compasse and caste
To taken other folkis thyng   195

---

115 **stif:** strong
118 **Seyne:** the river Seine
119 **strayghter wel away:** much more spread out
129 **Beet:** touched, bordered upon
134 **costeiyng:** following the edge of the water
139 **enbatailled:** with battlements
140 **entailled:** carved
142 **peyntures:** paintings
148 **onde:** envy
149 **mynoresse:** a Franciscan nun (?); see n.

152 **By semblaunt:** in appearance
155 **Frounced:** wrinkled
156 **grennyng:** grimacing
160 **writhen:** encircled
161 **towayle:** cloth, towel
162 **entayle:** shape
163 **A lyft half:** on the left side
179 **norture:** nurture, good manners
182 **eggith:** incites, eggs on
191 **smale harlotes:** petty criminals
194 **compasse:** plot

Thorough robberie or myscounting.
And that is she that makith trechoures,
And she makith false pleadoures
That with hir termes and hir domes
Doon maydens, children, and eek gromes   200
Her heritage to forgo.
Ful croked were hir hondis two,
For Coveitise is evere wod
To gripen other folkis god.
Coveityse, for hir wynnyng,   205
Ful leef hath other mennes thing.
     Another ymage set saugh I
Next Coveitise faste by,
And she was clepid Avarice.
Ful foul in peyntyng was that vice;   210
Ful fade and caytif was she eek,
And also grene as ony leek.
So yvel hewed was hir colour,
Hir semed to have lyved in langour.
She was lyk thyng for hungre deed,   215
That ladde hir lyf oonly by breed
Kneden with eisel strong and egre,
And therto she was lene and megre.
And she was clad ful porely
Al in an old torn courtepy,   220
As she were al with doggis torn;
And bothe bihynde and eke biforn
Clouted was she beggarly.
A mantyl heng hir faste by,
Upon a perche, weik and small;   225
A burnet cote heng therwithall
Furred with no menyver,
But with a furre rough of her,
Of lambe-skynnes hevy and blake.
It was ful old, I undirtake,   230
For Avarice to clothe hir well
Ne hastith hir never a dell.
For certeynly it were hir loth
To weren ofte that ilke cloth,
And if it were forwered, she   235
Wolde have ful gret necessite
Of clothyng er she bought hir newe,
Al were it bad of woll and hewe.

This Avarice hild in hir hand
A purs that heng by a band,   240
And that she hidde and bond so stronge,
Men must abyde wondir longe
Out of that purs er ther come ought.
For that ne cometh not in hir thought;
It was not, certein, hir entente   245
That fro that purs a peny wente.
     And by that ymage, nygh ynough,
Was peynted Envye, that never lough
Nor never wel in hir herte ferde
But if she outher saugh or herde   250
Som gret myschaunce or gret disese.
Nothyng may so moch hir plese
As myschef and mysaventure,
Or whan she seeth discomfiture
Upon ony worthy man falle,   255
Than likith hir wel withalle.
She is ful glad in hir corage,
If she se any gret lynage
Be brought to nought in shamful wise.
And if a man in honour rise,   260
Or by his wit or by his prowesse,
Of that hath she gret hevynesse.
For, trustith wel, she goth nygh wod
Whan any chaunce happith god.
Envie is of such crueltee   265
That feith ne trouthe holdith she
To freend ne felawe, bad or good.
Ne she hath kyn noon of hir blood,
That she nys ful her enemy;
She nolde, I dar seyn hardely,   270
Hir owne fadir ferde well.
And sore abieth she everydell
Hir malice and hir maltalent,
For she is in so gret turment,
And hath such [wo] whan folk doth good   275
That nygh she meltith for pure wood.
Hir herte kervyth and so brekith
That God the puple wel awrekith.
Envie, iwis, shal nevere lette
Som blame upon the folk to sette.   280
I trowe that if Envie, iwis,
Knewe the beste man that is
On this side or biyonde the see,
Yit somwhat lakken hym wolde she;
And if he were so hende and wis   285
That she ne myght al abate his pris,

196 **myscounting**: embezzlement
198 **pleadoures**: lawyers
199 **domes**: judicial decisions
200 **gromes**: young men
217 **eisel**: vinegar **egre**: bitter
218 **megre**: thin
220 **courtepy**: jacket
223 **Clouted**: wrapped in rags
225 **perche**: a horizontal pole put up in rooms for hanging
clothes
226 **burnet cote**: coat made of coarse brown cloth
227 **menyver**: fine, gray fur
235 **forwered**: worn out

239 **hild**: held
273 **maltalent**: evil disposition
276 **for pure wood**: from sheer madness
278 **puple**: people **awrekith**: protects (literally, avenges)
284 **lakken hym**: disparage him

Yit wolde she blame his worthynesse
Or by hir wordis make it lesse.
I saugh Envie in that peyntyng
Hadde a wondirful lokyng,   290
For she ne lokide but awry
Or overthwart, all baggyngly.
And she hadde a [foul] usage:
She myght loke in no visage
Of man or womman forth-right pleyn,   295
But shette hir [oon] eie for disdeyn.
So for envie brenned she
Whan she myght any man se
That fair or worthi were, or wis,
Or elles stod in folkis prys.   300
   Sorowe was peynted next Envie
Upon that wall of masonrye.
But wel was seyn in hir colour
That she hadde lyved in langour;
Hir semede to have the jaunyce.   305
Nought half so pale was Avarice,
Nor nothyng lyk of lenesse;
For sorowe, thought, and gret distresse,
That she hadde suffred day and nyght,
Made hir ful yelow and nothyng bright,   310
Ful fade, pale, and megre also.
Was never wight yit half so wo
As that hir semede for to be,
Nor so fulfilled of ire as she.
I trowe that no wight myght hir please   315
Nor do that thyng that myght hir ease;
Nor she ne wolde hir sorowe slake,
Nor comfort noon unto hir take,
So depe was hir wo bigonnen,
And eek hir hert in angre ronnen.   320
A sorowful thyng wel semed she,
Nor she hadde nothyng slowe be
For to forcracchen al hir face,
And for to rent in many place
Hir clothis, and for to tere hir swire,   325
As she that was fulfilled of ire.
And al totorn lay eek hir her
Aboute hir shuldris here and ther,
As she that hadde it al torent
For angre and for maltalent.   330
And eek I telle you certeynly
How that she wep ful tendirly.
In world nys wight so hard of herte
That hadde sen her sorowes smerte,

That nolde have had of her pyte,   335
So wo-begon a thyng was she.
She al todassht herself for woo
And smot togyder her hondes two.
To sorowe was she ful ententyf,
That woful recheles caytyf.   340
Her roughte lytel of playing
Or of clypping or kissyng;
For whoso sorouful is in herte,
Him luste not to play ne sterte,
Ne for to dauncen, ne to synge,   345
Ne may his herte in temper bringe
To make joye on even or morowe,
For joy is contrarie unto sorowe.
   Elde was paynted after this,
That shorter was a foot, iwys,   350
Than she was wont in her yonghede.
Unneth herself she mighte fede.
So feble and eke so old was she
That faded was al her beaute.
Ful salowe was waxen her colour;   355
Her heed, for hor, was whyt as flour.
Iwys, great qualm ne were it non,
Ne synne, although her lyf were gon.
Al woxen was her body unwelde,
And drie and dwyned al for elde.   360
A foul, forwelked thyng was she,
That whylom round and softe had be.
Her eeres shoken faste withalle,
As from her heed they wolde falle;
Her face frounced and forpyned,   365
And bothe her hondes lorne, fordwyned.
So old she was that she ne wente
A foot, but it were by potente.
The tyme that passeth nyght and day,
And resteles travayleth ay,   370
And steleth from us so prively
That to us semeth sykerly
That it in oon poynt dwelleth ever —
And certes, it ne resteth never,
But goth so faste, and passeth ay,   375
That ther nys man that thynke may
What tyme that now present is
(Asketh at these clerkes this),

292 **overthwart:** askance, sidewise **baggyngly:** with a leer
305 **jaunyce:** jaundice
311 **megre:** thin
323 **forcracchen:** scratch badly
325 **swire:** face
330 **maltalent:** evil disposition

342 **clypping:** embracing
351 **yonghede:** youth
356 **for hor:** because of age
357 **qualm:** evil (literally, plague)
358 **synne:** a pity, shame
359 **unwelde:** feeble
360 **dwyned:** withered
361 **forwelked:** very wrinkled
365 **forpyned:** wasted away
366 **lorne:** lost (useless) **fordwyned:** shriveled up
368 **potente:** crutch

For [er] men thynke it, redily
Thre tymes ben passed by —   380
The tyme, that may not sojourne,
But goth and may never retourne,
As watir that doun renneth ay,
But never drope retourne may;
Ther may nothing as tyme endure,   385
Metall nor erthely creature,
For alle thing it fret and shall;
The tyme eke that chaungith all,
And all doth waxe and fostred be,
And alle thing distroieth he;   390
The tyme that eldith our auncessours,
And eldith kynges and emperours,
And that us alle shal overcomen,
Er that deth us shal have nomen;
The tyme that hath al in welde   395
To elden folk had maad hir elde
So ynly that, to my witing,
She myghte helpe hirsilf nothing,
But turned ageyn unto childhede.
She had nothing hirsilf to lede,   400
Ne wit ne pithe in hir hold,
More than a child of two yeer old.
But natheles, I trowe that she
Was fair sumtyme, and fresh to se,
Whan she was in hir rightful age,   405
But she was past al that passage,
And was a doted thing bicomen.
A furred cope on had she nomen;
Wel had she clad hirsilf and warm,
For cold myght elles don hir harm.   410
These olde folk have alwey cold;
Her kynde is sich, whan they ben old.
     Another thing was don there write
That semede lyk an ipocrite,
And it was clepid Poope-Holy.   415
That ilk is she that pryvely
Ne spareth never a wikked dede,
Whan men of hir taken noon hede,
And maketh hir outward precious,
With pale visage and pitous,   420
And semeth a simple creature;
But ther nys no mysaventure
That she ne thenkith in hir corage.
Ful lyk to hir was that ymage,

That makid was lyk hir semblaunce.   425
She was ful symple of countenaunce,
And she was clothed and eke shod
As she were, for the love of God,
Yolden to relygioun,
Sich semede hir devocioun.   430
A sauter held she fast in honde,
And bisily she gan to fonde
To make many a feynt praiere
To God and to his seyntis dere.
Ne she was gay, ne fresh, ne jolyf,   435
But semede to be ful ententyf
To gode werkis and to faire,
And therto she had on an haire.
Ne, certis, she was fatt nothing,
But semed wery for fasting;   440
Of colour pale and deed was she.
From hir the gate ay werned be
Of paradys, that blisful place;
For sich folk maketh lene her face,
As Crist seith in his evangile,   445
To gete hem prys in toun a while;
And for a litel glorie veine
They lesen God and his reigne.
     And alderlast of everychon
Was peynted Povert al aloon,   450
That not a peny hadde in wolde,
All though she hir clothis solde,
And though she shulde anhonged be,
For nakid as a worm was she.
And if the wedir stormy were,   455
For cold she shulde have deyed there.
She nadde on but a streit old sak,
And many a clout on it ther stak:
This was hir cote and hir mantell.
No more was there, never a dell,   460
To clothe hir with, I undirtake;
Gret leyser hadde she to quake.
And she was putt, that I of talke,
Fer fro these other, up in an halke.
There lurked and there coured she,   465
For pover thing, whereso it be,
Is shamefast and dispised ay.
Acursed may wel be that day
That povere man conceyved is;
For, God wot, al to selde, iwys,   470

387 **fret** = *freteth*, devours
391 **eldith:** ages, makes old
395 **in welde:** in (its) power, control
396 **elden:** age
401 **pithe:** vigor
408 **nomen:** taken (put on)
413 **don there write:** written there (literally, caused to be written there)
415 **Poope-Holy:** hypocrisy

427 **shod:** provided with shoes
429 **Yolden:** dedicated, joined (a religious order)
433 **feynt:** feigned
438 **haire:** hair shirt
450 **Povert:** poverty
451 **in wolde:** in (her) possession
458 **stak:** was fastened, stuck
464 **halke:** corner, nook
465 **coured:** cowered

Is ony povere man wel fed,
Or wel araied or [wel] cled,
Or wel biloved, in sich wise
In honour that he may arise.
   Alle these thingis, well avised,   475
As I have you er this devysed,
With gold and asure over all
Depeynted were upon the wall.
Square was the wall, and high sumdell;
Enclosed and barred well,   480
In stede of hegge, was that gardyn;
Com nevere shepherde theryn.
Into that gardyn, wel wrought,
Whoso that me coude have brought,
By laddre or elles by degre,   485
It wolde wel have liked me.
For sich solas, sich joie and play,
I trowe that nevere man ne say,
As was in that place delytous.
The gardeyn was not daungerous   490
To herberwe briddes many oon.
So riche a yer[d] was never noon
Of briddes song and braunches grene;
Therynne were briddes mo, I wene,
Than ben in all the rewme of Fraunce.   495
Ful blisful was the accordaunce
Of swete and pitous song thei made,
For all this world it owghte glade.
And I mysilf so mery ferde,
Whan I her blisful songes herde,   500
That for an hundred pound nolde I
(If that the passage openly
Hadde be unto me free)
That I nolde entren for to se
Th'assemble — God kepe it fro care! —   505
Of briddis whiche therynne ware,
That songen thorugh her mery throtes
Daunces of love and mery notes.
   Whan I thus herde foules synge,
I fel fast in a weymentynge   510
By which art or by what engyn
I myght come into that gardyn;
But way I couthe fynde noon
Into that gardyn for to goon.
Ne nought wist I if that ther were   515
Eyther hole or place [o-]where
By which I myght have entre.
Ne ther was noon to teche me,

For I was al aloone, iwys,
Ful wo and angwishus of this,   520
Til atte last bithought I me
That by no weye ne myght it be
That ther nas laddre or wey to passe,
Or hole, into so faire a place.
Tho gan I go a full gret pas   525
Envyronyng evene in compas
The closing of the square wall,
Tyl that I fond a wiket small
So shett that I ne myght in gon,
And other entre was ther noon.   530
   Uppon this dore I gan to smyte,
That was fetys and so lite,
For other wey coude I not seke.
Ful long I shof, and knokkide eke,
And stood ful long and of[t] herknyng,   535
If that I herde ony wight comyng,
Til that [the] dore of thilk entre
A mayden curteys openyde me.
Hir heer was as yelowe of hewe
As ony basyn scoured newe,   540
Hir flesh tendre as is a chike,
With bente browis smothe and slyke.
And by mesure large were
The openyng of hir yen clere,
Hir nose of good proporcioun,   545
Hir yen grey as is a faucoun,
With swete breth and wel savoured,
Hir face whit and wel coloured,
With litel mouth and round to see.
A clove chynne eke hadde she.   550
Hir nekke was of good fasoun
In lengthe and gretnesse, by resoun,
Withoute bleyne, scabbe, or royne.
Fro Jerusalem unto Burgoyne
Ther nys a fairer nekke, iwys,   555
To fele how smothe and softe it is;
Hir throte, also whit of hewe
As snowe on braunche snowed newe.
Of body ful wel wrought was she;
Men neded not in no cuntre   560
A fairer body for to seke.
And of fyn orfrays hadde she eke
A chapelet — so semly oon
Ne werede never mayde upon —

520 **angwishus:** anxious
540 **basyn:** copper basin **scoured:** polished
541 **chike:** young bird
542 **slyke:** sleek, shining
551 **fasoun:** fashion, shape
552 **gretnesse:** size
553 **bleyne:** blemish **royne:** roughness
554 **Burgoyne:** Burgundy
562 **orfrays:** gold embroidery

472 **cled:** dressed
482 **shepherde:** a rustic
485 **degre:** step, stairway
489 **delytous:** delightful
490 **daungerous:** reluctant, disdainful
510 **weymentynge:** lamentation

And faire above that chapelet   565
A rose gerland had she sett.
She hadde [in honde] a gay mirrour,
And with a riche gold tressour
Hir heed was tressed queyntely,
Hir sleves sewid fetisly,   570
And for to kepe hir hondis faire
Of gloves white she had a paire.
And she hadde on a cote of grene
Of cloth of Gaunt. Withouten wene,
Wel semyde by hir apparayle   575
She was not wont to gret travayle,
For whan she kempt was fetisly,
And wel arayed and richely,
Thanne had she don al hir journe,
For merye and wel bigoon was she.   580
She ladde a lusty lyf in May:
She hadde no thought, by nyght ne day,
Of nothyng, but if it were oonly
To graythe hir wel and uncouthly.
    Whan that this dore hadde opened me   585
This may[de] semely for to see,
I thanked hir as I best myghte,
And axide hir how that she highte,
And what she was I axide eke.
And she to me was nought unmeke,   590
Ne of hir answer daungerous,
But faire answerde, and seide thus:
"Lo, sir, my name is Ydelnesse;
So clepe men me, more and lesse.
Ful myghty and ful riche am I,   595
And that of oon thyng namely,
For I entende to nothyng
But to my joye and my pleying,
And for to kembe and tresse me.
Aqueynted am I and pryve   600
With Myrthe, lord of this gardyn,
That fro the land of Alexandryn
Made the trees hidre be fet
That in this gardyn ben set.
And whan the trees were woxen on highte, 605
This wall, that stant heere in thi sighte,
Dide Myrthe enclosen al aboute;
And these ymages, al withoute,
He dide hem bothe entaile and peynte,
That neithir ben jolyf ne queynte,   610
But they ben ful of sorowe and woo,

As thou hast seen a while agoo.
And ofte tyme, hym to solace,
Sir Myrthe cometh into this place,
And eke with hym cometh his meynee   615
That lyven in lust and jolite.
And now is Myrthe therynne to here
The briddis how they syngen clere,
The mavys and the nyghtyngale,
And other joly briddis smale.   620
And thus he walketh to solace
Hym and his folk, for swetter place
To pleyen ynne he may not fynde,
Although he sought oon in-tyl Ynde.
The alther-fairest folk to see   625
That in this world may founde be
Hath Mirthe with hym in his route,
That folowen hym always aboute."
    Whan Ydelnesse had told al this,
And I hadde herkned wel, ywys,   630
Thanne seide I to dame Ydelnesse,
"Now, also wisly God me blesse,
Sith Myrthe, that is so faire and fre,
Is in this yerde with his meyne,
Fro thilk assemble, if I may,   635
Shal no man werne me to-day,
That I this nyght ne mote it see.
For wel wene I there with hym be
A fair and joly companye
Fulfilled of alle curtesie."   640
And forth, withoute wordis mo,
In at the wiket went I tho,
That Ydelnesse hadde opened me,
Into that gardyn fair to see.
    And whan I was inne, iwys,   645
Myn herte was ful glad of this,
For wel wende I ful sikerly
Have ben in paradys erthly.
So fair it was that, trusteth wel,
It semede a place espirituel,   650
For certys, as at my devys,
Ther is no place in paradys
So good inne for to dwelle or be
As in that gardyn, thoughte me.
For there was many a bridd syngyng,   655
Thoroughout the yerd al thringyng;
In many places were nyghtyngales,
Alpes, fynches, and wodewales,

569 **queyntely:** elaborately, elegantly
574 **Gaunt:** Ghent **wene:** doubt
579 **journe:** day's work
584 **graythe hir:** dress herself **uncouthly:** strikingly
590 **unmeke:** proud, disdainful
602 **Alexandryn:** of Alexandria, source of Eastern luxuries
609 **entaile:** carve

619 **mavys:** song thrush
624 **in-tyl:** into, as far as
634 **yerde:** enclosed garden
636 **werne:** forbid
648 **paradys erthly:** Garden of Eden
656 **thringyng:** thronging
658 **Alpes:** bullfinches **wodewales:** woodpeckers (?), song birds (?); see n. to 657–65

That in her swete song deliten
In thilke places as they habiten.   660
There myghte men see many flokkes
Of turtles and laverokkes.
Chalaundres fele sawe I there,
That wery, nygh forsongen were;
And thrustles, terins, and mavys,   665
That songen for to wynne hem prys,
And eke to sormounte in her song
That other briddes hem among.
By note made fair servyse
These briddes, that I you devise;   670
They songe her song as faire and wel
As angels don espirituel.
And trusteth wel, whan I hem herde,
Ful lustily and wel I ferde,
For never yitt sich melodye   675
Was herd of man that myghte dye.
Sich swete song was hem among
That me thought it no briddis song,
But it was wondir lyk to be
Song of mermaydens of the see,   680
That, for her syngyng is so clere,
Though we mermaydens clepe hem here
In English, as is oure usaunce,
Men clepe hem sereyns in Fraunce.
        Ententif weren for to synge   685
These briddis, that nought unkunnynge
Were of her craft, and apprentys,
But of song sotil and wys.
And certis, whan I herde her song,
And saw the grene place among,   690
In herte I wex so wondir gay
That I was never erst, er that day,
So jolyf nor so wel bigoo,
Ne merye in herte, as I was thoo.
And than wist I and saw ful well   695
That Ydelnesse me served well,
That me putte in sich jolite.
Hir freend wel ought I for to be,
Sith she the dore of that gardyn
Hadde opened and me leten in.   700
        From hennes forth hou that I wroughte,
I shal you tellen, as me thoughte.
First, whereof Myrthe served there,
And eke what folk there with hym were,
Withoute fable I wol discryve.   705

And of that gardyn eke as blyve
I wole you tellen aftir this
The faire fasoun all, ywys,
That wel wrought was for the nones.
I may not telle you all at ones,   710
But, as I may and can, I shall
By ordre tellen you it all.
Ful fair servise and eke ful swete
These briddis maden as they sete.
Layes of love, ful wel sownyng,   715
They songen in her jargonyng;
Summe high and summe eke lowe songe
Upon the braunches grene spronge.
The swetnesse of her melodye
Made al myn herte in reverye.   720
And whan that I hadde herd, I trowe,
These briddis syngyng on a rowe,
Than myght I not withholde me
That I ne wente inne for to see
Sir Myrthe, for my desiryng   725
Was hym to seen, over alle thyng,
His countenaunce and his manere —
That sighte was to me ful dere.
        Tho wente I forth on my right hond
Doun by a lytel path I fond   730
Of mentes full, and fenell grene,
And faste by, without wene,
Sir Myrthe I fond, and right anoon
Unto Sir Myrthe gan I goon,
There as he was hym to solace.   735
And with hym in that lusty place
So fair folk and so fresh had he
That whan I saw, I wondred me
Fro whennes siche folk myght come,
So faire they weren, alle and some;   740
For they were lyk, as to my sighte,
To angels that ben fethered brighte.
This folk, of which I telle you soo,
Upon a karole wenten thoo.
A lady karolede hem that hyghte   745
Gladnesse, [the] blissful and the lighte;
Wel coude she synge and lustyly,
Noon half so wel and semely,
And make in song sich refreynynge:
It sat hir wondir wel to synge.   750
Hir vois ful clere was and ful swete.

660 **habiten:** live, frequent
662 **laverokkes:** larks
663 **Chalaundres:** larks
664 **forsongen:** all sung out
665 **thrustles:** thrushes **terins:** siskins **mavys:** song thrushes
676 **man that myghte dye:** mortal man
684 **sereyns:** sirens
687 **apprentys:** unskilled, like an apprentice

708 **fasoun:** appearance, fashion
716 **jargonyng:** twittering
720 **reverye:** gladness, joy in the spring season
731 **mentes:** mints **fenell:** fennel, the herb
741 **as to my sighte:** from my point of view
744 **karole:** a dance
745 **karolede:** sang the accompaniment to the *karole*
749 **make . . . sich refreynynge:** invent such (skillful) refrains
750 **sat:** suited

She was nought rude ne unmete
But couthe ynow of sich doyng
As longeth unto karolyng,
For she was wont in every place   755
To syngen first, folk to solace.
For syngyng moost she gaf hir to;
No craft had she so leef to do.
   Tho myghtist thou karoles sen,
And folk daunce and mery ben,   760
And made many a fair tournyng
Upon the grene gras springyng.
There myghtist thou see these flowtours,
Mynstrales, and eke jogelours,
That wel to synge dide her peyne.   765
Somme songe songes of Loreyne,
For in Loreyn her notes bee
Full swetter than in this contre.
There was many a tymbestere,
And saillouris, that I dar wel swere   770
Couthe her craft ful parfitly.
The tymbres up ful sotily
They caste and hente full ofte
Upon a fynger fair and softe,
That they failide never mo.   775
Ful fetys damyseles two,
Ryght yonge and full of semelyhede,
In kirtles and noon other wede,
And faire tressed every tresse,
Hadde Myrthe doon, for his noblesse,   780
Amydde the karole for to daunce;
But herof lieth no remembraunce,
Hou that they daunced queyntely.
That oon wolde come all pryvyly
Agayn that other, and whan they were   785
Togidre almost, they threwe yfere
Her mouthis so that thorough her play
It semed as they kiste alway —
To dauncen well koude they the gise.
What shulde I more to you devyse?   790
Ne bede I never thennes go,
Whiles that I saw hem daunce so.
   Upon the karoll wonder faste
I gan biholde, til atte laste
A lady gan me for to espie,   795
And she was cleped Curtesie,

The worshipfull, the debonaire —
I pray to God evere falle hir faire!
Ful curteisly she called me:
"What do ye there, beau ser?" quod she,   800
"Come and, if it lyke you
To dauncen, dauncith with us now."
And I, withoute tariyng,
Wente into the karolyng.
I was abasshed never a dell,   805
But it to me liked right well
That Curtesie me cleped so
And bad me on the daunce go.
For if I hadde durst, certeyn
I wolde have karoled right fayn,   810
As man that was to daunce right blithe.
Thanne gan I loken ofte sithe
The shap, the bodies, and the cheres,
The countenaunce and the maneres
Of all the folk that daunced there,   815
And I shal telle what they were.
   Ful fair was Myrthe, ful long and high;
A fairer man I nevere sigh.
As round as appil was his face,
Ful rody and whit in every place.   820
Fetys he was and wel beseye,
With metely mouth and yen greye;
His nose by mesure wrought ful right;
Crisp was his heer, and eek ful bright;
His shuldris of a large brede,   825
And smalish in the girdilstede.
He semed lyk a portreiture,
So noble he was of his stature,
So fair, so joly, and so fetys,
With lymes wrought at poynt devys,   830
Delyver, smert, and of gret myght;
Ne sawe thou nevere man so lyght.
Of berd unnethe hadde he nothyng,
For it was in the firste spryng.
Ful yong he was, and mery of thought,   835
And in samet, with briddis wrought,
And with gold beten ful fetysly,
His body was clad ful richely.
Wrought was his robe in straunge gise,
And al toslytered for queyntise   840
In many a place, lowe and hie.
And shod he was with gret maistrie,

752 **unmete:** displeasing
763 **flowtours:** flute players
764 **jogelours:** entertainers
766 **Loreyne:** Lorraine, in northern France
769 **tymbestere:** female tambourine players
770 **saillouris:** dancers
772 **tymbres:** tambourines **sotily:** skillfully
777 **semelyhede:** comeliness, grace
778 **kirtles:** frocks
791 **bede:** desired (literally, prayed)

800 **beau ser:** good sir
824 **Crisp:** curly
826 **smalish:** slender **girdilstede:** belt line
830 **at poynt devys:** exactly, to perfection
831 **Delyver:** agile **smert:** brisk, nimble
836 **samet:** samite (rich silk)
840 **toslytered:** cut with slashes (to reveal the lining)
queyntise: elegance

With shoon decoped, and with laas.
By druery and by solas
His leef a rosyn chapelet   845
Hadde mad, and on his heed it set.
    And wite ye who was his leef?
Dame Gladnesse there was hym so leef,
That syngith so wel with glad courage,
That from she was twelve yeer of age   850
She of hir love graunt hym made.
Sir Mirthe hir by the fynger hadde
Daunsyng, and she hym also;
Gret love was atwixe hem two.
Bothe were they faire and bright of hewe.   855
She semed lyk a rose newe
Of colour, and hir flesh so tendre
That with a brere smale and slendre
Men myght it cleve, I dar wel seyn.
Hir forheed, frounceles al pleyn;   860
Bente were hir browis two,
Hir yen greye and glad also,
That laugheden ay in hir semblaunt
First or the mouth, by covenaunt.
I not what of hir nose descryve,   865
So fair hath no womman alyve.
Hir heer was yelowe and clere shynyng;
I wot no lady so likyng.
Of orfrays fresh was hir gerland;
I, which seyen have a thousand,   870
Saugh never, ywys, no gerlond yitt
So wel wrought of silk as it.
And in an overgilt samit
Clad she was, by gret delit,
Of which hir leef a robe werde —   875
The myrier she in hir herte ferde.
    And next hir wente, on hir other side,
The God of Love that can devyde
Love, and as hym likith it be.
But he can cherles daunten, he,   880
And maken folkis pride fallen;
And he can wel these lordis thrallen,
And ladyes putt at lowe degre,
Whan he may hem to p[r]oude see.
    This God of Love of his fasoun   885
Was lyk no knave ne quystroun;
His beaute gretly was to pryse.

But of his robe to devise
I drede encombred for to be;
For nought clad in silk was he,   890
But all in floures and in flourettes,
. . . .
And with losenges and scochouns,
With briddes, lybardes, and lyouns,
And other beestis wrought ful well.   895
His garnement was everydell
Portreied and wrought with floures,
By dyvers medlyng of coloures.
Floures there were of many gise
Sett by compas in assise.   900
Ther lakkide no flour, to my dom,
Ne nought so mych as flour of brom,
Ne violete, ne eke pervynke,
Ne flour noon that man can on thynke;
And many a rose-leef ful long   905
Was entermedled theramong.
And also on his heed was set
Of roses reed a chapelett,
But nyghtyngales, a ful gret route,
That flyen over his heed aboute,   910
The leeves felden as they flyen.
And he was all with briddes wryen,
With popynjay, with nyghtyngale,
With chalaundre, and with wodewale,
With fynch, with lark, and with archaungell.   915
He semede as he were an aungell   916
That doun were comen fro hevene cler.
    Love hadde with hym a bacheler
That he made alweyes with hym be;
Swete-Lokyng cleped was he.   920
This bacheler stod biholdyng
The daunce, and in his hond holdyng
Turke bowes two had he.
That oon of hem was of a tree
That bereth a fruyt of savour wykke;   925
Ful crokid was that foule stikke,
And knotty here and there also,
And blak as bery or ony slo.
That other bowe was of a plante

843 **decoped:** cut in open-work patterns
844 **druery:** love
845 **leef:** sweetheart   **rosyn chepelet:** garland made of roses
860 **frounceles:** unwrinkled
868 **likyng:** agreeable, pleasing
869 **orfrays:** gold embroidery
873 **samit:** samite garment
878 **devyde:** distribute
886 **quystroun:** scullion
887 **pryse:** praise

891 **flourettes:** little flowers
892 Not in MS. Thynne has: *Ypaynted al with amorettes* (pure lovers or love-knots).
893 **losenges:** diamond-shaped figures   **scochouns:** escutcheons
894 **lybardes:** leopards
896 **garnement:** garment
900 **by compas in assise:** by design in position
902 **brom:** broom bush
903 **pervynke:** periwinkle
906 **entermedled:** mixed
912 **wryen:** covered
913 **popynjay:** parrot
914 **chalaundre:** lark   **wodewale:** woodpecker
915 **archaungell:** a bird (The word does not appear elsewhere; the French has *mesenges,* titmouse.)
928 **slo:** sloe (a plum-like fruit)

Withoute wem, I dar warante, 930
Ful evene and by proporcioun
Treitys and long, of ful good fasoun.
And it was peynted wel and thwyten,
And overal diapred and writen
With ladyes and with bacheleris, 935
Ful lyghtsom and glad of cheris.
These bowes two held Swete-Lokyng,
That semede lyk no gadelyng.
And ten brode arowis hild he there,
Of which fyve in his right hond were. 940
But they were shaven wel and dight,
Nokked and fethered right,
And all they were with gold bygoon,
And stronge poynted everychoon,
And sharpe for to kerven well. 945
But iren was ther noon ne steell,
For al was gold, men myght it see,
Out-take the fetheres and the tree.
    The swiftest of these arowis fyve
Out of a bowe for to dryve, 950
And best fethered for to flee,
And fairest eke, was clepid Beaute.
That other arowe, that hurteth lesse,
Was clepid, as I trowe, Symplesse.
The thridde cleped was Fraunchise, 955
That fethred was in noble wise
With valour and with curtesye.
The fourthe was cleped Compaignye,
That hevy for to sheten ys.
But whoso shetith right, ywys, 960
May therwith doon gret harm and wo.
The fifte of these and laste also,
Faire-Semblaunt men that arowe calle,
The leeste grevous of hem alle,
Yit can it make a ful gret wounde. 965
But he may hope his soris sounde,
That hurt is with that arowe, ywys,
His wo the bet bistowed is,
For he may sonner have gladnesse —
His langour oughte be the lesse. 970
    Five arowis were of other gise,
That ben ful foule to devyse,
For shaft and ende, soth for to telle,
Were also blak as fend in helle.
The first of hem is called Pride. 975
That other arowe next hym biside,

It was cleped Vylanye;
That arowe was al with felonye
Envenymed, and with spitous blame.
The thridde of hem was cleped Shame. 980
The fourthe Wanhope cleped is;
The fifte, the Newe-Thought, ywys.
    These arowis that I speke of heere
Were alle fyve on oon maneere,
And alle were they resemblable. 985
To hem was wel sittyng and able
The foule croked bowe hidous,
That knotty was and al roynous.
That bowe semede wel to shete
These arowis fyve that ben unmete 990
And contrarye to that other fyve.
But though I telle not as blyve
Of her power ne of her myght,
Herafter shal I tellen right
The soothe and eke signyfiaunce, 995
As fer as I have remembraunce.
All shal be seid, I undirtake,
Er of this book an ende I make.
    Now come I to my tale ageyn.
But aldirfirst I wol you seyn 1000
The fasoun and the countenaunces
Of all the folk that on the daunce is.
The God of Love, jolyf and lyght,
Ladde on his hond a lady bright,
Of high prys and of gret degre. 1005
This lady called was Beaute,
As an arowe, of which I tolde.
Ful wel thewed was she holde,
Ne she was derk ne broun, but bright,
And clere as the mone lyght 1010
Ageyn whom all the sterres semen
But smale candels, as we demen.
Hir flesh was tendre as dew of flour,
Hir chere was symple as byrde in bour,
As whyt as lylye or rose in rys, 1015
Hir face, gentyl and tretys.
Fetys she was, and smal to se;
No wyndred browis hadde she,
Ne popped hir, for it neded nought
To wyndre hir or to peynte hir ought. 1020

930 wem: blemish warante: swear
933 thwyten: carved
934 diapred: decorated with small geometric patterns
938 gadelyng: scoundrel
942 Nokked: notched
948 Out-take: except tree: wood
954 Symplesse: simplicity
966 sounde: heal, make sound

979 spitous: hateful
981 Wanhope: despair
985 resemblable: similar
986 sittyng: suitable, fitting
988 roynous: rough
990 unmete: displeasing
1008 wel thewed: well behaved, of good character
1014 byrde: young girl
1015 rys: twig
1016 tretys: well formed
1018 wyndred: plucked, painted (?); see n.
1019 popped hir: adorned herself, used cosmetics
1020 wyndre: embellish

Hir tresses yelowe and longe straughten,
Unto hir helys doun they raughten.
Hir nose, hir mouth, and eye, and cheke
Wel wrought, and all the remenaunt eke.
A ful gret savour and a swote   1025
Me toucheth in myn herte rote,
As helpe me God, whan I remembre
Of the fasoun of every membre.
In world is noon so fair a wight,
For yong she was, and hewed bright,   1030
Sore plesaunt, and fetys withall,
Gente, and in hir myddill small.
    Biside Beaute yede Richesse,
An high lady of gret noblesse,
And gret of prys in every place.   1035
But whoso durste to hir trespace,
Or til hir folk, in word or dede,
He were full hardy, out of drede,
For bothe she helpe and hyndre may.
And that is nought of yisterday   1040
That riche folk have full gret myght
To helpe and eke to greve a wyght.
The beste and the grettest of valour
Diden Rychesse ful gret honour,
And besy weren hir to serve,   1045
For that they wolde hir love deserve:
They cleped hir lady, gret and small.
This wide world hir dredith all;
This world is all in hir daunger.
Hir court hath many a losenger,   1050
And many a traytour envyous,
That ben ful besy and curyous
For to dispreisen and to blame
That best deserven love and name.
Bifore the folk, hem to bigilen,   1055
These losengeris hem preyse and smylen,
And thus the world with word anoynten;
And aftirward they prikke and poynten
The folk right to the bare boon,
Bihynde her bak whan they ben goon,   1060
And foule abate the folkis prys.
Ful many a worthy man and wys,
An hundred, have [they] do to dye.
These losengers thorough flaterye
Have made folk ful straunge be,   1065
There hem oughte be pryve.
Wel yvel mote they thryve and thee,
And yvel aryved mote they be,

These losengers, ful of envye!
No good man loveth her companye.   1070
    Richesse a robe of purpur on hadde —
Ne trowe not that I lye or madde,
For in this world is noon it lyche,
Ne by a thousand deell so riche,
Ne noon so fair; for it ful well   1075
With orfrays leyd was everydeell,
And portraied in the ribanynges
Of dukes storyes, and of kynges,
And with a bend of gold tasseled,
And knoppis fyne of gold ameled.   1080
Aboute hir nekke of gentyl entayle
Was shet the riche chevesaile,
In which ther was full gret plente
Of stones clere and bright to see.
    Rychesse a girdell hadde upon,   1085
The bokel of it was of a stoon
Of vertu gret and mochel of myght,
For whoso bar the stoon so bright,
Of venym durst hym nothing doute,
While he the stoon hadde hym aboute.   1090
That stoon was gretly for to love,
And tyl a riche mannes byhove
Worth all the gold in Rome and Frise.
The mourdaunt wrought in noble wise
Was of a stoon full precious,   1095
That was so fyn and vertuous
That hol a man it koude make
Of palasie and toth-ake.
And yit the stoon hadde such a grace
That he was siker in every place,   1100
All thilke day, not blynd to ben,
That fastyng myghte that stoon seen.
The barres were of gold ful fyn
Upon a tyssu of satyn,
Full hevy, gret, and nothyng lyght;   1105
In everich was a besaunt-wight.
    Upon the tresses of Richesse
Was sette a cercle, for noblesse,

1031 **Sore plesaunt:** extremely (?) agreeable; see n.
1032 **Gente:** graceful
1050 **losenger:** flatterer; see n.
1058 **poynten:** stab
1067 **thee:** prosper
1068 **yvel aryved mote they be:** may they have an unhappy landing (i.e., bad luck)

1071 **purpur:** purple cloth
1072 **madde:** go mad
1076 **orfrays:** gold embroidery
1077 **ribanynges:** ribbon-work, silk borders on trim
1079 **bend:** band
1080 **knoppis:** ornamental buttons, studs   **ameled:** enameled
1081 **entayle:** shape
1082 **chevesaile:** collar
1089 **durst hym:** he needed
1091 **for to love:** to be loved, prized
1092 **tyl . . . byhove:** for profit, advantage
1093 **Frise:** Frisia
1094 **mourdaunt:** trim; see n.
1098 **palasie:** palsy
1106 **besaunt-wight:** the weight of a bezant (a Byzantine gold coin)

Of brend gold that full lyghte shoon;
So fair, trowe I, was never noon.　1110
But he were kunnyng, for the nonys,
That koude devyse all the stonys
That in that cercle shewen clere.
It is a wondir thing to here,
For no man koude preyse or gesse　1115
Of hem the valewe or richesse.
Rubyes there were, saphires, jagounces,
And emeraudes, more than two ounces,
But all byfore, ful sotilly,
A fyn charboncle set saugh I.　1120
The stoon so clere was and so bright
That, also soone as it was nyght,
Men myghte seen to go, for nede,
A myle or two in lengthe and brede.
Sich lyght sprang out of the ston　1125
That Richesse wondir brighte shon,
Bothe hir heed and all hir face,
And eke aboute hir al the place.
　Dame Richesse on hir hond gan lede
A yong man ful of semelyhede,　1130
That she best loved of ony thing.
His lust was mych in housholding.
In clothyng was he ful fetys,
And loved well to have hors of prys.
He wende to have reproved be　1135
Of theft or moordre if that he
Hadde in his stable ony hakeney.
And therfore he desired ay
To be aqueynted with Richesse,
For all his purpos, as I gesse,　1140
Was forto make gret dispense,
Withoute wernyng or diffense.
And Richesse myght it wel sustene,
And hir dispence well mayntene,
And hym alwey sich plente sende　1145
Of gold and silver for to spende
Withoute lakking or daunger,
As it were poured in a garner.
　And after on the daunce wente
Largesse, that settith al hir entente　1150
For to be honourable and free.
Of Alexandres kyn was she.
Hir most joye was, ywys,

Whan that she yaf and seide, "Have this."
Not Avarice, the foule caytyf,　1155
Was half to gripe so ententyf,
As Largesse is to yeve and spende;
And God ynough alwey hir sende,
So that the more she yaf awey
The more, ywys, she hadde alwey.　1160
Gret loos hath Largesse and gret pris,
For bothe [wys] folk and unwys
Were hooly to hir baundon brought,
So wel with yiftes hath she wrought.
And if she hadde an enemy,　1165
I trowe that she coude tristily
Make hym full soone hir freend to be,
So large of yift and free was she.
Therfore she stod in love and grace
Of riche and pover in every place.　1170
A full gret fool is he, ywys,
That bothe riche and nygard is.
A lord may have no maner vice
That greveth more than avarice,
For nygart never with strengthe of hond　1175
May wynne gret lordship or lond,
For freendis all to fewe hath he
To doon his will perfourmed be.
And whoso wole have freendis heere,
He may not holde his tresour deere.　1180
For by ensample I telle this:
Right as an adamaunt, iwys,
Can drawen to hym sotylly
The iren that is leid therby,
So drawith folkes hertis, ywis,　1185
Silver and gold that yeven is.
Largesse hadde on a robe fresh
Of riche purpur Sarsynesh.
Wel fourmed was hir face and cleer,
And opened hadde she hir coler,　1190
For she right there hadde in present
Unto a lady maad present
Of a gold broche, ful wel wrought.
And certys, it myssat hir nought,
For thorough hir smokke, wrought with silk,
The flesh was seen as whit as mylk.　1196
Largesse, that worthy was and wys,
Hild by the hond a knyght of prys,
Was sib to Artour of Britaigne,
And that was he that bar the ensaigne　1200

1117 **jagounces:** jacinths, precious stones of reddish color
1118 **emeraudes:** emeralds
1120 **charboncle:** carbuncle (a precious red stone)
1130 **semelyhede:** comeliness, grace
1132 **housholding:** keeping a great house
1137 **hakeney:** small riding horse
1142 **wernyng:** refusal **diffense:** hindrance
1147 **Withoute . . . daunger:** with no holding back, freely
1148 **garner:** granary
1152 **Alexandres:** Alexander the Great's

1158 **sende:** sent
1161 **loos:** praise
1163 **to hir baundon:** into her control
1182 **adamaunt:** magnetic stone
1188 **Sarsynesh:** Saracen (cloth), cloth from the East
1194 **myssat hir nought:** was not unbecoming to her
1199 **sib:** related, kin
1200 **ensaigne:** standard

Of worship and the gounfanoun.
And yit he is of sich renoun
That men of hym seye faire thynges
Byfore barouns, erles, and kynges.
This knyght was comen all newely   1205
Fro tourneiynge faste by;
There hadde he don gret chyvalrie
Thorough his vertu and his maistrie;
And for the love of his lemman
He caste doun many a doughty man.   1210
    And next hym daunced dame Fraunchise,
Arayed in full noble gyse.
She was not broun ne dun of hewe,
But whit as snow fallen newe.
Hir nose was wrought at poynt devys,   1215
For it was gentyl and tretys,
With eyen gladde, and browes bente.
Hir heer doun to hir helis wente,
And she was symple as dowve on tree.
Ful debonaire of herte was she.   1220
She durst never seyn ne do
But that that hir longed to;
And if a man were in distresse,
And for hir love in hevynesse,
Hir herte wolde have full gret pite,   1225
She was so amiable and free.
For were a man for hir bistad,
She wolde ben right sore adrad
That she dide over-gret outrage,
But she hym holpe his harm to aswage;   1230
Hir thought it elles a vylanye.
And she hadde on a sukkenye,
That not of hempene heerdis was —
So fair was noon in all Arras.
Lord, it was ridled fetysly!   1235
Ther nas [nat] a poynt, trewely,
That it nas in his right assise.
Full wel clothed was Fraunchise,
For ther is no cloth sittith bet
On damysell than doth roket.   1240
A womman wel more fetys is
In roket than in cote, ywis.
The whyte roket, rydled faire,
Bitokeneth that full debonaire
And swete was she that it ber.   1245
    Bi hir daunced a bacheler.
I can not telle you what he highte,
But faire he was and of good highte,

All hadde he be, I sey no more,
The lordis sone of Wyndesore.   1250
    And next that daunced Curtesye,
That preised was of lowe and hye,
For neither proud ne fool was she.
She for to daunce called me
(I pray God yeve hir right good grace!), 1255
Whanne I com first into the place.
She was not nyce ne outrageous,
But wys and war and vertuous,
Of fair speche and of fair answere.
Was never wight mysseid of here;   1260
She bar rancour to no wight.
Clere broun she was, and therto bright
Of face, of body avenaunt —
I wot no lady so plesaunt.
She [were] worthy for to bene   1265
An emperesse or crowned quene.
    And by hir wente a knyght dauncyng,
That worthy was and wel spekyng,
And ful wel koude he don honour.
The knyght was fair and styf in stour, 1270
And in armure a semely man,
And wel biloved of his lemman.
    Faire Idilnesse thanne saugh I,
That alwey was me faste by.
Of hir have I, withoute fayle,   1275
Told yow the shap and apparayle;
For (as I seide) loo, that was she
That dide to me so gret bounte
That she the gate of the gardyn
Undide and let me passen in.   1280
    And after daunced, as I gesse,
[Youthe], fulfilled of lustynesse,
That nas not yit twelve yeer of age,
With herte wylde and thought volage.
Nyce she was, but she ne mente   1285
Noon harm ne slight in hir entente,
But oonly lust and jolyte;
For yonge folk, wel witen ye,
Have lytel thought but on her play.
Hir lemman was biside alway   1290
In sich a gise that he hir kyste
At alle tymes that hym lyste,
That all the daunce myght it see.
They make no force of pryvete,
For who spake of hem yvel or well,   1295
They were ashamed never a dell,
But men myght seen hem kisse there

1201 **gounfanoun:** banner
1227 **bistad:** in trouble
1229 **over-gret outrage:** violence, excessive cruelty
1232 **sukkenye:** a loose frock
1233 **hempene heerdis:** coarse parts ("hards") of flax (hemp)
1235 **ridled:** gathered or pleated as a curtain
1240 **roket:** frock

1250 The son of the Lord of Windsor; see n.
1263 **avenaunt:** pleasing
1270 **stif in stour:** bold in battle
1284 **volage:** flighty, foolish

As it two yonge dowves were.
For yong was thilke bacheler;
Of beaute wot I noon his per.   1300
And he was right of sich an age
As Youthe his leef, and sich corage.
　　The lusty folk thus daunced there,
And also other that with hem were,
That weren alle of her meyne;   1305
Ful hende folk and wys and free,
And folk of faire port, truëly,
There weren alle comunly.
Whanne I hadde seen the countenaunces
Of hem that ladden thus these daunces,   1310
Thanne hadde I will to gon and see
The gardyn that so lyked me,
And loken on these faire loreres,
On pyntrees, cedres, and oliveris.
The daunces thanne eended were,   1315
For many of them that daunced there
Were with her loves went awey
Undir the trees to have her pley.
　　A, Lord, they lyved lustyly!
A gret fool were he, sikirly,   1320
That nolde, his thankes, such lyf lede!
For this dar I seyn, oute of drede,
That whoso myghte so wel fare,
For better lyf durst hym not care;
For ther nys so good paradys   1325
As to have a love at his devys.
　　Oute of that place wente I thoo,
And in that gardyn gan I goo,
Pleyyng along full meryly.
The God of Love full hastely   1330
Unto hym Swete-Lokyng clepte;
No lenger wolde he that he kepte
His bowe of gold, that shoon so bright.
He bad hym bende [it] anoon ryght,
And he full soone [it] sette an-ende,   1335
And at a braid he gan it bende,
And tok hym of his arowes fyve,
Full sharp and redy for to dryve.
Now God, that sittith in mageste,
Fro deedly woundes he kepe me,   1340
If so be that he hadde me shette!
For if I with his arowe mette,
It hadde me greved sore, iwys.
But I, that nothyng wist of this,
Wente up and doun full many a wey,   1345
And he me folwed fast alwey,

But nowhere wold I reste me,
Till I hadde in all the gardyn be.
　　The gardyn was, by mesuryng,
Right evene and square in compassing: 1350
It as long was as it was large.
Of fruyt hadde every tree his charge,
But it were any hidous tree,
Of which ther were two or three.
There were, and that wot I full well,   1355
Of pome-garnettys a full gret dell;
That is a fruyt full well to lyke,
Namely to folk whanne they ben sike.
And trees there were, gret foisoun,
That baren notes in her sesoun,   1360
Such as men notemygges calle,
That swote of savour ben withalle.
And alemandres gret plente,
Fyges, and many a date-tree
There wexen, if men hadde nede,   1365
Thorough the gardyn in length and brede.
Ther was eke wexyng many a spice,
As clowe-gelofre and lycorice,
Gyngevre and greyn de parys,
Canell and setewale of prys,   1370
And many a spice delitable
To eten whan men rise fro table.
And many homly trees ther were
That peches, coynes, and apples beere,
Medlers, plowmes, perys, chesteynes,   1375
Cherys, of which many oon fayn is,
Notes, aleys, and bolas,
That for to seen it was solas.
With many high lorer and pyn
Was renged clene all that gardyn,   1380
With cipres and with olyveres,
Of which that nygh no plente heere is.
There were elmes grete and stronge,
Maples, assh, ok, asp, planes longe,
Fyn ew, popler, and lyndes faire,   1385
And othere trees full many a payre.
　　What shulde I tel you more of it?
There were so many trees yit,

1356 **pome-garnettys**: pomegranates
1359 **foisoun**: plenty
1360 **notes**: nuts
1361 **notemygges**: nutmegs
1363 **alemandres**: almond trees
1368 **clowe-gelofre**: clove
1369 **Gyngevre**: ginger **greyn de parys**: grain of paradise, cardamom seed
1370 **Canell**: cinnamon **setewale**: zedoary, a ginger-like spice used as a condiment and stimulant
1374 **peches**: peaches **coynes**: quinces
1375 **Medlers**: medlars (a fruit) **plowmes**: plums **perys**: pears **chesteynes**: chestnuts
1376 **Cherys**: cherries
1377 **Notes**: nuts **aleys**: service berries **bolas**: wild plums
1380 **renged**: arranged in rows
1381 **olyveres**: olive trees
1385 **ew**: yew

1313 **loreres**: laurel trees
1314 **oliveris**: olive trees
1335 **an-ende**: upright
1336 **at a braid**: suddenly
1341 **shette**: shot

That I shulde al encombred be
Er I had rekened every tree.   1390
   These trees were set, that I devyse,
Oon from another, in assyse,
Fyve fadome or sixe, I trowe so;
But they were hye and great also,
And for to kepe out wel the sonne,   1395
The croppes were so thicke ronne,
And every braunche in other knet
And ful of grene leves set,
That sonne myght there non discende,
Lest [it] the tender grasses shende.   1400
There myght men does and roes se,
And of squyrels ful great plente
From bowe to bowe alway lepynge.
Conies there were also playinge,
That comyn out of her clapers,   1405
Of sondrie colours and maners,
And maden many a tourneying
Upon the fresshe grass spryngyng.
   In places saw I welles there,
In whiche there no frogges were,   1410
And fayr in shadowe was every welle.
But I ne can the nombre telle
Of stremys smal that by devys
Myrthe had don come through condys,
Of whiche the water in rennyng   1415
Gan make a noyse ful lykyng.
   About the brinkes of these welles,
And by the stremes overal elles,
Sprang up the grass, as thicke set
And softe as any veluët,   1420
On which men myght his lemman leye
As on a fetherbed to pleye,
For the erthe was ful softe and swete.
Through moisture of the welle wete
Sprong up the sote grene gras   1425
As fayre, as thicke, as myster was.
But moche amended it the place
That th'erthe was of such a grace
That it of floures hath plente,
That bothe in somer and wynter be.   1430
   There sprang the vyolet al newe,
And fressh pervynke, riche of hewe,
And floures yelowe, white, and rede —
Such plente grew there never in mede.
Ful gay was al the ground, and queynt,   1435

And poudred, as men had it peynt,
With many a fressh and sondri flour,
That casten up ful good savour.
   I wol nat longe holde you in fable
Of al this garden dilectable.   1440
I mot my tonge stynten nede,
For I ne may, withouten drede,
Naught tellen you the beaute al,
Ne half the bounte therewithal.
   I went on right hond and on left   1445
About the place; it was nat left,
Tyl I had [in] al the garden ben,
In the estres that men myghte sen.
   And thus while I wente in my play,
The God of Love me folowed ay,   1450
Right as an hunter can abyde
The beest, tyl he seeth his tyde
To sheten at good mes to the der,
Whan that hym nedeth go no ner.
   And so befyl, I rested me   1455
Besydes a wel, under a tree,
Which tree in Fraunce men cal a pyn.
But sithe the tyme of Kyng Pepyn,
Ne grew there tree in mannes syghte
So fayr, ne so wel woxe in highte —   1460
In al that yard so high was non.
And springyng in a marble ston
Had Nature set, the sothe to telle,
Under that pyn-tree a welle.
And on the border, al withoute,   1465
Was written in the ston aboute,
Letters smal that sayden thus,
"Here starf the fayre Narcisus."
   Narcisus was a bacheler
That Love had caught in his danger,   1470
And in his net gan hym so strayne,
And dyd him so to wepe and playne,
That nede him must his lyf forgo.
For a fayr lady that hight Echo
Him loved over any creature,   1475
And gan for hym such payne endure
That on a tyme she him tolde
That if he her loven nolde,
That her behoved nedes dye;
There laye non other remedye.   1480
   But natheles for his beaute
So feirs and daungerous was he
That he nolde graunten hir askyng,
For wepyng ne for fair praiyng.

1392 **assyse:** position
1404 **Conies:** rabbits
1405 **clapers:** dens, warrens
1413 **devys:** a contrivance, device
1414 **condys:** conduits, water pipes
1420 **veluët:** velvet (to be pronounced as trisyllabic)
1426 **myster:** need, necessity
1432 **pervynke:** periwinkle
1435 **queynt:** pleasing

1436 **poudred:** adorned (with flowers)   **peynt:** painted
1448 **estres:** inner parts, nooks and crannies
1453 **at good mes:** from a favorable vantage point (a good range; a hunting term)
1458 **Kyng Pepyn:** father of Charlemagne
1472 **playne:** lament

And whanne she herde hym werne [her] soo,
She hadde in herte so gret woo,　　　　　　　1486
And took it in so gret dispit,
That she, withoute more respit,
Was deed anoon. But er she deide,
Full pitously to God she preide　　　　　　　1490
That proude-hertid Narcisus,
That was in love so daungerous,
Myght on a day ben hampred so
For love, and ben so hoot for woo,
That never he myght to joye atteyne,　　　　1495
And that he shulde feele in every veyne
What sorowe trewe lovers maken,
That ben so vilaynsly forsaken.
　　This prayer was but resonable;
Therfore God held it ferme and stable.　　　1500
For Narcisus, shortly to telle,
By aventure com to that welle
To reste hym in that shadowing
A day whanne he com fro huntyng.
This Narcisus hadde suffred paynes　　　　　1505
For rennyng alday in the playnes,
And was for thurst in gret distresse
Of heet and of his werynesse
That hadde his breth almost bynomen.
Whanne he was to that welle comen,　　　　1510
That shadowid was with braunches grene,
He thoughte of thilke water shene
To drynke, and fresshe hym wel withalle.
And doun on knees he gan to falle,
And forth his heed and necke he straughte　1515
To drynken of that welle a draughte.
And in the water anoon was seene
His nose, his mouth, his yen sheene,
And he therof was all abasshed.
His owne shadowe had hym bytrasshed,　　1520
For well wende he the forme see
Of a child of gret beaute.
Well kouthe Love hym wreke thoo
Of daunger and of pride also,
That Narcisus somtyme hym beer.　　　　　1525
He quytte hym well his guerdoun ther,
For he musede so in the welle
That, shortly all the sothe to telle,
He lovede his owne shadowe soo
That atte laste he starf for woo.　　　　　　1530
For whanne he saugh that he his wille
Myght in no maner wey fulfille,
And that he was so faste caught
That he hym kouthe comfort nought,

He loste his wit right in that place,　　　　1535
And diede withynne a lytel space.
And thus his warisoun he took
For the lady that he forsook.
　　Ladyes, I preye ensample takith,
Ye that ageyns youre love mistakith,　　　　1540
For if her deth be yow to wite,
God kan ful well youre while quyte.
　　Whanne that this lettre of which I telle
Hadde taught me that it was the welle
Of Narcisus in his beaute,　　　　　　　　1545
I gan anoon withdrawe me,
Whanne it fel in my remembraunce
That hym bitidde such myschaunce.
But at the laste thanne thought I
That scatheles, full sykerly,　　　　　　　1550
I myght unto the welle goo.
Wherof shulde I abasshen soo?
· · · · · · · · · · · ·
And doun I loutede for to see
The clere water in the stoon,　　　　　　　1555
And eke the gravell, which that shoon
Down in the botme as silver fyn,
For of the well this is the fyn:
In world is noon so cler of hewe.
The water is evere fresh and newe,　　　　　1560
That welmeth up with wawis brighte
The mountance of two fynger highte.
Abouten it is gras spryngyng,
For moiste so thikke and wel likyng
That it ne may in wynter dye　　　　　　　1565
No more than may the see be drye.
　　Down at the botme set saw I
Two cristall stonys craftely
In thilke freshe and faire welle.
But o thing sothly dar I telle,　　　　　　1570
That ye wole holde a gret mervayle
Whanne it is told, withouten fayle.
For whanne the sonne, cler in sighte,
Cast in that well his bemys brighte,
And that the heete descendid is,　　　　　　1575
Thanne taketh the cristall stoon, ywis,
Agayn the sonne an hundrid hewis,
Blew, yelow, and red, that fresh and newe is.
Yitt hath the merveilous cristall
Such strengthe that the place overall,　　　1580
Bothe flour and tree and leves grene

1498 **vilaynsly**: cruelly, churlishly
1513 **fresshe**: refresh
1515 **straughte**: stretched
1520 **bytrasshed**: betrayed

1537 **warisoun**: payment, requital
1540 **mistakith**: transgress, do wrong
1542 **youre while quyte**: repay (wreak revenge on) you
1550 **scatheles**: without harm
1553 Not in MS. Thynne has: *Unto the welle than wente I me.*
1558 **fyn**: main point
1561 **welmeth**: swells
1562 **mountance**: amount
1564 **moiste**: moisture

And all the yerd in it is seene.
And for to don you to undirstonde,
To make ensample wole I fonde.
Ryght as a myrrour openly 1585
Shewith all thing that stondith therby,
As well the colour as the figure,
Withouten ony coverture,
Right so the cristall stoon shynyng
Withouten ony disseyvyng 1590
The estrees of the yerd accusith
To hym that in the water musith.
For evere, in which half that he be,
He may well half the gardyn se,
And if he turne, he may right well 1595
Sen the remenaunt everydell.
For ther is noon so litil thyng
So hid, ne closid with shittyng,
That it ne is sene, as though it were
Peyntid in the cristall there. 1600
This is the mirrour perilous
In which the proude Narcisus
Saw all his face fair and bright,
That made hym sithe to ligge upright.
For whoso loketh in that mirrour, 1605
Ther may nothyng ben his socour
That he ne shall there sen somthyng
That shal hym lede into lovyng.
Full many worthy man hath it
Blent, for folk of grettist wit 1610
Ben soone caught heere and awayted;
Withouten respit ben they baited.
Heere comth to folk of newe rage;
Heere chaungith many wight corage;
Heere lith no red ne wit therto; 1615
For Venus sone, daun Cupido,
Hath sowen there of love the seed,
That help ne lith there noon, ne red,
So cerclith it the welle aboute.
His gynnes hath he sette withoute, 1620
Ryght for to cacche in his panters
These damoysels and bachelers.
Love will noon other bridde[s] cacche,
Though he sette either net or lacche.
And for the seed that heere was sowen, 1625
This welle is clepid, as well is knowen,
The Welle of Love, of verray right,

Of which ther hath ful many a wight
Spoken in bookis dyversely.
But they shull never so verily 1630
Descripcioun of the welle heere,
Ne eke the sothe of this matere,
As ye shull, whanne I have undo
The craft that hir bilongith too.
Allway me liked for to dwelle 1635
To sen the cristall in the welle
That shewide me full openly
A thousand thinges faste by.
But I may say, in sory houre
Stode I to loken or to poure, 1640
For sithen [have] I sore siked.
That mirrour hath me now entriked,
But hadde I first knowen in my wit
The vertu and [the] strengthe of it,
I nolde not have mused there. 1645
Me hadde bet ben elliswhere,
For in the snare I fell anoon
That hath bitrasshed many oon.
In thilke mirrour saw I tho,
Among a thousand thinges mo, 1650
A roser chargid full of rosis,
That with an hegge aboute enclos is.
Tho had I sich lust and envie,
That for Parys ne for Pavie
Nolde I have left to goon and see 1655
There grettist hep of roses be.
Whanne I was with this rage hent,
That caught hath many a man and shent,
Toward the roser gan I go;
And whanne I was not fer therfro, 1660
The savour of the roses swote
Me smot right to the herte-rote,
As I hadde all enbawmed be.
And if I ne hadde endouted me
To have ben hatid or assailed, 1665
My thankis, wolde I not have failed
To pulle a rose of all that route
To beren in myn hond aboute
And smellen to it where I wente;
But ever I dredde me to repente, 1670
And lest it grevede or forthoughte
The lord that thilke gardyn wroughte.
Of roses ther were gret wone,

1591 **accusith:** reveals
1598 **shittyng:** shutting
1601 **mirrour perilous:** the well and its crystals
1604 **ligge upright:** lie flat on his back; i.e., dead
1611 **awayted:** waylaid
1612 **baited:** tormented
1620 **gynnes:** traps (devices)
1621 **panters:** bird snares
1624 **lacche:** snare

1642 **entriked:** ensnared
1648 **bitrasshed:** betrayed
1652 **enclos:** enclosed
1654 **Pavie:** Pavia
1659 **roser:** rose bush
1663 **enbawmed:** perfumed
1664 **endouted me:** feared
1666 **My thankis:** willingly
1667 **pulle:** pluck
1671 **forthoughte:** displeased

So faire waxe never in rone.
Of knoppes clos some sawe I there;   1675
And some wel beter woxen were;
And some ther ben of other moysoun
That drowe nygh to her sesoun
And spedde hem faste for to sprede.
I love well sich roses rede,   1680
For brode roses and open also
Ben passed in a day or two,
But knoppes wille [al] freshe be
Two dayes, atte leest, or thre.
The knoppes gretly liked me,   1685
For fairer may ther no man se.
Whoso myght have oon of alle,
It ought hym ben full lief withalle.
Might I [a] gerlond of hem geten,

For no richesse I wolde it leten.   1690
Among the knoppes I ches oon
So fair that of the remenaunt noon
Ne preise I half so well as it,
Whanne I avise it in my wit.
For it so well was enlumyned   1695
With colour reed, [and] as well fyned
As nature couthe it make faire.
And it hath leves wel foure paire,
That Kynde hath sett, thorough his knowyng,
Aboute the rede roses spryngyng.   1700
The stalke was as rishe right,
And theron stod the knoppe upright
That it ne bowide upon no side.
The swote smelle sprong so wide
That it dide all the place aboute —   1705

Fragment B

Whanne I hadde smelled the savour swote,
No will hadde I fro thens yit goo,
Bot somdell neer it wente I thoo,
To take it, but myn hond, for drede,
Ne dorste I to the Rose bede   1710
For thesteles sharpe, of many maneres,
Netles, thornes, and hokede breres,
For mych they distourbled me,
For sore I dradde to harmed be.
    The God of Love, with bowe bent,   1715
That all day set hadde his talent
To pursuen and to spien me,
Was stondyng by a fige-tree.
And whanne he saw hou that I
Hadde chosen so ententifly   1720
The botoun, more unto my pay
Than ony other that I say,
He tok an arowe full sharply whet,
And in his bowe whanne it was set,
He streight up to his ere drough   1725
The stronge bowe that was so tough,
And shet att me so wondir smerte
That thorough myn ye unto myn herte
The takel smot, and depe it wente.
And therwithall such cold me hente   1730
That under clothes warme and softe
Sithen that day I have chevered ofte.

Whanne I was hurt thus, in [a] stounde
I felle doun plat unto the grounde.
Myn herte failed and feynted ay,   1735
And longe tyme a-swoone I lay.
But whanne I come out of swonyng,
And hadde witt and my felyng,
I was all maat, and wende full well
Of blood have loren a full gret dell.   1740
But certes, the arowe that in me stod
Of me ne drew no drope of blod,
For-why I found my wounde all dreie.
Thanne tok I with myn hondis tweie
The arowe, and ful fast out it plighte,   1745
And in the pullyng sore I sighte.
So at the last the shaft of tree
I drough out with the fethers thre.
But yet the hokede heed, ywis,
The which [that] Beaute callid is,   1750
Gan so depe in myn herte passe,
That I it myghte nought arace;
But in myn herte still it stod,
Al bledde I not a drope of blod.
I was bothe anguyssous and trouble   1755
For the perill that I saw double:
I nyste what to seye or do,
Ne gete a leche my woundis to;
For neithir thurgh gras ne rote
Ne hadde I help of hope ne bote.   1760
But to the botoun evermo

1674 **rone**: thick bush
1675 **knoppes**: buds
1677 **moysoun**: harvest, crop

1713 **distourbled**: disturbed
1721 **botoun**: rosebud
1729 **takel**: arrow
1732 **chevered**: shivered

1695 **enlumyned**: made bright
1696 **well fyned**: delicately made
1701 **as rishe right**: straight as a rush, reed

1733 **stounde**: moment

Myn herte drew, for all my wo;
My thought was in noon other thing,
For hadde it ben in my kepyng,
It wolde have brought my lyf agayn.   1765
For certis evenly, I dar wel seyn,
The sight oonly and the savour
Alegged mych of my langour.
Thanne gan I for to drawe me
Toward the botoun faire to se;   1770
And Love hadde gete hym, in a throwe,
Another arowe into his bowe,
And for to shete gan hym dresse.
The arowis name was Symplesse,
And whanne that Love gan nygh me nere,   1775
He drow it up, withouten were,
And shet at me with all his myght,
So that this arowe anoon-right
Thourghout [myn] eigh, as it was founde,
Into myn herte hath maad a wounde.   1780
Thanne I anoon dide al my craft
For to drawen out the shaft,
And therwithall I sighed eft.
But in myn herte the heed was left,
Which ay encreside my desir   1785
Unto the botoun drawe ner;
And evermo that me was woo,
The more desir hadde I to goo
Unto the roser, where that grew
The freysshe botoun so bright of hew.   1790
Betir me were to have laten be,
But it bihovede nedes me
To don right as myn herte bad,
For evere the body must be lad
Aftir the herte, in wele and woo;   1795
Of force togidre they must goo.
But never this archer wolde feyne
To shete at me with all his peyne,
And for to make me to hym mete.
The thridde arowe he gan to shete,   1800
Whanne best his tyme he myght espie,
The which was named Curtesie.
Into myn herte it dide avale;
A-swoone I fell bothe deed and pale.
Long tyme I lay and stired nought,   1805
Till I abraide out of my thought,
And faste thanne I avysede me
To drawe out the shaft of tree.

But evere the heed was left bihynde,
For ought I couthe pulle or wynde,   1810
So sore it stikid whanne I was hit,
That by no craft I myght it flit.
But anguyssous and full of thought,
I felte sich woo my wounde ay wrought,
That somonede me alway to goo   1815
Toward the Rose that plesede me soo,
But I ne durste in no maner,
Bicause the archer was so ner.
"For evermore gladly," as I rede,
"Brent child of fir hath myche drede."   1820
And, certis yit, for al my peyne,
Though that I sigh yit arwis reyne,
And grounde quarels sharpe of steell,
Ne for no payne that I myght feell,
Yit myght I not mysilf witholde   1825
The faire roser to biholde,
For Love me yaf sich hardement
For to fulfille his comaundement.
Upon my fete I ros up than,
Feble as a forwoundid man,   1830
And forth to gon [my] myght I sette,
And for the archer nolde I lette.
Toward the roser fast I drow,
But thornes sharpe mo than ynow
Ther were, and also thisteles thikke,   1835
And breres, brymme for to prikke,
That I ne myghte gete grace
The rowe thornes for to passe,
To sen the roses fresshe of hewe.
I must abide, though it me rewe,   1840
The hegge aboute so thikke was,
That closide the roses in compas.
But o thing lyked me right well:
I was so nygh, I myghte fel
Of the botoun the swote odour,   1845
And also se the fresshe colour,
And that right gretly liked me,
That I so neer myghte it se.
Sich joie anoon therof hadde I
That I forgat my malady.   1850
To sen I hadde sich delit,
Of sorwe and angre I was al quyt,
And of my woundes that I hadde thore;
For nothing liken me myght more
Than dwellen by the roser ay,   1855

1768 **Alegged:** relieved
1774 **Symplesse:** simplicity
1775 **nygh me nere:** draw near to me
1776 **withouten were:** without warning
1791 **laten be:** let (it) be
1797 **feyne:** cease
1803 **avale:** sink down

1812 **flit:** escape
1823 **quarels:** crossbow bolts
1827 **hardement:** daring
1836 **brymme:** fierce
1838 **rowe:** rough
1853 **thore:** there

And thennes never to passe away.
But whanne a while I hadde be thar,
The God of Love, which al toshar
Myn herte with his arwis kene,
Castith hym to yeve me woundis grene.   1860
He shet at me full hastily
An arwe named Company,
The whiche takell is full able
To make these ladies merciable.
Thanne I anoon gan chaungen hewe   1865
For grevaunce of my wounde newe,
That I agayn fell in swonyng
And sighede sore in compleynyng.
Soore I compleyned that my sore
On me gan greven more and more.   1870
I hadde noon hope of allegeaunce;
So nygh I drow to desperaunce,
I roughte of deth ne of lyf,
Wheder that Love wolde me dryf.
Yf me a martir wolde he make,   1875
I myght his power nought forsake.
And while for anger thus I wok,
The God of Love an arowe tok —
Ful sharp it was and pugnaunt —
And it was callid Faire-Semblaunt,   1880
The which in no wise wole consente
That ony lover hym repente
To serve his love with herte and alle,
For ony perill that may bifalle.
But though this arwe was kene grounde   1885
As ony rasour that is founde,
To kutte and kerve, at the poynt
The God of Love it hadde anoynt
With a precious oynement,
Somdell to yeve aleggement   1890
Upon the woundes that he had
·   ·   ·   ·   ·   ·   ·   ·   ·   ·   ·   ·   ·
To helpe her sores, and to cure,
And that they may the bet endure.
But yit this arwe, withoute more,   1895
Made in myn herte a large sore,
That in full gret peyne I abod.
But ay the oynement wente abrod;
Thourghout my woundes large and wide
It spredde aboute in every side,   1900
Thorough whos vertu and whos myght
Myn herte joyfull was and light.
I hadde ben deed and al toshent,

But for the precious oynement.
The shaft I drow out of the arwe,   1905
Rokyng for wo right wondir narwe;
But the heed, which made me smerte,
Lefte bihynde in myn herte
With other foure, I dar wel say,
That never wole be take away.   1910
But the oynement halp me wel,
And yit sich sorwe dide I fel
That al day I chaunged hewe
Of my woundes fresshe and newe,
As men myght se in my visage.   1915
The arwis were so full of rage,
So variaunt of diversitee,
That men in everich myghte se
Bothe gret anoy and eke swetnesse,
And joie meynt with bittirnesse.   1920
Now were they esy, now were they wod;
In hem I felte bothe harm and good;
Now sore without alleggement,
Now softenyng with oynement;
It softnede heere and prikkith there: 1925
Thus ese and anger togidre were.
    The God of Love delyverly
Com lepande to me hastily,
And seide to me in gret rape,
"Yeld thee, for thou may not escape!   1930
May no defence availe thee heer;
Therfore I rede make no daunger.
If thou wolt yelde thee hastily,
Thou shalt rather have mercy.
He is a fool in sikernesse,   1935
That with daunger or stoutnesse
Rebellith there that he shulde plese;
In sich folye is litel ese.
Be meke where thou must nedis bow;
To stryve ageyn is nought thi prow.   1940
Com at oones, and have ydoo,
For I wol that it be soo.
Thanne yeld thee heere debonairly."
And I answerid ful hombly,
"Gladly, sir, at youre biddyng,   1945
I wole me yelde in alle thyng.
To youre servyse I wol me take,
For God defende that I shulde make
Ageyn youre biddyng resistence.

1858 **toshar:** cut through
1871 **allegeaunce:** alleviation
1879 **pugnaunt:** piercing
1892 Not in MS. Thynne has: *Through the body in my herte made.*
1898 **abrod:** all over

1906 Rocking it (in order to free the barbed head of the arrow)
very slightly to avoid the pain (*wo*)
1917 **variaunt:** changeable
1920 **meynt:** mingled
1927 **delyverly:** nimbly
1928 **lepande:** leaping
1929 **rape:** haste
1936 **stoutnesse:** pride
1940 **prow:** profit, advantage

I wole not don so gret offence,   1950
For if I dide, it were no skile.
Ye may do with me what ye wile,
Save or spille, and also sloo.
Fro you in no wise may I goo.
My lyf, my deth is in youre hond;   1955
I may not laste out of youre bond.
Pleyn at youre lyst I yelde me,
Hopyng in herte that sumtyme ye
Comfort and ese shull me sende;
Or ellis, shortly, this is the eende,   1960
Withouten helthe I mot ay dure,
But if ye take me to youre cure.
Comfort or helthe how shuld I have,
Sith ye me hurt, but ye me save?
The helthe of love mot be founde   1965
Where as they token first her wounde.
And if ye lyst of me to make
Youre prisoner, I wol it take
Of herte and will, fully at gree.
Hoolly and pleyn Y yelde me,   1970
Withoute feynyng or feyntise,
To be governed by youre emprise.
Of you I here so myche pris,
I wole ben hool at youre devis
For to fulfille youre lykyng   1975
And repente for nothyng,
Hopyng to have yit in som tide
Mercy of that I abide."
And with that covenaunt yelde I me
Anoon, down knelyng upon my kne,   1980
Proferyng for to kisse his feet;
But for nothyng he wolde [me] let,
And seide, "I love thee bothe and preise,
Sen that thyn aunswar doth me ease,
For thou answerid so curteisly.   1985
For now I wot wel uttirly
That thou art gentyll by thi speche.
For though a man fer wolde seche,
He shulde not fynden, in certeyn,
No sich answer of no vileyn;   1990
For sich a word ne myghte nought
Isse out of a vilayns thought.
Thou shalt not lesen of thi speche,
For [to] thy helpyng wole I eche,
And eke encresen that I may.   1995
But first I wole that thou obay
Fully, for thyn avauntage,
Anoon to do me heere homage.

And sithe kisse thou shalt my mouth,
Which to no vilayn was never couth   2000
For to aproche it, ne for to touche;
For sauff of cherlis I ne vouche
That they shull never neigh it nere.
For curteis and of faire manere,
Well taught and ful of gentilnesse   2005
He muste ben that shal me kysse,
And also of full high fraunchise,
That shal atteyne to that emprise.
And first of o thing warne I thee,
That peyne and gret adversite   2010
He mot endure, and eke travaile,
That shal me serve, withouten faile.
But ther-ageyns thee to comforte,
And with thi servise to desporte,
Thou mayst full glad and joyfull be   2015
So good a maister to have as me,
And lord of so high renoun.
I bere of love the gonfanoun,
Of curtesie the banere.
For I am of the silf manere,   2020
Gentil, curteys, meke, and fre,
That whoever ententyf be
Me to honoure, doute, and serve,
And also that he hym observe
Fro trespas and fro vilanye,   2025
And hym governe in curtesie
With will and with entencioun.
For whanne he first in my prisoun
Is caught, thanne must he uttirly
Fro thennes forth full bisily   2030
Caste hym gentyll for to bee,
If he desire help of me."
    Anoon withouten more delay,
Withouten daunger or affray,
I bicom his man anoon,   2035
And gaf hym thankes many a oon,
And knelide doun with hondis joynt
And made it in my port full queynt.
The joye wente to myn herte rote,
Whanne I hadde kissed his mouth so swote;
I hadde sich myrthe and sich likyng,   2041
It cured me of langwisshing.
He askide of me thanne hostages:
"I have," he seide, "taken fele homages
Of oon and other, where I have ben   2045
Disceyved ofte, withouten wen.
These felouns, full of falsite,

1972 **emprise:** rule
1984 **Sen:** since
1992 **Isse:** issue, come forth
1994 **eche:** add

2002 **sauff of cherlis I ne vouche:** I do not vouchsafe to churls
2003 **neigh it nere:** draw any nearer
2018 **gonfanoun:** banner
2047 **falsite:** deceit

Have many sithes biguyled me
And thorough falshed her lust achieved,
Wherof I repente and am agreved.   2050
And I hem gete in my daunger,
Her falshede shull they bie full der.
But for I love thee, I seie thee pleyn,
I wol of thee be more certeyn;
For thee so sore I wole now bynde   2055
That thou away ne shalt not wynde
For to denyen the covenaunt,
Or don that is not avenaunt.
That thou were fals it were gret reuthe,
Sith thou semest so full of treuthe."   2060
    "Sire, if thee lyst to undirstande,
I merveile the askyng this demande.
For why or wherfore shulde ye
Ostages or borwis aske of me,
Or ony other sikirnesse,   2065
Sith ye wot, in sothfastnesse,
That ye have me susprised so,
And hol myn herte taken me fro,
That it wole do for me nothing,
But if it be at youre biddyng?   2070
Myn herte is youres, and myn right nought,
As it bihoveth, in dede and thought,
Redy in all to worche youre will,
Whether so turne to good or ill,
So sore it lustith you to plese,   2075
No man therof may you disseise.
Ye have theron sette sich justice,
That it is werreid in many wise;
And if ye doute it nolde obeye,
Ye may therof do make a keye,   2080
And holde it with you for ostage."
    "Now, certis, this is noon outrage,"
Quod Love, "and fully I acord.
For of the body he is full lord
That hath the herte in his tresor;   2085
Outrage it were to asken more."
    Thanne of his awmener he drough
A litell keye, fetys ynowgh,
Which was of gold polisshed clere,
And seide to me, "With this keye heere   2090
Thyn herte to me now wole I shette.
For all my jowelles, loke and knette,
I bynde undir this litel keye,
That no wight may carie aweye.
This keye is full of gret poeste."   2095

With which anoon he touchide me
Undir the side full softely,
That he myn herte sodeynly
Without anoy hadde spered,
That yit right nought it hath me dered.   2100
    Whanne he hadde don his will al oute,
And I hadde putte hym out of doute,
"Sire," I seide, "I have right gret wille
Youre lust and plesaunce to fulfille.
Loke ye my servise take at gree,   2105
By thilke feith ye owe to me.
I seye nought for recreaundise,
For I nought doute of youre servise,
But the servaunt traveileth in vayne,
That for to serven doth his payne   2110
Unto that lord, which in no wise
Kan hym no thank for his servyse."
    Love seide, "Dismaie thee nought.
Syn thou for sokour hast me sought,
In thank thi servise wol I take,   2115
And high of degre I wol thee make,
If wikkidnesse ne hyndre thee.
But, as I hope, it shal nought be;
To worshipe no wight by aventure
May come, but if he peyne endure.   2120
Abid and suffre thy distresse;
That hurtith now, it shal be lesse.
I wot mysilf what may thee save,
What medicyne thou woldist have.
And if thi trouthe to me thou kepe,   2125
I shal unto thy helpyng eke,
To cure thy woundes and make hem clere,
Where so they be olde or grene —
Thou shalt be holpen, at wordis fewe.
For certeynly thou shalt well shewe   2130
Wher that thou servest with good wille
For to complysshen and fulfille
My comaundementis, day and nyght,
Whiche I to lovers yeve of right."
    "A sire, for Goddis love," seide I,   2135
"Er ye passe hens, ententyfly
Youre comaundementis to me ye say,
And I shall kepe hem, if I may;
For hem to kepen is all my thought.
And if so be I wot hem nought,   2140
Thanne may I [erre] unwityngly.
Wherfore I pray you enterely,

2052 **bie**: buy, pay for
2058 **avenaunt**: pleasing
2067 **susprised**: surprised
2087 **awmener**: alms-purse
2092 **loke and knette**: locked and knitted up
2095 **poeste**: power

2099 **spered**: barred
2100 **dered**: harmed
2101 **al oute**: utterly, completely
2107 **recreaundise**: cowardice
2126 **unto . . . eke**: add to, increase
2132 **complysshen**: accomplish
2141 **unwityngly**: unknowingly

With all myn herte, me to lere,
That I trespasse in no manere."
    The God of Love thanne chargide me   2145
Anoon, as ye shall here and see,
Word by word, by right emprise,
So as the Romance shall devise.
    The maister lesith his tyme to lere,
Whanne that the disciple wol not here;   2150
It is but veyn on hym to swynke
That on his lernyng wol not thinke.
Whoso luste love, lat hym entende,
For now the Romance bigynneth to amende.
Now is good to here, in fay,   2155
If ony be that can it say,
And poynte it as the resoun is
Set; for other-gate, ywys,
It shall nought well in alle thyng
Be brought to good undirstondyng.   2160
For a reder that poyntith ille
A good sentence may ofte spille.
The book is good at the eendyng,
Maad of newe and lusty thyng;
For whoso wol the eendyng here,   2165
The craft of love he shall mowe lere,
If that ye wol so long abide,
Tyl I this Romance may unhide,
And undo the signifiance
Of this drem into Romance.   2170
The sothfastnesse that now is hid,
Without coverture shall be kid
Whanne I undon have this dremyng,
Wherynne no word is of lesyng.
    "Vilanye, at the bigynnyng,   2175
I wole," sayde Love, "over alle thyng,
Thou leve if thou wolt [not] be
Fals, and trespasse ageynes me.
I curse and blame generaly
All hem that loven vilany,   2180
For vilanye makith vilayn,
And by his dedis a cherl is seyn.
Thise vilayns arn withouten pitee,
Frendshipe, love, and all bounte.
I nyl resseyve unto my servise   2185
Hem that ben vilayns of emprise.
But undirstonde in thyn entent
That this is not myn entendement,
To clepe no wight in noo ages

Oonly gentill for his lynages.   2190
But whoso is vertuous,
And in his port nought outrageous,
Whanne sich oon thou seest thee biforn,
Though he be not gentill born,
Thou maist well seyn, this is in soth,   2195
That he is gentil by cause he doth
As longeth to a gentilman;
Of hem noon other deme I can.
For certeynly, withouten drede,
A cherl is demed by his dede   2200
Of hie or lowe, as we may see,
Or of what kynrede that he bee.
Ne say nought, for noon yvel wille,
Thyng that is to holden stille;
It is no worshipe to myssey.   2205
Thou maist ensample take of Key,
That was somtyme, for mysseiyng,
Hated bothe of olde and ying.
As fer as Gaweyn, the worthy,
Was preised for his curtesy,   2210
Kay was hated, for he was fell,
Of word dispitous and cruell.
Wherfore be wise and aqueyntable,
Goodly of word, and resonable
Bothe to lesse and eke to mare.   2215
And whanne thou comest there men are,
Loke that thou have in custome ay
First to salue hem, if thou may;
And if it fall that of hem som
Salue thee first, be not domm,   2220
But quyte hem curteisly anoon,
Without abidyng, er they goon.
    "For nothyng eke thy tunge applye
To speke wordis of rebaudrye.
To vilayn speche in no degre   2225
Lat never thi lippe unbounden be.
For I nought holde hym, in good feith,
Curteys, that foule wordis seith.
And alle wymmen serve and preise,
And to thy power her honour reise;   2230
And if that ony myssaiere
Dispise wymmen, that thou maist here,
Blame hym, and bidde hym holde hym stille.
And [set] thy myght and all thy wille
Wymmen and ladies for to please,   2235
And to do thyng that may hem ese,
That they ever speke good of thee,
For so thou maist best preised be.

2157 **poynte:** punctuate
2158 **other-gate:** otherwise
2161 **poyntith ille:** mispunctuates, misinterprets
2168 **unhide:** reveal
2170 **Romance:** Romance language; i.e., French
2183 **vilayns:** peasants, churls
2188 **entendement:** intention

2213 **aqueyntable:** affable
2222 **abidyng:** delay
2231 **myssaiere:** slanderer

"Loke fro pride thou kepe thee wel;
For thou maist bothe perceyve and fel   2240
That pride is bothe foly and synne,
And he that pride hath hym withynne
Ne may his herte in no wise
Meken ne souplen to servyse.
For pride is founde in every part   2245
Contrarie unto loves art.
And he that loveth, trewely,
Shulde hym contene jolily
Without pride in sondry wise,
And hym disgysen in queyntise.   2250
For queynt array, without drede,
Is nothyng proud, who takith hede;
For fresh array, as men may see,
Withouten pride may ofte be.
"Mayntene thysilf aftir thi rent   2255
Of robe and eke of garnement,
For many sithe fair clothyng
A man amendith in myche thyng.
And loke alwey that they be shape —
What garnement that thou shalt make —   2260
Of hym that kan best do,
With all that perteyneth therto.
Poyntis and sleves be well sittand,
Right and streght on the hand.
Of shon and bootes, newe and faire,   2265
Loke at the leest thou have a paire,
And that they sitte so fetisly
That these rude may uttirly
Merveyle, sith that they sitte so pleyn,
How they come on or off ageyn.   2270
Were streite gloves with awmenere
Of silk; and alwey with good chere
Thou yeve, if thou have richesse;
And if thou have nought, spende the lesse.
Alwey be mery, if thou may,   2275
But waste not thi good alway.
Have hat of floures as fresh as May,
Chapelett of roses of Whitsonday,
For sich array ne costeth but lite.
Thyn hondis wassh, thy teeth make white,
And let no filthe upon thee bee.   2281
Thy nailes blak if thou maist see,
Voide it awey delyverly,
And kembe thyn heed right jolily.
Fard not thi visage in no wise,   2285

For that of love is not th' emprise;
For love doth haten, as I fynde,
A beaute that cometh not of kynde.
Alwey in herte I rede thee
Glad and mery for to be,   2290
And be as joyfull as thou can;
Love hath no joye of sorowful man.
That yvell is full of curtesie
That laughith in his maladie;
For ever of love the siknesse   2295
Is meynd with swete and bitternesse.
The sore of love is merveilous;
For now the lover [is] joyous,
Now can he pleyne, now can he grone,
Now can he syngen, now maken mone;   2300
To-day he pleyneth for hevynesse,
To-morowe he pleyeth for jolynesse.
The lyf of love is full contrarie,
Which stoundemele can ofte varie.
But if thou canst mirthis make,   2305
That men in gre wole gladly take,
Do it goodly, I comaunde thee.
For men shulde, wheresoevere they be,
Do thing that hem sittyng is,
For therof cometh good loos and pris.   2310
Whereof that thou be vertuous,
Ne be not straunge ne daungerous;
For if that thou good ridere be,
Prike gladly, that men may se.
In armes also if thou konne,   2315
Pursue til thou a name hast wonne.
And if thi voice be faire and cler,
Thou shalt maken [no] gret daunger
Whanne to synge they goodly preye —
It is thi worship for t' obeye.   2320
Also to you it longith ay
To harpe and gitterne, daunce and play,
For if he can wel foote and daunce,
It may hym greetly do avaunce.
Among eke, for thy lady sake,   2325
Songes and complayntes that thou make,
For that wole meven in hir herte,
Whanne they reden of thy smerte.
Loke that no man for scarce thee holde,
For that may greve thee many folde.   2330
Resoun wole that a lover be
In his yiftes more large and fre
Than cherles that ben not of lovyng.

2244 **souplen:** bend, yield
2250 **queyntise:** finery
2256 **garnement:** garment
2263 **Poyntis:** laces   **sittand:** fitting
2269 **sitte so pleyn:** fit so tightly
2271 **awmenere:** alms-purse
2285 **Fard:** use cosmetics on

2304 **stoundemele:** from time to time
2322 **gitterne:** play the cithern, a guitar-like instrument
2325 **Among:** from time to time
2326 **that thou make:** (see) that you compose
2329 **scarce:** miserly

For who therof can ony thyng,
He shal be leef ay for to yeve,   2335
In Loves lore whoso wolde leve;
For he that thorough a sodeyn sight,
Or for a kyssyng, anoonright
Yaff hool his herte in will and thought,
And to hymsilf kepith right nought,   2340
Aftir swich gift it is good resoun
He yeve his good in abandoun.
    "Now wol I shortly heere reherce
Of that I have seid in verce
Al the sentence by and by,   2345
In wordis fewe compendiously,
That thou the better mayst on hem thynke,
Whether so it be thou wake or wynke.
For the wordis litel greve
A man to kepe, whanne it is breve.   2350
Whoso with Love wole goon or ride,
He mot be curteis, and voide of pride,
Mery, and full of jolite,
And of largesse alosed be.
    "First I joyne thee, heere in penaunce,   2355
That evere, withoute repentaunce,
Thou sette thy thought in thy lovyng
To laste withoute repentyng,
And thenke upon thi myrthis swete,
That shall folowe aftir, whan ye mete.   2360
    "And for thou trewe to love shalt be,
I wole, and comaunde thee,
That in oo place thou sette, all hool,
Thyn herte withoute halfen dool
Of trecherie and sikernesse;   2365
For I lovede nevere doublenesse.
To many his herte that wole depart,
Everich shal have but litel part;
But of hym drede I me right nought,
That in oo place settith his thought.   2370
Therfore in oo place it sette,
And lat it nevere thannys flette.
For if thou yevest it in lenyng,
I holde it but a wrecchid thyng;
Therfore yeve it hool and quyt,   2375
And thou shalt have the more merit.
If it be lent, than aftir soon
The bounte and the thank is doon;
But, in love, fre yeven thing
Requyrith a gret guerdonyng.   2380

Yeve it in yift al quyt fully,
And make thi yift debonairly,
For men that yift holde more dere
That yeven [is] with gladsom chere.
That yift nought to preisen is   2385
That man yeveth maugre his.
Whanne thou hast yeven thyn herte, as I
Have seid thee heere openly,
Thanne aventures shull thee falle,
Which harde and hevy ben withalle.   2390
For ofte whan thou bithenkist thee
Of thy lovyng, whereso thou be,
Fro folk thou must departe in hie,
That noon perceyve thi maladie.
But hyde thyne harm thou must alone,   2395
And go forth sool, and make thy mone.
Thou shalt no whyle be in o stat,
But whylom cold and whilom hat,
Now reed as rose, now yelowe and fade.
Such sorowe, I trowe, thou never hade;   2400
Cotidien ne quarteyne,
It is nat so ful of peyne.
For often tymes it shal falle
In love, among thy paynes alle,
That thou thyself al holly   2405
Foryeten shalt so utterly
That many tymes thou shalt be
Styl as an ymage of tree,
Domm as a ston, without steryng
Of fot or hond, without spekyng.   2410
Than, soone after al thy payn,
To memorye shalt thou come agayn,
As man abasshed wonder sore,
And after syghen more and more.
For wyt thou wel, withouten wen,   2415
In such astat ful ofte have ben
That have the yvel of love assayd
Wherthrough thou art so dismayd.
    "After, a thought shal take the so,
That thy love is to fer the fro.   2420
Thou shalt saye, 'God! what may this be,
That I ne may my lady se?
Myn herte alone is to her go,
And I abyde al sol in wo,
Departed fro myn owne thought,   2425
And with myne eyen se right nought.
Alas, myne eyen sende I ne may
My careful herte to convay!

2342 **yeve . . . in abandoun:** give freely
2350 **breve:** brief
2354 **alosed:** praised
2355 **joyne:** enjoin, command
2364 **halfen dool:** with a half portion, half-heartedly
2372 **flette:** flit, pass away
2373 **in lenyng:** as a loan

2384 **gladsom:** cheerful
2386 **maugre his:** in spite of himself
2396 **sool:** alone
2401 **Cotidien:** a fever recurring daily   **quarteyne:** a fever recurring every four days
2428 **careful:** sorrowful   **convay:** guide (back)

Myn hertes gyde but they be,
I prayse nothyng, whatever they se.   2430
Shul they abyde thanne? Nay;
But gon and visyten without delay
That myn herte desyreth so.
For certainly, but if they go,
A fool myself I may wel holde,   2435
Whan I ne se what myn herte wolde.
Wherfore I wol gon her to sen,
Or eased shal I never ben,
But I have som tokenyng.'
Than gost thou forth without dwellyng;   2440
But ofte thou faylest of thy desyr,
Er thou mayst come her any ner,
And wastest in vayn thi passage.
Thanne fallest thou in a newe rage;
For want of sight thou gynnest morne,   2445
And homward pensyf thou dost retorne.
In greet myscheef thanne shalt thou bee,
For thanne agayn shall come to thee
Sighes and pleyntes with newe woo,
That no ycchyng prikketh soo.   2450
Who wot it nought, he may go lere
Of hem that bien love so dere.
  "Nothyng thyn herte appesen may
That ofte thou wolt goon and assay
If thou maist seen, by aventure,   2455
Thi lyves joy, thin hertis cure;
So that, bi grace, if thou myght
Atteyne of hire to have a sight,
Thanne shalt thou don noon other dede,
But with that sight thyne eyen fede.   2460
That faire fresh whanne thou maist see,
Thyne herte shall so ravysshed be
That nevere thou woldest, thi thankis, lete,
Ne remove for to see that swete.
The more thou seest in sothfastnesse,   2465
The more thou coveytest of that swetnesse;
The more thin herte brenneth in fir,
The more thin herte is in desir.
For who considreth everydeell,
It may be likned wondir well,   2470
The peyne of love, unto a fer;
For evermore thou neighest ner,
Thou, or whooso that it bee,
For verray sothe I tell it thee,
The hatter evere shall thou brenne,   2475
As experience shall thee kenne:
Whereso [thou] comest in ony coost,

Who is next fyr, he brenneth moost.
And yitt forsothe, for all thin hete,
Though thou for love swelte and swete,   2480
Ne for nothyng thou felen may,
Thou shalt not willen to passen away.
And though thou go, yitt must thee nede
Thenke all day on hir fairhede
Whom thou biheelde with so good will,   2485
And holde thisilf biguyled ill
That thou ne haddest noon hardement
To shewe hir ought of thyn entent.
Thyn herte full sore thou wolt dispise,
And eke repreve of cowardise,   2490
That thou, so dul in every thing,
Were domm for drede, withoute spekyng.
Thou shalt eke thenke thou didest folye
That thou were hir so faste bye,
And durst not auntre thee to saye   2495
Somthyng er thou cam awaye;
For thou haddist no more wonne,
To speke of hir whanne thou bigonne.
But yitt she wolde, for thy sake,
In armes goodly thee have take —   2500
It shulde have be more worth to thee
Than of tresour gret plente.
Thus shalt thou morne and eke compleyn,
And gete enchesoun to goon ageyn
Unto thi walk, or to thi place   2505
Where thou biheelde hir fleshly face.
And never, for fals suspeccioun,
Thou woldest fynde occasioun
For to gon unto hire hous.
So art thou thanne desirous   2510
A sight of hir for to have,
If thou thin honour myghtist save,
Or ony erande myghtist make
Thider for thi loves sake,
Full fayn thou woldist, but for drede   2515
Thou gost not, lest that men take hede.
Wherfore I rede, in thi goyng,
And also in thyn ageyn-comyng,
Thou be well war that men ne wit.
Feyne thee other cause than it   2520
To go that weye, or faste by;
To hele wel is no foly.
And if so be it happe thee
That thou thi love there maist see,
In siker wise thou hir salewe,   2525
Wherewith thi colour wole transmewe,

2450 **ycchyng**: itching
2475 **hatter**: hotter
2476 **kenne**: teach

2484 **fairhede**: beauty
2495 **auntre thee**: take a risk
2497 **wonne**: won, obtained
2522 **hele**: conceal

And eke thy blod shal al toquake,
Thyn hewe eke chaungen for hir sake.
But word and wit, with chere full pale,
Shull wante for to tell thy tale.   2530
And if thou maist so fer forth wynne
That thou resoun durst bigynne,
And woldist seyn thre thingis or mo,
Thou shalt full scarsly seyn the two.
Though thou bithenke thee never so well,   2535
Thou shalt foryete yit somdell,
But if thou dele with trecherie.
For fals lovers mowe all folye
Seyn, what hem lust, withouten drede,
They be so double in her falshede;   2540
For they in herte cunne thenke a thyng,
And seyn another in her spekyng.
And whanne thi speche is eendid all,
Ryght thus to thee it shall byfall:
If ony word thanne come to mynde   2545
That thou to seye hast left bihynde,
Thanne thou shalt brenne in gret martir,
For thou shalt brenne as ony fir.
This is the stryf and eke the affray,
And the batell that lastith ay.   2550
This bargeyn eende may never take,
But if that she thi pees will make.
And whanne the nyght is comen, anoon
A thousand angres shall come uppon.
To bedde as fast thou wolt thee dight,   2555
Where thou shalt have but smal delit.
For whanne thou wenest for to slepe,
So full of peyne shalt thou crepe,
Sterte in thi bed aboute full wide,
And turne full ofte on every side,   2560
Now dounward groff and now upright,
And walowe in woo the longe nyght.
Thine armys shalt thou sprede a-bred,
As man in werre were forwerreyd.
Thanne shall thee come a remembraunce   2565
Of hir shap and hir semblaunce,
Whereto non other may be pere.
And wite thou wel, withoute were,
That thee shal se[me] somtyme that nyght
That thou hast hir that is so bright   2570
Naked bitwene thyne armes there,
All sothfastnesse as though it were.
Thou shalt make castels thanne in Spayne
And dreme of joye, all but in vayne,
And thee deliten of right nought,   2575

While thou so slombrest in that thought
That is so swete and delitable,
The which, in soth, nys but fable,
For it ne shall no while laste.
Thanne shalt thou sighe and wepe faste,   2580
And say, 'Dere God, what thing is this?
My drem is turned all amys,
Which was full swete and apparent;
But now I wake, it is al shent!
Now yede this mery thought away!   2585
Twenty tymes upon a day
I wolde this thought wolde come ageyn,
For it aleggith well my peyn.
It makith me full of joyfull thought;
It sleth me, that it lastith noght.   2590
A, Lord! Why nyl ye me socoure
The joye, I trowe, that I langoure?
The deth I wolde me shulde sloo
While I lye in hir armes twoo.
Myn harm is hard, withouten wene;   2595
My gret unese full ofte I meene.
  " 'But wolde Love do so I myght
Have fully joye of hir so bright,
My peyne were quyt me rychely.
Allas, to gret a thing aske I!   2600
Hit is but foly and wrong wenyng
To aske so outrageous a thyng;
And whoso askith folily,
He mot be warned hastily.
And I ne wot what I may say,   2605
I am so fer out of the way;
For I wolde have full gret likyng
And full gret joye of lasse thing.
For wolde she, of hir gentylnesse,
Without and more, me oonys kysse,   2610
It were to me a gret guerdoun,
Relees of all my passioun.
But it is hard to come therto;
All is but folye that I do,
So high I have myn herte set,   2615
Where I may no comfort get.
I wote not wher I seye well or nought,
But this I wot wel in my thought,
That it were better of hir alloone,
For to stynte my woo and moone,   2620
A lok on hir I caste goodly,
Than for to have al utterly
Of an other all hool the pley.
A, Lord! Wher I shall byde the day
That evere she shall my lady be?   2625

2531 **so fer forth wynne:** get so far
2561 **groff:** face down
2563 **a-bred:** wide open
2564 **forwerreyd:** defeated

2583 **apparent:** evident
2592 **langoure:** languish (for); see n.
2596 **meene:** complain

He is full cured that may hir see.
A, God! Whanne shal the dawnyng spring?
To liggen thus is an angry thyng;
I have no joye thus heere to ly,
Whanne that my love is not me by.　　2630
A man to lyen hath gret disese,
Which may not slepe ne reste in ese.
I wolde it dawed, and were now day,
And that the nyght were went away;
For were it day, I wolde uprise.　　2635
A, slowe sonne, shewe thin enprise!
Sped thee to sprede thy beemys bright,
And chace the derknesse of the nyght,
To putte away the stoundes stronge,
Whiche in me lasten all to longe.'　　2640
　　"The nyght shalt thou contene soo
Withoute rest, in peyne and woo.
If evere thou knewe of love distresse,
Thou shalt mowe lerne in that siknesse,
And thus enduryng shalt thou ly,　　2645
And ryse on morwe up erly
Out of thy bedde, and harneyse thee,
Er evere dawnyng thou maist see.
All pryvyly thanne shalt thou goon,
What weder it be, thisilf alloon,　　2650
For reyn or hayl, for snow, for slet,
Thider she dwellith that is so swet,
The which may fall a-slepe be,
And thenkith but lytel upon thee.
Thanne shalt thou goon, ful foule afeered,
Loke if the gate be unspered,　　2656
And waite without in woo and peyn,
Full yvel a-coold, in wynd and reyn.
Thanne shal thou go the dore bifore,
If thou maist fynde ony score,　　2660
Or hool, or reeft, whatevere it were;
Thanne shalt thou stoupe and lay to ere,
If they withynne a-slepe be —
I mene all save the lady free,
Whom wakyng if thou maist aspie,　　2665
Go putte thisilf in jupartie
To aske grace, and thee bimene,
That she may wite, without wene,
That thou [a-]nyght no rest hast had,
So sore for hir thou were bystad.　　2670
Wommen wel ought pite to take

Of hem that sorwen for her sake.
And loke, for love of that relyk,
That thou thenke noon other lyk,
For whom thou hast so gret annoy,　　2675
Shall kysse thee, er thou go away,
And holde that in full gret deynte.
And for that no man shal thee see
Bifore the hous ne in the way,
Loke thou be goon ageyn er day.　　2680
Such comyng and such goyng,
Such hevynesse and such wakyng,
Makith lovers, withouten ony wene,
Under her clothes pale and lene.
For Love leveth colour ne cleernesse;　　2685
Who loveth trewe hath no fatnesse.
Thou shalt wel by thysilf see
That thou must nedis assayed be.
For men that shape hem other wey
Falsly her ladyes for to bitray,　　2690
It is no wonder though they be fatt;
With false othes her loves they gatt.
For oft I see suche losengours
Fatter than abbatis or priours.
　　"Yit with o thing I thee charge,　　2695
That is to seye, that thou be large
Unto the mayde that hir doth serve,
So best hir thank thou shalt deserve.
Yeve hir yiftes, and get hir grace,
For so thou may thank purchace,　　2700
That she thee worthy holde and free,
Thi lady, and all that may thee see.
Also hir servauntes worshipe ay,
And please as mych as thou may;
Gret good thorough hem may come to thee
Bicause with hir they ben pryve.　　2706
They shal hir telle hou they thee fand
Curteis, and wys, and well doand,
And she shall preise well the mare.
Loke oute of londe thou be not fare,　　2710
And if such cause thou have that thee
Bihoveth to gon out of contree,
Leve hool thin herte in hostage,
Till thou ageyn make thi passage.
Thenk long to see the swete thyng　　2715
That hath thin herte in hir kepyng.
　　"Now have I told thee in what wise
A lovere shall do me servise.
Do it thanne, if thou wolt have
The meede that thou aftir crave."　　2720
　　Whanne Love all this hadde boden me,
I seide hym: "Sire, how may it be

2628 **liggen**: lie
2641 **contene**: bear, endure
2647 **harneyse thee**: dress yourself
2656 **unspered**: unbarred, unlocked
2660 **score**: crack, hole
2661 **reeft**: rift, crack
2667 **bimene**: bemoan
2670 **bystad**: beset, oppressed

2708 **well doand**: well doing, acting well

That lovers may in such manere
Endure the peyne ye have seid heere?
I merveyle me wonder faste   2725
How ony man may lyve or laste
In such peyne and such brennyng,
In sorwe and thought and such sighing,
Ay unrelesed woo to make,
Whether so it be they slepe or wake,   2730
In such annoy contynuely —
As helpe me God, this merveile I
How man, but he were maad of stele,
Myght lyve a month, such peynes to fele."
    The God of Love thanne seide me: 2735
"Freend, by the feith I owe to thee,
May no man have good, but he it by.
A man loveth more tendirly
The thyng that he hath bought most dere.
For wite thou well, withouten were,   2740
In thank that thyng is taken more,
For which a man hath suffred sore.
Certis, no wo ne may atteyne
Unto the sore of loves peyne;
Noon yvel therto ne may amounte,   2745
No more than a man [may] counte
The dropes that of the water be.
For drye as well the greete see
Thou myghtist as the harmes telle
Of hem that with love dwelle   2750
In servyse, for peyne hem sleeth.
And yet ech man wolde fle the deeth,
And trowe thei shulde nevere escape,
Nere that hope couthe hem make
Glad, as man in prisoun sett,   2755
And may not geten for to et
But barly breed and watir pure,
And lyeth in vermyn and in ordure;
With all this yitt can he lyve,
Good hope such comfort hath hym yive,   2760
Which maketh wene that he shall be
Delyvered, and come to liberte.
In fortune is [his] fulle trust,
Though he lye in strawe or dust;
In hoope is all his susteynyng.   2765
And so for lovers, in her wenyng,
Whiche Love hath shit in his prisoun,
Good hope is her salvacioun.
Good hope, how sore that they smerte,
Yeveth hem bothe will and herte   2770
To profre her body to martire;
For hope so sore doth hem desire

To suffre ech harm that men devise,
For joye that aftirward shall aryse.
    "Hope in desir caccheth victorie;   2775
In hope of love is all the glorie;
For hope is all that love may yive;
Nere hope, ther shulde no lover lyve.
Blessid be hope, which with desir
Avaunceth lovers in such maner!   2780
Good hope is curteis for to please,
To kepe lovers from all disese.
Hope kepith his bond, and wole abide,
For ony perill that may betyde;
For hope to lovers, as most cheef,   2785
Doth hem endure all myscheef;
Hope is her helpe whanne myster is.
    "And I shall yeve thee eke, iwys,
Three other thingis that gret solas
Doth to hem that be in my las.   2790
The firste good that may be founde
To hem that in my las be bounde
Is Swete-Thought, for to recorde
Thing wherwith thou canst accorde
Best in thyn herte, where she be —   2795
Thenkyng in absence is good to thee.
Whanne ony lover doth compleyne,
And lyveth in distresse and in peyne,
Thanne Swete-Thought shal come as blyve
Awey his angre for to dryve: 2800
It makith lovers to have remembraunce
Of comfort and of high plesaunce
That Hope hath hight hym for to wynne.
For Thought anoon thanne shall bygynne,
As fer, God wot, as he can fynde,   2805
To make a mirrour of his mynde;
For to biholde he wole not lette.
Hir persone he shall afore hym sette,
Hir laughing eyen, persaunt and clere,
Hir shape, hir forme, hir goodly chere,   2810
Hir mouth, that is so gracious,
So swete and eke so saverous;
Of all hir fetures he shall take heede,
His eyen with all hir lymes fede.
    "Thus Swete-Thenkyng shall aswage   2815
The peyne of lovers and her rage.
Thi joye shall double, withoute gesse,
Whanne thou thenkist on hir semlynesse,
Or of hir laughing, or of hir chere,
That to thee made thi lady dere.   2820
This comfort wole I that thou take;
And if the next thou wolt forsake,

2737 **by**: earn, pay for
2740 **were**: doubt
2757 **barly breed**: an inexpensive bread

2787 **myster**: need, necessity
2795 **where**: wherever
2809 **persaunt**: piercing

Which is not lesse saverous,
Thou shuldist ben to daungerous.
   "The secounde shal be Swete-Speche,   2325
That hath to many oon be leche,
To bringe hem out of woo and wer,
And holpe many a bachiler,
And many a lady sent socour,
That have loved paramour,   2830
Thorough spekyng, whanne they myghte heere
Of her lovers to hem so dere.
To hem it voidith all her smerte,
The which is closed in her herte.
In herte it makith hem glad and light,   2835
Speche, whanne they [ne] mowe have sight.
And therfore now it cometh to mynde,
In olde dawes, as I fynde,
That clerkis writen that hir knewe,
Ther was a lady fresh of hewe,   2840
Which of hir love made a song
On hym for to remembre among,
In which she seyde, 'Whanne that I here
Speken of hym that is so dere,
To me it voidith all smert,   2845
Iwys, he sittith so ner myn hert.
To speke of hym, at eve or morwe,
It cureth me of all my sorwe.
To me is noon so high plesaunce
As of his persone dalyaunce.'   2850
She wist full well that Swete-Spekyng
Comfortith in full myche thyng.
Hir love she hadde full well assayed;
Of him she was full well apaied;
To speke of hym hir joye was sett.   2855
Therfore I rede thee that thou gett
A felowe that can well concele,
And kepe thi counsell, and well hele,
To whom go shewe hoolly thine herte,
Bothe wele and woo, joye and smerte.   2860
To gete comfort to hym thou goo,
And pryvyly, bitwene yow twoo,
Yee shall speke of that goodly thyng
That hath thyn herte in hir kepyng,
Of hir beaute and hir semblaunce   2865
And of hir goodly countenaunce.
Of all thi stat thou shalt hym sey,
And aske hym counseill how thou may
Do ony thyng that may hir plese;
For it to thee shall do gret ese   2870

That he may wite thou trust hym soo,
Bothe of thi wele and of thi woo.
And if his herte to love be sett,
His companye is myche the bett,
For resoun wole he shewe to thee   2875
All uttirly his pryvyte;
And what she is he loveth so,
To thee pleynly he shal undo,
Withoute drede of ony shame,
Bothe tell hir renoun and hir name.   2880
Thanne shall he forther, fer and ner,
And namely to thi lady der,
In syker wise; yee, every other
Shall helpen as his owne brother,
In trouthe withoute doublenesse,   2885
And kepen cloos in sikernesse.
For it is noble thing, in fay,
To have a man thou darst say
Thy pryve counsell every deell;
For that wole comforte thee right well,   2890
And thou shalt holde thee well apayed,
Whanne such a freend thou hast assayed.
   "The thridde good of gret comfort,
That yeveth to lovers most disport,
Comyth of sight and of biholdyng,   2895
That clepid is Swete-Lokyng,
The whiche may noon ese do
Whanne thou art fer thy lady fro;
Wherfore thou prese alwey to be
In place where thou maist hir see.   2900
For it is thyng most amerous,
Most delytable and saverous,
For to aswage a mannes sorowe,
To sen his lady by the morwe.
For it is a full noble thing,   2905
Whanne thyne eyen have metyng
With that relike precious,
Wherof they be so desirous.
But al day after, soth it is,
They have no drede to faren amys;   2910
They dreden neither wynd ne reyn,
Ne noon other maner peyn.
For whanne thyne eyen were thus in blis,
Yit of hir curtesie, ywys,
Alloone they can not have her joye,   2915
But to the herte they [it] convoye;
Part of her blisse to hym they sende,
Of all this harm to make an ende.
The eye is a good messanger,
Which can to the herte in such maner   2920
Tidyngis sende that [he] hath sen,

2827 **wer:** doubt
2833 **voidith:** removes
2842 **among:** always
2857 **concele:** conceal
2858 **hele:** hide

2899 **prese:** press forward
2916 **convoye:** convey, guide

To voide hym of his peynes clen.
Wherof the herte rejoiseth soo,
That a gret party of his woo
Is voided and put awey to flight.   2925
Right as the derknesse of the nyght
Is chased with clernesse of the mone,
Right so is al his woo full soone
Devoided clene, whanne that the sight
Biholden may that freshe wight   2930
That the herte desireth soo,
That al his derknesse is agoo.
For thanne the herte is all at ese,
Whanne the eyen sen that may hem plese.
    "Now have I declared thee all oute   2935
Of that thou were in drede and doute;
For I have told thee feithfully
What thee may curen utterly,
And alle lovers that wole be
Feithfull and full of stabilite.   2940
Good-Hope alwey kep bi thi side,
And Swete-Thought make eke abide,
Swete-Lokyng and Swete-Speche —
Of all thyne harmes thei shall be leche,
Of every thou shalt have gret plesaunce.   2945
If thou canst bide in sufferaunce,
And serve wel withoute feyntise,
Thou shalt be quyt of thyn emprise
With more guerdoun, if that thou lyve;
But at this tyme this I thee yive."   2950
    The God of Love whanne al the day
Had taught me, as ye have herd say,
And enfourmed compendiously,
He vanyshide awey all sodeynly,
And I alloone lefte, all sool,   2955
So full of compleynt and of dool,
For I saw no man there me by.
My woundes me greved wondirly;
Me for to curen nothyng I knew,
Save the botoun bright of hew,   2960
Wheron was sett hoolly my thought.
Of other comfort knew I nought,
But it were thorugh the God of Love;
I knew not elles to my bihove
That myght me ease or comfort gete,   2965
But if he wolde hym entermete.
    The roser was, withoute doute,
Closed with an hegge withoute,
As ye toforn have herd me seyn;
And fast I bisiede, and wolde fayn   2970

Have passed the hay, if I myghte
Have geten ynne by ony slighte
Unto the botoun so faire to see.
But evere I dradde blamed to be,
If men wolde have suspeccioun   2975
That I wolde of entencioun
Have stole the roses that there were;
Therfore to entre I was in fere.
But at the last, as I bithought
Whether I shulde passe or nought,   2980
I saw come with a glad cher
To me, a lusty bacheler,
Of good stature and of good highte,
And Bialacoil forsothe he highte.
Sone he was to Curtesy,   2985
And he me grauntide full gladly
The passage of the outter hay,
And seide: "Sir, how that yee may
Passe, if youre wille be
The freshe roser for to see,   2990
And yee the swete savour fele.
Youre warrant may [I be] right wele;
So thou thee kepe fro folye,
Shall no man do thee vylanye.
If I may helpe you in ought,   2995
I shall not feyne, dredeth nought,
For I am bounde to youre servise,
Fully devoide of feyntise."
    Thanne unto Bialacoil saide I,
"I thanke you, sir, full hertely,   3000
And youre biheeste take at gre,
That ye so goodly profer me.
To you it cometh of gret fraunchise
That ye me profer youre servise."
    Thanne aftir, full delyverly,   3005
Thorough the breres anoon wente I,
Wherof encombred was the hay.
I was wel plesed, the soth to say,
To se the botoun faire and swote
So freshe spronge out of the rote.   3010
    And Bialacoil me served well,
Whanne I so nygh me myghte fel
Of the botoun the swete odour,
And so lusty hewed of colour.
But thanne a cherl (foule hym bityde!)   3015
Biside the roses gan hym hyde,
To kepe the roses of that roser,
Of whom the name was Daunger.
This cherl was hid there in the greves,

2945 **every**: everyone, each
2947 **feyntise**: faint-heartedness
2960 **botoun**: rosebud
2964 **bihove**: profit
2966 **hym entermete**: concern himself, intercede

2971 **hay**: hedge
2984 **Bialacoil**: "Fair Welcome"
3018 **Daunger**: Disdain, standoffishness; see n.
3019 **greves**: branches

Kovered with gras and with leves,   3020
To spie and take whom that he fond
Unto that roser putte an hond.
He was not sool, for ther was moo,
For with hym were other twoo
Of wikkid maners and yvel fame.   3025
That oon was clepid, by his name,
Wykked-Tonge — God yeve hym sorwe! —
For neither at eve ne at morwe,
He can of no man good speke;
On many a just man doth he wreke.   3030
Ther was a womman eke that hight
Shame, that, who can reken right,
Trespas was hir fadir name,
Hir moder Resoun; and thus was Shame
Brought of these ilke twoo.   3035
And yitt hadde Trespas never adoo
With Resoun, ne never ley hir by,
He was so hidous and so ugly,
I mene this that Trespas highte;
But Resoun conceyveth of a sighte   3040
Shame, of that I spak aforn.
And whanne that Shame was thus born,
It was ordeyned that Chastite
Shulde of the roser lady be,
Which, of the botouns more and las,   3045
With sondry folk assailed was,
That she ne wiste what to doo.
For Venus hir assailith soo,
That nyght and day from hir she stal
Botouns and roses overal.   3050
To Resoun thanne praieth Chastite,
Whom Venus hath flemed over the see,
That she hir doughter wolde hir lene,
To kepe the roser fresh and grene.
Anoon Resoun to Chastite   3055
Is fully assented that it be,
And grauntide hir, at hir request,
That Shame, by cause she [is] honest,
Shall keper of the roser be.
And thus to kepe it ther were three,   3060
That noon shulde hardy be ne bold,
Were he yong or were he old,
Ageyn hir will awey to bere
Botouns ne roses that there were.
I hadde wel sped, hadde I not ben   3065
Awayted with these three and sen.
For Bialacoil, that was so fair,
So gracious and debonair,

Quytt hym to me full curteisly,
And, me to plese, bad that I   3070
Shulde drawe me to the botoun ner;
Prese in, to touche the roser
Which bar the roses, he yaf me leve;
This graunt ne myght but lytel greve.
And for he saw it liked me,   3075
Ryght nygh the botoun pullede he
A leef all grene, and yaff me that,
The whiche ful nygh the botoun sat.
I made [me] of that leef full queynt,
And whanne I felte I was aqueynt   3080
With Bialacoil, and so pryve,
I wende all at my will hadde be.
Thanne wax I hardy for to tel
To Bialacoil hou me bifel
Of Love, that tok and wounded me,   3085
And seide, "Sir, so mote I thee,
I may no joye have in no wise,
Uppon no side, but it rise.
For sithe (if I shall not feyne)
In herte I have had so gret peyne,   3090
So gret annoy and such affray,
That I ne wot what I shall say;
I drede youre wrath to disserve.
Lever me were that knyves kerve
My body shulde in pecys smale,   3095
Than in any wise it shulde falle
That ye wratthed shulde ben with me."
"Sey boldely thi will," quod he,
"I nyl be wroth, if that I may,
For nought that thou shalt to me say."   3100
    Thanne seide I, "Ser, not you displease
To knowen of my gret unese,
In which oonly Love hath me brought;
For peynes gret, disese, and thought
Fro day to day he doth me drye;   3105
Supposeth not, sir, that I lye.
In me fyve woundes dide he make,
The soore of whiche shall nevere slake,
But ye the botoun graunte me,
Which is moost passaunt of beaute,   3110
My lyf, my deth, and my martire,
And tresour that I moost desire."
    Thanne Bialacoil, affrayed all,
Seyde, "Sir, it may not fall;
That ye desire, it may not arise.   3115
What? Wolde ye shende me in this wise?
A mochel fool thanne I were,
If I suffride you awey to bere
The fresh botoun so faire of sight.

3030 wreke: vengeance
3044 lady: mistress
3052 flemed: driven away
3066 Awayted with: waylaid by

3079 made [me] . . . full queynt: took great pleasure
3088 but it rise: unless it comes to pass (?); see n.

For it were neither skile ne right, 3120
Of the roser ye broke the rynde,
Or take the Rose aforn his kynde.
Ye are not curteys to aske it.
Late it still on the roser sitt
And growe til it amended be, 3125
And parfytly come to beaute.
I nolde not that it pulled were
Fro the roser that it bere,
To me it is so leef and deer."
    With that sterte oute anoon Daunger, 3130
Out of the place were he was hid.
His malice in his chere was kid;
Full gret he was and blak of hewe,
Sturdy and hidous, whoso hym knewe;
Like sharp urchouns his her was growe; 3135
. . . .
His nose frounced, full kirked stood.
He com criand as he were wood,
And seide, "Bialacoil, telle me why
Thou bryngest hider so booldely 3140
Hym that so nygh [is] the roser?
Thou worchist in a wrong maner.
He thenkith to dishonoure thee;
Thou art wel worthy to have maugree
To late hym of the roser wit. 3145
Who serveth a feloun is yvel quit.
Thou woldist have doon gret bounte,
And he with shame wolde quyte thee.
Fle hennes, felowe! I rede thee goo!
It wanteth litel I wole thee sloo. 3150
For Bialacoil ne knew thee nought,
Whanne thee to serve he sette his thought;
For thou wolt shame hym, if thou myght,
Bothe ageyns resoun and right.
I wole no more in thee affye, 3155
That comest so slyghly for t'espye;
For it preveth wonder well,
Thy slight and tresoun, every deell."
I durst no more there make abod
For the cherl, he was so wod, 3160
So gan he threte and manace,
And thurgh the haye he dide me chace.
For feer of hym I tremblyde and quok,
So cherlishly his heed it shok,
And seide, if eft he myght me take, 3165
I shulde not from his hondis scape.
    Thanne Bialacoil is fled and mat,
And I, all sool, disconsolat,

Was left aloone in peyne and thought;
For shame to deth I was nygh brought. 3170
Thanne thought I on myn high foly,
How that my body utterly
Was yeve to peyne and to martire;
And therto hadde I so gret ire,
That I ne durst the hayes passe. 3175
There was noon hope; there was no grace.
I trowe nevere man wiste of peyne,
But he were laced in loves cheyne;
Ne no man [wot], and sooth it is,
But if he love, what anger is. 3180
Love holdith his heest to me right wel,
Whanne peyne he seide I shulde fel;
Noon herte may thenke, ne tunge seyn,
A quarter of my woo and peyn.
I myght not with the anger laste; 3185
Myn herte in poynt was for to braste,
Whanne I thought on the Rose, that soo
Was thurgh Daunger cast me froo.
A long while stod I in that stat,
Til that me saugh so mad and mat 3190
The lady of the highe ward,
Which from hir tour lokide thiderward.
Resoun men clepe that lady,
Which from hir tour delyverly
Com doun to me, withouten mor. 3195
But she was neither yong ne hoor,
Ne high ne lowe, ne fat ne lene,
But best as it were in a mene.
Hir eyen twoo were cleer and light
As ony candell that brenneth bright; 3200
And on hir heed she hadde a crowne.
Hir semede wel an high persoune,
For round enviroun, hir crownet
Was full of riche stonys frett.
Hir goodly semblaunt, by devys, 3205
I trowe were maad in paradys,
For Nature hadde nevere such a grace,
To forge a werk of such compace.
For certeyn, but if the letter ly,
God hymsilf, that is so high, 3210
Made hir aftir his ymage,
And yaff hir sith sich avauntage
That she hath myght and seignorie
To kepe men from all folye.
Whoso wole trowe hir lore, 3215
Ne may offenden nevermore.
    And while I stod thus derk and pale,
Resoun bigan to me hir tale.

3135 **urchouns:** hedgehogs
3136 Not in MS. Thynne has: *His eyes reed sparclyng as the fyr glowe.*
3137 **frounced:** wrinkled   **kirked:** crooked, aslant
3144 **maugree:** ill will, reproach
3155 **affye:** trust

3178 **laced:** snared
3203 **round enviroun:** all around   **crownet:** coronet
3204 **full of . . . frett:** thickly set with

She seide, "Al hayl, my swete freend!
Foly and childhood wol thee sheend,   3220
Which the have putt in gret affray.
Thou hast bought deere the tyme of May,
That made thyn herte mery to be.
In yvell tyme thou wentist to see
The gardyn, whereof Ydilnesse   3225
Bar the keye and was maistresse,
Whanne thou yedest in the daunce
With hir, and haddest aqueyntaunce.
Hir aqueyntaunce is perilous,
First softe, and aftir noious;   3230
She hath [thee] trasshed, withoute wen.
The God of Love hadde the not sen,
Ne hadde Ydilnesse thee conveyed
In the verger where Myrthe hym pleyed.
If foly have supprised thee,   3235
Do so that it recovered be,
And be wel ware to take nomore
Counsel, that greveth aftir sore.
He is wis that wol hymsilf chastise.
And though a yong man in ony wise   3240
Trespace among, and do foly,
Late hym not tarye, but hastily
Late hym amende what so be mys.
And eke I counseile thee, iwys,
The God of Love hoolly foryet,   3245
That hath thee in sich peyne set,
And thee in herte tourmented soo.
I can [nat] sen how thou maist goo
Other weyes to garisoun;
For Daunger, that is so feloun,   3250
Felly purposith thee to werreye,
Which is ful cruel, the soth to seye.
    "And yitt of Daunger cometh no blame,
In reward of my doughter Shame,
Which hath the roses in hir ward,   3255
As she that may be no musard.
And Wikked-Tunge is with these two,
That suffrith no man thider goo;
For er a thing be do, he shall,
Where that he cometh, overall,   3260
In fourty places, if it be sought,
Seye thyng that nevere was don ne wrought;
So moche tresoun is in his male
Of falsnesse, for to seyne a tale.
Thou delest with angry folk, ywis;   3265
Wherfore to thee bettir is

From these folk awey to fare,
For they wole make thee lyve in care.
This is the yvell that love they call,
Wherynne ther is but foly al,   3270
For love is foly everydell.
Who loveth in no wise may do well,
Ne sette his thought on no good werk.
His scole he lesith, if he be a clerk.
Of other craft eke if he be,   3275
He shal not thryve therynne, for he
In love shal have more passioun
Than monk, hermyte, or chanoun.
The peyne is hard, out [of] mesure;
The joye may eke no while endure;   3280
And in the possessioun
Is myche tribulacioun.
The joye it is so short lastyng,
And but in hap is the getyng;
For I see there many in travaille,   3285
That atte laste foule fayle.
I was nothyng thi counseler,
Whanne thou were maad the omager
Of God of Love to hastily;
Ther was no wisdom, but foly.   3290
Thyn herte was joly but not sage,
Whanne thou were brought in sich a rage
To yelde thee so redily,
And to leve of is gret maistry.
    "I rede thee Love awey to dryve,   3295
That makith thee recche not of thi lyve.
The foly more fro day to day
Shal growe, but thou it putte away.
Tak with thy teeth the bridel faste,
To daunte thyn herte, and eke thee caste,   3300
If that thou maist, to gete thee defence
For to redresse thi first offence.
Whoso his herte alwey wol leve,
Shal fynde among that shal hym greve."
    Whanne I hir herd thus me chastise,   3305
I answerd in ful angry wise.
I prayed hir ceessen of hir speche,
Outher to chastise me or teche,
To bidde me my thought refreyne,
Which Love hath caught in his demeyne: 3310
"What? Wene ye Love wol consent,
That me assailith with bowe bent,
To drawe myn herte out of his hond,
Which is so qwikly in his bond?

3231 **trasshed:** betrayed
3235 **supprised:** seized
3241 **among:** therewith
3250 **feloun:** ill willed
3254 **In reward of:** compared to
3256 **musard:** sluggard

3284 **in hap:** by chance
3288 **omager:** liege, one who does homage
3294 **leve of:** leave off
3300 **daunte:** defeat
3303 **leve:** believe
3310 **demeyne:** control

That ye counseyle may nevere be,   3315
For whanne he first arestide me,
He took myn herte so hool hym till,
That it is nothyng at my wil.
He taught it so hym for to obeye,
That he it sparrede with a keye.   3320
I pray yow, late me be all stille.
For ye may well, if that ye wille,
Youre wordis waste in idilnesse;
For utterly, withouten gesse,
All that ye seyn is but in veyne.   3325
Me were lever dye in the peyne,
Than Love to me-ward shulde arette
Falsheed, or tresoun on me sette.
I wole me gete prys or blame,
And love trewe, to save my name.   3330
Who that me chastisith, I hym hate."
    With that word Resoun wente hir gate,
Whanne she saugh for no sermonynge
She myght me fro my foly brynge.
Thanne dismaied, I lefte all sool,   3335
Forwery, forwandred as a fool,
For I ne knew no chevisaunce.
Thanne fell into my remembraunce
How Love bad me to purveye
A felowe to whom I myghte seye   3340
My counsell and my pryvete,
For that shulde moche availe me.
With that bithought I me that I
Hadde a felowe faste by,
Trewe and siker, curteys and hend,   3345
And he was called by name a Freend —
A trewer felowe was nowher noon.
In haste to hym I wente anoon,
And to hym all my woo I tolde;
Fro hym right nought I wold witholde.   3350
I tolde hym all, withoute wer,
And made my compleynt on Daunger,
How for to see he was hidous,
And to me-ward contrarious,
The whiche thurgh his cruelte   3355
Was in poynt to [have] meygned me.
With Bialacoil whanne he me sey
Withynne the gardeyn walke and pley,
Fro me he made hym for to go.
And I, bilefte aloone in woo,   3360
I durst no lenger with hym speke,

For Daunger seide he wolde be wreke,
Whanne that he saw how I wente
The freshe botoun for to hente,
If I were hardy to come neer   3365
Bitwene the hay and the roser.
    This freend, whanne he wiste of my thought,
He discomforted me right nought,
But seide, "Felowe, be not so mad,
Ne so abaysshed nor bystad.   3370
Mysilf I knowe full well Daunger,
And how he is feers of his cheer,
At prime temps, love to manace;
Ful ofte I have ben in his caas.
A feloun first though that he be,   3375
Aftir thou shalt hym souple se.
Of longe passed I knew hym well;
Ungoodly first though men hym feel,
He wol meke aftir in his beryng
Been, for service and obeysshyng.   3380
I shal thee telle what thou shalt doo.
Mekely I rede thou go hym to,
Of herte pray hym specialy
Of thy trespas to have mercy,
And hote hym wel, here to plese,   3385
That thou shalt nevermore hym displese.
Who can best serve of flatery,
Shall please Daunger most uttirly."
    Mi freend hath seid to me so wel
That he me esid hath somdell,   3390
And eke allegged of my torment;
For thurgh hym had I hardement
Agayn to Daunger for to go,
To preve if I myght meke hym soo.
    To Daunger came I all ashamed,   3395
The which aforn me hadde blamed,
Desiryng for to pese my woo,
But over hegge durst I not goo,
For he forbed me the passage.
I fond hym cruel in his rage,   3400
And in his hond a gret burdoun.
To hym I knelide lowe adoun,
Ful meke of port and symple of chere,
And seide, "Sir, I am comen heere
Oonly to aske of you mercy.   3405
That greveth me full gretly
That evere my lyf I wratthed you;
But for to amenden I am come now,

3320 **sparrede:** locked
3326 **in the peyne:** by torture
3336 **Forwery:** exhausted **forwandred:** exhausted from wandering
3337 **chevisaunce:** remedy
3351 **wer:** doubt
3356 **meygned:** maimed, injured

3372 **feers:** fierce
3373 **At prime temps:** for the first time
3376 **souple:** humble, yielding
3377 **Of longe passed:** since long ago
3380 **obeysshyng:** obedience
3385 **hote:** promise
3397 **pese:** appease, alleviate
3401 **burdoun:** stick, club

With all my myght, bothe loude and stille,
To doon right at youre owne wille.   3410
For Love made me for to doo
That I have trespassed hidirto,
Fro whom I ne may withdrawe myn hert.
Yit shall [I] never, for joy ne smert,
What so bifalle, good or ill,   3415
Offende more ageyn youre will.
Lever I have endure disese,
Than do that you shulde displese.
    "I you require and pray that ye
Of me have mercy and pitee,   3420
To stynte your ire that greveth soo,
That I wol swere for ever mo
To be redressid at youre likyng,
If I trespasse in ony thyng.
Save that I pray thee graunte me   3425
A thyng that may not warned be,
That I may love, all oonly;
Noon other thyng of you aske I.
I shall doon elles well, iwys,
If of youre grace ye graunte me this.   3430
And ye may not letten me,
For wel wot ye that love is free,
And I shall loven, sithen that I will,
Who ever like it well or ill;
And yit ne wold I, for all Fraunce,   3435
Do thyng to do you displesaunce."
    Thanne Daunger fil in his entent
For to foryeve his maltalent;
But all his wratthe yit at laste
He hath relesed, I preyde so faste.   3440
Shortly he seide, "Thy request
Is not to mochel dishonest,
Ne I wole not werne it thee,
For yit nothyng engreveth me.
For though thou love thus evermor,   3445
To me is neither softe ne soor.
Love where that the list — what recchith me,
So [thou] fer fro my roses be?
Trust not on me, for noon assay,
If ony tyme thou passe the hay."   3450
    Thus hath he graunted my praiere.
Thanne wente I forth, withouten were,
Unto my freend, and tolde hym all,
Which was right joyful of my tall.
He seide, "Now goth wel thyn affaire.   3455
He shall to thee be debonaire;
Though he aforn was dispitous,
He shall heere aftir be gracious.

If he were touchid on som good veyne,
He shuld yit rewen on thi peyne.   3460
Suffre, I rede, and no boost make,
Till thou at good mes maist hym take.
By sufferaunce and wordis softe
A man may overcome ofte
Hym that aforn he hadde in drede,   3465
In bookis sothly as I rede."
    Thus hath my freend with gret comfort
Avaunced [me] with high disport,
Which wolde me good as mych as I.
And thanne anoon full sodeynly   3470
I tok my leve, and streight I went
Unto the hay, for gret talent
I hadde to sen the fresh botoun
Wherynne lay my salvacioun;
And Daunger tok kep if that I   3475
Kepe hym covenaunt trewely.
So sore I dradde his manasyng,
I durst not breke his biddyng;
For, lest that I were of hym shent,
I brak not his comaundement,   3480
For to purchase his good wil.
It was [nat] for to come ther-til;
His mercy was to fer bihynde.
I wepte for I ne myght it fynde.
I compleyned and sighed sore,   3485
And langwisshed evermore,
For I durst not over goo
Unto the Rose I loved soo.
Thurgh my demenyng outerly
Than he had knowledge certanly   3490
That Love me ladde in sich a wise
That in me ther was no feyntise,
Falsheed, ne no trecherie.
And yit he, full of vylanye,
Of disdeyn, and cruelte,   3495
On me ne wolde have pite,
His cruel will for to refreyne,
Though I wepe alwey, and me compleyne.
    And while I was in this torment,
Were come of grace, by God sent,   3500
Fraunchise, and with hir Pite.
Fulfild the bothen of bounte,
They go to Daunger anoon-right
To forther me with all her myght,
And helpe in worde and in dede,   3505
For well they saugh that it was nede.
First, of hir grace, dame Fraunchise
Hath taken [word] of this emprise.

3437 **fil in his entent:** decided
3438 **maltalent:** ill will

3462 **at good mes:** from a favorable vantage point
3489 **demenyng:** judgment
3497 **refreyne:** bridle, restrain

She seide, "Daunger, gret wrong ye do,
To worche this man so myche woo,   3510
Or pynen hym so angerly;
It is to you gret villany.
I can not see why, ne how,
That he hath trespassed ageyn you,
Save that he loveth, wherfore ye shulde   3515
The more in cherete of hym holde.
The force of love makith hym do this;
Who wolde hym blame he dide amys?
He leseth more than ye may do;
His peyne is hard, ye may see, lo!   3520
And Love in no wise wolde consente
That he have power to repente,
For though that quyk ye wolde hym sloo,
Fro love his herte may not goo.
Now, swete sir, is it youre ese   3525
Hym for to angre or disese?
Allas! what may it you avaunce
To don to hym so gret grevaunce?
What worship is it agayn hym take,
Or on youre man a werre make,   3530
Sith he so lowly, every wise,
Is redy, as ye lust devise?
If Love hath caught hym in his las,
You for t'obeye in every caas,
And ben youre suget at youre will,   3535
Shuld ye therfore willen hym ill?
Ye shulde hym spare more, all out,
Than hym that is bothe proud and stout.
Curtesie wol that ye socoure
Hem that ben meke undir youre cure.   3540
His herte is hard that wole not meke,
Whanne men of mekenesse hym biseke."
    "That is certeyn," seide Pite;
"We se ofte that humilite
Bothe ire and also felonye   3545
Venquyssheth, and also malencolye.
To stonde forth in such duresse,
This cruelte and wikkidnesse.
Wherfore I pray you, sir Daunger,
For to mayntene no lenger heer   3550
Such cruel werre agayn youre man,
As hoolly youres as ever he can;
Nor that ye worchen no more woo
Upon this caytif, that langwisshith soo,
Which wole no more to you trespasse,   3555
But putte hym hoolly in youre grace.
His offense ne was but lite;
The God of Love it was to wite,

That he youre thrall so gretly is,
And if ye harme hym, ye don amys.   3560
For he hath had full hard penaunce,
Sith that ye refte hym th'aqueyntaunce
Of Bialacoil, his moste joye,
Which alle his peynes myght acoye.
He was biforn anoyed sore,   3565
But thanne ye doubled hym well more;
For he of blis hath ben full bare,
Sith Bialacoil was fro hym fare.
Love hath to hym do gret distresse,
He hath no nede of more duresse.   3570
Voideth from hym youre ire, I rede;
Ye may not wynnen in this dede.
Makith Bialacoil repeire ageyn,
And haveth pite upon his peyn;
For Fraunchise wole, and I, Pite,   3575
That mercyful to hym ye be;
And sith that she and I accorde,
Have upon hym misericorde.
For I you pray and eke moneste
Nought to refusen oure requeste,   3580
For he is hard and fell of thought,
That for us twoo wole do right nought."
    Daunger ne myght no more endure;
He mekede hym unto mesure.
    "I wole in no wise," seith Daunger,   3585
"Denye that ye have asked heer;
It were to gret uncurtesie.
I wole he have the companye
Of Bialacoil, as ye devise;
I wole hym lette in no wise."   3590
    To Bialacoil thanne wente in hy
Fraunchise, and seide full curteisly,
"Ye have to longe be deignous
Unto this lover, and daungerous,
Fro him to withdrawe your presence,   3595
Which hath do to him gret offence,
That ye not wolde upon him se,
Wherfore a sorouful man is he.
Shape ye to paye him, and to please,
Of my love if ye wol have ease.   3600
Fulfyl his wyl, sith that ye knowe
Daunger is daunted and brought lowe
Through help of me and of Pyte.
You dar no more afered be."
    "I shal do right as ye wyl,"   3605
Saith Bialacoil, "for it is skyl,
Sithe Daunger wol that it so be."
Than Fraunchise hath him sent to me.

3511 **pynen:** torture
3516 **cherete:** fondness
3547 **duresse:** distress
3548 **This** = *This is*

3564 **acoye:** soothe
3579 **moneste:** admonish
3584 **mesure:** moderation
3593 **deignous:** haughty
3604 **You dar:** you need (impersonal)

Byalacoil at the begynnyng
Salued me in his commyng.   3610
No straungenesse was in him sen,
No more than he ne had wrathed ben.
As fayr semblaunt than shewed he me,
And goodly, as aforn dyd he;
And by the hond, withouten doute,   3615
Within the haye, right al aboute
He ladde me, with right good cher,
Al envyron the verger,
That Daunger hadde me chased fro.
Now have I leave overal to go;   3620
Now am I raysed, at my devys,
Fro helle unto paradys.
Thus Bialacoil, of gentylnesse,
With al his payne and besynesse,
Hath shewed me, only of grace,   3625
The estres of the swote place.

I saw the Rose, whan I was nygh,
Was greatter woxen and more high,
Fressh, roddy, and fayr of hewe,
Of colour ever yliche newe.   3630
And whan I hadde it longe sen,
I saw that through the leves gren
The Rose spredde to spaunysshing;
To sene it was a goodly thyng.
But it ne was so spred on bred   3635
That men within myght knowe the sed;
For it covert was and close,
Bothe with the leves and with the rose.
The stalke was even and grene upright,
It was theron a goodly syght;   3640
And wel the better, withoute wene,
For the seed was nat sene.
Ful fayre it spradde (God it blesse!),
For such another, as I gesse,
Aforn ne was, ne more vermayle.   3645
I was abawed for marveyle,
For ever the fayrer that it was,
The more I am bounden in Loves laas.
Longe I abod there, soth to saye,
Tyl Bialacoil I gan to praye,   3650
Whan that I saw him in no wyse
To me warnen his servyse,
That he me wolde graunt a thyng,
Which to remembre is wel syttyng;
This is to sayn, that of his grace   3655
He wolde me yeve leysar and space,

To me that was so desyrous,
To have a kyssynge precious
Of the goodly fresshe Rose,
That so swetely smelleth in my nose.   3660
"For if it you displeased nought,
I wolde gladly, as I have sought,
Have a cos therof freely,
Of your yefte; for certainly,
I wol non have but by your leve,   3665
So loth me were you for to greve."
He sayde, "Frend, so God me spede,
Of Chastite I have such drede;
Thou shuldest nat warned be for me,
But I dar nat for Chastyte.   3670
Agayn her dar I nat mysdo,
For alway byddeth she me so
To yeve no lover leve to kys,
For who therto may wynnen, ywis,
He of the surplus of the pray   3675
May lyve in hoope to get som day.
For whoso kyssynge may attayne
Of loves payne hath (soth to sayne)
The beste and most avenaunt,
And ernest of the remenaunt."   3680
Of his answere I sighed sore;
I durst assaye him tho no more,
I hadde such drede to greve him ay.
A man shulde nat to moche assay
To chafe hys frend out of measure,   3685
Nor putte his lyf in aventure;
For no man at the firste strok
Ne may nat felle down an ok,
Nor of the reysyns have the wyn,
Tyl grapes be rype, and wel afyn   3690
Be sore empressid, I you ensure,
And drawen out of the pressure.
But I, forpeyned wonder stronge,
Thought that I abood right longe
Aftir the kis, in peyne and woo,   3695
Sith I to kis desired soo;
Till that, rewyng on my distresse,
Ther to me Venus the goddesse,
Which ay werreyeth Chastite,
Cam of hir grace to socoure me,   3700
Whos myght is knowe fer and wide,
For she is modir of Cupide,
The God of Love, blynde as stoon,
That helpith lovers many oon.
This lady brought in hir right hond   3705

3611 **straungenesse**: distance, aloofness
3618 **Al envyron**: all around
3626 **estres**: inner parts, interior
3633 **spaunysshing**: expanding, extending
3637 **covert**: covered
3646 **abawed**: disconcerted
3652 **warnen**: refuse

3663 **cos**: kiss
3680 **ernest**: pledge
3689 **reysyns**: grapes
3690 **wel afyn**: thoroughly
3691 **empressid**: pressed
3692 **pressure**: wine press

Of brennyng fyr a blasyng brond,
Wherof the flawme and hoote fir
Hath many a lady in desir
Of love brought, and sore het,
And in hir servise her hertes set.   3710
This lady was of good entaile,
Right wondirfull of apparayle.
Bi hir atyr so bright and shen
Men myght perceyve well and sen
She was not of religioun.   3715
Nor I nell make mencioun
Nor of robe, nor of tresour,
Of broche, neithir of hir riche attour,
Ne of hir girdill aboute hir side,
For that I nyll not longe abide.   3720
But knowith wel that certeynly
She was araied richely.
Devoyd of pryde certeyn she was.
To Bialacoil she wente apas,
And to hym shortly, in a clause,   3725
She seide, "Sir, what is the cause
Ye ben of port so daungerous
Unto this lover and deynous,
To graunte hym nothyng but a kis?
To werne it hym ye don amys,   3730
Sith well ye wote how that he
Is Loves servaunt, as ye may see,
And hath beaute, wherthrough [he] is
Worthy of love to have the blis.
How he is semely, biholde and see,   3735
How he is fair, how he is free,
How he is swoote and debonair,
Of age yong, lusty, and fair.
Ther is no lady so hawteyn,
Duchesse, ne countesse, ne chasteleyn,   3740
That I nolde holde hir ungoodly
For to refuse hym outterly.
His breth is also good and swete,
And eke his lippis rody, and mete
Oonly to pleyen and to kisse.   3745
Graunte hym a kis, of gentilnysse!
His teth arn also white and clene;
Me thinkith wrong, withouten wene,
If ye now werne hym, trustith me,
To graunte that a kis have he.   3750
The lasse to helpe hym that ye haste,
The more tyme shul ye waste."
Whanne the flawme of the verry brond,

That Venus brought in hir right hond,
Hadde Bialacoil with hete smete,   3755
Anoon he bad, withouten lette,
Graunte to me the Rose kisse.
Thanne of my peyne I gan to lysse,
And to the Rose anoon wente I,
And kisside it full feithfully.   3760
Thar no man aske if I was blithe,
Whanne the savour soft and lythe
Strok to myn herte withoute more,
And me alegged of my sore,
So was I full of joye and blisse.   3765
It is fair sich a flour to kisse,
It was so swoote and saverous.
I myght not be so angwisshous
That I [ne] mote glad and joly be,
Whanne that I remembre me.   3770
Yit ever among, sothly to seyne,
I suffre noy and moche peyne.
    The see may never be so stille
That with a litel wynde it nille
Overwhelme and turne also,   3775
As it were wood in wawis goo.
Aftir the calm the trouble sone
Mot folowe and chaunge as the moone.
Right so farith Love that selde in oon
Holdith his anker, for right anoon   3780
Whanne they in ese wene best to lyve,
They ben with tempest all fordryve.
Who serveth Love can telle of woo;
The stoundemele joie mot overgoo.
Now he hurteth, and now he cureth;   3785
For selde in oo poynt Love endureth.
    Now is it right me to procede,
How Shame gan medle and take hede
Thurgh whom fele angres I have had,
And how the stronge wall was maad,   3790
And the castell of brede and lengthe,
That God of Love wan with his strengthe.
All this in romance will I sette,
And for nothyng ne will I lette,
So that it lykyng to hir be,   3795
That is the flour of beaute,
For she may best my labour quyte,
That I for hir love shal endite.
    Wikkid-Tunge, that the covyne
Of every lover can devyne   3800

3706 **blasyng**: blazing
3709 **het**: heated
3711 **entaile**: shape
3715 **of religioun**: of a religious order
3728 **deynous**: haughty
3739 **hawteyn**: proud, haughty

3755 **smete**: smitten, struck
3758 **lysse**: be relieved
3762 **lythe**: smooth
3763 **Strok**: struck
3772 **noy**: harm, distress
3784 **stoundemele**: momentary
3799 **covyne**: deceit

Worst, and addith more somdell
(For Wikkid-Tunge seith never well),
To me-ward bar he right gret hate,
Espiyng me erly and late,
Till he hath sen the grete chere   3805
Of Bialacoil and me ifeere.
He myghte not his tunge withstond
Worse to reporte than he fond,
He was so full of cursed rage.
It sat hym well of his lynage,   3810
For hym an Irish womman bar.
His tunge was fyled sharp and squar,
Poignaunt, and right kervyng,
And wonder bitter in spekyng.
For whanne that he me gan espie,   3815
He swoor, affermyng sikirlye,
Bitwene Bialacoil and me
Was yvel aquayntaunce and pryve.
He spak therof so folily
That he awakide Jelousy,   3820
Which, all afrayed in his risyng,
Whanne that he herde janglyng,
He ran anoon, as he were wood,
To Bialacoil, there that he stod,
Which hadde lever in this caas   3825
Have ben at Reynes or Amyas;
For foot-hoot, in his felonye,
To hym thus seide Jelousie:
"Why hast thou ben so necligent
To kepen, whanne I was absent,   3830
This verger heere left in thi ward?
To me thou haddist no reward,
To truste (to thy confusioun!)
Hym thus, to whom suspeccioun
I have right gret, for it is nede;   3835
It is well shewed by the dede.
Gret faute in thee now have I founde.
By God, anoon thou shalt be bounde,
And faste loken in a tour,
Withoute refuyt or socour.   3840
For Shame to longe hath be thee froo;
Over-soone she was agoo.
Whanne thou hast lost bothe drede and feere,
It semede wel she was not heere.
She was bisy in no wyse   3845
To kepe thee and chastise,
And for to helpen Chastite
To kepe the roser, as thenkith me.
For thanne this boy-knave so booldely

Ne shulde not have be hardy,   3850
[Ne] in this verger hadde such game,
Which now me turneth to gret shame."
    Bialacoil nyste what to sey;
Full fayn he wolde have fled awey,
For feere han hid, nere that he   3855
All sodeynly tok hym with me.
And whanne I saugh he hadde soo,
This Jelousie, take us twoo,
I was astoned, and knew no red,
But fledde awey for verrey dred.   3860
    Thanne Shame cam forth full symply
(She wende have trespaced full gretly),
Humble of hir port, and made it symple.
Weryng a vayle in stide of wymple,
As nonnys don in her abbey.   3865
By cause hir herte was in affray,
She gan to speke withynne a throwe
To Jelousie right wonder lowe.
First of his grace she bysought,
And seide, "Sire, ne leveth nought   3870
Wikkid-Tunge, that false espie,
Which is so glad to feyne and lye.
He hath you maad, thurgh flateryng,
On Bialacoil a fals lesyng.
His falsnesse is not now a-new;   3875
It is to long that he hym knew.
This is not the firste day,
For Wikkid-Tunge hath custome ay
Yonge folkis to bewreye,
And false lesynges on hem leye.   3880
    "Yit nevertheles I see among,
That the loigne it is so long,
Of Bialacoil, hertis to lure,
In Loves servyse for to endure,
Drawyng suche folk hym to,   3885
That he hath nothyng with to doo.
But in sothnesse I trowe nought
That Bialacoil hadde ever in thought
To do trespas or vylonye,
But for his modir Curtesie   3890
Hath taught hym ever to be
Good of aqueyntaunce and pryve.
For he loveth noon hevynesse,
But mirthe and pley and all gladnesse;
He hateth alle trecherous,   3895
Soleyn folk, and envyous;
For ye witen how that he
Wol ever glad and joyfull be

3811 **Irish womman**: angry woman (?); see n.
3813 **Poignaunt**: piercing
3826 **Reynes, Amyas**: Rennes (in Brittany), Meaux
3832 **reward**: regard

3855 **he**: Jealousy
3863 **made it symple**: behaved with simplicity (R.)
3882 **loigne**: leash
3896 **Soleyn**: solitary, sullen

Honestly with folk to pley.
I have be negligent, in good fey,   3900
To chastise hym; therfore now I
Of herte crye you heere mercy,
That I have been so recheles
To tamen hym, withouten lees.
Of my foly I me repente.   3905
Now wole I hool sette myn entente
To kepe, bothe lowde and stille,
Bialacoil to do youre wille."
    "Shame, Shame," seyde Jelousy,
"To be bytrasshed gret drede have I.   3910
Leccherie hath clombe so hye
That almoost blered is myn ye;
No wonder is, if that drede have I.
Overall regnyth Lecchery,
Whos myght growith nyght and day   3915
Bothe in cloistre and in abbey.
Chastite is werreyed overall;
Therfore I wole with siker wall
Close bothe roses and roser.
I have to longe in this maner   3920
Left hem unclosid wilfully;
Wherfore I am right inwardly
Sorowfull, and repente me.
But now they shall no lenger be
Unclosid; and yit I drede sore,   3925
I shall repente ferthermore,
For the game goth all amys.
Counsell I must newe, ywys.
I have to longe tristed thee,
But now it shal no lenger be,   3930
For he may best, in every cost,
Disceyve, that men tristen most.
I see wel that I am nygh shent,
But if I sette my full entent
Remedye to purveye.   3935
Therfore close I shall the weye
Fro hem that wole the Rose espie,
And come to wayte me vilonye,
For, in good feith and in trouthe,
I wole not lette for no slouthe   3940
To lyve the more in sikirnesse,
To make anoon a forteresse,
T'enclose the roses of good savour.
In myddis shall I make a tour
To putte Bialacoil in prisoun,   3945
For evere I drede me of tresoun.
I trowe I shal hym kepe soo
That he shal have no myght to goo

Aboute to make companye
To hem that thenke of vylanye;   3950
Ne to no such as hath ben heere
Aforn, and founde in hym good chere,
Which han assailed hym to shende,
And with her trowandyse to blende.
A fool is eythe to bigyle;   3955
But may I lyve a litel while,
He shal forthenke his fair semblaunt."
    And with that word came Drede avaunt,
Which was abasshed and in gret fere,
Whanne he wiste Jelousie was there.   3960
He was for drede in sich affray
That not a word durste he say,
But quakyng stod full still aloon,
Til Jelousie his weye was gon,
Save Shame, that him not forsok.   3965
Bothe Drede and she ful sore quok,
That atte laste Drede abreyde,
And to his cosyn Shame seide:
"Shame," he seide, "in sothfastnesse,
To me it is gret hevynesse   3970
That the noyse so fer is go,
And the sclaundre of us twoo.
But sithe that it is byfalle,
We may it not ageyn calle
Whanne onys sprongen is a fame.   3975
For many a yeer withouten blame
We han ben, and many a day;
For many an Aprill and many a May
We han passed, not shamed,
Till Jelousie hath us blamed,   3980
Of mystrust and suspecioun,
Causeles, withoute enchesoun.
Go we to Daunger hastily,
And late us shewe hym openly
That [he] hath not aright wrought,   3985
Whanne that [he] sette nought his thought
To kepe better the purprise;
In his doyng he is not wise.
He hath to us do gret wrong,
That hath suffred now so long   3990
Bialacoil to have his wille,
All his lustes to fulfille.
He must amende it utterly,
Or ellys shall he vilaynesly
Exiled be out of this lond;   3995
For he the werre may not withstond

3904 lees: leash
3912 blered is myn ye: I have been deceived.

3954 trowandyse: fraudulence
3955 eythe: easy
3987 purprise: enclosure
3994 vilaynesly: cruelly, like a churl

Of Jelousie, nor the greef,
Sith Bialacoil is at myscheef."
  To Daunger, Shame and Drede anoon
The righte weye ben goon.   4000
The cherl thei founden hem aforn,
Liggyng undir an hawethorn;
Undir his heed no pilowe was,
But in the stede a trusse of gras.
He slombred, and a nappe he tok,   4005
Tyll Shame pitously hym shok,
And grete manace on hym gan make.
"Why slepist thou, whanne thou shulde wake?"
Quod Shame; "Thou doist us vylanye!
Who tristith thee, he doth folye,   4010
To kepe roses or botouns,
Whanne thei ben faire in her sesouns.
Thou art woxe to familiere,
Where thou shulde be straunge of chere,
Stout of thi port, redy to greve.   4015
Thou doist gret folye for to leve
Bialacoil hereinne to calle
The yonder man to shenden us alle.
Though that thou slepe, we may here
Of Jelousie gret noyse heere.   4020
Art thou now late? Ris up in hy,
And stop sone and delyverly
All the gappis of the haye.
Do no favour, I thee praye.
It fallith nothyng to thy name   4025
To make faire semblaunt, where thou maist
     blame.
Yf Bialacoil be sweete and free,
Dogged and fell thou shuldist be,
Froward and outrageous, ywis;
A cherl chaungeth that curteis is.   4030
This have I herd ofte in seiyng,
That man [ne] may, for no dauntyng,
Make a sperhauk of a bosard.
Alle men wole holde thee for musard,
That debonair have founden thee;   4035
It sittith thee nought curteis to be.
To do men plesaunce or servise,
In thee it is recreaundise.
Let thi werkis fer and ner
Be like thi name, which is Daunger."   4040
  Thanne, all abawid in shewing,
Anoon spak Drede, right thus seiyng,

And seide, "Daunger, I drede me
That thou ne wolt bisy be
To kepe that thou hast to kepe: 4045
Whanne thou shuldist wake, thou art aslepe.
Thou shalt be greved, certeynly,
If the aspie Jelousy,
Or if he fynde thee in blame.
He hath to-day assailed Shame,   4050
And chased awey with gret manace
Bialacoil out of this place,
And swereth shortly that he shall
Enclose hym in a sturdy wall;
And all is for thi wikkednesse,   4055
For that thee faileth straungenesse.
Thyn herte, I trowe, be failed all;
Thou shalt repente in speciall,
If Jelousie the soothe knewe;
Thou shalt forthenke and sore rewe."   4060
  With that the cherl his clubbe gan shake,
Frounyng his eyen gan to make,
And hidous chere; as man in rage
For ire he brente in his visage,
Whanne that [he] herd hym blamed soo. 4065
He seide, "Out of my wit I goo!
To be discomfyt I have gret wrong.
Certis, I have now lyved to long,
Sith I may not this closer kepe.
All quyk I wolde be dolven deepe,   4070
If ony man shal more repeire
Into this gardyn, for foule or faire.
Myn herte for ire goth a-fere,
That I let ony entre heere.
I have do folie, now I see,   4075
But now it shall amended bee.
Who settith foot heere ony more,
Truly he shall repente it sore;
For no man moo into this place
Of me to entre shal have grace.   4080
Lever I hadde with swerdis tweyne
Thurghoute myn herte in every veyne
Perced to be with many a wounde,
Thanne slouthe shulde in me be founde.
From hennes forth, by nyght or day,   4085
I shall defende it, if I may,
Withouten ony excepcioun
Of ech maner condicioun.
And if I it eny man graunt,
Holdeth me for recreaunt."   4090
  Thanne Daunger on his feet gan stond,
And hente a burdoun in his hond.

4015 **Stout:** proud
4028 **Dogged:** currish, surly
4032 **dauntyng:** taming (by threats)
4033 **bosard:** buzzard
4034 **musard:** sluggard
4038 **recreaundise:** cowardice
4041 **abawid:** disconcerted

4056 **straungenesse:** distance, aloofness
4069 **closer:** enclosure
4092 **burdoun:** stick, club

Wroth in his ire, ne lefte he nought,
But thurgh the verger he hath sought.
If he myght fynde hole or trace,   4095
Wherethurgh that me mot forth-by pace,
Or ony gappe, he dide it close,
That no man myghte touche a rose
Of the roser all aboute.
He shitteth every man withoute.   4100

    Thus day by day Daunger is wers,
More wondirfull and more dyvers,
And feller eke than evere he was.
For hym full ofte I synge "Allas!"
For I ne may nought, thurgh his ire,   4105
Recovere that I moost desire.
Myn herte, allas, wole brest a-twoo,
For Bialacoil I wratthed soo.
For certeynly, in every membre
I quake, whanne I me remembre   4110
Of the botoun, which I wolde
Full ofte a day sen and biholde.
And whanne I thenke upon the kiss,
And how myche joye and bliss
I hadde thurgh the savour swete,   4115
For want of it I grone and grete.
Me thenkith I fele yit in my nose
The swete savour of the Rose.
And now I woot that I mot goo
So fer the freshe floures froo,   4120
To me full welcome were the deth.
Absens therof, allas, me sleeth!
For whilom with this Rose — allas! —
I touched nose, mouth, and face;
But now the deth I must abide.   4125
But Love consente another tyde
That onys I touche may and kisse,
I trowe my peyne shall never lisse;
Theron is all my coveitise,
Which brent myn herte in many wise.   4130
Now shal repaire agayn sighinge,
Long wacche on nyghtis, and no slepinge,
Thought in wisshing, torment and woo,
With many a turnyng to and froo,
That half my peyne I can not telle.   4135
For I am fallen into helle
From paradys, and wel the more
My turment greveth; more and more
Anoieth now the bittirnesse,
That I toforn have felt swetnesse.   4140
And Wikkid-Tunge, thurgh his falshede,

Causeth all my woo and drede.
On me he leieth a pitous charge,
Bicause his tunge was to large.
    Now it is tyme, shortly, that I   4145
Telle you som thyng of Jelousy,
That was in gret suspecioun.
Aboute hym lefte he no masoun,
That stoon coude leye, ne querrour;
He hirede hem to make a tour.   4150
And first, the roses for to kep,
Aboute hem made he a diche deep,
Right wondir large, and also brood;
Upon the whiche also stod
Of squared stoon a sturdy wall,   4155
Which on a cragge was founded all;
And right gret thikkenesse eke it bar.
Aboute, it was founded squar,
An hundred fademe on every sid;
It was all liche longe and wid.   4160
Lest ony tyme it were assayled,
Ful wel aboute it was batayled,
And rounde enviroun eke were set
Ful many a riche and fair touret.
At every corner of this wall   4165
Was set a tour full pryncipall;
And everich hadde, withoute fable,
A porte-colys defensable
To kepe of enemyes, and to greve,
That there her force wolde preve.   4170
And eke amydde this purprise
Was maad a tour of gret maistrise;
A fairer saugh no man with sight,
Large and wid, and of gret myght.
They dredde noon assaut   4175
Of gyn, gunne, nor skaffaut.
The temperure of the morter
Was maad of lycour wonder der,
Of quykke lym, persant and egre,
The which was tempred with vynegre.   4180
The stoon was hard, of ademant,
Wherof they made the foundement.
The tour was round, maad in compas;
In all this world no riccher was,
Ne better ordeigned therwithall.   4185

4096 **me:** one (impersonal)
4102 **dyvers:** hostile
4103 **feller:** more terrible
4116 **grete:** lament

4149 **querrour:** quarry worker
4156 **founded:** built
4159 **fademe:** fathoms
4162 **batayled:** notched with crenellations
4168 **porte-colys:** portcullis
4176 **gyn:** war engine (catapult) **gunne:** canon **skaffaut:**
scaffold, a shed on wheels used to cover the approach of a
battering ram
4177 The mixing of the mortar
4179 **egre:** sharp
4181 **ademant:** hardest of stones

Aboute the tour was maad a wall,
So that bitwixt that and the tour
Rosers were sette of swete savour,
With many roses that thei bere;
And eke withynne the castell were   4190
Spryngoldes, gunnes, bows, and archers;
And eke above, atte corners,
Men seyn over the wall stonde
Grete engynes, who were nygh honde.
And in the kernels, heere and there,   4195
Of arblasters gret plente were;
Noon armure myght her strok withstonde;
It were foly to prece to honde.
Withoute the diche were lystes maad,
With wall batayled large and brad,   4200
For men and hors shulde not atteyne
To neigh the dyche over the pleyne.
Thus Jelousie hath enviroun
Set aboute his garnysoun
With walles rounde and diche dep,   4205
Oonly the roser for to kep.
And Daunger, erly and late,
The keyes [kepte] of the utter gate,
The which openeth toward the eest.
And he hadde with hym atte leest   4210
Thritty servauntes, echon by name.
   That other gate kepte Shame,
Which openede, as it was couth,
Toward the partie of the south.
Sergeauntes assigned were hir to   4215
Ful many, hir wille for to doo.
   Thanne Drede hadde in hir baillie
The kepyng of the conestablerye
Toward the north, I undirstond,
That openyde upon the lyft hond;   4220
The which for nothyng may be sure,
But if she do bisy cure,
Erly on morowe and also late,
Strongly to shette and barre the gate.
Of every thing that she may see   4225
Drede is aferd, wherso she be;
For with a puff of litell wynd
Drede is astonyed in hir mynd.
Therfore, for stelyng of the Rose,
I rede hir nought the yate unclose.   4230

A foulis flight wol make hir flee,
And eke a shadowe, if she it see.
   Thanne Wikked-Tunge, ful of envye,
With soudiours of Normandye,
As he that causeth all the bate,   4235
Was keper of the fourthe gate,
And also to the tother three
He wente full ofte for to see.
Whanne his lot was to wake anyght,
His instrumentis wolde he dight,   4240
For to blowe and make sown
Ofter thanne he hath enchesoun,
And walken oft upon the wall,
Corners and wikettis overall
Full narwe serchen and espie;   4245
Though he nought fond, yit wolde he lye.
Discordaunt ever fro armonye,
And distoned from melodie,
Controve he wolde, and foule fayle,
With hornepipes of Cornewaile.   4250
In floytes made he discordaunce,
And in his musyk — with myschaunce! —
He wolde seyn, with notes newe,
That he fond no womman trewe,
Ne that he saugh never in his lyf   4255
Unto hir husbonde a trewe wyf,
Ne noon so ful of honeste
That she nyl laughe and mery be
Whanne that she hereth, or may espie,
A man speken of leccherie.   4260
Everich of hem hath som vice:
Oon is dishonest, another is nyce;
If oon be full of vylanye,
Another hath a likerous ye;
If oon be full of wantonesse,   4265
Another is a chideresse.
   Thus Wikked-Tunge — God yeve him
      shame! —
Can putt hem everychon in blame,
Withoute desert and causeles;
He lieth, though they ben giltles.   4270
I have pite to sen the sorwe
That waketh bothe eve and morwe,
To innocentis doith such grevaunce.
I pray God yeve him evel chaunce,
That he ever so bisy is   4275

4191 **Spryngoldes:** catapults
4194 **who:** the reference could be to the men or the engines
4195 **kernels:** battlements
4196 **arblasters:** crossbow-men
4198 **prece to honde:** come close (within range)
4199 **lystes:** palisades, outer defensive walls
4204 **garnysoun:** garrison
4208 **utter:** outer
4217 **baillie:** control
4218 **conestablerye:** ward of the castle
4229 **for stelyng:** to prevent stealing

4234 **soudiours:** mercenary soldiers
4235 **bate:** strife
4248 **distoned from:** out of tune with
4249 **Controve:** compose   **foule fayle:** fail miserably (in his musical inventions)
4250 **hornepipes:** pipes made of horn   **Cornewaile:** probably a town in Brittany (rather than Cornwall)
4251 **floytes:** flutes
4266 **chideresse:** scold

Of ony womman to seyn amys!
Eke Jelousie God confound,
That hath maad a tour so round,
And made aboute a garisoun,
To sette Bealacoil in prisoun,   4280
The which is shet there in the tour
Ful longe to holde there sojour,
There for to lyve in penaunce.
And for to do hym more grevaunce,
Ther hath ordeyned Jelousie   4285
An olde vekke, for to espye
The maner of his governaunce;
The whiche devel in hir enfaunce
Hadde lerned of loves art,
And of his pleyes tok hir part;   4290
She was expert in his servise.
She knew ech wrench and every gise
Of love, and every wile;
It was [the] harder hir to gile.
Of Bealacoil she tok ay hede,   4295
That evere he lyveth in woo and drede.
He kepte hym koy and eke pryve,
Lest in hym she hadde see
Ony foly countenaunce,
For she knew all the olde daunce.   4300
And aftir this, whanne Jelousie
Hadde Bealacoil in his baillie,
And shette hym up that was so fre,
For seur of hym he wolde be,
He trusteth sore in his castell;   4305
The stronge werk hym likketh well.
He dradde not that no glotouns
Shulde stele his roses or botouns.
The roses weren assured all,
Defenced with the stronge wall.   4310
Now Jelousie full well may be
Of drede devoid in liberte,
Whether that he slepe or wake,
For his roses may noon be take.
    But I — allas! — now morne shall;   4315
Bicause I was withoute the wall,
Full moche dool and moone I made.
Who hadde wist what woo I hadde,
I trowe he wolde have had pite.
Love to deere hadde soold to me   4320
The good that of his love hadde I.
I wende a bought it all queyntly;

But now, thurgh doublyng of my peyn,
I see he wolde it selle ageyn,
And me a newe bargeyn leere,   4325
The which all-oute the more is deere,
For the solas that I have lorn,
Thanne I hadde it never aforn.
Certayn, I am ful lik in deed
To hym that cast in erthe his seed,   4330
And hath joie of the newe spryng,
Whanne it greneth in the gynnyng,
And is also fair and fresh of flour,
Lusty to seen, swoote of odour;
But er he it in sheves shere,   4335
May falle a weder that shal it dere,
And make it to fade and falle,
The stalke, the greyn, and floures alle,
That to the tylyer is fordon
The hope that he hadde to soon.   4340
I drede, certeyn, that so fare I;
For hope and travaile sikerly
Ben me byraft all with a storm;
The flour nyl seeden of my corn.
For Love hath so avaunced me,   4345
Whanne I bigan my pryvite
To Bialacoil all for to tel,
Whom I ne fond froward ne fel,
But tok a-gree all hool my play.
But Love is of so hard assay,   4350
That al at oonys he reved me,
Whanne I wende best aboven to have be.
It is of Love, as of Fortune,
That chaungeth ofte, and nyl contune,
Which whilom wol on folk smyle,   4355
And glowmbe on hem another while.
Now freend, now foo, [thow] shalt hir feel,
For [in] a twynklyng turneth hir wheel.
She can writhe hir heed awey;
This is the concours of hir pley.   4360
She can areise that doth morne,
And whirle adown, and overturne
Who sittith hyest, but as hir lust.
A fool is he that wole hir trust;
For it is I that am come down   4365
Thurgh change and revolucioun!
Sith Bealacoil mot fro me twynne,
Shet in the prisoun yond withynne,
His absence at myn herte I fele;
For all my joye and all myn hele   4370

4282 **sojour:** dwelling place
4286 **vekke:** hag
4292 **wrench:** trick
4302 **baillie:** control
4305 **sore:** extremely
4307 **glotouns:** gluttons (used as a general term of abuse)
4322 **I wende a bought:** I thought to have bought

4339 **tylyer:** tiller, farmer
4340 **to:** too
4349 **tok a-gree:** took in good part, graciously
4354 **contune:** continue
4356 **glowmbe:** scowl
4360 **concours:** course

Was in hym and in the Rose,
That but yon wal, which hym doth close,
Opene that I may hym see,
Love nyl not that I cured be
Of the peynes that I endure,   4375
Nor of my cruel aventure.

    A, Bialacoil, myn owne deer!
Though thou be now a prisoner,
Kep atte leste thyn herte to me
And suffre not that it daunted be;   4380
Ne lat not Jelousie, in his rage,
Putten thin herte in no servage.
Although he chastice thee withoute
And make thy body unto hym loute,
Have herte as hard as dyamaunt,   4385
Stedefast and nought pliaunt.
In prisoun though thi body be,
At large kep thyn herte free;
A trewe herte wole not plie
For no manace that it may drye.   4390
If Jelousie doth thee payn,
Quyte hym his while thus agayn,
To venge thee, atte leest in thought,
If other way thou maist nought;
And in this wise sotilly   4395
Worche, and wynne the maistry.
But yit I am in gret affray
Lest thou do not as I say.
I drede thou canst me gret maugre,
That thou enprisoned art for me;   4400
But that [is] not for my trespas,
For thurgh me never discovred was
Yit thyng that oughte be secree.
Wel more anoy is in me,
Than is in thee, of this myschaunce;   4405
For I endure more hard penaunce,
Than ony can seyn or thynke,
That for the sorwe almost I synke.
Whanne I remembre me of my woo,
Full nygh out of my witt I goo.   4410
Inward myn herte I feele blede,
For comfortles the deth I drede.
Owe I not wel to have distresse,
Whanne false, thurgh hir wikkednesse,
And traitours, that arn envyous,   4415
To noyen me be so corajous?
A, Bialacoil, full wel I see
That they hem shape to disceyve thee,
To make thee buxom to her lawe,

And with her corde thee to drawe   4420
Where so hem lust, right at her will.
I drede they have thee brought thertill.
Withoute comfort, thought me sleeth;
This game wole brynge me to my deeth.
For if youre goode wille I leese,   4425
I mot be deed, I may not chese.
And if that thou foryete me,
Myn herte shal nevere in likyng be,
Nor elleswhere fynde solas,
If I be putt out of youre gras —   4430
As it shal never been, I hope —
Thanne shulde I falle in wanhope.
    Allas, in wanhope? Nay, pardee!
For I wole never dispeired be.
If hope me faile, thanne am I   4435
Ungracious and unworthy.
In hope I wole comforted be,
For Love, whanne he bitaught hir me,
Seide that Hope, whereso I goo,
Shulde ay be relees to my woo.   4440
But what and she my baalis beete,
And be to me curteis and sweete?
She is in nothyng full certeyn.
Lovers she putt in full gret peyn,
And makith hem with woo to deele.   4445
Hir faire biheeste disceyveth feele,
For she wole byhote, sikirly,
And failen aftir outrely.
A, that is a full noyous thyng!
For many a lover, in lovyng,   4450
Hangeth upon hir, and trusteth faste,
Whiche leese her travel at the laste.
Of thyng to comen she woot right nought;
Therfore, if it be wysely sought,
Hir counseill foly is to take.   4455
For many tymes, whanne she wole make
A full good silogisme, I dreede
That aftirward ther shal in deede
Folwe an evell conclusioun.
This put me in confusioun.   4460
For many tymes I have it seen,
That many have bigyled been
For trust that they have set in Hope,
Which fell hem aftirward a-slope.
    But nevertheles, yit gladly she wolde   4465
That he, that wole hym with hir holde,
Hadde alle tymes his purpos cler,
Withoute deceyte or ony wer —

4384 loute: bow
4389 plie: bend
4399 canst me: bear me   maugre: ill will
4416 noyen: harm, injure

4432 wanhope: despair
4438 bitaught: entrusted
4441 what and: what if   baalis beete: amend my sufferings
4464 a-slope: askew

That she desireth sikirly.
Whanne I hir blamed, I dide foly.   4470
But what avayleth hir good wille,
Whanne she ne may staunche my stounde ille?
That helpith litel that she may doo,
Out-take biheest unto my woo.
And heeste certeyn, in no wise,   4475
Withoute yift, is not to prise.
Whanne heest and deede a-sundry varie,
They doon a gret contrarie.
Thus am I possed up and doun
With dool, thought, and confisioun;   4480
Of my disese ther is no noumbre.
Daunger and Shame me encumbre,
Drede also, and Jelousie,
And Wikked-Tunge, full of envie,
Of whiche the sharpe and cruel ire   4485
Full ofte me putte in gret martire.
They han my joye fully let,
Sith Bialacoil they have bishet
Fro me in prisoun wikkidly,
Whom I love so entierly   4490
That it wole my bane bee
But I the sonner may hym see.
And yit moreover, wurst of alle,
Ther is set to kepe — foule hir bifalle! —
A rympled vekke, fer ronne in age,   4495
Frownyng and yelowe in hir visage,
Which in awayt lyth day and nyght,
That noon of him may have a sight.
    Now mote my sorwe enforced be.
Full soth it is that Love yaf me   4500
Three wonder yiftes of his grace,
Whiche I have lorn now in this place,
Sith they ne may, withoute drede,
Helpen but lytel, who taketh heede.
For here availeth no Swete-Thought,   4505
And Sweete-Speche helpith right nought.
The thridde was called Swete-Lokyng,
That now is lorn, without lesyng.
    Yiftes were faire, but not forthy
They helpe me but symply,   4510
But Bialacoil loosed be,
To gon at large and to be free.
For hym my lyf lyth all in doute,
But if he come the rather oute.
Allas, I trowe it wole not ben!   4515
For how shuld I evermore hym sen?
He may not out, and that is wrong,
By cause the tour is so strong.

How shulde he out? By whos prowesse,
Out of so strong a forteresse?   4520
By me, certeyn, it nyl be doo;
God woot, I have no wit therto!
But, wel I woot, I was in rage,
Whonne I to Love dide homage.
Who was in cause, in sothfastnesse,   4525
But hirsilf, Dame Idelnesse,
Which me conveied, thurgh my praier,
To entre into that faire verger.
She was to blame me to leve,
The which now doth me soore greve.   4530
A foolis word is nought to trowe,
Ne worth an appel for to lowe;
Men shulde hym snybbe bittirly,
At pryme temps of his foly.
I was a fool, and she me leeved,   4535
Thurgh whom I am right nought releeved.
She accomplisshid all my will,
That now me greveth wondir ill.
Resoun me seide what shulde falle.
A fool mysilf I may well calle,   4540
That love asyde I had [nat] leyd,
And trowed that Dame Resoun seid.
Resoun hadde bothe skile and ryght,
Whanne she me blamed, with all hir myght,
To medle of love that hath me shent;   4545
But certeyn, now I wole repent.
    And shulde I repente? Nay, parde!
A fals traitour thanne shulde I be.
The develes engynnes wolde me take,
If I my lord wolde forsake,   4550
Or Bialacoil falsly bitraye.
Shulde I at myscheef hate hym? Nay,
Sith he now, for his curtesie,
Is in prisoun of Jelousie.
Curtesie certeyn dide he me,   4555
So mych that may not yolden be,
Whanne he the hay passen me let,
To kisse the Rose, faire and swet.
Shulde I therfore cunne hym mawgre?
Nay, certeynly, it shal not be;   4560
For Love shal nevere, yif God wille,
Here of me, thurgh word or wille,
Offence or complaynt, more or lesse,
Neither of Hope nor Idilnesse.
For certis, it were wrong that I   4565
Hated hem for her curtesy.
Ther is not ellys but suffre and thynke,
And waken whanne I shulde wynke;
Abide in hope, til Love, thurgh chaunce,

4472 **staunche:** heal   **stounde ille:** evil time
4474 **Out-take biheest:** except promise
4479 **possed:** tossed
4495 **rympled:** wrinkled   **ronne in age:** advanced in age
4499 **enforced:** increased, made stronger

4533 **snybbe:** rebuke
4534 **At pryme temps:** at first
4559 **cunne hym mawgre:** show him spite, ingratitude

Sende me socour or allegeaunce,   4570
Expectant ay till I may mete
To geten mercy of that swete.
   Whilom I thenke how Love to me
Seide he wolde take att gree
My servise, if unpacience   4575
[Ne] caused me to don offence.
He seide, "In thank I shal it take,
And high maister eke thee make,
If wikkednesse ne reve it thee;
But sone, I trowe, that shall not be."   4580
These were his wordis, by and by;
It semede he lovede me trewely.
Now is ther not but serve hym wel,
If that I thenke his thank to fel.
My good, myn harm lyth hool in me.   4585
In Love may no defaute be,
For trewe Love ne failide never man.
Sothly the faute mot nedys than —
As God forbede! — be founde in me;
And how it cometh, I can not see.   4590
Now late it goon as it may goo;
Whether Love wole socoure me or sloo,
He may do hool on me his will.
I am so sore bounde hym till,
From his servise I may not fleen;   4595
For lyf and deth, withouten wen,
Is in his hand — I may not chese —
He may me doo bothe wynne and leese.
And sith so sore he doth me greve,
Yit, if my lust he wolde acheve,   4600
To Bialacoil goodly to be,
I yeve no force what felle on me.
For though I dye, as I mot nede,
I praye Love, of his goodlyhede,
To Bialacoil do gentylnesse,   4605
For whom I lyve in such distresse
That I mot deyen for penaunce.
But first, withoute repentaunce,
I wole me confesse in good entent,
And make in haste my testament,   4610
As lovers doon that feelen smert:
To Bialacoil leve I myn hert
All hool, withoute departyng,
Doublenesse of repentyng.

     Coment Raisoun vient a l'amant.

   Thus, as I made my passage   4615
In compleynt and in cruel rage,
And I not where to fynde a leche
That couthe unto myn helpyng eche,
Sodeynly agayn comen doun
Out of hir tour I saugh Resoun,   4620
Discret and wis and full plesaunt,
And of hir port full avenaunt.
The righte weye she took to me,
Which stod in gret perplexite,
That was posshed in every side,   4625
That I nyst where I myght abide,
Till she, demurely sad of cher,
Seide to me, as she com ner,
"Myn owne freend, art thou yit greved?
How is this quarell yit acheved   4630
Of Loves side? Anoon me telle.
Hast thou not yit of love thi fille?
Art thou not wery of thy servise,
That the hath [greved] in sich wise?
What joye hast thou in thy lovyng?   4635
Is it swete or bitter thing?
Canst thou yit chese, lat me see,
What best thi socour myghte be?
   Thou servest a full noble lord,
That maketh thee thrall for thi reward,   4640
Which ay renewith thy turment,
With foly so he hath thee blent.
Thou fell in myscheef thilke day
Whanne thou didist, the sothe to say,
Obeysaunce and eke homage.   4645
Thou wroughtest nothyng as the sage,
Whanne thou bicam his liege man.
Thou didist a gret foly than,
Thou wistest not what fell therto,
With what lord thou haddist to do.   4650
If thou haddist hym wel knowe,
Thou haddist nought be brought so lowe;
For if thou wistest what it wer,
Thou noldist serve hym half a yeer,
Not a weke, nor half a day,   4655
Ne yit an hour, withoute delay,
Ne never han loved paramours,
His lordshipp is so full of shours.
Knowest hym ought?"
   L'amaunt   "Ye, dame, parde!"
   Raisoun "Nay, nay."
   L'amaunt   "Yis, I."
   Raisoun   "Wherof? Late se."   4660
   L'amaunt "Of that he seide I shulde be
Glad to have sich lord as he,
And maister of sich seignorie."

4570 **allegeaunce:** alleviation
4584 **fel:** feel, experience
Coment Raisoun, *etc.*: How Reason comes to the Lover

4618 **eche:** aid, help
4630 **quarell:** suit
4658 **shours:** hardships (literally, showers, storms, or battles)

Raisoun "Knowist hym no more?"
L'amaunt   "Nay, certis, I,
Save that he yaf me rewles there,   4665
And wente his wey, I nyste where,
And I abood, bounde in balaunce."
    Raisoun "Lo, there a noble conisaunce!
But I wille that thou knowe hym now,
Gynnyng and eende, sith that thou   4670
Art so anguisshous and mate,
Disfigured out of astate;
Ther may no wrecche have more of woo,
Ne caytyf noon enduren soo.
It were to every man sittyng   4675
Of his lord have knowleching;
For if thou knewe hym, out of doute,
Lightly thou shulde escapen oute
Of the prisoun that marreth thee."
    L'amant "Ye, dame, sith my lord is he,   4680
And I his man, maad with myn hond,
I wolde right fayn undirstond
To knowe of what kynde he be,
If ony wolde enforme me."
    Raisoun "I wolde," seide Resoun, "thee ler,
Sith thou to lerne hast sich desir,   4686
And shewe thee, withouten fable,
A thyng that is not demonstrable.
Thou shalt [wite] withouten science,
And knowe withouten experience,   4690
The thyng that may not knowen be,
Ne wist, ne shewid, in no degre.
Thou maist the sothe of it not witen,
Though in thee it were writen.
Thou shalt not knowe therof more,   4695
While thou art reuled by his lore;
But unto hym that love wole flee,
The knotte may unclosed bee,
Which hath to thee, as it is founde,
So long be knet and not unbounde.   4700
Now set wel thyn entencioun,
To here of love discripcioun.
    "Love, it is an hatefull pees,
A free acquitaunce, withoute relees,
A trouthe, fret full of falsheede,   4705
A sikernesse all set in drede.
In herte is a dispeiryng hope,
And full of hope, it is wanhope;
Wis woodnesse, and wod resoun;
A swete perell in to droun;   4710
An hevy birthen, lyght to bere;
A wikked wawe, awey to were.

It is Karibdous perilous,
Disagreable and gracious.
It is discordaunce that can accorde,   4715
And accordaunce to discorde.
It is kunnyng withoute science,
Wisdom withoute sapience,
Wit withoute discrecioun,
Havoir withoute possessioun.   4720
It is sike hele and hool seknesse,
A thurst drowned in dronknesse,
And helthe full of maladie,
And charite full of envie,
And hunger full of habundaunce,   4725
And a gredy suffisaunce;
Delit right full of hevynesse,
And drerihed full of gladnesse;
Bitter swetnesse and swete errour,
Right evell savoured good savour;   4730
Sin that pardoun hath withynne,
And pardoun spotted withoute [with] synne.
A peyne also it is, joious,
And felonye right pitous;
Also pley that selde is stable,   4735
And stedefast [stat], right mevable;
A strengthe, weyked to stonde upright,
And feblenesse full of myght;
Wit unavised, sage folie,
And joie full of turmentrie;   4740
A laughter it is, weping ay;
Reste that traveyleth nyght and day;
Also a swete helle it is,
And a soroufull paradys;
A pleasant gayl and esy prisoun,   4745
And, full of froste, somer sesoun;
Pryme temps full of frostes whit,
And May devoide of al delit,
With seer braunches, blossoms ungrene,
And newe fruyt, fillid with wynter tene.   4750
It is a slowe, may not forbere
Ragges, ribaned with gold, to were;
For also wel wol love be set
Under ragges, as riche rochet;
And eke as wel be amourettes   4755
In mournyng blak, as bright burnettes.

4667 **bounde in balaunce:** held in suspense
4668 **conisaunce:** understanding, knowledge
4672 **astate:** good or normal condition
4685 **ler:** teach
4705 **fret full of:** set thickly with (as an ornament)

4713 **Karibdous:** Charybdis, the dangerous whirlpool near Italy
4720 **Havoir:** possession
4728 **drerihed:** sadness
4732 **withoute:** on the outside
4737 **weyked:** (too) weakened
4739 **unavised:** thoughtless
4745 **gayl:** jail
4747 **Pryme temps:** spring
4749 **seer:** sere, withered
4751 **slowe:** sluggard
4754 **rochet:** cloak
4755 **amourettes:** lovers, pretty girls; see n.
4756 **burnettes:** dresses

For noon is of so mochel pris,
Ne no man founden so wys,
Ne noon so high is of parage,
Ne no man founde of wit so sage,   4760
No man so hardy ne so wight,
Ne no man of so mochel myght,
Noon so fulfilled of bounte,
That he with love [ne] may daunted be.
All the world holdith this wey;   4765
Love makith all to goon myswey,
But it be they of yvel lyf,
Whom Genius cursith, man and wyf,
That wrongly werke ageyn nature.
Noon such I love, ne have no cure   4770
Of sich as Loves servauntes ben,
And wole not by my counsel flen.
For I ne preise that lovyng
Wherthurgh men, at the laste eendyng,
Shall calle hem wrecchis full of woo,   4775
Love greveth hem and shendith soo.
But if thou wolt wel Love eschewe,
For to escape out of his mewe,
And make al hool thi sorwe to slake,
No bettir counsel maist thou take   4780
Than thynke to fleen wel, iwis.
May nought helpe elles, for wite thou this:
If thou fle it, it shal flee thee;
Folowe it, and folowen shal it thee."
L'amant Whanne I hadde herde all Resoun
        seyn,   4785
Which hadde spilt hir speche in veyn,
"Dame," seide I, "I dar wel sey,
Of this avaunt me wel I may
That from youre scole so devyaunt
I am, that never the more avaunt   4790
Right nought am I thurgh youre doctrine.
I dulle under youre discipline.
I wot no more than [I] wist er,
To me so contrarie and so fer
Is every thing that ye me ler,   4795
And yit I can it all *par cuer.*
Myn herte foryetith therof right nought,
It is so writen in my thought;
And depe greven it is so tendir
That all by herte I can it rendre,   4800
And rede it over comunely;
But to mysilf lewedist am I.
But sith ye love discreven so,
And lak and preise it, bothe twoo,
Defyneth it into this letter,   4805

That I may thenke on it the better;
For I herde never diffyne it er,
And wilfully I wolde it ler."
  Raisoun "If love be serched wel and sought,
It is a syknesse of the thought   4810
Annexed and knet bitwixe tweyne,
Which male and female, with oo cheyne,
So frely byndith that they nyll twynne,
Whether so therof they leese or wynne.
The roote springith thurgh hoot brennyng
Into disordinat desiryng   4816
For to kissen and enbrace,
And at her lust them to solace.
Of other thyng love recchith nought,
But setteth her herte and all her thought
More for delectacioun   4821
Than ony procreacioun
Of other fruyt by engendring,
Which love to God is not plesyng;
For of her body fruyt to get   4825
They yeve no force, they are so set
Upon delit to pley in-feere.
And somme have also this manere,
To feynen hem for love sek;
Sich love I preise not at a lek.   4830
For paramours they do but feyne;
To love truly they disdeyne.
They falsen ladies traitoursly,
And swern hem othes utterly,
With many a lesyng and many a fable,   4835
And all they fynden deceyvable.
And whanne they han her lust geten,
The hoote ernes they al foryeten.
Wymmen, the harm they bien full sore;
But men this thenken evermore,   4840
That lasse harm is, so mote I the,
Deceyve them than deceyved be;
And namely, where they ne may
Fynde non other mene wey.
For I wot wel, in sothfastnesse,   4845
[What man] doth now his bisynesse
With ony womman for to dele,
For ony lust that he may fele,
But if it be for engendrure,
He doth trespas, I you ensure.   4850
For he shulde setten all his wil
To geten a likly thyng hym til,
And to sustene, if he myght,
And kepe forth, by Kyndes right,
His owne lyknesse and semblable;   4855

4759 **parage:** birth, lineage
4766 **myswey:** astray
4767 **they of yvel lyf:** homosexuals
4768 **wyf:** woman
4796 **par cuer:** by heart

4808 **ler:** learn
4816 **disordinat:** excessive
4831 **For paramours:** with passionate love
4838 **ernes:** passion

. . . .
And faile shulde successioun,
Ne were ther generacioun
Oure sectis strene for to save.
Whanne fader or moder arn in grave,   4860
Her children shulde, whanne they ben deede,
Full diligent ben, in her steede,
To use that werk on such a wise
That oon may thurgh another rise.
Therfore sette Kynde therynne delit,   4865
For men therynne shulde hem delit,
And of that deede be not erk,
But ofte sithes haunt that werk.
For noon wolde drawe therof a draught,
Ne were delit, which hath hym kaught.   4870
Thus hath sotilled dame Nature;
For noon goth right, I thee ensure,
Ne hath entent hool ne parfit;
For her desir is for delyt,
The which fortened crece and eke   4875
The pley of love for-ofte seke,
And thrall hemsilf, they be so nyce,
Unto the prince of every vice.
For of ech synne it is the rote,
Unlefull lust, though it be sote,   4880
And of all yvell the racyne,
As Tulius can determyne,
Which in his tyme was full sage,
In a bok he made 'Of Age,'
Where that more he preyseth eelde,   4885
Though he be croked and unweelde,
And more of commendacioun
Than youthe in his discripcioun.
For youthe set bothe man and wyf
In all perell of soule and lyf;   4890
And perell is, but men have grace,
The tyme of youthe for to pace
Withoute ony deth or distresse,
It is so full of wyldenesse,
So ofte it doth shame or damage   4895
To hym or to his lynage.
It ledith man now up, now doun,
In mochel dissolucioun,
And makith hym love yvell company,
And lede his lyf disrewlily,   4900

And halt hym payed with noon estat.
Withynne hymsilf is such debat,
He chaungith purpos and entent,
And yalt [him] into som covent,
To lyven aftir her emprise,   4905
And lesith fredom and fraunchise,
That Nature in hym hadde set,
The which ageyn he may not get,
If he there make his mansioun,
For to abide professioun.   4910
Though for a tyme his herte absente,
It may not fayle, he shal repente,
And eke abide thilke day
To leve his abit, and gon his way,
And lesith his worshipp and his name,   4915
And dar not come ageyn for shame;
But al his lyf he doth so mourne,
By cause he dar not hom retourne.
Fredom of kynde so lost hath he
That never may recured be,   4920
But if that God hym graunte grace
That he may, er he hennes pace,
Conteyne undir obedience
Thurgh the vertu of pacience.
For Youthe sett man in all folye,   4925
In unthrift and in ribaudie,
In leccherie and in outrage,
So ofte it chaungith of corage.
Youthe gynneth ofte sich bargeyn,
That may not eende withouten peyn.   4930
In gret perell is sett youthede,
Delit so doth his bridil leede.
Delit thus hangith, dred thee nought,
Bothe mannys body and his thought,
Oonly thurgh Youthe, his chaumberere,   4935
That to don yvell is customere,
And of nought elles taketh hede
But oonly folkes for to lede
Into disport and wyldenesse,
So is [she] froward from sadnesse.   4940
    "But Eelde drawith hem therfro;
Who wot it nought, he may wel goo
Demande of hem that now arn olde,
That whilom Youthe hadde in holde,
Which yit remembre of tendir age,   4945
Hou it hem brought in many a rage,

4856 Not in MS. Thynne has: *For bycause al is corrumpable* (corruptible).
4859 **strene:** strain, race
4867 **erk:** weary
4871 **sotilled:** subtly arranged
4875 **fortened crece:** stimulated procreation
4881 **racyne:** root
4882 **Tulius:** Tully, Cicero
4884 **Of Age:** Cicero's *De senectute* (especially ch. 12)
4886 **unweelde:** feeble
4900 **disrewlily:** irregularly

4901 **halt hym payed:** considers himself satisfied
4905 **emprise:** rule
4910 **abide professioun:** live under vows
4914 **abit:** monastic habit
4920 **recured:** recovered
4923 **Conteyne:** contain his dissatisfaction
4926 **unthrift:** nonsense
4935 **chaumberere:** personal servant
4936 **customere:** accustomed

And many a foly therynne wrought.
But now that Eelde hath hem thourgh-sought,
They repente hem of her folye,
That Youthe hem putte in jupardye, 4950
In perell, and in myche woo,
And made hem ofte amys to do,
And suen yvell companye,
Riot and avouterie.
  "But Eelde can ageyn restreyne 4955
From sich foly, and refreyne,
And sette men by her ordinaunce
In good reule and in governaunce.
But yvell she spendith hir servise,
For no man wole hir love neither prise; 4960
She is hated, this wot I wel.
Hir acqueyntaunce wolde no man fel,
Ne han of Elde companye;
Men hate to be of hir alye.
For no man wolde bicomen old, 4965
Ne dye whanne he is yong and bold.
And Eelde merveilith right gretly,
Whanne thei remembre hem inwardly
Of many a perelous emprise,
Which that they wrought in sondry wise, 4970
Houevere they myght, withoute blame,
Escape awey withoute shame,
In youthe, withoute damage
Or repreef of her lynage,
Loss of membre, shedyng of blod, 4975
Perell of deth, or los of good.
Wost thou nought where Youthe abit,
That men so preisen in her wit?
With Delit she halt sojour,
For bothe they dwellen in oo tour. 4980
As longe as Youthe is in sesoun,
They dwellen in oon mansioun.
Delit of Youthe wole have servise
To do what so he wole devise;
And Youthe is redy evermore 4985
For to obey, for smert of sore,
Unto Delit, and hym to yive
Hir servise, while that she may lyve.
  "Where Elde abit I wol thee telle
Shortly, and no while dwelle, 4990
For thidir byhoveth thee to goo.
If Deth in youthe thee not sloo,
Of this journey thou maist not faile.
With hir Labour and Travaile
Logged ben, with Sorwe and Woo, 4995

That never out of hir court goo.
Peyne and Distresse, Syknesse and Ire,
And Malencoly, that angry sire,
Ben of hir paleys senatours;
Gronyng and Grucchyng, hir herbejours.
The day and nyght, hir to turmente, 5001
With cruell Deth they hir presente,
And tellen hir, erliche and late,
That Deth stondeth armed at hir gate.
Thanne brynge they to her remembraunce
The foly dedis of hir infaunce, 5006
Whiche causen hir to mourne in woo
That Youthe hath hir bigiled so,
Which sodeynly awey is hasted.
She wepeth the tyme that she hath wasted,
Compleynyng of the preterit, 5011
And the present that not abit,
And of hir olde vanite,
That, but aforn hir she may see
In the future som socour, 5015
To leggen hir of hir dolour,
To graunte hir tyme of repentaunce,
For her synnes to do penaunce,
And at the laste so hir governe
To wynne the joy that is eterne, 5020
Fro which go bakward Youthe hir made,
In vanite to droune and wade.
For present tyme abidith nought;
It is more swift than any thought.
So litel while it doth endure 5025
That ther nys compte ne mesure.
But hou that evere the game go,
Who list to have joie and mirth also
Of love, be it he or she,
High or lowe, who it be, 5030
In fruyt they shulde hem delyte;
Her part they may not elles quyte,
To save hemsilf in honeste.
And yit full many on I se
Of wymmen, sothly for to seyn, 5035
That desire and wolde fayn
The pley of love, they be so wilde,
And not coveite to go with childe.
And if with child they be, perchaunce,
They wole it holde a gret myschaunce; 5040
But whatsomever woo they fele,
They wole not pleyne but concele;
But if it be ony fool or nyce,

4954 **avouterie:** adultery
4964 **of hir alye:** associated with her
4979 **sojour:** dwelling place
4995 **Logged:** lodged

5000 **herbejours:** harbingers (who go before to arrange lodging)
5012 **abit** = *abideth*
5016 **leggen:** alleviate
5026 **compte:** number
5042 **concele:** conceal

In whom that Shame hath no justice.
For to delyt echon they drawe,   5045
That haunte this werk, bothe high and lawe,
Save sich that arn worth right nought,
That for money wole be bought.
Such love I preise in no wise,
Whanne it is goven for coveitise.   5050
I preise no womman, though she be wood,
That yeveth hirsilf for ony good.
For litel shulde a man telle
Of hir, that wole hir body selle,
Be she mayde, be she wyf,   5055
That quyk wole selle hir, bi hir lif.
Hou faire chere that evere she make,
He is a wrecche, I undirtake,
That loveth such on, for swete or sour,
Though she hym calle hir paramour,   5060
And laugheth on hym, and makith hym feeste.
For certeynly no such beeste
To be loved is not worthy,
Or bere the name of druery.
Noon shulde hir please, but he were wood,
That wole dispoile hym of his good.   5066
Yit nevertheles, I wol not sey
That she, for solas and for pley,
[Ne] may a jewel or other thyng
Take of her loves fre yevyng;   5070
But that she aske it in no wise,
For drede of shame of coveitise.
And she of hirs may hym, certeyn,
Withoute sclaundre yeven ageyn,
And joyne her hertes togidre so   5075
In love, and take and yeve also.
Trowe not that I wolde hem twynne,
Whanne in her love ther is no synne;
I wol that they togedre go,
And don al that they han ado,   5080
As curteis shulde and debonaire,
And in her love beren hem faire,
Withoute vice, bothe he and she,
So that alwey, in honeste,
Fro foly love they kepe hem cler,   5085
That brenneth hertis with his fer;
And that her love, in ony wise,
Be devoide of coveitise.
Good love shulde engendrid be
Of trewe herte, just, and secre,   5090
And not of such as sette her thought
To have her lust and ellis nought —
So are they caught in Loves las,
Truly, for bodily solas.

Fleshly delit is so present   5095
With thee, that sette all thyn entent
Withoute more (what shulde I glose?)
For to gete and have the Rose,
Which makith [thee] so mat and wood
That thou desirest noon other good.   5100
But thou art not an inche the nerre,
But evere abidist in sorwe and werre,
As in thi face it is sene.
It makith thee bothe pale and lene;
Thy myght, thi vertu goth away.   5105
A sory gest, in goode fay,
Thou herberest than in thyn inn,
The God of Love whanne thou let inn!
Wherfore I rede, thou shette hym oute,
Or he shall greve thee, out of doute;   5110
For to thi profit it wol turne,
If he nomore with thee sojourne.
In gret myscheef and sorwe sonken
Ben hertis that of love arn dronken,
As thou peraventure knowen shall,   5115
Whanne thou hast lost thy tyme all,
And spent thy youthe in ydilnesse,
In waste and wofull lustynesse.
If thou maist lyve the tyme to se
Of love for to delyvered be,   5120
Thy tyme thou shalt biwepe sore,
The whiche never thou maist restore;
For tyme lost, as men may see,
For nothyng may recured be.
And if thou scape yit, atte laste,   5125
Fro Love, that hath thee so faste
Knytt and bounden in his las,
Certeyn I holde it but a gras.
For many oon, as it is seyn,
Have lost and spent also in veyn,   5130
In his servise, withoute socour,
Body and soule, good and tresour,
Wit and strengthe, and eke richesse,
Of which they hadde never redresse."
  L'amant Thus taught and preched hath
Resoun, but Love spilte hir sermoun,   5136
That was so ymped in my thought,
That hir doctrine I sette at nought.
And yitt ne seide she never a del
That I ne undirstod it wel,   5140
Word by word, the mater all;
But unto Love I was so thrall,
Which callith overall his pray,
He chasith so my thought alway,
And holdith myn herte undir his sel   5145

5064 **druery:** lover

5137 **ymped:** implanted

As trust and trew as ony stel;
So that no devocioun
Ne hadde I in the sermoun
Of dame Resoun, ne of hir red.
It tok no sojour in myn hed,   5150
For all yede out at oon ere
That in that other she dide lere.
Fully on me she lost hir lore;
Hir speche me greved wondir sore.

   Than unto hir for ire I seide,   5155
For anger, as I dide abraide:
"Dame, and is it youre wille algate
That I not love, but that I hate
Alle men, as ye me teche?
For if I do aftir youre speche,   5160
Sith that ye seyn love is not good,
Thanne must I nedis ay with mood,
If I it leve, in hatrede ay
Lyven, and voide love away
From me, [and ben] a synfull wrecche   5165
Hated of all [that love] that tecche.
I may not go noon other gate,
For other must I love or hate.
And if I hate men of-newe
More than love, it wol me rewe,   5170
As by youre preching semeth me,
For Love nothing ne preisith thee.
Ye yeve good counsel, sikirly,
That prechith me alday that I
Shulde not Loves lore alowe.   5175
He were a fool, wolde you not trowe!
In speche also ye han me taught
Another love, that knowen is naught,
Which I have herd you not repreve,
To love ech other. By youre leve,   5180
If ye wolde diffyne it me,
I wolde gladly here, to se,
At the leest, if I may lere
Of sondry loves the manere."

  Raisoun "Certis, freend, a fool art thou,
Whan that thou nothyng wolt allow   5186
That I for thi profit say.
Yit wole I sey thee more in fay,
For I am redy, at the leste,
To accomplisshe thi requeste.   5190
But I not where it wole avayle;
In veyn, perauntre, I shal travayle.
Love ther is in sondry wise,
As I shal thee heere devise.

For som love leful is and good —   5195
I mene not that which makith thee wood,
And bringith thee in many a fit,
And ravysshith fro thee al thi wit,
It is so merveilous and queynt;
With such love be no more aqueynt.   5200

Comment Raisoun diffinist amiste

  "Love of freendshipp also ther is,
Which makith no man don amys,
Of wille knytt bitwixe two,
That wole not breke for wele ne woo;
Which long is likly to contune,   5205
Whanne wille and goodis ben in comune;
Grounded by Goddis ordinaunce,
Hool, withoute discordaunce;
With hem holdyng comunte
Of all her good in charite,   5210
That ther be noon excepcioun
Thurgh chaungyng of entencioun;
That ech helpe other at her neede,
And wisely hele bothe word and dede;
Trewe of menyng, devoide of slouthe,   5215
For witt is nought withoute trouthe;
So that the ton dar all his thought
Seyn to his freend, and spare nought,
As to hymsilf, without dredyng
To be discovered by wreying.   5220
For glad is that conjunccioun,
Whanne ther is noon susspecioun
[Of blame in hem], whom they wolde prove
That trewe and parfit weren in love.
For no man may be amyable,   5225
But if he be so ferme and stable
That fortune chaunge hym not, ne blynde,
But that his freend allwey hym fynde,
Bothe pore and riche, in oo state.
For if his freend, thurgh ony gate,   5230
Wole compleyne of his poverte,
He shulde not bide so long til he
Of his helpyng hym requere;
For good dede, don thurgh praiere,
Is sold and bought to deere, iwys,   5235
To hert that of gret valour is.
For hert fulfilled of gentilnesse
Can yvel demene his distresse;
And man that worthy is of name
To asken often hath gret shame.   5240

5150 **sojour**: dwelling place
5156 **abraide**: speak
5162 **mood**: anger
5166 **tecche**: quality

Comment Raisoun, *etc.*: How Reason defines friendship
5201 **Love of freendshipp**: love between friends
5217 **the ton**: the one
5230 **thurgh ony gate**: in any circumstance
5238 **demene**: control

A good man brenneth in his thought
For shame, whanne he axeth ought.
He hath gret thought and dredeth ay
For his disese, whanne he shal pray
His freend, lest that he warned be,   5245
Til that he preve his stabilte.
But whanne that he hath founden oon
That trusty is and trewe as ston,
And assaied hym at all,
And founde hym stedefast as a wall,   5250
And of his freendshipp be certeyn,
He shal hym shewe bothe joye and peyn,
And all that [he] dar thynke or sey,
Withoute shame, as he wel may.
For how shulde he ashamed be   5255
Of sich on as I tolde thee?
For whanne he woot his secre thought,
The thridde shal knowe therof right nought;
For tweyne of noumbre is bet than thre
In every counsell and secre.   5260
Repreve he dredeth never a deel,
Who that bisett his wordis wel;
For every wise man, out of drede,
Can kepe his tunge til he se nede;
And fooles can not holde her tunge;   5265
A fooles belle is soone runge.
Yit shal a trewe freend do more
To helpe his felowe of his sore,
And socoure hym, whanne he hath neede,
In all that he may don in deede,   5270
And gladder [be] that he hym plesith,
Than his felowe that he esith.
And if he do not his requeste,
He shal as mochel hym moleste
As his felow, for that he   5275
May not fulfille his volunte
Fully, as he hath requered.
If bothe the hertis Love hath fered,
Joy and woo they shull depart,
And take evenly ech his part.   5280
Half his anoy he shal have ay,
And comfort [him] what that he may;
And of his blisse parte shal he,
If love wel departed be.
    "And whilom of this amyte   5285
Spak Tulius in a ditee:
'Man shulde maken his request
Unto his freend, that is honest;

And he goodly shulde it fulfille,
But it the more were out of skile,   5290
And otherwise not graunte therto,
Except oonly in causes twoo:
If men his freend to deth wolde drive,
Lat hym be bisy to save his lyve;
Also if men wolen hym assayle,   5295
Of his wurshipp to make hym faile,
And hyndren hym of his renoun,
Lat hym, with full entencioun,
His dever don in ech degre
That his freend ne shamed be.   5300
In thise two caas with his myght,
Taking no kep to skile nor right,
As fer as love may hym excuse,
This oughte no man to refuse.'
This love that I have told to thee   5305
Is nothing contrarie to me;
This wole I that thou folowe wel,
And leve the tother everydel.
This love to vertu all entendith,
The tothir fooles blent and shendith.   5310
    "Another love also there is
That is contrarie unto this,
Which desir is so constreyned
That [it] is but wille feyned.
Awey fro trouthe it doth so varie   5315
That to good love it is contrarie;
For it maymeth, in many wise,
Sike hertis with coveitise.
All in wynnyng and in profit
Sich love settith his delit.   5320
This love so hangeth in balaunce
That, if it lese his hope, perchaunce,
Of lucre, that he is sett upon,
It wole faile and quenche anoon;
For no man may be amerous,   5325
Ne in his lyvyng vertuous,
But he love more, in mood,
Men for hemsilf than for her good.
For love that profit doth abide
Is fals, and bit not in no tyde.   5330
[This] love cometh of dame Fortune,
That litel while wol contune;
For it shal chaungen wonder soone,
And take eclips, right as the moone,
Whanne she is from us lett   5335
Thurgh erthe, that bitwixe is sett
The sonne and hir, as it may fall,
Be it in partie, or in all.

5274 He will be troubled as much as his fellow
5278 **fered:** inflamed
5280 **evenly:** equally
5284 **departed:** shared
5286 **ditee:** literary work

5290 **out of skile:** unreasonable
5299 **dever:** duty
5330 **bit** = *bydeth*

The shadowe maketh her bemys merke,
And hir hornes to shewe derke,   5340
That part where she hath lost hir lyght
Of Phebus fully, and the sight;
Til, whanne the shadowe is overpast,
She is enlumyned ageyn as fast,
Thurgh the brightnesse of the sonne bemes,
That yeveth to hir ageyn hir lemes.   5346
That love is right of sich nature;
Now is faire, and now obscure,
Now bright, now clipsi of manere,
And whilom dym, and whilom clere.   5350
As soone as Poverte gynneth take,
With mantel and wedis blake
Hidith of love the light awey,
That into nyght it turneth day,
It may not see Richesse shyne   5355
Till the blak shadowes fyne.
For, whanne Richesse shyneth bright,
Love recovereth ageyn his light;
And whanne it failith he wol flit,
And as she groweth, so groweth it.   5360
Of this love — here what I sey! —
The riche men are loved ay,
And namely tho that sparand ben,
That wole not wasshe her hertes clen
Of the filthe nor of the vice   5365
Of gredy brennyng avarice.
The riche man full fonned is, ywys,
That weneth that he loved is.
If that his herte it undirstod,
It is not he, it is his good;   5370
He may wel witen in his thought,
His good is loved, and he right nought.
For if he be a nygard ek,
Men wole not sette by hym a lek,
But haten hym; this is the soth.   5375
Lo, what profit his catell doth!
Of every man that may hym see
It geteth hym nought but enmyte.
But he amende hym of that vice,
And knowe hymsilf, he is not wys.   5380
Certys, he shulde ay freendly be,
To gete hym love also ben free,
Or ellis he is not wise ne sage
Nomore than is a goot ramage.
That he not loveth, his dede proveth,   5385

5343 overpast: passed by
5344 enlumyned: made bright
5346 lemes: rays
5349 clipsi: eclipsed
5363 sparand: miserly
5367 fonned: foolish
5384 goot ramage: horned goat

Whan he his richesse so wel loveth
That he wole hide it ay and spare,
His pore freendis sen forfare,
To kepen ay his purpos,
Til for drede his yen clos,   5390
And til a wikked deth hym take.
Hym hadde lever asondre shake,
And late alle his lymes asondre ryve,
Than leve his richesse in his lyve.
He thenkith parte it with no man;   5395
Certayn, no love is in hym than.
How shulde love withynne hym be,
Whanne in his herte is no pite?
That he trespasseth, wel I wat,
For ech man knowith his estat;   5400
For wel hym ought to be reproved
That loveth nought, ne is not loved.
"But sith we arn to Fortune comen,
And han oure sermoun of hir nomen,
A wondir will Y telle thee now,   5405
Thou herdist never sich oon, I trow.
I not where thou me leven shall,
Though sothfastnesse it be all,
As it is writen, and is soth,
That unto men more profit doth   5410
The froward Fortune and contraire
Than the swote and debonaire.
And if thee thynke it is doutable,
It is thurgh argument provable;
For the debonaire and softe   5415
Falsith and bigilith ofte;
For lyche a moder she can cherish,
And mylken as doth a norys,
And of hir goode to hem deles,
And yeveth hem part of her joweles,   5420
With gret richeses and dignite;
And hem she hoteth stabilite
In a stat that is not stable,
But chaungynge ay and variable;
And fedith hem with glorie veyn,   5425
And worldly blisse noncerteyn.
Whanne she hem settith on hir whel,
Thanne wene they to be right wel,
And in so stable stat withalle,
That never they wene for to falle.   5430
And whanne they sette so highe be,
They wene to have in certeynte
Of hertly freendis so gret noumbre,
That nothyng myght her stat encombre.
They trust hem so on every side,   5435
Wenyng with hem they wolde abide

5388 forfare: perish

In every perell and myschaunce,
Withoute chaunge or variaunce,
Bothe of catell and of good;
And also for to spende her blood,   5440
And all her membris for to spille,
Oonly to fulfille her wille.
They maken it hool in many wise,
And hoten hem her full servise,
How sore that it do hem smerte,   5445
Into her naked sherte!
Herte and all so hool they yive,
For the tyme that they may lyve,
So that with her flaterie
They maken foolis glorifie   5450
Of her wordis spekyng,
And han therof a rejoysyng,
And trowe hem as the Evangile;
And it is all falsheede and gile,
As they shal aftirward se,   5455
Whanne they arn falle in poverte
And ben of good and catell bare;
Thanne shulde they sen who freendis ware.
For of an hundred, certeynly,
Nor of a thousand full scarsly,   5460
Ne shal they fynde unnethis oon,
Whanne poverte is comen upon.
For this Fortune that I of telle,
With men whanne hir lust to dwelle,
Makith hem to leese her conisaunce,   5465
And norishith hem in ignoraunce.

"But froward Fortune and pervers,
Whanne high estatis she doth revers,
And maketh hem to tumble doun
Of hir whel, with sodeyn tourn,   5470
And from her richesse doth hem fle,
And plongeth hem in poverte,
As a stepmoder envyous,
And leieth a plastre dolorous
Unto her hertis, wounded egre,   5475
Which is not tempred with vynegre,
But with poverte and indigence,
For to shewe, by experience,
That she is Fortune verely,
In whom no man shulde affy,   5480
Nor in hir yeftis have fiaunce,
She is so full of variaunce —
Thus kan she maken high and lowe,
Whanne they from richesse arn throwe,

Fully to knowen, without were,   5485
Freend of affect and freend of chere,
And which in love weren trewe and stable,
And whiche also weren variable,
After Fortune, her goddesse,
In poverte outher in richesse.   5490
For all she yeveth here, out of drede,
Unhap bereveth it in dede;
For Infortune lat not oon
Of freendis, whanne Fortune is gon;
I mene tho freendis that wole fle   5495
Anoon as entreth poverte.
And yit they wole not leve hem so,
But in ech place where they go
They calle hem 'wrecche,' scorne, and blame,
And of her myshappe hem diffame;   5500
And namely siche as in richesse
Pretendith moost of stablenesse,
Whanne that they sawe hym sett on lofte,
And weren of hym socoured ofte,
And most yholpe in all her neede.   5505
But now they take no maner heede,
But seyn in voice of flaterie,
That now apperith her folye,
Overall where so they fare,
And synge, 'Go, farewel, feldefare.'   5510
All suche freendis I beshrewe,
For of trewe ther be to fewe.
But sothfast freendis, what so bitide,
In every fortune wolen abide;
Thei han her hertis in such noblesse   5515
That they nyl love for no richesse,
Nor for that Fortune may hem sende
Thei wolen hem socoure and defende,
And chaunge for softe ne for sore;
For who is freend, loveth evermore.   5520
Though men drawe swerd his freend to slo,
He may not hewe her love a-two.
But, in cas that I shall sey,
For pride and ire lese it he may,
And for reprove by nycete,   5525
And discovering of privite,
With tonge woundyng, as feloun,
Thurgh venemous detraccioun.
Frend in this cas wole gon his way,
For nothyng greve hym more ne may;   5530
And for nought ellis wole he fle,
If that he love in stabilite.
And certeyn, he is wel bigon,

5443 **maken it hool:** perform their all (?); see n.
5465 **conisaunce:** understanding, knowledge
5474 **plastre dolorous:** painful medicinal plaster
5475 **egre:** painfully
5480 **affy:** trust
5481 **fiaunce:** faith

5486 **Freend of affect:** friend by (true) inclination, true friend
5502 **Pretendith:** claims, professes to have
5504 **socoured:** saved
5507 **in voice of flaterie:** in the voice of a flatterer
5511 **beshrewe:** curse

Among a thousand that fyndith oon.
For ther may be no richesse 5535
Ageyns frendshipp, of worthynesse;
For it ne may so high atteigne
As may the valour, soth to seyne,
Of hym that loveth trew and well.
Frendshipp is more than is catell. 5540
For freend in court ay better is
Than peny in purs, certis;
And Fortune myshappyng
Whanne upon men she is fallyng,
Thurgh mysturnyng of hir chaunce, 5545
And casteth hem out of balaunce,
She makith, thurgh hir adversite,
Men full clerly for to se
Hym that is freend in existence
From hym that is by apparence. 5550
For Ynfortune makith anoon
To knowe thy freendis fro thy foon,
By experience, right as it is,
The which is more to preise, ywis,
Than is myche richesse and tresour. 5555
For more doth profit and valour
Poverte and such adversite
Bifore, than doth prosperite;
For the toon yeveth conysaunce,
And the tother ignoraunce. 5560
　"And thus in poverte is in dede
Trouthe declared fro falsheede;
For feynte frendis it wole declare,
And trewe also, what wey they fare.
For whanne he was in his richesse, 5565
These freendis, ful of doublenesse,
Offrid hym in many wise
Hert, and body, and servise.
What wolde he thanne ha yove to ha bought
To knowen openly her thought, 5570
That he now hath so clerly seen?
The lasse bigiled he shulde have ben,
And he hadde thanne perceyved it;
But richesse nold not late hym wit.
Wel more avauntage doth hym than, 5575
Sith that it makith hym a wise man,
The gret myscheef that he receyveth,
Than doth richesse that hym deceyveth.
Richesse riche ne makith nought
Hym that on tresour set his thought; 5580
For richesse stont in suffisaunce
And nothyng in habundaunce;
For suffisaunce all oonly
Makith men to lyve richely.

5559 conysaunce: understanding, knowledge
5563 feynte: feigned, false

For he that at mycches tweyne 5585
Ne valued [is] in his demeigne,
Lyveth more at ese, and more is riche,
Than doth he that is chiche,
And in his berne hath, soth to seyn,
An hundred mowis of whete greyn, 5590
Though he be chapman or marchaunt,
And have of gold many besaunt.
For in the getyng he hath such woo,
And in the kepyng drede also,
And set evermore his bisynesse 5595
For to encrese, and not to lesse,
For to aument and multiply.
And though on hepis it lye hym by,
Yit never shal make his richesse
Asseth unto his gredynesse. 5600
But the povre that recchith nought,
Save of his lyflode, in his thought,
Which that he getith with his travaile,
He dredith nought that it shall faile,
Though he have lytel worldis good, 5605
Mete, and drynke, and esy food,
Upon his travel and lyvyng,
And also suffisaunt clothyng.
Or if in syknesse that he falle,
And lothe mete and drynke withalle, 5610
Though he have noght his mete to by,
He shal bithynke hym hastily,
To putte hym oute of all daunger,
That he of mete hath no myster;
Or that he may with lytel ek 5615
Be founden, while that he is sek;
Or that men shull hym beren in hast,
To lyve til his syknesse be past,
To som maysondew biside;
He cast nought what shal hym bitide. 5620
He thenkith nought that evere he shall
Into ony syknesse fall.
　"And though it falle, as it may be,
That all betyme spare shall he
As mochel as shal to hym suffice, 5625
While he is sik in ony wise,
He doth [it] for that he wole be
Content with his poverte
Withoute nede of ony man.
So myche in litel have he can, 5630
He is apaied with his fortune;

5585 mycches: loaves of bread
5586 demeigne: domain
5588 chiche: miserly
5590 mowis: stacks
5592 besaunt: bezant, a Byzantine gold coin
5599–5600 make . . . Asseth: give satisfaction
5611 by: buy
5619 maysondew: hospital

And for he nyl be importune
Unto no wight, ne onerous,
Nor of her goodes coveitous,
Therfore he spareth, it may wel ben,   5635
His pore estat for to susten.
　　"Or if hym lust not for to spare,
But suffrith forth, as noght ne ware,
Atte last it hapneth, as it may,
Right unto his laste day,   5640
And taketh the world as it wolde be;
For evere in herte thenkith he,
The sonner that deth hym slo,
To paradys the sonner go
He shal, there for to lyve in blisse,   5645
Where that he shal noo good misse.
Thider he hopith God shal hym sende
Aftir his wrecchid lyves ende.
Pictigoras hymsilf reherses
In a book that 'The Golden Verses'   5650
Is clepid, for the nobilite
Of the honourable ditee: —
'Thanne, whanne thou gost thy body fro,
Fre in the eir thou shalt up go,
And leven al humanite,   5655
And purely lyve in deite.'
He is a fool, withouten were,
That trowith have his countre heere.
'In erthe is not oure countre,'
That may these clerkis seyn and see   5660
In Boece of Consolacioun,
Where it is maked mencioun
Of oure contre pleyn at the ye,
By teching of Philosophie,
Where lewid men myght lere wit,   5665
Whoso that wolde translaten it.
If he be sich that can wel lyve
Aftir his rente may hym yive,
And not desireth more to have
Than may fro poverte hym save,   5670
A wise man seide, as we may seen,
Is no man wrecched, but he it wen,
Be he kyng, knyght, or ribaud.
And many a ribaud is mery and baud,
That swynkith, and berith, bothe day and
　　nyght,   5675
Many a burthen of gret myght,
The whiche doth hym lasse offense
For he suffrith in pacience.
They laugh and daunce, trippe and synge,
And ley not up for her lyvynge,   5680

But in the taverne all dispendith
The wynnyng that God hem sendith.
Thanne goth he, fardeles for to ber
With as good chere as he dide er.
To swynke and traveile he not feynith,   5685
For for to robben he disdeynith;
But right anoon aftir his swynk
He goth to taverne for to drynk.
All these ar riche in abundaunce
That can thus have suffisaunce   5690
Wel more than can an usurere,
As God wel knowith, withoute were.
For an usurer, so God me se,
Shal nevere for richesse riche be,
But evermore pore and indigent,   5695
Scarce and gredy in his entent.
　　"For soth it is, whom it displese,
Ther may no marchaunt lyve at ese;
His herte in sich a were is sett
That it quyk brenneth [more] to get,   5700
Ne never shal ynogh have geten,
Though he have gold in gerners yeten,
For to be nedy he dredith sore.
Wherfore to geten more and more
He set his herte and his desir;   5705
So hote he brennyth in the fir
Of coveitise, that makith hym wood
To purchace other mennes good.
He undirfongith a gret peyne,
That undirtakith to drynke up Seyne;   5710
For the more he drynkith, ay
The more he leveth, the soth to say.
Thus is thurst of fals getyng,
That last ever in coveityng,
And the angwisshe and distresse   5715
With the fir of gredynesse.
She fightith with hym ay, and stryveth,
That his herte asondre ryveth;
Such gredynesse hym assaylith
That whanne he most hath, most he failith.
Phisiciens and advocates   5721
Gon right by the same yates;
They selle her science for wynnyng,
And haunte her craft for gret getyng.
Her wynnyng is of such swetnesse   5725
That if a man falle in siknesse,
They are full glad for her encres;
For by her wille, withoute lees,
Everich man shulde be sek,
And though they die, they sette not a lek.   5730
After, whanne they the gold have take,

5639 **hapneth:** happens
5649 **Pictigoras:** Pythagoras
5673 **ribaud:** laborer, churl
5674 **baud:** jolly, lively

5683 **fardeles:** bundles
5696 **Scarce:** miserly
5710 **Seyne:** the river Seine

Full litel care for hem they make.
They wolde that fourty were seke at onys,
Ye, two hundred, in flesh and bonys,
And yit two thousand, as I gesse,   5735
For to encrecen her richesse.
They wole not worchen, in no wise,
But for lucre and coveitise.
For fysic gynneth first by *fy*,
The physicien also sothely;   5740
And sithen it goth fro *fy* to *sy*:
To truste on hem is foly;
For they nyl, in no maner gre,
Do right nought for charite.
    "Eke in the same secte ar sett   5745
All tho that prechen for to get
Worshipes, honour, and richesse.
Her hertis arn in gret distresse
That folk lyve not holily.
But aboven all, specialy,   5750
Sich as prechen [for] veynglorie,
And toward God have no memorie,
But forth as ypocrites trace,
And to her soules deth purchace,
And outward shewen holynesse,   5755
Though they be full of cursidnesse.
Not liche to the apostles twelve,
They deceyve other and hemselve.
Bigiled is the giler than,
For prechyng of a cursed man,   5760
Though [it] to other may profite,
Hymsilf it availeth not a myte;
For ofte good predicacioun
Cometh of evel entencioun.
To hym not vailith his preching,   5765
All helpe he other with his teching;
For where they good ensaumple take,
There is he with veynglorie shake.
    "But late us leven these prechoures,
And speke of hem that in her toures   5770
Hepe up hir gold, and faste shette,

And sore theron her herte sette.
They neither love God ne drede;
They kepe more than it is nede,
And in her bagges sore it bynde,   5775
Out of the sonne and of the wynde.
They putte up more than nede ware,
Whanne they seen pore folk forfare,
For hunger die, and for cold quake.
God can wel vengeaunce therof take!   5780
Three gret myscheves hem assailith,
And thus in gadring ay travaylith:
With myche peyne they wynne richesse,
And drede hem holdith in distresse
To kepe that they gadre faste;   5785
With sorwe they leve it at the laste.
With sorwe they bothe dye and lyve,
That unto richesse her hertis yive;
And in defaute of love it is,
As it shewith ful wel, iwys.   5790
For if thise gredy, the sothe to seyn,
Loveden and were loved ageyn,
And good love regned overall,
Such wikkidnesse ne shulde fall;
But he shulde yeve that most good had   5795
To hem that weren in nede bistad,
And lyve withoute false usure,
For charite full clene and pure.
If they hem yeve to goodnesse,
Defendyng hem from ydelnesse,   5800
In all this world thanne pore noon
We shulde fynde, I trowe, not oon.
But chaunged is this world unstable,
For love is overall vendable.
We se that no man loveth now,   5805
But for wynnyng and for prow;
And love is thralled in servage,
Whanne it is sold for avauntage.
Yit wommen wole her bodyes selle;
Suche soules goth to the devel of helle!"   5810

Fragment C

Whanne Love hadde told hem his entente,
The baronage to councel wente.
In many sentences they fille,
And dyversely they seide hir wille;
But aftir discord they accorded,   5815
And her accord to Love recorded.
"Sir," seiden they, "we ben at on,
Bi evene accord of everichon,

Out-take Richesse al oonly,
That sworen hath ful hauteynly,   5820
That she the castel nyl not assaile,
Ne smyte a strok in this bataile,
With darte, ne mace, spere, ne knyf,
For man that spekith or berith the lyf,

5739 *fy*: trusting
5741 *sy*: sighing

5778 **forfare**: perish
5783 **myche**: much

5820 **hauteynly**: arrogantly (or loudly)

And blameth youre emprise, iwys,   5825
And from oure hoost departed is,
Atte leste wey, as in this plyt,
So hath she this man in dispit.
For she seith he ne loved hir never,
And therfore she wole hate hym evere.   5830
For he wole gadre no tresor,
He hath hir wrath for evermor.
He agylte hir never in other caas,
Lo, heere all hoolly his trespas!
She seith wel that this other day   5835
He axide hir leve to gon the way
That is clepid To-Moche-Yevyng,
And spak full faire in his praiyng;
But whanne he praiede hir, pore was he,
Therfore she warned hym the entre.   5840
Ne yit is he not thryven so
That he hath geten a peny or two
That quytly is his owne in hold.
Thus hath Richesse us alle told,
And whanne Richesse us this recorded,   5845
Withouten hir we ben accorded.
     "And we fynde in oure accordaunce
That Fals-Semblant and Abstinaunce,
With all the folk of her bataille,
Shull at the hyndre gate assayle,   5850
That Wikkid-Tunge hath in kepyng,
With his Normans full of janglyng.
And with hem Curtesie and Largesse,
That shull shewe her hardynesse
To the olde wyf that kepte so harde   5855
Fair-Welcomyng withynne her warde.
Thanne shal Delit and Wel-Heelynge
Fonde Shame adown to brynge;
With all her oost, erly and late,
They shull assailen that ilke gate.   5860
Agaynes Drede shall Hardynesse
Assayle, and also Sikernesse,
With all the folk of her ledyng,
That never wist what was fleyng.
     "Fraunchise shall fight, and eke Pite,   5865
With Daunger, full of cruelte.
Thus is youre hoost ordeyned wel.
Doun shall the castell every del,
If everich do his entent,
So that Venus be present,   5870
Youre modir, full of vasselage,
That can ynough of such usage.
Withouten hir may no wight spede

This werk, neithir for word ne deede;
Therfore is good ye for hir sende,   5875
For thurgh hir may this werk amende."
     "Lordynges, my modir, the goddesse,
That is my lady and my maistresse,
Nis not [at] all at my willyng,
Ne doth not all my desiryng.   5880
Yit can she som tyme don labour,
Whanne that hir lust, in my socour,
Al my nedes for to acheve,
But now I thenke hir not to greve.
My modir is she, and of childhede   5885
I bothe worshipe hir and eke drede;
For who that dredith sire ne dame,
Shal it abye in body or name.
And, natheles, yit kunne we
Sende aftir hir, if nede be;   5890
And were she nygh, she comen wolde;
I trowe that nothyng myght hir holde.
     "Mi modir is of gret prowesse;
She hath tan many a forteresse,
That cost hath many a pound, er this,   5895
There I nas not present, ywis.
And yit men seide it was my dede;
But I com never in that stede,
Ne me ne likith, so mote I the,
That such toures ben take withoute me.   5900
For-why me thenkith that, in no wise,
It may ben clepid but marchandise.
     "Go bye a courser, blak or whit,
And pay therfore; than art thou quyt.
The marchaunt owith thee right nought,   5905
Ne thou hym, whanne thou it bought.
I wole not sellyng clepe yevyng,
For sellyng axeth no guerdonyng:
Here lith no thank ne no merit;
That oon goth from that other al quyt.   5910
But this sellyng is not semblable;
For whanne his hors is in the stable,
He may it selle ageyn, parde,
And wynnen on it, such hap may be;
All may the man not leese, iwys,   5915
For at the leest the skyn is his.
Or ellis, if it so bitide
That he wole kepe his hors to ride,
Yit is he lord ay of his hors.
But thilke chaffare is wel wors,   5920
There Venus entremetith ought.
For whoso such chaffare hath bought,
He shal not worchen so wisely
That he ne shal leese al outerly

5833 **agylte:** offended
5843 **quytly:** freely
5857 **Wel-Heelynge:** Well-Concealing, Secrecy
5858 **Fonde:** try, attempt
5871 **vasselage:** prowess

5894 **tan:** taken

Bothe his money and his chaffare;   5925
But the seller of the ware
The prys and profit have shall.
Certeyn, the bier shal leese all.
For he ne can so dere it bye
To have lordship and full maistrie,   5930
Ne have power to make lettyng,
Neithir for yift ne for prechyng,
That of his chaffare, maugre his,
Another shal have as moche, iwis,
If he wol yeve as myche as he,   5935
Of what contrey so that he be —
Or for right nought, so happe may,
If he can flater hir to hir pay.
Ben thanne siche marchauntz wise?
No, but fooles in every wise,   5940
Whanne they bye sich thyng wilfully,
There as they leese her good fully.
But natheles, this dar I saye,
My modir is not wont to paye,
For she is neither so fool ne nyce   5945
To entremete hir of sich vice.
But truste wel, he shal pay all,
That repent of his bargeyn shall,
Whanne poverte putte hym in distresse,
All were he scoler to Richesse,   5950
That is for me in gret yernyng,
Whanne she assentith to my willyng.
  "But [by] my modir, seint Venus,
And by hir fader Saturnus,
That hir engendride by his lyf —   5955
But not upon his weddid wyf —
Yit wole I more unto you swer,
To make this thyng the seurere —
Now by that feith and that leaute
That I owe to all my britheren fre,   5960
Of which ther nys wight undir heven
That kan her fadris names neven,
So dyverse and so many ther be
That with my modir have be prive!
Yit wolde I swere, for sikirnesse,   5965
The pol of helle to my witnesse —
Now drynke I not this yeer clarre,
If that I lye or forsworn be!
(For of the goddes the usage is
That whoso hym forswereth amys   5970
Shal that yeer drynke no clarre.)
Now have I sworn ynough, pardee,
If I forswere me, thanne am I lorn,
But I wole never be forsworn.

Syth Richesse hath me failed heere,   5975
She shal abye that trespas ful dere,
Atte leeste wey, but [she] hir arme
With swerd, or sparth, or gysarme.
For certis, sith she loveth not me,
Fro thilke tyme that she may se   5980
The castell and the tour toshake,
In sory tyme she shal awake.
If I may grype a riche man,
I shal so pulle hym, if I can,
That he shal in a fewe stoundes   5985
Lese all his markis and his poundis.
I shal hym make his pens outslynge,
But they in his gerner sprynge.
Oure maydens shal eke pluk hym so
That hym shal neden fetheres mo,   5990
And make hym selle his lond to spende,
But he the bet kunne hym defende.
  "Pore men han maad her lord of me;
Although they not so myghty be
That they may fede me in delit,   5995
I wol not have hem in despit.
No good man hateth hem, as I gesse,
For chynche and feloun is Richesse,
That so can chase hem and dispise,
And hem defoule in sondry wise.   6000
They loven full bet, so God me spede,
Than doth the riche, chynchy gnede,
And ben, in good feith, more stable
And trewer and more serviable;
And therfore it suffisith me   6005
Her goode herte and her leaute.
They han on me set all her thought,
And therfore I forgete hem nought.
I wol hem bringe in gret noblesse,
If that I were god of richesse,   6010
As I am god of love sothly,
Sich routhe upon her pleynt have I.
Therfore I must his socour be,
That peyneth hym to serven me,
For if he deide for love of this,   6015
Thanne semeth in me no love ther is."
  "Sir," seide they, "soth is every deel
That ye reherce, and we wote wel
Thilk oth to holde is resonable;
For it is good and covenable   6020
That ye on riche men han sworn.
For, sir, this wote we wel biforn:

5966 pol of helle: the river Styx
5967 clarre: spiced and sweetened wine

5978 sparth: battle-axe gysarme: long-shafted battle-axe, halberd
5984 pulle: pluck
5987 outslynge: cast out
5988 sprynge: spring up, grow
5998 chynche: miserly
6002 chynchy: miserly gnede: stingy person

If riche men don you homage,
That is as fooles don outrage;
But ye shull not forsworn be, 6025
Ne lette therfore to drynke clarre,
Or pyment makid fresh and newe.
Ladies shull hem such pepir brewe,
If that they fall into her laas,
That they for woo mowe seyn 'allas!' 6030
Ladyes shullen evere so curteis be
That they shal quyte youre oth all free.
Ne sekith never othir vicaire,
For they shal speke with hem so faire
That ye shal holde you paied full wel, 6035
Though ye you medle never a del.
Late ladies worche with her thyngis,
They shal hem telle so fele tidynges,
And moeve hem eke so many requestis
Bi flateri, that not honest is, 6040
And therto yeve hem such thankynges,
What with kissyng and with talkynges,
That, certis, if they trowed be,
Shal never leve hem lond ne fee
That it nyl as the moeble fare, 6045
Of which they first delyverid are.
Now may ye telle us all youre wille,
And we youre heestes shal fulfille.
   "But Fals-Semblant dar not, for drede
Of you, sir, medle hym of this dede, 6050
For he seith that ye ben his foo;
He not if ye wole worche hym woo.
Wherfore we pray you alle, beau sire,
That ye forgyve hym now your ire,
And that he may dwelle, as your man, 6055
With Abstinence, his dere lemman;
This oure accord and oure wille now."
   "Parfay," seide Love, "I graunte it yow.
I wole wel holde hym for my man;
Now late hym come" — and he forth ran. 6060
"Fals-Semblant," quod Love, "in this wise
I take thee heere to my servise,
That thou oure freendis helpe alway,
And hyndre hem neithir nyght ne day,
But do thy myght hem to releve, 6065
And eke oure enemyes that thou greve.
Thyn be this myght, I graunte it thee,
My kyng of harlotes shalt thou be;
We wole that thou have such honour.
Certeyn, thou art a fals traitour, 6070
And eke a theef; sith thou were born,

A thousand tyme thou art forsworn.
But natheles, in oure heryng,
To putte oure folk out of doutyng,
I bidde thee teche hem, wostow how, 6075
Bi som general signe now,
In what place thou shalt founden be,
If that men had myster of thee;
And how men shal thee best espye,
For thee to knowe is gret maistrie. 6080
Telle in what place is thyn hauntyng."
   "Sir, I have fele dyvers wonyng,
That I kepe not rehersed be,
So that ye wolde respiten me.
For if that I telle you the sothe, 6085
I may have harm and shame bothe.
If that my felowes wisten it,
My talis shulden me be quytt;
For certeyn, they wolde hate me,
If ever I knewe her cruelte. 6090
For they wolde overall holde hem stille
Of trouthe that is ageyne her wille;
Suche tales kepen they not here.
I myght eftsoone bye it full deere,
If I seide of hem ony thing 6095
That ought displesith to her heryng.
For what word that hem prikke or biteth,
In that word noon of hem deliteth,
Al were it gospel, the evangile,
That wolde reprove hem of her gile, 6100
For they are cruel and hauteyn.
And this thyng wot I well, certeyn,
If I speke ought to peire her loos,
Your court shal not so well be cloos
That they ne shall wite it atte last. 6105
Of good men am I nought agast,
For they wole taken on hem nothyng,
Whanne that they knowe al my menyng;
But he that wole it on hym take,
He wole hymsilf suspecious make, 6110
That he his lyf let covertly
In Gile and in Ipocrisy
That me engendred and yaf fostryng."
   "They made a full good engendryng,"
Quod Love, "for whoso sothly telle, 6115
They engendred the devel of helle!
But nedely, howsoevere it be,"
Quod Love, "I wole and charge thee
To telle anoon thy wonyng places,
Heryng ech wight that in this place is; 6120

6027 **pyment:** spiced, sweetened wine
6028 **brewe:** make, contrive
6044 **leve hem:** remain to them
6045 **moeble:** personal property
6068 **kyng of harlotes:** king of rascals; see n.

6103 **peire her loos:** injure her reputation
6104 **cloos:** discreet
6111 **let** = *ledeth*, leads **covertly:** secretly
6117 **nedely:** necessarily
6120 **Heryng:** in the hearing of

And what lyf that thou lyvest also.
Hide it no lenger now; wherto?
Thou most discovere all thi wurchyng,
How thou servest, and of what thyng,
Though that thou shuldist for thi soth-sawe
Ben al tobeten and todrawe —   6126
And yit art thou not wont, pardee.
But natheles, though thou beten be,
Thou shalt not be the first that so
Hath for sothsawe suffred woo."   6130
"Sir, sith that it may liken you,
Though that I shulde be slayn right now,
I shal don youre comaundement,
For therto have I gret talent."

Withouten wordis mo, right than,   6135
Fals-Semblant his sermon bigan,
And seide hem thus in audience:
"Barouns, take heede of my sentence!
That wight that list to have knowing
Of Fals-Semblant, full of flatering,   6140
He must in worldly folk hym seke,
And, certes, in the cloistres eke.
I wone nowhere but in hem tweye,
But not lyk even, soth to seye.
Shortly, I wole herberwe me   6145
There I hope best to hulstred be,
And certeynly, sikerest hidyng
Is undirnethe humblest clothing.
Religiouse folk ben full covert;
Seculer folk ben more appert.   6150
But natheles, I wole not blame
Religious folk, ne hem diffame,
In what habit that ever they go.
Religioun umble and trewe also,
Wole I not blame ne dispise;   6155
But I nyl love it, in no wise.
I mene of fals religious,
That stoute ben and malicious,
That wolen in an abit goo,
And setten not her herte therto.   6160

"Religious folk ben al pitous;
Thou shalt not seen oon dispitous.
They loven no pride ne no strif,
But humbly they wole lede her lyf.
With swich folk wole I never be,   6165
And if I dwelle, I feyne me.

I may wel in her abit go;
But me were lever my nekke a-two,
Than lete a purpos that I take,
What covenaunt that ever I make.   6170
I dwelle with hem that proude be,
And full of wiles and subtilte,
That worship of this world coveiten,
And grete nedes kunnen espleiten,
And gon and gadren gret pitaunces,   6175
And purchace hem the acqueyntaunces
Of men that myghty lyf may leden;
And feyne hem pore, and hemsilf feden
With gode morcels delicious,
And drinken good wyn precious,   6180
And preche us povert and distresse,
And fisshen hemsilf gret richesse
With wily nettis that they caste.
It wole come foule out at the laste.
They ben fro clene religioun went;   6185
They make the world an argument
That [hath] a foul conclusioun.
'I have a robe of religioun,
Thanne am I all religious.'
This argument is all roignous;   6190
It is not worth a croked brere.
Abit ne makith neithir monk ne frere,
But clene lyf and devocioun
Makith gode men of religioun.
Natheles, ther kan noon answere,   6195
How high that evere his heed he shere,
With resoun whetted never so kene,
That Gile in braunches kut thrittene;
Ther can no wight distincte it so,
That he dar sey a word therto.   6200

"But what herberwe that ever I take,
Or what semblant that evere I make,
I mene but gile, and folowe that;
For right no mo than Gibbe oure cat,
· · · · · · · · · ·   6205
Ne entende I but to bigilyng.
Ne no wight may by my clothing
Wite with what folk is my dwellyng,
Ne by my wordis yit, parde,
So softe and so plesaunt they be.   6210
Bihold the dedis that I do;
But thou be blynd, thou oughtest so;
For, varie her wordis fro her deede,
They thenke on gile, withoute dreede,

6126 todrawe: pulled to pieces
6127 wont: accustomed (to telling the truth)
6130 sothsawe: speaking the truth
6134 talent: desire
6141 in worldly folk: among the laity
6144 lyk even: equally
6146 hulstred: hidden
6150 appert: open (not secretive)
6154 umble: humble
6158 stoute: proud

6174 espleiten: perform, carry out
6175 pitaunces: gifts, alms
6190 roignous: scurvy, rotten
6198 braunches . . . thrittene: thirteen types of sophistical reasoning; see n.
6205 Not in MS. Thynne has: *That awayteth mys and rattes to kyllen.*

What maner clothing that they were,   6215
Or what estat that evere they bere,
Lered or lewde, lord or lady,
Knyght, squyer, burgeis, or bayly."
    Right thus while Fals-Semblant sermoneth,
Eftsones Love hym aresoneth,   6220
And brak his tale in his spekyng,
As though he had hym told lesyng,
And seide, "What, devel, is that I here?
What folk hast thou us nempned heere?
May men fynde religioun   6225
In worldly habitacioun?"
    "Ye, sir; it folowith not that they
Shulde lede a wikked lyf, parfey,
Ne not therfore her soules leese
That hem to worldly clothes chese;   6230
For, certis, it were gret pitee.
Men may in seculer clothes see
Florishen hooly religioun.
Full many a seynt in feeld and toun,
With many a virgine glorious,   6235
Devout, and full religious,
Han deied, that comun cloth ay beeren,
Yit seyntes nevere the lesse they weren.
I cowde reken you many a ten;
Ye, wel nygh [al] these hooly wymmen   6240
That men in chirchis herie and seke,
Bothe maydens and these wyves eke
That baren full many a fair child heere,
Wered alwey clothis seculere,
And in the same dieden they   6245
That seyntes weren, and ben alwey.
The eleven thousand maydens deere
That beren in heven hir ciergis clere,
Of whiche men rede in chirche and synge,
Were take in seculer clothinge   6250
Whanne they resseyved martirdom,
And wonnen hevene unto her hom.
Good herte makith the goode thought;
The clothing yeveth ne reveth nought.
The goode thought and the worching,   6255
That makith the religioun flowryng,
Ther lyth the good religioun,
Aftir the right entencioun.
    "Whoso took a wethers skyn,
And wrapped a gredy wolf theryn,   6260
For he shulde go with lambis whyte,

Wenest thou not he wolde hem bite?
Yis, neverthelasse, as he were wood,
He wolde hem wery and drinke the blood,
And wel the rather hem disceyve;   6265
For, sith they cowde not perceyve
His treget and his cruelte,
They wolde hym folowe, al wolde he fle.
    "If ther be wolves of sich hewe
Amonges these apostlis newe,   6270
Thou hooly chirche, thou maist be wailed!
Sith that thy citee is assayled
Thourgh knyghtis of thyn owne table,
God wot thi lordship is doutable!
If thei enforce [hem] it to wynne   6275
That shulde defende it fro withynne,
Who myght defense ayens hem make?
Withoute strok it mot be take
Of trepeget or mangonel,
Without displaiyng of pensel.   6280
And if God nyl don it socour,
But lat [hem] renne in this colour,
Thou most thyn heestis laten be.
Thanne is ther nought but yelde thee,
Or yeve hem tribut, doutelees,   6285
And holde it of hem to have pees,
But gretter harm bitide thee,
That they al maister of it be.
Wel konne they scorne thee withal;
By day stuffen they the wall,   6290
And al the nyght they mynen there.
Nay, thou planten most elleswhere
Thyn ympes, if thou wolt fruyt have;
Abid not there thisilf to save.
    "But now pees! Heere I turne ageyn.   6295
I wole nomore of this thing seyn,
If I may passen me herby;
I myghte maken you wery.
But I wole heten you alway
To helpe youre freendis what I may,   6300
So they wollen my company;
For they be shent al outerly,
But if so falle that I be
Ofte with hem, and they with me.
And eke my lemman mote they serve,   6305
Or they shull not my love deserve.
Forsothe, I am a fals traitour;

6264 **wery:** worry, strangle
6267 **treget:** trickery
6275 **enforce:** try
6279 **trepeget:** trebuchet, catapult for hurling large stones
mangonel: catapult for hurling stones and other missiles
6280 **displaiyng of pensel:** showing the banner, giving the signal
to attack
6290 **stuffen:** fortify
6291 **mynen:** undermine
6293 **ympes:** seedlings

6218 **bayly:** steward of a lord's manor
6220 **aresoneth:** reasons with
6226 In secular dwellings
6241 **herie:** praise
6247 **eleven thousand maydens:** St. Ursula and the eleven
thousand virgins martyred in the fifth century
6248 **ciergis:** wax candles
6259 **wethers:** sheep's

God jugged me for a theef trichour.
Forsworn I am, but wel nygh non
Wot of my gile, til it be don.   6310
    "Thourgh me hath many oon deth resseyved,
That my treget nevere aperceyved;
And yit resseyveth, and shal resseyve,
That my falsnesse shal nevere aperceyve.
But whoso doth, if he wis be,   6315
Hym is right good be war of me,
But so sligh is the deceyvyng
. . . .
For Protheus, that cowde hym chaunge
In every shap, homly and straunge,   6320
Cowde nevere sich gile ne tresoun
As I; for I com never in toun
There as I myghte knowen be,
Though men me bothe myght here and see.
Full wel I can my clothis chaunge,   6325
Take oon, and make another straunge.
Now am I knyght, now chasteleyn,
Now prelat, and now chapeleyn,
Now prest, now clerk, and now forster;
Now am I maister, now scoler,   6330
Now monk, now chanoun, now baily;
Whatever myster man am I.
Now am I prince, now am I page,
And kan by herte every langage.
Som tyme am I hor and old;   6335
Now am I yong, stout, and bold;
Now am I Robert, now Robyn,
Now Frere Menour, now Jacobyn;
And with me folwith my loteby,
To don me solas and company,   6340
That hight Dame Abstinence-Streyned,
In many a queynte array feyned.
Ryght as it cometh to hir lykyng,
I fulfille al hir desiryng.
Somtyme a wommans cloth take I;   6345
Now am I a mayde, now lady.
Somtyme I am religious;
Now lyk an anker in an hous.
Somtyme am I prioresse,
And now a nonne, and now abbesse;   6350
And go thurgh alle regiouns,
Sekyng alle religiouns.

But to what ordre that I am sworn,
I take the strawe, and lete the corn.
To gyle folk I enhabit;   6355
I axe nomore but her abit.
What wole ye more in every wise?
Right as me lyst, I me disgise.
Wel can I wre me undir wede;
Unlyk is my word to my dede.   6360
[I] make into my trappis falle,
Thurgh my pryveleges, alle
That ben in Cristendom alyve.
I may assoile and I may shryve,
That no prelat may lette me,   6365
All folk, where evere thei founde be.
I not no prelat may don so,
But it the pope be, and no mo,
That made thilk establisshing.
Now is not this a propre thing?   6370
But, were my sleightis aperceyved
. . . .
As I was wont, and wostow why?
For I dide hem a tregetry.
But therof yeve I lytel tale;   6375
I have the silver and the male.
So have I prechid, and eke shriven,
So have I take, so have me yiven,
Thurgh her foly, husbonde and wyf,
That I lede right a joly lyf,   6380
Thurgh symplesse of the prelacye —
They knowe not al my tregettrie.
    "But forasmoche as man and wyf
Shulde shewe her paroch-prest her lyf,
Onys a yeer, as seith the book,   6385
Er ony wight his housel took,
Thanne have I pryvylegis large,
That may of myche thing discharge.
For he may seie right thus, parde:
'Sir preest, in shrift I telle it thee,   6390
That he to whom that I am shryven
Hath me assoiled, and me yiven
Penaunce, sothly, for my synne,
Which that I fond me gilty ynne;
Ne I ne have nevere entencioun   6395
To make double confessioun,
Ne reherce eft my shrift to thee.
O shrift is right ynough to me.
This oughte thee suffice wel;

6318 Not in MS. Eds. read: *That to hard is the aperceyving.*
6319 **Protheus:** god of the sea
6329 **forster:** gamekeeper
6332 **myster man:** sort of man
6337 **Robert, Robyn:** gentleman, common man; see n.
6338 **Frere Menour, Jacobyn:** Franciscan, Dominican
6339 **loteby:** paramour
6341 **Abstinence-Streyned:** Constrained Abstinence
6348 **anker:** anchorite
6352 **alle religiouns:** all religious orders

6355 **enhabit:** dwell (with them)
6372 Not in MS. Eds. read: *Ne shulde I more ben receyved.*
6384 **shewe . . . her lyf:** make confession
6386 **housel:** communion
6389 **he:** the parishioner making his annual confession to his curate

Ne be not rebel never a del.   6400
For certis, though thou haddist it sworn,
I wot no prest ne prelat born,
That may to shrift eft me constreyne;
And if they don, I wole me pleyne,
For I wot where to pleyne wel.   6405
Thou shalt not streyne me a del,
Ne enforce me, ne not me trouble,
To make my confessioun double.
Ne I have non affeccioun
To have double absolucioun.   6410
The firste is right ynough to me;
This latter assoilyng quyte I thee.
I am unbounde — what maist thou fynde
More of my synnes me to unbynde?
For he, that myght hath in his hond,   6415
Of all my synnes me unbond.
And if thou wolt me thus constreyne
That me mot nedis on thee pleyne,
There shall no jugge imperial,
Ne bisshop, ne official,   6420
Don jugement on me; for I
Shal gon and pleyne me openly
Unto my shrifte-fadir newe
(That hight not Frere Wolf untrewe!),
And he shal cheveys hym for me,   6425
For I trowe he can hampre thee.
But, Lord, he wolde be wrooth withalle,
If men hym wolde Frere Wolf calle!
For he wolde have no pacience,
But don al cruel vengeaunce.   6430
He wolde his myght don at the leeste,
Nothing spare for Goddis heeste.
And, God so wys be my socour,
But thou yeve me my Savyour
At Ester, whanne it likith me,   6435
Withoute presyng more on thee,
I wole forth, and to hym gon,
And he shal housel me anoon.
For I am out of thi grucching;
I kepe not dele with thee nothing.'   6440
   "Thus may he shryve hym, that forsaketh
His paroch-prest, and to me taketh.
And if the prest wole hym refuse,
I am full redy hym to accuse,
And hym punysshe and hampre so   6445
That he his chirche shal forgo.
   "But whoso hath in his felyng
The consequence of such shryvyng,

Shal sen that prest may never have myght
To knowe the conscience aright   6450
Of hym that is undir his cure.
And this ageyns holy scripture,
That biddith every heerde honest
Have verry knowing of his beest.
But pore folk that gone by strete,   6455
That have no gold, ne sommes grete,
Hem wolde I lete to her prelates,
Or lete her prestis knowe her states,
For to me right nought yeve they.
And why? It is for they ne may.   6460
They ben so bare, I take no kep,
But I wole have the fatte sheep;
Lat parish prestis have the lene.
I yeve not of her harm a bene!
And if that prelates grucchen it,   6465
That oughten wroth be in her wit
To leese her fatte beestes so,
I shal yeve hem a strok or two,
That they shal leesen with force,
Ye, bothe her mytre and her croce.   6470
Thus jape I hem, and have do longe,
My pryveleges ben so stronge."
   Fals-Semblant wolde have stynted heere,
But Love ne made hym no such cheere
That he was wery of his sawe;   6475
But for to make hym glad and fawe,
He seide, "Telle on more specialy
Hou that thou servest untrewly.
Telle forth, and shame thee never a del;
For, as thyn abit shewith wel,   6480
Thou semest an hooly heremyte."
   "Soth is, but I am an ypocrite."
"Thou gost and prechest poverte."
"Ye, sir, but richesse hath pouste."
"Thou prechest abstinence also."   6485
"Sir, I wole fillen, so mote I go,
My paunche of good mete and wyn,
As shulde a maister of dyvyn;
For how that I me pover feyne,
Yit alle pore folk I disdeyne.   6490
   "I love bettir th'acqueyntaunce,
Ten tyme, of the kyng of Fraunce
Than of a pore man of mylde mod,
Though that his soule be also god.
For whanne I see beggers quakyng,   6495
Naked on myxnes al stynkyng,

6425 **cheveys hym:** sustain himself
6434 **Savyour:** communion
6438 **housel:** give communion
6440 **kepe not dele:** care not to deal

6452 **this** = *this is*
6470 **croce:** crozier
6476 **fawe:** pleased
6484 **pouste:** power
6496 **myxnes:** dung hills

For hungre crie, and eke for care,
I entremete not of her fare.
They ben so pore and ful of pyne,
They myght not oonys yeve me dyne,   6500
For they have nothing but her lyf.
What shulde he yeve that likketh his knyf?
It is but foly to entremete,
To seke in houndes nest fat mete.
Lete bere hem to the spitel anoon,   6505
But, for me, comfort gete they noon.
But a riche sik usurer
Wolde I visite and drawe ner;
Hym wole I comforte and rehete,
For I hope of his gold to gete.   6510
And if that wikkid deth hym have,
I wole go with hym to his grave.
And if ther ony reprove me,
Why that I lete the pore be,
Wostow how I mot ascape?   6515
I sey, and swere hym ful rape,
That riche men han more tecches
Of synne than han pore wrecches,
And han of counsel more mister,
And therfore I wole drawe hem ner.   6520
But as gret hurt, it may so be,
Hath a soule in right gret poverte
As soule in gret richesse, forsothe,
Al be it that they hurten bothe.
For richesse and mendicitees   6525
Ben clepid two extremytees;
The mene is cleped suffisaunce;
Ther lyth of vertu the aboundaunce.
For Salamon, full wel I wot,
In his Parablis us wrot,   6530
As it is knowe to many a wight,
In his thrittene chapitre right,
'God thou me kepe, for thi pouste,
Fro richesse and mendicite;
For if a riche man hym dresse   6535
To thenke to myche on richesse,
His herte on that so fer is set
That he his creatour foryet;
And hym that begging wole ay greve,
How shulde I bi his word hym leve?   6540
Unnethe that he nys a mycher
Forsworn, or ellis God is lyer.'
Thus seith Salamones sawes.
Ne we fynde writen in no lawis,

And namely in oure Cristen lay,   6545
(Whoso seith 'ye,' I dar sey 'nay')
That Crist, ne his apostlis dere,
While that they walkide in erthe heere,
Were never seen her bred beggyng,
For they nolden beggen for nothing.   6550
And right thus was men wont to teche,
And in this wise wolde it preche
The maistres of divinite
Somtyme in Parys the citee.
    "And if men wolde ther-geyn appose   6555
The nakid text, and lete the glose,
It myghte soone assoiled be;
For men may wel the sothe see,
That, parde, they myght aske a thing
Pleynly forth, without begging.   6560
For they weren Goddis herdis deere,
And cure of soules hadden heere,
They nolde nothing begge her fode;
For aftir Crist was don on rode,
With ther propre hondis they wrought,   6565
And with travel, and ellis nought,
They wonnen all her sustenaunce,
And lyveden forth in her penaunce,
And the remenaunt yave awey
To other pore folkis alwey.   6570
They neither bilden tour ne halle,
But ley in houses smale withalle.
A myghty man, that can and may,
Shulde with his hond and body alway
Wynne hym his fode in laboring,   6575
If he ne have rent or sich a thing,
Although he be religious,
And God to serven curious.
Thus mot he don, or do trespas,
But if it be in certeyn cas,   6580
That I can reherce, if myster be,
Right wel, whanne the tyme I se.
    "Sek the book of Seynt Austyn,
Be it in papir or perchemyn,
There as he writ of these worchynges,   6585
Thou shalt seen that noon excusynges
A parfit man ne shulde seke
Bi wordis ne bi dedis eke,
Although he be religious,
And God to serven curious,   6590
That he ne shal, so mote I go,
With propre hondis and body also,
Gete his fode in laboryng,
If he ne have proprete of thing.

6498 **entremete:** meddle
6500 **dyne:** (something) to eat
6505 **spitel:** hospital
6509 **rehete:** cheer, console
6516 **ful rape:** hastily
6541 **mycher:** thief

6556 **nakid text:** literal text **glose:** interpretation
6557 **assoiled:** disproven
6583 **Austyn:** Augustine

Yit shulde he selle all his substaunce,   6595
And with his swynk have sustenaunce,
If he be parfit in bounte.
Thus han tho bookes told me.
For he that wole gon ydilly,
And usith it ay besily   6600
To haunten other mennes table,
He is a trechour, ful of fable;
Ne he ne may, by god resoun,
Excuse hym by his orisoun.
For men bihoveth, in som gise,   6605
Somtyme leven Goddis servise
To gon and purchasen her nede.
Men mote eten, that is no drede,
And slepe, and eke do other thing;
So longe may they leve praiyng.   6610
So may they eke her praier blynne,
While that they werke, her mete to wynne.
Seynt Austyn wole therto accorde,
In thilke book that I recorde.
Justinian eke, that made lawes,   6615
Hath thus forboden, by olde dawes:
'No man, up peyne to be ded,
Mighty of body, to begge his bred,
If he may swynke it for to gete;
Men shulde hym rather mayme or bete,   6620
Or don of hym apert justice,
Than suffren hym in such malice.'
They don not wel, so mote I go,
That taken such almesse so,
But if they have som pryvelege,   6625
That of the peyne hem wole allege.
But how that is, can I not see,
But if the prince disseyved be;
Ne I ne wene not, sikerly,
That they may have it rightfully.   6630
But I wole not determine
Of prynces power, ne defyne,
Ne by my word comprende, iwys,
If it so fer may strecche in this.
I wole not entremete a del;   6635
But I trowe that the book seith wel,
Who that takith almessis that be
Dewe to folk that men may se
Lame, feble, wery, and bare,
Pore, or in such maner care —   6640
That konne wynne hem never mo,
For they have no power therto —
He etith his owne dampnyng,
But if he lye, that made al thing.

And if ye such a truaunt fynde,   6645
Chastise hym wel, if ye be kynde.
But they wolde hate you, percas,
And, if ye fillen in her laas,
They wolde eftsoonys do you scathe,
If that they myghte, late or rathe;   6650
For they be not full pacient
That han the world thus foule blent.
And witeth wel that [ther] God bad
The good-man selle al that he had,
And folowe hym, and to pore it yive,   6655
He wolde not therfore that he lyve
To serven hym in mendience,
For it was nevere his sentence;
But he bad wirken whanne that neede is,
And folwe hym in goode dedis.   6660
Seynt Poul, that loved al hooly chirche,
He bad th'appostles for to wirche,
And wynnen her lyflode in that wise,
And hem defended truandise,
And seide, 'Wirketh with youre honden.'   6665
Thus shulde the thing be undirstonden:
He nolde, iwys, have bidde hem begging,
Ne sellen gospel, ne prechyng,
Lest they berafte, with her askyng,
Folk of her catel or of her thing.   6670
For in this world is many a man
That yeveth his good, for he ne can
Werne it for shame; or ellis he
Wolde of the asker delyvered be,
And, for he hym encombrith so,   6675
He yeveth hym good to late hym go.
But it can hym nothyng profite;
They lese the yift and the meryte.
The goode folk, that Poul to preched,
Profred hym ofte, whan he hem teched,   6680
Som of her good in charite.
But therof right nothing tok he;
But of his hondwerk wolde he gete
Clothes to wryen hym, and his mete."
    "Telle me thanne how a man may lyven,
That al his good to pore hath yiven,   6686
And wole but oonly bidde his bedis
· · · · · · · · · · · · · · · ·
May he do so?"
              "Ye, sir."
                        "And how?"
"Sir, I wole gladly telle yow: 6690
Seynt Austyn seith a man may be
In houses that han proprete,

6611 blynne: cease
6615 Justinian: Emperor of Constantinople, who had the Roman
laws collected and codified

6687 bidde his bedis: say his prayers
6688 Not in MS. Thynne has: *And never with hondes labour his
needes.*

As Templers and Hospitelers,
And as these Chanouns Regulers,
Or White Monkes, or these Blake —   6695
I wole no mo ensamplis make —
And take therof his sustenyng,
For therynne lyth no begging;
But other weyes not, ywys,
Yif Austyn gabbith not of this.   6700
And yit full many a monk laboureth,
That God in hooly chirche honoureth;
For whanne her swynkyng is agon,
They rede and synge in chirche anon.

    "And for ther hath ben gret discord,   6705
As many a wight may bere record,
Upon the estat of mendience,
I wole shortly, in youre presence,
Telle how a man may begge at nede,
That hath not wherwith hym to fede,   6710
Maugre his felones jangelyngis,
For sothfastnesse wole none hidyngis.
And yit, percas, I may abeye
That I to yow sothly thus seye.

    "Lo, heere the caas especial: 6715
If a man be so bestial
That he of no craft hath science,
And nought desireth ignorence,
Thanne may he go a-begging yerne,
Til he som maner craft kan lerne,   6720
Thurgh which withoute truaundyng,
He may in trouthe have his lyvyng.
Or if he may don no labour,
For elde, or syknesse, or langour,
Or for his tendre age also,   6725
Thanne may he yit a-begging go.
Or if he have, peraventure,
Thurgh usage of his noriture,
Lyved over deliciously,
Thanne oughten good folk comunly   6730
Han of his myscheef som pitee,
And suffren hym also that he
May gon aboute and begge his breed,
That he be not for hungur deed.
Or if he have of craft kunnyng,   6735
And strengthe also, and desiryng
To wirken, as he hadde what,
But he fynde neithir this ne that,
Thanne may he begge til that he

Have geten his necessite.   6740
Or if his wynnyng be so lite
That his labour wole not acquyte
Sufficiantly al his lyvyng,
Yit may he go his breed begging;
Fro dore to dore he may go trace,   6745
Til he the remenaunt may purchace.
Or if a man wolde undirtake
Ony emprise for to make
In the rescous of oure lay,
And it defenden as he may,   6750
Be it with armes or lettrure,
Or other covenable cure,
If it be so he pore be,
Thanne may he begge til that he
May fynde in trouthe for to swynke,   6755
And gete hym clothes, mete, and drynke,
Swynke he with his hondis corporell,
And not with hondis espirituell.

    "In al thise caas, and in semblables,
If that ther ben mo resonables,   6760
He may begge, as I telle you heere,
And ellis nought, in no manere,
As William Seynt Amour wolde preche,
And ofte wolde dispute and teche
Of this mater all openly   6765
At Parys full solempnely.
And, also God my soule blesse,
As he had, in this stedfastnesse,
The accord of the universite
And of the puple, as semeth me.   6770

    "No good man oughte it to refuse,
Ne ought hym therof to excuse,
Be wroth or blithe whoso be.
For I wole speke, and telle it thee,
Al shulde I dye, and be putt doun,   6775
As was Seynt Poul, in derk prisoun;
Or be exiled in this caas
With wrong, as maister William was,
That my moder, Ypocrysie,
Banysshed for hir gret envye.   6780

    "Mi modir flemed hym Seynt Amour;
The noble dide such labour
To susteyne evere the loyalte,
That he to moche agilte me.
He made a book, and lete it write,   6785

. . . .

6693 **Templers and Hospitelers:** Knights Templars and Knights
Hospitallers, members of military religious orders
6694 **Chanouns Regulers:** secular clergy who live by a monastic
rule
6695 **White Monkes:** Cistercians   **Blake:** Benedictines
6707 **mendience:** mendicancy
6713 **percas:** perchance   **abeye:** suffer
6721 **truaundyng:** idling, shirking

6749 **rescous:** rescue   **lay:** faith
6751 **lettrure:** learning
6763 **William Seynt Amour:** a doctor of the Sorbonne
(mid-thirteenth century)
6781 **flemed hym Seynt Amour:** drove this Seynt Amour away
6785 **a book:** *De periculis,* by William of Seynt Amour
6786 Not in MS. Thynne has: *Wherin his lyfe he dyd al write.*

And wolde ich reneyed begging,
And lyved by my traveylyng,
If I ne had rent ne other good.
What? Wened he that I were wood?   6790
For labour myght me never plese.
I have more wille to ben at ese,
And have wel lever, soth to seye,
Bifore the puple patre and preye,
And wrie me in my foxerie   6795
Under a cope of papelardie."
     Quod Love, "What devel is this that I heere?
What wordis tellest thou me heere?"
"What, sir?"
          "Falsnesse, that apert is;
Thanne dredist thou not God?"
                    "No, certis;   6800
For selde in gret thing shal he spede
In this world, that God wole drede.
For folk that hem to vertu yiven,
And truly on her owne lyven,
And hem in goodnesse ay contene,   6805
On hem is lytel thrift sene.
Such folk drinken gret mysese;
That lyf may me never plese.
But se what gold han usurers,
And silver eke in garners,   6810
Taylagiers, and these monyours,
Bailifs, bedels, provost, countours;
These lyven wel nygh by ravyne.
The smale puple hem mote enclyne,
And they as wolves wole hem eten.   6815
Upon the pore folk they geten
Full moche of that they spende or kepe.
Nis non of hem that he nyl strepe
And wrien hemsilf wel atte fulle;
Withoute scaldyng they hem pulle.   6820
The stronge the feble overgoth.
But I, that were my symple cloth,
Robbe bothe robbed and robbours
And gile giled and gilours.
By my treget I gadre and threste   6825
The gret tresour into my cheste,
That lyth with me so faste bounde.
Myn highe paleys do I founde,
And my delites I fulfille
With wyn at feestes at my wille,   6830

And tables full of entremees.
I wole no lyf but ese and pees,
And wynne gold to spende also.
For whanne the grete bagge is go,
It cometh right with my japes.   6835
Make I not wel tumble myn apes?
To wynnen is alwey myn entente;
My purchace is bettir than my rente.
For though I shulde beten be,
Overal I entremete me.   6840
Without me may no wight dure;
I walke soules for to cure.
Of al the world cure have I;
In brede and lengthe boldely
I wole bothe preche and eke counceilen.   6845
With hondis wille I not traveilen,
For of the Pope I have the bulle —
I ne holde not my wittes dulle.
I wole not stynten, in my lyve,
These emperoures for to shryve,   6850
Or kyngis, dukis, lordis grete;
But pore folk al quyte I lete.
I love no such shryvyng, parde,
But it for other cause be.
I rekke not of pore men —   6855
Her astat is not worth an hen.
Where fyndest thou a swynker of labour
Have me unto his confessour?
But emperesses and duchesses,
Thise queenes, and eke countesses,   6860
Thise abbessis, and eke bygyns,
These grete ladyes palasyns,
These joly knyghtis and baillyves,
Thise nonnes, and thise burgeis wyves,
That riche ben and eke plesyng,   6865
And thise maidens welfaryng,
Wherso they clad or naked be,
Uncounceiled goth ther noon fro me.
And, for her soules savete,
At lord and lady, and her meyne,   6870
I axe, whanne thei hem to me shryve,
The proprete of al her lyve,
And make hem trowe, bothe meest and leest,
Hir paroch-prest nys but a beest
Ayens me and my companye,   6875

6787 **reneyed:** renounced
6794 **patre:** recite the Pater Noster
6796 **papelardie:** hypocrisy
6811 **Taylagiers:** tax collectors **monyours:** money dealers, bankers
6812 **bedels:** officers of the law **provost:** magistrate
countours: lawyers (auditors)
6820 They do not scald them before skinning (as a butcher does a hog).

6831 **entremees:** delicacies
6834 **is go:** is empty
6835 **It cometh right:** i.e., it is replenished
6838 **purchace:** total income **rente:** proper income
6857 **swynker of labour:** laborer, simple working man
6861 **bygyns:** Beguines; see n.
6862 **palasyns:** of the palace
6863 **baillyves:** bailiffs (stewards)
6867 **clad or naked:** in all circumstances
6875 **Ayens:** in comparison with

That shrewis ben as gret as I;
Fro whiche I wole not hide in hold
No pryvete that me is told,
That I by word or signe, ywis,
[Ne] wole make hem knowe what it is,   6880
And they wolen also tellen me;
They hele fro me no pryvyte.
And for to make yow hem perceyven,
That usen folk thus to disceyven,
I wole you seyn, withouten drede,   6885
What men may in the gospel rede
Of Seynt Mathew, the gospelere,
That seith, as I shal you sey heere:
  " 'Upon the chaire of Moyses' —
Thus is it glosed, douteles,   6890
That is the Olde Testament,
For therby is the chaire ment —
'Sitte Scribes and Pharisen;'
That is to seyn, the cursid men
Whiche that we ypocritis calle.   6895
'Doth that they preche, I rede you alle,
But doth not as they don a del;
That ben not wery to seye wel,
But to do wel no will have they.
And they wolde bynde on folk alwey,   6900
That ben to be begiled able,
Burdons that ben importable;
On folkes shuldris thinges they couchen,
That they nyl with her fyngris touchen.' "
  "And why wole they not touche it?"
                    "Why?   6905
For hem ne lyst not, sikirly;
For sadde burdons that men taken
Make folkes shuldris aken.
And if they do ought that good be,
That is for folk it shulde se.   6910
Her bordurs larger maken they,
And make her hemmes wide alwey,
And loven setes at the table,
The firste and most honourable;
And for to han the first chaieris   6915
In synagogis, to hem full deere is;
And willen that folk hem loute and grete,
Whanne that they passen thurgh the strete,
And wolen be cleped 'maister' also.
But they ne shulde not willen so;   6920
The gospel is ther-ageyns, I gesse,
That shewith wel her wikkidnesse.
  "Another custome use we:
Of hem that wole ayens us be,

We hate hem deedly everichon,   6925
And we wole werrey hem, as oon.
Hym that oon hatith, hate we alle,
And congecte hou to don hym falle.
And if we seen hym wynne honour,
Richesse, or preis, thurgh his valour,   6930
Provende, rent, or dignyte,
Ful fast, iwys, compassen we
Bi what ladder he is clomben so;
And for to maken hym doun to go,
With traisoun we wole hym defame,   6935
And don hym leese his goode name.
Thus from his ladder we hym take,
And thus his freendis foes we make;
But word ne wite shal he noon,
Till alle his freendis ben his foon.   6940
For if we dide it openly,
We myght have blame redily;
For hadde he wist of oure malice,
He hadde hym kept, but he were nyce.
  "Another is this, that if so falle   6945
That ther be oon amonge us alle
That doth a good turn, out of drede,
We seyn it is oure alder deede.
Ye, sikerly, though he it feyned,
Or that hym list, or that hym deyned   6950
A man thurgh hym avaunced be;
Therof all parseners be we,
And tellen folk, whereso we go,
That man thurgh us is spronged so.
And for to have of men preysyng,   6955
We purchace, thurgh oure flateryng,
Of riche men of gret pouste
Lettres to witnesse oure bounte,
So that man weneth, that may us see,
That alle vertu in us be.   6960
And alwey pore we us feyne;
But how so that we begge or pleyne,
We ben the folk, without lesyng,
That all thing have without havyng.
Thus be we dred of the puple, iwis.   6965
And gladly my purpos is this:
I dele with no wight, but he
Have gold and tresour gret plente.
Her acqueyntaunce wel love I;
This is moche my desir, shortly.   6970
I entremete me of brokages,
I make pees and mariages,
I am gladly executour,

6902 **importable:** unbearable
6911 **bordurs:** borders of their garments (bearing phylacteries)

6928 **congecte:** plan, conjecture
6948 **oure alder deede:** a deed of us all (as if each of us had
done it)
6952 **parseners:** partners
6971 **brokages:** use of go-betweens, making deals
6973 **executour:** executor of wills

And many tymes procuratour;
I am somtyme messager,   6975
That fallith not to my myster;
And many tymes I make enquestes —
For me that office not honest is.
To dele with other mennes thing,
That is to me a gret lykyng.   6980
And if that ye have ought to do
In place that I repeire to,
I shal it speden, thurgh my witt,
As soone as ye have told me it.
So that ye serve me to pay,   6985
My servyse shal be youre alway.
But whoso wole chastise me,
Anoon my love lost hath he;
For I love no man, in no gise,
That wole me repreve or chastise.   6990
But I wolde al folk undirtake,
And of no wight no teching take;
For I, that other folk chastie,
Wole not be taught fro my folie.
    "I love noon hermitage more.   6995
All desertes and holtes hore,
And grete wodes everichon,
I lete hem to the Baptist John.
I quethe hym quyt and hym relesse
Of Egipt all the wildirnesse.   7000
To fer were alle my mansiounes
Fro citees and goode tounes.
My paleis and myn hous make I
There men may renne ynne openly,
And sey that I the world forsake,   7005
But al amydde I bilde and make
My hous, and swimme and pley therynne,
Bet than a fish doth with his fynne.
    "Of Antecristes men am I,
Of whiche that Crist seith openly,   7010
They have abit of hoolynesse,
And lyven in such wikkednesse.
Outward, lambren semen we,
Fulle of goodnesse and of pitee,
And inward we, withouten fable,   7015
Ben gredy wolves ravysable.
We enviroune bothe lond and se;
With all the world werreyen we;
We wole ordeyne of alle thing,
Of folkis good, and her lyvyng.   7020

    "If ther be castel or citee,
Wherynne that ony bouger be,
Although that they of Milayn were
(For therof ben they blamed there);
Or if a wight out of mesure   7025
Wolde lene his gold, and take usure,
For that he is so coveitous;
Or if he be to leccherous,
Or theef [or] haunte symonye,
Or provost full of trecherie,   7030
Or prelat lyvyng jolily,
Or prest that halt his quene hym by,
Or olde horis hostilers,
Or other bawdes or bordillers,
Or elles blamed of ony vice   7035
Of which men shulden don justice:
Bi all the seyntes that me pray,
But they defende them with lamprey,
With luce, with elys, with samons,
With tendre gees and with capons,   7040
With tartes, or with cheses fat,
With deynte flawnes brode and flat,
With caleweis, or with pullaylle,
With conynges, or with fyn vitaille,
That we, undir our clothes wide,   7045
Maken thourgh oure golet glide;
Or but he wole do come in haste
Roo-venysoun, bake in paste;
Whether so that he loure or groyne,
He shal have of a corde a loigne,   7050
With whiche men shal hym bynde and lede,
To brenne hym for his synful deede,
That men shull here hym crie and rore
A myle-wey aboute, and more;
Or ellis he shal in prisoun dye,   7055
But if he wole oure frendship bye,
Or smerten that that he hath do,
More than his gilt amounteth to.
But, and he couthe thurgh his sleight,
Do maken up a tour of height,   7060
Nought rought I whethir of ston, or tree,
Or erthe, or turves though it be,

6974 **procuratour:** agent, attorney
6977 **enquestes:** inquests, legal inquiries
6996 **holtes:** woods
6998 **Baptist John:** John the Baptist
6999 **quethe hym quyt:** declare him free
7013 **lambren:** lambs
7017 **enviroune:** surround

7022 **bouger:** sodomite (bugger), heretic
7032 **quene:** trollop, whore
7033 **horis hostilers:** innkeepers for whores
7034 **bordillers:** brothel-keepers
7037 **me pray:** one may pray to (impersonal)
7039 **luce:** pike
7042 **flawnes:** flans, custard puddings
7043 **caleweis:** a kind of pear   **pullaylle:** poultry
7044 **conynges:** rabbits
7046 **golet:** gullet
7049 **groyne:** complain
7050 **loigne:** leash
7057 **smerten:** smart for

Though it were of no vounde ston,
Wrought with squyre and scantilon,
So that the tour were stuffed well   7065
With alle richesse temporell,
And thanne that he wolde updresse
Engyns, bothe more and lesse,
To cast at us by every side,
To bere his goode name wide,   7070
Such sleghtes [as] I shal yow nevene,
Barelles of wyn, by sixe or sevene,
Or gold in sakkis gret plente,
He shulde soone delyvered be.
And if [he have] noon sich pitaunces,   7075
Late hym study in equipolences,
And late lyes and fallaces,
If that he wolde deserve oure graces;
Or we shal bere hym such witnesse
Of synne and of his wrecchidnesse,   7080
And don his loos so wide renne,
That al quyk we shulden hym brenne;
Or ellis yeve hym such penaunce,
That is wel wors than the pitaunce.
    "For thou shalt never, for nothing,   7085
Kon knowen aright by her clothing
The traitours fulle of trecherie,
But thou her werkis can aspie.
And ne hadde the goode kepyng be
Whilom of the universite,   7090
That kepith the key of Cristendom,
· · · · · · · · · · · ·
Suche ben the stynkyng prophetis;
Nys non of hem that good prophete is,
For they thurgh wikked entencioun,   7095
The yeer of the Incarnacioun,
A thousand and two hundred yeer,
Fyve and fifty, ferther ne neer,
Broughten a book, with sory grace,
To yeven ensample in comune place,   7100
That seide thus, though it were fable:
'This is the gospel perdurable,
That fro the Holy Goost is sent.'
Wel were it worth to ben brent!
Entitled was in such manere   7105
This book, of which I telle heere.
Ther nas no wight in all Parys,
Biforne Oure Lady, at parvys,

· · · · · · · · · · · ·
To copy if hym talent tok.   7110
There myght he se, by gret tresoun,
Full many fals comparisoun:
'As moche as, thurgh his grete myght,
Be it of hete or of lyght,
The sonne sourmounteth the mone,   7115
That troublere is, and chaungith soone,
And the note-kernell the shelle
(I scorne not that I yow telle),
Right so, withouten ony gile,
Sourmounteth this noble evangile   7120
The word of ony evangelist.'
And to her title they token Crist.
And many a such comparisoun,
Of which I make no mencioun,
Mighte men in that book fynde,   7125
Whoso coude of hem have mynde.
    "The universite, that tho was aslep,
Gan for to braide and taken kep;
And at the noys the heed upcaste,
Ne never sithen slept it faste,   7130
But up it stert, and armes tok
Ayens this fals horrible bok,
Al redy bateil [for] to make,
And to the juge the book to take.
But they that broughten the bok there   7135
Hent it anoon awey, for fere.
They nolde shewe more a del,
But thenne it kept, and kepen will,
Til such a tyme that they may see
That they so stronge woxen be   7140
That no wyght may hem wel withstonde,
For by that book [they] durst not stonde.
Awey they gonne it for to bere,
For they ne durst not answere
By exposicioun ne glose   7145
To that that clerkis wole appose
Ayens the cursednesse, iwys,
That in that book writen is.
Now wot I not, ne I can not see
What maner eende that there shal be   7150
Of al this [bok] that they hyde;
But yit algate they shal abide
Til that they may it bet defende.
This, trowe I best, wol be her ende.
    "Thus, Antecrist abiden we,   7155
For we ben alle of his meyne;
And what man that wole not be so,
Right soone he shal his lyf forgo.

We wole a puple upon hym areyse,
And thurgh oure gile don hym seise,   7160
And hym on sharpe speris ryve,
Or other weyes brynge hym fro lyve,
But if that he wole folowe, iwis,
That in oure book writen is.
    "Thus mych wole oure book signifie,   7165
That while Petre hath maistrie,
May never John shewe well his myght.
Now have I you declared right
The menyng of the bark and rynde,
That makith the entencious blynde;   7170
But now at erst I wole bigynne
To expowne you the pith withynne:
· · · · · · · · · · · · ·

And the seculers comprehende,
That Cristes lawe wole defende,
And shulde it kepen and mayntenen   7175
Ayenes hem that all sustenen,
And falsly to the puple techen.
And John bitokeneth hem that prechen
That ther nys lawe covenable
But thilke gospel perdurable,   7180
That fro the Holy Gost was sent
To turne folk that ben myswent.
    "The strengthe of John they undirstonde
The grace, in which they seie they stonde,
That doth the synfull folk converte,   7185
And hem to Jesus Crist reverte.
Full many another orribilite
May men in that book se,
That ben comaunded, douteles,
Ayens the lawe of Rome expres;   7190
And all with Antecrist they holden,
As men may in the book biholden.
And thanne comaunden they to sleen
Alle tho that with Petre been;
But they shal nevere have that myght,   7195
And, God toforn, for strif to fight,
That they ne shal ynowe fynde
That Petres lawe shal have in mynde,
And evere holde, and so mayntene,
That at the last it shal be sene   7200
That they shal alle come therto,
For ought that they can speke or do.
And thilke lawe shal not stonde,
That they by John have undirstonde,
But, maugre hem, it shal adown,   7205
And ben brought to confusioun.
But I wole stynt of this matere,
For it is wonder longe to here.

But hadde that ilke book endured,
Of better estat I were ensured,   7210
And freendis have I yit, pardee,
That han me sett in gret degre.
    "Of all this world is emperour
Gyle my fadir, the trechour,
And emperisse my moder is,   7215
Maugre the Holy Gost, iwis.
Oure myghty lynage and oure rowte
Regneth in every regne aboute;
And well is worthy we maistres be,
For all this world governe we,   7220
And can the folk so wel disceyve
That noon oure gile can perceyve.
And though they don, they dar not seye;
The sothe dar no wight bywreye.
But he in Cristis wrath hym ledith,   7225
That more than Crist my britheren dredith.
He nys no full good champioun,
That dredith such simulacioun,
Nor that for peyne wole refusen
Us to correcte and accusen.   7230
He wole not entremete by right,
Ne have God in his eye-sight,
And therfore God shal hym punyshe.
But me ne rekketh of no vice,
Sithen men us loven comunably,   7235
And holden us for so worthy
That we may folk repreve echoon,
And we nyl have repref of noon.
Whom shulden folk worshipen so
But us, that stynten never mo   7240
To patren while that folk may us see,
Though it not so bihynde be?
    "And where is more wod folye
Than to enhaunce chyvalrie,
And love noble men and gay,   7245
That joly clothis weren alway?
If they be sich folk as they semen,
So clene, as men her clothis demen,
And that her wordis folowe her dede,
It is gret pite, out of drede,   7250
For they wole be noon ypocritis!
Of hem, me thynketh, gret spite is;
I can not love hem on no side.
But beggers with these hodes wide,
With sleighe and pale faces lene,   7255
And greye clothis not full clene,
But fretted full of tatarwagges,
And highe shoos, knopped with dagges,

7169 **bark and rynde:** literal sense; see n.
7172 A couplet translating the French line "By 'Peter' it signifies
the Pope," is lacking after this line; see n.
7187 **orribilite:** horrible thing

7215 **my moder:** i.e., Hypocrisy
7252 **spite:** envy
7254 **beggers:** mendicants; see n.
7257 **fretted full of:** set thickly with   **tatarwagges:** tatters
7258 **knopped:** ornamented   **dagges:** ornamental cut-outs

That frouncen lyke a quaile pipe,
Or botis rivelyng as a gype;   7260
To such folk as I you dyvyse
Shulde princes, and these lordis wise,
Take all her londis and her thingis,
Bothe werre and pees, in governyngis;
To such folk shulde a prince hym yive,   7265
That wolde his lyf in honour lyve.

    "And if they be not as they seme,
That serven thus the world to queme,
There wolde I dwelle, to disceyve
The folk, for they shal not perceyve.   7270
But I ne speke in no such wise,
That men shulde humble abit dispise,
So that no pride ther-undir be.
No man shulde hate, as thynkith me,
The pore man in sich clothyng.   7275
But God ne preisith hym nothing,
That seith he hath the world forsake,
And hath to worldly glorie hym take,
And wole of siche delices use.
Who may that begger wel excuse,   7280
That papelard, that hym yeldith so,
And wole to worldly ese go,
And seith that he the world hath left,
And gredily it grypeth eft?
He is the hound, shame is to seyn,   7285
That to his castyng goth ageyn.

    "But unto you dar I not lye.
But myght I felen or aspie
That ye perceyved it no thyng,
Ye shulde have a stark lesyng   7290
Right in youre honde thus, to bigynne;
I nolde it lette for no synne."

    The god lough at the wondir tho,
And every wight gan laugh also,
And seide, "Lo, heere a man aright   7295
For to be trusty to every wight!"
"Fals-Semblant," quod Love, "sey to me,
Sith I thus have avaunced thee,
That in my court is thi dwellyng,
And of ribawdis shalt be my kyng,   7300
Wolt thou wel holden my forwardis?"
"Ye, sir, from hennes forwardis;
Hadde never youre fadir heere-biforn
Servaunt so trewe, sith he was born."

"That is ayenes all nature."   7305
"Sir, putte you in that aventure.
For though ye borowes take of me,
The sikerer shal ye never be
For ostages, ne sikirnesse,
Or chartres, for to bere witnesse.   7310
I take youresilf to recorde heere,
That men ne may in no manere
Teren the wolf out of his hide,
Til he be flayn, bak and side,
Though men hym bete and al defile.   7315
What! Wene ye that I nil bigile
For I am clothed mekely?
Ther-undir is all my trechery;
Myn herte chaungith never the mo
For noon abit in which I go.   7320
Though I have chere of symplenesse,
I am not wery of shrewidnesse.
My lemman, Streyned-Abstinaunce,
Hath myster of my purveaunce;
She hadde ful longe ago be deed,   7325
Nere my councel and my red.
Lete hir allone, and you and me."
And Love answerde, "I truste thee
Withoute borowe, for I wole noon."
And Fals-Semblant, the theef, anoon,   7330
Ryght in that ilke same place,
That hadde of tresoun al his face
Ryght blak withynne and whit withoute,
Thankyth hym, gan on his knees loute.
    Thanne was ther nought but, "Every man
Now to assaut, that sailen can,"   7336
Quod Love, "and that full hardyly!"
Thanne armed they hem communly
Of sich armour as to hem fel.
Whanne they were armed, fers and fel,   7340
They wente hem forth, alle in a route,
And set the castel al aboute.
They will nought away, for no drede,
Till it so be that they ben dede,
Or til they have the castel take.   7345
And foure batels they gan make,
And parted hem in foure anoon,
And toke her way, and forth they gon,
The foure gates for to assaile,
Of whiche the kepers wole not faile;   7350
For they ben neithir sike ne dede,
But hardy folk, and stronge in dede.

7259 **frouncen:** squeak (literally, creased, wrinkled) **quaile pipe:** pipe used to lure quail by imitating their call
7260 **rivelyng:** puckering (i.e., with elaborate folds, pleats) **gype:** smock
7268 **queme:** please
7281 **papelard:** hypocrite
7286 **castyng:** vomit
7290 **stark:** flat, outright
7300 **ribawdis . . . kyng:** see 6068 and n.

7307 **borowes:** pledges, security
7321 **chere of symplenesse:** appearance of sincerity
7323 **Streyned-Abstinaunce:** see 6341.
7324 **myster:** need (or benefited from?)
7336 **sailen:** assail, attack
7346 **batels:** battalions

Now wole I seyn the countynaunce
Of Fals-Semblant and Abstynaunce,
That ben to Wikkid-Tonge went.   7355
But first they heelde her parlement,
Whether it to done were
To maken hem be knowen there,
Or elles walken forth disgised.
But at the laste they devysed   7360
That they wolde gon in tapinage,
As it were in a pilgrimage,
Lyke good and hooly folk unfeyned.
And Dame Abstinence-Streyned
Tok on a robe of kamelyne,   7365
And gan hir graithe as a Bygyne.
A large coverechief of thred
She wrapped all aboute hir heed,
But she forgat not hir sawter;
A peire of bedis eke she ber   7370
Upon a las, all of whit thred,
On which that she hir bedes bed.
But she ne bought hem never a del,
For they were geven her, I wot wel,
God wot, of a full hooly frere,   7375
That seide he was hir fadir dere,
To whom she hadde ofter went
Than ony frere of his covent.
And he visited hir also,
And many a sermoun seide hir to;   7380
He nolde lette, for man on lyve,
That he ne wolde hir ofte shryve.
And with so great devocion
They made her confession,
That they had ofte, for the nones,   7385
Two heedes in oon hood at ones.

  Of fayre shap I devyse her the,
But pale of face somtyme was she;
That false traytouresse untrewe
Was lyk that salowe hors of hewe,   7390
That in the Apocalips is shewed,
That signifyeth tho folk beshrewed
That ben al ful of trecherye,
And pale through hypocrisye;
For on that hors no colour is,   7395
But only deed and pale, ywis.
Of such a colour enlangoured
Was Abstynence, iwys, coloured;
Of her estat she her repented,
As her visage represented.   7400

She had a burdown al of Thefte,
That Gyle had yeve her of his yefte;
And a skryppe of Faynt Distresse,
That ful was of elengenesse;
And forth she walked sobrely.   7405
And Fals-Semblant saynt, *je vous die,*
Had, as it were for such mister,
Don on the cope of a frer,
With chere symple and ful pytous.
Hys lokyng was not disdeynous,   7410
Ne proud, but meke and ful pesyble.
  About his necke he bar a byble,
And squierly forth gan he gon,
And, for to rest his lymmes upon,
He had of Treason a potente;   7415
As he were feble, his way he wente.
But in his sleve he gan to thringe
A rasour sharp and wel bytynge,
That was forged in a forge,
Which that men clepen Coupe-Gorge.   7420
  So longe forth her way they nomen,
Tyl they to Wicked-Tonge comen,
That at his gate was syttyng,
And saw folk in the way passyng.
The pilgrymes saw he faste by,   7425
That beren hem ful mekely,
And humbly they with him mette.
Dame Abstynence first him grette,
And sythe him Fals-Semblant salued,
And he hem; but he not remued,   7430
For he ne dredde hem not a del.
For whan he saw her faces wel,
Alway in herte him thoughte so,
He shulde knowe hem bothe two,
For wel he knew Dame Abstynaunce,   7435
But he ne knew not Constreynaunce.
He knew nat that she was constrayned,
Ne of her theves lyve fayned,
But wende she com of wyl al free,
But she com in another degree,   7440
And if of good wyl she began,
That wyl was fayled her than.
  And Fals-Semblant had he sayn als,
But he knew nat that he was fals.
Yet fals was he, but his falsnesse   7445
Ne coude he nat espye nor gesse;

7353 **countynaunce:** outward appearance
7361 **tapinage:** disguise
7365 **kamelyne:** a fabric of wool mixed with silk and other fibers
7366 **graithe:** clothe **Bygyne:** see 6861.
7372 **hir bedes bed:** said her prayers
7397 **enlangoured:** made weak or pale by illness

7401 **burdown:** pilgrim's staff
7403 **skryppe:** bag, traveling pack **Faynt:** feigned, false
7404 **elengenesse:** sadness
7406 **saynt:** girded (?) *je vous die:* I tell you
7413 **squierly:** like a squire (?); see n.
7415 **potente:** staff, crutch
7417 **thringe:** thrust
7420 **Coupe-Gorge:** Cut-Throat
7430 **remued:** moved

For Semblant was so slye wrought,
That Falsnesse he ne espyed nought.
  But haddest thou knowen hym beforn,
Thou woldest on a bok have sworn,   7450
Whan thou him saugh in thylke aray,
That he, that whilom was so gay,
And of the daunce joly Robyn,
Was tho become a Jacobyn.
But sothly, what so men hym calle,   7455
Freres Preachours ben good men alle;
Her order wickedly they beren,
Suche mynstrelles if they weren.
So ben Augustyns and Cordyleres,
And Carmes, and eke Sacked Freeres,   7460
And alle freres, shodde and bare
(Though some of hem ben great and square),
Ful hooly men, as I hem deme;
Everych of hem wolde good man seme.
But shalt thou never of apparence   7465
Sen conclude good consequence
In non argument, ywis,
If existens al fayled is.
For men may fynde alway sophyme
The consequence to envenyme,   7470
Whoso that hath the subtelte
The double sentence for to se.
  Whan the pylgrymes commen were
To Wicked-Tonge, that dwelled there,
Her harneys nygh hem was algate;   7475
By Wicked-Tonge adown they sate,
That bad hem ner him for to come,
And of tidynges telle him some,
And sayd hem, "What cas maketh you
To come into this place now?"   7480
  "Sir," sayde Strayned-Abstynaunce,
"We, for to drye our penaunce,
With hertes pytous and devoute
Are commen, as pylgrimes gon aboute.
Wel nygh on fote alwey we go;   7485
Ful dusty ben our heeles two;
And thus bothe we ben sent
Throughout this world, that is miswent,
To yeve ensample, and preche also.
To fysshen synful men we go,   7490
For other fysshynge ne fysshe we.
And, sir, for that charyte,
As we be wonte, herborowe we crave,

Your lyf to amende, Christ it save!
And, so it shulde you nat displese,   7495
We wolden, if it were youre ese,
A short sermon unto you sayn."
And Wicked-Tonge answered agayn:
"The hous," quod he, "such as ye see,
Shal nat be warned you for me.   7500
Say what you lyst, and I wol here."
  "Graunt mercy, swete sire dere!"
Quod alderfirst Dame Abstynence,
And thus began she her sentence:
  "Sir, the firste vertu, certayn,   7505
The greatest and moste soverayn
That may be founde in any man,
For havynge, or for wyt he can,
That is his tonge to refrayne;
Therto ought every wight him payne.   7510
For it is better stylle be
Than for to speken harm, parde!
And he that herkeneth it gladly,
He is no good man, sykerly.
  "And, sir, aboven al other synne,   7515
In that art thou most gylty inne.
Thou spake a jape not longe ago,
(And, sir, that was ryght yvel do)
Of a young man that here repayred,
And never yet this place apayred.   7520
Thou saydest he awayted nothyng
But to disceyve Fayr-Welcomyng;
Ye sayde nothyng soth of that.
But, sir, ye lye, I tel you plat.
He ne cometh no more, ne goth, parde!   7525
I trowe ye shal him never se.
Fayr-Welcomyng in prison is,
That ofte hath played with you, er this,
The fayrest games that he coude,
Withoute fylthe, stylle or loude.   7530
Now dar he nat himself solace.
Ye han also the man do chace,
That he dar neyther come ne go.
What meveth you to hate him so,
But properly your wicked thought,   7535
That many a fals leasyng hath thought
That meveth your foole eloquence,
That jangleth ever in audyence,
And on the folk areyseth blame,
And doth hem dishonour and shame,   7540
For thyng that may have no prevyng,
But lyklynesse, and contryvyng?
  "For I dar sayn that Reson demeth
It is nat al soth thyng that semeth,

7454 **Jacobyn:** Dominican friar
7456 **Freres preachours:** Dominicans
7459–60 **Augustyns, Cordyleres, Carmes, Sacked Freeres:** the
four orders of Friars—Augustinian, Franciscan, Carmelites, and
Friars de Penitentia (see n.)
7468 **existens:** reality
7469 **sophyme:** sophism, subtle argument
7470 **consequence:** conclusion
7475 **harneys:** gear, arms

7520 **apayred:** damaged
7542 **contryvyng:** invention

And it is synne to controve   7545
Thyng that is to reprove.
This wote ye wel, and sir, therfore
Ye arn to blame the more.
And nathelesse, he recketh lyte;
He yeveth nat now therof a myte.   7550
For if he thoughte harm, parfay,
He wolde come and gon al day;
He coude himselve nat abstene.
Now cometh he nat, and that is sene,
For he ne taketh of it no cure,   7555
But if it be through aventure,
And lasse than other folk, algate.
And thou her watchest at the gate,
With spere in thyn arest alway;
There muse, musard, al the day.   7560
Thou wakest night and day for thought;
Iwis, thy traveyle is for nought;
And Jelousye, withouten fayle,
Shal never quyte the thy traveyle.
And skathe is that Fayr-Welcomyng,   7565
Withouten any trespassyng,
Shal wrongfully in prison be,
There wepeth and languyssheth he.
And though thou never yet, ywis,
Agyltest man no more but this,   7570
(Take nat a-gref) it were worthy
To putte the out of this bayly,
And afterward in prison lye,
And fettre the tyl that thou dye;
For thou shalt for this synne dwelle   7575
Right in the devels ers of helle,
But if that thou repente thee.''
   "Ma fay, thou liest falsly!" quod he.
"What? Welcome with myschaunce now!
Have I therfore herbered yow,   7580
To seye me shame, and eke reprove?
With sory hap, to youre bihove,
Am I to day youre herberger!
Go herber yow elleswhere than heer,
That han a lyer called me!   7585
Two tregetours art thou and he,
That in myn hous do me this shame,
And for my soth-sawe ye me blame.
Is this the sermoun that ye make?
To all the develles I me take,   7590
Or elles, God, thou me confounde,
But, er men diden this castel founde,

It passith not ten daies or twelve,
But it was told right to myselve,
And as they seide, right so tolde I,   7595
He kyst the Rose pryvyly!
Thus seide I now, and have seid yore;
I not wher he dide ony more.
Why shulde men sey me such a thyng,
If it hadde ben gabbyng?   7600
Ryght so seide I, and wol seye yit;
I trowe, I lied not of it.
And with my bemes I wole blowe
To alle neighboris a-rowe,
How he hath bothe comen and gon.''   7605
   Tho spak Fals-Semblant right anon:
"All is not gospel, out of doute,
That men seyn in the town aboute.
Ley no deef ere to my spekyng;
I swere yow, sir, it is gabbyng!   7610
I trowe ye wote wel, certeynly,
That no man loveth hym tenderly
That seith hym harm, if he wot it,
All he be never so pore of wit.
And soth is also, sikerly   7615
(This knowe ye, sir, as wel as I),
That lovers gladly wole visiten
The places there her loves habiten.
This man yow loveth and eke honoureth;
This man to serve you laboureth,   7620
And clepith you his freend so deere:
And this man makith you good chere,
And everywhere that [he] you meteth,
He yow saloweth, and he you greteth.
He preseth not so ofte that ye   7625
Ought of his come encombred be;
Ther presen other folk on yow
Full ofter than he doth now.
And if his herte hym streyned so
Unto the Rose for to go,   7630
Ye shulde hym sen so ofte nede,
That ye shulde take hym with the dede.
He cowde his comyng not forbere,
Though me hym thrilled with a spere;
It nere not thanne as it is now.   7635
But trusteth wel, I swere it yow,
That it is clene out of his thought.
Sir, certis, he ne thenkith it nought;
No more ne doth Fair-Welcomyng,
That sore abieth al this thing.   7640

7545 **controve**: invent
7553 **abstene**: restrain
7572 **bayly**: (place of) custody
7578 *Ma fay*: by my faith
7582 **bihove**: profit

7600 **gabbyng**: idle gossip
7603 **bemes**: horns
7618 **habiten**: live, frequent
7626 **come**: coming
7634 **me**: one (impersonal)   **thrilled**: pierced

And if they were of oon assent,
Full soone were the Rose hent;
The maugre youres wolde be.
And sir, of o thing herkeneth me,
Sith ye this man that loveth yow   7645
Han seid such harm and shame now,
Witeth wel, if he gessed it,
Ye may wel demen in youre wit
He nolde nothyng love you so,
Ne callen you his freend also,   7650
But nyght and day he wolde wake
The castell to destroie and take,
If it were soth as ye devise;
Or som man in som maner wise
Might it warne hym everydel,   7655
Or by hymsilf perceyven wel.
For sith he myght not come and gon,
As he was whilom wont to don,
He myght it sone wite and see;
But now all other wise doth he.   7660
Thanne have [ye], sir, al outerly,
Deserved helle, and jolyly
The deth of helle, douteles,
That thrallen folk so gilteles."
  Fals-Semblant proveth so this thing   7665
That he can noon answeryng,

And seth alwey such apparaunce
That nygh he fel in repentaunce,
And seide hym, "Sir, it may wel be.
Semblant, a good man semen ye,   7670
And, Abstinence, full wise ye seme.
Of o talent you bothe I deme.
What counceil wole ye to me yiven?"
  "Ryght heere anoon thou shalt be shryven,
And sey thy synne withoute more;   7675
Of this shalt thou repente sore.
For I am prest and have pouste
To shryve folk of most dignyte
That ben, as wide as world may dure.
Of all this world I have the cure,   7680
And that hadde never yit persoun,
Ne vicarie of no maner toun.
And, God wot, I have of thee
A thousand tyme more pitee
Than hath thi preest parochial,   7685
Though he thy freend be special.
I have avauntage, in o wise,
That youre prelatis ben not so wise
Ne half so lettred as am I.
I am licenced boldely   7690
To reden in divinite,
And longe have red. . . ."

Explicit.

7643 **maugre:** ill will

7682 **vicarie:** vicar
7689 **lettred:** learned
7691–92 Thynne has this conclusion:
In divynite for to rede
And to confessen out of drede
  If ye wol you newe confesse
And leave your synnes more and lesse
Withoute abode / knele downe anon
And you shall have absolucion.
  FINIS.

APPENDIX

GENERAL BIBLIOGRAPHY

THE EXPLANATORY NOTES provide specific bibliographic references, but they are necessarily concentrated on particular problems of the individual texts. The following bibliography is intended to provide guidance for more general study. It includes many works cited in the notes and listed among the frequently cited works (pp. 779–93 below), but it also lists broader studies that are not often cited in the notes on individual works and books and articles that deal with a variety of background and ancillary matters. The studies listed are classified (with inevitable overlapping and some duplication) under general subject headings, which are intended for guidance rather than restriction, since many of the works listed concern matters other than that of the heading under which they appear. These are, of course, intended for advanced students; a reader just beginning the study of Chaucer should first turn to the introductory materials in this volume. Among the other many good introductions to Chaucer are Derek S. Brewer's *Chaucer* (3rd ed., 1973), George L. Kittredge's still valuable *Chaucer and His Poetry* (55th Anniversary Edition, intro. Bartlett J. Whiting, 1970), *An Introduction to Chaucer,* by Maurice Hussey, A. C. Spearing, and James Winny (1965), and George Kane's *Chaucer* (1984).

BIBLIOGRAPHIES AND SURVEYS OF SCHOLARSHIP

Baird, Lorrayne Y., *Bibliography of Chaucer, 1964–1973,* 1977.

Crawford, William R., *Bibliography of Chaucer, 1954–1963,* 2nd corr. printing, 1967.

Griffith, Dudley David, *Bibliography of Chaucer, 1908–1953,* 1955.

Hammond, Eleanor P., *Chaucer: A Bibliographical Manual,* 1908.

Annual annotated Chaucer bibliographies are printed in *Studies in the Age of Chaucer,* beginning with volume 1 (bibliography for 1975–76), edited first by John H. Fisher, then by Lorrayne Y. Baird, and now (beginning with volume 6) by Lorrayne Y. Baird-Lange and Cynthia Dobrich Myers, and in the *Year's Work in English Studies* (beginning in 1921), formerly edited by Joyce Bazire, now by David Mills and J. David Burnley. Annual bibliographies of work on Chaucer are included in *The Annual Bibliography of English Language and Literature* (1920–),

published by the Modern Humanities Research Association, and the MLA International Bibliography (1921–, under varying titles) published first in *PMLA* and new separately by the Modern Language Association of America. A report on Chaucerian research in progress appears annually in the bibliography compiled by Thomas H. Kirby in *The Chaucer Review.*

The volumes of the *The Variorum Edition of the Works of Geoffrey Chaucer,* gen. ed. Paul G. Ruggiers and Donald C. Baker, now in progress, will contain full bibliographies for each work. A new series, The Chaucer Bibliographies, first under the general editorship of H. J. Colaiaine and R. M. Piersol, now of Russell A. Peck, will eventually supply fully annotated bibliographies for each of the works. Among the selected bibliographies available is Albert C. Baugh, *Chaucer* (Goldentree Bibliographies, 2nd ed., 1977). Especially useful because of its full annotations is John Leyerle and Anne Quick, *Chaucer: A Bibliographical Introduction,* Toronto Medieval Bibliographies 10, 1986.

Caroline F. E. Spurgeon's *Five Hundred Years of Chaucer Criticism and Allusion, 1357–1900* (2nd ed., 1925, 3 vols.) provides a fascinating collection of early allusions to Chaucer and his works (see also the checklist of supplements by William L. Alderson, PQ 32, 1953, 418–27). Derek S. Brewer's *Chaucer: The Critical Heritage* (1978, 2 vols.) contains generous excerpts from many of the works Spurgeon quotes or cites; it is an anthology of comments on Chaucer from Deschamps's ballade addressed to Chaucer (c. 1385) to an excerpt from Rosamund Tuve's *Seasons and Months* (1933), and it thus provides a broad view of Chaucer criticism from the beginning to the year in which Robinson's *Chaucer* first appeared. Hammond's *Chaucer: A Bibliographical Manual* contains a survey of scholarship in the nineteenth century. The first half of this century is covered by Albert C. Baugh in "Fifty Years of Chaucer Scholarship," Speculum 26, 1951, 659–72). For reviews of more recent criticism, see those listed at the end of the section on "Critical Approaches" below. Among other surveys are:

Benson, L. D., "A Reader's Guide to Writings on Chaucer," pp. 321–72 in *Geoffrey Chaucer: Writers and Their Background,* ed. Derek S. Brewer, (1974; referred to below as Ch: Writers and Background)

Brewer, Derek S., "The Criticism of Chaucer in the Twentieth Century," pp. 3–28 in *Chaucer's Mind and Art,* ed. A.C. Cawley (1969).

Ridley, Florence, "The State of Chaucer Studies: A Brief Survey," SAC 1, 1979, 3–16.

The Companion to Chaucer Studies, ed. Beryl Rowland (rev. ed., 1979) contains chapters, with bibliographies, reviewing the state of scholarship on a variety of specific topics.

EDITIONS OF CHAUCER

The early editions of Chaucer are listed and discussed in Hammond's *Bibliographical Manual.* The first collected edition is available in a facsimile: William Thynne, ed., *Geoffrey Chaucer: The Works, 1532, with Supplementary Materials from the Editions of 1542, 1561, 1598, and 1602,* intro. Derek S. Brewer, 1969 (rpt. 1976). The first modern edition of Chaucer is that of Thomas Tyrwhitt, *The Canterbury Tales* (1775–78), which is still interesting for its critical and scholarly commentary. Skeat's *Oxford Chaucer* (1894–97) was the first scholarly edition and it remains one of the most useful, mainly because of its extensive notes and full glossary.

CANON AND CHRONOLOGY

Studies of the authenticity and dates of the individual works are cited wherever appropriate in the notes. Hammond's *Chaucer: A Bibliographical Manual* contains discussions of these problems and summaries of earlier opinions. Among the more important general studies are:

Brusendorff, Aage, *The Chaucer Tradition,* 1925.
Koch, John, *The Chronology of Chaucer's Writings,* Ch Soc, 2nd ser. 27, 1890.
Skeat, Walter W., *The Chaucer Canon, with a Discussion of the Works Associated with the Name of Geoffrey Chaucer,* 1900.
Tatlock, John S. P., *The Development and Chronology of Chaucer's Works,* Ch Soc, 2nd ser. 37, 1907 (rpt. 1963).

On the lost works:

Brown, Carleton, "Chaucer's Wreched Engendring," PMLA 50, 1935, 917–1011 (see reply by Dempster in MLN 51, 1936, 284–95).
Dear, F. M., "Chaucer's Book of the Lion," MAE 7, 1938, 105–12.
Lewis, Robert E., "What Did Chaucer Mean by 'Of the Wretched Engenderynge of Mankynde'?" ChR 2, 1968, 139–58.
McCall, John P., "Chaucer and the Pseudo Origen *De Maria Magdalena:* A Preliminary Study," Spec 46, 1971, 491–509.
Moore, Arthur K., "Chaucer's Lost Songs," JEGP 48, 1949, 198–208.

On the *Equatorie of the Planetis:*

Herdan, G., "Chaucer's Authorship of the *Equatorie of the Planetis:* The Use of Romance Vocabulary as Evidence," *Language* 32, 1956, 254–59.

North, J. D., "Kalenderis Enlumyned Ben They: Some Astronomical Themes in Chaucer," RES n.s. 20, 1969, 132–33 (a note on the *Equatorie*).
Price, Derek J., ed., *The Equatorie of the Planetis, With a Linguistic Analysis by R. M. Wilson,* 1955.
Smith, Roland M., Review of Price's edition, JEGP 57, 1958, 533–37.

On the apocryphal works see, in addition to Hammond's *Bibliographical Manual* and volume 7 of Skeat's *Oxford Chaucer* (where most of the texts are printed):

Bonner, Francis W., "The Genesis of Chaucer Apocrypha," SP 48, 1951, 461–81.
Brusendorff, Aage, *The Chaucer Tradition,* 1925 (rpt. 1965).
Hammond, Eleanor P., "Omissions from the Editions of Chaucer," MLN 19, 1904, 35–38.

LANGUAGE

The only full dictionary of Chaucer's language remains the glossary in Skeat's *Oxford Chaucer* (vol. 6). For a selected glossary see Norman Davis, Douglas Gray, Patricia Ingham, and Anne Wallace-Hadrill, *A Chaucer Glossary,* 1979. The best source of information on Chaucer's language is *The Middle English Dictionary,* ed. first by Hans Kurath, Sherman M. Kuhn, and John Reidy, and now by Robert E. Lewis (1956–), which has proven invaluable in the preparation of the present edition and its glossary. The *Oxford English Dictionary* (1884–1933), with the new *Supplement* ed. by R. W. Burchfield (1972–86) remains the best source for the study of those words not yet covered by the *Middle English Dictionary.* For proper names, see Francis P. Magoun, Jr., *A Chaucer Gazetteer* (1961) and Bert Dillon, *A Chaucer Dictionary: Proper Names and Allusions, Excluding Place Names* (1974). For a concordance and indices to rhymes, see:

Marshal, Isabel, and Lela Porter, *A Ryme-Index to MS Texts of Chaucer's Minor Poems,* Ch Soc, 1st ser. 78, 1887 (rpt. 1967).
Masui, Michio, *The Structure of Chaucer's Rime Words: An Exploration into the Poetic Language of Chaucer,* 1964 (contains indices of the rhyming words in the Tales, based on the Manly-Rickert edition, and Troilus, based on Root's edition).
Tatlock, John S. P., and Arthur G. Kennedy, *A Concordance to the Complete Works of Geoffrey Chaucer and to the Romaunt of the Rose,* 1927 (rpt. 1963). (Based on the Globe edition.)

Albert C. Baugh's *History of the English Language,* 3rd ed. with Thomas Cable (1978), contains a good discussion of the state of the English language in Chaucer's time. Ferdinand Mossé's *Handbook of Middle English,* tr. James A. Walker (1952), provides a thorough linguistic discussion. Some other helpful studies of Middle English are:

Brunner, Karl, *An Outline of Middle English Grammar,* tr. Grahame K. W. Johnston, 1963.
Luick, Karl, *Historische Grammatik der englischen Sprache* [1921–40], ed. Friedrich Wild and Herbert Koziol, 1964.

Moore, Samuel, *Historical Outlines of English Sounds and Inflections,* rev. Albert H. Marckwardt, 1951 (rpt. 1966).

Mustanoja, Tauno F., *A Middle English Syntax,* 1: *Parts of Speech,* Mémoires de la Société Néophilologique de Helsinki, 23, 1960.

Visser, Karl, *Historical Outlines of English Syntax,* 3 vols., 1963–73.

Wright, Joseph and Elizabeth M., *Elementary Middle English Grammar,* 2nd ed., 1928 (rpt. 1972).

A good general introduction to Chaucer's language is provided by J. David Burnley, *A Guide to Chaucer's Language* (1983). Among many other studies on specific aspects of Chaucer's language are:

Burnley, J. David, *Chaucer's Language and the Philosophers' Tradition,* 1979.

Davis, Norman, "Chaucer and Fifteenth-Century English," in Ch: Writers and Background, 58 – 84.

Elliott, Ralph W. V., *Chaucer's English,* 1974.

Héraucourt, Will, *Die Wertwelt Chaucers: Die Wertwelt einer Zeitwende,* 1939.

Kerkhof, Jelle, *Studies in the Language of Geoffrey Chaucer,* 2nd ed., 1982.

Kittredge, George L., *Observations on the Language of Chaucer's Troilus,* Ch Soc, 2nd ser. 28, 1894.

Mersand, Joseph E., *Chaucer's Romance Vocabulary,* 2nd ed. 1939 (rpt. 1968).

Roscow, Gregory H., *Syntax and Style in Chaucer's Poetry,* 1981.

Schlauch, Margaret, "Chaucer's Colloquial English: Its Structural Traits," PMLA 67, 1952, 1103–16.

For the pronunciation of Chaucer's English, Helge Kökeritz, *A Guide to Chaucer's Pronunciation,* rev. ed. 1962 (rpt. 1978), is especially helpful when used with Kökeritz's recorded *Chaucer Readings* (EVA Lexington LE 5505 B). Among the many other good recordings now available are the reading of the General Prologue and the Nun's Priest's Tale by Nevill Coghill, Norman Davis, and John Burrow (Argo RG 401, 466), *The Parliament of Fowls* and six lyrics by J. B. Bessinger, Jr. (Caedmon TC 1226) and the dramatic reading of extensive selections from *Troilus and Criseyde* by Gary Watson, Prunella Scales, Richard Marquand, Derek S. Brewer, and Peter Orr (2 LP records; Argo Stereo ZPL 1003–4).

METER AND VERSIFICATION

Many of the studies listed in the previous section are concerned at least in part with matters of prosody. There is a full survey of this subject, with bibliography, by Tauno F. Mustanoja in the *Companion to Chaucer Studies,* ed. Beryl Rowland (1979), 65–94. Among other important studies are:

Baum, Paull F., *Chaucer's Verse,* 1961.

Donaldson, E. Talbot, "Chaucer's Final -e," PMLA 63, 1948, 1101–24; and 64, 1949, 609.

Everett, Dorothy, "Chaucer's Good Ear," RES 23, 1947, 201–8 (rpt. in her *Essays on Middle English Literature,* ed. Patricia Kean, 1955).

Gaylord, Alan T., "Scanning the Prosodists: An Essay in Metacriticism," ChR 11, 1976, 22–82 (review of theories of Chaucer's metrics).

Halle, Morris, and Samuel J. Keyser, "Chaucer and the Study of Prosody," CE 28, 1966, 187–219. (See Wimsatt below.)

Lewis, C. S., "The Fifteenth-Century Heroic Line," E&S 24, 1930, 28–41.

Pyle, Fitzroy, "Chaucer's Prosody," MAE 42, 1973, 47–56 (a critical review of Ian Robinson's book).

Robinson, Ian, *Chaucer's Prosody: A Study of the Middle English Verse Tradition,* 1971.

Southworth, James G., "Chaucer's Final -e in Rhyme," PMLA 62, 1947, 910–35; and 64, 1949, 609–10 (but see Donaldson above).

———, *Verses of Cadence: An Introduction to the Prosody of Chaucer and His Followers,* 1954.

ten Brink, Bernhard, *The Language and Meter of Chaucer,* tr. by M. B. Smith from the 2nd rev. ed. edited by F. Kluge, 1901. (See also *Chaucers Sprache und Verskunst,* rev. 3rd ed. by E. Eckhardt, 1920.)

Wimsatt, W. K., "The Rule and the Norm: Halle and Keyser on Chaucer's Meter," CE 31, 1970, 774 – 88.

STYLE AND RHETORIC

Most general studies of Chaucer touch on matters of style, as do most of the studies of his language, cited above. Among more specialized studies are:

Baum, Paull F., "Chaucer's Puns," PMLA 71, 1956, 225– 46.

———, "Chaucer's Puns: A Supplemental List," PMLA 73, 1958, 167–70.

Birney, Earle, "The Beginnings of Chaucer's Irony," PMLA 54, 1939, 637–55.

———, "Is Chaucer's Irony a Modern Discovery?" JEGP 41, 1942, 303–19.

Bloomfield, Morton W., "Authenticating Realism and the Realism of Chaucer," *Thought* 29, 1964, 335–58 (rpt. in his *Essays and Explorations,* 1970).

Brewer, Derek S., *Toward A Chaucerian Poetic,* Sir Israel Gollancz Lecture, PBA 60, 1974.

Crosby, Ruth, "Chaucer and the Custom of Oral Delivery," Spec 13, 1938, 413–32.

Donaldson, E. Talbot, "Chaucer the Pilgrim," PMLA 69, 1954, 928–36 (rpt. in his *Speaking of Chaucer,* 1970).

Eliason, Norman E., *The Language of Chaucer's Poetry: An Appraisal of the Verse, Style, and Structure,* Anglistica 17, 1972.

Fichte, Joerg O., *Chaucer's "Art Poetical": A Study in Chaucerian Poetics,* 1980.

Howard, Donald R., "Chaucer the Man," PMLA 80, 1965, 337–43.

Kolve, V. A., *Chaucer and the Imagery of Narrative: The First Five Canterbury Tales,* 1984.

Lawler, Traugott, "Chaucer," in *Middle English Prose: A Critical Guide to Major Authors and Genres,* ed. A. S. G. Edwards, 1984.

Muscatine, Charles, *Chaucer and the French Tradition: A Study in Style and Meaning,* 1957 (rpt. 1965).

Rowland, Beryl, "Pronuntiatio and Its Effect on Chaucer's Audience," SAC 4, 1982, 33–52.

Schaar, Claes, *The Golden Mirror: Studies in Chaucer's Descriptive Technique and Its Literary Background,* 1955 (rpt. 1967).

Schlauch, Margaret, "Chaucer's Prose Rhythms," PMLA 65, 1950, 568–89.

——, "The Art of Chaucer's Prose," in *Chaucer and Chaucerians,* ed. Derek S. Brewer, 1966, 140–63.

Wenzel, Siegfried, "Chaucer and the Language of Contemporary Preaching," SP 73, 1976, 138–61.

On the general influence of the rhetorical tradition, see Robert O. Payne, "Chaucer and the Art of Rhetoric," in the *Companion to Chaucer Studies,* ed. Beryl Rowland (1979), 42–64 (with bibliography). For texts and a discussion of the use of rhetoric in earlier French poetry, see Edmond Faral, *Les arts poétiques du XIIe et du XIIIe siècle* (1924; rpt. 1958). Stephen Knight, *Rymyng Craftily* (1973), provides a list of rhetorical figures illustrated by examples from Chaucer's poetry. Among other important studies are:

Everett, Dorothy, "Some Reflections on Chaucer's 'Art Poetical,' " PBA 36, 1950 (rpt. in her *Essays on Middle English Literature,* ed. Patricia Kean, 1955).

Kökeritz, Helge, "Rhetorical Word Play in Chaucer," PMLA 59, 1954, 937–52.

Manly, John M., *Chaucer and the Rhetoricians,* Warton Lecture on English Poetry, 17 (PBA 12, 1926; rpt. in Richard J. Schoeck and Jerome Taylor, *Chaucer Criticism: The Canterbury Tales,* 1960).

Murphy, James J., "A New Look at Chaucer and the Rhetoricians," RES n.s. 15, 1964, 1–20.

——, *Rhetoric in the Middle Ages,* 1974.

Naunin, Traugott, *Der Einfluss der mittelalterlichen Rhetorik auf Chaucers Dichtung,* 1930.

Payne, Robert O., *The Key of Remembrance: A Study of Chaucer's Poetics,* 1963.

CHAUCER'S LIFE

Indispensable to the study of Chaucer's biography is *Chaucer Life-Records,* ed. Martin M. Crow and Clair C. Olson from materials compiled by John M. Manly and Edith Rickert with the assistance of Lilian J. Redstone and others (1966). All known contemporary records appear in this volume (for a description of the project see Crow, Univ. Texas Studies in English 31, 1952, 1–12). This supersedes the *Life Records of Chaucer,* ed. W. D. Selby, F. J. Furnivall, E. A. Bond, and R. E. G. Kirk (Ch Soc, 2nd ser. 12, 14, 21, 32; 1875–1900), though that work remains useful for a number of supplementary documents necessarily omitted from the *Chaucer Life-Records.* For an index, see E. P. Kuhl, MP 10, 1913, 527–552.

The early lives of Chaucer are examined by Thomas R. Lounsbury, *Studies in Chaucer* (1892; rpt. 1962), vol. 1, chs. 1–2; Hammond, *Chaucer: A Bibliographical Manual,* 1–39 (where the early brief lives are printed); and, especially valuable, Clair C. Olson, *The Emerging Biography of a Poet* (1953). For modern lives, see Marchette Chute, *Geoffrey Chaucer of England* (rev. ed. 1962) and Derek S. Brewer, *Chaucer,* 3rd rev. ed. (1973). Donald R. Howard is preparing a new biography, now in press.

Albert C. Baugh, in the *Companion to Chaucer Studies,* ed. Beryl Rowland, (1979), 1–20, provides a judicious discussion of the biographical problems and a useful select bibliography. Some important studies on special problems are:

Baugh, Albert C., "The Background of Chaucer's Mission to Spain," in *Chaucer und seine Zeit,* ed. Arno Esch, 1968, 55–69.

DuBoulay, F. H., "The Historical Chaucer," in Ch: Writers and Background, 33–57.

Garbáty, Thomas J., "Chaucer in Spain, 1366: Soldier of Fortune or Agent of the Crown?" ELN 5, 1967, 81–87.

Honoré-Duvergé, Suzanne, "Chaucer en Espagne? (1366)," *Recueil de travaux offert à M. Clovis Brunel,* 1955, 2:9–13 (announces the discovery of the record of Chaucer's trip to Spain).

Hulbert, J. R., *Chaucer's Official Life,* 1912 (rpt. 1970).

Kane, George, *The Autobiographical Fallacy in Chaucer and Langland Studies,* 1965.

Kern, Alfred A., *The Ancestry of Chaucer,* 1906.

Leland, Virginia E., "Chaucer as Commissioner of Dikes and Ditches, 1390," *Michigan Academician* 14, 1981, 71–79.

Pratt, Robert A., "Geoffrey Chaucer, Esq., and Sir John Hawkwood," ELH 15, 1949, 188–93.

Redstone, Vincent B. and Lilian J., "The Heyrons of London: A Study in the Social Origins of Geoffrey Chaucer," Spec 12, 1937, 182–95.

Rickert, Edith, "Was Chaucer a Student at the Inner Temple?" in *Manly Anniversary Studies in Language and Literature,* 1923 (rpt. 1968), 20–31.

Rudd, Martin B., *Thomas Chaucer,* 1926.

On the portraits of Chaucer, see:

Brusendorff, Aage, *The Chaucer Tradition,* 1925, 13–27.

Call, Reginald, "The Plimpton Chaucer and Other Problems of Chaucerian Portraiture," Spec 22, 1947, 135–44.

Galway, Margaret, "The *Troilus* Frontispiece," MLR 44, 1949, 161–67 (cf. Salter below, and Pearsall in the section, Chaucer's Literary Environment, below).

Lam, George L., and Warren H. Smith, "George Vertue's Contributions to Chaucerian Iconography," MLQ 5, 1944, 303–22.

Rickert, Margaret, "The Ellesmere Portrait of Chaucer," in the Manly-Rickert ed. of *The Canterbury Tales* 1:587–90.

Salter, Elizabeth, in Troilus and Criseyde: *A Facsimile of Corpus Christi College Cambridge MS 61,* intro. M. B. Parkes and Elizabeth Salter, 1978.

Spielman, M. H., *The Portraits of Geoffrey Chaucer,* Ch Soc, 2nd ser. 31, 1900.

HISTORICAL AND SOCIAL CONTEXTS

C. S. Lewis's *The Discarded Image: An Introduction to Medieval Literature* (1964; rpt. 1971), is a useful introductory discussion of the medieval world view, and Derek S. Brewer, *Chaucer in His Time* (3rd rev. ed., 1973) provides a good introduction to Chaucer's social milieu. For the general historical background see:

Ackerman, R. W., "Chaucer, the Church, and Religion," in Comp to Ch, 21– 41 (with bibliography).

Barnie, John, *War in Medieval Society: Social Values and the Hundred Years War 1377–99,* 1974.

Bloomfield, Morton W., "Fourteenth Century England: Realism and Rationalism in Wyclif and Chaucer," *English Studies in Africa 16,* 1973, 59–70.

Coulton, G. G., *The Medieval Panorama: The English Scene from Conquest to Reformation,* 1938.

——, *Chaucer and His England,* with a new bibliography by T. W. Craik, 1963.

DuBoulay, F. R. H., *The Age of Ambition: English Society in the Late Middle Ages,* 1970.

Froissart, Jean, *Chronicles,* tr. Geoffrey Brereton, 1978 (selections).

Jusserand, J. J., *English Wayfaring Life in the Middle Ages,* tr. Lucy Toulmin Smith, rev. and enl. ed. 1920 (4th ed. rpt. 1950).

Leff, Gordon, *The Dissolution of the Medieval Outlook: An Essay on Intellectual and Spiritual Change in the Fourteenth Century,* 1976.

McKisack, May, *The Fourteenth Century, 1307–1399,* Vol. 5 of the *Oxford History of England,* 1959.

Myers, Alec R., *London in the Age of Chaucer,* 1972.

Oberman, Heiko A., "Fourteenth-Century Religious Thought: A Premature Profile," Spec 53, 1978, 80–93.

Olson, Clair C., "Chaucer and Fourteenth-Century Society," in Comp to Ch, 20–37 (1968 ed. only, with bibliography).

Pantin, William A., *The English Church in the Fourteenth Century,* 1955 (rpt. 1980).

Rickert, Edith, *Chaucer's World,* ed. Clair C. Olson and Martin M. Crow, 1948 (rpt. 1968). (A collection of documents illustrative of contemporary life.)

Strutt, Joseph, *Sports and Pastimes of the People of England,* enl. and corr. ed. J. Charles Cox, 1903.

Thrupp, Sylvia L., *The Merchant Class of Medieval London (1300–1500),* 1948.

Whitmore, Sister M. Ernestine, *Medieval English Domestic Life and Amusements in the Works of Chaucer,* 1937.

For the arts in Chaucer's time, see:

Evans, Joan, "Chaucer and Decorative Art," RES 6, 1930, 408–12.

——, *English Art, 1307–1461,* 1949.

Kolve, V. A., "Chaucer and the Visual Arts," in *Geoffrey Chaucer: Writers and Their Background,* 290–320.

Loomis, Roger Sherman, *A Mirror of Chaucer's World,* 1965.

Olson, Clair C., "Chaucer and the Music of the Fourteenth Century," Spec 16, 1941, 64–91.

Pevsner, Nicholas, "Late English Medieval Architecture," in *The Age of Chaucer,* ed. Boris Ford, Pelican Guide to English Literature 1, rev. and expanded ed., 1982.

Rickert, Margaret, *Painting in England: The Middle Ages,* 2nd ed., 1965.

Smyser, Hamilton M., "The Domestic Background of *Troilus and Criseyde,*" Spec 31, 1956, 297–315.

Stone, Lawrence, *Sculpture in Britain: The Middle Ages,* 1955.

Wilkins, Nigel E., *Music in the Age of Chaucer,* 1979.

Wood, Margaret, *The English Medieval House,* 1965.

Reproductions of the art of Chaucer's time are found in some of the works listed above and in Maurice Hussey, *Chaucer's World: Pictorial Companion* (1968), as well as in such richly illustrated studies as Derek S. Brewer's *Chaucer in His Time,* D. W. Robertson's *Preface to Chaucer,* and V. A. Kolve's *Chaucer and the Imagery of Narrative.*

CHAUCER'S LEARNING

On the Properties of Things: John Trevisa's Translation of Bartholomaeus Anglicus' De proprietatibus rerum (ed. M. C. Seymour, et al., 1975), provides a convenient and fascinating compendium of the general scientific knowledge of Chaucer's time. For studies of popular lore in Chaucer's works, see Beryl Rowland, *Blind Beasts: Chaucer's Animal World* (1971), and Bartlett J. Whiting, *Chaucer's Use of Proverbs* (1934; rpt. 1973). For general studies of Chaucer's learning, see Thomas R. Lounsbury, *Studies in Chaucer* (1892; rpt. 1962), vol. 2, ch. 5, and R. W. V. Elliot, "Chaucer's Reading," pp. 46–68 in *Chaucer's Mind and Art,* ed. A. C. Cawley (1969). Among the many special studies see:

Curry, Walter Clyde, *Chaucer and the Mediaeval Sciences,* rev. ed., 1960.

Kohl, Stephan, *Wissenschaft und Dichtung bei Chaucer: Dargestellt hauptsächlich am Beispiel der Medizin,* 1973.

Manzalaoui, M., "Chaucer and Science," in *Geoffrey Chaucer: Writers and Their Background,* 224–61.

Plimpton, George A., *The Education of Chaucer: Illustrated from the English Schoolbooks in Use in His Time,* 1935.

Pratt, Robert A., "The Importance of Manuscripts for the Study of Medieval Education, as Revealed by the Learning of Chaucer," *Progress of Renaissance and Medieval Studies* 20, 1949, 509–30.

Rickert, Edith, "Chaucer at School," MP 29, 1932, 257–74.

Shepherd, Geoffrey, "Religion and Philosophy in Chaucer," in *Geoffrey Chaucer: Writers and Their Background,* 262–89.

On astronomy, see Chauncey A. Wood, "Chaucer and Astrology," in Comp to Ch, 202–20 (with bibliography) and:

Eade, J. C., " 'We ben to lewed or to slowe': Chaucer's Astronomy and Audience Participation," SAC 4, 1982, 53–85.

North, J. D., " 'Kalenderes Enlumyned Ben They': Some Astronomical Themes in Chaucer," RES n.s. 20, 1969, 129–54, 257–83, 418–44.

Smyser, Hamilton M., "A View of Chaucer's Astronomy," Spec 45, 1970, 359–73.

Wedel, Theodore O., *The Medieval Attitude toward Astrology, Particularly in England,* 1920 (rpt. 1968).

Wood, Chauncey A., *Chaucer and the Country of the Stars: Poetic Uses of Astrological Imagery,* 1970.

For additional discussion and bibliography, see the introductory note to the Explanatory Notes to *A Treatise on the Astrolabe.*

CHAUCER'S LITERARY ENVIRONMENT

For surveys of fourteenth-century English literature, see:

Burrow, John A., *Medieval Writers and Their Work: Middle English Literature and Its Background, 1100–1500,* 1982.
Pearsall, Derek, *Old English and Middle English Literature,* 1977.

Full bibliographies are supplied in *A Manual of the Writings in Middle English, 1050–1500,* ed. first by J. Burke Severs, now by Albert E. Hartung (1967–). For studies of the period, see:

Burrow, John A., *Ricardian Poetry: Chaucer, Gower, Langland, and the Gawain-Poet,* 1971.
Muscatine, Charles, *Poetry and Crisis in the Age of Chaucer,* 1972.
Salter, Elizabeth, *Fourteenth-Century English Poetry,* 1983.

For Chaucer's relation to the English tradition:

Boitani, Piero, *English Medieval Narrative in the 13th and 14th Centuries,* tr. Joan Krakover Hall, 1982.
Brewer, Derek S., "The Relationship of Chaucer to the English and European Traditions" in his *Chaucer and Chaucerians,* 1966, 1–38.
Kean, Patricia M., *Chaucer and the Making of English Poetry,* 1: *Love Vision and Debate;* 2: *The Art of Narrative,* 1972 (a shortened, one-vol. ed., 1982).

For Chaucer's audience and the literary milieu of London and the court:

Fisher, John H., *John Gower: Moral Philosopher and Friend of Chaucer,* 1964.
Giffin, Mary E., *Studies on Chaucer and His Audience,* 1956.
Green, Richard F., *Poets and Princepleasers: Literature and the English Court in the Late Middle Ages,* 1980.
McFarlane, Kenneth B., *The Nobility of Later Medieval England,* 1973.
Mathew, Gervase, *The Court of Richard II,* 1968.
Middleton, Anne, "Chaucer's 'New Men' and the Good of Literature" in *Literature and Society, Selected Papers from the English Institute* [*1978*], ed. Edward W. Said, 1980, 15–56.
Pearsall, Derek, "The *Troilus* Frontispiece and Chaucer's Audience," YES 7, 1977, 68–44.
Strohm, Paul, "Chaucer's Audience," *Literature and History* 5, 1977, 26–41.
Tout, T. F., "Literature and Learning in the English Civil Service in the Fourteenth Century," Spec 4, 1929, 365–89.
Wimsatt, James I., ed., *Chaucer and the Poems of "Ch" in University of Pennsylvania MS French 15,* 1982; French poems of the sort the young Chaucer would have known and perhaps written.

On the general literary temper of the period:

Allen, Judson B., *The Friar as Critic: Literary Attitudes in the Later Middle Ages,* 1971.
de Bruyne, Edgar, *The Aesthetics of the Middle Ages,* tr. Eileen Hennessey, 1969.

Curtius, Ernst Robert, *European Literature and the Latin Middle Ages,* tr. Willard R. Trask, 1953 (rpt. 1967); a survey of the literary "topoi" (commonplaces) available to Chaucer.
Glunz, H. H., *Die Literarästhetik des europäischen Mittelalters: Wolfram, Rosenroman, Chaucer, Dante,* 1937.
Huizinga, Johan, *The Waning of the Middle Ages,* tr. R. Hopman, 1924 (rept. 1954); an important work, though some of its basic assumptions are now questioned.
Jordan, Robert M., *Chaucer and the Shape of Creation: The Aesthetic Possibilities of Inorganic Structure,* 1967.
Olson, Glending, "Deschamps' *Art de dictier* and Chaucer's Literary Environment," Spec 48, 1973, 714–23.
———, *Literature as Recreation in the Later Middle Ages,* 1982.
Poirion, Daniel, *Le poète et le prince: L'évolution de lyricisme courtois de Guillaume Machaut à Charles d'Orleans,* 1965.
Robertson, Durant W., Jr., *A Preface to Chaucer: Studies in Medieval Perspective,* 1962.
Smalley, Beryl, *English Friars and Antiquity in the Early Fourteeth Century,* 1960.

For two contemporary views of the literary environment, see:

The Goodman of Paris (Le Ménagier de Paris): *A Treatise on Moral and Domestic Economy by a Citizen of Paris, c. 1393,* tr. (with omissions) Eileen Power, 1928. This shows, along with fascinating glimpses of contemporary life, the literary tastes of an educated citizen of the late fourteenth century (and includes versions of the tales Chaucer used for his Melibee and Clerk's tales).
The Love of Books: The Philobiblion of Richard de Bury, tr. E. C. Thomas, 1888 (rpt. 1966), a charming work by a learned contemporary.

SOURCES AND INFLUENCES

The Chaucer Library, under the direction of a committee chaired first by J. Burke Severs, then Robert A. Pratt, and now by Robert E. Lewis, is publishing a series of editions of classical and medieval texts in versions closest to those known by Chaucer; Robert E. Lewis's edition and translation of Pope Innocent's *De miseria condicionis humane* and Sigmund Eisner's edition (with translation) of the *Kalendarium* of Nicholas of Lynn have now appeared.

Detailed discussions of Chaucer's literary sources are given in the introductory notes to each work, and the relevant bibliographies are cited there. For texts of the sources, see:

Bryan, W. F., and Germaine Dempster, eds., *Sources and Analogues of Chaucer's Canterbury Tales,* 1941.
Havely, N. R., *Chaucer's Boccaccio —Sources of Troilus, and The Knight's and Franklin's Tales,* 1980.
Windeatt, Barry A., *Chaucer's Dream Poetry: Sources and Analogues,* 1982.

The *Companion to Chaucer Studies* contains chapters on the French influence by Haldeen Braddy (pp. 134–59), the Italian by Paul G. Ruggiers (pp. 160–84), and the classical by Richard L. Hoffman (pp. 185–201), each with a full bibliography. *Geoffrey Chaucer: Writers and Their Back-*

ground contains useful chapters on Chaucer and French poetry by James I. Wimsatt (pp. 109–36); the Latin classics by Bruce Harbert (pp. 137–54); the Medieval Latin poets by Peter Dronke and Jill Mann (pp. 154–83); and Italian poetry by Howard Schless (pp. 184–223). See also the following studies of the influence of specific authors and works.

The Bible

Landrum, Grace W., "Chaucer's Use of the Vulgate," PMLA 39, 1924, 75–100.

Thompson, W. Meredith, "Chaucer's Translation of the Bible," in *English and Medieval Studies Presented to J. R. R. Tolkien,* ed. Norman Davis and C. L. Wrenn, 1962, 183–99.

The Latin Poets

Ayres, Harry M., "Chaucer and Seneca," RomR 10, 1919, 1–15 (see Pratt, Spec 41, below).

Clogan, Paul M., "Chaucer's Use of the *Thebaid,*" English Miscellany 18, 1967, 9–31.

Fyler, John M., *Chaucer and Ovid,* 1979.

Hazelton, Richard, "Chaucer and Cato," Spec 35, 1960, 357–80.

McCall, John F., *Chaucer among the Gods,* 1979.

Minnis, Alistair J., *Chaucer and Pagan Antiquity,* 1982.

Pratt, Robert A., "Chaucer's Claudian," Spec 22, 1947, 419–29.

———, "Chaucer and the Hand that Fed Him," Spec 41, 1966, 619–42.

Shannon, Edgar F., *Chaucer and the Roman Poets,* 1929.

Wetherbee, Winthrop, *Chaucer and the Poets: An Essay on Troilus and Criseyde,* 1984.

Wise, Boyd A., *The Influence of Statius upon Chaucer,* 1911 (rpt. 1967).

Wrenn, C. L., "Chaucer's Knowledge of Horace," MLR 18, 1923, 286–92.

Boethius

Jefferson, Bernard L., *Chaucer and the* Consolation of Philosophy *of Boethius,* 1917 (rpt. 1968).

The French Poets

Fansler, Dean S., *Chaucer and the* Roman de la rose, 1914 (rpt. 1965).

Lowes, John L., "Chaucer and the *Ovid moralisé,*" PMLA 33, 1918, 302–25.

Wimsatt, James I., *Chaucer and the French Love Poets: The Literary Background of the* Book of the Duchess, 1968.

The Italian Poets

Boitani, Piero, *Chaucer and Boccaccio,* 1977.

Lowes, John L., "Chaucer and Dante," MP 16, 1916–17, 705–35.

Pratt, Robert A., "Chaucer's Use of the *Teseida,*" PMLA 66, 1947, 419–29.

Schless, Howard, *Chaucer and Dante: A Revaluation,* 1984.

Wallace, David, *Chaucer and the Early Writings of Boccaccio,* 1985.

Young, Karl, "Chaucer's Use of Boccaccio's *Filocolo,*" MP 4, 1906–07, 169–77.

COURTLY LOVE

The subject of courtly love, the style of aristocratic courtship that informs much of Chaucer's poetry, has become a subject of much critical debate in recent years. See especially:

Benson, Larry D., "Courtly Love in the Later Middle Ages," in *Fifteenth Century Studies,* ed. Robert Yeager, 1984, 237–57.

Benton, John F., "Clio and Venus: An Historical View of Medieval Love," in *The Meaning of Courtly Love,* ed. F. X. Newman, 1968.

Boase, Roger, *The Origin and Meaning of Courtly Love: A Critical Study of European Scholarship,* 1977.

Donaldson, E. Talbot, "The Myth of Courtly Love," in *Speaking of Chaucer,* 1970, 154–63 (rpt. of essay in *Ventures: Magazine of the Yale Graduate School* 5, 1965).

Kane, George, "Chaucer, Love Poetry, and Romantic Love," in *Acts of Interpretation,* ed. Mary J. Carruthers and Elizabeth D. Kirk, 1982, 237–55.

Kelly, Henry Angsar, *Love and Marriage in the Age of Chaucer,* 1975.

Lewis, C. S., *The Allegory of Love: A Study in Medieval Tradition,* 1936 (rpt. 1958).

Lowes, John L., "The Loveres Maladye of Hereos," MP 11, 1913–14, 491–546.

Robertson, Durant W., Jr., "Courtly Love as an Impediment to the Understanding of Medieval Texts," in *The Meaning of Courtly Love,* ed. F. X. Newman, 1968.

Steadman, John M., "Courtly Love as a Problem of Style," in *Chaucer und seine Zeit: Symposium für Walter F. Schirmer,* ed. Arno Esch, 1968, 1–33.

Walsh, P. G., ed. and tr., *Andreas Capellanus: De Amore,* 1982.

CRITICAL APPROACHES

Scholarship on Chaucer in the early part of the twentieth century was primarily historical in approach, dealing mainly with the search for his sources and the study of the biographical details of his life. Interpretation was informed by this approach (as in John M. Manly's *Some New Light on Chaucer,* 1926) or by an appreciation for Chaucer's realism (best exemplified in George L. Kittredge's *Chaucer and His Poetry,* first pub. 1915). The work of these critics is still useful, as the Explanatory Notes show; if their aesthetic preference for Chaucer's cheerful realism sometimes led them to ignore or condemn those works that did not embody that quality, they nevertheless illuminated much and defined many of the problems (for instance, the dramatic qualities of Chaucer's poetry; the marriage group in *The Canterbury Tales*) that still concern critics and readers.

By the 1960s studies of Chaucer could be said to be dominated by three approaches, the old historical, the

New Critical, and the new historical or "exegetical" schools (see William R. Crawford, *A Bibliography of Chaucer 1954–1963,* xiv–x1). The New Criticism in theory flatly "eschewed the historical approach" and was "reluctant to invoke historical data from outside the poem to explain what is in it" (Donaldson, *Chaucer's Poetry,* 2nd ed., 1975, vi). In the hands of its most distinguished practitioners, such as E. Talbot Donaldson, the New Criticism's aim was not to ban historical considerations from criticism but "to make history serve Chaucer's poetry rather than be served by it." The older historical critics were less historical than the critical disputes of the 1950s made them seem: at their worst their criticism was merely appreciative and uninformed by historical considerations; at their best—in Kittredge's genial criticism, for example—they concentrated on the text at hand and seldom invoked historical data as a means of interpretation, though the qualities they sought in the text were not those ironies, ambivalences, and verbal complexities that fascinated the New Critics and are today widely accepted as characteristic of Chaucer's works. The historical approach today is at once more historical and more aesthetic than that exemplified in the works of Kittredge or even in Manly's still useful *Some New Light on Chaucer.* Derek S. Brewer, who modestly classifies himself with "the traditional or even naive reader within the English tradition" (*Chaucer,* 3rd ed., 1973, 1), is now perhaps the foremost exponent of the historical approach. This is the consideration of *Chaucer in His Time* (the title of one of Brewer's books), "which attempts to re-create the 'culture-patterns,' at once generally historical and highly personal," of Chaucer's imaginative world (Brewer, in *Tradition and Innovation in Chaucer,* 1982, preface).

The attempt to make literary and cultural history serve Chaucer's poetry and thus to understand Chaucer in his time has characterized almost all the criticism in the past quarter-century, which has been dominated by the attempt to come to an understanding of Chaucer's own poetics. Charles Muscatine's *Chaucer and the French Tradition* (1957) provided a powerful impulse by showing that convention and originality, which once seemed the touchstones of literary merit, had a much different function in Chaucer's time than in the nineteenth century, and it gave a new impetus to studies of Chaucer's style. This impetus is most obvious in the important new studies of Chaucer's poems, treated in the light of medieval rhetoric, which began to appear in the 1950s and 1960s (see the section on Style and Rhetoric above, and especially Robert O. Payne, *The Key of Remembrance: A Study of Chaucer's Poetics,* 1963). The same impetus is evident in studies such as Robert M. Jordan's *Chaucer and the Shape of Creation* (1967), Patricia M. Kean's *Chaucer and the Making of English Poetry* (1972), Alfred David's *Strumpet Muse* (1976), Donald R. Howard's *Idea of The Canterbury Tales* (1976), and Robert B. Burlin's *Chaucerian Fiction* (1977). Many other works might be cited; all attempt in their various ways to come to an understanding of Chaucer's poetics and to read his works in the light of that understanding.

The new historical or exegetical criticism likewise attempts to define a Chaucerian poetic. It was first exemplified in an article by Durant W. Robertson, Jr., "The Doctrine of Charity in Mediaeval Literary Gardens: A Topical Approach through Symbolism and Allegory," *Speculum* 26, 1951, 24 – 49 (rpt. in his *Essays in Medieval Culture,* 1980), and fully developed in his *Preface to Chaucer* (1962). In this learned survey of medieval art, mythography, and biblical exegesis, Robertson attempts to define a "medieval aesthetic," allegorical and iconographic, derived from late classical allegorists and Pauline interpretations of the Scriptures. Chaucer, he argues, employs a literary iconography by which the reader can discover the *sentence* of the texts, which is always some aspect of *caritas*—love of the divine or its aberrations. This approach, the most controversial since Robinson's second edition appeared, has attracted much comment. See, for example:

Besserman, Lawrence, "Glossyng is a Glorious Thyng: Chaucer's Biblical Exegesis," in *Chaucer and Scriptural Tradition,* ed. David L. Jeffrey, 1984, 65–73.
Critical Approaches to Medieval Literature: Selected Papers from the English Institute 1958–59, ed. Dorothy Bethurum, 1960; see E. Talbot Donaldson, "Patristic Exegesis in the Criticism of Medieval Literature: The Opposition," 1–26; Robert E. Kaske, "The Defense," 27–60; Charles Donahue, "Summation," 61– 82.
DeNeef, A. Leigh, "Robertson and the Critics," ChR 2, 1968, 205–34.
Utley, Frances J., "Robertsonianism Redivivus," RPh 19, 1965, 250–60 (rpt. in A. C. Cawley, *Chaucer's Mind and Art,* 1969).

Chaucer's works seem to respond to almost any critical approach (see John H. Fisher, "Chaucer's Prescience," SAC 5, 1983, 3–15), perhaps because, as some modern theorists hold, the text is as much a creation of the reader as of the poet (see Chauncey Wood, "Affective Stylistics and the Study of Chaucer," SAC 6, 1984, 21– 40). In very recent years, a great variety of interdisciplinary approaches to Chaucer has been developed—sociological, Marxist, feminist, to name but a few—and there has been considerable interest in the relevance of contemporary literary theories—*Rezeptionsästhetic,* reader response, semiotics, deconstruction, speech act theory—to the reading of Chaucer's works. For reviews and discussions (with bibliographical references) see Florence Ridley, "Questions without Answers —Yet or Ever? New Critical Modes and Chaucer," ChR 16, 1981, 101– 06; and Morton W. Bloomfield, "Contemporary Literary Theory and Chaucer," in *New Perspectives in Chaucer Criticism,* ed. Donald M. Rose, 1981, 23–36 (with a response by Florence Ridley, 37–51, and further essays by Alastair J. Minnis, 53– 69, and Winthrop Wetherbee, 71– 81). The volume of such works testifies to the continuing vigor of Chaucer criticism and to the appeal of the poet to readers of all critical persuasions.

ABBREVIATIONS

CHAUCER'S WORKS

WHERE NECESSARY, the following abbreviations are used in combination with Pro (= Prologue), Epi (= Epilogue), and Intr (= Introduction). Ch (= Chaucer) is used in the citation of secondary works, as is CT (= *The Canterbury Tales*).

ABC	An ABC
Adam	Chaucers Wordes Unto Adam, His Owne Scriveyn
Anel	*Anelida and Arcite*
Astr	*A Treatise on the Astrolabe*
Bal Comp	*A Balade of Complaint*
BD	*The Book of the Duchess*
Bo	*Boece*
Buk	Lenvoy de Chaucer a Bukton
CkT	The Cook's Tale
ClT	The Clerk's Tale
Compl d'Am	Complaynt D'Amours
CT, Tales	*The Canterbury Tales*
CYT	The Canon's Yeoman's Tale
For	Fortune
Form Age	The Former Age
FranT	The Franklin's Tale
FrT	The Friar's Tale
Gent	Gentilesse
GP	General Prologue
HF	*The House of Fame*
KnT	The Knight's Tale
Lady	A Complaint to his Lady
LGW	*The Legend of Good Women*
MancT	The Manciple's Tale
Mars	The Complaint of Mars
Mel	The Tale of Melibee
MercB	Merciles Beaute
MerT	The Merchant's Tale
MilT	The Miller's Tale
MkT	The Monk's Tale
MLT	The Man of Law's Tale
NPT	The Nun's Priest's Tale
PardT	The Pardoner's Tale
ParsT	The Parson's Tale
PF	*The Parliament of Fowls*
PhyT	The Physician's Tale
Pity	The Complaint unto Pity
Prov	Proverbs
PrT	The Prioress's Tale
Purse	The Complaint of Chaucer to his Purse
Ret, Retr	Chaucer's Retraction (Retractation)
Rom	*The Romaunt of the Rose*
Ros	To Rosemounde
RvT	The Reeve's Tale
Scog	Lenvoy de Chaucer a Scogan
ShipT	The Shipman's Tale
SNT	The Second Nun's Tale
SqT	The Squire's Tale
Sted	Lak of Stedfastnesse
SumT	The Summoner's Tale
Tales, CT	*The Canterbury Tales*
Thop	Tale of Sir Thopas
Tr	*Troilus and Criseyde*
Truth	Truth
Ven	The Complaint of Venus
WBT	The Wife of Bath's Tale
Wom Nobl	Womanly Noblesse
Wom Unc	Against Women Unconstant

EDITIONS OF CHAUCER

Only editions frequently cited in the Explanatory and Textual Notes are included here; other editions are listed in the notes to the individual works.

Baugh, Bgh   Albert C. Baugh, ed., *Chaucer's Major Poetry*, 1963.

Donaldson, Don   E. Talbot Donaldson, ed., *Chaucer's Poetry: An Anthology for the Modern Reader*, 2nd ed., 1975.

Fisher, Fsh   John H. Fisher, ed., *The Complete Poetry and Prose of Geoffrey Chaucer*, 1977.

Globe, Glb   A. W. Pollard, M. H. Liddell, H. F. Heath, W. S. McCormick, eds., *The Globe Chaucer*, 1898 (rpt. 1953).

Heath, Hth   *Globe Chaucer* as above.

Koch, Kch   John Koch, ed., *Geoffrey Chaucer: Kleinere Dichtungen*, 1928 (rpt. 1947).

Liddell, Lid   *Globe Chaucer* as above.

Manly, CT   John M. Manly, ed., *Canterbury Tales by Geoffrey Chaucer*, 1928.

Manly-Rickert, M-R   John M. Manly and Edith Rickert, eds., *The Text of* The Canterbury Tales, *Studied on the Basis of All Known Manuscripts*, 1940. 8 vols.

McCormick, Mck   *Globe Chaucer* as above.

Pace-David   George B. Pace and Alfred David, eds., *Geoffrey Chaucer: The Minor Poems: Part One* (Vol. 5 of the *Variorum Chaucer*), 1982.

Pollard, Pol   *Globe Chaucer* as above.

Pratt, Tales; Prt   Robert A. Pratt, ed., *The Tales of Canterbury*, 1974.

Robinson, R., Rob F. N. Robinson, ed., *The Works of Geoffrey Chaucer,* 2nd ed., 1957.

Root, Rkr Robert K. Root, ed., *The Book of* Troilus and Criseyde, *ed. from All the Known MSS,* 1926.

Skeat, Skt Walter W. Skeat, ed., *The Complete Works of Geoffrey Chaucer,* 1894. 6 vols., with a Supplementary vol. 7, containing the apocryphal works, 1897 (the Oxford Chaucer).

Thynne, Th William Thynne, ed., *Geoffrey Chaucer: The Works, 1532, with Supplementary Material from the Editions of 1542, 1561, 1598, and 1602* (facsimile ed. Derek S. Brewer, 1969, rpt. 1976).

Tyrwhitt Thomas Tyrwhitt, ed., *The Canterbury Tales,* 1775–78. 5 vols.

JOURNALS AND SERIES

ABR	*American Benedictine Review*
Acad	*The Academy* (London)
AFP	*Archivum fratrum praedicatorum*
AHDLMA	*Archives d'Histoire Doctrinale et Littéraire du Moyen Age*
AmN&Q	*American Notes and Queries*
Anglia	*Anglia: Zeitschrift für englische Philologie*
AnM	*Annuale mediaevale*
ArAA	*Arbeiten aus Anglistik und Amerikanistik*
Archiv	*Archiv für das Studium der neueren Sprachen und Literaturen*
Athenaeum	The Athenaeum (London)
BSUF	*Ball State University Forum*
CC	Corpus Christianorum
CE	*College English*
CFMA	Classiques français du moyen âge
ChR	*Chaucer Review*
Ch Soc	Chaucer Society, London
CL	*Comparative Literature*
Criticism	*Criticism: A Quarterly for Literature and the Arts*
CritQ	*Critical Quarterly*
CSEL	Corpus Scriptorum Ecclesiasticorum Latinorum
DAI	*Dissertation Abstracts International*
E&S	*Essays and Studies* (by members of the English Association, London)
EDS	English Dialect Society
EETS	Early English Text Society (Original Series)
EETS e.s.	Early English Text Society, Extra Series
EETS, SS	Early English Text Society, Supplementary Series
EIC	*Essays in Criticism*
ELH	*ELH* (English Literary History)
ELN	*English Language Notes*
EngR	*English Record*
ES	*English Studies*
ESC	*English Studies in Canada*
ESt	*Englische Studien*
EtAng	*Etudes anglaises: Grande-Bretagne, Etats-Unis*
Expl	*The Explicator*
FFC	Folklore Fellows Communications (Helsinki)
GSLI	*Giornale storico della letteratura Italiana*
HLQ	*Huntington Library Quarterly*
JEGP	*Journal of English and Germanic Philology*
JMRS	*Journal of Medieval and Renaissance Studies*
Lang&S	*Language and Style*
LeedsSE	*Leeds Studies in English*
Loeb	The Loeb Classical Library
M&H	*Medievalia et Humanistica*
MAE	*Medium Ævum*
MLN	*MLN* (Modern Language Notes)
MLQ	*Modern Language Quarterly*
MLR	*Modern Language Review*
MP	*Modern Philology*
MS	*Mediaeval Studies* (Toronto)
MSE	*Massachusetts Studies in English*
N&Q	*Notes and Queries*
Neophil	*Neophilologus*
NM	*Neuphilologische Mitteilungen*
OL	*Orbis litterarum*
PAPS	*Proceedings of the American Philosophical Society*
PBA	*Proceedings of the British Academy*
PG	Patrologia Graeco, ed. J.-P. Migne
PL	Patrologia Latina, ed. J.-P. Migne
PLL	*Papers on Language and Literature*
PLPLS-LHS	*Proceedings of the Leeds Philosophical and Literary Society, Literary and Historical Section*
PMASAL	*Papers of the Michigan Academy of Science, Arts, and Letters*
PMLA	*PMLA* (Publications of the Modern Language Association)
PQ	*Philological Quarterly*
RBPH	*Revue belge de philologie et d'histoire*
RES	*Review of English Studies*
Rolls, Rolls Series	Rerum Britannicarum Medii Aevi Scriptores
Romania	*Romania*
RomR	*Romanic Review*
RPh	*Romance Philology*
RUO	*Revue de l'Université d'Ottawa*
SAC	*Studies in the Age of Chaucer*
SATF	Societé des Anciens Textes Français
SB	*Studies in Bibliography*
SELit	*Studies in English Literature* (Tokyo)
SHF	Societé d'Histoire de France
SMC	*Studies in Medieval Culture*
SMed	*Studi medievali*
SN	*Studia neophilologica*
SP	*Studies in Philology*
Spec	*Speculum: A Journal of Medieval Studies*
STS	Scottish Texts Society

TLF   Textes Littéraires Français
TLS   *Times Literary Supplement* (London)
TPS   *Transactions of the Philological Society* (London)
TRHS   *Transactions of the Royal Historical Society*
TSE   *Tulane Studies in English*
TSL   *Tennessee Studies in Literature*
TSLL   *Texas Studies in Literature and Language*
TWA   *Transactions of the Wisconsin Academy of Sciences, Arts, and Letters*
UMSE   *University of Mississippi Studies in English*
UTQ   *University of Toronto Quarterly*
YES   *Yearbook of English Studies*
ZRP   *Zeitschrift für romanische Philologie*

DICTIONARIES AND OTHER REFERENCE WORKS

Aarne-Thompson   Antti Aarne, *Types of the Folk Tale,* tr. and enlarged by Stith Thompson, FFC 3, 1928.

Acta Sanctorum, ed. Joanne Carnadet, 1863–1919. 60 vols. (The lives of the saints; for English versions see Butler's *Lives of the Saints*.)

Davis, Ch Glossary   Norman Davis, Douglas Gray, Patricia Ingham, and Anne Wallace-Hadrill, *A Chaucer Glossary,* 1979.

Dict. of M.A.   *The Dictionary of the Middle Ages,* gen. ed. Joseph R. Strayer, 1982–.

DNB   *Dictionary of National Biography,* ed. Leslie Stephen (vols. 1–22) and Sir Sidney Lee (with Stephen, vol. 23), 1885–1901.

Düringsfeld, Sprichwörter   Ida von Düringsfeld and Otto Freiherr von Reinsberg-Düringsfeld, *Sprichwörter der germanischen und romanischen Sprachen,* 1872–75, 2 vols.

EDD   *English Dialect Dictionary,* ed. Joseph Wright, 1896–1905, 6 vols.

Emden, BRUO   Alfred B. Emden, *A Biographical Register of the University of Oxford to 1500,* 1957–59, 3 vols.

Godefroy   *Dictionnaire de l'ancienne langue française,* ed. Frédéric Godefroy, 1881–1902, 10 vols.

Hassell   James Woodward Hassell, *Middle French Proverbs, Sentences, and Proverbial Phrases,* 1982.

Magoun, Ch Gazetteer   Francis P. Magoun, Jr., *A Chaucer Gazetteer,* 1961.

Manual ME   *A Manual of the Writings in Middle English, 1050–1100,* ed. J. Burke Severs and Albert E. Hartung, 1967–. (Replacing Wells's Manual.)

MED   *Middle English Dictionary,* ed. Hans Kurath, Sherman M. Kuhn, John Reidy, Robert E. Lewis (Editor in Chief, Q–), 1954–.

Morawski, Proverbes français   Joseph de Morawski, *Proverbes français antérieurs au XVe siècle,* CFMA, 1925.

OED   *Oxford English Dictionary,* ed. James H. A. Murray et al., corr. reissue, 1933 (rpt. 1978). 13 vols. *Supplement,* ed. R. W. Burchfield, 1972–86.

Oxford Latin Dictionary, ed. P. G. W. Glare, 1982.

Pauly-Wissowa, Real-Ency.   *Real-Encyclopädie der classischen Altertumswissenschaft,* ed. August F. von Pauly, rev. Georg Wissowa, Wilhelm Kroll, and Karl Mittelhaus, 1894–1972, 46 vols. (incl. suppl.).

Singer, Sprichwörter   Samuel Singer, *Sprichwörter des Mittelalters,* 1944–47, 3 vols.

Skeat, E. E. Proverbs   Walter W. Skeat, *Early English Proverbs, Chiefly of the Thirteenth and Fourteenth Centuries, with Illustrative Quotations,* 1910.

STC   A. W. Pollard and G. R. Redgrave, comps., *A Short Title Catalogue of Books Printed in England, Scotland, and Ireland and of English Books Printed Abroad, 1475–1610,* 1926. 2nd rev. and enl. ed. W. A. Jackson, F. S. Ferguson, and K. F. Pantzer, 1976–77.

Thompson, Motif-Index   Stith Thompson, *Motif-Index of Folk Literature: A Classification of Narrative Elements in Folk-Tale, Ballads, Myths, Fables, Medieval Romances, Exempla, Jest-Books and Local Legends,* rev. and enl. ed., 1955–58 (rpt. 1975). 6 vols.

Tilley   Morris P. Tilley, *A Dictionary of the Proverbs in England in the Sixteenth and Seventeenth Centuries,* 1950.

Tobler-Lommatzsch   *Altfranzösiches Wörterbuch: Adolf Toblers nachgelassen Materialien bearbeitet und mit Unterstützung der Preussischen Akademie der Wissenschaft,* ed. Erhard Lommatzch, 1925–.

Walther   Hans Walther, *Proverbia sententiaeque Latinitatis medii aevi,* 1963–69. 9 vols. (Vols. 7–9 ed. Paul Gerhard Schmidt.)

Whiting   Bartlett J. and Helen W. Whiting, *Proverbs, Sentences, and Proverbial Phrases from English Writings Mainly Before 1500,* 1968.

PRIMARY TEXTS

Following are abbreviations and shortened forms for the primary texts frequently cited in the notes, along with some other texts of special interest or importance. For the convenience of students, translations are noted wherever possible, but these are not necessarily the translations used in the notes, which are often those of the annotators.

Collections of Texts

Analecta hymnica medii aevi, ed. Guido Maria Dreves and Clemens Blume, 1866–1922. 55 volumes.

The Babee's Book: Early English Meals and Manners, ed. Frederick J. Furnivall, EETS, 32, 1868.

Benson and Andersson, Lit. Context   Larry D. Benson and Theodore M. Andersson, eds., *The Literary Context of Chaucer's Fabliaux: Texts and Translations,* 1971.

Bode, Scriptores Rerum Myth   See Scriptores rerum mythicarum.

Child, Ballads   Francis J. Child, *The English and Scottish Popular Ballads,* 1883–98. 5 vols. in 10 (rpt. 1965).

Ch Life Records   *Chaucer Life Records,* ed. Martin M. Crow and Clair C. Olson, 1966.

Curye on Inglysch   *Curye on Inglysch: English Culinary Manuscripts of the Fourteenth Century (Including the Forme of Cury),* ed. Constance B. Hieatt and Sharon Butler, EETS SS 8, 1985.

EHD   *English Historical Documents, 1327–1485,* ed. Alec R. Myers, 1969.

Faral, Les arts poétiques   Edmund A. Faral, *Les arts poétiques du XIIe et du XIIIe siècle: Recherches et documents sur la technique littéraire du moyen âge,* 1924.

Hammond, Engl. Verse   Eleanor P. Hammond, *English Verse Between Chaucer and Surrey,* 1927 (rpt. 1965).

Harley Lyrics, ed. Brook   *The Harley Lyrics,* ed. George L. Brook, 4th ed., 1968.

Hist. Poems, ed. Robbins   *Historical Poems of the XIVth and XVth Centuries,* ed. Rossell Hope Robbins, 1959.

Miller, Ch: Sources   Robert P. Miller, Jr., *Chaucer: Sources and Backgrounds,* 1977.

Montaiglon and Raynaud   Anatole de Montaiglon and Gaston Raynaud, *Recueil général des fabliaux,* 1872–90. 6 vols.

Mythographi Latini, ed. Thomas Muncker, Amsterdam, 1681.

Originals and Analogues   *Originals and Analogues of Some of Chaucer's* Canterbury Tales, ed. F. J. Furnivall, E. Brock, and W. A. Clouston, Ch Soc. 2nd ser. 7, 10, 15, 20, 22; 1872–87.

Poems of "Ch," ed. Wimsatt   *Chaucer and the Poems of "Ch" in University of Pennsylvania MS French 15,* ed. James I. Wimsatt, 1982.

Rel. Lyrics, ed. Brown   *Religious Lyrics of the XIVth Century,* ed. Carleton Brown, 2nd ed. rev. G. V. Smithers, 1952.

Rickert, Ch's World   Edith Rickert, *Chaucer's World,* ed. Clair C. Olson and Martin M. Crow, 1948.

S&A, Sources and Analogues   *Sources and Analogues of Chaucer's* Canterbury Tales, ed. W. F. Bryan and Germaine Dempster, 1941 (rpt. 1958).

Scriptores rerum mythicarum Latini tres, ed. G. H. Bode, 1834.

Sec. Lyrics, ed. Robbins   *Secular Lyrics of the XIVth and XVth Centuries,* ed. Rossell Hope Robbins, 2nd ed., 1955.

Two Fifteenth Century Cookery Books, ed. Thomas Austin, EETS 91, 1888 (rpt. 1964).

Windeatt, Ch's Dream Poetry   Barry S. Windeatt, *Chaucer's Dream Poetry: Sources and Analogues,* ed. and tr. Barry A. Windeatt, 1982.

Individual Authors and Works

ADENET LE ROI (*Adenès le Roi, 13th century*)

Berte aus grans piés, in *Œuvres,* ed. Albert Henry, 1951–71. 5 vols. Tr. in *The Medieval Myths,* ed. Norma L. Goodrich, 1961.

Cléomadès, in *Oeuvres,* as above.

AENEID

Aen., Aeneid   See Virgil.

ALANUS DE INSULIS (*Alain de Lille, 1125/30–1203*)

Anticlaudianus, ed. R. Bossuat, Textes Philosophiques du Moyen Age, 1955. Tr. as *Anticlaudianus, or the Good and Perfect Man,* James J. Sheridan, 1973.

Liber parabolarum, PL 210.

De planctu naturae, ed. Nikolaus Häring, SMed, 3rd ser.,

19.2, 1979. Tr. as *The Plaint of Nature,* James J. Sheridan, 1980; and as *The Complaint of Nature* in Barry A. Windeatt, *Chaucer's Dream Poetry* (extracts only).

ALBERTANUS OF BRESCIA (*Albertanus Brixiensis, ?1193–1270*)

De arte loquendi et tacendi, ed. Thor Sundby in *Brunetto Latinos levnet og skrifter,* 1869.

Liber de Amore Dei   *Liber de amore et dilectione Dei & proximi,* Coni, 1507.

Liber Cons.   *Liber consolationis et consilii,* ed. Thor Sundby, Ch Soc., 2nd ser. 8, 1873 (rpt. 1973).

AMIS AND AMILOUN

Amis and Amiloun, ed. MacEdward Leach, EETS 203, 1937.

ANCRENE WISSE (*Ancrene Riwle*)

The English Text of the Ancrene Riwle, *ed. from MS Corpus Christi College 402,* ed. J. R. R. Tolkien, EETS 249, 1962. Tr. as *The Ancrene Riwle,* Mary B. Salu, 1955.

ANDREAS CAPELLANUS (*c. 1174–1233*)

De amore libri tres, ed. E. Trojel, 2nd ed., 1964. Tr. as *The Art of Courtly Love,* John J. Parry, 1941 (rpt. 1959), and more recently by P. G. Walsh (1982). (Also known as *De arte honeste amandi.*)

ANSELM (*archbishop of Canterbury, saint, 1033–1109*)

Opera omnia, ed. F. S. Schmitt, 1938–61. 6 vols.

AQUINAS (*Thomas Aquinas, Saint, 1224/25–1274*)

Summa Theol.   *Summa theologica,* vols. 4–12 in *Opera omnia iussu Leonis XIII P. M. edita,* 1882–. Tr. by the Fathers of the English Dominican Province, rev. Daniel J. Sullivan, 1955.

JOHN ARDERNE (*fl. 1370*)

Treatises of Fistula in Ano, ed. D'Arcy Power, EETS 139, 1910 (rpt. 1968).

ARISTOTLE (*384–322 B.C.*)

De Caelo: *Aristotle on the Heavens,* ed. and tr. W. K. C. Guthrie, Loeb, 1939.

Nichomachean Ethics, ed. and tr. H. Rackham, Loeb, rev. ed., 1934.

Physics, ed. and tr. Philip E. Wicksteed and Francis M. Cornford, Loeb, rev. ed., 1957–60. 2 vols.

AUGUSTINE (*Aurelius Augustinus, saint, bishop of Hippo, 354–430*)

De Civ. Dei   *De civitate Dei contra paganos,* ed. B. Dombart and E. Kalb [1928–29], CC Ser. Lat. 47–48. 1955. Tr. as *The City of God against the Pagans,* George McCracken et al., Loeb, 1957–72, 7 vols.

Confessions   *Confessionum, libri tredecem,* ed. P. Knöll, CSEL 40, 1899–1900. Ed. and tr. W. Watts, Loeb, 1950–51. 2 vols.

AYENBITE OF INWIT

See Dan Michel.

BARTHOLOMAEUS ANGLICUS (*fl. 13th century*)

De proprietatibus rerum, London, 1601 (rpt. in facs. 1964). Tr. as *On the Properties of Things: John Trevisa's Translation of Bartholomaeus Anglicus'* De proprietatibus rerum: *A Critical Text,* ed. M. C. Seymour et al., 1975. 2 vols.

BENEDICT (*Benedict of Nursia* [*Benedictus Cassiensis*], *saint, c. 480–c. 550*)

Rule   Regula, ed. Rudolphus Hanslik, CSEL, 1960. Ed. and tr. as *The Rule of St. Benedict,* Justin McCann, 1952.

BENOÎT DE SAINTE-MAURE (*Benoît de Sainte-More, fl. late 12th century*)

Roman de Troie, ed. Leopold Constans, SATF, 1904–12. 6 vols. Tr. in *The Story of Troilus* by Robert K. Gordon, 1934 (rpt. 1980), with important omissions (see Gretchen Mieszkowski, ChR 15, 1981, 127–37). Excerpts tr. in N. R. Havely, *Chaucer's Boccaccio* (see under Boccaccio).

BERNARD OF CLAIRVAUX (*saint, c. 1090–1153*)

Opera, ed. Jean Leclercq et al., 1957–; vols. 1–2, *Sermones super Cantica canticorum;* vol 3, *Tractus et opuscula;* vol. 4, *Sermones.* Trs.: *Sermons on Cant.,* tr. a priest of Mt. Melleray, 1920 (2 vols.); *Letters,* tr. B. S. James, 1953; *Of Conversion,* tr. Watkins Williams, 1938; *On Consideration,* tr. George Lewis, 1908; *On the Love of God,* tr. T. L. Connolly, 1937; *The Steps of Humility,* tr. G. B. Burch, 1940.

BERNARDUS SILVESTRIS (*Bernard S., fl. 1136*)

Megacosmos   In *Cosmographia,* ed. Peter Dronke. Tr. as *The Cosmographia,* Winthrop Wetherbee, 1973.

BIBLIA SACRA IUXTA VULGATAM VERSIONEM

Biblia sacra iuxta vulgatam versionem, ed. Robertus Weber et al., 2nd rev. ed., 1975. See the Douai version for a translation. The King James translation of the Bible is most often cited in the notes.

BOCCACCIO (*Giovanni Boccaccio, 1313–75*)

Ameto, ed. Antonio E. Quaglio in vol. 2 of *Tutte le opere di Giovanni Boccaccio,* gen. ed. V. Branca, 1964–.
De casibus virorum illustrim, Paris, 1520 (rpt. in facs., ed. Louis B. Hall, 1962). Tr. as *The Fates of Illustrious Men,* Louis B. Hall, 1965.

De claris mulieribus, ed. V. Zaccaria in vol. 10 of *Tutte le opere.* Tr. as *Concerning Famous Women* by Guido A. Guarino, 1963.
Il Comento alla Divina commedia, ed. Domenico Guerri, Scrittori d'Italia, 1918. 2 vols.
Decameron, Dec.   *Il Decamerone,* ed. V. Branca, 1958. Tr. G. H. McWilliam, 1972.
Il Filocolo, ed. Antonio E. Quaglio in vol. 1 of *Tutte le opere.* Tr. (selections) in N. R. Havely, *Chaucer's Boccaccio —Sources of* Troilus *and the Knight's and Franklin's Tales,* 1980. Also tr. Donald Cheney and Thomas G. Bergin, 1985.
Filostrato, Fil.   *Il Filostrato,* ed. V. Branca in vol. 2 of *Tutte le opere.* Tr. with original text, Nathaniel E. Griffin, intro. Arthur B. Myrick, 1929, and in N. R. Havely, *Chaucer's Boccaccio.*
De gen. deor.   *De genealogia deorum,* ed. V. Romano, Scrittore d'Italia, 1951. Preface and Bks. 14 and 15 tr. as *Boccaccio on Poetry,* Charles G. Osgood, 1930.
Teseida, Tes.   *Il Teseida,* ed. A. Limentani in vol. 2 of *Tutte le opere.* Tr. as *The Book of Theseus,* Bernadette M. McCoy, 1974; and (selections) in N. R. Havely, *Chaucer's Boccaccio.*

BOETHIUS (*Anicius Manlius Severinus Boethius, 480–524*)

Consolation, Cons.   *De consolatione Philosophiae,* ed. Ludwig Bieler, CC Ser. Lat. 94.1, 1957. Tr. in *Tractates and Consolation of Philosophy,* ed. H. F. Stewart and E. K. Rand, rev. H. F. Stewart, 1968; also *The Consolation of Philosophy,* tr. V. E. Watts, 1969.

BOOK OF THE KNIGHT OF LA TOUR LANDRY

Book of the Knight of La Tour Landry, ed. Thomas Wright, EETS 33, rev. ed. 1868; as tr. by William Caxton, *The Book of the Knight of the Tower,* ed. M. Y. Offord, EETS, SS 2, 1971. (ME tr. of *Le Livre du chevalier de La Tour Landry pour l'enseignement de ses filles,* ed. A. de Montaiglon, 1854.)

JOHN BROMYARD (*Johannes de Bromyard; fl. 1390*)

Summa praedicantium, Venice, 1586. 2 vols.

CATO (*Attr. Marcus Porcius Cato, 234–149 B.C.; formerly attr. to "Dionysius Cato"*)

Distichs   *Disticha Catonis,* ed. M. Boas and H. J. Botschuyver, 1952. Tr. in *Minor Latin Poets,* ed. J. Wright and Arnold M. Duff, Loeb, 1984.

CHRÉTIEN DE TROYES (*Chrestien de Troyes, Christian of Troy, fl. late 12th century*)

Cligés, ed. Alexander Micha, CFMA, 1958 (rpt. 1970). Tr. L. J. Gardiner, 1912.
Erec et Enide, ed. Mario Roques, CFMA, 1952 (rpt. 1970). Tr. in *Arthurian Romances* by W. Wistar Comfort, 1914, rpt. 1975 with intro. and notes by D. D. R. Owen.
Lancelot   *Le Chevalier de la charette,* ed. Mario Roques,

CFMA, 1958 (rpt. 1972). Tr. as *Lancelot, or, The Knight of the Cart,* William W. Kibler, 1981.

Perceval   *Le Roman de Perceval ou Le conte du Graal,* ed. William R. Roach, TLF, 2nd ed., 1959. Tr. as *Perceval, or The Story of the Grail* by Ruth H. Cline, 1983.

Yvain   *Le Chevalier au lion (Yvain),* ed. Mario Roques, CFMA, 1960. Tr. Ruth H. Cline, 1975.

CICERO (*Marcus Tullius Cicero, 106–43 B.C.*)

Epist.   *Letters to His Friends,* ed. and tr. W. Glynn Williams, Loeb, 1927, 3 vols.

Disp. Tusc.   *The Tusculan Disputations,* ed. and tr. J. E. King, Loeb, 1927.

De Officiis   Ed. and tr. Walter Miller, Loeb, 1913.

De senectute, De amicitia, De divinatione, ed. and tr. William A. Falconer, Loeb, 1928.

Somnium Scipionis   In *De re publica,* ed. and tr. Clinton W. Keyes, Loeb, 1928. Tr. Derek S. Brewer, ed., *Parlement of Fowles,* 1960, App. 3; and in Barry A. Windeatt, *Chaucer's Dream Poetry.* See also Macrobius, *Commentarii in som. Scip.*

CLANVOWE (*Sir John Clanvowe, 1341?–91*)

The Works of Sir John Clanvowe, ed. V. J. Scattergood, 1975.

CLAUDIAN (*Claudius Claudianus, d. 408?*)

De IV consulatu honorii, in *Works,* below.

De raptu Proserpinae, in *Works,* ed. and tr. Maurice Platnauer, Loeb, 1922 (rpt. 1956). 2 vols.

CLÉOMADÈS

See Adenet le Roi.

CONFESSIO AMANTIS

Conf. Aman., Confessio Amantis   See Gower.

CYRURGIE OF GUY DE CHAULIAC

Cyrurgie of Guy de Chauliac, ed. Margaret S. Ogden, EETS 265, 1971. (ME translation of Guy de Chauliac (1300 –68), *La grande chirurgie,* ed. E. Nicaise, 1890.)

DANTE (*Dante Alighieri, 1265–1321*)

Convivio, ed. Maria Simonelli, 1966. Tr. William W. Jackson, 1909.

Divine Comedy   *La divina commedia,* ed. G. H. Grandgent, rev. Charles S. Singleton, 1972. Tr. Charles S. Singleton, 1970–73. 3 vols.

Vita nuova, ed. Fredi Chiappelli, 2nd ed., 1965. Tr. Mark Musa, 1973.

De vulgari eloquentia, ed. Aristide Marigo in vol. 6 of *Opere,* 1961. Tr. as *Literature in the Vernacular,* Sally Purcell, 1981.

DARES PHRYGIUS (*fictional eyewitness of Trojan war*)

De excidio Troiae historia, ed. F. Meister, 1873. Tr.

Richard M. Frazer, Jr., in *The Trojan War: The Chronicles of Dictys of Crete and Dares the Phrygian,* 1966.

EUSTACHE DESCHAMPS (*1340?–1406?*)

Œuvres complètes, ed. Auguste H. E. Queux de Saint-Hilaire and Gaston Raynaud, SATF, 1878–1903, 11 vols.

Miroir   *Miroir de mariage,* in vol. 9 of *Œuvres.*

DICTYS CRETENSIS (*fictional eyewitness of Trojan war*)

Ephemeridos belli Troiani, ed. Werner Eisenhut, 2nd ed., 1973. Tr. Richard M. Frazer, Jr. (see Dares, above).

DISTICHS

See Cato.

DIVES AND PAUPER

Dives and Pauper, ed. Priscilla H. Barnum, EETS 275, 280, 1977–80. 1 vol. in two parts.

EARLY SOUTH ENGLISH LEGENDARY

Early South English Legendary, ed. C. Horstmann, EETS 87, 1887.

ENÉAS

Enéas   *Roman d'Enéas,* ed. J.-J. Salverda de Grave, CFMA, 1964. 2 vols. Tr. John A. Yunck, 1974.

EPISTOLA VALERII AD RUFINUM

See Walter Map.

THE FLOURE AND THE LEAFE AND THE ASSEMBLY OF LADIES

The Floure and the Leafe and The Assembly of Ladies, ed. Derek A. Pearsall, 1962.

FROISSART (*Jean Froissart, 1338?–1410?*)

Ballades et rondeaux, ed. Rae S. Bauduoin, TLF, 1978.

Chronicles, Chroniques   *Chroniques,* ed. Siméon Luce, Gaston Raynaud, Léon Mirot, SHF, 1869 –1931. 12 vols. in 14. Older ed.: Baron Kervyn de Lettenhove, 1867–77. 25 vols. in 26. Tr. as *The Chronicles of Froissart,* Thomas Johnes, 1803–05, rev. ed., 1901. 4 vols. Selections tr. as Froissart, *Chronicles,* Geoffrey Brereton, 1978.

L'Espinette amoureuse, ed. Anthime Fourrier, TLF, 1963.

Joli Buisson de Jonece, ed. Anthime Fourrier, TLF, 1975.

Méliador, ed. Auguste Lognon, 1895–99. 3 vols.

Poésies   *Œuvres de Froissart: Poésies,* ed. August Scheler, 1870–72. Rpt. 1977. 3 vols. Selections tr. in Barry A. Windeatt, *Chaucer's Dream Poetry.*

FULGENTIUS (*Fabius Planciades Fulgentius, fl. c. 500; sometimes identified with Claudius*

Gordianus Fulgentius, saint, bishop of Ruspe, 467–533)

Opera, ed. Rudolphus Helm; new ed. with additions ed. Jean Préaux, 1970. Tr. as *Fulgentius the Mythographer,* Leslie G. Whitbread, 1971.

SIR GAWAIN AND THE GREEN KNIGHT

SGGK *Sir Gawain and the Green Knight,* ed. J. R. R. Tolkien and E. V. Gordon, 2nd ed. rev. Norman Davis, 1967; and in *Poems of the Pearl Manuscript,* ed. Malcolm Andrew and Ronald Waldron, 1978.

GEOFFREY OF MONMOUTH (*Galfridus Monemutensis, bishop of St. Asaph, c. 1100–1155*)

Historia regum Britanniae *Together with a literal trans. of the Welsh MS N. LXI of Jesus College, Oxford,* ed. Acton Griscom, tr. Robert E. Jones, 1929. Lat. text tr. as *History of the Kings of Britain,* Lewis Thorpe, 1966.

GEOFFREY OF VINSAUF (*d. 1210*)

Documentum de modo et arte dictandi et versificandi, ed. in Edmond Faral, *Les arts poétiques du XIIe et du XIIIe siècle,* 1924. Tr. as *Instruction in the Method and Art of Speaking and Versifying,* Roger P. Parr, 1968.
Poetria nova, ed. in Faral, *Les arts poétiques.* Tr. Margaret F. Nims, 1967.

GESTA ROMANORUM

Gesta Romanorum, ed. H. Oesterle, 1872. Modernized vers. Charles Swan, rev. W. Hooper, 1905. For ME translations see *The Early English Versions of the* Gesta Romanorum, ed. Sidney H. Herrtage, EETS e.s. 33 (re-ed. of EETS e.s. 33, ed. Sir Frederic Madden), 1879.

GIRALDUS CAMBRENSIS (*de Barri; ?1146–?1220*)

Itinerarium Cambriae: in vol 6 of *Giraldi Cambrensis opera,* ed. J. S. Brewer et al., Rolls Series, 1861–91. 8 vols. (rpt. 1964–66). Tr. Richard C. Hoare, 1806. 2 vols.

GOWER (*John Gower, 1325?–1408?*)

Conf. Aman. *Confessio amantis* in *Complete Works of John Gower,* ed. G. C. Macaulay, 1899–1902. 4 vols.
Mirour *Mirour de l'omme,* in *Works,* above.
Vox Clam. *Vox clamantis,* in *Works,* above. Tr. as *The Major Latin Works of John Gower: The Voice of One Crying and The Tripartite Chronicle,* Eric W. Stockton, 1952.

GRANDSON

See Oton de Grandson.

GRATIAN (*Gratianus, 1st half of 12th century*)

Decretum, ed. Emil Friedberg, Corpus Iuris Canonici, 1, 1879.

GREGORY (*Pope Gregory I, saint, "Gregory the Great," c. 540–604*)

Opera in PL 75–79.
Past. Care *Cura pastoralis,* PL 77. Tr. as *Pastoral Care,* Henry Davis, 1950.

GUIDO DELLE COLONNE (*13th century*)

Historia destructionis Troiae, ed. Nathaniel E. Griffin, 1936. Tr. Mary Elizabeth Meek, 1974.

GUILLAUME DE DEGUILLEVILLE (*14th century*)

Le pelerinaige de vie humaine, ed. J. J. Stürzinger, Roxburghe Club, 1893. Tr. B. M. Pickering, 1859.

GUILLAUME DE LORRIS (*fl. 1230*)

Roman See *Le Roman de la rose.*

HIGDEN (*Ranulph Higden, d. 1364*)

Polychronicon *Together with the English Translations of John Trevis [1387] and an Unknown Writer of the Fifteenth Century,* ed. Churchill Babington (vols. 1–2) and Joseph R. Lumby (vols. 3–9), Rolls Series, 1365–86 (rpt. 1964). 9 vols.

THOMAS HOCCLEVE (*1370?–1430?*)

The Minor Poems, ed. F. J. Furnivall and Israel Gollancz, EETS e.s. 61, 73; rev. A. I. Doyle and Jerome Mitchell, 1970.
The Regement of Princes and 14 of Hoccleve's Minor Poems, ed. F. J. Furnivall, EETS e.s. 72, 1897.

HORACE (*Quintus Horatius Flaccus, 65–8 B.C.*)

Opera, ed. Fr. Klinger, 1959. *Odes and Epodes* tr. C. E. Bennett, Loeb, rev. ed. 1927; *Satires, Epistles, Ars Poetica* tr. H. Rushton Fairclough, Loeb, rev. ed. 1929.

HYGINUS (*Attr. Gaius Julius Hyginus, c. 64 B.C.– 17 A.D.*)

Fabulae, ed. H. J. Rose, Oxford, 1934.

INFERNO

Inf., Inferno See Dante, *Divine Comedy.*

INNOCENT III (*Lotario dei Segni, pope, 1160/61–1216*)

De Contemptu Mundi Lotario dei Segni, *De miseria condicionis humane,* ed. and tr. Robert E. Lewis, Chaucer Library, 1978.

ISIDORE OF SEVILLE (*Isidoris, saint, bishop of Seville, c. 570–636*)

Etym., Etymologies *Etymologiae,* ed. Wallace M. Lindsay, 1911. 2 vols. Selections tr. as *An Encyclopedia of the Dark Ages,* Ernest Brehaut, 1912.

JACOBUS DE VORAGINE (*Varagine; Jacobus Januensis, 1228/30–1298*)

Legenda aurea, ed. Th. Graesse, 1850. Tr. and adapted by Granger Ryan and Helmut Ripperger, 1941; tr. as *The Golden Legend, or Lives of the Saints,* by William Caxton, ed. in modern spelling, F. S. Ellis, 1900.

JEAN DE MEUN (*Jehan de Meun, called Clopinel; d. 1305?*)

Roman, RR   See *Le Roman de la rose.*
Testament   in *Le Roman de la rose,* ed. M. Méon, 1814, vol. 4.

JEROME (*Eusebius Hieronymus, saint, 350–420*)

Opera in PL 22–30.
Adv. Jov.   *Epistola adversus Jovinianum* in his *Epistolae,* below.
Epistolae, ed. I. Hilberg, CSEL: 54–56, 1910–18. Tr. as *Letters* by Charles G. Mierow, 1960 (vol. 33 of *Ancient Christian Writers: The Works of the Fathers in Translation*).

JOHN OF SALISBURY (*Johannes Sarisburiensis, c. 1115–80*)

Metalogicon, ed. Clement C. H. Webb, 1929. Tr. Daniel C. McGarry, 1955.
Policraticus   *Policratici sive De nugis curialium et vestigiis philosophorum,* ed. Clement C. J. Webb, 1909. 2 vols. Bks. 1, 2, 3, with selections from 7 and 8 tr. as *The Frivolities of Courtiers and Footprints of Philosophers,* Joseph B. Pike, 1938. Bks. 4, 5, 6, with selections from 7 and 8 tr. as *The Statesman's Book,* John Dickinson, 1927.

JOSEPH OF EXETER (*Exoniensis; Joseph Iscanus, fl. 1190*)

Frigii Daretis Ylias: De bello Troiano, in *Werke und Briefe von Joseph Iscanus,* ed. Ludwig Gompf, 1970. Tr. as *The Iliad of Dares Phrygius,* Gildas Roberts, 1970.

JUVENAL (*Decimus Junius Juvenalis, c. 50–c. 127 A.D.*)

Satires, in *Juvenal and Persius,* ed. and tr. G. G. Ramsay, Loeb, rev. ed., 1940 (rpt. 1950).

KALENDARIUM

See Nicholas of Lynn.

KNIGHT OF LA TOUR LANDRY

See *Book of the Knight of La Tour Landry.*

LANGLAND (*William Langland, 1330?–1400?*)

PP A   *Piers Plowman, The A Text,* ed. George Kane as vol. 1 of *Piers Plowman: The Three Versions,* gen. ed. George Kane, 1960–.

PP B   *Piers Plowman, The B Text,* ed. George Kane and E. Talbot Donaldson as vol. 2 of *Piers Plowman: The Three Versions.*
PP C   *Piers Plowman, The C Text,* ed. Walter W. Skeat, 1886; 10th rev. ed., 1924; also ed. Derek Pearsall, 1978.

THE LAY FOLKS MASS BOOK

The Lay Folks Mass Book, ed. Thomas F. Simmons, EETS 71, 1879.

LEGENDA AUREA

See Jacobus de Voragine.

LIBER ALBUS

Liber Albus   The White Book of the City of London; *Compiled 1419 by John Carpenter* [*and*] *Richard Whittington,* ed. and tr. Henry T. Riley, 1861.

LIVY (*Titus Livius, 59 B.C.–17 A.D.*)

Livy, ed. and tr. B. O. Foster, F. G. Moore, E. T. Sage, and A. C. Schlesinger, Loeb, 1919–59. 14 vols.

LOTARIO DEI SEGNI

See Innocent III.

LUCAN (*Marcus Anneaus Lucan, 39–65 A.D.*)

De bello civili, ed. A. E. Housman, 1926. Tr. in Lucan, *The Civil War,* J. D. Duff, Loeb, 1926. (Also known as the "Pharsalia".)

LYDGATE (*John Lydgate, 1370?–1451?*)

The Fall of Princes, ed. Henry Bergen, EETS e.s. 121–24, 1924–27. 4 vols.
Minor Poems, ed. Henry N. McCracken, EETS e.s. 107, 192, 1911–34. 2 vols.
The Siege of Thebes, EETS e.s. 108, 125, ed. Axel Erdmann, 1911–30. 2 vols.
The Troy Book, ed. Henry Bergen, EETS e.s. 97, 103, 106, 126, 1906–35. 4 vols.

MACHAUT (*Guillaume de Machaut, d. 1377*)

Chaucer's Dream Poetry, tr. Barry A. Windeatt. (Windeatt translates selections from Machaut in this volume.)
Œuvres   *Œuvres,* ed. Ernst Hoepffner, SATF, 1908–21. 3 vols.
Œuvres, ed. Tarbé   *Œuvres,* ed. Prosper Tarbé, 1849.
Poésies lyriques, ed. Vladimir-Fedorovich Chichemaref, 1909. 2 vols.
Voir Dit   *Le Livre de Voir Dit,* ed. Paulin Paris, 1875.

MACROBIUS (*Ambrosius Macrobius Theodosius, fl. 400 A.D.*)

Commentarii in somnium Scipionis, ed. James Willis, 1970.

Tr. as *Commentary on the Dream of Scipio*, William H. Stahl, 1952.

MALORY (*Sir Thomas Malory, fl. c. 1470*)

Le Morte Darthur   Ed. as *Works*, Eugène Vinaver, 2nd ed. with corr., 1967. 3 vols.

MANDEVILLE (*Sir John Mandeville, d. 1372*)

Mandeville's Travels, ed. P. Hamelius, EETS 153, 159, 1919–23; ed. Michael C. Seymour, EETS 253, 1963.

ROBERT MANNYNG (*Robert Mannyng of Brunne, c. 1288–1338*)

Handlyng Synne, ed. Frederick J. Furnivall, EETS, 119, 123, 1901–03. 2 vols. Rpt. 1973.

WALTER MAP (*c. 1140–1209*)

Epistola Valerii ad Rufinum, in *De nugis curialium*, below.
Latin Poems, ed. Wright   *Latin Poems Commonly Attributed to Walter Map*, ed. Thomas Wright, Camden Society 16, 1841.
De nugis curialium: Courtier's Trifles, ed. M. R. James, rev. ed. and tr. C. N. L. Brooke and R. A. B. Mynors, 1983.

MARIE DE FRANCE (*12th century*)

Fables, ed. Karl Warnke, 1898. Tr. as *Medieval Fables*, Janet Beer, 1983.
Lais, ed. Karl Warnke, 3rd. ed., 1925. Tr. as *The Lais of Marie de France*, Robert Hanning and Joan Ferrante, 1978.

MARTIANUS CAPELLA (*beg. of 5th century A.D.*)

De nuptiis Philologiae et Mercurii, in *Martianus Capella*, ed. A. Dick, rev. ed. Jean Préaux, 1969. Tr. as *The Marriage of Philology and Mercury*, William H. Stahl et al., 1977.

MATHEOLUS (*fl. late 13th century*)

Lamentations   *Les Lamentations de Matheolus et le Livre de leesce de Jehan le Fèvre: Edition critique accompagnée de l'original latin des Lamentations*, ed. A. G. van Hamel, 1892–1905. 2 vols.

LE MÉNAGIER DE PARIS

Le Ménagier de Paris, ed. Georgina E. Brereton and Janet M. Ferrier, 1981. Tr. (with omissions) as *The Goodman of Paris* by Eileen Power, 1928.

METAMORPHOSES

Met., Metamorphoses   See Ovid.

DAN MICHEL OF NORTHGATE (*fl. 1340*)

Ayenbite of Inwit, or Remorse of Conscience, ed. Richard

Morris, EETS 23, 1866; Vol. 2 (intro. and notes) ed. Pamela Gradon, EETS 278, 1979.

MINOT (*Laurence Minot, 1300?–1352?*)

Poems, ed. Joseph Hall, 3rd ed., 1914.

MIRK (*John Myrc or Mirk, Johannes Mirkus, fl. 1403*)

Festial: A Collection of Homilies by Johannes Mirkus, EETS e.s. 96, ed. Theodore Erbe, 1905.
Instructions for Parish Priests, ed. Edward Peacock, EETS 31, rev. ed., 1902; ed. Gillis Kristenson, 1974.

MIROIR DE MARIAGE

See Eustache Deschamps.

ALEXANDER NECKAM (*1157–1215*)

De naturis rerum, ed. Thomas Wright, Rolls Series, 1863.

NICHOLAS OF LYNN (*fl. 1386*)

Kalendarium, Kal.   *The Kalendarium of Nicholas of Lynn*, ed. Sigmund Eisner, tr. Gary Mac Eoin and S. Eisner, Chaucer Library, 1980.

NICOLE DE MARGIVAL (*13th century*)

Panthère d'Amours   *Le dit de la panthère d'amours*, ed. Henry A. Todd, SATF, 1883. Tr. in Barry A. Windeatt, *Chaucer's Dream Poems* (extracts only).

NIGEL WIREKER (*Nigel de Longchamps, Nigellus Wirekerus; c. 1130– c. 1200*)

Speculum stultorum, ed. John H. Mozley and Robert R. Raymo, 1960. Tr. as *The Book of Daun Brunel the Ass: Nigellus Wireker's* Speculum stultorum, Graydon W. Regenos, 1959; and as *The Mirror for Fools*, J. H. Mozley, 1963.

OTON DE GRANDSON (*Othe or Otes de Graunson, d. 1397*)

Oton de Grandson: Sa vie et ses poésies, ed. Arthur Piaget, Mémoires et Documents Publiés par la Societé d'Histoire de la Suisse Romande, 3rd ser., 1941.

OVID (*Publius Ovidius Naso, 43 B.C.–17/18 A.D.*)

Ars Amatoria, Ars Am.   In *The Art of Love and Other Poems*, ed. and tr. J. H. Mozley, Loeb, rev. ed., 1957.
Her.   *Heroides and Amores*, ed. and tr. Grant Showerman, 2nd ed. rev. G. P. Gould, Loeb, 1977.
Met.   *Metamorphoses*, ed. and tr. Frank J. Miller, Loeb, 3rd ed. rev. G. P. Gould, 1957.

OVIDE MORALISÉ

Ovide Moralisé   Ovide moralisé: *Poème de commence-*

ment du quatorzième siècle, ed. C. de Boer et al., 1915–38. 5 vols.

PAMPHILUS
Pamphilus: *Prolegomena zum* Pamphilus (*de amore*) *und kritische Textausgabe,* ed. Franz G. Becker, 1972, and ed. Keith Bate, in *Three Latin Comedies,* 1976. Tr (from ed. of Jacobus Ulrich, 1893) Thomas J. Garbáty, ChR 2, 1968, 108–34.

PANTHÈRE D'AMOURS
See Nicole de Margival.

PARADISO
Par., Paradiso   See Dante, *Divine Comedy.*

PARTONOPE OF BLOIS
Partonope of Blois, ed. A. T. Bödtker, EETS e.s. 109, 1912.

PEARL
Pearl   Ed. E. V. Gordon, 1953 (rpt. 1966), and in *Poems of the Pearl Manuscript,* ed. Malcolm Andrew and Ronald Waldron, 1978.

PERSIUS (*Aulus Flaccus Persius, 34–62 A.D.*)
Satires   Ed. in *Juvenal and Persius,* ed. and tr. G. G. Ramsay, Loeb, rev. ed. 1940 (rpt. 1950).

PETER LOMBARD (*Petrus Lombardus, bishop of Paris, c. 1095–1160*)
Sentences, Sententia   *Sententiae in IV libris distinctae,* ed. Patres Colegii S. Bonaventurae, 3rd ed., Editiones Colegii S. Bonaventurae ad Claras Aquas (Quaracchi), 1977–81.

PETER OF RIGA (*Petrus Rigae, d. 1209*)
Aurora   Aurora, Petri Rigae Biblia versificata: *A Verse Commentary on the Bible,* ed. Paul E. Beichner, 1965. 2 vols.

PETRARCH (*Francesco Petrarca, 1304–74*)
Prose, ed. G. Martellotti et al., 1955.
Rime et trionfi, ed. Ferdinando Neri, 2nd ed., 1966. Tr. as *Triumphs,* Ernest H. Wilkins, 1962.

PETRUS ALPHONSUS (*1062–1110*)
Disciplina clericalis, ed. Alfons Hilka and Werner Söderhjelm, Acta Societas Scientiarum Fennicae 38.4–5, 49.4; 1911. 3 vols. Tr. as *The Scholar's Guide,* Joseph R. Jones and John E. Keller, 1969.

PETRUS COMESTOR (*P. Manducator; c. 1100–c. 1179*)
Opera in PL 198, 1053–1844.

PHAEDRUS (*1st half of 1st century A.D.*)
Fables   In *Babrius and Phaedrus,* ed. and tr. Ben Edwin Perry, Loeb, 1965.

PHARSALIA
See Lucan.

PLINY (*Gaius Plinius Secundus, "the Elder," 23–79 A.D.*)
Hist. Nat.   *Historia naturalis,* ed. and tr. H. Rackham (vols. 1–5, 9) and W. H. S. Jones (vols. 6–8), Loeb, 1938–63. 9 vols.

PIERS PLOWMAN
PP, Piers Plowman   See Langland.

PROMPTORIUM PARVULORUM
Promptorium parvulorum, ed. A. L. Mayhew, EETS e.s. 102, 1908. (Fifteenth century Latin-English dictionary.)

THE PRYMER
The Prymer or Lay Folk's Prayer Book, ed. Henry Littlehales, EETS 105, 109, 1895–97. 2 vols.

PSEUDO-HYGINUS
See Hyginus.

PTOLEMY (*Claudius Ptolemaios, c. 100–179 A.D.*)
Almagest   In *Claudii Ptolomaei opera quae extant omnia,* ed. J. L. Heiberg, 1898–1919. 3 vols. Tr. Robert Catesby Taliaferro in *Great Books of the Western World,* ed. Robert M. Hutchins, 1952, vol. 16, pp. 1–478. *Tetrabiblos,* ed. and tr. F. E. Robbins, Loeb, 1940 (rpt. 1964).

PURGATORIO
Purg., Purgatorio   See Dante, *Divine Comedy.*

RAYMOND OF PENNAFORTE (*Raimundo de Peñafort, saint, c. 1180–1275*)
Summa de poenitentia et matrimonio, Rome, 1603 (rpt. 1967).

RHETORICA AD HERENNIUM
Rhetorica ad Herennium: Ad C. Herennium Libri VI de ratione dicendi [*M. Tulli Ciceronis ad Herennium Libri VI*],

ed. and tr. Harry Caplan, Loeb, 1954 (formerly attr. to Cicero).

RICHARD OF WALLINGFORD (*abbot of St. Albans, 1292?–1334*)

Exafrenon pronosticacionum temporis, in *Richard of Wallingford: An Edition of His Writings,* ed. and tr. John D. North, 1976, 1:179–243.

ROMAN DE ENÉAS

See *Enéas.*

ROMAN DE THÈBES

Roman de Thèbes, ed. Leopold Constans, SATF, 1890. 2 vols.

ROMAN DE LA ROSE

RR, Roman de la rose   Guillaume de Lorris and Jean de Meun, *Le Roman de la rose,* ed. Ernest Langlois, SATF, 1914–24. 5 vols. Tr. as *The Romance of the Rose,* Harry W. Robbins, 1962 (verse), and Charles Dahlberg, 1971 (prose).

SARUM MISSAL

The Sarum Missal, ed. J. W. Legg, 1916. Selections tr. in Miller, *Ch: Sources.*

SECRETA SECRETORUM

Secreta secretorum: Lydgate and Burgh's Secrees of Olde Philisoffres, ed. Robert Steele, EETS e.s. 66, 1894.
Secretum secretorum, ed. Mahmoud A. Manazaouli, EETS 276, 1977. (Other ME versions of the above.)
Secreta Secretorum, ed. Robert Steele, tr. James Yonge, EETS e.s. 74, 1898.

SENECA (*Lucius Anneaus Seneca, 3/4–65 A.D.*)

Epist., Epistles   *Moral Essays,* ed. and tr. John W. Basore, Loeb, rev. ed., 1951. 3 vols.
Ad Lucilium   *Ad Lucilium epistulae morales,* ed. L. D. Reynolds, 1965. Tr. R. M. Gummere, Loeb, 1917 (rpt. 1953). 3 vols.
Tragedies, ed. and tr. Frank M. Miller, Loeb, rev. ed., 1917 (rpt. 1927). 2 vols.

SENESCHAUCY

See Walter of Henley.

SERVIUS (*Maurus Honoratus Servius, fl. late 4th century*)

In Vergilii Carmina commentarii, in *Opera,* ed. Georgius Thilo and Hermannus Hagen, 1878–1902 (rpt. 1961). 3 vols. Ed. E. K. Rand et al., *Servianorum in Vergilii Carmina commentariorum editionis Harvardianae,* 1946–65. 3 vols.

THE SEVEN SAGES OF ROME

The Seven Sages of Rome, ed. Karl Brunner, EETS 191, 1933.

SOUTH ENGLISH LEGENDARY

South English Legendary, ed. Charlotte D'Evelyn and Anna J. Mill, EETS 235–36, 244, 1956. 3 vols.

STATIUS (*Publius Papinius Statius, c. 45–96 A.D.*)

Theb., Thebaid   In *Statius,* ed. and tr. J. H. Mozley, Loeb, rev. ed., 1955–57. Tr. John B. Poynton, 1971–75. 3 vols.

THEOPHRASTUS

Theophrastus, *Liber aureolus de nuptiis,* in Jerome, *Epistola adversus Jovinianum.* (See Jerome.)

THOMAS USK (*d. 1388*)

Testament of Love, in vol. 7 of Skeat's *Oxford Chaucer,* pp. 1–145.

VALERIUS FLACCUS (*Gaius Valerius Flaccus, d. c. 90 A.D.*)

Argonautica   *Argonauticon,* ed. O. Kramer, 1913 (rpt. 1967); ed. and tr. J. H. Mozley, Loeb, 1934.

VALERIUS MAXIMUS (*1st half of 1st century A.D.*)

Facta et dicta memorabilia, ed. Carolus (Karl F.) Kempf, 1888 (rpt. 1982).

VEGETIUS (*Flavius Vegetius Renatus, fl. c. 400 A.D.*)

De re militari, ed. C. Lange, corr. ed. H. D. Blume, 1967. Tr. into French by Jean de Meun as *Art de chivalerie,* ed. Ulysse Robert, SATF, 1897.

VINCENT OF BEAUVAIS (*Vincentius Bellovacensis, 1184/95–c. 1264*)

De eruditione filiorum nobilium, ed. Arpad Steiner, 1938.
Spec. Nat.   *Speculum naturale,* in Bibliotheca Mundi Vincenti Burgundi, Douay, 1624. 4 vols. (rpt. 1964).
Spec. Hist.   *Speculum historiale,* in *Bibliotheca,* as above.

VIRGIL (*Publius Vergilius Maro, 70–19 B.C.*)

P. Vergilii Maronis opera, ed. Roger A. B. Mynors, corr. rpt., 1972. Tr. H. Rushton Fairclough, Loeb, rev. ed., 1935. 2 vols.
Aen., Aeneid   *Aeneid,* in *Opera,* above.
Ecl., Eclogues   *Eclogues,* in *Opera,* above.

WALTER OF HENLEY (*fl. 1250*)

Walter of Henley, ed. Oschinsky   *Walter of Henley and Other Treatises on Estate Management and Accounting,* ed. Dorothea Oschinsky, 1971.

WALSINGHAM (*Thomas Walsingham, c. 1360–1420*)

Historia Anglicana, ed. Henry T. Riley, Rolls Series, 1863–64. 2 vols.

WIREKER

See Nigel Wireker.

WYCLIF (*John Wycliffe, c. 1320–84*)

English Works of Wyclif, Hitherto Unprinted, ed. F. D. Matthew, EETS 74, 2nd ed. rev., 1902 (rpt. 1973).
Select English Works, ed. Thomas Arnold, 1869–71. 3 vols.

CRITICAL STUDIES

The following book-length studies and collections of essays, with their shortened and abbreviated forms, are those frequently cited in the Explanatory Notes.

Acts of Interpretation   *Acts of Interpretation: The Text in Its Contexts, 700–1600: Essays in Medieval and Renaissance Literature in Honor of E. Talbot Donaldson,* ed. Mary J. Carruthers and Elizabeth D. Kirk.
Aers, Ch, Langland   David Aers, *Chaucer, Langland and the Creative Imagination,* 1980.
Allen and Moritz, A Distinction of Stories   Judson B. Allen and Theresa A. Moritz, *A Distinction of Stories: The Medieval Unity of Chaucer's Fair Chain of Narratives for Canterbury,* 1981.
Ames, God's Plenty   Ruth M. Ames, *God's Plenty: Chaucer's Christian Humanism,* 1984.
Baum, Ch: A Crit. Appreciation   Paull F. Baum, *Chaucer: A Critical Appreciation,* 1958.
Baum, Ch's Verse   Paull F. Baum, *Chaucer's Verse,* 1961.
Bennett, Ch at Oxford   Jack A. W. Bennett, *Chaucer at Oxford and at Cambridge,* 1974.
Bennett, Ch's Bk of Fame   Jack A. W. Bennett, *Chaucer's Book of Fame: An Exposition of the "House of Fame,"* 1968.
Bennett, PF   Jack A. W. Bennett, The Parlement of Foules: *An Interpretation,* 1957.
Blair, European Armour   Claude Blair, *European Armour circa 1066 to circa 1700,* 1959.
Bloomfield, Essays   Morton W. Bloomfield, *Essays and Explorations: Studies in Ideas, Language, and Literature,* 1970.
Boitani, Ch and Boccaccio   Piero Boitani, *Chaucer and Boccaccio,* 1977.
Boitani, Ch and Fame   Piero Boitani, *Chaucer and the Imaginary World of Fame,* 1984.
Boitani, Engl. Med. Narrative   Piero Boitani, *English Medieval Narrative in the 13th and 14th Centuries,* tr. Joan Krakover Hall, 1982.

Bowden, Comm. on GP   Muriel A. Bowden, *A Commentary on the General Prologue to* The Canterbury Tales, 2nd ed., 1973.
Boyd, Ch and Liturgy   Beverly Boyd, *Chaucer and the Liturgy,* 1967.
Braddy, Geoffrey Ch   Haldeen Braddy, *Geoffrey Chaucer: Literary and Historical Studies,* 1971.
Brewer, Chaucer   Derek S. Brewer, *Chaucer,* 3rd ed., 1973.
Brewer, Ch in his Time   Derek S. Brewer, *Chaucer in His Time,* 3rd rev. ed., 1973.
Bronson, In Search of Ch   Bertrand H. Bronson, *In Search of Chaucer,* 1960.
Brooks, Ch's Pilgrims   Harold F. Brooks, *Chaucer's Pilgrims: The Artistic Order of the Portraits in the Prologue,* 1962.
Brusendorff, Ch Trad.   Aage Brusendorff, *The Chaucer Tradition,* 1925 (rpt. 1965).
Burlin, Ch Fiction   Robert B. Burlin, *Chaucerian Fiction,* 1977.
Burnley, Ch's Language   J. David Burnley, *Chaucer's Language and the Philosophers' Tradition,* 1979.
Burnley, Guide to Ch's Lang.   J. David Burnley, *A Guide to Chaucer's Language,* 1983.
Burrow, Ricardian Poetry   John A. Burrow, *Ricardian Poetry: Chaucer, Gower, Langland, and the Gawain-Poet,* 1971.
Clemen, Ch's Early Poetry   Wolfgang Clemen, *Chaucer's Early Poetry,* tr. C. A. M. Sym, 1963.
Ch and Chaucerians   *Chaucer and Chaucerians: Critical Studies in Middle English Literature,* ed. Derek S. Brewer, 1966.
Ch and ME Sts.   *Chaucer and Middle English Studies in Honor of Rossell Hope Robbins,* ed. Beryl Rowland, 1974.
Ch and Trecento   Piero Boitani, ed., *Chaucer and the Italian Trecento,* 1983.
Ch at Albany   *Chaucer at Albany,* ed. Rossell Hope Robbins, 1975.
Ch the Love Poet   *Chaucer the Love Poet,* ed. Jerome Mitchell and William Provost, 1973.
Ch Problems   *Chaucerian Problems and Perspectives: Essays Presented to Paul E. Beichner,* ed. Edward Vasta and Zacharias P. Thundy, 1979.
Ch's Mind and Art   *Chaucer's Mind and Art,* ed. A. C. Cawley, 1969.
Ch's Troilus   *Chaucer's* Troilus: *Essays in Criticism,* ed. Stephen A. Barney, 1980.
Ch und seine Zeit   *Chaucer und seine Zeit: Symposium für Walter F. Schirmer,* ed. Arno Esch, 1968.
Ch: Writers and Background   *Geoffrey Chaucer: Writers and Their Background,* ed. Derek S. Brewer, 1974.
Comp to Ch   *Companion to Chaucer Studies,* ed. Beryl Rowland, rev. ed., 1979.
Cooke, OF and Ch Fabliaux   Thomas D. Cooke, *The Old French and Chaucerian Fabliaux: A Study of Their Comic Climax,* 1978.
Cooper, Structure of CT   Helen Cooper, *The Structure of* The Canterbury Tales, 1983.
Corsa, Ch, Poet of Mirth   Helen S. Corsa, *Chaucer, Poet of Mirth and Morality,* 1964.
Craik, Comic Tales   Thomas W. Craik, *The Comic Tales of Chaucer,* 1964.
Crampton, Condition of Creatures   Georgia R.

Crampton, *The Condition of Creatures: Suffering in Chaucer and Spenser,* 1974.

Cummings, Indebtedness of Ch   Hubertis M. Cummings, *The Indebtedness of Chaucer's Works to the Italian Works of Boccaccio,* 1916 (rpt. 1965).

Curry, Ch and Science   Walter Clyde Curry, *Chaucer and the Mediaeval Sciences,* rev. ed., 1960.

Curtius, European Lit.   Ernst Robert Curtius, *European Literature and the Latin Middle Ages,* tr. Willard R. Trask, 1953 (rpt. 1967).

David, Strumpet Muse   Alfred David, *The Strumpet Muse: Art and Morals in Chaucer's Poetry,* 1976.

Delany, Ch's HF   Sheila Delany, *Chaucer's "House of Fame": The Poetics of Skeptical Fideism,* 1972.

Dempster, Dramatic Irony   Germaine Dempster, *Dramatic Irony in Chaucer,* 1932. Rpt. 1959.

Donaldson, Speaking of Ch   E. Talbot Donaldson, *Speaking of Chaucer,* 1970.

Dugdale, Monasticon   Sir William Dugdale (1605–1686), *Monasticon Anglicanum,* English, enl. edition, ed. John Caley, Sir Henry Ellis, Bulkeley Bandinel, 1846. 6 vols. in 8.

Economou, Goddess Natura   George Economou, *The Goddess Natura in Medieval Literature,* 1972.

Editing Ch   *Editing Chaucer: The Great Tradition,* ed. Paul G. Ruggiers, 1984.

Eliason, Lang. of Ch   Norman E. Eliason, *The Language of Chaucer's Poetry: An Appraisal of the Verse, Style, and Structure,* Anglistica 17, 1972.

Elliott, Ch's English   Ralph W. V. Elliott, *Chaucer's English,* 1974.

Essays on Tr   *Essays on Troilus and Criseyde,* ed. Mary Salu, 1979.

Fansler, Ch and RR   Dean S. Fansler, *Chaucer and the Roman de la rose,* 1914 (rpt. 1965).

Fichte, Ch's Art   Joerg O. Fichte, *Chaucer's "Art Poetical": A Study in Chaucerian Poetics,* 1980.

Finucane, Miracles and Pilgrims   Ronald C. Finucane, *Miracles and Pilgrims: Popular Beliefs in Medieval England,* 1977.

Fisher, John Gower   John H. Fisher, *John Gower, Moral Philosopher and Friend of Chaucer,* 1964.

Frank, Ch and LGW   Robert W. Frank, Jr., *Chaucer and The Legend of Good Women,* 1972.

French, Ch Handbook   Robert D. French, *A Chaucer Handbook,* 2nd ed., 1947.

Furnivall, Temp. Pref.   F. J. Furnivall, *A Temporary Preface to the Chaucer Society's Six-Text Edition of Chaucer's* Canterbury Tales, Ch Soc, 2nd ser., 3, 1868.

Fyler, Ch and Ovid   John M. Fyler, *Chaucer and Ovid,* 1979.

Gardner, Poetry of Ch   John C. Gardner, *The Poetry of Chaucer,* 1977.

Gerould, Ch Essays   Gordon Hall Gerould, *Chaucerian Essays,* 1952.

Giffin, Sts. on Ch   Mary E. Giffin, *Studies on Chaucer and His Audience,* 1956.

Haeckel, Sprichwort   Willibald Haeckel, *Das Sprichwort bei Chaucer,* 1890.

Hamilton, G. L.   *The Indebtedness of Chaucer's* Troilus and Criseyde *to Guido delle Colonne's* Historia Trojana, 1903.

Hammond, Ch: Bibl. Man.   Eleanor P. Hammond, *Chaucer: A Bibliographical Manual,* 1908.

Hammond, Engl. Verse   See under Collections of Texts, above.

Haskell, Ch's Saints   Anne S. Haskell, *Essays on Chaucer's Saints,* 1976.

Héraucourt, Wertwelt   Will Héraucourt, *Die Wertwelt Chaucers: Die Wertwelt einer Zeitwende,* 1939.

Hinckley, Notes on Ch   Henry B. Hinckley, *Notes on Chaucer: A Commentary on the Prologue and Six* Canterbury Tales, 1907.

Hoffman, Ovid and CT   Richard L. Hoffman, *Ovid and* The Canterbury Tales, 1966.

Howard, Idea of CT   Donald R. Howard, *The Idea of* The Canterbury Tales, 1976.

Huppé, Reading of CT   Bernard F. Huppé, *A Reading of* The Canterbury Tales, 1964.

Huppé and Robertson, Fruyt and Chaf   Bernard F. Huppé and Durant W. Robertson, Jr., *Fruyt and Chaf: Studies in Chaucer's Allegories,* 1963.

Hussey, Chaucer   S. S. Hussey, *Chaucer: An Introduction,* 2nd ed., 1981.

Jefferson, Ch and the Consolation   Bernard L. Jefferson, *Chaucer and the Consolation of Philosophy of Boethius,* 1917 (rpt. 1968).

Jordan, Ch and the Shape of Creation   Robert M. Jordan, *Chaucer and the Shape of Creation: The Aesthetic Possibilities of Inorganic Structure,* 1967.

Kean, Ch and Poetry   Patricia M. Kean, *Chaucer and the Making of English Poetry,* 1: *Love Vision and Debate;* 2: *The Art of Narrative,* 1972; shortened one-vol. ed., 1982.

Kellogg, Ch, Langland   Alfred L. Kellogg, *Chaucer, Langland, Arthur: Essays in Middle English Literature,* 1972.

Kelly, Love and Marriage   Henry Ansgar Kelly, *Love and Marriage in the Age of Chaucer,* 1975.

Kenyon, Syntax of Infinitive   John S. Kenyon, *The Syntax of the Infinitive in Chaucer,* Ch Soc, 2nd ser., 44, 1909.

Kittredge, Ch and His Poetry   George L. Kittredge, *Chaucer and His Poetry,* 55th Anniversary Edition, with an intro. by Bartlett J. Whiting, 1970.

Kittredge, Date of Tr   George L. Kittredge, *The Date of Chaucer's* Troilus *and Other Chaucer Matters,* Ch Soc, 2nd ser., 42, 1909.

Kittredge, Observations   George L. Kittredge, *Observations on the Language of Chaucer's* Troilus, Ch Soc, 2nd ser., 28, 1894.

Kittredge Anniversary Sts   *Anniversary Papers by Colleagues and Pupils of George Lyman Kittredge* [no editor listed], 1913.

Knight, Poetry of CT   Stephen T. Knight, *The Poetry of* The Canterbury Tales, 1973.

Knight, Rymyng Craftily   Stephen T. Knight, *Rymyng Craftily: Meaning in Chaucer's Poetry,* 1974.

Koch, Chronology   John Koch, *The Chronology of Chaucer's Writings,* Ch Soc, 2nd ser., 27, 1890 (rpt. 1972).

Kohl, Wissenschaft   Stephan Kohl, *Wissenschaft und Dichtung bei Chaucer: Dargestellt hauptsächlich am Beispiel der Medizin,* 1973.

Kolve, Ch and Imagery of Narrative   V. A. Kolve, *Chaucer and the Imagery of Narrative: The First Five* Canterbury Tales, 1984.

Koonce, Ch and Fame   B. G. Koonce, *Chaucer and the*

Tradition of Fame: Symbolism in The House of Fame, 1966.

Lawler, One and the Many   Traugott Lawler, *The One and the Many in* The Canterbury Tales, 1980.

Learned and Lewed   *The Learned and the Lewed: Studies in Chaucer and Medieval Literature,* ed. Larry D. Benson, 1974.

Lewis, Allegory of Love   C. S. Lewis, *The Allegory of Love,* 1936 (rpt. 1958).

Lewis, Discarded Image   C. S. Lewis, *The Discarded Image: An Introduction to Medieval and Renaissance Literature,* 1964 (rpt. 1971).

Lounsbury, Sts. in Ch   Thomas R. Lounsbury, *Studies in Chaucer,* 1892 (rpt. 1962). 3 vols.

Lowes, Art of Ch   John L. Lowes, *The Art of Geoffrey Chaucer,* Sir Israel Gollancz Memorial Lecture, British Academy, 1930.

Lowes, Geoffrey Ch   John L. Lowes, *Geoffrey Chaucer and the Development of His Genius,* 1934 (rpt. as *Geoffrey Chaucer,* 1958).

Loxton, Pilgrimage   Howard Loxton, *Pilgrimage to Canterbury,* 1978.

Lumiansky, Of Sondry Folk   Robert M. Lumiansky, *Of Sondry Folk: The Dramatic Principle in* The Canterbury Tales, 1955.

M. Madeleva, Lost Language   Sister Mary Madeleva, *A Lost Language and Other Essays on Chaucer,* 1951.

Malone, Chapters on Ch   Kemp Malone, *Chapters on Chaucer,* 1951.

Manly, New Light   John M. Manly, *Some New Light on Chaucer: Lectures Delivered at the Lowell Institute,* 1926.

Manly Anniv. Sts.   *Manly Anniversary Studies in Language and Literature,* [no ed. listed] 1923 (rpt. 1968).

Mann, Ch and Estates   Jill Mann, *Chaucer and Medieval Estates Satire: The Literature of Social Classes and the General Prologue to* The Canterbury Tales, 1973.

McAlpine, Genre of Tr   Monica E. McAlpine, *The Genre of* Troilus and Criseyde, 1978.

McCall, Ch among the Gods   John P. McCall, *Chaucer among the Gods: The Poetics of Classical Myth,* 1979.

McKisack, Fourteenth Cent.   May McKisack, *The Fourteenth Century, 1307–1399.* Vol. 5 of the *Oxford History of England,* 1959.

Med. Lit. and Folklore   *Medieval Literature and Folklore Studies: Essays in Honor of Francis Lee Utley,* ed. Jerome Mandel and Bruce A. Rosenberg, 1970.

Meech, Design in Tr   Sanford B. Meech, *Design in Chaucer's* Troilus, 1959 (rpt. 1970).

Mersand, Ch's Rom. Vocabulary   Joseph P. Mersand, *Chaucer's Romance Vocabulary,* 1937 (rpt. 1968).

Minnis, Ch and Antiquity   Alastair J. Minnis, *Chaucer and Pagan Antiquity,* 1982.

Muscatine, Ch and Fr Trad.   Charles Muscatine, *Chaucer and the French Tradition: A Study in Style and Meaning,* 1957 (rpt. 1965).

Mustanoja, ME Syntax   Tauno F. Mustanoja, *A Middle English Syntax,* 1: *Parts of Speech,* Mémoires de la Société Néophilologique de Helsinki, 23, 1960.

Myers, London   Alec R. Myers, *London in the Age of Chaucer,* 1972.

Neilson, Origins of the Court of Love   William A. Neilson, *The Origins and Sources of the Court of Love,* [Harvard] Studies and Notes in Philology and Literature 6, 1899.

New Perspectives   *New Perspectives in Chaucer Criticism,* ed. Donald H. Rose, 1981.

Norton-Smith, Geoffrey Ch   John A. Norton-Smith, *Geoffrey Chaucer,* 1974.

Nykrog, Les Fabliaux   Per Nykrog, *Les Fabliaux: Etude d'histoire littéraire et de stylistique médiévale,* 1957 (new ed. 1973).

Owen, Pilgrimage and Storytelling   Charles A. Owen, Jr., *Pilgrimage and Storytelling in* The Canterbury Tales: *The Dialectic of "Ernest" and "Game,"* 1977.

Owst, Lit and Pulpit   Gerald R. Owst, *Literature and the Pulpit in Medieval England,* 2nd rev. ed., 1961.

Owst, Preaching in Med. Engl.   Gerald R. Owst, *Preaching in Medieval England,* 1926 (rpt. 1965).

Pantin, Eng. Church   William A. Pantin, *The English Church in the Fourteenth Century,* 1955 (rpt. 1980).

Patch, Goddess Fortuna   Howard R. Patch, *The Goddess Fortuna in Medieval Literature,* 1927.

Patch, On Rereading Ch   Howard R. Patch, *On Rereading Chaucer,* 1939.

Patch, Trad of Boethius   Howard R. Patch, *The Tradition of Boethius: A Study of His Importance in Medieval Culture,* 1935.

Payne, Ch and Menippean Satire   F. Anne Payne, *Chaucer and Menippean Satire,* 1981.

Payne, Key of Remembrance   Robert O. Payne, *The Key of Remembrance: A Study of Chaucer's Poetics,* 1963.

Poirion, Le Poète   Daniel Poirion, *Le poète et le prince: l'évolution du lyricisme courtoise de Guillaume de Machaut à Charles d'Orleans,* 1965.

Preston, Ch   Raymond Preston, *Chaucer,* 1952.

Provost, Structure of Tr   William A. Provost, *The Structure of Chaucer's* Troilus and Criseyde, Anglistica 20, 1974.

Richardson, Blameth Nat Me   Janette Richardson, *"Blameth Nat Me": A Study of Imagery in Chaucer's Fabliaux,* 1970.

Robertson, Ch's London   Durant W. Robertson, Jr., *Chaucer's London,* 1968.

Robertson, Pref to Ch   Durant W. Robertson, Jr., *A Preface to Chaucer: Studies in Medieval Perspectives,* 1962.

Root, Poetry of Ch   Robert K. Root, *The Poetry of Chaucer: A Guide to Its Study and Appreciation,* rev. ed., 1922 (rpt. 1957).

Root, Text. Trad.   Robert K. Root, *The Textual Tradition of Chaucer's* Troilus, Ch Soc, 1st ser. 99, 1916.

Roscow, Syntax and Style   Gregory H. Roscow, *Syntax and Style in Chaucer's Poetry,* 1981.

Ross, Ch's Bawdy   Thomas W. Ross, *Chaucer's Bawdy,* 1972.

Rowland, Blind Beasts   Beryl Rowland, *Blind Beasts: Chaucer's Animal World,* 1971.

Ruggiers, Art of CT   Paul G. Ruggiers, *The Art of* The Canterbury Tales, 1965.

Ruggiers, Editing Ch   Paul G. Ruggiers, ed., *Editing Chaucer: The Great Tradition,* 1984.

Salter, Ch: KnT and ClT   Elizabeth Salter, *Chaucer: "The Knight's Tale" and "The Clerk's Tale,"* 1962.

Schless, Ch and Dante   Howard Schless, *Chaucer and Dante: A Revaluation,* 1984.

Seznec, Survival of the Pagan Gods   Jean Seznec, *Survival of the Pagan Gods: The Mythological Tradition and Its Place in Renaissance Humanism and Art,* tr. Barbara F. Sessions, 1953. Rpt. 1972.

Shannon, Ch and Roman Poets   Edgar F. Shannon, *Chaucer and the Roman Poets,* 1929.

Signs and Symbols   *Signs and Symbols in Chaucer's Poetry,* ed. John P. Hermann and John J. Burke, Jr., 1981.

Skeat, Ch Canon   Walter W. Skeat, *The Chaucer Canon, with a Discussion of the Works Associated with the Name of Geoffrey Chaucer,* 1900.

Spearing, Crit. and Med. Poetry   Anthony C. Spearing, *Criticism and Medieval Poetry,* 2nd ed., 1972.

Spearing, Med. Dream Poetry   Anthony C. Spearing, *Medieval Dream Poetry,* 1976.

Speirs, Ch the Maker   John Speirs, *Chaucer the Maker,* 2nd rev. ed., 1960.

Steadman, Disembodied Laughter   John M. Steadman, *Disembodied Laughter: Troilus and the Apotheosis Tradition: A Re-examination of Narrative and Thematic Contexts,* 1972.

Stevens, Music and Poetry   John E. Stevens, *Music and Poetry in the Early Tudor Court,* 1961.

Strutt, Sports and Pastimes   Joseph Strutt, *Sports and Pastimes of the People of England,* enl. and corr. ed. J. Charles Cox, 1903.

Sts. in Hon. of Baugh   *Studies in Medieval Literature in Honor of Professor Albert Croll Baugh,* ed. MacEdward Leach, 1961.

Sts. in Lang., ed. Atwood and Hill   *Studies in Language, Literature, and Culture of the Middle Ages and Later,* ed. E. Bagby Atwood and Archibald A. Hill, 1969.

Sumption, Pilgrimage   Jonathan Sumption, *Pilgrimage: An Image of Medieval Religion,* 1975.

Sypherd, Sts. in HF   W. O. Sypherd, *Studies in Chaucer's "House of Fame,"* Ch Soc, 2nd ser., 39, 1907.

Tatlock, Dev. and Chron.   John S. P. Tatlock, *The Development and Chronology of Chaucer's Works,* Ch Soc, 2nd ser. 37, 1907 (rpt. 1963).

Thorndike, Hist of Magic   Lynn Thorndike, *The History of Magic and Experimental Science,* 1923–64. 6 vols.

Thrupp, Merchant Class   Sylvia L. Thrupp, *The Merchant Class of Medieval London (1300–1500),* 1948.

Tupper, Types of Society   Frederick Tupper, *Types of Society in Medieval Literature,* 1926.

Tuve, Seasons and Months   Rosemond Tuve, *Seasons and Months: Studies in a Tradition of Middle English Poetry,* 1933.

Twycross, Med. Anadyomene   Meg Twycross, *The Medieval Anadyomene: A Study in Chaucer's Mythography,* 1972.

Wetherbee, Ch and Poets   Winthrop Wetherbee, *Chaucer and the Poets: An Essay on Troilus and Criseyde,* 1984.

Whittock, A Reading of CT   Trevor Whittock, *A Reading of The Canterbury Tales,* 1968.

Wimsatt, Ch and Fr Poets   James I. Wimsatt, *Chaucer and the French Love Poets: The Literary Background of The Book of the Duchess,* 1968.

Wimsatt, The Poems of "Ch"   James I. Wimsatt, ed., *Chaucer and the Poems of "Ch" in University of Pennsylvania MS French 15,* 1982.

Winny, Ch's Dream-Poems   James Winny, *Chaucer's Dream-Poems,* 1973.

Winternitz, Musical Instruments   E. Winternitz, *Musical Instruments and Their Symbolism in Western Art,* 2nd ed., 1979.

Wisdom of Poetry   *The Wisdom of Poetry: Essays in Early English Literature in Honor of Morton W. Bloomfield,* ed. Larry D. Benson and Siegfried Wenzel, 1982.

Wise, Infl. of Statius   Boyd A. Wise, *The Influence of Statius upon Chaucer,* 1911 (rpt. 1967).

Wood, Ch and the Stars   Chauncey Wood, *Chaucer and the Country of the Stars: Poetical Uses of Astrological Imagery,* 1970.

Wood, Elements of Tr   Chauncey Wood, *The Elements of Chaucer's Troilus,* 1984.

Young, Origin of Tr   Karl Young, *The Origin and Development of the Story of Troilus and Criseyde,* Ch Soc, 2nd ser., 40, 1908 (rpt. 1968).

EXPLANATORY NOTES

INTRODUCTION

THE EXPLANATORY NOTES are intended to provide the reader with the information needed for understanding Chaucer's text. References not dealt with in the glosses are explained, sources noted, difficult passages explicated, and, as space allows, illustrative materials are quoted. Bibliographical references are supplied so that the interested reader can explore the problems of the texts in greater detail. Where relevant, the more important critical interpretations are noted

and the state of critical opinion is described. There is, however, no attempt to provide full bibliographies of the sort that Robinson gave in his 1933 edition. The number of bibliographical aids has grown so greatly in the intervening years as to render that unnecessary, and the volume of critical publication has so increased as to make it impossible.

The emphasis in the notes differs according to the nature of each work, but in general we have concentrated on the factual rather than the speculative and on the historical rather than the interpretative; our conviction is that we best serve our readers by recording what is known and providing the references for further study, so that they can arrive at their own interpretations of Chaucer's often elusive works.

In citing illustrative materials, we have tried to empha-

size the proximate rather than ultimate sources of Chaucer's ideas and to cite, wherever possible, the most accessible texts. In the notes we have included (in translation) the more important Latin glosses found in the margins of the manuscripts of Chaucer's works; some of the glosses in the Canterbury Tales (where glossing is most frequent) may be Chaucer's own (see p. 797 below) and almost all of them provide important information about Chaucer's sources. Even those that are clearly not Chaucer's show that Chaucerian scholarship is at least as old as the earliest surviving texts.

We have used abbreviated forms for the critical books and primary texts that are most often cited; full bibliographical information is provided in the list of frequently cited works.

We have ordinarily translated references in foreign languages, and in citing Middle English texts we have usually regularized the spellings of "u" and "v," and used modern forms for thorn and yogh. "U" and "v" have likewise usually been regularized in the Latin texts quoted in the notes.

Occasionally Robinson's notes are retained or quoted; these are identified by the notation "Robinson" or "R."

LARRY D. BENSON

The Canterbury Tales

The work that Chaucer and his early scribes called *The Tales of Canterbury* (ParsT X.1086 and Pratt, PQ 54, 1975, 19–25) was begun in the late 1380s and occupied Chaucer's attention until at least the late 1390s, perhaps until the end of his life. Information on the probable dates of composition of the individual tales is in the explanatory notes to each.

The idea of a narrative framework for a collection of tales could have come to Chaucer from a great variety of sources (Cooper, Structure of CT, 8–26; Pratt and Young, in S&A, 1–11; Clawson, UTQ 20, 1951, 137–54), though earlier literature offers no exact analogue. The discovery that Chaucer visited Spain has led to speculation about his knowledge of Spanish literature (e.g., Waller, Spec 51, 1976, 292–306) and a renewal of interest in Juan Ruiz's *Libro del buen amor,* the resemblance of

which to the Tales has long been known (George Ticknor, Hist. of Span. Lit., 1849, 1:84–86). The parallel that has most interested scholars is offered by Boccaccio's *Decameron* (see Andersen, OL 27, 1972, 179–201). *The Tales of Canterbury* does resemble collections of novelle such as Boccaccio's (Robert J. Clements and Joseph Gibaldi, Anatomy of the Novella, 1977); Guerin (ES 52, 1971, 412–19), Biedler (Italica 50, 1973, 266–83) and McGrady (ChR 12, 1977, 1–26) have argued for Chaucer's direct knowledge of the *Decameron.* The evidence for Chaucer's direct use of the work is circumstantial and remains unproven (see Tedeschi, Studia Romanica et Anglica Zagrabiensia 33–36, 1972–73, 849–72; for a survey and bibliography see Ruggiers, Comp. to Ch, 161–84). Nevertheless, it is likely that Chaucer did know of the *Decameron,* at least indirectly, and it may have offered some suggestions for the *Tales*. Yet the differences between the two works are considerable, and the *Decameron* could have offered Chaucer little more than the bare suggestions for his plan (Pratt and Young, S&A, 19–20).

The *Novelle* of Giovanni Sercambi (ed. Giovanni Sinicropi, 1972; summary in S&A, 36–81) provides a closer analogue. Sercambi frames his tales with a pilgrimage-like journey (like that in the *Decameron*, a journey to avoid the plague) set in February 1374; the travelers are a diverse group and Sercambi himself serves as leader and tells all the tales. It was once believed that this work was first written in 1374 (it survives only in a later version) and that Chaucer knew and drew upon it (McGrady, Italica 57, 1980, 3–18). However, it seems clear that Sercambi's realistic framework and exact date are fictional and that the work must date from after 1400 (ed. Sinicropi, 779–86, and GSLI 141, 1964, 548–56; cf. the ed. of Luciano Rossi, 1976, xix–xx, and Nicholson, Italica 53, 1976, 201–13).

Chaucer may have drawn the suggestions for his pilgrimage from life. Pilgrimages were common (Jonathan Sumption, Pilgrimage, 1975; Howard Loxton, Pilgrimage to Canterbury, 1978; Ronald C. Finucane, Miracles and Pilgrims, 1977) and telling tales was an ordinary pastime for travelers (cf. GP I.771–74 and Brown, MLN 52, 1937, 28–31). Chaucer may also have been influenced by the travel literature and accounts of pilgrimages then becoming popular (Christian K. Zacher, Curiosity and Pilgrimage, 1976; Donald R. Howard, Writers and Pilgrims, 1980). Nevertheless, Chaucer makes little attempt to depict an actual pilgrimage (Howard, Idea of CT, 159–62), and many critics today assume that his pilgrimage, like Sercambi's, is intended as a metaphor rather than a direct reflection of life.

The assumption that Chaucer did attempt to portray an actual pilgrimage spurred efforts to determine the precise date and itinerary of his pilgrims' journey. The traditional date, 1387, was established by Skeat (3:373–74), who assumed that 18 April (IntrMLT II.5–6) was the second day of a four-day journey and consulted calendars for the years 1386–90 (having ruled out 1385 as too early and 1391 as too late). He eliminated 1386, when 18 April fell in Holy Week (and the Parson would have been needed at home), 1388 and 1390, which would have necessitated Sunday travel and, at the least, attendance at Mass would have prevented an early start, and 1389, when 18 April was Easter, a day unsuitable for telling tales. This left only 1387, which was also the year to which Skeat assigned The Knight's Tale. However, the Introduction to The Man of Law's Tale may belong to the first day rather than the second (Stevens, LeedsSE n.s. 1, 1967, 1–5); Sunday Mass need not have prevented an early start (see the itinerary of the Count of Ostrevant printed by Flügel, Anglia 23, 1901, 239–41); religious festivals were no bar to "honest mirthes" (Dives and Pauper, ed. Barnum, EETS 275, 296–97); a date of 1387 for The Knight's Tale would seem to indicate a later date for the General Prologue; and, most important, there is no indication in the text that Chaucer had any particular day in mind.

F. J. Furnivall in 1868 (Temp. Pref., 12–18, 26, and 39–41), influenced by Henry Bradshaw (see Baker, Ch Newsletter 3, 1981, 2–6), first advanced the theory that Chaucer's pilgrimage to Canterbury took three to four days. The roads, he explained, were a "swampy mess" in April, and three royal itineraries all showed a four-day journey (Temp. Pref., 119–32). Flügel (Anglia 23:239–41) gathered itineraries from Froissart that showed the journey between London and Canterbury ranged from one to four days, though the one-day journey was the dowager queen's flight from Jack Straw's rebellion. To these should be added the journey of the Londoner, cured by Becket and "so pleased that he walked fifty miles to Canterbury in one day, so the registrar wrote, to strip, show himself cured, and challenge all comers to a foot race" (Finucane, Miracles, 101).

A three- to four-day journey is still widely assumed (e.g., Baugh, 233, and French, Ch Handbook, 196–98). The only surviving record of a nonroyal pilgrimage (aside from the enthusiastic walker) is that made in 1415 by two Aragonese ambassadors (F. J. Furnivall and R. E. G. Kirk, Analogues to Ch's Pilgrimage, Ch Soc., 2nd ser., 36, 1908), who made a comfortable one-night, two-day journey. The reference to "prime" in The Squire's Tale may indicate that more than one day was intended; the time of The Manciple's Prologue seems also to have been early morning (IX.15–16). One could argue that the pilgrims spend two nights and three days on the road, which fits the usual rate of fourteenth-century travel, twenty to thirty miles a day (Thorold Rogers, Hist. of Agriculture and Prices in Eng., 1866, 1:506–7, 2:610–14). However, it is not clear that Chaucer paid much attention to this matter. The related question of the stopping places on the journey cannot be answered with certainty either, since it hinges on the order of the tales (on which see Textual Notes).

Speculation about their proper sequence is based on the assumption that Chaucer left his work unfinished, the apparent fact that he made changes in plan and arrangement as he worked, and the inference that other changes were intended but never effected. Initially, the Host's plan (GP I.790–801) calls for 120 stories, two from each of the thirty pilgrims (twenty-nine plus Chaucer) on the way to Canterbury and two on the return trip; in The Franklin's Prologue, the plan has apparently been reduced to "a tale or two" (V.698), and by the time of The Parson's Prologue another pilgrim has been added, the Canon's Yeoman, and the plan now calls for but one tale each (X.16, 24). Apparently the return trip has been abandoned. Some critics assume that a homeward journey was still intended (Root, MLN 44, 1929, 493–96; Manly, SP 28, 1931, 613–17; Owen, Pilgrimage and Storytelling, 1977). The continuations of the *Tales* in Lydgate's *Siege of Thebes* and in the anonymous *Tale of Beryn* (ed. F. J. Furnivall and W. G. Stone, EETS e.s. 105, 1909) are both set in Canterbury and initiate a homeward journey, as if both authors assumed that Chaucer had not taken his pilgrims that far and were attempting to complete the plan announced in the General Prologue (see Bower, SAC 7, 1985, 23–50).

Chaucer apparently also made changes in the order and assignment of the tales. At an early stage of the composition, the Man of Law evidently told The Tale of Melibee and the Wife of Bath told what is now The Shipman's Tale (Dempster, PMLA 68, 1953, 1142–59; Pratt, in Sts. in Hon. of Baugh, ed. McEdward Leach, 1961, 45–79). Some believe that The Merchant's Tale was originally assigned to another pilgrim (see introductory note to MerT) and other revisions have been suspected; on the general problem see Fisher, MLR 67, 1972, 241–51, and Owen in Comp. to Ch, 221–42.

Nineteenth-century criticism sometimes treated *The Tales of Canterbury* as a mere collection of tales whose main interest lay in the framework rather than in the stories "patched up by fits and starts" (G. G. Coulton, Ch and His England, 3rd ed., 1908, 144). Studies such as Kittredge's discussion of the "marriage group" (MP 9, 1912, 435–67) helped focus attention on the interplay among the tales, and his emphasis on the dramatic relation between tale and teller (Ch and His Poetry, 146–218) encouraged a dramatic reading of the work as a whole, most thoroughly in Robert M. Lumiansky, Of Sondry Folk, 1955.

Lumiansky's study led him to the conclusion that, though unfinished, the work is nearly complete as it stands (TSE 6, 1956, 5–13). Ralph W. Baldwin, while rejecting the "roadside drama" approach, likewise argued for the integrity of the work as it stands: that its narrative frame is essentially complete, with a clearly defined beginning and end and with a primarily metaphoric, rather than dramatic or narrative, function (Unity of CT, Anglistica 5, 1955). These views underlie a striking change in critical thinking about the *Tales*. Studies written since the early 1950s show a new appreciation of the fact that modern ideas of literary form do not necessarily apply to medieval works (Robert M. Jordan, Ch and the Shape of Creation, 1967, 111–31), a shift of attention from the dramatic interplay among the pilgrims, where the unfinished character of the *Tales* is most obvious, and a tendency to treat the *Tales* as a thematically unified whole. Helen S. Corsa (Ch, Poet of Mirth and Morality, 1964), Bernard F. Huppé (Reading of CT, 1964), Paul G. Ruggiers (Art of CT, 1965), P. M. Kean (Ch and Poetry, 1972, 2:153–75), and Judson B. Allen and Theresa A. Moritz (A Distinction of Stories, 1981) all find some degree of thematic unity in the work. That they do so, even though none treats the tales in a sequential order, may be explained by the theory that the tales are organized not as a straightforward story of pilgrimage but in the "interlaced" manner of medieval romance (Leyerle, E&S, 1976, 107–21; Howard, Idea of CT, 1976, 210–332; Cooper, Structure of CT, 69–72).

Even critics who find more variety than thematic unity in the work tend to treat the tales in a sequential order, (e.g., Whittock, A Reading of CT, 1968, and David, Strumpet Muse, 1976). Some recent critics even regard the sequence of the tales (in the Ellesmere order) as an integral part of Chaucer's meaning (David R. Pischke, Movement of CT, 1977; Gardner, Poetry of Ch, 1977, 227–37). Given the increasingly broad consensus that the tales are somehow unified and the recent tendency to accept even the order in which they appear in the manuscripts as Chaucer's own, it is perhaps not surprising that some critics regard the work as complete and finished as it stands. John Norton-Smith argues that the *Tales* was intended to be an "imperfect work" (Geoffrey Ch, 1974, 79–159); Howard emphasizes that the plan for four tales is the Host's rather than Chaucer's and that the "unfinished quality" of the *Tales* "is a feature of its form, not a fact of its author's career" (Idea of CT, 1 and 162); Lawler argues that the apparently unfinished quality is calculated, that Chaucer intended but one tale for each pilgrim from the beginning and that the Host's ambitious plan is part of a "pattern of diminishment" (One and the Many, 1980, 118). This shift to the consideration of the *Tales* as an artistically unified whole has been one of the most remarkable features of Chaucerian criticism in the last three decades. At the same time, there has been a strong attack on the whole assumption that the tales are dramatic in any way (Robertson, Pref to Ch), and some critics have stressed variety rather than unity (Payne, Ch and Menippean Satire), while, as these notes show, much of the most valuable criticism of the *Tales* treats each tale in isolation, as parts of a single fragment, or as expressions of themes independent of any particular order or theory of a unified whole. Moreover, some recent studies have emphasized the fragmentary nature of the *Tales* and argued that the apparent unity of the work is most likely the achievement of an early editor or literary executor (see Blake, E&S 32, 1979, 1–18, and ed. CT Edited from the Hengwrt MS, 1980; Doyle and Parkes, in Med. Scribes, MSS and Libraries: Essays Presented to N. R. Ker, ed. M. B. Parkes and A. G. Watson, 1978, 163–210; cf. Owen, PMLA 97, 1982, 237–50).

Studies of individual tales are cited in the notes that follow. The full annotation in Skeat's edition remains valuable, and Donaldson's edition provides very useful interpretative commentary. Derek Pearsall, CT, 1985, provides a good survey of critical and scholarly problems. Perhaps the earliest commentaries on the tales are to be found in the marginal Latin glosses in such manuscripts as the Hengwrt and Ellesmere; they are especially frequent in The Man of Law's Tale, The Wife of Bath's Prologue and Tale, the tales of the Summoner, Clerk, Merchant, and Franklin, and The Pardoner's Prologue. Owen (PMLA 97, 1982, 240–41) argues from the crowding of the glosses on the pages in the Hengwrt manuscript that they were added later by the Hengwrt scribe, but at least some of the glosses are most likely Chaucer's own (M-R 3:483–587; Dempster, MLN 52, 1937, 20, and MP 41, 1943, 6; Silvia, SP 62, 1965, 28–39; see introductory note to The Man of Law's Tale and the note to line 41 of the Clerk's Prologue). The more important marginal glosses (almost all those from the Ellesmere manuscript) are translated from Manly and Rickert's text (M-R:483–525) in the following notes.

LARRY D. BENSON

FRAGMENT I

The General Prologue and the tales of the Knight, Miller, Reeve, and Cook form a dramatically unified group which, though unfinished, is so tightly knit that it was almost never broken up in the scribal rearrangements. In addition to its obvious dramatic unity, critics have found a variety of unifying themes. Besides the works cited in the preceding section, note might be taken of studies of the themes of rivalry (Frost, RES 26, 1949, 289–304), betrayal and deception (Owen, ES 35, 1954, 49–56), justice (Olsen, MLQ 24, 1963, 227–36), human and divine judgment (Delasanta, MLQ 31, 1970, 298–307), "herbergage" (Joseph, ChR 5, 1970, 63–96), and time and space (Blodgett, Spec 51, 1976, 477–93).

LARRY D. BENSON

General Prologue

Chaucer probably wrote the General Prologue in the late 1380s, but a precise date cannot be determined. The only clear historical reference, to the sea route between Middelburg and Orwell, is of little help (see 276, 277 below). Probably Chaucer began work on the *Tales* in 1387–88, but we cannot know whether he first composed a number of tales or began with the General Prologue. Nor can we determine when Chaucer finished the Prologue, since it is likely that he revised it from time to time. No completely convincing case has been made for any specific revision, such as Hammond's theory that the Miller, Manciple, Reeve, Summoner, and Pardoner were added in a later draft (Ch: Bibl. Man. 254–55), nor for the theories that the Squire or the Five Guildsmen are later additions (see 101 below and the introductory note on the Guildsmen), though Pratt (in Sts. in Hon. of Baugh, 45–79) offers good support for Hammond's suggestion (Ch: Bibl. Man., 254) that the Wife of Bath's portrait was not given its final form until her present prologue was finished. If it is true that Chaucer intended to compose portraits of the Second Nun and Nun's Priest (see 164 below), there is further reason to believe that he did revise from time to time and that the Prologue as we have it contains some of his latest work.

The form of the General Prologue is original with Chaucer, though it owes much to the convention of the dream vision (Cunningham, MP 49, 1952, 172–81). The portraits are indebted to the medieval rhetorical tradition (Haselmayer, in S&A, 3–5), as transmitted both by rhetorical treatises (Faral, Les arts poétiques; Claes Schaar, Golden Mirror, 1955), and in previous poetry, especially that of Benoît de-Sainte-Maure (Lumiansky, JEGP 55, 1956, 431–38) and the *Roman de la rose* (Baedendyck, EngR 21, 1970, 113–25), as well as in conventional descriptions of Vices and Virtues (Patch, MLN 40, 1925, 1–14). Chaucer also drew on his knowledge of the medieval sciences (Curry, Ch and Science) and on life itself (Manly, New Light). The most valuable recent study of the literary background of the portraits is Jill Mann's Ch and Med. Estates Satire, 1973, which considers them from the standpoint of "estates satire"—satire of the estates (occupations) of medieval society—and provides a useful analysis of the methods by which Chaucer employed traditional materials to create characters "to whom we respond as individuals" (189).

Mann's resolution of the old problem of whether the portraits represent "individuals" or "types" (for which she provides a useful bibliography, p. 289 n. 1) has been challenged (Morgan ES 58, 1977, 381–83). Indeed, the question has been broadened in recent years by D. W. Robertson's vigorous advocacy of his theory that Chaucer does not create characters in the ordinary sense: such a character as the Wife of Bath, he maintains, is not intended to be individualized but is rather an "elaborate iconographic figure designed to show the manifold implications of an attitude," a philosophical rather than a psychological construct (Preface to Ch, 330–31).

The General Prologue is sometimes regarded as deliberately disordered, as a means of adding verisimilitude (Nevill Coghill, The Poet Ch, 1949, 116), and, since it is an introduction we might not expect it to stand alone as a unified work in itself. Nevertheless, the question of its unity and the related problem of the order of the portraits have concerned many critics. The influential article by Hoffman (ELH 21, 1954, 1–16) focused attention on tone and theme as the major sources of unity. Muscatine suggests that the sequence of portraits has the form of a rhetorical catalogue (in Ch and Chaucerians, 95; see also Martin, ELH 45, 1978, 1–17). Others have found the organizing principle to be that of artistic con-

trasts (Harold F. Brooks, Ch's Pilgrims: The Artistic Order of the Portraits in the Prologue, 1962), the "three estates"—the traditional division of society into "Those who fight, those who pray, and those who work"—(Corsa, Ch, Poet of Mirth, 85–87; David, Strumpet Muse, 58–76), or of more complex contemporary ideas of rank and order (Swart, Neophil 38, 1954, 127–36; Reidy, PMASAL 47, 1962, 593–603; Morgan, ES 59, 1978, 481–98; Higgs, HLQ 45, 1982, 155–73), or of the pilgrims' occupational and economic concerns (Nevo, MLR 58, 1963, 1–9); Lenaghan, Comp. Sts. in Soc. and Lit. 12, 1970, 73–82). Gardner argues, unconvincingly, that the order of the portraits reflects the theory of the tripartite soul (Poetry of Ch, 232–41), and Howard proposes a mnemonic arrangement (Idea of CT, 148–58). Kirby (in Comp. to Ch, 249–53, 264) provides a helpful survey of the problem.

The question of the relation of the narrator of the Prologue to Chaucer himself has much concerned critics in recent years. Few today would accept the old assumption that Chaucer was writing autobiographically (cf. Manly, CT, 497). Kittredge's rejection of the related assumption of a "naive" Chaucer ("a naïf Collector of Customs would be a paradoxical monster," Ch and His Poetry, 45) and his emphasis on Chaucer's dramatic method underlies much of the modern concern with the dramatic stance of the narrator and the resulting irony, a subject little considered in previous criticism (Derek S. Brewer, Ch: Crit. Heritage, 1978, 2:11). Though some have argued that the narrator is so little developed that he is without a consistent point of view (Kimpel, ELH 20, 1953, 77–86, and Duncan, in Essays in Hon. of Walter C. Curry, 1955, 77–110), there is no doubt of the importance of the narrator's viewpoint in shaping the reader's response to the portraits (Woolf, CritQ 1, 1959, 150–57); Mann's discussion (Ch and Estates, 190–202) is especially valuable. Donaldson's thesis that the narrator is an ironic literary persona—"Chaucer the pilgrim"—distinct from the author (PMLA 69, 1954, 928–36, rpt. in Speaking of Ch) has been widely influential (e.g., Huppé, A Reading, 21–29, and Fisher, Works, 7) but also much disputed by critics such as Bertrand H. Bronson (In Search of Ch, 28), who rejects the notion of a "schizoid Chaucer," and Majors (PMLA 75, 1960, 160–63), who finds the narrator "shrewd and clever" rather than naively inept. Still others argue that the poet and narrator cannot be so sharply distinguished (Baum, Ch: A Crit. Appreciation, 62 and 219 n. 3; Howard, PMLA 80, 1965, 337–43; Garbáty, PMLA 89, 1974, 97–104). Donaldson himself was more cautious about this matter than many who have adopted the thesis.

A useful survey of the critical problems of the Prologue is provided by Kirby in Comp. to Ch, 243–70. Muriel Bowden's Comm. on GP remains the most useful compendium of information on the historical background of Chaucer's pilgrims, and Mann's Ch and Estates the best treatment of their literary backgrounds. The celebrated Ellesmere portraits are well reproduced in Ellesmere Miniatures of Cant. Pilgrims, ed. Theo Stemmler, 1977, which also contains a useful discussion and bibliography.

LARRY D. BENSON

1–11 Skeat (5:1–2) noted the striking similarities to Guido delle Colonne, *Historia destructionis Troiae,* a work which Chaucer knew well (see Intro. to Explanatory Notes to *Troilus*): "It was the time when the aging ("maturans") sun in its oblique circle of the zodiac had already entered ("cursum suum") into the sign of Aries, in which the equal length of nights and days is celebrated in the Equinox of Spring; when the weather begins to entice eager mortals into the pleasant air; when the ice has melted and breezes ("Zephiri") ripple the flowing streams; when the springs burst forth in fragile bubbles; when moistures exhaled from the bosom of the earth are raised up to the tops of trees and branches, for which reason the seeds sprout, the crops grow, and the meadows bloom, embellished with flowers of various colors; when the trees on every side are decked with renewed leaves; when earth is adorned with grass, and the birds sing and twitter in music of sweet harmony. Then almost the middle of the month of April had passed when . . . the aforesaid kings, Jason and Hercules, left port with their ship" (ed. Griffin, 1936, 34–35; tr. Meek, 1974, 33–34). Chaucer knew Adenet le Roi's *Cléomadès*, a thirteenth-century romance (S&A, 366), and Rea (PQ 46, 1967, 128–30) suggests that he may have also known that author's *Berte aus grans piés* (ed. Holmes, 1946); this romance opens with a description of April that inspires the author to visit the shrine of St. Denis in Paris, where he meets a monk who gives him a book containing the romance that he then relates. The April opening of Creton's *Hist. of Richard King of Eng.,* which also involves a journey that provides the matter to be related (ed. Webb, Archeologia 20, 1824, 13), may be indebted to the *Tales,* since Creton, who wrote after Chaucer's death, had connections with the English court. Numerous parallels have been found in other works—among the most suggestive being the *Pervigilium veneris,* a second-century Latin poem celebrating an April festival (Hankins, MLN 49, 1934, 80–83)—for the description of Spring was a literary commonplace. See Rosemond Tuve, Seasons and Months, 1933 where the tradition of describing the seasons in encyclopedias is given particular prominence (see also Tuve, Spring in Ch, MLN 52, 1937, 9–16); Nils E. Envist, The Seasons of the Year, Societas Scientiarum Fennica (Helsinki), Commentationes Hum. Litt. 22.4, 1957, 109–14; and James J. Wilhelm, The Cruelest Month: Spring, Nature, and Love, 1965. Chaucer most likely owed the idea of beginning his narrative with a description of Spring to the dream vision; cf. Rom 52–90, BD 291–303, PF 183–210, ProLGW, and see Cunningham, MP 49:173–74.

1   Aprill: Skeat printed a final *-e* and scanned *Whan that Aprílle*. Robinson printed the *-e* in his first edition but warned that it was not pronounced; he dropped it from his second edition, influenced by Manly's scansion *Whán that Áprill* (CT, 495); Evans (N&Q 202, 1957, 234–37) makes a case for the *-e* and the scansion *Whán that Aprílle.*

   soote: Fisher (JEGP 50, 1951, 326–31) notes that *soote* and *swote* were used to translate Lat. *suavis* and thus means "gentle, fragrant"; *swete* was used to translate *dulcis,* sweet. The distinction is not uniformly observed; cf. KnT I. 2427, Form Age 42.

2   The dryness (**droghte**) of March has been attributed to literary convention but is a fact (Hart, TSLL 4, 1962–63, 525–29; Daley, ChR 4, 1970, 171–79); the phrase "drought of March" (*sekernesse de mars*) is used in Walter of Henley, ed. Oschinsky, 326–27. A dry March, necessary for sowing, promised a good crop; cf. Whiting

B611: "A bushel of March dust is worth a king's ransome."

5–6   Cf. BD 402–3, Bo 1.m5.22–23, LGW F 171–73.

7–8   The sun is **yonge** (Guido: "maturans") because the solar year has just begun with the vernal equinox (then 12 March; cf. Astr 2.1.7). Aries, **the Ram,** is the first sign of the zodiac, through which the sun passed from 12 March to 11 April. On the face of it, these lines fix the time at the beginning of April, when the sun was a bit more than halfway through Aries. However, since 18 April is specified in the IntrMLT II.5–6, **halve cours** is usually taken to mean the second half of the sun's course through Aries that falls in April. By 16 or 17 April the sun was five or six degrees into Taurus. Chaucer is usually more precise in such references, and Lydgate perhaps corrects him in the Prologue to the *Siege of Thebes* (vv. 1–2; Lydgate's dating fixes the time as 28 April, the reading of many MSS in IntrMLT II.5; see Parr, PMLA 67, 1952, 254–57). Prins (in Ch and ME Sts., 342–45) argues that Chaucer here refers to the stellar zodiac (rather than the terrestrial, which he ordinarily used), on which the equinox would have been 2 April, with half its course in Aries completed on 17 April. For Chaucer's knowledge of the stellar zodiac see FranT V.1280n.

   Chaucer first uses the specification of time by astronomical periphrasis (chronographia) in *Troilus,* influenced by Boccaccio (see Tr 1.155–58n.), Statius, and perhaps mainly Dante, who was very fond of the device (Curtius, European Lit., 275–76). He uses the device frequently in the *Tales* (IntrMLT II.6, MerT IV.1885–87, 2219–24, SqT V.48–51, 263–65, FranT V.1245–49, ParsPro X.2–12); cf. FranT V.1017–18 and Tr 2.904–6. See Wood, Ch and Stars, 70–102.

10   That birds sleep with open eyes is apparently original with Chaucer; the line is imitated in the *Sowdone of Babylon*: "Loveres slepen with open ye / As nightingales on grene tre" (ed. Emil Hausknecht, EETS e.s., 38, 1881 41–48). If Chaucer does refer to nightingales, **slepen . . . with open ye** may be a sort of litotes meaning "sleep not at all," since nightingales were said to sing continuously day and night in the mating season (see 98 below). Skeat suggests a parallel with the modern expression "sleep with one eye open," sleep very lightly (5:3). Baugh (237) quotes R. C. Murphy, who supports that explanation: "The reference [is] to the fact that most birds are light sleepers and . . . take their slumbers in snatches rather than in the human manner" (Ch's Maj. Poetry, 237). R. C. Paynter of the Museum of Comparative Zoology, Harvard University, kindly informs us that one can rarely see a bird with its eyes closed, since most birds have two sets of eyelids, and that which they use for blinking is transparent.

11   **nature:** The personified goddess Natura (Magoun, MLN 70, 1955, 399; cf. PF 303n.).

13   **palmeres:** Carried a palm branch as a sign they had been to the Holy Land. Many were perpetual pilgrims, sworn to poverty, who journeyed from one shrine to another, often as paid substitutes for deceased persons (cf. Rickert, Ch's World, 267–68) or for those who could not find time to go themselves (Sumption, Pilgrimage, 298–99).

17   **martir:** Thomas Becket was martyred in 1170, canonized in 1173. His shrine at Canterbury was rivaled only by Walsingham as an object of pilgrimage until the Reformation. See Loxton, Pilgrimage to Cant., 92–115. St. Thomas was especially associated with healing, and the water from a miraculous well near his shrine was highly prized for its curative powers; see Finucane, Miracles, 153–72.

17–18   seke . . . seeke: A *rime riche,* or identical rhyme, much admired in ME and OF poetry; see Kökeritz, PMLA 69, 1959, 937–52; Ito, SELit 46, 1969, 29–44; Machui Masui, Structure of Ch's Rime Words, 1964, 28–30.

20   Southwerk: A borough south of London, across London Bridge at the beginning of the road to Canterbury, it was known not only for its many inns but also for its numerous brothels (Myers, London, 11; cf. 719 below). The **Tabard** was an inn so called from its sign, shaped like a tabard, a sleeveless smock embroidered with armorial bearings (the word was also applied to a laborer's smock; see GP I.541). There was an actual inn of this name in Southwark (Manly, CT, 498). A sixteenth-century inventory (Norman, Surrey Archaeol. Soc., Collections 13, 1897, 28–38) shows it was as commodious as Chaucer indicates (GP 28–29). On its later history see William Rendle and P. Norman, Inns of Old Southwark, 1888, 181–201. Though a public house of this name now stands on the site, the original inn was destroyed by fire in 1676.

24   On the number of pilgrims see 164 below. There has been speculation about this number (which recurs in ParsPro X.4). Keenan notes that 29 December is Thomas Becket's saint's day (AMN&Q 16, 1978, 66–67), and it has been explained by medieval number theory as emblematic of imperfection (Peck, ES 48, 1967, 207) and of "the approach to perfection" (Reiss, SP 67, 1970, 304).

33   The subject of **made** is "we" implied in the preceding line. When the context makes the subject clear, the pronoun is frequently omitted (cf. lines 529, 786, 811). For a full discussion see Mustanoja, ME Syntax, 138–45.

37   resoun: Probably used here in its technical sense of "ordo" (proper order, suitable arrangement); see Goffin, MLR 21, 1926, 13–18.

The Knight

The Knight is usually considered an experienced and distinguished professional man-of-arms, motivated by religious ideals (Hoffman, ELH 21, 1954, 5–7; Bowden, Comm. on GP, 44–73; David, Strumpet Muse, 59) and genuinely admired by the poet. William Blake (Desc. Catalogue [1809] in Compl. Writings, ed. Keynes, 1966, 566) takes him as the universal "guardian of man against the oppressor"; Donaldson (881) as the pattern of perfection "against which all the other pilgrims may be measured." Thus it is appropriate that he appears first in the series (Harold F. Brooks, Ch's Pilgrims, 1962, 13). Some recent critics judge him more harshly: Mitchell (MLQ 25, 1964, 66–75) finds the portrait ambiguous, with touches of excess, and Terry Jones (Ch's Knight, 1980) regards the Knight as a mere mercenary adventurer; cf. Burrow, TLS, 15 Feb. 1980, 163; Maurice Keen, Ch's Knight, the Engl. Arist., and the Crusade, in Scattergood and Sherborne, eds., Engl. Court Culture, 1983, 45–61.

On the Knight's campaigns, see Manly, Trans. and Proc. Amer. Philol. Assoc. 38, 1907, 89–108; Cook, Trans. Conn. Acad. of Arts and Sci. 20, 1916, 165–240;

Engel, Rev. des sciences humaines 30, 1965, 577–85; and cf. Jones, Ch's Knight, 31–140. The records of the controversy between Sir Richard Scrope and Sir Robert Grosvenor (ed. Nicolas, 1832; excerpts in Rickert, Ch's World, 147–50) show a number of knights who campaigned in the same places as Chaucer's Knight, and attempts have been made to identify a real-life prototype (see Manly, as above, 104–6, and Cook, as above, 192–212), although Mann, Ch and Estates, 110–13, notes that such lists of campaigns are a literary convention in descriptions of chivalric heroes.

Richard Hakluyt (Princ. Navigations [1598], Hakluyt Soc., 1903, 1:307–8) considered the Knight's campaigns a proud example of English crusading. Modern critics, however, tend to view his career as anachronistic; see Manly, as above, 90; Kahrl, in The Holy War, ed. Thomas P. Murphy, 1972, 2; Howard, Idea of CT, 94; but cf. Coghill, Ch's Idea of What is Noble, Pres. Address to the Eng. Assoc., 1971, 9. Although by Chaucer's time the Holy Land was long lost to Christianity, and crusading was no longer considered an essential function of an exemplary knight (John Barnie, War in Med. Eng. Soc., 1974, 65), the crusading ideal nonetheless remained strong, encouraged by numerous fourteenth-century propagandists, especially the zealous Peter of Cyprus (see 51 below); see Atiya, in Hist. of the Crusades, ed. Harry Hazard, 1975, 3:3–27, and D. Sandberger, Studien über das Rittertum in Eng., 1937, 224–41. Such zeal largely abated after the disastrous Christian defeat at Nicopolis in 1396 (see Aziz Suryal Atiya, Crusade of Nicopolis, 1934, 113–25).

The Knight's unostentatious appearance, although considered by Ebner (in Imagination and Spirit, ed. Charles A. Huttar, 1971, 94–95) to be due merely to pilgrimage custom and by Jones (Ch's Knight, 27) as suggestive of the Knight's poor status as a footloose adventurer, has been more generally viewed (Bowden, Comm. on GP, 50; Charles Moorman, A Knight Ther Was, 1967, 82) as a virtuous corrective to the excesses of knightly display bemoaned by the satirists. Mann, Ch and Estates, 104–05, sees in the Knight's array the union of chivalric and monastic ideals advocated for the crusading order of Templars by St. Bernard of Clairvaux (1090–1153).

VINCENT J. DiMARCO

44–45   That . . . he: The use of a general relative **that** or **which** followed by a personal pronoun or another relative to clarify its referent is common in Middle English; cf. I.604, KnT I.2710; ParsPro X.39, HF 1099, Tr 2.318. See Mustanoja, ME Syntax, 202–3.

45–46   chivalrie: Probably "prowess" as well as the ethical code of knighthood (see Mathew, in Sts. Pres. to Frederick M. Powicke, ed. R. W. Hunt et al., 1948, 356–57). **Trouthe** (modern "troth") means fidelity to one's pledged word (cf. FranT V.1479). **Honour** means good reputation, the opposite of shame (cf. ParsT X.187), as well as good character. **Fredom** means generosity of goods and spirit; Brunetto Latini (Livres dou Tresor, ed. Carmody, Univ. of Calif. Pubs. in Mod. Philol. 22, 1948, 2.23) relates this virtue to an aversion to speaking villainously (see lines 70–71). **Curteisie** denotes refinement of manners and spirit as well as a command of courtly usages; Héraucourt (Wertwelt, 72–73) notes that in Chaucer's late works it also has the sense of tender, charitable comportment. See also Mitchell, MLQ 25, 1964, 66–75.

47   Though Chaucer specifies that the Knight has fought in Christendom as well as in heathendom, only campaigns against Moslems, schismatics (Russian Orthodox), and pagans are enumerated. Loomis (in Essays and Sts. in Hon. of Carleton Brown, 1940, 136–37), finds this an implied criticism of the Hundred Years' War; Hatton (ChR 3, 1968, 81–84) and Olson (Mediaevalia 5, 1979, 65–68) suggest the influence of Philippe de Mézières's plea that Christians stop fighting one another and join in a new chivalric order for a crusade (Le songe de vieil pelerin, ed. and tr. Coopland, 1969, and Philippe de Mézières, Letter to King Richard II, ed. and tr. Coopland, 1976); also see John J. N. Palmer, Engl., France, and Christendom, 1377–99, 1972, 180–82, on plans for an Anglo-French crusade.

49   Apparently a line of eleven syllables. Christopherson (ES 45, Suppl. 1964, 146–47) suggests phonetic shortening of **cristendom** to two syllables, but elsewhere in Chaucer's verse it is trisyllabic.

51   Alisaundre (Alexandria, in Egypt) was conquered by Peter I (Lusignan) of Cyprus on 10 October 1365 and abandoned a week later, after great plundering and a massacre of its inhabitants; see MKT VII.2392n.; Guillaume de Machaut, La Prise d'Alexandrie, ed. Mas Latrie, 1877; Aziz Suryal Atiya, Crusade in the Later MA, 1938, 345–71; and George Hill, Hist. of Cyprus, 1948, 2:336–37. The campaigns against *Satalye* and *Lyeys* (GP I.58) were also led by Peter of Cyprus, the foremost crusader of the century; see MkT VII.2391–96.

52   he hadde the bord bigonne: He was accorded the place of honor. There may be an association with the *Ehrentisch* (Table of Honor), a feast periodically proclaimed by the Teutonic Knights to honor preeminent warriors (Cook, JEGP 14, 1915, 375–78).

53   Pruce: Prussia, the area along the Baltic shore roughly between the Vistula and the Niemen; by Chaucer's time it was largely used as a base of operations by the Teutonic Order for its *reysen* ("raids"; cf. *reysed*, GP I.54) into Lithuania and Russia; see Eric Christiansen, Northern Crusades, 1980, 100–104, 157–58. Sandberger, Das Rittertum, 234–39, lists numerous Englishmen who crusaded with the Order. The Knight's campaigns in the Baltic are usually considered his most recent, from which he has just returned, though DiMarco (RBPH 46, 1978, 654–55) notes an English ban on all travel to the Baltic in 1385–88.

54   Lettow, Lithuania, was a large area south of present-day Latvia, including part of the Ukraine (Magoun, Ch Gazetteer, 101). The conversion to Christianity of Crown Prince Jagailo in 1386 did not mean the end of hostilities with the Teutonic Order; see Christiansen, North. Crusades, 132–70, and Górski, M&H 17, 1966, 32–33. **Ruce** (Russia) is perhaps used here to mean the principalities of Pskov, on the Livonian frontier, and Novgorod, on the Volkhov; but cf. Urban, ChR 18, 1984, 347–53, who identifies it as Rossenia, between Livonia and Prussia. In 1378 Pope Urban VI authorized indulgences for those aiding the crusade against the Russian Orthodox, but nothing of consequence ensued (see Christiansen, 191).

57   Algezir: Algeciras, a seaport of the kingdom of Granada (*Gernade*, GP I.56), near Gibraltar. Its conquest by Christians led by Alphonso IX of Castile in 1344

ended the influence in Spain of the Moslem Merenid dynasty (*Belmarye*). On English participation, see P. E. Russell, Eng. Intervention in Spain and Portugal, 1955, 6–7.

Belmarye: Belmarin, Banu Merin, in the fourteenth century the powerful Berber dynasty ruling what is now Morocco, here called by the dynasty's name. The Knight's activity *in Belmarye* may refer to attacks on Merenid towns by Christian (mostly Castilian and Aragonese) privateers; see Jamil E. Abun-Nasr, Hist. of the Mahgrib, 1971, 127–28.

58   Lyeys: Ayash, a seaport near Antioch, in the medieval kingdom of Cilicia, or Lesser Armenia, was captured by Peter of Cyprus in 1367; see Machaut, Prise d'Alexandrie, 201–12, 7008–140. Peter began the expedition with English knights in his company (Hill, Hist. of Cyprus 1:352) and along the way was joined by others (Chronique des quatre premiers Valois, ed. Luce, 1862, 187–90).

Satalye: Antalya (the ancient Attaleia), an independent Turcoman principality in southern Anatolia, which Peter of Cyprus attacked on 23–24 August 1361; for the ME form of the name, see Sedgwick, RES 2, 1926, 346. Machaut (Prise d'Alexandrie, 20–21, 641–60) describes the campaign as an unqualified success, but cf. Charles Stubbs, Lectures on Med. and Mod. Hist., 1887, 221–22.

60   armee: "military expedition." Some MSS read *aryue*, ("landing of an armed force"), but that word seems to be known in only one other ME example (Görlach, N&Q 218, 1973, 363–65). See also Donaldson, in Med. Sts. in Hon. of L. H. Hornstein, ed. Jess B. Bessinger, Jr., and Robert R. Raymo, 1976, 99–103.

62   Tramyssene: Tlemcen, in northwest Algeria.

63   Duels between champions of opposing Christian and Moslem armies were fought as late as the sixteenth century: Captain John Smith claimed to have killed three Saracens in the lists on three successive days (General Historie of Virginia, etc., 1907, 2:128–30). Since no Christian army is known to have attacked Tlemcen during the fourteenth century, Jones (Ch's Knight, 78) speculates that the Knight was there as a mercenary serving the Arabs. Abun-Nasr (Hist. of Maghrib, 154–55) shows that there were such mercenaries. They were condoned by the Church; see Norman Daniel, Arabs and Med. Europe, 1978, 222.

65–66   Palatye: Balat, near the site of ancient Miletus on the southwest coast of Turkey, was an independent emirate ruled by a Seljuk Turk. The "Lord of Palatye" paid homage to Peter of Cyprus in 1365 but is not known to have campaigned with him against other Turks. Engel, Rev. des sciences humaines 30:581–82, suggests a reference to the late 1340s when Hizir, "Turchus qui domine Palatia" (The Turk who is lord of Palatye) promised to aid the Christians in Smyrna against the Turk Umur, who had been besieging them intermittently. But by 1350 Hizir was apparently threatening to attack Smyrna himself. Baugh (238) suggests that the Knight fought in the service of Sultan Yakoub, then lord of Palatye, against Saroukhan, Sultan of Magnesia, in 1355 (citing Mas Latrie's Trésor de chronologie, col. 1801).

68   worthy . . . wys: A common collocation (see Tr 2.180 and Minot, Pol. Poems, 5.38). *Worthy* may mean "distinguished" here, but more probably means "brave" (as in MLT II.579 and probably Thop VII.917). The paired terms reflect the commonplace "fortitudo et sapientia" (see Curtius, Europ. Lit. 176–80, and cf. KnT I.865).

74 The horses may be his, the Squire's, and the Yeoman's (French, MLN 76, 1961, 293–95), or, since "Knights regularly travelled with extra horses" (Baugh, 239), they may be his own.

The Squire

The Squire is generally considered an attractive figure, and some critics, noting that Chaucer himself had been a squire and fought in Artois and Picardy (GP I.86) and that the Squire is the only pilgrim said to write poetry (GP I.95), have suggested autobiographical overtones (Bowden, Comm. on GP, 74–75). But the portrait owes much to the *Roman de la rose,* especially the descriptions of Mirth and Love (Rom 820–35, 890–910) and the catalogue of courtly accomplishments (Rom 2310–30; Wood, ES 52, 1971, 116–18). Rosemond Tuve (Seasons and Months, 1933, 186–88) notes similarities to MS illustrations of the month of May (92), the iconography of which draws on courtly customs (Derek Pearsall and Elizabeth Salter, Landscapes and Seasons of the Med. World, 1973, 131–35, 140). The conventionality of the topics of description in the portrait is illustrated by Gallo (PAPS 118, 1974, 53–54).

The Squire's youthful, romantic enthusiasms, many critics have believed, will later develop into his father's sober virtues (Patch, On Rereading Ch, 157; Whittock, A Reading of CT, 51; Hoffman, ELH 21, 1954, 6), while Speirs (Ch the Maker, 103) and William Blake (Desc. Catalogue [1809], in Compl. Writings, ed. Keynes, 1966, 566) assert the value of the Squire's vitality and artistic interests in comparison with his father, an aging warrior. Some recent critics have been less admiring: Philippa Tristram (Figures of Life and Death in Med. Eng. Lit., 1976, 27) suggests he is viewed with ironic realism; Hatton (SMC 4, 1974, 452–57) with amusement and tolerance. His future is ambiguous to Raymond Preston (Ch, 1952, 156) and Nevo (MLR 58, 1963, 6); Fleming (N&Q 212, 1967, 48–49) and Wood (ES 52:116–18) see his conformance to the ideals of courtly love as evidence of lechery; and Howard (Idea of CT, 95–96) sees him as, however attractive, a representative of a degenerate chivalry. Donaldson (883) and Mann (Ch and Estates, 106, 116–19) view the portraits of the Squire and the Knight as alternative formulations of the romantic and religious aspects of chivalry, with prejudice to neither.

VINCENT J. DiMARCO

79–80 A **squier** held the first degree of knighthood, with the privileges of a **bacheler** but not those of a banneret, who could lead knights under his own banner. The Squire serves as an attendant to his father, who has perhaps instructed him in chivalry, as advised by Ramon Lull (Mann, Ch and Estates, 115). Although there are instances of sons serving on campaigns with their fathers (Froissart, Chronicles, tr. Johnes, 1:161), we need not assume with Stillwell and Webb (MLN 59, 1944, 45–47) that the Squire ordinarily did so.

82 Cf. Rom 21–23. Pearsall regards the Squire as "a very young, young man" travelling among his elders (UTQ 34, 1964, 82). Baum points out, however, that the Squire is "no timid inexperienced youth" (MLN 32, 1917, 376–77). As Hatton indicates (SMC 4, 1974, 452–58), at twenty Richard II exercised adult responsibilities.

85 **in chyvachie** has no article because it is an anglicized imitation of OF *en chevaucie* (Prins, ES 30, 1949, 42–44). On such raids, perhaps the typical tactic of the English during the Hundred Years' War, see John Barnie, War in Med. Soc., 1974, 9–10.

86 The reference is probably to the "crusade" of 1383, led by Henry Despencer, bishop of Norwich, against the largely orthodox Flemish and their schismatic French overlords. Gaylord (PMASAL 45, 1960, 341–61) and Kahrl (ChR 7, 1973, 208–9) take the reference as evidence of the degenerate ideals of the Squire's chivalry; contemporary criticism of this campaign, however, was directed at its failure, rather than its motive (plunder), and Despencer was back in Richard II's favor by 1385 (see DNB s.v. Despencer or Spencer, Henry le).

90 Fehrenbach (ELN 15, 1977, 4–7) notes the use of white (for purity) and red (for sacrifice for the Church) in the ceremony of knightly investiture. The **whyte and reede** flowers, however, may simply be daisies (cf. ProLGW F 42).

91 **floytynge:** Probably "playing the flute" rather than "whistling," which is an uncertain medieval usage. Cf. MED s.v. *flouten.*

93 ParsT X.416–30 criticizes such extravagance, but Amor in RR distinguishes the pursuit of fashionable elegance from Pride (Rom 2251–54).

95 **endite:** As Fleming (N&Q 212:48–49) notes, the source of the passage in the *Roman de la rose* does not mention poetry-making; it is alluded to, however, in Rom 2325–28.

96 **purtreye:** Nicholas Orme (From Childhood to Chivalry, 1984, 175) argues that the term is here used in the sense of "representing in speech or writing," since noble education made no provision for training in art.

98 Nightingales were believed to sing all night in the mating season: they "synge plesauntly day and night"; "whanne they haue reioysed thaire amerous desyre and plesaunces, thei make abace melodye, for thei synge no more" (Book of the Knight of La Tour Landry, EETS 33, 156). Pliny compares their song to the music of a flute (Hist. Nat. 10.43).

99–100 Squires customarily carved for their knights; cf. SumT III.2243–45 and MerT IV.1772–73. It was an honorable duty (see Froissart's account of the Black Prince serving the captive King John of France, in Chronicles, tr. Johnes, 1:167, and Madeleine P. Cosman, Fabulous Feasts, 1976, 26) and an honor to carve for one's father (Kuhl and Webb, ELH 6, 1939, 282–84).

The Yeoman

A yeoman was a free servant, ranking in feudal households next below a squire. This yeoman is a forester (*forster*), a gamekeeper (Emerson, RomR 13, 1922, 115–20) charged with guarding his lord's game (cf. PhysT VI.83–85), skilled in *wodecraft* (the ceremonies of the hunt; cf. SGGK 1605–6) and dressed in the *cote and hood of grene* appropriate to a huntsman (cf. FrT III.1380–82 and Emerson, RomR 13:141). Though Birney (REL 1, 1960, 9–18) finds him overly elegant and his portrait therefore ironic, he seems clearly admirable. Manly (CT, 503) conjectured that Chaucer intended to adapt for him the *Tale of Gamelyn* (in Skeat 4:645–47), found in some MSS of the *Tales* (and assigned to the Cook), but there is little basis for this supposition.

LARRY D. BENSON

101   he: The Knight, who leads the minimum knightly retinue ("a squire and servant that may take hede to his horse," Wm. Caxton, Bk of the Ordre of Chyvalry, ed. Byles, EETS 168, 1926, 19). The separation of the pronoun from its referent led Brown to speculate that the portrait of the Squire was a later addition (MLN 49, 1934, 216–22); Birney (and others) argue that *he* refers to the Squire (REL 1:9–18).

104   Peacock feathers were prized for arrows (Bowden, Comm. on GP, 86–87), and still are by modern archers (Test, AMN&Q 2, 1964, 67–68).

107   Low feathers cause an arrow to fall (*droup);* see Roger Ascham, *Toxophilus* [1545], ed. Arber, 1868, 133.

115   The image of St. Christopher is a talisman against death, injury, and weariness (Waller, Surrey Archeol. Soc., Collections 6, 1874, 60–64, 296). The saint has no special associations with foresters, though Waller finds a tenuous connection with archers in the sixteenth century. The sumptuary law of 1363 (Statutes of the Realm 1:380), which attempted to regulate the degree of luxury in clothing allowed to each class, forbade the wearing of silver ornaments by yeomen. The law, however, was widely ignored, never enforced, and repealed the next year (see Francis E. Baldwin, Sumptuary Legislation in Engl., 1926, esp. 55).

The Prioress

The Prioress has attracted more critical commentary and controversy than almost any other character in the General Prologue. She has the appearance and manners of a traditional courtly lady, though she is a bit large for the ideal beauty (156) and a bit too provincial to attain *cheere Of court.* Yet she is a nun, professing *love celestial,* and though many of the attributes of the ideal secular lady-love were incorporated in the ideal nun, the bride of Christ (Mann, Ch and Estates, 128–37), the exact degree of "the engagingly imperfect submergence of the feminine in the ecclesiastical" (John L. Lowes, Convention and Revolt in Poetry, 1919, 60–61) has been the subject of much debate. She clearly violates many of the rules of her order (Rule of St. Benedict, ed. and tr. Justin McCann, 1952; Eileen Power, Med. Eng. Nunneries, 1922, and Med. People, rpt. 1954, ch. 3; Sister Mary-of-the-Incarnation Byrne, Trad. of Nun in Med. Eng., Diss. Cath. Univ. of Am., 1932; Quinn, in Chaucer, ed. George D. Economou, 1976, 60–61). Yet such rules, including that which forbade nuns to go on pilgrimages, were frequently ignored or waived by dispensation, and M. Madeleva (A Lost Language, 31–60) defends, not altogether convincingly, all of the Prioress's apparent violations of religious discipline. Frank (ChR 13, 1979, 346–62) argues that Chaucer and his contemporary audience would have interpreted every aspect of her characterization as a reflection of veneration of Mary. For a detailed comparison of the Prioress and Second Nun as characters shaped by Chaucer's medieval Christian views, see Ruth Ames, God's Plenty, 1984.

The Prioress is associated with an actual Benedictine nunnery, St. Leonard's, adjoining *Stratford atte Bowe,* about two miles from London. Chaucer knew this nunnery (see HF 117), and had gone there as a boy when the Countess of Ulster and her husband, Prince Lionel, visited the Prince's aunt, Elizabeth of Hainault, who was a nun there (cf. Manly, New Light, 204–6).

Like the neighboring nunnery at Barking, it may have served as a kind of finishing school for daughters of rich London merchants (Manly, New Light, 204–5). Though not so aristocratic as Barking (where Chaucer's sister or daughter, Elizabeth, was a nun; see p. xvi above), it was relatively prosperous, with thirty nuns in 1354 (including Elizabeth of Hainault, sister of Queen Philippa) and probably at least that many when Chaucer was writing (Hamilton, in Philologica, ed. Thomas A. Kirby, 1949, 179–90). Manly (CT, 504) suggests that Chaucer's Prioress was modeled on an actual person, but no such model has been found. The Prioress of St. Leonard's at this time was Mary Syward (or Suhard); see Manly, TLS, 10 Nov. 1927, 817.

Though most critics formerly agreed with Robinson that Chaucer's "satire—if it can be called satire at all—is of the gentlest and most sympathetic sort," and though she lacks most of the failings traditional in satiric portraits of nuns (Mann, Ch and Estates, 129), many critics today take a much harsher view of the Prioress than did Robinson, Lowes, and Kittredge. The primary cause is the anti-Semitism of her tale, which, though long recognized (Wordsworth noted her "fierce bigotry," Works, ed. A. J. George, 1932, 263–66), has only in recent years become an important critical issue (see introductory note to PrT). For an appraisal of the evidence and arguments, see Florence H. Ridley, The Prioress and The Critics, Univ. of Calif. Pubs., Eng. Sts. 30, 1965, and the criticism cited in the following notes.

FLORENCE H. RIDLEY

119   symple and coy: The phrase is common in French courtly poetry (Lowes, Anglia 33, 1910, 440 n. 1 and cf. Rom 7321 and n.), though in religious verse "symple, coyes" was also applied to ideal nuns (Mann, Ch and Estates, 136, 272 n. 48). *Coy* means "quiet" or perhaps "silent" (Brennan, MLQ 10, 1949, 451–53). It has no coquettish connotations.

120   ooth: Even a mild oath would have earned the disapproval of a strict moralist, though swearing was common (see EpiMLT II.1171 n.). Skeat (5:14) cites a tradition that to swear by St. Loy, who refused to take an oath, became no oath at all. *Seinte Loy* has been identified as St. Eulalia, "sweet spoken" (Lynch, MLN 72, 1957, 242–49), or St. Louis (Bell, ed. Wks. of Ch, 1895, 1:82). Cutts, Sts. in Humanities 7, 1979, 34–38, argues that the oath combines references to St. Louis and St. Eligius, reflecting a balance between the Prioress's human and ecclesiastical tendencies, but *Seinte Loy* is generally agreed to be St. Eligius (588–629), in French Éloi, in English Loy, a goldsmith and master of the royal mint who became Bishop of Noyan and later the patron saint of metalworkers, carters, and farriers (cf. FrT III.1564n.). For his life see Acta Sanctorum, December 1, and Butler's Lives of the Saints, 4:455–58. His "attrib-

utes'' of bread, austerity, and charity have been seen as
an ironic contrast to the Prioress (Haskell, Ch's Saints,
1–2, 32–37). He was renowned for his beauty, courtliness, and skill in working precious metals (Lowes, RomR
5, 1914, 368–81; Wainwright, MLN 48, 1933, 34–37),
founded convents for women (Gerould, Ch Essays,
1952, 16), and betrothed a Benedictine abbess to Christ
with his own ring, perhaps a parallel to the Prioress's
brooch (Steadman, Neophil 43, 1959, 54–57). Manly
suggests (CT, 505) that there was a cult of St. Loy at the
royal court and notes that the Countess of Pembroke
gave an image of the saint to Grey Friars, a fashionable
London church. For any or all of these reasons, the Prioress may swear by St. Loy, though Kittredge (Ch and
His Poetry, 177) believes the saint was chosen because
his soft, ladylike name did not distort the lips, and Baugh
(240) follows Brusendorff (Ch Trad, 483) in suggesting
that the name merely serves to meet the exigencies of the
rhyme.

121   Eglentyne: "briar rose" (MED, s.v. *eglentin*). It
probably connotes heroines in romance (Lowes, Anglia
33:440–41) or the Virgin (Wood, in Signs and Symbols,
82, 255), though curiously similar to Argentyn, the
name of an actual nun at St. Leonard's (Manly, New
Light, 204–11). Besides its obvious association with
flowers (Eliason, Names 21, 1973, 143), the name may
be suggestive of *esglantiers* in RR (Engelhardt, MS 37,
1975, 294), or *eglentier,* Christ's third crown (Kuhl,
MLN 60, 1945, 325–26); but see also Davies (MLN 67,
1952, 400–402), who in refuting Kuhl cites an historical
nun with the romantic name Idoine.

122   service dyvyne: Liturgy of the canonical hours—
Matins (cf. WBT III.876), Lauds (MilT I.3655), Prime
(PardT VI.662), Sext, Nones, Vespers, and Compline
(RvT I.4171); see Boyd, Ch and the Liturgy, 61–62.
Owen (Pilgrimage and Story-Telling, 57–60, 119) notes
the humor which derives from the rhyme with *Eglentyne*
and the irony suggested by other rhymes and sounds in
the portrait.

123   Entuned . . . ful semely: Evidence of Chaucer's
familiarity with the manner in which the Divine Office
was to be said (M. Madeleva, Lost Language, 37–38); the
nasal intonation was commonly employed to avoid strain-
ing the throat in singing long liturgies (Kirby, in Sts.
Pres. to W. A. Read, 1940, 33, but see Brennan, MLQ
10:455). The music could signal a harmonious moral
state, yet *ful semely* links the Prioress's singing with her
table manners (see 127–136 below) and emphasizes her
concern with external appearances (Knoepfelmacher,
ChR 4, 1970, 180–83).

124–26   The Prioress's French is apparently Anglo-Norman, as opposed to the *Frenssh of Parys* spoken at the
royal court (cf. Hinckley, Notes on Ch, 10–11). For
discussions of the French used in England in the fourteenth century, see Rothwell, MLR 80, 1985, 39–54,
and Suggett, TRHS, 4th ser. 28, 1946, 61–83. Short
(RPh 33, 1980, 467–79) discusses English attitudes toward native French and notes that the author of the *Vie
d'Edouard le Confesseur* (ed. Södergård, 1948), a nun,
apologizes because "I know only the false French of
England" (vv. 7–8; see also H. J. Chaytor, The Troubadours and Engl., 1923, 18–19). Walter Map (De nugis
curialium, ed. Thomas Wright, 235–36) tells of a school
("fons") at Marlborough that taught its students a barba-
rous French, "Gallicum Merleburgæ" (cf. Nicholas

Orme, Eng. Schools in the M.A., 1972, 310). Donaldson, in New Perspectives, 195–96, notes the heavy use
of French idioms in the Prioress's portrait; Hughes
(Standpunte 137, 1978, 2) argues that she is created in
the language of frenchified cliché. Manly (New Light,
219–220) suggests that the French at St. Leonard's was
the Flemish-tinged dialect of Hainault, introduced by
Elizabeth of Hainault (and presumably spoken by Chaucer's wife). Kuhl (PQ 2, 1923, 306–08) believes a contrast is intended with the better dialect at the wealthy
convent of Barking. Cf. SumT III.1832n.

127–36   The Prioress's table manners are modeled directly on the advice of La Vieille in RR, in a speech
derived from Ovid, *Ars amatoria,* advising a young
woman how to attract men (RR 13408–32), and are thus
possibly ironic (Hoffman, Ovid and CT, 26–28; Simons,
Coll. Lang. Assoc. Jour. 12, 1968, 79; Brown, in Ch, ed.
George D. Economou, 1975, 47–48). However, the
manners are those of a well-bred lady (Kirby, Sts. Pres.
to Read, 33), prescribed in courtesy books of the time
(Manly, CT, 504), and are perhaps a necessary part of a
nun's caring for her habit (M. Madeleva, Lost Language,
39). Nothing the Prioress consumes is explicitly forbidden by her rule, though the care with which her eating
and drinking are described suggests improper concern
with food and drink, as well as with manners, which may
explain line 156.

132   curteisie: This word has associations with faithfulness to a way of life ordained by God as well as with an
aristocratic refinement of manners and spirit (see n. 45–
46 above, and Evans, MS 29, 1967, 143–57), though it
frequently connotes merely ceremonious behavior or affability (see Burnley, Ch's Language, 153), as its restriction here to table manners suggests.

134   hir coppe: "her cup." "Their (communal) cup"
(Bowles, Expl 35, 1976, 5–6) is possible but unlikely.

  ferthyng: "speck" or "farthing" (quarter-penny),
perhaps related to a French pun involving "spot" and
"coin" (John Orr, OF and Mod. Eng. Idiom, 1962, 8–9;
Reid, N&Q 209, 1964, 373–74).

139–40   countrefete cheere/Of court: Imitate the
manners appropriate to the court, or show proper concern for behavior (Kittredge, Ch and his Poetry, 176–
77). Either would be mildly satirical; but Wood (in
Signs and Symbols, 92) finds more intense satire, citing
MED s.v. *countrefete* 3(a), "to pass oneself off as," and
argues that the Prioress counterfeits a lady and thus fal-
sifies her religious calling. Alfred David, on the other
hand, sees stylistic analogies between the Prioress and
the Virgin as depicted in Chaucer's ABC ("An ABC to
the Style of the Prioress," in Acts of Interpretation, 147–
57).

141   digne of reverence: The Benedictine Rule specifies that the heads of houses must remember their positions and illustrate the dignity of their titles in their acts
(ed. McCann, 17). Yet the Prioress's self-consciousness
is perhaps intended satirically (Wood, in Signs and Symbols, 92–93).

142–50   conscience: Both "moral sense, awareness of
right and wrong" and "solicitude, anxiety" (MED s.v.
conscience 2, 4). Mice and dogs are obviously inadequate
objects of a nun's compassion (Burnley, Ch's Language,
160) and may indicate that her conscience is mere sensibility (Kaske, ELH 30, 1963, 175–92) and that her tender heart and conscience are misdirected (Knoepfel-

macher, ChR 4:182–83; Steadman MP 54, 1956, 1–6). On conventions of fourteenth-century sensibility, see the headnote to her tale. On the difference between her conscience and that of the Nun's Priest, see Rex, MP 80, 1982, 53–54.

144   mous: The anti-climactic mouse has been variously interpreted: an ironic, bathetic substitute for an image of human suffering (Wood, in Signs and Symbols, 89); an attribute of St. Gertrude, whose austerity contrasts with the Prioress's garb (Haskell, Ch's Saints, 34–37); the devil (Witte, PLL 13, 1977, 227–37, and Brumble, Expl 37, 1978, 45). Both Witte and Brumble note the associations of the mousetrap with the devil; for illustrations of medieval mousetraps, see Roth, Bodleian Lib. Rec. 5, 1946, 244–51.

146   smale houndes: Whether Chaucer loved dogs (H. W. Garrod, Study of Good Letters, 1963, 193–94) or scorned them (Rowland, Blind Beasts, 154–65), they were favored by fashionable ladies of the time (cf. Bk. of the Knight of La Tour Landry, EETS 33, 28–29). Nuns were ordinarily forbidden to keep animals (The Ancrene Riwle, a thirteenth-century handbook for female anchorites [tr. Salu, 186], allows only a cat; and see Kuhl, PQ 2, 1923, 303–44); Baugh (240) believes the dogs show that the Prioress had a dispensation, evidence for her influence or that of her house, but they are usually taken as an indication of the discrepancy between her profession and her inclinations (Mann, Ch and Estates, 132, 271 nn. 30, 31, 32, 33; Steadman, MP 54:1–6). For a survey of the evidence, see Ridley, The Prioress and The Critics, Univ. Calif. Pubs., Eng. Sts. 30:19–21.

147   rosted flessh: The Benedictine Rule forbade meat (*flessh*) except to the ill or infirm (cf. The Ancrene Riwle, 183). Whether she fed the dogs from her own table or had their food specially prepared, such expensive fare was not for animals (cf. ParsT X.222).

wastel-breed: The most expensive bread in ordinary use, half the price of the special *payndemayn* (Thop VII.725) but more expensive than the third-grade *Fraunceis* or *pouf* and the fourth-grade *tourte,* the dark bread eaten by the poor widow in NPT VII.2843–44. See Liber Albus, ed. Riley, 1:1xvii, RS 12, pt.1; Kuhl, PQ 2:302–3.

151   The Ancrene Riwle (tr. Salu, 186) warns nuns against wearing a wimple, and, though M. Madeleva (Lost Language, 41) notes that it was a customary part of the Benedictine habit, the emphasis on its being *semely* pleated (*pynched*) relates it to traditional satiric criticisms of nuns' concern with worldly fashions (Mann, Ch and Estates, 130).

152–56   The Prioress is described in the "descending (head-to-toe) catalogue" conventional for beautiful women in courtly poetry here left incomplete, perhaps out of deference to her calling. Her features—well-proportioned nose, grey eyes, pretty mouth, fair forehead—are those of standard romance beauties (cf. Rom 539–74, BD 855–865 and note 817–1040, Kiernan, ChR 10, 1975, 1–10, and Brewer, MLR 50, 1955, 257–69). Chaucer utilizes prescribed rhetorical devices to increase the interest, realism and dynamism of the portrait (Parr, SMC 4, 1974, 433–36, and Sklute, SN 52, 1980, 35–46). Yet his inversion of conventional rhetorical description and manipulation of the order of detail produce irony (Morgan, ES 62, 1981, 418–20, and Wood, in Signs and Symbols, 82–101).

152   greye: A favorite color for the eyes of beautiful women (Rom 546, 862) and men (Rom 822) in Chaucer's time and later (cf. Shakespeare, Two Gentlemen of Verona, 4.4.197). The color intended is uncertain. Chaucer first uses it in Rom 862 to translate Fr. *vair* (variable, expressive). Middle English poets describe eyes as black, brown, green, or grey, never blue. It may be that *greye* includes shades of blue (Kinney, RomR 10, 1919, 339–43), though Moore (PQ 26, 1947, 307–12) makes a good case for hazel, greyish.

155   spanne brood: The high and broad forehead, which should have been covered by the Prioress's wimple, is that of a courtly beauty (Knight, Neophil 52, 1968, 178–80), though a *spanne* is about seven to nine inches. In the context of line 156 this forehead can be seen as proportionate to the Prioress's stature and with favorable physiognomical implications; see Clark, PQ 9, 1930, 312–14.

156   nat undergrowe: The humor of the understatement is made more piquant by the Prioress's love of small things (Kelly, PLL 5, 1969, 362–74) and is obvious, but it has been subjected to interpretations ranging from "not spiritual" to "well proportioned," "mature," "corpulent," and "fat" (Wood, in Signs and Symbols, 95–96; Bowden, Comm. on GP, 95; Engelhardt, MS 37:291; Harper, PQ 12, 1933, 308–10).

157   fetys: Another indication of the Prioress's concern with worldly fashion, though Benedictines were to wear cloaks of better than ordinary quality when they traveled (Böddeker, ESt 2, 1879, 87, ll. 2093–96).

158   coral: Deemed a protection against "the feendes gyle" and various other evils (Bartholomaeus Anglicus 16.32, tr. Trevisa 2:842). Manly (MLN 74, 1959, 385–88) notes the stone's ambiguity, suggesting that it may traditionally have been a love charm. Such coral rosaries were fashionable; see Friedman, MAE 39, 1970, 301–5, who also notes the reputed apotropaic power of coral.

159   The rosary has large green dividers (*gauds*), marking the Paternosters and separating sets of ten Ave Marias, or meditations on Mary; on medieval rosaries see Boyd, MLQ 11, 1950, 404–16. The modern "gaudy," which Baum (PMLA 73, 1958, 168) uses to detect a pun here, is not attested in Middle English.

160   brooch of gold: Nuns were forbidden to wear brooches (Kuhl, PQ 2:305). Cawley (MLR 43, 1948, 74–77) suggests a parallel to Criseyde's brooch (Tr 4.1370–71) and a parallel between the two women. Smith (West Va. Univ. Bull., Phil. Papers 6, 1949, 1–11) finds further resemblances between them.

161   crowned A: A flat capital "A" surmounted by a crown was a contemporary emblem for Queen Anne (Lowes, PMLA 23, 1908, 285–99; Braddy, MLN 58, 1943, 18–23; rpt. in Geoffrey Ch, 97–98).

162   Amor vincit omnia: "Love conquers all." The motto is secular in origin (Virgil, Eclogue 10.69) and application (RR 21332), but was commonly used by monastics (M. Madeleva, Lost Language, 43). Its ambiguity has occasioned much commentary. Steadman notes that *vincit* means "binds," as well as "conquers" (ES 44, 1963, 350–53), suggesting that the Prioress's dedication to religion is significant, even heroic. See also Wainwright, MLN 48, 1933, 36–37. *Amor* could be God's love, which can conquer her misdirection (Hoffman, ELH 21, 1954, 10), though Jacobs (ChR 25, 1980) notes biblical allusions that distinguish between "amor" and "caritas" and admonish against worldly ornaments such as those the Prioress wears. The possibility of secular interpretation remains, strengthening the portrait's ambiguity (Adams, Lit and Psych. 18, 1968, 215–17). Still applicable is Lowes's comment: "Which of the two loves does 'amor' mean to the Prioress? I do not know; but I think she thought she meant love celestial" (Convention and Revolt, 66).

The Second Nun and Nun's Priest

Neither the Second Nun nor the Nun's Priest are described, though each is later assigned a tale. Critics usually assume that Chaucer intended in a final revision to add portraits of these characters.

FLORENCE H. RIDLEY

164   chapeleyne: A nun serving her prioress as secretary, amanuensis, and attendant at festivals; see MED s.v. *chepelain* 2 (b), Förster, Archiv 132, 1914, 399–401, Kuhl PQ 2:304–5. Engelhardt takes the word as meaning "mentor" (MS 37:294–96). In both the Hengwrt and Ellesmere MSS the marginal notation reads "Nonne Chapelayne."

preestes thre: This phrase has occasioned much comment. In line 24 Chaucer specifies that *Wel nine and twenty* pilgrims arrived at the Tabard. If three priests accompany the Prioress, the number of pilgrims listed in the GP is thirty-one; if Chaucer meant the Prioress to have but one attendant priest, the total is twenty-nine. It is usually believed that Chaucer left the line unfinished after *chapeleyne* and that, as Bradshaw suggested, the text was carelessly patched by someone else. Rickert (M-R 3:428) suggested that *and the preest is three* was added first, then *preest is* was miscopied as *preestis,* but the MED does not record this meaning of *is* ("adds up to"). For good reviews of opinions about the number of pilgrims, see Eckhardt, YES 5, 1975, 1–18, and Brosnahan, ChR 16, 1982, 293–309.

The Monk

The older view that Chaucer admired and lightly satirized his Monk (P. V. D. Shelly, The Living Ch, 1940, 197–99) is still current (Lumiansky, Of Sondry Folk, 97–101; Ussery, TSE 17, 1969, 1–30), but many now regard the portrait as heavily ironic (Donaldson, 1046; Kaske, ELH 24, 1957, 251–58; Gillmeister, NM 69, 1968, 222–32) or bitterly satiric (Robertson, Pref. to Ch, 253–56; Reiss, ChR 2, 1967–68, 254–72 and 3, 1968–69, 12–28; and White, JEGP 70, 1971, 13–30). Beichner defends the Monk as a successful administrator (Spec 34, 1959, 611–19). His vices are those commonly attacked by satirists and reformers (Bowden, Comm. on GP, 107–18; Mann, Ch and Estates, 17–37), but his worldliness, lordly air, and love of horses, hounds, and hare hunting are faults that Gower attributes specifically to monastic officers and "keepers" (cf. 172), whose duties take them outside the monastery (Mirour, 20953–21158; cf. Wyclif, Eng. Works, 126).

The hunting cleric was a familiar figure (Gower, Vox Clam. 3.1490–1512; Wyclif, Eng. Works, 212, 249; Owst, Preaching in Med. Engl., 279), and the visitation of Selborne Abbey in 1387 by William Wykeham,

Bishop of Winchester, found monastics of the time keeping hounds, hunting, and indulging in rich food and clothing (see Gilbert White, Nat. Hist. and Antiq. of Selborne, ed. Buckland, 1875, 509–15; George G. Coulton, Med. Village, 1925, 215–17, 508–12, offers many further examples). The pious and affable William de Clowne, Abbot of Leicester (1345–78) was the most famous hare hunter in England (Henry Knighton, Chronicon, ed. Lumby, Rolls, 1895, 2:125–27; tr. EHD 4:785). Each year he held a hare hunt for Edward III and such nobles as John of Gaunt and, in 1363, Peter of Cyprus (MkT VII.2391–98). Bressie suggests that Clowne was the model for the Monk (MLN 54, 1939, 477–90). Tatlock objects that Clowne was an Augustinian canon rather than a Benedictine monk (MLN 55, 1940, 350–54), but see David Knowles, Rel. Orders in Engl., 1955, 2:185–86, 365–66.

SUSAN H. CAVANAUGH

165   for the maistrie: OF *pour la maistrie*, "surpassing all others." Ussery (TSE 17:9) notes that keepers of cells (see 172) were sometimes designated *maisters.*

166   outridere: Cf. ShipT VII.65–66n. For the suggestion that the term is used pejoratively, see Ussery, TSE 17:13–26. Note the echo of line 45 above, and the implied contrast of Knight and Monk; see R. E. Kaske, The Knight's Interruption of the Monk's Tale, ELH 24, 1957, 249–68.

venerie: Baum (PMLA 71, 1956, 245–46) detects a pun on "hunting" (OF *venerie*) and "sexual activity" (Med. Lat. *veneria*), but the OED does not record the latter meaning until 1497.

167   manly: Cf. ShipT VII.43n.

168   On monks as collectors of fine horses, see Mann, Ch and Estates, 23–24, and cf. ParsT X.432.

169–70   Bridles adorned with bells were fashionable (see Sir Gawain and the Green Knight, 195; Wyclif, Select Eng. Works, 3:520), and Canterbury pilgrims often had clusters of bells on their bridles; the Lollard William Thorpe scornfully described the "jangling of their Canterbury bells" (in Eng. Garner, ed. Alfred W. Pollard, 1903, 97–104; rpt. Rickert, Ch's World, 264–65). These bells later gave their name to the flowers called Canterbury bells (Bowden, Comm. on GP, 111).

172   celle: A monastic establishment subordinate to a great monastery or abbey and governed by a prior or *custos cellae* (keeper of the cell; see Ussery, TSE 17:6–13). Derocquigny (Revue germanique 6, 1910, 203–6) suggests, however, that the cellarer (person in charge of storehouses or storerooms) is meant; cf. ProMkT, VII.1936.

173   reule: The Benedictine *Rule* (ed. and tr. Justin McCann, 1952), written by **Beneit**, St. Benedict (480–c. 550), who was regarded as the father of Western monasticism. His disciple **Maure**, St. Maurus, was believed to have brought the Benedictine Rule to France in 543.

175   Since the construction begun in 173–74 is left unfinished, various other interpretations have been offered to avoid the anacoluthon (Mark H. Liddell, ed., Pro to GP, 1910; Prins, ES 30, 1949, 83–86, 133–34; Visser, ES 30, 1949, 133). However, such anacoluthons are common in colloquial speech; cf. CkT I.4391–94, Tr 5.281, and see Elliott, Ch's English, 185; Schlauch, PMLA 67, 1952, 1103–16.

176   space: Probably "course, direction" (Lat. *spatior*, "to walk"); see Tatlock, MLN 50, 1935, 294. Given the possible contrast with *streit* (174), *space* may have one of its more common meanings: "room, space." Visser glosses it as "greater liberty" (ES 30:84).

177   text: The reference here may be to Augustine, De civ. Dei 16.4, as Crawford suggests (TLS, 13 Nov. 1930, 942); or to the legend of Nimrod in Gen. 10.9, as Skeat (5:21) suggests; or, more probably, to the *Decretum* of Gratian (cf. Emerson, MP 1, 1904, 105–10, based on St. Jerome's *Tractatus de Psalmo* 90.3 (CC 78:127). "Esau was a hunter; therefore he was a sinner. And indeed we do not find in holy scripture any virtuous hunter. We do find virtuous fishermen" in Psalms 90.3 (91.3 in AV). Fleming (ChR 15, 1981, 287–94) notes an implicit parallel between lines 177–82 and the prologue to Peter Damian's (1007–72) *De divina omnipotentia*, where the emblem of the hunter occurs in conjunction with the figure of the fish out of water in a passage enjoining monks to shun worldly affairs.

pulled hen: Such indications of worthlessness, most often in the form of a negative comparison (*nat worth an hen*, WBT III.1112; *naught worth a beene*, Tr 3.1167) are common in Chaucer and throughout Middle English; see Hein, Anglia 15, 1893, 41–186, 396–472, and the index to Whiting, Proverbs, s.v. *not worth*. The construction was influenced by French; see Frederick H. Sykes, Fr. Elements in ME, 1899, 24–39, and note the French parallel to *nat worth an oystre* quoted below (182). For the similar *dere ynough a myte, jane*, etc., see CYT VIII.795n. Lumiansky (in Sts. in Hon. of Margaret Schlauch, 1966, 229–32), Grennen (NM 69, 1968, 573) and Mann (Ch and Estates, 20) note that the Monk's comparisons reveal his concern with food.

179   recchelees, var. *cloisterlees*: Both terms are somewhat unusual. See Donovan, PQ 31, 1952, 440–41; Macaulay, MLR 4, 1908, 14–15; Emerson, MP 1:110–15.

180   a fissh that is waterlees: A commonplace; cf. Wyclif, Eng. Works, 449; Langland, PP C 6.146–52; Gower, Vox Clam. 4.281–82, Mirour, 20845–51; and Whiting F233. Langland attributes it to Pope Gregory I, Gower to Augustine. Ellershaw (Acad, 6 Dec. 1890, 531) finds its earliest use in the *Life of St. Anthony*, which is ascribed to St. Athanasius (c. 296–373); see *Vitae patrum*, PL 73:858.

181–82   cloystre . . . oystre: Skeat (5:22) notes the resemblance, with the meaning reversed, to Jean de Meun, *Testament*, 1165–67: "Let whosoever wishes to find them [monks] seek them in their cloister. . . . For they do not reckon this world at the value of an oyster" (Car ne prisent le munde la muntance d'une oistre).

187   Austyn: [St.] Augustine [of Hippo] (354–430) was the reputed author of a monastic rule (Études Augustiniennes, ed. Luc Verheijen, 1967) used by Augustinian canons, though Gower applies it to monks (Mirour, 20885–90). The reference may be to Augustine's *De opera monachorum* (CSEL, 41:529–96; tr. Coulton, Life in MA, 4:32–39), which, Baugh notes (241), is mentioned by name in some MSS of the RR; see Langlois's note in his edition of RR 3:316.

How shal the world be served: Clergymen frequently took secular employment, a practice too worldly for the Clerk (GP I.292) and condemned by Gower (Mirour, 20245–56) and Wyclif (Eng. Works, 212–13). In 1395 a group of Lollards petitioned Parliament to abolish this practice (EHD 4:848–50), which was defended by Richard II's chaplain, Roger Dymmok (Liber contra XII errores et hereses Lollardorum, ed. Cronin, Wyclif Soc., 1922, 145–59). "Chaucer ironically asks how these valuable services are to be rendered if the clergy confine themselves to their religious duties and manual labor" (Robinson).

191   prikyng: Tracking a hare by its pricks or footprints (OED s.v. *pricking* vb. sb., 2). Baum (PMLA 71: 242) finds an obscene pun here. The MED offers no support and the OED records no obscene meaning of the verb and none of the noun until 1592 (s.v. *prick* sb. V. 17). RvT I.4231 offers no support; see Eliason, Lang. of Ch, 110. Robertson, Pref to Ch, 255, finds an even less likely pun on "hare," a traditional symbol of lechery (Wailes, Seminar 5, 1969, 92–101); see FrT III.1327n. Hare hunting was highly esteemed (Manly, CT, 510, cites Machaut, Roy de Navarre, 510–12) and Chaucer refers to it in ShipT VII.104, ProThop VII.696; for a description see Edward, Duke of York, Master of Game, ed. W.A. and F. Baillie-Grohman, 1909, 181–86; rpt. Rickert, Ch's World, 221–23.

194   grys: An expensive gray squirrel fur that was expressly forbidden to all cloistered clergy (Bennet, E&S 31, 1945, 11); see Gower, Mirour 21018; Chapters of the Augustinian Canons, ed. H. E. Salter, Cant. and York Soc. 29, 1922, 247.

197   The use of such expensive pins by monks was frequently attacked (Bowden, Comm. on GP, 113; Gower, Mirour, 21020–22). Bressie (MLN 54:487–88) notes that Thomas Usk allegorizes the love knot as the *summum bonum* (Testament of Love, 7:61).

200   in good poynt: This translates the OF *en bon point*. Manly (CT, 510) compares Fr. *embonpoint* (stoutness).

201   stepe: Either "large, prominent" (Robinson) or "bright" (Skeat). The Ashmole version of the *Secretum secretorum* (EETS 276, 97) takes eyes "sette high and bolnyng out" as a bad sign; if "whirlyng about," they show one to be impatient and "to women and belly plesaunce and lustis all yoven." However, they could also be considered an attractive feature; see 753 below.

202   Skeat notes that stemed is related to ME *stem*, a bright light. Grennen (NM 69:574) argues that the line refers to the Monk's head, steaming from overindulgence.

203   On monks' fondness for elegant footwear, see Mann, Ch and Estates, 21–23, and Alphabet of Tales, ed. Mary M. Banks, EETS 126, 1904, 9.

206   swan: A chicken cost two and a half pence, "but a swan for the earl's dinner cost 6s., and for the judge's dinner 7s." (Bressie, MLN 54:488). The Benedictine Rule forbade monks to eat the flesh of quadrupeds (Gilmeister, NM 69:224–25).

207   broun as is a berye: Cf. CkT I.4368 and Whiting B259. See also HF 139 and n. where *broun* may mean "blackened," and cf. NPT VII.2843–44. Eichler (ESt 70, 1935, 102–05) proposes that the hawberry, which ripens to a brownish color, is meant, and he points out that red and brown sometimes overlap as color terms for animals.

The Friar

The mendicant orders founded in the first half of the thirteenth century are represented by the friar of The

Summoner's Tale as well as the pilgrim Hubert. Both reflect common charges directed against the orders in the extended controversy that resulted from the friars' early modification of their founders' ideal of Apostolic poverty and from their competition with the secular clergy as preachers and confessors. Williams (Spec 28, 1953, 499–513) shows that the Friar's cultivation of the rich (particularly women), his giving of easy penance, and his successful begging echo the antifraternalism of William of St. Amour's *De periculis novissimorum temporum* (1256) and the various censures of Richard FitzRalph, archbishop of Armagh (mid-14th c.). Similar condemnations of friars appear in later Lollard texts (Wyclif, Eng. Works, 1–27, 47–51, 294–324, and Sel. Eng. Works, 3:366–429). See also Pantin, Eng. Church, 123–26, 155–63, 267–68; Owst, Preaching in Med. Engl., 71–77, 85–91; and for excerpts from antifraternal texts, Miller, Ch: Sources, 237–68.

Manly's identification of the Friar as a Franciscan (New Light, 104) has been refuted by Fleming (JEGP 65, 1966, 688–700), who is probably correct in asserting that Chaucer's satire is not limited to a specific order. That Faus Semblant in the *Roman de la rose* (see Rom 6082–7696) is a literary ancestor of the Friar has long been recognized, and such matters as the Friar's winning speech and fine clothing, as well as his abuses of his office, were traditional in later satire of the orders (Mann, Ch and Estates, 37–54; Bowden, Comm. on GP, 119–45).

JANETTE RICHARDSON

208   wantowne: "Jovial, light-hearted." Later references to the Friar's association with women, however, suggest that "lascivious" is also appropriate.

209   lymytour: Each convent had its own assigned limits (for begging) and these districts were sometimes subdivided into smaller "limitations." For a friar to hear confessions, he had to be licensed by the bishop of the diocese (Williams, SP 57, 1960, 463–78; AnM 1, 1960, 22–95).

210   ordres foure: The four orders were the Carmelites, Augustinians, Jacobites or Iacobites (Dominicans), and Minorites (Franciscans), the first letters of which formed, according to antifraternal satirists, the word CAIM (the medieval spelling of Cain).

212–13   Although providing dowry was a charitable act encouraged by merchant guilds (Havely, ChR 13, 1979, 339–40), these lines are generally thought to refer to finding husbands for victims of the Friar's own seduction. For other instances, see Young, MLN 50, 1935, 83–85; Pearcy, N&Q 215, 1970, 124–25. Cf. WBT III.880–81.

214   Cf. the phrase, "a pillar of the church" and Galatians 2.9.

216   For franklins, see GP I.331–60.

219   Friars were sometimes given special penitential commissions not entrusted to local parish priests (Williams, SP 57:477); cf. Rom 6364–65.

220   A papal bull of 1300, Boniface VIII's *Super cathedram,* required the orders to specify which of their friars could be licensed as confessors.

233–34   Wyclif (Eng. Works, 638) complains that friars have become peddlers and that they carry knives, pins, and other small goods "for women . . . to gete love of hem, and to have many giftis for little good or nought."

M. Förster, Archiv 135, 1916, 401, prints a scrap of verse: "Fratres cum knyvis goth about and swivyt mennis wyvis."

235–37   St. Francis called his followers "joculatores Domini" (God's minstrels), but the Friar is a worldly minstrel (Mann, Ch and Estates, 45); **yeddyng** is defined in the *Promptorium parvulorum* (EETS e.s. 102, 548) as "geeste (romawnce)." See Rom 7457–58.

238   nekke whit: A white neck was regarded as a sign of lecherousness by the physiognomists (Horton, MLN 48, 1933, 31–34).

239   champioun: In certain cases in English law a final appeal could be made to a trial by arms, in which the two parties or their representatives (champions) would determine the case by the ordeal of battle. The theory was that God would assure victory to the rightful side. Such judicial duels were common in the fourteenth century and Chaucer frequently alludes to them. Cf. KnT I.1713, MLT II.631, FrT III.1662, ParsT X.698, ABC 85. The right to an appeal to arms remained a part of English law, at least in theory, until the early nineteenth century. See William A. Nielson, Trial by Battle, 1890.

241–42   In **tappestere** and probably in **beggestere** the suffix -*stere* (OE -*estre*) has its proper feminine signification, as in the Mod. Eng. "spinster"; so also doubtless in *hoppesteres* (KnT I.2017), *chidestere* (MerT IV.1535, and *tombesteres* and *frutesteres* (PardT VI.477–78). But the distinction of gender was often lost in early English (Robinson).

244–45   By contrast, ministering to lepers specifically was what St. Francis practiced (Bowden, Comm. on GP, 129).

252 a–b   This couplet is found in only a few MSS. Williams (SP 57:478) suggests that it may have been canceled because of inaccuracy. No English records show that friars paid a fee (*ferme*) for rights, exclusive or otherwise, to operate within a district, or "limitation."

254   In principio: Gen. 1.1 and John 1.1. Here the reference is to the latter, since the first fourteen verses of this Gospel were popular for devotions (Law, PMLA 37, 1922, 208–13) and were often used by friars when entering a home. The verses were also thought to have magical power, especially against demons (Bloomfield, MLN 70, 1955, 559–65).

256   purchas, rente: A proverbial comparison (Whiting P438; cf. RR 11566, Rom 6838) implying ill-gotten gains. Greenlaw (MLN 23, 1908, 142–44) suggests that what the Friar "gathered by questionable means" (his *purchas*) "far exceeded his income properly collected" (his *rente*). Slightly different interpretations are given by Pollard in Globe, 1898, 4; Flügel, Anglia 23, 1901, 233–39, and Jeffrey, JEGP 70, 1971, 600–606. Cf. FrT III.1451.

258   love-dayes: Occasions for reconciliation and settlement of disputes out of court. For historical instances and protests against abuses practiced by the arbitrators, see Bennett, Spec 33, 1958, 351–70, and Heffernan, ChR 10, 1975, 174–76.

261   maister: Presumably Master of Arts (cf. SumT III.2185–88) a degree that was "of considerable dignity and was obtained only after lavish expenditure of money" (R), but see introductory note to the portrait of the Clerk.

262   semycope: This vestment was a specific topic in the dispute of the early 1380s between Richard Maidstone, a Carmelite, and John Ashwardby, a Wyclifite (Williams, MP 54, 1956, 117–18).

263 presse: Casting mold. For Chaucer's possible knowledge of bell-founders, see Frank, MLN 68, 1953, 524–28.

269 Huberd: According to Manly (Tales, 513), the name is not common in English records of the fourteenth century. Why it was chosen for the only pilgrim named in the Prologue besides the Prioress is unknown. Bowden (Comm. on GP, 119) suggests a possible personal allusion; Lumiansky (Of Sondry Folk, 132) etymological appropriateness; Muscatine (MLN 70, 1955, 169–72) derivation from Hubert, the kite, in the *Roman de Renart;* Reiss (JEGP 62, 1963, 481–85) associations with thieving concepts of the man in the moon; and Owen (MLN 76, 1961, 396) mere metrical exigency to provide a rhyme for the first line of the Merchant's portrait.

The Merchant

In Chaucer's day, the term *merchant* applied primarily to wholesale exporters and importers, dealers in such commodities as wool, cloth, and wine. The Merchants of the Staple, exporters of wool, woolfells, and skins, were perhaps the most important single group of fourteenth-century English merchants, but the Merchant Adventurers, who dealt in cloth and other items, were gaining power throughout the period. The activities of English merchants in international trade involved them in the flow of bullion into and out of the country—a matter of special concern to the Crown, given its frequent need of capital for the Hundred Years' War, and the rapid inflation and growing money economy of the time. The large scale of the merchants' operations also enabled them to act as moneylenders to the king and other magnates. For the general economic and historical contexts of the Merchant's portrait, see Thrupp, Merchant Class; John H. A. Munro, Wool, Cloth, and Gold, 1972, 1–63; Terrence H. Lloyd, Eng. Wool Trade in the MA, 1977; Cahn, SAC 2, 1980, 81–119; and Eberle, ChR 18, 1983, 161–74.

For the details of the portrait, Knott's historical essay (PQ 1, 1922, 1–16) remains a useful starting point. It is complemented by the documents published by Rickert (MP 24, 1926, 111–19, 249–56) and drawn from the account book of Gilbert Maghfeld, a powerful London merchant from whom Chaucer apparently borrowed money, and whom she proposes as a possible model for the Merchant. See also M. K. James (Econ. Hist. Rev. 8, 2nd ser., 1956, 364–76) for details of Maghfeld's career. Other links between Chaucer's personal background and his description of the Merchant have also been noted: Chaucer's father was himself a merchant with family roots in Ipswich, near Orwell, the English port mentioned in the portrait, and Chaucer's own work at the Custom House would have brought him into close contact with many important merchants (Manly, New Light, 198; Ch Life Records, 2–3, 148–270; Brown, ChR 13, 1979, 255–56).

The portrait also matches traditional satiric and homiletic descriptions of the merchant class (Mann, Ch and Estates, 99–103). Typical elements in such descriptions are accusations of avarice, deceit, and usury; to a lesser extent, one finds allegations of self-important behavior

and of the concealment of debts. Opinions on how sharp or explicit a critique Chaucer intends in the Merchant's portrait have ranged from defenses of the Merchant's financial dealings as normal business operations (Park, ELN 1, 1964, 167–75; Cahn, SAC 2:81–119) to suggestions that even his garb and bearing may signify moral flaws (Crane, ELN 4, 1966, 84; Delasanta, ChR 3, 1968, 30, 35; Jennings, Archiv 215, 1978, 366). Compare Chaucer's characterization of the merchant of Saint-Denis in The Shipman's Tale.

M. TERESA TAVORMINA

270 forked berd: A mark of fashion; see C. Willett and Phillis Cunnington, Hdbk. of Eng. Med. Cost., rev. ed., 1969, 117. The portraits of Chaucer show him wearing such a beard (see Frontispiece).

271 mottelee: Variegated or parti-colored cloth, often in a figured design. Knott (PQ 1:9–10) shows that parti-colored and figured garments were customarily worn by members of various London guilds and companies on state occasions and notes that the Merchants of the Staple wore a distinctive livery.

hye on horse: Perhaps implying ostentation; see MED, s.v. *heighe* adv. 1b.

272 Flaundryssh bever hat: Beaver-skin hats were sufficiently elegant to have been worn by the upper nobility and by important officials in formal processions (Rickert, MP 24:249; Manly, CT, 514). Cahn argues that the hat suggests the Merchant's familiarity with Flanders, where he probably engaged in trade and foreign exchange (SAC 2:93–94).

275 Constant talk of one's profits was a fault stereotypically attributed to merchants (Mann, Ch and Estates, 101).

276 kept for any thyng: Pirates and foreign privateers were a genuine threat to English seatrade (Knott, PQ 1:7–8; Walker, MLN 38, 1923, 314), and powerful merchants like Gilbert Maghfeld were sometimes charged with the "keeping of the sea" (Rickert, MP 24:112). Manly (New Light, 197–98) and Crane (ELN 4:83–85) suggest that the Merchant may also be interested in the opportunities that such protection afforded for certain questionable moneymaking schemes.

277 Middelburgh: A Dutch port on the island of Walcheren, opposite the English port of Orwell. Middelburg was the foreign staple port (the port through which wool was allowed to be exported) from 1384 to 1388. If Chaucer's Merchant is a Merchant of the Staple, this line suggests a date of composition for the portrait not much later than 1388 (John W. Hales, Folia Litteraria, 1893, 100), though Knott (PQ 1:6) observes that wool could be and was exported to Middelburg by royal license in other years as well. Moreover, Chaucer's character may be one of the Merchant Adventurers, who made Middelburg their headquarters from 1384 to 1444 (Manly, New Light, 186–90); see also DiMarco, RBPH 56, 1978, 650–55. Middelburg was near Bruges, the Flemish banking center, where the Merchant could have carried out some of his transactions (Cahn, SAC 2:119).

278 sheeldes: = OF *escu,* but here it probably refers to the Flemish *écu,* a fictional "money of account," valued at 24 silver groats in real Flemish currency (Cahn, SAC 2:85). The Merchant's sale or exchange of foreign currency was for a long time taken as an illegal activity (Knott, PQ 1:10–11). Park, however, observes that some forms of exchange were lawful and in fact common in international commercial circles (ELN 1:168–70). Cahn similarly asserts that "selling shields in exchange" was a legal way of borrowing money, usually at a cost to the seller because of slightly worse exchange rates in London—where the shields were sold—than in Bruges—where the bill of sale or exchange was redeemed (SAC 2:82–98). But Park also notes that seemingly legal exchanges could conceal usury, and it is still often argued that traffic in foreign currency, even when technically legal, was associated with dubious business practices (Mann, Ch and Estates, 100).

280   The syntactic ambiguities of this line are analyzed by Johnson, JEGP 52, 1953, 50–57, and Stillwell, JEGP 57, 1958, 192–95. Cahn (SAC 2:118) notes that a regular seller of shields would regularly be in debt, and would thus need to take special care to seem like a good credit risk—prosperous, dignified, and debt-free (cf. ShipT VII.289). See ShipT VII.230–34 and n. for merchants who go on pilgrimages to escape their creditors (though that is not necessarily the case here). The merchant with hidden debts is found elsewhere in estates satire (Mann, Ch and Estates, 102).

282   bargaynes . . . chevyssaunce: Although the literal senses of these words are value-neutral, the terms can connote improper financial dealings; *chevyssaunce* is often associated with usury, though the *Promptorium parvulorum* (EETS e.s. 102, 80) glosses it as *providencia* (resource, remedy, shift; cf. MED s.v. *chevisaunce* n. 2, 6). See Knott, PQ 1:12–15; Baum, PMLA 71, 1956, 233; Park, ELN 1:170–71; Crane, ELN 4:85; and Mann, Ch and Estates, 99–100.

284   The Merchant's anonymity has been taken as a sign of Chaucer's tact or scorn (Knott, PQ 1:15–16; Manly, CT, 515); moreover, it might be compared to the nameless indistinguishability of the avaricious and spendthrift in Dante, Inf. 7.49–54. It is also an authenticating detail: for the author not to know a pilgrim's name implies that he in fact has one.

The Clerk

The word *clerk* generally denoted any man who could read or write, that is, any man of learning, and specifically an ecclesiastic, whether a student or a man in holy orders; see MED s.v. *clerk*. For a full semantic history of the word, see Karl Krebs, Der Bedeutungswandel von ME Clerk und damit zusammenhängende Probleme, Bonner Studien 21, 1933, 11–62. Education at Oxford and Cambridge was primarily intended as preparation for the priesthood; ultimately, however, many graduates were not ordained (see 291–92 below).

A student normally entered the university at fourteen or fifteen and completed his undergraduate studies about four years later (see 286 below). The student, now called a bachelor, could study three more years and receive the M.A. He would be twenty or twenty-one years old when he became a master. Bachelors and masters were expected to teach as well as study; for the curriculum, privileges, and duties of both undergraduates and advanced students at Oxford, as well as other relevant matters, see Weisheipl, MS 26, 1964, 143–85; and Rashdall, in Universities of Eur. in the MA, ed. Frederick M. Powicke and A. B. Emden, 1936, 3:153. On life at medieval Oxford, see Jones, PMLA 27, 1912, 106–15, Rickert, Ch's World, 128–36, and Bennett, Ch at Oxford.

The Clerk is usually taken as an ideal figure (Green, ELH 18, 1951, 1–6; Ussery, TSE 16, 1968, 1–18), though some (Mann, Ch and Estates, 76, 83; Ginsberg, Criticism 20, 1978, 307–23) find a note of ambiguity amid the general approbation. The Clerk certainly does not indulge in drinking, gambling, whoring, and similar vices, which satirists regularly accused students of making their primary objects of study (Mann, Ch and Estates, 74–85; cf. MilT I.3200–20). Chaucer stresses the Clerk's devotion to learning, even if we hear nothing of the ultimate purpose of that study, knowledge of how to please God (Mann, 76). Brevity and concise speech are virtues particularly commendable in clerks (see PP B 10.163–67; Gower, Mirour, 14665–670); almost by definition they ought to be poor, their clothes threadbare (Mann, 80).

The Clerk has often been identified with well-known schoolmen of Chaucer's time. Ussery (TSE 18, 1970, 1–15) reviews thirty-six prominent Oxford logicians of the fourteenth century. Most possible models were associated with Merton College, probably including Ralph Strode (see Tr 5.1856–59 and n.); see further, Bennett, Ch at Oxford, 58–85.

WARREN S. GINSBERG

286   logyk: The most important course of study of the Trivium (grammar, rhetoric, logic), the basic curriculum of the (generally) four-year undergraduate education. The Quadrivium (arithmetic, geometry, astronomy, music) provided the basic curriculum that led, usually in three years, to the master of arts. Both degrees stressed the study of Aristotle and logic.

290   thredbare: Cf. GP 260.

291–92   The Clerk has not been offered an ecclesiastical living (**benefice**), which would require him to perform the pastoral duties of a priest, yet he would not accept secular employment (**office**), frequently as a secretary or member of a government office. Benefices were of two kinds, ecclesiastical and academic. The ecclesiastical benefice required its recipient to be in orders; many logicians at Oxford, however, put off entering even minor orders until a benefice was assured (Ussery, TSE 18:12). For the disbursement and uses of such benefices, see Pantin, Eng. Church, 30–46. The effect of the Black Death on the availability of benefices has been debated, but Courtenay (Spec 55, 1980, 712) shows that the pattern of distributing ecclesiastical livings worsened for university graduates. This was partly because priests who had benefices flocked to London to "sing for silver" (PP B Pro 83–86; cf. Mann, Ch and Estates, 82–83). They would hire substitute curates to discharge the parish duties and pay them as little as possible, in order to keep the rest of the parish income for themselves; cf. the Parson, who would *sette nat his benefice to hyre* (GP 507). Such positions were available, but to accept one, as Wyclif says (Eng. Works, 250), effectively ended a man's intellectual activity. As for academic benefices, Wyclif himself was supported by one at Oxford. Kellogg (Ch, Langland, 324), and Mann (Ch and Estates, 83) suggest this may be the kind of benefice the Clerk is waiting for. But Pantin (Eng. Church, 108) says that academic benefices were given for study leading to the doctorate of divinity (ten years after the master's) or of canon law (eight years). To be eligible, the Clerk would have to have studied more than Aristotle and his logic, whether he acquired that knowledge at Oxford or at Padua.

294 Twenty bookes: Because large personal libraries were unusual, the size of the Clerk's collection has drawn much comment, even though Chaucer says (LGW G 273) he owned sixty books. Prices of books varied greatly, but the average cost of a volume of Aristotle was about two pounds; each book might have cost the Clerk three times his annual income (Schramm, MLN 48, 1933, 145). The Clerk, however, does not have twenty books: he would "rather have them."

clad in blak or reed: Perhaps a tag meaning "of all forms," "in any kind of cover," rather than sumptuously bound volumes (cf. MED s.v. *blak,* adj. 2b: *blak and broun;* also *blak or whit,* adj. 1b). Cf. HF 1074–78 and Bennett (Ch at Oxford, 13), who says that by the turn of the fourteenth century, Oxford bindings were usually white.

296 Cf. MilT I.3213n.

297 philosophre: Chaucer puns on "philosopher" and the other sense of the word, "alchemist" (CYT VIII.1427). The study of philosophy has not brought the Clerk the "philosopher's stone," which transmutes base metals into gold. This is one of the few puns in Chaucer that Robinson accepted; he noted "other more or less clear cases of word-play" in line 514, SumT III.1916–17, WBPro III.837–38, SqT V.105–6, CYT VIII.730, Tr 1.71, and Purse 3–4. On Chaucer's puns see Tatlock, Flügel Memorial Volume, 1916, 228–32; Kökeritz, PMLA 69, 1954, 937–52; Baum, PMLA 71, 1956, 225–46, and PMLA 73, 1958, 167–70; Hinton, AmN&Q 2, 1964, 115–16; Ross, Ch's Bawdy. However, many of the puns proposed depend on meanings not attested in Chaucer's time and it is often difficult to determine whether or not a pun is intentional.

299–302 *Pauperes scholares,* students who were aided by contributions from friends and family, were familiar figures. See MilT I.3220; PP C 6.36–38; Jones, PMLA 27:109–12; and Bennett, Ch at Oxford, 117–19. Clerks who received support were obliged to pray for the souls of their benefactors (Mann, Ch and Estates, 81–82).

305 forme and reverence: The word *forme* would have particular resonance for a schoolman. Requirements at Oxford were *pro forma* or *secundam formam.* The term, borrowed from Roman law, here conveyed the idea of a legal norm, pattern, or standard of specification. The Clerk's speech conforms to the established rules. See further Weisheipl, MS 26:149–50.

307 Sownynge in moral vertu: Candidates for both the B.A. and the M.A. were examined on their "knowledge and their morals" (Weisheipl, MS 26:157, 163). For the relation of logic to morals, see Taylor, in Petrarch: A Symposium, ed. Aldo Scaglione, 1975, 364–83.

308 gladly . . . lerne and gladly teche: Similar expressions are found in Seneca (c. 3/4 B.C.–65 A.D.): "gaudeo discere, ut doceam" ("I rejoice to learn, that I might teach"; Beale, ELN 13, 1974, 81–86); John of Salisbury (c. 1115–80): "Rare is the philosopher who walks the ways of knowledge with charity and humility, ut doceatur aut doceat . . ." ("that he may be taught or teach"; Fleming, ELN 2, 1965, 5–6); RR 7099–7103: Plato taught that man was given speech "Pour faire noz vouliers entendre,/Pour enseignier e pour apprendre" ("to make us willingly study, to teach and learn"; Wood,

ELN 4, 1967, 166–72); *Sermones nulli parcentes* 500–504: "Constantly be now learning, now teaching (*iam doceri, iam docere*) how you can please God" (Mann, Ch and Estates, 76).

The Sergeant of the Law

Sergeants were the most prestigious and powerful lawyers of Chaucer's time; they ranked above esquires, and were the equals of knights. Their group, called the Order of the Coif, was small (only twenty-one sergeants were created during Richard II's reign), chosen from among the most accomplished apprentices who had spent at least sixteen years studying and practicing law. They had exclusive rights to plead cases in the Court of Common Pleas, and all judges were chosen from this group. Their lengthy education presupposed a wealthy background, and their profession was lucrative. Although satirists such as Gower (Mirour 24181–24624, Vox Clam. 6.1–5) attack their wealth as evidence of greed, Sir John Fortescue, in his classic account of the order of sergeants (*De laudibus legum Angliae* [1468–71], ed. Chrimes, 1942, 50–51), celebrates their prosperity as evidence of the "great pre-eminence" justly accorded to their expert knowledge of English common law. (Theodore F. T. Plucknett, Concise Hist. of Common Law, 1929, ch. 6.; Warren, Va. Law Rev. 28, 1942, 911–50; Manly, New Light, 131–57; McKenna, RUO 45, 1975, 244–62.)

Critical opinion has traditionally viewed the portrait as satiric (Bowden, Comm. on GP, 165–72, citing parallels with Wyclif, Eng. Works, 234, 237–38, and Langland, PP C 3.63–64; see also Donaldson, 889–90). However, McKenna (RUO 45:244), citing evidence from legal history, sees the sergeant as a "model of excellence" for his profession. Mann (Ch and Estates, 86–91) points out that Chaucer omits traditional censures of greed or dishonesty and instead notes lesser faults, such as the sergeant's desire to appear *bisy* (321) and *wise* (313).

Chaucer may have studied law at the Inner Temple (see p. xviii and the introductory note on the Manciple, below). He certainly had first-hand experience with sergeants in the course of various kinds of litigation in which he was involved (see Ch Life Records). Manly suggests (New Light, 147–57) that the word *pynche* (326) involves a pun on the name of Thomas Pynchbek, a sergeant who often served as justice of assize between 1376 and 1388 and who was known for his acquisition of land, as well as for his learning; in 1388, as chief baron of the Exchequer, he signed a writ for Chaucer's arrest in a case of debt.

PATRICIA J. EBERLE

310 Parvys: The portico of a church (cf. Rom 7108) but here usually understood to mean the portico in front of St. Paul's Cathedral (Bowden, Comm. on GP, 166–67; Warren, Va. Law Rev. 28:936–37). Fortescue (De laud. leg. Ang., 51) says that clients were accustomed to consult sergeants "at the Parvys" (Lat. *ad pervisam*); a contemporary lyric makes similar reference to the "parvis" (Robbins, Sec. Lyrics, No. 59).

314 justice . . . in assise: Only a sergeant of law could serve as justice in the assizes (Warren, Va. Law Rev., 28:914). These were originally courts held in the various counties to determine questions of land tenure, but by

Chaucer's time assizes heard all civil cases originating in the counties over which they had jurisdiction. As a result, the justices of assize "exercised a jurisdiction practically co-extensive with the court of common law" (William Holdsworth, Hist. of Eng. Law, 6th ed., 1938, 1:275–80).

315 patente: (Lat. *patere,* to be open). An open letter of appointment from the king; *pleyn commissioun* authorizes jurisdiction in all cases (Bowden, Comm. on GP, 167); see also McKenna (RUO 45:253–54), who argues that *patente* refers to special status as king's sergeant, ranked above the solicitor general and with special powers as counsel to the king.

317 fees and robes: The phrase reflects the Latin formula, *cum robis et foedis,* used to designate recurrent rather than one-time, payments of clothing and money; cf. "robes and fees of an hundred shilling the term of life by yere" (John Arderne, Treatises of Fistula in Ano, EETS 139, 6). A king's sergeant typically received from the king a salary of twenty pounds yearly, plus a robe at Christmas (McKenna, RUO 45:256).

318–20 Transactions involving property, usually heard in the Court of Common Pleas, were a special province of sergeants, who were often engaged as **purchasours** of land for a client. Purchasing land in the technical legal sense meant obtaining a writ, and the process often involved litigation to remove entails, or legal conditions, limiting the right to dispose of a property (David Mellinkoff, Lang. of Law, 1963, 108). The most desirable writ was **fee symple** (Lat. *in feodo simpliciter*), which granted the right to sell, transfer, or bequeath property directly. As moralists such as Gower charged (Mirour, 24537–40; Vox Clam., 6.2), sergeants often purchased land for themselves, but Mann (Ch and Estates, 88–89) argues (against Manly, New Light, 131–57) that these lines leave ambiguous whether the Sergeant is acting for his client or for himself. The lines may be paraphrased as follows: "There was no one better at real estate transactions: he found ways to transform the most complex entails into writs granting fee simple; as for his writs, no one could invalidate them" (William Holdsworth, Hist. of Eng. Law, 3rd ed., 1923, 2:490–92). See also Lambkin, Comitatus 1, 1970, 81–84, and Munroe, New Law Jour. 120, 1970, 1189–90, for arguments that the lines imply illegal activity.

323–24 Reports of cases in the Court of Common Pleas (now called Year Books), probably made for the use of sergeants, were called **termes,** because the reports were ordered under headings according to law terms, the main divisions of the legal year, such as *De terminio Michaelis* (cases from Michaelmas term). Although popular opinion may have assumed that the Year Books extended as far back as William I's reign (1066–87), extant manuscripts begin with Edward I (1272). See William C. Bolland, The Year Books, 1921, 6–7; Baugh, ed., Mélanges . . . offerts à Jean Frappier, 1970, 1:65–76; and Plucknett, Law Quart. Rev. 48, 1932, 336–37. For a similar use of *termes,* see Gower, Mirour, 24493–95.

326 pynche: Cases could be dismissed because of a flaw in the wording of a writ (Albert K. R. Kiralfy, A Source Book of Eng. Law, 1957, 49). Manly believed this was a pun on the name Pynchbek (see introductory note).

327 Although this is doubtless an exaggerated description of his memory, sergeants were, nevertheless, regarded as the pre-eminent authorities on the statutes;

they were frequently summoned to Parliament to resolve difficult questions of law (Warren, Va. Law Rev. 28: 914).

328 medlee: A cloth of one color or of different tones of one color, made of wool dyed before being spun, it was usually not worn by classes above the rank of knight (Linthicum, JEGP 34, 1935, 39–41). The Sergeant's **hoomly,** unpretentious, dress does not indicate his official status; no mention is made of the white coif (a close-fitting cap) characteristic of his order, and his official parti-colored robes would usually have been made of more expensive materials. The Ellesmere illumination depicts his white coif and a short, parti-colored gown, which seems to have been the official traveling costume for sergeants (see McKenna, RUO 45:258; the most detailed account of sergeants' ceremonial dress is Alexander Pulling, Order of the Coif, 1897, 217–62).

The Franklin

The Franklin was a provincial gentleman, an early example of the English country squire. His offices and appointments were commonly held by men of that rank (Gerould, PMLA 41, 1926, 262–79; Noel Denholm-Young, Country Gentry in 14th Cent., 1969, 23–26) as part of the warp and woof of rewards and responsibilities that gave form to the practical operations of government (Kenneth B. McFarlane, Nobility of Later Med. Eng., 1973, 268–78). For a thorough discussion of the Franklin's particular situation, see Henrik Specht, Ch's Franklin in CT, Pubs. of the Dept. of Eng., Univ. of Copenhagen 10, 1981. Manly proposes a Lincolnshire knight, Sir John Bussy, as the possible historical model for Chaucer's Franklin (New Light, 162–68). Bussy was a neighbor of Thomas Pynchbek, whom Manly proposes as the historical model for the description of the Franklin's companion, the Man of Law (New Light, 151–57). Wood Leigh suggests instead Stephen de Hales, another acquaintance of Pynchbek's (RES 4, 1928, 145–51). The detail of these identifications illuminates the nature of the biographical records for such men even if the identifications themselves are inconclusive. Bowden presents the Franklin as a straightforward exemplar of the social type (Comm. on GP, 172–77), but there is disagreement about his social and intellectual sophistication. Although The Franklin's Tale is the focus of the disagreement, reference is sometimes made to his description in the General Prologue. In one reading he is intelligent and dignified, linked by some of his offices with Chaucer himself (Blenner-Hasset, Spec 28, 1953, 791–92); in another, satiric, reading he is ignorant, even corrupt, like others of the moneyed "middle class" (Robertson, Pref. to Ch, 276, and Costerus n.s. 1, 1974, 2–7, 26), and insecure in his social position (Burlin, Neophil 51, 1967, 55–59). Mann considers the details of the Franklin's description in the context of a number of satiric texts and differentiates Chaucer's treatment as nonsatiric (Ch and Estates, 152–59).

R. T. LENAGHAN

332 dayesye: The English daisy (*Bellis perennis*) often affords marked contrasts of red and white (cf. LGW 42–43), which make it an especially appropriate simile for the Franklin.

333   Complexioun: An individual's temperament, or "complexion," was thought to be formed by the four humors of the body (see 420 below). The idea of medieval medicine was to keep the humors in balance, but in each individual one humor tends to dominate. A *sangwyn* person like the Franklin (cf. KnT I.2168) is ruddy in complexion, dominated by blood and loves "Ioye and laghynge . . . he shal be . . . of good will and wythout malice . . . he shall haue a good stomake, good dygescion . . . he shall be fre and liberall." The phlegmatic temperament (dominated by phlegm) is "slowe sadde . . . piteuouse, chaste, and [shall] lytill desyre company of women." The choleric (cf. 587 below), dominated by choler or red bile, is "lene of body . . . hasty of worde and of answere; he louyth hasty wengeaunce; Desyrous of company of women moore than hym nedyth." The melancholy temperament, dominated by black bile, "sholde bene pensyf and slowe . . . of sotille ymagynacion as of hand-werkys" (Secreta Secretorum, EETS e.s. 74, 219–20).

334   sop in wyn: A light breakfast consisting of bits of bread in wine; cf. MerT IV.1843.

336   Epicurus owene sone: "He was, as we should say, an epicure. The philosophy of Epicurus was associated (somewhat unjustly) then as now with luxurious living" (Robinson). Cf. Bo 3.pr2.77–80 and MerT IV.2021–30. John Russell's *Book of Nurture* lists the menu for a Franklin's feast (The Babee's Book, EETS 32, 170–71).

340   Seint Julian: Julian the Hospitaller, a mythical saint associated with hospitality (David H. Farmer, Oxford Dict. of Saints, 1978, 226–27). For versions of his legend, see *Legenda aurea,* 142–43 (tr. Ryan and Ripperger, 130–31), *Gesta romanorum,* 311–13 (tr. Swan, 114–16), *South English Legendary,* EETS 235, 32–37.

345–46   Keenan sees reflections of the miracle of the manna (which was represented as snow) and Eucharistic typology in the description of the Franklin's bounty (NM 79, 1978, 36–40).

347   sondry sesons: Medieval medical theory held that seasonal adjustment of the diet would maintain a healthy balance of the humors (Bryant, MLN 63, 1948, 318–25; cf. 435–37 and n. below). Mann, on the other hand, sees this as a gourmet's pleasure in seasonal variety (Ch and Estates, 279 n. 30).

351–52   As a context for such a cuisine and for sauces in particular, see Two Fifteenth-Cent. Cookery Bks., EETS 91, viii and index; and Hieatt, in Ch Problems, 139–63.

353   table dormant: A table left in place and thus differentiated from a table set up in the hall and taken down after use. It is presumably a table dormant, though a grander example of the type, that is depicted in the illustration for January in *The Très Riches Heures de Jean, Duke of Berry* (Facsimile ed., 1969). At such a table a lord could readily dispense hospitality, and perhaps justice (cf. 355).

355   sessiouns ther . . . lord and sire: He presided at a judicial session, presumably as a justice of the peace (Putnam, in Eng. Govt. at Work, 1327–36, ed. James Willard, William Morris, and William Dunham, Jr., 1940–50, 3:185–217). It is also possible, since *session* has a more general sense and the sessions were *ther* in the Franklin's hall, that he presided as a feudal lord like the one in the SumT III.2162–67. Chaucer was a Justice of the Peace in Kent from 1386–89 (Ch Life Records, 348–63; see above pp. xxii–xxiii).

356   knyght of the shire: Member of Parliament (Plucknett, in Engl. Govt. 1:94–105). Chaucer was knight of the shire for Kent in 1386 (Ch Life Records, 364–69; see above p. xxiii).

357   anlaas and . . . gipser: Sumptuary legislation (see 115 above) and church monuments indicate that the dagger and purse marked a gentleman's social standing (Specht, Ch's Franklin, 119–23).

359   shirreve: The sheriff was the principal officer of the Crown in a shire (Morris, in Engl. Govt. 2:41–108).

contour: An officer charged as an accountant to oversee the collecting and auditing of taxes in a shire (Johnson, in Eng. Govt. 2:201–05). The term can also refer to one who pleads in court, a lawyer.

360   vavasour: A term of feudal tenancy, literally the vassal of vassals, in Romance usage the lowest rank of nobility (Marc Bloch, Feudal Society, tr. L. A. Manyon, 1961, 177, 322). Coss reviews both literary and legal use of the term (Lit. and Soc. Terminology: The Vavasour, in *Soc. Relations and Ideas,* ed. T. H. Aston et al., 1983, 109–50). The primary reference for Chaucer's use of the term is probably literary. In romances *vavasours* often have a status appropriate to provincial gentlemen (see Frankis, N&Q 15, 1968, 46–47; and for more extensive discussion, Pearcy, ChR 8, 1973, 33–59).

The Five Guildsmen

Each guildsman represents a different trade, chosen tactfully, Kuhl argues (TWA, 18, 1916, 652–75), from trades that remained neutral in the political struggles among the London crafts at this time (on which see Myers, London, 85–105; and Goodall, MAE 50, 1981, 289–91). Camden (PQ 7, 1928, 314–17) argues that the guildsmen were added to the General Prologue after the political strife had calmed, but Herndon (Florida State Univ. Sts. 5, 1952, 33–44) refuted this on textual grounds. Their great *fraternitee* is probably not one of the craft guilds, which were usually composed of practitioners of a single trade. McCutcheon (PMLA 74, 1959, 313–17) notes that the Drapers admitted nondrapers, mainly from the related cloth trades, to which four of these five Guildsmen belong, but the Carpenter would be an unlikely member of the Drapers. Instead, they are probably members of one of the parish guilds, fraternal and charitable organizations, which were then gaining power; see George Unwin, The Gilds and Companies of London, 1908, 110–11. Attempts to identify the exact guild have been made by Fullerton (MLN 61, 1946, 515–23) and Garbáty (JEGP 69, 1960, 691–709). Garbáty makes a strong case for the guild of St. Botolph's in Aldersgate, but such identifications can be only speculative.

Some critics read the description of the Guildsmen as a satiric attack on middle-class pretensions (Lisca, MLN 70, 1955, 321–24; Robertson, Ch's London, 79–81; Morgan, ES 59, 1978, 481–98). Mann notes that the Guildsmen have none of the traditional mercantile vices, such as fraud, usury, and avarice (Ch and Estates, 104). Chaucer seems more amused than indignant at their bustling self-importance.

LARRY D. BENSON

361–62   There is no basis for William Blake's theory, revived by Nathan (MLN 67, 1952, 533–34), that Chaucer wrote *Web dyer* and hence intended four, rather than five, guildsmen.

363 lyveree: The members of each guild were entitled to wear its distinctive attire, usually a cape and hood, on ceremonial occasions.

366–67 Skeat (5:36) noted that the sumptuary law of 1363 (see n. 115 above) forbade the use of silver ornamentation to ordinary tradesmen, and Morgan (ES 59:494) regards the Guildsmen's silver-mounted knives as a satiric detail. However, the law (which had been repealed) specifically allowed such ornamentation to "Merchants, Citizens and Burgesses, artificers, people of handy-craft" who had property to the value of five hundred pounds, a criterion these prosperous would-be aldermen probably meet.

370 a yeldehalle: The guildhall was the seat of municipal government; the mayor and aldermen, the highest ranking civic officials, sat on the **deys** (dais). The use of the indefinite article **a** seems to indicate that the reference is not necessarily to the Guildhall in London.

371–73 An alderman was required to be "wise and discreet in mind, rich, honest, trustworthy, and free" (Liber Albus, 29). None of the trades of these Guildsmen was represented in the aldermancy of London for another hundred years (Kuhl, TWA 18:652–757; see also Goodall, MAE 50:284–92).

376 "madame": Aldermen's wives were accorded this title (see Thrupp, Merchant Class, 18). The Liber Albus styles aldermen "barons" (45) and claims that as late as 1350 aldermen were buried with baronial honors (29).

377 vigilies: Skeat (5:37) quotes Speght's note: "It was the manner in time past, upon festival events, called *vigiliae,* for parishioners to meet in their church-houses or church-yards and there to have a drinking fit for the time. . . . Hither came the wives in comely manner, and they that were of the better sort had their mantles carried before them, as well for show as to keep them from cold at the table." Cf. WBPro III.555–59.

goon . . . bifore: cf. 449–51 below.

The Cook

The Cook's portrait is "a concoction of culinary superlatives," telling us nothing of his personality, "except what is suggested by his knowledge of London ale" (Donaldson, 891). The reference to his ulcerous sore—so quietly slipped in—is startlingly dramatic. Langland (PP B Pr 225–26) gives a vivid picture of "cokes and here knaves," which Mann (Ch and Estates, 163) thinks may have been a stimulus for Chaucer's description. In his prologue (4336) the Cook calls himself *Hogge* (a nickname for Roger; see CkPro I.4345). Possibly a real person lurks behind him. Rickert (TLS, 20 Oct. 1932, 761) discovered a contemporary Roger Knight de Ware of London, Cook. He may be the same Roger Knight de Ware, Cook, named in a plea of debt in 1384–85; if so, there would be a joke in *a fair chyvachee of a cook* (MancPro IX.50) and possibly in *gentil Roger* (CkPro I.4353; see Emerson, Expl 16, 1958, 51). Lyon finds a reference (probably 1373) to a Roger de Ware, Cook, accused of being a common night-walker, i.e., one who broke curfew (MLN 52, 1937, 491–94). For information on cooks in medieval England, see Bowden, Comm.

on GP, 185–89. Curry, (Ch and Science, 37–53) discusses the medical aspects of the characterization.

DOUGLAS GRAY

379 for the nones: Probably "for the occasion." He was a shopkeeper (cf. CkPro I.4325–64), who had been engaged to cook meals for them on the pilgrimage. It is possible, though less likely, that the phrase is here used either intensively—"especially skillful"—or as a simple line-filler. See the discussion of the phrase by Lumiansky, Neophil 35, 1951, 29–36; however, his claim that the primary meaning is usually discernible is not convincing in a number of cases he cites.

381 poudre-marchant tart: A sharp spice or flavoring powder (Two Fifteenth-Cent. Cookery Bks., EETS 91, 25; Curye on Inglysch, EETS, SS 8, 208).

galyngale: A sweet spice, the powdered root of sweet cyperus (a sedge of the genus cyperus), resembling ginger; see Curye on Inglysch, EETS, SS 8, 190.

382 London ale was stronger and more expensive than other varieties. It was "famous as early as the time of Henry III. In 1504 it was higher priced than Kentish ale by five shillings a barrel" (A. J. Wyatt, ed., CT: GP and SqT, 1904). An ability to judge its quality was important, and each London ward elected "the Aleconners of the ward" to determine if each batch brewed was "so good as it was wont to be" (Liber Albus, 277, 312).

384 mortreux: Both "mortrewes de chare" (meat) and "mortrewes of fysshe" are mentioned (cf. Two Fifteenth-Cent. Cookery Bks., 14, xliii; Babees Book, EETS 32, 151, 170, 172; Liber Cure Cocorum, ed. Morris, 9.19; Curye on Inglysch, EETS, SS 8, 202). One recipe is for finely ground pork seasoned with saffron, salt, and ginger mixed with ale, egg yolks and bread; another is for chopped boiled fish seasoned with sugar, salt and ginger. It is hard to be sure of the pronunciation of the *-x* in words where it represents etymologically an *-s* or *-us.* In the case of *mortreux* spellings like *mortrels, mortrewes* point to a final *-s.* *Lybeux* (Thop VII.900), Fr. *li biaus,* doubtless also had an *-s.* For *Amphiorax* (WBPro III.741; Anel 57; Tr 2.105, 5.1500) Chaucer must have been familiar with the Lat. form *Amphiaraus,* though there may have been a corrupt English pronunciation in *-x* (Robinson).

386 mormal: (Fr. *mortmal*), defined in the *Cyrurgie* of Guy de Chauliac, EETS 265, 333, as "a filty scabbe." It is a species of dry scabbed ulcer, gangrenous rather than cancerous. For medicinal theories on the subject, see Curry, Ch and Science, 47–52. He quotes Bernardus de Gordon: "*Malum mortuum* is a species of scabies, which arises from corrupted natural melancholia . . . the marks of it are large pustules of a leaden or black color, scabbed, and exceedingly fetid. . . . In appearance it is most unsightly, coming out on the hip-bone and often on the shin-bones." Mann, however, points out that the authorities Curry cites attribute mormals to generally intemperate or unclean habits, rather than to any specific pattern of behavior (Ch and Estates, 285). See also Braddy, who argues that it is a runny, not a dry, sore MLQ 7, 1946, 265–67. A mormal could smell strongly (Cook, MLN 33, 1918, 379). Bennett (Ch at Oxford, 8) finds a reference to a cook with a mormal in the early rolls of Merton College. There is a contemporary account of the treatment of an ulcerated leg in John Arderne's *Treatises of Fistula in Ano,* EETS 139, 52–54.

387 blankmanger: A kind of thick stew or mousse

made of chopped chicken or fish, richly spiced (cf. Liber Cure Cocorum, 9; Two Fifteenth-Cent. Cookery Bks., EETS 91, 85; Curye on Inglysch, EETS, SS 8, 172; and Ch Problems, 149–63).

The Shipman

"The shipman plays a very minor role in estates literature" (Mann, Ch and Estates, 170). In the absence of any obvious stereotype, scholars have sought to identify the Shipman with individual fourteenth-century sailors from the *weste* of England (388), particularly from *Dertemouthe* (389), though Chaucer perhaps mentions Dartmouth (Devon) simply because it was a notorious haunt of pirates (Bowden, Comm. on GP, 192–93). Karkeek pointed out records of a ship called the *Maudelayne* (410), sailing out of Dartmouth; in 1379 the master was George Cowntree, in 1391 Peter Risshenden (Essays on Chaucer 5, Ch Soc, 1884). Manly identified Risshenden with Piers Risselden, involved with the famous buccaneer John Hawley in the controversial capture of three foreign wine-ships in 1386, an action that resulted in a court case lasting until 1394 (New Light, 169–81). But Galway draws attention to the Shipman's similarities in career and character to John Piers, who lived *fer by weste* (though at Teignmouth, not Dartmouth), went on expeditions to Bordeaux, and in 1383 captured a ship called the Magdeleyn (MLR 34, 1939, 497–514).

J. A. BURROW AND V. J. SCATTERGOOD

390   rouncy: Perhaps "hackney" or "nag," or "large, strong horse" (Lat. *roncinus*, OF *ronci*). The Ellesmere MS portrait shows the Shipman riding something similar to a cart horse.

395   good felawe: Literally, the phrase means "good companion" but is used by Chaucer with connotations of rascality; cf. GP I.650 and 648, and FrT III.1385. Chaucer's contemporary Clanvowe takes a less sympathetic view: "But now swiche as been synful men and wacches [look-outs] of the feend been cleped of the world 'good felawes' " (The Two Ways, 575–77, in Works, ed. V. J. Scattergood, 1975).

396–97 The Shipman apparently stole wine, perhaps by drawing some from each barrel in the cargo or, as Stobie holds, by misappropriation of the "courtesy-wine" merchants were required to supply for crews (PMLA 64, 1949, 565–69). A Latin poem laments the thieving habits of sailors: "Sailors and peasants, who used to be honest, are so corrupted by fraud that hardly one of them is upright" (Mann, Ch and Estates, 171). Bordeaux (**Burdeux**), in English Gascony, was a great source of imported wine.

399–400 "He drowned his prisoners" (Robinson). Mann cites a fourteenth-century manual for confessors: sailors "not only kill clerks and laymen while they are on land, but also when they are at sea they practise wicked piracy, seizing the goods of other people and especially of merchants as they are crossing the sea, and killing them mercilessly" (Ch and Estates, 171). Bowden notes that Edward III drowned the crew of a captured ship and does not seem to have been criticized for doing so (Comm. on GP, 194).

401–09 For a comparable list of the skills required by a good seaman, see Vegetius in his popular treatise on

military training: "The expertise of sailors and steersmen lies in knowing the places where they are to sail and the harbors, so that they can avoid dangerous shallow waters, with rocks jutting out or hidden, and also sandbanks" (*De re militari*, ed. Lang, 1967, 4.43).

404   Hull is on the Yorkshire coast. **Cartage** is Carthage elsewhere in Chaucer (e.g., FranT V.1400, NPT VII.3365), but here may possibly be Cartagena in Spain (Magoun, Ch Gazetteer, 46).

408   **Gootlond:** Probably Gotland, an island off the Swedish coast (Magoun, Ch Gazetteer, 80–81), though Danish Jutland is another possibility.

Fynystere: Probably Cape Finisterre, Galicia, Spain (Magoun, 72–73; and Malone, MLN 45, 1930, 229–30), rather than Finistère in Brittany.

410   **barge:** If Chaucer is using the word precisely, he probably had in mind a vessel such as that described by Alan Moore from the reign of Edward III: single-masted, but with oars, undecked but with fore- and after-castles and perhaps a top-castle, about eighty feet long on the keel with raked bows and stern, and about twenty feet wide (Mariner's Mirror 6, 1920, 229–42; also 4, 1914, 169–70).

The Doctor of Physic

The most complete accounts of the Physician in relation to fourteenth-century medical theory and practice are Curry, Ch and Science, 3–36 (a slight reworking of PQ 4, 1925, 1–24) and Huling Ussery, Ch's Physician, TSE 19, 1971. The portrait is a mixture of apparent praise and satiric hints with the result that "we cannot be absolutely sure about anything in the Doctor's character" (Curry, 36). As with the portrait of the Sergeant of Law, this complexity is caused by Chaucer's "transforming the features which other writers attack into evidence of professional skill" (Mann, Ch and Estates, 91).

A few critics have found Chaucer's attitude toward the Physician essentially admiring (Manly, CT, 524; O'Neill, Jour. Amer. Medical Assoc. 208, 1969, 78; Ussery, Ch's Physician, 102–17; Cosman, N.Y. State Jour. Medicine 72.2, 1972, 2439–44); some others take an equally negative view, seeing the pilgrim as an "Arabist and astrologer" (Tupper, Nation 96, 1913, 640), "society doctor" (Lumiansky, Of Sondry Folk, 195), unprincipled thief (James Winny, ed., GP to CT, 1965, 106–7), or irreligious quack (Robertson, Ch's London, 1968, 207–8). Most critics, while usually conceding the pilgrim's professional competence, follow Curry in emphasizing the elements of satire, especially a love of gold and concern with only the physical (Nicholls, Dalhousie Rev. 12, 1932, 219–21; Bowden, Comm. on GP, 199–213; Donaldson, 1053–54; Regenos, in Classical, Medieval and Renaissance Studies in Honor of Berthold L. Ullman, 1964, 2:45–46; Stephan Kohl, Wissenschaft und Dichtung bei Chaucer, 1973, 127–48; Howard, Idea of CT, 335; Gardner, Poetry of Ch, 238; and Skerpan, Jour. Rocky Mtn. Med. and Ren. Assoc. 5, 1984, 41–56).

Manly suspected that the portrait was based on a real person but could supply no name (New Light, 260–61); Ussery (Ch's Physician, 61–89) dismisses earlier suggestions that Chaucer may have had in mind John of Gaddesden (Bashford, Nineteenth Century 104, 1928, 247–48) or John Arderne (Bowden, Comm. on GP, 208; Hodgson, GP to CT, 114) and offers five contemporary candidates of his own, none especially convincing. There is perhaps no need for an actual model since so much of the portrait is conventional (see, especially, Mann, Ch and Estates, 91–99). Ussery (Ch's Physician, 29–31, 95) argues that the Physician is a cleric, since most fourteenth-century physicians, especially eminent ones, were secular clerics, and cites the Host's comment that the Doctor is *lyk a prelat* (PardT VI.310). However, clerics were forbidden to draw blood; if the Doctor is also a surgeon (see line 413 and n.), he must be regarded as a layman.

Further information about medicine in the period can be found in C. H. Talbot, Medicine in Med. Engl., 1967. See also Jones, Bull. Inst. Hist. Medicine 5, 1937, 405–51, 538–88; Bullough, Spec 36, 1961, 600–12; and Alford, Centennial Rev. 23, 1979, 377–96.

C. DAVID BENSON

411   Doctour of Phisik: The Physician is no ordinary *medicus* or *leche* but one of the relatively few holders of an advanced degree, which at this period might require as many as fifteen or seventeen years of study and residence at a university (Talbot, Medicine in Med. Engl., 70; Ussery, Ch's Physician, 7–11).

413   To speke of: Curry's suggestion that this phrase and the list of authorities below indicate that the Physician is good only at speaking about medicine (Ch and Science, 28–29) has been attacked by Manly (CT, 524) and Ussery (Ch's Physician, 111–12).

phisik and of surgerye: Ussery (Ch's Physician, 6–21) notes that physic and surgery were two distinct professions and only rarely practiced by the same person (cf. Jones, Bull. Inst. Hist. Medicine 5: 407–8) and interprets the line to mean that the Physician's skill is greater than that of other physicians and also of surgeons (94–95). But Guy de Chauliac styles himself "Cirurgien, doctoure of phisik" (Cyrurgie of Guy de Chauliac, EETS 265, 9), and Ussery (Ch's Physician, 59–60) notes that others in England so designated themselves.

414   astronomye: Astronomy, the influence of planetary forces (what we would call astrology), was an important part of medieval medical practice. Some critics suggest that the physician's reliance on astronomy is intended pejoratively (Bowden, Comm. on GP, 204; Robertson, Ch's London, 207–8), but the following lines do not describe "judicial astronomy" (cf. Astr 2.4.57–59) but rather the use of astronomy to foretell physical events, as in meteorology or medicine, which was regarded as legitimate by Thomas Aquinas (Summa Theol. 2.2.95.5) and many others (though some churchmen were uncomfortable even with this; cf. Dives and Pauper 1:141). In the *Astrolabe*, Chaucer notes that each of the twelve zodiacal signs "hath respect to a certeyn parcel of the body of a man, and hath it in governaunce" (Astr 1.21.71–73). Some medical writers ignore planetary influences, but most stress its importance: "As Galian the full wies leche saith, and Isoder the gode clerk, hit witnessith that a man may not perfitely can the sciens and crafte of medessin but yef he be an astonomoure" (Secreta secretorum, EETS e.s. 74, 195; cf. also John Arderne, Treatises of Fistula in Ano, EETS 139, 16–20). See Thorndike, Hist. of Magic; Talbot, Jour. Hist. of Medicine 16, 1961, 213–33; Robbins, Spec 45, 1970, 395–98; Braswell, SAC 8, 1986, 145–56.

In the lines that follow Chaucer seems to derive much of his information about the use of astronomy in medicine from the *Kalendarium* of Nicholas of Lynn, which he knew and used (Astr Pro 84–86 and n.). See C. D. Benson, AmN&Q 22, 5–6, 1984, 66–70. In Canons 11 and 12 of the *Kalendarium* especially, Nicholas makes clear the importance of the position of the moon when letting blood or giving medicine: "And if a physician should neglect to look at these things [the sign in which the moon is] when giving medicine, he will be deprived very often of a cure, because the power of heaven will work to the contrary" (Kalendarium, 211).

415–16 The "hours" during which the Physician watched over (**kepte**) his patient might refer to the *hora* or stages of a disease described by Vincent of Beauvais (Aiken, SP 53, 1956, 22–24). More likely, the reference is to the twenty-four astrological hours, which varied according to the time of year, in which different planets reigned (cf. Astr 2.12), and also to the six-hour periods of the day in which one of each of the four humors was dominant (see 420 below). Nicholas of Lynn provides a table (Kalendarium, 176–77) by which this information can be determined "for each hour of the day and night" (60).

416   magyk natureel: As opposed to black magic; cf. HF 1266, FranT V.1125. See Thorndike's discussion of legitimate and forbidden astrology in Roger Bacon (Hist. Magic 2:668–70) and cf. Gower, who uses similar terms, sometimes apparently pejoratively (Conf. Aman. 6.1338; 7.649, 1301, 1471).

417   fortunen the ascendent: Calculate the planetary position, especially that of the "lord of the ascendent" (cf. Astr 2.4), in order to make the *ymages* (talismatic images) when the planets are in a favorable position. For a similar reference see HF 1265–70. Nicholas of Lynn (Kalendarium, 164–75) provides a chart for discovering the ascendent (eighth canon) and explains (twelfth canon) the making of such talismans: "For, as Thebith says, images and sculptures are made in stones so that they might receive the worth of precious stones from the influence of heaven. However, they do not have the power except from the aspect of the planets at the time when they were sculpted. . . . the supercelestial power gives them the power they possess" (210). For the making of images for medicine as discussed by Thebit ibn Corat and others, see Curry, Ch and Science, 20–25, and Thorndike, Hist. Magic 1:663–66; 2:*passim*, and 3:519.

420   hoot, or coold, or moyste, or drye: The four qualities, or contraries, linked to the four elements, air (hot and moist), fire (hot and dry), earth (cold and dry), water (cold and moist). According to the theory popularized by Galen (see 429–34 below) from ideas he attributed to Aristotle and Hippocrates, the body is composed of these four elements, which correspond to the four humors (bodily fluids): blood, phlegm, choler (yellow or red bile), and melancholy (black bile). "The blood is hot and moist to the likeness of the air; phlegm is cold and moist after the kind of the water; choler hot and dry after kind of fire; melancholy cold and dry after kind of earth" (Secreta Secretorum, EETS e.s. 74, 219–20; modernized). The humors of an individual could be affected by the planets and signs of the zodiac, each of which is characterized by elemental qualities (thus Aries is a fiery hot and dry sign, Mars a hot and dry planet), by seasons of the year (spring is hot and moist, like blood; summer hot and dry, like choler; autumn cold and dry, like melancholy; winter cold and moist, like phlegm), by the time of day (see 415–16 above), and by diet. An imbalance of the humors was thought to cause illness, and the physician's task was to keep the humors "in evene proporcioun in quantite and qualite" (Bartholomaeus Anglicus, De proprietatibus rerum, 4.6, tr. Trevisa 1:148). If the humors were out of balance, the physician attempted to determine the nature of the imbalance and its origin (as described in line 421) and offered compensating treatment with medicines of the proper elemental qualities: "Also therfore [the medical man] nedith to knowe the qualitees of herbes and of othir medicinal thinges and diversite of degrees, what is hote and drye, what is colde and moiste, in what degree, yif he wil nought erre in his office" (Barth. Ang., 7.69, tr. Trevisa 1:435).

425–28   The implication of collusion between druggists and doctors is traditional (see Gower, Mirour, 25621–80, and Mann, Ch and Estates, 95).

426   letuaries: Electuaries, medicine in the form of paste or syrup (MED s.v. *letuarie* a), often mixed with honey (Lanfrank's Science of Cirurgie, ed. Robert v. Fleischacker, EETS 102, 1894, 263). Chaucer also refers to electuaries at PardT VI.307, Tr 5.741, and (as aphrodisiacs) MerT IV.1809.

429–34   This list of eminent medical authorities contains more names than similar lists in RR, 15959–61, or Dante, Inf. IV.143–44. **Esculapius** (Aesculapius) is the legendary founder of medicine in ancient Greece to whom many works were attributed in the Middle Ages. **Deyscorides** (Dioscorides, fl. 50–70 A.D.) is the author of *Materia medica,* the largest pharmaceutical guide in antiquity. **Rufus** (of Ephesus, probably fl. c. 25 B.C. to 50 A.D.) is a Greek who wrote widely on medical topics. The eminent **Ypocras** (Hippocrates) was born at Cos about 460 B.C. and moved Greek medicine from superstition toward science. **Haly** is almost certainly Haly Abbas (Ali ibn Abbas, d. 994), a Persian who wrote a widely circulated work on medical theory and practice known in the West as the "Royal Book," but the reference might also be to Haly Eben Rodan (Ali ibn Ridwan, fl. c. 1050), an Egyptian whose most famous medical works were commentaries on Galen and Hippocrates. **Galyen** (Galen, c. 129–99 A.D.) wrote works that were central to the curriculum of medieval medical schools. Chaucer refers to him in ParsT X.831 and (with Hippocrates) in BD 572. **Serapion** could be the Alexandrian Serapion (c. 200–150 B.C.), founder of the empirical school of medicine; Serapion the Elder (Yahya ibn Sarafyun, ninth century), a Christian of Damascus whose works were translated into Latin; or a mysterious Arab known as Serapion the Younger (probably twelfth century) to whom is attributed the popular *Liber medicamentis simplicibus.* **Razis** (Rhazes, c. 854–930) wrote the *Liber ad almansorem* and a comprehensive medical manual known in the West as "Continens." **Avycen,** Avicenna (Ibn Sina, 980–1037), is the influential philosopher whose most important medical work was the encyclopedic *Book of the Canon of Medicine* (cf. PardT VI.889–90). **Averrois** (Averroës, 1126–98) was a Spanish Moslem philosopher and astronomer whose major medical work was translated into Latin as "Colliget." John of Damascus (**Damascien**) was an important Syrian theologian of the eighth century, but the name Johannes (or Janus) Damas-

cenus was given to works by Serapion the Elder and Yuhanna ibn Masawayn (Mesuë, d. 857). **Constantyn** (Constantine the African, fl. 1065–85), called the "cursed monk" in MerT IV.1810, translated a number of medical works and was an important transmitter of Greco-Arabic science to the West. **Bernard** (of Gordon, fl. 1283–1309) taught medicine at Montpellier and wrote the famous *Lilium medicinae,* which contains possibly the earliest reference to eyeglasses. The last two authorities are English. **Gatesden** (John of Gaddesden, probably died c. 1349) was a fellow of Merton College and author of the medical text *Rosa anglica.* **Gilbertyn** (Gilbertus Anglicus, fl. 1250) was an English physician, author of the *Compendium medicinae.*

Despite claims for Vincent of Beauvais (Aiken, Spec 10, 1935, 287) no single source for this list has been found. Robbins (in Sts. Lang. and Lit. in Hon. of Margaret Schlauch, 1966, 335–41) shows that all of the names could not have come from Vincent and concludes that "Chaucer's list contains just those names that an educated doctor of his day would have cited."

435–37   The importance of such a diet for health is repeatedly stressed in medieval writing, as in Langland, PP B 6.259–76, and all versions of the Secreta secretorum (cf. GP I.347, NPT VII.2838). Mann (Ch and Estates, 252, n. 41) suggests that the actual vocabulary of these lines may be drawn from Gower, Mirour, 8338–43. On diet, see also Ussery, Ch's Physician, 113–14; Robbins, Spec 45, 1970, 404; and Jones, Bull. Inst. Hist. Medicine 5, 1937, 561–64.

438   The conventional association of medicine with atheism can be found in Petrarch's *Invective contra medicum* and was still current in the time of Sir Thomas Browne as can be seen from the beginning of *Religio medici.* Curry (Ch and Science, 30) cites John of Salisbury's charge in *Polycraticus* 2.29 that physicians "while they attribute too much authority to Nature, cast aside the Author of Nature." The implication of this line has influenced much recent criticism of the pilgrim and his tale; see especially Hoffman, ChR 2, 1967, 20–31.

439–40   For other examples of doctors clad in rich clothing, see Langland, PP B 6.269–70 and B 20.176; and Henryson, Testament of Cresseid, 250–51.

443–44   "Among metalle is nothing so effectuelle in vertue as golde" for, among many other medical uses, it "helpeth . . . agens cardeakle passioun" (Bartholomaeus Anglicus 16.4, tr. Trevisa 2:829). Both Arnald of Villanova (Thorndike, Hist. Magic 2:864) and Raymond Lully (or Lull) (Lowes, MP 11, 1914, 30) give directions for preparing "aurum potabile." The irony of the last line depends on the common belief in the greediness of doctors (Bowden, Comm. on GP, 209–10, Mann, Ch and Estates, 97–98). John Arderne stresses the importance of arranging for the fee, which he advises should not be too low, before performing an operation (Treatises, EETS 139, 5–6, 15). On fees, see Alford, Centennial Rev., 23, 1979, 391–96.

The Wife of Bath

The portrait of the Wife is expanded by the Wife herself in the prologue to her tale. Chaucer knew the city of Bath, through which he would have passed to North Petherton as Forester in 1391 and later. Manly (New

Light, 225–34) believes that Chaucer may have based the portrait on an actual woman of St. Michael's parish there, in which cloth-weaving was a principal occupation (see 460 below) and which had an unusual number of women named Alison (CT, 527). For some more exotic suggestions about the significance of Bath, see Weissman, in ChR 15, 1981, 11–36. Puhvel (SN 53, 1981, 101–6) attempts to identify her with Alice Kyteler, an Irish woman tried for witchcraft. However, her portrait is shaped by a number of literary sources, principally La Vieille's monologue in the *Roman de la rose* (echoed in GP I.461 and 476). Chaucer also drew on Jankyn's *Book of Wicked Wives* (cf. WBPro III.669–81), other Latin and French anti-feminist texts, estates satire (Mann, Ch and Estates, 121–27), and astrological and physiognomical lore (Curry, Ch and Science, 91–118, and PMLA 37, 1922, 30–51; Wood, Ch and the Stars, 172–80). On the rich critical literature the Wife has inspired, see the notes to her Prologue.

CHRISTINE RYAN HILARY

445   biside Bathe: Probably the parish of St. Michael's "juxta Bathon," just outside the north gate of the walls of Bath (Manly, 231–33; Magoun, Ch Gazetteer, 29–30). Robertson argues that the phrase could refer to any village near Bath (ChR 14, 1980, 409).

446 See WBPro III.668.

447–48 Weaving and spinning are the occupations traditionally assigned to women in medieval estates theory, and, since nothing more is said of the Wife's occupation, Mann suggests this traditional association as the chief reason for mentioning **clooth-makyng** (Ch and Estates, 121–22). However, many women of the time were engaged in the trade of weaving, which was the principal occupation in St. Michael's "juxta Bathon" (Manly, New Light, 227–29). On this trade, see Robertson (ChR 14: 403–20).

448   Ypres . . . Gaunt: Ypres and Ghent were celebrated for their cloth; Edward III persuaded Flemish weavers from this area to settle in England (Magoun, Ch Gazetteer, 78 and 92). Manly suggests that Chaucer's praise of the Wife's weaving is exaggerated, "perhaps ironical," since West-country weavers were not in good repute; a statute of Richard II notes that some of their cloth was so bad that English merchants abroad were in danger of their lives (Manly, CT, 527; cf. Boren, NM 76, 1975, 247–56).

449–51 At the **offrynge** (Offertory) of the Mass, the worshipers went individually to the altar to give their offerings to the priest or (as in MilT I.3350) the clerk; see The Lay Folks Mass Book, EETS 71, 232–44. Worshipers went to the altar in order of rank, and arguments over precedence were common; e.g., Matheolus, Lamentations, tr. Le Fèvre, 2.1431–40; and Deschamps, Miroir, 3262–90. See also the Book of the Knight of La Tour Landry, EETS 33, 150 (on women who "be envyeusis whiche shalle go furst up on the offerande"), ParsT X.407; GP I.377; and Bo 3.pr.8.12.

452   out of alle charitee: Taken by Hoffman (ELN 11, 1974, 165–67) as indicative of the Wife's spiritual state (cf. ParsT X.1043); Elliott (Ch's English, 291) finds it merely idiomatic and compares KnT I.1623.

453   coverchiefs: Possibly kerchiefs, more likely linen coverings for the head, worn severally over a wire framework. Elaborate headdresses were made fashionable by

Queen Anne (Wretlind, MLN 63, 1948, 381–82, but see also Mann, Ch and Estates, 266–67, n. 86); cf. WBT III.1017–18. Women's headdresses were frequent objects of satire (Mann, 124–25). For an illustration of the Wife's headgear, see A Facsimile of Cambridge MS Gg.4.27, 1979–80.

456 See RvT I.3954–55n.

460   at chirche dore: From the tenth century until the sixteenth, marriage was a two-part ceremony. The legally binding pledge took place at the church door, in the presence of witnesses, and was followed by a nuptial Mass in the church; cf. MerT IV.1700–8n. In the ceremony at the church door, the wife was legally endowered by the husband to protect her financially in the event of his death. The frequently widowed Wife thus accumulated substantial assets with which to attract subsequent husbands, who then had the legal right to control but not to own her property; see Margulies, MS 24, 1962, 210–16, and Robertson, ChR 14:403–20.

461   Withouten: On the deliberate ambiguity, see Tatlock, Flügel Memorial Volume, 1916, 229. Cf. Tr 2.236.

oother compaignye: Cf. RR 12781, "autre compaigne."

463–67 A love of pilgrimages, for illicit purposes, is typical of women in estates satire (Mann, Ch and Estates, 123); cf. Matheolus, Lamentations, 1012–15 (tr. Le Fèvre, 2:1003–8); Deschamps, Miroir, 3500–15, 3729–31; and Golias de Conjuge non Ducenda, 93–100, in Lat. Poems Commonly Attr. to Walter Mapes, 81. In her prologue (III.551–62), the Wife makes clear that her pilgrimages are not for devotional purposes. On the pilgrimage to **Jerusalem,** see Shumacher (ELH 18, 1951, 77–89), who compares the Wife's itinerary with the contemporary account in the Book of Margery Kempe (ed. Sanford M. Brown and Hope Emily Allen, 1940, 67–68 and 74–75), and Bowden (Comm. on GP, 224–25), who compares it with Mandeville's *Travels,* EETS 153, 48–66.

465   Rome: For the objects of pilgrimage in fourteenth-century Rome, see the *Stacions of Rome,* ed. Furnivall, EETS 25, 1–34 (summarized in Bowden, Comm. on GP, 221–22).

Boloigne: At Boulogne-sur-Mer, on the French Atlantic coast, a miraculous image of the Virgin, which had arrived in a rudderless vessel, was a popular object of pilgrimage (Magoun, Ch Gazetteer, 35–6).

466   Galice at Seint-Jame: The shrine of St. James at Compostela in Galicia, in northwestern Spain, then a part of the kingdom of Castile. It was, with Jerusalem and Rome, one of the three most important objects of pilgrimage in Christendom. Bowden summarizes the account given in the *Legenda aurea* of how the body of St. James the Apostle was miraculously transported to Galicia in a rudderless boat (Comm. on GP, 222–23). For a description of medieval Compostela, see Liber IV Sancti Jacobi Apostoli, partially summarized by Bowden (Comm. on GP, 222–23).

Coloigne: At Cologne, on the Rhine, pilgrims visited the shrines of the three Magi, St. Ursula, and the Eleven Thousand Virgins, said to have been massacred there (Magoun, Ch Gazetteer, 57).

468   Gat-tothed: "with teeth set wide apart" (Robinson); *gap-tothed* in some MSS. The word is derived from OE *gaet,* gate, rather than *gat,* goat, as Skeat held (5.44). Curry shows that in medieval physiognomy such teeth indicated an envious, irreverent, luxurious, bold, faithless, and suspicious nature (Ch and Science, 109). The Wife's red face (458) indicates immodesty, loquaciousness, and drunkenness (Curry, 108). In the satiric tradition, such traits are commonly attributed to women but not necessarily as associated with appearance and physique (Mann, Ch and Estates, 125, 268 n. 95).

469 amblere: A pacing horse lifts both feet on a side simultaneously (unlike a trotter) and is therefore comfortable for riding long distances. The Ellesmere illustration shows the Wife riding astride, as did most women in her day. The Prioress and the Second Nun are shown riding sidesaddle; the sidesaddle was "used only by a limited court circle" (Dent, PLPLS-LHS, 1959, 9).

472 foot-mantel: Apparently an apronlike overskirt, as illustrated in the Ellesmere drawing.

475 remedies of love: means of remedying (curing or satisfying) love-sickness, with a possible reference to Ovid's *Remedia amoris.*

476 art: Hoffman (N&Q 209, 1964, 287–88) takes this as a reference to Ovid's *Ars amatoria,* but it may mean simply "craft," as in Rom 4289.

the olde daunce: "la vieille daunce" RR 3938 (Rom 4300). In French the phrase implies artfulness and skillfulness and was not originally restricted to sexual matters (see Rom 4300n.). Chaucer was apparently the first to use it in English (Whiting L535), and he always applies it to matters of love or sex; cf. PhysT VI.79; HF 639–40; Tr 1.517, 2.1106, 3.695. Rabelais later used it as a euphemism for "copulation" (see the "Erotica verba" in App. to vol. 3 of Rabelais, Oeuvres, Paris, 1820).

The Parson

Chaucer's portrait of the Parson is usually understood to depict an ideal priest. It is devoid of irony, and what satire can be found in it is directed against those common failings of the profession from which the Parson is free. Doris Ives (MLR 27, 1932, 144–48) and Loomis (in Essays in Hon. of Carleton Brown, 1940, 141–44) argued that the portrait reflects Wyclifite (Lollard) ideals, but earlier, Ezra K. Maxfield (PMLA 39, 1924, 64–74) and Looten (Ch, Ses modèles, ses sources, sa religion, 1931, 215–43) had rejected a Wyclifite interpretation. Though the Host accuses the Parson of Lollardy (EpiMLT II.1173 and n.), all the elements of the portrait can be found in contemporary discussions of the ideal requirements and failings of spiritual shepherds.

E. P. Kuhl thought that the portrait parallels a royal remonstrance of 1390 and might have been composed at that time (MLN 40, 1925, 321–38).

SIEGFRIED WENZEL

486 cursen for his tithes: The practice could be abused; Wyclif attacks "worldly clerkis" who "cruely" curse for tithes (Eng. Works, 144), but so too does the orthodox Robert Mannyng (Handlyng Synne, 10882). The Lambeth Constitutions of 1281, reiterating decrees of earlier synods, required every parish priest to pronounce the sentence of excommunication before his congregation four times a year; see Frederick M. Powicke and Christopher R. Cheney, Councils and Synods, 1964, 905; and John Mirk, Instr. for Parish Priests, ed. Kristens-

son, 104 ("twies or thries in the yere"). The "great sentence" includes those who withhold tithes; see Mirk, ed. Kristensson, 104, v. 15. A list of specific tithes can be found, in English, in Mirk, Instructions, EETS 31, 64–65.

489 For an account of a parson's income, see John R. H. Moorman, Church Life in Engl. in Thirteenth Cent., 1946, 110–37.

492 but: Eamon Grennan (ChR 16, 1982, 195–200) regards the unusually frequent occurrence of *but* in this portrait as "a deliberate rhetorical strategy."

497–98 Cf. Matt. 5.19. Said of Christ in Gower, Conf. Aman. 5.1825.

500 A commonplace based on Lam. 4.1 and its use by Gregory, Pastoral Care, 2.7 (PL 77:40). Chaucer's wording is exactly paralleled in French: Le Renclus de Moiliens (late twelfth century), Romans de carité, ed. van Hamel, 1885, st. 62. Fleming (N&Q 209, 1964, 167) notes a quotation by Grosseteste.

504 The thought of this alliterative line is a commonplace, but parallels in Latin (Gower, Vox Clam. 3:1063) and French (Romans de Carité, st. 71) lack its forceful diction.

507–14 Absenteeism was a major topic of late medieval criticism directed at the clergy; cf. Gower, Mirour, 20209–832, and ParsT X.721.

510 chaunterie: A provision for a priest to chant the office for the dead or to say or sing Mass for the repose of a soul, usually that of the founder of a chantry. Such endowments were especially numerous at St. Paul's, London. Cf. PP B Pro 83–86 and n. in J. A. W. Bennett ed., Langland: Piers Plowman, 1972; and Robertson, Ch's London, 110.

511 Or . . . withholde: Chantries were often founded by wealthy guilds. See Tatlock, MLN 31, 1916, 139–42.

514 Cf. John 10.12. "He is a hireling (*mercenarius*) not a shepherd" who "leaves the sheep and flees."

518 discreet: Here, "courteous, civil." See Dustoon, RES 13, 1937, 206–9.

523 snybben: The word is similarly used in Eng. Metr. Homilies, ed. Small, 1862, 147 and 168.

The rhyming of two words with one (*nonys : noon ys*), often a variety of "rime riche" (see 17–18 above), is sometimes called "broken" rhyme and was a regular feature of ME verse; for other examples, see GP I.671–72, KnT I.1323–24, IntrMLT II.102–3, SqT V.675–76, Tr 1.5n. On such rhymes see Kökeritz, PMLA 69, 1954, 937–52; and Elliott, Ch's English, 85.

526 spiced conscience: Cf. WBPro III.435. The basic meaning of *spiced* as "seasoned" has been variously interpreted in relation to the Parson's character: "overscrupulous . . . The Parson was reasonable and not too fastidious in his dealings with his flock" (Robinson); "[he did not] lay flattering unctions to their souls" (Hinckley, Notes on Ch, 40); "he [did not] harden his heart . . . render himself insensitive" (Biggins, ES 47, 1966, 174); "he [did not] cultivate highly refined feelings" (Macaulay, MLR 4, 1908, 16); he did not give way to "hot" or "easily aroused moral indignation" (Rockwell, N&Q, n.s. 4, 1957, 84); "he would not quibble over minutiae with regard to ceremonial" (Boyd, Ch and Liturgy, 47).

528 Cf. Acts 1.1 ("facere et docere").

529 was his brother: The omission of the subject pronoun is common; see 33 above.

The Plowman

The Plowman is apparently a free skilled laborer who owns some property (*catel;* cf. Horrel, Spec 14, 1939, 87–88). In the labor shortage following the Black Death such laborers sometimes demanded high wages, and incurred criticism for doing so. Contemporary preachers attacked the laborer "that goth to the plow" and formerly worked for ten or twelve shillings a year but now "musten have xx or thritti and his liverei also" (Owst, Lit and Pulpit, 369). Gower complains of the laziness of "servants of the plow" (Vox Clam. 5.9) and of the peasantry in general (Mirour 26425–508). Chaucer's *trewe swynkere* has been seen as a tacit criticism of contemporary peasants (Stillwell, ELH 6, 1939, 285–90; David, Strumpet Muse, 91). However, "the trewe laborer" (Wyclif, Eng. Works, 370) was also a traditional symbol of the ideal Christian (Barney, MS 35, 1973, 161–93). The Plowman's resemblance to Piers Plowman has often been remarked (Coghill MAE 4, 1935, 89–94), and it may be that Chaucer was influenced by Langland's work. See J. A. W. Bennett, Ch's Contemporary, in Piers Plowman: Crit. Approaches, ed. S. S. Hussey, 1969, 310–24.

LARRY D. BENSON

530 Coghill (MAE 4:93) compares PP C 4.148: "Lawe shal ben a labourer and lede a-felde dong."
533–35 Cf. Matt. 22.37–39.
534 **thogh him gamed or smerte:** One of a number of such phrases denoting "in all circumstances." On such "merisms" in ME see Besserman, AnM 17, 1976, 58–69.
536 Coghill (MAE 4:92) compares PP B 5.522–23: "I dyke and I delve . . . and some tyme I thresch." In the *Seneschaucy* it is specified that plowmen "ought to dig, make enclosures, and thresh; they ought to remove earth or dig trenches to dry the land and drain off the water" (Walter of Henley, ed. Oschinsky, 282–83). **Dyke and delve** is also a common collocation meaning "work hard" (MED s.v. *dichen* 1a).
539–40 The plowman pays his tithes (a tenth) both on his earnings (**propre swynk**) and on profits derived from his stock (**catel**); cf. Bowden, Comm. on GP, 241.
541 **mere:** The mare is commonly said to be a humble mount (Garkeek, Essays on Ch 5, Ch Soc, 2nd ser. 9, 1884, 486), but few of the pilgrims would have ridden stallions, since for inexperienced riders mares and geldings are usually much easier to control.

The Miller

The ruggedness, brutal strength, and grossness of the Miller are evident from the details of his portrait; his overwhelming physical presence is emphasized by the absence of such details from the following description of the Manciple and by the contrast with the portrait of the Reeve (Brooks, Ch's Pilgrims, 43–44), as well as by his powerful voice (MilPro I.3124); the account that the Reeve gives in his tale of the miller Simkin alludes to and develops these characteristics.

Curry notes that the Miller's short-shouldered, broad, and thick figure, red beard, nose with a wart, and wide mouth were believed by the physiognomists to denote variously a shameless, talkative, lecherous, and quarrelsome character (PMLA 35, 1920, 189–209). Chaucer may have been drawing on familiar physiognomical notions rather than the learned scientific treatises cited by Curry. As Mann observes, "the redhead is a widespread figure of deceit and treachery. Conventional descriptions of ugliness feature red hair, bristly hair, hair on the face, a huge mouth, and a prominent beard, and they also make full use of the animal imagery which is so striking in the Miller's portrait" (Ch and Estates, 160–62, 282–83). She notes two references to millers in Piers Plowman (B 2.111 and 10.43–44) suggesting that Langland associated them with dishonesty and "a low kind of entertainment." On the popular image of millers, see Jones, MLQ 16, 1955, 3–15. Bowden (Comm. on GP, 246–49) illustrates the importance of the miller to a medieval manor. There is a wealth of fascinating information on millers and mills in Bennett, Ch at Oxford, especially ch. 4 and app. B. Attempts to find a possible historical model for Chaucer's Miller, for Robin in MilT and Simkin in RvT (Manly, New Light, 94–101; Galway, N&Q 195, 1950, 486–88) are unconvincing.

DOUGLAS GRAY

545 **for the nones:** "Here apparently in the intensive sense" (Robinson); cf. GP I.379n.
548 **ram:** The prize for winning a wrestling match; cf. Thop VII.740–41 and The Tale of Gamelyn (ed. Skeat, 4:172, 184, 280–81), where a ram and a ring are offered as prizes. For further examples, see Strutt, Sports and Pastimes of the People of Engl., ed. W. Hone, 1830, 82–83.
550–51 Individuals who excelled in breaking doors with their heads from the fourth to the nineteenth century (including, in the fourteenth, Thomas Heyward of Berkeley) are listed in Whiting, MLN 52, 1937, 417–19, and MLN 69, 1954, 309–10; Wiley, MLN 53, 1938, 505–7; and Utley, MLN 56, 1941, 534–36.
552 The animal images of sow and fox may suggest lasciviousness and lechery (Rowland, Archiv 201, 1964, 110–14).
559 **greet forneys:** A number of critics and editors (e.g., Fisher, Works, 559) detect a suggestion of the gaping hell-mouths depicted in medieval painting (see LGW 1104n.). The physiognomists regarded a large mouth as a sign of a "glotonous and bold" personality (cf. Secretum secretorum, EETS 276, 105).
560 **janglere:** Mann (Ch and Estates, 161) notes hints that tale telling was traditionally connected with millers (and the mill itself is used as a figure for a wagging tongue in ClT IV.1200 and ParsT X.406). A **goliardeys** is a "buffoon" (MED s.v. *goliardeis*) or "a windbag, teller of dirty stories" (Fisher, 559). In its origin the word is probably related to "Goliardi" or "Goliardenses," the wandering clerics who purportedly wrote goliardic verse, satiric and convivial Latin poetry and who were supposed to be followers of the fictitious "Bishop Golias" (cf. Helen Waddell, The Wandering Scholars, 1927). The word lost its literary associations and came to be applied to tellers of coarse tales. Mann (Ch and Estates, 281) notes that it is recorded elsewhere only in PP B Pro 139 and in Robert Mannyng, Handlyng Synne, EETS 23, 4701. Possibly a popular association with either or both the vaunting OT giant Goliath and the Lat. word *gula* (gluttony) may be in the background (see

Manly, MP 5, 1907, 201–9; and Thompson, SP 20, 1923, 83–98). Hornstein (recorded by Baum, PMLA 73, 1958, 168) suggests a play on the possible etymology from *gula*: Langland's "a goliardys, a glotoun of wordes" (PP B Pro 139) makes the association.

562   tollen thries: The toll (a fraction of the grain ground) was exacted in addition to the usual money payment. It might range from a twentieth to a twenty-fourth or a sixteenth part; see H. S. Bennett, Life on the Eng. Manor, 1948, ch. 6.

563   thombe of gold: Possibly an ironic reference to a proverb "an honest miller hath a golden thumb" (i.e., there are no honest millers), though it is not recorded until after Chaucer's time (Whiting M559–61; Tilley M954–59; Bächtold-Stäubli, Handwörterbuch des deutschen Aberglaubens, 1927–42 s.v. Müller, 4a, n. 15). Skeat notes that the Miller's thumb may be called golden in reference to the profit that comes from his skill in judging grain by feeling samples with the thumb and forefinger. Lines 562–63 may be taken together as "The miller was a thief yet he had the mark of honest millers, the reputation of being honest."

565   baggepipe: Essentially a folk instrument; see Winternitz, Musical Instruments, especially 66–85, and 129–36. The medieval bagpipe inherited from antiquity the Dionysiac associations of wind instruments with passion and drunkenness (Winternitz, 153, 156–62), and critics often associate the Miller's bagpipe with gluttony and lechery (Jones, JEGP 48, 1949, 209–28; Block, Spec 29, 1954, 239–43; Scott, RES 18, 1967, 287–90). However, it is not necessary to regard the Miller's playing as a *discordia,* as opposed to the *concordia* of the Christian "New Song" (Robertson, Pref. to Ch, 243). The symbolic associations of bagpipes were not rigidly fixed; as Winternitz notes, angels sometimes played them. When the accused Lollard William Thorpe attacked pilgrims and the noise they make as they go through towns—some, he said, will have bagpipes— Archbishop Arundel defended this sort of "solace" (D. Gray, ed., Oxford Bk. of Late Med. Verse and Prose, 1985, 17–18).

The Manciple

A manciple was a subordinate official who purchased provisions for a college or "inn of court" (law school); the *temple* was either the Inner or Middle Temple near the Strand. The manciple does not appear in traditional estates satire, and it may be that Chaucer is here drawing on his own personal experience (see p. xviii). The tradition that Chaucer, as well as Gower, studied at the Inner Temple derives from Speght: "It seemeth that both these learned men were at the Inner Temple . . ." (Works of Chaucer, 1598, Biii, rpt. in Derek Brewer, Ch: The Crit. Heritage, 1978, 1:142–43). For a discussion of this evidence, see Rickert, Manly Anniv. Sts., 1923, 20–31; and Bland, ES 33, 1952, 145–55. Chaucer "connects the Manciple with the Reeve, for the former is, like the latter, over-shrewd in business dealings" (Bowden, Comm. on GP, 255). He "may be linked with the dishonesty Langland assigns to manorial officials, lawyers, and those who . . . look after provisions" (Mann, Ch and Estates, 174). Cf. PP B 2.59–60.

V. J. SCATTERGOOD

567   gentil: On the ironic application of the epithet, see Birney, NM 61, 1960, 257–67.

570   by taille: On a tally stick the amount of a debt was kept in notches and the stick then split, with debtor and creditor each retaining half as a record. See Jenkinson, Archaeologia 74, 1925, 289–351.

**573–75   Perhaps based on an ironic reversal of the proverb "Many wits are better than a man's wit" (Whiting W409).

579   stywardes: Stewards, or seneschals, were the managers of estates, and usually had direct responsibility to the lord of the manor.

586   sette hir aller cappe: Deceived them all. Cf. MilPro I.3143, RvPro I.3911. Apparently the phrase occurs only in Chaucer (Whiting C32); the idea seems to be tilting somebody's cap or hood to make him seem foolish.

The Reeve

"A reeve acted as a kind of general foreman on a manor, seeing to the condition of fields, woods, and pastures, responsible for all work done, for collecting his lord's dues, and for presenting the annual account" (Phyllis Hodgson, ed. GP). The duties of the reeve are fully discussed (with copious references) by Bowden, Comm. on GP, 249–55; Robertson, Spec 52, 1977, 573–76; and H. S. Bennett, Life on the Eng. Manor, 1937, 155–78. McKisack (The Fourteenth Cent., 317–19) points out that the social status of reeves had improved in Chaucer's time, and that they were usually capable men, holding positions of importance and trust. Bennett discusses their work and remarks that when all the duties were discharged by necessity rather than by choice, and "reeves were so closely watched by the auditors on the one hand, and on the other by their neighbors whose work they had to supervise . . . it is not surprising that Chaucer depicts his reeve as thin, worn, tetchy, and uncompanionable" (Ch at Oxford, 88–92).

In some respects (e.g., in cheating his lord without detection), the Reeve resembles the Manciple; they are "two characters of the most consummate worldly wisdom" (William Blake, Compl. Writings, ed. Keynes, 1966, 601). In physique and in personality, the Reeve is in complete contrast to the Miller, with whom he later has an altercation. The description should be compared with that which he gives in his own prologue (I.3867– 98). The physical characteristics of the Reeve are those the physiognomists regularly attributed to the choleric complexion and associated with a sharp wit, a quick temper and wanton disposition (Curry, Ch and Science, 71– 90). Mann (Ch and Estates, 163–67) remarks that Curry does not give a total view of the choleric man, who is often (unlike the Reeve) impulsive and emotional. However, astuteness and fraudulence were often attributed to a choleric person (cf. Sec. Lyrics, ed. Robbins, no. 76.- 11). Reeves had a reputation for thieving (cf. the saying "thefe is reve," Mann, Ch and Estates, 164); in Piers Plowman B 2.111 "Rainalde the Reve of Rotland sokene" is a witness to Meed's wedding (cf. also 10.466– 67; 19.466–64). Preachers and moralists refer to the dishonesty of reeves and bailiffs (Owst, Preaching in Med. Engl., 324–25). Mann (Ch and Estates, 165) notes the careful ambiguity of Chaucer's treatment: "the sugges-

tion of dishonesty runs right through the portrait, but its phraseology is constantly as ambiguous as the statement that the Reeve could please his lord 'subtilly.' "

The description is highly individualized (we are given not only the name of the Reeve's town but the situation of his house), and this has suggested to some that Chaucer based his portrait on an actual official. (See Manly, New Light, 84–94; Powley, TLS, 14 July 1932, 516; Redstone, TLS, 27 Oct. 1932, 789–90; and also Rickert, TLS, 27 Sept. 1928, 684.) *Baldeswelle* (620), the modern Bawdeswell in northern Norfolk, lay partly in the manor of Foxley, which belonged to the earls of Pembroke. Chaucer certainly had connections with Sir William de Beauchamp, cousin of the second earl, who had the custody of the estates in Kent. There is evidence that some of the Pembroke estates were mismanaged, and Beauchamp's own management was investigated in 1386–87. Manly (New Light, 70–94) speculates that through his connections with Beauchamp Chaucer may have learned about this rascally Norfolk reeve. However, as Mann points out (Ch and Estates, 166), there seems to have been a tradition that Norfolk people were crafty and treacherous, and, moreover, Chaucer, like Langland, may be using specific names to give an illusion of concrete reality.

DOUGLAS GRAY

587   **colerik:** Dominated by the humor choler (yellow or red bile). See 333 and 420 above.

589   **ful round yshorn:** Close-cut hair is probably not a sign of a servile station (Curry, Ch and Science, 72) but rather, as Mann notes (Ch and Estates, 284 n. 70), it makes him look like a "clerk." She notes too (284) that Langland seems to class clerks and reeves together (cf. PP B 10.466–67) and that Chaucer twice compares the Reeve to a cleric (GP I.590, 621), and wonders if he is hinting at the pretensions of his class to "clergy" (clerkly skills and status).

594   **Ther was noon auditour:** On the careful accounting a reeve was required to make to his auditors, see Seneschaucy, ch. 73, in Walter of Henley, ed. Oschinsky, 290–91.

605   **the deeth:** Probably "the plague," but possibly "death" in general. On the occasional use in ME of the definite article in constructions similar to French "la mort," see Mustanoja, ME Syntax, 257.

606–7   **His wonyng:** A dwelling at the cost of the lord and a robe (cf. the *cote and hood* in line 612) were apparently regular perquisites of the bailiff, in addition to his salary (Robinson). Redstone noted that there was still a heath at Bawdeswell shaded by the trees of Bylaugh Wood (TLS 1932, 789–90).

616   **Scot:** Apparently a common name of horses in Norfolk in modern times (and in Suffolk according to EDD, and George E. Evans, Where Beards Wag All, 1970, 162); Manly (CT, 533), notes its occurrence in a fourteenth-century inventory (Oxf. Hist. Soc. Collectanea, 3, 1896, 60 n. 12). It is the name of a horse in FrT III.1543.

621   **Tukked:** Skeat notes that the Ellesmere illustration shows both the Reeve and the Friar with girdles and rather long coats (cf. SumT III.1737).

622   **hyndreste:** The detail seems significant. It may indicate an "instinctive craftiness" and lack of gregariousness, in striking contrast to the position and behavior of

the Miller, as Robinson believed. Or perhaps the Reeve has chosen the place farthest from his professional enemy. Some critics believe that the quarrel between them is an old one (see Pratt, MLN 59, 1944, 47–49; Owen, MLN 67, 1952, 336–38), and Tupper (JEGP 14, 1915, 265) argues that millers and reeves were traditional enemies. But Mann (Ch and Estates, 284–85) remarks that the evidence shows only that a clash of interests was likely, not that it was proverbial. Donaldson (Ch's Poetry, 1057) suggests that the Reeve rides last because of his "habitual watchfulness," for the rear is "the best position from which to watch what is going on among any band of travellers."

The Summoner

The summoner, or *apparitor,* was a minor nonclerical officer of the ecclesiastical courts who delivered citations for people to appear before the tribunal and acted as usher, or beadle, while sessions were in progress. Haselmayer (Spec 12, 1937, 43–57) shows that historical documents in England contain only minimal evidence for the corrupt practices that Chaucer attributes to his pilgrim and the summoner of The Friar's Tale (III.1321–1442). According to Mann (Ch and Estates, 274, n. 60), the office does not appear in estates satire much before Langland, who links summoners with Lady Meed and refers scornfully to them in various contexts (e.g., PP B 2.58, 169; 3.133; 4.167). However, attacks on the venality of the ecclesiastical courts in general were numerous in sermons and moral literature, as well as in popular poetry (Bowden, Comm. on GP, 269–72; Mann, Ch and Estates, 139–40; Owst, Lit and Pulpit, 251–54, 280–82; Haselmayer, Spec 12:55).

In terms of medieval medical treatises, the Summoner's disease is a form of leprosy called *alopicia* (Curry, Ch and Science, 37–53), which, Garbáty (Medical Hist. 7, 1963, 348–58) argues, was actually syphilis. Aiken (SP 33, 1936, 40–44), referring to the thirteenth-century *Speculum doctrinale* of Vincent of Beauvais, diagnoses scabies. Whatever the case, the pilgrim's debauchery seems to account for the condition, and the remedies listed as ineffectual (629–31) were common medieval treatments. For the metaphorical appropriateness of the disease in the light of Wyclif's *Tractatus de simonia,* see McVeigh, Classical Folia 29, 1975, 54–58.

JANETTE RICHARDSON

624   **fyr-reed cherubynnes face:** The usual explanation that cherubim, the second order of angels in the Dionysian hierarchy, were painted red is inaccurate. Red was the conventional color for seraphs, and blue the color for cherubim, until the end of the fifteenth century. Some confusion about the hierarchy apparently existed in popular thinking, however, for the late twelfth-century *De sex alis cherubin,* ascribed to Alanus de Insulis, is actually about seraphs (Pelota, NM 69, 1968, 560–68). Morris (CL 10, 1958, 36–44) suggests that the thirteenth-century *De proprietatibus rerum* of Bartholomaeus Anglicus may have caused Chaucer's error (though there it is said only that all angels are clothed in red). Because the color symbolism was based on the idea of being inflamed with divine love, the ironic intention of the image is nonetheless evident. Whitbread suggests that the fire-red face involves word play on a Latin phrase *fieri facies,* the name of a writ (NM 79, 1978, 41–43).

625   saucefleem: With pimples caused by an excess of salty phlegm (*de salso flegme*) in the system (Skeat 5:53), which makes the face red. The condition, also called *gutta rosacea,* was taken as a symptom of leprosy (Cyrurgie of Guy de Chauliac, EETS 265, 435). The **eyen narwe,** swollen eyelids, accompany *alopicia,* according to Gilbertus Anglicus (see 429–34 above and Curry, Ch and Science, 44).

626   One afflicted with *gutta rosacea* should abstain "fro lecherie and fro all excessive hete" (Cyrurgie of Guy de Chauliac, 435). The sparrow "is a ful hoot bridde and lecherous" (Bartholomaeus Anglicus 12:33, tr. Trevisa 1:639). See PF 351. The sparrow's association with lechery dates back to antiquity; see Pliny, Nat. Hist. 10.107 and, for further references, Denys Page, Sappho and Alcaeus, 1955, 7–8.

627   Loss of eyebrows and beard is listed as a symptom of *alopicia* by Arnaldus de Villa Nova, who is mentioned in CYT VIII.1428 (Curry, Ch and Science, 43). The scanty eyebrows are black, and Pace suggests that black hair was associated with lecherousness (Traditio 18, 1962, 417–20).

629–30   All these remedies were recommended by medieval physicians for the Summoner's malady; see Cyrurgie of Guy de Chauliac, 435, which lists all that are here mentioned.

631   oynement: A caustic ointment composed chiefly of arsenic (Curry, Ch and Science, 47).

634   The Summoner should likewise abstain "fro alle sharpe thinges, as fro garlik, fro onions, fro pepper" (Cyrurgie of Guy de Chauliac, 435). Kaske (MLN 74, 1959, 481–84) suggests an allusion to Num. 11.5 and medieval interpretation of the passage as symbolic of moral corruption. See also Biggins, N&Q 209, 1964, 48; and Wood, ChR 5, 1971, 240–44.

635   Skeat (5:53) cites Prov. 33.31 and quotes The Book of the Knight of La Tour Landry, EETS 33, 116: wine "maketh the visage salce flemed [misprinted falce flemed] rede and full of white welkes."

637–38   The notion of speaking Latin when intoxicated was commonplace. See Hinckley, MP 14, 1916, 317; Manly, CT, 534; and the fabliau "Du prestre et de la dame" in Benson and Andersson, Lit. Context, lines 97–107.

643   clepen "Watte": Say "Walter." Caged jays were taught to imitate human speech. Cf. Gower, Vox Clam. 1.679–92 (tr. Stockton, 65 and 352 n.).

646   "Questio quid iuris": For one explanation of when this tag would have been heard by the Summoner in court, see Spargo, MLN 62, 1947, 119–22.

650–51   Chaucer's contemporary, the Dominican John Bromyard, mentions such a case in his *Summa praedicantium* (Owst, Lit and Pulpit, 253). Woolf, however, suggests that the concubine is the Summoner's own (MLN 68, 1953, 118–21). On good felawe see 395 above.

652   Kittredge's explanation (MP 7, 1910, 475–77) of "to pull (i.e., pluck) a finch" as a crude expression for the Summoner's own lecherous behavior is generally accepted, but see also Ericson, ES 42, 1961, 306; Biggins, ES 44, 1963, 278; Cawley, PLPLS-LHS 8, 1957, 173–74. MED (s.v. *finch*) defines the phrase as "to do something with cunning, to pull a clever trick."

656–57   For the image of being punished in the purse,

cf. Gower, Mirour, 20108–9, and Vox Clam. 3.193–202 (tr. Stockton, 121).

659–61   The narrator's opinion here has been variously interpreted, depending upon what one senses as its tone. Tatlock's moderate view (MP 14, 1916, 257–68) is now generally accepted; if the lines imply doubt of the efficacy of absolution, they are written in the same spirit as Wyclif's attacks on excommunication (see 486 above) and are part of Chaucer's general criticism of avariciousness in the clergy.

662   Significavit: The first word of the writ that authorized civil officers to imprison a person who had not made reparation within forty days after being excommunicated. In the approximately ten thousand writs preserved from the thirteenth to the fifteenth century, nonpayment of tithes is the most common offense specified, followed by matrimonial and testamentary cases, fornication, adultery, perjury, and defamation (Fowler, TRHS, 3rd ser., 8, 1914, 113–17). Cf. FrT III.1304–12.

664   girles: The term is used for youths of both sexes, but young women may be intended here, as in MilT I.3769; see Bloomfield, PQ 28, 1949, 503–7.

666–68   Fleming finds the garland and buckler grotesque, with the buckler perhaps reflecting an incident in the *Roman de la rose* (in New Perspectives in Ch Criticism, 121–36).

667   ale-stake: See PardPro VI.321–22n.

The Pardoner

The Pardoner (officially, *questor*) was a churchman, usually a cleric, empowered to transmit "indulgences" to the faithful. The forgiveness of sin requires penance, which consists of "Contricioun of herte, Confessioun of Mouth, and Satisfaccioun" (ParsT X.108). Contrition and confession remove the moral guilt (*culpa*) of sin, but the need for punishment (*poena*) must also be satisfied, either on earth or in purgatory. This satisfaction can be achieved, the Parson says, by giving alms or performing such penitential acts as going "naked in pilgrimages, or barefot" (X.105). The church, however, is guardian of a "treasury of merit" (earned by Christ and the saints), on which the pope and bishops may draw to provide dispensations from a part of purgatorial punishment to the truly penitent. The giving of alms to the church was the required evidence of true penitence. Thus funds could be raised for the maintenance of hospitals, the building of churches, the repair of bridges, and other worthy causes. To raise such money, religious foundations would hire professional fund raisers, pardoners, who would undertake to obtain pardons, and, with the permission of the archdeacons of the dioceses (who required a fee), travel about a given area, appearing in churches to offer their indulgences to those willing and able to pay. The system was easily abused, as detailed in the following lines and in The Pardoner's Prologue, and both church and state attempted, without much success, to control the more flagrant abuses. See Henry C. Lea, Hist. of Confession and Indulgences, 1896, 3:54–82; Jusserand, Ch's Pardoner and the Pope's Pardoners, Ch Soc Essays 5:13, 421–36; Bowden, Comm. on GP, 274–90; Williams, in Univ. of North Carolina Sts. in Rom. Lang. and Lit. 56, 1965, 177–207; Kellogg and Haselmayer, PMLA 66, 1951, 251–77.

The pardoners were frequent objects of satire (Mann, Ch and Estates, 145–52), though Bowden (Comm. on GP, 283) notes that this is the only fully developed and individualized satiric portrait in the fourteenth century (cf. Langland, PP B Pro 68–77, 2.219–22, 5.648–49).

Chaucer's Pardoner is in the employ of the Hospital of St. Mary Rouncesval at Charing Cross in London, a dependency (cell) of the Augustinian Hospital of Our Lady of Roncesvalles, in Spain on the pilgrim road to Compostela (see 466 above) at the mountain pass where Roland is said to have died (see BD 1123n.); see William Dugdale, Monasticon Anglicanum [1655–73], 1846, VI, 2:677. The cell was very active in the sale of indulgences and was specifically criticized for this (cf. PP C 20.18 and the Reply of Friar Daw Topias, in Political Songs, ed. Wright, Rolls Series, 1859–61, 2:78–79). In 1382 and 1387 unauthorized sales of pardons were made by those professing to be working for this house; in the 1390s it was raising money through the sales of indulgences for a building fund; see James Galloway, Hospital and Chapel of St. Mary Roncevall, 1913; and Moore, MP 25, 1927, 59–66. Manly believes Chaucer has some particular pardoner in mind (New Light, 122–130), and Kellogg and Haselmayer point out that the carrying of false relics was an abuse so rare that it may suggest some particular individual (PMLA 66:275). However, Mann notes that the satirizing of false relics was common (Ch and Estates, 150).

Pardoners were customarily clerics, and this Pardoner's participation in the Mass (line 708) seems to indicate that he has clerical status, but the exact nature of that status is unclear. Jusserand holds that he is a complete fake and therefore perhaps not in orders at all (Ch Soc 2nd ser. 19, 421–36). Hamilton argues that he is an Augustinian canon (JEGP 40, 1941, 48–72); Miller and Bosse suggest that he assumes a priestly role during parts of the Mass (ChR 6, 1972, 173); and the Pardoner himself seems to suggest that he is a friar (PardPro VI.416; see also I.683 and n.).

A great deal of critical attention has been devoted to the Pardoner's sexual nature. Curry (Ch and Science, 59–70) argues that the Pardoner was a born eunuch, "eunuchus ex nativitate," a position widely accepted until recent years. Miller (Spec 30, 1955, 180–99) regards him as spiritually and morally sterile, the opposite of the "eunuchus Dei" (Matt 19.12). Rowland (Neophilol 48, 1964, 56–60) draws on modern medical texts to define him as a "testicular pseudo-hermaphrodite of the feminine type." Howard (Idea of CT, 338–45) sees him as a grotesque "feminoid" or "hermaphroditic" male. Recent critics have tended to see him as a homosexual (McAlpine, PMLA 95, 1980, 8–22), who, unlike the eunuch, was a frequent figure of medieval satire (Mann, Ch and Estates, 145–48). In two mutually supporting articles in Mediaevalia 1985 (for 1982), C. D. Benson and R. F. Green present a strong case for the idea that the Pardoner is an effeminate heterosexual like Absolom in The Miller's Tale. It should be noted that a eunuch would have been ineligible for holy orders (Deut. 23.1) and that in the fifteenth-century Prologue to the Tale of Beryn (ed. F. J. Furnivall and W. G. Stone, EETS e.s. 105), the Pardoner is depicted as the lecherous (but woefully unsuccessful) seducer of the barmaid Kit.

For reviews of critical opinion, see Sedgwick, MLQ 1, 1940, 431–58; Halverson, ChR 4, 1970, 184–202; Ewald Standop, "Chaucers Pardoner," in Geschichtlichkeit und Neuanfang in sprachlichen kunstwerk: Studien zur englischen Philologie zu Ehren von Fritz W. Schulze, ed. Peter Erlebach, Wolfgang G. Müller, and Klaus Reuter, 1981, 59–69. McAlpine (PMLA 95:8–22) summarizes more recent criticism.

CHRISTINE RYAN HILARY

670   Rouncivale: The Hospital of St. Mary of Rouncesval at Charing Cross (see introductory note). Tatlock, Flügel Memorial Volume, 1916, 228–32, suggests a pun on "rouncival," a mannish woman, or "rouncy," a riding horse (see 691 below), which is unlikely, though accepted by Baum (PMLA 73, 1958, 169–70). On St. Mary's Hospital, see in addition to Galloway and Moore (both cited above), Friend, JEGP 53, 1954, 387–88; and Bloomfield, PQ 35, 1956, 60–68.

671   court of Rome: Only the pope would grant the highly prized, and therefore expensive, plenary indulgence, which freed the recipient from all punishment. Though during the Schism (1378–1417) there was also a pope at Avignon, England was loyal to Urban in Rome. Hamilton suggests that papal licenses, even if genuine, may not have been welcome in England, where their importation was repeatedly forbidden (JEGP 40:71).

672   "Com hider, love, to me!": Skeat (5:55) compares ME Pearl (ed. E. V. Gordon, 1953, 763–64), "Com hider to me, my lemman swete, For mote ne spot is non in the," echoing Cant. 4.7. On the unusual rhyme *Rome: to me,* see 523 above.

673   stif burdoun: In musical terms, the bass (*cantus firmus*) part; cf. RvT I.4165. *Burdoun* has also been taken to mean staff or phallus, and Biggins (N&Q 204, 1959, 435–36, following a suggestion by Baum, Ch: A Crit. Appreciation, 218 n. 20) and Miller (N&Q 205, 1960, 404–6) see the connotation of a homosexual relationship between the Pardoner and the Summoner. However, Howard (Idea of CT, 344) and Brady (Southern Folklore Quart. 32, 1968, 4) argue against this interpretation. On the meaning of *bourdoun,* see Dieckmann, MP 26, 1929, 279–82. The Summoner, an official of the archdeaconry, and the Pardoner may have worked in collusion; see Sleeth, MLN 56, 1941, 138.

675–79 The "Ashmole" version of the Secretum secretorum notes: "Heres yelow and whitissh untechable and wild maners thei shewen. . . . And the thynner the heeres ben, the more gileful, sharp, ferefull, and of wynnyng covetous, it sheweth" (EETS 276, 92). Clerics were forbidden long hair; Hamilton (JEGP 40:60) quotes the archbishop of Canterbury in 1342 complaining of clerics who dress fancily and scorn the tonsure, "making themselves conspicuous by hair spreading almost to the shoulders in feminine fashion"; cf. also Owst, Lit and Pulpit, 262.

683   cappe: Hamilton argues that this is the "biretta" worn by Augustinian canons, who were supposed to wear their hoods on journeys (JEGP 40:62).

684   glarynge eyen: Such eyes indicate "a man given to folly, a glutton, a libertine, and a drunkard," according to the physiognomist Palemon (Curry, Ch and Science, 57; cf. Secreta secretorum, EETS e.s. 66, 82). The **hare** was believed to sleep with its eyes open and thought to be hermaphroditic: "it is yseid that he gendreth withoute bothe male and hath both sexus, male and femele" (Bartholomaeus Anglicus, 18.68, tr. Trevisa 2:1221); cf. Schweitzer, ELN 4, 1966, 247–50.

685 vernycle: A medal struck with a representation of St. Veronica's veil, upon which an image of Christ's face was said to have been imprinted. Such medals were a badge of the pilgrimage to Rome (Sumption, Pilgrimage, 222, 249–56).

688–89 A high (**smal**) voice and beardlessness were signs of eunuchry; if the testicles are cut away, "mannes strengthe passith and manly complexioun chongith into femel complexioun . . . [they lose their hair . . . their voices] beth as voys of wommen" (Bartholomaeus Anglicus 5.48, tr. Trevisa, 1:261). The **goot** was, and still popularly is, considered a lecherous beast (Barth. Angl. 18.24, tr. Trevisa, 2:1163).

691 geldyng, mare: *geldyng* suggests a eunuch, while *mare* may imply a homosexual—a somewhat unusual meaning, but see Mann, Ch and Estates, 146, who compares Walter of Chatillon's "Equa fit equus" (the horse becomes a mare); and Rowland (Neophil 48:56–60), and McAlpine (PMLA 95:8–22). As McAlpine points out, the narrator avoids specifying the Pardoner's condition too precisely. Scheps suggests that the comparison of the Pardoner to the two kinds of horses links him with the sin of avarice (Acta 4, 1977, 107–23). Schweitzer regards the *hare* in line 684 (see note above) as an anticipation of hints of sexual abnormality in line 691 (ELN 4:247–50).

692 fro Berwyk into Ware: From Berwick-upon-Tweed (the northernmost spot in England) to Ware in Hertfordshire or in Kent; i.e., from one end of the Great North Road in England to the other. Cf. Whiting B260 and Magoun, Ch Gazetteer, 31–32. See also WBPro III.824n.

696–98 Cf. Matt. 14.29.

699 latoun: A metal (*auricalcum*) alloy "of copper and of tynne and of auripigment and with other metalles" that has the appearance of gold but not its value or durability (Bartholomaeus Anglicus 16.5, tr. Trevisa, 2: 830). It was used for ornaments (MilT I.3251) and for armor (Thop VII.877).

701–4 On legislation against the use of false relics by pardoners, see Owst, Preaching, 108–10. For satirists' comments, see Mann (Ch and Estates, 150–52); she compares Boccaccio's story of Fra Cipolla (Decameron 6.10), who claims to have one of the angel Gabriel's feathers, though actually it is a parrot's.

706 apes: Fools, dupes; cf. MilT I.3389, ShipT VII.440, CYT VIII.1313 (Robinson). Proverbial; cf. Whiting A148 and MED s.v. *ape* 2.(b).

709 lessoun: An excerpt from the Bible or other sacred writings, perhaps here the Epistle (see Lay Folks Mass Book, EETS 71, 96). **Storie** has a variety of liturgical meanings (Robinson; see Young, MLN 30, 1915, 97–99), but here is probably a series of lessons "covering a story in the Bible or the life of a saint" (Manly, CT, 537). Miller and Bosse (ChR 6:173) suggest that it is instead the Gospel, noting the use of *stories* in PardT VI.488 to refer to the Gospels of Matthew and Mark.

710 offertorie: That part of the Mass, sung by the priest "with his ministers" (Lay Folks Mass Book, 98–99), while the faithful make their offerings. In England, unlike the continental usage, the sermon ordinarily followed either the Offertory or the Bidding Prayer, or Prayer of the Faithful (Lay Folks Mass Book, 317–19).

712 affile: Cf. Tr 2.1681n.

719 the Belle: Southwark contained over half a dozen taverns and inns called the Bell; William Rendle and P. Norman note that one stood across from the Tabard, though there is no record of its existence before 1600 (Inns of Old Southwark, 1888, 420). Baum (MLN 36, 1921, 307–9) rejects that identification and speculates that it may have been one of the many "allowed stew-houses" (licensed brothels) mentioned by John Stow, Survey of London [1598], ed. Kingsford, 1908, 2:53–55, which operated under regulations dating back at least to Henry II and whose licenses dated back to Edward III.

725–42 The apology offered here is similar to that in RR 7103–20 and 15159–92; for a second apology which relates to subject matter, see MilPro II.3167–86 and cf. MancT IX.207–10 and n., and, for the same general idea, Lak of Stedfastnesse 4–5. Chaucer quotes Plato (Timaeus 29 B) in I.741–42, but, like most of his contemporaries, he knew Plato only indirectly and he probably derived the quotation from Boethius (Bo 3.pr.12.206–7), though the application may have been suggested by the *Roman de la rose* (Root, ESt 44, 1911, 5 n. 2). The expression became proverbial (Whiting W645). See Taylor, Spec 57, 1982, 315–27, esp. 319.

746 The topos of "affected modesty," in which an author disclaims any skill or protests inadequacy to the subject, is common in classical and medieval literature (Curtius, Europ. Lit., 83–85) and frequently used by Chaucer (e.g., BD 896–901, MerT IV.1736–37, SqT V.105–6, and FranPro V.716–27).

The Host

The Host is called Herry Bailly in The Cook's Prologue (I.4358); the Subsidy Rolls for Southwark in 1380–81 list "Henri Bayliff ostlyer" (innkeeper) and his wife "Christian." He was a man of substance who represented his borough in Parliament in 1376–77 and 1378–79 and held other public offices (Manly, New Light, 79–83). Malone (Chapters on Ch, 187–92) rejected the identification partly because in The Monk's Prologue the Host's wife is called not "Christian" but *Goodelief* (VII.1894). Nevertheless, there is no reason to doubt that the Host is related to the actual Henri Bayliff. (See also Rickert, TLS 16 Dec 1926, 935.) The Host has been the subject of considerable comment. See, in addition to most general studies of the Tales, B. Page, ChR 4, 1969, 1–13 (with summary of previous opinions), C. C. Richardson, TSLL 12, 1970–71, 325–44 (on the Host as representative of an uncritical contemporary audience), Pichaske and Sweetland, ChR 11, 1977, 179–200 (on the host as *governour*), and E. D. Higgs, MHLS 2, 1979, 28–43 (on the relation of the Host to the narrator).

LARRY D. BENSON

752 marchal in an halle: The marshall had the exacting task of managing protocol and directing the service at feasts; see A Fifteenth-Century Courtesy Book, ed. Chambers, EETS 148, 1914.

753 eyen stepe: Either "bright" or "large, prominent" eyes (see note 201 above); Keen shows that the phrase is frequently used of bold, attractive heroes in ME romances (Topic 17, 1969, 9–10).

754   Chepe: The modern Cheapside, where the most prosperous shops were located (Myers, London, 23–24).

785   make it wys: Raise difficulties. The idiom *make it* plus an adjective is common in Middle English (MED s.v. *maken* 14) and in Chaucer (RvT I.3980, FranT V.1223, ShipT VII.379n., BD 531, Tr 2.1025n., Rom 2038); it is probably derived from French constructions with *faire* (see A. A. Prins, Fr. Infl. on Engl. Phrasing, 1952, 203).

791   to shorte with: For the construction, cf. I.3119, VI.345, VII.273.

796–801   Laila Gross of Fairleigh Dickinson University notes that a free dinner was the prize for the best poem at the festivals of the London "Pui" (an association of amateur poets) in the thirteenth century; excerpts from its regulations are translated by D. W. Robertson, Jr., The Lit. of Med. Engl., 1970, 285–87.

805–6   Kuhl compares an instance in which an alderman who disobeyed a rule about wearing special garments to a feast had to pay for a dinner for all the others (TWA 18, 1916, 652–75).

811   "We" is the understood subject of **preyden,** perhaps also of *swore* in the preceding line. Cf. note 33 above.

817   In heigh and lough: "In every respect," a translation of the Lat. legal formula *in alto et basso* (Hinckley, PMLA 46, 1931, 98–99). On similar expressions, see 534 above.

819   Wine was drunk as a nightcap; cf. Tr 3.671.

826   the Waterynge of Seint Thomas: A brook at the second milestone on the Old Kent Road from London to Canterbury. On the road to Canterbury, see Loxton, Pilgrimage, 125–43.

830   Proverbial (cf. Whiting E160).

843   shortly for to tellen: A common formula; cf. KnT I.875–88n.

844   aventure: This word, meaning "chance," regularly contrasts with words such as **cas** ("destiny"); cf. ClT IV.812, MerT IV.1967, and Tr 1.568. **Sort** may mean something more like "luck." The words are, however, near synonyms and thus emphasize the inexplicability of what has happened. Many critics (e.g., Donaldson, 1061) suspect that Harry Bailey rather than these mysterious forces arranged that the *cut* should fall to the knight.

849   what nedeth wordes mo: A rhetorical formula (*occupatio*); cf. KnT I.1029, 1715, and BD 189–90n.

The Knight's Tale

The Knight's Tale is a free adaptation of Boccaccio's *Il Teseida delle nozze d'Emelia* (*The Story of Theseus concerning the Nuptials of Emily*), written around 1339–41. Chaucer could have obtained a manuscript of this work on either of his trips to Italy in 1372–73 and 1378, though it is usually held that Chaucer did not know Boccaccio's work until the later trip (see Pratt, SP 42, 1945, 762–63). Coleman (MAE 51, 1982, 92–101) notes that many MSS of the *Teseida,* including Pavia MS 881 representing the tradition Chaucer may have known, lack an attribution to Boccaccio (whom Chaucer nowhere names).

The explanatory notes to The Knight's Tale were written by Vincent J. DiMarco.

A reference in the Prologue to *The Legend of Good Women* to *the love of Palamon and Arcite / Of Thebes, thogh the storye ys knowen lyte* (F 420–21) shows that Chaucer made a version of the tale sometime before that prologue was composed (1386–88). In his 1775 edition Tyrwhitt first posited a lost translation of the *Teseida* by Chaucer, which he later revised as the first of the tales. However, the old theory of a lost version in rime-royal stanzas (ten Brink, Ch Studien, 1870, 36–69) was proven both needless and improbable by detailed arguments (not all of equal worth) by Tatlock (Dev. and Chron., 45–66; see also Mather, in Eng. Misc. Presented to F. J. Furnivall, 1901, 301–13, and Hammond, Ch: Bibl. Man., 271–72), and most likely The Knight's Tale as we have it does not essentially differ from the earlier "Palamon and Arcite." A few lines of The Knight's Tale show revision to accommodate the earlier version to the Tales (see KnT I.875–92 and n.), and occasionally a detail different from Boccaccio seems particularly appropriate for the Knight as narrator (e.g., I.2630; cf. GP I.57), but elsewhere (I.1201) Chaucer seems to have neglected the minimal revision one might have expected in his adaptation of the work to its new setting and purpose.

The tale cannot be dated precisely. Line 884 is often taken as an allusion to Queen Anne's arrival in England on 18 December 1381, but the allusion is by no means certain (see 884 below). Cook (Trans. Conn. Acad. 20, 1916, 166–74) saw in the description of Emetrius a reminiscence of the return to London of Henry, Earl of Derby (and future Henry IV) on 5 July 1393, and Olson (Mediaevalia 5, 1979, 61–87) relates the characterization of Theseus as peacemaker to the peace movement of the early and mid 1390s. Both theories assume a more thorough and a later revision of the earlier version than seems likely.

That the tale of Palamon and Arcite was *knowen lyte* when the Prologue to *The Legend of Good Women* was written may indicate that it was a recent work. Manly (CT, 540, 549–50) argued for 1381, before the *Troilus.* Pratt (PMLA 62, 1947, 618–19) shows that lines 1491–96 are original and replace *Teseida* 4.73, which Chaucer had used in *Troilus* (2.64–70), and he argues therefore that *Troilus* must have preceded this tale, which would then date after *Troilus* (written 1385–86; see critical introduction to *Troilus*) and before the F Prologue to *The Legend of Good Women* (written 1386–88). The fact that The Knight's Tale shares a number of lines with both *Troilus* (see 1010 and 1101 below) and *The Legend of Good Women* (see 1035–36, 1223, 1502, 1761 below) lends some support to such a date.

Skeat (5:70, 75–76) attempted to date the work by reference to the calendar: Arcite escapes from prison on the night of 3 May (I.1462–67); he meets Palamon the next day, a Friday (I.1528–38), and their duel is on the next day, Saturday, 5 May. In 1386, 5 May was a Saturday. The tournament is held a year later on Tuesday, 7 May according to Skeat's calculations, and in 1387, 7 May was a Tuesday. Mather (Eng. Misc. . . . F. J. Furnivall, 308–10) used the same arguments for 1380–81, the other years in the decade that fit the supposed calendrical references. Manly (CT, 547) interprets *thridde night* (I.1463) as "the night preceding the third day" and the duel would thus fall on Saturday, 4 May (which fits 1382 and 1388). North (RES n.s. 20, 1969, 149–54) accepts Skeat's date of 1387, since Saturn was in the sign of Leo (I.2461–62) during this decade only in 1387 and 1389, and only in 1387 was either 3 May or 4 May a Friday.

Chaucer's main source, the *Teseida,* is a poem of 9904 lines (9896 lines, the exact length of the *Aeneid,* in the family of manuscripts known to Chaucer), written in an elaborate, pseudo-classical style, and divided in epic fashion into twelve books. Boccaccio wrote copious glosses to the work (printed in Limentani's edition and translated by McCoy, *The Book of Theseus*) but they seem not to have been in the manuscript family available to Chaucer and it is not clear that he knew them. The case for his knowledge of Boccaccio's glosses is made by Boitani (Ch and Boccaccio, 190–97; see 2895 below). The glosses are of some interest for interpretation but represent, on the whole, conventional learning such as Chaucer might well have possessed or have acquired from various other sources (Pratt, SP 42:745–63).

Chaucer handled his source freely, omitting much of Boccaccio's narrative and adding much of his own. Of the 2249 lines in The Knight's Tale only about 700 correspond, even loosely, to lines in the *Teseida.* For comparisons of the two narratives, see Cummings, Indebtedness of Ch, 123–46; Wilson, UTQ 18, 1948, 131–46; Salter, Ch: KnT and ClT, 1962, 9–36, and Fourteenth-Century Engl. Poetry, 1983, chap. 6; A. Kent Hieatt, Ch, Spenser, Milton, 1975, 29–45; and Boitani, Ch and Boccaccio, esp. pp. 76–189, and Ch and Trecento, 1983, 194–99. The line-by-line relation of the two poems is indicated by H. L. Ward's marginal notations in the Six-Text Edition (Ch Soc 1, n.d.; minor corrections by Wise, Infl. of Statius, 78). The main correspondences are shown by the following table, based on one devised by Skeat:

Knight's Tale	Teseida
865–83	Bks. 1;2
893–1027	2.2–5, 25–95
1030–1274	3.1–11, 14–20, 47, 51–54, 75
1361–1448	4.26–29, 59
1451–1479	5.1–3, 24–27, 33
1545–1565	4.13, 14, 31, 85, 84, 17, 82
1638–1641	7.106, 119
1668–1739	5.77–91
1812–1860	5.92–98
1887–2022	7.108–110, 50–64, 29–37
2102–2206	6.71, 14–22, 65–70, 8
2222–2295	7.43–49, 68–93, 23–41, 67, 95–99, 7–13, 131, 132, 14, 100–102, 113–18, 19
2275–2360	7.71–92
2600–2683	8.2–131
2684–2734	9.4–61
2735–2739	12.80, 83
2743–2808	10.12–112
2809–2962	11.1–67
2967–3102	12.3–19, 69–83

Chaucer almost certainly had direct access to a glossed manuscript of Statius's *Thebaid* (see Wise, Infl. of Statius, 46–54, 78–115, and Clogan, SP 61, 1964, 599–603; and Eng. Misc. 18, 1967, 8–15, 25–31). He may also have used the *Roman de Thèbes* (Wise, 129–36) and he made extensive use of Boethius's *Consolation of Philosophy,* which he himself had translated (see in particular Jefferson, Ch and the Consolation, 130–32, 142–44; Lumiansky, TSE 3, 1952, 47–68; Elbow, ChR 7, 1972,

97–112; Payne, Ch and Menippean Satire, 223–40; and 2987–3089 below).

Chaucer's condensation, even elimination, of much of Boccaccio's epic machinery suggests to many readers that The Knight's Tale is best considered a chivalric romance of a philosophical complexion (though the usefulness of generic categories such as "romance" is thoughtfully questioned by Jordan, in Ch at Albany, 83–86). Haller (ChR 1, 1966, 67–84) argues that Chaucer retains the manner and purpose of the epic in this tale (see also Patch, On Rereading Ch, 201–10), and C. D. Benson (ChR 3, 1968, 107–23) finds in Chaucer's handling of the story the techniques and historical perspective of the late medieval chronicle. Elements of realism and contemporary courtly practices, many introduced in the tale by Chaucer, are collected by Stuart Robertson (JEGP 14, 1915, 226–55), though Chaucer also seems to attempt to "distance" the story from his audience by using a pre-Christian setting with occasional archaic features (Cowgill, PQ 54, 1975, 670–74).

The characterizations of Palamon and Arcite have been the subject of much debate. Fairchild (JEGP 26, 1927, 285–93) argued that they represent active (Arcite) and contemplative (Palamon) character types, but Marckwardt (U. Mich. Contr. in Mod. Philol. 5, 1947, 1–23) exactly reversed this polarity. Lumiansky (TSE 3:47–68) argued that they reflect the uninformed (Palamon) and educated (Arcite) voices of the imprisoned Boethius (see also Halverson, SP 57, 1960, 606–21; but cf. Delasanta, NM 70, 1969, 683–90). Hulbert (SP 26, 1929, 375–85) argued for the essential equality of the young men (but cf. Baker, MLN 45, 1930, 460–62), and this view has been developed by a number of critics (e.g., Frost, RES 25, 1949, 289–304). Baum (Ch: A Crit. Appreciation, 1958, 88–104) and van Boheemen (Dutch Qtly Rev. of Anglo–Amer. Letters 9, 1979, 176–90) view Palamon and Arcite as complementary halves of a world view fundamentally antagonistic to that of Theseus. Brooks and Fowler (MAE 39, 1970, 123–46), enlarging on Curry's work (Ch and Science, 119–23), argue that Arcite is astrologically dominated by Mars and is thus morally inferior to Palamon, dominated by Venus; but see Schmidt, EIC 19, 1969, 107–17, on this question.

Emelye, much diminished in vivacity from Boccaccio's more lifelike heroine, was seen by Dodd (Courtly Love in Ch and Gower, 1913, 234–46) as a device to focus attention on the love-rivalry of the young knights; see also Pratt, PMLA 62:598–621. Spiers (Ch the Maker, 1951, 122) stressed the fresh naturalness of her description, perhaps at the expense of the conventionality of the portrait (Robinson, Ch and the Eng. Trad., 1972, 114–15) and its place in a rhetorical tradition (Brewer, MLR 50, 1955, 257–69). She may well symbolize the regenerative forces of nature adapted to a chivalric milieu (Cameron, Sts. in Short Fict. 5, 1968, 119–27), as an individual whose identification with the month of May affects by contrast our reading of the character of that name in The Merchant's Tale (Cooper, in Med. Sts. for J. A. W. Bennett, ed. P. L. Heyworth, 1981, 65–79). Donaldson (Speaking of Ch, 46–64) sees her as one of chivalry's idealizations that make the real world tolerable; to Weissman (in Geoff. Ch, ed. George D. Economou, 1975, 93–110) she is emblematic of the grand courtly impulse to transmute nature into art.

The traditions available to Chaucer regarding Theseus (who also appears in *The House of Fame, Anelida and Arcite,* and *The Legend of Good Women*) are summarized by Scheps (LeedsSE 9, 1976–77, 19–34). The Theseus of The Knight's Tale is usually seen as an idealized ruler characterized by wisdom and justice (e.g. Robertson, Pref. to Ch, 260–66); more specifically, Burnley (Ch's Language, 11–28) considers him the antithesis of the tyrant figure. Some critics, however, have seen him as a cruel conqueror and tyrannical autocrat (Webb, RES 23, 1947, 289–96; Jones, Ch's Knight, 1980, 192–202), or a figure of glamorized violence (Aers, Ch, Langland, 174–95). But emphasizing Theseus's development and education in the course of the story, Reidy (in Epic in Med. Soc., ed. Harald Scholler, 1977, 391–408) justly assesses the seemingly contradictory elements in Theseus's character; see also Crampton, Condition of Creatures, 45–75; and McCall, Ch among the Gods, 64–68, 72–86.

Most interpretative criticism of the tale has turned on the problems of order in an apparently unjust universe. Muscatine, in an influential article (PMLA 65, 1950, 911–29; see also Ch and Fr Trad., 175–90), discusses the relation of cosmic order to the ordering function of ritual, ceremony, noble ideals, and the formal symmetries of the poem (see also Frost, RES 25: 289–304, and Halverson, SP 57:606–21). Underwood (ELH 26, 1959, 455–69), Salter (KnT and ClT, 9–36), Westlund (PQ 43, 1964, 526–37), Blake (MLQ 34, 1973, 3–19), and Herzmann (PLL 10, 1974, 339–52) have in varying ways argued that the impulses toward order are frustrated and the encouraging philosophy of Theseus's great speech on order is belied by reality, while others (e.g., Herz, Criticism, 6, 1964, 212–24, and Hanning, Lit. Rev. 23, 1980, 519–41) explain the tensions in the story as symptomatic of the split between the ideals and the realities of fourteenth-century chivalry. Some critics (e.g., Neuse, UTQ 31, 1962, 299–315, and Paul J. Thurston, Artistic Ambivalence in Ch's KnT, 1968) even argue that such tensions render the tale consistently comic and ironic. Yet the dominant approach remains sympathetic, recognizing the complexities of the tale (see, e.g., Howard, Idea of CT, 230–36) but most often admiring its incorporation of elements of imperfection in a structurally perfect artifact (Fichte, Anglia 93, 1975, 335–60).

The relation of The Knight's Tale to the rest of the First Fragment has been explored by Stokoe (UTQ 21, 1952, 120–27) and Owen (ES 35, 1954, 49–56) in noting the dramatic interplay of the Knight, Miller, Reeve, and Cook as narrators; by Howard (Idea of CT, 227–47) under the theme of civil conduct; by Blodgett (Spec 51, 1977, 477–93), focusing on the motif of "privetee"; and by Allen and Moritz (A Distinction of Stories, 119–36) with reference to the topic of human justice and authority. Westlund (PQ 43:526–37) profitably considers the story as an appropriate "impetus for pilgrimage" in its representation of pagan mankind's tragic state, partially counterbalanced by some larger design; and Kolve (Ch and the Imagery of Narrative) studies the first five tales as a sequence of the genres of romance, fabliau, and chronicle, dealing with, respectively, pagan Greece, fourteenth-century England, and the transitional period of sixth-century Europe.

PART ONE

Part One of The Knight's Tale is mainly dependent on Tes. Bks. 1–3, and rapidly summarizes in I.865–83 much

of the first two books of Boccaccio's poem. Chaucer omits such topics as the history of the Amazons' crimes against their husbands and men from other lands (which prompts Teseo's invasion); Ipolita's spirited defense of the Amazons' past action; their stout resistance to Teseo's attack; his harangue of the troops; Ipolita's admission that the Amazons have sinned against Venus; the re-emergence of their feminine qualities; Ipolita's espousal to Teseo; Teseo's decision to award Emilia to his kinsman Acate; Peritoo's appearance before Teseo to shame him out of the lethargy to which love has subjected him; the personal combat of Teseo and Creonte; the latter's haughty defiance; and his burial by order of Teseo.

The motto, *Iamque domos patrias, Scithice post aspera gentis Prelia, laurigero, &c,* found in many MSS of all groups and perhaps included as a gloss by Chaucer himself (M-R 2:484–85, 527), is from Statius, Theb. 12.519–20, which likewise describes the hero's victorious return to Athens. An expanded form of the gloss is found in three MSS of *Anelida and Arcite,* before the stanza beginning at Anel 22, also dependent on Statius. Cf. Tes. 2.19–24.

860 Theseus, properly speaking king of Athens, is called duke by Dante (Inf. 12.17), by Boccaccio (Tes. 1.5–6), and elsewhere by Chaucer in Anel 29 and LGW 2442–43. This is not the characteristic medieval anachronism it may seem. There was a duke of Athens; the title was established by Louis IX of France, c. 1260. See Kenneth M. Setton, Catalan Dom. of Athens, 1311–88, 1948, 17; and Nicolas Cheetham, Med. Greece, 1981, 166–88.

866 Femenye: An OF form from Lat. *Femina, land of women; see Benoît de Saunte-Maure, *Roman de Troie* 23283, 25663–704; Gower, Conf. Aman. 4.2140, 5.2548. Earlier sources tend to locate the Amazons (Gr. Ἀμαζών, breastless) on the southern shore of the Black Sea. Boccaccio, following Statius, places them in the region of the Don and Lake Maeotis, to which the name Scythia was also applied (see Bartholomaeus Anglicus, 15.12, tr. Trevisa, 2:730, and cf. Anel 23). See also Magoun, Ch Gazetteer, 71.

875–92 Tatlock (Dev. and Chron., 66) suggests this entire paragraph was added when the original *Palamon and Arcite* was revised into The Knight's Tale. Wager (MLN 50, 1935, 296–307) finds support for the suggestion in a tense-system different from that of the immediate context, as well as a repetition of rhymes (I.865–66/877–78; 867–68/881–82) that one might not expect if the passages had been written continuously.

875–88 The rhetorical figure here employed is *occupatio* or *praeteritio,* a refusal to describe or narrate that often has the effect of describing or narrating (see Geoffrey of Vinsauf, *Poetria nova,* 1159–62, ed. Faral, 233; tr. Nims, 59). Other examples in this tale of the figure—described by Manly (PBA 12, 1926, 106) along with the absolute construction—as Chaucer's two favorite methods of abbreviation—are I.994–99, 2197–207, 2919–66 (the account of Arcite's funeral). Haller (MP 62, 1965, 288) sees the use of the device in The Knight's Tale as wholly functional, in introducing matters that must, for the sake of brevity, be dispensed with; Knight, Rymyng Craftily, 136–45, distinguishes degrees of rhetorical elaboration and heightening of style that correspond with various functions of the narrator: sometimes speeding up the action, sometimes intensifying the emotion. He notices a matter-of-fact use of the device, along with that of *continuatio* (pithy expression of a thought) and *dubitatio* (doubting what to say or how to say it) in I.1187–89, 1199–201, 1216–18, 1340–42, 1353–54, 1377–80, 1417–18, and 1459–61.

884　tempest: There is no mention by either Statius or Boccaccio of a storm on Theseus's homecoming, prompting Tyrwhitt to substitute the reading of two MSS, *temple,* on the basis of Tes. 2.23. Wise (Infl. of Statius, 49) argued for emending to *feste.* Lowes (MLN 19, 1904, 240–43) sees here a reference to the storm that destroyed the ship that brought Anne of Bohemia, fiancée of Richard II, to England on 18 December 1381 (Walsingham, *Historia Anglicana,* 2:46). Curry (MLN 36, 1921, 272–74), and Wager (MLN 50:296), and Parr (PMLA 60, 1945, 315) argue instead that the word is used metaphorically to describe the excitement of the Athenians (cf. "tomolto," Tes. 2.24); see OED, s.v. *tempest, sbst.* 2.

885–86　Skeat compares RR 21215–17.

894　Both Statius and Boccaccio place the Temple of Clemence (I.928) within the city; and both introduce the suffering widows in the narrative before Theseus arrives.

912–13　The eldeste lady: Identified by Boccaccio as Evadne. She does not swoon in either Theb. or Tes.

915　Wise (Infl. of Statius, 49–50) suggests the influence of Theb. 12.547, explicitly linking Fortune to Theseus's victory; but the conception is wholly conventional. For comprehensive treatments of the medieval idea of Fortune, see Patch, Goddess Fortuna; Jefferson, Ch and the Consolation, 49–60; Barbara Bartholomew, Fortuna and Natura, 1966, 9–45; see also 1663–72 below.

924　caytyves: Miserable wretches, perhaps from the Roman de Thèbes, 9994 ("chaitives"). For the word as a motif in the tale, see Crampton, Condition of Creatures, 92–104.

925–26　For Fortune and her wheel, see Bo 2.pr2.51–57 and Tr 1.138–40n.

932　The impious **Cappaneus,** one of the "Seven against Thebes," was struck with a thunderbolt from Zeus; see Tr 5.1485–510 and n.

938　the olde Creon: As Wise (Infl. of Statius, 130) notes, a familiar epithet in the Roman de Thèbes; see 5190, 5799, 8341, etc.; and cf. Anel 64. In Tes. 2.61 Creon is of mature age, but he is nowhere described by Boccaccio as old.

949–57　Wise (Infl. of Statius, 131–32) notes similarities to the Roman de Thèbes: Theseus's arrival on a horse (instead of in a chariot); the suppliants falling prostrate to make their plea; Theseus raising them to their feet. Cf. I.949 and Thèbes 9944; I.952 and Thèbes 9946; I.957 and Thèbes 9997–98.

952　This gentil duc: On the use of *this,* see Language and Versification, p. xxxviii.

966　His baner he desplayeth: To display one's banner before an enemy was formally to declare war (Maurice Keen, Laws of War in the MA, 1955, 106).

968　go ne ride: A common collocation; see, e.g., I.1351, 2252.

969–70　Statius (Theb. 12.661), but not Boccaccio, includes the detail of a night-march to Thebes. Clogan (SP 61:611) suggests that Chaucer's phrasing shows knowledge of the gloss on the line in the Thebaid.

971–74　In Tes. 2.41–42, Ipolita willingly leaves Teseo after courteously offering to accompany him to Thebes. Statius explains her not going by the fact that she is pregnant.

975–77　The description of Mars as red (see also I.1747, 1969; Anel 1n.; LGW 2589) is from Tes. 1.3 (*rubicondo,* ruddy).

feeldes: Plains, not, as Skeat has it, heraldic fields; see Gibbs (MLN 24, 1909, 197–98) and Kittredge (MLN 25, 1910, 28).

979　ybete: Probably "embroidered" here and in Tr 2.1229, Rom 837; cf. MED s.v. *beten* 6. (b).

980　Mynotaur: Not mentioned in Tes., the minotaur is depicted as defeated by Theseus on the hero's shield in Theb. 12.668–73. Chaucer recounts the exploit in LGW 1886–2150. McCall (Ch among the Gods, 171) notes that in Boccaccio, De genealogia deorum 4.10, killing the beast is explained as the prudent man's victory over bestiality; see also Green, in Crit. Approaches to Med. Lit., ed. Dorothy Bethurum, 1960, 131–32.

989　For the destruction of the city by assault, Chaucer may have been influenced by the Roman de Thèbes, 10073–75.

990　The wholesale destruction of the captured city, apparently consistent with fourteenth-century practice (S. Robertson, JEGP 14:227–28), finds a macabre analogue in Tes. 2.81, where the widows themselves set fire to Thebes.

993–94　The detailed description of these rites can be found in Tes. 2.79–80. Chaucer has also omitted the women's search among the rotting corpses for the remains of their husbands.

1006–7　By the laws of medieval warfare, "reasonable pillage" of a defeated enemy was permitted; see Keen, Laws of War, 135–55; Gower (Mirour, 24037–49) distinguishes those who fight primarily for the love of justice from those motivated by hope of material gain.

As Robinson points out, however, Chaucer omits Teseo's courteous dispatch of men to bury the dead and treat the wounded.

1010　Almost identical with Tr 4.627.

1013–14　An example of *commutatio,* a repetition of words or phrases in reverse order (Geoffrey of Vinsauf, Poetria nova, 1174). See also I.1736, 2843–44; and BD 597.

1013–24　The names **Palamon** and **Arcita** are derived from Boccaccio. *Palaemon* occurs in Statius: he is the son of Ino, hence the grandson of Cadmus, founder of the "dreadful race" of Thebes (Theb. 1.12–14, 115–22). His mother jumped with him into the sea as a result of Oedipus's curse on the city. Boccaccio's *Arcita* may derive from the Greek poem *Digenes Akrites,* or a version of that story known to Boccaccio; technically it refers to Byzantine knights who defended against Muslim incursions (see Metlitzki, Matter of Araby in Med. Engl., 1977, 145).

1024　he nolde no raunsoun: Theseus's refusal to ransom his captives (like his later release of Arcite *withouten any raunsoun,* I.1205) is proof of his unmercenary character (Robertson, JEGP 14:229), not, as Palamon says (1111) of his tyranny. Perpetual imprisonment for prisoners who have not surrendered and who pose a threat of further war was an acceptable practice; see Reidy, in Epic in Med. Soc., 399–402. The topic of ransom is not raised by Boccaccio; for Theseus's behavior here, see Kolve, Ch and the Imagery of Narrative, 98–101.

1035–36　Cf. LGW 2425–26.

1039　The device of *dubitatio* (see 875–88 above). Cf. I.1459–60 (mixed with *interrogatio,* a question); and I.2227–32.

1047   For May-day and maytime customs depicted here and in I.1500–12, see John Brand, Observations on the Pop. Antiq. of Gt. Brit., ed. Ellis, 1849, repr. 1969, 212–34; Mitchell, MLN 71, 1956, 560–64; Floure and the Leafe, 27–29; and cf. Halverson, SP 57:608–9.

1049–50   In Tes. 3.10, Emilia's blond hair is wound about her head, rather than worn in a braid (cf. Tr 5.808–12). Renoir (N&Q 203, 1958, 283–84) cites Apuleius, *Metamorphoses* 2.10, and compares Virgil, Aen. 1.318–20 (Venus with her hair falling loosely).

1053–54   Emelye makes her garland of flowers, Arcite makes his of leaves (I.1508). This may be an allusion to the fashionable courtly debates between the adherents of the flower and of the leaf; see ProLGW 72n.

1074–79   In Tes. 3.11–14, Arcita spies Emilia first; and both he and Palemone think she is Venus.

1077–97   The motif of love's fatal glance, probably founded upon the Empedoclean theory of vision accepted by Plato, whereby the eye transmits light through beams that join the eye to the viewed object, and the eyes, as agents (not merely perceivers), strike through the eyes of the beloved into the heart, passed from Greek literature into medieval vernaculars through the agency of the Arabs. It is hardly known in classical Latin literature. See Cline, RPh 25, 1972, 263–97; and Donaldson-Evans, Neophil 69, 1978, 202–11. In Tes. 3.15–16, Boccaccio associates the "Aggressive Eyes" topos with the iconography of Cupid's arrows. Cf. KnT I.1567, Tr 2.533–35, MercB 1–13, Compl d'Am 41–42.

1077–79   In Tes. 3.18–19, Emilia notices that the youths are watching her and shows off a bit.

1087–91   For medieval "astrologizing" of the classical gods see Seznec, Survival of the Pagan Gods, 37–83, 149–83. On the astrology of The Knight's Tale, see Curry, Ch and Science, 119–38; also Brooks and Fowler, MAE 39, 1970, 123–46. Chaucer's attitude toward astrology, or "judicial astronomy," is not altogether clear. See MLT II.295–301n.; Astr 2.4n and 2.4.57–69n. For **Saturne** (I.1088), see 2443–78 below.

1089   For the construction cf. SqT V.325; Tr 4.976; but cf. also KnT I.1666, where the negative idea is expressed, rather than (as more frequent) implied.

1101   Cf. Tr 1.425.

1116–24   In Tes. 2.85–89, the noble youths need not be disarmed, and Teseo acts quickly to have their wounds treated. See 1024 above.

1129–32   For these lines and 1169–70 and 1172–76, Chaucer draws from the conversation of Arcita and Palemone in the grove (Tes. 5.53ff.) where the jealousy motif is allowed to surface more gradually.

1132   Palamon and Arcite were not only cousins, but "sworn brothers"; i.e., united through oath and formal ceremony in a legally binding relationship, ordinarily for the duration of the lives of the contracting parties, in which each pledged to the other military assistance in time of danger, ransom in the event of capture, the right to share in the spoils of war, the duty to avenge the other's death, and even the privilege of marrying his widow. Classical examples of the compact recognized in the Middle Ages include Achilles and Patroclus, Orestes and Pylades, and Theseus and Pirithous (see I.1191–1201). The development of the institution from the earlier blood-brotherhoods exemplified by Odin and Loki, Hadding and Lysir, and the Gislasaga is sketched by Gerould, ESt 36, 1906, 193–208; MacEdward Leach

(Intro., Amis and Amiloun, EETS 203, 1937); A. McI. Trounce (Athelston, EETS 224, 1951, 11–14); and Keen, History 47, 1962, 1–17.

The relationship of Arcite and Palamon is extraordinary in that its primary aim (I.1135–39) is the furtherance of a brother's love-suit; ordinarily, romantic concerns are much subordinated to "feudal" or heroic impulses. But more representative of the institution as practiced in the OF *chansons de geste* and the ME romances is the assumption (I.1134) of the duration of the bond; the formal abrogation of the oath (I.1604–5) when one party recognizes treacherous behavior in the other; and even the reconciliation of the compact (I.2783–97; cf. Amis and Amiloun) when such alleged treachery has been proven to rest on a misunderstanding.

1133   **for to dyen in the peyne:** On this concessive use of *for* see Language and Versification, p. xlii, and Mustanoja, ME Syntax, 536. Hinckley (Notes on Ch, 64–65) sees here a reference to *peine fort et dure*, strait and close confinement. Note that Theseus rejects the idea of torture in I.1746, Arcite having confessed.

1155   **For paramour:** As a mistress, hence, opposed to Palamon's love of Emelye as a goddess (I.1157).

1163–64   Translates "Quis legem det amantibus?/ Maior lex amor est sibi," quoted as a gloss, from Boethius, Cons., 3.m12.52–55 (see n.), though the sentiment is proverbial (Whiting, L579; Walther 25383). Cf. Tr 4.618 and 1606 below. As Chaucer's glosses in Boece make clear, Boethius intends his lines as a criticism of lovers. Cf. Tr 1.236–38.

1165   **by my pan:** Elliott (Ch's English, 247, 252) remarks upon Arcite's predilection for swearing. Swearing by one's head (I.2670, Tr 5.283), crown (RvT I.4041) or *pan* is common.

1167   **positif lawe:** Human, legislated law *(lex civilis),* as opposed to natural law *(lex naturalis).* We are disposed by natural law to love; and any human law that tries to prevent our obeying natural law, Arcite argues, will be broken.

1169–70   In Tes. 5.51, Arcita implies he would sooner die than leave off loving Emilia, and reminds Palemone that no true lover can promise not to love.

1169   **maugree his heed:** In spite of his resistance, in spite of all he could do about it. See also I.2618, and cf. *maugree . . . yen,* WBPro III.315. (OF *maugre,* from *mal,* bad, difficult + *gré,* permission, will.) Cf. Tr 3.989–90.

1177–80   For the somewhat similar Aesopic fable (Augustana recension, no. 147) of the lion and the bear who fight over the body of a fawn, only to lose it to a fox, see Halm's ed. of Aesop, 1854, no. 247; and cf. LaFontaine, "Les voleurs et l'ane," (Fables, ed. Robert, 1825, 1, no. 13) and Thompson, Motif-Index, K348. Helterman (ELH 38, 1971, 493–511) notes that Arcite ignores the moral of the fable: to avoid useless toil for the benefit of a scoundrel. Wenzel (SP 73, 1976, 145) cites a comparison of foolish lovers fighting over a corpse, from a treatise for preachers which Chaucer seems to have known (Wenzel, Traditio 30, 1974, 351–78).

1181–82   Proverbial after Chaucer; Whiting M73.

1191–1208   For Pirithous's visit to Athens, and his supplication on Arcite's behalf, see Tes. 3.47–53. The friendship of Theseus and Pirithous was legendary; their daring but unsuccessful attempt to ravish Proserpina from the Underworld to be Pirithous's bride is alluded to in Theb. 1.475–76 and 8.53–54, where the description of Theseus as "iuratus amico" (sworn to [his] friend) may have suggested to Chaucer describing them here as *felawes;* i.e., sworn brothers. See also Plutarch, Theseus, 30–31 (in Lives, ed. and tr. Bernadotte Perrin, Loeb, 1914, 1:69–73). According to Plutarch (35) Heracles once intervened with Aidoneus to secure the release of Theseus from prison. See also Hoffman, Ovid and CT, 52–56.

That Theseus sought his dead companion in hell follows no classical account, and considerably enhances the adventure. As Skeat notes, Chaucer's source is most probably RR 8148–51.

1196　Cf. SNT VIII.236.

1201　Sometimes considered a line unaltered from the original Palamon and Arcite; Manly, however, compares WBPro III.224–25 as a similar violation of narrative decorum.

1210　**hym Arcite:** For the demonstrative use of the third person pronoun Mustanoja, ME Syntax, 135–36.

1223–50　Haller, ChR 1:70–71, notes the similarity of this lament to Polynices' resentment of his brother Eteocles, in Theb. 1.316–23.

1223　Cf. LGW 658.

1238　The figure of dice was commonly applied to the vicissitudes of Fortune. Cf. MkT VII.2661 and Tr 2.1347; and see Patch, Goddess Fortuna, 81.

1242　Proverbial; Whiting F523.

1247　On the four elements, see GP 333 and n.

1251–67　Arcite's lament is derived from Boethius (Bo 3.pr2), who asserts that true happiness can be found only in the possession of the Supreme Good; but men, driven by folly and error, mistake such transitory goods as power, fame, and riches for the Supreme Good. Arcite speaks only of the vanity of human wishes. His failure adequately to distinguish between Providence and Fortune should be compared with Bo 4.pr6; pr7; and Dante, Inf. 7.70–96. I.1255 may echo Bo 3.pr2.25–28; and I.1258–59 Bo 2.pr5.90–95. I.1260 is probably an echo of Romans 8.26, which contrasts present miseries with God's providence.

1261　Proverbial; cf. WBPro III.246 and Whiting M731.

1261–67　Cf. Bo 3.pr2.82–88, which compares the soul that no longer recognizes the true good with a drunken man who cannot find his home.

1272　Cf. Bo 1.pr6.75–6.

1279　grete is perhaps to be taken with **fettres,** though Pratt takes the phrase **shynes grete** (not corresponding with anything in Tes.) as "swollen shins."

1299　In Tes. 3.77–79, Palemone's envy of Arcita's freedom is tempered by sincere fellow-feeling, and at this point stops well short of jealousy.

1301–2　For the comparison of the (yellowish) color of the boxtree *(Buxus sempervirens),* cf. LGW 866 (from Ovid, Met 4.134–35).

1303–27　Palamon's lament echoes the sentiments of the imprisoned Boethius (Bo 1.m5) who takes the suffering of the innocent as a contradiction of God's otherwise benevolent governance of the universe, a position that Lady Philosophy then refutes. Cf. MLT II.813–16; FranT V.865–93; Mars 218–26; Tr 3.1016–19; and LGW 2228–35; and see Jefferson, Ch and the Consolation, 69–71.

1305　atthamaunt: Cf. 1990 below.

1307–9　The figure of the sheep cowering in the fold is not in Boethius; for Chaucer's metaphoric use of the animal, see Rowland, Blind Beasts, 141–52; and cf. WBPro III.431–36. Chaucer's inspiration here may have been Eccles. 2.18–20, quoted by Innocent III, De miseria condicionis humanae, 1.2.

1313–14　Cf. Tr 3.1016–19, Bo 1.m5.

1315–21　For the familiar idea that brutes may be happier than men, Hinckley cites the Dialogus inter corpus et animam, 227–30 (Lat. Poems Attrib. to Walter Map, 103) (Robinson). Cf. also Bo 3.pr7.12–16.

1323　Cf. ParsT X.957n.

1323–24　For the rhyme *dyvynys : pyne ys* see GP I.523n.

1329–31　The anger of Juno against Thebes was due to Jupiter's adultery with the Theban women Semele and Alcmena. See Anel 51n.

1331　Cf. Statius, Theb., 12.704.

1347　This is a typical love-problem *(demande d'amour* or *questione d'amore),* familiar to French, Provençal, and Italian literature of the Middle Ages, of a genre given vogue by the *De arte honesti amandi* of Andreas Capellanus (tr. Parry, 167–77). For other examples see WBT III.904–5 and FranT V.1621–22. For its prevalence as a topic of literature, see Neilson, Origins of the Court of Love, 246 (from Boccaccio's *Filocolo,* tr. Donald Cheney, 1985, bk. 4) and John Stevens, Music and Poetry, 154–64. Manuals apparently designed to teach the art of amorous conversation in court (see I.2203) and containing series of such questions (with responses) were very popular. See *Les adevineaux amoreux,* ed. James W. Hassell, Jr., 1974; and The Demaundes off Love, ed. W. L. Braekman, Scripta: Med. and Ren. Texts and Sts. 7, 1982.

PART TWO

The principal omissions from the *Teseida* in Part Two are: the wanderings of Arcita in Corinth and Maecena; his worshiping in the Athenian temple of Apollo; his recognition by Emilia after he joins Teseo's household; his identification, as he laments aloud in a grove, by Palemone's servant Panfilo; and the discovery by Emilia alone of the two youths fighting.

1355–76　Chaucer here elaborates upon Tes. 4.26–29, adding such symptoms as Arcite's chronic swooning and his changing complexion, while omitting the fearsome appearance rendered by Arcita's thick brows and shaggy hair. Both Boccaccio and Chaucer describe the malady as melancholic; Lowes (MP 11, 1914, 491–546) shows that the symptoms Chaucer adds are those of the **loveris maladye of Hereos** (from Gr. ἔρως but influenced in form and meaning by Lat. *heros,* hero, and *herus,* master), a mental disease (love sickness) regularly recognized and discussed by medieval medical authorities. Robertson (Pref to Ch, 456–60) translates relevant portions of Bernard of Gordon's *Lillium medicinae* (see GP I.429–34 and n.). For a full discussion see Ciavollella's study of *aegritudo amoris,* GSLI 147, 1970, 498–517; Kohl, Wissenschaft und Dichtung bei Ch, 218–308; and Schweitzer, SAC 3, 1981, 20–27. The Third Partition of Robert Burton's *Anatomy of Melancholy* is an encyclopedic discussion of "heroick love."

1374–76　manye: Mania is a form of madness to which *amor hereos* could lead; it could be fatal. The brain was thought to have three cells, or ventricles: in the front is the **celle fantastik**, which controls the imagination, in the middle cell judgment, and in the rear memory (cf. Bartholomaeus Anglicus 5.3, tr. Trevisa, 1:173). The **humour malencolik** (cf. GP I.333n.), engendered in some cases by passions of the soul such as "grete thoughtes of sorwe, and of to grete studie and of drede" (in this instance love), could lead to melancholia, which affects the middle cell and deprives one of judgment and reason; or to mania, which deprives one of the imagination (i.e., he can perceive no new images but thinks continually of his beloved); see Bartholomaeus Anglicus 7.6, tr. Trevisa, 1:349.

1379   daun: A title of respect, derived from Lat. *dominus,* lord or master, but used very loosely and applied to priests, who were also called "sir" (cf. ProNPT VII.2820), to monks (cf. ShipT VII.43 and the modern title Dom, used for Benedictines), to historical figures, authors, poets, and classical gods. In MilT I.3761 it is used for the blacksmith Gervays, in NPT VII.3334 for the fox, and in VII.3312 for *'Daun Burnel the Asse.'* Spenser was apparently the first to apply the title to "Dan Chaucer" (OED s.v. *dan*).

1381   a yeer or two: Boccaccio communicates a sense of Arcita's gradual physical transformation; see Tes. 4.19, 21, 27.

1384–92 In Tes. 4.31–34, Arcita is motivated to return to Athens when a crewman of a ship bound there speaks to him of Emilia. Skeat, following Lounsbury (Sts. in Ch, 2:382), felt Chaucer's inspiration for Mercury's appearance was Claudian, *De raptu Proserpinae* 1.77; Wilkins (Spec 22, 1957, 522) suggests Berchorius, *Ovidius moralizatus* and the *Libellus de deorum imaginibus;* but the description of Mercury, largely conventional, is perhaps closer to Ovid, Met. 1.671–72 (Shannon, Ch and Roman Poets, 303; Richard L. Hoffman, Ovid and CT, 61–62). Bachman (ELN 13, 1976, 168–73) notes, however, a closer parallel of situation in Mercury's appearance to the sleeping Aeneas in Aen. 4.556–70; while Taylor (Classical Folia, 30, 1976, 40–56) suggests parallels with Laius's nighttime visit to Eteocles in Theb., 2.102–27, and argues for Chaucer's dependence upon the larger epic tradition of the descent of an other-worldly figure to exhort a hesitant hero to action.

1387   slepy yerde: Mercury's *somniferam virgam,* with which he put the hundred-eyed Argus to sleep and then killed him (Ovid, Met. 1.670). Mercury's command perhaps absolves Arcite of breaking his parole by returning to Athens.

1400–1 Cf. Tr 4.864–65.

1422 Cf. Jos. 9.21.

1426–43 Arcite's promotion from **Page of the chambre** of a lady, to squire of the chamber of a duke—not paralleled in the Teseida—has been explained autobiographically with reference to Chaucer's having served while a youth perhaps as a page in the household of Elizabeth, Countess of Ulster, in the time around 1357–59, then in 1368 as a squire attached to the household of Edward III (see Lowes, MP 15, 1918, 692n.; Brewer, Spec 43, 1968, 290–91); but the autobiographical correspondence is doubted, with good reason, by Green (ELN 18, 1981, 251–57), who sees in Arcite's meteoric rise an idealization of a court that recognized true merit, perhaps with the implication of the venality of court life as Chaucer knew it.

1428 In the Teseida, Arcita assumes the name Penteo;

Chaucer took the name **Philostrate** from Boccaccio's Filostrato, the primary source of the *Troilus. Philostrato,* from the Greek, means "army lover," but Boccaccio, and probably Chaucer, took it to mean "overthrown by love" (Lat. *stratus,* past participle of *sterno*).

1439   neer: "Near," though the form usually is comparative ("nearer") in Chaucer.

1442–45 There is nothing in Tes. to correspond with this realistic touch.

1453   Forpyned: In Tes. 5.1 Palemone is also dejected because of the absence of his companion.

1459–60 Chaucer frequently refers to his lack of **Englyssh:** cf. MLT II.778–79; SqT V.37–38; BD 898–99; LGW 66–67; these contexts are highly rhetorical and the references may be merely variants on the "modesty" or "inexpressibility" topos (cf. GP I.746n.) but they may also reflect a concern about the state of literary English; cf. Ven 80 and introductory note to Venus.

1460 RR and LGW regularly refer to those who die for love in the language of martyrdom. See also I.1562.

1462–64   of May/The thridde nyght: Boccaccio says only that the action took place when the moon was in Sagittarius. Chaucer specifies 3 May here and in NPT VII.3187–91 (when Chauntecleer encounters the fox) and Tr 2.50–56 (when Pandarus suffers a *teene* for love). Manly, who takes *thridde nyght* as referring to the night of 2 May and thus specifying 3 May as the day of the duel, notes the occurrence of 3 May on lists of "Egyptian" or "dismal" days (see BD 1206–7 and n.). Robertson (ELH 19, 1952, 9) notes that on 3 May, the Feast of the Invention of the Holy Cross, St. Helena cast down the idol of Venus and that the day may therefore be unlucky for lovers. McCall (MLN 76, 1971, 201–5) argues that this is a day on which Love has a special force, since it is the climax of the festival in honor of Flora, mistress of Venus (Ovid, Fasti 5.183–93, 331–75). See further Kellogg and Coxe in Kellogg, Ch, Langland, 155–98. Clark (RUO 52, 1982, 257–65) notes that since Palamon escapes after midnight (I.1467) the duel is on 4 May (the day on which Pandarus visits Criseyde) and argues that the reference is not specifically to May but to the lunar month. In medieval *lunaria* such as Pandarus apparently consults (Tr 2.74n.) the third day of the month is inauspicious, the fourth favorable for a new beginning. Clark quotes John Metham's *Days of the Moon* (in Works, ed. Hardin Craig, EETS 132, 1916, 149): "The thryd day of the mone ys noght fortunat to begynne ony werke upon" and "the fourthe day is gode to begynne euery worldly occupacioun." Cf. MLT II.306–8, MilT I.3515n.

1465 Cf. I.844 and n.

1466 Proverbial; Whiting T171.

1471   clarree: Clary, a spiced, sweetened wine; see also MerT IV.1807 and Form Age 16. Skeat's recipe (5:70), from London, British Library MS Sloane 2584, fol. 173, calls for mixing one gallon boiled honey to eight gallons of red wine, then adding one pound of cinnamon, half a pound of powdered ginger, and a quarter pound of pepper. See Curye on Inglysch, EETS, SS 8, 178.

1472   opie of Thebes: The reference is to Egyptian Thebes (Hg and El gloss "opium Thebaicum"). Palamon may have had the drug with him because it was one of the recognized remedies for the *loveris maladye of Hereos* (Emerson, MP 17, 1919, 287–91). See also Burton's Anat. of Melan., 3.2.5.1 (1977 ed., 194).

1479   With dredeful foot: Cf. LGW 811 and n.

1491 Bawcutt (YES 2, 1972, 5–12) traces the idea of the lark greeting the dawn to Alexander Neckam, *De naturis rerum,* 1.68. Often understood in a moral sense as a type of zeal and industry, it is frequently turned into an amorous symbol, as in I.2209–15.

1494 Cf. Dante, Purg., 1.20, "Faceva tutto ridere l'oriente," ([Venus] was making the whole east smile), which Bennett (MAE 22, 1953, 114–15) suggests was associated in Chaucer's mind with Tes. 3.5–8.

1502 **courser:** A hunting horse, invariably used by Chaucer in knightly contexts (Rowland, Blind Beasts, 116). This line is nearly identical with LGW 1204.

1506–7 On the observance of May, see 1047 above and Savage, MLN 55, 1940, 207–9.

1509 Cf. SqT V.53 and Tr 2.920.

1521 Proverbial; Whiting F127; and in a Latin form, "Campus habet lumen, et habet nemus auris acumen," Walther 2272.

1524 Proverbial; Whiting M210; for the use of *men* as the singular indefinite pronoun (as in Germ. *Man sagt*), cf. GP I.149 and see Language and Versification, p. xxxvi.

1529 **roundel:** The lines quoted from Arcite's song, 1510–12, rhyming *abb,* could conceivably be the beginning of a roundel; see PF 675n.

1531 **thise:** see Language and Versification, p. xxxviii.

1533 Proverbial; see Patch, Goddess Fortuna, 53–54, and ESt 65, 1930, 352–53; and Whiting B575.

1539 For proverbial and folk wisdom that Friday is different from the other days of the week, see Neckam, De nat. rerum 1.7; Lowes, MLR 9, 1914, 94; and Whiting F622.

1545 Theb. 1.17 calls the Theban dynasty a "confusa domus" of Oedipus.

1546–49 **Cadme:** Cadmus, father of Semele (see 1329–31 above) was said to have founded Thebes with the warriors produced when he sowed the teeth of a dragon he had slain. **Amphioun** was said to have built the walls of Thebes with the sound of his lyre; see MerT IV.1716n.

1566 Cf. Tr 3.733–35; LGW 2629–30; and see Whiting D106. Hibbard (PQ 1, 1922, 222–25) connects the figure of the shirt with the thread of life, spun by the Fates (see Tr 4.1546, 5.3–7) but the similarity may be merely coincidental, and the expression as Chaucer uses it may mean nothing more than that one's fate is determined before one's first garment is made.

For **erst,** superlative, where the comparative would be more natural in Mod. English, cf. NPT VII.3281; ClT IV.336; Rom 692.

1579–1613 In the Teseida, where Palemone is not surprised to find Arcita in the grove, Palemone wishes not to awaken his sleeping friend, so peaceful does he seem. Chaucer, who has gained much through the surprise meeting of the youths (Boitani, Ch and Bocc., 130), must put off to the next day the combat that occurs in Tes. soon after their meeting.

1598 A commonplace; Whiting L311.

1606 Proverbial after Chaucer; see Whiting L516 and cf. FranT V.767; Rom 3432.

1609 **darreyne:** Lat. *derationare* (OF *deraisner*) originally meant to disprove an argument, but later acquired the meaning to prove or decide (by battle). Cf. I.1853 and 2097; and see GP I.239n.

1625–26 Proverbial in English after Chaucer (Whiting L495), and a common sentiment in classical literature, with analogues in Ovid, Ars Am. 3.564 (addressed ironically to women; cited by Matthew of Vendôme, *Ars versificatoria* 3.10, in Faral, Les arts poétiques, 170); Ovid, Met. 2.846–47; RR 8449–54; and Tes. 5.13, where Boccaccio refers to such feelings as "the poison that has power to divide." Cf. FranT V.764–66. Skeat (5:73) took RR as Chaucer's source here, but Hoffman (Ovid and CT, 63–67, 105–8) distinguishes two related proverbs, with the formulation of the KnT and Tes. deriving from Ars Amatoria.

Haller (ChR 1:74–79) sees the tale as a whole presenting an alternative to the sentiment here expressed by the narrator, in that the qualities of love are shown to be transferable to the public life of a ruler.

1626 **his thankes:** Willingly; adverbial genitive of *thank* in the primary sense of "thought," hence "will," "wish." Cf. lines 2107, 2114, Rom 2463 (Robinson). Cf. also WBPro III.272.

1633 **allone as he was born:** Perhaps proverbial (Whiting B465), though the phrase is found only in Chaucer (WBT III.885; Tr 4.298).

1636–1707 The single combat of Palemone and Arcita is conducted quite differently in Boccaccio, where (Tes. 5.66–67) Palemone falls unconscious from a blow by Arcita who, thinking that he has perhaps slain his beloved friend, manages to revive him to consciousness; the two youths then resume the battle, only to be discovered by Emilia and then interrupted by Teseo.

1638–46 See Tes. 7.106, 119; and cf. Theb. 4.494.

1642 **breketh:** Wise (Infl. of Statius, 91) notes that the phrase *rami rompendo* (Tes. 7.119) ought better to yield *breking,* parallel with *come russhyng* (I.1641).

1658 The duel between Eteocles and Polynices (Theb. 11.530–31) is likened to the combat of wild boars. The simile is not in Tes. See Whiting B405.

1663–72 The distinction that Chaucer here makes between Destiny and Providence is dependent on Boethius 4.pr6: Providence is the government of all mutable nature as it exists in the mind of God; Destiny is that plan as it is worked out on changeable things in time. Chaucer also seems indebted to Dante, Inf. 7.73–96, where Fortune, described in terms analogous to Destiny, is referred to as "general ministra" of Providence; cf. *ministre general* (I.1663; no corresponding term in Boethius). For background, see W. C. Greene, Moira, 1944; and V. Cioffari, Conception of Fortune and Fate in the Works of Dante, 1940.

In Tes. 6.1–5, Boccaccio discusses the inexplicability of Fortune, without suggesting God's providential plan.

1668 From Tes. 5.77, but also proverbial; see Whiting D56.

1675 **the grete hert:** For the occurrence of the term in books of hunting, see Emerson, RomR 13, 1922, 140.

1676–78 Cf. LGW 45–47 and n.

1697 **Under the sonne:** "Theseus looked under the low lying sun, perhaps (as Professor Child used to suggest) shielding his eyes as he swept the field in his observation" (Robinson). See Tatlock, MLN 37, 1922, 120–21; and van Roosbroeck, MLN 38, 1923, 59; but cf. the fifteenth-century Robin and Gandelyn (Child Ballad 115), 35, cited by Smith, MLN 51, 1936, 318, where the meaning clearly is "in every direction," and see also Smith, MLN 37, 1922, 120–21.

1712 **juge:** Theseus objects to the irregularity of the duel, which should be conducted by the rules for judicial combat or for duels of honor; for a set of such rules, see those drawn up by Thomas of Woodstock, Constable of England, in Chaucer's time (ed. Henry Arthur, Viscount Dillon, Archaeologia 57, 1900, 61–66) and cf. Maurice Keen, Laws of War, 1965, 54–59.

1721   The form **seinte** (with final -*e*) might be explained as a case of inflected adjective with a proper name, or as a dative, or as a French feminine (Robinson).

1724   In Tes. 5.86–87, each of the young knights confesses his identity to Teseo.

1736   it am I: The usual ME idiom (Robinson). Cf. LGW 314.

1742–60   There is nothing in Tes. to correspond to the intercession of the ladies at this point. Teseo, though angry, has pledged his word that the youths will not be harmed if they identify themselves. Parr (PMLA 60:307) sees an allusion to Queen Anne's intercession for Sir Simon Burley (1388); Hinckley (Notes on Ch, 75) suggests Queen Philippa's successful appeal to Edward III on behalf of six condemned citizens of Calais.

1747   Mars the rede: See 975–77 above.

1761   Chaucer's favorite line; see MerT IV.1986; SqT V.479; LGW F 503 (G 491); and cf. MLT II.660. It became proverbial after Chaucer (Whiting P243). Lowes (MP 14, 1917, 718) proposed as Chaucer's source Dante, Inf. 5.100, "Amor, ch'al cor gentil ratto s'apprende" (Love, which is quickly kindled in the gentle heart), but the immediate context (the sinful passion of Paolo and Francesca) and the fact that Dante is describing love, not pity, make more likely Shannon's suggestion (Ch and the Roman Poets, 178) that the source is Ovid, Trist. 3.5.31–32, "Quo quisque est maior, magis est placabilis irae / Et facile motus mens generosa capit" ("The greater a man, the more his wrath can be appeased; a noble mind is easily capable of kindly impulses"). As in The Knight's Tale and *The Legend of Good Women*, Ovid uses the line with reference to a nobleman who is fully justified in inflicting punishment on an offender. For Chaucer's **pitee**, see Gray, in J. R. R. Tolkien, ed. Salu and Farrell, 1979, 173–203.

1774–81   Loomis (Essays and Studies . . . Carleton Brown, 1940, 147) sees here a suggestion of Chaucer's counsel that King Richard exercise magnanimity and mercy. Cherchi (MP 76, 1978, 46–48) traces the sentiments as a topos from Aen. 6.851–53.

1785–1825   The speech is Chaucer's addition.

1785   benedicite: A mild oath, meaning something like "bless us" or "bless my soul," etc.; from the 2nd pl. imper. of Lat. *benedicere,* to bless. *Benedicite* was usually pronounced with three syllables but could have as few as two *(benste),* or as many as five, as in this case, unique in Chaucer's works.

1799   See Whiting F459; and cf. Walther 918, "Amare et sapere vix deo conreditur [for conceditur]" ("To love and be wise is hardly granted by God") and Tilley L558.

1808   Kan hem . . . thank: For the idiom, cf. I.3064 and Rom 4559.

1810   cokkow or an hare: Some MSS have *cokkow of an hare* (i.e., knows nothing about it). The reference is to the foolishness of the cuckoo (cf. PF 612 and Alexander Neckam, *De naturis rerum,* ed. Wright, 393, lines 865–66 on its inane song), and the proverbial madness of the hare (cf. SumT III.1327 and n., and Whiting H116). The figure is not in the Teseida.

1817   Cf. I.1951; LGW 600; RR 15108–9.

1838   Cf. Tr 5.1433 (with Root's parallels) and MilT

I.3387. Proverbial after Chaucer; see Whiting I72 and Tilley I110.

1850   fifty wykes, fer ne ner: A full year is probably intended (Tes. 5.98 "un anno intero").

1852   at alle rightes: Cf. I.2100. The phrase, of obscure origin, also occurs in the forms *to alle rightes, at hire right,* and *at right(s).*

PART THREE

Part Three of The Knight's Tale, drawn from Tes. 6–7, omits the return of the youths to Athens after their interrupted combat in the grove; the renewal of their old friendship as they prepare for the tournament; the description of many of the champions on their arrival in Athens; the reception of these warriors by Ipolita and Emilia; the high estimation these heroes put on Emilia's beauty and person; and the knighting by Teseo of Palemone and Arcita as a prelude to the tournament.

1884   From his treatment of Boccaccio's amphitheater (Tes. 7.108–10), Chaucer has omitted the marble walls and the number of rows of seats (**degrees,** I.1890, 1891, 2579) specified as 500; he has retained, however, the colossal dimensions of a mile in circumference, and has thus produced accommodations for upwards of 200,000 spectators (Herben, MLN 53, 1938, 595; Magoun, Ch Gazetteer, 25–27). (Cf. the population of London in 1377 estimated by J. C. Russell, Brit. Med. Pop., 1948, 285, as approximately 35,000.) The theater in The Knight's Tale differs from that in Teseida: Chaucer's theater is constructed especially for the tournament; see Kolve, Ch and the Imagery of Narrative, 106–12. As Clerk of the Works, Chaucer was commissioned to have scaffolds constructed for the jousts at Smithfield, May, 1390; see F. J. Furnivall and R. E. G. Kirk, Anal. of Ch's Cant. Pilg., Ch Soc., 2nd ser. 36, 1890, 21–31. As opposed to the "fayre building of stone" for the lists in Cheapside, the often-used wooden Smithfield lists were not a permanent structure.

Chaucer's introduction of the oratories within the amphitheater is analyzed by Pratt, PMLA 52:617–18. Entrances thus situated at the eastern and western ends of the field are shown to conform with customary practice by George Neilson, Trial by Combat, 1891, 185, while the layout of the three oratories is considered a zodiacal chart by North, RES n.s. 20:149–54; and Brooks and Fowler, MAE 39:129–30.

1912   Dyane of chastitee: The chaste Diana. The genitive is used as an adjective (the genitive of description or quality; see Mustanoja, ME Syntax, 80–81). The construction is common in ME, both with the inflected genitive (*any lyves creature,* any living being, I.2395) and with the analytical (as here and in *diluge of pestilence,* pestilential deluge, Scog 14).

1913   doon wroght: Caused (to be made). The causative *don* is ordinarily used with the infinitive, but for parallels to this construction with the past participle see MLT II.171; ClT IV.1098; HF 155. Cf. Mustanoja, ME Syntax, 605–6 and see Language and Versification, p. xl–xli.

1918–66   The description of the Temple of Venus is derived from Tes. 7.51–62, a passage which, along with Tes. 7.63–66, furnished the source of PF 183–294. Chaucer has eliminated, largely through the addition of painted and sculptured images, Boccaccio's fiction of Arcita's personified prayer, delivered in Athens, arriving at Mt. Cithaeron (I.1936–39), where the allegorical, historical, and mythological characters are imagined to be present.

For the tradition of the "children" of a planetary deity, i.e., those engaging in the trades, professions, and activities that come under its influence and patronage, see Seznec, Survival of the Pagan Gods, 70–75; and Kolve, Ch and the Imagery of Narrative, 114–26.

1925–35 Chaucer derives from Boccaccio *Ydelnesse* (who becomes, under the influence of RR 515–82, porter of the house), **Foolhardynesse, Beautee, Youthe, Bauderie, Richesse, Lesynges** and **Flaterye** (both from "Lusinghe"?), and **Jalousye**. Boccaccio's *Arte* may have become Chaucer's **Charmes**; **Hope** and **Bisynesse**, not in Teseida, are probably from RR. Omitted from Chaucer's version are "Memoria," "Leggiardia" (Grace, Loveliness), "Affabilitate," "Pace" (Peace), "Pazienza," "Gentilezza," and "Cortesia."

1929 gooldes: Marigolds (St. Mary's Gold). The yellow color here symbolizes jealousy (cf. RR 21772–73). Cf. the use of red for anger (KnT I.1997), blue for fidelity (SqT V.644 and cf. azure in Anel 330), green for disloyalty (SqT V.646), and white for virtue (SNT VIII.115, Tr 2.1062).

1930 cokkow: A symbol of cuckoldry; see MancT IX.243n.

1936–37 Citheroun: The confusion of the island Cythera and the mountain Cithaeron, Robinson notes, may be partly due to Aen. 10.51 or 86, and is found also in RR 15563 ("Cytheron") and Boccaccio's Ameto ("Citerea").

1940 Cf. Rom 593, ParsT X.714.

1941 For Narcisus (not in Boccaccio's treatment), see RR 1439–1614; Ovid, Met. 3.407–510; and Hoffman, Ovid and the CT, 79–81.

1942 For the folye of . . . Salomon, see WBPro III.35 and n.

1943 Ercules: Hercules is mentioned as a victim of love in Tes. 7.62. Cf. MkT VII.2095–142.

1944 Medea and Circes: Perhaps a reminiscence of RR 14404–6, where Medea and Circe are examples of those who could not hold their loves by magic. Cf. HF 1271n.

1945 Turnus: See Aen. 8.1 and passim.

1946 Cresus: Croesus was not a victim of love; see MkT VII.2727–66. J. A. W. Bennett, ed., Parl. of Foules, 1957, 101n., suggests that Chaucer's inspiration here is Alanus de Insulis, *De planctu naturae,* m.5, where Croesus serves as an example of character traits changing to their opposites, through love's power.

1955–66 With this description, and that of HF 132–39, cf. PF 260–79, which is translated directly from Tes. 7.64–66. Robertson, Pref. to Ch, 124–27, sees Chaucer's version in The Knight's Tale as illustrative of the mythographic tradition of Fulgentius, Mythologies 2.1, tr. Whitbread, 66–67, according to which Venus's nakedness and (thorny) roses symbolize the effects of lust; her doves, lecherousness. Bennett, however (ed. PF, 95–98), identifies her as the "good" and "lawful" Venus, and differentiates her from the Venus of lascivious enticement of the *Parliament of Fowls,* Teseida, and Boccaccio's gloss on Tes. 7.50. (For Venus as the goddess of carnality, see also Robert Hollander, Bocc.'s

Two Venuses, 1977, 158–60.) But Boitani (Ch and Boccaccio, 89–95) sees the deity in both Tes. and KnT as incorporating honorable and voluptuous elements. Meg Twycross, Med. Anadyomene, 1972, 4–11, suggests that Chaucer's source was Bersuire's (Berchorius's) *Ovidius moralizatus* (ed. J. Engels, *De formis figurisque deorum,* Werkmateriaal 3, 1966). Chaucer's substitution of a citole for the traditional conch is explained by Steadman (Spec 34, 1959, 620–24) with reference to the second of the moralizations provided, where Bersuire speaks of the conch as if it were a musical instrument, in making an analogy of Venus to the harlot of Isaiah 23.10, 16. Twycross (Med. Anadyomene, 51–68) presents numerous examples of the astrological Venus playing a stringed instrument and argues that Chaucer need not have been carrying over Bersuire's interpretation. Cf. HF 130n.

1958 Cf. Bo 1.m 7.6–7.

1963–65 Cupid is traditionally represented as blind here and in MerT IV.1598; HF 137–38, 617; Tr 3.1808; for examples see Whiting C634 and for the tradition see Erwin Panofsky, Studies in Iconology, 1939, 95–128.

1967–2050 The account of the Temple of Mars is derived mainly from Tes. 7.29–37, with occasional details taken from Boccaccio's source, Theb. 7. 34–73.

1971–74 Cf. Anel 2–3 and nn.

1979 Boitani (Ch and Boccaccio, 84) notes that these sounds, like those of I.1985–86, are literally impossible to have been represented in a painting. He compares Dante, Purg. 10.28–96. See also HF 1201–3.

1985 veze: An extremely rare word in ME (MED, s.v. *fese;* cf. *bewese*). Glossed "impetus," violent motion, in seven MSS (including Hg and El), probably with reference to Theb. 7.47, "primis salit Impetus amens" (from the outer gate wild Passion leaps). But the rendering in Tes. 7.33, "li l'Impeti dementi parve a lei veder" (mad Impulses coming forth proudly), is similar.

1987 The northren lyght: Not the aurora borealis but rather derived from Theb. 7.45, "adversum Phoebi iubar" (the brightness of the sun opposite), indicating that the temple is oriented toward the north.

1990 adamant: The adamant was thought to be the hardest of stones (Bartholomaeus Anglicus 16.8, tr. Trevisa, 2:833) and later came to be identified with the diamond. It was also thought to have magnetic powers. Cf. PF 148, Rom 1182.

1995–2041 From Tes. 7.33–35 (cf. Theb. 7.48–53), Chaucer derived Ire, Dread, Conflict (**Contek**), Menace, Misfortune (**Meschaunce**), Madness, and Death. He omits "cieco Peccare" (Blind Sin), "ogni Omei" (Every Alas), "Differenza" (Difference), and "Stupore" (Bewilderment). **Conquest** seems to be Chaucer's own addition.

1995 Ther saugh I: This formula, probably derived from the first-person account in Boccaccio ("vedivi") and frequently used here (I.2011, 2017, 2028, 2062, 2067, 2073) is literally inappropriate for a third-person narrator but seems, like *maystow se* (I.1918), a device for achieving vividness of expression rather than a survival of an earlier, more literal version of Boccaccio's story, the "Palamon and Arcite," as Skeat believed.

1999 Skeat (5:79) suggests the possible influence of the description of Fals Semblant, RR 12093–94 (Rom 7417–18).

2005–6 For the association of wrath with suicide, see

Prudentius, *Psychomachia* 1.145–53 (ed. and tr. H. R. Thomson, Loeb) and Sachs, MS 26, 1964, 239–40.

2007   Cf. the killing of Sisera by Jael in Judges 4.17–22.

2012   Chaucer's **Compleint** and **Outhees** (Outcry), which are not in Theb. 7.53, may have been derived from Lactantius (Clogan, SP 61:612).

2017   **shippes hoppesteres:** Dancing ships (*hoppestre,* a female dancer). Chaucer apparently mistook "bellatricesque carinae" (Theb. 7.57: and ships of war) or "le navi bellatrici" (Tes. 7.37) as a form of "ballatrices" or "ballatrici." For the conversion of nouns into adjectives in ME, see Mustanoja, ME Syntax, 642–43. OED, s.v. *dance,* v.3, cites ships dancing on the water from the sixteenth century; on the suffix *-ster* cf. GP I.241–42n.

2022–24   Cf. Theb. 7.58–59: "et vacui currus protritaque curribus ora, paene etiam gemitus." ("And empty chariots and faces ground by chariot wheels, ay, almost even their groans!")

2024–26   The scribal variant *laborer* for **barbour** is accounted for by MacCracken (MLN 28, 1913, 230) by knowledge of Vegetius, *De re militari,* 1.3, where laborers are deemed fit for war, barbers not.

2027–30   As Wise, Infl. of Statius, 53–54, points out, Chaucer's lines are closer to Theb. 7.55–57 than Tes. 7.36; but Clogan (SP 61:612–23) finds an even closer parallel in a gloss to Statius's lines.

2029   Perhaps an allusion to the sword of Damocles (See Cicero, Tusculan Disputations, 5.21), which Chaucer knew from Boethius (3.pr5).

2031–34   Cf. MLT II.190–203, where the glosses refer to Bernardus Silvestris, Megacosmos.

2031–32   The death of Julius Caesar (**Julius**) is related in MkT VII.2695–726; that of **Nero** in MkT VII.2519–50; and that of **Antonius** (Marc Antony) in LGW 624–62.

2041–50   The figure of Mars, in a chariot, accompanied by a wolf, reflects the iconographical tradition of Albricus Philosophus, *De deorum imaginibus* (1681; 2.302; quoted by Skeat, 5:82) with the detail of the wolf devouring a man perhaps suggested by Albricus's etymology "Mavors" (Mars) from "mares vorans" (devouring males). For the iconography, see Seznec, Survival of the Pagan Gods, 190–94.

2045   **Puella** and **Rubeus** are figures in geomancy, or divination by means of lines and figures. One would quickly jot down four rows of dots, then count the dots in each row to determine whether the number of dots is odd or even; the rows would then be represented by one dot for an odd-numbered row and two dots for an even-numbered row. Sixteen possible figures can thus be drawn, each with its name and each with astrological significance, and the resulting figures can then be used to cast a horoscope for predicting the future. One figure, Rubeus, consistently signifies Mars direct (a fortunate aspect). Another, Puella, sometimes indicates Mars retrograde (unfortunate), as in MS Bodley 581, prepared for Richard II in March, 1393 (illustrated in Manly, CT, after p. 552), though sometimes she indicates Venus (Skeat, Acad, 2 March 1889, 150–51). For geomantic procedures, see Lynn Thorndike, Hist. of Magic 2:837–88; and Thérèse Charmasson, Recherches sur une technique divinitoire: La géomancie dans l'Occident médiévale, 1890.

The practice of geomancy was deplored by churchmen such as Thomas Aquinas and Nicholas Oresme (Thorn-

dike, 2:606; 3:417). Twycross (Med. Anadyomene, 50–51) sees a strong likeness to the figures over Mars's head in Oxford MS Bodley 266, the Introductorium of Michael Scot, fol. 115v.

2053–88   Tes. 7.72 says merely that the temple of Diana was clean and adorned with beautiful hangings.

2056–61   **Calistopee:** The story of how **Diane** punished Callisto is related by Ovid, Fasti 2.156–82; Met. 2.409–507; and by Boccaccio, in his gloss to Tes. 7.50 (Callisto herself being mentioned in Tes. 7.61, the source of PF 281–87, where Chaucer calls her *Calyxte*). According to the usual account, Callisto was transformed into Arctus, Ursa Major (she is thus glossed in Hg, El and other MSS) and her son, Arcas, into Boötes, sometimes (incorrectly) identified with Ursa Minor, where is located the **loodesterre** (2059), or Polestar. Chaucer may have known a version of the story similar to that in Boccaccio's De gen. deor., 5.49, where Callisto is identified with Ursa Minor, her son with Ursa Major. But in either account, Boötes is a constellation, rather than, as Chaucer may be implying, a star. Skeat (5:83) took Chaucer's use of the word *sterre* to refer to a constellation, as in Boece 4.m5 and 4.m6, where he follows Boethius in correctly distinguishing Boötes and Ursa Major. Pratt (SP 42:758) and Hoffman, Ovid and CT, 84–85, suggest as a source of these lines in The Knight's Tale the account in Metamorphoses, where Arcas and his mother are referred to as "sidera," "stellas" (stars); but the *loode-sterre* is not mentioned. And although Chaucer elsewhere (Tr 5.232) uses *lode-sterre* in the sense of a guide, his reference here is specific; by the Middle Ages, this was what we now know as alpha, Ursa Minor (see Allen, Star Names, 453–58).

2062–64   **Dane:** Chaucer's source for the legend of Daphne, turned into a laurel tree by her father, the river-deity Peneus, is Ovid, Met. 1.452–567. Chaucer makes no mention of who effected the metamorphosis, however, and although Boccaccio (gloss to Tes. 3.16) believes it was Apollo, he elsewhere (gloss to Tes. 3.25) identifies the agent correctly. Boccaccio does not link Daphne directly with Diana (I.2063), as does Ovid in Met. 1.474–76, 486–87 (Hoffman, Ovid and CT, 86–87) and Froissart (Smith, MLN 66:27).

2063–64   With the Knight's insistence on being correctly understood, cf. the Pardoner's careful distinction between *Samuel* and *Lamuel* in PardT VI.585. The figure is similar to "expeditio" (Geoffrey of Vinsauf, Poetria nova, 1187–1201), in which the writer presents several choices, only to reject all but one; cf. BD 855–58. For the use of **I mene,** see MLT II.261n.

2065   **Atheon:** For the story of Actaeon, the grandson of Cadmus, see Ovid, Met., 3.138–252. For the phraseology, see also Roman de Thèbes, MSS B and C, 9127–30 (ed. Constans, 2:78–79); and Froissart, L'Espinette amoureuse (Smith, MLN 66:28). In the corresponding passage in Tes. 7.79, Emilia herself invokes Actaeon in praising Diana.

2070–72   **Atthalante, Meleagre:** For Atalanta and Meleager, see Ovid, Met. 8.260–444, where the former is referred to as Tegeaea (but cf. Heroides 4.99–100). For the story of the Calydonian boar, see Tr 5.1464–84.

2075   **seet:** An unusual occurrence of the preterite plural vowel *(seeten)* in the 3rd sing. pret., perhaps employed for rhyme.

2085   **Lucyna:** Lucina, a title given to Juno and Diana in their character as goddesses of childbirth through identification or confusion with a goddess of that same name, the daughter of Jupiter and Juno, who was born without her mother feeling pain. Chaucer uses the name to refer to Diana (signifying the moon) in FranT V.1045; Tr 4.1591; and cf. Tr 5.655–56 and n.

2119   Som: With a singular noun, a certain, or one. Cf. 2187, 2761.

2125 See Whiting G494. On the face of it, this proverbial expression seems to contradict the Knight's attitude toward pagan customs elsewhere in the tale (e.g., I.993, 2279, 2911, 2941) where Boitani (Ch and Boccaccio, 193–94) suspects Chaucer's knowledge of Boccaccio's glosses.

2129   Lygurge: Lycurgus of Nemea (Tes. 6.14), the father of the child Opheltes who was killed by a serpent while his nurse, Hypsipyle, saw to the refreshment of Adrastus and his army on their way to serve Polynices at Thebes. Chaucer apparently confuses this Lycurgus with Lycurgus of Thrace, mentioned in Theb. 4.386 and 7.180, and explicitly referred to as king of that region in the Thebaid glosses (Clogan, SP 61:613). Chaucer and Gower make Lycurgus the father of Phyllis, deserted by Theseus's son Demophoon (LGW 2425 and Conf. Aman. 4.738). His description in The Knight's Tale shows similarities to that of Agamemnon (Tes. 6.21–22) and Evander (Tes. 6.35–40). Curry (Ch and Science, 134–37) argues that the details of his physiognomy suggest he is a type of Saturn, who has taken up Palamon's cause.

2133   grifphon: The griffin, a beast with the head of an eagle, wings, and the body of a lion, renowned for its ferocity and said to dwell in Sicia (far Northern Europe); Bartholomaeus Anglicus 18.56, tr. Trevisa, 2:1207. Sir Thomas Browne (Pseudodoxia epidemica [1666], 3.9) says the beast is especially appropriate for generals and heroic commanders.

2140–42 The practice of gilding an animal's claws when its hide was worn as a cloak is referred to in Theb. 6.722–24, 9.685–86. Both Agamemnon (Tes. 6.22) and Evander (Tes. 6.36) are fitted out in this way.

2142–44   for old, for blak: Probably "with, because of age, blackness" (see Language and Versification, p. xxxix), though in ME for may sometimes function as an intensifying prefix (see Mustanoja, ME Syntax, 381–82).

2148   alauntz: The alan (or alaunt), a large hunting dog, was so called because the breed was supposedly introduced into Western Europe by the Alani in the fourth century; see Cook (Trans. Conn. Acad. 21, 1916, 128–40; 23, 1919, 30); Master of Game, ed. William A. and F. Baillie-Grohman, 1919, 116–19, 202–3; and Rowland, Blind Beasts, 155.

2155–86   Emetreus, the kyng of Inde: Not in Boccaccio or Statius. Hinckley (MLN 48, 1933, 148–49) suggests the name may have derived from that of the Graeco-Bactrian prince Demetrius. Bivar (Journ. Royal Asiatic Soc., 1950, 7–13) shows that Justin's tradition of Emetrius's humiliating defeat by a numerically inferior army was recorded in the Middle Ages by Boccaccio, De casibus virorum illustrium, 6.6. Curry (Ch and Science, 131–34) sees his physiognomy as wholly Martian; Brooks and Fowler (MAE 39:132–33) find both Martian and Solar attributes in his description, representative of the choleric personality of the years between twenty and forty. Even the **frakenes** (freckles, 2169), which Cook

(Trans. Conn. Acad. 20:16) saw as a specific reference to the pock-marks of Henry, Earl of Derby, are paralleled in the astrological descriptions of the planet-deities; see Brooks and Fowler, MAE 39:130–34.

2178 Another white eagle appears in Tr 2.926; since they are not generally believed to exist in nature, it has been assumed that Chaucer here uses **egle** generically, as in PF 332–36. But Marco Polo (Travels, ed. Yule, 1871, 3.19) describes white eagles in the kingdom of Mutfili, in India.

2200 The detail is not in Boccaccio; see S. Robertson, JEGP 14:235.

2215   Citherea: Venus, so called from her association with the island Cythera (see 1936–37 above)

2217   hir houre: Each of the twenty-four houres inequal (see 2271 below) was thought to be dominated by one of the planets in the order "in which they sitten in hevene," from the outmost inward—Saturn, Jupiter, Mars, Sun, Venus, Mercury, Moon (see Astr 2.12), with the hour beginning at sunrise assigned to the planet for which the day was named. Thus on Sunday the first hour after sunrise was that of the Sun, the second that of Venus, and the twenty-third (when Palamon arose) was again Venus's hour. The twenty-fourth hour was Mercury's, and the first hour of Monday, when Emelye arose (I.2273), belonged to the moon; the fourth hour of Monday belonged to Mars, and it was then (I.2367) that Arcite went to pray. The Kalendarium of Nicholas of Lynn (176–77) contains a table showing the planetary hours.

2224   Adoon: Adonis; see Ovid, Met. 10.

2236 Venus is traditionally at war with chastity; see Seznec, Surv. of the Pagan Gods, 109. In RR 20785–816, Venus herself leads the attack on the Tower of Shame; in RR 21083–108 Pygmalion prays to Venus when he deserts Chastity and joins Venus's forces.

2243 There is no basis for the idea (Braddy, Arlington Qtly. 2, 1969, 130) that **dye** had a sexual connotation in the fourteenth century. The verb did not acquire that meaning until the sixteenth century.

2271   houre inequal: Hours by the clock are "equal," since each has sixty minutes. When night and day are each divided into their twelve planetary hours, the hours of the day and those of the night are of differing lengths—inequal—save at the equinox. See Astr 2.10–11.

2273–94 Chaucer is here dependent on Tes. 7.71–76, though his attribution to Statius (I.2294) may reflect his knowledge of what was probably Boccaccio's model for the passage, the description of the rites of Tiresias and his daughter Manto in Theb. 4.43–72. Wise (Infl. of Statius, 92–102) also suggests hints from Theb. 9.570–604, Atalanta's morning-time observances in honor of Diana.

2273 An example of compar (Geoffrey of Vinsauf, Poetria nova, 1128–29), clauses or phrases of similar length and structure; and repetitio (Poetria nova, 1098), repeating a word or phrase at the beginning of successive clauses.

2281   Smokynge the temple: It is usually assumed that Chaucer read Fumando il tempio for Boccaccio's "Fu mondo il tempio" (The temple was clean); Bennett (ed. KnT) suggests that Chaucer's line represents an intentional abbreviation of Boccaccio's longer, more detailed account (Tes. 7.71–76), which goes on to describe the sacrifice filling the temple with smoke.

For other uses of the absolute participle, see I.2421 and 2877.

2302   **As keepe:** See Language and Versification, p. xxxix.

2313   The **thre formes** of the goddess (cf. Lat. *triformis dea*) are those of Luna, in the heavens; Diana, on earth; and Proserpina, in the underworld (FranT V.1074–75). See Ovid, Met. 7.94; Horace, Odes 3.22.4; Cicero, De nat. deorum, 3.

2333–37   There is no indecent pun on *queynt(e)* here, pace Bolton, ChR 1, 1967, 224; see Benson, SAC, Proceedings 1, 1984, 23–47, esp. 45–46.

2339–40   The conception of the bleeding twigs (Tes. 7.92) is doubtless derived from the Polydorus episode in Virgil's *Aeneid,* 3.19–76. Cf. the transformation of Phaeton's sisters into trees in Met. 2.325–66, and the forest of suicides in Inf. 13.31–34. The gloss to Tes. 7.91 explains the action of the fires as the rekindling of Palemone's hopes after the accident that befell Arcita.

2367   **nexte houre of Mars folwynge:** The next planetary hour ruled by Mars, the fourth after sunrise on this day (see 2217 above).

2388–90   Boccaccio refers to Mars as "rinchiuso," trapped, by Vulcan. Chaucer could have derived the idea of the **las** from the account in RR, 13835–74 (especially 13860, "prise et laciee," captured and netted); cf. Ovid, Ars am. 2.561–92; or Met., 4.171–89.

2397   Proverbial (Whiting F268); cf. Anel 182; PF 7; Pity 110.

2399   **in the place:** As opposed to the *lystes,* which refer to the entire structure, Dean (N&Q 211, 1966, 90–92) argues that *place* here and elsewhere corresponds to Lat. *platea* and refers to the specific space where the action took place.

2410–17   The vows of Arcite (from Tes. 7.28) have parallels in Theb. 2.732–43; 6.193–200, 607–13; 8.491–94. For the dedication in antiquity of hair and beard, see James G. Frazer, Golden Bough, 3rd ed., 1911, 1:25, 28; Lewis R. Farnell, Greek Hero Cults and Ideas of Immortality, 1921, 64–66.

2432–33   For **murmurynge Ful lowe and dym:** Tes. 7.40.6 has "con dolce romore" (with a pleasing sound); Lowes (MP 15:707–8) suggests that Chaucer's paraphrase echoes "un tacito mormorio" in Filocolo 1.207–8, where Florio and Ascalione visit the temple of Mars.

2437   Proverbial; Whiting B292; F561, 566; cf. ShipT VII.51; CYT VIII.1342; Tr 5.425; and Rom 74–77. See Scattergood, ChR 11, 1977, 211, who notes that in Chaucer the phrase "almost always connotes a trust that turns out to be misplaced."

2443–78   With **pale Saturnus the colde,** cf. *olde colde Saturnus* of Bo 4.m1.12–13. On the hostile *(colde)* aspects of Saturn, see Gower, Conf. Aman. 7.935–46; Bartholomaeus Anglicus 8.12, tr. Trevisa, 1:479; and cf. Astr 2.4.35. But Saturn was often interpreted as signifying wisdom and prudence born of experience and time (see Kean, Ch and Poetry 2:28–33; and Bethurum, in Ch und seine Zeit, 149–61). The planet's malefic aspects were thought to be ameliorated by time in their effects on life and natural functions (Bernardus Silvestris, *Cosmographia,* tr. Wetherbee, 100) or by the influence of Jupiter (Curry, Ch and Science, 127–29; Gaylord, ChR 8, 1974, 171–90 [quoting Ptolemy, *Tetrabiblos* 2.8]). Gower (Vox Clam. 2.5) held that man's conformance with divine law would result in Saturn's becoming beneficial to mankind. The deity is Chaucer's addition.

2447–48   A commonplace; see Whiting E61 and cf. M118.

2449   Proverbial; Whiting O29; cf. Tr 4.1456 (there applied to the wise).

2453   Chaucer knows that Venus is the daughter of Jupiter, not of Saturn; see I.2222. **Doghter** is used here, as in I.2346–48 and PF 447–48, as a term of address to a woman or girl by an older person (Brooks, MLN 49, 1934, 459–61).

2454   Saturn's **cours,** orbit, was the largest known in the Middle Ages.

2456–62   For a similar list of calamities ascribed to Saturn's influence, see Ptolemy, *De judiciis,* 339.

2459   Perhaps a reference to the Peasants' Revolt of 1381 (cf. NPT VII.3393; Tr 4.183–86), although Parr (MLN 69, 1954, 393–94) notes that Albohazen Haly (1485 ed.) and Guido Bonatus (1491 ed.) ascribe to Saturn influence over rebellion and discord.

2462   **leoun:** Liddell quotes a paraphrase of Ptolemy to the effect that Saturn caused destruction by felling buildings while the planet passed through the signs of the quadrupeds (i.e., Leo, Taurus). Skeat quotes Hermetis Aphorismorum Liber, no. 66, on Leo's influence: "Leo works terrible evils with evils; for he increases their badness."

2466   For **Sampsoun** (Samson), see Judges 13–16; cf. MkT VII.2015–94. He is introduced in a similar context of astrological determinism in MLT II.201.

2475   **compleccioun:** See GP I.333 and n.

PART FOUR

Part Four of The Knight's Tale greatly compresses the material of Tes. 7–12, omitting from the tournament such matters as the speeches of Arcita and Palemone to Emilia; a catalogue of the various fates that befell many of the champions in battle; Arcita's encouragement from the sight of Emilia and then from the appearance of Mars; and Emilia's complaint of her own fatal beauty. Chaucer likewise omits Palemone's formal surrender to Emilia and her release of him; Emilia's marriage to Arcita; funeral rites for the fallen champions; Emilia's vow to the dying Arcita always to remain a widow; Arcita's prayer to Mercury, confessing his error in fighting Palemone; the journey of Arcita's spirit after death to the eighth sphere, from which he censures the vanity of mankind; the construction by Palemone of a temple depicting the main scenes of Arcita's life as recounted in the poem; and, finally, the details of the nuptials of Palemone and Emilia.

2491–656   For tournaments involving opposing troops of combatants (*mêlées*), which were perhaps more in vogue in the thirteenth century than in Chaucer's time, see Cowgill (PQ 54:670–77); and Denholm-Young, in Sts in Med Hist . . . Frederick M. Powicke, ed. R. W. Hunt et al., 1948, 240–68. Cowgill (676–77) cites two proposed combats in the time of Edward III of one hundred versus one hundred; neither passed beyond the stage of challenge. For parallels with the 1390 Smithfield tournament, see S. Robertson, JEGP 14:239–40, and Parr, PMLA 60:317–19.

2491   Tuesday, Mars's day, ought to have been propitious to Arcite. It is specifically alluded to as a day of battle in the ME *Partonope of Blois,* EETS e.s. 109, 3067–72; see Garvin, MLN 46, 1931, 453–54.

2499   **testeres:** Head-armor for war horses; see Ackerman, MLN 49, 1934, 397–400.

2519 **he:** That fellow. Sometimes in ME the 3rd pers. sing. pronoun has indefinite force; see also I.2612–19.

2528–29 The comparison of Theseus to a god is original with Chaucer; in Tes. 7.1–2 the duke remains in the theater with the visiting warriors.

2528 **was . . . set:** A passive construction expressing reflexivity; see Mustanoja, ME Syntax, 154–55, and cf. Tr 3.1681; LGW 208.

2549 **sharpe ygrounde spere:** Teseo prohibits the more injurious lances, but allows swords, maces, and two-edged hatchets.

2558 **Gooth forth:** Joseph Strutt, Sports and Pastimes of the People of Engl., 1801, ed. 1969, 119, quoting London, British Library MS Harley 69, notes the traditional call of the heralds to "come forth" (*hors chevaliers*) as a prelude to the tournament; equally traditional is the heralds' call *Do now youre devoir* (I.2598).

2568 **sarge:** Serge, in the Middle Ages referring to a woolen fabric apparently held in low esteem, was used primarily for hangings, covers, etc. Cf. the disparaging reference in Chrétien de Troyes, *Erec et Enide*, 6667–72.

2601–16 Although the Parson disparages alliterating poetry (X.43), Chaucer frequently uses alliterating phrases (cf. *holt and heeth*, GP I.6) and here and in the account of the Battle of Actium in *The Legend of Good Women* (629–653), the only other extended account of a battle in his work, he uses alliteration heavily. See Everett, RES 23, 1947, 201–8; Jacobs, Spec 47, 1972, 695–719; Baum, Ch's Verse, 55–59. Elliott (Ch's English, 103) notes that only I.2605, 2612, and 2615 are regular alliterative lines. Blake (ChR 3, 1969, 163–69) argues that too much has been read into Chaucer's use of alliteration and that he may not have known the alliterative romances. Elliott notes that **shyveren** as a verb (I.2605), **herte-spoon** (I.2606), and **tronchoun** (2615) are not ordinary Chaucerian usages, and that the passage is remarkable for its syntactic inversions. Smith (MLN 51: 320–22) cites parallels in Ipomedon A, ed. E. Kölbing, 1899, 220–21 (cf. introductory note to Thop) and Partonope of Blois, ed. EETS e.s. 109, 11137–39 (neither of which are alliterative poems and both of which may postdate Chaucer).

2613–14 The game of football was well established from at least the time of Edward II; see Magoun, Amer. Hist. Rev. 35, 1929, 33–45; and Strutt, Sports and Pastimes, 93–97, which mentions a 1389 statute forbidding the game.

2621–22 Such pauses for rest and refreshment are not uncommon in depictions of medieval tournaments.

2621 For the causative use of **dooth**, see Language and Versification, p. xl–xli.

2626–28 Chaucer's figure of the tiger bereft of her whelp was probably inspired by Tes. 8.26, which compares Diomed, hearing that Ulisse has been captured, to a lioness that has lost her cub. Hinckley (Notes on Ch, 108) would also compare Met. 13.547–49 which, like Chaucer's image, stresses the young age of the lost whelp.

2626 **Galgopheye:** Probably a distortion of Lat. *Gargaphia*, a valley near Plataea in Boeotia, sacred to Diana, where Actaeon (see I.2065) was slain (Met. 3.156). See Pratt, SP 42:7; and Magoun, Ch Gazetteer, 27.

2630 **Belmarye:** Roughly corresponding to present-day Morocco; cf. GP I.57 and n. Cf. also LGW 1214 where, as Magoun (Ch Gazetteer, 30–31) notes, Chaucer also associates lions with north Africa.

2636 Proverbial; see Whiting T87, and cf. I.3026; LGW 651; and Tr 3.615.

2638–42 Jones, Ch's Knight, 180–81, sees the conditions of Palamon's capture as a violation of the rules of fair play; but cf. S. Robertson, JEGP 14:240. It is, after all, a *mêlée*.

2652–53 These lines are echoed in MilT I.3747–49; see MilT I.3119n.

2663–70 For the source of this scene, unparalleled in Teseida (in which Venus summons the fury with Mars's polite permission), Hinckley (Notes on Ch, 109) suggests Aen. 1.223–96, in which Venus receives consolation from Jupiter for the sufferings of her son Aeneas. The situations and their resolutions are wholly different, however.

2664–66 Bennett (ed. KnT) compares this conceit with Scog 8–12. See also Mars 89.

2680–83 In Tes. 8.124–27, Emilia's change of heart takes place as soon as Palemone is indisposed, even before the tournament is concluded. I.2681–82 are lacking in many MSS, including Hg, El, and Gg; their relatively weak support, and the fact that they interrupt the sentence, suggests to Manly-Rickert (3:434) that they may have been meant to be canceled.

The reading of 2683, and hence the interpretation, is problematic. Perhaps (with Skeat and Robinson), "she was all his delight, as regarded his heart." Bennett (ed., KnT) plausibly suggests that in Tes. 8.124, "l'animo suo sanza dimoro / a lui voltò" (her heart forthwith turned towards him), Chaucer may have understood *volto*, countenance.

2685 The Fury here and in Tes. 9.4 is borrowed from Theb. 6.495–506, where a similar being is sent by Phoebus to frighten Arion, one of the horses drawing Polynices' chariot. Polynices is flung backward, head over heels, and barely survives. Chaucer adds the detail (I.2676–79) that Arcite rides bareheaded, looking up at Emelye, when the accident occurs.

2689 Skeat (5:90) cites from Walsingham's *Historia Anglicana* (2:177) an account of an accident rather similar to Arcite's, which occurred in Cambridge, 1388: ". . . the horse falls, and almost all the interior organs of the rider are torn asunder; nevertheless, he prolongs his life until the morrow."

2710 **That . . . his:** See GP I.44–45n.

2712 **salves:** Sage (Lat. *salvia,* from *salveo,* I am well) was a respected remedy for paralysis, convulsions, and nervous disorders; see Med. Health Handbook, ed. Luisa C. Arano, 1976, no. 36; Teresa McLean, Med. Eng. Gardens, 1980, 177; and cf. Walther 4696, "Why should a man die when sage grows in the garden?"

2731 For **leet** as a causative, see Mustanoja, ME Syntax, 601.

2743–56 According to the physiology developed from Galen, there were three kinds of virtues (otherwise called spirits) that operate most of the body's vital processes: the **natural**, situated in the liver; the *vital*, localized chiefly in the heart; and the **animal**, operating through the brain (Bartholomaeus Anglicus 3.14, tr. Trevisa, 1:103). For the physiological principles involved, see G. Verbeke, L'évolution de la doctrine du pneuma, 1945, esp. 518–28; and Dorothee Metlitzki, Matter of Araby, 64–73.

2747 **veyne-blood:** Drawing off the blood by opening a vein (Cyrurgie of Guy de Chauliac, EETS 265, 534).

ventusynge: Bleeding by means of a cupping glass,

partially evacuated by heating, being locally applied to the skin (Guy de Chauliac, 545).

2749 Corrupted blood must be expelled from the body or it turns into **venym** (Barth. Ang. 4.7, tr. Trevisa 1:151). The **vertu expulsif**, which expels what is grievous (Barth. Ang 3.8, tr. Trevisa, 1:97), is a function of the natural virtue, which "moves the humors of the body" (ibid 3.12, tr. 1:99), but is here controlled by the animal virtue, which governs the motions of breathing (Aiken, PMLA 51, 1936, 361–69) or coughing (Curry, Ch and Science, 138–45). Since Arcite's lungs are infected (I.2752–54) he cannot effect such a purgation, and this impairment of the lungs prevents them from expelling the smoky air thrown off from the blood and tempering the heat of the heart. The venom accordingly spreads through his body; neither emetics nor laxatives avail, and death results. Schweitzer (SAC 3:20–31) considers Arcite's injury and death a parallel to his earlier love-sickness.

2759–60 Proverbial; Whiting N30. Cf. Tr 5.741–42n.

2768 Cf. Tr 4.785–87.

2775 In Tes. 9.83, Arcita and Emilia are wed in a formal ceremony. Chaucer here and in I.3062 is no doubt using **wyf** merely as a term of endearment, as in Tr 3.106, 1296.

2779 A regular formula in both ME and OF poetry; cf. MilT I.3204 and Mel VII.1560. Hammond (Engl. Verse, 471) compares OE *Dream of the Rood* (ed. B. Dickens and A. S. C. Ross, 1966), 123–24, and lists examples from Gower, Machaut, Christine de Pisan, Dante, and Petrarch.

2780 **sweete foo:** For this and similar uses of oxymoron in medieval love poetry, see Tr 1.411 and n.

2789–91 Bennett (ed. KnT) notes that these qualities, representing a considerable expansion of Boccaccio's "gentile e bello e grazioso" (Tes. 10.63), are almost all attributed to the Knight in GP.

2801 **And yet mooreover:** And still further. Chaucer may have seen *ed ancor* in Tes. 10.3 for the MS reading *e acciò*. Robinson compares Bo 2.pr6.76–77 where *And yit moreover* translates "ad haec" and Rom 4493 where it corresponds to "ensurquetot."

2809–15 The narrator's remarks on the destination of Arcite's soul replace the description by Boccaccio (Tes. 11.1–3) of Arcita's journey through the spheres, his disparagement of worldly vanities, and his arrival at the place chosen for him by Mercury the psychopomp, which Chaucer used in his account of the death of Troilus (Tr 5.1807–27). Tatlock and Robinson both held that the passage from Boccaccio was rejected as inappropriate to the spirit of The Knight's Tale. Mary E. Thomas, Med. Skepticism and Ch, 1950, 64–71, 104–7, suggests Chaucer's decision not to incorporate this material indicates his reluctance to decide categorically on a controversial topic of the times, the salvation of the righteous heathen; but this hardly explains his use of the passage in the *Troilus.*

The tone of these lines is lightly derisive. It is characteristic of Chaucer's attempts throughout the story to forestall, even undercut, high pathos, and of the Knight's grim humor; Lounsbury (Sts. in Ch, 2:513–16) goes too far in seeing these lines as evidence of Chaucer's own agnosticism. Boccaccio's Athenian elders, it should be noted, utter blasphemous indictments of the gods (Tes. 11.38, 42). Such anticlimactic moments in the KnT,

often humorous, are discussed by Howard (Idea of CT, 229–34) as a satire of knightly mentality; see also Foster, ChR 3, 1968, 88–94.

2815 **ther:** See Language and Versification, p. xxxix.

2817 For such shrieking and howling over the dead, see John Brand, Observ. on the Pop. Antiq. of Gt. Brit., 1849 ed., repr. 1969, 2:269–72.

2821 Cf. the reactions of Dorigen to the absence of her husband Arveragus in FranT V.814–25.

2837–52 In Tes. 11.9–11, Boccaccio tells how no one could console the Greek heroes but, because Egeo was a wise man who well understood the vicissitudes of the world, he was able to restrain his grief and offer eternal truths, "that one sees deaths, changes, sorrows, and songs, one after the other." No one pays heed, however. Chaucer is able to introduce the more comprehensive, elevated Boethian speech of Theseus (I.2987–3089) by moving some of the platitudinous comments of Teseo's later speech (Tes. 12.6) to Aegeus (I.2843–49) and by emphasizing the consolation that such remarks of Aegeus bring about.

2841 Cf. I.3068; and see Whiting J61. Pratt (JEGP 57, 1958, 416–23) explores this statement as a major theme and organizing principle of the story.

2847–49 The idea of life as a pilgrimage to death may have been suggested by such Biblical passages as Eccles. 7.1, Hebrews 11.13, Psalm 119 (Smith, MLN 65:441–47). Parr, MLN 67, 1952, 330–41, notes the same figure in the ME lyric "Lolla, litil child" (ed. Carleton Brown, Relig. Lyrics of the 14th Cent., 1924, 35–36). Cf. also Truth 20; and see Whiting W663. For the figure of humans as pilgrims in the world, see also Whiting P200; and for I.2849, Whiting D94. For a general treatment of pilgrimage as idea and metaphor, see Ladner, Spec 42, 1967, 233–59.

2868 **they:** For the pleonastic use of the personal pronoun in ME, see Mustanoja, ME Syntax, 137–38.

2874 This detail, not in the Teseida, may reflect folk-customs for the funeral of an unmarried person of either sex, and of an infant; see Brand, Pop. Antiq. 2:282–83.

The line, it should be noted, apparently lacked two syllables in the archetype of all extant texts. Manly-Rickert (3:435) suggest the emendation *putte he* before *hondes.*

2895 **bowe Turkeys:** Cf. RR 913 and Rom 923 and n. This may be the strongest evidence that Chaucer saw some of Boccaccio's glosses, for as Boitani (Ch and Boccaccio, 195–96) shows, Boccaccio glosses Tes. 11.35.7 "farete" as "turcassi" (both meaning quivers). Chaucer, if he had seen the gloss, might have thought that "turcassi" referred to "archi," bows. By Caxton's time, *tarcays* meant quiver (OED s.v. *Tarcays*).

2919–62 This is the longest sentence in Chaucer's poetry; for other extended sentences, see Tr 1.22–51, 3.127–47.

2919–24 For the rhetorical topos of the catalogue of trees, see PF 176–82n. Chaucer's immediate source in The Knight's Tale is probably Tes. 11.22–24, where the forest, unspoilt until the time of Arcite's funeral, functions as a symbol of peace, security, and permanence through natural change.

2921 **holm:** Although *holm* is the medieval word for holly bush (genus *Ilex*), this most probably refers to the holm-oak *(Quercus ilex),* so named because of the resemblance of its dark evergreen foliage to that of the holly.

2925–27 Skeat (5:93) and Wise (Infl. of Statius, 54) saw the influence of Theb. 6.110–13; Clogan (SP 61:614) notes that in glosses on the Thebaid the nymphs and **amadrides** (i.e., Hamadryades) are the living spirits of the trees.

The tone of the passage seems lightly comic, rather than (Neuse, UTQ 31:301) burlesque. Crampton (Condition of Creatures, 90) suggests that Chaucer aims here at a sense of detachment from the generally hyperbolic depiction of the funeral by reminding us that the natural world and its guardians are merely inconvenienced by the death which elsewhere seems so important.

2933–38 Cf. Theb. 6.56–65.

2986 he seyde his wille: Lawler (One and the Many, 87) suggests "spoke as his desire moved him," rather than "pronounced his royal will."

2987–3089 In place of the sentiments that he has transferred from Teseo's speech to that of Aegeus (I.2843–49), Chaucer draws in I.2987–3016, 3035–40 from Bo 2.m8; 4.pr6; and 3.pr10. For the fair chain of divine love, joining together the potentially discordant universe, see specifically Bo 2.m8 and cf. PF 380–81 and n. For the guarantee such ordered change based on love provides (I.3111–16), as well as the necessity of each thing returning to its source in God's love and guidance, see Bo 4.m6. The entire concept is analyzed in detail by Arthur O. Lovejoy, Great Chain of Being, 1950; see also Nature's confession in RR, 16707–81 (especially 16786–87, "la bele chaeine doree / Qui les quatre elemenz enlace").

The examples of the oak, the stone, and the river (I.3017–24) are from Tes. 12.7, with Chaucer adding that of the **grete tounes** (3025), perhaps from Met. 15.287–306. From Boccaccio also is the catalogue of ways in which one can die (I.3031–33; cf. Tes. 12.10), the emphasis on the folly of opposing the fact of death, and the value of a life of fame, though Chaucer wisely suppresses Teseo's disparagement of living to "oscura vecchiezza piena d'infiniti guai" (an obscure old age full of misfortunes).

This important speech has elicited wide critical commentary, with the traditional position, that Theseus's words serve as a fitting and convincing answer to the problems raised in the story, perhaps best articulated by Kean, Ch and Poetry 2:41–48. A trend of recent criticism explores unsatisfactory aspects of Theseus's discourse: Donaldson (902–3) emphasizes Theseus's lack of an explanation of the fates that have befallen Arcite and Palamon, while Theseus insists on the necessity of believing that a benevolent will directs all. Salter (KnT and ClT, 19–36) argues that the activities of the First Mover cannot be reconciled with those of Venus, Mars, and Saturn, and that Chaucer seems here to have posed questions he could not himself answer (cf. her Fourteenth-Century English Poetry, 1983, ch. 6). Herzman (PLL 10, 1974, 346–47) sees the speech as symptomatic of the tale's emphasis on flawed human capability in relation to the divine, yet worthy to be celebrated nonetheless. Cozart (in Med. Epic to the "Epic Theatre" of Brecht, ed. R. Armato and J. Spalek, 1968, 30–36) sees in the failure to reconcile God's justice and the arbitrariness of human destiny the influence of nominalism; so too does Fichte, Anglia 93, 1975, 342–52. Underwood (ELH 26:465–66) notes the absence of a human dimension in the speech, which Neuse (UTQ 31:305–6) believes to end

on a note of practical political realities (I.3042); see also Spearing, KnT, 1966, 76–79; but for a contrary view, cf. Ian Robinson, Ch and the Eng. Trad., 1972, 137–44. Westlund (PQ 43:533–35) and Fifield (ChR 3, 1968, 95–96) compare aspects of the speech to its Boethian source and context, to the disadvantage of Chaucer's treatment, which seems to ignore the Boethian possibility of escaping fortune and destiny in divine contemplation; see also Schweitzer, SAC 3:30–45, and Pearsall, CT, 1985, 124–37. Justman (MLQ 39, 1978, 10) sees the Boethian authority of Theseus's utterance liable to, and compromised by, the stresses of contingency, while Minnis (Ch and Pagan Antiquity, 125–31) and Burlin (Ch Fiction, 105–11) understand the limitations of Theseus's vision as those of a pagan world view.

2994–3015 Cf. Bo 4.pr6.42–47.

2994 quod he: So too in PrT VII.581 does Chaucer call attention to the speaker, even at the expense of dramatic consistency. In I.3075, *quod he,* thus inserted, has the effect of breaking up an extended monologue.

3000–3002 Cf. WBPro III.1–2n.

3005–10 Cf. Bo 3.pr10.25–30.

3011–15 Cf. Bo 4.pr6.149–53.

3025 The ruin of great cities (a detail not found in Tes.) is a conventional topic of consolation; see Cross, Neophil 45, 1961, 68–69.

3030 See Whiting D101.

3031–32 Som: Singular; cf. BD 304n.

3034 Proverbial; Whiting D243.

3035–38 Cf. Bo 4.m6.47–54; 3.m9.41.

3041–42 Chaucer's source is Tes. 12.11, but the phrase is proverbial. It is not recorded in English before Chaucer (Whiting V43) but was common in French (Hassell V49). See Jerome, Adv. Rufinum 3.2 (PL 23:458): "Facis de necessitate virtutem," and cf. SqT V.593 and Tr 4.1586.

3061 Cf. PF 53–54n.; SNPro VIII.71–74n.

3064–65 For the folk-belief that excessive mourning harms the departed, see F. J. Child's notes to "The Unquiet Grave"; Ballads, no. 78 (2:234–36).

3089 Proverbial; cf. Tr 3.1282n.; LGW 162. Robinson notes the underlying notion of the Christian doctrine of grace, in the familiar courtly idea that the lover is dependent on his lady's mercy.

The Miller's Prologue

The continuation of Fragment I from The Miller's Prologue through the Cook's fragment is a consecutive composition clearly written for the place it occupies after The Knight's Tale. There is no external evidence of the date of its composition, and attempts to date it on internal and aesthetic grounds may be challenged. However, the sophisticated adaptation of The Miller's Tale and The Reeve's Tale to the dramatic framework of the *Tales* has inclined many scholars to place them in the later years of Chaucer's work on the *Tales*.

3115 unbokeled is the male: Cf. ParsPro X.26; Rom 3263; and MED s.v. *mal(le)* n (2) 1.c.

The explanatory notes to The Miller's Prologue and Tale were written by Douglas Gray.

3119   Somwhat to quite with the Knyghtes tale: That is, a story that will "repay" or "match" the Knight's tale (for the word order see GP I.791n.). There are certainly some verbal echoes of The Knight's Tale (most obviously in I.3204); Wordsworth, MAE 27, 1958, 21, points out a possible parodic echo of the rhetorical questions found in KnT (I.1454–56, 1870–71, 2652–53) in 3747–49. The Miller's Tale is often taken as an intentional and elaborate parody or burlesque of its predecessor (e.g. Donaldson, 906–7: "The Miller takes the same triangle and transfers it . . . to contemporary Oxford . . . he retains, however, some of the conventions of the courtly romance—though, of course, he does so only to make them ridiculous"). Others see it as a fundamental criticism or parody of the values of The Knight's Tale. However, J. Norton-Smith (Geoffrey Ch, 137–38) argues against these interpretations: by the time he announces his subject (I.3141–43) "all notions of quitting the Knight . . . have fled from the Miller's tipsy mind."

3120   for dronken: See also I.4150. Some editors (e.g., Skeat, Baugh) have taken this as *fordronken,* a past participle with intensive *for-*. This is one of the cases in which it is difficult to determine whether *for* is a preposition or an intensive prefix. See Language and Versification, p. xxxix and cf. 2142–44 above.

3124   Pilates voys: A voice like that of the ranting Pilate in some mystery plays; cf. his entry in the Towneley Scourging, ed. England and Pollard, EETS e.s. 71, 243, and Parker, Spec 25, 1950, 237–44. Ellinwood Spec 26, 1951, 482, argues from Palsgrave's gloss "In a pylates voyce; a haulte voyx" that it is rather an allusion to the falsetto singing of the subdeacon in a Gospel narrative, but "a haulte voyx" can surely mean "in a loud voice." Skeat (5:95) quotes Udall's translation of Erasmus's *Apothegms:* "speaking out of measure loude and high, and altogether in Pilates voice." See Whiting P196. This is the first of a number of references to mystery plays, but the suggestion that Chaucer meant the whole tale to be a parody of the mysteries (Harder, MLQ 17, 1956, 193–98) is unconvincing.

3125   See PardT VI.651–54.

3129   Robyn: Mann, Ch and Estates, 282, cf. "Robyn the rybaudoure" and his "rusty wordes" in Piers Plowman B 6.73. See Rom 6337 and n.

3134   a devel wey: A common oath: "in the devil's name." See Whiting D219; for the variant *a twenty devel way,* see below I.3713, 4257; CYT VIII.782; LGW 2177. For similar expressions, see MED s.v. *devel* 6.

3141   a legende and a lyf: This phrase might suggest a saint's life (cf. SNPro VIII.25–26) and, indeed, a challenge to the Monk, who has been displaced (Coffman, MLN 50, 1935, 311–12), and a playful claim by the Miller that he will be a good substitute. The ensuing tale is clearly not a straightforward "parody" of a saint's legend, but it has perhaps something of the lively "legendary" style of the Golden Legend (which contains comedy of a decidedly uncourtly kind and splendidly fantastic exaggerations, as well as edification) of which de Negri, RomR 43, 1952, 166–89, detects some influence in the Decameron.

3143   Cf. GP I.586 and n.

3144–48   Cf. RvPro I.3860–81. The Reeve is a carpenter.

3152   The idea is proverbial; Whiting M321. Skeat

quotes Mannyng, Handlyng Synne, 1893–94, "Men sey, ther a man ys gelous / That "ther ys a kokewolde at hous." Cf. RR 9129–35.

3154–56   Cf. ProLGW G 273–77 and Deschamps, *Miroir de mariage,* 9097–100.

3161   that I were oon: That is, a cuckold (thought to have had horns; cf. Lydgate, Fall of Princes 2.3363)—and like one of his horned oxen (cf. Leontes's punning on "neat" in Shakespeare's *Winter's Tale* 1.2.123–25).

3164   pryvetee: There is possibly a play on the differing senses: "mysteries" and "privy parts" (Baum, PMLA 71, 1956, 242). Neuss, EIC 24, 1974, 325–40, argues that double-entendre of this kind is sustained throughout the tale (cf. I.3200–3201, 3454, 3493, 3558).

3165   Goddes foyson: A proverbial expression (Whiting G228).

3170–86   There is a strikingly similar apology by Boccaccio at the end of the Decameron ('Conclusione,' 760–64; tr. McWilliam, 829–33), which Chaucer may well have known (see Root, ESt 44, 1912, 1–7); cf. GP I.725–42 and n. W. J. Brown (Univ. of Colorado Studies, Series in Lang. and Lit. 10, 1966, 15–22) argues that The Miller's Prologue constitutes a "double apology" in which "dramatic action between the Miller and the Reeve anticipates every important argument of Chaucer's formal defence" (of realism and ribaldry). Perhaps the fact that Chaucer places his apology at the beginning rather than at the end of these stories serves also to whet the reader's appetite.

3186   Proverbial; see Whiting E18 and cf. HF 822n.

The Miller's Tale

No direct source for this tale is known; its three principal motifs—the man who is made to fear a prophesied second flood, the misdirected kiss, and the branding with a hot iron—are widely distributed in medieval and modern anecdotes, occurring both individually and in combination. Chaucer may have found them combined in a single source, perhaps a French fabliau, or he may have combined them himself from various other versions, written or oral. For discussions of the analogues, see S&A, 106–23 (with copious references and texts of a number of versions) and Benson and Andersson, Lit. Context, 3–77 (with texts and translations of eleven versions).

On the fabliau as a literary form, see Joseph Bédier, Les fabliaux, 1893; Per Nykrog, Les fabliaux, 1957 (which argues strongly against Bédier's theory of bourgeois origins; but cf. C. Muscatine, Genre 9, 1976, 1–19); Jean Rychner, Contribution à l'étude des fabliaux, 1960; Jürgen Beyer, Schwank und Moral, 1969; Muscatine, Ch and the Fr Trad., 1957. A large collection of French fabliaux is Anatole de Courde de Montaiglon and Gaston Raynaud, Recueil général des Fabliaux des XIIIe et XIVe siècles, 1872–90; for a selection see R. C. Johnson and D. R. Owen, Fabliaux, 1966. Chaucer's use of the genre is discussed by Hart in PMLA 23, 1908, 329–74, and in Kittredge Anniversary Studies, 1913, 209–16; Brewer in Comp to Ch Studies, 247–67; Rowland, SN 51, 1979, and others. There are full-length studies by Craik, Comic Tales; Richardson, Blameth Nat Me; and Thomas D. Cooke, OF and Chaucerian Fabliaux, 1978. Most critics find that Chaucer "transformed" the fabliaux, especially in the Miller's and Reeve's tales. McGrady (ChR 12, 1977, 1–16) argues that Chaucer knew the Decameron and constructed the Miller's and Reeve's tales by combining motifs in the manner of the Italian *novellieri.* The treatment of the Miller's and Reeve's tales is so ambitious and individual that some have wondered if they can still be called fabliaux; see Bennett, Ch at Oxford, passim, and Norton-Smith, Geoffrey Ch, 144.

Among the many critical studies of The Miller's Tale may be mentioned some that discuss questions of poetic justice (Olson, MLQ 24, 1963, 227–36; Bloomfield, in Med. Lit. and Folklore Studies, 205–11), characterization (Beichner, in Ch Crit: the CT, ed. Richard Schoeck and Jerome Taylor, 1960, 117–29), and bawdy and double-entendre (Braddy, Geof Ch; Neuss, EIC 24:325–40). Donaldson (in Speaking of Ch, 13–29) discusses the ironic use of such words as *hende* and *derne* (cf. 3199 below); on the ironic use of the language of elegant love in the French fabliaux, see Stillwell, JEGP 54, 1955, 693–99, and cf. Nykrog's chapter on parody, Les Fabliaux, 72–104. V. A. Kolve, Ch and Imagery of Narrative, 158–216, gives an account of the tale in the light of traditional iconography and visual imagery.

3187   at Oxenford: See Bennett (Ch at Oxford, Chapter 2) for the many details of Oxford life in the tale.
3188   gnof: "Churl, boor, lout" (OED compares the Frisian word *gnuffig,* "Ill mannered, coarse"). It is not recorded elsewhere in Middle English and is probably a colloquialism (Davis, Ch Glossary).
3189   a carpenter: Cf. I.3144–48. On Oxford carpenters, see Bennett, Ch at Oxford, 26–31 (figs. 2a and 2b reconstruct John's house [see 36–39]: he is rich enough to afford both a serving-boy or apprentice for himself and a maid for his wife).
3190   poure scoler: Probably formulaic (see RvT I.4002 and n.); if not, then ironic, since Nicholas "is not too poor to have a room to himself" (Bennett, Ch at Oxford, 31). Students in academic halls regularly shared rooms, though the early fifteenth-century regulations of King's College, Cambridge, specified that each scholar "shall have a separate bed" (Rickert, Ch's World, 131). Beds themselves were not in great supply, especially in humbler areas (cf. E. Le Roy Ladurie, Montaillou, tr. Bray, 1978, 39, 46, 145). Nicholas's shelf full of books, psaltery, and astrolabe give us "the fullest inventory of a scholar's belongings before the sixteenth century" (Bennett, Ch at Oxford, 32–34). It has been suggested that some similarities with the description of the Clerk in the General Prologue may indicate the Miller's unsympathetic estimate of a clerk's qualities (Simmonds, N&Q 207, 1962, 446–47). Certainly, astrological prognostications, a favorite hobby of clerks, was likely to provide a focus for a plain man's suspicion of all learning "as having to do with the arcane, the mystifying, the magical" (Bennett, Ch at Oxford, 83). Cf. I.3451–61 and RvT I.4002 and n.
3191–215: Coffman (MLN 67, 1952, 329–31) argues that this is a deliberate burlesque of the Seven Liberal Arts. However, although Nicholas is doing the "course," any irony and satire is surely directed at him, rather than at the Liberal Arts. Cf. Bishop's discussion of The Nun's Priest's Tale, RES n.s. 30, 1979, 257–67.
3193   a certeyn: A definite but unspecified (number);

see MED s.v. *certain* n. 2(a), quoting this, and cf. *certain* adj. 2(a).

conclusiouns: The technical term for propositions or problems. Here the reference is to astrological operations undertaken to obtain answers to horary questions. Possibly the implication of the phrase is that Nicholas's astronomical knowledge is limited—he can work out only a certain limited number of *conclusiouns* (Bennett, Ch at Oxford, 33).
3195   certein houres: Cf. GP I.415–16n.
3199   hende Nicholas: Chaucer plays on the various meanings of the epithet, repeated eleven times: "courteous, gracious," "gentle," "nice," and perhaps "handy, near at hand" (Beichner, MS 14, 1952, 151–53); it was conventional and perhaps had become worn (Donaldson, Speaking of Ch, 17–18). **Nicholas** was the patron saint of clerks; attempts to find further significance in the name and parallels with the saint's legends (Haskell, in Ch at Albany, 105–23, Blechner NM 79, 1978, 367–71) are not convincing.
3200   deerne love: The "secret" love of courtly tradition. Donaldson, Speaking of Ch, 125–27, claims that it was a common phrase in earlier verse (cf. MED s.v. *derne* 5), but, since Chaucer uses it only here and in I.3278 and 3297, suggests that Nicholas's aptitude parodies an ideal already devalued through misuse in the vernacular.
**3204   The line is identical with that used by Arcite in KnT I.2779 (see n.), but it is also found in Mel VII.1560.
3205   herbes swoote: Bennett (Ch at Oxford, 33) quotes Burton's remark that juniper "is in great request with us at Oxford, to sweeten our chambers."
3207   cetewale: Bennett, Ch at Oxford, 8, mentions a payment for "zedewaude" in the early records of Merton College.
3208   Almageste: The word (OF *almageste*) is derived ultimately from Arabic *al-majistī,* where *al-* is the article, and *majistī* represents the Greek μεγίστη "greatest." It was the name given to the great astronomical treatise of the Greek astronomer Ptolemy (Claudius Ptolomaios, c. 100–170), and was then applied loosely to other textbooks of astrology.
3209   astrelabie: See the discussion in Astr. Astrolabes were not cheap: "even the Fellows of Merton had at this time only three between them" (Bennett, Ch at Oxford, 33–34).
3210   augrym stones: Stones or counters with the numerals of algorism (Arabic numerals) and intended for use upon an abacus. On "algorism" (derived from the name of the ninth-century Arab mathematician Al-Khwārizmī), see Karpinsky, MLN 27, 1912, 206–9; and F. A. Yeldham, Story of Reckoning in M.A., 1926, 36–45; cf. BD 435–42 and n.
3213   sautrie: Psaltery, a harp-like instrument, triangular or trapezoidal in shape, held against the breast or on the lap and plucked with quills (Stevens, in Med Ses. for J. A. W. Bennett, ed. P. L. Heyworth, 1981, 297); for illustrations, see Winternitz, pl. 61a; F. W. Galpin, Old Eng. Instruments of Music, 4th ed. rev. Thurston Dart, 1965, 42–48, pls. 11, 12, and 52. The Clerk of the General Prologue would rather have books than a psaltery (GP I.296). Such musical instruments were forbidden to the clergy, though frequently used by the goliardic clerks (Mann, Ch and Estates, 75, citing Helen Waddell, The Wandering Scholars, 1927, app. E.). Though the instrument is sometimes associated with

David and sacred song (Gellrich, JEGP 73, 1974, 178), its playing is clearly associated with thoughts of sex in 3304–6. For varying interpretations of the musical imagery, see Gellrich, as above; Robertson, Pref. to Ch, 127–33; and David, Strumpet Muse, 96–97.

3216   Angelus ad virginem: A song on the Annunciation, beginning "Angelus ad virginem/Subintrans in conclave/Virginis formidinem/Demulcens inquit, 'Ave.'" (The angel, secretly entering her chamber, softly overcoming the virgin's fear, says to her "Hail!") For a full account of this text and its music and English translations, see Stevens, in Med. Studies for J. A. W. Bennett, 207–328. It was originally a song and, though in liturgical use by the fifteenth century, was never completely taken over by liturgical officialdom. It was the collegiate custom to sing an antiphon to the Virgin after compline or the evening collation (Bennett, Ch at Oxford, 31); if the song had already become part of the liturgy, Nicholas's singing gains "additional piquancy and point" (Stevens, 323). The mention of the song has led some critics (Rowland, in Ch and ME Sts., 43–45; Ross, ELN 13, 1976, 256–58) to find an extensive parody of the Annunciation, with Nicholas in the role of the angel Gabriel (cf. Decameron 4.2) and John in the fabliau role attributed to Joseph the carpenter in the plays of "Joseph's trouble"), but this is surely to exaggerate. Perhaps we are meant to pick up some ironic echoes, and certainly the choice of this song has an ironic appropriateness. Nicholas might be expected to respond with particular relish to the song's delicately sub-erotic undertones (cf. Douglas Gray, Themes and Images in the ME Religious Lyric, 1972, 104).

3217   the Kynges Noote: This piece has not been identified. For various attempts (including "Kyng Villzamis Note" in the Complaint of Scotland (1549), the Welsh Ton y Brenhin, "The King's Tune," and a sequence on St. Edmund which begins "Ave rex gentis anglorum," Hail King of the English people), see Collins, Spec 8, 1933, 195–97; Frost, Spec 8, 1933, 526–28; Gellrich, ELN 8, 1971, 249–52; and Olson, Spec 16, 1941, 78n.

3218   To anyone who has had to live in the proximity of students, this line seems clearly ironical.

3219–20   In contrast to the Clerk of the General Prologue (cf. 301–2), Nicholas squanders his friends' or family's money, as do the students in Deschamps, Miroir de mariage, 2081–89 (Bennett, Ch at Oxford, 31).

3224   narwe in cage: Wives and young girls in fabliaux are often kept in a (literal or metaphorical) prison, to which there is usually some unexpected way of entry (see Nykrog, Les fabliaux, 77); cf. Joseph, ChR 5, 1970, 83–96.

3225   old: A senex amans; cf. introductory note to MerT.

3226   lik: Perhaps "like," i.e., "considered himself to be like a cuckold" (Hench, ELN 3, 1965, 88–90, following Skeat), rather than "likely to be."

3227   Catoun: "Dionysius" Cato, the supposed author of a collection of Latin maxims, usually called Disticha de moribus ad filium (but also known as Liber Catonis, Dicta Catonis). It was widely current in the Middle Ages and was used in elementary school (see Curtius, Europ. Lit., 1953, 48–51; Nicholas Orme, Eng. Schools in the M.A., 1973, 102–3). It was frequently translated into the vernaculars. See Brusendorff in Sts. in Eng. Philol. in Hon. of Frederick Klaeber, ed. Kemp Malone and M. B. Rudd, 1929, 320–39. The proverb referred to here does

not form part of the Disticha proper, but similar maxims are found in the Facetus (see C. Schroeder, Der deutsche Facetus, Berlin, 1911 (Palaestra 86), 16), and that of Walter Burley, and in other collections (Disticha diversorum, etc.) associated with Cato (Brusendorff, St. in Ch, 338). For a full study of Chaucer's use of Cato, see Hazelton, Spec 35, 1960, 357–80. (Hazelton suggests that since this tag comes from the Facetus, not Cato, the implication for Chaucer's audience would be that the Miller knows no more of Cato than does the ignorant carpenter he is making fun of, but this rests on the assumption that they would have retained an extraordinarily clear recollection of a text they had studied many years before.)

3231   snare: This word is used of love in Tr 1.507, 663, 5.748; and Rom 1647. When the Merchant uses it of marriage, MerPro IV.1227, it has distinctly misogynistic overtones (it is an image which is frequently and sardonically used in the Quinze joies de mariage (ed. J. Crow, 1969)). There may be a hint of this here.

3233–70   Critics have often praised and analyzed the portraits of Alison and Absolon (cf., e.g., Lowes, Art, of Ch, 176–79). Haselmayer (RES 14, 1938, 310–15) discusses the portraits in the French fabliaux (usually brief and conventionalized) and in the Latin comoedia (where the formal rhetorical description of effictio is used). Chaucer's treatment here is different: the conventional description is translated into a naturalistic "Oxford context" (Muscatine, Ch and the Fr Trad., 229). Cf. also Kiernan, ChR 10, 1975–76, 1–16. See Donaldson's discussion of the language in Speaking of Ch, 22–25. He suggests that perhaps it was from the conventionalized portraits in the fabliaux that Chaucer got the idea of using conventional poetic idiom in ironic contexts. See also Hill, NM 74, 1973, 665–72; and Brewer, MLQ 50, 1955, 267–68, who notes resemblances to "The Fair Maid of Ribbesdale" (Harley Lyrics, No. 7, 37–39).

3234   gent: Possibly "a stale adjective" (Donaldson, Speaking of Ch, 22); cf. 3199 above and Thop VII.715.

3248   pere-jonette: Early-ripe pear. Skeat compares Piers Plowman C 13.221, where "pere-Ionettes" are mentioned as fruit that is sweet and ripens early (and that soon become rotten). It is a succulent and swelling fruit and (not surprisingly) appears elsewhere with erotic suggestions, in the lyric "I have a new garden" (Secular Lyrics, ed. Robbins, No. 21).

3251   latoun: See GP I.699n.

3256   noble: A gold coin worth 6s 8d (see PardT VI.907n.). The principal London mint was in the Tower. Pratt (Tales, 81) notes that Chaucer had charge of the upkeep of the Tower in 1389–91.

3258   The pardoner, in his Prologue (VI.397), compares the movement of his neck and head to a dove sittynge on a berne. The swallow is proverbially swift of flight and associated with summer; its insistent twittering (or cheterynge, which in Tr 2.68–70 is yerne enough to wake Pandarus) is not the most beautiful of bird songs, but it is attractive, and very rural.

3261   bragot: Bragget (Welsh bragawd), a drink made of ale and honey fermented together.

3268   a prymerole, a piggesnye: Both names probably have the implication of "poppet" (cf. popelote I.3254), and both seem to be flower names, although the identification of the flowers is difficult. Prymerole is variously glossed a "primrose," "cowslip," or "daisy"; the evidence from early usage is inconclusive. In a Harley lyric

(No. 3, 13) it is one of the flowers that the beauty of Annot surpasses. If *piggesnye* is a flower it may be the cuckoo-flower (called "pig's eyes" in Essex, EDD) or the hyophthalmos (Hill, NM 74:669–70), known as "swine's eye," "sow's eye"; in some parts of America the name is applied to the trillium (cf. Garrett, Dialect Notes 5, 1923, 245). As a term of endearment it is commonly recorded from the time of Skelton on. The early uses (e.g. in Skelton's "Womanhood wanton ye want"; cf. OED s.v. *pigsney*) suggest that it is a "low," or at least a very familiar term of endearment, suitable no doubt for a *wenche* (cf. MancT IX.212–20). (Later, in the nineteenth century, the EDD records it once in Devon as a term of contempt for an immodest woman.)

3274   Oseneye: There was an abbey of Augustinian canons at Osney, now part of Oxford, but then some distance from the city. Its splendid buildings ("the fabric of the church was more than ordinary excelling" [Wood]) fell into ruin; the site is now occupied by the cemetery near the Oxford railway station. See Cline, HLQ 26, 1963, 135–39; and Bennett, Ch at Oxford, 54–55. See 3659 below.

3276   queynte: A euphemism, the absolute adjective, "elegant, pleasing (thing)," used here for pudendum, with a pun on the obscenity, which was the same in Middle English as in modern speech. For a fourteenth-century illustration (from the Taymouth Hours) of this lecherous and distinctly uncourteous gesture, see Robertson, Pref to Ch, plate 5, and J. B. Trapp, Med. Eng. Lit. (Oxf. Anth. of Eng. Lit., 1973), fig. 39.

3280   Lemman: Cf. 3199 above and MancT IX.204–6n.

3291   Seint Thomas of Kent: St. Thomas Becket (cf. GP I.17 and n.). Cline (HLQ 26:135) suggests that the oath (which is also used twice by the carpenter [I.3425, 3461]) may have a local appropriateness, because the parish church of St. Thomas in Osney.

3312 On the duties of parish clerks, see Bennett, Ch at Oxford, 42–45.

3312–38 The formally organized portrait of Absolon "immerses us in the life of Oxford parishes and Oxford streets"; the name **Absolon**, however, is rare (Bennett, Ch at Oxford, 42). The OT Absolon (2 Sam. 14.26) was a traditional example of male beauty in medieval literature (Beichner, MS 12, 1951, 222–33); the famous rhetorical description of his beauty in Peter of Riga's *Aurora* may have supplied the detail of his golden hair, or Chaucer may have derived it from RR 13870; cf. LGW 249. The name is appropriate to this youth with his luxuriant hair. Cline (HLQ 26:140–45) says that a surpliced clerk should have been tonsured, though the practice seems to have been lax; cf. the Archbishop of Canterbury's complaint quoted in note to GP I.675–79.

3318 His shoes were "windowed," i.e., the uppers were cut and latticed so that they resembled the windows of St. Paul's Cathedral in London. Cf. Rom 842–43 and for illustrations, see Frederick W. Fairholt, Costume in England, 3rd. ed., London, 1885, 2:64–65. Whitbread (N&Q 183, 1942, 158) makes the unconvincing suggestion that such decorations may have suggested those on the shoes of prostitutes, with a pun on *Poules* and "poulaine" (prostitute).

3326 Being a parish clerk was a part-time occupation, and Absolon was also a barber-surgeon. There was a guild of university barbers ("a shave was an expensive luxury, and few university men shaved more than once a week"); see Bennett, Ch at Oxford, 45–46. A barber was often a blood-letter, though clerics were forbidden to draw blood (see note on Physician in GP).

3327 See Bennett (Ch at Oxford, 46) for references to conveyancing and business teaching in Oxford: "Absolon might earn substantial fees for engrossing, and perhaps too for procuring witnesses." See also Richardson, Amer. Hist. Rev. 46, 1941, 259–80; Emden, Bibliog. Register Univ. of Oxford s.v. Thomas Sampson.

3329   scole: Cf. GP I.125. It is not clear that the reference to Oxford dancing, like that to Stratford French, is to be taken satirically. Bennett (Ch at Oxford, 48) suggests that it seems to be "townish" (possibly with the bravura of dancing in the Morris style).

3331   rubible: See the illustrations in F. W. Galpin, Old Eng. Instruments of Music, fig. 14 and plates 15, 16, 43 (cf. 59–63).

3333   giterne: Cf. Piers Plowman B 13.233. For illustrations, see R. S. Loomis, Mirror of Ch's World, 1965, No. 164; and Galpin, fig. 15, plate 7 (cf. 16–19).

3339   jolif: This word is applied to Absolon a number of times, as *hende* is to Nicholas. It is also used of the clerk Jankyn in a song describing a similar scene at church (also, apparently, involving an Alison). See R. L. Greene, Early English Carols, 2nd ed., Oxford, 1977, No. 457.

3341 The scene is set in church, not (Baugh, 294, following Cutts, Scenes and Characters of the M.A., 219) in a perambulation of the parish, since the women come forward to make their offerings (I.3350; cf. GP I.449–51n.). The women may be seated separately, or they may be attending one of the feasts to be kept by women (Bennett, Ch at Oxford, 43–44).

3349   love-longynge: Another idiom of popular verse; cf. 3199 above and Thop VII.772n.

3369   Yis: The emphatic form of assent. The modern *yes* is equivalent to Chaucer's *ye* (Robinson).

3377 Bennett compares the carol cited in 3339 above, where Jankyn "cracks" his notes, and Wyclif's criticism of "smale brekynge" (Sisam, Fourteenth Cent. Verse and Prose, 123). Cf. MerT IV.1850.

3379   wafres: Thin crisp cakes baked in wafer irons over an open flame. They were made "of cheese, eggs, milk, sugar, ginger, and the belly of a pike" (Bennett, Ch at Oxford, 45) and sold by waferwomen, who were often employed in amatory intrigues (cf. PP C 16.199 and PardT VI.479n.).

3382 Some MSS have the marginal gloss "Unde Ovidus: Ictibus agrestis," but the quotation is not from Ovid. One glossator finishes the line "Ictibus agrestem civilem munere vince colloquio nobilem commoditate loci" (M-R 3, 490), though this may have been suggested by Chaucer's line. Hoffman, N&Q 209, 1964, 49–50, suggests the phrase may be due to a misreading of Ovid, Fasti 2.193, 1–2: "Idibus agrestis fumant altaria Fauni" (On the Ides, smoke issues from the altars of Faunus).

3384   Herodes: The part of Herod in a mystery play, the role of the blustering tyrant (Bennett, Ch at Oxford, 48–51). In a Coventry play (Two Coventry Corpus Christi Plays, ed. H. Craig, EETS e.s. 87, 1957, 27) a rubric says "here Erode ragis in the pagond and in the strete also" (cf. "out-herods Herod," Hamlet 3.2.15). The **scaffold hye** is probably the upper story of a pageant wagon (Bennett) rather than a simple outdoor stage (Baugh, Fisher). The *Ludus Coventriae* (ed. K. S. Block, EETS 120, 283) has "herowdys scafald xal un-close shewynge Herowdes in astat," i.e., seated on a throne above the crowd. There were enough guilds in Oxford to stage a complete cycle of mystery plays, but no text has survived.

3387   blowe the bukkes horn: "Go whistle." Cf. the phrase *Pipe in an ivy lef* (Tr 5.1433) and see KnT I.1838 and n.

3389 Cf. GP I.706n.

3392–93 Proverbial; see Whiting S395. Cf. the modern "out of sight, out of mind."

3396   stood in his light: Also proverbial; see Whiting L264.

3404   sely: Reed (PQ 41, 1962, 768) notes that this adjective is used of the carpenter five times (cf. *hende* and *joly*), and that Chaucer plays ironically on its different senses, such as "happy, fortunate, blessed," "innocent," "simple, hapless," "pitiable, unfortunate." Cooper (JEGP 79, 1980, 1–12) discusses the semantic range of the word in Chaucer's poetry, and the way he uses polysemy to create ironic effects.

3428 An expansion of the common proverbial type "here today, gone tomorrow" (Whiting T351). Cf. Norton-Smith, Geoffrey Ch, 139.

3430   That . . . hym: "Whom." Cf. GP I.44–45n.

3449   Seinte Frydeswyde: The virgin saint (d. eighth cent.) is appropriately invoked, since she was noted for her healing powers, especially the casting out of devils (Cline, MLN 60, 1945, 480–81; Leyland, N&Q 219, 1974, 126–27). There was a monastery of St. Frideswide in Oxford; its church became the present cathedral; see Stenton, Oxoniensia 1, 1936, 103–12; and E. F. Jacob, St. Frideswide the Patron Saint of Oxford, 1953.

3451–54 For the popular belief that those who follow the craft of astronomy are trying to pry into **Goddes pryvetee**, see Dives and Pauper (EETS 275, 117 and 140), where Acts 1.7 and Isaiah 14.16 are quoted; cf. Whiting G198.

3451   astromye: The form is sometimes taken as a malapropism and an indication of the carpenter's speech (cf. *Nowelis flood* I.3818). However, the form *astromien* (found, for instance, in *Kyng Alisaunder*) is a genuine one, and *astromye* may have been a genuine variant form. See Tolkien, TPS, 1934, 3n.; Blake, N&Q 224, 1979, 110–11.

3457–61 A familiar fable, related by Plato of Thales in the *Theaetetus,* 174A; also in Diogenes Laertius, 1.34. Cf. Aesop's Fables, ed. E. Chambry, 1925, 1960, No. 65; and Cento Novelle Antiche, no. 38, both telling it of an astrologer. Bennett (Ch at Oxford, 53) suggests that Chaucer has substituted a "marl-pit" for the well into which the Greek philosopher fell, because he has in mind the "Campus Pits" of marl or clay at the east end of Milham Ford, beside the Cherwell (where the present St. Hilda's College stands).

3478   thenk on Cristes passioun: The recalling of Christ's passion is a traditional remedy against despair (I.3474). (It is used thus in the Ars Moriendi or Craft of Dying, ed. F. M. Comper, London, 1917, 12–14.) John quickly slips into the practices of popular religion by making the sign of the cross against elves and wightes. The sign of the cross was traditionally of great spiritual efficacy (cf. Ancrene Wisse, EETS 249, 28), and in more humble and more popular belief it was regarded as having magical power.

3480–86   nyght-spel: A magic charm against the demons of the night. (The carpenter makes the boundaries of the house secure by saying it at the four sides and at the threshold.) The **white** *pater-noster* is a traditional and ubiquitous charm, which survives into modern times (e.g., in the nursery-rhyme "Matthew, Mark, Luke, and John / Bless the bed that I lie on"—still implying a protective "marking" of the corners; see I. and P. Opie, Oxf. Dict. of Nursery Rhymes, 1951, 303–5 (with full references). On the charm, see Thoms, Folklore Record 1, 1878, 145–54; Carrington, ibid. 2, 1879, 127–34; Barb, Folklore 61, 1950, 15–30 (esp. 18); on ME charms in general, Gray, in Ch and ME Sts., 56–71. It is *white* because it is not in any way connected with the black magic of the devil (cf. ParsT X.508). Like other charms, it is rough in meter and not always clear in sense (for some attempts at scribal improvement, see Manly and Rickert 3:142). **Seinte Benedight** is presumably St. Benedict (d. c. 547), the patriarch of Western monks, to whom a spectacular series of miracles is attributed in the *Dialogues* of St. Gregory the Great. A Latin charm involving both the saint and the cross—"Vade retro Satana; nunquam suade mihi vana" (Englished as "Avaunt foul fiend, vain are thy tempting charms; / The cross shall ward me from thy poysonous harms" in The Effects and Virtues of the Crosse or Medal of the Great Patriarch St. Benedict, 1660) is often engraved on St. Benedict medals and crosses (it is popular from the seventeenth century, but seems to go back to the Middle Ages). (See Bächtold-Stäubli, s.v. *Benediktussegen,* with full references); P. Guéranger, The Medal or Cross of St. Benedict, tr. anon., London, 1880). It is also possible that he has been manufactured here out of the word *benedight* ("blessed"; see OED).

The nearest equivalent in ME to this night-spell is probably that spoken by the third shepherd in the Towneley Prima Pastorum (EETS e.s. 71, 109): "for ferde we be fryght / a crosse lett vs kest, / Cryst crosse, benedyght / eest and west, / ffor drede. / Ihesus onazorus, / Crucyefixus / Morcus, Andreus, / God be oure spede!"

3485   For nyghtes verye: The meaning is uncertain. The best suggestion is "against the evil spirits of the night" (Skeat and others); possibly the mysterious *verye* is a derivative or a corruption of OE *we(ar)g* "evil spirit." It would not be surprising to find an old word preserved in a charm. Donaldson (MLN 69, 1959, 310–13) suggests an emendation to another old form, *nerye* "save." Paleographically, this change is an easy one, but the resulting syntax seems awkward.

3486   Seinte Petres soster: St. Peter's brother appears in a White Paternoster quoted by J. White, The Way to the True Church, 1610, c. 2 (cf. N&Q 8, 1853, 612–13). St. Peter's sister appears in a charm quoted by Grosseteste: "Grene pater noster / Petres leve soster" (Wenzel, N&Q 215, 1970, 449–50). Skeat notes (5:106) that St. Peter's daughter, St. Petronilla, was invoked for healing of a quartain ague.

3512   by hym that harwed helle: The story of the Harrowing of Hell (from the apocryhyal Gospel of Nicodemus, ed. H. C. Kim, Toronto, 1973) was immensely popular in the Middle Ages (see R. P. Wülker, Das Evangelium Nicodemi in der abendländischen

Literatur, Paderborn, 1872; Craigie, in An English Miscellany Presented to F. J. Furnivall, Oxford, 1901, 52–61; cf. Piers Plowman B, 18). John would have been familiar with it from wall-paintings and from mystery-plays.

3515 **in the moone:** On prognostication by the moon, or "the days of the moon," see Farnham, SP 20, 1923, 70–82. Sometimes recourse was had to astronomical calculations of the position of the moon; sometimes the mere day of the moon was considered as being favorable or unfavorable for an undertaking. Cf. Tr 2.74. On medieval moon-books or *lunaria,* see Thorndike, Hist. of Magic 1:680–82. Hirsh (ELN 13, 1975, 86–90) argues that the tale's emphasis on Monday (I.3430, 3516, 3633, 3659) is significant. Nicholas's choice of the day is partly determined by his interest in the moon; Monday is associated by etymology with the moon (the ruling planet of that day) and shares its reputation for instability; Monday is also sometimes associated with the unlucky "Egyptian" or "dismal" days (see BD 1206–7 and n.). On the astrological background to the tale, see O'Connor, Spec 31, 1956, 120–25; cf. Wood, Ch and the Stars, 170–72. There was a tradition that Noah was a skillful astrologer who was aware of the approaching deluge through his study of the stars as well as through divine revelation. For Noah's esoteric knowledge, see also Utley, Spec 16, 1941, 450.

3521 **hir lyf:** See Language and Versification, p. xxxv.

3530 See Ecclus. 32.24. ("My son, do nothing without counsel, and you will not repent later.") It is a very common proverb; see Whiting C470. The form and attribution to Solomon here and in MerT IV.1483–86 are due to Albertanus of Brescia, *Lib. consolationis et consilii,* translated in Mel VII.1003. See Bühler, Spec 24, 1949, 410–12.

3538–43 This is a clear reference to the comic scenes in the mystery plays in which Noah's wife refuses to enter the ark (**Noe with his felaweshipe,** Noah and his sons). For an illustration (from a window in Malvern Priory), see M. D. Anderson, Drama and Imagery in Eng. Med. Churches, 1963, pl. 14a (a ladder, like those which are to figure in the tale, can be seen clearly in the background). See also Sir Israel Gollancz, The Caedmon MS, 1927, xlv, 66. There are delicate hints of parallels in matters both small and great: Noah was frequently pictured as a carpenter (see Olson, SP 59, 1962, 4n.) (and the play about him was sometimes performed by the shipwrights), and the Flood was regarded as an apocalyptic event, a typological anticipation of the end of the world and the Last Judgment. It may be noted that Noah's Flood took place (Gen. 7:11) on the seventeenth day of the second month (17 April, March being the first month; cf. NPT VII.3187–88), the date traditionally assigned to the first day of the Canterbury pilgrimage.

3548 **kymelyn:** On the word, see Bennett, Ch at Oxford, 3–5: occurrences of the term in early Oxford accounts suggest that kimlins were trays or troughs used in college halls, kitchens, brewhouses, etc.

3590–91 An allusion to the traditional teaching that there was no copulation on the ark. Bennett (Ch at Oxford, 37) compares Mirk, *Festial,* EETS e.s. 96, 72. The idea is an old one, and widespread (see Utley, Germanic Rev. 16, 1941, 242–44).

3598 Proverbial; cf. "a word to the wise" and Whiting W399.

3611–13 **affeccioun . . . impressioun:** On the idea of perception through the *affeccioun,* see Bo 5.m4.6–19 and cf. Tr 1.295–98 and n., MerT IV.1577–87n.

3624 **His owene hand:** For the idiom (which occurs in a number of late ME works), see Mustanoja, ME Syntax, 106. The construction is probably a descendant of the OE inflectional instrumental, but the notion of instrumentality has become rather faint.

3628 **jubbe:** "A fairly large container for liquor"; so MED, which cites the accounts for the 1392 expedition of the Earl of Derby (later Henry IV): "et pro uno pare jobbes de iiij galonibus."

3637 **furlong way:** A measure of time, 2½ minutes, one eighth of a *mile wey* (twenty minutes); cf. Astr 1.16 and Isaacs, N&Q, 8, 1961, 328–29.

3645 **corfew-tyme:** At dusk, probably 8 P.M. (fires were then covered for the night). By being out after curfew, Absolon lays himself open to suspicion (Bennett, Ch at Oxford, 40–41).

3655 **laudes:** The second of the seven canonical hours (services), following matins and preceding prime; sometime, then, before day had broken (I.3731).

3659 **Oseneye:** Probably Osney Mead or Bulstake Mead, which was held by the Abbey (Bennett, Ch at Oxford, 54). See 3274 above.

3682–83 Absolon's interpretation follows popular tradition: divination from involuntary itching, burning ears, etc., was a widespread practice. See Beibl, Anglia 27, 1916, 61–62; C. S. Burne, Shropshire Folklore, London, 1883, 269–70; cf. W. Henderson, Notes on the Folklore of the Northern Counties, London, 1879, 112–13. To itch, then as now, could also mean "to have an irritating desire or uneasy craving provoking to action" (OED s.v. *itch* v.1.2).

3690 **greyn:** Grain of Paradise, or cardamom seed (a sweetener of the breath).

3692 **trewe-love:** A four-leafed sprig of herb paris (*Paris quadrifolia*) in the shape of a fourfold true-love knot.

3698–707 Kaske (SP 59, 1962, 479–500, esp. 481–83) notices in Absolon's speech some parodic echoes of the Song of Songs (e.g., **hony-comb, bryd:** "favus distillans labia tua, sponsa," thy lips, O my spouse, drop as the honeycomb, 4.11; **my sweete cynamome:** "cinnamomum," 4.14). Not all of the parallels he adduces are convincing, however, and it is far from certain that Chaucer had the Song of Songs in mind in the earlier descriptions of Alison and Absolon. Cf. the more obvious parody in MerT IV.2138–45.

3703 Cf. Rom 2480.

3709 **'com pa me':** *Pa* or *ba* is a rarely recorded word but one that was perhaps a familiar affectionate term for "kiss," possibly originating in the nursery (OED s.v. *ba*) or as a playful adaptation of Fr. *baiser* (MED s.v. *ba*). It is probably used mockingly here (perhaps echoing Absolon's more childish remarks, e.g. I.3704); cf. WBPro III.433.

3713 Cf. I.3134 and n.

3718–22 Beidler (ChR 12, 1977, 90–102) discusses the differences between the Flemish version and Chaucer's of this episode. Chaucer is unique among early tellers of the story in having the woman execute the trick; he also intensifies the affront to Absolon by stressing his sensitivity to smells and sounds (I.3337–38). The episode, and particularly the roles of Gervase and of the fart, has been the subject of some absurdly earnest symbolic and moralizing criticism; the curious may find the references in Beidler's notes.

3723   This Absolon: This use of *this* (and the plural *thise,* RvT I.4100), "mainly a feature of vivid, colloquial and often chatty style, is particularly common in Chaucer's and Gower's works. It is current even today in lively but less educated speech" (Mustanoja, ME Syntax, 174). See Language and Versification, p. xxxviii.

3725   Cf. RR 3403–8 (Rom 3674–76); Ovid, Ars Am. 1.669.

3726   The whole line may be meant to sound hackneyed. See Donaldson, Speaking of Ch, 26–27 (**bryd** is a trite form of endearment). For **oore,** cf. "ledy, thyn ore," Harley Lyrics, No. 32, 16–17, and the refrain of a love song quoted by Giraldus Cambrensis (Rolls Series, 2.120).

3728   com of: The phrase is frequent in Chaucer (e.g., RvT I.4074; FrT III.1602; PF 494), though not attested before him; cf. MED s.v. *comen* 1b.(c).

3742   a berd: Possibly (Baugh) also with a play on the sense of *joke* (in the phrase make a man's beard, i.e., "delude him, hoodwink him," which is used in WBPro III.361, and—in what seems to be a deliberate echo of this line—in RvT I.4096).

3747–48   See 3119 above.

3755–58   This is a more effective and more instantaneous remedy for the *loveris maladye / Of Hereos* (KnT I.1374–75) than anything suggested in the medical books or in Ovid's *Remedium amoris* (see KnT I.1355–76 and n.).

3756   kers: On these proverbial phrases, see GP I.177n.

3761–63   An entertaining alliterative poem (ed. Sisam, Fourteenth Cent. Verse and Prose, 169–70) complains about the noise blacksmiths make at night; see Salter, Lit. and Hist. 5, 1979, 194–215. Kuhl (MLN 29, 1914, 156) draws attention to a reference in 1394 to the nuisance, noise, and alarm experienced by the neighbors of blacksmiths in London. Perhaps Gervase is preparing a plough or ploughs for use in the morning, which would suggest that his smithy is near the edge of town, perhaps in Smithgate, "a small gate closing a foot-passage near the north end of Catte Street" (Bennett, Ch at Oxford, 41–42).

3761   daun: The title was used very loosely, though only here is it applied to a lower class character. (It is used for the fox *daun Russell* in NPT VII.3334.) See KnT I.1379n.

3770   upon the viritoot: The origin and meaning of this (presumably colloquial) phrase is obscure. The best suggestion seems to be (Skeat 5:110–11) "astir." The first element may represent OF *virer* (Skeat notes Cotgrave's *virevoulte,* "a veere, whirle a round, gambol, friske or turne"). Spitzer, Language 26, 1950, 389, suggests that Chaucer's word is connected with *virevoulte,* and means "on the prowl," but the rhyme is on *o* and not on *u:* (this would also tell against McDonald's suggestion, Neophil 48, 1964, 237, that Gervase innocently keeps Absolon's anger on the boil because the word may have reminded him of the word *toute* in I.3812, 3853). Gillmeister (Poetica 4, 1976) suggests that it may represent OF *viretost,* "early riser, early rising." Another suggestion, that the second element may represent OE *totian,* ME *tote(n),* "to peer," or "to look inquisitively, to pry" (cf. Gower, Conf. Aman. 3.29, "he pireth And

toteth on hire wommanhiede") might be added, but without much conviction.

3771   Seinte Note: Apparently St. Neot, a ninth-century saint. Why Gervase swears by this obscure saint is not clear, though there is a town, St. Neot's, near Cambridge. It is just possible that Chaucer might have heard of the tradition (Cline HLQ 26, 1962–63, 131–35) associating St. Neot with King Alfred's legendary foundation of Oxford University. It has been suggested that there may be some ironical reference to the saint's practice of rising in the dead of night to pray (McDonald, Neophil 48:235–37; Richards ChR 9, 1975, 212–15), but this would imply that his legends were more widely known than the evidence indicates.

3774   He hadde moore tow on his distaf: A proverbial expression; see Whiting T432. There may be a more specific allusion here: Revard (ELN 17, 1980, 168–70) points out evidence (Liber Albus, 1:459) that in London the carrying of a distaff with a tow in it was statutory punishment for a person guilty of crimes of sex and violence (those attainted as a *tensurere* or *tensuresse,* [?] "wrangler, brawler," were to be led to the pillory carrying a distaff with a tow, accompanied by minstrels, presumably to make a parade of their shame). Cf. Robertson, Ch's London, 103.

3782   Cristes foo: Probably "the devil!" rather than an intentional substitution for *foot* (as Robinson held) to avoid open profanity (as in *cokkes bones,* MancPro IX.9).

3818   Nowelis: This seems to be a malapropism, implying a confusion of "Noe" and "Nowel," Christmas. However, "Noels" for "Noe" does appear in Froissart's *Chroniques,* ed. George T. Diller, TLF, 1972, 37.

3821–22   Cf. the Fr. "ne trouva point de pain a vendre" (Tyrwhitt, quoted by Skeat), which appears in the fabliau Aloul, 591–92 (Barbazan, Fabliaux, 1808, 3.344).

3822–23   That is, John falls from the roof of the hall to the floor (*celle* [=*selle*], "flooring"). The tubs hang from the *balkes* (I.3626), beams of squared timber, which serve as tie beams.

3850–54   Fabliaux often have a neatly pointed ending.

The Reeve's Prologue

3857   Proverbial; see Whiting H230 and Walther 26216, "Quot homines, tot sententiae" (as many opinions as men). Chaucer may have derived the phrase, which he uses also at MLT II.211; MerT IV.1469; SqT V.203, from RR 10684: "Diverse diverses chose distrent" (Fansler, Ch and RR, 121).

3860   Osewold: The name, Manly says (CT, 560) was rare in fourteenth-century Norfolk, "though common enough farther north." St. Oswald (d. 642) was a Northumbrian saint; cf. David Knowles, Monastic Orders in Eng., 1940, 55.

3864   So theek: The suffixed *ik,* "I" (cf. I.3867), is a Northern and East Midland form, appropriate to a Norfolk man. Although Chaucer took great care with the dialect of the students in the tale (see 4022 below), he does not consistently represent the speech of the Reeve in his own person; only a few indications of pronuncia-

The explanatory notes to The Reeve's Prologue and Tale were written by Douglas Gray.

tion (e.g., *lemes, abegge*) suggest East Anglia (Davis, RES 27, 1976, 336–37).

3865 With bleryng of . . . ye: A common expression; cf. I.4049 below; CYT VIII.730; MancT IX.252; Rom 3912; and Whiting E217.

3868 Gras time is "the time when a horse feeds himself in the field" (Skeat 5:113). Bennett (Ch at Oxford, 87) notes that the Reeve, whose business keeps him constantly in the saddle, talks "in 'horsly' terms"; cf. I.3888.

3873 mullok: Bennett (Ch at Oxford, 90) notes this is "an earthy dialect word." It is recorded in Middle English only here and in CYT VIII.938. It emphasizes the strong impression of ripeness passing into rottenness that is given by many words in this speech.

3876 Cf. Luke 7.32.

3877 Possibly an echo of 2 Cor. 12.7 ("stimulus carnis mea").

3878 Exactly this image is put in the mouth of the old man in the Decameron, Introduction to the Fourth Day (see McWilliam, 329). It may have been proverbial—it certainly was after Chaucer's time: see Whiting H240.

3882 See Whiting F185. The idea appears in Alanus de Insulis, *Liber parabolarum*, cap.1, 61–62, PL 210: 582.

3883–85 There is a general similarity with Jean de Meun, *Testament*, 1733–36. With 3885, cf. Tr 4.1369.

3888 Proverbial; see Whiting C377. Cf. WBPro III.602. The phrase is discussed by Whiting in Med Stud. in Hon. of J. D. M. Ford, ed. Urban T. Holmes and A. J. Denomy, 1948, 321–31. It is not recorded in English before Chaucer, who may have found it in Deschamps, Balades 865, 1282 (Œuvres 5:43–44, 7:24).

3890–97 On the imagery of the wine-cask, see MacLaine, MAE 31, 1962, 129–31. In a medieval cask (tonne), the tappe was a tapered stick used to plug the tap-hole, located on the head of the cask somewhere close to the chymbe (the rim, formed by the ends of staves protruding beyond the head). A new cask would require the boring of a tap-hole for the insertion of the tap; there is therefore probably a pun on the word bore, "born" (Pratt, recorded in PMLA 73, 167). There is possibly (Pratt, ibid.) another word play in 3895–96 on rynge and *chymbe,* and probably on tonge (with the "tongue" of a bell); MacLaine explains that when the cask is full "the stream of wine flows silently and strongly, but at the end it splashes on the rim, just like the foolish tongue of a garrulous old man." There may also be a suggestion of the "ringing sound caused by the dropping of the liquid on the rim," and perhaps the red stream emerging from the tap-hole could suggest the human tongue and mouth.

3904 Cf. Phaedrus, Fables 1.14: "ex sutore medicus."

3906 half-wey pryme: Usually taken to mean about 7:30 A.M. Block (Spec 32, 1957, 826–33), argues that it is 6:30 A.M. (according to monastic time).

3907 Grenewych: Greenwich, about half a mile past Deptford. Chaucer was probably then living there.

3911 Cf. GP I.586.

3912 In the Ellesmere MS this is glossed by the Latin equivalent, "vim vi repellere" (given in its full form in other MSS, "licitum est vim vi repellere"), which is a well-known legal maxim (to be found in the *Digesta* of Justinian, and many other sources; see Montgomery, PQ 10, 1931, 404–5; Myers, MLN 49, 1934, 222–26).

3919 stalke: Cf. Matt. 7.3 (Lat. *festucam*). It was proverbial; see Whiting M710.

The Reeve's Tale

The Reeve's Tale is based on a traditional fabliau story (the "cradle-trick" is especially wide-spread; see Aarne-Thompson, No. 1363). No precise source has been found, but there are some close analogues, six of them early (five of these are printed with translations and discussion in Benson and Andersson, Lit. Context, 79–201; two French texts of *Le meunier et les ii clers* are printed in S&A 124–47). Of these, two French fabliaux, *Le meunier et les ii clers,* and, to a lesser extent, *De Gombert et les ii clers* by Jean Bodel (d. 1210), are especially close to Chaucer. There are some close similarities also with Boccaccio's *Decameron,* Ninth Day, 6 (see McGrady ChR 12, 1977, 9–10). The analogues account for every part of the plot, but none for Chaucer's masterful characterization and skillful union of plot and character. For additional discussion of the analogues and Chaucer's treatment of the story, see Hart, PMLA 23, 1908, 1–44; Dempster, JEGP 29, 1930, 473–88; Burbridge, AnM 12, 1971, 30–36; G. Olson, MLR 64, 1969, 721–25; and Goodall, Parergon 27, 1980, 13–16. Kirby, in Chaucer and ME Studies, 381–83, draws attention to a parallel in a modern Appalachian ribald story. On fabliaux in general, see the introductory note to The Miller's Tale. Among a number of critical studies, see P. A. Olson, SP 59, 1962, 1–17; Copland, MAE 31, 1962, 14–32; G. Olson, MLQ 35, 1974, 219–30; Lancashire, ChR 6, 1972, 159–70 (on the sexual innuendos, especially of milling); Bennett, Ch at Oxford, 19–20, discusses the echoes and parallels that bind it closely to the MilT, which it is evidently intended to "quit" (I.4324) and (esp. in ch. 4) the local Cambridgeshire references and the use to which they are put. There is much useful critical comment in the edition of RvPro and RvT with CkPro and CkT, by A. C. and J. E. Spearing, 1979; and in Kolve, Ch and Imagery of Narrative, 217–56.

3921–23 The topographical details are accurate. At Trumpyngtoun (Trumpington), three miles from Cambridge (Cantebrigge), the Rhee river becomes the Cam; it is "something more than a brook" but here is "joined by the Bourn, which has always been called a brook" (Bennett, Ch at Oxford, 110–14). The bridge was perhaps higher up than the present bridge (built in 1790). There was a mill at the place now called Byron's Pool, but previously Old Mills (Bennett, 111–13, and App. B). Cf. 4065n. Bennett (109) notes that Trumpington was then a small village that probably had no inn (hence the clerks' need for lodging) but only an ale-house or two (thus the Miller can send Malin to buy ale). Chaucer may have had some local knowledge through Sir Roger de Trumpington, who was in the King's household (Manly, New Light, 97–101; Bennett, 110–11); he was responsible for the last of Edward III's annuities to Phillipa Chaucer; John of Gaunt gave New Year gifts to Philipa and "Blanche de Trompyngton" (Ch Life Records, 90).

3925–41 The correspondence of some details in the Reeve's description (e.g., the references to playing the bag-pipe, wrestling) with those singled out in the description of the pilgrim Miller in the GP is no doubt deliberate and provocative.

3928 turne coppes: Usually explained as "make wooden cups in a turning-lathe." However, a very attractive suggestion by Pratt (JEGP 59, 1960, 208–11) is that there may be a reference to some country drinking-game such as that with a communal chant "The cup is turned over," recorded in Sussex in 1862. This would be a more appropriate activity for this miller; the absence of early evidence is an objection, but probably not an insuperable one. Perhaps *turne* simply has the sense of "invert," "turn over" (i.e., empty), but the placing of the phrase may suggest a more distinctive and specialized activity.

3933 Sheffield (**Sheffeld**) was already famous for its steel. The word **thwitel** is poorly attested, but there are examples in fourteenth-century records, which "all concern brawls (one actually at Trumpington)" (Bennett, Ch at Oxford, 5).

3936 **market-betere:** One who loiters around a market place (MED s.v. *market* n. [1].4a), probably with the implication of quarrelsomeness; cf. the phrase in Minot 2.25 (in Sisam, Fourteenth Cent. Verse and Prose, 153), "the Skottes gase in Burghes and betes the stretes," where the implication is that Scots are quarrelsome swaggerers.

3941 **hoote:** "Called." Baum (PMLA 71, 1956, 239) claims that there is a pun with *hoot* "hot."

Symkyn: A diminutive of Symond (the form was used in East Anglia; see Bennett, Ch at Oxford, 92n.). Steadman (MLN 75, 1960, 4) suggests that the name together with the emphasis on the *camus* nose may involve a pun with the Latin word *simus* "flat-nosed, snub-nosed." Biggins (SP 65, 1968, 44–50) extends this further to an allusion to the simian qualities of Symkyn's appearance (cf. I.3935) and his moral qualities (which he shares with those unflatteringly attributed to apes—lasciviousness, pride, drunkenness, lying, and treachery). Cf. H. W. Janson, Apes and Ape Lore in the M. A. and the Ren., Sts. of the Warburg Inst. (London) 20, 1952.

3943 She was an illegitimate daughter of the parson, who consequently paid her dowry. On priests and concubinage, see G. G. Coulton, Five Centuries of Religion, 1928, 2, 182; P. Heath, The Eng. Parish Clergy on the Eve of the Reformation, 1969, 104–8. Cf. Piers Plowman B 5.160–61. One of the parsons of Trumpington, Ricardus dictus Berde de Ledbury, was in 1343 succeeded by his son (and a similar situation is recorded at nearby Grantchester). See Bennett, Ch at Oxford, 109–110.

3954–55 For evidence (mainly from French and German) that the wearing of red hose was thought to be inappropriate to the lower classes, because it was associated with nobility, see the discussion of sartorial symbolism by Jones, MAE 25, 1956, 65–66. Symkyn and his wife are proud of his *estaat of yomanrye* (I.3949). Absolon, in the MilT (I.3319), and the Wife of Bath (GP I.456) also affect red hose; the Wife of Bath also wears *scarlet gytes* (WBPro III.559).

3964 A proverbial comparison. Cf. Whiting D268.

3974 **kamus nose:** She is her father's daughter. For an attempt to explain the significance of this physiognomic detail (cf. Curry, Ch and Science, 85), see Turner (N&Q 199, 1954, 232), who quotes the remark (from Scriptores Physiognomici, ed. R. Foerster, 1893, 2:203) "whoever has a snub-nose is lustful and loves intercourse." Emerson (N&Q 202, 1957, 277–78) objects that this is not the simplest or the easiest explanation; she notes that lines 4022–23 may indicate that Alan knew Malin of old, and notes that she is twice called a *wenche*,

which may have the connotation of "wanton, light girl" (cf. MancT IX.215, 220).

3980 For the idiom, see GP I.785n.

3983–86 Eliason (MLN 71, 1956, 162) claims that Chaucer is punning on the word *holy*. But Copland, (MAE 31:22n) rightly objects that "it is not the sense of the word that changes, but the varying *appropriateness* with which the same adjective is applied."

3987 **sokene:** "Feudal jurisdiction," but here the right of a mill-owner, in exchange for a fixed rent, to grind and take toll of all grain of the manor or town in which the mill stands (Bennett, Ch at Oxford, 91–92).

3990 **Soler Halle:** A name for King's Hall, an important college that grew out of a society of scholars founded by Edward II; it was later merged in Trinity College. See A. B. Cobban, The King's Hall, 1969; and Brewer, ChR 5, 1971, 311–17. Kuhl (PMLA 38, 1923, 123) notes that the members of Parliament that met at Barnwell Abbey in 1388 were entertained at the college. The name *Soler Hall* (referring to the number of solars [rooms admitting sunlight] it contained) is not found in a King's Hall document; Bennett (Ch at Oxford, 94–96) suggests that Chaucer's phrase **Men clepen** may indicate that it is not the official name, and that by choosing an apt, but noncommittal epithet the poet is avoiding any risk of libel (he notes similar obfuscations in the choice of the titles *wardeyn* and *manciple*).

3991 **malt:** Because colleges brewed their own ale (Bennett, Ch at Oxford, 6, 106).

4002 **povre scolers:** Probably formulaic (they can offer silver for a night's lodging): "they are called poor simply because scholars without exhibitions or benefices were assumed to be so" (Bennett, Ch at Oxford, 98–99). Their equivalents in the two French fabliaux are actually poor; cf. MilT 3190 above.

4014 **Strother:** The town cannot be identified with certainty. There is a Castle Strother in Northumberland. "The name, both as a simplex and as an element, is now found only north of the Tees," but a "Lange Strothere" is recorded in the thirteenth century, so that "strother" (meaning a place overgrown with brushwood) "may have been more widely distributed then than now" (Bennett, Ch at Oxford, 101).

4022 Chaucer clearly wished the language of the two clerks to sound Northern. It is apparently the first case of this kind of joking imitation of a dialect recorded in English literature. Bennett (Ch at Oxford, 99–100) notes that no college in Cambridge drew so many members from the North as King's Hall did. On the dialect forms, see Tolkien, TPS, 1934, 1–70; cf. also, Blake, Lore and Lang. 3, 1979, 1–8; C. Elliott, N&Q 209, 1964, 167–70 (who discusses some cases where the Hengwrt manuscript has preserved northernisms better than the Ellesmere); R. W. V. Elliott, Ch's English, 390–93. The most distinctive features are: the reflex of OE ā appears as a/aa instead of Chaucer's usual o/oo (*gas, swa, ham*); the OE consonant group *-lc* (usually *-lch, -ch*) appears as *-lk* in *swilk, whilk;* the initial consonant of *shall* appears as *s-* (*sal*); the 3rd sg. and plural pr. ind. of verbs appears as *-(e)s*. The pronominal form *thair,* which Chaucer uses only here, although it later became accepted in London English, was presumably still felt to be northern. Also suggestive of the North are a number of words, for instance: *heythyng, heythen, ille, ymel, lathe* (all of Scandinavian origin), and *boes, pit* (for *put*), *gif* (for *if*), and *taa* (for *take*).

4026 nede has na peer: Cf. "Necessity knows no law"; see Whiting N51, N52.

4027 The remark sounds proverbial; cf. Whiting S919 (only ME example).

4029 hope: "Expect" but possibly with a pun on "hope for"; both meanings are well attested (MED s.v. *hopen* v.(1) 1 and 2).

4030 wanges: Probably "back teeth, molars" (cf. OED, EDD s.v. *wang*; G. E. Evans, Where Beards Wag All, London, 1970, 162–63). Bennett, Ch at Oxford, 103, cites A Fifteenth-Century Schoolbook, ed. W. A. Nelson, Oxford, 1956, 29: "It were better to eny of us all to be dede than to suffre such thynge as the maister hath sufferyde these thre dais agone in the totheache."

4038 by my fader kyn: Spearing (ed. RvT) notes the appropriateness of the common oaths here (the miller's pride in ancestry); in 4041 *by my croun* (a reference to the clerks' tonsure), in 4049 *by my thrift* (since the miller prospers by dishonesty), in 4099 *by my croun* (the miller's baldness, recalling the clerks' tonsure).

4049 blere hir ye: Proverbial; cf. 3865 above.

4054 Proverbial; see Whiting C291. A very ancient statement of the idea is credited to Heraclitus, ed. H. Deils, 1909, fragment 40[16].

4055 The mare told the wolf, who wanted to buy her foal, that the price was written on her hind foot. When he tried to read it she kicked him. The fable and its variants are fully discussed by Baum, MLN 37, 1922, 350–53; cf. Aarne-Thompson, No. 47B. The proverb quoted in 4054 is found in the later versions of the fable by Caxton, Hist. of Reynard the Fox, ed. Blake, EETS, 263, 1970, 59; and Henryson, ed. Fox, 1981, Fables 1064.

4056 noght a tare: That is, "nothing" (cf. GP I.177n), but appropriate to a miller, "accustomed to find vetch seeds in corn" (Bennett, Ch at Oxford, 102).

4065 fen: Probably Lingay fen, a stretch of open country to the south of Trumpington, then frequently flooded (I.4106–7; this was before the fens were drained). Horses abounded in the wilds of Cambridgeshire; about ten miles to the south is a place called Horseheath (Bennett, Ch at Oxford, 113–14).

4066 "wehee": "The whinny of sexual desire" (Bennett, Ch at Oxford, 114, cf. PP B 7.91–92).

4087 Blake (N&Q 222, 1977, 400–1) points out that the Hengwrt and Ellesmere manuscripts have the uninflected gen. sg. *god* here (in 4187 Ellesmere, supported by other MSS, also has it), and suggests that this is a Northernism.

4096 Proverbial; Whiting B116. Cf. 3742 above.

4100 Thise sely clerkes: On this "vivifying" use of *thise* see MilT I.3723n.

4101 Jossa: Recorded only here in ME. EDD s.v. *joss* records it in Suffolk as a "command to a horse to sidle up to a block or gate that the rider may easier mount." Skeat (5:124) compares OF *jos, jus,* and quotes Cotgrave, "*jus,* down on the ground."

4114 by the way: This may suggest that "they found a track going back to the mill: 'the way' was a local term for such tracks: compare Derham Way, Millway in Grantchester Hundred" (Bennett, Ch at Oxford, 114).

4115 Bayard: A name for a horse (cf. CYT VII.1413n., Tr 1.218); Bennett (Ch at Oxford, 8) draws attention to an occurrence of it in the early records of Merton College.

4122–26 Cf. 4049–54. The miller has no compunction

about "rubbing in" his advantage. His satirical scorn for the schools seems to have been a fairly common joke at the expense of university students (cf. the Cook's repetition of *argument,* I.4329). Wenzel (Anglia 97, 1979, 310) quotes a jest by John Waldeby about an Oxford student who wanted "to prove to his father that his room had two doors. So the father closed the one door and started to beat him until he could find the other." Wenzel (SP 73, 1976, 144) cites another such joke, appearing in Giraldis Cambrensis's *Gemma ecclesiastica,* II.350, and in *The Hundred Merry Tales* ("Of the scholar of Oxford that provyd by sophestry ii checkyns iii"). On the treatment of space in the tale, see Brown, ChR 14, 1980, 225–36.

4127 Cutberd: St. Cuthbert, bishop of Lindisfarne (d. 686); his remains were buried in Durham Cathedral. He was a well-known saint throughout England, but his connection with the North makes him an appropriate figure for John to swear by. Cline (MLN 60, 1945, 481–82) suggests, less convincingly, that he is associated also with the notion of hospitality, since on one occasion he entertained angels unaware and was rewarded by having food miraculously supplied to him. The form *Cutberd* is sometimes taken to represent a comic mispronunciation or malapropism (like the carpenter's *Nowelis*), but it is probably a current form (Bennett, Ch at Oxford, 101 n., notes it in a Godstow document).

4129–30 Proverbial (cf. "Take as one finds," Whiting T15), but the saying turns out to have unexpected application, since the students do indeed take both what they find and what they bring (Spearing, ed. RvT).

4134 Also proverbial; see WBPro III. 415 and Whiting H89. Cf. RR 7518–20 and John of Salisbury, *Policraticus* 5.10. See also FrT III.1340n.

4140 chalons: Blankets, taking their name from Chalons in France, where they were manufactured. See Magoun, MS 17, 1955, 124.

4149 vernysshed his heed: The phrase is closely associated with drunkenness (cf. Fr. *être verni*) and may be virtually a synonym for being "well oiled." We should probably think of the literal meaning as well: his bald head shines with perspiration and later reflects the moonlight (Spearing, ed. RvT).

4155 The expression "to wet one's whistle" is still heard. For examples from Chaucer on, see Whiting W225 and OED s.v. *whistle* sb., 2.

4171 complyn: Compline, the last canonical hour, the service sung before retiring (and appropriately here bringing the musical passage to a conclusion).

4172 wilde fyr: Usually taken to be erysipelas, an infectious disease with inflammation of the skin, as in MerT IV.2252, but it is just possible that as in other uses of the word in imprecations (see OED s.v. *wild* 5b), the allusion is more generally to the inflammable "wild fire" used in medieval warfare (see WBPro III.373).

4174 the flour of il endyng: Baum (PMLA 71:237) notes a pun; cf. Spearing, ed. RvT, 39–41.

4179 esement: Cf. I.4186. Baum (PMLA 71:237) suggests a pun on the legal sense and on the simpler enjoyment ("comfort, entertainment") that he obtains.

4181–82 In the margin of MSS Ha⁴ and Ht is noted the equivalent Latin legal maxim: "Qui in uno gravatur in alio debet relevari." This legal phrase, and the use of words such as *amendement* and *esement,* support Bennett's conjecture (Ch at Oxford, 105) that the two clerks were reading law (books of civil law made up half of the library of King's Hall).

4210   Proverbial; see Whiting U3 (cf. "Fortune favors the brave," Whiting F519, or "Nothing venture, nothing win," Whiting N146). Cf. Tr 4.600–601n.

4231   **priketh:** On the supposed obscene pun noted by Baum (PMLA 71:242), see GP I.191n. Even the metaphoric usage of this verb for the sexual act is rare (see Robbins, Sec. Lyrics 28.28).

4233   **the thridde cok:** Near dawn. Skeat (5:109) notes that Tusser's *Husbandrie,* EDS, 1878, 165, says that cocks crow at midnight, at three o'clock, and an hour before day.

4235–40   It seems likely (Kaske, ELH 26, 1959, 295–310) that this exchange is parodying the courtly tradition of the "aube," the parting of lovers by the dawn, of which Chaucer offers a notable example in Tr 3.1422–1533 and n.

4248   **almoost:** If the scene is in some sense a "parody," it is by no means a savage one. This carefully chosen word is delicately pathetic (see Copland, MAE 31:20) as well as ironic.

4253   **toty:** Probably (Davis, Ch Glossary, 83) a colloquial word. This is the first recorded occurrence, and the only one in Chaucer.

4257   Cf. I.3713.

4264   For the formulaic pattern, cf. ShipT VII.227.

    Seint Jame: St. James the Great, one of the Apostles (d. 44 A.D.). He was a popular saint in the Middle Ages (especially because of his relics at Santiago de Compostela in Spain, a great place of pilgrimage), but there seems no special significance in mentioning him here.

4271   **disparage:** "Dishonor," but the word probably also has its more specific (and etymological) sense of being dishonorably matched to someone of inferior rank (cf. WBT III.1069); the miller's main concern is not the seduction but the low social rank of the seducer (Muscatine, Ch and the Fr Trad., 204).

4278   Proverbial; cf. Whiting P190.

4286   **hooly croys of Bromeholm:** A supposed relic of the true cross, known as the Rood of Bromholm, was brought to Norfolk from Constantinople between 1205 and 1223. It was famed for its miraculous powers, and was an object of pilgrimage; see W. Sparrow Simpson, Jnl. of Br. Archaeol. Ass. 30, 1874, 52–59; Wormald, Jnl. of the Warburg and Courtauld Institutes 1, 1937, 31–45 (with examples of popular prayers and illustrations [plates 7a, b] of the kind of representations of it that were sold to pilgrims); J. A. W. Bennett, ed., Piers Plowman, Oxford, 1972, 165. Langland's Avarice (Piers Plowman, B 5.229) says that he will pray to it to bring him out of debt. Pratt (MLN 70, 1955, 324–25) suggests that the miracles attributed to it—e.g., freeing from demonic possession (cf. I.4288), restoring life to the dead (cf. 4289)—make the mention of it here particularly appropriate.

4287   **In manus tuas:** Luke 23.46. The formula was used as a prayer before sleep, or at the hour of death (cf. Havelok the Dane, ed. Skeat, rev. K. Sisam, 1929; 228; Everyman, ed. W. W. Greg, 1909, 886–87); for English verses based on it, see Gray, Selection of Religious Lyrics, 1975, No. 53(e) and note.

4320–21   It was a common rhetorical convention to end a tale with a proverb or a *sententia* or a general moral idea ("moral" sometimes in a rather popular, fabliau-like way; cf. Gombert, in Benson and Andersson, Lit. Context, 99: "This tale shows us by its example that a man who has a pretty wife should never allow . . . a clerk to

sleep in his house, for he will do this same thing. The more one trusts them, the more one loses"). Cf. Chaucer's ShipT, MancT. Here we are given two proverbs: "He that does evil need not expect well" (see Whiting E185; cf. PrT VII.632) and "the guiler is beguiled" (see Rom 5759 and Whiting G491).

The Cook's Prologue

There is an apparent inconsistency between The Cook's Prologue and that of the Manciple (IX.1–55) where, as Tyrwhitt noticed, "when the Coke is called upon to tell a tale, there is no intimation of his having told one before" (Canterbury Tales, Intro. Discourse, 1775, 4:144). The problem remains unsolved. Luminansky (MS 17, 1955, 208–9) attempts to defend the status quo, arguing that the antagonism there expressed between the Cook and the Host would have seemed natural to Chaucer's audience, and that his question (IX.11) "Is that a cook of Londoun," etc., does not imply that he has just noticed him, but is simply a "japing" reference—"can it be this man, a London cook, is overcome by drink?" Nevertheless it remains odd that there is no reference either to "another tale" by the Cook (which would imply that Chaucer was thinking of the plan that each pilgrim should tell two tales) or to an unfinished attempt at a tale. A more probable explanation seems to be that either the MancPro was composed later and Chaucer meant to cancel the Cook's Fragment and perhaps to introduce the Cook later, or that the Cook's Fragment was written after the MancPro and Chaucer intended to adjust that. There is no sure way to decide the priority of composition. Possibly (Stanley, Poetica 5, 1976, 45) "the business may be the result of scribal reluctance to abandon one or other of the passages (whichever Chaucer cancelled) knowing it to be genuine and not wishing to lose any part of Chaucer's writings." See Tupper, PMLA 29, 1914, 113–14; Root, Poetry of Ch, 179–80.

4327   **For Cristes passion:** Spearing (ed. RvT) compares John's oath (I.4084) and remarks that Chaucer almost invariably puts such over-emphatic (and apparently vulgar) oaths in the mouths of lower-class characters. See Elliott, Ch's English, 253, and ch. 5.

4328–29   **conclusioun / Upon his argument:** The joking use of the technical language of the schools suggests that the Cook has the Miller's words in I.4122–24 in mind. On the theme of **herbergage** in Fragment I see Joseph, ChR 5, 1970, 83–96.

4331   Ecclus. 11.29 "Bring not every man into thine house; for many are the plots of the deceitful man." For the attribution of Ecclesiasticus to **Salomon;** see 3530 above.

4334   There is possibly (Spearing, ed. RvT) a pun on **pryvetee.** Cf. 3164 above.

4336   **Hogge of Ware:** See note on the portrait of the Cook in GP. Ware is a town in Hertfordshire, some thirty miles from London.

4345–52   Tupper (JEGP 14, 1915, 256–70) suggests that there is a reference here to the professional enmity between cooks and hostelers.

The Explanatory Notes to The Cook's Prologue and Tale were written by Douglas Gray.

4347 **Jakke of Dovere:** The meaning is not certain, but the expression is usually explained as a twice-cooked pie, i.e., one that is stale and has been warmed up. Skeat compares "Jack of Paris," used in this sense by More (Works, London, 1557, 675E) and Fr. *jacques.* Robinson records a suggestion of Kittredge that the name (like "poor John," "John Dory") might have been applied to a fish. Tancock (N&Q ser. 8.3, 1893, 366) gives evidence that in the thirteenth-century cooks and pastry-makers warmed up pies and meats on the second and third days. For references to ordinances against bad food (pies "not befitting, and sometimes stinking"), see Bowden, Comm. on GP, 188.

4352 **many a flye:** They presumably found their way into the parsley stuffing.

4355 Proverbial; Whiting S488; cf. ProMkT VII.1964.

4357 Proverbial; cf. Whiting P257. The use of the Flemish adjective *quaad* (bad) may suggest that Chaucer knew the proverb in Flemish form (although *quade* appears in ProPrT VII.438). J. Grauls and J. F. Vanderheijden, RBPH 13, 1934, 748–49, quote the saying in the form "Waer spot, quaet spot," and suggest that it may have been current with the word *spel* instead of *spot,* which would account for the variant *spel* for the second *pley* in some Chaucer MSS. For another Flemish proverb, see MancT IX.349–50. There were many Flemings in London (cf. D. W. Robertson, Ch's London, 22, 78), and Chaucer's wife was the daughter of a Flemish knight.

4358 It is only now that we hear the name of the Host. It corresponds to that of an actual innkeeper of Southwark, "Henri Bayliff, Ostyler." See note on the portrait of the Host in GP.

The Cook's Tale

The Cook's Tale stops suddenly, apparently in mid-career. The Hengwrt MS leaves the rest of the page blank, and notes "Of this cokes tale maked Chaucer na moore." The tale is long enough to show that it was likely to have been of the same general type as the Miller's and the Reeve's (and apparently with a firmly established London setting to match those of Oxford and Cambridge), but too short to disclose the plot, or consequently, the source. See the discussion by Lyon in S&A 148–54, who suggests that Chaucer may have had no literary source, but may have started out to fictionalize contemporary persons and events. A number of MSS have inserted after The Cook's Tale the Tale of Gamelyn, also ascribed to the Cook. This tale (ed. Skeat, 4:645–57), however, is certainly not by Chaucer, and does not seem at all appropriate to the Cook. It is often assumed, without evidence, that this tale was among Chaucer's papers and that he intended to work it over for one of the other pilgrims. The inconsistency between the Cook's Prologue (see introductory note) and the Manciple's may also suggest that Chaucer had not finally decided what he wished to do at this point. There are a number of ways in which the incompleteness of The Cook's Tale may be accounted for: that more of it existed, but has been lost (but the Hengwrt scribe seems to have decided that there was no more); that Chaucer was by some circumstance or other prevented from completing it, or that for some reason he decided not to do so. Stanley (Poetica 5:36–59) argues persuasively that the tale is complete as it stands. The Cook, he notes, reduces all to its lowest essentials; he sees the three preceding tales simply as "consequences of incautious *herbergage,*" which he answers by the formula of the situation at the end of his tale ("the recipe for carefree *herbergage*"); hence, "there is no more for him to say on the subject." Yet it might be argued that the careful setting of the London scene, as well as the obvious interest in a number of forms of "riot," suggests the story was meant to continue. Kolve, Ch and Imagery of Narrative, 257–85, questions the assumption that the tale has to be a fabliau, and points out that there are other latent narrative possibilities in the fragment (e.g., of a prodigal-son story).

4365 **A prentys:** By the time of Deloney and Dekker, in the late sixteenth to early seventeenth century, London apprentices had become notorious for merriment and revelry.

4367 Goldfinches are lively, brightly-colored, and sing gaily. The imagery used of Perkin (cf. I.4368, 4373) perhaps recalls that used of Alison in MilT; one or two points of appearance (hair *ykembd ful fetisly*) or activity (e.g., dancing) perhaps recall the description of Absolon.

4377 **Chepe:** Cheapside, a busy thoroughfare, with many shops; cf. GP I.754n. It was a favorite place for processions and festivals; see W. Kelly, Notices . . . of Leicester, London, 1865, 38–51; W. Herbert, Hist. of the Twelve Great Livery Companies, London, 1834, 1.90–99. Perhaps the kind of **ridyng** most likely to attract Perkin would have been the processions of "summer kings" or Lords of Misrule, which were sometimes accompanied by riotous behavior.

4383 **setten stevene:** Cf. KnT I.1524.

4388 **place of pryvetee:** It seems likely here (Spearing, ed. RvT) that the phrase "may carry a vague suggestion of immoral purposes."

4391–92 An anacoluthon; see GP I.175n.

4394–96 **he** in 4394 refers to the master, and it seems likely (Baugh, 312) that **he** in 4396 also does: he has no share in the "minstrelsy" even though he may know how to play a guitar or a rebec (see 3331 above; possibly this is the Cook's adaptation of the musical imagery of the MilT). Biggins (PQ 44, 1965, 117–20) takes I.4395 as a parenthesis, suggesting that the master himself is not above reproach, an appropriate touch "from a cook talking about a victualler."

4399 Apprentices regularly lived in their masters' houses.

4402 **lad with revel:** Another ironic kind of "minstrelsy" and "riding." Disorderly persons, when carried off to prison, were preceded by minstrels, to proclaim their disgrace. See 3774 above. On **Newgate** (where there was a celebrated prison), see Robertson, Ch's London, 20–26.

4404 **his papir:** Probably his written certificate of service and release; see Blenner-Hassett, MLN 57, 1942, 34–35; Call, MLQ 4, 1943, 167–76. Skeat took *papir* to refer to the master's accounts (where the results of Perkin's wickedness would appear).

4406–7 Proverbial; see Whiting A167.

4415 Proverbial; see Whiting T73.

4422 The scribe of the Hengwrt MS wrote in the space he left after these lines "Of this cokes tale maked Chaucer na moore."

FRAGMENT II

Introduction to the Man of Law's Tale

Although the Man of Law's Introduction, Prologue, and Tale appear together consistently in the MSS, their relationships have appeared problematic to critics. The Man of Law says *I speke in prose* (II.96), though both his prologue and tale are in rime royal. Stevens (PMLA 94, 1979, 62–76) argues that *prose* can refer to stanzas of equal length (but note that Chaucer himself describes the Melibee and The Parson's Tale as *prose* in VII.937 and X.46). Elliott (Ch's English, 96) accepts Skeat's tentative proposal that *I speke in prose,* in contrast to *I wol yow telle a litel thyng in prose* (Thop VII.937; cf. ParsPro X.46), means "I normally speak in prose." Mustanoja (ME Syntax, 482–83) may offer some support for this interpretation in his observation that in ME the use of the present to refer to habitual action becomes increasingly common as the future is increasingly expressed by auxiliaries such as *wol.*

Most critics have inclined to the view that the reference to *prose* indicates a prose tale was to follow. Lowes (PMLA 20, 1905, 794–96) suggested it was to be "the Wreched Engendrynge of Mankynde" (cf. LGW Pro G 414–15 and n.), but most have accepted the older view that it was to be the Melibee (see Pratt, PMLA 66, 1951, 1141–67; Lewis, PMLA 81, 1966, 488). Some references in the Epilogue to The Man of Law's Tale have been taken to support this view (see 1188–90 and n.). On the other hand, Wickert (Anglia 69, 1950, 89–104) holds that the Introduction was written for the present tale, on the basis of the references to The Legend of Good Women (see 60–76 and nn.) and the argument that Custance is also a *seint* of Love, though here of celestial rather than earthly love. The supposed references to Gower may also indicate a link between the Introduction and the Tale since he also tells the story of Constance in his *Confessio amantis* 2.587–1598.

The date of the Introduction is uncertain. The use of the *Kalendarium* of Nicholas of Lynn (see II.1–14 and n.) makes 1386 the earliest possible date. Further evidence for dating is sometimes based on the references to *Canacee* and *Tyro Appollonius,* which have usually been viewed, following Tyrwhitt's account in the introductory discourse to his edition of Chaucer, as references to stories in Gower's *Confessio amantis* (see 77–89 below). The story of Appollonius is the concluding tale in the Confessio, and this evidence would seem to suggest a date after 1390, when Gower's poem was completed (Fisher, John Gower, 116). Since Gower and Chaucer were on friendly terms as early as 1378, when Chaucer gave Gower his power of attorney, however, Chaucer would not have needed to wait until the first complete version of the Confessio was issued to know about the planned inclusion of Appollonius. A related hypothesis, as presented by Tatlock, is that Gower saw these references as negative criticisms and reacted by removing a flattering reference to Chaucer from his own poem (Confessio Amantis 8.2941*–57*) in a revised version dated c. 1391. The grounds for this hypothesis are not firm, how-

ever; no other evidence for the supposed quarrel between Chaucer and Gower is extant (Fisher, John Gower, 27–32, 117–21, reviews the question), and recent work on the manuscripts of the Confessio has raised questions about when the reference to Chaucer was removed (Peter Nicholson, ChR 19, 1984, 123–43). See the introductory note to the *Tales* for further discussion of the date.

Opinions differ on the significance of the attitudes toward literature expressed in the Introduction. The view that the Man of Law speaks for Chaucer in censuring tales of incest, perhaps as an indirect defense of Chaucer's own fabliaux (Fisher, John Gower, 289), is contested by David (PMLA 82, 1967, 217–25), who sees the Man of Law as representative of self-appointed critics of poetry with whom Chaucer disagreed. Some critics (e.g., Sullivan, MLN 68, 1963, 1–8; and Wood, Traditio 23, 1967, 149–90) see the account of the *Seintes Legende of Cupide* here as designed to undercut the Man of Law's claim to a prodigious memory (GP I.327 and n.), since the tales of good women mentioned include some not in *The Legend of Good Women* as we have it, while others who do appear in the Legend are not named here (see 63–76 below). Another explanation is that the Introduction was written while the *Legend* was still in progress; on the basis of discrepancies between the account of Medea in the *Legend* (LGW 1580–1678), Root (PMLA 24, 1909, 124–53; 25, 1910, 228–40) suggests that the Introduction was written before the tale of Medea in the *Legend* (but cf. Kittredge, PMLA 24, 1909, 343–63). On one matter, however, the Man of Law's views have not been identified with Chaucer's own: the Man of Law's disparaging remarks on Chaucer's versification (II.47–49), which echo Harry Bailly's comments on Sir Thopas (VII.919–31). Scheps (PMLA 89, 1974, 287) relates this passage to Chaucer's tendency to ironic self-deprecation, as seen also in *The Book of the Duchess* and *The House of Fame.*

1–14 The Host's calculations of time, purportedly "off-hand and empty handed," could only have been made with astronomical instruments and tables (Smyser, Spec 45, 1970, 360, 362–63). Here and in NPT VII.3187–97 and ParsPro X.11, Chaucer used the *Kalendarium* of Nicholas of Lynn (ed. Eisner, 29–34; cf. Astr Pro 84–86 and n.). It showed that on 18 April at precisely 10 A.M. the shadow of a six-foot-tall man would be exactly six feet long (Kalendarium, 86–87), a neat congruence so rare (it occurs again only at 9 A.M., 28 June) that North (RES 20, 1969, 424) believes Chaucer chose 18 April for that reason. The Host's other means of calculating time, by reference to the **artificial day** (the time the sun is above the horizon; cf. Astr 2.7) presents problems. On 18 April the sun rose at 4:47 and the artificial day had 14 hours 26 minutes (Kalendarium, 83, 86), and **The ferthe part, and half an houre and moore** would be closer to nine than to **ten of the clokke.** Brae (ed. Astr, 1870, 68–71) argues that Chaucer mistook the azimuthal day for the artificial day, an explanation which Eisner rejects as unlikely (Kalendarium, 31), noting that the Host was **nat depe ystert in loore.** Whether one accepts Brae's explanation or uses Nicholas's tables, the error remains (Eade, SAC 4, 1982, 82–85). It is unlikely that many of Chaucer's listeners noticed it.

18 Seint John: Author of the Fourth Gospel, also

The explanatory notes to The Man of Law's Tale were written by Patricia J. Eberle.

known as the apostle of truth (Skeat 5:134 and note to SqT V.596, 5:385).

20–31 Many of these remarks on time are proverbial and literary commonplaces. The continual passage of time (20–21) echoes Rom 369–71 (cf. RR 361–65 and see also ClT IV.118–19). The comparison with falling water echoes Rom 383–84 (cf. RR 371–74) as well as Ovid (Met. 15.179–84 and Ars Am. 3.62–64). The general idea that lost time cannot be recovered is proverbial (Whiting T307; cf. HF 1257–58 and Tr 4.1283n.). The comparison of lost time and lost goods (25–29) attributed to Senec (Seneca the Younger, ca. 4 B.C.–65 A.D.) probably refers to Epistulae morales 1.3 (ed. Gummere, Loeb, 1979) although the wording is not exact: for a closer parallel see Conf. Aman. 4.1485–87. The comparison of lost time to **Malkynes maydenhede** (30) combines several proverbial elements. Malkin, a diminutive of Maud (ME Malde, Lat. Matilda), was often used for a woman of the lower classes (NPT VII.3384) or of loose morals (MED s.v. malkin). In this sense, Malkin's maidenhead, as used in PP A 1.157–58, is proverbial for something "no man desirith" (see Whiting M511). Here, however, the reference is to the proverb that virginity, once lost, cannot be recovered (Whiting, M20, citing Conf. Aman. 5.5646–49 and 5.6208–11). Stevens (Leeds SE, n.s. 1, 1967, 1–5) takes it as an allusion to Malyne in RvT (I.4236).

32 ydelnesse: Pratt (PMLA 66:1147) notes the parallel with ParsT X.715 and suggests that the word may refer to the type of tale represented by MilT, RvT, and CkT.

33 Sire Man of Lawe: According to Lumiansky (Of Sondry Folk, 63), this form of address suggests that the Host does not recognize the special status of the Sergeant, perhaps because he is misled by his hoomly coat (GP I.328; cf. the Host's remarks on the Canon's clothing, CYPro VIII.627–39); note, however, that Gower in his account of sergants du loy (Mirour de l'omme, 24421) also calls them gens du loy (note following 24180), so that the terms sergeant and man of law seem to have been interchangeable.

33–38 In addressing the Man of Law, the Host uses a number of legal terms: forward, submytted, cas, juggement, acquiteth, biheeste, devoir (Elliott, Ch's English, 357).

39 depardieux: De par (OF de part, on the side of) is a common formula in French legal language (Skeat 5:135–36).

41 Biheste is dette: Proverbial (Whiting B214); especially appropriate to a Sergeant, who had exclusive right to plead cases of debt in the Court of Common Pleas (see GP I.309–28 and n.).

43–45: Proverbial (Whiting L107), but **oure text** may refer to the Digesta of Justinian (ed. Mommsen, 1870; trans. Munro, 1904–9), 2.2 rubric, "Whatever law someone imposes on another, let him make use of it himself."

46–49 "I cannot tell any profitable tale now that Chaucer . . . has not told." ME idiomatic usage omits the second negative (see Tr 1.456–57), using **hath** (49) instead of nath. Lumiansky (Of Sondry Folk, 65) sees this reference to Chaucer's tales as evidence that the Man of Law recognizes Chaucer among the pilgrims; Coghill and Tolkien (eds. MLT, 1969, 14) argue that it shows only that he knows Chaucer's literary reputation.

55 Episteles: Lat. "letters." Ovid's Heroides, a collection of letters attributed to famous heroines (cf. HF 379);

in Ars amatoria (3.345), Ovid refers to one of the books of Heroides as an epistola.

61 Seintes Legende of Cupide: See the introductory note to LGW for this description of the work.

62 large woundes: Lucrece committed suicide out of shame over her rape (LGW 1854–55); Thisbe killed herself for love of Pyramus (LGW 913–15 and 893).

63–76 This catalogue of Cupid's saints (cf. a similar catalogue of wronged women in HF 388–426) omits two of the figures in The Legend of Good Women, Cleopatra and Philomela, and includes others whose tales are not in LGW although they are in Ovid's Heroides. Many are also in Gower's Confessio amantis: **Dianire** (Deianira, wife of Hercules, Heroides 9 and Conf. Aman. 2.2145–2307); **Hermyon** (Hermione, lover of Orestes, Heroides 8); **Erro** (Hero, lover of Leander, Heroides 18); **Eleyne** (Helen of Troy, lover of Paris, Heroides 16 and Conf. Aman. 5.7195–7596); **Ladomya** (Laodamia, lover of Protesilaus, Heroides 13); and **Penelopee** (Penelope, wife of Ulysses, Heroides 1 and Conf. Aman. 4.146–233). **Brixseyde** (Briseis, Heroides 3 and Conf. Aman. 2.2451–55) is a Trojan girl captured by Achilles, as described in the Iliad (1.184) and referred to in HF (398); in the Roman de Troie of Benoît de Sainte-Maure (twelfth cent.), she is the lover of Troilus, the woman whom Chaucer in Troilus calls Criseyde, after his source, Boccaccio's Filostrato. **Alceste** (Alcestis, wife of Admetus) is not in Heroides; Chaucer tells her story briefly in LGW (F 511–16, G 499–504; cf. Conf. Aman. 7.1917–1949). All the others do appear in LGW: **Lucresse** (LGW 1680–1885, cf. Conf. Aman. 7.4754–5130); **Babilan Tesbee** (Babylonian Thisbe, LGW 706–923, cf. Conf. Aman. 3.1331–1494); **Dido** (LGW 924–1366, cf. Heroides 7); **Phillis** (LGW 8, cf. Heroides 2 and Conf. Aman. 4.731–886); **Adriane** (Ariadne, LGW 1886–2227, cf. Heroides 10 and Conf. Aman. 5.5231–5495); **Isiphilee** (Hypsipyle) and **Medea** (LGW 1368–1679, cf. Heroides 6 and 12, and Conf. Aman. 5.3246–4222); and **Ypermystra** (Hypermnestra, LGW 2562–2733, cf. Heroides 14).

64–65 Dido killed herself with the sword of Aeneas (LGW 1351 and Aeneid 4.646), and Phyllis hanged herself from a tree (not mentioned in LGW or Heroides; see Conf. Aman. 4.856–60; on the Latin sources, see Conrad Mainzer, MAE 41, 1972, 223).

66–67 The reference is to a formal complaint against a faithless lover, a regular feature of the Heroides that is sometimes adapted in LGW (see p. 632 for "complaint" as a literary form). This account of the complaints in LGW is misleading: only **Adriane** (Ariadne) has a complaint in LGW (2185–2217, following Heroides 10); no complaint is given Hypsipyle in LGW (although 1564–74 refer to one); and Deianira and Hermione do not appear in LGW at all.

68 The bareyne yle: The island where Theseus abandoned Ariadne (LGW 2163–77).

72–74 The reference to Medea's hanging her children by the hals has no parallel, either in The Legend of Good Women, book 4 (which stresses her kyndenesse, 1664) or in Heroides 12 (but there is a prophecy that she will murder them in Heroides 6.159–60 and LGW 1574). In Gower's version (Conf. Aman. 5.3246–4242), Medea slouh (4215) the children, but the means are not specified; in RR (13229–62) she strangled them (estrangla, 13259). See also BD 725–77.

77–89 Because the stories of **Canacee** and **Tyro Appollonius** (Apollonius of Tyre), which are rejected by the Man of Law, are included in Gower's Confessio Amantis (Canace, 3.143–336; and Apollonius, 8.271–2028), this passage has been viewed as a slighting reference to Gower (see the note to the Man of Law's Introduction). The possibility of a reference to Gower here involves some complexities since the Man of Law's literary criticisms involve two main points: one about the poor taste of telling **cursed stories** of incest such as Canace and Apollonius and a second about the lack of originality in telling stories already told by Chaucer. The first criticism need not have been directed at Gower, since both stories were available in other versions. The incestuous father who throws his daughter **upon the pavement** is not in Gower's version of the story of Apollonius, but the detail may have been suggested by a misreading of a passage in a Latin version (Fisher, John Gower, 289 and 370 n. 18); the Apollonius story is extant in over 100 MSS in Latin and was also told in the *Pantheon* of Godfrey of Viterbo (Rickert, MP 2, 1904–5, 385 n. 1). The tale of Canace is told by Ovid (Heroides 2) as well as Gower, and Chaucer himself may once have planned to include it in LGW as a reference in the Prologue of that work (F 265, G 219) suggests. The second criticism is implied in the list of tales the Man of Law gives as told in Chaucer's *Seintes Legende of Cupide,* ten of which also appear in Gower's Confessio (see 63–76 above). If the Man of Law is understood to be criticizing Gower's lack of originality, this criticism has an ironic application to the Man of Law himself: his own tale of Custance is a version of one of the most popular stories of the period and one that is also retold by Gower (Confessio 2.587–1598; see introductory note to MLT).

91–92   Pierides: The nine Muses, so called from their birthplace, Pieria (Ovid, Tristia 5.3.10), are here confused with the daughters of King Pierus, who unsuccessfully challenged the Muses to a singing contest and were changed into magpies (Ovid, Met. 5.293–678). The implied comparison between Chaucer and the Muses is flattering but it does not sort well with the Man of Law's rejection of stories of incest (II.79). The Muses' song of the rape of Proserpina is filled with examples of incest among the gods: Proserpina is the daughter of the incestuous liason between Ceres and Jupiter, while Dis, who rapes Proserpina, is the brother of Jupiter and hence her uncle as well.

93   *Methamorphosios:* The form is the genitive singular, dependent on *liber,* a common form for referring to Ovid's *Metamorphoses* in medieval MSS (Shannon, Ch and the Roman Poets, 307–8). For other examples of the use of the genitive as the title, see MkT VII.2046, NPT VII.3359, HF 378, LGW 1457. This usage is perhaps related to Chaucer's use of the oblique form of the source in translating Latin names; see Bo 2.pr3.59n.

96   prose: See introductory note.

The Man of Law's Prologue

Lines 99–121 are a condensed translation of a part of *De miseria condicionis humane* (1.14) by Pope Innocent III (late twelfth cent.). Chaucer's additions are the image of the wound of need (102–3), the imagined speech of the poor man (110–12), and the caution against poverty

(119). The denunciation of riches that concludes the section in Innocent is replaced here with praise of wealthy merchants (122–32), a passage which demonstrates a habit of thought Innocent condemns, whereby "a person is valued according to his wealth." (Manly-Rickert note parallels with Mel VII.1567–71; Miller, Costerus 3, 1975, 49–71, notes a similar denunciation of poverty in RR 7921–8206.) Both the praise of merchants and the passage from Innocent link the Prologue with the Man of Law's Tale. The Tale opens with an account of merchants (134–40), and several passages in it, as well as glosses to these passages in many MSS, are based on Innocent's treatise (see MLT introductory note below).

The use of *De miseria* offers some evidence for dating the Prologue and Tale (or its revision). In ProLGW (G 414–15) Chaucer adds to the list of his works in the F Prologue, the title "Of the Wreched Engendrynge of Mankynde / As man may in pope Innocent yfynde" (see LGW introductory note on dating Prologues G and F). Lewis (ed. De miseria, 1978, 16–31) reviews the evidence and argues that Chaucer was working simultaneously on a translation of *De miseria* and the Man of Law's Prologue and Tale during the period from 1390 to 1394–95.

The connections of the Prologue to the Tale and to the Man of Law are problematical. Manly-Rickert find the Prologue unnecessary since the Introduction (II.98) implies that the Man of Law's Tale begins with the next line. Alfred David (PMLA 82:221) notes that the rime royal verse form suggests the Prologue and Tale were meant to be joined but agrees with Tatlock (Dev. and Chron., 188) that the praise of wealth in the Prologue sorts oddly with a tale of Custance's material deprivations (Strumpet Muse, 127). Tupper (The Nation 99, 1914, 41, and PMLA 29, 1914, 93–128) notes that lawyers were traditionally associated with grumbling against poverty. Scheps (PMLA 89:287–88) connects the Prologue with the portrait in the General Prologue of the Sergeant's material success, and he notes that a Sergeant might well feel resentment against the poor, since he was pledged to defend them without a fee.

102–3 On the rhyme of two words with one (a type of rime riche), see GP I.523n.

114 Ecclus. 40.29, quoted in Mel VII.1571–72; see also Haeckel, Sprichwort, 44, no. 151, 152.

115 Proverbs 14.20.

118 Proverbs 15.15.

120–21 See Proverbs 19.7 and Whiting P295; cf. Mel VII.1559.

124–25 The references are to a game of **chaunce** played with dice (see PardT VI.653 and n.). Gower (Mirour 24226–28) discusses in similar terms how the covetousness of lawyers leads them to pervert justice: "For you will never maintain a just cause aginst a six if you have a double ace (*ambesaas*)." (See also MkT VII.2661).

The Man of Law's Tale

Though earlier scholars believed The Man of Law's Tale was an early composition (see Skeat; Cowling, RES 2, 1926, 316–17; and cf. Coghill and Tolkien, ed. MLT,

1969, 41), most scholars now agree with Tatlock (Dev. and Chron., 172–88) that Chaucer's use of Innocent III's *De miseria* and of Gower's *Confessio amantis* (see below) indicate a "rather late date (about 1390)" (Robinson). Lewis, in the most recent discussion of the problem (ed. De miseria, 16–31), assigns it to the period from about 1390 to 1394–95.

Chaucer's principal source for this tale is a lengthy section of an Anglo-Norman chronicle of world history written around 1334 by the Dominican Friar Nicholas Trevet (or Trivet) for Marie, daughter of Edward I. The full text has not been edited, but Originals and Analogues (2nd ser., 7, 10, 15, 22) contains an edition of the section on the life of Constance with a modern English translation (1–84), a fifteenth-century English version (221–50), and selected analogues (365–414). Schlauch (in S&A, 165–81) printed another edition of Trevet's Constance with an English summary. French (Ch Handbook, 220–31) provides a detailed summary of Trevet. Robert M. Correale is preparing an edition of a text of Trevet for the Chaucer Library that is closer to Chaucer's version at many points than any previous edition. This text will take into account the fresh analysis by Ruth J. Dean of the MSS of the *Chronicles* (M&H, 14, 1962, 95–105; see also her account of Trevet as historian in J. J. G. Alexander and M. T. Gibson, eds. Med. Learning and Lit., 1976, 328–52).

Trevet's story is based on a widely popular story derived from two tale types: the story of a princess exiled for refusing to marry her father, and the story of a queen exiled for giving birth to a monster (Margaret Schlauch, Ch's Constance and Accused Queens, 1927). The story was very popular and appears in several versions in Middle English (see Hornstein, Manual ME 1:120–32), in the *Decameron* (see 519 below), and elsewhere. A noteworthy analogue, because of the author's legal background, is *La manekine* by the noted jurist Philippe de Remi, Sire de Beaumanoir (c. 1250–96; in Oeuvres poétiques, ed. Suchier, SATF, 1884, 1:3–263). For full discussions see Schlauch (Ch's Constance, and in S&A, 155–62) and Rickert (MP 2:355–61). Trevet apparently knew the story in a form that combined central motifs from both tale types, the motif of incest and the motif of monstrous birth. He omitted the element of incest, added circumstantial details, and attached the fabulous story to historical events: the heroine became Constantia, daughter of the Byzantine emperor Tiberius Constantinus (d. 582); and Mauricius Flavius Tiberius (c. 539–602), who succeeded Tiberius as emperor (and was historically Constantia's husband) became in Trevet's account her son. Trevet also added motifs more typical of a saint's life, such as the healing of the blind man and the intervention of God at Constantia's trial (Schlauch, S&A, 158–59).

Most scholars agree that Chaucer also knew the adaptation of Trevet's tale in Gower's *Confessio amantis* (2.587–1598). Though Skeat and Macaulay (ed. Conf. Aman. 1:482–84) believed that Chaucer's work was written first, Schlauch (Ch's Constance, 132–34, and S&A, 155–56) and Block (PMLA 68, 1953, 600–2) argue convincingly for Gower's priority (see also Lücke, Anglia 14, 1892, 77–122, and Tatlock, Dev. and Chron., 172–88). According to Block, Chaucer's direct borrowings from Gower are limited to nine passages (cf. II.430 with Conf. Aman. 2.689; 439 with 2.709; 535 with 2.749–51; 561–

62 with 2.766; 599 with 2.828; 683 with 2.987; 721 with 2.932; 799 with 2.1031; and 825 with 2.1055–57). To these should be added the most important parallel between Gower's and Chaucer's versions, the pathetic scene with Custance and her child as she leaves Northumberland (see 834–68 and n.).

According to Block's detailed analysis (PMLA 68: 572–616) only one-third of The Man of Law's Tale is based closely on Trevet. Although Chaucer adopts all the main episodes and adds none of his own, very few lines are direct translations from Trevet. He omits about two-thirds of Trevet's version, including most of the historical and circumstantial details and all of the episodes not directly involving Custance. He also changes the order of the narrative so that the episode of the renegade Christian (II.915–45) comes just before Custance returns to Rome. His principal additions are: the description of the merchants (II.134–54) and of Custance (155–70); the astrological commentary (190–203) and the Sultan's council (204–31); the direct discourse and comments on Custance's departure (245–52, 256–94, 316–22); the council of the Sultan's mother (326–43) and comments on it (348–74); preparations for the banquet (386–420) and comments on it (421–28, 432–34); Custance's prayers and the narrator's comments on her departure (446–62); the formal hearing before the king (606–89); comments on the marriage to Alla (701–14, 719–21); direct discourse and comments in the episode of Alla's mother and the messenger (731–43, 760–63, 766–84, 803–5, 810–18); the scene of Custance with her child (825–75); comments on the renegade Christian (925–52); direct discourse and comments in the recognition scenes (1103–13, 1116–42); and the comments at the end (1149–62).

The sources for many of these additions are indicated by the marginal glosses that appear in several manuscripts, including Ellesmere and Hengwrt, and are translated in the notes of the Manly-Rickert edition (M-R 3:492–96). Manly-Rickert, along with Brusendorff (Ch Trad., 127–28), Tatlock (PMLA 50, 1935, 103), and Lewis (SP 64, 1967, 1–16), hold that the glosses from Innocent III's *De miseria* at II.421, 771, 925, 1132, and 1135 (see notes to these lines, below) are most likely Chaucer's (but see Owen, PMLA 97, 1982, 240–41, for a contrary view).

Criticism of the tale has focused on the use of rhetoric, the relation of the tale to the teller, and the pathos in the characterization of Custance. Bloomfield (PMLA 87, 1972, 384–90) argues that the rhetorical apostrophes distance the audience from the story, while Bestul (ChR 9, 1974–75, 216–26) holds that such appeals are intended to arouse sympathetic feelings in the audience. See also Wurtele (Neophil 60, 1974, 577–93). On the use of legal terms and practices in the tale, see Hamilton (in Sts. in Lang. and Lit. in Hon. of Margaret Schlauch, ed. M. Brahmer et al., 1966, 153–63), Scheps (PMLA 89:285–95), and Elliott (Ch's English, 398). Against the view of Wood (Traditio 23:149–90) that the tale reveals its teller's inadequacies, Loomis (in Ch Problems, 207–20) defends the lawyer's view of the relation of providence to the power of the stars. (On the psychology of the teller see Finnegan, NM 77, 1976, 227–40; and Farrell, in J. R. R. Tolkien: Essays, ed. Mary Salu and R. Farrell, 1979, 159–72.) Delany (ChR 9, 1974–75, 63–72) criticizes Custance as a flawed ideal of womanliness, but Clogan (M&H 8, 1977, 217–33) takes her as a typical heroine of hagiographical romance. Clasby (ChR 13, 1978–79, 221–39) defends her as a Boethian heroine. Against Bloomfield's view (PMLA 87:384–90) that the tale delicately balances comedy and tragedy, Weissman (JMRS 9, 1979, 133–53) argues that it is a critique of late Gothic pathos. On pathos and religious sensibility in the tale, see also Yunck, ELH 27, 1960, 249–61, and Windeatt, M&H 9, 1979, 143–69. V. A. Kolve (Ch and Imagery of Narrative, 1984, 297–358, 360–71) discusses the rich iconographical tradition that informs the central image of the rudderless ship; he argues that The Man of Law's Tale is a "provisional palinode" (369) that speaks to many of the philosophical and moral issues raised by Fragment I of *The Canterbury Tales* and that it serves as a fitting conclusion to the tales of the first day.

134 **Surrye:** Trevet, "la grande Sarazine" (S&A, 165); Gower, "Barbarie" (Conf. Aman. 2.599).
161 Lat. gloss: "Europe is the third part of the world." On the three parts of the world (Europe, Asia, Africa), see Conf. Aman. 7.520–86.
162–68 Paull (ChR 5, 1970–71, 181–82) notes similarities with descriptions of romance heroines.
171 **han doon fraught:** For the construction see KnT I.1913n.
190–203 The source of this passage is suggested by the Lat. gloss: "The sceptre of Phoroneus, the conflict of the brothers at Thebes, the flames of Phaeton, the flood of Deucalion. In the stars [are] Priam's pomp, the boldness of Turnus, the cleverness of Ulysses, and the strength of Hercules. (Bernardus Silvester, *Megacosmos*.)" (For the full passage, see Bernardus Silvestris, Megacosmos, in Cosmographia, 3.39–44; tr. Wetherbee, 76; see also Dronke in Brewer, Geoffrey Ch, 1975, 156–60.) In adapting Bernardus, Chaucer takes over his image of the heavens as a **book** (see Megacosmos 3.33–34) in which future events are written, but he changes the emphasis so that only evil fates, **strif** and **deeth**, are foretold. Chaucer omits from his catalogue the good fortunes described by Bernardus (Phoroneus was honored as the founder of Argos; Deucalion survived a universal flood and helped to reestablish the human race; Ulysses was widely celebrated as the embodiment of wisdom; and Priam was revered as the last ruler of Troy.) Except for **The strif of Thebes** (200; see also Tr 5.1485–1510), Chaucer changes those references he does adopt from a positive to a negative emphasis: Bernardus stresses the "boldness" of **Turnus** (the Rutulian prince betrothed to Lavinia and a fierce opponent of Aeneas; see Aeneid 12.887–952 and HF 457–58 for his death); the "strength" of Hercules (**Ercules**, see MkT VII.2095–2140); and the fighting of **Achilles** (cf. Megacosmos 3.51; on his death see Guido delle Colonne, Hist. dest. Troi., 27.30–50, and Benoît de Sainte Maure, Roman de Troie, 21838–22500). Chaucer stresses their deaths. Other deaths in the catalogue are Chaucer's additions, sometimes suggested by a line in Bernardus: **Ector** (Hector, see Tr 5.1804–6); **Pompei** and **Julius** (the Roman general Pompey and Julius Caesar, at first allies then opponents; cf. "the Roman wars," Megacosmos 3.50, and see MkT VII.2671–2726); **Sampson** (the Biblical Samson, see MkT VII.2015–94); and **Socrates** (the death of the Athenian philosopher 469–399 B.C., described in Plato's Apology and Phaedo, is referred to

in Bo 1.pr.3, 26–28). Chaucer's conclusion (202–3) that men cannot read what is written in the stars is a marked change from Bernardus's conclusion: "Thus the Creator wrought, that ages to come might be beheld in advance, signified by starry ciphers" (Megacosmos 3.58–59).
211 Proverbial; see RvPro I.3857 and n.
220–21 **diversitee/Bitwene hir bothe lawes:** A loose translation of Lat. *disparitas cultus,* a technical term in canon law (apparently introduced by Peter Lombard, Sententiarum 4.39.1, PL 192:934), referring to the difference in religion between the baptized and the unbaptized, which created an impediment to marriage (Beichner, Spec 23, 1948, 70–75).
224 **Mahoun:** Mohammed (570?–632 A.D.), prophet and founder of Islam. Although Mohammed is not mentioned in Trevet's life of Constance, there are two paragraphs on him in the section of Trevet's *Chronicles* dealing with the later career of Maurice (Pratt, in Sts. in Lang., ed. Atwood and Hill, 303–11).
236 **mawmettrie:** In ParsT X.749, this word (OF *Mahumet,* Mohammed) is a synonym for *ydolatrie,* despite the fact that the Koran, like the Bible, forbids idolatry.
261 **I seye:** For the use of this and similar expressions (e.g., *I mene,* KnT I.2063) see Hammond, Engl. Verse, 447. "Sometimes they serve merely for emphatic repetition, sometimes they are rather a scholastic formula (like Dante's use of 'dico' in Inf. 4.66 and elsewhere)." (Robinson.)
281 **the Barbre nacioun:** Probably equivalent to "the pagan world"; (Gr. *barbaros,* one who speaks a foreign language; cf. FranT V.1452). See Magoun, Ch Gazetteer, 29.
285–87 In calling herself a **wrecche** (OE *wrecca*), Custance is probably using the word in its original sense, an outcast or exile, since she feels herself to be cast out of her homeland, and since her next words echo God's reproach to Eve before casting her out of Eden (Genesis 3:16). In Bo 1.pr5.6, *wrecche* translates Lat. "exilium."
288 **Pirrus:** Pyrrhus, son of Achilles and Deidamia; his breach of the walls of Troy and the ensuing loud laments are vividly described in Aeneid 2.469–90. See also NPT VII.3355–59.
289 **Ilion:** Ilium, the Greek name for Troy, but used by Chaucer and other medieval writers for the citadel of Troy; see Magoun, Ch Gazetteer, 91, and cf. NPT VII.3356; BD 1248; HF 158; LGW 936.
  Thebes: See 190–203 above.
290 **Hanybal:** The great Carthaginian general, invader of Italy during the second Punic War (see Livy, Ab urbe condita, Bks. 21–30). "Hannibal ad portas!" (Hannibal is at the gates!) is a proverbial Latin cry of alarm (Lewis and Short, Latin Dict., 1879).
295–301 Lat. gloss: "Whence Ptolemy in Book I, Chapter 8: 'the primary motions of the heavens are two, of which the first is that which continually moves the whole from east to west in one way, above the spheres' and so forth. 'Moreover, there is indeed a second motion which impels the spheres of the moving stars [*stellarum currencium,* i.e. the planets], running contrary to the first motion, that is to say, from west to east above the two other poles' and so forth." The gloss is a paraphrase of a passage from Bk. 1, chap. 8 of the *Almagest* of Ptolemy (c. 100–c. 178 A.D.). See MilT I.3208 and WBPro III.183, 324–25, for references to the *Almagest.* The Ptolemaic

system of the universe referred to here is a series of seven concentric transparent spheres, each bearing one of the seven planets (Saturn, Jupiter, Mars, sun, Venus, Mercury, moon), surrounding a stationary earth. Two other spheres surround the whole: the eighth, bearing the fixed stars, moves slowly from west to east (thus accounting for the gradual shift, or precession, of the date of the equinox); and the ninth (or the first, counting from the outside, often called the *primum mobile,* Chaucer's **firste moevyng;** cf. Astr 1.17.35–41 and n.), which revolves daily from east to west, causing what appears to be the daily rising and setting of the sun, moon, and other heavenly bodies. The "second motion" referred to in the gloss is, as the rest of Ptolemy's ch. 8 makes clear, the west to east movement "contained by the first, and embracing itself all the planetary spheres," i.e., all eight inner spheres, which revolve at differing speeds and cause what appear to us to be the movements of the planets through the signs of the zodiac. This second movement is referred to by Chaucer as occurring **naturelly** (298), probably because it characterizes each sphere individually (cf. the use of *kyndely* in HF 730–36), in contrast to the movement of the *primum mobile,* which compels them all to revolve as a group in the opposite direction. Loomis (in Ch Problems, 207–20) cites a parallel passage from *The Sphere of Sacrobosco* (ed. and tr. Lynn Thorndike, 1949, 119–20): "The first movement carries all the others with it in its rush about the earth once within a day and night, although they strive against it, as in the case of the eighth sphere one degree in a hundred years." The main point of this stanza is thus to lament the daily revolution of the *primum mobile,* which was responsible for the configuration of the heavens, making it possible for **crueel Mars** to doom Custance's marriage to the Sultan from the moment she set out. Jill Mann (Lit. in 14th-cent. England, ed. Piero Boitani and Anna Torti, 1983, 169–71) points out that this lament is highly untraditional; the movement of the *primum mobile* was usually viewed as a force making for cosmic harmony.

302–8   This stanza gives a more particular account of the unfavorable configuration of the heavens at Custance's departure, using more technical terminology (see Elliott, Ch's English, 302–4, for Chaucer's innovative poetic use of technical terms) and assuming some knowledge of basic astrological concepts. In order to plot the location of the planets and signs of the zodiac, astrologers envisioned the annual pathway of the sun, the ecliptic, as a belt around the earth, which was divided into twelve "houses." These were numbered so that the sun, moving through them in order, began at one, also known as the **ascendent** (302; cf. Astr 2.4.16) from its location on the eastern horizon, and ended, after its course of twenty-four hours, by coming full circle to twelve, the house just below the horizon, also known as *carcer* (Lat.) or "prison" and thought of as the **derkeste hous** (304). These houses are also classified according to three types: an **angle** (304; cf. Astr 2.4.46n.) refers to houses 1, 4, 7, and 10; succedants are 2, 5, 8, and 11; and cadents are 3, 6, 9, and 12. The power of a planet or sign is affected by the type of house in which it is located; an *angle* reinforces the power of the planet or sign, and the *ascendent* is the most powerful of the angles. Hence the *ascendent* (the sign located in the ascendant house at a given moment) was the most important single point of any

astrological configuration. The configuration here is ill-omened because the *ascendent,* a **tortuous** sign (one of the six that rise obliquely on the horizon; cf. Astr 2.28 and n.), is one that happens to be ill-omened for Custance and her plans.

Each planet's power is also enhanced when it is in one of the two signs of the zodiac (the sun and moon each have only one sign) over which it is said to be **lord** (303). In this case the planet that is *lord* of the sign presently in the ascendant is not in that sign; it has fallen out of the *angle* (probably the ascendant, most powerful of the angles) into the *derkeste hous,* probably number twelve or *carcer* ("prison"), where its power is thwarted. The moon's situation is similarly **unhappy** (ill-omened): she is **fieble** because her power is thwarted by her location, having been **weyved** (moved) from a place that would enhance her power to one where she is **nat receyved,** a technical expression meaning that she is received unfavorably in a sign that does not enhance her power.

The ill-omened configuration of the *ascendent* and its *lord* (cf. Astr 2.4.32), coupled with the *unhappy* situation of the moon (which had special influence on travel, particularly on the sea, Conf. Aman. 7.721–54), add to the unfortunate astrological indications for Custance. She apparently has Mars as her **atazir,** probably meaning "the planet which is the characteristic sign of a nativity (*significator nativitatis*)," as the word was defined by John Walter, an Oxford master in 1383. Walter compiled a set of tables for determining astrological houses, which Chaucer may have known. North (RES 20:430–31) doubts that the original and technically accurate meaning of *atazir,* from Persian *tasyīr* translated by late Latin *directio,* was known to Chaucer, since it required an understanding of the complex calculations required to forecast the "direction" of each of the five key points in a nativity and to plot their locations at a precise time in the future. Eade (SAC 4:76–82) argues for the technical sense of *atazir;* MED and OED base their definitions on this unique use in Middle English. North's definition fits the grammatical construction best, with *atazir* in apposition to Mars.

Various attempts have been made by Skeat, Manly, Curry (Ch and Science, 164–94), North (RES 20:427–31), Wood (Ch and Stars, 200–34), and Loomis (in Ch Problems, 214–15) to give a detailed account of a specific astrological configuration based on this stanza. Their conflicting results suggest, however, as Eade argues (SAC 4:76–82), that this stanza does not provide sufficient information to reconstruct in detail the particular configuration Chaucer envisioned, if indeed he did have a specific one in mind. (A related problem is that astrological terminology is itself sometimes ambiguous; "house," for example, can refer to a sign of the zodiac as well as to one of the divisions of the ecliptic.)

309–15   The Latin gloss at 309 explains the rationale behind this lament that no **philosophre** (astrologer) was consulted in order to make an **eleccioun** (selection of an astrologically propitious moment) for the beginning of her journey: " 'All are agreed that elections are defective except in the case of the rich; indeed, it is permissible [to make an election] for these people because they, even if their elections be weak, have a "root" i.e., their nativities, which reinforces every planet that is weak in respect to the journey,' et cetera." The source of the gloss, as Tyrwhitt first noted, is the Jewish authority on astrological elections, Zahel Benbriz (Sahl ben Bishr ben Ḥabîb ben Hânî al-Isrâ'îlî, Abû 'Uthmân, d. c. 822–850; see Francis J. Carmody, Arab. Astronom. and Astrol. Sci. in Lat. Trans., 1956, 41–46). The passage is the incipit of his *De electionibus* (On Elections), a work sometimes attributed to Ptolemy or Mâshâ'allâh and often printed in early editions of collected works on astrology (e.g., Iulius firmicus maternus . . . astronomicorum libri VIII, by Nicolaus Pruckner, Basel, 1551, 102–14; see Carmody, 42–43, for MSS of the work and for other early editions). The rest of the opening section of Zahel's work clarifies the meaning of this passage in terms that explain MLT 313–14. In Zahel's view, elections are not valid unless they take into account the most important astrological influence on any individual, one's "root," (Chaucer's **roote . . . of a burthe**), i.e., the configuration of the heavens at the moment of one's birth. Since determining the root requires the services of expensive experts, only the rich are likely to know their root and consequently only they can have accurate elections made. The Man of Law laments that *eleccioun* on this basis was not made for Custance's journey, since she was of **heigh condicioun** and her *roote* was presumably known. Although the information in these lines is insufficient to reconstruct the exact configuration of the heavens at the moment of Custance's departure, the three negative signs described are sufficient, according to Zahel's treatise, to indicate that the moment is unpropitious for her journey: the *ascendent* is tortuous (302); the *atazir* is not favorable (305); and the position of the moon is unfavorable (306–8). The evidence of Zahel's treatise confirms the view of Eade (SAC 4:76–82) that the passage is intended as an accurate account of the process of making an election.

According to Smyser (Spec 45:371–72), this passage is evidence of Chaucer's own "real commitment to astrology," an "avowal of faith" in the use of astrology to make elections. (See Loomis, Ch Problems, 207, for a similar view.) Astr 2.4, however, contains Chaucer's explicit denunciation of the astrological uses of the ascendant for making *eleccions of tymes,* as "rytes of payens, in which my spirit hath no feith," and which are, moreover, too imprecise to be fully accurate. It is worth noting, following Curry (Ch and Science., 188–90) and Wood (Ch and the Stars, 192–244), that the Man of Law's astrologically-inspired dire predictions are not fully accurate—Custance does survive her voyage—and they do not take into account the workings of the divine providence in which Custance places her faith.

321–22 Paull (ChR 5:179–94) notes that passages of abrupt transition like this (cf. II.897–900, 953–54, 1124–25) characterize Chaucer's reshaping of Trevet and call attention to Custance as the main focus; Crosby (Spec 13, 1938, 413–32) takes them as marks of oral delivery.

358 In many MSS a marginal note *auctor* (either "author" or "authority") appears at this point. Robinson suggests that its purpose is to call attention to a "noteworthy utterance," called an *auctoritee* (see also WBPro III.1; MerT IV.1783; NPT VII.3050).

359 **Semyrame:** Semiramis, the militant queen of Babylon (cf. LGW 707), who was celebrated for her lust (cf. PF 288 and n.). Parr (ChR 5, 1970, 57–61), however, argues that here the reference is to the *Bibliotheca historica* of Diodorus Siculus (2.1–21, ed. Oldfather, Loeb, 1933, 349–424): after Semiramis persuaded her husband, King Ninus, to yield power to her

for five days, she gave a banquet during which she won over his enemies and had him thrown in prison. In Boccaccio's *De mulieribus claris* (chap. 2), where she is also described as lustful, she usurps the throne from her son. (On other medieval references to Semiramis, see Samuel, M&H 2, 1943, 24–44.) If the reference is to Semiramis as usurping power, then **Virago** is probably to be understood not as OED defines it, citing II.358, "a bold, impudent, (or wicked) woman," but in the sense defined by Gavin Douglas, describing Juturna in his translation of the Aeneid, "a woman exersand a mannis office" (12.8.56–58, Aeneid, ed. Coldwell, STS, 1960, 4:107); cf. the similar censure of Donegild as *mannysh* (II.782).

360–61 According to a tradition transmitted by Petrus Comestor (*Historia scolastica libri Genesis,* chap. 21; PL 198:1072), Satan "chose a certain type of serpent (as Bede says) having the face of a maiden" for the temptation of Eve. The snake in Paradise is frequently so depicted in late medieval art. Cf. PP B 18.335.

361 The brief allusions to the chaining of the fallen angels in 2 Peter 2.4, Jude 1.6, and Apoc. 20.1–2 are more fully developed in the account of the descent into hell that forms the second part of the apocryphal Gospel of Nicodemus. Spencer (Spec 2, 1927, 187–88) discusses some medieval treatments of the idea. See also II.634 and Buk 9–10.

365 On the envy of Satan, see Morton W. Bloomfield (Seven Deadly Sins, 1952, 382 n. 16), who cites Wisd. Sol. 2.24: "by the envy of the devil, death came into the world." Cf. ParsT X.492.

383 Chaucer adds to Trevet the gesture of the Sultan's kneeling to show devotion to his mother. On this and other key gestures added by Chaucer, see Windeatt, M&H 9:143–69, and Robert G. Benson, Med. Body Lang., Anglistica 21, 1980, 61–62, 130–33.

400–401 Lucan (Marcus Annaeus Lucanus, 39–65 A.D.) does not make a **boost** (clamor) about the triumph Julius Caesar held after his defeat of Pompey, because Caesar did not hold one (Pharsalia 3.73–79). Lucan does, however, record Caesar's own boast about the triumph he is planning (Pharsalia 4.358–62 and 5.328–34; see Shannon, Ch and Roman Poets, 114–15). In his work on the Trevet MSS for the Chaucer Library (see introductory note), Robert M. Correale has found a MS which says that after Caesar conquered Pompey, he "held a triumph for three years" (*tenoit la victoire trois aunz;* quoted in a talk at the 20th International Congress on Medieval Studies, Western Michigan Univ., 1985). See also MkT VII. 2719–20; HF 1499.

404 The scorpion was a common symbol of treachery; see BD 636–41 and n.

421 Lat. gloss (largely translated in the text): "Nota de inopinato dolore. Semper mundane leticie tristicia repentina succedit. Mundana igitur felicitas multis amaritudinibus est respersa; extrema gaudii luctus occupat. Audi ergo salubre consilium: 'In die bonorum ne immemor sis malorum.' (Innocent, De contemptu mundi 1.23.)" Innocent is quoting Ecclus. 11.27. The third sentence partially quotes Boethius (cf. II.422 and Bo 2.pr4.118–19) and Prov. 14.13 (Skeat 5:154). The sentiments are commonplace. See KnT I.1255–67; NPT VII.3205; Tr 3.813–33n., 1625–28n., and 4.836n.

448 Cf. KnT I.1662–73.

449–62 Skeat (5:155) quotes from a hymn of Venantius

Fortunatus ("Lustra sex qui iam peregit") as a source for the description of the Cross red with the blood of the Lamb (452) and alone worthy to bear the King of Heaven (457–58). Rosenfeld (MLN 55, 1940, 359–60) shows that this hymn and "Pange lingua gloriosi" were used for offices for the feast of the Exaltation of the Cross and for the Mass of the Presanctified on Good Friday. She suggests that Custance's prayer to the Cross before beginning her voyage reflects the votive Mass invoking the aid of the Cross for protection for travelers.

460–61   Skeat cites a parallel reference in Piers Plowman (B 18.429–31) to the cross as a talisman to ward off evils.

463–90   Farrell (NM 71, 1970, 239–43) notes that except for a reference to Noah (for whom Chaucer substitutes Jonas, 486) this passage is not based on Trevet. The figures cited—Daniel in the lions' den (Dan. 6.16–24), Jonah in the whale (Jon. 2:11), the passage through the Red Sea (Exod. 14:21–23)—are often found together in early Christian art and in the liturgy, as part of the rites administered to those near death. In art, the group is often joined by the figure of a woman praying. Yunck (ELH 27:249–61) notes that a similar speech on the help of God was frequently uttered by saints before their martyrdom. Schlauch (Kwartalnik Neofilologiczny 20, 1973, 305–6) notes that some versions of the *Gesta Romanorum* make parallels between Jonah and heroines like Custance.

482–83   On divine **purveiance** and human ignorance, see Bo 4.pr6, 5.pr4.

491–94   On the **foure spirites**, see the four angels who held back the winds in Apoc. 7.1–3.

500   **Egipcien Marie:** St. Mary the Egyptian, a prostitute in fifth-century Alexandria who repented her sins while on a pilgrimage to Jerusalem. She subsequently lived in the desert for 47 years, subsisting on weeds and grasses, having taken only two and one half loaves of bread into the desert with her (South Eng. Legendary, EETS 235, 1:136–48). Her legend was widespread in literature and in visual art. See Clogan, M&H 8:217–31.

502–3   For the miracle of the loaves and fishes, see Matt. 14.14–21, Mark 6.30–44, Luke 9.10–17, and John 6.1–13.

507–8   Smith (JEGP 47, 1948, 347–48) argues that Chaucer suppresses Trevet's "castle . . . near the Humber" because it might have suggested John of Gaunt's Pontefract and given rise to comparisons between Custance and Constance of Castile; Block (PMLA 68:599 n. 73) argues that the omission is part of a larger pattern of omissions of circumstantial details in Chaucer's adaptation of Trevet.

508   **Northhumberlond:** Chaucer follows Trevet in assigning this title to Alla's kingdom of Deira, which came to form part of Northumbria. Magoun (Ch Gazetteer, 115) suggests, however, that Chaucer probably was thinking of the modern county of Northumberland.

510   **of al a tyde:** See MED s.v. *of* prep. 5b.

519   Trevet, who notes that Constance had learned many languages, says she spoke Saxon. Chaucer's **Latyn corrupt** may refer to a similar incident in Boccaccio's version of the Constance story (5th Day, 2nd Tale; see McNeal MLN 53, 1938, 257–58) or it may be used as it is in the Alliterative Morte Arthure, where it seems to mean "Italian" (Benson ed., 3478–79). Burrow, MAE 30, 1961, 33–37, notes the tradition, common to all

these texts in Isidore's *Etymologiae* (9.1.6–7), that one of the four branches of Latin is the corrupt form called "mixed Latin."

532   ClT IV.413 and Tr 1.1078 are nearly identical.

557   **furlong wey:** Cf. MilT I.3637n.

578   **Alla:** the Old English king of Deira, Aella (regn. 560–588; Magoun, Ch Gazetteer, 115).

609   Cf. Tr 4.357.

610–68   Hamilton (in Stud. in Lang. and Lit. in Hon. of M. Schlauch, 153–63) notes that unlike Trevet and Gower, Chaucer makes the trial a formal judicial inquest before the king.

620   **Berth hire on hond:** accuses her falsely; the phrase is common in Middle English. See MED s.v. *beren* v. 13, Whiting H65; cf. WBPro III.226, 232 and n., 293, Anel 158, Tr 4.1404.

631–43   These lines suggest the custom of trial by the ordeal of battle; cf. GP I.239n. Hamilton (in Stud. . . . in Hon. of M. Schlauch, 153–66) notes in the breviary (in the order for the last rites; see "Ordo commendationis animae" in Breviarium monasticum, 1880, 260) a parallel reference to Susannah's divine rescue from a false charge (**Susanne**), which was also used in rituals associated with ordeals.

641   **Seint Anne:** The mother of Mary; see FrT III.1613n.

641–42   Cf. SNT VIII.69–70.

660   See KnT I.1761n.

676   Trevet (S&A, 172): "These things hast thou done, and I was silent" (hec fecisti et tacui), probably from Ps. 49.2 (AV 50.2).

701–2   See NPT VII.3443n.

754   **elf:** "An evil spirit in the form of a woman" (Trevet, S&A, 173). Cf. Promptorium parvulorum, EETS e.s. 102, 144: *"Elf, spyryt:* lamia-e." Elves, however, could also be male; cf. WBT III.873–74 and 880n.

771–77   Lat. gloss: "What is worse than a drunk, in whose mouth is a stench, in whose body a trembling; who utters foolish things, betrays secrets; whose mind is gone, whose face is transformed? 'For there is no secret where drunkenness reigneth' (De contemptu mundi, ii, 19)" (Innocent III, De miseria condicionis humanae, 2 19. 1–4, quoting Prov. 31.4, also quoted in Mel VII.1194).

778–79   Cf. KnT I.1459–60n.

782   **mannysh:** That is, devoid of feminine virtues; cf. MerT IV.1536n.; Tr 1.284.

784   Dante refers to a similar tradition that the souls of those who betray friends or guests go to Hell while their bodies continue to live (Inf. 33.124–32); see also LGW 2066–67. (Tatlock, MLN 29, 1914, 97–98, citing also John of Salisbury, Policraticus 3.8.)

786   **the kynges moodres court:** Edwards (PQ 19, 1940, 306–9) and Smith (JEGP 47:343–51) suggest that Chaucer omits the name Knaresborough, which occurs in Trevet and Gower, because it belonged to John of Gaunt and was associated with his difficulties with his wife, Constance of Castile (see also Giffin, Sts on Ch, 67–88); Block (PMLA 68:594 n. 58) argues that Chaucer suppresses most of the place names and circumstantial details in Trevet.

813–16   Echoes Bo 1.m5.34–46 and 4.pr1.19–31.

834–68   This pathetic scene between Custance and her child owes nothing to Trevet, whose brief, sardonic note sets another tone altogether: "Then, on the fourth day she was exiled with Maurice her dear son, who (thus) learned sailing at a tender age" (S&A, 175). It probably was inspired by a similarly pathetic scene of mother and child in Gower's version (Conf. Aman. 2.1054–83).

837–38   Brunt (N&Q n.s. 214, 1969, 87–88) cites Bartholomaeus Anglicus (De proprietatibus rerum 6.4; tr. Trevisa 1:299): children should be protected from bright light, "for a place that is to bright departith and todelith the sight of the smale eiye that bes right ful tendre"; cf. Vincent of Beauvais, Spec. Nat. 31:79. Lancashire (ChR 9, 1975, 324) notes that in many of the cycle plays Abraham covers Isaac's eyes as he prepares to sacrifice him.

841   Cf. ProPrT VII.467.

848–9:   Kean (Ch and Engl. Poetry 2:192) cites as a parallel a Middle English lyric (no. 7 in Carleton Brown, Relig. Lyrics of the 15th C., 1938, 5–8).

852   Cf. SNPro VIII.75n.

896   with meschance: Cf. FrT III.1334n.

925–31   Lat. gloss: "O extreme foulness of lust, which not only weakens the mind but also enervates the body; sorrow and repentance always follow afterwards (De contemptu mundi, ii, 21)" (Innocent III, De miseria condicionis humanae, 2.21.5–8, 12–13).

934   Golias: The Philistine giant Goliath, killed by David's slingshot (1 Sam. 17.4–51).

940   Olofernus: See MkT VII.2571–74.

946–47   Septe refers to the ridge of seven peaks, opposite Gibraltar in former Spanish Morocco, called "the seven brothers" (*septem fratres*); cf. Magoun, Ch Gazetteer, 142–43. Ceuta, an ancient seaport, lay at its foot.

981   Chaucer may have misunderstood Trevet's use of "nece" for cousin.

1009   In both Gower and Trevet, Constance tells the child how to act before Alla at the feast.

1126   olde Romayn geestes: Apparently a reference to Roman history in general, as used in WBPro III.642 and MerT IV.2284, rather than the *Gesta Romanorum,* where the life of Maurice does not appear.

1132–38:   Lat. gloss: " 'From the morning until the evening the time shall be changed.' [Ecclus. 18.26.] 'They take the timbrel and rejoice at the sound of the organ.' " [Job 21.12.] At 1135, Lat. gloss: "Who has ever passed an entire delightful day in his own pleasure, whom, in some part of the day, the guilt of conscience or the impulse of anger or the agitation of concupiscence has not disturbed? or the spite of envy or the burning of avarice or the swelling of pride has not vexed? Whom some loss or offense or passion has not upset, and the rest (De contemptu mundi i, 22)." Both glosses are from Innocent III, De miseria condicionis humane (1.20, "Of Brief Joy").

1140–41   Cf. BD 211.

1142   Cf. ParT X.762. Whiting (D101) cites this as proverbial.

1161   Joye after wo: Cf. Tr 1.4n.

The Man of Law's Epilogue

The Epilogue, or Endlink, of The Man of Law's Tale appears in 35 MSS; it is omitted from 22 MSS, including the Hengwrt, the Ellesmere, and all those with the "Ellesmere" arrangement (see introduction to textual notes to *The Canterbury Tales*).

In those MSS in which the Epilogue does appear, it almost invariably follows The Man of Law's Tale and it usually introduces The Squire's Tale. It was apparently composed at the same time as the Introduction to MLT, which it echoes in the repeated *thrifty tale* (46, 1165). As noted above (Introductory note to IntrMLT), the Man of Law's announcement that he speaks in *prose* has been explained by the plausible theory that he was originally assigned the prose tale of Melibee, and certain lines in the Epilogue (see 1188–90 below) do seem more suitable to Melibee than to the tale of Custance. It thus seems likely that the Epilogue was composed to follow The Man of Law's (then) Tale of Melibee. It is also probable that it was composed to introduce what is now The Shipman's Tale. The speaker who interrupts the Parson refers to *my joly body,* a phrase that is echoed in ShipT VII.423 and that seems to imply a female speaker (Pratt, PMLA 66:1141–67), and The Shipman's Tale was almost certainly written for a female speaker, most likely the Wife of Bath (see introductory note to ShipT below). There is, moreover, some evidence (see Pratt, cited below) that the speaker in II.1179 was originally the Wife of Bath, whose name was erased, leaving the space that scribes later filled with "Summonour/Sompnour," "Squier," or "Shipman" (see Textual Note to II.1179).

The Man of Law's Epilogue thus seems to bear witness to an early stage in the composition of the *Tales* when this sequence appeared: IntrMLT–Melibee–EpiMLT–ShipT. First the Wife of Bath was assigned a new tale and her name erased from II.1179 (see Pratt in Sts. in Hon. of Baugh, 45–79). Then the Melibee was reassigned, and the Man of Law was given the Tale of Constance. Editors differ on what happened next. One school (Furnivall, Skeat, Pollard, Baugh, Pratt) holds that Chaucer's final intention was to use the passage as a link to The Shipman's Tale; accordingly, they read *Shipman* in line 1179, and in their editions Fragment VII immediately follows. The other school believes that the passage was canceled. Manly (ed. CT) printed it in an appendix; Robinson printed it as it stands here, in brackets. Fisher, while believing the Epilogue was cancelled (81) prints it with *Wif of Bath* in line 1179, thus using it as a link to her Prologue. Donaldson had first adopted that solution, noting that it "does not represent Chaucer's final intention—if he had one" (1074).

1168   ye lerned men: Shipley (MLN 10, 1895, 136, 140) took the plural as referring to the Physician, Pardoner, Parson, and Man of Law, and thus as an argument for ordering the fragments I(A), VI(C), II(B); Furnivall agreed (Acad 2, 1895, 296). However, the reference to men of learning (which should perhaps include the Monk and Chaucer himself; Manly, CT, 572) need not imply they have told their tales, and the reference could be merely general, "all you learned men."

1169   Can moche good: Literally "know much good," a phrase of general application, meaning to be capable or competent, to know one's profit or advantage. Cf. WBPro III.231; BD 998, 1012; LGW 1175. Essentially the same idiom occurs in English as early as the Beowulf (nát he pára góda, line 681) (Robinson).

1171   swere: Swearing was endemic, even, as Manly notes (CT, 505), among Church dignitaries such as Sampson, the Abbot of Bury St. Edmunds, who swore "By the face of God" (Jocelyn of Brakeland, Camden Soc, 1844, 35, 169). The Host assumes that the Parson's objection to swearing indicates he is a Lollard, but though the Lollards raised special objections to the taking of oaths (Russell, Amer. Hist. Rev., 51, 1946, 668–84), orthodox preachers were equally opposed to casual swearing and cursing (Owst, Lit. and Pulpit, 416; cf. VI.629–59; X.587–99). The Host is the most enthusiastic swearer on the pilgrimage (Elliott, Ch's English, 256–59). Tupper (Types of Soc., 50) offers little evidence for his suggestion that inn-keepers were traditionally given to swearing, but the Pardoner does associate swearing with taverns (VI.472–76).

1172 **Jankin:** The diminutive of *Sir John* (cf. ProNPT VII.2810), a derisive name for a priest; MED s.v. *Jon.*

1173 **Lollere:** Lollard, a heretical follower of Wyclif's doctrines; see May McKisack, The Fourteenth Cent., 1959, 517–22; Gordon Leff, Heresy in the Later Middle Ages, 1967; and Anne Hudson, ed., Selections from Eng. Wycliffite Writings, 1978. "The Twelve Conclusions of the Lollards," setting forth their program, are printed in EHD, 848–50. Religious zealots of whatever persuasion were frequently accused of Lollardy; cf. Poems of John Audelay, ed. Whiting, EETS 184, 1939, 15: "Yif ther be a pore prest and spirituale in spiryt . . . thay likon him to a lollere and to an epocryte"; and The Bk. of Margery Kempe, ed. Meech and Allen, EETS 212, 1940, 28–29, 111–12, 135. Chaucer had friends who were Lollards, and he may have been sympathetic to some aspects of the movement (Brewer, Ch in His Time, 236). Loomis (in Essays and St. in Hon. of Carleton Brown, 1940, 141–44) and Bowden (Comm. on GP, 238) argue that the Parson is meant to be an actual Lollard. The Parson's Tale, however, is perfectly orthodox and, since Lollards were almost unanimously opposed to pilgrimages (cf. Walsingham, Historia Anglicana 2:188 and the eighth of the "Twelve Conclusions"), an actual Lollard would probably not have been on the pilgrimage.

The word *Lollard* is derived from the Dutch *lollaert,* "mumbler (of prayers)," which was applied to members of a lay order of mendicants, regarded as heretics by the clergy (H. B. Workman, John Wyclif, 1926, 1:327; Ekwall, ES 28, 1947, 108–10). The already existing word *lollere,* "a lazy vagabond, fraudulent beggar" (MED s.v. *lollere* 1.), was deliberately confused with the newly introduced *Lollard* (cf. PPC 10.213–29 and Skeat's note). "Zizannia: Ysider, lib. xiiii°, seith that poetes clepith this herb infelix lollium [cf. Virgil, Ecl. 5.37; Horace, Sat. 2.6.89], ungracious cokil other weed," and Thomas Wright, ed., Political Songs and Poems, 1859, 1:232: "Lollardi sunt zizania / Spinae vepres ac lollia / Quae vastant hortum vinea" (Lollards are tares, / Thorns, briars, and weeds / That destroy the vines in our garden).

1179 **Shipman:** Of the thirty-five MSS in which the EPiMLT appears, six read "Sommonour/Sompnour," twenty-eight "Squier," and one (the late Selden) "Shipman," which most editors have taken as the most probable reading. All three readings, however, are most likely scribal inventions (see textual note).

1180 **glosen:** Cf. SumT III.1792–94. The speaker is more worried about the prospect of hearing a sermon than being informed about Lollardry; Wyclif and his followers were much opposed to "glossing," preferring literal interpretation of the Bible (Sel. Eng. Wks. 1:376; Owst, Lit. and Pulpit, 61–62).

1183 **cokkel:** A common pun was made on *Lollard,* Lat.

lollium (weed), and the tares sown among the wheat in the parable of the tares (Matt. 13.24–30); cf. Gower, Conf. Aman. 5:1880–83, and Bartholomaeus Anglicus, tr. Trevisa (1:627).

1186–87 Cf. ProNPT VII.2794–98.

1188–90 It has often been noted that the references to philosophy, legal terminology, and Latin are more descriptive of Melibee than of the tale of Constance (e.g., Manly, CT, 572). Some scribes may have agreed; in a number of MSS line 1188 is changed to "Ne of art ne of astronomye," probably referring to lines 190–203, 295–315 in MLT.

1189 **phislyas:** The word (which does not appear elsewhere in English) apparently puzzled the scribes, who produced many variants (*phisilias, fisleas, philyas phillyas, (of) phisik, phisicians, speke, physices*). "The reading of O¹ was apparently 'phislyas' or 'phyllyas' (whether spelled with *ph* or *f* is doubtful)" (M-R 3:453). Skeat (5:167) suggested the original reading was *physices,* "with reference to the Physics of Aristotle, here conjoined with 'philosophy' and 'law' in order to include the chief forms of medieval learning." Shipley (MLN 10:134–35) relates *phislyas* to an Anglo-Saxon gloss "phisillos leceas" (leeches, physicians), which may explain the variants *(of) phisik, phisicians,* and *physices* but has not been accepted as the original reading. Manly and more recently Fisher have accepted the suggestion by Goffin (MLR 18, 1923, 335–36) that *phislyas* represents an uneducated speaker's attempt to use the legal term *filace,* "files" or "cases" (from OF *filaz,* med. Lat. *filacium,* late Lat. *chartophylacium*). The word seems clearly a corruption (whether the scribe's or the speaker's) of some more difficult form, but none of the explanations thus far offered is entirely convincing.

FRAGMENT III

The Wife of Bath's Prologue and Tale are generally regarded as the beginning of a "Marriage Group": her views on marriage provoke the responding tales of the Clerk, Merchant, and Franklin, with the intervening tales of the Friar, Summoner, and Squire serving as "interludes" in the continuing debate (Kittredge, MP 8, 1912, 435–67; cf. Hammond, Ch: Bibl. Man., 256–57; Kittredge's essay is reprinted in Ch Criticism, ed. Robert Schoeck and Jerome Taylor, 1960; on p. 158, n. 1, the editors provide a bibliography of the main discussions since Kittredge's essay appeared). This theory has had a powerful influence on criticism, though few critics accept Kittredge's theory without qualification, and it has been rejected by some; see Hulbert (SP 45, 1948, 565–77) and, most recently, Allen and Moritz (A Distinction of Stories, 106–7 and 116 n. 43), who place the Clerk's and Merchant's tales in a "moral" group and put the rest in a group of tales dealing with magic. Those who accept the "Bradshaw shift," by which Fragment VII precedes Fragments III–IV–V, would extend the "Marriage Group" so that it begins with the Melibee and Nun's Priest's Tale (W. W. Lawrence, Ch and CT, 1950, 125–36; Dempster, PMLA 68, 1953, 1142), or would read The Second Nun's Tale as its conclusion (Preston, Chaucer, 1952, 279–80; see also Howard, MP 57, 1960, 223–32, though he modifies his position in Idea of CT, 247 n. 36). Those who read the *Tales* in the order printed in this edition sometimes argue that the group begins with The Man of Law's Tale (see Huppé, A Reading of CT, 107). Owen (Pilgrimage and Storytelling, 144–210) would include the tales of the Physician and Pardoner within a group with the fragments in the order III–VI–IV–V. As the arguments of these critics show, a concern with the problems of marriage is not restricted to the tales of Fragments III–IV–V, and those tales concern problems broader than that of who shall be sovereign in marriage—the relation of authority to sexuality in the context of marriage (Kaske, in Ch the Love Poet, 45–65), the position of women in society (Cooper, Structure of CT, 222–24; cf. Diamond, on Authority of Experience: Essays in Feminist Crit., ed. Arlyn Diamond and Lee R. Edwards, 1977, 60–83), and the broader issues of the need for mutual respect and forgiveness in human relations (Richmond, Viator 10, 1979, 323–54). Kittredge's belief that the Franklin speaks for Chaucer in resolving the problem of sovereignty has frequently been challenged (see introductory note to The Franklin's Tale below). For general discussions see David (Strumpet Muse, 182–92) and Kean (Ch and Poetry 2:139–64).

That Fragment III has a unity independent of the concerns of the "Marriage Group" is argued by East (ChR 12, 1977, 78–82), who sees the three tales as explorations of the problems of experience versus authority posed by the Wife, and by Wasserman (Allegorica 7, 1982, 65–99), who finds a thematic unity in the philosophic opposition of the Wife of Bath and Summoner to the Friar.

LARRY D. BENSON

The Wife of Bath's Prologue

The date of composition of this prologue cannot be precisely determined. Chaucer seems to have developed his conception of the Wife of Bath and the stylistic devices he uses in her prologue over a considerable period of time (see Pratt in Sts. in Hon. of Baugh, 45–79, and, for a modification of Pratt's view, Boren, NM 76, 1975, 247–56). A reference to the Wife in the Lenvoy de Chaucer a Bukton (Buk 29) indicates her Prologue was in existence when that Envoy was written, but its date, usually taken as 1396, is not certain. The references to the Wife in The Merchant's Tale (IV.1685) and in the conclusion to The Clerk's Tale (IV.1170) show that her Prologue preceded the final versions of these tales, but their dates are likewise undetermined. The heavy use of Jerome's Epistola adversus Jovinianum here and in the Merchant's and Franklin's tales may help indicate a date, since Chaucer's earlier works show no direct knowledge of Jerome (the quotations in the Melibee come from its source in Albertanus of Brescia); Jerome, who is not mentioned in the first version of the Prologue to The Legend of Good Women, is cited directly in the revised Prologue (see LGW G 268–312 and n.). That revised Prologue is usually dated around 1395–96 and the Wife of Bath's Prologue is therefore assigned to a date before that. Lowes (MP 8, 1911, 305–34) argued that Chaucer

The explanatory notes to The Wife of Bath's Prologue and Tale were written by Christine Ryan Hilary.

was also heavily indebted to Deschamps's Miroir de mariage, a copy of which, Lowes believed, Chaucer obtained in 1393. Chaucer's use of the Miroir has been seriously questioned by Thundy (see below) and that Chaucer obtained a copy of that work in 1393 is mere conjecture. Yet a date in the early to mid 1390s seems probable and is accepted by most scholars. Blake (Leeds SE 13, 1982, 42–55) argues that both Prologue and Tale were revised; if so, the composition may have extended over a considerable period.

The character of the Wife is principally derived from that of La Vieille, and secondarily from that of Le Jaloux, in the Roman de la rose, one of the most influential of Chaucer's sources throughout the Prologue (see Fansler, Ch and RR, 168–74). La Vieille is one of the numerous tribe of "old bawds" in Western literature (Garbáty, Jnl. of American Folklore 81, 1968, 342–46), and Chaucer may have been influenced by some of her ancestors (such as Ovid's Dipsas; see Matthews, Viator 5, 1974, 413–43). Muscatine (Ch and Fr Trad., 65) notes resemblances to the prostitute-heroine Richeut (ed. Lecompte, RomR 4, 1913, 261–305) and to the widow in the fabliau Le Veuve (see Rom. Sts. in Memory of Edward B. Ham, 1967, 109–14, and Charles H. Livingston, Le jongleur Gautier le Leu, 1951, 159–83.). Carter Revard (SP 79, 1982, 122–46) notes resemblances to the preaching bawd, Gilote, in the Anglo-French Gilote et Johane in Harley 2253, ed. in Achille Jubinal, Nouveau recueil de contes, dits, fabliaux, 1842, 2:28–39. On Chaucer's use of his French antecedents, see Muscatine (Ch and Fr Trad., 204–13).

Most of Chaucer's other sources for the Prologue come from antifeminist literature. In addition to the Roman de la rose, his principal sources are Jerome's Adversus Jovinianum, Theophrastus's Liber aureolus de nuptiis (preserved in Jerome, Adv. Jov. 1.48), Walter Map's Epistola ad Rufinum de non ducenda uxore (in De nugis curialium 4.3–5), and, perhaps, Deschamps's Miroir de mariage. Deschamps's unfinished work may not have been known to Chaucer; though Lowes (MP 8:329) believed that he obtained a copy of it, Thundy (in Ch Probs, 49–53) argues that it was not in circulation until after Deschamps's death in 1406 and that the resemblances between the Miroir and the Wife of Bath's Prologue derive from their common source, the Lamentationes of Matheolus, which Chaucer probably used in Jehan Le Fèvre's French translation (see van Hamel's intro. to his edition; Manly, CT, 579–81; Moore, N&Q 190, 1946, 245–46). Thundy overstates his case but does show direct borrowing in a number of instances, as noted below. On the antifeminist satiric tradition in the earlier Middle Ages, see A. Wulff, Die frauenfeindlichen Dichtungen des Mittelalters bis zum Ende des XIII Jahrhunderts, 1914, and, for the ME and Scots tradition, see Francis J. Utley, The Crooked Rib, 1944. The most important passages from Chaucer's antifeminist sources are collected, with other analogues and bibliographical notes, by Whiting in S&A, 207–22. On Chaucer's use of medieval antifeminism, see Patterson, Spec 58, 1983, 656–95. The Prologue is also notable for its heavy use of proverbs; see MacDonald, Spec 41, 1966, 453–65, and Whiting, Ch's Use of Proverbs, 92–100.

The form of the Prologue is that of a literary confession, like that of La Vieille in the Roman. Duncan argues for the use of rhetorical amplificatio in the shaping of the

Prologue (MP 66, 1969, 199–211). The Pardoner and Friar seem to regard the Wife's performance as a kind of sermon (III.165, 1277), and she does draw on pulpit rhetoric (Shain, MLN 70, 1955, 241, pulpit literature Owst, Lit. and Pulpit, 389, and exempla (Miller, ELH 32, 1965, 442–56). Patterson makes a good case that the Prologue is a mock sermon, a "sermon joyeux" (Spec 58:674–80).

The character of the Wife of Bath has fascinated readers and critics and has elicited a considerable volume of critical literature. Alyson explains herself by reference to astrological influences, and these have been studied in detail (Curry, Ch and Science, 91–118; Wood, Ch and the Stars, 172–80). Since 1912, however, the major approach to the study of her character has been from the standpoint of, or in reaction to, Kittredge's theory of the "Marriage Group" (see note on Fragment III above). According to this theory, the Wife sets forth an unorthodox doctrine of marriage to which the other tellers in the "Marriage Group" respond. Most critics agree that her position in the matter is indeed unorthodox, even heretical (see Robertson, Preface to Ch, 317–31), yet Howard notes that she is less radical than she has been made out to be (Idea of CT, 248–52), and David argues that her basic position is one that many of the time would have accepted, that indeed it represents Chaucer's own feelings (Strumpet Muse, 158). Some critics have raised the question of whether the Wife really wants sovereignty after all (see introductory note to her tale, below).

Such criticism takes the Wife as a sympathetic figure, one of the great comic characters in our literature (Donaldson, 1075) and one of Chaucer's most masterful creations (see esp. Muscatine, Ch and Fr Trad., 204–13), yet with a touch of the tragic (Root, Poetry of Ch, 236) and all the more human for her frailties and inconsistencies (Jordan, Ch and the Shape of Creation, 208). Against this is the view, gaining in strength in recent years, that she has no personality of her own but is a universalized representation of some aspect of womankind (Shumaker, ELH 18, 1951, 77–89), an allegorical or typological construct (Robertson, Pref to Ch, 317–30; Delasanta, ChR 12, 1978, 218–35; cf. Donaldson, TSL 22, 1979, 1–16), or a prostitute-martyr to patriarchy (Weissman, ChR 15, 1980, 11–36; cf. Delaney, Minnesota Rev. n.s. 5, 1975, 104–15). To some recent critics, far from being a sympathetic character, Alyson has become a monster—androgynous, spiritually corrupt in both sexes (Rhodes, Jnl. of Women's Studies in Lit. 1, 1979, 348–52), a frigid nymphomaniac (Rowland, NM 73, 1972, 381–95) and a "sociopath" (Sands, ChR 12, 1978, 171–82). The Wife has indeed attracted critical extremes, including the attempts in recent years to revive the theory—first advanced as an elegant joke by Hall (Baker Street Journal 3, 1948, 84–93)—that she murdered her fourth husband; for a review and refutation, see Hamel, ChR 14, 1979, 132–39. The volume of recent studies—from sociological, economic (e.g., Robertson, ChR 14, 1979–80, 403–20), and feminist (e.g., Aers, Ch, Langland, and the Creative Imagination, 1980; Carruthers, PMLA 94, 1979, 209–22) as well as literary points of view—shows that she has imbued criticism and scholarship with some of her own unflagging energy.

The Prologue is one of the most heavily glossed parts of the *Tales,* most often with quotations from Chaucer's sources in Jerome, *Adversus Jovinianum* (see Caie, ChR 10, 1976, 350–60). The Latin marginal glosses quoted below are from the Ellesmere and related manuscripts, unless otherwise noted.

1–2 Cf. RR 12804–5: "Mais je sai tout par la practique:/Esperiment m'en ont fait sage" (I know all by practice: Experiment has made me wise); see KnT I.3000–3001. Chaucer frequently appeals to experience (e.g., FrT III.1517; SumT III.2057; HF 876–78), and his Parson notes, on the subject of women, "Ther neden none ensamples of this; the experience of day by day oghte suffise" (see X.927 and n.). Many critics have explored the conflict between experience and authority, most recently Burlin, Ch Fiction, 3–22; Justman, ChR 11, 1976, 95–111; and Lawler, One and the Many, 83–108.

4 **twelve yeer:** In canon law, the legal age of marriage for girls (Manly, CT, 575); cf. ClT IV.736.

6 Cf. GP I.460n.

9–24 The Wife closely follows the argument of Jerome, Adv. Jov. 1.14 (S&A, 209).

11 Lat. gloss: "In Cana Galilee" (John 2.1, from Jerome, Adv. Jov. 1.40). The argument in lines 11–34 is from Adv. Jov. 1.14 (S&A, 209).

13 Lat. gloss: "For by going once to a marriage he taught that men should marry only once" (Jerome, Adv. Jov. 1.40).

15 John 4.6, 18 (so glossed in Egerton 2864—Additional 5140).

23 Lat. gloss: "The number of wives is not defined since, according to Paul, those who have wives be as though they had none," alluding to Jerome, Adv. Jov. 1.15, and quotes 1 Cor. 7.30 as in Adv. Jov. 1.13.

28 Lat. gloss: "Increase and multiply" (Gen. 1.28, from Jerome, Adv. Jov. 1.3). This was the text on which the Brothers and Sisters of Free Love, a continental heretical sect known in England, based their pantheistic doctrines of sexual license; see Mahoney, Criticism 6: 144–55. Critics have often noted that the Wife is apparently childless; cf. NPT VII.3344–45.

30–31 Matt. 19.5, as cited by Jerome, Adv. Jov. 1.5.

33 **bigamye and octogamye:** Successive (second and eighth) marriages (from Jerome, Adv. Jov. 1.15, S&A 209). Jerome specifically allows widows remarriage, but clerics (such as the Wife's fourth and fifth husbands) who married widows were guilty of bigamy; see Matheolus, Lamentationes, 1–8 (Le Fèvre 1.59–60), and Dives and Pauper, EETS 280, 2:112–16.

35 **Salomon:** Cf. 1 Kings 11, where Solomon is said to have had seven hundred wives and three hundred concubines, and cf. MerT IV.2242n.

38 **refresshed:** See Higdon, cited in 144–45 below.

44a–f Although Chaucer may have meant to cancel lines 44a–f, Manly and Rickert argue that the most reasonable hypothesis concerning these and lines 575–84, 605–12, 619–26, and 717–20 is that Chaucer inserted them in a later revision (see Textual Notes). Baugh (383), however, notes that lines 44a–f were omitted in the best MSS and offers the opinion that they break "the nice continuity between lines 44 and 45." For lines 44c–e, cf. MerT IV.1427–28n.

46 **chaast:** The reference is to "chaste widowhood," that of the widow who does not remarry and remains celibate for the rest of her life. Nowhere is it explicitly stated that the Wife is a widow, though most critics agree that she is. See 503–14 below.

46–51 The marginal Lat. glosses quote 1 Cor. 7.28 (from Jerome, Adv. Jov. 1.13), 7.39 (Adv. Jov. 1.14), and 7.9 (Adv. Jov. 1.9).

52 From 1 Cor. 7.28; it became proverbial (Whiting, W162).

54–56 Lameth, Abraham, Jacob: The marginal Lat. gloss quotes 1 Cor. 7.9 from Jerome, Adv. Jov. 1.9, and notes "Lamech, a man of blood and a murderer, was the first to enter bigamy etc., Abraham trigamy, Jacob quatrigamy," which approximates Jerome, Adv. Jov. 1.14, 5, (S&A 209, 208). For the story of Lamech and his two wives, see Gen. 4.19–23. Cf. SqT V.550–51 and Anel 150.

64–65 Th'apostel: St. Paul, 1 Cor. 7.25; cf. Jerome, Adv. Jov. 1.12 (S&A, 208–9), where Jerome, citing this verse, makes clear there is no absolute commandment to virginity. When the definite article is used with *apostel*, the reference is almost invariably to Paul.

67 Proverbial; Whiting C472. Howard points out that by undermining virginity the Wife of Bath is also undermining a medieval notion of personal perfection (MP 57, 1960, 223–32). For a clear, if perhaps overly sympathetic, discussion of virginity as a concept in St. Jerome's notion of the holy life, see Dumm, The Theological Basis of Virginity according to St. Jerome, 1961.

71–72 Jerome, Adv. Jov. 1.12 (S&A, 209): "If the Lord were to decree virginity . . . whence would virginity be born?" (Cf. also Jerome, Epistolae 22.20 in CSEL 54, 143–211, tr. F. A. Wright, Select. Letters, 1933, 94–97.)

73 Poul: St. Paul. The marginal Lat. gloss quotes 1 Cor. 7.25 as in Jerome, Adv. Jov. 1.12.

75 Lat. gloss: "He invites candidates to the course, He holds in His hand the prize of virginity, (virginitatis bravium) [saying] he that is able to receive it, let him receive it, etc.," from Jerome, Adv. Jov. 1.12, (S&A, 209). Egerton 2864–Additional 5140 gloss Rom. 15.18 and 1 Cor. 9.24, whence Jerome derives *bravium* (Gr. βραβεῖον), a prize in a footrace. Skeat (5:293), following Tyrwhitt, suggests that a *dart* was a common prize in footraces and compares the similar use of *spere* in Lydgate, Fall of Princes 1.5108–9.

76 Proverbial; Whiting C112.

77–78 "Perhaps suggested by Matt. 19.11–12" (Robinson).

81 1 Cor. 7.7; quoted in the Lat. gloss from Jerome, Adv. Jov. 1.8.

84 1 Cor. 7.6.

87 The Lat. gloss quotes 1 Cor. 7.1 as in Jerome, Adv. Jov. 1.7, omitting "homini." MSS Additional 35286 and Egerton 2864–Additional 5140 quote the verse correctly at line 95.

89 Proverbial (Whiting F182), and glossed in MSS Egerton 2864–Additional 5140 by Prov. 6.27–29 and 1 Cor. 7.1, which is the source of line 87 above.

91 From Jerome, Adv. Jov. 2.22.

99–101 From Jerome, Adv. Jov. 1.40 (S&A, 210), echoing 2 Tim. 2.20.

103 The marginal Lat. glosses quote the last part of 1 Cor. 7.7 as in Jerome, Adv. Jov. 1.8. The gloss is preceded by 1 Cor. 12.4 in MSS Egerton 2864–Additional 5140.

105 Lat. gloss: "The [hundred and] forty-four thou-

sand who sing will follow the lamb," from Rev. 14.3–4 as in Jerome Adv. Jov. 1.40.

107–12 This reference to Matt. 19.21, and the rejection of its message by the speaker, is paralleled in the speech of Faux Semblant in RR 11375–79. See also Jerome, Adv. Jov. 1.34 and 2.6. For a brief but lucid explication of the grades of chastity as a component of perfection, i.e. marriage, widowhood, and virginity in ascending order, see Howard, MP 57:224–25: See also 67 above.

110 The Ellesmere MS has an explanatory gloss to **foore**, ".i. [=i.e.] steppes" (M-R 3:502), which suggests "footsteps." See Matt. 19.21 and SumT III.1935.

112 Almost identical with Mel VII.1088 and MerT IV.1456.

113 Baum (PMLA 71, 1956, 230) finds here a pun on "age," lifetime of experience, and "age," day and generation. Sanders (PLL 4, 1968, 192–95) finds an intricately developed pun on "flour," meaning "virginity," involving the grinding of meal on a grindstone. See also 477–78 below.

115–23 For the argument here, see Jerome, Adv. Jov. 1.36 (S&A, 210), and RR 4401–24.

129–30 The reference is to 1 Cor. 7.3, quoted in the gloss of several MSS. Moore (N&Q 190:245–48) finds a parallel to these lines and to lines 152–57 and 197–202 in Matheolus, Lamentationes, 2073–78 and 582–84 (Le Fèvre, 2.3277–94 and 1.1337–43). For an explanation of the conjugal debt, see 198 below.

132 sely instrument: Thundy (in Ch Probs, 36) compares Le Fèvre 2.1879 "beauls instrumens," sexual organ (of either sex).

135–41 Cf. Jerome, Adv. Jov. 1.36 (S&A, 210).

144–45 It is not Mark but John 6.9 that mentions barley loaves in the miracle of the loaves and fishes. Cf. Jerome, Adv. Jov. 1.7 (S&A, 208). Robertson, Pref to Ch, 328–29, would take **barly-breed** as an identification of the Wife with the Old Law. It is mentioned as humble fare, fit for horses, asses, and beggars in 1 Kings 4.28, Judg. 7.13, and 2 Kings 4.42. RR 2755–57 suggests that it was prison food. But Rowland, referring to Eustathius, *Commentarii ad Homeri Iliadem et Odysseam,* 1.134.22 and 3.948.48 (ed. Hildesheim, 1960), Martial (14. ep. 69 and 9. ep. 2), and folk songs and customs, argues that *barly-breed* here may recall Priapic loaves offered as love tokens, sometimes associated with magic (Neophil 56, 1972, 201–6). Higdon (PLL 8, 1972, 199–201) notes the miracle of the loaves and fishes is read as the Gospel for "Dominica Refectionis," mid-Lent Sunday, known also as "Refreshment Sunday." He suggests that this, along with Jerome's use of white and barley breads as metaphors for chastity and incontinence, suggested *refresshed* in lines III.37–38.

147 Cf. 1 Cor. 7.20, quoted from Jerome, Adv. Jov. 1.11 in the marginal Lat. gloss.

152–57 See 129–30 above.

154–60 The Wife of Bath misuses Paul's notion of the conjugal debt (1 Cor. 7.4), to which these lines allude, and his notion of the subordination of wives, Eph. 5.22, throughout. The **tribulacion** in line 156 refers to 1 Cor. 7.28.

155 Lat. gloss: "He who has a wife is regarded as a debtor, and is said to be uncircumcised, to be the servant of his wife, and like bad servants to be bound," (Jerome, Adv. Jov. 1.12); MSS Egerton 2864-Additional 5140 gloss the entire verse from 1 Cor. 7.3, of which only the first part was quoted at line 130.

158	Lat. gloss: "And although you are the slave of a wife, do not on account of this grieve. If you marry you have not sinned, but such shall have tribulation in the flesh, etc. He does not have power over his own body, but his wife (does). Husbands, love your wives," from Jerome, Adv. Jov. 1.13, 16, alluding to 1 Cor. 7.28 and 7.4 and to Eph. 5.25 or Col. 3.19.

165–68	On the Pardoner's interruption here and other digressions from the narrative in the Prologue and Tale, see Moore, MLQ 10, 1949, 49–57, and Silverstein, MP 58, 1961, 153–73.

170	**another tonne:** Cf. Bo 2.pr2.74–76: " . . . in the entre or in the seler of Juppiter ther ben cowched two tonnes, the toon is ful of good, and the tother is ful of harm?" From these, Fortune serves all with sweet or bitter drinks (RR 6813–54); cf. Gower, Conf. Aman. 6.330–48,

8.2253–58. The ultimate source of the idea is Homer, Iliad 24.527. However, cf. ParsT X.859, and for another possible explanation see 199 below.

180–83	**Ptholomee:** His **Almageste** originally contained neither this proverbial saying (Whiting A118, M170; cf. Tr 3.329n.) nor the quotation in lines 326–27. They appear in a collection of apothegms (probably written by the twelfth century "Albuguafe," Emir Abu 'l Wafâ Mutaskshir ben Fatik; see Boll, Anglia 21, 1899, 222–30) that appear as a preface in the Latin translation of the *Almagest* by Gerard of Cremona (cf. the edition printed in Venice, 1515). Chaucer may have known a manuscript of the *Almagest* (Young, SP 34, 1937, 1–7) or taken the references from some collection (see Flügel, Anglia 18, 1896, 133–40). Cf. MilT I.3208. The Wife of Bath's antifeminist sermon follows a conventional pattern like that in "Golias de conjuge non ducenda" (see 489–90 below) and other works: first the question of taking a wife, then evidence of women's defects, and finally examples of men injured by marriage. See Moore, MLQ 10:49–57, and Sanders, SMC 4, 1974, 437–45.

197–202	See 129–30 above.

198	**the statut:** The *debitum,* the conjugal debt, whereby sexual relations were acknowledged as legitimately due both marriage partners (cf. ParsT X.375, 940; MerT IV.2048). This idea was widely disseminated; see, for instance, Peter Lombard, *Sententiae* (PL 192: 922), and St. Thomas Aquinas, *Summa theologiae,* "Supplementum Tertiae Partis," Q.64, a.1 (see also Mogan, ChR 4, 1970, 123–141, and Rowland, NM 73:2, 1972, 388). The Wife of Bath, however, would ordinarily forfeit her right to sexual relations in view of the elderly or otherwise disabled or abused condition of her husbands; on *debitum,* see Cotter, ELN 6, 1969, 169–72. On the subject of marriage as the *iurata fornicatio,* another possible meaning of *statut,* see Harwood, MLQ 33:257–73. For lines 198–202 and 213–16, cf. Miroir de mariage, 1576–84 (S&A, 217).

199	Lat. gloss: "The high priests of Athens to this day emasculate themselves by drinking hemlock," from Jerome, Adv. Jov. 1.49. Silvia (SP 62, 1965, 28–39) suggests that this gloss may have been a note by Chaucer to himself to amplify the Wife's veiled threat to the Pardoner in lines 169–78.

207–10	La Vieille expresses a similar idea in RR, 13269–72.

218	"At Dunmow, near Chelmsford in Essex, a flitch [a side] of bacon was offered to any married couple who lived a year [and a day] without quarrelling or repenting of their marriage" well into the twentieth century (Robinson); see also Steer, Essex Record Office Publication 13, Chelmsford, 1951; Shaver, MLN, 50, 1935, 322–25; Hench, Southern Folklore Qtly. 16, 1952, 128–31.

222–34	Lowes (MP 8:317–18) finds a parallel in Miroir de mariage, 3634–35 and 3544–55 (S&A, 221–22).

227–28	This is almost literally from RR 18136–37, "Plus hardiement que nus on/Certainement jurent e mentent" (Certainly they swear and lie more boldly than any man) and is glossed in MS Cambridge Dd., "Verum est" (It is true!).

231	For the idiom, see MLT II.1169n.

232	**beren hym on honde:** Deceive him (cf. III.226 and 393), a variant of *bere on honde,* accuse falsely (see MLT II.620n.). For a study of its use here and elsewhere see Duncan TSL 11:19–33.

  cow: An allusion to the widespread tale of the talking bird; when it tells a husband of his wife's adultery, the wife, usually with the collusion of the maid (cf. III.233), persuades him that the bird is mad. Chaucer may have known the version in the *Seven Sages of Rome* (cf Benson and Andersson, Lit. Context, 366–71); he tells another version in the MancT.

235–47	Cf. Miroir de mariage, 1589–1611 (S&A, 217–18), which is based in turn upon Theophrastus *Liber de nuptiis,* preserved in Jerome, Adv. Jov. 1.47. See also Matheolus, *Lamentationes,* 1107–14 (Le Fèvre, 2.1452–59).

236	Cf. lines 265–70 and ClT IV.1207–10.

246	**dronken as a mous:** Cf. KnT I.1261n.

248–75	This passage is paralleled in Deschamps's *Miroir de mariage,* 1625–48 (based on Theophrastus *Liber de nuptiis,* preserved in Jerome, Adv. Jov. 1.47; S&A, 211), and is supplemented by RR 8579–8600 (S&A, 213–14). In the passage parallel to lines 257–61, Theophrastus tells by what means men woo women, but the Wife of Bath gives reasons why women are desired. Lowes (MP 8:314) suggests that the discrepancy may be due to Chaucer's following Deschamps's "pour son gent corps" instead of Theophrastus's "forma." Pratt (MLN 74, 1959, 293–94), however, suggests that Theophrastus's "alius forma, alius ingenio, alius facetiis, alius liberalitate sollicitat" may have reminded Chaucer of similar reasons why men desire women that were widely circulated by Isidore of Seville: "pulchritudo, genus, divitiae, mores" (Etymologies, 9.7.29); Isidore apparently develops this from a passage in Donatus on Terrence in which are listed "forma, probitas, dos, nobilitas" (P. Wessner, ed., Aeli Donati commentum Terenti, 2, 1905, 381).

253–56	Cf. RR 8587–92 (S&A 213): "S'el rest bele, tuit i acueurent/ . . . Tuit li vont entour, tuit la prient" (If she is beautiful, all will come running . . . all will surround her, beg her). With this and III.265–70, cf. ClT IV.1207–10.

263–64	Cf. RR 8595–96 (S&A, 213–14), "Car tour de toutes parz assise/Enviz eschape d'estre prise," (For a tower besieged on all sides can hardly escape being taken).

265–70	Cf. RR 8597–8600, "S'el rest laide, el veaut a touz plaire;/E coment pourrait nus ce faire/Qu'il gart chose que tuit guerreient,/Ou qui veaut touz ceus qui la veient?" (If on the other hand, she is ugly, she wants to

please everybody; and how could anyone guard something that everyone attacks [guard one] who wants all
those who see her?). The sentiment is ultimately from
Theophrastus, Liber de nuptiis (PL 23.277); see Lowes,
MP 8:314.

269–70 Possibly proverbial, though unrecorded before
Chaucer; see Whiting G382.

271–72 This directly translates: "Molestum est pos-
sidere, quod nemo habere dignetur"; it is from Theophrastus as quoted in Jerome, Adv. Jov. 1.47 (S&A, 211).

272 his thankes: On the construction, see KnT-
I.1626n.

273 lorel: The word appears only here and in Bo
1.pr4.308, translating "perditissimum," one who is utterly lost (see Elliott, Ch's English, 225).

278 Proverbial; cf. Mel VII.1086n. In a number of
MSS the glosses note its source in Prov. 9.13 and
27.15–16. See Taylor, Hessische Blätter für Volk-
skunde, 1925, 24, 130ff.

282–92 Chaucer is again following Theophrastus (in
Jerome, Adv. Jov. 1.47; S&A, 211) along with RR 8667–
82 and either Deschamps's Miroir, 1538–59, 1570–75
(S&A, 216–17), or, more likely, Matheolus, Lamentationes, 2425–34 and 800–811 (Le Fèvre 3:265–68 and
2:393–418). In III.285–89, Chaucer translates directly
from Theophrastus.

293–302 This passage is also from Theophrastus in
Jerome, Adv. Jov. 1.47 (S&A, 211); cf. Deschamps's
Miroir (1765–77; S&A, 219).

303 Lat. gloss: "And the curled darling who manages
her affairs, etc.," from Jerome, Adv. Jov. 1.47 (S&A,
211), indicating that Chaucer was still following Theophrastus. The name **Janekyn** is common in ME lyrics for
rustic lovers, especially clerks (since it is a diminutive of
"Sir John," a contemptuous term for a priest; cf. II.1172
and n.); see Elliott, Ch's English, 203, and Mustanoja in
Med. Lit. and Folklore, 65–66.

308–16 See Duncan, MP 66:199–211, and with 310 cf.
MerT IV.1300.

311 Oure dame: An instance of what Tatlock (SP 18,
1921, 425–28) termed the " 'domestic *our*,' an extension
of the ordinary possessive to cases where it involves taking the point of view of the person addressed and finally
becomes stereotyped." Cf. III.432, 595, 713, 719; SumT
II.1797, 1829, 2128; FranT V.1204; ShipT VII.69, 107,
356, 363; NPT VII.3383.

312 Seint Jame: Cf GP I.466n.

327 Lat. gloss: "Among all men he is higher who does
not care in whose hand rests the world." See III.180 and
Young, SP 34:1–7.

332 queynte: Elegant, pleasing thing; a euphemism,
here referring to either sexual activity or the female sexual organ. Cf. III.444 and MilT I.3276 and n.

333–34 Cf. BD 963–65n. The idea is proverbial (Whiting C24), but here is probably from RR 7410–14,
where, as here, it has sexual implications. Cf. the widespread tale of Virgil's revenge on his mistress, in which
she supplies fires for the whole city of Rome "in a way
better left undescribed" (Domenico Comparetti, Virgil
in the M.A., tr. E. F. M. Benecke, 1895, 326–36).

337–39 Cf. Miroir de mariage, 1878–84 (S&A, 219–
20) and 8672–91.

341 The Lat. gloss quotes 1 Tim. 2.9 from Jerome,
Adv. Jov. 1.27.

348–54 This figure appears in Deschamps's Miroir,

3208–15 (S&A, 220), and in Matheolus, Lamentationes,
1939–44 (Le Fèvre, 2.3071–80). For other parallels see
van Hamel's introduction to Matheolus, 2:clxiv.

354 a-caterwawed: For the form, see PardPro
VI.406n.

357–60 Cf. RR 14381–84 and 19393–94 and Matheolus, Lamentationes, 1800–1801 (Le Fèvre, 2.2979–
80). **Argus** was the hundred-eyed son of Jupiter and
Niobe, commissioned by Juno to watch over Io, whom
Zeus loved and had transformed into a heifer (Ovid,
Met. 1.622–723). He was famed for watchfulness and
cunning, though the idea that women could trick him was
widespread; see Tr 4.1459n. and cf. MerT IV.2111.

361 make his berd: Proverbial; cf. RvT I.4096 and n.

362–64 Lat. gloss: "eciam odiosa uxor si habeat virum
bonum et cetera" from Jerome, Adv. Jov. 1.28, quoting
Prov. 30:21–23. Cf. Duncan, MP 66:199–211.

371 Lat. gloss: "Her love is compared to hell, to the
burning earth and to fire etc. Hell and woman's love, and
the earth that is not satisfied with water, and the fire, saith
not enough, etc.," from Jerome, Adv. Jov. 1.28 (S&A,
210), quoting Prov. 30:16. Jerome has "amor mulieris"
for the Vulgate's "os vuluae" (Skeat 5:301).

373 wilde fyr: "Greek fire," a flammable preparation,
composed mainly of naphtha, used as a weapon in naval
warfare; it could not be quenched with water.

376 Lat. gloss: "Like a worm in wood, so a (wicked)
woman destroyeth her husband," from Jerome, Adv.
Jov. 1.28 (S&A, 210), quoting Prov. 25.30.

378 Lat. gloss: "No one can know better than he who
suffered through them, what a wife or woman is," which
closely approximates Jerome, Adv. Jov. 1.28.

382–94 Cf. Matheolus, Lamentationes, 686–88 and
1045–46 (Le Fèvre, 2.77–83, 1080–84, and 1099–
1106).

386 Cf. also Anel 157; probably proverbial though not
recorded before Chaucer (Whiting H530).

387–92 Cf. Miroir de mariage, 3600–3608, 3620–22,
3629–32 (S&A, 220–21).

389 Proverbial; see Whiting M558 (the first use in English); it is known in Latin (Walther, 1142) and Swedish
(S. B. Ek, Scripta Minora Regiae Societatis Humaniorum
Litterarum Lundensis, 1963–64:1) and remains current
in "First come, first served." Rowland (Expl 24, 1965,
Item 14) notes a Biblical and classical tradition of the
association of miller, grain, grinding, and mill with sexual relations, the "mill" representing woman. See also
144–45 above.

393 For the technique here, cf. RR 13828–30 and Miroir 3920–35 (S&A, 222).

398 Baum (PMLA 71:236) finds a pun on "dight,"
with the Wife implying that one of her old husbands has
"done" better for his paramour than for her in providing
finery, though the first meaning here is the sexual one
(for which cf. III.767, MancT IX.312, and PP C 2.27–
28).

401 Many MSS (not the Ellesmere group) have the
gloss "ffallere flere statuit deus in mulier" (Lying and
weeping, God gave unto woman); cf. Walther, 8751,
and Whiting D120.

407–10 Cf. RR 9091–96.

414 Possibly proverbial, though this is the only recorded example in Middle English (Whiting W286).
The commercial imagery is notable; cf. III.447, where
the Wife is portrayed as selling her *bele chose,* and 478

where she sells the *bren;* see Rowland, Archiv 209, 1972, 278 n.

415   Proverbial; see RvT I.4134 and n.

418   bacon: Bacon; may refer to old meat, "and so here for old men" (Robinson). Hoffman, referring to the "Dunmow flitch" (cf. 218 above), argues that the Wife's admission she does not delight in bacon means she has "never striven for a happy marriage" (N&Q 208, 1963, 9–11).

432   Wilkyn, oure sheep: Baugh (389) takes *Wilkyn* (a diminutive for William) as the name of a pet sheep; it is more likely the name of the husband whom the Wife addresses with a variant of the "domestic plural" (see 311 above) and to whom she uses the infantile *ba* for "kiss" (see Elliott, Ch's English, 224, and MilT I.3709n.). Her William is as meek as a sheep.

435   spiced conscience: Probably "scrupulous, fastidious conscience" (cf. GP I.526 and n.) (Robinson). But Rockwell (N&Q 202, 1957, 84) interprets the phrase here as meaning "a bland, gentle disposition, to be recommended to all husbands," and not the same as GP I.526; also see Rex, MP 80, 1982, 53–54.

455–56   Cf. MerT IV.1847–48.

460   Lat. gloss: "Valerius 6.3: Metellius killed his own wife whom he had struck with his staff because she had drunk wine," referring to Valerius Maximus, Factum et dictorum memorabilium (ed. Kempf, 1888). The story is also told in Pliny, Hist. Nat. 14.13, with the name Mecenius. For Chaucer's further use of the same chapter from Valerius, see 642 and 647 below.

464   Cf. Ovid, Ars Amat. 1.229–44, and, on the association of wyn and **Venus,** see PF 275–76n.

466   Proverbial, though this is the first appearance in English (Whiting M753, Tilley T395).

467–8   The Lat. gloss in MSS Egerton 2864–Additional 5140 quotes Ecclus. 26.11: "A drunken woman is filled with great anger and pride, and has no defense against sin." The source may rather be RR 13452–53, "And when a woman is drunk she has no defense at all." But the idea is common enough; cf. Whiting C619, R92; Ovid, Ars Amat. 3.765; and 464 above.

469–73   Chaucer follows RR 12932–48 very closely: "Par Deu! si me plaist il encores/Quant je m'i sui bien pourpensee;/Mout me delite en ma pensee/E me resbaudissent li membre/Quant de mon bon tens me remembre/E de la joliete vie/Don mes cueurs a is grant envie;/Tout me rejovenist le cors/Quant j'i pens e quant jou recours;/Touz les biens dou monde me fait/Quant me souvient de tout le fait,/Qu'au meins ai je ma joie eüe,/Combien qu'il m'aient deceüe. /Jenne dame n'est pas oiseuse/Quant el meine vie joieuse,/Meïsmement cele qui pense/D'aquerre a faire sa despense." (O God! But it still pleases me when I think back on it. I rejoice in my thought and my limbs become lively again when I remember the good times and the gay life for which my heart so strongly yearns. Just to think of it and to remember it all makes my body young again. Remembering all that happened gives me all the blessings of the world, so that however they may have deceived me, at least I have had my fun. [tr. Dahlberg, 224])

477–78   Perhaps proverbial, though this is the only recorded instance (Whiting, F299); cf. 113 above.

483   Seint Joce: St. Judocus (Josse), a seventh-century Breton saint, symbolically identified by the pilgrim's staff (see Haskell, ChR 1, 1966, 85–87). His relics were at Hyde Abbey, whose Abbot owned the Tabard Inn and had lodgings adjacent to it; Reisner (Ch Newsletter 1, 1979, 19–20) suggests the saint is named as a "bit of local lore." The name appears in the *Testament* of Jean de Meun, 461ff. "When dame Katherine sees the proof of *Sir Joce,* who cares not a prune for his wife's love, she is so fearful that her own husband will do her a like harm that she often makes for him a staff of a similar bit of wood (d'autel fust une croce)"; (Skeat, 5:303, who offers this as the source of the *Joce/croce* rhyme).

487   The proverb (Whiting G443) is still current.

489–90   The notion of marriage as earthly purgatory is common enough to make ascribing it to a certain source unlikely. A particularly appropriate parallel is to be found in Matheolus, Lamentationes, 3024–29 (Le Fèvre, 3.1673–95), in which Christ appears in a dream and announces: "O peccatorum quia mortem nolo, redemptor/Et pugil ipsorum, cum res non debeat emptor/Emptas tam care pessundare, jamque parare/circo volui sibi purgatoria plura,/Ut se purgarent; egros sanat data cura;/Inter que majus est conjugium." (O, since I who am the redeemer and scourge of sinners do not desire their death—for the buyer should not destroy goods bought so dearly—I wanted to provide for them many torments so that they might purify themselves. The prescribed cure heals the sick; among these [torments] the greatest is marriage.)

Lines 197–98 of "Golias de conjuge non ducenda" in Latin Poems, ed. Wright, 84, have: "Quid dicam breviter esse coniugium?/Certe vel tartara, vel purgatorium." (What shall I say, in brief, is marriage?/Certainly either hell or purgatory!) Cf. MerT IV.1332, 1670.

492   The proverb (Whiting S266) is still common, but this probably echoes Jerome, who tells of the Roman sage who, blamed for divorcing his wife, said that only the wearer of an ill-fitting shoe knew where it pinched (Adv. Jov. 1.48; S&A, 212); see also Map's letter of Valerius, 152, and 672 below. The same story (to which Chaucer also alludes in MerT IV.1553) is told in John of Salisbury, Policraticus, 5.10; and in Walter Map, De nugis curialium, 4.3 (S&A, 213).

495   Cf. GP I.463.

496   roode beem: "The beam, usually between the chancel and the nave, on which was placed a crucifix" (Robinson). Such burial within the church itself was reserved for the very prosperous.

498–99   Lat. gloss: "Appelles wrought a wonderful work in the tomb of Darius, in Alexandreid 6." Appelles was a Jewish craftsman whom Darius's fictional but elaborate tomb is ascribed in lines 6.381ff. of Gaultier de Chatillon's twelfth-century *Alexandreid* (ed. Mueldener, 1863, summary in Lounsbury, Sts. in Ch 2:354).

503–14   Compare this with La Vieille's more leisurely recollections of a satisfying but destructive relationship, RR 14472–546. Most readers take line 504 to mean that Janekyn is dead. Silvia (N&Q 212, 1967, 8–10) is nearly alone in arguing that he is alive, but that the Wife of Bath, following her pattern, has lost interest in him and is actively seeking a replacement before she becomes a widow again. See 46 above.

516–24   For the idea that something given too freely is despised, see RR 13697–708. For the proverb in 517–20, see Whiting W549.

522   Perhaps proverbial, though this is the only occurrence in Middle English (Whiting P368).

534–38   For women's inability to keep secrets of any kind, see RR 16347–75, but the idea is commonplace. See 950 below.

543–49   Cotter (PLL 7, 1971, 293–97) argues for an ironic interpretation of the Wife of Bath's violations of the spirit and letter of Lent in her sexual interest in Janekyn, her clothing, and her general demeanor. But Boyd (AmN&Q 1, 1963, 85–86) suggests the word **Lente** may here be used in its older sense, "springtime," though this is doubtful. See Bo 2.pr5.67n.

552   There is a close parallel to this line in Deschamps's Miroir de mariage, Ch. 43, rubric. Chaucer's direct source may have been RR 9029–30: "E vont traçant par mi les rues/ Pour voeir, pour estre veües" (they go strolling through the streets in order to see, in order to be seen), which is based on Ovid, Ars Am., 1.99.

555–58   See RR 13522–28 and Matheolus, Lamentationes, 988–91 (Le Fèvre 2.947–52). On **vigilies,** see GP I.377n.

557   Cf. RvT I.3954–55.

559   **wered upon:** *upon* is adverbial as *upon* in III.1382 and *on* in 1018. Cf. Mod. Eng. "What did she have on" (Robinson).

560–62   Cf. Matt. 6.19–20.

570–74   For a widow thinking of a new husband at her late husband's funeral, as here and at III.587–92 and 617–29, see Matheolus, Lamentationes, 862–65 and 953–55 (Le Fèvre 2.597–601, 847–52).

572–74   Chaucer echoes RR 13150–52, and possibly Matthieu de Vendôme, *Ars versificatoria* (Manly, Ch and the Rhetoricians, 1926, 12). MS Egerton 2864 glosses line 573: "It is a miserable mouse who hides in only one hole." Cf. Whiting M739.

575   **enchanted:** For this sense, cf. RR 13691 and PP B 2.42.

576   The reference here and in III.583 to **My dame** is debatable. It may be to La Vieille in RR (Koeppel, Anglia, 14, 1892, 253); to Dame Alys, her *gossyb,* in line 548 (Wood, Expl 23, 1965, Item 73); possibly, but not likely, to Venus (Curry, PMLA, 37, 1922, 32); or, more likely, to her own mother, as suggested by "la mere" in Chapters 34–37 of Deschamps's Miroir and Matheolus, Lamentationes, 1362. PardT VI.684 and MancT IX.317, however, seem to indicate that the phrase was of loose or general application.

581   Rowland (Archiv 209:277n.) cites Artemidori Daldiani, *Onirocriticon,* 5, ed. Roger A. Pack, 1963, 42.6 and 67.24, in illustration of this belief. See also Arnoldus de Villa Nova, *Expositiones visionum,* in *Opera,* 1524, 1.4 and 2.2, as cited by Curry, Ch and Science, 212.

587–92   See 570–74 above.

593–99   For sentiments similar to those here and at III.627–31, see Miroir 1966–77 (S&A, 220) and Ovid, Ars Am. 3.431.

602   **coltes tooth:** See RvPro I.3888n.

603   **Gat-tothed:** see GP I.468n.

604   **Venus seel:** Most likely a violet or purplish birthmark located upon the "loins, testicles, thighs, or perhaps upon the neck" (Curry, Ch and Science, 106, quoting Les Oeuvres de M. Jean Belot, Lyon, 1654, 225).

608   *quoniam*: A Lat. conjunctive adverb ("since, therefore") or a relative ("that") introducing a clause, here used as a euphemism for pudendum, as in Matheolus 1237 and as translated by LeFèvre (2.1748–49), in which men and women rush "Pour faire charnelment

congnoistre/Leur quoniam et leur quippe" (To make carnally acquainted their *quoniam* [female genitals] and *quippe* [male genitals]); see Thundy, Ch Probs, 36. The phrase *quoniam bonum,* meaning "female genitals," appears, along with a number of the Wife's other euphemisms, in Rabelais (see the list of Erotica Verba in Vol. 3 of Oeuvres, Paris, 1820).

613   At the time of the Wife's birth the zodiacal sign of Taurus, a domicile of Venus, was ascending, and the planet Mars was in it. The Lat. gloss (at 609) reads, "Mansor Amphorisoun [i.e., aphorismorum] 14: 'Whenever they are in ascendance unfortunately one will bear an unseemly mark upon the face. At the nativities of women when a sign is ascending from one of the houses of Venus while Mars is in it, or vice versa, the woman will be unchaste' [from Almansoris Propositiones, printed in Astrologia Aphoristica, Ptolomaei, Hermetis, . . . Almansoris, etc., Ulm, 1641, 66.] 'She will be the same if she has Capricorn in ascendance; thus Hermes in his trustworthy book, the 24th aphorism' [in the volume cited above, though the section quoted is the 25th]."

615   **inclinacioun:** The Wife of Bath justifies her conduct by astrological determinism. Curry (PMLA 37:48) describes her as "a fair Venerian figure and character imposed upon and oppressed, distorted and warped by the power of Mars." The Wife's horoscope is imprecise; Wood (Ch and the Stars, 172–80) modifies Curry's analysis and holds that Mars and Venus were not in conjunction at the Wife's birth. He suggests that the Wife uses astrology to set herself against clerks, whom she disparages with so common but so antiestablishment an idea as that of the stars' mitigating moral responsibility. Dives and Pauper (EETS 275, 125) presents the orthodox view: one "is enclyned be the werkyngge of the bodyes abouyn," but by virtue may overcome this inclination and so "euery wys man is lord and mayster of the planetys." See MLT II.295–315nn. and Astr 2.4.57–69n.

615–26   The Wife of Bath proudly claims some of the worst practices charged to women in medieval antifeminist literature. See, for example, "Golias de conjuge non ducenda," in Walter Map, Latin Poems, ed. Wright, 77–85, reviewed in Utley, The Crooked Rib, 136–37.

618   **chambre of Venus:** From RR 13336.

619   **Martes mark:** Cf. the gloss cited in 609. Skeat notes the more precise statement in Ptolemy *Centum dicta,* 74 (in Almansoris Propositiones, etc.): "Whoever has Mars ascending will indeed have a mark (cicatricem) on the face." For the form *Martes,* see SqT V.50n.

624   From RR 8516, "Ne vous chaut s'il est cours ou lons" (It doesn't matter to you if he is short or long).

627–29   See 570–74 above.

630–33   Legally, the Wife was in no way bound to surrender ownership of her property to her husband; he was, however, required to provide a dower for his wife. See Margulies, MS 24, 1924, 210–16, and GP I.460n.

642   Lat. gloss: "Valerius lib. VI. fo. 14," i.e., Valerius Maximus, *Facta et dicta memorabilia* 6.3, to which the incidents here and in 647 refer. In this case *Romayn geestes* does not refer to the *Gesta Romanorum;* cf. MLT II.1126n.

647   **Another Romayn:** P. Sempronius Sophus, from Valerius Maximus 6.3.

648   This may be a reference to the revels on Midsummer Eve (A. C. Cawley, ed., CT, 1958, 175), which

Robert Mannyng, Handlying Synne, EETS 119 and 123, 4681–86, implies were indecent.

651–57   Ecclesiaste: Ecclesiasticus. At line 657 the Lat. gloss has "[Nor] allow a bad wife to say what she likes" (Ecclus. 25.31, in part); MSS Egerton 2864-Additional 5140 have the fuller form along with Prov. 14.25 at line 638.

655–58   This might be a popular jingle, though these lines are its first appearance (Whiting H618). Some verses from the Lansdowne MS (c. 1417) printed in *Reliquiae antiquae* I.233 repeat, with minor changes, III.655–57 and are probably based on Chaucer. Cf. Skeat 5:308.

660   For this and the lines following, MSS Egerton 2864–Additional 5140 gloss Prov. 3.11; 9.7; 10.17; 12.1; 13.18; 15.10, 12, and 32, all of which concern the value of discipline but none of which is appropriate, except possibly 12.1 ("He who hates rebukes is foolish") for line 662. These MSS add: "Qui enim impatiens est odit disciplinam."

662   RR 9980 has, "Si het quiconques la chasteie" (She hates whoever corrects her). This is perhaps based upon Ovid, Rem. am. 123–24, which circulated separately as a proverb (Walther, 11556). On the Wife's possible knowledge of the *Remedia amoris*, see GP I.475 and n.

669–75   Janekyn's *book of wikked wyves* is a fictional collection of antifeminist and antimatrimonial works written to encourage young men to choose celibacy. Chaucer most likely created it from his own collection of similar materials, possibly bound in one volume according to the usage of the time (on medieval collections of "classics" similarly preserved see Harbert in Ch: Writers and Background, 139–41), to which he added "a few other authors and titles so as to give the imagined volume an appropriate and distinctive personality"; see Pratt, in Memoir of Karl Young, 1946, 45–56, in Sts. in Hon. of Baugh, 45–79, and in AnM 3, 1962, 5–27.

671   Valerie and Theofraste: Valerius, the supposed author of Walter Map's famous letter (c. 1180), *Dissuasio Valerii ad Rufinum Philosophum ne uxorem ducat* (The Advice of Valerius to Rufinus the Philosopher not to Marry; De nugis curialium, 4.3); and Theophrastus, the author of *Aureolus liber Theophrasti de nuptiis* (The Golden Book of Theophrastus on Marriage), a vitriolic antimarriage tract preserved only in Jerome, Adv. Jov. 1.47 (see Schmitt, Viator 2, 1972, 251–70). On the *De nuptiis* and related treatises see Pratt, AnM 3, 1962, 6–12.

674–75   Jerome . . . book agayn Jovinian: Jerome's *Epistola adversus Jovinianum.* Jerome writes from the standpoint of Christian asceticism. But Delahaye (MS 13, 1951, 65–86) suggests he also draws on classical philosophy and particular medieval anti-feminist texts. See also Pratt, Criticism 5, 1963, 316–22.

676   Tertulan: Tertullian (c. 150–c. 230) did not write a specific book against marriage but his *De exhortatione castitatis, De monogamia,* or *De pudicitia* could have found a place in Janekyn's imaginary book.

677   Crisippus: Probably the antifeminist writer mentioned by Jerome, Adv. Jov. 1.48. Hamilton (Ch's Indebtedness to Guido della Colonna, 190) suggests that Chaucer may have had in mind the stoic Chrysippus mentioned in Cicero's *De divinatione* 2; Pratt (JEGP 61, 1962, 244–48) suggests he may have known a work by Chryssipus on marriage through its quotation in a treatise by a later Stoic (in Iohannes ab Arnum, ed. Stoicorum veterum fragmenta, vol. 1, 1905, and vol. 4, 1924).

Trotula is probably Trotula di Ruggiero, an eleventh-century female physician of Salerno, the reputed author of treatises on gynecology (known as *De begritudinibus mulieribus* or *De passionibus mulierum,* the *Trotula Major*) and on cosmetics (*De ornatu mulierum,* the *Trotula Minor*), neither of which appears in antifeminist MS collections. There is no evidence that Chaucer knew Trotula directly.

Helowys is Heloise, the eager lover but reluctant wife of Abelard, who expressed her antimatrimonial ideas in her letters to her husband, which were translated by Jean de Meun (see Schultz, La Vie et les Epistres de Pierres Abaelart et Heloys sa fame, A Trans. by Jean de Meun, etc., Ph.D. diss., University of Washington, 1969). Chaucer probably did not know the letters directly; he could have known of Heloise from RR 8759–8832.

679   Parables of Salomon: Owst (Lit and Pulpit, 285–86) finds the ultimate source of the Wife of Bath in Prov. 7.10–12. Boren (NM 76:247–56) suggests the perfect wife of Prov. 31.10–31 may have been an "up-so-doun" influence on Chaucer's characterization of the Wife.

680   Ovid's *Ars amatoria* was sometimes included in antifeminist manuscript collections.

688   an impossible: Perhaps simply "an impossiblility" (so MED), one of the "impossibles" (adynata); cf. Tr 3.1495–98n.; but more likely referring to *impossibilia,* school exercises in dialectic consisting of the logical proof of impossible propositions (e.g., "God does not exist," "The Trojan war is now in progress"). See the *Impossibilia* in Siger de Brabant, Ecrits de logique, de morale et de physique, ed. Bernardo Bazan, 1974; and Paul V. Spade, The Medieval Liar: A Catalogue of the Insolubilia-Literature, 1975. Cf. SumT III.2231n., FranT V.1009.

692   This allusion, possibly proverbial, is to the fable, originally Aesopian, of the man and the lion: a peasant shows a lion a likeness of a peasant killing a lion with an axe, and the lion asks, did a man or a lion make this likeness? But the painting of the lion (rather than sculpting, as in Aesop) suggests Marie de France's version of the fable as the source of the allusion (Fables, No. 37; see Pratt, Tales, 269, n. 692). See Malvern, SP 80, 1983, 238–52.

702   The Lat. gloss has: "The one falls where the other is exalted" and then explains at 705, quoting Almansoris Propositiones, 2 (see 613 above): "In Book One of Mansor, the exaltation of a planet is said to be that place in which another suffers the contrary etc., as Mercury in Virgo, which is the fall ["casus," or dejection] of Venus; the one, Mercury, signifies knowledge and philosophy, the other [Venus] song, lively joys, and whatever is pleasant to the body." That is, the **exaltacioun** of Venus (the sign of the zodiac in which she exerts her greatest influence; see Astr 2.4.47n.), which is in Pisces, is the "dejection" ("casus," fall) of Mercury, of **diverse disposicioun** to Venus; Virgo is the "dejection" of Venus, the "exaltation" of Mercury.

707–10   Cf. LGW G 261–63.

715–26   Eva (Eve), **Sampson** (Samson), and **Dianyre** (Deianira) are all named in Epistola Valerii (De nugis curialium, 4.3). For Samson, see also RR 9203–6 and MkT VII.2015–94; for Hercules and Deianira, see MkT VII.2119–35 and RR 9195–98.

727–32   This story of **Socrates** and **Xantippa** is from Jerome, Adv. Jov. 1.48 (S&A, 212), where the dirty water ("aqua immunda") is not necessarily **pisse**. Line 732 is proverbial, but Chaucer's use of it is the earliest example (Whiting T267). On Socrates as a model of patience, see BD 718 and For 17.

733 Lat. gloss: "Why should I refer to Pasiphae, Clytemnestra, and Eriphyle, the first of whom, the wife of a king and swimming in pleasure, is said to have lusted for a bull, the second to have killed her husband for the sake of an adulterer, the third to have preferred a gold necklace to the welfare of her husband, etc., thus Metellius Marrio according to Valerius" (from Jerome, Adv. Jov. 1.48).

Phasipha, Pasiphae, was wife of Minos of Crete and mother of the Minotaur, fathered upon her by a bull. Cf. Ars amatoria 1.295–326.

737 **Clitermystra:** Clytemnestra committed adultery in the absence of her husband, Agamemnon, whom, on his return from Troy, she murdered in his bath.

741 **Amphiorax:** Amphiaraus was betrayed by his wife *Eriphilem.* Eriphyle, into joining the war against Thebes, the fatal result of which he foretold. When he was about to be killed, Jupiter made him immortal. Chaucer adds details from Statius, Thebaid 4. For the spelling, see GP I.384n.

747 **Lyvia** and **Lucye** appear in the Epistola Valerii (De nugis curialium 4.3, S&A, 213). The former poisoned her husband, Drusus, at the instigation of her lover, Sejanus (23 A.D.); the latter, known also as Lucilla, accidentally poisoned her husband, the poet Lucretius (d. 55 B.C.), with a love potion.

757 The story of a hanging-tree appears in the Gesta Romanorum, chapter 33; in the Epistola Valerii (De nugis curialium 4.3, S&A, 212–13), which is notably Chaucer's source here; and in Cicero, *De oratore* 2.69, the ultimate source (where only one wife is mentioned). The original of the name **Latumyus** is uncertain; it appears in none of the other versions.

765–68 Possibly an allusion to the story of the Widow of Epheseus (Petronius, Satyricon, 91), who succumbed to a lover's advances in the presence of her husband's corpse, though she did not murder him. Pratt (MLN 65, 1950, 243–46) notes that this story, the one alluded to in III.769–70, and the mention of poison in 771 are all paralleled in John of Salisbury, Policraticus, 7.20.

769–70 Probably an allusion to the story of Jael and Sisera (Judg. 4.21).

775–77 Ecclus. 15.16; cf. Mel VII.1087n. MSS Egerton 2864–Additional 5140 gloss with Ecclus. 25.23: "A bad wife brings humiliation, downcast looks, and a wounded heart. Slack of hand and weak of knee is the man whose wife fails to make him happy."

778–79 Prov. 21.9–10.

782–83 From Jerome, Adv. Jov. 1.48 (S&A, 212), but ultimately from Herodotus 1.8.

784–85 Lat. gloss: "Circulus aureus in naribus suis Mulier formosa et fatua .i. impudica," quoting Prov. 11.22 and adding ".i. impudica," ("i.e., unchaste"). The same passage is quoted in ParsT X.156.

794 **wood leoun:** A common comparison; cf. SumT III.2152 and Whiting L326, L327.

800–810 Walter Map's *De nugis curialium* 2.26 contains an anecdote about a wounded man who begs his attacker to take a kiss to his wife and children. When the attacker kneels for the kiss, the wounded man stabs him. Tatlock (MLN 29, 1914, 143) suggests that this anecdote supplied Chaucer with the Wife of Bath's stratagem.

813 For the figure of the bridle, see Bo 1.m.7.20 and 2.m.8.17, and Robertson, Pref to Ch, 22–23 and fig. 6.

824 **Denmark unto Ynde:** That is, throughout the whole world; cf. Tr 5.971. Such collocations were common in both French and English (Whiting C63, I36, L427); cf. PardT VI.722; BD 889–90; Rom 624 and Hassell J6: "Pareille n'a, d'Inde jusqu'à Saint Jame."

829–49 The historical enmity between mendicants and possessioners, here represented by the Friar and Summoner, was a long-standing professional rivalry. See Williams, Spec 28, 1953, 499–513, and AnM 1, 1960, 22–95. Braswell, ESC 2, 1976, 373–80, suggests some tales in the *Legenda aurea* as a source for the anti-mendicant satire here and in the tale.

831 **preamble:** This word—like **preambulacioun** in III.837—is new to English from French and peculiar to Chaucer in his day. See Elliott, Ch's English, 386, and Davis, in Ch: Writers and Background, 74. Tatlock (in Flügel Memorial Volume, 1916, 230) finds a pun on *preamble.*

834–36 Proverbial; Whiting F336.

847 **Sydyngborne:** See ProMkT VII.1926 and n.

The Wife of Bath's Tale

Most scholars agree that what is now The Shipman's Tale was originally intended for the Wife of Bath. (For an objection see Blake, Leeds SE 13, 1982, 42–55.) The tale she now tells is sometimes said to differ markedly in style from her prologue, but it is just as often said to accord with the Wife's notion of female dominance in marriage and to embody her fantasies of sexual and emotional satisfaction with a young man even late in life (see, for example, Owen, JEGP 52, 1953, 303–4, and Townsend, MLR 49, 1954, 1–4). The opening and closing passages (III.862–81 and 1257–64), obviously written with the Wife in mind, seem to stand out for their aggressiveness and sexual preoccupation from the rest of the tale, and it may be that Chaucer never completed an intended integration of tale and teller. The tale in its present form was probably written about the same time as the prologue, around the early to mid 1390s. It is usually classified as a romance (see Severs, in Comp. to Ch, 271–95, with bibliography), though Finlayson argues against this (ChR 15, 1980, 168–81).

Chaucer's exact source is unknown. The story of the disenchantment of a "loathly lady" is widespread (see George H. Maynadier, WBT: Its Sources and Analogues, 1901) and was known in a variety of forms, such as that in the popular "Fair Unknown" romances, in which the lady is transformed into a serpent. The particular form that Chaucer used, that in which the disenchantment is connected with the theme of sovereignty, apparently originated in Ireland (Sigmund Eisner, A Tale of Wonder, 1957). It occurs in an Arthurian setting in two brief Middle English romances, The Marriage of Sir Gawain and The Weddynge of Sir Gawen and Dame Ragnell, and (without the Arthurian setting) in the ballad King Henry and in the Tale of Florent in Gower's *Confessio amantis* (all four versions are printed by Whiting in S&A, 223–68). Chaucer knew and probably echoes Gower's version (see III.1081 and n.). None of the analogues includes the rape with which the Wife's tale begins; Coffman (MLN 59, 1944, 271–74) adduces an Irish analogue and suggests that it derives from the Life of St.

Cuthbert; Loomis (SP 38, 1941, 29–31) suggests it may come from the Middle English Romance Sir Degare, in which a princess, lost in a forest, is raped by a knight from Fairyland. It could as easily have been suggested by Gawain's casual seduction of a damsel (told in the Middle English Jeaste of Syr Gawayne), in which he fathers the hero of the "Fair Unknown" romances, or it may be Chaucer's own invention.

The majority of the analogues concern the disenchantment of the "Loathly Lady." Roppolo (CE 12, 1951, 263–69) presents the plausible argument that Chaucer combined this motif with that of the "Converted Knight," since the tale concerns the knight's reformation as much as the Hag's transformation.

The choice offered to the hero, a wife foul and faithful or fair and possibly faithless, is unique to Chaucer's version (fair by night and foul by day or vice versa is the usual formulation) and perhaps derives from satirical antimarriage tracts (see Schlauch, PMLA 61, 1946, 416–30, and Hoffman, AmN&Q 3, 1965, 101). Murtagh (ELH 38, 1971, 473–92) argues that Chaucer uses the tale to allow the Wife to free herself from the ungenerous notion of womanhood (beautiful and unchaste or undesirable and chaste by necessity) in the satiric antifeminist tradition. Chaucer's version is also unique in that the hero grants the woman sovereignty before her transformation, swayed by her arguments rather than her beauty.

The concern with *gentillesse* and the Hag's sermon on that subject are likewise found only in Chaucer's version. Malone (MLR 57, 1962, 481–91) believed that this feature may have resulted partly from the "Arthurization" of the original tale. Chaucer's principal sources for the discussion of *gentillesse* were Dante, Boethius, and RR (see 1109 below), though the idea is commonplace; the Hag's defense of her ugliness and low birth is somewhat similar to the defense offered by an ugly, middle class man in one of the dialogues in Andreas Capellanus's *De amore* (tr. Parry, 53–62).

Until recent years most studies of the tale concerned its sources. Critical studies in the past decades have concerned the problem of the knight and courtly love (see the summary of criticism in Cary, PLL 5, 1969, 375–88); the significance of the rape (Gerould, Ch Essays, 75–76; Malone, MLR 57:481–91; Huppé, MLN 63, 1948, 378–81); the meaning of the "curtain lecture" (see, among many others, Roppolo, CE 12:263–69, and Albrecht, ibid., 459); the moral and literary ironies of the tale (Miller, ELH 32:442–56); and its Jungian characteristics (Brown, ChR 10, 1976, 303–15, and ChR 12, 1978, 202–17; Atkinson, Southern Rev.: An Australian Journ. of Lit. Sts. 13, 1980, 72–78).

Kittredge saw the tale as an extension of the Wife's argument, and it is most frequently studied in light of the Wife's character and argument as presented in the prologue. The dominant opinion is that it is a projection of her desire to dominate the male (Allen and Moritz, A Distinction of Stories, 152; Derek Traversi, The CT: A Reading, 1983, 120–21; Donaldson, 1077–78), or, in feminist criticism, the twisted result of her domination by males (Bolton, in Gender and Lit. Voice, ed. Janet Todd, 1980, 54–65). However, a number of critics have considered the question of whether the Wife really wants sovereignty after all; see Harwood, MLQ 33, 1972, 257–73; Howard, Idea of CT, 252–55; Berggren, MSE 6, 1979, 25–36. See also Patterson, Spec 58:2, 656–95.

880 **incubus:** An evil spirit that appears "in manys lycnesse & womannys to don lecherye with folc" called "elves" in English and *incubus* in Latin when male, *succubus* when female (Dives and Pauper, EETS 280, 118). Note *elf* in 873, though Chaucer also uses the word for females; cf. MLT II.754n. and Thop VII.788n.

881 "The friar brought only dishonor upon a woman; the incubus always caused conception" (Robinson).

884 **ryver:** See Tr 4.413n.

885 **allone . . . born:** Cf. KnT I.1633n.

887 Baum (PMLA 71:239) notes a possible pun here on "head" and "maiden-head."

889 The word **oppressioun** may give some slight support to Coffman's argument (MLN 59:271–74) that the *Libellus* about St. Cuthbert's conception by rape is an analogue to WBT.

890 There is a possible pun here in **pursute**, technically meaning "prosecution," and "pursuit," the knight's having been driven to appear before the king (Baum, PMLA 71:243).

904–5 Cf. KnT I.1347n.

929–30 For an elaboration of this idea, see RR 9945–58. MS Cambridge Dd glosses "verum est," "it is true"!

939–40 Proverbial; Whiting G7, H505.

950 From RR, 19220, "Car fame ne peut riens celer" (For a woman can hide nothing), but also proverbial; Whiting, W534. Cf. Mel VII.1062.

951–82 Ovid, Met. 11.174–193, has the story of Midas, but Chaucer's version is different: in Ovid, Midas's barber knows his secret, which escapes in the wind blowing through reeds growing over a hole the barber dug in which to bury the secret—no inference is drawn about women as gossips. The Wife of Bath's misrepresentation of her sources here is stylistically consistent with her prologue (Hoffman, N&Q 211:48–50).

961–63 For the general idea, see RR 16521–30.

965–68 RR 16366–68 has, "To her thinking she would be dead if the secret did not jump out of her mouth, even if she is in danger or reproached" (tr. Dahlberg, 278).

972 **bitore:** The bittern, a type of crane known popularly as the "mire drum" because of the booming sound it makes in the mating season (OED s.v. *bittern*). Bartholomaeus Anglicus 12.28, tr. Trevisa 1:635, says that "The mirdrommel . . . is a bridde that maketh soun and voys in watir."

1004 The idea is proverbial; cf. Whiting A70, O29. MSS Egerton 1864–Additional 5140 gloss Ecclus. 25.7–8, "I can think of nine men I count happy, and I can tell you of a tenth: a man who can take delight in his children, and one who lives to see his enemy's downfall; happy the husband of a sensible wife, the farmer who does not plough with ox and ass together, the man whose tongue never betrays him, and the servant who has never worked for an inferior!"

1013 Cf. Gower, Conf. Aman. 1.1587 (S&A, 229).

1018 **on:** Cf. 559 above.

1028 The setting here and the question the knight is required to answer in line 905 are reminiscent of the courts of love supposedly presided over by such ladies as Eleanor of Aquitaine and her daughter Marie of Champagne. See Neilson, Origins of the Court of Love; such a court was, so it seems, actually held in Paris in 1400; see Piaget, Romania 20, 1891, 417–54; Straub, Zeitschrift für romanische Philologie 77, 1961, 1–14.

1081 Cf. Gower, Conf. Aman. 1.1727–31 (S&A, 232).

1062 Almost identical with NPT VII.1062.

1067   Tatlock (Anglia 37, 1913, 107 n.) compares similar antitheses in Boccaccio, and Robinson cites Purg. 6.78, but no source is needed for this common rhetorical figure.

1109   gentillesse: The doctrine that gentility depends on character, not inheritance—"virtus, non sanguis"—was a commonly received opinion. It might be described as the Christian democracy regularly taught by the church (cf. ParsT X.460–74), though not regularly exemplified in Christian society (Robinson). The immediate influences here seem to be the canzone preceding Dante's Convivio 4 and 4.3, 10, 14, 15; for III.1117–18 see RR 6579–92, 11607–896 (Lowes, MP 13:19–33), and Bo 2.pr6 for 1160–76 (Dempster, MLN 57, 1942, 173–76). Lumiansky (Italica 31, 1954, 1–7) cites parallels in Il Filostrato 7.86–100, and Tupper (PMLA 29, 1914, 101) notes similar ideas in Wyclif (Sel. Eng. Works 3:125–27) and Gower, Mirour de l'omme 12073–74. Cf. also ClT IV.155–61, Gentilesse, and Rom 2189–92.

1110   old richesse: Cf. Dante, "antica richezza."

1118–24   Cf. RR 18620–34.

1126   Dant: III.1127–23 closely parallel Purgatorio 7.121–23: "Rade volte risurge per li rami/l'umana probitate; e questo vole/quei che la da, per che da lui si chiama" (see Lowes, MP 13:19–33).

1133–38   Cf. Dante, Convivio 5.15.19–38.

1139–45   Cf. Bo 3.pr4.64–69. Lowes (MP 15, 1917, 198–99) suggests, as Chaucer's source for the comparison with fire, Servius, Commentarium in Vergilii Carmina (ed. Thilo and Hagen, 1883–84, 2.101.15–21), or possibly Servius's source. Cf. also Macrobius, Commentarium in Somnium Scipionis, 2.16.6.

1152–58   For similar sentiments, see Dante's Canzone (preceding Convivio 4, vv.34–37 and the prose comment in Convivio 4.7, 87–92.

1158   RR 2083–86 (Rom 2175–86).

1161   Cf. Bo 2.pr5.70.

1165–68   Valerius: Valerius Maximus, 3.4 (cf. also Seneca, Ep. 44). The legendary Tullius Hostillius (673–642 B.C.) started life as a herdsman, but became the third king of Rome and enjoyed the highest honors and dignities in his old age.

1168–76   Senek: Ayres (RomR 10, 1919, 8–9) compares Seneca's Ep. 44.2–5, "[the] practice of virtue is open to all and . . . regardless of one's station in life, is the immediate and the only source of true nobility"; cf. also Convivio 4.1.101–2.

1170   For the relationship between behavior and nobility, see RR 18802–5.

1178–79   Cf. 2 Cor. 8.9.

1183–84   Proverbial (Whiting P331); but from Seneca's Ep. 2.4, which is quoted in the marginal Lat. gloss: "Seneca in epistola: Honesta res est leta paupertas." The whole of III.1183–90 is a paraphrase of the Senecan passage. John of Salisbury (Policraticus 7.13) is a secondary source here, as is "Seneca's" De Paupertate, a tract made up of citations from Seneca's works. Pratt (Spec 41, 1966, 619–42) shows that all of Chaucer's Senecan passages appear in the Communiloquium sive summa collationum of John of Wales.

1186   Lat. gloss: "He is poor who desires what he does not have but he who has nothing and covets nothing is rich, according to that which is said in the Apocalypse 3 [17] 'You say that I am rich . . . and know not that you

are wretched and miserable and poor.' " The gloss seems dependent upon the Chaucerian text, which generally follows Seneca.

1187   Cf. RR 18566: "Covetousness makes poverty"; cf. Walther 1884.

1193–94   Lat. gloss: "Cantabit vacuus coram latrone viator et nocte ad lumen trepidabit Arundinis umbram" (Juvenal, Sat. 10.22, 21). The same line is quoted in Chaucer's gloss in Bo 2.pr5.181–84 and in Langland, PP B 14.305; the idea was commonplace (Whiting M266).

1195–1200   Lat. gloss: "Secundus Philosophus Paupertas est odibile bonum [cf. III.1195] sanitatis mater curarum remocio [cf. 1196] sapientie reparatrix [cf. 1197] possessio sine calumpnia [cf. 1200]" (Vincent of Beauvais, Spec. Hist. 10.71). The philosopher Secundus is the supposed author of a collection of gnomae; see Fabricius, Bibl. Graeca, 6.10 (1726, 13.573). The first clause is quoted in Latin in PP B 14.275, the next phrase (in English) in PP B 14.298.

1202   Lat. gloss: "Crates the famous Theban, after throwing into the sea a considerable weight of gold, exclaimed, 'I will drown you that you may not drown me,' " from Jerome, Adv. Jov. 2.9. Robinson observes that this note "probably indicates that Chaucer meant to add lines on Crates."

1203–4   For the idea, see RR 4949–56 (Rom 5551–60); for variations, see Bo 2.pr8.32–48 and For 9–10, 33–34.

1210–13   Cf. PardT VI.739–47.

1219–27   Schlauch (PMLA 61:416–30) cites for these lines Ovid's Heroides 16.290; Hoffman, AmN&Q 3:101 cites Amores 3.4.41–42 on the incompatibility of beauty and marital fidelity.

1258–60   Cf. ShipT VII.173–77 and n.

The Friar's Prologue

The Friar's Prologue and Tale, and the following Summoner's Prologue and Tale, are dramatically linked to those of the Wife of Bath and were probably written shortly after them. To explain the quarrel that develops from the Summoner's attack upon the Friar (WBPro III.829–49), Robinson and others have conjectured that the two were enemies before the pilgrimage began. As Tyrwhitt first pointed out, however, their animosity reflects the rivalry between mendicants and secular clergy that arose in Paris in the mid-thirteenth century and later spread to England. See introductory note for the portrait of the Friar, GP I.208–69. The specific controversy over mendicants hearing confession is probably an adequate basis for the Summoner's hostility, for, as Faus-Semblant asserts in an interpolated passage in the Roman de la rose, one who is given absolution by a friar cannot be charged again with the sin (printed in the notes to Langlois's ed. 3:311–15; tr. Robbins, 228–31), and the threat that such a situation poses to the Summoner's success at extortion (GP I.649–65) could certainly account for his initial charge that friars meddle in everything. The topic of confession, moreover, figures significantly in each of the rivals' tales, and critics have found other links in the series, such as parody (Szittya, PMLA 90, 1975, 386–

The explanatory notes to The Friar's Prologue and Tale were written by Janette Richardson.

94), structural parallels (Richardson, ChR 9, 1975, 227–36), concern for proper glossing (Carruthers, Journ. of Narrative Technique 2, 1972, 208–14), and use of Jerome's *Epistola adversus Jovinianum* (Correale, ELN 2, 1965, 171–74).

1265   lymytour: See GP I.209n.

The Friar's Tale

The tale of the heart-felt curse is probably of folk origin, and numerous analogues found across northern Europe indicate that any avaricious type might be used for the role here played by a summoner. Taylor (PMLA 36, 1921, 35–59) discusses three groupings of the tale and prints various examples. See also: S&A, 269–74, and Lutz Röhrich, Erzählungen des späten Mittelalters, 1967, 2:251–78. One of the earliest recorded versions, an exemplum in Caesarius of Heisterbach's thirteenth-century *Libri VIII miraculorum*, concerns an *advocatus*, a judicial administrator for church estates whose position was comparable in some ways to that of a summoner (Benson and Andersson, Lit. Context, 362–65). Chaucer's tale, however, more nearly resembles the two extant examples from England in that the victim fails to realize his own danger (Nicholson, ELN 17, 1979, 93–98), and, in the one from a contemporary sermon by Robert Rypon, the victim is a bailiff (Owst, Lit and Pulpit, 162–63; tr. Nicholson, Ch Newsletter 3:1, 1981, 1–2). See also Wenzel, SP 73, 1976, 142–43. In amplifying the anecdote, Chaucer incorporated common demonological lore found not only in sermons (Owst, Lit and Pulpit, 112), but also in such thirteenth-century Dominican works as Vincent of Beauvais's *Speculum naturale* (Aiken, SP 35, 1938, 1–9) and Thomas Aquinas's *Summa theologica* (Mroczkowski, Eng. Sts. Today, 2nd ser., 1961, 107–20). Chaucer's masterful characterization and handling of dialogue are totally lacking in the analogues. Mroczkowski (N&Q 207, 1962, 325–26) points out a similar use of effective, though less fully developed, dialogue in the *Roman de Renart*, Branch 1b, the tale of Renart li Teinturier. On the historical context of the satire of the ecclesiastical courts, see Hahn and Kaeuper, SAC 5, 1983, 67–101. For analyses of narrative and ironic techniques, see Birney, MS 21, 1959, 17–35; Bonjour, EIC 11, 1961, 121–7; Richardson, Blameth Nat Me, 73–85; and Lenaghan, ChR 7, 1972–3, 281–94.

1302   erchedeken: Archdeacons, second in rank to bishops, conducted ecclesiastical courts for assigned areas while the bishop (see III.1317) did likewise for the entire diocese. Satiric contemporary reference in this portrait has been suggested by Kuhl (MLN 40, 1925, 321–38) and Manly (New Light, 102–22). Assuming Holderness in Yorkshire to be the Friar's contree, because it is specified as the setting for the Summoner's retaliatory tale about a friar, Kuhl points to Walter Skirlawe, archdeacon (c. 1359–c. 1385) of the archdeaconry of the East Riding, in which Holderness was a rural deanery, as a notorious absentee holder of many benefices. Manly points to Richard de Ravenser, a canon of Beverley and archdeacon of Lincoln (1368–86), as a prelate who acquired great wealth from his positions. Manly's claim for a northern flavor in the diction of the

tale, however, has been refuted by Malone (MLR 26, 1931, 75–77).

1308   On the obligation to confess and take communion at least once a year, see ParsT X.1027n.

1309   usure: Collecting interest on loans, prohibited by canon law. symonye: Buying or selling ecclesiastical positions, named after Simon Magus (Acts 8.9–24), who wanted to purchase the power of bestowing the Holy Ghost.

1314   That is, the archdeacon never failed to impose fines rather than other penances. Cf. GP I.656–58; Gower, Mirour, 20089–208. See also the references in the introductory note to the Summoner's portrait, GP I.622–68.

1317   hook: A bishop's staff, symbolic of the pastoral office, resembles a shepherd's crook.

1327   wood were as an hare: Proverbial (Whiting H116), often "mad as a March hare," referring to erratic behavior during the breeding season. In iconographic representations, the hare was frequently symbolic of lechery. See Rowland, Blind Beasts, 65, 89–91; Robertson, Preface to Ch, 113, 255; Richardson, Blameth Nat Me, 75–76, 83–84.

1329   Friars were answerable to the superiors general of their orders, not to the ecclesiastical courts.

1334   with myschance and with mysaventure: Basically "bad luck to you," but as an imprecation *with myschance* varies considerably in forcefulness. Cf. MLT II.896, SumT III.2215, MancPro IX.11, MancT IX.193.

1340   Cf. RvT I.4134, WBPro III.415. The lure, made of feathers to resemble a bird and attached to a thong for twirling, was a device from which hawks were fed and thus trained to return to the falconer's hand.

1349   atte nale: For *atten ale*, at the ale house. Such false word division was not uncommon, e.g., PP C 1.43, 8.19.

1350–51   Judas, according to John 12.6, was keeper of the Disciples' purse and stole from it.

1356   Priests rather than knights may be intended here; they were often addressed as "sir" out of courtesy. See ProNPT VII.2810, 2820.

1365   Cf. Wyclif, Sel. Eng. Works, 3:166.

1369   dogge for the bowe: Proverbial; Whiting D303. Cf. MerT IV.2014.

1377   ribibe: Literally, a kind of fiddle, but used derisively for "old woman," perhaps because of the carved head on the instrument (Ross, Expl 34, 1975, 17) rather than Halliwell's conjecture (in his Dictionary) of confusion of Lat. *vetula*, old woman, and *vitula*, viol.

1380–83   Cf. GP I.103–4. The green garb here may hint at the yeman's origin. The color was traditional in Celtic mythology for underworld spirits who walk the earth (Garrett, JEGP 24, 1925, 129), and Pierre Bersuire's fourteenth-century scriptural dictionary draws a parallel between hunters wearing green as camouflage and the manner in which the devil approaches mortals (Robertson, MLN 69, 1954, 470–72). See also Baird, NM 69, 1968, 575–78. Birney (MS 21, 1959, 21) suggests that the unusual frenges blake, which may be bindings on the hat (Baugh), provide a color always associated with devils. Cf. III.1622.

1382   upon: Cf. 559 above.

1399   bretherhede: Cf. III.1528 and see KnT I.1132n.

1408   venym: Thorns upon which shrikes or butcherbirds impale their prey were believed to be poisonous thereafter (Harrison, N&Q 199, 1954, 189).

1413 Infernal regions in both biblical tradition and Germanic mythology were often thought of as in the north. See Isaiah 14.13–14; Jer. 6.1; Gregory's commentary on Job, 17.24 (PL 76:26; tr. Marriott, Library of Fathers, 1844–50, 21.300); Augustine, Epis. 140 (PL 33:561; tr. Parsons, Fathers of the Church, 1953, 11.103–4); Kellogg, Spec 24, 1949, 413–14; Piers Plowman (ed. Pearsall), note to C.I.110. See also Gummere, Haverford Col. St. 1, 1889, 118–24, and Founders of Eng., 1930, 418 n.

1436 Proverbial (Whiting H316).

1451 Cf. GP I.256 and n.

1475 Proverbial (Whiting T88, Hassell C198), derived from Eccles. 3.1. See also ClPro IV.6; MerT IV.1972; Tr 3.855.

1491 Job 1.12, 2.6. Cf. PardT VI.848.

1502 Lives of St. Dunstan, Archbishop of Canterbury (d. 988), contain various instances of his power over devils (Sr. Mary Immaculate, PQ 21, 1942, 240–44). Aiken (SP 35:8–9) notes an episode related by Vincent of Beauvais (*Speculum historiale* 24.73) that may be relevant.

1503 See Acts 19.11–17. Legends showing power over devils were also told of other Apostles. For James and Bartholomew, see Early South English Legendary, ed. Horstmann, EETS 87, 35–37, 369–72; for Andrew, Thomas, Peter, Simon, and Jude, see Jacobus de Voragine, *Legenda aurea*, 15–21, 38–39, 372–73, 710; tr. Ryan and Ripperger, 1:10–16, 45, 336; 2:638–39.

1510 Phitonissa: The name in the Vulgate for the Witch of Endor (1 Paralipomenon 10.13). When consulted by Saul, she raised the spirit of Samuel, who foretold the victory of the Philistines (1 Sam. 28.7–20).

1511 som men: As Baugh notes, the theological question about whether it was Samuel who appeared goes back at least to the fourth century when Eustathius, bishop of Antioch, argued that the apparition was merely a hallucination. For other references see Cath. Encyc. 10.736. The idea of St. Basil, and other early churchmen, that Samuel was impersonated by the devil was equally current in the late Middle Ages, e.g., John of Salisbury, *Policraticus* 2.27 (PL 199:461–70).

1518 Professors in medieval universities lectured from chairs, while their students sat about them on the floor. See the illustration from Aberdeen Univ. Library MS 109 in N. R. Ker, MAE 39, 1970, 32–33.

1519–20 Virgile: Cf. the description of the underworld in Bk. 6 of the *Aeneid;* Dant: Dante's *Inferno.* Cf. HF 445–50.

1528 Cf. 1399 above.

1543 Hayt: Skeat (5.328) quotes modern and medieval examples of *hayt* (go) and *ho* (whoa) as commands to draft animals. Scot was apparently a common name for a horse (see GP I.616n.); Brok ("badger") was commonly used for gray farm animals (cf. *lyard boy,* III.1563).

1553 For German ballad versions of the devil appearing to take what is consigned to him, see Child, Ballads, 1.219–20.

1561 On this use of *ther,* see Language and Versification, p. xxxix.

1564 Seinte Loy: See GP I.120 and n. St. Eligius is called upon here as the patron of carters. Lowes (RomR 5, 1914, 382–85) discusses the saint's connection with horses.

1570 upon cariage: A feudal lord had the right to use the horses and wagons of his tenants, but he could collect a payment of "carriage" instead. Cf. ParsT X.752; Bo 1.pr4.71.

1573 rebekke: Like *ribibe,* the word means "fiddle"; cf. 1377 and n. Skeat's suggestion that the slang term arose from a pun on Rebecca is elaborated by Hatton (JEGP 67, 1968, 266–71), who sees the widow as a type of the Church.

1582 virytrate: Another term of contempt, perhaps related to "old trot"; cf. Gower, Mirour, 8713 and 17900 (ed. Macaulay, 1:101 and 208).

1587 Up peyne of cursyng: Echoes of the formulas for anathema are found by Work (PMLA 47, 1932, 428) and Cawley (PLPLS-LHS 8, 1957, 175) in the passage that follows.

1602 Com of: See MilT I.3728n.

1613 Seinte Anne: According to the apocryphal Gospel of the Birth of Mary, Anne was the mother of the Virgin. See Benjamin H. Cowper, Apoc. Gospels, 6th ed., 1897, 85–90; *Legenda aurea,* 586–88, 934–35 (tr. Ryan and Ripperger 2.520–23).

1630 stot: Literally a horse (see GP I.615) or a bullock, but used here as another term of abuse.

1636 Pratt (Tales, xxx) notes an inverted echo here of Christ's words to the repentant thief (Luke 23.43).

1645–55 This concluding admonition perhaps derives from the office of compline in the Breviary (Sutherland, PQ 31, 1952, 436–39).

1647 and is supplied by the editors for this defective line. Havely (Fr.'s, Sum.'s and Pard.'s Tales, 1976, 134) suggests as appropriate texts for the three allusions: Matt. 8.12, 13.42, and 22.13; the apocryphal Vision of St. Paul; Rev. 19 and 20.

1657–58 See Ps. 10.8–9; 10.8 is quoted in the Lat. gloss, with some MSS adding 1 Peter 5.89. Correale (ELN 2:171–74) cites Jerome's Adv. Jov. 2.3 as a source for applying the biblical phrasing to the devil and notes that the two subsequent biblical echoes are also found there.

1659–60 Ecclesiasticus 2.1–2: "If you aspire to be a servant of the Lord, prepare yourself for testing/ Set a straight course, be resolute."

1661 1 Cor. 10.13.

1662 champion: See GP I.239n.

The Summoner's Prologue

For this scurrilous anecdote about the final abode of friars, Chaucer seems to have inverted a tale, first recorded in Caesarius of Heisterbach's *Dialogus miraculorum* (thirteenth century), about the vision of a Cistercian monk who found his brothers in heaven dwelling under the cloak of the Virgin. The concept became a common iconographic theme in Marian representations and was used particularly by the mendicant orders and, in the fourteenth century, by the lay confraternities associated with the Dominicans and Franciscans (Fleming, ChR 2, 1967, 95–107). The change in the story may have been suggested by a fresco in Pisa, Francisco Traini's *The Last Judgment,* which Chaucer could have seen when he trav-

The explanatory notes to The Summoner's Prologue and Tale were written by Janette Richardson.

eled from Genoa to Florence in 1373 (Pratt, Tales, 295; see also Spencer, Spec 2, 1927, 196–97), or merely by vulgar jokes or curses. For earlier recorded instances of the punishment, see Brusendorff, Ch Trad., 411; Fansler, Ch and RR, 165.

1667　Cf. Tr 3.1200n.
1685　**Yis:** Used sarcastically, to negate the proposal that there are no friars in hell.
1688　Cf. Dante's description of Satan's wings, Inf. 34.48.
1690　The same image in Rom 7576 may be the translator's erroneous reading of the Fr. "cul [var. "puis"] d'enfer," or it may derive from Chaucer's usage here.
1692　**furlong wey:** See MilT I.3637n.
1693　Cf. Tr 2.193n.

The Summoner's Tale

The Summoner's tale of a hypocritical friar has neither a known source nor any close analogues (see Pearcy, Fabula 15, 1974, 103–13). Two somewhat similar narratives that involve humiliating gifts, Jacques de Basieux's "Li Dis de la Vescie a Prestre" and "How Howleglas Deceived His Ghostly Father," are printed in Benson and Andersson, Lit. Context, 339–61. See also S&A, 275–87. If the idea for the story came from a current joke, as Robinson thought, Chaucer's creation of a character for whom the punishment is absolutely apt is nonetheless strikingly original, however much the begging friar may reflect common criticism of the mendicant orders (see introductory note for the portrait of the Friar, GP I.208). See also, for discussion of narrative and ironic techniques, Birney, Anglia 78, 1960, 204–18; Adams, EIC 12, 1962, 126–32; Zeitlow, ChR 1, 1966, 4–19; Richardson, Blameth Nat Me, 147–58.

1710　**Holdernesse:** A rural deanery in the southeast corner of Yorkshire. Manly held that a jurisdictional dispute between the Friars at Beverley, the principal town in the district, and the cathedral clergy accounts for Chaucer's choosing this locale (New Light, 102–22), but this has been challenged by Fleming (JEGP 65, 1966, 688–89). *Holdernesse* was also the home of Sir Peter Bukton, one of the two possible addressees of the Envoy to Bukton. See the introductory note to Bukton.
1711　**lymytour:** See GP I.209n.
1714　Friars could preach in parish churches only by obtaining the permission of the local priest or by being licensed by the bishop of the diocese (Williams, AnM 1, 1960, 39–41).
1717　**To trentals:** For a story of the origin of trentals, see The Trental of St. Gregory (Polit., Relig., and Love Poems, ed. Furnivall, EETS 15, 1866, 83–92, and 1903, 114–22).
1722　**possessioners:** The monastic orders and the secular clergy, both of whom had income from endowments and land, whereas the friars subsisted entirely on alms. Friar John's later use of the term designates chantry priests specifically.
1726　**hastily ysonge:** Friars sometimes assembled to perform all thirty masses in one day (see English Gilds, ed. Smith, EETS 40, 1870, 8), a practice which Friar John asserts produces speedier delivery from purgatory than a priest's singing the office over thirty consecutive days.

1730　Except for mention of fire, most descriptions of purgatorial torments are vague. This use of meathooks and awls, however, does appear in the various versions of St. Patrick's Purgatory (Stanford, JEGP 19, 1920, 377–81).
1734　*qui cum patre:* Part of the formula invoking Christ's blessing at the end of prayers and sermons ("Who with the Father and the Holy Spirit lives and reigns for ever and ever").
1737　**scrippe and tipped staf:** Cf. Christ's command that his disciples go into the world with neither bags nor staffs (Matt. 10.9–10; Luke 9.3, 10.4).
1740　**His felawe:** Friars traveled in pairs, in accord with Christ's direction to his disciples (Luke 10.1).
1741　**peyre of tables:** A folding set of writing tablets. Wax coating on the inner surfaces of the ivory could be inscribed with the point of a stylus and smoothed out with the other end. Such writing materials date back to classical antiquity (see E. M. Thompson, Intro. to Gr. and Lat. Paleog., 1912, 14–20). For possible iconographic meanings attached to horn and ivory, see Kaske, NM 73, 1972, 122–26.
1745　**Ascaunces:** Cf. Tr 1.205n.
1755　**hostes man:** Skeat proposed "servant to the guests at the friar's convent," but Hartung (ELN 4, 1967, 175–80) argues well for "servant borrowed from the host at whose inn the two friars are staying" (cf. III.1779). The man's function is reminiscent of the "bursarius," or spiritual friend, who received contributions of money, which Franciscans were forbidden to touch (Williams, Spec 28, 1953, 506–7).
1768　**goode man:** Cf. ShipT VII.29n.
1770　*Deus hic:* God be here. The prescribed Franciscan blessing when entering a home was *pax huic domui* (peace to this house), Matt. 10.12.
1778　**was go walked:** For the construction, see BD 387n.
1792　**glose:** The interpretation of the "spirit" of a biblical text in contrast to its literal meaning (see Robertson, Pref to Ch, 331–32). For Chaucer *glose* is usually pejorative: "From the original sense of 'gloss,' 'interpret,' the word passes to the idea of irrelevant or misleading comment, and so to outright deception" (Robinson). See, as examples, WBPro III.509, MancT IX.34 (to mislead verbally), MkT VII.2140, ParsPro X.45 (to mislead, deceive).
1794　2 Cor. 3.6.
1803–4　Although the kiss of peace was a normal greeting, the action here is rendered suspect by the comparison to the sparrow, a common symbol of lechery (see GP I.626 and n.). See also Kellogg, Scriptorium 7, 1953, 115.
1820　Cf. Matt. 4.19, Luke 5.10, and Rom 7.90–91. On Friar John's claim for apostolic stature, see Levy, TSL 11, 1966, 45–60; Szittya, SP 71, 1974, 30–41.
1832　*je vous dy:* I tell you. Although this was a commonly used phrase (Skeat, 5:334), ability to speak French generally indicated social or educational superiority: "Oplondysch men wol lykne hamsylf to gentil-men and fondeth with gret bysynes for to speke Freynsh, for to be more ytold of" (John of Trevisa's translation of Higden's *Polychronicon,* ed. C. Babington and J. R. Lumby, Rolls Series, 1865–66, 1:59). See GP I.124–26n. The use of French by the merchant in the Shipman's Tale is apparently for local color; see ShipT VII.214n.
1854–58　On the belief in such visions as divine revelation, see Curry (Ch and Science, 207–17), who refers to

Augustine, Gregory, Vincent of Beauvais, and Thomas Aquinas, among others.

1862   jubilee: Anniversary of fifty years of service, marked by such privileges as the right to travel without an accompanying friar.

1866   *Te Deum:* A song of praise that regularly concluded matins, but is supposedly sung here to honor the miraculous vision. See Tatlock, MLN 29, 1914, 144.

1872   burel: Cf. FranPro V.716n.

1877   See Luke 16.19–31. This example and the following references to Moses, Elijah, Aaron, and Adam all appear in Jerome's Adv. Jov. 2 (Koeppel, Angl 13, 1891, 177). Tupper, MLN 30, 1915, 8–9, cites the parallel passages.

1880   Lat. gloss: "Melius est animum saginare quam corpus" (It is better to fatten the soul than the body), from Jerome, Adv. Jov. 2.6.

1881–82   Lat. gloss: "Victum et vestitum hiis contenti sumus." (Cf. 1 Tim. 6.8).

1885–90   Exod. 34.28.

1890–93   1 Kings 19.8.

1898   Lev. 10.8–9.

1915–16   Cf. PardT VI.504–11 and n.508–11; ParsT X.819.

1923   Matt. 5.3.

1929   Jovinyan: The heretical fourth-century monk who provoked Jerome's Adv. Jov. (cf. introductory note to WBPro) and is there (1.40) sarcastically described as "iste formosus monachus, crassus, nitidus, dealbatus, et quasi sponsus semper incedens"—that beautiful monk, fat, sleek, whitewashed (i.e., simulating sanctity), and always parading like a bridegroom (PL 23:268).

1934   *cor meum eructavit:* The opening of Ps. 44 (Vulgate; 45 in A.V.), but *eructare* also means to belch. For an explanation of why Chaucer's audience would have recognized the pun, see Beichner, MS 18, 1956, 135–44. See also Hamilton, MLN 57, 1942, 655–57.

1935   foore: Cf. WBPro III.110n.

1937   James 1.22; also in Adv. Jov. 2.3 (Correale, ELN 2:173–74).

1943   Seint Yve: See ShipT VII.227 and n.

1944   See III.2126–28 and n.

1967   Cf. the final scene of the tale.

1968–69   Lat. gloss: "Omnes virtus unita forcior est seipsa dispersa."

1973   Lat. gloss: "Dignus est mercede et cetera" (Luke 10.7).

1980   Thomas lyf of Inde: A legendary account of the life of Thomas the Apostle, who is said to have converted thousands in India. (For the word order, see Language and Versification, p. xxxviii.) The usual story of the death and restoration of the king's brother suggests that the churches accredited to Thomas were congregations, not buildings (see Jacobus de Voragine, *Legenda aurea,* 32–39; tr. Ryan and Ripperger 1:39–46), but the account in the South English Legendary (EETS 236, 577) seems to indicate literal construction of the sort mentioned by Friar John (III.2102–6). Thomas is, of course, the "doubting" Apostle (John 20:26–30). See also Szittya, SP 71:34; Clark, ChR 11, 1976, 164–78.

1989–91   Lat. gloss: "Noli esse sicut leo in domos tua, evertens domesticos tuos opprimens subiectos tibi" (Ecclus. 4.35).

1994–95   Cf. RR 16591–604, where Virgil's "snake in the grass" (Ecl. 3.93) is paraphrased. Proverbial after Chaucer; Whiting S153. Cf. SqT V.512.

2001–3   Cf. RR 9800–9804, which incorporates Ovid, Ars Am. 2.376–78. Cf. also Virgil, Aen. 5.6; Seneca, Medea, 579–82.

2018   Senek: Seneca. The exemplary tale of the wrathful potentate is from *De ira* 1, 18. Chaucer probably knew it, and the later anecdotes about Cambyses (*De ira* 3, 14) and Cyrus (*De ira* 3, 21) from the *Communiloquium sive summa collationum* of the thirteenth-century Franciscan, John of Wales, rather than Seneca (Pratt, Spec 41, 1966, 627–31). See also S&A, 286–87; and for comparison of the exempla with Seneca, Zeitlow, ChR 1:12–13.

2042   dide doon sleen: A rare use of the double causative; see Language and Versification, p. xl.

2075   *Placebo:* "I shall please," from Ps. 114.9 (Vulgate; 116.9 in AV), well known because of its use as an antiphon in the Office for the Dead. The word came to denote flattering complaisance. See MerT IV.1476 and n., ParsT X.617n.

2079   Cirus: Cyrus the great (see MkT VII.2728n).

2080   Gysen: The river Gyndes, a tributary of the Tigris (Magoun, MS 15, 1953, 119).

2085   See Prov. 22.24–25.

2090   squyre: Carpenter's square, the iconographic symbol of Thomas of India (Clark, ChR 11:168). The phrase was proverbial (Whiting S645), but cf. III.2243–80.

2093   On the power of friars to hear confession, cf. GP I.218–20 and Rom 6364–65.

2094   Seint Symoun: Possibly a reference to St. Simon, the disciple (Mark 3.18), but Simon Magus (Acts 8.9–24) may be intended (Haskell, ChR 5, 1971, 218–24).

2095   Cf. ParsT X.1006.

2098   Cf. ParsT X.1008n.

2106   By contrast, St. Francis prescribed humble buildings of wood and mud (Fleming, JEGP 65:696–97). For criticism, see Wyclif, Eng. Works, 5 and 14. Cf. Rom 6571.

2107   See MilT I.3512n.

2108   The hoarding of MSS bought with profits from begging was one of FitzRalph's charges against the mendicant orders (Birney, Anglia 78, 1960, 215). See also Fleming, JEGP 65:697–98.

2113   For this image, cf. Cicero, *De amicitia,* 13.47, which also appears in John of Wales's Comm. (Pratt, Spec 41:631).

2116   Elye, Elise: Although the Carmelites received their first rule in 1209 or 1210 and were endorsed by the papacy in 1226, they claimed that their founders were Elijah, who destroyed the prophets of Baal on Mt. Carmel (1 Kings 18.19–40), and his disciple Elisha. See Koch, Spec 34, 1959, 547–60; Williams, MP 54:188–19.

2126–28   youre brother: Thomas and his wife were members of a lay confraternity attached to Friar John's convent. These penitential associations, sponsored by various religious and civic organizations, flourished in the late Middle Ages. A census ordered by Richard II in 1389 found 507 such confraternities in England, and Philippa Chaucer received a letter of fraternity from Lincoln Cathedral in 1386. See Fleming, ChR 2:101–05. For Wycliffites, such letters were but another deceptive way of obtaining money. See Wyclif, Sel. Eng. Works, 3:377–78, 420–29.

2149   For connection of this action with practices of exorcism, see Wentersdorf, Sts. in Short Fiction 17, 1980, 249–54.

2152   Proverbial; cf. WBPro III.794n.

2163   Manly (New Light, 119) suggests identifying the lord with Michael de la Pole.

2186–87   **that honour:** That is, although Friar John has a Master of Arts degree (required at Oxford by a statute of 1251 for those seeking subsequent graduation in theology), he here follows St. Francis's dictum (Mann, Ch and Estates, 39) that his followers not be called masters (**Raby:** rabbi); but cf. 1781, 1800, 1836. This concept derived from Christ's criticism of the scribes and Pharisees (Matt. 23.5–11), who were anti-types of the Apostles in medieval tradition (Szittya, SP 71:41–43).

2196   Matt. 5.13.

2215   **with meschaunce:** Cf. FrT III.1334n.

2222   **ars-metrike:** Literally, art of measurement (i.e., arithmetic), but with an obvious pun.

2228   **with harde grace:** A common imprecation; cf. CYT VIII.1189 and MED s.v. grace 3(b)(d).

2231   **an inpossible:** For the relation of the problem to the class of logical exercises known as *impossibilia* in late scholastic teaching (WBPro III.688n.), see Pearcy, N&Q 14, 1967, 322–25.

2234   Cf. HF 765–821n. Albertus Magnus's *Liber de sensu et sensato* may be the source for Jankyn's remarks on the spreading of sound and odor (Pratt, PQ 57, 1978, 267–68).

2244   Cf. GP I.100, MerT IV.1773.

2255   **cartwheel:** The squire's solution seems to parody iconographic representations of the descent of the Holy Spirit to the twelve Apostles at Pentecost. See Levitan, UTQ 40, 1971, 236–46; Levy, TSL 11:52–56; Clark, AnM 17, 1976, 48–57; Szittya, SP 71:22–29.

2259   In imitation of the Apostles, convents were composed of twelve members and a principal. Larger religious houses were considered to consist of several convents (Skeat, 5:341).

2289   **Ptholomee:** See MilT I.3208 and n. A corrupt spelling in nearly all MSS, *Protholomee*, might account for the loss of *dide*, here supplied by the editor.

2294   **at towne:** Perhaps Sittingbourne (see WBPro III.845–47), but see Greenfield, MLR 48, 1953, 51–52.

FRAGMENT IV

This fragment, consisting of the Clerk's and Merchant's prologues and tales, is not explicitly connected at the beginning with The Summoner's Tale, and in some MSS The Merchant's Tale is separated from The Clerk's Tale and precedes that of the Wife of Bath, with which it is connected by a spurious link (see introduction to the textual notes to *The Canterbury Tales*). Nevertheless, the integrity of Fragment IV has never been doubted and the order of Fragments III, IV, and V is widely accepted.

LARRY D. BENSON

The Clerk's Prologue

2–3   Cf. GP I.840–41; Rom 1000. The Clerk's demeanor ought to be maidenly: "A maidenly simplicity is fitting for clerks" (Totum regit saeculum, 145; Mann, Ch

The explanatory notes to The Clerk's Prologue and Tale were written by Warren S. Ginsberg.

and Estates, 76); William of Wheatley (fl. 1305–31), commenting on Boethius's *Disciplina scholastica,* says: "The scholar . . . ought to be so chaste and modest in word and action, that he may resemble a virgin newly spoused" (Ussery, TSE 15, 1967, 15).

5   **sophyme:** By the fourteenth century, *sophisma* had come to mean not merely an enigmatic proposition or a fallacious argument or conclusion, but any question disputed in logic. For earlier meanings, as well as the place of disputations *de sophismatibus* in the curriculum of Oxford, see Weisheipl, MS 26, 1964, 154, 177–81. For a fourteenth-century collection, see John Buridan, Sophisms on Meaning and Truth, tr. Theodore K. Scott, 1966.

6   Eccles. 3.1. Cf. FrT III.1475 and n.

7   **as beth:** On this use of the hortatory *as,* see Language and Versification, p. xxxix.

10   Cf. the French proverb, "Ki en jeu entre jeu consente" (he who joins a game consents to its rules): Skeat, 5.343; cf. Whiting, P256.

12–14   This reference to friars fits the preceding tale, whether or not it was written with that in mind (R.). Sermons in the fourteenth century often tended to neglect their message for the sake of rhetorical extravagance; Wyclif was the chief spokesman against such bombast (Owst, Preaching in Med. Engl., 133–34); his followers, variously called poor priests or poor clerks, wandered about England preaching Wyclif's ideas in unadorned, vernacular sermons (McKisack, Fourteenth Cent., 519). Lent, one should note, was the time at Oxford when undergraduates would begin their determination (the resolving by scholastic disputation of questions of grammar and logic) for the bachelor's degree (Weisheipl, MS 26:157–59). Harry's words would have had particular resonance for the Clerk.

16   **colours . . . figures:** Rhetorical ornaments; cf. HF 853–59. In general, colors refer to figures of speech (metaphors, similes, etc.), figures to patterns of thought; cf. SqT V.39n, FranPro V.723–26n. Rhetoric was one of the subjects of the Trivium; cf. BD 817–1040n.

18   **Heigh style . . . kynges write:** The *ars dictaminis,* the medieval manual of epistolary technique, taught that a letter should be written in low, middle, or high style depending on its subject and on the status of its recipient.

27   **at Padowe of a worthy clerk:** Oxford clerks frequently studied at Padua (Bennett, Ch at Oxford, 61). Petrarch was archdeacon of Padua and canon of Parma. From 1368 until his death in 1374, he lived in Padua or in his country house at Arqua, two miles from the city. Like Livy before him, Petrarch was sometimes known as *patavinus,* "of Padua" (ClT, ed. Sisam, 47); the association of the man with the town is hardly evidence that Chaucer met Petrarch in Italy.

29   Petrarch in fact was "placed in a sarcophagus of red stone, after the ancient manner" (Cook, RomR 8, 1917, 222–24). **Nayled in his cheste** here means nothing more than "dead and buried."

31   **Petrak . . . the lauriat poete:** Both here and in MkT VII.2325, the best MSS support the spelling *Petrak* rather than *Petrark.* There are parallels for it in French, Latin, and Italian documents. By 1340 both the University of Paris and the Roman Senate offered Petrarch the poet's bays. On Easter Sunday, 1341, having stood a public examination before King Robert of Naples, Petrarch was crowned laureate in Rome amid great pomp.

34   **Lynyan:** Giovanni da Lignano (or Legnano) (c.

1310–83), an eminent professor of canon law at Bologna, wrote on law, ethics, theology, and astronomy, but was best known in England for his defense of the election of Urban VI. Chaucer was in Italy when the Great Schism broke out; after 1378 the English court was intimately involved in the Schism on Urban's side. Lignano was known also to favor simple dress and to befriend young, poor scholars; in his will he left an endowment for impoverished Milanese students at Bologna (McCall, Spec 40, 1965, 484–89; Cook, RomR 8:353–82).

philosophie: For the three philosophies at Oxford, natural, moral, and metaphysical, see Weisheipl, MS 26: 173–76.

41 heigh stile: Cf. IV.18; here almost certainly derived from the misreading of "stylo . . . alto" (the form that appears in the Latin gloss of IV.1077) for Petrarch's "stylo . . . alio" (a different style); cf. Severs in S&A, 330. The Ellesmere, Hengwrt and ten other MSS contain a number of marginal glosses from Petrarch's tale; many are of textual significance. For transcriptions of these glosses, which may be Chaucer's own, see M-R 3:505–8. The forms in the gloss vary in minor and major ways from Severs's text (S&A, 296–330); the gloss to IV.281, for example, has "expeditis" for "expedita"; "videndum" for "visendam"; "prepararet" (that she might get ready) for "properaret" (that she might go quickly). Dempster (MP 41, 1943, 6–16) discusses the most important variants; she concludes they derive from a more corrupt version of Petrarch's tale than that printed by Severs (see introductory note to ClT). Significant glosses are recorded at the appropriate places in the notes to the ClT.

43–51 prohemye: Petrarch's *prohemium* is as follows: "There stands in Italy, toward the western side, Mount Viso, one of the highest of the Apennines, whose summit, surpassing the clouds, thrusts itself into the pure ether. This mount, noble in its own right, is most noble as the source of the Po, which, issuing in a little spring from its side, flows eastward toward the rising sun. Descending a short distance, it soon swells with great tributaries, so much so that it is not only one of the greatest rivers, but is called king of rivers by Virgil; it cuts Liguria violently with raging waters; then, bounding Emilia, Ferrara and Venice, it finally empties through many great mouths into the Adriatic Sea." (The Lat. gloss quotes the first two sentences.) All fourteenth-century translations of Petrarch's tale lack this proem; most French versions, including the one Chaucer used, substitute a passage commending the story as a model for married women.

54 impertinent: Ginsberg (Criticism 20, 1978, 311–14) argues for the relevance of the prologue.

The Clerk's Tale

As acknowledged in the prologue, the source of The Clerk's Tale is Petrarch's Latin story *De obedientia ac fide uxoria mythologia* (A Fable of Wifely Obedience and Faithfulness); this in turn is a translation of the last story of Boccaccio's *Decameron* (10.10). Petrarch first wrote his version in 1373 and placed it as the last letter of his final work, the *Epistolae seniles* (17.3). War in Italy, however, prevented this letter, which was dedicated to Boccaccio, from being delivered to him; one year later, Petrarch recopied his translation, revising it here and there,

and added another letter (17.4), in which he made some further comments on the tale. J. Burke Severs (The Literary Relationships of Ch's ClT, 1942) has shown that Chaucer made use of a MS containing Petrarch's final (1374) version of the story. Dempster (MP 41:6–16) has argued strongly that Chaucer's MS of Petrarch is not closest to the one Severs chose as the base text for his edition, but to a lost version that stems from a different, more corrupt family, which, however, also preserves the 1374 version of the story.

Boccaccio's and Petrarch's versions of the tale served as exemplars for other Italian, Latin, and French translations in the fourteenth century: see Severs, Lit. Relationships, 3–37, 135–80; Elie Golenistcheff-Koutouzoff, L'histoire de Griseldis en France au XIVe et au XVe siècle, 1933; Käte Laserstein, Der Griseldisstoff in der Weltliteratur, 1926. Chaucer made extensive use of one of the French translations of Petrarch; Severs (Lit. Relationships, 190–211) establishes the text, based on Paris, Bibliothèque Nationale, MS fr. 12459 (a translation, one should note, of the 1373 version). This text, as well as Severs's edition of Petrarch's letter, are printed in S&A, 288–331. French, Ch Handbook, 291–311, translates Petrarch's Latin. A number of studies have emphasized Chaucer's handling of his sources. For how both religious and worldly elements are simultaneously emphasized, see Severs, Lit. Relationships, 215–48; Elizabeth Salter, Ch: KnT and ClT, St. in Engl. Lit. 5, 1962, 37–68; Kellogg, Ch, Langland, 276–329; Ginsberg, Criticism 20:307–23; Middleton, SAC 2, 1980, 121–50.

The Griselda story is one of the most familiar and popular in European literature. Boccaccio's seems to have been the first written rendering of the tale; he at least gave it the literary form by which it has been known all over the world. But Petrarch implies that Boccaccio drew upon Italian popular tradition; many elements of the story have indeed been found widely dispersed in folklore. Dudley D. Griffith, The Origin of the Griselda Story, 1931, and Cate (SP 29, 1932, 389–405) associate the story with the myth of Cupid and Psyche and the fairy tale "East of the Sun and West of the Moon." See as well Aarne-Thompson, 133, no. 887; 68, no. 425A (The Monster Bridegroom). More recently Bettridge and Utley (TSLL 13, 1971, 153–208) have argued that Boccaccio's source was not a variant of the "Monster Bridegroom," but rather a version of a folktale known in Turkey and Greece, which they call "The Patience of a Princess."

The extravagant, not to say "monstrous," behavior of both Walter and Griselda has been the subject of much discussion. Older attempts to discern survivals of a supernatural character in Chaucer's figures have been superseded for the most part by a new generation of psychological readings of Griselda and Walter. Many, however, still find the tale's central idea "too revolting for any skill in description to make it palatable" (Lounsbury, Sts. in Ch 3:341). Kittredge (MP 9, 1912, 435–67) defended the aptness of the tale in the marriage debate, but the artistic merit of the tale itself had its first true defender in Sledd (MP 51, 1953, 73–82), and it has attracted considerable attention in the years since. It has often been read as a tale in which allegorical meaning and realistic treatment are in conflict (e.g., Salter, Ch: KnT and ClT, 39–65), though its allegorical character has been doubted (Allen and Moritz, A Distinction of Stories, 191–92), and its exemplary rather than allegorical nature stressed (Morse, SAC 7, 1985, 51–86).

Most such studies have attempted to read the poem in the light of the medieval concepts that inform Chaucer's telling (see, e.g., Spearing, Criticism and Med. Poetry, 76–106; Middleton, SAC 2:121–50; Mann, SAC 5, 1983, 17–47.). Heninger (JEGP 56, 1957, 382–95) discusses the idea that the obedience a wife owes her husband is part of the order of things that stems ultimately from God: cf. ParsT X.930–31. Part Four of the Ancrene Riwle, ed. Mabel Day, EETS 225, 1952, 97, discusses Temptation and presents something similar to the narrative of the ClT: "When a man has just brought home his new wife, he watches her ways tolerantly. Although he may notice in her some traits he doesn't like . . . he behaves cheerfully . . . doing all he can to make her love him deeply, with her whole heart. When he is quite certain that her love is really fixed upon him, then indeed he feels able to correct her faults openly. . . . He becomes very stern, and shows his displeasure in his looks, trying to see whether her love for him can be weakened. At last, when he is convinced that she has been properly trained—that, whatever he does to her, she loves him not the less . . .—then he reveals to her that he loves her tenderly, and does all she wants. . . . Then all that sorrow is turned to joy. If Jesu Christ, your husband, acts thus towards you, do not be surprised. . . ." (See Salter, Ch: KnT and ClT, 38–39.) McCall (MLQ 27, 1966, 260–69) cites Phil. 2.8 ("He humbled himself, becoming obedient unto death") as biblical sanction for submission to authority, which is seen as a death of the will in preparation for death itself. McNamara (ChR 7, 1973, 184–93) discusses the use of the Epistle of St. James in the tale.

A number of studies have related the philosophy taught at Oxford, particularly Ockham's, to the tale. See Morse, MLQ 19, 1958, 3–20. Stepsis (ChR 10, 1976, 129–46) and Steinmetz (ChR 12, 1977, 38–54) discuss the nominalist doctrine of "potentia dei absoluta et ordinata" (God's absolute power and his power to actualize possibilities and leave others forever unactualized). Grennen (ChR 6, 1971, 81–93) relates Walter and Griselda to medieval theories of motion. Taylor (in Francis Petrarch: A Symposium, 364–83) assesses the logic of the tale.

The question whether Chaucer revised the tale is discussed in M-R 2:500–501; Severs, Spec 21, 1946, 295–302; Dempster, PMLA 61, 1946, 385–86 and PMLA 68, 1953, 1142–59. Kriser (Manuscripta 17, 1973, 159–77) argues that the MSS do not allow any firm conclusion that the tale was composed separately from its links. See further IV.1177n. Most probably composition of the tale should be assigned to the Canterbury period.

58 roote: Lat. gloss: "At the root of Vesulus (ad radicem Vesuli) is the land of Saluces with its [many] villages and castles."

colde: The adjective is not in Petrarch nor the Fr. version. Mt. Viso (Vesulus, 12,400 ft.) is permanently covered with snow (ClT, ed. Sisam, 48).

72 Lumbardye: Cf. IV.46, 945. Not in Chaucer's sources. Hardman (RES 31, 1980, 172–78) has shown that fourteenth-century Lombardy was infamous for its tyrants, particularly the Visconti of Milan. See Gower, Mirour, 23233–236, 23257–59; LGW 374; and the char-

acterization of Bernabò Visconti, MkT VII.2400. While there is no indication that we should identify Walter with the proverbial tyrants of Lombardy, the association of tyranny with the area is consistent with elements of Walter's future behavior. Cf. MerT IV.1245, LGW 374.

92 Lat. gloss: "'Tua,' inquid, 'humanitas, optime Marchio'" (Severs 1.28; trans. in text).

101 ye: Cf. IV.316–22, 483–92, 876–79, 890–93, etc. On Chaucer's subtle use of the second person pronoun in the tale, see Wilcockson, Use of English 31, 1980, 37–43. But see 508 below.

106 us liketh yow is inconsistent in construction, the pronoun *yow* apparently standing as an object of the impersonal *us lyketh* (Robinson); see Language and Versification, p. xli.

110–40 The Prince's marriage to the social body was a popular political metaphor in the late fourteenth century. See Johnson, ChR 10, 1975, 17–29.

155–61 With the discussion of heredity here, cf. the treatment of *gentillesse* in WBT III.1109–76. See Baker, SP 59, 1962, 631–40; Levy, ChR 11, 1977, 306–17.

174–75 Chaucer's addition.

Explicit prima pars: In all likelihood, Petrarch wrote his tale without division. The MS Severs chose as his base text for the French translation, however, coincides exactly with the first four divisions of Chaucer's rendering, and somewhat later for the fifth. (Ellesmere and most MSS have only five sections.) Chaucer probably followed the example of his French model (Severs, Lit. Rel., 192–96).

197 Lat. gloss: "ffuit haut procul a palacio et cetera" (Severs 2.1, trans. in text).

207, 291–94 oxes stalle: See Luke 2.7–16 and Isa. 1.3; the image is not in Chaucer's sources. Sr. Rose Marie (Commonweal 43, 1941, 225–27) argues that Griselda is associated with Mary at both the Annunciation and the Nativity. For Griselda's resemblance to the "mulier fortis" (woman of valor) of Prov. 31.10–31, see Kellogg, Ch, Langland, 286–88.

212 oon the faireste: "The fairest of all"; see Language and Versification, p. xxxviii, and on the intensifying "one" with a superlative adjective, Matti Rissanen, The Uses of One in Old and Early ME, Memoires de la Soc. Néophilologique de Helsinki 31, 1967, 194–96.

215–17 Chaucer's addition.

223 The Virgin Mary was often pictured both as a shepherdess and as a spinner. (Utley, ChR 6, 1972, 220–21.) Cf. WBPro III.401.

227 Petrarch has "she prepared food suited to her station," the French translation "she brought cabbages or other kinds of herbs for their sustenance" (S&A 2.12). Chaucer keeps the basic structure of Petrarch, adds details from the French, and makes the scene his own with matter of his own invention.

249–52 Chaucer's addition.

260–94 Considerably expanded in Chaucer.

262–64 On the structure and internal arrangement of houses in Chaucer's time, see Smyser, Spec 31, 1956, 297–315.

266 last: Either "to farthest Italy" (taking *last* as superlative adj.: cf. Bo 4.m1.24) or "as far as Italy extends" (taking *last* as the contracted third person of *lasten:* see PF 49).

276–94 The well and water are often found at the threshold of the fairy world, but the scene also recalls

Rebecca and Rachel (Gen. 24.13–67; 29.1–2) and the Annunciation (Utley, ChR 6:224).

281   Lat. gloss: "So that, her other duties done, she might with her friends prepare to see the wife of her lord" (Severs 2.33–35).

295   Lat. gloss: "Walter, deep in thought, drew near and addressed her by name" (Severs 2.35–36).

336   **erst:** For the idiom see KnT I.1566 and n.

337   Lat. gloss: "And he found her astonished at the unexpected coming of such a guest" (Severs 2.50).

344   Lat. gloss: " 'Et patri tuo placet,' inquid, 'et mihi vt uxor mea sis, et credo idipsum tibi placeat sed habeo ex te querere et cetera" (Severs 2.51–53, trans. in text).

350   **yow avyse:** "Consider the matter," with the implication of refusal. Compare the legal formula *le roy s'avisera* for expressing royal refusal to a proposed measure (Skeat 5:346).

356   Lat. gloss: "Sine vlla frontis aut verbi inpugnacione" (Severs 2.56–57, trans. in text).

362–64   Lat. gloss: "I will never knowingly do or even think anything that may be contrary to your will nor will you do anything, even though you order me to die, that I will take ill" (Severs 2.59–62).

365   **ynogh:** Mann (SAC 5, 1983, 31–33) notes that this word is repeated at IV.1051 and discusses its thematic importance.

372–76   Lat. gloss: "Then, that she not bring any remnant of her old fortune into her new home, he ordered her stripped" (Severs 2.65–66). Griselda's clothing and unclothing, a motif not as prominent in Chaucer's sources, has received much comment. See Gilmartin, RUS 62, 1976, 99–110. Note also the emphasis on clothing in the Envoy (Rothman, PLL 9, 1973, 115–27), the Clerk's own threadbare attire (GP I.290, 296), and the Wife of Bath's constant reference to clothes.

381   **corone:** Dives et Pauper, EETS 280, Commandment 6.2.45–47: "Thre ornamentis longyn principaly to a wyf: a ryng on hyr fyngyr, a broche on hyr breste, & a garlond on hyr hefd."

385   **translated:** Grennen (ChR 6:90) argues that the technical philosophical sense of *translatio,* "change of place," not "transformation" of moral being, applies here.

406   Lat. gloss: "And to all she became dear and respected beyond belief, so that those who had known her birth and lineage (originem) could hardly persuade themselves that she was Janicola's daughter, so gracious was her life and the way she lived it, so weighty and sweet were her words, by which she had bound all the people to her with a bond of great love" (Severs 2.79–84).

413   MLT II.532 and Tr 1.1078 are nearly identical.

422   **honestetee:** Cf. the gloss: "Sic Walterus humili quidem set insigni ac prospero matrimonio honestatis summa dei in pace . . . [vivebat]. (Thus Walter, in humble indeed but renowned and prosperous marriage with honor, lived in God's highest peace.)" Hendrickson (MP 4, 1907, 191) points out that "honestatis" is awkward and probably corrupt; he suggests "honestatus." Severs (Lit. Rel., 266) shows that Petrarch did in fact write "honestatus." The line then would read "Thus Walter, honored by certainly a humble yet renowned and prosperous marriage . . ." Most Petrarch MSS also read "domi," "at home," for "dei." (Cf. the French translation "en . . . maison.") On the significance of the confusion, see Dempster, MP 41:8, 10. In glosses at 425,

428, 435, and 449, Ellesmere quotes continuously the end of the second part of Petrarch's tale and the beginning of the third. The text, with some minor variations, is the same as Severs's, and Chaucer's translation of it is full and accurate.

431   **commune profit:** Cf. PF 47n.

432   Cook (PQ 4, 1925, 27) notes that the corresponding passage in Petrarch draws on Pilatus's Latin translation of Odyssey 7.73–78.

441   Cf. Matt. 1.21. Haldman (RES 31:172–78) compares the following passage from the Apocryphal Gospels of the Infancy: "And when the multitude saw it, they were astonished, and said: This young child is from heaven: for he hath saved many souls from death, and hath power to save them all his life long" (The Apoc. New Test., ed. James, 1924, 54).

444   **Al had hire levere:** The phrase is a confusion of the impersonal *hire were levere* and the personal *she levere had;* see Language and Versification, p. xl, and Mustanoja, ME Syntax, 531–32.

449   Lat. gloss: "Meanwhile, as it happened, when the baby girl had been weaned, Walter was seized with a desire as wondrous as laudable to test more deeply the fidelity of his dear wife, already well proven, and to test it again and again" (Severs 3.1–4).

452   **tempte:** In ParsT X.322–57, 1054–55, Chaucer distinguishes between internal and external temptation. McNamara (ChR 7:184–93) argues that Griselda is tested by external temptation; Walter, far more grievously, by internal temptation.

459–62   Chaucer's addition.

499   Lat. gloss: "Nec verbo nec vultu et cetera" (Severs 3.15–16, trans. in text).

508   **save oonly yee:** Hengwrt and Ellesmere read *thee* with *vel yee* (or yee) in the margin: Petrarch: "nisi te"; Fr.: "que toy." Of the other MSS, some have *thee,* some *yee.* The Hengwrt and Ellesmere scribes were perhaps confused by the fact that "tonality" here demands the plural, rhyme the singular: see Mustanoja, ME Syntax, 125 for *ye* as an unstressed form of *you,* though this is rare in Chaucer, occurring only here and Tr 1.5.

538–39   Cf. Isa. 53.7.

540–43   Lat. gloss: "Suspecta viri fama, suspecta facies, suspecta hora, suspecta erat oratio" (Severs 3.32–33, trans. in text).

554–67   Chaucer's addition.

581   Chaucer's comment.

588   **whenne:** By the late fourteenth century *when* = "whence" (from OE *hwanon*) was rare, having been displaced by *whennes.* This is the only use in Chaucer.

590   Pearsall (MLN 67, 1952, 529–31) identifies Panik as Panico, a castle and family situated 18–20 miles south of Bologna. The identification, however, is not certain.

603–6   Lat. gloss: "Per alacritas atque sedalitas solitum obsequium idem amor nulla filie mencio" (Severs 3.53–54, trans. in text).

610   Lat. gloss: "Transiverant hoc in statu anni .iiij.^{or} dum ecce gravida et cetera" (Severs 4.1, trans. in text).

621–23   Chaucer's addition.

624–25   Lat. gloss: " 'Et olim,' ait, 'audisti populum meum egre nostrum ferre connubium' et cetera" (Severs 4.5–6, trans. in text; **sikly berth** = egre . . . ferre).

647–49   Chaucer's addition.

651   Cf. Petrarch "preter laborem" (Severs 4.16), "except childbirth."

664–65   Lat. gloss: "If it would please you that I should die, I would willingly die" (Severs 4.25).

666–67   Cf. Cant. 8.6 (Kellogg, Ch, Langland, 287).

687   **evere lenger the moore:** See Mustanoja, ME Syntax, 281–82.

722   Lat. gloss: "Slowly an evil rumor about Walter began to spread" (Severs 4.53–54).

736   Cf. WBPro III.4n.

811–12; 839–40; 851–61:   Chaucer's additions.

812   **Fortune, aventure;** see GP I.844n.

834–38   Kean (Ch and the Making, 2.126) detects an echo here of Paul's counsel on marriage, widowhood, and virginity in 1 Cor. 7.1–40. Cf. PP C 19.84–90.

871   Cf. Job 1.21: "Naked came I out of my mother's womb, and naked shall I return thither."

880–82   Chaucer's addition. A stock comparison; Whiting W672. (Cf. Rom. 454, *nakid as a worm,* Fr. "nu comme un ver"), but also Ps. 21.7 and Richard Rolle, Meditations on the Passion, 1.54–55, who applies this verse to Christ (Kean, Ch and the Making, 2.128).

890   **The smok:** For discussion of Walter's switch from "ye" to "thou" from this point onward in addressing Grisilda, see Wilcockson, Use of English 31, 3, 1980, 37–43; because the singular pronoun contains the opposite potentials of affection and alienation, Walter, by this mode of address, can simultaneously both conceal and reveal his love for Grisilda. See Language and Versification, p. xxxix.

902–3   Chaucer's addition. Cf. Job 3.3: "Let the day perish wherein I was born, and the night in which it was said: A manchild is conceived."

932–38   Chaucer's addition. See Job 42.6: "Therefore I reprehend myself, and do penance in dust and ashes"; James 5.11: "You have heard of the patience of Job"; cf. WBPro 436, 688–96. Severs (MLN 49, 1934, 461–62) reports one Petrarch MS (Cambridge, Corpus Christi College, MS 458) that refers to Job at exactly the point where the Job stanza appears in Chaucer; it is, however, the only MS that does so. On the figure of Job in medieval literature, see Lawrence Besserman, The Legend of Job in the MA, 1979.

990–91   Chaucer's addition.

995–1001   Cf. Bo 4.m5.31–37, Tr 4.183n.

995–1008   Chaucer's addition. Several MSS have "auctor" in the margin, but IV.1002 shows that Chaucer has not interrupted the Clerk. See MLT II.358n.

999   A jane is a Genovese coin worth a halfpenny. The phrase "not worth a jane" also appears in Provençal: "non prezo un genoi," in V. Crescini, Studi Romanzi, 1892, 50 (Robinson). Cf. CYT VIII.795n.

1037   Lat. gloss: "One thing I pray and advise you in all good faith: that you do not drive this woman with those goads you have driven another, for she is younger and more delicately nurtured, and would not, I think, be able to suffer as much as I have" (Severs 6.39–40).

1079–1106   Much expanded in Chaucer's version.

1098   **Hath doon yow kept:** For the construction see KnT I.1913n.

1138–40   Cf. Form Age.

1141–62   Lat. gloss at 1142: "This story it seemed good to weave anew in a high style [*stilo alto;* see 41 above] not so much that the matrons of our time might be moved to imitate the patience of this wife, which seems to me inimitable, but that the readers might be stirred at least to imitate this woman's constancy, that what she did for

her husband they might dare to do for God, for, as says the Apostle James, 'God cannot be tempted by evil, and He tempts no man' (James 1.13); yet he tests us and often allows us to suffer grievous scourgings, not that he might know the state of our souls, for he knew that before we were created etc." (Severs 6.69–78). The gloss omits Petrarch's final sentence: "Therefore I would add to the list of constant men whosoever he be who suffers without murmur for his God what this rustic wife suffered for her mortal husband."

1153–55   James 1.13: "Let no man when he is tempted say that he is tempted by God. For God is not a tempter of evils and he tempteth no man." Cf. 1141–62 above.

1163   The translation of Petrarch and the French version ends here.

1164–69   Dean (ELH 44, 1977, 401–17) argues that the references to gold and brass allude by extension to the decline of the Golden Age.

1170   **Wyves love of Bathe:** A group genitive; see Language and Versification, p. xxxviii. The second application of the tale that follows is the Clerk's direct reply, in satirical vein, to the Wife of Bath. It was obviously written when the plan of the Marriage Group was well under way. Whether any considerable time elapsed between the writing of the tale and the addition of this ending (or, for that matter, the addition of the ClPro), is unknown. See Kriser (Manuscripta 17:159–77) for a review of critical opinion.

1170–76   In 16 MSS this stanza is omitted. See 1177 below.

1171   **secte:** The possible range of meanings: "sect" (category of persons; a methodological rather than a doctrinal distinction: cf. Galen's *De sectis,* which discusses different schools of physicians, and Grennen, ChR 6: 81–93); "sex" (Kökeritz, PQ 26, 1947, 147–51); "oath-helper, compurgator" (Hornstein, ChR 3, 1968, 65–67); "petition, action, lawsuit" (Baird, ChR 6, 1971, 117–19; cf. PP B 5.495–98). Baird argues that there is a legal coloring to the term that should not be overlooked.

1177   The song, as the scribe's heading **Lenvoy de Chaucer** indicates, is Chaucer's independent composition. But it belongs dramatically to the Clerk and is entirely appropriate (Robinson). For the opposing view see Skeat (5.351), Koch (Anglia 50, 1926, 65–66), and Baugh (439). The meter changes to six-line stanzas with only three rhymes (-ence, -aille, -inde) throughout the series; it is thus a double ballade in form (see the Introduction to the Short Poems, p. 632). The *envoy* in the ballade is a brief stanza, usually differing in form from the main body of the poem, which addresses the recipient directly (see, e.g., Womanly Noblesse); it is not necessarily the logical conclusion to the poem but often is rather a means of connecting the action to actual life, by establishing a realistic context for the abstract ideas of the poem (Poirion, Le poète, 373). Chaucer also uses *envoy* to designate a verse epistle, as in the Envoys to Bukton and Scogan, though here it seems apparent an ordinary *envoy* is apparently meant.

In sixteen MSS the fourth stanza of the *envoy* (IV.1195–1200) stands last. On the question of whether Chaucer rearranged the stanzas, see M-R 2.244, 500–501; Covella, ChR 4, 1970, 267–83; and Kriser, Manuscripta 17:159–77.

1188   **Chichevache:** Literally, "lean cow," perhaps a corruption of "chiche face" (lean face); a cow which fed on patient wives and consequently had little to eat. Sometimes Chichevache is contrasted to Bicorne ("two-horned"), which fed on patient husbands and was "always fat and in good case" (Skeat 5.351–52). See Mystères inédits du XVe siècle, ed. Achille Jubinal, 1837, 1.281, 390; Lydgate, Bicorne and Chichevache, Minor Poems, EETS 192, 433–38. For a good account of the recorded forms of the name see Hammond, Engl. Verse, 113–15.

1191   bidaffed: Usually glossed "tricked," "made a fool of," but Stevens (ChR 7, 1972, 124–25) plausibly suggests "deafened."

1196   camaille: Camel, but also a punning reference to *aventaille*, IV.1204. Claude Blair, Eur. Armour, 1958, 52, notes that in fourteenth-century England the piece of armor called a *ventaille* was in France called the *camail*, though both words were occasionally used in both countries.

1200   Proverbial; see ParsT X.406n.

1204   aventaille: A wide strip of chainmail that formed the lower half of the moveable part of the helmet and served to protect the neck and upper chest. See Blair, Eur. Arm., 52–53, and Hamilton, MP 3, 1905, 541–46.

1207–10   Cf. WBPro III.253–56 and n., 265–70 and n.

1212a–g   The Host's stanza is generally held to have been written early and canceled when Chaucer wrote new lines for The Merchant's Prologue containing an echo of 1212. It is found in Ellesmere, Hengwrt, and 20 other MSS. See the works cited in 1177 above and Stevens (ChR 7:130–31). Cf. MkT VII.1889–94, perhaps a reworking of this canceled link.

The Merchant's Prologue

On the date of The Merchant's Prologue and Tale see the introductory note on The Wife of Bath's Prologue. Although in the scribal arrangement of the tales, The Merchant's Prologue and Tale are sometimes separated from The Clerk's Tale, the echo of line 1212 in the first line of The Merchant's Prologue and the direct reference to Griselda leave no doubt that this prologue should directly follow The Clerk's Tale. The Merchant's autobiographical account of his own unhappy marriage has led many critics to read his tale as a bitter comment on himself (see introductory note to The Merchant's Tale).

1226–27   Cf. Buk 13–16, MilT I.3231n.

1230   Seint Thomas of Ynde: St. Thomas the Apostle. See SumT III.1980n.

The Merchant's Tale

The Merchant's Tale has three parts: first, January's deliberations on marriage (1245–1688); second, from January's wedding to the understanding reached by May and Damian (1689–2020); and third, the deception story proper (2021–2418). Many of the arguments and images

The explanatory notes to The Merchant's Prologue and Tale were written by M. Teresa Tavormina.

of the first part of the tale have parallels in Eustache Deschamps's *Miroir de mariage* (Oeuvres 9; S&A, 333–39). The debt to the *Miroir* is argued in detail by Lowes, MP 8, 1910, 167–86; see also McGalliard, PQ 25, 1946, 193–220; Cherniss, ChR 6, 1972, 245–51; and Altman, RPh 29, 1976, 514–18. Thundy (Ch Problems, 24–58), however, has cast doubt on Chaucer's knowledge of the *Miroir,* and the resemblances may be due to a common source in the *Lamentationes* of Matheolus.

The opening arguments also draw on two works of Albertanus of Brescia, the *Liber de amore Dei* and the *Liber consolationis et consilii,* the ultimate source of Chaucer's Melibee. Other influences are Jerome's *Adversus Jovinianum* (PL 23:221–352; S&A, 208–13) and the homiletic commonplaces used in the discussion of *luxuria* in The Parson's Tale. Parallels with these materials are noted below, and see Patterson, Traditio 34, 1978, 363–66.

In the second section of the tale, the depiction of January's lovemaking may be taken from Giovanni Boccaccio's *Ameto* (ed. Quaglio, 772–76; S&A, 339–40), which describes the aged, impotent husband of a young nymph. For the third part of the tale, Chaucer uses a common fabliau plot: the story of the blind husband and the fruit tree. The nearest extant analogue, perhaps a source, of Chaucer's version is an Italian tale (S&A, 341–43); the possibility of a lost, auxiliary source, probably French, has been suggested as well (Schlauch, MLN 49, 1934, 231–32; Dempster, MP 34, 1936, 140–54). Wentersdorf (SP 63, 1966, 619–29) argues for the influence, direct or through a French version, of a Celtic analogue featuring fairies as the story's dei ex machina. The possible influence of *Decameron* 2.10 and 7.9 has also been defended (Beidler, Italica 50, 1973, 266–84; McGrady, ChR 12, 1977, 11–12). For other analogues, see S&A, 343–56. The early MSS contain a number of Latin marginal glosses, the most important of which are quoted in the following notes from M-R 3:508–11.

The tale illustrates the familiar topos of the *senex amans,* or aged lover, also found in The Miller's Tale, The Reeve's Prologue, and The Wife of Bath's Prologue. On Chaucer's handling of the topos here and in the MilT, see Boothman, Thoth 4, 1963, 3–14. In addition to the treatment in the *Ameto* of the subject, Chaucer would have known the elegies of Maximianus, which focus on the misery of aged desire (Hartung, MS 29, 1967, 10–25). Further examples can be easily found in fabliaux, medieval lyrics (e.g., the *chansons des malmariées*), and other satiric pieces. For the religious and medical contexts of medieval ideas on old age, see Brown, NM 74, 1973, 92–106. Kean (Ch and Poetry 2:156–64) suggests that January is modeled in part on Le Jaloux in the RR 8455–9492. Helen Cooper (Structure of CT, 227–30) compares the tale's techniques, themes, and basic plot situation ("the girl with two lovers") with those of the Knight's, Miller's, and Franklin's tales. On the tale as a critique of contemporary values concerning love and marriage, see Schlauch, ELH 4, 1937, 201–12; Holman, ELH 18, 1951, 241–52; and David Aers, Ch, Langland, 151–60. R. A. Shoaf discusses relations between the tale and medieval theories of monetary and domestic economies (Dante, Ch, and the Currency of the Word, 1983, 185–209).

The degree to which the tale reflects its teller has been a matter of significant critical disagreement, mainly on the basis of lines 1251 and 1322. Some critics have suggested that Chaucer originally intended the tale for a clerical narrator, probably the Monk or Friar, perhaps as a *quiting* of The Shipman's Tale, which was probably first assigned to the Wife of Bath (Manly, CT, 596, 624; Baugh, MP 35, 1937, 15–26; Garbáty, MP 67, 1969, 18–24; Rowland, SN 51, 1979, 211). Others have argued that it was always meant for the Merchant, who might also have taken offense at The Shipman's Tale (Dempster, MP 36, 1938, 1–8; Sedgewick, UTQ 17, 1948, 339–40; Gates, NM 77, 1976, 374–75). Whether first assigned to the Merchant or not, the tale does seem to have been composed around the same time as The Wife of Bath's Prologue and in deliberate connection with it, The Clerk's Tale, and the Melibee, judging from the various echoes among the pieces, and thus to belong to Chaucer's general response to the issues of marriage and governance raised by his reading of Albertanus and other sources.

The traditional reading of the tale, put forth by Kittredge, Tatlock, Sedgewick, and others, is that it is a dramatic unfolding of the Merchant's character as revealed in the prologue—newly wed and bitterly unhappy. A number of later critics argue that, taken by itself, the tale is a rather lighthearted jape at women and human folly. They have also offered a general critique of too close an identification of the Merchant and January, and of unexamined acceptance of Kittredge's dramatic principle for all the *Tales*. (Bronson, SP 58, 1961, 583–96; Jordan, PMLA 78, 1963, 293–99; Craik, Comic Tales, 133–53; Stevens, ChR 7, 1972, 118–29.) The new view of the tale as a light farce, unrelated to its prologue, was soon opposed (Elliott, TSL 9, 1964, 11–17; Hartung, MS 29:16–25), most definitively by Donaldson (Speaking of Ch, 30–45) and Harrington (PMLA 86, 1971, 25–31). While recent critics tend to accept the older, darker view of the tale, certain perspectives offered by proponents of the lighter reading continue to influence commentary on it (Beidler, Costerus 5, 1972, 7–13; David, Strumpet Muse, 179–81; Aers, Ch, Langland, 224).

The debates over the tale's ascription to the Merchant, the degree to which it reflects his character, and the quality of its humor, are part of a still larger problem—the tale's apparent failure of decorum, its mixing of genres, styles, voices, and tones, of pagan and Christian elements, even of narrative levels (cf. IV.1685–87). Critics have long noted these tensions and dramatic improprieties, explaining them variously as marks of the Merchant's or Chaucer's loss of artistic control or as instances of Gothic juxtaposition (Kittredge, MP 9, 1912, 453–56; Sedgewick, UTQ 17:337–45; Jordan, PMLA 78:293–99; Brewer, in Comp. Ch St., 309–10). Most recently, they have also been seen as Chaucer's testing of the bounds of fiction or his deliberate manipulation of audience response to the tale (Bloomfield, 37–50, in Med. and Ren. St. 7, ed. Siegfried Wenzel, 1978; Schleusener, ChR 14, 1980, 237–50). For a more detailed review of scholarly controversies over the tale, see Brown, ChR 13, 1978–79, 141–56 and 247–62.

1245 Lumbardye: The Lombards were active in international trade and finance and would have been professional rivals of the Merchant; Lombardy also had a thriving commercial aristocracy by Chaucer's time, the ancestry and values of which often differed from those of the traditional feudal aristocracy represented by the Clerk's Marquis Walter (Olson, TSLL 3, 1961, 259–63). Lombard rulers were known as well for lechery, tyranny, and avarice; see ClT IV.72n.

1246 Pavye: Pavia, a Lombard city famous at the time for usury, wealth, and amorous sensuality (Olson, TSLL 3:263; Brown, NM 71, 1970, 654–58).

1248 sixty yeer: Authorities differed on when old age began (see Coffman, MLN 52, 1937, 25–26; Philip, MLN 53, 1938, 181–82); "Medill Elde" is sixty in The Parlement of the Thre Ages (EETS 246, lines 150–51). Vincent of Beauvais (Spec. Nat. 31.75) quotes Avicenna, who takes the years from thirty-five or forty to sixty as "senectus," a time of diminishing powers, and sixty as the beginning of senility and the end of life ("senium et finis vitae").

1251 seculeer: "Lay" (Baugh, Donaldson, Fisher, Davis, Blake); perhaps "of the secular clergy" (Skeat, Robinson, Pratt). Critics who favor a cleric as the original teller of the tale take the meaning "lay" as evidence for their case (Baugh, MP 35:20; Garbáty, MP 67:22–23). Those who favor the Merchant either take *seculeer* as a direct or ironic attack on the clergy or argue that a layman could gibe at lay follies as easily as a cleric (Dempster, MP 36:1–2; Sedgewick, UTQ 17:339–40; Keiser, Manuscripta 17, 1973, 176n.; Howard, Idea of CT, 261).

1259–60 Cf. FranT V.803–5.

1267–1392 The question of whose voice is heard in these lines, commonly called the "marriage encomium," is a major interpretative crux. A review of critical opinion on the problem and a detailed analysis of the passage are given by D. R. Benson, ChR 14, 1979, 48–60.

1286–92 Burnley notes echoes of vernacular parts of contemporary marriage vows in this passage as well as in IV.1333–36 (YES 6, 1976, 19–20).

1294 Theofraste: Cf. WBPro III.671n. The Miroir also draws on Theophrastus (Lowes, MP 8:177–78, 306–15).

1296–1306 Adv. Jov. 1.47 (S&A, 212).

1296 housbondrye: "Domestic economy," with a possible play on "husband" (Baum, PMLA 71, 1956, 239; MED, s.v. *husbondrie* n. 1b, 4).

1300 Cf. WBPro III.310.

1305–6 The variant readings of this couplet suggest that Chaucer did not complete it. See textual note.

1311–14 Lat. gloss: "A wife is to be loved because she is a gift of God. Jesus son of Sirach [error for Prov. 19.14]: 'House and riches are given by parents, but a good or prudent wife is properly from the Lord'" (quoting Albertanus, De amore Dei, fol. 40r).

1315 shadwe upon a wal: Proverbial; see Whiting S185; ShipT VII.9; and ParsT X.1068n.

1319 Cf. ParsT X.918.

1325–29 Lat. gloss: "'Let us make a helpmate for him'; and having taken a rib from Adam's body, He made Eve, and said, 'For this reason shall a man leave father and mother and cleave, etc.; and they shall be two in one flesh'" (Gen. 2.18, 24, as quoted in De amore Dei, fol. 39v; cf. Mel VII.1103–4).

1332 paradys terrestre: For the notion of marriage as an earthly paradise or an earthly purgatory, cf. IV.1265, 1647, 1670–73; and WBPro III.489–90 and n. On the image of paradise in the tale, see Richardson, Blameth

Nat Me, 133–35; Cherniss, ChR 6:244–54; Bleeth, in Learned and Lewed, ed. Benson, 45–60. Connected with the paradisal imagery are the garden images later in the tale; cf. IV.2028–41 and nn. Also relevant is the common justification of marriage as the only sacrament established in paradise. Cf. ParsT X.918–21; Mirk's Festial, EETS e.s. 96, 289; Peter Lombard, Sentences 4.26.1.

1334–36   Cf. RR 16435–44 and Gen. 2.24.

1341   Cf. Tr 4.1695–96n.

1343   Cf. ShipT VII.243–44.

1345   Cf. ClT IV.355.

1362–74   The examples of **Rebekke** and **Jacob** (Gen. 27.1–29), **Judith** and **Olofernus** (Judith, chapters 11–13; apocryphal in A.V.; cf. MkT VII.2551–74), **Abigayl** and **Nabal** (1 Sam. 25.1–35), and **Ester, Mardochee,** and **Assuere** (Esther 7.1–10) are from Albertanus's *Liber consolationis* and appear also in Mel VII.1098–1102, which this passage may echo. Details not in Albertanus or Melibee may come from Deschamps (IV.1366–68 from Miroir 9107–16; IV.1371–74 from Miroir 9135–49, in S&A, 338) or directly from the Bible (**the kydes skyn** from Gen. 27.16, **whil he slepte** from Judith 13.4). See Lowes, MP 8:181–83.

Because the counsels of these women were variously deceitful, many critics read the exempla as sharply satiric (Turner, ELN 3, 1965, 93–94; Owen, Pilgrimage and Story, 192; Besserman, Hebrew Univ. Sts. in Lit. 6, 1978, 19–20). But some recent critics have also observed the positive typological value of these women for medieval exegetes and liturgists, and argue for reading them in a positive sense (Otten, ChR 5, 1971, 278–83; Burnley, YES 6:22–23; Harty, BSUF 19, 1978, 67–68; Ames, 90–91, in Acta IV, ed. Paul E. Szarmach and Bernard S. Levy, 1978); for an interpretation that includes both positive and negative viewpoints, see Brown, Viator 5, 1974, 410–12.

1375   Lat. gloss: "Seneca [error for Fulgentius, Mythologies 1.22]: 'As nothing is better than a humble wife, nothing is more savage than an aggressive woman'" (Albertanus, Lib. Cons., 18).

1377   Catoun: "Dionysius" Cato, Distichs 3.23, quoted in Lib. Cons., 19, which appears as a marginal Lat. gloss: "Be mindful to suffer your wife's tongue, if she is worthy." See Hazelton, Spec 35, 1960, 376.

1380   Lat. gloss: "A good wife is a good and faithful keeper of the household" (Albertanus, De amore Dei, fol. 40v).

1381–82   Cf. Ecclus. 36.27: "Where there is no hedge, possessions will be spoiled; and where there is no woman he who is needy *(egens)* will mourn." The change of the Bible's "needy" *(egens)* to "sick" *(eger)* betrays Chaucer's debt to Albertanus's *De amore Dei* (see introductory note to Melibee), which quotes the verse with the variant "eger" (fol. 40r).

1384–88   Eph. 5.25, 28–29, 33, a selection of verses already made by Albertanus in the *De amore Dei,* fols. 39v–40r, and quoted in the Lat. gloss: "The Apostle Paul to the Ephesians: 'Love your wives as Christ loved the Church, etc.' The Apostle [says]: 'So ought men to love their wives as their own bodies, because he that loveth his wife [loveth himself]. No man ever hated his own flesh, but nourisheth it and cherisheth it.' And later, 'Let every man love his wife as himself.'" Cf. ParsT X.929.

1393   January: Chaucer's name for his *senex amans* may

have been suggested by the January-April marriage in Deschamps's ballade "Contre les mariages disproportionnés" (Oeuvres 5:63–64). See Matthews, MLR 51, 1956, 218; Brown, NM 74:92–93; Eliason, Names 21, 1973, 140. January is etymologically connected with the two-faced god Janus, associated with gates, trade, doubleness, and other matters appropriate to the tale (Brown, Names 31, 1983, 79–87). Cf. 1693 below.

1401   pittes brynke: Cf. the Biblical use of "pit" as a figure for death or hell, e.g., Ps. 87.5 (A.V. 88.4), Ezek. 31.14, Rev. 9.1–3.

1417   twenty: *Sixteen* is the reading of some MSS and editors (see textual note), which may add to the humor. But *twenty* is still young; cf. Anel 78.

1418–20   Cf. Whiting F236.

pykerel: A young pike; however, not all authorities consider an old pike better eating (Donovan, PQ 31, 1952, 441).

1424   Wades boot: Cf. Tr 3.614. Robinson noted that Speght's comment on this (in his 1598 ed.) "has often been called the most exasperating note ever written on Chaucer: 'Concerning Wade and his bote called Guingelot, as also his strange exploits in the same, because the matter is long and fabulous, I passe it over.' If Speght really knew the story and understood the allusion, he was more fortunate than later editors. For though there are a number of references in medieval literature which indicate he was a famous hero, they do not suffice for the reconstruction of the narrative as it was known to Chaucer." Detailed reviews of the available evidence on Wade and speculation on this reference may be found in Wentersdorf, JEGP 65, 1966, 274–86, and Peeters, Amsterdamer Beiträge zur älteren Germanistik 1, 1972, 51–88. Baugh (135) takes *tolde tale of Wade* in Tr 3.614 to mean "told a tall story," and perhaps here the reference merely connotes deceit; see also Bennett, MLR 31, 1936, 202–3.

1425   broken harm: Probably "to do harm or mischief" (MED, s.v. *brouken* v. 2b); cf. Cassidy, MLN 58, 1943, 23–27.

1427–28   Cf. WBPro III.44c–e; Whiting S90. On the differences between the Merchant's and the Wife's expressions of the idea, see Harrington, N&Q 11, 1964, 166–67.

1441–55   the cause why: Cf. ParsT X.883, 939–43 and note 939. The views of medieval theologians and canonists on the motives for marriage and intercourse are discussed in relation to the MerT by Mogan, ChR 4, 1970, 123–36; Kelly, Love and Marriage, 1975, 245–74; and Patterson, Traditio 34:363–66.

1454   Cf. ParsT X.861.

1456   Cf. WBPro III.112, Mel VII.1088 (almost identical).

1461   On the iconographic contexts of the Merchant's literal and figural trees, see Annunziata, in Acta IV, ed. Szarmach and Levy, 1978, 128–33.

1469   See RvPro I.3857 and n.

1476   Placebo: Lat. "I will please." The word is often associated with flattery, especially in the phrase "to sing Placebo," meaning "to flatter." Cf. SumT III.2075n. and ParsT X.617n.; Whiting P248. On the probable source of the phrase, see Fleming, N&Q 12, 1965, 18. Given January's advanced age, it may also be relevant that *Placebo* is the first word of an antiphon based on Ps. 114.9 (A.V. 116.9), sung at the beginning of Vespers for the

Dead, and applied by extension to the vespers office itself. See Langland, PP C, ed. Skeat, 4.467 and n.

1485–86 A common proverb; see MilT I.3530n.

1514 **stapen is in age:** Cf. NPT VII.2821.

1516 **hangeth on a joly pyn:** Perhaps with connotations of amorous desire (Pratt).

1523–25 A paraphrase of "Cui des, video" ("Consider to whom you give"), Distichs of Cato, Sententia 17. Cf. PP C 10.69n. The proverb is given without attribution and followed by the sentiment of IV.1526–29 in Map's letter of Valerius to Rufinus (in De nugis curialium, ed. James, 146). Misattribution of ethical maxims to Seneca was common in the Middle Ages.

1530–39 On inquiring into the qualities of a wife before marriage, cf. WBPro III.285–92, and see Adv. Jov. 1.47 (S&A, 211) and Miroir 1553–75 (S&A, 216–17).

1536 **mannyssh wood:** See MED, s.v. *mannish* adj. 2; and Utley, MLN 53, 1938, 359–62; cf. MLT II.782, Tr 1.284.

1553 Cf. WBPro III.492n.

1561 Cf. RR 13851–52.

1568–69 Perhaps an ironic allusion to an episode in the Life of Aesop, in which Aesop's master's learning is less effective than Aesop's common sense at explaining the nature of such a basket (von Kreisler, ChR 6, 1971, 30–37).

1577–87 The ME term **fantasye** was applied variously to the mental faculties involved in the reception or retention of sensory impressions or to the formation, perhaps deluded, of mental images and ideas (MED s.v. *fantasie* n. 1a). See Tr 1.295–98n. For the mirror image here, cf. the mirrors of Bo 5.m4.26–7 and Tr 1.365. Economou notes similarities between January's mental mirror and the fountain-mirror of Narcissus in the RR (CL 17, 1965, 251–57). See also Robertson, Pref to Ch, 110–11; Schroeder, Criticism 12, 1970, 168–71; and Burlin, Ch Fiction, 209–10.

1598 On Cupid's traditional blindness see KnT I.1963–65n.

1662 **right of hooly chirche:** The burial service (Wichert, Expl 25, 1966, Item 32; OED s.v. *right* sb. 11c); or perhaps the solemnization of the marriage (so Robinson and others).

1670 **purgatorie:** Cf. 1332 above and WBPro III.489–90 and n.

1685–87 This intrusive reference to the Wife has exercised critics since Skeat (5:359); it is often taken as a mark of carelessness, either on the Merchant's part or on Chaucer's (Bronson, SP 58:587; Baugh, 447; Elliott, TSL 9: 15–16; Eliason, Lang. of Ch, 148–49). More positive evaluations are given by Grove (Critical Rev. 18, 1976, 29–30) and Bloomfield (see introductory note).

1686 **we:** *ye* in many MSS; see M-R 3:391. Baird suggests that *ye* was Chaucer's initial choice, which he revised to *we* for a more complex and multileveled ambiguity in the passage (AmN&Q 11, 1973, 100–102).

1693 **Mayus:** "A masculine form, because the name of the month is so" (Skeat 5:359); "used for the sake of the meter" (Baugh, 448; see also Eliason, Names 21:140). Brown suggests a deliberate allusion to the month because of traditions associating it with healing, a theme of the tale (ChR 2, 1968, 273–77).

1700–1708 While not complete, this sketch of the wedding service matches surviving fourteenth-century English marriage rites fairly well. The priest's "coming forth" refers to the wedding proper, performed at the church door before the nuptial Mass (see GP I.460 and n.). See also the Sarum Missal (tr. in Miller, Ch: Sources and Backgrounds, 374–84).

1702 **the hooly sacrement:** Probably marriage (Sr. M. Immaculate, MLQ 2, 1941, 62–64), but the Eucharist has also been suggested, since the bride and groom received it at the nuptial Mass (Tatlock, MLN 32, 1917, 374).

1704 **Sarra and Rebekke:** Referring to the prayer in the marriage service that the wife be "wise as Rebecca, long-lived and faithful as Sara" (tr. in Miller, Ch: Sources and Backgrounds, 381).

1716 **Orpheus:** See Bo 3.m12 and n.

Amphioun: Ruler of Thebes who moved rocks for the city walls by the power of his music; Statius, Theb. 1.9–10, 8.232–33, 10.873–77; Ovid, Met. 6.178–79; Horace, Ars poetica, 394–96; Boccaccio, De genealogia deorum 5.30. Cf. KnT I.1546; MancT IX.116–17. See also Hoffman, Ovid and CT, 151–54.

1719 **Joab:** See 2 Sam. 2.28, 18.16, 20.22. For Joab and Theodomas, see also HF 1245–46.

1720 **Theodomas:** Augur for the Argive besiegers of Thebes after Amphiaraus's death; his first prayer as augur was followed at once by the trumpets of the attacking Thebans, and more trumpets followed a raid on the Thebans that he later inspired (Theb. 8.275–347; 10.160–553).

1727 **fyrbrond:** Associated with Venus in RR 3424–26 (Rom 3705–10), 15778, 21251–54, and PF 114; or, the torch of the marriage procession, usually carried by Hymen.

1730 **Ymeneus:** Cf. LGW 2250; RR 21016, 21020.

1732 **Marcian:** Martianus Capella (fifth century), who wrote The Marriage of Philology and Mercury; cf. HF 985 and n.

1734 **hym Mercurie:** For the construction, see Mustanoja, ME Syntax, 135–36.

1736–37 The rhetorical "inexpressibility" topos; cf. Tr 3.1310–37.

1744–45 **Ester:** Esther; on her eyes, beauty, and meekness before King Ahasuerus, see Esther 15.4–19 (Vulg.); also 1.15–20, 2.7–20, 5.1–8. Cf. BD 986–87, LGW 250; and see Harty, BSUF 19:65–68.

1762–63 January's thoughts and words here and in IV.1855–56 parody traditional formulas in lovers' aubes (Kaske, MLN 75, 1960, 1–4); cf. RvT I.4236–39 and Tr 3.1422–1533n.

1772 **Damyan:** Griffith (Expl 16, 1957, Item 13) argues that St. Damian was a patron saint of physicians and suggests that by naming January's squire Damian, Chaucer may have been underlining the theme of healing in the tale. Against this view, see Eliason, Names 21:140.

1773 Cf. GP I.100, SumT III.2243–44.

1777 Cf. PF 113–14 and note 113.

1783 The Ellesmere, Hengwrt, and several other MSS have the gloss "Auctor" in the margin here and at IV.1869, 2057, 2107, and 2125, indicating scribal awareness of the narrator's intrusions at these places. Cf. MLT II.358n.

1786 Proverbial phrase based on a common fable of a man warming a snake in his bosom, only to have it turn and poison him. Whiting A42; Gesta Romanorum, Ch. 174.

1793–94   **pestilence . . . hoomly foo:** For the sentiment expressed here and in IV.1784 (*famulier foo*), see Bo 3.pr5.68–70.

1795–99   An elaborate "chronographia"; see GP I.7–8n. For **ark diurne** see Astr 2.7; for **latitude** see IntrMLT II.13; and for **hemysperie** see Astr 1.18.8–10.

1807   **ypocras:** Wine mixed with sugar and spices and drained through a strainer, called by apothecaries "Hippocrates' sleeve" (MED s.v. *ipocras* n.); for directions for making the beverage, see The Babees' Book, EETS 32, 125–28, and Curye on Inglysch, EETS s.s.8, 196–97.

clarree: Wine mixed with honey and spices; see I.1471n.

vernage: "Vernaccia," a strong Italian wine; see ShipT VII.70–71 and n.

1808   **t'encreessen his corage:** Delany notes that the spiced wines January drinks were thought to give the body heat and moisture, necessary for lusty, fertile intercourse, and to stimulate the heart, which produced a "windy spirit" responsible for erection (PQ 46, 1967, 561–62; see also Brown, NM 74:100–102). However, spices and wines were ordinarily taken before retiring (the *voide*); cf. Tr 3.671n.

1810–11   **Constantyn:** Constantinus Afer, or Africanus, eleventh-century translator of Arabic medical texts; cf. GP I.433 and I.429–34n. For his life and work, and the possible intent of the epithet **cursed,** see Bassan, MS 24, 1962, 127–40. His treatise *De coitu* (tr. Delany, ChR 4, 1970, 55–65) describes the nature of intercourse and prescribes foods and potions *(letuaries)* for male sexual disorders, especially impotence. On the use of the title **daun,** see KnT I.1379n.

1819   The blessing of the wedding chamber and bed was a common though not essential feature of later medieval English weddings. See Tatlock, MLN 32:374, and the Sarum Missal (tr. in Miller, Ch: Sources and Backgrounds, 383–84).

1825   **houndfyssh:** The skin of the dogfish was used by medieval carpenters as a sort of sandpaper or rough polishing cloth (Burrow, Ricardian Poetry, 137). Older men at this time generally wore beards; younger men were clean-shaven; cf. Thop VII.730–31n. See also Tkacz, ChR 18, 1983, 127–36, for possible sexual connotations of barbering here and elsewhere in the *Tales.*

1832–33   Cf. Whiting W652.

1840   **owene knyf:** Cf. ParsT X.859n. On the sources of the expression, and the canonists' views on sexual sin in marriage, see Field, N&Q 17, 1970, 84–86; Kelly, Love and Marriage, 245–85; Patterson, Traditio 34: 359–60; and Andrew, ELN 16, 1979, 273–77.

1843   **sop in fyn clarree:** Bread soaked in wine; perhaps a morning-after restorative (Birney, N&Q 6, 1959, 347), though a *sop* was the usual light breakfast (cf. GP I.334).

1847–48   Cf. RvPro I.3888; WBPro III.455–56, 602. On **coltissh,** see Whiting, in Med. St. in Hon. of J. D. M. Ford, ed. Urban T. Holmes, Jr. and Alexander J. Denomy, 1948, 321–31.

1862   Cf. SqT V.349, RR 19731–32; Whiting L5.

1893   May's four days in *hire chambre* (IV.1860) have been reckoned from noon of the wedding day (Skeat 5:363) and from noon of the day after (North, RES 20, 1969, 274); such reckonings involve taking *into Cancre* (IV.1887) as 1° of Cancer, which is likely but not certain.

1967   **destynee or aventure:** Cf. GP I.844n.

1969   **constellacion:** See WBPro III.615n.

1972   **alle thyng hath tyme:** Eccles. 3.1; cf. FrT III.1475n.

1986   Cf. KnT I.1761n. On May's *gentilesse* and *pitee,* see Holman, ELH 18:241–52; Levy, ChR 11, 1977, 309–16.

2014   **dogge for the bowe:** Cf. Whiting D303. Cf. FrT III.1369.

2021–22   Cf. GP I.335–38, Bo 3.pr2.77–80.

2029–37   On January's garden, and its well and laurel, see, among others, Burrow, Anglia 75, 1957, 203–5; Donovan, PQ 36, 1957, 55–56; Kellogg, Spec 35, 1960, 276–79; Kee, MS 23, 1961, 154–61; Bleeth, in Learned and Lewed, 45–60; and Heffernan, PLL 15, 1979, 346–50. The enclosed garden itself recalls the "hortus conclusus" of the Song of Songs, commonly taken as a symbol of the Virgin. Cf. PF 122n.

2032   **Romance of the Rose:** The *Roman de la rose* opens with an elaborate description of a walled garden, which contains the fountain of Narcissus; see Rom 475–700, 1349–1468.

2034–35   On **Priapus,** cf. Ovid, Fasti 1.391–440, 6.319–48. The phrase **god of gardyns** may be due to Boccaccio's "(id)dio degli orti," in the "chiose" to the *Teseida* (ed. Limentani, 403, 466); Priapus was also a phallic god, associated with comically frustrated lust. Cf. PF 253–59, and see Hoffman, ELN 3, 1966, 169–72, and Brown, ChR 4, 1970, 31–35.

2038–41   Chaucer's identification of **Pluto** and **Proserpina** with the rulers of Faerie has been explained as an extrapolation from the romance *Sir Orfeo,* which he may have known (Loomis, SP 38, 1941, 27–29); a reflection of a Celtic analogue to the fruit-tree episode involving the fairies (Wentersdorf, SP 63:619–21); and a reminiscence of traditional connections between the triple goddess Luna-Diana-Proserpina and the Queen of Faerie (Donovan, in Ch Probs, 60–62 and nn. 9–10). Cf. KnT I.2313n.

2045–46   **clyket** and **wyket** may be a double entendre for male and female genitalia. See Bugge (AnM 14, 1973, 55–58), citing the OE Riddle 44, "Key" (Exeter Book, ed. Krapp and Dobbie, Anglo-Saxon Poetic Records 3, 1936, 204–5, 346), the obscene sense of *guichet, wyket*'s OF cognate, in the Roman d'Eneas 8575, and other medieval parallels.

2048   1 Cor. 7.3: "Let the husband render the debt *(debitum)* to the wife and likewise the wife to the husband." Cf. WBPro III.198n.

2058–68   The scorpion was a common symbol of treachery. See BD 636–41n.

2106   Cf. Tr 3.125.

2111   **Argus:** The hundred-eyed guardian of Io; cf. WBPro III.357–60 and n., Tr 4.1459n.

2115   Proverbial; cf. Whiting P44.

2126–27   Cf. LGW 742; Ovid, Met. 4.68: "What does love not see?"

2128   **Piramus and Tesbee:** Ovid, Met. 4.55–166; cf. LGW 706–923.

2133   See textual note.

2138–48   An assemblage of phrases from the Song of Songs (cf. 1.14, 2.10–12, 4.1, 7–12), the details of which derive from Jerome, Adv. Jov. 1.30–31. On Chaucer's use of the Song here and elsewhere in the tale, see Wimsatt, in Ch the Love Poet, 84–90; Bleeth, in Learned and

Lewed, 54–59; and Wurtele, ChR 13, 1978, 66–79, and AnM 21, 1981, 91–110.

2176   covenant: An echo of the OT term for the union between the "jealous" Yahweh and Israel (Rosenberg, ChR 5, 1971, 270–71); commonly used in ME Biblical translations (OED, s.v. *covenant* sb. 7a; MED, s.v. *covenaunt* n. 1c).

2217   pyrie: On the phallic symbolism of the pear, see Olson, ELH 28, 1961, 207n.; and MilT I.3248n.

2222   V. A. Kolve, in a paper delivered at the 1980 MLA Meeting in Houston, and in subsequent personal correspondence, notes that depictions of Gemini (the Zodiacal sign for May in medieval calendars) develop from pictures of two wrestling youths (as in Oxford, Bodleian Library, MS Douce 144, fol. 10r) to pictures of an embracing couple, often surrounded by trees and bushes (as in Oxford, Bodleian Library, MS Douce 72, fol. 3r)—a posture and setting not unlike those of May and Damian later in the poem.

2223–24   Cf. Astr 1.17.5–10, FranT V.1246.

2225–2319   Some critics see the Pluto and Proserpina episode as a digression or intrusion (e.g., Kittredge, MP 9:455; Bronson, SP 58:595), while others, usually more recent, argue that it plays an integral part in the whole tale (e.g., Wentersdorf, PMLA 80, 1965, 524–27; Dalbey, NM 75, 1974, 408–15).

The two gods are often interpreted negatively, as counterparts of January and May, or as representing Satan, avarice, lust, idolatry, materialism, or sterility (Sedgewick, UTQ 17:342–43; Donovan, PQ 36:59–60; Wentersdorf, PMLA 80:525–27; Cherniss, ChR 6:251; Dalbey, NM 75:409–12; Gates, NM 77:370–71; Whitlark, AnM 18, 1977, 65–67). A smaller group of critics notes the positive features of the two gods, such as their keeping of promises, judgment of souls, appreciation of beauty, and bringing of fertility back to the earth (Loomis, SP 38:28–29; Donovan, PQ 36:57–58; Bronson, SP 58:594).

The argument between Pluto and Proserpina is sometimes read as the bitter, vindictive result of an unhappy marriage (Brown, Viator 5:401; Dalbey, NM 75:414), but more often as an amusing, relatively good-natured squabble between a couple that has learned to disagree amicably (Tatlock, MP 33:372–73; Jordan, PMLA 78: 298; Schroeder, Criticism 12:177; Otten, ChR 5:283–84; Schleusener, ChR 14:248).

2230   Ethna: Although Proserpina was actually abducted from the fields of Enna, Claudian frequently describes those fields in terms of the relatively nearby Mt. Etna—e.g., as the countryside or valleys of Etna. Most MSS read *Proserpyna* here, which makes no sense; Pratt has suggested that Chaucer may have written *Trynacryna* (i.e., Sicily) and then canceled it, and that *Ethna* is a scribal completion of the line (Spec 22, 1947, 426–28). See textual note.

2232   Claudyan: Claudius Claudianus (d. 408? A.D.), author of the unfinished poem, The Rape of Proserpine. Cf. HF 1507–12. The work was part of the common school anthology known as the *Liber Catonianus.* On Chaucer's use of Claudian, see Pratt, Spec 22:419–29; Donovan, in Ch Probs, 59–69. Chaucer could also have known the story from Ovid, Met. 5.346–571, and Fasti 4.417–620.

stories: The MSS appear to support the plural here, but it is still unclear why Chaucer would choose the

plural; Donovan suggests a "loose usage" in which *stories* refers to the books or even smaller divisions into which The Rape of Proserpine is organized (in Ch Probs, 63).

2242   Solomon was known to the Middle Ages as the author of the Song of Songs and Proverbs and for his wealth, wisdom, idolatry, magical skill (cf. SqT V.250), and lechery (cf. WBPro III.35n.). On the Merchant's references to him, see Rosenberg, ChR 5:270–71; Gates, NM 77:371–75; Wurtele, RUO 47, 1977, 481–87; and Ames, in Acta IV, 94–100.

2247–48   Eccles. 7.29 (A.V. 7.28); cf. Mel VII.1057.

2250–51   Ecclesiasticus, in the Vulgate OT, is ascribed to Jesus son of Sirach; for its misogyny, see 9.1–13, 26.5–15, 42.9–14.

2257   lechour: Main (Expl 14, 1955, Item 13) and Griffith (Expl 16:13) argue for a play on the word *lecher* "healer."

2265   Saturn was the father of Ceres, Proserpina's mother. See Ovid, Fasti 6.285–86.

2277–90   Cf. Mel VII.1075–79. IV.2280–83 may recall Miroir 9064–67, which immediately precedes a list of virgin martyrs, followed by the references to Judith and Esther, which Chaucer may have drawn on for IV.1366–68, 1371–74; IV.2284–85 may stem from Jerome's list of virtuous Roman wives in Adv. Jov. 1.46.

2284   Romayn geestes: Cf. MLT II.1126.

2290   Cf. Mark 10.18.

2298–2302   1 Kings 11.1–13.

2321–22   Cf. RR 10097–98. Cf. ShipT VII.369, Thop VII.767n.

2330–37   May's alleged craving for fruit and the pregnancy implied thereby have been compared to Mary's hunger in the Cherry-Tree Carol (Child, Ballads, no. 54). McGalliard (PQ 25:203) notes that the Miroir has a long passage (3782–843) on the appetites of pregnant women. The Bairds (ChR 8, 1973, 162–67) have suggested further parodic parallels of May and January with Mary and Joseph.

2365   Ovid, Rem. Am. 127–30, referred to in Mel VII.976 (Robinson), though the resemblance is slight.

2367   stronge: Brown (Viator 5:406) sees an allusion here to the "mulier fortis" of Prov. 31.10.

stoore: Kean suggests that *stronge lady stoore* ironically echoes the abusive colloquial epithet *stronge hore*, found in the Paston letters and the Sultan of Babylon (Ch and Poetry 1:19–20); four MSS and some early editions in fact alter *stoore* to *hore* (M-R 6:495; Thynne, Speght, Urry).

2414   wombe: Robbins notes that ME *wombe* can mean pudendum, as well as belly or uterus, and suggests that January's caress is more intimate than a gentle pat on the stomach (LHR 10, 1968, 3–6).

The delicate question of whether May has conceived by Damian or not appears to be irresolvable. For differing views, see Miller, PQ 29, 1950, 437–40; Brown, ChR 4:36–38; and Beidler, ChR 6, 1971, 38–43.

Epilogue to the Merchant's Tale

2422   Proverbial; see SNT VIII.195n.

2426   as trewe as any steel: Proverbial; cf. PF 395, LGW 334, 2582, Tr 5.831, Rom 5146, Whiting S709.

2427–34   Cf. ClT IV.1212b–d, ProMkT VII.1889–923.

2436–38 "The reference to the Wife of Bath is sufficiently clear" (Robinson); for IV.2438, cf. III.521.

FRAGMENT V

In some MSS The Squire's Tale is placed immediately after the Man of Law's Epilogue and before the Wife of Bath's Prologue, with a spurious link (see textual note to SqT V.650). Likewise, in some MSS The Franklin's Tale is preceded by The Clerk's Tale with a spurious link (see textual notes on the Host's Stanza IV.1212a-g), and in Tyrwhitt's edition The Franklin's Tale is linked by a spurious transition to The Physician's Tale (see textual notes following FranT V.1455–56, 1493–98). In the "scribal" orders Fragments IV and V are the most frequently disarranged (see the introduction to the textual notes to The Canterbury Tales). In the MSS with the "Ellesmere" order, however, the integrity of these fragments is maintained, and in the Ellesmere MS the passage from IV.2419 through V.3 is written as one continuous speech by the Host; this and the Squire's reply (V.4–8) are headed The Prologe of the Squieres Tale. Many scholars therefore consider Fragments IV and V a single unit.

LARRY D. BENSON

Introduction to the Squire's Tale

2 On the character of the Squire and the appropriateness of the request here, see GP I.79–100 (Robinson).

The Squire's Tale

Robinson believed that The Squire's Tale was late and that the " 'note of time' in line 73 suggests that Chaucer was writing with the Canterbury scheme in mind." Wager (MLN 50, 1935, 306) considered that "note of time" superfluous and argued for a pre-Canterbury version, as have more recent critics (Moseley, Archiv, 212, 1975, 124–27; Larson, Rev. des langues vivantes 43, 1977, 598–607), but there is no clear evidence on this matter. Older attempts to establish a date by supposed allusions to contemporary events (Brandl, ESt 12, 1889, 161–86; tr. Ch Soc Essays, part 6, 1894, 625–41; refuted by Kittredge, ESt 13, 1890, 1–24; and Tupper, PMLA 36, 1921, 186–222) were unsuccessful.

Though Chaucer implies he is working from a source (V.67–72, 655), none has been discovered nor is likely to be. The tale is a miscellany of various motifs, allusions, story-patterns, pseudo-scientific lore, and reminiscences of travelers and merchants. For the details of Cambyuskan's court Chaucer may have drawn upon accounts of the Mongols by missionaries such as John of Plano Carpini and Simon of St. Quentin (included in Vincent of Beauvais, Speculum historiale, bk. 31). The famous letter of Prester John (see Lowes, Wash. Univ. Sts. 1, no. 2, 1913, 3–18), which mentions a king of Arabia and India who owns a magic mirror and sends another monarch a magic ring, offers closer parallels of setting than the Trav-

The explanatory notes to the Squire's Prologue and Tale were written by Vincent J. DiMarco.

els of Marco Polo, which appears to have been a rare book in fourteenth-century England (Manly, PMLA 11, 1896, 349–62). The Travels of Sir John Mandeville may have supplied some details of the Mongols' eating habits (see 67–71 below). It also provided Chaucer's audience with a convenient account of the Mamluk kingdom of Egypt, in The Squire's Tale apparently identified with that of Arabe and of Inde. Pratt (Tales, 375n.) suggests that the poem may reflect some actual diplomatic relations between the Mamluk court and the Mongols at Sarai, the Golden Horde.

The four magic gifts of the tale are common in medieval literature (see W. A. Clouston, Magical Elements in the SqT, Ch Soc, 2nd ser. 26, 1889), but the closest analogues to the magic horse in Chaucer's tale are in the two late thirteenth-century romances, the Cléomadès of Adenet le Rois (ed. Albert Henry) and the Roman du Cheval de Fust, ou de Méliacin of Girard d'Amiens (selections ed. Paul Aebischer, TLF, 1974). Jones (JEGP 6, 1906, 221–43, and S&A, 364–74) favored Cléomadès as an analogue over the then unedited Méliacin, but in the Asian setting, the sudden arrival of noble visitors bearing gifts, the demonstration of the flying horse, and the absence of lengthy "enfances" of the hero, the Méliacin is closer to Chaucer's tale.

In situation and often phrasing the falcon episode resembles Chaucer's own Anelida and Arcite. Ultimately the story of the falcon may be of oriental origin: Braddy (MLR 31, 1936, 11–19) and Jones (S&A, 372–76) discuss some distant analogues in the Thousand and One Nights, and Friend (M&H n.s. 1, 1970, 57–65) adduces some oriental stories known in England that he believes might explain how the bereaved falcon would come to be reunited with her beloved. Galway's explanation of the episode (MLR 33, 1938, 180–81) as referring to the love affair of Joan of Kent and Thomas Holland does not persuade.

No close analogues have been found for the story of Canacee and her brothers. Braddy (JEGP 41, 1942, 279–90), taking line 664 as an indication that the promised story was to deal with incest, suggests that Chaucer's source was an oriental tale with this motif and that Chaucer abandoned the tale when he came upon the offensive matter. Dorothee Metlitzki (Matter of Araby in Med. Engl., 1977, 144–52) notes some similarities to the eleventh-century Greek poem Digenes Akrites (ed. John Mavrogordato, 1956). Since the tale is unfinished, such analogues are of limited relevance.

In form the poem is a romance, though many critics have found it either satiric (Grace Hadow, Ch and His Times, 1924, 82) or atypical of the genre (Stillwell, RES 24, 1948, 177–88; Jordan in Ch at Albany, 83–86). Recently, however, Goodman (SAC 5, 1983, 127–36) has shown the poem's affinities in structure and matter, including even the possible incest motif, to the late "composite romances," such as Valentine and Orson, and Generides (see Hornstein, Manual ME 1:147–67).

With the exception of the fifteenth-century Jean of Angoulême (Strohm, NM 72, 1971, 69–76) readers of the tale until well into the twentieth century had been warmly admiring. Recent critics regard it as unsatisfying except as a means of satirizing its teller as excessively rhetorical and immature; see Pearsall (UTQ 34, 1964, 82–92; but cf. Pearsall, CT, 1985, 141), Berger (ChR 1, 1966, 88–102), Göller (in Ch und seine Zeit, 189–93) and McCall (ChR 1, 1966, 103–9). Haller (MP 62, 1965, 285–95) reads the tale as designedly superficial, and Kahrl (ChR 7, 1973, 194–209) sees it as a revelation of the decline of late medieval court culture (but on this cf. Bloomfield, Poetica 8, 1981, 28–35, and Goodman, SAC 5:127–36). Most critics today find the satire gentle (e.g., Howard, Idea of CT, 264–68), but almost none unreservedly admires the tale in the manner of a Spenser or Milton (Il Penseroso, 109).

The poem abruptly ends after a promise of a narrative that would have continued for perhaps several thousand lines, even longer than the tale told by the Squire's father. Chaucer may even have intended the tale to remain unfinished, perhaps with the Franklin delicately interrupting a narrative that was certain to continue for too long. There is a spurious brief conclusion in the Lansdowne MS (see textual notes). Continuations were written by Spenser (Faerie Queene, bk. 4) and John Lane, whose work was licensed in 1614–15 but first printed in 1887 (ed. F. J. Furnivall, Ch Soc, 2nd ser. 23).

9   Sarray: The modern Tsarev, near Volgograd in southeastern Russia; see Yule, Cathay and the Way Thither, Hakluyt Soc., 1914, 3:53; and Magoun, Ch Gazetteer. The city was founded by Berke Khan (1257–66) and made the capital of the Golden Horde by Uzbek (Öz-Beg, 1313–41); see Ibn Battuta, Travels, ed. H. A. R. Gibb, Hakluyt Soc., 1959, 2:515–16.

Tartarye: The Mongol or "Tartar" empire, though sometimes used loosely for outer Mongolia (see BD 1025 and n.).

12   Cambyuskan: In form, probably corresponding to Genghis (Chingiz) Khan, Latinized Camius Khan, as first suggested by Francis Thynne, Animadversions [1599], ed. G. H. Kingsley, rev. F. J. Furnivall, EETS 9, 1875, 54. Skeat (5:33) felt the description better suited Genghis's grandson Kublai, whose court at Cambaluc (Beijing) Marco Polo visited; and Robinson notes that it was Batu, another grandson of Genghis, who *werreyed Russye* (see John of Plano Carpini, Hist. of the Mongols, tr. Dawson, 29–30). The Russians never peacefully accepted Mongol suzerainty, and in the 1330s the city of Smolensk rose in revolt against Uzbek, knowledge of whom Chaucer might well have possessed. In an astrological explanation, more ingenious than convincing, North (RES, n.s. 20, 1969, 257–62) identifies Cambyuskan with the planet Mars; but cf. Manzalaoui, in Ch: Writers and Background, 242–43.

16–27 On Cambyuskan as an example of a pagan who displays the noble virtues of natural (non-Christian) man, see Bloomfield, Poetica 8:29–30.

17–18   his lay: Uzbek's conversion to Islam, it should be noted, made it the official religion of the Golden Horde. He was, moreover, renowned for his religious piety.

22   centre: For the center (of a circle) linked to the idea of stability, see Bo 4.pr6.116–29.

29–33 The names of **Elpheta, Algarsyf, Cambalo,** and **Canacee** offer intriguing possibilities. Manly's suggestion that the name *Elpheta* corresponds in medieval starlists to alpha Coronae Borealis ("Alphecca" in Richard Hinckley Allen, Star Names, 1899 [1963], 178–79) has been endorsed by North (RES 20:259–62) and Metlitzki (Matter of Araby, 78) who notes the "familial" aspects of the constellation. *Algarsyf* may derive from *saif al-jabbar* (Metlitzki, 79–80), "the sword of the giant," cor-

responding to eta of Orion (Allen, Star Names, 316); and, less probable, *Cambalo* may correspond (North, RES 20:257–62) to *cabalcet,* or alpha Leonis (Allen, Star Names, 256). Hinckley (Notes on Ch, 215) noted the similarity in form of *Algarsyf* to the Russian noble family Iaroslav; perhaps Chaucer knew of Iaroslav I, father of Alexander Nevsky, who enjoyed special favors from Batu (see John of Plano Carpini, tr. Dawson, 15, 62, 65; and George Vernadsky, Mongols and Russia, 1953, 61, 142–43, 381). Skeat thought Cambalo derived from Cambaluc, Kublai's capital; Robinson preferred as a source Kambala (properly, Kammala), the grandson of Kublai. But closer to Chaucer's concern in the tale is Cembalo, modern Balaclava on the Crimean peninsula, an important trading center ceded by Uzbek to the Genoese (Michel Balard, La Romanie Génoise, 1978, 1:157). Chaucer's use of the name *Canacee* (Gr. Κανάκη) may be explained by the incest-motif possibly suggested in SqT V.667 (cf. IntrMLT II.77 and note 77–89); but Bushnell (Blackwood's 187, 1910, 655) notes the Mongol word for *princess* can be transliterated *kanaki;* while North (RES 20:259–61) suggests an astrological identification with the star Cauda Ceti, in Chaucer's time found in the zodiacal sign Pisces.

The Tale of the Enchanted Horse in the *Thousand and One Nights,* the *Cléomadès,* and the *Méliacin* all describe a royal family in which there are three daughters and one son. Ibn Battuta, however (Travels, tr. Gibb, 1959, 2:486), notes that Uzbek and his principal wife Taitughli had two sons, Jani Bak and Tina Bak, and one daughter, It Kujujuk.

31   Cambalo: Cf. Cambalus (V.656), apparently referring to the same person. For the "Italian" form in -*o,* see MkT VII.2345n.

35–41 An elaborate example of the "inexpressibility" topos. See KnT I.1459–60n. and cf. V.105–6 and n. below.

39   colours: James J. Murphy (Rhet. in the MA, 1974, 189–90) notes the use of the word *color* as a medieval innovation, superseding *exornation* and *figura.* He suggests that to Chaucer it meant any kind of decorated language. Cf. ClT IV.16n. and FranPro V.723–26n.

45–46   leet. . . Doon cryen: The double causative is rare in Chaucer; see Mustanoja, ME Syntax, 605.

48–51 Since it is exactly 15 March (line 47), three days after the vernal equinox (see Astr 2.1.6–14), the sun is about three degrees into Aries. This is an especially elaborate "chronographia" (see GP I.7–8n.), so elaborate that Wood (Ch and the Stars, 98–99) holds it is a parody. Since it is Cambyuskan's birthday, it is also a horoscope, as the use of face makes clear (see Astr 2.4.60–69). Marco Polo (ed. Yule, 1903, 1:386–88) says the Great Khan's birthday is in September. Skeat (5:372) suggests that Chaucer noted that the "White Feast was on New Year's day, which he took to mean the vernal equinox, or some day near it," and thus conflated the two celebrations.

50   Martes: Possibly a Latin genitive; Chaucer frequently employs the Latin oblique forms when translating (see Bo 2.pr3.59n.) and perhaps here as elsewhere (KnT I.2024; WBPro III.619; HF 1844; Tr 3.437) was also influenced by Latin usage. He also uses the Italian form *Marte* (KnT I.2021, 2581; Tr 2.435, 988; LGW 2244), and *Martes* may represent an anglicization. *Mars* is Chaucer's usual form, but it never appears as a genitive save in analytical constructions (with *of*).

52–57   Cf. Rom 71–77 and, for the **swerd of wynter,** LGW 127 and n.

67–71   European reports often mentioned the strange foods of the Mongols; see Bertold Spuler, Hist. of the Mongols, tr. Drummond and Drummond, 1972, 92–93, 176–77. On the basis of **knyghtes olde** Bennett suggests (MLN 68, 1953, 531–34) that Chaucer's source may be Mandeville's *Travels* (ed. Seymour, 1967, 180–81).

73   **pryme:** In ecclesiastical usage, corresponding to the first hour of the day, or sunrise (cf. PardT VI.662), but here used for the period between the first hour and tierce, which began after "full prime" or "prime large" (see V.360), or about 9:00 A.M.

75–294   Chapman (MLN 68, 1953, 521–24) notes parallels with *Sir Gawain and the Green Knight* in the interruption of a royal meal at a specified moment (here the third course, the first in *Sir Gawain*) by a strange visitor on horseback, the suggestion that the horse is of **Fairye,** and the subsequent resumption of the feast. But there is no clear indication that Chaucer knew this romance (cf. Moseley, Archiv 212:124–27).

80   For numerous instances of the riding of a horse into hall in romances, see Whiting, MS 9, 1947, 232.

90–97   The passage may be modeled on RR 2087–114 (cf. Rom 2209–22); those lines praise Gawain for his courtesy (V.95) and emphasize the duty to salute nobles in a polite and courtly fashion (V.91–93).

95–96   For Gawain's reputation for courtesy, see Whiting, MS 9:189–234; for his association with Arthur in the faerie-land Avalon, see Loomis, MLN 52, 1937, 413–16. WBT III.857 similarly associates the Arthurian court with **Fairye,** there used in the general sense of magic and enchantment; Chaucer's reference here may be no more pointed.

99–104   Classical and medieval rhetorical theory described the appropriate delivery *(pronuntiatio)* of speeches with respect to voice, countenance, and gesture; see the *Rhetorica ad Herennium* 3.11; Geoffrey of Vinsauf, *Poetria nova,* 2031–66, and *Documentum de modo et arte dictandi et versificandi,* 94–95; and see also Ernest Gallo, Poetria Nova and Its Sources in Early Rhet. Doctrine, 1971, 221–23. Cf. Tr 1.12–14, and, for *pronuntiatio* in Chaucer, see Rowland, SAC 4, 1982, 33–52.

105–6   The rime riche (see GP I.17–18n.) is clearly intended as a pun; cf. the Franklin's pun on *colours* (FranPro V.723–26). For the "affected modesty" topos employed here see GP I.746n.

110   The kingdom **of Arabe and of Inde** refers (Pratt, Tales, 375n.) to what was variously called India Minor or Middle India, now southern Arabia. Benjamin of Tudela (Travels, tr. Manuel Komroff, in Contemp. of Marco Polo, 1928, 312) identifies Middle India with Aden, which both he and Marco Polo (ed. Yule, 1903, 2:425–33) seem to place on the western side of the Red Sea. During most of the fourteenth century, Arabia was under the control of the Bahri Mamluks at Cairo, who were engaged in active diplomacies with the Golden Horde at Sarai (see Henry H. Howorth, Hist. of the Mongols from the 9th to the 19th Century, 1880, 2:-149–51).

115–342   The magic **steede of bras** is described primarily as a mechanical aeronautical contrivance, controlled by the manipulation of various pegs (V.127, 314–30) and perhaps by the action of the rein (312–13) and bridle (340–42); it is no mere appearance or delusion (201,

218). There is a wide range of classical, medieval, and Renaissance speculation on flying contrivances; see Berthold Laufer, Prehist. of Aviation, 1928, 19–22. For literary parallels see W. A. Clouston, Magical Elements, and Lowes, Univ. of Washington Sts. 1, 1913, 3–18.

129–31   **constellacion:** Cf. KnT I.1088, WBPro III.616. One would make a **seel** (cf. GP I.417n.) when the stars were in the right position. **Bond** refers to the controlling force of the practitioner's knowledge (MED, s.v. *Bond* 5[a]), unless used in a more technical sense (elsewhere unattested) related to this natural magic. Lynn Thorndike (Hist. of Magic and Exper. Science, 1923, 2:164–65) notes that in denying the efficacy of such seals, John of Salisbury may be alluding to allegedly magic automata. For a list of treatises on seals and images, see Joan Evans, Magical Jewels of the MA and the Ren., 1922, 95–120.

132–36   For the magic mirror, see 228–35, below.

146–55   Canacee's ring gives her the power to understand and speak the language of birds. Such a ring is cited by W. A. Clouston, On the Mag. Elements in the SqT, 188, 348. It also gives her an expert knowledge of medicinal herbs. For the (extremely common) use in medieval England of medicinal herbs and flowers, see Teresa McLean, Med. Eng. Gardens, 1980, 140–47, 172–82. The magic ring is later associated with Moses and Solomon (see 250–51 below).

156   For the magic sword, see 236–40 below.

166   **glose:** Cf. SumT III.1792n.

171   Proverbial; Whiting S772.

184   "By no device of windlass or pulley." Just so in the Méliacin, lines 541–52, the horse cannot be moved except through the manipulation of the pins.

193–95   **Poilleys:** For accounts of the high esteem in which the Lombardian and Apulian (later known as the Neapolitan) horses were held, see Rowland (Blind Beasts, 123), who suggests that the Ellesmere illustration of the Squire may picture him on a Lombardy steed.

203   See RvPro I.3857 and n. Chaucer elsewhere (Tr 4.183–89, ClT IV.995–1001) shows no great faith in the common opinion of the crowd; Burrow (Ricardian Poetry, 122–25) sees an interest in crowd reactions as typical of the literature of the period.

207   **the Pegasee:** Glossed in Ellesmere and several other MSS as "equ[u]s Pegaseus," from which adjectival form derives Chaucer's form in *-ee.* The Pegasus was the fabulous winged horse of Bellerophon, the Muses, and Zeus.

209   Dictys agrees with Virgil's account in describing a wooden horse; but Guido delle Colonne (Historia, 30, 81) describes it as brass—perhaps, as Mary Elizabeth Meeks speculates (Historia Destructionis Troiae, 1974, 305n.), the result of a confusion of planks of fir *(abiete)* with *aerum,* bronze. But Hinckley (MLN 23, 1908, 157–58) notes that Pausanias twice refers to brazen images of the horse in Greece. Gower, in *Confessio amantis* 1.1131, following Guido delle Colonne, describes a horse of brass, as does Caxton, *Recuyell of the historyes of Troye* [1474?], 3.28.

219   For illusionists in Chaucer's time, see HF 1277n. and FranT V.1141n.

220–24   Cf. Tr 2.271n. and Ovid, Tristia, 4.2.25–26.

224   **gladly:** Habitually; cf. NPT VII.3224n.

226   **maister-tour:** Cf. *maister strete,* KnT I.2902, and *mayster-toun,* LGW 1591.

228–35 The discussion of optics is based on RR 17993–18298, where a magic mirror such as described in V.132–36 and alluded to here is mentioned and where both **Alocen** (Lat. Alhazen, Ibn al-Haitham, c. 965–1039, author of an influential treatise on optics) and **Aristotle** are mentioned (the latter perhaps because of his *Meteorologia* 3.2–4, where rainbows are explained as reflections). Chaucer adds **Vitulon** (Lat. Vitello), the Polish Witelo, author of a treatise on perspective (ante 1278) that drew on Alhazen's work. See Thorndike, Hist. of Magic 3:602–5, 707, and Lindberg, Spec 46, 1971, 66–83.

231 **in Rome was swich oon:** Virgil was believed to have built and placed on a tower or pillar a magic mirror that showed the image, whether by day or night, of approaching enemies, even if many miles distant. The story was widespread and Chaucer could have known versions in Gower's *Confessio amantis* (5.2031–2224), in some version of the *Seven Sages of Rome,* in *Renart le contrefait* (ed. Raynaud and Lemaitre, 1914, 1.29391–400), a poem which Chaucer perhaps used (Pratt, Spec 47, 1972, 422–44, 646–69), in Cléomadès (lines 1691–96), and elsewhere, though it seems likely that the discussion of such a mirror in RR (see preceding note) accounts for this allusion. On Virgil's medieval reputation as a magician, see John Webster Spargo, Virgil the Necromancer, 1934, esp. 1–68.

235 **herd:** The practice of reading a book aloud to a group remained popular (see Tr 2.82–84, 80–109n.), though private reading was increasing (Parkes, in Med. World, ed. David Daiches and Anthony Thorlby, 1973, 555–77). Perhaps here there is a slight condescension to those who have heard but not studied these technical treatises.

236–40 The sword (here **spere**) with which **Achilles** wounded **Thelophus** (Telephus) and which had the power to heal the wound it inflicted is alluded to in Ovid, Met. 12.112, 13.171–72; Tristia 5.2, 15; Rem. Am. 44–48; and Dante, Inf. 31.4–6. See also Tr 4.927.

243–46 On the medicinal properties of certain prepared metals, see Pliny, Hist. Nat. 34.43–45 (DiMarco, ChR 16, 1981, 178).

250 **he Moyses:** That Moses. For the use of the personal pronoun as a demonstrative, see Mustanoja, ME Syntax, 135–36. Perhaps here *he* has the sense of Lat. *ille:* that well-known Moses.

250–51 Moses was said to have made a Ring of Memory and, for his Egyptian wife Tharbis, a Ring of Oblivion when he wished to return to Zipporah (see Gower, Conf. Aman. 4.647; Peter Comestor, Historia scolastica, Exodi 6, in PL 198:1144). The legend was based on Numbers 12.1; Moses's knowledge of Egyptian magic is mentioned in Exodus 7.11 and Acts 7.22. The *Chronicon Angliae* (ed. E. M. Thompson, Rolls, 1874, 98) accuses Alice Perrers of maintaining her influence over Edward III with such Mosaic rings.

Solomon was also thought to be adept in the magical sciences (cf. 1 Kings 4.33) and to have made a magical ring (see Clouston, Magical Elements, 334–40).

Moses and Solomon are mentioned together in a discussion of magic in Roger Bacon's *Opus Maius* (ed. J. H. Bridges, 1897, 1:392) and possibly this is Chaucer's immediate source (DiMarco, Anglia 99, 1981, 399–405).

253–61 For the idea that phenomena whose causes are

known to the expert seem a wonder to others, see Bo 4.m.5, and pr6.199–210.

254–58 Glass was made from the ashes of ferns; see Tollenaere, ES 31, 1950, 97–99, and, for detailed instructions, the medieval additions to Eraclius, *De coloribus et artibus romanorum* (ed. and tr. M. P. Merrifield, Original Treatises, 1849, 1:212–13 [3.7]). Chaucer's source may be RR 16096–105, which presents the making of glass as a wonder (in a defense of alchemy) and also mentions thunder; see Magoun, RomR 17, 1926, 69–70.

258–59 The phenomena listed have no obvious causes. Isidore of Seville (Etymologiae, 13.9) held that **thonder** was caused by colliding clouds, Aristotle that the noise was produced by the impact of forcibly ejected vapor from cooling clouds striking other clouds (see Bartholomaeus Anglicus 11.13, tr. Trevisa 1:591–92). The **ebbe and flood** were explained by Macrobius (Comm. on the Dream of Scipio, tr. Stahl, 214) as the product of the collision of ocean currents, by Aristotle (as quoted in Barth. Ang. 13.21, tr. Trevisa 1:666) as resulting from the influence of the moon (see Astr 2.46). Of **gossomer,** spider web, Bartholomaeus Anglicus (18.10, tr. Trevisa 2:1139) writes "It is wonder how the matiere of the thredes that cometh of the wombe of the spithere may suffice to so gret a werk and to the weuynge of so gret a webbe." **Myst** was thought to be caused by disintegrating clouds (Barth. Ang. 11.12, tr. Trevisa 1:590).

263–65 **angle meridional:** The celestial sphere was divided into twelve astrological "domiciles" (see Astr 2.4.46n.), of which the four principals were called *angles* (see Astr 2.4.36n.). The *angle meridional* is the tenth, through which the sun would pass on 15 March between 10 A.M. and noon. The constellation Leo, the **beest roial,** would also have begun its two-hour ascent above the horizon at about noon on that day. Allen (Star Names, 1899, 234) notes Al Dhira'an (Chaucer's **Aldiran**) as the name of Castor and Pollux, in Gemini; Skeat takes it to be the relatively minor star Hydra, in Leo's forepaws, which was perhaps confused with alpha Leonis, a star of the first magnitude.

272 **Venus children:** Those born under the influence of the planet Venus are, of course, lovers. See Seznec, Survival of the Pagan Gods, 70–76.

273–74 **Fyssh:** Pisces is the "exaltation" of Venus, the sign in which she is most powerful. See WBPro III.702n.

287 **Launcelot:** Lancelot was famous as the lover of Guinevere in Arthurian romance, but there is no apparent basis (other than the idea that a perfect knight is also a perfect courtier) for the narrative skill the Squire here attributes to him.

291–94 **spices . . . wyn:** Spices were taken with wine (see Joseph of Arimathea, ed. Skeat, EETS 44, 1871, n. to line 698), but *spice* could also mean spiced cakes (Skeat 2:506), and the mention of eating in 294 implies that is the case here. Cf. LGW 1110.

300 **Hath plentee:** Some MSS (including the Ellesmere) omit *at* in the previous line, thus making *kynges feeste* the subject of *Hath.* Robinson follows Skeat (5: 381) in taking *Hath* as parallel to Fr. *il y a,* often written as simply *a* in Old French.

302 **At after-soper:** The construction may be construed with *at-after* as a compound preposition ("after supper") or with *after-soper* as a compound noun ("at, during the time after supper"), though the difference in meaning is slight. See Mustanoja, ME Syntax, 366–67, and cf. FranT V.918, 1219; ShipT VII.255.

347 Possibly proverbial (though not recorded before Chaucer); Whiting S377. The Ashmole version of the Secretum Secretorum, EETS 276, 54, explains that sleep after a meal provides the stomach with the greatest amount of bodily heat and thus aids digestion.

349 Proverbial; see MerT IV.1862n.

351–52 Skeat (5:382) notes that the Shepherdes Kalender (ed. 1656, ch. 29) describes the six hours after midnight as under the influence of the sanguine humor (cf. V.347).

353 Healthy blood was regarded as the source of bodily well-being; cf. Batholomaeus Anglicus 4.7, tr. Trevisa 1:153.

358–59 **fumositee:** Fumes that derive from wine drinking (cf. PardT VI.567); for the worthlessness of dreams thus produced see NPT VII.2923–39 and cf. Macrobius, Commentary on the Dream of Scipio, 1.3.4. John of Plano Carpini, History (tr. Dawson, 15–16) remarks upon the fondness of Mongol men for the cup and notes that Mongol women were renowned for temperance and chastity.

371 **impressioun:** Cf. HF 39, Tr 5.372–74.

376 The sentence is poorly constructed; for **This** designating a class, see Language and Versification, p. xxxviii, for this use of **gladly** see NPT VII.3224.

386 Nicholas of Lynn's *Kalendarium,* 77, shows that on 16 March (see 48–51 above) the sun at noon was at 4 degrees 35 minutes in Aries (the **Ram**); since the sun is also only four degrees above the horizon, it is about 6:15 A.M. North (RES 20:261) identifies Canacee with the star Cauda Ceti, which on 16 March 1390, would have been rising when the sun was at four degrees.

399–400 Cf. Rom 714–16.

401 **knotte:** Used in the same sense in V.407 and ParsT X.494. Cf. ParsPro X.28n. and Göller, in Ch and seine Zeit, 168–69.

404–5 Cf. Tr 2.1564n.

409 The significance of the dry tree is not clear. Skeat suggested a reference to the *Arbre Sec* that was said to have withered at Christ's crucifixion and would bloom again only when a Christian prince conquered the Holy Land (Mandeville's Travels, EETS 253, 50–51; Yule's Marco Polo, 1871, 1:119–31).

419 For the tiger as an image of cruelty, see KnT I.1657, 2626–28.

428 The **faucon peregryn,** according to Brunetto Latini (Livres dou Tresor, 1.148, ed. Francis Carmody, U. Cal. Publ. in Mod. Philol. 22, 1948), is so named because the young of this species were taken while on their flight, or "pilgrimage" from their breeding place, rather than from the nest. The ME form is an anglicization of Med. Lat. *falco peregrinus.*

448 **furial:** Related to the Furies; cf. Tr 1.1–14n.

479 Cf. KnT I.1761.

491 For the proverb in Latin, French, German, and English, see Holthausen, Archiv 14, 1892, 320; Tatlock, MLN 38, 1923, 506–7; Frank, MLN 55, 1940, 481; Whiting W211; and cf. *Othello* II.iii.262. The actual medieval practice of teaching the lion by beating the dog is illustrated by Brown and West, MLN 55, 1940, 209–10.

496 Proverbial; cf. Tr 3.115n. For the omission of finite verbs of motion, see Mustanoja, ME Syntax, 510.

504 **tercelet:** The male hawk, especially the peregrine falcon or the goshawk. So named (Cotgrave's French and English Dictionary, 1611, s.v. *tiercelet*) because it is one-third smaller than the female, or (OED, s.v. *tercellene* [1682]) because the third egg in the nest was believed to be smaller and to produce a male bird.

511 To dye **in greyn** is to dye in a fast color; see NPT VII.3459n. *Coloures* is a pun, for the tercelet deceives through the use of his rhetorical devices ("colors").

512 Cf. SumT III.1994–95n.

514–19 Cf. Christ's denunciation of the hypocritical Pharisees, Matt. 23.27.

535 Cf. Criseyde's dream of an exchange of hearts, Tr 2.925–31.

537 Proverbial; Whiting W259. Cf. LGW 464–65 and Anel 105n., where other parallels with SqT are noted.

543 For the association of tigers with deceit, see Rowland, Blind Beasts, 14–15, and Storm, ELN 14, 1977, 172–74.

550 **Lameth:** Cf. WBPro III.54 and n., Anel 150–54.

555 An echo of Mark 1.7; see also Luke 3.16 and John 1.27. Cf. LGW 1039–43n.

558 Cf. Tr 2.637.

593 See KnT I.3041–42 and n.

596 **Seint John to borwe:** Bethurum (ed.) notes that lovers' rites were associated with St. John the Baptist's Day, 21 June, and Skeat (5:385) notes that he was the apostle of truth; however, the reference may conceivably be to one of the other St. Johns. Cf. Mars 9.

602–3 Proverbial after Chaucer (Whiting S639).

607–20 **thilke text:** Cf. 608–9 with Bo 3.m2.39–42, and 610–17 with Bo 3.m2.21–31 (see also RR 13941–66). Chaucer uses the image of the caged bird again in MancT IX.163–74 (cf. MilT I.3224). Economou notes the humor of the Squire's comparison of a bird to a bird (PQ 54, 1975, 679–84). Göller, in Ch und seine Zeit, 184–86, finds irony in the use of Boethius here, as does Haller, MP 62:285–95; but cf. Greene, N&Q 12, 1965, 446–48.

618–20 Cf. WBT III.1109 and n. Osgerby (Use of Eng. 11, 1959, 102–7) takes **gentillesse** as the main theme of the story.

624 For the **kyte,** considered a cowardly type of hawk, see PF 349; for its predatory habits, see Rowland, Blind Beasts, 51, and cf. KnT I.1177–80.

644 **blewe:** The color symbolizing constancy; see Tr 3.885n.

648 **tidyves:** Small birds, apparently, of contested identification. Skinner (Entymolog. Voc. Antiq., 1671) suggests a *tidyf* is the titmouse; Holmes (PQ 16, 1937, 65–67) thinks it is the small owl, Athene noctua; but cf. Wilson, PQ 17, 1938, 216–18. Chaucer again refers to the *tidyf* as inconstant in LGW F 154.

650 **Pyes:** Cf. HF 703n.

664 **Theodora:** Metlitzki, Matter of Araby, 156–59, speculates this character may recall the wise maiden Tawaddud (known in the West variously as Teodor, Teodora, Theodora), who, like Canacee, knows the language of birds and the secrets of medicine. But with this Greek name, Chaucer might be announcing his attention to portray a marriage between a prince of the Golden Horde and the royal house of Byzantium, such as occurred in the 1260s between Nogay and Euphrosyne, the illegitimate daughter of Michael VIII. Vernadsky (Mongols and Russia, 168–70) relates another political marriage, between Prince Gleb of the Russian house of Rostov and a princess of the Great Khan Mongka in Mongolia; the bride was baptized Theodora, and the couple were received in (Old) Sarai in 1257–68 and 1271.

667 The plot here sketched, as Robinson noted, is obscure. It is sometimes assumed that this **Cambalo** is a different character from Canacee's brother (V.31, 656), but this seems unlikely. "Chaucer may have intended that Canacee should be abducted and then won back by Cambalo. . . . Spenser (Faerie Queene IV.5) represents three brothers as suitors for Canacee, fighting against Cambello her brother."

671–72 These lines, apparently genuine, set the time in May, when (on 12 May) the sun enters Gemini, a mansion of Mercury (though Virgo, which the sun enters in August, is the other mansion of Mercury).

The Introduction to the Franklin's Tale

675–76 For the rhyme yowthe:allow the, see GP I.523n.

The Franklin's Prologue and Tale

The concern with mastery and marriage, the use of Jerome's *Adversus Jovinianum,* and some echoes of The Merchant's Tale all suggest that The Franklin's Prologue and Tale were composed about the same time as the other tales in the "Marriage Group." Lowes (MP 15, 1918, 689–728) argued for an earlier date on the basis of parallels to the *Teseida* and The Knight's Tale, and North (RES n.s. 20, 1969, 262–67) argued for 1389 or 1392 on the basis of the astrological allusions. Neither is completely convincing in his argument and, though the precise date remains uncertain, most scholars continue to assign the work to the middle 1390s.

The basic story in The Franklin's Tale is the folklore motif of the "rash promise" (Aarne-Thompson M223), which is widespread not only in Europe but also in the Orient (see 989–98 below). The oldest versions survive in the Sanskrit Vetāla stories, though the magician appears only in the European versions. Thus, the similar stories in Chaucer, Boccaccio, Boiardo's *Orlando innamorato,* Juan Manuel's *Conde Lucanor,* and Jean de Condé's *Chevalier à la manche* all include the rash promise, the magician, and the *demande* ending. (For a review of the analogues see A. Aman, Die Filiation der FranT, Munich Diss., 1912, and J. Schick in Studia Indo-Iranica, Ehrengabe für Wilhelm Geiger, 1931, 89–107.) Schofield (PMLA 16, 1901, 405–49) noted the frequent use of the "rash promise" in Celtic literature and Arthurian romance (*Sir Orfeo,* the Welsh *Mabinogi of Pwyll,* the Irish *Tochmare Etaine,* and some versions of the *Tristan* romance), but none of these resembles The Franklin's Tale in any other significant way.

No single literary source completely accounts for the plot, characters, scene, and form of the tale. Boccaccio's *Filocolo* is usually regarded as Chaucer's primary source (Rajna, Romania 32, 1903, 204–67; N. R. Havely, Ch's

The explanatory notes to the Franklin's Prologue and Tale were written by Joanne Rice.

Boccaccio, 1980). However, the Franklin's claim that a Breton lay is his source complicates the problem. The Breton setting and names do distinguish Chaucer's version from those in the *Filocolo,* the *Decameron* 10.5, and other possible Latin sources, though Schofield's claim (PMLA 16:405–49) that Chaucer drew solely on Geoffrey of Monmouth, Celtic tradition, and Breton lays can be dismissed (see Tatlock, Scene of the FranT, Ch Soc, 2nd ser. 51, 1914, 55–77). In its brevity, apparent simplicity, idealism, and concern with love and the supernatural, Chaucer's tale does resemble the "Breton lays" written by Marie de France in the twelfth century, though Chaucer probably knew only English examples of this genre. The relevant analogues are printed by Dempster and Tatlock in S&A, 377–97.

The Franklin's Tale contains many narrative and thematic elements that are not found in any of the analogues. The removal of the rocks, for instance, is Chaucer's own invention, possibly suggested by Geoffrey of Monmouth's account of Merlin's magical transportation of rocks from Ireland to Stonehenge (Schofield, PMLA 16:417); by the well-known legend of St. Balred, who lived on Bass Rock performing miracles, the best known of which was the removal of dangerous rocks at sea (T. A. Reisner and M. E. Reisner, SP 76, 1979, 1–12); by Medea's recounting her feats of magic in Ovid, Met. 7.202–5 (Bleeth, AmN&Q 20, 1982, 130–1); or by the actual rocks off the coast of Brittany (Tatlock, Scene of the FranT, 5–9, 44–54, and Frank Cowper's Sailing Tours: Yachtman's Guide to the Cruising Waters of the Eng. Coast, 3: Coasts of Brittany, 1894, 156–58).

The most striking differences between The Franklin's Tale and any possible antecedents center on Chaucer's preoccupation with marriage, *gentillesse,* and troth. Traditionally, the tale has been seen as Chaucer's resolution of the "Marriage Debate" (Kittredge, MP 9, 1912, 435–67; Lyons, ELH 2, 1935, 252–62; Dempster, PMLA 68, 1953, 1142–59; Olson, in Ch and ME Sts., 164–72; and, with some reservations, Ruggiers, Art of the CT, 226–37). But this view has been questioned by critics who see the Franklin as a self-important man whose "middle-class" values clash with Christian ones or as a storyteller who does not fully understand the implications of his own tale (e.g., Lumiansky, UTQ 20, 1951, 344–56; Howard, MP 57, 1960, 223–32; Robertson, Pref to Ch, 470–72; Burlin, Ch Fiction, 197–207; Miller, Mediaevalia 6, 1980, 151–86; Allen and Moritz, Distinction of Stories, 148–50; and Mathewson, MAE 52, 1983, 27–37). Blenner-Hassett, however, notes similarities between Chaucer and the Franklin (Spec 28, 1953, 791–800), and Henrik Specht clears the Franklin of many unjust criticisms (Ch's Franklin in the CT, 1981), including the idea that he is a socially ambitious member of the "middle class."

The themes of *gentillesse* and troth have also proved controversial. Some critics claim that no character is gentle or honorable and that the tale ultimately focuses on delusion, illusion, or appearance versus reality (Gaylord, ELH 31, 1964, 331–65; Wood, PQ 45, 1966, 688–711; Bachman, ChR 12, 1977, 55–67; and Luengo, JEGP 77, 1978, 1–16). But others argue that the tale in fact reflects the values of truth and gentility as well as the Franklin's idealism (Holman, ELH 18, 1951, 241–52; Corsa, Ch, Poet of Mirth, 168–81; White, PMLA 89, 1974, 454–62; Frazier, South Atlantic Bulletin 43, 1978, 75–85;

Carruthers, Criticism 23, 1981, 283–300; and Mann, New Pelican Guide to Eng. Lit., Vol. I, Part 1, ed. Ford, 1982, 133–53).

Recently, a number of critics have offered a different perspective by taking into account the apparent contradictions and arguing that the multiplicities in the tale are a deliberate function of its meaning (Hatton, PLL 3, 1967, 179–81; Milosh, Wis. Sts. in Lit. 5, 1970, 1–11; Kaske, in Ch the Love Poet, 62–65; F. N. M. Diekstra, Ch's Quizzical Mode of Exemplification, 1974; Bloomfield, 189–98, in Acts of Interpretation; and Traversi, Literary Imagination, 87–119). They especially focus on the significance of the *demande* ending as an invitation to debate rather than a means of resolving all the problems raised by the text.

Other approaches broaden the context of the tale by focusing on its various connections with other tales, especially The Wife of Bath's Prologue, and the Squire's, Merchant's, and Nun's Priest's tales (Holman, ELH 18: 241–52; Neville, JEGP 50, 1951, 167–79; Pratt, Criticism 5, 1963, 316–22; Hodge, ES 46, 1965, 289–300; Hoffman, ChR 2, 1967, 20–31; Beidler, ChR 3, 1969, 275–79; and Murtaugh, ELH 38, 1971, 473–92). A slightly different view (Cooper, in Med. Sts. for J. A. W. Bennett, 65–80) connects this tale with the Knight's, Miller's, and Merchant's tales through the motif of the girl with two lovers.

The MSS contain many Latin glosses, most of them quotations from Chaucer's source for Dorigen's complaint (M-R 3:512–15); these are quoted, usually in translation, in the following notes.

The Franklin's Prologue

709   Britouns: Bretons, inhabitants of Brittany, although the word is also used for the Celtic inhabitants of Great Britain (cf. MLT II.545). The collocation of *olde, gentil,* and *firste Briton tonge* may suggest the golden age and the Franklin's image of an "ideal, or rather idyllic, life" (Berger, ChR 1, 1966, 98–99).

710   layes: OF *lai,* originally a short lyric or song, but here as "Breton lay," a brief narrative poem with an idealized, romantic content (see Foulet, ZRP 30, 1906, 698–711 and MLN 21, 1906, 48–49; and Mortimer J. Donovan, The Breton Lay, 1969, 44–64). Although Marie de France's twelve lays, written before 1189, are the earliest extant examples of this genre, they claim unknown and unverified Breton sources. Most likely Marie originated the literary type whose popularity continued into or was resurrected in fourteenth-century England. Loomis (SP 38, 1941, 15–18) and Burlin (Neophil 51, 1967, 59–60) claim the genre's popularity had waned, so that the Franklin tells an old-fashioned tale. For opposing views, see Donovan, Breton Lay, 173–75; and Hume, PQ 51, 1972, 373–79. Like Marie, Chaucer claims to follow an unknown Breton source, but this may be nothing more than a literary artifice since the tale has affinities to Boccaccio's *Filocolo* and *Teseida.* Some scholars see a connection to the lay tradition in general and to Marie's *Equitan* in particular, especially in terms of courtly love, magic, and idealized characters (Schofield, PMLA 16:426–32; Claes Schaar, Golden Mirror, 1955, 82, 231, 347; and Michael Stevens, Ch's Major Tales, 1969, 84). Since it is doubtful that Chaucer knew Marie's

work, he probably relied on the English tradition, especially *Sir Orfeo, Lay le Freine,* and *Sir Degare,* all represented in the Auchinleck MS (Loomis, SP 38:14–33; Heydon, PMASAL 51, 1965, 529–45; and Beston, in Learned and Lewed, 319–36). Carl Lindahl, in an unpublished paper, argues that Chaucer deliberately molded the tale to conform to the structural patterns and basic plot elements shared by all the known ME lays.

716   burel man: Unlearned man or layman (see MED, s.v. *burel,* 1b), derived from *burel,* a coarse, woolen cloth. Cf. ProMkT VII.1955; SumT III.1872, 1874.

**716–28   This passage fits the dramatic context following the Host's attack (Lumiansky, Of Sondry Folk, 185–86) and echoes SqT V.36–41 (Berger, ChR 1:101). The Franklin follows the "affected modesty" topos, using the rhetorical device *diminutio* (Knight, ChR 4, 1970, 17). For discussion of rhetoric in general, see Baldwin, PMLA 42, 1927, 106–12; and for the modesty topos, see GP I.746n.

721   Pernaso: Cf. HF 521, Anel 16, Tr 3.1810. Lat. gloss: "From Persius: '[Never] did I wet my lips in the Castillian well nor dreamed that I slept on twin-peaked Parnassus.'" (Persius, Satires, Pro 1–3). The form of the quotation is a bit garbled, possibly showing that Chaucer did not know Persius directly. This seems to be the only allusion to Persius in Chaucer's work (Wrenn, MLR 18, 1923, 291; and Wright, PQ 52, 1973, 739–46).

722   Scithero: Cicero. The form Cithero is also found in Latin MSS, possibly reflecting confusion with Mt. Cithaeron (Pratt, Progress of Med. and Ren. Sts. in U.S. and Canada, Bull. 20, 1949, 48). Apparently, this is Chaucer's only use of "Cicero"; elsewhere he uses "Tullius" or "Marcus Tullius." Peck interprets the Franklin's use of this form of the name as an affectation (ChR 1, 1967, 257).

723–26   Donovan suggests the description of Rhetoric in Anticlaudianus 3.3 as a source (JEGP 56, 1957, 52–55). Chaucer plays on the three meanings of **colour in rhetoric, painting, and nature, producing the rhetorical device of *traductio* (Harrison, SP 32, 1935, 56; Kökeritz, PMLA 69, 1954, 950). Cf. ClPro IV.16n.

The Franklin's Tale

729   Armorik: Armorica (from *Ar vor,* land by the sea), ancient name of Brittany, usually used as a conscious and scholarly archaism (Tatlock, Scene of the FranT, 17; Burlin, Neophil 51:59).

734   oon the faireste: Cf. Language and Versification, p. xxxviii, and ClT IV.212n.

740   penaunce: Distress or suffering; with pain, pity, service, and obedience, it is part of the stock vocabulary of courtly love. Cf., e.g., Venus 46.

**740–42   Cf. KnT I.3080–83.

752   for shame of his degree: In order not to bring shame upon him in his status as a knight and possibly as a husband and lord (see OED, s.v. *shame,* 13).

**764–66   Cf. RR 9424–42; Ovid, Met. 2.846–47; KnT I.1625–26n.

**767   Proverbial; cf. KnT I.1606n.

**768–70   Paralleled in the Duenna's speech in RR 13959–66 (see Overbeck, ChR 2, 1967, 75–94). Cf. MancT IX.148–54.

**773–76   Proverbial; Whiting P61. The scribe of MS En3

glosses "pacientes vincunt," which appears in Piers Plowman B 13.135 and 14.33. The idea is commonplace in Latin proverbs (cf. "patientia vincit omnia," Walther 20833; Cato, Distichs 1.38). Cf ParsT X.661n., Tr 4.1584n.

781   constellacioun: Cf. WBPro III.615n.

782   complexioun: Cf. GP I.333n.

792–98 Cf. RR 9449–54; Enfances Gauvain, 275–80, ed. Paul Meyer, Romania 39, 1910, 1–32; and Cligès, 6753–61 (Loomis, Philologica, 1949, 191–94). The Franklin's idealization of a marriage that tries to combine the courtly servant-in-love with the traditional Pauline image of lord-in-marriage has often been criticized as an epicurean and faulty ideal (Robertson, Pref to Ch, 472; Howard, Idea of CT, 269; and Allen and Moritz, Distinction of Stories, 148), or as a utopian indulgence that the Franklin really does not intend to allow to threaten male supremacy (Aers, Chaucer, Langland, 1980, 160–69). Most critics, however, following Kittredge's lead (MP 9:435–67), see this mutual tolerance and regard as a basis for a happy marriage (Neville, JEGP 50:179; Hussey, Chaucer, 138; and Olson, in Ch and Med. Sts., 166), as a triumph over selfishness, weakness, or evil (Holbrook, Quest for Love, 125; Ruggiers, Art of CT, 226; and Mann, SP 63, 1966, 25), as a leveling of inequalities (David, Strumpet Muse, 187), or as Chaucer's only tale in which neither mate asserts sovereignty to the disadvantage of the other (Silvia, Rev. des langues vivantes 33, 1967, 228–36). Other critics, examining the function of the passage, find it a digression (Frazier, South Atlantic Bulletin 43:75–85), a necessary preparation for the ending's unconventional idealism (Severs, Schlauch Essays, 389), or an introduction to various incongruities and conflicts in the story (Lumiansky, UTQ 20:350–52; R. Howard, BSUF 8, 1967, 40; and Kearney, EIC 21, 1971, 109).

801   Pedmark: Penmarch, referring to the Breton cape or the commune in the southwest corner of the department of Finistère near Quimper, south of Brest. Manly (New Light, 170–73) suggests that this locale was well-known after 1386 because of a celebrated case in which John Hawley and his men seized three ships there. In the fourteenth century the village that now stands nearby was evidently a baronial seat (Tatlock, Scene of the FranT, 1–9). The description of both a high shore and the grisly, outlying rocks, however, fits no known site in Brittany. The rugged coast of Penmarch perfectly fits the description of the treacherous rocks, but the nearest high shore is at Concarneau, 35 km. away. If this site at Penmarch is intended, then the shoreline description must be Chaucer's invention.

805–6 Echoes MerT IV.1259–60; cf. MerT IV.1340–41.

808   Kayrrud: Welsh *Caer-rhudd,* "red house" or "red town." Although several villages with the modern name "Kerru" exist in Brittany, none fits the description in the tale. According to Tatlock, the adjective could refer to the red Roman bricks, and in fact Gallo-Roman remains are abundant in the vicinity of Penmarch rocks. The form of the name, however, is neither Breton nor a Breton form in French. It probably represents an English approximation of a Breton pronunciation.

Arveragus: A Latinized form of a Celtic name. See Schofield (PMLA 16:405–49) for the story of Arviragus and Genuissa found in Geoffrey of Monmouth, Hist.

Brit. 4.12. Archer (PMLA 65, 1950, 318–22) argues against Geoffrey of Monmouth as a source. Another Arviragus is one of the sons of Cymbeline and is mentioned in Juvenal, Satires, 4.127.

809–14 Verbal echo of Chrétien de Troyes's Cligès, 14–17 (Hamel, ChR 17, 1983, 316–17).

815   Dorigen: The source and pronunciation of the name are uncertain, but it has a Celtic appearance. Dorguen or Droguen is the late medieval spelling for Ohurguen (or Orgain, Oreguen, Ohurgen), the wife of Alain I of Brittany (G. A. Lobineau, Histoire de Bretagne, 1707, 1:70). Droguen is also the name of a prominent rock among the Rochers de Penmarch. Elsewhere, Dorgen or Dorien is a male personal name and occasionally a place name (Tatlock, Scene of the FranT, 37–41).

818 Possible allusion to the grief expressed in SqT V.412–22.

819 Cf. KnT I.2822–26.

829–31 This unusual engraving of an image seems closer to the sculpturing of Nature's reason in Anticlaudianus 1.1 (Donovan, JEGP 56:55) than to the corresponding image in Filocolo 2.49, which alludes to "gutta cavat lapidem" in Ovid, Ex Ponto, 4.10.5. Cf. Walther 5599a: "Dicit Aristoteles: 'Lapidem cavat ultima gutta.'"

861 Cf. Anel 177.

865–93 This passage echoes Book 4, De Consolatione (Bachman, ChR 12:55–59) and recalls Palamon's questioning in KnT I.1303–24 (Stevens, Ch's Major Tales, 90). Some critics see Dorigen's questioning as self-indulgence, impatience, or failure to accept the natural order (Baum, Ch: An Appreciation, 123–24; Benjamin, PQ 38, 1959, 119; and Gray, TSLL 7, 1965, 217). Hume (SN 44, 1972, 289–94), however, argues against such critical readings because the intentional pagan setting allows a philosophy not necessarily Christian.

865–67 Cf. Teseida 9.52–53 and Bo 1.m5.31–33.

879 Cf. Bo 1.m5.52–53.

880   merk: Cf. Gen. 1.27 "ad imaginem suam" (in his own image). *Merk* is a ME translation of Latin "imago" (the impression on a coin). Cf. Matt. 22.20; Bo 3.m9.12–15.

886 "All is for the best" is a popular rendering of Romans 8.28 (Whiting A93.1). Cf. FrT III.1496 and ClT IV.1161.

886–89   argumentz, causes, conclusion: Cf. CkPro I.4328–29n.

899   places delitables: Essentially a translation of Latin *locus amoenus* and used here both as a simple description and as an allusion to the rhetorical topos (Burnley, Neophil 56, 1972, 93). For the plural adjective, rare in the verse, see Language and Versification, p. xxxv.

900   tables: Backgammon, a game of chance played with dice, from Latin *tabularum ludus.* The medieval form of the game was much like the modern one (see Joseph Strutt, Sports and Pastimes, 319–22).

902–19 The May garden was a conventional setting for courtly love, derived ultimately from RR (cf. KnT I.1505–39 and MerT IV.2029–41). Although Rajna believed the specific source to be Filocolo 2.23–25, this scene is similar to Teseida 3.5–7, and especially close to Machaut's *Dit dou vergier.* Cummings points out that the garden descriptions in Filocolo (2.27–32 and 2.119) do not occur within its version of this scene (Indebtedness of Ch, 190), but Lowes (MP 15:702, 714–15) dismisses

913–14   Cf. SqT V.395–96.

925–34   The conventional descriptions of a courtly lover here and later in V.943–52 echo that of the Squire in the GP I.79–100 and of Arcite in Teseida 4.62. Holman sees a parallel to the courtly-love triangle in the Merchant's Tale (ELH 18:241–52). Lowes (MP 15:689–728) compares V.925–32 to Teseida 4.62.1–6; 933–34 to KnT I.1423–43; 935–43 to Teseida 4.60.5–6; 944–45 to Teseida 4.66.6–8; 946 to Teseida 4.68.2; 947–49 to Teseida 4.78.1–2; 959 to Teseida 4.62.7–8.

932   beste farynge: Most handsome (cf. MED, s.v. *faren,* 15a; Patch, ESt 65, 1931, 355–56).

938   Aurelius: A Roman name used among the Britons (see Gildas, De excidio Brit., ch. 30; Geoffrey of Monmouth, Hist. Brit. 6.5). Royster (SP 23, 1926, 380–84) calls attention to the Latin name of Orleans ("Aurelianus") and quotes a passage from *Maniere,* a fourteenth-century handbook possibly written by an Englishman, under the heading for the city, which describes Orleans as the site for the activities of necromancy and "Colle tregetour" (see HF 1277n.).

942   Withouten coppe: This is usually interpreted as "copiously" but Whiting (C628) gathers examples that show that "to drink without cup" means "to suffer intensely." For the idea of drinking woe (penaunce), see HF 1879–80n., Tr 2.784n.

943   A possible misreading (*É disperava*) of the phrase "Ed isperava" in Teseida (Lowes, MP 15:692n.).

947–48   layes: Loosely meaning song or lyric, rather than its specialized sense in V.710.

compleintes: A common troubadour form applied to love songs and religious poems, but later a genre used often by Chaucer in his short poems (see Introduction to The Short Poems, p. 632).

roundels and virelayes: Originally French dance songs with refrains, but later also used of stanzaic poems; see PF 675n.

949–50   Chaucer's conception of the furies here and in V.1101 may be colored by Dante, Inferno 9.37–51 (Lowes, MP 14, 1917, 719–20). Cf. Tr 1.1–14n; 4.22–24; Claudian, De raptu 1.226; and Bo 3.m12.33–37 (Spencer, Spec 2, 1927, 185). Some MSS have *fuyre,* which Skeat takes as "fire," but a similar form, *fuires,* clearly refers to the furies and appears in Roman d'Eneas 1919 and as *fure* in Roman de Thèbes 510. Other MSS of this line read *fuyre* and *fyr* for furies (see MED, s.v. *furie,* 2).

951–52   Ekko . . . Narcisus: Echo, a nymph who fell in love with the arrogant Narcissus, wasted away in grief until only her voice remained. The allusion is no doubt to Ovid's story in Met. 3.353–401, as the Latin marginal gloss, "Methamorphosios," suggests. Cf. BD 735.

989–98   Dorigen's promise, a version of a folklore motif called the "rash promise," is also the imposing of an impossible task since she clearly intends it as a refusal. Many critics see the promise as a rhetorical way for Dorigen to affirm her love for Arveragus (e.g., Hinckley, MP 16, 1918, 44; and Robertson, Costerus n.s. 1, 1974, 19–20).

Burlin (Neophil 51:59) notes the parallel in the legalistic promise to Arveragus, and Joseph (ChR 1, 1966, 26) sees a facetious echo of Dorigen's earlier questioning of natural law. Gaylord (ELH 31:331–65) not only

doubts the legitimacy of a promise made *in pley* and never intended as a vow, but claims that a rash promise should not be kept according to moral treatises and medieval law. Dorigen's stipulation is unlike any in the other analogues. (Cf. Filocolo, in which the lady asks for a garden blooming in January.)

999–1000   On the authority of only three inferior manuscripts, Manly and Rickert place these lines after line 1006 (see M-R 2:314 for an explanation).

1009   inpossible: Cf. WBPro III.688n.

1016–17   Lowes (MP 15:695–96) suggests that the May morning scene is reminiscent of Teseida 3.12.1–2 and 7.68.1–2, possibly recalling a line from Dante, Purgatorio 7.60. He also compares the use of **reft** to Teseida 3.43.1–2, 4.72.5–6, and 10.14.5–6.

1017–18   Hammond (MLN 27, 1912, 91–2) describes this as a rhetorical device similar to the prose line ("et, ut in verba paucissima conferam, nox erat") following eleven flowery lines of verse in Fulgentius, *Liber mitologiarum,* book 1, ed. Helm, 1898, 13. Hodgson's note cites this as a humorous anticlimax after *circuitio* as in Tr 2.904–5 (see note 905), but Harrison (SP 32: 58–59) claims the line is neither burlesque nor humorous, but an example of *expolitio,* a common device to explain a preceding assertion.

1031–37   Apollo, as the god of herbs, is suggested by two passages from Ovid, Met. 1.521–24, 2.23–30 (see Hoffman, Ovid and the CT, 170).

1033   The sun's declination (distance from the plane of the celestial equator) determines the changes of seasons according to whether its position is low (winter) or high (summer) in the sky.

1045   Lucina: Luna, as goddess of the moon, controls the tides and hence the sea. Instead of praying directly to her, Aurelius prays to Apollo, her brother, because Lucina is also Diana, goddess of virginity (Hunter, MLN 68, 1953, 174). Lowes (MP 15:721–22) compares Aurelius's prayer to Florio's in Filocolo 1.166.

1049–54   This passage refers not only to the moon's dependence on the sun, but also to the tide's dependence on the moon. Robinson notes a possible parallel to Anticlaudianus 2.3, though, as he notes, the idea was commonplace (cf. Bartholomaeus Anglicus 1.8, tr. Trevisa, 489–94).

1053   as she that is: Although the accusative is expected, the nominative is used in this construction. Cf. V:1088 and KnT I.964.

1057–70   Highest tides occur when the moon is either full or new (in opposition or in conjunction with the sun). The sun would exert its greatest power in its own astrological mansion, Leo, with the moon in opposition (V.1057) in Aquarius, the zodiacal sign of water especially appropriate for this miracle. Since it is only early May (cf. 906) and the sun is in Taurus, Aurelius asks Apollo to grant his prayer that when the sun is next in Leo (1058), the moon slow her course to move at the same rate as the sun (1066) so that for two years (1068) the moon will remain full (1069), thus keeping the tides high (1070) and the highest rock covered (1059–61).

1073–74   A variation on Dorigen's own words in V.891–92. Lucina is here seen as Proserpina, goddess of the underworld. Cf. KnT I.2081–82 and I.2313n.

1077   Delphos: Delphi, from the Latin accusative form (cf. Tr 4.1411n.) or perhaps confused with Delos, the birthplace of Apollo.

1110   Pamphilus: Lat. gloss: "Pamphilus to Galatea: 'I

am wounded and bear the arrow deep in my breast,' "
from *Pamphilus de amore,* a thirteenth-century Latin poem
(ed. Becker, 1972). Garbáty (PQ 46, 1967, 457–70)
argues that Chaucer first became acquainted with this
work in *El libro de buen amor,* written by his Spanish
contemporary Juan Ruiz. Cf. Mel VII.1556 and n.

1113 sursanure: This image derives from the line
quoted above from *Pamphilus de amore.*

1118 Orliens: Orleans, the seat of the University of
Orleans, famous for its law school (Rashdall, Univ. of
Europe in MA, 1936, 2:139–51). In the fourteenth cen-
tury, it was an important center of astrological studies
(Royster, SP 23:383–84).

1119–28 Deschamps, Chaucer's friend, describes his
own student days at Orleans in *Miroir de mariage,* which
Lowes (RomR 2, 1911, 125–26) believed was a possible
influence on this passage.

1125 magyk natureel: See GP I.416n.

1130 mansiouns: Mansions or stations of the moon,
referring to the twenty-eight equal divisions of the
moon's path in a lunar month, often used to forecast
natural phenomena and favorable times for specific
human activities. See MilT I.3515n.

1133 On Chaucer's attitude toward astrology or "judicial astronomy," see MLT II.295–315nn. and Astr
2.4.57–69n.

1139–51 Witke sees a parallel to OF *Floire et Blancheflor,*
first version, 805–91 (ChR 1, 1966, 33–36).

1141 tregetoures: Although Skeat and Robinson gloss
the word as "juggler," it more likely means "magician"
(Fisher, Donaldson, Davis Glossary). Cf. HF 1277n.
Since Chaucer repeatedly refers to illusions or appearances (V.1140, 1141, 1143), Prins suggests a magician
who causes "hallucinations or collective apparitions" (ES
35, 1954, 161), but Loomis (Spec 33, 1958, 244) argues
for "craftsmen, artisans mécaniques, who, in effective
unison, produced spectacular results." Some parallels for
V.1190–91 appear in the marvels offered as entertainment in the court of the Great Khan, as reported in
Mandeville's *Travels,* EETS 153, 140–45, 156–57. Loomis (Spec 33:242–55) noted similarities to actual entertainments at the royal palace in Paris in 1378. See also
Fifield, PLL 3 Supplement, 1967, 64–66.

1196 Thise: Used in a general sense; see Language and
Versification, p. xxxviii.

ryver: Hawking ground, or hawking. See Tr 4.413n.

1203–4 By clapping his hands, the clerk may be signaling his stage assistants or breaking the magic spell as in
the epilogue of the *Tempest.* Cf. the verbal echo in *Tempest*
4.1.148 (Thompson, Archiv 212, 1975, 317).

1219 At after-soper: For the construction see SqT
V.302n.

1222 Gerounde: The river Geronde; **Sayne,** the Seine.
This would indicate the southwest coast from Geronde to
Brest and the northwest coast to Honfleur.

1223 made it straunge: For the idiom see GP I.785n.

1228 That the earth is round was common knowledge;
see, e.g., The Life of St. Michael, Early South English
Legendary, ed. C. Horstmann, EETS 87, 1887, 311.

1245 laton: Cf. GP I.699n.

1248 Cf. Astr 2.1.18–19, 23.

1250–51 Cf. Teseida 3.44.2–4 (Robinson).

1252 Janus: The two-faced god, referred to as "double-
bearded," who was also the god of gates (ingress and
egress) as well as of beginnings and endings (Adams, Sts.
in Med. Culture 4, 1974, 447). The Latin marginal note

reads "Janus biceps," a reference to Ovid, Fasti 1.65.
Rosemond Tuve (Seasons and Months, 1933, 186) demonstrates the similarities between this passage and familiar seasonal motifs found in medieval manuscript illuminations in Books of Hours and Calendars.

1254 brawen: Boar's meat, a ceremonial dish for
Christmas festivities. The boar's head appeared in illuminations for January in medieval calendars.

1255 Nowel: Noel (Lat. *natalem,* birthday). To "cry
Noel" originally meant to sing a Christmas carol, but
came to mean a cry of rejoicing. Cf. Sir Gawain and the
Green Knight, 64–65.

1273 tables Tolletanes: Astronomical tables adapted
around 1272 for the city of Toledo, under the direction
of Alphonso X, King of Castile. These Alfonsine Tables,
which corrected and superseded earlier, eleventh-century tables compiled by Al-Zargali, were then adapted
for longitudes of London and other medieval cities. See
Astr 2.44–45n.

1274 corrected: Corrected for errors or for a given
longitude. See Tatlock, Kittredge Anniv. Papers, 346,
for discussion of the inaccuracy of the tables.

1275 expans yeeris: Tabulated values for a planet's
position in single-year periods; **collect:** Tabulated values
for a planet's position in twenty-year periods from 20
A.D. to 2000 A.D. The values from these two tables could
then be added to the root computation to determine a
planet's position for any year. See Astr 2.44–45n.

1276 rootes: Root, the first date for which a table is
given and the basis for calculating a planet's motion. Cf.
MLT II.314 and Astr 2.44.

1277 centris: Although Skeat and Robinson gloss
"centre" as part of an astrolabe, it more likely refers to
the table of centers, which shows "distances from the
centre equant and centre defferent from the centre of an
equatorie for each of the planets" (MED, s.v. *centre,* 7c).
Thus both *centris* and **argumentz,** angles or arcs used in
calculating the position or motion of a planet (MED), are
astronomical figures.

1278 proporcioneles convenientz: Most often
glossed as tables of proportions for computing the motions of planets; Dictionnaire Astrologique, 1935, 357,
defines "proportion" as a mathematical formula used in
astrology for calculating motion.

1279 equacions: Method of dividing a sphere into
equal houses for astrological purposes (MED). Cf. Astr
2.36n.

1280 his eighte speere: The eighth sphere or the
sphere of the fixed stars, by the usual reckoning (cf. Tr
5.1809n). The precession of the equinoxes could be ascertained by observing the distance from the true equinoctial point (the head of the fixed Aries in the ninth
sphere) and the star Alnath (α Arietis) in the head of
Aries in the eighth sphere.

1283 ninthe speere: The Primum Mobile; see Astr
1.17.35–41n.

1285 his firste mansioun: The first mansion of the
moon is called Alnath (Ellesmere gloss at 1281). Cf.
1130 above.

1288 face . . . terme: Astronomical terms; each zodiac
sign was divided equally into faces of ten degrees and
unequally into terms; both divisions were assigned to
particular planets. See Astr 2.4.60–69.

1311–22 Skeat (5:395) notes similarities between this
complaint and the complaint of Anelida, especially
V.1318 with Anel 288.

1325   but youre grace: This idea of relying on the unmerited favor of the lady was the counterpart of the Christian doctrine of grace. Cf. KnT I.3089n.

1340   Skeat (5:395) compares this line to Anel 173 and V.1348 to Anel 169.

1354   compleynt: See 947–48 above.

1355–1456   Dorigen's complaint summarizes six chapters of Jerome, *Adversus Jovinianum* (more briefly summarized in ProLGW 281–304). Gatherings of such lists of exempla were common, though Chaucer may have been influenced by Machaut (see Oeuvres, ed. Hoepffner, intro. lxxiii). Critics generally complain about the passage's inordinate length, rhetorical excesses, apparent disorganization, and display of learning for its own sake (Manly, Ch and the Rhet., Brit. Acad., 1926, 12; Dempster, MLN 52, 1937, 16–23; Tatlock, PMLA 50, 1935, 103; and Sledd, MP 45, 1947, 44). The complaint, however, has also been viewed as an effective narrative device for postponing the tale's denouement (Stevens, Ch's Major Tales, 87) or as an appropriate rhetorical device generalizing Dorigen's experiences (Brewer, PBA 60, 1974, 242). Other critics focus on its content as an illumination of the Franklin's idea of marriage (Baker, JEGP 60, 1961, 56–64), as a testing and discarding of courtly-love ideas (Lumiansky, UTQ 20:354), or as a complete alienation from Christian principles by its toying with the pagan virtue of honor through suicide (Golding, MAE 39, 1970, 309). The passage also reflects Dorigen's psychological state of mind in subtle and accurate ways, according to Sledd, MP 45:42–43; Benjamin, PQ 38:123; and Hoffmann, ChR 2:27–28.

Though Chaucer follows Jerome closely, he places his examples in a different order. Morgan (MAE 46, 1977, 77–97) argues that this produced a coherent exposition of chastity (V.1367–1418), fidelity (1424–41), and honor (1442–56). Baker (JEGP 60:56–64) argues that the exempla are organized into: women who commit suicide to avoid rape (1367–1404), women who commit suicide after being raped (1405–38), and notably faithful wives (1439–56).

Some critics have seen the passage as presenting Dorigen as a foil to the Wife of Bath (Pratt, Criticism 5: 316–22; Murtaugh, ELH 38:479–92) or to Virginia in The Physician's Tale (Tupper, PMLA 29, 1914, 97; Hoffmann, ChR 2:26–31; Beidler, ChR 3:279).

Those who object to its length tend to see Chaucer as ridiculing rhetorical practices (M–R 4:487; Spearing, 45–46) or transforming the tale's incipient tragedy into comedy (Sledd, MP 45:44). Yet Chaucer may have intended to make the list of good women even longer (see 1455–59 below).

1356   Possibly suggested by Teseida 3.32.5.

1360   have I levere: For this idiom, see Mustanoja, ME Syntax, 531–32.

1364   Lat. gloss: "When the thirty tyrants of Athens slew Phidon at a feast, they ordered his virgin daughters to come to them, stripped naked in the manner of prostitutes, and dance with shameless gestures on the floor stained with their father's blood. When they saw the drunken feasters, they, concealing their grief, went out as if for the needs of nature and straightway embracing one another, leapt into a cistern so that they might by death preserve their virginity" (Jerome, Adv. Jov. 1.41; S&A, 395).

1379–80   Mecene . . . Lacedomye: Lat. gloss: "When

the Messenians tried to violate the Lacedemonian [Spartan] maidens," [they willingly chose to die rather than consent] (Jerome, Adv. Jov. 1.41; S&A, 395). (The portion of the text not included in the MS gloss is in square brackets.)

1387   Lat. gloss: "When Aristoclides, the tyrant of Orchomenos, after killing her father, desired the virgin Stymphalis (Stymphalides), she fled to the temple of Diana" [to whose statue she clung until stabbed to death]. (Jerome, Adv. Jov. 1.41; S&A, 395.)

1399   Lat. gloss: "As to Hasdrubal's wife, when, the city taken and set fire," [she was about to be taken captive by the Romans, she snatched up her children in both arms and threw herself into the burning house] (Jerome, Adv. Jov. 1.43; S&A, 396). Cf. NPT VII.3362–68.

1405   Lucresse: Lat. gloss: "And first I put Lucretia who, unwilling to survive her shameful rape, wiped out her body's stain [*maculam*] with her own blood" (Jerome, Adv. Jov. 1.46; S&A, 397). Cf. LGW 1680–1885.

1409   sevene maydens of Milesie: Lat. gloss: "Who could pass over in silence the seven virgins of Miletus, who [when all was laid waste by the attack] of the Gauls (or Galatians) [*Gallorum*]" [escaped dishonor by death]? (Jerome, Adv. Jov. 1.44; S&A, 396).

1412–13   Cf. Miroir de mariage 9153.

1414   Lat. gloss: "Xenophon in the [book on] the boyhood of great Cyrus [Cyropaedia, 7.3] writes that when Habradate [Abradates] was killed" [his wife Panthea committed suicide alongside him] (Jerome, Adv. Jov. 1.45; S&A, 396–97).

1426   Demociones doghter: Lat. gloss: "The virgin daughter of Demotion, prince of the Ariopagites" [killed herself on learning of the death of her betrothed rather than marry another, which would have seemed like bigamy to her] (Jerome, Adv. Jov. 1.41; S&A, 395).

1428   Lat. gloss: "By what words are to be praised the daughter of Scedasus" [who killed herself rather than survive rape] (Jerome, Adv. Jov. 1.41; S&A, 395).

1432   Lat. gloss: "Nichanor, when Thebes was taken, was overcome by love for a captive virgin" [who killed herself] (Jerome, Adv. Jov. 1.41; S&A, 396).

1434   Another Theban mayden: Lat. gloss: "Greek writers tell of another Theban virgin" [who, when violated by a Macedonian enemy killed her rapist then herself] (Jerome, Adv. Jov. 1.41; S&A, 396).

1437   Lat. gloss: "What should I say of the wife of Niceratus, piously unable to bear the death of her husband" [who killed herself to escape the lust of the Thirty Tyrants] (Jerome, Adv. Jov. 1.44; S&A, 396).

1439   Lat. gloss: "Alcibiades, the Socratic, vanquished by the Athenians" [was killed and later buried by his mistress at the risk of death] (Jerome, Adv. Jov. 1.44; S&A, 396).

1442–43   Lat. gloss: "They made a fable of Alcestis, who died willingly for Adametus, her husband, and the poem of Homer is of chaste Penelope" (Jerome, Adv. Jov. 1.45; S&A, 397). Cf. LGW F 499–504n.

1445   Lat. gloss: "Lacedoma [for Laodamia] is also sung by the mouths of poets, she who when Protesilaus [for Protesolao] was killed at Troy," [did not wish to survive him] (Jerome, Adv. Jov. 1.45; S&A 397). Cf. LGW F 264 and note F 263–68.

1448   Lat. gloss: "Portia could not live without Brutus" (Jerome, Adv. Jov. 1.46; S&A, 397).

1451   Lat. gloss: "Also Artemesia, the wife of Mausolus is said to have been famous for her chastity" [she built a tomb for her husband so elaborate that "to this day every precious sepulcher is called 'Mausoleum' from his name"] (Jerome, Adv. Jov. 1.44; S&A 396).

1453   Lat. gloss: "Teuta, queen of Illirica" [was famous for her chastity] (Jerome, Adv. Jov. 1.44; S&A, 396).

1455–59   On these lines appear the Lat. glosses: "Memorandum Strato Regulus" (referring to Adv. Jov. 1.45); "Vidi et omnes pene Barbares capitulo xxvj° primi" (referring probably to Adv. Jov. 1.42); "Item Cornelia et cetera" (Adv. Jov. 1.49); and "Imitentur ergo nupte Theanam Cleobiliam Gorgim Thymodiam Claudias atque Cornelias in fine libri primi" (Adv. Jov. 1.49). Skeat (5:399), assuming the glosses are Chaucer's, notes that "Chaucer seems to have contemplated adding more examples to the list."

1455   **Bilyea:** Bilia, wife of Duillius, whose fame was being able to tolerate her husband's bad breath: "She said 'I thought the mouths of all men smelled like that'" (Jerome, Adv. Jov. 1.46; S&A, 397).

1456   **Rodogone:** Rhodogune, who killed her maid for suggesting a second marriage (Jerome, Adv. Jov. 1.45; S&A, 397). **Valeria:** Another woman who refused to remarry (Jerome, Adv. Jov. 1.46; S&A, 397).

1472   Proverbial; see Tr 3.764 and n. Cf. Whiting H569.

1486   **of yow:** Concerning you, rather than from you. Arveragus is concerned with protecting his wife's reputation (Morgan, MAE 46:97).

1504–12   The emphasis on the movement toward the garden (through repetition) becomes significant since the characters never reach the garden and thus avoid the implications of the fall, according to Kee, MS 23:162.

1533   Aurelius uses the legal language of a medieval release or quit-claim. These words, though this may be sheer coincidence, resemble those of Cecilia Chaumpayne to Chaucer (Blenner-Hassett, Spec 28:796–800), when releasing him from the charge of "raptus" (see Chaucer's Life, pp. xxii–xxiii).

1534   **serement:** The reading in the Ellesmere and Hengwrt MSS (from Latin *sacramentum,* meaning oath). Three other MSS have *seuerte* (from Latin *securitas,* meaning surety); all the other MSS have *surement:* assurance, pledge.

1541–44   Although in most MSS these lines are part of Dorigen's speech, they seem more appropriate to the Franklin (Baum, MLN 32, 1917, 377; Severs, Schlauch Essays, 395; Magoun, MLN 70, 1955, 173). Manly transfers them to the Franklin, but after line 1550 (MR 4:488).

1547   **sayd:** An unusual use of the past participle in place of an infinitive, which occurs in both Middle and Modern English (heard tell, heard told), especially when the context is preterite. See Mustanoja, ME Syntax, 554, for examples.

1549   **wryte:** Seems to be used here by oversight. Cf. KnT I.1201 and n. (Robinson).

1552   **sovereyn blisse:** Contrasted to simple *blisse* in V.802 (Kearney, EIC 19, 1969, 251).

1580   **a-begged:** For the form see PardT VI.406.

1614   Donovan (JEGP 56:59) compares the description of the furies in Anticlaudianus.

1621–22   Some critics view this question as a kind of joke since they see no character as noble (Baum, Ch, 128–

33; R. Howard, BSUF 8:44; Wood, PQ 45:688–711). However, this *demande* ending is a common medieval device for ending a courtly narrative by calling for further discussion. Cf. KnT I.1347 and n.; Filocolo 2.60. It is also a common folklore motif, "Which was the Noblest Act?" (Aarne-Thompson Type 976).

FRAGMENT VI

This fragment has no explicit connection with the tales that precede and follow it, and its position varies in the manuscripts. In some it follows The Franklin's Tale, in others The Canon's Yeoman's Tale; in such manuscripts the scribes supplied spurious links (see M-R 4:488–89). Furnivall placed it after Fragment VII, and Skeat adopted this Chaucer Society order in his edition, though he protested that there was no good reason for this placement of VI (4:434). Pollard, the Globe editor, followed this order as well. Pratt (PMLA 66, 1951, 1141–67), however, has shown the validity of the order V–VI–VII, which has been adopted by all twentieth-century editors. Biedler (ChR 3, 1968–69, 275–79) and Dewey Faulkner (ed., The Pardoner's Tale: A Collection of Essays, 1973, 5–6) argue for deliberate parallels and thematic continuities between the Franklin's and Physician's tales.

Critics have argued that the fragment is unified, though there is little agreement on exactly how its two tales are related. Trower (ABR 29, 1978, 67–86) finds a theme of spiritual sickness unifying the fragment; Joseph (ChR 9, 1975, 237–45) and Haines (ChR 10, 1976, 220–35) find the unity in the theme of the gifts of Nature and of Fortune (see VI.295 and n.). Barney (in Faulkner, ed., as above, 84–87) argues for a dramatic relation, with The Physician's Tale and the Host's comment on it providing the basis for the Pardoner's performance.

LARRY D. BENSON

The Physician's Tale

The Physician's Tale is usually assigned to a date before or at the beginning of the Canterbury period (Tatlock, Dev and Chron, 150–51; Baugh, 485; Fisher, 214). Tatlock developed the argument that its first composition was either for or under the influence of *The Legend of Good Women,* and this view has been widely accepted (see most recently Middleton, ChR 8, 1973, 27–30, and Kinney, Lit. and Psych. 28, 1978, 76), though disputed by Overbeck (ChR 2, 1967, 92–93). As often with Chaucer, the evidence for dating the work is almost wholly inferential. Ten Brink (Hist. Eng. Lit. 2:121) believed the conclusion refers to political events of 1388. Developing a suggestion from Kittredge, Tatlock (see 72–104 below) argued that the warning to guardians was prompted by a contemporary scandal, the elopement of John of Gaunt's daughter Elizabeth in 1386, and that the tale was most likely written when the couple returned to England in 1388. Though this theory has been widely accepted,

The explanatory notes to The Physician's Tale were written by C. David Benson.

it remains little more than a guess. A date no earlier than 1386 has been assumed because the poem does not appear in the list of Chaucer's works in the Prologue to *The Legend of Good Women* and a date no later than 1390 because it betrays no influence of Gower's version of the story in *Confessio amantis.* Recent attempts to see the tale as a reflection of the personality of the Physician assume that the work in its present form was composed expressly for *The Canterbury Tales.*

For many years the majority view of the critics, expressed most eloquently in silence, has been that the tale is poorly written and motivated (Brewer, Chaucer, 136; Muscatine, Poetry and Crisis, 138–39) or, at best, an example of Chaucer "working rather routinely" (see, e.g., Donaldson, 927; Waller, Spec 51, 1976, 303). Coghill found it a work of "false values and improbable circumstances" (in Ch and Chaucerians, 126–28), and critics have frequently objected to the tale's apparent unsuitability to its teller (e.g., Knight, Poetry of CT, 119–21; but cf. Huling Ussery, Ch's Physician, 1971, 119–34; Rowland, ELH 40, 1973, 165–78, who argues that the tale reflects the traditional animosity between law and medicine; and Kempton, ChR, 19, 1984, 24–38, who sees the tale expressing the limitations of medicine itself). In various ingenious, if not wholly convincing, ways, some critics have found value in the poem's apparent failures. The disparity between the tale and its teller has seemed to some a source of comedy (Longsworth, Criticism 13, 1971, 223–33) or irony, either because a promoter of lechery tells a tale of chastity (Lumiansky, Of Sondry Folk, 195–200) or because of the Physician's inability to recognize the real cause of the tragedy he tells (Brown, PQ 60, 1981, 129–49). Middleton (ChR 8: 9–32) holds that the inadequacies of the narrative are deliberately designed to evoke the reader's recognition of the tale's moral complexity. See also Ramsey, ChR 6, 1972, 185–97; McCall, Ch among the Gods, 105–8; and Allen and Moritz, Distinction of Stories, 158–63. Gardner (Poetry of Ch, 293–98) and Whittock (A Reading of CT, 179–83) insist that Chaucer's art is here deliberately "bad," intended to reveal the moral failings of the teller.

Though few would agree with Tupper (JEGP 15, 1916, 61–62) that the tale is wholly successful except to a "critic running amuck" (cf. Root, Poetry of Ch, 222; and Fansler, Ch and RR, 35), some limited respect has been forthcoming. It has been read as a work about sexual maturation (Kinney, Lit. and Psych. 28:76–84) or the relations of men and women (Mathewson, AnM 14, 1973, 35–42), and it has been admired for its pathos (Gerould, Ch Essays, 85–86), use of rhetoric (Rowland, ELH 40:166–68), and religious and moral seriousness (Kean, Ch and Poetry, 2:179–85; Barbara Bartholomew, Fortuna and Natura, 1966, 46–57; Mandel, ChR 10, 1976, 316–25).

Tyrwhitt (4:305, n. to line 12074) was the first to recognize that the principal source for The Physician's Tale is the brief account of Virginia in the *Roman de la rose,* 5589–658. The reference to Livy (VI.1) imitates RR 5594, and thus Chaucer may not have known the original account in Livy's history (3:44–50, 56–58). Shannon (S&A, 398–407) argued that Chaucer drew directly on Livy for some details, and many have echoed this assertion, though, as earlier critics recognized (e.g., Skeat 3:435–37), the case for Chaucer's use of the Latin author is weak (Harbert, in Ch: Writers and Back-

ground, 142–43). The tale was popular in medieval literature (versions appear in Bersuire, in Boccaccio's *De claribus mulieribus,* and in Gower's Conf. Aman. 7:5131–306) and was almost always told as an exemplum of evil government. For the tale as Chaucer's "transformation of history," see Fichte, *Florilegium* 5, 1983, 189–207. Delany (SAC 3, 1981, 47–60) attributes the failure of the tale to Chaucer's inability to deal with the political themes, especially popular revolt, implicit in the story. There is no convincing evidence that Chaucer drew on any earlier version except RR, and, perhaps most striking in a tale not highly regarded, most of the material and treatment are original (see, especially, Fansler, Ch and RR, 31–35, and Brown, PQ 60:131–37). The minor sources are identified in the notes to specific lines below.

6 Hoffman (ChR 2, 1967, 24) and, earlier, Grace W. Landrum (Chaucer's Use of the Vulgate, Radcliffe Diss., 1921, 2:21–22) suggest that in making Virginia an only child, Chaucer is following the story of Jephtha's daughter (see 240 below) rather than his sources, but Virginia is also apparently an only child in Livy (see R. M. Oglivie, Commentary on Livy, 1965, 479).

9–117 These lines are essentially original with Chaucer.

9–13 Chaucer elsewhere presents the goddess Nature as the creator of beautiful women (Anel 80, BD 871, PF 374), a conceit common in medieval French poetry (Knowlton, MP 20, 1923, 310). Kean (Ch and Poetry 2:59–60) notes the discussion of art and nature in RR 20817ff. and elsewhere in Chaucer; and George Economou (Goddess Natura in the M.A., 26–27) finds the conception of the goddess here in accord with a tradition that goes back to antiquity.

14 Lat. gloss: "Look in Metamorphoses." For the story of Pygmalion, see Ovid, Met. 10:243–97. The medieval allegorization is discussed by Robertson (Pref to Ch, 99–103) and Hoffman (Ovid and CT, 179–81; rpt. from AmN&Q 5, 1967, 83–84). Pygmalion is cited in a similar context in *Pearl* (749–50).

16 Lat. gloss: "Apelles made a marvelous work on the grave of Darius, see in the first [other MSS give fifth or sixth] book of Alexander; for Zanzis in the book of Tulius" (i.e., Cicero). Apelles, Darius, and a similar gloss occur at WBPro III.498–99. The *Alexandreis* (1178–82) of Gautier de Châtillon, a widely renowned medieval Latin epic (see George Cary, Medieval Alexander, 1956, 63–64; Lounsbury, Sts. in Ch 2:353–55), describes the elaborate tomb of Darius constructed by the fictional Jewish artist Apelles (7:383–97; cf. 4.176–79; ed. Mueldener, 1863). The Athenian artist Zeuxis (**Zanzis**) and the historical painter Apelles are both cited in Cicero's De oratore 3.26, but the specific reference in the gloss is to the story of Zeuxis's method of portraying feminine beauty in Cicero, De inventione 2.1–3. Despite the learned allusions in the glosses, however, Chaucer's immediate source is almost certainly RR 16177–210, which mentions Pygmalion, Apelles, Zeuxis (and, indeed, Cicero's story of Zeuxis) in a discussion of art versus nature.

20 **vicaire general:** Cf. PF 379 and n.

32–34 Although both Skeat and Robinson cite RR 16242–44, Fansler (Ch and RR, 89) notes how common these flower comparisons are in descriptions of beauty.

37–38 Cf. Tr 4.736 and 5.8.

41–71 This detailed description of Virginia's "maidenly virtues" is unparalled in earlier versions. Many critics have noticed the greater prominence Chaucer has given Virginia in the story and her resemblance to Christian virgin martyrs. See Crowther, Eng. St. in Canada 8, 1982, 125–37. Chaucer is undoubtedly drawing on material common to medieval treatises on virginity, but no single source can yet be accepted unquestionably as the poet's own. Tupper (MLN 30, 1915, 5–7) found many specific parallels to the "consecrated virgin" type discussed by St. Ambrose in his *De virginibus* (PL 16:183–232; the most striking passages are given in Shannon, S&A, 407–8). Young (Spec 16, 1941, 340–49) argued instead for a more ample compilation like Vincent of Beauvais's *De eruditione filiorum nobilium,* which includes much from Ambrose in addition to other parallels not in the older work. Waller (Spec 51:292–306) insists that everything not from RR in these lines and elsewhere in the tale can be accounted for by Juan García de Castrojeriz's Castillian version of Aegidius Romanus's *De regimine principum,* the presentation copy of which might have been in the possession of John of Gaunt's second wife, Constance. In a second article, Tupper (JEGP 15:61n.) noted resemblances to Virginia's virtues in treatises on the sins such as the *Ayenbite of Inwit.* Kean (Ch and Poetry 2:180–82) suggested that not virginity but chastity, as part of Nature's plan, is discussed here, and he finds parallels with the four cardinal virtues.

49　Pallas: Pallas Athena, goddess of Wisdom (cf. Aeneid 5.704).

54　See GP I.307n.

58–59　The association of wine (**Bacus**) with sexual desire (**Venus**) is commonplace; cf. PF 275–76n.

59–60　Proverbial; Whiting, W359; cf. Ovid, Ars Am. 1.243–44; Horace, Sat. 2.3.321; and PardT VI.484, 549.

65–66　Vaguely reminiscent of Ovid, Ars Am. 1:229 and RR 13522–28.

72–104　This digression on the responsibilities of parents and guardians has often been regarded as unduly obtrusive, and historical explanations have been sought. In a brief note, Kittredge (MP 1, 1903, 5n.) first suggested that Chaucer might have had in mind his sister-in-law, Katherine Swynford, who was governess to the daughters of John of Gaunt and also his mistress before becoming his third wife. Tatlock (Dev and Chron, 152–55) argued for a specific allusion to the elopement in 1386 of John's second daughter, Elizabeth, then married to the young Earl of Pembroke, with John Holland. They returned to England in 1388. This explanation has been widely accepted; and Cowling (Chaucer, 1927, 165–66) suggested a reference to a second scandal, the abduction of Isabella atte Halle in 1387 (Ch Life Records, 375–83). Others, for a variety of reasons, have doubted that Chaucer was thinking specifically of Katherine and Elizabeth (see, most recently, Brown, PQ 60, 133–34), and there is no necessity to seek an actual event behind sentiments that are quite conventional, however awkwardly introduced.

79　Cf. GP I.476 and n.

83–85　Proverbial; Whiting T76.

98　Cf. Prov. 13.24; Langland, PP B 5.39–40; and Whiting Y1.

101–2　Proverbial in both English (Whiting S242) and Latin (Walther 30542). The Latin gloss in a single MS (Oxford, Christ Church 152) has the variant Lat. prov-

erb: "Whence [the saying] of an improper man—under a soft shepherd, the wolf shits wool and the flock perishes"; see Langland, PP C 10.264–66, Whiting S241, and Walther 30541.

107–8　Cf. 2 Cor. 3.2.

114–17　**The Doctour:** Lat. gloss: "Augustinus." St. Augustine offers a brief definition of envy in his *Enarrationes in Psalmos* (PL 37:1399): "Envy is the hatred of another's good fortune." Owen (MLN 71, 1956, 86) points out that the longer definition here was commonly attributed to Augustine, as in a short poem on Envy from Harley 7322: "De isto malo dicit Augustinus, quod est aliene felicitatis tristicia, et aduersitatis leticia" (Political, Religious, and Love Poems, ed. Furnivall, EETS 15, 257). The longer definition appears again in ParsT X.484 (see n.).

135　Chaucer begins again to follow the general story in RR.

140　The MSS are divided between **cherl** and *clerk,* the former being perhaps a translation of the Fr. *ribauz* (RR 5599).

153–54　Chaucer follows Jean de Meun in calling Appius Claudius simply Apius and Marcus Claudius simply Claudius.

156–57　Cf. LGW 702.

168–70　This closely follows RR 5612–14: "And if Virginius denies it, I am ready to prove everything, for I can find good witnesses."

207–53　Many critics are disturbed by the account of Virginia's death, which is original with Chaucer; instead of killing his daughter instantly and publicly under extreme pressure, as in Livy and RR, Virginius deliberately plans and announces the execution, which is carried out at home.

225　**For love, and nat for hate:** Cf. RR 5635: "Car il, par amour, senz haïne" (put her to death).

229–30　A common formula; see BD 189–90n.

240　Lat. gloss: "Iudicum capitulo xi° fuit illo tempore Iepte Galaandes" [for Galaadites] (Judges 11.1). In exchange for victory, Jephtha vows to sacrifice whatever first comes out of his house on his return; the victim turns out to be his only daughter who asks for two months respite to bewail her wasted virginity. Tupper (MLN 30:7) believed the reference to the story of Jephtha and his daughter resulted from its prominence in one of Ambrose's treatises on virginity. Hoffman (ChR 2:20–31), perhaps making too much of a casual reference, argues that the Physician misunderstands the story both literally and figuratively, thus proving his little study of the Bible (GP I.438); see Hanson (ChR 7, 1972, 132–39) and Lancashire (ChR 9, 1975, 323) for arguments that the teller elsewhere misuses Christian material. Longsworth (Criticism 13:228–31), finds the allusion to Jephtha's daughter "comically maladroit," but Huling Ussery, Ch's Physician, 1971, 127–28, defends the Physician's learning. Hoffman (25–26), Brown (PQ 60:139) and Allen and Moritz (Distinction of Stories, 161–62) note that Jephtha's vow was widely condemned in the Middle Ages.

255–76　This closely follows RR 5635–58. The beheading of Virginia and the bringing of her head to Apius are narrated in RR but not in Livy.

277–86　Several critics (most notably Kean, Ch and Poetry 2:182–83; Ramsey, ChR 6:195–96; Donaldson, 1091; Brown, PQ 60:136) have questioned the appro-

priateness of the final moral since it could only apply to
Apius, who is not the primary focus of the tale. Whatever
the intended effect, Chaucer presents standard medieval
thinking about sin, especially as expressed by Innocent
III, who mentions the "worm of conscience" ("vermis
conscientiae tripliciter lacerabit") in the work most commonly known as the *De contemptu mundi* (*De miseria condicionis humane* 3.2). As do these lines, Innocent warns that
death may be unexpected (3.1) and that the damned
suffer not only physically but also inwardly from the
knowledge of their sin (3.2). For the Augustinian doctrine of the secret punishment that sin inflicts upon its
perpetrator, see Kellogg (Spec 26, 1951, 465–81).
286   An old and common proverb (Whiting S335; cf.
ParsT X.93). Hanson (ChR 7:137) finds the advice
ironic because only Virginia is forsaken, but the reference is to spiritual not physical death. In the same section
of the work cited above (3:2), Innocent warns that it is
too late to repent when one is no longer capable of
sinning.

Introduction to the Pardoner's Tale

288   **Harrow:** Here simply "alas"; originally a cry for
help (*clameur de haro*). Cf. MED and I.3286, 3285, etc.
    by nayles and by blood: See VI.651 and n. below.
295   On the gifts (or goods) of Fortune (riches and
social position) and of Nature (endowments of the body
and the soul), see ParsT X.449–56, Bo 2.pr5.71ff., Tr
4.386–92. Omitted here are the gifts (or goods) of
Grace (mental powers and spiritual strength). The idea
of the three gifts of God apparently derives from Frère
Lorens's *Somme des vices et des virtues* (see the translations
by Dan Michel, *Ayenbite of Inwit*, ed. Morris, EETS 23,
1866, 24–25, and The Book of Vices and Virtues, ed.
Francis, EETS 217, 1942, 19–21), though the distinction
between the powers of Fortune and those of Nature is
older (see Patch, Goddess Fortuna, 65–66, and 75, for
further references).
305   **jurdones:** Glass vessels with bulbous bodies and
rimmed necks, used by physicians; so called because of
their resemblance to flasks of the water from the River
Jordan brought from the Holy Land (see OED s.v. *Jordan* 1).
306   **ypocras . . . galiones:** Skeat (5:266) notes the
resemblance to the names of the medical authorities Hippocrates and Galen (cf. BD 571–72). *Ypocras* is a drink
made of wine and spices (see MerT IV.1807n.). *Galiones*
is not elsewhere recorded and may be a malapropism for
"Galen," often spelled *Galien;* however, Guy of Chauliac describes medicines that are "Galiens" (Cyrurgie,
EETS 265, 631, 636), and perhaps the reference is to
one of these. Despite January's use of *ypocras* and *lectuar-
ies* (MerT IV.1805–12), there is no reason to assume
with Tupper (JEGP 15, 1916, 56–106) that they are
here meant to be aphrodisiacs.
310   **Seint Ronyan:** Taken by Skeat (5:266–67) as a
reference to St. Ronan: the Pardoner's pronunciation in
line 320 (see n.) lends this some support. Haskell (Ch's
Saints, 17–25) argues for the appropriateness of this

The explanatory notes to the Pardoner's Introduction,
Prologue, and Tale were written by Christine Ryan Hilary.

saint, a Celt venerated in Brittany. However, the name
may be a popular variant pronunciation of "Ninian," a
Scottish saint widely known in the fourteenth century;
see Sledd, MS 13, 1951, 226–33. The OED offers no
support for Tupper's idea (JEGP 14, 1915, 257 n., and
15:66–67) that there is a pun on Fr. *rognan,* kidney, and
runnion, the male sexual organ; there are no citations for
this form before Shakespeare nor for this sense before
1635.
311   **in terme:** Cf. I.323.
313   **cardynacle:** A malapropism confusing *cardinal*
with *cardiacle,* "herte quakyng" (see Dempster, PMLA
68, 1953, 1152), which may be caused by melancholy
and for which "comfortives" should be given (Bartholomaeus Anglicus 7.32, tr. John of Trevisa 1:377–
78); hence, perhaps, the Host's need for a drink.
314   **By corpus bones:** The Host confuses "by Corpus
Domini" (By Our Lord's Body) with "by Christ's
Bones." Cf. MkPro VII.1906.
    triacle: Cf. Elliott, Rev. of Eng. Lit. 7, 1966, 61–73.
318   **beel amy:** "Fair friend," but most often used with
contemptuous or derisive overtones; see MED s.v. *bel
ami* (b).
320   **Ronyon** is here rhymed with *anon* and is apparently to be pronounced with two syllables, like "Ronan."
When the Host uses the word in VI.310, it rhymes with
man and has three syllables.
321–22   **alestake:** A pole projecting from a roadside
public house, decked with an evergreen garland, as a sign
that liquor is sold on the premises. For details concerning
such signs see Jusserand, Eng. Wayfaring Life in the
M. A., rev. ed., London, 1925, 132–33. Tupper (JEGP,
13, 1914, 553–65) understands this to mean that the
Pardoner's performance takes place in a tavern. The theory was attacked by Sedgewick (MLQ 1, 1940, 431–58)
and by Gordon H. Gerould (Ch Essays, 1952, 57–59),
who suggested that the *alestake* may be the Summoner
(see GP I.667) and that the *cake* in line 322 is the flat
circular piece of bread that he carries as a buckler. Gerould's explanation has been widely accepted, though it
is only speculation and has been rejected by some scholars (e.g., Baum, Ch: An Appreciation, 49; Howard, Idea
of CT, 164 n. 1). Nichols (PMLA 82, 1967, 498–504)
takes the cake and ale as a foreshadowing of the theme
of gluttony in the tale and an ironic reference to the
eucharist, a device, he argues, that unifies the Introduction, Prologue, and Tale.
324   Indulgence in ribald tales, not surprisingly, is a
trait associated with gluttony by medieval moralists; see,
for example, PP B 5.383 and C 7.433.

The Pardoner's Prologue and Tale

The Pardoner's Prologue and Tale, which will be discussed together here since they are so closely linked by
Chaucer, seem clearly to date from the Canterbury period. The use of Innocent III's *De miseria condicionis humane* (see 483 below) associates the work with the Man
of Law's Prologue, which is thought to have been written
around 1390. The work could probably not be any earlier than that, and its assured art has been taken as an
indication of a later date. The extensive use of Jerome's
Adversus Jovinianum associates this work with The Wife of
Bath's Prologue and The Merchant's Tale, and it is most

likely that it was composed at about the same time as those works, around the middle of the decade.

The Pardoner's Prologue, like that of the Wife of Bath, has the form of a "literary confession" and was most likely modeled on the confession of "Faus Semblaunt" in the *Roman de la rose* (11065–11974; the relevant passages are in S&A, 409–411; see Rom 6082–7292 and 403). On the use of the *Roman* here see Fansler, Ch and RR, 162–66; Currie, LeedsSE 4, 1970, 11–22; and especially Kean, Ch and Poetry 2:96–108, who discusses the development from the allegorical self-exposure of Faus Semblant to the greater naturalism of the Pardoner. On parallels with false religious confessions see Patterson, M&H 7, 2nd ser., 1976, 153–73.

The genre of the whole performance is problematical; the Pardoner offers it as an example of his preaching, and it has often been understood to be a sermon, including a brilliant exemplum framed by a fabliau-like situation; see Chapman (MLN 41, 1926, 506–9; Nancy Owen, JEGP 66, 1967, 541–49; Merrix, ChR 17, 1983, 235–49). Manly (CT, 614) identified in the prologue and tale three or four of the six usual parts of a formal sermon: the theme (VI.334); the protheme, a kind of introduction (lacking); the dilation on the text (lacking); the exemplum or illustrative anecdote (463–903); the peroration, or application (904–15); and the closing formula (perhaps 916–18). However, such formal divisions are characteristic of learned sermons (see intro. to ME Sermons, ed. Woodburn O. Ross, EETS 209, 1940, xliii–lv), and vernacular sermons were often looser in structure. Sedgewick (MLQ 1:431–58) argued that Chaucer had no intention of creating a sermon, and recent critics (Shain, MLN 70, 1955, 235–45; Wenzel, SP 73, 1976, 138–61; Gallick, Spec 50, 1975, 456–76) have agreed that the work employs the elements and techniques of a sermon but does not have its structure. The Pardoner's skill as a preacher has often been noted (see Elliott, REL 6, 1966, 61–73; and Knight, Sydney Sts. in Engl. 9, 1983–84, 21–36; for a qualified view see Cespedes, ELH 44, 1977, 1–18). The Pardoner's preaching has been found wanting by those who argue that it lacks spiritual insight (e.g., Ginsberg, Mediaevalia 2, 1976, 77–99), especially when compared to The Parson's Tale (Adelman, in Twentieth-Century Interpretations, ed. Dewey Faulkner, 1973, 103–6).

The sins that the Pardoner denounces—false oaths, gambling, gluttony—are the "tavern sins," a popular topic in medieval sermons (Owst, Lit and Pulpit, 425–49), in which, as in The Pardoner's Tale, the tavern is the scene of gluttony and gambling, which leads inevitably to blasphemy (417–18).

The story the Pardoner tells has the form of an exemplum and is generally regarded as one of Chaucer's most powerful narratives, a "matchless short-story" (Kittredge, Ch and His Poetry, 21). Kittredge's characterization is not altogether anachronistic, since the classic short story, the fabliau, and the exemplum are all dependent on the same sort of economy of narrative, with, in the case of the exemplum, didactic power (for a good analysis see Bishop, MAE 36, 1967, 15–24). The tale of the three rioters is based ultimately on a folk-tale of the *märchen* type (Aarne-Thompson, no. 763), and consequently it has many analogues, from ancient Buddhist, Persian, and other Oriental texts (see Clouston in Originals and Analogues), to African tales (see e.g., Hamer N&Q 214, 1969, 335–36), and even to Hollywood (Kirby, MLN 66, 1951, 269–70, cites *The Treasure of Sierra Madre*). Studies of such analogues are listed in Lynn K. Morris, Chaucer Source and Analogue Criticism, 1985, 156–59.

The story was common in medieval novelle and exempla (see Tupper, S&A, 415–23), and, though none of the surviving versions could have been Chaucer's direct source, they share enough common elements (the quest-for-death motif, the rioters' scorn for the old man, the mention of rats when the poison is purchased) to render it probable that Chaucer knew some related version (S&A, 415–16). The setting in Flanders (see 463–84 below), the theme of the plague (see Beidler, ChR 16, 1982, 257–69), and some aspects of the old man's character are unique to Chaucer's version.

In the analogues the figure who directs the young men to the treasure is sometimes Christ, sometimes a hermit or philosopher whose advanced age is implied but not much emphasized. Critics have associated Chaucer's old man with many figures: the Wandering Jew (Bushnell, SP 28, 1931, 450–60; Anderson, JEGP 45, 1946, 237–50); Elde, the messenger of Death (Ruggiers, Art of CT, 129); a personification of Death (Kittredge, Ch and His Poetry, 215; Dempster, Dramatic Irony, 77–78; see Thompson, Motif-Index C11 and Z111); even a realistic, individualized character (Owen, RES n.s. 2, 1951, 49–55). Steadman (MAE 33, 1964, 121–30) strikes a balance between the allegorical and literal readings, and many critics rightly warn against imposing a single narrow interpretation on the figure (e.g., A. C. Spearing, ed. PardPro and T, 1965, 40). For a summary of opinions see Hatcher, ChR 9, 1975, 250 n. 1. There has also been considerable debate over whether the old man represents good or evil. He has been seen both as a reflection of God's mercy and justice (Dean, ChR 3, 1968, 44–49; cf. Calderwood, ES 45, 1964, 306–7) and, on the other hand, as St. Paul's "vetus homo," fallen man (Miller, Spec 30, 1955, 180–99), or even as a devil (Olsen, NM 84, 1983, 367–71). Yet other critics have stressed the deliberate ambiguity of the figure; see, e.g., David, CE 27, 1965, 39–44; Schmidt, SFQ 30, 1966, 249–55; and Patterson, M&H 2nd ser., 7:153–73, who believes the figure embodies the Pardoner's own contradictions.

Many aspects of the tale have received critical attention, especially the religious symbolism (see, in addition to Miller, Spec 30:180–99; Nichols, PMLA 82:498–504; Delasanta, AnM 14, 1973, 43–52) and the tensions between appearance and reality, both literal and spiritual (see, e.g., Pittock, EIC 24, 1974, 107–23; Adelman, in Twentieth Century Interpretations, 96–106).

The main critical problems of this prologue and tale, however, are those raised by the Pardoner's motives and character. It was once believed that the Pardoner's performance took place in a tavern (see 321–22 above)—thus in the early morning, before the travelers had resumed their journey; the Pardoner's insistence on having a drink (VI.321–28) was therefore an indication that he, like the Miller in the General Prologue, is drunk. Older critics frequently offered this explanation for the extraordinary degree of self-revelation in his Prologue; for a summary of these views see McNamara, PMASAL 46, 1961, 597–98. The theory is still popular (see e.g.,

Ruggiers, Art of CT, 124; Spearing, ed., 22; Faulkner, in Twentieth Century Interpretations, 11), but it has been attacked by Elliott, Rev. of Eng. Lit. 6:63–64, and Halverson, ChR 4, 1970, 185–86, who point out that the text offers no support for the idea that the Pardoner is drunk. Some have seen the Pardoner's confession as too excessive to be believed and have argued that the Pardoner is indulging in self-parody (Calderwood, ES 45:-302–9) or an elaborate "put on" (Halverson, ChR 4: 196–97). Beichner argues instead that the Pardoner is simply trying to entertain his hearers (MS 25, 1963, 160–72). Yet others believe that he is motivated by a need for approval (Condren, Viator 4, 1973, 177–205), acceptance (McNamara, PMASAL 46:603–4), or compassion (David, Strumpet Muse, 201).

Such psychological explanations of the Pardoner have dominated criticism since the time of Kittredge, and he has been generally regarded as "the ultimate example of Chaucer's subtle handling of human psychology" (Ruggiers, Art of CT, 123); Howard's study (Idea of CT, 339–70) is the most important recent example of this approach. Objections to the excesses of the psychological approach have been raised, most recently by Pearsall (ChR 17, 1983, 358–65; see also Bronson, In Search of Ch, 79–87), and the idea that medieval literature has characters in the modern sense has been vigorously attacked (Robertson, Pref. to Chaucer, 34–37; cf. Morgan, MLR 71, 1976, 241–55). In an important essay, Kellogg (Spec 26, 1951, 465–85; rpt. in Ch, Langland, 245–68) studies the Pardoner as an exemplification of the Augustinian theory of sin, and Miller's exegetical study of the implications of the presentation of the Pardoner as a eunuch (Spec 30:180–99; see also Curry, Ch. and Science, 54–70) has been widely influential (see also Leicester, in Acts of Interpretation, 25–50).

The idea that the Pardoner is evil—the "one lost soul" on the Pilgrimage (Kittredge, Ch and His Poetry, 180)—is widely accepted (e.g., Huppé, Reading of CT, 209–20); to some he has seemed a personification of vice (Peterson, ChR 10, 1976, 326–36; Scheps, Acta IV, 1977, 107–23). Recent critics, such as Howard, have been more sympathetic toward him (see also McAlpine, PMLA 95, 1980, 8–22). Reiss (CE 25, 1964, 260–66) argues that he is misunderstood by the pilgrims, and Mitchell that, because of his lack of hypocrisy, he is their moral superior (CE 27, 1966, 437–44; see also Rhodes, ChR 17, 1982, 40–61).

The question of the Pardoner's motivation comes to focus on his attempt to sell his admittedly fake relics to the Host. Kittredge's explanation that the Pardoner suffers from a "paroxysm of agonized sincerity" is still widely quoted, but a great many other explanations have been offered (for summaries of opinions see Halverson, ChR 4:189–90; Reiss, CE 25:260–66). Lumiansky (Of Sondry Folk, 220) argues rather that the Pardoner has foolishly reverted to his usual sales pitch, and this has been taken as a gross insult to the pilgrims (Bronson, In Search of Ch, 86), an elaborate joke (Beichner, MS 25: 170–72), mere forgetfulness (Stockton, TSL 6, 1961, 56), and as a cynical attempt to reduce the pilgrimage to nonsense (Curtis, Crit. Rev. 11, 1968, 15–31). Howard (Idea of CT, 353) regards the Pardoner's offer of his relics as an extravagant gamble motivated perhaps by an unconscious will to lose. The Host's reaction has likewise been explained in a variety of ways—disgust at the Par-

doner's effrontery (Gerould, Essays, 71), an expression of the reader's feelings toward the Pardoner (Brewer, Chaucer, 159), and as an angry reaction to a personal attack (Kean, Ch and Poetry 2:104).

As the above shows, the critical bibliography is formidable and the range of disagreement broad indeed. The reviews by Sedgewick (MLQ 1:431–58) and Halverson (ChR 4:184–202), both of whom make valuable contributions of their own, are good starting points for the reader intent on studying this criticism. *Twentieth Century Interpretations of The Pardoner's Tale*, ed. Dewey Faulkner, 1973, contains excerpts from older criticism as well as some significant original essays.

The Pardoner's Prologue

331 For the phrasing, cf. Tr 2.1615 and Whiting B234.

333 **theme:** The biblical text for a sermon, often subdivided into three (as here: gluttony, gambling, swearing). See headnote.

334 *Radix malorum est Cupiditas:* 1 Tim. 6.10; cf. Mel VII.130. Morton W. Bloomfield (The Seven Deadly Sins, 1952, 74 and 95) notes that greed was increasingly seen as the root of evil in the later Middle Ages. Friend (MLQ 18, 1957, 305–8) argues that this is a dangerous text to choose: a secular clerk, Robert Lynclade, was arrested in 1395 by Richard II for using this text as a sermon against churchmen who preached for money. On the relation of this theme to gluttony, gambling, and swearing, see Robertson, Pref. to Ch, 332–34.

336 **bulles:** Bulls, papal letters (here indulgences) bearing the round leaden seal, or *bulla,* stamped with the figures of Sts. Peter and Paul on the obverse and the name of the pope who gave it on the reverse. Cf. Rom 6847.

337 Cf. PP B Pro 66–67: "Ther preched a Pardoner, as he a preest were/And broughte forthe a bull with bishopes seles." **Oure lige lordes** may also be the bishop, though Hamilton (JEGP 40, 1941, 70), agreeing with Brown (ed., 27), regards this as a royal seal.

patente: letter patent ("open," to be shown publicly; cf. GP I.315n.), containing the Pardoner's authorization.

342–43 Popes, cardinals, patriarchs, and bishops could all grant indulgences (Kellogg and Haselmayer, PMLA 66, 1951, 251–77). Patriarchs here are metropolitans such as those of Venice and Lisbon.

347–49 Owst (Preaching in Med. Engl., 109–10) quotes a contemporary sermon attacking "theves" who "with fals letters and seeles, with crosses and reliques that thei bere abowten them, . . . sei that thei be of seyntes bones or of holy mens clothinge, and bihoteth myche mede that will offre to hem." On the display of relics in sermons, see Owst, 349–51.

347 **cristal stones:** Cf. GP I.700. See, on the relation of *cristal stones* to lapidary lore, Henkin, Bull. of the Hist. of Medicine 10, 1941, 504–12.

350 **latoun:** See GP I.699n. On the use of a sheep's bone in divination (spatelmancy), see ParsT X.602, Higden's Polychronicon, tr. John of Trevisa 1.cap.60, and Andersen, NM 75, 1974, 630–39.

351 **hooly Jewes:** The epithet *hooly* has led to attempts to identify this Jew with one who lived before the incarnation; Skeat (5:271) suggests Jacob (Gen. 30.31–43), noting this would add force to VI.365; others (Rutter,

MLN 43, 1928, 536) suggest Gideon (Judges 6.13–40). Henkin (MLN 55, 1940, 254–59) argues that no specific individual is intended and that the reference is rather to the common association of Jews with magic. Andersen (NM 75:630–39) discusses the use of relics as part of agrarian witchcraft, appropriate to the Pardoner's rural audience.

372   miteyn: Said by Brown (ed. PardT, 28) to be a mitten worn by farmers when sowing grain.

377   For analogues to the trick of telling parishioners that sinners may not offer to his relics, see Whiting, MLN 51, 1936, 322–27, and S&A, 411–13; see also 652 below on the blood of Hayles, which was visible only to the truly penitent.

390   A mark was worth two-thirds of a pound (13s. 4d.). In his last years Chaucer himself had official annuities amounting to only £46 13s. 4d. (Ch Life Records, 533), considerably less than the Pardoner's claimed income. Baugh (Ch's Maj. Poetry, xv) estimates that in his most affluent years Chaucer's annual income was about £99.

391   lyk a clerk: Beichner (MS 25:160–72) argues that this implies the Pardoner is not a cleric. His clerical status is uncertain (see introduction to notes to his portrait in the General Prologue).

392   doun yset: Manly (CT, 614) notes that this and Gower, Mirour de l'omme, 5245–56, show that there were seats in English churches for the congregation, though none have survived.

397   Cf. MilT I.3258. Huppé (Reading of CT, 213) finds an allusion to the Holy Ghost; see also Rowland, N&Q 209, 1964, 48–49.

403   See Rom 6837 (RR 11565; S&A 410). Morgan (MLR 71:241–55) agrees with Brusendorff (Ch Trad, 402–4) that Chaucer followed the English Romaunt rather than RR here and at VI.407–08 and 443–44.

406   a-blakeberyed: Play truant (Cross, RES, n.s., 2, 1951, 372–74). Kökeritz (cited in Baum, PMLA 71, 1956, 231) finds this a pun on beryed (buried) (VI.405) and blakeberyed. Skeat (5:272–74) explains the form as based on an analogy with forms such as ME an hunteth, ahunted, from OE on huntoþ, with the ME forms in -ed taken as past participles rather than as abstract nouns (OE suffix -oþ, as in modern strength, etc.). Cf. III.354, V.1580, and (without a-) III.1778.

407–8   Parallel to Rom 5763–64 (RR 5113–14); cf. 403 above. See also Rom 5745–57, discussed by Morgan, MLR 71:241–55. Jungmann (Ch Newsletter 1, 1979, 16–17) compares Augustine (De doctrina 4.27.59), who says that the wicked may preach what is right and good. Yet contemporary opinion held that a preacher must be of good character. Cf. Mirk's Instructions for Parish Priests, EETS 31, 19–68; GP I.505–6.

415–20   Cf. SumT III.2212 for another example of a preacher's using the pulpit for revenge.

416   my bretheren: This suggests to some readers that the Pardoner is a mendicant friar (see Hamilton, JEGP 40:48–72); cf. 391 above; VI.443; and GP I.683n.

435   ensamples: Exempla, illustrative anecdotes used by preachers, found in collections such as Petrus Alphonsus, Disciplina clericalis (c. 1110); Robert Holkot, Libri sapientiae (c. 1340); and the Gesta Romanorum (c. 1300).

441   in poverte wilfully: see WBT III.1178–79 and n.

443–44   Cf. Rom 6845–46 (RR 11571–72; S&A, 410).

445   Cf. PP B 15.263–70. Both Chaucer's text and

Langland's seem to confuse St. Paul the Apostle, a tent-maker, with St. Paul the Hermit, who appears in medieval art clad in a mat of palm-leaves (see Jerome, Vita S. Pauli, PL 23:27). However, these passages very likely derive from Jerome, Ad rusticum, advising him to "weave a little basket from rushes, or weave a basket from supple osiers" by way of providing for himself (CSEL 56:130). See Hemingway, MLN 32, 1917, 57–58; Pratt, Expl 21, 1962, Item 14; and Fleming, Christianity and Lit. 28, 1979, 21–22, who argues there is no confusion here.

447–48   See Mark 6.7–10.

The Pardoner's Tale

463–84   For the Flemish setting cf. S&A, 437. Manly (CT, 619) suggests that Chaucer set the tale in Flanders because of the Flemings' reputation for drunkenness; for English attitudes toward Flanders, see Norris, PMLA 48, 1933, 636–41. Morgan (MLR 71:241–55) finds the company of young folk given to excess reminiscent of Rom 4925–28, but the resemblance is slight.

468–71   For the conception of gluttony in the Middle Ages and its links with blasphemy and heresy, esp. in Chaucer and Gower, see Yeager, SP 81, 1984, 42–55. Lewis, ed. 1978, 8, notes possible parallels in lines 467–69 and 481–82 to Innocent III, De miseria condicionis humane 2.18.11–12[46] and 12[47].

470   develes temple: Cf. The Ayenbit of Inwit (S&A, 438): "The taverne ys the scole of the dyeuele . . . and his oghene chapele . . . ther huer he maketh his miracles . . . vor huanne the glotoun geth in the taverne he geth opright, huanne he comth a-yen, he ne heth not thet him moghe sostyeni ne bere." Cf. Jacob's Well (S&A, 438); the Ménagier de Paris, 1.48; Tupper JEGP 13: 553–65.

474–75   Cf. ParsT X.591; EpiMLT II.1171 and n.

479   wafereres: Cf. MilT I.3379 and n. According to OED (s.v. waferer), wafereres were apparently employed as go-betweens and bawds.

481–82   Association of lechery and gluttony, and of wine and lust, is commonplace; cf. PF 275–76n. and 468–71 above.

483   hooly writ: Lat. gloss: "And do not become drunk with wine, in which is lechery" (Eph. 5.18), quoted from Innocent III, De miseria 2.19.12–13, which work Chaucer probably translated as the lost Of the Wrecched Engendrynge of Mankynde (cf. LGW G 414–15 and Lewis, ed., 1978, 20–30). Skeat (3:444–45) notes parallels between Innocent's work and VI.485–87 (2.20.1[48]); 505–7 (2.18.5–7[49]); 513–16 and 521–23 (2.17.21–26[50]); 517–20 (2.17.2–5, 14[51]); 534–36 (2.18.2–5); 537–46 (2.17.5–14[52]); 547–48 (2.17.19–21[53]); 549–50 (2.19.14[54]); 551–52 and 560–61 (2.19.1–4[55]). See also Skeat 3:444–45.

485   Looth: See Gen. 19.30–36. Langland uses Lot as an example of drunkenness and lechery in Piers Plowman B I.27–33. See 483 above.

488   Herodes: Herod and Lot are listed together as examples of drunkenness in Piers Plowman, ed. Skeat, C 11.176–79. Stories may refer to the Historia evangelica, part of the Historia scholastica of Peter Comestor (Skeat 5.278; Taitt, N&Q 216, 1971, 284–85). Robinson doubted this, since Peter's account of Herod does not mention his drunkenness (PL 198:1574–75). Brown (ed., 32) believes the reference is to the expanded version in Vincent of Beauvais, *Speculum historiale* 7.22, where it is specified that Herod "diem natalis sui super bibiendo celebravit." *Stories* could also refer to the biblical account (Matt. 14.3–12, Mark 6.17–29), though the drunkenness of Herod is not mentioned. Cf. GP I.709.

492   Senec: Identified in the gloss as Seneca, from whose epistle 83.18 lines 493–97 are roughly translated. Ayers (RomR 10, 1919, 5–7) finds further reminiscences of Seneca (esp. from Epist. 95.19–25) in VI.513–548. Skeat finds parallels instead in Innocent's *De contemptu mundi* (esp. 2.17, 18), which he believes reflect Chaucer's prose translation (see PL 218:723 and Skeat 3:445, where the relevant passages are printed).

498   For gluttony associated with taverns, see PP B 5.296–305 and 470 above.

504–11   Cf. SumT III.1915–16, ParsT X.819.

505   From Jerome, Adv. Jov. 2.15 (PL 23:305).

508–11   Lat. gloss: "Jeronimus contra Jovinianum: 'Quamdiu jejunavit Adam in Paradiso/fuit: comedit et ejecit est statim duxit uxorem' " (Adv. Jov. 2.15), translated in the text. Cf. ParsT X.819.

512–16   Cf. Ecclus. 37.29–31: "Do not be greedy for every delicacy or eat without restraint. For illness is a sure result of overeating, and gluttony is next door to colic. Gluttony has been the death of many; be on your guard and prolong your life." Brown (ed., 32) compares VI.513–14 to Seneca, Epist. 95.19: "Many courses make for many diseases."

517–20   Cf. Jerome, Adv. Jov. 2.8: "Because of the brief pleasure of the throat lands and seas are ransacked" (PL 23:297). See 483 above.

522–23   Lat. gloss: "Meat for the belly, and the belly for meat, but God shall destroy both the one and the other" (1 Cor. 6.13). See 483 above.

527–28   Jerome, Adv. Jov. 2.17.

529–35   Lat. gloss: "Ad Philipenses capitulo 3°" (Phil. 3.18–19; cf. ParsT X.820). See also 483 above.

538–39   Cf. Innocent III, De miseria 2.17.5–14[52]: "Alius contundit et colat, alius confundit et conficit, substantiam vertit in accidens, naturam mutat in artem." The "substance into accident" figure (the essential nature and the outward quality by which a thing is identified and apprehended) as applied to cookery appears also in Latin Poems Commonly Attributed to Walter Map, page liii: "fiant per accidents quod esse non potuere per substantiam." Robinson notes that Chaucer could hardly have failed to relate this to the controversy over transubstantiation, a lively topic in Chaucer's time (Manly, CT, 619), and to have been reminded of Wyclif's facetious remark that the faithful should forbid friars to enter their cellars lest the wine be transubstantiated into nothing (Wyclif, Sermones, ed. Iohann Loserth, Wyclif Soc., 1887–90, 194). On allusions to the Eucharist in the work, see Nichols, PMLA 82: 501–2. Cf. Tr 4.1505 n.

547–48   Lat. gloss: "[She] who lives in pleasure is dead while living" (1 Tim. 5.6). Quoted in Jerome (Brown, ed., 34).

549–50   Lat. gloss: "Luxuriosa res vinum et contumeliosa ebrietas" (Prov. 20.1, with "contumeliosa" for Vulgate "tumultosa," as in Jerome, Adv. Jov. 2.10 [PL 23: 299]). Lewis notes it is also quoted by Innocent. See 483 above.

554–55   Sampsoun: Sampson, as a Nazarite, abstained from wine (Judges 13.5 and Num. 6.3). Skeat suggests the name was chosen for its sound and that it should be pronounced with a nasal intonation.

558–59   Cf. MLT II.773–74, ParsT X.822.

560–61   Proverbial; cf. Mel VII.1194n. See 483 above.

564–66   Fysshstrete: Fish Hill Street, off Thames Street, just below London Bridge. **Chepe:** probably Cheapside, one of the principal shopping streets in the London of Chaucer's day (cf. I.754 and n.), though here perhaps Eastcheap; see Magoun, Ch Gazetteer, 105–6.

565–71   That the wine of Spain could creep subtly into other wines produced nearby is a reference to the illegal diluting of better wines with cheaper varieties, a practice common enough that in the Liber albus, 615–18, there are regulations specifying that different kinds of wine are to be kept in different cellars. Manly (CT, 619) quotes Letter Book H. 145 on the price of wines from Bordeaux (**Burdeux**) and La Rochelle (**Rochele**) set at ten pence, and wines from Spain, such as those produced at **Lepe** (northwest of Cadiz), set at eight pence. See further Hench, MLN 52, 1937, 27–28. Bronson (In Search of Ch, 82) takes the reference to adulterating wines as a dig at the Host.

579   Attila, king of the Huns, died (453) of a nosebleed brought on by excessive drinking on a night when he had just wed a new wife; see Jordanes, *De getarum gestis,* 49, and Paul the Deacon, *De Gestis Romanorum,* 15.

584   Lamuel: Lat. gloss: "Noli vinum dare," from Prov. 31.4: "Do not to kings, O Lamuel, do not to kings give wine, for there is no secret where drunkenness reigns." For the rhetorical device used here, see Geoffrey of Vinsauf, *Poetria nova,* 668–86.

591   Lat. gloss: "Policraticus, Book I: 'Dicing is the mother of lies and perjuries' " (John of Salisbury, Policraticus 1.5).

603   Stilboun: Chaucer draws the story in VI.603–20 from John of Salisbury's Policraticus 1.5.1 (S&A, 438) but substitutes *Stilboun* for Chilon. Some MSS (not in the Ellesmere or Hengwrt traditions of glossing) gloss the name with "i.e., Mercurius," since this is the Greek name ($\sigma\tau\iota\lambda\beta\omega\nu$) for that planet. But Chaucer may have been thinking of the philosopher Stilbo, mentioned in Seneca Epist. 9, 18–19, 10.1 (Ayers, RomR 10:5) or in Seneca's Dialogues 2.5.6 (Hinckley, Notes on Ch, 175–76).

621   Demetrius: His story appears in John of Salisbury's Policraticus 1.1.5 (S&A, 438), immediately following that of Chilon (Chaucer's *Stilboun*).

622   Parthes: See Magoun, Ch Gazetteer, 123.

631–32   Cf. ParsT X.600n. Swearing is associated with gluttony in PP B 2.92–93, 6.92, 5.314, and 13.400. Drunkenness, a branch of gluttony, was associated with gambling. See Tupper, JEGP 13:553–65; Owst, Lit and Pulpit, 414–25.

631–50   Cf. ParsT X.587–93 and 474–75 above.

633–34   Mathew: Lat. gloss: "Do not swear at all" (Matt. 5.34).

635   Lat. gloss: "Jeremiah 4: 'You shall swear in truth, in judgment, and in righteousness' " (Jer. 4.2, omitting "that the Lord lives" after "swear"). The same text is quoted in ParsT X.592 (Brown, ed., 36).

639   the firste table: The first three commandments, setting forth the duties owed to God, the other seven being those owed to mankind; see Dives and Pauper, EETS 275, 1:304.

641   seconde heeste: "Thou shalt not take the Lord's

name in vain" (reckoned as the third commandment in most Protestant usages).

649–50 Ecclus. 23.11 has "A man given to swearing is lawless to the core; the scourge will never be far from his house . . . his house will be filled with trouble."

651 **nayles:** Either Christ's fingernails or the nails of the cross. The former seems most likely in the light of Wyclif (Select Engl. Works 3.483): "It is not leeful to swere . . . by Godds bonys, sydus, naylus, ne arms, or by ony membre of Cristis body, as tho moste dele of men usen." As Skeat notes (5:284), however, the rioters were probably not concerned with the distinction.

652 **Hayles:** Hayles Abbey in Gloucestershire, founded in 1246, where there was a vial containing what was said to be the blood of Christ; the blood was visible only to those with pure consciences; see Horstmann, Altenglische Legenden, 275–81.

653 **chaunce:** In the game of hazard (*hasard,* VI.465), which is played with two dice, the thrower calls a number (his "main") and throws the dice; if his main appears, he wins; if two aces (*ambes as*), ace-deuce, or (if seven is the main) twelve appear, he loses; if seven is the main an eleven will also win, as will a twelve if six is the main. If any other number appears on the first roll, this is the thrower's *chaunce,* and the thrower casts the dice until either his *chaunce* appears and he wins, or his main reappears and he loses (see Charles Cotton, The Compleat Gamester, 1674, ed. in Games and Gamesters of the Restoration by Cyril H. Hartman, 1930, 82–84). Obviously modern "craps" is "hazard" with seven always the main. In this case the speaker's main was eight (**cink and trey**); on his first throw he cast a seven, which is now his winning number, his *chaunce,* while an eight will win for his opponent. For accounts of medieval dicing see Deschamps (Oeuvres 7:253–65 and 4:286–87) and Franz Semrau (Würfel und Würfelspiel im alten Frankreich, Beih. zur ZRP, 23, 1910).

656 **bicched bones:** "Cursed dice" (MED s.v. *bicched* ppl). Brown (MLN 23, 1908, 126) compares "ossibus caninis" (dog's bones), used for "dice" by Vincent of Beauvais in *Speculum morale* 3.8.4, though it is not clear whether this refers to the material of which the dice were made or is also an opprobrious epithet.

661 Sometimes taken as a clumsy transition back to the tale of the rioters; for a refutation see Osselton, ES 49, 1968, 37–38.

662 **prime:** The first of the canonical hours (cf. GP I.122n.); the bell is rung at 6 A.M. for the singing of the office of prime.

664–65 Skeat (5:286) notes the custom of ringing a handbell before a corpse on its way to burial and cites Mirk's Instructions for Parish Priests, EETS 31, line 1964.

679 **pestilence:** Possible reference to the plagues of 1348–50, 1361–62, 1376, and 1379, though there were minor outbreaks throughout the century. For contemporary accounts of riotous behavior in plague times, see Philip Ziegler, The Black Death, 1969, 160, 164, and 270–71; for the decline of morals after the plague, see Élisabeth Carpentier, Une ville devant la peste: Orvieto et la Peste Noir de 1348, 1962, 195–96; both are cited in Beidler's discussion of the plague background to The Pardoner's Tale, ChR 16, 1982, 257–69. For a contemporary description of the plague, see Boccaccio, *Decameron,* 1, intro., and PP B 20.52–182. The hospital at

Charing Cross (see GP I.670 and n.) was particularly hard hit.

710 Cf. Hosea 13.4 and PP B 18.35.

713 **oold man:** On the literary definition of old age in Chaucer's day, see Lowes, PMLA 20, 1905, 782–85; Coffman, MLN 52, 1937, 25–26; and Philip, MLN 53, 1938, 181–82. See also 727–36 below.

717–20 Morgan (MLR 71:241–55) finds a source for the hostility of the rioters toward the old man in Rom 2925–28, 4955–58, 4961; Harris (SFQ 33, 1969, 24–38) cites Old Norse analogues; but this may have been part of the story as Chaucer received it (cf. the contempt for the old man shown by Tagliagambe in the Rappresentazione di Sant' Antonio, S&A, 423–24).

719 The contemporary Geoffrey le Baker writes "The pestilence seized especially the young and strong, commonly sparing the elderly and feeble." Other chroniclers say the same (Beidler, ChR 16:260).

721–24 Cf. Rom 4964–66.

722 **Ynde:** Cf. WBPro III.824n.

727–36 The Old Man's desire for death is not found in any of the analogues; it is based on the first elegy of Maximian, in which the aged man knocks on the ground and pleads, "Receive me, mother, take pity on the hardships of age; I seek to warm my tired bones in your bosom" (vv. 227–28; S&A, 437). Chaucer may have read Maximian in school (Coffin, Spec 9, 1934, 269–71). Nitecki (ChR 16, 1981, 76–84) shows that the lament of an old man, based on Maximian's elegy, was the subject of a number of Middle English poems; she notes the closest analogue is "Le regret de Maximian," in Carleton Brown, Rel. Lyrics of XIII Cent., 1932, 92–100.

730 Steadman (N&Q 5, 1958, 323) derives the knocking on the gate, not in Maximian, from a Spanish proverb.

743–44 Lat. gloss: "Stand up in the presence of a gray head" [and honor the face of an old man] (Lev. 19.32).

745 Cf. Ecclus. 8.6: "Despise no man for being old."

765 **ook:** The oak does not appear in the analogues. Candeleria (MLN 71, 1956, 321–22) connects this with the ancient folk custom of burying an image of death under an oak tree. Chaucer was robbed in 1390 at a place called "fowle ok" in Kent, an execution site (Kuhl, MLN 36, 1921, 157–59, and Ch Life Records, 477–89). Collette (ChR 19, 1984, 39–45) argues that the oak is a complex exegetical symbol of death and idolatry.

770 **floryns:** Either coins in general or German or Flemish florins, worth three shillings and struck in imitation of the Florentine florin, the standard gold coin of the later Middle Ages. An English florin was minted briefly in 1344 but then recalled and replaced by the "noble" (Baker, Spec 36, 1961, 282–86).

779 "Treasure is believed to be a gift of Fortune . . . of ancient time it was by natural law the property of the finder, [but] it is now by the law of nations the property of the lord king himself" (Henri de Bracton, De legibus et consuetudinibus Angliae, ed. George E. Woodbine, 1915–42, 2:338–39). This is quoted by Roache (JEGP 64, 1965, 1–6), who shows that the rioters commit theft by keeping the treasure.

781 Proverbial; Whiting C384.

793 See GP I.835.

845 On poison lore see Hallissy, MSE 9, 1983, 54–63.

848   he hadde leve: On God's permitting the devil to tempt an individual, see Job 1.2, 2.6 and cf. FrT III.1482–96.

889–90   Avycen: Avicenna, the authority on medicine (see GP I.432 and note 429–34), whose work included **canons** or rules of procedure; in his book a chapter is called a **fen** (Arabic *fann,* a division of a science). His work treats of poisons in Bk. 4, Fen 6.

907   nobles: First struck in the reign of Edward III, they were worth six shillings eight pence (Baker, Spec 36: 284–86, with illustrations).

sterlynges: The name is said to derive from the Easterlings, Norwegians and Danes, once brought to England to undertake the purification of the minting of English money (Drennen and Wyatt, ed. PardT, 79).

916   Cf. Psalms 146.3 (A.V. 147.3).

946   On complicit audiences' sharing the guilt of fraudulent pardoners, see Mitchell, CE 27:437–44.

949   Knapp (ELH 39, 1972, 1–26) suggests there is an allusion here to the hair breeches worn by St. Thomas, an object of veneration at Canterbury.

951   On St. Helen's discovery of the cross, see Acta Sanctorum, 18 Aug.

952–53   Possibly an echo of RR 7108–9 where there is a word play on "coillons" and "reliques" (**relikes**). This is usually taken as a crude reference to the Pardoner's eunuchry (e.g., Curry, Ch and Science, 67), but cf. GP I.691 and n. Baum (Ch, 54) and Faulkner (Twentieth-Century Interpretations, 11) argue that this indicates that the Pardoner is not a eunuch.

953   seintuarie: Taken by the OED as "shrine," but perhaps here rather "sacred relic" as in Roman de Troie, 25515; Cligés, 1194–96; Yvain, 6630–33.

968   they kiste: They exchange the kiss of peace as a formal sign of reconciliation; on the custom see Nicholas J. Perella, The Kiss: Sacred and Profane, 1969, 130. Some critics have doubted that the Host and Pardoner are actually reconciled; see Burlin, Ch Fiction, 169–75.

FRAGMENT VII

Fragment VII usually follows Fragment VI in the MSS with the Ellesmere order, but in the Chaucer Society order, which Skeat adopted for his edition, VII was joined with II, forming Fragment B, to correct a geographical inconsistency (see VII.1926 and n. and the introduction to the textual notes to *The Canterbury Tales*). Seventeen MSS contain lines linking The Pardoner's Tale with the Shipman's, and three other MSS contain lines that link The Nun's Priest's Tale with the Second Nun's Prologue and Tale (see textual notes to VI.944 and EpiNPT), but both links are clearly spurious.

Fragment VII is the longest and most varied of the fragments and lacks any very clear unifying theme. Paull F. Baum (Ch: A Crit. Appreciation, 1958, 74–84) argues that the tales of this fragment form a "Surprise Group," since, though the tellers tell stories that on reflection are seen to fit their characters, they often surprise the Host's expectations. Bernard F. Huppé (A Reading of CT, 1964, 231) emphasizes the dramatic refusal of the clergy to provide the Host with the sort of "mirth" he demands. Gaylord (PMLA 82, 1967, 226–35) suggests instead that the tales form a "literary group," with Harry Bailly acting as a kind of editor. Howard (Idea of CT,

271–88) finds rather a sort of "retrospective" unity supplied by The Nun's Priest's Tale read as a skeptically ironic comment on the tales that have gone before. Though the tales that make up the fragment are of varying dates of composition, the fragment itself was assembled rather late in the composition of *The Canterbury Tales* (see Dempster, PMLA 68, 1953, 1142–59) and perhaps never received a final revision.

LARRY D. BENSON

The Shipman's Tale

The Host's words to the *gentil maryneer,* which follow this tale (VII.435–42), show Chaucer intended it for the Shipman. The textual history of EpiMLT II.1179, however, suggests that the tale may originally have been intended for another narrator (see note to that line). Furthermore, the pronouns *we* and *us* suggest a married female speaker. The tale may therefore have been originally intended for the Wife of Bath (Lawrence, Spec 33, 1958, 56–68, and Pratt, Sts. in Hon. of Baugh, 45–79). However, the Shipman may be mimicking a female speaker; see Copland (MAE 35, 1966, 25–26), comparing Skelton's *Magnificence,* 461.

The tale is a fabliau, like others of the *Tales,* but "nearer to the pure fabliau-type" (Brewer, in Companion to Ch, 259). The setting in St.-Denis, the snatch of French at VII.214 and several oaths might suggest a French source; but the nearest known French analogue is not very close: *Le bouchier d'Abevile* (Benson and Andersson, Lit. Context, 282–311). The story belongs to a well-known folktale type, "the lover's gift regained": see J. W. Spargo, Ch's ShipT, The Lover's Gift Regained, FFC 91, 1930, and S&A, 439–46. The closest extant analogue is Boccaccio's *Decameron* 8.1 (8.2 is a similar story). A version preserved in Sercambi's Novella 19 (text and trans. in Benson and Andersson, Lit. Context, 312–19) perhaps gave Chaucer some ideas (see Pratt, MLN 55, 1940, 142–45). Guerin (ES 52, 1971, 412–19) suggests that he used all three Italian versions. If these were Chaucer's sources, however, he altered a great deal—particularly the ending where, in his version, the merchant's wife excuses herself with a ready answer (VII.400–426).

Uncertainty about the tale's narrator and the lack of any definite source have contributed to difficulties of interpretation. Lawrence (Spec 33:56–68) compares the tale with its analogues, and finds in Chaucer's untypical ending a profeminist tendency; but Tupper sees only the standard antifeminism (JEGP 33, 1934, 352–72). The tale may be read as simply cynical, "an immoral tale told by an immoral man" (Howard, Idea of CT, 273); but Richardson (Blameth Nat Me, 100–122) finds traditional Christian standards "embedded in the imagery," by which the behavior of the characters is measured and found wanting. According to Silverman (PQ 32, 1953, 329–36) the equation in the tale between sex and money shows that in the Shipman's world human relations are reduced to the level of financial transactions. Many critics see a basic irony directed at the merchant in the tale (e.g.,

The explanatory notes to The Shipman's Tale were written by J. A. Burrow and V. J. Scattergood.

Dempster, Dramatic Irony in Ch, 1932, 39–42). He is "a success as a merchant and a failure as a human being" (Craik, Comic Tales, 50). But Stillwell (RES 20, 1944, 1–18) points out that the merchant has such admirable characteristics as "substantiality, prosperousness, probity perhaps, and sober good manners"; and Scattergood (ChR 11, 1977, 210–31) sees the tale as a sympathetic but not uncritical examination of the bourgeois mercantile ethos.

1   **Seint-Denys:** Saint-Denis, north of Paris, famous for its abbey and fair. The cloth trade was carried on there in the fourteenth century. Perhaps the *ware* in which the merchant dealt (VII.56) was cloth: see OED s.v. *ware* sb³ 3b., though this meaning is first recorded in 1442.

4–19   Compare WBPro III.337–56 and 543–62; but neither passage mentions cost, the main point here. On the pronouns suggesting a feminine speaker in VII.12, 14, 18, 19, see introductory note.

9   Proverbial; see MerT IV.1315n.

13   The wife claims here and at VII.421 that she dresses extravagantly to manifest her husband's social status; see Thrupp, Merchant Class, 147–50.

20   **heeld a worthy hous:** MED s.v. *holden* v. (1) 15(b).

22   **largesse:** A noble quality not always characteristic of merchants in medieval literature. This merchant's *largesse* appears at VII.281–86 (see Copland, MAE 35: 17–23), though he uses *large* reproachfully (431) and his wife complains of his *nygardye* (172).

26   **a thritty wynter:** About thirty years (the age of Youth in Parlement of the Thre Ages 133; cf. *yonge,* VII.28). On this use of the indefinite article, see Language and Versification, p. xxxix.

29   **the goode man:** The master of the house; see MED s.v. *god man* phr. and n. 2(a). Compare VII.33, 107, and *goode weyf* at 92 and cf. SumT III.1768. The phrase is used quite frequently in contexts of cuckoldry: "Ye xall goo . . . Onto the goodewyff when the goodeman ys owte" (Mankind, ed. Eccles, EETS 262, 1969, 703–4); cf. Tilley G332.

35   **village:** The word suggests humble origins for both men; compare ClT IV.483.

36   **cosynage:** The words *cosyn* and *cosynage* are frequent in the tale. Though Fisher (N&Q 210, 1965, 168–70) argues for a pun on *cozen,* "cheat," that word is not recorded before 1453 (MED s.v. *cosin* n.).

38   A proverbial comparison (Whiting F561); cf. VII.51 and KnT I.2437n. In Chaucer it usually "connotes a trust that turns out to be misplaced" (Scattergood, ChR 11:211).

42   **bretherhede:** In KnT, Palamon and Arcite are both cousins by birth (cf. VII.36) and sworn brothers: see KnT I.1132n.

43   **daun John:** Practically a generic name for a cleric: compare ProMkT VII.1929 and see EpiMLT II.1172 and n.

     manly: Generous (compare Piers Plowman B 5.257, 10.90); cf. GP I.167. See Donaldson, in Geoffrey Ch, ed. Brewer, 106–7: "the adjective *manly* does double duty for the monk's generosity and his virility."

51   Cf. 38 above.

55   **Brugges:** Bruges, the great Flemish mercantile center where many alien merchants had dealings. See van Houtte, Econ. Hist. Rev. 19, 2nd Ser., 1966, 29–47.

65–66   **officer:** The monk holds some office in his mon-

astery, probably that of cellarer, which requires him to do business with the outside world (compare VII.272–73). See Ussery, TSE 17, 1969, 13–26. The cellarer would normally supervise monastic **graunges**; see Colin Platt, The Monastic Grange in Med. England, 1969, 12. John is, like the Monk on the pilgrimage, *an outridere* (GP I.166n.).

69   **Oure deere cosyn:** The "domestic *our*" (see WBPro III.311n.) is unusually frequent in this tale; see also VII.107, 356, 363.

70–71   **malvesye:** Malmsey, a sweet wine originally produced at Monemvasia in the Morea (*malvesie* in French). **vernage:** Probably a white Italian wine (*vernaccia).* See Curye on Inglysch, EETS, SS 8, 1985, 221.

79   **thilke yeer:** The merchant apparently draws up his annual accounts before setting off on his principal buying trip.

91   See 131 below.

95–97   Like other gentlewomen, merchants' wives sometimes had a girl to wait on them. Thrupp (Merchant Class, 151) quotes the demands of a retired tailor to his son: "At all due tymes whan that I or my wyf walketh oute that my said sone shall late me have an honest man chyld to wayte upon me and an honest mayde chyld to wayte upon my wyf."

104–5   This perhaps implies a contrast between monks' virility and laymen's feebleness; cf. ProMkT VII.1945–61.

108   **laboured:** Compare MerT IV.1842.

111   Compare Tr 2.652.

113   **God woot al:** A proverbial expression (Whiting G245), here suggesting that the truth is different.

131   **portehors:** Chaucer probably wrote this trisyllabic French form here and at 135 (though the MSS have *porthors, portos,* etc.). This restoration makes for a regular ten-syllable line and adds a touch of local color (compare 214). A *portehors* is a breviary that priests carry (*porte)* out (*hors)* with them. This monk has just said his devotions (*thynges,* VII.91) from it.

136   Perhaps an allusion to the fate of *Genylon of France* (194), torn apart by four warhorses for betraying Roland at Roncesvalles (Chanson de Roland 3964ff). Compare BD 1121; and MkT VII.2389; NPT VII.3227.

145   **legende:** Properly the story of the life and sufferings (compare VII.146) of a saint. The wife dramatizes herself as a "martyr" to her husband; see Thro, ChR 5, 1970, 106–8.

148   **Seint Martyn:** St. Martin, bishop of Tours (d. 397), founder of the first monastery in Gaul.

151   **Seint Denys:** St. Denis (Dionysius), bishop of Paris and patron saint of France (d. 272). His remains were preserved in the monastery at Saint-Denis, so the reference is particularly apt.

155   **professioun:** Monastic vows (which included chastity). The monk prepares for his assignation on the Sabbath (VII.307) by having his tonsure (which marked his acceptance of monastic vows) and beard *al fressh and newe yshave* (309).

158–71   Compare WBPro III.531–42 and WBT III.961–80 (especially III.979–80 with VII.159–60).

171   Proverbial: Whiting F345. On the theme of male sexual inadequacy in French fabliaux see Nykrog, Les fabliaux, 189. But VII.377–79 suggest that the wife is lying.

173–77   Compare NPT VII.2912–17 (2914 resembles

176 here) and WBT III.1258–64 (1259 resembles 177 here), and also WBT III.925–48. But none of these passages numbers the qualities desired in a husband. Perhaps the hexadic form derives indirectly from Irish lists of "the six excellences": see Smith, Journal of Celtic Studies 1, 1949–50, 98–104.

181   An hundred frankes: About £15 sterling, a considerable sum. The "franc à cheval" was first issued in 1360, and established itself as a common French gold coin in Chaucer's lifetime, valued at approximately half an English noble (i.e., 3s 4d).

194 See 136 above.

202–3 For another courtly speech accompanied by an indecorous embrace, see MilT I.3277–81.

205–6 Dinner was usually taken some time between pryme (9 A.M.) and noon: compare Tr 2.1095 and 1163, 2.1555–60, 5.1129–30. Monks' liking for food was a satirical commonplace; compare GP I.206 and see Mann, Ch and Estates, 18–20 and 34–35.

chilyndre: "A portable sun dial in the shape of an upright cylinder with a conical top" (MED s.v. *chilindre*). Two thirteenth-century treatises on the instrument are edited by E. Brock in Essays on Chaucer 1, Ch Soc, 1868, and 2, Ch Soc, 1874. Thorndike lists other descriptions: Isis 13, 1929, 51–52.

214   *Quy la*: This is Chaucer's only use of foreign speech in a foreign setting as local color (contrast SumT III.1832, 1838).

Peter: The wife swears by St. Peter, the porter of heaven, in the face of the locked door (see 85). Compare Sir Gawain and the Green Knight, 813.

219   Goddes sonde: The wife piously suggests that her husband be content with what God provides.

224–48 Merchants were notorious worriers about their property and profits. Compare VII.76 and Winner and Waster, ed. I. Gollancz, 1921, rpt. 1974, 246–62; and for a preacher's disapproval, see Owst, Lit and Pulpit, 352. See also Stillwell, RES 20:1–18. Cf. GP I.274–75.

227   Seint Yve: More likely a reference to St. Ivo of Chartres than to St. Yves of Brittany or St. Ives of Huntingdonshire: Cline, MLN 60, 1945, 482. Compare SumT III.1943.

228   tweye: See textual notes. "The confused mass of readings here seems to have originated in efforts by the scribes to adjust the proportion of thrivers to their ideas of the facts" (M-R 4:497).

230–34 A difficult passage. For different interpretations, see Baugh (337) and Copland (MAE 35:19). pleye/ A pilgrymage may mean either that merchants seek relaxation on pilgrimages (some MSS read *on* for *a*), or else, if *pleye* is transitive, that they pretend to go away on pilgrimages in order to escape creditors. Jonathan Sumption, Pilgrimage, 1975, 168, speaks of the pilgrim's immunity in courts of law (Glanvill, De legibus Angliae, ed. Hall, 1965, 16–17).

238 Medieval merchants justified their profits by emphasizing the risks (hap, fortune) that they took: R. H. Tawney, Religion and the Rise of Capitalism, 1926, 33.

243 Compare MerT IV.1343. On the responsibilities of merchants' wives, see Thrupp, Merchant Class, 169–74.

255   At after-dyner: For the construction, see SqT V.302n.

261–62 Medical authorities recommended moderation in eating during hot weather; see Avicenna, Libri canonis

quinque, Venice, 1486, 1.3.5, and Bartholomaeus Anglicus, 6.20, tr. Trevisa 1:324. Cf. GP I.347.

277–78 The monk, who does not want the wife to hear of the loan, seems to suggest that any disclosure of it may prejudice his impending purchase.

287–90 On the power of ready money, see poem no. 51 in Robbins, Hist. Poems, especially 31–32: "At al tymys the best ware ys/Ever redy money." In fact "supplies of ready money were low," Thrupp, Merchant Class, 143.

304 Compare the dicing and dancing apprentice in CkT I.4370, 4384.

317 On merchants abroad as likely cuckolds, see Mann, Ch and Estates, 254–55.

328–34 In Bruges, where merchandise proved unexpectedly dear, the merchant had spent 20,000 shields on credit. The **sheeld** was a unit of account in the Bruges money market (cf. GP I.278 and Cahn, SAC 2, 1980, 81–119). Having entered into a formal pledge (**reconyssaunce**) for early repayment, he accordingly returned to Saint-Denis, collected what French francs he had there, and went to Paris to borrow the rest from **certeine freendes** in order to redeem his *bond* (VII.368). At the end of the fourteenth century, the London-Bruges exchange rate was 25d sterling to the shield, so the value of the merchant's loan would have been nearly £2000, a very large sum. See generally R. de Roover, Money, Banking and Credit in Medieval Bruges, 1948, chap. 4.

334   certeyn: See MilT I.3193n.

355   Seint Jame: See RvT I.4264n.

359   tokenes: Compare MancT IX.258.

367   Lumbardes: The merchant redeems his *bond* (368) from the Paris branch of the Italian bank that lent him the 20,000 shields in Bruges. For a different analysis, see Cahn, SAC 2:116–17. Italian bankers "practically dominated the money market" in Bruges, according to de Roover, Money, Banking and Credit, 55.

369 Compare MerT IV.2322.

379   maketh it ful tough: The phrase occurs in ME in various senses (see GP I.785n. and Whiting T431). In Chaucer's works it means "put on airs, be haughty" (BD 531) or "be bold, swagger" (see Tr 2.1025 and n.). It is not elsewhere applied to sexual activity.

384   yow: The merchant addresses his wife with the reproachfully formal plural pronoun from here to 389, reverting at 395 to his customary *thou*.

400–401 Compare MerT IV.2264–75.

413–17 The wife here uses mercantile terminology (compare VII.397–99) in its traditional Pauline application to sex: "Uxori vir debitum reddat, similiter autem et uxor viro" (1 Cor. 7.3). Compare WBPro III.130, 153; MerT IV.1452, 2048; ParsT X.375, 940; and cf. WBPro III.198n.

416   taille: A tally was a stick in which notches were cut to record debts (compare GP I.570). *Tail* means "sexual member" in WBPro III.466 (see OED s.v. *tail* sb.¹ 5c), and a pun is clearly intended here: Jones, MLN 52, 1937, 570, and Caldwell, MLN 55, 1940, 262–65. On the interchangeability of sex and money in the tale, see especially Silverman, PQ 32:329–36. Compare VII.434.

423   my joly body: Compare EpiMLT II.1185.

432   thy: Variant readings *my* and *our* miss a subtle point. The merchant, seeing no profit in anger, accepts the wife's claim that she thought the money was given to her personally (VII.406–7), and simply suggests that she should not spend so much of her money on dress (418–19).

434 Taillynge: For the pun, see 416 above.

The Introduction to the Prioress' Tale

435 *corpus dominus*: The Host's blunder for *corpus Domini,* the body of the Lord. See Elliott, Ch's English, 270–73.

440–41 Compare GP I.706n. and HF 1809–10.

442 French fabliaux writers often draw morals of this knowing sort (Nykrog, Les fabliaux, 100–103, 248–52). The Cook draws a similar conclusion from RvT: CkPro I.4330–34. Compare the end of the fabliau Gombert, quoted in note to RvT I.4320–21.

447 youre: The Host uses *thou* to address the Shipman (VII.436), but shifts to the formal plural when he speaks *curteisly* to the Prioress (446).

The Prioress's Prologue and Tale

The stanzaic form, rhetorical style, and sources of The Prioress's Prologue and Tale seem to place this work in Chaucer's Italian period, but it cannot be dated precisely. The prologue appears to be later than The Second Nun's Prologue, from which it apparently "borrows" (see 474–80 below). Lines 460–80, for which the Second Nun's Invocacio seems to be a rough draft (Burlin, Ch Fiction, 278 n. 11), smoothly condense and repeat themes used less skillfully in SNPro VIII.29–77 and ABC 89–94 (Knight, Poetry of CT, 139–40). Though the tale is adapted for a female speaker (cf. VII.454, 581 and nn.), it was not necessarily written with the Prioress of the General Prologue in mind, since it fits her portrait only in being a celebration of the Virgin with stress upon a tenderness for small creatures, without reference to her courtly elegance and expensive tastes, and it has nothing about it of the idealized romance hero or satirized nun. Ferris (ChR 15, 1981, 295–321) offers some evidence that the tale may have been written to be read on the occasion of a visit to Lincoln by Richard II and Queen Anne on 26 March 1387. The revision of the tale must have come relatively late in the Canterbury period, after The Shipman's Tale, to which it refers (see 642–43 below), and before The Nun's Priest's Tale, which echoes it a number of times (see VII.570 and n.).

The Prologue is made up of details from Scripture and the Liturgy, especially the Little Office of the Virgin (Boyd, Ch and the Liturgy, 68–75; M. Madeleva, Lost Language, 52–53) and Dante (Par. 33.1–21), with echoes as well of the Mass of the Holy Innocents (Childermas, 28 Dec; cf. the Sarum Missal and 453–59 below). Ferris (ABR 32, 1981, 232–54) discusses Chaucer's use of systematic and doctrinal theology in this prologue and tale. On the use of sources, in addition to Boyd (as cited above) see Kean, Ch and Poetry 2:195–96. A prologue such as this is conventional in saints' lives and miracles of the Virgin.

The tale belongs to the large and varied genre of Mira-

cles of the Virgin, on which see A. Mussafia, Sitzungberichte der Philosophisch-Historichen Classe, 113, 1886, 917–94; 115, 1888, 5–92; 119, 1889, pt. 9; 123, 1891, pt. 8; 139, 1898, pt. 8; W. M. Hart, Univ. of Calif. Publ. in Mod. Philol. 11, 1922, with emphasis on the Old French collection of Gautier de Coincy; and R. W. Southern, Med. and Ren. Sts. 4, 1958, 176–216, with emphasis on twelfth-century English collections. Middle English versions are edited by Beverly Boyd, Miracles of the Virgin, 1964.

Carleton Brown provides a history of the legend Chaucer used and a study of the analogues, classified and printed in three groups, assigning Chaucer's tale to Group C (A Study of The Miracle of Our Lady, Ch Soc, 2nd ser. 45, 1910; S&A, 477–85; see also Statler, PMLA 65, 1950, 896–910). Chaucer's version is unique in such details as the little *clergeon's* age (see 503 below), the friend who teaches him the antiphon, and the *greyn* that Mary puts on his tongue. The tragic ending is characteristic of Group C but may also have been influenced by legends such as that of St. Hugh (see 684 below) embodying the ritual murder libel (for which see Child, Ballads, 3:233–54, and Langmuir, Spec 47, 1972, 459–82). The theme of a child murdered by enemies of his faith is ancient and widespread; it apparently first appeared in English in the story of William of Norwich (see Life of William of Norwich, ed. A. Jessop and M. R. James, 1896), and it persists even today (Ridley, Western Folklore Qtly. 26, 1967, 153–56).

Brennan (SP 70, 1973, 243–51) finds three stages of composition in the tale: first, the creation of a version close to the "C" analogues (S&A, 450–57); second, the addition of pathos by making the victim so young (see 495 below) and providing allusions to the Mass of the Holy Innocents; and third, emphasizing the exalted state of virginity, to make the Prioress contrast with the Wife of Bath and thus integrate her tale more fully into the thematic plan of the CT.

The anti-Semitism of the tale has been a difficult problem for readers and critics, especially in recent years, and has deeply affected critical attitudes toward both the Prioress and her tale. Some critics, reluctant to ascribe the anti-Semitism to Chaucer himself, regard the tale as a satiric revelation of the Prioress's character and see both it and her portrait in the General Prologue as harshly satiric. Yet the Parson also regards the Jews as "cursed" and links them with the Devil (X.599), and the Prioress's pitiless attitude toward the murderers is no different from the Man of Law's fierceness toward the unbelieving Saracens (II.960–65). The miracles of the Virgin were frequently fiercely anti-Semitic, as was liturgical drama (see R. W. Frank, in Wisdom of Poetry, 177–88; Karl Young, Drama of the Med. Church, 1933, vols. 1, 2, cf. index, s.v. *Jews*), and contemporary tales of compassionate treatment of Jews were offset by others of violence toward them (see EETS 46, 1871, ed. R. Morris). For the attitude of the Church, see S. Grayzel, Church and Jews, 2nd ed., 1966, and for representative Christian polemics, A. L. Williams, Adversus Judaeos, 1935. On the characterization of the Prioress as a reflection of her veneration of Mary and the whole question of medieval anti-Semitism in the miracles of the Virgin, see Frank, ChR 13: 346–62 and in Wisdom of Poetry, 1982, 177–88. But see also Donaldson, 933–34. It should be noted that the tale has little connection with English life of the time;

The explanatory notes to The Prioress's Prologue and Tale were written by Florence H. Ridley.

Jews had been banished from England since 1290; see C. Roth, Hist. of the Jews in Eng., rev. ed., 1970. On the whole, Chaucer's characteristic ambiguity defies final definition of either his own attitude or his intent regarding the Prioress.

The tale appears to be one perfectly adapted to its teller (Ruth Ames, God's Plenty, 1984, especially 192–203), but critics have regarded it as a fairy tale (David, Strumpet Muse, 209), a sentimental experiment (Payne, Key of Remembrance, 164–69), a model of official culture whose exemplary structure is fixed by tradition (Piero Boitani, Eng. Med. Narrative, trans. Joan K. Hall, 1982, 246, 257–258), a sincere expression of piety (Kean, Ch and Poetry 2:187, 204–9), a comedy (Mills, Paunch 27, 1966, 49–51), an excessive realization of the role of the Virgin as New Woman (Hope E. Weissman, in Ch, ed. Economou, 1975, 94–104), a distortion of sentimentality (Charles Owen, Pilgrimage and Storytelling, 1977, 119–21), or a psychotic study (Rudat, Amer. Imago 35, 1978, 407–18). On the tale's relation to others, see Hawkins, JEGP 63, 1984, 621–24 (those around it); Russell, in Med. Lit. and Civ., ed. Pearsall and Waldron, 1969, 211–27 (the Shipman's); Broes, PMLA 78, 1963, 156–62 (the Nun's Priest's); and Hamel, ChR 19, 1980, 251–59 (Sir Thopas). The tender treatment of the clergeon and his mother relate The Prioress's Tale to those of the Man of Law and Clerk. For discussion of such pious tales and affective poetry as a conventional type, see Gray, in J. R. R. Tolkien, ed. Salu and Farrell, 1979, 173–203; Stugrin, ChR 15, 1980, 155–167; and Collette, ChR 15, 1980, 138–50. Burlin (Ch Fiction, 181–194) discusses the Prioress's skillful use of language, finding it, combined with her portrait, a means of extending the ambiguity of her presentation. On her anti-Semitism, see R. J. Schoeck, rpt. in Ch Criticism, ed. R. J. Schoeck and J. Taylor, 1960; Preston, N&Q 206, 1961, 7–8; Robinson, Crit. Rev. 10, 1967, 20–21; Haskell, Ch's Saints, 51–57; David, Strumpet Muse, 212–14, all of whom see her as an anti-Semite. For other views, see Friedman, ChR 9, 1974, 118–29; Hirsch, ChR 10, 1975, 30–45; Ruggiers, Art of CT, 175–83; J. Winny, ed., ProPrT and PrT, 1975, 21–32. For a survey see Ridley, Univ. of Calif. Publs., ES 30.

The Prioress's Prologue

453–59 Paraphrase of Psalm 8.1–2 (Vulgate 8.2–3), the opening lines of matins in the Little Office of the Virgin, though Chaucer may have had in mind the introit of the Mass of the Holy Innocents (Hamilton, MLR 34, 1939, 3; Wenk, MS 17, 1955, 216).

454 quod she: This follows smoothly from line 451; cf. VII.581 and n.

457–59 mouth of children . . . heriynge: Literal translation of "Ex ore infancium deus . . . perfecisti laudem" from the Mass of the Holy Innocents (children two years old and under). See Sarum Missal, 32; cf. Boyd, Ch and Liturgy, 67–75.

458 on the brest soukynge: Perhaps an allusion to St. Nicholas (VII.514), who as an infant would suckle but once on Wednesdays and Fridays.

461 lylye: Cf. SNPro VIII.27. The lily and burning bush (VII.468) are Marian symbols, the first of purity, the second an Old Testament anticipation of the Virgin

Birth (Exodus 3.2). In one version of the tale a lily rather than a *greyn* is placed on the child's tongue (S&A, 457; for an illustration see Pratt, Tales). For the lily's appropriateness to the tale, see Bernard, Sermon 48:2, tr. K. Walsh and I. Edwards, Cistercian Fathers Ser. 31, 1979, 12–13.

467–72 Cf. MLT II.841; SNPro VIII.36–42; ABC 89–94. Kean compares the passages with the Fr. source of ABC (Ch and Poetry 2:193–96). Kolve comments on the burning bush as a commonplace of medieval devotion (in New Perspectives, 153, n. 34), M. Madeleva on the passage's relation to the liturgy (Lost Lang., 53).

469–72 "Through humility you ravished from God the Holy Spirit which alighted within you, from whose potency Christ, the Wisdom of God, was conceived." Burrow (ed., Eng. Verse 1300–1500, 1977, 223) finds an allusion to Dante, Inferno 3.4–6: "Justice moved my high Creator; divine Power made me, supreme Wisdom (Sapienza) and primal Love," which defines the Trinity: Power (Father), Wisdom (Son), Love (Holy Spirit). Compare **Fadres sapience** to PP B 16.36–37: "*sapiencia-dei-patris, / That is, the passioun and the power of oure prince Iesu.*"

474–80 Based on Dante, Par. 33.16–21, which Chaucer used earlier in SNPro VIII.50–56 and recalled here (Pratt, MLQ 7, 1946, 259–61). There are also echoes of the prayer and absolution of matins; cf. Kean 2:188–89.

481–86 This stanza is regarded by many critics as the key to the Prioress's character and tale, whether the tale is considered as an expression of childlike innocence or of wisdom and the inexpressible expressed by a child or as emotionally and intellectually immature (e.g., Ruggiers, Art of CT, 175–76; Fritz, ChR 9, 1974, 166–81; Gaylord, PMASAL 47, 1962, 613–36). The piety is sincere but naive; the kindness verges on sentimentality; the morality is the justice of fairy tale (David, Strumpet Muse, 209; but cf. Hostia, CE 14, 1953, 351–52). In keeping with these sentiments, as well as with her actors and theme, the Prioress echoes throughout the liturgy of the Holy Innocents. Cf. VII.453–59.

The Prioress's Tale

488 Asye: Most versions of the tale either leave the country unspecified or set it in some remote country (Brown, Miracle of Our Lady, 55). Burlin (Ch Fiction, 191–92) believes the exotic setting provides the tone of an archetype, though Hamilton believes it might link the *clergeon* with Asiatic child martyrs (MLR 34:3).

489 Jewerye: Apparently the Jewish quarter of the city, a ghetto (see MED s.v. *Jeuerie* 2 (c)), although Burrow takes it to be a street (Eng. Verse, n. 489).

490–91 lucre of vileynye: Glossed in the Ellesmere and Hengwrt MSS with "turpe lucrum," a term (derived from 1 Tim. 3:8) in canon law meaning "shameful (excessive) profits" (Yunck, N&Q 205, 1960, 165–67). Jewish colonies were protected for the taxes they provided and for money lending, **usure,** forbidden in canon law, but essential for business (Roth, Hist. of the Jews, 192–97, 207).

495 litel scole: Apparently a village school (Brown, MP 3, 1906, 467–91), though its enrollment (*children an heep*) may imply it was modeled on the song schools of London (A. F. Leach, Schools of Med. Engl., 1915, 137)

such as St. Paul's, near which Chaucer lived as a child (Brewer, Ch in His Time, 127). F. W. Bateson contends that the frequency of diminutives such as *litel* makes the tale the sort to be expected from the Prioress, a pastiche half-way between pathos and satire (Scholar Crit., 1972, 18–20); but cf. MLT II.834–40; Brewer, REL 5, 1964, 52–60; and Root, Poetry of Ch, 197–98. See also Gaylord, PMASAL 47:632, and Kelly, PLL 5, 1969, 362–74.

503   clergeon: Used in the general sense of a young clerk rather than a chorister, as Skeat suggested (Brown, MP 3:467–71). On the effectiveness and realism of the child's description, see Owen, ChR 16, 1981, 72–73, and Brewer, REL 5:58–60.

seven yeer: The child is ordinarily ten in the analogues; Chaucer's change increases both the pathos and the realism. Seven is the first year of childhood, the "threshold of accountability" (Hamilton, MLR 34:1–2). See Bartholomaeus Anglicus 6.5, tr. Trevisa 1:300, who notes that seven is the age at which children entered school; the **clergeon** is in his first term, which ends at Christmas (S&A, 465).

508   *Ave Marie*: The first prayer in the primer printed by Plimpton (517 below): "Hail mari full of grace the lord is with the. blessed be thow among women & blessid be the frute of thi wombe jesus. amen." Cf. Luke 1.28, 42.

512 Proverbial: Whiting C219.

514   Seint Nicholas: Bishop of Myra, first half of fourth century; for his legend see Jacobus de Voragine, Legenda aurea, tr. Ryan and Ripperberger, 16–24; and Early South Eng. Legendary, EETS 87, 1887, 240–55. St. Nicholas was renowned for his infant piety (cf. 458 above) and his precocious learning, which made him the patron of schoolboys and clerks (cf. Wace's Vie de Saint Nicholas, ed. Einar Ronsjö, 1942, 127). His providing doweries for poor girls (S. E. Leg., 33–64) is perhaps the basis for his modern transformation into Santa Claus. His feast, 6 Dec., is closely related to Childermas (Hamilton, MLR 34:6). On his further appropriateness to the tale, see Haskell, Ch's Saints, 47–55, and Blechner, NM 79, 1978, 370, who cites a legend of the saint's resurrecting three dead clerks.

517   prymer: An elementary school book, usually containing the alphabet, basic prayers, elements of the faith (creed, seven deadly sins, etc.) and simple devotions such as the Hours (little Office) of the Virgin Mary (Nicholas Orme, Eng. Schools in the M. A., 1973, 62). Possibly it was of the sort represented by The Prymer or Lay Folks' Prayer Book (ed. Henry Littlehales, EETS 105, 109, 1895–97) or the fourteenth-century English primer reproduced in George A. Plimpton, Ch's Education, 1935, plates IX.1–IX.15. Plimpton also reproduces a fifteenth-century French primer that includes a selection of hymns, among which is the *Alma Redemptoris Mater* (plates XIII.1–XIII.39).

518   *Alma redemptoris*: An antiphon to Mary in liturgical use from Advent to Candlemas (2 Feb.). It begins, "Alma Redemptoris Mater, quae pervia caeli/ Porta manes, et stella maris, succurre cadenti,/ Surgere qui curat, populo." For full text and translation, see Matthew Britt, Hymns of the Breviary, rev. ed., 1955, 64–65. On the origin of the anthem's text and tune and its appropriateness, see Davidson, SMC 4, 1974, 459–66. This is the song usually sung in the "C" versions; for a ME translation see S&A, 469; in the Vernon MS it is summarized:

"Godus Moder, Mylde and Clene/ Hevene yate and Sterre of se,/ Saue thi peple from synne and we" (woe). The frontispiece to Brown, Miracle of Our Lady, reproduces the musical notation from an early MS. In the "A" and "B" versions of the tale the song is "Gaude, Maria," "with the line 'Erubescat Judaeus infelix' specially suited to irritate Jewish auditors" (S&A, 448), thus perhaps providing a better motivation for the murder (cf. Hawkins, JEGP 63:611).

523   Noght wiste he: Since he used the antiphoner, perhaps he sang with the clergy, learning to chant the Latin before he could translate it (Boyd, Radford Rev. 1, 1960, 3).

534   help and socour: Synonyms with accrued connotations, whose order had become stereotyped (Porter, NM 73, 1972, 313).

540   Cristemasse: The end of the feast of Christmas is the beginning of the next school term.

558–64 Ferris discusses Chaucer's developing art of alliteration, citing this stanza as a tour de force of onomatopoeia used to convey the malevolence of Satan (NM 80, 1979, 164–68). For an explication of the passage in terms of the doctrinal antagonism between Christian and Jew, church and synagogue, see Hawkins (JEGP:602–24), who cites John 8.43–44. On the Jews as a fallen people who, like Adam, listen to Satan and die, see Hirsch, ChR 10:41.

564   youre lawes: In several MSS *oure lawes,* contrasting the law of Satan and the Jews with that of Christians; see Textual Notes.

570   hym hente: Cf. NPT VII.3335, and see note to VII.3052 for other possible echoes of this tale in that of the Nun's Priest.

572   wardrobe: A euphemism for privy or *gong* (MED s.v. *gang* 3 [a]), deriving from the practice of having one place serve as both clothes room and latrine (Draper, ESt 60, 1925–26, 238–39).

576 Proverbial (Whiting M806); cf. NPT VII.3052, 3057.

578 Cf. Gen. 4.10, referring to the ancient belief that the blood of one murdered would cry out unless it were covered (Wenk, MS 17:217).

579 Singled out, with VII.649–55, by Matthew Arnold to illustrate the virtue of Chaucer's poetry (Eng. Poets, ed. T. H. Ward, 1880; rpt. in EIC, 2nd ser., 1888, 29–31).

580–85 Lat. gloss (M-R 3:518) reads: "Let us look in the Apocalypse of John and there we shall find a lamb and with him 144 thousand of those with the sign, etc. [cf. Rev. 14.1]. These are those who have not polluted themselves with women; those indeed who have remained virgins, who follow the lamb wherever he goes, etc. [cf. Rev. 14.4]." The gloss is from Jerome's *Adversus Jovinianum* (PL 23:281) and may indicate an intent to develop an ironic connection between the Prioress and the Wife of Bath, based on their divergent views of virginity (Brennan, SP 70:243–51). The passage from Revelation was read at the Feast of the Holy Innocents (Hamilton, MLR 34:4; Boyd, Ch and Liturgy, 69–70).

581   quod she: This suggests adaptation of the tale to its context. The phrase echoes ProPrT VII.454 and emphasizes the speaker's presence. It has been seen as a means of indicating the Prioress's limitations, questioning her tale, making clear its expression of innocent belief, or the poet's desire to dissociate himself from its moral taint (Trevor Whittock, A Reading of CT, 1968, 204–5; Spitzer, Traditio 2, 1944, 454; Nist, TSL 15, 1966, 96–97).

583   **Pathmos:** Patmos, an island in the Aegean, where the apostle *Seint John* was believed to have written the Revelation in a cave that is still pointed out today.

585   **flesshly:** Glossed in Hengwrt and Ellesmere MSS with "carnaliter," i.e., in a carnal sense.

586–96   On the mother's suffering as an instance of affective tone, see Hirsch, ChR 10:37–39.

607–8   Cf. VII.453–59. Chaucer has replaced "propter inimicos tuos" of the Introit with **lo, heere thy myght,** perhaps because he is about to reveal how God confounded his enemies through the voice of a child (Wenk, MS 17:216).

609–10   **emeraude:** Emerald, whose color may be an echo of GP I.159 (Engelhardt, MS 37, 1975, 292), is a gem that guards against lechery (see J. Evans and M. S. Serjeantson, Eng. Med. Lapidaries, EETS 190, 1933, 20–21, 40–41, 121). The **ruby,** since it shines in the dark (LGW 1119), betokens the light of Christ, and if it can serve as a metaphor for the blood of the Passion, it is doubly fitting for a martyr (Friedman, MAE 39, 1970, 304). On the qualities of the gems, see also Lynch, MLN 59, 1942, 440–41.

616   **provost:** In reference to foreign cities, the officer charged with punishment of offenders (OED s.v. *provost* 6). Since both Christians and Jews are alien in this place, Kelly argues the murderers' punishment (vv. 268-33) is no indication of anti-Semitism (PLL 5, 1969, 368), but see Owen (Pilgrimage and Story, 230 n. 7) and Archer (ChR 19, 1984, 52).

627   The Lat. gloss (M-R 3:518) reads "Rachel weeping for her children would not be consoled, etc." (Matt. 2.18), part of the gospel for the Mass of the Holy Innocents (Hamilton, MLR 34:4). Matthew here refers to Jeremiah 31.15 and thus relates the Massacre of the Innocents to Jeremiah's prophecy. David (Strumpet Muse, 210, 212–13) argues that such reminiscence of Old Testament material suggests Chaucer's awareness that Jews were not only legendary monsters but children of the promise (Gen. 9.9, 17.1–7) and thus an ironic contrast is created between the Prioress's view and his own. But see Ames, MS 19, 1957, 37–47.

632   Proverbial; Whiting E178. Cf. Exod. 21.1, 23, 24. This is the old law by which the Jews are punished; the new law (cf. Matt. 5.38–41) was to have displaced it. On the use of doctrinal conflicts in the tale, see Hawkins, JEGP 63:603–4, and Archer, ChR 19:46–54.

635   Hengwrt and 4 other MSS have here as a gloss (M-R 3:518) verses from John of Garland's "Miracula Beatae Virginis"; see Brown, Miracle of Our Lady, 7.

639   **hooly water:** The ceremonial sprinkling of the body with holy water regularly follows the Requiem Mass; here perhaps it implies the child's release from the flesh, symbolized by the filth in which he had been thrown (Wenk, MS 17:218; Boyd, Ch and Liturgy, 51).

642–43   Apparently a reference to the monk in The Shipman's Tale rather than to the Monk in the General Prologue, whom the Prioress has no reason to reprove. Russell finds the tale a sensitive rejoinder to the Shipman (in Med. Lit. and Civilization, 211–27).

649–55   The manner of dying is reminiscent of Cecilia's; cf. SNT VIII.526–34. The calm authority of the child's

speech contrasts with his earlier innocence (Russell, Med. Lit. and Civilization, 223–34).

662   **greyn:** Unique to Chaucer's version; a lily, gem, and white pebble occur in three analogues (S&A, 457–58). The grain has been explained in a great variety of ways: as medicine a "loving mother" might administer to relieve her child's injured throat, since *greyn* is glossed in the Promptorium Parvulorum as "grain of paradise" (cardamom), used as a breath-sweetener (MilT I.3690) and to relieve an aching throat (Beichner, Spec 36, 1961, 302–7); as a particle or prayer bead (M. Madeleva, Lost Lang., 59); as a pearl, symbol of the Virgin (Robinson); as the spirit (Hill, Spec 40, 1965, 63–73); as the blood of martyrs, seed of the Church (Engelhardt, MS 37:293); as the pippins placed under Adam's tongue by Seth (Cursor Mundi, EETS 57, 1874, lines 1373–75, p. 87, cited by Skeat, 5:180); as the smallest, least valuable object, symbolizing the worthlessness of earthly existence (Wenk, MS 17:219); as a symbol of immortality (Fritz, ChR 9:176–78); as a means of detaining the bird soul (Taylor, Southern Folklore Qtly., 34, 1970, 82–89); as a sweetener, necessary after immersion in a privy (Bratcher, N&Q 208, 1963, 444–45). Friedman surveys the theories, suggesting that the *greyn* is important as a prop rather than a symbol (ChR 11, 1977, 328–33). But Maltman (ChR 17, 1982, 163–70) points out further links between The Prioress's Tale and the Sarum Breviary, and finds the source of the *greyn* in a commemoration of St. Thomas sung during second Vespers of the Feast of the Holy Innocents, where it is a symbol of both martyrdom and the soul winnowed from the body. A miracle is not meant to be understood, and perhaps *greyn* was left deliberately ambiguous (Steadman, MS 24, 1962, 388–91; Hawkins, JEGP 63:614–17).

675   On the suggestiveness of the line's sound see Gaylord, PMASAL 47:632.

684   **Hugh of Lyncoln:** The young Hugh of Lincoln was said to have been martyred by Jews in 1255. His story is preserved in the ballad "Sir Hugh or the Jew's Daughter" (Child, Ballads, no. 155). For the legend, see Butler's Lives of the Saints 3:421–22; and J. W. F. Hill, Med. Lincoln, 1948, 217–38. Ironically, another Hugh of Lincoln was conspicuous in defense of the Jews (see Butler 4:370–74). Hugh was regularly listed among martyred saints until recent times (see Bk. of the Saints, 5th ed., 1966, 351), though it is clear that the boy was not murdered by Jews (Langmuir, Spec 47, 1972, 459–82). Lincoln Cathedral, where a plaque commemorated his supposed martyrdom until 1959 (Lachs, Western Folklore Qtly. 19, 1960, 61–62), was the center of his cult. On 19 Feb. 1386, Chaucer's wife, together with Henry, Earl of Derby, and other members of John of Gaunt's family, was admitted to the Fraternity of Lincoln Cathedral (Ch Life Records, 91–92), so Chaucer may have had a special interest in Hugh. Boyd (Radford Rev. 14:1–5) suggests that the "saint," who was honored with a feast, 27 August, in an ecclesiastical calendar in the diocese of Lincoln, is invoked to make the tale liturgically complete.

687   **Preye eek for us:** From the point of view of the victims of the Prioress's justice, ironic; but as acknowledgment of God's power, a fitting close to a tale celebrating the triumph of the innocent and weak which that power made possible (cf. Knight, Poetry of CT, 142–43; Russell, in Med. Lit. and Civilization, 227).

Prologue to Sir Thopas

"This Prologue is noteworthy as conforming in meter to the rime-royal stanza of the preceding tale. The regular meter of the headlinks, or talks by the way, is the heroic couplet, even when they connect tales in stanzaic form or in prose" (Robinson).

696–97 Kellogg (MAE 29, 1960, 119–20) compares Virgil's reproach to Dante, "Che hai, che pure in ver la terra guati?" (Why do you keep your eyes fixed on the ground?) Purg. 19.52.

700–702 Chaucer jokes about his stoutness and consequent unattractiveness to women in Scog 31. Compare MercB 27.

703–4 Because the Host's description of Chaucer as abstracted (**elvyssh**) and unsociable appears to conflict with the gregariousness of GP I.30–34, Knott (MP 8, 1910, 135–39) took the description to refer, not to permanent characteristics, but to a temporary mood of seriousness induced by The Prioress's Tale. But Chaucer portrays himself as generally unsociable in HF 644–60; and 694–95 here suggest that the Host is noticing him for the first time. Harry's condescension to Chaucer, as an obscure and unpromising participant in the tale-telling, provides an apt introduction to the ensuing tale. See also Lumiansky, PQ 26, 1947, 313–20.

Sir Thopas

For his own tale of Sir Thopas Chaucer pointedly departs from his normal poetic usage ("as though he himself were not the author but only the reporter of the rest," Speght, ed., 1598). He imitates the popular poetry of his day in meter, rhyme, and diction.

The tail-rhyme stanza is employed in many ME romances (see Trounce, MAE 1, 1932, 87–108, 168–82; 2, 1933, 34–57, 189–98; 3, 1934, 30–50), but Chaucer uses it only here. The metrical peculiarity of Thopas is indicated in many MSS (including the Ellesmere and Hengwrt) by conspicuously drawn lines bracketing the rhymes, a device unusual in MSS of the *Tales* but quite common in other ME verse MSS (Stanley, NM 73, 1972, 417–26). Most tail-rhyme romances have a twelve-line stanza; but Chaucer's basic stanza has six lines, rhyming either *a a b a a b* (18 stanzas) or *a a b c c b* (8 stanzas), as in the first part of the romance of *Bevis of Hampton* in the Auchinleck MS. The remaining five stanzas incorporate a one-stress line or "bob" (first at VII.793), perhaps in imitation of the English *Sir Tristrem*, and four of them follow the bob with an extra section of three lines, variously rhymed (VII.797–826, 881–90). Perhaps Chaucer had in mind the pointless metrical variations to be found in some popular romance texts (e.g., the Auchinleck *Bevis*). He also imitates their loose rhyming technique, allowing himself several uncharacteristic licenses: identical rhyme (*contree,* 722; *goon,* 805), rhyme requiring a silent final *-e* (*entent,* 712; *plas,* 781; *gras,* 831; *chivalry,* 902; *well,* 915; and see 806, 819, and 902 below), and facile rhyme tags (*verrayment,* 713; *it is no nay,* 766; *In*

The explanatory notes to The Prologue and Tale of Sir Thopas were written by J. A. Burrow.

towne, 793; *In londe,* 887, etc.). The diction of Thopas has a distinct popular coloring, drawn from contemporary English romance, ballad, and song. The pilgrim-poet addresses his audience as *lordes* (712, 833), divides his narrative into fits (888), calls his hero *child Thopas* (830, cf. 810, 817, 898), and employs several other expressions not found elsewhere in Chaucer's work: *listeth* (listen, 712 and 833), *spray* (770), *downe* (hill, 796), *myrie men* (839), *dappull gray* (884), *love-drury* (895), *auntrous* (909), *worly* (917). See Scheps, NM 80, 1979, 69–77. A group of words shared with The Miller's Tale has a similar popular character (Donaldson, Speaking of Ch, 13–29): *gent* (715, MilT I.3234), *rode* (727, MilT I.3317), *love-longynge* (772, MilT I.3349, etc.), and *lemman* (788, MilT I.3278, etc.).

The stereotyped style of common ME narrative verse, in tail-rhyme, short couplet, and ballad stanza, makes it difficult to determine exactly which poems Chaucer had in mind. The standard collection of parallels, taking account of all previous work, is by L. H. Loomis in S&A, 486–559. The most striking verbal similarities are with *Guy of Warwick* (Thop VII.772–73, 804–6), *Bevis of Hampton* (Thop VII.730–31, 833–35), *Lybeaus Desconus* (Thop VII.730–31, 869–70), *Sir Launfal* (Thop VII.794–95), *Perceval of Gales* (Thop VII.915–16), *Sir Eglamour* (Thop VII.722, 888–90), and *Thomas of Erceldoune* (Thop VII.878–84). Chaucer refers to Guy, Bevis, and Lybeaus, together with *Horn child* and *Ypotis,* in his list of heroes of *romances of prys* at VII.897–900. His chief model appears to have been *Guy of Warwick* (see 899 below). The tail-rhyme version of this popular story survives only in the Auchinleck MS, along with *Bevis of Hampton* and the unique copy of *Horn Childe.* This manuscript, dating from 1330–40, would be an appropriate source for the *rym I lerned longe agoon* (VII.709); see the facsimile, ed. D. Pearsall and I. C. Cunningham, 1979, and the study by L. H. Loomis in *Essays and Studies in Honor of Carleton Brown,* 1940, 111–28. *Lybeaus Desconus* and *Sir Launfal,* however, were the work of Chaucer's contemporary, Thomas Chester. Chaucer perhaps read these in a lost antecedent of the fifteenth-century MS B.L. Cotton Caligula A.ii, in which they both appear along with *Sir Eglamour* and *Ypotis* (see 898 below). Yet these two MSS as they stand (Auchinleck is mutilated) cannot account for all that Chaucer knew. *Perceval of Gales* appears only, and *Thomas of Erceldoune* first, in the Lincoln Thornton MS. Chaucer had no doubt read and heard much English narrative verse (probably ballads as well as romances, see 739, 740–41, and 839 below); see D. S. Brewer in Ch and Chaucerians, 1–15, and Kean, Ch and Poetry 1:1–30. He also draws on the *Roman de la rose* (see 760–65 below).

The plot of Sir Thopas consists of several familiar motifs of romance—the adventurous knight, the hero in love, the giant adversary, the arming of the hero—combined into a deliberately inconclusive and shapeless whole. No single source is to be looked for, although Magoun (PMLA 42, 1927, 833–44) proposed an episode in *Lybeaus Desconus.* The cowardly nature of the hero and his prosaic origins in Flanders (VII.718–20) push the poem towards the burlesque. Of the many Latin and vernacular burlesques surviving from the Middle Ages, nearest to Thopas is the anonymous thirteenth-century *Prise de Nuevile* (ed. Auguste Scheler, Trouvères Belges II, 1879, 170–75). This poem describes, in a ludicrous mixture of Flemish and corrupt French, how a group of Flemish artisans assemble to assault the Castle of Nuevile. Meter and style are those of the French epic, with lists of heroes, arming scenes, vaunting speeches, etc.; but the warriors' preparations, like those of Thopas, come to nothing, and the poem, like Chaucer's, breaks off before the real action begins. See Burrow, YES 14, 1984, 44–55. The burlesque genre was well understood by most early readers of Thopas; witness the imitations by Dunbar (*Schir Thomas Norny*) and Drayton (*Nimphidia*). Like Drayton, Richard Hurd in his *Letters on Chivalry and Romance,* 1765 ed., 319, compared Chaucer with Cervantes: "Sir Topaz is all Don Quixote in little."

Sir Thopas contains no clue to its date. Manly suggested that it was composed before the Canterbury period, at the time of a Flemish embassy in 1383 (E&S 13, 1928, 52–73); but his reading of the whole poem as a satire on the Flemish bourgeoisie is not convincing (see 719 below). In any case, the structure of the tale, insofar as it depends on a pilgrim interrupting at VII.918 (see 833–35 below), shows that Chaucer had the Canterbury journey in mind.

712   The appeal for attention, here and at 833 and 893, is in the minstrel manner. See 833–35 below for an example and Loomis (S&A, 496–503) for other parallels from the romances.

Listeth: The word occurs in Chaucer only here and at 833. His usual word is "hark/hearken"; but "list(en)" occurs more commonly with "lord(ing)s" at the beginning of ME poems (Burrow, Essays on Med. Lit., 1984, 66–69).

entent: The rhyme with *verrayment* (a word Chaucer uses only here) requires *entent* rather than the regular Chaucerian *entente*. On rhymes in Thopas requiring irregular forms without the final *-e,* see introductory note.

715   gent: A "stale adjective," used also of Alisoun in MilT I.3234 (see n.), and in PF 558 (see n.), and presumably inappropriate here: "elegant"?

717   sire Thopas: "An excellent title for such a gem of a knight" (Skeat 5:183). The topaz, a bright gem, is used as a type of superlative excellence in the Bible (Job 28.19, Psalms 118.127) and also in medieval French poetry, where it is applied to both men (S&A, 493) and women (Machaut, Jugement dou Roy de Behaingne, 1861); see Conley, SP 73, 1976, 42–61. Besides ironical eulogy, other implications of the name have been proposed: effeminacy (Smith, MLN 51, 1936, 314–15, notes "Topyas" as a female name) and chastity (Ross, MLN 45, 1930, 172–74). Some lapidaries credit the topaz with effect against lust: see English Medieval Lapidaries, ed. Evans and Serjeantson, EETS 190, 1933, 19, 106, 122. The title *sire,* prefixed to *Thopas* whenever the name occurs (except VII.830), as also to *Gy* (899), *Lybeux* (900), *Percyvell* (916), and even *Olifaunt* (808), imitates the promiscuous use of titles in popular English romances. Except in Thopas, Chaucer avoids prefixing *sire* to a knight's name, thus following contemporary French practice, which confined the usage to wealthy bourgeois; see Foulet, Romania 72, 1951, 330–33, 346–53. Froissart refers to a Flemish bourgeois as "sire Ghisebert Grute" (Foulet, 348). See Burrow, Essays on Med. Lit., 69–74.

719   Flaundres: Flanders was familiar to many Englishmen as a center of industry and trade just across the Channel. The use of Flanders as a comically mundane setting for knightly feats does not, however, imply that Thopas as a whole is to be understood as a satire on the Flemings, as Manly proposed (E&S 13:52–73). See the decisive objections of Lawrence, PMLA 50, 1935, 81–91; also Burrow, YES 14, 1984, 44–55.

720   Poperyng: A Flemish town noted for its cloth and (Skelton, Speke Parrot, 70) its pears, no doubt selected by Chaucer for its comic-sounding name and commonplace associations (Lawrence, PMLA 50:86).

in the place: "Interpreted by Skeat 'in the mansion, manorhouse'; but it may be a mere rime-tag, meaning 'right there'" (Robinson).

722   Compare Eglamour (Cotton MS, 934–36): "I was born in Artas;/Syr Prymsamour my fadyr was,/The lord of that countre" (ed. Richardson, EETS 256, 1965). Thopas's father was presumably lord of the Poperinge region, not of Flanders as Lawrence suggested (PMLA 50:82). Manly (CT, 630) notes that the lord of Poperinge was the Abbot of St. Bertin, though this may not have been known to Chaucer or his audience.

724–35   For ME parallels to the description of Thopas and his dress, see Loomis, S&A, 504–7.

724   swayn: A word used in the romances of young gentlemen attendant on knights, sometimes equivalent to "squire": Bevis of Hampton, ed. Kölbing, EETS e.s. 46, 48, 65, 1885–94, Auchinleck MS, 571, 3586; Lybeaus Desconus, ed. Mills, EETS 261, 1969, Cotton MS, 1748. But Chaucer uses it elsewhere only as a Northern word for "servant" (RvT I.4027).

725–27   Poetic praise of a pink-and-white complexion is normally reserved for women and children, as in the stock simile "red as rose" (Whiting R199), sometimes coupled with the equally common "white as (lily) flower" (Whiting L285, compare VII.867). But the comparison with **payndemayn,** fine white bread, is unparalleled. Loomis (S&A, 504) suggests that "punning on the word 'flour' probably led Chaucer to his own variant" (for the pun, compare WBT III.477–78).

rode: Complexion. A word used elsewhere by Chaucer only of Absolon (MilT I.3317) and generally applied to women (Donaldson, Speaking of Ch, 20–21).

scarlet in grayn: Deep-dyed scarlet cloth; *grayn* was the most effective and expensive of red dyes. NPT VII.3459n.

730–31   Compare the dwarf in Lybeaus (Cotton MS, ed. Mills), 127–28: "Hys berd was yelow as ony wax,/To hys gerdell henge the plex [plaits]," and Bevis of Hampton disguised as a begging palmer: "His berd was yelw, to is brest wax,/And to his gerdel heng is fax [hair]," Bevis (Auchinleck MS, ed. Kölbing), 2243–44. Bevis's golden locks are admired (2246–47), but by the reign of Richard II long hair and long beards were no longer in fashion; see Richard Corson, Fashions in Hair, 1965, 104.

saffroun: Used in cooking for color and flavor. Compare the domestic similes in VII.725 and 727 and the romance parallel in S&A, 507.

733   Brugges: Bruges, the main commercial center in Flanders (see ShipT VII.55, etc.), from which a Poperinge man might get good-quality stockings.

734   syklatoun: A fine and costly material (patterned silk?) from the East: see Guy of Warwick, ed. Zupitza, EETS e.s. 42, 49, 59, 1883–91, Auchinleck MS, 2835.

735   jane: Cf. ClT IV.999n.

736–41   For ME parallels to the description of Thopas's pastimes, see Loomis, S&A, 508–15.

737   See Tr 4.413n.; river (OF *rivere,* used here in a technical sense) is stressed on its second syllable.

738   goshauk: A kind of hawk much used in England. "Not a hawk for a knight" notes Manly, following the Boke of St. Albans, which assigns the goshawk to yeomen; but Hands (N&Q 216, 1971, 85–88) shows that the Boke is unreliable here, citing correspondence about a goshawk between Sir John Paston and a relative.

739   Archery was a pastime not practiced by knights in romance (S&A cites no parallels). It suggests rather the yeoman heroes of greenwood ballads (compare GP I.104–10). See 740–41 and 839 below.

740–41   By Chaucer's time, wrestling was not considered a knightly sport. Yeomen wrestle in the Gest of Robyn Hode (Child, Ballads, no. 117) st. 135, and the greenwood hero Gamelyn (Tale of Gamelyn, 171–72), like Chaucer's Miller (GP I.548), wrestles for the prize of a ram.

742   bright in bour: Thirty "maidens bright" fall in love with Guy of Warwick, but he cares only for Felice: Guy (Auchinleck MS, ed. Zupitza), 235–43. The stock phrase, *bright in bour,* is found only here in Chaucer, but is common in the romances; compare Guy (Auchinleck) 11.6, where it rhymes with "par amoure," as here.

745   For this rhetorical device, *contrarium,* the reinforcement of a word by adding the negative of its opposite, see also VII.882; MancT IX.20; Rom 310; BD 143; and BD 817–1040n. The emphasis upon Thopas's chastity (compare 717 above) is unexpected and hard to explain. Loomis, S&A, cites no convincing parallels from the romances. Donaldson (935) speaks of "downright effeminacy." Edmund Spenser introduced Thopas into his allegory of chastity: Faerie Queene (1590 ed. only) 3.7.48.

746–47   The dog-rose was distinguished in ME from other kinds of "bramble" by appellations such as "red bramble" and "hip bramble"; see MED s.v. *brembel* 2(a).

748–49   Compare Amis and Amiloun (Auchinleck MS), 1885–86: "So it bifel that selve day,/With tong as y you tel may," ed. Leach, EETS 203, 1937. See 918 below.

751   worth: Probably present tense "gets" (a contraction of *wortheth;* see Language and Versification, p. xxxvi). Past-tense forms in some MSS *(worthed, warth)* smooth the sequence of tenses.

752   launcegay: Thopas is not fully armed for knightly combat (see VII.819), nor is he out hunting, so his purpose in "riding out" is not clear.

756   Deer and especially the timid hare provide an anticlimax (in the short tail-line, as often) after *many a wilde best,* though they are both technically "wild" or undomesticated (Tucker, RES n.s. 10, 1959, 54–56). Rowland (ELN 2, 1964, 6–8) finds sexual innuendos, convincingly disposed of by Greene, N&Q 211, 1966, 169–71.

760–65   The plants (herbes) mentioned are all spice-bearing exotics, not to be found in Flanders: licorice, cetewale or zedoary (with a root like ginger), clove, and nutmeg. See Loomis (S&A, 550–55) for similar catalogues of spices, and compare MilT I.3207. The passage belongs to a tradition of descriptions of paradisal woods and gardens best represented by the Roman de la rose. See RR 1331–44 (Rom 1359–72), which includes all four spices mentioned here among the exotic trees and plants growing in Love's garden. Their association with love is relevant in Thopas.

767   papejay: The parrot's voice is a type of ugliness in Thomas Hoccleve's Praise of his Lady, 19–20: "Hir comly body shape as a foot-bal;/And shee syngith ful lyk a pape-Iay," Sec. Lyrics, ed. Robbins, 223. So also in another ME burlesque, ed. Wright and Halliwell, Reliquiae Antiquae, 1841–43, I 82 (item 1116 in Brown-Robbins Index of ME Verse): "Tho throstyll and tho popegey notyd full clene." Compare MerT IV.2321–22n.

769   hir: This reading, found in Ellesmere and seven other MSS (the rest have *his*), sustains the comedy of incongruous birds, to which the male thrush would otherwise not contribute.

770–71   Manly (CT, 631) sees a joke here: "The sweet notes of the sparrowhawk and the parrot well offset the loud, clear voice of the wooddove."

   spray: Only here in Chaucer. "On the spray" is a stock poetic phrase; see OED s.v. *spray* sb.[1] 1c.

772   love-longynge: This compound (cf. *love-likynge,* VII.850) occurs elsewhere in Chaucer only in MilT I.3349, 3679, 3705. It belongs to the idiom of popular poems such as Bevis (Auchinleck MS, ed. Kölbing), 897 (Donaldson, Speaking of Ch, 26).

773   Bird-song provokes love-longing in several romances (S&A, 516–26), notably Thomas of Erceldoune, ed. Murray, EETS 61, 1875, 29–33, and Guy of Warwick (Auchinleck MS, ed. Zupitza), 4519–20: "So michel he herd tho foules sing,/That him thought he was in gret longing."

774   Compare Guy (Auchinleck MS, ed. Zupitza), 181.10: "And priked right as he wer wode" (see S&A, 512–13). See also RvT I.4231. Repetition of the verb *prick* eight times in Thopas, five between 754 and 779, comically suggests the limited diction of ME romance.

781   plas: Like *gras* (831) this word always has a final *-e* in rhyme elsewhere in Chaucer; but it commonly rhymes with *was* in Guy (S&A, 517).

783   yaf hym good forage: "May mean 'turned him out to graze': but *forage* usually is 'dry fodder' and Sir Thopas was quite capable of the absurdity implied" (Manly, CT, 631). The suggestion gains support from Chaucer's two other uses of *forage,* MerT IV.1422 and especially RvPro I.3868: *Gras tyme is doon; my fodder is now forage.*

784   The first fit falls into three sections, each of six stanzas: introductory descriptions (st. 1–6), Thopas in the forest (st. 7–12), and the quest for the fairy queen (st. 13–18). Here, as at 748, the new section begins abruptly. Presumably Thopas makes this speech after waking from a night's sleep (787) in the clearing. For parallels to his forest nap, see S&A, 514–15.

785   eyleth: See MED s.v. *eilen* 3(b).

788   elf-queene: Line 814 here and WBT III.872–73 show that Chaucer made no distinction between elf and fairy. His fairy queen probably owes something to Thomas Chester's Launfal (see 794–95 below) and to Thomas of Erceldoune, in both of which poems the hero encounters a fairy woman in a forest and loves her; Launfal, 220 ff. and Thomas of Erceldoune, 25 ff. See S&A, 516–26. Spenser probably derived Prince Arthur's vision of the Fairy Queen from Chaucer's episode; Faerie Queene 1.9.9–15.

   lemman: A common ME word for "mistress," used by

the mature Chaucer only in contexts degraded morally or socially or both; see MancT IX.204–22.

789 goore: Originally a triangular piece of cloth inserted in a garment, but here a cloak. See Donaldson, Speaking of Ch, 23–24.

793 Single-stress lines ("bobs") occur in two other ME romances, neither in tail-rhyme: Sir Gawain and the Green Knight, and Sir Tristrem. Chaucer perhaps knew the latter in the Auchinleck MS. Bobs often take the form of a prepositional phrase with indistinct meaning: compare *in londe* at 887 and *in toune,* Sir Gawain and the Green Knight, 614. See Stanley, NM 73:417–26.

794–95 Chaucer is probably imitating Launfal, 316–18, where the fairy princess says to the hero: "Yf thou wylt truly to me take,/And alle wemen for me forsake,/Riche I wyll make the" (ed. Bliss, 1960).

796 A stock alliterative phrase. The word *down,* "hill," is found only here in Chaucer.

797 "A knight would surely have leapt or vaulted, not climbed, into his saddle" (Robinson). See S&A, 511–13.

798 stile and stoon: Unlike *dale* and *downe* (796), this collocation is not recorded elsewhere in ME. It looks like a fake traditional phrase, created by Chaucer on the analogy of "stick and stone" and "still as stone."

805 This line, found only in eight manuscripts, may have been missing in the archetype, and its authenticity is questionable. But, although the passage is perhaps acceptable in meter and meaning without it, it is hard to believe that a corrector could have hit on the echo of Guy of Warwick 148.7–9: "In this warld is man non/That ogaines him durst gon,/Herl, baroun, no knight" (and cf. Guy 236.9–11). The identical rhyme on **goon** must be deliberately bad, like that on *contree* (722).

806 childe: Outside prepositional phrases such as *with childe,* the word does not have a final *-e* elsewhere in Chaucer (a possible exception is MLT II.919). The form here may be a deliberate mock-poetic departure from Chaucer's normal usage.

807 Giants are common in ME romances; see S&A, 530–41, and Gerald Bordman, Motif-Index of the English Metrical Romances, FFC 190, 1963, under F531. Three are especially relevant to Thopas: the Saracen Sir Amoraunt and the African Colbrond, both adversaries of the hero in Guy of Warwick (Auchinleck MS, ed. Zupitza), st. 95–133, 253–69; and Maugys in the Île d'Or episode of Lybeaus Desconus (Cotton MS, ed. Mills), 1225–1395. Magoun (PMLA 42:833–44) proposes the latter work as a major source for the plot of Thopas; but the relationship of giant and lady is quite different in Chester's poem.

808 sire Olifaunt: Sir Elephant. The comic name is modeled on giants' names such as *Sir Amoraunt* in Guy 98.1 (with similar promiscuous use of "sir," see 717 above), or *Guymerraunt* in Octovian Imperator, ed. McSparran, 1979, 921, both names rhyming conveniently with *geaunt* and *Tervagaunt.* Spenser borrows Chaucer's name in Faerie Queene 3.7.48, 3.11.3–6.

810 Child: "A youth of noble birth, esp. an aspirant to knighthood; also, a knight or warrior," MED s.v. *child* 6(a). The usage is common in romance and ballad, but confined in Chaucer to Thopas (also at VII.817, 830, 898).

Termagaunt: Supposed to have been a god of the Saracens, along with Apollo, Mahomet, and others. Amoraunt swears by Tervagaunt (the OF form of the name) in Guy (Auchinleck MS, 121.2, 126.7); and the giant in Lybeaus "levede yn Termagaunt" (Cotton MS, 1301).

812 It was considered unsporting to set out to kill an opponent's horse. Bevis calls the act "gret vileinie" (Bevis of Hampton, 1891). Compare Guy of Warwick 101.2, 260.10 (Auchinleck MS, ed. Zupitza), and Lybeaus 1316 (Cotton MS, ed. Mills).

815 In Thomas of Erceldoune (Thornton MS, ed. Murray), 257–60, the castle of the fairy mistress is full of "all manere of mynstralsye."

symphonye: Probably a hurdy-gurdy, a sort of mechanized fiddle. See H. H. Carter, Dictionary of ME Musical Terms, 1961, s.v. *simphonye;* and Susann and Samuel Palmer, The Hurdy-Gurdy, 1980. By Chaucer's time the instrument was becoming associated with blind street entertainers and losing its former dignity. See also E. Winternitz, Musical Instruments and their Symbolism in Western Art, 2nd ed. 1979, chap. 4.

819 armoure: The original ME form, normal in Chaucer, was *armure* (with ŭ, not ū) from OF. The modern *armour (armor)* is due to substitution of the suffix *-our* for *-ure,* and occurs at VII.866. Here the two suffixes have been blended to give *-oure,* rhyming with *soure* "sourly." The alteration of suffix was probably, at this time, a vulgarism.

829 Unlike the *mace* or club (813), the **staf-slynge** does not figure in the armory of ME giants; see Bordman, Motif-Index, F531.4.5. Loomis (MLN 51, 1936, 311–13, and S&A, 531) suggests that it is transferred from the Biblical David to the Chaucerian Goliath. In a larger form (such as Olifaunt might have used), the "staff-sling" was a kind of siege-engine.

831–32 The double explanation of the hero's success is most closely matched in Bevis of Hampton (Auchinleck MS, ed. Kölbing): "Thourgh godes grace and is vertu" (812, cf. 2490) and "Thourgh godes grace and min engyn" (2003). See also Loomis, S&A, 533.

gras: An irregular form without *-e,* required by rhyme.

833–35 Evidently an imitation of the opening of Bevis of Hampton: "Lordinges, herkneth to me tale!/Is merier than the nightingale,/That y schel singe;/Of a knight ich wile yow roune" (Auchinleck MS, ed. Kölbing, 1–4). Chaucer's lines recall the opening of Thopas (see 712 above). They themselves open a new fit, the second. This structural division is indicated, here as at 891, by a paragraph mark or extra-large capital letter in about a quarter of the MSS, including the Ellesmere and Hengwrt. See Burrow (Essays on Med. Lit., 1984, 61–65; RES n.s. 22, 1971, 54–58), noting that the three fits contain 18, 9, and 4½ stanzas respectively, each halving the length of its predecessor until vanishing point is nearly reached.

835 rowne: A word that usually in ME and always elsewhere in Chaucer denotes private or whispered speech, but here refers to open discourse: "tell." Chaucer seems to have been amused by Bevis, 4 (see previous note).

836 sydes smale: Perhaps a feminine touch (cf. VII.702), like those in the third stanza (Donaldson, Speaking of Ch, 22).

839 myrie men: OED s.v. *merry man* 1, "companion in arms." The expression occurs in Gamelyn, 774, and in many early Robin Hood ballads, e.g., Gest of Robyn Hode (Child, Ballads, no. 117), sts. 205, 281, 316, 340,

382. Here as at VII.739, Chaucer's burlesque seems to glance at greenwood balladry.

842 Many-headed giants appear in Irish and Icelandic stories (Thompson, Motif-Index, F531.1.2.2), and there is a five-headed specimen in the ballad Sir Cawline (Child, Ballads, no. 61), st. 30; but there are none in surviving ME romances. Chaucer's failure to mention the extra heads earlier may reflect either upon the narrator's competence or upon the hero's veracity.

845–46 The word mynstrales most often denoted musical entertainers in Chaucer's day, whereas geestours recited stories of stirring deeds (gestes, Latin gesta). Compare HF 1197–98: alle maner of mynstralles,/And gestiours that tellen tales.

848–50 romances: The term romance was broadly applied in ME: see Strohm, Spec 46, 1971, 348–59. The MS collections freely mix tales of chivalry and love with stories concerning religion and the church. Loomis (S&A, 488–89) points out that B.L. MS Cotton Caligula A.ii contains, besides romances such as Lybeaus and Launfal, the pious tale of Ypotis (see VII.898 and n.) and also "the extraordinary Trentals of St. Gregory, and a life of St. Jerome, two fourteenth-century poems which may account, since Gregory was called a pope and Jerome was, to the contemporary mind, a cardinal, for the diverting romances of popes and cardinals." Yet Chaucer certainly intends some incongruity here.

848 roiales: "Royal" only in a vague sense, here as at 853 and 902. For the French plural adjectival ending, rare in verse, cf. FranT V.899 and see Language and Versification, p. xxxv.

853 spicerye: Delicacies and tidbits ("spices") were often served with sweet wines before retiring to bed (MerT IV.1807–8) or, as here, for daytime refreshment (cf. Tr 5.852).

854 gyngebreed: For a recipe, see Curye on Inglysch, EETS SS 8, 154.

856 Sugar is mentioned, with licorice, ginger, and cumin, among the "spices" in the Harley lyric Annot and John, st. 4.

857–87 The account of the arming of Thopas is not, as Manly suggested (E&S 13:70), full of deliberate mistakes and comic absurdities. Rather it is "a fairly realistic description of the successive stages of arming. If there be any satire intended it must reside in the overelaboration of detail and in the emphasis upon the obvious" (Herben, Spec 12, 1937, 475–87). See also Linn, MLN 51, 1936, 300–11. Brewer, in Ch Problems, 221–43, comments on this problem and presents as well ME parallels (accounts of arming are common in epic and romance); see also S&A, 526–30. The best general work of reference is Claude Blair, European Armour, 1958.

859 The arming of Lybeaus Desconus begins with "a scherte of selk" (Cotton MS, ed. Mills, 223). Such underclothing, of silk or fine linen (cloth of lake), was commonly worn by knights (Blair, European Armour, 53).

860 aketoun: A quilted jacket, worn under armor as an added defense and to prevent chafing (Blair, European Armour, 33, 75).

863 hawberk: Plate armor (plate, 865) for breast and back, worn over the chainmail shirt or haubergeoun, and providing the main body-defense in Chaucer's day. See Herben, Spec 12:480; and Blair, European Armour, 55–61, 74, and fig. 28.

864 Jewes werk: A fine Saracen hauberk in one French chanson de geste is said to have been forged by "Ysac de Barceloigne," presumably a Spanish Jew (La Prise d'Orange, ed. Régnier, 1969, 969). Ficke's non-literary evidence for the Jews as armorers is not impressive (PQ 7, 1928, 82–85), nor is Loomis's attempt to derive Jewes from an obscure word in Guy of Warwick (S&A, 528). Skeat suggested an allusion to some form of decorative work, such as damascening, but this is more characteristic of later armor (Blair, European Armour, chap. 8).

866 cote-armour: A surcoat worn over the armor, often decorated with the wearer's armorial bearings (Blair, 75–76, and figs. 25 and 27). For the rhyme with flour, see 819 above.

867 A proverbial simile: Whiting L285. No heraldic absurdity need be supposed, as by Manly. The line refers, in a general eulogistic way, to the whiteness of the fabric.

869–71 Compare Lybeaus: "Hys scheld was of gold fyn,/Thre bores heddes ther-inne/As blak as brond y-brent" (Cotton MS, ed. Mills, 1567–69); and also Sir Degarré ed. Schleich, 1929, Auchinleck MS, 1006–8. Boars' heads are a common heraldic bearing, most often in threes as in Lybeaus and Degarré and the arms of the Booth family. The charbocle is not precisely located, and may not be on the shield at all (see next note); but the reference is probably to the heraldic escarbuncle, a rayed bearing held to represent the precious stone carbuncle, best known as the traditional arms of the Plantagenets' county of Anjou. Cf. Allit. Morte Arthure 2523. Thopas's escutcheon is therefore not ludicrous (quite unlike those in burlesques such as Tournament of Tottenham; but the unusual combination of boar's head and escarbuncle on a gold ground has not been traced and is doubtless fanciful.

871 charbocle: The previous note suggests a heraldic interpretation; but this is not certain. Melton (PQ 35, 1956, 215–17) notes the reading by his syde for bisyde in about half the MSS, and sees a reference to an actual precious stone on the hilt of the sword at the knight's side; cf. Guy 167.2.

872–74 For parallels to the hero's braggart vows here and at 817–26, see Loomis, S&A, 541–44. Skeat suggested that the oath on ale and bread was a "ridiculous imitation of the vows made by the swan, the heron, the pheasant, or the peacock, on solemn occasions," as in the Voeux du Paon (Vows of the Peacock) of Jacques de Longuyon. Loomis, S&A, 541, recalls "familiar vows of popular phraseology, never to take meat or drink, or, specifically, never to eat bread." White (NM 64, 1963, 170–75) suggests polite substitution for a blasphemous oath by the eucharistic wine and bread. The effect is in any case deliberately flat and commonplace.

875 quyrboilly: Leather hardened by soaking in heated wax (Fr. cuir bouilli, boiled leather). It was much used by fourteenth-century armorers for pieces such as Thopas's lower leg-defenses (jambeux). See Blair, European Armour, 19, 41.

877 latoun: Latten, a brass-like alloy (cf. I.699n.), used by armorers. A pair of gauntlets of gilded latten belonging to the Black Prince survives at Canterbury. See Blair, European Armour, 41, 66. Blair (171) refers to headpieces mounted in latten. It would not be unsuitable for helmets, as has been suggested.

878 rewel boon: Ivory, from walrus or whale. Ivory was employed as a luxury in saddles and sheaths (VII.876). The fairy mistress in Thomas of Erceldoune has a saddle of *roelle bone* (Thornton MS, ed. Murray, 49). See also Ipomadon A 6456, and, for ballad instances, the glossary to Child's Ballads, s.v. *roelle-bone.*

879 Compare the fairy mistress in Thomas of Erceldoune: "als clere golde hir brydill it schone" (Thornton MS, ed. Murray, 63). The parallels with Thomas hereabouts (cf. VII.878 and 884) suggest that Chaucer may have had that romance, or a lost early ballad version, in mind.

881–83 Spears of cyprus wood are mentioned in Wars of Alexander, ed. Skeat, EETS e.s. 47, 1886, Dublin MS, 790. Spear-points were commonly ground before combat, whence the customary description **sharpe ygrounde** (cf. KnT I.2549; Tr 4.43; Bevis 3401).

884 **dappull gray:** Perhaps another touch of romance or ballad diction, but first recorded in English here. The palfrey of the fairy mistress in Thomas of Erceldoune is "a dappill graye" (Thornton MS, ed. Murray, 41). Chaucer elsewhere uses more Gallic forms: *pomely grey* (GP I.616) or *pomely grys* (CYPro VIII.559).

885 **an ambil:** Ambling is a soft gait, associated with mules and ladies' horses (GP I.469n.), not with warhorses.

888–90 Such minstrelish indications of the ending of a **fit** (an ancient Germanic term for a section of a poem, equivalent to Latin *passus*) occasionally appear in the text of romances and ballads. See Loomis, S&A, 496–503; and Baugh, Spec 42, 1967, 24–26. In Sir Eglamour they form a three-line supplement to the regular tail-rhyme stanza on three occasions, rather as here: Cotton MS, ed. Richardson, 343–45, 634–36, 904–6. The expression "here [is] a fit" is similarly used in Thomas of Erceldoune (Thornton MS, ed. Murray, 307), the ballad Adam Bell (Child, Ballads, no. 116) sts. 51 and 97, and Ipomedon B 1524.

891–93 Each of the poem's three fits begins with an appeal for attention, in the minstrel manner, coupled with an announcement of subject. See 712 and 833–35 above. **holde youre mouth** is even ruder than the "hold your tongue" cited by Loomis (S&A, 497) from Gamelyn, 169: compare MancPro IX.37.

895 **love-drury:** A compound unique in Chaucer (see 772 above). *Drury,* "love, courtship," itself occurs only here and in Rom 844 in Chaucer.

897–902 Other lists of heroes and romances are cited by Loomis, S&A, 556–59. Those in Richard Coer de Lyon (Caius MS, 7–32, and 6725–41) and Laud Troy Book (11–30) resemble Thopas in seeking to exalt a protagonist by preferring him to other heroes. Both, like Thopas, include Bevis and Guy (Richard, 6730; Troy Book, 15).

898 **Horn child:** The English hero Horn figures in two ME romances (ed. Hall, King Horn, 1901). He is frequently called "Horn child" in the older couplet poem; but Chaucer probably knew the inferior tail-rhyme version, preserved only in the Auchinleck MS and headed there "Horn Childe and Maiden Rimnild." For this use of *child,* see 810 above.

Ypotys: The hero of a ME verse legend Ypotis, in which the pious child (the name is that of Epictetus, the Stoic philosopher) instructs the emperor Hadrian in the Christian faith (ed. Horstmann, Altenglische Legenden, 1881). The poem appears together with romances in B.L. Cotton Caligula A.ii (see introductory note). Like the other three major MSS containing ME romances

(Lincoln Thornton, Auchinleck, Cambridge Ff.ii.38), Cotton Caligula freely mixes romances with didactic and religious matter such as Ypotis. See Everett, RES 6, 1930, 446–48, and Dieter Mehl, The ME Romances of the 13th and 14th Cents., 1968, 13–22. Chaucer does not imitate Ypotis in Thopas. The allusion may have been prompted by the hero's youth (prominent in all the romances mentioned in this stanza).

899 The English Bevis of Hampton (**Beves**) and Guy of Warwick (**Gy**) are both versions of Anglo-Norman "ancestral romances"; see M. Dominica Legge, Anglo-Norman Lit. and Its Background, 1963, chap. 7. Both appear in the Auchinleck MS, and their heroes are often cited together (see 897–902 above). Chaucer drew on both poems for Thopas, especially on Guy: see Strong, MLN 23, 1908, 73–77 and 102–6; and Loomis, in Carleton Brown Essays, 111–28.

900 **Lybeux:** "Lybeaus Desconus" (The Fair Unknown) is the name assumed by young Guinglain, Gawain's son, in the tail-rhyme romance of that title composed by Thomas Chester, an English contemporary of Chaucer. See 730–31, 807, and 869–71 above. For the spelling with *-x* see GP I.384n.

Pleyndamour: An obscure knight called Sir Playne de Amoris is overthrown by La Cote Male Tayle in Malory (ed. Vinaver, 472); but there is no evidence of any such romance hero worthy to rank with Guy and the rest. Chaucer may have been provoked into inventing the name by passages such as "Syr Prynsamour the erle hyght;/Syr Eglamour men call the knyght" (Eglamour, Cotton MS, ed. Richardson, 19–20). As an invented name *Pleyndamour* would stand to *Prynsamour* and *Eglamour* much as *Olifaunt* stands to *Amoraunt* and *Guymerraunt.* (See 808 above.)

902 **Chivalry** rhymes without the regular final *-e* here, as do *chivalry* and *love-drury* at 894–95 if the MS spellings are to be trusted there.

903 A typical conventional romance line: S&A, 511–13. Guy (Auchinleck MS, ed. Zupitza, 6411) has "His gode stede he bistrod." Chaucer's **al** is a choice example of the redundant or meaningless *all,* cultivated in Thopas: cf. VII.715, 719, 773, 831.

905 ME poets commonly compare rapid actions to sparks leaping from fire or flint; see Whiting S561–69.

906 Helmets often bore distinctive crests (though **creest** here refers not to the crest itself but to the top of the helmet to which it is fixed; see MED s.v. *creste* 3[a]). The heraldic crest may or may not carry the same device as the shield. In this case it does not (cf. VII.869–71). See J. Woodward, Treatise on Heraldry, 1896, 2.235–36.

tour: Towers frequently figure in crests; see Fairbairn's Book of Crests, ed. A. C. Fox-Davies, 1892, plates 156–57.

907 **lilie flour:** Guy of Warwick has an unspecified flower as his crest (Auchinleck MS, 250.1–3). The royal house of France sported a fleur-de-lis or lily (helmet illustrated in Blair, European Armour, fig. 86). But the lily stuck in the tower is unparalleled and probably, like Thopas's escutcheon, fanciful.

909 **knyght auntrous:** This semi-technical phrase, frequent in romances (S&A, 547–50), involves a reduced form of the adjective *aventurous* not found elsewhere in Chaucer.

911 To "lie in one's hood" is to sleep dressed, as knights errant do (cf. Sir Gawain and the Green Knight,

729); **hoode** may refer to the coif of mail: MED s.v. *hōd* 3(a).

912   Knights errant use their helmets as a pillow (**wonger**, a rare word) in Malory, ed. Vinaver, 253, 563.

915–16   A clear imitation of the lines from the opening stanza of the tail-rhyme romance of Perceval of Gales: "His righte name was Percyvell,/He was fosterde in the felle,/He dranke water of the welle:/And yitt was he wyghte" (5–8), ed. French and Hale, ME Metrical Romances, 1930.

well: The word normally has a final -*e* in Chaucer's English, but the rhyme is carried over from the Northern romance.

917   **worly under wede:** Chaucer elsewhere consistently avoids this type of alliterating phrase, very common in ME poetry ("lovely under linen," "comely under kell," etc.). The form *worly,* in place of *worthy* (which some MSS read), derives from *worthly* (also present as a MS variant). It is a rare and deliberately un-Chaucerian form; see Burrow, Essays on Med. Lit., 1984, 74–78.

918   The analogy of VII.748 and of many similar lines in ME romances suggests a phantom conclusion to this interrupted line: "Til on a day [it so bifel]."

The Prologue to Melibee

923   **drasty:** This word (from OE *draestig,* Lat. *feculentus*) has all the connotations of Modern English "crappy" (cf. Elliott, Ch's English, 173): crude, vulgar, like excrement, worthless (cf. Cullen, Expl 32, 1974, 35, and MED s.v. *drasty*).

933   **in geeste:** *Geeste* usually means "exploit," "deed," or "tale," as in III.642 and elsewhere. Here it seems to designate a literary form distinct from *ryme* or *prose.* The Parson uses the corresponding verb to designate alliterative verse (*I kan nat geeste 'rum, ram, ruf,' by lettre,* ParsPro X.43), which he likewise distinguished from *rym* (X.44) and *prose* (X.46); probably here *in geeste* means "in alliterating verse" (cf. Bone, MAE 7, 1938, 226).

937   **litel:** The adjective here and in 957 and 963 is a modest deprecation of the tale's importance (Olson, ChR 10, 1975, 147–53). See ParsT X.1081; Astr Pro 42; and, for similar usages, HF 1093; Tr 5. 1786, 1789.

943–52   Robertson (Pref to Ch, 367–69) explains that all the Evangelists tell the same story "when they are read spiritually rather than literally"; assuming that *tretys* in 957 and 963 "is obviously the Canterbury Tales itself," he asserts that Melibee affords a clue to the *sentence* of all the tales that preceded it. Huppé (A Reading of the CT, 235–36) agrees, but the view is refuted by Clark, ChR 6, 1971, 152–54, and Olson, ChR 10:147–53. Cf. ParsT X.1081n.

947   Cf. ParsPro X.58.

951   The line lacks a syllable, perhaps due to a pause after *Mark.*

955   "Chaucer's remark about proverbs is odd, as Professor Tatlock has observed, for the French version of Melibee which he followed was considerably more condensed than the Latin original" (Robinson). See however Palomo (PQ 53, 1974, 314–15), who agrees with

The explanatory notes to The Prologue and Tale of Melibee were written by Sharon Hiltz DeLong.

Albert H. Hartung's hypothesis that Chaucer may have produced an earlier version of the tale and that the present tale is actually a revision by Chaucer of this earlier version (A Study of the Textual Affiliations of Ch's Mel Considered in Its Relation to the Fr. Source, diss., Lehigh U., 1957, 1).

958   Cf. Whiting M264.1. For the word order, see GP I.791n.

963–64   **tretys lyte . . . murye tale:** Though Olson argues that two versions are here implied (ChR 10: 149–51), identical terms are applied to The Parson's Tale: *myrie tale* (X.46), *litel tretys* (X.1081; cf. 943–52 above). *Tale* is apparently the more general term, comprehending treatises such as the Melibee and The Parson's Tale (Strohm, MP 68, 1971, 321–28).

The Tale of Melibee

Chaucer's Tale of Melibee is a close translation of the *Livre de Melibée et de Dame Prudence,* written by Renaud de Louens sometime after 1336 (ed. Severs, S&A, 560–614). Renaud's work was apparently popular, since it was included in the *Ménagier de Paris* (compiled 1392–94), which also includes a version of the Griselda story. The *Livre de Melibée* is a translation of the *Liber consolationis et consilii* (ed. Thor Sundby, Ch Soc, 1873), written in 1246 by Albertanus of Brescia (?1193–?1270), as one of three moral treatises that he presented to his three sons as each came of age (the others are *De amore et dilectione Dei* and *De arte tacendi et loquendi*). Renaud handled his Latin text very freely, cutting it to about two-thirds its original length (Severs, S&A, 561). Yet he made additions, at several points drawing upon Albertanus's *De amore et dilectione Dei et proximi et aliarum rerum et de forma vitae* (ed. Hiltz, diss., U. of Pennsylvania, 1980). There is no evidence that Chaucer knew either the *De amore Dei* or the *Liber consolationis;* he relied solely on the French (Severs, S&A, 563 and n. 2), which he closely followed. His few deviations, noted by Severs, are recorded in the following notes.

The date of the Melibee is uncertain. Nineteenth-century critics tended to assign this, along with Chaucer's other religious and didactic pieces, to an early period. However, Chaucer apparently made his translation of Innocent III's *De miseria condicionis humane* in the late 1380s (ed. Lewis, see pp. 30–31), and The Parson's Tale is now often assigned to his later years (see introductory note to ParsT). Tatlock, Dev. and Chron., 188–98, argued for a date after 1376 on the basis of a deliberate omission (see 1199 below), and he argued that it came after *Troilus* and The Knight's Tale, which it seems to quote (Tr 1.956, Mel VII.1054; KnT I.2779, Mel VII.1559), and before the Man of Law's Prologue, written to introduce a tale in prose generally believed to have been Melibee. A date early in the Canterbury period (1386–90) seems most likely. See also Owen, ChR 7: 268.

Various attempts have been made to read the work as a political allegory, concerning John of Gaunt's proposed campaign in Spain (Hotson, SP 18, 1921, 429–52; Williams, New View, 162) or as generally applicable to English affairs at the time (Stillwell, Spec 19, 1944, 433–44). Scattergood, in Court and Poet, ed. Glyn S. Burgess, 1981, 287–96, argues that Sir Thopas and Melibee

were written, probably in the late 1380s, to form together an anti-war tract. The relevant passages, however,
are nearly all in Chaucer's French original; its general
concern with matters of war and peace was relevant to
almost any time and place from Albertanus's time to
Chaucer's (cf. Lawrence, in Essays and Sts. in Hon. of
Carleton Brown, 1940, 100–110). Other critics have
stressed the religious aspects of Melibee (Huppé, A
Reading of the CT, 1964, 237–39), and yet others its
possible relation to the themes of the "Marriage Group"
(W. W. Lawrence, Ch and CT, 1950, 131–33).

The style of Melibee has been regarded as an overly
elaborate rhetorical style intended as parody (Palomo,
PQ 53:304–20; Elliott, Ch's English, 173–74), though
Schlauch finds it consciously artistic (in Ch and Chaucerians, 153–56) and Bornstein (ChR 12, 1978, 236–54)
sees it as an example of a sophisticated *style clergial* that
she says was in vogue in the fourteenth and fifteenth
centuries. The idea that the tale is a comic parody stems
ultimately from the old idea that the Melibee is Chaucer's
revenge on the Host for interrupting Sir Thopas
(Mather, Ch's GP, 1899, xxxi; Lumiansky, Of Sondry
Folk, 94) and survives in various comic readings (Whittock, A Reading of CT, 209–17; Gaylord, PMLA 82,
1967, 226–35). Preston perhaps exaggerates when he
says that the Melibee can be a joke only to those who skip
it (Ch, 1952, 212), but David (Strumpet Muse, 220) is
surely right in maintaining that whereas Sir Thopas is
short enough to be a joke, the Melibee is simply too long
to be either a parody or an intentionally dull piece intended as a characterization of its teller.

The tale has been defended on the grounds that it is
typical of its time (Manly, CT, 634—though he, like
Baugh and Donaldson, omitted it from his edition) and,
more recently, that it is a serious and important work in
itself (Thundy, NM 77, 1976, 582–98). A number of
recent critics regard it as having a central thematic function in the *Tales*. Howard (Idea of CT, 309–16) considers it a "major structural unit" in the *Tales*, part of the
"address to the ruling class" that is a recurrent theme of
the *Tales*. Ruggiers (in Ch Probs, 83–94) considers the
tale's emphasis on prudent action, the taking of wise
counsel, and the right use of the intellect part of the
main concerns of *The Canterbury Tales*. Traugott
Lawler, One and the Many, 102–8, regards it as a pivo-
tal tale, a specifically Christian complement to the philosophical Knight's Tale and an anticipation of The Parson's Tale.

The notes that follow emphasize Chaucer's departures
from his French source, as identified by Severs, and the
sources of Albertanus's proverbs and sentences, mainly
as identified by Sundby and Skeat. Obviously, works
known to Albertanus were not necessarily known to
Chaucer, and the notes show not Chaucer's own reading
but the ultimate sources of bits of learning that came to
him at third hand in Renaud's French version. Renaud is
cited by page and line number from Severs's edition in
S&A, Albertanus by page and line number in Sundby's
edition. Quotations from the Vulgate, including the
Apocrypha, are here translated only where they differ
from the RSV.

Notice that the line numbers for the text of The Tale
of Melibee appear at the *end* of the respective lines.

967   Melibeus: *A man that drynketh hony* (Mel 1410); a
false etymology from the Lat. *mel bibens.*

Prudence: Lat. "prudentia." Albertanus has taken the
name from Cassiodorus, *Variarum* 2.15 (ed. Mommsen,
Monumenta Germaniae Hist. 12, 1972).

Sophie: From the Gr. σοφία, wisdom. Melibee's
wounded daughter is not named in the Latin or French
texts. Thundy (NM 77:596) suggests that the naming
illustrates Chaucer's concern with the theme of wisdom
in the tale: Sophie is Melibee's own wounded wisdom
which needs to be healed.

968   into the feeldes: This is Chaucer's addition; it appears in neither the Latin nor French texts (Severs, S&A,
568.10). Scattergood (in Court and Poet, ed. Burgess,
288) suggests this is intended to recall Thopas VII.909–
15 and thus establish the continuity between the two
works.

970   olde foes: The three enemies of man: the world,
the flesh, and the devil, as explained in VII.1421. See
Donald R. Howard, The Three Temptations, 1966, 61–
65.

972   feet: Fr. "piez," an error for *yeux* (Lat. "oculis,"
Liber Cons. 218); Severs, S&A, 568.14.

976   Ovide . . . Remedie of Love: Ovid, Remedia
amoris, 127.

984   Senek: Seneca, Ad Lucilium 74.30.

989   See Romans 12.15.

991   Seneca, Epist. 63.1.

993   See also Seneca, Epist. 63.11.

995   Jhesus Syrak: Jesus, son of Sirach, author of Ecclesiasticus, though this is from Prov. 17.22; the error is
due to the French.

996   Ecclus. 30.23.

997   Prov. 25.20 (Vulg.): "Like a moth in a garment or
a worm in wood, sorrow injures the heart of a man."
Moths were thought to be bred in the fleece of sheep (see
Vincent of Beauvais, Spec. Nat. 20.124).

998   goodes temporels: The French adjective plural,
-(e)s, is relatively rare in Chaucer except in his translated
prose; see Language and Versification, p. xxxv.

1000   Job 1.21.

**1003   Cf. MilT I.3530 and n., MerT IV.1485–86. From
Ecclus. 32.24; Whiting C470. The confusion of Solomon
and the author of Ecclesiasticus here and elsewhere derives from Albertanus (Liber Cons. 6.11; S&A, 570.64).

**1017   Proverbial; cf. Whiting C414 and Walters (Nova
series) 35738b "Contrariis medici curant contraria."

1028   to moeve werre: From the Fr. "de mouvoir
guerre," (Severs, S&A, 571.104).

**1030   A commonplace: "Ad paenitendum properat, cito
qui iudicat," from Publius Syrius (1st century A.D.), Sententia, 32 and 59, ed. Meyer, 1880. See Mel VII.1135
and cf. Whiting D143, J78.

**1031   Proverbial; cf. Whiting J75, Tilley J75.

**1032   Cf. Whiting T44, "In long tarrying is noys."

**1033   Cf. John 8.3–8.

**1036   Proverbial: Whiting I60, Hassell F51; cf. Tr
2.1276.

**1045   Ecclus. 22.6.

**1047   Cf. ProNPT VII.2801–2. Ecclus. 32.6 (Vulg.):
"Do not lavish your words where there is no audience."

**1048   Publius Syrius, Sent., 594; see Whiting C458.

1050   weren accorded: Most of the French MSS add
"et conseilloit" here. It is likely that Chaucer's source MS
omitted these words since he does not translate them.
The Latin text does not have their equivalent (S&A,
573.147).

1053   Piers Alfonce: Petrus Alphonsus, a Spanish Jew

who was baptized in 1106; the reference is to his Disciplina clericalis 25.15 (ex. 24).

1054 Proverbial: Tr 1.956 is identical; cf. Tr 4.1567–68. See also Whiting H171, H166. Chaucer has added this sentence, which is not present in the Latin or French texts (S&A, 573.154).

wikked haste: Cf. ParsT X.1003.

1057 Eccles. 7.28; cf. MerT IV.2247–48.

1059 Ecclus. 25.30 (Vulg.): "If a woman has primacy, she is contrary to her husband." Cf. ParsT X.927.

1060 Ecclus. 33.20–22 (AV 19.21).

1060–61 The French reads: "For it is written, 'The chattering of women can hide nothing except what she does not know.' Further, the philosopher says, 'In bad advice women outdo men. For these reasons I must not use your advice.'" Omitted by Chaucer, though in both the French and Latin texts.

1062 Seneca, Controversiarum 2.13.12. Cf. WBT III.950 and n.

1063 Publius Syrius, Sent., 324.

1067 Seneca, De beneficiis 4.38.1.

1070 **save youre grace:** From the Fr. "sauve vostre reverence" (S&A, 575.189); Lat. "salva reverentia tua" (Liber Cons., 14.3).

1071 **Senec:** An erroneous attribution in the Latin text; actually from Martinus Dumiensis, Formula honestae vitae 3 (PL 72:26). The misattribution is repeated throughout.

1075 Mark 16.9.

1075–79 Cf. MerT IV.2277–90n.

1076 Possibly alluding to Prov. 31.10.

1079 Cf. Matt. 19.17; Luke 18.19.

1084 Cf. Whiting W534, W485.

1086 This common proverb (Whiting T187) appears also in WBPro III.278–80, and though it here derives from Albertanus, Chaucer may have known it in Innocent III, *De miseria condicionis humane* (ed. Lewis, 1.16.33) or Jerome's *Epistola adversus Jovinianum* 1.28. ParsT X.631 quotes Prov. 27.15, the ultimate source of the saying, which may also conflate Prov. 10.26, 19.13.

1087 Cf. WBPro III.775–77; Prov. 21.19, Ecclus. 25.16.

1088 Almost identical with MerT IV.1456, WBPro III.112.

1090 Cf. Whiting W545.

1094 Chaucer omits the Fr. "For often when men want to work by evil counsel, women dissuade them from it and convince them," which is also in the Latin (S&A, 576.229–31).

1096 Cf. Whiting C473, and cf. NPT VII.3256.

1098–1102 These examples of womanly counsel appear in the same order in MerT IV.1363–74; they derive from Gen. 27, Judith 8, 1 Sam. 25, Esther 7.

1104 See Gen. 2.18.

1106 Cf. NPT VII.3164n. and Whiting W529.

1107–8 Lat. gloss: "Quid melius auro? Jaspis. / Quid Jaspide? Sensus. / Quid Sensu? Mulier. / Quid mulier? Nihil" (translated in the text, with the addition of the qualification *good*). See Hervieux, Les fabulistes latins, 1884–99, 5:622. The verses were popular (Walther 24980) and had many variants. (For example, "Quid levius flamma? Flumen. / Quid flumine? Ventus. / Quid vento? Mulier. / Quid mulier? Nihil." Walther 25064; see also Walther 1584, 25065.)

1113 Prov. 16.24.

1121–23 Cf. VII.1246–48; see Haeckel, 27.88; "Cae-

cilius Balbus," De nugis philosophorum 28.5, ed. Wölfflin, 1855; Whiting T184.

1124 **may nat do:** Chaucer omits "et pour ce son conseil surmonte tousjours sa force." The passage is also present in the Latin (S&A, 578.275–76).

1125 Cf. Whiting I62, Walther 12913.

1127 From Publius Syrius, Sent., 281; not from Seneca.

1130 1 Tim. 6.10. Cf. VII.1840; PardPro VI.334; ParsT X.739; Whiting C491.

1135 Publius Syrius, Sent., 32. Cf. 1030 and 1054 above.

1141–42 Ecclus. 19.8, 9.

1143 **Another clerk:** Not identified in the source ("Et alius dixit").

1144 **The book:** Cf. Petrus Alphonsus, Disc. cler. 4.3; Ecclus. 8.22 (AV 8.19).

1147 Martinus Dumiensis, De moribus 16 (PL 72:29); not from Seneca. Cf. Whiting C462.

1153 Proverbial; Whiting M273.

1158 Prov. 27.9.

1159 Ecclus. 6.15.

1161 Ecclus. 6.14.

1162 **the book:** Cf. Prov. 22.17; Tobias 4.19 (AV 18); Ecclus. 9.14.

1164 Cf. Job 12.12; Whiting C452, M118.

1165 **Tullius:** Cicero, De senectute 6.17.

1167 Ecclus. 6.6.

1171 Prov. 11.14.

1173 Ecclus. 8.20 (AV 17). Cf. Whiting C465.

1174 Cicero, Tusculan Disputations 3.30.73.

1176 Cicero, De amicitia 25.91.

1177 Cf. Martinus Dumiensis, Form. honest. vir. 3. See also Prov. 28.23.

1178–79 Prov. 29.5.

1180 Cicero, De officiis 1.26.91.

1181 **Caton:** "Dionysius," Cato, Disticha 3.4, ed. Boas, 1952.

1183 Publius Syrius, Sent., 91.

1184 **Isope:** "Ysopus," the Latin version of Aesop's Fables, here quoted by the Latin text "Ne confidatis secreta nec hiis detegatis, / Cum quibus egestis pugnae discrimina tristis" (Liber Cons., 49). See Walther 15973; Whiting S123.

1185 Not from Seneca, but Publius Syrius, Sent., 389; cf. Whiting F194, R77.1.

1186 Ecclus. 12.10. Cf. Whiting F364, F367, C467.

1189 **Peter Alfonce:** Petrus Alphonsus, Disc. cler. 4.4. Albertanus's "deviabunt" (Liber Cons., 50.6) for *devitabunt* may account for the French "pervirtiront," Chaucer's *perverten*.

1191 **a philosophre:** Unidentified in either the French or the Latin.

1192 Cf. Cicero, De officiis 2.7.23.

1194 Prov. 31.4 (Vulg.): "Quia nullum secretum est ubi regnat ebrietas." The idea is proverbial (Whiting D425); cf. PardT VI.560–61; and see MLT II.771–77n.

1196 **Cassiodorie:** Cassiodorus (Flavius Magnus Aurelius Cassiodorus, fl. first half of sixth cent.), Variarum 10.18.

1197 Publius Syrius, Sent., 354. Cf. Prov. 12.5.

1199 Both the French and English versions omit about 2 pages of the Latin text at this point (Liber Cons., 53–55). Another passage (Liber Cons., 57–58) is omitted after VII.1210. After VII.1199, Chaucer omits "And Solomon says, 'Woe to the land that has a child as a lord and whose lord dines in the morning'" (Eccles. 10.16;

S&A, 581.381–83). Tatlock (Dev. and Chron., 192) argues that Chaucer was thinking of the young king Richard II and that, though the middle eighties would best fit with the omission, such a reference would have been tactless "at any time from 1376 to (say) 1395."

1200 **folwe:** Fr. "fuir." This word may be the result of a confusion of *suir* with *fuir;* it does not appear in the Latin original (S&A, 582.385).

1201–10 **doctrine of Tullius:** Cf. Cicero, De officiis 2.5.18.

1215 Cf. Chaucer's Proverbs 5–8; Whiting M774.

1216 Cato, Dist. 3.15.

1218 Petrus Alphonsus, Disc. cler. 6.12 (ex. 4).

1219 Proverbial; cf. PF 514–16; Whiting T366.

1221 Cicero, De officiis 1.9.

1225 Proverbial: A legal aphorism (Walther 3180), which Albertanus quotes from no particular source. Cf. Tr 4.416n.

1226 Not identified in Seneca. Cf. Whiting C467.

1229 Cf. Justinian (483–565), Digesta 45.1.26, ed. Mommsen, Schöll, Kroll, 1954.

1230 **parfourned or kept:** Chaucer omits the French "et en moult d'autres manieres" here, which conflates a longer passage in the Latin text (S&A, 583.428–29).

1231 Cf. Publius Syrius, Sent., 362.

1246 Cf. 1121–23 above. See also "Caecilius Balbus," De nugis 28.5.

1250 **They han espied . . . enclyned:** Chaucer's addition, found in neither the Latin nor French texts (S&A, 584.458).

1257 **cast . . . hochepot:** This phrase is not found in the Latin or French versions (S&A, 585.465). *Hochepot* is a legal term meaning a gathering of properties together for equal distribution—i.e., treating all claimants as equal. See OED s.v. *hotchpot* 3.

1264 Sundby compares St. John Chrysostom (?345–407), Adhortatio ad Theodorum lapsum 1.14 (PG 47–64); Vincent of Beauvais, Spec. Hist. 17.45; but cf. Augustine, Serm. 164.10.14: "Humanum est errare, diabolicum est in errore perse[ve]re" (Walther 112676).

1269 Cf. Gregory IX, Decretals 1.37.3 (Frankfort, 1586). Gregory applies the aphorism to priests, not physicians.

1277 Cf. 1017 above.

1283 Cf. Whiting M75.

1292 See Rom. 12.17; cf. also 1 Pet. 3.9; 1 Thess. 5.15; 1 Cor. 4.12.

1304 Ps. 126.1 (AV 127.1).

1306–7 Cato, Dist. 4.13.

1309 Petrus Alphonsus, Disc. cler. 18.10 (ex. 17).

1316–17 Prov. 28.14; cf. Whiting M83.

1320 Publius Syrius, Sent., 542, 607, 380, 116; not from Seneca. Cf. Whiting M338.

1324 Publius Syrius, Sent., 255.

1325–26 Ovid, Rem. amor. 421–22: "The little viper will slay a huge bull with its bite/ And a dog, which is not large, holds back the wild boar." Chaucer omits the title of the reference, which is given in the Latin and French texts (S&A, 588.541; Liber Cons., 71.3), and adds **and the wilde hert** and **A litel thorn may prikke a kyng ful soore.** Skeat (5:214) explains Chaucer's **wesele** as the result of a confusion of Fr. "vivre" (= Lat. "vipere," viper) with Lat. *viverra,* a ferret.

1328 Seneca, Epist. 3.3.

1330 Albertanus, De arte loquendi et tacendi, ed.

Sundby in Brunetto Latinis Levnet og Skrifter, 1869; also Liber Cons., 72.2–3.

1336 **olde and wise:** Chaucer omits "and at great expense" (S&A, 589.560; Liber Cons., 73.4–5).

1339–40 Not from Cicero, but from Seneca, De clementia 1.19.6, ed. Haase, 1873.

1344 Cicero, De officiis 1.21.73.

1347 Not from Cicero. Cf. Publius Syrius, Sent., 125.

1348 Cassiodorus, Variarum 1.17.

1355 Cicero, De officiis 2.5. Cf. VII.1200–1210. Chaucer departs here from both the French and the Latin, perhaps because his source was "faulty or incomprehensible at this point" (S&A, 599.581–82).

1360 Cf. Cicero, "quid consentaneum cuique" (De officiis 2.5).

1364 **ne been nat youre freendes:** Chaucer's addition (S&A, 590.591–92).

1380 **the lawe:** Cf. Justinian, Corpus iuris civilis 8.4.1.

1387 **consequent:** "Quid consequens" (Cicero, De officiis 2.5).

1390 **engendrynge:** "Ex quo quidque gignatur (Cicero, De officiis 2.5).

1395 *Oriens:* Not in the Latin or French texts. Chaucer apparently uses it as the equivalent of "longinqua." Although Chaucer may have misread the French ("Deux causes ouvrières et efficiens"), he may have been responsible for the Latin terms, none of which, aside from "efficiens," is in the Latin (Liber Cons., 85.5–6); cf. M-R 4:304; S&A, 591.628–29.

1404 Gratian (fl. 1140), Decretum 2.1.1.25, ed. Friedberg, Corpus iuris canonici, 1, 1879.

1406 The Latin text refers expressly to 1. Cor 4.55, "but Chaucer has accommodated it to Romans 11.33" (Skeat 5:216).

1410 See 967 above; the allegory of the opening, which had not been developed, is here resumed. See Strohm ChR 2, 1967, 32–42, and Owen, ChR 7, 1973, 267–80.

1415 Ovid, Amores 1.8.104.

goodes of the body: See ParsT X.452.

1416 Prov. 25.16; Chaucer adds **and be nedy and povre** (S&A, 592.655–56).

1421 **three enemys:** See 970 above.

1424 See the ParsT for a treatment of the seven deadly sins.

1433–34 Chaucer omits the French: "And to this dame Prudence replied: 'Certainly,' she said, 'I grant you that from vengeance comes much good; but to take vengeance does not belong (is not proper) to anyone except only judges and to those who have jurisdiction over evil-doers.'" The lines seem necessary to the sense, but Severs thinks it likely they were missing from Chaucer's source manuscript (S&A, 593.677–80).

1437 The Latin is "Bonis nocet qui malis parcet": He who spares evil-doers does harm to the good (Martinus Dumiensis, De moribus 114), accurately translated in the French as "Celui nuit aus bons que espargne les maufais" (S&A, 593.682–83). Perhaps, as Robinson suggested, Chaucer's source manuscript was here corrupt.

1438 Cassiodorus, Variarum 1.4.

1439 Publius Syrius, Sent., 528.

1440–43 Romans 13.4.

spere: A mistake for *swerd* (Fr. "glaive"; Lat. "gladium").

1449 Publius Syrius, Sent., 320.

1450 Publius Syrius, Sent., 189.

1455 Publius Syrius, Sent., 172.

1460 Romans 12.19.

1463 Publius Syrius, Sent., 645.

1466 Publius Syrius, Sent., 487.

1473 "Caecilius Balbus," De nugis 41.4.

1481–83 Seneca, De ira 2.34.1, ed. Haase, 1873; cf. Whiting M86.

1485 Prov. 20.3.

1488 Publius Syrius, Sent., 483.

1489 Cato, Dist. 4.39.

1496 the poete: Identified only as "le poëte" in the French text, and not mentioned at all in the Latin. Skeat compares Luke 23.41. Possibly he was a versifier of the De duodecim utilitatibus tribulationis ascribed to Peter of Blois (Kreuzer, MLN 63, 1948, 54).

1497 Seint Gregorie: The passage has not been located in Gregory's works.

1502–4 1 Pet. 2.21–23.

1509 epistle: Chaucer omits the name of the epistle (2 Cor. 4.17), which is present in the French text. The Latin original lacks the passage altogether (S&A, 597.772).

1510 Cf. 2 Cor. 4.17.

1512 Prov. 19.11 (Vulg.): "Doctrina viri per patientiam noscitur" (tr. in text).

1513 Prov. 14.29 (Vulg.): "Qui patiens est multa gubernatur prudentia" (tr. in text).

1514 Prov. 15.18.

1515–16 Prov. 16.32.

1517 Cf. James 1.4.

1519–20 Cf. WBPro III.111–12.

1524 Cf. Whiting O56.

1528 Cassiodorus, Variarum 1.30.

1531 Cf. Martinus Dumiensis, De moribus 139. Not from Seneca.

1539 Prov. 19.19.

1541 Cf. Justinian, Digesta 1.17.36.

1542 Prov. 26.17.

1550 Eccles. 10.19; cf. Whiting M633.

1553 1 Tim. 4.4 is quoted by Albertanus.

1554 Skeat notes that "Homo sine pecunia est quasi corpus sine anima" is written on the flyleaf of a MS (5:219); see his intro. to PP C, xx. Cf. Whiting M235.

1556 Pamphilles: Hero of a twelfth-century Latin poetic dialogue, Pamphilus de Amore, ed. Becker, 1972. Cf. FranT V.1110n. The lines quoted here are 53–54: "Dum modo sit dives cuiusdam nata bulbuci,/ Eliget ex mille quem libet [or, volet] illa virum."

1558 Not from Pamphilus. Cf. Ovid, Tristia 1.9.5–6, though the idea is common (see Whiting R108).

1559 Proverbial; cf. ProMLT II.120. The quotation does not appear in the Latin text (S&A, 600.838).

1560 alloone . . . compaignye: Identical to KnT I.2779 (see n.) and MilT I.3204.

1561 Not from Pamphilus. Cf. Petrus Alphonsus, Disc. cler. 6.4 (ex. 4): "Ut ait versificator: Glorificant [var. Clarificant] gaze privatos nobilitate." The versifier has not been identified.

1562 Cf. Horace, Epistles 1.6.37.

1564 See Cassiodorus, Variarum 2.13. Chaucer has mooder of ruyne for the Fr. "mère de crimes," Lat. "mater criminum"; his source MS may have been corrupt here (S&A, 600.843).

1566 Petrus Alphonsus, Disc. cler. 4.4 (ex. 2).

1567 eten: An accurate translation of the Fr. "men-

gier," but that is a scribal error for mendier or demander; the Lat. has "postulare"; Severs, S&A, 601.845.

1568–70 Innocent III, De miseria condicionis humane 1.16; cf. MLT II.99–121.

1571 Cf. ProMLT II.114; Ecclus. 40.28 (Vulg. 29).

1572 Cf. Ecclus. 30.17.

1578 Prov. 28.20.

1579 Prov. 13.11.

1583 The source for this quotation, added by Renaud, is not known.

1584 no man: For the construction see 1757 below.

1585–88 Cicero, De officiis 3.5.21.

1587 The Fr. reads "Et pour ce que tu puisse acquerre plus loyaument," the Lat. "Opes igitur bonas et Deo placentes acquiras manibus operando" (from De amore et dilectione Dei, cited but not quoted in Liber Cons. 101.15–102.4); Chaucer's version seems to have been due to a corruption in his French source (S&A, 602.869).

1589 Ecclus. 33.27; cf. SNPro VIII.1n.

1590–91 Prov. 28.19.

1593 versifiour: Unidentified. Cf. Prov. 20.4; Whiting M110.

1594 Cato, Distichs 1.2.

1595 Jerome: Cf. SNPro VIII.6–7. Although this idea is attributed to St. Jerome in the Ayenbite of Inwyt (ed. Morris, EETS 23, 1866, 206) and in Jehan de Vignay's introduction to his French translation of the Legenda aurea, the reference has not been traced. Cf. Jerome, Epist. 125.11.

1602–3 Cato, Distichs 4.16.

1605 Cato, Distichs 3.21.

1612 This quotation does not appear in the Latin text, and has not been identified. Cf. Whiting D94.

1617 Seint Austyn: Not identified in Augustine's works; cf. Prov. 27.20.

1621 Cicero, De officiis 2.15.55.

1628 Prov. 15.16.

love of God: For "fear of God" (Fr. paour, Lat. timore) is probably due to an erroneous reading "amour" in Chaucer's source manuscript (Severs, S&A, 603.910).

1630 Ps. 36.16.

the prophete: That is, David; "philosophe" in the French text.

1634 2 Cor. 1.12.

1635 Ecclus. 13.30 (AV 24).

1638 Prov. 22.1.

1639–40 Ecclus. 41.12.

Chaucer's freend for "name" apparently results from a French MS which had "ami" instead of "nom" (M-R 4.506).

1642 Cassiodorus, Variarum 1.4: "Est enim indigni [var. digni] animi signum, famae diligere commodum." Albertanus inserts this sentence, as if it were his own, between two other quotations from Cassiodorus (3.12 and 9.22). But for "indigni" (or "digni") he substitutes "ingenui," which explains gentil in Renaud's and Chaucer's versions (Robinson).

1643–45 Austyn: St. Augustine, Sermo 355.1 (PL 39: 1568), apparently added by Renaud.

1644 This explanation is not in the French or Latin and may be Chaucer's addition.

1651 The philosophre has not been identified.

1653 Eccles. 5.11 (Vulg. 10).

1661–63 1 Macc. 3.18–19.

1664 Cf. Eccles. 9.1 (Vulg.): "There are just men and

wise, and their works are in God's hand; yet none knows if he is worthy of God's love or displeasure." After **victorie** the French reads: "any more than he is certain whether he is worthy of the love of God."

1666 Cf. Whiting M42, K49.

1668 **seconde Book of Kynges:** See Liber secundus regum (AV 2 Samuel) 11.25, where the Vulgate has "Varius enim eventus est belli; nunc hunc et nuncillum consumit gladius."

1671 Ecclus. 3.27 (AV 26); here as elsewhere Solomon and Jesus son of Sirach are confused.

1676 **Seint Jame:** "Saint Jaques" in Chaucer's source, an error for *Seneques* (S&A, 606.968); see Seneca, Epist. 94.46, which quotes Sallust, Jugurtha 10.6.

1678 **oon of the gretteste:** See Language and Versification, p. xxxviii, on this construction. Manly and Rickert (4:506) suggest that the addition of *unytee* in the English text where the French has only "paix" may stem from an interest in unity in fourteenth-century England and cite Passus 19 of PP B.

1680 Matt. 5.9.

1686 Proverbial: cf. "Familiarity breeds contempt;" Whiting H426.

1691 Martinus Dumiensis, De moribus 3; Whiting D265.

1692 Ps. 34.15 (AV 34.14).

1696 Prov. 28.14.

1701 Chaucer has **prophete** for Fr. "philosophe," but no literary source of the quotation is known; Whiting E225.

1704 Prov. 28.23.

1707–08 An expansion of Eccles. 7.4 (Vulgate): "Sadness is better than laughter;" VII.1709–10 expand the rest of the verse: "because through sadness the countenance corrects the wayward soul" (Skeat 5:222).

1719 Prov. 16.7.

1735 Ps. 20.4 (Vulg.): "You have come before him with sweet blessings; you set a crown of precious stones on his head."

1740 Ecclus. 6.5 (Vulg.): "Verbum dulce multiplicat amicos et mitigat inimicos" (tr. in text).

1753–56 Ecclus. 33.19–20 (RV 18–19).

1757 **that man sholde nat yeven:** The negative construction here may be due to the French. Cf. Bo 3.pr10.14. See also Tr 2.716–18n. for similar constructions in English.

1775–76 Martinus Dumiensis, De moribus 94.

1777 Cf. Publius Syrius, Sent., 489.

1783 **the lawe:** Justinian, Digesta 50.17.35.

1794 Proverbial; Whiting T348. Cf. ProLGW 452.

1815 Chaucer begins at this point to paraphrase the French version more freely.

1825–26 These lines are Chaucer's addition (S&A, 612.1125).

1840 1 Tim. 6.10.

1842 Publius Syrius, Sent., 479.

1846 Publius Syrius, Sent., 293.

1850 Gregory, Decretals 3.31.18.

1857 Cf. Seneca, De clementia 1.24.1.

1859 Publius Syrius, Sent., 64.

1860 Cicero, De officiis 1.25.88.

lord: Fr. "seigneur," the reading of Chaucer's source MS. All other MSS have "homme"; Lat. "viro" (Liber Cons., 123.11). Cf. S&A, 613.1160.

1866 Publius Syrius, Sent., 366.

1869 James 2.13.

1884–88 Cf. 1 John 1.9. Not in the Latin or French texts (S&A, 614.1179).

The Monk's Prologue

The opening words of the Host in the Monk's Prologue correspond closely to part of a single stanza, usually designated "The Host stanza," which appears in twenty-two MSS at the end of The Clerk's Tale (see IV.1212a–g above). Apparently, Chaucer first wrote the speech for the latter position, but transferred it to the Monk's Prologue when he developed at length the characterization of the Host and his wife.

The words of the Host to the Monk (VII.1941–62) are similarly repeated in substance in the Epilogue to the Nun's Priest's Tale (VII.3447–62), which is preserved in only nine MSS and which perhaps Chaucer canceled when he wrote the present link.

Dempster (PMLA 68, 1953, 1142–59) argues that Chaucer was consciously leading up to the Marriage Group when he revised this prologue. She also notes (1151) the comic characterization of the Host here and in the Nun's Priest's Prologue, the Shipman-Prioress link, and the Physician-Pardoner link, all of which she would date near to one another.

1892 **corpus Madrian:** No St. Madrian is known, and this is probably another of the Host's malapropisms; he has trouble with any oath involving *corpus* (see 1906 below, PhysT VI.314, ShipT VII. 435) and with saints' names (cf. PardPro VI.310). *Madrian* means "spice, or sweetmeat" (MED; cf. Frost, MLN 57, 1942, 177–79). Materne and Mathurin have been proposed as the saint intended but neither seems likely. Haskell (JEGP 67, 1968, 430–40) reviews these and other suggestions and argues instead for a reference to St. Hadrian or Adrian, an officer of the imperial Roman court who, upon his conversion to Christianity, suffered martyrdom; he was sustained and encouraged during his ordeal by his wife Natalia (see Jacobus de Voragine, Legenda aurea, 597–601; tr. Caxton 5:112–19; tr. Ryan and Rippberger, 531–35). Byers (ELN 4, 1966, 6–9) notes the contextual suitability of this saint, whose wife had the persistence and concern of Dame Prudence and the persistence and pride of Goodelief. Two late scribes wrote *Adrian* for *Madryan* (M-R 7:464). Haskell offers no contemporary proof for her assertion that Adrian was known in the fourteenth century as the patron saint of brewers.

1894 **Goodelief:** Printed as two words, *gode lief,* in some editions, and taken as an epithet (cf. WBPro III. 431), but now generally accepted as a proper name whose popularity in the mid-fourteenth century is demonstrated by Rickert (TLS 16 Dec. 1926, 935; MP 25, 1927, 79–82; see also Richardson, TLS 20 Jan. 1927, 44). In Southwark records the wife of the real Harry Baily (or Bailly) is named Christian (Manly, New Light, 79–81); Rickert (MP 25:81) believes that the name was chosen from "ironic malice," and Malone (ES 31, 1950, 209–15) that it was meant for comic effect. Seaton (MLR 41, 1946, 196–202) notes the existence of a Flemish

The explanatory notes to the Monk's Prologue and Tale were written by Susan H. Cavanaugh.

saint, Godeleva (variant, Goodelief), the theme of whose legend centers on her wifely patience.

1901-4   Cf. GP I.449–52.

1906   **corpus bones:** Another of the Host's blunders, this time attributed to his wife.

1907   **distaf:** See 2374 below.

1922   **mysdooth or seith:** Cf. MilT I.3139.

1926   **Rouchestre:** Since Sittingbourne, mentioned in WBPro III.847, is ten miles farther on the road to Canterbury, the order of tales in the MSS, in which Fragment III precedes Fragment VII (with IV through VI intervening), has seemed to many unsatisfactory (see the introduction to the textual notes to *The Canterbury Tales*).

1929   **daun John:** The name of the monk in The Shipman's Tale (cf. VII.43 and n.). The Host addresses the Monk by his right name, *daun Piers,* in ProNPT VII.2792. On the title *daun,* see KnT I.1379n.

1934   Cf. GP I.205.

1955   **borel:** Cf. FranPro V.716n.

1956   **wrecched ympes:** The expression is proverbial; Whiting T465. Cf. Matt. 7.17, LGW 2395, and WBT III.1128–32.

1962   **lussheburghes:** Coins of inferior metal imported into England from Luxemburg during the reign of Edward III. Cf. Langland, PP B 15.349: "In lussheburwes is a luther alay, and yet loketh he lik a sterlyng."

Robinson notes that while the Host's banter here is simply a variation on the old theme of the Goliardic poets: "clerus scit diligere virginem plus milite" (a cleric knows more about pleasing a maiden than a knight), sacerdotal celibacy was much discussed in England at the end of the fourteenth century. Wyclif and his followers were skeptical of the validity and efficacy of restraint upon clerical marriage, and in the decade or so after Wyclif's death the Lollards openly attacked the regulation. "The particular argument of the Host, however, seems to have been seldom used. In the century-long controversy about compulsory celibacy the opponents of the law have laid emphasis chiefly on the weakness of human nature and the licentiousness of the clergy when living under unnatural restraint. They have rarely referred to the effect on the population of the withdrawal of the clergy from parenthood" (Robinson). On the opinions of Wyclif and the Lollards, see Henry C. Lea, Hist. of Sacerdotal Celibacy, 1907, 1:474–76; Herbert B. Workman, John Wyclif, 1926, 2:45.

1964   Proverbial; cf. CkPro I.4355.

1970   **Seint Edward:** Probably Edward the Confessor (c. 1004–66), king of England, whose veneration as a saint was supported by his reputation for religious devotion and generosity and by a number of miracles attributed to him. Richard II had a special devotion to this saint, whom he had depicted alongside himself in the Wilton Diptych. His *Life* was known in Latin and in several French versions (M. Dominica Legge, Anglo-Norman Lit., 1963, 60, 246–48) and is included in the South English Legendary.

1973   **Tragedie:** Used not in the modern sense, but as explained in the lines that follow. A similar definition of tragedy occurs in the gloss on Bo 2.pr2.70. Cf. also VII.1991–94 and 2761–65. This limited definition may not, however, reflect Chaucer's own view. See the introductory note to The Monk's Tale below and Tr 5.1786n.

1985   The Monk's apology for departing from chronological order is sometimes held to apply to the "Modern

Instances" (see introductory note to Monk's Tale below), but it should be noted that the ancient tragedies themselves fail to follow a strict chronological arrangement.

1986   **popes, emperours, or kynges:** Pratt (in Sts. in Lang., 308) notes the similarity between this line and the running head of the final and longest section of Nicholas Trevet's Chronicles, "les gestes des Apostoiles, Emperours et Rois."

The Monk's Tale

The most thorough discussions of the date of The Monk's Tale and the probable circumstances of its composition remain those of Tatlock (Dev. and Chron., 164–72) and Kittredge (Date of Tr, 1909, 38–50). The Monk's Tale, like that of the Second Nun has usually been taken to be one of Chaucer's earlier works, written, perhaps, shortly after his first Italian journey and adapted at a later stage for its position in the Tales. The Bernabò stanza, which cannot have been written before 1386 (Bernabò died 19 December 1385), has been recognized as a later interpolation, and the other so-called Modern Instances—the two Pedros and Ugolino—have been similarly regarded by Skeat, Kittredge, and others (see also Baugh, Ch's Maj. Poetry, 355). Tatlock, who opposes the theory of interpolation, takes the whole tale as a product of the Canterbury period, though he gives no decisive reason in support of the late date. Socola (JEGP 49, 1950, 159–71), who compares Chaucer's passages on Fortuna with their sources, detects a progressive development of the personification of the goddess. His thesis, if correct, would argue for all the tragedies having been composed at approximately the same time and therefore after the date of the latest of the Modern Instances (i.e., December 1385). Positive evidence in support of any of these theories, however, is lacking. The general character of the tragedies suggests that they may have been written in the early part of Chaucer's career, perhaps in the early 1370s, when the Italian influence was first making itself evident in his works, though a later date cannot be ruled out.

The general plan of the tale is due to Boccaccio's *De casibus virorum illustrium* (apparently acknowledged in the subtitle), and to the *Roman de la rose* (5829–6901). The Fortune motif appears to have come from the *Roman,* where modern as well as ancient instances are used to illustrate the capricious workings of the goddess, while the prevailing tone, set out in 1973–77 of the introductory link and the first stanza of the tale, is partially indebted to certain passages of Boethius's *De consolatione philosophiae* (2.pr2; 3.pr5). Many of the tragedies themselves are so brief that establishing their sources is both impossible and unimportant, except for the light they would throw on Chaucer's reading. The tragedies of Adam, Hercules, Nero, and Samson have commonly been held to show the influence of the *De casibus,* and the Zenobia that of the *De claris mulieribus.* The tragedy of Hercules comes in part from Boethius, *De consolatione philosophiae* (4.m7), with some details possibly derived from Ovid (Hoffman, Ovid and CT, 186–92); Ugolino from Dante's *Inferno* 23, perhaps with collateral use of an Italian chronicle; and Lucifer, Samson, Nebuchadnezzar, Belshazzar, Holofernes, and Antiochus all derive in substance from the Old Testament or the Apocrypha. For evidence that the accounts of Samson, Nero, and perhaps Caesar (for which Chaucer himself cites Lucan, Valerius, and Suetonius) may have been influenced by the *Speculum historiale* of Vincent of Beauvais, see Aiken, Spec 17, 1942, 56–68. There are also possible, though hardly demonstrable, borrowings from the *Speculum* in the accounts of Adam, Belshazzar, Alexander, and Croesus. Johnson (PMLA 66, 1951, 827–43) suggests the *Bible historiale* of Guyart Desmoulins as a likely source for some of Chaucer's variations from Boccaccio and the Vulgate. For the accounts of the two Pedros and of Bernabò, Chaucer doubtless drew on his own knowledge and recollections. Other parallels to the various tragedies that have been noted are mentioned in the notes that follow. The more important analogues have been assembled and printed by Root in S&A, 615–44.

The Monk's tragedies center on the workings of the ancient Roman goddess Fortuna, whose capricious turnings of a great wheel were thought to govern the fates of men. Whether this concept, literally applied as it is in The Monk's Tale, reflects the genuine application of a theory of tragedy as Chaucer understood it, or whether it reflects the "philosophical inadequacy" of the Monk is a matter of dispute; see, e.g., Oruch, Criticism 8, 1966, 288; Berndt, SP 68, 1971, 435–36; Howard, Idea of CT, 280–81. Babcock (PMLA 46, 1931, 205–13) has assembled an extensive list of Roman and medieval stories and collections similar to Chaucer's tale, and classifies it, along with the *Roman de la rose*, in a non-clerical medieval tradition, where the goddess Fortuna operates independently of a divine plan. Patch (MLR 22, 1927, 377–88) detects a belief in divine providence elsewhere in the writings of Chaucer and is supported by other critics who have stressed the discrepancy between the fatalistic viewpoint of the Monk and a more genial attitude towards man's destiny expressed in Chaucer's other writings (see especially Kaske, ELH 24, 1957, 249–68). For other discussions of tragic theory in Chaucer, see Robertson, ELH 19, 1952, 1–37; Mahoney, AnM 3, 1962, 81–99; Ruggiers, ChR 8, 1973, 89–99; Dean MAE 44, 1975, 1–13; Bornstein, Expl 33, 1975, item 77. Lepley (ChR 12, 1978, 162–69) maintains, in contrast to most scholars, that the tale is philosophically sound in Boethian terms. Still standard is Willard Farnham, The Med. Heritage of Elizabethan Tragedy, 1956 (esp. 129–36).

A major textual problem in the tale relates to the placement of the Modern Instances, which differs in various MSS. In the best group, including the Ellesmere MS and most of its nearest relatives, they stand at the end. But in most copies they come between Zenobia and Nero. A natural ending of the whole tale is suggested by the definition with which the tragedy of Croesus closes, and by the echo of the final line of Croesus in the Nun's Priest's Prologue (VII.2782–83). Whether the Ellesmere order is simply due to an officious scribe, desirous of mending the chronology, or preserves Chaucer's own intention, is perhaps impossible to determine. The Monk's apology for the chronological confusion does not settle the matter (see 1985 above), and a slight inconsistency exists, on any assumption, in the final state of the text, since if the tragedy of Croesus stands at the end, as the following headlink appears to require, then the tale has so good a formal conclusion that the Knight's interruption (ProNPT VII.2767) seems out of place. The question is still further complicated by the Nun's Priest's Prologue itself, which exists in several MSS in a short form omitting all reference to the Croesus passage (see introductory note to the Nun's Priest's Prologue). For a discussion of the question, see Walter W. Skeat, The Evolution of the CT, Ch Soc, 1907, 21–22, 29; Tatlock, Dev. and Chron., 170–72; Brusendorff, Ch Trad., 77–78; and M-R 2:406–13, 4:512. For a recent discussion of the problem, see Fry (JEGP 71, 1972, 355–68), who advocates the final placement of the Modern Instances. Fry argues that the Knight's interruption is motivated by his distress at hearing the misfortunes of his old military commander, Peter of Cyprus. The interruption would, therefore, be most appropriate if Pedro's tragedy had only recently been recounted. The placement adopted here, with the Modern Instances following the account of Zenobia and that of Croesus at the end, follows the order of most MSS and modern editions.

1999   Lucifer: "Light-bearer," the name of the morning star. It was applied to the rebel archangel because of an interpretation by the Church Fathers of Isa. 14.12, which was thought to apply to Satan: "How art thou fallen from heaven, O Lucifer, son of the morning."

2007   Damyssene: The notion that Adam was created in a field where Damascus later stood occurs in Boccaccio's De casibus, Book 1; in Peter Comestor's Historia scholastica, Genesis, 13; and in Vincent of Beauvais's Speculum historiale 1.41 (Aiken, Spec 17, 1942, 57). Lydgate writes in Fall of Princes 1.500: "Off slym off therthe in Damascene the feeld/ God made hem fairest a-boue ech creature."

2009   sperme unclene: The phrase was commonplace. It occurs in Innocent III's *De miseria condicionis humane* 1.3: "Formatus est homo . . . de spurcissimo spermate" and in Vincent of Beauvais's Spec. Hist. 29.115: "Homo autem noster exterior de immundo semine conceptus est" (Aiken, Spec 17:57).

**2015   The story of Samson occurs in Boccaccio's De casibus 1.17, but Chaucer appears to have based his account primarily on Judges 13–16. Robinson notes the probable influence of RR 16677–688 and the Spec. Hist. (see Fansler, Ch and RR, 30–31, and Aiken, Spec 17: 58–59).

2044   wang-tooth: A detail taken from the Vulgate, Judg. 15.19: "And thus the Lord opened a molar tooth in the jaw of an ass."

2046   *Judicum*: Liber Judicum, the Book of Judges, where the story of Samson is told. Titles of books were frequently cited in the genitive case; see ProMLT II.93n.

2047   Gazan: The form appears to be a corruption of the accusative *Gazam* in Judg. 16.1.

2063   Dalida: The form *Dalida* for the Vulgate *Dalila* is taken by Fansler (Ch and RR, 31) to be due to RR. Landrum (PMLA 39, 1924, 89) shows, however, that this spelling occurs in Vincent of Beauvais's Spec. Hist., in the Cursor mundi, the Confessio amantis, and Le pélerinaige de la vie humaine. Cf. BD 738, Wom Unc 16.

**2091–94   The moral, which departs from the emphasis on fortune in the other tragedies, is paralleled in RR 16541–700. Grennen (NM 67, 1966, 121) notes a similar moralistic emphasis in the account of Samson in Le Livre de la Chevalier de La Tour-Landry ch. 74 (ed. de Montaiglon, 1854; Eng. tr. ed. Wright, EETS 33, 1868).

**2095   The story of Hercules was widely known, but

Chaucer's account appears to have been based on Boethius's Cons. 4.m7, with details perhaps from Ovid's Metamorphoses 9 or Heroides 9 (Hoffman, Ovid and CT, 186–92). Boccaccio's De claris mulieribus 22 includes a short account of Deianira (S&A, 629–30).

2096 The werkes of Hercules are taken from the Cons. 4.m7.13–31 (cf. Bo 4.m7.28–62), whose list corresponds only in part with the traditional twelve labors.

2098 rafte: The first of the traditional twelve labors of Hercules was the slaying of the Nemean lion, whose skin Hercules afterwards wore. Cf. Bo 4.m7.30–32.

2099 Centauros: Probably a reference to the centaur Pholus, whom Hercules slew after the labor of the Erymanthian boar. He also inadvertently killed Chiron, the centaur son of Saturn and Philyra (Skeat 5:232). Cf. Bo 4.m7.29–30.

2100 Arpies: Hercules's sixth labor was the killing of the Harpies, the Stymphalian birds who ate human flesh. Cf. Bo 4.m7.32–34.

2101 dragoun: Hercules's eleventh labor was to bring back from the garden of the Hesperides the golden apples guarded by the dragon Ladon. Cf. Bo 4.m7.34–35.

2102 Cerberus: Hercules's twelfth labor was to bring to the upper world the three-headed dog Cerberus, who guarded the gates of Hades. Cf. Bo 4.m.7.36–37.

2103 Busirus: Here Chaucer conflates two stories, that of Busirus, a king of Egypt who killed and sacrificed all foreigners who came to his land, and that of Diomedes, a king of Thrace who fed his mares on human flesh until Hercules killed him as his eighth labor and fed his body to the horses (cf. Bo 4.m7.37–41). Shannon (MP 11, 1913, 227–30; Ch and Roman Poets, 312–17) suggested that Chaucer's error arose from a misunderstanding of Ovid's Heroides 9.67–70, where the two tyrants are mentioned together. Hoffman (N&Q 210, 1965, 406–9; Ovid and CT, 186–89) notes, however, that confusion of the two occurs in the gloss to an eleventh century MS copy of Ovid's Ibis: "Busiris hospites suos equis suis dedit ad comendum. Vel dicamus esse Diomedem, quem Hercules peremit." (Busiris gave his guests to his horses to be eaten. Or let us say that it was Diomedes, whom Hercules killed.)

2105 firy serpent: The Lernaean hydra. McDermott (Classica et Medievalia 23, 1962, 216–17) notes Chaucer's epithet, which lacks classical parallel, arose from a misreading of Aeneid 6.288, where "flammisque" applies to Chimaera rather than Hydra.

2106 Acheloys: Cf. Bo 4.m7.48–50: *Hercules brak oon of his hornes, and he for schame hidde hym in his ryver.*

2107 Cacus: Hercules slew the monster Cacus to appease Evander.

2108 Antheus: The wrestler Antaeus, giant son of Neptune and Ge, increased in strength each time his body touched the ground.

2109 the grisly boor: As his fourth labor, Hercules captured (but did not slay) the Erymanthian boar.

2117–18 The Pillars of Hercules on the Strait of Gibraltar were famous in the fourteenth century, as were the Pillars of Hercules at the limits of the Oriental world (Kittredge, in Putnam Anniversary Volume, 1909, 545–66). Pratt (Sts. in Hon. of Ullman, 1960, 118–25) cites statements that Hercules erected pillars in both the east and west, from an anonymous Irish account of the destruction of Troy, the Togail Troi, and also from commentaries on Walter Map's Epistola Valerii ad Ruffinum

de non ducenda uxore, a work certainly known to Chaucer.

Trophee: The identity of Trophee remains uncertain. Kittredge (Putnam Vol., 555–56, 559) conjectured that the noun *tropaea, trophea,* "pillars," came to be misunderstood as the name of a book. Skeat (5:233), Tupper (MLN 31, 1916, 11–14), and Emerson (MLN 31:142–46) identified *Trophee* with Guido delle Colonne on the grounds that the same noun *(tropaea)* furnished a play on his name *(de Columpnis),* and that his Historia destructionis Troiae may have been a source for the passage on the pillars of Hercules. Pratt (Sts. in Hon. of Ullman, 121–23) refutes the identification, noting that Chaucer habitually refers to the author of the Hist. Troiae as *Guido* or *Guydo de Columpnis* and maintaining that Chaucer probably believed in the existence of a commentator named Tropheus.

Several MSS, including the Ellesmere MS and Hengwrt are here glossed "Ille vates Chaldeorum Tropheus." Tupper (MLN 31:11–13) disposes of this nonsensical gloss as a scribal conflation of a gloss "Tropheus" at line 2117 with a gloss "ille vates Chaldeorum" for Daniel at lines 2154–56. Tupper conjectures that the two notes stood on contiguous margins of a manuscript and were subsequently combined. Pratt, who accepts Tupper's conjecture (Sts. in Hon. of Ullman, 122–23) suggests that if the ancestral MS had double columns, the fusion may have occurred in the space between the columns. The gloss is thus of no help in determining the identity of *Trophee.*

Lydgate, Fall of Princes 1.283–87, cites *Trophee* as the source of Chaucer's *Troilus.*

2120 Dianira: Deianira, second wife of Hercules, gave her husband the poisoned shirt of the centaur Nessus, believing that it had the power to restore waning love. For the account of the poisoned shirt from Ovid's Metamorphoses, see S&A, 630–31.

2136 Proverbial; Whiting F546.

2137 world of prees: See Language and Versification, p. xxxviii, for the construction.

2139 Proverbial; Whiting K100.

2140 glose: Cf. SumT III.1792n.

2143–2246 The accounts of Nabugodonosor (Nebuchadnezzar), king of Babylon (c. 605–652 B.C.), and of his son Balthasar are based on the Book of Daniel 1–5. For the suggestion that Chaucer used the Bible Historiale of Guyart Desmoulins, see Johnson, PMLA 66: 832–39.

2147 See 2 Kings 24–25.

2152 leet do gelde: A double causative; see Mustanoja, ME Syntax, 605. This statement does not occur in the Vulgate. Aiken (Spec 17:59) suggests it may be due to Vincent of Beauvais's Spec. Hist. 2.121, where Daniel is stated to be a eunuch and also "the wisest child of every one." Johnson (PMLA 66:834) cites Peter Comestor's more explicit statement (Hist. Scholastica, Liber Danielis 1) that Nebuchadnezzar ordered the emasculation of Daniel and other youths: "cum Nabuchodonosor duxisset in Babylonem nobiliores pueros Judaeorum et quosdam de semine regio, pulchriores inter eos et doctiores, qui stare possent in palatio regis, ut ait Josephus, castravit" (PL 198:1447). The statement also occurs in Desmoulins's Bible Historiale.

2155 wiseste child: Skeat glosses *child* as "young man," but J. A. Burrow notes (by letter) that *child* has its modern meaning here, since Daniel is one of the most frequently cited biblical examples of the *puer senex;* see Christian Gnilka, Aetas Spiritalis, 1972, 236–39.

2157   Fisher (285) notes that Babylonians were traditionally versed in occult learning.

2166   **tweye:** An error for three: Shadrach, Meshach, and Abednego. Daniel does not play a part in the fiery furnace episode in the Vulgate (Dan. 3). For the idea that he was himself in the fiery furnace, Johnson (PMLA 66: 836) suggests a misreading of the passage in the Bible Historiale: "Donc aourerent tout lymage fors les iii compaignons daniel ananies et misael et asaries" (New York, Morgan Library, MS. 394, fol. 194r), while Aiken (Spec 17:60) suggests a misreading of Vincent of Beauvais.

2177   **a certeyn yeres:** That is, until God revoked for him a certain number of years of punishment; for the construction see MilT I.3193n.

2244–45   This proverb (Whiting F667, cf. F635) occurs also in Bo 3.pr5.66.

2247   **Cenobia, Palymerie:** Zenobia was queen of Palmyra, a city in the desert just east of Syria, in the third century A.D. Chaucer based his account of her on Boccaccio's De claris mulieribus 98 and apparently made some use also of his De casibus 6.6 (S&A, 632–36).

2248   No Persian account of Zenobia is known. For the suggestion that Chaucer misread Boccaccio's "priscis testantibus literis" (ancient letters testifying) as "persis testantibus literis" (Persian letters testifying), see Lüdeke, 98–99, in Festschrift zum 75. Geburtstag von Theodor Spira, ed. H. Viebrock and W. Erzgräber, 1961.

2252   **Perce:** Persia, apparently a mistake. Boccaccio says she was of the race of the Ptolemies of Egypt.

2256   **Office of wommen:** The phrase closely follows Boccaccio's "a pueritia sua, spretis omnino muliebribus officiis" (printed in S&A, 633).

2289   **fourty wikes:** All manuscripts except two of dubious authority read "dayes." Boccaccio writes "post partus purgationes," indicating the period of gestation. Manly (M-R 4:510) notes that forty weeks is the common term for the period of gestation.

2307   Zenobia knew several languages, was familiar with Egyptian literature, and studied Greek under the philosopher Longinus.

2325   **Petrak:** Chaucer's source was Boccaccio, not Petrarch, although Petrarch devotes ten lines to Zenobia in the Trionfo della Fama 2.107–17. "Why Chaucer refers here to Petrarch rather than to Boccaccio is unknown. From the fact that he never names Boccaccio it has even been inferred that he attributed to Petrarch (or to Lollius) all the writings of Boccaccio that he knew" (Robinson).

2345   In Boccaccio the names are "Heremianus" and "Timolaus." "Chaucer's forms in *-o* might be thought to indicate that he had a source or intermediary in Italian. But he changed a number of names in various works to an Italian form. Cf. *Cambalo,* V.667; *Danao,* LGW 2563; *Iulo,* HF 177; *Lyno,* LGW 2569; *Myda,* III.951; *Sytheo,* LGW 1005; *Vulcano,* HF 138; and *Pernaso, Parnaso,* passim. Some of the instances in LGW have been explained as due to Chaucer's use of an Italian translation of Ovid" (Robinson).

2347   Proverbial; Whiting F517.

2351   **Aurelian:** Aurelianus, emperor of Rome, 270–75 A.D., defeated Zenobia in 272.

2372   **vitremyte:** Probably a woman's headdress of linen or light canvas. The meaning of this word, which occurs only once in Chaucer, has invited considerable speculation. Most editors follow Skeat, who postulated that it was a coined word, formed on the Lat. *vitream mitram,* meaning a glass and therefore fragile headdress, as opposed to a strong helmet. The expression "head of glass" occurs as a proverbial symbol of vulnerability in Tr 2.867; Debate of Body and Soul, 13–14; and Boccaccio's De genealogia deorum 14.18 (Tatlock, MLN 21, 1906, 62); see Whiting H218. Young (SP 40, 1943, 494–501) concurs with Skeat, adding that the proverbial glass headdress also carried the implication of delusion or deception of the wearer (as in Tr 5.469; PP B 20.168–71).

Generally neglected, however, has been the double parallel offered by Boccaccio, De casibus 8.6 and approached by Chaucer: "Haec nuper *galeata* concionari militibus assueta, nunc *velata* cogitur muliercularum audire fabellas! Haec nuper Orienti praesidens *sceptra* gestabat, nunc Romae subiacens *colum* sicut ceterae baiulat!" (She who, recently *helmeted,* was accustomed to be roused by soldiers, now *veiled* is thought to listen to the tales of little women. She who recently bore the *scepter* in command of the Orient, now lying in subjection to Rome, carries a *distaff* just as the rest. [Printed in S&A, 633.]) The parallel was first noted by Jenkins (141–47, in Mélanges de linguistique et de littérature offerts à M. Alfred Jeanroy, 1928), who proposed a derivation from OF *vite* or *vete* (Lat. *vitta,* "band," or "fillet") and OF *mite* (Lat. *mitra,* "a woman's headdress"), concluding that the word denotes simply a feminine head covering. Pratt, in an unpublished note, suggests a derivation of the first element from ME *vitry* (OF *Vitré*), meaning vitre canvas, a light durable canvas made at Vitré, Brittany; and the second element from OF *mite* (Lat. *mitra*), "headdress." Pratt's solution makes complete sense and preserves the parallelism offered by Boccaccio.

2373   **ful of floures:** Baugh (362) conjectures that Zenobia's scepter was ornamented with gold flowers.

2374   **distaf:** The staff of a hand spinning wheel, upon which the flax to be spun is placed; figuratively, women's work or occupation (OED s.v. *distaff*). Cf. the parallelism with Boccaccio's De casibus 8.6 discussed in 2372 above.

2375–98   King Pedro of Castile and León was assassinated in 1369 by his illegitimate half-brother, Don Enrique of Trastamare, who was aided by Bertrand du Guesclin, Oliver de Mauny, and others. "Chaucer had various reasons for interest in Pedro of Spain. The Black Prince fought with him against Enrique in 1367. Then John of Gaunt married Constance, Pedro's daughter, in 1371, and assumed in her right the title of King of Castile and León. And for about two years after Constance came to England Chaucer's wife, Philippa, appears to have been attached to her household" (Robinson). Chaucer is now known to have traveled to Spain in 1366, and it has been conjectured that he went on an embassy to Pedro's court (see Chaucer's Life, p. xvii). For historical background, see P. E. Russell, The Eng. Intervention in Spain and Portugal in the Time of Ed. III and Rich. II, 1955.

Chaucer's stanzas on Pedro are generally held to be based on oral information. Braddy (PMLA 50, 1935, 69–80; rpt. in Braddy, Geoffrey Ch, 23–36) argues convincingly that Chaucer's informant was his friend and Pedro's partisan, Sir Guichard d'Angle. Savage (Spec 24, 1949, 357–75), who gives a detailed account of the murder, suggests that his informant was Don Fernando de

Castro, an eye witness of the event who was later in the service of John of Gaunt (but see Braddy, MLQ 13, 1952, 3–5; rpt. in Geoffrey Ch, 124–27).

2378 Manly (M-R 4:511) notes that many MSS read "Thy bastard brother made the to flee," perhaps an earlier reading changed after the reconciliation of the two factions by the marriage in 1386 of Constance of Castile's daughter, Katharine, and the grandson of Don Enrique of Trastamare.

2383–84 These lines refer to the arms of Bernard du Guesclin, who lured Pedro into Enrique's tent where he was murdered. Brusendorff (Ch Trad., 489) quotes a ballade attributed to Deschamps and written after the death of du Guesclin in 1380: "Lescu dargent a une aigle de sable / A deux testes un roge baton / Portoit . . . le bon bertran de Clesquin" (A silver shield with a black two-headed eagle carried on a red baton . . . the good Bernard du Guesclin). The **feeld of** snow corresponds to the silver, the black **egle** on a **lymrod** (a stick smeared with birdlime) glowing red (**as the gleede**) corresponds to the eagle on the red baton.

2386 **wikked nest:** Skeat (5:239) notes a play on the name of Oliver Mauny (OF *mau ni,* i.e. *mal nid,* "bad nest"), another of Pedro's betrayers.

2388 Armorica was the home of Oliver de Mauny.

2389 **Genylon-Olyver:** Cf. ShipT VII.136n. and line 194 and NPT VII.3227n.

2391 Pierre de Lusignan, king of Cyprus, was assassinated by three of his own knights on 17 January 1369. "Like Peter of Spain he was well known to the English court, having been entertained by Edward III in 1363 and having numbered many Englishmen among his followers. His reputation for chivalry, as Chaucer says, was of the highest, but his murder can hardly be ascribed to jealousy of his fame. It was due rather to resentment at his personal misconduct and his oppressive rule" (Robinson). See Nicolas Jorga, Philippe de Mézières, 1896, 385–91.

Braddy (PMLA 50:78–80; MLN 62, 1947, 173–75; rpt. in Braddy, Geoffrey Ch, 23–36; 124–27) points out that Chaucer's account of Pierre's death is at variance with historical fact, and suggests that it may be derived from Machaut's fictitious account in La prise d'Alexandrie (see also S&A, 636–7).

2392 **Alisandre:** Peter's celebrated victory at Alexandria on 10 October 1365, was accomplished with the aid of English knights. See GP I.51n. Fry (JEGP 71:356) notes that the event was well known to the English court because of the participation of Sir Stephen Scrope and Nicholas Sabraham and through Machaut's La prise d'Alexandrie, as well as Froissart's Chronicles.

2399 Bernabò Visconti, lord of Milan, fell from power on 6 May 1385, when he was arrested by his nephew and son-in-law, Gian Galeazzo. In December of the same year he died suddenly in prison, and current opinion attributed his death to poison. Like the two Peters, Bernabò was a figure of special interest to Chaucer and the English court. His niece, Violanta, married Chaucer's first patron, Lionel, duke of Clarence; his daughter Caterina had been offered in marriage to Richard II; and his daughter Donnina married the English condottiere, Sir John Hawkwood. Furthermore, Chaucer knew Bernabò personally, for he visited his court on an embassy to treat with him and Hawkwood in 1378 (Pratt, ELH 16, 1949, 188–93).

Kittredge (Date of Tr, 46–50) maintains that the stanza on Visconti was written as soon as news of the latter's death reached England. He conjectures further that the news was brought by one of Hawkwood's men, whose arrival in England in January 1386 is chronicled in Malverne's continuation of Ranulph Higden's Polychronicon 9:78.

2401 **acounte:** Generally taken to mean "recount" or "relate" (MED s.v. *accounten* v. [4]). Kittredge (Date of Tr, 50), who favors the sense "reckon in" or "take into account" (OED s.v. *account* I, 2b), cites the latter meaning as evidence that the Bernabò stanza is a later insertion. Cf. also Mel VII.1315. The line could bear either meaning.

2406 Kittredge (Date of Tr, 50) notes the curious parallel between the uncertainty of this line and a marginal entry in Malverne's continuation of Higden's Polychronicon (9:78n.): "Quo in tempore dominus Barnabos moriebatur in carcere, qua morte an gladio aut fame aut veneno ignoratur."

2407 Ugolino della Gherardesca, also known as Ugolino da Pisa, conspired first with his grandson Nino and later with Nino's rival, Archbishop Ruggieri, to seize control of Pisa. For his supposed betrayal of Pisan interests he was put in prison where he died of starvation in 1289.

Chaucer's account of Ugolino is based primarily on Dante's Inferno 33.1–90, but variations (see Spencer, Spec 9, 1934, 295–301) suggest that Chaucer either wrote from memory or had additional information. Dante makes no mention of Archbishop Ruggieri's betrayal of Ugolino, and gives the number of children imprisoned with him in the tower as four. For the suggestion that these variations originated in Chaucer's use of Villani's Chronicle 121 and 128 (quoted by Charles Singleton, ed. Inferno, 1970, 2:607–9), see Baddeley and Toynbee, N&Q, Ser. 8:11, 1897, 205–6, 369–70. Chaucer omits Dante's reference to Ugolino's dream, as well as Ugolino's cannibalism, but expands the narrative in other places, emphasizing the pathos (see Spencer, Spec 9:295–301; Schless, in Ch: Writers and Background, ed. Brewer, 220–23, and Ch and Dante, 1984, 209–12; also Boitani, MAE 45, 1976, 54–64.). The reference to Fortune, which brings the story into accord with the scheme of The Monk's Tale, is absent in Dante but occurs in Villani.

Robbins (Trivium 2, 1967, 1–16) prints a late fifteenth-century analogue of the legend of Ugolino from Corning, New York, Corning Museum of Glass, MS 6.

2416 **Roger:** Ruggieri degli Ubaldini, Archbishop of Pisa (1278–95), conspired with Ugolino, but later betrayed him (see previous note).

2455 **starf:** The word appears not to have acquired the meaning "to die of hunger" until after Chaucer's time (OED s.v. *starve*).

2462 **Fro point to point:** Burrow (Ricardian Poetry, 69–78) observes that in the late fourteenth century "pointing" meant to describe in detail. Cf. Tr 3.491–97.

2463 Chaucer's information on **Nero** appears to be based on Jean de Meun's passage on Fortune in Le roman de la rose 6183–6488, which accounts for all but the second stanza of the tragedy. Socola, however (JEGP 49:163), maintains that in RR the emphasis is on Fortune's perversity rather than Nero's wickedness. Skeat notes the possible influence of Boethius (Bo 2.m6 and

3.m4), but as Fansler (Ch and RR, 26) points out, the RR follows Boethius so closely in places that it is practically impossible to determine which was Chaucer's original.

Whether Chaucer actually relied on Suetonius remains uncertain. Fansler (Ch and RR, 24–25) notes that the reference to Suetonius may itself have been taken from RR 6458: "Si cum Suétonius l'escript." As possible sources for the second stanza, with its emphasis on Nero's extravagance, see Root (S&A, 640), who suggests Boccaccio's De casibus, Suetonius's De vita Caesarum and Boethius's De consolatio philosophiae; and Aiken (Spec 17:60–62), who maintains that all the details not accounted for in the RR occur in Vincent of Beauvais's Spec. Hist. 8.7, where the material borrowed from Suetonius is duly attributed to him. Waller (Indiana Soc. Sts. Qtly. 31, 1978, 47–48) shows that the particular detail of Nero's golden nets in VII.2475 is found in numerous histories from Suetonius and Orosius down to and including, in the fourteenth century, Ranulph Higden and Boccaccio.

2465   Swetonius: The De vita Caesarum by Suetonius (ed. and tr. J. C. Rolfe, rev. ed. 1928–30, 2 vols.) was an ultimate source for both Jean de Meun and Chaucer, but it is questionable whether either of them relied directly on this work. See Fansler (Ch and RR, 24–26) and note above.

2467   south: *South* is Skeat's emendation. The Hengwrt, Ellesmere, and related MSS read "north," but that quarter is represented by **septemtrioun**. The error seems more likely to be a scribe's than Chaucer's.

2475   Nettes of gold threed: See 2463 above.

2477   Singleton (ed. Inferno n. to 5.52–60) notes this is a nearly direct translation from Orosius's account of Semiramus: "ut cuique libitum esset liberum fieret."

2479–95   Skeat notes the similarity between this passage and Boece 2.m6. Fansler (Ch and RR, 26) points out that much of the similarity is contained in Chaucer's glosses to Boethius, which might have been derived from the RR.

2495   a maister: That is, Seneca. Cf. Bo 1.pr3.57, 3.pr5.40–60.

2503, 2515   This Seneca: Chaucer describes Seneca's death twice, with a different motive in each case. Aiken (Spec 17:61–62) suggests Chaucer may have been following two different sources. Baugh (365) notes that the actual reason for Seneca's death, not given by Chaucer, was an accusation against him for conspiring to assassinate Nero. On the use of *this* see Language and Versification, p. xxxviii.

2550   Cf. Bo 2.m1.10–14.

De Oloferno For the story of Holofernes, see the Vulgate Book of Judith.

2553   Nor was stronger in every respect on the field of battle.

2565   Bethulia: The location of Biblical Bethulia remains unidentified. For the suggestion that it may be Shechem (Sichem), see Robert H. Pfeiffer, The Hist. of New Testament Times, 1949, 296–97 and n. 15.

2566   Lat. gloss: "Et fecerunt filii Israel constituerat eis sacerdos domini Eliachim" (Judith 4.7).

2575–2630   The story of **Anthiochus**, Antiochus IV, king of Syria (175–163 B.C.) is found in 2 Macc. 9.

2591   Nichanore . . . Thymothee: Two of the generals who fought against the Jews and were defeated by Judas Maccabeus. See 2 Macc. 9.13: "And while he (Antio-

chus) was at Ecbatana, news came to him of what had happened to Nicanor and the forces of Timothy."

2631   Alisaundre: The story of Alexander the Great (356–323 B.C.), king of Macedon, was **commune** in the Middle Ages because Alexander was the hero of a popular cycle of romances as well as of a historical tradition represented by the works of Quintus Curtius, Justin, and Orosius. While Chaucer appears to be writing in the historical tradition, his account of Alexander is so brief and general that no specific source for his material has been identified. For an account of the writings on Alexander, see Francis P. Magoun, The Gests of King Alexander of Macedon, 1929; George Cary, The Medieval Alexander, 1956; David J. A. Ross, Alexander Historiatus, 1963; Lumiansky, 1:104–5 in Manual ME.

2655   Machabee: See 1 Macc. 1.1–7.

2660   "This account of Alexander's death, given as an alternative tradition by Diodorus Siculus 17.118, and adopted by Quintus Curtius, is usually followed by medieval writers. See, for example, Vincent of Beauvais, Spec. Hist. 4.64–65" (Robinson).

2661   sys . . . aas: For the figure, see ProMLT II.124–25; Gower, Miroir de l'omme, 22103, 23399.

For another of the many uses of Alexander as a victim of Fortune, see Boccaccio's Amorosa visione 35.

2671–2726   Chaucer's account of **Julius** Caesar (c. 100–44 B.C.) is so full of generalities widely current in the Middle Ages that scholars have been unable to agree on its sources. Certain passages derive ultimately from such classical writers as Lucan, Suetonius, and Valerius Maximus (see VII.2719–20), but it is uncertain whether Chaucer relied directly upon them. Shannon (MP 16, 1919, 609–14; Ch and Roman Poets, 334–39) believed that Chaucer used Lucan's Pharsalia, though the two accounts differ. Robinson notes that certain features peculiar to Chaucer's tragedy: "the triumph, the epithet *lauriat,* the account of Pompey's death, are closely paralleled in the French Ly Histore de Julius Cesar of Jehan de Tuim" (fl. 1240; ed. F. Settegast, 1881). MacCracken (ed., John Lydgate, Serpent of Division, 1911, 42–43) and Aiken (Spec 17:67) note parallels between Chaucer's Caesar and Vincent of Beauvais's Spec. Hist. 6.35–42. For a complete discussion, see Root, S&A, 642–44.

Lock (ELN 12, 1975, 251–55) cites discrepancies between the Monk's account of Caesar and its putative authorities as evidence of the Monk's intellectual inferiority, but he overlooks the probability that much of Chaucer's own information came from a corrupt secondary source. See Harbert, 137–53 in Ch: Writers and Background.

2672   From humble bed: The tradition of Caesar's humble birth, which occurs in Ranulph Higden's Polychronicon 3.42 and later English writers, is at variance with historical fact. Waller (Indiana Soc. Sts. Qtly. 31: 48–55) shows how the tradition may have arisen by the confusion of Suetonius's account of Augustus Caesar's ancestry.

2673   he Julius: For the use of *he,* see Mustanoja, ME Syntax, 135–36.

2677   Caesar was never emperor of Rome, but in the Middle Ages he was regarded as the first of the Roman emperors. See Brunetto Latini, Trésor, ed. Carmody, 1948, 27.6: "Julle Cesar fu empereour des romains, par qui tot li autre empereour de Rome furent apelé Cesar," and 38.1: "Et ensi Julle Cesar fu li premier empereor des romains."

2680　Pompeus: Pompey the Great was actually Caesar's son-in-law. Baugh notes that writers before Chaucer seem to have confused Pompeius Rufus (who was Caesar's father-in-law) with Gnaeus Pompeius (Pompey the Great), who married Caesar's daughter, Julia, and was famous for his campaigns in the East. See Ranulph Higden's Polychronicon and Trevisa's translation (4:188–89, 192–93), where the same error occurs twice.

MacCracken (ed., Lydgate's Serpent of Division, 43) suggests the ultimate source of this mistake is perhaps the statement in Suetonius's Historia XII Caesarum 27 that Caesar proposed for the hand of Pompey's daughter. Fisher cites the mistake as evidence that Chaucer was working from general knowledge.

2697　Brutus Cassius: Chaucer was not the first medieval writer to make Brutus and Cassius into one person. The error occurs in an anonymous ninth-century commentary on Virgil's Bucolics and Georgics (Montpellier, École de Médecine de Montpellier, MS 358, fol. 27) and in chapter 19 of the Alfredian translation of Boethius's De consolatio philosophiae 2.m7 (ed. Sedgefield, 1899, 46). See Silverstein, MLN 47, 1932, 148–50; Hammond, Ch: Bibl. Man., 292.

Lydgate repeats Chaucer's error at least four times; see Hammond, Eng. Verse, 450. MacCracken (ed., Lydgate's Serpent of Division, 43) suggests the misunderstanding arose originally in the scribal omission of an *et* sign between Brutus and Cassius in a phrase such as "dolo Bruti et Cassii," in Vincent of Beauvais, Spec. Hist. 6.42. Hammond (Eng. Verse, 450) notes also Philargyrius's fifth-century commentary on Virgil: "Tiberius Caesar Iulius et Antonius contra Cassium Brutum civile bellum gesserunt."

2703　Capitolie: Capitol, the Temple of Jupiter on the Tarpeian (later Capitoline) Hill of Rome, where some medieval writers, including Vincent of Beauvais, placed the assassination of Caesar (see Aiken, Spec 17:67). Pratt notes the assassination actually took place in the Curia of Pompey in the Campus Martius.

2721　word and ende: A common ME corruption of the older idiom *ord and ende,* "beginning and end." Cf. Tr 2.1495; 5.1669. Skeat notes that it is not uncommon to find a *w* prefixed to a word where it is not required etymologically, especially before the vowel *o.*

2727　Cresus: Croesus, last king of Lydia, reigned c. 560–546 B.C. Chaucer's primary source for his tragedy is Jean de Meun's passage on Fortune in RR 6489–6622, though the first stanza echoes Boethius, Cons. 2.pr2.34–36 (Fansler, Ch and RR, 28–30; S&A, 644; cf. Bo 2.pr2.58–63). For the suggestion that Chaucer may have been influenced by a similar account of Croesus in Vincent of Beauvais's Spec. Hist., see Wimsatt, Spec 12, 1937, 379–81, and Aiken, Spec 17:67–68.

2728　Cyrus the Great (550–530 B.C.), founder of the Persian Empire, overthrew Croesus in 547 B.C.

2740　Croesus's dream was a medieval fabrication. It appears to have arisen by the conflation of Herodotus's accounts of Croesus (1.87) and Polycrates (3.124) and occurs in its present form in RR and Vincent of Beauvais's Spec. Hist. (Crawford, TLS, 26 June 1924, 404).

2761　With the definition here, cf. VII.1973–77, 1991–94 above, and Bo 2.pr2.67–72. Note especially *unwar strook* (VII.2764 and Bo 2.pr2.69).

The Nun's Priest's Prologue

The Nun's Priest's Prologue exists in two forms. The shorter and probably earlier version does not have lines 2771–90. It survives in fourteen MSS, ten of which have the Host as interruptor of the Monk. The long form of the prologue, printed here, appears to represent Chaucer's latest intention. In it he adds the Host's echo of the Monk's definition of tragedy and makes the Knight interrupt the speaker, thereby removing what would have been a monotonous repetition of the Host's interruption of Chaucer just before the Melibee. See M-R 4:513–14; 2:410–13; Dempster, PMLA 68, 1953, 1147; Hammond, Ch: Bibl. Man., 241–43. On the dramatic fitness of the Knight as interruptor, see Kaske, ELH 24, 1957, 249–68, and Fry, JEGP 71, 1972, 355–68.

2782–85　Cf. MkT VII.2766, 1993, 2762.
2801–2　See Mel VII.1047 and n.
2810　sir John: A common and rather contemptuous designation for a priest but apparently the Nun's Priest's actual name. See VII.2820 and II.1172 n. The familiarity of the Host's address is shown in the use of the second person singular.
2816　Yis: The emphatic form; cf. MilT I.3369n.

The Nun's Priest's Tale

The Nun's Priest's Tale was probably composed with its narrator in mind. The homiletic material and method are highly appropriate to the teller, while the digressions on dreams, the advice of women, and predestination reveal a character intimately acquainted with matters of current intellectual interest. Chaucer's deliberate pairing of the Nun's Priest's brilliant tale with the pedestrian Monk's Tale is now generally acknowledged. First noted by Hemingway (MLN 31, 1916, 479–83), the relationship between the tales is further explored by Watson (Sts. in Short Fiction 1, 1964, 277–88), who shows how the Nun's Priest's Tale parallels and parodies the concept of the falls of great men, and by Delasanta (TSL 13, 1968, 117–32), who claims the Monk's simplistic attitude towards fortune is dramatically refuted by the Nun's Priest (see also Kean, Ch and Poetry, 129–39). There are also satiric allusions to The Prioress's Tale and Melibee (see 3052, 3057 below). Howard (Idea of CT, 287) believes that by such means The Nun's Priest's Tale may supply a "retrospective" unity to all of Fragment VII.

This lends support to Robinson's assertion that the tale was composed "when the scheme of the Canterbury pilgrimage was well under way." There are, however, no clear indications of date. The only sure historical allusion is to Jack Straw and the revolt of 1381 (see 3394 below). Hotson's theory that the work is an allegorical representation of the duel between Mowbray and Bolingbroke in September of 1397 (see 3215 below) is now almost universally rejected. Rand (see 3123–24 below) argues for a date before 1386 on the basis of the mistaken reference to Macrobius. On the basis of calendrical allusions, North (RES n.s. 20, 1967, 418–22) dates the tale in

The explanatory notes to the Nun's Priest's Prologue and Tale were written by Susan H. Cavanaugh.

1392: Chauntecleer is seized by the fox on 3 May (VII.3190 and note 3187–90), which is a Friday (VII.3352), and 3 May was a Friday in 1381, 1387, 1392, and 1398; North argues, on the basis of the astronomical situation on that date, that 1392 is most likely.

Chaucer's tale ultimately derives from the fable "Del cok e del gupil," by Marie de France (ed. A. Ewert and R. C. Johnston, 1942, 41–42; tr. Coghill and Tolkien, eds., NPT, 1959, 51–52), from the corresponding episode by Pierre de Saint Cloud in Branch II of the OF beast epic, the *Roman de Renart* (ed. Ernest Martin, 1882, 1:91–104; rpt. S&A, 646–58), and perhaps from the corresponding episode by an unknown "clerc" of Troyes in Branch VI of *Renart le Contrefait* (ed. Gaston Raynaud and Henri Lemaître, 1914); see Pratt, Spec 47, 1972, 422–44, 646–68. Chaucer's combining of features from both the fabular and epic traditions has led to considerable debate concerning his sources. While Tyrwhitt early recognized Chaucer's indebtedness to Marie (Originals and Analogues of Ch's CT, Part II, ed. F. J. Furnivall, Ch Soc, 2nd ser., 1875, 116), later investigators have concentrated on the tale's relationship to the *Roman de Renart* (Lecompte, MP 14, 1917, 737–49; Kenneth Sisam, ed., NPT, 1927, 23–28; Fish, College Lang. Assoc. Journ. 5, 1962, 223–28). In her classic study, *On the Sources of the Nonne Prestes Tale* (1898), Kate Petersen carefully analyzed the many forms of the tale and placed it in the beast epic tradition of the *Roman de Renart* rather than the fabular tradition of Marie. More recently, Maveety (College Lang. Assoc. Journ. 4, 1960, 132–37) has reasserted the influence of Marie with the claim that Chaucer's tale "is not so much a departure from the fable as an extension of it." Both influences are present, and, as Shallers (ELH 42, 1975, 319–37) points out, much of the tale's dynamism arises from Chaucer's combining two genres, the moral fable, and the amoral beast epic. The central episode or fabular section of the tale, beginning with Chauntecleer's crow to the sun in Taurus and ending with the *moralite,* corresponds with Marie's fable, while the overall frame, including the dream section, the hen, and the old woman on whose farm the action takes place, follows the pattern of the *Roman de Renart.* The hen's skepticism, her denunciation of fear and cowardice, the debate on woman's counsel, and the absurdly inflated and expanded style of the narrative are to be found in *Renart le Contrefait.* While earlier scholars (Petersen, Sources of NPT; Hulbert, S&A, 645–46) have postulated a lost source for the tale, all the details relevant to Ch's narrative are to be found in these three poems (Pratt, Spec 47:667).

Only a small part of Chaucer's tale is taken up with the central episode. The narrative is expanded with anecdotes and moral applications and is enriched with literary allusions and verbal extravagances. The use of homiletic material is discussed by Petersen, who notes that the commentary of Robert Holcot (d. 1349), *Super Sapientiam Salomonis* furnished much of Chaucer's information on dreams. For a full account of the influence of the Wisdom commentary on this tale, see Pratt, Spec 52, 1977, 538–70; for the use of sermon techniques in the tale see Gallick, Spec 50, 1975, 471–76.

The extent to which the moralizations in the tale are to be taken seriously is much debated. A number of critics have advanced allegorical views. Speirs interprets the tale as an allegory of the Fall of Man, (Ch the Maker,

185–93), as do Huppé (A Reading of CT, 174–83), and Levy and Adams (MS 29, 1967, 178–92), whose interpretations, however, carry a more heavily moralistic bias. Donovan (JEGP 52, 1953, 498–508) sees the tale as a sermon on alertness to moral obligation, with Chauntecleer representing the holy man and Daun Russell the devil. Dahlberg (JEGP 53, 1954, 277–90) detects an allegory on the controversy between the secular clergy and the friars, with Chauntecleer representing the cock priest in a state of sloth and the fox representing the friar who will beguile him. Allen (SP 66, 1969, 25–35) sees the tale as a mock allegory, with Chauntecleer representing the exegetical figure of the cock preacher. All these interpretations are more ingenious than convincing. Widely accepted, however, is the view that the tale is ultimately serious in its intent (see, for example, Corsa, Ch, Poet of Mirth, 211–20; Hieatt, SN 42, 1970, 3–8; Bloomfield, in Ch Problems, 70–82). Manning (JEGP 59, 1960, 403–16) points out, however, that fables were controversial in the Middle Ages, particularly as a means of preaching (see also Owst, Preaching in Med. Engl., 80) and suggests that Chaucer is ridiculing the rhetorical and poetic practice of his day.

While the issue of morality remains in question, the interpretation of the tale as a parody of the excesses of rhetoric (see 3347 below) is generally acknowledged (see, e.g., Donaldson, 1104–8; Lenaghan, PMLA 68, 1963, 300–307; Donaldson, Speaking of Ch, 146–50; Gallick, ChR 11, 1977, 232–47). The digressions from the central episode, the anecdotes and moralities, the literary allusions and verbal extravagances, constitute the major stylistic feature of the narrative and a main point of the tale.

Chaucer's conception of the person and character of the Nun's Priest, who is not described in the General Prologue, has been the subject of much discussion (Sherbo, PMLA 64, 1949, 236–46; Broes, PMLA 78, 1963, 156–62; Watkins, ELH 36, 1969, 455–69). Lumiansky, who reviews the discussion (PMLA 68, 1953, 896–906), argues that the Host's remarks are cynical. Pratt (Spec 47:667–68) notes an interesting parallel between the character of the Nun's Priest as revealed in the tale and epilogue and that of the unknown "clerc de Troyes" who wrote *Renart le Contrefait.*

Why Chaucer gave so splendid a tale to a pilgrim so sketchily described elsewhere can only be guessed. Several critics (Root, Poetry of Ch, 208; Sisam, ed., NPT, 1927, xlii; Craik, Comic Tales, 81 n.) see in this tale the revelation of Chaucer the poet in *propria persona.* Donaldson (1108) offers the more sophisticated explanation that "in the personality of the satirist will always exist grounds for rebutting the satire." He maintains that Chaucer deliberately refrained from describing the Priest in order to maximize the comic effect of his tale. Whatever Chaucer's motive in hitherto obscuring the character of the Priest, the Priest's own tale of the cock and hen ultimately reveals a personality as engaging as the tale itself.

2821   stape in age: Cf. MerT IV.1514 and *ronne in age* Rom 4495.
2832   Robinson finds "humorous exaggeration" in ascribing a **bour** and **halle** to the widow's cottage. Manly (CT, 637) compares Froissart's description (Chroniques, tr. Johnes, ch. 95) of a "small house, dirty and smoky, and as black as jet. There was in this place only one poor

chamber, over which was a sort of garret that was entered by means of a ladder." The house is **sooty** because there is no chimney. Chauntecleer and the other chickens roost in the *halle* (see VII.2884).

2838 Cf. PP B 6.265, 268–69: "Lat noght sire Surfet sitten at thi borde/ . . . And if thow diete thus I dar legge myne armes/That Phisik shal his furred hood for his fode selle." On the importance of diet in medieval medicine see GP I.435–37.

2842 Whit ne reed: Cf. PardT VI.562; Tr 3.1384.

2844 broun breed: The cheapest variety; cf. GP I.147n.

in which she foond no lak: Either "with which she found no fault" or "of which she had no lack," since *lak* can mean either "fault" (cf. BD 958) or "lack" (PF 87).

2845 Seynd: Broiled or smoked (pp. of *senge*); the suggested derivation from OF *saim/sain,* "fat" (Dickens, Leeds SE 4, 1935, 76–77), has not found acceptance.

2851 orgon: Organs, like clavichords and virginals later on, were referred to as a pair, like scissors and trousers today (C. Clutton and A. Niland, The British Organ, 1963, 46), hence the plural verb *gon*. Bishop (RES n.s. 30, 1979, 259) suggests Chaucer was distinguishing between the high-pitched portative and the larger positive or great organ of a church. Cf. SNT VIII.134–35n.

2854 clokke: This was a recent loan-word in English, and the clock was itself an object of wonder. The famous clock at Wells Cathedral was constructed in about 1390, and the clock at Salisbury in 1386. Their basic timekeeping was notoriously inaccurate (Bishop, RES 30:259–60). The cock as timekeeper and astrologer was a common metaphor; cf. PF 350n.; Tr 3.1415n.

2857–58 It was commonly believed that the cock crowed on the hour (Hinckley, Notes on Ch, 128) and this belief fostered the idea of the cock's instinctive knowledge of astronomy (Steadman, Isis 50, 1959, 242). See RvT I.4233n.

2859–64 Coghill and Tolkien (eds., NPT, 1959, 17, 46) note that Chauntecleer's description follows precisely the rules for describing a beautiful woman as set down in Geoffrey of Vinsauf's Poetria nova, 598–99 (see 3347 below). Various allegorical interpretations have been applied to Chauntecleer's colors (Hotson, PMLA 39, 1924, 762–81; Dahlberg, JEGP 53:286), but Boone (MLN 64, 1949, 78–81) suggests that the description fits an actual breed of rooster, the Golden Spangled Hamburg. A similar description of a cock occurs in a ME lyric, "My Gentle Cock" (Robbins, Sec. Lyrics, 41–42).

2870 Pertelote: A departure from the French analogues, where the hen is called Pinte. *Pertelote* means "one who confuses (Fr. *perte*) someone's lot or fate" (Pratt, Spec 47:655).

2879 "My lief is faren in londe!": A popular song. The text is printed by Robbins (Sec. Lyrics, 152): My lefe ys faren in londe;/Allas! why ys she so?/And I am so sore bound/I may nat com her to./She hath my hert in hold/Where euer she ryde or go,/With trew love a thousand-fold.

2882 Medieval theory held that morning was a propitious time for prophetic dreams. See Curry, Ch and Science, 207–8, and HF 4n.

2914–17 The qualities Pertelote mentions were regularly demanded of courtly lovers; cf. LGW 1526–31 and

also the qualities of the ideal husband enumerated in ShipT VII.173–77. Cf. also WBT III.1258–60.

2917 Men who boast of their conquests in love were held in particular contempt by those who observed the chivalric code of conduct; cf. Tr 2.724–28; 3.306–22.

2918–20 aferd: The cock was known as a "bold and hardy" fighter (Bartholomaeus Anglicus, De prop. rerum 12.17; tr. Trevisa 1:627).

berd: Alexander Neckham writes in his De naturis rerum (ed. Wright, 121) that a cock's wattles were commonly known as beards (vulgo dicuntur barbae); see Steadman, Isis 50:243.

2922–3157 "Chaucer's writings give abundant evidence of his interest in dreams. Several pieces, BD, HF, PF, ProLGW, purport to be the records of dreams, and though this might be a mere case of conformity to literary fashion, the poems themselves show more than a passing consideration of the dream experience. Then in at least three passages of some length, HF 1–65, Tr 5.358–85, and the present debate of Chauntecleer and Pertelote, the medieval theories on the subject are explicitly discussed" (Robinson). Information on dreams would have been available to Chaucer in such works as Macrobius's *Commentarii in somnium Scipionis* (see 3123–24 below) or one of its many borrowers (see HF 1–52n.), and the standard medical treatises. Most of the discussion between Chauntecleer and Pertelote is based, however, on Robert Holcot's *Super Sapientiam Salomonis,* lectiones 103 and 202 (Pratt, Spec 52:538–70).

Medieval theory distinguished between two types of dreams, those arising from natural causes, which had no prophetic value, and those of prophetic significance. Pertelote, a skeptic like Pandarus (Tr 5.358–64), identifies Chauntecleer's dream as a *somnium naturale,* one which arises from an imbalance of humors and has no significance. Chauntecleer maintains, however, that his is a celestial or prophetic dream. For a discussion of medieval opinion concerning the validity of various kinds of dreams, see Curry, Ch and Science, 195–232; Constance B. Hieatt, The Realism of Dream Visions, 1967, 23–49.

2923–32 Cf. Bartholomaeus Anglicus, De prop. rerum 6.27, tr. Trevisa 1:336–37: "Somtyme such sweuenes cometh of to moche replecioun . . . somtyme of complexioun, as he that is . . . colericus [dreams] of fire and firy things." Cf. HF 21–22.

2924 Fumes were thought to be the result of overindulgence; see PardT VI.567. **complecciouns:** see GP I.333n.

2928 youre rede colera: The cock is naturally hot and dry (i.e. choleric) of complexion (Barth. Angl. 12.17, tr. Trevisa 1:627). See also Steadman, Isis 50:236–37. An excess of red choler gives off a fiery smoke that ascends to the brain and brings on dreams of fiery things (Barth. Angl. 4.10, tr. Trevisa 1:159).

2933–36 humour of malencolie: "Blake colera"; one with an excess of this humor dreams "dredeful sweuenes and of derknes, griselych to se" (Barth. Angl. 4.11, tr. Trevisa 1:161). See BD 445n.

2940–41 As noted in the marginal gloss in some MSS (but not Ellesmere or Hengwrt; cf. M-R 3:521), the quotation "somnia ne cures," is from Disticis 2.3., attributed to Marcus Porcius Cato (**Catoun;** see also MilT I.3227). Pertelote omits the second half of the proverb, "nam fallunt somnia plures" (for dreams deceive many).

2942–67 Pertelote's advice is in accord with her diagnosis and standard medical practice. Chaunticleer is naturally choleric (VII.2928), hot and dry, and must therefore avoid too much of the hot and dry sun which would increase his choler and lead to a **fevere terciane**, a fever that recurs every third day and is caused by choler. The patient must first be administered digestives (VII.2961) and then laxatives (2962); see Bartholomaeus Anglicus, De prop. rerum 7.39, tr. Trevisa 1:386–88, and, for other authorities, Curry, Ch and Science, 226–27, and Aiken, Spec 10, 1935, 282–83.

2953   purge bynethe and eek above: Vincent of Beauvais (quoted by Aiken, Spec 10:282) recommends purging "aut superius aut inferius" (either above or below); Pertelote enthusiastically recommends both.

2961–66   wormes: In Dioscorides, De medica materia 2.72 (ed. Curtius Sprengel, 1829–30, 1:195; ed. Max Wellmann, 1906–14, 1:142), earthworms are prescribed for tertian fever (Lowes, Geoffrey Ch, 26–27n.). **lawriol** *(lauris nobilis)* is a hot and dry herb with "virtue of purging" (Barth. Angl. 17.48, tr. Trevisa 2:942; see also R. H. Robbins, ChR 3, 1968, 68); **centuare** *(centuaria)* is a "most bitter herb, hot and dry" that "unstopeth the spleen and the reins" (Barth. Angl. 17.47); **fumetere** *(fumus terre)*, a hot and dry herb with "horrible sauoure and heuy smell . . . clensith and purgith melancholia" (Barth. Angl. 17.59); **ellebor,** "a full violent herb," hot and dry, never to be used except "warly" (Barth. Angl. 17.55); **katapuce,** "setteth on fire and scorcheth . . . the whole body" (John Gerarde, The Herball, 1597, quoted by Kauffman, (ChR 4, 1970, 45); **gaitrys beryis,** identified by Skeat (5:252) as the buckthorn, whose berries "purge downwards mightily flegme and choller with great force, much troubling the body" (Langham, Garden of Health, 1633, 99); **herbe yve,** an extremely nauseous herb (Manly, CT, 640), but strong "though he be bitter" (Barth. Angl. 17.53). Pertelote seems to overprescribe (Aiken, Spec 10:284); since almost all are hot and dry and taken together would increase Chaunticleer's hotness and dryness, her prescription could endanger his very life (Kauffman, ChR 4, 1969, 41–48).

2967 "The conversational effect of the meter is surely intentional, and it is not necessary to regularize the line by omitting *hem* or *up*" (Robinson).

2984   Oon of the gretteste auctour: One of the greatest authors; see Language and Versification, p. xxxviii, and Tr 5.832n. on this construction. The superlative may refer to Cicero or Valerius Maximus, both of whom tell the stories (Cicero, De divinatione 1.27; Valerius, Facta et dicta memorabilia 1.7). Petersen (Sources of NPT, 109–10) argues the latter is meant, as Chaucer appears to have found the stories in Holcot's Super Sapientiam Salomonis, where they are quoted from Valerius. However, opposite this line in some manuscripts is the marginal gloss "Tullius" (M-R 3:520), indicating, perhaps, that Cicero is intended (Pratt, Spec 52:562–63 and n. 56). Baum (PMLA 73, 1958, 169) detects a possible pun on the name of Valerius Maximus.

3050 The marginal gloss "auctor" is written here in the Ellesmere MS. Cf. MLT II.358n.

3052, 3057   Mordre wol out: The phrase is proverbial (Whiting M806) and echoes PrT VII.576. See also VII.3335.

3065 This statement does not apply to Cicero, Valerius, or Holcot (Petersen, Sources of NPT 109–10; Pratt,

Spec 52:562 and n.). "Manly remarks that Chaunticleer is perhaps 'deceiving Pertelote by a pretense of scrupulous accuracy.' In l. 3164 he is certainly not above taking advantage of her ignorance of Latin!" (Robinson).

3076   herkneth!: Hypermetrical *herkneth* is found in most manuscripts, including Ellesmere and Hengwrt. Manly suggests it was inserted for dramatic effect in reading.

3078   agayn the day: See 2882 above.

3092   of owles and of apes: Rowland (MS 27, 1965, 322) notes that owls and apes signify evil in Greek dream books though there is no reason to think Chaucer knew them. She notes they were often used with pejorative meanings in medieval art. The owl is traditionally an evil portent (cf. PF 343, Tr 5.316–20, LGW 2253–54); the ape an emblem of foolishness (cf. GP I.706, CYT VIII.1313). Shaver (MLN 58, 1943, 106–7), noting later collocations of owls and apes, suggests the phrase means something monstrous and absurd. Regan (ChR 17, 1983, 278–80) cites further evidence for a tradition associating the two creatures.

3110–12   Kenelm: Legend maintained that *Kenelm* (Cenhelm), son of *Kenulphus* (Cenwulf, d. 821) king of Mercia, succeeded his father at the age of seven, but was murdered at the instigation of his sister. Shortly before his death, Kenelm dreamed that he climbed a beautiful tree which was cut down beneath him by his attendant, whereupon his soul flew to heaven as a little bird. (Early South Eng. Legendary, EETS 87, 345–55; Jacobus de Voragine, Legenda aurea, tr. Caxton 4:60–66).

3123–24 The Somnium Scipionis (**Cipioun**) was originally a chapter of the De republica of Cicero. It was edited with an elaborate commentary by Macrobius in about 400 A.D. (see PF 29–84 and nn.). Chaucer here makes the common medieval error of attributing the book to Macrobius instead of Cicero, an error which he repeats in BD 284–86 and Rom 7–10, although he attributes the book correctly to Cicero in PF 31 (see n.). Rand (AmN&Q 7, 1969, 149–50) concludes on this basis that NPT was written before PF, but this argument is not convincing.

3128   Daniel: Dan. 7–12 describes the visions in which the fate of the Jews was revealed to Daniel. Crider (AmN&Q 18, Oct. 1979, 18–19) notes that in Dan. 4 is described the dream of Nebuchadnezzar cited in MkT VII.2154–56.

3130–35   Joseph: Joseph as a master interpreter of dreams was a medieval commonplace; cf. BD 280. Chauntecleer's exempla occur in Gen. 37, 40, and 41. Lines 3130–32 closely parallel the corresponding passage in Holcot's Super Sapientiam Salomonis, lectio 202: "Therefore some dreams are worthy of credence" (Ergo aliqua sunt sompnia digna fide), where the exemplum of Joseph is also used (Pratt, Spec 52:559).

3141   Andromacha: Her dream of the death of **Ector** (Hector), which has no ancient authority, is recounted in Dares Phrygius's De excidio Troiae historica, ch. 25. Chauntecleer's anecdote may be based on Pinte's use of this exemplum in Renart le Contrefait, 31323–40 (Pratt, Spec 47:648).

3163   *In principio:* The first words of the Gospel of St. John and of the Book of Genesis. The first words of St. John's gospel were the object of special devotion in Chaucer's time (see GP I.254n.), and the line probably means "for as sure as gospel truth." An allusion to Genesis is not, however, inappropriate in this context; see Baum, PMLA 73:169.

3164   *Mulier est hominis confusio*: Part of a comic definition of woman so widely known that it was almost proverbial. The definition occurs in the Altercatio Hadriani Augusti et Secundi (ed. Suchier, Ill. Studs. in Lang. and Lit. 24, pt. 2, 1939, 156) from which it was taken over verbatim by numerous later compilers. A list of analogues is given by Brown, MLN 35, 1920, 479–82.

3167   your softe syde: Cf. Bartholomaeus Anglicus, De prop. rerum 12.17, tr. Trevisa 1:627, on the domestic cock: "And settith next to him on rooste the henne that is most fatte and tendre and loueth hire best and desireth most to haue hire presence. In the morwetide whanne he fleeth to gete his mete, furst he leith his side to hire side and bi certeyne tokenes and beckes, as it were loue tacchis, a woweth and prayeth hire to tredinge."

3173–75   Cf. Barth. Ang. (as above): "And whenne he fyndeth mete he clepith his wifes togedres with a certeyn voys and spareth his owne mete to fede therwith his wifes."

3187   According to medieval belief, the world was created at the vernal equinox; see Bede, De ratione temporum (ed. Charles W. Jones, 1943) 6.6–7.

3187–90   This elaborate *chronographia* (see GP I.7–8 and n.) is meant to establish the date as 3 May, the date of Palamoun's escape from prison (see KnT I.1462–64 and n.) and of Pandarus's dream the night before he woos Criseyde for Troilus (see Tr 2.56 and n.).

3190   Syn March [was gon]: For *was gon* the MSS read *bigan*, but this makes little sense (Adolphus and Skeat, N&Q ser. 10, 8, 1907, 202–3, 252). The present editor proposes that Chaucer wrote *was gon* and that scribal miscopying from 3187 led to the mistaken repetition of *bigan* in 3190.

3194–99   The Kalendarium of Nicholas of Lynn, which Chaucer probably used here (cf. Astr Pro 84–86n.) shows that on 3 May the sun was at 21° 6′ of **Taurus** (the bull, the second sign of the zodiac) and that at 9 A.M. in the latitude of Oxford the sun was at a height of 41° 17 ′. (See Eisner, ed., 89, 93.)

3196–97   See 2857–58 above.

3205–6   A medieval commonplace, attributed to Solomon in a marginal gloss (cf. Prov. 14.13). See MLT II.421n. Lumiansky (in Sts. in Lang. and Lit. in Honour of Margaret Schlauch, ed. Irena Dobrzycka, 1966) and Dean (MAE 44, 1975, 4) argue that the Nun's Priest is parodying the idea, which had become a cliché by Chaucer's time. Young (MP 41, 1943–44, 180) detects a gibe at Geoffrey of Vinsauf, who elaborated the theme at length in his Poetria nova.

3208   The name "Petrus Comestor," author of a widely read chronicle, is written here in the margin of five MSS, including Ellesmere and Hengwrt, but no reference to him in the NPT has been traced.

3212   the book of Launcelot de Lake: The story of Lancelot, knight of Arthur's court and lover of Queen Guinevere. "Who" was not in use as a relative in Chaucer's time, so *that* in the following line may refer either to Lancelot or to the book. This is the story that Paolo and Francesca were reading when they were inspired to commit adultery (Dante, Inferno 5.117–38). In his Comento alla divina commedia, Boccaccio remarks that Lancelot was "composed rather for approval than to ac-

cord with truth" (più composte a beneplacito che secondo la verità) (ed. Guerri 2:144). Hinckley (Notes on Ch, 141) quotes from Hugh of Rutland's Ipomedon: "Sul ne sai pas de mentir lart / Walter Map reset ben sa part." Walter Map was the supposed author of the prose Book of Lancelot.

3215   col-fox: Hotson (PMLA 39:762–81) argued elaborately that Chaucer uses a *col-fox* instead of the usual red fox of the Reynard cycle to suggest the name of Nicholas Colfax, a supporter of Mowbray; his colors are those of Mowbray's truncheon as earl marshal; his name, *daun Russell*, suggests Sir John Russell, a minion of Richard II. Hotson takes Chauntecleer's colors as suggesting the arms of Henry Bolingbroke and sees the confrontation of the cock and the fox as representing the duel between Mowbray and Bolingbroke on 16 September 1398. The identification with Bolingbroke is very unlikely, as is the rest of the theory.

3217   By heigh ymaginacioun forncast: The line has been taken to be either a reference to Chauntecleer's dream or to God's foreknowledge, and to mean "foreseen by the exalted imagination," (i.e. in Chauntecleer's prophetic dream), or "foreordained by the high vision of God." Hamm (MLN 69, 1954, 394–95) notes that Dante uses the phrase "alta fantasia" in connection with his ecstatic visions in Purgatorio 17.25 and Paradiso 33.142 (see also Pratt, Spec 47:666 and n. 36). However, Davis (MAE 40, 1971, 79) and Wentersdorf (SN 52, 1980, 31–34) make it clear that the phrase refers to the fox's cunningly premeditated attack on Chauntecleer.

3222   undren: Strictly speaking, *undren* meant 9 A.M., but the term was loosely used to cover the entire period from 9:00 until noon.

3224   gladly: For this extension of meaning, see V.224; X.887, and MED s.v. *gladlī* adv. (4).

3227   Genylon: Ganelon, the traitor in the Chanson de Roland, betrayed Charlemagne's army at Roncesvalles; cf. MkT VII.2389, ShipT VII.194.

3228   Synon: See Aen. 2.57–267; HF 152–56; SqT V.209–10.

3240–42   Cf. ParsT X.957.

3241–50   The question of predestination versus free will and the issue of divine grace were much debated in the universities during Chaucer's time. **Augustyn**, St. Augustine (354–430), bishop of Hippo, one of the four original Doctors of the Church, was an exponent of the orthodox doctrine on the subject, which held that free will was granted to man by God to be used to the extent that God allowed. **Boece**, Boethius, discusses the problem (see Boece 4.pr6 and Bk. 5, esp. pr6.140ff.) and makes the distinction between "simple" and "conditional" necessity mentioned here. Thomas **Bradwardyn** (c. 1290–1349) was an Oxford theologian who became archbishop of Canterbury. In his treatise De causa Dei (ed. Savile, 1618), he reaffirmed the (orthodox) doctrine of predestination and grace (VII.3242–45); see Gordon Leff, Bradwardine and the Pelagians, 1957. The subject is treated at length in Tr 4.953–1078. See also Payne, ChR 10, 1976, 201–19.

3245–50   symple necessitee . . . necessitee condicioneel: See Bo 5.pr6.178–83. "Simple" necessity is direct, as in *it byhovith by necessite that alle men ben mortal*. "Conditional" necessity is inferential: *yif thou wost that a man walketh, it byhovith by necessite that he walke*. Thus

God's foreknowledge, Boethius argues, is not a necessary cause of man's actions. See Payne, ChR 10, 1976, 201–19.

3256   colde: Proverbial (Whiting W505), cf. Mel VII.1096, LGW 762. Severs (SP 43, 1946, 30) maintains the passage reveals an antifeminist attitude on the part of the Nun's Priest.

3260   Cf. RR 15195–210: "If you ever find set down here any words that seem critical of feminine ways, then please do not blame me for them nor abuse my writing, which is all for our instruction. I certainly never said anything, nor ever had the wish to say anything . . . against any woman alive."

3266   Since kan may mean "am able" or "know," and **divyne** may be read as either a verb or an adjective, the sentence has several possible meanings. For a complete analysis of what Muscatine (Ch and Fr Trad., 239) calls "the most deliciously ambiguous line in Chaucer," see Besserman, ChR 12, 1977, 68–71.

3271–72   Phisiologus: "The Naturalist," the title or the supposed author of a popular compilation in which descriptions of imaginary and real animals, birds, and stones were allegorized to illustrate points of Christian doctrine. The descriptions are introduced by the formula: "Physiologus says" (Physiologus dicit). The Latin Physiologus circulated in numerous versions, for which see Florence McCulloch, Med. Lat. and Fr. Bestiaries, Univ. of North Carolina Sts. in the Romance Langs. and Lits., 33, revised ed., 1962. See also Theobaldi, *Physiologus,* ed. P. T. Eden, 1972.

The mermaid or siren (*mermayde*) appears in several versions of Physiologus, where she is characterized by a sweet voice that leads sailors to destruction (McCulloch, s.v. *siren and onocentaur*; Meredith, Neophil 54, 1970, 81–83; Schrader, ChR 4, 1970, 285–86; Friedman, ChR 7, 1973, 250–66; cf. Rom 680–82; Bo 1.pr1.69).

3280:   Robinson notes that according to the old philosophy every object or creature had its contrary toward which it felt a natural antipathy. Professor Jon Whitman of the University of Virginia, in a letter, quotes Fulgentius, Mitologia 1.6 (tr. Whitbread, 51–52): "Quarrels are brought about in a threefold fashion, that is, by nature, cause, and accident. Hate is natural, as between dogs and hares, wolves and sheep, men and snakes."

3281   erst: For the idiom see KnT I.1566 and n.

3294   Boece: Boethius's treatise De musica (ed. G. Friedlein, Leipzig, 1867) was a standard medieval university text. In it, he advocated a mathematical rather than instinctual approach to music. Chaucer's couplet, therefore, may have an ironic meaning (Dieckmann, MLN 53, 1938, 177–80; Chamberlain, MP 68, 1970, 188–91).

3306   wynke: Coghill and Tolkien (eds., NPT, 125) note this older meaning of *wink* is the origin of the expressions "I'll wink at it," and "I couldn't sleep a wink."

3312   'Daun Burnel the Asse': The comic beast tale (c. 1180) of Nigel Wireker or Nigel of Longchamps entitled Burnellus, or Speculum stultorum; for the story to which Chaucer refers, see lines 1251–1502. "A young man named Gundulfus broke a cock's leg by throwing a stone at it. Later, when Gundulfus was to be ordained and receive a benefice, the cock crowed so late that Gundulfus overslept and lost his living" (Robinson). On the literary relationship between this poem and The Nun's

Priest's Tale, see Schrader, ChR 4, 1970, 284–90; Mann, ChR 9, 1975, 262–82.

3320   seinte: For the form see KnT I.1721n.

3325   Allas, ye lordes: This passage, which is inappropriate to the pilgrimage framework (Sisam, ed., NPT, 1927) is taken almost verbatim from John of Wales's preaching manual, the Communiloquium 1.8.2 (Pratt, Spec 41, 1966, 635–36). The interpolation may be meant as a parody of the sort of intrusiveness found in Chaucer's sources, the Roman de Renart and Renart le Contrefait (Pratt, Spec 47:665), although Fisher finds it appropriate to the court situation in which Chaucer may have read his tales. Cf. also ProLGW F 352–56.

3329   Ecclesiaste: Skeat and Robinson cite Ecclesiasticus 12.10, 11, 16; 27.26, while Sisam notes that *Ecclesiastes* may stand for *Solomon* in any of his works and may refer to Prov. 29.5, quoted in Chaucer's Melibee in the section on flattery (VII.1177). Steadman (MAE 28, 1959, 178) suggests the allusion is not to a single passage, but to a theme expressed in various texts cited above, including perhaps Eccles. 7.6 and other sections of the Book of Proverbs.

3338   Cf. Bo 5.pr3.189–90.

3341   Friday: Friday, Venus's day, was traditionally associated with bad luck. The Expulsion, the Deluge, the Betrayal, the Crucifixion, and the fatal wounding of Richard I all occurred on a Friday. See also KnT I.1534–35.

3345   Cf. RR 4385–88: "A lover thinks of nothing else; he takes no account of bearing fruit, but strives only for delight."

3347   Gaufred: Geoffrey of Vinsauf, author of the Poetria nova (c. 1210), the standard text on medieval rhetoric (i.e., poetics) (see BD 817–1040n.) gives artificial rules, with flamboyant illustrations of his own composition. In VII.3347–52 Chaucer parodies the most famous of these, the lamentation on the death of Richard the Lion-Hearted, which begins (Poetria nova, 375–76): O Veneris lacrimosa dies! O sidus amaram!/Illa dies tua nox fuit et Venus illa venenum. (O tearful day of Venus! O bitter star!/That day was your night and that Venus your venom.) In VII.3355–73 Chaucer elaborately expands a simple statement in accord with the rules set down by Geoffrey. Chaucer quotes Geoffrey again in Tr 1.1065–71; both that passage and this one circulated independently from the Poetria nova (see Tr 1.1065–71n., and Young MP 41:172–82).

3357   Pirrus: Pyrrhus, son of Achilles, seized Priam by the hair (not the beard) and killed him with his sword. The laments he caused are narrated in Aeneid 2.469–90. Cf. MLT II.288.

streite swerd: Cf. Aeneid 2.333–34, "acies stricta"; OF *estreit.*

3359   Eneydos: Aeneid 2.533–58. For the form *Eneydos* (gen. sing. dependent on *Liber* in the full title) see IntroMLT II.93n. Chaucer may have found the hint for his references to Troy, Carthage, and Rome in the five lines (363–68) of the Poetria nova just preceding those parodied in VII.3347–52 (Pratt, MLN 64, 1949, 76–78).

3363   Hasdrubales wyf: Hasdrubal was king of Carthage when the Romans captured and burned it in 146 B.C. Chaucer tells of his wife's suicide in FranT V.1399–1404, from Jerome, Adversus Jovinianum 1.43 (see V.1399n.). He may also have known other versions, such as Orosius 4.23.

3375–3401 The chase of the fox was a stock scene in medieval poetry and art. An example occurs in the poem The Fals Fox (Sec. Lyrics, ed. Robbins, 44–45). See also Varty, Nottingham Med. Sts. 8, 1964, 62–81, and Varty, Reynard the Fox, 1967, 34–42.

3381 Ha, ha!: The regular cry to frighten away wolves and other marauding animals. The thirteenth-century Dominican, Nicholas Biard, says in a sermon: "There is no wolf disguised as a sheep, that will not flee if the shepherds go on shouting Ha! Ha!" (Non est lupus incarnatus in ove quin fugiat si pastores continuent clamare Ha! Ha!) (Tatlock, MLN 29, 1914, 143).

3383 Colle oure dogge: The "domestic plural"; see WBT III.311n. For Colle as a dog's name in a fifteenth-century poem, see R. H. Robbins, ed., Hist. Poems, 1959, 189, 355n.

Talbot and Gerland: Dogs' names. For other instances of Talbot as a dog's name and the observation that a particular kind of hunting dog called a talbot was introduced into England by the Talbot family, see Hinckley, MP 16, 1918, 42. There is a list of names of hounds in one MS of the Roman de Renart (ed. Martin, 1882–87, 5:1187; rpt. S&A, 656:412–13).

3384 Malkyn: A typical name for a country girl or serving-maid; see IntroMLT II.30 and II.20–31n. In medieval art, it was a regular feature of the chase of the fox for the woman to carry a distaff as a weapon (Varty, Nottingham Med. Sts. 8:62–81).

3394 he Jakke Straw: A supposed leader of the Peasants' Revolt of 1381. The Flemings, prosperous foreigners engaged in the wool trade, were the victims of a particularly ruthless attack by the mob. See Charles W. Oman, The Great Revolt of 1381, 1906; Robertson, Ch's London, 143–49; R. B. Dobson, ed., The Peasants' Revolt of 1381, 1970.

For the demonstrative use of he meaning here "that famous," or "that notorious," see Mustanoja, ME Syntax, 135–36.

3398 box: Cf. PF 178 and n.

3416 delyverly: Nimbly; with a possible pun on the idea of being set free.

3426 Almost identical with WBT III.1062.

3438 Cf. ParsPro X.31–34.

3441 Seint Paul seith: Rom. 15.4: "For whatever was written in former days was written for our instruction, that by steadfastness and by the encouragement of the scriptures we might have hope." Sisam notes that the quotation in its context is not as sweeping as this paraphrase. Chaucer's Retraction, X.1083, is nearly identical.

3443 For the familiar figure, see MLT II.701–2; ParsPro X.35–36; ProLGW G 312, G 529; Jean de Meun, Testament, 2167 (in RR, ed. Méon, 4:115), and cf. Whiting C428. The comparison derives from Matt. 3.12 (Luke 3.17). Manning (JEGP 59:414) notes the similarity between the Nun's Priest's words and the introduction to the versified Romulus collection attributed to the twelfth-century writer, Walter of England: "If the fruit is more pleasing than the flower, gather the fruit, if the flower more than the fruit, the flower; if both, take both" (Si fructus plus flore placet, fructum lege; si flos/ Plus fructu, florem; si duo, carpe duo; Léopold Hervieux, ed., Les Fabulistes Latins, 1894, 2:316). See also Robertson (Pref to Ch, 58 and 316–17) on the chaff image in Augustine and other patristic writers.

3445 As seith my lord: It is uncertain who is meant. If the ascription applies to the phrase if that it be thy wille, there may be an allusion to the prayer of Jesus in Gethsemane (Matt. 26), but in that case oure lord would be more natural than my lord. A marginal gloss in the Ellesmere MS (M-R 3:520) reads: "scilicet Dominus archiepiscopus Cantuariensis" (that is the Lord Archbishop of Canterbury) and a considerable, but so far unsuccessful, search has been made to find a similar benediction associated with that prelate (then William Courtenay). Manly observes that the Nun's Priest's "lord" was the bishop of London, Robert Braybrooke. While VII.3444–46 may echo an episcopal blessing, many ME secular compositions, including a good number of Chaucer's Tales, conclude with a prayer. Correale (Expl 39, 1980, 43–45) notes the similarity between these lines and the ending of a homily for the Feast of the Conversion of St. Paul. He argues that the "lord" intended is St. Paul, mentioned in VII.3441.

The Nun's Priest's Epilogue

These lines occur in a group of nine MSS generally taken to be of inferior authority and may have been canceled by Chaucer when he wrote lines 1941–62 of the Monk's Prologue, where the same ideas are repeated (M-R 2:422–23; Dempster, PMLA 68:1147–49). Tatlock (PMLA 50, 1935, 113–15) defends retention of the link, however, on the grounds that repeated language and ideas are characteristic of Chaucer's style, and that in the best MSS, link passages pointing to lacunae in the text would have been suppressed to give semblance of completeness to the work. For the suggestion that Chaucer originally meant the lines to introduce the wife of Bath, see Gibbons, SP 51, 1954, 21–33. His hypothesis is refuted by Brosnahan, SP 58, 1961, 468–82.

3451 trede-foul: Cf. ProMkT VII.1945. Pearcy (N&Q 213, 1968, 43–45) shows the parallel between a man in a religious house and hens in a hen-run was traditional in the Middle Ages.

3459 brasile: A red dye derived from the wood of an East Indian tree (OED s.v. Brazil, 1.2). Among its uses was the rubrication of books (Baugh, 382n.). The name was afterwards applied to Brazil in South America because a similar dye-producing tree was found there.

greyn of Portyngale: Another crimson dye-stuff, obtained from the dried bodies of the insect coccus ilicis, which were thought to be seed grains; also known as "kermes berries." See Magoun, Ch Gazetteer, 129.

3461–62 These lines, with the indefinite and hypermetrical reference to "another" may be a spurious attempt at patchwork (M-R 2:422). For a clearly spurious link with The Second Nun's Tale see Textual Notes.

FRAGMENT VIII

Though editors have differed on whether Fragment VI or Fragment VII should precede Fragment VIII, none has printed the last three fragments in any other order than VIII–IX–X. Howard (Idea of CT, 305) and Lawler (One and the Many, 145–46) argue that these three fragments form a coherent group that recapitulates earlier themes of the whole work, providing a sense of closure.

The two tales of this fragment are explicitly linked (by line 554), though there is no other explicit relation between the tales, and the attribution of the first to the Second Nun occurs only in the rubric (some scribes of manuscripts with the Ellesmere order remedied this deficiency by supplying a spurious link with The Nun's Priest's Tale; see Textual Notes. Critics have nevertheless often remarked on the thematic unity of the two tales (Muscatine, Ch and Fr Trad., 216–17). The thematic link is most often found in the use of alchemical imagery (Grennen, JEGP 65, 1966, 466–81; see also Gardner, in Signs and Symbols, 201–7) or in the manipulation of contrasts, such as those of reason versus revelation, sight versus blindness, and contrasting imagery and attitudes (see Rosenberg, ChR 2, 1968, 278–91; Peck, AnM 8, 1967, 17–37; Taylor, ES 60, 1979, 280–88). Olson explains the unity of theme and imagery in the context of Dante's influence (ChR 16, 1981, 222–36) and supplies a summary of commentary viewing the two tales as complementary, as does Brown (ES 64, 1983, 481–90), who finds the lesson that the Canon's Yeoman learns the same as that which Cecilia offers to Almachius.

LARRY D. BENSON

The Second Nun's Prologue and Tale

The reference to the *lyf of Seynt Cecile* in the Prologue to *The Legend of Good Women* (ProLGW F 426) shows that The Second Nun's Tale was written before 1386–87, and its borrowings from Dante (see notes to 36–58 below) and use of rime royal show that it probably belongs to Chaucer's Italian period. Older scholars put it very early in that period, around 1373, since they regarded it as a close translation of its source (e.g., Skeat 3:485, but cf. Lumiansky, Of Sondry Folk, 224) and therefore as an immature work. But the charge of immaturity is unwarranted; the versification of the prologue and tale have been rightly praised (Knight, Poetry of CT, 175–79), and on the whole a date in the mid- rather than the early period is more likely. Peck (AnM 8, 1967, 17) argues that the tale was later revised to create a unit with The Canon's Yeoman's Tale.

The prologue and tale seem to have been composed at the same time, although occasionally a critic finds them ill-matched (e.g., Brusendorff, Ch Trad, 131; Burlin, Ch Fiction, 278) and Skeat (5:403) argued that lines 36–56 of the Invocacio were a later interpolation. However, the prologue and tale are linked both thematically and by their use of similar sources; cf. Clogan, M&H n.s. 3, 1972, 213–40; and Boyd, Ch and the Liturgy, 26–33.

This prologue (on which the Prioress draws; cf. introductory note to the Prioress's Prologue) and tale are eminently suited to a nun and seem to suggest a definite personality (Engelhardt, MS 37, 1975, 295–96), but it is clear that the tale was never completely revised (see VIII.62, 78, 139 and nn.). Since there is no portrait of the Second Nun in the General Prologue, and since the tale is assigned to her only in widely varying scribal

The explanatory notes to the Second Nun's Prologue and Tale were written by Florence H. Ridley.

rubrics (see Brusendorff, Ch Trad., 131), Eliason (MLQ, 3:9–16) conjectures that the Nun herself was a creation of the scribes, suggested by the heading *Second Nonnes Tale,* meant to designate the second tale told by the Prioress, but his theory has not been widely accepted. The lack of any clear integration with the *Tales* may indicate that David is correct in his conjecture that it was spontaneously linked to The Canon's Yeoman's Tale (Strumpet Muse, 234). Though recent criticism has found close thematic relationships between The Second Nun's Tale and The Canon's Yeoman's Prologue and Tale (see introductory note to Fragment VIII above) or has seen it as an inspiration (Peck, AnM 8:17–37) or illumination for what follows (Kolve, in New Perspectives, 156), the tale was apparently allowed to stand as written, without revisions to adapt it to its context.

Almost nothing is known of the historical Cecilia, whose martyrdom is assigned to various times from the reign of Marcus Aurelius (c. 177 A.D.) to the persecutions of Julian the Apostate (362 A.D.). An error in the *Liber pontificalis* (ed. L. Duchesne, 2nd ed., 1955, 1:143) associates Cecilia with Pope Urban I, making him a martyr under Diocletian (c. 245–316). On the history of the legend, see Butler's Lives of the Saints 4:402–5; Karl Künstle, Ikonographie der christlichen Kunst, 1926, 2: 146–50; Agostino Amore, I Martiri di Roma, Spicilegium Pontificii Athenaei Antoniani 18, 1975, 144–56; and Kolve, in New Perspectives, 137–58.

The idea for lines 1–28, on idleness, may have come from the introduction to the French translation of the *Legenda aurea* by Jean de Vignay (1282/85–1348), though such a prologue is conventional. The *Invocacio ad Mariam* (VIII.29–84) is based mainly on Dante (Par. 33.1–39), though it contains numerous commonplaces and echoes and paraphrases from other sources (see Clogan, M&H n.s. 3:221–31). The *Interpretacio nominis Cecilie* and the tale, to about line 345, are drawn from the *Legenda aurea* of Jacobus de Voragine (ed. Gerould, in S&A, 671–77). It was once believed that the second half of the tale was based ultimately on a late tenth-century Greek version of the legend by Simeon Metaphrastes (Kölbing, ESt 1, 1877, 215–48), but it is now generally agreed that Chaucer drew on a source descended from some longer Latin life of the saint. Gerould was inclined toward the *Passio* by Mombritus (which he printed in S&A, 677–84). Reames (MP 76, 1978, 111–35) argues persuasively that the second half of the tale was based on some version of a Latin life close to that used by Antonio Boso in his *Historia passionis beatae Caeciliae* (ed. G. Laderchii, 1722, 1:1–39). Yet the question of whether Chaucer combined this version with material from the *Legenda aurea* or worked from a source in which the combination had already been made remains unanswered.

Some critics have found the tale dull (e.g., Donaldson, 1108–9; Rosenberg, ChR 2, 1968, 278), but this may simply reflect a modern aversion to saints' lives. It is the finest saint's life in Middle English verse (Kolve, in New Perspectives, 139). Boitani (Eng. Med. Narrative, 246) finds it a model of official culture whose exemplary structure is fixed by tradition, and recent critics have increasingly recognized the power and complexity of both the prologue and the tale (e.g., Kean, Ch and Poetry 2:201–4). In the past few years the work has attracted an increasing body of commentary, not only on its relation to The Canon's Yeoman's Prologue and Tale but on such matters as the relations between Chaucer's two nuns and their tales, the themes of marriage and sight, and the interpretations of Cecilia; see, among others, Hostia (CE 14, 1953, 351–52), Knight (Poetry of Ch, 175–79), Howard (MP 57, 1960, 223–32), Collette (ChR 10, 1976, 337–49), Reames (Spec 55, 1980, 38–57), and Hirsch (ChR 12, 1977, 129–44). For a detailed appraisal of Chaucer's probable attitude toward both the Second Nun and the Prioress, see Ames, God's Plenty.

1–28 The idea for the stanzas on idleness may derive from de Vignay's introduction, with the theme of **bisynesse** deriving from Jacobus de Voragine, Sermones aurei, ed. Rudolph Clutius, 1760, 2:361–62 (Lowes, PMLA 30, 1915, 294) and that of idleness from Boccaccio's Ameto, 58–59. However, the ideas are conventional; Whittock (A Reading of CT, 252) notes how the lines develop a proverb (see 1 below).
1   norice unto vices: Proverbial; Whiting 16. Cf. Mel VII.1589.
2–3   Ydelnesse: Cf. Rom 593, KnT I.1940. Malina (Expl 43, 1984, 3–4) discusses the thematic word play of *ydelnesse* and *ydoles.* Cf. ParsT X.714.
4–6   bisynesse: Cf. Gent 10–11. Cecilia is the antitype of sloth (Tupper, PMLA 29, 1914, 106); the stress on her *bisynesse* (VIII.195) is appropriate for one also noted for charity (118), which is, according to St. Thomas, the opposite of sloth (Rosenberg, ChR 2:285). Giffin finds in this contrast a major theme (Sts. on Ch, 40–48).
4   contrarie: The principle in medicine (Mel VII.1017n.) was applied to the deadly sins (*vices*, line 1) each of which has as its remedy a particular virtue (cf. ParsT, Part I); there the remedy for *ydelnesse (Accidie)* is *fortitudo or strengthe* (X.728); cf. Tupper, PMLA 29: 98–99.
6–7 Cf. Mel VII.1595 and n.
10–11   trappe: On idleness as the Devil's trap, see Wycliffe, Selected Eng. Works 3:200.
14   werche: Cf. VIII.2–5, 64–66, 77, 84, 384–85. Rosenberg and Grennen trace the theme, ChR 2:282–91; JEGP 65:466–81.
19   syn: Hengwrt and other MSS read *seen,* syntactically better.
19–21 Sloth holds idleness on a leash, causing men to sleep, eat, drink, and devour the produce of others.
25–26   legende . . . lif . . . passioun: In early ME *lif* indicates a brief biography, emphasizing a saint's passion; *legende* is most often applied to the lives in the *Legenda aurea,* though the word could be used satirically; cf. MilPro I.3141 (Strohm, ChR 10, 1975, 154–71). On medieval hagiography, see Hippolyte Delehaye, Legends of the Saints, tr. Donald Attwater, 1962; for Chaucer's use of the genre, see Gerould, Ch Essays, 3–32. In the Retraction, X.1087, Chaucer seems to imply he wrote more than one saint's life, though only the life of Cecilia has survived.
27   rose . . . lilie: The rose symbolizes martyrdom, the lily purity; cf. Ambrose's commentary on the Song of Songs, PL 15:1966–67, and Bernard's (see 29–30 below), Clogan, M&H n.s. 3:233. Cf. ProPrT VII.461.
29–77   Invocacio: The resemblance to ProPrT VII.467–80 and to ABC is striking. On the form of such prayers, see Clogan, M&H n.s. 3:222.
29–30   flour of virgines: The figure of flower-virgo-virga is frequent (Clogan, M&H n.s. 3:223–24), possibly

ultimately due to Bernard of Clairvaux (c. 1090–1153), who was noted for his devotion to the Virgin. Cf. On the Song of Songs, tr. Kilian Walsh and Irene M. Edwards, Cistercian Fathers ser. 31, 1969, 6–7; Homilia 2, tr. Marie-Bernard Saïd and Grace Perigo, Cistercian Fathers ser. 18, 1979, 18–19.
36–56 Based on Dante, Par. 33.1–51; Skeat took the passage as a late addition (5:403), but Brown argues effectively for the unity of the *Invocacio* (MP 9, 1911, 1–11).
36–42 Cf. ProPrT VII.467–72n.
36 Translation of Par. 33.1: "Vergine madre, figlia del tuo figlio." On the concept, see Augustine, De sancta virginitate, tr. John McQuade, Treatises on Marriage, 1955, 149. For analysis of the stanza, see Whittock, A Reading of CT, 253; Clogan, M&H n.s. 3:224–25.
37   welle of mercy: Cf. ABC 177–8 and Bernard's image of "aquaeductu" for Mary as mediatrix (Opera, ed. LeClercq et al. 5:275–88).
39 Translation of Par. 33.2: "Umile e alta più che creatura." Cf. Luke 1.28.
40–41 From Par. 33.4–6: "Che l'umana natura nobilasti che il suo Fattore non disdegnò di farsi sua fattura" (to become its making). On modification of the Immaculist view, cf. Clogan, M&H n.s. 3:226.
43–49 Cf. Par. 33.7: "Nel ventre tuo is raccese l'amore" (in your womb was rekindled the love). The phrase **cloistre blisful** may derive from Par. 25.127, but the passage as a whole is close to the *Quem terra* by Venantius Fortunatus (Analecta Hymnica II.38, No. 1, 27, 1–4): "The womb (claustrum) of Mary bears Him, ruling the threefold fabric (trinam machinam), Whom earth, stars, sea, honor, worship, proclaim."
50–51 Cf. Par. 33.19–20: "In te misericordia, in te pietate, In te magnificenza." Pity is a traditional attribute of Mary (on which see Gray, in J. R. R. Tolkien, ed. Mary Salu and Robert T. Farrell, 1979, 184–85).
52   sonne: At times applied to Mary (Brown, MP 9:7). Skeat (5:404) suggests it may have had a feminine reference in Chaucer's day. Clogan (M&H n.s. 3:228) suggests the figure was inspired by Par. 33.10–11: "Qui sei a noi meridiana face, di caritate" (Here you are to us the meridian torch [i.e., sun] of love). Olson (ChR 16, 1982, 231) notes a similar usage in Purgatorio.
53–56 Cf. Par. 33.16–18: "La tua benignità non pur soccorre, a chi domanda, ma molte fiate, liberamente al domandar precorre" (Your kindness not only helps those who ask but many times generously anticipates the asking). This passage is echoed also in ProPrT VII.477–80 and *Troilus.*
58   flemed wrecche: Banished exile; possibly suggested by the Lat. source for VIII.62 (see n.) and "wraeca," "exile." Lounsbury (Sts. in Ch 2:389) compares Bernard's *Tractatus ad laudem gloriosae Virginis* (PL 182: 1148), "in exsilio filios Evae" (sons of Eve in exile).
   galle: Bitterness; Skeat (5:404) sees a possible allusion to the name "Mary" and the Heb. *mar,* fem. *marah,* "bitter"; cf. ABC 50n., Exodus 15.23.
59   womman Cananee: Cf. Matt. 15.22 ("mulier Chananaea").
62   sone of Eve: Perhaps suggested by Bernard (see 58 above) or by the antiphon Salve Regina, 3, exsules filii Hevae (Matthew Britt, Hymns of the Breviary and Missal, 2nd ed., 1955, 67). The antiphon contains other phrases which may be echoed here: "In hac lacrimarum

valle," 4: *desert of galle* (VIII.57); "Eia ergo advocata nostra," 5: *Be myn advocat* (VIII.68); "O clemens, o pia, o dulcis virgo," 10: *thow meeke and blisful fayre mayde* (VIII. 57). See Brown, MP 9:7. Tupper (MLN, 30, 1915, 9–11) argues *sone of Eve* is well suited to a nun, since it occurs in Compline service of the Hours of the Virgin as *exiled sones of Eue* (Prymer or Lay Folks Prayer Book, ed. Henry Littlehales, EETS 105, 1895, 34). Brown (MLN 30, 1915, 231) prints another version somewhat closer to Chaucer's from the Mateyns of Oure Lady (Oxford, Bodleian Libr. MS Ashmole 1288). Yet "filii" is the inclusive pl., and a nun would more naturally refer to herself as "doghter." The masc. sg. probably is evidence that the tale was composed without thought of the Second Nun (see introductory note).

64 James 2.17.

69–70 Cf. MLT II.641–42. Perhaps reminiscent of Par. 32.133–34.

70 **Anne,** mother of Mary; see FrT III.1613n.

71–74 For the concept of the body as prison, weighting the soul down with lust, cf. KnT I.3061; the passages are indebted to Macrobius, Som. Scip., 1.11.2–4, 1.10.9, tr. Stahl, 130–31, 128. However, Chaucer probably did not know Macrobius directly until the time of *The Parliament of Fowls* and may have taken this passage from the long chapter on Pluto in *Albericus philosophus* (the Mythographer, in Bode, Scriptores Rerum Mythicarum, 1834, 1: 178, 180); cf. Lowes, MP 15, 1917, 200–201.

72 **contagioun:** Cf. "contagione corporis" (Macrobius, Som. Scip. 1.11.11). This is the earliest use of the word in this sense in English; MED s.v. *contagion,* n.

75 **havene of refut:** Cf. ABC 14, MLT II.852. There are similar scriptural expressions, cf. Ps. 46.1, 48.3, 107.30, but the epithet is common in hymns from Chaucer's day to the present. For Latin examples see Brown, MP 9:10.

78 **reden:** This reference to reading material supposedly delivered orally seems obvious evidence of lack of revision, but has been explained variously: Giffin, Sts. on Ch, 29–48, argues that Chaucer composed the poem in 1383 for presentation to an audience of monks who could read it later; Clogan (M&H n.s. 3:214–15) argues that *reden* could mean "interpret," "study," and the line be taken as "you who interpret," "you who read later," etc.; Whittock's suggestion (A Reading of CT, 252–53) that the Nun reads aloud from a manuscript that reflects her hours of "busyness" strains the text; David's suggestion (Strumpet Muse, 232) that Chaucer here signed his poem as an artist might paint in his own face, is more engaging than plausible.

79 **Foryeve me:** Chaucer frequently employs the "modesty topos" (see GP I.746n.), though it may be especially appropriate to a hagiographer, whose purpose is not to excel in narration, but to instruct (Clogan, M&H n.s. 3:216).

84 Cf. Tr 5.1856–59n.

85–119 The *Interpretacio* is based on Jacobus (S&A, 671): "coili lilia" (**hevenes lilie**); "caecis via" (**wey to blynde**); "caelo et lya" (**hevene and Lia,** the active life); "caecilia quasi caecitate carens" (**Wantynge of blyndnesse**—as non-light suggests light); "coelo et leos" (**hevene of peple**). These etymologies are all wrong, the name perhaps deriving from *caecus* (blind) (Robinson). However, such etymologies were considered a legitimate means of expressing the moral significance of words

(Hanning, Names 16, 1968, 325–26) or finding the appropriateness of a name to its bearer (Robinson, Anglia 86, 1968, 14). Medieval etymologists held that the origin of a word was related to its force or function; see Isidore of Seville, Etymologiae, ed. Lindsay, 1.1.29, and Curtius, Europ. Lit., 497. Moreover, things, particularly names, were considered signs representing more than their literal referents (Collette, ChR 10:342), here, the characteristics of Cecilia, cf. VIII.86–91.

87 Cf. VIII.29, 220–21.

96–98 **hevene . . . bisynesse:** Thought of heaven may signify the contemplative life, thought of Leah, the active life (Skeat, 5:406; for the biblical account of Leah, see Gen. 29.16–35).

104 **hevene of peple:** In her, people (Gk. λᾱός) see virtues as they see sun, moon, stars in heaven.

114, 118 **brennynge:** The references to fire throughout symbolize the saint's later imperviousness to flames. Possibly she reflects Mary; cf. ABC 90–91 for the *brennynge* bush as symbol of immaculate conception.

The Second Nun's Tale

127–30 Cecilia's marriage is part of a consistent metaphor wherein her fruitful teaching brings an increase in the Christian community (Kolve, New Perspectives, 152; Whittock, A Reading of CT, 255, 259), but is variously seen as representing the highest degree of perfection (Howard, MP 57:223–32, and Idea of CT, 288–89); an alchemical wedding (Grennen, JEGP 65:466–81); mystical union of Christ with his church (Clogan, M&H n.s. 3:237); one of the two poles between which the varied experiences of human love can be studied (Fichte, Ch's Art, 99); or as providing dramatic motivation (Glasser, TSL 23:1–11). She is removed from human relationships (Reames, Spec 55:38–57), yet in her tale there is a strong sense of family. On her virginity, see Ames, God's Plenty, 139–44.

134–38 The tradition of Cecilia in music apparently originated in this episode (Kirsch, Cath. Encyc. 3:473; Butler, Lives of the Saints 4:404). Albert P. de Mirimond (Sainte-Cécile, 1974) prints relevant illustrations ranging from a fresco attributed to Lorenzo di Bicci (c. 1373–1452) to examples from the nineteenth century. A fifteenth-century manuscript shows Cecilia playing a small portative organ (Gustave Reese, Music in the M.A., 1940, 372–73).

134–35 **organs:** Cf. NPT VII.2851n. The plural may result from translation of "cantantibus organis" (S&A, 672), although "pair of organs" was sometimes applied to one instrument (see Percy M. Young, Hist. of Brit. Music, 1967, 50–51; Montgomery, Music Qtly. 17, 1931, 443–44). The song of Cecilia probably indicates harmony and rightness, but has been interpreted as the "New Song" of Christian charity (Robertson, Pref to Ch, 127–33; see also Chamberlain, in Signs and Symbols, 60–61, 74–75). On the theme, see Miller, Spec 30, 1955, 186; Hoffman, in Crit. Approaches to Six Maj. Eng. Works, ed. R. M. Lumiansky and Herschel Baker, 1968, 57–58.

139 Mistranslation of "biduanis ac triduanis ieiuniis" (with two and three-day fasts, S&A, 672). Small errors such as this indicate that Chaucer never completely, if at all, revised the tale (Reames, Spec 55:55).

152 aungel: Perhaps from Ps. 91.11 (M. Madeleva, Lost Lang., 59), but reminiscent of the demon lover of Sarah, OT Book of Tobit (Vulgate).

159 clene love: A number of saints renounced marriage (Baudouin de Gaiffier, Analecta Bollandiana 65, 1947, 157–95), but Cecilia's marriage distinguishes her legend from that of other virgin martyrs (Glasser, BL 23:3, 12). The account may have been influenced by the concept of mystical marriage (Clogan, M&H n.s. 3:237; see H. Achelis, Encyc. of Relig. and Ethics, 177–80, s.v. *Agapēta*). The significance of Cecilia's continence, however, may lie in its reflection of an Augustinian tradition of moderation (Reames, Spec 55:40–41) or in asserting a theme of unity through bodily integrity (Grennen, JEGP 65: 473).

172–73 Via Apia: The road, which runs past catacombs where early Christians hid, is not **miles three** from the city; Chaucer mistranslates "tercium miliarum ab urbe" (the third milepost from the city, S&A, 672). The Roman setting is taken by McCall as creating an air of historical authenticity (Ch among the Gods, 88–110); but see Boitani (Eng. Med. Narrative, 253), who finds the setting entirely romantic and fabulous.

177 Urban: Pope Urban I, 222–30. An error in the Liber pontificalis (ed. L. Duchesne, 2nd. ed., 1955, p. 143) makes him a martyr under Diocletian (c. 245–316), associating him with Valerian and Cecilia. For his legend, see Jacobus de Voragine, Legenda aurea, 341–42. Urban VI was pope of Rome at the probable time of the tale's composition (1378–89), during the Great Schism, but the theory that Chaucer modified his sources to reflect English support of Urban and imply an allegory of the reunion of the church (Hirsch, ChR 12, 1977, 129–33) is not convincing.

186 seintes buryeles: "Sepulcra martirum" (S&A, 672), i.e., the catacombs.

192–94 The saint's virtuous counsel and steadfast chastity inspired by Christ have resulted in the birth of a convert, Valerian, fruit of the seed sown within her. On the imagery of procreation, see Whittock, A Reading of CT, 255, 259; Kolve, New Perspectives, 152. On the tradition of spiritual multiplication and virtues or good works as the fruit of the righteous, see Miller, Spec 30: 185–86.

195 bisy bee: Cf. EpiMerT IV.2422. The comparison could derive from a sermon by Jacobus de Voragine (Tupper, PMLA 29:99), the liturgy (Lowes, PMLA 30: 293), or, most likely, a translation of "apis argumentosa" (S&A, 672). "Argumentosa," is " 'assiduous' or 'busy,' the latter an epithet of the bee" (R. E. Latham, Dict. of Med. Lat., 1975, 124); Chaucer may have coined the English phrase, which became proverbial, Whiting B165.

201 oold man: Cf. VIII.207–9 (tr. from Eph. 4.5–6). Probably St. Paul. Reames takes his appearance before mention of Valerian's faith as one indication among many of Chaucer's modifying his source to lessen human participation and emphasize God's grace in conversion (Spec 55:36–57).

207–9 A paraphrase of Ephesians 4.5–6.

208 Cristendom: Cf. "baptisma" (S&A, 672).

221 Corones two: For an illustration, see Kolve, New Perspectives, 141, fig. 5. In the Life of St. Cecilia in the Early South Eng. Legendary, EETS 87, 490–96, the angel explains "the lilie betokeneth youre maydenhood . . . the rose betokeneth youre martirdom" (lines 77–78).

For studies of the background of this common symbolism, see Lowes, PMLA 29:129–33, 315–23; Emerson, PMLA 41, 1926, 252–61; Cornelius, PMLA 42, 1927, 1055–57; Tatlock, PMLA 45, 1930, 169–79; and Campbell, Spec 8, 1933, 471–73. Crowns of victory or glory are frequently mentioned in the Bible (e.g., Prov. 4.9, 1 Cor. 9.25, 2 Tim. 4.8), and crowns of lilies for good works and of red roses for martyrdom had been noted as early as the third century, in Cyprian (c. 250), PL 4:255. Nuptial garlands and crowns were also an ancient custom (garlands for brides were still used in England; see ClT IV.381n.). An incident in the fictitious sixth-century life of St. Amato (bishop of Auxerre, d. 418), in which nuptial garlands and celestial crowns are apparently combined (see the Bollandist Acta Sanctorum, Antwerp, 1679, May 1, 52–53), parallels the situation involving Cecilia's and Valerian's crowns: the young Saint Amato was compelled to marry a virgin, but on their wedding night the couple took vows of virginity "And behold an angel, who carried two garlands for them, appeared, praising their intention and exhorting them to persevere in it." Both in this episode and in the life of St. Cecilia "husband and wife each receive a garland. It seems natural to regard the crowns as celestial substitutes for the nuptial crowns of an earthly marriage" (Robinson). On nuptial crowns, see Tr 2.1735n.

229 soote savour: The repeated references to smell convey the sweetness of sanctity and contrast with the rankness in CYT VIII.885–90; cf. Taylor, ES 60, 1979, 380–88, who deals particularly with sight and smell.

236 Cf. KnT I.1196.

240 palm of martirdom: Martyrdom is seen as the victor's prize; cf. PF 182. The phrase is from the preface to the Ambrosian mass for St. Cecilia's day, quoted in the Legenda aurea (S&A, 673) and tr. in VIII.274–33.

271 Seint Ambrose: Bishop of Milan, d. 347. The reference is to the preface proper to the mass attributed to him. For the original, see Henshaw, MP 26, 1928, 16.

277 Valerians: Most MSS have "Ceciles," but Jacobus names Valerian and Tyburce, and modern editors have adopted this emendation. **shrifte:** In view of Jacobus's "Tiburcii . . . confessio" (S&A, 673), "confession" seems the correct meaning; but see Fisher: "conversion" (315).

283 Devocioun . . . to love: Jacobus has "devocio castitatis" (S&A, 673). The most plausible reading is the simplest: "the world knows what chastity's devotion to love (i.e., Christ or love of him) is worth." But Clogan (M&H n.s. 3:237, 240) would translate: the world knows "what devotion to chastity is capable of effecting." Emerson (Ch Essays, 1929, 416–17) argues for the special sense of "to" as "against"; Donaldson argues for "to" as "in terms of" (525n.).

290 kisse his brest: Peck suggests that with this conversion another spiritual marriage occurs, symbolized by Cecilia's gesture (AnM 8:31).

338–39 Chaucer slightly modifies Jacobus: "in una hominis sapientia sunt tria, scilicet ingenium, memoria et intellectus" (in the one wisdom of man are three things, imagination, memory, and judgment). The idea that the mind consisted of these three faculties (**sapiences**) was common; see Bartholomaeus Anglicus 3.10, tr. Trevisa 1:98, and for the history of the theory, Wolfson, Harvard Theol. Rev. 28, 1935, 69–133. Cf. Bo 5.pr4.153–54, where the three faculties are wit, reason, and intelligence.

345-48 A summary rather than a direct translation of Jacobus (S&A, 674). The remainder of the tale is based on a Latin legend descended from one close to that represented in Bosio (see introductory note). Summarizing his sources is characteristic of Chaucer (cf. HF 447-50; Tr 1:140-47), but he may have modified his material from this point forward to lessen the roles of Valerian and Tiburce (Hirsh, ChR 12:131; Reames, Spec 55:42-54).

352 cristned: Reilly (MLN 69, 1954, 37-39) argues that the sacrament of Confirmation, appropriate here as in VIII.217, as well as baptism is meant. However, he also believes that Tiburce was instructed for a week prior to being *cristned*, which could not apply to Valerian, who is baptized immediately after his confession of faith.

353 Goddes knyght: This common image of the Christian (cf. 2 Tim. 2.3 and PP B 11.304) marks a shift to military imagery; cf. VIII.383-86.

369 corniculer: A subordinate officer who wears a corniculus, a horn-shaped helmet ornament, as a sign of rank. The term does not appear in Jacobus and may derive from the lives of Valerian and Tiburtius (Bollandist Acta Sanctorum 10, Antwerp, 1675, 203) or the Metaphrastes version of the legend published by Lipomanus (Kölbing, ESt 1:221), both of which have "praefecti corniculario."

384-85 Cf. Romans 13.12.

386-88 Cf. 2 Tim. 4.7-8.

421-512 Although every martyrdom can be seen as an analogue of the Crucifixion (Whittock, A New Reading of CT, 260), Cecilia's confrontation with Almachius is an apparent reflection of Christ's confrontation with Pilate (John 18.33-38; 19.9-11; cf. Carol Ann Breslin, diss., Temple Univ., 1978, DAI 39:2246A). Chaucer here manipulates his source, perhaps to emphasize the conflict and difference between the saint and her judge (Hirsch, ChR 12:134-37). On the ironies of the encounter see Birney, PMLA 54, 1939, 648.

437 In her defiance of Almachius, Cecilia resembles the "mulier fortis," valiant woman, of Prov. 31.17, in terms of whom St. Bernard praises the Virgin (Homilia 2, Opera, ed. Leclercq, et al. 4:24; tr. Saïd and Perigo, 18). To interpret the figure as a "spiritual Amazon or virago" and Cecilia's courage as an expression of the Second Nun's pride (Engelhardt, MS 37:295-96) is at odds with both scripture and legend. But see Luecke, ABR 33, 1982, 335-48, who offers a feminist interpretation, identifying Cecilia with the Second Nun as a strong-willed woman who utilizes virginity to effect freedom of action.

462 laughe: Chaucer either follows a source that gives "ridens" (Reames, MP 76:119) or modifies one that gives "surridens" (possibly Mombritus, S&A, 683). By having Cecilia laugh instead of smile, he intensifies her scorn of Almachius and anticipates her witty reply in VIII.463-65 (Beichner, ChR 8, 1979, 202). On laughter in the tale, see Eggebroten, ChR 19, 1984, 55-61.

463-65 Closely parallel to the Sarum Breviary (Rosenfeld, MLN 55, 1940, 358).

490 philosophre: Also a term for medieval alchemists, one of the several links to The Canon's Yeoman's Tale that critics have noted (see introductory note to Fragment VIII). SNT and CYT are related through images of the philospher's stone and stone idols; night and blindness; the bath of flames and the tempering of metals; sweat and coolness; failure to multiply metals, and the multiplication of converts.

515 bath: A caldarium, pot for boiling water. The Roman hypocaust, bathing room heated from below, might be meant (Fisher, 319); such a room is preserved in the church of Santa Cecilia in Trastevere (Mary Sharp, Guide to the Churches of Rome, 1966, 65). But a medieval tradition of illustration shows the saint naked, in a cauldron, with fire blazing beneath (Kolve, New Perspectives, 141).

521 Because of her holiness, expressed by affinity with the burning empyrean and burning charity, Cecilia is safe from physical fire (Peck, AnM 8:25-26). Kolve finds in the erotic suggestiveness of many depictions of the saint, naked in a bath surrounded by flames, and the licentious associations with public baths, a further implication that she is safe from the heat of lust. But see Miller, who reproduces an illustration of her in a high-necked dress (Ch: Sources, 114). Kolve draws parallels with the children in the fiery furnace (Dan. 3), who also refused to worship an idol and were thought to have been preserved by their virginity, and with St. Eulalia, who remained a virgin and though thrown into fire did not burn (New Perspectives, 152-54).

533-38 Wenk (MS 17, 1955, 215) finds here an expression of the doctrine of willfully assumed suffering, similar to PrT VII.611-13, 649-55.

540 The bequest of her movable goods and property to the spiritual children whom she has fostered, VIII.539, reaffirms the idea of a family and maternal love (Kolve, New Perspectives, 157-58).

550 Chaucer may have seen the church of Santa Cecilia in Florence, razed in 1367, rebuilt soon after near the Piazza della Signoria (Pratt, Tales, 442), which contained an altarpiece depicting scenes from the life of the saint, reproduced by both Pratt (443) and Kolve (New Perspectives, figs. 7, 8). However, the church referred to here is probably that of St. Cecilia in Trastevere (Sharp, Guide to the Churches of Rome, 63-66).

The Canon's Yeoman's Prologue and Tale

The Canon and his Yeoman do not appear in the General Prologue, and whether Chaucer had the Canon's intrusion in mind from the beginning, we cannot know. It is generally agreed that the tale was written late in the Canterbury period though Owen (Pilgrimage and Story, 151) would date it before The Wife of Bath's Tale. Norman Blake's argument that the tale is spurious (ed., CT, 1980, 6, 9) depends on a rigid adherence to a textual theory (the sole authority of the Hengwrt MS) that few accept.

Tyrwhitt believed (4:181) that the occasion for Chaucer's tale was "some sudden resentment." Richardson (TRHS ser. 4, 5, 1922, 38-40) showed that a chaplain, William de Brumley, confessed in 1374 to having made counterfeit gold pieces according to the teaching of William Shuchirch, a canon of the King's Chapel at Windsor. In 1390 Chaucer was responsible for the repairs to Windsor chapel, and if Shuchirch was still alive and practicing, Chaucer would have known him. Manly (New Light, 245-52) is inclined to agree with Richardson that Chau-

The explanatory notes to the Canon's Yeoman's Prologue and Tale were written by John Reidy.

cer lost money in dealings with Shuchirch, and he lists occasions in the 1390s when Chaucer borrowed small sums. French (Ch Handbook, 328) dismisses this as an "amusing speculation" but agrees that Chaucer must have had some particular person in mind.

Manly further argues (New Light, 246–47) that the tale was not written for the Canterbury series but for an audience that included canons of Windsor (see also Baum, MLN 40, 1925, 152–54, and 992n.). This view is not widely accepted, but the case for separate composition is well made by Hartung (ChR 12, 1977, 111–28), on the basis of manuscript evidence as well as the address to *chanons religious* (VIII.992–1011).

No source is known for the tale, and the closest analogue so far unearthed for the tricks in part 2 is a story by Ramón Lull (d. 1315), in which a swindler adds to molten gold a mixture purporting to be an herbal electuary, but actually containing much gold, so that the amount of gold found at the end is greater than was originally melted down (see Folch-Pi, N&Q 212, 1967, 10–11). Spargo cites, together with other illustrative material, a somewhat similar trick from the *Novelle* of Sercambi (S&A, 685–98). Later analogues are given by Andrae, Anglia, Beiblatt 27, 1916, 84–85, and de Vocht, ESt 41, 1910, 385–92. De Vocht believes that Erasmus used the canon's first trick in the dialogue *Ptochologia,* "Beggars' Talk" (Colloquies of Erasmus, tr. Bailey, ed. Johnson, 1878, 1:417–23; see also "The Alchemist," 1:402–11). None of these match Chaucer's version for precision, specificity, or plausibility.

Only a brief note on alchemy as it relates directly to The Canon's Yeoman's Tale can be given here. For further information see the standard works, Marcelin P. E. Berthelot, La chimie au moyen âge, 1893, and Edmund O. von Lippmann, Entstehung und Ausbreitung der Alchemie, 1919–54, and the more recent F. Sherwood Taylor, The Alchemists, 1949, and Erik J. Holmyard, Alchemy, 1957. A brief sketch is also available in Thomas Norton's *Ordinal of Alchemy,* ed. Reidy, EETS 272, 1975, 1ii–1xvii.

Western Europe in the twelfth century, through translations from Arabic into Latin, inherited a large body of alchemical theory and practice, which Islamic writers had in turn received from Greek writings of Hellenistic Egypt and which they further developed. From Greek alchemy came the notions of a precious metal, gold or silver, in an alloy with base metals, acting as "ferment" to leaven base metals with its own properties (see VIII.817), and that of coloring metal alloys white or yellow with arsenic or sulphur to look like silver or gold (the canon's *silver citrinacioun,* 816, is only a more elaborate version of this).

Another important element in Greek alchemy was the color sequence, in which a "dead" mass of "first matter" (apparently lead or an alloy heated and hence blackened with surface oxydization) was "revived" and perfected (see Taylor, Journ. Hellen. Sts. 50, 1930, 133–37). The sequence, in Chaucer's time, was black, white, red, the final color being that of the perfected "philosophers' stone." The Yeoman's face has undergone a reverse sequence (VIII.727–28).

Among the Arabs, from the late eighth century, was added a sulphur-mercury theory of metals, developed from Aristotle's theory that metals originated in the earth from a blend of two vapors. A perfect blend resulted in

gold, an imperfect one in a base metal; this left the possibility of correcting a faulty blend and transmuting a base metal into gold. Since real sulphur and mercury were known to combine to produce mercuric sulphide, cinnabar, alchemists claimed that the sulphur and mercury they meant were something secret and different. This theory appears briefly in lines 1438–39. Another important feature first found in Arabic writings was based on the theory of the four elements, each containing two of the four qualities, hot, cold, moist, dry. If the qualities could be calculated and isolated, mixtures or medicines could be produced to correct imbalances in sick people, or in substances. These would be elixirs, and the idea developed (probably influenced by Chinese alchemy) of a perfect elixir that would prolong life besides "curing" base or sick metals into gold (VIII.862–63). The attempt to isolate qualities and to separate and recombine elements led to numerous experiments involving repeated distillation of organic and sublimation of inorganic substances; repetition of such processes was thought to enhance their effects and to produce purer end-products. In The Canon's Yeoman's Tale we have frequent mention of *sublymyng* (770) as well as *amalgamyng* (771), *enbibyng* (814) or soaking the residue of a dried-off solution with the liquid distillate, and *encorporyng* (815). The theory of the division of minerals into spirits, metals, stones, etc., (see 820 below) also belongs to this period.

The art was supposed originally to be a secret revelation from the Egyptian god of wisdom, Thoth, corresponding to the Greek Hermes (VIII.1434); the chosen few were therefore to guard its holiness from the profane, hence the numerous "cover names" (see VIII.844–45, 1435–40, 1447, 1463–66, 1467–71). This tradition passed on to western Europe, where alchemical treatises were attributed to holy men such as Moses and St. Dunstan; ancient sages such as Plato (VIII.1448) were alleged to have received advance revelation of Christian doctrines, as well as of the secrets of alchemy, and the alchemical process was made analogous to the Christian mysteries of the death and resurrection of Christ (see Finkelstein, Archiv 207, 1970, 260–76, and esp. 273–74; Reidy, PMLA 80, 1965, 33–34; Grennen, SP 62, 1965, 546–60). As a result, there were alchemists who believed that they had been taught the true secret—and who wrote alchemical treatises—and those who were called "puffers" or "Geber's cooks" (after the author of a well-known alchemical treatise) and who, however learned, experimented forever in vain, like the Yeoman's master. There were also out-and-out swindlers like the canon of part 2.

Despite the vastness of the corpus of Latin alchemical literature, no account of the process of making the philosophers' stone or the elixir, or white or red tincture, is intelligible; how could it be? The process usually called for "calcination" (VIII.804) of the original material by heating and pounding or by attacking with acids ("mercury") or both; this reduced the material to ash, or dead matter. Then repeated distillations were to separate and purify the elements, which were then to be recombined, by imbibing, or soaking, and successive sublimations. A color sequence of whitening and reddening is thus finally obtained. Thus far one can follow or partially guess the operations, but the later stages are always too vague to be understood. The final product, a red elixir for gold and a white for silver, was spoken of as a stone, a liquid, a powder, a tincture, and the phrases *watres rubifyng* (VIII.797) and *watres albificacioun* (805) may refer to these elixirs, which finally reddened or whitened the baser metals into gold or silver.

Though authorities such as Vincent of Beauvais and Ramón Lull, following Avicenna (980–1037), denied that any real change could be made in metal, they could not defeat the plausibility and attractiveness of alchemical theory. There was an outburst of writings and apparently of practice, with the inevitable swindling that the promise of gold-making would induce. Religious orders attempted to suppress alchemy, and Pope John XXII (1316–34) condemned it, principally because of swindling and counterfeiting (see Duncan, Spec 43, 1968, 635–37). But this did not stop it; manuscripts of old and new works were produced, and we have direct evidence of alchemists such as Canon William Shuchirch and of victims such as the Prior of Binham, William of Somerton, who became apostate from his order and was arrested in secular dress through trusting an alchemist (Hamilton, Spec 16, 1941, 107; Coulton, Med. Garner, 518–21).

It is not clear how much alchemical literature Chaucer knew. Aiken (SP 41, 1944, 371–89) thinks he could have obtained all he needed for The Canon's Yeoman's Tale from Vincent of Beauvais's *Speculum naturale,* but Duncan (Spec 43:641–46) believes that he had read or scanned not only those works of Arnaldus de Villanova (c. 1240–1311) that he refers to and quotes (VIII.1428–47) and the *book Senior* (see 1448–71 below), but also the *Sum of Perfection* of Geber, of whom nothing is known but whose very practical book was widely read. It is hoped that Duncan's edition and translation of alchemical texts illustrative of Chaucer's alchemy will shortly be published in the Chaucer Library series.

In 1477 Chaucer was quoted as an alchemical authority (in Norton's Ordinal, 1162–66, referring to CYT VIII.1454–57), and Elias Ashmole printed the tale "to shew that *Chaucer* himself was a *Master* therein" (Theatrum Chemicum Britannicum, 1652, 467). There are also alchemical pieces attributed to him (see Dunleavy, Ambix 13, 1965, 2–21). Damon (PMLA 39, 1924, 782–88) and Rosenberg (Cent. Rev. of Arts and Sci. 6, 1962, 578) believe that Chaucer knew and respected the great secret. The majority, however, holds that Chaucer is skeptical (Kittredge, Ch and His Poetry, 15); unconsciously prophetic in warning against an incipient dehumanizing technology (e.g., Speirs, Ch the Maker, 196–97; Muscatine, Ch and Fr Trad., 213–21); or convinced of the evil of the science (e.g., Gardner, PQ 46, 1967, 2–3, who identifies the canon of part 2 as a fiend, and Rosenberg, Cent. Rev. 6:566–80, who identifies him with the antichrist). It has been held that Chaucer found alchemy absurd (Grennen, SP 62:547; Whittock, Theoria 24, 1965, 17; Harrington, AnM 9, 1968, 93). Against this are the calmer views of Brewer (Geoffrey Ch, 150) that Chaucer does not take an extreme position but has objections on the practical and religious grounds that the ignorant non-scientist should leave the science alone, and of Ruggiers (Art of CT, 132, 138, 140) who sees the sinister aspects of the tale but insists that the Yeoman's views must not be confused with Chaucer's, whose final view of alchemy and technology cannot be exactly known. An assessment of Chaucer's attitude will be partly determined by how much weight we allow to

the thematic parallels with and contrasts to The Second Nun's Tale proposed by Rosenberg (ChR 2, 1968, 278–91).

The character of the Yeoman has been much studied, especially since Lumiansky examined his continuing two-mindedness towards alchemy (Of Sondry Folk, 227–35); see, besides those studies already mentioned: Baldwin, JEGP 61, 1962, 237–40; Herz, MP 58, 1961, 236–37; Ryan, ChR 8, 1974, 301–5; and especially Howard, Idea of CT, 294–96.

There is likewise the problem of the unity of the work, since the tale of part 2 is thought to be imperfectly adapted to its setting (see Craik, Comic Tales, 96–97, and Baum, Ch's Verse, 136), though the general structure of the tale, a prologue and two parts, is shown by McCracken (MP 68, 1971, 289–91) to be an example of a developing pattern in Chaucer's confessional tales. The problem of unity is also raised by the puzzle over the existence of two canons. Baldwin attempted to solve this by identifying the two, and also the Yeoman with the gulled priest (JEGP 61:236–40); Olmert (AnM 8, 1967, 80–82) unifies the tale by making the second canon anagogically equivalent to the fiend, who is the first canon; and see also Reidy, PMLA 80:36–37. Grennen succeeds best in arguing a unity of theme and diction that shows the involvement of the characters in a kind of meta-alchemical process of degeneration (Criticism 4, 1962, 225–40; Journ. Hist. Ideas 25, 1964, 279–84). Manzalaoui (Ch and Sci., in Brewer, ed. Geoffrey Chaucer, 1975, 224–61) deals succinctly with Chaucer's attitude toward alchemy, which he considers mainly satirical, and with the scholarship to 1975; see 256–57 and notes.

The Canon's Yeoman's Prologue

556   Boghtoun: Boughton was five miles beyond Ospring, a regular stopping place, where the pilgrims had presumably spent the night; they were now some five miles from Canterbury.

557   A man: The Canon, identified as a Canon Regular of St. Augustine, or Black Canon, by Hamilton (Spec 16:103–8); he wears a cassock, *overslope* (VIII.633), a surplice over it (558), and outermost a black cloak with hood attached (557, 571).

565   He: Coffman (MLN 59, 1944, 269–71) argues that the Yeoman's horse must be meant, in view of *his croper* (566), since a crupper must be a horse's.

566   male tweyfoold: A double bag; frequently taken to imply folded over and hence almost empty.

580   as a stillatorie: On the appropriateness of the comparison with an alchemical process, see Grennen, Journ. Hist. Ideas 25:280.

581   Were ful: The relative pronoun *that* is omitted.

583–86   Brewer (Geoffrey Ch, 149) finds the Canon's explanation of his arrival inadequate, and indeed it certainly does not account for his headlong speed. With a three-mile gallop, the pair would overtake the slow-moving pilgrims in about ten minutes; at a canter or even a trot they could have caught up in half an hour or less and arrived in a more decent condition. Chaucer clearly wishes to have them make a dramatic and striking entrance.

587   Kittredge (Trans. Roy. Soc. Lit. 30, 1910, 88–90) sets out the received opinion that the Yeoman, in collusion with his master, here begins an attempt at a confidence-trick but is exposed and broken down by the Host's skillful probing. This version is generally accepted, usually without question, by, for example, Manly, New Light, 235–38; Lumiansky, Of Sondry Folk, 229–30. For a different view, see John Read, Alchemist in Life, Lit. and Art, 1947, 29–35; Baldwin, JEGP 61: 234; and Reidy, PMLA 80:32.

611 leye in balaunce: See MED s.v. *balaunce* 5.

612 Al that I have: For the Yeoman's possessions, see VIII.733–36.

635–38 Cf. George Ripley, Compound, in Ashmole, Theatrum, 153: "Their Clothes be bawdy and woryn threde-bare." For standard responses to this question, see Read, Alchemist in Life, 30–31, and Reidy, PMLA 80:32; the Yeoman knew at least one of these (VIII.892–97, and cf. VIII.1371–74).

645–46 The Lat. gloss quotes the common proverb (Walther 19859) "Omne quod est nimium vertitur in vitium" (Everything that is too much turns into a vice); cf. Whiting E199, 200, 203 and Tilley E224. Grennen (Journ. Hist. Ideas 25:284) sees in Chaucer's version an extra meaning referring to an alchemical process continued too long, so that the product fails at its final testing. For this sense of **preeve**, see MED s.v. *preven* 13 (b).

664 discoloured: See 727–28 below. According to Kittredge (Trans. Roy. Soc. Lit. 30:90), it is this reminder of his lost fresh complexion that finally exasperates the Yeoman into open hostility towards his master.

669 multiplie: See MED s.v. *multiplien* 4 (a), (b), and *multiplicacioun* (d); this latter sense of increase in the quantity or potency of the elixir is the subject of Ripley, Compound, ch. 11 in Ashmole, Theatrum, 181–83; Grennen (Criticism 4:227–28) sees an ironic pun on the usual sense of *multiplie,* "to increase," "to thrive," since alchemy produces poverty; cf. VIII.1400–1401.

673–79 The Yeoman admits to borrowing, though not necessarily to intentional fraud. For the strictness of the alchemical code with regard to borrowing, see Reidy, PMLA 80:35–36.

681 Cf. KnT I.1089.

685 drough hym neer: Owen (Pilgrimage and Story, 7) thinks that here Chaucer admits the implausibility of a company on horseback all hearing a tale; if the Canon had heard al thyng before he came close, he would have intervened earlier.

688–89 Catoun: Dicta Catonis 1.17, quoted in the Lat. gloss: "Concius ipse sibi de se putat omnia dici" (The self-conscious man thinks everyone is talking about him).

695–96 The Canon accuses his Yeoman of *calumnia, slander,* and *detractio,* detraction, i.e., unnecessarily revealing truth that is detrimental to someone's reputation.

707 For peny ne for pound: For examples of such phrases, see MED s.v. *peni* 1 (c).

The Canon's Yeoman's Tale

726 an hose upon myn heed: The illustration in the Ellesmere manuscript shows the Yeoman thus adorned; Piper (PQ 3, 1924, 253) gives a lively description and wonders whether Chaucer or the illuminator knew the proverb "A man's a man though he wear a hose upon his head," of which this is the first recorded version (see Whiting H549).

727–28 Grennen (Journ. Hist. Ideas 25:279–80) notes that the Yeoman's face has changed from red to a dull leaden color—the reverse of the alchemical color sequence.

730 blered is myn ye: Proverbial; cf. RvPro I.3865n.

746–47 A Latin marginal note in Ellesmere and one other MS have the beginning of the common Latin proverb "The solace of the wretched is to have companions in grief" (Walther 29943), quoted in a slightly different form (Walther, Nova Series, 35687) in some other MSS; cf. Tr 1.708n.; Whiting, W715; Hassell S111.

757 silver: From the Yeoman's haphazard account, Duncan (MP 37, 1940, 248–54) pieces together an account of the sublimation of orpiment and mercury, preliminary to a process of *silver citrinacioun* (VIII.816), or yellowing of silver, similar to those described by Geber and Arnaldus de Villanova (see VIII.1428 and n.).

759 orpyment: Probably arsenic trisulphide; one of the four "spirits" (see 820 below), to be sublimed along with quicksilver (VIII.772).

brent bones, iren squames: These, together with the *salt* and *papeer* (762), were "feces," which were supposed to retain the grosser earthy impurities in the "spirits" when these were sublimed (Duncan, MP 37:251).

761–66 For an account of an **erthen pot**, its enlutyng, and its surmounting by a **lampe of glas,** the whole constituting a vessel for sublimation, see Duncan, MP 37:250–51.

764 lampe: See MED s.v. *laumpe* (g); the definition is not wholly certain, but presumably a glass vessel placed over the *erthen pot* (761), and cemented or luted on.

768 Fires and furnaces of different temperatures for different processes were of great importance to alchemists. See Norton's Ordinal, 2831–96, 2983–3086; and Duncan, MP 37:252. For an account with illustrations, see The Works of Geber, Englished by Richard Russell, London, 1678, ed. Holmyard, 1928, 229–42.

775 grounden litarge: See 907 below.

776 a certeyn: See MilT I.3193n.

778–79 spirites ascencioun . . . fix adoun: "Spirits" were volatile, that is, they vaporized when heated and were deposited on the top or lid of the vessel; the residue remaining solid at the bottom was "earthy", or "fixed."

782 a twenty devel waye: See MilT I.3134n.

795 deere ynough a leek: Expensive enough at the price of a leek (i.e., worthless). Proverbial (Whiting L182); for similar expressions see ClT IV.999 and n.; Thop VII.735; Tr 3.1161; LGW 741; and MED s.v. *dere* adj. (1) 3(d).

797–818 For similar lists of materials, see Ripley, Compound in Ashmole, Theatrum, 189–93, and Norton's Ordinal, 1051–68.

797 Watres rubifiyng: Liquids capable of reddening substances, of turning them to gold. For the redness of the elixir, see reproduction of Brit. Lib. MS Sloane 2560 f.15 in Stanislas K. de Rola, Alchemy, 1973, plate 26; also f.14, plate 63 for the white elixir (see 805 below).

798 Arsenyk, sal armonyak, and brymstoon: See 820 below.

799 herbes: Many alchemists scoffed at ignorant workers who attempted to obtain the elixir or philosophers' stone from vegetable substances; see, e.g., Norton's Ordinal, 1051–58; Petrus Bonus, The New Pearl of Great

Price, tr. Waite, 1894, 243–44; and Duncan, MP 37: 260. Roger Bacon took a different view: "a vegetable substance is better, such as fruit and parts of trees and herbs" (Notes on pseudo-Aristotle, Secreta Secretorum, in Robert Steele, Opera Hactenus Inedita Rogeri Baconi 5, 1920, 117).

800   lunarie: Moonwort; its use in alchemy and witchcraft is testified by John Gerarde (The Herball or Generall Historie of Plantes, London, 1636, 407); he condemns such "drowsie dreames and illusions." A poem printed by Ashmole in Theatrum, 348–49, describes the alchemical process by relating its stages to the parts of this plant.

804   fourneys . . . of calcinacioun: Geber (Works, tr. Russell, 229) prescribes a rectangular furnace, four feet by three feet, for calcination.

805   watres albificacioun: Possibly "whitening by liquids," but probably a mistake for "watres albifiyng," (liquids which whiten metals and turn them to silver) caused by confusing the present participle form with a gerund; cf. 797 above.

809   wode and cole: See 768 above.

820   foure spirites . . . bodies sevene: Al-Razi (Abu Bakr Muhammad ibn Zakariyya, c. 826–925), known to the Latin West as Rhazes, divided minerals into six classes (see Holmyard, Alchemy, 89), of which the two most important for alchemists were spirits (i.e., volatile substances like camphor and the four in VIII.822–24) and bodies (i.e., the six metals, gold, silver, lead, tin, iron, and copper). The Latin Geber follows this, treating quicksilver—which boils easily—as a spirit; but he includes "Mundification" of quicksilver among his chapters on preparation of metals, or "Metallick Bodies" (Works, tr. Russell, 62, 124, 126–28, 146, 157–58; cf. Aiken, SP 41:378–79). This might lead to confusion, and the Yeoman names quicksilver in both categories (VIII.822, 827).

838   Ascaunce: The meaning varies slightly with the punctuation; if the sentence is a question, the meaning is "Do you imagine," "Perhaps"; but with a comma after *philosophre* (837), and not regarded as a question, the meaning is "as if," "as though." Cf. Tr 1.205n.

844   lerne: The verbs *leren,* "teach," and *lernen,* "learn," were frequently confused in ME; cf. MLT II.181, and see MED s.v. *leren* 4, *lernen* 4a (a). Chaucer rarely uses *lernen* to mean "teach", but he uses *leren* to mean "learn" frequently (see VIII.838).

861   To reyse a feend: For a comical list of names of spirits to be conjured, and the conjuration itself, see The Bugbears, Act 3, Sc. 3, ed. Grabau, Archiv 99, 1897, 29–31.

874   to seken evere: Cf. the negative form in GP I.784.

884–91 Grennen (Journ. Hist. Ideas 25:281) suggests that Chaucer may have had in mind a passage from an alchemical work, Consilium conjugii, in Jean J. Manget, Bibliotheca Chemica Curiosa, Geneva, 1702, 2:251.

889   infecte: Grennen (Journ. Hist. Ideas 25:281–82) notes an alchemical double meaning with the technical sense of Lat. *inficere,* used of corrupting of metals and acids by inferior substances.

907   The pot tobreketh: Duncan (MP 37:253–54) suggests that the explosion is caused by adding ground-up litharge (VIII.775) to the mixture and using saltpeter for the salt required.

916–19 For the Canon as devil, see introductory note and cf. VIII.885–86.

938   mullok: See RvPro I.3873n.

962–65 Lat. gloss: "Do not think that all that shines is gold nor any apple good that looks nice," from Alanus de Insulis, Liber parabolarum (PL 210:585). See also Whiting A155, G282; HF 272.

967–69   wiseste: This seems to apply to the Yeoman's master, while the **trewest** who proves a thief would be the canon of part 2.

970   er that I fro yow wende: Chaucer seems not to intend retaining the Yeoman in his company of pilgrims.

971 The Yeoman has not been asked to tell a tale, and he has already fulfilled his promise to the Host (VIII.717–19). The scheme of tale-telling has been only hinted to him (VIII.597–98).

984   as hymselven is: See 916–19 above; but there is no need to take the Yeoman literally.

992–1011 This address to **chanons religious** was a reason for Manly's suggestion that part 2 was read to an audience of canons at the King's Chapel at Windsor; see the introductory note. Robinson, however, thinks the passage could be merely rhetorical, cf. PhysT VI.72, NPT VII.3325; Hartung (ChR 12:111–28) argues strongly that part 2 was originally complete in itself, on the basis of certain textual variants and also of inconsistencies he finds between part 2 and the Prologue and part 1. Herz (MP 58:235) suggests that the Yeoman is casting "an unsure eye at the monk and friar," ignorantly supposing that they might be canons.

1048   in good tyme: A formula to avert evil consequences, similar to "touch wood."

1066–67 Proverbial; see Whiting S167 and cf. PF 518.

1090   another chanoun: For opinions on the two canons, see introductory note.

1095–97 Cf. 727–28 above. For a possible parallel in an alchemical process, see Grennen, Journ. Hist. Ideas 25: 280–81.

1117   crosselet: The crucible containing one ounce of quicksilver (VIII.1120–21) is put on the fire, and the canon throws in the purported "powder of projection." The canon has the priest build up the charcoal (1157), but, pretending to correct him, sets a special piece above the crucible (1189–91). This contains silver filings in a hole stopped with wax (1160–64); when the wax melts the silver drops into the crucible. The trick depends on the fact that the quicksilver boils and vaporizes at about 357° C, leaving only the silver, which melts at 962° C (1196–1200). The canon pours the molten silver into an ingot or mold, which he has cut to measure out of chalk (1222–23, 1232–33), and drops it into cold water. The result is a one-ounce bar of silver, to all appearances transmuted from quicksilver (see Baum, MLN 40:154).

1126   mortifye: Meaning apparently that the fluid quicksilver will harden into silver, losing its volatile "spiritual" quality; cf. VIII.1436. The *quyk* in **quyksilver** means "alive," and the canon will "kill" (**mortifye**) it.

1174–75 The canon's lack of a fixed address suggests to Herz (MP 58:232) the protean nature of alchemy, which can never be attained; she finds the same symbolism in the rapidity of the Canon's and Yeoman's gallop and the Canon's abrupt departure.

1185   by Seint Gile: For the implications of this oath, see Haskell, ChR 7, 1973, 221–26.

1189   with sory grace: Cf. SumT III.2228.

1238–39 See Hartnung, PMLA 77, 1962, 508–9.

1265   An holwe stikke: This second trick is almost the same as the first, only the silver filings are now concealed in a hollow stick, with which the canon stirs the fire.

1296   The third trick is simple sleight of hand. The canon melts the copper, pours it into his ingot, immerses it in water to solidify it, and while apparently feeling for it, substitutes for it the *teyne* of silver which we know him to have had up his sleeve (VIII.1225).

1313   ape: "Dupe"; cf. GP I.706n.

1342–49   On the language of romance in this passage, see Herz, MP 58:234–35.

brid gladder agayn the day: Proverbial; cf. KnT I.2437n.

1371–74   Cf. 635–38 above.

1407–8   See Whiting C201, H53, M160. Grennen (Criticism 4:230–32) sees a reference to the alchemical understanding of "spirits" that flee from the fire while the earthly parts remain (cf. 759 above). For the perfect work, however, the spirit and body must be united and the spirit fixed with the body in the fire.

1410   See Whiting L89, T211.

1411   Proverbial, though this is the only citation in Whiting, T256; see further references there.

1413   Bayard: A bay-colored horse; the name of a horse given by Charlemagne to Renaud. See MED s.v. *batard* n.(1), esp. (c) *as blind as Baiard;* and Whiting B71, 72, 73; cf. RvT I.4115n., Tr 1.218 and n. See Burnley, N&Q 221, 1976; and Rowland, Blind Beasts, 127–28.

1422   rape and renne: Literally "seize and run," but then both verbs cannot be syntactically related in the same way to **al that.** Various forms of the phrase occur, perhaps all deriving by confusion of the verbs from *repen and rinen* (OE *hrepian* and *hrinan,* touch and seize); see MED s.v. *rennen* v.(1) 6 (a), *rappen and rennen,* and 26 (d), *rapen and rennen, repen and rennen;* s.v. *repen* v.(2) (b) *repen and rinen, ?repen and rinen;* also s.v. *rapen* v.(2) (e), *rappen* v.(2) (a); and s.v. *rinen* v.(1) (e).

1428   Arnold of the Newe Toun: Arnaldus de Villanova (c. 1240–1311).

1429–40   Rosarie: Arnaldus's Rosarium philosophorum, "Rosary (or Rose Garland) of the Philosophers" (Manget, Bibl. Chem. 1:662–76); but Lowes (MLN 28, 1913, 229) shows Chaucer's source is his De lapide philosophorum, "On the Philosophers' Stone," better titled "On the Secrets of Nature" (Opera, Lyons, 1532 [rpt. Basel, 1585], fol. 304r); the relevant passage is given in S&A, 698.

The dragon (VIII.1435) is mercury, which is not hardened (mortified) except with his brother, sulphur, derived from gold and silver. On the Arabic origin of these ideas, see Finkelstein, Archiv 207:263–66.

1434   Hermes: Hermes Trismegistus, "Thrice-great Hermes," was the Greek name for Thoth, the Egyptian god of wisdom. He is the alleged author of a number of theological, mystical, and magical books, the Corpus Hermeticum, written in the early centuries A.D. (see Arthur D. Nock and André J. Festugière, ed. and tr., Corpus Hermeticum, 1945). These contain no alchemy, but Hermes was claimed by Greek alchemists as the author of their art, and later Greek alchemists quote works attributed to him. The most famous work in the Middle Ages to bear his name was the Emerald Table of Hermes, which goes back to ninth-century Arabic writings or earlier Syriac or Greek sources, and is quoted in Holmyard, Alchemy, 95. For Hermes' medieval reputation, see Thorndike, Hist. Magic 2:214–20.

1441–47   These lines are also derived from Arnaldus's De lapide philosophorum (Duncan, MLN 57, 1942, 31–33; Young, MLN 58, 1943, 102–5). Young goes on to show that **secree of the secretes** (VIII.1447) is not the pseudo-Aristotle, Secreta Secretorum, "Secret of Secrets" (see 799 above), but simply a phrase meaning "best of secrets," a common name for alchemy, as proposed by Manly, CT, 653. On the origin of the term, see Finkelstein, Archiv 207:272–76.

1448–71   This dialogue between Plato and a disciple is based on a passage in a Latin translation of an Arabic commentary on an allegorical alchemical poem, Epistle of the Sun to the Crescent Moon. The passage Chaucer used is printed in Lazarus Zetzner, Theatrum Chemicum 5, 1622, 249, under the title Senioris Zadith fil. Hamuelis Tabula Chimica, "The Chemical Table of Senior Zadith, Son of Hamuel," Ch's book **Senior** (VIII.1450). (In the 6-vol. edition, 1659–61, the passage is in 5:224.) Ruska (Anglia 61, 1937, 136–37) shows that Chaucer freely invented most of the dialogue, drawing on a few sentences of the Latin. In Zetzner's version the teaching of VIII.1454–55, 1459, is given by King Solomon, but Ruska says neither Solomon nor Plato appears in the original Arabic, where their place is taken by an unidentified philosopher, Qualimus. **Senior** is Muhammad ibn Umail (10th cent.); for his works and commentary, see Ruska, Angl 61:136n. In a paper at the MLA meeting, 1971, Edgar Hill Duncan pointed out that in Trinity Coll. Cambridge MS 1122, in the prologue to the work, fol. 39r, the word "senior" is annotated "i. Plato," (i.e., Plato) in a contemporary hand. At the beginning of the work, fol. 40r, a later hand wrote opposite the title "Liber hic dicitur Senior" (This book is called Senior), and further down the leaf a third hand wrote "liber Platonis" (The book of Plato). From this fourteenth-century English manuscript we can see how Chaucer may have come by both Plato and his title for the work.

1454   Titanos: From Greek, a white earth, probably gypsum, but also possibly chalk or lime; here, of course, a cover name.

1455   Magnasia: Magnesia, now magnesium oxide, but here a cover name, and variously described, but always of a brilliant whiteness. The pseudo-Lull, Testamentum in Manget, Bibl. Chem. 1:727, calls it a white earth and equates it with the special alchemists' quicksilver; elsewhere it is an amalgam of tin and mercury.

1463–71   On the holiness and necessary secrecy of the art, see the introductory note and Finkelstein, Archiv 207:260–76.

FRAGMENT IX

Fragment IX occurs regularly before, and is explicitly connected to (X.1), The Parson's Prologue and Tale in most early manuscripts (see Textual Notes). This fragment is usually taken by editors to contain the penultimate story on the journey to Canterbury, though there are difficulties, and some critics have questioned this assumption (see introductory note to Fragment X below). Several critics, such as Owen (JEGP 57, 1958, 449–76), have suggested that The Manciple's Tale is the first story on the homeward journey. But Fragment IX is clearly involved in some of the confusions produced by the unfinished condition of the *Tales:* the Cook is introduced at IX.11 as if for the first time. Perhaps Chaucer intended to cancel the Cook's Prologue and the fragmentary Cook's Tale.

LARRY D. BENSON

The Manciple's Prologue and Tale

The date and the relationship of the Manciple's Prologue to his tale have provoked much discussion. "The Manciple's Tale is held to be early chiefly on the grounds of its slight story, its evident rhetorical padding and its lack of any obvious relation to its narrator or even its own prologue" says Hussey (Chaucer, 2nd ed., 1981, 137), summarizing a position assumed by several critics. That there are stylistic differences between the Manciple's Prologue and his tale is stressed by Knight, Rymyng Craftily, 161–83; but recently most critics have accepted Severs's contention that it is logical that the dishonest Manciple of the General Prologue should be involved in a discreditable incident with the Cook and tell a tale that "exalts expediency rather than morality" (JEGP 51, 1952, 1–16). It is now usually assumed that both the prologue and the tale "issue from Chaucer's most sardonic maturity" (Coghill in Ch and Chaucerians, ed. Brewer, 1966, 138).

The Manciple's Tale consists of the fable of the "tell-tale bird" followed by a fifty-four-line moralitas recommending restraint in speech: ironically, according to several critics. Indeed, Hazelton (JEGP 62, 1963, 1–31) argued that the whole performance was parodic, in particular of Gower's Confessio amantis, where a moralized version of the story appears at 3.768–817. Hazelton stresses the way in which Chaucer alters his sources to emphasize the pettiness and sordidness of the incident, as do others: see McCall, Ch among the Gods, 129–31. The story derives from Ovid's Metamorphoses 2.531–632, but Chaucer ignores "all reference to cornix and her story, to corvus's journey to Phoebus, to the pregnancy and lament of Coronis, to Phoebus's vain attempts to save Coronis, to the cremation of Coronis and to the birth of Aesculapius" (Work, in S&A, 701). There is a version in Ovide moralisé, 2130–2548; one in Machaut's Voir dit, 7773–8110; and another in The Seven Sages of Rome, EETS 191, 2193–2292, any or all of which Chaucer may have used. See Cadbury (PQ 43, 1964, 538–48), who discusses Chaucer's modifications of his received material. The exempla of the caged bird, cat, and she-wolf can be found in Le roman de la rose and elsewhere (see notes to 175–86, below), and the main sources for the concluding aphorisms seem to be the Bible and Cato's Distichs (see notes to 325–60, below).

The interpretation and evaluation of The Manciple's Prologue and Tale have varied a great deal over the years. But few recent critics have shared Manly's dismissiveness (PBA 12, 1926). Tupper stressed the coherence of the fragment in terms of its concern with the sin of anger and "the sins of the tongue" (PMLA 29, 1914, 93–128). Donner (MLN 70, 1955, 245–49) and others have argued that it is a sermon on careless speech; Birney (NM 21, 1960, 261) agrees but detects an "irrepressible savoring of his own slyness by the talkative Manciple." A number of scholars, such as Harwood (ChR 6, 1971,

The explanatory notes to the Manciple's Prologue and Tale were written by V. J. Scattergood.

268–79), consider "the subject of the tale is language." Scattergood (EIC 24, 1974, 124–46) agrees, but thinks that the tale demonstrates how by verbal dexterity one can try to avoid the consequences of what one says; he stresses it is a tale about a servant who has to be careful about how he tells the truth. Fradenburg (ELH 52, 1985, 85–118) likewise sees it as about the problems of inferiors in their relation to authority, but interprets it on more general political lines: "The Manciple's Tale suggests the limitations of ideology; it presents to us the psychology of a culture unable to go beyond the prince as the personification of identity and the means by which the court imagines its survival." Trask (Sts. in Short Fict. 14, 1977, 109–16) considers the tale reveals the "utter moral blindness of the Manciple," but Davidson (AnM 19, 1979, 5–12) argues, like the majority, that the Manciple's simple-minded confession is deliberately assumed to cloak his roguery. Delany (Writing Women, 1983, 47–75) argues that the killing of Python is the double of Apollo's murder of Coronis and that the whole story represents Chaucer's "profound ambivalence towards his wife and her distinguished lover-patron." Many recent critics, such as Howard (Idea of CT, 304), see The Manciple's Tale as part of the preparation for the close of the Tales: "The Manciple's Tale fastens upon fallen nature and makes all ideals—of thought, word, and deed, seem impossible," but this is transcended by the orthodox moral stance of The Parson's Tale. Chauncey Wood (Medievalia, 6, 1980, 209–29) also argues that the association is more in terms of contrast than similarity: "as we observe this contrast between the proper and improper uses of speech our attention is drawn to the even larger question of text and gloss, fruit and chaff, the contest for tales of 'best sentence and moost solaas.'"

The Manciple's Prologue

2–3   Bobbe-up-and-doun: Probably Harbledown, two miles north of Canterbury on the old road from London, though "Up and down field" in the parish of Thannington (Athen 1868, II:866) and Bobbing, two miles west of Sittingbourne (N&Q 167, 1932, 26), have both been suggested.

5   Dun is in the myre: Proverbial; Whiting D434. The reference is to a rural game that imitates the freeing of a horse (dun = dark colored horse) from the mud: the participants test their ability to move some unwieldy object (for references see Tilley D642). Brusendorff's suggestion (Ch Trad., 484) that it means "the fat is in the fire" is unlikely; the Host is complaining of the Cook's slow progress (al bihynde, IX.7) and because the story-telling has come to a temporary halt.

6   for preyere ne for hyre: Cf. Whiting L480.

8   Trask (Sts. in Short Fict. 14:109–16) interprets this line symbolically: the **theef** may be the devil who might capture the unvigilant Cook were he not rescued by his companions. But the reference could simply be to the danger from highwaymen; Chaucer himself was robbed in 1390 (Ch Life Records, 477–89).

9   cokkes bones: Cf. ParsPro X.29 and n.

11   a cook of Londoun: Identified by Rickert (TLS, 20 Oct. 1932, 761) as Roger Knight of Ware on the basis of CkPro I.4336.

with meschaunce: Cf. FrT III.1334n.

12–13 For difficult literary composition as a **penaunce**, cf. Complaint of Venus 79.

14 **nat worth a botel hey:** Proverbial; Whiting B470. Cf. GP I.177n.

20 For the rhetorical structure, see Thop VII.745n.

24 **Chepe:** Cf. GP I.754n.

38 "A curse; apparently with reference to the belief that the devil entered through the open mouth" (cf. Andrae, Anglia, Beiblatt 13, 1902, 306). But Pearcy (ELN 11, 1974, 167–75) suggests that the devil entered the Cook through the drink he had, and that he failed in temperance and sobriety—virtues that should guard the mouth (cf. Gower, Mirour, 16453–86). Pearcy also suggests that Chaucer may have in mind the iconography of the hell-mouth.

39 Particularly in plague years it was thought that infection was carried through foul air; see Nohl, The Black Death: A Chronicle of the Plague, trans. Clarke, 1961, ch. 4.

40 An apt comparison, and not only in terms of smell. The pig was traditionally associated with the Cook's other failings; for sleepiness (IX.7, 16, 22–23) cf. Whiting G467, H408, S539, S970, and for drunkenness (IX.44, 57, 67) cf. Whiting S532, 534, 955, 968.

42 **justen atte fan:** "The vane (*fan*) or board was at one end of a cross-bar, which swung round on a pivot. At the other end hung a bag or club. The jouster had to strike the fan and avoid the stroke of the bag" (Robinson). Originally this was an exercise designed to sharpen military skill: the target was sometimes dressed as a Saracen. To joust at the quintain successfully demanded horsemanship and manual dexterity that were beyond the inebriated Cook.

44 The different stages of drunkenness, or its effects on different men, were sometimes compared to four animals: the lamb (meek), the lion (bold), the ape (foolish), and the sow (wallowing). See Gesta Romanorum, ch. 159. For the idea that the different states were appropriate to men of different humors, see Kalendrier et compost des bergiers, rpt. 1925, xli. To be ape-drunk was to be playful; see Lydgate, Troy Book 2.5779–81: "And with a strawe pleyeth like an ape,/ And devoutly gynneth for to gape,/ And noddeth ofte . . . ," and cf. IX.35, 45, 47. But Norton-Smith (Geoffrey Ch, 152) argues on the basis of IX.40 that the Cook is "sow-drunk."

46–47 For the traditional enmity between cooks and manciples, see Tupper, JEGP 14, 1915, 256–70. For another angry cook, see PP B 5.155.

48 Cf. I.3121 where the drunken Miller can *unnethe* sit his horse; see also Delasanta, ChR 3, 1968, 29–36.

50 Certainly ironic, this may be allusively humorous, too, if the Cook is identified with Roger Knight; see Brodie, NM 72, 1971, 62–68; and Rickert, TLS, 20 Oct. 1932, 761.

60 **oold or moysty ale:** "Old or new ale." *Moist* as an adjective could mean "damp," or as noun refer to "must," or new wine. Cf. Sir Tristrem, 2492: "No hadde thei no wines wat, No ale that was old."

72 The metaphor is from falconry: the **lure** was sometimes a small piece of meat, or a more elaborate apparatus made of leather or feathers by which the falconer attracted his flying bird down so that he could **reclayme** it.

74–75 Cf. GP I.586, where it is implied that the Manciple may have been deceiving his superiors over his accounts.

78 **mare:** "The mare was rarely the mount of a person of quality" (Rowland, Blind Beasts, 117), but cf. GP I.541n.

90 "And when he had blown upon this horn . . . ," i.e., drunk from the horn-like mouth of the wine flask (*gourde*, IX.83). But the sense "blown upon this wind instrument" is also present, and Baum (PMLA 73, 1958, 168) suggests a pun on "broke wind," though OED (s.v. *poop* v.¹) offers no support.

97–99 Norton-Smith (Geoffrey Ch, 150–51) suggests that lines IX.97–98 derive from Ovid's Ars Amatoria 1.238 "Cura fugit multo diluiturque mero" (Care flees and is dissolved in a lot of wine); and that IX.99 refers to Ars Amatoria 1.543–44 where Silenus, drunk, falls off his ass in a religious procession that is followed by Bacchus in his chariot.

The Manciple's Tale

105–8 The **olde bookes** are probably Ovid's Met. 1.438–567 or 2.531–632, and possibly Ars Amatoria 2.239–40, where Phoebus's life on earth is recounted.

109 **Phitoun:** Python, the fabled serpent sprung from the mud and stagnant waters remaining after Deucalion's flood, was killed by Phoebus with his arrows (Met. 1.438–51).

110 **Slepynge agayn the sonne:** Perhaps parodic, suggesting that Phoebus's exploit was not particularly magnificent; see Hazelton JEGP 62:9. But according to Marshall ". . . a serpent . . . superimposed upon the sun illustrates the *mercurias noster,* the *prima materia* of the alchemical process" (Ch Newsletter 1, 1979, 18).

116 **Amphioun:** See MerT IV.1716n.

121–24 In representational art Phoebus was the ideal type of young, but not immature, manly beauty. His traditional associations with music and archery (cf. IX.108–18, 129) meant that he was usually depicted with a lyre or bow. Cf. Met. 1.559.

130 **crowe:** In classical versions of the story, usually a raven; but in *Seven Sages of Rome,* 2201, a "pie."

139 **a wyf:** According to Ovid (Met. 2.542), Coronis of Larissa is meant. Chaucer's sources do not describe Phoebus as married to her, so *wyf* may here mean "woman" (cf. I.445; III.998, VI.71, etc.). Yet Chaucer gives this tale a very domestic setting.

148–54 A gloss appearing only in the Hengwrt MS (M-R 3:523) suggests that the passage is based on Theophrastus's Liber aureolus de nuptiis, as quoted by Jerome in Adv. Jov. 1.47; see PL 23:277. See also RR 14381–84, 14393–94; and WBPro 357–61 for similar ideas. Whiting (W240) says the whole passage is proverbial, but cites only this instance. With IX.148–52, however, cf. "Femme garder point se veult; bonne ne doit, male ne peut" (Hassell F31), which echoes Jerome ("uxor impudica servari non possit impudica non debeat"), and with IX.153–54, cf. "Fous est cis qui feme weut gaitier" (Morawski, Proverbes Français, Nos. 769, 800). The **olde clerkes** are probably Theophrastus and Jerome.

160–62 Cf. Horace's Epistolae 1.10.24, which Chaucer may have known by way of RR 10427–30.

163–74 Cf. Boethius (Bo 3.m2.21–31), which Chaucer followed in SqT V.610–17; but here he probably used RR 13941–58.

175–80 Cf. RR 14039–52. For a fragmentary debate between "nurture" and "kynde" that uses the same exemplum, see Scattergood, N&Q 215, 1970, 244–46; for the traditional story on which this is based, see Braekman and Macaulay, NM 70, 1969, 690–702.

183–86   Cf. RR 7761–66, the probable source. But Reid (MAE 24, 1955, 16–19) demonstrates that the exemplum was widespread.

187–88   Cf. Tr 5.1779–85.

193   with meschaunce: Cf. FrT III.1334n.

199   man of litel reputacioun: In some versions of the story the *man* is identified as Ischys, son of Elatus, an Arcadian; but Ovid (Met. 2.599) has simply "cum iuvene Haemonio" (with a young Thessalian). The stress on social differences (cf. IX.253, and also 190, 211–22) led Whittock to detect "something akin to modern class bitterness" (Reading of CT, 284).

204–6   The word **lemman** in Chaucer usually has connotations of "adultery, lust, treacherous love, and rape"; see Elliott (Ch's English, 232), where the other uses are analyzed. But the word was not held to be coarse, and the Manciple is the only pilgrim to apologize for it; he reuses it at 238. Perhaps Chaucer felt that the word had lower-class connotations and was somewhat old-fashioned. To Nicholas and Absolon it may have meant "sweetheart" (MilT I.3280, 3700), but elsewhere it had come down in the world. Burnley (ES 65, 1984, 195–204) argues that the word has connotations of moral disapproval: he cites its presence in a fifteenth-century glossary in a section entitled "Nomina reprehensibiliorum mulierum" where it translates *concubina*. For the *lemman/lady* contrast see Cleanness, 1351–52, in Poems of the Pearl MS, ed. Andrew and Waldron.

207–10   Cf. GP I.725–42n. The idea is ultimately from Plato's Timaeus, 29B; but Chaucer probably derived it from Boethius (Bo 3.pr12.205–7) or from RR 7099–7102, 15190–92.

211–37   Cf. Reason's excuse for lewd speech in RR 6987–7184.

220   wenche: "Not a respectable word in Chaucer's eyes" (Donaldson, Speaking of Ch, 25n.). It is usually applied to lower-class women, especially servants; see Elliott, Ch's English, 206–8. Cf. *I am a gentil womman and no wenche* (MerT IV.2202).

222   There is an obvious pun on "lay" meaning "to have sexual intercourse"; see Ross, Ch's Bawdy, 130. Cf. MilT I.3269–70.

226   The anecdote about Alexander was familiar; Chaucer could have read it in Cicero's De republica 3.12; Augustine's De Civ. Dei 4.4; John of Salisbury's Policraticus 3.14; Gesta Romanorum ch. 146; or elsewhere.

235   textueel: Cf. also IX.316. But 314–62 are almost entirely based on "textes." Cf. the similar claim at ParsPro X.57.

243   Cokkow: That the cuckoo/cuckold pun was known at this time is clear from Jean de Condé's Messe des oiseaux, 310–12, or Clanvowe's Boke of Cupide, ed. Scattergood, 1975, 183–85. See also Whiting C603. The cuckoo was thought to lay its eggs in the nests of other birds; see PF 358 and n.

252   blered is thyn ye: Proverbial; cf. RvT I.3865n.

260   Cf. Ovide moralisé, 2352: "La vilonnie et la grante honte."

271   The scorpion was a common symbol of treachery. See BD 636–41n.

279   O ire recchelees: For similar denunciations, cf. SumT III.2005–88, ParsT X.537–650.

295–96   The metamorphosis from white to *blake* (IX.308) is the point of the story in most of the analogues; but to deprive the crow of its **song** is Chaucer's innovation, as is the earlier destruction of Phoebus's bow, arrows, and instruments (IX.267–69); see Harwood, ChR 6:268–79.

301   Cf. PF 363, which may be based on Virgil's Georgics 1.388. The closest analogue is the Integumenta Ovidii: "The raven is said to be sacred to Jupiter . . . because he is able to foretell tempests as Phoebus can" (S&A, 716).

307   which: For the syntax, cf. Tr 2.1418.

311–13   Mustanoja suggests Carmen ad astralabium filium, attributed to Abelard, as source; see Franciplegius, ed. Bessinger and Creed, 1965, 250–54.

314   Cf. Prov. 21.23; Ps. 34.13.

317   Cf. WBPro III.576, PardT VI.684.

318   My sone: Cf. Prov. 23.15, 19, 26. For this form of address in other wisdom literature, see Tatlock, MLN 40, 1935, 296.

319   Proverbial; Whiting T373.

320   Proverbial; Whiting T402 (but the only instance).

322–24   Proverbial; cf. Tilley T424.

325–28   Cf. Cato's Distichs 1.12; Albertanus de Brescia's De arte loquendi et tacendi, xcviii. Cato and Albertanus may be the **clerkes** of IX.326.

329–31   Cf. RR 7037–43.

332–33   Distichs 1.3 (quoted as a gloss in some MSS; M-R 3:523): Albertanus, xcvi; RR 12179–83 (Rom 1705–9); cf. Tr 3.294n. See Hazelton Spec 35, 1960, 357–80 for a discussion.

338   Cf. Prov. 10.19 (quoted as a gloss in some MSS; M-R 3:523); cf. Albertanus, cxv; Ovide Moralisé, 2522. Whiting S608 cites other examples.

340–42   Cf. Ps. 57.4. See Whiting T385, 388.

343   Prov. 6.16–18.

344–45   Perhaps the Manciple has in mind Prov. 10.19, 31, 17.20, 26.28; and Ps. 10.7, 12.3, 52.2, 54.3–8, 120.2–3. Chaucer uses Seneca's De ira in SumT III.2017–88, where three exempla against anger are cited.

349–50   Cf. the Flemish proverb "Luttel onderwinds maakt groote rust" (Grauls and Vanderheijden, RBPH 13, 1934, 745–49). For English sayings see Whiting J13, M482. Cf. CkPro IV.4357.

355–56   Probably from Horace's Epistolae 1.18.71. See also Albertanus, cxviii; RR 16545. Cf. Whiting D287, H134, T198 for proverbs making similar points.

357–58   Cf. Albertanus, cvi.

359–60   From Distichs 1.12; "Rumores fuge, ne incipias novus auctor haberi" (quoted as a gloss to some manuscripts; see M-R 3:523).

FRAGMENT X

Since the first line of The Parson's Prologue explicitly links it with the preceding tale, the Manciple's and Parson's prologues and tales actually form a single fragment. They have traditionally been divided into two fragments because of doubt that Chaucer could have intended The Parson's Tale, which begins at four in the afternoon (X.5), immediately to follow the brief Manciple's Tale, which begins in the morning (IX.16). From the fact that in the early Hengwrt MS the word *Maunciple* is written over an erasure and some later manuscripts here give the names of other Pilgrims (see textual note to X.1), it has been conjectured that Chaucer originally left a blank space where *Maunciple* was later inserted by some scribe or scribal editor. More recent critics have accepted the reading *Maunciple,* ignoring the temporal inconsistency (cf. Howard, Idea of CT, 165–66) and finding artistic justification for the juxtaposition of these two tales (see introductory note to Manciple's Tale).

Whatever doubt may exist about which tale was intended to precede Fragment X, there is no question that its three component parts, the Parson's Prologue, Parson's Tale, and the Retraction, are firmly linked together by speaker and repeated theme (*wey*: ParsPro, ParsT; *penitence*: ParsT, Retr). Nor is there any doubt that the fragment was intended as the final section of the *Tales,* a position it indeed holds in all the manuscripts. The length, prose form, dullness, and somber tone of The Parson's Tale, leading to a statement of authorial remorse and the retraction of what generations of readers have experienced as the best of Chaucer's poetry, all pose the most serious questions about the relation of Fragment X to the preceding tales, its function in the *Tales,* and the unity of the entire poem. The view that the Parson's is only accidentally the last tale in an unfinished work cannot be seriously held in light of the carefully crafted Parson's Prologue, with its repeated stress that The Parson's Tale is to be the last on the fictional pilgrimage and with its seemingly deliberate use of verbal echoes and of literary motifs. A convenient discussion of the latter is Wenzel, in Europäische Lehrdichtung, ed. H. G. Rötzer and H. Walz, 1981, 86–98. David discusses the parallels between The Parson's Prologue and the Introduction to the Man of Law's Tale in Strumpet Muse, 131–34; and Lawler, The One and the Many, 153–72, analyzes the elements of closure found in Fragment X.

The early suggestion by Tupper that the description of vices and virtues in The Parson's Tale announces the moral principles of which the tales and their characters are narrative exempla (PMLA 22, 1914, 93–128) was demolished by Lowes (PMLA 23, 1915, 237–371). In his seminal Unity of the CT, 1955, Baldwin again pointed to the fact that many moral statements made by the Parson can be applied to individual pilgrims and their characters, and argued that *The Canterbury Tales* is unified by the image of pilgrimage, which first refers to the fictional journey to Canterbury, and is then, in Fragment X, elevated to the religious metaphor for human life.

Among the many critics who have followed Baldwin in this view there is much diversity of opinion about precisely how the relation of The Parson's Tale to the preceding tales is to be conceived and described. The attempt to relate specific passages in The Parson's Tale to specific pilgrims, exemplified by Baldwin and by Huppé, Reading of CT, and others, is more often rejected in favor of taking the moral values of The Parson's Tale as only a general comment on the world of the pilgrims and their stories, or of taking Fragment X as an invitation to view the entire poem from a higher perspective than that offered by the preceding pilgrims and the narrator. Some representative expressions of this view are: Baldwin, Unity, 90–95; Ruggiers, Art of CT, 251–52; Jordan, Ch and the Shape of Creation, 227–41; Norton-Smith, Geoffrey Ch, 159; Patterson, Traditio 34, 1978, 370–80; and Wenzel, in Europ. Lehrd., 86–98.

The attempt to evaluate specific tales in the light of the Parson's pronouncements was wittily chastised by Donaldson, Speaking of Ch, 164–74. A different perspective on the view that assigns to The Parson's Tale a higher function in the *Tales* comes from critics who argue that in this tale Chaucer creates an ironic picture of the Parson, whose view of reality therefore holds no superiority over that of other tellers; thus Finlayson, ChR 6, 1971, 94–116; Allen, JMRS 3, 1973, 255–71; and C. V. Kaske, 147–77, in Ch at Albany. Arguments for such an ironic reading have in turn been rebutted by Delasanta, PMLA 93, 1978, 240–47; and Wenzel, in Europ. Lehrd., 86–98.

SIEGFRIED WENZEL

The Parson's Prologue

1   Maunciple: See introductory note to Fragment X.
2–11   For the elaborate specification of time Chaucer again, as in IntrMLT II.1–14 (see n.), draws on the Kalendarium of Nicholas of Lynne, according to which the sun is descended from the meridian (**south lyne**) not quite 29° and a man's shadow is eleven times one-sixth the height of his body (cf. X.6–9) at four P.M. on 16 or 17 April. And at four P.M. on 15 through 17 April, to an observer in London, the zodiacal sign **Libra** (the Scale) was beginning to rise (**ascende**) above the horizon (North, RES 20, 1969, 424–26). This contradicts the date given in IntrMLT II.5–6, 18 April, as well as the traditional assumption that the pilgrimage began on 17 April and ended with The Parson's Tale on 20 April. Eisner (E&S 29, 1976, 20–21) suggests Chaucer was not bothered by the temporal contradiction and chose to set The Parson's Prologue and Tale on 17 April because in 1394, 17 April was Good Friday.
4   nyne and twenty: Cf. GP I.24. On the possible symbolism of this number, see Peck, ES 48, 1967, 205–15.
10–11   moones exaltacioun: The *exaltacioun* of the moon (the zodiacal sign in which a planet exerts its greatest influence; see Astr 2.4.47n.) is Taurus rather than Libra, which is the exaltation of Saturn. The first of the three "faces" of Libra (the first 10°; see Astr 2.4.60–69) was the "face" of the moon, and Skeat suggests Chaucer confused "exaltation" with "face" (5:445). Wood (Ch and the Stars, 272–97) argues that Chaucer mentions Libra for a symbolic allusion to divine justice.
12   at a thropes ende: No village is known to have existed between Harbledown (cf. IX.2) and Canterbury, which may provide an argument for the view that The Parson's Prologue and Tale were written for the fictive return journey to Southwerk.
26   Cf. MilPro I.3115 and n.
28   knytte up: Possibly a rhetorical term, also in preaching; see Wenzel, SP 73, 1976, 155–61.
29   cokkes: A euphemism for *Goddes*; cf. MancPro IX.9 and X.591.
32–34   See 1 Tim. 1.4, 4.7; 2 Tim. 4.4.
35–36   Cf. NPT VII.3443n.
39   that: Here used in place of *if*; cf. Bo 1.m3.7, 9 (*that*

The explanatory notes to the Parson's Prologue and Tale were written by Siegfried Wenzel.

for *when*). For the more frequent use of *that* as a pronoun, see GP I.44–45 and n.

42–43 Allusion is made here to the contemporary alliterative poetry mainly written in the north and west of England. Parallels to **rum, ram, ruf** are listed in Skeat 5:446, and Biggins, PQ 42, 1963, 558–62. On Chaucer's use of alliteration and possible knowledge of alliterative poetry see KnT I.2601–16n.

43   geeste: Apparently this refers to alliterative verse (cf. ProMel VII.933 and n.).

44 The predominant metrical feature in non-alliterative poetry is **rym.**

46 On the widening meaning of **myrie tale** in Chaucer and Lydgate, see Ebin, ChR 13, 1979, 316–36.

51 For the "heavenly" or New Jerusalem, see Rev. 21.2. Life is a way "towards the high Jerusalem" and is beset by the beasts of the seven deadly sins, in Ancrene Riwle, tr. Salu, 86. The connection between penance, pilgrimage and man's way to the heavenly Jerusalem is made in a sermon by Peraldus; see Wenzel, in Europ. Lehrd., 98.

57   textueel: Cf. MancT IX.235, 316.

58   sentence: Cf. ProMel VII.947.

67   hadde the wordes for us alle: Tyrwhitt notes the fourteenth-century Anglo-French description of the Speaker of Parliament as one who "avoit les paroles pur les Communes" (Rot. Parl., 51 Edward III, no. 87).

73–74 In all MSS this couplet follows upon X.68. See Textual Notes.

The Parson's Tale

Though spoken by a parish priest to a group of listeners, The Parson's Tale is formally not a sermon or homily but a handbook on penance; see Wenzel, ChR 16, 1982, 248–51. A good general account of penitential manuals is Pfander, JEGP 35, 1936, 243–58; see also Patterson, Traditio 34, 1978, 331–51. Some earlier critics were dubious about Chaucer's authorship because of the tale's style and subject matter, but modern critics fully accept the work as Chaucer's. For a review of earlier discussion of this question and arguments for Chaucer's authorship, see Spies, in Festschr. für L. Morsbach, 1913, 626–721.

The problem of authorship is intimately linked with the question of sources. Basically, The Parson's Tale uses material from the *Summa de poenitentia* or *Summa casuum poenitentiae* (1222/29) by the Dominican St. Raymund of Pennaforte for lines 80–386 and 958–1080, and from the *Summa vitiorum* (1236) by the Dominican friar William Peraldus (or Peyraut) for a large part of lines 390–955. It should be noted that Peraldus wrote the *Summa vitiorum* before and separately from his *Summa virtutum;* see Dondaine, AFP 18, 1948, 184–87. The Latin *summae* of Pennaforte and Peraldus were immensely popular and were utilized in many Latin and vernacular handbooks. Parallel passages from the two *summae* were given by K. O. Petersen, The Sources of the ParsT, 1901. In her summary of intervening scholarship on the sources, G. Dempster in 1941 (S&A, 723–60) reproduced representative extracts from both *summae* as well as parallels from two French manuals, the Anglo-Norman *Compileison* (fourth quarter of thirteenth century) and Frère Laurent's *Somme le Roy* (1279), which had been suggested as possible influences on Chaucer. The linking of material from the two *summae,* especially at X.387, was felt by some critics to be inorganic, mechanical, and crude, and led Manly and Rickert to reaffirm the possibility that The Parson's Tale is the work of someone other than Chaucer, even though they found no textual support for genuine doubt of Chaucer's authorship (M-R 4:527, in contradiction to 2:454–55). But the linking of the treatment of the deadly sins to the discussion of penance is logical and paralleled in other handbooks. Likewise, the startling disproportion of Chaucer's section on the sins and their remedies to the remainder of the tale is neither unique nor a good argument against his authorship.

The probability that instead of mechanically combining two Latin treatises The Parson's Tale embodies material intelligently from a larger number of sources has received support from Wenzel's discovering a source for the "remedies" for the seven deadly sins (referred to as Postquam; see Traditio 27, 1971, 433–53; superseded in his edition of *Summa virtutum de remediis anime,* Chaucer Library, 1984) as well as from his identifying two redactions of Peraldus's *Summa vitiorum* (referred to as Quoniam and Primo) that are close to Chaucer (Traditio 30, 1974, 351–78) and from presenting different sources or analogues for several other passages (ChR 16:237–56). Though the possibility that the tale is but the translation of a single source that already combined all these materials remains open, it is equally possible to think that Chaucer himself made a purposeful compilation and translation from divers sources.

The diction of the tale in general and some instances of phraseology in particular (lines 79, 572, 898) may suggest that Chaucer's immediate source was in French rather than Latin; see Mersand, Ch's Romance Vocabulary; Robinson, 766; Fisher, 345 and 362n.; Pratt, Tales, 490; Pfander, JEGP 35:257; Norton-Smith, Geoffrey Ch, 155. But no French treatise significantly close to The Parson's Tale has been identified. In addition, one should bear in mind that French usage exerted a profound influence, indirect as well as direct, on the development of English prose in Chaucer's time; see A. A. Prins, French Infl. in Eng. Phrasing, 1952; and Davis, Langue et litt., Bibl. de la Fac. de Philos. et Lettres de l'Univ. de Liège 161, 1961, 165–81.

Stylistically, the tale is frequently uninspiring and awkward, with faulty or incorrect transitions (e.g., X.916, 939) and blatant errors (870, 1073, perhaps 679, 692); cf. Patterson, Traditio 34:351–53. Often only comparison with the suggested sources will clarify Chaucer's meaning, and its compositional flaws may be due to hasty work or a faulty source text or Chaucer's extracting material from a much longer work of complex structure (Wenzel, Traditio 27:451–53, and S. virtutum, 12–30). Balanced evaluations of Chaucer's prose are Schlauch, in Ch and Chaucerians, 148–53; Eliason, Lang. of Ch, 75–80; and Elliott, Ch's English, 132–80.

No external or internal-external evidence is available to determine the date of the tale. Dating it on internal grounds depends on one's view about Chaucer's relation to his sources and about the development of his prose style. Langhans (Anglia 53, 1929, 243–68) argued a date of 1358 (he assumed Chaucer was born earlier than now believed; see Chaucer's Life, p. xvi above) on the basis of vocabulary, style, and Chaucer's personal development. His argument for a very early date has been followed by many scholars and may find support in the use of pronouns of address studied by Nathan, MS 21, 1959, 193–201. But comparison of specific phrases and verses not found in Chaucer's suggested sources with parallels in other parts of the *Tales* has led some scholars to the view that The Parson's Tale was composed after the other tales; thus Owen, MLN 71, 1956, 84–87, and especially Patterson, Traditio 34:356–70.

References to Pennaforte are to *Summa de poenitentia et matrimonio,* Rome, 1603, repr. 1967. The section "De poenitentiis et remissionibus" forms title 34 of Book 3 (pp. 437–502).

Notice that the line numbers for the text of The Parson's Tale follow the practice established in the Six-Text edition and appear at the *end* of the respective line.

State super vias . . . : Jer. 6.16, translated in lines 77–78. Chaucer's phrase *de viis antiquis* normally reads *de semitis antiquis* in the Vulgate Bible and medieval sermons. The verse is connected with penance in a sermon by John Felton, vicar of St. Mary Magdalen, Oxford, 1397, and after; see Wenzel, ChR 16:251–52.

75   that no man wole perisse: Probably an awkward rendering of "nolens aliquos perire" (wishing no one to perish) of 2 Pet. 3.9, although Chaucer's clause could also mean "who wishes to destroy no one." For the following phrase, cf. 1 Tim. 2.4.

79   espirituels: The plural in -*s* of the adjective imitates French usage (Mustanoja, ME Syntax, 277). See Language and Versification, p. xxxv.

80–386   For parallels in Pennaforte, see Petersen, Sources, 4–18 and 34–35 n. 2.

82–83   The six divisions or parts of the tale, which begin respectively at X.84, 86, 95, 102, 107, and 1057, to which a seventh part on *the fruyt of penaunce* is added at 1076.

84   Pseudo-Ambrose, Sermon 25, 1 (PL 17:677).

85   Pennaforte attributes the quotation to "Augustinus." The source is Pseudo-Augustine, De vera et falsa poenitentia 8.22 (PL 40:1120); see Correale, ELN 19, 1981, 96.

86   This sentence probably corresponds to the topic *whennes it is cleped Penitence,* announced at 82, i.e., the etymology of *penitence.* Pennaforte gives it at this very point: "Dicitur autem poenitentia quasi poenae tentio" (Penitence is so called as if it were the holding of sorrow) (3.34.1).

87–88   These two sentences do not occur in Pennaforte and are stylistically different from the authorities previously quoted.

89   Isidore, Sententiae 2.16.1 (PL 83:619).

92   Gregory, Morals 4.27.51–52 (PL 75:662–64).

93   forlete synne er that synne forlete hem: Since one condition of true penitence and forgiveness is the penitent's firm intention not to commit again those sins of which he repents (*and namoore to do . . .*), sinners who repent at a time in their lives when they can no longer commit their former sins (that is, when "sins leave them") therefore cannot be certain (**siker**) that their repentance will be genuine. The same thought and image occur at PhysT VI.286. They derive from a sermon attributed to Augustine (Sermo 393, PL 39:1715: "peccata te dimiserunt, non tu illa") and to Caesarius (Sermo 63, CC 103:274) and reappear in the theological literature of the later Middle Ages in two different forms. One is in Compendium theologicae veritatis 6.21 (in Albertus Magnus, Opera 34.220: "peccata te dimiserunt, non tu illa"); the other is in De vera et falsa poenitentia 17.33 (PL 40:1127: "prius a peccatis relinquitur quam ipse

relinquat"), from which it passed into Peter Lombard's Sentences 4.20.1 (with omissions) (2:372) and Gratian's Decretum, De poen. 7.

95–101   three acciouns of Penitence: Though Chaucer's wording is awkward, especially because of the shifting of terms from **gilt** (98) to **defaute** (99, 100), this section, in agreement with Pennaforte, declares that penitence, i.e., sorrow for one's personal sins, can occur in three situations: (98) before baptism received in adulthood, for any sins that were committed; (99) after baptism, for any mortal sins; and (100) further for any venial sins. **Acciouns** here means "acts" or "functions." The distinction comes from Augustine, Sermo 351 and Epistola 265, excerpted in Gratian, Decretum 1.33.3.1.81 (ed. Friedberg 1:1181), and further digested in Pennaforte, 3.34.5.

97   Augustine, Sermo 351, 2 (PL 39:1537).

101   Augustine, Epist. 265, 8 (PL 33:1089).

109–10   From a Sermo de poenitentia formerly attributed to John Chrysostom (?345–407); see Correale, N&Q 225, 1980, 101–2.

112–27   Not in Pennaforte. The image of the tree of Penitence, X.112–16 and 126, occurs in Compileison de Seinte Penance, in Anglo-Norman and Latin, where it is attributed to Chrysostom; see Wenzel, ChR 16: 240–43.

115   Matt. 3.8, spoken by John the Baptist.

116   Matt. 7.20.

118   The grace of this seed: Perhaps a mistake for *the egernesse of this seed;* cf. Patterson, Traditio 34:352.

119   Prov. 16.6.

125   Ps. 118.113 (AV 119.113).

126   Dan. 4.7–15.

127   Perhaps Prov. 28.13.

130–32   Nicholas of Clairvaux, Sermo in festo sancti Andreae, 8 (PL 184:1052–53); see Correale, AmN&Q 20, 1981, 2–3.

133   causes: Pennaforte similarly discusses "six causes that lead to contrition" (3.34.9), but they are only in part like Chaucer's, and the development is quite different. For an Anglo-Norman analogue, see Dempster, S&A, 751–56.

134   Prov. 12.4. Pennaforte also mistakenly refers to "Job."

135   Isa. 38.15, words of King Hezekiah (**Ezechie**).

136   Rev. 2.5.

138   Cf. Prov. 26.11 and 2 Pet. 2.22.

141   Ezek. 20.43.

142   John 8.34; cf. 2 Pet. 2.19. Pennaforte also refers to "Peter."

143   Perhaps a reference to Job 30.28, "moerens incedebam," or Ps. 42.2, "tristis incedo." Not in Pennaforte.

144   Unidentified. Pennaforte also attributes the quotation to Seneca.

145   Seneca, Epist. morales 65.21. Pennaforte refers to "Philosophus."

150   Robinson refers to Augustine, Sermo 9, 16 (PL 38:87).

151   Pennaforte quotes and attributes this sentence to Augustine.

155–57   Prov. 11.22; cf. WBPro III.784–85. The application (X.157) appears in Quoniam; see Wenzel, ChR 16:237–38.

159–60   Jerome: A conflation of passages from Jerome, Epist. 66, 10 (CSEL 52:660), and Pseudo-Jerome, Regula monacharum, 30 (PL 30:417).

162   Romans 14.10.
166   Pseudo-Bernard, Sermo ad prelatos in concilio, 5 (PL 184:1098).
168   Cf. Prov. 6.34–35.
169–73   Cf. Anselm, Meditatio 1 (Opera 3:78–79).
174   Unidentified.
175–230   The discussion of fear of the suffering in hell is a homiletic exegesis of Job 10.20–22, quoted in X.176–77.
189   1 Sam. 2.30.
191   Job 20.25.
193   Cf. Ps. 75.6. (AV 76.5).
195   Deut. 32.24 and 33.
198   Isa. 14.11.
201   Cf. Micah 7.6.
204   Ps. 10.6. (AV 11.5).
208   Cf. Matt. 13.42 and 25.30.
209   Isa. 24.9.
210   Isa. 66.24.
214–15   Gregory, Morals, 9.66.100 (PL 75:915).
216   Rev. 9.6.
220   Cf. Ps. 106.34–35 (AV 107.34–35).
221   Basil, Homiliae in Psalmos, on Ps. 28.7 (PG 29:298).
227   Prov. 11.7.
229   Cf. Ecclus. 1.17–18.
230   Unidentified.
231–54   The fourth consideration that may move a person to contrition concerns the notion that mortal sin annuls the spiritual or eternal merit a person gains by performing good deeds. This has two aspects (X.232): (a) Merits once gained by good works but since canceled by mortal sin may again be "activated" through penance (235–41); and (b) good works performed in the state of sin will never have spiritual merit with regard to man's eternal life, though they may be helpful in lesser ways (242–45). Pennaforte's fifth "causa," meditating on the loss of heaven, has little bearing on Chaucer's **fourthe point.**
236–37   Ezek. 18.24 and also 20.
238–40   Gregory, Homiliae in Hiezech. 1.11.21 (CC 142:178).
248   The same line is quoted in Fortune 7. French proverbs and snatches appear frequently in the Latin Summa praedicantium by the English Dominican John Bromyard; similarly, the English Franciscan John of Grimestone (1372) quotes a French song and several French proverbs in his commonplace book.
253–54   Unidentified; based on Luke 16.2 and 21.8. Line X.254 is also used in The Pricke of Conscience, ed. Morris, 1863, 5653–62; and Spec. Christiani, ed. Holmstedt, EETS 182, 1933, 54.
255–82   Christ's passion, the fifth incentive to contrition, is here presented as the consequence of a triple disorder or insubordination (X.260–63), which was the result of sin. No parallels in Pennaforte. The notion that sin consists in a disordering of man's inner faculties is taken up by the Parson again at 322–32.
256–59   Bernard, Sermo in quarta feria hebd. sanctae, 11 (Opera 5:64); see Sanderlin, MLN 54, 1939, 447–48.
261–62   Witlieb, N&Q 215, 1970, 202–7, presents parallels from Ovide moralisé to this medieval commonplace.
269   Unidentified.
273   Words placed in the mouth of the suffering Christ,

from an unidentified source, perhaps based on Ps. 68 (AV 69).
274   Unidentified.
281   Isa. 53.5.
284   See John 19.19.
285   For the etymology see Jerome, Lib. interpret. hebr. nominum 13.28 (CC 72:76).
286   Matt. 1.21.
287   Acts 4.12.
288   See Jerome, Lib. interpret. hebr. nominum 62.24 (CC 72:137).
289–90   Rev. 3.20.
291   in the gospel: E.g., Matt. 3.8; Luke 15.7.
303   Pseudo-Augustine, De vera et falsa poen. 24 (PL 40:1121).
304   Jonah 2.8.
307   Ps. 96.10 (AV 97.10).
309   Ps. 31.5 (AV 32.5). The gloss **I purposed fermely** also occurs in Pennaforte, 3.34.11, end.
313   Cf. Eph. 2.3.
317   The parts of this division are treated as follows: (a) nature of confession, X.318–979; (b) its necessity, 980–81; (c) its conditions, 982–1027. The three topics also occur in Pennaforte, 3.34.13–27.
318–979   The definition of "confession" given in X.318 is developed in the following lines. In 321 three subtopics on "sin" are announced, whose discussion takes up 322–957. The following section, 958–79, returns to a definition of "sin" and a discussion of the circumstances of sin. Though this entire section has occasional parallels in Pennaforte, it is unlikely that Chaucer used the latter as his direct source here.
319   condiciouns that bilongen to his synne: Chaucer may seem to confuse "circumstances of sin" (which he treats later, 960–79) and "conditions of (a valid) confession" (which he also treats later, separately, at 982–1027), both common topics in penitential literature; see Patterson, Traditio 34:349, n. 46. However, "circumstances" and "conditions" of sin could be used synonymously, and the terminology of X.319–20 (not in Pennaforte) may be less muddled than has been suggested; see Wenzel, ChR 16:239–40.
320   True confession must be complete, open, and self-accusing. **Al moot be seyd** is a translation of the etymology of con-fessio (saying together or all at once). Thus according to Pennaforte (3.34.13), who adds: "ille confitetur qui totum fatetur" (he confesses who says all).
322–49   the spryngynge of synnes: The origin of sin (in Adam and Eve) is meant, as well as its effect, present in all mankind (Original Sin) as concupiscence, which in scholastic terminology is called the fomes peccati (norissynge of synne, X.338), i.e., the root from which all actual sins spring. The Parson's teaching here is commonplace, based on Augustine and transmitted through Peter Lombard and many other scholastic theologians and handbooks for preachers. See 331–32 below, and Kellogg, Traditio 8, 1952, 424–30.
322   Romans 5.12.
325–30   Cf. Gen. 3.1–7.
331–32   The moralization of the Fall, in which the serpent, Eve, and Adam are interpreted as the devil, the flesh, and reason, and their actions respectively as the three stages in committing a sin (suggestion, delight, and consent), is standard medieval teaching. It derives from Augustine, De trinitate 12, and can be found condensed,

for instance, in Peter Lombard, Sent. 2.24.9. See Robertson, Pref to Ch, 69–75.

333–49 For the topics of Original Sin, its transmission to all mankind, and concupiscence as the lasting effect ("poena") of the Fall, see Peter Lombard, Sent. 2.30.

336 Cf. 1 John 2.16.

342 Gal. 5.17.

343 Cf. 2 Cor. 11.23–27.

344 Romans 7.24.

345–46 Jerome, Select Letters, Epist. 22 ad Eustochium, 7.

348 Jas. 1.14.

349 1 John 1.8.

350–56 The Parson gives two series of steps in the progression of sin. For the second series (X.355–56), Kellogg pointed to a similar passage in the Summa de officio sacerdotis by Richard de Wetheringsett (before 1222): RBPH 31, 1953, 61–64; repr. in Kellogg, Chaucer, Langland, 339–42. But Wetheringsett in fact furnishes two different lists, as does Chaucer, who retains the pattern of the earlier list, probably under the influence of the theological considerations stated by Wetheringsett in the same context; see Wenzel, ChR 16:243–45.

351 subjeccioun: The expected word is *suggestion,* which is found in some MSS.

bely: "Bellows." The image of the devil as a blacksmith blowing his bellows of evil suggestion and eliciting *a flambe of delit* (353) also occurs in the Summa by Wetheringsett; see Wenzel, ChR 16:245.

355–56 Quotation of Exod. 15.9 with gloss. From Wetheringsett's Summa (see 350–56 above).

358–955 Development of *whiche* (i.e., what kinds of), sins there are as announced at X.321. The initial distinction between venial and mortal ("deadly") sins (358–70) is followed by an illustrative list of venial sins (371–81), by a series of remedies for venial sins (382–86), and then by the long discussion of the seven deadly sins and their individual remedies (387–955).

362 See Whiting S397. A Latin form: "Levia multa faciunt unum grande," appears in Augustine, In epist. Joannis ad Parthos 1.6 (PL 35:1982).

363–64 The example of the ship derives from Augustine, Epist. 265, 1 (PL 33:1089), quoted by Peter Lombard, Gratian, Pennaforte, and others; see Petersen, Sources, 7, n. 1.

368 Free translation of the standard scholastic definition of sin: "aversio a bono incommutabili ad bonum commutabile," which is based on Augustine, De libero arbitrio 1.16 (PL 32:1240). See Kellogg, Traditio 8: 426, and Petersen, Sources, 34–35, n. 2. The quoted formulation is used in Quoniam, where the following explanation of "bonum incommutabile" (unchanging good) as everything created (X.369) likewise appears.

371–81 The list of venial sins derives verbally from the pseudo-Augustinian sermon In lectione apostolica, 3 (PL 39:1946–47), which is referred to or quoted by Gratian (ed. Friedberg, 1:93–94), Pennaforte (3.34.21), and others.

376 Cf. Matt. 25.43.

383–84 Cf. Petersen, Sources, 35, n. 2.

385–86 The same remedies against venial sins occur in Pennaforte; see Petersen, Sources, 30.

386 *Confiteor*: "I confess," first word of the general confession of sins recited at the beginning of Mass as well as during compline, the canonical prayer before bedtime.

Rubric *Dependencia* (or *dependenciae*) is an unusual word in this context.

387 the sevene deedly synnes: The topic of deadly sins was announced at X.359. The term "deadly sin" can refer to both mortal sins (*peccata mortalia,* as used in X.359) and the seven chief vices or sins (*vitia* or *peccata capitalia* or *principalia,* as in 387). The ambiguity, in both Latin and vernacular languages, is characteristic of some scholastic theologians and generally of preachers from the thirteenth century on. See Bloomfield, Seven Deadly Sins, 1952, 43–44. Chaucer's rendering of *vitia capitalia* with **chieftaynes of synnes** may have been influenced either by French usage ("chevetain vice" in the Somme le Roi; see Eilers, Essays on Ch, Ch Soc, 1868, 509) or else by the common notion that these vices are captains or leaders in the army of vices ("duces" in Gregory, Morals 31.45.87, PL 76:620; "capteyns" in Lydgate's Assembly of the Gods, passim).

Alle they renne in o lees: Either literally "they all run together on one leash," as hunting-dogs, or figuratively in the sense of "they all are connected in one chain." For the notion that the capital vices are psychologically concatenated, see Wenzel, Spec 43, 1968, 4–5.

An Anglo-Norman analogue to X.387–90 is given by Dempster, S&A, 745–47.

388 Of the roote of thise sevene synnes: Apparently a rubric wrongly shifted into the text.

braunches: The image of the capital vices as branches of a tree whose root is pride was commonplace. See Bloomfield, Seven Deadly Sins, 70 and passim.

390–474 For parallels to X.407–9, 411–14, 416–19, 422, 432–35, 437, 439, 441, 444–46, 450–73 in Peraldus, S. Vitiorum, see Petersen, Sources, 36–45. An Anglo-Norman analogue to the branches of pride (X.391–408) is given by Dempster, S&A, 747–48.

406 clappeth as a mille: see ClT IV.1200, and Whiting C276 and M557.

407–8 Apparently without parallel in the suggested sources. Lowes suggested possible models in Deschamps's Miroir de Mariage (MP 8, 1910–11, 322n.), but the vice was common. Cf. GP I.449–51n.

kisse pax: For the custom see Maskell, Ancient Liturgy of the Church of Engl., 3rd ed., 1882, 170–73, n. 76; for pictures of a *pax,* see Braun, Das christliche Altargerät, 1932, plates 116–20.

411 leefsel: Perhaps a "leafy bower" or "arbor" as in I.4061 (Elliott, Ch's English, 148–49), but the meaning "bush for a tavern sign" (MED s.v. *lef* n.[1] 1[b]) is substantiated by the use of a tavern sign as a symbol for pride in clothing by Peraldus and derived treatises; see Wenzel, ChR 16:238.

413 Cf. Luke 16.19.

414 Cf. Gregory, Hom. in Ev. 2.40.3 (PL 76:1305), but the reasons why precious clothing is sinful are derived from Peraldus.

415 For condemnations of pride in clothing by contemporary preachers, see Owst, Lit. and Pulpit, 390–411, and index under *costume.*

418 daggynge of sheres: Cf. Rom 840.

422–29 Complaint at the shortness or scantiness of clothes as a sign of pride does not occur in Peraldus or derived Latin treatises. For similar remarks in French, see Liddell, Acad 49, 1896, 509.

424 According to medieval encyclopedias, in the full of the moon apes display their posteriors: Biggins, MAE 33,

1964, 200–203. Rowland suggests a reference to estrus: ChR 2, 1968, 159–65.

434 Zech. 10.5.

435 See Matt. 21.7.

437–43 For contemporary complaints at unruly retainers, see Owst, Lit. and Pulpit, 324–26, and the Harley lyric Satire on the Retinues of the Great (Hist. Poems, ed. Robbins, 27–29).

441 **houndes:** Peraldus speaks of wolves instead of dogs.

442 Ps. 54.16. (AV 55.15).

443 Cf. Gen. 31 and 47.7.

450 On the gifts of fortune and nature, see PardPro VI.295n.

459 Cf. Gal. 5.17.

461 **gentrie:** Peraldus speaks of "nobilitas generacionis," Quoniam of "stema, idest nobilitas generis." The view here expressed is paralleled in WBT III.1109–76 and in Gentilesse.

467–68 Seneca, De clem. 1.3.3 and 1.19.2, as quoted by Peraldus. On Chaucer's substituting **pitee** for "clementia," see Burnley, Ch's Language, 100.

470 Cf. Gregory, Morals 33.12.25 (PL 76:688); see Correale, ELN 19:97.

473 Cf. ClT IV.995–1001.

475–83 For the source of Chaucer's remedy for pride, see Wenzel, S. virtutum, 13–14.

484–514 Parallels in Peraldus are given by Petersen, Sources, 45–47. They are discussed, and a closer source is presented, by Wenzel, Traditio, 30:354–62.

484 **Philosophre:** Fox suggests Aristotle, Rhetoric, 2.10 (N&Q 203, 1958, 523–24); perhaps, rather, John Damascene, De fide orth. 2.4 (ed. Buytaert, Franc. Inst. Pub. 8, 1955, 121).

Seint Augustyn: Augustine, En. in Ps. 104, 17 (CC 40:1545), Sermo 353, 1 (PL 39:1561), and elsewhere. The sorrow-joy definition is used again in ParsT X.491–92 and PhysT VI.114–17 (see n.).

485 **bountee:** Translates "bonitas."

489 **bountees:** Translates "bonum, bona."

493–97 For an Anglo-Norman analogue, see Dempster, S&A, 748–49.

494 The knot image appears in John de Grimestone's commonplace book; see Wenzel, Traditio 30:359, n. 27.

502 See John 12.4–6.

504 See Luke 7.39.

508 **the develes** *Pater noster:* Perhaps suggested by Peraldus. A *Pater Noster* of misers or usurers is often mentioned in sermons; see also J. Mourin, ed., Six sermons français inédits de Jean Gerson, 1946, 299.

509 **prive hate:** "Odium occultum," a species of envy in Quoniam, which also contains, at this point, a reference to the later section on wrath; see Wenzel, Traditio 30:361. Chaucer mentions hate again at X.562.

512 Cf. Rev. 12.10.

515–32 For the source of the remedy for envy, see Wenzel, S. virtutum, 14–16 and 27–28.

517 Matt. 22.39.

526 Matt. 5.44.

532 **paas:** The usual interpretation "step" or "passage, section" leaves the sentence entirely cryptic. Wenzel (ChR 16:245–48 and notes) suggests a meaning of "way, progression, process" and relates the sentence and its context to the notion that the remedial virtues are linked as stages in a process of healing (see X.530), just as the vices are linked in a psychological concatenation (see 387 above).

533–653 For parallels see Petersen, Sources, 49–61; Wenzel, Traditio 30:362–64.

535 Augustine, City of God 14.15.2.

536 **Philosophre:** Ultimately Aristotle, On the Soul 1.1.24 (cf. Schmidt, N&Q 213, 1968, 327–28), whose definition is taken up by Seneca, De ira 2.19.3 (cf. Fox, MLN 75, 1960, 101–2). Chaucer's **fervent** has cognates in the medieval Latin translations of Aristotle as well as in Seneca. Chaucer's definition actually combines the two definitions between which Aristotle distinguishes.

539 **wys man:** Ecclus. 7.4.

540 Ps. 4.5.

551 **tree:** The juniper; cf. Isidore, Etym. 17.7.35.

552 Perhaps a reference to the kindling of the new fire in the liturgy of the Easter vigil; or else to the mandatory annual confession, usually made before Easter Sunday; cf. X.1027.

562 The definition of hate as **oold wratthe** comes from Augustine, Sermo 58, 7.8 (PL 38:397).

564–79 The discussion of homicide, not in Peraldus, is ultimately derived from Pennaforte, 2.1.2–3; see Johnson, PMLA 57, 1942, 51–56.

565 The **sixe thynges** are: hatred, backbiting, giving evil counsel, withholding or reducing wages, usury, and withdrawing alms, as listed in X.566–69. Pennaforte lists only five kinds.

Seint John: 1 John 3.15.

566 Cf. Prov. 25.18.

568 Prov. 28.15.

569 **the wise man:** Cf. Prov. 25.21, but probably quoting Gratian, Decretum 1.86.21 (ed. Friedberg 1:302).

571 The four kinds of bodily manslaughter are: by law, for necessity, by accident, and through contraception, onanism, and abortion. In Pennaforte the fourth kind is "voluntary manslaughter," without specification (2.1.3), though abortion is taken up later (2.1.6). See Johnson, PMLA 57:55–56, and John T. Noonan, Contraception, 1965, 215–16 and 235–36.

572 **in his defendaunt:** Seemingly a French construction. For its currency, see MED s.v. *defendaunt* n. 3.

580–653 As stated in 653, at this point Chaucer turns to "sins of the tongue." Partial parallels occur in Peraldus (Petersen, Sources, 53–61), but in a separate *tractatus,* "De Peccato Linguae," which follows upon but is not verbally linked to the *tractatus* on wrath. Treatises derived from Peraldus, such as Quoniam, distribute his "sins of the tongue" among various deadly sins including wrath. Chaucer seems to be aware of different traditions; see 618 and, of course, 653, and cf. Yeager, SP 81, 1984, 42–55.

580 Gambling and blasphemy are connected in both Peraldus (people "play and blaspheme" in the devil's temple, the tavern: S. vitiorum, 9.2.1) and Quoniam (the punishment for blasphemy can especially be seen "de lusoribus et aleatoribus": MS Durham, Cathedral, B.I.18, fol. 62r).

582 Cf. Ps. 144.9 (AV 145.9).

583–86 The sin of defending one's sins is partially derived from Peraldus: Petersen, Sources, 53.

587–607 **sweryng:** The few parallels on "perjurium" in Peraldus (Petersen, Sources, 53–54) only concern parts of Chaucer's biblical quotations.

588 Exod. 20.7.

589–90 Matt. 5.34–37.

591 Cf. PardT VI.472–75 and 629–59, EpiMLT II.1171n.

592 Jer. 4.2.

593 Ecclus. 23.12.

597 Acts 4.12.

598 Phil. 2.10.

599 Cf. Jas. 2.19.

600 Cf. PardT VI.631–32 and discussion by Patterson, Traditio 34:361–62.

603–7 Various kinds of divination and incantation are usually included in the sin of *sortilegium.* The latter is a species of avarice in Quoniam (together with swearing and lying), whereas Peraldus had treated similar sins under pride. Chaucer's subsuming *sortilegium* under swearing (603), a branch of wrath, is peculiar. See also Owst, in Sts. Pres. to Sir H. Jenkinson, ed. J. C. Davies, 1957, 272–303.

603 **shulder-boon of a sheep:** For this practice, see Rowland, Blind Beasts, 149–52, and cf. PardPro VI.350–70 and 350n.

605 **gnawynge of rattes:** For the belief that the gnawing of mice is a bad omen, see Handwörterbuch des deutschen Aberglaubens, ed. Bächtold-Stäubli, 6.47–48 and 44–45.

608–11 The definition and kinds of lying derive from Augustine, De mendacio, 5 and 25 (PL 40:491, 505) by way of Peraldus (Petersen, Sources, 54–55); see also Augustine, Contra mendacium, 26 (PL 40:537).

612–18 Largely derived from Peraldus ("adulatio"; Petersen, Sources, 55), with some parallels in Quoniam (under envy). Lines not found in either treatise are X.612, 617b, 618.

614 While Peraldus and Quoniam cite in this context several verses from Proverbs that contain the milk image of X.613 (Prov. 16.29, 24.28), none of them is close to the quotation attributed to **Salomon** in 614. But Peraldus and Quoniam link flattery to backbiting as follows: "And it seems that flattery is worse than backbiting, because backbiting lowers a man, but flattery raises him up" (Peraldus, S. vitiorum 9.2.7, not noticed by Petersen). Chaucer's "Salomon" quotation clearly indicates a misreading of Peraldian material.

617 *Placebo:* Lat. "I shall please"; see also SumT III.2075, and MerT IV.1476n. "To sing *placebo*" appears as a synonym for "to flatter" in Somme le Roi and its English translations (e.g., Book of Vices and Virtues, ed. Francis, EETS 217, 1942, 58).

619–21 Cursing, "maledictio," derives from Peraldus: Petersen, Sources, 55–56. Chaucer's definition **Malisoun . . . harm** seems to be corrupt.

619 1 Cor. 6.10.

620 The bird image derives from Prov. 26.2, via Peraldus.

622–34 **chidynge and reproche:** Derived from Peraldus ("convitium" and "contentio"; Petersen, Sources, 56–58).

623 See Matt. 5.22.

624 The examples of abuse given here and in 626 do not occur in the suggested sources.

627 **a vileyns herte:** Peraldus has: "In veritate rusticus est, qui rusticitatem libenter dicit" (he is truly a boor who willingly speaks boorish things) (S. vitiorum 9.2.9, not noticed by Petersen), following the quotation of Matt. 12.34.

after the habundance . . . : Matt. 12.34.

629 Prov. 15.4.

deslavee: Lat. *immoderata;* cf. X.834.

630 **Seint Augustyn:** Thus quoted in Peraldus.

Seint Paul: 2 Tim. 2.24 (unidentified in Peraldus).

631 Prov. 27.15. Compare WBPro III.278–80 and Mel VII.1086n.

633 Prov. 17.1.

634 Col. 3.18. Compare WBPro III.160–61. The quotation does not appear in Peraldus or Quoniam, although the latter expands Peraldus's treatment of chiding between husband and wife with a few remarks on how a husband should chastise an unruly wife, concluding: "If she does not experience the fear of God in her frequent disturbance, he should do as Solomon orders him: 'Strike her with a hard staff!' " (MS Durham, Cathedral, B.I.18, fol. 32v.).

635–53 The remaining "sins of the tongue" are also derived from Peraldus; Petersen, Sources, 58–61.

639 For Achitophel's bad counsel, see 2 Sam. 17.

640 The quoted saying is actually Peraldus's text, which also cites Ecclus. 27.29–30 and Prov. 26.27. **Every fals lyvynge** renders "omnis injusticia" (every injustice).

642 Cf. Prov. 6.16–19, and Eph. 2.14–16.

648 Cf. Matt. 12.36.

649 Eccles. 5.2.

650 The **philosophre** is unidentified, as in Peraldus.

651 See Eph. 5.4.

653 See 580 above.

654–76 For the source of the remedy for wrath, see Wenzel, S. virtutum, 16–18 and 28.

657 Unidentified, thus quoted in Postquam.

658 Aristotle, On Interpretation, 11.

660 Moralium dogma philosophorum, ed. Holmberg, 1929, 30.

661 **Crist:** Cf. Matt. 5.9.

the wise man: Part of a common Latin distich; see Walther 16974. Cf. Tr 4.1584n.

664 Prov. 29.9.

665 See Matt. 27.35.

669–73 The story is unidentified, but Wenzel notes a possible analogue in Peraldus: S. virtutum, 28.

674 Cf. Hebr. 13.17.

677–727 For parallels, see Petersen, Sources, 61–66, and Wenzel, Traditio 30:364–66.

678 **Accidie** is, properly, only **anoy of goodnesse** (taedium boni) according to standard scholastic definitions followed by Quoniam; see Wenzel, Sin of Sloth, 1967, 218, n. 17. The expansion **joye of harm** belongs to the definition of envy (see 484 above).

679 **Salomon:** Probably result of a misreading of "Paral." (Chronicles) in the source text; Quoniam here quotes 2 Chron. 19.7 (omnia facite cum diligentia).

680 Jer. 48.10, quoted in Quoniam with "negligenter" (as here) rather than "fraudulenter."

686 **The fourthe thyng:** Comparison with the source text shows that the preceding three "things" are arguments for scorning the vice, here advanced without numbering in 678 (two) and 681.

687 Rev. 3.16.

688 Prov. 18.9.

690 William of Saint-Thierry (d. c. 1148), Epist. ad fratres de Monte Dei 1.8.23 (PL 184:323); cf. Sanderlin, MLN 54:447–48.

692 **Gregorie:** In Quoniam "Gregorius" seems to

refer to the preceding sentence not translated by Chaucer.

694 **Seint Augustin:** Quotation unidentified; thus also in Quoniam.

696 **Judas** hanged himself in despair, Matt. 27.5.

698 **creant:** The cry of surrender in combat. Chaucer's image is of a spineless participant in judicial combat (see GP I.239n.) who surrenders (**coward champioun recreant**). "To say *creant*" is a commonplace expression in ME homiletic literature for "giving up"; see MED s.v. *creaunt* (b).

700–703 Luke 15.7, 11–24; 23.42–43; all are commonplaces in treatments of despair in penitential literature.

709 Prov. 8.17.

712 Eccles. 7.19.

714 **yate:** see SNPro VIII.2–3, and KnT I.1940.

716 Ps. 72.5 (AV 73.5).

720–21 Without parallel in the suggested sources at this point, this passage has given rise to speculations that Chaucer may allude to the government takeover by Gloucester in 1388 (Robinson) or to a court scandal involving Katherine Swynford (Owen, MLN 71:84–87). But the condemnation of negligent pastors (X.721) is a homiletic commonplace: Owst, Lit. and the Pulpit, and Preaching in Med. Engl. 41–47, 139; and Rowland, Blind Beasts, 105. In Peraldus and derived works, clerical absenteeism is treated under avarice.

723 Bernard, Serm. super Cant., 54 (Opera 2:107–8).

725 2 Cor. 7.10.

728–38 For the source of the remedy for accidie, see Wenzel, S. virtutum, 19–20. X.729 and 733 may be derived from Peraldus's S. virtutum, and 738 from his S. vitiorum; see Wenzel, 28.

733 **discrecioun:** Heiner Gillmeister suggests that Chaucer began using the word only in his later works (Discrecioun. Ch und die Via Regia, 1972, 69); it first appears in *Boece* and *Troilus* and is common in the *Tales*.

739–803 For parallels, see Petersen, Sources, 66–70, and Wenzel, Traditio 30:367–70.

739 **Seint Paul:** Tim. 6.10. Cf. Mel VII.1130, PardPro VI.334.

741 Augustine, City of God 14.15.2.

748 Eph. 5.5.

749 The notion that an idolater has only one idol, but an avaricious person many, occurs also in Dante, Inferno 19:112–14; see Schless, Dante and Chaucer, 218.

750–51 Exod. 20.3–4.

752 **cariages:** Cf. FrT III.1570n.

754–56 Augustine, City of God 19.15, with ref. to Gen. 9.25–27.

759 Seneca, Epist. morales 47.1.

760–62 Inspired by Seneca, Epist. morales 47.10, 11, 17; cf. Ayres, RomR 10, 1919, 4.

762 Compare MLT II.1142.

766 Gen. 9.25–27, as at X.755.

768 The reference to Augustine may be the result of misunderstanding the source; see Wenzel, Traditio 30:368.

773 Cf. Romans 13.1.

commune profit: Cf. PF 47n.

775 **mercy or mesure:** On the synonymy, see Burnley, Ch's Lang., 126.

782 "Irregularity," in canon law, is a condition that permanently prevents a person from receiving Holy Orders or from exercising them; see G. Oesterlé, Dict. de droit canon., 1957, 6:46.

783 **Simon Magus:** Cf. Acts 8.18–24.

788 **Damasie:** Pope Damasus I, 366–84. The quotation, attributed to Damasus in Peraldus, occurs in Gratian, Decretum 2.1.7.27 (ed. Friedberg 1:438).

795 Some of these branches, notably **lesynges,** were already treated under wrath (608). In Quoniam all occur here, under avarice.

comaundementz: the conventional seventh and eighth commandments of the Decalogue, Exod. 20.15–16.

797 See Dan. 13.

801 **hurtynge of hooly thynges:** translates "sacri ledium," the supposed etymology of "sacrilegium": "sacrum laedere," to hurt something holy.

804–10 For the source of the remedy for avarice, see Wenzel, S. virtutum, 20–21.

806 Moralium dogma philosophorum, ed. Holmberg, 27.

811–17 Perhaps suggested by Peraldus, S. vitiorum 4.4–5; see Wenzel, S. virtutum, 28–29.

816 Rowland refers to Aristotle's observation that the horse prefers muddy water (Blind Beasts, 125); Peraldus likens the prodigal to dirty water.

818–30 For parallels, see Petersen, Sources, 70–71, and Wenzel, Traditio 30:370–71.

819 Cf. PardT VI.504–11 and n.

820 Phil. 3.18–19; quoted also in PardT VI.529–32.

822 **sepulture of mannes resoun:** Used also in PardT VI.558–59.

828–30 Gregory, Morals 30.18.60 (PL 76:556). The corresponding passages in Peraldus and the Anglo-Norman Compileison are reproduced in S&A, 742–44 and 749–50.

831–35 For the source of the remedy for gluttony, see Wenzel, S. virtutum, 21–22.

831 **Galien:** Galen, the Greek physician (see GP I.429–34n.); thus quoted in Postquam. Perhaps from Pseudo-Galen, De dinamidis, in Galeni ascripti libri, Venice, 1541, fol. 18v.

832 Attributed to Augustine, De vera innocentia, in the source, but not found in modern editions.

836–914 For parallels, see Petersen, Sources, 71–76, and Wenzel, Traditio 30:371–77, with discussion of Chaucer's peculiar structure. A French analogue to X.852–64, by Frère Laurent, is given by Dempster, S&A, 759–60.

837 Exod. 20.14.

838 See Deut. 22.21 and Lev. 21.9.

839 See Gen. 6.5–7 and 19.24–25.

841 See Rev. 21.8.

842 Cf. Gen. 1.28 and 2.18–25; Matt. 19.5.

843 Cf. Eph. 5.25.

844 Cf. Exod. 20.17 and Matt. 5.28.

845 Cf. Augustine, De sermone Domini in monte 1.36 (PL 34:1247).

gospel: Matt. 5.28.

850 Quoniam quotes Ecclus. 9.10 and Jer. 2.36 in support of "famam tollit," **bireveth . . . hir goode fame.**

853 The basilisk was supposed to kill at a glance; see Bartholomaeus Anglicus 18.16, tr. Trevisa 2:1153, and Rowland, Animals with Human Faces, 1973, 28–31.

854 Ecclus. 26.10 and 13.1.

858 This memorable image occurs verbatim in Quoniam and was borrowed by Dunbar, Tretis of the Tua Mariit and the Wedo, 185–87 (Bawcutt, N&Q 209, 1964, 332–33). Bromyard applies a very similar image

to slanderers: "They lift their leg over higher and green places, wishing to foul them," Summa praedicantium, D.5.9 (before 1330). The emendation to **bushes** is supported by "virgultum" in Quoniam. See Textual Notes.
859   sleen hymself with his owene knyf: Cf. MerT IV.1840n. The expression is proverbial, apparently popularized by Somme le Roi: Whiting M.154.
   dronken of his owene tonne: Cf. WBPro III.170.
861   Not in the suggested sources. Cf. MerT IV.1454 and Patterson, Traditio 34:365.
865–914   The section on the species of lechery is somewhat obscure in structure but essentially follows the five species discussed by Peraldus and Quoniam: 1. "Fornicatio" (X.865–67); 2. "stuprum" (868–72); 3. "adulterium" (873–906); 4. "incestus" (907–9); 5. "vitium contra naturam," Chaucer adds a section on "luxuria clericorum," which furnishes material for X.891–903. The discussion of adultery here seems to be divided into three subspecies: (a) between partners one of whom or both are married to someone else (X.873–90); (b) between a man in holy orders and a married or unmarried woman (891–903); and (c) between husband and wife (904–6, already treated at 859). After the fifth species, "vitium contra naturam," Chaucer adds as another synne "pollutio nocturna" (912–14), which is not treated in the suggested sources, but is otherwise a traditional topic.
867   God: Exod. 20.14 and Matt. 5.27–28.
   Seint Paul: Gal. 5.19–21. Chaucer's text should read: "Saint Paul denies them the reign, which is not denied to anyone but those who commit deadly sin."
869   Cf. Matt. 13.8. The three degrees of the parable were traditionally related to the states of married life, widowhood, and virginity.
872   Loss of virginity does not prevent people from regaining the state of grace; but the original state of inviolate virginity cannot be restored.
874   approchynge of oother mannes bed: Translates the etymology of "adulterium" given by Peraldus: "ad alterius thorum accessio."
875   Ecclus. 23.32–33, listing four "harms," which Chaucer treats in 875–85 (the fourth biblical "harm" appearing as two harms in 884–85).
879   1 Cor. 3.17.
880–81   Gen. 39.8–9.
883   See Gen 1.27–28, already mentioned in 842 above.
887   Exod. 20.13–15.
888   Lev. 20.10.
889   John 8.11.
890   The pains of hell were already listed at X.864.
895   2 Cor. 11.14.
897   1 Sam. 2.12.
898   withouten juge: "Without judge," for the biblical "absque iugo" (without yoke) (Judg. 19.22). Chaucer's wording has been explained as a misreading of Old French *sans ioug* as *sans iuge* and has been taken as evidence that he used a French source (Skeat 5:471; Fisher).
898–99   free bole: See Homans, RES 14, 1938, 447–49. The image occurs in Quoniam. Bradwardine applied the simile to the king of Scotland, in his Sermo epinicius (1346), ed. Oberman and Weisheipl, AHDLMA 25, 1958, 328.
900   the book: 1 Sam. 2.13–17.
904   Jerome, Adv. Jov. 1.49 (PL 23:293–94).
906   Tobit 6.17.

907   affynytee: In canon law, the relationship between persons established by marriage, excluding that between the spouses themselves; to be distinguished from **kynrede**, or consanguinity.
910   See Romans 1.26–27 and elsewhere.
911   the sonne . . . mixne: Proverbial, see Whiting S891, and Wenzel, Traditio 30:376, n. 117.
912–14   For the (traditional) four causes of nocturnal pollution, see Müller, Divus Thomas 12, 1934, 457.
915–55   Some parallels occur in Peraldus (Petersen, Sources, 76–78); for a closer source see Wenzel, S. virtutum, 22–26 and 29–30.
916   two maneres: At 948 Chaucer adds a third, virginity. His source has three species, in the same order; but the variant readings at ix.12 in the S. virtutum may explain his mistake.
918   Eph. 5.32.
   as I have seyd: See 842 and 883.
919   See John 2.1–11.
921   Augustine, De bono coniugali, 20–21 (PL 40: 387); Sanderlin (MLN 54:448) suggests De nuptiis et concup. 1.9 (PL 44:419).
922   Cf. Eph. 5.22–32; 1 Cor. 11.3.
925–29   Cf. Gen. 2.22. This moral interpretation of Eve's being created from Adam's rib was a commonplace. See for instance: Peter Lombard, Sent. 2.18.2; Holcot, In Sapientiam, lect. 44 (ed. Hagenau 1494); Gower, Mirour, 17521–32.
927   Preachers' references to daily experience were commonplace in Chaucer's time, as in Bromyard's Summa praed. or the sermons by Rypon or Mirk.
929   Eph. 5.25.
930   1 Pet. 3.1–4.
931   Gratian, Decretum 2.33.5.17 (ed. Friedberg 1: 1255), cited by Pennaforte, 2.8.9.
933   Seint Jerome: Cyprian, De habitu virginum, 13 (PL 4:464).
   Seint John: Rev. 18.16–17.
934   Gregory, Hom. in Ev. 2.40.3 (PL 76:1305). The three quotations of X.933–34 occur in Peraldus, S. vitiorum 6.3.10 and 14, and in Quoniam, in the section on pride of clothing.
935   Perhaps derived from Peraldus, S. vitiorum 6.3.12; also in Quoniam.
939   thre: Actually four reasons for sexual intercourse are discussed. For Chaucer's position in the late medieval moral evaluation of sexual intercourse, see Noonan, Contraception, 246–57; Mogan, ChR 4, 1970, 123–41; and Kelly, Love and Marriage, 245–85.
941   decree: Perhaps Gratian, Decretum 2.33.5.1 (ed. Friedberg 1:1250), cited by Pennaforte, 4.2.13.
946   For complete abstinence in marriage, exemplified by Joseph and Mary, see Gratian, Decretum 2.33.5.4 (ed. Friedberg 1:1251–52), cited by Pennaforte, 4.2.15.
947   Magdelene: Cf. Matt. 26.7.
948   Sister Mary Immaculate (MLQ 2, 1941, 65–66) suggested emendation of **lyf** to *lyk,* on the basis of Mark 12.25 ("sicut angeli") quoted in Somme le Roi and its English translations. But notice that Chaucer's source, in commending virginity, makes a series of statements about "ipsa," which may refer to either a virgin ("she") or virginity ("it"). To consider virginity **the lyf of angeles** *(vita angelica* or *v. angelorum)* is an ancient Christian commonplace: Augustine, De sancta virginitate, 24 and 54 (PL 40:409 and 427); Sermo 132, 3 (PL 38:736). Chaucer's source here has "vivere angelicum est."

951–55   All special remedies here listed and the examples occur in Peraldus, S. vitiorum 2.3.1 and 3.4.1–2; the material of X.953–55 also appears in Quoniam. See Wenzel, S. virtutum, 29–30. For an Anglo-Norman analogue, see Dempster, S&A, 750–51.

956–57   The Parson's discussion of the deadly sins contains clear quotations of or allusions to the first (X.750–51), second (588), fifth (887), sixth (837, 867, 887), seventh (795, 798, 887), eighth (795), and ninth (844) commandments.

957   Cf. the similar expression at KnT I.1323; NPT VII.3240–66; HF 12–15, 52–58.

958   seconde partie: See X.316, and 318–979 above.
firste chapitre: See Textual Notes.

958–1075   For parallels from Pennaforte, see Petersen, Sources, 18–34.

959   Augustine, Contra Faustum 22.27 (PL 42:418), quoted in Quoniam as follows: "Est autem peccatum, ut dicit Augustinus, dictum vel factum vel concupitum contra legem Dei . . . . Et tangit generaliter omne peccatum quod est aut peccatum oris aut peccatum operacionis aut cogitacionis" (MS Durham, Cathedral, B.I.18, fol. 14r). The application of Augustine's definition to sins of heart, mouth, and deed, and its further expansion to the five senses, are common in penitential literature. Cf. Kellogg, Traditio 8:426.

960   agreggen: According to penitential theology, the circumstances of a sinful act may increase (or occasionally diminish) its seriousness; cf. Pennaforte, 3.34.29, marg. note g. In discussing the circumstances, Chaucer follows the standard list formulated in the hexameter "Quis, quid, ubi, per quos, quoties, cur, quomodo, quando," quoted in Pennaforte.

977   This sentence apparently treats the circumstance of time ("quando"); see 960 above.

980–81   These lines apparently discuss the second major section of confession, whether it is necessary (cf. X.317).

982–1027   The condition for a **trewe**, i.e., valid, confession, the third topic on confession announced at X.317. Though the structure of this section is confusing, it essentially follows Pennaforte's exposition (3.34.22–26). Pennaforte announces four necessary qualities: "amara," "festina," "integra," and "frequens" (in his treatment the last two are reversed). Chaucer follows the same conditions: **sorweful** (X.983), **hastily** (998), **alle** (1006), and **ofte** (1025), but fails to introduce the last two by number. The framework taken from Pennaforte is often expanded, particularly with the **foure thynges** of 1003–5. The **certeine condiciouns** of 1012–24 correspond to Pennaforte's nine subsidiary aspects of "integra," in the same order: "voluntaria" (X.1012), "fidelis" (1014–15), "propria" and "accusatoria" (joined, 1016–18), "vera" (1019–20), "nuda" (1021–22), "discreta" (1023: **discreet**), "pura" (1023: **nat . . . for veyne glorie,** etc.), and "morosa" (1024). The confusing failure on Chaucer's part to label the third and fourth qualities by number also follows Pennaforte exactly, who, after introducing the first quality (amara) with "prima," introduces the other three with "item" (also).

983   Isa. 38.15.

984–97   fyve signes: As in Pennaforte (3.34.22), with expansions.

985   Pseudo-Augustine, De vera et falsa poen. 10.25 (PL 40:1122).

986   See Luke 18.13.

987   The source in Augustine is unidentified.

988   1 Pet. 5.6.

994   Matt. 26.75.

996   See Luke 7.37.

997   Phil. 2.8.

998   For parallels to this image, see Petersen, Sources, 20, n. 1, and 26.

1000–1002   The (five) reasons for speedy confession also occur in Pennaforte, 3.34.23.

1003–5   The **foure thynges,** which are common requirements for a valid confession and absolution, may have been added here to qualify, or avert wrong application of, the quality of speediness (cf. X.998 and 1003).

1003   wikked haste: Cf. Mel VII.1054.

1008   For repeating one's confession out of humility, see SumT III.2098 and discussion by Patterson, Traditio 34:366–69.

1012–24   See 982–1027 above.

1014–15   The two sentences translate the distinction Pennaforte makes of "fidelis" as meaning "of the true faith" and "having faith in Christ's forgiveness." Cain (**Caym**) and Judas are standard types of religious despair.

1020   Augustine, Sermo 181, 5 (PL 38:981).

1026   The entire line stems from Pseudo-Augustine, De vera et falsa poenit. 10.25 (PL 40:1122); see Regan, N&Q 209, 1964, 210.

1027   laweful: "Decreed by law." Reference to the church decree that every adult Christian must confess his or her sins and receive Holy Communion at least once a year ("Omnis utriusque," Friedberg 2:887). Cf. FrT III.1308.

1029   The thridde partie: Cf. 108. The section on satisfaction (X.1029–56) generally follows Pennaforte: Petersen, Sources, 27–30.

1030   defaute: Pennaforte speaks of "adversities" (3.34.34).

1031–33   Allusion to the conventional "seven works of mercy," not included in Pennaforte but commonly treated in religious handbooks; e.g., Spec. Christiani, ed. Holmstedt, EETS 182, 40–47. Works of mercy are identified with almsgiving by Thomas Aquinas, Summa theol. 2–2.32.2.

1033   day of doom: Cf. Matt. 25.31–46.

1035–36   Matt. 5.14–16.

1039   Pater noster: See Matt. 6.9–13.

1040–44   Not in Pennaforte; for analogues see Petersen, Sources, 28, n. 1; Book of Vices and Virtues, ed. Francis, EETS 217, 97–98. The term **privyleged** is used in a commentary by Bonaventure ("privilegiata"; see Wenzel, ChR 16:238–39).

1044   That praying the Our Father deletes venial sins is common teaching: Augustine, Enchiridion, 71 (PL 40:265); Gratian, Decretum 2.33.3.20 (ed. Friedberg 1:1214).

1047   Seint Jerome: The quotation appears in the Glossa Ord. on Mark 9.28 (PL 114:215) and in Pennaforte, 3.34.35, in both cases attributed to Jerome.

1048   Matt. 26.41.

1052   disciplyne: The twofold meaning of "teaching" and "mortification," both used by Chaucer, is common for medieval Latin "disciplina"; see Wenzel, ChR 16: 239. Pennaforte has the noun "flagella" instead.

1054   Col. 3.12.

1055   Pennaforte includes "the affliction of pilgrimage" here.

1057–75 The impediments to Penance, the sixth major topic announced at X.83. For parallels in Pennaforte, see Petersen, Sources, 31–34.

1068 **passen as a shadwe:** An image with a strong biblical background (Job 14.2; 8.9; etc.), but **on the wal** seems to be Chaucer's addition; cf. MerT IV.1315n.

1069 Gregory, Morals 34.19.36 (PL 76:738).

1073 **Agayns the seconde wanhope:** A manifest slip. Chaucer speaks of the second cause (thinking that he has sinned *so ofte*, 1071) of the first kind of despair.

1076–80 The topic of **the fruyt of penaunce** was neither announced at X.83 nor treated by Pennaforte. Chaucer loosely uses material from the conventional Joys of Heaven (X.1076–79) and perhaps the beatitudes (1080). The former appear often at the end of religious manuals, such as Bonaventure's Breviloquium, The Pricke of Conscience, or Fasciculus morum. The beatitudes are treated last in Peraldus's S. virtutum.

Chaucer's Retractation

This final section, usually referred to as Chaucer's Retractation or Retraction (cf. X.1085), appears in this position in practically all manuscripts that contain The Parson's Tale complete (M-R 2:471–72). Chaucer's authorship has often been questioned; it is supported by the manuscript evidence and by Thomas Gascoigne's report of Chaucer's death-bed repentance (between 1434 and 1457; reproduced and discussed by Wurtele, Viator 11, 1980, 335–59), though Gascoigne's report could, of course, have been derived from the Retraction itself. Such repentance is not without precedent; Augustine, Bede, Giraldus Cambrensis, Jean de Meun, Sir Lewis Clifford, and others down to the time of Tolstoy experienced similar conversions (Kittredge, MP 1, 1903–4, 12–13; Tatlock, PMLA 28, 1913, 521–29). The alternatives to reading the Retraction as an expression of the poet's personal remorse are: either to see it as an application to the poet-narrator of the Parson's call to penitence, the concluding step in a poem on the theme of the pilgrimage of life (see introductory note to Fragment X),

The explanatory notes to Chaucer's Retractation were written by Siegfried Wenzel.

or to see it as Chaucer's utilization of the *retractatio* as a literary convention that includes establishing a canon of his authentic works (see Sayce, MAE 40, 1971, 230–48). Convenient surveys of critical opinions are James D. Gordon, in Sts. in Hon. of Baugh, 81–96; and Wurtele, Viator 11:335–59.

1081 **Now preye I:** If the title or rubric *Heere taketh the makere of this book his leve* is authentic (see Textual Notes), the speaker here is clearly Chaucer the poet, as he is in lines 1085–89. Otherwise, 1081–84 and 1090 (or 1091)–92 can be read as spoken by the Parson and would thus form the expected conventional conclusion to his treatise on penance, which is lacking at 1079. In this case, 1085–90 have to be an insertion into the original form of The Parson's Tale, made either by Chaucer or someone else. Such a reading has been accepted by a number of critics from Tyrwhitt (3:277) to Eliason (Lang. of Ch, 209–10) and Wurtele (Viator 11:431–43).

this litel tretys: The phrase, also used in ProMel VII.957 and 963, is normally taken to refer to The Parson's Tale, primarily because of the meaning of *tretys;* cf. Work, MLN 47, 1932, 257–59; Clark, ChR 6, 1971, 152–56; and Wurtele, Viator 11:340–41. But critics who read the *Tales* as a work of moral instruction take the phrase to refer to the entire poem; see esp. Robertson, Pref to Ch, 268–69, for parallels. Cf. ProMel VII.943–52n.

1083 Romans 15.4; also quoted in NPT VII.3441–42.

1086 **book of the XXV. Ladies:** Evidently LGW. "XXV" may be a misreading for "XIX"; see Hammond, MLN 48, 1933, 514–16.

1087 **book of the Leoun:** Unknown and presumably lost. It could have been a redaction of Machaut's Dit dou Lyon (Langhans, Anglia 52, 1928, 113–22) or of Deschamps's Dit du Lyon (Brusendorff, Ch Trad, 429–30), perhaps freely adapted as a compliment to Prince Lionel on the occasion of his marriage (Dear, MAE 7, 1938, 105–12). Neither conjecture can be proven.

1092 *Qui cum Patre . . . Amen:* The conventional ending (which reads *per omnia saecula saeculorum*) of liturgical prayers and sermons.

Rubric compiled: The medieval concept of *compilatio* and notions of authorship are discussed by Parkes, 115–41, in Med. Learning and Lit. Essays Pres. to Hunt, ed. Alexander and Gibson, 1976.

Though in none of the manuscripts do the copyists assign *The Book of the Duchess* to Chaucer, his authorship has never been questioned. He lists it among his works as "the Deeth of Blaunche the Duchesse" in the Prologue to *The Legend of Good Women* (418, G 406) and as "the book of the Duchesse" in his Retraction (Tales X.1086). Chaucer's authorship is also attested in Lydgate's *Fall of Princes* (bk. 1, Pro 304–5). In the Introduction to the Man of Law's Tale (II.57) we are told that in his youth Chaucer wrote of Ceys and Alcione; while this could refer to another (unknown) work of Chaucer's, the likelihood is that the reference is to BD 62–220.

The Fairfax MS has a note, evidently in the hand of John Stowe, stating that Chaucer wrote the poem at the request of the Duke of Lancaster "pitiously complaynynge the deathe of the sayd dutchess blanche" (see 905 below, and John Norton-Smith's intro. to the facsimile of the Fairfax MS, 1979). For internal evidence supporting a dedication to Gaunt and Blanche, see BD 1318–19 and the note below on 1314–29, though there is an apparent discrepancy with regard to Gaunt's age at the time of Blanche's death (445 below). For further information on the historical context, see Sydney Armitage-Smith, John of Gaunt, 1904, especially 74–78 (death of Blanche and her memorial services) and 420 (Gaunt's will, where, in the first clause, he directs that he be interred in St. Paul's Cathedral "juxte ma treschere jadys compaigne Blanch illeoq's enterre," next to my beloved former wife Blanche where she is buried).

For the old theory that the narrator-persona contains autobiographical details of a hopeless love affair, see Furnivall, Trial Forewords, 35–36; Bernhard ten Brink, Geschichte der engl. Litt. vol. 2, bk. 4, 1893, 49–50; and note 30–43 below; on such theories see George Kane, Autobiographical Fallacy in Ch and Langland, 1965.

The Book of the Duchess was strongly influenced by French poetry, notably *Le roman de la rose* and the works of Froissart and Machaut. A number of passages are closely translated, and the form of *The Book of the Duchess* owes much to Machaut's *Jugement dou Roy de Behaingne,* where the narrator overhears the stories of bereaved or forsaken lovers. The notes indicate these source-passages, as well as debts to Ovid, Statius, and others. See further, Kitchel, Vassar Med. Studies, 1923, 217–31; Rosenthal, MLN 48, 1933, 511–14; Braddy, MLN 52, 1937, 487–91; Max Lange, Untersuchungen über Ch's BD, 1883; Sypherd, MLN 24, 1909, 46–47; Windeatt, Ch's Dream Poetry. For additional discussions of the dream-vision tradition, see W. O. Sypherd, Studies in Ch's HF, 1907, and n. 291–343 below.

An outline account of the critical history of the poem by D. W. Robertson, Jr., is in Comp. to Ch, 403–13. Recent criticism has included interpretations of the poem along exegetical, allegorical lines (see references to Huppé and Robertson in 30–43, 309–10, 388–97, 1314–29 below). James Winny, Ch's Dream-Poems, 1973, also puts forward some theories of interpretation. Some notable studies not mentioned in the notes are: *On rhetoric:*

The explanatory notes to *The Book of the Duchess* were written by Colin Wilcockson.

Harrison, PMLA 49, 1934, 428–42; Manly, Brit. Acad., 1926, 95–113. *On meter:* Malone, in Ch und seine Zeit, 71–95. *On structure:* Baker, SN 30, 1958, 17–26; Crampton, JEGP 62, 1963, 486–500; Ebel, CE 29, 1967, 197–206. *On literary background:* Wimsatt, Ch and Fr Poets; Boitani, Eng. Med. Narrative, 140–49. *Edition:* Helen Phillips, ed., Ch: The BD, 1982.

1–15 Closely modeled on Froissart, Paradys d'amours, 1–12. Kittredge (ESt 26, 1899, 321–36) demonstrated that BD was written after Paradys. D. S. Brewer (in Ch and Chaucerians, 2–8) analyzes both passages, concluding that though Chaucer's subject-matter is from Froissart, the style is that of the native rhyming romances. Barbara Nolan (in New Perspectives, 203–22) argues that, through the Narrator, Chaucer transformed the style of his French exemplars, freeing himself from the demands of familiar mythologies "by his refusal to embrace authoritative stances in relation to his audience, matter, and meaning." Severs (MS 25, 1963, 355–62) draws attention to similarities in Machaut, Dit dou vergier, and in the anonymous Songe vert (ed. Constans, Romania 33, 490–539).

Some of Chaucer's knowledge of dreams came from glosses on the common school text, Cato's Distichs; see Hazelton, Spec 35, 1960, 369. For further references see HF 1–52n. For discussion of the Narrator's state of mind and its similarity to that described by Petrus de Abano as a likely prelude to a "somnium animale," see Clemen, Ch's Early Poetry, 26; Curry, Ch and Science, 233–37; Kittredge, Ch and his Poetry, 58–60. The "somnium animale" grows out of "much worry of the waking mind" (Petrus de Abano). Gardner (Lang. and Style 2, 1969, 143–71) argues that the dream is open to both a sexual and a religious interpretation: on one level a "somnium animale," on the other a "somnium coeleste." A. C. Spearing (Med. Dream Poetry, 55–62) considers that the dream could be classified as a "somnium naturale," "animale," or "coeleste." (The "somnium naturale" "originates in the dominion of bodily complexions and humors"; the "somnium coeleste" derives "from the impressions made by celestial minds or intelligences which are said to direct the heavenly bodies in their courses" tr. from Petrus de Abano, Liber conciliator differentiarum philosophorum precipueque medicorum appelatus, 1472, dif. 157 fol. 208r).

14 **ymagynacioun:** Douglas Kelly (Med. Imagination, 1978, 57) suggests that the confused state of mind here described as *sorwful ymagynacioun* derives ultimately from Macrobius's classification of dreams: the narrator's *fantasies* (28) correspond to Macrobius's "visum," in which fantastic images appear between waking and sleeping and have no prophetic significance (Macrobius, Commentarii in somnium Scipionis 1.3.3.).

16–21 There are many similarities here to the beginning of Machaut's first Complainte (Poésies lyriques, ed. Chichemaref 1:241). See Kittredge, PMLA 30, 1915, 1–24.

23 **melancolye:** Paradys d'amours, 7, refers to this condition; so, too, Machaut, Jugement dou Roy de Navarre (Oeuvres 1:109–12), where there are further parallels to BD 23–29. See Kittredge, PMLA 30:2–4. Cf.

445 below. On the melancholic humor, see GP I.333n. and 420n.

30–43   The eight-year sickness and the physician of these lines have been the subject of considerable debate. There has been much critical concern about whether Chaucer is writing autobiography, spiritual allegory, or simply repeating the common convention of the love-sick poet and unresponsive mistress. The eight-year sickness has been attributed to Chaucer's supposedly unhappy married life (Frederick G. Fleay, Guide to Ch and Spenser, 1877, 36–37) or to some bereavement (Lumiansky, TSE 9, 1959, 5–17; also see Condren, as cited in 1314–29 below). The "physician" has been identified as Joan of Kent, mother of Richard II, who, the critic supposes, was Chaucer's patron (Galway, MLN 60, 1945, 431–39); as sleep, which could assuage melancholy (Hill, ChR 9, 1974, 35–50); as God (Severs, PQ 43, 1964, 27–39); and as Christ (Huppé and Robertson, Fruyt and Chaf, 32–34; cf. Cherniss in 544 below); Gardner (Lang. and Style 2:148–49) argues that all these various interpretations are simultaneously present. However, the situation and the sentiments are conventional in French poetry of the period, and Sypherd (MLN 20, 1905, 240–43) argues for the love/unresponsive mistress motif and suggests that the eight-year period is simply to give the appearance of verisimilitude; see also Loomis (MLN 59, 1944, 178–80) and the "seven or eight years" of love-devotion in BD 759–804 (see n.). With *physicien,* cf. BD 571 and 920; Tr 2.1065–66; and Gower, Confessio amantis 8.3092.

44–45   Cf. Paradys d'amours, 13–14, "n'a pas lonc terme/Que de dormir oi voloir ferme" (it was not long ago that I deeply desired to sleep). For an argument that reading a book was not a regular convention of love visions until after Chaucer, see Stearns, MLN 57, 1942, 28–31. Spearing, Med. Dream Poetry, 58, taking the dream as a "somnium animale" (which reflects the experience of waking life), notes that Chaucer is innovative in making that experience the reading of a book. For discussion of medieval theory of the therapeutic powers of literature (and hence, by extension, of the consolatory potential of BD for Gaunt), see Glending Olson, Lit. as Recreation, 1982, 85–89.

48   A romaunce: Ovid, Met. 11.410–749. Wimsatt (MAE 36, 1967, 231–41) notes the similarity of treatment of the Ceyx story in Machaut's Dit de la fonteinne amoreuse (hereafter Font. amor.), 543–698. Ovid's description of the storm is reduced drastically in BD (omitted in Font. amor.), and only brief mention is made (Font. amor.) or there is total omission (BD) of the metamorphosis into sea-birds (cf. 215 below). Wimsatt also notes that Chaucer probably used the Ovide moralisé, as did Machaut, as well as Ovid's original work; Minnis (MAE 48, 1979, 254–57) supports this in remarking that *romaunce* usually referred to a work in French, not Latin.

56   lawe of kinde: Probably implies the gentle dealings between people in the unbrutalized Golden Age. (See Fyler, Ch and Ovid, 65–81.)

62–220   Many critics regard the Ceyx and Alcione story as a tactful encouragement to Gaunt to come to terms with Blanche's death. The mirror-image (death of a husband) politely distances the hint. See, for example, Spearing, Med. Dream Poetry, 53–58.

68   To tellen shortly: A common formula in Chaucer: e.g., GP I.843; KnT I.1000; cf. KnT I.875–88n. But the

reference could be to Chaucer's abbreviations of Ovid's tale; see 48 above. In the Metamorphoses, the storm and shipwreck occupy 77 lines.

70   gan to rise: Although *gan* is from OE *onginnan* (= to begin), the use of the verb in the preterite in ME is often for dramatic, intensive purpose and does not necessarily imply the commencement of an action. See Mustanoja, ME Syntax, 610–15, especially 613, where he notes, "In his earlier poems written under strong French influence, like BD, Chaucer makes sparing use of periphrastic *gan* . . . [in Chaucer] the *gan-* periphrasis is particularly used when the action takes place unexpectedly or in haste." Cf. BD 193, 536, etc.

73   telles: The third person singular present indicative in *-es* (properly of Northern or West Midland dialect) occurs very rarely in Chaucer. Here and in line 257 it is clearly established by the rhyme. On such forms, see Burnley, Guide to Ch's Language, 127. Cf. RvT I.4022n.

108–17   Alcione uses both the singular and the plural pronouns to Juno. It was common to use *thou* in prayers to a deity (see KnT I.2221–2260, where the singular is used), though the plural is also used (cf. Sir Gawain and the Green Knight, 756). In Font. amor., Alcione addresses Juno using the singular pronoun. See Language and Versification, p. xxxix.

137–87   The peremptory tone of the speeches of Juno to the messenger and of the messenger to Morpheus does not appear in Ovid or Machaut. For discussion, see Clemen, Ch's Early Poetry, 104; Lowes, Geoffrey Ch, 96; Muscatine, Ch and Fr Trad., 104. The singular pronoun *thou* emphasizes this tone; see 519 below.

142   For the word order, see Language and Versification, p. xxxviii.

153–65   Though Chaucer borrows from the Ceyx and Alcione stories in Ovid and Machaut (see 48 above), including the account of the messenger's journey to the god of sleep, he also takes some details from Statius, Theb 10.84–99, and 10.121–31, where Iris is sent to the cave of sleep to deliver a command from Juno. See Clogan, Eng. Miscellany 18, 1967, 16, n. 17, and cf. BD 242–69 and n.

154–56   Imitated from Font. amor., 590–92, "Tant se traveille/Que venue est en une grant valee,/De deus grans mons entour environnee" (He put such effort into his journey that he arrived in a large valley completely enclosed by two high mountains).

154   hys: The messenger in Ovid and in Machaut, however, is Iris.

164   under a rokke: Shannon (Ch and Roman Poets, 6–7) argues that this corresponds to a variant reading in some MSS of Met. 11.591, "sub rupe" instead of "sub nube." However, Wimsatt (MAE, 36:231–41) agrees with Wise (Infl. of Statius, 41) that the phrase derives from Statius, Theb. 10.86–87, "Subterque cavis grave rupius antrum/it vacuum in montem" (And under the hollow rocks the deep cave runs into the empty mountain); even though Chaucer would have understood the Latin, "cavis grave" may have suggested the rhyme of BD 163–64, and Wimsatt doubts whether Ovidian MSS available to Chaucer contained "rupe" (for "nube").

167   Eclympasteyr: The name occurs only here and in Froissart's Paradys d'amours, 28, where he is a son of the "noble dieu dormant." "The source of the name is uncertain. Derivation has been suggested from Icelon plastera (πλαστήρ), or from Icelon and Phobetora (corrupted into Pastora) which occur in Met. 11.640" (Robinson). Cartier (Revue de la littérature comparée 38, 1964, 18–34) discusses the many attempts to account for the name. Froissart, he shows, invented names by twisting them or forming anagrams. The probable derivation, he suggests, is "Enclin + postere" = "supine," thence "Lazy-bones."

171   helle-pit: Spencer (Spec 2, 1927, 177–200, esp. 180–81) notes that the "pit" of hell is a medieval rather than a classical concept. In Met. 11.594–96 Ovid says that the sun never enters and that there is "doubtful light"; Thebaid, 10.84, speaks of "nebulosa cubilia noctis," (cloudy couches of the night). (See references to Ovid and Statius in 48 and 153–65 above.)

174   Machaut, Font. amor., 607, (describing the god of sleep): "ses mentons a sa poitrine touche," (his chin touches his chest). Met. 11.619–20 has "Knocking his breast with his nodding chin."

184   oon ye: The comedy derives from Font. amor., 632, where the god of sleep "Un petiot ouvri l'un de ses yeus" (opened one of his eyes a little). Ovid, 619, has "oculos" (eyes).

189–90   As I have told yow: A commonplace formula. (Cf., for example, FranT V.1465–66, 1593–94; PhyT VI.229–30; GP I.849; and in RR 7243–45 we find, "And I told him, just as you have heard—there is no purpose in repeating it to you.")

201–5   Wimsatt (MAE 36:237–38) suggests that the speech of Ceyx to Alcione is imitated from Aeneid 2.776–84, where Creusa appears to Aeneas as a ghost and "very much as if in a dream" ("simillima somno," 794). Chaucer tells the story in HF 174–92.

202–10   your sorwful lyf: For the use of the plural pronoun, see 108–17 above and 519 below.

215   But what she sayede more: Chaucer omits the rest of the story, including the metamorphosis into seabirds. Delasanta (PMLA 84, 1969, 245–51, esp. 249) suggests that though a hint of afterlife reunion is inherent, the Narrator has at this point insufficient spiritual maturity to see anything but death at the end of man's existence. Shannon (Ch and Roman Poets, 10) commends Chaucer's sound taste in omitting an "irrelevant device of pagan mythology." Gower, Conf. aman. 4.3088–123, includes the metamorphosis. Chaucer ordinarily omits the metamorphosis in stories adapted from Ovid (e.g., the legend of Philomela in LGW).

222–23   Cf. Paradys d'amours, 19–22, where the narrator says that he would still be sleepless had he not sacrificed a gold ring to Juno; cf. BD 243.

242–69   Chaucer is conflating Font. amor., 807–10, where the poet promises the god a hat and a feather bed, with Paradys d'amour, 15–18, where the poet prays to Morpheus, Juno and Oleus. Kittredge (PMLA 30:2) suggests that Chaucer "shied at Oleus": hence *som wight elles, I ne roghte who.* "Oleus" appears nowhere else. Perhaps the confusion is with Aeolus. In Met. 11.444, 573, Alcione is referred to as the "daughter of Aeolus" (god of the winds), and in 747–48, after the metamorphosis of Ceyx and Alcione into seabirds, Aeolus imprisons the winds so that their chicks may be safe. In Statius, Theb. 10.55–60, a beautiful cloth is offered to Juno shortly before the visit of Iris to the cave of sleep. Cf. BD 153–65 and n.

255   cloth of Reynes: A kind of linen made at Rennes, in Brittany. Skeat (1:469–70) cites medieval examples of sheets and pillow cases made of Rennes linen. It was evidently fine cloth. Skelton, Complete English Poems, ed. Scattergood, 1983, 254 (Collyn Clout, 314) uses the phrase "fyne raynes" in a passage about worldly luxury.

265–66   Morpheus . . . moo feës thus: For the rhyme, see 309–10 below.

272–75   Cf. Paradys d'amour, 14 (see note 44–45 above), and 30–31, where the narrator says he falls asleep he knows not how.

280   Joseph: For his interpretation of the Pharaoh's dream, see Gen. 41.

282   The kynges metynge Pharao: "The dream of king Pharaoh" (see Gen. 41). For the structure, see BD 142 and n.

284   Macrobeus: The reference to Macrobius is perhaps secondhand and due to similar citation in RR 7–10 (Rom 7–10). On the Somnium Scipionis, which was written by Cicero and expanded with a commentary by Macrobius, see PF 31n., and notes 1–15 and 14 above.

286   kyng Scipioun: Scipio was not a king; the error is due to RR (see 284 above and HF 916–18n.).

291–343   The description of May is largely indebted to the Roman de la rose, and there is a kind of acknowledgement of this fact in BD 332–34. For particular resemblances, cf. BD 291–92 with RR 45–47, 88 (Rom 49–51, 94); 304–5 with RR 705, 484–85 (Rom 717, 496–97); 306–8 with RR 667–68 (Rom 675–76); 309–11 with RR 487–92 (Rom 499–501); 318 with RR 74–102 (Rom 78–108); 331–32 with RR 20831–32; 339–43 with RR 124–25 (Rom 130–31), though in this case the Dit dou Roy de Behaingne, 13–14, is closer where the conventional May morning is described: "Et li jours fu attemprez par mesure,/Biaus, clers, luisans, nès et purs, sans froidure" (And the day was perfectly temperate, beautiful, clear, bright, fine and cloudless, without chill). For discussions of the convention see, for example, Bennett, PF, ch. 2; Lewis, Allegory of Love, ch. 3; Muscatine, Ch and Fr Trad., 15–17.

293   al naked: At 125 is another reference to the common custom in the Middle Ages of sleeping naked. For references to night attire see Tr 3.738, 1099, 1372, 4.92–96.

304   som: Probably singular, as often elsewhere in this construction, and referring back to 301 *everych,* cf. KnT I.3031–32. See Mustanoja, ME Syntax, 259–63.

309–10   entewnes: Usually taken as a noun, "tunes." Emerson suggests (PQ 2, 1923, 81–96, esp. 81–82) that it is the Northern form of the present tense of the verb, third person singular, substituted for the preterite in rhyme. For other Northern forms, see BD 73, 257. Kökeritz (PMLA 69, 1954, 937–52) discusses the influence on Chaucer of French word-play: a "punning or jingling effect" common in the French poets is seen here, and in 265–66 where, Kökeritz suggests, Robinson's diaeresis in *feës* is probably unwarranted. (The diaeresis is, however, metrically desirable, and the "jingling" remains.) See also BD 813–14, *pervers . . . clepe hir wers.* For exegetical interpretations of BD as a religious allegory and holding that the *toun of Tewnes* suggests "tune of tunes" (i.e., Song of Songs) and also "Town of Towns" (i.e., the New Jerusalem), see Huppé and Robertson, Fruyt and Chaf, ch. 2, esp. 46–47; so also Gardner, Lang. and Style, 2:153. Robinson translates, with comment: " 'Certainly, even to gain the town of Tunis, I would not have given up hearing them sing.' The choice of Tunis was probably due to the rime.''

326–31 the story of Troy: Chaucer refers to the whole history of Troy as told by either Benoît de Sainte Maure or Guido della Colonne, probably the former, rather than the story of the siege and fall of the city as told by Homer and Virgil or as summarized in RR, which does not associate Medea with the Troy story. See 1117–23 below and introductory note to *Troilus*. See *Troilus* for the characters named (**Lamedon,** Laomedon, is there called Lameadoun, Tr 4.124), with the exception of **Medea** and **Jason,** for which see LGW 1580–1679.

333–34 bothe text and glose: Perhaps simply a formula meaning ''the whole story.'' Possibly Chaucer had in mind some manuscript in which both text and commentary were illustrated by pictures, though no such MS of RR is known. The search for rhyme might account for ''glose/Rose'' (cf. LGW, F 328–29). But the scribal *explicit* to one MS may provide a clue: ''Cy gist le Romant de la Rose,/Ou tout l'Art d'Amours se repose,/La fleur des beaulx bien dire l'ose,/Qui bien y entend texte et glose.'' (Ernest Langlois, Les MSS du RR, 1910, 211.) This MS contains miniatures (but no commentary on the text). It would suit the idea of a mural decoration if *glose* here meant ''illustrations'' (the *significacio* sometimes of the allegory) and *text* referred to brief descriptions of these illuminations which commonly appear in the MSS, either above or below the pictures. But the suggestion is tentative, as *glose* normally means ''textual commentary'' (MED s.v. *glose* n.).

344–86 The accuracy of Chaucer's hunting terminology is attested by Emerson, RomR 13, 1922, 115–50. Lowes, (PMLA 19, 1904, 648 n. 1) compares the huntsmen of the God of love in Paradys d'amours, 916–64. For possible word-play on ''hart/heart'' from BD 351–1313, see Kökeritz, PMLA, 69:951; and Marcelle Thiébaux, Stag of Love, 1974, especially 116–17 and n. 35. Baum (PMLA 71, 1956, 225–46, esp. 239) suggests that the hart represents Blanche; Huppé and Robertson, Fruyt and Chaf, 49–92, believe the Black Knight of *The Book of the Duchess* represents the Narrator's alter ego, whose heart must be hunted until it recognizes that the loss of the virtuous Blanche must be seen ''not as the loss of a gift of Fortune, but as an inspiration''; Grennen (MLQ 25, 1964, 131–39) discusses medical treatises on heart diseases, and suggests that the Dreamer's offers in lines 553 and 556 are in accordance with the comforting recommended in the treatment; Shoaf (JEGP 78, 1979, 313–24) draws attention to some confessional literature where huntsman = ''confessor,'' and hart = ''penitential self.'' He suggests that specific parallels on the theme in Le livre de seyntz medicines by Blanche's father might honor his memory and also that of his daughter.

346 horn: The detail, and several others, may have been suggested by a passage in Machaut, Roy de Navarre, where the passing of the outbreak of the plague was celebrated by the playing outside the poet's window of ''Cornemuses, trompes, naquaires,/Et d'instrumens plus de set paires'' (Bagpipes, horns, drums,/And more than seven pairs of instruments) (463–64); Guillaume, delighted, mounted his horse (488, cf. BD 356–57) and went swiftly to the fields to hunt with a hound (491, 520; cf. BD 359, 362). Spearing (Med. Dream Poetry, 58–59) sees the horn blown by Juno's messenger (BD 182) and the horns blown by the huntsmen as examples of the

reflection in his subsequent dream of the book the Narrator had read earlier. See 44–45 above.

351 with strengthe: Kill in regular chase with horses and hounds (Fr. ''à force,'' see Emerson, RomR, 13: 117).

353 embosed: MED (s.v. *embosen* v.) interprets ''exhausted from being hunted'' (MED has one other reference only, where this meaning seems confirmed). So also Emerson, RomR, 13:117. Baugh (Language 37, 1961, 539–41) argues for ''to go to or to hide in the woods'' (see OED s.v. *enboss* v.[2]).

357–58 Took my hors: The inconsequentialities of riding a horse from a bedroom here, the lack of surprise on hearing about Octavian (368), the unremarked disappearance of the puppy encountered at 389, and so on, may be evidence that Chaucer is accurately describing dream-psychology (see, for example, Kittredge, Ch and His Poetry, 68–71; Clemen, Ch's Early Poetry, 41; Lowes, Art of Ch, 122–23; Spearing, Med. Dream Poetry, 63). Muscatine (Ch and Fr Trad., 102) disagrees, considering that incoherence of plot sequence is characteristic of narrative of this kind.

365 oon, ladde a lymere: ''One who was leading a hound on a leash.'' This construction of a relative clause without a subject pronoun first appears in the later fourteenth century. See Mustanoja (ME Syntax, 204–5), who notes that it is rarer in Chaucer's prose than in his verse, which implies that he uses it for metrical purposes.

368 Octovyen: The original name of Augustus Caesar, adopted son of Julius Caesar (63 B.C.–14 A.D.). Skeat suggests that there may be an oblique compliment to Edward III (see reference to *this king* at 1314); Condren (ChR 5, 1971, 195–212, esp. 210) also favors the Octovyen/Edward III equation. Carson (AnM 8, 1967, 46–58) suggests that Chaucer had in mind the story, in the Welsh Mabinogion, of Eudav, who is king of the Other World, and is found carving chess pieces. (In the Welsh Dingestow Brut, a translation of Geoffrey of Monmouth's Historia regum Britanniae, ''Octavian'' is rendered ''Eudav.'') For the medieval romance of Octavian, who is befriended by a lion and has many adventures, see Laura A. Hibbard, Med. Romance in Engl., 1924, 267–73; Lillian H. Hornstein, in Manual of ME 1:127–29. Two (probably fourteenth-century) English versions exist. In Behaingne, 421, a lover says, ''If I had all of Octavian's wealth''; this may have caught Chaucer's eye.

370 in good tyme: Possibly a formula to avert evil; cf. CYT VIII.1048n.

386 forloyn: See Emerson, RomR 13:130–32.

387 I was go walked: ''The construction of *walked* appears to correspond to that of the past participle in German (*kam gelaufen,* etc.). But there may be involved a confusion with nouns in -ed, earlier -eth, -ath. See the note in *a-blakeberyed,* Pard. Prol, VI, 406'' (Robinson). But Mustanoja (ME Syntax, 558 and 582) considers it more likely that the construction exemplifies a semantic weakening of *go,* and is roughly equivalent to ''was walked'' (*walked* and auxiliary *is* occurs in KnT I.2368). See also SumT III.1778.

389–96 The lines were suggested by Machaut's Behaingne, 1204–15 (a lady's little dog runs barking to Guillaume, thus revealing that he has accidently overheard sad accounts of love; with which situation cf. BD 443–86), but more particularly by a passage about a lion, who is compared with a little dog and ''joined his ears'' when patted, in Machaut's Dit dou lyon, 325–31 (see Kittredge, PMLA 30:7). Steadman (N&Q 201, 1956, 374–75) draws attention to dogs representing fidelity in medieval literature and, specifically, marital fidelity on tombs; thus the **whelp** may suggest Chaucer's fidelity to Blanche and Gaunt and the fidelity between the married couple; Rowland (NM 66, 1965, 148–60) points out that Chaucer never bestows commendatory adjectives on dogs, that *whelp* does not necessarily denote smallness (cp. NPT VII.2932), and she finds a possible association with ghostly huntsmen or snarling emissaries of hell; Huppé and Robertson (Fruyt and Chaf, 53–55, 97) refer to hunt symbolism where hounds = "preachers," and the whelp is here taken as symbolic of the elucidation of the cares of the soul; Friedman (ChR 3, 1969, 145–62) concludes that the existence of such various literary treatment of dogs in the Middle Ages means that the particular context must be taken into account, and that, here, traditional roles of leading, healing, and wisdom are relevant. Many agree, however, with Kittredge's view (PMLA 30:7) that we have here simply a "charming picture of the lost puppy."

402–33 For both Flora and Zephirus . . . : Probably modeled on RR 8411–30, where Flora and Zephirus are associated and where earth with its flowers is seen to be striving to outdo the sky in "stars." See ProLGW F 171; cf. BD 410–15 with RR 53–66: "La terre . . . oblie la povreté/Ou ele a tot l'iver esté" (The earth . . . forgets the poverty/Which it has endured throughout the winter) and see also Rom 59–62 and ProLGW F 125–26; cf. 416–33 with RR 1361–82 (Rom 1391–1403) where the trees in the idyllic "hortus inclusus" are evenly spaced, providing shade where deer roam and there are many squirrels; cf. also RR 12790–96.

408 swiche seven: On the idiom, see Klaeber, MLN 17, 1902, 323, and Mustanoja, ME Syntax, 309.

410–15 Cf. Rom 57–62, LGW 125–29 and n.

435–42 That thogh Argus, the noble countour . . . : More commonly called Algus, which is in turn an Old French adaptation of the Arabic surname Al-Khwārizmī (native of Khwārizm) of the ninth-century mathematician Abū 'Abdallāh Muhammad ibn Mūsā. See MilT I.3210n.

figures ten: Arabic numerals and the decimal system were introduced into Europe through translations of this mathematician's works. Chaucer may well have had in mind RR 12790–96, where the La Vieille tells Bel Acueil (Fair Welcome) that even Algus with his ten figures could not reckon up the number of squabbles that arose among her suitors. The matter is different, the phraseology similar.

438 ken: "Kin, mankind. The form *ken* (riming with *ten*) is properly Kentish" (Robinson). On such forms, see Burnley, Ch's Language, 128–29, and cf. Tr 1.229n.

443–617 There are many close paraphrases of Machaut in this passage (Kittredge, MP 7, 1910, 465–83, especially 465–71; and Kittredge, PMLA 30:7–9). Chaucer draws chiefly on Behaingne. BD 475–86 has similarities to Machaut's third Motet, 475–86, and to Behaingne, 193–200. In Behaingne 208–28, the lady faints after her lament (with which cf. BD 487–99).

445 a man in blak: It is usually agreed that the Knight represents Gaunt, but the age discrepancy poses a difficulty: Gaunt was twenty-nine at Blanche's death (if she died in 1369); the Knight is twenty-four (see 455). (For

a suggestion that Gaunt was twenty-eight when Blanche died, see reference to Palmer in 1314–29 below.) Viktor Langhans (Untersuchungen zu Ch, 1918, 280–302) argues against the Knight/Gaunt identification on grounds of the discrepancy in age. Skeat (1:476) considers it a mere slip on Chaucer's part, though he also quotes a Mr. Brock's suggestion that xxiiij could be a scribal error for xxviiij and notes a similar scribal confusion in IntrMLT II.5 (see textual note). Schoenbaum (MLN 68, 1953, 121–22) suggests that the apparent discrepancy results from Chaucer's universalizing the theme of loss: though Blanche's death probably provided the impulse to write the elegy, the details are not limited to a specific historical context, and twenty-nine was not considered young (cf. BD 454). Nault (MLN 71, 1956, 319–21) quotes the nearly contemporary poem, Parlement of the Thre Ages, where thirty is described as young; Nault agrees with the scribal error theory, though extant MSS of *The Book of the Duchess* have *foure and twenty,* not xxiiij. Fisher (550) suggests that the underestimation of age might have been intended as a compliment. That the melancholy Narrator should dream of a mourning figure in black is in accord with medieval medical theory: Petrus de Abano (in Liber conciliator, dif. 157, fol. 208r) remarks that the melancholy man is likely to dream "of black things that strike terror into us, weeping and wailing, accidents, places of the dead." Cf. notes 1–12 and 23 above, and see NPT VII.2933–36 and n.

464 The compleynte, which begins at 475, has eleven lines. There is no fixed form for the "complaint" (see p. 632). However, the rhyme-scheme appears to be faulty, *a a b b a c c d c c d*. All MSS agree, though Thynne (ed. 1532) adds a line after 479 and rearranges the lines. Most modern editors omit Thynne's line, but number as if the line were present. Dickerson (Papers of Bibliograph. Soc. America 66, 1972, 51–54) argues for reinstatement of Thynne's line 480. Blake (ES 62, 1981, 237–48) sees no conclusive authority for Thynne's line: none of the scribes leaves a space for later completion and Thynne's 480 adds little to the sense of the *compleynte.* Perhaps on the "lectio difficilior" principle, the eleven-line *compleynte* should stand. See further, textual note to BD 480; cf. also 1155–57 below. In Fonteinne amoureuse, Machaut overhears his patron reciting a complaint. The lord subsequently takes the poet into his confidence and asks him to write a love poem. Machaut delivers the poem that the lord had composed aloud and confesses its origin. His patron is amazed and delighted.

479 That the Dreamer hears that the lady is dead, yet is apparently ignorant of the fact when he later questions the Black Knight has been the cause of much debate. Kittredge (Ch and His Poetry, esp. 52–53) suggests that the Dreamer understands that the lady is dead, but feigns ignorance so that the Knight may disburden himself by opening his heart. Lawlor (Spec 31, 1956, 626–48) takes this further: the Dreamer understands, but needs to know the precise nature of the love between the Knight and the lady as in the *débat* poems on which *The Book of the Duchess* is modeled (Machaut's Behaingne and Navarre); the consolation lies in the Knight's recognition that his grief is over the removal by death of a faithful love fulfilled, not unfulfilled through infidelity. For discussion of the similarity of consolatory functions of the (often comic) dreamer-narrator in BD and Behaingne, see Calin, A Poet at the Fountain, 1974, 48–50. However, French (JEGP, 61, 1957, 231–41) maintains that love-laments were conventional exercises not intended to be taken literally, and thus the Dreamer is not certain that the Knight is describing an actual occurrence. Diekstra (ES 62, 1981, 215–36) argues that Chaucer juxtaposes comedy and courtly conventions, particularly in the exchanges between the Dreamer and Black Knight, as a testing of the conventions, in the tradition of Jean de Meun in RR; but Chaucer leaves untouched the praise of Blanche and the technique does not invalidate elegiac elements. Kreuzer (PMLA 66, 1951, 543–47) would distinguish the Narrator of the opening lines from the Dreamer-persona. Zimbardo (in ChR 18, 1984, 329–46) suggests that the Black Knight/Dreamer relationship is akin to the traditional relationship of King and Fool: the Dreamer-Fool educates the Knight so that he may question the boundaries of philosophy and of art.

502–62 Behaingne, 56–109, has many similarities: the young man salutes the lady who is so absorbed in her grief that she does not observe him; there are mutual apologies and he begs her to tell the cause of her sorrow. Some phrases that read awkwardly in the Chaucer passage may have been influenced by the French constructions in the Behaingne: BD 504 **argued with his owne thoght** corresponds to Beh. 61, "la dame que pensée argua" (the lady, exercised by her contemplation). Similarly, BD 509–10 is evidently modeled on Beh. 70–71, "Certes, sire, pas ne vous entendi/Pour mon penser qui le me deffendi" (Indeed, sir, I did not hear you/Because of my preoccupation which prevented me from so doing). BD 509–10 apparently means, "Thus, because of his sorrow and unhappy contemplation, he was in such a mental state that he did not hear me at all." Perhaps, if the MS he used had the abbreviation *pr* at this point, Chaucer incorrectly assumed it to represent *par* (hence his translation *throgh*) instead of *pour* (Mod. Fr. *à cause de*).

512 Pan . . . god of kynde: The idea may have come to Chaucer from Servius, Comentarii in Aeneidem, ed. Georg Thilo and Hermann Hagen, 1884, 2:99: ". . . quod graece τὸ πᾶν dicitur, id est omne quod est" (which is called "*to pān*" in Greek, that is everything which is); and more particularly Servius, In Vergilii Bucolicon librum commentarius, ed. Thilo and Hagen, 1887, 3:23: "Pan . . . totius naturae deus" (Pan . . . the god of all nature). Similarly, Isidore, Etym. 8.11.81–83; and Vincent of Beauvais, Spec. doctrinale, 1624, liber 17, ch. 10, fol. 1556: "Pan . . . Quem volunt rerum et totius naturae Deum" (Pan . . . whom they [i.e., the Greeks and the Romans] make the god of everything and of all nature). See also Bode, Scriptores rerum mythicarum 1:40–41, 91, 200; and Wetherbee, Platonism and Poetry in the 12th Century, 1972, 136, n. 25.

519 I prey the: The relative social positions of the Dreamer and the Black Knight are indicated by the consistent use of *thou/thee* (Knight to Dreamer) implying the Dreamer's inferiority and the respectful *ye/you* (Dreamer to Knight) in their forms of address. (See Mustanoja ME Syntax, 126–28, for discussion of ME usage.) Cf. the use of the plural pronoun between persons of high rank in the address of Alcione to Ceyx in BD 202–10, and see also ClT IV.890n.

531 For the idiom see ShipT VII.379n., Tr 2.1025n.

544–57 Elliott (Ch's English, 242–44) draws attention to the large number of tags, oaths, and coordinating

conjunctions in the Dreamer's speech, which convey a sense of his well-intentioned but incoherent outpouring of counsel.

544 The dialogue between the Dreamer and the Black Knight has been considered by some critics to be modeled on Boethius, Consolation of Philosophy. D. W. Robertson, Jr. (in Med. Sts. in Hon. of Urban T. Holmes, Jr., ed. J. Mahoney and J. E. Keller, 1966, Univ. of North Carolina Sts. in Romance Lang. and Lit., 56, 169–95) equates the Black Knight with Boethius, the Dreamer with the Confessor, arguing that the Black Knight, who does not suffer wisely and bravely, cannot represent Gaunt, but rather "a certain aspect of almost everyone in the audience." See also Cherniss (JEGP, 68, 1969, 655–65), who considers that the physician of BD 39 is the "medicine" of philosophy, so described in Cons. A detailed comparison of the structure of Cons. with that of BD is given by Russell A. Peck (in Silent Poetry: Essays in Numerological Analysis, ed. A. Fowler, 1970, 73–115), who sees throughout the passage a Boethian "combination of confession and recollection." Bronson (PMLA 67, 1952, 863–81) suggests that the Black Knight represents both Gaunt and the Dreamer's surrogate. Shoaf (Genre 14, 1981, 163–89) suggests that the dialogue between the Dreamer and the Black Knight echoes the terminology of confessional literature; in particular, he notes the similarity between BD 746–48 and 1126–36 and the references to *circumstantiae peccati* of penitential writings. Shoaf argues that the Black Knight's "sin" in the early part of the dialogue had been "to try to live *in* the past—not *with* it."

569–72 Ovid, Met. 10.40–44, describes the power of **Orpheus**'s music to bring rest to those tortured in the Underworld; cf. Bo 3.m12n. **Dedalus** (Daedelus) represents mechanical skill; his story is told in Met. 8.183–262. For **Ypocras** (Hippocrates) and **Galyen** (Galen) see GP I.429–34n.

571 Cf. 39–40 and note 30–43 above.

583 Identical sentiments are expressed in Behaingne, 196–97.

589 Cesiphus: "Sisiphus, mentioned along with Orpheus in Met. 10.44. But *that lyeth in helle* is applicable rather to Tityus, who is referred to (but not named) by Ovid in the same place. Perhaps Chaucer's memory was confused for the moment" (Robinson). But see Textual Notes (MSS read *Tesiphus/Thesiphus*).

597 Rhetorical *commutatio;* see 817–1040 below.

599–616 Hammerle (in Anglia 66, 1942, 70–72) suggests that this may have been inspired by Chaucer's recollection of the first couplet of Alanus de Insulis, De planctu Naturae, "In lacrymas risus, in fletum gaudia verto; In planctum plausus, in lacrymosa jocos" (I turn my laughter into tears, my joy into weeping; my applause into complaint, my jokes into grieving); Behaingne, 177–87, is also a likely source, which itself may be modeled on the long list of paradoxes describing the state of being in love ("Esperance desesperee," hopeless hope, etc.) of RR 4293–334. With BD 600 cf. Machaut's Remede de fortune, 1198, "en grief plour est mué mon ris" (my laughter is turned to sad weeping). Cf. Tr 5.1375–79.

617–709 Kittredge, PMLA 30:10–14, discusses Chaucer's indebtedness to four Machaut poems in this passage: Remede de fortune (Oeuvres, ed. Hoepffner, lines 918, 1052–56, 1138, 1162, 1167–68); Behaingne (1072–74,

1078–80); the eighth Motet (Poésies lyriques, ed. Chichemaref 2.497–98); and Confort (Poésies lyriques, ed. Chichemaref, 2.415, lines 10–13—where Machaut remarks that there is no element or planet in the firmament that does not give him the gift of weeping, with which cf. BD 693–96). Many phrases are translated word for word by Chaucer. With the scorpion figure Kittredge (PMLA 30:11) compares Machaut's ninth Motet; cf. also RR 6744–46; MLT II.361, 406; and MerT IV.2058–64. Chaucer may have also recalled the discussion of the duplicity of Fortune in Remede de fortune, 2379–2452, where she is described as two-faced, both bitter and sweet, etc.

629–33   As fylthe over-ystrawed with floures: Cf. RR 8908–13, where the sentiment is expressed that a dunghill covered with silk or flowers still smells; the idea is proverbial (Whiting F146): Machaut's eighth Motet, 6–8, is the immediate source, however, describing Fortune as "Sans foy, sans loy, sans droit et sans mesure" (Faithless, lawless, unjust and extreme; cf. BD 632–33) and as dung covered with rich cloth. See 811–13 below.

636–41   The scorpion was a common symbol of treachery; cf. MLT II.404; MerT IV.2058–65; MancT IX.271; and Whiting S96, who quotes a gloss from Ecclesiasticus 26.10 in the Wycliffite Bible: "A scorpion that maketh fair semblaunt with the face and pricketh with the tail; so a wickid woman draweth by flateryngis, and prickith til deth"; cf. Ayenbite of Inwit, EETS 23, 62. The idea is traditional and occurs in Aesop's Fables 4.3. According to Vincent of Beauvais, the scorpion's face is "somewhat like a maiden's," and it never ceases seeking occasions to strike (Spec. nat. 20.95, col. 1549).

652–71   With the chess allegory, cf. RR 6620–726, from which Chaucer takes some phrases (see 660–61 and 663 below); in RR the "games of chess" are the actual battles between Charles of Anjou and his enemies, though their discomfiture is seen to be due to Fortune. See also Remede de fortune, 1190–91; the trope was a common one, however. **fers** originally meant "wise man, counsellor" (Arabic firzan) and the name was given to a chess piece with restricted movement (one square diagonally), which kept close to the King (see H. J. R. Murray, A Hist. of Chess, 1913, esp. 423). Alongside fers as the name of the piece, there developed in Europe other names which were feminine, domina, regina, etc. Cooley (MLN 63, 1948, 30–35) suggests that the medieval strategy was to keep the queen (fers) in close attendance on the king, so that it is likely to be the last piece taken before the king is mated. French (MLN 64, 1949, 261–64) is of the view that the losing of the queen is in itself not serious, but that the Black Knight takes no further interest in the game when his fers is lost and is thus easily checkmated.

660–61   the myd poynt of the chekker: Apparently refers to the four central squares of the board, where the checkmate often took place (Murray, Hist. of Chess, 428–29, 474, 605). **Poun errant** (traveling pawn) was frequently the title given to the mating pawn (Murray, 751). Cf. RR 6652–59, where all these phrases occur, "Eschec e mat . . . /D'un trait de paonet errant/Ou milieu de son eschequier" (Check and mate . . . With a move of the traveling pawn in the middle of the chessboard).

663   Than Athalus, that made the game: Attalus the Third, Philometor, king of Pergamos, described in RR

6691–92 as the inventor of chess. (See Murray, Hist. of Chess, 502.)

667   Pictagores: Pythagoras; Baugh (15) notes that John of Salisbury says that Pythagoras was interested in games that have a numerical basis.

669   And kept my fers the bet therby: See 772 below.

708   Proverbial, Whiting D287; cf. HF 361 and Tr 2.789n.

709   Tantale: Tantalus, who is mentioned along with Ixion and Sisyphus in Met. 10.41. Cf. 589 above. Ixion, Tantalus, and Sisyphus are also named near together in RR 19279–99.

710–58   In the following conversation Chaucer made considerable use of RR; cf. for example, BD 717–19 with RR 5847–56 (Socrates' indifference to Fortune); 726–34 with RR 13174–262, where La Vieille (the Duenna) gives examples (Dido, Phyllis, Oenone, Medea) of women who have committed suicide when forsaken by their lovers; 735–37 with RR 1439–56 (Rom 1469–89—the death of Echo); 738–39 with RR 9203–6 and 16677–88, though in these references to Samson the deceit of Dalilah (rather than Samson's death) is stressed.

717   Socrates: Cf. note WBPro III.727–32 and For 17 and note 17–20.

723   the ferses twelve: The number twelve presents a problem to which no completely convincing solution has been found. The RR passage (see 652–71 and 660–61 above) does not mention a number. Murray, Hist. of Chess, 452, shows that by medieval rules "a game was won by checkmating the opponent's king, or by robbing or denuding him of his forces—an ending called Bare King." Stevenson (ELH 7, 1940, 215–22) suggests that the Dreamer refers to draughts or checkers, though finds no evidence of a draughtsman ever being called a fers. Cooley (MLN 63:30–35) suggests that, as the fers was so important (cf. 652–71 above) ferses twelve could, by metonomy, mean "twelve games"; though all MSS have the ferses, Cooley advocates the omission of the definite article to resolve the difficulty; twelve might, he suggests, be used because of its associations with companions, e.g., apostles and douzepers. Bronson (PMLA 67:874–75) also favors the association with the Twelve Peers of Charlemagne and suggests that Doucepers might sometimes have been corrupted into Doucefers. Skeat (1:481–82) counts eight pawns (referring to Caxton's Game of Chesse to prove the individual character of each pawn—laborer, smith, clerk, etc.) and one each of (the duplicated) bishop, knight, and rook; this, with the addition of the queen, totals twelve. He argues, "As the word fers originally meant counsellor or monitor of the king, it could be applied to any of the pieces." But, while a pawn could become a fers by reaching the eighth square, there is no reason to believe that fers could apply to "any" piece. Rowland (Anglia 80, 1962, 384–89) points out that boards of 12 by 8 squares existed (particularly in a German version of chess) with twelve pawns; she also suggests an improbable astrological link involving a pun on fers/Lat. ferus (ME fer, OF fier, fer)—"wild beast" (cf. Astr 1.21.49–62), which might give the meaning "even if you were not under the influence of the twelve signs of the zodiac and could choose your own destiny and kill yourself as you wish, you would be condemned because it is foolish to die for love." For an interpretation of the pawn image as an oblique reference to Chaucer himself in a struggle for promotion, see Rowland, AmN&Q 6, 1967, 3–5. See also 946 and n. below.

728–29　The idea that **Phyllis** hanged herself is probably from RR 13414–17; see LGW 2484–85n.

735　**Ecquo:** See 710–58 above. Echo's hopeless love for Narcissus is told in Ovid, Met. 3.370–401.

738　**Dalida:** For the form of the name, see MkT VII.2063–70.

749–52　Cf. Behaingne, 253–56.

759–804　Many details and a good deal of the vocabulary are taken from Behaingne, 125–33, 261–73; Remede de fortune, 23–60; and RR 1881–2022, 12889–92 (Kittredge, PMLA 30:16–17). The account is thoroughly conventional. Von Kreisler, MP 68, 1970, 62–64, compares the formula in BD 768 with 116, and also with PF 417 and KnT I.3078. Although he suggests that the formula originates in Matt. 22.37, and that in the BD passages Chaucer stresses physical absence, it should be noted that in Behaingne, 125–32, the lady says that she has for seven or eight years (cf. BD 37) given her devotion to Bonne Amour; and that since her first childhood knowledge of love she has "Cuer, corps, pooir, vie, avoir et puissance/Et quanqu'il fu de moy, mis par plaisance/En son servage" (joyfully placed in her [Bonne Amour's] service heart, body, strength, life, possessions and might, and whatever else was mine). A similar formula occurs in Behaingne, 502–3: the lover adores the lady above everything else, "With heart, body, true desire, and soul."

793–98　Cf. 445 above. Gaunt married Blanche in 1359 when he was nineteen. Much of the phraseology is directly from Remede de fortune (see 759–804 above), e.g., "Et l'entrepregne en juene aäge . . . juenesse me gouvernoit" (Let him undertake it when young . . . youth governed me).

797–98　Cf. Rom 593.

805–9　Modeled on Behaingne, 281–90 (Kittredge, MP 7:467–68); cf. Dit dou vergier (Oeuvres 1:155–58).

810–11　For the rhetorical devices used here see 817–1040 below.

811–13　**Nay, but Fortune . . . :** This reversion to the tirade against Fortune (see 617–709 and n.; 629–33n.) is a blend of Behaingne, 284–85: "Fortune,/Qui de mentir a tous est trop commune" (Fortune who lies to everyone all too often) and the eighth Motet, 17, where Fortune is described as "Fausse, traitre, perverse" (False, treacherous, perverse).

813–14　For the rhyme, see 309–10 above.

817–1040　For the long description of the lady, Chaucer drew very largely upon Behaingne, with frequent incidental use of the Remede de fortune, and occasional reminiscences from the Lay de confort and the Roman de la rose. Even some of the most individualizing traits in the picture are paralleled in the French sources. Yet it is hard to believe that the passage does not contain a real portrayal of the Duchess of Lancaster. Clemen (Ch's Early Poetry, 54–57) remarks that Chaucer shortens the catalogue of physical features found in Machaut and stresses Blanche's sympathy, friendliness, and goodness of heart; by interspersing his conventional material with protestations, questions, and so on, freshness and a personal effect are created. For another contemporary portrait emphasizing Blanche's unspoiled nature, see Froissart, Le joli Buisson de Jonece, 241–50, ed. Anthime Fourrier, 1975. For further discussion, see Anderson,

MP 45, 1948, 152–59. Cf. BD 817–32 with Behaingne, 286–96; 833–45 with Remede de fortune, 71–72, 95–99, 102–3, 197–99 (and also with RR 1681–83); 844–45 with Confort, 164–66; 848–74 with Behaingne, 297–330; 871–72 with Rom 543 and Behaingne, 321–22; 904–6 with Behaingne, 356–58 and Remede de fortune, 1629–30; 907–11 with Behaingne, 397–403, 582; 912–13 with Behaingne, 411–14; 918 with Behaingne, 580–81; 919–37 with Remede de fortune, 217–38; 939–47 with Behaingne, 361–63; 948–51 with Remede de fortune, 54–56; 952–60 with Behaingne, 364–83; 966–74 with Remede de fortune, 167–74; 985–87 with Remede de fortune, 123–24; 1035–40 with Behaingne, 148–53, 156–58.

There is in many of these passages a very close modeling: cf. for example, BD 848–54 with Behaingne, 297–301: "car je la vi dancier si cointement/Et puis chanter si trés joliement,/Rire et jouer si gracieusement,/Qu'onques encor/Ne fu veü plus gracieus tresor" (For I saw her dance so prettily,/And then sing so very charmingly,/Laugh and play so graciously,/That since then,/There has never been seen so gracious a treasure); Chaucer is also influenced by Machaut's rhyme-scheme. This mode of describing a lady feature by feature from head to foot was conventional in medieval love-poetry. A rhetorician's specimen known to Chaucer (cf. NPT VII.3347 and n.) was furnished by Geoffrey of Vinsauf, Poetria nova, 562–599. For a number of other examples, see Faral, Les arts poétiques, 75–81; Rom 817–1302; Hammond, Eng. Verse, 405, 452; see also Brewer, MLR 50, 1955, 257–69; Rudolfo Renier, Il tipo estetico della donna nel medio evo, 1885; Kohn, Das weibliche Schonheitsideal in der ritterlichen Dichtung, 1930; Muscatine, Ch and Fr Trad., 17–18. See also Tr 5.799–840n. Chaucer also follows the Poetria nova (ultimately derived from the pseudo-Ciceronian Rhetorica ad Herennium) in particulars. Geoffrey of Vinsauf describes thirty-five "plain colors" of rhetorical devices. Many can be seen in the Black Knight's speeches: e.g., 810, *dubitatio* and *interrogatio* (rhetorical question); 811, *ratiocinatio* (a question addressed to and answered by the speaker) and *expeditio* (elimination of all but one possibility); 829, *praecisio* or *aposiopesis* (unfinished sentence); 830, *interrogatio* again; 832, *conclusio* (brief summing-up); 848–51, *similiter cadens* (successive clauses with the same inflectional endings); 855–56, 896–70, *contrarium* (denying the contrary of an idea before affirming it). For Chaucer's use of rhetoric, see the works cited in the Bibliography, pp. 773–74. Murphy (RES n.s. 15, 1964, 1–20) has challenged the idea that Chaucer knew Geoffrey of Vinsauf directly, but see Dronke in Ch: Writers and Background, 170.

869–73　Cf. PhyT VI.9–13n.

889　**Ynde:** I.e., the end of the earth; cf. Rom 624; WBPro III.824n.

895–901　Perhaps a use of the topos of "affected modesty" (see GP I.746n.), though cf. KnT I.1459–60n.

905　**Was whit, rody, fressh, and lyvely hewed:** Against this line (and against 942 and 948) the word "blanche" has been written in the Fairfax MS, probably by John Stowe. Lines 905 and 942 are hypermetric. Some editors have omitted *whit* (see Textual Notes), but Peck (in Silent Poetry, 94) suggests that the extra foot is intended "to heighten the metaphysical import of 'White' when she is actually named in 948"; Peck believes that Stowe's marginal notes show that he understood the riddle.

946   a round tour of yvoyre: The detail does not appear in Machaut or RR. This may be a continuation of the chess-piece image, BD 652–741, and see also 975 (Rowland, N&Q 208, 1963, 9). Song of Songs 7.4 has "Collum tuum sicut turris eburnea" (Thy neck is as a tower of ivory, AV). The association of Mary with the "turris eburnea" was common (see Yrjö Hirn, The Sacred Shrine, 1912, 444–45). Wimsatt (JEGP 66, 1967, 26–44) notes a number of details in the description of Blanche that are associated with the Virgin (e.g., the phoenix, 982–83; Esther, 985–88, who was sometimes seen as a prefiguring of Mary; and the spotless mirror in Wisdom 7.26, which was taken to represent Mary, and with which cf. BD 974). Wimsatt concludes that the poem's consolatory function is thus effected: "Chaucer by means of the Black Knight's description raises her to Heaven where she is no longer an imperfect figure of Mary."

963–65   lyk to torche bryght: A common simile, cf. LGW 2419 and Whiting C24. The idea is proverbial and appears in Ennius, as quoted by Cicero, De officiis 1.16 (Skeat 5:300), though here probably drawn from RR 7410–14. Cf. WBPro III.333–34.

982   The soleyn fenix: The ancient tradition about the phoenix was familiar in both learned and popular writings of the Middle Ages. Passages that Chaucer may have had in mind are Met. 15.392–407, and RR 15975–98, both of which emphasize the solitariness of the bird. Cf. also Gower's Balade no. 35, 8–11 (Works, ed. Macaulay, I:366), where the lady is compared with "la fenix souleine . . . En Arabie" (The one and only phoenix . . . In Arabia). See also note 946 above.

987   Hester: Cf. MerT IV.1370–71, 1744–45n.

1019   "It gave her no pleasure to keep anyone's interest in her by raising false expectations." See Tr 3.773n.; cf. also Tr 5.1615, 1680. For an example of similar usage in Shakespeare, see Much Ado, 4.1.304.

1024–32   Cf., for the general tenor of this passage, the Dit dou lyon, 1368–504, where long journeys are compared by lovers who are anxious to prove their worthiness of ladies' affections; and Gower's Confessio amantis 4.1615–82, where the Confessor enjoins the task of military travel "over the grete Se," etc., to win the love of "worthi wommen," though the Lover adduces arguments to the contrary. For illustrations of the young knight's wanderings, see Lowes, RomR 2, 1911, 113–28, esp. 121–23. Lowes quotes from Jean de Condé's Li dis dou levrier, where a lady commands her lover to spend seven years acquiring honor in Scotland, England, France, and Germany. Cf. GP I.85–88.

1024–25   Walakye: Wallacia, an independent Romanic-speaking country between the Danube and the Transylvanian Alps in South Romania.

Pruyse: See GP I.53n.

Tartarye: Probably used here loosely for Outer Mongolia (see SqT V.9n.; Magoun, MS 17, 1955, 117–42, esp. 140 and 142).

1026   Alysaundre: Cf. GP I.51n.

1028–29   the Drye Se: Probably the great Desert of Gobi in Central Asia; the **Carrenar** (or Carrenare), the Kara-Nor, or Black Lake, is on its eastern side. This region lay on a main trade route between China and the West. That it was known to medieval Europeans is proved by the mention of it by Marco Polo (ed. Sir Henry Yule, 3rd ed., 1903, 1:196–203). Chaucer and his contemporaries may have confused it with the great shoals at the mouths of the Dwina and the Petchora in Russia, which bore similar names and lay along the course of another Asiatic trade route. On the whole subject, see Lowes, MP 3, 1905–6, 1–46; for other explanations see 2–5 there.

hoodles probably implies a "romantic disregard for comfort" (Lowes, RomR 2:121).

1056–74   With this list of worthies cf. the Remede de fortune, 107–34. "Even if I were as wise as Solomon etc. . . . I would never love anyone but my lady," and also Machaut's thirty-eighth Balade notée (Poésies lyriques, ed. Chichemaref 2:560–61) where the poet says that he has no interest in seeing the beauty of Absalon, or in testing Samson's strength, because, "Je voy assez, puisque je voy ma dame" (I see enough because I see my lady), and Behaingne, 421–25. The sentiment was commonplace.

1057–60   Alcipyades: Alcibiades was commonly celebrated for his beauty; cf. RR 8943, Bo 3.pr8.44–45. The strength of **Ercules** (Hercules) was proverbial (Whiting H358), as was the worthiness of **Alysaunder** (Alexander, Whiting A83).

1061–63   Babylon (Babyloyne), Carthage **(Cartage),** Macedonia **(Macedoyne), Rome,** and the biblical Nineveh **(Nynyve)** are examples of great cities and empires now fallen.

1069   Antylegyus: A corruption of Antilogus (Antilochus), which is in turn a mistake for Archilochus. He and **Achilles** (1066) were slain by ambush in the temple of Apollo, where they had gone so that Achilles might marry **Polixena** (1071). The plot was laid against them in revenge for the deaths of Hector and Troilus. This episode is briefly related by Dares, ch. 34; but Chaucer may have got it rather from Benoît (see Le roman de Troie 21838–22334; Dares is cited in some MS readings of 22306) or from Joseph of Exeter, De bello Troiano 6.402–50. It is also in Guido delle Colonne (ed. Griffin, 207–8).

1070   Dares Frygius: On Dares Phrygius and his place in the history of the Trojan legend, see the introduction to the notes to *Troilus.* See also 1117 below.

1081–85   Penelopee and **Lucrece** were famed for their virtues (cf. IntrMLT II.63, 75; FranT V.1443; Anel 82; LGW 1680–1885). Cf. RR 8605–12, where **Tytus Lyvyus** is also mentioned. See also PhyT VI.1 and the introductory note to that tale.

1088–1111   Cf. Remede de fortune, 64–65, 89–94, 135–66, 295–302.

1089–90   The rhyme say (preterite indicative) and say (a clipped form of the infinitive) is very unusual in Chaucer; cf. introductory note to Proverbs. Possibly, as Skeat suggested, the former should be *seye* (preterite subjunctive), though the indicative seems more natural. Perhaps Chaucer was attracted by the "rime riche." See GP I.17–18n.

1100   slouthe: In the later Middle Ages, sloth (accidia) in descriptions of the Seven Deadly Sins related primarily to laziness in the performance of religious duties. (See Bloomfield, Seven Deadly Sins, 1952, esp. 217.) This association is appropriate in the context of the Black Knight's *worship and servise* (1098).

1108–11   Cf. Dit dou lyon, 207–12.

1113–25 Perhaps a development of Behaingne, 1140–47.

1114 **shryfte wythoute repentaunce:** Some critics have taken this to mean that the Dreamer considers the Black Knight has "got off without penance," or has "sorrow with nothing to repent." More likely, however, is "It seems to me that you have as much chance of being shriven as if you were to confess without being contrite." (For discussion, see Diekstra, ES 62:215–36, esp. 224.) Cf. RR 6924, "Confession senz repentance."

1117–23 **Achitofel:** Achitophel counseled Absolon to rebel against David (2 Sam. 17). **Anthenor** (Antenor) betrayed Troy by sending the statue of Pallas Athena, on whose safety Troy depended, to Ulysses. Cf. Tr 4.202–6 and n.; Benoît, Roman de Troie, 24397–824 (where both Dares and Dictys are referred to); and Guido delle Colonne, Historia destructionis Troiae, 226–29.

Genelloun: The notorious traitor of the Chanson de Roland (cf. ShipT VII.136n.). **Rowland and Olyver,** whose friendship was celebrated, were the most famous of Charlemagne's knights (cf. MkT VII.2387).

1146–50 Cf. Remede de fortune, 357–66.

1152–53 Cf. RR 1996–97: "Il est assez sires dou cors/ Qui a le cuer en sa comande" (He who possesses the heart can be sure enough of the body). This is turned about in BD 1154: "and if any one has that [his heart], a man may not escape."

1155–57 Cf. Remede de fortune, 401–6. The making of complaints in song was of course the regular procedure under such circumstances. See, for example, Machaut's Confort d'ami, 2057–2102, Font. amor., 235–1034. For discussion of Machaut's "complaints," see Calin, Poet at the Fountain: references are given under "complainte" on 256 there. Cf. FranT V.943–49.

1162 **As koude Lamekes sone Tubal:** "In Gen. 4.21 it is Jubal, not Tubal, who is called the 'father of all such as handle the harp and the organ.' The ascription to Tubal, however, is not peculiar to Chaucer. It occurs in Peter Comestor's Historia scholastica (Lib. Gen. cap. 28) and Vincent's Speculum doctrinale 17.25, as well as in the Aurora of Petrus de Riga, which Chaucer in 1169 acknowledges as his source. (All these passages were printed by Young, Spec 12, 1937, 299–303.) They all mention also the Greek attribution of the invention of music to Pythagoras (Pictagoras)" (Robinson). Machaut, Remede de fortune, 2318, makes the Pythagoras/music attribution also. Lamech took two wives: from Ada was born Jubal (father of harpists and organists); from Sella was born Tubalcain (hammerer and artificer of brass and iron). Beichner (in Texts and Studies in Hist. of Med. Educ. 2, 1954, 5–27) gives a detailed history of medieval traditions about the original discoverer of music and demonstrates that there was a common misreading of "tubal" for "iubal," paleographically understandable, particularly with the proximity in the context of "tubalcain" (in Latin MSS of the Middle Ages, proper names were seldom capitalized). Of twenty copies of the Aurora studied by Beichner, only two read "tubal" instead of "iubal"; he concludes that Chaucer writes " 'Tubal', . . . either because he was using one of the rare copies of the Aurora with this spelling, or because he changed 'iubal' to 'tubal' thinking it was right. The latter, I believe, is more probable because by this time 'tubal' was rather common."

1180–1312 In the following passages Chaucer again makes frequent use of Behaingne and the Remede de fortune. Cf. BD 1181–82 with Remede de fortune, 681–82; 1183–91 with Behaingne, 453–56; 1192 with Behaingne, 466; 1195–98 with Behaingne, 461–62 and Remede de fortune, 1671–83; 1203–18 with Behaingne, 467–76; 1216 with Remede de fortune, 696; 1219 with Behaingne, 504–5; 1226–28 with Behaingne, 656–58; 1236–38 with Behaingne, 509–12; 1239–44 with Behaingne, 541–48; 1250–51 with Remede de fortune 751–52; 1258–67 with Behaingne, 610; 1273 with Remede de fortune, 4074–75; 1275–78 with Behaingne, 642–43; 1285–86 with Remede de fortune, 139–40; 1289–297 with Behaingne, 166–76. Many of these Machaut passages are quoted in columns with BD in Kittredge, PMLA 30:20–24.

1200 **With sorwe:** Probably imprecatory rather than descriptive. For the construction, see FrT III.1334n.

1206–7 **I trowe hyt was in the dismal/That was the ten woundes of Egipte:** MED derives *dismal* from OF *dis mal* (unlucky days). A thirteenth-century Anglo-French poem defines *dismal* as "maljours" (which, Skeat states, confirms the etymology from Lat. *dies mali*). But Spitzer (MLN 57, 1942, 602–13) argues that this etymology is philologically impossible, that the genuine origin is Lat. *decem mala* (ten evils), and that the idea links with Gregory's instruction that a tenth of the year should be given over to self-mortification. The connection between *dismal* and the *ten woundes of Egipte* is complex: two days each month were designated as "Egyptian days" and were thought to be unlucky. (Vincent of Beauvais, Speculum naturale 15.83, explains that there were minor plagues in addition to the major ten.) These Egyptian days were sometimes called "dismal days" (MED s.v. *dismal,* a reference to Wyclif, "egipcian daies that we call dysmal"; MED, s.v. *Egipcien,* quotes the Cyrurgie of Gui de Chauliac [c. 1425]: "Of egipcianez daiez, i.diez malez days"). Spitzer demonstrates that medieval writers were not averse to using more than one "etymology" of a word, and that Chaucer here plays on both Lat. *dies mali* (OF *dis mal*), "evil days" and Lat. *decem mala* (OF *dix mals*), "ten evils." Skeat (1.493) believes that *woundes* is an over-literal translation of Lat. "plagae" (see Vulgate, Exodus 7–12, headings), usually translated "plagues," but Promptorium parvulorum, EETS e.s. 102, gives Lat. "plaga" as a definition for *wound.* On the tradition of the "Egyptian" or "dismal" days, see Hirsch, ELN 13, 1975, 86–90.

1246 For the lamentation of **Cassandra,** see Benoît, Roman de Troie, 26113–122.

1248 **Ilyoun:** See MLT II.289n.

1270 This phrase occurs twice in Behaingne, 641, 670.

1312 **to strake:** See Emerson, RomR 13:135–37 and cf. Sir Gawayn and the Green Knight, 1363–64, and 1922–23. In Master of Game by Edward, second duke of York, written between 1406 and 1413 (ed. W. A. and F. Baillie-Grohman, London, 1904, 110 and 112) two types of straking are described, each with a distinct sequence of notes. One indicates that the king no longer wishes to hunt and it is used "for all huntynges save when the hert is slayn with strength" (see 351 above). The other note-sequence for straking indicates that a hart has been "slayn with strength" in the king's hunt. As Chaucer does not say which of the two horn-calls was used, he leaves ambiguous whether the hart was slain. See Tilander, Cynegetica 4, 1957, 228–33;

and Marcelle Thiébaux, Stag of Love, 1974, 115–27, esp. 126 and n. 40.

1314–29   this kyng: It seems likely that the *emperour Octovyen* of line 368, the Black Knight, and **this kyng** all represent Gaunt. Skeat (1:422), following an earlier suggestion, considered that *this kyng* "plainly intended" Edward III. Condren (ChR 5, 1970, 195–212) suggests that the poem may have been composed for an anniversary service of Blanche's death (for details of which see Lewis, Bulletin of John Rylands Library 21, 1937, 176–92) and in ChR 10, 1975, 87–95, Condren proposes a date post-1371, because only after Gaunt's marriage to Constantine (September 1371) did he assume the title of King of Castile and León; Condren sees the eight-year sickness (cf. 30–43 above) as Ch's period of grief after Blanche's death, and favors accordingly a 1376 date for the composition of BD. See also discussion of the possible date of composition by Palmer (ChR 8, 1974, 253–61), who demonstrates that Blanche's death was not the hitherto accepted 12 September 1369, but 12 September 1368. For further evidence supporting the 1368 date, see Ferris (ChR 18, 1983, 92–93). There appear to be several examples of word play which connect the poem with Gaunt and Blanche: *long castel* = "Lancaster" (also called "Loncastel," "Longcastell"), *walles white* is probably an oblique reference to "Blanche" (cf. the translation pun in 948); *seynt Johan* is Gaunt's name-saint; *ryche hil* = "Richmond." Gaunt, at the age of two, was created earl of Richmond in Yorkshire and it belonged to him until 1372. (See Tupper, MLN 31, 1916, 250–52 and MLN 32, 1917, 54; Skeat's letter in Acad 45, 1894, 191, where he accepts the above interpretations and would emend his own note on Richmond accordingly; Kökeritz, PMLA 69:951). Exegetical, allegorical interpreters of the poem (see references to Huppé and Robertson and to Gardner in 309–10 above) take the lines to imply also the "white city of Jerusalem, on the rich hill of Sion, which St. John described." Similarly, Peck (in Silent Poetry, 76) considers that the general archetype of counsellor-healer occurs in various manifestations in the poem, "and ultimately emanates from the vision *'be seynt Johan'* of the homeward bound king, where Christ is indeed immanent."

1324–34   At the end of the poem Chaucer reverts to the Paradys d'amours, from which he took the suggestion of his opening lines. With BD 1324–25, cf. the Paradys, 1685–92; and with 1330–34, cf. Paradys, 1693–95 and 1722–23.

The House of Fame

The House of Fame, like The Book of the Duchess, is not ascribed to Chaucer in the manuscripts, but its authenticity is sufficiently vouched for by Chaucer's own reference in the Prologue to The Legend of Good Women (F 417, G 405)—where it is named as one of Chaucer's poems in praise of love—and in the Retractation at the end of The Canterbury Tales. In the poem itself, moreover, the eagle addresses the narrator as Geffrey (729).

Because Lydgate does not include The House of Fame in his list of Chaucer's works in the Fall of Princes, several scholars have argued that his phrase "Dante in Inglissh" refers to the poem indirectly. Robinson (Journ. of Comp. Lit. 1, 1903, 292–97), among others, effectively refuted the extreme theory that the poem is more or less a parody of the Divine Comedy (see, e.g., Rambeau, ESt 3, 1870, 209–68). But Chaucer does use a number of passages from Dante, and there are several correspondences, some more striking than others, between the two works: Nevill Coghill (The Poet Ch, 1949, 48) remarks on the division into three books, the use of invocations, the precise dating of the visions, and the presence of deserts, eagles, steep rocks, and lectures. Leyerle (UTQ 40, 1971, 250) suggests that in 1379 or 1380 Chaucer would have been 35 years old, Dante's age in the Divine Comedy (but this analogy becomes less likely, of course, if Chaucer was born in 1340). B. G. Koonce (Ch and Fame, 73–88) argues that the two poems are related allegorically, and tries to correlate Chaucer's three books with Dante's Hell, Purgatory, and Paradise. At any rate, the Divine Comedy may indeed be thought of as a divinely ordained House of Fame, in which Dante keeps alive the renown of the souls whose eternal reward he has witnessed: see Cacciaguida's remarks in Paradiso 17.136–42, on the souls known to fame (fama).

Chaucer also owes a great deal to the love visions that abounded in French literature for a century after the Roman de la rose. W. O. Sypherd's Sts. in HF, 1907, is still useful as an account of Chaucer's debt to Le roman de la rose itself, and to the works of Machaut, Froissart, and other poets; but Wolfgang Clemen (Ch's Early Poetry, 68–69) rightly disputes Sypherd's contention that The House of Fame is essentially another such love vision. Chaucer may also have used Boccaccio's Teseida, but despite the parallels that have been adduced, there is little persuasive evidence that he was influenced by Boccaccio's Amorosa visione or by Petrarch's Trionfo della fama (but see Wallace, Ch and the Early Writings of Boccaccio, 1985).

The most pervasive influences in the poem are Virgil's Aeneid and several works of Ovid: especially the Metamorphoses, Heroides, and Ars amatoria. See Shannon, Ch and Roman Poets, 48–119. Chaucer probably made use of such translations as the Ovide moralisé, and such commentaries as Servius's on Virgil and Pierre Bersuire's Ovidius moralizatus. But there is no doubt that he knew Virgil and Ovid at first hand, and thoroughly; for, in essence, The House of Fame is an extended meditation on Fame,

expanding on the descriptions of the goddess in Aeneid 4.173–90 and Metamorphoses 12.39–63.

This prolonged look at Fame and the concepts she personifies is Chaucer's most noticeable innovation, since Fame is much less common than Fortune as a theme in medieval literature. In Latin as in Middle English, "fame" can mean either "reputation" and "renown," or "rumor"; and Chaucer conflates its meanings. Kittredge (Ch and His Poetry, 106) sensibly argues that Chaucer has not confused, but harmonized the two senses of the word, since the "substance or material" of fame or reputation "is nothing but rumors." For further information on the meanings and literary descriptions of Fame, see: María Rosa Lida de Malkiel, La idea de la fama en la edad media castellana, 1952 (translated as L'idée de la gloire dans la tradition occidentale, 1968); Cawley, REL 3, no. 2, 1962, 10–14; Koonce, Ch and Fame, 13–45; Watts, JMRS 3, 1973, 87–113; and Piero Boitani, Ch and Fame, 1984. See also the briefer remarks by Clemen, Ch's Early Poetry, 102–3; and John Norton-Smith, Geoffrey Ch, 42–43.

"The HF belongs of course to the literary type which describes an intellectual or mental flight. Numerous examples of this type are cited by F. Cumont, Le mysticisme astral dans l'antiquité, Acad. Roy. de Belgique, Bull. (Lettres), 4th series, 1909, 256–86. For additional references see Nock and Festugière, Corpus Hermeticum (Hermès Trismégiste), 1:66" (Robinson). Chaucer also alludes to passages, and sometimes to the original contexts of such passages, in earlier visionary literature: 2 Corinthians, Revelation, Martianus Capella, Boethius, and Alanus de Insulis.

Nineteenth-century critics tended to read The House of Fame as an allegory of Chaucer's own life; Sypherd (Sts. in HF, 156–63) gives an account of various theories, and rightly rejects them. Early in the present century such readings were replaced by attempts to explain the work as an occasional poem, meant to rebuke John of Gaunt for indecency or—more plausibly—to celebrate a royal marriage or betrothal; Robinson seems correct in stating that "the poem seems at best inappropriate" for such a purpose. Manly (in Kittredge Anniv. Sts., 1913, 73–81) argues that the vision was meant to introduce a collection of tales, but that the scheme was abandoned in favor of the Canterbury pilgrimage; cf. Sypherd's objections to this argument (MLN 30, 1915, 65–68). All these theories are lucidly categorized and discussed by Bronson, Univ. of Calif. Pubs. in Eng., 3, no. 4, 1934, 171–77. See also 2158 below.

More recent critics have tried, with varying degrees of success, to find a unifying theme in The House of Fame. The poem has been explained as a Boethian rejection of earthly mutability (Ruggiers, SP 50, 1953, 16–29; and Stillwell, ES 37, 1956, 149–57); as an art of poetry (Allen, JEGP 55, 1956, 393–405; and Shook, in Comp. to Ch, 414–27); as a plea for patronage (Simmons, MLQ 27, 1966, 125–35); and as a rejection of the via moderna in fourteenth-century philosophical thought (Eldredge, NM 71, 1970, 105–19). Koonce, Ch and Fame, argues for an allegorical reading of the poem; and J. A. W. Bennett, Ch's Book of Fame, offers an extended gloss on

The explanatory notes to The House of Fame were written by John M. Fyler.

many matters of detail. There are comments on Chaucer's pervasive skepticism about books, dreams, and experience in Robert O. Payne, Key of Remembrance, 129–39; and more extensively, in Sheila Delany, Ch's HF, and John M. Fyler, Ch and Ovid, 23–64, which notes (30–31) that dreams, Fame, and Virgil had all been described as "of fals and soth compouned."

Chaucer wrote *The House of Fame* while he was comptroller of the wool custom (1374–85), as lines 652–53 show; but the poem "contains no precise indication of date. Inferences drawn from the biographical and allegorical interpretations are all uncertain. Those based on literary relations are also not very secure. The assumption, for example, that the poem is the 'Comedy' announced by Chaucer at the end of the *Troilus* is both unwarranted and improbable." *The House of Fame* is usually dated about 1379–80. "In general, the probabilities favor the early years" of the so-called "Italian period, before the composition of the Palamon or the *Troilus.* The use of the octosyllabic couplet would have been more natural at that time than later. This date would account also for the transitional character of the poem" —indebted to the French love-vision, but also "clearly written under the influence of Dante" (Robinson). See Tatlock, Dev. and Chron., 34–40; Lowes, PMLA 20, 1905, 854–60; and Kittredge, Date of Tr, 53–55. Fisher (564) believes *The House of Fame* to be later than *The Parliament of Fowls,* but the evidence seems to point the other way: see Pratt, MLQ 7, 1946, 259–64.

BOOK I

1–52   This extended *dubitatio* on the types, causes and effects of dreams, "one long, eager, and breathless sentence" (Kittredge, Ch and His Poetry, 75), contrasts with the confident openings of the RR and other French dream visions, which were "often prefaced . . . with theories, to prove that dreams were worthy of belief" (Clemen, Ch's Early Poetry, 74). It owes most to Nature's discourse in the RR (18299–514), both in its adoption of key words—*visions* and *revelacions,* 18509–10; *fantosmes,* 18424; *complexions,* 18506; *figure,* 18350—and in its phrasing: compare HF 24–31 and RR 18343–49; HF 33–35 and RR 18357–60; HF 36–40 and RR 18394–402; and HF 41–42 and RR 18365–66. Chaucer also drew on Macrobius's influential classification of dreams, either directly from Somnium Scipionis 1.3 or, more probably at this time in his life, from one of its many borrowers: see John of Salisbury, Policraticus 2.15; Vincent of Beauvais, Spec. nat. 26.11–25 and 32–65; Bartholomaeus Anglicus, 6.24–27; and Robert Holkot, Liber sapientiae (Basel, 1586), Lectio 102. For a listing of relevant passages, see Sypherd, Sts. in HF, 74–76; see also Curry, Ch and Science, 202–18. Hazelton (Spec 35, 1960, 357–80) finds that many of Chaucer's ideas about dreams are also current in school commentaries on Cato's Distichs, a common elementary textbook (see MilT I.3227n.). Cf. the discussions of dreams in PF 99–105, Tr 5.358–85, NPT VII.2922–3157.

Chaucer's use of dream terminology is confusing, apparently on purpose: "too much information is as fatal to certainty as too little" (Delany, Ch's HF, 41). The confusion is inherited: terms are often ambiguous or contradictory (Chalcidius's "somnium" is equivalent to Ma-

crobius's "insomnium"); a single dream may belong to several categories (Som. Scip. 1.3), and its prophetic value is hard to establish before the event. Macrobius lists five kinds of dreams: "somnium," "visio," "oraculum," "insomnium," and "visum" (also called "phantasma"); this list provides Chaucer's **avision, oracle,** and **fantome.** But the argument that **drem** corresponds to "somnium" and **sweven** to "insomnium" (ten Brink, Chaucer, 1870, 101; Lewis, Discarded Image, 64; Newman, ELN 6, 1968, 8) is unconvincingly tidy; Chaucer seems to use the words interchangeably. Moreover, **avisions** may be either prophetic, delusory, or meaningless dreams (see MED). **Revelacion** is not on Macrobius's list, though a twelfth-century treatise does give it as a synonym for "oraculum" (AHDLMA 38, 1963, 157); the word probably comes, by way of the RR, either from 2 Cor. 12.1 ("visiones et revelaciones Domini") or, as Lewis argues (Discarded Image, 54), from Chalcidius, ch. 256.

4   Morning dreams were thought to be true, evening dreams unreliable; for sources, including the Divine Comedy, see Newman, ELN 6:6.
12–15   Cf. ParsT X.957 and n.
18   **gendres:** May refer (Skeat) to Macrobius's five species of the "somnium" or "enigmatic dream" ("proprium," "alienum," "commune," "publicum," "generale"), or as likely, to the five kinds ("genera") of dreams.
18–19   **distaunce/Of tymes:** The interval between dreams, or, perhaps, between a prophetic dream and the event it prophesies.
21–51   The origins of dreams are listed here, in a catalogue progressing from inward states to exterior spiritual forces, and from the less to the more veridical (see Koonce, Ch and Fame, 48).
21–22   On the **complexions** of humors (cf. GP I.333) as causes of dreams, see NPT VII.2923–36 and note to VII.2923–32.
26   **Prison-stewe:** *Stewe* is usually glossed here as "brothel," but Prof. John Reidy of the MED informs us that in Middle English this sense seems to occur only with the plural. The singular is wrongly glossed as "brothel" in Lydgate's Fall of Princes 9.609, 623, where its meaning is "bath" (Fr. *tandis que . . . se baignoit,* Lat. *in balneo*). In Troilus 3.601, 698 it means "small room, closet." For its use as a compound here, Reidy compares *prisoun-stie* meaning "prison enclosure" (cf. MED s.v. *prisoun,* sense 5).
36–40   Macrobius and John of Salisbury name Dido as the preeminent lover besieged by the "insomnium" (Aen. 4.9).
39   **impressions:** Cf. SqT V.371, Tr 5.372–74.
48   **figures:** Probably refers to Macrobius's "somnium," which conceals its meaning "with figures and ambiguities" (figuris et . . . ambagibus); also see Numbers 12.6–8, which Koonce (Ch and Fame, 50) cites. Curry (Ch and Science, 206–7) identifies *figures* as the sense-images or "simulacra" originating in the imagination of a dreamer; see Vincent of Beauvais, Spec. nat. 26.41.
53   **Wel worthe:** *worthe* is a verb here, as in Tr 2.1011, 5.379; cf. also the biblical "Woe worth the day" (Ezekiel 30.2).
55–56   Cf. RR 18513: "De tout ce ne m'entremetrai" (None of this will I discuss).

63　The conventional time for a medieval dream vision, especially concerning love, is an indeterminate day in the spring; but there are precedents for Chaucer's precise dating and unusual choice of season: the Divine Comedy of course, but also Machaut's Dit dou lyon (2 Apr. 1342) and Jugement dou Roy de Navarre (9 Nov. 1349), and Froissart's Joli Buisson de Jonece (30 Nov. 1373).

Earlier speculation about "10 December" tried to link HF to preparations for a royal marriage (1380 or 1381), or the hoped-for betrothal of John of Gaunt's daughter Philippa (1384). But "in none of these three cases . . . has December tenth been shown to have been actually a significant day, and the allegorical interpretations of the poem are themselves altogether doubtful" (Robinson).

Recent critics argue for the poetic appropriateness of the heavens on 10 December. Bevington (Spec 36, 1961, 292) notes that in the late fourteenth century, 10 December is just before the winter solstice (12 Dec.; cf. Astr 2.1.18): "the obtuse narrator" has picked the day least "suggestive of love and springtime," though why the tenth rather than the twelfth is not clear. Leyerle (UTQ 40:249) states that the sun in December approaches the constellation Aquila, "the Eagle," and on 10 December is in Sagittarius, "the house of dreams, tidings, and travels," and "the night domicile of Jupiter, the most benevolent of the planets." Also see Koonce, Ch and Fame, 65–66.

66–84　"There has been considerable discussion as to the source of the three invocations. The second and third (518–28, 1091–1109) clearly come from Dante, and it has been held that the whole idea of invocations was suggested by the Divine Comedy. But their use was common in poetry of various kinds and not unexampled in love-visions. In fact the particular address to Morpheus in the present passage seems to have been suggested by Froissart's Trésor Amoureux, 615–24 (Oeuvres 3.71)" (Robinson), which is not, however, an invocation. Bevington (Spec 36:291) points out that Morpheus "is a ridiculous deity to invoke" when the narrator is about to request the attention of his audience.

69–70　For the God of Sleep's cave, see BD 163–77; ultimately based on Ovid, Met. 11.592–615.

71, 73　The three MSS quote Latin verses from Ovid in the margin: Met. 11.602–3 ("But from the bottom there flows the stream of Lethe") and 11.592 ("Near the land of the Cimmerians there is a deep recess"). For the association of Lethe with **helle unswete**, Spencer (Spec 2, 1927, 182) cites Claudian, De raptu Pros. 1.282.

81　From Dante, Par. 1.1: "La gloria di colui che tutto move." Solari (Revista de literaturas modernas 1, 1956, 223–24) notes resemblances, and argues that Chaucer is indebted to Machaut's Confort d'ami, 53–70.

82　An echo of the Gloria Patri; cf. Tr 1.245.

105　For the story of **Cresus** (Croesus), see MkT VII.2727–60; Chaucer's source is RR 6489–622.

112–14　Cf. Rom 23–25.

115　**wery . . . forgo:** On this construction, see MED s.v. *forgon* 4(a) and Samuels, ES 36, 1955, 313.

117–18　**corseynt Leonard:** The presumed joke here is hard to decipher. "St. Leonard was the patron saint of captives and might therefore be expected," as he is in RR 8833–38, "to release the wretched who were in the prison of married life" (Robinson). Koonce (Ch and Fame, 71) notes that the Legenda aurea gives, as an etymology of the saint's name, "the odor of good fame."

Smyser (MLN 56, 1941, 205–7) notes that Chaucer lived approximately two miles from St. Leonard's nunnery of Stratford-atte-Bowe.

120　This line gave Lydgate the title of his Temple of Glas. Bennett (Ch's Bk of Fame, 11) remarks that the glass of Venus's temple—like the ice of Fame's house and the brittle twigs of Rumor's—denotes insubstantiality.

130　"The temple of Venus here resembles her temple, which is much more fully described, in KnT. No model has been found for either description. For the idea of the paintings on the walls there would have been sufficient suggestion in the temple of Juno in Aen. 1.446–65. Medieval poetry provides numerous other examples, and Chaucer must have been familiar with many actual decorations of the sort" (Robinson). See Sypherd, Sts. in HF, 81–86, and Bennett, Ch's Bk of Fame, 10–12. Braswell (JMRS 11, 1981, 103–9) argues that this *temple of glas* was inspired by the Sainte-Chapelle in Paris.

On the portrait of Venus, the fullest account (with a summary of earlier scholarship) is Meg Twycross, Med. Anadyomene. Chaucer takes some of its details from Pierre Bersuire's Ovidius moralizatus (see Twycross, 14) and perhaps also from "Albricus Philosophus," De deorum imaginibus libellus, 903–4.

The mythographers' supposition of two Venuses (see, e.g., Boccaccio's "chiose" [gloss], Teseida 7.50, and R. Hollander, Boccaccio's Two Venuses, 1977) has been adopted by some critics. Brewer (Chaucer, 74) argues that this temple belongs to the lascivious Venus of "painful betrayed love"; also see Koonce, Ch and Fame, 89–107. But Loomis argues sensibly (in Philol. Essays in Hon. of Herbert Dean Meritt, ed. James Rosier, 1970, 192–93) that Venus is a single ambiguous goddess. Virgil's narrative reveals her double nature: she is at once the benevolent mother of Aeneas and the destroyer of Dido. Cf. KnT I.1955–66n.

136　**comb:** On Venus's shell, comb, and *citole* (KnT I.1959), see Twycross, Med. Anadyomene, 70–88.

137–38　**daun Cupido/Hir blynde sone:** Cupid is traditionally blind; see KnT I.1963–65n. On the title **daun**, see KnT I.1379n., and on the Italianate form of **Cupido** and **Vulcano**, see MkT VII.2345n.

139　As Bennett remarks (Ch's Bk of Fame, 21), Vulcan's darkened face is a detail taken from RR 13864–68 ("charbonez de sa forge"); **ful broun** may thus mean "blackened" (cf. GP I.207n.).

142　**bras:** Either "copper" or "brass" (an alloy of copper and tin or zinc); copper is Venus's metal (see CYT VIII.829). Koonce (Ch and Fame, 104) quotes Boccaccio's comments on this matter (in his gloss to Teseida 7.50).

143　Chaucer begins his summary of the opening books of Virgil's Aeneid. The first two lines, here translated, are quoted in the margins of the Fairfax and Bodleian MSS.

synge: Edwards, Expl 44.2, 1986, 4–5, argues for the superiority of the Fairfax/Bodleian reading *say,* on the grounds that Chaucer's intention here is "ironic and deflationary."

yif I kan: Adds an un-Virgilian tentativeness to Virgil. Fyler (Ch and Ovid, 33) argues that the phrase implies "the uncertain ability of art to be true to the facts," specifically the facts in the story of Dido and Aeneas. See also Dane, AmN&Q 19, 1981, 134–36.

The dreams in BD and PF reflect and expand on Chaucer's bedtime reading. Here the book is inside the dream, but in other respects its role is analogous.

148   Lavyne: In the Aeneid, "Lavinium." But the scribes of the Fairfax and Bodleian MSS, as their marginal notes show, read "Lavinia": "Filia regis Latini."

151   First sawgh I: Norton-Smith (Geoffrey Ch, 49) observes that Chaucer had acquired this formula in translating RR, where the dreamer describes the painted figures on the wall of the garden (e.g., Rom 147, 164). Also see the descriptions of the temples in KnT (e.g., I.1995, 2056).

155   Made the hors broght: Causative *made* is rare in Chaucer; see Mustanoja, ME Syntax, 601–2.

161   The margins of the Fairfax and Bodleian MSS quote in Latin from Aen. 2.526–28, on the death of Polites: "But lo! escaping from the sword of Pyrrhus, through darts, through foes, Polites, one of Priam's sons, flees down the long colonnades."

177   Iulo: "Iulus, who was the same person as Ascanius. The blunder, if it be one, may be due to the wording of Aen. 4.274–75 ('have regard for growing Ascanius and the promise of Iulus thy heir'), or possibly to a misinterpretation (by Chaucer or a predecessor) of the Historia Miscella (formerly ascribed to Paulus Diaconus), 1.2; after Aeneas, 'regnum suscepit Ascanius, qui et Iulus, eiusdem Aeneae filius' (Ascanius, who is also Iulus, the son of the same Aeneas, took up the royal authority) (ed. Eyssenhardt, Berlin, 1869, 2). For evidence of a confusion in the Latin tradition itself, see Rand, Spec 1, 1926, 222–24" (Robinson).

184   Aeneas does not know (Aen. 2.738–40) and Virgil does not say how Creusa died.

191   The wordes: The Fairfax and Bodleian MSS quote the "verba Creuse" in the margin: "And now farewell, and guard thy love for our common child" (Aen. 2.789).

198–238   Chaucer summarizes the first book of the Aeneid, but alters the story to augment Venus's role: according to Virgil, Neptune—acting alone—calms the winds that Juno and Aeolus have unleashed. Friend (Spec 28, 1953, 320) notes that the Ilias of Simon Aurea Capra is midway between Chaucer's version and Virgil's: Neptune intervenes on Venus's behalf.

219   Joves: "Jupiter. This peculiar form, which seems to be formed on an OF nominative, occurs again in lines 586, 597, 630, and in Tr 2.1607, 3.15" (Robinson).

229   an hunteresse: The Fairfax and Bodleian MSS quote in Latin from Aen. 1.318–20 with omissions: "For from her shoulders in huntress fashion she had slung the ready bow and had given her hair [to the winds to scatter]; her knee [bare, and her flowing robes gathered in a] knot."

240–382   Chaucer complicates Virgil's account of Dido and Aeneas by adopting Ovid's perspective (in Heroides 7), which wholeheartedly takes Dido's view of the affair: he cites his two sources in lines 378–79. In LGW Chaucer exaggerates Aeneas's guilt by conspicuously omitting exculpatory details (see Fyler, Ch and Ovid, 112–13); "My mastir Chauser gretly Virgill offendit," Gavin Douglas charges, because "he was evir (God wait) all womanis frend" (Aeneid trans., ed. David F. C. Coldwell, 1957, 2:14, 16). In HF, though Chaucer omits some of Virgil's excuses for Aeneas (see Bennett, Ch's Bk of Fame, 42), the effect is more balanced between the dreamer's sympathy for Dido and the book's full pardon for its hero (HF 427–28).

To some degree, Chaucer reflects medieval emphases in his handling of the story (though see Delany, Ch's HF, 1972, for a more elaborate explanation). The influential Roman d'Enéas treats the Aeneid as a romance with Dido as its heroine; for later medieval versions, see Eberhard Leube, Fortuna in Karthago, 1969. Aeneas's reputation as one of the betrayers of Troy (implicit in Tr 2.1474) no doubt weakens his claims for sympathy: on the tradition of the deceitful "unhero Aeneas," see Reinhold, Classica et mediaevalia 27, 1966, 195–207; and Clemen, Ch's Early Poetry, 84. Virgil's truthfulness is called into question, just as Homer's is (see HF 1477–80): John of Salisbury (Policraticus 8.14), Ranulph Higden, Petrarch, and Boccaccio all insist that the story of Dido and Aeneas is a fiction, since Aeneas died several hundred years before Dido was born (for references, see Fyler, Ch and Ovid, 34). Also see Macrobius, Saturnalia 5.17.5–6.

265–66   Cf. RR 12139–42 (Rom 7465–68), and Whiting A152.

269–85   McPeek (MLN 46, 1931, 295–99) notes similar reflections on men as deceivers in Heroides 17.191–96, and RR 4391–96 (Rom 4828–39).

272   Proverbial; see CYT VIII.962–65n.

273   Cf. MerT IV.2308; NPT VII.3300; ProLGW F 194.

290–91   This proverb is common in both English and French; see Whiting H356 and Hassell H25.

305   The gloss in the margins of the Fairfax and Bodleian MSS warns: "Cavete vos innocentes mulieres" (Beware, you innocent women).

314   Non other auctour: Norton-Smith (Geoffrey Ch, 50) remarks that of the sixty lines in Dido's lament, only six or so have any parallel in Virgil; Chaucer is indeed his own *auctour,* since most of this lament appears to be original. The originality is presumably inspired by his aroused sympathy for Dido; for a similar claim see Tr 1.393–99, where the narrator professes to be more accurate than his *auctour* Lollius, upon whom he is wholly dependent elsewhere. The dreamer's response to the love story has become increasingly subjective (so argue Clemen, Ch's Early Poetry, 80, and Fyler, Ch and Ovid, 36–38); such subjectivity has a precedent in Aeneas's response to the paintings in Juno's temple (Aen. 1.446–65). Child (MLN 10, 1895, 191–92) compares Dido's lament in Boccaccio's Amorosa visione, 28. Also see Miller, ChR 17, 1982, 109.

346   my name: Cf. Aen. 4.321–23, where Dido laments that her "fama prior" (former reputation) is now lost, and Criseyde's similar lament (Tr 5.1058–64).

350   The gloss in the Fairfax and Bodleian MSS quotes Aen. 4.174 (incorrectly): "Rumor (Fama) of all evils the most swift."

351   Cf. Luke 12.2: "Nichil occultum quod non reveletur," also quoted in the marginal gloss in the Fairfax and Bodleian MSS. See also Whiting E167.

358–59   The gloss in the Fairfax and Bodleian MSS quotes the second half of the following couplet, with "fieri" and "turpia" reversed: "Rumor de veteri faciet ventura timeri; cras poterunt fieri turpia sicut heri" (Rumor about the old will make things to come be feared; tomorrow, just as yesterday, shameful things will be able to happen). The lines, which allude to Helen, are from "the so-called Versus magistri Hildeberti, a short elegiac poem on Troy. The couplet was widely circulated; see Walther 26973. The second line, quoted by the glossator, itself circulated as a proverb (Walther 3619, 5043 with variations). The text is printed by Hauréau, Notices et extraits, 28.2.438–40, and by Du Méril, Poésies populaires latines antérieures au XIIe siècle, Paris, 1843, 309–13. Fourteen lines are quoted at the end of Caxton's Recuyell of the Historyes of Troye (ed. Sommer, London, 1894, 2:703). For further references see Hamilton, MLN 23, 1908, 63'' (Robinson).

361 Proverbial; Whiting D287; cf. BD 708 and Tr 2.789.

367 hir suster Anne: The gloss in the Fairfax and Bodleian MSS quotes, with errors, Aen. 4.548–49: "O Anna, thou, my sister, wert first to load my frenzied soul with these ills."

378 On the form **Eneydos** (genitive) see ProMLT II.93n.

381–82 A rhetorical *occupatio.* See KnT I.875–88n.

388–426 The list of false lovers comes from the Heroides and, as Bennett notes (Ch's Bk of Fame, 44), is "in much the same order": Heroides 2 (Phyllis), 3 (Briseis), 5 (Oenone), 6 (Hypsipyle), 12 (Medea), 9 (Deianira), and 10 (Ariadne). The marginal gloss of the Fairfax and Bodleian MSS quotes the opening verses of Heroides 2, 3, 12, 9, and 10. Chaucer's knowledge of these epistles is direct, though Meech (PMLA 45, 1930, 110–28) argues that he may also have used an Italian translation attributed to Filippo Ceffi. A few details come from RR, Machaut, or the Ovide moralisé. For **Demophon**'s betrayal of **Phillis,** see LGW 2394–2561, and for the idea that she hanged herself, see LGW 2485–86n. **Breseyda** was the captive for whom **Achilles** sulked when she was given to Agamemnon. **Paris** deserted **Oenone** when he went to kidnap Helen (see Tr 1.652–56). For **Jason's** desertion of **Isiphile** and **Medea,** see LGW 1368–1679; on **Ercules's** desertion of **Dyanira** for **Yole,** see Ovid, Met. 9, Her. 9, and cf. MkT VII.2119–35; the story of **Adriane** and **Theseus** is told in LGW 1886–2227.

392 This phrase is similar to RR 13213, "Pour le terme qu'il trespassa," but also to Her. 2.2, "Ultra promissum tempus abesse queror" (I complain that the promised day is past).

405–26 Several details in this account of **Theseus** do not appear in Heroides 10. Chaucer may have borrowed from Machaut's Jugement dou Roy de Navarre, 2741–69, or from Machaut's source, the Ovide moralisé. See Lowes, PMLA 33, 1918, 324–25, and Meech, PMLA 46, 1931, 183–85. Cf. LGW 1886–2227.

405 he Theseus: See Mustanoja, ME Syntax, 135–36, for the construction.

409 That is, liked it or not. For expressions of this type see GP I.534n.

426 tellis: On the form, see BD 73n.

429 The book seyth: See Aen. 4.252–76, where **Mercurie** brings Jove's command that Aeneas leave for Italy.

435–38 The tempest is described in Aen. 5.8–22, and the death of Palinurus, the **sterisman,** in 5.838–71. (The Bodleian MS names "Palinurus" in the margin of HF 436.)

439–46 Book six of the Aeneid describes Aeneas's consulting the **Sybile;** the **yle** is Crete, which Skeat (3:252) notes is not **besyde** but far from Cumae. Aeneas then visits the underworld where he sees his father, **Anchyses, Palinurus** the steersman (see above note), **Dido,** and **Deiphebus,** a son of Priam who married

Helen after the death of Paris and was betrayed by her when Troy fell. See Tr 2.1398n.

449 Claudian: The author of the De raptu Proserpinae is named, with **Virgile** and *Daunte* (Dante), as an authority on the underworld. See MerT IV.2232 n.; cf. line 1509 and note 1508–12, and ProLGW G 280.

451–65 Chaucer's summary of the last six books of the Aeneid is noticeably brief.

458 Lavina: Lavinia; *Lavyne* in HF 148, BD 331, and ProLGW F 257; its form may be due to either French or Italian. Cf. RR 20831 and Dante, Purg. 17.37.

482–88 Cf. BD 157–59. Chaucer's description of the **feld . . . of sond** may be influenced by Inf. 1.64—where Virgil comes to Dante's aid in a desert, "nel gran diserto"—or Inf. 14.8–13. "In the latter passage Dante refers to the desert of Libya, also described by Lucan in Pharsalia 9.431–37. Chaucer may have drawn directly upon Lucan or (as Professor Lowes has suggested to the editor)" (Robinson) upon Jehan de Tuim's OF translation of Lucan, Li hystore de Julius Cesar, which is closer in detail (see 152–53 of that work).

The dreamer's situation is also similar to that of Aeneas, in several respects. Steadman (MLN 76, 1961, 196–201) notes the associations of Libya with Jupiter and the many references to it in the Aeneid. Aeneas meets Venus there; and she calls his attention to an eagle, the bird of Jove (Aen. 1.394). Fama carries the rumor of the love affair "through Libya's great cities" (4.173); and Mercury comes "to Libya's sandy shore" (litus harenosum ad Libyae, 4.257) to tell Aeneas that he must depart.

There are also many wastelands in French love visions. Patch (MLN 34, 1919, 321–28) cites the Panthère d'amours, Machaut's Dit dou lyon, Froissart's Temple d'onnour, and Deschamps's Lay du desert d'amours; in these poems the desert "seems to be the realm of despair for the lover" (Patch, 328). Among more recent critics, Koonce (Ch and Fame, 126) has discussed "the sterile desert of carnal love" (cf. Norton-Smith, Geoffrey Ch, 55); Bennett (Ch's Bk of Fame, 47) comparing PF 243, argues that sand symbolizes "the decadent and the illusory"; and Leyerle (UTQ 40:258) suggests that the lifeless desert shows that "private love cannot be fruitful without revealing itself."

Several critics have described the apparent disillusionment as primarily literary: a response to the story of Dido and Aeneas (Clemen, Ch's Early Poetry, 89), especially to its unreconciled viewpoints (Delany, Ch's HF, 59; Fyler, Ch and Ovid, 41); see also Miller, ChR 17:111. *Sond* may imply fragmentation as much as sterility: cf. HF 691 where *greynes . . . of sondes* describes a nearly boundless multiplicity.

493 "The **fantome,** or 'phantasm,' was often explained as produced by the operation of demons on the mind of the sleeper, and the term **illusion** was applied to their false revelations. (See Curry, Ch and Science, 209, 214)" (Robinson). See also Vincent of Beauvais, Spec. nat. 26.56 and 26.61. Delany (Ch's HF, 60–66) argues that *fantomes* may refer to literary illusions as well as false dreams, and that they may be especially hazardous for a poet.

Steadman (MLN 76:200) compares Aen. 1.407–8: Aeneas accuses Venus of mocking him "with lying phantoms" (falsis . . . imaginibus).

499–508 In part reminiscent of the eagle with plumes of gold of which Dante dreams in Purg. 9.19–20; also cf.

2.17–24, and Dante's description of the eagle in Par. 18–20. Chaucer alludes in 589 to Ganymede, carried up to heaven by Jupiter's eagle (Aen. 5.252–57) or by Jupiter in the form of an eagle (Met. 10.155–61). The eagle is a traditional symbol of contemplative thought (Steadman, PMLA 75, 1960, 153–59) and, in bestiary lore, is "famed for its acute, unblinking eyesight and for the rigorous education given to its fledglings" (Leyerle, UTQ 40:251).

504–6 These lines seem to echo Par. 1.61–63: "And suddenly it seemed day was added to day, as if He who could had adorned the sky with another sun." See Dilts, MLN 57, 1942, 26–28. The echo is less distant in Thynne, who has *god* for *gold* (see Textual Notes).

BOOK II

511 listeth: Burrow's reading (N&Q 213, 1968, 326) has been adopted though construed as the imperative plural of "listen" (as in Thop VII.712 and 833), rather than the third person singular "desires" (CYT VIII.1056 or MilT I.3176). Cf. MED s.v. *listen* (2) (generally replaced by *listenen* in the fifteenth century).

514–17 For the dream of **Isaye**, Isaiah, see Isa. 1 or 6. Chaucer summarizes Cicero's dream of **Scipion**, Scipio, at the beginning of PF. On **Nabugodonosor**, Nebuchadnezzar, see Dan. 1–4, and MkT VII.2143–82; and on the dream of **Pharoo**, Pharaoh, see Gen. 41.1–7. Iris visits **Turnus** to warn him of Aeneas's arrival (Aen. 9.1–13); but Tatlock argues (MLN 36, 1921, 95n.) that the reference is to his nightmare (Aen. 7.413–59), in which the Fury Alecto appears to him. The identity of **Elcanor** is uncertain. Skeat mentions Alcanor (Aen. 9.672 and 10.338), and Heath suggests Elkanah (Vulg., Elcana), the father of Samuel; but neither is associated with any dream. Tatlock (MLN 36:96n.) gives a list of more far-fetched suggestions, none of whom appears to have had a vision. His own explanation (MLN 36:95–97) is the most likely. He refers to the OF Roman de Cassidorus (ed. Joseph Palermo, SATF, 1963–64), a sequel to the Sept Sages de Rome. (For an account of this work, see Speer, RPh 27, 1974, 479–87.) "Helcana, the heroine of the story, is forced to live in man's disguise, and takes the name Helcanor. When her lover is counseled not to marry, she appears to him twelve times in dreams and tells him stories to show that he should. As Professor Tatlock remarks, there is a difficulty in the identification in the fact that Helcana-Helcanor is not herself the dreamer. But Chaucer may have forgotten this, or may have thought the inaccuracy added to the humor of the allusion. Tatlock thinks there was intentional anticlimax in the addition of this rather absurd figure to the list of famous dreamers of antiquity" (Robinson).

518 Cipris: Venus, so called because of her association with the island of Cyprus; cf. Tr 3.725 and *Cypride* in PF 277; she, along with the Muses, is invoked in Boccaccio, Tes. 1.1–3.

519–22 Cf. Tes. 1: "O sorelle castalie, che nel monte/Elicona contente dimorate,/dintorno al sacro gorgoneo fonte." Since Chaucer took Elicon as the name of a well rather than a mountain (in 522), Bennett (Ch's Bk of Fame, 53) argues that he did not yet know the Teseida (the first line of Tes. 1 correctly identifies Helicon as a

mountain); it is, however, definitely called a fountain in Tes. 11.63. On the relation of these lines to PF 113–19, see Pratt, MLQ 7:262–64.

519 favour: See MED s.v. *favour* 2 (c).

520–26 Cf. Inf. 2.7–9: "O muses, O high genius, now aid me! O memory (mente) who has written what I saw, here will be shown thy nobility." Chaucer's "thought" should perhaps be taken here as "memory."
     This is, Bennett notes (in Ch and Trecento, 108), the first appearance of the muses in English poetry.

521–22 Parnaso, Elicon: Parnassus and Helicon are mountains about twenty-five miles apart (see Magoun, Ch Gazetteer, 65–66). Chaucer here and in Anel 16 and Tr 3.1810 takes Helicon as a well *in* (or *on*) *Parnaso*. Here the Italian spellings in *-o* may be due to recollections of Tes. 11.63 or of Par. 1.16 and Purg. 29.40, though cf. *Cupido* and *Vulcano* in HF 137–38 and see MkT VII.2345n. Skeat believed that Dante's dubious language in Purg. 29.40 led Chaucer to take Helicon as a well rather than a mountain, but Robinson noted that in the Teseida it is definitely a fountain ("fonte," though Boccaccio correctly identifies it as a mountain in 1.1.1–2) and Guido's Hist. dest. Troiae, 15, "scientie inbibens Elyconia" (drinking in the Helicon of science), carries the same implication. Contemporary French poets likewise took Helicon as a well: "la fontaine Helye" (Poems of Ch, ed. Wimsatt, 1982, 54). See Lowes, MP 14, 1916–17, 725–33.

524–25 Cf. Par. 1.10–12: "Truly that of the holy realm which I could store as treasure in my memory (ne la mia mente potei far tesoro) shall now be the matter of my song."

528 Cf. Par. 18.87: "let thy might appear in these brief verses."

534–39 The descent of the eagle is imitated from Purg. 9.28–30: "Then it seemed that, having wheeled about, he descended, terrible as a thunder-bolt (folgor) and snatched me up to the fiery sphere." Dante compares himself to Ganymede (9.22–24). Also see Machaut's Jugement dou Roy de Navarre, 301–2, and Confort d'ami, 1889–90, for the *fouder/powder* rhyme.

543 swap: Glossed by Robinson, Baugh, and Fisher as "swoop (of a bird of prey)." But Grennen (AnM 8, 1967, 41n.) argues that this relatively unusual word always seems to mean "stroke"; and Davis, Ch Glossary, gives as its definition "blow, stroke."

557 Skeat compares Purg. 9.46, where Virgil tells Dante not to be afraid, after he has awakened from his vision of the eagle; also cf. Bo 1.pr2.12–15. Chaucer's eagle may also be reminiscent of Virgil as a guide; they are, Clemen notes (Ch's Early Poetry, 93), both mind-readers: see HF 595.

561–62 The familiar **vois** and **stevene** no doubt belong to Chaucer's wife (as Skeat suggests) or servant (see Bennett, Ch's Bk of Fame, 58). Koonce (Ch and Fame, 143) suggests, implausibly, Christ and the apostles, or Lady Philosophy.

574 noyous for to carye: Here, as in lines 660 and 738–41, Chaucer seems in danger of being dropped: the eagle was thought so to punish recalcitrant eaglets (Leyerle, UTQ 40:251).

588–92 Compare this expression of modesty with Inf. 2.32. Dante asks why he should be granted a supernatural journey, since "I am not Aeneas, I am not Paul" (the founders of the Empire and the Church). On **Ennok**

(Enoch), see Gen. 5.24; on **Elye** (Elijah), see 2 Kings 2.11. **Romulus** was carried to heaven by Mars (Met. 14.816–28). On **Ganymede**, see Aen. 1.28, and the references in 499–508 above. Enoch and Elijah were constantly associated, and they, as well as Ganymede, are mentioned in the Ecloga Theoduli (65–68, 217–19, 77–80; ed. Osternacher, 1902), which Chaucer uses in 1227. But Steadman (Archiv 197, 1960, 16–18) argues that Chaucer's phrasing comes from Pierre Bersuire, Ovidius moralizatus, which describes how Ganymede was abducted by Jupiter in the form of an eagle, stellified ("stellificatus") in heaven, and made the **botiller** (cup-bearer) of the gods ("pincerna deorum").

608–9   Leyerle (UTQ 40:250) argues for a hidden astronomical reference: the planet Jupiter was in Capricorn and Aquarius (i.e., near the constellation Aquila) in 1379–81.

617   On Cupid's blindness, see 137–38 above.

623   **cadence:** The meaning is uncertain; perhaps, as MED suggests, "Rhythm of prose in poetry." "Skeat suggested that perhaps *ryme* is used for couplets, and *cadence* for longer stanzas. From the contrast with rime one might also infer that the reference is to unrimed or alliterative verse" (Robinson). Brewer (in Ch and Chaucerians, 37) argues for the meaning "rhythmic prose"; this is the usual meaning of *cadence* in the fifteenth century (see Hammond, Eng. Verse, 457; and Morgan, MLR 47, 1952, 156–64). "Possibly no precise contrast was intended. Cf. the note on *drem* and *sweven,* lines 1–52 above; also that on *sort, cas,* and *aventure* in GP I.844" (Robinson). Indeed, Baum (Ch's Verse, 5–6) argues that *cadence* is merely a synonym for *ryme.*

Also see Saintsbury, Hist. of Eng. Prosody, 1908, 1:160n.; and Schlauch, PMLA 65, 1950, 577–78; and cf. Gower, Conf. aman. 4.2414: "Of metre, of rime and of cadence."

627–40   Chaucer adopts his usual pose as a love poet who is not a lover (at least not a successful one): cf. PF 8–9, 157–68; Tr 1.15–21, 2.13–21, 3.40–42, 3.1331–36; and Scog 25–42.

639–40   On the "dance of love," cf. Tr 1.517–18, and GP I.476n.

652–53   As comptroller of the wool custom in the Port of London, Chaucer was required to keep records "manu sua propria" (in his own hand): see Ch Life-Records, 148.

660   **thyn abstynence ys lyte:** Cf. Thop VII.700 and Scog. 27–31. The eagle's reproach negates one of the possible causes for Chaucer's dream (see line 25). Bevington (Spec 36:295) compares HF 738–41, on the propensity of heavy things to fall when dropped, as a joke on the precariousness of Chaucer's position.

670   Bennett (Ch's Bk of Fame, 69) compares PF 112.

675–76   Cf. MancT IX.360.

681   Proverbial; see Whiting M37.

689   **berdys:** Cf. RvT I.4096 and n.

691   **greynes . . . of sondes:** Bennett (Ch's Bk of Fame, 6) suggests that Chaucer takes this simile and two others (*cornes in graunges,* 698; *leves in trees,* 1946) from Ovid's numbering of the dreams in the cave of sleep (Met. 11.614–15).

692   **holdynge in hondes:** Cf. Tr 3.773n. Cf. *berth hire on hond,* MLT II.620 and n.

695   On love-dayes, see GP I.258n.

696   **cordes:** "Cords, strings," not "musical chords."

See Colvert (MLN 69, 1954, 240), who suggests that Chaucer is referring to a bass lute or harp.

703   **pies:** Magpies were often thought to speak, and they supposedly spread rumors; cf. the well-known tale of the magpie in the Seven Sages of Rome (see also WBPro III.232 and introductory note to MancT).

706   **yis:** The emphatic affirmative; cf. MilT I.3369 and n.

712   **thyn oune bok:** Ovid's Metamorphoses, which describes the House of Fame (12.39–63). Clemen (Ch's Early Poetry, 98) remarks on the joke of proving the reality of a fiction: "real factual observation is used to substantiate a castle in the air."

720   **every soun:** Fry (Ch at Albany, 31–32) observes that this includes written learning, "since medieval readers seem generally to have read to themselves aloud." But cf. HF 656.

734   **kyndely enclynyng:** "Natural inclination." The idea (stated again in lines 826–29) that every natural object has a natural place it tries to reach, and in which it tries to remain, the predecessor of the principle of gravitation, received its classic statement in Aristotle, Physics 8.4; and it also appears in Augustine, Confessions 13.9, and De civ. Dei 11.28. Chaucer's sources are probably Bo 3.pr11.95–187, and Dante, Par. 1.103–41; also see Purg. 18.28, and RR 16761–67. Like Augustine, Boethius and Dante use the doctrine to explain the soul's yearning for Heaven; Chaucer may imply, by ironic analogy, that the poet's *kyndely stede* is the House of Fame.

For further discussion and references, see Bennett, Ch's Bk of Fame, 77n., and Lewis, Discarded Image, 92–93.

765–81   This theory of sound was familiar; Chaucer probably knew its statement in Boethius's De musica 1.3; even closer to Chaucer's phrasing is that of Vincent of Beauvais, Spec. nat. 4.14: "Sonus est aeris percussio indissoluta, usque ad auditum." Also see Macrobius, Som. Scip. 2.4.2; and Grennen (AnM 8:42) who quotes an analogous passage in Grosseteste. For similar remarks in medieval grammatical theory, see Boitani, ChR 17, 1983, 212–14, and Irvine, Spec 60, 1985, 850–76.

Leyerle argues (UTQ 40:255) that this proof is "an elaborate joke on flatulence"; and he mentions the evidence of SumT III.2233–35 and of the phrasing in Vincent of Beauvais's description of sound produced "aeris constrictione, sicut . . . per flationem intra fistulam" (Spec. nat. 4.15), which could be misconstrued in a scatological sense. See SumT III.2234n. The eagle's proof does have the effect of reducing language to the physical equivalent of any other noise or sound; and the eagle often pairs *speche* and *soun,* thus blurring the distinction between them (HF 783, 819, 824, 832). "From his point of view the Aeneid and flatus are essentially the same thing" (Fyler, Ch and Ovid, 54). Cf. the Aeolists' syllogism in Swift's Tale of a Tub, ed. A. C. Guthkelch and D. Nichol Smith, 1920, 153: "Words are but Wind; and Learning is nothing but Words; Ergo, Learning is nothing but Wind."

788–821   This illustration for the movement of sound appears in Boethius's De musica 1.14, and Vincent of Beauvais, Spec. nat. 4.18 and 25.58. Sypherd (Sts. in HF, 97–99) quotes relevant passages from these works and from Macrobius, for comparison with lines 765–821. Also see Bennett (Ch's Bk of Fame, 79), who points out that this illustration also appears in Vitruvius, De architectura 5.3.6.

822 Take yt in ernest or in game: For another occurrence of the same formula, see ClT IV.609 and cf. MilPro I.3186. A number of phrases of similar import were current in Middle English. Cf. *foul or fair,* in HF 833, and 409 and n. above.

826 fele: See Lewis (Discarded Image, 189), who compares *felyngly,* in KnT I.2203; and the eagle's promise of a proof *be experience* (HF 788).

845–46 Cf. Met. 12.39–40: "There is a place in the middle of the world, 'twixt land and sea and sky, the meeting-point of the threefold universe."

847 conservatyf the soun: Robinson notes that this construction, in which the adjective takes an object like a participle, is most peculiar. Grennen (AnM 8:44) argues that Chaucer is indebted to Walter Burley's commentary on Aristotle's Physics, because Burley uses a similar construction (analogous to the objective genitive in classical Latin).

858–59 Teager (PMLA 47, 1932, 410–18) points out that the eagle has in fact used a great many tropes and rhetorical figures in his proof.

861–63 Cf. Astr Pro 45–46.

868 shake hem be the biles: Kittredge notes (Ch and His Poetry, 91) that the eagle here "drops unexpectedly into the bird-idiom." The effect, as Skeat implies (3: 261), is to remind us that Chaucer is a captive audience (see HF 872–74).

888–89 Cf. Par. 22.128–29: "Look down and see what a great world I have already put beneath your feet"; and see Norton-Smith, Geoffrey Ch, 58.

907 There are similar passages, comparing the distant earth to a "punctum," in the Som. Scip. 3.7 and Bo 2.pr7.22–30. Cf. Tr 5.1807–27n.

911 Bennett (Ch's Bk of Fame, 83) compares Som. Scip. 2.1. Africanus asks, pointing out Carthage, "Do you see that city . . . ?" He later moralizes on the vanity of earthly fame (6.1), as does Bo 2.m7.

914–20 Delany (Ch's HF, 80) argues that these four celestial travelers were often used to point a moral: "that men must acknowledge limits to their understanding of nature."

914 half so high: In fact, Chaucer, unlike several of his visionary predecessors, never rises above the sublunary world; the House of Fame is in the air, which in the medieval universe is below the element of fire, and very definitely below the moon.

915 Alixandre Macedo: In the romances of Alexander, he is carried in a car in the air by four gigantic griffins. See the ME Wars of Alexander, ed. Skeat, EETS e.s. 47, 1886, lines 5515–30; also the Latin Historia de Preliis, ed. G. Landgraf, 1885, 131. For further references, see F. P. Magoun, Gests of King Alexander of Macedon, 1929, 41 n. 3; and George Cary, The Medieval Alexander, 1956, 134–35. Sypherd (Sts. in HF, 93) mentions an Ethiopic version, in which Alexander flies on the back of an eagle.

916–18 In RR 18363–70, Nature mocks those who claim that their self-reflecting dreams are like Scipio's vision; they, too, think they see "hell and paradise, and heaven and air and sea and earth." Scipio, the hero of Cicero's Somnium Scipionis (see PF 29–84), did not see hell, and was not a king. The former error may be due to RR 18365–69; see PF 32n. The latter error is proba-

bly due to RR 10 (Rom 10); it is repeated in BD 286. These errors may imply that Chaucer's knowledge of the Somnium Scipionis (as edited by Macrobius) was as yet second-hand, though the possible allusions to it may suggest otherwise. Fisher adopts Caxton's and Thynne's correction, which resolves the difficulty by making Alexander, not Scipio, the king. See Textual Notes.

919–20 Dedalus (Daedalus) made wings of feathers fixed to a framework with wax that he and his son **Ykarus** (Icarus) used to escape from Crete; Icarus flew too near the sun, which melted the wax, and he drowned in the sea. The story is mentioned in RR 5526–27, but Chaucer certainly knew Ovid's account in Met. 8.183–236; see also Ars amatoria 2.21–98. For the conventional moral readings of the story, see Koonce, Ch and Fame, 162, and cf. Dante, Inf. 17.109–14.

930–34 many a citezeyn . . . eyryssh bestes: Chaucer may refer here to the signs of the zodiac (as Skeat, Baugh, and Fisher hold). Francis (MLN 64, 1949, 339–41) points out that Ovid's story of Phaethon (Met. 2.-47–332), briefly mentioned in HF 941–56, clearly refers to the signs of the zodiac as "formas ferarum" and "simulacra ferarum," equivalent to Chaucer's *bestes;* see also Astr 1.21.52n.

Nonetheless, *many a citezeyn* and *eyryssh bestes* most likely refer to the demons of the air. Skeat compares *citezeyn* to "cives" in the Anticlaudianus of Alanus de Insulis, where the reference is to the aerial powers; see 4.274 ("aerios cives"); 5.407 ("cives superi"); and 5.471 ("superos cives"). Since Chaucer clearly identifies *best* with *citezeyn,* the same interpretation probably applies to the beasts. W. P. Ker notes the term "animalia . . . corpore aeria" (animals with body composed of air) in Augustine's De civ. Dei, 8.16; in 8.15 Plato is acknowledged as an authority on these powers. Ker further suggests that Apuleius's De deo Socratis, which was one of Augustine's sources, may also have been known to Alanus and to Chaucer. He compares particularly HF 925–34, 964–66, with sentences in Apuleius; see his note, Mod. Quart. 1, 1899, no. 5, 38–39. On Apuleius, see Lewis, Discarded Image, 41. The demons of the air, which Alanus de Insulis describes as "falsi uerique sophyste" (sophists of false and true), are especially germane if Chaucer's vision is an *insomnium:* "multo phantasmate brutos deludunt homines" (they delude dull-witted men with many an apparition): see Anticlaudianus 4.283–84.

936–39 Cf. PF 56n.

939 Watlynge Strete: See Magoun, Ch Gazetteer, 170–71: "the old native name for the Roman road running from near London through St. Albans . . . to Wroxeter and Chester, and from the twelfth century on also applied to the road running SE from London to Canterbury and on to Dover."

942 Pheton: See Met. 2.31–332; and Dane, JMRS 11, 1981, 71–82, for the medieval commentaries on the story.

950 for ferde: "In this phrase *ferd(e)* seems to be a substantive, but its original construction is uncertain. Possibly it was a participle after *for,* but this again would be easily confused with the compound *forfered"* (Robinson). See Textual Notes, and MED s.v. *ferd(e)* 1 (b).

966–68 Cf. Anticlaudianus 4.332–40; also Apuleius, De deo Socratis, 10. Alanus de Insulis contrasts the noisy air with the ether, "where all things are still" (4.338);

and the difference is described more fully by Bernardus Silvestris, Cosmographia 2.5.193–205. (See Fyler, Ch and Ovid, 49–50.)

972   Cf. Bo 4.m1.1–7n. Boethius "describes the soul's ability, using the wings of Philosophy, to ascend beyond the elements and reach its proper home. . . . Chaucer glaringly marks off the modest limits of his own journey by cutting Boethius off in mid-sentence" (Fyler, Ch and Ovid, 46).

978   **Cloude:** Interestingly, Macrobius says that the "visum" or "phantasma" occurs in the "first cloud" (prima nebula) of sleep. The dreamer "imagines he sees specters rushing at him or wandering vaguely about, differing from natural creatures in size and shape, and hosts of diverse things, either delightful or disturbing." See Som. Scip. 1.3.7.

981   Cf. 2 Cor. 12.2: Paul hears "secret words" (arcana verba) "that man may not repeat," when he is lifted up to the third heaven. Also see Dante, Par. 1.4–9 and 73–75.

983–84   Clemen (Ch's Early Poetry, 97) argues that these lines echo Dante, Purg. 4.76–77: "Certainly, master, I never saw so clearly as I discern there."

985   **Marcian:** Martianus Capella (fifth century). His De nuptiis Philologiae et Mercurii, 8, contains an extended discussion of astronomy; and Bennett (Ch's Bk of Fame, 93) notes that book 1 describes a flight to the heavens. Chaucer also refers to Martianus, in a quite different context, in MerT IV.1732–37.

992   Cf. Beatrice's rebuke (Par. 1.88–90); she goes on to explain the principle of *kyndely enclynyng.*

993–94   Bennett (Ch's Bk of Fame, 94) notes a similar exchange in Froissart's Joli Buisson de Jonece, 1721–26: the poet prefers a spring walk to an astronomy lesson.

1015–17   Africanus compares the music of the spheres (too great for human ears) with the sun (too bright for human eyes): see the Som. Scip. 5.3. Similar remarks on the dazzling brilliance of the heavens appear in Bernardus Silvestris (Cosmographia 2.3. 108–9), Alanus de Insulis (Anticlaudianus 6.3–14), and Bartholomaeus Anglicus, tr. Trevisa 1:458: "But for defaute of oure heringe and for passinge mesure of that noise this armony is nought iherd of vs, as we may nought se the sonne meue, they he meue, for the clernes of bemes ouercometh the sharpnesse of oure sight."

In bestiary lore, the eagle's distinctive quality is its ability to look directly at the sun (cf. PF 331 and n.); it slays or drives its fledglings from the nest if they refuse to do so (Bartholomaeus Anglicus, tr. Trevisa 1:603). Dante mentions this ability (Par. 20.31–33), and he discovers that he can stare at the sun, following Beatrice's eagle-eyed example (Par. 1.48, 52–54).

1022   On St. Julian, the patron saint of hospitality, see GP I.340n.

1025   Cf. the Som. Scip. 5; and Met. 12.48: "There is no quiet, no silence anywhere within."

1029   **of fals and soth compouned:** A traditional attribute of Fama. See Aen. 4.188; Met. 9.138 and 12.54–55; and Anticlaudianus 8.305–12. Cf. Tr 4.659–60.

1034   This oath by St. Peter also appears in line 2000, and in WBPro III.446, FrT III.1332, and ShipT VII.214.

1037–41   Cf. Met. 12.50–52: "like the murmur of the waves of the sea if you listen afar off, or like the last rumblings of thunder when Jove has made the dark clouds crash together."

1044   Cf. Tr 3.737 and PF 157–59.

1063   **lives body:** "Living body." On this use of a genitive as an adjective, see Language and Versification, p. xxxviii, and KnT I.1912n.

1066   **Seynte Clare** (1194–1253), an abbess and a disciple of St. Francis. Her mention may be dictated by the rhyme; but see Neville (JEGP 55, 1956, 429), who argues that the allusion makes "a clear contrast between clamorous speech and silence."

1068–82   There are several possible sources for this explanation of the conversion of words into images. Shannon (Ch and Roman Poets, 82), notes that Ovid personifies the rumors in Fame's house (Met. 12.53–58); the same is true of the dream-shapes in the cave of sleep (Met. 11.613–14). Ziegler (MLN 64, 1949, 73–76) compares Bo 4.pr1 and m1; Leyerle (UTQ 40:263n) argues that the embodied sounds are analogous to the eagle "as the poetic incarnation of a Boethian metaphor" (the feathers of philosophy). Ruggiers (MLN 69, 1954, 34–37) argues that Chaucer is influenced by the words of Beatrice in Par. 4.37–48, explaining the appearance of spirits on the various planets. Bennett (Ch's Bk of Fame, 98) suggests that the images "correspond to those shades in Dante that embody the mental state of men in life"; and Koonce (Ch and Fame, 158) argues that Chaucer thus prepares an "elaborate inversion of the Last Judgment."

There are also some resemblances to Vincent of Beauvais, Spec. nat. 2.57, which explains the process by which speech becomes intelligible. (Also see Koonce, Ch and Fame, 172n., who quotes Anselm and Augustine on the sense in which words are themselves images; and see Rowland, RUO 51, 1981, 170.)

BOOK III

1091–1109   The invocation is imitated from Par. 1.13–27. With HF 1091–93 cf. 1.13–15: "O good Apollo for this final labor make me such a vessel of your merit as you require for giving the beloved laurel." With 1101–9 cf. 1.22–27: "O divine Power, if you lend yourself to me that I may show the image (ombra) of the blessed realm that is marked in my head (segnata nel mio capo) you shall see me come to the foot of your beloved tree and crown myself with its leaves." The laurel is Daphne, Apollo's beloved.

1093   **This lytel laste bok:** This phrase validates the division of *The House of Fame* into books, as it appears in Caxton and Thynne but not the three MSS. Burrow (Ricardian Poetry, 59) argues that this division into books is "a definite neoclassical or learned feature," and was apparently "a complete novelty in English poetry around 1380" (it appears in Gower's Confessio amantis as well). Chaucer uses it again in *Troilus.*

1098   "This seems to be a definite acknowledgment on Chaucer's part of his practice of writing verses without the full number of syllables. He may have in mind particularly those which begin with an accented syllable—the seven-syllable lines in the octosyllabic, and the nine-syllable lines in the decasyllabic, measure. Or is it simply a prayer for indulgence with imperfect verses?" (Robinson).

1099   **that:** On the construction, see GP I.44–45n. and cf. ParsPro X.39.

1116   Cf. Met. 12.43: "Rumour (Fama) dwells here, having chosen her house upon a high mountain top."

1116–17   Smith (MLN 60, 1945, 39–40) compares RR 2437–47, Rom 2573–74 (see 2573n.): "Thou shalt make castles thanne in Spayne,/And dreme of joye," and refers to OED on "castles in the air." But Chaucer is now known to have visited Spain in 1366, and the reference may be to actual places. Baugh (45) suggests the Rock of Gibraltar, but there is no indication Chaucer went that far south.

1130   Sypherd (Sts. in HF, 114–20) shows that Chaucer's description of Fame derives from the much more common medieval portraits of Fortune. He cites particularly the Panthère d'amours of Nicole de Margival, in which Fortune's house is situated on a rock of ice (1963–75). This detail is apparently original; otherwise, Nicole's description copies the details of RR 5921–6118, which is itself a translation of Anticlaudianus 7.405–8.14. See Baugh (in Britannica: Festschrift für Hermann M. Flasdieck, ed. W. Iser and H. Schabram, 1960, 57–58), and Norton-Smith, Geoffrey Ch, 44.

1147   Proverbial; see Whiting L87.

1170   The word "compace, riming with **place,** ought to be the infinitive, and not the noun 'compass.' It is probable, therefore, that we should either emend the MS reading *no* to *ne* or interpret *no* as 'nor' (for which there is slight authority). See Kenyon, The Syntax of the Infinitive in Ch, Ch Soc, 1909, 91, n. 1" (Robinson). Baugh (45) suggests "to lay out a plan" or "exercise any amount of ingenuity" as the meaning of **casten no compace,** if the noun is intended. Fisher (601) interprets the phrase as "couldn't go to the extent."

1183   **Seynt Gyle:** St. Aegidius. See Legenda aurea, ch. 130.

1184   **beryle:** On its suitability as the material for a palace of Love, Sypherd (Sts. in HF, 133n.) quotes L'Intelligenza, st. 25: "Per sua vertude fa crescer l'amore" (Through its power it makes love grow). Bartholomaeus Anglicus 16.20, tr. Trevisa 2:837, notes that the beryl "maketh a man gret of state, and loueth wel loue of matrimonie." The word was sometimes used to mean "crystal" or "glass"; but the reference in HF 1288, as here, seems to be to the gem. In 1288–91, beryl has a magnifying power, and Norton-Smith (Geoffrey Ch, 53), citing Marbodus's Lapidarium, suggests a possible pun on "magnificare" (to glorify). For further notes on the symbolic meaning of *beryle,* see Patch, MLN 50, 1935, 312–14.

1189   **Babewynnes:** From OF *babouin,* "baboon, dunce." Bennett (Ch's Bk of Fame, 119) quotes Robert Holkot on *babewynnes* as symbols of "pretense and self-importance."

1191–1200   With the description here Whiting (MP 31, 1933–34, 196–98) compares a similar one in Li biaus descouneus of Renaud de Beaujeu. Williams (MLN 72, 1957, 6–9) notes similarities with the Maison des Musiciens in Reims.

1203–6   Orpheus was the most famous musician of antiquity, called *god of melodye* in BD 569; Chaucer doubtless knew Ovid's long account of him in Met. 10 and 11; cf. Bo 3.m12n. **Orion** (Arion) was a legendary poet of Corinth and another famous harper; for his story, see Ovid, Fasti 2.79–118. **Eacides Chiron** (Chiron the Centaur), who was Achilles' tutor in music and other subjects, was the grandson of Aeacus. Chaucer's genitive

form is apparently from Ars amatoria 1.17, "Aeacidae Chiron" (for the use of the genitive here see Bo 2.pr3.59n.). Shannon, Ch and Roman Poets, 88, notes that Chiron is mentioned as a musician in Fasti 5.385–86.

1208   **Glascurion:** "A British bard. He is probably the same as the Glasgerion of a well-known ballad (Child, Ballads 3:136, no. 67). The name may go back to the Welsh 'y Bardd Glas Keraint (or Geraint),' the Blue Bard Keraint, supposed to have lived in the tenth century. This identification was proposed by T. Price, Literary Remains, 1854–55, 1:151–52, and has been received favorably by most commentators both on Chaucer and on the ballad. Unfortunately the accounts of the Welsh bard thus far pointed out are modern and of very little authority. According to the Iolo MSS (ed. Taliesin Williams, 1848, 623), he was a brother of Morgan Hên, King of Glamorgan; 'he collected ancient records of poetry and bardism.' He is also credited with having compiled the first Welsh grammar (see William Owen Pughe, Cambrian Biography, 1803, 128–29). A few pieces of prose and verse, attributed to him, are published in the Myvyrian Archaiology of Wales, 1801–7, 3:100–15. The Iolo MSS also record that he went to King Alfred to London as his domestic bard; they say that many other Welsh bards accompanied him, and that to them was due an improvement in learning and knowledge among the Saxons. . . . Nothing is known of the Blue Bard to account for Chaucer's mention of him here, and the source of Chaucer's information is undiscovered. Possibly he got it from some of his Welsh friends. See the note on line 1925 below" (Robinson).

1212–13   Cf. RR 16029–31; also see Delany, ELN 11, 1973, 1–5.

1218–24   There are similar lists of musical instruments in RR 21030–52, Machaut's Remede de fortune, and other French poems. See Smith, MLN 65, 1950, 522–23; and Norton-Smith, Geoffrey Ch, 42.

1221   A **doucet** is "a wind instrument resembling a flute" (OED).

1224   **pipes made of grene corn:** See Rom 4250.

1227–28   Atiteris is probably a corruption of Tityrus, the shepherd singer of Virgil's first Eclogue; but see Norton-Smith, Geoffrey Ch, 41. **Pseustis,** whose name means "falsehood," is a shepherd who enters a poetic contest with Alithia in the Ecloga Theoduli, a well-known medieval textbook, which Holthausen argued (Anglia 16, 1894, 264–66) may have influenced Chaucer here.

1229   **Marcia:** Marsyas, the satyr whom Apollo defeated in a musical contest and then flayed alive. The feminine form here may be due to Chaucer's having been misled by the Italian "Marsia," which appears in Par. 1.20 (in a passage that Chaucer uses in HF 1091–1109), and in Teseida 11.62. Chaucer also seems to use details from Ovid's account (Met. 6.382–400). David (in Learned and Lewed, 19–29) argues that the source of Chaucer's error may be an anonymous interpolation in the RR.

1235–36   **sprynges, Reyes:** Smith (MLN 65:521–22) notes that this is apparently the first occurrence of these terms in English. *Reyes* (translating a Dutch word) are ring dances.

1239   **blody soun:** Cf. KnT I.2512.

1243   **Messenus:** Misenus, son of Aeolus. See Aen. 3.239; 6.162–65.

1245 Joab: Named as a trumpeter in 2 Sam. 2.28, 18.16, and 20.22.

1246 Theodomas: Mentioned again with Joab in MerT IV.1719–21, which makes clear that Chaucer is referring to Thiodamas, the augur of Thebes. After he exhorts the besiegers of Thebes, there is a great sound of trumpets (Thebaid 8.342–43); but Statius does not say that he himself is a trumpeter. Smith (MLN 65:526–27) suggests that Chaucer takes the spelling *Theodomas* from the Roman de Thèbes.

1247–48 Trumpet playing was a great feature of ceremonial life in Catalonia and Aragon, at least in the thirteenth century: cf. Higini Anglès, La Musica a Catalunya fins al segle XIII, 1935, 88.

1257–58 Proverbial; see Tr 4.1283n.

1261 Phitonesses: The word is based on *Phitonesse,* the Witch of Endor; see FrT III.1510n. and OED s.v. *Pythoness.*

1268 ascendentes: That part of the zodiacal circle which appears to be ascending above the eastern horizon at a given moment. See Astr 2.4.

1271 Skeat compares RR 14397–406, where Balenus, Medea, and Circe are mentioned together; Fansler, Ch and RR, 74, notes that the last two and Calypso are all named in Ars amatoria 2.101–25.

quene Medea: By notorious expertise in magic she restored her father-in-law's youth; see Met. 7.162–293 and cf. LGW 1650.

1272 Circes: Cf. Met. 14.8–74. "Chaucer's form with *-s* may be due to the frequent occurrence of the genitive 'Circes' in Ovid" (Robinson); cf. Bo 2.pr3.59n. On Circe, see Bo 4.m3.

Calipsa: See Ovid, Ars amatoria 2.123–42, and Ex ponto 4.10.13.

1273 Hermes Ballenus: Belinous (Balanus), the disciple of Hermes Trismegistus "who discovered, beneath a statue of Hermes, a book containing all the secrets of the universe" (Skeat 3:272). *Hermes* is apparently either a possessive genitive or an epithet. On Hermes Trismegistus, see CYT VIII.1434n. On *Ballenus* see Langlois's note to RR 14399: further references are given, and mention is made of a possible identification of Belinous with Apollonius of Tyana.

1274 Limote: Skeat (3:273), following Hales, takes this name (*Limete* in the Fairfax MS) as the sorcerer in Acts 13.8.

1277 Colle tregetour: "Probably an English magician mentioned in a French manual of conversation composed in 1396, and declared to have practiced his art recently at Orléans. He is described as 'an Englishman who was a powerful necromancer, whose name is Colin T., who knew how to create many marvels by means of necromancy.' The manual is attributed, doubtfully, to an Englishman, M. T. Coyfurelly. Royster (SP 23, 1926, 380–84), who proposed the identification, suggested very reasonably that 'T.' in the French may stand for Tregetour. He called to mind further the reference in FranT to Orléans as a seat of magic arts" (Robinson).

1315 shoken nobles and sterlynges: Poured out nobles (coins worth 8s. 6d.) and silver pennies (see PardT VI.907n.) in a lavish display of largesse (*larges,* see HF 1309) of the sort associated with great nobles.

1316 kynges: This is usually taken as kings-of-arms (chief heraldic officers), who would proclaim the exploits

of their masters; cf. A. R. Wagner, Heralds and Heraldry in the M.A., 1956, 39.

1321–22 Watts (JMRS 3:90n.) compares ParsT X.813 and John of Salisbury, Policraticus 8.2, on the vainglory of paying heralds to buy renown.

1329–35 Cf. RR 6738–40: "But I don't want to say more of them because to tell all their deeds would require a large book." This is a common form of the rhetorical *occupatio,* enlivened by Chaucer's humorous overstatement; cf. 381–82 and n. above.

1352 the Lapidaire: A well-known treatise on precious stones and their virtues, Marbodus of Rennes's (1035–1123) De lapidibus, ed. John M. Riddle, 1977. The form of the title probably indicates that Chaucer knew the work in some French translation; cf. Tr 2.344n.

1363 carbuncle: Bartholomaeus Anglicus 16.23, tr. Trevisa 2:839, lists some twelve varieties of carbuncle, all of which are a shade of red; Vincent of Beauvais, Spec. nat. 8.51, gives "rubith" as the vernacular name for "carbunculus."

1368–92 Boccaccio presents a goddess of Renown ("la Gloria del popol mondano") in the Amorosa visione, 6; but there is no persuasive evidence that Chaucer knew this poem. As Sypherd argues (Sts. in HF, 16–17, 112–32), Chaucer's debts are most likely to the association of fame and fortune in Boethius and to earlier descriptions of Fortune and Love. Chaucer expands on some details in Virgil's description of Fama (Aen. 4.173–90); his goddess also parodies the appearance of Philosophy (Bo 1.pr1.4–42). Several critics have noted that Fame's judgment of her petitioners is an ironic version of the Last Judgment (see Henkin, MLN 56, 1941, 583–88; Koonce, Ch and Fame, 158, 210–11; Delany, CL 20, 1968, 254–64; and Norton-Smith, Geoffrey Ch, 43–44).

1383–85 See Rev. 4.6.

1392 Partriches wynges: This seems to be a misreading of Virgil's "pernicibus alis" (Aen. 4.180) (or Chaucer may have had a MS which read "perdicibus"). The Latin phrase is correctly rendered in Tr 4.661, *with preste wynges.*

There have been several attempts to explain Chaucer's phrase, noting the partridge's reputed fraudulence (Norton-Smith, Geoffrey Ch, 43) or fearfulness (Koonce, Ch and Fame, 212); also see Magoun and Mustanoja, Spec 50, 1975, 48n., and Newman, Mediaevalia 6, 1980, 231–38.

1419–28 Kendrick (SAC 6, 1984, 123) argues that this hall, with pillars **on eyther syde,** copies the Great Hall of the Palais de Justice in Paris.

1431 led and yren: Lead and iron, the metals of Saturn (HF 1449) and Mars (1446); see CYT VIII.820, 827–28.

1432–36 "**Josephus,** author of the Historia Judaeorum, probably said to be of the **secte saturnyn** because of the astrological doctrine that the Jewish religion, as the root of all others, is signified by 'the father of the planets' " (Robinson). See Miller (MLN 47, 1932, 99–102), who cites Roger Bacon, Opus majus, tr. Burke 1:277–78. Cf. Bennett, Ch's Bk of Fame, 139.

1457 yren piler: Bennett notes (Ch's Bk of Fame, 140) that Thebes was Mars's city, and iron is Mars's metal (see HF 1446).

1459 tigres blod: Two tigers, sacred to Bacchus, broke loose and killed three men, and were mortally wounded themselves. As a result, the war at Thebes was renewed (Thebaid, 7).

1460   Stace: Statius (d. 96 A.D.), the author of the Thebaid and of the Achilleid. He is called the **Tholosan** because he was incorrectly supposed to have been a native of Toulouse. Cf. Purg. 21.89, where he is called "Tolosano."

1467–69   See the introductory note to *Troilus,* for information on all these writers and on their part in the transmission of the Troy legend.

1470   Gaufride: Geoffrey of Monmouth (d. 1154), author of the celebrated Historia regum Britanniae, which is the source of a great body of literary material on the legendary history of Britain. Since he deals with the tradition that makes the Britons the descendants of Aeneas, he is properly reckoned among the writers who "bore up Troy." It was popularly believed that London was originally called "Troynovant," New Troy (cf. the ME St. Erkenwald), and that English history was a continuation of Trojan history (cf. Robertson, Ch's London, 2–4). It is unlikely that Chaucer, as E. K. Rand suggests (Spec 1, 1926, 225), meant himself to be recognized as the *Englyssh Gaufride;* John S. P. Tatlock (Mind and Art of Ch, 1950, 64), repeats Rand's suggestion. Bennett (Ch's Bk of Fame, 30) argues that this reminder of a special British interest in Troy serves to link Book 3 with the account of Dido and Aeneas in Book 1.

1477–80   For this attack on Homer's truthfulness and objectivity, which comes from Dares Phrygius, cf. Benoît, Roman de Troie, lines 45–70, 110–16; and Guido delle Colonne, Historia destructionis Troiae 4.204, and 276.

1482   The significance of the **tynned yren** of Virgil's pillar is not quite clear. Elizabeth Nitchie (Vergil and the English Poets, 1919, 57–59) points out that tin was the metal of Jupiter, and interprets "tinned iron" to imply that Mars controlled and directed Jupiter in the Aeneid. Also see Bennett, Ch's Bk of Fame, 142. Copper is Venus's metal, and thus appropriate for Ovid; and Claudian's pillar is made of sulphur because of its associations with the lower world (but cf. Pratt, Spec 22, 1947, 425).

1494–96   See, on the magnifying power of fame, Aen. 4.189; Met. 12.54–57; and Alanus de Insulis, Anticlaudianus 8.305–12. Also cf. HF 2077.

1499   Lucan: See MLT II.400–401 and n.

1508–12   Claudian, author of the De raptu Proserpinae (cf. 449 above), mentions his poetic "Furor" (**lyk as he were wood**) in De raptu 1.5, and narrates the ravishing by **Pluto,** god of the underworld, of **Proserpyne;** see Shannon, Ch and Roman Poets, 357–58; and Pratt, Spec 22:425. With 1512 cf. Dante, Inf. 9.44: "regina de l'eterno pianto," queen of eternal lamenting.

1521–25   Rambeau (ESt 3:259) compares the sound of bees in Inf. 16.3. Manzalaoui (N&Q 207, 1962, 86) argues that the simile is more reminiscent of Aen. 6.706–9. Cf. also Tr 2.193 and 4.1356.

1526–48   Robinson notes that in the descriptions of the groups of supplicants and the awards that they receive there may be reminiscences of Dante, but adds that the passage on Providence in Bo 4.pr6 may also have been in Chaucer's mind and that the whole conception of the arbitrary goddess seems to have been most influenced by the characteristics of the divinities of Love and Fortune (cf. Sypherd, Sts. in HF, 117–32). Clemen notes that

Fame was not one of the common medieval allegorical figures and that it does not appear in art until the end of the Middle Ages (Ch's Early Poetry, 102, citing R. van Marle, Iconographie de l'art profane, 1932, 124ff.).

1530   alleskynnes: "Really a genitive singular, dependent upon **condiciouns**" (Robinson) rather than a plural adjective.

1547–48   Fame and Fortune are frequently associated, but no source has been found for the statement they are sisters; this was apparently Chaucer's invention.

1571   Lounsbury (Sts. in Ch 2:382) notes that **Eolus** (Aeolus) is described as having two trumpets by "Albricus Philosophus," De deorum imaginibus, 920–21. Shannon (Ch and Roman Poets, 97 and 341–43) explains the connection with Thrace as deriving from Valerius Flaccus, Argonautica 1.597–613; and Bennett (Ch's Bk of Fame, 150) suggests that its source may be one of Horace's Odes (4.12.1–2), which is quoted in Servius's commentary on Aen. 1.57. Skeat notes also Ovid's phrase "Threicio Borea" (Thracian Boreas) in Ars amatoria 2.431.

1573–82   There is a striking parallel to the trumpets **Clere Laude** and **Sklaundre** in Gower's Mirour de l'omme, 22129–52, in which Fortune has "deux ancelles," Renomée and Desfame, each of whom carries a great horn around her neck. This was first noted by Tatlock (Dev. and Chron., 38–40), who regarded Gower as the borrower and, partly on this base, inferred a date "about 1379" for HF. Patch (Goddess Fortuna, 111–12) argued instead for a common source, noting a similar conception of the trumpets (called "Eur" and "Malheur") in the fifteenth-century Dance aux aveugles of Pierre Michault (ed. Douxfils, 1748, 32–35). However, Bennett (Ch's Bk of Fame, 150–53) makes a good case for the priority of Chaucer's invention of the names.

1596   Triton: Triton and his shell-trumpet are mentioned in Met. 1.333. He is referred to as a trumpeter twice in the Aeneid (6.171–74; 10.209).

1598   The use of **to** after **let** is unusual, and Skeat (3: 280) suggests the possibility of reading *to-goo* here (and *to-glyde* in FranT V.1415) but does not adopt that suggestion in his text.

1611   in honour of gentilesse: Bennett (Ch's Bk of Fame, 155–56) glosses as "as due, that is, to their rank, ancestry, and breeding," and compares HF 1311; cf. Bo 3.pr6.12–40; and WBT III.1109–12.

1643   pelet: Usually glossed as "stone cannonball"; but Robert C. Rice, Asst. Research Editor of the MED, notes (by letter) that they were frequently made of lead. (See MED s.v. *pelote.*)

1649   tuel: See Leyerle (UTQ 40:255) and 765–81 above, for the possible scatological sense of this word (for which see SumT III.2148).

1702   clew: Chaucer's only use of the strong preterite of *clawen,* "claw, rub"; elsewhere he uses *clawed.*

1708   a lek: A common expression denoting worthlessness; see Whiting L185 and GP I.177n.

1747   for wod: Cf. *for pure wood* (Rom 276), and on this use of *for* with an adjective, see Language and Versification, p. xxxix.

1758–62   Cf. Ovid, Ars am. 2.632–34: "Some say there is no woman with whom they have not lain. If bodies escape them, they take hold of names, and though the body escape, the name retains the charge" (Famaque non tacto corpore crimen habet). Cf. RR 9855–58.

1768   **lese:** For the figure of the pasture, cf. Tr 2.752.

1783–85   The proverb of the cat who would eat fish but would not wet her feet was widely current. See Whiting C93; and cf. Gower, Conf. aman. 4.1108–9. Skeat (3:282) also cites Macbeth 1.7.45.

1794   **noskynnes labour:** Cf. the similar construction in HF 1530.

1796   **bele Isawde:** Cf. PF 290n.

1803   Cf. Inf. 5.28–33, where "mugghia" in 29 (che mugghia come fa mar per tempesta) corresponds to Chaucer's beloweth: this is as Dante approaches the punished lechers, including Paolo and Francesca, whirled about in the wind. Cf. Spencer, Spec 2:192–93.

1810   See Tr 2.1109–10; and cf. the phrase "to put an ape in a man's hood," ShipT VII.440. See Whiting G25.

1840–41   On the garb of medieval court fools, see Enid Welsford, The Fool: His Social and Lit. Hist., 1961 [rpt. of 1935 ed.], 123. Sandra Billington, A Social History of the Fool, 1984, 9, suggests that Chaucer here refers to a rustic dance of fools.

1844   **Ysidis:** Isis; this is probably a reference to Herostratus, who in order to win fame set fire to the temple of Diana at Ephesus. The story is told by John of Salisbury (Policraticus 8.5), who takes it from Valerius Maximus, Facta et dicta memorabilia 8.14. Why the temple of Isis at Athens is substituted is unknown. For the use of the Lat. genitive see SqT V.50n.

1871–72   The Frend's query suggests that he takes Chaucer to be an embodied sound (see HF 1074–82); his misapprehension may be reminiscent of the repeated comments on Dante as a living, corporeal soul. See, e.g., Inf. 3.88–93; 8.27; 12.80–82; 15.46–48; and esp. 27.61–66 where Guido da Montefeltro expresses his fear of infamy (infamia). Koonce argues (Ch and Fame, 245–48) that the friend is satanic, and leads Chaucer "to the snare or cage of the world."

1879–80   Stillwell (ES 37:153–54) mentions Bo 2.pr4.128–49 and 2.pr6.20–27 as analogues to this proverbial expression. Cf. Gower, Conf. aman. 3.1626–27; and see Whiting D405, and Tr 2.784n.

1907–9   This passage may have suffered some corruption in its transmission (see Textual Notes); its meaning is, in any case, not altogether clear. The form **brynges** (for *bryngest*), supported by the rhyme, appears elsewhere only as the Northern third person singular in RvT I.4130. "It seems better to let the irregularity stand than to remove it by emendation" (Robinson).

1920–21   Daedalus built a maze of chambers (the **Domus Dedaly**) to imprison the Minotaur (cf. Met. 8.156–58); the name "labyrinthus" (**Laboryntus**) is applied to it in Aen. 5.588 and, as Baugh notes (56), in Trevisa's translation of Higden's Polychronicon ("laborintus," "Dedalus hous"). Bo 3.pr12.156 refers to the *hous of Dedalus*, which is glossed "Domus Dedali"; the intricate structure is described in LGW 2012–14 as a maze. In Bo 3.pr12.155–57, the house is described as *so woven* and *so entrelaced that it is unable to ben unlaced*, and Winny (Ch's Dream Poems, 102n.) argues that Chaucer may have supposed the Labyrinth to have had "an interwoven structure rather than an intricate ground-plan." See also Magoun, Ch Gazetteer, 86–88. For the symbolic implications of this labyrinth, see Leyerle (UTQ 40:259–60) and Howard, in Milton and the Line of Vision, ed. Joseph A. Wittreich, 1975, 14.

1925–85   For the House of Rumor Chaucer draws on Ovid's account of the dwelling of Fame (Met. 12.39–63), especially its countless entrances, open night and day (44–46), and the absence of silence anywhere within (47–48). There is, however, no classical precedent for a whirling house made of twigs. Whirling houses are fairly common in romance and entrance to them is often gained by the aid of a guide, sometimes a helpful animal (cf. Cigada, SMed, ser. 3, 2, 1961, 576–87; Sypherd, Sts. in HF, 144–51; Tuve, MLN 45, 1930, 518). For buildings of wicker, Robinson speculated that Chaucer drew on his own observation or on reports of such actual houses among the Irish and Welsh, since he may have visited Ireland (see Ch Life-Records, p. 21), he did have Welsh friends (Kittredge, MP 1, 1903–4, 16, and PMLA 16, 1901, 450–52), and he seems to have had some knowledge of Welsh lore (see 1208 above). Bennett (Ch's Bk of Fame, 168–69) retorts that Chaucer "would not need to wander in Wales or Ireland to find such dwellings," and also points out Chaucer's debt to the descriptions by Alanus de Insulis (Anticlaudianus 8.10–12) and Jean de Meun (RR 6108–14) of the ruined half of Fortune's house. David (PMLA 75, 1960, 339) suggests that the House of Rumor "has a nightmarish resemblance to the customs house." Bennett notes (Ch's Bk of Fame, 176) that it is the exact antithesis of the cave of sleep (see HF 70–76, and BD 153–77). And Delany argues (Ch's HF, 106) that it is the locus of experience, "the raw material of tradition," just as Fame's palace is the locus of literary tradition: Book 3 thus recapitulates the themes of Books 1 and 2.

1926   Possibly a reminiscence of Inf. 3.53–54, which describes a banner that came so fast, whirling about, "that it seemed it might never have rest."

1928   **Oyse:** "It was doubtless chosen here for the rime" (Robinson), but see Smith, MLN 65:527–28.

1942   **gygges:** Defined by the MED s.v. *gigge* n. (2), as "?a squeaking sound, a creak." Though this is the only occurrence, the MED compares the equally rare verb *gigen*, "to make a creaking sound" (see also Smith, MLN 65:529). Baugh (56), deriving the word from OF *gigue*, a fiddle, notes that in Par. 14.118 the sound of the fiddle, "giga," is "dolce."

1966   **bildynges:** See MED s.v. *belding*.

2011   For the order of words, cf. GP I.791.

2034–40   Cf. Inf. 3.55–57: "And behind it came so long a train of people that I would not have believed death had undone so many."

2053   **Thus shal hit be:** "Probably in the sense, 'Thus it is reported to be.' This use of *shal,* like Ger. 'soll,' is known in early English. LGW 1725 appears to be another example" (Robinson).

2060   There is a discussion of the spreading of report in Dante's Convivio 1.3, though Chaucer's primary source here is Met. 12.56–58: "Some of these fill their idle ears with talk, and others go and tell elsewhere what they have heard; while the story grows in size, and each new teller makes contribution to what he has heard."

2078–80   See Whiting S559; and, in the Bible, James 3.5–8. Also see Koonce, Ch and Fame, 259–61. Bennett (Ch's Bk of Fame, 179) compares Aen. 4.666–71.

2108–9   Cf. Ovid, Met. 12.54–55: "Mixtaque cum veris passim commenta vagantur Milia rumorum" (And everywhere wander thousands of rumours, falsehoods mingled with the truth).

2119   Cf. SumPro III.1695.

2122–23   On the proverbial mendacity of shipmen and pilgrims, see Whiting S251 and P18. Also cf. D246: "Ther is no difference bi-twene a lier and a grete teller of tidingis."

2139–40   Cf. Whiting S199.

2152   The reading is uncertain. The line means either "And lifted up their noses on high" or "And lifted up their noses and eyes." See Textual Notes.

2154   "Editors have in general refrained from commenting on this line, either because its meaning seems clear or because the custom was familiar. But Professor Magoun has had the curiosity to collect instances of catching eels by 'stamping' or by 'treading,' and the editor is indebted to him for the following references. From Dr. Alfred C. Redfield of the Woods Hole Oceanographic Institution he cites the information, on the testimony of Mr. Harold Backus, chief engineer at Woods Hole, that the custom still exists in Norfolk Broads, England, where the term for treading is 'stomping.' Mr. Jan Halin, of the publicity department at Woods Hole, testifies that the fishermen in the Zuider Zee have a similar method of driving eels into nets. The one published reference Mr. Magoun has found is in Mourt's Relation or Journal of the Plymouth Plantation (ed. H. M. Dexter, 1865, 97) where Squanto (an Indian) is described as treading eels out with his feet" (Robinson). See also Donovan (PQ 31, 1952, 439–40), who cites Izaak Walton.

2158   *A man of gret auctorite:* When readings of HF as an occasional poem were more in fashion, the *man* was identified with a historical figure, such as Richard II or John of Gaunt. Leyerle (UTQ 40:259–60) rightly questions whether either "would be flattered to be described as cornered in a whirling bird cage by a gabbling rush of eel-stampers." More recent suggestions seem as incongruous, if safely beyond a concern with the nuances of flattery: Boethius (see Ruggiers, SP 50:28); Boccaccio (Goffin, MAE 12, 1943, 44); Christ (Koonce, Ch and Fame, 266–68); and Amor (Overbeck, MP 73, 1975, 157–61). Schoeck, who reads HF as a holiday entertainment, suggests "the Constable-Marshal of the Christmas revels" at the Inner Temple (UTQ 23, 1954, 190). Several critics have suggested ironic possibilities: A. C. Spearing (Med. Dream Poetry, 82) finds the word *semed* (HF 2157) suspicious, since "Fame's world is one of seeming"; and Bennett (Ch's Bk of Fame, xii–xiii), who reminds us that the dreamer himself could not identify the *man* (2156), notes that *auctorite* has "a deeply ironical color" elsewhere (see Tr 1.65).

"The fragment ends in the middle of a sentence. Caxton's copy breaks off at line 2094, after which he adds twelve lines of his own; see the Textual Notes [2157]. Thynne prints lines 2095–2158 and then appends Caxton's ending slightly altered. What Chaucer's own intentions were with regard to continuing the poem is entirely unknown. Brusendorff argued (Ch Trad., 156) that the unfinished form is due merely to bad MS tradition. He held Chaucer to have composed a very short ending, which has been lost. This appears to be also Manly's opinion (Kittredge Anniv. Papers, 79)" (Robinson). Also see Blake, Archiv 221, 1984, 65–69. But the Fairfax and Bodleian MSS, it should be noted, end in mid-page. Accordingly, several critics have argued that *The House of Fame* breaks off as a deliberate fragment, either because Chaucer is censoring "a conclusion of dubious credit to the person celebrated" (Bronson, Univ. of Calif. Pub. in Eng. 3, no. 4, 186–90), or as a final joke on "the unreliability of transmitted secular knowledge" (Fry, in Ch at Albany, 27–28). Baum (ELH 8, 1941, 255) and Bevington (Spec 36:289) argue that no serious item of current news could be expected. L. D. Benson, in Ch in the Eighties, ed. J. N. Wasserman and R. J. Blanch, 1986, 3–22, notes payment on 10 December to a messenger coming from Cardinal Pileo da Prato with news that the proposed marriage of Richard II to Caterina Visconti was definitely off. He argues that the poem is deliberately unfinished and speculates that the man of "great authority" is a joking reference to Nicolò, the messenger. Also see Dickerson, TSLL 18, 1976, 178, and Stevenson, ES 59, 1978, 26.

Anelida and Arcite

The *Anelida,* which Chaucer does not mention in his own lists of his works, is ascribed to him in three manuscripts (two written by John Shirley), as well as by Lydgate (*Fall of Princes* Pro 1.320–21); it is of unquestioned authenticity.

The composition has been dated from as early as 1373–74 (Langhans, Anglia 44, 1920, 235–44) to as late as circa 1390 (ten Brink, Hist. of Engl. Lit., tr. Kennedy, 1901, 2:189). Langhans's date assumes too early a time (1374) for *The Parliament of Fowls;* nevertheless, the transitional character of the *Anelida's* fusion of French and Italian influences, its largely decorative use of pseudo-epic material from Boccaccio's *Teseida,* its occasional similarities to *The House of Fame* (Clemen, Ch's Early Poetry, 197–203), and even what appear as occasional difficulties with the use of the rime-royal stanza (Knight, Rymyng Craftily, 3–10), combine to suggest a possible date in the mid- to late-seventies, not far removed from Chaucer's first exposure to Boccaccio and Italian literature. The poem's "continuation stanza" (Anel 351–57) clearly promises material that we find only in The Knight's Tale, and this, plus the use of the name *Arcite* in the *Anelida* for a character so radically different from the noble youth of The Knight's Tale, is difficult (though perhaps not impossible) to understand if the first of the *Tales of Canterbury* were already completed.

Attempts to relate the poem to events in the 1380s have not been successful. Bilderbeck's theory that the poem concerns Robert de Vere's desertion of his wife (N&Q, 8th ser. 9, 1896, 301–2) was refuted by Tatlock (Dev. and Chron., 84). Tupper's theory that Anelida is to be identified with the Countess of Ormonde (sometimes Latinized as Ermonia) is unconvincing (PMLA 36, 1921, 186–222), despite some similarities in the names. George C. Williams offers no real support for his proposal that the poem is related to John of Gaunt (A New View of Ch, 1965, 123–24).

No overall source has been found for the poem, though the story of the deserted falcon in The Squire's Tale has similarities to Anelida's situation (see 105 below). Chaucer's claim that he follows *Stace and after him Corynne* (21) implies that he is using Statius's *Thebaid,* though Boccaccio's *Teseida* is his primary source for the opening lines (here as elsewhere Chaucer does not name Boccaccio); and there is no parallel to the story of Anelida and Arcite in the *Teseida,* Statius's *Thebaid,* or the *Roman de Thèbes.* But Wimsatt (MAE 47, 1978, 66–70) has shown an indebtedness of situation and phrasing in the Complaint to Guillaume de Machaut's chant royal, "Amis, je t'ay tant amé et cheri."

The reference to *Corynne* has never been satisfactorily explained. Skeat proposed Corrinus, supposed author of a lost pre-Homeric work on the Trojan war (1:531). Robinson, cautiously, suggested the Theban poetess Corinna, mentioned by Statius (Silvae 5.3.156–68) and Propertius (Elegies, ed. and tr. Butler, Loeb, 1929, 2.3.21) and said by Pausanias (Desc. of Greece, ed. and

tr. Jones, Loeb, 1935, 9.22.3) to have overcome Pindar in a poetic competition (see D. L. Page, Corinna, 1953). She is one of the nine poetesses praised as early counterparts to the Muses (Antipater, Anthologia Palatina 9.26), and Appolonios Dyscolos cited a lost work of hers, elsewhere unattested, on the Theban story. Yet Chaucer may have known none of these references. Shannon (Ch and Roman Poets, 20–44) notes the frequent post-medieval designation of Ovid's *Amores* (addressed to his mistress Corinna) as *Corinna* and speculates that a text of this poem, thus titled, might have suggested the name. Bush (Spec 4, 1929, 106–7) cites Lydgate's use of *Corynne* (Troy Book 4.3008–36) in a list of authors, referring to *Amores* 2.6, a lament for the death of a parrot Ovid gave to his mistress. This may merely be Lydgate's attempt to explain Chaucer's reference, or it may suggest how Chaucer, coming upon a similar reference to Corinna associated with a lamentation, might have enlisted her as an authority. Wise's suggestion (Infl. of Statius, 67–68) that Chaucer intended a reference to Boccaccio (Ital. *corina,* wry face) can be safely disregarded.

The name *Arcite* was taken from the Teseida, as was that of *Emelye* (38), whose part in this poem is difficult to understand, unless she is to be identified as Arcite's second mistress (Cherniss, ChR 5, 1970, 20–21). No convincing source has been found for the name *Anelida;* see, e.g., Galway's fanciful suggestion (MLR 33, 1938, 180) that the name refers to Joan of Kent, known as Lady Wake of Liddel (hence, perhaps, Joh-*ann-a Liddel*). Cowell, enlarging on a suggestion by Bradshaw, explains the name as a possible misreading of Latin *Anaetidem* or *Anaetidos* (for Gr. Ἀναῖτις), a Persian goddess (Essays on Ch, Ch Soc, 2nd ser., 617–23). Wise (Infl. of Statius, 70) attempts to explain it as a form of Latin *analuta,* in a reference to the Brooch of Thebes (see Mars 245–62), here passed on to Anelida, the queen of *Ermony,* which he takes not as Armenia (see 72 below) but as an allusion to Harmonia, the first recipient of the brooch. Perhaps more significant is the occurrence of "la bella Analida" in a list of noble lovers in the (late thirteenth-century?) Italian allegorical romance *L'intelligenza* (ed. Mistruzzi, 1928, stanza 75), referring to Laudine, wife of Yvain in Chrétien de Troyes's romance *Yvain ou le chevalier au lion.* The name *Laudine* appears in a variety of forms, such as "la belle Alydés" in Froissart's *Dit dou bleu chevalier* (ed. Fourrier, TLF, 1979, 301) and "Alundyne" in the Middle English *Ywain and Gawain* (ed. Friedman and Harrington, EETS 254, 301–8). There is, however, no strong resemblance in character between Chaucer's Anelida and any of the proposed sources for her name.

In form the *Anelida* is a "complaint" (see introductory note to the text), and shows some general correspondences to French examples of the genre, such as Machaut's *Lay de pleur* and *Lay de souscie* (Fabin, MLN 34, 1919, 266–72; Emile Legouis, Chaucer, 1910, 2:434, 459). The combination of a complaint with a narrative (here and in *The Book of the Duchess,* The Franklin's Tale, and the *Troilus*) has been compared to works such as Machaut's *Fonteinne amoureuse* and *Remede de fortune* and Froissart's *Paradys d'amours,* in which the situation de-

The explanatory notes to *Anelida and Arcite* were written by Vincent J. DiMarco.

scribed in a complaint is remedied by a "comfort." Wimsatt, who notes these resemblances (ChR 5, 1970, 1–9), suggests that had the *Anelida* been completed, Anelida would have been comforted by the return of Arcite. However, the authenticity of the final stanza, in which the continuation is promised, has been questioned (Brusendorff, Ch Trad., 259–60, and Norton-Smith, in Med. Sts. for J. A. W. Bennett, 1981, 81–99). If the final stanza is a scribal addition, Chaucer may not have intended a continuation, but rather a complaint introduced by a brief "story" as in The Complaint unto Pity and The Complaint of Mars.

The work has received little critical attention aside from studies of possible sources and historical allusions in The Story, though the technical virtuosity of the Complaint has often been noted.

1–6   Thou ferse god of armes, Mars the rede . . . Be present: Cf. Tes. 1.3.1–2: "Siate presenti, o Marte rubicondo, nelle tue armi rigido e feroce." On *Mars the rede* see KnT I.975–77n. To Statius, Mars is "cruentus," stained with blood (Theb. 8.231); to Virgil (Aen. 12.332) and Ovid (Rem. amoris, 153) he is "sanguineus," bloody; cf. Tr 3.724.
2   Trace: Thrace (corresponding to the area in northern Greece around the Rhodopian range). In his gloss on Tes. 1.15, Boccaccio explains: "wrath and fury are more violently and more easily enkindled in men in whom there is much blood than in those in whom there is little . . . the men of Magna are under a cold sky and are full-blooded and wild and eager for war: for this reason the poets excellently conceived that the house of Mars, that is the appetite for war, is in Thrace" (Book of Theseus, tr. McCoy, 49).
3   grisly temple: Cf. KnT I.1971 and Tes. 7.29.3 ("orribile ospizio").
5   Bellona, the sister of Mars and goddess of war, is distinguished from **Pallas** Athena (who is sometimes, as in Tr 5.308, considered a goddess of war) by Statius and Boccaccio in the Teseida. They are confused, as they appear to be here, in Boccaccio, De gen. deorum 5.48; in glosses on Statius's Achilleid (Pratt, Prog. of Med. and Ren. Sts. in U.S. and Canada, 20, 1949, 49); in glosses on the Thebaid (Clogan, SP 61, 1964, 606); and in the Ovide moralisé (Witlieb, N&Q 17, 1970, 203–4).
8–14   Cf. Tes. 1.2: "con pietosa rime" (**With pitous hert**), "una istoria antica" (**This olde storie**), and Dante, Par. 1.8: "nostra intelletto si profonda tanto" (**hit ful depe is sonken in my mynde**); cf. also Par. 1.11, "la mia mente potei far tesoro." On the theme of poetry as preserver of the past, cf. Bo 2.pr7.86–92; and see Payne, Key of Remembrance, 68–72, and Norton-Smith, in Med. Sts. for J. A. W. Bennett, 88–99. Cf. Lowes, MP 14, 1917, 727–28.
15   Polymya: Polymnia (or Polyhymnia), one of the nine Muses born of Zeus and Mnemosyne (Memory). Polymnia ("she who is rich in hymns") was the muse of sacred song and is so invoked by Dante (Par. 23.55–57) in a passage that likewise treats the inadequacy of memory (Lowes, MP 14:730). McCall, Ch among the Gods, 16, 168, suggests that Chaucer's association here of Polymnia with the *vois memorial* (18) is sufficiently explained by the etymological tradition that "defined" her as memory; e.g., Fulgentius, Mythologies 1.15: "The fifth is Polyhymnia, for *polymnemen,* as we say, making much

memory, because memory is necessary after growth [in knowledge]."
17   Cirrea: Cirra, which Chaucer, like Isidore (Etymologies 14.8), locates near *Parnaso* (Mt. Parnassus), one of the traditional homes of the Muses), though this is a confusion of Crisa (Crissa) with its ancient port, Cirrha. On the idea that *Elycon* is a well on Parnassus, see HF 521–22n.
20   On the use of nautical metaphors for literary composition, here suggested by Tes. 12.86 and Theb. 12.809, see Tr 2.1–4n.
21   Stace: Statius. On **Corynne,** see introductory note.
22–28   The Latin is quoted (in medieval spelling) from Statius, Theb. 12.519–21, and is translated in the following stanza. On Chaucer's translation, see Wise, Infl. of Statius, 45–46. The first line and part of the second of this passage from Statius are also quoted at the beginning of The Knight's Tale, which may echo Anelida (cf. Anel 24, KnT I.1027, 979; see also Tr 5.1107, Anel 25, KnT I.869, and notes 29–35, 36–42 below).
29–35   Based on Theb. 12.522–32, the lines following those quoted above; cf. "ante ducem spolia et duri Mavortis imago" (Theb. 12.523), and Anel 31 and the heralding of Theseus's arrival with **trompes** (Theb. 12.522). Anel 30–31 seems to be partially echoed in KnT I.975–76. Clogan (SP 61:606–7) shows that such details as the **bright helm** and **targe** are from a glossed MS of Statius.
36–42   Based on Tes. 2.22; Emelye does not appear in Statius. Lines 36–37 may be echoed in KnT I.881–82; 38 is nearly identical to KnT I.972.
49–70   These lines translate Tes. 2.10–12, a summary of the earlier part of the Thebaid, necessary to motivate Theseus's campaign against Creon in the Teseida (and The Knight's Tale), but here decorative.
51   For Juno's wrath against Thebes, see Theb. 1.250–82. Boccaccio (gloss on Tes. 3.1) explains: "This was for the adulteries committed by Jove, her husband, with the Theban women, with Semele, by whom he had Bacchus, and Alcmena, by whom he had Hercules."
57   Amphiorax is the common form for Amphiarus in the OF Roman de Thèbes; on *-x* for *-us* in French words see GP I.384n.
59   The spelling **Campaneus** for Cappaneus (as in KnT I.932, Tr 5.1504) is, as Francis Thynne noted in 1598 (Animadversions, ed. Furnivall, EETS 9, rev. 1875, 43), the usual Italian form; it appears in Boccaccio's autograph MS of the Teseida (Pratt, PMLA 62, 1947, 605).
60   The word **wrecched** may be an echo of Statius's "miseri" (Theb. 11.552).
61   Adrastus: King of Argos and father-in-law of Polynices; he left the war when he was unable to dissuade Eteocles and Polynices from their single combat (Theb. 11.425–46).
72   Ermony: Armenia; see introductory note. For knowledge of Armenia in fourteenth-century England, see Cowell, Essays on Ch, 619–21; and Lowes, Wash. Univ. Sts. 1, 1913, 17–18.
80   Nature's satisfaction in an exemplary creature is a conventional topic of description; see PhysT VI.9–13n.
82   Penelope and Lucresse: Common examples of womanly constancy; see BD 1081–85n.
85   Arcite (found in no MS) is added for sense and meter; even so, the transition in thought is unexpected

and abrupt, and the repetition of *knyght* in 85–86 is far from felicitous (Knight, Rymyng Craftily, 85).

105 Proverbial; see Whiting F43 and cf. SqT V.537. Skeat (1:534) and Tupper (PMLA 36:196–97) note, besides the general similarity of the situation here to that of the falcon and tercelet of The Squire's Tale, a number of parallels in thought and language. Of these, perhaps the most significant are Anel 119, SqT V.569; Anel 141, SqT 610; Anel 146, SqT 644–46; Anel 169, SqT 412, 417, 430, 631. For Chaucer's use of the story of betrayed love here and in The Squire's Tale, see David, SAC, Proceedings 1, 1984, 105–15.

146 Blue, the color of constancy (see 330 and n., below) is not included here. Wimsatt (ChR 5:83) notes that in Machaut's Le livre de voir dit the male lover dreams that his lady wears green, and hence has been untrue.

154 For Lamech (*Lamek*), as the first bigamist, see WBPro III.54–56n. and SqT V.550. But it was Jabal, son of Lamech, who **found tentes first** (see Gen. 4.20), a misidentification on Chaucer's part which Pratt (in Sts. in Lang., 306) suggests was due to the poet's carelessness in reading only the last four words of a line from Nicholas Trevet's Chronicles: "Cist Jubal le fitz lamec contreva primes tentes" (London, British Library, MS Arundel 56, fol. 3r).

157 Cf. WBPro III.386 and n.

158 **bar her on honde:** Cf. MLT II.620n.

162–64 For the rhetorical commonplace of inexpressibility, here turned to a sentimental purpose, see GP I.746n.

182 Proverbial; cf. KnT I.2397n.

183–87 The figure describes holding the animal by the bridle and keeping him at the end of a stick, perhaps by beating him. See OED s.v. *staff,* 5b, and Rowland, Blind Beasts, 135–36; and cf. Mars 41–42; Tr 1.218–24.

194 Cf. BD 1024–32 and n.

197 Cf. Tr 5.1784–85; LGW 2559–61.

201–3 A commonplace, but cf. Ovid, Amores 3.4.13–17, where the thought is related to the figure of a restrained horse.

211–350 The form of the Complaint has been analyzed by Paull F. Baum (Ch's Verse, 99–101) and Green, UMSE 2, 1962, 55–63. After an introductory stanza (211–19) rhyming *a a b a a b b a b* (the *a*-rhymes of which are matched in the *b*-rhymes of a metrically similar concluding stanza, 342–50), the Complaint is divided into two matched halves of six stanzas each (220–80; 281–341), described by Skeat as the Strophe and Antistrophe. The first four stanzas of each part (220–55; 281–316) retain the *a a b a a b b a b* rhyme scheme in pentameters, while the matching fifth stanzas, elaborating on this basic measure in a way almost to resemble a virelay, introduce a scheme of *a a a b a a a b* and its reverse, *b b b a b b b a,* with the *a*-lines of the basic pattern reduced to four stresses while they are increased in number, and then continued in reverse rhyme. Then the matching sixth stanzas return to the basic metrical pattern, but include two internal rhymes in each of their lines. Although Chaucer infrequently repeats actual rhyming words in the Complaint, the repetition of rhyme-syllables artfully connects stanzas throughout. The third stanza of the Antistrophe (299–307) shows especial technical accomplishment, as it balances the two rhymes of the third stanza of the Strophe (238–46, regular pattern) with

nine rhymes in *-ede,* apparently observing in the rhyme scheme the distinction of open and close *e*'s. *Rime riche* (cf. GP I.17–18n.) is especially heavy. See lines 229, 230, 233, 236; 240, 246, 342, 343; 299, 307; 310, 313; 330, 331; and 333, 336.

Wimsatt (Ch and Fr Love Poets, 173) notes Machaut's and Froissart's use in complaints of a sixteen-line stanza with a rhyme scheme identical to that of Anel 256–71, 317–32, though with line-lengths different from Chaucer's. *Anelida*'s nine-line stanza, nowhere else used by Chaucer, became popular in fifteenth-century Scots poetry; it is found in Henryson's Testament of Cresseid, the anonymous Quair of Jelousy, Dunbar's Golden Targe, the Prologue to Book III of Douglas's Eneydos, and his Palace of Honour, where it appears with internal rhyme.

211 **poynt of remembraunce:** Cf. "la puntura della rimembranza" of Dante, Purg. 12.20 (Schless, Ch and Dante, 87–8), and the image of the piercing sword in Machaut's chant royal (Wimsatt MAE 47:69).

214 Cf. Lady 51.

222 Cf. Lady 31 (nearly identical); for the possible source in Machaut, see Wimsatt MAE 47:67.

237 Cf. Lady 46 (exactly the same).

272 For **swete foo,** see Lady 37, and cf. Oton de Grandson, ed. Piaget 1:464, "tresdoulce ennemye"; on similar uses of oxymoron, see Tr 1.411n.

284–348 Of the numerous general correspondences of the *Anelida* with Ovid's Heroides cited by Shannon, Ch and Roman Poets, 38–43, perhaps the most interesting are Anel 284–89 and Her. 3.139–42 (effects on the heroine of the lover's separation); Anel 328–34 and Her. 15.123–27 (appearance of the lover in a dream); and Anel 342–48 and Her. 7.3–6 (heroine's comparison to the dying swan; see note 346–47 below).

309 For April's proverbially wet weather, see GP I.1–2 and Tr 4.750–51. For Chaucer's use of the rhetorical device of "impossibility" (listing events which ordinarily cannot happen) see Brookhouse, MAE 34, 1965, 40–42.

315–16 **tame:** Cf. RR 9913–14, where the same figure is used to describe women's unfaithfulness.

320 *Chaunte-pleure:* A thirteenth-century French poem, entitled La pleurchante (see Meyer, Romania 6, 1877, 26–27; Romania 13, 1884, 510–11; and Bull. de la SATF 9, 1883, 101) contrasts sinful joys in this world with weeping hereafter; but the term took on proverbial force to describe that which begins in joy and ends in woe, or vice versa. See Morawski, Proverbes français 1279; and, for its frequent use by Lydgate, Whiting C146.

323–24 **keye:** Cf. Tr 5.460n.

330 **asure:** Blue, the color of constancy; cf. 146 and n., above, and Tr 3.855n.

333–34 Cf. Lady 8–9.

346–47 It was widely believed that the swan, otherwise mute, sings at its death. See PF 342n., and cf. LGW 1355–56.

351–57 The description of the Temple of Mars is in Statius, Theb. 7.40–62; Boccaccio, Tes. 7.29–39; and KnT I.1967–2050.

353 **betwixe pale and grene:** Norton-Smith (Med. Sts. for J. A. W. Bennett, 85–86), who doubts the authenticity of this stanza, finds an un-Chaucerian distinction between the virtually identical qualities denoted by *pale* and *grene* (see MED s.v. *grene* adj. 1 [b]); cf. *hewes pale and grene* in Tr 4.1154 and compare 5.243.

The Parliament of Fowls

Chaucer acknowledges his authorship of *The Parliament of Fowls* in the Prologue to *The Legend of Good Women* F 419 (G 407) and in the Retraction to the *Tales;* it is confirmed by Lydgate in his *Fall of Princes* 1.311–15. Its exact date is unknown. The genre, theme, and style, and the use of the rime-royal stanza, suggest a position between *The House of Fame* and *Troilus,* that is, in the late 1370s or early 1380s. Attempts at more precise dating have usually been based on the possibility of personal allegory in the parliament scene, and on the reference to the planet Venus as *north-north-west* (see 117 below).

Although the meaning and value of the poem do not depend on its being read as an occasional poem, the studied preference accorded in the poem to the royal tercel as a suitor for the formel's hand suggests an occasion involving a royal suitor, whom most investigators identify as King Richard II (born 1367). The various attempts to arrange a match for Richard began in 1377, and ended in January 1382 with his marriage to Anne of Bohemia, daughter of Emperor Charles IV. The most plausible theory, offered over a century ago by Koch, and many times attacked and defended, is that the *Parliament* is related to the match between Richard and Anne. Various noble suitors have been proposed for the roles of the second and third tercels. Larry D. Benson (in Wisdom of Poetry, 123–44), has recently renewed the claims of Friedrich of Meissen as the second tercel (who is of lesser rank but who claims longevity of service) with new evidence that Friedrich was Anne's fiancé from 1377 until her betrothal to Richard in 1381. The Dauphin (and future Charles VI of France) was regarded, at least in Clementist quarters, as a candidate for Anne's hand in mid-1380 (after negotiations to join Anne and Richard had begun), thus suggesting him as the third tercel, who cannot boast of long service. In this theory the most likely date for the *Parliament* is about June 1380; it provides for a *respit* of about a year between the first "courtship" of Anne and the actual betrothal. For references to the many other speculations on the date and occasion of the poem, see Robinson, and Benson in the essay cited above. If the poem reflects the style and flavor of actual national parliaments of the time, it does so only very lightly (see D. S. Brewer, ed., PF, 1960, pp. 37–38).

The Parliament of Fowls is a highly complex and original work, but it is related to genres and subjects already familiar in medieval literature. Along with *The Book of the Duchess, The House of Fame,* and the Prologue to *The Legend of Good Women,* it belongs to the class of dream visions (see, e.g., Spearing, Med. Dream Poetry, chap. 1), many of which from the thirteenth century onward were devoted to love and brought together such conventional traits as "the lover-poet, the dream . . . , the May morning, the enclosed orchard or garden, the guide, and the love-problem debated before the god or goddess of Love by a council of birds" (Brewer, MLR 53, 1958, 323). The parliament of birds was itself a familiar genre

(Seelmann, Jahrbuch des Vereins f. niederdeutsche Sprachforschung 14, 1888, 101–47; Farnham, Univ. Wisc. Sts. Lang. and Lit. 2, 1918, 358–65). Chaucer also draws on the tradition of the *demandes d'amours,* questions of love involving two or three rival solutions, presented to a fictional judge or to the actual audience for a verdict (Manly, Studien zur engl. Philol. 50, 1913, 283–85, and cf. KnT I.1347n.). The situation in the parliament scene has been likened to that in the widespread folk tale of the Contending Lovers (see Farnham, PMLA 32, 1917, 492–518). But in *The Parliament of Fowls,* the original question of the three suitors' rivalry is soon dropped for a larger question; and there are many other alterations of love vision and debate convention.

The *Parliament* is one of the earliest known Valentine poems (see 309 below); on its probable setting as part of court entertainment, see Brewer, ed., PF, 3–7.

The essays of B. H. Bronson (Univ. of Calif. Pubs. in Eng. 3, 1935, 193–224; ELH 15, 1948, 247–60) initiate modern investigation of *The Parliament of Fowls* as a work of art; critics have since offered a whole spectrum of interpretations of its tone, structure, and morality. The chief critical problem has been to explain the apparent discordances among its successive parts: the dour summary of the *Somnium Scipionis* suggests allegiance to "common profit" and to transcendental values; the temple of Venus and Nature's comic assembly of birds suggest different and conflicting sublunary and private values. Depending on critical emphasis, the poem may thus be seen as a sober philosophical tract (Lumiansky, RES 24, 1948, 81–89); as a comedy of manners (Stillwell, JEGP 49, 1950, 470–95); as a Christian allegory (Huppé and Robertson, Fruyt and Chaf, chap. 3); and as a "great civic poem" (Olson, SAC 2, 1980, 53–80). Baker, in Comp. to Ch, 428–45, summarizes many other interpretations. Perhaps the dominant stream in modern criticism is that which embraces the poem's discordances, dwelling in one way or another on irony, indirectness, disharmony, and inconclusiveness as part of its design. See, e.g., Bronson; Clemen, Ch's Early Poetry, chap. 3; Wilhelm, ChR 1, 1967, 201–6; McCall, ChR 5, 1970, 22–31; Winny, Ch's Dream-Poems, chap. 4; Leicester, ChR 9, 1974, 15–34; Reed, RUO 50, 1980, 215–22; L. Sklute, ChR 16, 1981, 119–28.

Valuable comment on the text will be found in J. A. W. Bennett, PF, 1957, and in the editions of Skeat and Brewer.

1 This proverbial phrase (Whiting, L245; Walther 1417), often quoted in its Latin form—*Ars longa, vita brevis*—goes back to Hippocrates, who applied it to medicine. Here applied to love, it is used as a rhetorical device, the beginning of a poem with a proverb or sententious remark. On the rhetoric of the opening, see Manly, Ch and Rhetoricians, PBA, 1926, 99–100; Dorothy Everett, Essays on ME Lit., 1955, 103–6, 153–54; and Brewer, ed., PF, 48–50. The significance of the alternation of rhetorical and plain speech in the opening is discussed by Bateson, EIC 11, 1961, 256–61; Manzalaoui, EIC 12, 1962, 221–22; Knight, Rymyng Craftily, 1974, 25–28; and Jordan, ESC 3, 1977, 379–80.

The explanatory notes to *The Parliament of Fowls* were written by Charles Muscatine.

3 dredful joye: Criseyde uses the same phrase in Tr 2.776. The paradoxical and unstable quality of human love is an ancient literary commonplace; see Bennett, PF, 26–29.

7 Proverbial; cf. KnT I.2397n.

8 Chaucer usually represents himself as either unsuccessful or a complete outsider in the affairs of love; cf. PF 158–63; BD 30–40; HF 628–40; Tr 1.15–18; ProLGW F 490; ProThop 700–702.

10, 15–25 For Chaucer's love of reading, see HF 652–58 and ProLGW 29–39.

12–14 Manzalaoui (EIC 12:222–24) calls attention to the substantially different meanings produced by different punctuation of these verses (and by the reading *sey* for *can* in 14) in the editions of Skeat, Bilderbeck, Koch, and Brewer. The main issue is whether (as, e.g., in Brewer) **his strokes been so sore** is to be enclosed in quotation marks, to produce the meaning "I dare not say his inflictions (in my case) have been grievous; all I can do is to give him royal honors." The present punctuation, defended by Manzalaoui, produces "Since he is apt to give severe treatment to those who oppose him, I am too frightened to do anything but propitiate him by expressing my homage and good wishes. And that is all I know about the matter."

12 lord and syre: Love is here personified as the powerful and tyrannical Cupid, the god of love familiar in poetry since Ovid (e.g., Amores 1.1.21–26, 1.2; Ars amatoria 1.9–10; Met. 1.453–73). In the classical tradition he is a young boy armed with bow and arrow, but Chaucer may also have in mind here a more mature figure, resembling a feudal lord, as in RR 866–903, 1681–2050 (Rom 885–917, 1715–2144), who first wounds then exacts fealty from the Lover. Cf. ProLGW F 311–454, where the lordship of the God of Love is treated at length. Cupid appears again in lines 211–217, in a passage based on Boccaccio, Teseida 7.54.

31 The Dream of Scipio (Somnium Scipionis) is the brief final part of M. Tullius Cicero's Republic (De re publica), a work of political and moral philosophy. The Republic was not known in the Middle Ages except for the Somnium Scipionis, which was preserved by Macrobius (c. 400) in the course of his writing a long commentary on it. Chaucer had probably read the combined Dream and Commentary, but in 36–84 he summarizes only the Dream, which opens with the mission of Scipio Africanus the Younger (Roman general and statesman, c. 184–129 B.C.) to Massinissa, king of Numidia, in 149 B.C. Massinissa was an old family ally and admirer of Scipio's adoptive grandfather, Scipio Africanus the Elder (c. 235–183 B.C.), one of Rome's greatest generals, and they speak of him late into the night. The elder Scipio, whom Chaucer calls *Affrycan*, then appears to his grandson in the dream related in the rest of the work; it consists mainly of a philosophical dialogue in which the elder Scipio is the principal speaker.

The Commentary, over sixteen times the length of the Dream, uses successive passages from the latter as occasion for an exposition of neoplatonic doctrine and an encyclopedia on such subjects as arithmetic, astronomy, the music of the spheres, geography, and the immortality of the soul. It was a very important intellectual influence on the Middle Ages and beyond. Chaucer refers to it particularly as an authority on dreams in Rom 6–10 (trans. of RR 7–10), in BD 284–87, HF 916 (Scipio is erroneously called a king in all three), HF 514, and NPT VII.3123–26.

For texts, see Som. Scip. in Cicero, De re publica, ed. and tr. Keyes, 260–83; Macrobius, Som. Scip., ed. J. Willis; William H. Stahl, tr., Macrobius, Commentary on the Dream of Cicero (including Som. Scip.), 1952; Som. Scip., trans. Brewer, ed., PF, app. 3. For a summary of opinion on Chaucer's knowledge of Macrobius, and on the latter's identity, sources, and influence, see Stahl, Comm., intro.

32 Anderson, PAPS 33, 1902, xcviii–ix, notes that neither Cicero nor Macrobius wrote in chapters, and that Som. Scip. contains no reference to hell. He suggests that **Chapitre**, parallel to the contemporary use of the Latin term *capitulum,* could have meant "main topic." Gower so uses it in Conf. aman. 5.1959, 6.617; cf. MED s.v. *chapitre,* 1(d). Bennett (in Ch Problems, 132) offers a list of the work's seven main themes. Chaucer also makes reference to Scipio's seeing *helle and erthe and paradys* in HF 917; both are possibly based on misreading of RR 18365–69: "Ausinc con de l'ome qui songe, / Qui veit . . . en leur presences / Les esperitueus sustances, / Si con fist Scipion jadis; / E veit enfer e paradis" (Just as with the man who dreams, who sees . . . spiritual substances in their actuality, as Scipio did formerly; and sees hell and paradise).

33 soules: On medieval doctrine on the fate of heathen souls, see Bennett, in Ch Problems, 133–35.

47 commune profyt: Cf. 75. This phrase is often cited in the criticism of the poem. Cicero here (Som. Scip. 6.13) reads, "all those who have preserved, aided or enlarged their country." Bennett, PF, 33–34, notes that the phrase, often used in the proceedings of the Plantagenet parliaments, has elsewhere in Chaucer the extended "suggestion of peace and general harmony." See ClT IV.431, 1194; ParsT X.773; cf. Bo 1.pr4. Olson, SAC 2:53–80, discusses the relevant medieval political theory.

53–54 Som. Scip. (6.14) reads, "Surely all those are alive . . . who have escaped from the bondage of the body as from a prison; but that life of yours, which men so call, is really death" (tr. Keyes, 267). Benson (in Wisdom of Poetry, 125–29) shows that Chaucer's rendition tempers somewhat the contempt for earthly life (*contemptus mundi*) found in Som. Scip. Cf. KnT I.3061, SNPro VIII.71–74.

56 Galaxye: The Milky Way, referred to in Som. Scip. 16 as the habitation of the virtuous dead, but described by Macrobius, who regards it as the locus of Scipio's dream (Comm. 1.4.5), also as the pathway taken by souls between earth and sky (1.12.2). See also HF 936–39.

57–58 Cf. Bo 2.pr7.

59–63 Ancient and medieval thought commonly represented the universe in the form of the immovable earth surrounded by eight or nine revolving concentric spheres. Cicero (Som. Scip. 6.17) describes the outer one as that of heaven, in which the stars are fixed. The next seven are those of Saturn, Jupiter, Mars, the sun, Venus, Mercury, and the moon. (For Cicero the earth is in the ninth sphere; other commentators exclude the earth but count the *primum mobile* as the outermost sphere. Chaucer's view seems to vary; cf. Astr 1.17.38–39, FranT V.1283.) The movement of the spheres was supposed by some to produce a perfectly harmonious music, often related to the tones of a diatonic scale. Cicero, for example, says that the eight revolving spheres produce seven different sounds (two of them precisely producing the same note an octave apart; see Anderson, PAPS 33:xcix). Although it was itself inaudible on earth, this harmony was regarded as the source and prototype of all music, i.e., all harmony or proportioning, in the universe. Cf. Tr 5.1809–13; RR 16947–54; Macrobius, Comm. Som. Scip. 2.1–4. Chamberlain (ChR 5, 1970, 32–56) provides a valuable analysis of the ample references to music and harmony in PF, along with some debatable numerological speculations.

67–69 The reference is to the "great year," the period, variously estimated, in which all the heavenly bodies go from a definite position and return to it. Macrobius (2.11.11) gives 15,000 solar years, Jean de Meun (RR 16816) 36,000 years. See Stahl, Comm., 221n. On the cyclical patterns of time in PF, see Entzminger, JMRS 5, 1975, 1–11.

80–84 Som. Scip. reads, "their spirits, after leaving their bodies, fly about close to the earth, and do not return to this place except after many ages of torture" (6.26; tr. Keyes, 283). Chaucer adds Christian coloration to this suggestion of Purgatory with that blysful place (83) and with the concluding prayer. Cf. Bennett, PF, 41–44; Clemen, Ch's Early Poetry, 133–34.

85–86 Based on Dante, Inf. 2.1–3: "Lo giorno se n'andava, e l'aere bruno / togliera li animai che sono in terra / da le fatiche loro."

90–91 Based on Boethius (Bo 3.pr3.33–36), these lines may refer specifically to the reading of Som. Scip. (cf. PF 20: *a certeyn thing to lerne*) or, more likely, they may simply express a state of general discontent. See also Pity 99–104; Lady 43–45; Tr 3.445.

95–96 Cf. Tr 3.1255, and see 260–79 below.

99–105 This stanza is closely parallel to Claudian (d. 408?), De IV consulato honorii (ed. and tr. Platnauer), 3–10: "venator defessa toro cum membra reponit, / mens tamen ad silvas et sua lustra redit. / iudicibus lites, aurigae somnia currus / vanaque nocturnis meta cavetur equis. / furto gaudet amans, permutat navita merces / et vigil clapsas quaerit avarus opes, / blandaque largitur frustra sitientibus aegris / iniguus gelido pocula fonte sopor" (The huntsman stretches his weary limbs upon the couch, yet his mind ever returns to the woods where his quarry lurks. The judge dreams of lawsuits, the charioteer of his chariot the nightly steeds of which he guides past a shadowy turning point. The lover repeats love's mysteries, the merchant makes exchange of goods, the miser still watchfully grasps at elusive riches, and to thirsty sufferers all-pervading sleep offers from a cooling spring idly alluring draughts). Pratt (Spec 22, 1947, 421–23) has shown that the passage occurs in Liber Catonianus, a widely used medieval schoolbook. The idea was commonplace. Cf. Macrobius, Comm. 1.3, a very popular source of medieval dream lore; Boccaccio, De genealogia deorum 1.31; Bartholomaeus Anglicus, De proprietatibus rerum 6.27, tr. Trevisa 1:337–38. Chaucer discusses dreams elsewhere, in HF 1–52, Tr 5.358–79, NPT VII.2970–3148. The explanation offered by the narrator here puts his dream into the medieval medical category of the *somnium animale,* a dream brought on by mental activity or disturbance; cf. Curry, Ch and Science, 207; and BD 1–15n.

109–12 Africanus here takes on the role, traditional in vision literature, of the narrator's guide. Cf. Dante, Inf. 1.61–114; HF 605–71.

111 Macrobius says in the concluding sentence of his Commentary that, because the Som. Scip. takes up all three of the branches of philosophy—moral, physical, and rational—"there is nothing more perfect than this work."

113–19 Cf. HF 519–20n.

113 Cytherea: An epithet for Venus, from the island of Cythera (now Cerigo), where she was said to have risen from the foam of the sea (cf. KnT I.1936–37n.). She is here personified as the goddess carrying a firebrand (cf. Rom 3705–10, 3753–57; MerT IV.1777), and in PF 117 as the planet. Dante uses "Citerea" to denote the planet in Purg. 27.

117 north-north-west: The meaning of this term has been widely debated. If it means that the planet Venus was actually visible in the north-northwest, it is inaccurate, since from the latitude of London, Venus is never visible north-northwest, nor indeed even as far north as northwest. If *north-north-west* were meant as a rough approximation, meaning Venus's "extreme northern position" (Manly, Stud. Engl. Phil. 50:288) or if an uncorrected sighting had been taken by magnetic compass with a variation of over 20° westward of true bearing due to the earth's magnetic field (Lange, Anglia 58, 1934, 333–44), then the reference could be used to help date the poem. Venus at her most northwesterly position was brightly visible in April and May of 1374, 1377, and 1382, and clearly visible in May and June of 1380 (see Lazarus, in Wisdom of Poetry, 145–51). But Chaucer's use of the clearly more precise term *north-*northwest as an approximation for northwest is unlikely, and it is also unlikely that the future author of the Astrolabe, even though he knew the mariner's magnetic compass (cf. Astr 2.31), would not habitually have used the easily determined true bearings rather than magnetic bearings for celestial observation.

Manly remarks (parenthetically) that the term may simply be a reference to the proverbially evil associations of the north, here meaning "in an unpropitious position"; he compares Hamlet 2.2.396: "I am but mad north-north-west" (Studien zur engl. Philol. 50:288; cf. FrT III.1413n.). Garbáty (Romance Notes 9, 1968, 330) gives references from Andreas Capellanus (late 12th-c.) and Boccaccio (cf. KnT I.1903–12) suggesting that the most propitious direction for Love is the east, and that the north in this respect signifies aridity or chastity. Bronson (Univ. of Calif. Pubs. Eng. 3:204–8), after reviewing the astronomical uncertainties, follows Manly, suggesting that in the usage of a narrator who proclaims himself detached from love, Venus north-northwest means "hardly at all"; elsewhere (ELH 15:252) Bronson suggests that the allusion is "geographical rather than astronomical"; it points to a locale where "Cytherea was exerting her influence." Cf. Malone, Chapters on Ch, 78–79. One MS (Gg) reads "north nor west," usually accepted as a variant of *north-north-west.* Two MSS of lesser authority (R, Ff) read "northewest." Manzalaoui (in Geoffrey Ch, 234) notes that "for *north-east* and *south-east* the *Astrolabe* (II, 31, 2–3) makes use of the terms *northe the est* and *south the est:* thus *north the west* or, by apocopation, *northewest,* could be a straightforward description of the most northerly evening position of the planet."

122 The walled park or garden is a version of the "pleasance" (*locus amoenus*) common in poetry from classical times; see Curtius, European Lit., 195–202; as a setting for erotic love it was most familiar to Chaucer in RR (Rom 136–39; cf. MerT IV.2029–37). In the Middle Ages this tradition merges with that of the paradise of Genesis, and of the enclosed garden ("hortus conclusus") of the Song of Solomon (Cant. 4.12), with the possibility of religious signification. See below, 204–10. For a view of the garden in PF as an allegorical representation of the church, see Huppé and Robertson, Fruyt and Chaf, 110–15.

123–141   The picture is that of a single gateway having two contradictory inscriptions over its entrance, one in gold, the other in black. The repeated *Thorgh me men gon* clearly echoes "Per me si va," thrice repeated in the inscription over the portal of Hell in Dante's Inferno (3.1–9). Dante's inscription, written in dark ("oscuro") color, has of course no optimistic note; it ends: "Abandon every hope, you who enter." Both narrators (Inf. 3.12; PF 142) respond with perplexity. Chaucer's lines are probably meant simply to express the paradoxical character of earthly love; but they have also been interpreted as contrasting different types of love (good and bad, natural and courtly, divine and human). Clemen, supporting the former view, observes that since there is only one gate, no choice is possible: "Whoever goes through the gateway accepts both possibilities" (Ch's Early Poetry, 140).

132   thow redere: Cf. Tr 5.270 and n.

136   Disdayn and Daunger: *Daunger* appears in RR (cf. Rom 3015–30, 3130–66), the personification of something akin to disdain: "the rebuff direct, the lady's 'snub' launched from the height of her ladyhood, . . . and perhaps her anger and contempt" (Lewis, Allegory of Love, 124). Cf. Rom 3018n.

140   Cf. RR 16616: "Seul foir en est medecine" (The only medicine for it is flight).

148   adamauntes: The *adamant* was thought to be the hardest of substances (cf. KnT I.1305, 1990n.) and was later identified with the diamond; it was also thought to have magnetic powers greater than those of a magnet (cf. Rom 1182–86) and the power of controling emotions as well (Bartholomaeus Anglicus, 16.8, tr. Trevisa 2:833).

154   shof: "Pushed, thrust," but with perhaps less connotation of rudeness than modern English "shoved."

155–56   Possibly influenced by Dante, Par. 4.10–12, "my desire was painted on my face."

159   Loves servaunt: Cf. 12 above.

169–70   Cf. Inf. 3.19–21, referring to Dante's guide: "E poi che la sua mano alla mia puose / con lieto volto, ond' io mi confortai, / me mise dentro a le segrete cose." (And when he [Virgil] had placed his hand on mine, with a cheerful look that comforted me he led me in to the hidden things.)
This is the last reference to Africanus in PF.

176–82   Here is a "mixed forest," "a subspecies of the 'catalogue,' which is a fundamental poetic form that goes back to Homer and Hesiod" (Curtius, European Lit., 195). Curtius cites examples of mixed forests from Ovid to Spenser and Keats. The tradition was by no means bound by the observation of nature. Chaucer's list, notable for its "almost total absence of botanic description" (Bennett, in Ch Problems, 139), identifies the trees by their uses. Chaucer owes some of the trees and epithets to his reading, particularly in Tes. 11.22–24; Joseph of Exeter's Iliad 1.505–10; RR 1353–60 (Rom 1379–86);

Ovid, Met. 10.90–108. For detailed comparison with those in earlier authors, see Boitani, Reading Medieval Studies 2, 1976, 28–44; Root, MP 15, 1917, 18–22; see also Barney, in Wisdom of Poetry, 189–223. Chaucer's epithets for the oak, elm, holm-oak, yew, and aspen appear to be original.

176   hardy asshe: Cf. Joseph of Exeter: "fraxinus audax." Barth. Angl. explains (17.62, tr. Trevisa 2:951) that it grows in rough places and mountains.

177   piler: "Pillar"; perhaps a support for vines. Cf. Tes. 11.24; Ovid, Met. 10.100.

cofre unto carayne: Elm was used for making coffins.

178   pipere: Boxwood is excellent for making pipes and horns. Cf. Joseph of Exeter: "cantatrix buxus"; NPT VII.3398.

179   saylynge: Fir was used for ships' masts and timbers; cf. Claudian, De raptu Proserp. 2.107: "Apta fretis abies."

deth to playne: Vincent of Beauvais reports (Speculum nat. 1.12.57) that the cypress was "consecrated to death among the pagans" and is "placed on houses as a sign of a funeral." Cf. Joseph of Exeter: "cupris flebilis."

180   The yew was used to make bows (Barth. Angl., 17.161, tr. Trevisa 2:1056); the aspen to make shafts or arrows (cf. Vegetius in MED s.v. *aspe* 1).

181   dronke vyne: Cf. Joseph of Exeter: "ebria vitis."

182   victor palm: Cf. Boccaccio Tes. 11.24: "d'ogni vincitore / premio, la palma" (the palm, prize of every victor).

to devyne: The ancient sibyls, or prophetesses, were supposed to have been inspired by eating laurel; cf. Tibullus, ed. Postgate, Loeb, 1962, 2.5.63–64.

183–294   This passage, which contains reminiscences of RR and of the Divine Comedy, is mostly a close adaptation of Boccaccio, Tes. 7.51–56 (tr. Brewer, ed., PF, app. 4) describing the visit of Palemone's personified Prayer to the temple of Venus. For detailed comparison of the two passages, see Pratt, PMLA 62, 1947, 606–7; Bennett, PF, 74–106.

187   nothyng dede: Bennett, PF, 74n. suggests that Chaucer may have read in Tes. 7.51.6 "fonti vive," (lively fountains) for "fonti vide" (she saw fountains).

188–89   These brilliant images are Chaucer's.

204–10   This stanza is not based on the Teseida. Temperate climate, healthful spices and plants, health and everlasting life, indescribable joy, and eternal day are all conventional in medieval descriptions of paradise or heaven. See von Kreisler, PQ 50, 1971, 16–22. With 204–5, cf. BD 341–42.

214   Wille: "Carnal desire or appetite," translating "Voluttà" (Tes. 7.54.4); cf. Malone, MLR 45, 1950, 63. On the possibility that *Wille* translates "Voluntà" (found in some MSS), see Pratt, SP 42, 1945, 755–56.

215–16   wile . . . couchede: The sense is probably that with her "skill" she "placed" or "arranged" the arrows. But cf. OF *cochier*, "to notch (an arrow)." Some MSS support the reading *file . . . touched*.

217   Brewer (ed. PF, 108) notes that in RR (Rom 949–82) some of Cupid's arrows inflict less grievous wounds than others.

218–19   Chaucer follows Boccaccio closely but not exactly in his list of personifications. **Lust** and **Plesaunce** replace "Leggiadria" (comeliness, grace) and "Affabilitate" (affability), Tes. 7.55.

223–24   Translating Tes. 7.55.7–8: "e Van Diletto /

con Gentilezza vide star soletto" (and she saw Vain Delight standing alone with Nobility).

225–29   Follows Tes. 7.56, but replaces "Piacevolezza"
(Charm) and "Ruffiana" (Pandering) with **Desyr, Messagerye** (Message-Sending), **Meede** (Bribery), and the
unnamed **other thre**.

230–94   In describing the temple architecture and paintings, Chaucer and Boccaccio are following a tradition of
literary pictorialism or iconic poetry that goes back to
Homer. Cf. HF 120–467, 1112–1519; KnT I.1886–
2088; Virgil, Aeneid 1.446–93; Ovid, Met. 2.1–30,
6.70–128, Fasti 5.551–68; Dante, Purg. 10.34–93; RR
129–470. On the tradition in classical antiquity and the
Christian period, see Jean H. Hagstrum, Sister Arts,
1958, 3–56. On the temple of Venus particularly, see
Boitani, Studi Inglesi 2:9–29.

230–31   **jasper . . . bras:** Boccaccio writes (Tes. 7.57.1–
2): "in su alte colonne / di rame un tempio vide" (she
saw a temple of copper on tall columns). Chaucer makes
the columns of jasper and the temple of *bras*. The brass
is explained by Boccaccio himself, in his long note (*chiosa*)
to Tes. 7.50.1 (ed. Limentani, 465–66), where he says
that copper and brass, although they differ in particular
respects, are both in general the same metal, "born of the
planet Venus," and that by "copper" he means copper
and brass; the terms are interchangeable. See also Bartholomaeus Anglicus, 16.36, tr. Trevisa 2:844. On Chaucer's knowledge of Boccaccio's *chiose*, which occur in
only certain MSS of Tes., see Pratt, SP 42:745–63, and
Boitani, Ch and Boccaccio, 113–16. If Chaucer did not
know this *chiosa* he apparently shared the common
medieval linking of the two metals (Pratt, SP 42:753–
55). For jasper used in idealizing architecture, see Rev.
21.18–19; Claudian, Epithalamium de nuptiis honorii
Augusti, ed. Platnauer, 90–91.

240   **curtyn:** Of uncertain significance. In Tes. (7.58.3–
4), Peace holds up a curtain ("cortina") "lightly in
front of the temple's portals." Boccaccio explains (ed.
Limentani, p. 465) that Peace is present to show that
the desires that can be called loving require harmony
on both sides. Samuel C. Chew (Virtues Reconciled,
1947, 119–123) suggests that "the object held by
Peace is a Curtana, the truncated, pointless sword"
which was borne before the kings of England at their
coronation (MED s.v. *curtana*). Robert A. Pratt, agreeing, cites (in a letter) Ch Life Records, 296–99, on
Chaucer's awareness of the coronation swords. In
medieval Italian the word is *cortana* (from Old French
cortain, the sword of Ogier the Dane and other epic
heroes). But the spelling *cortina* in Tes. is supported by
the rhyme, and the English coronation sword was traditionally regarded as the emblem of Mercy rather
than of Peace. Perhaps Chaucer (and Boccaccio) visu-
alized Peace as holding up a temple-curtain or veil
such as may have been familiar from Biblical references to the curtains of the Tabernacle (Exodus 26.1–
6, 36.9–11) and the veil of the Temple (Matt. 27.51,
Mark 15.38, Luke 23.45); or, Peace may be lifting before the temple of Venus simply but not inappropri-
ately a bed-curtain.

242–43   Boccaccio (Tes. 7.58.5–7) gives Patience a pale
face, but the hill of sand appears to be Chaucer's. On the
conventional attributes of Patience in the Middle Ages,
see Hanna, in Triumph of Patience, ed. Gerald J. Schiff-
horst, 1978, 65–87.

246–94   Chaucer describes the interior of this Boccac-
cian temple of Venus again in KnT I.1918–66.

253–59   Based on Tes. 7.60 and Ovid, Fasti 1.415–40,
with additions by Chaucer. Boccaccio tells the story of
Priapus and the ass in fuller detail in his *chiosa* to Tes.
7.50.1 (ed. Limentani, 466–67). Ovid's version takes
place at an outdoor festival of the gods, where Priapus
loses his heart to the nymph Lotis, who scorns him. At
night he tiptoes to where she is sleeping: "He joyed, and
drawing from off her feet the quilt, he set him, happy
lover! to snatch the wished-for hour. But lo, Silenus's
saddle-ass, with raucous weasand braying, gave out an
ill-timed roar! The nymph in terror started up, pushed off
Priapus, and flying gave alarm to the whole grove; but,
ready to enter the lists of love ["obscena nimium quoque
parte paratus," literally: his obscene member only too
well-prepared], the god in the moonlight was laughed at
by all" (trans. J. G. Frazer, Loeb, 1951). For a study of
the connotations of Chaucer's passage, see Brown, SP 72,
1975, 258–74.

256   **sceptre:** Chaucer's addition to the picture; for *scep-
tre* used in an erotic sense, cf. Carmina Priapea 25, in
Petronii Saturae et liber Priapeorum, ed. F. Buecheler
and G. Heraeus, Berlin, 1922, 154; and Matthew of
Vendome, Milo, 139 (ed. Abraham in Gustave Cohen,
La comédie en France au XIIe siècle, Paris, 1931, vol. 1).

257–59   Not in Ovid, and Boccaccio merely mentions
garlands as decorating the temple. Brown (SP 72:263)
notes that the use of statues of Priapus in fertility worship
sometimes involved garlands of flowers.

260–79   Critics disagree on the significance of Venus in
this passage. Brewer, ed., PF, pp. 30–31, relying on the
tradition of the allegorist Fulgentius (6th c.) and on connotations of details found in Tes., reads the passage as "a
moral allegory, signifying selfish, lustful, illicit, disastrous love." Dorothy Bethurum Loomis, leaning more
heavily on the possible influence of Alanus de Insulis (see
316 below), regards Venus as representing "sexual desire in rather pure form, but . . . not . . . as necessarily
evil or corrupt" (in Philological Essays, ed. James L.
Rosier, Janua Linguarum, ser. major, 37, 1970, 192); cf.
P. Dronke in N&Q 206, 1961, 475–76. Bennett, PF, 98,
is perhaps closest to the mark: "The ambivalence of the
concept is part of the very theme of our poem." Cf.
Clemen, Ch's Early Poetry, 147; and see also E. Salter,
Fourteenth-Century English Poetry, 1983, 132–39.

272   **Valence:** The French town of Valence, on the
Rhone near Lyon; it still has a textile industry.

275–76   Cf. the proverb, "Without Ceres and Bacchus
(Libero) Venus is cold" (Terence, Eunuchus, 4.5.732).
The idea is common; cf. WBPro III.464, PhysT VI.58–
59, PardT VI.481–82, ParsT X.836, Tr 5.208; and
Whiting C125, W359.

277   **Cypride:** Venus, so called from her worship in
Cyprus. Cf. Tr 4.1216, 5.208; Alanus de Insulis, De
planctu Naturae 18.87.

281   **Dyane the chaste:** Cf. KnT I.1912n.

284–94   Lists of famous unhappy lovers were common
in medieval literature. Chaucer's is based on Tes. 7.61–
62 and Dante, Inf. 5.58–67, with the addition of **Candace, Isaude, Troylus, Silla,** and **the moder of Romulus.** For other such lists by Chaucer, see HF 388–426;
ProLGW F 249–69; and of course, LGW itself. Brewer
(ed. PF, 111) cites lists by Machaut and Froissart "which
Chaucer certainly knew."

286   Calyxte: Callisto, a nymph of Diana who was raped by Jupiter, bore a son, and was transformed into a bear by the jealous Juno. Cf. KnT I.2056–61n.

Athalante: Won in marriage by Hippomenes, who defeated her in a running race, Atalanta and her husband were turned into lions for making love in a sacred place; see Ovid, Met. 10.560–707. Not the same as Atalanta the boar-hunter, cited in KnT I.2070.

288   Semyramis: Legendary queen of Assyria, to whom medieval writers variously attributed the building of Babylon, the invention of trousers, and incest with her son. She became a type of pagan sinfulness. Dante (Inf. 5.52–60) puts her into the circle of carnal sinners. See Samuel, M&H 2, 1944, 32–44. Cf. MLT II.359 and n.; LGW 707.

Candace: Possibly Candace the Indian queen of the Alexander legend; in the late thirteenth-century Kyng Alisaunder (ed. Smithers, EETS, 1952–57, 6648–6733, 7578–7727) she offers Alexander fabulous gifts, then outwits and seduces him. Cf. the Anglo-Norman Alexander, ed. Foster, Anglo-Norman Text Soc., 1976–77, 6934–7018, 7611–7894. But the name may be intended rather to be that of Canace, daughter of Aeolus, who fell in love with her brother and bore him a child. Aeolus then forced her to kill herself. See Ovid, Heroides 11. Cf. IntrMLT II.77–80. Skeat (1:515) finds Candace for Canace in LGW 265 in one MS.

Hercules: His jealous wife Deianira, thinking that it would revive his love for her, sent him as a present the blood-stained tunic of a centaur he had killed. But the blood had been poisoned by Hercules' arrow, and the tunic caused him to suffer horribly. See Ovid, Heroides 9; Met. 9.198–238; MkT VII.2119–34.

289   Biblis: She fell desperately in love with her own brother; after he repulsed her and fled, she went mad. See Ovid, Met. 9.454–655.

Dido: Cf. Virgil, Aen. 4; Ovid, Heroides 7; HF 239–432.

Thisbe, and Piramus: Cf. Ovid, Met. 4.55–106.

290   Tristram, Isaude: The earliest known version of their celebrated love-story is a fragment by the trouvère Thomas (c. 1160), Tristan, ed. Wind, 1960; the best version is that of Gottfried von Strassburg (c. 1210), Tristan, ed. Weber, 1967. Chaucer uses the English form Tristram, as in Malory (Morte Darthur, ed. Vinaver as Works, 1967); cf. Sir Tristrem (late 13 c.), ed. G. P. McNeil, STS, 1886. Cf. HF 1796, LGW 254.

Paris: The story of Paris's abduction of Helen (*Eleyne*), which led to the Trojan War, was well known in the Middle Ages. Cf. Tr 1.61–63; Ovid, Heroides 16 and 17; Benoît de Sainte-Maure, Roman de Troie, 4315–4865.

Achilles: The medieval tale of Achilles' death as a result of his love for Polyxena is mentioned by Chaucer in BD 1067–71. Cf. Benoît, Roman de Troie, esp. 17511–18472, 20691–812, 21838–22334, where the story is told in elaborate detail.

291   Eleyne: Helen of Troy. Often cited with disapproval by medieval writers, she is nevertheless a sympathetic character in Chaucer's Tr.

Cleopatre: Her tragic romance with Antony is told in LGW 580–705.

Troylus: On Chaucer's sources for his version of the story, see the Explanatory Notes to Tr.

292   Silla: Scylla betrayed her father and his city,

Megara, for love of the attacking King Minos. Minos was horrified by the deed, and spurned her. See Ovid, Met. 8.1–151.

the moder of Romulus: Rhea Silvia (Ilia) was condemned to eternal virginity by her uncle, lest she bear a male avenger to punish the usurpation of her father's power. Imprisoned in a wood sacred to Mars, she produced the twins Romulus and Remus. She was weighted with chains and died. Ovid's account in Fasti 3.9–45 emphasizes Mars's captivation with Silvia and his possession of her. Cf. Justinus (3rd c.), Epitoma historiarum Philippicarum, ed. Seel, 1935, 43.2.1–4, in which the paternity of the twins is more doubtful.

303   Nature: The personification of Nature was commonplace in the Middle Ages. In his conception of Nature, Chaucer was particularly indebted to Alanus de Insulis (see 316 below) and to Jean de Meun, RR 15891–20667 (with many digressions). Nature is characterized as a queen and goddess, vicar of God (PF 379), representing the forces of both generation and order in the universe. On the medieval treatment of Nature, see Lewis, 90–111; Curtius, European Lit., chap. 6; Bennett, PF, 107–112, 194–212; Brewer, ed., PF, 26–30; Economou, Goddess Natura.

309   Seynt Valentynes day: The tradition of St. Valentine as patron of mating birds (and humans) may have been an invention of Chaucer and his literary circle. At any rate, there is no convincing evidence of a prior popular cult, or of other connection between any of the several Saint Valentines and the subject of erotic love or fertility before Chaucer. Valentine poems were written by Chaucer's friends Gower and Clanvowe, and by the French poet Oton de Grandson, whose work Chaucer knew, but their relative chronology has not been established. On the whole subject see Oruch, Spec 56, 1981, 534–65. Oruch suggests that "What relationship Valentine did have with fertility probably came through the simple coincidence of his feast day with events in nature and farming practices. . . . February 14 came, after all, shortly after the first and most ancient date for the beginning of spring and at the time when, by tradition, the birds began singing and mating" (562). The day is mentioned again in Mars 1–28, ProLGW F 145–47, and Compl d'Am 85.

310   Brewer cites here, as a possible indication of beliefs of educated persons in Chaucer's day, John Trevisa's translation (c. 1400) of the thirteenth-century Bartholomaeus Anglicus, De prop. rerum 12.1 (tr. Trevisa 1:597–98): "Among alle bestis that ben in ordre of generacioun, briddes and foules [folwen] most honest[ee] of kynde. For by ordre of kynde males seche femalis with bisynesse and loueth hem whanne they beth ifounden. . . . And briddes and foules gendrynge kepith couenable tyme, for in springinge tyme whanne the generacioun cometh inne, briddes crien and singen. Males drawen to companye of females and preyen iche othir of loue and wowith by beckes and voys. . . ."

316   Aleyn, Pleynte of Kynde: Alanus de Insulis (1125/30–1203), teacher, philosopher and theologian, member of the "humanist," platonizing "School of Chartres," was best known for his Anticlaudianus, a long allegorical poem on the perfection of virtue and knowledge, and his De planctu Naturae (The Complaint of Nature, or Pleynte of Kynde). The latter, which has been called a Menippean satire, is cast in the form of an allegorical dream vision, in which Nature, the main character, complains of man's failure to live by her laws; she gives an account of her own role in the universe, and of contemporary vices. The work is extremely rhetorical in style, and contains much elaborate description; Chaucer alludes to the most notable description, that of Nature herself, in PF 316–18. On her dress, writes Alanus, "was a packed convention of the animals of the air," after which follows a long list of birds. Alanus must thus have been among the influences suggesting the motif of a bird-parliament to Chaucer, but Chaucer's list in lines 330–64 does not particularly follow that of Alanus. See De planctu Naturae 2.145–95.

323–29   The division of birds into groups according to their eating habits goes back to Aristotle, Hist. animalium 8.3 (592b–593b). Chaucer may have found it in Vincent of Beauvais, Spec. nat. 1.16.14: "Some eat flesh, some seed, some various things; . . . some eat worms, like the sparrow. Some . . . fall upon thorns and feed from them. And some live on fruit, like doves and turtledoves. Some live on the banks of the waters of lakes or the sea and feed from them." While Chaucer's birds of prey clearly suggest the knightly class, and while it is certain that he plays in PF with social distinctions among the birds and thus with socially characteristic attitudes towards love, his four groups—birds of prey, worm-fowl, seed-fowl, and water-fowl—cannot be precisely identified with any medieval social classes or political interest-groups. On suggested identifications of this sort (e.g., with the nobles, the bourgeoisie, the agricultural class, and the great merchants, respectively), see Robinson 323n.; Olson, SAC 2:62–64.

331   Bartholomaeus Anglicus (12.2, tr. Trevisa 1:603) reports that in the eagle "The spirit of sight is most temporat and moost sharpe in acte and dede of seyinge and byholdynge the sonne in roundenes of his cercle withouten any blenchinge of yghen (eyes)." The eagle's medieval reputation for clear-sightedness was supported by the etymology of Isidore of Seville, cited by Vincent of Beauvais, Spec. nat. 1.16.32; "Aquila ab acumine oculorum vocata est" (the eagle gets its name from the keenness of its eyes). Cf. HF 1015–17n.

332–33   Pliny, Nat. Hist. 10.3 lists six kinds of eagles.

334   tiraunt: This epithet may have been suggested by Alanus, De planctu 2.150, describing the hawk's extortion of tribute from its subjects "with violent tyranny" (uiolenta tirannide); cf. Barth. Angl., 12.3, tr. Trevisa 1:607: "he[o] is a coueytous foul to taken othir foules" and "is iclepid aucipiter, 'a raptour and ravischere.' "

337–38   In falconry, a sport much favored by the nobility, the bird is carried on the hunter's hand or fist. Cf. Barth. Angl., 12.21, tr. Trevisa 1:630.

338–40   The sparrowhawk and the merlin prey on smaller birds. Cf. Barth. Angl., 12.4, tr. Trevisa 1:609; Tr 3.1191–92.

341   Chaucer distinguishes the dove here from the turtledove (turtil) in 355. The beauty of doves' eyes is alluded to in the Song of Solomon, e.g., 1.14, whence MerT IV.2141: thyn eyen columbyn. Barth. Angl. (12.7, tr. Trevisa 1:615) characterizes doves as "mylde briddes and meke."

342   Cf. David A. Bannerman, Birds of the Eng. Isles, 1953–61, 6:187 (cited by Rowland, Blind Beasts, 58): "A pair of swans are very jealous of their ownership [of the nest] and an intruder in the form of another swan is

quickly driven away." The idea of the swan song was very common though Pliny (Nat. Hist. 10.12.63) denied it; cf. Vincent of Beauvais, Spec. nat. 1.16.49–50; Barth. Angl., 12.12, tr. Trevisa 1:623; Alanus, De planctu 2.157–58. See also Anel 346–47, LGW 1355–56.

343   Cf. Alanus, De planctu 2.167–68 (tr. Sheridan, 89–90): "There the horned owl, prophet of grief, sang in advance psalms of lamentation for the dead"; cf. Barth. Angl., 12.6, tr. Trevisa 1:614. See also Tr 5.319n.

344   geaunt: Cf. Alanus, De planctu 2.162–63: "grus . . . in gigantee quantitatis euadebat excessum" (tr. Sheridan, 88–89): "the crane . . . rose to the size of the oversized giant."

345   thef: The chough's thievery was a traditional trait; see Alanus, De planctu 2.171–72.

janglynge: Cf. Vincent of Beauvais, Spec. nat. 1.16.131: "loquax," "garrula."

347   false lapwynge: The lapwing pretends its wing is broken to distract predators from its nest. Bennett, in Ch Problems, 140, suggests that the lapwing here is identified with "the false Tereus, the villain who raped Philomela," of Ovid, Met. 6, citing Conf. aman., where in Gower's retelling Tereus is changed into a "lappewinke," which remains "the bird falseste of alle" (5.6041–47). A flock of lapwings was called in the fifteenth century a "deceit"; cf. MED s.v. lap-wink.

348   The starling can be taught to speak; cf. The Manciple's Tale where a speaking bird betrays a secret.

349   coward kyte: Traditional; cf. Barth. Angl., 12.27, tr. Trevisa 1:634; Vincent of Beauvais, Spec. nat. 1.16.108.

350   orloge: Alanus says: "the barnyard cock, like a common man's astronomer, with a crow for a clock (horologio) announces the hours" (De planctu 2.163–64; trans. Sheridan, 89); cf. NPT VII.2855–58 and note VII.2857–58, Tr 3.1415n.

351   Venus sone: The sparrow was reputed to be lecherous. Cf. GP I.626 and n.

352   Bennett, in Ch Problems, 140, suggests that this is a reference to the shame of Philomela, raped by Tereus and changed into a nightingale (cf. 347 above). He cites Gower, Conf. aman. 5.5960–75, where the nightingale awaits the new green leaves in order to hide herself among them. For the story of Philomela, see LGW 2228–2393.

353–54   The reference is to the swallow's reputation as an eater of bees; see Vincent of Beauvais, Spec. nat. 1.16.97. In 353 two MSS read flyes for foules, but medieval authorities sometimes classified bees and other insects as birds; cf. Barth. Angl., 12.5, tr. Trevisa 1:609.

355   Chaucer elaborates on the faithfulness of the turtledove in lines 582–88. Cf. Alanus, De planctu 2.179–81; Barth. Angl., 12.35, tr. Trevisa 1:641.

356   On the long tradition, in various arts and crafts, of representing angels' wings with the design of peacock feathers, see Giffin, Sts. on Ch, 49–50.

357   Chaucer may be attributing to the pheasant a trait of the wild cock (gallus silvestris), which Alanus (De planctu 2.164–65) describes as scorning the inactivity ("deridens desidiam") of the domestic cock. Vincent of Beauvais, Spec. nat. 16.72, describes the pheasant as a wild cock (gallus sylvaticus). But it has also been noted that "a pheasant will breed with a common hen" (Skeat, 1:519). See also Rowland, Blind Beasts, 58.

358　waker goos: The watchfulness of geese was often illustrated by the story (alluded to in Pliny, Nat. hist. 10.23; Vincent of Beauvais, Spec. nat. 1.16.29) that their cackling awoke the defenders of the Roman Capitol (c. 389 B.C.) just in time to save it from the enemy.

unkynde: "Unnatural"; cf. 612–15. Some cuckoos are parasitic. They lay eggs in the nests of other birds, and the young eject the young of their hosts. Cf. Alanus, De planctu 2.184–85; King Lear 1.4.215–16: "The hedge-sparrow fed the cuckoo so long, / That [it] had it head bit off by it young."

359 The parrot was reputed to be luxurious, and fond of wine; cf. Vincent of Beauvais, Spec. nat. 16.15, 16.135.

360 Vincent of Beauvais, Spec. nat. 16.27, reports that drakes sometimes kill the female in the fury of their wantonness.

361 On the stork killing its female if she is unfaithful, see Vincent of Beauvais, Spec. nat. 1.16.48; Barth. Angl., 12.9, tr. Trevisa, 1:619; and Skeat (1:520).

362 The **cormeraunt** is still commonly known for its gluttony. Skeat (1:520) compares Shakespeare, Richard II, 2.1.38.

363 The raven is **wys** because it makes predictions; cf. Barth. Angl., 12.11, tr. Trevisa 1:622. The crow has a **vois of care** because it cries out when rain is approaching (cf. MancT IX.301) with a sorrowful voice "greding and crying, as this verse [Virgil, Georgics 1.388] meneth: 'Nunc cornix pluvium vocat improba voce' " (Barth. Angl., 12.10, tr. Trevisa 1:620).

364 ". . . with its beard-like white chest beneath its brown face, the [thrush] looks old. . . . the fieldfare has a frosty appearance, particularly in flight, when the white axillaries and underwings are conspicuous" (Rowland, Blind Beasts, 58). But Skeat (1:521) suggests that **frosty** is an allusion to the fieldfare's being a winter bird in England.

371　formel: MED lists this as the earliest use in English. It is a technical term from hawking and means "the female bird of prey" (as *tercel*, 529 and 596, means the male). On the proposed identification of the *formel* and her three *tercel* suitors, see the introductory note.

372–75 Cf. PhysT VI.9–13n.

379　vicaire: Mention of Nature as God's deputy (vicaria) is found in Alanus, De planctu 13.224, 16.187, 18.44; and in RR 16782, 19507; cf. PhysT VI.20.

380–81 This philosophical commonplace is found in Boethius, Cons. 3.m9 (Bo 3.m9.18–24), where the light (fire) and the heavy are mentioned along with the four primary qualities: hot, cold, moist, and dry (see GP I.420n.). Cf. Macrobius, Comm. Som. Scip. 1.6.24–28; Alanus, De planctu 6.46–48; RR 16958–64; Tr 3.-1751–54; KnT I.2991–93; and see Bennett, PF, 133, 161; Kean, Ch and Poetry 1:75–77.

387–90　statut . . . ordenaunce: Technical terms in constitutional law. "Nature's *statute* has the sacred character of law, and refers to the general mating; her *ordenaunce* is a particular act or decision within the scope of the *statute*, and is a mode of putting it into practice" (Brewer, ed., PF, 119).

395　secre: In the sense of "discreet," "not a gossip or booster," one of the qualities of a good courtly lover; as in Tr 1.744; listed also in NPT VII.2914–15 and LGW 1528. See Brewer, ed., PF, 119–20.

trewe as stel: Proverbial; see MerT IV.2426n.

411　This is: Pronounced as a monosyllable, *this,* and often so written; cf. 620, 650.

485　ple: "Appeal"; the legal terminology is continued in the next two stanzas.

491　delyvered: Probably a technical term for the dissolving of a parliament; see Bennett, PF, 166.

507　charge: "A frequent parliamentary word" (Brewer, 123).

510–11 These lines have been very variously interpreted by editors, and punctuated accordingly. Skeat (1:523), followed by Brewer, interprets: "If it be *your* wish for anyone to speak, it would be as good for him to be silent." Robinson suggests the possibility of "If you please (with your permission), a man may say what he might as well keep silent about." Baugh (70) (in the context of the stanza following) offers "Granted that a person may speak, nevertheless it would be as well for him to keep quiet." Fisher (576), regarding 509–10 as a separate sentence, interprets 511 as "Some people talk who might better be quiet." B. H. Bronson's reading, recorded in the gloss, seems the most probable.

512–18 A. J. Gilbert, N&Q 217, 1972, 165, points out similarities in situation, attitude, and expression between the turtledove here and the "faucon pelerin" of Oton de Grandson's Le songe Saint Valentin, esp. 390–98, noting the co-occurrence of Grandson's "entremis," "tel office," and "ne sçay chanter ne lire" beside Chaucer's **entermeten, such doinge,** and **neyther rede can ne synge.** The direction of borrowing between Grandson and Chaucer cannot, however, be determined with any certainty.

518 This proverbial expression is equivalent to *profred servyse / Stynketh* (CYT VIII.1066–67 and n.), **uncommytted** meaning "not commissioned, not delegated." Cf. Dante, Purg. 10.57: "officio non commesso."

521 Cf. Thop VII.891–93n.

529　tercelet: Cf. SqT V.504n.

530–32 On **termyne, presente,** and **accepteth** as possible parliamentary terms see Brewer (ed. PF, 123) and Bennett, PF, 140, 168.

558　gent: A term from popular poetry, here used mockingly, as in Thop VII.715 (see n.); see Brewer, ed., PF, 124.

574 Proverbial; Whiting F397.

587–88 The puzzling shift in person and gender is perhaps best explained as the turtledove's quotation either of a snatch of lyric or of what she would advise a lover to say. Hence, the punctuation (following Donaldson).

595 Proverbial; Whiting S680.

599–600 Cf. Bo 4.pr4.186–87: *thei ben lyk to briddes of whiche the nyght lightneth hir lokynge and the day blendith hem.*

609　recorde: Cf. Tr 3.51.

612 See 358 above.

632　If I were Resoun: The poet's going out of his way here and in 553–54 to emphasize the arguments for the superiority of the royal tercel makes a personal reference likely.

647–48 Bennett, in Ch Problems, 142–43, compares the similar conclusion of the matches in Shakespeare's Love's Labours Lost; he gives other examples of the use of **respit** in the formal sense of a period of delay.

675　roundel: A French lyric form, the rondel, in which one or more of the opening lines may recur as a refrain in the middle and/or at the end. It uses only two rhymes. In Chaucer's time its length varied from eight to fourteen lines or more, depending on the number and extent of the refrains. None of the MSS of PF indicate how the refrains should go, and only one (Gg) gives a full text (but in a later hand). The present version is that reconstructed by Skeat, on a model used by Machaut and others; the scheme is *ABB' abAB abb ABB'* (*A, B,* and *B'* are the lines used for the refrain).

677   Chaucer seems to be referring to an actual French tune to which the *roundel* was set. Some MSS have after 679, in place of the *roundel,* the words "Qui bien aime a tard oublie" (who loves well forgets slowly), which may indicate that a song of that name could be sung at this point. The line (a proverb: Morawski, Proverbes français, 1835; Hassell A63; Whiting L65) is found in several French lyrics. It is the first line of Guillaume de Machaut's "Le lay de plour" (in Oeuvres 1:283), and of a hymn to the Virgin by Moniot d'Arras (fl. 1213–39; see H. P. Dyggve, Moniot d'Arras et Moniot de Paris, Memoires de la société neophilologique de Helsinki, 13, 1938, 69–73). It is part of the refrain of Eustache Deschamps's Balade 1345 (in Oeuvres 7:124–25); and it appears in two anonymous secular lyrics (see Dyggve, Moniot, 145–50; Edward Järnström, Recueil de chansons pieuses du XIIIe siècle, 1910, 141). It is possible that the French line indicates simply a tune suitable for the *roundel.* Tunes used with the Moniot and Machaut lyrics have been preserved; see, for Moniot, Hendrik van

der Werf, Trouveres-Melodien II, Monumenta monodica medii aevi, 12, 1979, 381–83; and for Machaut (per advice of Cinny Little), see Works, ed. Leo Schrade (Polyphonic Music of the Fourteenth Century, 2), 1956, 90–93. *Now welcome, somer* is set to the music of Machaut's rondeau, "Dame, se vous n'avez aperceü," in Wilkins, Ch Songs, Ch Studies 4, 1980, 29. Perhaps Chaucer first intended to use a French song, then later inserted a *roundel* in English. The *roundel,* with its references to the birds in the third person (687–89; cf. 684), may possibly have been first composed for another occasion. See the next note.

680   **Now welcome, somer:** It is on the first of May that the birds in ProLGW F 171 (having in 145 just offered blessings to St. Valentine) sing "Welcome, somer." Perhaps *somer* is used in the present passage "for the warm season in general" (Robinson; see Bo 2.pr5.67n. and Moore, N&Q 194, 1949, 82–83); or perhaps this is an indication that, as suggested above, the song was first composed for another occasion.

688   **recovered:** Brewer suggests that the meaning is simply "to get or obtain." Bennett, in Ch Problems, 144, prefers " 'found again, got back': the suggestion being that they all separated while the parliament was in session." A. J. Gilbert, MAE 47, 1978, 301, accepts the OED's "to get back or find again" (s.v. *Recover* [v.] I.3.9) in the Boethian and neoplatonic sense of cyclical renewal. Cf. Bo 3.m2.40–42: *and alle thynges rejoysen hem of hir retornynge ayen to hir nature.*

Boece

Chaucer refers to his translation of Boethius's *De consolatione Philosophiae* three times—in the stanza to Adam Scriveyn (2), and in the comprehensive canons provided in the Prologue to the Legend of Good Women (F 425) and in the Retraction (CT X.1088). Lydgate also asserted that Chaucer "Off Boeces book, the Consolacioun,/ Maad . . . an hool translacioun" (Fall of Princes 1:291–92). The translation here edited is universally accepted as Chaucer's on the basis of internal evidence, early borrowings, and later ascriptions. Thomas Usk borrowed from it (and from *Troilus* as well) in his *Testament of Love* (probably 1387, though see introductory note to *Troilus*), and so did John Walton in his poetic translation (c. 1410). See Skeat 7:xxv–xxvi; Mark Science, Boethius, 1927, pp. xlii–lxii, and TLS, 22 March 1923, 199–200. *Boece* is thus a work that circulated during Chaucer's lifetime. The only ascriptions attached to the work itself, however, occur in John Shirley's verse table of contents (Brown and Robbins, Index of Middle English Verse, 1943, 1426), rubrics, and running titles in British Library MS Additional 16165 (A²), and at Cambridge, Pembroke College MS 215 (P), fol. 1r, in a hand of c. 1500 (not that of the scribe), "Istud opus est translatum per Chawcers [sic] armigerum Ricardi Regis 2di." Copies of Former Age and Fortune in Cambridge Univ. Lib. MS Ii.iii.21 (C²), but not *Boece* itself, are ascribed to the poet.

Like most of the canon, the *Boece* can be dated only approximately, and then only by such evidence as its association with, and use in, other works provides. It is most probably a labor of the late 1370s or early 1380s. *The House of Fame*, especially Book 2, shows a close knowledge of some portions of Boethius's work, notably 4.m1, although not a knowledge that necessarily implies that Chaucer had translated it. In the poems traditionally assigned to the early and middle 1380s, *Troilus* and The Knight's Tale, Chaucer shows a wide and detailed interest in topics Boethian (not simply the issues of causation discussed in 5; see 3.m12.52–55n., for example). This interest may well have coincided with his decision to give the work broader dissemination in England through a translation. In any event, a clear *terminus ad quem* is provided by Usk's borrowings: *Boece* must have achieved some degree of circulation by around 1387, even though the oldest surviving manuscripts (C², Hn, perhaps C¹) are thirty years later. (Our independent examination of Usk convinces us that he did indeed use *Boece*, although Skeat exaggerates the extent of that use; we disagree with Virginia Jellech's conclusion [cf. DAI 31, 1971, 6060A] that he used only Jean de Meun.)

Nearly all critical commentary on the *Boece* has been concerned with either Chaucer's prose style or the mechanics of his translation. This latter topic involves three separate issues—the nature of Chaucer's Latin text, his use of a French "pony" to aid in the translation (typical of nearly all his Latin translations), and his reliance upon commentaries. In the literature, these issues have usually

been discussed separately and the best current opinion on any single topic has never conveniently meshed with that on another. One major purpose of both our Explanatory Notes and our Textual Notes is to coordinate information relevant to all three problems.

False assumptions about Chaucer's Latin source text and his reliance upon it have bedeviled discussions of the work and have produced some extraordinarily negative comments on Chaucer's abilities as a Latinist. Furnivall long ago made the genial injunction to his readers to buy a two-shilling copy of Boethius to compare with Chaucer's text (Ch Soc 1st ser. 75, page v): he assumed that Chaucer should have had access to and used exclusively the same text of Boethius as that printed in modern critical editions. This same assumption has governed a number of discussions of Chaucer's failure as a Latinist, usually accompanied by lists of his blunders; see Hugh F. Stewart, Boethius, 1891, 222–26; Mark Liddell, Nation 64, 1897, 124; Liddell's notes to his edition in the Globe Ch; most extensively, Jefferson, Ch and the Consolation, 16–25; and Robinson's notes.

Chaucer may in fact have been ignorant of many specifically classical locutions, but his Latinity is not nearly as bad as these early studies claim. Liddell himself (Nation 64:124) saw half the answer to the problem: fourteenth-century texts of Boethius had lost, in many places, the readings of the traditional text. Major advances on this matter were made in two still unpublished Yale dissertations. Edmund Taite Silk, DAI 31, 1970 (diss. 1930), 2355A, showed that Chaucer's Latin text was most probably the version of Boethius that typically accompanies the commentary composed by Nicholas Trivet in the early fourteenth century; and Barnet Kottler, DAI 31, 1971 (diss. 1953), 6013A–14A, showed that such texts constitute a later medieval "Vulgate" tradition of the *Consolation*. (See further MS 17, 1955, 209–14.)

In our notes, we rely on Silk's and Kottler's findings. We use as our basic Latin text (and cite as Lat.) an early fifteenth-century English "vulgate" manuscript, the Latin text intercalated with manuscript C² (Kottler's Ca) and edited with scrupulous care by Silk. This text often presents Chaucer's supposed errors in a new light; for example, at 1.pr1.70 Chaucer plainly had a text that, like C², read "usque in exitum" (glossed "mortem"), not the traditional "usque in exitium." And yet often enough we have found that Chaucer's Latin text resembled not C² (and those readings typifying the "vulgate" tradition) but the traditional Latin (for which we use the most recent critical edition by Ludwig Bieler, 1957).

Thus the "errors" are only half explained by reference to the vulgate Latin tradition. A number of them, upon inspection, are neither errors, nor based upon variant Latin readings, but direct translations from a second source that Chaucer used side-by-side with his Latin: the French prose translation by Jean de Meun (for its authorship, see Langlois, Romania 42, 1913, 331–69). Its relevance was first noted by Stewart, Boethius, 202–6; his findings were seconded by Liddell, Acad 48, 1895, 227, who printed some readings from Jean in the Globe Ch. John L. Lowes demonstrated Chaucer's reliance on Jean

The explanatory notes to *Boece* were written by Ralph Hanna III and Traugott Lawler.

in a sample passage, RomR 8, 1917, 383–400; and V. L. Dedeck-Héry, in a series of articles, showed definitively that Chaucer used the whole work and, moreover, a copy resembling a small subfamily of manuscripts; see PMLA 52, 1937, 967–91; Spec 15, 1940, 432–43; PMLA 59, 1944, 18–25. Dedeck-Héry's contributions culminated in his posthumous edition of Jean's text, MS 14, 1952, 165–275, from which we draw the majority of our French readings.

Our investigations confirm Dedeck-Héry's claim that the closest surviving copy to that used by Chaucer is Besançon MS 434 (B); they further show that Chaucer translated literally, and from both Latin and French simultaneously. 1.m3.1–2 *discussed and chased* for Latin "discussa," French "chaciee," is but one example of several hundred that might be cited. Chaucer, then, regularly combined Latin and French readings, sometimes by doublets, more often by following the more explicit French syntax while preserving Latin lexis. Thus many of Chaucer's supposed misunderstandings of Latin are direct translations of the French.

A good deal of Chaucer's text, however, reproduces neither the Latin nor the French. In many places Chaucer translated not what was before him as the text of Boethius, but the explanatory commentary that frequently accompanied the text in manuscripts. Liddell first noticed Chaucer's reliance on explanatory, rather than textual, materials; in Nation 64:124–25, he identified the explanatory text Chaucer used as "the pseudo-Aquinas commentary," which occurs in a number of early prints. This identification was refuted by Petersen (PMLA 18, 1903, 173–93), who showed that Chaucer relied rather upon the commentary of Nicholas Trivet. Petersen's selective demonstration is extended in Silk's dissertation, cited above. We are indebted to Professor Silk for kindly supplying us with a typescript of his edition of Trivet and for allowing us to quote from it; we regret that he died without publishing it and before we could show him how much he had helped us.

Our study of this commentary has, in the main, confirmed Silk's conclusion that Chaucer is indebted to Trivet. But in a small minority of instances Chaucer follows, not Trivet, but Trivet's source, the commentary of Guillaume de Conches (we cite BL MS Royal 15B.iii, which lacks some portions of Book 3 and the last third of 5.pr5). In a few isolated cases Chaucer used other commentaries: an ancestor of the pseudo-Aquinas (for which we cite the Huntington copy of Anton Koberger's 1476 Nuremberg edition; see, for example, 4.m5.5n.); an unidentified commentary that appears attached to C^2 (see, for example, 3.pr12.182n); and one gloss (see 3.pr5.57–58n) from the commentary of William of Aragon (for which we use the copy in C^2). This small minority of readings reflects, we believe, the Latin manuscript from which Chaucer worked: like C^2, which contains an abbreviated copy of Trivet but other glosses as well, Chaucer's Latin text gave eclectic annotation of Boethius.

Given all these facts and suppositions, it is reasonable to suppose further, following Petersen and, in recent unpublished papers, Jerome Taylor, that Chaucer used a manuscript that contained all three of his sources together: a Latin text with commentary and French translation. Six of the seventeen surviving copies of Jean's translation in fact contain a Latin text and a commentary, and in two (P^2 and P^3) the commentary is Trivet's. But none

of these augmented texts has a version of the French with the specific readings of Chaucer's source, and Petersen's and Taylor's suggestion remains attractive but beyond substantiation.

Apart from discussions of the mode of translation, scholars have shown only moderate interest in the *Boece.* Jefferson, Ch and Cons., and Koch, Anglia 46, 1922, 1–51, collect passages elsewhere in the canon influenced by the *Consolation,* and critics who cite the translation typically do so as historical evidence to bolster interpretations of the individual poems (notably of *Troilus*). For a general introduction to the *Consolation,* one might consult Edward K. Rand, Harvard Sts. Class. Phil. 15, 1904, 1–28; and the translations by Richard Green, 1962; V. E. Watts, 1969; and S. J. Tester, 1973. For the literary influence of the work, see Patch, Goddess Fortuna, 1927, and Tradition of Boethius, 1935; the latter is now superseded by the exhaustive study of Pierre Courcelle, La Consolation, 1967. For notable critical readings, see Lewis, Discarded Image, 75–90; Winthrop Wetherbee, Platonism and Poetry, 1972, 74–82; and Dronke, SMed 6, 1, 1965, 389–422. On the practice of translation in the Middle Ages, see Jacques Monfrin, Jour. des savants 148, 1963, 161–90, and 149, 1964, 5–20. On Chaucer's prose, see Baum, JEGP 45, 1946, 38–42; Schlauch, PMLA 65, 1950, 568–89, and in Ch and Chaucerians, 140–63; Elliott, Ch's English, 132–80; and Lawler in Edwards, ed., ME Prose, 1984, 291–313. For Chaucer's and Jean's reliance on the gloss tradition, see Minnis, in Gibson, ed., Boethius, 1981, 312–61. For the best recent scholarship on Boethius, see the essays in Gibson's collection; Henry Chadwick, Boethius, 1981; and Edmund Reiss, Boethius, 1982. See also Peck's comprehensive annotated bibliography on Boece, 1986; Seth Lerer, Boethius and Dialogue, 1985; and Tim Machan, Techniques of Translation, 1985, which appeared too late to be of use here.

The notes that follow, in addition to the customary function of identifying sources and references to historical figures and paraphrasing difficult passages, are intended to provide a thorough commentary on the mode of Chaucer's translation. We take as normal—and so do not comment on—any reading that adequately reflects the Latin or French or both, although occasionally, where Chaucer's reliance on the French has seriously distorted Boethius's meaning, we comment on that fact. We attempt to identify all palpable mistranslations: our silence on a number of readings commonly thought to be mistranslations is to be taken as our sense that Chaucer has indeed accurately rendered the text (usually either the French or a reading from the Latin vulgate tradition) before him.

In addition, we identify readings where Chaucer's translation rests upon what we take to be a scribal error in or corruption of the source text. In many cases, the error occurs in either C^2 or the Latin cited by Trivet and is so identified. Where we hypothesize an error in Chaucer's French source, and where the reading occurs in an extant manuscript as reported by Dedeck-Héry, we direct the reader to his edition by page and line. But Dedeck-Héry's variants are incomplete. We have made our own collation of B, and, in many places where he is silent, we add the notation "as B" to indicate "the reading of B and, perhaps, of other extant MSS." By "Chaucer's Lat. MS" and "Chaucer's Fr. MS" we mean not simply the actual reading of Chaucer's hypothetical source, but also "Chaucer's perception of the form of his source"—which may have been erroneous, as at 2.pr8.15 ("$\overline{spe}$"), or 5.pr6.229 ("ncc^{te}," not "nat^{2e}").

Finally, we have tried to indicate everything Chaucer took from Trivet and other commentaries and glosses. Departing from previous editions of Robinson, we use italics in the text only to indicate clearly extratextual phrases and sentences not parallelled in either the Latin or the French. (Many readings that Robinson italicized as if they were glosses are simply Chaucer's effort to provide, parenthetically, the French reading.) All italicized phrases and sentences not explicitly commented upon in these notes are from Trivet. Of the remainder, most are Chaucer's original efforts at annotating the text or his mode of translating it (see 1.pr4.229–30n., 1.m5.25–26n., 5.pr4.36–37n.); a few others are from sources other than Trivet, and are also noted below. We do not italicize, but do note, numerous short additions grammatically integrated with the text. Some of these are derived from Trivet, but the greater number, marked "a Middle English addition," are without parallel in the source texts. Many may be by scribes, though at least some may be glosses by Chaucer.

Space has precluded extensive discussion of other potentially Chaucerian glosses (some Latin) found in the English manuscripts. All the manuscripts except HΘ have at least some interlinear annotation (most extensive in B). We are particularly struck by the relevance of those glosses common to C¹C²Hn (sometimes A¹) and believe these may be by Chaucer. We have cited these glosses, however, only when they have been of use in illustrating or explaining a point about the text we have wished to make on other grounds.

Summary of special abbreviations:

B	MS Besançon 434 of Jean de Meun's French translation of Boethius. "As B" means as MS Besançon 434 actually reads.
Chaucer's Fr. MS	The manuscript Chaucer used of Jean de Meun's translation
Chaucer's Lat. MS	The manuscript Chaucer used of Boethius
Fr.	Jean de Meun's French translation as edited by Dedeck-Héry
Guillaume	Guillaume de Conches's commentary on Boethius
Lat.	The "vulgate" text of Boethius in MS C²
MSt 14	*Mediaeval Studies,* vol. 14 (Dedeck-Héry's edition of Jean de Meun's translation)
Trivet	Nicholas Trivet's commentary on Boethius
Trivet's Latin	The text of Boethius that Trivet cites in his commentary

For the abbreviations used for manuscripts of *Boece,* see the introduction to the Textual Notes.

Title: At Adam 2 Chaucer uses *Boece* as the title of the book; this and ProLGW F 425 *(he hath in prose translated Boece)* seem to imply that at times "Boece" was to Chaucer synonymous with "The Consolation of Philosophy," even though he surely knew of Boethius's other works.

The form "Boece" is the normal English development, through French, of med. Lat. "Boetius" (like "Horace" from "Horatius"). Chaucer says *Boece of Consolacioun* at Rom 5661 (if he wrote it) and *Boece de Consolacione* in the Retraction, CT X.1088; and he alludes to the *De musica* at NPT VII.3294.

BOOK 1

Metrum 1

12　sorwful wyerdes: From Trivet's Latin "mesta fata mei senis," not Lat. "mesti . . . senis."
18–23　Cf. Tr 4:501–4; PardT VI.727–38.
20　to wrecches: Mistranslating Lat. "mestis," correctly interpreted by Trivet as modifying "annis," and glossed "id est tempore tristicie." But Guillaume's gloss "qui sunt in adversitate" (short version, MS Vat. lat. 5202) may lie behind Chaucer's translation.
28　to meward: Chaucer's Fr. MS (as B) added "vers moy."
30　wherto: Chaucer ignores Lat. "tociens," Fr. "tant de fois."

Prosa 1

12–17　The details are transposed into the description of Fame, HF 1368–76.
22, 25　clothes: Chaucer's Fr. MS (as B) added "robes."
30–32　The letters represent the traditional division of philosophy into two parts, "practica" (π) and "theorica" (θ). See Boethius's In Porphyrium dialogi 1 (PL 64:11).
41　this forseide womman: Chaucer's Fr. MS added "la devant dite fame" (Fr. "Elle"). In 42, the ordering of the phrases *smale bokis* and *in hir right hand* also follows Chaucer's Fr. MS; cf. MSt 14:173/22. Fr. has the phrases in reverse order.
56　fructifyenge: Chaucer's Fr. MS (as B) read "fructefians" (Fr. "fructueuses," Lat. "infructuosis").
63　I . . . suffre: Lat. "ferendum putarem," Fr. "je le deusse souffrir."
69　mermaydenes: Lat. "Sirenes," where the mythological allusion is clearer. Cf. NPT VII.3270–72.
75　wrothly: An adjective modifying 74 *companye* (Lat. "mestior"); Chaucer keeps Fr. word-order, in which "plus courrouciee" follows the verb.
79　so that y: Chaucer's Fr. MS (as B) read "a ce qui ie" (Fr. "ne," Lat. "nec").

Metrum 2

14　comprehendid al this: Lat. "comprensam" (sc. "stellam"), Fr. "compris . . . quelconque estoille." Perhaps Chaucer's Lat. MS read "comprensa."
14–15　of . . . astronomye: From Trivet "per computacionem parcium temporis"; cf. Guillaume "comprehendebat numero quando stella debet stare, quando retroire. Astronomia enim constat numeris. Oportet enim astronomum scire quot annis, quot diebus explet unusquisque planeta cursum suum."
24　maketh: Chaucer's Fr. MS read "fait" (Fr. "a donné que," Lat. "dedit"); cf. MSt 14:174/13.

Prosa 2

19–20 Cf. Tr 1.730.
27 **the lappe of:** A ME addition.

Metrum 3

5 **clustred:** The confusing gloss reflects Trivet "nubibus inuoluuntur."
7 **that²:** On the repetition of *when* by *that,* cf. ParsPro
X.39n.
17 **in:** Chaucer's Fr. MS (as B) read "es" (Fr. "les,"
Lat. "oculos . . . ferit").

Prosa 3

53 **So yif:** *But yif* would yield better sense; cf. Lat.
"Quodsi," Fr. "Mais se." This is a key transition in the
paragraph.
53ff. For the trial of Anaxagoras, see Diogenes Laertius
2.12–14; for the trial and death of Socrates, see Plato's
Apology and Phaedo; for accounts of Zeno of Elea,
see Diogenes 9.26–28 (including the anecdote of
2.pr6.53ff.) and Valerius Maximus 3.3.ext.2.
57 **the Senecciens . . . Soranas:** Roman examples to
parallel the preceding Greek examples. It is not clear
whether Chaucer understands Boethius's figure of
speech; the translation *Senecciens* especially seems to reflect Trivet "discipulos Senece" (Fr. "Seneciens"). Chaucer describes Seneca's death as one of Nero's crimes at
MkT VII.2495–518 (and see 3.pr5.40ff.). For the death
of Julius Canius, condemned by Caligula, see Seneca, De
tranquilitate 14.4–10 (and 1.pr4.178ff.). For the trial of
Barea Soranus during Nero's tyranny, see Tacitus, Annales 16.23 and 30–33.
58 **renoun:** Chaucer's Fr. MS read "renommee" (Fr.
"memoire," Lat. "memoria"); cf. MSt 14:176/29.

Metrum 4

1 **cleer of vertue:** From Trivet "clarus virtute."
6 **hete:** Lat. "estum"; cf. 1.m7.4–5.
11 **thonderleit:** Cf. Lat. "ardentis . . . fulminis," Fr.
"foudre ardent." Chaucer apparently found that the
compound, with its second element related to OE *līeg*
(flame), rendered the adjective of the source unnecessary.
18 **stable of:** Chaucer's Fr. MS read "estables de" (Lat.
"stabilis suique," Fr. "estables et de"); cf. MSt 14:176/
10.
21 **hym in:** A ME addition.

Prosa 4

2–3 Cf. Tr 1.731–35. A common Greek proverb; see
the examples assembled by Adrian Fortescue, De consolatione, 1925, note ad loc., and cf. Tr 1.731n.
2 **like:** From Trivet "asinis similes sunt homines" (Lat.
"Esne asinus").

4–6 Cf. Tr 1.857–58.
4 **teeris:** So Chaucer and Fr., but Lat. adds "Exonio
logo me id est confitere mihi" (Trivet "confitere mihi, ne
abscondas"). The first three words are a garbled form of
Boethius's Greek, Ἐξαύδα, μὴ κεῦθε νόῳ, (speak out,
do not conceal in mind; Homer, Iliad 1.363).
7 **Tho:** Lat. "Boecius Tunc"; cf. ε B. Tho; such speech
directions are normal in εθ(−P), sporadic in other MSS.
8 **answeride and:** A ME addition.
22–23 **my¹ . . . hevene:** See Plato, Republic 9.591–92.
24 **noght:** Cf. Lat. "Heccine," one of a number of
places in which Chaucer inverts the sense of a question.
Similar mistranslations occur at 2.pr5.11–12; 3.pr4.2–6,
78–80; 3.pr9.127–29; 5.pr4.31–36.
    gerdouns: Chaucer's Lat. MS had "premia," the tradi-
tional reading, not Lat. (as other "vulgate" texts)
"gracias," Fr. "loiers." According to Barnet Kottler, MS
17:209–14, the retention here and there of a traditional
reading is perfectly typical of vulgate manuscripts; we
normally do not note it.
27 **Plato:** Republic 5.473d; 6.487e; and Epist. 7.326b;
the reference at 33 is to Republic 1.347c.
37 **turmentours:** Cf. Fr. "aus mauvais àngres et tor-
menteurs citeiens," and, for the plural adjective, see Language and Versification, p. xxxv.
51 **liberte . . . fredom:** Chaucer translated both Lat.
"libertas" and Fr. "franchise" in order to specify the
reference of **this**; the word-order is inverted and *fredom*
the subject of *hath.*
55ff. The figures mentioned here and at 92 and 99ff.
are known only from passing references in Cassiodorus's
Variae epistolae. To the account given here of Boethius's
fall, the "Anonymus Valerii" adds only a few facts; see
Stewart, Boethius, 1891, 30ff.
71 **cariages:** Cf. FrT III.1570n.
72–92 The two sentences of gloss precede the text they
explain. For an account of the gradual development
of this gloss, see Dwyer, Boethian Fictions, 1976, 33–
35.
86 **unplitable:** Derived from Lat. "inexplicabilis" on
the same principle as 2.pr8.2 *untretable* from Lat. "inex-
orabilis."
86–87 **that . . . endamagen:** Chaucer's Fr. MS read "la
quele si comme l'en veoit bien devoit trop domagier et
tormenter" (Fr. "fust veuz a degaster et a tormenter par
souffreté et par mesaise"; Lat. "profligatura inopia . . .
videretur"); cf. MSt 14:178/45–46.
89 **for:** Chaucer's Fr. MS read "pour le" (Fr. "pour la
raison du"); cf. MSt 14:178/47–48.
90–91 **of it, Y overcom it:** Chaucer's Fr. MS read "les-
trif et vainqui" (Fr. "estrivé et vainqui," Lat. "contendi
et . . . euici"); cf. MSt 14:178/48.
103 **ayens:** "Before" (Lat. "apud," Fr. "envers").
106 **nothyng:** Five MSS (C¹ B δ A¹) add the gloss
affinite.
125 **hoot iren:** Cf. Trivet "ustione cauterii."
127 **likned:** Lat. "adstrui," added; Fr. "pareillé,"
which Chaucer apparently took as past participle of "pa-
reillier," resemble.
149 **And:** Lat. "Et." The traditional Lat. and Fr. lack
the conjunction; in them the sentence is interrogative
("Shall I confess?"), the counterpart of the questions at
146 and 152.
159–62 Cf. Theaetetus 151d (and Republic 6.485c).

172   lettres: Chaucer's Fr. MS had the addition "lettres"; cf. MSt 14:179/91.

176   nedes: Chaucer's Fr. MS (as B) read "besoings" (needs); Lat. "negociis," Fr. "besoingnes" (tasks).

182   and consentynge: Chaucer's Fr. MS (as B) read "consentant" (Fr. "consachable," Lat. "conscius").

198–201   Epicurus, frag. 374 (quoted by Lactantius, De ira Dei 13, PL 7:121).

206–7   hadde . . . disservyd: Chaucer's Fr. MS read "n'avions nous pas desservi" (Fr. "desservions nous," Lat. "num . . . merebamur"); cf. MSt 14:180/110. Chaucer thus follows his Fr. MS in turning a question into a statement.

208–9   that . . . destruccioun: From Trivet "ut ipsi deberent velle nos perire."

229–30   that . . . hath: Chaucer's gloss, although cf. Fr. "a juigier." One of several original glosses; see also notes to 1.m5.25–26, 2.m3.5–8. Other original glosses add no facts but provide English synonyms or rephrasings; cf. 1.pr4.63, 2.pr4.158–60, m5.37–38, 2.pr6.65–67, 3.pr10.166–67 (inspired by 3.pr10.187), 4.pr2.41–44, 4.pr3.29–30, 5.pr3.107–9 and 113–15.

245–46   as . . . nay: Chaucer's explanation of Trivet "reos" glossing "meritos"; C¹δ add Guillaume's gloss "yrronice."

246   of hem: Chaucer's Fr. MS added "d'eus"; cf. MSt 14:180/131.

259–62   Boethius cites ἕπου θεῷ (serve God); see Seneca, De vita beata 15.5. Chaucer incorporates the Lat. and Fr. addition "et non diis."

266–67   the . . . hous: Lat. "penetral innocens domus" (i.e., my stainless private life).

277–80   And . . . offencioun: One source of opaqueness in this awkward sentence is 279 of thy free wil, translating Fr. "de ton gré" but mistranslating Lat. "ultro" (further). The error recurs at 2.pr6.103.

282   bytideth: Chaucer's Lat. MS read "accidit" (Lat. "accedit," Fr. "s'aproiche et se conjoint").

288–94   Glose . . . folk: Largely Chaucer's paraphrase joining material on adversity from Trivet (directly translated in 291–92) and material on prosperity from Fr. See also Guillaume: "illos tantum dicunt . . . bonos qui utuntur prosperitate, quo fit ut . . . infortunatos dicant malos . . . unde dicunt homines deus dereliquit eos."

311–12   every luxurious turmentour: Lat. "flagiciosum quemque," as glossed by Trivet "flagiciosi dicuntur libidinosi."

316   to God: A ME addition, anticipating Lat. "conditor."

Metrum 5

1   wheel: See Astr 1.17.35–41n.

13   cometh: Chaucer's Fr. MS (as B) read "vine" (Fr. "mue," Lat. "mutet").

21   sesouns of the: Cf. Trivet "secundum quattuor tempora," with further elaboration later in the gloss; see also Guillaume "illas quattuor diversas partes anni; cum enim hyems et estas sunt contraria, temperantur per ver et autumpnum que sunt interposita."

22–23   Cf. GP I.5–7.

25–26   that . . . somer: Chaucer's explanation of his

own neologism (similarly at m6.16–17). Similar glosses occur at 2.pr3.41 (*masculyn*), 2.pr6.56–57 (*conjuracioun*), 3.pr6.3–4 (*tragedien*), 5.pr3.128 (*egaly*, in the Latinate sense "impartially, neutrally"), 5.pr6.37 (*futuris*), 5.pr6.38–39 (*preteritz*), 5.pr6.56–59 (*coeterne*). Such explanations (as well as the indication of a normal form of translation at 1.pr3.31–32) imply that Chaucer translated for purposes other than private consultation; they aid a potentially confused reading audience. See also 5.pr4.36–37n.

27   Arcturus: The brightest star in Bootes; at 4.m5.2, Chaucer uses *Arctour* to refer to the whole constellation. *Syrius* at 28 is the Dog-Star in Canis Major, ascendant in the "dog days" of late summer.

saugh: Chaucer's Lat. MS (as Trivet) had "vidit," the traditional reading (Lat. "videt," Fr. "vit").

31–33, 52–53   Cf. FranT V.865–66, 871, and 879–80.

34–46   Cf. MLT II.813–16 and below 4 pr1.17–31.

44–45   and kembd: Chaucer's addition; cf. SqT V.560.

51   alle: A ME addition.

53   but . . . partie: Cf. Trivet "immo valde nobilis pars."

57   thilke boond: Cf. KnT I.2987–93.

Prosa 5

9–11   thy cuntre . . . amys: Cf. Truth 19–20 (where *lat thy gost thee lede* looks ahead to 4.m1).

18   governement: Chaucer's Fr. MS (as B) read "gouvernement" (Fr. "commandement").

20   o lord and o kyng: Boethius gave the words in the form of Homer's Greek from Iliad 2.204–5.

37   I seie that: Based on Trivet "quasi respondens ad illud quod Boecius supra prosa quarta [see 1.pr4.14] plangendo quesiuit . . . dicit."

48   gode: A ME addition.

54   ryghtfully and schortly: Better *ryghtfully schortly*, i.e., you rightly thought it was to be touched briefly. Perhaps *and* is scribal.

58–59   wrongdede: Perhaps Chaucer's Lat. MS. read "iniustum (factum)"; cf. Lat. "iniusti (senatus)."

68ff.   Philosophy imagines Boethius's errors as a tumor or boil, hard yet tender, which she must foment, or soften with warm applications, before she can lance it. The process of fomenting takes all of 2; although at 2.pr5.2, 3 she says her applications (Lat. "fomenta"; Chaucer follows Fr. "norissement") *descenden now into the* so that she can use *a litel strengere* remedies, these are perhaps to be thought of as merely a hotter application. She is not ready to lance the wound until 3.pr1.6ff., where Boethius himself declares that the process of fomenting is complete (*thow hast remounted and norysshed me*; Lat. "me refovisti"), and that he is eager for the *ryght scharpe* remedy. In the first stage of fomenting, she demonstrates that Fortune is mutable, in the second that even good fortune is worthless; she lances the wound, and heals Boethius fully, by demonstrating that the source of perfect happiness is God. On medical imagery in the Consolation, see Peter von Moos, Consolatio, 1972, 3: 215.

73   medicynes: From Trivet "remediis."

75–76   into thy thought: Cf. Trivet "inflacionem animi" (glossing 75 **swellynge**) or Guillaume "ad aufe-

rendum tumorem perturbationum ab animo Boecii"
(glossing the whole *so that* clause).

Metrum 6

22   of doynge: A ME addition.

Prosa 6

21   doutedest the: Chaucer's Lat. MS read "uerebare"
(Lat. "mouebare," Fr. "estoies . . . esmeuz").
40   tolde: Chaucer's Fr. MS read "dire" (Fr. "dis je,"
corresponding to Lat. "inquam," Chaucer's *quod 1*); cf.
MSt 14:185/23.
60   thyng: Chaucer's Fr. MS (as B) added "chose."
75–76   Cf. KnT I.1272.
96   desceyved: A ME clarification.

Metrum 7

6–7   Cf. KnT I.1958.

BOOK 2
Prosa 1

16–18   Cf. Tr 4.2–3.
31   entre: Lat. "aditu" (entrance) for traditional
"adyto" (sanctuary), reflected in Fr. "secré." For the
gloss, cf. Trivet "idest informacione nostra per quam
homo adit veritatem."
32–33   mutacioun: Chaucer's Fr. MS (as B) lacked
equivalents for Lat. "rerum," Fr. "des chosez."
41ff.   Recalling the banishment of the sirenlike Muses
(1.pr1.68ff.) and the promise of *lyghtere medicynes* at
1.pr5.73.
46   moedes or prolacions: See Hollander (MLN 71,
1956, 397–99), whom we follow in translating "rhythms
and tunes." Hollander suggests that Chaucer took Lat.
"modos" (Fr. "vers") in the sense used by fourteenth-
century composers ("rhythms") and added *prolacions* as
an explanatory gloss. Trivet's commentary discusses at
some length the relation of rhythm and harmony.
70–73   Glose . . . forsake: The Trivet gloss distinguishes the two variant readings "quam non relicturam"
and "qua non relicta."
93   floor: That is, threshing-floor (Lat. "ariam"), a
confined space filled with violent activity; cf. pr7 and m7.
Chaucer maintains Boethius's metaphor, as Dante does
in Paradiso 22.157, where he looks down on "the little
threshing-floor that makes us so fierce." Trivet's gloss
similarly captures the vivid irony: "mundum ubi tor-
quentur homines"; as does Guillaume's "in hoc mundo
ubi fortuna terit segetes suas, id est animos amancium res
temporales."
113–14   Cf. Tr 1.848–49.

Metrum 1

10–14   Cf. MkT VII.2550 and Tr 4.7.

Prosa 2

Together with some reminiscences from 2.pr4, this section is a major source of Fortune. That poem, along with
The Former Age, is copied into the text of C² following
the translation of 2.m5. Patch (Goddess Fortuna, 149–
51, 176) discusses the historical importance of Boethius's
description.
10   ever any: A single intensive pronoun (cf. *whoso* and
whosoever); cf. Lat. "cuiusquam," Fr. "aucun de."
11   resceyved: Chaucer's Fr. MS (as B) read "receu"
(Fr. "riens," corresponding to Lat. "quid," Chaucer's
ony).
51   whirlynge: A ME addition; Chaucer may not have
understood the difficult metaphor in Lat. "rotam volubili
orbe versamus"; but see Guillaume "hic probat illud
idem per collationem [i.e., comparison] ad rotam volubi-
lem."
58–63   Cf. MkT VII.2727–32 (ultimately Herodotus
1.86–87).
65   of Percyens: From Trivet and Fr., but note Lat.
"Persi regis," (of king Perseus [of Macedonia]); see Livy
45.7–8. The only actual weeping Livy reports is by Perseus, not by Paul; what Boethius presumably has in mind
is Paul's pious lament over the reversal of Perseus's fortune at 45.8.6–7.
67–72   Cf. ProMkT VII.1973 and n. Cf. Trivet
"tragedia est carmen de magnis iniquitatibus a prosperitate incipiens et in aduersitate terminans."
73   in Greek: Boethius quotes Iliad 24.527–28, which
Trivet renders "duo dolia, unum quidem malum, al-
terum bonum."
84–86   Cf. Tr 4.391–92.

Metrum 2

We punctuate as if Philosophy speaks this poem, but it
may well be Fortune.
2–3   withdraweth: HθHn *withdrawe*, but in shifting
mood (present subjunctive to indicative), Chaucer follows Fr. "donnoit . . . sans retraire," rather than Lat.
"fundat . . . retrahat."
19–21   Cf. Rom 5699–5716.
20   ay: A ME addition (*εθ om.*) to improve parallellism
of the construction.
21–23   Cf. Rom 5693–96, 5703.

Prosa 3

4   And: Lat. "aut," Fr. "ou"; *or* would yield better
sense.
13–16   From Guillaume: "profundius intrant dolores
quam pulchra dicta, id est ista verba"; and again, "quasi
dicit, ea que dicis dulcia sunt valde ad audiendum; tamen
non possunt ita profunde descendere ut possint omnino
meum dolorem removere, tamquam demulcent et delec-
tant cum audiuntur."
41   over al this: Chaucer's Lat. MS read "preterea," as
some Trivet MSS (Lat. "pretereo"); 42 *how* must be
construed as parallel with 28 *how*.
59   Circo: That is, the Circus. When translating proper
names, Chaucer frequently uses oblique forms created by

the syntax of the source; cf. *Busyrides* 2.pr6.67 (but *Busirus*, MkT VII.2103); *Tyrie* 3.m4.3 (Lat "tyrio" a.); *Euripidis* 3.pr7.25; and *Tyresie* 5.pr3.134.

63–65   that . . . hir: Chaucer's dramatic condensation of Trivet "quasi diceret decipisti eam. . . . Promittens aliquid alicui et non implens uerbum suum decipit dando [ironically reflected in 64 **feffedestow**] ei solum uerba et non rem."

68   that . . . guerdoun: Cf. Trivet "bona," Fr. "beneurté"; but Chaucer's Lat. MS may have had a gloss "premia."

75–79   Cf. Tr 1.846–47.

80–81   schadowe or tabernacle: Lat. "scenam"; Guillaume "umbraculum, quia vita mundi non est nisi quoddam umbraculum preteriens"; Trivet "scenos enim tabernaculum significat quod transitorium est." This is particularly strong evidence that Chaucer, or the compiler of his Lat. MS, supplemented Trivet with material from other commentaries.

87–88   Cf. Fort 71.

90   dar: That is, "what do you think you need care?" (cf. Fr. "cuidez tu"); cf. Rom 1324. MSS in group ι (see textual notes) have the more explicit spelling *thar* (B *ther*). Skeat urges the reading *thar thee,* seconded mildly by Liddell and Robinson; but for *thar* used personally, see Mel VII.1068.

Metrum 3

1–5   Cf. Tr 5.274–78.

5   the sterre lyght: A ME clarification based on Trivet's gloss to 3 *ydymmed,* "a uigore lucis proprie."

5–8   This . . . sonne: Although 7–8 reflect Trivet (and Fr. "clarté du soleil"), for the most part the gloss is Chaucer's effort to express Boethius's figurative language more directly.

13   of: "From," following Fr. "des."

Prosa 4

4–5   ne . . . me: Perhaps Chaucer's Fr. MS read "vait en" (Fr. "n'ait eu"); cf. MSt 14:192/2.

5–9   Cf. Tr 3.1625–28 (and more distantly, 4.481–83); see also Francesca's words to Dante, Inferno 5.121–23.

31–32   and . . . hym: Lat. "securus suarum," Guillaume "qui suis propriis iniuriis sibi illatis non ingemiscit." But Symmachus was executed shortly after Boethius.

42   two: A ME addition, following 2.pr3.51.

67–68   so . . . fortune: Chaucer's addition. For **tempeste the nat,** see Truth 8.

75–78   Cf. Tr 3.816–19.

94   is in: Apparently a calque translation of Lat. "inest" (which glosses *is in* in C¹Hn); *somwhat* is predicate nominative, not object of *in*. Liddell's translation, "something is therein," presupposes emendation to *is therin* or *is in it* (cf. B *is in hym*). At 5.pr4.161 "inest" again is translated *is in.*

97   so that: Lat. and Fr. "et."

99   is inpacient or: From Trivet "impaciens."

102–3   or the perfeccioun: From Trivet "perfeccionem."

110–13   As . . . corage: Combines Guillaume "nichil est

miserum nisi reputes esse miserum" and Trivet "nisi ex reputacione animi."

118–23   Cf. Tr 3.813–15; with 118–19, cf. MLT II.421–22.

134–38   Cf. Tr 1.891–93.

140   thynges: Lat. "his rebus," Fr. "ces choses" make the point more clearly.

150–66   Cf. Tr 3.820–33.

155–56   that . . . chaungeable: From Guillaume "eam esse mutabilem."

159–60   Cf. GP I.44–45n.

162–63   he² . . . forleten: Better, "does he think that a negligible matter?" (Lat. "an . . . neglegendum putat?"). Chaucer seems to have been misled by Fr. "il en cuide estre cheuz en despit et en vilté," which turns the question into a statement, and perhaps also by his Fr. MS, which may have had "il cuide" for "il en cuide." The mistranslation mars the link with the next sentence, which answers the question.

Metrum 4

7   moyste: From Fr. "moistez," which inverts the sense of Lat. "bibulas" (thirsty; Trivet "aridam et sitibundam paupertatem").

12   that . . . werld: Perhaps suggested by Trivet "uita presens."

13–14   of . . . sete: In Lat. and Fr. modifies *aventure* 12 (cf. Lat. "sortem sedis amene"); but Chaucer follows Trivet's rearranged word-order "domum sedis amene."

18   cler: Lat. "serenus," modifying the subject (Chaucer's *thou* 16), not "euum": did Chaucer's Lat. MS read "serenum"?

Prosa 5

32–33   Cf. Lat. "illos quos relinquunt," Fr. "ceulz que elles delaissent."

46–47   a fair creature: Chaucer's Fr. MS read "bele creature" (Fr. "bele a creature"); cf. MSt 14:195/29.

49   laste: Lat. "postreme"; cf. Trivet "pulchritudo . . . ultima." Guillaume explains the chain of being here: he lists six beauties, ranging from the first, in God, through angels, men, animals, and plants, to the sixth and last, in stones.

62   The order of the nouns follows Chaucer's Fr. MS "les estoilles et le solail et la lune" (not Fr. sun-moon-stars or Lat. stars-moon-sun); cf. MSt 14:196/37–38.

67   spryngynge . . . first somer sesoun: Chaucer's typically expansive translation of Lat. "vernis," Fr. "en prin temps"; cf. 1.m2.22, 1.m5.23, 2.m3.9. The fact is that Chaucer had no one word for the season; *spring* (springtide, springtime) did not emerge until the sixteenth century (cf. OED s.v. *spring,* sb.¹ II.6b), and the older word *lent* he uses only in its liturgical sense (cf. WBT III.543 and note 543–49); cf. PF 680 and n.

71ff.   Cf. the discussion of the gifts of fortune, nature, and grace at ParsT X.449–456 and see PardPro VI.295n. See further 3.pr2.55ff.

78–80   Cf. Truth 2 and 3.pr3.94–96.

84   to the: A ME addition.

108   alle thyne: Combines the reading of Chaucer's Fr. MS (as B) "toutes" and Lat. "tuis" (Fr. "tes").

113   desirestow: In Lat. and Fr. the construction shifts here to plural (cf. 116 *you*).

126   subgit: Chaucer's Lat. MS read "suppositis" (Lat. "sepositis," Fr. "dessevrees").

127–32   Cf. Lak of Stedfastnesse 5–6.

148–52   A reference to the Socratic dictum γνῶθι σεαυτόν (cf. the Latin "Scito te ipsum"), inscribed on the temple at Delphi. Cf. Philebus 48c, Phaedrus 229e ff., Protagoras 343b, and Macrobius, Com. 1.9.2.

156–57   but . . . hemself: Chaucer retranslates Lat. "sese ignorare" for clarity.

163–64   as . . . aparayled: Chaucer's restatement of Trivet's brief exemplum: "Unde probe respondit clericus quidam uni domine querenti utrum esset pulchra: domina, inquit, pulchra sunt tibi appensa."

173–74   and . . . wikkidnesse: Cf. Lat. "eoque," Fr. "et par sa mauvaistié."

179–81   From Juvenal 10.22, which Trivet and Guillaume quote; with 181–84 cf. WBT III.1192–94.

Metrum 5

This poem, especially indebted to Metamorphoses 1.88–152, Georgics 1.125ff., and the Fourth Eclogue, is the major impulse behind The Former Age, a copy of which appears in C² following the translation of this poem. Petersen (PMLA 18:190–93) prints the full texts of Lat., Fr., and Trivet. Chaucer would also have known RR 8355–8454, an extensive reworking of this poem.

10–11   fleezes . . . Seryens: Lat. "uellera serum," "the fleeces of the Chinese," i.e., silk, gives the proper air of decadent opulence. Boethius here recalls Georgics 2.121. Chaucer follows Fr. "toisons des Sirians."

15–16   They . . . gras: As Hammond points out (MLN 41, 1926, 534), Chaucer basically follows Fr. "il se dormoient sur les herbes"; however, Lat. "sompnos dabat herba salubres" probably means that a vegetable diet made for healthful sleep.

Prosa 6

12   the imperie of consulers: Lat. "consulare imperium," a feature of the Republic, following upon the abolition of the monarchy (cf. 18–19 and 2.m7.18–19n).

53–62   For the anecdote, see Diogenes Laertius 9.27 (of Zeno), or 9.59 (of Anaxarchus). See 1.pr3.53ff.

53   confownde / 54   constreyne: Chaucer's expansion based on Lat. "acturum" (traditional "adacturum," Trivet "compulsurum"), Fr. "contraindre."

54   of corage: From Trivet "animo." Thus the whole phrase *a . . . corage* means "a man of independent spirit."

67–75   Busirus, an Egyptian king, is mentioned as a type of savagery at Georgics 3.5; Ovid, Tristia 3.11, 39; and MkT VII.2103–4 (partly confused with Diomedes). M. Atilius **Regulus**, a Roman consul, was taken prisoner after victorious campaigns against Carthage in 255 B.C.; rather than urge on the Senate actions of which he disapproved, he returned to Carthage to endure death by torture. (See Cicero, De officiis 3.26.99–100.)

68–69   that . . . hous: Chaucer's addition, inspired by Trivet's citation of Metamorphoses 9.183 "domui."

75–78   Wenestow . . . othere: Liddell and Robinson find this nonsensical and wish to move 76 *a thyng* to

follow 77 *doon*. But construe as in the page gloss, correlating *that* 77 with *a thyng that* 76.

79   And yit moreover: Cf. KnT I.2801n.

111   it: Chaucer reverts to the singular of the source; cf. Lat. "dignitas," Fr. "dignité" for 109 *dignytees*.

Metrum 6

3–12, 12–27   Cf. MkT VII.2479–90, 2466–67, respectively.

6   blood: Chaucer ignores Lat. "effuso."

Prosa 7

14   to governaunce: Loosely translating the Fr. addition "a dignité et a puissance," derived from Trivet's gloss to 4 which mentions "sapiencia," "auctoritas," and "potencia" as necessary for successful action.

16   nat drawen / 17   as ben: A mistranslation; Lat. "nondum" should produce *drawen, as ben nat yit*. Did Chaucer's Lat. MS read "non"? The passage is the source for Milton's "last infirmity of noble mind."

17–18   to the ful perfeccioun: From Trivet "ad summam perfectionis" (Lat. "ad extremam manum . . . perfeccione," Fr. "a la derreniere euvre par perfection").

19–20   to han . . . thynges: A ME addition, apparently Chaucer's explanation or alternative translation of the following phrase.

23–27   Cf. HF 906–7; PF 57–58; Tr 5.1815; and Macrobius's description of the earth as a "punctum," Com. 2.5.10.

31   of²: Chaucer's Fr. MS (as B) read "de" (Fr. "en," Lat. "in").

32   the ferthe: Chaucer simplifies Lat. "quarta fere," Fr. "la quatre . . . et encore moins."

34   Tholome: See Almagest 2.1.

60   Marcus Tulyus: See Republic 6.20.22 and Macrobius, Com. 2.10.3.

61   in his book: Perhaps Chaucer's Fr. MS read "en sien livre" (Fr. "en un sien livre," Lat. "quodam loco").
   that: Otiose, apparently prompted by *writ*.

78–80   he . . . spreden: A mistranslation; cf. Lat. "huic . . . proferre nullo modo conducat" (Trivet "conueniat"), it may not in any way serve him to spread.

87–88   nedy . . . writeris: Mistranslates Lat. "scriptorum obliuio inops," oblivion for lack of writers, accurately rendered in Fr.

90–92   Contrast LGW F 17–28.

120–21   Have . . . undirstand: Lat. "accipe," Fr. "recoif et entent." For the Chaucerian idiom "have here," cf. Tr 1.1061, 3.885, 4.1366.

122ff.   The anecdote exemplifies the assertions of Macrobius (Saturnalia 7.1.10) and Plutarch (who quotes Euripides, Moralia 7.532f.) that the philosopher may practice his art in silence. See also Prov. 11.12, 17.28; Ecclus. 20.5–7.

123   swich vanyte: Chaucer's Fr. MS (as B) read "vanité" (Fr. "un autre"), supplying an object for Lat. "illuserit" (Trivet "quendam dicentem se esse philosophum").

149–50   for . . . ben: A ME addition.

152–57   Cf. Tr 5.1807–19.

Metrum 7

8–10   Cf. the similar extension of the idea of pride at Tr 1.211–24.
9–10   of this world: A ME addition.
18–19   trewe Fabricius: The hero of the war with Pyrrhus (c. 280 B.C.), renowned for his incorruptibility (see Cicero, Paradoxa 48). **Brutus** is either Lucius Junius Brutus, traditionally the founder of the Roman republic (c. 509 B.C.), or the later tyrannicide. **Stierne Catoun** is the conservative censor, M. Porcius Cato (234–149 B.C.).
28   cruel: Chaucer's Lat. MS read "seua" (Lat. "sera," Fr. "derreniers," Trivet "ultima").

Prosa 8

14   falsly byhetynge: Chaucer's addition; cf. Guillaume "promittendo felicitatem quod non facit."
15   hope: Chaucer's Lat. MS read "spe" (Lat. "specie," Fr. "semblance").
24   alwey: Chaucer translated Lat. "semper" twice; cf. 25 *evere*.
36ff.   Cf. Fortune 9–10, 33–34.

Metrum 8

With this poem generally, cf. Tr 3.1744–64 and KnT passim, esp. Theseus's final speech.
9   to flowen: Reflecting Trivet "ad exeundum sicut videtur quando fluit."
12   erthes: Cf. Lat. "terris . . . uagis," Fr. "la terre."
18   contynuely: A slight mistranslation; cf. Lat. "continuo" (correctly glossed "statim," immediately), Fr. "tantost."
23   of[2]: Chaucer's Fr. MS (as B) read "de" (Fr. "par," Lat. "castis . . . amoribus").

BOOK 3

Prosa 1

18   to . . . remedies: A clarifying expansion; cf. Fr. "que tu les (sc. remedes) me dies."
48   thilke . . . goodes: Lat. "eā" (sc. "causā"), Fr. "celle"; cf. Guillaume "ista falsa felicitate."

Metrum 1

5ff.   Cf. Tr 1.638–39, 631–44n., 3.1219–20. For the topic of knowledge by contraries, see 4.pr2.10–12n.
14   of erthely affeccions: Chaucer's specification; cf. Trivet "false felicitatis," glossing "iugo."

Prosa 2

3   streyte: Lat. "augustam," read as "angustam" (cf. Fr. "estroit"); the error recurs at 3.m9.40.
9   blisfulnesse: Perhaps following Trivet "qui est

beatitudo," which glosses 8 *oon ende.* The result is a mistranslation; the sentence should begin, "And the good is that which, once one has it . . ."
25–28   Cf. KnT I.1255.
49   al: A ME addition.
55–59   But . . . delyt: Better, "As for friends, the holiest kind of friendship comes under the heading of virtue, not fortune; but all other kinds of friendship are taken up for the sake of power or pleasure."
77–80   Cf. GP I.336–38 and MerT IV.2021–22; the source is Epicurus, frag. 348 (from Augustine, De civitate Dei 19.1; see also 14.2).
81–82   byrefte awey . . . from the herte: Chaucer's Lat. MS read "animo . . . auferre" (Lat. "animo . . . afferre," Fr. "aportent au corage").
82–88   Cf. KnT I.1261–67.
99–100   wel . . . folk: Cf. Lat. "omnium [Chaucer's Lat. MS "omnis"?] fere mortalium . . . intencio."
109–10   For . . . saie: Interrogative in Lat. and Fr. (cf. Lat. "quid attinet dicere"); but Trivet "quasi diceret hoc de se palam est."

Metrum 2

21–31   Cf. SqT V.610–17, MancT IX.163–74.
31   desyrynge: From Trivet "appetit."
39–42   Cf. SqT V.608–9, MancT IX.160–62 (distantly).
40   alle: Chaucer's Fr. MS read "toutes" (Fr. "chascuns," Lat. "singula"); cf. MSt 14:209/25.
44   cours: Chaucer's Fr. MS (as B) read "cours" (Fr. "tour," Lat. "orbem").

Prosa 3

33–36   Cf. PF 90–91 and, far more distantly, Pity 99–105 and Lady 43–45.
59   wel: Chaucer's Fr. MS (as B) added "bien."
63   alle: A ME addition, likely a scribal intensifier. Liddell and Robinson omit.
79   maken suffisaunce: Chaucer's Fr. MS read "feissent souffisance" (Fr. "les feissent suffisans," Lat. "sufficientes sibi facere"); cf. MSt 14:210/43.
87   slaken: Chaucer's addition; in Lat. and Fr. *thurst* parallels *cold.*

Metrum 3

2   hadde: Cf. Lat. "cogat . . . opes" (might constrain riches [in]), Fr. "a . . . amoncelle richeces" (might heap riches up to); but Chaucer apparently confused the Fr. preposition "a" with "a" (has). This error is responsible for the further difficulty, 3 *sholde . . . staunchen* (cf. Lat. "expleturas," Fr. "li acompliront," the riches should never fulfill).
   ryver or a goter: Lat. "gurgite" (Trivet "locus altus id est profundus in flumine"), Fr "gort"; cf. MED *goter* n. 1.3(a).
5   Rede See: For the gems of the Red Sea, see Pliny, Nat. Hist. 9.54.106ff.

Prosa 4

11 Catullus: At Carmen 52.2; cf. Pliny, Nat. Hist. 37.21.81.

16 of: Chaucer's Fr. MS read (as B) "de la" (Fr. "de sa").

21–22 as² . . . suffren: Cf. Trivet "quot incurristi."

22 thow woldest: Chaucer allows the modal to convey the force of Lat. "putares," Fr. "cuidoies."

23 Decorat: Like the figures at 1.pr4.54ff., known only through Cassiodorus; cf. Variae 5.3 (PL 69:646).

24–25 by offence of: Trivet "offendendo regem."

36 quod I / 37 quod sche: ME additions; cf. Trivet "Et quasi respondens pro Boecio dicit 'minime.'"

37–40 Cf. Gent 5–6 (more distantly paralleled at 2.pr6.24–27).

59 transitorie: From Trivet "transitorias ad modum vmbre."

64–69 Cf. WBT III.1139–45 and n.

71 to folk: Properly "to dignities"; cf. Lat. "eis," Trivet "dignitatibus."

81 provostrye: Apparently the office of the *praefectus annonae* (Lat. "prefectura"), an officer created by Augustus, responsible for providing Rome with grain at a reasonable price; cf. the Praetorian prefect's usurpation and abuse of this responsibility mentioned at 1.pr4.88–89.

83–84 and . . . charge: Better, "and a great burden on the senatorial wealth"; Chaucer, following Trivet, who interprets "census" (rent) as nominative plural instead of genitive singular, takes this as a second example of a change in political status; but Boethius is saying that the prefecture is now merely a burden.

93 usaunces: Chaucer's Fr. MS read "usances" (Lat. "vtencium," Fr. "usans," users); cf. MSt 14:212/46.

95 of hir wil: Lat. "vltro" (moreover); a persistent confusion (here reinforced by the Lat. gloss "sua aptitudine"); see also 1.pr4.279, 2.pr6.103.

Metrum 4

1–4 Cf. MkT VII.2468–70 (distantly).

3–4 white peerles: Lat. "niueis lapillis" (Trivet "albis margaritis"), Fr. "preciuesez pierres." See the similar specification based on Trivet at 3.m8.13. Chaucer relies heavily on glosses in translating this poem; in addition to the first two lines of explicit gloss, 8 *of dignytees,* 11 *resonably,* 12 *blisfulnesse were in,* and 13 *vycious schrewes* all represent Trivet.

7 yaf: Lat. has a second subject, "improbus," rendered unnecessary by 6 *wikkide* (Trivet "uiciosus").

9–11 Although arguably a reflection of Trivet "ex hoc quod ab indigno dabantur," the lines more closely resemble Guillaume "indecoras autem vocat eas quia ab illo dabantur qui easdem dignitates dehonestabat."

Prosa 5

23 A tyraunt: Dionysius of Syracuse showed the sword to his flatterer Damocles; see Cicero, Disp. Tusc. 5.21.61–62.

25 schewede by simylitude: From Trivet "similitudine demonstrauit" (Fr. "fainst et monstra").

27 of his: Chaucer's Fr. MS (as B) read "du sien" (Fr. "d'un sien," not in Lat.).

32 and yit: Lat. "dehinc," Fr. "aprés" (therefore); Chaucer obliterates the irony.

41 or servantz: Chaucer's explanatory addition, although perhaps an effort at resolving the ambiguity between Fr. "familiers" (from Lat. "familiaribus") and the reading "famularibus" in Chaucer's Lat. MS.

42 myself: A ME addition, perhaps scribal dittography based on 43 *hemself.*

47 Nero: See 1.pr3.57n.

49 Antonyus: Fr. "Antonius" (Lat. "Antoninus" [Caracalla]). Caracalla in 212 ordered the great jurist Aemelius Papinianus executed for his support of Caracalla's brother Geta, whom Caracalla murdered; see Spartianus, Historia Augusta (ed. David Magie), Caracalla 4.1 and 8.

56 gon into solitarie exil: Chaucer's Fr. MS read "aler seulz . . . en essil" (Fr. "aler s'en . . . en essil," Lat. "se . . . in ocium conferre"; Trivet glosses "ocium" "in vitam solitariam et priuatam"); cf. MSt 14:213/33.

57–58 that . . . fortune: Chaucer's elaboration of William of Aragon "dominii imperatori" (i.e., -torii).

64–65 whethir . . . nede: Chaucer's awkward fusion of Lat. "An presidio sunt amici," Fr. "li ami . . . aident il au besoing" (Are friends an aid who, in need . . . ?).

66–68 Certes . . . enemys: Singular in Lat. and Fr.; cf. MkT VII.2244–45 and n.

68–70 Cf. MerT IV.1784, 1793–94.

Metrum 5

6–7 the laste . . . Tyle: Lat. "vltima tyle," glossed by Trivet "que est insula ultra Britanniam"; *that highte* modifies *ile,* not *see.*

8–9 foule dirke desires: Cf. Lat. "atras curas" (Trivet "sollicitudines uiciosas"), Fr. "mauvais desiriers."

Prosa 6

2–3 a tragedien: Euripides, Andromache 319–20, quoted in Greek by Boethius; Chaucer translates the rather free version in Lat.

27–31 Liddell and Robinson object that there is an extra negative. Chaucer might have negated only the subordinate clause; but he decided to negate the main clause, and then followed the standard idiom after a verb of thinking by negating the subordinate clause as well.

32ff.[and m6] Ultimately the source of the ideas, although not the diction, of the poem Gentilesse. With 34–37, cf. WBT III.1159–61, although most of that speech came to Chaucer through Dante.

36 of lynage: Cf. Trivet "nobiles."

50 forlynen: Lat. "degenerat," Fr. "forlignent"; cf. m6.12 *forlyned* (Lat. "degener," Fr. "forlignablez"). See Mark Science, TLS 22 March 1923:199–200.

Metrum 6

1 ben²: Chaucer's Fr. MS read "sont" (Fr. "sourt," Lat. "surgit"); cf. MSt 14:215/1.

Prosa 7

16   jolyte: Chaucer's Lat. MS read "lasciuiam" (as Trivet), rather than Lat. "lacunam" (glossed "voluptatem"), Fr. "le parfont ventrail."
25   Euripidis: See Andromache 420.

Metrum 7

3   flyes . . . clepen: A ME addition; cf. Fr. "les ees . . . la mouche," the latter corresponding to **4 be.** On bees as *foules,* i.e., flying things, see PF 353 and note 353–54.

Prosa 8

11–12   yif . . . folk: Cf. GP I.449–51n.
24   coveyten: Apparently a modification of Chaucer's usual translation of "nituntur," *enforcen hem* (see 4.pr4.248n.); but Boethius's sense is "rely on, depend on" (cf. Fr. "s'apuient").
30–31   swyft cours: Cf. Lat. "celeritatem," Fr. "l'inesleté"; the effect of Chaucer's particularization is to mute Boethius's paradox.
39–46   For . . . foul: Apparently from Aristotle's lost Protrepticus; a closely similar passage is preserved by Iamblichus in his Protreptikos 8 (ed. Pistelli, 47.12–15), published as Fragment 59 by Valentin Rose, Aristotelis fragmenta, 1886. See Chroust, Aristotle: New Light, 1973, 2:88.
41   a . . . highte: Chaucer's effort to explain Fr. "lins" (but Lat. "Lyntheis," i.e., Lynceus, the sharp-eyed Argonaut; see Apollonius, Argonautica 1.151–55, and Pindar, Nemean Ode 10.161ff.).

Metrum 8

9   of . . . highte: Cf. Trivet "Tyrreni maris." But 18 *fyssches that hyghten* is simply a ME addition.

Prosa 9

23–24   that hym ne lakketh nothyng: Chaucer follows Fr., inverting the sense of Lat. "quod nihilo indigeat egere potencia," (what lacks nothing, lacks power).
39–40   that . . . reverenced: From Trivet "quin . . . sit ueneracione dignissima."
50–51   as . . . that: At 22–50; the *as-*clause should follow 53 *honour,* and *that* is superfluous.
55–56   for . . . cleernesse: A ME addition.
**78–80   In the traditional text, but not Lat. and Fr., the conclusion of Boethius's speech.
105–6   wasteth and scatereth: Lat. "profligat" (Trivet "quod idem est quod destruere, dispergere").
110   of manye: Chaucer's Fr. MS read "de assez de" (Fr. "d'avoir ses"); cf. MSt 14:219/58.
161–62   that . . . seyn: A ME addition.
182   lyen falsly: Lat. "menciantur," Fr. "mentent que vraie beneurté soit en eulz".
190   Plato: Cf. Timaeus 27c. The following poem has

often been taken as an epitome of early portions of this dialogue.

Metrum 9

For a very full commentary, see Klingner, De Boethii, 1966, 38–67. For medieval commentaries, see Huygens, Sacris Erudiri 6, 1954, 372–427.
**11–14   Cf. LGW 2228–30.
14–15   Thou . . . and: In both Lat. and Fr., follows 11 *frely.*
16–17   world . . . absolut: Primarily from Trivet "mundum perfecte creatum . . . absolute continere."
**18–24   Cf. PF 380–81 and KnT I.2987–93 (a rather distant resemblance, also shared by 4.m6.22–28).
18–19   proporcionables: Cf. Trivet "proporcionibus numeralibus."
25–26   the mene . . . kynde: Cf. Trivet *"mediam,* scilicet existentem, *triplicis nature,* scilicet quia de tribus naturis, quarum prima est eiusdem substancie, alia diuerse substancie, tercia ex duabus commixta anima est media." Trivet responds to the difficult description of Timaeus 35, in which the world soul forms a third substance as a mean combining the indivisible (the world of ideas) and the divisible (the temporal, material, and multiple expression of the idea).
34   ablynge hem heye: Lat. "sublimes . . . aptans." Trivet glosses "sublimes" as "animas racionales" and explains the **waynes or cartes** as "uigorem anime immortalem per quem dissoluto corpore euolat."
**40–41   Cf. KnT I.3035–38.
40   streyte: Lat. "augustam," read as "angustam" (Fr. "royal"); see 3.pr2.3.

Prosa 10

**15   For the negatives see Mel VII.1757n.; Tr 2.716–18n.; pr.6.27–31n. above; and cf. line 34.
**25–30   Cf. KnT I.3005–10.
83   by nature: See 72 textual note; Chaucer here introduces the second part of the distinction made there but omitted in his translation, following his Fr. MS.
84   wenynge: Chaucer's addition. Cf. the uses of *wene* in 70, 77, and 78.
**114–17   Cf. MerT IV.1638.
130   than: Better *of;* cf. Fr. "plus digne de dieu."
137   or . . . coroune: From Fr. but ultimately from Trivet: "correlarium est premium alicuius certaminis et dicitur a corolla quod est diminutiuum a corona."
159–60   it . . . witen: Chaucer's addition, turning the question in Lat. and Fr. into a statement.
166   blisfulnesse: Lat. "ad hoc," Fr. "a lui" indicate that the reference is to 163 *ony* and 164 *it.*
182   of alle: Chaucer's Fr. MS read "de toutes" (Fr. "toutez," Lat. "omnia"); cf. MSt 14:224/101.
184   thanne: Chaucer's Fr. MS (as B) read "ainsi" (Fr. "aussi").
**198–200   In Lat. and Fr., Philosophy's speech continues, but Fr. is at least susceptible to Chaucer's interpretation.
215–16   sovereyn: A ME addition.
234   grace: This literal translation of the Lat. construction, genitive + "gracia," for the sake of (here "boni

gracia''), follows Fr. ''grace de'' (similarly 5.pr1.67, 5.pr4.44). But at 3.pr2.54 Chaucer translates accurately.

Metrum 10

1   **ye that:** Chaucer's Fr. MS (as B) read ''vous qui'' (Fr. ''qui'').
12–15   The golden sands of the Iberian **Tagus** are mentioned at Metamorphoses 2.251; Amores 1.15.34. **Hermus,** a river in Lydia, also has a **rede brinke** because of gold deposited by the stream; see Georgics 2.137.
12   **thinges:** Chaucer's Fr. MS read ''choses'' (Fr. ''richecez,'' Lat. ''quicquid''); cf. MSt 14:225/4.

Prosa 11

20   **of hem:** Chaucer's Fr. MS read ''en'' (Fr. ''uns''); cf. MSt 14:225/10.
56–73   Cf. Tr 1.960–61.
63   **of a wyght:** Chaucer's addition, necessitated by the translation *beestes* 56 for Lat. ''animalibus,'' living beings.
109–14   Cf. Tr 4.767–70 (perhaps only a fortuitous resemblance).
158   **while we slepyn:** Chaucer's expansion of Fr. ''lors.''
165–68   **That . . . sore:** An apparently vapid gloss, but perhaps expanding Trivet ''ut patet in martiribus.''
182   **here lif:** Chaucer's Fr. MS read ''leur vie'' (Fr. ''leur vivre et leur estre''); cf. MSt 14:228/95–96.
186   **perdurable:** Chaucer's Fr. MS (as B) read ''perdurable'' (Fr. ''perdurablement''); contrast 193.
188, 189   **wel:** ME additions.
220   **prykke:** For the sense ''bull's eye'' see OED, s.v. *prick* sb.10. Cf. Trivet ''Loquitur ad similitudinem eorum qui nituntur aliquid figere telo uel alio instrumento quorum iste reputatur melius facere qui directe figit medium eius. Sic Boecius acie mentis penetrando non fixit ueritatem a latere sed recte in medio.''
224   **That . . . noght:** Chaucer's addition.

Metrum 11

10   Cf. Tr 4.200.
13–27   Petersen (PMLA 18:181–83) gives the commentaries of Trivet and pseudo-Aquinas on these lines to exemplify Chaucer's reliance on the former.
44   **Plato:** For the doctrine of remembered preexistence (anamnesis), see Phaedo 76a.

Prosa 12

29   **answeren:** Chaucer's Fr. MS read ''respondrai'' (Fr. ''espondre,'' Lat. ''exponam''); cf. MSt 14:229/13.
40   **brynge forth:** Chaucer's Fr. MS omitted the first verb in the phrase Fr. ''n'iroit pas . . . ne ne despleroit'' (Lat. ''procederet nec . . . explicaret''); cf. MSt 14:229/19.
43   **stedfaste:** From Trivet ''immobiliter.''
44   **moevynges:** Chaucer's Lat. MS read ''mocionum,''

a variant recorded in early MSS (Lat. ''mutacionum,'' Fr. ''muances'').
46   **ilad:** Chaucer's Fr. MS read ''menees'' (Fr. ''meues,'' Lat. ''agitantur''); cf. MSt 14:229/22.
73, 88   **keye:** Chaucer's Lat. MS read ''clauis'' and ''claue'' (Lat. ''clauus'' and ''clauo,'' Fr. ''clos'' and ''clo et . . . gouvernail'').
99   **of mysdrawynges:** Chaucer's Lat. MS read ''detractacionum,'' perhaps the basis also of Fr. ''se traioient'' (Lat. ''detrectancium'').
   ne: Lat ''non'' (not); i.e., ''if government consisted of the yoking of the recalcitrant, instead of the welfare of people of good will.'' But the syntax follows Fr.
100   **obedient:** From Trivet ''obediencium'' (Lat. ''obtemperancium'').
117–18   **alle . . . softly:** Cf. Wisd. Sol. 8.1. Trivet ascribes Boethius's delight in these words (122–23) to the scriptural echo.
133   **the fables:** Chaucer's Fr. MS read ''les'' (Lat. ''in,'' Fr. ''es''); cf. MSt 14:230/63. Boethius refers to the revolt of the Titans, described at Metamorphoses 1.151–60, Georgics 1.277–83.
134   **with:** Either ''against'' or ''and''; cf. Fr. ''o les diex'' (lacking in Lat.).
142   **Wenestow:** Chaucer's Fr. MS added ''Cuides tu''; cf. MSt 14:231/68.
155–59   Cf. HF 1920, where Chaucer actually uses the phrase *Domus Dedaly* (Trivet ''domus Dedali,'' Fr. ''la maison Dedalus''), and goes on to describe the issuing rumors. For the labyrinth, see Aeneid 5.588, 6.24ff.
168–69   **covenable:** Chaucer's Fr. MS read ''couvenable'' (Fr. ''coronable''); cf. MSt 14:231/83. See 3.pr10.137.
171   **the forme:** Chaucer's Fr. MS read ''la forme'' (Fr. ''la forme meismes,'' Lat. ''ipsam . . . formam''); cf. MSt 14:231/84.
177   **governementis:** Chaucer's Fr. MS read ''gouvernemens'' (Fr. ''governaus,'' Lat. ''gubernaculis''); cf. MSt 14:231/88.
182   **in cercles:** From the Lat. gloss ''in circulis'' (Lat. ''insitis,'' Trivet ''intrinsecis''). The Lat. gloss is based upon Trivet's explanation of the labyrinth reference at 156ff.: ''faciendo raciones circulares que nichil probant''; although as 161–62 and Philosophy's speech show, the issue is not circular reasoning but the peculiar nature of the divine essence.
191   **uttreste:** Chaucer's Lat. MS read ''extrema'' (Lat. ''externa,'' Fr. ''estrangez'').
193   **Parmanydes:** A pre-Socratic philosopher; see his frag. 8.
   in Grees: Cf. Lat. ''Greca,'' replacing Boethius's Greek quotation; Trivet ''auctoritate . . . quam primo ponit in Greco deinde sensum eius subiungit in Latino.'' But Trivet is wrong to say that Boethius gives the sense of the Greek. The missing quotation is a simile: ''like the mass of a sphere well-rounded on all sides,'' which Boethius incorporates in his Latin sentence. That sentence is based roughly on the remainder of Parmenides' sentence, but is Boethius's own.
198–99   **that . . . thinges:** From Trivet, but Chaucer twice translates forms of ''mutare'' *moeve* to accord with the language of the text.
205–6   **sentence of Plato:** At Timaeus 29b. Cf. GP

I.741–42 and 725–42n., and see Wood, ELN 4, 1967, 166–72.

Metrum 12

Boethius knew the Orpheus story from Georgics 4.454–527 and Metamorphoses 10.1–85, and his account is equally influential in the Middle Ages. For discussion of its use, see John B. Friedman, Orpheus, 1970, esp. 90–117; and Gros Louis, Spec 41, 1966, 643–55.

13   so: Chaucer's Fr. MS added "si"; cf. MSt 14:232/7.
25   with . . . wepynge: Lat. "quod luctus dabat impotens"; Chaucer follows Fr. "de tout quenque puissance de pleur," but seems to misunderstand the Fr. syntax, in which "donnoit" *(myghte yeve)* goes with "puissance de pleur" as well as with "amour."
30   of relessynge: Lat. "veniam," Trivet "relaxacionem."
33   And: Chaucer's Fr. MS (as B) added "et."
33–34   thre . . . and: From Trivet "tres furias." Trivet's commentary on this poem is printed by Denton Fox, Poems of Henryson, 1981, 384–91.
41–42   Cf. Tr 1.786–88.
52–55   Cf. KnT I.1163–66. But note the contrary statement about love at 2.m8.24–25, which Arcite ignores.
58   abakward: From Trivet "respiciendo in tergo."
59   was deed: Cf. Fr. "et la perdi et fu morte" (and lost her and she was dead), which is apparently what Chaucer means; but Lat. "perdidit occidit" (he lost her and was undone).

BOOK 4

Prosa 1

18–19   so as: Lat. "cum"; 19, 21 yif that (reflecting Fr. "se . . . ou se") are otiose. The sentence means, "It distresses me that evil exists despite God's goodness."
18–31   Cf. MLT II.813–16, and 1.m5.34–46.
25–26   to . . . uppon: From Trivet "admirandum."
27   richesses: Chaucer's Fr. MS omitted the addition "et des autres prosperitéz"; cf. MSt 14:233/16–17.

Metrum 1

1–7   Cf. HF 972–78. The description follows a pattern typical of journeys of vision or apotheosis. The soul first leaves behind the material world of the elements (4 *erthes*, 5 *ayr*, 6 *clowdes* (i.e., water), 7 *fir*; see HF 975 and Tr 5.1810); then passes the spheres of the planets (11 *Phebus*, 12–13 *Saturnus*) and of the stars (17–23; see Tr 5.1809, 1811–13), as well as the Primum Mobile (26 *firmament*); finally it reaches direct cognition of deity. For studies of the tradition, see Bloomfield, Seven Deadly Sins, 1952, 12ff.; Steadman, Disembodied Laughter; Delany, Ch's HF, 69ff; and Tr 5.1807–27n. The poem thus inverts the pattern of descent of 3.m12 and recalls Boethius to his "true country" first mentioned at 1.pr5.9ff.
2   the heighte: Chaucer's Fr. MS (as B) read "la hau-

tesce" (Fr. "les haulteces," Lat. "celsa"); cf. MSt 14:234/1.
13   imaked: From Trivet "effecta" (similarly 26–27 *and he schal be makid*).
28   of God: From Trivet "dei."
39   fastne my degree: Cf. Lat. "sistam gradum."

Prosa 2

10–12   According to J. Norton-Smith (Lydgate, 1966, 177) the source of the venerable topos of knowledge through contraries; cf. Tr 1.638–45 and 631–44n.; Mel VII.1276–94; and see also 3.m1.5ff.n.
18   ferme: Apparently translating Fr. "grant."
97   thanne: Chaucer's Fr. MS added "donques"; cf. MSt 14:236/48.
128   jugement: From Fr. "jugemens," a misreading of Lat. "indicium."
133   schewe: Chaucer's Fr. MS read "monstre" (Fr. "amonceleré," Lat. "coaceruabo"); cf. MSt 14:236/67.
156   of sovereyn good: From Trivet "summo bono" (Lat. "in eo"); similarly 158 *the . . . good* represents Trivet "assecucione boni" (Lat. "qua re").
161   myghty: Chaucer's Fr. MS (as B) lacked Fr. "tres" (Lat. "potentissimum"). Contrast 164–65 *ryght myghty* (Fr. and B "tres," Lat. "potentissimum").
168   power . . . folk: A ME clarification.
171   vertus: Chaucer's Fr. MS (as B) read "vertus" (Fr. "vertu," Lat. "virtute").
180   wel: Chaucer's Fr. MS (as B) added "bien."
208   certes²: Chaucer's Fr. MS read "certes" (Fr. "ceste," Lat. "hec"); cf. MSt 14:237/106.
220   power: Chaucer's Fr. MS omitted Boethius's response: Lat. "Perspicuum est inquam," Fr. "C'est cler"; cf. MSt 14:238/113.
226   sovereyn good: From Trivet "summum bonum."
234   schrewes: Chaucer's overspecific identification of the subject (Trivet "homines"; cf. *men* 230).
261–62   sentence of Plato: Gorgias 466b–481b, paraphrased in this and the following prose.

Metrum 2

3   here chayeres: Chaucer's Fr. MS read "leurs chaieres" (Fr. "leur chaere," Lat. "solii culmine"); cf. MSt 14:238/2.
9   hem: Lat. "corda," Fr. "leur cuer," but Chaucer, after translating Fr. "leur corage" for Lat. "intus" in the preceding line, may have sought to avoid repetition.

Prosa 3

28 (and 29–30, 31)   goodnesse: From Fr., but Boethius's sense is "reward"; cf. Trivet "premio." Chaucer's sense and Boethius's finally correspond at 34 *mede*.
40–41   schal . . . gerdoned: Chaucer's clarification.
63   to schrewes: Chaucer's clarification (similarly 69, 93, 98), perhaps suggested by Guillaume's "malis" in gloss to 63.

Metrum 3

8–9   hir gestes: From Trivet "hospites" (Lat. "quos," Fr. "les").

11   For other North African lions, see 3.m2.8 *Pene.*

30   chaungynge: From Trivet "mutacionem."

42   of vices / 44   vices: From Trivet "vicia."

Prosa 4

30   and . . . don: Chaucer's Fr. MS read "et pooir faire" (Fr. "et pooir et faire"); cf. MSt 14:242/15–16.

49–50   moost . . . lengest: In Lat. and Fr., comparatives.

103   solitarie: Lat. "pura ac solitaria," Fr. *om.*

112   more: Chaucer's Fr. MS read "plus" (Fr. "moult plus," Lat. "multo"); cf. MSt 14:243/58. Contrast *Moche more* 128 (Fr. and B "Moult . . . plus," Lat. "Multo").

116–31   Chaucer and Fr. here follow the Lat. manuscript order which modern editors emend; see Bieler, ed., Consolatio, 74, 52–63n. The emended order is 115, 132–39, 116–31, 140. Thus the immediate referent of 140–142 is the conclusion reached in 129–31, and *herebyforn* 142 refers to lines 30–33.

125–26   for . . . felonye: Better "on the score of injustice" (Lat. "iniquitatis merito").

153   nat: Chaucer ignores Lat. "nunc," Fr. "maintenant."

153   peynes: From Trivet "penis" (Lat. "his").

163–64   and that: Chaucer's Fr. MS read "et que" (Fr. "que"; cf. MSt 14:244/82), a scribal error that destroys the parallelism necessary to this unwieldy sentence.

178   studies: Lat. "iudicia," Fr. "jugemens."

182–87   Cf. PF 599–600.

182   so it es: Lat. "ita est" (yes, they should believe and hearken); but Chaucer follows Fr. in translating disjunctively.

197   thing: Plural, answering 195 *thinges* (Lat. "excellentioribus").

215–17   now . . . blynd: Cf. Trivet (whose Latin = Lat.) "videntes cecos esse [glossed 'illos'] putaremus eadem [glossed 'que ipsi putant']" (would we, seeing that they are blind, think the same things as they do?). Trivet does not comment on the shift from singular to plural. Fr. "nos qui verrions ces meismes chosez ne cuiderons pas que cil et ceulz qui seroient de semblable opinion ne fussent avugle," taking "eadem" as object of "videntes," not of "putaremus," and spelling out shift of number. Chaucer follows Fr.; his MS may have omitted "et . . . opinion."

248   enforced: Cf. Lat. "nitentibus," Fr. "apuiees" (dependent upon). See the similar translation at 3.pr8.24 and the somewhat better doublet at 4.pr7.87.

249   that: Otiose, and lacking in Lat. and Fr.

255   don: Chaucer ignores Lat. "nunc," Fr. "ore."

281   whiche . . . lost: A ME addition.

284   hemself: Chaucer's Fr. MS (as B) lacked equivalent for Lat. "totos," Fr. "touz."

290   overmochel: Chaucer's Fr. MS read "trop" (Fr. "tres," Lat. "stultissimus"); cf. MSt 14:245/148.

Metrum 4

1   What: Lat. "Quid," Fr. "Pour quoy."

3   the . . . deth: Lat. "fatum," Trivet "fatalem disposi-

cionem siue mortem aliorum hominum" and "desideratis siue uestram siue aliorum" (sc. "mortem," *deth* 5).

Prosa 5

8   flouren: Simplifying Lat "pollens . . . florere," Fr. "fleurir resplendissans de."

10–19   That is, in order to be happy, and have scope for his wisdom, a wise man must live not only in society, but in a just society (and since societies are regularly governed unjustly, in fact no one's life, wisely led though it may be, is unmixed with care). Justice can come about only if the people have as much chance for happiness as the rulers, and if criminals are punished, not good men. 14 **syn** (from Fr. "comme") should be *whanne*, paralleling 12 *whanne.* 12 **pouste** comes from Chaucer's Fr. MS "poesté," rather than Fr. "proece" (cf. MSt 14:246/8), and 15 **lawe** is evidently based on Lat. "lex," Fr. "lai," rather than the traditional "nex" (death).

21   the: Chaucer's Fr. MS (as B) read "les" (Fr. "ces," Lat. "hec").

29   thise: Chaucer's Fr. MS (as B) added "les."

Metrum 5

5   passeth or gadreth: Lat. "legat" (Trivet and Guillaume "colligat," pseudo-Aquinas "pertranseat").

10   And . . . that²: Chaucer's addition.

17   basyns of bras: Mention of beating upon brass to dissipate an eclipse is a commonplace in classical literature; see Tibullus, 1913, 1.8.22n. The Trivet and Fr. references to the Coribantes conflate this practice with the noisy rituals of Cybele.

30   that . . . hevene: Cf. Guillaume "in cursu et ratione celi"; Guillaume glosses 28 *her* (Lat. "hic") "in istis terrenis."

31–33   Cf. ClT IV.995–1001, Tr 4.183n.

Prosa 6

17   determined: From Trivet "soluta."

36   noryssynges: Chaucer's Lat. MS read "alimenta" (Lat. "oblectamenta").

42–47   Cf. KnT I.2994–3015.

70–72   departeth . . . in moevynges in places: Chaucer's Fr. MS (as B) read "depart . . . au mouvement en lieux" (Fr. "depart . . . en mouvement . . . en lieus," Lat. "digerit in motu [traditional "motum"] locis," ordains in movement by places).

71   and: Chaucer's Fr. MS read "et"; for sense, cf. Lat. "singula . . . distributa" (all individual things which are divided); cf. MSt 14:249/39.

82–88   Cf. Tr 1.1065–71.

114   ben: Chaucer's Fr. MS added "sont"; Lat. and Fr. lack verb and combine this sentence with the next: "and those, fixed . . . , surmount"; cf. MSt 14:249/63.

121   cerklis: Chaucer follows Fr. in ignoring Lat. "extra locatorum" (placed outside it).

149–53   Cf. KnT I.3011–15 (and more distantly, 2294–99).

152   of sexes: Cf. the erroneous Fr. "de sexes . . . de naturez maslez et femeles" (Lat. "fetum" [of offspring]).

166   that: Chaucer's Fr. MS read "que" (Lat. "vt

tametsi''; Fr. "que ja soit ce que," where this sentence and the next are one); cf. MSt 14:250/93.

178   unreste: Cf. Lat. "inquies" (you will say), construed as a noun; **thou mayst seyn** translates Fr. "tu diras."

188   manere: A ME specification (cf. Lat. "in hoc").

191   I pose: A ME addition.

198–99   or . . . atempraunces: A specification (as is 196–97 *of atempraunce*) suggested by Fr. "parler des qualitéz et des atemprancez."

224   constreyne: Cf. Lat. "perstringam" (touch lightly upon).

231   Lucan: At Pharsalia 1.128.

236   wikkid: Lat. "peruersa (confusio)"; perhaps Chaucer's Lat. MS read "peruerse (opinioni)."

240–41   is . . . yif: Cf. Lat. "est . . . cui si," Fr. "est . . . et si."

243   continue: Chaucer's Fr. MS read "continuer" (Lat. "colere," Fr. "cultiver"); cf. MSt 14:251/135.

254   a philosophre: From Trivet "philosophus"; Trivet identifies the author as Parmenides.

255–56   he . . . that: Chaucer's addition, based on Trivet, signaling Boethius's Greek quotation, represented in Lat. by gibberish; Chaucer actually translates part of Trivet's explanation (included in Lat.) "viri sacri corpus edificauerunt virtutes et reddiderunt fortem."

263   prosperites and adversites: Chaucer's Fr. MS (as B) read "prosperitéz et adversitéz" (Fr. singular, Lat. lacks).

284   adversite: Chaucer's Fr. MS (as B) read "adversité" (Fr. "adversitéz," Lat. "tristia").

299   to: Chaucer's Fr. MS read "au" (Fr. "en"); cf. MSt 14:252/168.

303   to yeven: Chaucer's Fr. MS (as B) read "pour donner" (Fr. "par donner," by giving).

309   ne . . . nat: Idiomatic after 307 *dredith* in the main clause but not negating the subordinate clause; i.e., he dreads that the loss will be painful.

317   contynuacioun: Chaucer's Fr. MS read "continuance" (Fr. "acoustumement"); cf. MSt 14:252/177.

321   ne[1]: Cf. Lat. "ita," Fr. "certez aussi," lacking in Chaucer's Fr. MS; cf. MSt 14:252/179.

323   whiche: Like Fr., Chaucer associates the pronoun with *vices*, but the proper antecedent is 322 *schrewes*.

332–33   wrongfully: A ME addition.

351–53   syn . . . world: Based on Fr. and Trivet explanation of Boethius's Greek (Iliad 12.176), garbled as usual in Lat.

355   the . . . disposiciounis: Lat. "machinas," Fr. "les soutivez ordenancez," Trivet "vel disposiciones."

376   questions or: A ME addition.

Metrum 6

8   the sterre yclepid: A ME addition, as are 13–14 *the see of the,* 15 *in the see,* 17 *the sterre.*

14   Occian: The great sea that encircles the known world.

16   nyghtes: Chaucer ignores Lat. "vicibus temporum equis," Fr. "par igalz muancez de temps."

19   entrechaungeable: Cf. Lat. "alternus amor."

22–28   See 3.m9.18–24n.

47–54   Cf. KnT I.3035–38.

51   contynued: Chaucer's Fr. MS read "continuees" (Lat. "continet," Fr. "contenuez"); cf. MSt 14:254/26.

The reading in MS A[2], *conteyned,* is an error accidentally corresponding to Lat. and Fr.

Prosa 7

19   resouns: Chaucer's Lat. MS, as Trivet, read "racionibus" (Lat. "viribus").

26   this . . . fortune: Chaucer's expansion of Lat. "id," Fr. "en."

27   seyn: The shift of subject follows Fr. "(parole) use . . . et (hommes) dient."

54   and: So Fr., but better omitted, as in Lat.

60   War now and: From Trivet "caue."

62   and concluded: From Trivet "concluserimus."

63   to the peple: From Trivet "apud vulgus," incorporated in Fr. at 23–24.

65   folweth or: From Trivet "sequitur."

77, 79   semeth: Chaucer follows Fr. "se doit . . . doit" in removing the Lat. variation "decet . . . debet."

86–87   it . . . 'vertu': That is, "the noun *uirtus* is derived from 'uires' (strength)." The correct etymology, from "vir" (man), was known to Cicero; see Disp. Tusc. 2.18.43.

90   or in the heyghte: From Fr. "en la hautece," not an adequate equivalent of Lat. "prouectu" (cf. 68).

103   is levest: Chaucer's Fr. MS lacked equivalent for Lat. "formare," Fr. "que vous forméz en vous"; cf. MSt 14:255/49.

Metrum 7

3–4   purgide in wrekynge: From Trivet "vlciscendo purgauit." For the sacrifice of Iphigenia, see Metamorphoses 12.1–45.

12   yeveth in sacrifyenge: From Trivet "sacrificando dat."

13   kuttynge of throte: From Trivet "incisionem gutturis."

28–62   Cf. MkT VII.2095–2110, a listing of the twelve labors; Boethius follows such sources as Hercules' lament, Metamorphoses 9.181ff.

BOOK 5

Prosa 1

2   resoun: Chaucer's Lat. MS read "racionis" (Lat. "oracionis," Fr. "parole").

8   by the same thing: That is, by your authority (cf. 4–5, where Chaucer omits *youre,* but Lat. "tua," Fr. "de toi").

16   axest: Chaucer's Fr. MS (as B) read "demandes" (Fr. "me demandez," Lat. lacks phrase).

23   togidre: Mistranslating Lat. "simul," which goes with 26 *whan,* not with *knowen.*

43–44   Cf. Tr 2.798; King Lear 1.2.90; see Walther 8299 (with cross-references); Whiting N151; F. P. Wilson, Oxford Dictionary of English Proverbs, 579.

47   God . . . wirkynge: Lat. "principio [Trivet 'deo creatore'] operante," Fr. "dieu qui est commencement et premiers ouvrans." Perhaps Chaucer's Lat. MS read "principe"; perhaps also O had *begynnyng wirkynge.*

48   casten: Lat. "iecerint"; Chaucer maintains the

building metaphor, but 46 *undirstoden ne meneden* also translates "iecerint"; cf. modern *construct,* with the same range of physical and intellectual reference. One might add, as Skeat suggests, *it* (Lat. "id").

62   Myn Aristotle: See Physics 2.4-5, 195bff.

81   abregginge . . . hap: Fr. "l'abregement du cas fortunel," a misunderstanding of Lat. "fortuiti . . . compendii" (of the chance profit), but defensible as a metaphor implying the bridging or foreshortening of the gap between two remote possibilities. In a coincidence, two events "come together"; that is, the distance between them is shortened.

83-84   to hemself: Chaucer's Fr. MS read "s'en entre" (Lat. "sibi," Fr. "s'-"); cf. MSt 14:258/46.

Metrum 1

Boethius's rather lame poem builds on the comparison of providential order to a flowing stream with which the first prose ends. The *o welle* from which the Tigris and Euphrates spring represents God, the two rivers any two diverse currents of causation. Should the rivers converge (as in fact they do), they and the things they convey would mingle by chance, and yet be "governed" by such things as the slope of the land and the direction of the current. Thus chance combines accident and order. Boethius's use of the conditional form seems arch; apparently he uses it because he is considering the rivers from the point of view of their upper reaches: a person who observes the point of divergence cannot regard it as necessary that they will converge again. Chaucer (following Fr.) obscures the conditional form by writing the indicative 14 *wrappeth or emplieth* for Lat. "implicet" (would wrap).

3   Achemenye: Persia, called so after Achaemenes, founder of the great dynasty eventually destroyed by Alexander. Boethius apparently uses the name loosely to include Armenia, where the two rivers rise separately. *The fleinge bataile* refers to the tactics of the Parthians who shot arrows at their enemies while riding away from them; see Georgics 3.31.

9, 13   moten: From Trivet "oportebit," "necesse est."

Prosa 2

42   joyned: Lat. "inuexere" (brought on), read as "innexere" (Fr. "aportee").

43-49   Cf. Tr 4.960-66.

47-49   and . . . herith: Although modern editions place these lines at the start of m2, with Greek quotation of Iliad 3.277, traditionally they occur here.

Metrum 2

1   Homer: See Iliad 1.605.

Prosa 3

7   fredom of liberte: Lat. "arbitrium libertatis"; cf. pr2.3 *liberte of fre wille* (Lat. "libertas arbitrii").

8-99   Cf. Tr 4.974-1078.

40-41   as . . . travailed: Boethius's sense was "as if the question were" (Lat. "quasi . . . laboretur").

47-48   But I ne enforce: Cf. Lat. "ac non . . . nitamur" (and as if we were not striving), continuing the previous sentence and dependent on "quasi." Chaucer follows Fr. in translating as indicative and thus reversing the sense utterly.

73   of God: A ME addition.

75-76   and . . . nat: The negatives surrounding the verb *bytide* do not negate it but rather reinforce the negation of the entire clause.

92   yit this thing: Chaucer's Fr. MS read "encore aucune chose," a locution arising from the loss of a clause by eyeskip; cf. Fr. "encores que aussi comme quant je sai que aucune chose." Chaucer simply drew the lost clause from Lat. "sicuti cum quid esse scio," but retained this phrase from his Fr. MS; cf. MSt 14:261/53.

94   and: Otiose, and lacking in Lat. and Fr.

134   Tyresie: See Horace, Satires 2.5.59; the poem is a conversation parodying the epic encounter of Odysseus with the blind Theban seer in Odyssey 11.

140   domes of men: Chaucer's Fr. MS read "de quoy" (sc. "l'oppinion") (Fr. "des quiex," Lat. "quorum"); cf. MSt 14:262/78. Boethius's intended antecedent is *thinges uncertayn* 138-39.

157   purposed and byhyght: Chaucer's Fr. MS read "proposés et promis" (Fr. "proposéz," Lat. "proponuntur"); cf. MSt 14:262/86.

176   the ordre: Chaucer's Fr. MS read "l'ordre" (Fr. "touz li ordres," Lat. "omnis ordo"); cf. MSt 14:262/96.

180-81   to . . . nothing: Fr. "valoir" (some manuscripts "voloir"); cf. MSt 14:262/97. Perhaps Chaucer was uncertain of the reading of his Fr. MS and gave alternative translations.

181   oure vices: Lat. "vicia quoque nostra," Fr. "nos vicez meismes" (even our vices).

188, 189   to God: ME additions.

189-90   Cf. NPT VII.3338.

191   and streyneth: Chaucer's Fr. MS read "constreint" (Fr. "contient").

**194-205   Chaucer follows Fr. in these two sentences without quite achieving full sense. 194 But should be "if in fact" (Lat. "si quidem")—a qualification of the previous statement. 199 oonly the manere means "the only manner." 200-201 for whiche means "by which." 202-5 and . . . it² might be better rendered "and be joined to that inaccessible light before they obtain it [i.e., before reunion with God after death]—by means of supplication."

207   iresceyved: Lat. "recepta" (being granted). C² has interlinear gloss *graunted.*

Metrum 3

9-10   But ther nis: Better, "or is there no?" (Lat. "An nulla est," Chaucer's Lat. MS perhaps "at nulla est"). Lines 9-17 should be a single question: "Is the problem not in things but in our faulty perception of them?" Indeed, the entire poem through 47 *singularites* should be a series of questions.

18   so: A ME addition, very likely scribal.

38-40   byholdeth . . . seeth . . . knoweth: These verbs should be in the past tense; cf. 42-43 *But now* and Lat. "cerneret," "norat"; Fr. "regardoit," "avoit . . . cogneu."

44   of the body: A ME addition, as is 50–51 *of things.*

Prosa 4

3   Marcus Tullius: See De divinatione 2.8.20.
10   and of this difficulte: Chaucer's addition; cf. the parallel insertion of "ignorance" in Fr.
20   resoun . . . difficulte: Chaucer's clarification.
22   I . . . ispendid: Lat. "expendero" (I shall have weighed, considered). Perhaps *ispendid* is a scribal representation of a Chaucerian neologism, *expended.*
36   that¹ . . . betide: Chaucer's explanation of the double negative (an intended Latin positive, not an English intensified negative); cf. the similar glosses at 2.pr4.158–60 and 5.pr6.163–64.
46–47   Thanne . . . sche: Chaucer's addition.
61   algate . . . wey: Two alternative translations of Fr. "toutevois."
152   wit: "The senses" (Lat. "sensus," here glossed by Trivet "exterior," the basis of Chaucer's *withoute-forth* 155, 188). The source of Boethius's faculty psychology is Aristotle, De anima 3.3, 427b. See SNT VIII.338–39n.
164   over that: A ME addition, repeating the idea in *surmountith;* 165 *forme* is direct object of *loketh.*
208   resoun, resoun: Fr. "raison," but Lat. "racione" here means "manner, mode," as it does at pr5.60.

Metrum 4

1   The porche: The colonnade of the Stoa Poikile in Athens, where Zeno of Citium taught and whence (Greek στοά, "porch") the Stoic philosophers derived their name.
**6–20   Echoed occasionally in the poetry to describe perception through the *affecciouns* alone; see Tr 1.295–98 and n., 361–66; MilT I.3611–13; MerT IV.1577–87, 2178; Rom 2806.
7   sensibilities: Lat. "sensus"; Trivet (the source of the subsequent gloss) includes the words "sensibiles" and "sensibilium"; Lat. gloss "sensibilia"; Guillaume "virtutem senciendi et ymaginandi."
36   the: Chaucer's Fr. MS read "la" (Fr. "sa"); cf. MSt 14:268/15.
46   manere of: From Fr. "maniere de," but Lat. "modo" here means "merely."
54   imoevid and: A ME addition, following 48–49.

Prosa 5

1   But what yif / 3   and albeit so: Lat. "quod si . . . quamuis." Liddell suggests that 3, 13 *and* are only intensive; cf. Fr. "Mais se . . . ja soit ce que" (and 13 "se"). But 13 *and yif* is correlative with 3, 6 *albeit;* all three clauses present conditions or objections.
24   ther comen: Chaucer's Fr. MS read "en viennent" (Fr. "avindrent," Lat. "cessere"); cf. MSt 14:268/14.
26   the whiche wit: Chaucer's Fr. MS read "li quiex sens" (Fr. "li quiex seus," Lat. "sensus enim solus"); cf. MSt 14:268/15.
29   her and ther: Based on Trivet's gloss to 32–33 *remuable bestis,* "que mouentur motu progressiuo."

45   thilke universel thingis: Chaucer's Fr. MS (as B) read "celles choses universeles" (Fr. "celle chose universele," Lat. "illud vniuersale").
46–47   For . . . seyn that: Cf. Trivet "hoc arguendo."
55   universel: Chaucer's Fr. MS read "universel" (Fr. "un universel," Lat. "quiddam vniuersale"); cf. MSt 14: 269/31.
56   two: A ME clarification (Lat. "hec," Fr. "ces chosez"), perhaps suggested by 62 *thilke two* (Fr. "ces deus").
72   seyn: Chaucer's Fr. MS read "dire" (Fr. "dire de comprendre") and thus omitted the phrase that gives point to the gloss; cf. MSt 14:269/40.
73   we scholde: In Lat. and Fr. a question, expecting a positive answer (cf. Lat. "nonne").
102   alle: Chaucer's Fr. MS (as B) read "toutes" (Fr. "toutevois," not in Lat.); cf. MSt 14:269/56.

Metrum 5

8   by moyst fleynge: Lat. "liquido [smooth, flowing] volatu." Chaucer retains the metaphor of swimming, if awkwardly.
**9–19   Perhaps cf. Truth 18–19.

Prosa 6

**15–26   Reflected vaguely at Tr 5.746–49.
30   Aristotile: See De caelo 1.10, 279bff.
52   Plato: See the general argument of Timaeus 28–29.
**56–59   Chaucer's gloss.
77   the lif: Lat. "sue," Fr. "sa"; but Chaucer simply repeats the construction of 69.
97   Plato: See Timaeus 37de.
106   and considereth alle: Chaucer translates "omnia . . . considerat" twice; cf. 107–8 *lokith . . . alle thinges.*
108   of preterit: Chaucer's Fr. MS (as B) added "du temps passé."
109   presently: From Trivet "presencialiter."
**140ff.   Cf. the burlesque at NPT VII.3234–50.
157   to be: Chaucer's simplification of Lat. "exstaturum esse," Fr. "a estre ou a avenir."
**162–68   Cf. Tr 2.622–23.
214   What: In Lat. and Fr. merely Philosophy's rhetorical question and not a separate speech, with no parallel for *Boece* or *quod I.*
229   nature: Lat. "necessitate," Fr. "necessité"; apparently either Chaucer or a Latin scribe misread an abbreviation, perhaps turning "ncc^{te}" into "nat^{2e}."
245   he: Chaucer shifts the antecedent to *God* (B has interlinear gloss "deus"); cf. Lat. "illa," Fr. "elle (sc. prouidencia)." The change surely represents an intentional decision to personify, linked to the inclusion in 243 of Fr.'s addition *of God.*
259   prescience: From Trivet "presciencia."
310   thinges: One English MS, C², adds "To whom be goye [i.e., glorye] and worshipe bi infynyt tymes amen," perhaps by Chaucer, reflecting Trivet "qui est dominus deus iesus christus cui est honor et gloria in secula seculorum amen." Or perhaps the C² scribe himself translated the prayer from the Latin text he had copied (Lat.), which includes it (reading "dominus noster iesus" and "sit").

Troilus and Criseyde

Chaucer names the poem *the book of Troilus* in his Retraction (X.1086) and *Troylus* in his poem to Adam Scriveyn. Of the allusions to *Troilus* in the Prologue to *The Legend of Good Women* (F 441, 469; G 264–65, 431, 459), one (F 441, G 431) seems to be Alceste's title for the work, *Creseyde.* Those manuscripts that name the poem divide evenly between simply "Troilus" and "Troilus and Criseyde" (in various spellings, in Latin and English). The Morgan and St. John's manuscripts have "Liber Troili et Criseid(is)"; the equally authoritative Corpus MS has "Liber Troily." Thomas Usk (d. 1388) makes the earliest known reference to the poem, calling it "the boke of Troilus" (Testament of Love, 3.4.258–59). Another early allusion, probably to Chaucer's poem (see 5.90n.), in the alliterative *Destruction of Troy* (ed. G. A. Panton and David Donaldson, EETS 39, 56, 1869–74) calls it "Troilus" (line 8054). Lydgate calls the poem "Troilus and Cresseide" (Pro to The Fall of Princes, 287), and editors since the sixteenth century have named both principal characters in the title, as have early critics (Puttenham, The Arte of English Poesie, 1589; Sidney, An Apologie for Poetrie, 1581, 1595). See Root, xi–xii; and G. Gregory Smith, Eliz. Crit. Essays, 1904, 1:196, 2:64.

The date of the poem is unknown. Tatlock (Dev. and Chron., x, 15–34) lists earlier opinions giving dates from 1378 to 1385, and his own proposal for 1377, later demolished by Kittredge (Date of Tr), as Tatlock came to admit (MLN 50, 1935, 277–96) while still resisting a date as late as 1385. Of recent editors, variously doubtful, Robinson gives 1385; Baugh, after 1378, leaning toward 1382–85; Donaldson, 1385 or 1386; Fisher, 1382–85. Root provides the fullest commentary on the problem and argues (xiv–xx) that Chaucer completed the poem "between the spring of 1385 and the end of the year 1386, or, at the very latest, the early months of 1387."

The only firm date derives from that of the death of Usk on 4 March 1388 (John Malvern's continuation of Higden's Polychronicon, ed. Lumby, Rolls Series 9: 169). Usk names the poem and alludes specifically to Troilus's monologue on necessity (Tr 4.958–1078), but he borrows as well from other parts of the poem, as shown by passages cited by Skeat (7:xxvii), Tatlock (Dev. and Chron., 20, 23), Bressie (see below), and Root (xv, n. 10). It seems improbable that Usk knew only parts of the poem before its completion; most likely *Troilus* was finished before Usk's death. Tatlock argued that Usk imitates as well passages from the Prologue to *The Legend of Good Women* (Tatlock, 22–23), which clearly postdates the completed *Troilus*, but the evidence is not wholly persuasive. Usk's *Testament* may have been composed before Skeat thought, during an earlier imprisonment than his last, that is, December 1384 to June 1385, which if true would set back the date of *Troilus* to early 1385 at the latest (and if Tatlock is right, would set back the date of the *Legend* as well). See Bressie's persua-

sive argument, MP 26, 1928, 17–29; Bressie's findings are seconded by John Leyerle, who kindly showed me the discussion of these dates in his forthcoming edition of Usk's *Testament.* Virginia B. Jellech reports that she dates the *Testament* September 1384 to July 1385 in her 1970 Washington University dissertation, an edition of the work (DAI 31, 1971, 6060–61A).

Another dating-point was first advanced by Root and Russell (PMLA 39, 1924, 48–63), who observed that the planetary conjunction described in Tr 3.624–25 actually occurred in the late spring of 1385. See the note to the passage for an account of the controversial facts. Chaucer may have anticipated the conjunction by use of an almanac, or he may possibly have described a potent conjunction *ex vacuo*, for poetic effect; still the coincidence is remarkable, and gives us reason to believe Chaucer was working on the poem around 1385.

Lowes (PMLA 23, 1908, 285–306) proposed that Tr 1.171 *Right as oure firste lettre is now an A* compliments Queen Anne, who married Richard II on 14 January 1382. The word *now* strengthens Lowes's case, although (Tatlock, MLN 50:279) it may be merely pleonastic (see MED s.v. *nou* 7[f]; and Tr 2.878 for an example). See 1.171n. A conjecture of the same sort, but less compelling, supposes that the unwise *parlement* of Tr 4.141–217 alludes to the Peasant's Revolt of the late spring of 1381, and possibly that the *blase of straw* (4.184) puns on the name of a leader of the revolt, Jack Straw, named in NPT VII.3394, whose name is played upon in Latin by Gower, *Vox clamantis* 1.652, 655 (see Brown, MLN 26, 1911, 208–11). Following Tatlock (MLN 50:277–78), McCall and Rudisill (JEGP 58, 1959, 276–88) argue that the Trojan *parlement* is a parliament, not a mob in revolution. They propose that Chaucer was rather thinking of the stormy English Parliament of October 1386, in which the poet served, and they assign the completion of the poem, within Root's limits, to 1387. Lerch (Romanische Forsch. 62, 1950, 67–68) thought the word "Pandras," in the ballade that Eustache Deschamps sent to Chaucer, refers to the Pandarus of *Troilus.* Mieszkowski (ChR 9, 1975, 327–36), persuasively supports this view, but she points out that the date often assigned to the ballade, 1386, is unsupported tradition.

Chaucer directs his poem to Gower and *philosophical Strode.* If this Strode is in fact, as seems likely, the Ralph Strode whose will was proved in London in 1387, the poem was dedicated before that date. The identity of Strode is not certain: see 5.1856–59n. North (RES 20, 1969, 134n.) contends that Chaucer dedicated *Troilus* to Strode after his death, but Chaucer asks Strode and Gower to correct his work, and we cannot admit of posthumous editing.

In sum, *Troilus* was completed before March, 1388. A date of composition 1382–85 seems likely, but the reasons for assigning the poem to this period are such that new evidence would easily controvert them. Among Chaucer's works, *Troilus* certainly precedes the Retraction and *The Legend of Good Women. Troilus* has enough features in common with the Complaint of Mars to suggest that they are linked in date. Probably it follows or accompanies Chaucer's work on *Boece*, because of the

The explanatory notes to *Troilus and Criseyde* were written by Stephen A. Barney.

abundant Boethian material embedded in the poem. Whether it follows or precedes The Knight's Tale, in many ways a companion-piece, has been disputed: see Expl. Notes to KnT, introductory note. Since both *Troilus* and The Knight's Tale derive from poems of Boccaccio and adopt material from Boethius, it is tempting to assign their composition to the same period: Chaucer may well have been at work on *Troilus,* The Knight's Tale, and *Boece* simultaneously (see Tr 5.748n.). J. A. W. Bennett observes that Chaucer's giving Arcite the pseudonym *Philostrate* (KnT I.558) indicates that he at least knew of the *Filostrato* as he worked on KnT (in Boitani, ed., Ch and Trecento, 1983, 92).

The main source of the *Troilus* is Giovanni Boccaccio's *Filostrato,* written in the late 1330s. On the sources of the *Filostrato,* see Gozzi, Studi sul Bocc. 5, 1969, 123–209, and Pernicone, Studi di Filol. Ital. 2, 1929, 77–128. An edition (based on Moutier, 1827–34, and Savj-Lopez, 1912) with facing-page English translation and a good introduction on the sources of the poem is by Nathaniel E. Griffin and Arthur B. Myrick. Other translations are by Robert K. Gordon, The Story of Troilus, and N. R. Havely, Ch's Boccaccio, 1980. Havely includes relevant passages from Benoît de Sainte-Maure and Guido delle Colonne; Gordon offers passages from Benoît, supplemented by Mieszkowski, ChR 15, 1980, 127–37.

The particulars of the relation of *Troilus* to the *Filostrato* have been often examined, especially since William M. Rossetti printed a transcription of a *Troilus* MS (Harley 3943) in parallel columns with a translation of the Italian (Ch Soc, 1st ser., 44 and 65, 1873–83). Among the most thorough studies are: Meech, Design in Tr, (with good bibliographies of many aspects of Tr); Rudolf Fischer, Zu den Kunstformen des mittelalt. Epos, 1899; Cummings, Indebtedness of Ch; a series of studies by Robert P. apRoberts, PMLA 77, 1962, 373–85; Spec 44, 1969, 383–402; JEGP 69, 1970, 425–36; ChR 7, 1972, 1–26; Windeatt, in Boitani, ed., Ch and Trecento, 163–83. Most influential has been C. S. Lewis, "What Chaucer Really Did to *Il Filostrato,*" E&S 17, 1932, 56–75. I refer in the notes below to several hitherto unnoticed borrowings from the *Filostrato* kindly communicated to me by D. J. Wallace.

Robert A. Pratt presents substantial evidence that Chaucer used a French prose translation of the *Filostrato, Le roman de Troilus* (or, *Troyle*), along with the Italian (SP 53, 1956, 509–39); see L. Moland and C. d'Héricault, ed., Nouvelles françoises en prose du XIVe siècle, 1858, 117–304. They based their text, it seems, on a poor manuscript (Paris, Bibl. Nat. MS fr. 1467), and emended it eclectically from five other Paris manuscripts they knew. Pratt lists fourteen manuscripts. William Provost, who kindly informs me that he concurs with Pratt's conclusions about Chaucer's use of this translation, has undertaken to edit the French text. For a few of the more striking examples from the 309 parallels Pratt adduced to support his argument, see the notes to Tr 1.109, 124, 141, 675; 2.541; 3.415, 1115; 4.514, 575, 623, 1223–25; 5.430–31, 1270. In his prefatory remarks the author of the *Roman* calls himself Beauvau, seneschal of Anjou (and he attributes the *Filostrato* to Petrarch—in some manuscripts corrupted to Petre Arane—not Boccaccio). Traditionally the translation has been assigned to Pierre or his son Louis de Beauvau in the first half of the fifteenth century. See Carla Bozzolo, Manuscrits des tra-

ductions franç. d'oeuvres de Boccace: XVe siècle, 1973; and Brian Woledge, Bibliog. des romans et nouvelles en prose franç. antér. à 1500, 1954, and Supplément, 1975, No. 119. Unaware of Pratt's findings, Bozzolo argues for the authorship of Louis de Beauvau, working between 1442 and 1458. An edition of the *Roman de Troyle* of Beauvau by Gabriel Bianciotto has appeared (diss., Univ. of Paris, Catalogue des thèses de doctorat, 1977, no. 16823). A notice of this edition reports that it "argues from linguistic evidence that Pratt's hypothesis is wrong" (SAC 7, 1985, 297). New editions of both the Italian and the French texts, aimed at locating variant readings available to Chaucer, and further study of the questions of authorship and date of the *Roman* are required before the matter can be definitively settled. Because the French translation is close and faithful, it is hard to prove that Chaucer used it, and granting that he did, his use does not substantially alter our sense of how he reshaped Boccacio's poem. There is no question that the *Filostrato* is Chaucer's prime source.

Comprehensive studies of the sources of *Troilus* other than the *Filostrato* are Young, Origin of Tr; and Root, xx–xlviii. Young's argument that Chaucer used Boccaccio's *Filocolo* seems plausible in spite of its rejection by Cummings, Indebtedness of Ch, 3–12.

Materials from the Trojan legends, often conflicting among themselves, were abundant and widespread through the Middle Ages. Details of Chaucer's particular knowledge as displayed in his poems can often be traced to particular sources, but because we have to do with a poet's retentive, combining, and inventive mind, we cannot always determine whence he derived some individual bit of information. Such borrowings and close analogues as can be ascertained are pointed out in the notes.

Chaucer certainly knew Benoît de Sainte-Maure's *Roman de Troie* (ca. 1160), or at least one of the French prose redactions of it (surveyed by Williams, MAE 53, 1984, 59–72), and Guido delle Colonne's *Historia destructionis Troiae* (completed 1287). See George L. Hamilton, The Indebtedness of Ch's Tr to Guido delle Colonne's Hist. Trojana, 1903; and C. D. Benson, ChR 13, 1979, 308–15.

We have no evidence that Chaucer used, except indirectly, the major Latin sources that the Latin-reading West took for authentic and ancient histories of Troy. These are the *De excidio Troiae historia* by "Dares the Phrygian" (?6th century A.D.); the *Ephemeridos belli Troiani* by "Dictys of Crete" (4th century A.D.); the *Ylias Latina* by Baebius (?) Italicus, formerly attributed to "Pindarus the Theban" (?1st century A.D.), ed. Fredericus Plessis, 1885, Martín de Riquer, 1959; and the anonymous *Excidium Troiae* (before the 9th century), ed. E. Bagby Atwood and Virgil E. Whitaker, 1944, with an introduction referring to many of the medieval accounts of Troy. Probably Dares and certainly Dictys were translated from Greek originals of the first century A.D. For further comment, see Nathaniel E. Griffin, Dares and Dictys, 1907. Chaucer thought he knew (see below) and names Dares (Tr 1.146; 5.1771; HF 1467), and he also names Dictys (Tr 1.146; possibly HF 1467), probably at second hand from Guido, as like Lollius (see below) a notable *auctoritee* on the matter of Troy.

Root showed (MP 15, 1917–18, 1–22; see note to Tr 5.799–840) that Chaucer used the *Frigii Daretis Ylias* by Joseph of Exeter (Iscanus), dated 1188–90 by its editor,

Ludwig Gompf. Gompf demonstrates that Joseph's redaction of Dares' *De excidio* was often known through the Middle Ages as "Dares"; Chaucer may well have taken Joseph's work as the actual *De excidio* or at least as an authoritative redaction of it.

Besides works already mentioned, for general studies of the medieval Troy material see C. David Benson, Hist. of Troy in ME Lit., 1980; Atwood, Spec 9, 1934, 379–404; MP 35, 1937, 115–28; SP 35, 1938, 36–42; U. of Texas Stud. in Eng., 1938, 5–13; Griffin, JEGP 7, 1908, 32–52; Parsons, MLR 24, 1929, 253–64, 394–408; Wilhelm Greif, Die mittelalt. Bearbeitungen der Trojanersage, 1886; Egidio Gorra, Testi inediti di storia trojana, 1889; Hugo Buchthal, Historia Troiana: Stud. in the Hist. of Med. Secular Illustration, 1971.

Incidental borrowings from various authors—especially Ovid, Statius, Dante, Petrarch, Boethius, and the authors of *Le roman de la rose*—are recorded in the notes. The deep influence of Boethius on *Troilus* has been the subject of much comment: see Jefferson, Ch and the Consolation, 120–32, 137–40; Koch, Anglia 46, 1922, 6–30; Patch, Trad. of Boethius, 69–73, JEGP 17, 1918, 399–422, Spec 6, 1931, 225–43; Stroud, MP 49, 1951–52, 1–9; Eldredge, Mediaevalia 2, 1976, 49–75; Gaylord, PMASAL 46, 1961, 571–95; McAlpine, Genre of Tr; Payne, Ch and Menippean Satire, chs. 4 and 5. On Chaucer's use of other sources, see Wise, Infl. of Statius; Clogan (on Ch's use of the *Thebaid*), Eng. Misc. 18, 1967, 9–31; Shannon, Ch and Roman Poets; Mieszkowski, Reputation of Criseyde: 1150–1500, 1971; Fansler, Ch and RR, esp. 149–57; Wimsatt (on Machaut and Tr), MAE 45, 1976, 277–93; and Schless, Ch and Dante, 1984.

Chaucer refers to his source as a Latin work (see 2.14 and n.) by *myn auctour called Lollius* (1.394; see 5.1653; HF 1468), and he nowhere names Boccaccio, nor does he name Petrarch in the *Troilus*, although he translates one of Petrarch's sonnets (1.400–420) and he may have thought, like the French translator of the *Filostrato,* that Petrarch was the author of Boccaccio's poem. The question of Lollius's identity has aroused much speculation. Kittredge summarized earlier opinion in a brilliant essay, "Chaucer's Lollius," Harv. Sts. in Class. Philol. 28, 1917, 47–133, which includes a survey of "touches of antiquity" in *Troilus* (see also Tatlock, MP 18, 1920–21, 625–59; Boughner, ELH 6, 1939, 200–210) and extended appendices on Chaucer's reference to his sources and on the use of Boccaccio's *Teseide* in the *Troilus* (see also Pratt, PMLA 62, 1947, 598–621). Kittredge argued that Chaucer erroneously believed that there was a Lollius who was an authority on the Trojan War, and he accepted the suggestion by R. G. Latham (Athenaeum 2136, 3 Oct. 1868, 2:433) and ten Brink, Ch Studien, 1870, 87–88, that Chaucer followed some medieval misunderstanding of the opening of Horace, Epist. 1.2.1–2: "Trojani belli scriptorem, Maxime Lolli, / Dum tu declamas Romae, Praeneste relegi" (While you declaim at Rome, Maximus Lollius, I have been reading again at Praeneste the writer of the Trojan War—that is, Homer). Reading "scriptorem" as "scriptorum" (and taking "Maxime" as an adjective rather than a proper noun) would give, "Lollius, greatest of authors of the Trojan War." Pratt, MLN 65, 1950, 183–87, proved that this error was current in Chaucer's time. Chaucer may have known Horace's lines only from John of Salis-

bury's *Policraticus* 7.9 (ed. Webb 2:128; see Pratt, MLN 65:243–46) or some other medieval quotation. Pratt found the reading "scriptorum" in a manuscript of the *Policraticus,* and further he found, in a French translation of the *Policraticus* done by Denis Foullechat in 1372, the statement, "Car il dit, que lolli fu principal ecrivain de la bataille de troye" (For he says that Lollius was the principal writer of the battle of Troy). No better evidence that Kittredge was right could be desired. Chaucer may have claimed Lollius as his *auctor* in keeping with a medieval preference for antique and Latin over "modern" and vernacular sources of historical information.

Lydgate speaks of *Troilus* as "a translaccioun / Off a book, which callid is Trophe, / In Lumbard tunge" (Fall of Princes, Pro 283–85). He correctly speaks of the source as Italian, but why he called it "Trophe" is not known. Chaucer also mysteriously cites *Trophee,* either as an author or as a work, in The Monk's Tale (VII.2117), and various interpretations are discussed in the note to that passage.

The critical and interpretative literature on *Troilus* is substantial. Along with the usual bibliographical sources, reference may be made to the summaries and bibliography, not always accurate, in Alice R. Kaminsky, Ch's Tr and the Critics, 1980. A list of some books devoted to *Troilus* but not mentioned above will indicate the quantity of commentary: Thomas A. Kirby, Ch's Tr: A Study of Courtly Love, 1940; Sister Anne Barbara Gill, Paradoxical Patterns, 1960; Ida L. Gordon, The Double Sorrow of Tr, 1970; John M. Steadman, Disembodied Laughter, 1972; William Provost, Structure of Ch's Tr, 1974; Donald W. Rowe, O Love, O Charite!, 1976; Ian Bishop, Ch's Tr: A Critical Study, 1981; Chauncey Wood, Elements of Tr, 1984; Wetherbee, Ch and Poets, 1984. Two anthologies, mainly of reprinted essays by various hands, include many of the more influential treatments of *Troilus*: Richard J. Schoeck and Jerome Taylor, eds., Ch Crit., Vol. 2, 1961; Stephen A. Barney, ed., Ch's Troilus, 1980. Mary Salu edited a collection of new essays on Troilus and Criseyde, 1979. The notes that follow can record only those findings from this mass of literature that would aid a fundamental understanding of the poem.

Much attention has been paid to the characters of Criseyde and Pandarus. Criseyde's name is derived from the Greek Χρυσηΐδα, Chryseida, accusative of Χρυσηΐς, Chryseis, daughter of Chryses. She is referred to only by this patronymic in Homer (Iliad 1.13, etc.), and known as Astynome in later classical tradition (see Pauly-Wissowa, Real-Ency. s.v. *Chryseis*). Boccaccio, perhaps taking the name Criseida from Armannino's *Florita,* written 1325 (see Griffin, ed., Filostrato, Intro., 26), applies it to the character known formerly in medieval tradition as Briseida, another figure in the *Iliad* (see Pauly-Wissowa, Real-Ency., s.v. *Briseis*—her classical name was Hippodameia). On the development of her name and character in the tradition, see E. H. Wilkins, MLN 24, 1909, 65–67; Mieszkowski, Reput. of Cris.; and Donaldson, in Ch Problems, 3–12. The story of the love of Troilus and Briseida is wholly the invention of Benoît in the twelfth century.

Much of what has been written about Criseyde's character follows issues broached by Kittredge in Ch and His Poetry, 108–45; by C. S. Lewis, E&S 17:56–75; and by Arthur Mizener, PMLA 54, 1939, 65–81. These essays focused on the causes of her betrayal of Troilus, and especially on whether the early indications of her character in the poem gave sufficient notice of her later actions. Recent critical thought tends to exculpate her in the light of her situation (e.g., Saintonge, MLQ 15, 1954, 312–20; McAlpine, Genre of Tr, chs. 6 and 7; Lambert, 105–125, and David, 90–104, in Essays on Tr; Aers, ChR 13, 1979, 177–200), or to treat her as emblematic of instability, as the moon, or sublunary Nature, or Fortune, wallowing seas, contrary winds, or simply frail humanity (e.g., Berryman, ChR 2, 1967, 1–7; Durham, ChR 3, 1968, 1–11; apRoberts, Spec 44:383–402; Knapp, ChR 13, 1978, 133–40), or to consider her especially in the light of the narrator's admiration and pity for her (e.g., Käsmann, in Ch und seine Zeit, 97–122; Donaldson, Speaking of Ch, 46–83).

Pandare or *Pandarus* (the name usually varying with the exigencies of meter) is based on Boccaccio's Pandaro, whose name derives ultimately from the *Iliad* and Virgil (a Lydian archer, known to Plato as a violator of oaths—Repub. 379E), but whose character is Boccaccio's invention, modeled on numerous go-betweens in classical and medieval literature. For the Homeric Pandaros, see Pauly-Wissowa, Real-Ency. For accounts of the tradition of go-betweens, friends, and procurers, see Young, Origin of Tr, 43–66; Neilson, Origins of Court of Love, ch. 5; Kirby, Ch's Tr, ch. 6; and Griffin, ed. Fil., Intro., 42–47. Medieval literary characters of special interest are Galehout, in the French *Lancelot du Lac,* and four characters in Boccaccio's *Filocolo* who in one way or another serve as go-betweens. Fansler (Ch and RR) notes connections of Pandarus with both Ami (Friend) and Raison (Reason) in *Le roman de la rose.* Several scholars find a resemblance between Pandarus in *Troilus* and Lady Philosophy in Boethius (Jefferson, Ch and the Consolation, 124; Gaylord, PMASAL 46, 1961, 571–95). Other analogues, none very likely as immediate sources, are Spurius in Guillaume de Blois's Latin farce *Alda,* of the twelfth century (Renoir, N&Q 203, 1958, 421–22); Anus (Old Woman), the go-between in the widely popular *Pamphilus de Amore,* which Chaucer probably knew in the Latin or a French version (see FranT V.1110n., Mel VII.1556n.; Garbáty overstates the probable influence of this work on *Troilus* (PQ 46, 1967, 457–70 and ChR 2, 1967, 108–34)); Houdée, the garrulous, pedantic go-between in the expanded French version of Pamphilus by the same author (Mieszkowski, ChR 20, 1985, 40–60); Ovid's Dipsas, the Old Woman of the *Roman de la rose,* and the Lady Esperance in Machaut's *Remède de fortune* (all adduced, along with Anus of Pamphilus, by Wimsatt, in Essays on Tr, 43–56, and MAE 45, 1976, 277–93).

From Pandarus's name the common noun *pandare* (procurer) is first attested in a poem written in about 1440, "The Chance of Dice," ed. Hammond, ESt 59, 1925, 1–16, line 160 (see Mieszkowski, Rep. of Cris., 131). The mid-fifteenth century (so Root) MS H⁴ has in the margin beside Tr 3.396–97 the words "Nota nomen P" (for "Pandari"); the context indicates that the annotator connects lines 395–397, which speak of *bauderye* (procuring), with an already common noun *pander.*

Pandarus's character has been considered in terms of four topics: his function as "friend," and Chaucer's use of the literature of friendship deriving ultimately from Cicero (Gaylord, ChR 3, 1969, 239–64; Cook, JEGP 69, 1970, 407–24; Freiwald, ChR 6, 1971, 120–29); his role

as courtier attendant on a prince (Stanley, E&S 29, 1976, 84–106); his role as artist, manipulator, catalyst in the poem (Bloomfield, PMLA 72, 1957, n. 14; Rutherford, AnM 13, 1972, 5–13; Donaldson, Mich. Quart. Rev. 14, 1975, 282–301); and, a favorite recent theme, his role in the "Treason in *Troilus*" (Bolton, Archiv 203, 1966, 255–62) as traitorous, manipulating, deceptive, evil—a view ultimately associated with D. W. Robertson, Jr. (who refers to Pandarus as "priest of Satan"—ELH 19, 1952, 1–37), more subtly explored by Carton, PMLA 94, 1979, 47–61; Newman, in Ch's Troilus, 257–75; and Fyler, MLQ 41, 1980, 115–30.

On Pandarus's age, the opinion advanced by Rossetti and often assented to (perhaps under the influence of his successor Polonius) that he is of middle age (older than the youth in Boccaccio), distinctly avuncular to Criseyde, has been challenged (Slocum, PQ 58, 1979, 16–25); the issue cannot be decided on the facts. See 3.293 and n., 5.826n.

A few topics of special interest to *Troilus* should be noticed. Important treatments of the theme of "courtly love" are William G. Dodd, Courtly Love in Ch and Gower, 1913, and Lewis, Allegory of Love. The validity of the theme has recently been disputed (Benton, 19–42, and Robertson, 1–18, in Meaning of Courtly Love, ed. F. X. Newman, 1968; Donaldson, Ventures 5, 1965, 16–23, repr. in Speaking of Ch, 154–63) or discounted with respect to *Troilus* specifically (Kleinstück, Archiv 193, 1957, 1–14); the opposition has drawn forth defenders of the usefulness of the concept of courtly love for understanding medieval literature (Utley, M&H n.s. 3, 1972, 299–324; Ferrante, Spec 55, 1980, 686–95). For a full survey and bibliography of the controversial literature on the subject, see Roger Boase, Origin and Meaning of Courtly Love, 1977. A sensible essay on the form of love in *Troilus* as seen in its proper context—late medieval French love-literature—is Green, ChR 13, 1979, 201–20. No better introduction to the subject can be had than the work that Chaucer would have taken as authoritative on love, *Le roman de la rose.*

On the remarkable painting of Chaucer reciting his work before a courtly audience, the frontispiece to the Corpus manuscript, see Elizabeth Salter's introduction to the facsimile of the manuscript, published by Brewer, 1978, and Pearsall, YES 7, 1977, 68–74 (who rightly observes, contrary to many published descriptions, that Chaucer has no book before him); and, with many extravagant conjectures, Brusendorff, Ch Trad., ch. 1; Galway, MLR 44, 1949, 161–77; Williams, MLR 57, 1962, 173–78.

The origins and name of the rime royal stanza adopted for *Troilus* are examined by Stevens, PMLA 94, 1979, 62–76. On the relation of the poet to his audience, see Crosby on oral delivery, Spec 11, 1936, 88–110 and 13, 1938, 413–32; Bronson, "Ch's Art in Relation to His Audience," Univ. of Cal. Publ. in Eng. 8, 1940, 1–53; Pearsall, YES 7:68–74; Robert M. Durling, Figure of the Poet in Renais. Epic, 1965; Dieter Mehl, in Ch and ME Sts., 173–89, and Geoffrey Ch: Eine Einführung in seine erzählende Dichtungen, 1973.

The significant use of proverbs in the poem can be studied by way of Whiting, Proverbs, often cited in the notes. See also his Ch's Use of Proverbs, 1934; Hassell, Middle French Proverbs; Lumiansky, TSE 2, 1950, 5–48; Newman, 257–75, and Taylor, 277–96, in Ch's Troilus. The style of the poem is the subject of studies by Lanham, SMC 3, 1970, 169–76; Eliason, Lang. of Ch's Poetry, esp. 126–36; Knight, Rymyng Craftily; Elliott, Ch's English; Taylor, Spec 51, 1976, 69–90, revised in Ch's Troilus, 231–56; Dahlberg, ChR 15, 1980, 85–100.

Studies of the structure of the poem include: (scenic or dramatic structure) Price, PMLA 11, 1896, 307–22; Fischer, Kunstformen, 217–370; Utley, Sts. in Hon. of Baugh, 109–38; Norton-Smith, Geoffrey Ch, ch. 6; (general structure) a thorough survey by Provost, Structure of Tr, ch. 1; Brenner, AnM 6, 1965, 5–18, revised in Ch's Troilus, 131–44; Rowe, O Love, esp. ch. 4; McCall, MLQ 23, 1962, 297–308; McAlpine, Genre of Tr; Meech, Design in Tr; Payne, Key of Remembrance, ch. 6. The temporal sequence of the poem, especially the chronology of Book 5, has called for much comment. See Root, xxxiii–xxxiv; Graydon, PMLA 44, 1929, 141–77; Sams, MLN 56, 1941, 94–100; Meech, Design in Tr, 226–33; Longo, MLQ 22, 1961, 37–40; Durham, ChR 3:1–11; Bessent, SN 41, 1969, 99–111; North, RES 20:142–49; Hussey, MLR 67, 1972, 721–29; Provost, Structure of Tr, ch. 3; Bie, ELN 14, 1976, 9–13; Tavormina, BSUF 22, 1981, 14–19.

For references to marginalia in the manuscripts of *Troilus,* I am indebted to an unpublished study by Barbara Hurwitz.

Barry A. Windeatt's edition, Troilus & Criseyde: A New Edition of "The Book of Troilus," 1984, presents the manuscript variants more fully than ever before, and prints in parallel with *Troilus* the text of the *Filostrato* from the edition of V. Pernicone, 1937. This fine work came into my hands long after I completed these notes, but I have been able to include some information gleaned from its commentary. Conscious of an obligation to distinguish carefully my own work from Windeatt's recent and laborious enterprise, I have labeled matters derived from his edition with his name or "Wdt."

The following table, compiled by Robinson, shows the main parallels between the *Troilus* and the *Filostrato*. A more thorough examination would require consultation of the works listed above that compare the two poems, especially Windeatt's edition. The numbers refer to lines in *Troilus,* and to stanzas in the *Filostrato* (with line numbers occasionally added after commas).

Troilus	Filostrato
1.21–30	1.5–6
57–140	7–16
148–231	17–25
267–73	26
281–329	27–32, 6
354–92	32, 7–37
421–546	38–57
547–53	2.1
568–630	2–10
646–47	11, 1
666–67	13, 7–8
673–86	11, 7–8; 12
701–3, 708–14	13
722–24	15, 1–2
856–65; 874–89	16–17; 20–22
967–94	24–25; 27–28
1009–64	29–34

Troilus	Filostrato
2.148–52	35
274–91	35–36; 44
316–20	46
393–99	54–55
407–20	47–48
501–9, 519–22	55–57
540–41	61, 1–2
554–78	62–64
584–88	43
596–604	68
659–65; 704–7	72
733–35	70
746–63; 768–88	69; 73; 75–77
960–81	79–81; 89
995–1009	90–91
1044–64	93–95
1065–92	97; 105; 107
1100–1104	108–9
1120–58	109–13
1173–78	114
1195–1200	118
1205–9	119
1212–26	120–28; 134
1321–51	128–31
3.1–38	3.74–79
239–87	5–10
330–36	9–10
344–441	11–20
1310–23	31–33
1338–65	34–37
1373–86	38–39
1394–1426	40–43
1443–52	44
1471–93	44–48
1499–1555	49–56, 1
1588–1624	56–60
1639–80	61–65
1695–1701	70
1709–43	71–73
1772–1806	90–93
4.1–10	94
29–35	4.1
47–112	2–11
127–68	12–16
211–322	17; 22; 26–36
330–57	38–43
365–85	44–46
393–406	47–48
415	49
439–51	50
452–628	52; 54–58; 60–75
631–37	76
645–795	77–93
799–821	95–96
841–926	97–107
939–48	108–9
1083–95	109–10
1108–1253	110; 112–27
1303–6; 1324–27	133
1331–48	131–34
1359–72	132, 2; 134, 2; 135–36
1422–46	137–40
1464–1542	141–46

Troilus	Filostrato
1555–1659	147–63
1667–1701	164–67
5.15–90	5.1–6; 10–13
190–261	14–21; 24–28
280–95	22–23
323–36; 353–64	29–32
386–686	33–38; 40–61; 67–71
687–93; 708–43	6.1–6
750–55	7
766–805	8; 10–11; 33; 24
841–47	9
855–942	12–25
953–58	26–27
967–91	28–31
1100–1354	7.1–32; 40–41; 48–55
1373–1421	60; 62; 72; 75
1422–39	76; 105; 77
1513–22	27; 89–90
1523–37	100–102; 104
1562–86	8.1–5
1632–1764	6–26
1800–1806	27
1828–36	28–29

BOOK I

1–14 Boccaccio invokes, not Jove or Apollo or the Muses, but his lady; Chaucer, retaining the epic machinery but consistent with his stance as an outsider in matters of love (see 2.13), invokes **Thesiphone,** the Fury Tisiphone, perhaps influenced by Statius, Theb. 1.56–59, 85–87; 8.65–71, 686. The satiric *Lamentationes* of Matheolus likewise has an invocation to the Furies, rejecting the Muses because of the sorrowful matter (ed. van Hamel, 6). On Chaucer's use of Matheolus, see Thundy, in Ch Problems, 24–56. Tisiphone was regularly interpreted as voice (vox) of the Furies: see McCall, Ch Among the Gods, 16, 29. The MS H⁴ glosses line 6 "fure d'enfer" (Fury of hell), a phrase found in the Roman de Thebes, 510. That the Furies themselves suffer blends the classical notion of them as agents of torment with Dante's conception (Inf. 9.37–51) of their own torment. But Virgil's Fury Alecto is herself "luctifica" (meaning, ambiguously, causing woe or doleful), and he speaks of "tristis Erinys" (the sad Fury, Aen. 7.324, 2.337). See Tr 4.22–24; SqT V.448; FranT V. 950, 1101 (Lowes, MP 14, 1917, 718; Spenser, Spec 2, 1927, 185). Schless persuasively argues that Chaucer need not have had Dante in mind here, noting (with Spenser) the passage from Bo cited below (Ch and Dante, 103–5). Thomas E. Maresca notes that the Furies' cheeks are wet with tears in response to Orpheus's lament in Ovid, Met. 10.45–46 (Three English Epics, 1979, 158). Boethius, 3.m12.26, 36–37, adapted the passage from Ovid and refers to the doubled sorrow of Orpheus and the weeping Furies. Nearly all the classical lore found in this poem by Boethius is used in Troilus.

1 **double sorwe:** May recall Dante's "doppia tristizia," (Purg. 22.56), speaking of Statius as author of "the double sorrow of Jocasta." Maresca (see previous note) suspects that Chaucer has in mind the theologians' descrip-

tion of hell as "duplex poena" (the double torment of mind and body; e.g., Haymo of Halberstadt, PL 118: 946; Paschasius Radbertus, PL 120:868). Cf. Fil. 4.118, "doppia doglia" (Wdt).

4 **wo and wele:** Commonly associated (OED s.v. *woe* B.1.b; Whiting W132–40), and their alternation ascribed to the influence of Fortune, as in the lyric "Lady Fortune and Her Wheel": "She turnes wo al into wele, and wele al into wo" (Brown, Relig. Lyrics, no. 42). Compare the sentences on "joy after woe" (Whiting J61, Hassell D47), and Fort 2, MLT II.1161.

5 Chaucer here, as often, presents himself both as writer for readers and as reader before an audience. See the studies by Crosby and Bronson cited in the introductory note above. With the rhyme *Troye : fro ye* cf. *Rome : to me,* GP I.523 and n.; for other examples of broken rhyme, see Tr 1.687–89 and n., 2.20–21, 5.382–83, 1161, 1376–77. See also Mustanoja, ME Syntax, 125.

7 Fil. 1.6: " 'l mio verso lagrimoso," and Boethius, Cons. 1.m1.2, "maestos modos" (sorrowful meters, perhaps playing on his "elegiac" Latin meter and the sad content of elegy; Chaucer translates *vers of sorwful matere*). **Vers** is plural with *wepen*.

12–14 For this rhetorical commonplace, see SqT V.103 and note 99–104, and Whiting W254.

15–21 For Chaucer's pose as servant to Love and to lovers, see HF 615–40. His stance partly conforms to the rhetorical topos of "affected modesty" (see GP I.746 and n.). As servant of the servants of the God of Love he alludes to the papal title ("servus servorum Dei," servant of the servants of God), a title itself derived from humility formulas (Curtius, Europ. Lit., 407–13): see ParsT X.773. Chaucer as pope of Love may recall Ovid as helmsman and charioteer of Love (Ars Am. 1.3–8). In the Troilus Chaucer frequently draws from the medieval convention of the "religion of love." See the note to 29–46 below, and see also Tr 1.42 (an allusion to despair as the sin against the Holy Ghost), 336–40; 2.523–41, 1503; 3.15–17, 704, 1267, 1282; cf. KnT I.3089 and n., and William G. Dodd, Courtly Love in Chaucer and Gower, 1913, 190–204; Meech, Design in Tr, 262–70; Dunning, in Eng. and Med. Sts. presented to J. R. R. Tolkien, ed. Davis and Wrenn, 1962, 164–82. G. H. Roscow, Syntax and Style, 42, draws attention to the modern form of group genitive here, as opposed to Chaucer's usual split group (as in line 2). See Language and Versification, p. xxxviii.

22–52 For the address to an audience of lovers cf. Ovid, Amores 2.5–10. If these lines are taken as a single sentence, only KnT I.2919–62 is a longer one in Chaucer's poetry. See also 3.127–47. For an account of the various audiences addressed in the poem, see Dieter Mehl's essay in Ch and ME Sts., 173–89.

29–46 Root observes that these lines imitate the form of the "bidding prayer" of the Mass, when the priest requests prayers for various people. See the account in Joseph A. Jungmann, Mass of the Roman Rite, trans. F. A. Brunner, 1950, 1:488–89, and for English examples, Lay Folks Mass Book, EETS 71, 61–80 and 315–46.

39 **wikked tonges:** Cf. 2.785, 5.1610 and *Wikked-Tunge,* Rom 3257.

58, 60 The **thousand shippes** and **ten yer** were traditional figures, derived from Aen. 2.198 and Ovid, Her. 13.97. Benoît and Guido give different numbers of ships.

62   Eleyne, Helen of Troy, wife of Agamemnon, abducted by Paris. The Greeks besieged Troy to win her back. Cf. PF 290n.

66   In Homer (Iliad 1.69, etc.) **Calkas,** Calchas, is a Greek, but the medieval tradition made him a Trojan, taking the place of Homer's Chryses. On the classical lore about him, see Pauly-Wissowa, Real-Ency. s.v. *Kalchas.* His role in medieval writers before Chaucer is examined by Lumiansky, TSE 4:5–20. On the character in Chaucer see Greenfield, MAE 36, 1967, 141–51 and Knight, Rymyng Craftily, 50–56.

68–70   This consultation of the Delphic oracle is not mentioned in the Filostrato. Chaucer may draw from Benoît (Roman de Troie, 5817–92) or Guido (Historia, p. 98). Apollo has the epithet **Delphicus,** from his oracle at Delphi, in Ovid, Met. 2.543 and Fasti 3.856. See Tr 4.1411 and n. There is perhaps a baleful paranomasia on **Troie . . . destroied** here and in 76–77.

71   by calkulynge: By astrological computation (see FranT V.1284) or some other form of divination (perhaps *by sort,* 76; see ParsT X.603–5), with a play on the name *Calkas.*

86, 88, 90   On the construction, see GP I.33n.

96   As she that: According to Kerkhof, p. 278, a calque on the French *com cil qui* meaning "for she." See Tr 5.1413.

97   allone: But we learn later that she has a friend in Pandarus (on friendship in the poem, see Gaylord, ChR 3:239–64).

99   On Criseyde, see the introductory note.

101   forpassynge: More likely one word (so Fisher) than two (Rob).

109   The French translation of the Filostrato (p. 122), and not the Filostrato itself (1.12), specifies that her habit was a **widewes** (de veufvage).

110   Ector: On his role, see Kiernan, AnM 16, 1975, 52–62, who perhaps overemphasizes the superiority of Hector's conduct over Troilus's.

124   The French (p. 123) has "moult humblement," corresponding to **with ful humble chere,** lacking in the Filostrato (1.14).

126   hom, "went home." Such ellipses are common in Chaucer. See 3.548, 691; 5.1825; Elliott, Ch's English, 72; and, with further citations, Roscow, Syntax and Style, 98; Kerkhof, p. 84; Mustanoja, 510.

132–33   Boccaccio (1.15) expressly says Criseida had neither son nor daughter, and Benoît (13111) calls her "la pucele" (the virgin). On the references to sources in Chaucer's narratives see H. Lüdeke, Die Funktionen des Erzählers in Chs epischer Dichtung, 1928, 52–71. He notes that in only five works does Chaucer name a source (Tr, Anel, PhyT, MkT, ClT). For examples of references to their sources by medieval English authors, see F. R. Amos, Early Theories of Translation, 1920, 19–46. On a medieval tendency to cite false sources, see Beryl Smalley, English Friars, 1960, 18 (Wolfram von Eschenbach) and Flint, Spec 54, 1979, 447–68 (Geoffrey of Monmouth).

138–40   On the common conception of Fortune and her wheel, see Tr 4.1–11; Bo 2.pr2.51–57; KnT I.925–26; Lady 35; For 45–46; Patch, Goddess Fortuna; Doren, Vorträge der Bibliothek Warburg 2:1, 1922–23, 71–144; Whiting F506; Hassell F123, R85.

141–47   An example of the rhetorical device *occupatio* or

praeteritio (see KnT I.875–88n.). See also 2.965, 1264, 1299, 1595; 3.1576; 5.1032; and 2.1071n.; and Lüdeke (132–33 above).

141   destruccion: The use of this word may reflect the French translation of the Filostrato, "destruction" (p. 124); Pratt notes that in Troilus it occurs only here.

146   Omer, Dares, Dite: Homer, Dares the Phrygian, and Dictys of Crete, supposed ancient authorities on the Trojan War (cf. HF 1466–67), none of whom Chaucer knew directly. See introductory note. Like Chaucer, Benoît and Guido regularly spell Dictys's name without the *c.* Griffin, ed. Filostrato, intro., 25, lists other redactors of Troy material who refer to early authorities such as Dares and Dictys but not to their proximate sources.

153   Palladion: Sacred to the Trojans; in some accounts, its loss caused Troy's doom. See Aen. 2.166–70. Chaucer may have derived its spelling from the Ovide moralisé (Witlieb, N&Q 215, 1970, 202–7), but it seems to be a common French spelling (see Greif, Trojanersage, 1886, 71).

155–58   For the influence of the Teseida on these "heightened time descriptions" (chronographiae), see Kittredge, Harv. Stud. in Class. Philol. 28: append. 2; Pratt, PMLA 62:598–621; and Provost, Structure of Tr, 103–6. See GP I.7–8 and n.

162–315   Boccaccio apparently drew suggestions for his account of Troilus's enamorment from an episode in Benoît (17489ff.) telling of Achilles' love for Polyxena, and from his own Filocolo. Chaucer may have independently reverted to these accounts for details in his own version. See Young, Origin of Tr, 35–44, 167–70. The first sight of one's beloved in a church or temple is conventional: Paris first met Helen in a temple; Dante first saw Beatrice in a church in Florence; Petrarch first saw Laura at a service in Avignon; Pamphilus first conversed with Galatea outside a church; cf. also MilT I.3340–43, WBPro III.593–99. Classical precedent may be found in Aeneas's first sight of Dido (Aen. 1.496), and in Ovid's account of the love of Acontius and Cydippe (Her. 21. 91–107). See Griffin, ed. Fil., intro., 15, and König, Die Begegnung im Tempel, 1960.

171   is now an A: Lowes (PMLA 23:285–306; see introductory note) explained this as a compliment to Queen Anne, whom Richard II married in January 1382. Perhaps Chaucer alludes to the Latin phrase *a per se,* which became proverbial in English after his time in the sense "unique, outstanding person" (Whiting A3) and which is so used of Cresseid by Henryson (Testament of Cresseid, ed. Wood, 1958, lines 78–79). Beverly Boyd's suggestion that the *A* refers to the "dominical letter" of the year 1385, which was an *a,* implausibly has Chaucer dating his poem in code (Ch and Liturgy, 12–14).

183   This Troilus: On the "vivifying" or "epideictic" use of *this,* common in Troilus, see Language and Versification, p. xxxviii. Coghill notes that in Tr *this Troilus* occurs forty-two times, *this Pandarus* eleven times, and *this Criseyde* not at all (Ch and Chaucerians, 135).

203   Cf. 3.329 and n.

205   Ascaunces: As if (Ital. "quasi dicesse," as if she said); cf. 292 below, and SumT III. 1745, CYT VIII.838, LGW 2203. On the form of the word, see Livingston, MLR 20, 1925, 71–72, and Spitzer, PQ 24, 1945, 23.

206–10   On the widespread topic of the vengeful Cupid, see Lewis, E&S 17:69–70; Ovid, Met. 1.452–74. For the plucking of the proud bird, cf. 5.1546. Peacocks are proverbially proud: Whiting P210.

211   blynde world: From Fil. 1.25 ("O blindness of worldly minds"), but the phrase may recall Dante's "mondo cieco" (Inf. 27.25, Purg. 16.66); cf. Tr 5.1824 and n., Theb. 5.718–19.

214–16   An elaboration of the proverb, "Pride will have a fall" (Whiting P393).

217   Cf. the Scottish proverb, "All fails that fools think." See Whiting F448. Cf. Usk, Testament 2.8.122.

218   Bayard: A common name (from its bay color—see Tr 2.624) for a horse; the over-bold "blind Bayard" was proverbial: see CYT VIII.1413 and n. The name was too common to support Fisher's development of Root's idea (South Atlantic Quart. 60, 1961, 71–79) that it has mock epic resonance, here and in RvT I.4115, CYT VIII.1413, as the name of the steed given by Charlemagne to Renaud. Horses were proverbially proud: see Walther, 16856, 19031a; Düringsfeld, Sprichwörter, no. 741; and Whiting H521. Matthew Abbate in an unpublished study observes that Chaucer rarely uses elsewhere (see KnT I.1637, PF 148) the formal, extended similes found here and in several other stanzas in the Troilus (2.764, 967; 3.351, 1233, 1240; 4.225, 239, 1432).

228   stere: Probably "steer, control" (as in 3.910). See Read, JEGP 20, 1921, 397–98, and Baugh; but Davis (Ch Glossary), Donaldson, and Windeatt gloss it "stir, disturb."

229   a-fere: The spelling is Kentish; so too is lest (330). Cf. 3.978, 1129. Cf. BD 438n.

232–66   Generally Chaucer's addition to the Filostrato. On the commonplace notion of the power of Love, see Roman de Troie 18443–59, Filocolo 1.5–6 and 96–98, Gower's Confessio amantis 6.78–99.

234   To scornen: In an instance of the scribal tendency toward easier readings, four copyists wrote "To serven."

236–38   Cf. KnT I.1163–66 and note 1163–64, Tr 3.1744–71.

241–43   None is so wise as to avoid love (e.g., Solomon, Virgil, Aristotle, as in Gower, Conf. Aman. 6.78–99); the strongest too succumb (Samson, Hercules, as in WBPro III.721–26). See 1.976–79; Rom 4757–64; Whiting M224.

245   This echoes the Gloria Patri; see also HF 82 and cf. Ovid, Met. 1.517–18.

250–52   Chaucer repeats the notion that Love stimulates courage and virtue at 1.1072–85; 3.22–25, 1716–29, and 1772–1806; the latter passages are based on Filostrato 3.90–93. See Dante, Vita nuova, 11 for the commonplace; also Ovid, Amores 1.9.46.

257   Proverbial. Cf. 2.1387–89, and Aesop's fable of the Oak and the Reed. See Whiting B484 and the essays by Newman and Taylor in Ch's Troilus. For similar Latin proverbs, see Walther, 3343, 27292, 27336.

264   cares colde: A phrase repeated ten times by Chaucer. Glossing "carefull cold" in Spenser's Shepherd's Calendar, "E. K." reports that "care is said to cool the blood" (Poet. Works, ed. J. C. Smith and E. de Selincourt, 1912, 467). On care in Troilus, see Steadman, Disembodied Laughter, 106–7.

268   This Troilus: On the use of this see 183 above.

281   nat with the leste: Corresponds to "Ell' era

grande" (she was tall—Fil. 1.27); cf. the somewhat different description, derived from other sources, given in 5.806.

295–98   A close parallel, perhaps a source, of this passage is Machaut's Jugement dou Roy de Behaingne 411–13, cited by Wimsatt, MAE 45:279. The conception of the lady's figure as imprinted in the heart was commonplace; Young, Origin of Tr, 169 gives examples from Boccaccio. See Tr 1.365–66, 2.1238–39, 3.1499; MerT IV.1577–87. Stearns traces the idea of imprinted sensory images back to Aristotle: SP 43, 1946, 15–21. Boethius's reaction to the idea, which he attributes to the Stoics, appears in Bo 5.m4.6–20 (see note). Further on impressioun, see Burnley, Ch's Lang., 102–15.

300   Like a snail, Troilus withdraws into his shell. The figure was proverbial: Whiting (H491) cites the early fourteenth-century romance Richard Coer de Lyon (in the Auchinleck and six other MSS): "And gynne to draw in here hornes / As a snayl among the thornes" (ed. Karl Brunner, Wiener Beiträge zur englischen Philologie 42, 1913, 3863–64). A related simile (of a turtle's, not a snail's, collapsed pride) is in the preachers' manual Fasciculus morum, where the image is preceded by the image of an ox goaded, as Chaucer had referred to Bayard under the lash; see Wenzel, SP 73, 1976, 138–61. Hassell (C310) cites a French proverb, "Baisser les cornes" (lower the horns).

307   See KnT I.2743–56n.

309   She . . . likynge is more probably an absolute nominative (Mustanoja, ME Syntax, 116) than a loose use of she for hire. She, this renders Boccaccio's "questa" (Mustanoja, 137).

336–40   Troilus alludes to religious orders (ordre), subservient to their "rules," with their "observances" of devotion. Their religion is a lay, a law of belief (see MED s.v. lei 2.; MLT II.223, SqT V.18). See note to 15–21 above; and 4.782.

365–67   See 1.295–98 above, Rom 2804–7, Bo 5.m4.6–20 and n. The punctuation adopted here has the narrator remarking on Troilus's good aventure, but the sense is nearly the same as that of the alternative, with a full stop after 366 and a comma after 367, because the narrator assumes Troilus's attitude.

390   Possibly "And he began to overcome his sorrow aloud." For "win on," see OED s.v. win 10; GP I.594; **loude** (aloud) as in HF 810. Fowler's suggestion that **wynne** here means "complain" (cf. its use as "remonstrate" in Piers Plowman A 4.53) is likewise possible (MLN 69, 1954, 313–15). Chaucer may use the word awkwardly for the sake of rhyme.

392   Cf. Rom 1974–76; Machaut, Font. amor., 2231 (Wdt).

394   On Lollius see the introductory note above, and especially the study by Kittredge cited there. Lollius is the Latin author from whom Chaucer professes to derive his story and whom he pretends faithfully to follow. Lüdeke observes that when Chaucer names a source he usually names it earlier in the work (see 1.132–33 above).

396   Root, alone of recent editors, makes good sense of this passage by placing a comma after in al, implying that he reads the line: "I make bold to say, in its entirety, what Troilus. . . ." Chaucer's use of that for "that which" is common. In any case, the stanza seems to mean that

Chaucer will give not only the gist of Troilus's complaint as Lollius records it, but he will reproduce it fully (*pleinly*) as Lollius records it, word-for-word, as far as the different languages permit it. However, Chaucer possibly means for us to understand that Lollius (as it were, Boccaccio) gave only the gist, whereas Chaucer can give the whole song (from Petrarch: see below).

400–420   The **Canticus Troili** is a fairly close rendering of Petrarch's Sonnet 88 (In Vita), no. 132 in the Canzoniere, "S'amor non è," in the form in which Petrarch released it after 1359. A few variants seem due to Chaucer's misunderstanding of the Italian. See Wilkins, ELH 16:167–73, and Thomson, CL 11, 1959, 313–28. On the medieval use of lyrics inset into narrative, see Moore, CL 3, 1951, 32–46; and on Chaucer's particular use, see Payne, Key of Remembrance, 184–87, 192, 201–9, and Provost, Structure of Tr, 102–3. Several separate copies of all or part of this poem are extant. See below, and see Pace, Spec 26, 1951, 306–16, esp. n. 46.

400–406   This stanza is quoted (with minor variants) in a fifteenth-century moral treatise for women religious, the Disce mori. The quotation of the stanza, discovered by Carleton Brown, was first discussed by Wager, MLR 34, 1939, 62–66, and definitively treated by Patterson, Spec 54, 1979, 297–330. The writer of the treatise also quotes and translates a widely known Latin distich that begins "Nescio quid sit amor" ("I wote not what is love"). The distich resembles the opening of Petrarch's "S'amor non è" (if this be not love), which Chaucer (deliberately generalizing?) mistranslates as **If no love is**. For the distich see Walther, 16532 (cf. 16531), and Walther, Initia carminum, no. 11741 (Patterson, 303–4). The Disce mori erroneously attributes the distich to Ovid's De arte amandi; a similar phrase ("nescit, enim, quid amor," for he knew not what love was) occurs in Ovid, Met. 4.330.

406   **thurst:** Marcelle Thiébaux, Stag of Love, 1974, 159, discusses the convention of "amorous hydropsy."

409   **If harm agree me;** Petrarch, "S'a mal mio grado" (if against my will), for which Root suggests Chaucer's MS may have read, "Se mal mi agrada" (if evil gives me pleasure).

411   **quike deth:** For such oxymorons, see 2.1099, 5.228. The figure has always been considered a distinguishing sign of "Petrarchan" amorous lyric, though it is common in earlier poetry, and is subjected to parodic explosion in RR 4293–4334 (Rom 4703–56), a passage derived from Alanus de Insulis, De planctu Naturae, 9. Alanus there calls the figure "antiphrasis."

412   **How . . . quantite:** Probably mistranslating Petrarch's "Come puoi tanto in me" (how do you have such power over me).

416   The ship without rudder was proverbial; Whiting S247, Hassell N9.

417   On the persistent imagery in Troilus of wallowing among contrary "winds of fortune," see Stevens, ChR 13, 1979, 285–307.

420   Root notes that this line is closer to Petrarch, Rima 182.5, than to the end of his Sonnet 88.

425   See KnT I.1101, Fil. 1.38, Aen. 1.327.

449   Proverbial: RR 2358 (Rom 2478); Machaut, Behaingne, 1743; Whiting F193.

455   **Polixene:** See 1.162–315 above.

456–57   For the construction, see IntrMLT II.47–49. The omission of the negative was idiomatic. See

Zupitza's ed. of the fifteenth-century version of Guy of Warwick, EETS, e.s. 25–26, 1875–76, 368.

464   **savacioun:** From the Italian "salute" (Fil. 1.44), hence probably "safety" rather than spiritual "salvation."

465   The striking figure with **fownes** is not in Fil.

470   **of armes preve:** Could be set off by commas as appositional.

474   The verb **abiden** (with short *i*) cannot be an infinitive; it could be a past participle used as an adjective (cf. "well-spoken"), or used as an infinitive (Mustanoja, ME Syntax, 554), or simply with "have" elided: "he was found to have remained the longest time." Less likely (as Skeat took it) it could be an elliptical past plural, "found (one of those who) longest remained."

483   **the deth:** The plague; see GP I.605, PardT VI.675; or simply "death" (as in line 536). See Kerkhof, p. 362.

484–87   For these regular symptoms of love-sickness, see KnT I.1355–76 and n.

507   **snare:** Cf. 1.663, 5.748; Rom 1647; MilT I.3231n.

517   See GP I.476 and n.

532   **that fol:** If a specific figure (such as Till Eulenspiegel) is intended, it has not been identified. Arntz's suggestion that Chaucer refers to Tristan disguised as a fool (Am N&Q 3, 1965, 151–52) is based on parallels too remote.

543   On drowning in tears, see Mars 89; Machaut, Remède, 1489 (Wdt); Tr 4.510, 930; Scogan 12.

548   On **Pandare**, see the introductory note.

550–875   This dialogue, corresponding to Filostrato 2.1–20, resembles the scene in the Filocolo (1.214–22) in which Duke Feramonte extorts from Florio a confession of love. On the pronouns of address (*ye* or *thou*) used by the characters in Troilus, see Schmidt, Archiv 212, 1975, 120–24, and the studies cited there, and Mustanoja, ME Syntax, 126–28.

552   Elliott, Ch's English, 251, notes that of some two hundred oaths in the poem, Pandarus utters the most (over eighty) and Criseyde more (over sixty) than Troilus (about forty).

559   **leye . . . on presse:** "Lay away, shelve" as in a clothing or book cupboard. MED's reference to a hair curler (s.v. *leien* 1b.(a) "put a crimp in") seems whimsical (cf. GP I.81).

560   **holynesse:** For the meaning "religious observance, piety," as often in Chaucer, rather than "sanctity," see Tatlock, SP 18, 1921, 422–25.

568   See GP I.844 and n.

623   **How devel:** Probably "how the devil," but possibly Troilus calls Pandarus *devel* in exasperation (as Root's commas imply). The phrase is not paralleled elsewhere (although *what devel*, "what the devil," is common). Because the same mood of annoyance could occasion either interpretation, Robertson's demonic reading of Pandarus is unwarranted (see introductory note, and cf. D'Evelyn, PMLA 71, 1956, 275–79, and Stanley, in Ch und seine Zeit, 123–48).

628–30   For these proverbs, see Hyder E. Rollins, Paradise of Dainty Devices, 1927, 267ff.; Whiting F404. Compare Ovid, Ars Am. 2.547–48: "I am, I confess, not perfect in this art; what am I to do? I am less than my own maxims."

631–44   The comparison to a whetstone is also proverbial. See Rollins, Paradise, 268, and Whiting W217.

Chaucer may have known it from Horace, Ars Poet. 304–5. This whole passage, which does not follow the Filostrato, contains echoes of *Le roman de la rose*: compare 637 with RR 21573–83, and 638–44 with RR 21559–72. Skeat compares also Piers Plowman, C 20.210–20. Line 637 is proverbial (Whiting C415, T110). Cf. also Bo 3.m1 and its Latin gloss, cited by Robinson: "For all good is known by its opposite"; see also Bo 4.pr2.10–12. See Tr 3.329 and n.; and cf. Mel VII.1275–94, Tr 3.1219–20. Lines 638–39 are proverbial: Whiting S943. Likewise 642–43: Whiting W231. The "whetstone stanza" was copied as an independent poem in the fifteenth century: see Variorum Chaucer, the Minor Poems, Part One, ed. Pace and David, p. 198.

645 Proverbial: Whiting C415.

652–700 The citation of "ensamples" here, for which there is no parallel in the Filostrato, may derive from the similar use of exempla by Duke Feramonte, a go-between figure in the Filocolo 1.219 (see Young, Origin of Tr, 162).

659–65 From Ovid, Her. 5.151–52 (the passage is probably an interpolation into Ovid's text), perhaps expanded by the use of glosses or of the Italian translation attributed to Filippo Ceffi (see Meech, PMLA 45, 1930, 112–13). **Phebus** Apollo was known as the inventor of medicine (Ovid, Met. 1.521). For a time he acted as shepherd for King **Amete**, Admetus, of Thessaly (see 5.1527–33n.) and fell in love with Admetus's daughter. There may also be influence from Tes. 3.25. The conception of the physician who cannot heal himself is of course proverbial: see Whiting L171; Luke 4.23. Phoebus complains that he cannot heal himself of love for Daphne in Met. 1.524.

674 For the phrase see KnT I.1133 and n., Tr 3.1502.

675 **discoveren**: Recalls "descouvert" used by Boccaccio's French translator (Moland and d'Héricault, ed., 138).

687–88 A proverbial conception (see Walther 32756c) ultimately from Seneca, Epist. 3.4: "Utrumque enim vitium est, et omnibus credere et nulli" (for either is a vice, to believe everyone or no one). The sentence is quoted in a gloss to Boethius 3.m8 cited by Robinson. For many Chaucerian examples of the chiastic order of 688, see Roscow, Syntax and Style, 43–46.

689 **vice is**: A "broken rhyme"; see lines 1.4–5 and note 5 above.

694–95 Pandarus quotes Ecclesiastes (4.10), commonly attributed to Solomon.

699–700 This "classicizing" touch, not in the Filostrato, derives ultimately from Ovid, Met. 6.312. **Nyobe**, Niobe, wife of Amphion, King of Thebes, was turned to stone while grieving for the slaughter of her fourteen children by Apollo; the stone still weeps. See also pseudo-Hyginus, Fabulae 9 (ed. Bunte, 1857).

704–7 A gloss in MS R ("Require in Metamorphosios") may be a misplaced reference to *Nyobe* above, or it may refer to a passage in the account of Procris (Met. 7.720): "Quaerere quod doleam statuo" (I determine to seek out something I may grieve for) with a variant "studeo" (I am zealous), which better fits Chaucer's passage. But a closer parallel is Seneca, Epist. 99.26: "For what is worse than to snatch pleasure in grief itself, indeed from grief, and even to seek out what is pleasing among tears."

708 For the proverb "Misery loves company," cf. CYT VIII.746–47n. Latin versions of the proverb are quoted in the margins of MSS R and S[1]; see Walther 29943 and the further references cited there.

712–14 A gloss in MS R again refers to Ovid, probably to Epist. ex Ponto 2.7.41–42: "Sic ego continuo Fortunae vulneror ictu, / vixque habet in nobis iam nova plaga locum" (I am so wounded by the continual blows of Fortune that there is scarcely room on me for a new wound). See also ex Ponto 4.16.51–52. A question mark could be placed after *for-why* in 714 or 733 (cf. *"and whi?"*).

730 **litargie**: See Bo 1.pr2.18–21.

731 **asse to the harpe**: From Bo 1.pr4.2–3; MS R has a marginal gloss referring to Boethius. See also Rowland, Blind Beasts, 32, for a preacher's use of the simile; and Whiting A277, Hassell A137. Walther 27969, etc., cites many variants; see also Curtius, Europ. Lit., 95. The proverb is ancient Greek (ὄνος λύρας; see Liddell/Scott, Lexicon s.v. ὄνος).

738–39, 755, 806, etc. With these references to solitary complaints, cf. Fil. 2.1, 6, 13, 16, etc.

740–42 Proverbial: Whiting S652.

744 **secree**: Cf. PF 395n.

747–48 Cf. RR 7557–58 (Rom 4783–84 and n.).

760 Perhaps recalling Ovid, Rem. Am. 451: "Quid moror exemplis quorum me turba fatigat?" (Why do I dwell on examples, the crowd of which fatigues me?).

764 **ther**: Taken by Mustanoja (ME Syntax, 337) as an "existential," anticipatory adverb, as in "there is . . . ," but it may simply mean "in that direction, in this matter."

774 The words And whi may be spoken by Pandarus, but see Tr 2.895, 3.1613, 5.1278.

780–82 Cf. Filocolo 1.220.

786 **Ticius**: Tityus, the giant whose eternal punishment in Hades is described in Bo 3.m12.41–43. Cf. also Aen. 6.595; Met. 4.457, 10.43; Theb. 6.753. Roscow discusses the Chaucerian idiom *he Ticius* in Syntax and Style, 62. Cf. 5.212.

809 Unknowe, unkist was proverbial, although it is not recorded before Chaucer (Whiting U5, citing among others Gower's Conf. Aman. 2.467, who quotes it as what "men sein").

810–12 Probably from RR 20889–92.

813–19 Kittredge (MLN 30, 1915, 69) and Wimsatt (MAE 45:283) compare Machaut's Remède de fortune 1636–51, 1662.

813 Robinson put a question mark after **What**, but "What should" for "Why should" is common: see 2.292, 965, 1264, 1299, 1614, 1622, 5.946.

825 That wite here is the noun *blame* and not the infinitive *to know* is indicated by its long *i*, rhyming with the adverb lite (cf. 2.1279, 1648, 3.739).

834–56 Unparalleled in the Filostrato; cf. RR 5842–93 and (as Jefferson, Ch and the Consolation, 49–60, noted) the opening of Bo 2.

837 Whiting (F529) cites Piers Plowman B 11.61: "And thanne was Fortune my foo."

843–44 Cf. Tr 4.391–92, HF 1547–48.

846–47 See Bo 2.pr3.75–79.

848–53 Cf. Machaut's Remède de fortune 2531–38, and for the *torne/sojourne* rhyme, Remède 912–14 (Wimsatt, MAE 45:283). See also Bo 2.pr.1.110–15.

857–58 Cf. Bo 1.pr4.4–6; also Ovid, Rem. Am. 125–26; Whiting L173.

859   Cerberus: See Bo 3.m12.31–33.

860–61   Cf. 3.407–13.

890–966   Mainly Chaucer's, with occasional echoes of Boccaccio. The stanza 890–96, missing in many manuscripts, was according to Root canceled in Chaucer's revision. Scribal eyeskip from *And* (890) to *And* (897) as easily explains the loss, but see Textual Notes.

891–93   Cf. Seneca, Epist. 2.1; Bo 2.pr4.134–38.

894–95   Cf. Dante, Purg. 17.97–99, and Schless, Ch and Dante, 108–12.

897–900   Cf. the closely parallel Remède de fortune 1671–83. Fil. 2.23 is partly parallel, though the argument differs. Wimsatt (MAE 45:282–84) argues that Pandarus's speeches generally reflect those of Esperance (Hope) in Machaut's Remède. That the **vertuous** have **pitee** is a favorite Chaucerian sentiment (see KnT I.1761 and n.).

916   blaunche fevere: "Fievres blanches" (the white sickness) is a French technical term for a form of lovesickness, characterized by paleness and chills (see Gower, Conf. Aman. 6.239–46; MED s.v. *fever* 3. [a]).

918   took on hym: Either "fussed" (OED s.v. *take* 84.j) or, more likely, "put on clothing" against the chills.

927–28   For faylyng: see MED s.v. *for* 8 and Language and Versification, p. xxxix.

932–38   See lines 421–27.

946–49   Ultimately from Ovid, Rem. Am. 45–46. See Alanus de Insulis, Liber parabolarum, PL 210:582 (Walther 9909). Whiting (G478) quotes a similar passage from Higden's *Polychronicon* 6:460/61.

948–52   For an elaborate series of such antitheses, see the Liber parabolarum (PL 210:582–83; Walther 22030). Other examples are cited by Skeat, EE Prov., no. 154; Haeckel, Sprichwort, 67; Morawski, Proverbes français, 5; Hammond, Eng. Verse, 467. A similar series, including night/morning, is quoted by Whiting (N108) from the Orologium sapientiae (ed. Horstmann, Anglia 10, 1887, 352).

950   Cf. Filocolo 2.276.

953–54   Possibly recalling Fil. 2.23, 7–8; see Bo 5.m1.18–20 for the figure of the bridle. **Suffre** as "yield" is unique in Chaucer and has no exact parallel in OED: Chaucer's word may be due to the Italian "soffrire." Windeatt may be right, that the sense is "suffer until the time (of success)."

956   Proverbial: see Mel VII.1054n.

960–61   Cf. RR 2245–46 (Rom 2367–68); Seneca, Epist. 2.2–3; Bo 3.pr11.62–69.

964–66   See Albertanus of Brescia, De amore Dei 3: "For Seneca [Epist.2.3] said, a plant often transplanted does not thrive" (Coni, 1507, fol. 60 verso). See also Walther 17403a and Whiting T474.

969   Cf. 1.526; Anel 20; RR 12759–60; Whiting P309.

976   The wyse lered have not been identified, but the sentiment of 977–79 resembles that of Virgil in Dante, Purg. 17.91–93: "Never was Creator or creature . . . without love, either natural or of the spirit (o naturale o d'animo)." In the corresponding passage in the Filostrato, Pandaro refers to the amorousness of widows (2.27). See Tr 1.241–43 and n. The contrast between heavenly (*celestial*) and earthly or natural (*of kynde*) love was commonplace: for further references, see Schless, Ch and Dante, 112–14, esp. n. 21.

998–1008   The zeal of converts is exemplified by Paul and Augustine.

1000   post: See GP I.214 and n.

1021   for the manere: "For appearance's sake" (cf. 1.313) or "for the sake of propriety" (cf. 1.880, MED s.v. *maner* 5.) or "in accordance with the custom" (MED s.v. *maner* 7. [c], citing this passage) or "considering the circumstances" (Baugh, Fisher). Cf. Fil. 2.30: "per mostrarti / D'essere onesta" (to show you that she is respectable). Alternatively, the meaning may be "and also she would wish to hear no such thing because of the behavior of you, her uncle," construing *of the* with *manere,* not with *here.*

1024   The spots on the moon were thought to represent an old man with a bundle of thorns. Details of the legend are treated by Menner, JEGP 48, 1949, 1–14 in connection with the Middle English lyric, "The Man in the Moon" (who fears he will fall) from Harley Lyrics, no. 30. Cf. also Inf. 20.126, Par. 2.49–51, where Dante refers to the common belief that the man in the moon is Cain; Walther 27033; English references collected by Whiting M138; Emerson, PMLA 21, 1906, 840–45.

1038   "And I thy surety?" That is, with me as agent guaranteeing decency? Besides, every lover behaves as you do (or, everyone behaves honorably in such situations; or, everyone speaks in this way). See 2.134.

1065–92   Without parallel at this point in the Filostrato, though the passage may recall later passages in the Italian poem. Cummings, Indebtedness of Ch, 53, cites Fil. 3.90 and 7.80.

1065–71   These lines are from the *Poetria nova* of Geoffrey of Vinsauf, 43–45: "Si quis habet fundare domum, non currit ad actum / Impetuosa manus: intrinseca linea cordis / Praemetitur opus" (If anyone sets out to build a house, his rash hand does not rush to action; the inward line [plumb-line, plan] of his heart measures out the work beforehand). Chaucer may have read in some manuscript, instead of "praemetitur," the word "praemittitur" or "praemittetur" (will be sent out). The topic was traditional: see Bo 4.pr6.86–93 and Luke 14.28–30. Teresa Tavormina points out to me a similar passage in Augustine's Enarrationes in Psalmos (CSEL 38:496 on Ps. 44.4); see also Dionysius of Halicarnassus, On Literary Composition, ed. W. Rhys-Roberts, 1913, 107. Murphy (RES 15, 1964, 1–20) argues that Chaucer may not have known Geoffrey of Vinsauf directly and that he could have taken this passage from a compilation such as the Englishman John de Briggis's *Compilatio de arte dictandi* (Oxford, Bodleian MS Douce 52, fols. 82v–89v). The passage likewise appears in Vincent of Beauvais's *Speculum doctrinale* 4.93 (see Norton-Smith, Geoffrey Ch, p. 2, n. 3) and in a fourteenth-century collection of Latin sentences preserved at Kremsmünster (Walther 29021). Chaucer could have known the passage from some such collection; in The Nun's Priest's Tale (see VII.3347 and n.) he shows knowledge of another passage from the *Poetria nova*, which itself circulated independently (see Young, MP 41, 1943, 172–82). See further BD 817–1040n.

1078   ClT IV.413 and MLT II.532 are nearly identical.

1081   oon the beste knyght: See Language and Versification, p. xxxviii, and 3.781–82n.

BOOK II

1–4   From Dante, Purg. 1.1–3, although the figure is familiar (see Curtius, European Lit., 128–30; cf. Anel 20,

Tr 1.969). Two of the invocations in The House of Fame are from Dante (see HF 66n.). Cummings, Indebtedness of Ch, 53, compares Boccaccio, Ninfale Fiesolano 7.65, and Sonnet 95; Tes. 11.12; Fil. 9.3; and Petrarch's Canzone 8 (In morte). See also Ovid, Ars Amat. 1.772; 3.26, 748; Rem. Am. 811–12. **the boot . . . Of my connyng** translates "la navicella del mio ingegno," Purg. 1.2. See Schless, Ch and Dante, 114–15.

7 **kalendes:** See 5.1634 and n.

8 In invoking **Cleo,** Chaucer follows Statius, Theb. 1.41, rather than Dante, who invokes the Muses generally and Calliope (Purg. 1.8–9); cf. Tr 3.451. A gloss in MS H[4] calls her "domina eloquentie" (mistress of eloquence).

13 The claim of writing "de sentemente" was a commonplace among the French poets: Windeatt cites Machaut, Remède, 407–8; Froissart, Par. d'amours, 1604–6; L'Espinette am., 919–21 and 3925–30.

14 Skeat followed Kynaston and Tyrwhitt in thinking **Latyn** here means "Latino volgare" (Tes. 2.2.4), that is, the Italian of the Filostrato, but Kittredge (Harv. Sts. in Class. Philol. 28:50) rightly rejected the notion as unfounded. Romancers conventionally claimed a "livre du latin" as a source (see Larry D. Benson, Malory's Morte Darthur, 1976, 8–9; Thorpe, Nottingham Med. Sts. 5, 1961, 57).

17 A characteristic Chaucerian disclaimer: cf. GP I.725–46, MilPro I.3181.

21 Proverbial: "Caecus non judicat de coloribus" (a blind man is no judge of colors). See Whiting M50; Walther 2208a, 2214a. It is used similarly in Dante, De vulgari eloquentia 2.6.27, and in L'Intelligenza (ed. Gellrich, 1883) st. 5. See Kittredge, MP 7, 1909–10, 477–78, and Lowes, MP 14:710–11.

22–28 Ultimately from Horace, Ars poetica 70–71 (a passage that circulated independently: see Walther 15417), with perhaps further debt to Seneca, Epist. 114.13. The Horatian passage is quoted by John of Salisbury, Metalogicon 1.16, 3.3, and by Dante, Convivio 1.5.55–66, 2.14.83–89. The former citation in Dante speaks of "mille anni," Chaucer's **thousand yeer,** and is therefore closest (so Lowes, MP 14:710–11; cf. Schless, Ch and Dante, 115–17). On Chaucer's sense of history, and on the Troilus narrator's distance from his story, see Bloomfield, JEGP 51, 1952, 301–13, and PMLA 72: 14–26.

28 Proverbial: Whiting T63; see below, 42 and n.

36–37 Cf. Alanus de Insulis, Lib. par. (PL 210:591): "Mille viae ducunt homines per saecula Romam" (a thousand ways lead men through the centuries to Rome—Walther 14873). Walther also cites another relevant proverb: "Mille vias et mille modos mens querit amantum" (the mind of lovers seeks a thousand roads and a thousand ways—14873a). Prudentius represents Symmachus as arguing similarly that men seek God by many paths, and "suus est mos cuique genti" (every nation has its own custom), in Contra orationem Symmachi, ed. H. J. Thomson, 1961, 2.87–89. See also Astr Pro 39–40; Whiting P52, T63.

41 **seyde:** Can be construed as parallel with *ferde* in line 39, or perhaps better (Elliott, Ch's English, 72, and Donaldson's gloss), as loosely for the gerund, "saying." A comma after **visityng** is possible, in which case **in forme** would mean "in formal etiquette." Cf. 3.1674.

42 Also proverbial. See the note to lines 36–37 above, and Haeckel, Sprichwort, 34, no. 113. For similar prov-

erbs, see Walther 22657, 23133, 4176 (when in Rome, do as Romans do), and 33849, and Hassell C29. See Bo 2.pr7.72–77.

50–55 Cf. Tes. 3.6–7; RR 45–66 (Rom 49–70)

55 **Bole: Taurus.** On 3 May, the sun (*Phebus*) would have reached 21 degrees and six minutes of Taurus according to the *Kalendarium* of Nicholas of Lynn, 89; cf. NPT VII.3195 (see Eisner, ed. Kalendarium, 32). Taurus may be white as the bull whose shape Jupiter took when he ravished Europa (Met. 2.852; see Tr 3.722–23); or (Clayton, N&Q 224, 1979, 103–4) Chaucer may have remembered Virgil's "candidus . . . Taurus" (Georgics 1.217–18), quoted by Macrobius, Comm. on the Dream of Scipio, ed. Willis, 72, a bull presumably white as the bulls used by Romans in sacrifices. Supporting the former interpretation is the medieval notion that the white bull that abducted Europa was the origin of the zodiacal sign Taurus. See the Third Vatican Mythographer 15.2 (ed. Bode, Scriptores Rerum Myth., 253); Wood, Chaucer and Stars, 148; Pauly-Wissowa, Real-Ency., s.v. *Tauros;* Mars 86.

56 **Mayes day the thrydde:** Chaucer mentions this date in KnT I.1462–63 (the night of Palamon's escape from prison) and NPT VII.3189–90 (the day of Chanticleer's capture by the fox). See KnT I.1462–64n.

64–70 **Proigne,** Procne, sister of Philomena and wife of **Tereus,** was metamorphosed into a swallow, and Philomena into a nightingale, after they avenged Tereus's rape of Philomena. Cf. Tes. 4.73; Purg. 9.13–15 (a probable source); and Petrarch's Sonnet 42, In morte, "Zefiro torna." For the story of Procne, see Ovid, Met. 6.412–674, to which a gloss in MS R refers, and LGW 2228–2393.

74 Cf. MLT II.306–8. Pandarus's "casting" might involve merely consulting a moonbook or Lunarium. See MilT I.3515n., KnT I.1462–64n.

77 **Janus:** A gloss in MS R refers to Ovid's Fasti, probably especially to 1.125–27, 139.

80–109 The scene in which a maiden reads aloud to the three ladies is not from the Filostrato, and represents a practice current in Chaucer's age. See Crosby, Spec 11:88 and Spec 13:413, and cf. SqT V.235 and n. Crosby notes similar scenes in Chrétien's *Yvain* (5356–63) and in *Li chevaliers as deus espees* (ed. Foerster, 1887, 4266ff., 8951ff.). See also the familiar story of Robert Bruce reading *Fierabras* to his men (Barbour's Bruce, ed. Skeat, EETS, 1870–89, 3.435–66) and Havelock, ed. Skeat and Sisam, 1915, 2327.

84, 100–108 Chaucer's classical authority for the story of Thebes was the *Thebaid* of Statius, of which a Latin summary is inserted in the Troilus MSS after 5.1498. See the note to 5.1485–1510. The term "romance" could be applied in Chaucer's time to any narrative of adventure, not merely to a narrative written in a Romance vernacular such as French (see Strohm, Spec 46, 1971, 348–59, and Genre 10, 1977, 1–28). Nevertheless, Chaucer could have had in mind the French Roman de Thèbes, which as Renoir points out was regularly associated with the Roman de Troie and sometimes bound with it in the same codex (SN 32, 1968, 14–17). **Romaunce . . . of Thebes** (line 100) seems almost a translation of its title. Evidence that Chaucer knew the French poem is assembled by Wise, Infl. of Statius, 127–37. The mention of **bookes twelve** (108) suggests rather the *Thebaid*.

103 **lettres rede:** The rubrics that regularly set off titles and sections of works in medieval manuscripts. She seems to quote the rubric in 104–5; such rubrics often began, "How . . . ."

104–5   The death of **Amphiorax** (Amphiaraus) is told at the end of Theb. 7 and in Roman de Thèbes 4711–4842. The use of **bisshop** here may have been suggested by "evesque" and "arcevesques" in the Roman de Thèbes 4791, 5053, etc.; Chaucer's spelling *Amphiorax* is the French spelling of this Latin name (see GP I.384n.). Baugh notes that Lydgate speaks of him as bishop. The references to the bishop here and to saints' lives in line 118 are among the few anachronisms Chaucer permits himself in the Troilus, and even these two can be taken in context as non-Christian terms (see MED s.v. *bishop* 3; OED s.v. *saint* B.2.c.), as can *religious* (a nun, Tr 2.759): the three words are after all of classical origin. For *gospel*, see note to 5.1265. See also 1.15–21n., 2.1735n., 3.1165.

110   The **barbe**, a piece of white pleated linen passed over or under the chin and reaching to the breast, was worn by nuns and widows, and was a sign of mourning. See MED s.v. *barbed*, and 222 below.

112   May . . . observaunce: See KnT I.1047n.

113–19   Cummings (Indebtedness of Ch, 54) compares Fil. 2.49, and, for the whole scene of Pandarus's visit to Criseyde, Fil. 2.108.

113   That I is an interjection, not the pronoun, is confirmed by 3.761.

157–61   Cf. the Roman de Troie 3991–92, 5393–96.

158   **Ector the secounde:** Perhaps an echo of Guido's phrase (Historia, p. 86) "alius Hector uel secundus ab ipso" (another Hector or the second to him). Benoît calls Troilus most valiant "fors que sis frere Hector" (except for his brother Hector—5439–40). See 3.1775 and 1.110n.

160–61   On such lists of chivalric virtues, see Jill Mann, Ch and Estates, 257–58; Davis, Leeds SE, n.s.1, 1967, 17, n. 57; and Barney, in Wisdom of Poetry, 211–12.

167–68   From RR 5660–62, citing Lucan, which in turn goes back to a Latin sentence, "Virtue and great power do not coexist" (Walther 33667) from Lucan, Pharsalia 8.494–95. A marginal gloss in MS S² refers to Lucan ("Luceanis"). Cf. Whiting E148.

180   wis and worthi: Cf. GP I.68 and n.

191–203   Not from the Filostrato, Benoît, or Guido.

193   For the figure, see SumPro III.1693, Tr 4.1356, RR 8721–22; and Whiting B167.

197–203   Apparently influenced by Tes. 8.81.

198   Alternatively a full stop could follow **blood** or **Troilus.** Further, *Troilus* could be a genitive.

205   my lyve: Accusative of extent (Mustanoja, ME Syntax, 111). Cf. 5.334.

215–16   On the lack of privacy in medieval households, see Smyser, Spec 31, 1956, 297–315, and Russell, N&Q 211, 1966, 50–52; for its significance, see Windeatt, ChR 14, 1979, 116–31.

225–26   Cf. Fil. 2.37. The next fifty lines are mainly independent of Boccaccio.

236   Withouten paramours: Cf. GP I.461 for a similarly ambiguous use of *withouten*. Taking it as referring to Criseyde's being "without lovers" strains the sense.

260   Proverbial. See Whiting E78, E75, E81, W598; Walther 9536: "Finis coronat opus" (the end crowns the work); Hassell F89, "La fin couronne l'oeuvre"; Dante, Convivio 2.9 (see Wenzel, in Europäische Lehrdichtung: Festschr. f. Walter Naumann, 1981, 89). Petrarch ob-

served that Boccaccio put his tale of Griselda at the end of the Decameron "where, according to the principles of rhetoric, the most effective part of the composition belongs" (Decam., ed. Musa and Bondanella, 1977, 185, from Ep. Sen. 17.3).

267–69   The idea is commonplace: "Know that no tale can bear a long delay" (Albert von Stade, Troilus, ed. Th. Merzdorf, 1875, 2.607; see Walther 27644a).

271   Cf. SqT V.221–24; Whiting W411.

281–82   See 2.989n.

315–85   Mainly Chaucer's independent work: see Fil. 2.42, 43, 44, 46.

318   Which . . . his: For the construction, see GP I.44–45n.

331   "Troilus the true" was perhaps already proverbial; the phrase was certainly current soon after Chaucer's time (Whiting T483).

343   Proverbial: Whiting A62.

344–47   Baum, Ch's Verse, 74, observes the regressive caesura in this anaphora: the pause follows the seventh, sixth, fifth, and fourth syllable in the four lines.

344   vertulees: Lacking the magical power a gem was thought to possess. Accounts of medieval lapidaries may be found in L. Pannier, Les lapidaires français, 1882; Thorndike, Hist. of Magic 2:387–92. On jewels in Troilus and Chaucer's use of lapidaries, see Bass, CE 23, 1961, 145–47; Doob, ChR 7, 1972, 85–96; and Jennings, N&Q 221, 1976, 533–37. Cf. HF 1352n.

348   crop and roote: Cf. 5.25.

353   baude: See MED; ParsT X.886; and Levy, PQ 32, 1953, 83–89. Cf. Tr 3.254, 397.

366   doute of resoun: For the construction, see KnT I.1912.

367   I sette (as a hypothesis). On this use, and the more technical term of Criseyde, *Now sette a caas* (2.729; see also *pose*, 3.310, 571), related to the Latin phrase "pono casum," see Wenzel, SP 73, 1976, 138–61.

370   fool of kynde: Congenital fool (MED s.v. *fol* n. 1[a]); cf. 1.913 and the studies by Wenzel cited in 400–405 below.

371   love of frendshipe: Cf. 962 and Rom 5201.

379–80   Either line might conclude with a comma or a semicolon to give slightly different sense. As punctuated here, the sense would be: "Amity prevails in Troy; cloak yourself always in the mantle of that friendly trustfulness."

384   daunger: Cf. 1376 below.

393–405   For the common sentiments, see Ars Am. 2.113–18; Fil. 2.54.

398   Hazlitt, English Proverbs, 1907, records two similar proverbs: "Too late to grieve when the chance is past" (p. 501) and "He is wise that is ware in time" (p. 193). See also Skeat, E. E. Prov., no. 160; Whiting B155.

400–405   On royal fools, see Enid Welsford, The Fool, 1935, 113–27; Wenzel, in Wisdom of Poetry, 225–40, and SP 73:138–61; MED s.v. *fol* n. 3; Sandra Billington, Social Hist. of the Fool, 1984.

403   No earlier use of the figure of crow's-feet has been identified.

406   bidde: Cf. Rom 1793, and see Smithers, Eng. and Ger. Sts. 1, 1948, 101–13. Putting a comma after *bidde,* and reading: "(Niece,) I pray, wish for yourself no more sorrow" (Donaldson, Fisher), seems less likely. See textual note.

409–27 With Criseyde's speeches, cf. that of Helen in Ovid's Her. 17, a tissue of sentences on false love.

410–11 An example of the unusual rhyming open and close *o:* see Skeat 6:xxxv.

424 **paynted proces:** Manipulative and deceptive discourse, with reference to the "colors" of rhetoric (cf. ClT IV.16n.) and paint's quality of concealing; see MED s.v. *peinten* 6.(c); Piers Plowman B 20.115: "And with pryvee speche and peyntede wordes"; Whiting (W611) citing Barclay's Ship of Fools (ed. T. H. Jamieson, 1874, 2:40): "So paynted wordes hydeth a fals intent." See William Empson, Seven Types of Ambig., 1930, 62–63; Burnley, YES 7, 1977, 53–67; and on *proces,* Barney, ChR 16, 1981, 18–37. For *proces* as an orderly argument in the terminology of preachers' manuals, see Wenzel, SP 73:153–54 (and see line 268).

425 **Pallas:** Cf. 1.153, 5.977, 999.

428–500 Mainly Chaucer's own; see Fil. 2.52, 66, 121.

435–36 See Tes. 1.58 (O fiero Marte, o dispettoso iddio) and 3.1, and Tr 4.22–24 and n. On the forms **Marte** here and in 988 and *Martes* in 3.437, see SqT V.50n.

468–69 Cf. 4.1560–61; Roscow, Syntax and Style, 23–25, comments on the "broken order" of sentence parts and its effect in these passages.

470 Proverbial: see Whiting E193.

477 **holden hym in honde:** Cf. 3.773 and HF 692 and n.

480 On the issue of preserving the lady's honor, see 2.468, 727–28, 762, 3.941–44; Fil. 2.121; Her. 17.17–18.

483 Proverbial medical doctrine: see GP I.423–24. Whiting C121, cites the sentence: "Cessante causa, cessat effectus" (when the cause ceases, the effect ceases). See also Hassell C17.

484–89 Wrenn (MLR 18, 1923, 289–92) suggests this passage was influenced by Horace, Odes 3.3.1–8, but the passages are not very similar.

507–53 It is possible that this episode took place, and that Pandarus concealed his knowledge when he first spoke with Troilus (1.551ff.), just as the dreamer in the Book of the Duchess seems to conceal, shrewdly or obtusely, what he has overheard before he speaks with the Black Knight. To overhear a noble lover's complaint or debate (as in Machaut's Dit de la fontaine amoreuse and Jugement dou Roy de Behaingne), and then to pretend ignorance of what has been learned, was a conventional strategy in amatory literature, particularly in such genres as the *pastourelle* and complaint. In another place in the Filostrato that Chaucer does not adopt, Boccaccio adopts this convention (7.77–78). Cf. also KnT I.1497–1577. But a more likely explanation of the present passage is that Pandarus concocts the whole episode in order to impress Criseyde; this second interpretation better fits the characters of the two men, Pandarus's guile and consciousness of proper love-conventions, and Troilus's less studied grief. In the Filostrato the first interpretation is made explicit (2.56–62).

508 **gardyn, by a welle:** A typical situation for a complaining lover. See, especially for Machaut, William Calin, A Poet at the Fountain, 1974; and Rom 1456.

513–16 **fro . . . fro:** Rime riche consists of a rhyme upon separate meanings of homophones (see GP I.17–18n.), but here, and in 5.975–78 and perhaps 3.191–93 (see textual note 3.193–94), Chaucer simply rhymes with a repeated word.

525 *mea culpa:* A familiar phrase from the Confiteor, or form of confession. Hutson (MLN 69, 1954, 468–70) notes that the muttering and smiting of the head (540–41) correspond to the act of contrition. Thus Chaucer develops the situation of the penitent before his confessor: "it is a *confessio amantis*" (Root, alluding to the title of Gower's poem). See 1.15–21 above. For examples of such extended metaphors, see Neilson, Origins of the Court of Love, 220–25.

530 **disesperaunce:** See 1.15–21 above.

533–35 See KnT I.1077–97n.

538–39 Cf. Ovid, Met. 4.64, which became proverbial (Walther 26157; A. J. V. le Roux de Lincy, Proverbes, 2nd ed., 1859, 1:71; see LGW 735–36 and note 735).

541 **motre:** Seems to reflect the French translation of the Filostrato, "disant . . . entre ses dents" (saying between his teeth—p. 152), not in Fil. 2.61.

542–50 Not in the Filostrato; some details may be drawn from the Filocolo 1.238.

584–85 The image of the gem set in the ring is from Fil. 2.43. See 344 above, and 5.549.

596–931 On the process of Criseyde's falling in love, see Howard, in Med. Lit. and Folklore, 173–92.

602 **hire:** A "sympathetic dative" (Mustanoja, ME Syntax, 98–99), associated with the datives of possession regularly used with parts of the body in earlier English ("the hand to him").

611–44 The description of Troilus's triumphant entry is Chaucer's invention, but the idea is drawn from an episode in which Criseida gazes from her window at Troiolo and Pandaro (Fil. 2.82); cf. also Tr 2.1247–70. Some features of the triumph may derive from Benoît's account of Hector's return from battle (10201–18; cf. also 20597–627, 3147–48, 10283–301, and 10609). But the best parallel, as Lowes pointed out in an unpublished study cited by Robinson, is the account of Aeneas and Lavinia in the Roman d'Eneas, 8047–8126, 8381–98 (tr. Yunck, 215–16, 221–22). Cf. also Ovid, Met. 8.14–54.

617–18 **yate . . . Of Dardanus:** Cf. Benoît (3147–48) and Guido (p. 127); both tell that Hector ordered the gate Dardanides opened to let his army through. According to Guido (p. 47), the first of the city's six gates was Dardanides; in Benoît it was the second (3148). Chains were used to block off streets from horsemen.

622–23 Cf. Bo 5.pr6.162–68.

628–30 Cf. Aen. 4.149–50.

632 The passive sense of the infinitive **to seen,** active in form, is a common Chaucerian usage. See Mustanoja, ME Syntax, 520; Kerkhof, 105–6.

637 Cf. SqT V.558.

651 Perhaps, as Skeat (with Root and Robinson concurring) says, Criseyde refers to a love-potion (cf. the story of Tristan and Isolde), but it seems simpler and better to take **drynke** as any intoxicating beverage (so Baugh). See Gower on "love-drunkenness," Conf. Aman. 6.76–529.

652 Cf. ShipT VII.111.

656 **for pure ashamed:** For the construction, see Language and Versification, p. xxxix, and Mustanoja, ME Syntax, 381–82, 647–48.

657 For the emphatic use of **and that,** see Mustanoja, ME Syntax, 171, and many Chaucerian examples in Roscow, Syntax and Style, 55.

666–67 Boccaccio says, "And so suddenly was she caught" (E sì subitamente presa fue; Fil. 2.83).

671   Proverbial: Whiting E164.

681   The term **hous** here (as Skeat remarks) probably refers not to the zodiacal sign, but to one of the twelve divisions of the celestial sphere made by great circles passing through the north and south points of the horizon. See Astr 2.37 and 35.24–26n. on the equations of the houses. The first and seventh houses, just below the eastern horizon and just above the western, were deemed fortunate. Wood, Ch and Stars, 76, n. 40, holds that *hous* does refer to the zodiacal sign (Libra), but he observes that either interpretation would give the same astrological sense.

715   Proverbial: Whiting M464.

716–18   From RR 5744–45: "If I forbid drunkenness, I have no wish to forbid drinking." We would translate **forbet** as "enjoins, requires"; in Middle English idiom, "to make a prohibition" (MED s.v. *forbeden* 1a.[a], 2.[a]) is frequently followed by a negative (as "God forbade them, that they should not eat of the tree"), here expressed by the negative implication of *drynkeles.* Cf. ABC 26; Mel VII.1584, 1757n.; Bo 3.pr10.14–16, 33.

724   Boasters are condemned at 3.306–22; cf. NPT VII.2917.

726–27   Taking **als** as "also" rather than "as" would require heavier punctuation after **cause.** Six MSS read "also," two read "as."

752   Most editors take **lusty leese** to mean "pleasant pasture," but Donaldson may rightly gloss it as "i.e., love's leash."

754   The figure from chess occurs in RR 6652 and BD 659–60. It was commonplace in the French poets: see BD 617–709n. See also Whiting C169 and Hassell E15 for many instances.

756   Cf. SqT V.619.

766–67   See Bo 1.m3.

776   Cf. PF 3 and n.

784   **wo to drynke:** For the idiom (from French), see MED s.v. *drinken* 2. and 3. Cf. 3.1035, 1215 and note 1212–16; FranT V.942; HF 1879–80n.

789   Proverbial: See Whiting H134 and cf. HF 361, BD 708.

791   Proverbial. MS S¹ has the gloss: "Acriores in principi[o] franguntur in fine" (those [who are] very sharp or ardent in the beginning are broken in the end). Wenzel finds the same Latin saying in a fourteenth-century collection of preaching material, British Lib. Harl. 7322, fol. 54v (SP 73:147). Hassell cites a French version (A48): "Ceulx qui sont trop aigres au commaincement en la fin se treuvent tous froissez." For similar sayings, see Whiting B200, and the references given there, and B191–210; also Walther 18425.

798   "Ex nihilo nihil fit" (from nothing comes nothing). See Bo 5.pr1.43–44 and n.

807–8   "Nothing ventured, nothing gained." See 5.784, Whiting N146, and Hassell A17, A218, E53.

811   Cf. RR 2278 (Rom 2398).

813–931   The garden scene and Antigone's singing are not in Chaucer's sources, but he may have derived a suggestion from Fil. 3.73–89, where Troiolo leads Pandaro into a garden and sings a love song.

816   The origin of the names of Criseyde's nieces is unknown. Chaucer would know the name **Antigone** from the story of Thebes; or Ovid, Met. 6.93–97 (Wdt). Hamilton, Indebt. to Guido, 94–96, would derive **Tharbe** from "rex Thabor" in Guido's Historia, p. 115,

and **Flexippe** from Ovid's Plexippus, the uncle of Meleager (Met. 8.440); neither guess carries conviction.

827–75   Parallels to Antigone's song, none so compelling as to prove they are Chaucer's sources, may be found in Machaut's Paradis d'amour and his Mireoir amoureux (Poésies lyriques 2:345–51, 362–70). See Young, Origin of Tr, 173–76; Kittredge, MLN 25, 1910, 158; and Wimsatt, MAE 45:288–91, who cites further parallels from other poems of Machaut. Koeppel (ESt 20, 1895, 156) compared Gower's 46th Balade, but the resemblance is slight. Sister Borthwick (MLQ 22, 1961, 227–35) observes that the song answers point for point Criseyde's objections to loving; see also Dempster, Dramatic Irony, 24, and Knight, Rymyng Craftily, 59–65.

827–28   This use of **Ben** as past participle with **have** and infinitive with **shal,** paralleled in 3.1001 (and cf. 1.593–95), is first recorded in Chaucer, according to Roscow, Syntax and Style, 101–2.

841–47   See Venus 1–24.

861   A proverb (Whiting R156) referred to in MSS H⁴ and Ph, "of robyn hod."

862   A comma or question mark might follow **What.**

867   For the figure of a glass head or cap, cf. 5.469. The modern proverb, "People who live in glass houses shouldn't throw stones," is not recorded before Chaucer (Whiting H218) in English, but was current in Italian proverbs about glass heads or helmets (Düringsfeld, Sprichwörter 1, no. 600).

872–73   Windeatt compares the mutual grafting image in Machaut, Moult sui de bonne heure née, 26–29.

884–86   The only clear case in Chaucer of an assonance in place of a full rhyme. Skeat suggested emending to *syte,* "be anxious." Root thought the latter word too northern in provenance for Chaucer's dialect.

888   **han or ben:** On the constuction, see Mustanoja, ME Syntax, 503.

904   The sun as "eye of the world": Ovid, Met. 4.228.

905   Compare, for the humorous turn, FranT V.1017–18 and n. It is an old joke: see Curtius, European Lit., 275–76, and Payne in Comp. to Ch, 49–50.

908   See Dante, Par. 22.93.

918–22   The love songs of nightingales were conventional in French lyrics. See R. Dragonetti, La technique poétique des trouvères, 1960, 169ff.; GP I.97–98; Tr 2.64–70n.

920   Cf. KnT I.1509; SqT V.53–55.

925–31   This dream, not in the Filostrato, may be related to Fil. 7.23–24 and Dante, Purg. 29.108 (and following cantos): see Praz, Monthly Criterion 6, 1927, 29–31. See also Purg. 9.19–20, HF 496ff. A remote analogue in Old Icelandic is noted by Renoir, in Ch Problems, 180–206. On the dream, see Mudrick, Hudson Review 10, 1957, 88–95, and Gallagher, MLQ 36, 1975, 115–32. For the notion of an exchange of hearts, see Leyerle, in Learned and Lewed, 127–28, 138–42; see also 871–73 above.

926   **egle . . . whit:** See KnT I.2178n.

936   **yeden:** Imperfect rhyme.

954   **don thyn hood:** Probably "get ready to go" (to sleep), "call it a day" (Davis, Ch Gloss.); possibly with *hood* as "nightcap" (unattested elsewhere); or with a figurative sense like "keep your shirt on!"; or "cover your face," be quiet or go to sleep as a hooded falcon. Baugh proposes "be at ease," said to someone who has courteously doffed his hat. See Cassidy, JEGP 57, 1958,

739–42. Sadleck (ChR 17, 1982, 62–64) suggests that *hood* here means "battle helmet," so "prepare for action."

964 **hameled:** The term was used of both dogs and deer; here it is applied to the sorrow of Troilus, conceived as a pursuing hound. On such figurative uses of lame feet, see Freccero, Harv. Theol. Rev. 52, 1959, 245–81. Emerson suggests it refers to Criseyde, conceived as game in flight but now half captured (RomR 13, 1922, 147–48). For a similar figure, see 1.465.

967–71 Chaucer's source (Fil. 2.80) follows Dante, Inf. 2.127–32.

989 Proverbial; cf. 281–82 above and FrT III.1475n.

1001 For the idiom **along,** cf. CYT VIII.922.

1022 One's ears are said to glow (mod. Eng. "burn") when one is being talked about. See Whiting E12.

1023 The suggestion for the letter is from Fil. 2.91. For the directions about how to write it, see Ovid, Ars Am. 1.455–68. See also below, 5.1317–1421n.

1025 **make it . . . tough:** Here probably means not "make it difficult" but "put on airs, make a display, swagger." See also 3.87 and 5.101. See ShipT VII.379n., GP I.785n., and, for a discussion of the idiom, Roscow, Syntax and Style, 60–61, citing Palsgrave's (sixteenth century) Lesclarcissement, p. 624: "I make it tough, I make it coye, as maydens do, or persons that be strange if they be asked a questyon. Je fais le dangereux . . . ." Baugh here prefers to gloss *tough* as "difficult."

1027 Cf. 1.7; Ovid, Her. 3.3: "Whatever blots you will see, tears have made"; Propertius 5.3.3–4.

1030–36 "To harp on one string" was a proverbial phrase; Chaucer may have known the parallel passage in Horace, Ars poet. 355–56. See Whiting S389.

1041–43 Ultimately from the familiar passage in Horace, Ars poet. 1–5, which is partly quoted in John of Salisbury's Policraticus 2.18 (ed. Webb, 2.103).

1071 Francis observes, in his excellent article on abbreviation in Chaucer, that here (and in line 1219) the claim of brevity is true: Chaucer shortens the account in the Filostrato (PMLA 68, 1953, 1126–41).

1077 **leigh ful loude:** Although MED (s.v. *laughen* 1.[b]) takes the word to mean "laughed" here, editors since Skeat have correctly glossed it "lied," following the interpretations of early scribes (MSS R and A read "logh, lough"; the rest read "leigh, ley, ligh," and in seven authorities "lied, lyed"). Chaucer's preterite form of "laugh" is *lough*, rhyming with *ynough*; his regular preterite of "lie" is *lied*, but he may have used the strong form *leigh* here for the meter. An instance of *thou liest loude* (you lie palpably, shamelessly) is recorded in MED s.v. *loude* 3, dated circa 1390.

1086–87 On the moistening of the seal with tears, see Filocolo 1.274.

1093 Pandarus enacts a typical function of the go-between, conveying letters, like the "most faithful servant" of the Filocolo (1.267–75).

1099 For the use of oxymorons, see 1.411n.

1104 Proverbial: Whiting W343.

1106 On **loves daunce,** see GP I.476n.

1108 **to laughe:** Best taken as an absolute "historical infinitive" (Skeat 6:403; Mustanoja, ME Syntax, 538–39; and Donaldson, in Sts. . . . in Honour of Margaret Schlauch, ed. I. Dobrzycka et al., 1966, 106), and translated "laughed"; see LGW 635 and 653. Other explanations take the phrase causally, "for laughter" (J. S. Ken-

yon, Syntax of the Inf., Ch Soc, 2nd ser. 44, 1909, 80–81); or as a compound, *to-laugh* (laughed exceedingly; Root, Baugh, Fisher). Baugh observes that in this last construction, the form should be *to-lough* (MSJ reads "to laught"). Finally, there may be ellipsis of such a verb as *gan* (Elliott, Ch's English, 72).

1109–10 **fynde Game in myn hood:** Proverbial. See Whiting G25 and MED s.v. *game* 6.(b), and cf. ShipT VII.440.

1120–79 Cf. the similar situation in Fil. 2.109–14.

1145 This was the fate of Capaneus. See 5.1504–5 and Theb. 10.888–939.

1177–78 **Avysed** and **fond** are probably past participles, "having deliberated . . . and having found"; if the verbs were preterites with "she" understood from the preceding stanza, an "and" would probably follow lak. Cf. 2.1726.

1178 **koude good:** Cf. 2.503, 5.106, EpiMLT II.1169n.

1201 **to medes:** "In return" (MED s.v. *mede,* noun 4, 2.[d]), Pandarus will stitch the parchment letter closed. On folding and sewing letters, see Norman Davis, Paston Letters, 1971, I:xxxiv.

1205–14 Criseyde is literate but lacks matter. She had never before required the privacy of inscribing a letter for herself.

1213–14 Helen swears similarly that the writing of love-letters is a new art for her (Her. 17.141–44).

1219–25 The letter is given at length in Fil. 2.121–27.

1229 **ybete:** See KnT I.979n.

1234–35 The contrary of this proverb, unrecorded elsewhere (Whiting T150), that "An evil beginning has a foul ending" (Whiting B199, etc.; Hassell F90), is common.

1238–39 A proverb unrecorded elsewhere in English (Whiting I26), but cf. the Latin gloss in MS H⁴: "Levis impressio, levis recessio" (light impression, light recession). The modern version is "Soon learned, soon forgotten."

1240–1304 Independent of Boccaccio.

1249 **with his tenthe som:** For the idiom, see Mustanoja, ME Syntax, 211–12; cf. "foursome."

1272–73 Cf. 3.1104–5; 2 Cor. 12.7 (stimulus carnis meae, the thorn of my flesh).

1274 **Mo** can be either an adjective ("God send more such thorns to be plucked at") or a pronoun ("God send others such thorns to be plucked at"); cf. 1.613, 3.1514. Supporting the latter sense are the MSS A and Gg, reading "yow" for "mo." In either case, the narrator expresses the wish that more ladies might be thus afflicted by love, including perhaps his own unresponsive mistress. For the word order, see Roscow, Syntax and Style, 121.

1276 Cf. "Strike while the iron is hot." Cf. Mel VII.1036 and n.

1298 That **yeres two** was considered an appropriate period of widowhood may have suggested Pandarus's specific number: see Kirby, MLR 29, 1934, 67–68, and 33, 1938, 402; Mason, MLR 42, 1947, 358–59. Fisher observes that Pandarus's willingness to wait two years "stretches credulity"; it is probably comic exaggeration.

1332–34 See Whiting W560; Fil. 2.85.

1335 See Alanus de Insulis, Lib. parab. (PL 210:583): "From a nut springs the hazel, from an acorn the mighty oak." See Walther 5105.

1347   On the use of dice in divination with regard to love matters, see "The Chance of Dice," ed. Hammond, ESt 59, 1925, 1–16, and Cicero, De divinatione 1.13.23, 2.21.48, 2.59.121; Gower, Conf. Aman. 4.2792–93. See also Johannes Bolte, ed., Georg Wickrams Werke, 1903, 3:276–348.

1349   **his gistes:** "His lodgings" (that is, his itinerary) seems the best interpretation (so MED, s.v. *giste*), with the sense, "flowed with the tide of events." *Gistes* as "deeds" (Skeat), gests, makes little sense, and as "casts of dice" (Root) is unattested elsewhere.

1376   **Daunger:** The use of personifications such as *Kynde* (natural inclination) and *Daunger* (disdain, stand-offishness) were made popular by the Roman de la rose (see Rom 3015–30, 3130–66). For *Daunger,* cf. Tr 2.384, 399, and Rom 3018n.

1380–83   See Rom 3687–88; cf. the Latin proverb, "The oak is felled with many blows" (Walther 433).

1385–86   Galileo disproved this bit of Aristotelian physics.

1387–89   See 1.257; Whiting R71.

1392   **stant:** May mean "(an undertaking) that stands" with a colloquial shift of syntax (see Schlauch, PMLA 67, 1952, 1103–16); or possibly the phrase is parenthetical: "it stands beyond a doubt," there can be no doubt.

1394–1757   This episode is Chaucer's invention, perhaps influenced by a passage in the Filostrato (7.77–85) concerning the special friendship of Troiolo and Deifebo. We learned of Criseyde's insecure situation in Troy in 1.85–108 (Fil. 1.12–13). Patch noted that a few lines near the end of the episode (2.1735–49) reflect lines from an earlier dialogue in Boccaccio's poem (Fil. 2.134–37; MLN 70, 1955, 9). Muscatine suggested that Chaucer may have borrowed the device of the feigned illness from the Biblical story of Amnon and Tamar in 2 Sam. 13.1–20 (MLN 63, 1948, 372–77). Several medieval commentators took the Biblical story as an example of improper friendship: see Cook, JEGP 69:407–24. For fourteenth-century illustrations of the Biblical story, see Robertson, Preface to Ch, figs. 93–95, 108.

1398   **Deiphebus** was third in age of the five sons of Priam and Hecuba according to Dictys and Benoît, Roman de Troie 2939. Dictys (but not Dares, Benoît, or Guido) reports that he married Helen after the death of Paris; Chaucer probably knew this tradition from Virgil, Aen. 6.511 (see Sundwall, MP 73, 1975, 151–56; and Fyler, MLQ 41:115–30, and Res Publ. Litt. 7, 1984, 79–82), but it would positively contradict other sources he knew (Benoît, Joseph of Exeter's Dares), and Lambert may be right in finding the idea "unattractive as well as unnecessary" here (in Essays on Tr, 105–25).

1418   **Which:** For the syntax, Mustanoja (ME Syntax, 97) compares MancT IX.307.

1462   **arise:** The infinitive form (with long *i*), not the past participle.

1467   **Poliphete** does not appear in the Filostrato. Chaucer may have derived his name from that of a Trojan priest (a Greek in Homer), Polyphœtes (var., Polybœtes), in the Aeneid (6.484; Hamilton, Ch's Indebt., 97, n. 3), or from two characters, both Greeks, named Polibetes in the Roman de Troie.

1474   See 4.202–6 and n.

1495   **word and ende:** See MkT VII.2721n.

1503   Another application of terms of theology to matters of love: see Luke 8.48, 18.42.

1533   The metaphor has a proverbial homeliness, but is not recorded elsewhere; see Whiting H553.

1554   A superfluous request, since running was taken as a sign of madness; cf. "to run mad," MED s.v. *mad* 1. (b); and "Dote renne aboute and breyde wod," Body and Soul, ed. Emerson, ME Reader, 1915, p. 50, line 30.

1557   Ten in the morning, the hour of dinner (ShipT VII.205–6), the first full meal of the day. See 2.1095 and 1163; 5.1126.

1564   From RR 18298: "Bon fait prolixité foïr"; cf. SqT V.404–5 and Whiting P408.

1610   Cf. 5.651.

1615   For the phrasing, cf. PardPro VI.331 and Whiting B234.

1638   **beere:** Funeral bier (perhaps with a pun on the sense "pillowcase": Lounsbury, Compl. Works of Ch, 1900; Preston, Ch, 86; Baum, PMLA 71, 1956, 225–46; and doubtfully, Kökeritz, PMLA 69, 1954, 937–52), here, with sexual meaning, Criseyde. Cf. 4.863, 1183.

1675   **brother:** Might refer to Deiphebus or Troilus.

1681   **his tong affile:** File (probably "smooth" rather than "sharpen") his tongue. See GP I.712; Whiting T378.

1699   **swych a man:** C. D. Benson (PQ 58, 1979, 364–67) argues that some of Chaucer's audience would recognize the unspecified criminal as King Thoas (*Toas*), about whom (according to Benoît and Guido) the Trojans argued when he was taken prisoner. He is later exchanged, along with Criseyde, for Antenor (see 4.138 and n.). However, it seems most likely that had Chaucer meant his readers to recognize Thoas he would have been more explicit.

1732   Perhaps "And thus (he said to Criseyde) on the way in"; or perhaps more likely, "And (he said to himself or Criseyde) privately thus" (see MED s.v. *inward,* adv., 3., 4.). What Pandarus said, in the latter interpretation, would include either the two, or better, the three following words. Donaldson plausibly takes the whole line as continuing the direct discourse from the preceding lines, as: "And thus let us begin (to go) very softly in." Fisher takes the whole line as outside the discourse, implausibly construing *bygynne* as "began." Child suggested to Kittredge (Observations, 88) that the text may read *by gynne* "by contrivance."

1735   The **corones tweyne** have not been satisfactorily explained. For surveys of opinion, see Malarkey (Spec 38, 1963, 473–78) and Doob (ChR 7:85–96). Skeat connected them with the *corones tweye* of roses and lilies in SNT VIII.220–21, 270 (see note VIII.221), which are traditionally associated with martyrdom and virginity. Patch (MLN 70:8–12) noted that in a passage from the Filostrato not taken over by Chaucer Criseida had spoken of "the crown of my virtue" (la corona dell'onestà mia; Fil. 2.134), and that this phrase may have drawn Chaucer's attention to the idea from The Second Nun's Tale. But as Robinson says, "it is hard to believe that Chaucer's readers, without some further hint, would have thought, at this point, of the crowns of Cecilia and Valerius." Patch advances another guess that may be right, that Pandarus says in effect: "By the power of a crown—nay, two crowns." There may further be a play on "crown" (royal power) and "crown" (head) in the common asseveration *by my croun* (see RvT I.4041, 4099, and MED s.v. *coroune* 10.[b]).

In his edition of Chaucer's works (1854–56, 3:115),

Bell suggested that the reference was to the crowns of Priam and Hecuba, a guess only faintly supported by the reference to *thise worldes tweyne* in 3.1490, but this phrase is also of uncertain meaning (see note), and the guess lacks any support in the context. Malarkey's suggestion is similar: the two crowns refer to the second crown of the papal tiara added by Boniface in 1300, perhaps to represent the pope's temporal power (the third crown was added, for unknown reasons, before 1316), and hence to the spiritual and temporal powers of church and state. Along the same lines it may be noted that the royal coronation in Chaucer's time involved a double crowning ceremony, and that Lydgate (in 1432) mentions Henry VI's "crounes tweyne" (Minor Poems, 630–48, line 133; see MED s.v. *coroune* 1a); but this also seems very unlikely.

Robinson thought the reference might be to the nuptial crowns for bride and groom still used in the "steven-ing" (crowning) ceremony in the Greek Orthodox nuptial rite, a ceremony apparently still a part of the Latin ritual in some parts of Europe (see Léon Gautier, La chevalerie, 1884, 416, 420, and the nuptial garland in ClT IV.381 and n). Teresa Tavormina kindly brings to my attention evidence that the Greek ceremony was known in the Latin West; see Pope Nicholas I's letter of 866 A.D. to the Bulgari (PL 119:979–80), partially quoted in Gratian's Decretum among the canons forbidding clandestine marriage (Decretum 2.30.4.3, ed. Friedberg 1:1103). If Chaucer knew of the ancient Greek practice, Robinson suggests, he may have been aiming at a bit of "local color." Dunning (in Eng. and Med. Sts. for Tolkien, ed. Davis and Wrenn, 164–82) takes the words *whan ye be oon* in 1740 as solid support for the notion that Pandarus refers to nuptial crowns; those who regard the relation between Troilus and Criseyde as a "clandestine marriage" (see 4.554–55n.) would perhaps agree. But this explanation still does not account for Pandarus's request not to slay Troilus "by the virtue of *corones tweyne.*" The reference to the *duplicem coronam* of a perfect husband—chastity and martyrdom—in Matheolus's satiric *Lamentationes* likewise seems inapplicable in context (see Thundy, NM 86, 1985, 343–47).

Root suggested, tentatively, that the crowns stand for either Pity and Bounty (see Pity, 58, 71–77) or Justice and Mercy (see ABC 137–44). Agreeing with Root that the context suggests that *vertu* is pity or mercy, Robert E. Kaske, in a talk before the New Chaucer Society (16 April 1982), drew attention to the medieval interpretation of the "diadem" of Canticles 3.11 as a "corona duplex," double crown. Kaske notes that Gulielmus Durandus (Rationale divinorum officiorum, 1859, 1.3.19, p. 26) calls this diadem "corona misericordiae" (a crown of mercy), and that Sicard of Cremona (PL 213:43) and (confusedly) Hugh of St. Cher make the same interpretation. But a double crown is not quite the same as two crowns, and Robinson's objection to Skeat's interpretation applies here as well.

Doob proposed (ChR 7:85–96) that *corones* means, not "crowns" (as most of the scribes took it—but one wrote "his reignes" and one, "owre goddis," in place of the word), but two kinds of the gem named "ceranius" (see MED), supposedly of magical properties (which explains Pandarus's use of *vertu;* see 2.344 and n.); but Doob cannot explain why the ceranius is relevant here, nor why Pandarus should refer to two of them.

Wetherbee's suggestion (Ch and Poets, 94n.) that Ch may allude to the twin boys, Coronae, of Ovid, Met. 13.692–99, and their interpretation by Bernard Silvestris as instruments of generation (Cosmographia 2.14.157–62) seems too obscure.

Possibly Pandarus's oath is deliberately obscure, playfully portentous like the charm in MilT I.3483–86. Perhaps the *vertu of corones tweyne* is mere impressive nonsense.

1745 devyne at waggyng of a stree: See OED s.v. *wagging,* and Whiting W4. Gnerro (N&Q 207, 1962, 164–65) wrongly suggests the reference is to the movement of a divining rod.

1749 Las, tyme ilost: See textual note.

1750 One manuscript adds some lines here; see textual note.

1752 The word **kankedort** is unexplained; from the context it seems to mean a difficult situation or a state of suspense. The efforts at discovering the etymology of the word have proved fruitless. Among them: Swedish *kanka* (to be unsteady) and *ort* (place); *canker* (cancer) and Lowland Scottish *dort* (sulkiness); Old French *quant que dort* (whenever he sleeps) or *chien qui dort,* Provençal *can que dorm,* early Anglo-Norman *ken ke dort* (sleeping dog—which should not be wakened; see Tr 3.764); Old French *calembour(d)* (joke, pun—a word perhaps associated with the later English word *quandary*). These guesses are surveyed by Gillmeister, ES 59, 1978, 310–23. The word *cangen,* meaning "make a fool of," is attested mainly from the Middle English Katherine Group of texts, in an early dialect remote from Chaucer's; perhaps its past participle *canged* (made a fool of), or related words *cang* (from OE *canc,* scorn), *acangen,* play some part in the formation of *kankedort.* See MED for these words. Root noted what seems to be a corruption of the word, in the form "crank dort," in Henry Medwall's Nature (late fifteenth century; Plays, ed. A. H. Nelson, 1980, 1.1285).

BOOK III

1–49 The elaborate invocation to Venus is based mainly on Fil. 3.74–79, where it is part of a song sung by Troiolo, derived partly from Boethius (2.m8), perhaps with suggestions from Dante, Par. 8.1–15. At that point in the story (Tr 3.1744–71), Chaucer supplies a new song derived directly from the same poem in Boethius. In "astrologizing" the gods, Chaucer follows common medieval practice (see KnT I.2217n.). Venus, the **blisful light** (1) and **Joves doughter** (3), is the planet of the third sphere (2); she is **sonnes lief** (3) because the planet accompanies the sun as morning star and evening star (cf. Dante, Par. 8.11–12). As goddess of love she represents both sexual attraction and the cosmic "love" that binds the elements of the universe (see KnT I.2987–93, Tr 1.237). On the background of the medieval philosophical conception of love, see Cook, Archiv 119, 1907, 40–54 and Bloomfield, Classical Philology 47, 1952, 162–65. For Venus in the mythographic tradition, see Schreiber, JEGP 74, 1975, 519–35; on Chaucer's use of mythography generally, see Twycross, Med. Anadyomene; Minnis, Ch and Antiquity; and McCall, Ch Among the Gods. Good general studies of medieval ideas about love are Arthur O. Lovejoy, The Great Chain of Being, 1936, and Dronke, SMed, 3rd ser., 6, 1965, 389–422.

5 Closer to this than Fil. 3.74.5 ("Benigna donna d'ogni gentil core": gracious mistress of every noble heart) or Dante, Inf. 5.100, is the famous line by Guido Guinizelli, "Al cor gentil rempaira sempre Amore" (Love always repairs to a noble heart; Canzone, ed. Gianfranco Contini, Poeti del duecento, 1960, 2:460), cited by Dante, Convivio 4.20. Cf. Tes. 3.27.

11 vapour: Fil. 3.75: "vapor"; Boccaccio may recall Dante, Purg. 11.6, where "vapore" was taken by early commentators to mean divine love. The term in Dante is now understood to refer to Wisdom (see Wisdom 7.25 in the Vulgate where "vapor" is equated with "emanatio" as an aspect of "sapientia," wisdom).

14 worth: Wood wrongly suggests "has being" from the verb *worthen* (ELN 11, 1973, 9–14), but the Italian and French sources that he cites in fact support the more obvious interpretation. See 2.866.

15 The shift to the respectful plural, **ye,** from here to line 38, is not paralleled in Fil., which continues with "tu." See 1.550–875n.

17–21 Chaucer seems to have in mind only the amorous powers of Venus, whereas Boccaccio speaks of Venus in terms applicable to Mercy as an attribute of God. Many of the **thousand formes** love caused Jove to assume (bull, golden shower, swan) are told in Ovid, Met.

22–28 Cf. 1.250–52 and n. For the influence of Venus on Mars, see also Mars 36–42.

33 jo: A word not attested elsewhere, it may derive (Skeat) from Old French *joer* (to play, to move); here, then, "come about, come to pass."

39–42 The language seems to echo expressions used in addressing the Virgin Mary. Cf. Tr 1.15; ProPrT VII.478; Dante, Par. 33.16.

43 Cf. 2.13.

45 The invocation of **Caliope,** Calliope, the Muse of epic poetry, may have been influenced by Dante, Purg. 1.7–9, or Statius, Theb. 4.34–35. See also Bo 3.m12.24, Aen. 9.525. McCall, Ch Among the Gods, 16, quotes medieval mythographers' interpretations of Calliope as "optima vox" (best voice).

50–238 Largely independent of the Filostrato, but with suggestions from Fil. 3.23–29. Troilus's vows (127–47) are commonplace, but comparable to passages in the letter of Criseida, Fil. 2.96–106.

60 curtyn, the canopy of the bed. See 659–67n. below.

81 See 3.957, LGW 1817.

86–88 Robinson, acknowledging an unpublished note by Kittredge, explains: "Criseyde liked him none the less for being abashed—(1) for not being malapert, (2) for not bearing himself with jaunty self-assurance, (3) for not being over-bold in flattery or in professions of love—in such 'fair words' as, according to the proverb, 'make fools fain.'" On **made it tough,** see 2.1025n. The phrase **to synge a fool a masse** seems to be proverbial, but no exact parallel has been found (Whiting F458). The line probably means, "nor was he too bold, as one who would sing a mass to a fool," that is, flatter deceptively. The other recorded use of the proverb, by Lydgate (Minor Poems 2:483.341), refers to the mad futility rather than the boldness of the act, like teaching an ass to harp (cf. Tr 1.731). MED (s.v. *fole* n., 1b.) seems unwarranted in rendering *fool* as "foal," although the words cannot be distinguished phonologically outside of

rhyme. The idiom *to bolde, to synge* is treated in John S. Kenyon, Syntax of the Inf. in Ch, Ch Soc, 2nd ser., 44, 1909, 67. Carson, AmN&Q 6, 1968, 135–36, suggests "too bold a fool to sing a mass," but the sense and grammar are unlikely.

90 resons . . . rymes: Perhaps playing on the proverbial "rhyme or reason" (Whiting R103, Hassell R46).

114 For the proverbial comparison, see LGW 1841; Whiting H277.

115 See SqT V.496 and Whiting W81.

125 Cf. MerT IV.2106.

150 natal Joves feste: Unexplained. Perhaps "the feast of Jupiter, who presides over nativities" (so Skeat, Robinson), in support of which Pratt cites Jerome, Adversus Jovinianum: "Jovem Gamelium & Genethlium," that is, "Jove, god of betrothals and procreation" (JEGP 61, 1962, 244–48). Pauly-Wissowa, Real-Ency. s.v. *Iuppiter,* knows no "natalis Iovis," but does mention the epithets Almus and Propagator. Root suggests "the festival of Jove's birth," hence "the pagan equivalent of Christmas," but as Baugh observes, Chaucer could then more clearly have written *Joves natal feste* without disrupting the meter. Latin *natalis* means "birthday, festival" as well as "natal"; some scribal confusion of *natal* and a gloss "feste" may underlie the passage. *Joves* could be a miswriting of *Junos:* Juno presides over childbearing, and the two words look very much alike in medieval script; Jove would be more familiar than Juno. In the only other places in Troilus where *Juno* appears in a context in which *Jove* would also make sense, some of the manuscripts in fact read "Jove" (4.1116, 5.601). Juno is addressed as "natalis Iuno" in citations in Pauly-Wissowa, Real-Ency. s.v. *Iuno,* col. 1115, and in the Oxford Lat. Dict. s.v. *natalis.* Chaucer may have been aware that Jove's feasts were on the Ides of every month, and Juno's on the Kalends (Macrobius, Saturnalia 1.14–15; Ovid, Fasti 1.55–56).

188–89 In romance, saints' lives, and ballad, bells are rung "without hand" to mark an event of special joy or solemnity. See for example Child, Ballads 1:173, 231; 3:235, 244, 519–10. See Hinckley, MP 16, 1918–19, 40; Tatlock MLN 29, 1914, 28; Barry, MLN 30, 1915, 28–29. Barry suggests that the origin of such stories is a story told by the eighth-century St. Willibrord about the monks of Fulda. See Vitae S. Bonifatii, ed. W. Levison, 1905, 53.

198 bere the belle: Either "lead the flock" as a bellwether or, more likely, "take the prize" in a race (see Flom, JEGP 6, 1906, 115, citing Camden's Remaines, 1605, 348; see also Faerie Queene 4.4.25.9); in either case, "take first place." See Whiting B230; MED s.v. *bell* 9(a).

273 traitour probably from a mistranslation (as if Chaucer read "traditore") of "trattator," Fil. 3.8, "procurer" (Rossetti, 115). The French translator of the Filostrato also misunderstood or bowdlerized "trattator," taking it from its etymological sense "agent" to mean "provider for all her needs" (conduiseur de toute la bisogne—p. 175). Griffin and Windeatt mistranslate it "guardian"; Branca correctly glosses the word as "mezzano," and Havely translates "go-between."

293 us yonge: Could imply that Pandarus is young, or it may mean "to us when we were young" (see Slocum, PQ 58:16–25 and the introductory note).

294 Ultimately from pseudo-Cato, Disticha 1.3: "Virtutem primam esse puta [var., puto] compescere linguam" (Consider the prime virtue to be to hold your tongue—Walther 33716). MSS S² and Dg have "Cato" in the margin by this passage. See MancT IX.332–33; also RR 7037, 7041–45, 7055–57; and Hazelton, Spec 35, 1960, 363. For several English versions of the sentence, see Whiting V41.

309   Also proverbial: Whiting A244.

329   Cf. RR 8003–4: "He who is chastized (se chastie) by others leads a happy life." Cf. also Tr 1.203, 630, 635. For other variants, see Whiting F449, W47, W391, C161; Hassell C101; Walther 8952, 8927; WBPro III.180–83 and n.

349   richesse: Abundance ("divizia": Fil. 3.11.5).

351–54   Besides Fil. 3.12, see RR 47–54, 78–80 (Rom 49–58, 82–84).

360   Aperil the laste: But whether one (or more) or thirteen (or more) months ago cannot be determined: see Provost, Structure of Tr, 37–39; Bie, ELN 14:9–14; and the other treatments of the time scheme listed in the introductory note.

385   See textual note.

404   Departe it: Pandarus's terms smack of scholastic philosophy; Root cites Thomas Aquinas, "Diversitas requirit distinctionem" (Diversity requires a distinction; Summa theol. 1–1.31.2).

409–10   Benoît, 2949–55, reports that Troilus's sisters are Andromache, Cassandra, and Polyxena.

413   and lat me thanne allone: Fil. 3.18: "Poi mi lascia operar con qual sia l'una" (then let me work it out with whichever one it may be).

415   for non hope of mede recalls "ne . . . point . . . en esperance de guerdon" (not at all in hope of reward) in the French translation of the Filostrato (p. 177); Boccaccio has no corresponding expression (Fil. 3.16).

442–1309   Chaucer largely departs from the Filostrato.

444–45   Cf. PF 90–91 and n.

451–52   Perhaps an echo of Fil. 2.84.7–8.

502   As usual, Chaucer refers to the fictitious work of Lollius (cf. 575); the statement is not in the Filostrato.

510   fulfelle: Kentish for fulfille (cf. 3.978, etc.), a reading that only four authorities preserve (R A S¹ Th).

512–1190   The account of the lovers' meeting, which differs from Boccaccio's, probably derives in part from the passage in Boccaccio's Filocolo (2.165–83) in which a meeting is arranged between Florio and Biancofiore (see Young, Origin of Tr, 139–61). In both stories are the concealment of the lover by a go-between, the motif of jealousy, the lady's exaction of oaths from her lover, the use of rings, and the exchange of more or less formal vows. Detailed comparisons are made in the notes below. The business of Troilus's jealousy of Horaste may be due to the account of Florio's jealousy earlier in the Filocolo (1.247–89). Cummings, Indebtedness of Ch, 65, rejects the theory of indebtedness to the Filocolo, and adduces slight parallels from various places in the Filostrato, but Young's arguments are the more convincing. See also Root's ed., xxix–xxx; Griffin, Fil., intro, 101; and 5.1786n. below.

526   cler was in the wynd: See OED s.v. wind 20.b; Whiting W314.

530   Cf. 1.1065–71.

540   Root notes that in Benoît (16635–44) Apollo's temple was located near the Trojan gate of Timbree.

587   moste: Probably "must," though Root and Robinson take it as the adverb "most," an interpretation that, as Baugh notes, is supported by 2.247 and possibly by 3.916, where the construction is again ambiguous. In the present context, however, "must" is clearly preferable: Criseyde finds it useful to assert her dependency on her uncle. The form most(e), if it is a verb, is preterite, but its force may be either preterite or present (see WBPro III.440, 442, and MED s.v. moten 6a.[b]). Two MSS read "mot," and four "must": see textual note, and Kittredge, Observations, 330. Triste on is common in Chaucer for "trust in."

593   For the story of Tantalus, condemned in Hades to stand thirsty in a pool of water that always eluded him, see Ovid, Met. 4.458–59.

596   a certein: See MilT I.3193n.

601   litel wyndow: Young (Origin of Tr, 144–45, and MP 4:169–77) compares the "piccolo pertugio" (little aperture) through which Florio observes a festive scene in Filocolo 2.172. See above, 512–1190n.

stewe: Chaucer is unique in using stewe as a small room or closet rather than a heated or heatable room. Cf. HF 26n.

614   On Wade see MerT IV.1424 and n. Wentersdorf (JEGP 64, 1966, 1274–86) elaborates Bennett's unpersuasive idea (MLR 31, 1936, 202–3) that the Wade of the thirteenth-century German epic Kudrun corresponds to Pandarus as go-between. The he, she, and he of line 614 probably refer not to Pandarus and Criseyde but to this and that member of the company (or paid entertainer) who could please Criseyde and make her laugh (613). For the use see 2.1747–48 and Mustanoja, ME Syntax, 136.

615   every thyng hath ende: Proverbial. See KnT I.2636n.

617–20   Cf. Bo 4.pr6.42–196; 5.m1.18–23; For 65–68; KnT I.1663–72 and n.; Tr 5.1541–45. Chaucer may have been influenced as well by Dante's discussion of the heavenly spheres in Convivio 2.4.

619   Kittredge (Observations, 380) rightly rejects Skeat's notion that hierdes here means "(shep)herdess." Chaucer metrically stresses the second syllable of the latter word (see Tr 1.653).

624–26   The conjunction of the planets Saturn and Jupiter, together with the moon, in the zodiacal house of Cancer (which was the moon's mansion), caused the rain. Pandarus may have predicted the rain (line 551 in context seems to imply it, but the inference is not certain), and Criseyde certainly foresaw it (562). In the Filostrato the night of the consummation is described as merely "dark and cloudy" (Fil. 3.24). For the moon and its horns, see Bo 1.m5.9–10. Root, in the article discussed below, noted (p. 49n.) that the idea of a lovers' consummation during a rainstorm may derive from the story of the affair of Dido and Aeneas (Aen. 4.160–62; cf LGW 1218–39). Maresca, Three English Epics, 1979, 180–83, presses the parallel too far. A faintly similar motif occurs in the story of St. Scholastica; see Farina, Lang Qtly. (Univ. of S. Florida) 10, 1972, 23–26.

The conjunction specified here has been used as evidence for the date of composition of Troilus (see introductory note). Root and Russell (PMLA 39, 1924, 48–63) showed that such a conjunction actually took place in 1385, and they dated it on 13 or 14 May. North (RES 20, 1969, 142–44) dates it 8 or 9 June 1385, and O'Neil

(Journ. Australasian Lang. and Lit. Assoc. 43, 1975, 50–52) dates it 9 June or, admitting that Saturn was not yet in Cancer, 12 May. (Saturn actually joined Jupiter in Cancer at 9:42 A.M., 17 May 1385.) All thus agree that the conjunction occurred in May or June of 1385; North and O'Neil differ from Root and Russell on the exact date because they use a more modern ephemeris (that of Bryant Tuckerman, 1964, 59:710). The contemporary chronicler Walsingham reports that the conjunction of Saturn and Jupiter in Cancer occurred in May (Root, xvii, citing from Rolls Series 2:126); Chaucer may have been thinking of May, or (knowing that the planetary conjunction lasted until 18 July) he may have thought precisely of 9 or 10 June, the only dates, as Sigmund Eisner (on whose calculations I depend) kindly informs me, when all the conditions of the conjunction are met, including the appearance in the evening of the crescent moon. The moon was new, according to Herman H. Goldstine (New and Full Moons, 1973, 199) at 12:13 P.M., 8 June, and at 3:33 A.M., 8 July.

Root and Russell assume that Chaucer wrote after the conjunction appeared, and that Troilus was thus composed sometime between May of 1385 and the date of Usk's execution (see introductory note). But Chaucer could have predicted the conjunction by using an almanac (Tatlock, MLN 50:280–82; O'Connor, JEGP 55, 1956, 556–62; North, RES 20:142) and may therefore have completed the poem before May 1385. Further research in almanacs available to Chaucer may show that he would have assigned the conjunction to another date than the correct one given by Tuckerman's tables. In any case, the allusion would have had more point around the time of the conjunction.

Such a conjunction is very rare (it had not occurred for six hundred years), and as a conjunction of the largest and most distant known planets it was considered especially portentous. Root and O'Connor note that astrologers may have regarded it as causing floods (and having caused Noah's flood). Bradwardine, whose work Chaucer knew (see NPT VII.3241–42 and note VII.3241–50), in his De causa Dei, says that the birth of Christ occurred during a conjunction of Jupiter and Saturn (Wood, Ch and the Stars, 49). As noted above, Walsingham mentions this conjunction prominently in his chronicles and says that it was followed by "a very great disturbance of kingdoms."

641   As good chep: On the idiom, see Kirby, MLN 48, 1933, 527–28.

659–67   On the arrangement of Pandarus's house and the other domestic backgrounds in Troilus see Smyser, Spec 31:297–315. The **travers** screen or curtain (674) would divide the hall into a **myddel chaumbre** and an **outer hous** or chamber. The latter, where Pandarus claims he will sleep, would be at the far end of the hall from the **litel closet**, his own bedroom, given over to Criseyde. Chaucer does not trouble to explain how Pandarus moves through his house, nor precisely how the *stewe* (601, see n.), the small room in which Troilus has been hiding, fits into the architecture. Troilus is present but unseen by Criseyde from line 742 to 953, presumably because of curtains enclosing her bed. Whether Pandarus passes the night in the bedroom, without the curtains, Chaucer does not say (see 914, 1189, 1555). The gutter and secret passage (787) are of course Pandarus's fictions, assuming that Troilus had hidden since midnight of the night before the dinner party (602).

671   Wine, the *voide* in line 674 (Fr. "voidé," withdrawal from a hall or chamber), was drunk before retiring; cf. GP I.819–21; Skeat, 2:506.

695   olde daunce: Cf. GP I.476 and n. Harvey suggests **point** here may mean not the obvious "particular" but "note" or "phrase" in music, OED s.v. *point* sb.¹ 4.a. and 9 (N&Q 213, 1968, 243–44).

711   Apparently proverbial: see Whiting G484.

712–32   Root observes that Troilus invokes all the planetary deities except Saturn.

716   Mars and Saturn both had an evil influence. See KnT I.1995–2038 and 2456–69. Root defines **Aspectes** as the angle between two planets as seen from the Earth; if Saturn and Mars were 45° or 90° apart at Troilus's nativity, the prognosis would be especially malignant. Venus, when *combust* by being too near the sun, lost its influence (see Astr 2.4.33–56).

718   Thy fader is correctly glossed by MS H⁴, "Iupiter."

720–21   Adoun, Adonis, beloved of Venus and slain by a boar (see Ovid, Met.10.715–16). Possibly suggested by Tes. 7.43. See Chaucer's translation of the passage in KnT I.2221–25. MS H⁴, in marginal glosses, cites this passage in Ovid, as well as the Ovidian passages referred to in the notes to lines 722, 726, and 729.

722   On **Jove** and **Europe,** see Met. 2.833–75; cf. ProLGW F 113–14, Tr 2.55n.

724   For Mars's **blody cope,** see Theb. 7.69–71, and the Lactantius gloss to the line in Statius cited by Clogan, SP 61, 1964, 599–615.

725   For the form **Cipris** (Venus, beloved of Mars), see also HF 518n. For the prayer to Mars by his love for Venus, see KnT I.2383–92.

726   On **Dane** (Daphne), see Met. 1.452–567, and KnT I.2062–64 and n.; pursued by **Phebus** Apollo, she escaped by metamorphosing into a laurel tree.

729–30   See Met. 2.708–832. **Pallas** Athene (Minerva), angry with **Aglawros,** Aglauros, caused her to envy her sister **Hierse,** Herse, and Mercury, enamored of Herse, turned Aglauros into a stone. Chaucer wrongly implies that Mercury's love for Herse caused Pallas's anger against Aglauros. For comment on the story, see Wetherbee, Ch and Poets, 102–9.

731   Troilus asks **Diane,** the moon, to favor his undertaking (cf. 2.74–75).

733   With the **fatal sustren** cf. 5.3; for the application of the term "sorores" to the Parcae, see Theb. 1. 632, 8.59, 9.323. Clogan finds a possible source for the gloss in MS H⁴, explaining the roles of the Parcae, in Lactantius's gloss to Theb. 2.249 (see 724 above). For the idea that a child's fate is spun before his first garment is made, see KnT I.1566 and n.

764   Proverbial: See Whiting H569, and cf. FranT V.1472.

773   Cf. 2.477, BD 1019, HF 692; and Whiting H75. Cf. MLT II.620 and n.

775   Cf. GP I.586n.

781–82   the worthieste knyght . . . world: For this intensive (rather than partitive) use of **Oon,** see Language and Versification, p. xxxviii, Mustanoja, The Engl. Syntact. Type *one the best man,* 1958, and his ME Syntax, 297–99. Other examples in Troilus are at 1.1081, 2.746–47, 3.1310, 5.1056–57. In each case the meaning is "the very X-est" and not "one of the X-est." Chaucer signals the latter partitive sense by adding *of,* as in Tr 5.1473.

787 Compare LGW 2705. **pryve wente**, secret passage, perhaps (Smyser, Spec 31:310) a latrine outlet (in which case the **goter** would be, not an eaves-trough, but a sewer: MED s.v. *goter* 2.[a]); see MED s.v. *prive*. The MED (s.v. *goter* 4., comparing LGW 2705) plausibly takes *goter* here to mean a window leading to the eaves-trough. See 3.659–67 above.

791 **shal**, "owe" here and in 3.1649 (Mustanoja, ME Syntax, 491).

797 The motif of jealousy is suggested in the Filocolo (2.175); see the note to line 512–1190. The character **Horaste** is Chaucer's invention. His name is taken from that of Orestes (spelled Orrestes and Horrestes in Guido, Horeste in Gower, Conf. Aman. 3.2176); MSS D H⁵ read *Orast(e)*. See Kittredge, Observations, 347; and Hamilton, Indebtedness, 97.

808 Filocolo (1.259–60) has the phrase "iniquo spirito" (wicked spirit) of jealousy; but then, in another place (7.18), the Filostrato has "e'l nemico / spirto di gelosia."

813–33 Drawn from Bo 2.pr4.75–78, 118–27, 150–55. The sentiments were commonplaces: see 1625–28n. and MLT II.421n.

837 A standard reification; see 3.1010, and Gower, Mirour 2641–45; Ovid, Met. 2.768–77 (parallels noted by Root).

850 **fair**: Either "a fine thing" (MED s.v. *fair* n., [b]) or "a to-do, a fine how-do-you-do" (from "affair": MED s.v. *faire* n., citing this line).

853 Glossed in MSS H¹ and H⁴: "Mora trahit periculum" (delay draws danger). See Whiting P145, and Walther 31436–38.

855 Proverbial; see FrT III.1475n., Tr 2.989.

861 **fare-wel feldefare**: "Good-by, thrush!" The meaning is either "all is over," or as Skeat and MED (s.v. *faren* 10b.[c]) take it, "good riddance," alluding to the fieldfare's welcome departure north at the end of winter. See Whiting F130; Rom 5510.

885 **blewe**: Symbolizing constancy: see Anel 146n.; SqT V.644; Wom Unc 7, 14, 21. See MED s.v. *bleu* 1.d, Whiting B384, and Hassell B112 for many instances.

890 Pandarus's exclamation is of uncertain meaning. Skeat took it as "yea, hazel-bushes shake," as a useless truism, to indicate the futility of sending the ring. Derek Pearsall (private correspondence) elaborates: "Hazel-bushes shake, meaning that this is no very exceptional thing for them to do (compared, for instance, with oaks)." In two later passages (5.505, 1174), themselves not entirely clear, references to hazelwood accompany an attitude of incredulity approaching a mocking skepticism: this may be the implication here. For similar expressions, see Whiting H213. Gnerro's idea that Pandarus refers to hazel as used in divining rods is unsupported (N&Q 207:164–65). Possibly the phrase should be construed differently, taking *ye* as the personal pronoun (and deleting Skeat's comma), hence "you shake hazels," perhaps "you merely go a-nutting." Fisher's gloss to the phrase, "nuts," presumably alludes to post-medieval slang ("nuts to you"), but the word "nut" was one of the terms indicative of things of little value (MED s.v. *note* 1.[b]), and the sense could be "you trifle." Along these lines Sturtevant suggests a specific reference to the shaking of hazels to provide mast for pigs; hence "you offer food for pigs!" (Expl 28, 1969, Item 5). MS R reads *haselnotes;* H⁵, "than hawe we fayre bakyn."

891 On the power of gems, see 2.344n.

896 See 4.1283 and n.

901 **white**: Specious, plausible. Cf. 3.1567, and OED s.v. *white* 10. For a parallel use of the French "blanche," see the *Testament* of Jean de Meun, line 1473 (ed. Méon 4:75). See also Tr 2.424 and n.; Whiting W627, Hassell P61. **feffe . . . with** (give) is also used with specious *wordes* as its object in Bo 2.pr3.64–65.

920–45 This passage may reflect earlier material in the Filostrato: Cummings refers to Fil. 2.133, 139, 121 (Indebtedness of Ch, 67–68).

931 **dulcarnoun**: A name for the 47th proposition of the first book of Euclid's geometry, the Pythagorean Theorem, hence a term for difficulty or perplexity. The word is originally the Arabic epithet ("Dhu 'l Karnayn," the two-horned) of Alexander the Great, who claimed descent from Jupiter Ammon, the horned god. The application to the proposition in Euclid probably came from the resemblance of the diagram to a figure with horns. In 933 Pandarus says Dulcarnon is called *flemyng of wrecches*. But that is a translation of "Fuga Miserorum" (MS H⁴ has the gloss, "Dulcarnon: fuga miserorum"), which corresponds to "Eleufuga," from the Greek for "flight of pity," a name actually applied to Euclid's 5th proposition, a proposition difficult enough to elicit the severity of the teacher and the rout of the weaker students. See Skeat, Athenaeum, Sept., 1871, 2.393; for full citation of sources and modern comment, see Hart, ChR 16, 1981, 162–63, nn. 23–25. For **at my wittes ende** see Whiting W412.

936 **fecches**: Cf. GP I.177n.

947 For the use of **Ther**, see Language and Versification, p. xxxix; and Roscow, Syntax and Style, 52.

978 **feere**: Fire (Kentish). Cf. 1.229n.

979 For the usage, see MED s.v. *countenaunce*, 4.

989–90 Cf. KnT I.1169, 1785–90.

1016–19 Cf. KnT I.1313–14, Bo 1.m5.

1035 See 2.784n.

1046–49 On ordeal (**ordal**) and purgation by oath (**oth**), see Pollock and Maitland, Hist. of Eng. Law, 1898, 2: 595–99; Dict. of the M. A., s.v. *Compurgation*. On **sorte**, see 1.76 and Taylor, Primitive Culture, 4th ed., 1903, 1:78ff.

1060–64 Cf. 1.946–52; see Whiting M693, W372, S277 (and cf. S278).

1088 **spirit**: See KnT I.2743–56n. and Tr 1.307. A fairly close parallel appears in Machaut, Remède de fortune 1490–93 (see Wimsatt, MAE 45:281–82).

1092 This episode is partly drawn from Fil. 4.18–19, where Troilus faints on learning the decision of the Trojan council. The swoon is not repeated in the corresponding passage in Tr 4.218.

1104–5 For the figure see 2.1272–73.

1115 **frote . . . his temples**: Appears to follow words of the French translation of the Filostrato, "frotoient" and "ses temples" (p. 204), where Boccaccio (Fil. 4.19) has "fregando" (rubbing) and "faccia" (face). Pratt notes that *frote* does not occur elsewhere in Troilus, and that *temples* in this sense occurs nowhere else in Chaucer.

1129 **keste**: A Kentish form adopted, as often, for rhyme. Cf. 1.229n.

1137 See Whiting L260.

1154 **bar hym on honde**: See MLT II.620n.; Tr 4.1404; MED s.v. *beren* 13.(g.,i.); and Duncan, TSL 11, 1966, 19–33.

1161 See GP I.177n. and CYT VIII.795.

1165 On the anachronism, see 2.104–5n.

1169 ye were ybete: The scribe of MS R comments in the margin, "Ye, with a fether."

1189 Whether Pandarus retires to the *outer hous* (see above, 659–67) at this point cannot be determined, although the phrasing here suggests that he remains.

1191 MS R has the marginal comment, "how bace phisik come in honde betwene Creysseyde & Troylys."

1192 For a similar comparison see Filocolo 2.165–66. See Whiting L84, and textual note.

1194 soot: Is bitter; cf. RR 10633–34, "more bitter than soot." See Whiting S480, Hassell S123.

1200 The simile seems not to be recorded before Chaucer: Whiting A216. See LGW 2648; SumT III.1667; MED s.v. *aspen.* The Latin name of the tree is "Populus tremula."

1203 goddes sevene: See Scogan 3.

1212–16 I.e., "Bitter pills may have sweet effects." See Whiting D393. Cf. 2.784.

1219–20 Proverbial. See Bo 3.m1.5–6; Alanus de Insulis, Lib. parab. (PL 210:592), also Walther 6407; Whiting S944.

1230–31 Root and McPeek (MLN 46, 1931, 293–301) and Young (Origin of Tr, 148) note several examples (e.g., Ovid, Met. 4.365) from classical and medieval poetry of the commonplace figure of tree and vine as lovers.

1255 The application of the name **Citheria** to the planet is paralleled, as Root notes, in Dante, Purg. 27.95. See KnT I.2215–16.

1257 See Dante, Purg. 1.19—but the conception of Venus as benevolent (**wel-willy** is a calque on "benevolens") is familiar; see Mars 31–32n.

1258 Imeneus: See 4.554–55n.

1261–67 Adapted from an address to the Virgin Mary in Dante, Par. 33.14–18, esp. verse 15: "sua disïanza vuol volar sanz' ali" (his desire wishes to fly without wings). For the currency of the phrase, see Michele Barbi, Problemi di critica dantesca, 1934, 254. To "fly without wings" became a common phrase in the sixteenth century (Whiting W363); Machaut used the phrase in French before Chaucer (Hassell V143). A similar Latin proverb, from Plautus (Poenulus 4.2.29), was widely known: "Without feathers it is scarcely easy to fly" (Walther, 29675). Schless (Ch and Dante, 207, 101, 122–23), following Pratt (MLQ 7, 1946, 261) notes the use of the same canto from Dante in ProPrT VII.474–80 and SNPro VIII.36–56, and suggests Chaucer may have memorized it. On the bond, or chain, of love, see 3.1744–71; Lovejoy, Great Chain of Being; Barney, Spec 47, 1972, 445–58; KnT I.2987–3089n. Lowes notes a series of borrowings from Dante from here to the middle of Book 4 (MP 14:705–35); see Wetherbee, in Ch's Troilus, 297–317.

1267 Another application of Christian sentiment to matters of Love; see also 1282, and KnT I.3089n.

1282 Proverbial (Whiting M508); cf. Machaut, Remède de fortune, 1686: "Pitez est dessus droiture" (pity is beyond righteousness—Wimsatt, MAE 45:284); KnT I.3089; ProLGW F 162.

1293–95 Cf. Machaut, Behaingne 665–67 (Wimsatt, MAE 45:286).

1309 Devereux (PQ 44, 1965, 550–52) suggests that this line imitates the address to the eucharistic host in Middle English poems called "levation prayers," but the idiom (*welcome* with vocative epithets) is too common to support the conjecture.

1310 See 3.781–82n.

1316 Chaucer slightly softens the Italian (Fil. 3.32): "D'amor sentiron l'ultimo valore" (Havely: "They felt love's power to the full"; or perhaps, "they felt the ultimate value of love"; Griffin: "the last delight"). The French translation (p. 182) has "sentirent le derrenier et parfait bien d'amours" (they felt the last and perfect good of love).

grete worthynesse (cf. 5.717) catches the etymological notion in "valore" of worth, but adds a connotation of dignity and omits the connotation of strength.

1324–37 On the position of these stanzas, see the Textual Notes.

1331–37 Cf. 5.1856–59n.

1368–69 See Filocolo 2.181; cf. 512–1190 above.

1370–72 This may be the same **broche** that Troilus later gave Criseyde (see 5.1661 and n.). It is not connected with the *broche of Thebes* (Mars 245; cf. Anderson, SAC 4, 1982, 127–28). On the gold and azure, see ClT IV.254. Leyerle draws attention to the fashion for heart-shaped pins in late medieval England, in Ch's Troilus, 209. On the *scripture* (line 1369), see Joan Evans, English Posies and Posy Rings, 1934.

1384 The absolute adjectives **white** and **rede** elsewhere in Chaucer (NPT VII.2842, PardT VI.526) refer to wine, but in view of the Italian of Fil. 3.39, "denar perderanno" (they will lose their money), it is possible that Chaucer here means white silver and red gold. See OED s.v. *white* 10.

1387–93 These lines, independent of Boccaccio, may have been suggested by Dante, Purg. 20.106–8, 116–17, where **Mida**, Midas (see WBT III.951 and n.) and **Crassus** are likewise associated in a discussion of avarice. See Lowes, MP 14:711ff.; and Schless, Ch and Dante, 123–25, arguing against specific derivation from Dante. On Midas, see Ovid, Met. 11.100–193. Crassus, slain in battle against the Parthians in 53 B.C., had molten gold poured into his mouth because of his greed. The historian Orosius called Crassus "a man of insatiable cupidity" (Historiarum 6.13.1, ed. Zangemeister, 1889). Lowes (p. 712) suggests that Chaucer may use here *Li hystore de Julius Cesar* by Jehan de Tuim. Shannon considers Boccaccio's *De casibus* 6.7 a sufficient source (Ch and Roman Poets, 133 and n.). The information was probably common knowledge.

1387 On Ch's use of *so* and *as* with asseverations, see Roscow, Syntax and Style, 50–51.

1415–26 Primarily from Fil. 3.42–43, with additions from Dante (see 1420 below).

1415 The epithet **comune astrologer** is from Alanus de Insulis, De planctu Naturae 2.163–64: "gallus . . . uulgaris astrologus." Six MSS of Troilus gloss the lines with the words "vulgaris astrologus," and MS H⁴ refers to Alanus. See PF 350, NPT VII.2855–58 and note VII.2857–58.

1417–18 For similar references to Lucifer, see Ovid, Amores 1.6.65–66, 2.11.55–56; Her. 18.112. North, too meticulously, is troubled by the fact that Venus was an evening star rather than a morning star (so identified in the margins of five MSS) through most of the year 1385 (RES 20:145).

1420 Cf. Dante, Purg. 19.4–5: "quando i geomanti lor Maggior Fortuna / veggiono in orïente, innanzi a l'alba" (when the geomancers see in the east, before dawn, their *Fortuna Major*). Whether Chaucer knew precisely what

Dante meant by *Fortuna Major* may be doubted. It is one of the figures from the occult art of geomancy, described in KnT I.2045n. The figure had the form of a four of diamonds placed above a two of diamonds. According to the fourteenth-century commentator on Dante, Benvenuto da Imola, the geomantic form corresponds to a group of six stars in the constellations of Aquarius and Pisces, and modern students of Dante accept this interpretation. In geomancy, the figure was connected with the Sun and with Aquarius; it is thus possible that Dante or Chaucer meant simply, "the sun rose." Root shows that the group of six stars would be rising in the east at dawn in mid-May. See Curry, MLN 38, 1923, 94–96; Root and Russell, PMLA 39:56–58; Schless, Ch and Dante, 125–27. Skeat, citing Gavin Douglas's notes to his translation of the Aeneid (ed. Small, Edinburgh, 1874, 2:288), thought *Fortuna Major* meant the planet Jupiter, but he later rejected this interpretation.

1422–1533 This passage, much developed from the corresponding passage in the Filostrato, derives from a tradition of lyric dawn-songs, "aubes," in European poetry that has its source in Ovid's Amores 1.13. Other, briefer aubades in Chaucer are Tr 3.1695–1712, RvT I.4236–39 (a parody), and Mars 90–91, 136–40. The tradition, represented in French (*aube, aubade*) and Provençal (*alba*) but most abundantly in the German (*Tagelied*), is ably summarized and connected with this place in the Troilus by Kaske, in Schoeck and Taylor, eds., Ch Criticism, 1961, 2:167–79. See also Arthur T. Hatto, Eos, 1965, and Jonathan Saville, The Medieval Erotic "Alba," 1972. Kaske makes the interesting observation that, as compared at least with the German tradition, Chaucer has Criseyde express the sentiments usually given to the man, and Troilus those given to the woman. The tone of chiding the sun, and some details, come directly from Ovid.

1423 William E. Mead traces the sentiment, "Alas, that I was born" from classical and Biblical sources, noting Chaucer's frequent repetition of it (ed. Squyr of Low Degre, 1904, 52); see also MED s.v. *alas* 1.d.

1428 A Latin gloss in five MSS reads: "Almena was the mother of Hercules" (by Jove, who miraculously extended the length of the night when Hercules was conceived); see Theb. 6.288–89; 12.300–301; Roman de Thèbes 2.88; pseudo-Hyginus, Fabulae, 29; Boccaccio, De gen. deorum 13.1; Ovid, Amores 1.13.45–46; Tes. 4.14.

1433–35 Cf. Amores 1.13.15–34.

1437 Ther: See 3.947.

1462 See Ecclus. 38.28.

1464 Titan: The sun, often confused with Tithonus, consort of Aurora, the dawn: cf. Tes. 4.72; Filocolo 2.222, 1.173. Root notes that Servius's commentary on Virgil's Georgics 3.48 says that Virgil "now puts Tithonus for the sun, that is for Titan," and that some MSS of Dante, Purg. 9.1 read "Titan," others "Titon" (Tithonus). For reference to Tithonus and Aurora and Lucifer in the context of a dawn-complaint, see Ovid, Her. 18.111–14; see also Petrarch, Sonnet 23, In morte.

1490 thise worldes tweyne: Perhaps "two worlds such as this" (Root). The Filostrato has "che 'l troian regno" (than the Trojan kingdom—3.47); perhaps Chaucer meant "the realms of both Greece and Troy."

1495–98 These lines, like 4.1548–54, are examples of the topic of "impossibles" (*impossibilia, adynata*), for which see Curtius, European Lit., 95–98; WBPro

III.688n., SumT III.2231, FranT V.1009. Many medieval Latin examples are gathered by Walther, Index s.v. *Unmöglichkeiten* and *Vergebliche Mühe*. Recent studies of Chaucer's *impossibilia*, especially these two instances, cite many classical examples (Brookhouse, MAE 34, 1965, 40–42; Schibanoff, JEGP 76, 1977, 326–33). The ultimate source of line 1496 is probably Ovid, Fasti 2.90: "et accipitri iuncta columba fuit" (and the dove was joined to the hawk). Wimsatt cites an example from Machaut, Lay des Dames 141–52 (Poèsies lyriques 2:352–61) in MAE 45:287, but the resemblance is slight: both poets employ the familiar topic.

1499 herte grave: See 1.295–98 and n.

1502 To dyen in the peyne: Cf. 1.674, KnT I.1133n. For the construction, see Language and Versification, p. xxxvi.

1514 For mo as "others," see 2.1274n.

1538 ther: Not redundant but part of a common Chaucerian negative construction: see 2.202, 1050; 4.1197; 5.146; and Roscow, Syntax and Style, 18.

1555–82 The visit of Pandarus to Criseyde here is not paralleled in the Filostrato. The now widespread view that Pandarus here seduces or rapes Criseyde, or that Chaucer hints at such an action, is baseless and absurd. The statement, for example, published in 1979, that "criticism has widely ignored or failed to appreciate the suggestiveness of this scene" is incorrect; all too much has been written about its "suggestiveness."

1577 The reference is ultimately to Luke 23.34. The expression was proverbial as an illustration of how far forgiveness should go. See Whiting G205 (citations all later than Chaucer, but not obviously derived from him) and many citations from earlier fourteenth-century French works of "Dieu pardonna sa mort" (God forgave his death) in Hassell D80.

1600 Flegitoun: Named in Aen. 6.551; Dante, Inf. 14.116, 131. On the spelling with *F* see Schless, Ch and Dante, 127.

1607 For the not infrequent elision of *be* in such constructions, see 5.832 and, with further examples, Roscow, Syntax and Style, 99–102.

1625–28 Cf. 3.816–19. The commonplace sentiment derives from Bo 2.pr4.5–9; see also Walther 6534, 31586; Dante, Inf. 5.121–23; Augustine, Conf. 10.14; Thomas Aquinas, Summa theol. 2–2.36.1: "The memory of past goods . . . insofar as they are lost, causes grief." See Rom 4138–40.

1634 Cf. RR 8261–64; ultimately from Ovid, Ars Am. 2.11–14, and proverbial (Whiting C518; Walther 16215).

1636–37 Instances of this commonplace sentiment are gathered by Whiting W671.

1642 rakle: Here taken by Skeat, the later editors, doubtfully by OED, and by MED for a verb, "behave rashly," but the word, of obscure etymology, is elsewhere attested only as an adjective. It seems best to assume ellipsis of "to be": "Nor do I wish (to be) so importunate as to annoy her." The scribes in three MSS supplied a "be," indicating their ignorance of a verb *rakle.*

1681 ben met: For the construction, see KnT I.2528n.

1688–94 Cf. Par. 19.7–9, 24.25–27 for the typically Dantesque conceit that the writer's pen cannot set down his ineffable vision. On "inexpressibility topoi" generally, see Curtius, European Lit., 159–62.

1691–92   Felicite: See Bo 3.pr2.8–11; Dante, Conv. 4.22

1703   For **Piros** (Pyrois), and Eous, Aethon, and Phlegon, the sun's other horses, see Ovid, Met. 2.153–54.

1716–19   A combination of Fil. 3.72 and 2.84.

1744–71   For Troiolo's song, as given at this point by Boccaccio, Chaucer substitutes a song based on Boethius 2.m8. See Tr 3.1–49 above. This passage is omitted in MS H² and appears on an inset leaf in MS Ph. Root and others have taken this as evidence that Chaucer wrote this song in a revision of Troilus. See, however, the cogent counter-argument by Windeatt, in Essays on Tr, 1–23. Baum, Ch's Verse, 87–90, gives a helpful analysis of the difficult grammar of Troilus's song. Steadman, Disembodied Laughter, 69, notes that one commentator interpreted the love addressed in Boethius's poem as "divine love" (Pseudo-Aquinas, Commentum duplex on 2.8).

1751–54   Cf. PF 380–81 and n.

1751   That, that: See De Vries, ES 52, 1971, 502–7. Comparison with the grammar of Boethius's Latin and Boece shows that Chaucer construed the *That, that* of line 1758 in the same way, referring now back to line 1757.

1752   Cf. Boethius: Concordes uariat uices (*varieth accordable chaungynges*).

1762–68   See the note to lines 1261–67 above.

1784   In an unpublished paper, Matthew Abbate observes how nicely Chaucer assimilates Boccaccio's comparison ("Come falcon ch' uscisse di cappello," like a falcon that emerged from its hood) to a proverbial English alliterating phrase (Whiting F25), *fressh as faukoun*. Boccaccio (Fil. 3.91) drew the figure from Dante (Par. 19.34), but in the Filostrato it is Troiolo, not Criseida, who is compared with a falcon. The association of falconry with courtship was common; see for example Machaut's Dit de l'alerion.

1807–10   Chaucer seems to combine reminiscences of Tes. 1.3 and 11.63, and Dante, Par. 8.7–8, or perhaps, as Schless argues (Ch and Dante, 128–29), merely relies on general knowledge. The reference to Venus as daughter of **Dyone** (Dione) may be due to Aen. 3.19, or Claudian, De rapt. Pros. 3.433, or Ovid (Ars Am. 2.593; 3.3; 3.769; Amores 1.14.33). Chaucer calls Venus **lady bryght** in 3.39, also.

1808   On Cupid's blindness, see KnT I.1963–65n.

1809–10   On the erroneous conception of (Mount) Helicon as a fountain or spring on Mount Parnassus, see HF 521–22n.

1811–13   By echoing his invocation to Venus and the Muse Calliope (3.39–48), Chaucer consciously encloses and sets off his third book. See Baum, Ch's Verse, 185.

1814–16   Cf. Fil. 4.24.

BOOK IV

1–11   Special studies of the structure and meaning of the fourth book are Wenzel, PMLA 79, 1964, 542–47, and Erzgräber, in Manfred Bambeck and H. H. Christmann, ed., Philologica Romanica, E. Lommatzsch gewidmet, 1975, 97–117. For the commonplace sentiments of the opening stanzas, see, besides Fil. 3.94, Bo 2.pr1.14–21 and m1.12–15; RR 8039–41; Machaut, Remède de fortune (Oeuvres 2:1049–62), and Jugement dou Roy de Behaingne (1:684–91). The phrasing of lines 1–2 recalls MLT II.1132–33, 1140–41. See also Tr 1.138–40n.

6–7   mowe: Seldom used by Chaucer (ParsT X.258, HF 1806); it may have occurred to him because of its use in French poems about Fortune's wheel. Patch, Goddess Fortuna, 160, cites several French poems which rhyme "roue," wheel, and "moue," grimace. RR 8039–40, cited above, is an example. For the rhymes in Machaut, see Wimsatt, MAE 45:284–85.

22–24   Herynes: See Pity 92n., and on the Furies as suffering pain, Tr 1.1–14n. Both passages may reflect Dante, Inf. 9.37–51, although Schless is skeptical of any use of Dante here (Ch and Dante, 129). The form **Alete** (Alecto) may be due to the Italian "Aletto." For the idea that the Furies are **Nyghtes doughtren thre,** see Met. 4.451–52; Aen. 12.845–47; Boccaccio, De gen. deorum 3.6–9. See 2.435–36 and n.

25   Quyryne: See Ovid, Fasti, 2.475–80. For the statement that he is son of Mars, see Fasti 2.419; Aen. 1.274–76; Met. 15.863; Dante, Par. 8.131–32. The epithet **cruel** recalls Theb. 7.703 ("saevi"); Mars is generally malefic in astrology (see 3.716 and n.). Boccaccio associates Mars and the Furies in Tes. 3.1.

32   Hercules lyoun: The zodiacal sign Leo is associated with Hercules because that hero killed the Nemean lion and is regularly depicted as carrying or wearing a lion skin. Chaucer adopts this *chronographia* from Ars Am. 1.68, where Ovid speaks of the sun approaching the back (not **brest**) of Herculean Leo ("Herculei terga Leonis"). Martial also calls Leo "Herculean" (8.55.15); for other instances see Pauly-Wissowa, Real-Ency., s.v. *Leo* (12:2, 1925) col. 1974, 1979–80. The sun was in Leo from about 12 July to the first part of August; Root surmises that by *brest* Chaucer means the first part of this period; Skeat takes Chaucer to mean the star Regulus in the constellation (not sign) of Leo, and hence about 1 August. For the use of *brest*, cf. LGW F 113.

38–42   Not from the Filostrato; cf. Benoît, Roman de Troie, 11996–12006. in the berd: See Whiting B117, and MED s.v. *berd* 4a.(c), Hassell B9. Lines 39–42 briefly imitate the alliterative battle-descriptions rendered with such virtuosity in KnT I.2602–16 and LGW 635–49. Robbins notes a similar use of alliteration in a rhyming poem in the romance Ywain and Gawain, 3531–55, again a battle-description (in Eleanor of Aquitaine, ed. William W. Kibler, 1976, 147–72).

50–54   Except for **Phebuseo,** who appears to have been invented by Chaucer (an Italianate name based on Apollo's name Phoebus), all these men are named in Fil. 4.3. According to Boccaccio, they were all taken prisoner; Chaucer's account (with **Maugre** in line 51) follows Guido and Benoît in specifying that only Antenor was captured (see 5.403 and n.). One MS, H³, reads "Palidomas and also Menestes" for line 51, which suggests, as Root notes, that Chaucer's drafts may at one time have agreed with Boccaccio. Antenor, Polydamas, Sarpedon, and Polymnestor are familiar names in the Trojan cycle. **Santippe** (Italian "Santippo") is Antiphus (spelled Antipus, Anthiphus, Xantipus in Guido; Antif or Xantif in Benoît), Priam's ally, king of Frisia. **Polite** (Polites, Aen. 2.526), **Monesteo** (Mnestheus, Aen. 5.166, etc.), and **Rupheo** (Ripheus or Rhipeus, Aen. 2.339) are names Boccaccio probably derived ultimately from Virgil. Pernicone would derive three of the names in Fil. 4.3 from the Roman de Troie, 12647–49 (Studi di filol. ital. 2, 1929, 96, 105).

57–58   Whereas Boccaccio here (Fil. 4.4) says Priam asked for a truce, both Benoît and Guido say that the Greeks sent Ulysses and Diomede to sue for a truce in order to bury those slain on the battlefield. See Roman de Troie, 12822–13120, and Historia, p. 160. Chaucer's account varies in the MSS (see Textual Notes). Perhaps one of Chaucer's drafts agreed with Boccaccio and was revised later in consideration of the earlier authorities (cf. the preceding note).

96   in hire sherte: Cf. ClT IV.886.

101   now or nevere: Proverbial: Whiting N178.

113–17   Lounsbury notes (Sts. in Ch, 1:374) that the distinction of rhymes in -y and -ye here is of a type made only by Chaucer and Gower. (Cp's spelling does not reveal the distinction.)

115   astronomye: That is, astrology. Calchas's prediction is based on an oracle, on astrological calculation, on the casting of lots, and on augury with birds.

120–26   The reference to Phebus (Apollo) and Neptunus is not in the Filostrato. Benoît (Roman de Troie, 25920–23) says that Neptune built the walls of Troy, and Apollo consecrated them, but omits the refusal of Lameadoun (Laomedon) to pay their wages. Chaucer may have known this part of the story from Ovid (Met. 11.199–206); that Apollo raised the walls with his music was common knowledge (Her. 16.181–82). The story is first told in Iliad 21.441–57; for other accounts see pseudo-Hyginus, Fabulae 89 (ed. Bunte, 1857, 82); Servius, Comm. in Aeneida 2.610; Boccaccio, De gen. deorum 6.6; Bode, Scriptores rerum mythicarum 1:43–44, 138, 174.

138   Toas: Thoas is not mentioned in the Filostrato. Chaucer may follow Benoît (13079–120) or Guido (pp. 160–61); Guido's account is closer to Chaucer's. See 2.1699n.

143   parlement: Used in the English sense, though the Italian "parlamento" in the corresponding passage (Fil. 4.13; French "conseil," p. 202) apparently means "parley." Guido's term is "consilium."

169–210   Again Chaucer departs from the Filostrato and follows Benoît and Guido. The speech of Hector may derive from Benoît's account of his protest against the truce with the Greeks (Roman 12965–98), developing the idea presented in Tr 1.106–26 that Hector is Criseyde's special protector, and the popular outcry it causes recalls Guido's account of the outburst against Calchas when he asked for his daughter (p. 161). But in Guido's Historia, the Trojans opposed the surrender of Briseida and were overruled by Priam; in Chaucer the Trojans urge the exchange of Criseyde for Antenor. For a detailed comparison of the different versions, see Brown, MLN 26:208–11. Brown suggests that Chaucer's lines condemning the noyse of peple (183–201) allude to the Peasant's Revolt of 1381, and that the phrase blase of straw alludes to Jack Straw (see introductory note for details, and see the essays by Tatlock and McCall and by Rudisill referred to there). A. M. Taylor's suggestion that the parlement is modeled on the trial of Jesus before Pilate cannot be admitted (Nottingham Med. Sts. 24, 1980, 51–56).

183   noyse of peple: Perhaps a satiric reference to the familiar phrase, "vox populi vox Dei" (the voice of the people is the voice of God); see Brennan, ELN 17, 1979,

15–18. See Whiting V54 and Hassell V140, citing a French version from Gower. MS H[4] bears the marginal gloss, "Vox populi in oppositum" (the voice of the people in opposition). Chaucer's tone here resembles that of ClT IV.995–1001; cf. Bo 4.m5.31–33. Distrust of popular opinion as mob unreason (as well as "vox populi vox Dei") was conventional. For many examples, see George Boas, Vox Populi, 1969. Comparing the estates of a city with the parts of a man, Peter the Chanter connects the common people with tumultuous thoughts ("plebs," "tumultuose cogitationes") in his Distinctiones Abel, s.v. In civitate est.

197–201   From Juvenal, Sat. 10.2–4; see Walther 20873.

200   See Bo 3.m11.10.

202–6   The treason of Antenor—his contriving to remove the Palladium, on which depended the preservation of Troy (see 1.153n.)—does not appear in the Filostrato. See Benoît, Roman de Troie, 24397–5713; Guido, p. 228–29.

210   here and howne: "The master and the members of his household alike," that is, "one and all." MED accepts this explanation, made by Smithers, Eng. and Germanic Sts. 3, 1949–50, 74–77. Brennan (ELN 17, 1979, 15–18), unaware of Smithers's study, takes here as "host" from OE here, but Smithers shows that a ME word here is attested as meaning "lord, master of a household." Howne, they agree, is cognate with OE hiwa, plural hiwan (servant), perhaps (Smithers) influenced by Middle Dutch huwen (members of a household). Brennan surveys earlier, less likely explanations.

225–27   From Dante, Inf. 3.112–14, itself based on Aen. 6.309–12. Schless argues against specific recollection of Dante here, but the verbal parallels are conclusive.

229   bark: Although Ch uses the form barge, the related word bark (= barque) meaning "ship," is not recorded by MED before 1420, and is unlikely here. MED glosses the word here, from an extension of the sense of treebark as a covering, as "shroud (of care)," but it is better to take it as simply the bark of a tree, developing the simile of 225–28 into a metaphor. For humans locked in trees, see 3.726 and n.; 4.1139 and note 4.1135–41; Aen. 3.22–48; Dante, Inf. 13; Ovid, Met. 2.358–66. Metamorphosis into a tree is frequently associated with grief.

236–37   Kökeritz notes the play on brest . . . Out breste (PMLA 69:950).

239–42   The simile, from Fil. 4.27, goes back to Dante, Inf. 12.22–24, itself from Aen. 2.222–24.

251–52   See 3.1423 and n., ClT IV.902–3; Job 3.3. For the adjectival use of the genitive lyves, see KnT I.1912n.

271–72   Troilus defines himself as "tragic" by the Monk's definition: ProMkT VII.1973–77.

279   combre-world: Chaucer may have in mind passages in Statius about the living death of Oedipus (and cf. the Old Man in The Pardoner's Tale): Theb. 1.46–48; 11.580–82; 11.698, "patriae quantum miser incubo terrae" (how wretched[ly] I encumber my native earth). The comparison to Oedipus becomes explicit in line 300.

298   Allone . . . born: See KnT I.1633, WBPro III.885.

300   Edippe: Oedipus blinded himself on learning that he had killed his father and married his mother. See

Theb. 1.46–48; Roman de Thèbes 497–500; Tes. 10.96.

305   unneste: Glossed correctly in MSS H¹ S¹ D: "go out of thi nest."

312   Stonden for naught: "Be worth nothing," perhaps with a pun (see Kornbluth, N&Q 204, 1959, 243) on *naught* as zero, shaped like an eye. Cf. Purg. 23.32, in which the letter *o* is compared with an eye.

313 For the form of the expression, see 5.546, and on the force of the postponed relative clause, see Roscow, Syntax and Style, 106.

316   sovereigne: Cf. LGW F 94, 275.

323–29 Perhaps recalling Ovid's epitaph as a lover (Tristia 3.3.73–76) by way of Tes. 11.91. The reference to Troilus's sepulchre may be due to Filocolo 1.266.

356–57 Cf. Fil. 4.43.8; 357 is nearly identical to MLT II.609.

386–92 See Bo 2.pr2.9–14, 84–86; RR 8023–26. **Swich is this world:** cf. Tr 5.1434, 1748. On the **yiftes** of Fortune, see IntrPardT VI.295 and n.

406 Cf. the sentiment of the goose, PF 567.

407–12 Cf. Ovid, Amores 2.4.9–48.

413   ryvere: Either "the sport of hawking" or "water-fowl." Since a **heroner** is a falcon (trained to strike herons), and a heron is a water-fowl, the distinction is not clear. See Thop VII.737n.

414–15 Boccaccio merely records line 415 as what he often has heard tell ("come io udii già sovente dire"; Fil. 4.49) without naming an author. The ultimate source of the line seems to be Ovid, Rem. amoris, 462: "Successore novo vincitur omnis amor" (every love is conquered by a new successor); cf. Rem. amoris, 484. Although Ovid's line circulated independently as a proverb in the Middle Ages (Walther 30604; Whiting L547), Chaucer probably knew it directly from Ovid: the passage in Ovid goes on to speak of the Homeric story of Chryseis, Briseis, Achilles, and Calchas; for Chaucer's possible use of the immediately preceding line 461 in the Remedia, see Tr 1.760. Kreuzer (N&Q 202, 1957, 237) notes a form of the maxim that is closer to Boccaccio's line in Andreas Capellanus's De amore, Rule 17: "Novus amor veterem compellit abire" (a new love forces the old to leave). Kittredge collects further reminiscences in this passage of Ovid's Remedia (Harv. Sts. in Class. Philol. 28, 1917, 70).

Zanzis (MS variants: Zansis, Zauzis, Zauzius, Zenes) has not been identified. Chaucer may have meant "Zeuxis," because in The Physician's Tale (VI.16) he seems to refer to the famous Greek painter Zeuxis as *Zanzis.* Kittredge suggested (as above) that Chaucer had in mind the wise courtier Zeuxis in the Alexander story, as reported in Julius Valerius 1.9 (ed. Kübler, 1888). Fry proposes that Chaucer meant the painter Zeuxis, who according to Cicero (De inv. 2.1; see RR 16155–70) assembled the best features of a number of maidens in order to achieve a likeness of Helen—a notion that faintly recalls lines at 4.407–13, the division of virtues among women (ELN 9, 1971, 81–85). Neither suggestion is convincing. Until a more likely Zanzis is discovered, it is best to assume that Chaucer made up the name of an authority (cf. "Lollius"), knowing his actual source was Ovid by way of Boccaccio, and avoiding anachronism.

416 Probably also proverbial. Kittredge, in a letter to Robinson, referred to Cicero, Pro lege Manilia 20:

"Semper ad novos casus temporum novorum consiliorum rationes adcommodasse" (Always to have fit to the new happenings of the times the plans of new counsels). Cf. Mel VII.1225n.

418–24 That time and absence cause love's decline are sentiments uttered by Troiolo, not Pandaro, in the Filostrato (4.59).

421–27 See Whiting S307. Lines 423–24 expand the proverb, "Seldom seen, soon forgotten" (Whiting S130).

428–31 Cf. 1.561–64.

432–34 The echo of RR 4640–41 (Rom 5151–52) suggests that Chaucer associates Pandarus with the figure Reason (see introductory note on Pandarus). The expression "in one ear and out the other" was probably already proverbial, although Whiting (E4) cites no earlier instance in English. The "deaf ears" of a lover are known in antiquity (Propertius 2.16.35; Walther 31975).

460   raket: Surely "rackets," a form of tennis or handball played off walls, like squash (see MED). The OED wrongly deduces from a citation in Lydgate that it was a dice game.

461   Nettle in, dok out: The words are part of a charm for curing the sting of a nettle (N&Q 3, 1851, 133). While rubbing the wound with the juice of a dock-leaf, one repeats such words as "Nettle in, dock out, dock in, nettle out, / Nettle in, dock out, Dock rub nettle out." Other forms and references are given in Skeat's note (2:488). Usk quotes the charm and mentions the game of rackets (Test. of Love 1.2.166–67), obviously imitating Chaucer. See Whiting D288. **Now this, now that** and similar proverbial phrases (cf. Tr 2.811) often associated with mutability and Fortune (dozens of examples in Whiting N179) are examined by Brosnahan, Learned and Lewed, 11–18.

466 For the commonplace, see Bo 2.pr4.109–13; Seneca, Epist. 78.13.

473   Proserpyne: Queen of the underworld; see HF 1508–12n., MerT IV.2038–41n. She is not mentioned here by Boccaccio (Fil. 4.54).

477   for fyn: "Finally," or "to the conclusion," or perhaps best, "with this end in mind." MS H⁴ glosses the word "final" or "finale" (final *l* barred). That Troilus, having enjoyed Criseyde's love, might now more readily give her up was not the last of Pandarus's arguments (line 395).

482–83 See 3.1625–28 and n.

503–4 From Bo 1.m1.18–20.

514   at my requeste: Reflects "à ma requeste" of the French trans. of the Filostrato (p. 215); there is no corresponding phrase in the Italian.

519–20 The figure probably derives from RR 6382–83; cf. CYPro VIII.580.

530 Alternative punctuations of this line are possible.

548   ravysshyng of wommen: Telamon abducted Hesione of Troy, and in retaliation Paris abducted Helen of Greece. See Benoît, 2793–804, 3187–3650, 4059–68; Guido, pp. 42, 74–75.

554–55 These lines apparently refer to a possible marriage of Troilus and Criseyde. As such, they constitute an obstacle to the idea, independently proposed by John B. Maguire and Henry Ansgar Kelly, that Troilus and Criseyde had joined in a "clandestine marriage" of a kind condemned but considered valid by medieval canon law.

In a clandestine marriage the couple exchange wedding vows privately, without witnesses. The institution would be well known to Chaucer's audience because the queen mother, Joan of Kent, was involved in a celebrated case of clandestine marriage. See Maguire, ChR 8, 1974, 262–78 and, with much valuable information, Kelly, Love and Marriage, esp. 49–67, 163–242, and Viator 4, 1973, 435–57. The principal evidence supporting this view is the series of events in Book 3 drawn from the affair in the Filocolo (see 3.512–1190n.). There is no doubt that, probably influenced by the Filocolo, Chaucer made the affair more solemn, perhaps more like a marriage, than it was in the Filostrato. The path of love will naturally resemble marriage. The purpose of a clandestine marriage is to conceal the marriage from the community, but Kelly and Maguire cannot explain why Chaucer should conceal the marriage from his readers. Further, the tradition before and after Chaucer never took the lovers as married—in two English redactions of the Troy material that followed Chaucer, the Laud Troy Book (13555) and the Gest Hystoriale of the Destruction of Troy (9952–53), Criseyde specifically observes that she cannot marry Troilus (see Mieszkowski, Reputation, 113–14). See Wentersdorf, ChR 15, 1980, 101–26; Brewer, RES n.s. 28, 1977, 194–97; Wood, Elements of Tr, 189–90.

556   "This would constitute an accusation against her" as it would make public her affair with Troilus (so Fil. 4.69). In the following lines, Chaucer omits from Boccaccio a second motive for Priam's hypothetical refusal: that Criseyde is not a suitable match for Troilus, not being of royal blood.

575   In Boccaccio the clause corresponding to this line is spoken by Troiolo: "Thus weeping, I dwell (dimoro) in amorous wandering" (Fil. 4.70). Chaucer follows the French translation (p. 217) in giving the words to the narrator: "Ainsy plourant en amoureuse doubtance se demouroit en disant . . ." (Thus weeping he . . . dwelt in amorous uncertainty, saying . . .).

588   Cf. the proverbial "nine days' wonder" (Whiting W555), and the Latin "novendiale sacrum" (nine days' festival) often mentioned by Livy (see Lewis and Short's Latin Dict. s.v. *novendialis*). The glossator of MS H[4] quotes in Latin the proverb, "A wonder endured only nine days."

600–601   On this favorite commonplace ("Fortes Fortuna adiuvat"; Fortune helps the strong—Walther 9804), cited as "Audaces fortuna juvat etc." (Fortune helps the bold; Walther 1687–88) in the margin of MS H[4], see Thop VII.831–32n.; Whiting F519; Hassell F120; Patch, Goddess Fortuna, 83; cf. RvT I.4210. Virgil's unfinished line (Aen. 10.284) "audentis fortuna iuvat," variously supplemented, appears in Seneca (Epist. 94.28) with the addendum "piger ipse sibi obstat" (the sluggard hinders himself).

607   of ferd: Compare *for ferde,* Tr 1.557, 4.1411. See Mustanoja, NM 56, 1955, 174–77, and ME Syntax, 396–97, for evidence supporting the interpretation "because of being frightened."

608–9   Fil. 4.74 has, "Let her put up with it as Helen does."

618   Closer to KnT I.1163–68 than to Fil. 4.75. The source is Bo 3.m12.52–53, and the idea was proverbial; see KnT I.1163–64n.

622   "But boldly put everything at risk" is clearly the

meaning, but the precise origin of the phrase **on six and sevene,** presumably from the dicing game of hazard (see PardT VI.653), is uncertain. See OED s.v. *six* 5.; Root's note; Whiting S359; and Isaacs, AmN&Q 5, 1967, 85–86.

623   Boccaccio (Fil. 4.75) merely says, "Then the gods would have to aid us." Chaucer seems to derive his line from the French translation, "and the gods who saw your martyrdom [voustre martire] would come to your aid" (p. 218). Chaucer refers to the doctrine that a martyr's death ensures immediate entrance to heaven. See Rev. 7.14 and Harnack, Lehrbuch der Dogmengeschichte, 1894, 1:425ff. That a lover's death is martyrdom was a common conceit, part of the whole topic of the religion of love: see Rom 1875; Tr 4.818.

626   A proverbial comparison: Whiting D329.

627   Nearly repeated in KnT I.1010.

659–60   From Fil. 4.78; cf. HF 2088–2109; Ovid, Met. 12.54–55; Aen. 4.188.

661   with preste wynges: "Con prestissim' ale," Fil. 4.78, ultimately from Virgil's "pernicibus alis" (Aen. 4.180). See Walther 29481 for another use of Virgil's phrase. Cf. HF 1392 and n.

683   pitous joie: "Compassionate well-wishing" (pietosa allegrezza; Fil. 4.80), but with perhaps a hint of Schadenfreude.

684   Cf. LGW 741n.

707   For wo and wery: Probably "out of grief and weariness"; for the adjective *wery* after *for* cf. PF 93, and see Language and Versification, p. xxxix. Alternatively, putting a comma after *wo, wery* could be a second complement after *felte.*

728   The Italian has "itch" (prudea), not *ache* (Fil. 4.85).

736–56   On the order of stanzas, see textual notes 750–56.

737–38   The detail of the wringing of hands is not in the Filostrato; roughly parallel are Guido, p. 162 and Filocolo 1.176.

745   in corsed constellacioun: A bad nativity; Cf MLT II.302–8n.

754   he: Ungrammatically induced into the nominative (cf. 2.81). MS A, probably correcting, alone reads *hym.*

762   Argyve: Criseyde's mother is not named by Boccaccio, Benoît, or Guido. The name *Argyve* (for Statius's Argia, Theb. 2.297) is used in 5.1509 for the wife of the Theban Polynices (there derived from a variant Argiva; see n.). Schibanoff's attempt (Spec 51, 1976, 647–58) to explain Chaucer's choice of a name from an etymology in pseudo-Fulgentius (Argia as "providence") fails for want of a plausible motive. Anderson (SAC 4:127–28) cannot support his conjecture that Criseyde's mother was the wife of Polynices.

765   Proverbial: see GP I.180n.

767–68   Cf. Bo 3.pr11.96–109.

770   Root cites Le Roux de Lincy, Prov. franç., 1859, 1:83: "Seiche racine de l'arbre la ruyne" (a dry root kills the tree). See also Whiting G453.

776   The image of unsheathing the soul from the breast may recall Dante's lines about the flaying of Marsyas (Par. 1.20–21), a passage Chaucer used in HF 1229–32.

782   ordre: Cf. 1.336–40 and n., 2.759. Chaucer has Criseyde wear black as a nun; Boccaccio's Criseida wore black as a widow (Fil. 4.90).

785–87   Cf. lines 470–76, KnT I.2768. Chaucer may

have in mind the joint damnation of Paolo and Francesca (Inf. 5).

788–91 Chaucer's idea of **Elisos** (Elysium), may be influenced by Dante, especially Inf. 4. Its definition as **feld of pite** may reflect Ovid's "arva piorum" (fields of the pious, the *pitous:* Met. 11.62, quoted in the margin of MS H⁴). There may be, further, an association of Elysos with the familiar "Kyrie eleison" (Lord have mercy upon us) of the liturgy: MS R reads *eleisos* in line 790. See Tatlock, MLN 29:97; Kittredge, Harv. Sts. in Class. Philol. 28:53, n. 10, and PMLA 24, 1909, 352, n. 14; and Root's note. Steadman (N&Q, n.s. 17, 1970, 470, and Disembodied Laughter, 41) has located medieval support for these interpretations in a Latin gloss on Lucan, Pharsalia 3.12 by Arnulf of Orleans (ed. Berthe M. Marti, 1958, 156): "*Elysian,* 'Eleison,' that is, 'to pity,' hence 'Elysian fields,' as it were 'fields of pity' (campi misericordie) where the pious (pii) rest, or *Elysian,* placed 'beyond injury' (extra lesionem)." Chaucer's phrase **out of peyne** may be connected with a gloss by Lactantius on Theb. 3.108–11, which speaks of Elysium as "extra lesionem": see Clogan, SP 61:599–615, and see the gloss by Arnulf quoted above. Witlieb finds possible sources for *feld of pite* and *out of peyne* in the Ovide moralisé, which speaks of the Champs Elisées as the place of repose of souls that have not deserved torment (Qui n'ont pas paine deservie; 14.830) and where Orpheus found his beloved among the piteous company (En la piteuse compaignie; 11.167): see N&Q 214, 1969, 250–51.

791 For the story of **Orpheus** who went to hell to rescue his wife **Erudice,** Eurydice, see Bo 3.m12 and n. In this poem, Boethius mentions a number of the infernal figures who appear in the latter books of Troilus.

813–19 Besides the corresponding passage in the Filostrato (4.96), Chaucer may have had in mind Guido's similar description (p. 163) or Filocolo 1.188.

829 **cause causyng:** The "causa causans" or primary cause in logic, as distinguished from a "causa causata" or secondary cause. MS H⁴ has the gloss, "Causa causans."

836 Ultimately from Prov. 14.13 (part of which is used as a gloss in MS H⁴), and proverbial (Whiting E80, J58, J61). See MLT II.421–22 and n., Bo 2.pr4.

841–47 In the Filostrato (4.97) and its French translation (p. 223–24) this stanza is spoken by Pandaro.

865 Cf. KnT I.1400–1401.

880 Root, following Fil. 4.102 (And how this is a harmful case for Troilus, "cosa molesta / A Troiolo"), plausibly takes **moleste** as a noun ("distress"; cf. Bo 3.pr9.103) and **Troilus** as the indirect object: "But how this situation causes injury to Troilus." Cf. 4.89, 487. Robinson's glossary indicates that he agrees with Root. MED (s.v. *molesten* v.) takes *moleste* (presumably with periphrastic *dooth,* rare, but see 2.54, 546; HF 1036; LGW 1288; Mustanoja, ME Syntax, 602–3; and Kerkhof, 86) as the infinitive: "does injure Troilus." SumT III.2092 and Tr 4.1618, 5.350 may similarly be construed in several ways, but see LGW 1728.

884 **into litel:** The phrase seems to be unique (MED s.v. *litel* noun 1b.[a]) and its construction is not clear; perhaps it should be *in to litel,* "it would have slain us both in too little (a time)." MS R reads *unto.*

918–38 With Pandarus's argument, cf. Filocolo 1.117–18 (Fil. 4.106–7).

927 **rather . . . of flat than egge:** Of a sword, that is,

rather of healing than wounding. For the conception, see SqT V.156–65 and 236–40 and n. Root notes a possible verbal echo in **Beth . . . cause** of Dante, Inf. 31.5, "esser cagione" (to be the cause), but Schless rejects the suggestion (Ch and Dante, 132–33).

934–38 In Fil. 4.107, Pandaro merely advises Criseida to control her own grief so as to be able to lighten Troilus's. Chaucer's Pandarus urges more positive action, and in line 1254 the advice is carried out (see Cummings, Indebtedness of Ch, 74). That "women are wise with brief deliberation" (cf. 4.1261–62) became proverbial after Chaucer (Whiting W531).

953–1085 The discussion of predestination derives from Bo 5.pr2 and pr3. It is not found in some MSS of Troilus, and this omission was taken by Root and most other scholars as primary evidence for the hypothesis that the manuscripts preserve stages of Chaucer's own revision of the poem (Root, Text. Trad., 216–21, and the intro. to his ed., lxxi–lxxii). But now see Windeatt's persuasive argument, seconded by Hanna (in Editing Ch, ed. Ruggiers, 191–205, 285–89), that the manuscript omissions are merely scribal (in Essays on Tr, 1–23). The stanzas that precede and follow the discussion (946–52, 1086–92) expand a single stanza of the Filostrato (4.109). Troilus's fatalistic conclusion and the appropriateness of the inclusion of his **argument** have been treated by Curry, PMLA 45, 1930, 129–68, and by Patch, JEGP 17:399–422; MLR 22, 1927, 384–88; and Spec 6:225–43. Troilus's argument closely follows that of Boethius, but he breaks off before presenting Boethius's defense of human free will. For a detailed comparison of the two passages, see Huber, NM 66, 1965, 120–25.

958 Apparently not proverbial until after Chaucer. Bennett, Ch at Oxford, 63n., observes the resemblance to Wyclif's "[nec] omnia que eveniunt de necessitate eveniunt" (not all things that come about come about from necessity).

968 For reference to such **grete clerkes** on the problem of predestination as Augustine, Boethius, and Bradwardine, see NPT VII.3241–42.

976 For the idiom see KnT I.1089n.

1009–10 The sense could rather be: "I labored, as it were (**I mene as though**), to inquire . . . ."

1027 Root in his note on this line calls it "probably the least poetical line that Chaucer ever wrote." Cf. PardT VI.648.

1029 **herkne:** Troilus or Chaucer has either forgotten the situation of soliloquy in the heat of the argument, or he deliberately adopts the Boethian dialogue form. Cf. *thyn* (1025), *the* (1030), etc.

1098 See 2.1347 and n.

1105–6 Whiting (M157) cites Piers Plowman B 11.36: "A man may stoupe tyme ynogh whan he shal tyne (must lose) the crowne (top of his head)."

1116 **Juno** is not mentioned here in Fil. 4.111–12.

1128–1701 Writing of the parting of the lovers in the Filostrato, Boccaccio took over details from his own Filocolo, including Criseida's promise to return on the tenth day, a fact not in Benoît. See Young, Origin of Tr, 66–103.

1135–41 The simile is Chaucer's. **Ligne aloes,** the medicinal aloe, was, like gall, proverbially bitter (see Juvenal, Sat. 6.181; Walther 33629). On **Mirra** (Myrrha), the daughter of Cinyras, king of Cyprus, who was changed into a myrrh tree, see Ovid, Met. 10.298–502.

Lines 500–501 of the Ovid passage are quoted in the margin in MS H⁴. Wetherbee associates the activity of Myrrha's nurse with that of Pandarus (Ch and Poets, 98–100).

1142   hire woful weri goostes: Apparently the souls of the lovers, whereas the Filostrato (4.116) has "gli spiriti affannati" (the exhausted spirits), meaning "spirits" in the physiological sense (see KnT I.2743–56n.).

1159 Fil. 4.117 reads "E gli occhi suoi velati" (and her eyes veiled, that is, closed). Root suggests that Chaucer's copy may have read "levati," cast up.

1166 To sing **weylaway** is proverbial: Whiting S469.

1174 Similar to GP I.301; not in the Filostrato.

1188 **Mynos:** Boccaccio does not mention Minos at this point. Chaucer may have in mind Dante's Minos, judge of carnal sinners (Inf. 5.4–6) and suicides (Inf. 13.94–96), or the pagan judge of the dead described in the classical authors (e.g., Aen. 6.431–33; Claudian, De raptu 2.332), or both combined. See Schless, Ch and Dante, 133–35.

1216 **Cipride:** Venus; the island Cyprus was sacred to Venus. Cf. 5.208 and PF 277.

1223–25 Chaucer may use the French translation of the Filostrato here, finding words—"ses yeulx" (her eyes) and "nue" (bare)—that have no counterpart in the Filostrato (p. 230; Fil. 4.125).

1237 **a forlong wey:** See MilT I.3637n.

1283 Chaucer repeatedly uses this proverb (Whiting T307): 3.896; HF 1257–58; ProMLT II.27–28 (see II.20–31n.); and see Rom 5123–24 (RR 4623–24); Ovid, Ars Am. 3.64: "Nor can the hour that has passed return." Wenzel cites instances (including a pair in John Bromyard's *Summa praedicantium*) of the Latin proverb (Walther 4893): "I weep for the loss of things, but I weep more for the loss of days" (SP 73:146).

1305–6 For the sentiment, see RR 2601–2 (Rom 2740–42).

1356 On the familiar comparison, see 2.193n.

1369 See RvPro I.3883–85n.; and Whiting C490.

1373–74 Apparently proverbial, meaning one cannot have it both ways, or have one's cake and eat it too, but not recorded elsewhere (Whiting W444). See Skeat, E. E. Proverbs, 81, for similar sayings.

1397–98, 1404–11 The passages about the gods have no exact counterpart in the Filostrato. Closer parallels are in Benoît (13768–73), and closer still in Guido (p. 165). Benoît and Guido represent Briseida as making such reproaches to her father; in Chaucer she intends to do so, but in fact is *muwet, milde, and mansuete* when she meets Calchas (5.194), as she is in the Filostrato (5.14.3). A possible source of her skepticism (Wise, Infl. of Statius, 16–17) is the portrayal in the *Thebaid* of Capaneus as "superum contemptor" (contemptuous of the gods). See Theb. 3.611–18, 648–69; 9.550, etc. Capaneus's presumption is elaborated by Gower, Conf. Aman. 1.1980–90. On the whole passage see apRoberts, MLN 57, 1942, 92–97.

1404 **beren hym on honde:** Cf. WBPro III.232n., MLT II.620n.

1406 **amphibologies:** From Latin *amphibologia,* a corruption of "amphibolia," a term used of the ambiguous utterances of oracles by Isidore, Etym. 1.34.13, Cicero, De div. 2.56, and Alexander de Villa Dei, Doctrinale (ed. D. Reichling, MGP 12, 1893), 2399–2403.

1408 The marginal gloss in MS H⁴, "Timor invenit

deos," may record the exact words of Chaucer's source. These words may be found in the Third Vatican Mythographer (Albericus of London?), ed. Bode, 1834, 152. Whiting (D385) finds no citation of **drede fond first goddes** before Chaucer. The statement in Latin was proverbial: in the form "Primus in orbe deos fecit timor" (fear first made gods in the world) it was early attributed to Petronius (ed. Buecheler, 1922, no. 27), and quoted by Statius (Theb. 3.661). In various forms it is quoted by pseudo-Fulgentius, Mitol. 1.32 (ed. Helm, 1898, 17); Peter the Chanter, Verbum abbrev., cap. 93 (PL 205:271); Holcot, Super libros sapientiae, lect. 164 (Reuthlingen, 1498, fol. H 3 recto); as from Virgil by Johannes de Alta Silva, Dolopathos (ed. Hilka, Heidelberg, 1913, p. 103, line 9); Servius, Comm. in Aen. 2.715 (quoting Statius). See Walther 22405. Robinson cites further variations of the theme from Lucretius, Cicero, Juvenal (Sat. 10.365), Orosius, Diogenes Laertius, Lucan (Pharsalia 1.486); see also Kittredge, MP 7, 1909–10, 480; Wise, Infl. of Statius, 18. See Minnis, Ch and Pagan, 39, 84–93.

1411 Benoît, Roman de Troie, 5817–5927, reports that Calchas, sent to Delphi by the Trojans, there met Achilles, who was consulting the oracle on behalf of the Greeks. When the oracle warned of the fall of Troy, Calchas went over to the Greeks. See 1.68–70n. On the form **Delphos,** see FranT V.1077n.

1415–21 The narrator's protestations of Criseyde's sincerity are not paralleled at this point in Boccaccio; but see Fil. 5.7, and Tr 5.19–21, and cf. Benoît, 13495–97, Guido, p. 163.

1453–54 The bear and his leader are of different opinions (Whiting B101). Hassell (A147) gives: "Un pense l'âne et autre l'ânier" (the ass thinks one thing, its leader another).

1456 A variant of the same proverb occurs in KnT I.2449 (see note).

1457–58 Proverbial (Whiting H50). Cf. "Il ne faut point clochier devant boiteux" (one ought not limp before a cripple), Hassell B127.

1459 On Argus's reputation as cunning and deceptive, see Ovid, Ars Am. 616–18; Whiting A180; Walther 1374 and Index, s.v. *Argus;* Hoffman, N&Q 210, 1965, 213–16, citing medieval mythographers; and Schoanoff, Spec 51:647–58. For the idea that women can trick even Argus, see WBPro III.357–61 and note III.357–60; MerT IV.2111–13; and the fabliau La bourgoise d'Orliens: "Woman has even surpassed Argus. By their wiles [engin] they have deceived wise men since the time of Abel" (ed. Montaiglon and Raynaud 1:120). Spenser writes, "For who wotes not, that womans subtiltyes / Can guilen *Argus,* when she list misdonne?" (FQ 3.9.7).

1478–82 Chaucer seems here to use Benoît (13803–9) and Guido (p. 166) as well as the Filostrato (4.142).

1505 MS H⁴ has, in Latin, the gloss, "It is not good to lose the substance for an accident." On the philosophical distinction between substance and accident, see PardT VI.538–39n. Troilus plays on other meanings of the terms: **accident** as "uncertainty" as opposed to *sikernesse* (4.1512); **substaunce** as "possessions," wealth" (4.1513, OED s.v. *substance* 16.).

1538–40 **Athamante:** Juno, angry with Thebes, crossed the Styx to persuade Tisiphone (see 1.1–14n.) to haunt Athamas and drive him mad. Chaucer may have recalled the story from Ovid (Met. 4.416–562) and from

Dante (Inf. 30.1–12) where Atamante appears among the falsifiers. On Juno and Athamante, see Fyler, Res Publ. Litt. 7, 1984, 79–82. **Stix** as the **put of helle** rather than a river or marsh is a medieval notion: see Spencer, Spec 2: 180–81; Dante calls it a "palude," a marsh (Inf. 7.106). See Schless, Ch and Dante, 136–37.

1541–45   From Met. 1.192–93. Cf. also Theb. 6.112–13.

1546   See 4.1208.

1548   Probably recalling Ovid, Amores 1.15.10: "dum rapidas Simois in mare volvet aquas" (as long as Simois will roll its swift waters to the sea). On the geographical inaccuracy, see Magoun, MS 15, 1953, 129.

1551–54   Another example of adynaton (see 3.1495–98n. and the studies cited there), this one from Met. 13.324: "ante retro Simois fluet" (sooner will Simois run backward—than the cunning of stupid Ajax be useful to the Greeks). The application of the "impossible" to treachery in love is closest to Ovid, Her. 5.29–30: if Paris can continue to breathe, having abandoned Oenone (see Tr 1.659–65n.), the water of the Xanthus will run back to its source (repeated in RR 13225–28). See also Theb. 7.553.

1560–61   Cf. 2.468–69 and n.

1562   **take:** Perhaps "take place" (so, doubtfully, OED *take* 27.b.) or perhaps some such sense as "take root, take effect" (OED 6., 15th cent.; 11., 17th cent.).

1568   Proverbial: Whiting M97, R32, H157–68. Cf. 1.956.

1584   Another proverb: "Qui patitur, vincit" (who suffers, conquers; Walther 24454). See FranT V.774–75 and note V.773–76; ParsT X.661 and n.; Rom 2775 and n.; Whiting S865, P61; Hazelton, Spec 35, 1960, 367–68 (pseudo-Cato).

1585   Proverbial; Whiting L233. Baugh and Donaldson (MLN 76, 1961, 1–4, 4–5) demolished Evans's proposal (MLN 74, 1959, 584–87) that **lief** here means "life," alluding to Matt. 10.39.

1586   Proverbial; see KnT I.3041–42 and n.

1590–95   The *chronographia* (see 1.155–58n.) here is, as usual, Chaucer's addition to his source. Before the sister of the sun (**Phebus**), Lucina (the moon; cf. FranT V.1045), pass out of the zodiacal sign Aries (**Ariete**), in which it is now, and through the three intermediate signs (Taurus, Gemini, Cancer), and beyond Leo (**the Leoun**), she will see him. This is more than one-third of the circuit of the skies made by the moon every twenty-eight days; hence, Criseyde says she will return on the *tenthe day* (1595); see 5.650–57, 1018.

1597–1603   Erzgräber (see 4.1–11n.) suggests that Troilus's many monosyllables here and in 1654–59 below signify his simple integrity.

1608   **Cinthia:** Criseyde swears by the emblem of fickleness.

1628   Proverbial. See Whiting H413, and for the sentiment cf. WBPro III.357–61, MancT IX.148–53, FranT V.768.

1645   For the proverb, see Ovid, Her. 1.12; Whiting L517; Walther 26666.

1667–82   The corresponding passage in the Filostrato (4.164–66) is spoken by Troiolo to Criseida.

1677   **poeplissh:** "Popolesco" (Fil. 4.165).

1695–96   A common formula: cf. 5.445, 1321; MerT IV.1341; Rom 3183. The fuller form here may be influenced by 1 Cor. 2.9.

BOOK V

1   Tes. 9.1.1: "Già s'appressava il doloroso fato" (Now approached the dolorous fate).

2   The Fates are subject to Jupiter: see Bo 4.pr6; Statius, Theb. 1.212–13; KnT I.1663–65.

3   **Parcas:** The Latin accusative or an anglicization of "Parcae," the Fates. The **sustren thre** are Clotho, who spins, Lachesis, who apportions, and Atropos, who cuts the thread of life. See RR 19768–75; Purg. 25.79; 21.25; Tes. 10.32—but the lore was common knowledge. See also 3.733–34, 4.1208, 1546. Chaucer here has Lachesis spin; the three functions were often confused.

8–11   From Tes. 2.1; cf. also Theb. 4.1–3. For such definitions of time, see Tr 1.155–58n. For **gold-tressed** MS H² has "Auricomus tressed," incorporating a gloss; MS H⁴ glosses "goldetressed" with "auricomus." The Latin adjective is applied to the sun in Valerius Flaccus, Argonauticon 4.92, and in Martianus Capella, De nupt. 1.12. Still closer, Phoebus himself is called "auricomus" in a distich cited by Walther (20109) from the Deliciae cleri (ed. Huemer, Roman. Forsch. 2, 1885, lines 264–65).

22–26   The *a*-rhymes are long open *o*'s from OE long *a*; the *b*-rhymes are long open *o*'s lengthened in open syllables from original short *o*'s (see Richard Jordan, Handbuch, sect. 35.3, trans. Eugene J. Crook, 1974, 61). Their sounds must have differed slightly, as Chaucer seldom rhymes them together (see Skeat 6:xxxi–xxxiv). The preceding stanza exemplifies the distinction of open and close *e* in rhyme.

25   **crop and more:** Cf. 2.348.

67   **valeye:** A mistranslation of "vallo" (rampart; Fil. 5.10). Neither word appears in the French translation.

88–175   Diomede's conversation with Criseyde has some basis in Fil. 6.10–12, 14–25, but it shows the influence of Benoît, 13529–712. In Benoît, Diomede is said to have a wife, Aigale, at home in Greece.

90   **by the reyne hire hente:** Chaucer may have mistranslated the Italian (5.13) "di colei si piglia" (idiomatic for "he takes a fancy to her") as Rossetti suggested (p. 235), but Sundwall, following Meech, persuasively argues that Chaucer here follows Benoît, 13529: "E li fiz Tydeus l'en meine" (and the son of Tydeus—Diomede—leads her), influenced by other lines in Benoît, such as 13425: "Troïlus a sa regne prise" (Troilus seized her rein), and three other such expressions (ChR 11, 1976, 156–63). The French translator of Fil. also mistranslates here, but not as Chaucer does. The detail was adopted in the Alliterative Destruction of Troy (ed. Panton and Donaldson, EETS 39, 56, 1869, 1874): "He (Diomede) rode to that Riall (Breisaid), and the Reyne toke" (8078). For this and an instance in Lydgate, see Sundwall, RES 26, 1975, 313–17. See also Anel 183–84.

98   The proverbial expression is not recorded in English before Chaucer (Whiting F437).

101   **make it tough:** See 2.1025n.

106   **koude his good:** See EpiMLT II.1169 and n., Tr 2.1178n.

113–16   Cf. Roman de Troie 13596–610.

155–58   See Roman de Troie, 13591–96.

158   **As paramours:** See KnT I.1155, 2112; Tr 2.236, 5.332.

164–65 See Roman de Troie, 13552–55.

176–92 Apparently influenced by passages in Benoît: 13617–18, 13637–40, 13676–78, 13713ff. See also Guido, pp. 164–65.

208 For the association of the gods of food, drink, and love, see PF 275–77 and note 275–76.

212 Ixion: See Aen. 6.601; Met. 4.461. Patch, Goddess Fortuna, 167, notes the medieval association of Ixion's and Fortune's wheels.

223–24 Boccaccio here (Fil. 5.20) may echo Ovid, Her. 10.12. See LGW 2186.

228–29 Cf. the apostrophes in Fil. 5.24.

270 The narrator's address specifically to a **redere**, unique in Chaucer (cf. PF 132), may reflect a characteristic usage of Dante: see, e.g., Inf. 8.94, 25.46, 34.23; Par. 5.109, 10.7; and Lüdeke, Funktionen des Erzählers, 95.

274–78 Closely following Tes. 7.94; see also Bo 2.m3.1–5 and Theb. 12.1–4.

280–322 This passage combines material in Fil. 5.22–23 with details from the account of Arcite's death in the Teseida (cf. 1807–27 and n. below). Chaucer may also have had in mind the pyre and funeral games of Archemorus in Theb. 6 (see 5.1499). For various parallels, some slight, see Tes. 7.4, 27 ("palestral gioco," athletic contest of the kind held at funerals in ancient times); 10.37, 89, 93–98; 11.13, 14, 35, 50, 52–62 (58: "urna d'oro," urn of gold), 69, 70. See also the corresponding episode in KnT I.2809–2966.

281 **This Pandare:** For the construction, see GP I.175n.

295 A marginal gloss in MS R, "The testament of Troilus," and similar glosses in MSS S¹ S², draw attention to Chaucer's use here of a common topic in medieval literature; MS H⁴ has "testamentum t." by line 306.

319 The owl *prophete is of wo and of myschaunce* (LGW 2254, see PF 343n.). The name **Escaphilo** derives from Ascalaphus, whom Proserpine changed into an owl, "the harbinger of imminent grief." See Ovid, Met. 5.539–50, 6.431–32, 10.453, 15.791. MS H⁴ in a gloss refers (wrongly) to Met. 2. On Chaucer's use of such Italianate forms as the spelling here (the name is not in Fil.), see MkT VII.2345n.

321–22 Mercury is traditionally the guide of souls (psychopomp). See 5.1827; Tes. 10.90.

332 **paramours:** "With passion"; see 5.158n.

343 Proverbial: Whiting F639.

350 Perhaps proverbial (Whiting T300); Usk takes it from Chaucer (135, 94–96).

358–85 Pandarus derogates Troilus's dream as a mere "somnium naturale," a physiologically induced fantasy, in this case caused by the melancholic humor. Chaucer expands on Boccaccio (Fil. 5.32) on a favorite topic: see NPT VII.2922n. and BD 1–15n. In Albert von Stade's Troilus 3.363–64, Hector expresses the familiar skeptical attitude: "Trust not dreams, says Hector, they know how to deceive; in this matter none should confide" (ed. Th. Merzdorf, 1875, 83). Hector was quoting Cato (2.71), and he was wrong. See Walther 30025b, 30026–28a, Whiting D387, Hassell S106. Root cites similar dream-lore from Albertus Magnus, Vincent of Beauvais, and John of Salisbury (see HF 1–52n.). Hazelton finds that Chaucer need not have used abstruse sources: many of his notions about dreams, found ultimately in the fourth book of Gregory the Great's *Dialogues,* are quoted

from Gregory in school commentaries on Cato's *Distichs* (Spec 35:357–80).

365–68 Besides Fil. 5.32, see RR 18509–12.

372 **impressiouns:** Cf. HF 39, SqT V.371. See also PF 99–105.

376 On the belief that dreams vary with the seasons, Curry (Ch and Science, 211) cites Vincent of Beauvais, Spec. nat. 26.63.

379–85 A resemblance to a passage in Mandeville's *Travels* (EETS 153, 110–11) noted by Lange, Archiv 174, 1938, 79–81, seems too slight to prove that Chaucer drew from it.

379 On **Wel worthe,** see HF 53n.; on the generalizing **thise,** see KnT I.1531 and Language and Versification, p. xxiv.

403 **Sarpedoun:** Boccaccio (5.38–49) omits explaining how he returned to Troy soon after his imprisonment; Chaucer, following Benoît and Guido, avoided the problem (see 4.50–54n.).

425 Proverbial; cf. KnT I.2437n.

430–31 In the Filostrato (5.38) Troiolo suggests a visit to Sarpedon's; Chaucer follows the French translation (p. 251) in attributing the suggestion to Pandarus.

445 See 4.1695–96 and n.

460 **of his herte . . . the keye:** A familiar figure. See Anel 323–24; RR 1991–2010 (Rom 2080–2100); Machaut, Livre du voir dit 3883–3900. Chaucer follows Fil. 5.43.

469 For the figure of the glass hood, see 2.867 and n.; Whiting H624.

484–85 A man who borrows hot coals to start his fire must hurry home with them. See Whiting F201.

505 **Ye, haselwode:** See 3.890 and n., 5.1174

523 **palais:** Boccaccio calls Criseida's house "casa" or "magione" (house). The French translator has "hostel, ostel," dwelling (and calls Troilus's home a "palaiz"), p. 255. Young (Origin of Tr, 172) suggests the influence of the term for Biancofiore's dwelling, "palagio," in the Filocolo. Cf. 5.528, *hous;* 2.1094 *paleis.*

540–53 The address to the palace, from the Filostrato (5.53), draws from a traditional topic, the "paraclausithyron" (apostrophe at the door): see Bloomfield (NM 73, 1972, 15–24) citing a fourteenth-century example from Holcot's Comm. on the Book of Wisdom, and many classical examples.

543 Frost rightly argues against reading a pun in **queynt,** Yale Rev. 66, 1977, 551–61; see MilT I.3276n.

549 The figure of the gemless ring, not in the Filostrato, perhaps recalls Dante, Purg. 23.31, but Schless (Ch and Dante, 138–39) rightly doubts the allusion. See 2.344n.

551–52 The kissing of the doors is not in the Filostrato, but occurs in Filocolo 1.124 and RR 2538; cf. Rom 2673–76 and n.

561–81 Troilus's ride about Troy is based on Fil. 5.54–55, itself reflecting the experiences Boccaccio describes in the Proem to the Filostrato. See also Filocolo 1.120, 263. Filostrato 5.54–55 may draw on Petrarch's Sonnet 112: see Wilkins, ELH 16, 1949, 167–73.

589–93 Troilus seems to wish Cupid will change from an Old Testament to a New Testament god (Hatcher, ELH 40, 1973, 307–24).

601 On the fury of Juno against Thebes, see Anel 51n. There may be an echo here of Dante, Inf. 30.1–2.

641 The figure of a voyage may be due (Rossetti) to a

misreading of Fil. 5.62: "disii porto di morte" (I carry desires of death). Chaucer could have taken "porto" for the noun, "port, harbor." The phrase is properly translated by the French translator. In developing the figure Chaucer may recall another passage, Fil. 4.143 (Patch, MLN 70:11–12).

644 **Caribdis:** Cf. Rom 4713; Aen. 3.420, 558; Met. 14.75.

655–56 All the MSS read "Lat(h)ona," which Caxton and Thynne emended to "Lucyna," perhaps correctly (see 4.1591). Scribes could easily confuse the words, and Chaucer shows elsewhere knowledge of Lucina. See KnT I.2085. Virgil and Ovid speak of the moon as "Latonia" (Aen. 9.405, 11.534; Met. 1.696, 8.394), and it is possible that the error is Chaucer's. In Dante it is clear that Latona is Diana's (the moon's) mother (Par. 29.1, 10.67–69, etc.): see Smyser, Spec 45:359–73. MS H⁴ glosses (in Latin), "Latona, that is, the moon"; MS S² has this confused gloss: "Latona is the sign of Virgo (signum virginis) when the sun or moon is in Virgo." A zodiacal sign has no **spere,** unless the sphere of all the fixed stars is meant. Or could the glossator mean "sign of a virgin"?

664–65 Chaucer tells the Phaeton story in HF 940–56, following Ovid, Met. 2, referred to in a gloss in MS H⁴.

671–79 The conceit of the wind blown from the beloved is from Fil. 5.70; see also the Proem to the Filostrato 19, 14–16 (ed. Branca); Filocolo 1.120; Tes. 4.32. Griffin, ed. Fil., intro., 68, compares the same conceit in a poem by the troubador Bernart de Ventadorn, 37:1 (ed. C. Appel, 1915, 212).

741–42 Proverbial: Root cites from Düringsfeld (Sprichwörter, 2, no. 122) an Italian version, "Dopo la morte non val medicina" (Medicine is worthless after death). See Whiting L168 and C51, Hassell M105; and KnT I.2759–60.

744–49 Chaucer probably derived the figure of the three-eyed Prudence from Dante, Purg. 29.130–32, and the early commentaries that identified Dante's figure as Prudence. For the idea that the faculty of prudence regards past, present, and future, see also Cicero, De inv. 2.53; Thomas Aquinas, Summa theol. 1–2.57.6; Dante's Convivio, 4.27.5; and pseudo-Seneca (Martinus Dumiensis), Formula honestae vitae, 1, quoted by Albertanus, Liber cons., 57–58 (in a passage omitted by Chaucer's Melibee and the French source). See Tatlock, MP 3:367–72. Saint Ambrose speaks of "sapientia" as interpreter of past, present, and future (PL 14:492); at the end of Boccaccio's *Decameron,* the human mind is said to consist not only of memory of the past and knowledge of the present, but also the greatest mental power, foresight of the future ("antiveder le future"): ed. Branca, 1234. Further references are collected by Schless, Ch and Dante, 141, nn. 75 and 76, and Matthews, NM 82, 1981, 211–13. For illustrations of three-eyed Prudence in Dante manuscripts, see Baugh's note and Matthews, ELN 13, 1976, 249–55; further see Seznec, Survival of Pagan Gods, 119–21 and fig. 40.

748 MED supports Jefferson's contention (Ch and the Consolation, 140) that Chaucer first used the word **future** in English, translating Boethius (e.g., Bo 5.pr6.19–20, where he glosses the word as if readers would be unfamiliar with it, *tyme comynge*). The special use suggests that the composition of Troilus followed the composition of Boece.

757–61 With these lines, not from Fil., Root compares the proverb, "Tous se mêlent de donner des avis, un sot est celui qui les tous suit" (All throng to give advice; who follows all is a fool; Düringsfeld, Sprichwörter, 2, no. 235). See Whiting W629.

763 See the discussion of **suffisaunce** in Bo 3.pr2.90–94, and generally 3.pr2 and pr3.

777 The traditional metaphor is elaborated in Mars 237–43. See Hultin, AnM 9, 1968, 70–72; Wood, Ch and Stars, 157–58; Amsler, Allegorica 4, 1979, 301–8. It may be influenced by the apostolic "fishers of men" (Matt. 4.19, etc.); cf. Rom 7490, SumT III.1820.

784 Proverbial. See 2.807–8 and n.

790–91 The precise **bookes** that contain this sentiment have not been identified. For the idea, cf. Ovid, Ars Am. 1.361–62: "When hearts are blithe and not pinched with grief, they are accessible—then Love sneaks in with alluring art."

799–840 The series of portraits of the principal characters conforms to a standard literary type, especially the feature-by-feature description of ladies so common in medieval love poetry, as recommended by the rhetoricians (see BD 817–1040n.). For extended examples, see Rom 817–1302. Background studies of the topic include Curry, Middle Eng. Idea of Personal Beauty, 1916; Haselmeyer, PQ 17, 1938, 220–23, based on his Yale dissertation, Mediaeval Verse Portraiture (1937); Brewer, MLR 50, 1955, 257–69.

Portraits of Diomede, Briseis, and Troilus are included in the series of portraits of the principal figures of the Trojan War in Dares, Benoît, and Guido. Chaucer's primary source, however, as indicated by marginal quotations in MSS J and Gg and fully set forth by Root, MP 15:1–22, was the *Frigii Daretis Ylias* of Joseph of Exeter (see introductory note), itself based on Dares. On Joseph of Exeter, see Riddehough, JEGP 46, 1947, 254–59, and the full introduction in Ludwig Gompf's edition of the Ylias. Observing that nearly all medieval retellings of the Trojan story include a portrait-series, Haselmeyer takes Chaucer as acknowledging a familiar convention. Excerpts of Joseph of Exeter's descriptions of the principals of the war circulated separately (ed. Gompf, 51–55), and paintings of the figures are included in manuscripts of Guido (e.g., Hugo Buchthal, Historia Troiana, 1971, plates 46–47).

799–805 The portrait of Diomede is mainly based on Joseph's Ylias 4.124–27. Lines 804–5 probably reflect Filostrato 6.33 and 24. **heir . . . of Calydoigne** seems to be due to miscopying of Joseph's "heros" (4.349) as "heres": MS J has "Calidonius heres" in the margin. See also Magoun, MS 15, 1953, 117. Diomede's **tonge large** may derive from Virgil's description of Drances as "Largus opum et lingua melior," lavish of wealth, even more of tongue (Aen. 11.338): Frost, N&Q 224, 1979, 104–5.

806–26 The description of Criseyde conflates traditional material as represented in Benoît (5275–86) and Joseph (4.156–62). Lines 818–19 are due to a misreading of Joseph's line, "Diviciis forme certant insignia *morum,"* (her signs *of good character* vie with the wealth of her beauty), of which the last word is copied "amorum" (of loves) in the margin of MS J. Tr 1.281 may imply that Criseyde was tall (see note), following Boccaccio there; here her height is **mene** in agreement with Dares (ch. 13), Joseph, Benoît (5276), and Guido (p. 85).

809–12   The description of Criseyde's hair fortunately departs from Joseph: "nodatur in equos / Flavicies crinita sinus" (Root translates: her hairy yellowness is knotted in equal folds).

813–14   Dares, Joseph, Benoît, and Guido all mention Briseis's joined brows, but only the last two consider it a lak; Curry shows (p. 48, see 799–840 above) that in ancient Greece joined brows were signs of beauty and passion. Hanson, surveying the numerous studies of Criseyde's brows, adds evidence from medieval physiognomic treatises that joined brows were thought to signify sadness, or such traits as sagacity, vanity, cruelty, envy, etc. (N&Q 216, 1971, 285–86). In the romance Guillaume de Dole, 706–7, the separation of brows is a sign of beauty (cited by Fansler, Ch and RR, 91n.); cf. also Rom 544 and n. and the Court of Love, in Skeat 7:430.

817   The closest parallel to this striking line is Dante, Par. 18.21 "chè non pur ne' miei occhi è paradiso" (for not only in my eyes is paradise); see also Fil. 1.27.3–4, 28.8, and 4.100.3. See Cook, RomR 8, 1917, 226.

825   Criseyde's famous slydynge of corage reflects Benoît, 5286 ("mais sis corages li chanjot"; but her purpose/intention wavered in her), and Guido, p. 85 ("animi constantiam non servasset"; she had not kept constancy of mind). For an effort to pin down the sense of slydynge, see Elliott, Ch's Eng., 324–25, and cf. line 769, and 3.1732–34; also Bo 1.m5.34.

826   hire age: Briseis's age was twenty-one at the time of the rape of Helen, according to Dictys and the Greek tradition (Griffin, JEGP 7:32–52); the Latin tradition from Dares is silent. Stanley, E&S 29:84–106, says this line "makes me suspect she is on the wrong side of whatever age it was best to be on the right side of in the fourteenth century." Troilus, the youngest of Priam's and Hecuba's sons (Dares, Benoît), is called "puer" by Virgil (Aen. 1.475) and Joseph of Exeter (Ylias 4.62). The first Vatican Mythographer reports that "if he had reached twenty, Troy could not have been destroyed" (ed. Angelus Maius, 1831, 75). See Pauly-Wissowa, Real-Ency., s.v. Troilus, and on the ages of the principal characters, Steadman, MLN 72, 1957, 89–90; Brewer, SELit 1, 1972, 3–13; and the introductory note, on Pandarus.

827–40   Partly from Joseph, Ylias 4.61–64; cf. also Benoît, especially 5393–5446.

831   Trewe as stiel: A common simile: cf. MerT IV.2426n.

832   Oon of the beste: See Tr 3.781–82n.; Mustanoja (ME Syntax, 299) regards this example as a hybrid construction, both intensive and partitive in force; see Language and Versification, p. xxxviii.

837   Cf. Ylias 4.62–63: "nullique secundus / Audendo virtutis opus" (second to none in daring a deed of courage). See 2.158 and n. On durryng don (see MED) and its later development into the noun-phrase "derring-do," see Manzalaoui, N&Q 207, 1962, 369–70.

841   The same kind of absolute infinitive appears in LGW 1959.

842   Boccaccio (Fil. 6.9) puts this episode on the fourth, not tenth, day.

852   spices: Cf. SqT V.291–94 and n.

892   Manes: The gods of the lower world, sometimes conceived in antiquity as the spirits of the departed or abstractly as punishment (as in Aen. 6.743, where the

term is glossed by Servius "supplicia," torments). Wise (Infl. of Statius, 24) suggests that Chaucer represents the spirits of the Trojans as avengers, but Root's interpretation is better: "The Greeks will strike terror even to the deities of hell." For discussion of the various possibilities, especially of the influence of glossed MSS of the Thebaid, see Clogan, SP 61:599–615. Windeatt cites Gower, Conf. Aman. 5.1361–64, on Manes as gods of the dead.

897   ambages: From Fil. 6.17.3, "ambage." Cf. 4.1406 and n. For definitions of the underlying Latin term see Isidore, Etym. 2.20, and William Brito's Summa (ed. L. and B. Daly, 1975), s.v. Ambigo.

932   Tideus: See Fil. 6.24; Theb. 7.538; Tr 5.1485–1510 and n.

971   Orkades and Inde: The ends of the earth; see WBPro III.824n.

975   See 1.97.

994   The proverb "a few words to the wise suffice" (sapienti pauca) is not recorded in English until the fifteenth century (Whiting W588).

1000–1004   Chaucer seems here to combine Benoît (13677–79) and Guido (p. 164): "Amoris tui oblaciones ad presens nec repudio nec admitto" (I neither repudiate nor admit at present the offers of your love).

1010–11   Cf. Roman de Troie, 15053–56.

1013   The taking of the glove, not in the Filostrato, appears in Benoît (13709–11) and Guido (p. 165); in both sources the glove business and much of the love-talk occur earlier, on the initial ride from Troy to Calchas's tent—Chaucer has delayed Criseyde's progress in shifting her affections.

1016–19   Criseyde had promised (4.1590–96) to return before the moon passed out of Leo. North argues (RES n.s. 20:147) that the configuration of the heavens in these two passages and 5.8–13, 652–53 suits the ten-day period of 3–13 May 1388. But Chaucer may merely have set forth a likely configuration, and not a particular one for any special date.

1020   Signifer: A common Latin term for the zodiac (see Oxford Latin Dict.); for instances in medieval glosses, see Pratt, Spec 22, 1947, 419–29. MS H4 has the marginal gloss "Zodiacum."

1023–29   See Fil. 6.33.6–8; this sodeyn Diomede is Chaucer's (see Barney, ChR 16:18–30).

1030   gostly: "Devoutly, solemnly, religiously," hence "truly." See MED s.v. gostli adv., 3.(b). Or perhaps Chaucer means something like "figuratively," drawing attention to the affected similitude of morning and Diomede (cf. KnT I.2273).

1033–36   See Fil. 6.34.

1039   he . . . wan: That is, Diomede won the horse in battle. According to the account in Benoît (not in Fil.) 15079–172, Diomede presented the horse to Briseida, and then requested it back when he lost his own (only partially recounted by Guido, 169).

1040–43   The broche corresponds to the "fermaglio" that, in the Filostrato (8.8–10), Troiolo saw on a garment captured from Diomede; perhaps the brooch mentioned in 3.1370 (cf. 1661 and n., below). The pencel of hire sleve is due to Benoît, 15176–79.

1044–50   Corresponding to Benoît, 20202–28; cf. also Guido, pp. 197–98.

1054–85   Criseyde's soliloquy, not in Boccaccio or Guido, follows in part the soliloquy of Briseida, Roman de Troie 20238–340, which opens, "Henceforth no good will be written of me, nor any good song sung." So the Homeric Helen recognized she would be the subject of songs (Iliad. 6.357–58).

1062   "My bell shall be rung," that is, my story shall be a subject of gossip, my dishonor proclaimed: see Whiting B233. The prophecy of Criseyde's bad fame is fulfilled in later English poetry, but her reputation as the emblem of fickleness and treachery is due less to Chaucer than to his predecessors and successors, beginning with Benoît and developed by Henryson. See Rollins, PMLA 32, 1917, 383–429, and Mieszkowski, Reputation of Criseyde.

1071   Criseyde's pathetic avowal of *trouthe* to Diomede, at least, occurs also in Benoît, 20277–78.

1085   al shal passe: Proverbial; see Scog 41.

1086–88   Root finds that "the total elapsed time can hardly be less than two years" in Benoît, but Chaucer deliberately leaves us in doubt. See the studies of the time-scheme of Troilus mentioned in the introductory note.

1107   Cf. "laurigero . . . Phoebo" (laurel-wearing Phoebus), Ovid, Ars Am. 3.389. MS H⁴ has the Latin word in its margin; H² incorporates it in the text.

1109   The morning sun would naturally warm the sea to the east; it is further possible that Chaucer thought the sea lay to the east of Troy, as he has it in LGW 1423–28, derived from Guido, p. 7 (Pratt, MLN 61:541–43).

1110   Nysus doughter is Scylla, who was changed into the bird "ciris" (Met. 8.11–151; cf LGW 1904n.). Like Troilus, she stood on the wall of a besieged town (LGW 1908). Meech (PMLA 46:189) shows that Chaucer may have found the explanation of "ciris" as "lark" in a gloss or in the Ovide moralisé.

1162   fare-carte: A cart for driving outside the manor, presumably of a rude sort for farmers and inappropriate to convey Criseyde ('Espinasse, N&Q 221, 1976, 295–96; Mills, SN 40, 1968, 43–44). MSS H² H⁴ read "soory" for "fare." Or it may be that Troilus mistakes the cart itself, in the distance, for Criseyde. Fil. 7.8 has merely "carro," cart.

1174   In Fil. 7.10 Pandaro's incredulity is differently expressed: "From Mongibello the fellow expects the wind!" With Chaucer's phrase cf. line 505. It seems to mean, "Your happiness will come from never-never-land." **Joly Robyn** was a common name for a shepherd or rustic. Skeat and Mustanoja (in Med. Lit. and Folklore, 64) cite instances of its occurrence. Or the reference may be to Robin Hood; see 2.861n. See also Mann, Ch and Estates, 222, for examples of the name Robin used in contexts of idle amusement, and cf. Rom 7453, MilT I.3129n.

1176   Last year's snow is a familiar symbol of the irrevocable past, as in Villon's refrain, "Mais où sont les neiges d'antan?" (But where are the snows of yesteryear?—Ballade des dames du temps jadis). See Italo Siciliano, F. Villon, 1976, 256–75; and David Kuhn, La poétique de Villon, 77–97.

1177–80   From Fil. 7.11.

1190   Troilus tries to persuade himself that Criseyde meant that the moon would pass wholly out of Leo, which would give her another day. It was in Aries when she made the promise. See 4.1592.

1238–41   In the Filostrato, Troiolo dreamed that the boar was tearing out Criseida's heart with its tusks, and that she took it as a pleasure (7.23–24). Cf. Tr. 2.925–31.

1265   gospel: Proverbial (Whiting G401 and G398–99, Hassell E90) as "truth"; practically a common noun (MED s.v. *gospel* 4.).

1266–67   Cf. Bo 3.pr5.68–70 and n., and Whiting E97.

1270   no remedye: Seems to derive from the French translation of Boccaccio, "remède nul" (p. 276); there is no corresponding term in the Filostrato (7.32).

1277   From Fil. 7.40. Cf. the opening of Rom, and the note to lines 358–85 above. See also Whiting D387, and Hazelton, Spec 35:357–80, who cites a gloss to pseudo-Cato, "nam fallunt sompnia plures" (for dreams deceive most people). For the incident of Troiolo's dream and Pandaro's encouraging advice, Boccaccio's source may have been the Italian Tristano (ed. E. G. Parodi, 1896, p. 187) or his own Filocolo (2.26–27).

1317–1421   Norman Davis shows that Troilus's letter contains many of the epistolary formulas found in French letters and in handbooks of letter-writing, as well as in later English letters (none survive from before 1390). See RES n.s. 16, 1965, 233–44; see also Davis, Leeds SE n.s. 1, 1967, 7–17; Taylor, Nottingham Med. Stud. 24:57–70; McKinnell, in Essays on Tr, 73–89; Norton-Smith, Geoffrey Ch, ch. 5, citing comparable French poetic epistles, e.g., Eustache Deschamps, Balades 1244 and 1245 (Oeuvres 7:122–25).

1321   See 4.1695–96n.

1345–46   The corresponding passage in the Filostrato (7.54) may derive from Ovid, Her. 3.5–6.

1348   The period forty days is named in Fil. 7.54.

1374–77   For the rhymes **welles : helle is : ellis**, see GP I.523n.

1375–79   With these antitheses, not in Fil., Root compares BD 599–616 and RR 4293–4330.

1415–16   Windeatt compares Ovid, Her. 4.1.

1433   See KnT I.1838n.

1434   Cf. 4.390, 5.1748, Whiting W665. The phrasing here is closest to the French proverb, "Ainsi va le monde" (Hassell M163).

1450–1519   Chaucer substitutes the divination of Cassandra, one of Priam's three daughters, for the altercation between her and Troiolo in Fil. 7.86–102. In Boccaccio's account Troiolo interprets his own dream (Fil. 7.25–28). **Sibille,** properly a generic term (sibyl, prophetess), Chaucer seems to take as a second name for Cassandra. Root cites other cases of the same misunderstanding. For the common conception of Cassandra as prophetess of evil, see Benoît, or Ovid (Her. 5.113–25; 16.121–26).

1464–84   For the story of the Caledonian boar, see Ovid, Met. 8.260–546, and Boccaccio, De gen. deorum 9, cap. 15 and 19. Witlieb (N&Q 215:202–7) argues for the influence of the Ovide moralisé. See Marcelle Thiébaux, Stag of Love, 70.

1480   The ancient authorities make Tydeus the half-brother, not a descendant, of Meleager. Chaucer was probably misled by "l'avolo" (grandfather) in Fil. 7.27, a stanza he translates in 5.1512–19. Root notes that Boccaccio gives the relationship correctly in De gen. deorum 9.21. Wetherbee observes that Lactantius Placidus in his Comm. on Statius Theb. 1.463 (ed. Richard Jahnke, 1898, 52) makes Meleager the ancestor of Tydeus (in New Perspectives, 77; see also Ch and Poets, 129–30).

1485–1510   Cassandra summarizes the Thebaid of Statius. In all but two MSS of Troilus, the Latin summary of the Thebaid appears after line 1498. It is treated in detail by Magoun, Traditio 11, 1955, 409–20. This poetic argument to Statius's poem, often copied and perhaps used as a mnemonic (see Berry, ELN 17, 1979, 90–93), was probably based on a series of similar arguments, one for each book of the poem, which appear in many MSS of the Thebaid. On these summaries, besides Magoun, see also Hamilton, MLN 23, 1908, 127; Clogan, SP 61:599–615 and Eng. Misc. 18, 1967, 9–31; and for an unpersuasive argument that Chaucer is also indebted to the Ovide moralisé here for details of his Theban material, Witlieb, ELN 11, 1973, 5–9. Magoun shows that Chaucer, in his English summary of the Thebaid, used both the brief and the longer forms of the post-Statian Latin arguments, as well as the Thebaid itself (see also Wise, Infl. of Statius, 26–35). Chaucer treats the Theban material also in KnT I.931–47 and Anel 50–70; he knew of course Boccaccio's Teseida and the French epic based on the Thebaid, the Roman de Thèbes.

Polynices (**Polymytes**) and Eteocles (**Ethiocles**), sons of Oedipus, were to rule Thebes alternately, but the latter expelled his brother. Adrastus, king of Argos, took up the cause of Polynices and conducted the war of the "Seven Against Thebes." With Adrastus and Polynices were associated Tydeus, Amphiaraus (**Amphiorax**), Capaneus, Hippomedon (**Ypomedoun**), and Parthenopaeus (**Parthonope**). All the seven except Adrastus were slain, and Creon, who seized control of Thebes, refused them burial. This led to the expedition of Theseus, king of Athens, mentioned at the beginning of The Knight's Tale.

1492 Eteocles sent **Hemonydes** (Maeon) with forty-nine others to waylay Tydeus. Tydeus single-handedly slew all but Maeon.

1494 The **prophecyes** may be those of Maeon (Theb. 3.71–77), of Amphiaraus (Theb. 3.640–45), or of Laius (Theb. 4.637–44). Magoun (Traditio 11:409–20) compares the "presagia" in the Latin argument to Book 3.1.8.

1497 A **serpent** sent by Jove stung the infant Archemorus (Opheltes) to death, while his nurse Hypsipyle was guiding the Greek host to the river (the **welle**) Langia (Theb. 5.505–40). The epithet **holy** may be due to the phrase "sacro serpente" in the metrical argument to Book 5; see Magoun, Traditio 11:409–20.

1498 Incited by the **furies**, the women of Lemnos killed all but one of the island's males.

1499 The funeral rites of **Archymoris** occupy Theb. 6. See textual note.

1500 On the death of Amphiaraus, see Theb. 6.794–823 and Tr 2.104–5. For the spelling **Amphiorax**, cf. 2.104 and see GP I.384n.

1501–5 The deaths of Tydeus, Hippomedon, Parthenopaeus, and Capaneus are told in Theb. 8–10. The drowning of Hippomedon is mentioned in only one Troilus MS of the brief Latin summary, H², which has the additional line, "Fervidus Ypomedon timidique [read "tumidoque"] in gurgite mersus" (raging Hippomedon immersed in the swollen stream). The line comes from the twelve-line argument to Book 9.

1508 The first combat of Eteocles and Polynices is described in Theb. 11.389–573.

1509 **Argyves**: Argyve, Argia, the wife of Polynices ("Argiva," a variant reading in the argument to Book 12). This seems to be the source for the name of Criseyde's mother: see 4.762n.

1510 The Thebaid does not make explicit the fact that Thebes was burned (and see KnT I.990), although it refers to the possibility of destruction by fire. Chaucer

may take this hint, or he may recall the Teseida (2.81) or the Roman de Thèbes (10131–39). Wetherbee plausibly suggests that Chaucer recalls the last word of the twelve-line argument of the Thebaid, "ignem" (fire), which actually referred not to the city's burning but to the cremation of the slain (in New Perspectives, 78; see also his Ch and Poets, 131–32).

1513–19 The interpretation of Troilus's dream, here transferred to Cassandra's mouth, corresponds to that in Fil. 7.27. In the Filostrato it is made clear that Troiolo's brothers and sisters learn of his love affair because Deifebo overheard him making a complaint (Fil 7.77–102).

1520–26 Cf. Fil. 7.89. In the Filostrato, Cassandra taunts Troiolo for loving Criseida (7.86–87); in the Troilus she angers her brother by her interpretation of the dream.

1523 **sestow**: "Do you see," a rhetorical question here. **fol of fantasie**: Dupe of fantastic delusions.

1527–33 **Alceste**: The heroine of the LGW (see ProLGW F 499–504n. and Tr 5.1778). MS H⁴ gives the kernel of her story in a Latin gloss: "Note, concerning the death of Alcestis for the love of her husband." Her husband was Admetus, king of Pherae in Thessaly (see 1.664).

1541–47 Cf. Inf. 7.78–82; Bo 4.pr6; Tr 3.617–20n. On the common idea of the transfer of the empire (translatio imperii; **regnes shal be flitted**) see Curtius, European Lit., 28–29, citing Biblical and classical precedent; Werner Goez, Translatio imperii, 1958. See Schless, Ch and Dante, 141–43.

1545 **smytted**: The regular past participle form deriving from the OE verb smittian (to sully; related to smut). But OED (s.v. smite vb.) cites a weak preterite form contemporary with Chaucer, from the Wyclifite translation of the Bible, of the regularly strong verb smiten (to smite). A weak by-form of the past participle of smiten would be smited (also possibly with short i). Because in the context "smitten" is much more obvious a sense than "sullied," it may be preferable (and Donaldson prefers it in his gloss); Ch nowhere else uses smitten with the meaning "to sully."

1548 **parodie**: Glossed "duracioun" in MSS H¹, H⁴, and Cp; it seems to be merely a corrupt form of the French word periode. See MED s.v. parodie.

1558 **aventaille**: See ClT IV.1204n.

1577 Historical and literary cases of the use of a pilgrim's dress for a disguise in wartime are given by Magoun, MLN 59, 1944, 176–78, and Whiting, MLN 60, 1945, 47–49.

1590–1631 Boccaccio indicates some kind of communication between Troiolo and Criseida at this point, but Criseyde's letter is Chaucer's invention, drawing on earlier letters in Fil.: 2.96, 122, 126. See Fil. 8.5–6 and Tr 5.1317–1421n.

1597–1600 See Fil. 2.122.4–8.

1634 **kalendes**: "Beginning, harbinger," as in 2.7. The phrase "calends of (ex)change" may have been current (see MED s.v. calendes 2., and OED s.v. calends). Possibly it was a commercial term: in Roman use, interest and debt were due on the Calends of the month (hence Horace's "sad Calends," Sat. 1.3.87). Chaucer then would be playing on a phrase that means "accounts book."

1637–38 **leve**: Must mean "believe" (see Day, RES 6, 1930, 73), as in Fil. 8.7.3 (crede), but the omission of an object for leve makes difficult syntax.

1639–40 Proverbial: Whiting S491.

1644–66 Cf. Fil. 8.8–10.

1661 This **broch** (see Fil. 8.9–10) is not mentioned by Chaucer or Boccaccio earlier in the account of the parting of the lovers. But see 3.1370–72 and note 3.1369–72, 5.1040–43 and n.

1669 **word and ende:** See MkT VII.2721n.

1689 On the order of words, cf. GP I.791.

1705 The detail of the bleeding sides, not mentioned in Fil. 8.16.4–7, may derive from Benoît, 20075. Cf. KnT I.2635.

1748 See 5.1434n.

1751–56 These lines allude to combats that are fully described in Benoît and Guido: see Roman de Troie, 19281–21189; Historia, pp. 197–203. Boccaccio dismisses the matter with a single line (Fil. 8.25.7).

1758–64 These lines, which correspond to Fil. 8.26.1–5, may be influenced by the account of Troilus in the Roman de Troie, 19955–21189.

1765–66 Chaucer here sets aside the epic theme announced at the opening of the Aeneid, to which he alludes (**armes . . . man;** cf. HF 144), as he seems (if he knew them) to recall the opening words of the Iliad in 1800–1801.

1771 **Rede Dares:** It is doubtful that Chaucer made direct use of Dares' prose Historia. Root shows that the material here referred to may be found in Joseph of Exeter's Frigii Daretis Ylias (see 5.799–840n.). Gompf, Joseph's editor, shows that Joseph's poem was often referred to in the Middle Ages simply as "Dares." Chaucer may speak here of a title, not an author.

1772–1869 The conclusion (or "epilogue" or "palinode") of the poem has occasioned much study, from Tatlock's fundamental article, "The Epilog of Ch's Tr," MP 18, 1920–21, 625–59, to John M. Steadman's book, Disembodied Laughter: Troilus and the Apotheosis Tradition, 1972. The older opinion that the ending (wherever it begins) is a contradictory (Tatlock) or inept (Curry, PMLA 45:129–68) rejection of the values of the poem has been superseded: some hold that the condemnation of pagan values and secular love makes explicit an ironic criticism of the lovers' behavior that has been implicit from the start (Robertson, ELH 19, 1952, 1–37; Farnham, ChR 1, 1967, 207–16); some argue that Chaucer balances the claims of secular and religious love in fine, regretful ambiguities (Muscatine, Ch and Fr. Trad., 161–65; Donaldson, in Early Eng. and Norse Stud. Pres. to Hugh Smith, ed. Brown and Foote, 1963, 26–45; cf. Dronke, MAE 33:47–52); some propose that the various tones of the different parts of the ending may be accounted for by considering the various audiences addressed (Covella, ChR 2, 1968, 235–45) or that the narrator remains distinct from the author and inept (Markland, MLQ 31, 1970, 147–59). For a study of the last six stanzas as separable and in the narrator's voice, see Shoaf, Dante, Ch, and the Currency of the Word, 1983, 143–57. In a sensible article on the closing of the poem, Dean argues that Chaucer emphasizes mutability and its partial subjection to aesthetic experience (PQ 64, 1985, 175–84).

1772 Lüdeke, Funktionen des Erzählers, 108, compares addresses to ladies at the end of works by Boccaccio and Machaut.

1778 **Alceste:** See Tr 5.1527–33n. Chaucer seems to have in mind the idea of LGW; see LGW 917–23. On

Penelope (Penelope) as a model of chastity, cf. BD 1080 and 1081–85n.

1779–85 Cf. MancT IX.187–88.

1784–85 Cf. LGW 2559–61, Anel 197.

1786 The formula **Go, litel bok** was traditional; its use from Ovid ("Parve, nec invideo, sine me, liber, ibis in urbem"; Little book, you will go without me into the city, nor do I grudge it; Tristia 1.1.1) to Chaucer is traced by Tatlock, MP 18:625–59, especially its appearance—for the first time at the end of a long narrative—in works by Boccaccio. Closest to Chaucer is the envoi in the Filocolo (2.376–78), where Boccaccio addresses his little book and mentions Virgil, Lucan, Statius, Ovid, and Dante, for the last of whom Chaucer may substitute *Omer* as more appropriate to a tale of Troy. Boccaccio also speaks of the Filostrato, in its proem, as a little book (p. 22). See Young, Origin of Tr, 178–79; Holzknecht, Literary Patronage, 1923, 116–23; and, for the "Go, little book" formula after Chaucer, Schoeck, N&Q 197, 1952, 370–72, 413.

On Chaucer's term **tragedye**, see McAlpine, Genre of Tr, and Ruggiers, ChR 8, 1973, 89–99, and the many references cited there; see also ProMkT VII.1973 and n. Chaucer may have known other definitions of tragedy than the Monk's; e.g., Ovid's, "Tragedy surpasses every kind of writing in gravity; also it always has as its subject love" (Tristia 2.381–82). See Walther 19819a.

1787–88 **Ther** is pleonastic before the subjunctive **sende** (see Language and Versification, p. xxxix, and Boys, MLN 52, 1937, 351–53). **Make in,** a phrase unattested in the sense "compose" elsewhere, is close enough to the last line of ProLGW F, "And ryght thus *on* my Legende gan I *make,*" to indicate that Boys and MED (s.v. *maken* v. 2) are wrong in glossing the word "match," a weakly attested sense that spoils the association with *makere* and *makyng* in the adjacent lines. On the distinction between the Middle English terms "making" and "poetry" (see line 1790), see Olson, CL 31, 1979, 272–90. Whether Chaucer had **som** specific **comedye** in mind we do not know: some have suggested The Legend of Good Women (see 1778 above), The Knight's Tale, The Canterbury Tales, The House of Fame. Like Chaucer, Joseph of Exeter promises a new work (his Antiocheis) before his address to his book and his "envy theme" (Ylias 6.961–79).

1789–92 The disavowal of envy was conventional: see Astr Pro 59–64n., and Tupper, JEGP 16, 1917, 551–72. Closest to Chaucer here is Statius, Theb. 12.816–17: "nec tu divinam Aeneida tempta, / sed longe sequere et vestigia semper adora" (nor aim to rival the divine Aeneid, but follow from afar and always worship its footprints). The naming of the company of great poets, probably suggested to Chaucer by the Filocolo (see 1786 above), was likewise conventional: Dante names the same poets (with Horace for Statius) as joined in Limbo (Inf. 4.88–90); with the addition of Claudian they appear on the pillars in The House of Fame (HF 1456–1512). See Curtius, European Lit., 263.

1793–98 Cf. Adam Scriveyn. Criticism of scribes was conventional: see Work, PMLA 47, 1932, 419–30; Flügel, Anglia 22, 1901, 207–9; and Root, Poetry of Ch, 1906, 69–70. "The *diversite,* which Chaucer rightly recognized as a cause of corruption, consisted partly in dialectical variations and partly in growing disregard of final *-e*" (Robinson).

1806 Boccaccio likewise dispatches Troilus in a single line (Fil. 8.27): "miseramente un dì l'uccise Achille" (wretchedly one day Achilles killed him).

1807–27 These stanzas are from Tes. 11.1–3, where the flight of Arcite's soul is described. Chaucer omits the account in his Knight's Tale (see KnT I.2809–15n.). Boccaccio's primary sources are Dante (esp. Par. 22. 151), Lucan's Pharsalia 9.1–14 (the flight of Pompey's soul), the Somnium Scipionis (see PF 31n.), and Bo 4.m1 and 2.pr7.152–57; Chaucer surely knew all these sources directly. On the sources, see especially Steadman, Disembodied Laughter; and Velli, "L'apoteosi d'Arcite," Studi e problemi di critica testuale 5, 1972, 33–66, and the many references cited there. The notion that the soul or mind ascends to the spheres at death (or in visionary ecstasy: cf. 2 Cor. 12.2, Bo 4.m1.1–7n. and HF 972–78) is widespread in Platonic and other antique and early Christian thought. On "sidereal eschatology" in classical thought, see Franz Cumont, Astrol. and Relig. among the Greeks and Romans, 1912, 95ff.; Lux Perpetua, 1949, ch. 3; Jones, Class. Philol. 21, 1926, 97–113. For early Christian sources, see Nock, Harv. Theol. Rev. 34, 1941, 103–9; Bousset, Archiv für Religionswissenschaft 4, 1901, 136–69 and 229–73; Fiske, Spec 40, 1965, 438–39; Pierre Courcelle, La Cons. de Philos. dans la trad. litt., 1967, 197–99 and append. 2 (with plates showing medieval depictions of the winged Boethius); Origen, De principiis 2.3.7 (Sources Chrétiennes 252, 1968, 272); Gregory the Great, Dialogi 2.35. Aside from the four major sources of Arcite's soul-journey named above, three influential examples of the ascended soul looking back on the earth with contempt or laughter are Statius, Silvae 2.7, on Lucan; Seneca, De consolatione ad Marciam, sect. 25 (Moral Essays, Loeb, vol. 2), on Marcia's son; Prudentius, Peristephanon 14.91–111 (Loeb, vol. 2), on St. Agnes, concluding with her contempt for the "foul clouds of paganism."

1808 is went: Cf. 5.546; OED s.v. went 17; Kerkhof, 142–44.

1809 holughnesse of the eighthe spere: Cf. Tes. 11.1: la concavità del cielo ottava. The important MS Gg lacks this passage; of the rest, only two (and Caxton's edition) read eighthe; the rest read "seventhe." Yet the evidence of the source (Boccaccio's ottava), the somewhat smoother meter with eighthe, and the ease of scribal corruption from "viij" to "vij," make eighthe preferable. For full surveys of opinion as to which of the heavenly spheres Chaucer (and Boccaccio) had in mind, see Steadman, Disembodied Laughter, 1–20; and Drake, PLL 11, 1975, 3–17. Given the variables seventh or eighth, and given the additional variables caused by our uncertainty as to whether Chaucer reckoned the number of a sphere from the earth outward (as in Tr 3.2 and elsewhere) or from outside inward (as in Mars 29 and Scogan 9), and given further our uncertainty as to where Chaucer would start his count (the primum mobile? the fixed stars? Saturn?) if he reckoned inward, it is impossible to specify Troilus's exact location. The traditions (see note 1807–27 above) would offer two likely places: the sphere of the moon (where Lucan places Pompey's soul) or the sphere of the fixed stars (where Cicero put Scipio, and where Dante was when he looked back to earth). None of the arguments offered for either choice has proved conclusive (see, for example, Dobson, Eng. and Ger. Sts. 1, 1947–48, 56–62; Clark, JEGP 50, 1951,

1–10; Scott, MLR 51, 1956, 2–5; Bloomfield, MLR 53, 1958, 408–10; Wood, Ch and Stars, 180–91; Conlee, ChR 7, 1972, 27–36; Schless, Ch and Dante, 1–3–46). Steadman offers substantial support for Root's and Robinson's preference for the sphere of the moon; nevertheless, Chaucer's abiding interest in Macrobius and Dante make it more likely that he was thinking of their location of the visionary soul among the fixed stars.

1810 In convers letyng: Boccaccio has "degli elementi i convessi lasciando" (leaving behind the convex surfaces [the outer surfaces] of the elements). Chaucer's Tes. MS may have read "conversi," or Chaucer may have written "convess" or "convex" (none of these words is elsewhere recorded in Middle English), or he may simply have altered Boccaccio, without altering the meaning. The line in the Teseida makes best sense if "elementi" means "planetary spheres" (as it can in medieval Latin) rather than the four elements of earth, water, air, and fire (although it is barely conceivable that Boccaccio thought of the four sublunar elements as themselves forming spheres and having convex surfaces). C. S. Lewis would translate "celestial spheres" (Discarded Image, 33). Chaucer's element therefore probably has here the less common sense, "planetary sphere," and MED (s.v. element 2.[a]) supports this interpretation. HF 975 is inconclusive support.

1812 armonye: Cf. PF 59–63n.

1818 pleyn felicite: Pleyn derives ultimately from Lat. plenus (full), with perhaps a shade of influence from the homophone "pleyn" from planus (plain, uncomplicated). The phrase is not from Tes. On "felicite," see 3.813–33 and n. Kellogg (MS 22, 1960, 204–13) calls attention to a parallel from a commentary on Isaiah 40 embedded in Frère Lorens's Somme le roi, trans. in the ME Book of Vices and Virtues (ed. W. Nelson Francis, EETS 217, 1942, 141): when the soul "is ravessched up to hevene, sche loketh agen to the erthe from feer, . . . and seeth it so little as to regard to that gret fairenesse . . . than despiseth he . . .''; and later (p. 164): "and hym thingeth al the world litel . . . to regard of thilk grete plente of ioye . . . ."

1824 blynde lust: Suggested by "tenebrosa cechitate" (shadowy blindness) in Tes. 11.3, the phrase may recall Dante's apostrophe to "cieca cupidigia," blind cupidity (Inf. 12.49; see P. M. Kean, Ch Poetry 1:160), but Dante refers to cupidity and wrath as motives of violence. Cf. Tr 1.211.

1827 Cf. 5.321 and n. Boccaccio is equally vague as to where Mercury allots the soul its final resting place.

1828–34 Chaucer returns to the Filostrato, 8.28.

1833–34 Cf. 1.55–56.

1837 Cf. KnT I.2847–49 and n.

1840–41 al nys but a faire: Proverbial (Whiting W662; MED s.v. cheri 2.[a]; Root's note), as in the late fourteenth-century lyric, "This world nis but a chirie-feire, / Nou is hit in sesun, nou wol hit slake" (Brown, Relig. Lyrics, 199.85–86). The cherry fair took place at cherry harvest. Instances of preachers' comparisons of the world to a fair (marketplace, "forum") are gathered in Owst, Lit. and Pulpit, 108, and Wenzel, SP 73:138–61. For examples of the proverbial passing like a flower, see Whiting F326 (and cf. F317–28). On the senses of faire, see further Donaldson (see note 1772–1869 above) and Ida L. Gordon, Double Sorrow, 1970, 54.

1849 Tatlock, MP 18:625–59, compares the disowning

of paganism at the end of Boccaccio's De genealogia deorum. Comparable passages are in Guido, pp. 93–97; Roman de Troie, 21715–40; Tes. 11.42. On paganism generally in Troilus, see Frankis, in Essays on Tr, 57–72, and Minnis, Ch and Antiquity.

1853 The antique gods are referred to as "raschaille" in the Roman de Thèbes, 4441.

1854 forme: Perhaps the "essential principle" that informs pagan poetry, that is, false gods and worldly appetite (so Root), or perhaps "style, literary form, poetic shape." See MED s.v. *forme* 6. and 14.

1856–59 For a writer to request criticism or correction was commonplace (see Wattenbach, Schriftwesen, 3rd ed., 1896, 224, 236, 340–41, etc.; also Holzknecht, Literary Patronage, 116–23). Tatlock collects examples (MP 18: 625–59), notably from Boccaccio, whom Chaucer probably followed. See Tr 3.1331–37 and SNPro VIII.84. On literary dedications of books, see also Holzknecht, 124–55. On **Gower** and his personal relations with Chaucer, see Chaucer's Life, p. xxiii, and John H. Fisher, John Gower, 1964. **Moral** became after Chaucer his epithet; see the characterization of him in John Walton's trans. of Boethius (ed. M. Science, EETS 170, 1927, p. 2, st. 5).

Some uncertainty remains as to the identity of **philosophical Strode.** Radulphus (Ralph or Randolph) Strode or Strood was a logician and fellow of Merton College, Oxford, before 1360. His principal treatise on logic is lost, but his Consequentiae and Obligationes are preserved (Oxford, Bodleian Canonici MS misc. 219; printed at Venice, 1493, etc.) and his theological opinions can be deduced from John Wyclif's friendly rejoinders: Responsio ad decem questiones magistri Ricardi Strode and Responsiones ad argumenta Radulfi Strode (Wyclif, Opera minora, 1913, 398–404 and 175–200). There can be little doubt that Chaucer refers to this Strode. A catalogue of Merton fellows, compiled in 1422, names Stroode, and a late fifteenth-century hand adds a Latin note: "He was a noble poet, and he composed a book in the elegiac meter called 'Ralph's Vision' (Phantasma Radulphi)." If this is correct, Chaucer had all the more reason to address him as, like Gower, a fellow poet. (Gollancz's speculation that Strode's poem is The Pearl is incorrect.)

Whether the Oxford Strode, whom Wyclif says he knew at Oxford, is the same man as the London lawyer Radulphus Strode is not certain. He was Common Serjeant of the City of London from 1373–85 and Standing Counsel for the City from 1386 to his death in 1387 (his will is lost, but recorded). He owned a house over Aldersgate in 1375, the year after Chaucer received his Aldgate residence. That Chaucer knew him is proved by a document of 1382, in which Strode and Chaucer are named as sureties for the peaceful behavior of John Hende, a wealthy London draper. Tout doubts the identity of the London and the Oxford Strode, arguing the improbability of a prominent university philosopher's giving up his career, establishing another, and marrying (the London lawyer had a wife, Emma, and a son, also named Ralph). Yet two documents support the view that Strode was an exceptional case. In one, Wyclif and the London Strode appear together as mainpernors (sureties for appearance in court) of a parson in 1374; in the other, preserved in Merton College records and in the Calendar of Fine Rolls (1926, 9:8), Strode on 18 August 1377 is named mainpernor in a transaction involving land near Oxford committed to John Bloxham, warden of "Mertonhalle" (see Rickert). It remains possible that there were two or more Ralph Strodes connected with Chaucer, but it is more probable that the Ralph Strode of Oxford, connected with Wyclif and with Merton, is the same man as the Ralph Strode of London, connected with Wyclif and with Merton. For the documents and discussion see: Israel Gollancz on Strode in DNB, and his ed. of Pearl, 1921, xlvi–xlix; J. T. T. Brown, Scottish Antiquary 12, 1897, 5–12 (sorting out the early scholarship); Brown, PMLA 19, 1904, 146–48; Herbert Brook Workman, John Wyclif, 1926, 2:125–29 and 412–14; Kuhl, PMLA 29, 1914, 270–76; Rickert, TSL, 4 Oct. 1928, 707; reply by Garrod, 11 Oct. 1928, 736; reply by Gollancz, 25 Oct. 1928, 783; Tout, Spec 4, 1929, 365–89; Lynn Thorndike, Sci. and Thought in the 15th C., 1929, 237–38; Emden, BRUO 3:1807–8; Fisher, John Gower, 61–62; Ussery, TSE 18, 1970, 1–15; J. A. W. Bennett, Ch at Oxford, 63–64. On a reference, perhaps untrustworthy, to N. (or R.) Strode as tutor of Chaucer's "little son" Lewis, see the Explanatory Notes to the Astrolabe.

1863–65 From Dante, Par. 14.28–30. Boccaccio also uses "circonscrisse" of God's creation: Fil. 2.41. For further parallels, see Tatlock, RomR 10, 1919, 275; Walther 31014 (the uncircumscript sun as Christ); and Singleton, ed., Dante, Purg., 1973, 11.2n.

The Legend of Good Women

On the title and subtitle see Textual Notes. Robinson's notes to the *Legend* are generally concise, clear, and complete. We have updated the scholarship, and occasionally paraphrased and compressed Robinson's language, but have otherwise retained many of the original notes. Direct quotation from Robinson is so indicated. The *Legend* is firmly established as one of Chaucer's authentic works: it contains internal evidence of Chaucer's authorship; Chaucer lists it among his works, as *the Seintes Legende of Cupide* in the Introduction to The Man of Law's Tale and again as *the book of the XXV.* [or XIX.] *Ladies* in the Retraction; and it is attributed to him in one of the manuscripts (Arch. Selden B.24).

Lydgate, in *The Fall of Princes,* says that Chaucer "wrot, at request off the queen, / A legende of parfit holynesse off Goode Women" (1.330–32). Speght makes a similar statement in his 1598 edition ("Argument" to the *Legend*), possibly with Lydgate as his sole authority. Lydgate's assertion was accepted by Brown (ESt 47, 1913–14, 59–62) and Tatlock (Dev. and Chron. 111–14) and by more recent critics as well (cf. Fisher, John Gower, 235–37). Chaucer may indeed have written at royal command, but Lydgate's report that the book was made at the queen's order may simply be an inference from Chaucer's statement that it was presented to her (Pro F 496–97).

The date of composition of the *Legend* cannot be established with certainty, for Chaucer seems to have been occupied with it over a period of several years, and a number of the legends may have been composed before the Prologue, the only portion that contains any indication of its date (see notes on the Prologue, below). Lowes (PMLA 20, 1905, 749–864) held that most of the legends were earlier than the Prologue, as did Tatlock (Dev. and Chron. 122–31) and Galway (MLR 33, 1938, 165–66), who believed the work was written for Joan of Kent. Root (PMLA 24, 1909, 124–53, and PMLA 25, 1910, 228–40), basing his argument mainly on the Medea, argued for a later date. More recently, Robert W. Frank, Jr. (Ch and LGW, 1972, 1–10) suggests that Chaucer began work on the *Legend* in 1386, partly as an experiment in writing short narrative. The fact that the *Legend* is Chaucer's first work in iambic pentameter couplets ("heroic couplets," the meter of *The Canterbury Tales*) may perhaps lend some weight to this suggestion, but the dating of the collection remains uncertain.

For the general conception of the legends, Chaucer was indebted to the lives of the saints (on Chaucer's use of hagiographic models, see Lisa J. Kiser, Telling Classical Tales: Ch and LGW, 101–11) and to the common poetic use of Christian imagery and forms in love poetry. Early commentators believed that Chaucer's model was Boccaccio's *De claris mulieribus* (Bech, Anglia 5, 1882, 313–38), and traces of both this work and Boccaccio's *De casibus* have been noted (see following notes). Although all the stories except Ariadne, Philomela, and Phyllis are in *De claris mulieribus* 5, "there are many differences in detail and scarcely any verbal echoes between the two

collections" (Fisher, Comp to Ch, 471). A more likely model is Ovid's *Heroides* (Connely, Classical Weekly, 18, 1924, 9–13; Eleanor J. W. Leach, Sources and Rhetoric of Chaucer's LGW and Ovid's Heroides, diss. Yale Univ., 1963; Shannon, Ch and Roman Poets, 176–301), which Chaucer seems to have used in a heavily annotated manuscript and perhaps read in conjunction with an Italian translation by one "Filippo," generally assumed to be Filippo Ceffi (Meech, PMLA 45, 1930, 110–28; Epistole eroiche di Ovidio Nasone volgarizzate, etc., ed. G. Bernardoni, 1842). It is possible, however, that Chaucer was unacquainted with this translation, and that both he and Filippo used manuscripts of the *Heroides* having the same tradition of glosses. For the individual legends Chaucer drew on a number of other sources, including Virgil, the *Metamorphoses,* the *Ovide moralisé,* Vincent of Beauvais, and others, as indicated in the notes to the individual legends below. For the thematic significance and artistic effectiveness of Chaucer's use of his classical sources, see Fyler, Ch and Ovid, esp. ch. 4, and McCall, Ch Among the Gods, ch. 4 and notes.

Two questions have concerned critics of the *Legend* for years; first is the question of mode. Is the poem a satire, or should it all be taken at face value? Second is the question of literary merit; is it in fact a bad and boring work with occasional flashes of lyric beauty, or is it an important and fine example of Chaucer's literary skills? Goddard (JEGP 7, 1908, 87–129, and 8, 1909, 47–111) finds the *Legend* a satire against women in which the phrase "good women" should be taken ironically. Lowes opposes this view (JEGP 8, 1909, 513–69). Garrett (JEGP 22, 1923, 64–74) offers a modified version of the "satire upon women" theory, which Robinson finds still too strong. The general issue of satire in the *Legend* is discussed by Baum (MLN 60, 1945, 377–81). McCall (Ch Among the Gods, 112–117) finds the *Legend* a satire not of good women, but of bad men, developing an idea first formulated by Lumiansky, MLN 62, 1947, 560–2. E. T. Hansen (JEGP 82, 1983, 11–31) has argued that the poem is an ironic attack on antifeminism, the narrator, and Cupid.

As to the literary merits of the *Legend,* early critics speak almost with one voice. They agree that the F Prologue contains some fine poetry; that the G Prologue is less warm, less emotional; and that the legends themselves are so boring that Chaucer wearied of his task and finally broke away from it. Skeat, in his 1889 edition of the *Legend,* cites line 2457 as evidence of this, and there are many lines in the *Legend* that, if taken as statements of fact rather than the rhetorical devices *abbreviatio* and *occupatio,* support such a conclusion. Certainly the *Legend* lacks some of the qualities that are so much admired in *Troilus and Criseyde* and *The Canterbury Tales:* vivid characterization, variety and complexity of plot, and strong emotional impact. It has not had great appeal to most modern readers and critics. Robert Burlin (Ch Fiction, 34), while acknowledging the excellence of the Prologue, calls the *Legend* "a colossal blunder." Charles Muscatine, in *Poetry and Crisis,* 132–33, finds little sustained pathos in the legends because of their extremely condensed matter. But the poem was both popular and

The explanatory notes to *The Legend of Good Women* were written by M. C. E. Shaner with A. S. G. Edwards.

influential in the fifteenth century. (For a partial list of early references to the *Legend,* see Caroline Spurgeon, Five Hundred Years of Ch Criticism, 1925.) It has not always been without admirers, and recently it has begun to receive more favorable critical attention.

Foremost among modern defenders of the *Legend* against the charge that Chaucer himself found it boring is Robert W. Frank, Jr. In Ch and the LGW (189–210), Frank emphasizes that Chaucer was sufficiently interested in the *Legend* to revise the Prologue nearly a decade after it was first written, and to list the *Legend* among his works in the Introduction to The Man of Law's Tale. He argues further that the "boredom" passages in the *Legend* have been misread, and dismisses, probably correctly, the unfinished state of the poem as evidence of Chaucer's abandonment of it. On the question of the poem's incompleteness, see Blake, Archiv 221, 1984, 71–74. Frank sees the work as in part a preparation for *The Canterbury Tales,* an exercise in compressing complex materials. See also Frank, ChR 1, 1966, 110–33, and in Ch at Albany, 63–76. Kiser, in Telling Classical Tales, argues for a unity of theme throughout the entire *Legend;* she sees the Prologue as an explication through the person of Alceste of the proper melding of Christian thought and classical matter. The legends themselves, Kiser believes, are parodies of the infelicitous practice of distorting classical stories in order to point a moral. Burrow, Ricardian Poetry, 73–74, defends Chaucer's use of the *via brevitatis* in the *Legend,* and briefly compares modern and medieval taste. Norton-Smith (Geoffrey Ch, 62–78) points out a number of contrasting polarities generated by the Prologue, and analyzes the rhetorical structure of the legends. Overbeck, ChR 2, 1967, 75–94, finds the "good women" impulsive rebels against authority, prototypes of the Wife of Bath. On the other hand, McCall, Ch Among the Gods, 112–117, finds the women generally helpless and pathetic.

The issue of the intended scope of the poem is perhaps irresolvable. In the MSS of the Retraction, the *Legend* is called *the book of the XXV. Ladies* (or XIX. or XV.; MSS vary), and Lydgate (The Fall of Princes, 1.330–33) says the number of women was to have been nineteen. The ballade in the Prologue (F 249–69; G 203–23) lists several women (Esther, Penelope, Marcia Catonis, Lavinia, Polyxena, Laodamia, and Canace), whose stories do not appear in the *Legend,* but of whom Chaucer may have intended to write. Similarly, the list given in the Introduction to The Man of Law's Tale goes beyond the contents of the extant *Legend.* Clearly Chaucer planned a larger body of legends, but what stories it would have contained must remain the subject of speculation. See also the notes to Pro F 249–69, below.

THE PROLOGUE

The Prologue exists in two forms, F and G, of which the latter survives in but one manuscript (Camb. Univ. Lib. Gg 4.27). It is generally agreed that lines 496–97 in Prologue F refer to Queen Anne and that this prologue must therefore have been written sometime after her arrival in England in early 1382 and before her death on 7 June 1394. Bernard ten Brink (Ch Studien, 1870, 147–50) suggested that the Prologue was written to express Chaucer's gratitude to the queen for the appointment of his deputy in the Customs office (17 February

1385). However, the petition for this assistance was signed by the king's favorite, the Earl of Oxford (Ch Life Records, 168–69), and there is no evidence of Anne's intervention. Lowes (PMLA 19, 1904, 593–683) argued that the Prologue was influenced by Deschamps's *Lai de franchise,* which was written for 1 May 1385; Deschamps wrote Chaucer a ballade (Oeuvres 2:138–39) in which he says he is sending him some poems by the hand of Sir Lewis Clifford. Lowes argued that the *Lai de franchise* was one of those poems and that Clifford brought it in the spring or summer of 1386, which would then be the earliest possible date for the poem. Lossing (SP 39, 1942, 15–35) questioned whether Chaucer did use the *Lai de franchise;* and Brown (MLN 58, 1943, 274–78) argued that Clifford was unlikely to have delivered the verses to Chaucer after 30 April 1385, when the truce between the English and French expired.

Nevertheless, the reference to *Troilus* in the Prologue shows that it could not have been written much earlier than 1385, about the earliest plausible date for that poem (see introductory note to *Troilus,* above), and the lack of any mention of *The Canterbury Tales* (the pilgrimage especially, not the earlier-written components) seems to indicate that the Prologue antedates that work. It is most probable that the F Prologue was composed sometime in the period 1386 at the earliest to 1388 at the very latest, since the General Prologue to the *Tales* would surely have been mentioned, in Alceste's catalogue of the poet's writings, after that date.

The dating of the G Prologue depends on whether or not one accepts the priority of F. When G was first printed by Furnivall, it was assumed to be an earlier version, and this was for years the accepted view (see for example, J. C. French, Problem of the Two Prologues to Ch's LGW, 1902). Though the old theory that F is the later version still has its adherents (e.g., Eliason, Lang. of Ch, 192n.), the arguments for the priority of F (see esp. Lowes, PMLA 19, 1904, 593–683, and 20:749–864, and in Kittredge Anniv. Sts., 95–104) have prevailed. Most modern critics and editors, while admitting the matter is still open to debate, accept G as the later version and date it 1394 (the year of Anne's death) or later, because of the deletion of all reference to Queen Anne. Fisher (South Atlantic Bulletin, 43, no. 4, 1978, 75–84) argues for 1396 as the date of the G Prologue.

The sources of the Prologue are most fully set out in Lowes's articles (PMLA 19:593–683; and 20:749–64). For the panegyric of the daisy, the principal suggestion probably came from Deschamps's *Lai de franchise,* with reminiscences of a number of other French poems on the marguerite. The vision of Love, with the accusation and defense of the offender against Love's laws (F 197–end) is indebted for its framework and some details to Machaut's *Jugement dou Roy de Behaingne.* See Wimsatt, Ch and Fr Poets, 94–96. For the general idea of a court of love no specific source was needed, since there was a rich tradition of such fictional proceedings. Neilson, Origins of the Court of Love, 390–401, provides a broad survey. For the underlying fiction of Chaucer's heresy against love, there are various literary parallels, in addition to Machaut's *Jugement dou Roy de Navarre* and *Jugement dou Roy De Behaingne* (on which see William A. Calin, Poet at the Fountain, 1974, chs. 2 and 6), including Jean de Meun's excuses (RR 15135–58; cf. F. Guillon, Jean Clopinell, 1903, 169–70).

The question of whether characters in the Prologue

are allegories of historical figures has been much debated. The identification of Alceste with Queen Anne and the God of Love with Richard II was first proposed by Tyrwhitt and developed by ten Brink (Ch Studien, 1870, 147–50), Lange (Anglia 39, 1915, 347–55), and Koch (ESt 55, 1921, 161–65, and Anglia 50, 1926, 62–69, 104–5). Lowes (PMLA 19:666) provides a list of the major supporters of this view to 1904. Bressie (MP 26, 1928, 28–29) argued that the *Legend*, Usk's *Testament of Love*, and even *Pearl* are to be associated with a marguerite cult in honor of the queen (Robinson). Burlin (Ch Fict., 43) cites Anne's historical record as an intercessor and conciliator as being appropriate to the Alceste-figure. The theory was opposed by Lowes (PMLA 20:749–64) and Kittredge (MP 6, 1909, 435–39), among others. Robinson thought the allegorical interpretation of the Prologue improper, as does Bronson (In Search of Ch, 54–59). Baugh, in his edition, argues that the God of Love's command to give the completed book to the queen at Sheene (F 496–97) renders it highly improbable that Alceste can be identified with the queen. Donaldson (Ch's Poetry, 958) protests that such views are based on "a mistaken notion of the consistency required by medieval allegory."

Other candidates have been proposed. Tupper (JEGP 21, 1922, 293–317) identified Alceste with one Alice Chester (or de Cestre), a theory neatly demolished by Manly's demonstration that Alice de Cestre was not a lady-in-waiting but an elderly washerwoman (MP 24, 1927, 257–59). George Williams (New View of Ch, 1965, 134) put forth the unlikely theory that Alceste was meant to represent the Duchess Blanche, and the God of Love, John of Gaunt. Margaret Galway saw in Alceste the princess of Wales, Joan of Kent, widow of the Black Prince and mother of Richard II (MLR 33:145–99; MLN 60, 1945, 431–39; and MLR 44, 1949, 161–77). Her view has seemed attractive to some (see, for example, Baugh's introduction to the *Legend* in his edition, and Wimsatt, UNC Sts. in Rom. Langs. and Lits., 87–89, 64 n. 15) but her method is doubtful (Huppé, MLR 43, 1948, 393–99), her evidence has been questioned (Weese, MLN 63, 1948, 474–77), and since Joan died on 7 August 1385, Galway's theory would push the composition of the Prologue back to 1385 or even 1384. Though Carleton Brown uses Galway's idea as a makeweight for his argument for an earlier date for the F Prologue, 1385 seems too early. None of the proposed identifications have, thus far, done much to further our understanding of the poem.

For discussion of Chaucer's artistic (as opposed to personal or political) reasons for revising the Prologue, see Gardner, JEGP 67, 1968, 595–611. For a critical analysis of the G Prologue, see Payne, ChR 9, 1975, 197–211, and Key of Remembrance, ch. 3. For treatments of the Prologue as the last of Chaucer's dream-visions, see C. Hieatt, Realism of Dream Visions, 1967, 84–86, and Spearing, Medieval Dream Poetry, 101–10. Bronson praises the G Prologue for better organization and tighter unity, the F Prologue for its warmer, more personal and emotional tone (In Search of Ch, 52–54). Frank (Ch and LGW, 12–36) discusses the unconventional qualities of the Prologue.

("Corresponding passages in the two versions will be found in the parallel columns of the text, except where the order was changed [by Chaucer] in revision"—Robinson.)

F 1   Froissart's Joli buisson de jonece, 786–92, offers a striking parallel to the opening lines (see Kittredge, ESt 26, 1899, 336). On the rhetorical character of these lines, a combination of the methods of *sententia* and *exemplum,* see Manly, Ch and the Rhetoricians, 1926, 8.

F 16   Proverbial; Whiting B255. The Latin form of the proverb is written in the margin of some MSS: "Bernardus monachus non uidit omnia." **Bernard the monk** is most probably Bernard of Clairvaux; see Smith, MLN 61, 1946, 38–44, and Hamilton, MLN 62, 1947, 190–91.

F 17–28   For a contrary view, see Bo 2.pr7.89–90.

F 27–39, G 27–39   Malone (PAPS 94, 1950, 317–20) compares the two versions of this passage to illustrate Chaucer's methods of revision.

F 40–65   Lowes pointed out (PMLA 19:593–683) that these lines contain numerous echoes of the French marguerite poems.

F 40–43   Cf. Froissart, Paradys d'amours, 1633–35, 1621–22, and his Prison amoureuse (ed. Fourrier: Bibliothèque Française et Romane 73, 1974), 898–99.

F 43   With this use of **our,** cf. line 1689; it is probably to be taken literally rather than as a "domestic our" (cf. WBPro III.311n.). Possibly it is a quasi-demonstrative (cf. CkT I.4365).

F 44–49   Cf. Deschamps, Lai de franchise (Oeuvres 2: 203–214), 14, 27–30; and Froissart, Dittié de la flour de la margherite (Oeuvres 2:209–15), 162–65.

F 45–47   Similar to KnT I.1676–78. Tatlock (SP 18, 1921, 419–28) notes, in addition to the verbal similarities, a parallel between the situation here and Duke Theseus's separating Palamoun and Arcite and then pardoning them at the queen's request.

F 50–52   Cf. Machaut, Dit de la marguerite (ed. Tarbé), 123–29.

F 53–55   Cf. Froissart, Le joli mois de may (Poésies 2: 194–209), 289–90; and Deschamps, Ballade no. 532 (Oeuvres 3:368–69), 15–16. **floures flour** in 53 and *flour of floures* in F 185 express a commonplace. Cf. ABC 4, and see Peter Dronke, Med. Lat. and the Rise of the Eur. Love Lyric, 1965–66, 1:181–82. Frank (Ch and LGW, 22) points out that "the hackneyed metaphor acquires a comic truth" since the poet is not speaking of a lady but of a daisy.

F 56–59   Cf. Froissart, Dittié, 81–82, 159–62.

G 58   "With this line, which is true to actual fact, Lowes (PMLA 19:617) compares, among other passages, Froissart's Dittié, 96–98, and his Paradys d'amours, 1636–38" (Robinson).

F 60–65   Cf. Deschamps, Lai de franchise (Oeuvres complètes, vol. 2), 44–50.

F 66–67   Cf. KnT I.1459–60n.

F 68–77   "This is addressed to contemporary poets such as Machaut, Froissart, and Deschamps and may be regarded as an acknowledgment on Chaucer's part of his debt to their poems on the 'marguerite' " (Robinson).

F 72   Courtiers in England and France, as part of their May Day festivities, playfully divided themselves into two parties, defenders respectively of the flower and of the leaf. Cf. Gower, Conf. Aman. 8.2468 (which may be an imitation of Chaucer); see Marsh, MP 4, 1906, 121–67, 281–327, and The Floure and the Leafe and the Assembly of Ladies, intro., 22–23 (cf. KnT I.1053–54n.).

F 74   **makyng:** That is, making poetry, especially in the vernacular and aimed at contemporary social interests and tastes, as opposed to *poesye* written in Latin on universal themes and classical subjects. See Olson, CL 31, 1979, 272–90; Wetherbee, in New Perspectives, 74–80; and Kiser, Telling Classical Tales, 136–41. The figure of gleaning after reapers may be an echo of Ruth 2.2, which was used in the intro. to Higden's Polychronicon. "The reference to reaping in Usk's Testament of Love (Prol., 97–101), generally associated with Chaucer's lines, has more resemblance to the passage in Higden" (Robinson). (See Bressie, MP 26:17–29.)

G 71–80 Lowes (in Kittredge Anniv. Sts., 95–104) compares this and G 93–106 and G 179–202 to F 188–96, F 197–211, and F 276–99, and concludes that F is the earlier.

G 76 "With the use of *witholde(n)* here and in F 192, cf. GP I.511" (Robinson).

F 84–96 Based on the opening stanzas of the Filostrato, lines Chaucer did not use in Troilus. Lowes (PMLA 19: 624–26) conjectures that Chaucer's transition to the Filostrato was suggested by certain lines near the end of Machaut's Dit de la marguerite (ed. Tarbé, 128), which are similar to Boccaccio in language and sentiment. Some phrases still echo the marguerite poetry: cf. 86–87 with Machaut's Dit de la marguerite (126–27) and **erthly god** (95) with "la déesse mondaine" in Deschamps's Lai de franchise, 52 (Robinson). Norton-Smith (Geoffrey Ch, 67–69) discusses the imagery of this passage and suggests (66 n. 17) that **sorwes** (96) is "a calque on the Latin usage *curae . . .* signifying writings."

F 94 **sovereyne:** Cf. F 275 and Tr 4.316.

F 108 "Note the change of date from the first of May in the F version to the end of the month in the G version (1.89)" (Robinson).

F 113–14 The sun entered Taurus about 12 April, and on 1 May it would have been at about 20° of Taurus; Chaucer apparently meant **brest** to specify the middle sector of the sign rather than the exact center (15°), as Skeat believed (3:294). Cf. Tr 4.32. **Agenores doghtre:** Europa, who was loved by Jupiter in the form of a bull and is called "Agenore nata" in Met. 2.858 (where her story is told). The image is from Boccaccio, Tes. 3.5.

G 96 "The G version introduces at this point the poet's return to the house and his dream, which do not occur in F until line 200. Professor Lowes (Kittredge Ann. Sts., 95–104) argues that G thus has more unity and avoids verbal repetitions, and is therefore the revised form. The remark about the house with the arbor (which occurs in both texts) perhaps furnishes an indication of the date of composition. It seems hardly applicable to Chaucer's house over the city gate," on which he is known to have surrendered his lease on or before 5 October 1386 (Ch Life Records, 146), "perhaps for the purpose of attending to new duties, either as a member of Parliament or as justice of the peace in Kent" (Robinson).

F 123 Robinson says the daisy is odorless, following Lowes (PMLA 19:627, n. 5). But Rowland (N&Q 208, 1963, 210) suggests that it depends on the type of daisy, and also possibly on one's sense of smell. Whatever the reality, Robinson is undoubtedly right that Chaucer is here following the tradition of the marguerite poets; cf. Machaut, Dit de la marguerite (Oeuvres, ed. Tarbé, 123–29), and Deschamps's Ballade 539, 66 (Oeuvres complètes, 3:379–80).

F 125–29 From RR 57–62; the French has "povrete,"

rendered **pore estat** here and in Rom 61. Brusendorff (Ch Trad., 398) points to the parallel with BD 410–12.

F 127 **swerd of cold:** Cf. SqT V.57. Possibly from Machaut, Roy de Navarre, 34–36; RR 5942–46; or the Anticlaudianus of Alanus de Insulis 8.8 (PL 210:557).

F 137 **sophistrye:** "Cf. 'sofime' in RR 21498, and the De planctu Naturae of Alanus, 'perdix . . . nunc venatorum sophismata . . . abhorrebat' (PL 210:436, as suggested by E. S. A., N&Q, 8th ser., 1893, 3.249–50)" (Robinson).

F 138–39 Cf. Jeremiah 5.26–27; Amos 3.5.

F 139–40 Cf. RR 703–4, Rom 715–16.

F 145 Cf. PF 683.

F 153–74 "This paragraph on the birds is replaced in G by the five lines (139–43) in which the lark heralds the approach of the God of Love. The passage in F is in the manner of RR and contains a number of verbal parallels of more or less uncertain significance. See Cipriani, PMLA 22, 1907, 594–95" (Robinson). Norton-Smith (Geoffrey Ch, 65, n. 13) discusses the philosophical orientation with which this passage invests the "pre-sleep ambiance" of the F Prologue.

F 154 **tydif:** Cf. SqT V.648n.

F 160 **Daunger:** Cf. Rom 3018n.

F 162 **Mercy passen Ryght:** The idea is commonplace (Whiting M508), as is the application of the Christian doctrine of grace to the affairs of love; cf. KnT I.3089 and Tr 3.1282n.

F 166 **Etik:** Possibly, as Skeat has it, Aristotle's Ethics (cf. Dante, Convivio, Canzone 3.85), but also possibly a person, perhaps Horace. Robinson notes that John of Salisbury in Policraticus 8.13 (ed. Webb 2:317) introduces a quotation from the Satires (1.2.24) and a paraphrase from the Epistles (1.18.9) with "ut enim ait ethicus." The idea of *vertu is the mene* (F 165) is proverbial; cf. Whiting M443, Walther 33673, and RR 11275–76 (Rom 6527–28), where the Aristotelian idea is attributed to Solomon.

F 171–74 Cf. BD 402–3, RR 8411–13.

F 184 Chaucer's etymology of *daisy* is quite correct. The Old English is *dægeseage* (eye of day) (Robinson).

F 208 **was leyd:** For the construction, see KnT I.2528n.

F 213 "Cupid leads in Alceste clothed in the likeness of a daisy. Her name is disclosed in F 432," but Chaucer, probably inadvertently, represents the narrator as ignorant of her identity until F 518. This slip is present in both texts. "In the G version, Alceste is named in 422, but the passage may possibly be regarded as an aside to the reader, and not inconsistent with what follows" (Robinson). On the story of Alceste, see F 499–504 below.

F 214–25 Wimsatt (UNC Sts. in Rom. Langs. and Lits. 87, 87–89, 63–4) finds a unique literary precedent for Alceste's attire in Machaut's Dit de la fleur de lis et de la marguerite.

F 215 **fret:** A headnet, sometimes decorated with flowers or jewels; sometimes, an ornament of intricate, net-like design. See Iris Brooke, Hist. of Eng. Costume, 1972, figs. 25 and 35.

F 217, 220 "The rare word **flouroun** [**flowroun,** 220] here used in the sense of 'petal,' must have been taken by Chaucer from Froissart's Dittié, where it is twice employed in the same sense (166, 187)." The MED gives only LGW as examples of the word's use. It can mean a flower-shaped ornament (see OED s.v. *flouron* 1).

"Lowes (PMLA 19:631–34) argues that its use in F, as opposed to the more familiar *floures* in G, is evidence of the priority of the former." But *floures* may not be an authorial emendation. Nonetheless, *flouroun* appears to have been Chaucer's first form. (Robinson.)

F 221   perle: A single pearl. **oriental:** Of superior value and brilliancy, as coming in ancient times from the East (MED, s.v. *Oriental,* adj. [d]). Cf. the ME Pearl, lines 2–3.

F 227   greves: The allusion to "sprays" or "branches" has been taken by Bilderbeck, Ch's LGW, 87, as a reference to one of Richard's favorite devices, the badge of the Plantagenets. "*Rose-leves,* rose petals" (Robinson).

F 230   Norton-Smith (Geoffrey Ch, 69–71 and nn.) considers both crowns examples of the ornate "Bohemian style," brought to England when Richard married Anne of Bohemia.

G 161   "The *lylye floures* in G replace a sun-crown in F. Those who hold the Prologue to be allegorical understand both, as they do the *grene greves* above, to refer to Richard. On his monument there is a representation of the sun ascending behind clouds; and the lilies, it is pointed out, may betoken his claim to the French throne. . . . Lange also recognized Christian symbolism in the sun-crown, and compared the title 'sol justitiae' given to Christ by Albertus Magnus. And again changing the symbol, he suggested that the sun, serving as a crown of gold, represents pure, heavenly love as opposed to the earthly passion celebrated in the Troilus. See Bilderbeck, Ch's LGW, 86–87; Lange, Anglia 44, 1920, 72–77; . . . and . . . Langhans, Untersuchungen, 216 and Anglia 50, 1926, 97–99; Koch, Anglia 50:64. . . . Kuhl, PQ 24, 1945, 35, has also argued for an allegorical interpretation of the fleur-de-lys. But the presence of any of this allegory in the passage is dubious, and the particular interpretations suggested are arbitrary and more or less inconsistent" (Robinson).

G 179–202   "These lines correspond to F 276–99. If G is the revised version, the shift has the advantage of bringing closely together the sternness of the God of Love and the comfort of Alceste. The new order may also have suggested the transfer of the ballade from the dreamer to the Ladies" (Robinson).

F 247   "In the F version the ballade is sung by the poet, like the corresponding song in the Paradys d'amours. The change in G makes it form a distinct part of the action" (Robinson).

F 249–69   The ballade in Froissart's Paradys d'amour sings the praises of the daisy and agrees in substance and language with other parts of the Prologue, but Smith (MLN 66, 1951, 27–32) notes that in some respects Froissart's Ballade 6 is closer to Chaucer's. The question of to what extent the lists of women in this ballade and the Intro to MLT can be taken as a projected list of contents for the Legend remains moot. Frank (Ch and LGW, 198, 209) concludes from the two lists that Chaucer did have a large number of stories in mind and that the allusion to the work in the Intro to MLT indicates his continuing interest in the project. The ballade is in the strict French form (see the Short Poems intro., p. 632), in rime royal, with refrain and the same two rhymes throughout.

F 249   Absolon: Cf. 2 Sam. 16.26, though this line is from RR 13870; cf. MilT I.3312–38n.

F 255, 262, 269   "My lady of version F corresponds to 'ma dame' in Froissart and Ballade no. 42, attributed to Deschamps" (Pièces attributables à Deschamps, 10.xlix–1), "and is probably the original reading" (Robinson). G has *Alceste,* which is probably Chaucer's revision, although it could possibly be a scribal emendation. Frank observes that Alceste is not the narrator's lady in a courtly love sense. On the subtleties of such a distinction, see Ch and LGW, p. 24 and n. 14.

F 250–54   Ester: The biblical Esther, a model of *debonairte* in BD 986–87 and of meekness in MerT IV.1744–45 (see n.). On **Jonathas,** see 1 Sam. 19.2. **Penalopee:** Cf. FranT V.1443. **Marcia Catoun:** Either the wife of Marcus Cato Uticensis, who, unwillingly divorced, returned at an advanced age to her husband (Lucan, Pharsalia 2.326–49; cf. Dante's comments in Convivio 4.28, and Kittredge, MP 7, 1910, 482–83), or the daughter, likewise true to her first love (Jerome, Adv. Jov. 1.46), as Lounsbury argued (Sts. in Ch 2:294). **Ysoude:** Cf. PF 290. **Eleyne:** Cf. Tr 1.57–63.

F 257   Lavyne: For the form see HF 458n.

F 258   Polyxena, daughter of Priam of Troy, was sacrificed on Achilles' tomb in order to be reunited with him; see Ovid, Met. 13.448.

F 263–68   Herro: See Ovid, Her. 18, 19; she appears on the Man of Law's list of Cupid's saints (II.69). **Laudomia:** Laodamia, wife of Protesilaus, whose dead husband was allowed to return to her and who, when he died a second time, died along with him; see FranT V.1445n. For her tale, see Ovid, Her. 13; she is also on the Man of Law's list (II.71).

F 265   The incestuous love of **Canace** (Ovid, Her. 11 and Gower, Conf. Aman. 3.147–360) is specifically rejected by the Man of Law as an unsuitable subject for Chaucer.

espied by thy chere: Canace's guilty love for her brother and resulting pregnancy were revealed to her nurse when the latter accused her of being in love and she blushed and dropped her eyes to her stomach (Her. 11.33–34).

F 314   it am I: Cf. KnT I.1736.

F 321   relyke: "Treasure, precious possession; applied primarily to the relics of a saint. The use of the word as a term of endearment is striking, but not unnatural. It occurs in both English and French (see Rom 2673, 2907)" (Robinson).

F 329   Here the god of Love states plainly that Chaucer translated the Roman de la rose. Whether he in fact finished this work, and whether the existing Middle English translation belongs to him wholly, in part, or not at all is unknown. See Rom, Introductory Note and Explanatory Notes.

F 334   Proverbial; cf. Whiting S709, LGW 2582 and MerT IV.2426n.

G 261–63   Cf. WBPro III.707–10.

G 268–312   The passage on books occurs only in the G version. Some critics condemn it as a digression and consider its omission from F evidence that F is the revised text. Those who consider G the revision defend the passage as relevant or even essential to the argument of the poem. Burlin (Ch Fiction, 36), who sees the Prologue as concerned with the division between "bookish authority and natural experience," and Payne (Key of Remembrance, ch. 3), who sees it as concerned with Chaucer's development as a writer, both argue for the artistic integrity of this passage.

G 268–69 Lowes (MP 8, 1911, 323) compares Deschamps, Miroir de mariage, 9081–82; other possible influences of this work on G may be apparent in G 276–77 (Miroir, 9097–9100) and G 301–4 (Miroir, 9063–67).

G 273   sixty bokes: Probably to be taken as a humorous exaggeration; sixty books on a single subject would imply a huge personal library (cf. GP I.294 and n.), even if *sixty* is an estimate (Mary Immaculate, MLQ 2, 1941, 59–66; Tucker, RES 25, 1949, 152–53). Pratt (Spec 41, 1966, 619–42) shows that Chaucer knew and used a compendium of moral anecdotes and exhortations from various authors, such as the Communiloquium of John of Wales, and he therefore need not have known as many authors and books at first hand as some scholars have believed.

G 280   Valerye: Probably the Valerius of the Epistola Valerii ad Rufinum, included among the works of Jerome (PL 30:254–61) but now ascribed to Walter Map (see De nugis curialium, ed. James; and trans. Tupper and Ogle, 183–98). The mention of Jerome in the next line supports this identification, and though the work is primarily antifeminist, it praises Penelope, Lucretia, and the Sabine women. Valerius Maximus has also been proposed (see Tatlock, Dev. and Chron., 100, for a brief defense of this view). "A third possibility is Valerius Flaccus, whose Argonautica (bks. 2 and 7) tells the stories of Hypsipyle and Medea" (Robinson) and who is cited in LGW 1457. However, Chaucer does not use this Valerius as a source for these stories and mentions the name only as an authority for the names of the Argonauts.

Titus: Titus Livius, the Roman historian (cf. PhysT VI.1) cited (1683) as an authority for the legend of Lucretia.

Claudyan: The author of De raptu Proserpinae (see MerT IV.2232n. and Pratt, Spec 22, 1947, 419–29).

G 281   Jerome agayns Jovynyan: St. Jerome's famous attack on marriage; cf. WBPro and nn. The work, however, also praises chaste women and Chaucer drew on it for Dorigen's complaint in FranT V.1355–1456, which mentions many of the examples alluded to here in lines 286–304.

G 307   Estoryal Myrour: The Speculum historiale of Vincent of Beauvais; the Speculum is used as a source in the Legend of Cleopatra. On Vincent's influence on Chaucer, see Aiken, diss. Yale Univ., 1934.

G 312   Cf. NPT VII.3443n., and G 529.

G 315   This may be a friendly jab at Gower, who suggested at the end of the Conf. Aman. (8.2941–57) that Chaucer, like himself, was too old for the service of love. This might explain the change from *wrecches* (F) to **olde foles** (G). Bilderbeck (Ch's LGW, 1902, 105–6), who believes F to be the revised version, uses the same passage in Gower to explain the removal of the lines about old age. See also IntrMLT, II.77–89 and n.

F 338   "With **Seynt Venus** cf. RR 10827, 21086. The use of the term here was probably traditional rather than the result of deliberate adaptation to the device of the legend. Cf. WBPro III.604" (Robinson).

F 341–408   Some scholars "see this speech as a serious lecture on the duties of a king addressed to Richard II by Anne in the person of Alceste. Cf. particularly Bilderbeck, Ch's LGW, 93–99; Moore, MLR 7, 1912, 488–93; and Lowes's criticism of the view in PMLA 20:773–79. The speech itself . . . can easily be applied to the circum-

stances of Richard's reign. In fact, such an application is supported by a passage of similar import in Lak of Stedfastnesse, and Chaucer's sympathy with the sentiment expressed may perhaps be inferred from the ParsT X.761–65" (Robinson). But the allegorical identification of the god of Love with Richard is not proven thereby; the content of the speech is appropriate to the fictional characters and situation in question, but would surely be highly improper for Chaucer to put into the mouth of the queen of England for delivery to the king. Galway (MLN 60:434) believes the speech is drawn from an actual speech made by Princess Joan to Richard. Huppé and Weese cast doubt on this theory (see the introduction to the Explanatory Notes on LGW, above) but Galway has some support from Fisher (John Gower, 243–44), who says the speech would have been appropriate to Princess Joan, though we cannot assert with certainty that this is the speech that she made. "For extended illustration of the political doctrines of the speech, drawn from medieval political writings, see Schlauch, Spec 20, 1945, 151–56" (Robinson).

G 326   Proverbial; cf. Whiting G401.

F 352   Speirs (Ch the Maker, 120n.) compares NPT VII.3325–26. Also cf. RR 1034 (Rom 1050).

F 360   thus seith Dante: Inf. 13.64–65. "The whore (meretrice) that never turns her adulterous eyes from the house of Caesar." As Skeat notes, the substitution of *lavendere*, laundress, washer of dirty linen, for "meretrice" is a nice touch.

F 372–75   Ruggiers (PQ 29, 1950, 445–48) compares this passage to Dante, Convivio 4.20. Fisher (John Gower, 181) compares Gower, Mirour, 23233.

F 374   tirauntz of Lumbardye: Cf. ClT IV.72n. Also see Hardman, RES n.s. 31, 1980, 172–78.

F 379–83   Fisher notes these lines echo the Secreta secretorum (ed. Steele, 36), which was attributed to Aristotle, and parallel Gower's Vox clam., 6.581, 1001, and Conf. Aman. 7.2695–3600. The resemblance is general rather than specific. Robinson notes that Chaucer may have known indirectly similar material in the Nichomachean Ethics, bk. 5, and compares Seneca, De clementia 1.3.3 and 5.4. The **Philosophre** in 381 is, as almost invariably when the definite article appears, Aristotle.

F 388–90   A commonplace in discussions of kingship; Fisher notes parallels to Conf. Aman. 7.2743–44 and Vox clam. 6.741.

F 391–95   Skeat compares Martial, Epig. 12.61.5–6 ("Libyan lions attack bulls; they do not bother butterflies"), and Pliny, Nat. Hist. 8.16.

F 411   Cf. RR 10923–24.

F 412–13   Cf. the close of Deschamps's Lay amoureux, 275–end (Oeuvres complètes 2:202) and Ovid's defense of himself at the beginning of the Remedia amoris (except Ovid always declared himself a lover and Chaucer usually declared himself an outsider in matters of love) (Robinson).

G 400–401   Kaut, MLN 49, 1934, 87, takes these lines as evidence of that Chaucer was advancing in years when he wrote the G version (Robinson).

F 422–23   The **ympne, balades, roundels,** and **virelayes** have for the most part been lost. Though Brusendorff argued that this statement was merely conventional (Ch Trad., 432–33), Gower, Conf. Aman. 8.2943–47, mentions the many "Diteés and songes glad" that Chaucer made in his youth, and in the Retraction Chaucer repents of *many a song and many a leccherous lay* (X.1087).

Among the surviving works there are no real *virelayes,* only two *roundels* (Merciles Beaute and PF 680–92), and only three or four *balades* that could properly be called *ympnes* (hymns) for Love's holidays.

G 414　Of the Wreched Engendrynge of Mankynde: Apparently a lost translation of all or part of a work by Pope Innocent III, De miseria condicionis humane. Skeat believed the translation was in seven-line stanzas but offered no adequate evidence for this. Lowes suggested (PMLA 20:790–96) that the translation was in prose and that at one time Chaucer meant to assign it to the Man of Law (see IntroMLT II.96 and n.). The use of material from De contemptu mundi in the Man of Law's Prologue and Tale suggests that Chaucer was occupied with this translation around 1390. Brown (PMLA 50, 1935, 997–1011) proposed to identify the *Engendrynge* with "An Holy Meditation" ascribed to Lydgate and printed in the Minor Poems of John Lydgate, ed. McCracken 1:43–48 (Robinson). Dempster objected to this (MLN 51, 1936, 284–95), as did Tatlock (MLN 51:275–84), and Brown replied (ibid., 296–300), but his conjecture has not been accepted. Lewis (ChR 2, 1968, 139–58) makes a strong case for identifying the *Engendrynge* with the whole De contemptu mundi, while providing a tidy summary of the earlier arguments.

F 428　Origenes upon the Maudeleyne: A lost translation of the pseudo-Origen homily De Maria Magdalena; see McCall, Spec 46, 1971, 491–509.

F 432　quene of Trace: On the confusion here between Thrace and Thessaly, see Magoun, MS 15, 1953, 132 (Robinson). The idea of a queen asking mercy for an offender is common in literature (cf. KnT I.1748–61, WBT III.894–98, Tr 2.1447–49) and not unknown in life, as in the intervention of Edward III's queen to save the burghers of Calais (Froissart, Chron., ch. 146) and Anne's intercession with Richard for the people of London (Higden, Polychronicon, 9.272).

F 451–2 Proverbial; Whiting G76. Cf. Mel VII.1794.

F 464–65 Cf. SqT V.537 and n.

F 483　legende: Cf. G 473, G 539, F 549, F 557, 2456; on the implications of this characterization of LGW, see Janet Cowen, SP 82, 1985, 416–36.

F 496–97 Eltham, seven miles from London; **Sheene,** now Richmond. Since these lines do not appear in G, Koch (ESt 55:178) and Langhans (Anglia 50:74), who held that G is the earlier version, argued they were a scribal interpolation in F. It is more reasonable to assume that G is the revised form and that Chaucer removed the couplet to avoid any reference to Anne after her death. Richard was so grief-stricken that he ordered his residence at Sheene completely demolished so that not a stone would stand to remind him of her. Apparently his orders were not completely carried out (see Lowes, MP 8:331n. and 334n.). Baugh holds that this couplet renders impossible the identification of Alceste with Queen Anne. Donaldson, 958, says it is perfectly possible for the queen to have an existence on an allegorical level within the poem and an objective "real" existence outside the poem to which the poet can refer.

F 499–504 The story of Alcestis *(Alceste),* faithful wife of Admetus, is told by Gower (Conf. Aman. 7.1917–43 and 8.2640–46), who omits the rescue by Hercules. Chaucer could have found the story in Hyginus, Fabulae, 51; Boccaccio, De gen. deorum, 13.1; or, the closest, according to McCall (Ch Among the Gods, 178, n. 40), Simon of Hesdin's translation of Valerius Maximus, Memora-

bilia, 4.6. See Wetherbee, Ch and Poets, 142. None includes the transformation into a daisy, which appears to be Chaucer's invention, perhaps inspired, as Sandras suggests (Etude sur Geoffrey Ch, 1859, 58; cf. Beck, Anglia 5:363), by Froissart's Dittié de la margherite, 69–80 (Oeuvres 2:2), lines in which Heres' tears for Cepheï were turned into daisies.

F 503 See KnT I.1761n.

F 504 "Lange finds in this line an allusion to the allegorical character of Alceste. According to his theory, she stands for the queen, whose name, 'Anna,' signifies (in Hebrew) *gratia* (grace, mercy). So she discloses by her action *what* she is. . . . See Anglia 44, 1920, 72–77, 373–85; and for objections, Langhans, Anglia 44:337–45, and 50:87–103; Koch, Anglia 50:62" (Robinson).

F 505, 518 The discrepancy between these lines and 432, where Alceste has already told her name, cannot quite be explained away. Possibly Chaucer was led into error by a too-close following of Froissart (Paradys d'amours, 358–60), but he did not correct the mistake in revision. Langhans suggests punctuating line 518 thus: "Is this good Alceste the daisy, etc.?" But this does not really solve the problem.

F 525–26 Skeat identifies **Agaton** with the Greek dramatist "Agatone" mentioned in Dante, Purg. 22.107. Etienne Sandras (Etude sur Ch, 115), followed by Bech (Anglia 5:364–65), suggests instead Plato's Symposium, in which the feast was held at the house of this dramatist. This work was sometimes known as Agatho's feast (cf. Macrobius, Saturnalia 2.1) and contains the story of Alcestis. There is, however, no mention of her becoming a constellation.

F 531　Cibella: Cybela or Cybele, a Phrygian goddess of nature and fertility, sometimes identified with Ceres. Both Skeat and Robinson suggest that Chaucer was possibly influenced to mention Cybele by Froissart's Dittié, 105–9, in which Ceres receives the daisies made from the tears of Heres. Clogan (PQ 43, 1964, 272–74) argues that the more likely source is the common classical cognomen for Cybele, Berecynthia, defined as "flower of spring" in the Liber imaginum deorum of Albericus I (Neckham?).

F 533　reed: The red tips of the petals. Mars is commonly associated with red; see LGW 2589 and KnT I.975–77n.

F 540 In the F version of the ballade (249–69) Alceste is not named; in Pro G she is, so this reprimand is deleted in G.

G 529 Cf. NPT VII. 3443n.

F 562 Cf. the comparable "situation in Machaut's Jugement dou Roy de Navarre and in the Tresor amoureux (ascribed to Froissart, Oeuvres 3:52, but of doubtful authority), where very special meters are prescribed" (Robinson). See Kittredge (MP 7:471–74), who suggests that "the line . . . may easily be explained as a reversal of the injunction which the King of Navarre lays upon . . . Machaut."

I. THE LEGEND OF CLEOPATRA

Chaucer's exact source is not known; see Frank, Ch and LGW, 38n., from which the following account of Chaucer's sources is derived. Skeat suggested some Latin version of Plutarch without specifying further; Bech (Anglia 5:314–18) suggested Florus's *Epitome rerum Romanorum,* but that is unlikely (see 654 below); Robinson, following Shannon (Ch and Roman Poets, 179–90), took the apparent source as Boccaccio's *De casibus* 6.15, or *De claris mulieribus,* ch. 86, or both; see further P. Goodman, in Ch and Trecento, 280–90. Ghosh (MLR 26, 1931, 332–36) suggested Orosius, and Vincent of Beauvais, *Speculum historiale* 6.5; Vincent has also been proposed by Wimsatt (Spec 12, 1937, 375–81), Aiken (Spec 13, 1938, 232–36), Schanzer (N&Q 205, 1960, 335–36), and, most recently, Frank (Ch and LGW, 39), who says, however, "the *Speculum historiale* provided not much more than a scenario." Wimsatt and Aiken (Spec 12:378; 13:232–33) print all of Vincent's brief account. The description of the Battle of Actium is based on some knowledge of contemporary sea battles, and no source has been found for such details as Cleopatra's death in the serpent pit (see 678–80 below). Gower's brief account of Cleopatra (Conf. Aman. 8.2571–77) is probably based on Chaucer's legend. Frank (Ch and LGW, 44) finds the legend "a failure . . . because it lacks imaginative unity," but he credits Chaucer with "the first serious treatment of Cleopatra in English" (37). For general discussion of the classical and medieval traditions available to Chaucer and the implications of his use of them, see Taylor, JMRS 7, 1977, 249–69. As Shannon points out (179n.), this is the only one of the legends not to include material from Ovid or Virgil.

580   Tholome: "Ptolemy, the name of Cleopatra's father and two brothers. The reference here is probably to the elder brother," with whom Cleopatra shared the throne after their father's death (51 B.C.). After that brother's death in the Alexandrine War, the younger brother became Cleopatra's co-ruler until she had him killed four years later (Robinson).
589   "For this commonplace doctrine about Fortune, cf. MkT, esp. VII.2136–42, 2763–66" (Robinson).
592   After the death of his first wife, Fulvia, Antony married Octavia, the sister of Octavius (*Octovyan,* 624), whom he deserted for Cleopatra (Robinson).
594   Only in the accounts of Vincent of Beauvais and Boccaccio does Antony marry Cleopatra (Aiken, Spec 13:233).
600   Cf. KnT I.1817.
614–15, 622–23   Examples of rhetorical *abbreviatio* (cf. KnT I.875–88 n.). Chaucer is following the god of Love's instructions as given in Pro F 576–77.
621   Proverbial; see Whiting S249.
627   Proverbial; see Whiting L308.
629–53   Chaucer describes not the actual Battle of Actium but a late fourteenth-century sea battle, much of which he may have learned by hearsay. W. P. Ker (intro. to Berners's Froissart, 1901–3, 1:1xxviii) believed Froissart's account of the battle of La Rochelle (1372) was Chaucer's source; Schofield (Kittredge Anniv. Sts., 139–52) notes similarities to the Battles of Sluys (1340) and Espagnols-sur-Mer (1350) and to the Romance of Richard Coeur de Lion (ed. Brunner, Wiener Beiträge 42, lines 2537–2684). The relevant passages in Froissart are bk. 1 chs. 50 and 303–5 of Johnes's translation and the addition (in Johnes 1:382–90). Schofield shows there was an intense interest in naval affairs in England between 1385 and 1387, when he believes the Legend was written.

The description of the battle is notable for the heavy use of alliteration, which Chaucer also uses for his account of the tournament in KnT I.2601–16 (see n.).
634   "On the **se,** the Sinus Ambracius or modern Gulf of Arta, see Magoun," Ch Gazetteer, 19 (Robinson).
636   "'And try to attack with the sun at their back.' The English followed precisely this method in the battle of Sluys (Froissart, ch. 50; Johnes 1:72)" (Robinson).
637   Cannon mounted on ships were known in England in Chaucer's time, although they were evidently small compared to later cannon, and fired a variety of missiles and feathered bolts as well as balls (J. Batchelor and I. Hogg, Artillery, 1972, 4). Their advent cannot be precisely dated, but in 1336 there were guns aboard ships sent against Antwerp by Louis de Male (Henrard, Annales de l'Académie d'Archéologie de Belgique 45, 1889, 240). J. Mordal (Twenty-five Centuries of Sea Warfare, trans. Ortzen, 1959, 41) says that in 1338 the French mounted four cannon on each of five captured English ships, at least two of which were recaptured by the English at the Battle of Sluys in 1340.
640   "The grapnels (hooks for laying hold of vessels) and the shearing-hooks (used to cut their ropes) are mentioned in the description of Sluys, Espagnols, and La Rochelle" (Robinson).
642   For a similar boarding, cf. Espagnols (Johnes 1:199). Compare this vivid battle scene with the alliterative Morte Arthur, in King Arthur's Death, ed. L. D. Benson, 1974, 4154–4346.
645–48   The repeated **he** is used demonstratively, meaning "this one . . . that one." Cf. KnT I.1210 and see Burnley, Guide to Ch's Language, 82–83.
645   "For the use of spears in sea-fights, cf. a battle off Guernsey (Johnes 1:91) and La Rochelle (1.305)" (Robinson).
648   pesen: Peas were apparently poured on the decks to make footing difficult, as Skeat explains. Furniss (MLN 68, 1953, 115–18) has found a parallel passage from Gascoigne that mentions a similar use of peas at the battle of Lepanto. Nevertheless, scholars have been reluctant to accept Skeat's interpretation. Smith (JEGP 44, 1945, 56–61) would emend to "peires" (*pierres;* stones), Mather (JEGP 43, 1944, 375–79) to "resyn" (crude turpentine, commonly, but incorrectly, says the OED, called "pitch"). Schofield believes the line refers to pitch poured on the deck to spread "Greek fire" (see Jean de Meun, Art de chevalerie, ed. Robert, SATF, 1897, 174), in which case *pesen* would be due to mistaking Fr. *pois* (pitch) for *pois* (peas). But this assumes Chaucer was using a French source, and none is known.
649   On the use of quicklime, see Gwavas N&Q, 5th ser., 1878, 10:188; and Aegidius Romanus, De regimine principium 3.3.23.
651   Proverbial; cf. Whiting T87, Tr 3.615, and KnT I.2636n.
653   to-go: Probably the third person plural present indicative of a compound with *to-,* meaning "scatter," although it might be the historical infinitive used in place of the finite verb. See Mustanoja, ME Syntax, 538–39, and Kenyon, Syntax of the Infinitive, 82–83. Cf. *to laughe* Tr. 2.1108.
654   purpre sayl: The purple sail was Bech's strongest argument for Chaucer's use of Florus as his source (Anglia 5:314–18), but it appears also in Boccaccio's De

casibus and De claris mulieribus (Shannon, Ch and Roman Poets, 186–87) and in Vincent of Beauvais (Ghosh, MLR 26:332–36).

655 For the simile, which was a commonplace, see RR 15621–22.

657–61 Aiken (Spec 13:235) notes that only in Vincent of Beauvais's account does Antony commit suicide as soon as he sees Cleopatra's sail. In Florus he commits suicide after the battle; in Boccaccio and Plutarch he flees and commits suicide much later.

658 Cf. KnT I.1223.

678–80, 696–702 No source has been found for Cleopatra's death in a snake pit, which appears only here and in Gower (Conf. Aman. 8.2573–75), who probably got it from Chaucer. Plutarch tells of Cleopatra's death by snake-bite (only one snake); Boccaccio says she opened her veins by applying serpents to them, as does Florus; Vincent says that she died of the bites of snakes in Antony's tomb. According to Jehan de Tuim's Histoire de Jules César (ed. Settegast, 1881), she went naked into a pit to meet her death; but there is no mention of the serpents. The motif is far from uncommon in medieval legend and literature, however. It occurs in the romance of Bevis of Hampton, for instance. "Other examples . . . have been collected by Tatlock (MLN 29, 1914, 99–100), Brown (ibid., 198–99), and Griffith (Manly Anniv. Sts., 38)" (Robinson). Many of these instances occur in the lives of the saints, and Chaucer, as Griffith suggests, may have been led to think of them by his representation of Cleopatra as a martyr. Tatlock suggests Chaucer may have devised this horrible form of death simply because he knew serpent pits to be common in Africa. Kiser (Telling Classical Tales, 108) believes the "descent into the snake pit" is a deliberate echo of Christ's descent into Hell.

II. THE LEGEND OF THISBE

Chaucer's legend is based closely on Ovid's Met. 4.55–166. Chaucer omits the mulberry tree and thus eliminates the metamorphosis (as usual in the tales he draws from Ovid), adds several passages of his own invention (719–20, 798–801, 814–16, 887, 905–12), and elsewhere expands Ovid's narrative. Gower tells the same story in Conf. Aman. 3.1331–1494; for a comparison of his version to Chaucer's, see Meech, PMLA 46, 1931, 201n., and Callan, RES 22, 1946, 269–81. Chaucer's and Gower's versions seem related, but it is hard to say which came first.

706 Babiloyne: Meech (PMLA 46:201n.) argues for the influence of Ovide moralisé, since Ovid does not mention Babylon, but in Met. 4.99, Ovid calls his heroine "Babylonia Thisbe" (Frank, Ch and LGW, 47n.). Cf. IntroMLT II.63.

707 Semyramus: "Semiramis, the mythical queen who was said to have built the walls of Babylon" (Robinson). See Parr, ChR 5, 1970, 57–61; and PF 288n.

719–20 The gossip of the matchmaking women is Chaucer's addition.

735 Proverbial; Whiting G154 and cf. Tr 2.538–39. Ovid has: "Quoque magis tegitur, tectus magis aestuat ignis" (Met. 4.64).

741 A myte is a small Flemish coin and it is frequently used in expressions denoting worthlessness (cf. Tr 4.684; and Whiting M596–611). The use of the stereotyped phrase *deere ynough a myte/leek,* etc. as a qualifier meaning "worthless, useless" (cf. CYT VIII.795) perhaps accounts for the singular usage here.

742 Ovid, "quid non sentit amor?" (Met. 4.68). Cf. MerT IV.2126–27.

745 "The comparison to the confessional is Chaucer's. Ovid has simply 'murmure . . . minimo' (Met. 4.70)" (Robinson).

762 colde: For this use, cf. NPT VII.3256 and n.

768 Frank (Ch and LGW, 52) points out that the detail of the colde wal is not in Ovid.

773–74 Phebus, Aurora: Chaucer follows Ovid, Met. 4.81–82, but seems to reverse their roles.

811 with dredful fot: "Timido pede" (Ovid, Met. 4.100). The phrase also appears in KnT I.1479.

853–61, 862–68, 869–82 In each of these passages, Chaucer has expanded on Ovid.

885 hevy, dedly yen: "Oculos a morte gravatos" (Ovid, Met. 4.145).

916–23 These lines are evidently original with Chaucer.

917–18 "Cf. RR 14145 (not closely parallel)" (Robinson).

III. THE LEGEND OF DIDO

The primary source is Virgil's *Aeneid,* with incidental use of Ovid's *Heroides* 7.1–8, 1312–16 for the last sixteen lines. The character and motivation of Dido is particularly influenced by Ovid. See Shannon, Ch and Roman Poets, 196–208. For an analysis of medieval adaptations of the story of Dido and Aeneas, see Hall, MS 25, 1963, 148–59. Hall compares the *Excidium Troiae,* the *Roman d'Eneas,* the *Primera crónica general,* Simon Aurea Capra's *Ilias Latina,* and *I fatti d'Enea* from Guido da Pisa's *Fiore d'Italia.* He then examines Chaucer's two versions of the story, this legend and HF 151–382, in the light of the other versions. It is not certain that Chaucer knew any or all of these versions, but he may have been influenced by the *Excidium Troiae* (see Atwood, Spec 13, 1938, 454–57, though this was doubted by Bradley, PQ 39, 1960, 122–25) or the *Roman d'Eneas.* Hall points out that Andrea Lancia's fourteenth-century Italian translation of the *Aeneid* would have given Chaucer the basic narrative. On the sources, see further Frank, Ch and LGW, 58, n.4. Chaucer's treatment of Aeneas in the legend is so harsh that in the fifteenth century Gavin Douglas objected, defending Aeneas. (Eneados, Prol. 410–49; see Burrow, Ricardian Poetry, 98–99.)

926 Skeat (3:317) compares Purg. 1.43 for the figure of the lantern.

930–47 These lines are Chaucer's summary of Book II of the Aeneid; for details and parallels, see Shannon, Ch and Roman Poets, 197, n.2.

931 Synoun allowed himself to be taken prisoner and persuaded the Trojans to accept the wooden horse (Aen. 2.57–267); cf. HF 152–56.

934 Hector's ghost advised Aeneas to flee (Aen. 2.268–97) (Robinson).

939   "The death of Priam at the hands of Pyrrhus is related in" Aen. 2.531–58 (Robinson). Cf. HF 159–61.

940   Cf. Aen. 2.619 and HF 162–65.

941–42   Cf. Aen. 2.723–24 and HF 177.

945   Cf. Aen. 2.738–39 and HF 183.

947   "He had gone back to seek Creusa. (But Chaucer omits the incident of Creusa's ghost.)" (Robinson).

950–55   "Chaucer passed rapidly over the contents of Bk. 3 of the Aeneid" (Robinson). Cf. HF 198–221.

958–1102   "These lines correspond in general to Aen. 1.305–642" (Robinson); for details of Chaucer's omissions and changes, see Shannon, Ch and Roman Poets, 198–200.

964–66   Cf. Aen. 1.312 and HF 226.

971   **an hunteresse:** Venus in the disguise of a huntress (Robinson). Cf. Aen. 1.314–20 and HF 229.

978–82   From Aen. 1.321.24.

983–93   From Aen. 1.325–40.

994–1014   Cf. Aen. 1.341–414.

1005   **Sytheo:** Sichaeus. The confusion of *c* and *t* is common in MSS; cf. *Ticius* for Titius, Tr 1.786. The ending in *o* is perhaps due to Italian influence; cf. Inf. 5.62, "Sicheo," and MkT VII.2345n. (Robinson).

1022   Cf. Aen. 1.412, 516, where Venus covers Aeneas and Achates with a cloud.

1039–43   "The audacity of this comparison is not to be explained away on the ground that" Chaucer has Jupiter in mind, "or that Virgil compares Dido to Diana. Medieval taste differed from modern in speaking of sacred persons and things. Cf. SqT V.555 and n." (Robinson).

1044–46   Chaucer's interpolation.

1044   Proverbial; cf. Whiting F 518.

1047–60   Cf. Aen. 1.509–612.

1061–79   On Chaucer's techniques for describing the process of Dido's falling in love with Aeneas, see Frank (Ch and LGW, 63–67), where he discusses Chaucer's handling of the time scheme to create "a kind of double time" to give "the impression that Dido falls in love at once" and also "that her love evolved gradually."

1061–65   From Aen. 1.613–14.

1066–74   From Aen. 1.588–91.

1077   Proverbial; Whiting T142.

1086–1102   From Aen. 1.617–42.

1103–27   "Chaucer here departs from Virgil and gives the description a decidedly medieval cast" (Robinson).

1104   **swolow:** Skeat cites Wycliffe, "Swolwis of the see and helle, that resceyuen al that thei may and yelden not ayen," and suggests "whirlpool" or "gulf." "Mouth" may be better in the light of medieval depictions of Hell as a great, toothed mouth (cf., e.g., The Hours of Catherine of Cleves, c. 1440, fols. 105v, 168v, in the Pierpont Morgan Library in New York, published in facsimile 1966, plates 47, 99).

1110   Cf. SqT V.291–94n.

1114–24   In the description of Dido's gifts, Chaucer again departs from Virgil. Atwood (Spec 13:454–57) suggests he used Aen. 5.570–92 and 7.274–79. Bradley (PQ 39:122–25) adds Aen. 4.260–64 and 9.263–66.

1122   **floreyns:** See PardT VI.770n.

1128–49   From Aen. 1.643–722.

1153   "With this brief remark, Chaucer passes over Virgil's second book" (Robinson).

1159–67   Dido's loss of color and health, her sighs and sleeplessness, are classical symptoms of lovesickness (see KnT I.1361–76 n.); the only other female so afflicted in

Chaucer's work is the sick falcon in The Squire's Tale; cf. SqT V.411–30, 472–74.

1162–1351   "These lines cover the ground of the fourth book of the Aeneid" (Robinson); for details see Shannon, Ch and Roman Poets, 200–207.

1170–81   From Aen. 4.9–29.

1182–83   Skeat (3:322) notes "Cf. Aen. 4.31–53: but Chaucer cuts it short"; Chaucer also represents Anna as opposing Dido's love, which is not the case in the Aeneid. Although Shannon (200–201) argues that Chaucer may have taken Anna's rhetorical questions in Aen. 4.31–53 to indicate opposition to Dido's marriage to Aeneas, it is difficult to see how he could have. The questions are intended to eliminate Dido's doubts and fears, and Anna's arguments in favor of the marriage are strong and unambiguous. Chaucer's alteration of Anna's role probably has more to do with his own aims in the Legend (perhaps it seemed unsuitable to have a woman give a woman bad advice in the Legend) than with any misunderstanding. Overbeck points out (ChR 2:83, n. 25, and 84) that, in HF 366–70, Dido accuses Anna of having encouraged the relationship.

1187   Proverbial; Whiting L543.

1188–1211   From Aen. 4.129–59.

1191   **An huntyng:** On hunting, a-hunting (as also in 1211). For the omission of the verb of motion after *wol,* see Mustanoja, ME Syntax, 543–44.

1204   This line is nearly the same as KnT I.1502. Proverbial; cf. Whiting F174.

1212–31   From Aen. 4.154–70.

1213   Common hunting terms of encouragement. See Emerson, RomR 13, 1922, 148–49.

1218–26   In the Aeneid, the storm was prearranged by Juno and Venus. Throughout Dido's story, Chaucer consistently minimizes the role of the gods, thus placing upon Aeneas the responsibility for his own actions.

1231   **gladnesse:** Chaucer appears to have mistaken Virgil's "leti" (4.169), meaning "of death," for some form of *laetus* (often *letus* in medieval MSS), meaning "joyful." See Skeat's note (3:323).

1232–37   Chaucer adds this scene. He emphasizes Aeneas's deceit and again ignores the role of the gods.

1242   Virgil's description of Fame, which Chaucer used in HF 1360–92, is here omitted, and Chaucer passes on to Aen. 4.195.

1244   "On the omission of the subject, implied in what precedes, see GP I.33n" (Robinson).

1245   **Yarbas:** Iarbas (Aen. 4.196).

1254–84   Original with Chaucer, but cf. HF 269–92 and 269–85n.

1294–95   Pollard and Koch in their editions both punctuate these lines as direct speech by Aeneas. This is an attractive reading since it avoids punctuating 1294 as an interrogative construction with a suppressed verb.

1295–99   Cf. Aen. 4.351–59.

1310   "The sacrifice is in Virgil (4.452–55); the saints' shrines (**halwes**) are Chaucer's medieval addition" (Robinson).

1311–24   Very little of this is in Virgil; Chaucer's inspiration here is Ovid, Heroides VII. See Shannon, Ch and Roman Poets, 205–6.

1312–13   Skeat (3:323) compares Her. 7.167.

1323   "The appeal of pregnancy is suggested by Ovid, though Virgil intimates that there was no child" (Robinson).

1329 "For the statement that Aeneas stole away while Dido was asleep—another departure from Virgil's account—Atwood (Spec 13:456) suggests that Chaucer was influenced by the Excidium Troiae" (Robinson).

1331 Lavyne: Lavinia (Aen. 7.359); cf. Pro F 257.

1332 On the cloth and the swerd, see Aen. 4.648, 507, and 646 (Robinson).

1338-40 From Aen. 4.651-53.

1346 hire norice: "Barce, the nurse of Sichaeus (Aen. 4.632)" (Robinson).

1352 myn auctour: Ovid. The lettre, in 1355-65, is based on Ovid, Her. 7.1-8.

1355-56 Proverbial; Whiting 5932. The swan was believed to sing only at the approach of its death; see PF 342n.

1360 The line is very closely paralleled in Filippo's translation; 1357 less so. Chaucer may well have consulted this Italian version (see Meech, PMLA 45:110-28). But it should be noted, as stated above, that the marginal scholia and interlinear glosses in medieval MSS of the Heroides are also similar to Chaucer's lines. Compare 1360 to this gloss from MS Balliol 143: "aduerso: id est, contrario deo."

IV. THE LEGEND OF HYPSIPYLE AND MEDEA

Hypsipyle

For this legend, Chaucer drew mainly upon Guido delle Colonne's Historia destructionis Troiae 1.1368-1455; and Ovid's Metamorphoses, bk. 7, and Heroides 6. He seems incidentally to have consulted Valerius Flaccus (see 1457 below) and may have used Statius's Thebaid, bk. 5, and Hyginus, Fabula 15. Shannon, Ch and Roman Poets, 211-13, points out strong similarities between Hypsipyle's story and Dido's in the Aeneid, and suggests Chaucer drew upon the Dido story for the means of developing the relationship between Jason and Hypsipyle.

1368-95 "The introductory lines on Jason are not in the sources" (Robinson).

1371-72 Robinson notes a slight resemblance to Dante, Inf. 18.85, 91-93.

1371 Cf. MancT IX.72.

1383 The image of the horn may come from Inf. 19.5, "where it refers to the public crying of the misdeeds of condemned criminals. But the phrase Have at thee suggests that Chaucer had in mind rather the hunter's horn, sounded to start the pursuit of the game" (Robinson).

1396 Guido: Guido delle Colonne. The Historia destructionis Troiae begins with the story of Jason, and Chaucer follows it, at least as far as 1.1461.

1397 Pelleus: Properly Pelias. See Oxford Classical Dictionary s.v. Jason. Guido has "Peleus."

1425 Colcos: Lat. Colchis, a district at the east end of the Black Sea, just south of the Caucasus. Magoun (Ch Gazetteer, 56-57) says it corresponds to the area Mingrelia of the Georgian S.S.R. of the Soviet Union.

1457 Bk. 1 of the Argonautica of Valerius Flaccus contains a long list of the Argonauts. "Possibly Chaucer took this reference at second hand from Dares (De excidio

Troiae historia, i): 'sedqui vult eos cognoscere, Argonautas legat.' But the accurate citation of the title supports the theory that he knew Valerius Flaccus at first hand, and the influence of the Argonautica is perhaps to be recognized also in HF 1572 and Tr 5.8." See Shannon, Ch and Roman Poets, 210, 345-48. (Robinson.) For the form of the title Argonautycon, see ProMLT II.93n.

1459 Philotetes: Guido's spelling for Philoctetes. But it also appears in medieval scholia on the Heroides, particularly on the Epistle of Medea; see, e.g., Florence, Biblioteca Laurenziana MS Plut. 24 sin. 8, fol. 28v.

1463 Lemnon: Lemnos. Cf. Heroides 6.50, 117, 136.

1467 Ysiphele: Hypsipyle, daughter of Thoas and queen of Lemnos. The story that follows contains details not derived from Ovid, and not in agreement with the accounts of Statius, Theb. bk. 5; Valerius Flaccus, Argonautica, bk. 2; and Hyginus, Fabula 15. Chaucer may have invented them (Skeat 3:326).

1479 In Valerius Flaccus (Argonautica 2.326-27) the messenger is a woman, Iphinoe. According to the ancient tradition, the Lemnian women had killed all the men on the island except Thoas, whom Hypsipyle saved (Robinson).

1480 Ercules: Hercules, most noted in myth for his performance of the Twelve Labors, tasks involving the defeat of monsters or the accomplishment of the impossible (cf. Bo 4.m7). It was he who brought Alcestis back from the underworld, although Chaucer does not tell that part of her story. He was one of the Argonauts, the heroes who sailed with Jason on the Argo. His role in the seduction of Hypsipyle appears to be original with Chaucer; perhaps the fact that Ovid's Heroides 9 is a very accusing letter from Deianira to Hercules may have brought this unattractive characterization into Chaucer's mind. See following note.

1524 Shannon (Ch and Roman Poets, 213) compares Chaucer's use of Hercules as an ally and messenger of Jason to the role of Achates in the story of Dido in the Aeneid. There is no known source for what Chaucer does with the character. Hercules' strategy is very like that of Pandarus. Cf. Tr 2.155-207.

1526-31 This is a conventional description of a courtly lover; cf. NPT VII.2914-17. Cf. also the description of an ideal ruler in SqT V.19-27.

1528 secre: Cf. PF 395n.

1529 thre poyntes: They are not the poyntes in 1528 (where there are four) but those following, in 1530-33.

1548 Proverbial; cf. Whiting M5, also ClT IV.2-3.

1558 Th'origynal: Heroides 6 is the letter referred to in 1564. But the question of whether Chaucer knew (and is here referring to) the other possible sources named above remains uncertain.

1571-74 These lines derive from Her. 6.153-56, as noted by Shannon, Ch and Roman Poets, 215.

Medea

In Medea's legend, as in Hypsipyle's, Chaucer used Guido delle Colonne's Historia destructionis Troiae, bks. 1-3; Ovid's Metamorphoses 7.1-396 (although Shannon, Ch and Roman Poets, 219, denies the influence of the Metamorphoses here), and Heroides 12. He may also have used Hyginus, Fabulae 22-26. For Gower's version of

Jason and Medea, one of his finest narratives, see Conf. Aman. 5.3227–4222.

1580–1655   These passages are mainly based on Guido's Historia, bk 2.

1582   Cf. Guido, "sicut appetit materia semper formam." But Guido is talking about the greedy lust of women.

1590   Jaconitos: According to Magoun (Ch Gazetteer, 94), historically Dioscuras was the chief town of Colchis. Chaucer's source is Guido delle Colonne: "Iaconites . . . caput regni pro sua magnitudine constituta, urbs valde pulcra . . ."

1605   Proverbial; cf. Whiting L319.

1609   *"As* seems here to be employed in the unusual causal sense, 'inasmuch as,' 'since'; perhaps, however, it means 'as if.' For the reference to Fortune, or fate, cf. Her. 12.35" (Robinson).

1644–45   Frank (Ch and LGW, 89n.) compares this *bedde : spedde* rhyme with MilT I.3649–50.

1653   At this point, Chaucer ceases to follow Guido save for 1662–66, and follows Ovid, Her. 12.

1661   Creon's daughter was named Creusa. See Her. 12.53–54, Gower, Conf. Aman. 5.4196.

1670–77   These lines come from Her. 12.11–12, slightly expanded. Meech (PMLA 45:115) suggests that Filippo's Italian translation of the Heroides is closer: "Deh! or perchè mi piacquero oltre agli onesti termini, li tuoi biondi capelli e la tua beltade e la infinita grazia della tua lingua?"

V. THE LEGEND OF LUCRECE

Though Chaucer refers both to Livy (1.57–59) and to Ovid (Fasti 2.685–852), the narrative closely follows Ovid and makes no apparent use of Livy. Perhaps he cited Livy merely for the authority of his name, as in PhysT, where the actual source is the *Roman de la rose,* but see 1839–49 below. Gower tells the tale in Conf. Aman. 7.4754–5130, using Ovid and some other source, perhaps Livy, at the end. For comparison of Chaucer's and Gower's versions, see Weiher, ELN 14, 1976, 7–9; on the use of Livy, cf. Harder, Pubs. of the Missouri Philol. Assoc. 2, 1977, 1–7. McCall, Ch Among the Gods, 178, n. 35, suggests Chaucer may have used Simon of Hesdin's translation of Valerius Maximus's *Memorabilia* 6.1 as a source for Lucretia. Simon expands Valerius to include Livy's account and a summary of Augustine's comment, so Chaucer would have needed only the one work. For a discussion of how Chaucer "Christianized" his material, see La Hood, PQ 43, 1964, 274–76.

1680–93   With 1680, Shannon (Ch and Roman Poets, 220) compares Fasti 2.685, "Nunc mihi dicenda est regis fuga." The rest of these introductory lines appear to be Chaucer's own addition.

1690   The grete Austyn: St. Augustine speaks of Lucretia in De civitate Dei, 1.19, and, while recognizing her nobility, condemns her suicide. Frank (Ch and LGW, 97, n. 7) suggests Chaucer may be referring to Gesta Romanorum, no. 135, in which Augustine is given as the source for the story of Lucretia. Frank further suggests that *oure legende* (1689), usually identified with the Legenda aurea, might be the Gesta Romanorum. On the

other hand, Kiser (Telling Classical Tales, 104–7) believes De civitate is the source, and that Chaucer's narrator is somewhat falsifying Augustine's attitude in order to force Lucretia into "the mold of a chaste Christian" (106).

1694   "From this point Chaucer closely follows Ovid, Fasti 2.721–852. **Ardea,** capital of the Rutuli, in Latium" (Robinson).

1705   Colatyn: Collatinus (Lucius Tarquinus, cousin of Tarquinus Sextus) is not directly named in Ovid's account, though Chaucer could easily have inferred the name from "cui dederat clarum Collatia nomen."

1706–7   Cf. Ovid, Fasti 2.734: " 'Non opus est verbis, credite rebus,' ait." Apparently proverbial; cf. Whiting W642, not, however, citing this occurrence.

1710   Chaucer locates events in Rome instead of Collatia, which is clearly the locale in Livy. Ovid is less explicit, and Chaucer may have misunderstood the implications of Fasti 2.735–41 and 785. Gower shows the same misunderstanding in Conf. Aman. 7.4911–12, taking Collatia as the name of a gate of Rome.

1716–17   Fasti 2.738: "Tecta petunt; custos in fore nullus erat."

1721   oure bok: "Ovid, who mentions the wool at 2.742" (Robinson).

1725   shal: Cf. HF 2053n.

1729   "This line (as Skeat noted [3:332]) is possibly due to a misunderstanding of Ovid's 2.751–52; 'sed enim temerarius ille / Est meus et stricto quolibet ense ruit' " (Robinson).

1773   The proverb (Whiting H96) is in the source (Fasti 2.782), and occurs in various forms; cf. Tr. 4.600–601n. and RvT I.4210n.

1778–86   In Ovid and in Livy, Tarquin comes openly to the house and is received by Lucretia, as he is in Gower, Conf. Aman. 7.4920–39. Shannon (Ch and Roman Poets, 224), suggests Chaucer made the change deliberately, to emphasize Lucretia's innocence.

1781   stalke: Cf. KnT I.1479; ClT V.525.

1812–26   Robinson notes, "These lines are Chaucer's; Ovid says simply: 'Succubuit famae victa puella metu' (2.810)" (she yielded out of fear for her reputation).

1839–49   This passage has no exact correspondence to Ovid; Skeat (3:333) notes that 1847–49 are rather closely paralleled in Livy: "Dant ordine omnes fidem; consolantur aegram animi, auertendo noxam ab coacta in auctorem delicti; mentem peccare, non corpus; et unde consilium afuerit, culpam abesse." Cf. Gower, Conf. Aman. 7.5048–57.

1839   impossible: Cf. SumT III.2231 and n.

1841–42   Proverbial; Whiting H277. Cf. Tr 3.114n.

1847–70   Cf. Ovid, Fasti 2.829–52.

1871   Lucretia's canonization here is not merely conformity to the design of the legend. "As Skeat observes (3:333), it was probably suggested to Chaucer by the fact that Ovid tells her tale in the Fasti under the date (24 Feb.) which was commemorated as 'Fuga Tarquinii Superbi.' Thus she appeared to have a place on the calendar, like a Christian saint. . . . Shannon notes further (Ch and Roman Poets, 227), as affording a kind of suggestion of the veneration of saints, that Brutus took oath by Lucretia's spirit, which would become a divinity to him ('perque tuos manes, qui mihi numen erunt'), to drive out the Tarquins" (Robinson).

1881   The reference is to the Syro-Phoenician woman (Matt. 15.28), though Skeat suggests Chaucer may have confused her story with that of the centurion (Matt. 8.10; Luke 7.9).

VI. THE LEGEND OF ARIADNE

The exact sources of this legend have not been determined. The beginning may be dependent on Ovid, Met. 7.456–58 and 8.6–176, and the end on *Heroides* 10. Hyginus's *Fabulae,* 39–43, could have suggested the general outline of the story. Though much of the material from the *Metamorphoses* could have been found in marginal glosses on MSS of the *Heroides* (e.g., Bern, Burgerbibliothek MS 512, fol. 63v), Meech (PMLA 45: 110–28, and esp. 46:182–204) has shown that many of the details of Chaucer's narrative can be explained by the *Ovide moralisé,* Filippo Ceffi's Italian translation of the *Heroides* (esp. the double intro. to the Epistles of Phaedra and Ariadne), and glosses on Ovid. Child, MLN 11, 1896, 482–87, argues that some other details may be due to Boccaccio, De gen. deorum, and Lowes has argued for the influence of the *Teseida* on the prison scenes (see 1960–2122 below). Lowes, PMLA 33, 1918, 302–25, also suggests the influence of Machaut's *Jugement dou Roy de Navarre.* Gower tells the story of Ariadne in Conf. Aman. 5.5231–5495; his account agrees in some respects with Chaucer's, though the two versions are independent of one another, and perhaps, as Bech suggests (Anglia 5:337–38), Chaucer and Gower used a common source. For discussion of sources, see Frank, Ch and LGW, 111–113 and nn. 1–7.

1886 "The confusion of Mynos, the judge of the lower world, with Minos, the king of Crete, who was usually regarded as his grandson, has been traced [by Child, MLN 11:483] to the De gen. deorum, 11.26. . . . Meech [PMLA 46:185] notes that the identification is made in numerous glosses on the Metamorphoses, [as it is in the *scholia* to Heroides 10], and suggests that Chaucer found it in his copy" (Robinson).
1887 "The mention of the lot was perhaps due to Aen. 6.431" (Robinson).
1891–92 "Shannon suggests that the idea of retribution sent upon Theseus by the gods . . . may have come from Catullus, Carmen 64.188–248, a poem which he thinks also influenced HF 269–85. But [although the lines are a bit ambiguous] it is Minos, not Theseus, upon whom the gods are here said to take vengeance, and Chaucer does not develop at all Catullus's idea of poetic justice in the fate of Theseus. See McPeek, MLN 46, 1931, 299–301, (quoting Kittredge)" (Robinson).
1894–99 Chaucer draws on the tradition (cf. Geoffrey of Vinsauf, Documentum de modo et arte dictandi et versificandi 2.3) that Androgeus was killed because of his attainments in philosophy; Gower reports that it was rather because of his pride in these attainments (Conf. Aman. 5.5234–45).
1902–21 Here Chaucer summarizes the material in Met. 8.6–151. He makes **Nysus doughter,** Scylla, a sympathetic character rather than the unnatural daughter she is in Ovid (Meech, PMLA 46:187).
1902 **Alcathoe:** The citadel at Megara, capital of Megaris on the isthmus of Corinth in Greece; from Alcathous, founder of the city. The name occurs in Met. 7.443.
1904 **Nysus:** Nisus, king of Megara; his daughter Scylla became enamored of Minos, and in order to win his love,

cut off the purple lock of her father's hair on which the safety of the kingdom depended. Chaucer omits, as so often, the metamorphoses (of Nisus and Scylla).
1919–20 Perhaps due to the Ovide moralisé: "Noyee fut, je n'en doubt mie, / Quant li dieux par leur courtoisie, / et non mie par sa desserte, / Ffirent la demonstrance apperte / Et leur puissance y demonstrerent. / En vn oyselet la muerent / Qui a nom aloe couppee / Pour la teste qui fut couppee. / En entreseigne du pechie / Porte vne houppe sur son chie." (Paris, MS Bibl. Nat. fr. 373, fol. 168v, quoted by Meech, PMLA 46:188.)
1922–47 At this point Chaucer departs from Ovid, as does Gower, who uses roughly the same material in Conf. Aman. 5.5254–5314. Many of the deviations can be explained by Boccaccio's De gen. deorum, but they are also paralleled in Machaut's version of the story in the Jugement dou Roy de Navarre, 2707–2808, and in the Ovide moralisé, which has been shown to be Machaut's source and which was possibly Chaucer's. On the French version, see de Boer, Rom 43, 1914, 342–43; Lowes, PMLA 33:320–25; Meech, PMLA 46:189–204 (Robinson.)
1928 The **monstre** was the Minotaur, half bull and half man, begotten by a bull on Pasiphaë, Minos's wife; he is therefore half-brother to Ariadne and Phaedra. He dwelt in the Labyrinth constructed by Daedalus; cf. Met. 8.155–68.
1932 **every thridde yeer:** Hyginus says that seven children were sent yearly (perhaps this underlies 1926), Gower that nine were sent each year. Chaucer may have gotten his idea of the three-year period from a misunderstanding of Ovid ("tertia sors annis domuit repetita novenis," Met. 8.171), or of Servius on Aen. 6.14. The Jugement dou Roy de Navarre makes the tribute annual; in the Ovide moralisé the period is left indefinite. See further Shannon, Ch and Roman Poets, 239–42.
1933 Meech insists (PMLA 46:194–95) that the medieval reading of "sors" (in "tertia sors annis") as "lot" instead of "tribute" is incorrect, but this is questionable. Although the Loeb translator uses "tribute" (Met. 8.171), "lot" is the more common meaning, and is exactly what Ovid means. Shannon, Ch and Roman Poets, 245–46, says that Lowes (PMLA 33:324, n. 96) implies misleadingly that Theseus's being chosen by lot is not Ovidian. But the "voluntary" quality of Theseus's going to Crete could lie in his acceptance of the lot. Chaucer's reading of "lot" is common to the Middle Ages; cf. Gower, Conf. Aman. 5.5309.
1944 **Egeus:** See Met. 7.402–4 and KnT I.2838, 2905.
1960–2122 In this sequence of Theseus's imprisonment, the entrance of Ariadne into the action, and the proposal that Theseus should enter her service in disguise, Chaucer seems to be following the account of Palamon and Arcite in Boccaccio's Teseida 3.11–75, 4.1–29 (Lowes, PMLA 20:803–5). See also Frank, Ch and LGW, 116 and n. 12; 117); cf. KnT I.1056–61.
1962 Theseus is apparently imprisoned in a privy (**foreyne**) "that may have served also as the pit for the garderobe tower, the upper part of which belonged to the princesses' suite. See Draper, ESt 60, 1926, 250–51" (Robinson).
1966 **Of Athenes:** The reading of ten of the twelve MSS of the Legend, but inaccurate, since Theseus is in prison in Crete, not Athens. Lowes (PMLA 20:808n.) suggests that the error is Chaucer's own, and was due to the influence of the Teseida, which Chaucer seems to

have used as a source in this part of the legend. The prison in the Teseida is in Athens, and Chaucer may have been thinking of it here.

1969 Adryane: Ariadne. For the spelling, cf. HF 407 and IntroMLT II.67 (Robinson).

2004 "The device of the ball of wax or pitch, which occurs also in Conf. Aman. 5.5349, is derived from the commentators on Ovid (Meech, PMLA 45:118n). Bech (Anglia 5:341) compared the story of Daniel and the Dragon (Dan. 14.26 in the Vulgate, or Bel and the Dragon 27 in the Apocrypha)" (Robinson).

2010–26, 2050–51 The gayler is a mysterious figure of no obvious source. He is not in Met. 8 or the Ovide moralisé. Meech (PMLA 45:117–18) suggests he is Daedalus, the architect of the Labyrinth, who, according to a tradition not recorded in Ovid, gave Theseus "instruments for conquering the beast and the intricacies of its dwelling." But the gayler does not do these things; Ariadne provides the ball of wax and the twine. The gayler leads Theseus to the Minotaur and provides the barge. If Chaucer derived the character from Daedalus, then he makes little use of Daedalus's possibilities. Perhaps the gayler merely represents Chaucer's common sense: the easiest way to break out of jail is to bribe the jailer.

2064 shames deth: For the construction, see Language and Versification, p. xxxviii.

2075 of a twenty yer and thre: On this construction, cf. PardT VI.771, SqT V.383.

2099 youre sone: Hippolytus. This suggestion does not seem consistent with the statement in 2075 that Theseus was only twenty-three. Skeat thought Ariadne was jesting. But Theseus is old enough to have a young son, and there is plenty of medieval authority for the betrothal of the very young; there is medieval authority for this particular betrothal as well. Cf. Boccaccio, De gen. deorum 11.29. Meech (PMLA 45:117n.) cites also Giovanni dei Bonsignori's paraphrase of the Metamorphoses (8.11), and Filippo's double preface to the Epistles of Ariadne and Phaedra. The betrothal is not found in the Ovide moralisé (Robinson).

2105–8 Swearing by parts of one's own body was common in medieval times, but swearing by one's own blood was particularly powerful because the blood is the life of the individual. See Lev. 17.10–14. Skeat (3:338) notes that to draw one's blood was a frequent mode of attestation and compares Marlowe's Faustus 2.1.

2122 of Athenes duchesse: Chaucer calls Theseus duc . . . of Athenes in KnT I.860–61 (Robinson).

2145 geth: Goeth, a Kentish form. Cf. BD 438n.

2146–49 Cf. Her. 10.71–72, 103; Met. 8.172–73.

2155 Ennopye: Oenopia; cf. Met. 7.472–73.

2163 yle: Not named in Ovid, but usually said to be Naxos. Gower has "Chyo" (Chios, an island off the west coast of Turkey), as do the marginal glosses in many MSS of the Heroides. For the description, see Ovid, Her. 10.59–63, 83–87.

2177 A twenty devel-wey: See MilT I.3134n.

2178 "The reference to Aegeus's death might come from De gen. deorum (10.48) or from Filippo's preface (see Meech, PMLA 45:118–19)," or from a gloss. "Chaucer does not tell the familiar incident of the black sail" (Robinson).

2185–2217 Chaucer here follows rather closely Her. 10. For exact correspondences, see Shannon, Ch and Roman Poets, 255–58, and Meech (PMLA 45:116n.).

2186 From Her. 10.12, "Perque torum moveo brachia; nullus erat." Cf. also Tr 5.223–24, where Chaucer follows Fil. 5.20.

2203 Ascaunce: Cf. Tr 1.205n.

2208–09 A mistranslation of Her. 10.53–54: "et tua, quae possum pro te, vestigia tango / strataque quae membris intepuere tuis."

2220 hire Epistel: Heroides 10.

2223–24 Bacchus, out of pity, placed the crown of Ariadne in the heavens as the constellation Corona Borealis, the Northern Crown (Ovid, Fasti 3.451–516, Met. 8.176–82). As it is almost completely opposite Taurus, in the signe of Taurus must mean when the sun is in that sign. Skeat (3:340) explains that when the sun is in Taurus, the Northern Crown is especially conspicuous.

VII. THE LEGEND OF PHILOMELA

The primary source is Ovid, Met. 6.424–605, which Chaucer supplemented at many points with Chrétien de Troyes, Philomela (Maunce de la hupe et de l'aronde et del rossignol), ed. de Boer, 1909. Chrétien's work has been incorporated into the Ovide moralisé, which is probably where Chaucer read it. He draws on Chrétien for vivid details but ignores Chrétien's psychological elaborations. See further Frank, Ch and LGW, 137, n.10.

Frank (Ch and LGW, 139 n.13) draws attention to the fact that Philomela is not mentioned in the ballade in the Prologue nor in the list in the Introduction to The Man of Law's Tale. Nor is she mentioned in the "Nine worshipfullest Ladyes," a fifteenth-century summary of LGW (Odd Texts of Chaucer's Minor Poems, pt. 1, ed. Furnivall, Ch Soc, ser. 1, 23, 1871). Yet there is no doubt as to the tale's authenticity.

Gower gives a much fuller version of the tale in Conf. Aman. 5.5551–6047, a version that Pearsall (PMLA 81, 1966, 478–79) argues is much superior to Chaucer's; Frank compares the two versions (Ch and LGW, 139–45) and concludes that Chaucer's version, "read as a tale of pathos, is competent narrative but nothing more."

Philomena for Philomela is common; it is the form used by Chrétien and Gower, and appears in medieval MSS of Ovid.

2228 In MS B the words "Deus dator formarum" (printed above as subtitle) follow the title; MS F, which also has the subtitle, reads "formatorum." Although the general Platonic doctrine of the passage can be found in many writers accessible to Chaucer, the source has not been identified with certainty. Boethius 3.m9.11–14 or RR 15995–16004 have been suggested. Karl Young (Spec 19, 1944, 1–13) shows that the idea is also expressed in the opening passage of the Ovide moralisé (1.71–97) and in several prefaces (accessus) to the Metamorphoses, of which he prints five specimens. Wien (MLN 58, 1943, 605–7) quotes a Latin translation of Avicenna in which the term "dator formarum" is used twice, and she cites Averroes's summary of Avicennian thought. Wien believes the phrase was a popular expression in the Middle Ages, and that the concept came from Avicenna. See also Moses, MLN 49, 1934, 226–29; and Bryant, MLN 58, 1943, 194–96.

2236 From this world, regarded as the center of the universe, up to the outermost sphere. The spheres were sometimes counted from the outermost inward, as here, sometimes from the earth outward, as in Tr 3.2.

2244 "At this point begins the account based on Ovid" (Robinson).

Marte: For the form, see SqT V.50n.

2248–54 Cf. Ovid, Met. 6.428–32.

2252 **Furies thre:** See Tr 1.138–40n.

2253–54 **oule . . . prophete is of wo:** See Tr 5.319n.

2259–68 Cf. Ovid, Met. 6.438–42.

2270–78 Cf. Ovid, Met. 444–50, then 475, 483.

2291 MSS F and B have "bounte" ("bounde") instead of **beaute,** but the latter corresponds to Ovid's "divitior forma." Lowes (PMLA 33:310) would have *bounte* because of Chrétien's "Ne fu pas mains sage que bele" (She was not less wise than beautiful; 172), but the correspondence is not great. See Shannon, Ch and Roman Poets, 268, from which the above is derived.

two so ryche: Twice as rich. Cf. 736.

2295–2301 Cf. Ovid, Met. 6.495–501.

2302–7 Cf. Ovid, Met. 6.488–89.

2307 "In saying that Pandion suspected no malice, Chaucer follows Chrétien's account (544–729). Ovid says: 'timuitque suae praesagia mentis' (Met. 6.510)" (Robinson).

2318–22 The images are from Ovid, Met. 6.527–30.

2325–26 Cf. WBT 3887–88.

2342–49 Cf. Ovid, Met. 6.563–70.

2350 "This statement that Philomela had learned to embroider in her youth is derived or inferred from Chrétien. It appears at an earlier point in the French poem (188–93), in a long description of which Chaucer uses only this significant detail" (Robinson).

2352 "**radevore** is uncertain both in meaning and derivation. Skeat's explanation, that it comes from 'ras de Vaur,' is open to the two-fold objection that 'ras' is not known before the sixteenth century and that the proper form of the place-name seems to have been Lavaur. The final -*e*, required by the rhyme with *yore*, is also unexplained. Lowes, PMLA 33, 1918, 314n., is even doubtful whether the term refers to a stuff or to a design. He also expresses uncertainty about the meaning of stol, usually interpreted as 'frame' " (Robinson).

2360 **a stamyn large:** "(Ovid, Met. 6.576, has 'stamina') a large piece of stamin or woolen cloth, such as was used for shirts. Cf. ParsT X.1052" (Robinson).

2361–63 "The description of the embroidery was probably added from Chrétien (1120–33), but his version is much fuller" (Robinson). Ovid says only that she wove the story of her wrongs (Met. 6.577–78).

2366 "In Chrétien the messenger is a woman, and in some MSS Ovid has the feminine pronoun 'illa' (Met. 6.579)" (Robinson). Shannon (Ch and Roman Poets, 279–80), however, points out that "ille" has the better authority and was doubtless the reading followed by Chaucer, and also by Gower, Conf. Aman. 7.5779.

2382–93 Chaucer, typically, omits the grisly meal at which the two sisters serve Tereus the flesh of his and Procne's son Itys. After this, the three are changed into birds by the gods, Philomela into a nightingale, Procne into a swallow, and Tereus into a hoopoe. Both Gower and Chrétien tell the entire story.

VIII. THE LEGEND OF PHYLLIS

The major source is Her. 2, but apparently both Chaucer and Gower, who tells the story in Conf. Aman. 4.731–878, used some other source as well. See further Frank,

Ch and LGW, 148, n. 4, and Shannon, Ch and Roman Poets, 283–91. Certain features thought by Child and Shannon to have been derived from Boccaccio's De gen. deorum are held by Meech (PMLA 45:119–23) to have come from Filippo's translation. They could also have come from the marginal *scholia* on the Heroides.

2395 Cf. Matt. 7.17; also MkTPro VII.1956.

2400 This allusion and that in 2446–51 to the treachery of Theseus are inspired by the reference in Her. 2.75–76 to the desertion of Ariadne. Filippo strengthens the allusion in his translation.

2404–10 That Demophoön was returning from the Trojan War may have been derived from Filippo, from the De gen. deorum, or from an *accessus* to Ovid's Epistle. For references, see Meech, PMLA 45:119–20.

2422 **Thorus:** Clogan, Expl 23, 1965, 61, suggests that Chaucer derived *Thorus* from *tori* (couches; commonly "thori" in medieval MSS) in the Achilleid of Statius, 1.109–10.

Triton: See HF 1596n.

2423 "Phyllis' lond was Thrace; the ancient authorities disagree as to the name of her father. Both Chaucer and Gower make her the daughter of *Ligurges* (Lycurgus), perhaps on the authority of Boccaccio, De gen. deorum 11, 25. But Meech (PMLA 45:119–23) shows that the same account appears in numerous glosses on Ovid and in Filippo's preface to his Italian version of the letter. The idea may have originally arisen by inference from Her. 2.111" (Robinson).

2425–26 Cf. KnT I.1035–36.

2448 Proverbial; Whiting F80. For the general idea that animals are true to the nature of their kind, cf. NPT VII.3276, MancT IX.160–86; Tr 1.218–24; and RR 14027–14103.

2454 This is one of the lines frequently cited as evidence that Chaucer (the man, not the persona) was bored by the Legend.

2484–85 The tradition that Phyllis hanged herself occurs elsewhere in Chaucer (cf. BD 728–29 and HF 394), but does not derive from Her. 2.131–42. Kittredge, Date of Tr, 23, suggests that Chaucer may have derived this belief from the Roman de la rose, 13414–17.

2496–2554 From this point onward, Chaucer follows Her. 2. For details, see Frank, 153, n. 6.

2501–3 On these lines, see Janet Cowen, N&Q, n.s. 31 (1984), 298–99, who points to an additional parallel with Filippo's translation and suggests a sexual pun on **haven** (2501).

2508 **strem of Sytho:** Chaucer's translation of "Sythonis unda" (Ovid, Her. 2.6); Ovid is calling the sea "Sythonian," that is, Thracian, because Sithon or Sitho, king of Thrace, was Phyllis's father. As Kane notes (in ME Sts. Presented to Norman Davis, ed. Gray and Stanley, 1983, 44), no MS reads *Sytho*. For the variant spellings, see Textual Notes.

2511 Meech (PMLA 45:120–21) compares Filippo: "E se tu annoveri bene li tempi, come annovero io e gli altri fini amanti, il nostro lamento non è venuto dinanzi al suo die."

2522–24 Meech (PMLA 45:121) compares Filippo: "che ciascuno di questi Iddii, per li quali tu se' spergiurato, vorrano prendere vendetta delle tue offese. Tu tutto non sarai sofficiente a tante pene."

2525–29 Meech (PMLA 45:121) compares Filippo: "io credetti alle tue lusinghevoli parole, delle quale tu eri molto copioso; e ancora credetti alla tua nobile schiatta, ed alli tuoi Iddii, ed alle tue lagrime. Or come tu potevi piangere per arte? Or possonsi le lagrime infingere si."

2536   "Ovid represents the ancestors as sculptured, but Meech cites two glosses which refer rather to painting. Ovid's 'Aegidas,' descendants of Aegeus, Chaucer renders **thyne olde auncestres,** which corresponds to Filippo's translation ('tuoi antichi')" (Robinson).

2544–49   Meech (PMLA 45:122–23) compares Filippo: "Di tante cose gloriose del tuo padre, una sola abbominevole n'appare cioé l'abbandonata Adriana, la quale egli ingannoe con quel falso ingegno che tu facesti me. In quella sola cosa tu lui seguiti, e per lui ti scuse, e solamente di tanta fellonia ti fai suo erede."

2559–61   Cf. Tr 5.1784–85, Anel 197.

IX. THE LEGEND OF HYPERMNESTRA

Most of the legend comes from Ovid's *Heroides,* 14; it is also in Hyginus, *Fabula* 168. "But Chaucer confines his story to Hypermnestra and Lynceus, disregarding the murder of the other brothers. He also departs from his original in a number of details, some of which are paralleled in Boccaccio's De gen. deorum 2.22" (Robinson), or in glosses on the *Heroides.* But Meech (PMLA 45: 123–28) argues that they are all derived from Filippo's translation of Ovid.

"Danaus and Aegyptus were twin brothers. The former had fifty daughters, the latter fifty sons. Fearing his nephews, Danaus fled with his daughters to Argos, but the sons of Aegyptus followed and asked for the girls in marriage. Danaus consented, but gave each daughter a dagger with which to kill her husband. Hypermnestra, however, spared her husband" Lynceus, who later killed Danaus (Robinson). Chaucer has reversed the names of the two fathers, giving Danaus *(Danao)* sons and Aegyptus *(Egiste)* daughters. This may just be a slip on Chaucer's part (although he is consistent in the error), or he may have used a mistaken source. Shaner (N&Q 220, 1975, 341) points out that the same error occurs in Lactantius Placidus's *Commentarius in Statii Thebaida,* which Clogan (SP 61, 1964, 599–615) argues that Chaucer knew. There is a possibility that Chaucer made his mistake on the authority of this or some similar tradition of commentary. Meech (PMLA 45:110–28) finds verbal resemblances between this legend and Filippo's Italian translation of the *Heroides* in several lines: 2610–12, 2616, 2682, 2706. The forms *Danao* and *Lyno* may be due to Filippo's translation, though "Lino" for "Lynceo" also occurs in MSS of Ovid, and both forms are given in the De gen. deorum. The other name-forms in the legend could easily come from either the Italian or the Latin. "The opening lines correspond closely to Filippo's translation" (Robinson).

2576–99   The nativity here described is original with Chaucer. Venus was in conjunction with Jupiter. Mars was enfeebled by Venus and **oppressioun of houses** (i.e., in an unfavorable zodiacal house, probably Taurus or Libra), but Saturn was in an evil aspect. Venus and Jupiter are "well-willed" planets, Mars and Jupiter "evil-willed," though the evil influence of Mars can be mitigated by the influence of Venus (cf. Mars 31–32n.). For more detailed discussion, see Curry, Ch and Sci., 164–71; Wood, Ch and Stars, 112; and North, RES n.s. 20, 1969, 257–83.

"To summarize the passage briefly, the influence of Venus accounts for Hypermnestra's beauty; the conjunction with Jupiter caused her gentleness and fidelity; and the unfavorable position of Saturn ultimately caused her death" (Robinson).

2580   **Wirdes:** The OE *wyrd* meant "fate"; the Middle English plural *wierdes* was occasionally used to translate the Latin *Parcae* (Robinson).

2582   "The forms of these adjectives are puzzling. Skeat's text, following some of the MSS, reads "Pitouse, sadde, wise, and trewe." *Trewe* is properly entitled to its final *-e* from OE, and *wise* (properly *wis* from OE *wis*) seems to have acquired an ME *-e* (perhaps from the weak form), which accounts for the modern pronunciation of *wise* [with a long *i*]. But *pitous* and *sad* regularly had no final *-e* in the strong nominative singular. Skeat's suggestion that the *-e* here is due to the treatment of the adjectives like French feminine forms is very dubious. The trisyllabic form *pyëtous* (or piteous) keeps the rhythm without requiring any irregular *-e*'s" (Robinson).

trewe as stel: Proverbial; Whiting S709; cf. Pro F 334 and EpiMerT IV.2426n.

2584   "Venus, Jupiter, Mars, and Saturn are planets here rather than gods" (Robinson).

2593   **Mars his venim:** On this form of the possessive, which occurs very early, see Mustanoja, ME Syntax, 159–62.

2597   "For the association of Saturn with imprisonment, see KnT I.2457" (Robinson).

2602   **was spared no lynage:** Canon law forbade the marriage of first cousins, but the consanguinity of Hypermnestra and Lynceus does not seem to have bothered Chaucer's known sources. The problem may have been brought to his mind by a note to the Heroides such as the one in the margin of Munich, MS Staatsbibl. Clm. 1237/4612, fol. 28r: ". . . Hipermestrae pater petiit Egistum ut filios suis filiabus suis secundam legem Mosaycum copularent." The forbidden degrees of kinship in Mosaic law are laid out in Leviticus 18 and elaborated in the Code of Maimonides, bk. 4, treatise 1 (ed. Klein, Yale Judaica Series 19). This law forbade marriage with aunts, but nieces and cousins were not specifically forbidden. St. Augustine (De civitate Dei 15.16) says that despite the absence of a formal prohibition against the marriage of first cousins in the Old Testament, Christians shrank from such unions as if by natural instinct. The formal prohibition of marriage for Christians within the first six degrees of kinship was promulgated at the Burgundian Council of Epaon in 517. See also Coulton, Med. Panorama, 1938, 629–46.

2610   Skeat (3:349) says Chaucer's source is Ovid, Her. 14.25–26. But Meech (PMLA 45:125) believes it is this passage in Filippo: "Quivi in ogni luogo ed in ogni parte risplendeano li torchi e le chiare lampade adorne di molto oro. Allora si cominciaro a fare li sagrificii, e gli empi incensi s'accendono negli sforzati fuochi."

2629   A familiar formula; see KnT I.1566n.

2638   "This line has been held to come from Dante, Inf. 7.64: 'For all the gold that is beneath the moon.' But the parallelism is not striking unless *good* be emended to *gold*" (Robinson).

2648 Cf. Tr 3.1200n.

2649 "Ovid reads, in modern texts: 'mentemque calor corpusque relinquit.' Chaucer's translation renders the variant 'color,' as does also Filippo's" (Robinson).

2654 "The **knyf** corresponds to Filippo's 'coltello' rather than to Ovid's 'ensis.' Here Chaucer is also in agreement with Boccaccio in both the De gen. deorum (2.22) and the De claris mul. (ch. 13)" (Robinson).

2656–62 The dream is not mentioned by Ovid. Shannon (Ch and Roman Poets, 294) thinks Chaucer followed the De gen. deorum, but Meech (PMLA 45:126) shows that the information is supplied by Filippo's prefatory note (Robinson).

2668–70 Ovid (Her. 14.42) makes only general mention of soporific wines. With Chaucer's lines, cf. KnT I.1472. Emerson (MP 17, 1919, 288) suggests he used the plural **opies** because he knew of the two kinds of opium, meconium ($\mu\eta\kappa\acute{\omega}\nu\epsilon\iota o\nu$) and opium proper ('$o\pi\acute{o}\varsigma$, '$\acute{o}\pi\iota o\nu$) (Robinson).

2680 Her. 14.44.

2681 **Zepherus:** cf. Her. 14.39–40 and GP I.5.

2682 Cf. Her. 14.34.

2683 Cf. Her. 14.46.

2690 Cf. Her. 14.55–56, 58.

2694 **devel:** "This idiomatic expletive has no equivalent in Ovid" (Robinson).

2705 "The details of the escape seem to be Chaucer's addition" (Robinson). Cf. Tr 3.787.

2723 The legend breaks off only a line or two short of completion. We have no way of knowing whether Chaucer meant to add the ending and never did, or actually completed it and the last few lines have been lost. See Hansen (JEGP 82:30–31), who argues that this line may be a genuine ending to the poem.

The Short Poems

The following short poems are printed in only a very approximate chronological order, since few can be dated with any precision. The notes to each comment on the dating, the sources and influences, and the principal scholarly and critical concerns. The most important recent work on these poems is the Variorium edition of Chaucer's Minor Poems, ed. Pace and David, part 1, which contains full commentaries and bibliography. Also very useful is Russell A. Peck's annotated bibliography, *Chaucer's Lyrics and* Anelida and Arcite, 1982.

The poems that appear here and the few lyrics incorporated in the longer works are all that have survived from what is usually assumed to have been a larger body of lyric poetry (though, for a contrary view, see Moore, JEGP 48, 1949, 196–208, and CL 3, 1951, 32–46). Chaucer probably also wrote lyrics in French (Robbins, ChR 13, 1978, 93–115; Wimsatt, in Ch: Writers and Background, 109–36), though none is known to have survived. The Univ. of Pennsylvania MS French 15, an anthology of French poetry written in England, contains fifteen poems attributed to "Ch." They have been edited and translated by James I. Wimsatt (Poems of "Ch"), who concludes that they cannot be proven to be by Chaucer. The manuscript, which also contains poems by Machaut and Grandson—those by Grandson closer to the text Chaucer knew than are the modern editions (see introductory note to Venus)—provide a good idea of the literary milieu in which Chaucer's lyrics were written.

The milieu was French and courtly (see Derek Pearsall, OE and ME Poetry, 1977; Salter, SAC 2, 1980, 71–79; Richard F. Green, Poets and Princepleasers, 1980); Green, ChR 18, 1982, 146–54; and Lenaghan, ChR 18, 1982, 155–60. Chaucer's favorite forms were the French ballade (see Helen L. Cohen, The Ballade, 1915, 222–99; and Friedman, MAE 27, 1958, 95–110) and the French "complaint" (see Green, UMSE 3, 1962, 19–34; Norton-Smith, Geoffrey Ch, 16–17; and Derek Pearsall, John Lydgate, 1970, 92–93). For contemporary attitudes toward these forms see Eustache Deschamps, *L'art de dictier* (Oeuvres 7:266–92), Ernest Langlois, ed., Recueil d'art de seconde rhétorique: Collection de documents inédits sur l'histoire de France, 1902, vol. 13; see also Glending Olson, Lit. as Recreation in the Later Middle Ages, 1982, 147–55. For a full discussion of the forms and social function of French courtly verse, see Daniel Poirion, Le poète.

Probably none of Chaucer's surviving lyrics (with the exception of the roundel in *The Parliament of Fowls*) was meant to be sung. Chaucer admired and imitated Machaut, whose lyrics were composed with music, but he followed the practice of his contemporary, Deschamps, who held in *Art de dictier* (Oeuvres 7:270) that the music of poetry should be "naturele," that is, spoken rather than sung. Nevertheless, Chaucer's lyrics can be sung; settings from contemporary French music, including Machaut, are provided for fourteen of the lyrics by Nigel Wilson (Ch Songs, 1980). See also Wilson's Music in the Age of Ch, 1979.

The explanatory notes to the short poems were written by Laila Z. Gross.

Most of the short poems have received relatively little critical attention. For useful surveys, see Reiss, ChR 1, 1966, 55–65; and Robbins, in Comp to Ch, 380–402.

AN ABC

Chaucer's source is a prayer in Guillaume de Deguilleville's *La pelerinaige de vie humaine* (first redaction 1331, second 1355), a very popular work (see Rosamund Tuve, Allegorical Imagery, 1966, 149). It was translated by Lydgate, who left space for Chaucer's prayer in his text. Besides this testimony, the poem is also attributed to Chaucer in four of the MSS. Its date of composition is unknown, but it is usually considered to be very early on the basis of the heading in Speght's edition of 1602, fol. 347r: "Chaucer's A.B.C. called La Priere de Nostre Dame: made, as some say, at the request of Blanche Duchess of Lancaster, as praier for her privat use, being a woman in her religion very devout." None of the MSS mentions Blanche and this report comes two centuries after Chaucer's death, but Pace (SB 21, 1968, 225–35) notes that Speght might have used a MS once owned by Humphrey, Duke of Gloucester, Blanche's grandson, and could therefore have recorded a family tradition. If this is true, An ABC was written before Blanche's death in 1368. Of course, the report may be untrue, and the poem may have been written much later; certainly its stanzaic form (see below) associates it with later works.

An ABC is the only completely devotional work among Chaucer's short poems, although the Virgin is addressed in The Second Nun's Tale, The Prioress's Tale, and elsewhere.

Most critics have dismissed this poem as one of the least interesting and most derivative of Chaucer's works, though in recent years it has received more sympathetic attention from Reiss (ChR 1, 1966, 55–65), Clemen (Ch's Early Poetry, 175–79), Crampton (Ch Newsletter 1, 1979, 8–10), and Haskell (Eng. Symposium Papers 3, 1972, 1–45).

In form the poem is an alphabetical hymn to the Virgin; for other examples in English, see Carleton Brown and Rossell Hope Robbins, Index of ME Verse, 1943, nos. 471, 604, 607, 664, 2201. It consists of a sequence of prayers, whose unity is provided by the alphabet. Chaucer did not include Deguilleville's last two stanzas for *et* and *c* (= *cetera*), and there are no stanzas for modern *j, u,* or *w*. On this matter, see Pace (Manuscripta 23, 1979, 88–98), who also notes the special visual effect of the poem in the MSS, where the first letter of each stanza is usually very large, often adorned in red.

Chaucer changed Deguilleville's twelve-line stanza to an eight-line stanza, *a b a b b c b c,* which also appears in The Monk's Tale, Former Age, Venus, and Bukton. The line is decasyllabic as in French (rather than the octosyllabic line of the early narratives), and it is used skillfully (Skeat 1:16). Chaucer also departs from his source by using more epithets for the Virgin and by placing much greater emphasis on legal language. The law court is a familiar source of imagery for penitential literature, but here it is so emphasized that the speaker often seems to be pleading in a court of law (cf. Pity). The imagery is more intensely visual than in the original, though, and as Patricia Kean observes (Ch and Poetry 2:197), each image stands alone.

Deguilleville's lines are conveniently printed in Skeat (1:259–71). Since there are so many differences between the two prayers, they will usually not be noted. For a detailed comparison of the two works, see Rogers, Anglistica 18, 1972, 82–106.

4   **floures flour:** A commonplace epithet for the Virgin, though not in Deguilleville; cf. ProLGW F 185. For a study of the tradition, see Dronke, Med. Latin and the Rise of the European Love-Lyric, 1965–66, vol. 1.
14   Cf. MLT II.852, SNPro VIII.75n.
20   **accioun:** Fr. "Contre moy font une accion." The idea is that sin is accusing the sinner before the bar of heaven.
25–32   Klinefelter (Expl 24, 1965, no. 5) points to the Allegory of the Four Daughters of God here.
26   **n'art:** For the construction, see Tr 2.716–18n.
29–30   For the figure, cf. Ps. 7.12.
38   Chaucer adds the biblical image of fruit (cf. Romans 7.4).
50   **bitter:** Fr. "amère." Word play on *Maria* and the Hebrew *marah* (bitterness; Exod. 15.23); cf. SNT VIII.58.
56   **stink eterne:** Stench as a part of the conception of hell is commonplace in medieval thought (Spenser, Spec 2, 1927, 191–92); cf. HF 1654.
59   **bille:** Chaucer's addition. Cf. Col. 2.14.
81   **sorwe:** Chaucer may have misread Deguilleville's "douceur" (sweetness) as *douleur* (sorrow).
85   **lystes:** In the terminology of the judicial duel, "in the arena" (MED s.v. *liste* 5[a]); that is, "in a judicial combat" (see GP I.239n.). It is usually glossed as "wiles," but there is no such meaning in MED (s.v. *list* n. [3]), only "a crafty person." Given the legalisms throughout the poem and the commonplace image of the devil, Christ, etc., "fighting in the lists" (e.g., PP B Passus 19), seems preferable as an interpretation.
88–89   Exod. 3.2. A familiar symbol for the Virgin; cf. PrT VII.467–72n.
100   **melodye:** This is usually taken as Chaucer's mistranslation of "tirelire" (money box), though Chamberlain (in Signs and Symbols, 88) argues that the change was deliberate, intended to characterize the Virgin as "true melody."
109   **ancille:** Echoing Luke 1.38, "Ecce ancilla Domini."
114–15   Not in the Fr. text.
140   **vicaire:** Not in the French text.
149–50   Cf. Gen. 3.18.
159   **bench:** Chaucer uses the common English legal term for the Fr. "court."
161   **Xristus:** Christ; in the MSS the word is abbreviated as "Xpc" or "Xpu" (the sigma in Greek Χριστός is represented by the *c;* the *u* is for the Latin ending -*us*).
163   **Longius:** See Legenda aurea, ch. 47.
169   Cf. Gen. 22, Heb. 11.17–19.
177   Zech. 13.1.

THE COMPLAINT UNTO PITY

This was ascribed to Chaucer by Shirley in MS Harley 78 and called "A Complaint of Pitee," as it was in MS Add.

34360, and some critics have argued for that title. As is true for all the short poems, there is no evidence for when Pity was written. It is usually considered to be an early poem on the familiar grounds: it is artificial and therefore must have been written when Chaucer was still learning his craft; it is derivative, although no exact source has been found (which is true for all the short poems except ABC and Venus). Brusendorff (Ch Trad., 270), among others, sees a strong influence of *il dolce stil nuovo* and assigns it to Chaucer's Italian period. Clemen (Ch's Early Poetry, 181) has led the argument against a notable Italian influence: "There is nothing in the least 'dolce' about it." Yet Clemen also notes that a date in the Italian period is not impossible, since Chaucer here uses rime royal—the seven-line iambic pentameter stanza rhyming *a b a b b c c,* which became the narrative stanza of most of Chaucer's major works, but which had been used previously in French only for lyric poetry (see Stevens, PMLA 94, 1979, 67–76; and Baum, Ch's Verse). Chaucer may have chosen the rime royal stanza under the influence of Boccaccio's narrative stanza, *ottava rima* (eight iambic lines rhyming *a b a b a c c*), which closely resembles rime royal (the scheme is identical if the fifth line is omitted). The change from the octosyllabic couplets of *The Book of the Duchess* and *The House of Fame* to rime royal is usually attributed to Boccaccio's influence, and The Complaint unto Pity may be Chaucer's earliest use of the stanza, which he here already handles with great ease.

In form—a narrative introduction followed by a "complaint" (here *Bill*)—Pity resembles *Anelida* and The Complaint of Mars. Like ABC, Pity is notable for its heavy use of legal terminology and metaphors drawn from the law (Nolan, ChR 13, 1979, 363–72).

No exact source is known. Skeat argued that the personification of Pity was taken from Statius's *Thebaid,* bk. 12, but the parallel is very remote. There are some resemblances to the *Roman de la rose,* but they too are very vague, as are the poem's few parallels to the poems of Machaut (Wimsatt, MAE 47, 1978, 79–81). Poem IX in the Poems of "Ch" (ed. Wimsatt) contains a personification of Pity and bears some resemblance to this poem. However, the figure of Pity is commonplace in medieval poetry (Flügel, Anglia 23, 1901, 196) and the theme of pity was one of Chaucer's favorites (Gray, in J. R. R. Tolkien, Scholar and Storyteller, ed. Salu and Farrell, 1979, 173–203); the search for exact sources is probably unnecessary.

Norton-Smith (Geoffrey Ch, 21–23) gives the poem a very sympathetic reading, but no one else has made such great claims for its excellence as Pittock (Crit 1, 1959, 160–68), and most critics have simply ignored it. No "occasion" for the poem has been found, and there is no evidence for the older speculations that Chaucer here and in *The Book of the Duchess* refers to his own experiences in love.

11   Clemen (Ch's Early Poetry, 181) and Gray (in J. R. R. Tolkien, 174) identify **Cruelte** with Daungier in RR. Wimsatt (MAE 47:80–81) refutes this and cites analogues in Machaut's poetry for Chaucer's image of *Cruelte* in conflict with *Pite.* Nolan (ChR 13:371) sees Pity and Cruelty engaged in a legal contest.
14   Brusendorff (Ch Trad., 270) compares Petrarch's Sonnet 120: "Go, warm sighs, to the cold heart; break the ice that imprisons [*contende*] Pity," but the resemblance is slight.

15   herse: A frame for supporting lights as part of a funeral display. For an illustration, see fol. 142 of the Boucicaut Hours (repr. The Golden Age: Manuscript Painting at the Time of Jean, Duke of Berry, ed. Marcel Thomas, 1979, pl. 28). The body is lying in state.

38   It is not clear why **Bounte** should be **wel armed**.

The Bill of Complaint

This complaint is divided into three "terns," or groups of stanzas, each group ending with a couplet rhyming on -eyne. Nolan (ChR 13:364) shows how the tripartite division conforms with legal bills.

Complaint: This is, like bill (petition), a legal term, a formal complaint presented to a court or some other authority. Cf. ProLGW G 363; Bo 3.pr3.63–64; and MED s.v. complaint 4.

59   Sheweth: A term regularly employed in petitions.

64–72   The allegory here, as Robinson noted, is not quite clear. The meaning seems to be: "Cruelty, the opposite of Pity, has disguised herself as Womanly Beauty and allied herself with Bounty, Gentilesse, and Courtesy to usurp your rightful dwelling place, which is called the Beauty that pertains to Grace." Pittock (Crit 1:161) explains that "Chaucer is exploring the genre to see how far he can stretch it without breaking. That he succeeded can be gauged from its fifteenth-century imitations."

92   Herenus quene: A great deal has been written on this, but most readers agree with Robinson: "Herenus, which has the best MS support, is usually taken to be an error or corruption for 'Herines,' the Erinyes, the three Furies (cf. Tr 4.22). Chaucer's reason for calling Pity the Queen of the Furies is uncertain." Skeat argues for the influence of Statius's Pietas: "Pity may be said to be the queen of the Furies, in the sense that pity (or mercy) can alone control the vindictiveness of vengeance." Lowes (MP 14, 1917, 723) compares Inf. 9.43–45, where the furies ("Erine") are the handmaidens of Proserpina, "the queen of everlasting lamentation." See also Pittock, Crit 1:167. Various emendations have been suggested: "my hertes quene" (Flügel, Anglia 23, 1901, 205), "serenous" (Heath), "vertuous" (Koch), "Hesperus" (Ethel Seaton, Sir Richard Roos, 1961, 166).

99–104   Cf. PF 90–91n., Lady 43–45.

110   Proverbial; cf KnT I.2397n. and Anel 182.

119   This repeats line 2. Cf. Anel 211, 350. The Trinity MS has a colophon: "Here endeth the exclamacioun of the Deth of Pyte" (Skeat 1:457).

A COMPLAINT TO HIS LADY

This work is attributed to Chaucer by Shirley, and most critics, with the exception of John Norton-Smith (Geoffrey Ch, 20), accept it as genuine. In Shirley's MS Harley 78 and in MS Add. 34369, which is apparently derived from it, the poem is entitled "The Balade of Pyte" and treated as a continuation of the "Complaint unto Pite." Lowes (MP 14, 1917, 724) argues for a connection between the two works, but no one else has tried to do so.

The poem consists of four parts: I. two stanzas in rime royal; II. eight lines of what appear to be terza rima (Dante's meter—iambic tercets, aba bcb, etc.); III. another seventeen lines of terza rima; IV. ten stanzas, all but

the second consisting of ten decasyllabic lines rhyming a a b a a b c d d c. There is little relation between the parts, and Brusendorff (Ch Trad., 273) would have it printed as three separate poems. It is apparently a series of metrical experiments, which may, as Fisher (670) holds, have been written at different times. Clogan (M&H 5, 1974, 183–89), in the most sympathetic discussion of the poem, emphasizes its experimental and unfinished character and argues that editorial emendations to clarify and "improve" the text merely obscure its distinctive character. Clemen (Ch's Early Poetry, 185–88) praises the naturalness of parts of the work, but most critics have dismissed it as purely conventional.

Because of the apparent use of terza rima, this poem is usually dated after Chaucer's first Italian journey, though, of course, it is possible that Chaucer knew Dante's work before he went to Italy. The poem shows a number of close affinities with the Anelida; the stanza used in Part IV is similar to the nine-line stanza of Anelida, and the two poems show frequent resemblances in language and sentiment (see notes below and Wimsatt, MAE 47, 1978, 66–67).

1   On the narrator's sleeplessness, cf. the opening of BD, and with 1–3 cf. esp. BD 18–21.

8–9   Cf. Anel 333–34.

15   Skeat and Fisher repeat 14 in order to correct the rhyme.

18   The construction is doubtful. Apparently the sentence means, "And yet, though I were to die I cannot tear it (i.e., love) out of my sorrowful heart" (Robinson).

22   Skeat adds line 189 from The Complaint of Mars to complete the rhyme scheme.

27   Faire Rewthelees is a translation of "la belle dame sans merci," but this is contested by Timmer, ES 11, 1929, 20–22. The phrase does not occur in Machaut, Deschamps, or Grandson.

31   Cf. Anel 222 (nearly identical).

37   my swete fo: Cf. line 58 and Anel 272; Tr 1.874, 5.228; KnT I.2780. On such oxymorons, see Tr 1.411n.

40   Cf. KnT I.1565.

43–45   Cf. Pity 99–104, PF 90–91n.

46   Cf. Anel 237 (repeated exactly).

51   Skeat adds a line (Anel 182) after this and adds Anel 181 after 53 to make this eight-line stanza conform with the other, ten-line stanzas in this section.

118–27   Because this stanza is found in only one of the two MSS, its authenticity was questioned in the Globe edition. But there seems to be no reason to differentiate between the conventionalities in these lines and the rest.

124   Cf. KnT I.2392, FranT V.974.

THE COMPLAINT OF MARS

Chaucer's authorship is attested by Shirley and by Lydgate (Pro to Fall of Princes 1.322–23), who refers to the poem as "the broche which that Vulcanus / At Thebes wrouhte." It is also called "The Broche of Thebes" in MS Harley 7333 (see Brusendorff, Ch Trad., 261–64; see also Textual Notes).

None of Chaucer's other short poems has elicited so much and such varied critical commentary. The commentary generally falls into three categories: allegorical, astronomical, and interpretative-appreciative.

The allegorical approach, which takes the poem as

representing a court scandal, has its beginning with the copyist John Shirley, who states in the rubric to MS Trinity R.3.20 that this poem was "made by Geffrey Chaucier at the commandement of the renommed and excellent prince my lord the duc John of Lancastre." In the colophon Shirley writes: "Thus eondeth this complaint which some men sayne was made by my lady York doghter to the kyng of Spaygne [John of Gaunt] and my lord of huntyngdon some tyme duc of Exester." Then follows The Complaint of Venus, at the end of which Shirley writes "Hyt is sayde that Graunson made this last balade for venus resembled to my lady of York aunswering the complaynt of Mars." The poem has therefore been taken as representing a scandalous liaison between John Holland and Isabel of York (Skeat 1:65–66, 86) or another of John of Gaunt's daughters, Elizabeth of Lancaster (George Cowling, Ch, 1927, 1–64, 110–11). The allegorical reading remained popular until quite recent years (Haldeen Braddy, Ch and the Fr. Poet Graunson, 1947, 77–83) but has been vigorously attacked by recent critics such as Norton-Smith (Geoffrey Ch, 24–25), who argues that Shirley's "made by" cannot mean "composed concerning" (cf. MED s.v. *bi* 9 [a]) and that Shirley's statement "made by my lady of York . . . and my lord huntyngdon" records a rumor that the poem was "actually composed or recited by Isabel of York and John Holland." If so, it may have been recited as a courtly "disguising" (see Stevens, Music and Poetry, 169) or "mumming" (see Derek Pearsall, John Lydgate, 1970, 183–88), which were popular aristocratic entertainments of the time.

A number of critics have examined the poem only, or primarily, as a description of an astronomical event. This approach, like the allegorical, deals only with the story, not with the proem or complaint. Manly, refuting older theories, argued that the astronomical situation was purely imaginary (see 81–82 below). North (RES 20, 1969, 439–42) argued that the astronomical configurations described in the poem fit the year 1385; Parr and Holtz (ChR 15, 1981, 255–66) likewise argue for 1385, though noting discrepancies between the poem and the actual condition of the skies. Eade (SAC 4, 1982, 69–76) also provides a useful examination of the astronomy and argues that the references are simpler than they have seemed and would have been understood by many in Chaucer's audience (82). See also Wood, Ch and Stars, 100–117; Smyser, Spec 45, 1970, 359–73; Manzalaoui, in Ch: Writers and Backgrounds, 241–42.

Most interpretative and appreciative criticism has concentrated on the complaint itself. Stillwell (PQ 35, 1956, 69–89) was among the first to examine Mars for its poetic merits, reversing a long critical tradition of simply dismissing it out of hand (e.g., Root, Poetry of Ch, 63; and Lewis, Allegory of Love, 170). The poem has since received careful and sympathetic attention and has often been compared to *Troilus*. See, among others, Clemen, Ch's Early Poetry, 188–97; Lawlor, in Ch and Chaucerians, 39–64; Owen, SP 63, 1966, 535–36, and PQ 46, 1967, 434–35; Hultin, AnM 9, 1968, 58–75; Merrill, Lit. Monographs 5, 1973, 3–61; Laird, ChR 6, 1972, 229–31; Storm, PQ 57, 1978, 323–35.

Chaucer's ultimate source is the story of Mars and Venus, captured in Vulcan's net (Ovid, Metamorphoses 4.171–89 and Ars amatoria 2.561), one of the best-known classical stories. Peter Abelard used it to compare himself and Eloise to Mars and Venus (The Story of My

Misfortunes, tr. Henry A. Bellows, 1972, 20–21, where he also notes that they named their son Astrolabe), and Chaucer refers to it in KnT I.2383–92 and Tr 3.724–25. In this version, the lovers are discovered by the sun rather than by Vulcan with his net (Manzalaoui, in Ch: Writers and Background, 245, and Storm, PQ 57:326–27, argue that Vulcan is metaphorically present). Other Ovidian influences are found by Norton-Smith, Geoffrey Ch, 26–27, and Dean, CL 19, 1967, 1–27. Brewer (N&Q 199, 1954, 462–63) notes the possible influence of Boccaccio's *De genealogia deorum* 3.22 on the characterization of Venus. Wimsatt (MAE 47, 1978, 73–76) notes possible echoes of Machaut.

The story may be dated, hesitantly, around 1385, on the basis of the astronomical allusions, though there is the possibility that the story and the complaint were written at different times (see Owen, PQ 46:434, and Skeat 1: 65). The occasion may have been a Valentine's Day celebration at the court, perhaps involving a "disguising," but that is only conjecture.

"The proem and the story (1–154) are in Chaucer's customary seven-line stanza. The complaint consists of sixteen nine-line stanzas, one introductory stanza and five terns, or sets of three stanzas, on different subjects" (Robinson).

1   **gray:** MED s.v. *grei* 1(b), as used in referring to morning light; cf. KnT I.1492.
8   **blewe:** MED s.v. *bleu* 1(e), meaning, figuratively, "sad, sorrowful." Braddy (Geoffrey Ch, 78) argues that "blue" stands rather for "faithful," "loyal."
9   Cf. SqT V.596n.
12   Apparently proverbial, though this is the only recorded example in ME; cf. Whiting N103.
13–14   **Seynt Valentyne . . . thy day:** Cf. PF 309 and n.
29   **thridde hevenes lord:** Mars is in the third heavenly sphere, reckoned inward from Saturn, as here and in Scogan 9; in Tr 3.2 Chaucer counts from the earth outward and Venus is in the third heaven. Both methods of reckoning were common.
30–51   Venus and Mars are in "platic" conjunction, which occurs when the radius of their surrounding "rays" (a halo of 8° for Mars and 7° for Venus) touch one another; that is, when they are within 7½° of one another (see Richard of Wallingford, Exafrenon pronosticacionum temporis, in Works 1:227 and 2:115). In Richard's Canon supra kalendarium, the minimum distance is given as 15° (1:562).
30   **hevenysh revolucioun:** The orbit of Mars in his sphere, which brings him close to Venus. The addition of *by desert* (31) shows that the narrative has a non-astrological dimension.
31–32   **Venus . . . hath take him in subjeccioun:** Venus is a benevolent, "well-willed" planet (cf. Tr 3.1276), Mars "evil-willed" (Richard of Wallingford, Works 1:201). The benevolent influence of Venus tempers Mars's evil effects; see Tr 3.22–28.
42   **with scourging of her chere:** By her look; i.e., astrological aspect (Lat. *aspectus,* look).
45   **Who syngeth now but Mars:** Mars is in the zodiacal sign Aries, his house or domicile: "When a planet is in his hows . . . it is clepid his hows of joye" (Exafrenon 1:203). That Venus *regneth now in blysse* (43) could indicate she is in her exaltation at or near 27° Pisces: "When a planete is in his exaltation, he is likned til a kynge in

his see and in his joye emonge his men" (Richard of Wallingford, Works 1:203), but in both cases the joy may be due to love rather than astrology.

50–56   Mars and Venus, **knyt** in platic conjunction, agree to meet, join in exact conjunction, in **hir nexte paleys.** Venus's next house or domicile is the immediately following sign Taurus, the bull. Mars will await her there, since he is ahead of Venus and moves slowly through the sky as she, at her faster speed, overtakes him (see 69–70 below).

51   lokyng: Both astrological aspect and amorous glances.

58   my myschef: Taurus is an unfortunate sign for Mars (cf. 106–8); it is of opposite qualities to his house (Aries is "Masculyne, firye, orientale," Taurus "Feminyne, erthye, meredionale," Richard of Wallingford, Works 1:207) and in it he has no astrological "dignities" and thus no power; but in a conjunction "a planet of another takes greet strength and confort" (Richard of Wallingford, Works 1:227).

61   Cf. NPT VII.3160.

69–70   Mars was commonly said to complete his orbit in two years (actually 687 days): cf. Bartholomaeus Anglicus 8.3; tr. Trevisa 1:481. He thus moves about one-half degree a day; Venus moves almost a full degree.

71–72   Cf. MLT II.1075, 1114–15.

72   they be mette: Mars and Venus were in exact conjunction in 5° Taurus on 5 March 1385. Parr and Holtz (ChR 15:256) print a table of the planetary positions in 1385 (see 81–82 below).

79, 84, 85   chambre: North (RES 20:139) takes this as the first "term" (first 8 degrees) of Taurus, which was a dignity of Venus; Eade (SAC 4:73–74) takes it as the center (15°) of Taurus. The word may mean simply "bedroom," with a possible pun; see WBPro III.618.

81–82   Phebus . . . Within the paleys yates: The sun enters the sign of Taurus (on 12 April in Chaucer's time, see 139 below). In 1385, by 12 April Venus had already left Taurus and was 3° into Gemini. For this reason Manly rejected the year 1385 and judged the astronomical situation described as "entirely imaginary" (Harvard Sts. and Notes in Philol. and Lit. 5, 1896, 113); North (RES 20:138) and Parr and Holtz (ChR 15:259–60) regard the discrepancy as insignificant.

86   boles: The bull stands for Taurus, the *white Bole* (cf. Tr 2.55 and n.).

88   brenne hem: The sun, Phoebus, will destroy the influence of a planet, render it *combust* (cf. Tr 3.717; and 127–28 below) if it approaches closer than 15° (Richard of Wallingford, Works 1:562, 2:115), though 17° and 20° are given by some authorities. (North, RES 20:139.) Cf. Astr 2.4.33–36.

89   dreynt in teres: Venus is a "hot and moist" planet (cf. Scogan 11–12) and Mars, who reacts with *firi sparkes* (96), is "hot and dry." Cf. KnT I.2664–66.

90–91   A brief or dawn song; cf. 136–40, and Tr 3.1422–1533 and n.

104–5   The sun "can overtake Mars but not Venus because his sphere is between theirs and his motion is consequently slower than Venus; but faster than Mars" (Florence M. Grimm, Astro. Lore in Ch, 1919, 47): see North (RES 20:138) and the chart of transits in Parr and Holtz (ChR 15:256) for exact details.

104   Cf. KnT I.1949.

105   Cf. proem, 7.

111   half the stremes: Half the rays, or "halo" of Mars, extending 4° on each side of the planet. This would mean that the conjunction is ending, and Venus is beginning to move away. See Richard of Wallingford, Works 1: 562, 2:115.

113   Cilenios tour: Gemini, the sign of Mercury, who was born on Mt. Cyllene (Aen. 8:139). On *tour,* used for zodiacal house or domicile, see North (RES 20:139) and Laird (ChR 6:229–31). See Wood, Ch and Stars, pl. 21, for a zodiacal house depicted as a *tour.*

114   With voide cours: Venus moves through the last ten degrees of Taurus, which are "vacui" (Richard of Wallingford, Works 1:207). Emerson (PQ 2:83) argues for the meaning "cunning, artful," a recognized sense of Fr. *voide,* which is possible, though the astrological meaning is more plausible.

116   No other planet is in Gemini.

117   litil myght: Venus has but one "term" in Gemini and hence little power (Richard of Wallingford, Works 2:207).

119   cave: Skeat explains the cave within the gate as one of the caves or *patei* of Gemini, one of which was at 2°. The idea that she remains there *a naturel day* seems based on the idea that she moves 1° a day (see 69–70 above); see Smyser, Spec 45:368.

120   Derk . . . smokyng: "Does not accord with the standard allocation of *gradus tenebrosi, umbrosi,* and *fumosi.* Either Chaucer made a mistake (the degrees at the beginning of Gemini are actually *lucidi,* although followed by *fumosi*)" (North, RES 20:140).

127–28   The feebleness of Mars is due to the approach of the sun: "When he [a planet] begynnes to com towarde the sunne, so that he may not be seen (for owr mekill lighte of the Sonne), the planete is sayde to have his fallynge downe; and he is calid unhappy till domis" (Richard of Wallingford, Works 1:217).

129   steyre: Skeat (1:500) notes this exactly translates Lat. *gradus* (degree or stair).

139   twelfte daye of April: The day the sun enters Taurus, in which Mars remains (at 21° on 12 April 1385).

144   chevache: The planets are commonly depicted in illustrations as riding in chariots drawn by horses or birds (see Parr and Holtz, ChR 15:261).

145   valaunse: Most critics accept Skeat's explanation that this is a form of Fr. *faillaunce,* which he takes as a translation of the astronomical term *detrimentum.* The *detrimenta* of Venus (those signs opposite Venus's domiciles or mansions) were Scorpio and Aries, and Skeat takes the latter as intended here (1:501–2). Parr and Holtz (ChR 15:262) argue that Mercury must be in Taurus to see his *paleys* (Gemini, the next sign) and that *valaunce* must therefore be derived from Fr. *vaillaunce* (Lat. *valentia,* power), referring to Venus's power in her house, Taurus. Norton-Smith (Geoffrey Ch, 145) believes there is a wordplay with reference to Venus's headdress (cf. PF 272), but this is unlikely.

146–47   her receyveth: "A planet is 'received' by another planet if that planet being 'received' is in an essential dignity (i.e., house or exaltation of the other planet)" (Parr and Holtz, ChR 15:262). Since Gemini is the domicile of Mercury, *receyveth* is the astronomically precise term. The idea that Venus and Mercury become lovers, suggested by Stillwell (cf. Laird, PQ 51:486–89; Storm, PQ 57:329), is improbable.

155–298 Robbins (Comp to Ch, 390–91) regards the complaint as composed of five anti-complaints.

166 him that lordeth ech intelligence: God, who rules the "intelligences," angels, that govern each sphere. Cf. Dante, Convivio 2.5.1; and Bartholomaeus Anglicus 2.17, tr. Trevisa 1:83: "The philosopher clepith an angel *intelligencia.*"

185 hette: Here "promised," though the form usually means "was named." Apparently the weak intrans. pret. is used with the meaning of the strong trans. pret. for the sake of rhyme.

206 horowe: This is Chaucer's only use of this rare word.

221–22 The image is common; cf. ClT IV.37, and Whiting T547.

236–40 The image of the fishhook is common. Andreas Capellanus derives "amor" (love) from *hamus* (fishhook; De amore 1.1).

245 The broche of Thebes: From Statius, Thebaid 2.265–305. Cf. Ovid, Met. 4.563ff. Vulcan made it for Harmonia, the daughter of Mars and Venus, of whom he was jealous; it brought misfortune to all who coveted it. Skeat's complex theory that it referred to a real tablet of jasper (1:66) has not been found convincing. It was a powerful image and gave its name to the poem in one manuscript and in Lydgate's list of Chaucer's works (see introductory note). For various modern interpretations, see Hultin (AnM 9:66), Norton-Smith (Geoffrey Ch, 33), Dean (CL 19:19), Merrill (Lit. Monographs 5:40), and Wood (Ch and Stars, 159). Anderson (SAC 4, 1982, 127–28) connects this brooch with Criseyde's, but see Tr 3.1369–72n.

272, 281 If the poem was presented at a court entertainment or as a "disguising" (see introductory note), **knyghtes** and **ladyes** may be directly addressed to members of the Lancastrian household (Norton-Smith, Geoffrey Ch, 24–25).

285 emperise: Empress, here Venus, who rules the ladies as Mars rules the knights. The reference to Venus here and in the following stanza seems to imply a transition to The Complaint of Venus, which may account for its following Mars in some manuscripts.

286 desolat: Probably has its astrological meaning: "in an unfortunate position" (cf. WBPro III.703–5).

THE COMPLAINT OF VENUS

This poem is a free translation, or adaptation, of a triple ballade by the French knight-poet Oton de Grandson (d. 1397), whom Chaucer names as his source. In Shirley's manuscript and others it is treated as a continuation of The Complaint of Mars, though most editors reject that association and Robinson thought even the title, The Complaint of Venus, was "wholly inappropriate." However, Chaucer changes Grandson's speaker from a male to a female, and the envoy addresses some *princes* (see 73 below). There may thus be some basis for Shirley's report that the poem was associated with Isabel of York (see introductory note to Mars).

If that is the case, then the poem must have been written before Isabel's death in 1392, presumably about the same time as The Complaint of Mars, perhaps around 1385. Robinson dated it later, partly because of Chaucer's apparent reference to his advanced age (lines 76–

78), which, "though not to be dated too precisely, would have been most natural in the nineties," but mainly because on 17 November 1393 Grandson received a grant from Richard II "and about this time he and Chaucer may have been in personal contact." However, Piaget, Grandson's editor, believes the ballade Chaucer used dates from Grandson's early years, and the two poets must have met long before 1393. Grandson was an exemplar of international chivalry, who, over a period of twenty years, was a retainer of John of Gaunt, Richard II, and the future Henry IV. According to John of Gaunt's Register (ed. Sydney Armitage–Smith, item 1662) on 30 January 1375 John of Gaunt ordered Chaucer to be given 10 livres and Grandson 50 marks for the term of Easter. Their names appear separately on many occasions and on 11 May they appear together again, Grandson receiving 10 livres and Chaucer 100 "soldz" (John of Gaunt's Register, 1379–83, ed. E. C. Lodge and R. Sommerville, item 296). The Register ends in 1383, when Grandson is mentioned again on 8 April (item 847). He presumably continued in the family's employ, since from 1390 to 1393 he served with John of Gaunt's son Henry, the future king, then earl of Derby (see The Expedition to Prussia and the Holy Land Made by Henry Earl of Derby, ed. Lucy Toulmin Smith, 1894; rpt. 1965). Chaucer could have known Grandson's work at any time after about 1375. Grandson (c. 1340–1397) died in a judicial duel on the issue of his complicity in the death of the Count of Savoy. The best account of his life and works is that by Arthur Piaget, Oton de Grandson: Sa vie et ses poésies, 1941.

Chaucer did not translate *word by word* (81), as he claims, since the shift from a male to a female speaker necessitated omissions, additions, and alterations. Yet the lines remain close to the French, especially in the second and third sets of stanzas, and a good many lines are translated literally. For the text, see Wimsatt, Poems of "Ch," 70–74; these versions are closer to the text Chaucer used than those previously published by Piaget, Oton de Grandson; Braddy, Ch and the Fr. Poet Graunson, 1947, 61–62; and Skeat (1:400–404). Wimsatt points out that the first of the ballades originally bore the rubric "complainte," later effaced.

Chaucer's oft-quoted remark on the scarcity of rhymes in English (80) is true; that English has fewer rhymes than French is incontestable. Yet these ballades exhibit an apparent ease in finding the rhymes necessary in a strict ballade. The envoy of ten lines is both unusually long and unusually difficult, since it is built on but two rhymes, one of which (*-aunce*) had been used in the second set of ballades. Perhaps the apology for the *scarsete* of rhyme in English is at once a conventional use of the topos of "affected modesty" (see GP I.746n.) and a sly way of calling attention to the technical virtuosity of his poem.

Most discussions of this work have concerned its possible relation to a court scandal (see introductory note to Mars, and Braddy, Ch and the Fr. Poet Graunson, 77–83), and little attention has been paid to its aesthetic qualities. Robbins (in Comp. to Ch, 17–19) and Green (Univ. of Miss. Sts. in Eng. 3, 1962, 26–27) comment on Chaucer's improvement of his original; and Merrill (Lit. Monographs 5, 1973, 1–61) considers the relation of Venus to The Complaint of Mars and argues for the unity of the two poems.

14 For the common idea of beauty as the best work of Nature; cf. BD 908–11, PhysT VI.11–13. The idea is not in the French.

20 Cf. Wom Nobl 12.

22–23 aventure : honoure: This rhyme is not found elsewhere in Chaucer and is "not in accord with Chaucer's regular usage" (Robinson).

25–32 The stanza is closely translated from the French, though the ideas are common (cf. BD 599–615; KnT I.1375–76 and note 1355–76).

46 nouncerteyn: Fr. "sans nul certain." Cf. Tr 1.337.

50 las: Fr. "amoureux las," a commonplace in love poetry (cf. KnT I.1817, 1951).

71 compleynt or this lay: This again shows how loosely Chaucer uses these terms (cf. MerT IV.1881).

73 Princes: The plural in the envoy is very rare (see Fort 75). This could be a variant of "princesse"; see MED s.v. *princes(se* for examples. Two manuscripts read "princesse," but both are by Shirley, who reports the tradition that the poem was associated with Isabel of York, and the unambiguous form may be his attempt to make that association clear.

76–78 See Payne, Key of Remembrance, 83–84, on how these lines fit in the larger context of Chaucer's poetry. Cf. Scogan 35, 38.

TO ROSEMOUNDE

The sole copy of this poem (Bodleian MS Rawlinson Poet 163) was discovered by Skeat, who assigned it to Chaucer and gave it the present title (Athenaeum 1, 1891, 410). Brusendorff (Ch Trad., 439–40) rejected the ascription, but it has been accepted by most editors. In the MS To Rosemounde follows *Troilus,* and at the end of both works are written in a different script the words *chaucer* and *Tregentil,* as they are printed here. Skeat (1:81) argues that *Tregentil* is the name of the scribe; Kökeritz (MLN 63, 1948, 310–18) held instead that it was an honorific compliment *(très gentil).* Pace-David (1:170) note that the words are far separated in the manuscript, which suggests that they were intended to be taken separately rather than as a noun plus modifying adjective.

Because the ballade is so lively, some critics have assumed a real Rosemounde was addressed, though the name (which means "Rose of the World" or possibly, on the basis of line 2, "Rosy mouth") was fairly common in verse. Robbins (Sts. in Lit. Imagination 4, 1971, 73–81) reviews the candidates and endorses the conjecture by Rickert (MP 25, 1927, 255) that the poem was addressed to Richard II's child-bride, the seven-year-old Isabelle of Valois, on the occasion of her entry into London in 1396. There is no evidence for this and the poem may be much earlier; Vasta (in Ch Probs, 97–113) would put it as early as 1369–70.

In structure the poem is a highly conventional ballade (see R. T. Davies, Med. Eng. Lyrics, 1963, 133–34). Even its mock seriousness is not completely outside the tradition, since the courtly mode admitted a wide range of attitudes (see Stevens, Music and Poetry, 220–21; and Burrow in his edition of the poem in English Verse 1300–1500, 1977).

Vasta (as above) finds the major literary influence here the *Roman de la rose.* Wimsatt (MAE 47, 1978, 76–77)

argues for the influence of Machaut's "Tout ensement com le monde enlumine," but the resemblances are only general.

1 Madame: Robbins (Sts. in Lit. Imagination 4:79) notes this title was given to the eldest daughter of the king of France and suggests that, if Chaucer is addressing Isabelle of Valois, the word is used in its technical sense. However, *madame* is a common form of address in the ballades; see Against Women Unconstant 1.

2 mapamounde: Map of the world (Lat. *mappa mundi*); medieval maps were usually rounded (**cercled**); see Vasta, Ch Probs, 11–12.

3 cristal: A conventional comparison (Whiting C594); both crystal and rubies (line 4) were commonly used in shrines and reliquaries.

8 daliaunce: The meanings of this important word in love poetry range from "sociability" (GP I.211) to "sexual intimacy" (WBPro III.260).

9 tyne: A barrel holding four or five pails of liquid. Skeat (1:549) compares Chevalier au Cygne, "La jour i ot plore de larmes plaine tine" (That day he wept a barrel of tears). The rhyme *tine : galantine* was common in French verse (see Ernst Langlois, ed., Recueil d'art de seconde rhétorique, 1902, 13:137).

17 pyk walwed in galauntyne: A pike steeped in galantine sauce. Hieatt (in Ch Probs, 153) says this is a sort of aspic, a cold, jellied sauce. In Two Fifteenth Cent. Cookery Books, EETS 91, it is defined as a pickling sauce made of brown bread, vinegar, salt, and pepper; for "Pik in galentyne" the cook should "cast the same under him and above him that he be al yhidde in the sauce" (108). See Curye on Inglysch, EETS SS.8, 190.

20 Tristam: Tristan, the lover of Isolde, commonly cited as an ideal; Lowes (RomR 2, 1911, 128) compares Froissart, "Nom ai Amans, et en sornom Tristans" (Oeuvres, ed. Scheler 2:367). Cf. PF 290 and n.

21 refreyde: Kökeritz (MLN 63:317) takes the rarity of this word, which appears elsewhere only in Chaucer (Tr 3.1343, 5.507; ParsT X.341) and the works of Wyclif, as internal evidence for Chaucer's authorship.

affounde: "Decline, fail," according to MED s.v. *afounden* 2(a); possibly "be numb with cold" (Kökeritz, MLN 63, 1948, 316).

WOMANLY NOBLESSE

The single MS copy is in British Library Add. 34360, where it is headed "Balade that Chauncier made." The present title was taken by Skeat from line 24; Brusendorff (Ch Trad., 276–77) thinks it too abstract and suggests instead "Envoy to a Lady." That the work is Chaucer's is generally accepted, though Koch (ESt 27, 1900, 68) doubted its authenticity, and Helen L. Cohen (The Ballade, 1915, 246–47) argued against Chaucer's authorship on the basis of the looseness with which the form of the ballade is used here. Chaucer does depart from the usual form by omitting the refrain, but he increases the difficulty of the form by using only two rhymes (-*aunce,* -*esse*) rather than three throughout all three stanzas.

As in the case of Chaucer's other ballades, no one source is known. Wimsatt (MAE 47, 1978, 76–78) discusses Machaut's influence, particularly "Foy porter." He also points out the similarities between Womanly

Noblesse and To Rosemounde: the narrator praises the lady instead of complaining to her, and the diction is mainly derived from French, with the *-aunce* rhyme used in both.

12 To supply the missing line, Furnivall composed "Taketh me lady, in your obeisaunce," which Skeat printed.

13 souvenaunce: This is the only use of this word by Chaucer; Wimsatt (MAE 47:76) argues it was suggested by "souvenir" in the refrain of Machaut's "Dame, le dous souvenir."

25 outrance: According to the MED, this is the first use in English of this word.

ADAM SCRIVEYN

In Shirley's MS R.3.20 this poem bears the title "Chauciers words, ·a· Geffrey unto Adame his owen scryveyne." No one has doubted Chaucer's authorship, and critics have been mainly concerned with identifying the scribe Adam. For various suggestions, see Brusendorff, Ch Trad., 57; Hammond, Ch: Bibl. Man., 405, and MLN 19, 1904, 36, and MP 11, 1914, 223; Bressie, TLS 9 May 1929, 383; Manly, TLS 16 May 1929, 403; Wagner, TLS 13 June 1929, 474.

Kaske (in Ch Probs, 114–18) suggests that Chaucer may have been thinking of the popular Latin verses on Clericus Adam: "Beneath a certain tree, Adam the clerk wrote of how the first Adam sinned by means of a certain tree." Peck (PMLA 90, 1975, 467) had earlier suggested a relation between the first Adam and Chaucer's scribe. Root (Poetry of Ch, 69–70) compares Petrarch, who voices a similar exasperation with scribes in *Librorum copia* (ed. and tr. C. H. Rawskim, 1967, 34–37).

Since *Troilus* is mentioned, Robinson fixed the probable date around the middle 1380s, though the poem could have been composed any time after *Boece* and *Troilus* were finished. The poem is written in the same rime royal stanza as *Troilus,* and it reflects the same concern with accurate transmission of his text as Chaucer expressed in Tr 5.1793–98.

3 scalle: Modern English *scall,* which Fisher defines as "a parasitic skin infection (dermathophytosis)." "What that ever be, the commune use hath that the skalle is a scab of the hede with flawes and with crustes and with some moysture and with doynge away of heres and with an askisshe colour and with stynkynge smellynge and horrible lokynge" (The Cyrurgie of Guy de Chauliac, EETS 265, 416).

6 rubbe and scrape: Parchment was corrected by scraping off the old ink and then rubbing the surface smooth again. (MS illustrations of scribes and authors often show them with a pen in one hand and a scraper in the other.)

THE FORMER AGE

This and the four poems that follow are all ascribed to Chaucer in the MSS, and his authorship has never been questioned. They have been assigned to various dates between 1380 and the end of his life. They all show indebtedness to Boethius, but that influence cannot be reserved to any one period in Chaucer's life. The most thorough examination of this influence remains Bernard Jefferson, Ch and the Consolation, 1917. Norton-Smith (MAE 32, 1963, 117–24) has argued for the influence of Deschamps; many of Deschamps's ballades have themes similar to these "Boethian" poems (the whole first volume of his collected works consists solely of "ballades de Moralitez"), but the question of whether Deschamps influenced Chaucer or Chaucer influenced Deschamps has not received adequate study.

The theme of the Golden Age has been a commonplace since Hesiod (for a recent study, see Bodo Gatz, Weltalter: Goldene Zeit und sinnerverwandte Vorstellungen, 1967). Chaucer bases this poem on metrum 5 of book 2 of Boethius, with additions from Ovid and the *Roman de la rose* (as noted below).

Schmidt (EIC 26, 1976, 99–115) points out that this is the only poem in which Chaucer handles a myth that is not a story but an image, and he analyzes the unusual language, images, and rhythm of the poem.

Norton-Smith (MAE 32:117–24) approaches the work as a completely topical treatment of society under Richard II in 1398–99, but for the need to re-examine the whole notion of historical references in works such as this, see Cross, Saga-Book 16, 1965, 283–314. Brusendorff (Ch Trad., 293–94) regarded The Former Age as an unfinished rough draft; Pace (MS 23, 1961, 361–67) reaches the same conclusion from a study of the MSS.

In one of the MSS the poem is called "Aetas Prima," in the other "Chaucer upon the fyfte metur of the second book"; the present title was taken from the second line.

1–8 Closely follows Bo 2.m5.1–6. In Cambridge Univ. Library MS Ii.3.21, this poem is written in Boece, immediately following Bo 2.m5.

2 former: Norton-Smith (MAE 32:119) finds this usage, with the meaning "first," unusual. It does not appear in this sense elsewhere in Chaucer's works.

9–10 Cf. Ovid, Met. 1.109–10; RR 8381–84.

11 Cf. RR 8373.

15–18 Cf. Bo 2.m5.6–15.

16 clarre: See KnT I.1471 n.; galantyne: see Ros 17n.

21–25 Cf. Bo 2.m5.18–24; for 23–24 cf. Ovid, Met. 1.77–100.

27–40 Cf. Bo 2.m5.32–40; for 27–29 cf. Ovid, Met. 1.137–40.

33–37 The quotation from **Diogenes** is from Jerome, Adversus Jovinianum 2.11 (PL 23:300), possibly as quoted by John of Salisbury, Policraticus 8.6.

41–48 A very general expansion of Bo 2.m5.15–18, with suggestions from RR 8393–8402.

48–63 Expanded in part from Ovid; cf. Met. 1.128–31 (lack of faith), 113–15 (Jupiter), 151–53 (giants). For the characterization of Jupiter, see RR 20095–114 and Wittlieb, Ch Newsletter 2, 1980, 12–13.

55 A line is obviously missing; "Skeat skillfully composed a concluding line to this stanza: 'Fulfilled erthe of olde curtesye' " (Robinson). Koch and Brusendorff (Ch Trad., 293 n. 4) made other suggestions.

58 Nembrot (Nimrod) is not specifically connected with the Tower of Babel in chapter 11 of Genesis, but medieval tradition held that he was the builder; cf. Gower, Conf. Aman., Pro 1018–20. Schmidt (MAE 47,

1978, 304–7) notes that he was considered the first tyrant.

61–63   Cf. RR 9651–68; Preston (N&Q 195, 1950, 95) notes resemblances to Ovid, Met. 1.144–48, 224–29.

FORTUNE

In several MSS this poem—which received its present title in the Chaucer Society edition—is called "Balades de vilage (an error for "visage") sanz peinture," which could mean "ballads that paint portraits without using paint." Wimsatt (in Ch Probs, 124) suggests that the title means that Fortune is here presented "without her usual application of face paint." Fisher in his edition suggests it is rather an allusion to Bo 2.pr1.57–61, which refers to the *visage* of Fortune shown openly to the narrator. Norton-Smith (Reading Med. Sts. 2, 1976, 70) argues that the MS title originally read "deux visages" and notes Machaut's frequent use of "balades a deux visages," dialogues between two characters.

The pervasive influence of Boethius and echoes of the *Roman de la rose* are noted below. Wimsatt (in Ch Probs, 119, 124–27) argues for the influence of Machaut's "Il m'est avis" and, with Patch (MLR 22, 1927, 381), against Brusendorff's thesis (Ch Trad., 242–44) that two ballades by Deschamps were the source.

The poem is a strict triple ballade, organized as a dialogue between the complainant (*Pleintif*) and Fortune, with a concluding *envoy* in rime royal.

The envoi has been used to date the poem after 1390 by taking *princes* in line 76 to refer to the dukes of Lancaster, York, and Gloucester, and line 76 to refer to the ordinance of 1390, which specified that no royal gift or grant should be authorized without the consent of at least two of the three dukes. The *beste frend* of line 78, as well as of lines 32, 40, and 48, would thus mean King Richard.

There are, however, problems with this reading, since line 76 appears in only one of the ten MSS, and *beste frend* may be an echo of the *Roman de la rose* (see 32 below). It may be, as Patch argued (Goddess Fortuna, 74) that the poem belongs to the "friend in need" tradition: the consolation for bad fortune is that we discover who our friends are. If the poem does indeed refer to the three princes' power over grants, then it dates from the early 1390s; if not, given the use of Boethius, with possible echoes of Chaucer's own translation, some time around the later 1380s seems most likely.

1–4   For the common idea of the variability of Fortune, see Bo 2.m1 and RR 4901–4 (Rom 5479–82).
7   The same line is quoted as *a newe Frenshe song* in ParsT X.248 (Robinson).
9–16   Skeat compares this stanza to RR 4949–52, 5045–46, 4975–78. Cf. Bo 2.pr8.36–41, pr4.134–38.
10   mirour: An unusual attribute for Fortune, suggested by Bo 2.pr8.36–41; cf. Rom 5551–53 and n.
13–14   For the general idea, cf. Bo 2.pr4.134–38.
17–20   Socrates is a familiar example of indifference to Fortune and of patience in adversity; cf. BD 718, WBPro III.727n.
22   Cf. BD 630–31.
25   Fortune's response, the second ballade, was perhaps suggested by Bo 2.pr2.1–2, in which Philosophy replies

to Boethius's complaints *usynge the woordes of Fortune.* With 25–26, cf. Bo 2.pr4.109–10. Line 25 is very similar to Rom 5672.

32   beste frend: Cf. RR 8019–22, "Fortune m'ot ca mis, Je perdi trestous mes amis, fors ung" (Fortune has so treated me that I have lost all my friends, save one).
34   Cf. Rom 5486, *Freend of effect and freend of cheere;* for the idea see Bo 2.pr8.36–41.
35–36   Cf. Bartholomaeus Anglicus 10.61, tr. Trevisa 2:1211: the **galle** of the hyena "is ful medicinal and helpeth most ayens dymnesse of the yhen" (quoting Pliny, Nat. Hist. 28.8).
38   ancre: Cf. Bo 2.pr4.54.
43–44   Cf. Bo 2.pr1.95–100. Ross (Ch's Bawdy, 174) suggests a pun on the meanings of **quene**, "queen," and "harlot."
45–46   Cf. Bo 2.pr2.51–57.
55   Possibly proverbial; cf. Whiting A154, G167.
56   Cf. RR 19179–80: "Cest ruile est si generaus / Qu'el ne puet defaillir vers aus."
57–63   Echoes phrases from Bo 2.pr2.4–51; Cf. Tr 1.841–54.
65–67   Bo 4.pr6.51–56; cf. KnT I.1663–72 and n.
71   laste day: Bo 2.pr3.87–88, *The laste day of a mannes lif is a maner deth to Fortune.*
73–79   See introductory note.

TRUTH

No specific date, occasion, or source can be assigned to this moral ballade, which, if the number of surviving MSS (22 plus two early editions) is any indication, was Chaucer's most popular lyric. Shirley (in MS Cambridge, Trinity R.3.20) says it is a "Balade that Chaucier made on his deeth bedde," a title that is repeated in MS Hatton 73 and the burnt MS Otho A.xviii (see Brusendorff, Ch. Trad., 250 n. 4). The title seems to have been earlier than Shirley's copy (Pace, Spec 26, 1951, 313), but the implied date of composition has not been widely accepted. An earlier date, 1386–89, has often been based on the envoy addressed to *Vache*, whom Rickert (MP 11, 1913, 209–25) identified as Sir Philip (de) la Vache, whose career in the king's household extended over the reigns of Edward III, Richard II, and Henry IV. There was also a John le Vache mentioned in Joan of Kent's will (9 December 1385) with Lewis Clifford and John Clanvowe (John Nichols, ed., Collection of Wills of Kings and Queens of England, 1780, 80). However, the envoy in which Vache is addressed appears in only one of the manuscripts, and it may have been added at a later time (Pace-David 1:55).

In some of the MSS the poem is labeled "Balade de Bon Conseyl," which classes it with similar ballades on this fashionable theme. Brusendorff prints both a Middle English and a French example (Ch. Trad., 251–52), the latter of which is found in the same MS as Truth and resembles it in some details. "A Ballad of Good Counsel" is attributed to James I (in King's Quair, ed., Alexander Lawson, 1910, 102–3); its first five lines are generally reminiscent of Gentilesse (Skeat 1:554).

The influence of Boethius in Truth is to be found mainly in the general ideas (Jefferson, Ch and the Consolation, 104–9, 136), especially Bo 2.pr4 and m4; 3.pr11 and m11; and 4.pr6 and m6. The refrain is biblical (see

7 below), and Kean (Ch and Poetry 1:38–42) argues that the tone owes more to Seneca than to Boethius. Scattergood defines a tradition of curial satire and places Truth in it (Hermathena, 133, 1982, 29–45). Brusendorff (Ch. Trad., 251) believes that the chief inspiration for the poem was a passage from Gower (see 2 below).

The technical proficiency and poetic impact of Truth are very impressive. Chaucer makes excellent use of the tripartite ballade form (Green, UMSE 4, 1963, 80), of alliteration (Baum, Ch's Verse, 60), and of rhyme (Owen, SP 63, 1966, 534–35). The poem has been widely praised for its style (Basil Cottle, The Triumph of English, 1969, 39–40) and for "a metrical control in the imperative mood hardly to be met with before the close of the sixteenth century" (Kean, Ch and Poetry 1:38).

1 **prees:** See Flügel, Anglia 23, 1901, 209–10.
2 **Suffyce:** The notion is commonplace (see Flügel, Anglia 23:195–224, and the French ballade printed by Brusendorff, Ch. Trad., 252), but the use of *suffyce* is unusual and Robinson notes that it may be due to the Latin quoted in the margin of Gower's Conf. Aman. 5.7735–42 and attributed to Seneca (actually from Caecilius Balbus, De nugis philosophorum 11.3): "Si res tue tibi non sufficiant, fac ut rebus tuis sufficias." Gower translates "Bot if thy good suffice / Unto the liking of thy wille / Withdrawe thi lust and hold the still / And be to thy good sufficiant / For that thing appourtenant / To trouthe and causeth to be fre."
3–4 Possibly proverbial (Whiting H399); cf. Bo 2.pr5.15–16.
4 **Prees hath envye:** Proverbial; Whiting P369.
　　blent: Cf. "Prosperitas gentes cecat plus insipientes" (Walther 22707).
5 Romans 12.3: "Non plus sapere quam oportet sapere." Helen Kao, an editor of the MED, notes (by letter) the similarity of Chaucer's line to the Wycliffite translation: "That ye sauere no' more than it behoveth to sauere," Holy Bible . . . Made from the Latin Vulgate by John Wycliffe and his Followers, ed. Josiah Firshall and Frederic Madden, 1850, 4:328; similarly, A Fourteenth-Century Engl. Bible Version, ed. Anna C. Paues, 1904, 54.
7 John 8.32; cf. Conf. Aman. 5.7742, quoted in 2 above. The idea is proverbial (see Flügel, Anglia 23:215).
8–9 **Tempest thee noght:** Bo 2.pr4.66–69.
9 **hir . . . bal:** Cf. Bo 2.pr2.51–57.
11 Acts 9.5; cf. Whiting P377.
12 Proverbial; cf. Whiting W20, "Spurn not against the wall," and P319, "An earthen pot should not fight with a caldron."
15 Cf. Bo 2.pr1.91–94.
17–18 The idea of life as a pilgrimage is commonplace; cf. KnT I.2847–49n.; the comparison of man's lower nature with a **beste** is likewise common, as in KnT I.1309, Tr 3.620, For 68, and several times in Boethius (e.g., Bo 4.pr3.101–26 and m3).
19 **Know thy contree:** That is, heaven is your true home; cf. Bo 1.pr5.9–20, RR 5035.
　　look up: Beasts look downward, man upward; cf. Bo 5.m5.15–16. Skeat quotes Pol. and Love Poems, ed. Furnivall, 185, "But man, as thou witless were, / Thou lookest ever downward as a beast."
20 **the heye wey:** Cf. Bo 1.m7.13–15, 4.pr1.64 (Robinson).

lat thy gost thee lede: Cf. Romans 8.4, Gal 6.16. Pace and David compare Bo 1.m7.13–19.
22–28 The envoy has been held by some to be spurious, since it occurs in but one MS and, though it has the same rhymes as the ballade, is much different in tone. As noted above, it could be a later addition.
22 **Vache:** Fr. "cow" seems to follow from *beste* (line 18), but Rickert's argument that it is a proper name, referring to Sir Philip (de) la Vache (see introductory note) is now generally accepted. Vache was in disfavor in 1386–89, and the poem has been thus dated, before 1390 when Vache regained his emoluments. But the general exhortation to forsake worldly vanity and to turn to God would fit almost any time in Vache's (or anyone's) life.

GENTILESSE

Shirley's testimony to Chaucer's authorship of this moral ballade is supplemented by Henry Scogan (see Envoy to Scogan), who quotes all of Gentilesse in his own moral ballade (printed by Skeat 2:237–44). Chaucer's lines are also echoed in the moral ballade attributed to James I (in ed. Alexander Lawson, The King's Quair, 1910, 120–30; see Skeat 1:554).

The general idea is that expounded in WBT III.1109–64 and ClT IV.155–61 (see notes) and is based ultimately on Bo 3.pr6 and m6, but Chaucer was also influenced by RR 6579–92, 18607–896, and by Dante (Lowes, MP 13, 1915, 19–27). The ideas were commonplace (cf. Gower, Mirour, 17329–76). There are no indications of date, though Green (USME 4, 1963, 81–82) finds connections with Truth. Like that poem, in the MSS this poem is titled "Moral balade [or simply "balade"] of Chaucer."

1 **firste stok:** Interpreted as God by Scogan in introducing this ballade into his poem (lines 97–104). Brusendorff (Ch Trad., 257) quotes Lydgate's Thoroughfare of Woe, "Lord! what might thou gentilesse avail; / the first stokke of labour toke his price," where "first stokke" is Adam. Adam or Christ may be implied in line 8.
5 Cf. Bo 2.pr6.20–27, 3.pr4.37–38.
7 **mytre, croune, or diademe:** Brusendorff (Ch Trad., 256) quotes Boccaccio, Filostrato 7.94: "Non son re tutti quelli a cui vedete / Corona o scettre o vesta imperiale . . . re e colui il qual per virtu vale, / Non per potenza."
10–11 Cf. SNPro VIII.2–5.
15 **old richesse:** Cf. WBT III.1119; Dante, Convivio, "antica richezza" (4.3, etc.); RR 20313, "riches anciennes."
19–20 Cf. WBT III.1162–67.

LAK OF STEDFASTNESSE

In Shirley's MS R.3.20 the poem is called "Balade Royal made by our laureal poete then in hees laste yeeres" and the envoy is headed "Lenvoye to kyng Richard." The present title was first used in the Chaucer Society edition. MS Harley 7333, which has the notation that Chaucer wrote Truth on his death bed, has a notation that Chaucer sent the poem to Richard "thane being in his Castell of Windsore." On this basis, the poem has been dated

1397–99 (Brusendorff, Ch Trad., 274, 492), and has been read as a specific political comment (Schlauch, Spec 20, 1945, 133–56). Yet the ideas and phrases are commonplace (Cross, Saga Book 16, 1965, 283–84). ProLGW F 373–408, G 353–94, on the duties of a king, is generally similar to the admonition in the envoy, and Fisher (John Gower, 247–50) notes many parallels to the Prologue of Gower's *Confessio amantis,* which he attributes to friendship and conversation in 1385–86. Robinson believed that the association of Lak of Stedfastnesse with the other "Boethian" lyrics favored such an early date. The question of date is complicated by the possibility of two authentic texts (Norton-Smith, Reading Med. Std. 8, 1982, 3–10).

However, Boethius's description of the "bond of love" that established faith and order in the universe (cf. Jefferson, Ch and the Consolation, 106–7, 138) serves as a mere starting point. Other influences have been found in several ballades of Deschamps (Oeuvres 1:113, 209; 2:31, 63, 234; cf. Brusendorff, Ch Trad., 487), in a ballade by Grandson (Braddy, Ch and the Fr. Poet Graunson, 1947, 67–70, 88–89), and in Machaut's "Il m'est avis" (Wimsatt, in Ch Probs, 128). The contrasting picture of The Former Age seems also to have been in Chaucer's mind (Jefferson, Ch and the Consolation, 138). Green (UMSE 43, 1963, 79–82) notes that *trouthe* is mentioned three times in Lak of Stedfastnesse and argues for a relation to Truth. The obvious similarities may have been recognized by some of the scribes. In three MSS, Lak of Stedfastnesse immediately follows Truth and in one it immediately precedes that poem.

The conventionality of the ballade's ideas should in no way detract from one's admiration of Chaucer's expression of them and his technical virtuosity. Artistically it is a fine ballade, in the classic form with strong refrain and with the envoy having the same rhyme scheme as the three stanzas. Indeed, in this ballade, as in Fortune, the envoy is fully integrated and was probably composed at the same time as the poem.

4–5   word and deed: Proverbial (Whiting W642); cf. Bo 3.pr12.206–7; GP I.741–42 and 725–42n.
5   up-so-doun: Cf. Bo 2.pr5.127–32; for the tradition of "the world turned upside down" see Curtius (European Lit., 94–98).
7   Cf. Tr 3.1266, 1764, derived from Bo 2.m8.
21   For a spurious fourth stanza, see Skeat 1:556.
22   prince: The conventional form of address in the envoy, deriving from the *puys,* poetic clubs in which the members would gather to read their poems, which addressed the presiding officer directly as the *prince* (see Poirion, Le poète, 38–40, and, for an account of a late thirteenth-century London puys, see D. W. Robertson, Lit. of Med. Engl., 1970, 295–97). Cross (Saga Book 16:299–300) argues the address is merely conventional here; Pace and David hold that this and most of Chaucer's envoys were addressed to actual persons. The phrases *thy swerd of castigacioun* (26) and *thy folk* (22) make it most likely that an actual prince is concerned, though the ideas are so general that "Lydgate incorporated this envoy in his 'Prayer for England' (Hist. Poems, ed. Robbins, 389), where it satisfactorily dovetails into the whole poem" (Robbins, Comp. to Ch, 393).

LENVOY DE CHAUCER A SCOGAN

The authenticity of this work (which is attributed to Chaucer in all three MSS) has never been questioned. Here, and in the Envoy to Bukton, "envoy" means "letter," and both are extraordinary examples of epistolary verse. For a discussion of its genre and Chaucer's mastery of it, see Norton-Smith (in Essays on Style and Language, ed. Robert Fowler, 1966, 157–65, and Geoffrey Ch, 213–25). Norton-Smith argues for the pervasive influence of Horace's *Epistles,* and Wimsatt (MAE 47, 1978, 82) suggests Machaut's "Puis qu'amours faut" as a source, but neither offers any exact parallels to this, one of Chaucer's most inventive lyrics.

Scogan, who is addressed by name throughout and in the envoy (in the more familiar sense) is most likely Henry Scogan (1361?–1407), a squire in the king's household and lord of the manor of Haviles after the death in 1391 of his brother, John Scogan. He became a tutor to the sons of Henry IV, to whom he addressed "A moral Balade" (printed by Skeat 7:237–44); in his "Balade" Scogan quotes the entire text of Gentilesse, paraphrases part of it, and refers to Chaucer as his "maister." The copyist Shirley notes that Scogan's poem was read at a "souper" in the Vintry in London organized by a group of merchants and attended by the princes whom he addresses; Chaucer's poem may have been first read in similarly convivial circumstances.

The reference to *a diluge of pestilence* (14) caused by Scogan's recent renunciation of Love (at Michaelmas, 19) led Skeat to date the poem in late 1393, because of the floods around Michaelmas in that year. There were, however, other seasons of heavy rain (Brusendorff, Ch Trad., 219, suggests July and August 1391, and Fisher notes rains and floods in March 1390), and determining a precise date is impossible. To assume that the poem must be very late, on the grounds that *hoor* (31) is intended literally, is to ignore the bantering tone of the poem. The same might be said of the ingenious attempts to explain exactly what Chaucer wanted from Scogan, though French's suggestion (PMLA 48, 1933, 289–92) that Chaucer is refusing Scogan's request to compose a conciliatory letter to his lady is an attractive, though unprovable, possibility.

The poem is much admired, not least for the mastery with which the rime royal stanza is used. Among useful critical discussions are David (ChR 3, 1969, 265–74), Kean (Ch and Poetry 1:33–37), Lenaghan (ChR 10, 1975, 46–61), and Burrow (SAC 3, 1981, 61–75).

1–2   statutz hye . . . eternally: Skeat compares Purg. 1.76, "Non son gli editti eterni per noi gasti" (the eternal edicts are not broken by us).
3   bryghte goddis sevene: The seven planets, thought to be an important influence on the weather (cf. Tr 3.624–28 and Richard of Wallingford, in Works). Here, however, the rain is caused by the planets' tears rather than their heavenly positions.
9   the fyfte sercle: The sphere of Venus, counting from the outside inward (see Mars 29n.).
11   Venus was especially associated with rain (see Mars 89n.). Venus also weeps in KnT I.2664–66 and Mars 143.
14   For the construction, see KnT I.1912 and n.
15   goddis: Probably the seven in line 3 are meant.

Skeat's reading, "goddes" (i.e., Venus), is attractive but "the form *goddes* for *goddesse* in rime is hardly Chaucerian" (Robinson).

28   On the power of Cupid's arrows to harm or cure, see PF 215–17 and notes 215–16, 217.

31   **hoor and rounde of shap:** Chaucer seems to imply that he is stout in HF 574, ProThop VII.700, and MercB 27. Henry Scogan was probably only about 30 years old, and, taking *hoor* to imply a greater age, Brusendorff (Ch Trad., 291) identified the Scogan of this poem as Henry's elder brother John and dated it before his death (in 1391). However, Kittredge (Harvard Sts. and Notes 1, 1892, 116–17) and David (ChR 3:270) argue that *hoor* need not apply to Scogan.

32   Pace and David take **folk** as the object of **spede** and interpret, with Donaldson, "That are so able to help folk in love." But the humorous "That are such suitable folk to succeed in love" is equally possible.

35   **Grisel:** A gray-haired old man (MED) or, as in OF, a gray horse. For rhyme Caxton and Thynne have "renne," which may imply that "horse" is the better interpretation.

38–39   There has been much speculation on these lines, which are often taken as straightforward autobiography. Chaucer is said to be in his old age (French, PMLA 43:292; Kean, Ch and Poetry 1:33), to have ceased writing (Brusendorff, Ch Trad., 292), and to be not only old but neglected (Norton-Smith, in Essays on Style, 164) or, at the very least, to be middle-aged and, like many poets, fearful "that his poetic gift was deserting him" (Fisher). David notes (ChR 3:273) "It would be an error to take literally Chaucer's statement that he has given up poetry. This is simply another word to be broken, is in fact being broken in the writing of the *Envoy*."

39   **rusteth:** Robinson agrees with Kittredge (MP 7, 1910, 483) that the preface to Alanus de Insulis's Anticlaudianus, and Ovid's Tristia 5:12, 21, provided the metaphor. Norton-Smith (Geoffrey Ch, 217–18) argues that the source is Horace's Satires 2:39–44. Pace and David cite Merchie, Musée Belge 27, 1923, 83–89, who notes a parallel in Apuleius's Florida (17.31–32), and they conclude that the figure is a commonplace.

40   Cf. PF 603.

41   **al shal passe:** Proverbial; cf. Tr 5.1085 and Whiting T99.

43   **stremes hed:** In all three MSS this line is glossed "Windesor" (i.e., Windsor Castle) and line 45 is glossed "Grenewich," which is where Chaucer was probably living (Ch Life Records, 512–13). The *strem* is thus the Thames, though it may also have metaphorical meanings (see Preston, Ch, 123, and David, ChR 3:272).

47   **Tullius:** Possibly Tullius Hostillius, legendary king of Rome noted for his friendliness toward the poor; he is mentioned in WBT III.1116–66, lines quoted in Scogan's "Moral Balade," 166–67; see Phipps, MLN 58, 1943, 108–9. More likely this refers to Cicero, De amicitia, as cited in RR 4747–62 (Rom 5285–5304); see Goffin, MLR 20, 1925, 318–21.

LENVOY DE CHAUCER A BUKTON

This poem survives in but one MS, Fairfax 16, where it is given the title it bears, and one early print, Julian Notary's edition of Mars and Venus (1499–1501), but

its authenticity has not been seriously questioned. In the early collected editions, the title and the name Bukton in the first line were omitted, and it followed *The Book of the Duchess;* Urry thought it was an envoy addressed to John of Gaunt, and until the nineteenth century it was usually printed as an appendage to BD (see Hammond, Ch: Bibl. Man., 366–67).

The identity of Bukton is still doubtful, as there are two possibilities: Sir Peter Bukton, of Holdernesse in Yorkshire, first suggested by Tyrwhitt (see Kuhl, PMLA 38, 1923, 115–32). "His long and close association with the Lancasters brings him into association with Chaucer" (Robinson), and it is worth noting that The Summoner's Tale is set in Holdernesse (III.1709–10). Sir Robert Bukton, the other possibility (Tatlock, Dev. and Chron., 210–11; James R. Hulbert, Ch's Official Life, 1912, 54–55), was connected with the royal court as a squire of Queen Anne and later of the king. Most scholars are inclined to Peter, who was steward to the Earl of Derby, the future Henry IV, and, after Henry's coronation, guardian and later steward to his son, Thomas of Lancaster.

The poem is usually dated in 1396 because of the reference in line 23 to being taken prisoner at Frisia (though *Frise* is a common rhyme word; see 23 below); an expedition against Frisia was undertaken between 24 August and the end of September in 1396, and Froissart (Chronicles 4:98–99) remarks on the brutality of the Frisians, who killed their prisoners rather than ransoming them in the usual way. Yet Lowes (MLN 27, 1912, 45–48) notes that the brutality of the Frisians was a commonplace, and he argues that the reference to Frisia would have been appropriate at any time in the decade preceding 1396; he also argues that it would not have been appropriate after the defeat of the Frisians in that year, but this is doubtful. The reference to *The Wyf of Bathe* is of little further help, since the date of that prologue is not certain, nor is it clear whether Bukton was to read the work in its present, probably revised, form or in some earlier version. Finally, the reference to Bukton's proposed marriage is of no help; Robert Bukton was married sometime before 1397 (Tatlock, Dev. and Chron., 210–11) but when is not known; nothing is known of Peter Bukton's marriage.

The allegations against marriage are familiar and traditional. Kittredge (MLN 24, 1909, 14–15) and Brusendorff (Ch Trad., 487) note parallels in the ballades of Deschamps but none is especially striking.

The Envoy to Bukton, like that to Scogan, is a verse letter ending with an envoy to the addressee. It is a "near" ballade, having three stanzas of rime royal, though with a differing set of rhymes for each stanza and without a refrain.

1   **maister:** A respectful form of address (cf. GP I.837) rather than, as Rickert believed (Manly Anniv. Sts., 31), an indication that Bukton was a lawyer.

2   John 18.38. See SqT V.555n.

6   Cf. WBPro III.3.

8   **eft:** Chaucer's wife Philippa is believed to have died in 1387.

9   For the image of the bound Satan, common in literature and art, see MLT II.361n., and for gnawing on the chain (of love), see Tr. 1.509. For marriage as a chain or set of fetters, proverbial in antifeminist satire, see

Walther 10750, and Matheolus, Lamentations, 2287. Cf. the distich "Cur proprio caput ense secas, cur sponte cathenas / Demonis incurris, cur sua iussa facis" (Walther 4707), and see also John of Salisbury, Policraticus 8.11, cited by Tatlock, MLN 29, 1914, 98.

17   On love as a prison, see MercB 28 and n.

18   1 Cor. 7.9; also cited by the Wife of Bath (III.52). Proverbial (Whiting W162).

19–20   Cf. WBPro III.154–60. Brusendorff (Ch Trad., 487) compares Deschamps, Ballade 823 (Oeuvres 5: 343): "Car exil met son corps et sa vie / Et devient serfs, laches et espandu / Et d'une error fait seconde folie / Quant deux foiz est par femme confondue."

23   Frise is a common rhyme word in French courtly poetry; see Ernst Langlois, ed., Recueil d'art de seconde rhétorique, 1902, 13:141. Cf. Rom 1093.

25–28   The proverbs in 27–28 do not occur elsewhere in Middle English (cf. Whiting W134), though the sentiments survive in the modern saying "Leave well enough alone." Skeat notes that in Fairfax 16 the following proverb appears at the end of the poem: "Bettre is to suffre, and Fortune abide / Than [MS And] hastely to clymbe, and sodeynly slyde."

29   There is a similar reference in MerT IV.1685.

THE COMPLAINT OF CHAUCER TO HIS PURSE

This mock love complaint is attributed to Chaucer in the MSS (though labeled "a balade to kyng Richard" in Shirley's copy), and its authenticity has never been questioned.

The envoy can be dated, though not so precisely as was believed when it was assumed that the poem must have been written between 30 September 1399, when Henry was accepted as king, and 3 October (a mistake for 13 October), when the new king apparently granted Chaucer a pension of forty marks. Chaucer's annuity from Richard was terminated with his deposition and the regular installment of ten pounds, due on 29 September, was not paid. After Henry's acceptance as king on 30 September, in a document dated 13 October, his coronation day, he reconfirmed Richard's grant and granted Chaucer an additional forty marks a year (Ch Life Records, 525). Ferris (MP 65, 1967, 45–52) has shown that this document was antedated; it was actually issued around 16 February 1400. Chaucer may have been pressed for cash (Finnell, ChR 8, 1973, 147–58), though this is not certain (Scott, ELN 2, 1964, 81–87). On 18 October he appeared in the Exchequer to swear to the existence of the lost originals of Richard's grants, and these were confirmed (Ch Life Records, 525–27). Yet no payment was forthcoming. On 9 November, King Henry granted Chaucer ten pounds as a payment of the arrears of the annuity granted by Richard, specifying this was a gift ("de noustre doun," Ch Life Records, 530). This money, however, was not paid until 21 February 1400. Payment on the grant of 13 October, due 31 March, was not mandated until 11 May 1400, and no mandate for the further arrears of his grant from Richard was issued until 14 May. Chaucer finally received partial payment, five pounds, on 5 June 1400, the last he was to receive before his death later that year (Ch Life Records, 529–30). The plea for money could thus have been made at almost any time from 30 September 1399 until Chaucer's death. However, that the poem has a direct connection with these payments is only inference. There is no record showing that Chaucer sent the poem to Henry nor that the king responded with any payments.

The envoy in which the plea is made appears in only five of the eleven manuscripts, and it may be a later addition (see 17 below). Recent critics have defended the integrity of the whole work (e.g., Finnell, ChR 8: 154–55), though the tone and diction of the envoy, if not meant as mock serious, differ markedly from the preceding lines, and it is cast in an unusual stanzaic form (one also used by Clanvowe in his Boke of Cupide). If the envoy is an original part of the poem, Chaucer's Complaint to His Purse belongs to the category of "begging poems," such as that addressed by Deschamps to King Charles IV in 1381 (No. 247, Oeuvres 2:81) and that written by Machaut to John II (Oeuvres, ed. Tarbé, 78). Other such poems by Deschamps have been noted (Cook, Trans. Conn. Acad. 23, 1919, 33–38; Smith, MLN 66, 1951, 31–32). There are no striking similarities between any of these proposed models and Chaucer's poem, though Deschamps's Balade No. 247 offers an analogy to what may have been the circumstances—in Stanza 3 he complains that the king makes promises but all he gets is "you will be paid." Chaucer's poem is unique in its humorous application of the language of a lover's appeal to his mistress to this well-worn theme.

Without the envoy, Purse is not an overt "begging poem" and belongs rather to the popular tradition of poems about money. For English examples, see Lydgate's Letter to Gloucester, in Poems, ed. Norton-Smith, 1966, no. 1; Sec. Lyrics, ed., Robbins, nos. 57, 58, 59, 60; Hist. Poems, ed. Robbins, no. 51; and Sisam, Oxford Bk. of Med. Eng. Verse, rpt. with corr. 1973, no. 184, which cheerfully begins "Sing we all and say we thus: / Gramercy, myn owen purs!" Much more serious is Hoccleve's "Compleynt to Lady Money" (Minor Poems, ed. Furnivall, rev. Jerome Mitchell and A. I. Doyle, EETS e.s. 61 and 73). Chaucer probably knew two witty French poems, Froissart's "Dit dou florin" (Poésies 2: 220–34), where he bemoans the loss of a heavy purse, and Deschamps's uncharacteristically light "Se tout le ciel estoit de feuilles d'or" (text and tr. in Brian Woledge, Penguin Bk. of Fr. Verse, 1961, 1:236–38). On the relation between the poem and the envoy, see Lenaghan, ChR 18, 1982, 158–59.

1–2   Cook (Trans. Conn. Acad. 23, 1919, 35) notes a parallel to a well-known poem attributed to the Chatelaine de Coucy: "A vos, amant, plus k'a nule autre / Est bien raisons ke ma dolor complaigne" (To you, my love, more than to any other, my sadness rightly complains); in Chansons attr. au Chastelein de Couci, ed. Alain Lerond, 1964; tr. in Lyrics of the Troubadours and Trouvères, ed. Goldin, 1973, 350–53). The poem has no other similarities to Chaucer's Purse.

3–4   lyght . . . hevy: Both words had a wide range of meaning: lyght could mean "cheerful, fickle, wanton, giddy, or graceful" as well as "light" (in weight), and hevy could mean "sad, serious, clumsy, or pregnant" as well as "heavy."

13   **Quene of comfort:** An epithet of the Virgin in

ABC 77 (so Robbins, in Comp. to Ch, 394); Ludlum (N&Q 221, 1976, 391–92) discusses the religious imagery in the poem.

17   toune: Skeat takes this to refer to Chaucer's desire to get out of London to some cheaper place; Finnell suggests it refers to Westminster, where, he argues, Chaucer had taken sanctuary from his debtors (ChR 8:-147–58); Donaldson reads "tonne" and glosses "tun? predicament," as in OED s.v. *tone* 2(c). Pace (Papers of the Bibl. Soc., Univ. of Virginia 1, 1948, 119) notes the variant "this night" in the Morgan MS and takes it as evidence (as Skeat took the whole line) of the existence of an earlier version addressed to Richard II.

19   shave as nye as any frere: Robinson quotes Bell: "As bare of money as the tonsure of a friar is of hair." This is the OED's first example of *shave* in this sense (s.v. *shave* sb. 7), but it was common in French.

22–23   conquerour ... by lyne and free eleccion: The three bases of Henry's claim to the throne; Legge (MLN 68, 1953, 18–21) notes an exact parallel in Gower's Cronica tripertita: "Unde coronatur trino de jure probatur, / Regnum conquestat . . . / Regno succedit heres . . . / In super eligitur a plebe" (Works 4:338).

22   Brutes Albyon: The Albion (Britain) of Brutus, the descendent of Aeneas who first conquered Britain (Geoffrey of Monmouth, Hist. Reg. Brit. 1.16, ed. Griscom, 1929, 249).

PROVERBS

These stanzas are assigned to Chaucer in Fairfax 16 and Harley 7578, but not by Shirley in his copy (Add. 16165). Bradshaw (cited by Furnivall in Temp. Pref., 108) and Koch (Chronology, 78) rejected them from the canon mainly because of the troublesome rhyming of

compas (noun) with *embrace* (verb), which requires that the infinitival -*e* not be sounded. Hammond (Ch: Bibl. Man., 449) was persuaded by the rhyme and Shirley's authority to reject them, and Robinson found the rhyme suspicious enough to consign them to the "doubtful" category. Skeat (1:88, 564) and Brusendorff (Ch Trad., 285) defended the rhyme, noting the rhymes *gras : pas : solas* and *Thopas : Goddes gras* in Thop VII.779–82, 830–31, where in the latter case the organic -*e* in *grace (gras)* is omitted. But note that the substantive *grace (gras)* is not a good parallel to the infinitive *embrace,* and the rhymes in Sir Thopas may have been used for comic effect; see HF 1169–70 and the textual note to HF 1170 for a similar case. Pace (SB 18, 1965, 41–48) argued that the verses are genuine and suggested (an analogy with isolated fragments of *Troilus* in MSS) that they may be fragments of a lost longer work. John Fisher includes the proverbs among the authentic works in his edition.

Because of the possible echo of Melibee (6–7), Furnivall (Athenaeum, 1871, 2:495) dated the verses 1386–87, but this is mere conjecture. Brusendorff (Ch Trad., 285) notes the similarity of the form of the second quatrain (rhyming *a b b a*) to "Un proverbe bien notable" by Deschamps (Oeuvres 7:216); this may lend some justification to the editorial practice, lacking in the MSS, of dividing the verses into two stanzas.

3–4   The idea is commonplace; cf. Whiting C365; Kittredge, MP 7, 1910, 479; and Brusendorff, Ch Trad., 286.

7   Cf. Mel VII.1214–15; Skeat notes its occurrence in its French from "Qui trop embrasse, mal étreint" at the head of a ballade by Deschamps (Oeuvres, ed. Tarbé 1:132; cf. Oeuvres 5:383, with a similar proverb). This idea is commonplace (Whiting A91), and in this form is proverbial after Chaucer's time (Whiting M774).

Poems Not Ascribed to Chaucer in the Manuscripts

Some poems, not identified as Chaucer's by the scribes have been attributed to him by modern editors. The four printed here are those accepted as genuine in Skeat's Oxford Chaucer and printed by most subsequent editors. Of these, Merciles Beaute and Against Women Unconstant are generally accepted as genuine. The Complaynt D'Amours is more doubtful, and A Balade of Complaint (which Skeat later rejected in Ch Canon, 64–147) is most likely not Chaucer's.

A considerable number of short poems are ascribed to Chaucer in the MSS or were included by the early printers among his works. The principal discussions of these spurious attributions remain those of Skeat (1: 27–48; and Ch Canon, 90–142), Hammond (Ch: Bibl. Man., 406–603), and Brusendorff (Ch Trad., esp. 433–44). In Shirley's MS B.L. Add. 16165 are two poems, "The Balade of the Plough" and "A Balade of a Reeve," one of which Shirley heads "Balade by Chaucer." Furnivall was doubtful which ballade was meant,

and printed both with the title "A Balade or two by Chaucer" (in his ed. of Jyl of Brentford's Testament, 1871, 34–36). Hammond (MLN 19, 1904, 35–38) reprinted both and argued that the "Plough" was probably Chaucer's. Brusendorff (Ch Trad., 278–84) reprinted the "Reeve" parallel with another copy in Harl. 7578, arguing that it should be accepted as authentic. Neither has been so accepted by editors. "An Holy Meditation" (printed in Lydgate's Minor Poems, ed. McCracken 1:43–48), which Carleton Brown (PMLA 50, 1935, 997–1011) argued was Chaucer's lost "Of the Wreched Engendrynge of Mankynd," has likewise been rejected by the great majority of scholars.

AGAINST WOMEN UNCONSTANT

This was first ascribed to Chaucer in Stowe's edition of 1561; there is no ascription in the MSS, where it is called simply "Balade." The present title is Skeat's adaptation of Stowe's heading. Skeat (1:26–27, 86–88, and Ch Canon, 62–63) argues persuasively for Chaucer's authorship on the grounds of its quality and association with Chaucer's genuine works in the MSS. Koch was initially doubtful (Chronology, 41) but later accepted it (ESt 27, 1900, 60). Hammond rejected it (Ch: Bibl. Man., 440–41) as did Brusendorff (Ch Trad., 441), but Robinson noted that the language, meter, and subject matter are consistent with the theory of Chaucer's authorship, as are some details of the vocabulary (see 1 below). Skeat notes especially its resemblance in mood to Lak of Stedfastnesse.

The general idea of the poem is similar to a ballade of Machaut (in Voir Dit, 309), the refrain of which ("Qu'en lieu de bleu, Dame, vous vestez vert"; in place of blue, lady, you dress in green) is almost identical with line 27; Wimsatt (MAE 47, 1978, 83–84) argues that Chaucer is dependent directly on that poem. However, Machaut often used old refrains (see Gilbert Reaney, Machaut, 1971, 8) and the recurrence of the line of the old refrain in a close variant elsewhere in Machaut (Voir Dit, 4929) suggests it may have been proverbial.

The title, which Skeat adapted from Stowe, is unfortunate, since the speaker is specifically addressing one lady. The Fairfax MS calls it simply "Balade"; the other MSS have no heading. Furnivall's title "Newfangelnesse" in his Chaucer Society edition of the Minor Poems, which was adapted by Koch, seems more appropriate.

1 **Madame:** Cf. To Rosemounde.

newefangelnesse: Chaucer is the first to use this word (cf. MED s.v. *neufangelesse*) and he seems fond of it; it appears in SqT V.610, ProLGW F 154, and Anel 141, where it rhymes with *stidfastnesse*, while here with *unstedfastnesse;* in all its uses, except here, it applies to a male.
7 Proverbial (Whiting B384). See introductory note to this poem. Blue is explicitly symbolic of constancy, *(trouth)* and green of falsity in SqT V.644–47; cf. also Tr 3.885n., Anel 330–32. See especially Anel 145–47, the lines immediately following those noted above, as similar in rhyme to this stanza.
8 "Tatlock suggested (in a letter to the editor) that the similar use of the figure in MerT IV.1582 is perhaps evidence of the genuineness of the ballade" (Robinson). However, the image is commonplace; see MerT IV.1577–87n.
12 Proverbial; Whiting W160.
15–17 **brotelnesse : sikernesse:** The same rhyme is used in the discussion of faithless women in MerT IV.1279–80.
19 **If ye lese oon, ye can wel tweyn purchace:** Skeat compares the modern proverb "She has two strings to her bow"; cf. Whiting O39, "One lost and two recovered."

COMPLAYNT D'AMOURS

This poem, first printed by Skeat (Acad 33, 1901, 307) is not attributed to Chaucer in any of the MSS, including the one by Shirley. Since the MSS in which it appears contain genuine pieces, and because of its many echoes of Chaucer's works, Skeat concluded it was genuine. From Shirley's puzzling heading—"an amerowse com-

pleynte made at wyndesore in the laste may to fore nouembre"—he inferred it was an early work, associated with Chaucer's service in the royal court beginning in 1367. Koch first expressed doubts (ESt 15, 1891, 418) but then accepted it as genuine (ESt 27, 1901, 60; Chronology, 21) and conjectured 1374 as the date of composition. Robbins has questioned its authenticity (ChR 13, 1978, 386–87), but in Comp. to Ch, 386–87, he treats it without comment as one of Chaucer's lyrics. Lounsbury rejected it because "it has almost too many of his particular phrases" and "gives the impression of a cento collected from his various writings by an ardent admirer" (Sts. in Ch 1:452–53); Oruch (Spec 56, 1981, 559) is probably right in taking it as a fifteenth-century Valentine's Day poem inspired by Chaucer.

Braddy (Ch and the Fr. Poet Graunson, 1947, 56–57) sees a relation of this poem to Grandson's Complainte amoureuse de saint Valentin, which is disputed by Bennett in his review of Braddy's book (MAE 18, 1949, 35–37). Wimsatt (MAE 47, 1978, 71–73) finds a "family relationship" with some of Machaut's poems. Skeat notes its general resemblance to Aurelius's lament (FranT V.1311–25) and to various complaints in Troilus.

1 Cf. Tr 4.416.
6 Cf. Lady 49.
7 Cf. Lady 29, FranT V.1322.
12 **spitous yle:** Identified by Skeat as Naxos, where Ariadne was deserted by Theseus (cf. Tales II.68; HF 416; LGW 2163), but the reference is not certain (Bright, MLN 17, 1902, 278–79).
17–21 Cf. Lady 88–93.
24–25 This six-line song (perhaps a fragment of a longer complaint) was discovered and printed by Stanley (NM 60, 1959, 287–88, reprinted by Robbins in Comp. to Ch, 387).
31 Cf. Lady 113.
41–42 Cf. KnT I.1077–97n.
54 **whyl . . . dure:** Cf. PF 616.
70 Cf. FranT V.1313.
72 For the formula, cf. Tr 3.1501, LGW 1806.
77 Cf. Tr 3.1183, 5.1344.
79 Cf. Tr 3.141.
85 Cf. PF 309–10.
86 Cf. PF 419.
88 **song and . . . compleynte:** The words are used interchangeably and neither implies singing; in 67, it is clear the lady is to *rede* the poem.

MERCILES BEAUTE

This poem appears along with a number of undoubtedly genuine works in a single manuscript (Pepys 2006; see for a description Hammond, MLN 19, 1904, 196–98). It was first printed by Percy in his *Reliques* (2nd ed. 1767, 2:11) as "An Original Ballad by Chaucer" (though called "Merciles Beaute" in his list of contents of the MS). Skeat accepted it as genuine; Hammond (Ch: Bibl. Man., 437) and Brusendorff (Ch Trad., 440) rejected it. Though Robinson consigned it to the "doubtful" category because of the lack of MS attribution, he believed it "thoroughly Chaucerian."

The poem is divided by editors into three roundels (on the form, see PF 675n., and Daniel Poirion, Le poète,

318–60), with the form AB^1B^2 $abAB^1$ $abbAB^1B^2$. The refrains (indicated by the capitals) are editorial additions. In the MS the refrains are indicated only by "Your yen two &c; "So hath your beaute &c"; and "Syn I fro love &c"; and there is no way to determine how many lines were to be repeated.

Merciles Beaute is so thoroughly imbued with the attitudes and language of contemporary love poetry that it seems fruitless to search for analogues. Lowes (MLR 5, 1910, 33–39) suggested that the first roundel was based on Deschamps's Chanson baladée 541 (Oeuvres 3:382), beginning: "However my body suffers or endures the sweet looks of your beautiful eyes." The third he regards as a humorous paraphrase of Deschamps's Rondeau 570 (Oeuvres 4:29), "Puis qu'Amour ay servi trestout mon temps" (since I have always devoted my time to Love). However, the striking opening line of this section is exactly matched in a humorous ballade, the response of the Duc de Berry to the *Cent balades* (ed. Raynaud, SATF, 1905, 213), beginning "Puis qu'a Amours suis si gras eschape." Raynaud dates this ballade between 31 October and 6 November 1389. Which poem borrows from the other is not clear, and it could be that some common source accounts for the lines, though if borrowing is involved, the Duc de Berry is probably the debtor. Wimsatt (MAE 47, 1979, 67–88) argues for the strong influence of Machaut, but the parallels he adduces are commonplace. There is, however, a resemblance in the first roundel to Machaut's "Vo doulz regart, douce dame, m'a mort," which Deschamps quotes (without attribution) as an example of the roundel in his *Art de dictier* (Oeuvres 7:266–92).

Since for Machaut the roundel, like the ballade, was also a musical form and since in *The Parliament of Fowls* the birds are said to sing the roundel, it is possible that Merciles Beaute was also meant to be sung. Although "singing" and "song" were used loosely (see Moore, JEGP 48, 1949, 196–208), it is at least suggestive that the lover in To My Soverain Lady (Skeat 7:821, line 20)

describes himself as "singing evermore" the first line of Merciles Beaute.

Skeat entitled the three roundels "captivity," "rejection," and "escape." For the change from adoration to rejection as part of the game of love, see Stevens, Music and Poetry, 220–221, and Poirion, Le poète, 333–40.

1 The image is familiar in love poetry of the time (cf. KnT I.1096 and 1077–97n.).

16 **Daunger:** Cf. Rom 3018 and n.

27 **fat:** On this line, see introductory note above. Cf. Scogan 31. Skeat notes that lovers should of course be lean; cf. Rom 2684–86.

28 **prison:** A commonplace in love poetry; see Bukton 17, and Wimsatt, Ch and Fr. Poets, 32–36; Poirion, Le poète, 548–78; Stevens, Music and Poetry, 194.

29 **I counte him not a bene:** Proverbial; see Whiting B92, and GP I.177 and n. Poirion, Le poète, points out that Froissart, among others, frequently used proverbs in his roundels.

A BALADE OF COMPLAINT

Skeat greatly admired this poem and accepted it as Chaucer's because of its merits, though it is not attributed to him in the sole MS (by Shirley); he later denied its authenticity and attributed it to Lydgate (Ch Chron., 63–64). No one since then has argued for its authenticity, though with the exception of Koch, editors have usually included it among the "doubtful" poems. Norton-Smith (Geoffrey Ch, 20) regards it as a polished example of the complaint form, worthy of comparison to Chaucer's genuine works, but few others have shared Skeat's admiration. Though it is called a *balade,* it lacks the refrain and strict rhyme scheme. Robbins (Comp. to Ch, 386) notes that the *-ere* rhymes in all three stanzas may indicate that it was begun as a strict ballade.

A Treatise on the Astrolabe

The *Treatise* is ascribed to Chaucer in seven MSS of the fifteenth century, Dd¹ M¹ A¹ Cp Eg A² A³ (for sigla, see Textual Notes) and in Sl², which, however, is later than the first printed edition (Thynne's) of 1532. Lydgate refers to it in the Prologue to his *Fall of Princes* 1:293–95: "And to his sone that callid was Lowis / He made a tretis . . . Vpon thastlabre." Lydgate assumes that Lewis was Chaucer's son and despite some controversy, his assumption is now generally accepted. The Latin colophon at the end of the *Astrolabe* in MS Dd¹ (in a hand later than the text) tells us that at the time Lewis was in Oxford under the instruction of the philosopher N. (error for R.) Strode, but North (RES n.s. 20, 1969, 134 n.) points out that Strode had been a neighbor of Chaucer in London from 1383 and was dead in 1387, four years before the probable date of the *Astrolabe.* The colophon thus loses some credibility. However, earlier doubts that Chaucer had a son named Lewis have been dispelled by a document (West Wales Hist. Rec. 4, 1914, 4–8) showing two Chaucers, Thomas and Lewis, both of whom could be the poet's sons (see p. xvi above and Pro 1 below).

That Chaucer began to write this work in 1391 is highly probable; in 2.1.7 and 2.3.16 he refers to noon, 12 March 1391. Moore (MP 10, 1912, 203–5) argues that Chaucer was using the normal calendar, by which the new year began on 25 March, and that hence 12 March 1391 was really in 1392. North (RES n.s. 20:432–33) points out that 1392 was leap year, and on 12 March the sun would have been in the second, not the first, degree of Aries. In 2.40, Chaucer gives as an example Jupiter at 1° of Pisces, and Jupiter was there on 4 March 1393. North points out that these are only examples, and there is no proof that Chaucer was using current positions as he wrote—and indeed the latitude given in the examples does not correspond to the planet's actual latitude on the date suggested. Nonetheless it is probable that Chaucer's work extended over some time. The differing ways in which the MSS conclude the work may suggest that towards the end Chaucer was writing sporadically, perhaps adding sections from time to time. In fact 2.44 and 45 (Supplementary Propositions) refer to 1397, but these are very unlikely to be by Chaucer.

Sigmund Eisner, in an unpublished paper, argues that the *Astrolabe* cannot be dated by the references in the text to 1391, which is merely the third year after a leap year, when, according to Nicholas of Lynn (Kal. 77, 184), the sun at noon on 12 March would be closer than in the other three years of the four-year cycle to 0° of Aries, *a litel within the degre* (2.1.15). Now indeed the markings on the *cercle* of days indicated noon, so that Lewis could set his alidade very exactly, and have seen the *litel,* but only if his instrument were made for such a year, 1387, 1391, 1395, etc. For other years it would have been from a quarter to three quarters of a degree more. If Chaucer were concerned about this point, he would have made sure that the astrolabe that he supplied for Lewis was calibrated accordingly; it is more probable than not that he procured the astrolabe and began writing about the

The explanatory notes to *A Treatise on the Astrolabe* were written by John Reidy.

same time; hence Eisner's new consideration increases rather than diminishes the likelihood for a date of 1391, the year that Chaucer specifies, rather than four years later, or four years earlier, when Lewis would have been only six.

Some passages in Part 1 seem to be drawn from Johannes de Sacrobosco, *De sphaera,* a thirteenth-century work, cited in the Explanatory Notes from Lynn Thorndike, The Sphere of Sacrobosco and Its Commentators, 1949. For Chaucer's use of this work, see Harvey (JEGP 34, 1935, 34–38) and, for a brief account of Sacrobosco considered as a popularizer of astronomy, Veazie (Univ. of Colorado Sts. ser. B., Sts. in the Humanities 1, 1940, 169–82). But by far the most important source is Messahala (Māshā' Allah, c. 730–815), *Compositio et operatio astrolabii.* John Selden, in his introduction to Michael Drayton, Polyolbion, 1621, was the first to note Messahala as a major source, and Skeat confirmed this (3: lxx–lxxi; and ed. of Astrolabe, 1872, xxiv–xxvi); he printed a Latin version of part 2 of Messahala (EETS ES 16, 88–104). In the following notes reference is made by part and section, and also by page, to Robert T. Gunther, Ch and Messahala on the Astr, Early Sci. at Oxford, 5, 1929. Chaucer uses Messahala in detail in Part 2, basing thirty of the forty propositions (or conclusions) on this source, and 2.41 and 42 are also based on Messahala; however, the order of propositions is not identical with that in any known MS of the Latin source. Masi (Manuscripta 19, 1975, 36–47) makes a very good case for Chaucer's having read Messahala and other astronomical works in a particular manuscript, Bodleian Selden Supra 78; he points out Chaucer's varying use of his source, sometimes translating closely, at other times adding and omitting, and traces two additions (Astr 2.1 and 2.34) to the marginal notes in the Selden MS. He also alerts us to doubts that the *Compositio* is correctly attributed to Messahala, and to the reserve to be maintained in relying on Gunther. However, Gunther provides a translation, and Masi's own projected edition for the Chaucer Library has not yet appeared.

The varying ways in which the MSS end have already been mentioned and are detailed in the comments preceding the Textual Notes. From these, and also from other variations in the order of the conclusions, it seems likely that Chaucer began and wrote steadily through Part 1 and some way into Part 2, but later may have been interrupted and continued less steadily. Apart from the displacement in the J Group MSS, the sequence generally runs regularly until 2.35. But then must have come a break, witnessed by the erratic placement of 2.36, 37 in those MSS of the J Group that contain them. Another group of MSS ends at 2.36, perhaps because the original scribe thought 2.37 repetitious. Sections 2.38–40 appear in only 9 MSS and were probably on sheets detached from the rest, while the order of MSS M¹ and R is disturbed at the end. It therefore seems probable that towards the end Chaucer may have written sporadically and that the sheets became disordered; this might account for the difficulty of the text in 2.38–40, where even a very good MS, such as B1¹, is often unsatisfactory.

These indications of sporadic composition towards the end, together with the incomplete last sentence of 2.40

in six MSS (the α, β, and γ groups), would seem to show that Chaucer originally left the work unfinished, and consequently that the Supplementary Propositions, 2.41–46, are not his. But one group, π, concludes the last sentence of 2.40, and goes on to 2.43, thus adding the three sections dealing with the use of the scale or shadow-square. These are not very clearly expressed, but perhaps could be by Chaucer. The last two, on finding the *mene motus* of the sun, seem too breathless in style, are not easy to follow, and indicate a very late date, 1397. The very last, 2.46, found only in two MSS, is generally regarded as not by Chaucer; even if as a customs officer he may have been concerned with tides, it is out of keeping with what he had written for Lewis, the operations being neither new nor of much use.

The prose style has received some attention. Margaret Schlauch makes very slight reference to it, but allows the "sparing cadences and unobtrusive rhythms" to be as appropriate to purpose and reader as the more rhythmical prose of *Boece* and Melibee to theirs (PMLA 65, 1950, 589); Sister Mary Madeleva offers helpful comments on Chaucer's authorial tact in maintaining his delicate relationship with Lewis (Lost Language, 83–100). J. E. Cross stresses simplicity as part of the schoolmasterly craft of Chaucer's "functional prose for a junior boys' class" (English 10, 1955, 172–75), and Chaucer appears briefly as technical writer in Freedman, Journ. of the Soc. of Tech. Writers and Publishers 7, 1961, 14–15. On the other hand, the probability that Chaucer wrote for an audience of more than one and thought of the work as a literary project (as witness the careful arrangement of the Prologue), is persuasively argued by Elmquist (MLN 56, 1941, 530–34); and the long literary tradition Chaucer followed in his deprecation of envy is demonstrated by Tupper (JEGP 16, 1917, 551–72). Nagucka, Syntactic Component of Ch's Astr, 1968, finds the text suitable for study by transformational grammar theory, because of its simplicity and lack of foreign models. A recent survey of scholarship is in Lawler's chapter on Chaucer (in Middle Eng. Prose, ed. Edwards, 291–313; see 302–4, and bibliography, 308–13).

Part 1 is a description of the astrolabe. But Chaucer does not mention the theory, and he describes an instrument to a learner who has it in his hands. Since an editor's task is to make his author's meaning clear, some attempt must be made to sketch the theory and function of the principal parts. The attempt is made here in full consciousness of committing a *superfluite of wordes*, but also with the happy assurance that there is no risk of being guilty of stirring up envy in the reader.

An astrolabe (from Greek, meaning "star-catcher") could be of one, two, or three dimensions, linear, planispheric, or spherical. But commonly the word denotes the second kind, the planispheric, and this is Chaucer's meaning, too. A careful reading of Skeat's commentary is still the best means to understanding Chaucer's description and conclusions, though he uses the globe, an instrument no longer a common educational aid. The simplest complete modern account is Henri Michel, Traité de l'astrolabe, 1947, giving a clear account of the basic geometry of stereographic projection on which the instrument depends. Less complete but made clearer by excellent diagrams is J. D. North's account (Scientific American 230, 1974, 96–106). For anyone wanting to construct an astrolabe like little Lewis's, see Eisner (Journ. Brit. Astron. Assoc. 86, 1975, 18–29; 1976, 125–

32, 219–27), who gives a clear account, though the need to start from the beginning is obviated by the make-it-yourself kit sold by the Royal Maritime Museum, Greenwich, England; the Museum also publishes The Planispheric Astrolabe, amended impression, 1979. For a medieval work besides Messahala's, Raymond of Marseilles's eleventh-century treatise is edited by Emmanuel Poulle (SMed ser. 3, 5, 1964, 866–900), with a long note listing editions of pre-1500 western treatises on the astrolabe; on the geometry, see also Ron B. Thomson, ed. Jordanus de Nemore and the Math. of Astrolabes, MS 40, 1978, with a good bibliography.

The astrolabe has a long history: O. Neugebauer has shown that the instrument was known to Ptolemy (2nd century A.D.), and he believes that the theory of planispheric projection was known in the time of Hipparchus (2nd century B.C.); see Isis 40, 1949, 240–56. Photographs of Arabic and European astrolabes can be seen in The Planispheric Astr., and in Robert T. Gunther, Early Sci. in Oxf., 2, 1923, in which see especially the Merton College instrument, contemporary with Chaucer, plate 83, facing pages 210, 211. Much more comprehensive, and with many plates, is Gunther, Astrolabes of the World, 1932.

The body, called the "mother," of the instrument was a metal disk, usually brass, pierced by a small, central hole, and surrounded by a thicker metal rim so as to form a circular depression or well on one side, the front, or "womb" side. To the back was fastened the alidade, which Chaucer calls the *reule* (1.13). This was a sighting device free to revolve around a pin which passed through a hole in its center and the central hole of the "mother." It was also a pointer passing over the concentric series of graduations, namely the circles of degrees in four sets of 90, of degrees of the zodiac, of the days, the months, the holy days and the dominical letters described by Chaucer in 1.7–11. Two diameters were marked on the back, one from top to bottom, i.e., from south to north; the other at right angles to it from left to right (facing the instrument), i.e., from east to west. The four radii thus produced were called the south or meridional line (from top to center), the east line (from left to center), the line of midnight (from center to bottom), and the west line (1.4–5).

The pin holding the alidade (1.14) projected through the mother, and on to it, in the manner of phonograph records, could be slipped circular metal plates, and over them the "rete" *(riet)*, all made of a size to fit snugly into the central well. The plates were held in position with respect to the border by a tongue-in-groove device, but the rete was free to revolve around the pin. The front of the astrolabe had a revolving pointer, also held by the pin, which Chaucer calls the *label* (1.21.84). The pin was pierced by a slot, and into this a wedge was pushed to hold all the components together (1.14). The border on the front was graduated in degrees of arc, as a protractor, and by letters of the alphabet inscribed 15° apart; these marked the twenty-four hours of the day (1.16). A mounting at the top of the mother held an eye-bolt through which passed a ring by which the user held up the instrument on his right thumb; when so held the instrument hung straight and plumb, yet free to turn (1.1–2).

The important components were the plates and the rete. A plate represented the plane of the celestial equator, that is, the plane of the earth's equator extended to the celestial sphere. On it were inscribed lines representing the projections of certain celestial reference lines as seen by an imaginary eye at the south celestial pole, which is the point of projection. Viewed from this point, the north celestial pole would be projected at the center of the celestial equator, represented by the center of the central hole in the plate. Correspondingly, the two tropic circles and the celestial equator would appear as concentric circles, with centers at the projection of the north celestial pole; the northern tropic of Cancer would be the smallest, and the southern tropic of Capricorn the largest. The middle circle would represent the projection of the celestial equator, or equinoctial circle. As marked on the plate the circle of Capricorn was near or coincident with the edge of the plate. The north pole and the three circles thus projected formed a ground-plan for mapping a great portion of the sky, mostly the northern sky (with which an observer in northern latitudes would be mainly concerned).

Such an observer theoretically commands a view of half the universe, but his horizon is at an angle to the plane of the celestial equator, and he must make his observations with respect to that horizon and to his own zenith. (In astronomical theory his horizon was considered a plane passing through the center of the earth, terrestrial distances being negligible compared to stellar or planetary distances.) He can draw or imagine almucantars (Chaucer's *almykanteras*), lines of constant altitude, as a series of concentric circles on the great celestial hemisphere he observes. Their centers lie on a vertical line from him to his zenith, and the widest almucantar circle at the horizon, 0° of altitude; the other extreme is a point, his zenith, at 90° of altitude. These must be projected onto the plane of the celestial equator and marked on the plate. A line from the zenith to the south celestial pole will cut the equatorial plane at a point, and when transferred to the plate will represent the projection of the zenith. A series of lines from points on the circumference of an almucantar will project on the plate as a circle also. It is a feature of this kind of projection, stereographic projection, that circles on the surface of a sphere project on a plane through the center of the sphere as circles. The projections of the almucantars then will appear as circles on the plate, not concentric of course, but with their centers on the north-south line to the south of the zenith point. The smaller, higher-altitude almucantars will be completely projected, but the larger, lower-altitude almucantars will be cut off at the edge of the plate, the line of the horizon being the least complete. This line of 0° altitude, the observer's horizon, is called the oblique horizon, *horizon obliquus.* The lower the latitude of the observer, the less oblique his horizon, and the more this oblique horizon approaches the east-west line, the *horizon rectus.* The three circles on the plate are described by Chaucer in 1.17, and the zenith and almucantars in 1.18. In 1.19 he turns to the *azymutz.*

To locate or describe the position of a heavenly object one must know not only its altitude, measured on the almucantar lines, but also its bearing, or azimuth. Lines of equal azimuth are great circles from the zenith to the horizon cutting the almucantars and the horizon at right angles. These too are projected on the plate, and their projections will be arcs of circles from the projection of the zenith to the projection of the horizon. In accordance with another important feature of this kind of projection, the angles between the projections of intersecting circles on the surface of a sphere will be equal to the angles of intersection of the circles themselves. Hence the azimuth lines on the plate cut the almucantar lines at right angles. The plate is now almost complete. The azimuth lines end at the horizon, and the lower half of the plate is marked for the "unequal hours," each one-twelfth of the time from sunrise to sunset; hence the lines are curved, since the length of an "unequal hour" varies with the seasons (2.7–10).

Plates were made for a specific latitude, and it was common to have more than one, marked for different latitudes. This was not the case with the rete. On the rete (Lat. *rete,* a net) are the projections of a number of important stars, and, most important, of the ecliptic circle, the sun's apparent annual path through the heavens, which is inclined to the equator, or equinoctial, at an angle of 23½°. This circle is easy to make, for at its northernmost point, the summer solstice, it touches the circle of Cancer, and at its southernmost point, the circle of Capricorn. These two points will lie where the north-south line on the rete cuts these two circles at their points farthest from each other, and the ecliptic circle can be drawn with its center halfway between these two points. On this circle are marked the twelve signs of the zodiac, each graduated with 30 degrees. The six northern signs, Aries to Virgo, lie along the shorter arc to the north of the east-west line, with Gemini and Cancer occupying the smallest space; the other six lie on the longer, southern arc, Sagittarius and Capricorn taking up the greatest space (1.21). At 0° Capricorn is a small pointer, which Chaucer calls the *almury* (1.21.90).

In order that the plate beneath should be visible, the rete was cut away as much as possible, leaving only the edge, the ecliptic circle and enough of the cross lines to hold the pointers whose tips represent the projected positions of the major stars. Since the center of plate and rete represents the north celestial pole, and the rete turns around this point, the rete could be made to revolve over the plate around the pole as the sky appears to do above the observer, and on his grid of almucantars and azimuths, the user could plot the risings, settings, or other positions of the heavenly bodies on the rete. The astrolabe thus provided a means of fixing a position of a heavenly body in relation to the earth, and to calculate rapidly from one position those of others. Hence it was useful for an astrologer, who needed to know what degree of the zodiac was rising at a given time and, given from his tables what was the configuration of the planets, in what celestial houses they were at that time. By it one could tell the time from the sun or a star. In short, as Poulle sums up, the astrolabe enabled one to solve problems of astronomy and spherical trigonometry as by a diagram *(graphiquement)* and by means of the alidade to supply the data for the problems (Bibliothèque de l'Ecole des Chartes 112, 1955, 82).

For information on ancient and medieval scientific writers, consult Lynn Thorndike, Hist. of Magic and Exper. Sci., 1923–41 (the first four vols. cover the period to 1500), and George Sarton, Intro. Hist. Sci., 1927–48. A pleasant introduction to the men of science at Merton College, Oxford, with some of whose work Chaucer was familiar, is provided in J. A. W. Bennett, Ch at Oxford, 58–85. O. Neugebauer, The Exact Sciences in Antiquity, 2nd ed., 1957, provides a useful discussion of mathematics and astronomy and will help cure the somewhat contemptuous attitude towards older science that our modern cultural milieu instills. Important modern works bearing directly on Chaucer's astronomy and astrology are: The *Equatorie of the Planetis,* ed. Price and Wilson, tentatively ascribed to Chaucer, but never generally accepted as his; the *Kalendarium* of Nicholas of Lynn, ed. Eisner, tr. MacEoin and Eisner, 1980; Richard of Wallingford, an Edition of his Writings, ed. and tr. J. D. North, 1976; among the works of Richard, the *Exafrenon pronosticacionum temporis,* in English translation, is of especial interest. North has also edited a contemporary translation from Latin of instructions for making an elaborate sundial; see Little Ship of Venice, Journ. Hist. Med. 15, 1960, 399–407. To find the positions of planets in Chaucer's time, see Bryant Tuckerman, Planetary, Lunar, and Solar Positions, A.D. 12–A.D. 1649, Memoirs of the Amer. Philosoph. Soc. 59, 1964.

PROLOGUE

1 sone: Probably Chaucer's son (see introductory note). Kittredge (MP 14, 1917, 515) gives examples of a tutor or adviser using this word (cf. MancT IX.318 and n.). Elmquist (MLN 56:530–34) suggests that Chaucer had a larger audience in mind, and Bennett (Ch at Oxford, 33) even suggests that Lewis is a fiction to justify Chaucer's simplicity of style.

6 a philosofre: No certain source for this dictum is known. Skeat suggests Cicero, De amicitia, ed. Falconer, pp. 155–57: "Ask of friends only what is honourable; do for friends only what is honourable, and without waiting to be asked," but the sense in Cicero is that only honorable petitions should be acceded to.

frend: Kittredge (MP 14:516) argues that *frend* is less appropriate to a son than to someone else's son, or to a godson. However, the word is not appropriate for a mature man addressing a ten-year-old, and probably merely translates the source. Chaucer elsewhere uses the word to mean a kinsman or relation (e.g., KnT I.992, LGW 1827).

12–14 certein nombre . . . a certein of conclusions: For *certein* meaning a definite, though unspecified, number, see MilT I.3193n.

22 Treatises could contain erroneous information, and so give rise to misleading results. Raymond of Marseilles gives a wrong method for graduating the zodiac in the rete (Poule, SMed ser. 3, 5:869); most scribes of the Astrolabe give wrong figures in 2.23, 29–32, and have to falsify the result.

39–40 Cf. Tr 2.36–37, and Whiting P52.

42 redith or herith: For hearing read as well as reading, cf. the Retraction X.1081.

43 for excusid: This construction seems to have been much less common with a past participle than with an adjective. Many manuscripts omit *for,* and some substitute "ful." See MED s.v. *for* prep. 13a(b); also *haven* v. 6a(b)(c); and *holden* v. 27c(b).

45–46 Cf. HF 861–63.

56–57 lord of this langage: The earliest known occurrence of the notion of "the King's English." The first citation for the phrase in OED, however, is Shakespeare, *Merry Wives* 1.4.6.

59–64 In this passage Chaucer combines two longstanding literary traditions: the "affected modesty" prologue (cf. GP I.746n.) and the deprecation of envy (cf. Tr 5.1789–92n.).

65 The table of contents that begins here shows five parts, but we have only the first two extant, unless 2.40 and 44–45 are considered as parts of Part 4 (Skeat 3:1xv–1xviii). Chaucer's educational principles here require a good deal of practical experience with the instrument in Parts 1 and 2 before going on to theory in Parts 4 and 5.

74 smallist: Very small; cf. *thikkest* 1.3.1. On the absolute superlative in ME, see Mustanoja, ME Syntax, 285, 287–88. But note that the examples of Chaucer's rendering of Boethius's Latin absolute comparatives by superlatives may have been influenced by the French translation attributed to Jean de Meun (ed. Denomy, MS 14, 1952, 166–275).

75–76 Positions of the heavenly bodies in medieval tables are usually given in degrees and minutes of arc, much more *narwe* than an observer could achieve with an astrolabe. MS Dg refers to minutes and seconds as "calkelid in tabelis of astronomye." The word **cause** here seems to mean merely "purpose," so that **calculed for a cause** is "calculated for that purpose."

77–108 On the contents of the three parts which Chaucer did not write, see North, RES 20:436–37.

84–86 See Nicholas of Lynn, Kalendarium, 2–5, for facts and legends about **Frere N. Lenne.** He was a Carmelite friar at Oxford, and he made his calendar in 1386 for the latitude and longitude of that city; it covered the years 1387–1462, i.e., four Metonic cycles of 19 years each, and was dedicated to John of Gaunt, who is addressed as King of Castile. On Chaucer's use of this work, see IntrMLT II.1–14n.; NPT VII.3187, ParsPro X.5–9.

J. Somer (John Somer) entered the Franciscan order at Bridgwater, was at the Oxford convent in 1380, and was still there in 1395. He is credited with a short chronicle of Bridgwater convent, but was known principally as an astronomer. He wrote his calendar in 1380 for Joan, princess of Wales and mother of the young Richard II. Like Nicholas of Lynn's, it was for Oxford, and covered the same period. See Nicholas of Lynn, Kal., 8–9; A. G. Little, Greyfriars in Oxf., 1892, 244–46; and Emden, BRUO 1:1727.

103–6 Tables to find the beginnings of the first six houses for the latitude of Oxford, and tables of dignities of planets, are found in Nicholas of Lynn, Kal., 164–75 and 180–81. For the houses, see notes on 2.4.16, 46 and 2.36; for the dignities, see 2.4.47n. Chaucer in 2.36 and 2.37 gives instructions for ascertaining the houses for any time at which the ascendant is known.

PART I

§1.5 altitude: The angle between the celestial object and the observer's horizon; frequently confused by scribes with *latitude.*

§2 This seems to mean that the suspension ring passed through the eye of the torret (see OED s.v.)—mounted at the top of the astrolabe—which was sufficiently wide that the ring did not stick, but allowed the instrument to hang freely. Skeat's drawing (fig. 1) shows the device as an eye-bolt or swivel pin through a vertical hole in a metal handle riveted to the top of the instrument, which is therefore free to turn. This is the usual device in Western astrolabes; the part corresponding to Skeat's handle was called *armilla fixa,* the eye-bolt *armilla reflexa,* and the ring *armilla suspensoria* (see Planisph. Astrolabe, 10, illustration).

§5.7   centre: MS readings are divided, and slightly favor "oriental"; *centre* is, however, preferred as being more precise.

§6.10–12   This does not imply that the sun is considered always to rise due east; rather that the altitude of the sun is measured on the scale around the rim of the mother (described in 1.7), from 0° at the cross to 90° at the end of the meridional line; if the "rule" or alidade is pointed at the rising sun its point or edge will lie on the little cross, registering 0°.

§7.10   myle wey: Conventionally twenty minutes; cf. 1.16.15–16. Chaucer draws attention to the fact that each degree of arc in the outermost scale corresponds to four minutes of time, as the sun in its diurnal course moves fifteen degrees of arc per hour. In the next section he takes care to emphasize that though the word "minutes" used of the outer scale can refer to time, when used of the scale of the zodiacal signs it always means minutes of arc.

§8.5   Piscis: In MS Bl¹ the spelling Pisces also occurs; the singular form here may follow Nicholas of Lynn, Kalendarium, who in turn follows the Arabic, in which the name of the sign is singular, "al Ḥut."

13   Alkabucius: Alcabitius (Al-Qabīsī), tenth-century Muslim astrologer, for whom see Sarton, Intr. Hist. Science 1:669. Alcabitius's Introduction to Astrology was translated into Latin in the first half of the twelfth century by John Hispalensis (Alchabitii Abdilazi liber introductorius ad magisterium judiciorum astrorum interprete Joanne Hispalensi), and printed Bologna (1473), and Venice (five printings 1481–1521).

15–16   See 1.7.10n. Many scribes omit some or all of this, some probably by haplography, but some evidently because they felt the repetition was an unnecessary *superfluite of wordes.*

§10   The statements here are confused and partly erroneous. In the first place the names of the months are Roman, not Arabic. Secondly, Julius Caesar did not make the changes that Chaucer attributes to him. He did give July thirty-one days, but took none from February's twenty-nine, to which, on the contrary, he added a thirtieth in the bissextile year. It was Augustus Caesar who took one day (not two) from February, to give August as many days as July. It was only after this and other changes made during his reign that the calendar assumed the form in which Chaucer gives it.

21–22   At this point the scribe of MS Bl¹ adds a Latin note that the sun is in Cancer for thirty-two days and in Capricorn for only twenty-eight, at least according to the sun's true motion or true *motus;* however, if the sun's "mean *motus*" is considered, the sun spends an equal time in each sign. For an explanation of true and mean *motus,* see Equatorie, ed. Price and Wilson, 97–98. In the diagram on 98, note that the true *motus* of the sun corresponds to the true place.

§11.2–3   lettres of the A B C: See OED s.v. *dominical* 2b.

§14.6   The horse is usually taken to be named from its shape, but naming machines or their parts after animals is common, see e.g., OED s.v. *horse* 8. Yet the present example is the only one for *hors* in MED, and Messahala (Gunther, 147) says it may be in other animal shapes; Raymond of Marseilles says the wedge can have a horse's or a cock's head, "clavus latus equum vel gallinatum habens caput" (SMed ser. 3, 5:889).

§16.8   equinoxiall: The great circle where the plane of the earth's equator intersects the celestial sphere.

§17   See the introductory note. The three circles representing the orbits of the heads of the signs Cancer, Aries and Libra, and Capricorn, may be found in Messahala (Gunther, 168, and figure 64v). For the account of the tropics, see Sacrobosco (Thorndike, 127, 92).

9   Ptholome: MS J reads, "Ptolomeys almagest." See Heiberg 1, 80–81, last entry in the table, for the arc from ecliptic to equator at 90° from intersection, where the obliquity is given as 23°51′20″. The table follows chapter 14. Skeat notes that in Chaucer's time the true obliquity was about 23°31′. A detailed modern account of the Almagest is in Neugebauer, Hist. Anc. Math. Astron., 1975, 1:21–339.

14–24   Cf. Sacrobosco (Thorndike, 123, 86).

19   Chaucer may have had in mind Campanus of Novara, De sphaera solida, 1303 (Gunther, Early Sci. in Oxf. 2:31, 246), and may have used such an instrument.

21   weyer: This translates Latin *aequator* (OED s.v. *weigher,* and cf. Lat. *aequator monetae,* one who checks the weight of new coins). As may be seen from the Textual Notes, the MSS favor a reading such as: "the weyer i. (= i.e.) equator"; but it seems strange for Chaucer to explain an English word with a rare Latin word.

25–30   Any celestial body whose projection on the plate is inside the projection of the equinoctial circle must be north of the equinoctial circle. At the end of his discussion, however, Chaucer adds **as fro the equinoxiall,** since the height of a star, etc., may also be measured from the ecliptic circle and the projection of a star may be outside one circle and inside the other.

31   latitudes: Since Chaucer is using the equinoctial as his reference, the modern term would be "declination," but he elsewhere refers stellar latitudes to the equinoctial; see 2.17.29–31, 19.9.

35–41   Sacrobosco: "And 'tis called the 'belt of the first movement' . . . Be it understood that the 'first movement' means the movement of the *primum mobile,* that is, of the ninth sphere or last heaven, which movement is from east through west back to east again" (Thorndike, 123, 86). Since Chaucer (FranT V.1283) agrees with Sacrobosco in making the *primum mobile* the ninth sphere, the 8 in our text may be an error. North (RES n.s. 20:436n.) suggests that here Chaucer simply means that the *primum mobile* moves the eighth sphere, a suggestion apparently derived from Skeat. This forces the sense. In some MSS of Sacrobosco there are variants for "ninth": "eighth," "ninth or eighth," "of the eighth sphere or of the ninth, or of the firmament."

§18   See the introductory note.

2   almycanteras: See Gunther, Ch and Messahala, fig. 67v for a diagram showing the inscribing of the almucantars.

11   compowned by 2 and 2: Lewis's instrument was engraved with 45 almucantar circles, every two degrees from the horizon to 88, the zenith being a point. Bennett

(Ch at Oxford, 33n.) suggests that Chaucer's gift may have been a "mini" model, perhaps only a few inches in diameter.

§19.6 azimutz: See introductory note. In Lewis's instrument the lines of azimuth are marked for every 15°.

10–11 cenyth of the sonne and of every sterre: Here *cenyth,* unlike its meaning throughout 1.18 and 1.19.1, must mean "azimuth" (OED s.v. *azimuth* 1b).

§20.4 The hours of each day governed by the planets were "unequal hours," of which the daytime hours were each one-twelfth of the time from sunrise to sunset, and the nighttime hours one-twelfth of the time from sunset to sunrise; see further 2.12 and nn.

§21 On the rete, see the introductory note. Skeat in his note on this section gives the names of the stars marked in a diagram in Dd¹, which he reproduces as fig. 2. For other star lists, see Gunther, Early Sci. in Oxf., 2:192, 201, 205, 222–25.

10–15 Cf. 1.17.25–30 above. Stars whose projections on the rete are within the circle of the projection of the ecliptic are north of the ecliptic.

15–23 Aldeberan and **Algomeysa** (α Tauri and α Canis Minoris or Procyon) are south of the ecliptic but north of the equinoctial.

For an observer north of the equator, his horizon will be at an angle to the equatorial circle (i.e., the equinoctial); the two circles intersect at his east and west points, and the part of the equinoctial above his horizon will slope south of his zenith, and the part below will slope north of his nadir. Assume a star with a northerly declination is just on his eastern horizon; its right ascension is measured at the point where the great circle through the North Pole and the star cuts the equinoctial circle, and this point will be below the horizon to the east, and hence will rise some time later than the star. The star to the north, then, will rise sooner than "the degree of its right ascension" as Chaucer might put it. Correspondingly with the longitude of a star north of the ecliptic; its longitude is measured at the point where the great circle from the pole of the ecliptic through the star cuts the ecliptic circle. If the star is just rising, "the degree of its longitude" is below the horizon, and will rise later. The farther north the star, the earlier it rises.

It is of incidental interest that the scribe of B1¹ noted in the margin that *Aldeberan* and *Algomeysa* were on a Merton College Astrolabe, together with three others which he inserts in the text: "Menkar" (α Ceti), "Algevse" (? Castor and Pollux, or perhaps an error for "Rasalgeuse," β Geminorum, Pollux), and "Cor Leonis" (Regulus).

27–29 Chaucer does not reach this explanation of eclipses. For these lines, cf. Sacrobosco (Thorndike 125, 89), and for the explanation, Thorndike, 141–2, 115–6.

29–44 This refers to the zodiac circle on the rete. The heavenly zodiac is regarded as a band, 12° wide with the ecliptic in the center; in the rete, only the northern 6° are shown, the projection of the ecliptic circle being the outer circumference of the zodiac circle on the rete; its **large brede** is this 6° band, and the width of the band will vary with the size of the astrolabe.

52 The twelve signs of the zodiac (Gr. ζῴδιον, diminutive of ζῷον, living creature) are all named from **bestes** (which category can include humans), except Libra; however, the signs no longer correspond to the constellations for which they were named. The signs are marked out

with respect to the equinoxes, two points where the ecliptic and equinoctial circles intersect. Owing to the precession of the equinoxes the constellation Pisces is now in the sign of Aries, and so on round the twelve.

55–75 On astrology, see note on 2.4. For figures showing the relation of zodiacal signs to parts of the human body, see the reproduction from the Brussels MS in Pintelon (following 127), and Skeat, fig. 19.

78–83 Cf. Sacrobosco (Thorndike 124, 87).

90 almury: The edge of the rete at the first point of Capricorn (where the zodiac circle on the rete is nearest the border) is cut down to a small projecting tongue or pointer.

PART II

§1 Cf. Messahala 2.1 (Gunther, 169–70, 218).

The back of the mother has concentric scales of degrees of the ecliptic and of the days of the year. The degree of the sun, i.e., the sun's position in the ecliptic, can be read off for any day by the fiducial edge of the alidade.

7 12 day of March: In Chaucer's time this was the vernal equinox, and the sun was in the first degree of Aries. By new style the date is 20–21 March.

7–8 I wolde knowe: Chaucer is thinking about future readers, or, of course, he may have been writing of an event passed for him, however recent.

8–9 I soughte in the bakhalf of myn Astrelabie: This reference to the back side may have been suggested to Chaucer by a note in MS Selden Supra 78: "this may be done more easily if [the Astrolabe] is held in reverse so that on the circle of the days the tables may be better seen." (Masi, Manuscripta 19:42).

12–15 The divisions in the circle of days marked noon, not midnight; Lewis could set his **reule** precisely.

§2 Cf. Messahala 2.2 (Gunther, 170, 218).

2 thi lift syde: In this case the right or east side of the instrument would be toward the sun.

4–5 This procedure avoids the danger of looking directly at the sun; not possible or necessary for viewing the moon or a star.

§3 Cf. Messahala 2.2 (Gunther, 170–71, 218–19). This procedure for telling the time is given in Gunther, Early Sci. 2:186–87, and also in Plan. Astrol., 27. The actual altitude of the sun is taken, as in 2.2, and then the rete is turned until the degree of the sun for that day is on the almucantar for the sun's altitude, to the east of the meridian line if before midday, to the west if after. The label is then placed across this point and the hour of the day is read off in the border. Messahala reads the line from the nadir of the sun's degree of longitude, but Chaucer gets the same result by counting the hours from the line of midnight.

32–33 upon myn est orizonte: The ascending degree is that on the *horizon obliquus,* not on the east-west line.

63–81 Near the south line the edge of the zodiac circle in the rete is most nearly parallel to the almucantar lines; hence it is most difficult to determine the point where a particular degree of the circle touches a particular almucantar, and error is most likely to creep in.

Note that for the learner, this conclusion uses the skills acquired in 2.1 and 2.2. The degree of the sun is to be found on the back of the astrolabe; when this degree is to be set in some position, the degree on the ecliptic circle on the rete is meant.

§4   This conclusion, dealing with astrology, is not in Messahala. For medieval acceptance of astrology, see Theodore O. Wedel, Med. Attitude toward Astrology, 1920; for Chaucer and his use of it, see the references in the Bibliography (p. 775). The standard study of ancient astrology is Auguste Bouché Leclercq, L'astrologie grecque, 1899, and there is a brief account in Willy Hartner, Oriens-Occidens, 1968, 448–58. For Middle English accounts close to Chaucer's time, see Bartholomaeus Anglicus, De proprietatibus rerum, tr. John of Trevisa 1:441–506; also Richard of Wallingford, Exafrenon pronosticacionum temporis, ed. North 1:183–243, 2:83–126. For an unfavorable view, see Dives and Pauper, EETS 275, 1:1.117–43.

11–14   forseide degre . . . his longitude: Only the α group of two MSS contains this complete passage, which is necessary to the sense; the rest omit the passage almost entirely.

16   hous of the ascendent: On the astrological houses, see further 2.36n. and 2.37. The first house, the ascendant, was taken to begin at the ascending degree and stretch a varying number of degrees below the horizon. But Chaucer here seems to have a different system in mind, calling the ascendant or *horoscopus* a thirty degree arc of the zodiac running from 5° above to 25° below the horizon, as in Ptolemy, Tetrabiblos 3.10. The term "house" was also used for a sign of the zodiac in which a planet has special influence, or which he governs, but to avoid confusion this is better called a "domicile" of the planet (North RES n.s. 20:136–37).

25   25 degres: All MSS, except two that omit the figure, have "15 degres"; the error must go back to Chaucer.

32   lord of the ascendent: The planet whose domicile is the zodiacal sign that is ascending.

36   Tayl of the Dragoun: The moon's descending node, i.e., the point where the moon crosses the ecliptic, moving from north to south; this and the ascending node, the Head of the Dragon, were treated in some ways as planets in astrology (see Hartner, Oriens-Occidens, 349–404, esp. 359–82).

38   aspect of enemyte: Opposition or quartile aspect, a multiple of 90° away.

46   in an angle: In one of the principal houses, the first, tenth, seventh, or fourth, which began at the four principal points, i.e., on the eastern horizon (the ascendant), at the upper mid-heaven *(medium caelum),* on the western horizon (the descendant), and at the lower mid-heaven *(immum caelum).* (See Bouché-Leclercq, L'astrologie grecque, 257–59.)

46–47   in a succident: In one of the houses following the four principal houses, i.e., the second, fifth, eighth, and eleventh.

47   in hys dignite: Besides having domiciles in certain signs, planets had exaltations (and dejections) in specific degrees of signs; in addition each ten degrees of a sign was a "face" or "decan" (see 60–63) and was assigned to a planet; another system divided the signs irregularly into five parts, each part being assigned as a place of special influence for a planet. Thus a planet could have a number of "dignities." For details, see Willy Hartner, Oriens-Occidens, 451–57, or North RES n.s. 20:135–37.

48   frendly aspectes: These were trine and sextile aspects, 120° and 60° away from the point considered. Thus, for the second house the sixth and the tenth were in trine, and the fourth and the twelfth in sextile aspect.

57–69   Chauncey Wood (Ch and the Stars, 15–18) argues strongly from this passage against any real belief by Chaucer in astrological predictions, because of the wide margin the astrologers allowed themselves in plotting planetary positions. But Smyser (Spec 45, 1970, 359–73) asserts, on the basis of MLT II.295–315, that Chaucer, after translating Boethius in 1380, came fully to accept astrology as a rational way of understanding the universe. Certainly, despite his disclaimer, Chaucer slipped in information about "faces," and in 2.36–37 he gives methods for finding the twelve astrological houses. Lydgate (Fall of Princes 1.298–301) apparently believed that the main purpose of the Treatise on the Astrolabe was to teach the casting of horoscopes. See MLT II.295–315nn.

§5   Cf. Messahala 2.2 (Gunther, 170–71, 218–19).

Messahala considers almucantars as much as 6° apart, and obtains the true position by proportion rather than by a simple average of two readings.

§6   Cf. Messahala 2.4 (Gunther, 171, 219).

Twilight after sunset is due to refraction of the sun's light through the atmosphere. Chaucer follows Messahala in setting the beginning (or ending) of twilight when the sun is 18° below the horizon. Nicholas of Lynn (Kal., 12) sets it at about 20°.

1   the nadir of thy sonne: When the nadir of the sun is 18° above the western horizon, the sun will be 18° below the eastern horizon.

§7   Cf. Messahala 2.5 (Gunther, 172, 219).

The sun's longitude on the ecliptic circle in the rete is set on the eastern *horizon obliquus,* and the time, indicated on the border by the label, is marked; the same is done for the western *horizon obliquus,* and the intervening time is the time from sunrise to sunset, the artificial day.

19–22   The sun's **propre moeving** is its annual circle round the ecliptic, a movement of about 1° eastwards each day; hence it will cross the meridian about four minutes later each day; the *day naturall* is then the complete revolution of the equinoctial, and the four minutes due to the sun's own motion. Since Chaucer's method here uses the same *degre of the sonne* for sunrise and sunset, his two arcs will be slightly wrong.

§8   Cf. Messahala 2.6,9 (Gunther, 172, 173, 219, 220). One clock hour corresponds to 15° of the equinoctial circle (see 1.17,33–35).

§9   Not in Messahala.

4   day vulgar: From the beginning of morning twilight to the end of evening twilight, daybreak to dark.

§10   Cf. Messahala 2.6 (Gunther, 172, 219).

2   houres of planetes: See 2.12n.

§11   Cf. Messahala 2.8 (Gunther, 173, 220).

16–18   Chaucer never reached this promised fourth part.

§12   This section deals with an astrological system and is not in Messahala. The sequence of hours dominated by each planet follows the planetary order from the outermost, Saturn, to the innermost, the Moon. See Skeat's note, 3:196–98.

2–3   the nadir of the sonne: The unequal hours, or hours of the planets, are marked only on the lower part of the plate, from 1 to 12 (see 1.20.1–4); hence by day, if the sun's position on the ecliptic circle in the rete is set on the almucantar for the sun's height at any time, its nadir will show the unequal hour. After sunset the sun itself indicates the unequal hour; its position could be found, e.g., by the clock time on the equal hour scale.

7–8 North (RES n.s. 20:433) points out that 13 March fell on Saturday in 1389 and 1395. But Chaucer adds **peraventure**. It seems likely that he used Saturday in his example so that his explanation of the sequence of planetary hours could begin with the outermost planet, and work inwards. But note the statement of Robert Kilwardby, Archbishop of Canterbury 1273–78: "The reckoning of this successive dominance by hours they [i.e., astrologers] began from Saturn, which is the highest of the planets, and in the first hour of Saturday [or "of the Sabbath," Lat. "sabbati"] they made him 'dominant.' " (Dondaine, Le "De 43 questionibus" de Robert Kilwardby, AFP 47, 1977, 43, Qu. 40.) To begin on Saturday was a tradition, it seems.

11 it was but litel: Nicholas of Lynn (Kal., 77) gives the sun's position for 13 March as 1°38' of Aries.

§13 Cf. Messahala 2.10 (Gunther, 174, 220).

To check this without an astrolabe, take any diagram showing a plate marked with the three major circles and the almucantars, e.g., Skeat's fig. 5. For 12 March the first point of Aries on the rete will lie on the intersection of the *horizon obliquus,* the equinoctial circle, and the east-west line *(horizon rectus).* The degree of the sun will be 0° Aries, or very slightly more. Moving this point on the rete to the meridian will obviously bring it to where the meridian line cuts the equinoctial circle. On Skeat's diagram this is between the 35° and 40° almucantars, nearer the latter. Nicholas of Lynn (Kal., 81) shows the altitude of the sun at midday for 12 March to be 38°25', and the "degree of the sun," 0°39' (Kal., 77).

§14 Cf. Messahala 2.14 (Gunther, 175, 221).

The procedure is the reverse of that in the previous conclusion. Chaucer assumes that only two days in the year will have the same meridian altitude for the sun; which one, the observer can know from the season. If the date found is correct, the observer has a check on the accuracy with which the almucantars on his plate are engraved. Near the summer and winter solstices, 13 June and 13 December, the altitude of the sun varies only slightly each day, and measurement would be difficult. In fact, Nicholas of Lynn shows the noon altitude of the sun as 61°38' for 8, 9, 17, and 18 June, and 61°42' for 11, 12, 14, and 15 June. In December the change is more consistent, and only two consecutive days, the 12th and 13th, show the same altitude, 14°37' (Kal., 99, 135).

§15 Cf. Messahala 2.15 (Gunther, 175, 221).

1–3 The two degrees must be equidistant from either equinox.

8–10 Here the two degrees must be 180° apart, equidistant respectively from the head of Aries and of Libra. However, the phrase **in the opposyt parties** is not quite unambiguous, and could refer to two points an equal number of days or degrees before and after one equinox.

§16 Cf. Messahala 2.13 (Gunther, 175, 221).

§17 Cf. Messahala 2.34 (Gunther, 184–85, 227).

Messahala deals with finding the longitude of a planet. Chaucer tells us to take two measurements of the star's altitude, one before and one after it crosses the meridian great circle, such that the two measurements are equal. Immediately after each is taken, take the ascending de-

gree on the ecliptic by means of a known star on the rete, as in 2.3. The mid-point of these two ascendants is the ascending degree when the star crossed the meridian. This ascending degree on the ecliptic circle in the rete is now set on the eastern *horizon obliquus,* and the degree in the ecliptic circle that lies on the meridian is the longitude of the star. This method is faulty because, while the star has moved between the measurements through a number of degrees along a circle parallel with the equinoctial, the two ascensions and the final meridional position are measured on the ecliptic, which is oblique to the equinoctial. Of any two points on the ecliptic (apart from the two equinoxes), one will be north or south of the other with respect to the equinoctial. If the two measurements are made within a few degrees of the meridian, the error will be slight.

23–44 The distinctions Chaucer makes here are confusing. First he says that longitude is measured in the ecliptic, and latitude from the equinoctial; but then for the sun or a star, latitude is measured from the equinoctial, and for planets from the ecliptic. He concludes that both systems can be used, except for the sun, which (having no latitude from the ecliptic) has its latitude measured from the equinoctial.

§18 Cf. Messahala 2.16 (Gunther, 176, 221).

5–6 degre in which the sterre stondith: Skeat, in his commentary on this conclusion, notes that this is not the same as the star's longitude. He instances Sirius whose longitude is 12° of Cancer, but which crosses the meridian, or "souths" with 9° of Cancer. The ecliptic is inclined to the equinoctial, so that great circles of longitude and of right ascension will coincide only at the tropic points.

§19 Not in Messahala. See 1.21.15–23 and n., on a star rising earlier as it is farther north (for an observer in northern latitudes), and correspondingly later as it is farther south. Skeat, commenting on this passage, points out that Sirius, longitude 12° of Cancer, rises with 19° of Leo.

14–18 Here Chaucer makes the point explicit; only if a star is on the ecliptic will it rise together with the degree of its longitude.

§20 Cf. Messahala 2.20 (Gunther, 178, 223).

6–7 The first points of Aries and Libra (which lie on the equinoctial) should lie on the meridional line at exactly the point where the equinoctial circle cuts it. This method measures the altitude of any point on the ecliptic at noon and the altitude of the equinoctial at the same time. The difference is the declination.

11–14 If the declination of the point is south, it will lie outside the equinoctial circle on the plate.

§21 Cf. Messahala 2.23 (Gunther, 179, 223–24).

§22 Not in Messahala.

1–3 The angle between the southern horizon and the equinoctial equals the angle between the zenith and the north pole.

3–5 The angle between the northern horizon and the north pole equals the angle between the equinoctial and the zenith; **orisonte** is the southern horizon in 2, the northern horizon in 4.

§23 Not in Messahala.

For this operation the observer must know the direction of true north, and must choose two stars of high declination, which do not set, 180° of right ascension apart. He takes the altitude of one star both when it is at its southernmost point, directly above the pole, and again directly below the pole at its northernmost point. For this, a long clear winter's night is required. The average of the two altitudes is the altitude of the pole, the same as the observer's latitude. The second star and the plumb-line are for greater accuracy.

29–35 Since star A is 4° from the pole, Skeat took it that the pole-star, Polaris, was used by Chaucer for this example. Most MSS have figures of 62° and 21° for the first and second readings, making the height of the pole 42½°, in effect the latitude of Rome. But by juggling the calculation, that is, by adding half of 62 to 21, they obtain the required answer of 52.

§24 Cf. Messahala 2.22 (Gunther, 179, 223). This is the same, essentially, as 2.23, except that there is no need to know the direction of true north, which will be towards the star at its highest and lowest altitude.

§25 Cf. Messahala 2.21 (Gunther, 178–79, 223).

16   in the hevedes of Aries or of Libra: At the equinoxes the midday altitude of the sun is obviously the complement of the elevation of the pole.

§26 Not in Messahala, but see Sacrobosco (Thorndike, 130–33, 134–36; 97–100, 103–6).

1   the spere solide: See 1.17.19n. Liddell, in the Globe Ch, believes that Chaucer refers here to Sacrobosco's work.

5   These auctours: Authorities in general; for this use of *these,* see Language and Versification, p. xxxviii.

6   of right ascensioun: This refers not to the modern sense of the term, but to the fact that the signs so designated rise at a greater angle to the horizon, and so take longer to rise completely. See Skeat's commentary for details for each sign at latitude 52° north. Consider Aries: when its first point is rising, its last point is 30° east on the ecliptic, i.e., about 28° east on the equinoctial; this point on the equinoctial will rise after 1 hour and 52 minutes. But the last point of Aries is about 12° north, and so will rise sooner (see 1.21.15–23n.); in fact the whole sign will rise in 56 minutes, coming up obliquely, *embelif,* on the horizon. By contrast, Libra (or Virgo) with its last point 12° south of its first, takes 2 hours and 52 minutes to rise, more nearly perpendicular to the horizon.

11–23 The horizon of an observer at the equator has the two poles at the north and south points. For him the heavenly bodies will rise and set vertically; their daily circles round the poles will be bisected by the horizon, so that days and nights are equal in length. The almucantar lines on the plate for 0° latitude would be straight; the horizon would be the *horizon rectus,* the east-west line through the center (the pole); the zenith would be on the equinoctial circle, and the intervening almucantar lines would run parallel to the horizon.

The passage *Ferther-over . . . right orisonte,* 11–16, is found in only two MSS, though the connection of sense requires it (see Textual Notes).

24–25   ascensions of signes in the right cercle: In modern terminology, the right ascension of the signs (or of each part of a sign); Skeat explains the origin of the term "right ascension," as derived from measuring the elevation of stars from a position on the equator, hence in the right circle.

30–36   right orisonte: The horizon of an observer at the equator. This horizon is at right angles to the equator and the equinoctial. At other latitudes the pole is above the horizon—**enhaunced upon the orisonte**—which is oblique to the equinoctial.

§27 Cf. Messahala 2.28 (Gunther, 181, 225). The intention here is to find the number of degrees in the equinoctial corresponding to each zodiacal sign.

§28 Cf. Messahala 2.29 (Gunther, 182, 225).

In the previous conclusion the passage of a complete sign was measured on the equinoctial, using the meridian line as a reference point. Here, however, the reference point is the *horizon obliquus,* so that the position, north or south, of the ends of the sign will make a difference. Skeat gives the results in the table mentioned in 2.26.6n.

22–28 The oblique signs (**tortuose signes, or croked signes**) are, of course, those whose last point is north of the first point.

§29 Cf. Messahala 2.19 (Gunther, 177, 222).

Take the actual altitude of the sun by the alidade; then turn the astrolabe over and put the degree of the sun, i.e., its position on the zodiac circle in the rete, at the same altitude as shown by the almucantars, east or west of the meridian according to the time of day. This gives the projection of the sun's position on the rete and plate; its actual angular distance from the meridian is measured in the border by the **label** (7). Turning the instrument over again, put the alidade at this same number of degrees in the border from the meridian, and point the alidade at the sun; when the sun shines through both sighting holes, place the instrument flat on the ground, keeping the alidade pointing the same way. Then the meridian line will point south, and the other lines to their points of the compass.

§30 Cf. Messahala 2.35 (Gunther, 185, 227).

Rubric: wey of the sonne: Not the ecliptic, but the sun's apparent path that day, as Chaucer explains in 14–17.

2–3   of the same height that is the degre of the sonne: Of the same altitude as is the sun's position. The noon altitude of the sun can be found from the astrolabe; the planet's position can be set on the astrolabe from its longitude and latitude in a table.

§31 Cf. Messahala 2.18 (Gunther, 176–77, 222).

Rubric: cenyth: Here this must refer to the point of sunrise as measured by the azimuth lines on the plate.

The method is simply to set the degree of the sun for the date on the eastern *Horizon obliquus* and read off the degree of azimuth at this point.

§32 Not in Messahala.

Rubric: conjunccyoun: The Latin Rubric in MS J has "coniuncciones solis et lune" (the conjunctions of sun and moon). When the moon's and sun's longitudes are the same, they are in conjunction, and the moon is new.

3–4   fro the midday of the day precedent: The numbering of the equal hours (by letters, see 1.15.10–14) runs from the meridian line, corresponding to midday; hours before noon are then numbered from midday of the day before. See 2.3n. The method is to find the sun's azimuth at a stated, predicted time, but Chaucer's account is somewhat laconic. The label is laid over the predicted time of the conjunction, then the sun's position in the zodiac brought to the edge of the label; this will represent the sun's position at the time of conjunction, and its degree of azimuth can be read off. Then the bearing of the conjunction is known.

§33 Cf. Messahala 2.17 (Gunther, 176, 222).

The method is to proceed as in 2.29.1–7; when the position of the sun is set, its azimuth can be read off.

§34 Cf. Messahala 2.32 (Gunther, 183–84, 226).

The method is first to take the altitude of the moon with the alidade. Then the rete is to be set by means of one of its marked stars, which should be more or less above or below the moon. Having taken its altitude by the alidade, set the point of the star-marker in the rete at the correct almucantar. Then since the moon is always close to the ecliptic, the degree of the ecliptic circle that lies on the almucantar of the moon's altitude will be the longitude of the moon.

13–17 The inclination to the ecliptic of the moon's orbit has a maximum value of 5°18′, which is the maximum latitude of the moon; the very slight difference this would make in measuring the moon's longitude is ignored in Comoun tretes, as is the difference made by the position of the fixed star with respect to the moon. Masi believes this caveat about the moon's latitude could have been suggested to Chaucer by a marginal note in MS Selden Supra 78 (Manuscripta 19:42).

§35 Cf. Messahala 2.36 (Gunther, 185, 227).

A planet's motion is direct when it moves through the stars from west to east; the sun's path along the ecliptic is direct. As a planet moves east near the ecliptic, it will rise later and lose altitude with respect to a fixed star used as a point of comparison, so long as it is to the east of the meridian. West of the meridian, as both are sinking, the planet will sink later and later, thus gaining altitude compared to the star. If the planet is retrograde, moving east to west against the sun, the opposite will hold. However, the orbits of the moon and other planets are inclined at small angles to the ecliptic, and so can undergo changes in their declination north or south that will upset the observations described for this conclusion.

24–26 The motion of the moon on its epicycle is retrograde, as noted by Florence M. Grimm, Univ. of Nebraska Sts. in Lang., Lit. and Crit. 2, 1919, 44n. For a brief clear statement of the basic constituents of the moon's orbit in the Ptolemaic system, see Hartner, Oriens-Occidens, 328 (Ptolemy, Almagest, 5.2).

§36 Cf. Messahala 2.37 (Gunther, 186, 227–28).

For an account of how the twelve astrological houses are calculated, see Hartner, Oriens-Occidens, 449–51, which also contains a calculation of the houses for a certain time and date in 1527. Briefly, the sections of the daylight period from the ascendant to *medium caelum* (see 2.4.46n.) and from the ascendant to *immum caelum* were each divided into three. In summer, north of the equator, the three former arcs would be longer than the latter. The right ascensions of the division points were transferred to the ecliptic, which was now divided into six houses from *medium caelum,* eastward through the ascendant to *immum caelum;* these six were numbers 10, 11, 12, 1, 2, 3 starting from *medium caelum.* The other six were marked off symmetrically to the first six by lines passing through the center of the earth, giving houses numbered 4, 5, 6, 7, 8, 9, from *immum caelum* through the descendant and on up. Houses 1 and 7, 2 and 8, 3 and 9, 4 and 10, 5 and 11, 6 and 12, each were equal to the other in degrees of arc, but no pair would necessarily, or probably, have the same number of degrees as another pair. The houses varied not only with the time of day (the degree of the ascendant), but with the time of year. Nicholas of Lynn, as already noted, supplied a table for the beginnings of the first six houses for each degree of the zodiac (see Pro 103–6n.). In the example added to this section in Br (see Textual Notes), the variation in

size of the houses for a specified ascendant is immediately clear.

1–2 the degre that ascendith: The degree of the ecliptic rising at the time for which a horoscope or election is needed.

2 upon the ende of the 8 houre inequal: On the eighth unequal hour line.

8 ascended: The MSS favor "ascendith"; *ascended,* however, seems more natural. The same situation occurs in 12.

17 inequal: The MSS favor omission, narrowly. But since Chaucer is giving detailed and careful instructions, he most probably included the word.

§37 Cf. Messahala 2.38 (Gunther, 186–87, 228).

1–2 thy 4 angles: See 2.4.46n. Here the angles are the four principal points themselves.

15 in the zodiak: The MSS are much divided, but favor this reading; the meaning of the α reading is difficult, and the meaning of the others is similar to the chosen one.

24–26 the nader of these 3 houses: There is confusion here. The three houses following the fourth are numbers 5–7, but the nadirs of the beginnings of numbers 2, 3, and 4 will indicate the beginnings of the eighth, ninth, and tenth. The beginnings of 5, 6, and 7 are the nadirs of the eleventh, twelfth, and first.

§38 Not in Messahala. Gunther finds a similarity between this section and a method described in De mensura horologii, ascribed to Bede, and translates the passage (Gunther, Early Sci. in Oxf. 2;203, 26). The similarity is clear, and the method would be less subject to error. But Pintelon (Ch's Treat. on the Astrolabe, 1940, 10) rightly objects to calling it a source for Chaucer.

10–12 The height of the pin is half the radius of the circle, hence the sun's altitude when the shadow touches the circumference must be the angle whose tangent is ½, about 26½°. According to Nicholas of Lynn (Kal., 75, 117), on any day from 23 February to 30 September, the first observation would have to be made before 10 A.M.

§39 Cf. the description of the meridian in Sacrobosco (Thorndike, 126, 91).

17 longitude of the toun: Really the difference in longitude between two towns; there was no fixed accepted meridian from which terrestrial longitude could be measured.

22–24 thei chaungen her almykanteras: Since they differ in latitude, their almucantars and their astrolabe plates would differ.

25 longitude of a climat: Here by *longitude* Chaucer means the length (unspecified) of a zone or "climate," along a line of latitude perhaps (as Skeat suggests) through the place after which the climate is named. Sacrobosco (Thorndike, 138–40, 110–12) divides the habitable part of the northern hemisphere into seven "climata," and specifies their breadths and their central lines of latitude. They occupy altogether a band of latitude from 12¾° to 50½°.

27 latitude of a climat: The breadth of the zone, north to south.

§40 Once the latitude and longitude of a planet are known, this temporary position must be transferred to the rete with the help of the **label.** Take a pair of dividers (a **compas**), and set one point on the degree of longitude in the rete; set the other point the degree of latitude away along the ecliptic. The scale of degrees at a point on the ecliptic will be effectively the same for longitude and latitude, and in any case since no planet ever reaches a high latitude (Venus reaches almost 9°, Mars 7°, Mercury and the Moon about 5°, Jupiter and Saturn less than 3°) the error is quite negligible. Taking Chaucer's first example, set 1° of Capricorn on the *horizon obliquus,* lightly wax the *label,* and set it over this point. The dividers are open a distance corresponding to 4°; set one point on the edge of the *label* over the point 1° of Capricorn so that it pricks the wax. Set the other point of the dividers directly inwards on the ecliptic circle, that is to say northwards, so that it pricks the wax, too. Slightly turn the rete until this second prick, representing on the *label* the planet's position, is on the horizon, and then the degree with which it ascends will be the degree of the ecliptic on the horizon. In effect a temporary star, or rather planet, marker has been added to the rete by means of the *label;* if the rete were of a transparent substance like perspex, the mark could have been made in ink on the rete itself. This method may be compared with 2.19.

7   in general: No decision can be made for this on MS evidence; but there does seem a contrast implied with **in speciall** preceding.

22   heved: A slight confusion; should be 1°.

**44–50   The first point of Capricorn is on the tropic of Capricorn, which is inscribed very close to the edge of the plate or the rete; a more southerly latitude means outside the ecliptic circle, so that there is too little space for it if it is in Capricorn, or Sagittarius.

79   hir: Some MSS read "his"; the noun *mōna* is masculine in OE; *luna* feminine in Lat.

82–83   thou shalt do wel ynow: This ending was probably added by an ancestor of π, the only group going from 2.40 on to the Supplementary Propositions.

**§§41–43   *Umbra Recta:* This means the shadow cast by an upright object on a flat plane; *umbra versa* is the shadow cast on an upright wall by a style projecting from it at right angles. All three propositions here are methods to find the height of an upright tower; if the tower subtends an angle to the observer's eye of more than 45°, the alidade will register on the *umbra recta* side of the square, but if less, on the *umbra versa* side. All three propositions are based on the properties of similar right-angled triangles, the alidade and two sides of the square forming a triangle similar to that formed by the line of sight to the top of the tower, the distance to the tower, and its height. For geometrical proofs, see Skeat's commentary on these propositions.

**§41   Cf. Messahala 2.46 (Gunther, 190–91, 230–31). The Latin chapter is numbered 2.45.

5   ligge even in a poynt: The observer should move until the alidade falls exactly on one of the divisions of the square.

8–9   4 is to 12: The sides of the shadow squares are divided into 12, see 1.12.4.

9–10   right so . . . of the tour: Only one MS, J, has this passage, and it has a superfluous "and" in 10: "and to the altitude." It makes the sense clearer, but the other MSS change 11, and so make sense, probably considering the passage a *superfluite of wordes.*

17–19   than is 5 12-partyes . . . thee and the tour: The inverted sentence order makes the difficulty: "then the distance between thee and the tower is five twelfths the height" (of the tower). No MS makes sense, and *of* has been moved from before *the space.*

**§42   Cf. Messahala 2.47 (Gunther, 191–92, 231). The Latin chapter is numbered 2.46.

**21–23   All MSS get the figures reversed, but recover at 24.

**§§44–45   The Toledan Tables (see FranT V.1273–79) were edited by the eleventh-century astronomer Arzachel (Al-Zarqālī) of Cordova. They were calculated for the longitude of Toledo, Spain, to give the planetary positions for any given time. For an account, see Zinner, Osiris 1, 1936, 747–74. They would need adjustment for different places, and for an account of English activity in the fourteenth century on a later set of tables, the Alfonsine Tables, also originally calculated for the latitude of Toledo, see Gunther, Early Sci. in Oxf. 2:44–65. Specimens of Alfonsine Tables are printed from Peterhouse MS 75.I in Equatorie, 79–84. The examples here use only a table of mean *motus,* to find the mean position of a planet at any time. A figure would be given for the "root," the time from which the tables were calculated. Then the change by periods of time from twenty-year periods (*anni collecti*), one-year periods (*anni expansi*), or diurnal, could be looked up; these were given in signs, or 30°, degrees, minutes, and seconds, and even *smale fraccions infinite.* The user simply calculated the difference in years, days, etc., of the time he was concerned with from the root, then looked for the planet in the tables for the appropriate number of years and days, added them together, and added the total to or subtracted it from the figure for the root, according as his date was after or before the root date.

§44.14   in direct of the same yer: Directly in line with, or directly under; i.e., in the same column in a table.

§45.2   Arsechieles: Arzachel's; Merton College MS 259 contains a copy, formerly the property of William Rede, Bishop of Chichester (d. 1385) (Gunther, Early Sci. at Oxf. 2:384).

**§46   This procedure seems pointless. Knowing the moon's position or compass bearing, when the tide is full, set the label over the moon's place in the zodiac, and move label and rete together till the label points to the position of the moon's compass bearing. Moving the label to the sun's position in the zodiac will show a certain time of day when the tide is in. But since the tide does not come in again exactly 12 hours later, predictions of future high tides would not be very accurate for more than a day or two.

25   the tyme of the conjunccioun: At this point the sun and moon are in the same longitude.

The Romaunt of the Rose

The Middle English translation of the *Roman de la rose* covers roughly one-third of the original. Lines 1–5810, corresponding to 1–5154 of the French, comprise the whole of Guillaume de Lorris's 4058-line poem and the beginning of Jean de Meun's continuation; lines 5811–7696, corresponding to French 10679–12360, contain all but the beginning and end of the Faus-Semblant (False-Seeming) episode. The unique manuscript gives no indication of the abrupt break and gap of over 5000 lines, though the final section has a running title, "Fals-semblant." This manuscript was printed by William Thynne in his 1532 edition as Chaucer's translation (see the introduction to the Textual Notes for details about Thynne's use of the manuscript). The first leaf of the manuscript is now lost so that we do not know whether it contained any attribution; however, because Thynne included many spurious works, his testimony means little or nothing.

Thynne would have felt justified in assuming the translation to be Chaucer's because in the Prologue to *The Legend of Good Women* (F 329) the God of Love accuses Chaucer of heresy for translating the *Roman de la rose*. Lydgate also says that Chaucer translated the *Roman* (Fall of Princes 1.308), and Deschamps calls Chaucer "grand translateur" on the basis of his supposed translation (Ballade 285, Oeuvres, SATF 2.138). None of this is, of course, evidence for Chaucer's authorship of the extant fragmentary translation, nor is it even proof that Chaucer ever completed a translation of the *Roman*. Commentators note that the *Romaunt* does not include the bawdy and antifeminist portions that the God of Love might have found libelous. Few scholars have been willing to credit that Chaucer ever completed a translation of a work longer than *The Canterbury Tales*. The praise of Deschamps, whose knowledge of English is questionable, is probably based on hearsay. Lydgate's testimony could well be based entirely on what is said in *The Legend*, but the God of Love's remarks cannot be taken as external evidence about Chaucer's translation since he is a character in a work of fiction, and Chaucer's defense of himself is part of the fictional situation. If Cupid is being treated satirically, like the Man of Law who credits Chaucer with several stories that he seems never to have written, the comedy would be enhanced if Chaucer were not guilty, if he had translated only that part of the poem in which the God of Love is celebrated as the presiding deity in the garden of Mirth. Whatever the truth may be about Chaucer's translation, there is no mention of it in the one totally serious and straightforward itemization of his works—the Retraction.

Doubts about the language and versification of the *Romaunt* led in the nineteenth century to a controversy about authorship that has never been completely resolved. Dialect and style are by no means uniform throughout the text, and M. Kaluza (Ch und der Rosenroman, 1893) first set forth the generally accepted division into three fragments: A (1–1705), B (1706–5810),

and C (5811–7696). Fragment A, a very literal translation, is fairly close to Chaucer's practice with a few exceptions, notably several rhymes. Fragment B is set apart by many Northern forms (though its dialect is a curious mixture), by un-Chaucerian rhymes, by a much looser style of translation, and by its peculiar translation of two words: French "bouton" (rosebud) is rendered *knoppe* in Fragment A but *bouton* in B; the character "Bel Acueil," called *Fayre-Welcomyng* in C, is always referred to as *Bialacoil* in B. Fragment C, though again more literal and closer to Chaucer's practice than B, contains a greater number of uncharacteristic rhymes than does A.

The authorship of these fragments has been much disputed. Brusendorff was the last critic to attempt to claim the whole for Chaucer. His theory that Chaucer's translation survives in a badly corrupted memorial transmission by a Northerner is dismissed by Robinson as "a rather desperate measure to save Chaucerian authorship." Kaluza had made a case that both A and C were by Chaucer, though he acknowledged that the evidence was weaker for C. He persuaded Skeat to accept A, but not C. The most recent theory by R. Sutherland holds A to be the work of Chaucer and B and C to be that of a Northern translator but argues that all three fragments have been edited by a "reviser" (see the introduction to the Textual Notes).

Insofar as one can arrive at any consensus, the evidence argues most strongly that Fragment B cannot be by Chaucer. The evidence is also strong that Fragments B and C are by different authors and fairly strong that C is not by Chaucer. Fragment A is probably by a different author from C, and there is no persuasive evidence that the author of A is *not* Chaucer.

One might conjecture that the three fragments came to be joined thus. An attempt was made to continue Fragment A, probably believed to be by Chaucer, perhaps for commercial purposes. Two different translators worked on the continuation, perhaps simultaneously; neither completed his task. It is worth noting that had B carried on to the point where C begins and C continued to the end, B would have translated about ten thousand lines and C about eleven thousand. The project was finally abandoned, though someone combined the three fragments into one continuous text. Fragment A may thus be said to be either by Chaucer or by a "Chaucerian" who successfully imitated his style. Fragments B and C are also the work of "Chaucerians," a consideration that easily explains the many echoes of Chaucer's genuine works, which were formerly taken as evidence of Chaucer's authorship.

Hammond (Ch: Bibl. Man., 451–53) provides a summary of the debate over authorship with full references up to 1908. Brusendorff gives a detailed recapitulation (Ch Trad., 383–87), and the notes to his chapter contain very full references to discussion of specific points at issue in the controversy. Among the main contributions to the question of authorship discussed above are the following: Lindner, ESt, 11, 1888, 163–73; Lounsbury, Studies in Ch, 1892, 2:3–166; Kittredge, Harv. Stud. and Notes 1, 1892, 1–65; Kaluza, Ch und der Rosenroman, 1893; Skeat, Ch Canon, 1900, 65–93; Koch, ESt, 27, 1900,

The explanatory notes to *The Romaunt of the Rose* were written by Alfred David.

1103

61–73, 227–34, and 30, 1902, 450–56, and 46, 1912, 103–9, and 55, 1921, 161–74; Lange, ESt, 29, 1901, 397–405, and Anglia 35, 1911, 338–46; Schoch, MP, 3, 1906, 339–58; Brusendorff, Ch Trad., 296–425; Sutherland, Romaunt and Roman, Parallel-Text Edn., 1968.

Fragment A, if in fact it is Chaucer's, is generally thought to be apprentice work. Brusendorff (Ch Trad., 385), because the God of Love links Chaucer's translation with *Troilus,* believes those works to have been written in close proximity and suggests a date "a few years before 1380." Language and versification, however, point to an earlier period. Though closely following the French, the translation of Fragment A nevertheless uses much of the native idiom and imagery found in the English metrical romances as is evident in Kittredge's study of the authorship and as has been demonstrated by Ando (Sts. in Eng. Lit., 1970, 63–74). Eckhardt makes a close analysis of stylistic differences between the French and English of Fragment A in SAC, 6, 1984, 41–63.

Both in the Middle Ages and in recent times the *Roman de la rose* has been a subject of controversy. In the fourteenth century a famous literary "Querelle" took place between its partisans and detractors. In the twentieth century it has been interpreted as an erotic, a philosophical, and a moral allegory. C. S. Lewis's influential study, Allegory of Love, analyzes the poem as the allegory of the psychology and progress of an illicit affair of courtly love. A. M. F. Gunn (The Mirror of Love, 1952) finds an exposition of neoplatonic doctrines of love. In sharp contrast, Robertson (Preface to Ch, 91–104, 196–207) interprets the poem as an ironic condemnation of sinful love entirely consonant with Christian doctrine. His ideas are elaborated by J. V. Fleming in The Roman de la rose, 1969, and Reason and the Lover, 1984, and by C. R. Dahlberg in the introduction and commentary to a prose translation of the poem, 1971. On moral allegory, see also R. Tuve, Allegorical Imagery, 1966, 233–84. P. Badel, Le roman de la rose au XIVe siècle, 1980, gives a detailed account of the poem's reception in the Middle Ages and also places the modern criticism in historical perspective (see esp. 1–13). A useful introduction to the poem and the criticism, with a chapter on the *Romaunt* and excellent bibliographies, is M. Luria, A Reader's Guide to the Roman de la rose, 1982. Russell A. Peck, Ch Biblio: Romaunt, 1985, is an annotated bibliography on both the *Romaunt* and the *Roman de la rose.*

The *Roman* is among the most richly illuminated of medieval texts. Robertson, Tuve, Fleming, and Dahlberg all discuss the iconography of the manuscript illuminations and print reproductions. See also Alfred Kuhn, Die Illustration des Rosenromans, Jahrbuch der kunsthistorischen Sammlungen des allerhöchsten Kaiserhauses 31, 1913, 1–66.

The French edition cited in the notes, the one most fully annotated and that provides the greatest number of variants, is that of E. Langlois, SATF, 1914–24, 5 vols. More recently the *Roman* has been edited by F. Lecoy, 1965–70, 3 vols., and by D. Poirion, 1974. Kaluza, Ch Soc, ser. 1, 83, 1891, prints a parallel French text alongside a transcript of the unique manuscript of the *Romaunt.* Sutherland provides a parallel French text to his edition. Besides Dahlberg's translation (based on Langlois), there is a line-by-line modern French prose translation by A. Lanly, 1971–76, 2 vols. in 4 (based on Lecoy).

In the following notes there is no attempt to offer a detailed collation of the French and English texts, though the French text is frequently called on to elucidate the English and attention is drawn to the more interesting departures in the translation. A few references are made to important sources of the *Roman* and to parallels in other medieval literature, including, of course, Chaucer's works. The basic study of the influence of the *Roman* on Chaucer is Fansler, Ch and RR, 1914. For further information about the sources and the intellectual background of the French poem, see Langlois's notes and his Origines et sources du Roman de la rose, 1891. Also of great value, especially for the part of Jean de Meun, is G. Paré, Les idées et les lettres au XIIIe siècle, 1947.

On the principles followed in the edition of the English text, which, because of new evidence about the relationship between Thynne's edition and the Glasgow MS, differ from those of Robinson and other editors, see the introduction to the Textual Notes.

FRAGMENT A

1   The significance of dreams is a recurrent topic in Chaucer's poetry. See NPT VII.2922–3157 and n.; HF 1–52 and n.; Tr 5.358–85 and n.

7   **Macrobes:** Macrobius, author of the Commentary on Cicero's Somnium Scipionis (The Dream of Scipio), the source of much medieval dream lore. See PF 31n.

9   **undoth:** Fr. "escrist," but a variant has "espont," which corresponds to the English. In BD 284 and NPT VII.3123 Chaucer speaks of Macrobius as the author of the Somnium, but in PF 31 he names *Tullyus* as the author and shows firsthand knowledge of the work. Guillaume de Lorris, whose reference echoes Chrétien de Troyes's Erec (see Langlois's n.), may have known Macrobius only as a name. See next note.

10   **kyng Cipioun:** Fr. "roi Scipion." Scipio was not a king. This passage doubtless lies behind the same mistake in BD 286 and HF 916–18 (see n.).

22   **cariage:** Liddell's emendation of *corage;* Fr. "paage."

38   **rede you here:** Advise you to hear. An alternative meaning, "read to you here," is less likely because it violates the convention of *rime riche* (see GP I.17–18n.).

57–62   Cf. BD 410–15; ProLGW F 125–29 and n., G 113–17.

71–131   The description of the birds, the landscape, and the river and of the garden of Mirth below has many parallels in medieval poetry, including Chaucer's own. For illustrations and possible sources, see Langlois's notes. An especially close description is that of the emir's orchard in Floire et Blancheflor (see 140–42 below). On the topos of the *locus amoenus* (pleasance) in Latin poetry, see E. R. Curtius, European Lit., 195–200. Curtius (202n.) cites a fourteenth-century marginal gloss (quoted by Langlois, Fr. 78n.) that associates the whole description with Matthew of Vendôme's Ars versificatoria, as evidence of dependence on Latin rhetorical tradition. D. Thoss, Stud. z. Locus Amoenus im Mittelalter, 1971, 113–38, gives contrary evidence that the description derives independently from vernacular tradition and departs in significant ways from Matthew of Vendôme's model.

104   bastyng: The sleeves were fashionably sewn or laced. Cf. 570, the portrait of *Ydelnesse.* Langlois notes other examples in French. See also his article, Romania 33, 1904, 405–7.

119   straghter wel away: Much more spread out. From the pp. of *strecchen;* Fr. "plus espandue."

140–42   The images are wall paintings. **Portraied, entailled,** and **ymages,** taken over directly from the Fr., could suggest that the images are statues, but subsequent references are to paintings. Langlois notes the painted garden wall in Floire et Blancheflor, ed. Krüger, Rom. Stud. 45:86.

148   hir: In Fr. all these are female because of grammatical gender. The translation follows the original, but in English the same personifications could be male as *Enuye* and *Coveitise* are in Piers Plowman, B 5.75, 186.

149   mynoresse: A Franciscan nun? See MED s.v. *menouresse.* This instance is cited as a possible error for "meveresse" and glossed "? an anti Franciscan use." Previous eds., except Fisher, emend to "moveresse" (Fr. "moverresse"), a quarrelsome woman, stirrer-up of strife. But the reading probably derives from a variant "meneresse" (see Brusendorff, Ch Trad., 308) and is to be understood as referring to a nun. Cf. the quarrelsome convent whose abbess is the aunt of Wrath in Piers Plowman B 5.153–68.

191   these smale harlotes: *These* has a generalizing sense (Fr. "ces"); cf. 411 and see also KnT I.1531 and n.

225   perche: A horizontal pole put up in rooms for hanging clothes.

247–300   Based in part on Ovid, Met. 2.775–87.

276   for pure wood: Cf. *for hor,* 356; *For moiste,* 1564; *for wod,* HF 1747; *for pure ashamed,* Tr 2.656; and see KnT I.2142–44n.

292   baggyngly: Fr. "borgneiant." MED cites this as the sole instance.

325   tere hir swire: Not in the Fr.; added for rhyme.

356   for hor: This is the sole instance of *hor* as a substantive. See 276 above.

358   synne: Fr. "pechiez."

363   Fr. "Les oreilles avoit mossues [var. velues]," i.e., wrinkled. See Langlois's n.

366   her hondes lorne: Fr. "E toutes les denz si perdues." The English derives from a variant "mains" (hands) for "denz" (teeth).

369–99   Cf. IntrMLT II.20–24.

387   Cf. Ovid, Met. 15.234–36: "Tempus edax rerum" (Time the devourer of things).

413   don there write: Fr. "escrite," which Langlois glosses as "indicated by an inscription."

415   Poope-Holy: Fr. "Papelardie" (from *paper,* "eat," and *lard,* "bacon"). The English word is apparently a folk etymology, meaning "holy as the Pope." It occurs as an adjective in Piers Plowman B 13.283, "Was noon swich as hymself, ne noon so pope holy." Lange, Angl. 38:481–82, takes this as evidence of direct influence of Piers Plowman on the Romaunt.

429   Illustrations portray her as a nun.

446   Matt. 6.16.

468   Job 3.3.

481–82   gardyn : theryn: *Gardyn* rhymes six times in Fragment A but nowhere else in Chaucer nor in Fragments B and C. Within the line, Chaucer normally stresses the first syllable (except possibly MerT IV.2136). See Koch, ESt, 27:66.

482   shepherde: Fr. "bergiers."

490   daungerous: Fr. "desdeigneus (var. 'dangereus') ne chiches." Cf. 591, and see also 3018n.

505–6   On the rhyme **care : ware,** see textual note.

530–60   On the conventional details in this and other portraits, see D. S. Brewer, MLR 50, 1955, 257–69, and cf. BD 817–1040n.

540   basyn scoured newe: Fr. "bacins," which is copper according to Langlois.

544   The openyng of hir yen: Fr. "Li entriauz," i.e., the space between her eyes. Langlois's note gives instances of a "large entrueil" as a mark of beauty. Cf. Tr 5.813–14.

546   yen grey: A favorite color for the eyes (cf. 822, 862, and see GP I.152n.).

554   Burgoyne: Supplied in the translation for rhyme.

579   journe: Fr. "jornee." Lange, Anglia 38:480, cites Piers Plowman B 14.136: "And til he haue doon his deuoir and his dayes iournee."

593   Ydelnesse: Fr. "Oiseuse." The allegory is based on Ovid's Rem. am. 139, "Otia si tollas, periere Cupidinis arcus" (Take away leisure and Cupid's bow is broken). Cf. BD 797–98, KnT I.1940, SNT VIII.1–2.

602   of Alexandryn: The word is an adjective in French, and some editors omit *of.*

624   in-tyl Ynde: Not in the Fr. Cf. WBPro III.824n.

648   paradys erthly: The Garden of Eden, as distinct from the celestial paradise. On the relation of medieval notions of the earthly paradise to classical and Christian tradition, see A. B. Giammatti, The Earth. Par. and Renaissance Epic, 1966, 11–93, esp. 60–66 on the Roman de la rose.

657–65   There is no exact correspondence between the English and French lists of birds; the choice of names by both poets was to some extent determined by rhyme and meter. Skeat (1:421) identifies the **alpes** as bullfinches. The **wodewal** may be a small songbird of uncertain identity, "probably (as later) the Golden Oriole" (OED s.v. *woodwall*), or it may be a kind of woodpecker (Skeat, citing Promptorium parvulorum). Skeat identifies the **terins** as siskins and the **mavys** as song thrushes.

668   That other: For another instance of *that* modifying a noun in the plural, see 991.

676   man that myghte dye: Fr. "ome mortel."

680–84   According to the Fr. "sereines" (Sirens) get their name because their voices are "series" (clear) and "saines" (pure). In Bo 1.pr1.69 Chaucer translates Lat. "Sirenes" as *mermaydenes.* Lat. "serenus" is rendered as *cler* in Bo 1.m4.1 and 2.m4.18.

692   erst: For the idiom, cf. KnT I.1566 and n.

720   reverye: Fr. "reverdie." Skeat and Robinson emend to "reverdie," but this sense of the word is unattested in English. RvT I.4005, *revelrye,* which refers to the merriment, high jinks of the two clerks, has the var. "reverye." Thynne reads "revelrye."

744   karole: Originally a dance in a ring accompanied by a song. Illustrations show the dancers in a circle with hands joined.

745   karolede: Fr. "chantoit."

763–92   The flute players, minstrels, timbrel players, and dancers are professional entertainers hired by Mirth, as distinct from the aristocratic dancers in the *karole.*

768   in this contre: Fr. "en nul reine" (in any country). The translation perhaps refers to England.

840   toslytered: Slashing a garment to reveal the color of the lining was fashionable, especially in the late four-teenth century. Cf. ParsT X.418, and Mum and the Soth-segger, ed. Mabel Day and Robert Steele, EETS 199, 1934: "a gyse the queyntest of all / A wondir coriouse crafte ycome now of late, / That men clepith kerving the clothe all to pecis, / That seven goode sowers sixe wekes after / Moun not sett the seemes ne sewe hem ageyn" (lines 3.162–66).

843   shoon decoped, and with laas: Fr. "solers deco-pez a laz."

866–67 A couplet may be lost. Fr. "Ele ot la bouche petitete, E por baisier son ami prete" (She had a tiny little mouth ready to kiss her *ami*).

868   likyng: Fr. (variant) "plaisant" (Kaluza).

892 For the missing line Thynne reads: "Ypaynted al with amorettes." Fr. "Faite par fines amoretes," which must mean that the God of Love's robe was fashioned by "pure lovers"—perhaps young women who are "fines" or courtly lovers. Thynne, though, construes "amoretes" as an ornament of the robe like the *scochouns, briddes,* etc., in the lines following. Skeat and MED gloss "?love-knots." That the ME translator understood the word in its true sense is suggested by 878–79, where *The God of Love . . . can devyde Love* translates "depart Amoretes"; and see 4755 and note 4755–56 below. The translation in Thynne misses the distinction between Fr. "par" (was made *by*) and "a" (made *with*) in "A losenges, a es-cuciaus."

908   roses reed: The Fr. does not specify the color of the roses here or at the point corresponding to 1680. Kuhl, PQ 24, 1945, 33–38, suggests that by making the roses red the translator intended a compliment to Blanche of Lancaster and John of Gaunt whose family emblem was the red rose. However, it is altogether natu-ral to assume that the rose of love is red.

915   archaungell: No such bird name exists; Fr. "me-senges" is the titmouse. The word has been explained as a corruption of *acanthyllus* (goldfinch; Thompson, N&Q 175, 1938, 332) and of *wariangel* (used in FrT III.1408), the red-backed shrike (Kunstmann, MLN 55, 1940, 259–62). The right explanation, however, seems to be that of Whitteridge, Eng. and Ger. Sts. 3, 1950, 34–36, who cites "arcanges" (archangel) in a spurious line in a Fr. MS; some such variant would have misled the transla-tor into adding a new bird to the language.

923   Turke bowes: The Turkish bow is a powerful, short, composite, reflexed bow. See Webster, MLN 47, 1932, 260, and Herben, Spec 12, 1937, 485. The idea of two bows and two sets of arrows with opposite quali-ties comes from Ovid, Met. 1.468–71. Langlois cites other examples from medieval literature.

997 "The explanation here promised was never writ-ten" (Robinson).

1018   wyndred: The word, recorded only here and in 1020, must be an attempt to anglicize Fr. "guigniee" (spelled "wigniee" in some MSS), which the translator may not have understood. "Guignier" appears in for-mulaic expressions with "farder" and means roughly the same thing. Fr. "Ne fu fardee ne guignee" (She was not painted or made up). See also Fr. 2170, "ne te farde ne ne guigne," rendered in B 2285, "Fard not thi visage." The French does not mention "brows." The translation may introduce **browis** through misunderstanding "guig-nee" as "plucked."

1031   Sore plesaunt: The exact sense of *sore* is doubtful.

Fr. "Sade [var. sage], plaisant." Here "Sade" (agreea-ble) is simply another of Beauty's traits. As an adverb, *sore* qualifies words denoting pain, grief, or intense feel-ing. Perhaps here it has the force of colloquial modern "awfully," "terribly." See textual note for possible emendations. Cf. 4305.

1050   losenger: The traditional enemy of lovers in troubador poetry and romance.

1089   durst: The verbs *dar* and *tharf* were often con-fused. Cf. 1324. Precious stones were thought to be an antidote for poison and to have other medicinal proper-ties. Cf. Tr 2.344 and n.

1091–92   love . . . byhove: Northern rhyme. For its bearing on the question of authorship, see Kaluza, ESt 23, 1897, 336–38, and an exchange between Luick and Kaluza, ESt 24, 1898, 342–44.

1093   Frise: Not in the French. Cook, MLN 31, 1916, 442, would gloss as Phrygia, citing Rom. de Thèbes, 6630, "tot l'or de Frise," as evidence that the latter was considered a realm of gold, but Skeat is probably correct that the word here is merely a rhyme-tag. See Buk 23n.

1094   mourdaunt: A trim (usually metallic) fastened to the end of the girdle and causing it to hang down; here the material is another precious stone with medicinal properties. Cf. 1089–90.

1152 Alexander the Great was a type of liberality, an apt kinsman for *Largesse.*

1158   sende: The normal preterite *sente* is avoided for rhyme.

1182   adamaunt: Cf. KnT I.1990n., PF 148n.

1232   sukkenye: Fr. "sorquenie," a loose frock worn over the robe. It was made of fine material (probably linen), not of hempen hards (the coarse part of flax).

1235   ridled: Langlois believes the English translator misunderstood Fr. "cuillie," which he glosses as "ajusté" (fitted).

1240   roket: Fr. "sorquenie," therefore the same as *suk-kenye* in 1232 (see n.). It is said (1241–42) to be more becoming than a *cote,* a plain dress.

1250   The lordis sone of Wyndesore: At the time Guillaume de Lorris was writing, the lord of Windsor would have been Henry III, and his son, Edward (born 1239). But Langlois cites references associating Windsor with King Arthur; if Guillaume meant Arthur, though, he must have overlooked the fact that Arthur's only son is Mordred. For the word order, see Language and Ver-sification, p. xxxviii.

1324   durst: See 1089 above.

1352–66 On the "mixed forest" as a feature of the *locus amoenus,* see Curtius, European Lit., 194–95.

1353–54 The translator misunderstood the French, which says that there were at least one or two of every kind of fruit-bearing tree except a few that were too ugly.

1369   greyn de parys: Fr. "Graine de parevis." The English form derives from a Fr. biform in popular usage, "graine de parais (pareys, pareis)." By folk etymology this became "grain of Paris," but the translator recog-nizes it as the correct English equivalent for "parevis," and there is no reason to emend to "paradys." See Schöffler, Anglia Beibl. 29, 1918, 46–48.

1453   at good mes: A hunting term. Fr. "en bon leu."

1458   Kyng Pepyn: Fr. "puis Charle ne puis Pepin [var. Karles le fils Pepin]."

1469 See Ovid, Met. 3.356–503, for the story of Nar-cissus.

1537 warisoun: Fr. "guerredon," which Liddell suggests may have been confused by the translator with "guerison" (cure). Perhaps "cure" is intended here as an ironic "requital."

1553 For the line missing in the MS Thynne gives: "Unto the welle than wente I me." Fr. "De la fontaine m'apressai" (I drew near the well). A slightly more idiomatic version might be "To the welle than gan I drawe me." *Went* is rarely reflexive in Chaucer, but *draw* as a verb of motion is consistently so. Cf. 1546 and 3069–70.

1568 Two cristall stonys: These have been interpreted as the eyes of the lady (Lewis, Allegory of Love 117, 128–29); the dreamer's own eyes (Robertson, Preface to Ch, 95); and both of these together in the sense that the lady's eyes reflect back the essential self through the mirror of the other (Köhler, Journ. des savants, 1963, 95–100).

1601 mirrour perilous: On the aspects of hydromancy and crystallomancy in this passage, see Köhler, Journ. des savants, 1963, 98.

1652 enclos: A French form used for rhyme.

1674 rone: Fr. "soz ciaus" (beneath heaven). A Northern word, probably used for rhyme. OED cites Pistill of Susan 72: "the rose ragged on rys, richest on Rone."

1705 Fragment A is generally thought to break off here in mid-sentence, and the following line, which fails to complete the sense and makes a false rhyme, is attributed to the author of B seeking to continue the unfinished or truncated text of A. Kaluza's suggested emendation of "filde" for **dide** (Fr. "replenist") would complete the sentence. Koch, ESt 55:168, accepting the emendation, would credit the bad rhyme to the author of A (who he denies is Chaucer) and extend the first fragment to 1714. Thynne reads "dyed" for *dide,* taken by Reeves (MLN 38, 1923, 124) and Fisher as "dyed" (saturated). Skeat conjectured a lost portion of A, continuing with some such line as "Fulfild of baume, withouten doute." Liddell suggests that the present rhymes may have been substituted for a couplet like *swete* (vb.): *swete* (adj.); or *replete* (vb.): *swete;* he, too, believes Fragment A could extend to 1714. "In the case of such complete uncertainty it is best to let the MS. reading stand unaltered" (Robinson).

FRAGMENT B

Only a few typical examples of irregular rhymes and usage in Fragment B will be noted; see 1785–86 below. For comprehensive lists of such forms, see Skeat's edition 1:4–6.

1721 botoun: On the word (spelled variously in the MS) as a distinguishing feature of Fragment B, see introductory note.

1728 Love enters the heart through the eye; see KnT I.1096 and note 1077–97.

1766 certis evenly: Emended by Skeat and Robinson to "certeynly."

1776 withouten were: Fr. "senz menacier." Skeat notes that the excessive use of the tag *withouten* (*doute, drede, wene, were,* etc.) is characteristic of Fragment B.

1785–86 desir : ner: Imperfect rhyme. Other examples are 2037–38, *joynt : queynt;* 2441–42, *desyr : ner;* 2779–80, *desir : maner;* 4181–82, *ademant : foundement.*

1794–95 Not in the French. Proverbial; see Whiting H302, H303. Cf. 2084–85.

1797 feyne: Variant of "fine" for rhyme.

1802 The names of the arrows, as in the French, do not correspond exactly to those given in the earlier description, 949–63.

1811–12 The rhyme **hit** (pp.) **: flit** (inf.) is not Chaucerian; other instances of the infinitive without final *-e* in rhyme are 1873–74, 1939–40, 1981–82, 2615–16, 2627–28, 2629–30, 2645–46, 2755–56, 3099–3100.

1813–14 Another irregular rhyme, in which the final *-e* of the weak preterite, *wroughte,* is not present.

1818 ner: Positive here and in 1848, the form is normally comparative in Chaucer. KnT I.1439 is an exception to the rule.

1820 Proverbial; Whiting C201.

1849–50 I : malady (for *maladye*): An example of the un-Chaucerian *y : ye* rhyme, used by Skeat as a primary test of authenticity. Other instances are 1861, 2179, 2209, 2493, 2737, 3241, 4145.

1853–54 thore : more: Perhaps a substitution for the Northern forms *thar : mar* (Skeat), but possibly the translator simply changed the normal *there* to rhyme with *more.* For *thar* in rhyme, see 1857.

1892 The MS has a nonsensical line added by a later hand in a space originally left blank: "That he hadde the body hole made." Thynne substitutes: "Through the body in my herte made." This makes a kind of sense but has no equivalent in the French, which says that the God of Love made the ointment with his own hands to comfort pure lovers: "Amors l'avoit fait a ses mains Por les fins amanz conforter." Some word like "lovers" must be the antecedent of *her sores* and *they* (1893–94); therefore, an intervening couplet has perhaps been lost. A hypothetical reading (with the emendation "I" for *he* in 1891) would be: "Somdell to yeve aleggement Upon the woundes that I had. [To comfort lovers he had it maad]."

1906 Rokyng: Crouching, cowering? Or does the lover "rock" the shaft to extract the arrow? Skeat and Robinson take the word as a variant of *rouken,* as in KnT I.1308. Fisher glosses: "moving it back and forth slightly." Not in the French.

1928 lepande: A Northern participle; cf. 2263.

1965 For **love** possibly read "lovers," but the sense implied may be "[the wound] of love." In the French, the God of Love's hand, which gave the wound, must perform the cure. The motif of the magic weapon that alone can cure the wound it inflicts (as in the story of Achilles and Telephus) is applied to love; cf. SqT V.156–65.

1978 "Mercy of that [one] I await"(?). Punctuating after *Mercy,* editors obtain the sense: "For which [i.e., Mercy] I am waiting," close to the Fr. "la merci que j'atens"; but *of* is awkward in such a reading.

2002 sauff: See textual note.

2022–27 A verb is required to complete the sense. Liddell emends *And also* (2024) to "Nedes is." Fr. "Dedenz lui ne puet demorer Vilanie" (In him churlishness may not remain).

2028 prisoun: The French has nothing about Love's prison. Liddell suggests a misunderstanding of Fr. "mauvaise aprison" (ill breeding) for "aprisoner" (to make prisoner).

2037 The posture of the vassal performing homage before his feudal lord.

2038   For the idiom, see GP I.785n.

2077–78   justice: Guards? controls? (Liddell: punishments?). Fr. "Tel garnison i avez mise Qui le garde bien e justise" (You have set such a garrison over it as will guard it and rule over it well). A variant of the second line reads "Qui mout le guerroie et jostise." The translator may have taken "guerroie" (preserve) as a form of "guerreier" (to make war). Thus the sense of the English is probably that Love has set such enforcers of his law on the heart that it is in a state of siege.

2088   Langlois traces the image of the key to Chrétien de Troyes's Yvain, 4632–34, and Perceval, 3810–11.

2149–52   In the French, the God of Love speaks these lines to the lover.

2157–62   Not in the French.

2161   poyntith: The MSS were unpunctuated; hence the reader must construe both syntax and sense.

2181–82   Cf. WBT III.1158.

2185–2202   Not in the French. Sutherland's edition, xxx–xxxi, gives a parallel to the first six of these lines from additions made to the poem in a version by Gui de Mori. Skeat thought the passage was inspired by the sermon on *gentilesse* in WBT. Brusendorff, Ch Trad., 399–402, took the verbal similarities with the WBT as evidence of Chaucer's authorship of these lines. He points out that the whole passage derives ultimately from Jean de Meun, 18607–34; that text doubtless underlies the relevant passages in both Gui de Mori and the WBT. Brusendorff took the present passage to be an insertion by the transmitter into Fragment B of a bit of the rest of Chaucer's translation of the Roman, now lost.

2203–4   Cf. Ovid, Ars Am. 2.604. Much of the God of Love's advice is lifted directly from Ovid.

2206–12   For references to Kay and Gawain as types of *vilanye* and courtesy, respectively, see Langlois's notes. On Gawain, cf. SqT V.95.

2255–84   Cf. Ars Am. 1.513–24.

2263   sittand: A Northern participle; cf. 1928.

2273   yeve: The translator seems to be thinking here of alms-giving. The advice in the French is to dress up within one's means.

2285–88   The French explicitly describes such practices as effeminate: "Ce n'apartient s'as dames non, Ou a ceus de mauvais renon" (This pertains only to ladies or to men of ill repute).

2311–12   Fr. "Se tu te senz viste e legier, Ne fai pas de saillir dangier" (If you feel nimble and light, don't be reluctant to leap). The idea comes from Ovid, Ars Am. 1.596: "Et quacumque potes dote placere, place" (Please by whatever gifts you can).

2323   foote: Fr. "fleüter." Kaluza suggests the emendation "floyte."

2325–28   Not in the French.

2329   scarce: Fr. "aver."

2338   kyssyng: Fr. "ris" (a smile).

2345–48   Not in the French.

2363–65   Fr. "En un seul leu tot ton cuer mis, Si qu'il n'i soit mie demis, Mais toz entiers, senz tricherie" (Bestow your heart in just one place, that it be not only a part but entire, without treachery). The meaning of the English, which depends on Liddell's emendation "Of" for the MS *For,* is doubtful. Skeat, reading "For trecherie in sikernesse," translates, "Against treachery, in all security."

  halfen dool: From OE "healfne dæl," the Chaucerian *halvendel.*

2367–68   Cf. Tr 1.960–61n.

2383–86   Proverbial; Whiting G84.

2398   Cf. Tr 2.811.

2427–28   Proverbial; Walther 32036: "Ubi amor, ibi oculus" (Where love is, there is the eye); cf. Whiting L558.

2478   Proverbial; cf. Tr 1.449n.

2480   Cf. MilT I.3703.

2497–2502   Meaning unclear, but the manuscript reading has been retained with the following possible interpretation: The lover did not speak because (at the time) he told himself he would have gained no more than to speak of (to?) her; but yet she would (he thinks now) have greeted him with an embrace, which would have been worth more than a treasure. Liddell suggests the emendations [though] *thou* (2497) . . . *But* [that] (2499), yielding a meaning closer to the Fr. "Car se tu n'en peüsses traire Fors solement un bel salu, Si t'eüst il cent mars valu" (Because if you'd got nothing out of it except a fine salutation [i.e., a kiss of greeting], it would have been worth one hundred marks to you). Skeat, Robinson, and Fisher emend *But yitt* (2499) to "But yif," perhaps correctly.

2507–9   For fear of arousing attention, the lover cannot find occasion to visit her house.

2517–22   On the importance of secrecy in love, and especially concealment in visiting, cf. Tr 2.365–85.

2564   Fr. "Come ome qui a mal as denz" (Like a man with a toothache).

2573   The still proverbial "castles in Spain" first appears in Guillaume de Lorris and for the first time in English here. The proverbial meaning had not yet established itself. The reference is to the fantasy of a private retreat for lovers (a castle) in some distant place (Spain). "Spain" serves for the purpose of rhyme, not from any romantic associations, though Spanish castles placed high on rocks perhaps suggest the exotic (cf. HF 1117); the formula is found with other place names completing other rhymes. See Gallacher, Journal of American Folklore 76, 1963, 324–29, Whiting C77, and Hassell C100.

2592   Syntax and meaning are unsatisfactory. Liddell emends to "Fro joye" (Why will you not succor me [parted] from joy?). Robinson adopts the emendation, but divides the sentence differently (Why will you not succor me? From joy, I believe, I languish). MED s.v. *langouren* (b) renders the beginning of the line "For joy." Given the looseness of syntax and the vagueness of the Middle English translation at this point, it seems best to make whatever sense one can of the MS reading.

2619–21   "It were better of her alone . . . (that) I should cast a look on her in goodly fashion" (?). All editors emend 2621 to either "on me ycast" or "of hir ycast," making the translation conform to the French where it is the lady's look that might assuage the lover's woe: "d'un seul baisier Me deignoit la bele aaisier." However, given the rarity of the participle with the prefix *y-* in the MS (see the introduction to the Textual Notes), it seems proper to avoid substituting one poor translation for another. The phrase **of hir alloone** is an embarrassment to either version.

2628   liggen: Northern form; the alternate *lyen* occurs in 2631, and *ly*, in rhyme, at 2629, 2645. It is futile, however, to make Fragment B consistent with itself by emending the verb.

2641   contene: See MED s.v. *conteinen* 5(a). Fr. "contendras," which Langlois glosses "comport oneself."

2673–76   The text is unclear and departs from the

French. In the French the lover is told to kiss the door before he departs (cf. Tr 5.551–52), prompting Kaluza's suggestion that 2676 should read: "Thou kisse the dore er thou go away." The passage is probably corrupt. On the use of **relyk** as a term of endearment, cf. 2907 and ProLGW F 321 and n.

2684 Cf. Ovid, Ars Am. 1.729, 733.

2695 Cf. Ars Am. 2.251–60.

2710 Cf. Ars Am. 2.357–58, also the proverb "Out of sight, out of mind," for which Langlois cites several parallels; see also Whiting E213.

2737–39 Proverbial; Whiting G 356.

2775 Fr. "Esperance par sofrir vaint," from the proverb "Qui patitur, vincit," which is rendered in Tr 4.1584, *The suffrant overcomith* (see n.).

2778 Proverbial; Whiting H474.

2793–96 Fr. "C'est Douz Pensers, qui lor recorde Ce ou Esperance s'acorde" (That is Sweet Thoughts who reminds them of that which Hope agrees to). The translator has preserved the rhymes but garbled the sense: Sweet-Thought helps the lover remember whatever thing is most agreeable to his heart, wherever she (the lady) may be.

2806 Cf. Tr 1.365–66 and note 365–67.

2833–36 Not in the French.

2840–50 Langlois believes that Guillaume has followed a popular song. G. Paris, Hist. litt. de la France 28:373n., sees a literary allusion to the lady of Fayel. The translator has made a free and expanded version of the song, which is only four lines long in the French.

2984 **Bialacoil:** Fr. "Bel Acueil," rendered by the translator of Fragment C as *Fair-Welcomyng*. Allegorically he represents the lady's disposition to be open and receptive to the lover's presence. See Lewis, Allegory of Love, 122–23.

3018 **Daunger:** *Daunger* is the personification of something like disdain, standoffishness: "the rebuff direct, the lady's 'snub' launched from the height of her ladyhood . . . and perhaps her anger and contempt" (Lewis, Allegory of Love, 124). On the literary uses of "lufdaungere," see Barron, in Med. Misc. Pres. to Eugene Vinaver, ed. F. Whitehead et al., 1965, 1–18.

3024–32 The best French MSS name four guardians of the Rose at this point: "Daunger," "Male Bouche" *(Wykked-Tonge),* "Honte" *(Shame),* and "Peor" *(Drede).* The English translation comes from one of the great majority of French MSS designated by Langlois as Class II, which omit "Peor" and speak of only three guardians. Cf. 3060, 3066. See Les manuscrits du Rom. de la rose, 1910, 241–43.

3088 Not in the French. Cf. 3115, *it may not arise;* Fr. "ce qui ne puet avenir."

3130–37 *Daunger* is described as a typical *vilain* or peasant in romance literature with grotesque, animalistic features. See Langlois's notes for examples. Two notable examples are the ugly herdsman in Chrétien's Yvain and the peasant in Aucassin et Nicolette. See also A. M. Colby, The Portrait in 12th Cent. Fr. Lit., 1965, 72–88, 170–73.

3136 For the line missing in the MS Thynne gives, "His eyes reed sparclyng as the fyre glowe"; Fr. "S'ot les iauz roges come feus" (He had eyes red like fire). Note *eyes* in place of the usual *eyen.*

3137 **kirked:** See MED s.v. *croked* 1(d). Fr. "le nés froncié" (the nose wrinkled).

3146 Proverbial; Whiting F118.

3185 Not in the French.

3191 Reason belongs to the class of allegorical mentors who appear to the protagonist in distress as Philosophy does to Boethius, or Holy Church to Will in Piers Plowman.

3205–11 Nature as the creator of beauty is a common topos in descriptive portraits in Latin and Romance literature; see Curtius, European Lit., 181–82. This variant of the topos—not Nature, but only God Himself could create such beauty—occurs in Chrétien's Yvain, 1492–99. Langlois cites the latter as a parallel along with a poem in P. Meyer, Recueil d'anciens textes, 1874–77, 372.

3253–54 Fr. "E de Dangier neient ne monte Envers que de ma fille Honte" (And *Daunger* counts for nothing compared to my daughter Shame).

3256 Fr. "Con cele qui n'est pas musarde." Cf. 4235.

3294 Fr. "Mes au lessier [var. a l'issir] a grant mestrise," i.e., although it is easy to fall in love, it requires great mastery to extricate oneself again. See textual note for the MS reading and other emendations. Liddell reads, "And to leve of his gret maistrie, I rede thee Love awey to dryve." But in the MS *I* (3295) is a large initial beginning a new paragraph.

3326 **in the peyne:** Not in the French. Cf. KnT I.1133.

3346 **a Freend:** Fr. "Amis ot non" (He was called Friend). It is unclear whether the translator intended a proper name.

3356 **meygned:** Fr. "Qui par poi ne me vost mangier" (Who was about to eat me).

3422 **That:** Perhaps replace with "And"; Fr. "e."

3432 Proverbial; cf. KnT I.1606n.

3435 **for all Fraunce:** Fr. "por mon pois D'argent" (for my weight in money).

3437–38 Fr. "Mout trovai Dangier dur e lent De pardoner son mautalent" (I found *Daunger* very hard and slow to get over his ill will). The meaning of fil is obscure. Skeat: "condescended"; Liddell: "failed."

3454 **tall:** Unusual spelling for the sake of rhyme.

3462 **at good mes:** Fr. "en bon point." See 1453n.

3463 Cf. Prov. 15.1.

3489 Emended after Liddell. See textual note for the MS reading preserved by other editors.

3677 Proverbial; Whiting K69.

3687 Proverbial; Whiting T471.

3774 The emendation *nille,* for MS *wille,* may be unnecessary. Cf. IntrMLT II.49, Tr 1.456–57 and n.

3776–84 Not in the French. The translator has elaborated a commonplace about the vicissitudes of love.

3778 Proverbial; Whiting M655.

3811 **an Irish womman:** Fr. "iraise [var. irese]," which may mean simply an "angry woman." Langlois, 1.192n., suggests a pun in the French. On the reputation of the "Wild Irish" in the Middle Ages, see Snyder, MP 17, 1920, 687–725.

3826 **Reynes . . . Amyas:** Fr. "Estampes ou a Miauz."

3851 **[Ne]:** Robinson does not add the negative and translates *hadde,* "(that he) had."

3912 **blered is myn ye:** Cf. RvT I.3865n.

3931–32 Proverbial; Whiting E97.

3978 Proverbial in French. Langlois cites examples.

3995–96 The MS reads "londe" : "withstonde." Robinson wonders whether both final -*e*'s should perhaps be preserved. His practice is to normalize rhymes.

4030 Fr. "Vilains qui est cortois enrage" (A churl who is courteous has lost his wits).

4032–33 Proverbial in French. Langlois gives examples.

4137–40   Not in the French. This familiar topic has many parallels; see Tr 3.1625–28n.

4194   who: Skeat emends to [whiche] to clarify the reference.

4220   Fr. "L'autre porte, qui est assise A main senestre, devers bise" (The other gate, which is to the left facing north). The omission of "gate" in the English spoils the sense.

4247   Discordaunt: Evidently a mistranslation of Fr. "descorz," a type of song.

4250   hornepipes: Fr. "estives" (straw pipes).

4286   An olde vekke: Fr. "Une vieille" (an old woman). This character, greatly developed by Jean de Meun, becomes a prototype for the Wife of Bath. Langlois compares the description of the go-between in Pamphilus, 281–82, 425, but the figure has a long literary ancestry, including the bawd Dipsas in Ovid, Amores 1.8.

4300   Proverbial. Cf. GP I.476n. According to Langlois, the expression has a general sense of "to be cunning, shrewd" before it acquires its special application to the "dance of lovers."

4305   sore: Cf. 1031 above.

4322   I wende a bought: Fr. "Jes cuidoie avoir achetez."

4353–63   A typical complaint against Fortune, similar to several in Chaucer, e.g., BD 618–49, Tr 4.2–7, KnT I.925. Cf. Whiting L502.

4389–90   Proverbial; Whiting H298.

4429   Fr. "Que je n'ai mais aillors fiance." This is the last line of Guillaume de Lorris. The looseness of the translation, however, makes it difficult to fix the exact dividing point between Guillaume and Jean de Meun.

4446–48   Proverbial; Whiting H470.

4457–59   silogisme . . . conclusioun: Jean de Meun frequently uses analogies and scholastic terminology that reflect his university background. See G. M. Paré, Idées et lettres au XIIIe siècle, 1947.

4467   Fr. "le meilleur de la querele" (the better of the argument).

4472   stounde: Perhaps a mistake for "wounde."

4475–76   Proverbial; Whiting H371.

4478   They doon: Editors (except Liddell) supply "me have" from Fr. "Aveir me lait tant de contraires" ([Promise] has let me have so many disappointments). But the translator seems to have turned this into a general observation about the harm done when promise and deed fail to accord.

4493   And yit moreover: Fr. "Enseurquetout"; cf. KnT I.2801 and n.

4495   ronne in age: Cf. NPT VII.2821.

4499   enforced: Fr. "enforcera."

4510   Fr. "Il ne me vaudront riens jamais" (They will never be worth anything to me).

4559   cunne hym mawgre: Fr. "mal gré saveir." Cf. KnT I.1808 for a similar use of cunne.

4575–76   if unpacience . . . offence: Not in the Fr. The MS and all editors before Fisher omit Ne, but it seems essential for sense. Cf. 2117 and 4579.

4577–80   Cf. 2115–18. Jean de Meun is quoting Guillaume.

4587   Proverbial; Whiting L556.

4613–14   Fr. "Au departir mon cueur li lais. Ja ne seront autre mi lais." (At my death I leave him my heart. I shall make no other legacy.) At 4614, Thynne and editors

read "Or doublenesse," perhaps correctly. The translator seems to have taken Fr. "departir" (referring to the lover's death) in the sense of "division (of the heart)." Possibly his original read "Sans departir," though no such variant survives.

Doublenesse of repentyng is then in apposition with **departyng**: repenting of love is a falsehood or division of the heart. The passage echoes 2361–68.

4685–4784   This description of love is adapted from that given by Nature in Alanus de Insulis's De planctu naturae, T. Wright, Anglo-Latin Satirical Poets, Rolls, 1872, 2:471–74. Langlois prints the text from Migne in his n. to 4279.

4693–94   Not in the Fr.

4705   fret full: Cf. LGW 1117.

4712   Not in the Fr. Skeat glosses: "a wave, harmful in wearing away the shore." Liddell emends, "alwey to ware" (always to beware of).

4713   Karibdous: Charybdis, cf. Tr 5.644 and n. Previous editors, except Liddell, follow Thynne's learned spelling, "Carybdes" (or "Caribdis"), but something is lost in changing the MS form, which may well originate with the translator. On Thynne's corrections of the spellings of classical names, see J. E. Blodgett, Wm. Thynne, in Editing Ch, 48.

4715–20   From a passage interpolated in certain Fr. MSS and printed in Langlois's collations for 4302.

4717–18   Fr. "C'est sapience sans science, C'est science sans sapience" (It is wisdom without knowledge; it is knowledge without wisdom). Possibly kunnyng (4717) and Wisdom (4718) should be interchanged (Brusendorff, Ch Trad., 318, supported by Robinson's n.), but the MS also makes sense.

4732   Fr. "De pechié pardons entechiez" (Pardon spotted with sin).

4751   slowe: ?: sluggard (OED); vagabond (Liddell); Fr. "C'est teigne qui riens ne refuse, Les pourpres et les bureaus use" (It is a moth that rejects nothing, purple robes or coarse wool). The translation is doubtless based on the var. "caigne" (bitch) for "teigne," which could be used figuratively for a loose woman, a meaning that would fit the context but is not otherwise attested in English. Thus probably the word is to be taken as a general term of abuse. Skeat's gloss "moth," taking were to mean "wear away," is neither attested nor does it fit the context.

4753–54   Proverbial; Whiting L539.

4755–56   Proverbial; Whiting A119, "Amorets (love-knots) (may) be as well in black mourning as in bright burnet (cloth)." Fisher translates, "sweethearts are as good in black mourning as in bright robes." The latter is closer to the Fr. "ausinc bien sont amouretes Souz bureaus come souz brunettes" (pretty girls [lovers] may be found as well under coarse as under fine cloth). Langlois cites La Fontaine: "Sous les cotillons des grisettes Peut loger autant de beauté Que sous les jupes des coquettes." See 892 above. The interpretation of amourettes as "love-knots" rests on a misreading of the French in a line probably interpolated by Thynne for one missing in the MS.

4767–68   they of yvel lyf: The reference is to the excommunication pronounced against homosexuality at the end of De planctu naturae by Nature's priest Genius against "omnis qui legitimum Veneris obliquat incessum" (whoever turns awry the lawful course of love), or

"Qui a regula Veneris exceptionem facit anormalam" (who makes an irregular exception to the rule of love). On the history of Genius as an allegorical figure, see Nitzsche, The Genius Fig. in Antiq. and the Mid. Ages, 1975. Genius appears as Nature's priest in RR (16285ff.); as priest of Venus in Gower's Confessio amantis.

4783–84 Proverbial; Whiting L487. The Fr. follows Alanus's Lat. Cf. Tr 1.747–48.

4809 Langlois notes the similarity of this definition to that in Andreas Capellanus, De amore 1.1 and 1.2.

4821–24 Not in the Fr. though the lines elaborate the idea in 4825–27, which corresponds to "De fruit aveir ne fait il force; Au deliter senz plus s'efforce" (He cares not to have fruit; he takes pains for pleasure and nothing else). Cf. NPT VII.3344–45.

4831 paramours: With passionate love, in the manner of courtly love; Fr. "Mais par amour amer ne deignent" (But they deign not to love "paramours").

4838 ernes: Cf. LGW 1287.

4841–42 Proverbial; Whiting H137.

4856 For a line left blank in the MS Thynne and editors have "For bycause al is corrumpable"; Fr. "Pour ce qu'il sont tuit corrumpable." Something is needed to complete the thought, though "For" seems redundant with "bycause." See Textual Notes for different ways in which editors have punctuated the passage. The idea is proverbial (Whiting A93).

4875 fortened crece: Stimulated procreation (see MED s.v. fortenen and crese). Not in the Fr. Skeat's guess that the phrase refers to abortion is mistaken. The antecedent of which is desir. The desire for sexual pleasure caused by a kind of irritation (fortened) results in human reproduction.

4904 The English omits the reason for joining a religious order: "E cuide prendre au ciel la grue" (And thinks to grab the crane in the sky, i.e., to make a good bargain, to enjoy "pie in the sky").

4914–16 The English here conflates two choices confronting the man who has entered monastic life: he may leave the monastery ("s'en ist"), or he may stay because he is ashamed to leave ("Pour Honte qui l'i fait tenir").

4923 Conteyne: Fr. "sa mesaise li efface E le tiegne."

4933 hangith: Fr. "enlace e meine" (ties up and leads).

4943 Demande: See Textual Notes for MS reading and other interpretations.

4995–5000 Not in the Fr.

5022 The translator has forgotten the conclusion of the but clause beginning in 5014: "E qu'ele a sa vie perdue." Liddell suggests supplying "Al her lyf she hath forlorn."

5123–24 Not in the Fr. Perhaps influenced by HF 1257–58, though proverbial; see Tr 4.1283n.

5146 Proverbial; cf. MerT IV.2426n.

5151–52 Still Proverbial; cf. Tr 4.432–34n.

5162–66 An obscure passage. See Textual Notes for MS readings and possible emendations. Fr. "Ainz vivrai toujourz en haïnes; Lors si serai morteus pechierres, Veire, par Deu, pires que lierres" (Thus I should live ever in hatred; then I would be in mortal sin, truly, by God, worse than a thief).

5169–72 Obscure. Fr. "Mais espeir que je comparrai Plus la haïne ou darrenier, Tout ne vaille amour un denier" (But maybe I would in the end pay more for hatred, even though love be not worth a penny). Lines

5171–72 are either not in the Fr. or stem from a misreading.

5201 Love of freendshipp: Cf. Tr 2.371, 962; and for a similar construction, cf. KnT I.1912 and n. Reason's discussion of friendship draws upon Cicero's De amicitia, chaps. 5, 6, 13, 17. Citations are given in Langlois's notes.

5222–24 Obscure. The first half of 5223 is missing. Fr. "Senz soupeçon d'encusement. Teus meurs aveir deivent e seulent Qui parfaitement amer veulent" (Without suspicion of blame. Such must be and used to be the conduct of those who would love perfectly). The sense of the English is that the ones true and perfect in love suspect no blame in those (i.e., their friends) they would prove. The idea of testing friendship is proverbial. Cf. Whiting F656, "One true Friend should prove another."

5234–35 Proverbial; Whiting D130.

5259–60 Not in the Fr.

5266 Proverbial; Whiting F407. Not in the Fr.

5274 hym moleste: Liddell, noting that molest is not normally reflexive, suggests reading "That" or "It" for He.

5278 fered: A Kentish form used occasionally by Chaucer and others for the sake of rhyme.

5286 Direct reference to De amicitia. See chapters 12, 13, and 17.

5290 Obscure. Fr. "S'ele contient dreit e raison" (If it [the request] is just and reasonable).

5291 Fr. "Ne deit pas estre autrement faite" (It must not be done differently), i.e., the request must be performed if it is reasonable. This is perhaps the intended meaning of the English also, but the actual meaning is just the opposite, for if the request were other than unreasonable, it should be granted.

5351 take: Fr. "l'afuble" (muffles it). Poverty cloaks love with a dark mantle.

5353 Hidith: Some editors supply "It" as a subject.

5384 goot ramage: Fr. "cers ramages" (branched stag).

5409–5560 The argument is a greatly expanded version of Boethius 2.pr8.

5419 deles: Northern form.

5443 maken it hool: Perform their all (?) (cf. 5447); they perform it (their will) wholly (?) (Skeat).

5473–74 Perhaps And should be shifted to the head of 5473 to correspond to Fr. "E leur assiet, come marrastre, Au cueur un douloureus emplastre" (And, like a stepmother, lays a painful plaster on the heart).

5486 Freend of affect: "A friend by inclination, a loving friend" (MED, citing this passage). Not in the Fr. Skeat and Robinson emend to "effect," assuming imitation of Fortune 34, "Frend of effect, and frend of countenaunce," in which case the phrase means "a friend in deed, a true friend," as in 5549. The phrases may well have been confused. On verbal parallels between Fortune and Rom, see Brusendorff, Ch Trad., 404–7. The conclusion, however, need not be that Fragment B is a garbled version of Chaucer's translation, but that the translator was familiar with Chaucer's poetry and used it in appropriate places.

5507 in voice of flaterie: Fr. "a voiz jolie" (in a pleasant voice). The tone, not the substance of what is said, is flattering.

5510 For this proverb, not in the Fr., cf. Tr 3.861 and n.

5513–14   Perhaps from Prov. 17.17 (Skeat), but the parallel is very general. The tenor of the entire passage is proverbial. Cf. lines 5520, 5523, 5534, 5540, and notes 5534 and 5540 below.

5521–29   Cf. Ecclus. 22.21–22.

5534   Cf. Eccles. 7.28.

5540   Proverbial; Whiting F670.

5541–42   Proverbial; Whiting F633.

5551–53   Proverbial; Whiting F634.

5552   Cf. For 10.

5583–84   Proverbial; Whiting S867.

5649   **Pictigoras:** Pythagoras, whose works were lost. For the possible source of this reference to him in Chalcidius's commentary on the Timaeus, see Langlois's n. to 5025–32.

5659–60   Cf. Bo 1.pr5.8–25; 5.pr1.12–15. Cf. also Truth 17, 19.

5666   Both Jean de Meun and Chaucer translated Boethius.

5672   Cf. For 25.

5681   **dispendith:** A Southern plural form used for rhyme.

5706–7   Cf. Bo 2.m2.20–21.

5710   Proverbial; Whiting S140.

5739–44   Not in the Fr. Lounsbury (Studies 2:222) identified the source as La Bible de Guiot de Provins (in Fabliaux et Contes, ed. Barbazon and Méon 2:390). The passage is quoted in Sutherland, xxix, from La Fleur de la poésie française, ed. A. Mary, 288. The Fr. puns on *fi* ("fi"="fie!" "fier"="trust," "defie"="defy"). The Eng. carries over the play on *fy* (="fie," "trust") and adds a play on *sy* ="sigh" (Lounsbury) or on Fr. *si* ("if"), i.e., "the precariousness of trusting doctors" (Skeat).

5759   Proverbial; Whiting G491. Cf. RvT I.4320–21 and n.

5763–64   Cf. PardPro, passim (especially VI.407–8).

5781–86   Proverbial; Whiting R113.

5804   Proverbial; Whiting L525.

5810   Fragment B ends here. There is no break in the MS, but the translation passes from line 5154 to line 10679 of the Fr. In the omitted passage Reason continues her discourse, but fails to persuade the Lover to abandon the service of the god of Love. The Lover then consults L'Ami (Friend), who advises him to approach Belacueil's prison by a road called "Trop Doner" (i.e., large expenditure of money), constructed by Largesse. Ami also tells the Lover at length about the Golden Age, the corruption of society, and the proper treatment of one's mistress or wife. The Lover then approaches the castle, but Richesse bars his entrance. The god of Love now comes to his assistance, first calling a council of his barons. Among them are two new characters, False-Seeming and his female companion Constrained Abstinence. The god of Love opens the assembly with a speech in which he declares that his servant Guillaume de Lorris had begun and left unfinished the romance to be completed more than forty years after his death by Jean de Meun. He asks the barons' advice on how to conquer the castle. At this point Fragment C begins.

FRAGMENT C

5824   Fr. "Pour ome qui parler en sache, Ne de nule autre arme qui seit" (Notwithstanding anyone who might have something to say about it, nor with any other kind of weapon). Richesse refuses to fight in any way, no matter what anyone might say. The English is probably based on a variant for the second line: "Ne pour ame qu'el monde seit" (Nor for any soul on earth).

5837   **To-Moche-Yevyng:** Fr. "Trop Doner."

5856   **Fair-Welcomyng:** Called Bialacoil in Fragment B, one of the indications that a new translator is at work.

5857   **Wel-Heelynge:** Fr. "Bien Celer."

5869–70   **entent : present:** An un-Chaucerian rhyme. Chaucer regularly has *entente*. Other instances of the dropping of Chaucerian final *-e* in rhyme are 6105–6 (*atte last* [*e*] : *agast*); 6565–66 (*wrought* [pl.] : *nought*); and six instances of *I* or words ending in *-y*, rhyming with words in which Chaucer regularly has a final *-e*, at 6111–12, 6301–2, 6339–40, 6373–74, 6875–76, 7317–18.

5883   **nedes:** The translator has confused "besoignes" (affairs), with "besoinges" (needs). See also Textual Notes.

5919–20   **hors : wors:** An un-Chaucerian rhyme. Chaucer rhymes *wors* with *curs* (CkPro I.4349) and *pervers* (BD 813). Other irregular rhymes in Fragment C are *force : croce*, 6469–70; *pacience : vengeaunce*, 6429–30; *Abstynaunce : penaunce*, 7481–82 (Chaucer's form is *Abstinence*); *science : ignorence*, 6717–18. The last three instances, however, are taken directly from the Fr.

5954–56   Although there is an account (cited by Skeat) making Aphrodite (Venus) the daughter of Cronos (Saturn) and Euonyme, the Fr. text is probably alluding to a famous story told by Reason in the *Roman* after the point where Fragment B breaks off, how Venus was born from Saturn's genitals when Jupiter cut them off and cast them into the sea. A spurious passage interpolated in several Fr. MSS at this point (printed in Langlois's notes to 10830–31) refers the reader to the story ("Car maintes foiz oï l'avez"—For you've heard it many times) and proceeds to tell how Jupiter begot Cupid on Venus.

6024   Fr. "Il ne feront mie que sage" (They do not act wisely).

6041–42   Fr. "E leur donront si granz colees De baiseries, d'acolees" (And give them such great blows of kissings and embracings). The rhyme words *thankynges* and *talkynges* do not convey the sense that the ladies' flatteries are in reality "blows" dealt to their rich lovers. Kaluza suggested reading "thwakkynges" in 6041; Liddell, "wakynges" in 6042; but the translator has simply used rhymes to suggest flattering words that might accompany the "baiseries."

6044   **leve:** Fr. "leur demourra." The Fr. construction is impersonal, but possibly *ladies* is to be understood as the subject.

6045–46   After the rich lover has first been stripped of his liquid assets (**moeble**) he will give up land and rents.

6068   **kyng of harlotes:** Fr. "reis des ribauz," glossed in Lecoy's edition as a petty official of the king's retinue with jurisdiction over gaming places and houses of prostitution. Skeat's notion (derived from Méon's edition) that this functionary's duties were "to clear out . . . men of bad character" doubtless misinterprets his role and hardly accords with Skeat's further observation that the title was applied humorously to any notorious vagabond.

6090   Fr. "S'onques leur cruauté quenui."

6112   Fr. "De Barat et d'Ypocrisie." The vices practiced by Fals-Semblant and his kind are represented allegorically as his parents.

6135ff.   The self-portrait of Fals-Semblant, though draw-

ing generally on anticlerical satire common throughout
the thirteenth century, has as its special target the mendicant friars. Specifically it echoes the attacks of the secular
faculty at the University of Paris who were engaged in
bitter controversy during 1250–59 to deny the friars
chairs of public instruction that the secular clergy wished
to keep under their exclusive control. For a detailed
discussion of the parties, personalities, and issues, see
M.-M. Dufeil, Guillaume de Saint-Amour et la polé-
mique universitaire Parisienne, 1972. The facts are conveniently summarized by H. H. Lucas in the introduction
to Rutebeuf's Poèmes concernant l'Université de Paris,
1952. The confession of Fals-Semblant served Chaucer as
a source for the Pardoner as well as for certain touches
in the Friar's portrait.

6141 **worldly folk:** The laity as opposed to the clergy;
Fr. "au siecle ou en cloistre." Langlois, however, interpreted the phrase as specifying the secular clergy as opposed to the cloistered; in 6149–50, *Religiouse folk* and
Seculer folk may refer to the regular (cloistered) as opposed to the secular clergy; nevertheless, the secular
clergy, though living more in the world, are also "religious folk." Cf. 6232ff., where *seculer* definitely refers to
layfolk. The issue here and below is that good and evil
cannot be judged on the basis of one's estate or outward
appearance.

6149–50 Cf. 6141 and n.

6174 **nedes:** Fr. "besoignes"; cf. 5883.

6191 **a croked brere:** One of the many figures of
worthlessness. See GP I.177n. Fr. "un coutel troine" (a
knife of privet).

6192 Proverbial; Whiting H2.

6197–98 Fr. "Veire rere au rasoir d'elenches, Qui barat
trenche en treze branches" (Even though [he] shave with
the razor of De elenchis, which divides fraud into thirteen branches). The reference is to De elenchis sophisti-
cis in which Aristotle classifies thirteen types of sophistical reasoning. Thynne and editors emend *resoun* to
"rasour," taking the reference to be to a literal razor by
which a cleric is tonsured. The Fr. plays upon the literal
tonsure and the metaphorical razor of Aristotle, but the
translator has reduced the complicated figure of the
"razor of reason" to plain English.

6204 **Gibbe:** A common English name for a tomcat; Fr.
"dans Tiberz," also the name of the cat in the Roman de
Renard.

6205 For the line left blank in the MS Thynne and
editors (except Skeat) have "That awayteth myce and
rattes to kyllen"; Fr. "N'entent qu'a souriz et a raz."
Skeat declares that Thynne's line "will not rime, and is
spurious." He supplies "Fro myce and rattes went his
wyle" (i.e., the cat will not turn his wiliness from mice
and rats); and he emends 6206 to "begyle." Another
solution, not necessitating an emendation for rhyme
would be "But [= 'except'] to mys and rattes n'entendeth nothyng."

6226 **worldly habitacioun:** Fr. "En seculiere mansion." Lines 6234ff. show that the reference cannot be to
the secular clergy. Cf. 6141 and n., above.

6259–60 Fr. "dam Belin . . . Sire Isengrin," characters
from the Roman de Renard.

6281 Fr. "E se d'aus [var. d'eus] ne la veauz rescourre"
(And if you will not rescue it from them). The translator
has misread "d'eus" as "deus." In the Fr., the Church
apostrophized remains the subject.

6290 **stuffen:** Fr. "garnir."

6318 For the line left blank in the MS Kaluza and editors supply "That to hard is the aperceyving" from Fr.
"Que trop est grief l'aparcevance." Thynne has "That al
to late cometh knowynge," regarded by all editors as
spurious.

6319 Proteus's power of transformation has given its
meaning to the adjective *protean.* Proverbial; Whiting
P425.

6337 **Robert . . . Robyn:** Langlois notes that in Le jeu
de Robin et Marion, the knight is called Robert, and the
shepherd, Robin.

6341 **Abstinence-Streyned:** Fr. "Astenance Contrainte." She is portrayed as a nun. Her name indicates
that her chastity is not natural; nor, since she is the *lemman* of Fals-Semblant, is it real.

6354 Fr. "J'en lais le grain e preing la paille" (I leave
the grain and take the straw). Some MSS, however, transpose "lais" and "preing." Proverbial; Whiting S824.

6355 See Textual Notes for the MS reading and other
emendations of this line.

6360–6472 This passage is based on a spurious chapter
interpolated in many Fr. MSS—an attack on the "privileges," the licenses claimed by the mendicants. The text
is printed in Langlois's notes 11222–23.

6364–65 The license of the friars to hear confession was
a major point of contention. Cf. GP I.218–20 and SumT
III.2093–98.

6371–73 Fr. "Mais mes traiz ont aperceüz, Si n'en sui
mais si receüz Envers eus si con je souloie" (But they
have detected my treachery, and I am no longer received
by them as I used to be). For line 6372 left blank in the
MS and also omitted by Thynne, editors supply "Ne
shulde I more ben receyved (Skeat, Robinson); "Ne
shulde I ben so receyved" (Sutherland, Fisher). Liddell
(changing 6371) reads: "But where my sleight is aperceyved, Of hem I am nomore resceyved." It is noteworthy that the only blank line in the MS not filled in by
Thynne is from a spurious passage unlikely to have been
in Thynne's Fr. MS (see 6360–6472 above).

6381 The gullibility of the prelates who fail to detect
the friars' sharp practices.

6385 **Onys a yeer:** Annual confession to one's parish
priest, generally at Easter, was made mandatory by Innocent III at the Fourth Lateran Council in 1215. Cf. ParsT
X.1026.

6424 **Frere Wolf:** Fr. "frere Louvel." The name is, of
course, ironically appropriate.

6434 The priest might withhold Communion from
someone who had not been to confession.

6453–54 See Prov. 27.23, John 10.14.

6502 Proverbial; Whiting K92.

6532 Prov. 30.8, 9. See Textual Notes on the mistake
of *thrittene.*

6547–50 The mendicant orders claimed that their poverty and begging were modeled upon the example of
Christ and the apostles, thereby causing a bitter theological dispute over how Jesus and his followers made their
living. For his attack on mendicancy, Jean de Meun is
chiefly indebted to the Tractatus de periculis novissimorum temporum (Treatise concerning the dangers of
the most recent times) of Guillaume de Saint-Amour. On
Guillaume, see 6763 and n., below, where he is named.
With the present passage, cf. De periculis 12, pp. 50–51.
References to Guillaume's works are borrowed from
Langlois who gives the relevant passages from the Latin;
Lecoy's edition also contains full citations. De periculis is

cited by Langlois and Lecoy from the edition of Guillaume's works that appeared at Constance (actually Paris according to Lecoy [2:282]), 1632, pp. 17–72.

6556   The literal text as opposed to the interpretation. The Bible does not say that Christ and the disciples begged.

6565   **ther:** Possibly a scribal error for "her," but the C Fragment contains scattered Northern forms.

6571   No doubt a reproach to the mendicants for their fine buildings. Cf. SumT III.2099–2106.

6573–78   Cf. De periculis 12, p. 48.

6583–88   Based on a spurious passage in some Fr. MSS, printed in Langlois's notes 11316–27. The reference is to St. Augustine's De opere monachorum.

6589–90   Identical with 6577–78.

6595–96   Cf. Luke 18.22, cited in De periculis 12, p. 49. See also 6653–58.

6615   The Code of Justinian, eastern emperor, 527–65, became the basis of the civil and canon law. The passage referred to is bk. 11, tit. 24, De mendicantibus validis, and is cited in De periculis 12, p. 52.

6631–34   Langlois notes that Guillaume de Saint-Amour makes a similar disclaimer with regard to the authority of the pope and bishops, De periculis 12, p. 52. Lecoy observes that this caution applies specifically to the privilege of confession; Guillaume rejects any authority that would license mendicancy.

6636   Perhaps a general allusion to Matt. 23.14. The same idea is expressed in De periculis 12, p. 52 and in Collectiones catholice canonice scripture, another work attributed to Guillaume.

6644   Fr. "Se cil qui fist Adan ne ment" (If he who made Adam does not lie). Variation of the Pauline formula (Titus 1.2), "Qui non mentitur deus."

6653–58   Cf. 6595–96 and n., above.

6661–65   1 Thess. 4.11–12, quoted in De periculis 12, p. 48.

6671–78   Cf. De periculis 14, p. 64.

6679–84   Cf. Acts 20.33–35. Lecoy cites De periculis 12, p. 51.

6685–92   Cf. De periculis 12, p. 49–51.

6688   For the line left blank in the MS, Thynne and editors supply "And neuer with hondes labour his nedes" ("nede is," Liddell); Fr. "Senz jamais de mains labourer" (Without ever doing manual labor).

6691   **Seynt Austyn:** From a variant substituted in one family of Fr. MSS for "l'escriture" (Scripture). The reference to Augustine comes at second hand from De periculis 12, p. 48 and Responsiones 90–91.

6693–95   Communal property is permitted to those who have surrendered personal property to enter an order such as the following. The Knights Templars were founded in 1119, the Hospitallers, circa 1087. **Chanouns Regulers,** as distinguished from secular canons, are members of certain orders who follow a rule. The White Monks were Cistercians, a reformed order of the Benedictines; the Black, the unreformed.

6712   Proverbial; Whiting S490.

6757–58   The Fr. original probably called for illustrations (reproduced in Langlois), found in some MSS, of a hand labeled "manus corporalis" and a rectangular design containing the opening text of Genesis, labeled "manus spiritualis."

6763   **William Seynt Amour:** A doctor of the Sorbonne in the middle of the thirteenth century, the most

outspoken champion of the university against the mendicants. Jean de Meun's indebtedness to his works, especially the De periculis, has been indicated in the preceding notes. Guillaume's tract was condemned by Pope Alexander IV in 1256 and the author banished from France. For details of Guillaume's fall, see Langlois, n. to 11506. Guillaume continued to be a hero to Jean de Meun and, one may surmise, to the university community.

6782   **The noble:** Fr. "Le vaillant ome."

6784   **agilte me:** Fr. "Vers ma mere [var. A moi] trop mesprenait" (He committed too great an offense against my mother [me]). Since Fals-Semblant often directly expresses the views of Jean de Meun, one must recall from time to time that he is in fact a villain on the side of hypocrisy.

6786   For the line missing in the MS, Thynne and editors supply "Wherin his lyfe he dyd al write"; Fr. "Ou sa vie fist toute escrivre." Cf. Textual Notes.

6804   **on her owne:** Fr. "dou leur" (of their own possessions).

6824   Cf. 5759.

6834   **is go:** Fr. "seit vuiz" (be empty).

6837   Cf. PardPro VI.403.

6838   Cf. GP I.256 and n.

6841–48   Not in the Fr.

6845–46   Cf. PardPro VI.443–44.

6861   **bygyns:** Beguines, laywomen who led religious lives but took no vows except that of chastity and followed no fixed rule. Some lived in small groups, others in larger communities, still others alone. The movement sprang up in the latter half of the twelfth century, perhaps first at Liège, but almost simultaneously elsewhere in the low countries and the Rhine valley where it was concentrated. The name, probably given to it by its detractors, had previous associations of heresy. By the mid-thirteenth century the Beguines had acquired an unsavory reputation. Cf. 7254 below, and see E. W. McDonnell, The Beguines and Beghards in Med. Cult., 1954.

6862   Fr. "dames palatines" ("ladies of the court").

6867   **clad or naked:** See GP I.534n.

6871–72   Cf. De periculis 5, p. 32.

6875   Cf. De periculis 4, p. 12.

6887   Matt. 23.1–8, 13–15. A favorite text against hypocrites.

6911   **bordurs:** Fr. "philateres."

6923–36   Cf. De periculis 14, p. 69.

6948   **oure alder:** Cf. GP I.586.

6973   **executour:** Langlois cites Rutebeuf, Vie dou monde, 144–45 (Oeuvres 2:42).

6993–94   Cf. De periculis 1, p. 21.

6998   John the Baptist, because of his austere life in the wilderness, was regarded as the founder of asceticism.

7000   In place of Fr. "maneir e giste" (abode and lodging), the translation follows a variant "degipte."

7013   **lambren:** An interesting archaic form from OE lombru. (Cf. children from cildru.) Chaucer's plural was apparently lambes (Robinson).

7017   Matt. 7.15.

7022   **bouger:** Fr. "bougre." For references associating heresy with Milan, see Langlois, 11724–25n.

7037   **me pray:** Fr. "Par trestouz les sainz que l'en preie" (By all the saints prayed to).

7057   **smerten:** Fr. "Ou sera puniz dou mesfait" (Or he will be punished for the offense).

7059–74   The defenses of the castle depend not on the quality of the construction but on the bribes with which it is stocked.

7063   vounde ston: Fr. "Ne li chausist ja de quel pierre" (It matters not what sort of stone). Good building-stone, possibly "founde" (p.p. of *finden*) near the site of construction (Skeat).

7076   equipolences: The word, taken over directly from the Fr., seems to mean "equivalent arguments" (Langlois), i.e., in place of material bribes the friars might be bought off with flattering arguments instead of the usual attacks *(lyes and fallaces).*

7092   For the line left blank in the MS, Thynne and editors supply "We had ben turmented al and some." Cf. Textual Notes.

7093–7103   In 1254 (not 1255 as stated in both the Fr. and Eng. texts) the Minorite Gérard de Borgo San Donnino published an edition of the Concordia Novi et Veteris Testamenti of the Cistercian abbot Joachim di Fiore (d. 1202) under the title Evangelium Eternum sive Spiritus Sancti, which Gérard prefaced with an introductory book (Liber introductorius). The introduction created a sensation by claiming that this "Gospel of the Holy Ghost" would supersede that of the Son (the New Testament) as the latter had superseded the Gospel of the Father (the Old Testament). The book provided ammunition to the opponents of the friars. On remonstrance of the theologians of the university, the book was condemned in 1255 by Pope Alexander IV. Jean de Meun takes his information of the affair from De periculis, pp. 68–69.

7109   To fill a gap in the MS, editors supply "That he ne myghte bye the book." See Textual Notes on Thynne's efforts to patch two breaks in sense caused by the scrambling of four passages in the MS.

7135   The friars suppress the book until a more propitious time, presumably the advent of their leader, Anti-Christ. The Liber introductorius is in fact lost and known only through attacks upon it such as the De periculis.

7155   we: Fals-Semblant often speaks of the friars as *they,* but he is, of course, one of their party, and the *fals horrible book* (7132) is *oure book* (7164).

7166–70   The literal sense, **the bark and rynde** (7169), contains the fruit or the true sense, which states that the strength of John shall not be revealed while Peter is in power. Cf. next note.

7172–82   The English lacks a couplet necessary to the sense, which would translate Fr. "Par Pierre veaut le pape entendre" (By "Peter" it signifies the Pope). In other words, "Peter" stands for the present hierarchy, the secular clergy; "John" stands for the friars, the preachers of the eternal gospel, who would replace them.

7254   beggers: "A member of one of the mendicant orders," MED, s.v. *begger,* 2, citing this passage, but in context, 4, "rascal, knave," also applies. Fr. "beguins," a masc. form derived from "beguines" (see 6861 above). For the translator "beguins" was evidently synonymous with "begards" or "beguards" (New Eng. Beghards), a lay brotherhood, the male counterparts of the Beguines. The Beghards, founded like the Beguines in the twelfth century, were repeatedly condemned, and in French *begard* became a general term for "heretic." The use here in Rom is evidence for the etymological connection of *beggar* with OF *begard.*

7258–59   Fr. "Houseaus fronciez e larges botes, Qui re-

semblent bourse a caillier" (Pleated tights and big boots that look like a game bag for quail). The sound of a pipe imitating the call of the female quail to lure the male acquired the figurative sense (see OED, s.v. *quail-pipe*) of something enticing, likened here to the raffish effect of the beggars' boots. The translator has heightened the already vivid picture of the Fr. in a manner reminiscent of Langland's Prologue: "Grete lobies and longe that lothe were to swynke Clothed hem in copes to ben knowen from othere" (55–56).

7285–86   Prov. 26.11; cf. also 2 Pet. 2.22.

7300   See 6068 and n., above.

7311–15   Proverbial; Whiting W447.

7321   chere of symplenesse: Fr. "simple e queie," the formula applied to the Prioress's smile, GP I.119.

7323   Streyned-Abstinaunce: See 6341 above.

7327   you and me: Fr. "mei e li" (me and her).

7385–86   Proverbial; Whiting H242. Langlois gives examples in his note to 12063–64, among them "Rex, Papa, facti sunt una capa" with respect to the entente between Philip the Fair and Clement V.

7391   Rev. 6.8.

7406   saynt: Perhaps a variant spelling for "ceynt," i.e., girded like a Cordelier (Franciscan). Fr. "qui bien se ratourne" (who attires himself well).

7413   squierly: Fr. "Emprès s'en va senz [var. son] escuier" (Then he goes without a squire, or, His squire goes after him). Perhaps the Fr. copy-text read "con escuier." Or possibly change to "squierles."

7453   On Jolly Robin, see Tr 5.1174n.

7459–60   The Augustinians, Franciscans (**Cordyleres**), and Carmelites (**Carmes**), together with the Dominicans, comprised the four orders of friars. Cf. GP I.210. The **Sacked Freeres** were the friars "De Penitentia," also called "di Sacco" from the form of their robe.

7465–68   Proverbial; cf. HF 265–66 and n.

7490–91   Matt. 4.19, Luke 5.10. For its use by the friars, cf. SumT III.1820.

7505–09   Cf. MancT IX.332–33 and n.

7511–12   Proverbial; Whiting H133.

7517   Cf. 3815–18.

7544   Proverbial; Whiting T96.

7576   devels ers of helle: The ass of the devil of hell; Fr. "cul [var. puis] d'enfer" (the pit of hell). Cf. SumPro III.1665–1708.

7607   Proverbial; Whiting G401.

7634   Fr. "S'en le deüst tout vif larder" (Though one had roasted him alive).

7677–90   Cf. 6364–65 and n., above.

7691–92   Where the MS breaks off Thynne and editors have, "In diuynite for to rede / And to confessen out of drede / If ye wol you nowe confesse / And leaue your synnes more and lesse / Without abode knele downe anon / And you shal haue absolucion." Kaluza, ES, 18, 109–10, argued that this conclusion is spurious, tacked on by Thynne to prevent ending in mid-sentence. It is only very loosely related to the Fr. "J'ai de divinité congié, Veire, par Deu! pieç'a leü. Pour confesseur m'ont esleü Li meilleur qu'en puisse saveir Par mon sen e par mon saveir. Se vous voulez ci confessier E ce pechié senz plus laissier, Senz faire en jamais mencion, Vous avreiz m'assolucion." (I have license to teach theology, indeed, by God! I have been teaching it for a long time. The best people one could know of have chosen me as their confessor because of my intelligence and my knowledge. If you want to confess here and without more ado give up that sin, without ever further mention being made of it, you shall have my absolution.) The passage omits the MS's "And longe have red," which corresponds to "pieç'a leü"; it skips over the lines that Fals-Semblant has confessed the very best people; "senz plus laissier" is transformed into "more and lesse"; the particular sin of slander becomes generally *synnes.* Finally, "anon" : "absolucion" is a highly suspicious rhyme.

In the Fr., the episode concludes with Fals-Semblant using his razor to slit the throat and cut out the tongue of Male Bouche.

TEXTUAL
NOTES

THE TEXTUAL NOTES inevitably vary somewhat from text to text, since the nature of the problems in each text determines the notes' characteristics. In general, all are designed to show how the text was established, to list the important variant readings, and thus to provide the reader with the evidence (often recording the decisions of other editors) on which the readings of the more problematic lines were established. The reading of the text appears as the lemma, followed by the readings of other manuscripts and editions. Ordinarily only those that differ are listed; manuscripts and editions that do not appear after an alternate reading agree with the printed text. Occasionally, for clarity, those manuscripts and editions that do agree are listed immediately after the lemma, followed by a semicolon and then by the readings of those manuscripts and editions that differ from the text as printed.

Though the textual notes in this edition are much fuller than those in Robinson's edition, they are selective and do not attempt to record all variant manuscript and editorial readings. Only the most important variants are listed, and the reader is directed to other editions having full collations, where such exist. The volumes of the Variorum edition of Chaucer's works, now in progress, will carry much fuller lists of variants.

The authorities consulted are listed at the beginning of each set of textual notes. Almost all the authorities for the poetic texts are transcribed in the volumes of the Chaucer Society, though these must be used with caution, since they contain occasional errors. The following facsimiles of manuscripts are now available:

Bodley 638   *Manuscript Bodley 638: A Facsimile: Bodleian Library, Oxford University,* intro. Pamela Robinson. Variorum edition. Facsimile Series of the Works of Geoffrey Ch 2, 1981.

Camb., St. John's College MS L.1   *St. John's College, Cambridge, MS L.1: A Facsimile,* intro. Richard Beadle and Jeremy Griffiths. Variorum edition. Facsimile Series of the Works of Geoffrey Ch 3, 1983.

Camb. Univ. Gg.4.27   *Poetical Works: A Facsimile of Cambridge University Library MS Gg.4.27,* eds. M. B. Parkes and Richard Beadle. Cambridge, D. S. Brewer, 1979–80. 3 vols.

Camb. Univ. Ff.1.6   *The Findern Manuscript (Cambridge Univ. Library MS Ff.1.6),* intro. Richard Beadle and A. E.

Owen. London, Scolar Press, 1977.

Corpus Christi 61   *Troilus and Criseyde: A Facsimile of Corpus Christi College Cambridge MS 61,* intros. M. B. Parkes and Elizabeth Salter. Cambridge, D. S. Brewer, 1978.

Ellesmere   *The Ellesmere Ch: Reproduced in Facsimile,* intro. Alix Egerton. 1911. 2 vols.

Fairfax 16   *Bodleian Library MS Fairfax 16.* intro. John Norton-Smith. London, Scolar Press, 1979.

Hengwrt   *The Canterbury Tales: A Facsimile and Transcription of the Hengwrt MS with Variants from the Ellesmere MS,* ed. Paul Ruggiers, intros. Donald C. Baker, A. I. Doyle, and M. B. Parkes. The Variorum Edition of the Works of Geoffrey Chaucer, Vol. 1. 1979.

Pepys 2006   *Magdalene College, Cambridge, MS Pepys 2006: A Facsimile,* intro. A. S. G. Edwards. Variorum edition. Facsimile Series of the Works of Geoffrey Ch 6, 1985.

Tanner 346   *Minor Poems: A Facsimile of Oxford Bodleian Library MS Tanner 346,* intro. Pamela Robinson. Variorum edition. Facsimile Series of the Works of Geoffrey Ch 1, 1980.

Thynne   *Geoffrey Chaucer, The Works, 1532: With Supplementary Materials from the editions of 1542, 1561, 1598, and 1602,* ed. Derek S. Brewer. 1969 (rpt. 1976). (Thynne's edition, with the additions in Stowe and Speght.)

Facsimile editions of Morgan 817 (*olim* Campsall), Pierpont Morgan Library, New York, and of Trinity College, Cambridge, MS Trinity R.3.19, are scheduled to appear in the Variorum Chaucer Facsimile Series. Many of the other authorities are available on microfilm, which may in most cases be obtained from the libraries holding the manuscripts. Most manuscripts in British collections were filmed during the Second World War for the ACLS Microfilm Project (though the quality is not always of the best), and copies of these microfilms may be obtained from the Library of Congress.

LARRY D. BENSON

Authorities: There are eighty-two (or, if the Morgan fragment of The Pardoner's Tale is considered separately, eighty-three) manuscripts of the Tales, either complete or fragmentary. As Silvia suggests (Ch and ME Sts., 153–63), only fifty-five of them appear to have been intended as complete texts. Silvia discusses the purpose of the various selective versions; these are set off in the list below by appending a general indication of their contents.

The Tales exist not only in the manuscripts but in six early prints, all of which potentially have manuscript status. Clearly derived from a lost manuscript copy is the *editio princeps,* Caxton's text of 1478 (Cx¹, STC 5082). Caxton claims in the prologue to the second edition (Cx², STC 5083, c. 1484) to have revised the text on the basis of a different (and presumably better) manuscript supplied by a disappointed reader of the first edition; see EETS 176, 90–91.

The other four early editions are: Pynson, c. 1492 (STC 5084); de Worde, 1498 (STC 5085); Pynson, 1526 (STC 5086); and the first edition of Thynne's Works, 1532 (STC 5068). These derive in linear succession from either Cx² or their immediate predecessors. All include a certain amount of unique variation, either derived from spot consultation of manuscripts or from normal sixteenth-century editorial tinkering. Generally speaking, the later editions have no textual value. For further discussion, see Greg (PMLA 39, 1924, 737–61), the classic treatment; on Cx², see Kilgour, PMLA 44, 1929, 186–201 (and Greg's response, PMLA 44, 1929, 1251–53), as well as Charles F. Dunn's 1940 University of Chicago dissertation; on de Worde, Garbáty's findings (SB 31, 1978, 57–67) are flatly contradicted by those of Hutmacher (Wynkyn de Worde and Ch's CT, 1977); for Pynson, see White (DAI 39, 1978, 2926A).

Various textual witnesses are available in modern reproduction (see list on p. 1117). Eight manuscripts, designated by an asterisk in the list below, were printed in full by the Chaucer Society. Six are arranged in parallel in Ch Soc. 1st ser. 1+14 (Fragment I), 15+25 (II, VII, VI, III), 30 (IV), 31 (V), 37 (VIII, IX), 49 (X); to these, the society later added prints of Ha⁴ (vol. 73) and of Dd (vols. 95–96). The society also issued several numbers that contained photographic reproductions of leaves from various copies; see 1st ser. 48, 56, 74.

The list of surviving MSS follows:

Ad¹	Additional 5140, British Library
Ad²	Additional 25718, British Library
Ad³	Additional 35286, British Library (formerly Ashburnham 125)
Ad⁴	Additional 10340, British Library (a fragment, I.478–528, quoted from memory)
Ar	Arundel 140, British Library (Melibee only)
Bo¹	Bodley 414 (SC 27880), Bodleian
Bo²	Bodley 686 (SC 2527), Bodleian
Bw	Barlow 20 (SC 6475), Bodleian

The textual notes to *The Canterbury Tales* were prepared by Ralph Hanna III.

Ch	Christ Church 152, Oxford
Cn	Cardigan MS, formerly the property of the Brudenell estate, Deene Park, Nhants.; now University of Texas Library 143, Austin
*Cp	Corpus Christi College 198, Oxford
Ct	Chetham's Library 6709, Manchester
*Dd	Dd.iv.24, University Library, Cambridge (perhaps formerly Hodley or Hoadley)
Dl	Delamere MS (Urry's Cholmondeley), later Boies Penrose 10; now property of T. Takamiya, MS 32, Tokyo
Do	Douce d.4, Bodleian (a single leaf containing I.298–368).
Ds¹	Devonshire MS, formerly property of the Duke of Devonshire, Chatsworth House, Bakewell, Dbys.; sold Christie's, London, 6 June 1974, Lot 21, to House of LDF, New York; current location unknown
Ds²	Devonshire fragment, property of the Duke of Devonshire (two folios from The Man of Law's Tale); not sold in same sale as the preceding
Ee	Ee.ii.15, University Library, Cambridge (The Man of Law's Tale only)
*El	Ellesmere 26 C 9, formerly Lord Ellesmere's, now Henry E. Huntington Library, San Marino, Calif.
En¹	Egerton 2726, British Library (formerly Haistwell, and probably a Chandos MS)
En²	Egerton 2863, British Library (formerly the Norton, later a Hodson MS)
En³	Egerton 2864, British Library (formerly the Ingilby, later a Hodson MS)
Fi	McClean 181, Fitzwilliam Museum, Cambridge (formerly Ashburnham 127)
*Gg	Gg.iv.27 (1), University Library, Cambridge
Gl	Hunterian Museum U.1.1 (197), University Library, Glasgow
Ha¹	Harley 1239, British Library (five tales)
Ha²	Harley 1758, British Library
Ha³	Harley 7333, British Library
*Ha⁴	Harley 7334, British Library
Ha⁵	Harley 7335, British Library
Hl¹	Harley 1704, British Library (The Prioress's Tale only)
Hl²	Harley 2251, British Library (The Prioress's Tale only)
Hl³	Harley 2382, British Library (The Prioress's Tale and The Second Nun's Tale)
Hl⁴	Harley 5908, British Library (a single leaf containing IV.808–91)
He	Tollemache MS, Helmingham Hall, Suff.; now Princeton University Library MS 100
*Hg	Hengwrt 154 (Peniarth 392D), National Library of Wales, Aberystwyth
Hk	Holkham Hall MS 667, property of the Earl of Leicester, Wells-next-Sea, Nflk.
Hn	Huntington HM 144, Henry E. Huntington Library, San Marino, Calif. (formerly Huth; Melibee and The Monk's Tale only)

Ht	Hatton donat. 1 (SC 4138), Bodleian
Ii	Ii.iii.26, University Library, Cambridge
Kk	Kk.i.3 (20), University Library, Cambridge (a single leaf containing VII.460–529)
*La	Lansdowne 851, British Library
Lc	Lichfield Cathedral 2
Ld¹	Laud 600, Bodleian
Ld²	Laud 739, Bodleian
Ll¹	Longleat 257, property of the Marquess of Bath (The Knight's Tale and The Clerk's Tale)
Ll²	Longleat 29, property of the Marquess of Bath (The Parson's Tale only)
Ln	Lincoln Cathedral 110
Ma	English 113, John Rylands Library, Manchester (formerly Hodson 39)
Mc	Sir William S. McCormick's MS, University of Chicago Library 564 (formerly Ashburnham 126)
Me	Merthyr, formerly property of the Rev. L. C. Simons, Merthyr Mawr, Wales, and a National Library of Wales deposit; after resale (Bonham's, London, 16 Nov. 1983, Lot 13), again National Library, MS 21972D (three folios from The Nun's Priest's Tale)
Mg	Pierpont Morgan Library M249, New York (formerly Ashburnham 124). The last leaf contains an additional fragment of The Pardoner's Tale.
Mm	Mm.ii.5, University Library, Cambridge (formerly Ely)
Ne	New College 314, Oxford
Nl	Northumberland MS 455, property of the Duke of Northumberland, Alnwick Castle
Np	Royal Library XIII.B.29, Naples (The Clerk's Tale only)
Ox¹	English 63, John Rylands Library, Manchester (two folios from The Miller's Tale, part of next)
Ox²	Oxford MS, property of the Rosenbach Foundation MS f. 1084/2, Philadelphia (eleven folios)
Ph¹	Phillipps 6570, formerly property of A. S. W. Rosenbach Co., New York; later property of Louis H. Silver, Chicago; now University of Texas Library 46, Austin (24 folios)
Ph²	Phillipps 8136, formerly Canby, then property of A. S. W. Rosenbach Co., New York; now Foundation Bodmer, cod. 48, Cologny near Geneva
Ph³	Phillipps 8137, property of the Rosenbach Foundation MS f. 1084/1, Philadelphia
Ph⁴	Phillipps 8299, now HM 140, Henry E. Huntington Library, San Marino, Calif. (The Clerk's Tale only)
Pl	Plimpton MS 253, formerly property of George A. Plimpton, now Columbia University Library, New York (formerly Phillipps 9970; a single bifolium containing fragments from IV and V)
Pp	Pepys 2006, Magdalene College, Cambridge (Melibee and The Parson's Tale)
Ps	Fonds anglais 39, Bibliothèque Nationale, Paris
*Pw	Petworth House MS 7, property of Lord Leconfield, Petworth, Sussex
Py	Royal College of Physicians 388, London

Ra¹	Rawlinson poet. 141, Bodleian
Ra²	Rawlinson poet. 149, Bodleian
Ra³	Rawlinson poet. 223, Bodleian
Ra⁴	Rawlinson C.86, Bodleian (parts of The Prioress's Tale and The Clerk's Tale)
Ry¹	Royal 17 D.xv, British Library
Ry²	Royal 18 C.ii, British Library
Se	Arch. Selden B.14 (SC 3360), Bodleian
Si	Sion College, London, Arch. L.40.2/E.23; now property of T. Takamiya, MS 22, Tokyo
Sl¹	Sloane 1685, British Library
Sl²	Sloane 1686, British Library
Sl³	Sloane 1009, British Library (Melibee only)
St	Stonyhurst College B.xxiii, Whalley, Lancs. (Melibee only)
Tc¹	Trinity College R.3.3 (582), Cambridge
Tc²	Trinity College R.3.15 (595), Cambridge
Tc³	Trinity College R.3.19 (599), Cambridge (The Monk's Tale only)
To	Trinity College Arch. 49, Oxford

A great many other copies of the Tales are known to have existed. References to them appear in medieval wills, in the catalogues of medieval and later libraries, or in sales catalogues from various auctions. Many of these references have been gathered and arranged in chronological order in Manly and Rickert, The Text of The Canterbury Tales, 8 vols., 1940; see 1:606–45. A few further allusions to lost texts appear in R. M. Wilson, The Lost Lit. of Med. Eng., 1952, 147–48.

The watershed year for study of the text of the Tales was 1940. With the appearance in this year of Manly and Rickert's monumental eight-volume text, editing the poem could never proceed on the same footing as before. The Manly-Rickert text rendered some of Robinson's editorial procedures obsolete; this fact was chronicled in his second edition by a lengthy list of changed readings (see Robinson, 1957, 883–85).

Robinson, like all the editors who had preceded him, prepared a text after consulting only a few of the manuscripts. His primary source for readings was the Chaucer Society's transcript of the eight selected texts. Although the transcripts present several of the copies most important for any text of the Tales, manuscripts to be included in the volumes were chosen by procedures curious in the extreme; as a result, texts based on these copies alone tend to present rather skewed evidence. For discussion of Furnivall's choice of manuscripts for the Chaucer Society's transcripts, see Baker, in Editing Ch, 157–69.

In the light of more recent work, the Chaucer Society's transcripts overemphasize some sources of the text at the expense of others. Although the Chaucer Society prints Hg, probably the oldest surviving manuscript and since Manly-Rickert considered the most important, it appears as an isolated source of readings. Its readings are, in the Eight-Text Edition, ceaselessly compromised by masses of evidence from other sources. Three very important copies—El Gg Ha⁴—always appear numerically superior to Hg and often provide a different text. Moreover, the late Victorian editorial tradition inherited by Robinson frequently saw these codices as the central form in which Chaucer's text had been transmitted.

Further, within the Eight-Text Edition, Hg readings are isolated by variants from another source. The three texts Cp La Pw provide evidence for a tradition usually characterized as that of "shop manuscripts" (copies prepared by professional London scribes for sale). These copies are early representatives of a tradition that includes many of the copies of the poem produced in the period 1440–90. The mass of evidence in the Eight-Text Edition tends to denigrate Hg readings and to emphasize those of other copies, a tendency replicated in Robinson's text.

Perhaps the greatest apparent achievement of the Manly-Rickert Edition has been to elucidate the relationships of the various sources of evidence. This process proved to be exceptionally complicated, and not simply because of the great number of witnesses. The Chicago editors found themselves generally unable to describe consistent relations of manuscripts valid for the entire poem; they were reduced to offering a narrative account of changes in the relationships of the witnesses from tale to tale (and sometimes within individual tales; see IV.2318n below).

The early reviews of Manly-Rickert established the central pattern of response to the text. See in particular Brown, MLN 55, 1940, 606–21; Root, SP 38, 1941, 1–13; Everett, RES 18, 1942, 93–109. The reviewers were impressed by the labor involved in textual production but generally overwhelmed by the intricacy of the findings. Some expressed befuddlement at how a text could have been constructed out of the elaborate evidence. But, on the whole, no one seemed disposed to quibble with the results. This is surprising, especially given the editors' desire to create only the copy they called O', the ancestor of all surviving manuscripts (rather than O, the text of Chaucer's holograph). As a result of this choice, the text printed a number of readings the editors openly believed to be erroneous.

The original response to the work remained the received opinion for nearly forty years. Dempster, most notably in PMLA 61, 1946, 379–415, offered cogent clarifications of the fundamental problems that had troubled early reviewers, and, except for some marginal queries (see Stroud, MLN 68, 1953, 234–47; Ryland, NM 73, 1972, 805–14), the edition for years stood as an often unexamined but acknowledged monument.

Recently, the state of affairs has shifted radically. Scholars seem far more disposed than in the past to query Manly and Rickert's assumptions about the state of the text, their methodology, and the care with which they applied the methodology to the problem in hand. An early sally in this direction occurs almost as an aside in Donaldson, Speaking of Ch, 1970, 102–18. For more extensive revisionist readings of the text of the Tales, see Kane, in Editing Ch, 207–29, and Blake (perhaps most pregnantly in ES 64, 1983, 385–400). As a result of such analyses, the materials based on Manly and Rickert's analysis of manuscript relations should perhaps be taken as extremely tentative.

Most of Volume 2 of Manly and Rickert's text is given over to an elaborate classification of the manuscripts. They show, first, that a variety of "constant groups" occur—pairs and larger collocations of manuscripts that consistently share erroneous readings. These they are able to join into larger groups, though often groups with shifting membership. Rather than a transmission history of the Tales as a whole, the editors provide a series of histories, one for each part of the text.

To speak generally, Manly and Rickert conceive of the manuscripts as representing two broad groups. A number of texts that they judge to be independent join consistently with one of the constant familial groups (a) against the remainder of the texts. Manly and Rickert believe the independents joined with a "are for the most part derived from a better text" (2:44) than are the remaining copies. These remaining copies include at least one "independent" codex and three separate constant groups. But these constant groups often agree genetically to form a single "large composite group" of up to forty texts. A number of manuscripts remain that are thoroughly "independent" and alternate between agreement with the first group and with the large composite group.

An effort at presenting this information in a simplified schematic fashion follows.

Manly and Rickert's "better tradition":
  independent MSS: El (Ll² Sl³) Gg (Do Ph¹) Hg
  a Dd En¹ Ds¹ Cn Ma
    a joins with other copies, e.g., Ln Pp Ry¹ Tc¹, to form $a*$

Manly and Rickert's "large composite group":
  independent MS: Ha⁴
  b He (Ox¹ Ox²) Ne Cx¹ Tc²
    b joins with other copies, e.g., Ii Ha³, to form $b*$
  c Cp La Sl²
  d En² Ll¹ Lc Mg Pw Ph³ Mm Gl Ry² Ld² Dl Ha² Sl¹
    d joins with other copies, e.g., Bo¹ Ph² Bw Ht Ld¹ Ra² Se To, to form $d*$

Manly and Rickert's alternating manuscripts:
  (Ad³ Ha⁵) Bo² Ch (En³ Ad¹) Fi To

For our textual presentation, we adopt the same eclectic (and perhaps not completely consistent) procedures used in Robinson's second edition. The text of the Tales remains based, as was Robinson's, on El. However, in the light of Manly and Rickert's elaborate demonstration, one can no longer, as Robinson recognized, follow El for every lection. In response to Manly and Rickert, Robinson emended into his El text a substantial number of readings from other copies, particularly Hg.

We continue Robinson's procedures by introducing a substantial number of additional Hg readings. These are drawn to the reader's attention in the notes, which indicate all changes from the text of the second edition. But we believe the text we print still to be Robinson's; rather than switch copy texts or intercalate all possibly correct Hg readings, we prefer to present a hybrid. We are especially chary of deserting El completely because we remain unconvinced, as is Kane in the article cited above, by Manly and Rickert's argument that El represents a text "editorially sophisticated."

The extant manuscripts exhibit great variation in the order in which they present the Tales. Manly and Rickert discuss the problem and provide all the relevant manuscript information at 2:475–94 (with three unnumbered leaves of tables after p. 494). The various orders reflect two sides of a single problem regarding presentation of the poem; these difficulties were first addressed in the decade after Chaucer's death. One facet of the problem was the condition of the poem; although continuous in its general form, it was apparently not available for copying as a continuous whole. The text, whether in codex or fascicles, existed at the fullest in unlinked fragments; it lacked a complete set of links. Second, the editors responsible for the first copies wished to produce texts that gave the impression of completeness, and, in that process, the continuity suggested by consistent linking of the individual tales was important.

In considering this problem, two extreme views should be avoided: (a) that Chaucer left the Tales in a clear order, and (b) that Chaucer left the Tales in a completely disordered state.

The second of these views is enunciated by Manly and Rickert, who deny that Chaucer can be responsible for any of the orders in surviving manuscripts (see 2:475). The evidence for such a view, also argued by Pratt (PMLA 66, 1951, 1141–67), boils down to the references to place names in the poem; these do not appear in the text in an order corresponding to the actual order of the Canterbury road. But, as has frequently been argued, the poem is plainly incomplete. The Tales certainly never received a final revision. It is entirely possible that Chaucer expected to clean up messy details, such as the place-name references, in a final revision that he was never able to carry out. Barring new evidence, the view that no authorial order ever existed seems difficult to sustain; but see Owen, PMLA 97, 1982, 237–50; and Blake, Archiv 218, 1981, 47–58.

The opposite view, that Chaucer had a definite order in mind, seems equally subject to question. Such a view, argued, for example, in Benson's discussion of the order of the tales (SAC 3, 1981, 77–120), speaks to aesthetic values but not necessarily to values that are authorial. That is, the order that emerges as "Chaucerian" is not necessarily Chaucer's. A careful fifteenth-century editor, trying to create an acceptable order, could well have seen that The Clerk's Tale and The Merchant's Tale, to take one example, had to follow The Wife of Bath's Prologue. The joking references to the Wife in these two tales would lack their full savor, had she not already spoken.

The manuscripts of the poem, with the exception of some anomalous versions, can be reduced to four orders.

a (the order of El Gg En¹ Ad³):

   I II III IV–V VI VII VIII IX–X

b (the order of Ne and other *b* copies):

   I II SqT MerT III ClT FranT VIII VI VII
   IX–X

c (the order of Cp La Sl²):

   I Gamelyn II SqT III IV FranT VIII VI VII
   IX–X

d (the order of Pw and other *d* copies):

   I Gamelyn II SqT MerT III ClT FranT VIII VI
   VII IX–X

In addition, the orders in two very early copies with anomalous arrangements are important:

Ha⁴: I Gamelyn II III IV–V VIII VI VII IX–X

Hg: I III II SqT MerT FranT SNT ClT VI VII
   IX–X

Generally speaking, as Benson (SAC 3) and Donaldson (Med. Lit. and Folklore, 193–204) have suggested, the *a* order is apt to be as close as one can come to Chaucer's intentions. The insertion of Gamelyn in Ha⁴ and in *c* and *d* simply attempts to provide a full tale to follow the Cook's fragment. As Dempster suggested (PMLA 64, 1949, 1123–42), the *c* order, with its transposition of The Squire's Tale, presumably developed next, possibly by consultation of Hg or a direct descendent. Orders *d*

and *b* are both derivatives of *c*, the latter suppressing the spurious Gamelyn. The only real anomaly in the *a* order is the position of Fragment VIII; other than in copies with this order, the junction FranT-SNT is almost universal. It is possible that the *a* order was produced by moving Fragment VIII to bring its reference to a place far along the road to Canterbury near the end of the poem.

Surprisingly, the most volatile argument about the order of tales concerns a feature that occurs only in the disordered copy Se. A great many critics, among them Pratt, have sought to eliminate place-name discrepancies by the so-called Bradshaw shift. This maneuver, which assumes that The Man of Law's Epilogue should provide a link to The Shipman's Tale, involves moving Fragment VII toward the head of the poem so that it follows Fragment II. Such an arrangement is printed in the Globe edition, in Baugh, and in Pratt. (It is also responsible for the alternative alphabetical labeling of fragments, in which VII becomes B², attached to B¹; the moving up of Fragment VI to follow B² is responsible for its identification as C.) This textual order, in spite of the nearly complete absence of manuscript evidence to support it, has inspired a substantial critical literature; among recent discussions are: Baker, NM 63, 1962, 245–61; Gardner, PLL 3, summer sup., 1967, 80–106; Wilson, NM 74, 1973, 292–96; James, Rackham Lit. St. (Ann Arbor) 5, 1974, 118–20; Keiser, ChR 12, 1978, 191–201.

The notes below attempt a more detailed annotation of transmission difficulties than those in past editions of Robinson. We attempt to provide some notice of all those major readings about which editors in the past century have offered conflicting opinions. For Fragment I, in a series of summary notes, we address some variants of a sort scarcely major but common throughout the poem.

In creating these notes, we have chosen to avoid reliance on the Chaucer Society's Eight-Text Edition. For reasons suggested above, its evidentiary bases are too narrow. Instead, we have tried to put in practice a famous dictum stated by Manly and Rickert: "It is, then, possible to reduce the number of MSS whose behavior needs to be considered in establishing the text to the early MSS that were the ancestors of the groups we have called *a*, *b*, *c*, and *d*, and the single MSS El, Gg, and Hg, and in connection with them Ha⁴ and Ad³" (2:41–42). Manly and Rickert added the last of these manuscripts to provide some evidence from the "alternating manuscripts."

We typically cite nine, in some cases ten, copies—the five single manuscripts mentioned by Manly and Rickert and the alternating text Ch, together with representatives of the four families. We cite Pw to give readings of *d*, but only on those occasions when *d* provides readings different from *c* (for a listing of these passages, see M-R, 1:96); otherwise we cite only Cp to give *cd* readings. For *a* we cite En¹ and for *b* Ne, both identified by Manly and Rickert as the best examples of their families (see 1:102, 258, 382). Where the manuscripts cited to indicate familial readings lack textual material owing to damage, we cite closely affiliated copies—Cx¹ for *b*, La for *c*. Otherwise we provide only minimal references to omissions and damage in the manuscripts, particularly frequent in Gg. Since our texts include no repeated sigla, we drop all superscripts—for example, Ha⁴ becomes Ha. The phrase "only in Ch" indicates that, of the ten manuscripts normally cited, only Ch has the reading. Sometimes we cite texts other than those mentioned above; the phrase "five manuscripts," for example, indicates a reading not attested by any of the texts we normally cite but nonetheless recorded in that number of manuscripts. We bracket those few readings for which there is no evidence from the ten normally cited manuscripts, as well as such dubia as The Man of Law's Epilogue.

We cite the readings of seven major editions. In chronological order these are: Skt (Skeat, The Oxford Ch), Pol (Pollard, the Globe edition), Rob (Robinson's editions), M-R (Manly-Rickert), Don (Donaldson, Ch's Poetry), Bgh (Baugh), and Prt (Pratt). We distinguish Robinson's two editions, for we often cite the first as Rob¹ to indicate readings shared with the Victorian editors. Rob² then means, as context requires, either both earlier editions of Robinson or only Robinson's second edition. Fisher's edition of The Canterbury Tales is not cited here as it provides no material not available elsewhere.

Most of the notes follow one of two formats. The first we use in connection with readings we consider legitimately variant—that is, the readings contain errors which are nonetheless of interest either intrinsically or because they are printed in one of the seven editions we cite. In these notes, we provide, following the lemma, the variant reading, the sigla of those manuscripts which contain the variant (in alphabetical, not preferential, order), and an indication of the editions that print it.

The second type of note occurs with some frequency. It accompanies instances in which we retain Robinson's reading but recognize that substantial debate may surround it. Here, following the lemma, we cite, not a variant, but the sigla of those manuscripts that support the printed text (again in alphabetical order); we next cite any odd variants for the lemma; finally, we group all manuscripts with the competing reading under the heading "rest" and give the names of those editors who have been persuaded that the competing reading is the correct one. Many notes of this second type are extended further: We often give a brief comment suggesting why variation may occur here or what reasons might conduce acceptance of the competing, unprinted reading.

FRAGMENT I

The General Prologue

In this fragment, we provide a series of summary notes calling attention to variants persistent throughout the poem but scarcely major. See, for example, 288, 894, and 915 below.

1   Aprill] *Aprille* Skt Pol Rob¹; the *-e* appears unambiguously only in Ha Pw. One of numerous efforts by earlier editors to follow MSS that edited out Chaucer's headless or nine-syllable lines; cf. 217 below.
8   half] Nearly all MSS and M-R; *halve* Rob² Don Bgh Prt; *halfe* Ha Skt Pol. Cx En have *half* before *his*.
49   in²] Om. Ch Ha Hg Skt Don.
60   armee] *aryve* Cx En Gg Ha Skt Don; the variant is discussed further by Donaldson, Med. Sts. in Hon. of L. H. Hornstein, 1977, 99–110 (as are 252a-b; and III.44a-f, 838).
120   Seinte] Unambiguously in only Pw in the Eight

Text, but the form of all eds.; for discussion of this persistent difficulty, see Donaldson, SN 21, 1949, 122–30.
140   and to been] *and* Ch; *to been* Cx; *for to be* En; *and been* Ha Hg Skt Pol.
164   chapeleyne and preestes thre] *chapeleyne* Prt, who believes, with M-R (see 3:422–23), that O' was here deficient, although there are no variants for the line. Chaucer may have written "And her chapeleyne, the preest, is thre," although *is* "adds up to, makes" does not seem attested.
217   eek] Ad Ch Ha Hg; om. rest and M-R Don Prt, to create a headless line.
252a-b   In Ch Hg and three MSS (Ld² Py Tc²) only; merely noted in Pol M-R (see 3:424), on the assumption that Chaucer dropped the couplet in revision.
288   nas] Cp El Gg; *was* rest and M-R Don Prt. Alternation between double and simple negation occurs frequently, especially in the prose. For other examples, cf. 2125 **is]** El Gg Ne Pw Rob² Bgh; *nys* rest and eds.; and II.435 **was]** Ch El En Gg Ha Ne; *nas* rest and M-R Don Prt. See also notes I.1145, 3000, 3350, 3418, 4056, II.49, and 289 below.
338   verray] *verraily* Ha Skt Pol Rob¹.
342   nowher] Cx En Gg Ha; *nevere* rest and M-R Don Prt.
375   were they] El Gg; *hadde þei ben* Ha; *they were* rest and M-R Prt.
421   where they] El Gg Ha; *where it* Ad Ch Hg; *where* Cp Skt M-R Don Bgh Prt; *were* Cx; *whereof it* En.
430   Rufus] *Ruphus* Ad; *Rusus* Ch Cp En Ha Hg M-R (as an error in O'; see 3:424); *Platearius* Cx; *Risus* El; *Rufijs* Gg.
500   shal] Cp El Gg; *sholde* rest and M-R Prt.
514   noght a] *no* Ha Skt.
558   a²] Om. Cp Skt Rob² Bgh.
637–38   Om. Hg; bracketed Ne; 637 and 639 om. Ch.
660   him drede] Cp; *to drede* Ad En Ha Ne; *drede* rest and M-R (as an error in O'; see 3:425).
686   biforn] *lay biforn* En Ha Skt Pol Rob² Bgh. The line is headless, with stress on the second syllable of *walet*.
714   the murierly] *so meriely* Ad Cp Skt; *so mery* En; *full meriely* Ha; *the meryere* Ne.
715   soothly] *shortly* El Ha Ne Skt Pol Rob¹ Bgh.
741   whoso] *whoso þat* Ha Skt Pol Rob².
752   to been] *to han been* Ha Skt Pol Rob².
754   was] *is* Ad Ch Cp Gg Ha Ne Skt Pol Rob².
791   oure] *your* Cp En Ha Ne Skt Pol.
824   alle in] Cp El Ha Ne Skt Pol Rob² Bgh. But *alle* may be a scribal intrusion, partly inspired by a line that appears too short; the other MSS and M-R Don Prt omit the word.
829   I it yow] Cp Ha Skt Pol Rob² Bgh Prt; *ye it* En; *I yow* Ne. But the more probably correct reading *it yow* appears in the other MSS and M-R Don; see MED *recorden v.*, sense 1b "recall"; for the reflexive use, cf. Boece 4.pr2.59; Tr 3:1179.
858   as ye may heere] *in this manere* El En Ha Skt Pol Rob¹ (**in**] *on* En).

The Knight's Tale

Iamque &c. in Ad Ch Cp El En Hg only, om. Pol Don Bgh.
876   yow] El Ha; om. rest and M-R.

894 **unto**] El Ha; *into* Ne; *to* rest and M-R Don Prt. The harder variant *to* forces one to read the line as "Lydgatian," with juxtaposed stresses at the caesura. As in many medieval poems, variation among prepositions occurs throughout the textual tradition. Other such Fragment I readings that have provoked editorial discussion include: 2222 **of** Ad Ch El Gg] *to;* 3011 **of** El Ha Pw] *for;* 3187 **at** Ch Cp El Ha] *in;* 3470 **of** Ch Cp El En Gg Hg] *up;* 3810 **amydde** El Gg Ha Ne] *in;* 4074 **of** Cp En Gg Hg] *out,* etc.; and 4172 **upon** El Ha] *on.* See also 1810 below.

915 **She**] *And* El En Ha Skt Pol Rob[1]. Alternation between parataxis with *And* and more pointed connectives occurs widely in the textual tradition. Other such Fragment I readings that have provoked editorial discussion include: 927 **And** El En Ha] *Now;* 1154 **And** El En Hg] *But;* 1180 **And** Ad Ch El En Ne] *That;* 2488 **But**] *And* El En Gg Hg; 3501, 3620 **He** El Ne] *And.* See also 3813 below.

980 **wan**] *slough* El Gg Ha Skt Pol Rob[2] Bgh. For the sense, see OED *win* v., sense 2 "conquer."

992 **freendes**] *housbondes* El En Ha Ne Skt Pol Rob[2] Bgh. For the sense, see OED *friend* sb., sense 4 "lover," used of married persons at V.762.

1005 **bodyes**] Gg Ha Hg Ne; *the bodies* rest and M-R Prt. This second *the* has been generated by the first.

1031 **This Palamon**] Ad Ch El Gg Ha; *Dwellen this Palamon* rest and Skt M-R Don Prt (**this**] om. Ne). The reading here printed requires supplying *ben,* or *lyveth* from 1028.

his felawe] Ad Ch El En Gg Ha; om. Ne; *eek* rest and Skt M-R Don Prt. This reading and the preceding are linked.

1039 **fyner**] Ad Ch El Gg Ha; *fayrer* rest and Skt M-R Don Prt, a considerably more pointed reading.

1044 **it**] *hym* Ad Ch El En Ha Skt Pol Rob[2] Bgh.

1046 **maked**] Ad Ch El Ha; *meyde* En; *maketh* rest and M-R Don Prt. Variation involving alternation between normal narrative past and historical present (for immediacy) is widespread in the textual tradition. Other such Fragment I readings that have provoked editorial discussion include: 1876 **thonked** Cp En Gg Ha Ne Pw] *thonken;* 2528 **was** El Ha] *is;* 2982 **hadde** El Gg Ha] *hath;* 3063 **loved** El] *loueth;* 3761 **cleped** El Gg] *clepen,* etc.; 4001 **craketh** El En Gg] *craked;* 4104 **dide**] *do* El Gg. See also 500 and 754 above.

1095 **for**] Ad El En Gg Ha; om. rest and M-R Prt, a reading that creates a Lydgatian line.

1129 **quod he to thee**] El Ha Ne; *to thee quod he* rest and M-R Don Prt.

1145 **Nay**] Ad Ch El En; *Now* rest and Skt M-R Don Prt, possibly correctly, since this may be one of a number of examples of scribal supply of emphatic extra negation.

1156 **woost**] *wotist* Ch; *wist it* Cp; *wistest* El Skt Pol Rob[1] Don; *wost it* En Ha; *wyst* Gg.

1171 **or wydwe**] Ad Ch Cp El Gg; *or be sche widewe* Ha; *wydwe* rest and M-R Don Prt, perhaps correctly.

1179 **whil that**] Cp Gg Ha Hg; *whil* rest and M-R Prt. The supply of *that* may be authorial, assuming monosyllabic *kyte* and a Lydgatian line; but alternation of conjunction and conjunction plus *that* occurs throughout the variant corpus. For other such Fragment I readings that have provoked editorial discussion, see: 3070 **er that** El Gg Ha] *er;* 3876 **whil that**] *whil* Cp Ha. See also 741 above.

1223 **that day**] Cp El Gg; *the day* rest and M-R Don Prt. Such bits of scribal intensification are endemic in the textual tradition. Other Fragment I examples that have provoked editorial comment include: 1452 **This** El En] *This;* 2860 **that**[2] El Ne] *the;* 3850 **this** El] *the;* 3977 **This** El Gg] *The;* 4003 **this** El Gg Ne] *the.*

1248 **helpe**] *heele* Ad Ch El En Pol.

1260 **witen**] El; *woot* rest and M-R Don Prt.

thing] Ha Ne; om. El En; *thing that* rest and M-R Don Prt. Linked with the preceding lemma.

1320 **man after his deeth**] Ch Gg Ha Hg; *after his deeth man* rest and M-R Prt (**man**] *þe man* Cp; *a man* En).

1346 **ne shal**] *he shal* El En Skt Pol M-R Rob[2] Bgh; *he ne schal* Cp; *schal* Gg; *schal he* Ha Ne. The first *Ne* in the line is the coordinating conjunction, not the negation of the verb; confused scribes have suppressed the apparently otiose negation and provided an explicit subject.

1350 **he moot**] El Gg Ha (**he**] *ho* Gg); *moot he* rest and M-R Don Prt. After Fragment I, we generally do not note such minor transpositions.

1376 **Biforen in**] Ha; *Biforn* rest and M-R (as an O' error for the Ha reading, 3:429); *Bifore in* Don, to create a Lydgatian line.

his] *his owene* El En Gg Pol.

1424 **long**] El En Gg Ha; *strong* rest and Skt M-R Don; this assumes that Chaucer's construction is "strong . . . / To doon . . . ," with "and big of bones" as quasi-parenthetical, and that scribes have detached this line from the following, reading "strong and big" as a pair of parallel adjectives. The tendency to read lines as complete detached units is discussed by Windeatt, SAC 1, 1979, 119–41.

1573 **after he**] El; *aftirward* Ha Ne Pol Don; *afterward he* rest and M-R Prt.

1584 **told**] *seyd* El Gg Pol Rob[1].

1595 **or**] *for* Ha Skt Pol Rob[2] Bgh.

1608 **muche**] *muche as* En Hg (interlined) Ne Rob[1] Don; om. Ha.

1637 **To**] *Tho* Ha Skt Rob[2] Bgh; *They* En.

1810 **or**] Ch (a correction) En Gg Ha Ne Pw; *of* rest and M-R Don, the *lectio difficilior,* "(knows less about it than) a cuckoo does about a rabbit." Variation among *of, on,* and *or*—all assignable to varying scribal responses to MS *o*—is endemic in the textual tradition; cf. 1279 **on** Ch El En Ne] *of* rest and M-R Don Prt; see also note VIII.75 below.

1880 **Thebes with his**] Ch El En; *Thebesward with* Pw Prt; *Thebes with* rest and M-R, a headless line.

1906 **on the gate westward**] Ad; *on the westward gate* Don (cf. *on the west gate* Hk Ii Nl); *westward* En Ha Skt Pol (see the next lemma); *on þe westward side* Pw; *on the westward* rest and M-R (**on**] *of* Cp Ne). Manly and Rickert believe the line they print perhaps only octosyllabic and only the text of O' (Pw retains the correct O reading; see 3:431).

in] *in þe mynde and in* Ha Skt Pol.

1986 **gate**] *gates* Cp Ha Ne Pw Skt Pol. The plural has been inspired by *al,* but the sense should be singular, following 1983 *entree.*

2030 **twynes**] *twyned* Ad Ch Cp En Gg Ne Pw; *twyne* Ha.

2037 **sterres**] Ad Ch Ha; *cercles* Ne; *sertres* rest and M-R (as an error in O'; see 3:432).

2049 **was depeynted**] *depeynted was* Ha Pol Rob[2]; *was* *peynted* Ne; *was depeynt* two MSS (Ld¹ Se) and Skt Don Bgh.

2075   hye] *wel hye* Cp El Gg; *wel* Pw. **an]** om. Hg; **ful]** om. Gg Ne. Manly and Rickert believe Chaucer wrote *wel hye,* not *ful hye* (3:433).

2104   or] Cp El Ha Pw; *and* rest and M-R Don Prt. Similar alternation occurs at 2202, 3532 *(and).*

2202   dauncen] *chaunten* M-R (in note, 3:433) Prt; *karolle* two MSS (Ha³ Dl) and Koch. Manly and Rickert's conjecture assumes contamination from *daunsynge* in the preceding line; Donaldson retains *dauncen* but hypothesizes that *daunsynge* represents an unrecorded *daunselinge* "charming" (cf. MED *daunselen v.* "treat with kindness").

2212   right tho] *also* El Gg Ha Skt Pol Rob¹.

2420   victorie] Three MSS (Cn Ry¹ To) and Skt Rob²; *þy victorie* Ha; *the victorie* rest and eds. (including Rob¹; according to M-R, an O' error; see 3:433).

2427   the ground anon] Ad Ch Cp El; *anon the ground* rest and M-R Don Prt.

2513   peple] *peples* Cp El En Gg Hg Skt Pol Rob¹ Don.

2534   peple] El; *the peple* rest and Skt M-R Don Prt.

2536   Tho] El Gg; *Thus* rest and M-R Don Prt.

2559   mace] Ad Ch En Ha Hg Don Prt; *maces* rest and eds. But note **swerd]** *swerdes* Cp Ne Pw, perhaps suggesting that scribes have assimilated all forms to a single number—either singular or plural.

2602   in arrest] Cp El; *in the rest* En Ha Ne (**in]** *into* Ha); *in at rest* Gg; *in th'arest* Ad Ch Hg Pw M-R Don Prt (**in]** *into* Pw).

2642   ydrawen to] Ad Ch En Gg Hg M-R Don Prt (**to]** *unto* En); *drawe(n) to* Cp Ne Pw; *ydrawe vnto* El Ha and eds.

2657   no] El En Gg; *nat* rest and M-R Don Prt.

2671   trompours] *trompes* El En Gg Ha Skt Pol Rob¹.

2681–82 Om. Ad El Gg Hg.

2683   And] *And she* En Hg Skt Don; three MSS (Cn Ma To) and Pol Bgh add a syllable by reading **chiere]** *in chiere* (cf. **al]** *al in* Ne).

2684   furie] *fuyre* Ad; *fyre* Cp En Ha Ne Pw Pol.

2758   hath now] El En Ha; *bath* rest and M-R Don Prt, possibly restoring a Chaucerian headless line.

2779–82 Om. Hg.

2788   alle circumstances] El Gg Ha; *circumstances alle* rest and M-R Don Prt.

2825   swich] Ad Ch El Gg Ha Pw; *swich a* rest and M-R Don Prt.

2831   wepyng] *a wepyng* El Gg Ha Skt Pol Rob¹.

2840   chaunge bothe] Ad En Hg; *chaunge(n)* Ch Skt Pol; *torne* Ha; om. rest and M-R Prt, forming an octosyllabic (less likely a headless) line.

2842   ensamples] El Gg; *ensample* rest and M-R Don Prt.

2865   comande anon] El Gg Ha; *anon* Ne; *anon comande* rest and M-R Don Prt.

2874   hadde he gloves] El; *were his gloues* Ha; *two his gloves* Don; *his gloves* rest and M-R Prt. M-R suggests *putte he gloves* in note (3:435).

2892   that weren] Ha; om. rest and M-R Don Prt, to produce a Chaucerian headless line.

2904   is] *is al* Ha Skt Pol Rob¹.

2918   ful many] El Ha; *many* rest and M-R Prt.

2920   that] El; *what* Gg Ne; *how* rest and Skt M-R Don Prt.

2949   wyn and milk] Ad El Gg Ha; *milk wyn* Ne; *milk and wyn* rest and M-R Don Prt.

2956   And] *Ne* Cp Gg Ha Ne Pw Skt Rob² Bgh.

2963   eek how that they] El Gg Ha; *how they alle* Prt; *al(le) how they* rest and M-R Don.

2999   wel abregge] El Gg Ha; *abregge* rest and M-R Prt.

3000   noght] Cp El Rob²; om. rest and eds.

3003   by this ordre wel] El Gg; *wel by this ordre* rest and M-R Prt (**wel]** before *men* Ne; om. Pw).

3018   From] El Ha; *Fro the* rest and M-R Don Prt.

to sprynge] Cp En Gg Ha Ne Pw Rob² Bgh; *sprynge* rest (Ch corrected) and eds. Cf. **bigynneth]** *gynneth* Ad Ch Ha Hg.

3019   we] El Gg Ha; *ye* rest and M-R Don Prt.

3026   may ye se] El; *se ye* En Hg Don; *may y say* Gg; *may I see* Ha; *þe se* Pw; *ye se* rest and M-R Prt.

3028   nedes] Ad Ch En; *wendeþ* Ha; *nedeth* rest and Skt Pol Rob¹ Don.

3032   men] El Gg Ha; *ye* rest and M-R Don Prt.

3036   That] *The which* Ha Skt Pol Rob¹.

3052   up yolden is] El; *yolden is* Ad Ch En M-R; *yolden is vp* Cp Hg Pw Don (*y-yolden* Cp Pw); *is ʒoldyn vp* Gg Ha Prt; *so up yolden is* Ne.

3059   flour] *the flour* Ad Cp En Ha Ne Pw Rob².

3071   rede that] Ha; *rede* rest and M-R Prt. In the M-R construction, the line is Lydgatian.

3074   we] El Ha; om. Ch; *I* rest and M-R Don Prt. *I* is likely correct, given 3075 *my fulle assent.*

3090   the knight] *ful right* El Gg Ha Skt Pol.

3099   wyde world] El Gg Ha; *world* rest and M-R Prt.

3104   so] *al so* Ha Skt Pol Rob² Bgh. Don transposes *hire serveth* to make a line clearly headless.

The Miller's Prologue and Tale

3110   route] El Gg Ha; *compaignye* rest and M-R.

3155–56 Om. Ch Cp En Hg Ne Pw.

3170   M'athynketh] *Me thinketh* Ad En Gg Skt; *Me ouerthynketh* Ne; *Me forþenkeþ* Pw.

3183   Reve eek and othere] *Reue and othere manye* Ad El Gg Ha Skt Pol Rob¹ (**othere manye]** *monye othere* Ad).

3228   man] Ch El Ha; *a man* Ad Ne; *men* rest and M-R Don Prt. That Chaucer most likely intended the apparently plural indefinite pronoun *men* "one" is confirmed by En Gg, which have **his]** *her.* Rather than being a plural, the form is derived from the unstressed form of singular *man, me.*

3236   as¹] *eek as* Ha Skt Pol Rob² Bgh; the omission produces a Lydgatian line.

3285   she] *ich* Ch Cp El En Hg M-R Prt, a reading easier to defend were the text to read *quoth.*

3292   wol] El Ha; *wolde* rest and M-R Don Prt.

3350   took] *ne took* Ha Hg Skt Pol Rob¹ Don. The supply of *ne* seeks to avoid a Lydgatian line.

3403   hym] Ad Ch (corrected) El Gg Ne Pw, a spelling variant for the probably correct reading *hem,* in rest and M-R Don Prt. Cf. 4020 **hem]** El En Gg Ha] *hym.*

3418   thyng] El En Rob² Bgh; *nought* Ha Pw Pol; *nothyng* rest and eds., correctly.

3485   verye] Ch Cp Gg; *uerye* Ad El Hg M-R; *mare* En; *verray* Ha; *werry* Ne; most probably correct is Don *nerye,* M-R's reading and the unique Middle English example of *nerian* "protect" (see expl. note).

3519   an] El En Gg Ha; *in an* rest and Skt M-R Prt.

3541 be] Ad Ch El En Gg Ne; *wel* Ha; om. rest and M-R Don Prt, to form a headless line.

3566 espye] *spye* El Skt Pol Rob² Bgh.

3571 breke] *broke* Ch Cp El Skt Pol Rob¹ Don.

3672 to wake] *wake* El Ha Skt Pol Rob¹.

3721–22 Om. Ad Ch Cp En Gg Ha Hg, the result of returning to copy one paraph too far along; 3714, 3718, 3719, 3720, and 3723 all open with this MS punctuation in El Hg.

3767 for] Cp El; *what* with *for* supplied later Ha; *what* rest and M-R Don Prt.

3813 And] *That* Ad Ch En Hg M-R Don Prt; the result clause seems more pointed than does the simple parataxis.

3828 yet] El Gg Ne; om. rest and M-R Don Prt, a headless line. Note lay] *he lay* El Gg Skt.

The Reeve's Prologue and Tale

3864 thee] *yow* Ch El Skt Rob¹.

3876 whil that] *whil* Ad Cp Ha Ne Rob². Cf. alwey] *ay* El Skt Pol.

3931 in] *is in* Rob² (a misprint).

3953 wounde] *bounden* El Gg Ha Ne Skt Pol Rob² Bgh.

3990 Soler] *Scoler* Ne Prt, following Brewer, ChR 5, 1971, 311–17; see expl. note.

4005 revelrye] Ad En Ha Ne; *reverye* "wantonness, wildness" rest and M-R Don Prt.

4026 Symond quod John by God] El Gg Ne; *By God quod John Symond* rest and M-R Don Prt (Symond] om. Ad Ch; *nede must* En).

4027 boes] El; *muste* Gg; *falles* Ha; *bus* Ne; *bihoues* rest and M-R (an error in O'; see 3:443). An example of the varying representations of the students' dialect; see expl. note I.4022.

4037 howgates] Cp; *how that* El Ha Skt Pol Rob¹ Bgh, which confirms Cp; *how* rest and M-R.

4040 and] Cp Gg Ha; om. rest and M-R Don; the latter follows Koch in reading *Johan*.

4056 counte I] *ne counte I* Ha Ne Pol Rob² Bgh; *I counte* Gg Skt Rob¹.

4066 thurgh²] Ad Ch Cp El Gg; *eek þurgh* Ha; om. rest and M-R Don Prt.

4097 now] El Gg; *yet* Cp Ne; *ye* rest and M-R Don Prt. The form in Cp Ne, dependent on *ye*, probably confirms that the latter reading is Chaucer's.

4098 he gooth] *they goon* El En Ha Skt Pol Rob¹; the verb has been attached to the students (not the horse) under influence of subsequent *the children*.

4118 they hym bisoght] no variants, but to avoid a preterite plural without *-e*, Don, following Koch, emends by changing *hym* to *han*.

4127 John] El Gg; *this John* rest and M-R Don Prt.

4128 this] El Gg; *that* rest and M-R Don Prt. This variant and the preceding are linked, El Gg suppressing 4127 *this* to avoid apparent repetition.

4129 seyd] Ad Ch El Gg; *seye* rest and M-R Don Prt. Man] El; *men* rest and M-R Don Prt. Cf. 3228 above for similar difficulties with the indefinite.

4163 fnorteth] *snorteth* Cp En Gg Ha Skt Pol.

4166 two] El Gg; *a* rest and M-R Don Prt.

4184 al this] El Gg; *this* Ad Ch En Prt; *to* rest and M-R Don, perhaps correctly.

The Cook's Fragment

Following line 4422, in the inner margin, Hg notes "Of this Cokes tale maked Chaucer na moore." The absence of any conclusion produces a number of aberrations in the MSS (for example, the attempt to allow space for a conclusion implied by fascicle boundaries placed after The Cook's Tale in El Ha Hg). This sense of the need for some conclusion also motivates the bizarre supply of Gamelyn in the *cd* tradition.

FRAGMENT II

Introduction to the Man of Law's Tale

4 depe ystert] *deepe expert* Cp Skt Pol; *depe stert* En; *depe* Ha; *deppest stert* Ne.

5 eightetethe] The expansion printed by all eds. for *xviij*ᵗʰᵉ, in at least Hg Cp (M-R print Hg); *eighte and twentiithe* (*-ty* Ad Ch En) Ad Ch El En; *þe prettenþe* Ha. Both variants are from misread Roman numerals. The word must be read with four syllables (cf. Old English *eahtateoþa*).

14 of] Ad Ch Ha Ne; *at* rest and M-R Don Prt.

37 yow now of] *yow of* Ad; *ȝow and holdeþ* Ha Skt Pol.

49 Hath] *Nath* one MS (Ha³) and M-R (in note, 3: 447) Prt; *As* Gg.

102 with nede artow so] *so sore artow* Ch El En Pol.

The Man of Law's Tale

212 They argumenten] Ch El Gg Hg; *The argumentes* Cp Ha; *They argumentis* En Ne.

289 brende at] Gg; *brende* Ch El En M-R; *þat brende* Cp Ha; *brent hadde* Hg; *not brende* Ne; *brende n'at* Don.

409 And] Ha Ne; *He* rest and M-R Don Prt.

574 Converteth] *Conuertid* Gg Ha Skt Rob² Bgh; *Converted hath* Ne.

577 many a] Cp En Gg Ha Rob²; *many* rest and eds.

621 greet] a Lydgatian line, with no variants; *ful greet* Skt (so M-R in a note, 3:450); *there greet* one MS (Ps) and Don.

676 holde I] Ad Ch El En; *I moot holde* Cp; *I holde* rest and M-R Don Prt.

704 mariage] *mariages* Ad Ch El Hg Don, perhaps correctly; *the mariage* En; *this mariage* Ne.

714 no bet] Ad Ch El En; *noon oother* rest and M-R Don Prt.

728 taketh] Ch Gg Hg M-R Prt preserve what may be Chaucer's contracted form *tath* (cf. *takth* Skt Don); it is confirmed as archetypal by the erroneous *hath* Ad.

733 thanketh] *thanke* Cp En Ha Ne Skt; *thankid* Gg. The printed form is the imperative plural; cf. *ye* 732. However, Chaucer's use varies; see also III.1248 **Dooth** Skt Pol Rob² Bgh (and at least El Gg Ha)] *Do*.

756 wight] *man* Ha; om. Ad Ch El En Hg M-R (as an error in O'; see 3:451).

802 charge hire that she] *chargen hire she* El Pol Rob¹.

882 and eek] Ad En; *and* rest and Pol M-R Prt (in M-R, an error in O'; see 3:451).

1060 his] *alle his* Ha Skt Pol Rob² Don Bgh.

1121 was] *with* Rob² (a misprint).

1124   his] Cp El Gg Ha; *thyse* Ne; *this* rest and M-R Don Prt. The printed reading was probably inspired by 1125; such variation occurs frequently, for example at III.900.

The Epilogue of the Man of Law's Tale

The Epilogue appears in only Cp (our source for the text) Ha Ne. Given such phraseology as 1185 *My joly body,* the Epilogue probably goes back to a point in the development of the Tales when the Wife of Bath was still assigned the Shipman's fabliau; see Pratt, in Sts. in Hon. of Baugh, 45–79. Once such an assignment was dropped, the link was no longer needed but seems never to have been replaced; the editors behind some early manuscripts, in their attempt to create a continuous narrative through the Tales, used the Epilogue to provide a join with whatever story followed The Man of Law's Tale in their exemplars.

1170   him] *hem* Rob² (probably a misprint).
1174   Now] *How* Cp Skt.
1179   Shipman] One MS (Se, the single MS in which The Shipman's Tale follows); *Sompnour* Ha M-R; *Squyer* Cp Ne; *Wif of Bathe* Don. All these readings depend on and have been derived from the subsequent tale (in Ha, Fragment III, including Summoner's Tale, follows).
1189   phislyas] Cp Ne; *physices* Skt; *of phisyk* three MSS (Cx Fi Tc²; cf. *phisik* Ht Mc Ra¹ Ra²) and Pol.

FRAGMENT III

The Wife of Bath's Prologue

37   leveful were] *were leveful* El Ha Rob² Bgh.
44a-f   In Ch En Ne only, here supplied from Dd; not in Skt Pol; Manly and Rickert (3:454) argue that this and four other sparsely attested passages elsewhere in The Wife of Bath's Prologue (575–84, 605–12, 619–26, 717–20) are late Chaucerian insertions limited to a few textual traditions.
46   sothe] El Ha; a spurious line En Ne; *sith* rest and M-R Don Prt, taking the line as a subordinate clause joined with the next sentence.
56   ferforth as] El Ha; *fer as hieren* En (Ne similar); *fer as evere* rest and M-R Don Bgh Prt.
97   clene] El Gg; *clene in* rest and M-R Don Prt.
98   I nyl nat] El Gg; *I wole* Cp En Ne; *I nyl* Ha; *ne wol I* rest and M-R Don Prt.
117   And of so parfit wys] *And for what profit was* El Gg Skt Pol Rob¹; *And in what wise was* Ha. Confusion of *par-* and *pro-* abbreviations also occurs at 92.
   a wright] Three MSS (Ld² Ln Ry²) and Don Prt; *and why* Cp; *a wyf* Gg; *a wight* rest and eds. Donaldson explains the emendation in Speculum 40, 1965, 626–33.
127   That] *This* Cp Skt Pol Rob² Bgh.
189   yet] El Gg Skt Pol Prt; *that* rest and eds. (an O' error, in Manly and Rickert's opinion; see 3:456).
192   nys] Ad Hg; *is* Ch El En Gg Ne; *is not* Cp Ha Rob².
193   sire] *sires* En Ha La Ne Skt Rob¹; with the next, the product of confusion over whether Alison should address the Pardoner or the whole company.

now wol I telle] El Gg Ha; *thanne wol I telle yow* rest and M-R Don Prt.
210   love ye] *loue* El En Gg Ha Ne Skt Pol Rob¹.
231–32   if . . . / Shal beren . . . the] *schal if . . . / Bere . . . þat þe* Cp Rob².
280   houses] *hous* Gg Ha Skt Pol Rob² Bgh.
288   Spoones and] El Gg; *Spoones* rest and M-R Don Prt.
303   Janekyn] Trisyllabic, as also in 383; this form should also be used in 595, since it is more likely to be authorial than is disyllabic *ourë.*
316   helpith] *nedeth* El En Ne Skt Pol.
   to enquere or] El Gg Ha Ne; *enquere or* Ad Ch (**or**) corrected Ch); *to enquere and* En; *enquere and* Cp Hg M-R Don Prt.
327   nevere] El Gg; *nat* rest and M-R Don Prt.
331   certeyn] El Gg; *certes* rest and M-R Don Prt.
368   maner] Cp; *of þese* Gg; *of þy* Ha Pol; om. rest and M-R Don Prt (in M-R an O' error; see 3:458). Don also reads *ther nat;* cf. *ther now* Ne.
387   and yit] Gg; *thogh I* (**and was**] *were*) El En Ne Skt Pol; *and ʒet I* Ha; *and I* rest and M-R Don Bgh Prt.
391   blyve] El Gg Rob² Bgh; *belyue* En Ne; *ful blyve* rest and eds.
395   I] *it* El Skt Pol Rob¹.
457   How] *Lord how* Cp; *Wel* El En Gg Ne Skt Pol. The printed reading restores some of Alison's verbal energy and enthusiasm (as in note 210 above), while avoiding the scribal efforts at making them more intense.
501   soule] *soul* Rob² (a misprint?).
540   often] *ful often* El En Ne Skt Pol Rob¹.
575–84   Om. Cp Ha Hg; placed after 586 Ad.
580   ye] *he* Ad El Gg Skt Pol Rob² Bgh.
595   Jankyn] See 303 above.
600   twenty] *a twenty* El En Skt Pol Rob² Bgh.
605–12   Om. Ha; 609–12 om. Cp Hg.
619–26   Om. Ad Cp Ha Hg.
621   wys] El Gg; *wysely* rest and M-R Prt.
624   or long or] El Gg; *long* rest and M-R Prt.
717–20   Om. Ad Cp Gg Ha Hg.
727   care] *sorwe* El En Hg Ne Don; *penance* Cp Skt Pol.
836   eek] Cp; om. rest and M-R Prt.
838   pees] *pace* Prt (following Koch's conjecture, endorsed by M-R, 3:460); *pisse* En Ne Don, probably correctly. The scribes seem more often to reduce obscenity than to introduce it (cf. note VII.929–30 below).

The Wife of Bath's Tale

878   go] *go now* Ad Ch Cp Pol Rob² Bgh.
882   bifel] *bifel it* Ha Skt Pol Rob² Don; *fell it* Cp.
885   he] *she* Ch Cp Gg Ha Skt Pol, a piece of scribal sentimentality.
1038   to have] *haue* El Pol Rob¹; om. Ch.
1080   on] *on the* Ad Ch Rob²; *on a* Cp El Skt Pol Rob¹; *at a* En; *in the* Gg; *in a* Ha; *by the* Ne.
1091   and] *and eek* Cp En Ne Skt Rob² Bgh. The supply of *eek,* as frequently, seeks to avoid metrical embarrassment, here a Lydgatian line.
1096   tel] *tel me* En Gg Ha Ne Skt Rob².
1129   goodnesse] El En Ne; *prowesse* rest and M-R Don Prt, probably repeated from earlier in the line. In spite of M-R's note (3:461), *prowesse,* as an attribute of God, does not seem to make sense.

1191   it syngeth] El Gg; *synne is* Ad Ch; *is synne* Cp En Ha Hg M-R (as an O' error; see 3:461–62); *is an high ioye* Ne. The printed version is confirmed by the reading of Juvenal cited 1194.

1262   noght wol] *wol not* Cp Gg Ha Ne Skt Rob² Bgh; *nyl nat* En.

The Friar's Prologue and Tale

1277   scoles] Ha; *scole eek* Cp Skt Rob² Bgh; *scole* rest and Pol M-R Don. M-R claims (3:462) that the last reading is an O' error; rather, it creates a Lydgatian line.

1288   wol have] El En Ha Ne; *wol* rest and M-R Don Prt.

1295–96   In Ha Skt Pol misplaced after 1308.

1295   And] *And eek* Cp Ha Skt Pol Rob² Bgh, to avoid a headless line.

1300   leeve] *my leue* Cp Pol Rob² Bgh; *my* Ha; *myn own* En Ne.

1324   wel wher that] Rob² (cf. *wel wher* Dd); *where þat* Cp Skt Don Bgh; *wher* rest and Pol M-R Prt, identified by M-R as an O' error, 3:463.

1332   wommen] *þe wommen* Cp Ha Skt Pol Rob² Don Bgh.

1377   Rood for] Ad Ch Cp; *Wente for* Gg; *Rod forth* Ha Pol; *For* rest and M-R Prt. This variant is linked with the inclusion of 1379 **And** (so Ad Ch Cp Gg; *Hit* Ha; rest om.); several readings in these MSS later in 1377 attempt to adjust the meter.

1406   and pleye] *hir weye* Cp El Skt Pol, inspired by doubts as to whether *riden* is present or past tense.

1527   to] Cp El; *to thee* rest and M-R Don Prt (Gg adds *leue* later in the line).

1586   somonce here] Three MSS (Dd Nl Se); *somonce* Ch El En Hg M-R Prt; *somonaunce of* Ha Pol; *somounys in* Ad; *somonus of þe here* Cp; *somounys* Gg; *sompnour of þe* Ne.

1647   Crist] *Crist and* Skt (and M-R in note, 3:465); *Cristë* Pol. But probably a Lydgatian line.

1663   somonours] El En Hg (a correction); *somonour* rest and M-R Prt, with further changes to singular through 1664.

The Summoner's Prologue and Tale

1694   ther] Ad Ch El Hg; *they* rest and M-R Prt.

1784   I have] *haue I* Ch Cp En Gg Ha Ne Pw Skt Rob².

1838   now²] Om. Cp En Gg Ha Ne Pw Skt Pol Rob¹; cf. 1918 **now]** om. Cp El Hg Pol.

1864   trillyng] *triklyng* El Hg Skt Pol Rob¹ Don; *trynkelynge* Gg.

1983   sely] *holy* Ad Ch En Ha Ne Pw.

1991   nat] Ad Ch En Gg Ne; *fro* Ha Pol; *nat for* rest and M-R Bgh Prt.

1993   Ire] Ad Ch Pw Prt; *hire* rest and eds. (in M-R an O' error; see 3:467).

1999   hooly] *hooly and* Ha Skt Rob²; *holy and so* Cp. The scribal "and" produces the easier sense "holy and meek," rather than Chaucer's "completely meek"; although elsewhere in Chaucer, *hooly* only occurs with an adjectival possessive pronoun, cf. the Lydgate, *Life of Our Lady,* and Chauliac readings cited by MED *hooli adv.,* sense 3b.

2015   certes] *eek* Ad Ch El Gg Pw Rob¹; *also* Ha; om. En.

2125   yeve] *yeue you* En Ha Ne Rob²; *yeuen* El Gg Bgh.

2158   Pw ends, adding four spurious lines, the last pair derived from 2294.

2178   is noon] Cp El Ha; *nys non* Gg; *ther is* Ne; *ther nys* rest and M-R Don Prt.

2186   that] *swich* El Ha Skt Pol Rob¹.

2212   disclaundre] El; *sclaundre* Cp; *diffame* rest and Skt M-R Don Prt, more likely correct.

2235   evere] Ad Ch El Gg Ha; *therwiþ* Cp; *ther* rest and M-R Don Prt.

litel and litel] Cp El En Ne; *lite and lite* rest and Skt M-R Don Prt.

2289   dide or] Four MSS (Ii Ld¹ Ry¹ Si) and Rob² Don; *or elles* Ha; *or* rest and Pol M-R Bgh; *or as* Skt Prt.

Ptholomee] Ne; *Protholomee* rest and Pol M-R Bgh (in M-R as perhaps the Summoner's mispronunciation; see 3:468).

FRAGMENT IV

The Clerk's Prologue and Tale

17   be] *be that* Ch El En Ha Ne Rob² Bgh; om. Pw.

57   at] *right at* Ad La Rob² Bgh; *in* Ne.

128   youre] *thyn* Ad Cp Ha Pw Pol M-R Rob² Bgh (in M-R an error in O'; see 3:469).

137   lyne] *lynage* Ad Cp Ha Pw Skt Rob² Bgh Prt; *lif* Ch Gg Ne. The printed reading is confirmed by the Ch Gg Ne error, the result of misinterpreting minims and reading *lyue.*

165   What] *That what* Ad Cp Hg Skt Pol Rob² Don Bgh; *That* Ha Pw.

385   translated] *transmuwed* Ad Cp; *transformed* Pw, corresponding to Lat. *transformatam* (S&A 2:72).

413   on] *in* En Gg Ha Ne Rob².

429   hoomlinesse] Ad Cp, corresponding to Lat. *domestica* (S&A 2:92); *humblesse* Ha; *humblenesse* rest and M-R Don. The last reading may well be right, since it reflects the S&A variant *modestia* (cited from Har³, a codex related to Ch's source-text).

537   al²] Om. Ch Cp El Ne Skt Pol.

552–53   blisse : kisse] *kisse : blisse* El En Skt Rob¹.

583   softe] *ful softe* Ad Pw and eds. except M-R Prt; *ful ofte* Cp. According to M-R (3:472), *ful* is a scribal emendation.

588   whenne] Cp El; *when that* Ad; *whennes* rest and M-R Don Prt.

704   that] *a* Ad Cp En Ha Pw Skt Rob² Bgh Prt; *the* (changed to *a* later) Ne. The reading we print requires one to make a metaphoric connection between holding strongly to a purpose and being bound to a stake.

867–68   your . . . your] Ad Cp; *your . . . my* Pw; *my . . . my* rest and Pol Skt M-R. Manly and Rickert (3:472) report that McCormick insists that Pw preserves Ch's text: Grisilde surrenders the clothes as Walter's but insists that the ring he presented her is hers.

916   moore] Ad Ch Cp Pw; *she moore* rest and M-R Don Prt, perhaps correctly (although cf. the similar effort at marking Grisilde explicitly as actor in the next note).

1013   is] Ad Ch Cp Gg Pw; *is she* rest and M-R (perhaps as O' error; see 3:473).

1017   so konnyngly] *konnyngly* Ad Cp and eds. except

M-R Prt; *so benyngnely* Gg; *boxomly* Pw. Perhaps *so* echoes the preceding line.
1063   ne noon] Ad Ch Cp Gg Ha; *and noon* Pw; *noon* rest and M-R Prt.
1067   disposed] *purposed* Ad Ch Cp Ha Skt Pol; *supposed* El Gg Hg Don, repeated from 1065 according to M-R (3:473).
1170–76   Om. Pw, which also places 1195–1200 after 1212.
1181   trust] *hope* Ad Cp El Ha Skt Pol.

The Host's Stanza

Lines 1212a–g are omitted by Ad Ha La Pw Pol and printed in notes in Skt Bgh Prt. Past editors (see M-R, 3:473) have usually argued that the stanza formed the original link, and originally came after 1162 or 1169. In this view, Chaucer revised the conclusion of The Clerk's Tale by adding the envoy, directly linking the envoy and The Merchant's Prologue by the echo in 1213. But the echo is a real one, whether delayed by a stanza or not, and the stanza never appears earlier, but always after 1212. On the other hand, materials from the stanza do appear to have been absorbed elsewhere (see VII.1892–94), potentially a sign of cancellation.

The Merchant's Prologue and Tale

1213–44   Om. Hg La Pw; on a leaf now lost Gg.
1228   lyven] *lyue* M-R Don Bgh (and at least El Ha). For an outstanding recent examination of such variation, see Smithers, in ME Sts. Presented to N. Davis, Gray and Stanley, eds., 1983, 195–234.
1301   if] *if that* Cp Ch Ha Ne Pw Skt Pol Rob² Bgh, which avoids a Chaucerian headless line.
1305–6   The printed text follows El Gg; Don places all material after *wyf* in brackets to indicate either an incomplete O' line or a couplet subjected to scribal censorship. The couplet is omitted in Cp Ne. Other MSS offer rich variety:

And if thow take a wife of highe lynage
She shall be hauten and of grete costage (Ch En)

And if þat þou take a wif be war
(Cf. *be wel yware* in the three other copies Bo² Ha⁵ Ps.)
Of oon peril which declare I ne dar (Ha)

And if thow take a wyf she wole destroye
Thy good substance and thy body annoye
(Hg corrected; original hand stops at *wyf*, the form printed by M-R Prt.)

And if þou take a wif þat to þe is vntrewe
Ful ofte tyme it shal þe rwe (Pw)

1307   thynges] *siþes* Cp Ne Pw; *siþe* Ha; om. Gg.
1316   drede nat] *drede thow nat* Ad; *drede* Ch; *dredelees* El Gg Skt Pol; *drede it nouȝt* Pw.
1358–61   Om. El.
1417   twenty] *lx* Ch; *sixteen* Cp En Ha Ne Pw Don Prt.
1418   fayn] *ful fayn* Ch Cp Gg Ha Skt Rob² Bgh; *certayn* Pw.
1436   go streight] Ha Hg (a correction); *so streyt* Cp Ne Pw; *streight go* En; *streight* rest and M-R.

1523   amonges] *among hise* El En Gg Skt Pol Rob¹; *among* Ne.
1545   I have] El Ha; *I* Ne Pw (Pw reads *siþens* earlier); *that I* rest and M-R Don Prt.
1566   ysayd] *sayd* at least Gg Ha and Skt Pol Rob² Don Bgh; *al sayd* Cp Pw.
1776   ther] Cp El Ne; *as* rest and M-R Prt.
1780   at] *as at* Ha Skt Pol Rob² Bgh.
1960   He] *And* En Gg Skt Pol Rob² Bgh.
1967   by aventure] *aventure* Ha Skt Pol Rob² Don Bgh.
1998   oonly but] *but oonly* Gg Ha Ne Skt Pol Prt.
2011   preyneth] *proyneþ* Cp En Gg Skt Rob¹; *pruneth* Ha; *prayneth* Hg. Cf. IV.55, 391 **convey-]** *conuoy-* Ch El Hg.
2108   myghtest] *myghte* En Ha Rob².
2133   of¹] Eight MSS (Bw Cx Ha⁵ Ps Ra³ Ry¹ Tc¹ Tc²) and Don Prt; *er* rest and eds.
    Juyn] *Juyl* all MSS and Skt Rob¹ M-R Bgh (in M-R as an O' error; see 3:477). The emendation reflects 2222 *Geminis*, i.e., 11 May–11 June.
2140   with alle] Cp Ne; *with* rest and M-R Prt.
2218   myrie] *ful myrie* En Rob² Bgh.
2230   Ethna] Two MSS (Ha⁵ Ps); *Sithea* Ad; *Proserpyna* Cp M-R (as an O' error; see 3:477–78); *her pina* Ne. Most MSS have a spurious line: *Ech after oother right as any lyne* Ch El (later in blank) En Gg Ha Skt Pol; *Whos answer hath doon many a man pyne* Hg (later in blank). Koch conjectured *Sicilia* here to rhyme with 2229 *Proserpyna* (but note *Proserpyne* Ch El En Gg Ha Hg).
2233   fette] *sette* Ch El Gg Hg Ne.
2240   tales] A conjecture in Pol Rob² Don Prt; om. M-R (as an O' error; see 3:478); *stories* one MS (Ha⁵; in another, Ii, in 2241) and Skt Bgh; *samples* one MS (Bw; *ensamples* in two others, Cx Tc², in 2241); *historyes* one MS (Ps).
2290   but neither he ne she] *that sit in Trinitee* Ch El Gg Ha Ne Skt Pol Rob¹.
2300   if] *if þat* Cp Skt Pol Rob² Bgh.
2318   Cp ends; there is a change of ink in Hg and an irregular quire (the nineteenth) in Ha; according to M-R, substantial shuffling of relations of the manuscripts occurs here (see 3:375).
2380   fals] *al fals* Ad Gg Hg Skt Rob¹ Don.

Epilogue to the Merchant's Tale

Lines IV.2419–40 and V.1–8 constitute a single unit in all MSS in which they occur, although they do not always join the same tales (in Hg and some other copies they link Merchant and Franklin). In El, the rubric preceding 2419 reads "The Prologe of the Squieres tale." The division into two fragments, done by Victorian students of tale order, is simply misleading. The passage is omitted in Cp Ne.

2424   the soothe] Ch En Rob²; *a sooth* rest and eds.

FRAGMENT V

The Squire's Introduction and Tale

4   I wol seye] *suche thing* Ad Ch En.
6   lust] *heest* Ad; *wille* Ha Hg.
20   alwey] *and eueremore* Ch Hg Skt Pol Don. Manly

and Rickert read the line as we print it as headless (see 4:480).

94   contenaunce] *his contenaunce* En Rob² Bgh; *contynaunces* Ad Cp; *his cuntenaunces* Gg Hg Don. Probably a Lydgatian line.

105   be] *be it* Cp En Ha Ne Skt Pol Rob² Bgh.

128   ful many] Cp El Gg Ha; *many* rest and M-R Don Prt. Cf. IV.583n; this reading is treated as a similar scribal addition by M-R (4:480).

171   stille] *as stille* En Ha Skt Pol Rob² Don.

201   a] *of* Cp Ha Skt Pol Rob² Bgh; *as (fayr)* Gg; *of (feire)* Ne. Another example of varying scribal interpretations of archetypal *o* (cf. note I.1810 above); here the *lectio difficilior* involves taking *fairye* as a common noun ("marvel"), not the name of a mythical land.

202   they] El Gg Ha; om. Ch Ne; *han* rest and M-R Don Prt.

211   men] *men moun* En Ha Rob²; *men may* Skt Pol. An example of dittography; M-R takes the line as headless (see 4:481). *Men* is again indefinite "one."

266   Cambyuskan] *this Cambyuskan* Ha Skt Rob² Bgh. En adds *this* before *kyng*.

284   swiche] *so* Ad El Gg Ne Skt Pol Rob¹; *such a* Ha. A further example (cf. note I.1424 above) of reading the individual line as a single unit; on this basis some MSS erroneously emphasize the apparent parallelism.

291   the spices] Ha; *spices* rest and M-R Prt.

299   that] El En Gg Ha Ne Pol Rob¹ Prt; *that at* rest and eds.

317   yow telle] Ad Ch El Gg Hg Prt; *yow* Ne; *telle yow* rest and eds.

330   by day] Ha; *day* M-R Prt (in M-R apparently as an O' error; see 4:482).

**346   Between the first two parts, Cp reads *The Stag of an hert*.

357   now] *mowe* Ad Ch Cp; om. El Gg Ne Skt Pol.

419   noon] Om. Ad Ch En Hg Rob¹; om. phrase Cp Ne.

455   ire] *loue* El Gg Skt Pol Rob¹.

477   of hir swough gan breyde] El; *of (of hir* Gg) *swough gan abreyde (breyde* Ne) rest and M-R Don Prt.

491   chasted] *chastised* Cp En Gg Ha Ne Rob¹.

499   ilke] *harde* El Gg Skt Pol Rob¹; om. Ne. Manly and Rickert suggest (4:482-83) that the El Gg reading is a second generation error derived from the prior error *ille*.

514   loves] *love this* El En Gg Ha Ne Skt Pol Rob¹.

517   sownen] *sowneth* Skt Pol (and at least Cp El Ha), mistakenly construing the line as parallel to 516.

529   upon] *on* En Skt Rob² Don.

533   al my] Ad Ch En Gg Ha Ne; *my* rest and Pol M-R Don Prt, to form a Lydgatian line.

650   Pyes] *And pyes* Ad Ch El En Hg Skt Pol M-R (as an O' error; see 4:483) Don. Pol follows Tyrwhitt in inverting 649 and 650; Don places a semicolon after 648 *tidyves*.

657   which] *which that* En Rob² Bgh; in a more widely attested effort at avoiding this Lydgatian line, Ad Ch Hg read *yow]* *to yow*.

**671-72   Om. En and some others, including La, which adds a link to The Wife of Bath's Prologue, the first eight lines of which occur before 671-72 in Se:

Bot I wil here nowe maake a knotte
To þe time it come next to my lotte,
For here be felawes behinde an heþe treulye,

þat wolden talke ful besilye
And haue her sporte as wele as I,
And þe daie passeþ fast certanly.
Therefore Oste, takeþ nowe goode heede
Who schall next tell, and late him speede.

**673-708   Om. Ch Cp Ne; on a leaf now lost Gg Ha; in Hg links Squire and Merchant.

The Franklin's Prologue and Tale

726   to me] En; *me to* Cp Skt Pol Bgh; om. Ne; *to* rest and M-R Don Prt. **been]** *they ben* Hg. Manly and Rickert suggest (4:485) reading *rethorikë* with four syllables, as at IV.32, a reading perhaps correct.

**999-1000   These lines follow 1006 in Ne and nine MSS (Cx Gl Ha³ Ha⁵ He Hk Ii Ps Ra³) and Don Prt (Manly and Rickert recommend this change in a note 4:485-86).

1004   go] Ad Ch El En Gg Ne; om. Cp Ha Hg Don.

1050   lighted] *lightned* El Gg Ne Skt Pol Rob¹; *leteþ* Cp.

1067   seye] Ad Ch El En Gg; *say ȝou þus* Cp; *seye this* Hg Don; *seye thus* Ne M-R Prt.

1161   wowke] El Ne; *ȝeer* Cp; *day* rest and Skt M-R Don (apparently as O' error in M-R; 4:486 suggests *wowke* is correct in light of 1295).

1273   forth] *forth hath* Don (following Koch) to avoid a past tense without -*e;* one MS (Ph³) has **forth]** *hath*.

1358   or elles] Ad Ch En Gg Ha; *oþer elles* Cp; *or* rest and M-R Don Bgh Prt, which produces a Lydgatian line. Manly and Rickert suggest *or* is an error in O' (see 4:487).

1408   whan] *whan þat* Cp Rob² Don Bgh; to compensate for this suppressed syllable, we print *hadde* (in at least Gg Ha Hg). **hadde]** *had* at least Cp El and Rob² Bgh.

1430   swich] *swich a* Ch Cp Ne Pol Rob² Bgh.

**1455-56, 1493-98   In El Ad only, but genuine. The first lines Manly and Rickert found "so unpoetical" that they hoped they were written by the El scribe; but this view is qualified by their belief that Chaucer should have dropped (and may have intended to drop) the whole passage after 1423 (see 4:487-88).

1534   serement] Ad El Hg; *surement* rest and Skt Pol Rob¹.

**1541-44   These lines follow 1550 in two MSS (Gl Ra³) and Prt (Manly and Rickert recommend this change in a note 4:488). The variation (and the desire to move the lines) plainly reflects confusion over the boundary of Aurelius's speech; but the lines are not out of character in light of such a statement as 1610-12.

FRAGMENT VI

The Physician's Tale

2   called] *cleped* Cp Ha Ne; one of a number of instances in this tale where these copies agree in idiosyncratic readings; cf. 16 **Apelles]** *Apollus* Cp Ha Ne; **Zanzis]** *Zephirus* Cp Ha Ne; 204 **sentence]** *þe assent* Cp Ha Ne. In other readings below (e.g., 49, 59, 238), two of the three agree or all three agree with other MSS.

49   as] Cp Ne; om. rest and M-R (although said to be an O' error 4:489).

59   dooth] *doon* Ad Cp Ha Skt, a confusion over whether *Venus* or the noun doublet is the subject.

94 mo] *two* El Ne Skt.
97 if] El Hg; om. En Ne; *that* rest and Skt Rob² Bgh.
99 they ne] Ad Cp En Ha Ne; *they* rest and M-R Don Prt. As Manly and Rickert point out (4:489–90), this variant is grammatically linked to the preceding lemma; some MSS, however, show mixed forms.
100 deere] *sore* Cp Ha.
103–4 Om. El.
105 wol] *telle* Cp Ha Ne Don, forcing the more difficult reading of *express* as "specifically."
    this] *my* Ad Ch Cp Ha; om. phrase Ne.
238 leyser] *leue* Cp Gg Ha Ne.
252 wolde] *sholde* Ch Cp En Ha Ne Rob² Bgh.

The Words of the Host

Scholars (conveniently summarized in M-R, 4:490–91) generally have tended to discern two stages of composition in the link. In this theory, Chaucer originally wrote a short version of twelve lines (287–98), found in Cp Ha Ne; to this, once he decided which tale was to follow, he added the remainder. But like the variants shared by Ad Ha in 319–27, all forms of the link other than those printed here appear to be scribal products, readings derived by mechanical means from the lections we print.

291–92 Cp Ha Ne (spurious):

So falle vpon his body and his bones;
Þe deuel I bekenne him al at ones.

297–98 Another probably spurious couplet, derived from 292–93, in Ad (after 300) Cp Ha Ne only; om. M-R Don Prt.
299 *But hereof wil I not procede as now* Cp Ne (spurious); Ha om. 299–300, 305–6.
313 cardynacle] Ch El En Hg; *cardiacle* rest and Skt.
319–20 Ad Ha (spurious):

"Tel vs a tale, for þou canst many oon."
"It schal be doon," quod he, "and þat anoon."

326–27 Ad Ha (again spurious):

"Gladly," quod he, and sayde as ʒe schal heere:
"But in þe cuppe wil I me beþinke.

The Pardoner's Prologue and Tale

356 *Touche he þis boon anon he schal be sounde* Cp Ne; *About þe hert or ellis þe lunge* Pw (again spurious lines).
382 ymaked] *ymaad* Ad Cp Ha Ne Skt Pol Rob² Bgh; *maked* Ch En; *made* Pw.
386 a] *in* Cp Ha Ne Pw Skt Rob² Don Bgh; *on* El Pol.
392 *And schewe lewed poeple and doun þey sette* Cp Ne Pw **(and doun þey sette]** *synne ysette* Pw) (spurious lines).
492 Senec] *Seneca* Ha Pol; another effort at avoiding a headless line by providing an extra syllable is **seith]** *saiþ eek* Cp Ne Skt.
532 They] Ha; *That ther* Ad; *That they* one MS (Cx) and Skt Pol Rob² Bgh; *Ther* rest and M-R (Manly and Rickert, however, believe O may have read *They*; see 4:493).
544 leef and bark] Ch El Hg; *leef of bark* Ad En Gg; *leues bark* Cp Ha Ne Pw; *leef bark* most MSS and M-R.

581 ay] Om. Gg Hg Pw M-R Don Prt.
636 swere] *seye* El Ha Skt Pol.
646 knoweth] Cp Gg Ha Hg Ne; *knowen* rest and Skt Pol M-R Prt.
659 Lete] *Leueth* Cp Gg Ha Ne Pw Skt Pol.
663 to] *for to* Cp En Ha Pw Skt Pol Rob² Bgh.
709 they] *al* three MSS (Bo¹ Ds Ph²) and Rob²; *they all* En.
736 me] *in me* En Ha Ne Rob² Bgh.
777 what that] Ad Ch Gg Hg; *what* rest and Skt Pol M-R Bgh Prt.
817 woot] *woot wel* Ad Cp Ha Ne Pw Rob² Bgh; *woot how* El Skt Pol.
817–18 Cp Ne (spurious):

I woot wel þat þe gold is oure tuo;
What schulde we seye? what schulde we do?

Pw (a related spurious couplet):

I wold wel þat þe gold were oures twoo;
What shuld wee doo þat it myʒt be soo?

826 that right] *and þanne* Cp; *and þat* Ha Ne Pw; Skt Pol conjecture *and right.*
871 borwed of] Skt Rob² Don Bgh (and M-R in note 4:494), a conjecture. The MSS reading, *borwed,* without *of,* would mean "pledged."
941 heere] El Gg; om. rest and M-R Don Prt.
954 thee helpe] *the* Ch Hg; *with thee* El; *from the* Gg; *help* Ha Pw; *helpe thee* Ne.
968 Two spurious links, one attested in nineteen MSS, join The Pardoner's Tale and The Shipman's Tale; Manly and Rickert discuss these and provide texts at 4:495–96.

FRAGMENT VII

The Shipman's Tale

43 manly] Ha Hg Don; *namely* rest and eds. Cf. MED *manli adj.,* sense 4b "generous, hospitable." *Namely* was probably intended as a scribal clarification; there's muddled evidence that this word had the variant form *manely:* see *Piers Plowman* B 7.190, where *namely* apparently alliterates on *m-,* and Kane and Donaldson's discussion, PP B, 211 and n. 170.
59 to²] El Pw; *and* rest and M-R Don Prt.
78 wel] *as wel* Ad Ha Pw Skt Pol Rob². Don reads *himselvë,* an inflected dative (cf. *himselven* Ch Cp), and Manly and Rickert (see 4:496) suggest *himselven* was the O' reading.
131 I] *here I* Gg Ne Skt Pol Rob² Prt. The printed reading requires reading trisyllabic *portëhors.*
157 youre wey] Ad Cp El Ha Pw; *awey* rest and M-R Don Prt.
202 flankes] *shankes* Cp Ha Ne Pw.
214 Quy la] *Who ther* Ch El Gg Hg (*ys* interlined later); *Who is ther* En Ne. Ch El Hg have marginal gloss *qi la,* and probably reversed the two readings (so M-R, 4:497).
228 tweye] Cp; *two* Ad Ha Pol; *hundred twelue* Ne; *tweyn* Pw Don; *ten* rest and Skt M-R. The lower success rate suggested by the printed text seems correct, given *Scarsly,* but see expl. note.
306 his] *him* Rob² (misprint).

312 That] *For that* Ad Cp Ha Pw Skt Pol Rob² Bgh.
337 first gooth hym] *first* Ch; *ferst him goþ* Cp; *gooth hym first* El Skt Pol Bgh; *gooth first hym* Ne Rob²; *him first (he) goþ* Pw.
359 hire] Ad Cp Ha Pw Skt Rob²; *yow* rest and eds.
394 axen] Ad El Ha; *axe of* rest and Skt M-R Don Prt.
432 thy] *my* Cp Ha Pw Rob² Don Bgh; *oure* El Skt Pol. See expl. note.
433 endeth] *endeþ now* Cp Ha Pw Skt Pol Rob² Don Bgh.

The Prioress's Prologue and Tale

479 the lyght of] *to lyght þurgh* Cp Pw; *thurgh lyght of* El; *þe lyght þurgh* Ha Skt Pol Rob¹; *lyght of* Ne.
512 alday] Cp El Pw; *alwey* rest and M-R Prt.
553 than wolde] *wolde* Ch El En Hg Ne M-R Prt. (Manly and Rickert believe *than* was supplied by scribes to improve the meter; see 4:498.)
555 his] *hath his* Ad Cp Gg Ha Pw Skt Pol Rob² Don Bgh.
564 youre] *oure* Ch Cp El En Gg Hg Ne M-R Don Prt.
625 his] *the* Ad Cp Gg Ha Pw Skt Rob².
636 the masse] *masse* Ad Ch Cp Pw Skt Pol Rob²; *the high masse* Ne. Cf. **whil**] *whiles* at least Cp Ha Pw.
676 ben] *leyn* Ch El En Gg Hg, an echo of earlier *lay*.

The Prologue and Tale of Sir Thopas

691 al] Om. Ad Cp En Ha.
769 hir] Ch El En Pol (and noted approvingly in M-R, 4:499); *his* rest and eds. The reading gives a closer parallel to 771 *she*. See expl. note.
805 In Ch En only; several MSS have blanks, as if for an omitted line; line om. Prt (following M-R, 4:499). See expl. note.
824 Shal] *Thyn hauberk shal* El Gg.
833 [The Second Fit]] This division of the text is marked by large capitals in El Hg and by a paraph in Ch, decoration commensurate with their setting off the usually noted second fit (now our third fit) at 891. For discussion, see expl. note 833–35 and Burrow, RES 22, 1971, 54–58.
835 For now I] Cp; *I* rest and M-R Prt.
917 worly] Ch El Hg Don Prt; *worthly* Ad; *worþily* Cp (a correction) Ne; *worthy* En Ha and eds. See expl. note.

The Prologue and Tale of Melibee

929–30 Cp (a piece of scribal bowdlerization):

*"By God," quod he, "pleynly I þe say
þou schalt no lenger rymen heere today.*

951 Mark] *Markë* Skt Pol; *Mark and* Don (and M-R, in note, 4:500).
993 hast²] *has* Rob² (a misprint).
998 oure othere] Rob²; *oþere* El Pol; *oure* rest and Skt M-R Prt. (Don Bgh do not print Melibee.)
1000 Oure Lord hath yeve it me] Om. Ad El Gg Hg Ne, an eyeskip.
1026 persone²] El; *body* rest and Skt Pol M-R Prt.

1042 bigynne] El Gg Ne; *begonne* Ch; *be bigonne* rest and M-R Prt.
1058 God forbede] Cp El Ha Ne; *Goddes forbode* rest and M-R Prt, the *lectio difficilior.*
1062–63, 1433–34, 1664 (ne . . . Dieu)] These omitted passages, necessary to the sense, were first supplied in French by Tyrwhitt, followed by Rob² Prt; Skt Pol give English translations, while Manly and Rickert, noting the total absence of English MS evidence, omit the lines.
1070 and he . . . book] Om. El.
1098 good] Ch El En; *þe goode* Cp; *the* Ne; om. rest and M-R Prt. *Good* is probably confirmed by IV.1363.
1099 have al destroyed it] Cp El; *haue it destroied* Ne; *it al destroye* rest and M-R Prt.
1106 nevere] Cp El Ne; *neither* rest and M-R Prt.
1134 by] El Rob²; *of* Gg; om. rest and eds.
1138–71 Om. Cp, probably by skipping between paraphs.
1213 certes] Ch Cp El En; om. rest and M-R Prt.
1223 counseil] Ha; *conseillours* rest and M-R Rob² (in M-R as an O' error; see 4:503). Chaucer's French source reads *conseil* (S&A, 420).
1251 than] *that* Rob² (a misprint).
1276 encreesceden] *entreteden* two MSS (Lc Mg) and Skt; *han schewed ʒou* Ha; the source has *adjousterent* (S&A, 488).
1311 wolt] Three MSS (Ad¹ En³ Hk) and Rob²; *woldest go* Cp; *goost* El Skt Pol; *wel go* Gg; *wolt go* rest and M-R Prt.
1315 accompte] Cp El; om. phrase Ha; *attempt* rest and M-R (as an O' error, 4:503). Cf. French *desprises* (S&A, 529).
1324 Om. El Ne.
1335–36 apperteyneth . . . toures] Cp only; rest om. With the next, a case of eyeskip.
1336 and grete edifices] Two MSS only (Mc Ra¹; Cp om. *And . . . wise*); om. Pol.
1388 shalt] *shal* Rob² (a misprint?).
1556 which . . . housbonde] Om. El; 1556–57 which . . . men] om. Cp Gg.
1560 alloone] *al alloone* El Hg Pol.
1576 sokyngly] *sekyngly* Ch El Hg; *geytyngly* En. From French *a loisir* (S&A, 856–57); see OED *soakingly adv.*, sense 1 "gradually."
1593 greete²] Cp Gg Ha Rob²; om. rest and eds.
1594 yow nat] *nat yow* El Skt Pol Rob²; *yow* Ad.
1777 And he seith . . . remissioun] Om. Ad Ch El En Gg Ne. Within this passage: **place that he]** *place, 'He is worthy to have remissioun and foryifnesse* one MS (Fi) and M-R Prt; *place* Cp Ha Hg (which leaves a space of nearly a full line); **it is worthy remissioun]** two MSS (Mm Pw); *it.'* Cp Ha Hg M-R Prt. The French does not provide evidence for an absolute solution; the text we print is equivalent, except *is worthy remissioun* renders *est presque ignocent* (S&A, 1079–80).
1815 punyssement] Cp El Ha; *punysshynge* rest and M-R Prt.
1832 freyned] Ad Ch El En; *feyned* rest and M-R (as an O' error; see 4:507).

The Monk's Prologue and Tale

1889 my] *þe* Cp Ch Ne.
1895 For] Om. Ad Ch El En Hg Don.

1898 forth] El Ha Pw; om. rest and M-R Don Prt.
1957–58 Om. El.
2007–14 Om. Cp (space left) Hg (corrected later in margin) Ne. Apparently a case of eyeskip; the scribes returned to their archetypes at the subsequent Sampson stanza (2015), which also begins *Loo.*
2097 was] *bar* Ch Cp Ha Ne Pw, creating a set phrase.
2105 firy] Ad Ch El En Hg; *fery* Gg; *verray* rest and M-R. Although, as Manly and Rickert note (4:509–10), the Hydra wasn't fiery, the reading is probably authorial; cf. Bo 4.m7.42 *brende the venym,* which Chaucer may have misunderstood.
2192 bad] El Gg; *made* rest and M-R Don Prt.
2210 lente] Ch Hg; *sente* rest and Pol Rob[1] Don.
2275 Hadde] *Nadde* Don, a conjecture, which gives the expected negative sense; *Hath* Pw is the only variant, and no MS has any negation anywhere in the line.
2289 wikes] Two MSS (Py To); *dayes* rest and Skt Pol Rob[1] M-R (as an O' error; see 4:510).
2322 title had] Cp Ha Pw; *title she had* Ne; *title* rest and M-R (as an O' error; see 4:511).
2363 Biforen] *Biforn* M-R; *And biforn* Don.
2375–2462 These lines, presenting the so-called modern instances, appear at the end of the tale, after 2766, in Ad Ch El En Gg Hg Don; 2375–98 om. Ne. To this shift in position are linked a number of variants, especially in early portions of the passage: 2378 *Thy bastard broþer made þe to flee* Cp Ha Pw (taken by Manly and Rickert as an earlier version, later revised out); 2380 **bitraysed]** *betrayed* Cp Ha Pw Skt (a spurious line En); 2387 **took ay]** *ay took* Cp Ha Pw Skt (add *god* Cp Pw). Manly and Rickert (4:508) argue that the passage must belong in the midst of the tale, since moving it destroys both the Monk's apparent peroration (2761–66) and the echo of 2766 in 2782. But, as with the echo at the opening of The Merchant's Prologue, the juxtaposition need not be direct, and 2457 would offer an adequate reprise of the Monk's view, as well as a stimulus for the Knight's interruption. Differing placements of the passage do not necessarily reflect authorial revision (*pace* M-R, 2:406–9): the passage may have been on loose sheets inserted into the archetype diversely by various scribes.
2426 spak right] Ad Ch El En Hg; *ne spak right* Pol (*ne* in Bo[1] Ph[2]); *saugh it* Cp Ha Ne Pw.
2438 but] *sauf* Cp Ha Pw Skt Rob[2]; *than* Ne.
2467 south] Eds.; *north* Ad Ch El En Gg Hg Pol M-R; om. Cp Ha Ne Pw. As Koch noted, *north* suspiciously resembles the form for *south* in the source; cf. Bo 2.m6.23–27 and its reference to *the vyolent wynd Nothus.* But *north* may simply be a gloss that has become detached from *septemtrioun.*
2473 ilke] *like* Rob[2] (a misprint).
2477 al] *as* Cp En Ha Ne Pw Rob[1].
2544 greet] *ful greet* Cp Ha Pw Skt Rob[2] Bgh.
2563 adoured] *honoured* Cp En Ha Ne Pw.
2564 dorst] *dar* Cp En Gg Ha Ne Pw Skt Rob[2].
2662 And] *And ʒet* Cp Pw Skt Pol Rob[2] Bgh; *And right* Ha.
2720 Valerius] *Valirien* Ha; *Valerie* Ne Skt Rob[2].
2748 sentence] *science* El En Gg Ha Skt Pol Rob[1].
2757 ek] Ha Rob[2] Bgh; om. rest and eds. A similar effort at asserting a regular metrical pattern is **warned]** *warned sche* Ha Pw Skt Pol; *she warned* Ne. Don transposes *warned hym* to create a clearly headless line.

The Prologue of the Nun's Priest's Tale

The passage exists in two forms, the longer version, printed here, and a shorter version, lacking 2771–90, which appears in Cp Hg Ne.

2767 Knyght] *Hoste* Ch Ne; given the MSS in which it appears, there is no reason to associate this erroneous reading with the shorter version, as do Manly and Rickert (2:410–12). See Expl. Notes, introductory note to The Nun's Priest's Prologue.
2791 For therinne is ther no] Ad Ch El En Ha (ther) om. Ad Ha; *chere* Ch En); *Youre tales doon vs no* Cp Hg Ne, the remains of the original join with 2770.
2792 Monk] *Monk o* Ch En Hg Prt; *Monk or* seven MSS (He Ii Mc Ps Pw Se Tc[1]) and eds.

The Nun's Priest's Tale

2854 an] Ad El Ha; *any* rest and M-R Prt.
2855 knew] *krew* Ch El Hg Ne.
2870 Following this line, En inserts a couplet:

He fethered hir an hundred tyme a day
And she hym pleseth all þat euer she may.

Some critics have argued that these lines come from an early draft, since in The Nun's Priest's Tale, "The ancestor of *a* seems to be of independent origin, at times having correct readings as against the other MSS" (M-R, 4:257). But this couplet is a scribal derivative from 3177, perhaps done by anticipation. Similarly, many En readings viewed by Manly and other scholars as correct are in fact erroneous; cf. notes 3036, 3093, 3386, 3395 below.
2901 wolde han] Ad Cp Ha Ne; *han* rest and M-R Don Prt.
3036 wente as it were] *as he wente* Cp; *as it were* El Ne Skt Pol (and M-R, in note, 4:515); *for* En.
3042 he lith] Cp En Ne; *he lith heer* Ha; *heere he lith* rest and M-R Prt.
3076 herkneth] Om. En Skt Pol Rob[2] Don Bgh.
3085 byde] Ch El Hg; *abyde* rest and Skt M-R Prt. The two readings are in fact metrically equivalent, since *to* will elide. Cf. **to]** *for to* Gg Ne, the result of reading *preyde* as monosyllabic.
3093 And] *And eke* En Skt Pol Rob[2] Bgh.
3155 venymes] *venymous* Cp En Ha Ne Skt Rob[2].
3178 hire eke] En Rob[2] Bgh; *hire* four MSS (Ii La Nl Ra[2]) and Don; om. rest and eds. Cf. **er]** *er þat* Ha Skt Pol (and M-R, in note, 4:515), another effort at increasing the syllable count and thereby regularizing meter.
3190 was gon] Prt; *bigan* all MSS and eds.; *biran* Don ("passed"). In spite of the explanations offered by earlier editors, the MS reading seems a contamination inspired by *bigan* 3187.
3248 I] Ad Ch Gg Hg; om. one MS (Ii) and Rob[2]; *it* rest and Skt Pol M-R Bgh.
3386 So fered for the] Two MSS (Dd Ln) and Rob[2] Bgh Prt; *So fered for* Ad Ch El Hg M-R; *Sore aferde for* Cp Don; *So fered the* En; *Forfered for* Gg; *So were þey fered for* Ha Skt Pol; *For they so sore aferd were* Ne.
3395 shrille] *shille* El En Ne.
3411 I am] *am I* Ad Ch Cp Ne Skt Pol Rob[2].

3418   the cok] En Rob² Bgh; *he* rest and eds. See the efforts later in the line to compensate for lack of syllables: **gon]** *agoon* Ha Skt Pol; *agoon* two MSS (Cn Dl) and Don.
3428   ofter] Cp En Ne; *any ofter* rest and Pol Bgh Prt.

Epilogue to the Nun's Priest's Tale

The passage, here supplied from Dd, occurs in only nine MSS, among them Ch En. It has usually been considered canceled, its materials reworked in The Monk's Prologue (cf. 3451 and 1945).

3462   another] *the Nunne* four MSS (Ad¹ Cn En³ Ma), which also add six spurious lines to provide a direct link to The Second Nun's Tale (see the text provided in M-R, 4:516). The reading *another* presumably is original and reflects a rough-draft state in which Chaucer had not decided what tale was to follow. This reading may indicate why most MSS suppress the lines: if their purpose is to join two tales, as written they are of no use, since they do not link The Nun's Priest's Tale to anything.

FRAGMENT VIII

The Second Nun's Prologue and Tale

18   n'encrees] *encres* Ad Gg Ha La Ne Pw Skt Pol, the easier reading, since it allows one to construe *good* as adjective, not substantive.
19   syn] *seen* Ad El Gg Hg Skt Pol Rob¹ Don; om. Ch.
75   of] El En Gg Ha Ne; *o* rest and M-R (cf. note I.1810 above).
137   I] *it* El Rob² Bgh.
151   thus] El Ha; *þus* placed before *to* Cp Pw; om. rest and M-R.
183   Valerian] *This Valerian* Ad Ch En Gg Hg Ne Don.
185   olde] Om. Ch Cp En Ne Pw.
197   but] *right* El Ha Pol Rob¹.
216   this] *þe* Cp Skt Rob²; *þat* Pw.
277   Valerians] Three MSS (Gl Ra³ Tc¹) and eds.; *Cecilies* rest and M-R (as an O' error; see 4:520). Cf. Chaucer's source: *testis est Valeriani coniugis et Tyburcii prouocata confessio* (S&A, 673). But Chaucer may have construed the phrase *Valeriani coniugis* as *of Valerian's spouse*, i.e., Cecilia, and construed the reference as to 218–24, rather than to the subsequent martyrdoms.
280   made] *make* Rob² (a misprint?); om. Ne.
330   heigh] Ha; *he* Ad Ch En Gg Hg Don; om. El Skt Pol Rob¹; *by* Ne; line om. Cp Pw. The homeographic readings of Ne and Ha bracket the more probably correct reading of Ad.
405   bete] *tobete* Ch Cp En Ne Pw Skt Pol Rob² Bgh.
500   it is] El Ha; *is* rest and M-R Don Prt.
512   wordes] Cp El Gg Ha Pw (**wordes and swiche othere]** *and such oþer wordes* Cp Pw); om. rest and M-R.
534   he²] *is* Ad Ch En Gg Ne Skt Pol Rob².

The Canon's Yeoman's Prologue and Tale

The prologue and tale do not appear in Hg, probably owing to difficulties in the supply of copy. Such a prob-

lem is evident in the Hg presentation of The Second Nun's Tale; space in a double quire (the twenty-second, ff. 161–76, expanded to sixteen folia, rather than the usual eight) was saved to handle copy expected later by the scribe. For the most recent extensive discussion, see Doyle and Parkes, in The Cant. Tales, vol. 1 of the Var. Ed. (1979), esp. pp. xxxi–ii. *Pace* Blake (E&S 32, 1979, 1–18), the absence of The Canon's Yeoman's Tale in Hg provides no reason for doubting the Chaucerian authorship of the work. No other Middle English poet has either the narrative expertise or the scientific interest to have produced the poem.

558   undernethe] El En Ne; *under that* rest and M-R Don Prt.
562   hors] *hakeney* Ad El En Ne (line torn Gg); cf. the same MSS sharing common errors in note 558 above and notes 627 and 803 below and at 554 **ended]** *tolde* Ch El En Gg Ne Pol.
564–65   om. Ad El.
625   turnen] *turne it* Cp El Skt Pol Rob² Bgh; *turne* Don.
627   this tale] El En; *this* Gg; *thus* rest and Skt M-R Don Prt.
686   Which] *Which þat* Cp Ha Rob² Don Bgh; *With* Ad.
704   now] Ad El Gg Ha; *right* Cp; om. rest (line om. Ne).
765   of muche] *muchel* El Skt Pol Rob¹; *muche* En.
803   purpos if] Ad El En; *craft if* Ne; *craft if that* rest and Skt M-R Prt.
814   oure] Ch El En Ha; *othere* rest and Rob¹ M-R.
890   Lo] *And* El Rob² Bgh; *As* En. The rest of the Rob² line generally follows El; but **smellyng]** *smel* El En Rob²; *sellyng* Ne; **and]** *and by* Cp Ha Rob².
918   he is lord] *he lord is* El En Rob² Bgh.
944   And though] *Although* El Skt Pol Rob² Bgh.
963   herd] *herd it* Cp Skt Pol Rob² Bgh.
**1057   *I schal it schewe to ʒou anon-right heere* Cp.
1100   Rob² finds the line "metrically harsh" and, in a note, suggests emendation, either to *Consumed han and wasted* or to *Consumed and wasted haven.*
1157   as the] *as that the* Ad En Gg Rob² Bgh; *as that* El Pol.
1170   atwynne] *at wynne* Rob² (a misprint).
1189   sory] *harde* El Skt Pol Rob¹; **for the phrase with . . . grace]** *I schrewe his fas* Cp Ha.
1200   above] *aboven it* Ch El En Rob² Bgh; *abouen* four MSS (Gl Mm Ra² To) and Skt Pol Don.
1207   bryngeth] *brynge vs* Ad Ch El En Skt Pol Rob² Bgh; *brynge* Cp Ha.
1238–39   Om. El En.
1242   saugh] *saugh that* Ad Ch Cp Gg Skt Pol Rob² Bgh.
1260   faste] *faste he* El Skt Pol Rob² Bgh.
1283–84   Cp, a spurious couplet:

The prest supposede noþing but wel,
But busyed him faste and was wonder fayn

1303   werk] *herte* El En Skt.
1397   jayes] *þis iayes* Cp Ha Skt Pol Rob² Don Bgh; cf. the alternative additions **as]** *as that* Ad Ch El En; and **chiteren]** *chitre and iangle* Cp.
1427   What] Ch Ne and eds.; *What that the* rest and M-R (**the]** *ʒe* Gg).

1433   How be] Rob² Don Bgh, a conjecture (also suggested by M-R, in a note, 4:524); *How* MSS and eds.
1447   the secretes] Ch El Gg Prt; *secrees* Cp Skt Pol Rob² Bgh; *secretes* rest and M-R Don.

FRAGMENT IX

The Manciple's Prologue and Tale

99   Bacus] *thou Bacus* En Ha Skt Pol Rob² Bgh.
110   sonne] *soone* Rob² (a misprint).
147   in ydel] El Gg; *for naught* rest and M-R Don Prt. The printed reading may be a scribal effort to avoid apparent repetition.
157   for] Ad Ch Hg Rob²; *that* El En Gg; *thorow* Ne; *by* rest and eds. But *for* may be a scribal effort to increase parallelism with 158 *for.*
173   yif] *if that* En; *when* Cp Ha Ne.
263   And] *Him* Cp Ha Ne Skt M-R Don Prt.
310   ye] *I* El Gg Hg Ne Skt Pol Rob¹.
356   nevere so] *leef or* Ad Ch El En Gg Hg Skt Pol Rob¹.

FRAGMENT X

The Parson's Prologue and Tale

Since The Parson's Tale always occurs last, it frequently has been subjected to damage, especially lost leaves. Several of the MSS have lost the end of the text (and also the Retraction): Ad ends at 472, Ch at 1044, Cp at 290 (replaced, as usual, by La), Gg at 1080, Hg at 551.

1   al ended] Ad Ch El Hg; *ended* rest and M-R Prt.
5   Foure] Ch; *Ten* rest and M-R (as an O' error; see 4:528).
was tho] Ch El En Gg; *was* Ha; *was so* rest and M-R Don Prt.
**73–74   These lines occur in all the MSS after 68 and are printed in that position by Skt Pol M-R (although Manly in his 1928 edition suggests the transposition. Brown (ChR 10, 1976, 236–42) argues for a return to the MS order.
91   every] El En; *at every* rest and Pol M-R Prt. The Parson's Tale is not printed in Bgh; Don provides only 75–81, 915–43, 951–55.
94   laste] *laste ende* Ch Ha La Skt Pol Rob¹; *laste day* En. See MED *laste adj.,* sense 7b "last moments, end of life."
105   communly] Om. Ad Ch El En Gg Pol Rob¹.
126   of the kyng] El; *of* rest and Pol M-R Prt.
134   confusioun] En Ne; *confessioun* rest and Skt Pol Rob¹ M-R (as an O' error; see 4:529). Cf. the apparent source, Prov. 12:4 *confusione res dignas.*
185   as dooth] El Ha; *as* rest and M-R Prt.
190   ther . . . dignytee] Om. El, an eyeskip between the synonyms *lordshipe* and *dignytee.*
213   they¹] El; *men* (the indefinite) rest and M-R Prt.
232   lost] Cp Ne Pw; *left* rest and Skt Pol M-R (as an O' error; see 4:530). The sentence expands on 231 *lorn,* not *left to doon,* which requires no explanation.
254   in so muche] Four MSS (Bo¹ Mm Ph² Tc¹) and Skt Rob²; *nat so muche* rest and Pol M-R Prt, clearly harder, as Robinson says.

273   And² . . . manere] Gg; om. rest and M-R Prt. Perhaps an error, for seven other MSS have different additions at this point, all designed to suggest that what follow are Christ's words.
275   disordinaunces] A conjecture (based on 277 *this disordinaunce); disconcordaunces* El; *discordaunce* Gg; *discordauntes* Ne; *discordaunces* rest and Skt Pol Rob¹ M-R (as an O' error; see 4:530).
315   soothly] Ad Ch El En Gg; *certes* rest and M-R Prt.
320   thee of thy] Ad Ch El En Gg; *hym of hise* rest and Skt M-R Prt.
365   the love of¹] Rob² here follows, in part, Koch's conjecture; that scholar derived this phrase from the subsequent *that he loveth,* which he omitted. All other eds. print the version of the MSS and thus have no singular subject for subsequent *is.*
387   the sevene] La; *the* El Skt Pol; om. rest and M-R Prt. A scribal overspecification (as in 476 below).
spryng] Hg; *springers* Ha Skt; *spryngyng* Ne; *sprynген* rest and M-R. Ha Hg Ne appear efforts at accommodating the verb form to the syntax; if such is the case, the word has probably intruded from 388. Perhaps one should conjecture a phrase like *stremes hed,* which would fit the traditional metaphoric context for describing the generation of the vices and would provide some logic for the substitution.
443   Laban . . . Pharao] Three MSS (Cx Ra³ Tc²); *Pharao . . . Laban* rest and Pol M-R (as an error in O'; see 4:531). It's more likely that the two names in *J-* have been transposed; they occur in their correct position in four MSS (En³ [a correction] Ln Mm To).
476   the synne of Pride] Ch El En; *Pride* rest and M-R Prt. Probably another overspecification; cf. 475 and the source's *remedium superbie* (Wenzel, Traditio 27, 1971, 437).
487   malice] El En; *enuye* rest and M-R (probably as an O' error; see 4:531–32). Cf. the source: *Que malicia duas habet species. . . . Alia species est impugnatio* (Traditio 30, 1974, 356).
505   grucchyng] El; *it* rest and M-R Prt.
516   espiritueel] El; *spirituel* rest and M-R Prt; the following *and* occurs in Ch El En Ha only (om. rest and M-R Prt).
523   commandement] *comandement* Rob² (a misprint).
565   sixe] *thre* Prt, a conjecture based on the fact that lines 565–69 offer only three items. But *sixe* may be the remains of a more extensive *distinctio* Chaucer reduced.
568   cruel] *crueel* Rob² (a misprint).
576   wilfully] El; om. rest and Pol M-R Prt.
595   declaracioun] Ch El En; *declarynge* rest and M-R Prt.
605   nigromancie] Ne; *geomancie* Ch El En Ha Skt Pol Rob¹ (*recte?*); *griomancye* Gg; *ygromansy* La Pw.
609   disese and] El; om. rest and M-R Prt. The MSS that omit are probably correct; El tries to create too extensive a parallel with the preceding phrase (cf. notes 678 and 771 below).
612   flaterynge] Ch El En; *flaterye* rest and M-R Prt.
616   bitraysen] Addition *God and thise flaterers bitraysen* two MSS (Cx Tc²) and Skt Pol; *bitrayseth* En; *bitraysed* rest and eds. But the construction is "those who betray a man to sell him . . . are like Judas" (cf. Peraldus, the ultimate source, cited in M-R, 4:532), and both the addition and past tense are unnecessary.
649   sygne] *synne* El Gg Skt Pol.

651 japeres²] El Gg Skt Prt; *japes* rest and other eds. The error *japes* (printed by M-R because in O'; see 4: 532) is probably an echo of *apes.*

653 mo] Ch El En; om. rest and M-R Prt.

654 callen] Ch El En Gg; *clepen* rest and M-R Prt.

670 and broghte] All MSS and eds.; **and]** om. Rob². **scoure with]** El; *scourge* Ch Ne Skt Pol; *scourge with* Rob¹; *scoure* rest and M-R Prt. Cf. OED *scour v.*², sense 9 "beat, punish."

678 and joye of harm] El; blank left Ha; *and anoy of harm* rest and M-R (as an error in O'; see 4:532). The whole phrase may be a scribalism intended to balance the preceding; in any event, the source reads only *tedium boni* (Traditio 30:364), and no common late medieval definition includes such an addition. See Wenzel, The Sin of Sloth, 1960, 218, n. 17 (esp. definitions *f, i*).

698 that seith . . . recreant] Om. El (eyeskip); a similar eyeskip occurs in Ne.

716 labouren] *labourn* Rob² (a misprint).

748 the thraldom] Ch El En Ha M-R; *þral* La; *in his þraldom* Ne Pw (but read **is]** *haþ more hope*); *in the thraldom* eds. Rob¹ had the text as printed, which Manly and Rickert believed was an O' error (see 4:533). The use of *in* seeks to remove Paul's provocative metaphor; cf. Eph. 5:5 (and Traditio 30:367) *quod est idolorum servitus.*

769 ne¹] *no* Rob² (a misprint?).

771 and in his degree] Ha La Ne Pw (**his]** om. Ha Pw); om. rest and M-R Prt. Perhaps a scribal effort at increasing parallelism.

794 whiles . . . craft] Om. Ch El En Gg, a piece of scribal specification.

799 Corporeel] Ha; om. rest and M-R. The source has *corporale, aliud spirituale. Corporale subdividitur* (Traditio 30:369). There may have been a small eyeskip, only fully corrected in Ha through consultation of 799–800.

800 it agayn] El Gg; om. rest and M-R Prt.

812 and¹] El Gg; *and eek* rest and M-R Prt. **where ne how]** El Gg; om. rest and M-R Prt.

814 therof] El Gg; om. rest and M-R Prt. Cf. the effort at clarifying the construction **synne]** *do synne* La Ne Pw (**synne]** deleted Pw).

820 savouren] Ha La Pw; *seruyn* Ne; *devouren* rest and Pol Rob¹ M-R (as an error in O'; see 4:533). The reading printed is confirmed not simply by Ne but by Phil. 3:19 *terrena sapiunt.*

858 bushes] One MS (Ad¹) and Skt Pol Rob²; *benches* Ne; *beautees* rest and eds. Both Ne and the source (Traditio 30:372) confirm Rob²; cf. *rosetum vel virgultum.* The majority reading probably reflects an odd spelling like *bousses.*

864 grymnesse] El Gg; *grymlynes* Ch En; *grislynesse* rest and M-R Prt. *Grymnesse* "fierceness" does not answer so clearly as the majority reading the *horror demonum* of the source (Traditio 30:373). The preceding *and* appears in only five MSS (Ad¹ Cn En³ Ma Ph³) and Skt Pol Rob².

869 fructus] Ha adds *secundum Ieronimum contra Iouinianum* (see I.3, PL 23:213, alluding to Matt. 13:8). This reading is perhaps correct: the source has *premium,* not *fructum* (Traditio 30:373), and Chaucer's translation appears to depend on precise knowledge of Jerome's exegesis, not unlikely given his use of the work elsewhere.

890 if so be that] El Gg; om. Ha La Ne Pw; *if* rest and M-R Prt.

900 konne . . . knowe] *coude . . . knewe* Prt, to parallel later *helde, tooke.* But the present forms reflect Chaucer's awkward translation of *nescientes* (1 Sam. 2:12, Traditio 30:375). The scribes have generally been uncertain about where past forms should begin; past *helde* appears only in Gg Skt Rob² Prt (although here the common confusion of *e* and *o* may be at issue).

916 ardour] One MS (Ad¹) and Rob² Don Prt; *ordure* rest and eds. (for M-R, an error in O'; see 4:534). Cf. the source: *carnalis fomitis . . . incentivum* (Traditio 27: 446). A scribal intensification, aided by the prevalence of language encouraging the hatred of sin.

947 moste . . . mesurable] Om. El En Gg, but present in the source (Traditio 27:450).

and been] El; om. rest and Pol M-R Prt, perhaps correctly; cf. *honestas . . . abstinentia* (Traditio 27:450).

They been] El Gg; *And thanne is she* rest and M-R Prt. El Gg both follow on *Thise manere wommen* and recognize that the line does not describe a developmental process; cf. the source: *Continentia est quoddam vas. . . . Hoc vas figuratur in alabastro Magdalene* (Traditio 27: 450).

949 ne herte thynke] El Gg; om. rest and M-R Prt.

955 David] *Danyel* El Gg Pol.

958 firste] El Gg; *second* Ch; blank Ne; om. rest and M-R.

965 til . . . bysshop] Om. El En Gg M-R. The printed reading is probably a scribal clarification.

968 Wherfore] El Gg; *For* rest and M-R Prt.

983 Ezechias] *Ezechye* Ne (cf. Isa. 38:15); om. clause Gg; *Ezechiel* rest and Pol M-R.

997 for his synnes] El; om. rest and M-R Prt. Probably an eyeskip caused by the two proximate uses of *for.*

1000 no] El Gg; *in no* Ch; *at no* En; *not* Ha; *is in no* La Ne Pw Skt Pol. See MED *certein n.,* sense 4 "assurance."

1007 elles] Om. El En Gg Skt Pol Rob².

1013 and that] El Gg; om. rest and M-R Prt. This variant and the next are linked.

telle] El Gg; *shal telle* rest and M-R Prt.

1021 therfore] El Gg; *confesse* La; *confessioun* Ne; *confessir* Pw (**shame]** *same* La Ne Pw); om. rest and M-R Prt.

1027 certes²] El Gg; *soothly* rest and M-R Prt.

1029 moost] El En Gg; om. rest and M-R Prt.

1051 ete ete] Ha Rob²; *ete* rest and eds. The use of *untyme* later in the sentence indicates that *mesure* is shown by eating at a *resonable houre.* Thus the version with a single use of the verb *ete* is probably correct.

table to ete] El En; *mete* Ha; *table* rest and M-R Prt. *Table* is probably authorial and *to ete* an attempt to clarify an apparent paradox.

1053 swetenesse] *sikernesse* El Gg Skt Rob¹.

1066 hym semeth . . . come] El Gg (*thanne* also in En); *he may as hym semeth tymely ynough come* rest and M-R Prt.

Chaucer's Retraction

The Retraction occurs in twenty-eight MSS and the *editio princeps* Cx.

1086 xxv] *XIX* three MSS (Cn Ma Ry²) and Skt Rob¹; *XV* La.

Authorities: three manuscripts and Thynne's edition:

F   Fairfax 16, Bodleian, folios 130–147^v
B   Bodley 638, Bodleian, folios 110^v–141
T   Tanner 346, Bodleian, folios 102–119^v
Th Thynne's edition, 1532, folios cclxxii–cclxxvii^v

Transcriptions of all four copies are printed in Ch Soc. 1st ser. 21, pp. 1–38, and 60, pp. 215–51; all four are available in facsimile editions (see p. 1117).

Th is the only complete copy; F, B, and T all lack lines 31–96, 288, and 886, as well as 480 (which is probably not authentic). F has a gap at 31–96 (see n. below), filled by a seventeenth-century hand, drawing on some printed copy (most likely Stow's edition of 1561; see L. Inskip Dickerson, ed., BD, Diss. Univ. of North Carolina, 1968, 57–58). F and B leave gaps at 288 and 886 (both filled by a later hand in F). B also lacks 24–30 (no gap; 23 is the last line on the page, 97 the first line of the next; a leaf may have been lost at this point; see Robinson's facsimile, xxiii). B also lacks 791–92. T leaves no gaps; it also lacks 1283.

The textual relationships of the manuscripts have been most recently studied by Dickerson (28–56) and Blake (ES 62, 1981, 237–48; see also Brusendorff, Ch Trad., 186–92, and Heath, Globe edition, pp. xxxii–xxxiv). The shared omissions show that F, B, and T are related. However, F and B and T and Th frequently form contrasting groups: 160 *ther* F B; *that ther* T Th; 169 *slepe* F B, *slepte* T Th (so also 177); 173 *envye* F B, *vie* T Th; 397 *And I* F B, *as I* T Th; 418 *or thyck* F B, *of t.* T Th; 438 *mowe* F B, *new(e)* T Th; 446 *yturned* F B, *turned* T Th; 509 *hevy* F B, *holi* T Th; 689 *yet* F B, *ye* T Th; 811 *nay* F B, *not* T Th; 867 *fooles* F B, *fooly* T, *folly* Th; 904 *dar I* F B, *I dare* T Th; 993 *up* F B, *upon* T Th; 1045 *no wyght* F B, *noght* T Th; 1194 *sothe to* F B, *sothe for to* T Th. See also notes to 578, 628, 677, 750, 828, 888, 1046, 1064, 1226.

The agreement of T and Th (especially in errors, as noted above in 438, 509, 811, etc.) seems to indicate that they shared a common ancestor. The completeness of Th must be explained by Thynne's access to at least one other copy. Th contains many unique readings, some of which must be authentic, but there are also many editorial improvements (cf. 480 below), and the unique readings of Th must be used cautiously. Blake (ES 62:237–48) regards all lines attested only by Th as suspect, including lines 31–96. That these lines are genuine is convincingly demonstrated by Helen Phillips in a paper delivered at the meeting of the New Chaucer Society in York, 1984.

Robinson, like all editors, used F as the basis of his edition, regularizing its often erratic spellings (see "The Texts," p. xlvii above) and adopting the readings of the other manuscripts where F is deficient in sense or meter. Often all four authorities agree in lines that are metrically defective, and early editors heavily emended the text to produce more regular octosyllabic lines. Robinson, taking into account the freedom of the English tradition of four-beat verse, was more cautious than his predecessors and, aside from the regularization of final *-e*, he accepted few emendations for the sake of meter except the addition of final *-n* to avoid hiatus. (See 120, 350, 975, 1053, 1204, 1323, where the emendation is retained, and 73, 301, 903, where it is not.) Recent editors have been even more conservative. However, editorial opinion remains divided, and these notes therefore take account of the previous editions of Skeat (Skt), Heath (Hth), Koch (Kch), Robinson's second edition (Rob), Donaldson (Don), Baugh (Bgh), Dickerson (Dck), Fisher (Fsh), and Helen Phillips, ed., BD, Durham and St. Andrews Med. Texts 3, 1982 (Php). The editions of Dickerson and Phillips record full variants; only the most important are noted here, mainly those on which editors have disagreed. A number of unique readings of F rejected by all editors are listed at the end of the notes.

The textual notes to *The Book of the Duchess* were prepared by Larry D. Benson.

Title: *The Booke of the Duchesse* F B; *Chaucer's Dream* T (in a later hand); *The Dream of Chaucer* Th; cf. LGW 418 *the Deeth of Blaunche the Duchesse* and Ret X.1087 *the book of the Duchesse.*

19 **erthly]** *ertherli* F; *erþeli* T Don.

23 **thus]** *this* MSS and Th Hth Don Dck Php. The words are easily confused; cf. 1173 below.

31–96 From Th. Robinson, like all editors save Dickerson and Phillips, used the later addition to F (F^2); the only significant differences are 54 *poetes* (*poets* F^2), 90 *quod* (*quoth* F^2), and 96 *that* (*which* F^2).

73 **founde]** *founden* Skt Kch Rob to avoid hiatus (unnecessarily at the caesura).

76 **speke of Alcyone]** *spoken of* Skt Hth Rob Bgh; *Alcyone* is dropped to avoid a ten-syllable line and because it is regarded as a "gloss taken into the text" (Rob); and then *speke* is emended to make eight syllables. See Malone, in Ch und seine Zeit, 79.

80 **erme]** *yerne* Th F^2; all eds. so emend for rhyme.

82 **he dwelte]** *hir thoughte* Th F^2 Don Fsh Php, apparently a repetition from 81; *he taried* Kch.

87 **alas]** Om. Skt Hth Rob Bgh; Kch changes *alderbest* to *best.*

109 **to]** Om. F B T.

117 **wolt]** *wilt(e)* F T Bgh Don.

120 **knowen]** *know(e)* MSS Th Don Dck Fsh Php. The *-n* is added here and in 350, 975, 1053, 1204, and 1323 to avoid hiatus.

123 **as^1]** *and* F T.

142 **He]** *That he* F B T.

145 **Alcione]** *Alchione* F B T Dck Php, perhaps correctly here and in 196, 220, 264, 1327; Machaut has *Alchioine* (but see IntrMLT II.57).

156 **betwixe]** *bitwyx* B T; *betwex* F Php; *betwexe* Fsh; *bytwene* Th Skt Bgh Dck; *betwixen* Rob.

158 **noght]** *nothyng* Skt Hth Kch Rob, to avoid repetition; Don changes *ought* to *on live* and emends *noght* in 159 to *nothyng.*

179 how] *ho* Th and all eds. except Dck Php. *Ho* means "stop, hold" (MED s.v. *ho interj.*); *how* is a "call to attract attention" (MED s.v. *hou interj.* [2], b).

185 and axed] *axed* Skt Hth Kch Rob Bgh.

199 hyr] *hys* F B T.

204 am] *nam* Skt Kch Rob to restore the "usual idiom," but *nam but ded* means "am as good as dead"; cf. 1188 below.

207 for] Om. Hth Bgh; Bgh takes *such a tyde* as "at whatever time."

253 doutremer] *de owter mer* F B.

288 From Th.

298 as] *al* F B T.

301 songe everych] *song e.* T Don Php; *e. songe* Th; *songen e.* Skt Hth Kch Rob Bgh Dck Fsh. The emendation is unnecessary if a strong caesura is read after *songe.*

329 of kyng] MSS Dck Php; om. Skt Kch Rob Bgh; *of* Hth; *kyng* Don Fsh. Most editors omit on the assumption the phrase was repeated from the preceding line and makes the verse decasyllabic.

334 Of al] *And al* MSS Th Hth.

342 nas] *was* F B T.

343 a] *no* Th Rob.

350 speken] *speke* F B Th Don Dck Php; *spake* T.

364 I] Om. F B T.

378 yfounde] *founde* MSS Th Don; all other editors emend for meter.

383 overshote] *overshette* F T Fsh Dck Php, perhaps correctly (cf. *shette* Rom A 1341).

384 on] *vpon* F B Th.

420 or] *fro other* F B T.

422 or] Om. F B T Dck Php.

437 rekene] *rekened* Skt Rob Bgh. The emendation is attractive, but the reading of the authorities makes sense if *rekene* is taken as an infinitive dependent on *Sete* (Php) or as a subjunctive (Dck).

443 they] *I* Th Kch Don Dck Fsh, perhaps rightly, though cf. a similar use of *they* in line 1312 below.

479–80 After 479 Th has *And thus in sorwe lefte me aloon,* rejected by all eds. except Kch Dck. To retain the traditional numbering the next line is called 481. Dickerson in his edition (198–202) and in Papers of the Amer. Biblio. Soc. 66, 1972, 51–54, defends the authenticity of the line. However, in Th 486 is moved to follow 483, which violates the sense. The added line and this change of order converts the unusual rhyme scheme into the more common scheme used in 1175–80. Th is apparently "improving" the text.

509 throgh] Om. Kch; perhaps *So* should be emended to *And,* since the syntax of 508–11 is confused.

512 clepeth] *clepe the* F B; *clepe* T and all eds. except Dck Php. T is corrupt *(god vnkynde* for *god of kynde)* and the meter is rough in any case (since the *-e* of *clepe* must be apocopated to preserve it); *men* is the sing. impers. pro.

578 the] Om. F B Skt Kch Dck Fsh.

584 wolde not] *wyl n.* T Th Don Dck Fsh; *wull n.* B; *wol n.* Hth Kch Php.

589 Cesiphus] *Thesiphus* F B Kch Fsh Php; *Tesiphus* T Th Don; *Sesiphus* Skt; the confusion of *c* and *t* is common (cf. Tr 1.786).

599 song] *sorwe* MSS and Th, probably repeated from 597.

619 Atte] *Atte the* F Php; *At the* B T Th Don Dck; *At* Kch.

622 she halt] *she is halt* F B T; *is she halt* Don.

627 wrien] *varien* F B T.

628 monstres] *mowstres* F; *mowstrys* B.

640 he] *hyt* F B T.

660 in the myd] *in mid* Skt Kch Rob Bgh Fsh.

667 Pictagores] *Pictagoras* F T Php; *Pyttagoras* B; *Pithagoras* Th Skt Hth Rob Bgh; cf. 1167.

677 hadde] *as* F B.

721 good] Om. Hth Rob Bgh; Skt Kch retain *good* but omit *yis.*

722 say] Om. F B T.

723 the] Cooley (MLN 63, 1948, 34–35) makes a good case for the omission of this article.

745 Loo [sey] how that may be] *L. she t. m. be* F B T; *Howe t. m. be* Th; *L. sire h. t. m. be* Skt; *L. sire t. m. be* Don; *L. so t. m. be* Dck; *L. howe t. m. be* Php. The original cannot be determined.

750 the upon a] *hyt the vp a* F B Php; *thee up* Skt; *thee up a* Kch Don Dck; *hyt the upon* Fsh.

754 hereto] *here lo* F B T.

765 yive] *yeve* B Th; *yoven* T; *yiven* Skt Hth Rob Bgh Fsh; the *-n* is not necessary to avoid hiatus before a strong *r-.*

787 kend] *kende* F Fsh; *koude* B; *conde* T Th; *kenned* Hth; *koud* Skt Don Dck; *kond(e)* Kch Php; *koud* yields a somewhat better meaning, but *kend* is satisfactory.

828 of wel] *of so wel* F B (the *so* probably picked up from the next line); *and wel* Skt Kch.

830 more] Om. F B T.

832 as] *al* F B Th Kch Dck Fsh Php.

858 gold] Om. F B T.

884 lyte] *lytel* F Th Don Fsh Php.

886 From Th.

888 nas] *was* F B Don Dck Fsh Php.

903 comprehende] *comprehend* T; *comprehenden* Skt Hth Rob Bgh Fsh, to avoid hiatus, but probably *beaute* is here trisyllabic, as often in Chaucer (cf. KnT I.1926).

905 whit] Om. Skt Hth Don Fsh; Kch transposes *fressh* and *rody.*

916 Ne] *They ne* Skt Hth Bgh.

932 her] *hit* F; *hir* B T Th Fsh; *hire* Don Dck; *hir [ther]* Skt Hth Rob Bgh.

942 whit] Om. Hth Don Fsh; **pure]** om. Skt.

975 stonden] *stonde* MSS Th Don Php.

976 that] Om. F T B Kch Fsh Php.

1028 into] *to* Skt Kch Rob Bgh Php.

1039 blesse] *blysse* F B T Skt Hth Fsh Php. For other examples of *blesse* as a variant spelling of *blisse,* see MED s.v. *blis(e) n.* 2a(b) and 3(d). Most editors accept the spelling in Th for the rhyme.

1040 goddesse] *lisse* Skt; *good lisse* Hth; *goddysse* Fsh. The emendations follow on these editors' adoption of *blysse* in 1039.

1046 trowe hyt wel] *trowe* T Th Dck; *trowe hyt* all other eds. except Php. But *leve hyt wel* in 1047 depends on *trowe hyt wel* for its emphasis.

1053 sworen] *swore* MSS Th Don Dck Php.

1064 therto] *to* F B T. **also]** *also as* F B Hth Fsh.

1076 tellen] *telle* F and all eds. except Kch Rob; *tell* B T.

1137 seyde he] *he seyde* F B; *seyde the* T; *sayd* Th.

1147 nat never] *never* Skt Hth Kch Rob Bgh.

1159   thus] *this* F T Th.

1161   ne knewe] *the knowe* F; *to know* B; *ne know* T.

1173   this] *thus* F B T. the] Om. MSS Th Don Dck Php; the article appears with the only other adjectival usage of *altherferste* (Tr 3.97).

1174   werste] *first(e)* F B T.

1188   nam] *am* MSS Th Don Dck Php; here the idiom requires emendation (cf. 204 above).

1204   rehersen] *reherse* MSS Th Don Dck Php.

1226   gan hir hertely] *h. g. hir* T Th Rob Bgh, to avoid the cluster of h's.

1264   thynges] *thyng* Skt Hth Rob Bgh, to avoid a ten-syllable line; Skeat reads *al* for *alle* to make eight syllables.

1315   homwarde] Skeat noted that the line is too short (the *-e* is probably not sounded; *homward* is Chaucer's usual form), and he therefore added *quikly;* Kch adds *faste;* Hth Rob Don emend to *homwardes,* not used elsewhere in Chaucer and unrecorded before 1400 by the MED.

1323   smyten] *smyte* MSS Th Don Php.

  Explicit . . .] From F B; om. T Th.

Some readings from F adopted by no editor:

22   ne[2]] *no.*   **271**   as] Om.   **281**   he] *ho.*   **319** out] *out of.*   **418**   of leves] *of of* L (the second *of* seems canceled but possibly not by the scribe).   **422**   Of] *or.* **499**   lym] *hym.*   **509**   sorwe] *sorwes.*   **647**   she thus] *thus she.*   **670**   thogh] *thoght.*   **854**   so] *a so.* **889**   than] *that* (also B).   **1108**   in] Om.   **1149**   be ryght *r. be.*   **1155**   me] *so me.*   **1223**   al] *at.*   **1260** understonde] *vderstonde.*   **1282**   the] Om.

The House of Fame

Authorities: three manuscripts and the editions of Caxton and Thynne, which have manuscript authority (in the notes below, MSS refers to all five authorities). Robinson, following Koch, classified them as:

α {
  F   Fairfax 16, Bodleian, folios 154ᵛ–183ᵛ
  B   Bodley 638, Bodleian, folios 141ᵛ–193ᵛ
}

β {
  P   Pepys 2006, Magdalene College, Cambridge, pp. 91–114
  Cx   Caxton's edition, 1483
  Th   Thynne's edition, 1532, folios cccxiiᵛ–cccxxiiiᵛ
}

F B P and Th are accessible in facsimile editions. Transcriptions of all the authorities are available in Ch Soc. 1st ser. 23 and 57. All but Th lack many lines: F and B lack 504–7, 780, 911–12, 1546, 1572, 2028, and 2036; F also lacks 221, 340, and 1275–76. P Cx and Th lack 1291. P and Cx also lack 65–66, 793–96, 827–64, and 1541–42; P also lacks 136, 196, 988, 1264, 1432, 1457, 1572, and 1726, and it ends at 1843. As these losses and the notes below show, F and B are closely related, as are P and Cx. Th derives from Cx but makes use of at least one other authority; it often agrees with F and B even in errors (see notes 675, 1015, and others, below), and it is the sole authority for lines 280–83.

Except for the Globe editor, Heath, who held β to be superior, modern editors have preferred the readings of α in the majority of cases and have used F as the base text. "But as a matter of fact, whichever group is adopted, a good many readings of the other have to be substituted. In this text, too, as in the *Book of the Duchess,* the readings of all MSS. are unsatisfactory and considerable emendation is necessary" (R.). I have made only a few changes in Robinson's text, usually to restore manuscript readings where he and other editors have emended for metrical regularity. Otherwise, "though the spelling of F does not conform altogether to that of the best MSS. of the *Canterbury Tales* and the *Troilus,* most of its peculiarities (such as the double vowels in *too, froo, loo, mee,* etc.) have been allowed to stand. Forms that appear inconsistent with Chaucer's usage have been corrected, and inflectional endings have been made regular. In several instances *-n* has been silently added to infinitives to break a hiatus or mend the rhythm" (R.). I have provided a full list of such emendations (except for slight variations in spelling and for infinitives to which *-n* has been added with the warrant of one of the authorities); I have also noted the significant variants from the other authorities. The many departures from the base text, F, and from the α group, readings adopted by no editor, are listed separately at the end of the notes, as are most of the more significant readings from the β group rejected by all editors. I have also noted the significant variant readings from Skeat (Skt), Heath (Hth), Koch (Kch), Robinson's second edition (Rob), the partial edition of Donaldson (Don),

The textual notes to *The House of Fame* were prepared by John M. Fyler.

which omits lines 111–479 and all of Book III, Baugh (Bgh), Fisher (Fsh), and at several points Willert (ed., HF, Berlin, 1888). A full set of manuscript variants is available in Koch's edition.

The subdivisions Proem, Invocation, Story, and Dream, and the titles Book I, Book II, and Book III, are editorial, printed by all editors but Koch. The *explicits* and *incipits* are from Cx; Th has only the *explicits;* in F B and P the book divisions are indicated only by large capitals (see the expl. note to line 1093).

Title: *The House of Fame* F B Th; *The booke of ffame* P; *The book of Fame made by Gefferey Chaucer* Cx.

BOOK I

7–8   **avision, revelacion]** MSS; *-oun* eds.
8   **why this]** MSS Kch Don; *this* other eds.
14   **Devyne]** *Defyne* P Th Kch.
20   **Or why]** *For why* F B Skt Kch. **this]** *this is* MSS Don. **cause]** Om. Cx Th.
26   **Prison-stewe]** *Prison stewe* F B all eds.; *Preson stoe* P; *Pryson stryf* Cx Th. F has a punctuation slash after *stewe,* Cx Th a slash between *pryson* and *stryf.* Eds. read and punctuate as a series *(prison, stewe).* The evidence for *prison-stewe* and materials for this note were supplied by John Reidy; see Expl. Notes.
32   **bede]** *rede* P Cx Th Hth.
40   **Causeth]** *Causen* Cx Th Rob. **avisions]** *(to) have visions* P Cx Th Hth Rob.
54   **this and]** *that and of* P Cx Th; *that and* Hth.
63   **now]** Om. Cx; *dide* Skt Hth.
65–66   Om. P Cx.
85   **stonden]** *stonde* MSS Don, perhaps correctly.
92   **mysdemen]** *mysdeme* MSS Don, perhaps correctly.
104   **avision]** *vision* P Cx.
127   **olde]** *golde* P Cx Th Hth.
135–36   *Her roosgarland on her hede* P (next line missing); *Rose garlondes smellyng as a mede / And also fleyng aboute her hede* Cx.
143   **synge]** *say* F B; *singen* Rob Bgh Fsh.
153   **That]** Supplied by eds. "The ellipsis of the subject relative here is certainly difficult though perhaps not impossible" (R.).
160   **Polytes]** Th; *Polyte* F B Kch Fsh; *Plite* P; *Plyto* Cx.
174   **thys]** *hys* F B; om. Th.
191   **she to hym]** *to h. s.* P Cx Hth.
196   Om. P.
221   Om. F.
244   **Al that]** *That that* F B Skt Kch.
250   F B; *How (that) they first aqueynted were* P Cx Th Hth.
263   **herby]** *hertly* P Cx Hth.
278   **Or]** Th; *Of for* F; *Or for* B P Cx; *For* Skt.
280–83   Found only in Th.
284   **that]** Om. Cx Th Hth.
285   **or³]** Om. F B P Kch, "perhaps correctly: *privy double,* 'secretly double'?" (R.); *fals provyd or* Cx.
292   **this]** *that* P Cx Hth.

305   As] *And* P Cx Th Hth.
329   I] Supplied by eds.
330   have ye men] *m. h. ye* P Cx Hth Fsh.
340   Om. F.
347   alle] Om. P Cx Th Hth.
353   duren] *dure* F B; *endure* P Cx.
358   don] Th; om. rest.
362   Al] *But al* MSS Kch; "*But* perhaps repeated from l.361" (R.).
370   him] Th; om. rest.
381   hyt] Th; *h. were* rest Kch Fsh.
386   sen hyt] *se hyt* F B; *it is* P Cx.
402   And] Om. F B Hth Kch.
428   al] Om. P Cx Hth. **grete**] Om. F B Kch.
434   goo] *goo for* F B; *gan for* Th.
444   *And also Dido and Deiphebus* P Cx Th Hth.
480   at] *of* P Cx Th Hth. **dores**] *dore* P Cx Th.
483   that] *ever* P Cx Th Hth.
489   Ne no] Th; *Ne I no* rest Skt Kch Don.
491   I] Om. F B Skt Don.
497   as] F; *an* B P Cx; *on* Th.
504–7 Om. F B.

BOOK II

510   *That eny maner of englissh can* P Cx.
511   listeth] P Th Skt Hth; *listeneth* F Cx Kch Rob Bgh Fsh; *listneth* B Don. See Expl. Notes.
513   *So sely and (so) dred(e)ful a vision* P Cx Th.
514   Scipion] *Cipion* F B P.
527   tellen] *tel* F Th; *tell(e)* B Cx.
528   and] *and thy* P Th Don.
530   as] *alle* P Cx Th Hth.
536   smot] *smyte* P Cx Th Hth Bgh Fsh. **somtyme**] *son(n)e* P Cx Hth.
537   brende] *beende* F; *bende* B.
543   in] *at* P Cx Th Skt Hth.
552   That] *And* F B Kch.
557   agast so] *agast* F B Kch Don; *so agast* Skt Hth.
558   tho] Om. F B P.
566   nas] *was* F Cx; *as* P.
618   Venus] MSS Kch Rob Don Bgh Fsh; *V. [goddesse]* Skt; *[dame] V.* Hth. "The line may be headless, but it is suspiciously short" (R.).
621   lyte] *lytel* MSS; all eds. emend to *lyte*.
622   bookys songes dytees] *b. s. or d.* P Cx; *b. s. and d.* Th; *s. d. b.* F B; *s. ditis b.* Kch; *s. dites b.* Don.
635   in²] Om. P Cx Th Skt Hth.
642   this] *wel this* P Cx Th Hth.
646   noght] *nothyng(e)* P Cx Th Hth.
653   mad alle thy] *ymade* F B; *ymad thy* Skt Hth Kch Fsh.
675   And] P Cx Th Rob; om. F B and other eds. **folk**] P Cx Rob; *folkes* Don; *folke* F B Th and other eds. The reading of P Cx Th "makes the unusual dative *folkë* unnecessary" (R.).
680   ben] Om. F B Kch Don Fsh.
685   moo] *and mo* Cx Th Skt Hth.
705   she] Cx; *he* rest. **yet**] Om. Cx.
715   hevene and erthe] F Kch Don Fsh; *hevene erthe* rest and other eds.
717   either] *in* P Cx Th Skt Hth.
718   way] *aire* F B Don.

727   a worthy] *worth(e) a* F B Kch Don.
755   hit] Om. F; *he* P Cx Th.
756   Ther-as] P Cx Th Hth Rob; *As ther* F B other eds.; *but be kept* appears in the margin in F B.
766   speche that ys spoken] *spech that ys yspoken* F B Kch Fsh.
773   As] *Of* F B Don.
780   Om. F B.
793–96 Om. P Cx.
794   That whel] *That whele sercle* MSS.
797   Wydder] *Brod(d)er* P Cx Th Hth.
800   Causeth] P Cx Th Hth Rob Bgh; *Caused* F B Skt Kch Don Fsh.
803   That] *Til* F Don.
810   spoken] *yspoken* F B Th.
817   another] Em. Willert Kch Rob Don; *other* F B; *in other* P Cx Th Skt Hth Bgh Fsh.
823   thou have] *ye have in* F B Kch Fsh.
826   I preve] *ipreve* Fsh; *by preve* P Cx Th.
827–64 Om. P Cx.
827   same place] Hth Rob Bgh Fsh; *sum place stide* F; *som styde* B; *some stede* Th; *same stede* Don; *the mansioun* Skt; *every stede* Kch.
853   this now] Th; *thus* F; *this* B Skt Hth Kch.
872   [Quod he] A good] *A good* MSS Fsh; *A right good* Kch. The emendation is Skeat's, adopted by all eds. but Kch Fsh.
896   gan] Skt Hth Rob Bgh; *to* F B P Kch Don Fsh; *gan to* Cx Th; "conceivably an historical infinitive, but unlikely" (R.).
911–12 Em. Skt Kch Rob; Om. F B; *And seide seyst thou eny token / Or ought thow knowest yonder down* P; *And seyde seest thou ony token / Or ought that in the (this) world is of spoken* Cx Th Hth Bgh Fsh; *And saide seest thou any token / Of ought that in the world is spoken* Don. See Koch, ESt 27, 1916, 142.
916   kyng Daun Scipio] *Kynge ne of Rome dan Scipio(n)* Cx Th Fsh. See Expl. Notes. **Scipio**] *Cipio* F B; *Cupie* P.
919   wrechche] F B Th; *wryght* P Cx Hth Kch.
924   maked moch] *made a grete* P Cx Th Hth.
926   space] *place* F B Skt Hth Don.
935   thoo] Om. P Cx Th Don.
937   Which men clepeth] *The which men clep(e)* P Cx Th Hth.
946   gonne] *goome* P; *gan* rest Don. **launce**] *daunce* P Cx Hth; *praunce* Th.
950   for ferde] *for fer(e)* P Cx Th; *forfered* Don. See Expl. Notes.
957   gret] *mochil* F B Don.
961   alway upper] *upper alway for* F B Kch; *upper alway* Don Fsh.
964   y] *y to* F B Th Don.
978   Cloude] *Cloude and erthe* F B Th; *Cloude erthe* Don.
984   Nas me] *Nas* F B; *Nadde he me* P Cx Skt Hth.
988   Om. P.
991   gan] *began* F B Don.
1003 Bridd] *Briddes* F B Don.
1015 they shynen] *thy seluen* F B Th.
1034 lyk] Om. F B P Hth Kch Don; *lyke the* Cx Th.
1040 the] *a* F B Don Fsh.
1044 byten] B Th; *beten* F P Hth; *greve* Cx.
1063 And] Om. F B Don.
1078 hyt] *he* P Cx Th Hth Kch.

1079   hath] Om. F B Don. **verray]** P; *were* F B; *very* Cx
Th Bgh Fsh; *wereth* Don.
1088   lernen] *lere* B; *lern(e)* rest and Don, perhaps correctly.

BOOK III

1114   site] *cyte, cite(e)* MSS. All eds. emend.
1115   thys] *hys* F; *the* P Cx.
1119   it] Om. F Th Kch Fsh.
1124   alum de] *a thynge of* F B Skt; *alymde* P; *a lymed* Cx
Th; *alyned* Hth. Bradley's argument (Athenaeum 1,
1902, 563–64) for an original reading *alym de* ("alum de
glas," potash alum in its crystalline form) has been accepted by later eds. and the MED. Cf. *alum glas* CYT
VIII.813.
1136   al] Om. F B Kch Fsh.
1156   here] *there* P Cx Th Skt.
1161–62   Lines transposed in F B Th Skt Kch Fsh.
1170   no] *the* P Cx; *ne* Kch. "Reading doubtful; *compas*
(noun) ought not to have final *-e.* Either emend the rime-
word to *plas,* or take *no* as 'nor' and *compace* as infinitive"
(R.).
1177   craft] Om. MSS Kch Fsh. "All MSS. om. *craft* in
l.1177; β inserts in l.1178, from which the editors have
transferred it" (R.).
1189   Babewynnes] *Rabewyures* F; *Rabewynnes* B;
Babeweuries P; *As babeuwryes* Cx; *As babeuries* Th. All eds.
emend to the form printed.
1195   stoden] Om. F B; *stonden* P.
1204   his] P Cx; *the* F Kch; *this* B Th.
1208   Bret] *gret* F; *Bretur* P; *Briton* Cx Th.
1210   dyvers] Om. F B Skt Hth Kch.
1218   and] *or* B P Cx.
1227–28   Lines transposed in F B.
1227   Atiteris] *Cytherus* P Cx Th Hth; *Citharis* Kch.
1228   Pseustis] *Presentus* P; *Proserus* Cx Th Hth.
1234   the] *alle* F; *alle the* B Th.
1241   blod-shedynge] *blodeshedynges* F Th.
1242   clarionynge] *clarionynges* F Th.
1245   trumpe Joab] *J. t.* P Cx Th Skt Hth.
1264   Om. P; *And many other Invocacions* Cx; *And eke
subfumygacions* Th.
1272   Circes] *Artes* F; *Artys* B; *Cirtes* P. **Calipsa]** *Cali-
ophia* P Cx Th.
1274   Limote] *Limete* F Kch Fsh; *Lumete* B.
1275–76   Om. F.
1283   y ther] *that I* P Cx Th Skt Hth.
1287   eft imused] *oft I m.* F; *all I m.* B; *eft I m.* P Cx Kch
Fsh; *I amused* Th.
1291   Om. P; *And thenne anon after this* Cx Th.
1293   forth] *to* F B Kch.
1303   they hatte] Eds.; *they hat* F; *they hate* B; *the hack-
yng(e)* P Cx Th.
1304   ful of] B; om. F; *and* P Cx Th Kch.
1315   shoken] *shoon* F Fsh; *shone* B; *shoke* P Cx Th.
1351   Ful] P Cx; *Fyne* other MSS and Kch.
1356   lusty and ryche] *riche lusty* P Cx Skt Hth.
1372   So P Cx Th; *This was gret marvaylle to me* F B;
Robinson notes approvingly Heath's suggestion that the
original read *This was gret marvaylle to me, she.*
1374   erthe] *therthe* P Cx Th Skt Hth Fsh.
1406   or] *and* P Cx Th Skt Hth Fsh.

1411   th'] Om. F B P Cx; *the* Th.
1415   And thus] MSS; *Thus* eds.
1416   nobley] *noble* F B Th.
1425   hy and] Om. MSS; supplied by Heath from 1426
in Th; Kch inserts *ful;* Skt reads *greet [and hy].*
1432   Om. P.
1435   he bar on] *bare up on* P; *bare upon* Cx Skt Hth.
1456   stonden] *stonde* MSS, perhaps correctly.
1457   Om. P.
1477   that] Om. F B Skt Kch Fsh. **made]** *was* F B Fsh.
1483   The] P Cx Th Rob; *That* F B and other eds.
1484   a] Om. F B Hth Kch.
1491   this] *his* Rob Bgh Fsh.
1515   olde] *al of the olde* F; *of the olde* B Kch.
1541–42   Om. P Cx.
1542   thus] *this* Th Hth Kch.
1546   Om. F B.
1547   dame] *daun* F B P.
1568   messager] B Cx; *messangere* F; *masynger* P; *messenger* Th. "Spellings vary throughout *HF;* the older form
(without *n*) has been adopted" (R.).
1572   Om. F B P Kch (who adds a line after 1568).
1577   ypreised] *preised* F B.
1585   that] Om. F B Kch.
1594   clariouns] *clarioun* F B.
1595   forth] *fast(e)* P Cx Th Hth.
1599   That] *And* F B Hth Kch.
1603   to] *at* P Cx Skt Hth.
1623   So eds.; *Have do(o)n Eolus let se(e)* F B; *And thou dan
Eolus quod she* P Cx Th; cf. 1765 below.
1624   quod she] *let(e) se* P Cx Th.
1633   For] *That* P Cx Th Hth.
1668   Right] Om. F B Kch.
1675   Al] Om. F B Kch.
1683   than] *that* Cx Th Hth Kch; *at* P.
1685   it] P Cx Rob; om. rest and other eds.
1686   pot] *pot(te)ful* F B Th; *pitteful* P; *pyt ful* Cx. "To
avoid over-long line, editors om. *of* [Skt Kch Bgh Fsh]
or *ful* [Hth Rob] (perhaps repeated from l.1687)" (R.).
1701   your] *alle your* P Cx Hth Fsh.
1702   clew] *turned* P Cx Th Kch.
1709   For] *For no* F B Th Bgh Fsh. **ne for]** *for* F B; *ne*
P Cx Th.
1717   lyven] *lyen* F B Th Kch; *be* P; om. Cx; all eds.
except Kch emend.
1718   trumpes] *trumpe* P Cx Th Skt Hth Kch.
1720   werk] *werkes* MSS Kch.
1725   Also] *And so* P Cx Hth; *So* Skt. **kenely]** *kynd(e)ly*
P Cx Th.
1726   So F B; om. P; *That their fame was blowe a lofte* Cx
Th Hth.
1735   as] *so* P Cx Skt Hth.
1750   To] *The* F B Th.
1765   let se] *now let se* F B; *quod she* P Cx Th Hth; cf.
1623 above.
1775   ye] Supplied by eds.
1781   roughte] *thought* P Cx Th Hth.
1783   sweynte] *slepy* P Cx Th Hth.
1786   to] *on* P Cx Skt Hth.
1787   eke to] *on* P Cx Th Hth; *eke on* Skt.
1793   they] Om. F B Kch.
1813   grettest] Willert and all eds. but Kch; *gret(e)* MSS
Kch.
1818   a] Om. P Cx Th Skt Hth.
1821   to] Om. F B P.

1822   not] P; om. rest.

1843   End of P.

1847   thrift] *trouthe* Cx Th Hth.

1853   be] *be no(u)ght* F Th Hth Kch; *be [but]* Skt.

1883   But] Om. Cx Th Hth. **than**] Om. F B Kch Fsh.

1887   thinges] Eds.; *thing* MSS.

1897   wiste] Eds.; *wote* MSS.

1907   Whych] All eds. but Kch; *Why* MSS Kch.

1908   thus] Supplied by Skeat and adopted by all eds. but Kch, who omits the line as spurious.

1924   as swyft] Cx Th Rob Bgh; *so swift* F B all other eds.

1926   hyt stille] Th all eds. but Fsh; *still (h)it* rest Fsh.

1940   hottes] Eds.; *hattes* F B Cx; *hutches* Th.

1944   So Cx Th; om. B; "F starts the line *As ful this lo* (perhaps preserving a correct but uncompleted text)" (R.).

1946   in] *of* Cx; *on* Th Skt Hth.

1948   roof] Cx; *rove* F Kch; *rone* B; *rofe* Th; "perhaps a real dative" (R.).

1962   reste] Eds.; *restes* MSS. **of labour of viages**] *and of l. of v.* F B Th; *of l. and of v.* Cx.

1966   bildynges] *lesynges* Cx Th Kch Fsh.

1967   and] *And eke* MSS; om. Skt Hth Kch.

1984   of sprynges] *sprynges* Cx Th Skt Hth Kch.

2004   gynne] *the gyn(ne)* Cx Th. "Possibly *the gin,* 'the device,' riming with *therin*" (R.).

2009   these] MSS all eds. but Skt; "but *thesë* is not regular; Skeat em. *swiche*" (R.).

2010   syghtes] Th; *syght* F B Cx.

2017   fruit] All eds. but Hth; *frot* F; *foot* B; *swote* Cx Th Hth. Koch was doubtful about Skeat's emendation. Robinson suggests *rote,* "root," as another possibility.

2020   the an] Cx; *than* F Kch; *the* B Th Skt.

2021   yaf in] MSS; *yaf* eds.

2028   Om. F B.

2036   Om. F B; Koch thought the line spurious and suggested *Many a thousand in a route.*

2044   everych] Om. F B Kch; *ech* Skt.

2048   lo late or now] Om. F; *lo ryght now* Cx Th.

2049   "Metrically suspicious; Skeat em. *the other* for *he;* Koch supplies *sire* before *quod*" (R.).

2053   Thus¹] Eds.; *And thus* F B; *And thys* Cx Th. **Thus²**] Eds.; *and thus* MSS.

2061   forth ryght to] *forth unto* Cx; *streyght to* Th; *forth to* Skt Hth.

2063   to him was] *him was* F B Th; *w. to h.* Cx.

2067   So F B; *More than ever it spoken was* Cx Th Hth.

2069   Tho fro him that] *That he fro him thoo* F B.

2076   tydyng] Cx Th; *mouth* F B; *word* Skt; *thyng* Hth Kch.

2079   sparke] *sparcle* Cx Th.

2081   yspronge] *up spronge* Cx Th Hth.

2083   hit] Eds.; *and* MSS.

2090   drawe] *thrawe* F B Kch, "who interprets it as 'eilen,' hasten" (R.).

2094   "Rest missing in Cx, which adds, however, 12 lines apparently spurious. See below" (R.).

2103   they] *he* Th Skt.

2104   on [of us] two] Kch Rob; *on(e) two* F Th; *that oon* B; *that oon [of] two* Skt Hth Bgh; *that oon of us two* Fsh.

2129   boystes] F; *bowgys* B; *boxes* Th.

2152   nose and yën] B; *noyse an highen* F; *noyse on hyghen* Th; *nose on hye* Skt Kch.

2153   others] *other* F B Skt.

2156   nevene] Supplied by eds.; *Whiche that y nat (naught) ne kan* MSS; *ne wot ne kan* Hth.

2157   Cx adds at end:

And wyth the noyse of them wo
I sodeynly awoke anon tho
And remembryd what I had seen
And how hye and ferre I had been
In my ghoost and had grete wonder
Of that the god of thonder
Had lete me knowen and began to wryte
Lyke as ye have herd me endyte
Wherfor to studye and rede alway
I purpose to doo day by day
Thus in dremyng and in game
Endeth thys lytyl book of Fame.

Th alters the first three lines:

And therwithal I abrayde
Out of my slepe halfe a frayde
*Remembri*ng *wel what I had sene.*

Caxton labels his addition "Caxton" and adds "I fynde nomore of this werke to fore sayd / For as fer as I can vnderstonde / This noble man Gefferey Chaucer fy-nyshed at the sayd conclusion of the metynge of lesynge and sothsawe where as yet they ben chekked and maye not departe." Both the label and note were omitted in Th and his version of Caxton's conclusion was included in editions into the nineteenth century.

Readings from the α group rejected by all editors:

11   fantome] *ffamtome* F. **53   Wel**] *We* F. **64   now**] *yow* F. **77   And**] *That* F. **134   pardee**] *partee* F B. **148   Lavyne**] *Labyne* F B. **161   of**] *and* F. **172   goddes**] *goddesse* F B. **215   on**] *an* F B. **220   lysse**] *stent* F. **260   the**] Om. F. **291   saufly**] *savely* F. **305   oon**] *loue* F. **315   she**] *he* F. **322   have**] *ha* F. **347   myn**] *your(e)* F B. **352   be**] Om. F B. **363   Certeyn**] *Certeynly* F B. **371   And**] *As* F B. **381   nere**] *nor* F. **391   was**] Om. F B; **Trace**] *Tace* F. **403   for²**] Om. F. **410   al**] Om. F B. **426   as**] Om. F B; **us**] Om. F B. **433   how**] *how that* F B. **434   to sayle**] *to assayle* F B. **458   Lavina**] *Labina* F. **475   in**] Om. F B. **486   of**] Om. F B. **535   thyng**] *kynge* F B; **fouder**] *founder* F B. **536   to**] *of* F B. **545   caryinge**] *cryinge* F. **570   tho**] *that* F; **myn**] *my* F B. **575   it**] Om. F B. **651   ne**] *ner* F; *nor* B. **691   greynes**] *greyndes* F B. **696   cordes**] *acordes* F B. **789   Throwe**] *Thorwe* F B; **to**] om. F B. **798   thus**] *this* F B. **804   Although thou**] *Al thou* F. **805   alway**] Om. F B. **859   of**] *or* F B. **873   I**] *he* F B; **be**] *me* F B. **913   I sayde**] Om. F B. **931   speketh**] *seketh* F B. **932   the**] Om. F B. **956   fro**] *fer fro* F B. **973   A**] *Of* F B. **1014   As**] *Alle* F B. **1029   and soth**] *and that soth* F. **1077   Which**] *With* F. **1080   That¹**] *And* F B. **1101   thow**] *nowe* F B. **1102   me**] Om. F B; **now**] *yowe* F B. **1106   me**] *men* F B. **1109   entre**] *entreth* F B. **1113   the**] *thys* F B. **1127   I nyste**] *nyste I neuer* F B. **1142   by for**] *before* F B. **1155   tyme**] *tymes* F; **they**] *there* F. **1161   that**] Om. F. **1178   The¹**] *To* F. **1185   the¹**] Om. F B. **1197   of²**] Om. F B. **1201   on**] *vpon* F B. **1202   sowned**] *sowneth* F B. **1210   hem**] *hym* F. **1211   hem**] *hym* F B (so also 1212, 1214); **gape**] *iape* F B. **1233   famous**] *fames* F B. **1255   as now not**] *not now* F B.

1262 wicches] *wrechches* F.   **1273** I] Om. F.   **1286** yholde] *ycolde* F.   **1304** ymageries] Om. F.   **1328** Although] *As though* F B.   **1332** cotes] *cote* F B.   **1335** as] Om. F B.   **1349** lite] *litel* F B.   **1369** that] Om. F B.   **1371** semed be] Om. F B.   **1377** to] Om. F B.   **1404** songe] *synge* F.   **1422** cler] *chere* F.   **1436** up] Om. F B.   **1437** stoden] *stonden* F.   **1439** him] *hem* F B.   **1492** *And I hyt myght see myn ye* F.   **1494** highte length] *high the length* F.   **1498** sternely] *sturmely* F.   **1510** al] Om. F B.   **1544** of] Om. F B.   **1551** yit] *ryght* F B.   **1553** seyde] *quod* F B.   **1569** bad] Om. F B.   **1570** Upon] *Upon the* F B; anon] om. F B.   **1575** is] Om. F B.   **1576** wont] *wonde* F B.   **1582** do hem] *do him* F.   **1595** he] *hye* F B.   **1609** now] Om. F B.   **1614** ben] *ben wel* F B.   **1621** wel] Om. F B.   **1647** swartish] *swarte* F B.   **1661** han] *benen* F; trewely] *cruelly* F B.   **1707** To hide] *And hidden* F B.   **1719** thou] Om. F B.   **1734** But] *That* F.   **1735** a] Om. F B.   **1742** her] *hem* F; herte] Om. F B.   **1745** the] Om. F B.   **1748** as] *a* F.   **1749** as] *a* F.   **1779** Wher] *or* F B.   **1782** to] Om. F B.   **1792** thee] Om. F B.   **1834** vice] *vices* F B.   **1862** they] *this folke* F B.   **1864** it] Om. F B.   **1867** worldes] *wordes* F.   **1896** I] Om. F B.   **1906** the] Om. F.   **1931** that I] *I haue* F.   **1938** Swiche] *Whiche* F B.   **1941** twygges] *twynges* F.   **1946** as of leves] *of leues as* F.   **2018** Languisshe] *Laugh* F B.   **2029** And] Om. F B.   **2066** To] *Tho* F.   **2088** I] Om. F.   **2091** at] *to* F B.   **2115** wane] *wynne* F B.   **2118** Wynged] *Wenyed* F B.

Some readings from the β Group rejected by all editors:

19 Of] *Of the* P Cx Th.   **24** to] *the* P Cx Th.   **62** as I] *as dide* I P Cx.   **64** now] Om. Cx Th.   **96** vilanye] *felonye* P Cx Th.   **198** I thee] *I eke the* P Cx Th.   **208** any] *eny of hem* P; *any of her* Cx Th.   **223** arryvage] *a ryvage* P Cx Th.   **232** that] Om. P Cx Th.   **254** Tolde] *Tolde to* P Cx Th.   **271** be Cryste] *eny (every) trust* P Cx.   **279** this] *thus* P Cx.   **298** to] *in to* P Cx Th.   **333** any[2]] *a fals(e)* P Cx Th.   **362** ne al] *ne* P Cx Th.   **383** the routhe] *and routhe.* P Cx Th.   **397** lo] *loke* P Cx Th.   **548** nyste] *nyst(e) never* P Cx Th.   **991** this] *the* P Cx Th.   **1063** there] *her(e)* P Cx Th.   **1738** acheved] F B Th; *eshued* P; *eschewyd* Cx; lestes] *bestes* P Cx; *questes* Th.   **1761** gliwe] *blowe* P Cx.   **1803** beloweth] *belleth* P Cx Th.   **1812** trayterye] *trechery(e)* P Cx Th.   **1823** lepynge] *crepyng(e)* P Cx.   **1824** choppen] *clappe(n)* P Cx Th.   **1895** mene of] *mente* Cx; *ment of* Th.   **1967** wyndes] *wether* Cx Th.   **2026** here anoon] *here* Cx Th.

Anelida and Arcite

Authorities: twelve manuscripts and Caxton's early print:

Add Additional 16165, British Library, folios 256ᵛ–58ᵛ, 241ᵛ–43ᵛ (written by John Shirley)

B Bodley 638, Bodleian, folios 7ᵛ–11ᵛ, 5–7

D Digby 181, Bodleian, folios 39ᵛ–43ᵛ

F Fairfax 16, Bodleian, folios 32–35, 30–32

Ff Cambridge University Library Ff 1.6, folios 61–63ᵛ

Hl¹ Harley 372, British Library, folios 57–60ᵛ

Hl² Harley 7333, British Library, folios 134–35 (copied from Shirley)

Lt Longleat 258, in the possession of the Marquess of Bath, Longleat House, Warminster, Wilts., folios 76–83ᵛ

P Pepys 2006, Magdalene College, Cambridge, pp. 382–84

Ph Formerly Phillips 8299, now HM 140, Henry E. Huntington Museum and Art Gallery, San Marino, Calif., folios 85–87

R Trinity College, Cambridge R 3.20, pp. 306–10 (written by Shirley)

T Tanner 372, British Library, folios 59ᵛ–65

Cx Caxton's edition (1477–78?), folios 1–9

Several of the most important authorities are available in photographic facsimiles (see p. 1117); Cx is transcribed by Beverly Boyd, Ch according to William Caxton, 1978, pp. 29–38. Transcriptions of all MSS appear in Ch Soc. 1st ser. 57, 59, 77.

Ff P Ph and R contain only the Complaint (lines 211–350; Ff also has 351–57). Add B and F have the Complaint (211–350) before lines 1–210. The final or "continuation" stanza 351–57 is lacking in Add B F Hl¹ Hl² P Ph R and Cx (hence attested only by D Ff Lt and T). Lines 290–98 are lacking in Add Hl² P Ph R and Cx; Add also lacks 66–126, 141–47, 193–210, 335; Lt lacks 187; P 311–end (a leaf missing); Ph 237, 302–3; and R 265–68.

There is general agreement among previous editors that the authorities comprise two main groups, α and β. Koch distinguished further subgroups mainly on the basis of omitted lines, and Robinson, dependent on the uncompleted Harvard dissertation of Joseph Butterworth, further refined the classification of subgroups. The present editor would classify the MSS as follows:

α { α¹ F B Hl¹
    α² T Ff Lt D
β { β¹ Hl² R Add (Ph)
    β² P Cx

The notes below show that the α and β manuscripts are sharply distinguished; α¹ and α² are likewise distinguishable (see, for example, notes 82, 223, 351–57), as are β¹ (usually without Ph) and β² (see, for example, notes 241, 243, 253). F and B probably had a common parent

The textual notes to *Anelida and Arcite* were prepared by Vincent J. DiMarco.

that did not serve as the immediate ancestor of Hl¹ (see, for example, notes 77, 107, 109, 165, 198, 253). Robinson also distinguished T and Ff from Lt D, for which there is evidence (see notes 218, 283, 310, 332). Among the β manuscripts, Hl² and Add can be distinguished from R (225, 259, 299). Both Koch and Robinson place Ph with P Cx, but as Koch noted, it shows contamination from α (perhaps from L) and has few unique, shared errors with P Cx (note 241).

Furnivall (Ch Soc. 1st ser. 61) transcribed *Anelida* from Hl², with lines missing from that manuscript supplied from T. Skeat (Skt) relied on F B T Lt D Hl² Cx and Thynne's edition (1532), but mainly followed F, normalizing the orthography. Koch (Kch) based his edition on the α manuscripts, with substitutions from β when he thought them necessary for sense or meter. Heath (Hth) based his edition on β, which he considered superior. Robinson (Rob) was inclined to the same opinion but chose F as his base: "Perhaps there is a slightly larger number of good readings in β. But, for orthographical reasons, MS. F has been taken as the basis of the present text, and β readings have been substituted where they appear more probable" (R.). As usual, Robinson normalized some of the spellings. E. Spehar (diss. Univ. of Colorado, 1962) printed F unemended. Fisher (Fsh) based his text on F with corrections from Cx up to 210 and from P for the Complaint. The present text is based, with Robinson, on F, though, since there are clearly correct readings present in each of the two textual traditions, an editor must proceed line by line, with due attention to Chaucer's customary practice as well as to the habits of scribes, and without reliance on the authority of any one manuscript.

Some of the particular variants in α¹ (F B Hl¹) may represent Chaucer's own text (see, for example, notes 223, 229, 236, 257, 278–79). Yet for the most part the unique readings of these manuscripts appear to be scribal attempts to "correct" and sophisticate the text. Most of the unique readings of F and other members of this group, accepted by no editor, are listed at the end of the notes.

The notes that follow take into account all editions (except the one-text prints of Furnivall and Spehar) and the manuscript groupings listed above. Robinson's normalizations of spelling are not noted except in those cases that affect meter or sense. Significant variants are noted from both the α and β traditions. The contaminated manuscript Ph is noted separately when it deviates from β¹ (Hl² R Add). The notes, however, are selective; for a full set of variants, see Koch's edition. In the notes that follow "F+" means all manuscripts of the α group; and "Hl²+" means all manuscripts of the β group, in each case excluding manuscripts that lack the lines commented upon.

Title: *Anelida and Arcite* is supplied by eds. The printed subtitle is from F; *The boke of Anelida and fals Arcite* B; *Here begynneth the Compl. of A. and f. Arc.* Hl¹; *The Complaint of Annalada & Arcite the false Theban Knyght* Lt; *Balade of Anelyda Qwene of Cartage, made by Geffrey Chaucyer* Add; *Annilida and fals Arcyte* Cx.

Invocation] The headings—*Proem* (or *Invocation*), *The*

Story after line 21, *Proem* after 210, *Strophe* after 219, *Antistrophe* after 280, *Conclusion* after 341, and *The Story continued* after 350—are editorial, developed by Skeat from Furnivall and followed by Heath, Robinson, and Fisher (who uses *Narrative* for *Story*).

2   the] *thi* F B T Lt D Add (eyeskip to the following line?).

3   temple] *temples* F B Hl¹ T Lt Fsh.

14   oure] *my* Hl² Cx. The reference is probably to the collective memory, though *oure* may be an echo of *devoured.*

Iamque domos . . .] F B Hl¹ (all add *clamor* in the margin to complete the sentence); om. rest and Kch.

29   victorie] *hie v.* Hl² Skt Hth (*hy*); *his v.* Add Kch; the added syllable is unnecessary.

31   tokenyng] *token* F+ Skt Rob Fsh. Chaucer's consistent usage with *in* is *tokenyng,* here with two syllables, as in MancT IX.302, Tr 4.779, 870. and] Om. Add. in] Om. D Hl².

53   everich other to] *yche othir for to* Hl² (the most graceful reading; perhaps a fortuitous emendation by Shirley).

59   slayn] *slayne* Lt Add; *slayn and* Cx; *slayn* [*was*] Skt; *sla*[*we*]*n* Hth.

proude] *proud* Cx Fsh. As Robinson notes, the weak ending of *proude* (with the proper name) fills out the line.

63   fare] *care* F+ Skt Rob Fsh (for *fare* in the sense of "sorrowful condition" or "plight," see Tr 5.1366, Pity 62).

68   wonnen] Hl²; *women* Cx; *dwellen* F+ Skt Kch Rob Fsh. *Wonnen* is the harder reading; *dwellen* may have been suggested by *dwellynge,* four lines below.

76   is ther] *ther is* Lt Hth; *nis ther* Kch (perhaps to avoid hiatus).

77   the] *thes(e)* F B Fsh. worlde] *world* B Hl¹ Hl² Cx; the final *-e* is doubtful, though possibly, as noted by Robinson, a dative. Read *worold* (disyllabic)?

82   hath] *both(e)* F B Hl¹ Fsh.

85   Arcite] Skt Hth Rob Fsh; om. MSS Kch. soth] *for s.* Hl¹; *the s.* Hl² Kch.

91   trusted] *trusteth* T Hl²; *trust* (the contraction) Skt Hth; *truste* Kch.

101   swor] *sworne* F Fsh; *saide* Lt.

107   moche or] *both moche and* F B; *moche and* Kch Fsh.

109   then that] *than that* Hl² Cx Skt Hth Fsh; *than* Hl¹ Lt D; *then* F B T Kch.

110   nas] *was* F+ Skt Kch Fsh.

131   to him wedded] *w. to h.* F B Hl¹ Add Skt Fsh.

143   of] *for* F+ Skt Hth Kch Fsh.

156   wex] *was* Hl² Cx Hth.

157   pleyne] *whyne* D; probably a scribal "correction" based on a phrase associated with horses; see ProWBT III.386.

163   and] *or* F+ all eds. Chaucer's customary practice is to use *and* in this phrase; cf. RvT I.4200 and Tr 1.582.

165   mighte] Om. F B.

174   Non] *Ne non* F+ Fsh.

182   never wher] *never whether* (various spellings) B T Lt D; *no(ugh)t whether* Hl² Add Cx.

183   him so] Hl² Cx; *him vp so* rest.

187   or] *and* T Lt D Hl² Add Cx Kch.

193   fee or shipe] *mete or shipe* Hl²; *mete or sype* Cx.

194   sent] *sendith* Hl¹; *sende* T Lt D. londe] *lond(e) and* T D Hl² Cx; *london* Lt. *And* may have been added by scribes uncertain of the disyllabic dative *londe.*

198   of] Om. F B.

199   dere] Hl² Cx Skt Hth; *her der(e)* rest and Kch.

209   of] *with* F+ Skt Hth Kch Fsh Rob. Chaucer's consistent usage is *of . . . owne hond,* referring to writing; see also 352 below.

The compleynt . . .] F B Hl¹ have *feyre Anelida;* P Cx have *Anelida quene of hermenye;* rest vary.

214   in] *to* F+ Hth Fsh.

216   not for] *not* F B Hl¹ T Lt D; *the not* Ff; *no wight for* Hl².

217   hir] *him* F+ R.

218   her] *his* Lt D.

223   called] *cleped* F B Hl¹ Fsh, possibly correct as the harder form.

225   And when that] *When he was* Hl² Add.

227   hath] *had(de)* F B Hl¹ Skt Hth (perhaps correctly, although the ME historical perfect is used in place of the pluperfect to give a sense of strong emotion; see Mustanoja, ME Syntax, 506). plyght] *I plyght* F; *iplyght* Hl¹ Fsh.

229   *Alas now hath he left me causeles* F B Hl¹ Fsh.

236   For to] *That I ne* F B Hl¹ Skt Hth Fsh. For *restreyne for to,* see Tr 4.872–73.

237   me] *to* T Ff Lt D Cx. For the reflexive use of *pleyne,* see ProWBT III.336 and Bo 2.pr2.26.

241   Nay] *Now* F T Ff Lt D; *Ye* Ph. certis ferther] *for certes ther* Hl² R Add; *certes for ther* P Cx; *certes for that* Ph. I] Om. P Ph Cx.

founde] *be founde* all MSS. All eds. om. *be,* which may have been scribally introduced from the previous line or may be due to the scribes' mistaking the infinitive *founde* for the past participle of the verb *finde.* The reading of P Cx, *Nay certis for ther shal never be founde,* makes sense, but perhaps for that reason would make inexplicable the scribal introduction of *I* in all MSS but P Ph Cx.

242   sores] *sorowes* R Add.

243   shapen] *shape* P Cx. so] Om. F B Hl¹ Hl² R Add.

250   And your] F B Hl¹ Ph and all eds. but Kch; *Your* rest and Kch. awayting] *awaytinges* Hl² R Add.

251   calden] F B Hl¹ (various spellings); *called* T Ff Lt D Hl² P Ph Cx; *cleped* R Add.

252   in] *of* Hl²+. etc. here] *ne h.* F Hl¹.

253   Alas] *And* Hl² R Add; *Alas and* P Cx Skt Hth Kch Fsh.

ther now nother] *ther nother* (various spellings) F B T Ff Lt D Skt Hth Kch Fsh; *ther noon other* Hl¹; *ther nowe neyther* Hl² R Add Ph; *ther now no* P Cx. The reading here accepted, with Robinson against all other editors, is that of Ph.

254   vouchen sauf] Cx; *vouch(e)safe* F B T Skt Hth Kch Fsh; *vouchesauf* Hl¹ Lt; *vouche sauf* D; *vouchensauf* (various spellings) Hl² R Add; *vouchow sauf* P; *witsauf* Ph.

257   cause] *causer* F B Hl¹ Fsh.

259   hit] *it for* Hl² Add.

264–65   *But for I was so pleyn in all my werkes moche and lyte* Hl²+ Hth. The Hl²+ reading is attractive, since it increases the rime riche effect *(lyte : delyte);* see expl. note to 211–350. Moreover, it apparently echoes 115–16. On the other hand, it suppresses a direct reference to 113–15. The reading of F+, accepted by all eds. but Heath, is printed, but either could be right.

266   was] Om. Hl² P Ph Cx.

268   on] *in* F B.

269   And of me] *Alas ye* T Ff Lt D R Kch Rob; *And als ye* Hl² P; *And also ye* Cx; *Of my wo ye* Add; *And of my sorowe* Ph.

276   And do to me] *For to do me* Hl² R Add.

278   Yet] *nowe* Ph. **come]** *turne* T Ff Lt D Ph Skt Fsh.
   yet be pleyn] *be al pleyn* F B Hl[1] Skt Fsh; *me pleyne* Add; *be thou playn* Cx.

279   than shal] *turn al* F B Hl[1].
   now is] *hath be* F B Hl[1].

283   wey] *day(e)* Lt D.

286   ben] F+ Ph; *lithe* Hl[2]; *lyen* R; *lyn* Add; *lye* P Cx.
   newe] *new* Rob (a misprint?).

289   of] *on* D Hl[2]+ Rob.

290   y-soght] *so(u)ght* all MSS Fsh. Skeat's emendation is accepted by all eds. except Fsh, who prints *dethe soght.*

299   weyve] *venyme* Hl[2] R Add.

300   deth] *dye* Hl[2]+; it is perhaps easier to account for a scribe's change of *deth* to *dye* than vice versa.
   foul] *cruel* Hl[2]+ (except for Ph, which agrees with F+) Hth.

301   gilteles] *causeles* Hl[2]+ Hth.

303   *Then wol ye laugh I knowe hit out of drede* Hl[2]+ Hth. The Hl[2]+ reading seems consistent with Arcite's reaction in 305 and may possibly be correct.

309   holde] *kepe* Hl[2] R Add Ph.

310   yow] Om. T Ff. **be]** Om. Lt D.

316   fleen] *renne* F+ all eds. Chaucer's customary usage is *fleen away;* see LGW 941, 1223, 2020.

318   seyd oght amys I preye] *oght seyd out of the wey* T Ff Lt D Hl[2] R Cx Kch; *o. spoken o. of t. w.* Ph.

319   al] *half* Hl[2]+.

331   To profren eft] *To suere yet eft* F B Hl[1] Fsh; *Eft to profre* T Ff Lt D.

and] *a* F+ Skt Hth Rob Fsh.
   assure] *asure* F B; *ensure* Hl[2] Add Ph. The noun *asure* is not elsewhere attested in ME.

332   and merci me to preye] *and love me til I dye* Hl[2] (*ye* Ph; *he* Cx). **and]** *in* T Ff.

349   so] *to* F B Hl[1] Fsh.

351–57   Om. all MSS but T Ff Lt D; text from T, with adjustments in spelling. The authenticity of the stanza has been questioned; see expl. note 353.

352   ywriten] Rob; *writen* MSS and all other eds. **hand]** Rob; *hande* MSS and all other eds. Robinson's emendation is for meter, since the *-e* of dative *hande* is not elsewhere pronounced in Chaucer.

356   sorowful] *woful* Lt.

357   shal after] *may plainly* Lt.

Readings from the α[1] group rejected by all editors:

16   with] *hath(e)* F+.   **24**   With] *The* F B Hl[1] T.   **41**   the] Om. F+.   **58**   Parthonope] *Prothonolope* F B Hl[1]; *Pertynolope* Lt.   **86**   therwithal] *therto with al* F B Hl[1] T.   **112**   her] *here hert (an)* F+.   **119**   heste] *hert* F+.   **125**   nas] *was* F+.   **127**   so] *as* F B Hl[1].   **132**   So] *For so* F+.   **137**   alwey] *ay* F B Hl[1].   **156**   covere] *coveren* F B Lt.   **165**   mighte] Om. F B.   **178**   forth] *for* F B Hl[1] T.   **187**   liste] *lust* F B Hl[1] D.   **198**   of] Om. F B.   **203**   he[2]] *they* F+.   **210**   hit] Om. F.   **215**   in] *into* F B Hl[1] Ph.   **216**   for to] *to* F+ Cx.   **228**   evermore] *every more* F.   **234**   him] *me* F B.   **240**   myn] *my* B Ff P Ph Cx.   **304**   that] Om. F B Hl[1].   **315**   is[2]] *this* F Hl[1].

The Parliament of Fowls

Authorities: fourteen manuscripts and Caxton's early print:

B   Bodley 638, Bodleian, folios 96–109^v

D   Digby 181, Bodleian, folios 44–52

F   Fairfax 16, Bodleian, folios 120–129^v

Ff   Cambridge University Library Ff 1.6, folios 29–41

Gg   Cambridge University Library Gg 4.27, folios 480^v–490^v

H   Harley 7333, British Library, folios 129^v–132

Hh   Cambridge University Library Hh 4.12, folios 94–99^v

J   St. John's College, Oxford, LVII, folios 226–237^v

L   Laud 416, Bodleian, folios 288–289^v

Lt   Longleat 258, in the possession of the Marquess of Bath, Longleat House, Warminster, Wilts., folios 85–101

P   Pepys 2006, Magdalene College, Cambridge, folios 127–142

R   Trinity College, Cambridge R 3.19, folios 17–24^v

S   Arch. Selden B.24, Bodleian, folios 142–152

T   Tanner 346, Bodleian, folios 120–131

Cx   Caxton's edition, 1477–78, folios 1–16^v

Two of the manuscripts are fragmentary: Hh has only lines 1–365, L only 1–142. Most lack the roundel (see 680–92 below). In addition, a number of lines are missing from some of the manuscripts: B 1–22, 157–200; Ff 180; H 296–302, 680–end; P 192, 643, 688–end; S 1–14, 601–end. Several of the most important of these authorities are available in photographic facsimiles (see p. 1117); transcriptions of all appear in the Ch Soc. 1st ser. 21, 22, 23, 24, 60. Cx is transcribed in Beverly Boyd, Ch according to William Caxton, 1978, 1–19.

The manuscripts and early print by Caxton were classified by Eleanor P. Hammond (Univ. of Chicago Decennial Publs., 1st ser. 7, 1902, 3–25) as follows:

Group A:	α	Gg Ff
	β	H R S Hh Cx
	γ	P J L
Group B:	δ	F B
	ε	T Lt D

Koch (Ch: Kleinere Dichtungen, 1928, 24) divided Group A into a different set of subgroups: Gg; Ff (for which Koch assumes a double source); P Hh Cx S; H R; J L. Koch made considerable allowance for contamination among these groups.

Root (JEGP 5, 1903, 189–95) suggested, without adequate proof, that Group B represents Chaucer's earlier version. Although Skeat used F as the basis of his edition, most editors have regarded Group A as the superior group. However, Group A appears almost certainly to be imaginary, for the ten authorities so classified agree in what appear to be correct readings rather than in readings that are clearly wrong. Gg and Ff, in their preferable readings as well as their unique, shared errors, may constitute an independent line of descent from the original, though Gg often stands alone against all other manuscripts. P J and L clearly constitute a subgroup and often agree in unique, shared errors with Hammond's β subgroup (see, for example, 65 and 80 below), although Hh Cx and S often exhibit unstable textual relations. The traditional subgroupings of F B and of T Lt D, comprising Hammond's group B, are borne out. As with the readings unique to H R S Hh Cx P J L (for example, 18, 64, 65, 80, 148, 206), those readings unique to F B T Lt D (for example, 50, 71, 80, 221, 666) are seldom, if ever, correct.

Robinson followed the practice of most recent editors and based his text on Gg, though the relation is less direct than this implies, since he regularized the many bizarre spellings in Gg (and these are not listed in the textual notes). Moreover, though Gg often is alone in offering the right reading, it is even more frequently alone in error, and Robinson viewed its unique readings with skepticism. In this edition such readings have been even less often accepted unless supported by other manuscripts.

The textual notes do not take account of all the unique readings in Gg (most are listed at the end) nor in the other manuscripts; they attempt rather to show the manuscript evidence for the readings selected and to record the decisions of other editors in such cases. Along with the collected editions ordinarily cited in these textual notes—Skeat (Skt); the Globe editor, Heath (Hth), Koch (Kch); Robinson (Rob); Baugh (Bgh); Donaldson (Don); and Fisher (Fsh)—reference is made to the editions of Lounsbury (Lns), Parl. of Foules, 1883, Drennan (Drn), Ch's Parl. of Foules, 1911, and the valuable edition of D. S. Brewer (Brw), Parl. of Foulys, 1960, rev. ed. 1972. References to Brewer are to the second edition, unless otherwise noted. Since the textual problems are so complicated and editors have differed so greatly in their solutions, rather full textual notes are provided. Yet they are selective; for fuller listings of variants, see the editions of Koch and Brewer. Variants are listed in the order in which they appear in Hammond's groupings (Gg first, D last).

Title: That printed is from Gg; *The parlement of Foules* H P B Lt D; *The P. of Bridges* F T *(Byrdes); Here followeth the p. of Byrdes reduced to loue, etc.* R; *Of the assemble of þe byrdis on Seint Volantins day* L; see also note on the *explicit* below. Chaucer refers to the poem as *the Parlement of Foules* (LGW F 419) and *the book of Seint Valentynes day of the Parlement of Briddes* (Ret X.1086).

2   **so hard so sharp]** *so s. so h.* Gg Ff J L Lns Brw.

3   **slit]** *flit* H R Hh Cx T Lt D Lns.

7   **wher that]** *wher* Ff T; *whether* H R Hh P J L Lt; *whethir that* Cx. **flete or synke]** *wake or wynke* F T Lt Skt.

12   **There]** *That* Gg Don.

14   **can]** *sey* Gg Ff P J L Hth Kch Don Brw; *sey from seyn* in 13?

15   **lust]** *luste* F Skt Brw; *love* S. **and]** Om. Ff H R S Hh P J F T Lt D Skt Drn Brw.

18   **for to]** *to* H R S Hh Cx P J.

The textual notes to *The Parliament of Fowls* were prepared by Vincent J. DiMarco.

22   as men seyth] *as men sey(e)(n)* Gg Hh Ff Lns Drn Brw (the indefinite pronoun is not recognized); *quhere sowen sede is* S. Gg and Ff alter *feyth* to *fey* in 24 for rhyme.

26   as] Gg Hh J L; om. all other MSS.

27   hit gan me so delite] *so g. me to d.* Gg Lns Kch Don Brw; *I g. me so d.* Hh Cx J.

29   make] Ff P; *make of* all other MSS Don Fsh.

30   ther] *thus* Gg S Cx and all eds.; *here* L. Scribes could easily read an abbreviated *ther* (*th* plus the abbreviation for *-er,* which resembles an elongated apostrophe) as *thus,* a meaningless filler. *Ther,* like *therupon* in 20, refers to the actual book.

33   therinne] *ther(e)in(n)* all MSS Lns Fsh; eds. emend for meter.

34   it] Gg S Hh L; *of* J; om. all other MSS.

39   it] *he* all MSS Lns Hth Drn Don Brw Fsh; the reference is to *this bok* (29); *his* (35) is gen. neut. sing. **al]** *of* Gg Ff J L Lns Kch Don Brw.

40   the] *that* Gg Ff H L Don Brw.

46   seyde hym] *seyde* Gg Ff S Lns Kch Don Bgh Brw.

50   folk] *the folk(e)* F B T Lt D. **here]** *now* Gg Don.

53   that] Gg Ff all eds.; *how* H R Hh Cx P L D; *how that here* S; om. R J F B T Lt.

54   Nis] Gg Cx; *Ment* Hh P L; *Was* S; *In* J; *Meneth* all other MSS Brw. The source argues for *nis* (Cicero, Somnium Scipionis 6.14: "Vestra vero, quae dicitur, vita mors est").

64   bad] *seyd* (various spellings) H R S Hh Cx P J L.

65   disseuable and ful] *was sumdel disseyuable and ful* Gg (a hexameter); *was sumdel full* F B T Lt D; *wasse sumdell* Ff; *ful of turment and* H R S Hh Cx P J L Lns Skt Hth Drn Rob Bgh Fsh; *sumdel fals and ful* Kch. Brewer (p. 61) suggests that Chaucer originally wrote *And was sumdel ful of harde grace,* then later crossed out the feeble *was sumdel* and added *disseyuable* in the margin; Gg's exemplar picked up the substitution but not the cancellation, while other scribes ignored it and did the best they could. The emendation printed was suggested by Robinson in his textual note and adopted by Donaldson and Brewer.

71   to] Om. F B T D.

76   to²] Gg J and all eds.; *unto (into)* all other MSS. **that]** *this* Gg Lns Don.

77   of soules] *soules* Gg Hh J F B T Lt D.

80   whirle aboute th'erthe alwey] *alwey whirle aboute th(e) erthe* F B Lt D. **whirle]** Om. T. **th'erthe]** *ther(e)* Gg Ff; *the worlde* H R S Hh Cx J L (*wordel* P). The line as printed is found in no MS. *Worlde* is almost certainly an anticipation of the following line; the reading of Gg Ff, *ther(e),* probably derives from *th'erthe,* attested in F B T Lt D.

82   al hir] *is his* Gg; *is here* Lns Don.

83   that] *this* Gg Lns Kch Rob Don Brw; *a* Ff; *the* R.

84   the sende his] H Cx L; *synde us* Gg; *send vs* Ff; *sende the hys* J; *sende the* P; *vs sende his* R; *sende vs alle* S; *ye grant his* Hh; *sende ech lover* F B T Lt D.

85   faylen] *folwen* Gg Don.

91   ne hadde] *nadde* Rob (*ne hadde* is pronounced as one syllable). **that¹]** Om. Gg Ff F B T Lt D; *the* R S Cx.

96   selve] *same* Gg R Lns Hth Kch Don Brw; *ilk* S.

102   cart is] Gg Ff P J; *cartes* all other MSS and eds. Either variant could have produced the other. The parallelism with 101 argues for the plural, the source ("aurigae somnia currus") for the singular, though *currus* could be construed as plural after the verb understood. See expl. note 99–105.

114   the] *thow* Gg Ff H R Hh P J L Lt D Lns (the dative is necessary with the impersonal *lest*).

117   north-north-west] *north nor west* Gg Drn Brw; *north weste* Ff; *northewest* R. Added support for the majority reading is Gg's variant, taken to mean north-nor-west (for *nor* see MED s.v. *north* adj.) rather than "[neither] north nor west," as it is often understood (e.g., Bennett, PF, 60). Venus, however, never appears this far north (see Expl. Notes).

119   and endyte] Lt; *and ek tendite* Gg Lns Kch Rob Bgh Don Brw Fsh; *ek and endyte* Ff; *and to e.* P F B T; *(h)it and e.* H R Cx J L D Lns Skt Hth Drn; *it and to write* S. Apparently Chaucer left the line as printed, with a caesural pause after *ryme;* except in Lt, the scribes used *it, ek,* or *to* to fix the meter.

122   with] *of* Gg Fsh.

126   shal yow seyn] *shal now sey(n)* Gg T Lt D all eds. but Skt Drn; *shal yow telle* Hh Cx; *wyll yow sey* R; *now shal tell* Ff; *shal sey* P. *Now* is more likely a misreading of *you* than the opposite.

137   Ther nevere tre shal fruyt ne] *That n. yit s. f. ne* Gg; *Quhare n. t. s. f. ne* S; *ther t. s. neuyr f. ne* F B T Lt D Skt Drn.

143   For with] *Forwhi* Gg Don.

144   gan myn herte bolde] Gg all eds.; *g. m. h. to b.* Ff J F B T Lt D; *began m. h. b.* all other MSS.

148   Right as] *For right* H R S Hh Cx P J D.

152   bet] *best* Gg Hth.

155   stondeth] *stant* Gg H R P Don Brw.

158   nys] Gg; *is* all other MSS Skt Drn Brw.

165   Yet] *It* Gg T Lt D Lns Hth Rob Don Bgh Fsh.

at] *at the* F T Lt D Skt Drn Rob; *atte* J Bgh Fsh.

166   demen] Gg; *deme* S; *to deme* J; *demeth* all other MSS Skt Drn Rob Bgh.

167   And] *And there* Gg Lns.

169   in his he tok] *he t. in h.* Gg Ff Lns Kch Don Brw Fsh; *he hent in h.* S.

170   wente in] *that as* Gg Don.

183   blosmy] *blospemy* Gg; *bloussumede* Ff; *blossom(e)* R Cx; *blossumy* Hh; *blossomed* F T Lt D. See MerT IV.1463, Tr 2.821.

185   swetnesse] *ther s.* Gg Hth Kch; *that s.* S Hh P J Lns Skt; *the s.* Don.

186   blewe] *b. &* Gg Lns Don.

187   nothyng] *and n.* H R S P J; *quik and* S. The line is regular without the added syllable.

195   the³] *and* Gg Lns; om. F.

203   foules] *bryddis* Gg Lns Kch Drn.

205   was grevaunce] *w. ther g.* H R S J Rob Bgh Fsh; *w. g. therof* F B T Lt; *w. g. ther* D; *w. the g.* Hh; *ther w. g.* P.

206   wex] Gg L; *waxed* Ff; *was* H R S Hh Cx P J; *growen* F B T Lt D.

207   there waxe] *w. t.* Gg Brw; *t. may w.* Ff Lns.

210   mannes] *manys* Gg H D Lns Brw; *manes* Kch Bgh Rob; *man is* T Lt; *mannys* Ff R S Hh Cx P J F B.

214   Wille] *Wel* Gg Lns Skt; *Wele* Kch.

215   hire wile] *hard(e) file* F B T Lt D; *hir vyle* R; *hire file* Kch Rob. *File* was perhaps suggested by 212.

216   couchede] *touched(e)* Cx Kch Rob Brw; *touchyd* R B; *ordanyt* S. The variation results from the confusion of *c* and *t.* S's reading is an attempt to explain *couchede.*

after] *after as* S P F B T Lt D Lns Skt Hth Drn Bgh Fsh; *after that* R.

221 don by force] *don be fore* Gg Ff; *go(o) bifore* F B T Lt D.

223 hymself] *hemself* Gg Lns Kch Don Brw Fsh; *themself* Ff.

227 Flaterye] *And f.* Gg Hh Hth Lns Kch Don Fsh.

232 the] *that* Gg Lns Rob Don Bgh Fsh. daunsedyn] Gg; *daunsed* all other MSS Brw (1st ed.). Brewer, in his second ed. (109–10), defends the unique Gg reading.

241 by hire syde] *hir beside* F B T Lt D Skt Hth.

252 Cam] Gg; *cometh* Ff H R; *com(e)(n)* all other MSS.

256 hys sceptre in honde] *s. in his h.* Gg Fsh; *a ceptre in his h.* Ff.

259 freshe floures newe] *flourrys frosche & newe* Gg Lns Kch Don.

269 unto] *vp to* Gg Ff Don Brw; *to* Hh J D.

271 was wel kevered] *wasse couerede well* Ff; *was couerit wele* S; *coverd well* Hh; *wel covered* (various spellings) H Cx J F B T Lt D Skt Drn.

273 was] *nas* Gg all eds. but Skt Brw.

285 Ful] Gg Ff Cx Brw; *Of* rest and all other eds. (*Of* may be introduced in anticipation of the same word later in the line.)

295 into] *unto* Gg H Hh Lns Hth Kch Don Fsh.

298 that ther] Gg; om. Ff R; *ther* S Cx J F B T Lt D; *that* Hh. Possibly the unique Gg reading, adopted by all eds., "corrected" a headless line.

299 somer] *someris* Gg Ff Lns Kch Don Fsh.

303 Nature] *of Nature* S J F B T Brw Fsh.

305 cast] Gg Ff; *tast* Cx; *craft* all other MSS Hth Skt Drn.

307 they] *ther(e)* H S Cx P J F B T Lt D Kch.

310 foul] *bryd* Gg Ff Hh Cx Lns Skt Hth Drn Don Brw.

313 eyr and tre] Gg; *and tre* om. Ff; *see and tree* H P F B T Lt D; *see tree* R S Hh; *tree and see* Cx.

317 of] *in* Gg S Lns Kch Drn Don. aray] Gg Ff; *such aray* all other MSS (*such* may have come from the next line).

325 hem] Gg Cx; *them* Ff; om. J; *that* all other MSS.

327 And] Gg Ff Cx; *But* all other MSS.

342 his] *hire* Gg Ff S Lns.

344 the²] Om. Gg Ff Kch Don.

348 stare] *starlyng* Gg Lns Don; *sterlyng* S.

352 grene] Gg Ff Cx; *fresshe* all other MSS.

356 fetheres] *clothes* Gg Drn.

358 ever] *most* Gg Kch.

361 the²] Gg H R P J; om. all other MSS.

363 raven wys the crowe with] Gg; *ravon the crowe* Ff; *ravenes (and) (the) crow(e)s* all other MSS.

368 goddesse] Gg Ff; *g. of* all other MSS Rob Bgh Brw Fsh.

369 ech] *everich* Gg all eds.; *every* Ff J; *sche* S; the Gg ancestor "corrected" the Lydgatian line.

379 the¹] Om. Gg Kch Don. of] *o* Gg Brw.

381 by] *with* Gg Ff Lns Hth Kch Don Brw Fsh.

385 yow] Gg Ff Lt Cx; *me* all other MSS Skt Hth Drn Rob Bgh. Nature is speaking for the birds' benefit.

389 Youre] Gg Ff; *With y.* all other MSS.

391 lete] *breke* Gg Lns Kch Drn Don; *suffre* Ff.

393 tersel] *terslet* Gg Lns Don. wel] *ful w.* Gg Lns Don Fsh.

394 above yow in] *abovyn every* Gg Don.

396 Which] Gg Ff; *The* H; *The which* all other MSS; all MSS but Gg Ff omit *wel* later in this line.

400 ye] *they* Gg Ff.

406 the²] *yow* Gg S P J Kch Brw.

410 Whoso] *What so* Gg S Lns Fsh.

414 humble] *ful h.* H R S Cx F B T D Skt Rob Bgh Fsh.

424 may I] *I m.* Gg S Cx J Hth Kch Don Brw.

426 Havynge] *And h.* Gg Cx Lns Hth Kch Don Fsh. reward only] *o. r.* Gg D Lns Kch.

427 on] *of* Gg S Cx Lns Hth Kch Don Fsh.

428 I be founde to hyre] *that I to h. be f.* Gg all eds. (perhaps correct, but more likely Gg's attempt to "correct" a headless line; see Brewer, p. 121); *it be f. to h.* Lt.

432 I be al] *be I al* Gg Hth Don Fsh.

435 non loveth hire] *h. l. n.* Gg Lns Kch Don Fsh.

436 Al be she] *Al be it that he* Gg; *Although she* B T Lt D; *Al be that she* Cx P Don.

439 Ne] Gg Cx J; *Yit* S Kch; *And* Ff; *For* all other MSS (*for* perhaps from 438).

448 yow¹] *the* Gg J Lns Brw Fsh; *not* T.

455 allone] *ful longe* Gg Kch Rob Don Fsh; *al hole* S. *Ful longe* (i.e., long since) makes sense here, but Gg probably miscopied (influenced by *long* in the line above).

457 janglere] *or j.* Gg Don.

460 that] Gg; om. all other MSS.

461 in] Gg Ff H T Kch Brw; *to* rest Skt Hth Drn Rob Don Fsh.

462 she] *the* Gg Brw; *ye* H R Lns Don; *els* D.

473 wynter] *yeer* Gg Lns Drn Don. and] *and as* Gg Ff P J Lns Kch Drn Don Brw.

480 ese] Gg Ff S; *plese* all other MSS.

482 whether] *wer* Gg; *wher* Kch.

490 went] *drow* Gg all eds. but Brw. Given Gg's frequent unique errors, *drow* must be suspect despite its attractiveness.

493 toshyvered] *toslyvered* Gg Lns Kch Don.

494 criede] *criedyn* Gg; *criden* Don; *crieden* Fsh.

497 any] *othir* Gg S Lns Kch Don.

498 cokkow and the doke] Gg all eds.; *d. and the c.* all other MSS. As Brewer notes (p. 122) "Gg's word order corresponds to the cries in the next line, and gives the smoother metre, but may be suspect for these very reasons."

503 I] Gg S Cx; om. all other MSS.

505 seyde] *quod* Gg Hth Kch Don Fsh.

506 For] *And* Gg Lns Hth Don.

507 spede] *profit(e)* Gg J Drn. on the charge now] *no c. howe* Gg; *the c. now* R Skt Drn; *upon me the c. nowe* Ff; *on me this c. now* J; *on me the c. now* H S Cx P F B Lt D Lns Don Brw. The reading here adopted (Kch Rob Bgh Fsh) appears in no MS; *me* could easily have been added by scribes after the preposition.

520 behynde] Om. Gg; *blynde* H R Lns; *by kynde* Cx.

526 were] *was* Gg H R S P Don.

527 foules] Gg Lt; *the f.* all other MSS.

530 and as] *as* Gg R D Lns Hth Don Fsh. termyne] Ff Cx S; *to t.* all other MSS Lns Hth Don Fsh.

533 thanne] Om. Gg S Lt; *that* Ff J P.

537 non by skilles may be] Gg; *skilles noon* Lt; *by s. may n. be* all other MSS.

543 ne] Gg; om. all other MSS.

551 sittyngest] Gg; *best sittyng* S; *sittyng(e)* all other MSS.

553 it] *here* (corrected from *hre*) Gg; *hire* Don.

555 a short] *short* Ff S Cx P J F B T D Skt Drn.

560 God] Gg H R J; *to G.* all other MSS.

561 And] *As* Gg Don.

564 forth] Om. Gg Lns Skt Hth Kch Drn Don Brw; Gg has the more regular line if *herkeneth* is disyllabic.
571 yit] *now* Gg Don.
573 wit] *mygh* Gg; *might* Kch Don.
578 preyeden] *preyede* Gg; *pray(e)d* Ff H R Lt; *preyd(e)* P J; *preying* S; *prai(e)d* Cx Lt; *prayden* F B T D.
581 shewe] *it s.* Gg Don.
585 ever til] *til that* Gg Lns Kch Don.
593 **Who shulde recche of that**] *What s. I r. of hym that* Gg Kch Don Fsh; *who s. r. of hym that* S J Don Brw; *who s. r.* P.
594 **Ye queke**] Ff H Cx L F B T Lt; *Ye keke* J; *Kek kek* Gg Lns; *Ee kekyll* R; *ʒa (Ye) queke queke* S D; *Yet quek* P.
   yet] Gg Ff H S; om. all other MSS.
   seyde] *seith* Gg; *quoth (quod)* P F B; om. T.
   goos] *doke* (various spellings) Gg (over an erasure) Ff (over an erasure) Cx F B T Lt D; *goose* R P; *goss* S; *good* J (*d* corrected to *s*). Eds. have *Ye quek yit seyde the doke* Rob Drn (*quod*) Don Bgh Fsh; *Ye kek y. quod the d.* Skt; *Quek quek y. s. the d.* Kch; *Ye kek y. s. the gos.* The problems arose from confusion over whether *queke* is an interjection (by the duck) or a verb.
600 ful] *but* Gg Lns Hth Kch Don Fsh (perhaps correctly); om. Cx.
602 nouther] *nat* Gg Lns Skt Hth Drn Kch Rob Don Bgh Fsh; *not* Cx. Brewer notes (pp. 56–57; see also 125 and 97) that *nouther* is contracted to *nor* in pronunciation and that the scribe of Gg, not realizing this, substituted *nat*.
604 blyve] *blithe* Gg Hth.
613 reufullest] *reufulles* Gg Lns; *rowthful* P; *rewfull* all other MSS Fsh; *reufelle* Kch; *reweful* Don; *rewthelees* Skt Hth Drn Rob Bgh. The emendation adopted is Brewer's, who notes Gg's habit of omitting the final *-t* in consonant clusters.
616 whil] *w. that* Gg Lns Kch Don.
619 nevere] *not* Gg Kch.
621 hir] *the* Gg Cx Lns Skt Hth Kch Drn Don Bgh Fsh.
624 sith] *syn* Gg Lns Hth Kch Don Fsh.
626 hire this favour] Gg; *to h. this f.* H R; *this f. to h.* all other MSS.
629 Thus] Gg J; *This* all other MSS Skt.
632 thanne] *certes thanne* Gg all eds. but Brw. A headless line that Gg emends.
637 hit] Om. Gg Cx Skt Hth Drn Kch Bgh Brw Fsh; *it to you* H.
638 hire] *tho* Gg Lns Kch Rob Don Bgh Fsh; om. P.
641 everich other] *a nothir lyvis* Gg; *another lyves* Don.
642 whil] *while that* Gg Ff Lns Kch Don Fsh.
644 I wol yow sey right] *that wele I seyn wol* Gg; *you wel I s. r.* Ff P T Kch Brw Fsh; *I shall you seyn* B; *you wol I seyn wel* Don.
647 don] *gon* Gg Lns Hth Kch Rob Bgh Fsh; *goon* Don.
655 Quod] *Quod tho* Gg H all eds. Gg "corrects" a headless line.
661 is] *ne is* Gg Kch.
665 for] Gg Cx J; *fro(m)* all other MSS.
666 al brought was] *al wro(u)ght was* F B T Lt D.
670 in] *in his* Gg Ff H Lt Lns Hth Kch Drn Don Fsh.

672 goddesse] *queen* Gg Lns Kch Drn Don Fsh.
674 hir] *the* Gg Kch Don.
676 Nature] *to N.* Gg all eds. but Brw.
677 imaked was] *i. were* Gg; *made was* Ff Cx D; *makid was* (various spellings) H F B T Brw.
678 heer] Om. Gg Lns Kch Brw.
680–92 Complete only in Gg (in a later hand); D has all but 687 with the roundel turned into a stanza; J has only 683–84, 687–89; Ff T leave no gap; H leaves a gap (unfilled); F B R Cx have *qui bien ayme (a) tarde oublie* (no gap). Lines 685–86, 690–92 were conjecturally printed by Furnivall and followed by all editors except Donaldson, who repeats 680–82 after 684 and then, like Furnivall, 680–82 after the third stanza of the roundel. Thynne's edition (1532) has both the French line and 680–92. See expl. notes 675 and 677.
680 thy] Om. Gg.
681, 686, 691 thes] Gg; *this(e)* D all eds. but Brw.
682 longe] *large* Gg Don.
689 **Ful blissful mowe they synge when they wake**] *f. b. m. t. ben w. t. w.* Gg Drn (*awake*); *f. blissfully t. s. and endles ioy thei make* D.
697 I] *In* Gg Lns Hth Drn Don Fsh.
699 nyl] Ff T; *nele* Gg Brw Fsh; *wyl* all other MSS.
   Explicit . . .] So Gg; *Explicit tractatus de congregacione Volucrum dei sancti Valentini* F; *Explicit Parliamentum auium Quod W. Calverley* Ff; *Here endis the parliament of foulis Quod Galfride Chaucere* S; *Here endith the Parlement of foules* Lt D. *Explicit the temple of bras* Cx.

Gg readings rejected by all editors (unique to Gg unless otherwise noted):

7 flete] *slete.* **22** out] *ofte.* **31** Scipioun] *sothion.* **40** betwix] *betwixsyn.* **53** worldes] *wordis.* **57** litel] Om. **69** was first] *f. w.* **82** than foryeven al hir] *that f. is his.* **88** bed] *self* (also Ff). **90** which that] *that* (also Ff S P). **125** half] *syde* (also P). **132** of-caste] *ouercaste.* **138** the] Om. **140** Th'eschewing] *Th(er) shewynge* (*er* inserted). **175** joye] *sothe.* **204** Th'air] *The erthe.* **276** Ceres] *sereis.* **305** mesure] *mesuris.* **324** the] Om. (also S). **326** of which] Om.; no] *myn.* **345** chough] *crowe* (also Ff J). **354** of hewe] *& newe* (also Ff D). **400** ye] *they* (also Ff). **401** yow] *ye.* **404** sorest] *soryest.* **434** untrewe] *vntrere.* **438** knette] *arette.* **444** the] *hire* (also P). **450** and] Om. **471** But as] *That;* me] *to m.* **482** whether] *were.* **494** shende] *shynde.* **495** have] *havyn.* **506** For] *And.* **516** synge] *fynde.* **518** uncommytted] *onquit.* **520** behynde] Om. **524** of] *on.* **540** these] *this.* **558** gent] *so gent.* **560** hire] *hym.* **562** hire] *hys.* **563** She] *He.* **569** she] *he.* **573** wit] *mygh.* **577** turtle] *tersel.* **581** shewe] *it shewe.* **583** turtle] *tersel.* **596** fy] *sey* (also R). **611** the] *thanne a.* **614** wormes] *werm.* **623** as] *a.* **627** right] Om. **645** right] *that.* **658** hem] *hym.* **662** peyne him] *peignynge.* **663** quyt] *what.* **664** Fro] *For* (also P T D). **682** longe] *large.* **694** That] *That the.*

Boece

Authorities: nine extensive manuscripts, one brief manuscript fragment, a manuscript paraphrase of Bk. 1, and the early prints of Caxton and Thynne, classified, as the result of our full collation, as follows:

α	γ	A²	Additional 16165, British Library
		C¹	Cambridge Univ. Lib. Ii.i.38
	ε	B	Bodley 797, Bodleian Library
		H	Harley 2421, British Library
	θ	P	Pembroke College, Cambridge, MS. 215 (only fragments after 4.pr5)
		Cx	Caxton's edition, c. 1478
		Th	Thynne's edition, 1532
β	δ	C²	Cambridge Univ. Lib. Ii.iii.21
		Hn	Peniarth 393D (Hengwrt 328), National Library of Wales (breaks off in 3.pr10)
	η	Mo	Frag. MS. 150, Univ. of Missouri (brief portions of 2.m7 and 2.pr8)
	ι	A¹	Additional 10340, British Library
		Sal	Sarum 113, Salisbury Cathedral
		Auct	Auctarium F.3.5 (VII), Bodleian Library (a paraphrase of 1 only)

The work has been previously edited, always with C¹ or C² as base, in the various complete works of the poet: Skeat's Oxford Ch, the Globe Ch, earlier editions of Robinson, and Fisher. Of the editions, only that in the Globe, prepared by Mark H. Liddell, appears to have been based on collation of all manuscripts known to the editor. Two of the manuscripts have been printed in full: C² by F. J. Furnivall, Ch Soc. 1st ser. 75 (1886); and A¹ by Richard Morris, EETS e.s. 5 (1868; rep. as Ch Soc. 1st ser. 76, 1886). On the basis of these printed texts, L. Kellner provided a full collation of Cx (ESt 14, 1890, 1–53); more recently Cx has been printed in Beverly Boyd, Ch According to Caxton, 1978. Th has twice appeared in photographic facsimile: with an introduction by Walter W. Skeat (?1904), and with an introduction by D. S. Brewer (1969). Sal was identified as a copy and its version of 1.m1 printed by R. P. Wülcker (Anglia 2, 1879, 372–73). George B. Pace and Linda E. Voigts provided a full description and text of Mo in SAC 1, 1979, 143–50. Liddell (Academy 49, 1896, 199–200) successfully demonstrated that Auct is a paraphrase of Chaucer, not a separate translation (as Skeat claimed), that it was prepared to provide text for a commentary, and that it is associated with ι. Phillipps 9472, mentioned by Skeat as containing "a translation" (Oxford Ch 2:xliv) and assumed by Robinson (p. 903) to be Chaucer's version, is in fact a copy of Walton's verse translation; the manuscript is now Cambridge Univ. Lib. Additional MS 3573.

The textual notes to *Boece* were prepared by Ralph Hanna III and Traugott Lawler.

In our analysis, the textual situation resembles that of many Middle English prose translations. There has been a substantial loss of harder authorial readings between O, Chaucer's autograph, and O', the ancestor of all surviving manuscripts. Within the visible English textual tradition, variation has proved considerably less drastic: α and β, the archetypes of the surviving manuscripts, differed only occasionally. But at later stages in the tradition two distinctive, and usually corrupt, traditions emerged. The ι group has very frequent and highly distinctive variation: A¹ and Sal agree in unique errors nearly as often as all other manuscripts combined. This tradition (although Mo shows an early transitional form) seems to have fully developed about 1450, perhaps in the northeast Midlands. (Both Sal and Auct show traces of such a dialect.) In contrast, the tradition we identify as θ seems originally to have resembled H fairly closely; however, θ itself was sporadically conflated with a text most closely resembling Hn. A number of these readings were carried over into Cx and Th; but P's additional errors and agreements with Hn avoided by Cx and Th indicate either that Cx had access to a better θ manuscript or that P represents a less adequate derivative of θ than does Cx. Although Th used Cx for copy, a number of readings indicate consultation of an independent manuscript version, a text most closely resembling A² and B; see James E. Blodgett, Library 6th ser. 1, 1979, 97–113, and his paper on Th's text read at the 1979 meeting of the Midwest Modern Language Association.

In this edition we follow C¹ as copy-text. We chose this manuscript because it is complete, tolerably consistent in its spellings, and one of three manuscripts most faithful to O'. Of these three, Hn is incomplete and C² often idiosyncratic in its forms. Although, as Robinson noted (p. 904), the orthography of C¹ differs considerably from that of such early manuscripts of the *Tales* as Hg, we have retained its spellings and indeed have put all emendations into C¹ forms. Editors who have followed C² have, we believe, been somewhat misled by externals: that C² forms a Boethius anthology, provided with Latin text and a variety of commentaries, has led to some overestimation of the quality of the English text. Indeed, C² varies from O' slightly more frequently than does C¹; moreover, erroneous readings of C² are frequently substantial, in contrast to the quite incidental errors typical of C¹.

In the notes that follow we use a number of symbols to identify Chaucer's source texts—L for the Latin text of C², F for Dedeck-Héry's French, T for Trivet. We use the sigil Z to represent Chaucer's Latin manuscript, where that differs from L, and the sigil Y to represent Chaucer's French manuscript, where that differs from F. Where a reading of Y occurs in an extant manuscript, we identify that text in parentheses, using Dedeck-Héry's sigla. Thus Y (B) *sont* means "we suppose that Chaucer's French source read *sont*, as the manuscript B in fact does." The sigla Z and Y refer not simply to the actual reading of Chaucer's hypothetical manuscripts but also to Chaucer's perception of the form of his source—which may have been erroneous. (The abbreviations are summarized below.)

The symbol O' means "the latest common ancestor of

all surviving witnesses." But since the ordinary basis for positing the reading of O′ is agreement of all witnesses, we also use unqualified O′, in lieu of inventing some further symbol, to mean "all witnesses." Thus "om. O′′′" means "all witnesses omit, and we posit therefore that O′ omitted." In a few cases, however, we cite one witness in addition to O′; in such cases the cited manuscript stands as a factual exception to "all witnesses" but is not regarded as evidence against the posited reading of O′. Thus "of O′ (off B)" would mean "all witnesses but B read of, and we posit O′ of despite B off."

The notes that follow annotate our handling of the text. We give information on all readings we take to be cruces, places where the English manuscripts show various readings difficult of resolution and places where we have suggested (but not printed) emendations that would bring Chaucer's text into nearer accord with L and F. In addition, on the basis of our study of the traditional Latin, L, F, T, and Guillaume de Conches, we have printed a number of conjectural emendations. In all such places, which are bracketed in the text and marked with an asterisk in the notes, we believe the reading of Chaucer's holograph (O) has been lost in the archetype of all surviving English manuscripts (O′). Our consultation of Chaucer's sources has led us to conclude that Chaucer regularly consulted both Latin and French, that he translated very literally (though often preferring the syntax and wording of French), and that it is inherently unlikely that Z and Y agreed in the same corruption. Thus, agreement between L and F in the absence of a relevant French variant is of great value in positing what Chaucer probably wrote. Moreover, we find many readings that are far more simply explained as English scribal errors than as mistranslations or Chaucer's translation of errors in Z or Y (for example, 3.pr3.63 or 3.pr11.9–10).

Although for the sake of economy we usually merely cite L F as our basis for making or suggesting emendations, we have in fact satisfied ourselves in each case that the O reading we posit is likely to have produced O′ by some common sort of scribal error—most often eyeskip or *lectio facilior*. Furthermore, we cite only relevant sources; when F is cited without L, or T without L F, the sources not mentioned are to be understood as not contradictory but irrelevant.

In addition, we give selective examples of the different textual choices made by our predecessors, especially Robinson; since most past editors have simply printed C¹ or C², our silence often indicates that they reproduce the majority reading of the English manuscripts. Finally, at the end of the notes for each book we group all readings not elsewhere mentioned where we have departed from the text of C¹.

Summary of special abbreviations:

F Jean de Meun's French translation as edited by Dedeck-Héry

L The "vulgate" text of Boethius in MS C²

Lid Mark Liddell's edition in the Globe Ch

T Nicholas Trivet's commentary on Boethius

trad The reading of the oldest tradition of MSS of Boethius's Latin text, as represented by the edition of Ludwig Bieler, 1957

Y The MS Chaucer used of Jean de Meun's translation; letters in parentheses after Y represent actual French MSS, as reported by Dedeck-Héry

Z The MS Chaucer used of Boethius

BOOK I

Metrum 1 Hn lacks through pr1.72 (lost leaf).
29 in me] Om. α (−B) Rob; but *m'aloigne* F.

Prosa 1 *24–25 me The beaute [of] the] *me the beaute the* O′ (*off* [marg.] *the* H); L F begin new clause *Quarum speciem, la biauté des queles.*
38 and] *or* α (−B) Lid Rob; but *et* F.
45 aprochen] Probably contaminated from 48; *assistentes* L, *estans* F imply *stondynge* O.
50 nat] C² only; om. all others.
59 ye] C² Auct only; *þe* all others.
72 by] Hn begins.

Metrum 2 6 dryven] β (−Hn) Auct Rob add *to and fro,* without parallel in L F.
9 hevenliche] Hn lacks isolated readings from here to the end of m2 and also in m3 and pr3.1–2; the folio is torn.
*25 yere] *yeris* O′; but *pleno anno* L, *en plain an* F.

Metrum 3 8 with] C¹ Hn only; *by* all others.

Prosa 3 *4 whan that] Om. O′; but *ubi* L, *puis que* F.
66 whiche] δ Rob add *tempestes,* ι add *tempeste;* both readings have probably intruded from 65.

Metrum 4 13 o wrecches drede ye] Perhaps *han wrecches wondrede on* in O; cf. *mirantur* L, *merveillent* F.

Prosa 4 18 and] H θ (−P) ι Rob add *touchynge* (in C¹ Hn as an interlinear gloss preceded by *scilicet*). Robinson thus replicates a frequent variety of scribal error, the absorption of a gloss into the text; see for example, 2.pr4.94 *in,* where δ have interlinear gloss *inest* but ι read *inmest* in text.
21 nature] Cf. *cum mihi siderum vias radio describeres* L, *quant tu me escrivoies par ta verge les voies des estoilles* F. Chaucer may have written *whan thow descryvedest me the weyes of the sterres with thy yerde,* omitted in O′ by scribal eyeskip.
32 seidest] Perhaps *amonestedest* or *warnedest* in O; cf. *monuisti* L, *amonnestas* F.
56 propre] ι only; *prospere* all others (and Lid Rob) (*goodly* Auct); cf. *cuiusque fortunas* L, *biens de chascun* F (after *bona fortuna* T; but perhaps O *prospere* represents Z *bonas fortunas*).
79ff. Coempcioun] Skeat and Robinson split the gloss, moving this portion to follow *effect* in 92. We follow O′ and Lid, assuming that this portion of the gloss looks forward to subsequent material.
124 men] *me* C² may be authorial.
126 towne] *the towne* C¹ B θ (−P) C² Rob. We follow Lid in adopting Chaucer's normal usage.
138 in somme] Perhaps *the somme* in O; cf. *summam* L, *la somme* F.
*212–13 And wel thow remembrest] Om. O′; but *meministi inquam* L, *et bien te remembre* F.
218 al] Perhaps *the innocence of al* in O; cf. *uniuersi innocenciam* L, *l'innocence du tout* F.

224 conscience] Perhaps *conscience preysinge itself* in O; cf. *consciencie probantis* L (*laudantis* T) *se, la conscience loant soy meismes* F.
297 thynke] Perhaps *mynne* in O; cf. *reminisci* L, *remembrer* F.

the[1]] in θ (−P); om. C[1]. Perhaps in O *the rumours and the;* cf. *rumores* L, *les nouvelles* F. Possibly the otiose *ryght* is a remnant of this phrase.
***310 lien**] *ben* O'; but *iacere* L, *gisent* F.

Metrum 5 35 So] Perhaps *I see* in O; cf. *Je voy que* F.
49 peple] *the peple* θ Sal Lid Rob.

Prosa 5 18 emperoures] Perhaps *emperye* in O; cf. *imperio* L, *empire* F.
19 weren] Perhaps *weren whilom* in O; cf. *quondam* L, *jadis* F.
20 that[2]] *he* B Auct; om. Lid Rob.
27 cite] May represent an erroneous gloss taken into the text; cf. *qua* L (sc. *lege*), *par la quelle* F (sc. *loy*).
32 and the clos] C[2] only; *and þe closing* B; om. all others. Perhaps an English gloss taken into the text of C[2] B.
49 honestete] C[1] Hn only; *honeste* α (−C[1]) C[2]; *vnhonestee* ι Auct.
58–59 wrongdede] *wrongful dede* θ β Lid Rob.
***68 turbacions**] *tribulacions* O'; but *tumultus* L, *turbacions* F.

Metrum 6 20 devyded] *denyed* H; *dampned* Sal. Perhaps *brydeled* in O; cf. *cohercuit* L (*alligando eas propriis officiis* T), *refrenees* F. Chaucer routinely translated *coercere* with a doublet consisting of *constreyne* and a verb derived from F.

Prosa 6 *13 folie] Lid Rob; *fortune* O'; but *temeritate* L, *folie* F.
17 it is] C[1] Auct only; all others transpose.
***36 by**] Om. O'; but *robore* L, *par* F; *thorw* Lid Rob.
***37 and**] Lid Rob; *is* O'; but cf. *hiante* L, *derompue et ouverte* F.
***62 woot wel that I**] Om. O'; but *esse me sciam* L, *ne sai je bien que je sui* F.
***75 and despoyled**] Om. O'; but *exulem . . . et expoliatum* L, *exilléz et . . . despoilliéz* F.
87 noryssynges] Singular in θ (−P) Lid Rob (*fomitem* L), *trust* B. But Chaucer seems frequently indifferent to distinctions of number in the original.
***100 that**] Lid Rob; *and that* O'; but *hanc* L, *la* F.

Metrum 7 7 withstande] C[2] only; *withstant* all others (and Lid). Perhaps *wawe . . . was . . . withstant* in O; cf. *vnda . . . obstat* L, *l'unde . . . empeesche* F.
18 foure] Om. γ ε Lid.

Additional corrections of C[1]:

Metrum 1 24 the] *þe sil* (perhaps expunged). **26 for**] Om. **29 unagreable**] *vngreable.*

Prosa 1 11 nat] Om. γ. **16 the**[1]] Om. **19 the**] *ich.* **20 of right**] *riȝt of wol.* **34 ther**] *þei;* Om. ε. **54 tho**] *þe two.* **57 corn**] *cornes* C[1] ι. **76 schewynge**] *schewen.* **88 seyn**] *seyn off* (later).

Metrum 2 4 as[2]] Om. **8 wont**] *won.* **32 the**] Om. C[1] ε P ι. **fool**] *foule* α (−P Th) ι; *foltes* Auct.

Prosa 2 7 to] *into.* **23 yif**] *ȝif it.*

Metrum 3 7 that[2]] Om. C[1] H θ Auct.

Prosa 3 5 byholde] *byhelde* α (−P) Auct. **46 of men**] Om.; *of* θ (−P); *of some men* Hn. **tho**] *þe* (since *e* and *o* are frequently indistinguishable in C[1], subsequently such apparent variation of C[1] is not noted). **57 Soranas**] *Soronas* γ; *Soranos* θ (−P); *Sorans* δ; *Sorancis* ι Auct. **59 ne**] Om. γ B. **77 fro**] Om.; *for* B. **78 palys**] *paleys* γ H θ ι Auct.

Metrum 4 15 ne] *and.* **16 unmyghty**] *vnmyghty* (a common form for *-ght,* which, like the far rarer *-gth(t),* is not henceforth noted).

Prosa 4 7 I that] Transposed. **19 or**] *and* γ ε Sal. **30–31 so befille**] *be so fille.* **56 fortunes**] *fortune.* **65 tormentyde**] *tormentyden* C[1] B θ C[2]. **76 a**] Om. γ. **102 Is it**] Transposed. **102 nat**] Om. C[1] B. **108 tho**] *the* γ H P A[1] Auct Lid Rob. **124 on**] *in* C[1] Sal. **143, 151 accusour**] *accusours.* **148 I schal**] γ ε transpose. **181 by**] *byfore; of* θ Auct. **193 the**] Om. **195 as**] *and.* **204 wilned**] *wilnen; wil* H. **213 the**] Om. C[1] C[2]. **216 the**[1]] Om. C[1] H. **218 peril**] *gret peril.* **240 now**] Om.; added B. **243 studie**] *studies* C[1] H θ (−P) Auct. **254 thou**] *though.* **256 ne**[2]] Om. γ B Sal Auct. **262 goddes**] *goodes* γ. **was**] *is* γ B Auct; *nys* H; *nas* P Hn; om. C[2]. **275 am**] Om. γ H. **278 yif**] Om. **283 ne**] Om. C[1] Auct. **316 in**] *on.*

Metrum 5 2 art] *arn* γ H. **21 yer**] *eyr* C[1] B. **25 in**] Om. α Hn. **31 thou**] Om. γ ε. **32 refusestow**] *refusedestow.* **42 derke**] Om. γ B Auct. **58 governest**] *gouernedest.* **the**] Om. C[1] θ (−P).

Prosa 5 15 ne] Om. C[1] B. **29 founden**] *to founden.* **sete**] *cite.* **32 palys**] *palays* γ H θ A[1] Auct. **35 wil**] *wel* C[1] Auct. **38 so**] *as.* **39 axe**] *axen.* **41 sete**] *cite* C[1] Sal. **55 tho**] *the* C[1] θ Sal; *to* A[2]. **62 eschaufede**] *enchaufede; echaufed* A[2] P; *enchaced* θ (−P). **63 ne**] Om. C[1] B θ.

Metrum 6 18 offices] *office* C[1] Auct.

Prosa 6 28 with] *with the.* **55 Remem-**] *Reme-* (a common form, not henceforth noted). **76 of**] *fro* γ ε Auct. **76 whiche**] *swiche.* **the**] *how the.* **89 nis**] *is* C[1] B θ (−P) Lid Rob; *nil* A[2]. **90 underput**] *vnderupt.* **91–94 but . . . But**] *But* γ ε.

Metrum 7 4 medleth] *medleeth.*

BOOK II

Prosa 1 3 she seyde thus] Om. α Rob Lid; but *sic exorsa est* L (F is fully translated as the gloss).
10 desfeted] "Withered away"; other eds. emend to *deffeted,* but the form is a possible, if unique, reflex of OF *desfait* (F *te defaus*).
27–28 and despysen] Om. γ ε ι Lid; but *ostendendo eam contempnendam* T, *et la despisaies* F, both explaining the verb rendered as *pursuydest* in 30.
53 maneres] Perhaps O added *this is hir nature;* cf. *ista natura* L, *tele est sa nature* F.
***79 and**] Om. O'; but *et* L F.
88 fro adversite into prosperite] Perhaps *fro prosperite into adversite and fro adversite into prosperite* in O; cf. *tam in prosperitate quam in aduersitate* T and lines 89–91.

Prosa 2 ***34** hem] Lid Rob; om. O'; but *les* F.

57 it] Cf. *An tu mores ignorabas meos* L, *Ne cognoissoies tu pas donques mes meurs* F; *Wystestow nat thanne my maneris* Lid. Chaucer may have written *Wystestow nat my maneres,* omitted in O' by scribal eyeskip.

69 an] Om. A² Lid Rob.

72 Lernedest] *Textus. Lernedest* Lid Rob, but the rubric is unnecessary.

74 entre . . . seler] *limine* L, *sueil* F "threshold." Liddell suggests that O had *selle,* but presumably Chaucer here offers a more normal location for the tuns. *Sill* "threshold" is not recorded before the late sixteenth century.

Metrum 2 **21** thurst] *frust* A²; *desyre or thurst* B; *luste* θ (−P); perhaps O had *thurst or lust;* cf. *sitis* L, *desiriers* F.

Prosa 3 **12** is] *it is* C¹ B θ (−P) Lid Rob; but *altior sensus est* L.

59 Circo] P Hn only; *Circo and* all others.

86 fortunous] *fortunes* γ B Lid; *fortune* C²; but *fortuitis* L.

Metrum 3 **5** This] An accurate rendition of the pronunciation of *this is.* We regularly follow the spelling of C¹ (usually *this,* as also in C², though normalized in the other MSS to *this is*) without comment.

Prosa 4 **17** grete] δ only; om. all others; cf. trad. *pluribus maximisque.*

70 the] C¹ only; om. all others (and Lid Rob); but *te* F.

*109 is] Skt Rob; om. O'; but *est* L F.

*168 sewed] "Inserted, planted"; *schewed* O' (A² has *suwed,* a normal variant for this form, as also for *scheweth* in 147); but *persuasum atque insitum* L, *amonnesté et mis en cuer* F.

Prosa 5 **47** of] Perhaps *and* in O; cf. *-que* L, *et* F.

*57 fayr] *ryght fayr* O'; but *pulcra* L, *bele* F (in contrast to *pulcherimi, la tres belle* in the next phrase).

*78 with] *with ful* O'; but *paucis* L, *peu de* F. As in 57 above, a scribal distortion of positive-superlative distinction; cf. *minimis, tres petite* in the next phrase, and see note 3.pr1.15–16 below.

89 the werkman] Perhaps *the wit of the werkman* in O; cf. *ingenium artificis* L, *l'engin de l'ouvrier* F.

91 that] *that the* Th, perhaps reflecting *te* L F.

*114 affraie] *a fare* O'; but *effroy* Y (B) (*strepitu* L). F's *estroiz* appears unparalleled and is probably an error, scribal or editorial, for *effroiz.*

162–68 For yif . . . felthe] In L F, the pronoun represented by 162 *a wyght,* 163 *hym,* and 166 *he* is neuter (*quid* L, *riens* F), so that the phrase beginning *the thyng* (166–167) refers to the same thing, not something new. Chaucer began the sentence using personal pronouns but switched carelessly at *the thyng* back to the neuter referent (*illud* L, *la chose* F). Or perhaps he wrote *awght, hit,* and *hit,* and the personal forms are scribal, influenced by 164 *a man.*

174 the] *is the* B Rob Lid; in C¹ *is* has been expunged.

*176 weneth] *and weneth* O'; cf. *pessimus quisque . . . putat* L, *chascun tres mauvais . . . cuide* F; *weneth* Skt.

Metrum 5 **25** armures] Cf. *horrida . . . arma* L, *horribles chans* F (reflecting trad. *arua*).

Prosa 6 **17** doon] Hn lacking through pr7.74–75 *preysynge* (lost leaf).

*35–37 that . . . seye] Om. O'; but cf. the gloss as incorporated into F: *de vous* (sc. *hommes*) *qui li vilz hommes ont seigneurie sus les vilz hommes c'est a dire li corps* (*talis est potestas ista terrena que non nisi ad corpus se extendit* T).

62 it] F *les* suggests O *hem.*

72 after] *therafter* γ ϵ Lid Rob; but *mox* L (*cito post* T), *tantost* F.

*115 ethe] "Easily" (to be sure, only the parallel adjective occurs elsewhere in Chaucer); *ofte* O'; but *facile* L (*faciliter* T), *legierement* F. We posit O *ethe* rather than *esily* because we think it more likely to have produced *ofte.*

Prosa 7 ***14** o] *a* O'; but *hoc vnum* L, *une seule* F. A frequent error; cf. notes 3.pr6.23, 5.pr3.150, and 5.pr4.189 below.

20 comune] A² skips to 68 *glorie.*

27 gretnesse] *spacium* L, *l'espace* F, regularly translated *space,* suggest possible contamination from 29.

52 ben enhabited in] Perhaps *enhabiten in* in O; cf. *incolunt* L, *habitent en* F.

*56 of¹] *and* O'; om. ι; cf. *comercii insolencia* L, *faute de acoustumance de* F. The illogical *defaute of unusage* reflects Chaucer's awkward blending of F's construction and L's lexis; perhaps read *defaute or.*

83 thilke noble renoun] Cf. *preclara illa fame immortalitas* L, *celle perdurableté de noble renommee* F.

92 yow] *þoʒ ʒe* B; *þough* H P; *ye* θ (−P) ι. Yow is awkward; apparently Chaucer mixed two separate constructions—*it semeth yow that ye* and *ye men semen to.* Scribes have tried two different forms of improvement. The reading of H P implies confusion of *yow* and *þow;* that of θ (−P) ι is an attempt to precede *semeth* with a nominative pronoun—and that of B both together.

101 tho] *two* γ ϵ Lid Rob; *the* C²; om. Sal; but *vtrumque* L, *l'un et l'autre* F.

*101 yit] *for yit* O'; *for* Sal; cf. *si . . . conferatur, . . . habet tamen* L.

*124 assaillede] *assaiede* O'; but *adorsus* L (gl. *aggressus*), *assailli* F. O' presumably is contaminated from 129 *assaie.*

*156 usynge] *beynge in* O'; but *celo fruens* L, *usans du ciel* F (but note *est luisant au* Y [B]).

158 no glorye] *noon othir thyng ne* γ ϵ Lid Rob; om. ι in eyeskip; but *de la gloire de* F.

Metrum 7 **12** although] Mo present through 32 *the.²*

Prosa 8 ι lacking through 3.pr1; Mo has pr8 through 8 *undirstandestow.*

Metrum 8 ***13–14** accordaunce [and] ordenaunce] *accordaunce* γ H β Lid Rob; *ordenaunce* B θ; cf. *seriem* L (*concordiam* T), *ordenaunce* F.

Additional corrections of C¹:

Prosa 1 **Rubric** paulisper] Om.; *lisper* ι. **7** in] *on.* **14** and] Repeats. **27** were] Om. **33** manere] Adds *of.* **39** mowe] *mowen* C¹ θ (−P). **49** thyng] *thyngis.* **67** of²] Om. C¹ ι. **90** flaterynges] *flaterynge* α. **102** betakest] *takest* γ B. **105** the] Om. C¹ H.

Metrum 1 **13** wepynges] *wepynge* C¹ H θ Hn ι; om. A² B in eyeskips.

Prosa 2 **10** ever] *euery.* **25** of] Om. α (−P). **29** thinges] *goodes;* om. B. **38** tho] *the* C¹ H β (−C²)

Lid Rob; om. B in eyeskip. **48** that] *þ¹ the.* **50**
this] *swiche* C¹ H θ (−P); *thus* B. **63** out] *ought.*
76 of] Om. **80** yif] *rif.*

Prosa 3 **Rubric** pro] *proro; et pro ι.* **15** delites]
delices. **19** ne] Om. **23** and ajuste] Om. C¹ P
β; *and avise þe* B. **27** -nesse] *-nsse.* **59** the] Om.
64 feffedestow] *feddestow* C¹ Lid.

Metrum 3 **14** without] *with* α.

Prosa 4 **11** the] *thi;* om. Sal. **20** fortune] *for-
tyme.* **36** to] Om. α (−B). **52** yit] Om. **65**
or] *ne; and* Hn. **71** ther] Om. **74** and] *or* γ ι Lid
Rob. **87** zelily] *iolily.* **95** ne] Om. C¹ B Sal. **97**
that] Om. **99** is¹] Om. C¹ H β. **108** is] *is a.*
112 nis] *is* γ B. **138** it] Om. **158** leesen] *le-
seen.*

Metrum 4 **3** lowde] *lowe.* **14** sete] *site* C¹ ε C² A¹
Lid Rob; *cytee* A² Sal. **17** palys] *palays* α (−A²) Hn
Sal.

Prosa 5 **34** ne¹] Om. γ B ι. **35** withoute] *with* γ.
65 shynynge] *chynynge.* **71** ne] Om. C¹ B Hn ι.
77 no nede] *node.* **89** werkman] *werkmen* C¹ Cx.
93 a¹] *as.* **106** al so] *als so; als* A²; *as* B ι. **121**
of] *of ful.* **122** mesuren] *mesureth* γ H θ. **131** yif
] Om. C¹ Sal Lid Rob. **153** is it] γ ι Lid Rob transpose.

Metrum 5 **2** metes] *mete.* **19** ne²] Om. C¹ ι. **25**
yit] *hit;* om. A². **36** be] *by.*

Prosa 6 **5, 23** power(e)s] *powyer(e)s.* **8** Ethna] *of
ethna.* **9** ne²] Om. γ. **12** imperie] *imperier.*
consulers] *conseilers* γ θ Sal. **13** eldres] *eldren.* **18**
nolden] *wolden.* **20** if] *if it.* **23** tho] *the* γ ε. **41**
with] *by* C¹ θ (−P) Lid Rob. **63** thing] Om. **83**
contrarious] *contrarie.* **103** as] Om. γ ε. **110**
hem] Om. **119, 120** ben] *to ben* C¹ θ.

Metrum 6 **14** peples] *peple* C¹ H θ. **15** hide] *hidde*
C¹ B θ (−Th) ι. **17** peples] *peple* C¹ H. **21** sep-
tem-] *seven* γ β. **26** his] *þis* γ. **27** peples] *peple*
C¹ ε. **28** the] *to.*

Prosa 7 **3** hadde] *hadden* C¹ β. **5** to] *forto.* **7**
that³] *it.* **30** ne] Om. C¹ ε ι. **53** lytel] Om. C¹ H
θ. **58** ne] Om. **73** ek] Om. α. **90** writynges]
writynge. **95** comparysoun] *comparysons.* **116**
for] *byfore.* of] *of the* C¹ H θ (−P) Lid Rob. **152**
itself] *hymself* γ.

Metrum 7 **4** the] Om. C¹ C² Sal. **7** the²] Om. C¹
Sal. **23** nat] Om. C¹ Lid Rob. **26** ne] Om. C¹ Lid Rob. **30**
here] *hir* γ.

Prosa 8 **2** an] *and; a* A²; om. C². **5** whan]
what. **38** doutous] *doutes.*

Metrum 8 **3** qualites] *qualite* γ H C².

BOOK III

Prosa 1 **15–16** ryght scharpe] Perhaps *a lytel scharper*
in O; cf. *paulo acriora* L, *un pou plus aigres* F, and the
similar translation at 2.pr5.3. See also 1.pr5.71–72, 73,
77–78, 1.pr6.95, 2.pr1.45–46. Furthermore, Chaucer
regularly uses *ryght* to render a Latin superlative, never

(unless *here*) to render a comparative; see, however,
2.pr6.92, where *most digneliche* translates L's *dignius.*

Metrum 1 **Rubric** ingenuum] Hn Th only; *ingenium*
all others.

Prosa 2 **40** the] C¹ only; om. all others; but *li* F.
100 travayleth] *travaylen* O'; but cf. the English syntax and *laborat* L, *travaille* F. Scribes apparently construed
the adjacent *folk* as subject.
111 n'angwyssous] *angwyssous* O'; but *ne . . . pas* F.
Skeat inserts *nat;* Liddell and Robinson add *ne* before *be.*
We place the negative here as the most likely source of
error: *be nangwyssous* > *ben angwyssous* > *be angwyssous;*
cf. the variation at Tr 3.316.

Metrum 2 ***11*** maistre] *maistres* O'; but *magistrum* L,
maistre F. The form is probably influenced by the frequent neighboring plurals, but note *mayster* in 18.
19 assaieth] Liddell suggests *apaieth* (*imbuit* L, *abeuvre
de son sanc* F), but Chaucer follows T's *recipit uel experitur.*
25 hym] *hem* O'; but *huic* L, *li* F; cf. 21 *brid,* 27 *bryd.*
27 out] Hn lacking through pr3 (lost leaf).

Prosa 3 **54** yit] Om. β and L F.
63 forense] *foreyne* O'; but *forenses (querimonie)* L, *(com-
plaintez de) plaiz fors* F. Foreyne regularly represents *alien-
us* or *extrinsecus* in L (as at 80 and 70, respectively), and
Chaucer may have been guided, both in the legal sense
and in the construction of the doublet, by T's *forus enim
locus est exercendarum licium coram iudicibus.*
91–93 alwey . . . thyng] Perhaps *. . . gredy and axynge
anythyng be fulfild with richesses* in O; cf. *hians semper atque
aliquid poscens opibus expletur* L, *touz jours baians et re-
querans aucune chose dehors est raemplie ou saoulee par richeces* F.

Prosa 4 **48–51** the whiche . . . preysed] C¹ H θ ι Lid
Rob place *the whiche . . . folk* (48–49) at the end of the
passage, changing order of L F.

Prosa 5 **4** the²] Sal only; om. A²; *of* all others (and
Lid Rob); but *etiam* L, *et . . . li* F.
51 whiche] *whiche Papynian* O', apparently an interlinear gloss that has become part of the text.
65 consyled] *conseyled* O'; but *conciliat* L, *sont acordé* F.
Suggested by Robinson in an explanatory note *ad loc.*

Prosa 6 ***23*** o] *a* O'; but *vnius* L, *un* F.
50 forlynen] *degeneret* L, *forlignent* F; cf. m6.12 *forlyned*
(*degener* L, *forlignablez* F). See Mark Science, TLS 22 Mar
1923, 199–200.

Metrum 6 **10** eldres] Cf. *genus et proauos* L, *lignage et de
vos besaeus* F.
  thow . . . youre] *ye . . . youre* ε θ Hn; but *vestra
. . . spectes* L, *tu . . . vos* F.

Prosa 8 **48** or the feblesse] *of the feblesse* A² H θ
(−P) ι Rob; but cf. *et la foiblece* F.

Prosa 9 **32** o] Perhaps *o same* in O; cf. *vna . . .
eademque* L, *d'une meismes* F.
140 flytte] Perhaps *flytte ayeyn* in O; cf. the additions
in *aduersum* L, *d'autre part* F.
173 lyknesses] C²; all others (and Lid) singular.
197 thyng] ***198*** begynnyng] We posit here a
two-stage error. First, 198 *begynnyng* O (*exordium* L, *commencement* F) became *thyng* O', apparently by accidental
attraction to *thyng* in 197; then a later scribe changed 197

thyng O (*rerum* L, *chosez* F) to *goodes* O′ to forestall the repetition.

Metrum 9   1   soowere and] γ B only; *soueraign and* H θ; om. β.
12–13   formedest] Perhaps *formest* in O; cf. *formas* L (trad. *formans*), *formes* F.
***28   and]** *it* O′; cf. *cum secta . . . glomerauit* L, *quant elle est ainsi devisee et a assemblé* F.

Prosa 10   52   thing] C¹ only; om. all others (and Lid Rob); but *chose* F.
71   prince] *fader* θ (−P) Rob; but *principem* Z (*patrem* L), *princes* F.
72   hymself] From Y (B*b*), which omits *vel ita naturaliter habere* L, *ou s'il a naturelment en soy* F. Liddell suggests adding *or wenestow that he hath it naturely in himself.*
109   good] Appears to have intruded from 105; cf. *beatitudinem* L, *beneurté* F, implying *blisfulnesse* O.
***143   men ben maked just]** Om. O′; but *iusti . . . fiunt* L, *sont fait li homme juste* F. Suggested by Skeat; followed by Liddell and Robinson.
177   maked] *maked of* Lid Rob; but *fait* (*ceste* F) *beneurté* Y (B).
***178   is]** *that is* O′; but *est* L F.
***187   ben]** *that ben* O′; but *veluti ad verticem cuncta* L, *sont* F.
223   thei²] Hn ends.

Prosa 11   *9–10   undo] *do* O′; but *patefaciam* L, *monsterai* F; and cf. Chaucer's uses at Rom 9, BD 899.
***23   als]** *alle* O′; but *veluti* L, *aussi comme* F. A frequent error; see 5.pr4.176 and note below.
***90   and]** *that is to seyn that* O′; lacking in L F. The subsequent gloss 92–94 (and all that follows) shows that Chaucer had translated L in some approximately correct way and that this O′ reading, an otiose and meaningless gloss, is presumably scribal. Accidental loss of *as* from 91, subsequently restored, may have garbled the syntax sufficiently to produce O′.
***91   as]** *as herbes or trees* O′; but cf. *quid de inanimatis omnino . . . rebus* L, *et de toutez les chosez qui n'ont nulles ames* F.
102   mareys] A¹ lacking through pr12.3 *yet* (lost leaf).
***219   marke of the]** Om. O′; cf. *ipsam . . . medie veritatis notam* L. F misunderstood or translated as *notum: la cognoissance de comune verité.* The phrase is necessary to introduce the archery metaphor implied by *prykke* in 220.
***220–21   But in this . . . that]** *But this . . . in that* O′; but *Sed in hoc . . . quod* L, *Mais en ce . . . ceque* F. Suggested by Liddell.

Metrum 11   20   and] A² skips through pr12.9 *thow.*
***25   schewen]** *seen* O′; *seem* Th; but *apparebit* T. Chaucer renders *apparere* as *schewen* at 3.pr10.241, 4.pr2.258, and 4.pr4.251 (although as *apiere* at 5.pr4.68).

Prosa 12   113   mai or wole] β Lid Rob transpose, producing the order of L, but Chaucer apparently followed F.
155–56   woven] C² only; *wonnen* α (−H) A¹; *wounded* H; *voñnen* Sal.

Additional corrections of C¹:

Prosa 1   16   nat²] Om. C¹ B.   **20   that]** Om. γ ∈ Lid Rob.
Metrum 1   1   sowe] *haue* (added later).
Prosa 2   Rubric   Tum] *Cum* γ; *Tunc* ι.   **2   ryght]**

ryght eye (*eye* added later).   **25   some]** *þat some.*   **37 and]** Om.   **42   plowngen]** *plowgen.*   **47   or for]** *for þe.*   **55   ne]** Om. γ B Lid Rob.   **60   I]** Om.   **79 delyt]** *þe delyt.*   **87   not]** *noʒt; wote* Sal.   **98   nis]** *is* γ B P.   **106   that]** *thanne.*   **110   that]** *þ¹ þe.*   **114 the]** *thise* C¹ Lid Rob.

Metrum 2   26   studye] *studyes* γ P Hn.   **34   that¹]** Om. C¹ Lid Rob.   **39   t'aryse]** *aryse* C¹ H θ β Lid Rob.

Prosa 3   2   al-] *as* C¹ ι.   **18   yif]** *yif it* C¹ Lid Rob. ne] Om. C¹ B Lid Rob.   **25   the¹]** *þ¹;* om. A² B β Lid Rob; om. P in eyeskip.   **34   noldest]** *woldest* C¹ B Rob.   **38   desiredest]** *desirest* C¹ H Cx.   **76   That]** *This.* **90   ne]** Om. C¹ Lid Rob; added in B.   **96   ne]** Om. γ Lid Rob; B θ (−P) om. but add later negatives.   **97 ne]** Om.

Prosa 4   Rubric   dignitates] *dignitatibus* γ B ι.   **11 which]** *swich.*   **12, 15   Nonyus]** *Nomyus* α (−Th) δ; *Vomius* ι.   **17   Certes]** Adds *the.*   **45   wykkyd]** Om. α; om. ι in eyeskip.   **45–46   fowlere and the]** Om. α; om. ι in eyeskip.   **50   dignyte]** *dignytes* γ B ι .   **50–51   so much more]** Om. α; *more* ι.   **58   ne]** Om.   **63   worschipful]** *worschpful.*   **70   be holden]** *byholden;* be H θ.

Metrum 4   13   by] *to* C¹ H P Hn; *vnto* A².

Prosa 5   5   of] Om. C¹ C².   **8   fownden]** *fowden.* **9   yif]** Om.   **19   that]** *the* C¹ Sal Lid Rob.   **27, 47 familyer]** *familyler.*   **37   or]** *and.*   **46   ful]** *wol;* om. Cx.

Metrum 5   7   in] *into; of* B.

Prosa 6   2   which] *swich.*   **16   the³]** Om. γ.   **23 ne]** Om. C¹ P Sal.   **37–38   gloryfien]** *gloryfieden.*   **43 ne]** Om. C¹ B.   **49   imposed]** *inposed.*   **ne]** Om.

Metrum 6   14   forlete] *forleten.*

Prosa 7   Rubric   corporis] *corporibus* γ B β (−C²) Lid Rob.   **1   what]** Om.   **2   of]** Om. C¹ B θ (−Th). **9   that]** Om.   **20   fownden]** *fowden.*   **25   Euripidis]** *Euridippis* (-*pus*) C¹ B θ (−Th) β; *But dippus* A².

Prosa 8   4   byheeten] *byhighten.*   **11   tho]** *the* C¹ P. **15   anoyously]** *anoyous* γ ∈.   **44–45   Alcibiades]** *Altiades; Alcidiades* A² B P β; *Altibiadis* H Cx.   **48   the³]** *thyn.*   **52   the¹]** Om. γ C².

Metrum 8   2   fro] *to.*   **5   yowre]** *ʒow.*   **27   honours]** *honour.*

Prosa 9   14   knowen] *to knowen* γ Lid Rob.   **27   if]** *if it* C¹ H Lid Rob.   **62   Boece]** *Boce.*   **70   ne]** Om. **91   nis]** *is* γ Cx Sal.   **98   ben]** *to ben* γ P Lid Rob. **112   tho]** *the* γ H Sal.   **115   honours]** *honour* α (−P).   **116   delyces]** *delytes* C¹ H.   **120   the toon]** The original reading, altered to *that toon.*   **152   schalt]** *schat.*   **155   -nesse]** -*nsse.*   **160   that]** Om. C¹ Lid Rob.   **192   God]** *good* C¹ B.   **199   nis]** *is* C¹ B θ.

Metrum 9   Rubric   qui] *Quam* γ Lid Rob.   **5   duellest]** *duelledest* C¹ P.   **7   causes]** *cause* C¹ P.   **10 that]** *tha.*   **12   thy]** *thyn* (*þouʒt* over erasure, first letter originally *y*).   **22   ne¹]** Om. C¹ Lid Rob (but C¹ has caret).   **23   ne]** Om. C¹ ∈ Sal Lid Rob.

Prosa 10   12   ne] Om.; *and* P.   **13   thing]** *þinges.* **14   it]** *a.*   **22   yif]** *yif it.*   **29   into¹]** *into þe* C¹ H θ (−P).   **51, 53   God]** *good.*   **70   quod]** *sd* (?). this] *the* C¹ θ (−P) Lid Rob.   **83   so]** *it so* C¹ Lid Rob;

om. P.   **84**   it] Om. α (−P).   **89**   thilke] *ilke;* B *þat.*   **97**   ne] Om. C¹ B Lid Rob.   **110**   may] *may it.*   **119**   ne] Om. γ ι.   **140**   than] *þ¹.*   **146**   dyvinite] Has extra minim.   **172**   I] Om.   **177**   the] *thise* C¹ H Lid Rob.   **184**   thise] *alle thise.*   **219**   ne] Om. γ ε Sal.   **221**   that] Om.   **223**   thei¹] Om.   **225**   is it] α (−P) transpose.   **238–40**   thanne . . . desired] Om. γ H.

Metrum 10   **14**   Hermus] *Herinus* γ ε C²; *hernus* P.

Prosa 11   **20**   ne] Om. C¹ B Rob².   **57**   soule . . . body] *body . . . soule* C¹ Lid Rob.   **65**   yif] Om.   **89**   But] *Boece But* γ B β.   **132**   hirs] *his* α.   is] Adds *hic incipe,* an uncancelled scribal direction.   **153**   Ne] Om. C¹ B.   ne²] Om. γ Sal.   here now] C¹ θ (−P) Lid Rob transpose.   **159**   of] *is.*   **168**   ful] *wol; wel* P.

Metrum 11   **8**   tresors] *tresore.*   **17**   propretes] *proprete.*   **19**   thoughtes] *thoughte.*   **23**   he] Om.   **33**   wynde] *wyndes* C¹ θ Rob.   **39**   that] *what.*   **43**   if] *if it* C¹ Lid Rob.

Prosa 12   **2**   me] Om.   **10**   loke] *lokest; seke* H θ (−Th).   **30**   This] Om.   **39**   ne²] Om. C¹ Lid Rob.   **91**   may] *ne may* C¹ Lid Rob.   **109**   of] *ob.*   **112**   quod] *þ¹.*   **121**   the] Om. C¹ ι Rob.   **136**   destroyed] *destroyden.*   **144**   wyght] *wygh; man* B.   **154–55**   elles pleyestow] *el/lestow.*   **157**   it] Om.   **167**   God] *good* C¹ H θ (−Th) ι Rob.   **169**   nis] *is* γ θ (−Th) Lid Rob.   **171**   And] *& þou.*   **176**   the¹] Om. γ P ι.   **180**   ne] Om. C¹ θ (−P).   **185**   the] Om. C¹ H θ.   **187**   the²] Om. C¹ B θ; *to* ι.   **190**   that¹] *þ¹ it.*   **191**   into] *into þe.*   **201**   ne] Om. C¹ H θ (−P).

Metrum 12   **Rubric**   potuit] *poterit* γ Sal; *peterit* B.   **27**   hym²] Om.   **30**   soules] *solues.*   **42**   fulfild] *fulfuld.*   **58**   on] *on þe.*   **62**   to²] *into* C¹ Lid Rob.   **64**   so] Om. γ.

BOOK IV

Metrum 1   **1**   forthi] *forsothe* β. This is the first of a concentration of α/β disagreements through this meter (cf. 9, 14, 16). At 35, P alone of α agrees with β. In addition, C² stands alone at 17, and θ C² at 32. And in three places, at 23, 24, and 27, C² joins the entire α group in either generally or exactly following L, while ι very clearly follows F.
9   areyseth hym] C² only; *aryseth* α; *areyseth hir* ι; cf. *surgat* L, *se lieve* F.
14   whan] *þat* β.
16   trouthe] *cleer* (interlined in C¹) *trouthe* α Lid Rob; *cleer* has probably intruded from 13 (cf. *inuencionem ueritatis* T).
17   soule] *thoght* C² is perhaps preferable.
23   that he] *þe thought* γ ε Lid Rob; *he* θ C²; *þe soule* ι; cf. *elle* F. We insert *that* on the assumption that γ ε ι are responses to a corrupt reading *And whan the hath.*
23   gon] *don* α C² Lid Rob; cf. *alé* F, *transcendit ulterius* T (*exhausti fuerit* L).
24   point of the] Om. α C² Lid Rob; cf. *point du* F.
27–28   worschipful lyght or dredefulle clerenesse] *worschipful lyght* α C² Lid Rob (*verendi luminis* L); *dredefulle clerenesse* ι (*redoubtable clarté* F). We suppose a

Chaucerian doublet, of which half is preserved in α C², the other half in ι.
32   cart or wayn] only θ C²; *wayn* γ ε Lid Rob, *cart* ι (*currum* L, *cours* F).
34   thi] C¹ only; *this* all others (and Rob).
35   now] Om. α (−P) Lid Rob; cf. *nunc* L, *ores* F.
38   wel] L F have an additional clause, *patria est mihi* L, *c'est ci li miens pais* F, arguably translated *here is my country* by Chaucer and omitted by eyeskip in O'.

Prosa 2   **60**   gretly] Om. H θ; no parallel in L F; probably a scribal addition.
189   seien] Perhaps *seien whanne we seien* in O; cf. *a dire quant nous disons* F.

Metrum 2   **17**   tyranyes] *tyrauntes* ι, perhaps correct and scribally suppressed to avoid repetition; cf. *tyrannos* L, *tyrans* F.

Prosa 3   **45**   good hytself] *good hymself* ε C²; *god hymself* all others (*god in hymself* H); but *ipsum bonum* L, *biens meismes* F.
72   wikkidnesse] Perhaps O added *of al schrewednesse;* cf. the additions *omnium malorum* L, *et la fins de touz maulz* F.
90–92   forme . . . withowte] *forme of mankynde that is to seyn the forme of the body withowte* O'; but *humani corporis . . . species* L, *forme du corps humain* F. We suppose that the phrase *of the body* was moved from its proper place by scribal error.

Prosa 4   **7**   crwel] *cruel and wood* Cx Th. Perhaps *crwel and wikked* in O; cf. *atrox* (*crudelis* T) *scelerataque* L, *crueuse et felonnesse* F.
40   wene] ι adds *to lakken mowynge* (*mouyng* Sal) *to done yuel,* perhaps, as Liddell suggests, an O reading reflecting L's *esse carituros,* otherwise untranslated.
141   folwen that] Om. O'; but *consequencia sunt* L, *s'ensuit* F.
204–5   nere . . . erthe] C² only (but reads *heuenene*); *ne wer in neyþer* B Th; om. all others; cf. *ne fussez ne en ciel ne en terre ne ne veissez* F.
229   It accordeth] Cf. *Ita* L, *C'est voirs* F, usually translated *that is sooth;* perhaps a scribal error, influenced by 233 (*conuenit* L, *ce couvient il* F).
243   semeth it] Perhaps *semeth it the* in O; cf. *tibi* L, *t'- F.
249   of] *or* O'; but *de pechié* F.
250   it²] *and it* O'; but om L F.
266   seken] Perhaps *kerven* in O; cf. *resecarent* L, *retrenchassent* F, translated *kerve* at 2.m5.19, 3.m1.2; *seken* may be influenced by *syke* earlier in 266.

Metrum 4   **7–8**   serpent] C² only; *serpentz* all others; cf. *serpens* L, *li serpent* F, and the parallelism with the other singulars in the sentence.

Prosa 5   **11**   wise men] Perhaps *wisdom* in O; cf. *sapiencie* L, *sapience* F.

Metrum 5   **5**   the sterre] Perhaps *the slowh sterre* in O; but Chaucer may suppress *tardus* L, *tardis* F as repetitious of *late* (*sera* L) in 6.
15   folk] P ends, although the last leaf contains two fragments from 5.pr6.
16–17   the . . . maken] *maketh* O'; but *li Coribant en font sonner leurs tabours et lassent* Υ (B*b*). The subsequent gloss implies a previous reference to the Coribantes. We suppose that, after an initial eyeskip from *and* to *and,* scribes

altered *maken* to *maketh* to agree with the apparent subject *errour.*

17   thikke] *thilke* O', although B has *þ⁰*, perhaps expunged, with *thikke* in margin (B regularly substitutes *þo* for *thilke*); cf. *crebris* L, *espés* F. Cf. also line 23 below, where all MSS but B and A¹ again read *thilke.*

19   Coribantes] Th only; *Coribandes* all others.

***29   ther]** Om. O'; but *illic* L, *la* F; the contrast between *hic* (*her* in 28) and *illic* is the gist of Boethius's sentence.

Prosa 6   62   thinges] Perhaps *alle thinges* in O; cf. *omnium* L, *de toutez chosez* F.

70   certes] γ B only; *certeyne* H θ; om. β.

116   of] C² only; om. all others; cf. *orbium* L.

132   unfolden] Perhaps *infolden* in O; cf. *implicatur* L. *Unfolden* regularly translates *explicare* (e.g. 4.m5.7–8).

177   declyneth] B C² only; *enclyneth* all others.

207   sharpe] B C² only; *bittere* γ H θ (from 204); om. ι in eyeskip.

272   beren] θ adds *and somme despise that thei mowe nat bere.* O follows Y (B), which omits the clause corresponding to L's *alii plus equo dispiciunt quod ferre non possunt.* The θ group has probably reintroduced the clause by consultation with the source.

Metrum 6   15   the sterre] Perhaps *th'euesterre* in O; cf. *l'estoille du soir* F. See also 1.m5.11, 2.m8.8.

Prosa 7   *20   hyt] *hem* O' (*him* A²); but cf. *eam* L, *la* F (i.e., 18 *sentence*).

Metrum 7   28   travailes] C² only; all others singular. **42   slowh]** Cf. C² gloss (misplaced above *Arpiis* in 33) *in þe palude of Lyrne.* The unique example of a possible text reading that has become a gloss; cf. *in Lernea palude* T, *en la palu de Lerne* F. ***51   sondes]** *strondes* O'; but cf. *harenis* L, *gravellez* F, which Chaucer usually (four times in five other uses) translates *sondes.* Though *strondes* is an acceptable translation, it may have been influenced by 45.

Additional corrections of C¹:

Prosa 1   18   gret] Om. **20   eveles]** *þe eueles* C¹ Lid Rob. **27   nis]** *is* C¹ B Lid Rob. **35   and]** *and he* (*he* added later). **38   an]** Om. C¹ H Sal Lid Rob. **53   ne²]** Om. **67   arisen]** *areisen* C¹ C².

Metrum 1   19   schynynge] *schynnynge.* **27   be]** Om. **29   myght]** *nyght* C¹ B. **30   of]** Repeats.

Prosa 2   Rubric   inquam] Om. γ B Lid Rob (B leaves blank); *nequam* P. **13   yif]** *ȝif it.* **15   yif]** Om. **37   nilt]** *ne myght.* **40   that²]** Om. γ ε Cx C². **42   a]** Om. γ B Th C² Lid Rob. **44   that²]** Om. γ ε P Lid Rob. **49   the²]** Om. **67   ben men]** C¹ B Lid Rob transpose. **101   ne²]** Om. C¹ θ (−P) Sal Lid Rob. **119   coveytise]** *coueytises* γ θ. **142   alwey]** Om. γ ε; *awey* C². **150   ne²]** Om. **163   ne]** Om. C¹ B. **172   it]** Om. C¹ H.   **that]** *þat þ¹*; om. ε. **188   this]** *þise.* **191   but]** *but yit* γ ε. **196   seyn]** *seen.* **252   felonye]** *felononye.* **256   the]** Om. γ. **270   geten]** *geten nat* C¹ Lid Rob.

Metrum 2   10   trowblable] *trowbable* γ; *trowable* H. **11   floodes]** *flood* α. **17   ne]** Om. γ Sal Lid Rob.

Prosa 3   37   as] Om. **46   thanne]** *þ¹.* **it]** Om. **47   ben¹]** *is.* **54   thus]** *so.* **59   so]** Om. **60**

medes] *mede* C¹ Lid Rob. **65   is]** *is þe.* **66   that]** Om. γ θ (−P) Sal. **83   wel]** Om. **102   betidith]** *betitid.* **be]** *ben.* **107   if]** Om. **113   quakith]** *quake.* **125   syn]** *syn þ¹.*

Metrum 3   Rubric   Vela] *Vla* γ ι. **4   Cerces]** *certes* (all other uses, 32, 36, 44, *cirtes*), as generally the other MSS. **19   duc]** *duc of.* **20   unbownden]** *vnbowden.* **26   ne]** Om. γ. **30   chaungynge]** *chaunchynge.* **42   venyms]** *venym.* **43   to-]** *þ¹.*

Prosa 4   1   am] *I am* C¹ Sal. **5   al]** *& al.* **22, 23   yif]** *yif þat, yif it* C¹ Lid Rob. **25   it]** Om. C¹ C² Lid Rob. **30   mowynge]** *power* C¹ Lid Rob; *moeuynge* P ι. **31   that]** *that thei* C¹ H θ A¹ Lid Rob; *that the* A² Sal. **53   leste]** *laste.* **65   he]** *it.* **68   nis]** *is* C¹ Lid Rob. **75   that²]** Om. **82   ne¹]** Om. γ B. **I]** Om. **85   that]** Om. **102   that]** Om. **124   peyne]** *peynes* γ B Th. **142   a lytel]** Om. C¹ H θ (−Th); *a lyter* C². **155   that]** Om. C¹ Lid Rob. **162   that]** *&.* **189   and]** *and hir* C¹ H. **217   ne accordeth]** *it accordeth ne* (corrector's intent as per marginal instruction *ne accordeth it*). **218   that]** *þat þ¹* (recte) C¹ Cx. **239   doute]** *doute it.* **246   wel]** *it wel* (reflecting original *thanne,* corrected to *that*). **253   the²]** Om. C¹ Lid Rob; om. A² C² in eyeskips. **264   tho]** *the* γ A¹ Lid Rob; om. H θ (−Th). **268–69   the deffendours or]** Om. α. **269   fayle and]** Om. α. **276   forleten]** *forsaken.* **278   the]** Om. C¹ ι. **293   vices and synne]** *synnes and vice.*

Metrum 4   15   of] *of þe* C¹ H θ (−Th).

Prosa 5   13   is] Om. (perhaps erased). **26   the²]** Om. **29   medled]** *medleed.* **32   yyveth]** *yueth.* **35   hardnesses]** *hardynesses* γ; *hardnesse* B θ A¹; *hardynes* H; *asprenesse* Sal.

Metrum 5   5   the sterre] *sterre þe* (*þe* added). **6   and]** Rubbed. **10   ne]** Om. C¹ Lid Rob. **11   waxen]** *waxet.* **13   discovereth]** *disc. . . .th* (rubbed). **15   The]** Om. (rubbed). **23   thikke]** *thilke* α (−B) C² Sal. **31   brestes]** *brestees.*

Prosa 6   13   unethes] *vnuthes.*   **laven]** *lauent.* **68   that]** Om. γ θ Sal. **77   that]** *hem.* **109   subgitz]** *subigitz.* **111   is]** *it.* **116   cerklis]** *clerkis* γ. **118   cerkle]** *clerk.* **120   is]** *þ¹ is.* **121   cerklis]** *clerkis; cercle* A² H. **132   of]** *of* to γ ε ι.   **it is]** C¹ H transpose. **134   more]** *the more* C¹ H. **141   undirstondyng]** *vndirstonde* C¹ Sal. **157   fro]** *of.* **189   men that som folk]** *folk that som men* γ. **198–99   atempraunces]** *atempraunce* α (−A²) Sal. **213   corages]** *corage* γ H θ C². **222   thing, thing]** *thingis, thingis.* **225   a]** Om. **235   unwened]** *vnknowed* α. **271   thei]** *hem* γ ε. **273   ledeth]** *leueth.* **285   it]** Om. **334   eschaufed]** *escaufed; enchaufed* Sal; om. A². **348   nis]** *is* γ θ Lid Rob. **353   man]** *men* α. **372   Om. C¹ ε θ A¹ Lid Rob.

Metrum 6   1   wys] Om. γ ι. **16   the late]** Om. γ. **20   the]** Om. **50   -nesses]** *-nesse* C¹ H ι; *-es* Cx. **52   welle]** *wille* C¹ H; *weele* B.

Prosa 7   2   the] Om. **10   of¹]** Om.; *by* A². **42   quod sche]** Repeats (once by corrector). **82   to¹]** *two* γ; in C¹ marked to read *to.* **85   to³]** Om. C¹ ι Lid Rob. **88   it]** Om.; *is* Sal.

Metrum 7   19   the²] Om. γ ε. **34   applis]** *arplis* γ. **37–38   overcomer]** *ouercom* γ. **44   visage]** *visages.*

48 of] Om. γ Lid Rob. **67** ye] *ye the.* **70** that²] *the* C¹ H.

BOOK V

Prosa 1 4 by] Perhaps *by thy(n)* in O; cf. *tua* L, *de toy* F.
*14 the¹] Om. O'; but *tibi* L, *toi* F. As usual, scribes have simplified *the the.*
*36 but an idel] *ne duelleth but a* O'; cf. *inanem prorsus vocem esse* L, *c'est du tout vois vaine* F. The MSS version perhaps represents attraction to *duellynge* in 40, followed by a shift in position of *but a(n).*
46 undirstoden] B only; *vndirstonden* all others.

Prosa 2 3 of fre] *or fre* ι; perhaps *of oure fre* in O; cf. *nostri* L, *nostre* F.
27 loken] An adequate translation of L's *conseruant;* cf. OED *Look v.,* sense 6e. But more likely Chaucer wrote *kepen,* the normal translation of *conservare,* and the form was corrupted under the influence of *lokynge* in 28.
*40 helpen] *hepen* O'; but *adiuuant* L (*augmentant* T), *aident* F. Apparently scribes could not resist creating the doublet *hepen and encrecen.*

Prosa 3 47 comen] At this point, the end of fol. 56ʳ, the scribe of Sal apparently turned a leaf in his exemplar, as well as in his unfinished quire. As a result, he skipped ahead to 170 *Thanne,* a mistake he did not discover before filling fol. 56ᵛ and at least part of the next side with copy (the text is consecutive from fol. 56ᵛ to fol. 59ʳ). To repair this mistake, he inserted a bifolium after fol. 56 and left a note at the end of fol. 56ʳ: *sequitur in proximo folio.* Unfortunately, the piece omitted was too short for the bifolium: fol. 58ʳᵇ has only two lines, and fol. 58ᵛ is blank.
90 bytidden] C² only; all others (and Lid Rob) *bytiden,* the result of confusing Chaucer's sense of *whilom* ("formerly," not, as ι reads, *somtyme*).
 cause] H Cx only; all others plural; but cf. *causam* L, *cause* F; the plural form is a scribal reflection of *thinges* in 87 and 89.
*150 o] *a* O'; but *vnum* L, *un* F.
*159 and] Om. O'; but *ac* L, *et* F.
166 the . . . hir] O'; we retain the reading, believing *the whiche folk* simply Chaucer's consolidation of 164 *schrewes* and 165 *good folk* into a single, close antecedent for *hir.* He follows F (*puis que*) in writing an adverbial clause but retains the relative pronoun of L (*quos*). Conceivably O read *syn that the whiche folk hir,* which would be much clearer.

Metrum 3 MS A² presents the material from *the forme* in m3.37 to *striven ayein* in pr5.44 in a series of disordered blocks: pr4.82 *ne scholde*–182 *ben;* m3.37 *the forme*–pr4.82 *bytiden;* m4.55–56 *the speces*–pr5.44 *striven ayein;* m4.9 *thingis*–55 *moevyngis;* pr4.181 *that*–m4.8 *sensible.* The correct order resumes at pr5.44 *resonynge.* A²'s exemplar probably had two consecutive quires that had been folded backwards.

Prosa 4 *24–25 resoun] *resouns* O'; but *racionem* L, *raison* F; cf. the singular forms in 26–27, 27, 29.
*79 troweden] *trowen* O'; but *quasi . . . credamus* L, *aussi comme se nous cuidons* F.

*176 as] *al* O'; but *quasi* L, *aussi comme* F. A frequent scribal error, caused by confusing *l* with long upright *s.*
*189 o] *a* O'; but *uno* L, *un seul* F. See m2.11.

Metrum 4 26 ymages] Perhaps *ymages of thynges* in O; cf. *rerum* L, *des chosez* F.
52 hurteleth] B β only; *hurteth* γ (cf. *heurte* F); *hurleth* H θ. In the sense "dash against," Chaucer uses *hurtelen* on three other occasions (2.pr1.27; KnT I.2616; LGW 638) and never uses *hurten* except in the sense "injure."

Prosa 5 36 oonly] Perhaps *oonly to* in O; cf. *sola diuini* L, *seule . . . de* F, and 35 *oonly to the lynage,* to which this phrase should be parallel.
93 ryghtfull] Perhaps *ryght ryghtfull* in O, the normal translation of superlatives such as *iustissimum* L, *tres droituriere* F.
95–97 yif . . . us] Perhaps *Yif that we mowen, as enhaunse we us* (*as who seith that, if that we mowen, I conseile that we enhaunse us*) in O; cf. *si possumus erigamur* L, *se nous poons eslevons nous* F. To follow O', one must make 97 *we enhaunse us* part of the text yet grammatically dependent on the extratextual gloss. Between *mowen* and the gloss the sense requires a clause that means "let us elevate ourselves." Thus we suggest that Chaucer may have written *as enhaunse we us,* lost by eyeskip, and that the point of the gloss was to explain that rather colloquial exhortation with the plainer *I conseil that we enhaunse us.* Or perhaps the lost clause had, not *enhaunse,* but a slightly strange verb such as *elevate* or *erect.* In that case, the gloss would both specify the exhortation as Philosophy's counsel and replace the strange verb with *enhaunse.*

Metrum 5 Rubric terras] *figuris* γ ι Lid Rob; arguably a more lengthy citation, *terras animalia permeant figuris* (as B), has been shortened.
3 dust and] Perhaps *dust and meven hem to gon by the strengthe of hir brest and* in O; cf. *vi pectoris insita* (trad. *incitata*) L, *et s'esmeuvent a aler par la force de leur piz* F.

Prosa 6 *72 fro] *for* O'; but *ex* L, *de* F.
*74 and] Om. O'; but *et de* L.
*75 God] *God and* O'; the conjunction is unparalleled in L F and apparently misplaced from the preceding line.
124 sighte] Perhaps *lighte* in O; cf. *lumine* L. The reading may have been influenced by *yseyn* in 123 and *sighte* in 126. But *sighte* is a reasonable translation; cf. 5.m3.14 *lookynge* or 1.pr1.47 *eighen.*
134 this] Perhaps *this youre* in O; cf. *vestro hoc* L, *ycestui vostre* F.
196 have] P fol. 73, a fragmentary portion of the remaining text, begins (it ends at 262 *prescience* and lacks some readings in a large tear).
266 No] Liddell adds *quod I No;* cf. *Non. Certez non* F. But in L, Philosophy simply answers the putative objection herself, and Chaucer follows L T, merely adding *quod she* (om. B ι; *quod I* C² Rob). Chaucer realized that a negative answer from Boethius is wrong, since Philosophy has imagined him making an objection to which, had he made it, he would have expected the answer "yes." Cf. *soluit istam dubitacionem dicens "minime"* T.

Additional corrections of C¹:

Prosa 1 33 is] *is a* C¹ Lid Rob. **46** ne meneden] Om. α; *ne moeueden* ι. **54** it] Om. γ Lid Rob. **62**

Aristotle] *Aristotitle.* **86** undirstoden] *vndirstonden* C¹ ε Cx ι. **89** had] *þ¹ had.*

Metrum 1 **Rubric** Achemenie] *Aclemenie* γ; *achemenis* H; *achemenee* θ. **4** in] *into.* **7** if] Om.

Prosa 2 **8** Yis] *s* cancelled. **27** hem] *hym* γ. the] Om. C¹ B Cx.

Metrum 2 **Rubric** Puro] *Purum; Puto* A². **13** schollen] *scholden* γ H.

Prosa 3 **8** yif] *yif it* C¹ Lid Rob. **34** that¹] Om. C¹ B. **63** ne] Om. C¹ Lid Rob. **72** may] Om. semblable] *semblabe.* **76** yit] Om. α Lid Rob. **77** it] Om. **83** it] *it it.* wel] *wil.* **96** it] Om. C¹ H. **98** iwyste] *þ¹ I wyste* C¹ ε C² Lid Rob. **110** ne] Om. C¹ Lid Rob. **111** nat] Om. γ ι Lid Rob. than] *than than.* **135** ne] Om. C¹ ε Cx Lid Rob. **140** nis] *is* γ. **142** right] Om. **153** that¹] *this* C¹ B Th Lid Rob. **169** hem] Om. **171** ne¹] Om. **190** whiche] *þe whiche* C¹ Lid Rob.

Metrum 3 **5** two] *to.* **29–31** What² . . . right] Om. (marked for correction, but uncorrected). **33** ne] Om. γ B Lid Rob.

Prosa 4 **rubric** Tum] *Tunc; Tamen* A² ι. **8** and] *ne* C¹ Lid Rob. **29** ne] Om. γ Lid Rob. **30** that] *þ¹ the* γ. **42** the] Om. **44** posicioun] *possessioun* C¹ B β; *posessyoun and petissyoun* A². **67** ne²] Om. **72** thing] *thingis.* **73** isusteyned] *is susteyned.* **80** tho] *the* γ θ. **88** the] Om. and] *or* γ Rob. **100** men] *me* γ. **110** althoughe] *thoughe.* **121** that¹]

Om. C¹ Sal Lid Rob. **130** scholde deme] *schol/deme.* **162** of] *of þe* C¹ B Lid Rob. **173** ne²] Om. γ Lid Rob. **183** tho] *the* γ Rob². **193** ymaginacioun] *ymacon.* **195** diffynyscheth] *diffynys/scheth.* **198** nis] *is* γ Lid Rob. **212** or] *or of* C¹ ι. **213** so] Om.

Metrum 4 **5–6** that hyghten] Om. **6** Stoycienis] *stocyenis.* **7** sensibilities] *sensualities.* **11** the] Om. C¹ Lid Rob. **12** nakid] *makid* C¹ Sal. **18** smothnesse] *smothnesses.* **22** thryvynge] *vnthryuynge; thyving* A². **35** chesith] *chasith.*

Prosa 5 **2** the] Om. γ. **3** the] Om. C¹ Lid Rob. **25** and] *and to* C¹ θ Rob. **26** the²] Om. γ B. **32** to] *to þe.* **42** subjectz] *subject* C¹ B Lid Rob. **47** that³] Om. γ H θ Sal. **91** ymaginacioun] *ymacon.* **99** that²] Om. γ H.

Metrum 5 **1** be] *ben.* **13** walken] *walwen* C¹ ε; *wake* Sal.

Prosa 6 **12** that] Om. **18** fro] *fro the.* **19** into] *into the.* **23** hath] *hat.* **26** in] Om. γ ε. **32** no] *nat.* **45** it] *yit it* C¹ Lid Rob. **70** inmoevable] *moeuable* γ; *vnmoeuable* C². **75** disencresith] *discresith* C¹ Cx Lid Rob. **94** ne] Om. C¹ Lid Rob. **110** thinken] *diffine* γ. **123** and] *or.* **139** shollen] *sholden* α. **150** thanne] Om. **157** that] Om. γ. **185** ne] Om. C¹ Lid Rob. **209** of²] Sal. **212** that] Om. C¹ H θ. **217** the¹] Om. α (−A² P). **242** power] *ppower.* **260** entrechaunge] *entrechaungynge* C¹ ι. **284** ne] Om. nawht] *nat* γ.

Troilus and Criseyde

Authorities: sixteen manuscript copies; those three early printed editions that, in whole or in part, are not derived from earlier editions or extant manuscripts; and a number of fragments, quotations of Troilus in other works, and early redactions of small segments of the poem. The major authorities are as follows. Manuscripts:

A   British Library, Additional 12044
Cl   Pierpont Morgan Library, M 817 (formerly Camp-sall Hall, Doncaster; Robinson's sigil Cm)
Cp   Corpus Christi College, Cambridge, 61
D   University Library, Durham, Cosin MS V.ii.13
Dg   Digby 181, Bodleian Library, Oxford
Gg   Cambridge University Library, Gg.4.27 (Skeat's sigil Cm)
H^1 Harley 2280, British Library
H^2 Harley 3943
H^3 Harley 1239
H^4 Harley 2392
H^5 Harley 4912
J   St. John's College, Cambridge, L.1
Ph   Huntington Library, HM 114 (formerly Phillips 8252, Cheltenham, misnumbered 8250 by Root and Robinson)
R   Rawlinson Poet. 163, Bodleian
S^1 Arch. Selden B.24, Bodleian
S^2 Arch. Selden Supra 56, Bodleian

Editions:

Cx   Caxton, ca. 1483
Th   Thynne, 1532
W   Wynkyn de Worde, 1517, independent of Cx only up to 1.546

The notes also record the decisions of eight modern editors: Baugh (Bgh); Donaldson (Don), 2nd ed., 1975; Fisher (Fsh); McCormick (Mck); Root (Rkr); Robinson (Rob), second edition; W. W. Skeat (Skt), Complete Works (Oxford Ch), vol. 2, 2nd ed., 1900; and B. A. Windeatt (Wdt), Tr & Criseyde, 1984.

The fragments and other early sources are listed and enumerated F1 to F16 in Mr. Windeatt's edition. None is of value in establishing the text, and they are ignored in the notes below. Root, in Textual Tradition (Text. Trad.), Ch. 1, described and listed in detail the gaps in the authorities, and Windeatt (68–76) updates the information. In the notes below, manuscripts that are *out* are not noticed. Manuscripts A, D, Gg, H^1 H^2, H^3, R lack one or more leaves; Dg is *out* after 3.532 and H^5 after 4.686.

The Chaucer Society printed transcripts of Cp J Cl H^1 H^2 H^3 Gg. Photographic facsimiles of pages from the sixteen manuscripts were printed by Root, MSS of Ch's Tr, Ch Soc. 1st ser. 98, 1914 for 1911. Root also edited Specimen Extracts of all the authorities (Ch Soc. 1st ser. 99, 1916 for 1912, repr. 1967). Facsimiles of three com-plete manuscripts, with excellent introductions, have been issued: J, edited by R. Beadle and J. Griffiths and published for the Variorum Chaucer (who also promise a facsimile of Cl), 1983; Gg, edited by M. B. Parkes and R. Beadle (Vol. 1: Tr, 1979; Vol. 3: Introduction, 1981); Cp, edited by M. B. Parkes and Elizabeth Salter, 1978. Facsimiles of Thynne were edited by Skeat (1905) and Brewer (1969). A plate (of Ch's PF) from Dg is described (and dated "probably in the last quarter of the fifteenth century") in M. B. Parkes, English Cursive Book Hands, 1969.

The present edition is based on microfilm and other photographic copies of all the authorities, supplemented by reference to printed editions and discussions of the text, primarily Root and Windeatt. The goal has been to adopt the forms of Robinson's text, which is sensible and intelligent, while reconsidering "from scratch" the readings. The entire text was collated in full, with admirable accuracy, by Ardath McKee (Books 1, 2, and 4) and Sister Margaret Jennings (Books 3 and 5) for Mr. Robert Pratt, who originally planned to edit the text for this edition. Much of the analysis of the variants and many decisions about authentic readings presented here were made by Pratt, with whose judgment I usually and inde-pendently concurred.

When work on this text was far advanced, Mr. Win-deatt's excellent edition appeared, the first to be based, like this edition, on complete and direct collations of all the authorities. Windeatt largely agrees with Robinson, Pratt, and me about the appropriate methods of establish-ing the text, and for that reason Windeatt's text and this one differ little in substantial matters.

The principal issues in establishing the text of Troilus were raised by Root, following McCormick: whether, by the classic techniques of recension, manuscript families and their hyparchetypes can be determined, and whether we have evidence in the manuscripts of Chaucer's revi-sion, with discernible early and late authentic Chaucerian readings. In Textual Tradition, Root fully expounded his hypothesis that three states of the text are distinguisha-ble: α (represented by the rather corrupt Ph and other authorities), γ (represented by Cp Cl H^1 S^2 Dg and other authorities), and β (represented by R Cx, and other manuscripts). Root argued that the complex intermin-glings of readings from these three Chaucerian states of the text resulted from a hypothetical draft or two that Chaucer revised and from which copies were made over a period of time. He further argued (and in this he is supported, unpersuasively, by Cook, ChR 9, 1974, 51–62) that the β version is Chaucer's final version.

In fact, the obviously conflated readings of the manu-scripts present a situation so complex as to cast doubt on this entire hypothesis. Windeatt, later confirmed by Hanna, in the articles cited below, persuasively under-mined Root's argument. There is good evidence, espe-cially in Book 1, that we have two Chaucerian readings in some lines: Ph and its allies present a reading closer to the Italian source, and other manuscripts, generally more reliable, present a reading in no way differing from Chaucer's best usage. The abundant inconsistency and crossover of allegiance among the apparent groupings of

The textual notes to *Troilus and Criseyde* were prepared by Stephen A. Barney.

manuscripts, however, so much reduce the confidence we can place in recension and hypothetical authorial versions that in particular cases the fundamental principles of textual criticism—the exploitation of our knowledge of the author's general usage and the discovery of which reading (usually the more difficult according to the principle of *durior lectio*) most likely caused the others—will prevail. Editors generally agree in fact on the readings, whatever their hypotheses. Root follows J more often than does Windeatt, Robinson, or I, and Donaldson sometimes follows Cp or other manuscripts in very hard readings, but neither editor greatly alters the character of the text in doing so. For full discussion, see Root's fundamental Textual Tradition, his edition, Windeatt's edition, and Windeatt, in Essays on Tr, ed. M. Salu, 1979, 1–22; Windeatt, Poetica (Tokyo) 8, 1977, 44–60; Brewer, in Med. Sts. for J. A. W. Bennett, 1981, 121–38; Brewer, Poetica 12, 1981, 36–44; Cook, ChR 9, 1974–75, 51–62; Hanna, pp. 191–205, 285–89 (on Root), and Reinecke, pp. 230–51, 291–93 (on Robinson), in Editing Ch, ed. P. G. Ruggiers, 1984. Often cited in these notes is Kittredge, Observations on the Lang. of Ch's Tr, Ch Soc. 2nd ser. 28, 1894.

The text here presented, like Robinson's (and Donaldson's, Baugh's, and Windeatt's) is based on Cp. When Cp is rejected or deficient, this edition prints the readings of Cl or J, in that order. I have been slightly more conservative of Cp's forms than Robinson, but I have generally treated the spelling of the text as he did, altering some odd (*commeth*) or misleading (*on* for *oon*) spellings of Cp and suppressing (and occasionally adding) final *-e* in accordance with Chaucer's usage, especially when its pronunciation would affect the meter. It should be remembered that the scribes (and for all we know, Chaucer himself) did not mean for *-e* invariably to represent a sounded vowel or to display historically grammatical endings; the inclusion or omission of *-e* here is an editorial device intended to help readers grasp the grammar and meter. The availability of the facsimile of Cp makes any "diplomatic" transcription pointless. Perfect consistency in this editorial device is impossible and would be unhelpful. Many words sometimes had a sounded *-e*, sometimes not. The words *oure, hire/here* (pronoun), *here* (adverb), *youre,* and (plural) *thise,* rarely or never disyllabic, have been left with the *-e* written by Cp and other scribes. Cp often adds an otiose *-e* (sometimes doubling the final consonant) to such words as *wel, al, gret, frend, blynd, desir, lok, at, bet, wol, ded, out, virtu, hath, both, ech, tel* (some of these words sometimes require the form with *-e: alle, grete, atte* "at the," *bothe*). I have brought Robinson's punctuation into accord with lighter modern usage, particularly attending to places where the sense may be affected.

What follow are textual notes (not full reports of variants) meant to illustrate some of the remarkable variant readings and especially to explain the choice of readings here adopted. The notes are highly selective; many thousands of variants are not recorded.

In a note the citation of the authorities and the eight editors is complete, except for the (usually inconsequential) authorities that are *out,* which are not listed. Normally, then, manuscript or editors' sigils *not* listed agree with the lemma. Sometimes, as in 1.85, the authorities or editors that support a lemma are listed and the others are included under such terms as *rest* (for the authorities) or *all other editors.* For clarity, all the authorities are occasionally listed, especially where several groups are fairly evenly divided, as in 1.164, or where the array of variants is complex, as in 1.167. The order of sigils, Cp J Cl R H⁴ H¹ A D S² Dg S¹ H³ H² Ph Gg H⁵, is arbitrary. The printed authorities, Cx W Th, and the modern editors, Skt Mck Rkr Rob Bgh Don Fsh Wdt, are arranged chronologically.

In the explanatory comments, a statement such as "R + conceivably original" means "the reading represented by R and the authorities that agree with R may be the authentic (or an authentic) Chaucerian reading." I have tried to keep in mind that what Chaucer meant to write, what he wrote, and what the archetype of all the extant manuscripts reads are three different things. By a Lydgatian line I mean one in which two clearly stressed syllables in midline adjoin, contrary to an iambic rhythm and doubtfully within Chaucer's metrical practice.

Larry D. Benson and C. David Benson gave a meticulous and helpful review of these notes, for which I am in their debt. I owe great thanks to Stella Griffin, Kevin McGuirk, and Douglas Bradley for their help with this work.

BOOK I

20 Unto] *To* Cp H⁴ H³ H² Ph Cx W Th Skt Rob Bgh Don Wdt. Scribes were unlikely to change *To* to *Unto.* Readable as *Unt' any* (so Mck).

41 So] *To* Cp R A H² Skt Don; *He* W. *So* is less obvious.

60 neigh] *wel* J R H³ H² H⁵ Cx Mck Rkr. J+ is bland but could be construed as more accurate historically.

61 And¹] Om. Cp W Don.

and²] *and in* Cp R H⁴ H² Ph Don.

oon] Om. Ph. Possibly a headless original. Cf. Root, Text. Trad., 38.

83 In trust that he hath] *Hopyng in hym* H⁴ H² Ph W. H⁴+ is closer to the Italian (*Da lui sperando*) and the French (*pour ce que ilz esperoient de lui avoir*) and thus is perhaps a prior version.

85 Gret rumour gan] H² H⁴; *Grete rumour was* Ph; *The noise a roos* H⁵; *Grete noyse began* W; *Great rumour rose* Th; *Noyse up roos* Cx; *The noise up rose* rest and all eds. H²+ is closer to the Italian (*Fu ['l] romor grande*) and French (*Tresgrant rumeur fut*). The variant of Cp+ is well supported and may be a Chaucerian revision, as editors have taken it (but see Brewer, Poetica 12, 126–28). This variant, if scribal, imitates KnT 2660 and Tr 4.183. In 5.53 Chaucer uses *rumour* for the Italian *devisa* (fray), French *debat.* The French text at that place has the word *rumeur* a few lines above (p. 243). The first uses of *rumor* in English may have been in Chaucer's Boece; a minim confusion (like *riiiiior*) in an unfamiliar word may have elicited scribal substitution. Chaucer certainly wrote what is in H²+; he may also have written what is in Cp+.

99 al right] *a right* Cp H² Cx Th Skt Don; *fulle r.* S² Dg H⁵; *right* R. The weakly attested *a-right* is a suspiciously common rhyme in Chaucer. R is possible.

104 doth] *is* J R H³ Gg H⁵ Mck Rkr. (Cx Th vary.)

J+ is what Root termed a β version reading but is more likely an easier scribal substitution than Chaucerian.

111 H⁴ H² Ph W read *With chier and vois ful pitous and wepyng* (W *With clere voyce*), clearly inferior but closer to the Italian: *E con vece e con vista assai pietosa.*

118 Forth with meschaunce] *To sory hap* H⁴ H² Ph W. Windeatt observes that here the reading of Ph+ is more remote from the Italian *con la ria ventura.*

139 And under eft (*under eft* by a later hand on an erasure in J)] *Now up now down* Cp Don Fsh; *And wonder ofte* Cl A D S² Dg; *Right wondir ofte* H⁴; *And eyther oft* Gg. Perhaps Cp avoids the poor sense of the easy misreading in Cl+ and creatively supplies a Chaucerian tag (from KnT I.1533; see Whiting N179).

143 For] *For why* H⁴ S¹ H² Ph W.

were] *were here* J H³ Gg Cx and all eds.; *were right* R. A headless line that scribes "corrected" by adding *why, here,* or *right.*

164 Palladions] R H³ Gg H⁵ Th; *Palladion the* Cp Cl H¹ A D S² Dg S¹ Skt Rob Bgh Don Fsh Wdt; *Palladion* J Cx Mck Rkr. (W varies.) The reading of Cp+ is easier, and that of R+ more metrical. Cf. 1.1074 and n. below for another suspect stressed *the,* and cf. BD 1098. Servyce is rarely stressed on the first syllable—see 3.992 and note 1.315 below—and never unambiguously in rhyme. Herknen of is rare but attested at MerT IV.1699 (see Davis, Ch Glossary; MED *herkenen* 1b [a]). The ancestor of J and Cx probably read with R; the hard grammar was solved differently (it is unlikely that J+'s *Palladion* is a genitive in light of the metrical *Palladiones* in 1.161).

167 both meeste mene and leste] Rob, no MS (*moeste* Wdt); *b. moeste* (*o* written over an *e*) *meyne a. l.* Cp; *b. moste menne a. l.* D; *bothe meene meste a. l.* Cl; *bothe most mene a. l.* S¹; *the moost meyne a. l.* Ph; *the meste mene a. i.* H⁴; *bothe most meyne a. l.* H¹; *bothe the meste and the leste* J; *bothe most and lesse leste* R; *both most(e) a. l.* S² Dg Th; *bothe mest(e) a. l.* A Gg H⁵ Cx Skt Mck Rkr Bgh Fsh; *bothe tho moste a. l.* H³; *the moost and eke the l.* H² W; *bothe the moste a. l.* Don. It is hard to see why an original like *bothe meste and leste* would elicit the variants. All the words *bothe, meste, mene,* and *meyne* can be disyllabic; in Chaucer, *mene* (in this sense) and *meyne* always are disyllabic in unambiguous cases. Of these, *mene* is probably harder: *meyne* had occurred forty lines before; the context suggests a courtly company. *Bothe* might seem to (but does not in Chaucer) require a pair rather than a series of three. Chaucer avoids concluding a line with *bothe meste and leste* at Tr 5.440, KnT I.2198, LGW 2303. Root did not think of *mene* as meaning "middling" (Text. Trad., 44).

169 Among thise othere] *A. the which* H⁴ H² Ph W. H⁴+ is closer to the Italian (*Tra' quali*—or in Pernicone's ed., *Tra li qua*) and the French (*Entre lesquelles*).

195 seye] *seyde* Cp D S² Dg Gg Cx Don. Cp+ is possible but weakly attested.

253 Now] *And* Cp H¹ Don; *And now* S²; *A now* Dg. An ancestor of Cp H¹ may have read *And now,* which they "corrected" for meter, losing the logical force of *Now.*

261 Of] *As of* J R H⁴ H³ H² Ph Cx W Th and all eds. A headless line.

297 herte] *hertes* J Cl H¹ S² Dg S¹ H³ H² Ph Th and all eds. but Don. In Cp+, the rarer genitive (or compounding) form is supported by *herte-blod, herte-spoon,* and certainly by *herte roote* (ProWBT III.471, LGW

1993); but at 2.535 only A reads *herte botme.* See 3.1131 and n. below; Kittredge, Observations, 99; Kerkhof, Sts. in the Lang. of G. Ch., 2nd ed., 1982, 213.

314 thing] *thinges* Cp H⁴ S² Dg H³ W Don. The old plural without *-es* was probably harder in the fifteenth century; Cp+ is unmetrical.

his look som tyme] Cp Cl H¹ A; *s. t. h. l.* rest. Cp+ is preferred only because such simple transpositions are usually indiscriminable.

315 eft] *ofte* Cp H⁴ H¹ A H² Ph Don. Better sense.

that] Cp J H¹ Gg (W: *the while that*) Skt Mck Rkr; *the* Dg H⁵ Cx; *that the* rest and Rob Bgh Don Fsh Wdt. Cl+ perhaps emends for meter, wrongly stressing *servyse* on its first syllable (as only once elsewhere in Tr, at 3.992). Chaucer deliberately emphasizes *that.*

324 his] *the* J H⁴ H³ H² Ph Gg H⁵ W Mck Rkr. The Italian (*al palagio*) and French (*au palais*) seem to support J+, but to translate a Romance article with an English personal pronoun is common enough.

332 serveth] *serve(n)* Cp S² Dg W Don. In Cp+, the plural verb is conceivable, but more likely *serveth* accords with the singular *Hym* in 333.

338 sely fewe] Cp Cl H¹ H² Ph W Th Skt Rob Bgh Fsh Wdt; *sely feyre* Cx; *f. s.* rest and Mck Rkr Don. Cp+ has the less common word order.

363 a-temple] Cl Skt Rob Bgh Fsh; *and temple* Cp J H¹ A S¹ H³ Gg W Th Rkr Don Wdt; *at t.* R; *in t.* H⁴ H⁵ Mck; *in the t.* S² Dg H² Ph H⁵ (H⁵ added *the* interlinearly); *temple* Cx. Cl's hard reading readily explains the other variants. Cp+'s *and* oddly intrudes a vision of the setting between visions of her. The temple is not mentioned here in the Italian.

371 servantz] Cp J Cl; *servance* H³; *servantes* rest and Rkr Rob Wdt. Chaucer often has disyllabic *ellis; servant(e)s* is never unambiguously accented on the second syllable.

420 hote . . . hote] Cp S² Dg Don; *hote . . . hete* H¹; *heate . . . heate* Th; *hete . . . hete* rest. Cl+ is well attested, and H¹, making the clearest sense, could be authentic, but Donaldson's preference for Cp+, perhaps the hardest reading, is corroborated by the use of *hot* as a noun in PF 205 (see MED *hot* n.).

432 I here] Cp S² Dg H⁵ Cx; *here I* rest and Skt Mck Rkr Fsh. The original is indeterminable.

436 wherfro] *the wherfro* Cl J S¹ Rkr Rob Bgh Don Fsh Wdt; *ye w.* H¹ H⁵; *fro the wheche* A W; *wherefrom* Gg Cx. Disyllabic *love* (noun) is hard but possible (Tr 1.27, 1.421, 2.500, 546, 891, 922), or these lines may be Lydgatian or corrupt. See Kittredge, Observations, 14.

442 by] *fro* J R H⁴ H² Ph H⁵ Th W Mck Rkr; *from* Gg Cx. J+ is apparently not Middle English idiom (MED cites only this place for *dai fro dai*): perhaps an original "from day to day" (Italian *di giorno in giorno;* cf. 1.482) was corrupted.

455 were] Cp J H¹ D S¹ H² Gg Rkr Don Wdt; *was* rest. Cl+ may be "correcting" the grammar.

458 serve I] *I serve* A S² Dg Gg H⁵ Th; *to serve I* D (*whom to serven I laboure* Mck).

and] Cl R A Gg H⁵ Th W; *in* Dg S²; om. rest and McK Rkr. The editors' (and D's) emendations are tempting, but Cl+ makes good sense and meter. *Serve* (meaning "act as servant") followed by a *to* phrase occurs also at Bo 1.pr4.261, but it is rare enough to confuse scribes and editors (see OED *serve* v.¹ I.9).

465 fownes] *fewnes* Cp; *foules* D; *fode no(r)* S² Dg; *fantasie* H² Ph; *sownes* H⁴ Mck; om. H⁵.

466 his] *this* Cl H¹ D S¹ H² Ph W Skt Rob Bgh Fsh. Cp+, less obvious, emphasizes the authorship of the *conclusioun*. In line 480, all the authorities agree on *this*.

483 That] *T. all(e)* R H⁴ H² Ph W Skt Mck. A headless line, and R+ is more remote from the Italian *che li Greci* (French: *que les gens*).

496 it that] *it as that* J R H⁴ H⁵ W and all eds.; *it as* H² Ph. A Lydgatian line, unpopular with five authorities.

517 thanked] Cp J R H¹ S¹ Mck Rkr Don; *thankyth* H⁵; *thank* S² Dg; *thonked be* Cl H⁴ A D H² Ph Gg Cx W Th Skt Rob Bgh Fsh Wdt. The elision of *be* in this expression is unparalleled elsewhere in Chaucer (though found in variants at Tr 3.1400), but the rough meter with *be* is also unparalleled (though found in variants at ProWBT III.5). A headless reading "Now thank God," following the clue of S² Dg, is tempting, but "thank God" seems not to be a Chaucerian expression. H⁵ also is possible.

539 more thing] *no thing more* J H⁴ H² Ph Gg Cx W Mck Rkr (with other variants). Disyllabic *more*, though more frequent in Tr than monosyllabic, may have elicited the variants.

540 to] *mo* R H⁴ H² Ph H⁵ Th W Mck. Clearly *to* is better attested and less obvious, but whether its meaning "in addition," not standing before an adjective, is Chaucerian usage is not certain; cf. 3.194. OED lists a few Middle English examples. Skeat, troubled by the *to / wo* rhyme, with its close and open *o*, recommended *mo* here (Rime-Index Tr, Ch Soc. 1st ser. 84, 1892, 15, n.34), but accepted *to* in his edition, perhaps conscious of other off-rhymes or of the possibility that *wo*'s *w* could close its *o*.

563 angre] Cp H⁴ Don; *maugry* A; *hys angre* Cx Th; *an angre* rest, all eds. except Don. As headless, Cp H⁴ is harder; *an* was supplied (by dittography?) for meter. If Rom 3185 is Chaucer's, it would be his only use of *anger* with an article, but Kerkhof (Sts. in the Lang. of G. Ch., 2nd ed., 1982, 365–66) gives many instances of Chaucer's use of *a(n)* with such words as *envye, ire, peyne, sorwe, wo*—perhaps Cl+ is right.

wo to] *wo* Cl; *sorwe* J H⁴ H² Ph Gg H⁵ Cx Th Skt Mck Rkr; *evelle to* S² Dg. Cl+ seems metrically too hard, but perhaps it is original and elicited Cp+ *vs.* S² Dg. J+ is also possible.

568 or] *and* Cp Don. With the singular verb, Cp is perhaps harder, but poorly attested.

589 wol] *wolde* D Dg Mck; *wold* S²; *wyl* Cx; *wole* Cl R A S¹ Skt Fsh; *wele* Gg. A headless line, but it is tempting to conjecture an original *wol departen*, redividing D and Dg; cf. 1.960. Disyllabic *wole* isn't Chaucer's usage.

614 folwen] *fallen* Cp R H⁴ S² Dg Gg H⁵ Don. Cl+ agrees with the Italian, *seguire*.

640 may ben inly glad] *wot(e) what gladnesse is* J H⁴ H² Ph Gg H⁵ Th Mck. J+ is probably easier and may revert to the proverbial phrasing if Whiting's one citation of the proverb outside of Tr (M236) represents the common saying.

649 Ek] *And ek* J R H⁴ H³ H² Ph Gg H⁵ Cx Th Wdt; *Also* S² Dg. With regular elision of *ne aughte* (J has *noughte*), Cp+ produces a headless line, which scribes "improved."

681 And] *But* Cp S² Dg Don. Adversative is not required.

plat] *plat now* J R H⁴ H³ Cx Mck Rkr Rob Bgh Don Wdt.

th'enchesoun] *thyn enchesoun* Cl S² Dg Th Skt Fsh; *thy sorowe sone* H⁵; *thyn entencioun* Gg; *enchesoun* H⁴. The weakly attested *now* and *thyn* (the latter of poor sense and usage) appear to be scribal "improvements" on a Lydgatian, purposefully "plat" line. Cf. the clashing stresses in (hendecasyllabic) 680.

682 final] *finally* Cp J Cl H¹ A D S¹ H³ Gg Rkr; *the ffynelle* S² Dg H⁵. Cp+'s well supported reading, with less smooth meter, may be right: *finally* can mean "really" in Middle English. But the surrounding vocabulary is playfully legalistic and learned, and the philosopher's "final cause," perhaps unfamiliar to the scribes, is apt.

690 For] *For for* J H⁴ H¹ Gg Skt Mck Rob Bgh Fsh Wdt. A headless line, but *For for* may seem harder.

720 sith] *seist* J R H⁴ H³ H² Ph Gg H⁵ Cx Mck Rkr Rob Bgh Wdt; *sithen* Cl Fsh; *sen* S² Dg. Pandarus does not question Troilus's trust; the repetition of *sith* adds emphasis. But Cp+ may be easier, and Pandarus could be exaggerating Troilus's confidence, expressed in line 601.

726 he] Om. Cp S² Dg Don. Cp+ is perhaps right, but weakly attested.

747 a] Om. H⁴ H³ H² Ph Cx Th Skt Mck Don. The weakly attested H⁴+ is harder, has smoother meter, and is perhaps right. The usage with *craft* is unparalleled elsewhere in Chaucer or MED, but Chaucer does license the omission of the expected article on occasion (see Kerkhof, Sts. in the Lang. of G. Ch., 2nd ed, 1982, 372). Perhaps *it is* is to be pronounced *it's* or *'tis*: cf. the common *this* for *this is* (see Kittredge, Observations, 387).

761 quod] *quod tho* Cl H⁴ H¹ A D S¹ Skt Mck Rob Bgh Fsh Wdt. A headless line; the syllable count is "improved" but the meter worsened by *tho*.

767 Dorstestow] Cl R H¹ S¹ Gg Skt Mck Rob Fsh; *Dorst thow* J H⁴ D Dg H³ H⁵ Don; *Durste thow* Cp S² Cx Th Rkr Bgh Wdt; *Dorestow* A; *Trist thow* H² Ph.

tolde] *telle* Cl Fsh; *t. it* R A D S¹ H² Ph Cx Th; *t. her(e)* H⁴ H³ Mck. *t. hyr(e)* Gg H⁵ Rob Skt Bgh. *Dorstestow* is Chaucer's grammar; *tolde hit* is pleonastic, a scribal "improvement" of an already metrical line; *tolde hyre* is possible but weakly attested.

808 quyte it] J R H⁴ H² Ph Gg H⁵ Cx Th; *q. so* S¹; *quit the* H³; *quyte* rest and Skt Don Fsh. The verb *quyte* is regularly transitive in Chaucer, and the clause *that . . . fele* gives unsatisfactory sense as an object. Cp+ may be the exception but more likely omits *it* under the influence of the apparent parallel with 807.

820 Of] *And of* J R H⁴ H³ H² Gg H⁵ Th Mck Rkr Bgh Don Fsh Wdt. A headless line.

883 Ne nevere saugh] *Ny n. s.* J H¹ S¹ Mck Rkr Wdt; *Ne n. s.* I R H⁴ D H⁵ Fsh; *Ne n. man s.* A; *For n. s. I* S²; *For e n. s. I* Dg; *Ne I n. s.* H² Ph Skt Rob Bgh; *Ne n. ne s.* Gg; *Never sawe (I none)* Cx. As Cp+ and Donaldson realized, line 882 provides the subject of *saugh.* Cf. 3.1619 and 4.1219; and on such ellipses see Roscow, Syntax and Style, 85, and Kerkhof, Sts. in the Lang. of G. Ch., 2nd ed., 1982, 240–4.

884 n'a] Cp Mck Rob Bgh Wdt; *ne a* Cl Th Skt Fsh; *non* Gg; *ne* rest and Rkr Don. Cl Th and Cp are practically the same. It is hard to say whether Cp or J+ is harder, but in the next line J H¹ (and H⁴ H³ H² Ph) move from *ne* to the probably original *na.* Scribes often wrote the later members of a parallel series correctly without returning to correct the earlier members.

885   **n'a more]** *ne m.* R A D S² S¹ H⁵ Cx Th; *ne a m.* H⁴ H³ H² Ph Skt Fsh; *nor m.* Dg; *ne non m.* Gg. See preceding note.

886   **to²]** Om. Cp Don. Disyllabic *nede* is possible (see 3.1142 and probably 2.1553) but rare.

890–96   This stanza is found only in H⁴ H² Ph Th (and all eds.). The text follows H²; except that H² Ph om. *noht but* in 894 and *a* in 895. The *-e* in *oghte* (896) is editorial. Chaucer may have canceled the stanza in revision; it seems to intrude into Pandarus's argument (as it intrudes between stanzas drawn, much altered, from the Filostrato).

904   **evere that]** *ever* Cl R H⁴ D S² Dg H² Ph H⁵ Cx Th Skt Mck Fsh. Cl+ attempts to smooth meter, but *ever(e)* is more often slurred to a monosyllable before a consonant than pronounced as two syllables before a vowel (see Kittredge, Observations, 206–8).

914   **mucche]** *monche(n)* H² H⁴ Ph Th Skt Mck; *meche* A; *frete meche* Gg; *frete* H⁵. A gloss seems to intrude into Gg and H⁵, suggesting that *mucche / meche* was difficult. MED records *mucche,* but not *monche,* as occurring before Chaucer.

918   **hym]** *hem* J H² Ph Gg H⁵ Cx Th Skt Mck Rob Bgh Fsh Wdt; *tham* S² Dg S¹. The plural pronoun is possible, but *hym* is harder in the immediate context, and the singular *som* is supported by the preceding *som* in 916.

939   **Pandare]** *Pandarus* Cp J Cl H¹ A S² Dg Gg Rkr Fsh. The meter is rough in either case.

960   **departed]** *parted* J R H⁴ H² Ph Gg Cx and all eds. but Fsh. Some scribes "regularized" the meter. See Rom 2367–68.

976   **wyse]** *old(e)* R H⁴ H² Ph Mck; om. H³ Gg Cx. Root, Text. Trad., 53, thinks *wyse lered* tautological, but in his edition he followed the less bland, better attested reading in Cp+.

983   **sit hire]** *sit it* Cp Don; *sittis* S² Dg. An ancestor of Cp S² Dg probably omitted *hire. It sit it* is not used elsewhere by Chaucer.

1001   **to greve]** *greve* H⁴ H³ H² Ph Gg Th Rkr Don; *ay greve* J R S¹ Mck. H⁴+, metrically hard, was perhaps "corrected" by Cp+ and J+, but the meter seems too hard to be Chaucerian. Root improbably takes *moste* as a verb.

1002   **wise]** *grete* J R H⁴ H³ H² Ph Gg Cx Th Mck Rkr; om. A. J+ is tempting; cf. 1.976.

1006   **Thanne arn thise]** Cp Dg Don; *They are the* H² Ph; *Thanne ern they* J Cl R H¹ A S¹ Gg and all eds. except Don; *Than erthen* H⁴; *Then arn thi* D; *T. er this* S²; *T. ar thoo* H³. Cp+ (perhaps by way of S²) or H² Ph could have elicited the variants; Cp+ is slightly harder.

1047   **parde]** *Pandare* Cp Don. Cp misreads or "improves" on Chaucer, worsening the meter but avoiding "by God, God . . . ."

1050   **that]** Om. J R H⁴ H² Ph H⁵ Cx Mck Rkr. As *m'athenketh* is regularly disyllabic, Cp+'s meter is good.

1064   **place]** *space* R H⁴ H³ H² Ph H⁵ Mck Rkr Fsh. MS witness alone decides for Cp+.

1074   **tho]** *the* J R H⁴ D S² Dg H² H⁵ Cx Th Mck Rkr Rob Bgh Don Wdt; *as a* Ph; om. A. Chaucer sometimes has *leoun* without an article (KnT I.1598, LGW 627); in Tr 5.830, two MSS supply *a.* Cp+ is harder and continues emphasis on that particular time from 1072 to 1076.

Metrically stressed *the* is in any case suspect (see note 1.164 above).

1075   **a-day]** Cp J H¹ S¹ Mck Rkr Rob Bgh Don Wdt; *that day* rest. Cp+, the harder reading, gives a better sense of continuing action.

BOOK II

86   **youre book and all the]** Dg Cx Th; *al y. fayre b. and al the faire* Cp; *y. f. b. and al the* D S¹ Fsh; *al y. b. and al the* J S² H³ H² Ph Gg Skt Mck Rkr Bgh Don Wdt; *al y. f. b. and al the* Cl H¹; *al y. b. and eek the* R; *al y. bokes and y.* H⁴; *all y. b. and all youre* H⁵; *al the f. b. and your* A; *al y. f. b. and* Rob. A classic instance of scribal "correction" of a headless line by addition of monosyllables: *al* (from later in the line) and *fayr(e)* (invented). Cp ends up with a heptameter.

110   **barbe and]** *wympel and* J Gg H⁵ Cx Rkr; *wympill* R H³. More probably *wympel* is a scribal gloss of *barbe* than the reverse.

115   H⁴ H² Ph Gg H⁵ read *Ye make me bi Joves sore adrad*—possibly Chaucer's earlier draft.

143   **tyme that]** *tid* H⁴; *tyde that* Gg; *time* R Cx. In Tr, *tyme* is monosyllabic, if at all, in only one other line (see note 2.1211 below), but often enough elsewhere in Chaucer. The original here may be *tid that* or, with R Cx, *time.* See Kittredge, Observations, 3–4.

192   **He myghte]** Cp Cl H¹ A D S¹ Th; *Myghte* rest and Mck Rkr. J+ was troubled by the redundant pronoun, well within Chaucer's usage—or possibly Cp+ "corrects" a headless line.

194   **for]** Cp J D H³ Mck Don; *fro(m)* rest. The slightly harder reading printed here also avoids elision.

199   **hem . . . hem]** Cp H¹ H³ H⁵ Skt Don; *hem . . . hym* Th; *hym . . . hym* rest. Either the singular or the plural reading is plausible.

220   **tyme is that]** S² Dg S¹ Th; *is tyme that* H⁴ Ph; *is tyme* Cp J Cl H¹ A D Cx Rkr; *is it tyme* H³ H² Gg and all eds. but Rkr; *is it tyme that* H⁵. A transposition as in H⁴ Ph, making poor meter, could have caused the variants. H³+ is possible, but S²+ is a common Chaucerian expression (see 3.208, 4.517, 4.1687).

247   **I love moost]** *I m. l.* Cl H⁴ (H⁴: *leve*) H³ H² Gg H⁵ Skt Mck Rkr Wdt; *m. I l.* Fsh. Cp+ is better attested.

262   **peynte]** *poynte* Cp Cl H¹ Don Fsh; *poynthit* H⁵; *paynt* Th. Cp+ may be right: *poynte* is required by rhyme at 3.497, but even there Gg writes *peynte,* suggesting that *poynten,* meaning "to punctuate (rhetorically)" and hence "to describe" is harder than *peynten,* probably meaning "to provide with the 'colors' of rhetoric." Confirming the better witness of *peynte* is 2.424, where Criseyde seems to refer back to this line: there one MS, H⁵, improbably has *poyntid.* MED suggests *pointe* can be a variant spelling of *peinte* (Lat. *punctare* vs. *pingere*) but recognizes no sense "rhetorically adorn" of *pointen.*

283   **But]** *And* J R H⁴ H³ H² Ph Gg H⁵ and all eds. but Rob Don. Either reading is possible.

   if] Cp H⁴ S² Dg Gg Th; *if that* rest and all eds. Cp+ is headless, hence harder.

299   **the]** *tho* Cp S¹ H³ Don. Cp+ is less bland, but the presumed elision *th'othes* raises doubt. Chaucer may have written *thothes.*

309   Now] *And* Cp Don.
good] *my g.* J R H⁴ S² Dg H³ H² Ph Gg H⁵ Cx Th and all eds. but Don Fsh. A headless line.
322   Doth] Cp Cl H¹ A D S¹ Th Skt Don Fsh; *Do* rest. Cp+ has the less common form.
339   ye] Cp Cl H¹ A S² Dg Gg; *we* rest and Mck Rkr. Original is indeterminable.
349   ther] Om. Cp H⁴ H² Ph Cx; *ne* J Gg Th Don. Cp+ may be authentic, with scribes variously relieving a Lydgatian line.
372   wol] *wold* Cp (*wolde* Don); *wele* Gg. The *de-* of *demen* may have influenced Cp, or Cp could be right. Cl omits *What,* and the original may have been, with good meter, *wolde.*
380   wre] Cp Cl D S¹ Fsh; *wry(e)* J R H⁴ A H³ Gg H⁵ Cx Th and all eds. but Fsh; *were* H¹; *hille* S² Dg; *covere* H² Ph. The sense is clear; the forms of *wrien, wreen, wreyen* were much confused. S² Dg would be preferred, but H¹ shows that *wre* was sufficiently difficult to arouse variation—even the non-Chaucerian word *hille,* which poorly fits the meter.
406   I] J R H⁴ H³ H² Ph Gg H⁵ Cx Mck Rkr; *Nece I* rest and other eds. With *Nece* the line is hexametric. If *Nece* is authentic, *I bidde* is probably parenthetical and *wisshe* a (monosyllabic) imperative. See Expl. Notes. Cp+ may add *Nece* for clarity, or Chaucer may have left a rough line.
432   wel] *ful w.* Cp Cl H¹ A D S² Dg S¹ and all eds. but Mck Rkr. Cp+, perhaps missing the disyllabic *sette,* supplies a syllable for meter. Six MSS spell it *set(t),* and R, *setten.*
438   If . . . or] H⁴; *If that . . . or any* Cp Cl H¹ A S²; *Yif that . . . or* J R D Dg H³ Gg H⁵ Cx Th and all eds. but Rob Fsh; *Yf . . . or any* S¹ H² Ph Rob Fsh. A headless line, variously supplied by the scribes (Cp+ hexametrically).
465   lith in a] *lyth in* Ph Gg H⁵ Cx; *now lyth in* Cl Skt Fsh; *lith now in a* Cp H¹; *lith now in* A D S² S¹ Rob Bgh Don Wdt; *lyes now* Dg. J+ is probably hard in using the article with *jupartie* but is supported by 5.916.
491   to yow] *ther(e)to* Cp Cl H¹ A D S² Dg S¹ and all eds. but Mck Rkr. Cp+ avoids the hard idiom *truste to;* see 1.601 and note 5.410 below.
500   his love that] S² Dg H³; *h. l. whyche* Cx; *h. l. which t.* Cp Cl H¹ A D S² and all eds. but Skt Mck; *the l. which t.* H⁴; *l. of god weche that* J R Gg H⁵ Th Skt Mck; *l. of god* H² Ph. A headless line, with *love* disyllabic (see note 1.436 above) and various scribal "corrections." J+ and H² Ph look like scribal clarifications.
516   afer] J R (R's *affer* altered from or to *after*); *aftir* H⁴ A D H³ Gg H⁵ Cx Th Skt Don; *a fere* H² Ph; *ther after* Cp Cl H¹ S² Dg S¹. The hard reading of J R is confirmed by the Italian *non . . . vicin* and by the stress.
588   graunte us] Cp J Dg Don; *yet g. us* Cl R A D S² S¹ Gg Th and all other eds.; *yet let us* H⁵; *us g. to* H⁴ H³ H² Ph; *g. us that* H¹; *g. us to* Cx. A Lydgatian line, well supported and clearly effective, with a perfect spray of attempted metrical "corrections."
597   Lord] *L. so* J R H⁴ A D S¹ H³ Cx and all eds. but Skt; *L. how* Gg Th Skt; *L. that* H⁵. A less compelling example of the situation described in 588 above; the expression with *so* conceivably was thought hard and hence was original.
603   wex] H⁴ H² Ph Gg H⁵ Th Skt Rob Wdt; *was* rest and other eds. Scribes substituted the more obvious, blander word.

615   yates] *gate* D; *latis* H² Skt Mck Don. H² is perhaps harder, or an intelligent scribal effort to improve the sense.
617   to] *fro* J R H⁴ H³ H² Ph Gg H⁵ Cx Th and all eds. but Don. Original is indeterminable.
677   hire] *hire herte* S² Dg H³ H² Ph Cx and all eds. but Skt Rkr; *hire inwardly* R. The *-e* of *Made* is sounded, but beginning a headless line with a plural verb is rare enough to confuse scribes (H⁴ and S¹ omit the *-e*). If *herte* were better attested, its omission might be explained by a presumed ancestral dittographic reading *her herte.*
734–35   A (over erasure) H² Ph Gg H⁵ Th Skt read *al this toune aboute / Be they the wers (why) nay withoute doute.* This reading is faintly closer to the Italian; perhaps it is an earlier Chaucerian version.
735   byleve] *leve* J R H⁴ S² Dg H³ Cx Mck Rkr Don. Cp+ has the harder sense, but MED gives ample evidence of *bileven* in the sense "leave off, desist." J+ is possible—Cp+ may avoid rime riche.
737   al this] *a. t. ilk* Cp Cl H¹ D; *this ilke* A; *wommen in* J R H⁴ Mck. Conceivably A represents the original, perhaps revised by Chaucer. J+ varies widely in 736–38.
745   noon] *no man* J R H⁴ S¹ H³ H² Ph Gg Cx Mck Rkr. A headless line.
747   who that] Cp A D S¹ Don; *whoso that* Th; *who so* rest and other eds. Cp+ is distinctly harder but, also meaning "whoever," good Middle English (Mustanoja, ME Syntax, 192–93).
777   why] A Gg; *wey(e)* Cp J Cl R S² S¹ H³ Ph Cx Rkr Wdt; *way(e)* H¹ D Th; *cause* H⁵; *owith* H⁴ (*care and peyne* H²). Conceivably *wey* means (ironically) "means" or possibly "room," hence "cause" (so Windeatt); but the usage is not paralleled elsewhere in Chaucer. Root's suggestion that *wey = wo* is desperate.
781   that] *the* Cp R A D Gg H⁵ Cx Th Skt. Cp+ misses the continuing metaphor.
795   that it is ago] Cp H¹; *it is go(ne)* Cl H⁴ D H³ H² Ph Cx Th; *it is ago* J A H⁵ and all eds.; *that it is go* R S² S¹ Gg. Cp H¹ is preferred as hardest, requiring two elisions, *bycom'th* and *it's* or *'tis* (cf. 5.834).
800   dremen] *demen* R A S¹ H² Ph Gg Th Skt Mck; *demyth* H⁴. The context may suggest malicious deeming; but *dremen* is better attested, less bland, and (cf. 3.585) good sense.
815   ther] *they* J R H⁴ S¹ H² Ph Gg H⁵ Mck Rkr; *the* H³. J+ is an obvious substitution.
838   is moost] *that is m.* R S² S¹ H³ Gg Skt Rkr Rob Bgh Fsh; *that m. is* Cp H⁴ H¹ A Th Don Wdt. A headless line.
860   hym] J R H² Ph H⁵ Th; *it* rest and Rkr Don Wdt. The next line confirms the personification.
891   Why nay] Cp J Cl H¹ A S² Th; *We nay* D; *Nay nay* S¹; *Nay* rest and Mck. R+ is perhaps metrically harder, requiring disyllabic *love* (see note 1.436 above), but scribal omission of *why* before *nay* is more likely.
894   moste] *mosten* J R H³ and all eds. but Don; *mote* H⁴ Th; *most* A D S¹ H² Ph; *miste* (or *nuste*) Gg; *must* Cx. A headless line. Here *moste* is best taken as pret. subj. singular (*men* means "one"), meaning "would have to" (Kittredge, Observations, 331).
901   hire lasse] *l. h.* Cp H¹ D S² Ph Don; *it lessyd more* Cx. Cp has possible meter with disyllabic *love* (see note 1.436 above) but this is weak witness.
908   wexen dymme and] *gan to wax(en)* J R H⁴ H² Ph Gg Mck. Either alternative is suspect because of likely minim confusion; the grammar in J+ is perhaps easier.

914   til] *unto* J S¹ H² Ph H⁵ Mck Rkr Wdt; *into* H⁴ H³ Cx; *on to* Gg; *in* R; *to* A D S². Cp+ is perhaps slightly harder; when unambiguous, *soone* is always disyllabic in Tr.

947   unto] *and to* J R H⁴ H³ Gg H⁵ Cx Th Mck Rkr; *to her* H² Ph. J+ is possibly harder and right, as its version requires an understood verb.

963   therto] *also* Cp Cl H¹ A D S² Skt Rob Bgh Don Fsh; *therfore* Th. J+ is more specific, is well attested, and has better sense.

968   stalke] H⁴ D H³ Gg H⁵ Rob; *stalk* Cp Cl H¹; *stalkes* rest and all other eds. The harder singular is confirmed by the source, *in loro stelo*. The word is disyllabic.

976   al] *and* Cp H¹ A S² H³ H⁵ Th Don. Cp+'s blander reading is possible, with *al* drawn from 975.

1005   Of] *Right of* R H⁴ S¹ H³ H² Ph Gg H⁵ Cx Th Skt Mck Rkr Wdt. A headless line; see 2.1055.

1026   it] Om. J R H⁴ H³ Gg H⁵ Mck. J+ perhaps attempts to regularize the meter.

1043   were] *ner(e)* Cp J H¹ D S¹ H² Ph Gg H⁵ Cx and all eds. but Don Fsh; *where* H³. Cp+ is perhaps harder, but a sense "even if it were only a joke" or "then it would be only a joke" seems better than "unless it were only a joke" (Bgh, with *nere*).

1044   to] *unto* Cp Cl H¹ D S² H³ Th Don Fsh; om. J H⁵ Cx. Cp+ is metrically harder and would be preferred but that the archetype, not grasping the grammar, may well have read with J+; thus, both Cp+ and R+ may have supplied their readings independently for the more usual Chaucerian grammar, only R+ discovering the right word for meter. Chaucer nowhere has *unto* with *like*.

1055   Of] *Right of* J R H⁴ S¹ H² Ph Gg H⁵ Cx Th and all eds. but Don. A headless line; see 2.1005.

1077   leigh] Cp J H¹ S¹; *ley* Cl Gg H⁵ Skt Fsh; *logh* R; *lough* A; *lied* H⁴ S² H³ H² Ph Cx Th; *ligh* D. See Expl. Notes; *leigh/ley* is hardest and best attested.

1081   he ay] *ay he* Cp S¹ H³ Th Don Wdt. (Cx varies.) A difficult hiatus either way; Cl+ is better attested and has better emphasis.

1083   endeles] *infynyte* H² Mck; *infeint* H⁴; *enfayned* Gg; *infinyth* H⁵.

withouten hoo] *for ay and o* J R H⁴ H² Gg H⁵ Mck (H²: *that . . . oo* written by another scribe). The noun *ho* is rare enough to confuse: see MED (KnT I.2533 is a nominalized report of a verb or interjection). J+ further varies in 1084–85.

1093   tok the lettre] *up therwith* J R H⁴ H² Ph Gg Mck; *up tho with* H⁵; *toke* H³. Cp+ is closer to the Italian.

1095   J R H⁴ H² Ph Gg H⁵ Mck read *And seide slepe ye (yit) and it is prime*, an attractive Pandarism that, if it is Chaucer's, may have been revised as too abrupt.

1113   tydynges] *new tydynges* Cp Cl R H¹ D S² Dg Th Don Fsh; *suche thingis* H⁵. Cp+ attracts *new* from 1112, perhaps for meter, not recognizing disyllabic *telle.*

1119   that he spak] Cp R A S² Cx; *t. he spake* H¹ D Dg H³ Th Skt Rob Wdt; *t. he s. ther* J S¹; *that they spoke* Cl Fsh; *his woordis* H⁴ H² Ph Gg H⁵. (R varies.) *Spake* with *-e* sounded is ungrammatical, as the J S¹ Cl "corrections" show. Cp+ may be an imperfect Chaucerian revision of the headless H⁴+, leaving a Lydgatian line. Cl+ is also possibly original.

1132   bryng] *brynge* Cp J H⁴ H¹ D Dg H³ Cx Th and all eds. but Skt Mck; *bryngyth* Gg. Chaucer's monosyllabic imperative form, attested unambiguously only by

Tr 4.1082 and SumT III.2258, makes better meter. See Kittredge, Observations, 274, 283.

1148   it make] *to make* J Cl H⁴ D H² Ph H⁵ Cx Mck Rkr Fsh. J+, with no object for *make,* seems too hard.

1154   Refuse it] *Refuse* Cp Don; *Refusith* S¹; *Refuset(h) it* J Dg S³; *Refuse ye it* H² Ph. *Refuse* is always transitive elsewhere in Chaucer; Cp and S¹ may "correct" other variants for meter.

1202   sat on knowe] *fel on k.* J R H⁴ H² Ph Gg Cx Mck Rkr Fsh; *knelid lowe* H⁵. Cp+ is harder; cf. LGW 2028.

1211   tid] J H⁴; *tyde* H² Ph Gg; *tyme* rest and all eds. The less common word is preferred, here as a monosyllable for good meter (cf. note 2.143 above).

1225   wolde] *wolde ay* J R H⁴ S¹ Gg H⁵ Cx Mck Rkr Rob Fsh Wdt; *wold* H¹ D S²; *wole* A; *wold ay* H² Ph Th. J+ and H² Ph may be right or may for meter "correct" an ancestor such as H¹+.

1226   to Pandare in gan] *in to P. gan* Cp H¹ S² S¹ H⁵ Rob Bgh Don; *in to Pandarus gan* A D H³; *to Pandarus gan* Cl Skt Fsh; *to Pandaris in gan* Gg (with *-is in* on an erasure); *to P. gan* Cx; *to P. in to* H² Ph. Cp+ has rough meter; Cl is possible.

1227   into the] *in to* Cp J Th Skt Mck Don; *into a* Cl; *to the* R; *in the* S¹. Cp+ may be right or may have been troubled by a slurred *to th'.*

1231   dide] Cp; *dyd* R A; *did(e) a* rest and Mck Rkr Wdt. Cp, with (correct) *-e,* has slightly harder meter and sense; Chaucer seems to omit the article with *thing* more often than not.

1240   played] *p. the* J R H⁴ A H³ H² Ph Gg H⁵ Cx Th Mck Rkr Rob Bgh Wdt. Cp+ is harder; for disyllabic *played* and omission of the article see 1.1074.

1252   Pandare] J R H⁴ S¹ H² Ph H⁵ Cx Th Skt Mck Wdt; *Pandarus* rest and other eds. J+ has the better meter.

1280   lakked] Cp Cl H¹ S²; om. Dg; *lakke of* rest and Mck Rkr. Cp+ retains an impersonal verb that soon became personal only.

1284   Quod she Ye] *Ye q. s.* J R H⁴ S¹ H² Ph Gg H⁵ and all eds. but Skt Don; *q. s.* Cl D H³ Cx. Cp+ has better meter; Chaucer not infrequently preceded a quoted speech with *quod he/she.*

1291   speche] J R H² Ph Gg H⁵ Cx Mck Rkr; *this* H⁴; *shame* rest and all other eds. Cp+ may gloss (perhaps from 1286) the hard sense of *speche*—"malicious gossip" —or may be right.

1327   tho] Cp D S¹ Gg Don; *thas* S² Dg; *the* rest and all other eds. Cp+ is less bland and has somewhat better sense.

1333   encreese] no MS or ed.; *encrees(e) of* Cp Cl R H¹ A S¹ H³ H² Ph Cx Th Skt Rob Bgh Don Fsh Wdt; *thencres of* H⁴; *encresseth* J D Gg H⁵ Mck Rkr; *encreses of* S² Dg. McCormick suggested this emendation, which avoids poor grammar (with *Therwith* otiose or nonsensical in 1334) and which is hard enough at first sight (as subjunctive, spelled like the noun) to elicit the obvious variants. An exact parallel is 2.483, where Cl alters the subjunctive *cesse* to the indicative, just as J+ does here.

1347   thise] Cp Cl H¹ S² H³; *his(e)* rest and Mck Rkr Wdt. Cp+ is harder, probably meaning "the sort of dice lovers cast." The line is Lydgatian.

1349   gistes] J Cl H⁴; *giftis* A D S¹ Ph Cx; *gostes* Cp; *gestes* rest, Skt Mck Bgh. The J+ spelling best explains the rest. See Expl. Notes.

1353   ay tyl hym to pleyne] Cp Cl H¹ Skt Fsh; *ay to him to p.* H³ Rkr Rob Bgh Don Wdt; *ay unto hym p.* J S¹ Mck;

ay uppon hym p. R; *ay to him p.* H⁴ A S² Gg; *alwey to hym p.* H² Ph; *ay to him complein* D Dg H⁵; *unto hym p.* Cx; *aye on him to p.* Th. The best MSS avoid hiatus and retain good meter.

1395   thing now . . . shal] *t. . . . s. n.* J H⁴ D Mck Rkr Rob Bgh (now) om. R H² Ph Gg H⁵ Cx Th; *newe* A). Cp+'s less prosaic order is preferred.

1429   how thow woost of] J A Gg (Gg: *wolt*) H⁵ Mck Rkr; *thow that woost al(le)* Cp Cl H¹ S² (S²: *wote*) H³ and all other eds.; *h. for thow knowest* R; *h. t. w.* H⁴; *thou that w. of* D S¹; *(you me) that wote all* Dg; *for thou w. of* A; *howe for thou w.* Th; *for thou wost* Cx; *how for thou w. of* H² Ph. J+ with its abrupt parenthesis is hardest; the sequence *how thow* usually begins another construction and confused the scribes.

1430   It myghte] J H² Ph Gg H⁵ Mck Rkr; *It m. her* R; *myht* H⁴; *How m. I* H³; *I m. hyr* Cx; *I m.* Th; *How I m.* rest and all other eds. Only D and Gg read *mighte,* but the word is more often disyllabic than not in Chaucer. The only instance of a personal subject of *avaylen* in Chaucer is FrT III.1366, but the impersonal probably became harder in the fifteenth century. All points to the originality of J+ in 1429–30.

1436   preye] *p. yow* Cp Cl H¹ S² Dg H³ and all eds. but Skt Mck Rkr; *yow p.* S¹ Cx. The *yow* required for sense is in 1437; Cp+ anticipates, yielding an easier verse with poor meter.

1504   thow] *that thow* J S¹ H³ Gg H⁵ and all eds. but Skt Fsh, to "correct" Cp+'s headless or Lydgatian line.

1513   bylyve] *blyve* Cp Cl R H¹ A D H⁵ Mck Fsh; *as blyve* H⁴ S¹ H² Ph Cx Skt. Chaucer varies *bylyve* and *as blyve* at line ends; the former is a little less common and better attested, Cp+ in effect supporting it.

1517   Sone] *And* Cp Cl H¹ A D S² Dg H³ Don; *So* H² Ph. J+ is preferred as more specific; H² Ph is hard and perhaps original, requiring repunctuation to read with the preceding lines.

1600   that] Cp S¹ H² Ph Gg Cx Don; *this* rest and all other eds. Cl+ is better attested and perhaps right, but *that speche* seems less bland, an impatient "all that talk."

1602   If it] J R H⁴ S¹ H² Ph Gg H⁵; *If* rest and Skt Don Fsh. J+ makes better sense; *speke* is not the predicate complement of *be,* but the complement of *gon.*

1617   myghten] R; *myght(e)* rest and all eds. The plural form with *-en* (cf. 2.1624) is required for meter—unless *heynous* (*haignous/hyenous/haynous[e]*), used only here in Chaucer, is trisyllabic. (See Kittredge, Observations, 384, 412.)

1663   yow] *me* Cp Cl H¹ S² Dg Skt Don; *yt* R H⁴ Gg Th. R+ is conceivably original, eliciting the variants, but is pleonastic and more likely anticipates the *it* later in the line. Cp+ has poor sense.

1665   his] *this* Cp Cl H¹ D S² Dg S¹ Cx Skt Fsh. Cp+'s *this* would require a clearer antecedent.

1669   alweies] *algate(s)* J R H⁴ S¹ H² Ph Gg H⁵ Cx Th Mck Rkr Wdt; *all wise* D. Cp+ is probably harder in the sense "at all hazards, at any rate." MED reports that the form with *-s* is rare before 1400.

1735   of corones] Cp A S² Dg S¹ Ph Rob Bgh Wdt; *of corounes* J Cl H⁴ H² Gg Th Skt Mck Rkr Fsh; *of the coro(u)nes* H¹ D H³ Cx Don; *of his reignes* R; *owre goddis* H⁵. See Expl. Notes.

1749   Las tyme ilost] Cp Cl J H¹ Gg Rkr Wdt; *L. t. is ylost* A; *Lasse t. ylost* S¹; *Lasse t. is lost* Ph; *Lest t. ilost* H⁵ Skt Mck Rob (Rob reads *I loste*) Don; *Lest t. be lost* R H²

Th; *Last t. ilost(e)* S² H³; *Last t. is ilost* D; *Last t. ye lost* Dg; *Allas t. is lost* H⁴; *Thus t. I lost* Cx; *Allas t. iloste* Bgh Fsh. The archetype clearly read *ylost* or (Cp S²) *yloste,* without *is* or *be.* Internalized auditory confusion may account for the spray of spellings of the first word—because the second word begins with *t,* all the variants probably sound much the same. MED records spelling *lest* as *last; lesse* and *lasse* commonly alternate in Chaucer. The plausible alternatives are: 1. Cp+ *(A)las (for) lost time!* or *(A)las (that) time (be, is being) lost;* 2. S¹ Ph *(Let) less time (be) lost;* 3. H⁵+ *Lest time (be) lost* or *Lest I lost* (should lose, were to lose) *time.* Of these alternatives, the third is easiest in context, and MS support is weak, although the support of the *Last* readings should probably be added to that of *Lest.* Chaucer uses the expression *I lost(e)* (from OE *losode*) only twice elsewhere, but on the whole he prefers the weak to the strong (*lees,* from OE *leas*) preterite, and *I loste* is possible. Against it is the weak support for the expected *-e.* The first and second alternatives are hard enough to arouse variation: 1. The aphetic form of *allas* (recorded by OED no earlier than Marlowe) might have been unfamiliar to scribes. *Allas* derives from two OF words, *(h)a las* (Italian *lasso*); the aphesis would not seem strange to a French speaker. 2. Monosyllabic *lasse* ("less") is rare in Chaucer but occurs in BD 675 and (line initial) FranT V.1224. Chaucer might have spelled it without *-e* to signal its unusual pronunciation, confusing scribes. Against the "less" interpretation is that there is no parallel expression in Chaucer, and MS support is very weak. The most trustworthy MSS support the first alternative, and its form of expression is common in Chaucer: *O tyme ilost* (Tr 3.896); *For tyme ylost* (Tr 4.1283, HF 1257). Cf. variants at note 4.478 below.

1750   After line 1750, R repeats lines 1576–77 and follows them with a unique stanza: *For ye must outher chaungen your face / That is so ful of mercy and bountee / Or elles must ye do this man sum grace / For this thyng folweth of necessytee / As sothe as god ys in his magestee / That crueltee with so benigne a chier / Ne may not last in o persone yfere.* The stanza has, except for the bad meter of the first line, no non-Chaucerian features, and is probably genuine. The final couplet resembles 2.167–68—perhaps resembles it too much. The word *Vacat* appears (written perhaps by the main scribe) in the margin beside the repeated line 1577; the word usually means "to be canceled" but can mean "material is lacking." The stanza may have been meant originally to follow 1736. Chaucer may have canceled it, or it may accidentally have been canceled by scribal misinterpretation of *Vacat* as including not only the repeated lines but also the unique stanza.

BOOK III

17   him] no MS; *tham* S¹; *hem* rest and Rkr Wdt. Fil. has *il* (Jove); *hem* is nonsense, probably archetypal.

28   it] Rkr Wdt; om H⁴; *hym* H² Cx and all other eds. H² Cx is perhaps right, but the syntax of Cp+ is possible (*joies* construed collectively or *it* pleonastic with *myght;* see Mustanoja, ME Syntax, 63, 137–38, ParsT X.1039, LGW 1506, MerT IV.1268, Tr 1.608), and is harder and well attested.

91   yow wol] Cp Cl H¹; *w. y.* rest and Mck Rkr Rob Bgh Wdt. The less prosaic order is preferred.

101 ferforthly] *ferforth* H⁴ H⁵ Cx; *feithfully* Cp Cl H¹ A D S² Dg H³ Th Skt Don. J+, a less common bit of "love-talking," makes better sense in context.

110 youre wreththe may] J R H⁴ Ph H⁵ Rkr Wdt; *y may your hert* H²; *youre w. may y* Ph; *youre w. I may* Gg Mck Rob Bgh Fsh; *y. hert(e) may* rest and Don; *your herte I may* Skt. Cp+ draws *herte* from 109 (but see 3.887); H²+ was troubled by intransitive *apese*.

119 er] *er that* Cp Cl H⁴ H¹ A D S² Dg Th Skt Don Fsh (Cx: *or we hens*). Because *ones* is regularly disyllabic, Cp+ is hypermetric.

144 ben ylike] H³ H² Ph Cx Skt Mck; *ben ay lik* H⁴; *ben ay eke* R; *to ben(e) ay elike* S² Dg Th; *ay ben ilik* Gg; *ay ben in lyke* H⁵; *ben ay ylike* rest and all other eds. H³+ has good meter (*ylike* is regularly trisyllabic), but the archetype may read with Cp+.

158 softely] *sobrely* J R H⁴ S¹ H² Ph H⁵ Cx Mck Rkr; *sekyrly* Gg. Either Cp+ or J+ may be right.

188 the] Cp Cl H¹ S² Dg Don Fsh; om. rest and all other eds. Monosyllabic *sem'th* was misunderstood by some scribes. See 1.889 and Kittredge, Observations, 219.

189 merveille] Cp Cl H¹ S² Dg; *miracle* rest and Mck Rkr. Cp+ is perhaps harder but may, as seeming less specifically religious, be a pious alteration in the pagan and jocular context. Windeatt observes that Chaucer uses the terms interchangeably.

193–94 anon And to] Cp (*an oon*); *o(n) (n)one And to* S² Dg; *anon And eek* H⁴; *anon And the* Gg; *anon And* H⁵ Cx; *and oon And to* A Ph; *and one And* H²; *and oon And two* rest and all eds.   **thow¹**] *the* J A S² Dg H² H⁵ Cx Mck. Cp's reading is suspect because of the repeated rhyme word, *anoon*, but such rhymes are found elsewhere in Chaucer; e.g., Tr 2.513–16, 5.975–78. The J+ reading, glossed "both the one and the other" by editors, hardly makes sense. The vocative *thow* is harder than *the* in context, with ellipsis of *thee* unnecessarily repeated from 193. The sense of Cp is "I conjure you, Criseyde, forthwith, and (you) also, you Troilus. . . ." Cp makes good sense but is difficult enough to elicit variation.

214 wonder wel speken] *s. w. wel* J Gg H⁵ Skt Mck. J+ alters a Lydgatian line.

259 al shal ben] *al b. s.* Cp H¹ Don; *it s. b.* H⁴. Cl+ is supported by meter and MS witness.

267 as] Om. J Dg H² Ph Gg Mck; *es* S²; *is* Cx. J+ may be right (an easy error like those of S² and Cx, or taking *name* as monosyllabic, could elicit "correction"), but support is weak.

**269 **J H⁴ S¹ Gg H⁵ Cx Mck Rkr blandly read *For nevere was ther wight* (H⁵ *that wight;* Cx *yit wyght*), perhaps confused by *unbore* and deriving *nevere* from *evere* in 270.

**282 **All MSS but J R H⁴ H² Ph Cx and all eds. but Mck Rkr Wdt read *Yet eft I the beseche and fully seye* (J *preyen,* D *preye* for *seye;* H⁵ om. *eft, the*). J+ is slightly supported by the Italian *Per ch'io ti priego;* an error such as J's *preyen* could have confused scribes and elicited revision. Cp+ is a poor line but perhaps original; Hanna notes that *preye* could derive from 285, 287 (in Editing Ch, 288).

293 yet proverbed] *p. yet* H² Ph; *thus p.* Cp S² Dg Mck Rob Bgh Don; *this p.* H¹ Th; *this proverbe* H³. Perhaps a *y/thorn* error or a transposition like that in H² Ph, making poor meter, elicited *thus* in Cp+ and *this* in H¹ Th H³, or perhaps Cp+ is original. An error like H³'s, or the hard *proverbed,* or concern over dead clerks' still proverbing, may have caused the variant in J R H⁴ Cx

Rkr: *Han writen or this as men yit teche us yonge* (with minor variants).

303 Hath . . . ful] J R H⁴ H² Ph Cx; *Hastow* rest and Skt Don Fsh. Root saw that *O* in 302 means "one," and does not signal a vocative (H⁴ and Cx read *For* for *O*), as Cp+ took it to; J+ is harder. But one would expect some scribes to read *Oo* or *On(e):* none do.

315 lyere] *a l.* Cp Cl S² Dg S¹ H³ H² Ph Cx Don Fsh. Cp+ may take *avauntour* in 314 as article plus noun (H³ reads *vantour*) and unmetrically supply a "parallel" article here. Taking the line as headless and *lyere* as monosyllabic (see Hanna, in Editing Ch, 288) is unlikely: cf. 3.309 above.

319 nevere . . . bihyghte hem] *b. h. n.* Cp H¹ S² Dg H³ Th Don. Cl+ seems to have better emphasis, but either reading is possible.

324 wis-man] *wise men* Cp Cl H⁴ H¹ S² Dg Th Rob Bgh Fsh Wdt. The singular makes good sense and better meter, though the plural is supported by the parallel *foles nyce.*

355 to] *for to* Cp Cl H¹ S² Dg S¹ Cx Don Fsh. Cp+ perhaps reads *wise* as one syllable.

385 it liketh] Cl R H⁴ A; *it l. the* Cp J H¹ D Gg and all eds. but Skt; *the l. to* S² Dg; *it like the* S¹; *the l.* H³ Th Skt; *it lyke the to* H²; *it hit like to* Ph; *it likyth the to* Cx. In Tr, Chaucer never rhymes *here* in the sense "to hear" with words with lengthened open *e* like *swere,* nor *swere* with words with close *-e-.* Hence *here* in this place is the pronoun "her" (*swere*'s most common rhyme in Tr), which makes better but less obvious sense ("I'd rather die, if it please her, than tell") and better meter. The *-th* of *liketh* or the *the* of 384 may have contributed to the *the* confusion. See Skeat, Rime-Index, 10–11.

414 sith] *s. that* Cp Cl H¹ A Th Skt Don.   **don**] *idon* J R S¹ H² Ph and all eds. but Skt Don. A headless line. Possibly the original had disyllabic *sithe* (S¹ Gg) or *sithen;* cf. 3.1222 and n. above for comparable variation.

427 goode] *wyse* J R H⁴ H² Ph Gg H⁵ Cx Mck Rkr Wdt. Chaucer used both *wyse* (WBT III.1231) and *goode* (Tr 3.481) with *governaunce.* The latter is preferred because the (expected) weak form *goode* may have been missed by scribes (Cp D Dg S¹ read *good*), and J+ may hence "correct" for meter.

442 ful] R H⁴ S¹; om. rest and Skt Don. The word appears scribal (J+ has *laye,* perhaps hoping the *-e* would fill the meter), but the meter resulting from the omission of *ful* in Cp+ is too hard.

446 men is] *man is* Gg H⁵ Skt Rob Bgh Don Fsh; *men be(n)* J R H⁴ S² Dg S¹ H³ H² Ph Th Mck Rkr Wdt. Cp+'s *men* means "one"; Gg H⁵ and J+ make the obvious substitutions.

452 or] *and* Cl R H⁴ A D S¹ H³ H² Ph Th Mck Rkr Rob Bgh Fsh. Cp+ is harder, less bland, and better attested.

468 she] *hir(e)* J R H⁴ Mck Rkr Don Wdt; *he* Cp. J+ is not enough harder to seem original; Cp is probably a slip.

476 devyse] *avyse* Cp H¹ S² Dg H³ Don. J+ has better sense.

490 than he withouten drede] *to do(n) his frend to spede* J R H⁴ Cx Mck Rkr. J+ is less padded, but the repetition of *frend* from 489 is suspect.

527 Of] *From* Cl Rob Bgh Don Fsh. Cp+'s idiom is unobjectionable; Ch Soc. transcript of Cp reads *From.*

529 fremde] H⁵; *frend(e)* H² Ph Gg; *wild(e)* J R H⁴ S¹

H³ Cx Mck Rkr; *frem(m)ed* rest and all other eds. H⁵ and Cp+ are harder than J+; H⁵'s spelling makes better meter (cf. 2.248) and lies behind H²+ (OE forms: *fremde* and *fremede*).

546   J Cx Mck Rkr read *that he wolde hym spede* (so, with variants, do R H⁴), perhaps clarifying the concise construction of Cp+.

568   J R H⁴ Cx Mck Rkr read *And she agayne gan to hym for to rowne* (H⁴ *on game,* Mck *a-game;* H⁴ Cx om. *to*¹), plausibly compressing the sequence of the whispering; but Cp+ is better attested and suggests the snatched moments for privacy.

she to hym gan] *s. g. t. h.* D S¹ (S¹ *unto*) H² Ph Gg H⁵ Rob; *t. h. s. g.* Cl Skt. The original is indeterminable.

576   **whan]** *whan that* Cp Cl H² Ph Skt Don Fsh. Cp+ may take *thought(e)* as a monosyllable; the historically expected -*e* seems not to be sounded (or counted in the meter) in two of fourteen unambiguous occurrences of the preterite singular in Tr (3.468, 4.952).

585   **whiche as]** Cp H¹ Don; *the whiche* H⁵; *whiche* R; *which(e) that* rest and all other eds. Cp H¹ is distinctly harder, especially as it can suggest "things that were as if they never had been," whereas in fact they simply were not. But *which as* can mean simply "which" (ClT IV.331, Mustanoja, ME Syntax, 197–98). The *as* (or the R variant) further permits a metrically smooth -*e* on *whiche,* usual for the plural (e.g., KnT I.2972).

587   **moste]** Cp D; *must* R H² Ph H⁵ Cx Th *(muste); mot(e)* H⁴ Gg Skt; *most* rest and Rob Rkr Wdt. See Expl. Notes.

611   **herte]** Cp H¹; *hert* S² Th; *hertes* rest and all eds. J+ "improves" Chaucer's grammar, avoiding what Mustanoja terms "distributive number" (ME Syntax, 56–57).

686   **here]** Cp Cl H¹; *her* A H² Ph Mck; om. Gg; *to* (canceled) *you* H⁵; *soone* Cx Th; *bir(e)* rest and Rkr Don Fsh Wdt. Cp's form of the feminine accusative pronoun is regularly *hire.* Although the pronoun is redundant, it would be good Middle English grammar, and it is probably easier. The adverb *here* makes good sense.

705   **blisful]** *seint* J H⁴ S¹ Cx Mck Rkr; om. R. See note 712 below.

712   **blisful]** *seynt* H² Ph Gg H⁵. One or both occurrences of *seint* (as *seinte* Mck) may be right; scribes might think it blasphemous or might "correct" it in ignorance of Chaucer's disyllabic *seinte* (e.g., in ProWBT III.604). R rightly shows elision of *m'enspire.*

722   **O]** Om. Cp Cl A D S² Th Fsh. Possibly a headless line, but the parallel apostrophes and the usual form of address confirm *O.* Root suggests an ancestral MS left space for a decorated initial.

738   **Wy]** Cp H¹ S²; om. H⁴; *Why* rest and all eds. Perhaps a mere spelling variant, but *wy* (meaning *we*) and *why,* doubtless confused, may have different etymologies (see Mustanoja, ME Syntax, 628, 631); and *wy* is harder. At 1.1025 Gg and Ph read *W(h)e;* at 1.1026, Dg and S², *We;* at 5.907, H², *We* (these may be original). At 2.891, D reads *we* (in a variant; see note above). Also see 3.842.

758   **how]** *h. thus* J H⁴ S¹ H² Gg H⁵ Cx and all eds; *h. this* Ph. J+ may be right but seems a scribal "correction" of the meter. The Lydgatian line is here effective, and no reason appears for Cp+ to omit.

776   **while]** R H⁴ H² Ph Gg H⁵; *meen(e) w.* rest and Don. Cp+ seems to be a hypermetric scribal clarifica-tion, perhaps induced by the *meene* earlier in the line, possibly corrupt in the archetype—or it may be Chaucer's slip.

791   **that]** *the* Cp H¹ S² H³ H⁵ Cx Th Don. Cp+ is easy; *that* has sharper sense.

797   **hatte]** J R H²; *atte* H³; om. Cx; *that hat(te)/biht* rest and Skt Rkr Rob Wdt. Cp+ hypermetrically adds *that* for clarity; Cx is possible.

838   **mysbyleved]** *m. and* Cp H¹ S² Th Skt Rob Bgh Don Fsh. Cp+ clarifies and roughens the meter.

842   **Wy]** Cp; *What* Gg; *Why* rest and all eds. See note 3.738 above.

859   **How . . . is falle]** *How . . . dyde f.* Cx; *How is . . . ifall(e)* J R H⁴ S¹ H² Ph Skt Mck Rkr Bgh; *How is . . . fall(e)* H³ Gg H⁵. A headless line "corrected" by H³+ and "corrected" further by J+.

this] *the* Cp D S² Th Don. The original is indeterminable; J+ is better attested.

890   **haselwodes]** *haselnotes* R; *hasylwode is* H⁴ H² Ph Gg Cx; *hasylwod(e)* A D H³; *hasillwode ye* S². (H⁵ varies.) The sense being desperate, Cp+ is desperately preferred (by all eds.). A+ probably takes *ye* as a pronoun; H⁴+ takes it as an interjection; S² has one of each.

910   **o]** *a* Cp R H¹ S² H³ Gg H⁵ Th Don Wdt. The scribes often distinguished these etymologically equivalent words as we do (*one* and *a*); Cl+ is less common and has sharper sense.

928   **hadde grace to]** H⁴ H² Ph Cx (all with *had*); *h. a g. to* J R Don Fsh; *h. a g. for to* S¹; *a g. h. for to* Cp Th; *g. h. for to* H¹ A S²; *h. g. for to* Cl D H³ H⁵; *h. to* Gg. H⁴+ and J R are metrical; H⁴+ seems better idiom. An ancestral spelling of *hadde* without -*de* may have led to the confusion, but monosyllabic *had* here would make a good headless line.

940   **up first]** *f. up* Cp D S¹ Don; *first* H² Ph Cx. J+ is better attested and perhaps harder.

944   **honour may have]** *m. have honour* Cp Don. Cl+ is better attested.

950   **ese]** *eseth* Cp H¹ Th Don; *eses* S²; *is* Gg. The meter requires Cl+'s form, an imperative sg. or pl. without -*th,* or a subjunctive.

1049   **that]** Om. Cp H³ H² Don. Cp+ may be right, although only three headless lines in Tr begin with *And* (4.1244, 1.563, and 5.1446), and the last two of these are in some doubt. Robinson rightly commented on such lines (p. xxxvi), "When a preposition or conjunction gets this initial accent, there is perhaps more reason for the objections of the critics, but the evidence of the manuscripts makes it necessary to admit many such lines to the text."

1073   **that that]** Cp Don; *that tyme* S¹; *that* rest and all other eds. It is unlikely that Cp added a rather difficult *that* to make better meter (S¹ makes an easier "improvement" of this kind), but its meter is better, and the sense is good, though hard. (Either Troilus cursed, not the time that he was born [see Kerkhof, Sts. in the Lang. of G. Ch., 2nd ed., 1982, 278], but *that,* namely *that* he was born at all, or he cursed *that* time *in which* he was born.) Most scribes would presume *that that* was dittography (as several presumed in 3.1751, etc.). See OED *that* dem. pron., adj., adv. B.I.1.e. and B.I.6.

1096   **certeyn]** *alwey* J R H⁴ S¹ H³ Cx Rkr; *serteynli* Gg. J+ is perhaps right, as a hard sense of *alwey* ("at any rate"), but *certeyn* could have troubled scribes like Gg expecting the adverb form.

1106 is] Om. Cp H⁴ H¹ H³ Ph Cx Don. Cp+ continues the imperative mode from *Sey,* yielding rough meter.
1119 And] Cp Cl H¹ A D S² Th; *So that* H⁵; *So* rest and Rkr Wdt. The original is indeterminable.
1131 herte] Cp H¹ Skt Don; *hertes* rest and all other eds. The harder reading is preferred; see note 1.297 above.
1165 bought] *wrought* J R H⁴ S¹ H² Ph Gg H⁵ Mck Rkr. Cp+ is harder, possibly troubling scribes as blasphemous or anachronistic.
1192 it] *hym* Cp H¹ A D Th Don; *hir* S². Cl+ is better attested. If only one of the birds is to be considered female, it is not the *sperhauk* (*his* foot); in the Filocolo passage (see Expl. Notes), the hawks' names are of masculine, the preys' of feminine gender.
1203 bryghte] Mck Rkr; *blisful* Cp Cl H¹ A S² S¹ Th and all other eds.; om. D. J+ seems sharper here with its astral implication and is paralleled in Scog 3. Cp+ has an obvious term in context but is perhaps right.
1204 in] *to* Cl R H⁴ A H³ H² Ph Gg H⁵ Cx Th and all eds. but Mck. Cp+ is better attested, the less common usage, but Chaucerian (see Tr 1.31, MerT IV.2175, MED *in* prep. 8b.[f]).
1220 assaied was] *w. a.* Cp Don. Cp is poorly attested and has rougher meter.
1222 sithen] no MS; *sethen* H²; *sithe* Gg; *syn* Cp J H¹ S² Mck Rkr Don Wdt; *seth* Ph Skt; *sith that* Cl H³ Cx Fsh; *syn that* R H⁴ D S¹ Rob Bgh; *or that* A; *set that* H⁵; *sens* Th. Cp+'s Lydgatian meter seems pointless here, and the less common disyllable *sithen* (or *sithe*) could elicit the variants. Cf. 3.414.
1228 Line missing in Cp; text from Cl.
1268 koude leest] *l. k.* Cp Cl H¹ D S² S¹ Rob Bgh Fsh; *best k.* A; *k. best* Cx; *l. thonke k.* Th. J+ has the better meter.
1283 that] *this* J R H⁴ H³ Cx Mck Rkr Wdt. J+ is possibly right, and Cp+ influenced by surrounding *thats*, but it is less well attested and has no better sense.
1291 I mene he wol ye] A D S¹ H⁵; *I m. that ye wole/wil* Cl Ph Skt Fsh; *I m. ye w. ye* Cp H¹ S²; *he w. that ye* J R Cx; *he w. hou that ye* H⁴ H³ Mck; *I m. w. ye* Gg Th. A+, hard and metrical, appears to be the original of the radiating variants. Cl Ph is possible, but the sense is less apt.
1324–37 J R S¹ H³ Cx Rkr put these stanzas after 1414, and H⁴ copies them in both places. Line 1337 surely does not precede line 1415; in J R H⁴ S¹ H³ Cx the *But* of 1415 (from Fil. *Ma*) is omitted, which Root (Text. Trad. 157, 167, 169) took as evidence that J+ was a later, revised version. See Owen, MP 67, 1969–70, 125–32.
1360 a thousand] J R H⁴ S¹ H³ Cx Mck Rkr Wdt; *an hondred* rest and all other eds. The Italian has *mille sospiri.*
1365 nought bilynne] H¹; *nothynge blynne* Mck; *nevere blynne* A H⁵; *n. blynne* rest and Rkr Wdt. H¹ represents an authentic but rare Middle English variant of the word (see MED), and Cp+ is metrically unsatisfactory (as R A H⁵ saw).
1375 kecche] *kecche / ketche* J Cl Cx Th Skt Mck; *te(c)ch(e)* Cp H⁴ A H³; *the(c)che* R H¹ S² S¹ Ph; *crache* Gg; *cretthe* H⁵; *crecche* Rkr Bgh Don; *krecche* Rob Fsh; *cretche* Wdt. Two reliable MSS (J Cl) read "catch," and two more (Cp H⁴) read a word easily derived from *cecche* (the probable reading of the archetype) or *cetche* by the common *c/t* error. Only the Gg reading (and that in H⁵, if it derives from a similar reading) would also make sense

("scratch," as "scrape together"), but it appears to be a desperate scribal attempt.
1380 so] *so that* J Cl H⁴ A S¹ Gg and all eds.; *so what* R Ph. A Lydgatian line, as often in an exclamatory context, variously (and with poor idiom) "corrected."
1392–93 J R H⁴ Cx Mck Rkr Bgh read *To techen hem that covetise is vice / And love is vertu thogh men halde it nyce.* Cp+ is less explicit, harder.
1402 wo] *thyng* Cp Cl H¹ S² Th Skt Don Fsh. J+ makes better sense, especially with line 1407; Cp+ has the common phrase. Robinson's textual note accepts *thing;* his text, *wo.*
1420 that] all MSS; *than* Th (Skt, in brackets). Skeat's (and Thynne's) conjecture may be right. Root suggests —plausibly, in this distracting context—that Chaucer left an anacoluthon. Robinson suggests a "difficult ellipsis": perhaps "with that" or (as Baugh suggests) "it was then that."
1422 al] Cp H¹ A S¹ Th Don; *and all(e)* D S²; *and* rest and all other eds. J+'s substitution *and* was, as D S² show, inevitable in this context. Cf. notes 5.243 and 5.823 below for comparable variation.
1482 streyneth] *biteth* Cp A D S² Th Skt Rob Bgh Don Wdt; *brenneth* Cl Fsh; *bitleth* H¹. The Italian has *mi stringe.* Cl shows how scribes could invent in such a context; minim confusion (like *stretiieth*) could elicit the substitution. Cf. 3.1651.
1486 Were] *Yit w.* J R H⁴ S¹ H³ H² Ph Gg H⁵ and all eds. (*Yf it w.* Cx.) A headless line.
1488 so] *as* J R H⁴ S¹ H³ H² Ph Gg H⁵ Cx Mck Rkr Rob Bgh. Perhaps J+ "improves" the grammar; see MerT IV.1287, ShipT VII.68, MancT IX.167, OED s.v. *so* 21.b.
1518 at] *to* Cp H¹ A S² Cx Th Don. Chaucer regularly has *at* (once *in*) with *bringe . . . reste;* the idiom with *to* replaced it later.
1524 voys as though] *v. a. thoght* J; *wordes as* Cp Cl H¹ A D S² Th Skt Don; *voyse as* H⁵. R+ has the less common term; J may reflect an archetypal error, eliciting substitution.
1525 Farwel] *fare wel my(n)* Cp Cl H¹ A D S² H⁵ Th Fsh. The words *seyde, far(e)wel, dere,* and *herte* are all regularly disyllabic, hence *my* is unnecessary. Cp+ may result from confusion over the metrical stress on *far-:* cf. MLT II.863, MkT VII.2441.
1553 eft] *oft(e)* Cp A S² H² Ph H⁵ Th Don. Either reading is possible; *ofte* is more often disyllabic than not and is less well attested.
1576–82 Stanza from Cl; Cp omits. In 1577, Cl reads *an* for *and;* in 1578, Cl H⁴ D read *for to;* in 1579, Cl H³ H² Ph H⁵ Don Fsh read *but* for *than* (from 1580?).
1589 his] *the* Cp S² H² Ph Th Don. Original is indeterminable; Cp+ is weakly attested.
1595 and] *he* Cp H¹ A S² Th Skt Don. In the context, scribes (in J+) changed *hondred* to *thousand,* (the harder) *sythe* to *tyme(s),* and (consequently) *tyme* to *day to.* Here *he* is plausible, but less well attested, the enjambment of *An hondred sythe* with the preceding line perhaps harder, and beginning adjacent clauses with *he gan* awkward.
1617 thus] *hym* Cp Cl H¹ A D S² H³ Th Skt Don Fsh. Cp+ is easier; *hym* may come from 1616. The Italian is "cosí."
1621 now] Cp H¹ S² Gg Th Skt Don; *it* rest and all other eds. Cp+ is less obvious, as *it* (which is in fact

redundant) would seem at first to be required to produce a common idiom (cf. 3.862, etc.). In a similar construction in 4.613, two scribes likewise supplied an *it.*
Here scribes may have taken *tak(e)* as disyllabic (only
Cl Gg H⁵ spell it *tak*) and substituted *it,* with elision,
for meter.

1643   stere] R S¹ H³ Cx; *t(e)ere* rest and Skt. Cp+ seems
nonsense; Root compares Bo 3.pr12.200.

1660   this²] *that* Cp H¹ D S² S¹ Th Don. Here *that* is
immediately easier (as if to continue: for all *that* Troilus
said), but in the whole construction *that* would be an
otiose second object for *preisen* in 1662.

1665   ay was] Cp H¹ Gg; *was ever(e)* H³ H⁵; *was* H² Ph;
was alwey Cx; *was ay* rest and Rkr Rob Bgh Fsh Wdt.
Cp+ has the less prosaic order and better meter (*tale* and
newe are regularly disyllabic).

1675   and] Cp Cl H¹ D S² H³ Th Don; *and ek(e)* rest and
all other eds. The well-attested reading in Cp+ may, as
headless or possibly Lydgatian, have elicited "correction."

1681   to] Om. Cp Don. The attestation of Cp+ is weak,
but the line is odd. Following the hint of *It nedith not to
you* in H⁴, Donaldson conjectures *Nought it needeth you,*
perhaps rightly.

1693   writen] *iwrite(n)* Cp Cl D Don Fsh. Cp+ may
take *joie* as monosyllabic, but in unambiguous cases in Tr
it is so only once (4.1431).

1708   hire] Cp Cl H¹ D S²; *hym* rest and all eds. J+ may
have been influenced by the immediate context. Cp+ is
clearly harder but has good sense (the sun's and steeds'
sacrifice)—or does Cp+ fail to grasp the (not difficult)
pagan reference?

1723   was of hym] Cp Cl H¹ A D (D: *on* for *of*) S² S¹
Th; *of h. w.* rest and Mck Rkr Wdt. The original is indeterminable.

1725   yate] *yates* Cp D (Don: *gates*). Cp D has the worse
meter and perhaps reverts to a cliché.

1744–71 H² and Ph omit these stanzas, which are added
on an inset leaf in Ph; see Expl. Notes.

1745   hevene] *hevenes* J R H⁴ A S¹ Cx and all eds. but
Skt Don. J+ is not necessarily more pagan (and hence
harder), and the better witness of Cp+ is confirmed
by the singular *hevene* in the source, Bo 2.m8.16. Robinson's textual note indicates he intended to print *hevene.*

1748   knetteth] *enditeth* J R H⁴ Gg H⁵ Mck Rkr; *ken-
nyth* H³; *endith* H⁵; *endueth* Cx. Both terms are used in
Bo (that of J+ with *lawes*); Cp+ is better attested, is
perhaps harder, and continues the theme of joining—
perhaps a Chaucerian revision.

1805   Envye Ire] *E. and I.* J A S¹ Mck Rob Bgh; *and I.
E.* Cp H¹ Cx Th; *I. E.* D S² Don. Cp+ and J+ remove
the effective clashing stresses. D S² may be original but
is weakly attested.

BOOK IV

12   myn herte right now] *r. n. m. h.* J Cl H⁴ S¹ H³ H²
Ph H⁵ Cx and all eds. but Don. Cp+ has a less common
emphasis, but J+ is perhaps right.

37   they issen mente] J Mck; *t. issu m.* Ph; *the thus m.*
H²; *of assignement* H⁵; *t. fouhten m.* H⁴; *t. fight(e)(n) m.* rest
and all other eds. That *issen* is hard is confirmed by its

corruption in H² and H⁵; its originality is confirmed by
the Italian "uscì"; *fighten* is derived from 34.

39–40 These lines are transposed in J R H⁴ H³ H² Ph
Cx Mck Rkr; the original order is indeterminable.

42   hem faste] J H⁴ Cx Mck Rkr; *ful f.* R; *faste they* H³;
anon(e) hem Cp Cl H¹ A S¹ H⁵ Th and all other eds.;
anon(e) thei S² H² Ph; *thei* D. J+ is preferred to Cp+ for
alliteration; see Expl. Notes. R is possible (and even
more alliterative) if *Hir(e)/Her(e)* at the beginning of
the line is the adverb rather than the possessive pronoun:
only J Cp A spell it with *i,* and S² and S¹ read *There.* But
the action is *out* (39), and probably not *here.*

57–59 J R H⁴ S¹ Cx Mck Rkr read *But natheles a trewe
was ther take / At greke(s) requeste and tho they gonnen trete /
Of prisoners a chaunge for to make . . .* (in 58, J and H⁴ have
gret for *greke(s),* other minor variants). For *Of prisoners* in
Cp+, H³ and H⁵ read *To Pryamus.* In 57, S² and H⁵ (like
J H⁴) read *gret(e)* for *Grek(e);* H³ reads *his;* Cp H¹ S² H⁵
Th read *a* for *at,* nonsensically with *Of Priamus.* Along
with R (58), Cl A D H² Ph (57) read *Grekes* for *Grek;*
the latter is preferred as being harder and having better
meter. H³ and H⁵ are closest to the Italian; the lines may
have been revised. See Expl. Notes.

80   me yow] J S¹ H² Ph H⁵ Mck Rkr Rob Bgh Wdt;
it me Cp Cl H¹ S² Skt Don Fsh; *me* R Th; other variants.
Root shrewdly guessed an error like R's (caused by reading *herd* as *herde?*) caused the variation. Cp+ seems too
hard; *me it* is conceivable.

88   yow lordes for] Cp Cl H¹ S² Th; *my lordis yow* rest
and Mck Rkr Wdt. Neither reading is especially hard;
J+ may be right.

101   if that] *(y)if* J H⁴ H³ H² Ph H⁵ Cx Mck Rkr.
J+ may have resulted from trouble with the (normally)
slurred and elided *nevere.*

166   Lest for thi werk] *Yif thow debate it lest* J R H⁴ S¹
H³ Mck Rkr Wdt. (Cx varies.) J+ is perhaps harder and
right but looks like a scribal clarification.

191   to folk] Cp Cl D S² Th Don Fsh; *tolk* H¹; *of folkes*
H³; *of folk* rest and all other eds. The usage "have need
to some thing" is not found elsewhere in Chaucer but is
good Middle English (see MED s.v. *nede*) and is clearly
less common.

197   trewe] *soth* J R H⁴ H³ H² Ph Gg H⁵ Cx Mck Rkr
Wdt. Original is indeterminable.

200   let hem to] H³ Cx Don; *l. h. nat* J Cl A D S¹ Ph
Gg H⁵ Skt Rkr Rob Bgh Fsh Wdt; *l. h.* Cp H⁴ S² H² Th;
ne l. h. H¹; *lettyth h.* R Mck. *Letteth* meaning "hinders"
is harder; its contracted form *let* requires *to* (cf. 2.94–95,
etc.) or (with the easier sense "allows") *nat* for meter.
R may be right; H³ Cx best explains the rest.

220   Unto] Cp Cl H¹ A D S² Th; *Into* rest and Mck Rkr
Wdt. Original is indeterminable.

247 Ph Gg H⁵ read *So wep(t)yn that thei semyn well(is)
twey(e),* reflecting the Italian *parean* (French *sembloit*) and
perhaps Chaucer's earlier version. Could an original
semeden have elicited *stremeden?*

261   thus] *the* A D S² S¹ Th Rob. A+ seems closer to
the Italian (*che t'ho io fatto*), fuller; Cp+ was perhaps
influenced by repeated *thus* in 260, 263, 264. But the
hiatus *the agylte* is suspect; in 3.1457 the words are elided.

282   whiderward . . . me] J (*me* added by corrector);
whedyrward(es) R H⁴ H³ H² Cx Mck Rkr; *whidir . . . hit*
Ph; *whedyr . . . that* Gg; *whider/wheder . . . me* rest and
all other eds. Cp+'s stress pattern is poor, and scribes
may have shortened *whiderward,* not thinking of slurred

wold'st (cf. ProMkT VII.1945, NPT VII.3346). But Cp+ or R+ (with the easiest meter) may be right.

288	O²] J H¹ A S² S¹ Ph Gg Cx Th Mck Rob Bgh; *of* rest and all other eds. Scribes replaced the personification in J+ with the more familiar address to the lord of love. Cf. 3.1254.

295	shal I] *I may* Cp Cl H¹ A D S² Th Skt; *may I* Don Fsh. Cp+ makes good sense within 295 but poor sense in the larger context; J+ is closer to the Italian and would appear corrupt if not grasped as interrogative.

317	thilke] *this* Cp Cl H¹ A D S² Th Don; *that* H³ Cx; *ye ilke* Gg. Cp+ is possibly headless and right, but J+ is slightly harder and has good emphasis.

318	my] A D H² Ph Gg H⁵ Mck Rob; *thy* S¹ Th Don; *youre* H³; *the* rest and all other eds. A+ is closer to the Italian (*mie pene*); Cp+ may "correct" the grammar, taking *peyne* rather than *lady sovereigne* with *Of . . . soule.*

331	eiled] *eyleth* Cl R H⁴ H³ Gg Cx and all eds. but Rkr Don Wdt. Cl+ conforms to a cliché; the tense is preterite in the Italian source (*mosse*).

342	nor] *or* Cp H¹ S² Th Don; *ne* R A H³ H² Ph H⁵. J+ is harder than R+, is better attested and has better stress than Cp+.

434	At tother in H¹ makes sense of a spray of variants: *at oothir* Cp+ Don; *at the other* Cl Gg H⁵ Th Skt Bgh Fsh; *at(te) another* R A H³, *at that other* H⁴ D Cx; *atte other* S².

435	laste] Skt Mck; *l. he* Cl D S² S¹ H³ H² Gg H⁵ Cx Th and all other eds. Cp+ has the harder construction, taking 434 as parenthetical; Cl+ requires elision of the *-e* of *laste* for meter and would sound nearly like Cp+.

438	a wight] *hir(e)* J Cl A D H³ Ph Gg H⁵ Skt Mck Rob Bgh Fsh. Cp+'s less smooth but Chaucerian meter may have induced the alteration from the generalized *a wight* in a scribal clarification.

441	thus do] *do thus* D; *so do* J H³ Ph Mck Rkr; *do* Gg; *so werke* R H⁴ H². Original is indeterminable (Italian is *commetta*).

462	for thi wo that] J R H⁴ H² Ph Gg Cx Th and all eds. but Fsh; *f. t. w. t. woll* H⁵; *f. t. w. and* Cp H¹; *f. t. w. at* A; *that f. t. w. hath* Cl H³ Fsh; *that f. t. w.* D; *that f. t. w. wolde* S¹; *f. the wold wo or* S². J+ is hard enough to elicit the variation.

469	lightly] *wightly* Cp. Cp's rarer word is tempting but was probably induced by the nearby *w*'s. Chaucer seems to have used *wight* (swift, active) only in representing Northern dialect (RvT I.4086, and *wyghtly* in a variant at RvT I.4102).

478	a lasse] J Cl H⁴ D S¹ H³ Ph Cx; *lasse* Cp H¹ A S² Th Skt Don Wdt; *a(l)las* R H² Gg H⁵. R+ strengthens J+'s witness. Cf. note 2.1749 above.

481	unto] Cp H¹ A D S² Th Don Wdt; *arst to* Ph; *thus by* R; *thus to* rest and all other eds. Original is indeterminable.

484	now] *this* J R H⁴ H³ H² Ph Gg H⁵ Mck Rkr. Original is indeterminable.

491–532	Cp omits 6 stanzas; text from Cl.

498	Nay God wot] *Nay Pandar(us)* J H³ Ph Gg H⁵ Mck Don; *Nay nay g. w.* R H⁴ S¹ H² Cx Skt Rkr Wdt. R+ is attractive but probably, like J+, emends a headless line.

499	J H³ Ph Gg H⁵ Mck Don have *But douteles for aught that may bifalle,* an easier reading.

527	argumentz] J Cl H¹; *argument* A Gg H⁵; *argumentes* rest and Fsh.

to] Om. Cl R Th Fsh. Either J H¹ or R is right; *to* is well attested.

532	thi nyce fare] Cl H¹ A D S² Cx Th; *this n. f.* Ph Rkr; *this n. care* J R S¹ H³ H² Mck Don; *al thi n. care* H⁴; *thy(n) gret(e) care* Gg H⁵. Cl+, as rime riche, is probably harder than *care,* the attractive alternative.

570	moste] *have* J H³ Ph Gg H⁵ Mck.

	han] *yit* J H³ Ph Gg H⁵ Mck; *save* H² H⁴ Cx; *kepe* R. Cp+ has better sense than J+, better meter than H²+.

581	ther is but litel] *is t. b. l.* R H⁴ H² Cx Rkr; *is l. hertes* J H³ Ph Gg H⁵ Mck. J+ repeats from *herte,* 580.

590	preciously] J H³ Ph Gg H⁵ Mck; *preciently* R; *curyously* Cx; *corteisly* rest and all other eds. ProWBT III.148 and MerT IV.1962 prove J+'s word Chaucerian in this sense; R proves it hard (MED records no use in this sense outside of Chaucer); Cx may prove that Cp+ gives worse sense. The Italian has *sottilmente.* Root may be right that Cp+ corrupts Cx (Text. Trad., 200), but Cx may corrupt (correctly glossing) J+.

594	ifounde] *sownde* S²; *stounde* R H⁴ S¹ H² Cx Rkr. A very easy error like S²'s made nonsense and led to R+; the reverse sequence is unlikely.

596	rape in my dom] J H³ H⁵ Mck; *jape in my(n) dom(e)* Ph Gg; *shame unto yow* (with variants) rest and all other eds. The more striking J+ reading picks up *rapir* from the Italian. An error like that in Ph Gg could have caused Cp+'s variation, or Chaucer may have revised.

599	unto] Cp Cl H¹ A D S² Ph Th Fsh; *into* Gg (om. *thus*); *to* rest and all other eds. Cp+ is metrically harder and is well attested.

601	unto] Cp H¹ S² Th; *to* rest and all eds. As *-to his* would be slurred or elided, Cp+ has the better meter, and is harder. Cf. note 1.20 above.

630	it] R H¹ A S¹ H² H⁵; om. rest and Rkr Don. Chaucer nowhere else uses *recche* transitively (unless such phrases as *recche nat a bene* are examples), but enough scribes considered the grammar adequate and Cp+'s meter is poor; MED gives examples from Gower, etc., of transitive *recchen,* "take heed of" (s.v. *recchen* v. 2.a.).

638	J H³ Ph Gg H⁵ Mck: *Pandare answerde of that be as be* (H³ *it*; H⁵ *it be*) *may.*

	Pandare] J+ and R H⁴ A D S¹ H² Rkr Wdt; *Pandarus* rest and all other eds. Either version is attractive. R+'s form of Pandarus's name makes better meter.

657	in] Cp Cl H¹ A D S² S¹ Th; *of* rest and Mck Rkr Rob Bgh. Cp+ is perhaps harder but perhaps influenced by *in* in 658.

708–14	Cp Cl H¹ A D S² omit this obviously authentic stanza. Text from J.

728	ache] *eche* Gg. Conceivably Gg preserves an original *itch;* see Expl. Notes.

750–56	J H³ Ph Gg Mck set this stanza after line 735, perhaps representing an earlier version, closer to the Italian order. See comments in Windeatt (44) and Root (513).

751	ful] R Ph Gg; *dooth* S¹ Cx; om. rest and Rkr Don. A trisyllabic *Aperil* (H¹; *Aperille* Cl R; rest *April[le]*) and *ful* are needed for meter, but *ful* is very likely a scribal supplement to a corrupt ancestor. Chaucer once wrote *ful swithe* (PardT VI.796) but often uses the phrase *as swythe:* an ancestral *as* here, hard in sense and occurring earlier in the line, could have confused scribes.

791	and] Cp Cl H¹ A S² Th Skt Don; *is with* Cx; *with* rest and all other eds. Original is indeterminable.

820   shame] J H³ Ph Mck; *sowne* R; *sorwe* rest and all other eds. The Italian has *vergogna,* usually meaning "shame," but sometimes simply "embarrassment." Conceivably Cp+ is right; Chaucer may have revised for sense, as Criseyde has no special reason to feel shame here.

867   On] Cp H¹ S² Cx Th Don; *In* rest and all other eds. Chaucer normally has *finde in,* but see Tr 4.1165. Cp+ is harder, but perhaps too hard: MED offers no support for *finde on.*

876   ye] *wel ye* J R S¹ H³ Ph Gg Mck Rob Bgh Fsh. J+ supplies for meter, but *trowe* is sometimes disyllabic and *ye han* an unlikely elision.

882 Cp Cl H¹ A D S² S¹ Th and all eds. but Mck Rkr read *For verray wo his wit is al aweye.* J+'s deathliness seems better in a context of what earthly tongues cannot say, and its loose grammatical connection with the preceding lines or its corruption in some MSS (H⁴ H²: *shortly he that*) may have troubled scribes. The unusual sense of *As he that* here ("for he") is paralleled in Tr 1.96 and treated by Mustanoja, ME Syntax, 199. Cp+, if scribal, may draw its inspiration from 4.357. The expression in J+ is common (KnT I.2541, Tr 4.955, 5.1211), however, and Windeatt observes that J+ seems awkward before 883–84. J+ is closer to the Italian (*vuol morire,* "wishes to die").

903   his] *this* Cp R H⁴ H¹ A S² H² Th and all eds. but Mck Wdt. J+ makes obvious sense in context—perhaps too obvious, as Criseyde repeats her notion thrice.

907   I woot] Mck Rkr; *woot I* Cp Cl H¹ D S² S¹ Th and all other eds.; *I wote I* A. J+ avoids *I it* hiatus.

910   herte] R H⁴ H³ Gg Cx Th; *h. that* Ph; *h. he* rest and Rkr. An ancestral copy, perhaps the archetype, confused by the *goost* (vital spirit) beating (intransitively) in the heart, supplied *he,* to comic effect.

938   that that] J H³ Gg Mck Rkr; *that* R H⁴ H² Ph Cx; *what that* Cp Cl H¹ A D S² S¹ Th and all other eds. J+ is hardest and explains R+ and Cp+. Cf. note 3.1073 above.

944   his] Cl R H⁴ H² Gg Cx Rkr Wdt; *this* rest and all other eds. Cl+ has the sharper sense; cf. 903 variation above.

953–1078 H⁴ H³ Gg omit this passage; Ph contains it on an inset leaf. See Expl. Notes. H⁴ and H³ also omit 1079–85, contained on the inset leaf in Ph.

957   lorn] *l. so* J R D S¹ Cx Mck Rob Bgh Fsh Wdt. An effectively Lydgatian line.

1081   or] *and* J D S² H² Gg Cx Th and all eds. but Skt Don Fsh. For other *or . . . or* correlatives see 1.497, LGW 2698, etc. Most editors punctuate with a comma or nothing after *sorwe* and read *and,* perhaps rightly, as scribes might misconstrue before reading 1082. But Cp+ is hard and well attested.

1100   a] *my(n)* J R H⁴ H³ Ph Gg Cx Mck Rkr Rob Bgh Wdt; *and* A. (H² varies.) Original is indeterminable.

1107   of that that I shal] Cl A Skt Fsh; *of that I s.* Cp; *of that I s. the* R H⁴ H² Cx Rkr Rob Bgh Don Wdt; *of al that I s.* H¹ D S² Th; *of that I s. yow* S¹; *what that I s. the* J; *what I s. the* H³ Gg Mck; *what that I s.* Ph. Since *hede,* unusually, is treated as monosyllabic at 2.581, J is possible, but H³ Gg and Ph are better. Of MSS with well-attested *of,* Cl A is hardest and most likely to cause an error like Cp's, giving rise to the variants.

1110   mor] Cp H⁴; *mo* J Cl R H¹ S² S¹ Th and all eds. but Wdt; *more* rest. Monosyllabic *mor(e)* is harder and better attested than *mo.*

1120   this] *thi* J Cl H³ H² Th Mck Rob Bgh Fsh. The better-attested *this* gives slightly less obvious sense.

1143   oughte] J Cl R H² Skt Mck; *owe to* Cp S² Wdt; *owen to* H¹; *ought(e) to* rest and all other eds. The form in J+, with good meter, would elicit from scribes the more common expression with *to.* A singular verb would be expected in the impersonal construction; hence the Cp S² *owe* (for *oweth*) is anomalous in form as well as less apt in tense.

1178   for²] *and* J H³ Ph Gg Mck Rkr; *ne* R H⁴; om. H² Cx. The sense of Cp+ is harder. H² Cx could be right, with the reading *wiste* for *woot* (so J H³ Ph Gg).

1216   Cipride] J R S¹ H² Ph; *enpride* A; *Cupide* rest, Skt Don. J+ has the harder sense.

1218   conforte] J H³ Ph Gg Mck; *to glad(e)* rest and all other eds. (D: *he begladded hir.*) The Italian has *confortò;* Cp+ repeats at 1220.

1223   that] Om. Cp R H⁴ H³ H² Gg Cx Don; *she* Ph. Conceivably Lydgatian or caesural hiatus, but more likely Cp+ thought *as that* hard. The variant *as that* at note 1.496 above is not quite parallel; MED offers no support s.v. *as* for this use of *as that.*

1239   that] Cp R H¹ D S² S¹ Th Don Wdt; *the* rest and all other eds. Cp+ is arguably more expressive in context, and scribal substitution of *the* for *that* is more likely than the reverse.

1241   slawe] R Gg Mck Rob Don; *slayn(e)* rest and all other eds. (the *-e* of *slayne* in some MSS is inorganic); scribes regularly write the more modern *slayn* unless compelled by rhyme. See Kittredge, Observations, 317.

1303   this the] R H⁴ S¹ H² Rkr Rob Bgh Wdt; *that the* Cl D H³ Fsh Skt; *this that* J Ph (*this is that* Gg) Mck; *the* Cp H¹ A S² Th Don. R+ is slightly harder; Cl+ probably "corrects" the error of Cp+.

1324   oft-tyme] H¹ S² S¹ Th; *ofte tyme(s)* Cp Cl A D Rob Bgh Don Fsh Wdt; *ofte(n)* rest and Skt Mck Rkr. H¹+'s disyllable is unusual enough to elicit variants. MED gives *oft-time* as a variant of *ofte-time.*

1339   so] Om. Cp Gg Don. Cp Gg is possibly right in a headless line, but Chaucer has disyllabic and trisyllabic *coveiteth,* and *so* would be metrical even if the line were headless.

1344   neded] *nedede* Cl; *nedeth* Cp A S² H³ Gg Cx Mck Don. **nought to]** *nought* Cp H¹; *no thyng to* Cx. Cl's appropriate subjunctive form *nedede* (cf. 5.726) with the Cp H¹ omission of *to* would yield the right number of syllables, but the stress pattern is unlikely. With *nedeth,* Cp+ substitutes a more common expression.

1372   how] *now* Cp R H⁴ H³ H² Gg Th Rob Bgh Don. The Cp+ reading, the easier *now* (repeated from 1370), seems to ask Troilus to assent to listen rather than, with better sense, to assent to a certain conduct.

1388–1409 Cp omits from *but* in 1388 through *seyn* in 1409—an eyeskip. Text from Cl.

1424   him] *it* Cp H¹ D S² Th Don; *he* Ph; om. H² H⁴. J+ has the harder reading.

1461   so] Om. Cp R H⁴ A Cx Don. (H³ H² vary.) Possibly Lydgatian, but the sense is better with J+.

1535   for other] *for any o.* Cp S¹ Th; *of o.* Cl Cx Skt Rob; *of any o.* H¹ Gg; *any o.* S² Don; *othir* H⁴ H³. In the immediate context *of* is easier; the line with *any* is hypermetrical.

1541   this] *thus* Cp R D Ph Don. J+ is better attested and perhaps harder as redundant with *it* in 1542 (only R omits *it*).

1549   rennest] R Ph Gg Cx; *ay r.* J Cl A D H³ Mck Fsh Wdt; *r. ay* Cp H⁴ H¹ S² S¹ H² Th and all other eds. Cp+ is perhaps right, and rennest to be read as monosyllabic; but J+ seems to supply *ay* for a monosyllabic *Troy(e)* (in fact abnormal), and Cp+ transposes.

1694   hym] *he* Cp H¹ A S² Cx Th Don. J+ has the better grammar.

BOOK V

7   All the MSS (and Rkr) read *Lathesis;* Cx Th read *Lachesis.*

8   gold-tressed] Fsh; *goldetressed* D H³ Th Rkr Bgh Wdt; *golde dressed* A; *auricomus tressed* H²; *golden tressed* Skt; *gold-ytressed* Mck Rob Don. Cp+ is technically Lydgatian but satisfactory in rhythm. See Expl. Notes.

9   cleene] J Ph; *she(e)ne* R H⁴ S¹ H² Skt Mck Rkr; *clere* rest. R+ is easier; Cp+ is very easy but unrhymed.

26   heretofore] Cp H¹ S² Th Skt Don; *herebyfore* rest and all other eds. Cp+ is less common.

37   horse] S¹ H² Gg Th; *his hors* J; *hor* R; *hors* rest and Rkr Don Fsh. A "petrified dative" is presumed for meter; there are no other unambiguous cases with *horse* in Chaucer. See Kittredge, Observations, 36–37.

42   drye] *crye* Cp H¹ (D in a later correction) S² Th Don. J+, a less common word, gives better sense.

60–61   Cp Cl H¹ A D S² Th (and, with variation, Gg) transpose these lines. J+ (with Mck Rkr Wdt) has a better sequence of sense from 59 to 60 and avoids like beginnings of 59 and 60 (which probably caused the error); but Cp+ may be right. See Root, Text. Trad., 231. In 60, J Cl R A Cx have *nys,* perhaps correctly.

63   swete] *deere* J R H⁴ S¹ H³ H² Ph Gg Cx Mck Rkr Wdt. Original is indeterminable.

107   tyme was] Mck Rkr Wdt; *this was don* Cp Cl H¹ A D S² Th. J+ seems to give a little sharper sense, and Cp+ is perhaps influenced by *this* of 108, but either reading is possible.

183   thonketh] Cp Th Don Wdt; *thonked* rest and all other eds. The hard tense shift is still not accepted in 186 by five MSS.

202   nothyng] *no wight* J H³ Ph Mck Wdt; *non man* Gg (by corrector). J+'s arguably slightly better sense is too poorly attested.

211   walwith] H⁴ Gg Cx; *waltryth* R; *whieleth* J Don; *swellith* Ph; *weyleth* rest and Skt. Ph demonstrates that H⁴+ is hard; J (intelligently) and Cp+ (blandly) corrupt it. OED shows *waltryth* means the same; R is possibly right.

242   sustene] no MS; *this s.* Cp Cl H¹ A D S² S¹ Th Skt (*thus s.* Don); *ek(e) s.* rest and all other eds. J+ is possible, but hiatus before *how,* although rare, is Chaucerian (see 3.1102) and here effective; scribes "corrected" with words from 240 and 241.

243   pale] Cp H¹ S²; *p. and* rest and all eds. Cp+ has the less common usage; cf. note 3.1422 above and note 5.823 below.

277   for] J R H⁴ Mck Rob Bgh; om. rest. Chaucer ten times elsewhere concludes a line *wont to do(one):* scribes may revert to the cliché, producing poor meter. Cl's reading *wonted* possibly points to an original unsyncopated *woned* (see LGW 2353, dubiously BD 150).

306   That that] *That al* Cl H³ Skt Don Wdt; *That it* A D Gg. Scribes as usual avoid *that that.*

315   preyen hire kepe] *preyen h. to k.* Cp Cl H¹ A Th Fsh; *prei(e) h. to kepe* H⁴ D S² H³ Cx. Cp+'s *to is* unmetrical, but its slurred *preyen* is probably original. Reading it as a disyllable induced *to* for an iambic rhythm but produced a hexameter.

374   cometh] *comen* J R H⁴ Mck Rkr Rob; *come* H² Cx; *commes* S². J+ over-precisely alters the verb to plural.

409   jouken] *rowken* Cx Th Mck. Both words are rare and apt; Cp+ is better attested.

410   trust to] *trust(e)* J R H⁴ D H² Gg Mck Rkr Wdt; *thow trust to* Cl Fsh; *trust thou* S² H³ Cx. Cp+'s usage with *to* is Chaucerian (see 1.601, 2.491: variants aroused in both places) and harder; *trust* should have no *-e* here.

412   seyn] J R H⁴ H³ H² Ph Gg Cx Mck Rkr Wdt; *wene* rest. J+'s smoother meter is supported by the Italian *diria;* Cp+ is perhaps influenced by the *w* of *wol.*

417   smert] *smerte* Cp A D S² H² Skt Wdt; *smertith* Ph. The original is a contracted verb (see ABC 152).

436   largesse] J H⁴ H³ H² Ph Gg Cx (R out); *prowesse* rest and Skt Don. J+ is clearly more apt in context; scribes were influenced by the repeated line-ending *heigh* (2.632) or *excellent* (1.438, 2.660) *prowesse.*

459   pleye] D Cx Th; *to p.* Cp H⁴ Ph Gg Don; *so to p.* H³; *so p.* rest and all eds. but Don. D+'s reading (as a verb or—in the context, harder and with better sense—as a noun) explains the variation: *so* is not very apt, and *to* is an obvious supplement in the context of infinitives. J H⁴ S¹ H² Gg read *instrument,* and Cl H¹ read *instrumentz:* the trisyllable induced the error.

466   here] *there* Cp Cl S² Th Don. Cp+ attempts to improve the sense or avoids rime riche.

468   nat] Cp S¹; *is not* H⁴; *is* D; *was* S²; *nas* rest and all eds. Cp+ contracts *this is* to *this* (H⁴ expands the contraction) and is thus hardest. See Kittredge, Observations, 387. Roscow (Syntax and Style, 94–95) suggests that in such expressions *is* is elided rather than assimilated to *this.* See also Kerkhof, Sts. in the Lang. of G. Ch., 2nd ed., 1982, 83.

478   bleve] *beleve/bileve* H⁴ A S² H³ H² Ph Gg Cx Don. Kittredge suggests that the emphasis on *here* allows its rare non-line-end pronounced *-e* (Observations, 204). H⁴+ may be right, but the more common form *bleve* is better attested.

495   holden forth] Cp H¹ S¹ Th Don; *holde forth* Cl A D Skt Rob Bgh Fsh Wdt; *hold forth* S²; *hold(e)* J H⁴ H³ H² Ph Gg Rkr; *forth hold* Cx Mck. Cp+ and Cl+ are metrically equivalent. J+'s headless line is possible (Cp+ is perhaps influenced by *Holde forward* in 497) but more likely confused by the meter, in which Cp+ may (uniquely in Chaucer) slur *Lat us* as *Lat's. Holde forth* occurs also at 1.263, 5.1745.

498   Thus] *This* Cp H¹ D S² S¹ Cx Th Rkr Don. J+ has the better sense.

509   pleyde] H⁴ H³ H² Cx; *seyde* rest and Skt Don. Cp+ repeats the rhyme of 506; perhaps it represents an archetypal error.

565   last my lady] J R H³ H² Ph Gg Cx; *my lady last* H⁴; *myn owen(e) lady* rest and Skt Don Fsh. In Cp+, the loss of *last* (which complements *first* in 567 but is unlikely to have been introduced by scribes) was perhaps induced by the *la-* of *lady* and was compensated for by *owene.*

583   my] J R H³ H² Gg; om. rest and Fsh. Although Chaucer normally stresses *memorie* as a sdrucciolo (dactyl), confirmed here by the rhymes, Cp+ emends to get the more modern stressing.

662 do] Cp R A D H³ Cx Rob Bgh Don; *go* rest. J+ is an obvious substitution. Chaucer here seems to follow the French: *qu'il ne souloit faire. Do* fairly often rhymes with words with open *o* (Skeat, Rime-Index, 15).

670 tho] Cp Cl A S² S¹ H³ (D: *yonder tho the,* with *the* added interlinearly); *the* rest and Mck Rkr Rob Bgh. Cp+ is harder.

725 weep] R Skt Mck; *wepe* Ph; *wept(e)/wepid* rest and all other eds. The strong form is less common but has better meter; see 5.1046 and n. below and Kittredge, Observations, 250.

726 nedede] Cl; *neded* (Don)/*nede/nedit(h)* rest. See note 4.1344 above.

no] *non* J H¹; *none* Cp A Gg Don; *nat no* R. Cp+ and R compensate for disyllabic *neded.*

733 withinne] *w. tho* J Cl H¹ S¹ Rob Bgh Fsh; *w. the* Cp A H³ Don Wdt. Even as a preposition *withinne* can be trisyllabic (see 5.969 and Kittredge, Observations, 200), but it is uncommon enough to be hard and arouse the variants. All the variants are possible.

752 in] *on* Cl S¹ Ph Cx Th and all eds.; *be/by* H⁴ H². The idiom with *in* is rare (some scribes have it in variants to 1.321, 3.1735, etc.), but MerT IV.2226 proves it Chaucerian. Were the MS witness for *in* weaker, it might be taken as an error induced by the common phrase *in som maner(e).*

780 nevere] *ever(e)* Cp D H³ Don. Cp+, harder, is perhaps right, but it could arise from influence of the common phrase "ever since": Chaucer normally requires more negation than a simple *ne* in such contexts.

783 naught n'agreveth] No MS; *not agreveth* H⁴; *nought ne greveth* D (*ne* corrected from *ner*) Cx; *nought it g.* R S² Ph; *nought it ne g.* Cp H¹ Th Don; *it naught ne g.* J Cl A (A: *greved*) S¹ H³ and all eds. but Don; *it not me g.* H² (Gg varies). J+, H⁴, D Cx, and R+ are all possible; the conjecture adopted best explains the variants and parallels the forms in 784.

809 tymes] Cp D S¹ H³ H² Don; *tyme* rest (Cx *of-tyme*). The form in Cp+ is less common.

823 lusty] Cp J S² S¹ H² Ph Mck Don; *l. and* rest. The addition is easy (Ph adds *and* after *Charitable*); cf. 5.243, 3.1422.

924 kyng] Mck Rkr Wdt; *lord(e)* Cp Cl A D S² S¹ Th and all other eds. As the next stanzas show, the more specific title *kyng* is on Diomede's mind. Cp+ was perhaps influenced by line 889; J+ is supported by the Italian *re.*

938 Polymyte] Don Fsh; *Polomytes* R H⁴ H³ H² Ph Cx. Chaucer knew of the stress on the third syllable from the Latin (1498a) and so stresses it in 5.1507, but stresses on the second in 5.1488. The weakly attested form with *-s* may reflect scribal memory of the Latin form or an effort to "improve" a headless line.

944 Ye wol] *That ye* J R H⁴ H³ H² Ph Gg Cx Mck Rkr Wdt. The syntax is hard with either reading: if we can understand "I will seek your grace as long as (*So . . . [That]*) you (will) grant me . . . ," then J+ is slightly clearer and hence more likely scribal.

952 may] *mow(e)* Cp H¹ S² Th Don; *schul* Gg. Cp+ is harder but metrically inferior (elision is doubtful before *here,* "hear").

983 ysonder] Cp Rob Bgh; *in sonder* S²; *asonder* rest. The Cp by-form is less common. S² may be right—see MED *insonder.*

991 Peraventure so] Ph; *Peraunter so* Cp; *P. so than* S¹;

P. than(ne) so H⁴ A H² Gg Cx Th; *Peraunter then(ne) so* J Cl R H¹ D S² and all eds.; *Peraunter than* H³. Although the longer form *peraventure* is common in Chaucer, he uses the shorter form in all other instances in Tr; a pentasyllabic *peraventure* here would be less familiar and therefore perhaps harder and would explain the variants. A non-line-end *thanne* that is disyllabic is dubious, although some editors read it in 3.124 (Cp, Rob, etc.) and 5.1289—both, I think, headless lines scribally "improved." But see Kittredge, Observations, 198. So Cl R H⁴ A S² Gg read *thanne/thenne* here.

992 nevere yit I] H⁴ Ph Cx; *n. yit ne* Gg; *I n. yit* J; *I n.* R H³ H²; *I n. er(e)* Cp Cl H¹ A D Th Skt; *I n. are* S²; *n. ere* I S¹ Don. H⁴+ is preferred, doubtfully, as smoothest. An original sequence *never(e) er(e)* would easily lose *er* and elicit compensating *yit.* The intrusion of *er(e)/are* after *never* (A D S² Th) in line 993, if not original, may support Cp+ by indicating that an *er* in the vicinity caught a scribe's eye. Unattested but perhaps most likely would be an original third *that: That when I se that that I nevere er say* (or R+ or S¹).

1044 in] Rkr Don Fsh; *in the* Cp R H¹ D S¹ H³ Cx. A headless line.

1046 wep] J Gg Skt Mck Wdt; *wepe* H⁴ Ph; *wept(e)* rest and all other eds. See note 5.725 above.

1095 publysshed] R H² Ph Cx Th Skt Mck; *punysshed* rest. Cp+ may have a harder sense in context (so Windeatt), but the word itself is markedly more common—outside of Bo, Chaucer uses *publish* only twice elsewhere—and *publysshed* is apt: being rolled on tongues is punishment for a gentle lady. Some citations in MED *publishen* 1.(g) support a sense "to disgrace."

1102 often] J Cl R Ph; *oft* Cp H¹; *often tyme* S¹; *ofte* H⁴ and rest and Don. J+ (or H⁴+) is smoother, but the Lydgatian line of Cp H¹ is possible.

1133 that¹] Om. J A Ph. J+ is weakly attested but as headless is possibly right.

cape] Cp J Cl H¹; *gape* rest and Rkr Rob Bgh Fsh. Cp+ has the less common word.

1175 that²] J Cl R H⁴ S¹; *at* A; om. rest and Don. The common avoidance of *that that.*

1213 woode] *the w.* Cl D H³ Ph Rob Bgh Don Fsh. Some scribes wished to contract *clepeth* or read *wood.* Robinson, Baugh, and Donaldson were probably influenced by a Ch Soc. transcript error, Cp with *the.*

1214 this] Cp Cl H¹ S² S¹ Cx Th; *his* rest and Mck Rkr Wdt. Cp+ is slightly harder.

1224 But] Rkr Wdt; *And* Cx and all other eds. Editors were misled by errors in Ch Soc. transcripts of Cp and Cl.

1228 so] Om. Cp H⁴ H³ H² Gg Don. The line is conceivably headless, but more likely the scribes were confused by the *so so-* sequence.

1233–74 Cp omits six stanzas; text from Cl (in 1272, Cl alone reads *compleyne,* rest *to pleyne*).

1234 hym] *he* J R H⁴ H² Ph Cx Don. Cl+ seems to have slightly better sense and certainly is not easier.

1252 have I] *I h.* Cl R A H³ Skt Mck Fsh Wdt. J+ has the less prosaic order and (permitting elision) the better meter, and it is better attested.

1270 lith] J R H⁴ H³ H² Ph Gg Cx; *is* rest and Skt Rob Bgh Fsh. J+ is harder. See MilT I. 3525; Tr 5.60 for the meter.

1272 alwey than thus] *than thus a.* H⁴ Gg Cx Rob Bgh; *than a. thus* S² H³ Th Skt Don Wdt. Cl+ is hardest, requiring either the sense "at any rate" of *alwey* or a difficult word order.

1273   the] *my* Cl Skt Rob Bgh Fsh. J+'s harder reading is corroborated, but not proved, by the Italian *il morir.*

1295   of that thow art] *ther(e) thow art* J Cx; *ther thow art now* R H⁴ H² Ph Gg Mck Rkr Wdt. In Cp+, *that* means "that concerning which"; J Cx seems to clarify and R+ to smooth the resulting meter.

1327   yet] Om. Cp H¹ Don. A Lydgatian line (or disyllabic *whiche*) is unlikely here.

1367   wit] Cp J S² S¹; *man* H⁴; *wight* rest and Skt Rkr. Cp+ is hardest.

1390   owen] Bgh Don; *hertes* J Cl R H⁴ H² Ph Gg Cx and all other eds.; *one* H³. J+, perhaps right, may be a scribal intensification.

1413   she] J R H⁴ H³ H² Ph Gg Mck Rkr Wdt; *ye* rest (A: *As the lyf*). J+ is slightly harder and has slightly better sense with the quasi-comparative *As* (see expl. note 1.96 and note 4.882 above).

1440   ne word] Skt; *ne no w.* R H⁴ Cx Mck Rkr Rob Bgh Wdt; *ne w. ne* H³ Don Fsh (Gg: *drank ne no word he ne seyde*). Most scribes restrained themselves from "correcting" the clashing stresses in the final feet of this forceful line.

1444   outen] no MS; *out* D S¹ Gg; *ek out* Cl; *come(n) out(e)* rest and all eds. (Ph transposes, *come nevere*). The hard verb (used in ProWBT III.521, EpiMerT IV.2438, CYT VIII.834) recognized by no scribe; Cl and Cp+ alternately emend. In 3.1498, *out(e)* may also be the verb.

1446   that] *that that* J H⁴ Ph Gg Mck. J+ "improves" a headless line, making nonsense in the whole context, unless Kittredge's suggestion that the second *that* may be the demonstrative adjective is right (Observations, 411).

1498a–l   The Latin argument is found here in all MSS except H⁴ and R. All MSS corrupt 1498c *Hemoniden* (Skt Mck Rob): *Heiiiiioduden* (?) J; *Sinoduden* Gg; *Hemodiden* Ph; *Hermodien* Cx Th; *Homodeden* H³; *Hemoduden* rest and Rkr Wdt. H²'s added line is quoted in Expl. Notes. Skeat places the passage after line 1484 in his text; Windeatt, after 1498; McCormick, Root, and Robinson among the textual notes; Baugh, Donaldson, and Fisher ignore the lines. Conceivably the lines are entirely scribal. In this Latin passage the many shared errors of Cx and Th prove that Th sets directly from Cx. The typesetters had little Latin.

1499   brennynge] D Gg; *burying(e)* rest and all eds. Line 1498f *bustum* supports what would be a harder reading, for scribes unfamiliar with cremation, of better meter; a spelling like *brinnynge* (Cp has *brynnen* in 5.303) or even *burninge* (which would resemble *buriinge*) may lie behind the error. But possibly D Gg improves on Chaucer; Windeatt notes that Roman de Thèbes 2621–30 tells of the burying, not cremation, of Archemorus, and his ashes were interred in any case.

1567   for²] Om. Cp Cl R D H² Ph Mck. (Cx varies.) The meter in Cp+ is so poor and so easily corrected, and

the grouping of MSS so odd, as to suggest that the error was archetypal.

1585   that sithen] H³; *t. sith(e)* H⁴ Cx; *t. syn/sith that* J R D H² Ph Gg Skt Mck Rkr Don Wdt; *syn that* Cp Cl H¹ S² S¹ Th Rob Bgh Fsh. H³ best explains the variation.

1625   on] *an* Cp Cl H¹; *in* H⁴ D Don; *to* S². Chaucer's idiom is hard to determine. With *take* he has *for yvel* in 4.606. Also parallel are "for the best" and "in idle" with *take*. Closest are *take a-game* (Mars 277) and the common idiom *take a-grief.* These support *on/an/in yvel*: any of the three particles would be equivalent to *a-* before a vowel. Best attested is *on*; *an* would confuse the grammar, but as hardest may be right.

1631   Criseyde's signature appears, with small variations, in H¹ D S² S¹ Th and all eds. but Mck Don. Easily lost, but possibly scribal.

1674   myn] *bright* J R H⁴ H² Ph (Gg over erasure) Cx Mck Rkr Wdt. Both expressions are common, but it is easier to imagine a scribe "improving" on *myn*. (The Italian is *O Criseida mia.*)

1776   gilt] *giltes* Cp D Ph Rob Bgh Don. Cp+ unmetrically anticipates the plural *bokes.*

1777   yif] J Mck Rob; *yif that* H⁴ H³; *and* R D; *if* rest and all other eds. The *y-* avoids hiatus.

1791   pace] Cl (corrected from *space*) H⁴ Ph Th; *space* rest and Rkr Wdt. The archetype may have read *space,* anticipating the rhyme-word *Stace* in an *s*-filled context and producing a tongue-twister with a non-Chaucerian verb. Most scribes, not mindful of the whole context, probably took *space* for the noun, to comic effect (cf. 1.714). OED has no citation of *space* "walk" from French *espacer* (*expatiate,* Lat. *spatiari*) before 1572—then probably an inkhorn term. Prof. Robert E. Lewis kindly informs me that the MED files have one other ME citation of *space* as a verb, from before 1450. The expression there speaks of land "spased out by foot mesure." The sense of spatial measurement is more specific than the general sense "walk" in Tr, but it remains possible that some scribes took *space* for a verb.

1795   I] *I to* Cp H⁴ H¹ S² H² Th; *thi* A; *to* J H³ Ph Cx Mck. The sequence of variation is more likely Cl+ to Cp+ to J+ than the reverse, and Cl+ has the best sense in context.

1798   God I] *god* Cp J Cl A Mck; *I god* R Skt *god I the* H². Cp+ and R seem to "correct" for meter, unnecessarily in the exclamatory context, but R may be original. An absolute *god biseche* or an ellipsis of *I* subauded from 1795 is too hard.

1807–27   H² H⁴ omit these stanzas; Ph has them on an inset leaf.

1809   eighthe] J R Cx (spelled *viij, viij^th, eyght*); *seventh(e)* rest and Skt (spelled *vij^th* and *vij* in D and Ph; spelled out in the rest). Regular meter requires J+; *seventhe,* even if pronounced without the *-e* (as sometimes in Chaucer), does not permit elision with the preceding *the.* Kittredge, seeing this but not willing to admit J+, suggests an improbable syncope of the middle vowel of *holughnesse* (Observations, 380). See Expl. Notes.

The Legend of Good Women

Authorities: twelve manuscripts and Thynne's edition:

A¹ Additional 9832, British Library, fol. 4–5, 7–9, 11–14, 16–17, 19–21, 23–25, 27–30, 32–35, 37–39, 41–42ᵛ

A² Additional 12524, British Library, fol. 1–17ᵛ

A³ Additional 28617, British Library, fol. 1–38.

B Bodley 638, Bodleian, fol. 48–95ᵛ

F Fairfax 16, Bodleian, fol. 83–119ᵛ

Ff Cambridge Univ. Library Ff 1.6, fol. 64–67ᵛ

Gg Cambridge Univ. Library Gg 4.27, fol. 445–480ᵛ

P Pepys 2006, Magdalene College, Cambridge, pp. 53–88

R Rawlinson C.86, Bodleian, fol. 113–119ᵛ

S Arch. Selden B.24, Bodleian, fol. 152ᵛ–191ᵛ

T Tanner 346, Bodleian, fol. 1–40ᵛ

Tr Trinity College, Cambridge, R.3.19, fol. 114–150ᵛ

Th Thynne's edition (1532), fol. ccxx–ccxxxiiii

In addition, Arthur Sherbo (SB 35, 1982, 154–55) has drawn attention to a manuscript, now apparently lost, once owned by the eighteenth-century antiquarian Samuel Pegge. Thynne's 1532 edition (Th) must be regarded as an authority, because he had access to the manuscripts, though, since he so often "improved" his texts, his testimony must be regarded with caution.

None of the manuscripts is complete. A¹ has only lines 1–1985, A² only 1640–2723; A³ is a series of fragments, and only lines 513–610, 808–1106, 1156–59, 1306–1515, 1518–1801, 1852–2110, 2125–35, 2151–2723 are collated here; P contains lines 1–705, 777–1377; Ff has only the Legend of Thisbe, R only the Legend of Dido. There are losses through the excision of leaves in Gg (lacks 1836–1907) and S (lacks 2551–2616). Single lines and passages are missing from the other manuscripts as well (for details of the lacunae, see J. B. Bilderbeck, Ch's LGW, 1902, 45–71). Even fragmentary and late manuscripts provide valuable testimony; thus A³ P and R are the only manuscripts to support Gg in including 960–61.

Transcriptions of all the manuscripts have been published by the Chaucer Society: A¹ A² B P (Supp. Parallel Texts of Ch's Min. Poems, new ser. 59); Gg F T Tr S Th (Parallel-Text Ed. of Ch's Min. Poems, new ser. 58); Gg F (One-Text Print of Ch's Min. Poems, new ser. 61); A³ Ff R and the Prologues to F and Gg (Odd Texts of Ch's Min. Poems, new ser. 23). Facsimiles have been printed of B F Ff Gg P T and Thynne's edition (see p. 1117 above); a facsimile edition of Tr is in progress.

Detailed studies of the manuscripts of the Legend were done by Siegfried Kunz (Der Verhältnis der Handschriften von Ch's LGW, 1889), J. B. Bilderbeck (Ch's LGW, 1902), Ernest Amy (The Text of Ch's LGW, 1918; rpt. 1965), and John Koch (Geoffrey Ch: Kleinere Dichtungen, 1928). The formerly vexed question of whether the

Prologue of Gg is an earlier or later version was resolved by John Livingston Lowes in two important articles (PMLA 19, 1904, 593–683 and 20, 1905, 749–864), which argued that the Prologue of Gg is Chaucer's revision, and modern scholarship has generally endorsed this position.

Because of the fragmentary nature of many of the manuscripts, the fact that at least some of the legends circulated separately, and the likelihood of contamination, particularly among the later manuscripts, the exact relations of the manuscripts are obscure. Robinson defined the textual relationships as follows:

MS Gg stands by itself, since it contains the sole copy of the revised version of the Prologue. The other MSS fall into two groups:

$$
\alpha \begin{cases} 1 & Tr\ A^1 \\ 2 & S\ A^2 \\ 3 & Ff\ P\ R\ A^3 \end{cases} \\
\beta \begin{cases} 1 & F\ B \\ 2 & T \end{cases}
$$

In the α group, Tr and A¹ are closely related in shared errors (see, for example, note 1966 below); the relationship between S and A², though less pronounced, is also clear (see, for example, 1902n.), although obscured by the tendency of both scribes to make independent emendations. P and R show a very close connection in the single legend (Dido) that they share (for example, see notes 1058 and 1210 below). Ff and A³ are more problematic: Ff contains only Thisbe, and though it shows some agreements with P (for example, both insert *she* in 858), these are not striking. Likewise, A³, a series of fragments, shows no consistent agreements with any one manuscript or group of manuscripts.

In the β group F and B are closely related (see notes 40, 314, and 542, etc., below). They share a somewhat less pronounced link with T; these three manuscripts (together with A³) replace 2338 with a spurious line after 2339 (*Huges ben thy sorwes and wonder smert*). Thynne's edition shows close affinities with the β group (see notes on F Pro 129, 131, 164, etc., below), but, as is the case with other works, Thynne seems to have had access to more than one manuscript (Bilderbeck, 70, suggests "several"), and he occasionally supplies a striking unique reading (see note 1721 below).

Since Gg is the only manuscript to contain the revised version of the Prologue and since it is the earliest of the surviving manuscripts, dating around the first quarter of the fifteenth century, Robinson regarded it as having a "peculiar authority," though he rejected many of its unique readings. George Kane ("The Text of LGW in CUL Ms Gg.4.27," in ME Sts. Pres. to Norman Davis, ed. D. Gray and E. G. Stanley, 1983, 39–58) suggests a large number of emendations to Gg, some of which we have adopted. He is now preparing, in collaboration with Janet Cowen, a full edition. It is doubtful that Chaucer's revision went beyond the Prologue; Gg has around 250 unique readings throughout the legends but, as the notes

The textual notes to *The Legend of Good Women* were prepared by A. S. G. Edwards with M. C. E. Shaner.

show, most are clearly errors. There is no basis for treating Gg as having unique authority in determining the readings of the lines after the Prologue.

Robinson nevertheless chose Gg as the base text for his edition, and we have done the same. It is not only the earliest of the extant manuscripts, it is relatively complete. As is the case with *The Parliament of Fowls,* the unique readings of this manuscript have been viewed with caution and with an awareness of the scribe's tendency to "correct" his text. Its orthography, as Robinson observed, "departs widely from the usage of most Chaucer MSS," and he therefore normalized it throughout, albeit not with total consistency. Such normalizations are generally not recorded in the notes. The F and G Prologues are based on those respective manuscripts, with the orthography of F likewise normalized, often by the addition of final *-e* (again such adjustments are not recorded in the notes). Throughout, the notes attempt to record all important departures from the base manuscripts. In such cases the readings adopted by Skeat (Skt), the Globe edition, edited by Pollard (Pol), and Robinson (Rob, meaning both his first and second editions unless otherwise indicated) are noted. In the F Prologue occasional reference is made to the editions of Koch (Kch), Baugh (Bgh), and Fisher (Fsh). Amy's and Kane's studies of the text are frequently cited (by name and page number). We do not present full collations. A full set of manuscript variants will be provided in the edition by George Kane and Janet Cowen. Readings unsupported by any editor are generally grouped separately, although, occasionally, where a number of witnesses support Gg in a rejected reading, or where the variation among witnesses is striking, we have included it in the main textual notes.

The forms of the Latin incipits and explicits are those of F (occasionally silently emended). Of the complete, or substantially complete, manuscripts (Gg B F S T Tr) only F and B have complete sets of incipits and explicits. Tr has only incipits and S only explicits, including the only explicit to the Prologue apart from Gg's (*Here endis the prolog of the legendis of good wommen*). Gg provides the authority for the explicit to the Prologue, used here collectively for both forms. Otherwise, Gg has only a title for the Legend of Cleopatra: *Incipit legenda Cleopatrie regine* (fol. 452); *Explicit Cliopater Incipit Semiramus* (deleted; fol. 453 ᵛ).

Title: The traditional title derives from the Prologue, where Alceste exhorts Chaucer: "The moste partye of thy tyme spende / In makyng of a glorious legende / Of goode wymmen, maydenes and wyves" (F 482–84). The designation *legende* is used elsewhere in the Prologue (e.g., F 549, 557, 579). But in the Prologue to the Man of Law's Tale the work is cited as "the Seintes Legende of Cupide" (II.61), and in the Retraction it is described as "the book of the xxv. Ladies" (X.1086–87; some MSS give the number as *xv.* or *xix.*).

Not all MSS have titles; Gg has none. Those that do have titles vary. F and B both call it *The Prologue of .ix goode wymmen* (F also describes it in the table of contents as *The boke of the ix goode women*). Tr calls it *the legend of ladies,* while R, which contains only the Legend of Dido, calls it *The Complaynte of Dido* and ascribes it to Lydgate. Only Th and P call it *The legende of good women,* and, in

the case of P, the title is added in a later hand, possibly on the basis of Th or some later printed edition.

The traditional title is retained here. The characterization in the Prologue to the Man of Law's Tale appears as a subtitle.

PROLOGUE, VERSION F

1   tymes] *sythes* B Gg, probably a scribal variant.
I] om. P.
men] om. F B P.
5   nis] *is* A¹ F Tr Pol.
40   eek this] *suche a* F B Pol; *eke a* P; *lo this* S; *ek* T; *swiche a* Skt.
100   men] Om. F; *they* A¹ Tr Pol; *man* S.
103   thursteth] *trusteth* F A¹; *thrusteth* B S Skt.
129   him] *yt* F B Th Skt Pol Kch; *hem* A¹ Tr; om. P; *in* T.
131   from] *of* F B P T Th Pol.
146   his] *this* Rob (misprint in Rob¹ and Rob²).
164   clepe] *c. yt* F B P T Th Pol Kch; *c. that* S.
211–12   Order reversed in F.
211   so love] *l. so* F B P T Th Pol.
244–45   men . . . shulde] Om. F; supplied from T.
249   Om. F B T (also the heading *Balade*).
261   for] *of* B P T Th Skt Pol.
263–69   F B place after 277.
314   Sir] Om. F B Pol.
326   Om. F; supplied from T.
351   That] *Ther* Gg Skt Rob. *That* ("so that") is clearer, but either reading is possible.
404   dredeful] *sorweful* A¹ S Tr Gg Kch Rob. Kane (57) argues that the penitential *sorweful* is inappropriate in the context of the submission of a conquered rebel.
427   ys] *sithen* S Skt. *Sithen* may be correct, since *ys* is metrically suspect, but S frequently emends for meter.
435   swere] *sweren* F P S T Th Skt Pol Kch Rob.
447   I wol] *ye wolde* F; *I wold(e)* A¹ P Skt Pol Kch.
477   at] *of* F B P S T Th Skt Pol Bgh Fsh.
480   Understonde] *and u.* Gg S Skt Pol Kch Rob; Gg corrects a headless line (Kane, 57).
487   don] *do* Th Rob; *doth* A¹; *did* S; P om. phrase; F B T om. line; *doon* Skt Kch.
502–03   Conflated in F to read *That hast deserved soone in gentil herte.*
508   that] Gg S Tr Skt Pol Kch Rob; om. all other MSS and Fsh.
529   florouns] *floures* all MSS but F Th and all eds. but Pol Rob. Lowes (PMLA 19:593–683) notes that the F Prologue contains many French and French-derived forms, few of which survive in the revision of Gg.
542   so] Om. F B P T Th.
571   diden] *dide* F B S T Th Pol.

Readings from F rejected by all editors:

2   That] Om. (also B).   **6**   or] *or in* (also A¹ B P T Th).   **43**   our] *hir.*   **89**   werk] *werkes* (also B T Th).   **96**   in my] *my* (also P T Tr Th).   **102**   al] Om.   **108**   this] Om.   **124**   alle] *of.*   **126**   hym] *hem* (also B).   **202**   to sprede] *sprede* (also B).   **294**   stynten] *styten.*   **297**   To¹] *The.*   **329**   translated] Om. (also B T).   **364**   But] Om. (also B).   **366**   Or]

of.   **399**   **to]** *vnto* (also B T Th).   **403**   **if]** *it* (also B
P T Th).   **435**   **as]** Om. (also B P T Th).   **436**   **no]**
never (also B P T Th).   **442**   **thus]** Om. (also A¹.)
457   **ye the]** *thee.*   **459**   **yeve me]** Om. (also B P T
Th).   **461**   **put]** *put me* (also T).   **561**   **may]** *my.*
573   **Suffiseth]** *Suffith.*

PROLOGUE, VERSION G

17   **mote]** *motyn* Gg Pol.
34   **make]** *maketh* Pol. Gg may be in error but is retained as possibly an intentional subjunctive.
48   **sprede]** *to s.* Gg Pol. The *to* adds nothing to the
sense and makes the line too long.
51   **gynneth]** *begynnys* Gg Pol. Gg may be correct, since
Chaucer elsewhere uses *-ys* (e.g., BD 73, HF 426), a
recessive variant form in the London dialect (see Burnley, Guide to Ch's Lang., 127).
58   Gg places this line after 76.
63   **And¹]** Om. Gg; supplied by Skt Pol Rob from F 75.
66   **rehersen]** *reherse* Gg; editors emend to avoid elision.
116   **th'atempre]** *the tempre* Gg Pol; *a tempre* Tr A¹.
127–38   This passage is corrupt in Gg, and editors have
extensively revised it. Robinson observed "It looks as if
Chaucer's revision had been left incomplete, or had been
badly corrupted by a scribe." Kane (55–56) discusses the
passage and doubts that there was much revision; he
concludes that "the whole passage may be seen as the
sum of the sort of corruptions the G [Gg] scribe was
capable of." Emendation based on the assumption that
the passage was indeed revised may therefore be suspect.
In the MS it reads:

Some songyn on the brau nchis clere   127
Of love & that joye it was to here
In worschepe & in preysyng of hire make
And of the newe blysful somerys sake   130
That su ngyn blyssede be seynt volentyn
At his day I ches yow to be myn
With oute repenty nge myn herte swete
And therwithal here bekys gu nne mete
The honour & the humble obeysau nce   135
And aft er dedyn othere obseruau ncys
Ryht on to love & to natures
So eche of hem to cryaturys   138

127–28   Kane says that the Gg scribe omitted *And al his
craft* (F 139) through "And-and eyeskip" (55). Accordingly, we have emended from F 139–40.
127   *Some songen [layes] on the braunches clere* Skt Rob.
128   **Layes of love]** *Of love and [May]* Skt Rob; Pollard
also uses F 140 for this line.
130   **for]** *of* Gg Skt.
131   **They]** *That* Gg Skt; *And* Pol.
132   **For on]** *At* Gg; *For at* Skt Pol.
135   **Yelding]** *The* Gg; *They dide* Skt; Pollard and Robinson emend from F 149.
    and] *and the* Gg. **obeysaunces]** *obeysaunce* Gg.
135–36   J. C. McLaughlin (PQ 38, 1959, 515–16)
argues that these lines should be transposed.
137   **Ryht longing]** *R. plesing* Skt; Pollard and Robinson emend on the basis of F 151.
    nature] *natures* Gg Pol.

138   **doth wel]** Om. Gg Pol.
    creature] *cryaturys* Gg Pol.
189   **had]** Om. Gg; supplied by Pollard from F 286.
192   **wyde]** Om. Gg Skt; supplied by Pollard from F
289.
227   **enveroun]** *alle in veroun* Gg Skt Pol. Gg may be
right, though metrically unsatisfactory.
268   **han]** *a* Gg Pol.
271   **ne²]** *me* Rob² (misprint).
289   **wolde]** *wole* Gg Pol.
317   **worthyeste]** *worthyere* Gg Pol.
337   **nat]** Om. Gg Pol; Skt proposed this reading,
based on F 361, and it was adopted by Robinson.
358–93   Gg places these lines after 429.
372   **and most]** *most* Gg; editors supply *and* from F 386.
374   **he]** *be* Pol Rob. **and]** Om. Gg; supplied by Skt Pol
Rob from F 388.
375   **estat]** *stat* Gg Skt.
390   **But]** Om. Gg; supplied by Skeat from F 404.
398   **his]** *this* Rob² (misprint).
399   **wel]** Om. Gg Skt; supplied by Pollard from F 413.
412   **besynesse]** Pollard substitutes *holynesse* from F
424, but *besynesse* is probably a revision.
436   **betere non]** *nevere non betere* Gg; the emendation
is Skeat's, based on F 446.
440   **foryeve]** *foreyve* Rob² (misprint).
451   **put]** *put me* Gg Pol.
456   **to blame]** *blame* Gg Skt Pol.
472   **tyme]** *lyf* Gg Skt.

Readings of Gg rejected by all editors:

88   **seyn]** *s. and.*   **94**   **closed]** *clothede.*   **167**   **Two]**
Tho.   **233**   **mountaunce]** *mountenaunce.*   **293**
they] *thy.*   **314**   **reneyed]** *reneyist.*   **322**   **deite]** *dede.*
333   **preye]** *prere.*   **360**   **of]** *o.*   **367**   **Withouten]**
Which oughtyn.   **384**   **every thing]** *eueryth.*   **388**
ful] *wol.*   **410**   **your]** *thorw.*   **411**   **roundeles]** *r.
and.*   **456**   **oghte]** *may.*   **475**   **lovynge]** *leuynge.*
507   **hertes]** *herte is.*   **509**   **in]** *ek.*

I. THE LEGEND OF CLEOPATRA

587   **at]** *unto* Gg Skt; *under* A¹ Tr.
611   **hardynesse]** *of h.* Gg A¹ B F P T Th Pol.
623   **it]** Om. Gg A¹ S Pol; P omits line.
638   **heterly]** *hertely* A¹ B F P Tr Th.
639   **And]** Om. Gg; *That* A¹ Tr.
    come] *comyth* Gg B F T Th Skt Pol; *comen* S; *came* Tr.
641   **renne]** *rennyth* Gg; *raf(e)* A¹ Tr; *and* B F T Skt Pol;
thenn P; *than* S; *ran* Th. Amy (58) hypothesizes that S
and P mistook *r* for thorn.

Readings of Gg rejected by all editors:

588, 684   **Antonius]** *Antonrus.*   **593**   **falsly]** *falle.*
632   **wente]** *wentyn.*   **636**   **peynen]** *peynede.*   **643**
Byhynde] *Byhyndyn.*   **647**   **hem]** *hem to.*   **650**   **in
fyght]** *togedere.*   **664**   **is]** *is sche* (also A¹ P Tr).

II. THE LEGEND OF THISBE

718   **That estward in the world was tho dwellynge]**
That tho was in that lond e. d. Gg Rob, probably the Gg
scribe's correction for clarity (Kane, 45–46); *That aftirward in this w. was d.* S. **tho]** *non* A¹.

725   Tysbe] *And T.* Gg Skt Pol Rob; Gg "corrects" a headless line (Kane, 48).

738   cop] *top(pe)* A¹ B F S Tr Th Skt Pol Rob; *cop* is the harder reading, though *c* and *t* are easily confused.

788   this] *there* Gg; *his* Pol.

794   lykinge] *haste* Gg Ff P Rob, induced by *faste* and *laste* in 790, 791 (Kane, 50).

815   that that] Gg; *of that* Tr Skt Rob; *that* all other MSS and Th Pol.

825   he] Om. Gg; *men* B F T Th Pol Skt.

874   medeleth] *medeled* Gg; *medulth* Ff; *medled* P; *mellith* S; *medleth* A³ T Th Pol.

882   she] *he* P; *s*, *sc* scratched out before *he* Gg A¹.

890   My] *Myn* Gg Ff; rest *Thy.* Editors correct to *my* to accord with ordinary ME usage.

898   shalt] *schat* Gg; *shal* F Pol.

903   yfere] Tr; *in fere* A¹; om. all other MSS. *Yfere* is confirmed by the source (Met. 4.155–57).

911   in] *and* Gg A³ Ff F B T Th Skt; *of* P.

915   hireselven] *hire self* Gg A¹ B Ff P Tr.

Readings of Gg rejected by all editors:

713   nas] *was* (also Tr).   **725   hight the]** *brit te miade.*   **729   have]** *a.*   **730   nolde it]** *myghte.*   **737   which that]** *t. w.*   **750   the]** *that* (also Ff).   **759   but]** *b. if* (*ʒit* S).   **761   myghte]** *myghtyn;* **kyssen]** *kysse* (also A¹; *kys* Tr).   **765   ek]** *thour.*   **768   wolden]** *wele.*   **773   whan]** *that.*   **774   hire]** Om. (also A¹).   **785   under]** *out of.*   **791   hem]** *hym* (also Ff).   **796   nyght]** *nygh.*   **798   For¹]** *And.*   **800   woman]** Om.   **805   Than]** *there* (also S).   **831   heer]** *herte* (also P Th).   **840   slow]** *slayn.*   **848   shalt]** *schat.*   **870   now]** *tho.*   **871   turmente]** *turnemente* (also P).   **881   am]** *al.*   **887   noyse or]** *ony.*   **895   ek]** Om. (also A¹).   **897   departe]** *depare (part(e)* A¹ Ff Tr; *departen* S).   **904   this]** *his.*   **913   as]** *a.*   **916   are]** *is* (also A³ S).   **920   to us]** *for u.*

III. THE LEGEND OF DIDO

928   In thyn Eneyde and Naso] *In Naso and Eneydos* Gg Rob; *In t. suporte ovide and naso* R; *In t. Ouide and Naso* S. The reading printed was first adopted by Skeat and urged by Kane (46), who believes the Gg reading is likely an attempt to improve the grammar of the text.

932   offered unto] *iofferede to* Gg Skt; *offered to* P.

944   cleped] *iclepid* Gg Rob; *callid* R; *clepte* S.

960–61   Attested only by Gg A³ P R. The authenticity of the couplet is demonstrated by Amy (16–17).

1046   was ther yit so] *yit was so* Gg; *was ther so* A¹ A³; *was yit so* B F T; *was ther a* P R; *yit was sene so* S.

1058   biknew] *he knew* Gg; *tho knew* A¹ Tr; *they knew* P R.

1094   Ful] *Sche* Gg Skt. **she]** *he* canceled in Gg; om. Skt.

1099   beter at ese was in his] *at e. was b. in al hese* Gg; *beter at e. was his* B F S Skt; *b. at e. was he in his* A¹.

1102   Of] *And* all MSS and eds. but Gg Rob.

1107   ornementes] *pavement(e)s* all MSS but Gg Tr A¹; probably caught from the preceding rhyme-word.

1126   Thus can this quene honurable hire gestes calle] *Thus can this hon. q. hire g. c.* Gg B F Th; *Thus ganne this honorabyll q. hire g. to c.* A¹; *Thus can this hon. q. her*

gyftes c. P; *Thus gafe this hon. q. her gyftes all* R; *Thus kan this hon. q. his g. c.* T; *Thus gan this hon. q. hyr g. c.* S Tr. "No MS reading can be right" (Rob). Skeat emends to *Thus can this noble q. her g. c.;* Pollard, to *Thus gan this q. honoure hir g. talle,* suggesting as another possibility *Thus yaf this noble q. hir giftes talle.* Though *c* and *t* are frequently confused, *talle,* as Robinson notes, occurs only once elsewhere in Chaucer (*tal,* Mars 38). Robinson adopted the emendation proposed by Amy (62–63), who suggests the line reads "Thus, her guests have every reason to call this queen honorable," and it is printed here, though the syntax is very odd.

1145   take] *make* F B T Th Skt Pol.

1160   now to²] *now comyth* Gg.

1166   waketh, walweth] *wayleth and sche* Gg; *wakyth she waloweth* A¹; *walith w.* B; *waketh she waileth* P; *waikith she walieth* R; *waketh and waleweth* Tr.

1187   nothing] *no wight* all MSS but Gg P R and all eds. but Rob.

1202   she as] *she is* F B T Th Skt Pol.

1203   folk] *men* Gg; *folkes* A¹ F T Tr Th Pol.

1210   thus lat I] *this lady* Gg B F S T Th Pol; *doth* P R.

1215   ones mete hym] *hym onys mete* Gg; *ones mete hem* A¹; *hym ones meten* F B T Th Pol.

1216   seyn] *sey* Gg Rob; *seynge* P.

1235   hire] Om. all MSS but Gg P R and all eds. but Rob.

1246   hadde hir loved] *hadde ilouyd* Gg; *here rad l.* A¹; *euer hir l.* P; *ever l. her* R; *had l. hir* S; *hyr had l.* Tr.

1253   he] Om. Gg F B T Th Pol.

1292   hir] Gg; *his* all other MSS and all eds. **he]** *sche* Gg Rob. Robinson's *she* may be a misprint; Aeneas sighs, leading to Dido's question (1293).

1316   let] *and l.* Gg P R Rob, which creates a hypermetric line. The insertion of *and* could be a dittographic error (the line begins *And seyth*).

1330   he hath] *hath he* F B T Th Skt; *he* A¹ P R S Tr Pol; *hath* A³.

1338   Juppiter] Pollard emends to *Jove* to avoid the hexameter. In Tr and S the same effect is achieved by omission of *swete,* but this translates Lat. *dulces* (Aen. 4.651), and thus Chaucer probably wrote the hexameter as it stands.

1352   yit] *right* Gg S Skt; om. A¹ R P.

1360   contraire] *contrary(e)* Gg A¹ A³ P R Tr Pol; *contrarious(e)* B F T Th.

1366   who] *whoso* Gg A³ B F S Th.

Readings of Gg rejected by all editors:

941   awey] *away and.*   **944   olde]** *owene.*   **950   ful]** *wol.*   **951   with]** Om.   **963   ytake]** *take* (also A¹ Tr).   **964   called]** *clepid.*   **993   which]** Om. (also R).   **999   with him]** Om.   **1000   she]** *he.*   **1003   wolde]** *schule* (*shuld* A³ P R); **to]** *the.*   **1009   queenes]** *q. the* (*the* above line; also A¹ A³ S).   **1032   for to]** Om.   **1055   whan]** *w. that;* **told]** *t. of* (*of* possibly marked for deletion).   **1067   myght]** *mygh.*   **1071   braunes]** *braun* (also Th).   **1082   She¹]** *And.*   **1091   messageres]** *m. for* (also A¹ A³; *m. anon for* P; *m. anen to* R).   **1095   hem]** *hym* (also A¹ A³ S; om. T).   **1112   To¹]** *For* (with *tho* deleted following); **take]** Om.; **have]** *take* (also A¹ R).   **1115   the justing]** *to iuste* (*Iustynge* A¹; *the iuste* P; *the Iustis* R).   **1124   ne]** Om. (also P R).   **1131   broches, and ek]** *and ek brochis* (*b. and* P R).   **1132   for²]** Om. (also Th).   **1133   hire]** *hym* (also

A¹). thise noble] Om. **1138** his yonge] *this blysful.*
1143 noble] *holy.* **1149** thanked] *thankyth.* in]
with (also A¹). **1165** turmente] *turnemente.* **1170**
dere] *leue.* **1171** my drem] *myn slep.* **1173** For
that] Om. **1174** ek so] Om. **1175** therwithal] *ek
therto.* **1177** him telle] Om. **1189** hire] *oure.*
1193 hir] *his.* **1202** fair] *bright.* **1212** founden
is] *is ifounde.* **1213** Go] *bo.* **1231** gynning] *gyn-
nere.* **1240** this] Om. **1242** upros] *aros.* **1247**
to his] *as his.* **1248** hath] Om. (also P R). **1250**
as] Om. (also P R). **1251** at] *of.* **1255** and] *of*
(also Tr). **1259** they] *that ye.* **1263** may²] *may it*
(also A¹). **1267** privy] *trewe.* **1283** land] *landys;*
a] Om. **1313** degre] *gre.* **1316** Have] *Hauyth.*
1322 deyen] *deye* Gg (also A¹ R Tr). **1324** Have]
hauyth. **1339** unbynd me] *and brynge it.* **1341**
allas] Om. **1345** it] Om. (also A¹ R Tr). **1351** to
the] Om. **1352** But] *B. yit.* **1366** have] *hauyn.*
1367 Rede] *r. he.*

IV. THE LEGEND OF HYPSIPLE AND MEDEA

1370 gentil wemen tendre creatures] *tendere w. gentil
c.* Gg; *gentil w. gentil c.* A³ B F T Th Pol; *ientil w. and ientil
c.* P.
1382 sekte] *seeyte* A³; *sleight(e)* B F Skt Pol; *set* S Tr; *seite*
T; *disceyte* Th.
ff.1395 The Legend of Hypsipyle] The title here,
after 1395, and the one after 1579 are editorial additions
by Robinson.
1396 as Guido] *and G.* A³; *as Ouyde* Th; *and Ouyde* B
F T.
1404 gentilesse] *gentilnes(se)* Gg A¹ Tr.
1429 ther] Om. Gg Rob. Kane suggests (45) the Gg
error may be due to homoeoarchy.
1457 go] Om. Gg B F T Th.
1473 blyve] *blythe* Gg Rob; *belyve* A¹ S; *bliu* B. The odd
Gg rhyme may have been influenced by the ending of the
previous word, *sendyth;* a comparable error occurs in
lines 2176–77, where *swythe* is rhymed with *dryve.* The
retention of the false rhyme here in Robinson appears to
be an error.
1476 him] *hem* Gg B F Pol.
1499 fynt] *fyndeth* Gg A³ B F T Th Pol; *fynding* S.
1513 renone] *reno(u)me(e)* A³ B F S Th Skt Pol Rob;
renoune A¹ T Tr.
1523 Gg places this line after 1535.
1538 God] *almighty G.* S Skt Pol Rob. S corrects the
meter, but the line must have been short in the original
(Amy, 43).
1541 swich] *whiche* Gg; *suche* A¹ A³ B F S T Tr Th Pol.
1573 untrewe to hir] *ontrewe* Gg A³ T Th; *to hir untrewe* B F Skt Pol.
1607 al craft and art] *al the c. and art* Gg Th; *al the c.*
A³; *al the art and c.* A¹ S (om. *al*) Tr Rob.
1657 his] *hire* Gg A²; om. A¹ A³ B F T Th Pol.
1659 chef traytour] *thef and traytour* Gg; *theeff a t.* A³;
theffe traytour A¹ Tr; *traytour and theffe* A². The variants
arise from confusion of *t* and *c* (see Amy, 71–72).
1671 whan she of his falsnesse] *of his f. whan she* Gg
S (S: *whan that*) Pol; A¹ Tr om. *his.* (Tr adds *hym* after
she.)

Readings in Gg rejected by all editors:
1380 thow] *tow.* **1387** ful] *wol.* **1398** which]
Om. **1413** may] *myghte* (also S). **1414** And] Om.
1423 So] *Tho.* **1427** mighte] *may* (also A³). **1433**
moche] *meche othir.* **1435** thylke] *tylke (that ylke* A¹).
1437 boles] *bole.* **1449** And] Om.; wilt] *wit.*
1452 ilke] Om. (also A¹ Tr). **1454** With] *And with.*
1463 Lemnon] *lenoun* (also A¹ A³ S Tr; *leonon* B F T).
1468 whylom] Om. **1475** thider were] *w. t.;*
yblowe] *blowe.* **1477** and] *and to* (also A³ B). **1482**
and] *and for.* **1483** morwenynge] *morwynge (mor-
nyng* A¹ T Th; *morowynge* B; *morowyng* Tr). **1484**
hem] *hym* (also A¹ S). **1486** hem] *hym.* **1489**
For] *Or.* **1496** oure] *hire.* **1499** this other] *these
othere* (also A¹ F). **1526** half] Om. **1529** non] *no
man* (also A¹ Tr). **1536** He hadde lever] Om. **1540**
the] Om.; owher] *om.* **1543** on] *in.* **1560** hir] *it.*
1563 hir] *hym.* **1566** grete] Om. **1567** him]
Om. **1568** his] *hire.* **1579** sorwes] *sorwe.* **1581**
devourer] *deuoure.* **1591** of al] *iclepid.* **1596** as-
senteth] *assentede* (also S). **1599** which] Om. **1608**
with] *and.* **1613** yput] *put* (also A¹ Tr). **1643**
hereupon at] *here vp a.* **1647** stynten] *stynted.* **1660**
wedded] *weddyth.* **1663** receyved] *receyuyth* (also
Tr). **1677** mikel] *meche* (also A²).

V. THE LEGEND OF LUCRECE

1682 And] Om. all MSS but A², which reads *And specially.* The short line is possible but would require
emending *here* in 1681 to *the.*
1710 to-nyght to Rome] *to R. to-n.* A² B F S T Th Pol.
The reading adopted allows elision of the final *e* of *Rome*
(see Amy, 73).
1721 oure bok] Om. Gg Th (Th inserts *Liui* after
seyth).
1728 to] *sore* Gg Skt.
1730 on the sege] Om. Gg; *on these* F B T; *off the assege*
A²; *on that sege* A³; *of the sege* Tr; *on this* Th.
1738–39 Gg places these lines after 1743.
1764 newe] *now* Gg A³ S Skt; om. A¹ Tr.
1791 there] *that* A¹; *thou* B F T Th Skt Pol.
1809 swich] Om. Gg; *suche* A¹ A² B F T Tr Th Skt Pol;
this S.
1812 Romeyns] *Romeyn* Gg Skt Rob; the scribe was
perhaps trying to clarify the text (Kane, 45–46).
1815 bothe at ones] *at onys bothe* Gg Pol.
1824 vileyns] *vileyn* Gg; *vilenouse* A² B F T Th Pol.
1836–1885 Lacking in Gg; supplied from F.
1839 an] Om. F B T Th Skt.
1840 made] *make* F A² B T Th; *maden* Tr.
1846 wolde] *nolde* F B Pol.
1847 upon] *vnto* F B T Th; *by* A¹.
1857 she hede] *h. s.* F B T Th.
1862 by hir chaste blood hath] *hath by h. c. b.* F B T
Th.
1876 for the] *in hir* F A³ B T Th.
1879 himselve] *himself(e)* all MSS and Th Pol, rejected
by Robinson as "metrically difficult."
1881 al that] *al the londe* F B T Th Skt Pol, an error
caught from the preceding line (Amy, 78).
1882 and] Om. F A¹.
1883 men] *women* F.
  loke ye] *loketh* F B Skt Pol; *loke* S.

Readings from Gg rejected by all editors:

1684 cause] *c. ne.* **1685** to memorye] *to me m.*
1693 of] *of al.* I] *and.* **1695** Romeyns] *romeynys*
(*romanys* S). **1702** wyves] *w. and.* **1718** they] *t.*
gan. **1722** kepen] *kepe* (also A³ B Tr). **1726**
walles] *wal.* **1729** it stingeth] *me thynkyth that.*
1730 Whan I thynke] *It styngith me whan I thynke.*
1733 she] Om. **1734** she let hyre eyen] *h. e. l. s.*
1735 thilke] *tilke.* **1736** eek] Om. **1737** Embel-
ished] *Emblemyschid* (*Embeseled* A³). **1741** of him]
Om. **1752** was] *is.* **1753** For wel thoghte he] *for
he woste wel.* **1755** he coveyteth] *coueyth hire.* **1756**
His¹] *This.* **1763** this] *thus* (also A¹ B T). **1766**
That] *Yit;* ago] *agon.* **1770** But] Om. **1786** this]
the. **1788** is that quod she] *q. she is th.* (also A²); that
weyeth] *weyeth.* **1803** hath] *hast;* with] *w. a* (also
A¹). **1813** the] *here.* **1816** swogh] *(?)w(?).*
1821 verray] *worthi.* **1826** he] *this;* is] *be.* **1828**
yfeere] *in feere* (also A¹). **1830** used] *vsyn* (also A²).

VI. THE LEGEND OF ARIADNE

1886–1907 Supplied from F.
1886 Crete] *grece* F B T.
1888 Nat for thy sake] *Nat oonly for thy s.* F B Pol; *Nat
for thy s.* A³. oonly write I] *writen is* B F; *o. wryten ys* T
Th; *wryte I only* A³.
1891 the heven] *heven* F B T Th.
1895 hadde] *whan* F Pol; *wanne* B; om. T; A¹ omits the
line.
1902 Alcathoe he] *And the citee* F B; *Alcie* T; *All the Cyte*
A¹ Tr; *Alcitoe* A² S; *Alcyote* A³; *Alcathoe* Pol.
1922–23 Om. Gg; supplied from F.
1927 right] *right thus* S Rob. ye shal here] *ye s. after h.*
B F Th Skt Pol. *Thus* and *after* are scribal emendations
for meter, unnecessary since *slayne* can be disyllabic
(Amy, 79).
1933 com] *fil* Gg; *cam(e)* A² A³ B F T Tr Th Pol.
1934 on pore] *or p.* Gg Rob; *and p.* A¹ Th.
1936 Unto Minos] *To Thesius* Gg; *To M.* A² A³ B F S
T Th Pol.
1964 Mynos] *Thesius* Gg (cf. 1936); *king M.* S Skt Pol.
1966 Of Athenes] *In moche(ll) myrth(e)* A¹ Tr Skt; *Of the
towne* Th. See Expl. Notes.
1971 compleynynge] *compleynt* A³ B F T Th Pol.
stode] *stodyn* Gg A¹ Tr Pol.
1973 so] Om. Gg A² S Skt Pol.
1977 This] *Than* A² A³ B F S T Th Skt Pol; *That* A¹
Tr.
2052 so gwerdone] *to go.* Gg F Skt; *g. so* S.
2053 men] *man* Gg "which is grammatically possible;
see ClT IV. 212n." (Rob).
2059 therof] *therfore* Rob (probably a misprint).
2075 of a] Gg Skt Rob only. On this construction, see
Expl. Notes.
2083 lene] *leve* A² S Skt; *let* Tr.
2084 herte and sleyghte] *slyghte & herte* Gg; *sleyghte of
hert* A³ B F T Th Skt.
2086 leve] *leene* A³ B T Th Pol; *graunt* Tr; *lyve* S.
2094 no profre] *no(t) profyt* B F T Th Skt.
2134 us herof] *herof us* Gg Skt Rob; an example, according to Kane (48), of Gg's sophistication of the
meter.

2184 now pite] Gg Skt Rob; *gret(e) p.* Tr S; *pit(e)* rest
Pol Kch, perhaps correctly, since the scribes of Gg and
Tr S are most likely "improving" the meter.
2187 evere] *evere that* Gg Rob.
2215 ship or] Om. Gg A² A³ B F S T Th.

Readings from Gg rejected by all editors:

1911 caste] *caughte.* **1915** thilke] *tilke.* **1917**
whom] *hem.* **1924** And] *But.* **1932** yeer] Om.
1942 this] *the* (also A³). **1948** lad] *goa.* **1954**
this] *thus* (also T). **1955** whom] *hym.* **1965**
Dwellten] *Dwelledyn.* **1972** bryghte] *brygbe.* **1974**
hadde] *haddyn* (also Tr). **1977** syster] *systeryn.*
1978 Phedra leve syster] *l. s. P.* **1984** that] *euere.*
1986 any] Om. **1994** That if] *If.* **1999** hath]
hath bothe. eek] Om. (also A³). **2000** To] *And.*
2008 on] *as.* **2009** To] *And;* or] *as.* **2016**
clewe] *c(r.?)ewe.* **2027** Whan] *And w.* **2030**
ydampned] *dampnede* (also S Tr). **2038** If that] *If.*
2044 no man] *non.* **2049** to] Om. (also A² Tr).
2056 As] *So.* **2063** to yeve] *so y.* (also A² S); me]
yow. **2064** ther] *than.* **2077** He] *Ne.* have] *a.*
2088 yow] *the.* **2095** man] *men.* **2119** assure]
ensure. **2125** manere] *mane.* **2126** Now] Om.
(also Th). **2137** of hire hath] *hath of hire.* **2170**
for] *forth.* **2176** blyve] *swythe.* **2182** for] *with.*
2186 gropeth] *graspith* (also Tr; *gaspeth* A²; *grapid* S).
2188 and] *and al.* **2202** on] *vpon* Gg A³. up] Om.
Gg (also Th). **2208** rist] *rysith.* **2210** she] Om.
2215 thogh] *thow;* here] *h. ne.* **2216** to] *to to.*

VII. THE LEGEND OF PHILOMELA

2277 hyre wol] *hyre I wol* A² A³ B F S T Th Pol Rob².
If the *w* of *wol* functions as a half-vowel, permitting the
elision of *I,* Gg's reading appears metrically short. But
bothe can be disyllabic (see Amy, 85).
2286 she loveth] *hir longeth* B F T Th Skt.
2291 beaute] *bounte* B Skt; *bounde* F.
2314 Of] *For* Gg Rob, probably an error caught from
the previous line (Kane, 41–42).
2324 hath] *hat he* Gg; *hath he* Skt Rob. a] *that* Gg Skt
Rob. Amy (85) believes the Gg scribe emended for
meter; see also Kane (45, 48).
2359 that the] *the* Gg A² A³ B F T Th.
2379 The wo the compleynt] *the c. the w.* Gg; *the woo
constreynt* B F Th; *the wo conteynte* T.
2388 for²] *for his* Gg Pol.

Readings from Gg rejected by all editors:

2237 Corrumpeth] *Coruptyh.* **2241** last] *lestyth*
(also Tr Th). **2248** hire] *that.* **2253** aboute the]
a. te. **2263** gan] *be gan.* **2266** to] *with* **2267**
preyde] *preyeth.* **2269** al] Om. (also Tr). **2275**
but] *myghte.* **2293** that it go] *euere he do* **2294**
kneled and so preyde] *he so fayre hire preyede* **2314**
agros] *aros.* **2322** sat] *that* (also A² A³ T). **2345**
fond hir] *say his.* **2356** eek] Om. **2358** can]
coude. **2372** maner] *m. hire.*

VIII. THE LEGEND OF PHYLLIS

2422 Thorus] *Chorus* Th Skt Rob. See Expl. Notes.
2430 That] *And* all MSS but Gg, all eds. but Rob. Kane

(47) believes the Gg scribe "may have misread the line as a result clause." **he almost was**] *almost he was* Gg; *he ys all moste* A²; *ys he almost* Tr; *he was almoste* A³ B F S T Th Pol.

2483 **abought**] *abough* Gg; *yboghte* A² A³ B F T Th Pol; *sought* Tr.

2505 **Syn**] *Syn that* Gg B F S T Tr.

2506–7 Om. Gg; supplied from F.

2508 **Sytho**] *Sytoye* Gg A² B S Tr; *Cyteys* A³; *Sitoio* F T; *Scython* Th Pol. The emendation adopted is Skeat's.
　　ybrought] Tr Skt Pol Rob; *brought* all other MSS.

Readings of rejected by all editors:

2395 **of a**] *o.* **2396** **fynde**] *wete.* **it**] *Om.* **2432** **seken**] *seke* (also B Tr). **2445** **in**] *of.* **2449** **olde**] *owene.* **2456** **haste**] *hastyn.* **2469** **doth**] *don.* **2471** **al**] *Om.* **2484** **storyes**] *storye* (also B F T Th); **recorde**] *recordith.* **2487** **him prayed**] *she p.* **2496** **Thyn hostesse**] *Ostesse thyn.* **2500** **as**] *that.* **2501** **which**] *oure.* **oure**] *youre* (also Tr). **2508** **strem**] *storm.* **2513** **wryten**] *wryte* (also B Tr). **2517** **thoughte**] *thoughe;* **that**] om. **2525** **trusted I**] *truste.*

2536 **be**] *ben.* **2537** **se**] *sen.* **2539** **folk**] *men.* **2554** **is**] Om.

IX. THE LEGEND OF HYPERMNESTRA

2612 **fyre**] *fuyr out* Gg, perhaps correctly. **2666** **costret**] *costrel* B F T Th Skt Pol. **2668** **to¹**] Om. Gg B F T Tr Th. **2676** **ben**] *sone ben* Tr Skt Rob, probably a scribal emendation of a headless line. **2712** **he**] Om. Gg A³ B F T Th.

Readings of Gg rejected by all editors:

2570 **called was**] *w. c.* **2579** **sholde**] *shal.* **2590** **raft**] *be r.* **2593** **houses**] *h. that;* **his**] om. **2596** **tho**] *to* (also A² Tr). **2598** **deyen**] *turne.* **2613** **flour**] *flourys.* **2618** **And**] Om. **2620** **to**] *til.* **2625** **voyded**] *voyd(e)* (also A³). **2636** **nis**] *is* (*ne ys* Tr). **2639** **right**] *ful.* **2658** **it is**] *is it.* **2660** **which**] *wit.* **2676** **to**] *a.* **2683** **As**] *And.* **2686** **That**] *And;* **swich**] *this* (also A³ S; *that* A² Tr). **2712** **good**] *gret.* **2714** **fer**] *forth.*

The twenty-one poems of this section are found in fifty-three manuscripts and in a number of early printed books, of which five have been used for this edition. These authorities are designated by the sigils (with slightly different conventions of capitalization) of the extremely useful edition of George Pace and Alfred David, The Minor Poems: Part One, Vol. 5 in the Variorum Chaucer, which also provides some description of the manuscripts and printed books. The notes that follow are intended to show variants of both textual and literary interest. Although the authorities for the poems resist genetic classification, their variants do form manuscript groups, and these groups have been indicated in the notes to focus and simplify comparison of variants. The authorities for a particular variant are listed by groups and alphabetically within each group. Whole-word emendations without textual authority are bracketed and noted. In some instances emendations by the earlier modern editors, Skeat, Koch, Heath, and Robinson, have developed a sort of authority, and so their editions are occasionally noted: Skt, Kch, Hth, Rob. The following notes are selective; for more complete sets of variants, see Pace and David and Koch's edition.

AN ABC

Authorities: sixteen manuscript copies and Speght's edition of 1602:

α
Bod   Bodley 638, Bodleian
Cov   Coventry MS (Accession 325), City Record Office, Coventry
F   Fairfax 16, Bodleian
Gg   Gg.4.27, Cambridge University Library
H³   Harley 2251, British Library
H⁵   Harley 7578, British Library (lines 1–50 only)
P   Pepys 2006, Magadalene College, Cambridge (two copies, P₁ and P₂, lines 1–60 only)
Sp   Speght's second edition, 1602, STC 5080–81

β
A⁶   Additional 36983, British Library (formerly Bedford)
Ff²   Ff.5.30, Cambridge University Library
G   Hunter 239, Glasgow University Library
J   G.21, St John's College, Cambridge
L   Laud Miscellany 740, Bodleian
Mel   Melbourne MS, State Library of Victoria (Felton Bequest)
S   Arc. L.10.2/E.44, Sion College, London

Cos (Cosin MS.V.I. 9, Durham University Library), lines 1–16 only, is not classified. Ff², G J L Mel and S occur in a prose translation of Deguilleville's *Pelerinage de*

The textual notes to *The Short Poems* were prepared by R. T. Lenaghan.

la vie humaine. All texts have been published: fourteen by the Chaucer Society; Cov by Doyle and Pace (PMLA 83, 1968, 22–34), Mel by Doyle and Pace (SB 28, 1975, 41–61), Cos by Doyle (Durham Philobiblon 1, 1949–55, 54–55), and Sp in the Brewer facsimile. Ff² is the basis of the present text.

Title: *An ABC* is editorial (Skt Rob); the subtitle is from A⁶ Ff² S; om. Bod Gg H³ H⁵ P₁ G J L Mel; *Chaucers A.b.c.* F (in margin); *Here biginneth a preiour of our ladie that Geffrie Chaucer made after the ordre of the a b c* Cov *La priere de nostre Dame . . . per Chaucer* P₂; *Chaucers ABC called La Priere de Nostre Dame* Sp; S has a marginal attribution to Chaucer.

6   thou mighti] *thou* om. P₁ P₂; *al m.* Cov Gg H³ Sp; *O goodly* Cos.

33   been in thee] *in the be* α.

35   Hast thou to misericorde] *Unto mercy bestow* α.

38   fruit] *good* Bod F H⁵; om. G L Mel; *goodnesse* J.

39   correcte vice] *correcte me* α (except *correctie be* Cov) G L; *me chastyse* A⁶ Ff²; *correcte my folise* J; *help me that in syn lyse* Mel; *me wel chastyse* S Skt Hth Kch Rob. Severs (MLN 64, 1949, 306–9) argues for *correcte me,* the reading of most MS authority, in spite of its departure from the rhyme scheme. The present reading is the proposal of Avril Henry, ChR 18, 1983, 95–99.

40   wol me] *me wole* Ff² G; *will my w.* A⁶.

54   the] *ther* A⁶ Ff² G; *that* J.

55   if thou] *that thow* Bod F P₁ P₂; *if* om. Cov G J L Mel.

58   to have oure] *as for our* α (except *heere for us* in H³).

59   precious blood he wrot the bille] *blode h. w. t. bill* Bod; *p. bloode h. w. that bill* Cov; *bloode h. w. t. blisful bille* F; *blod h. w. that blisful bille* Gg P₁ P₂ Sp; *bloode h. w. a p. bille* H³.

83   bothes] Gg Sp A⁶ Ff² G S; *both* Bod Cov F L Mel; om. H³; *bather* J. *Youre bothes,* though supported by good MSS, is a strange construction. Perhaps the reading should be *youre bother* (supported by J), as in Tr 4.168 (R).

99   That cometh of thee thou Cristes] *Thow erte cristis awyn* J; *Thou art crystys* L; *That ert cristes our lordes awn* Mel.

115 to] *unto* A⁶ Ff² S.

132 is his rightful rekenynge] *his fulle rekenynge is* Gg Sp; *it is rightful rekenynge* A⁶ Ff² G; *it is the rightful rekennyng* S; *it is that rewfulle rekenynge* J L Mel.

133 merci] *joye* Gg Sp.

137 Soth is that God] *S. is t. he* α except *trowth it is G.* H³; *S. it is t. G.* J L Mel.

145 hath] *ches* Cov Gg Sp.
        his] Om. J.

151 so] Om. A⁶ Ff²; *soore* S.

158 court] *countrey* α except H³.

159 O freshe] *of fresh* α; *of a freshe* J Mel.

163 And eek that] All MSS have hypermetric *suffred: And suffred that* Bod F J; *And s. eek t.* Cov Gg Sp; *And s. eek* H³; *And eek s. t.* A⁶ Ff² G S; *And also s. t.* L Mel.

181 bryghte] Cov Gg Sp; om. rest.

183 palais] *place* H³ J L Mel.

THE COMPLAINT UNTO PITY

Authorities: nine manuscripts and Thynne's edition of 1532:

<table>
<tr><td rowspan="3">α</td><td>A⁵</td><td>Additional 34360, British Library (formerly Phillipps 9053)</td></tr>
<tr><td>H¹</td><td>Harley 78, British Library</td></tr>
<tr><td>H⁵</td><td>Harley 7578, British Library</td></tr>
<tr><td rowspan="7">β</td><td>Bod</td><td>Bodley 638, Bodleian</td></tr>
<tr><td>F</td><td>Fairfax 16, Bodleian</td></tr>
<tr><td>Ff¹</td><td>Ff.1.6. Cambridge University Library</td></tr>
<tr><td>Lt</td><td>Longleat 258, in the possession of the Marquess of Bath</td></tr>
<tr><td>R¹</td><td>R.3.19. Trinity College, Cambridge</td></tr>
<tr><td>T</td><td>Tanner 346, Bodleian</td></tr>
<tr><td>Th</td><td>Thynne's edition, 1532, STC 5068</td></tr>
</table>

All have been published: nine by the Chaucer Society and Th in Brewer's facsimile edition (see p. 1117). F is the basis of the present text.

Title: From Bod (colophon); *And now here folwith a complaynt of pite made bi Geffray Chauucier the aureat poete . . .* A⁵ H¹; om. H⁵; *Balade* F; *How pite is dead* T Th; *Pite* Ff¹; (colophon) *The exclamation of the dethe of pyte* Lt R¹.
4 **Withoute deth]** *W. the d.* α.
6 **crueltee and tirannye]** *cruel t.* α.
15 **that]** H⁵; om. rest.
16 **a]** Lt R¹ Th; om. rest.
  me] Om. α R¹.
19 **gan to]** H⁵; *came to* A⁵ H¹; *to* om. β.
21 **I was but]** H⁵ β; *Me thoughte me* A⁵ H¹; *nas* Skt Hth Kch Rob.
24 **hold]** *heve* α.
34 **first I hadde]** *I h. f.* β.
45 **when]** Om. β except Bod F.
50 **sauf]** *save only* β.
52 **of]** α; *and by* β except R¹ Th: *and* R¹; *unto* Th.
  The Bill of Complaint] *The complaynt in the bill* A⁵; om. rest.
59 **rial]** *souverayne* α.
61 **in]** Om. α.
  yfalle] Th; *in falle* α; *falle* β except Th.
67 **lo]** A⁵ H¹; om. rest.
69 **now]** A⁵ H¹; om. rest.
70 **hyghte]** *is high* β.
  to Grace] *of G.* H⁵; *to your G.* β.
76 **wanten]** Skt Hth Kch Rob; *want(e)* all MSS.
79 **Withoute yow, benygne creature]** *With yowe benigne and feyre creature* A⁵ H¹; *W. youre b. a. f. c.* H⁵.
80 **your]** *now oure* α.
83 **that perilouse alliaunce]** *of thoo persones a.* A⁵; *of thoo persones the a.* H¹; *these persones a.* H⁵.
86 **than]** H¹; *that* A⁵ H⁵; om. β.
  in] *with* α.
87 **well]** F; om. rest.
  Pite] *peyne* α.
88 **is falle]** *sholde be* α Rob.
89 **than]** *also* H⁵ β.
91 **seken]** *speken* F.
92 **Herenus]** *vertuous* α. See Expl. Notes.
113 **youres]** *youre* H⁵; om. Ff¹ Lt R¹ T.
117 **Sith ye be ded]** *Now pite that I have soughte so yore*

agoo α (repeating line 1); *S. ye be yet d.* β (*yet* om. Skt Hth Kch Rob).

A COMPLAINT TO HIS LADY

Authorities: two manuscripts and Stowe's edition of 1561.

<table>
<tr><td>A⁵</td><td>Additional 34360, British Library (formerly Phillipps 9053)</td></tr>
<tr><td>H¹</td><td>Harley 78, British Library</td></tr>
<tr><td>St</td><td>Stowe's Edition 1561, STC 5075–76</td></tr>
</table>

The copy in H¹ was written by Shirley; A⁵ and St seem to derive from it. A⁵ adds a unique stanza at the end. H¹ and A⁵ have been printed by the Chaucer Society, St in Brewer's facsimile edition. H¹ is the basis of the present text, but a number of readings present difficulties that have led to relatively frequent, and more or less traditional, emendation.

Title: Supplied by Skeat; *the balade of Pytee by Chauciers* A⁵ H¹. The MSS and Stowe present this poem as a continuation of The Complaint unto Pity.
2 **hir]** *theyre* MSS.
3 **hir]** *theyre* MSS.
15 Skeat repeats 14 here, before 15, to begin the terza rima.
16 **he]** Om. MSS.
  nevere wol] *wol n.* MSS.
22 After this line Skeat adds a line, Mars 189, to fill out the rhyme scheme. See Expl. Notes.
23 Before this line Skeat begins the new sequence of terza rima with two additional lines, a compound of Pity 22 and 17 and Anel 307.
40 **and]** Om. MSS.
41 **eek]** Om. MSS.
50 **than]** *lo than* MSS.
51 After this line Skeat adds a rhyming line based on Anel 182.
52 **lo]** Om. Skt Hth Rob.
53 After this line Skeat adds a rhyming line based on Anel 181.
62 **while]** *whil(e)st* H¹ St Skt Kch Hth Rob.
71 **noon fayner]** *f. n.* Hth Kch Rob.
73 **youre hevynesse]** *y. hyenesse* MSS; *you h.* Kch; *you distresse* Skt Hth Rob.
76 **livyng than]** *than l.* A⁵ Kch Rob; *than* om. Skt Hth.
79 **doon yow]** *y. don* A⁵.
86 **wil]** *may* St.
92 **ne wil]** *nil* Skt Hth Kch Rob.
94 **on yow in such manere]** *so by upon your whele* St.
97 **here]** Om. MSS.
110 **whyles]** *whyl* Skt Hth Rob.
114 **trewer verrayly]** *trewer so verrayly* A⁵ H¹.
118–27 The last stanza occurs only in A⁵.
120 **is]** Om. A⁵.
121 **Wel]** *For wel* A⁵.

THE COMPLAINT OF MARS

Authorities: eight manuscripts and the editions of Julian Notary (1499–1501) and of Thynne (1532):

α {
F　　Fairfax 16, Bodleian
Lt　　Longleat 258, in the possession of the Marquess of Bath (lines 43–298 only)
T　　Tanner 346, Bodleian
Th　　Thynne's edition, 1532, STC 5068
}

β {
H⁴　　Harley 7333, British Library (lines 1–176 only)
JN　　Julian Notary's edition, STC 5089
Pb　　Pepys 2006 (Hand B), Magdalene College, Cambridge
Pe　　Pepys 2006 (Hand E), Magdalene College, Cambridge (lines 1–84 only)
R²　　R.3.20 Trinity College, Cambridge
S²　　Arch. Selden B.24, Bodleian
}

Though the readings of β are preferable, no individual manuscript of that group claims preference. Therefore, because the spelling of F conforms with that of good manuscripts for other texts, F is the basis of the present text, but β readings are usually preferred where there is disagreement. All texts have been published: nine by the Chaucer Society and Th in Brewer's facsimile.

Title: Supplied by Skeat; *Complaint of Mars and Venus* F T Th; . . . *The Broche of thebes as of the love of Mars and Venus* H⁴ Pb (Hammond, 1908, Ch: Bibl. Man., 384); *The love and complayntes bytwene Mars and Venus* (caption) JN; om. Pe S²; . . . *the alliance . . . bytwene . . . Mars . . . and Venus . . . made by Geffrey Chaucier.* . . . R².
The Proem: This, *The Story* (after 28), and *The Proem* (after 154) were supplied by Skeat.
1 foules] *lovers* α; *floures* H⁴; *fooles* R².
2 yon] Th Skt Kch Rob; *yow* α (except Th) H⁴ JN Pe; *yonder* Pb; *your* R²; *the* S².
3 day] *may* H⁴ JN Pb S².
4 ye] *they* F Th Pb; *the* T; *he* H⁴.
16 F mistakenly has line 19 next.
17 yow] R² S²; om. α H⁴ Pb Pe; *ye* JN.
19 Displaced in F (16, 19, 17).
25 atte] *at the* T Th H⁴ Pb S²; *at* Pe R².
42 scourging] *stering* F; *schouryng* T; *scornyng* Th; *strenght* H⁴.
54 and ther abyde] *to a.* F Lt Th; *forto a.* T H⁴; *and* Pe.
67 ther] Om. α.
68 wo] *sorwe* α.
69 sped her] *her* om. Lt T Th.
76 lappeth] *happeth* Lt T Th.
84 knokkeden] *knokken* Lt T H⁴; *knokked* Lt T H⁴; *knokking* Pe; *gan kythe full grete light* S²; line missing R².
96 brosten] *sprangen* Lt T Th; *breken* JN.
105 Phebus] *Vlcanus* S².
115 ne] Om. α JN; *so* S².
139 twelfte daye] *xii dayes* α.
141 allone] *al alone* JN Pb.
143 Venus weping] F H⁴ S²; *w. V.* α except F; *wepyng* om. β except H⁴ S².
146 doth] *maketh* α; *did* S².
181 yshewed] *shewed* Th β.
182 it] Om. α JN.
186 I shal] *shal I* Lt T Th JN R².
191 than] R²; om. rest.
192 harm] *hert* Lt T Th S².
207 Depraven] *Departen* α except Th; *Depeynen* S².
208 non] *his* α.
216 wel oughte] *oghte wel* α.

218 the God] α S²; *he* β except S².
219 him] Om. F; *thame* S².
　other] *or* β except *ony* S².
228 seme] Om. β except *sum* S².
256 tresor] *jewel* Lt T Th.
293 had yow dere] *be to you d.* Lt; *be yow d.* T Th; *made you chere* S²; *yow* om. R².

THE COMPLAINT OF VENUS

Authorities: eight manuscripts and the editions of Julian Notary (1499–1501) and of Thynne (1532):

α {
A　　Ashmole 59, Bodleian
R²　　Trinity College, Cambridge, R.3.20
}

β {
F　　Fairfax 16, Bodleian
T　　Tanner 346, Bodleian
Th　　Thynne's edition, 1532, STC 5068
}

γ {
Ff¹　　Ff.1.6 Cambridge University Library
JN　　Julian Notary's edition, 1499–1501, STC 5089
Pb　　Pepys 2006 (Hand B), Magdalene College, Cambridge
Pe　　Pepys 2006 (Hand E), Magdalene College, Cambridge (lines 45–82 only)
S²　　Arch. Selden B.24, Bodleian
}

All texts have been published: nine by the Chaucer Society and Th in Brewer's facsimile. F is the basis of the present text.

Title: F S²; *Here begynneth a balade made by that worthy Knight of Savoye in frenshe calde sir Otes Graunson. translated by Chaucier* A R²; om. T Pe.
5 on] F Ff¹ S² only; but it prevents hiatus (Rob.).
7 blame] *to blame* A T Th; *to blamen* R²; *Therefore there suld blame* S². Lines 7 and 8 are transposed in A.
8 *Sith he is croppe and roote of gentylesse* A; *For he is c. and r. of g.* R² (from margin); *gentilnesse* T γ.
22 oghte I blesse wel] *aught me wele to blesse* α; *o. I w. blisse* Ff¹ JN; *wel* om. Pb; *o. I w. to b.* S².
27 and fasten] *and fastinge* α γ except *and om.* JN.
30 hewe] α Pb S²; *visage* rest, caught from previous line.
31 Pleyne] All eds.; *Pley* MSS.
33 by] *be* F Rob; *with* γ.
47 wele ofte] α Pe Kch; *ful often* F T Skt Hth Rob; *wele often* Th Ff¹ S²; *full ofte* JN; *ofte* Pb.
59 made] *maked* R² Ff¹ Pb Pe Rob; *caught* S².
63 wol I not] *ne shal I never* α; *wille I not* β; *wolde I not* γ.
64 him] *yow* F Ff¹ JN Pb. Cf. *hym* in lines 56 and 72.
67 in] *of* α γ except *on* S².
73 Princes] *Princesse* α Skt Hth Rob. See Expl. Notes.
　Here endith, *etc.* From F (which adds *And Mars*).

TO ROSEMOUNDE

Authority: Rawlinson Poet. 163, Bodleian. The manuscript has been printed by Skeat (Twelve Facsimiles of Old English Manuscripts, 1892, 36–37) and by Kökeritz (MLN 63, 1948, 310), who argues for a more conservative treatment of the manuscript than Skeat's.

Title: Supplied by Skeat on the basis of line 15; om. MS.
8   Thogh] *Thoght* MS.
11   smal] *fynall* MS.
20   trewe] *trew* MS.
21   not refreyde] *not be refreyde* MS; *be* is above the line in a different hand.

WOMANLY NOBLESSE

Authority: Additional 34360 British Library. The poem is printed by Skeat (Athenaeum, 9 June 1894, 742) and transcribed by Brusendorff (Ch Trad., 277–78).

Title: Supplied by Skeat, who took it from line 24; the subtitle is that in the MS (with *Chauncier* for *Chaucier*).
1   herte] *hert* MS.
8   trewe] *trieve* MS.
10   you] Om. MS.
**12   After this the syntax and rhyme scheme imply a missing line. Skeat supplied *I pray yow, do to me som daliaunce* in his edition in Athenaeum; Furnivall conjectured *Taketh me, lady, in your obeisance,* which Skeat adopted in the Oxford Ch.
14   herte] *hert* MS.
15   loke how humbly] *how h.* MS; *l. h. humblely* Skt Rob; *hoveth humbly* Hth; the emendation adopted is that of Fisher.
25   to] *til* MS.

CHAUCERS WORDES UNTO ADAM, HIS OWNE SCRIVEYN

Authorities:

R²   Trinity College, Cambridge, R.3.20
St   Stowe's edition, 1561, STC 5075–76

Both have been printed by the Chaucer Society. R² is transcribed without changes in Pace and David; St is available in Brewer's facsimile of Thynne. R² is the basis of the present text.

Title: From R²; St has *Chaucers woordes vnto his owne Scriuener.*

THE FORMER AGE

Authorities:

Ii   Ii.3.21 Cambridge University Library
Hh   Hh.4.12 Cambridge University Library

Both have been printed by the Chaucer Society. Ii is the basis of the present text.

Title: Supplied by Skeat; *Chawcer upon this fyfte meter of the second book* Ii.
18   his] *is* Ii.
20   was] *is* Ii.
23   No trompes] Eds.; *No batails trompes* MSS.
34   No wildnesse] *No places w.* Ii; *No place of w.* Hh.
40   for to asayle] *forto a sayle* MSS; *for t'assaile* Skt Kch Rob; *forto asayle* Hth.

41   was] *were* Hh.
42   wodes] *in w.* Skt Hth Kch Rob.
44   parfit quiete] *parfyt joye reste and quiete* Ii; *parfite joy and quiete* Hh.
50   voyd] *voyded* Ii.
**55   After this line, the syntax and rhyme scheme imply a missing line.
60   men] Om. Ii.
63   Poyson, manslawhtre] *P. & manslawtre* Ii.
    Finit, etc. Om. Ii.

FORTUNE

Authorities: ten manuscripts and the editions of Caxton (1477–78) and of Thynne (1532):

α	Ii	Ii.3.21 Cambridge University Library
β	A	Ashmole 59, Bodleian
	H³	Harley 2251, British Library
	R²	R.3.20 Trinity College, Cambridge
	Bod	Bodley 638, Bodleian
	Cx	Caxton's edition, c. 1477–78, STC 5068
	F	Fairfax 16, Bodleian
	Ld	Lansdowne 699, British Library
γ	Leyd	Vossius GG.qv.9, Leiden University Library
	P	Pepys 2006, Magdalene College, Cambridge
	S¹	Arch. Selden B.10, Bodleian
	Th	Thynne's edition, 1532, STC 5068

All texts have been published: ten by the Chaucer Society, Leyd by Nichols (Spec 44, 1969, 46–49), and Th in Brewer's facsimile. Ii is the basis of the present text.

Title: Supplied by eds. The subtitle occurs, with *vilage* for *visage,* in Ii Bod Cx F (*the village* Th); *. . . compleynte of the pleintyff ageynste fortune translated out of frenshe into Englysshe by . . . Geoffrey Chaucier* A; om. H³; *. . . a balade made by Chaucier of the lover and of Dame Fortune* R²; *. . . disputatio inter conquerulatorem et fortunam* Ld Leyd; *Paupertas conqueritur super fortunam* S¹.
    Le Pleintif Om. Ii R² Bod F Ld Leyd S¹.
2   or] *and* β γ except *as* Cx.
4   Fortunes errour] *Fortunes fals errour* A H³; *F. hye e.* R².
6   though I] *t. that I* A H³ Ld Leyd S¹ Th; *al though I* R².
8   thee] Om. β γ.
9   light] *sight* β γ.
11   whirling] *tournyng* β γ.
12   for] Om. β γ.
14   the] Om. A Cx Ld Leyd Th.
16   thee] Om. β γ.
18   never mighte] *myght never* A H³ γ; *might fortune not* R².
21   wel the] *ay weele* β; *wel om.* Cx Th.
24   thee] Om. β γ.
30   Why wolt thou] *thou shalt not* β γ.
35   noon] Om. MSS; all eds. emend to conform to Chaucer's usage.
    hyene] *hyve* β; *hen* S¹; *hyne* Th.
47   wikke is thy grevaunce] *wike is thy governaunce* H³; *thi wikkid governaunce* Ld Leyd S¹.
51   it thee] *to t.* Ii; *not t.* A; *it not t.* H³.

61   or] Ii A; *and* β (except A) γ.

62   or] *and* β γ.

64   **may nat**] *ne may nat* β. After this line all MSS introduce an erroneous subtitle, which attributes the next lines to the plaintif.

73–79   Om. Ld Leyd S[1].

75   **your**] *this* Bod Cx F P Th.

76   Ii only; om. β γ.

77   **And but**] *That but* Ii R[2]; *And yf* Cx Th.

TRUTH

Authorities: twenty-three manuscript copies, a transcript of a Cotton manuscript, and the editions of Caxton (1477–78) and of Thynne (1532):

α	A[1]	Additional 10340, British Library
	Ph	Phillipps 8299, now HM 140, Huntington Library, San Marino, Calif.
β	A[4]	Additional 22139, British Library
	C	Cotton Cleopatra D.VII, British Library
	Cov	Coventry MS (Accession 325), City Record Office, Coventry
	El	Ellesmere MS, Huntington Library, San Marino, Calif.
	Gg	Gg.4.27, Cambridge University Library
γ	A[6]	Additional 36983, British Library (formerly Bedford)
	Co	Cotton Otho A XVIII, British Library, from a transcript by William Thomas
	Cp	MS 203 Corpus Christi College, Oxford
	Cx	Caxton's edition, c. 1477–78, STC 5091
	F	Fairfax 16, Bodleian (two copies, F₁ and F₂)
	H[4]	Harley 7333, British Library
	Hat	Hatton 73, Bodleian
	Kk	Kk.1.5, Cambridge University Library
	Lam	MS 344 Lambeth Palace Library
	Ld	Lansdowne 699, British Library
	Leyd	Vossius GG.qv.9, Leyden University Library
	Nott	MS ME LM 1 (Mellish), Nottingham University Library
	P	Pepys 2006, Magdalene College, Cambridge
	R[2]	R.3.20, Trinity College, Cambridge (two copies, R[2-1] and R[2-2]).
	S[1]	Arch. Selden B.10, Bodleian
	S[2]	Arch. Selden B.24, Bodleian
	Th	Thynne's edition, 1532, STC 5068

A further manuscript, Phillipps 11409, is suggested in Brown and Robbins's Index of Middle English Verse, 1943, no. 809; but this seems to be a ghost (Nichols, Spec 44, 1969, 46). All texts have been published: eighteen by the Chaucer Society; Cov by Doyle and Pace (PMLA 83, 1968, 22–34), P and A[6] by Pace (MLN 63, 1948, 457–62), Nott by Doyle and Pace (SB 28, 1975, 41–61), Co by Pace (Spec 26, 1951, 306–7), and Leyd by Nichols (Spec 44, 1969, 46–50), and Th in the Brewer facsimile. The envoy is unique to A[1], which is the basis of the present text.

Title: The title is modern (Hammond, Ch: Bibl. Man., 1908, 403). The subtitle is from Cov Gg; om. α A[4] C El

A[6] F₁ Kk S[2]; MSS vary greatly, e.g.: *Balade* F; *B. that Chaucier made on his death bedde* Co R[2-1]; *Mora B. of C.* H[4]. See the Variorum edition or the published transcripts listed above for the full record.

2   **unto thy thing**] *thin owen t.* A[1]; *the thyne owne* Ph; *u. t. lyvynge* A[4]; *u. t. good* El γ (except Cx F Leyd Th) Rob; *(un)to the g.* Cx Leyd Th; *thee thy g.* F.

4   **blent**] *blindeth* β; *is blent* γ except F₂ Kk Nott R[2-1]; *ys blynd* F₂ Kk Nott; *blentethe* R[2-1].

6   **Reule**] *Werke* β; *Do* A[6] Co F H[4] Hat Lam R[2] S[2]; *Rede* Cp Cx Nott Th; *r. thy self* Ld Leyd P S[1]. Ek interchanges 13 for 6, γ (except Kk) 20 for 13, and α 6 for 20.

7   **trouthe thee shal delivere**] *thee* om. A[1] C El Gg; *t. s. the d.* A[4] Lam Nott; *t. s. d. the* Cov.

8   **Tempest**] *Restreyne* A[4]; *Peyne* γ except *Ne study* Cp.

10   **Gret reste**] *Myche wele* α; *Meche r.* Cp.

11   **Be war therfore**] *And eke bewar* β (except A[4], which has line 12 here and *Clymbe not to hye for fere thou fall* as line 12) Skt Hth; *b. w. also* γ (except Cp Kk) Rob; *Ne stomble not thy fotte* Cp; *also b. w.* Kk.

14   **trouthe thee shal delivere**] *thee* om. A[1] C El Gg; *t. s. the d.* A[4] Nott.

19   **Know thy contree**] *Loke up on hye and* γ (except Cp Kk); *Lyfte up thy heart* Cp; *Lyft up thyne* Ene Kk

20   **Hold the heye wey**] *Weyve thy lust* γ except (A[6] Co Kk Lam S[1]); *Wayse thy lust* A[6]; *Distreyne thy luste* Co; *Weye thy lust* Lam S[1]; *Ruell thi self thet other folk may rede* Kk. See note 6 above.

21   **trouthe thee shal delivere**] *thee* om. A[1] C El Gg; *t. s. the d.* Ph A[4] F₁ F₂ Nott S[1].

22–28   A[1] only.

28   **thee**] Om. A[1].

GENTILESSE

Authorities: ten manuscripts and the editions of Caxton (1477–78) and of Thynne (1532):

α	A[4]	Additional 22139, British Library
	C	Cotton Cleopatra D.VII, British Library
	Cov	Coventry MS (Accession 325), City Record Office, Coventry
	Cx	Caxton's edition, ca. 1477–78, STC 5091
	H[3]	Harley 2251, British Library
	H[5]	Harley 7578, British Library
	Nott	Nottingham University Library MS ME LM 1 (Mellish)
	R[4]	R.14.51, Trinity College, Cambridge (lines 1–7 only).
	Th	Thynne's edition, 1532, STC 5068
β	A	Ashmole 59, Bodleian
	H[4]	Harley 7333, British Library
	R[2]	R.3.20, Trinity College, Cambridge

All have been printed: nine by the Chaucer Society; Cov by Doyle and Pace (PMLA 83, 1968, 28), Nott by Davis (RES 20, 1969, 46), Th in Brewer's facsimile. C is the basis of the present edition.

Title: Supplied by Skeat. The subtitle is from H[4]; om. α except Cov. R[4]; *Balade* Cov R[4]; *Geffrey Chaucier made theos thre balades next that folowen* A; *B. by Chaucier* R[2]; Cx Th occur in the text of Henry Scogan's poem on gentilesse.

1   stok fader] *s. was f.* H³; *strooke f.* H⁵; *f. and foundour* A; *f. and fynder* H⁴; *f. fynder* R².
   gentilesse] A R²; *gentilnes(se)* rest.
2   desireth] *claymeth* Cx H³ Nott R⁴(?) Th A; *that coveytethe* A⁴ Cov.
4   love] *shewe* R⁴ H⁴; *suwe* A R²; *folowe* Cx; *loke* Th; *sewe* Skt Hth Rob.
13   he²] *him* β.
15   Vyce] *vices* A⁴ C Cov H⁵.
16   as men may wel see] *alle men may wele see* Cx Nott; *as every man se* H³; *al men may se* Th; *as thou maist wele seeme* A; *as yee may wel see* H⁴ R².
20   hem his heyres that] Rob; *his eires hem that can* A⁴ Cov Nott Th; *his heires hem that* C H⁵; *hem eyres that can* Cx; *his Eyre suche as can* H³; *his heyre him that wol* A Hth; *his heires hem that doone* H⁴; *heos heyres hem that wol* R²; *him his heir that can* Skt; *him his heir that wol* Kch. The emendation adopted was proposed by Robt. E. Brittain, MLN 51, 1936, 433.

LAK OF STEDFASTNESSE

Authorities: fourteen manuscripts, a transcript of a Cotton manuscript, and Thynne's edition of 1532:

	B	Advocates Library i.1.6, Edinburgh
	Co	Cotton Otho A XVIII, British Library, from a transcript by William Thomas
	Du	No. 432, Trinity College, Dublin
	H⁴	Harley 7333, British Library
α	**Hat**	Hatton 73, Bodleian
	Lam	No. 344, Lambeth Palace Library
	M	Pepys 2553, Magdalene College, Cambridge
	R²	R.3.20, Trinity College, Cambridge
	R³	R.3.21, Trinity College, Cambridge (two copies of lines 22–28, the envoy, only)
β	**R⁴**	R.14.51, Trinity College, Cambridge
	Th	Thynne's edition, 1532, STC 5068
	A⁴	Additional 22139, British Library
	C	Cotton Cleopatra D.VII, British Library
γ	**Cov**	Coventry MS (Accession 325), City Record Office, Coventry
	F	Fairfax 16, Bodleian
	H⁵	Harley 7578, British Library

All have been printed: ten by the Chaucer Society; Co by Pace (Spec 26, 1951, 306–7), Du by Pace (MLN 63, 1948, 460–61), Lam and R³ by MacCracken (MLN 23, 1908, 214), M by John Pinkerton (Ancient Scottish Poems, 1786), Th in Brewer's facsimile, and Cov by Doyle and Pace (PMLA 83, 1968, 28). C is the basis of the present edition.

Title: Adopted by Skeat from the Ch Soc. transcriptions; om. B Du M R³ Th A⁴ C; *Balade Ryalle made by Poetecall Chaucyer a Gaufrede* Co; *This b. made Geffrey Chaunciers the Laureall Poete of Albion and sente it to . . . Kynge Richarde* H⁴; *B. Royal made by oure laureal poete of Albyon in hees laste yeeres* R²; *Balade* R⁴ Cov F H⁵. For Hat titles, see MacCracken, MLN 23:214.
1   the] *this* α except M; om. H⁵.
5   Ben] H⁴ Hat Lam R²; *Is* Co β C F H⁵; *Ar* B M A⁴ Cov.

lyk] *oon* Co H⁴ Hat Lam R².
10   For among us now] γ; *For now adayes* Du H⁴ Hat Lam R²; *For* om. B Co M; *now* om. β.
11   collusioun] *conclusion* Lam γ; *ymaginacioun* Du.
   Lenvoy to King Richard] R²; *to Kyng Richard* om. H⁴ Hat Lam Th F; entire rubric om. Co Du M R³ R⁴ A⁴ C Cov H⁵.
26   swerd] *yerde* Du β.
28   wed] *bring* B; *dryve* Co H⁴ Hat Lam R² R³; *knyt to gydre* Du; *leid* M.

LENVOY DE CHAUCER A SCOGAN

Authorities: three manuscripts and the editions of Caxton (1477–78) and of Thynne (1532):

Cx	Caxton's edition, 1477–78, STC 5091 (lines 1–28 only)
F	Fairfax 16, Bodleian
Gg	Gg.4.27, Cambridge University Library
P	Pepys 2006, Magdalene College, Cambridge
Th	Thynne's edition, 1532, STC 5068

Cx F Gg and P have been printed by the Chaucer Society, Th in Brewer's facsimile edition. Because the variants determine no grouping among F Gg and P, they are treated as equally valuable. The variants do suggest that Cx and Th descend from P (cf. 10, 32, and 38 below), but because there are other variants with alternative implications (cf. 3, 16, 28 below), Cx and Th are represented in the notation. F is the basis of the present text.

Title: *Litera directa de Scogon per G. C.* Gg; om. Th, but *Lenvoye* is catchword on preceding page.
2   were] *weren* F.
3   Syth] *Syn* Cx Gg P.
5   erthe] *yerthe* P.
6   whennes] *hens* P.
8   it shape] *yshape* F Kch Rob; *it y-shape* Hth.
10   a drope] Om. Cx P Th.
15   Hastow] *Havesthow* F.
   the] *this* F.
16   rekelnesse] *rechelesnesse* Gg Kch; *reklesnesse* P Cx.
25   his] *thy* F.
27   oure] *youre* F.
28   him] *hem* P.
   ne] *nor* F.
32   in love] Om. P Th.
33   have] *han* Gg P Skt Hth Rob.
35   olde] *tholde* F.
38   to] Om. P Th.
   Envoy] Supplied by eds.; om. MSS.
43   stremes] *wellis* Gg.

LENVOY DE CHAUCER A BUKTON

Authorities: two MSS and the editions of Julian Notary (1499–1501) and of Thynne (1532):

α	**Cov**	Coventry MS (Accession 325), City Record Office, Coventry
	JN	Julian Notary's edition, 1499–1501, STC 5089

F   Fairfax 16, Bodleian
Th   Thynne's edition, 1532, STC 5068

This classification is somewhat uncertain, dependent upon taking the F readings in 13 and 24 as independent variants. All have been printed: three by the Chaucer Society; Cov by Doyle and Pace (PMLA 83, 1968, 28); Th is in Brewer's facsimile. F is the basis for the present text.

Title: from F; om. Th; *Balade* Cov; *Here foloweth the counceyll of Chaucer touchyng Maryag . . . sente to Bucketon etc.* JN.
1 **maister Bukton]** *maister Boughtoun* Cov; *Maister etc.* Th.
5 **highte to]** *highte you to* α.
9 **that]** Om. Cov. **yt]** Om. JN.
13 **eft]** *ofte* α F.
20 **these]** *the* α.
23 **lever to be]** *leve be* Cov; *lever be* JN.
24 **eft]** *ofte* α. **to]** Th; om. α F.
32 **hard]** *foule* Th.

THE COMPLAINT OF CHAUCER TO HIS PURSE

Authorities: eleven manuscripts, a transcript of a Cotton manuscript, and the editions of Caxton (1477–78) and Thynne (1532):

α {
F   Fairfax 16, Bodleian
Ff¹   Ff.1.6 Cambridge University Library

β {
A⁴   Additional 22139, British Library
Ca₂   MS.176, Gonville and Caius College, Cambridge (lines 15–26 only)
Cov   Coventry MS (Accession 325), City Record Office, Coventry
Cx   Caxton's Anelida and Arcite, 1477–78, STC 5090
P   Pepys 2006, Magdalene College, Cambridge
Th   Thynne's edition, 1532, STC 5068

γ {
A⁵   Additional 34360, British Library
Ca₁   MS.176, Gonville and Caius College, Cambridge (lines 1–14 only)
Co   Cotton Otho A.XVIII, British Library, from a transcript by William Thomas
H³   Harley 2251, British Library
H⁴   Harley 7333, British Library
Mg   MS.4, Morgan Library

With the addition of Cov and Th this is the classification proposed by Pace (SB 1, 1948, 103–12). For an alternative classification see Vinton A. Dearing, A Manual of Textual Analysis, 1959, 72–78. All texts have been published: eight by the Chaucer Society; Cov by Doyle and Pace (PMLA 83, 1968, 22–34), Ca₂ by Pace (MLN 63, 1948, 461–62), Ca₁ by MacCracken (MLN 27, 1912, 228–29), Th in Brewer's facsimile edition, Mg by Buhler (MLN 52, 1937, 5–9), and Co by Pace (Spec 26, 1951, 306–7). F is the basis of the present text.

Title: Om. Ff¹ A⁴ A⁵ H³; *Balade* Cov; *La c. de C. a sa Bourse voide* Cx P Th; *A Nother Balade* Ca₁; *Balade by C.*

etc. Co; *A supplicacion to Kyng Richard by chaucer* H⁴; *The c. o. C. unto h. p.* Mg.
4 **yf]** Om. β Skt Hth Rob².
7 **Beth]** *Be* β.
13 **good]** Om. γ except *all* Ca₁.
14 **Beth]** *Be* A⁴ Cov Cx Th Ca₁; *By* P.
16 **saveour]** *soverayn lady* A⁵ Co H⁴ Mg.
17 **thurgh your myght]** *by y. m.* Cx Th; *this night* Mg.
19 **as nye as any frere]** *as n. as is a f.* F; *as ys any f.* Ff¹.
21 **Beth]** *Be* β except Cov.
22–26 Om. A⁴ Cov A⁵ Co H³ Mg.
25 **oure]** *myn* F Ca₂; om. Cx P Th.

PROVERBS

Authorities: four manuscripts and the edition of Stowe 1561:

A²   Additional 10392, British Library (lines 5–8 only)
A³   Additional 16165, British Library
F   Fairfax 16, Bodleian
H⁵   Harley 7578, British Library
St   Stowe's edition, 1561, STC 5075–76

All have been published: three by the Chaucer Society and the entire set by Pace (SB 18, 1965, 43) F is the basis of the present edition.

Title: *Proverbs* is editorial; the subtitle *Proverbe of Chaucer* is from F H⁵; A³ has *Prouerbe,* St *A proverbe agaynst coviitse and negligence;* A² is untitled.
1 **shul]** *shal* A³ St; *shulde* H⁵.
3 **grete]** Om. A³.
5 **al]** Om A³.
   large] *wyde* A³.
6 **myn]** *my* A² F H⁵.
7 **so]** *that* A²; om. H⁵.

AGAINST WOMEN UNCONSTANT

Authorities: three manuscripts and Stowe's edition 1561:

α {
F   Fairfax 16, Bodleian
C   Cotton Cleopatra D.VII, British Library

β {
H⁵   Harley 7578, British Library
St   Stowe's edition, 1561, STC 5075–76

C is printed by the Chaucer Society, F by Pace (SB 28, 1975, 57–58), St in Brewer's facsimile edition of Thynne. F is the basis of the present edition.

Title: Supplied by Skt, adapting *A balade whiche Chaucer made ageynst women inconstaunt* St; *Balade* F H⁵ (F has *The Newfangilnes of A Lady* in MS table of contents); om. C.
1 **for]** *that throgh* F.
2 **ye]** Om. F.
   out of grace] *out of your grace* α St.
4 **ye have lyves]** *to lyve have* C St.
7 **thus may ye]** *ye may wel* F. This F reading is repeated as the refrain in line 14, but in line 21 F agrees with β.
8 **as a]** *as in a* F.
   nothing] *that nothinge* C β.
   impresse] *enpresse* C St Skt Hth Kch Rob.

10   **beren]** *bereth* C β Skt Hth Kch Rob.
12   **his]** *ay his* F.
14   **thus may ye]** *ye may wel* F. See 7 above.
16   **Bet]** *Better* MSS; all eds. emend for meter.
17   **stant]** *stondeth* MSS; all eds. emend for meter.
19   **oon]** *fone* H⁵.

COMPLAYNT D'AMOURS

Authorities: three manuscripts:

α { **F**   Fairfax 16, Bodleian
     Bod   Bodley 638, Bodleian
     H⁴   Harley 7333, British Library

F and Bod are available in facsimile editions (see p. 1117). H⁴ is the basis of the present edition.

Title: From F Bod; the subtitle is from H⁴: . . . *an amourouse compleynte made at wyndesore in the laste Maye tofore November.*
9   **Ne]** MSS Hth; *Nay* Kch Rob; *For* Skt.
14   **love you]** α Skt; *l. y. best* H⁴ Hth Kch Rob.
16   **that]** Om. H⁴.
17   **For to acompte]** *Tacompte* α.
24   **singe]** *say* H⁴. F lacks line endings 24 through 28 and Bod is corrupt.
58   **sore wolde]** *hem wolde* α; *hem soore wolde* H⁴.
66   **sorwes]** *shoures* H⁴.
76   **have pleyned unto you]** *on yow have pleyned* α.

77   **lady dere]** Skt Hth Kch Rob; *hert dere* α; *lady so dere* H⁴.
81   **of the]** *over the* α.
     and clere] Om. α.
82   **Alwey in oon]** *And I ay oon* H⁴.

MERCILES BEAUTE

Authority: One manuscript, Pepys 2006, Magdalene College, Cambridge (P). It has been printed by the Chaucer Society. There is a seventeenth-century transcription (Additional 38179, British Library), which lacks authority (see Pace and David, Minor Poems, 173). The poem was first printed in Bishop Percy's Reliques of Ancient English Poetry (1767).

Title: From the index in P. The subtitle added by Skt Hth Rob; Kch has *(Rondel);* on the subtitle, see further Pace and David, 175.
1   **yen two]** *two yen* P. When repeated in 6 and 11, the reading is *yen two.*
6   **Your yen two wol]** *Your yen etc.* P. All the repeated lines in the poem are abbreviated.
36   **ther]** All eds., beginning with Percy; *this* P.

A BALADE OF COMPLAINT

Authority: one manuscript, Additional 16165, British Library (A), printed by Skeat (Acad. 33, 1888, 1:292).

A Treatise on the Astrolabe

Authorities: Thirty-one manuscripts contain all or some of *A Treatise on the Astrolabe* in English, and one contains a Latin version of a small part. The sigla allotted are those that Professor Sigmund Eisner proposes for his forthcoming Variorum edition; the differences from those of Robinson's second edition are too slight to cause difficulty, and in the following list the sigla used by Skeat and Pintelon are added in parentheses.

Dd¹	Dd.3.53, Cambridge University Library	(A)
Dd²	Dd.12.51, Cambridge University Library	(P)
Cp	Corpus Christi College, 424, Cambridge	(F)
J	St. John's College, E.2, Cambridge	(M)
R	R.15.18, Trinity College, Cambridge	(G)
A¹	Ashmole 391, Bodleian, Oxford	(D)
A²	Ashmole 360, Bodleian, Oxford	(O)
A³	Ashmole 393, Bodleian, Oxford	(Q)
Bl¹	Bodley 619, Bodleian, Oxford	(E)
Bl²	Bodley 68, Bodleian, Oxford	(U)
Dg	Digby 72, Bodleian, Oxford	(N)
M¹	E. Museo 54, Bodleian, Oxford	(B)
M²	E. Museo 116, Bodleian, Oxford	(W)
Rl¹	Rawlinson D.913, Bodleian, Oxford	(C)
Rl²	Rawlinson D.3, Bodleian, Oxford	(K)
Ad¹	Additional 23002, British Library	(L)
Ad²	Additional 29250, British Library	(S)
Eg	Egerton 2622, British Library	(R)
Sl¹	Sloane 261, British Library	(I)
Sl²	Sloane 314, British Library	(H)
Sl³	Sloane 446, British Library	
Ph	Thompson Collection, no. 1 (formerly Phillipps 11955), Institution of Electrical Engineers, London	(T)
Hg	Peniarth 359 (Hengwrt 219), National Library of Wales, Aberystwyth	
Pu	3567B (Puleston 7), National Library of Wales, Aberystwyth	
W	3049D (Mostyn 146), National Library of Wales, Aberystwyth	
Ab	Aberdeen University Library 123	
N	Northumberland 460, Alnwick Castle	
Br	Brussels, Royal Library 4862/69	(X)
Hv	Harvard University, Houghton Library, English 920	(Z)
Pl	Plimpton 254, Columbia University Library	
T	Takamiya 9 (formerly Penrose), Toyko	(Y)
Bu	Formerly Marquess of Bute MS 13 (A.19); now in the United States	

The conclusion of N consists of second versions of 2.35 and 2.36, with 2.41–45 and the Spurious Conclusions (2.41a–42b, not included in this edition) sandwiched between, and, finally, 2.37. This conclusion is subsequently referred to as N², but does not constitute a separate manuscript.

The dates are: J Dd¹ Bl² Br and M¹, first quarter of the fifteenth century; Rl¹ Pl, about 1425; Bl¹ M², second

The textual notes to *A Treatise on the Astrolabe* were prepared by John Reidy.

quarter of the fifteenth century; Ab, about 1440 (Ker, Med. MSS in Brit. Libraries 2, 1977); Bu, after 1460; Ph Hg and T, probably the third quarter of the fifteenth century; Hv and probably N, last quarter of the fifteenth century; Ad² perhaps 1491 (this date appears in 2.1.7 instead of 1391). Dd² Cp R A¹ A² A³ Dg Rl² Ad¹ Eg and Sl² are dated ante 1500 by the MED, but though many of these are clearly late, the dating (accepted from catalogs) cannot be pressed further than "fifteenth century" in any individual case. Finally, Pu is dated probably 1551; Sl¹, 1555; W, last quarter of the sixteenth century; Sl³, second half of the sixteenth century. The earliest manuscript may be J, dated fourteenth century by James (Descript. Cat. of MSS in St. John's Coll. Cambridge, 1913), but this is surely too early.

Since Robinson's second edition was published, the former Penrose manuscript has been acquired by Professor T. Takamiya of Keio University, Tokyo; and seven others have been noticed, Hg Ab N Pu W Bu and Sl³. This last contains Latin instructions for establishing the twelve houses, based on 2.36 and 37, and a Latin version (not a translation) of 2.23, both attributed to Chaucer; it includes a horoscope for April 21, 1547, and also has instructions for finding the height of a tower, slightly resembling those in 2.41, and probably based on them, but not attributed in the manuscript to Chaucer. Hammond (Ch: Bibl. Man., 359) notes a Hatton manuscript mentioned in Edward Bernard, Catalogi manuscriptorum Angliae et Hiberniae in unum collecti, 1697, but this has never been identified.

The earliest edition was that of Thynne, 1532. Of subsequent editions the earliest still useful is Brae, 1870, using Sl¹ Sl² and Ad¹. Skeat (EETS e.s. 16, 1872 and Oxford Ch 3) is especially valuable; his text is based for the most part on Dd¹, and Oxford Ch 3 contains a brief account of twenty-two manuscripts in all. Mark R. Liddell, in the Globe Edition, 1898, based his text on Bl¹, which he set apart from the two groups described by Skeat. P. Pintelon, Ch's Treat. of the Astr., 1940, provides a photographic reproduction of Br and a very useful introduction, giving a table of the order of conclusions in twenty-two manuscripts and variant readings from seventeen manuscripts for Pro 1–64 and from Dd¹ and Rl¹ for the whole; Hv and T, and of course Hg Ab N and Pu, were not known to him. Robinson's second edition is based on Bl¹ up to 2.40, on J for 2.41–43, and on Dg for 2.43–45.

The present edition attempts to establish groups of manuscripts related by common variants and then to weigh the evidence of these groups in working towards an archetype. This archetype is then corrected towards what is probably nearer Chaucer's version by use of external evidence, such as the source, actual astrolabe readings, and consistency with astronomical fact, and of internal evidence, the necessity for the text to make sense, or a consideration of how an error might have developed. The textual notes supply the manuscript evidence where the archetype is thus changed or where there is difficulty in determining the archetype. It follows that the text is based on all manuscripts, regardless of date or general accuracy, except for A³ Sl¹ Sl³ Pu W and Bu; Sl¹ is an edition in itself, and Pu and W are evidently much affected by one of the first three editions of Thynne (1532, 1542, and about 1551). Sl³ is Latin, and A³ is too fragmentary to be useful; of Bu I have seen only one page. But though no manuscript is considered inherently preferable as to wording, one has to be used in providing a Middle English spelling, and Robinson's choice of Bl¹ has been retained for this purpose. However, Robinson modified the spelling not only in conformity to modern practice (for example, with regard to *u* and *v* and *th*) but also in accordance with Chaucerian grammar; this edition maintains this latter practice, though carrying it through more consistently.

The following table shows the contents of the manuscripts used, neglecting short omissions and insertions.

Bl¹ Ad²	Prologue–2.40, 2.46
Dd¹ M¹ Br Rl¹	Prologue–2.40
Pl Dd²	Prologue–2.40, 2.41–43
Ab R Sl²	Prologue–2.36 (Ab lacks 2.24–2.26.7 owing to a missing leaf)
Bl² Hg	Prologue–2.36 (omit Pro 1–64)
N	Prologue–2.36 (omits Pro 65–108, 2.15, 2.20–25)
Cp	2.16.1–2.36
A¹	Prologue–2.31.13 (lacks 2.3.46–2.25.25)
J	Prologue–2.38.9, 2.41–44, 2.41a–42b
Dg	Prologue–2.37, 2.41–45, 2.41a–42b
Eg Ad¹	Prologue–2.37, 2.41–45, 2.41a–42b (omit 1.15–21)
A²	Prologue–2.35, 2.41–45, 2.41a–b, 43a (omits 1.15–21)
T	Prologue–2.40, 2.41–45, 2.41a–42b
Hv	Prologue–2.37, 2.41a–42b
Ph Rl²	Prologue–2.35
M²	2.31.2–2.37, 2.41–45, 2.41a–42b
N²	2.35(2)–2.37, 2.41–45, 2.41a–42b

Of these, all the manuscripts from J to N² (with the exception of T) constitute a group, which is referred to as the J Group. Apart from T, only manuscripts of this group contain the Spurious Conclusions, 2.41a–42b, and the Supplementary Propositions, 2.44–45; and apart from this group only Pl Dd² and T contain 2.41–43. Furthermore, except for Hv, manuscripts of this group that contain 2.36–37 (and in J part of 2.38) place these conclusions at the end after the Spurious Conclusions. This distinctive ending enables us to place M² and N² in this group, which clearly represents a tradition in which 2.38–40 are missing, a break occurs after 2.35, the Supplementary Propositions and Spurious Conclusions follow, and 2.36–37 form the conclusion; in this tradition also 2.19–21 follow 2.12 (missing in M² and N²).

The T manuscript ends in the same way as this group, but as will be detailed later, it changes its affiliation twice and so does not misplace 2.19–21. Among the manuscripts outside the J Group, Sl² and A¹ are often close to J in their variants, though not in order or content; on the other hand Hv is close to Pl and Dd².

In the manuscripts outside the J Group, certain variations in order and content are noteworthy. M¹ ends with the order 2.34, 37–40, 35–36; and R with 2.35–36, 34. Bl¹ Ad² Dd¹ M¹ Br and Rl¹ leave the last sentence of 2.40 incomplete; Pl and Dd² complete it and go on to

2.43. T and N are more complicated. In Part 2, T begins with 2.2, followed by part of 3, 38–40, a spurious conclusion (found also following 2.2 in Dg A² Eg and Ad¹), part of 3, 4–35, 41–45, 41a–42b, and 36–37. N runs in order to 2.13, after which come 36, 35, 34, 33, 16–19, 26–32, and 14; there follow a second 35, 41–45, 41a–42b, a second 36, and finally 37; as mentioned, this ending, from the second 35 on, is called N². The scribe evidently followed an exemplar with a haphazard order ending at 2.36, and then found another exemplar to form a conclusion. It is interesting that Bu, judging from one page reproduced in Sotheby's Sale Catalog, is very close to T, and this closeness is borne out by its erratic order of conclusions in Part 2.

From a study of the variant readings the following clusters of manuscripts are clear: Bl¹ and Ad² (α); Dd¹ and M¹ (β); Br and Rl¹ (γ); Pl and Dd² (π); Dg A² Eg and Ad¹ (δ); Ph and Rl² (ϕ). Other pairs are Hg and R, Ab and N, Sl² and A¹, and for one stretch Cp and T. Larger groupings are discernible, especially J ϕ and δ, with which Sl² and A¹ are closely associated; M² and N² are very close to δ. Thus the manuscripts of the J Group, though varying among themselves, are much closer to each other than to any others, with the exception of Hv, which is close to π. The cluster ending at 2.36 seems as if it would be an obvious group, and indeed these manuscripts do share some readings unique to themselves (not all errors); but the pairs separate and coalesce too frequently for one label to cover them all. As noted, Sl² and A¹ are close to J and ϕ, and also Hg and R share a few unique variants with β. T is with δ, especially A² Eg and Ad¹ up to 1.14; but these three lack 1.15–21, and T follows another exemplar, similar to Ab and N until Cp begins at 2.16; from there T shares with Cp several strikingly aberrant readings until 2.31 rubric, after which it shifts back to close association with δ.

The following are the six groups used to establish an archetype, as explained above: α; β; γ; π (with or without Hv); Bl² Hg R Ab N Sl² A¹ Cp and T or a majority of these; and J ϕ and δ (with Sl² and A¹, T, M² and N², in parts). A case might be made for reducing these to four, namely: α and β; γ π and Hv (which have a number of readings against all others); the Bl², Hg, etc. group of manuscripts ending at 2.36, including the incomplete A¹; and the J Group. But α and β, though sometimes together against the rest, are also often split, leaving α against the rest; and γ differs from π and Hv as often as not. J ϕ and δ are at variance, but as a rule of thumb J with either ϕ or δ, or Sl² and A¹, is taken for the whole. The J Group tradition must be very old even if the fourteenth century date for J is not accepted (it includes 2.44, possibly written about 1397). J is not the ancestor of the others in this group but seems to attest one branch of the tradition against ϕ and δ.

Group α, and to a lesser degree β, provide the most consistently acceptable text, especially for numerical readings; α also contains two unique and necessary passages. Bl¹ particularly is most often correct in measurements on an astrolabe. However, it sometimes gives measurements too fine for a small astrolabe, and in 2.25 many of the figures in γ π and the J Group are accepted instead. Of the other groups, γ is most useful, though less often than α and β, except in 2.38–40, where it is more so. The evidence of the other three groups is mostly corroborative of readings accepted from α β or γ, though on a few occasions the group comprising Bl² Hg R, etc., together with some of the J Group, provides an accepted reading against the rest. Moreover, the six groups are split in two or three ways often enough for the corroboration of π; Bl² Hg R, etc.; and the J Group to be welcome in assessing the reading for the archetype. Withal there are still left a number of occasions (as may be seen in the Textual and Explanatory Notes) when the final appeal must be made to editorial judgment.

Title: *Tractatus de Conclusionibus Astrolabii* Dd¹ (colophon); *Explicit tractatus Astrolabij* Pl (at end); *Tractatus Astrolabii* Cp; *Heere begynneth the tretyyce of the declaracioun on the conclusiouns of the astrelaby* Hv; *The Tretys off* (? *the*) *Astrolabye* A³; *De Astrelabio* J; *Astrolabium* Ph Rl²; *Heir begynneth the knowlach of the Rewles of the Astrolabom* N; *Brede and milke for children* Bl¹ Bl² M¹ Ab.

PROLOGUE

28 suffise] α β R Sl² A¹; *it sufficeth* γ Ab N π Hv J φ δ T; Bl² Hg Cp M² out.
61 n'am] β R; *ne am* Br Ad² Sl² π Hv; *am* Bl¹ Rl¹ Ab φ δ T; *am not* J; illegible passage precedes *am* A¹; om. passage N; Bl² Hg Cp M² out.

PART I

§5.7 centre] γ π Hv φ; *hool* α; + β; *oriental* Bl² Hg Ab R Sl² A¹ J; om. passage N δ T; Cp M² out. See Expl. Notes.
§10.6 were clepid] Hg Ab R δ T; *w. c. thus* α; *w. c. in Arabyens* β; *w. cald* Bl²; *w. yeuen* γ; *w. yeue hem* π Hv; *ben considered* Sl² A¹ φ; *taken here namys* J; om. passage N; Cp M² out.
10.8 Arabiens] Bl² Hg Ab R δ T; *lordes A.* α; *lordes* (*bordes* M¹!) β; *emperours* γ π Hv; *clerkys* J φ; *charchus* Sl² A¹; om. passage N; Cp M² out. The variety of readings is probably due to scribal attempts to produce a satisfactory balance for *othre lordes of Rome.* Since none of the months has an Arabic name, *emperours* is the obvious reading; but if it had been what Chaucer wrote, who would have changed it? *Arabiens* occurs twelve words earlier in β (see note to 10.6 above), and was perhaps displaced from here owing to marginal or superscript insertion.
§12.7–9 *Umbra Versa* and *Umbra Recta* or *ellis Umbra Extensa* are transposed in all MSS; the confusion must be Chaucer's own; om. passage N; Cp M² out.
§17.2 3 cercles] Bl² Hg Ab R N Sl² A¹ J φ Dg; *tropik c.* α; *3 tropikal c.* β; *3 principal c.* γ π Hv T; Cp A² Eg Ad¹ M² out; Messahala has *tribus circulis.*
21 Equator that is the weyer] α Br; *the w. eq.* β R A¹; *the w. i. eq.* Bl² T; *the w. or eq.* Hg Ab; *the waye or eq.* N; *the very* (*weray* Dg) *eq.* Sl² Dg; *the even w.* π; *eq. t. is to saye on English tunge the even w.* Hv; *the w.* Rl¹ J; *the eq.* φ; Cp A² Eg Ad¹ M² out. See Expl. Notes. N.B.: The *i.* in the Bl² T reading is the normal ME form for our *i.e.*
§18.6 cenyth] The spelling *signet,* especially frequent in the MSS of the J Group, seems to be a simple confusion due to pronunciation; *cenyth* appears occasionally as *cynet* (e.g., M², 2.31.23) or *cenit* (e.g., Pl, 1.18.15), and the

gn in English words borrowed from French was not palatalized, but a simple *n.* In the Latin Rubric to 2.31, the scribe, or exemplar, of J renders *cenyth* as *signum.*

PART II

Between §2 and §3 in δ, and before §3 in T, a spurious short section, merely repeating §1, is printed by Skeat, 3:360.

§3.37–38 After *ascendent* occurs a long note in Bl¹, corresponding to Messahala 2.30 (Gunther, Ch. and Messahala on the Astr., 182, 225–26); printed by Skeat, 3:360–61. See introduction to Expl. Notes.
39–58 The MSS give basically two sets of readings for using *Alhabor* (Sirius) to find the time and the ascendent: altitude of Sirius 12°, time 9:40 P.M. (9 hours 10 degrees), ascendent 10° Scorpio; altitude 18°, time 5 (or 7 or 8) hours and 2 degrees, ascendent 20° Libra. In my instrument, using a plate for 51° north latitude, with 10° Scorpio on the eastern horizon, the time is 9 o'clock plus 10 degrees, i.e., 9:40 P.M., and Sirius is at about 13°. With 20° Libra ascending, the time is 7:44 P.M. (i.e., 7 hours and 11 degrees, as in many MSS), and Sirius is about 21°. I have chosen the first set of readings, against the weight of the evidence.
45 12] α β Hg (Dd² has *12* in red, underdotted, crossed out, *18* superscript); om. Bl² R (with space); Cp T M² out; rest *18.*
47 12] α M¹ (superscript by scribe) Hg; *18* Dd¹ (above erasure); om. γ R (with space); A¹ Cp T M² out; rest *18.*
55 9] α β (Dd¹ also *8* superscript) Hg; *5* Br; *ij* Rl¹ (apparently altered from *9* or *5*); *7* Bl² Ab Sl² J φ δ Hv; *8* π N; om. R (with space); A¹ Cp T M² out. 10] α β (Dd¹ also *2* superscript) Hg; *2* γ π Hv J; *11* Bl² Ab N Sl² φ δ; om. R (with space); A¹ Cp T M² out.
57 10] α β (Dd¹ underdotted, *23* superscript) Hg; *24* π; *12* φ; om. R (with space); A¹ Cp T M² out; rest *20.* Scorpius] α; *libra* (over erasure) Dd¹; *taurus* M¹; *libra* Hg (*taurus* superscript by scribe); A¹ Cp T M² out; rest *libra.*
§4.11–14 forseide degre than hath . . . of his longitude] α; *f. latitude h. l.* β; *f. same d. o. h. l.* γ; *f. same gree o. h. l.* π; *thilke same d. o. h. l.* Hv; *f. orizont* Bl²; *f latitude* Hg Ab R N T; *f. orysount assendent hys* (*is* Sl²) *l.* Sl² J Eg Ad¹; *f. orizont ascendyth his l.* φ; *f. latitude orizont ascendente his l.* Dg A²; A¹ Cp M² out. See Expl. Notes.
21 ascendith] α β; *a. on the* (*that* Hg) *est orizonte* γ Bl² Hg Ab R N Sl² J φ Dg Ad² T; *a. upon the e. o.* π Hv; *a. on the o.* Eg Ad¹; A¹ Cp M² out. The phrase *on* (*upon*) *the est orizonte* is otiose and is picked up from 9.
25 25] Om. π; A¹ Cp M² out; rest *15.* See Expl. Notes.
50 ascendent] α β Hg Ab R N δ T; *a. frendschiped* γ π Hv; *a. be frendschip* Bl² Sl² J φ; A¹ Cp M² out.
§9.2 3] *2* α; A¹ Cp M² out; rest om.
§11.9 parties] α Sl² J Ph Hv; *part(ye)* β γ Bl² Hg Ab π δ Rl² T; om. passage R N; A¹ Cp M² out.
§15.9 point] Ab π Hv; om. J N; A¹ Cp M² out; rest *pointes.* The MSS favor *pointes,* but Chaucer never elsewhere uses *either* to mean *both.*
§22.18 place] α Dd¹ Hg Cp T Ph; *planete place* π; om. (with space) Hv; Ab N A¹ M¹ out; rest *planete,* which must be an error.

§23.29   56] α β; N A¹ M² out; rest *62.* For this and next five notes, see Expl. Notes 23.29–35.

31   48] α β; N A¹ M² out; rest *21.*

    8 degrees] α; N A¹ M² out; rest om.

32   56] α β; N A¹ M² out; rest *62.*

33   8] α β; N A¹ M² out; rest *62.*

    48] α β; N A¹ M² out; rest *21.*

35   52. **Now hast thou]** α β; N A¹ M² out; rest om.

§25.23   **38 degrees]** Rl¹ Sl² J φ Eg Ad¹ Hv; *98 d.* Br; *38 grees* π, *38 d. and 10 minutes* β; *38 d. and 25 m.* α Bl² Hg R Cp T Dg A²; Ab N A¹ M² out.

24   **leveth there 52]** γ Sl² π J φ Eg Ad¹ Hv; *l. t. 51 degrees and 50 minutes* α β Hg R; *l. t. 51 d. and 15 m.* Bl²; *l. t. 51 d. and 51 m.* Cp T Dg A²; Ab N A¹ M² out. Chaucer has already given the latitude of Oxford as 51°50′ (2.22.5–8), and the β figures, 38°10′ for the sun's meridional altitude (making a latitude of 51°50′), render 25–28 otiose. The figures adopted, 38° and 52°, fit well with 25–28, but 38°25′ and 51°15′ (or 51′) are absurd. Chaucer in his examples usually keeps to whole numbers.

26   **latitude]** *by the l.* Hg R Cp T; *be t. altitude* Bl²; *altitude* A² Eg; Ab N M² out.

27   **is certeyn minutes lasse]** Om. Bl² Hg R Cp T; Ab N M² out.

27–28   **thow might preve the same]** *as y m. p.* Dd¹; *t. m. p. the* M¹; *t. may p. t. s.* Bl² Hg R Cp T; om. γ π A¹ Sl² φ δ Hv; Ab N M² out. The passage was probably an afterthought, added to challenge Lewis to very close observation, to *preve,* i.e., find out, or check this measurement. For Lewis to judge accurately 10′ would have been impossible, but he might perhaps with care have noticed a slight difference—*certeyn minutes.*

40   **10 degre of Leoun]** *first d. o. L.* α β Hg R Cp T; *d. of l.* φ; *10 degrees* (*gree* π) *of l.* γ Bl² Sl² A¹ π Hv J Eg Ad²; *first d. 10* (*10 d.* A²) *of l.* Dg A²; Ab N M² out.

41   **almost 56]** γ Sl² A¹ π Hv J φ Eg Ad¹; *58 degrees and 10 minutes* β; *58 d. and 17 m.* α Hg R; *toward 58 d. and 17 m.* Cp T; *56 d. and 17 m. almost* Bl²; *a. 56 58 d. and 17 m.* Dg A²; Ab N M² out.

42   18] γ Bl² Sl² A¹ π Hv φ Eg Ad¹; *16* J; *18* (*other* Dg) *20* Dg A²; Ab N M² out.

44   18] γ Bl² Sl² A¹ π Hv Eg Ad¹; *18.20* Dg A²; om. J φ; Ab N M² out.

45   **38 degrees]** γ Sl² A¹ π Hv J φ δ; *38 d. and odde minutes* α β Bl² Hg R Cp T; Ab N M² out. In 40–45 the MSS are about equally divided between those keeping to whole numbers and those with added minutes. The altitude of the sun as 58°17′ is taken from Nicholas of Lynn (*Kalendarium,* 105) and is much too precise for Lewis, besides the inconsistency of then giving the declination as *almost* 20°. The readings adopted are the most likely and consistent; the added phrase *and odde minutes,* perhaps an afterthought, still makes sense, because *almost* 56 less *almost* 18 might not be exactly 38.

§26.11–16   **Ferther-over** (*ffurthermore* Ad²) **they seyn . . . this** (*the* Ad²) **world . . . the right orisonte]** α; M² out; rest om. See Expl. Notes.

§28.32   **ende]** Bl² Hv; om. M¹ A²; M² out; rest *heved* or *heed.* The erroneous *heved* or *heed* may go back to Chaucer or to an early scribe spelling *ende* with initial *h,* leaving *n* to be mistaken for *u.*

§30 Rubric   **latitude]** α Cp T Hv; rest *altitude.*

17   All except α β add: *for on the morowe wole the sunne be in another degre and thanne & cet.* γ Ab R Sl²; om. *and t. & cet.* Bl² A¹ J φ; om. *& cet.* Hg; *f. in* (*the* Cp T) *m.*

. . . *degre* (*than* Cp T) *that tym* Cp T δ; *f. in t. m. . . . degre* (*gree* π) *and northere or souther* (*north or sowth* Hv) *peraventure* π Hv; M² out.

§33.8–9   **is the sterre]** Dd¹ R; *the s.* α M¹; *the s. is* Bl² Hg; *t. s. is in* Ab N; *the s. stondeth* γ Sl² π Hv φ δ T M²; *he ascendith* J; om. passage Cp; A¹ out. The choice of reading lies between *is* and *stondeth* (miscopied in J); *is* could be more easily lost.

§35.11   **tak]** β γ Hv J Rl²; rest om.

22   **west syde]** α β Hg J φ; *w. s. on the* (*thy* Br Hv) *lyne meridional* γ Sl² Hv δ M²; *w. s. of the l. m.* Bl² π T N²; *w. s. of thy m.* Ab N; *est syde* Cp R; A¹ out.

§36.8   **ascended]** α γ Bl² Hg Sl²; *ascendit* Dg; A¹ A² Ph Rl² out; rest *ascendith* (N.B.: *ascendid* Hv; this MS regularly illustrates the late ME sound change by which *-th* becomes *-d*).

12   **ascendid]** α γ Bl² Hg Sl²; A¹ A² Ph Rl² out; rest *ascendith.*

16–17   **4 houre inequal]** α γ π Hv; *4 h.* β Bl² Hg R Ab N; *4* Cp; *4 houus* J Sl²; *5 hows* δ T M² N²; φ A¹ Ad² out. See Expl. Notes.

26   At the end of this conclusion Br adds the following example, not found in any other MS:

Now for the more openere declaracioun I wole make an ensaumple to the forseid conclusioun of the equacion of houses. I sette caas that the sixte degre of Leo were ascendent in the firste hous. Thanne remeve thi zodiac and sette the sixte degre of Leo that ascendith upon the ende of the 8 houre inequale; thanne wole the 28 degre of Leo sitte upon the lyne of mydnyght, the whiche is the bygynnynge of the secunde hous. Remeve thanne the sixte degre of Leo that ascendith and sette hym upon the ende of the 10 hour inequal; thanne wole the 21 degre of Virgo sitte upon the lyne of mydnyght, which is the bygynnynge of the thridde hous. Bringe up ayen the sixte degre of Leo and sette hym upon the est orizonte ascendynge, and thanne wole the 14 degre of Libra sitte upon the lyne of mydnyght, which is the bygynninge of the fourthe hous. Thanne tak the nadir of the degre that ascendith, that is the sixte degre of Aquarie, and sette hym upon the ende of the secunde houre inequal; and thanne wole the 24 degre of Scorpio sitte upon the mydnyght lyne, which is the bygynnynge of the 5 hous. Take thanne the same nadir of the ascendent, that is the 6 of Aquarie, and sette hym upon the ende of the 4 hour inequal; thanne wole the 29 degre of Sagittarie sitte upon the lyne of mydnyght, whiche is the bygynnynge of the 6 hous. Now further more as it is seid in the conclusion bifore: The bigynnynge of the 7 hous is the nadir of the ascendent, that is the 6 degre of Aquarie, and the bygynnynge of the 8 hous is the nadir of the secunde hous right as ye may se by this present figure next folowynge.

§37.15   **in the zodiak]** γ π; *i. which degree of t. z.* β; *and be thy z.* J δ T Hv M² N²; *lith i. t. z.* α; rest out. See Expl. Notes.

17   **the begynnyng of the 12 hous next]** α β; *the 12 hous next* γ π; *the nex hous next* J δ Hv M² N²; A² out; rest out.

§38.12   **centre amiddes]** α; *c.* β; *pyn* γ π T; rest out.

31   **the opposit of the south lyne i.e. the north]** *t. o. o. t. s. l. is t. n.* γ; *t. nader o. t. s. l. is t. n. lyne* β; *than is the s. l. t. n. o.; the o. that is t. n.* π; *n.* T; rest out.

§40.7   **in general]** γ T; *for sonne* β; *in special* π; *treuly* Bl¹; *forsothe* Ad²; rest out. See Expl. Notes.

10–43   Of the MSS running only α, Dd¹, and occasionally M¹ have figures; the others omit them, sometimes leaving spaces. We must choose either the α readings—longitude 1° Capricorn, latitude 4° north, and the planet rises 8° from the head of Capricorn (i.e., 22° Sagittarius)—or the corresponding Dd[1] readings—6°, 2° north, rises with 24° Sagittarius *(the 6 degree in the heved of capricorne)*. Either set is hard to read, owing to the position near the edge of the rete and plate, but the α readings give an accurate result; the Dd[1] readings do not.

10 1] α; 6 Dd[1]; om. M[1] γ π T; rest out.

12 4] α; 2 Dd[1]; 3 M[1]; om. γ π T; rest out.

17 1] α; 6 Dd[1]; om. M[1] γ π T; rest out.

21 4] α; 6 Dd[1]; *3* (inserted) M[1]; om. γ π T; rest out.

22 4] α; 2 Dd[1]; 3 M[1]; om. γ π T; rest out.

41 4] *her* T; om. α β γ π; rest out.

42 8] α; 6 Dd[1]; om. M[1] γ π T; rest out.

53–73 Once again the choice of readings is between α, usually with M[1], and Dd[1], α having the latitude 2° south and the ascending degree 8° of Pisces, while Dd[1] has 3° and 14° of Pisces; the α readings again are more accurate.

53, 58, 59 2] α M[1]; *3* Dd[1]; om. γ π T; rest out.

66 endlong] γ π T; *evene* α β; rest out.

67 2] α; *3* Dd[1]; om. M[1] γ π T; rest out.

72 2] α M[1]; *3* Dd[1]; om. γ π T; rest out.

73 8] α; *14* Dd[1]; 6 M[1]; om. γ π T; rest out.

79 hir] *his* α β γ; *here* π; rest out.

82–83 thou shalt do wel ynow] π; om. α β γ; rest out. See Expl. Notes.

§41 Only π J δ T M[2] N[2] are now running, and notes will refer only to these (α resumes at §46). Spelling of text is based on J for §§41–43, on Dg for §44–45.

9–10 right so . . . of the tour] J; rest om. See Expl. Notes.

11 For 4 is] J; *and I finde that hit is* π; *and ye shull (thou schalt* T) *f. t. h. is* δ T M[2] N[2].

18 5 12-partyes of the heyght the space] *5* (om. Dg A[2]) *12-p. t. h. of t. s.* J δ T M[2] N[2]; *5 tymes 12 the heighte of the tour* π. See Expl. Notes.

§42.3 I see] *I sette* J; *thou sixt* π.

5 go I] *go* J π.

7 π has had second person throughout; all the rest but J change to second person here; J changes at 9.

11 12 passith 6 by the numbre] T N[2]; *12 p. 6 t. n.* δ; *12 6 t. n.* J; om. passage π M[2].

17 60 foot] *sex fett* J; *80 foot* π.

21 2] 6 MSS. See Expl. Notes.

22 3] *4* MSS.

23 2 is 6 partyes] *6 is 2 p.* MSS.

  3 is 4 partyes] *4 is the thrid p.* MSS; om. J.

§43 Rubric Recta] *Versa* J.

1 *recta*] *versa* J.

10 tour] *t. and so of all other & cet.* π; π ends here.

§46 Found only in α.

13 it] Om. Bl[1].

19 tyme] Om. Bl[1].

23 shalt] Om. Bl[1].

The Romaunt of the Rose

Authorities: MS V.3.7 in the Hunterian Museum, Glasgow (G), edited by Kaluza, Ch Soc. 1st ser. 83, 1891, and Thynne's edition of 1532 (Th), edited by Furnivall, Ch Soc. 1st ser. 82, 1890, and available in facsimile editions by Skeat (1905) and Brewer (1969). Until recently Th was regarded as an independent authority, though closely related to G. J. E. Blodgett (Library, ser. 6, 1, 1979, 97–113), however, demonstrated on the evidence of printer's marks in G that the manuscript was actually the copy-text used for Th. Someone marked off the lines in G systematically to indicate to the compositor precisely where each page and column of the printed text was to begin, a standard printer's practice of the time. That these marks are in fact connected with the printing of Th is clear from a few instances where they were adjusted to correct a mistake in counting off, to allow space for a missing line, or to change the layout. Blodgett describes similar markings in a copy of a Caxton *Boece* and in the manuscript Longleat 258, both also used in the printing of Th.

Th can therefore no longer be taken as a primary authority except where it preserves the text of eleven leaves and a few marginal words now lost from G. The close relationship between G and Th has often been noted, though the differences, especially several lines missing from G supplied in Th, have led editors to assume that Th was based on a sister manuscript or close relative of G. The two share many errors, the most remarkable of which is a misarrangement of four passages in Fragment C (comprising lines 7013–7304). Two leaves were accidentally displaced in binding an ancestor of G, and the resulting breaks in sense escaped the notice of G's scribe, of Thynne, and of every editor until Tyrwhitt first pointed out the error in a note to his edition of *The Canterbury Tales* (4:314). Skeat provided a full explanation of the error and its origin both in his edition (1:11–12) and in the Thynne facsimile (xxx).

It is of course possible that Thynne had access to a second manuscript of the Romaunt, which he used to emend G. A far likelier explanation of the differences between the two texts, however, is that Thynne edited G, just as modern editors have done, with the aid of the French original and according to his notions of Chaucerian usage. This was the opinion of Kaluza (ESt 18, 1893, 106–11; Ch und der Rosenroman, 1893, 2–3, 254), though he never kept his promise to publish the evidence on which he based his belief. William Thynne's son Francis, in his Animadversions on Speght's 1598 edition of Chaucer, taking Speght to task for some of his readings in the Romaunt, cites "the frenche verses that euer was (to be founde in Englande)," perhaps the same copy his father had used in editing the poem (Ch Soc. 2nd ser. 13, 1876, 74). On Thynne's editorial practices, see J. E. Blodgett, Wm Thynne, in Editing Ch, 35–52.

The notion that Thynne's editing accounts for most of the discrepancies between G and Th is supported by the

way those discrepancies are distributed throughout the text. If Thynne had merely reproduced a manuscript similar to G, occasionally correcting obvious errors, one would expect a more or less random distribution of the variants between the two texts, but this is not the case. Of the 7696 lines in previous editions (the present edition ends at 7692, the last four lines of what is believed to be a spurious conclusion by Thynne having been relegated to the notes), 417 differ substantively in G and Th; that is, they present variations ranging from the omission of whole lines in G to slight omissions, additions, or changes of single words or morphemes affecting sense, meter, or grammar. Of these 417 variants, 133 occur in the first 1300 lines. With adjustments made for the leaves lost from G, this means that 11 percent of the lines before 1300 show variation but only 4.7 percent of the lines after that point. The inference is that Thynne's interest and editorial initiative began to decline after some 1200 lines and that, although he or his printer continued to catch a few mistakes, and missing lines were filled in, more of the errors in G were repeated and fewer editorial changes introduced.

This pattern gains support if we examine one typical kind of variation. Skeat observed in his edition (1:14) that "the scribe of 'G' frequently dropped the prefix *y*- in past participles." The prefix occurs in G only once (*ydoo,* 1941); in addition, in three corrupted passages (2621, 4657, 5505), the pronoun *I* may represent a scribal misreading of the *y*- prefix. In contrast, Th has the prefix at 126, 135, 155, 160, 167, 471, 472, 480, 604, 718, 890, 897, 1063, 1214, 1238, 1396, 1419, 1510, 1610, 5505, and 6806. The inference is clearly not that the scribe omitted the prefix but that Thynne added it, mainly in the first 2000 lines, because he considered it to be a hallmark of Chaucer's style and found it a convenient device to add a metrical beat to the line.

The evidence, therefore, dictates a different approach to the text from that used in previous editions. Skeat, Liddell (Globe), and Robinson based their texts on G but made frequent use of variants from Th. Sutherland (1968) and Fisher (1979) based their editions on Th. Many of the readings in Th correct obvious errors in G and should be retained. Elsewhere, however, when G makes sense and does not show clear evidence of miscopying, its reading ought to be retained even when a variant in Th offers a stylistically more satisfactory choice. Such is particularly the case with meter. Robinson's policy in this respect is even more cogent than he had reason to suspect: "The editor has very sparingly adopted emendations to improve the meter. Many lines are easy to mend, as Skeat and other editors have done, by supplying words or changing their order. But in verse that is either non-Chaucerian or the work of Chaucer's youth it is hardly justifiable to introduce the smoothness of his later technique." Thynne may now be regarded as the first of those editors who sought to mend Chaucer's lines, and his efforts should not be taken as authentic in a problematic text like the Romaunt.

The present text therefore relies even more heavily on G than did previous editions. G's reading has usually been accepted where it makes sense and where it is not

The textual notes to *The Romaunt of the Rose* were prepared by Alfred David.

clear how a copying error could have resulted, even when a more attractive alternative is suggested by comparison with the French. The effect may not always be as smooth or as aesthetically pleasing as that in former editions; however, where the text seems deficient but not obviously in error, we often have no way of telling whether the supposed deficiencies are due to the scribe or to the author.

In order to provide readers with evidence for drawing their own conclusions about the dependence of Th on G, the notes record all departures from G and all substantive variants in Th. When the reasons for the variants in Th are not obvious, attempts have been made to account for them. Twelve lines missing from G have been omitted from the text. The corresponding lines in Th are given at the foot of the text page and in both the textual and explanatory notes, as is Th's conclusion. The traditional numbering of the lines is retained. Besides the complete collations for G and Th, the textual notes regularly collate the editions of Skeat (Skt), Liddell (Lid), Robinson (Rob), and Fisher (Fsh) for passages where G and Th differ and for many emendations these editors suggest. Notice is also taken of some readings suggested by Kaluza (Kal) and Sutherland.

Citations of the French are taken from Langlois's edition (SATF, 1914–24). Langlois's text does not rest on a base manuscript as does the edition of Lecoy (1965–70) but attempts rather to reconstruct the original through a comparison of the best thirteenth- and fourteenth-century manuscripts. More than 300 manuscripts of the *Roman de la rose* are extant, and of these Langlois described and classified 116 in *Les manuscrits du* Roman de la rose (1910). For the purpose of comparing the Middle English with the French, one would of course ideally wish to consult not a modern edition but a French manuscript similar to one or more of the fragments of the Romaunt and thus presumably close to one used by the translator(s). Although the literalness of the English translation, especially in Fragments A and C, frequently makes it possible to identify the original of individual lines in some variant reading of the French (many such variants are printed by Langlois), no single French manuscript or combination of manuscripts can be positively identified as the source for any of the three fragments of the Romaunt.

Kaluza's edition of G has a parallel text based on Michel's edition (1864) with variants corresponding to the Middle English inserted from four manuscripts and a black-letter edition of the French *Roman*. Sutherland (PMLA 74, 1959, 178–83, and parallel text edition, 1968, ix–xxxix) argued that Fragment A was made by one translator from an ancestor of the manuscript family Langlois classified as H; that Fragments B and C came originally from a different translation made from an R manuscript, possibly Ri (2775 Riccardi Library, Florence); and that the two translations were later combined by a third person who revised the entire text with reference to a manuscript from the G/B group. (The Guillaume de Lorris portion comes from a manuscript of the G family; the Jean de Meun portion, from the B family; many French manuscripts reveal different affiliations for the two parts.) Sutherland's French text is based on Ha (Fr. 1573, Bibliothèque Nationale, Paris) for Fragment A and Ri for Fragments B and C, with frequent substitutions from related manuscripts, especially He (Fr. LV,

Royal Library, Copenhagen) and Go/Bu (11019, Royal Library, Brussels). Some of these manuscripts, particularly Go/Bu, are of considerable interest for the text of the Romaunt; nevertheless, the hypothesis of two translators and a reviser does not explain all the facts and is open to serious objections, pointed out by David (Spec 44, 1969, 666–70). Above all, it fails to account adequately for the marked stylistic and linguistic differences between Fragments B and C that have led all modern scholars to assign these to different translators.

Given the evidence at our disposal, the best that can be said is that each of the three fragments probably derives from a separate, relatively contaminated French text or that parts of the English may depend on more than one French manuscript. To postulate a Middle English text somehow corrupted—through memorial transmission as Brusendorff proposed (Ch Trad., 1925, 382) or through the intervention of a reviser—is pure speculation and raises more problems than it solves.

Brusendorff (308–83) and Sutherland (in his introduction and notes) comment extensively on the relation between the English and French in individual passages. Lange provides textual notes and emendations (in support of Chaucer's authorship of Fragment A) in Anglia 35, 1911, 338–46; 36, 1912, 479–91; and 37, 1913, 146–62.

FRAGMENT A

1–44   From Th; missing in G.

3   **sweven[es]]** *sweuen* Th.

4   **that false ne ben]** *ne false been* Skt; Fr. *ne sont mie mençongier* (are not deceivers).

22   **cariage]** *corage* Th Skt. Liddell's emendation, from Fr. *paage* (toll), has been adopted. Th's reading could only arise from the rarer word, a literal equivalent of the French.

37   **this book which]** *[that]* t. b. *[the]* w. Skt; *[wil I]* t. b. w. Lid; t. b. *[the]* w. Rob; Fr. *je vueil que li romanz* (I wish that the romance). Many lines in G do not count out to eight syllables. In view of the different emendations, it seems best to follow the copy-text.

66   **hath]** *had* G Th.

69–71   The beginnings of these lines, torn off in G, are supplied from Th.

71   **briddes]** *byrdes* Th Lid Rob Fsh. The word is torn off in G, but G's spelling is regularly *briddes,* modernized in Th to *byrdes.*

haven] *han* Th and eds.; *han* is metrically preferable, but *-en* is visible in G.

72   **so]** *ful* Th Fsh.

80   **sithe]** *a sythe* Th Skt Fsh.

81   **papyngay]** *the popyngay* Th Skt Lid Fsh.

84   **saverous]** *fauerous* G. See 2902 below.

85   **the]** *his* Th Skt Fsh.

91   **affraieth]** *affirmeth* Th.

92   **a-nyght]** *one night* Th Fsh.

94–96   The ends of these lines, torn off in G, are supplied from Th.

101   **song]** *sowne* Th Skt Fsh.

102   **in]** *on* Th Skt Fsh.

103   **the]** Om. G (erasure between *in* and *swete*).

leef] *swete* G (over erasure); Liddell suggests *newe;* Fr.

novele. The reading *leve is* would make the best rhyme (: *slevis*), and that may well be the pronunciation intended, though *leef* cannot be construed as a weak adjective.

107   They] *That* Th and eds.; Fr. *Qui.*
109   Joly] *Jolif(e)* Th Skt Lid Rob Fsh.
117–20   The beginnings of these lines, torn off in G, are supplied from Th.
126   paved] *ypaued* Th Fsh.
128   medewe] *medowes* Th Fsh.
135   goon] *ygone* Th Fsh.
142   the peyntures] *peyntures* Th and eds.
146   in] Om. Th Skt Lid Fsh.
147   Hate] *a hate* G.
148   yre] *and y.* Th Fsh.
149   mynoresse] *moveresse* Skt Lid (rev. ed., 1928) Rob; *meveresse* Lid (1st ed.); Fr. *moveresse* (var. *meneresse*). See Expl. Notes.
155   Frounced] *Yfrounced* Th and eds.
160   writhen] *ywrithen* Th and eds.
163   faste] Om. G.
167   Clepid] *Ycleped* Th and eds.
176   ymage] *an ymage* Th Fsh. Thynne supplied the article because he did not pronounce the final *-e* and put the stress on the first syllable.
182   gise] *a gise* Th Fsh.
185   she] Om. G.
189   she that] *that* G; *she for* Th and eds. See 190 below.
190   Techith] *That techith* G Th and eds.; Fr. *semont d'embler* (incites [thieves] to [the act] of stealing). Omission of *That* (perhaps through dittography) yields better sense than the substitution of *for* in line 189. *Coveitise* is the one that teaches thieves to steal many pennies, not to steal *for* many pennies.
196   myscounting] *myscoveiting* G Th; Kaluza's emendation, from Fr. *mesconter,* has been adopted.
211   fade] *sade* G Th Skt; *fade* is Liddell's emendation from Fr. *maigre.* Liddell, however, is incorrect in saying that *fade* also translates *maigre* in 311, where it is a synonym for *pale.*
225   perche] *benche* Th. Th's reading may result from the printer's misreading the ligature between *r* and *c.*
236   necessite] *nycete* Th.
240   heng] *heng [doun]* Skt Lid Rob.
243   that] *the* Th Fsh.
244   not] Om. Th Fsh.
256   Than] *That* Lid; Fr. *Ice.*
    wel] *[ful] w.* Skt; Fr. *mout.*
259   shamful] *shynful* G; Fr. *aler a honte.*
264   chaunce] *chaunge* G Lid.
275   hath] *hate* Th (perhaps reading *such* as the object).
    wo] Om. G Th; Fr. *duel.*
293   foul] Om. G; Fr. *mauvais.*
295   or] *ne* Th.
296   [oon] eie] *eien* G; Fr. *un ueil.*
299   fair or worthi] *fairer or worthier* G; Fr. *preuz ou biaus.*
307   Nor] *Ne* Th.
310   ful] Om. Th.
314   of] *with* Th.
323   forcracchen] *cratchen* Th Fsh.
333–80   From Th; missing in G.
379   er] Om. G Th; Fr. *ainz.*
380   passed] *y-passed* Skt Lid Fsh.
408   cope] *cappe* Th.

421   simple] *semely* G; Fr. *sainte* (var. *simple*).
424   that] *thilke* Th Fsh.
435   ne fresh] Om. *ne* Th and eds. The omission does not greatly improve the meter and breaks the parallelism of the three negatives.
444   face] *grace* G Th; Fr. *vis.*
446   hem] Om. G Lid.
448   and] *and eke* Th and eds.; Fr. *Deu e son reine.*
451   wolde] *holde* Th Lid Fsh.
457   nadde] *ne had* Th.
471   fed] *yfedde* Th Rob *(yfed)* Fsh.
472   wel] Om. G Th; Fr. *bien.*
    cled] *cledde* G Lid; *ycledde* Th Fsh; *y-cled* Skt.
478   were] *newe* G.
480   barred] *ybarred* Th Skt Rob Fsh.
483   wrought] *ywrought* eds.
485   laddre] *laddres* G; *ladders* Th; Fr. *eschiele.*
492   yer[d]] *yeer* G Th; Fr. *leus.*
497   and] Om. Th.
501   nolde] *wolde* G Th; Fr. *n'en preïsse pas.*
505   God kepe it fro care] *god [it kepe and were]* (God keep and defend it) Skt; *God [it kepe fro were]* (God keep it from sorrow) Lange (Anglia 35:444–64, 36:479–91); Fr. *que Deus guerisse.* The emendations would convert the un-Chaucerian rhyme (with *ware*) into a normal rime riche; nevertheless, the MS reading is retained by all editors save Skeat as a possible dialectal variant.
516   [o-]where] *where* G Th. Kaluza suggests *any where;* Liddell suggests *there.*
520   Ful] *For* G Th; *For-wo* ("very weary") Lid; Fr. *mout.*
    angwishus] *anguisshe* Th.
523   or] *ne* Th.
526   Envyronyng] *Enuyron* Th.
532   fetys] *[so] fetys* Skt Lid.
535   and of[t]] *and of* G; *al* Th; Fr. *par maintes foiz.*
537   the] Om. G; Fr. *Le guichet.*
541   flesh] *f.* *[as]* Skt Lid Rob.
560   neded] *neden* Th Fsh.
567   in honde] Om. G Th; Fr. *en sa main.*
586   may[de]] *mayden* Skt Fsh; *may* G Th.
602   of Alexandryn] *Alexandryne* Lid Rob; Fr. *terre as Sarradins* (var. *t. Alexandrins*). See Expl. Notes.
604   set] *yset* Th and eds.
645   inne] *[ther]in* Skt Fsh.
662   and] *and [of]* Skt Lid.
673   wel] *me* Th; Fr. *bien.*
    whan] *that* G; Fr. *quant.*
674   lustily] *lusty* Th.
688   But] *For* G.
    song] *[hir] song* Skt Fsh.
716   her] *their* G Lid; *hir* Skt Rob. G's *their* is a unique instance of a Northern pronoun in Fragment A. The 3rd pers. pl. gen. pro. in G is consistently *her;* the 3rd pers. fem. gen. and acc. is *hir.* The sole exception is 199, which twice reads *hir* for the 3rd pers. pl., perhaps influenced by *she* in the preceding line. Th reads *her* for both these pronouns. For the bearing of G's Northernism on the question of authorship, see the exchange between Hinkley and Skeat, Acad 71, 1906, 2.640–41, 647; 72, 1907, 1.79.
    jargonyng] *yarkonyng* G.
718   spronge] *ispronge* Th and eds.
720   reverye] *reverdye* Skt Rob; *revelrye* Th Fsh; Fr. *reverdie.* See Expl. Notes.
743   This] *These* Th Fsh.

746   the¹] Om. G Th.
the²] Om. Th.
749   And make] *And couthe make* G Th; *Couthe mak* Lid
(with *noon* as subj. of *Couthe*). G's *couthe* is perhaps repeated by attraction to *coude* in 747.
761   made] *make* Skt Lid Fsh, perhaps correctly; Fr.
faire.
773   hente] *henten* [*hem*] Skt. Liddell suggests *casten* and
[*hem*] *bente.*
791   bede] *bode* G Th Lid; Fr. *ne me queisse.*
801   Come] *Come* [*neer*] Skt; *Come* [*here*] Lid; Fr. *ça
venez.*
847   leef] *sefe* Th.
858   slendre] *tendre* Th.
859–60   seyn : pleyn] *sey : pleye* Th; Fr. *blanc, poli* (var.
bel et plein). .
861   Bente were hir browis] *B. w. b.* [*browne*] *b.* Lid;
[*Broun and*] *b. w. b. b.* Kal; Fr. *bruns et enarchiez.*
865   not . . . descryve] *wot not . . . I shal descryue* G Th.
"If the reader prefers to keep *eleven* (or *twelve*) syllables
in this line, I am sorry for him" (Skt).
877   on] *in* G.
884   p[r]oude] *poude* G.
890   clad] *ycladde* Th and eds.
891   in flourettes] *flourettes* Th Skt Fsh.
892   Om. G (no gap in MS). *Ypaynted al with amorettes*
Th and eds. A marginal notation in a later hand in G
reads "Lat alyn" (probably "let [i.e., leave] a line"), and
a line is left empty at the bottom of the page. The note
looks like an instruction to the printer to allow space for
the missing line to be supplied. See Blodgett, Library,
ser. 6, 1:100–101, and Expl. Notes.
897   Portreied and wrought] *Ypurtrayed and ywrought*
(*wrought* Lid) Th and eds.
900   Sett] *Yset* Th and eds.
904   man] *men* Th.
923   bowes two] *b. t. full wel deuysed* G Th. The translator perhaps ended the line with *deuysed,* changed his
mind about the rhyme, and then forgot to cancel the
phrase.
932   ful] Om. Skt Lid Fsh; Fr. *de bone* (var. *gente*)
façon.
942   right] *aright* Th and eds.
944   poynted] *peynted* G. G's reading results perhaps
from attraction to 933.
947   it] Om. Th
959   sheten] *shoten* Th Lid Fsh. Cf. 989.
960   right] Kaluza suggests *nigh;* Fr. *de près.*
970   His] *Hir* G.
978   al] *as* G Th Skt; Fr. *toute.*
1007   As] *And* G Th; *As* [*was*] Skt; Fr. *Ausi come.*
1010   as] *as* [*is*] Skt Lid Fsh.
1018   wyndred] *wyntred* G Th; emended by Skeat to
conform with 1020.
1026   toucheth] *thought* G Th; *thinketh* Skt; Kaluza's
emendation, from Fr. *touche,* has been adopted.
1031   Sore] [*Wys*] Skt; *Sote* Fsh (suggested by Sutherland). Skeat also suggests *Queint* and *Fine;* Kaluza, *Sade*
("agreeable"). See Expl. Notes.
1034   An high] *And bight* G Th; Fr. *de grant hautece.*
1037   word] *werk* G Th; Fr. *par faiz ne par diz.*
1043   beste] *leste* Lid Rob; Fr. *li graignor e li menor* (var.
meilleur).
the grettest] *greattest* Th Skt Lid Fsh.
1055   Bifore] *To forne* Th Fsh.
1058   And¹] *But* Th Skt Fsh.

prikke] *prile* G; *prill* Th; *prille* Lid. Liddell suggests
prille may be an error for *thrill* (pierce).
1061   abate the folkis] *abaten folkis* Th.
1062   and wys] *ywys* G Lid.
1063   An hundred have [they] do] Om. [*they*] G Lid;
Han hyndred and ydon Th Rob Fsh. The reading is doubtful
and depends on the syntax of 1063–65. The addition of a
subject, as in Skeat, and a full stop after 1064 allows G's
lines to stand without further change. Th's line looks like
an attempt to make sense out of G (perhaps inspired by
hyndre in 1039), but it is difficult to see how Th's reading
could lead to G's. Neither closely matches Fr. *Mainz pro-
domes ont encusez Li losengier par lor losenges* (Many a good
man have the backbiters denounced with their calum-
nies). *An hundrid* may be a line-filler, translating *Mainz.*
Kaluza cites a var., *Mainz miles d'ommes ont rusez.*
1064   thorough] *with her* Th Fsh.
1065   Have made] *And maketh* Th Skt Fsh; *And make*
Lid Rob. G's reading is parallel with *have do* (1063),
though the French changes to present tense, *font.*
1066   There] *There as* Th Skt Fsh.
1068   aryved] *achyued* G; Fr. *arivé.*
1073   it] *hir* G.
1080   ameled] *enameled* G; *amyled* Th.
1084   bright] *fayre* Th Fsh.
1089   durst] *thurte* Skt. Liddell notes the confusion of
the forms of *durren* and *tharf;* cf. 1324.
1092   mannes] *man* G.
1094   wise] *gyse* Th Fsh.
1098   and] *and of* Th and eds.
1111   he] *she* G; Fr. *cil.*
1116   the] *that* G.
1117   jagounces] *ragounces* G Th.
1130   semelyhede] *pmelyhede* G.
1134   well to have] *to haue well* G.
1137   ony] *an* Th Skt Fsh; *on* Rob.
1141   Was] *And* G.
1142   or] *of* G.
1144   dispence] *dispences* Th Fsh.
1146   spende] *dispende* G; cf. 1157.
1147   lakking] *lakke* G.
1150   settith] *sette* Th and eds.
1158   ynough alwey] *alwaye ynowe* Th Fsh.
1162   wys] Om. G.
1166   tristily] *craftily* Th Skt Rob Fsh.
1168   yift and free] *yeftes a. wyse* Th Fsh.
1172   riche] *riche and poore* Th.
1176   wynne] *wynne hym* Th and eds.
1188   Sarsynesh] *Sarlynysh* G Th; Fr. *sarazinesche* (var.
sarradinesche).
1201   gounfanoun] *Gousfaucoun* G Th; Fr. *gonfanon.*
1207   There] *The* G.
1214   fallen] *falle* G; *yfallen* Th and eds.
1219   on] *of* G.
1221   never] *neither* Th Lid.
1231   elles] *al* Th.
1233   hempene] *hempen ne* G Lid.
1236   nat] Om. G.
1238   clothed] *yclothed* Th and eds.
1255   right] Om. Th.
1256   Whanne] *For whan* Th.
1259   of fair answere] *fayre answere* Th Skt Fsh.
1261   rancour] *no rancour* Th and eds.
1263   of body] *and body* Th.
avenaunt] *wenaunt* G; Fr. (var.) *Gente iert e bele e ave-
nant.*

1265   were] Om. G.
1279   That] Om. Th.
   the gardyn] *that g.* Th Fsh.
1282   Youthe] *And she* G Th; Fr. *Jonece;* emended by B. ten Brink, Ch Studien, 1870, 30.
1288   wel] *wole* G; Fr. *bien le savez.*
1295   who] *who so* Th Fsh.
1303   thus] *that* G Th; Fr. *ensi.*
1306   and wys] *wys* Th Fsh.
1313   loreres] *loreyes* G; *laurelles* Th; Fr. *loriers.*
1314   oliveris] *olmeres* Th Lid Rob Fsh; Fr. *moriers* (mulberry trees). Liddell suggests that *moriers* was read as *ormiers* (elms), but the printer has misread the minims in *iu* as *m.* Cf. 1381.
1332   he²] *she* G Th.
1334   bad hym bende [it]] *had(de) hym bent* G Th.
1335   it] Om. G Th Lid.
1341   hadde me shette] [*wol*] *me shete* Skt. In 1343, Skeat has [*wol*] *me greven.* The regular pp. of *shete(n)* is *shote(n);* Skeat's emendation thus provides the infin. for rhyme but breaks the sequence of tenses. G's *shette* may represent a variant form of the pp. Fr. *Se il fait tant que a moi traie.*
1348   in all the gardyn] *al the* [*yerde in*] Kal Skt; cf. 1447 and n. below.
1356   dell] *doll* Rob (misprint).
1359   gret foisoun] *of gret foisoun* G.
1365   wexen] *weren* Th Skt Fsh.
1369   parys] *paradys* Skt Lid Fsh; Fr. *Graine de paradis* (var. *parevis*). See Expl. Notes.
1379   lorer] *lorey* G; *laurer* Th.
1387–1482   From Th; two leaves missing in G.
1396   ronne] *yronne* Th and eds.
1400   it] Om. G Th.
1419   set] *yset* Th and eds.
1447   [in] al the garden] *a. t. g.* Th Fsh; *a. t.* [*yerde in*] Skt (suggested by Kaluza); *a. t. g.* [*in*] Lid. Cf. 1348 and n. above.
1448   estres] *efters* Th.
1453   sheten] *shete* Skt; *shoten* Th Lid Rob Fsh.
1485   her] Om. G.
1496   And that he shulde] *Than shulde he* Th Skt Rob Fsh; *Than he shulde* Lid.
1503   that] *the* Th and eds.
1508   heet] *herte* Th Fsh.
1510   comen] *ycomen* Th and eds.
1515   he straughte] *out straught* Th and eds.
1520   had] *was* G.
1528   all] Om. Th.
1534   comfort] *comforte* G Th. Possibly the infin. is intended, though more probably the n.
1538   For] *Fro* Lid; Fr. *de la meschine* (from the damsel).
1553   Om. G (no gap in MS); *Unto the welle than wente I me* Th and eds.; Fr. *De la fontaine m'apressai.* See Expl. Notes.
1581   flour] *foule* G Th; Fr. *flors.*
1586   stondith] *stant* Skt Fsh; *stont* Lid.
1591   estrees] *entrees* G Th; Fr. *l'estre.*
1593–94   he] *ye* G Th Lid; Fr. *il.*
1603   face fair and bright] *fayre face bright* Th Fsh.
1604   sithe] *swithe* G Lid.
1608   lovyng] *laughyng* G Th; Fr. *d'amer.*
1609   many] *many a* Th Skt Rob Fsh.
1610   Blent] *Yblent* Th and eds.

1611   awayted] *wayted* Th.
1623   bridde[s]] *bridde* G; *byrde* Th; Fr. *oisiaus.*
1641   have] Om. G Th.
1644   The vertu and [the] strengthe] *The vertue(s) and strengthes* G Th; Fr. *sa force . . . e sa vertuz.*
1652   enclos is] *enclosid is* G; Fr. *clos.*
1655   and] *att* G.
1663   be] *me* G Th. Corrected by Speght.
1666   My] *Me* G.
1673–74   wone : rone] *won : ron* Skt Rob.
1674   waxe] *ware* Th Fsh.
1683   al] Om. G Th Skt. Added by Kaluza from Fr. *tuit.*
1684   or] *or els* Th Fsh.
1689   a] Om. G Th Lid.
1694   it] Om. Th.
1696   and] Om. G Th; Fr. *e si fine.*
1700   roses] *rose* Skt; *Rose* Rob.
1705   Incomplete sentence and imperfect rhyme with 1706. For possible emendations, see Expl. Notes, but the most common view is that Fragment A breaks off and Fragment B, by a different author, begins with 1706.
   dide] *dyed* Th Fsh.

FRAGMENT B

1721   botoun] *botheum* G; *bothum* Th. The word is variously spelled (also *bothom, bothun, bothom*). Eds. normalize it on the basis of Fr. *bouton.*
1728   myn ye] *me nye* G.
1733   a] Om. G Th; [*that*] Kal Skt.
1749   yet] *atte* G.
1750   that] *it* G; om. Th Skt Fsh.
1757   do] *to do* G.
1758   to] *two* G.
1766   certis evenly] *certeinly* Skt Rob. Robinson thinks the MS may be correct and glosses " 'certainly in equal measure'?"
1771   a] *his* G Th; *this* Lid.
1779   myn] Om. G Th.
1786   drawe] *drowe* I Th Fsh.
1797–98   feyne : peyne] *fyne : pyne* Th Skt Rob Fsh.
1806   of] *on* G.
1811   stikid] *stikith* G.
1814   felte] *lefte* G Th.
1831   my] Om. G Th.
1851   sen] *sene* [*it*] Skt.
1860   Castith] *Cast* Skt Lid Rob.
1879   pugnaunt] [*ful*] *pugnaunt* Skt Lid.
1892   Om. G; but *That he hadde the body hole made* added, on the line originally left blank, by a different (Brusendorff says the same) hand; *Through the body in my herte made* Th and eds. See Expl. Notes.
1913–14   Following Skeat's suggestion, Robinson transposes these lines; but, though the order is closer to the French, there is no need for the change; all other eds. follow G.
1922   hem] *hym* G.
1924   softenyng] *softyng* G Th.
1925   prikkith] *prikked* Skt Lid.
1929   rape] *jape* Th.
1965   love] *lovers* Skt Fsh.
1978   Mercy] *The mercy* Lid; Fr. *la merci que j'atens.*
1982   me] Om. G.

1984 Written by a different (Brusendorff says the same) hand on a line originally left blank; Fr. *Don tu as respondu issi.*

1994 to] Om. G Th.

2002 Skeat suggests *to* in place of *of* as idiomatic with *vouche . . . sauff.* The sense seems, however, to be that the God of Love will not vouchsafe that his mouth be touched *of* (i.e., by) churls, nor that they draw near it. The construction seems mixed.

2003–4 nere : manere] *ner : maner* Rob.

2006 Robinson suggests *kysse* may represent a Kentish rhyme *(gentilnesse : kesse),* but with the number of imperfect rhymes in B, one cannot be sure.

2024 And also] *Nede is* Lid; Fr. *Dedenz lui ne puet demorer Vilanie ne mesprison.*

2036 Written by a different (Brusendorff says the same) hand on a line originally left blank.

2046 Disceyved] *Disteyned* G Th. The scribe has confused *c* for *t* and *u* for *n.*

2049 falshed] *her falshed* G Th.

2066 wot] *wole* G.

2067 susprised] *surprised* Skt; *suprised* Fsh.

2074 so] *so [it]* Skt Fsh; *to* Rob (1957, misprint).

2076 disseise] *desese* G; *disese* Th; Fr. *dissaisir.*

2092 jowelles] *iowell* G Th Lid.

2116 degre] *gre* Lid (after Skeat's suggestion).

2132 complysshen] *accomplysshen* Th Lid Fsh.

2141 erre] Om. G Th; *[sinne]* Skt; Fr. *issir hors de voie* ("go astray"). The emendation is from J. Urry, Works of Ch, 1721.

2148 Romance] *Romaunt* Th Fsh. Subsequently Th reads *Romance,* though the running title is *Romaunt.*

2150 that] Om. Th and eds.

2167 ye] *he* Th and eds.; Fr. *Por quoi il vueille tant atendre.* However, the French poet is addressing his audience, telling them what a patient reader may expect to learn (*Je vos di bien que il porra*—"I tell *you* indeed that *he* can"). The confusion of pronouns in the translation is, therefore, natural enough.

2176 sayde] *say(e)* G Th.

2177 not] Om. G Th.

2208 ying] *yong(e)* G Th Fsh.

2215 mare] *more* G.

2218 hem] *hym* G.

2234 set] Om. G.

2261 kan] *kan [hem]* Skt Lid.

2271 awmenere] *awmere* G; *aumere* Th. Scribal error for Fr. *aumosniere.*

2285 Fard] *Farce* G Th Lid; Fr. *farde.*

2294 laughith] *knowith* G Th; Fr. *rit.* Kaluza suggests *lowith,* and some such spelling doubtless accounts for the error.

2298 is] Om. G Th.

2302 pleyeth] *pleyneth* G Th.

2309 hem sittyng] *h. [best] s.* Skt Fsh; *[to] h. s.* Lid; Fr. *miauz li avient.*

2316 til] *to* G.

2318 no] Om. G.

2323 foote] Fisher and Sutherland have *flute,* after Kaluza's suggestion from Fr. *fleüter* (whistle). Brusendorff (419) suggests changing *he* and *hym* (2324) to the 2nd pers. to conform with the rest of the passage.

2333 ben] *can* Lid Rob, perhaps rightly, from Fr. *sot.*

2336 Loves] *londes* G Th; Fr. *d'amors.*

2341 swich gift] *this swiffte* G Th; *so riche gift* Fsh (suggested first by Liddell); Fr. *après si riche don.*

it] Om. Skt Lid.

2343 wol I] *woly I* G.

2355 heere] *that heere* G.

2365 Of] *For* G Th Skt Fsh.

trecherie and] *t., in* Skt; Fr. *Si qu'il n'i soit mie demis, Mais toz entiers, senz tricherie* (that it be not only a part but entire, without treachery).

2371–72 sette : flette] *sitte : flitte* G. *Sette* corresponds to Fr. *metes; flette* may be a variant of *flitte,* or *flitte* could be an imperfect rhyme with *sette.*

2384 is] Om. G.

2395–2442 From Th; missing in G.

2413 As] *A* Th Lid; Fr. *Ausi come.*

2427 sende] *sene* Th; Fr. *enveier.*

2472 thou] *tho* G.

2473 Thou] *Thought* G Th Skt; *That* Fsh. Skeat suggests "That swete."

2477 thou] Om. G Th Lid Fsh.

2493–94 folye : bye] *foly : by* Skt Rob. Though doubtless the final -*e* here is not pronounced, it seems best not to adjust the spellings of Fragment B in the interest of rhyme.

2499 yitt] *yif* Skt Rob Fsh. See Expl. Notes, 2497–2502.

2532 resoun] *[thy] r.* Kal Skt Lid Rob; Fr. *ta* (var. *tu*).

2541 a] *o* Th Rob Fsh; Fr. *un.*

2551 bargeyn] *batail* Kal Fsh; Fr. *guerre.*

2563 a-bred] *abrode* G; *a brede* Th.

2564 forwerreyd] *forweriede* G; *forwerede* Th.

2569 se[me]] *se* G Th.

2574 in] *it* Th.

2578 but] *b. a* Th Skt Rob Fsh.

2592 The] *Fro* Lid Rob; *For* MED (passage cited under *langouren*).

2610 Without] *Withouten* Th and eds.

kysse] *kesse* Th Rob Fsh. Given the character of B, the rhyme is doubtless at fault, not the spelling in G.

2617 wote not] *not* (= *ne woot*) eds.

2621 on hir] *on [me]* Skt Lid; *of hir* Rob Fsh; Fr. *de li.* I caste] *ycast* eds.; see Expl. Notes.

2622 Than] *That* G Th.

2628 liggen] *ly* Skt Lid (cf. rhymes at 2629, 2645).

2641 contene] *contynue* Th Fsh. See Expl. Notes.

2644 shalt] *shat* G; *shal* Th Fsh.

2645 enduryng] *endurying* Rob (misprint).

2650 weder] *whider* G Th.

2660 score] *shore* Th.

2664 the] *thy* Th Skt Rob Fsh; Fr. *la bele.*

2668 without] *withouten* Skt Rob; *withoute* Lid.

2669 [a-]nyght] *nyght* G Th.

2675 whom] *whanne* G Th Lid.

2676 Fr. *Au revenir* (var. *departir*) *la porte baise.* Kaluza suggests *Thou kisse the dore er thou go away.* See expl. note 2673–76.

2682 wakyng] *walkyng* G Th Skt.

2693 oft] *of* G.

2696 is] *it* G.

2699 grace] *gace* G.

2704 mych] *moche* Th Fsh; *muche* Skt; *mychel* Rob.

2709–10 mare : fare] *more : fore* G Th Fsh. Cf. 2215–16 and 2741–42. The B translator appears to use *mare/more* depending on the rhyme.

2746   may] Om. G Th.
2752   yet] *that* G Th Skt (though he suggests the emendation); Fr. *toutes-voies.*
2763   his] Om. G Th.
   trust] *trist* G.
2772   sore] *sore sore* G.
2775   caccheth] *cacche* G; *to cacche* Skt; *hathe* Lid.
2778   lover] *lenger* Th.
2783   bond] *londe* G Th Skt; Fr. *Iceste te garantira, Ne ja de toi ne partira.*
2796   Thenkyng] *Thought* Skt.
2824   ben] *not ben* G Th; Fr. *seroies.*
2833   hem] *me* G Th. Cf. 2845 below.
2836   ne] Om. G Th Skt; *have [no] sight* Lid.
2845   smert] *[my] smert* Skt Rob, perhaps correctly; cf. 2833 and 2848.
2854   him] *hem* G.
2895   of biholdyng] *beholdyng* Th Skt Rob Fsh.
2902   saverous] *faverous* G Th. Cf. note 84 above. The scribe of G misread long *s* for *f,* perhaps not understanding the word. Thynne emends above but not here nor in 3767. His editing has grown very casual.
2916   it] Om. G Th. **convoye]** *conveye* G.
2917   they] *thou* G Th.
2921   he] Om. G Th Lid.
2934   the eyen] *they* G Th Skt; Fr. *li ueil.*
   that] *that [that]* Skt.
2950   at] *all* G Th Skt; Fr. *a ja* (var. *des ja; des ore*).
   yive] *yeue* G Th.
2988   how] *nowe* Fsh (from Sutherland).
2992   I be] Om. G Th; Liddell and Fisher read *You warrante may [I];* Fr. *Je vos i puis bien garantir.*
3005   full] *fully* G.
3029   good] *[no] good* Skt Rob; *good [ne]* Lid.
3035   Brought] *[On lyve] b.* Skt. Robinson calls the line "defective" but does not emend it.
3040   conceyveth] *conceyved* Lid Rob.
3058   is] Om. G.
3079   me] Om. G Th; Fr. *me fis.*
3083   wax] *wext* Th Fsh.
3125   growe] *late it g.* G Th.
3127–28   Robinson notes that the rhyme should be *wer : ber,* though *bere* might be construed as subjunctive.
3130   sterte oute anoon] *a. s. o.* Th Fsh.
3136   Om. G (line left blank in MS); *His eyes reed sparclyng as the fyre glowe* Th and eds. (Skt Lid om. *sparclyng*); Fr. *S'ot les iauz roges come feus* (He had eyes red like fire).
3137   kirked] Possibly an error for *kroked;* Fr. *Le nés froncié, le vis hisdeus* (The nose wrinkled, the face hideous).
3141   is] Om. G Th; *[is] so nygh* Lid.
3150   I] *it* G; *he* Th; Fr. *je.*
3164   it] *he* Th Skt Rob Fsh. No emendation is needed; it is the head that shakes.
3175   hayes] *haye* Lid Rob; Fr. *la haie.*
3179   wot] Om. G Th; *not* Lid; *wiste* R. Morris (Works of Ch, 1866).
3186   braste] *barste* G.
3188   Was] *That was* G.
3201   on] *in* G.
3207–8   grace : compace] *gras : compas* Rob.
3217   thus] *this* Th.
3221   the] *ye* G.
3227   yedest] *didest* G.

3228   haddest] *hadde* G; *had* Th Fsh.
3231   thee] Om. G Th.
3248   nat] Om. G.
3264   seyne] *feyne* Skt.
3275   Of] *Or* Th Fsh.
   if] *if that* Th Fsh.
3279   of] Om. G.
3292   a rage] *arrage* G.
3294   leve of is] *loue of his* G Fsh; *Loue of his* Th Skt; *leve of his* Lid; Fr. *Mes au lessier* (var. *a l'issir*) *a grant mestrise.* The emendation adopted (from Kaluza) is closest to the French; *leue* is easily misread as *loue,* especially with the anticipation of *loue* in the next line.
3319   taught] *thought* G Th.
3337   chevisaunce] *cherisaunce* G Th; Fr. *chevissance.*
3356   have] Om. G.
   meygned] *meymed* Th Rob Fsh; MED *(maimen)* cites *meygned* in this line without *have,* taking it as a form of the infin. (from OF *mahaigner*). Perhaps read *meygne.* See Expl. Notes.
3372   his] Om. Th.
3379   meke] *make* G.
3385   hym wel] *him wel [him]* Skt; *well hym* Lid Rob.
3414   I] Om. G.
3418   you shulde] *s. y.* Th Skt Rob Fsh.
3429   elles well] *al wel* Th Fsh; *[al your wyl]* Rob (suggested by R. M. Bell, Works of Ch, 1854–56); Fr. *Toutes voz autres volontez.*
3433   sithen] *sichen* G; *such* Th; *sith* Skt Rob Fsh. The scribe confused *t* and *c* and may actually have intended to write *t;* Thynne or his printer, however, interpreted the word as a form of *such.*
3448   thou] Om. G Th.
3450   If] *I* G; *In* Th Skt; Fr. *Se tu passes jamais.*
3454   tall] = *tale,* with final *-e* apocopated for rhyme.
3468   me] Om. G.
3482   nat] Om. G Th; *[hard]* Morris Skt Fsh; Fr. *Mais ce me torne a grant contraire.*
3484   wepte] *kepte* Th.
3489   Thurgh my demenyng] *Thurghout my demyng* G Th Skt Rob Fsh; Fr. *Etant qu'il a certainement Veü a mon contenement.* Liddell's emendation, as printed here, makes sense of the passage: Daunger perceives the Lover's plight through his comportment *(contenement).*
3490   Than] *That* G Th; *Tyl* Skt Fsh; Fr. *E* (var. *a*) *tant.* The first words of 3490–91 have been reversed. The emendation *tyl* (from Sutherland), though closer to the French, does not fit the syntax. The entire line, however, has been entered by a different hand in a space originally left blank and may be spurious.
3491   That] *Thanne* G Th.
3498   Though] *Thou* G; *Tho* Th Fsh. The normal form in both G and Th is *though.* Th's exceptional *tho* indicates that it is a correction of the scribal error in G.
3502   bothen] *bothom* G Th; *botoun* Skt; Fr. *Car l'une et l'autre me voudroit.*
3508   word] Om. G Th; Fr. *parole.*
3522   he] *ye* G Th.
3525   is it] *it is* G Th.
3533   hath] *haue* Th.
3534   t'obeye] *to beye* G; *to bey* Th.
3543   That] *This* Th Fsh.
3552   he] *ye* G.
3569   do] Om. Th.
3588   he] *ye* G Th Skt Rob; Fr. *qu'il.*

3595–3690 From Th; two leaves are lost from G.

3643 God it blesse] *the god of blesse* Th; Fr. *Deus la beneïe.*

3676 May lyve] *My lyfe* Th.

3694 Thought] *Though* G Th.

3697 rewyng] *rennyng* G Th.

3698 to me] *come* G Th Lid.

3710 hertes] *herte is* G Th.

3730 werne] *worne* G; *warne* Th Rob.

3733 he] Om. G Th Lid.

3740 ne countesse] *countesse* Th Skt Fsh.

3745–46 kisse : gentilnysse] *k. : gentilnesse* Skt; *kesse : gentilnesse* Rob.

3745 pleyen] *pleyne* G Th Fsh.

3749 werne] *worne* G; *warne* Th Rob Fsh.

3751 to] *ye* G Th.

3752 The more] *And the more* Th.

3755 hete] *his h.* Th.

3756 bad] *bade me* G Th Lid.

3757 Graunte] *Grauntede* G.

3761 Thar] *There nede* Th. Thynne misunderstood *Thar* = "it needs."

3767 saverous] *fauerous* G Th. Cf. note 2902 above.

3769 ne] Om. G Th Skt.

3774 it nille] *it wille* G; *at wyl* Th.; *it wyl* Fsh.

3779 selde] *yelde* G.

3786 selde] *elde* G.

3832 reward] *regarde* Th Fsh.

3834 thus] *this* Th.

3846 chastise] [*to*] *c.* eds.

3851 [Ne] in] *In* G Th Rob.

verger] *verge* G Th.

3862 wende] *wente* G.

3864 vayle] *bayle* G.

3895 trecherous] *trechours* G Th Lid.

3896 envyous] *envyou*[*r*]*s* Lid.

3902 crye] *I crye* G Th Lid Fsh.

3907 lowde] *lowe* G Th.

3936 Therfore] *Wherfore* Th Fsh.

3942 To] *Do* G Th.

3943 T'enclose] *Thanne close* G Th; Fr. *clorra entour.*

3954 blende] *blynde* G Lid.

3967 That] [*Till*] *that* Skt; *Than* Lid.

3977 ben and many a day] *passed not ashamed* Rob (misprint from 3979).

3979 shamed] *ashamed* Skt Lid Rob.

3985 he] Om. G.

3986 he] Om. G.

4000 goon] *a-goon* Skt Rob.

4021 in hy] *an high (hye)* G Th Lid; Fr. *Levez tost sus.* Perhaps read *on hye.*

4032 ne] Om. G Th Lid; Fr. *ne puet.*

4059 knewe] *knowe* G.

4063 as] *a* G.

4065 he] Om. G.

4075–78 Sutherland and Fisher print 4081–84 as 4075–78 because the lines in G and Th do not follow the order of the French. Although 4081–83 thus fit the French sequence more closely, 4084, which corresponds to the end of Daunger's speech, is displaced by the shift. The translator has not followed the loose logic of Daunger closely, and the MS should stand.

4110 quake] *quoke* G.

4137 wel the more] *welthe the more* G Th Skt; *welthe. The more* Fsh.

4174 myght] *hyght* Sutherland Fsh; Fr. *grant e lee e haute.*

4175 dredde] [*ne*] *dredde* Skt Rob.

4177 The[1]] [*For*] *the* Skt Fsh; Fr. *Car.*

4188 Rosers] *Roses* G Th; Fr. *rosier.*

4191 bows and] *and bows* G; *bows* Skt.

4192 above] *about* Th.

4207 Daunger] *D. eek* Skt; *D. bere* Lid; *D. bereth* Kal.

4208 kepte] Om. G Lid.

4214 partie] *parte* G Th Skt.

4242 Ofter] *Ofte* G Lid Rob.

4267 him] *hem* G.

4269 desert] *disseit* G.

4272 waketh] *walketh* G Th.

4274 him] *hem* G.

4285 Ther] *Which(e)* G Th.

4291 expert] *except* G Th.

4294 [the] harder] *harder* G; *harde* Th.

4314 his roses] *of his roses* Th Skt Rob Fsh.

4320 to[2]] Om. Th Fsh.

4322 wende a bought] *wente aboute* G Th; Fr. *les cuidoie avoir achetez.*

4339 tyler] *tylyers* G; *tyllers* Th; Fr. *au vilair.*

4352 wende] *wente* G Th.

4357 thow] Om. G Th. shalt] *shaltow* Lid Fsh.

4358 in] Om. G Th. turneth] *turne* G Lid.

4361 areise] *arise* G Lid.

4363 but as hir lust] [*al*] *as hir list* Skt. Liddell prints the line as a rhetorical question.

4366 change] *charge* G Th.

4372 you wal] *yone wole* G; *you wol* Th.

4374 nyl] *wol* Th Fsh.

4401 is] Om. G Th.

4416 corajous] *curious* Kal Lid Fsh; Fr. *curieus.*

4465 nevertheles] *nathelesse* Th Skt Fsh.

4467 his] *her* G Th.

4472 ne] *no* G. Skeat suggests *wounde* for *stounde.*

4477 a-sundry] *a sondre* Th Fsh; *a-sundir* Skt; *asunder* Rob.

4478 doon] *doon* [*me have*] Skt Rob Fsh. See Expl. Notes.

4483 Drede] *Dre* G.

4495 age] *rage* Th.

4498 him] *hem* G Th Skt Fsh; Fr. *Qu'il n'ose nului regarder* (That he dares see no one).

4519 By] *or by* Th Fsh.

4520 Out] Om. Th Fsh.

4527 my] *faire* G Th Skt; Fr. *ma priere.* G's *faire* is probably an anticipation of *faire* in the next line.

4540 I may well] *I may well I may wel* G.

4541 asyde] *assayde* G. nat] Om. G.

4549 develes] *devell* G; *dyuels* Th.

4550 lord] *loue* G Th; Fr. *mon seigneur.*

4556 that] *that it* Th Fsh; *it* Skt.

4561 yif God wille] *yeve good wille* G Th; Fr. *se Deu plaist.*

4576 Ne] Om. G Th Skt Lid Rob.

4614 Doublenesse] *Or d.* Th Skt Lid Rob Fsh. See Expl. Notes.

4628 com] *came* Th Fsh.

4629 yit] Om. Th.

4631 me telle] *tel me* Th.

4634 greved] Om. G Th; [*pyned*] Skt Fsh; Lid: "Insert some word like *harmed*" (n.). Emended by J. Urry (Works of Ch, 1721); cf. 4530, 4538.

4641   thy] *thy thi* G.

4657   han loved] *I lovede* G Th; *ha lovede* Lid; *yloved* Rob Fsh.

4660   Wherof] *Wherfore* Th Fsh.

4672   Disfigured] *Diffigured* G.
    astate] *a state* G; *a-state* Lid; *astat* Rob.

4689   wite] Om. G Th; [*here lerne*] Skt; Fr. *savras.*

4700   be] *to* Th.

4705   A trouthe] *And thurgh the* G Th. Tyrwhitt's emendation.

4709   wod] *vode* G; *voyde* Th. Th's variant results from G's eccentric spelling.

4713   Karibdous] *Carybdes* Th Fsh; *Caribdis* Skt Rob. See Expl. Notes.

4720   Havoir] *Havior* Rob (misprint).

4721   sike] *like* G Th.

4722   thurst] *trust(e)* G Th; Fr. *seif.*
    in] *and* G Th.

4723   And] *An* Skt Lid Fsh.

4725   And] *An* Skt Lid Fsh.
    hunger] *anger* G Th; Fr. *fain.*

4728   drerihed] *dreried* G Th.

4731   Sin] *Sen* G Th Fsh; *Sinne* Skt Lid.

4732   withoute [with]] *withoute* G Th; *oute with* Lid.

4736   stat] Om. G Th; Fr. *estaz.* For *stedefast* Kaluza suggests *stedefastnesse.*

4755   be] *by* G Th Lid; Fr. *sont.*

4764   That] *But* Skt.
    he] *ne* Fsh (Sutherland).
    [ne] may] *may* G Th Skt Rob Fsh; Fr. *ne seit dontez.* All eds. except Robinson emend to give a negative sense. For Robinson's defense of the "inconsequent construction," see his explanatory notes here and at MLT II.49. Though he cites 3774 above as a parallel, there he follows Skeat and Liddell in changing *wille* to *nille.* Liddell's emendation is adopted here as the simplest.

4793   [I] wist] *wist(e)* G Th; *wist [I]* Lid Fsh.
    er] *euer* Th Lid; Fr. *devant.*

4796   *par cuer*] *by partuere* G Th.

4800   by] *myne* Th.

4807   diffyne it er] *diffyned he(e)re* G Th; Fr. *defenir onques.*

4812   Which] *With* G Th.

4813   byndith] *that b.* G Th.

4815   brennyng] *brennyg* G.

4823   engendring] *engendrure* G Th Lid Fsh.

4824   plesyng] *pleasure* Th Lid Fsh.

4839   they] Om. Th Fsh.

4846   What man] *That what* G Th; *That [who]* Skt Fsh; *What wight* Lid.

4856   Om. G (line left blank in MS); *For bycause al is corrumpable* Th and eds.; Fr. *Pour ce qu'il sont tuit corrumpable* (Because all are corruptible). Th's line closely renders the French except for *For,* which causes difficult syntax. Skeat and Fisher place a comma after 4855; Liddell, a period; Robinson, a semicolon. Although the clause should complete the thought as it does in the French (man should beget his likeness because all is corruptible), *For* seems to start a new period to which the *bycause* clause is subordinate.

4858   ther] *their* G Th Fsh. The form in G is unique (the adv. is normally *ther,* the pro. *hir*); its occurrence in Th would be a remarkable coincidence if it had not been taken over directly from G.

4859   strene] *sterne* Th Fsh; *stren* Rob.

4871   Thus hath sotilled] *This hadde sotille* G Skt; *This had subtyl* Th; Fr. *Ainsinc . . . soutiva.* Liddell's emendation.

4878   vice] *wise* G.

4892   tyme] *perell* G Lid; *parel* Th. Skeat's emendation.
    youthe] *yougth* G.

4904   him] Om. G Th; Fr. *se rent.*

4926   in²] Om. Rob. Mistakenly omitted in Kaluza's edition; Skeat also says in error "G om."; Liddell brackets.

4933   thus] *this* G Th; Fr. *ainsinc.*

4935   Youthe his chaumberere] *youthes chamb(e)re* G Th; Fr. *Jennece sa chamberiere.*

4940   is she] *is* G Th; [*she*] *is* Lid.

4943   Demande] *And mo(o)* G Th Lid; Fr. *demant.* Liddell suggests that *moo* means "ask" or is a corruption of a word with that meaning. Cf. 5290 and n. below.

4945   remembre] *remembreth* G Th.

4948   hem] *him* G Th.

4952   to do] *do to* G.

4955   can] *gan* G Th.

4960   neither] *ne* Skt Lid Fsh, perhaps correctly.

5004   stondeth] *stont* Skt Lid Rob.

5010   wepeth] *weped* G Th.

5021   hir] *he* G Th; *her* Lid Fsh.

5028   have] *love* G Th.

5051   she] *so* G Th; Skeat suggests *sho,* a Northern form, but *she* is the normal form throughout G.

5054   wole] *wel* Th.

5059   loveth] *loued* G Th.

5067   nevertheles] *nathelesse* Th Fsh.

5068   That] *But* Skt Rob Fsh.

5069   [Ne] may] *May* G Th Skt Rob Fsh. Liddell's emendation is adopted as preferable to Skeat's of 5068.

5085   they] *to* G Th; Fr. *se gardent.*

5099   thee] Om. G.

5107   herberest than] *h. hem* G; *herborest* Th; *herberedest t.* Skt Rob; *herborest hem* Fsh. *Than* is suggested by *whanne* in 5108, though it is difficult to see how G's *hem* originates. Perhaps Th is correct, and the verb should stand by itself.

5116   thy] *the* G Th; Fr. *ton tens.*

5117   thy youthe] *by thought* G Th; Fr. *ta jouvente.*

5124   recured] *recouered* Th Rob Fsh. Cf. 4920. OED cites this line (s.v. *recured*).

5135   *L'amant*] Skt Lid Rob om., though they print an identical rubric with 4785.

5144   alway] *ay(e)* G Th Fsh; *al day* Lid. There is an erasure between *thought* and *ay* in G.

5155   Than] *That* G Th; Fr. *Lors.* A large initial in both G and Th indicates a new paragraph.

5162   ay] *say* G Th and eds.; Fr. *Puis qu'amours ne sont mie bones, Jamais n'amerai d'amours fines, Ainz vivrai toujourz en haïnes* ("Since love is not good, I would never love according to 'fine amour,' thus I would live perpetually in hatred"). The verb *say* corresponds to nothing in the French and lacks an object. The *s* may be repeated from the final letter of *nedis.* Dropping it, *ay with mood* becomes parallel with *in hatrede ay* in 5163.

5165   and ben] Om. G Th; *wole I* Fsh (Sutherland); Fr. *serrai.* Skeat's emendation has been adopted here.

5166   that love] Om. G Th Fsh; not in the French. The emendation adopted was supplied by Skeat, but the whole passage is probably corrupt.
    that tecche] *t. vertu tetche* (teach) Fsh (Sutherland).

5223 Of blame in hem] Om. G Th; [*Ne lak in hem*] Skt Lid Rob Fsh; Fr. *Senz soupeçon d'encusement* (Without suspicion of blame).

5229–30 state : gate] *stat : gat* Rob

5253 he] Om. G Th.

5259 of] *in* Th Fsh.

5261 dredeth] *dreded* G.

5271 be] Om. G Th.

5282 him] Om. G Th.

5283 his] *this* G Th.

5284 wel] *wole* G Th Skt; Fr. *a dreit.*

5285 amyte] *vnyte* G Th Lid; Fr. *amitié.*

5287 Man] *And* G Th; *A man* Skt Fsh; Fr. *bien devons faire requeste.*

5290 But it the more] *But if the more* Lid. Liddell explains *more* as a noun meaning "request" or an error for some such word; he compares 4943.

5292 causes] *cause* G; *cases* Skt Fsh.

5301 caas] *cases* Skt Fsh; *causes* Lid.

5309 entendith] *attendith* Skt Fsh; Fr. *s'amort* (attaches itself). Cf. SqT V.689.

5314 it] Om. G Th.

5330 bit] *bydeth* Th.

5331 This] Om. G Th; Fr. *C'est.*

5335 she] *he* G Th Lid; cf. 5337, 5341.

5353 Hidith] *It h.* Skt Fsh.

5356 blak] *blacke* Th Fsh; *blakke* Skt; *blake* Rob.

5360 groweth . . . groweth] *greueth . . . greueth* G Th (possibly representing *grewith*).

5367 fonned] *fonde* Th Skt Fsh.

5376 his] Kaluza, Skeat, and Fisher mistakenly show G's reading as *this.*

5379 hym] *hym silf* G; *hym selfe* Th.

5389 kepen ay] *kepe [it ay is]* Skt; *kepen alway* Lid; Fr. *E toujourz garder la propose* (And always intends to keep it).

5393 asondre] Om. Rob (perhaps an error in 1st ed.).

5399 wat] *wote* G.

5401 For] *Ful* Fsh (suggested by Liddell from Fr. *mout*).

5403 sith] *se* G; *sithe* Th Rob Fsh; *sen* Lid.

5404 han] *hath* G Th Lid; *have* Fsh.

5408 it be all] *i. b. tt a.* G; *i. b. [in] a.* Skt; *i. b. at a.* Lid.

5419, 5420, 5425, 5427, 5436 hem] *hym* G Th.

5425 glorie veyn] *glorie and veyne* G.

5433 so] *to* G Th.

5446 naked] *very n.* Th Skt Rob Fsh.

5452 therof] *cheer of* G Th.

5463 this] *thus* G Th.

5465 hem] *men* G.

5470 Of hir] *Or with h.* G.

5486 affect] *effect* Skt Rob. See Expl. Notes.

5491 she] *that* G Th.

5502 Pretendith] *Pretendid* Lid Rob.

5503 they] *the* G.

5505 yholpe] *I hope* G.

5544 fallyng] *fablyng* G Th; Fr. *cheanz.*

5546 casteth] *caste* G Th Fsh.

5555 is] *in* G Th.

5556 doth] *depe* G Th.

5559 the toon] *that one* Th Fsh.

5569 yove] *yow* G; *you* Th; *yeve* Skt.

5577 receyveth] *perceyveth* G Th; Fr. *receit.*

5585 For] *Lor* G.

that at] *that hath* G Th; *that hath [but]* Skt.

5586 valued [is]] *value* G Th; [*more*] *value* Skt; Fr. *Car teus n'a pas vaillant deus miches* (For someone not worth two loaves).

5590 mowis] *mavis* G Th Fsh.

5598 it] *that* G Th Lid.

5611 noght] *not* G Lid; *nat* Th Fsh.

5617 beren] *berne* G Th Fsh.

5620 He] *Or he* Lid; Fr. *Ou.*

5624 Written by a later (but probably fifteenth-century) hand on a line originally left blank.

5627 it] Om. G Th Fsh; [*that*] Lid.

5633 wight] *witte* G.

5638 forth] *frost* Fsh.

noght] *not* G Th Lid; *hot* Fsh. The emendation *frost as hot ne ware,* suggested by Liddell and adopted by Sutherland and Fisher, is based on Fr. *Ainz viegnent li freit e li chaut* (Then come cold and heat), but it is not really parallel.

5641 taketh] *take* G Th.

5649 Pictigoras] *Pythagoras* Th Fsh. On the spelling of classical names in Th, see Expl. Note 4713.

5675 swynkith] *wynkith* G.

5685 feynith] *feyntith* G.

5686 For for] *For* Th Fsh.

disdeynith] *disdeyntith* G.

5699 were] *where* G Th.

5700 more] Om. G Th; Fr. *plus.*

5701 ynogh have] *though he hath* G Th; Fr. *assez aquis.*

5727 her] *ther* G Lid.

5740 sothely] *sorthely* G.

5741 sy] *fy* G; *fye* Th.

5742 is] *it is* Th and eds.

5751 for] Om. G Th; [*in*] Lid.

5755 shewen] *shewing* G Th Lid.

5761 it] Om. G Th.

5777 ware] *were* G.

5781 Three] *The* G Th.

5788 yive] *yeue* Th.

5791 thise] *this* G; *these* Th Fsh.

FRAGMENT C

5814 wille] *tille* G.

5821 That] *The* G. This line begins leaf 115 v., which has the heading, as do all the following leaves: ¶ *Falssemblant.*

5879 at] Om. G Th; Fr. *dou tout.*

5883 Al my nedes] *As my nede is* G Th Lid; Fr. *A mes besoignes achever.*

5900 withoute] *with* Th.

5906 it bought] [*hast*] *i. b.* Skt Rob.

5942 fully] *folyly* G Th; Fr. *tout perdent.*

5946 vice] *wise* G.

5953 by] Om. G Th.

5958 seurere] *sikerer* Kal Lid Rob (from analogy with 6147, 7308).

5959, 6006 leaute] *beaute* G Th.

5977 she] Om. G Th Lid.

5983 grype] *grepe* G.

5997, 5999 hem] *hym* G.

6002 gnede] *grede* G Th.

6009 wol] *wolde* Skt Lid Rob.

6019 Thilk] *Tilk* G; *Thilke* Th.

6037 worche] *worthe* G.

6041 hem] *hym* G Lid.

thankynges] See Expl. Notes.

6063 alway] *away* G.

6064 hyndre] *hyndreth* G Th Lid.

6082 fele] *ful* Th Fsh.

6165 swich] *which(e)* G Th Lid; Fr. *teus.*

6174 nedes] *nede* G Th Fsh; Fr. *besoignes.*

6187 hath] Om. G.

6197 resoun] *rasour* Th and eds. See Expl. Notes.

6205 Om. G (line left blank in MS); *That awayteth myce and rattes to kyllen* Th and eds.; Fr. *N'entent qu'a souriz et a raz.* See Expl. Notes.

6206 bigilyng] *begylen* Th Fsh; *bigilen* Lid Rob; *begyle* Skt.

6240 al] Om. G.

6264 the] *ther* Lid; Fr. *leur sanc.*

6271 be wailed] *biwailed* G.

6275, 6282 hem] Om. G Th.

6296 seyn] *feyne* G Th.

6317 deceyvyng] *aperceyuyng* G Th; Fr. *Mais tant est fort la decevance* (But the deception is so strong).

6318 Om. G (line left blank in MS); *That al to late cometh knowynge* Th; *That to hard is the aperceyving* eds. (following Kal); Fr. *Que trop est grief l'aparcevance* (That the detection is too difficult).

6340 solas] *salas* G; *solace* Th Fsh.

6341 Streyned] *and reyned* G Th; Fr. *Contrainte.*

6354 lete] *be(a)te* G Th; Fr. *J'en lais.*

6355 gyle] *Ioly(e)* G Th Lid; *[blynde]* Skt Rob; Fr. *Por gens embacler* (var. *avugler*) *i abit* (In order to cheat [blind] people I dwell with them). Sutherland's emendation has been adopted here.

I] *[ther]* I Skt Rob.

6359 wre] *were* G Skt; *beare* Th Fsh; Fr. *Mout est en me muez li vers* (I greatly change my tune). Liddell's emendation has been adopted.

6361–6472 From a spurious passage interpolated in several Fr. MSS. For the text, see Langlois, 11222–23n.

6361 [I] make into] *Make into* G; *Thus make I into* Th Rob Fsh; *Thus make I in* Skt.

6362 Thurgh] *The people t.* Th Fsh.

6371 were my sleightis] *where my sleight is* Lid.

6372 Om. G (line left blank in MS) Th; *[Ne shulde I more been receyved]* Skt Rob (from Morris); *Of hem I am no more resceyved* Lid (cf. 6371n.); *Ne shulde I ben so receyved* Fsh (from Sutherland); Fr. *Si n'en sui mai si receüz.*

6374 tregetry] *tegetrie* G.

6375 lytel] *a lytel* G Th.

6378 me] *I* G Th.

6392 assoiled] *assailed* G.

6393 Penaunce] *For p.* G Lid.

6424 not] Om. Th.

6425 cheveys] *chuse* Th.

6452 this] *this is* Th Fsh.

6460 Skeat, Robinson, and Liddell punctuate *And why* (or *And why it is*) as a question by Amor. But Fr. *Pour quoi?* sounds like a rhetorical question and is treated as part of Faux Semblant's speech in Langlois.

6465 grucchen] *gruc(t)che* G Th Lid.

6466 wroth] *woth* G Th.

6481 semest] *seruest* G Th; Fr. *sembles.*

6482 an] *but an* G Th.

6491 th'acqueyntaunce] *that queyntaunce* G.

6492 tyme] *tymes* Th Skt Rob Fsh.

6500 dyne] *a dyne* G Th.

6515 mot] *not* G Th.

6531 to] *of* Th Skt Fsh.

6532 thrittene] *thrittethe* Skt Rob. The allusion is to Prov. 30, but the reading probably comes from a Fr. var. *tresime.*

6538 foryet] *dothe foryette* Th Fsh.

6539 begging] *beggith* G Th.

6542 God is] *goddis* G; *goddes* Th.

6551 was] *were* Th Skt Rob Fsh.

6565 ther] *their* Th Fsh; *hir* Skt; *her* Rob.

6572 ley] *they* G Th.

6583 Sek] *Eke* G (initial *S* has been cut out).

6598 tho] *the* Th Fsh.

6599 For] *Fro* Rob (misprint).

6600 besily] *desily* G.

6601 To] *Go* G.

mennes] *mennes* G.

6606 Somtyme leven] *Ben somtyme in* G Th; *Blynne somtyme in* Lid Rob.

6616 dawes] *sawes* Th Fsh.

6633 comprende] *comprehende* Th Fsh.

6648 And] Om. Th.

6653 ther] Om. G Th; *wher* Skt (before *that*) Fsh; *though* Kal Lid; Fr. *la ou.* Liddell suggested *ther,* adopted by Robinson.

6677 hym] *hem* Lid Rob.

6682 therof] *therefore* G Th.

6684 wryen] *wryne* G Th.

6688 Om. G (line left blank). A later hand entered *And wole but only done that . . .* (last word illegible). Th and eds. have *And neuer with hondes labour his nedes* (*nede* is Lid); Fr. *Senz jamais de mains labourer* (Without ever doing manual labor).

6700 Yif] *Yit* G Th.

6707 mendience] *mediciens* G; *mendicience* Th Fsh.

6711 his] *this* (= these) Lid; Fr. *les.* felones] *felowes* Th.

6728 noriture] *norture* G.

6756 clothes] *clothe* G Th Lid.

6757 his] Om. eds. Mistakenly omitted from both Kaluza's and Sutherland's editions. Morris has it.

6782 The] *This* Th Skt Fsh.

6786 Om. G (line left blank). A later hand has entered *Of thyngis that he beste myghte.* Th and eds. have *Wherin his lyfe he dyd al write;* Fr. *Ou sa vie fist toute escrivre.* Kaluza suggests *endite* for *al write.* A better line would be *Wher he his lyf did al endite.*

6796 papelardie] *paperlardie* G.

6806 sene] *ysene* Th and eds.

6810 garners] *[hir] g.* Skt Rob; *[her] g.* Lid Fsh.

6819 wrien] *wrine* G Th.

hemsilf] *himsilf(e)* Skt Rob Fsh.

6823–24 robbed . . . giled] *robbyng . . . gilyng* G Th; Fr. *lobez . . . robez.*

6843 cure] *[the]* cure Rob.

6851 Or] *Of* Th. lordis] *and l.* Th Skt Rob Fsh.

6880 [Ne] wole] *Wole* G; *Nil* Skt Lid Rob.

6911 bordurs] *burdons* G Th; *burdens* Skt; Fr. *philacteres.*

6925, 6926 hem] *hym* G Th Lid.

6974 procuratour] *a p.* G Th Fsh.

6977 enquestes] *enqueste* Th Fsh.

6978 not honest is] *is nat honest* Th Fsh.

7002　citees] *al(le) c.* Th and eds.

7007　swimme] *swmme* G.

7013–7304　In G and Th 7110–58 are misplaced before 7013–7109, and 7159–7208 after 7209–7304.

7017　se] *fe* G.

7022　bouger] *begger* G; *bougerons* Th Skt Fsh; *bourgerons* Lid; Fr. *bogre.* Kaluza's emendation has been adopted.

7025　if] *of* Th.

7026　his] *her* Th.

7029　theef or] *these that* G Th Lid; Fr. *Ou lierres ou symoniaus.*

7037　me] *we* Th Skt Fsh.

7041　cheses] *cheffis* G Th.

7047　he] *we* G.

7056　oure] *his* G Th Lid; Fr. *S'il ne nous a bien procurez* (If he has not taken good care of us). Possibly *his* is correct, meaning "made his friendship (or peace) with us."

7071　as] Om. G Th.

7075　he have] Om. G.

7092　Om. G (line left blank). A later hand has entered *Of al that here axe juste their dome.* Th and eds. have *We (They* Skt) *had ben turmented al and some;* Fr. *Tout eüst esté tourmenté.*

7098　ne neer] *neuer* G.

7109–10　G om. 7109 (line left blank); Fr. *Qui lors aveir ne le peüst, A transcrivre s'il l'i pleüst* (Who could not then have acquired it [the book] to transcribe if he pleased). This passage is a good example of Thynne's efforts to reconstruct G. Because of the misplacements noted at 7013, 7110 comes out of sequence after 7012 and is followed by a blank line. To understand what happened in Th, it is necessary to place the readings of G and Th in their original contexts—not in the supposedly "correct" positions established by modern editors—for the readings in Th derive from misplacements already present in G.

G (7009–12, 7110–11):

Of antecristes men am I
Of whiche that crist seith openly
They have Abit of hoolynesse
And lyuen in such wikkednesse
To copy if hym talent took
[line left blank]
There myght he se by gret tresoun . . . .

The text in Th, except for minor spelling differences, is identical for 7009–12 but continues:

To the copye if him talent toke
Of the Evangelystes book
There myght he se by great traysoun . . . .

Th's next-to-last line, rejected by all editors as spurious, is an effort to patch the sense in this context. The verb *copy* (transcribe) becomes *the copye* of the Gospel, where, if one wished *(if him talent took),* one might see examples of hypocrisy and treason as that in Matt. 7.15, alluded to in 7110.

G (7107–8, 7207):

Ther nas no wight in all parys
Biforne oure lady at paruys
But I wole stynt of this matere . . . .

Th is identical for 7107–8 but continues:

That they ne myght the booke by
The sentence pleased him wel trewly.
But I wol stynte of this matere . . . .

The first of these three lines obviously renders the first half of the French couplet; the second, constructed to rhyme with it, is more obviously spurious. Editors reject the latter and print the former after Skeat's revision: *That he ne myghte bye the book,* providing a pairing with the genuine 7110. Skeat's reconstruction, however, though it is better Middle English and a good translation of the French, has no more textual authority than Thynne's. Though in G the blank line follows 7110, the French makes it clear that the lacuna must come before; accordingly, 7109 has been omitted.

7115　sonne] *same* G.

7116　troublere] *trouble* Lid; Fr. *plus trouble.*

7123　a] Om. Th Skt Lid Fsh.

7133　for] Om. G.

7134　to take] *they t.* Th Fsh.

7137　shewe] *s. it* Th Skt Rob Fsh.

　more] *no more* Th Fsh; *never* Rob (from Kal).

7138　will] *wele* Th Fsh.

7142　they] Om. G.

7143　Awey] *Alwey* G.

7145　ne] *no* G Th, possibly correct (= nor).

7151　bok] Om. G Th; *bokes* Lid; Fr. *cil livres.*

7172–73　Two lines are omitted or lost corresponding to Fr. *Par Pierre veaut le pape entendre.* Skeat makes up a couplet, thus changing his numbering for the remainder of the poem.

7178　And] *That* G Th Lid; *For* Fsh.

　bitokeneth] *betoketh* Th Fsh.

　that] *to* G Th Fsh; Fr. *Par Johan, les preescheurs* (By John [it signifies] the preachers).

7197　ynowe] *ynough* G Th Fsh; *enowe* Lid.

7219　maistres] *mynystres* G Th; Fr. *E bien est dreiz que nous reinons* (And it is entirely right that we should rule).

7234　rekketh] *rekke* G.

7242　bihynde] *b. hem* Th and eds.; Fr. *Tout soit il darriers autrement* (Though it be otherwise behind [their backs]).

7252　hem] *hym* G.

　gret spite] *it g. s.* Skt Lid; Kaluza suggests *g. despit.*

7253　hem] *hym* G.

7255　sleighe] *steight* G.

7270　The] *To* G.

7314　flayn] *slayn* G Th.

7315　al] *alto* G.

7316　nil] *wol(e)* G Th Skt Lid; *ne wole* Fsh; Fr. *ne triche.*

7323　Streyned] *streyneth* G.

7334　Thankyth] *Thankyng* Th Rob Fsh. Kaluza suggests *and on his knees gan loute.*

7340　they] *the* G.

7366　graithe] *gracche* G; *gratche* Th.

7369　sawter] *psaltere* Th Fsh.

7383–7574　From Th; missing in G.

7387　devyse] *devysed* Th Rob.

7392　tho] *to* Th.

7407　Had] *And* Th.

7423　at] *al* Rob (misprint).

7442　than] *thanne* Th; *[as] than(ne)* Skt Lid.

7456　Freres] *Frere* Th Fsh.

7471　hath] *h. hadde* Th Lid.

7485 nygh] *nyght* Th.
7486 dusty] *doughty* Th; Fr. *poudreus.*
7531 he . . . himself] *she . . . her self* Th.
7588 sawe] *saugh* G.
7593 passith] *passid* Rob.
7623 he] Om. G Th.
7634 me] *he* G Th Lid; *ye* Skt; *men* Fsh. *Me* is impersonal.
7635 It nere] *I nerer* G.
7651 wolde] *wol(e)* G Th Fsh.
7660 doth] *wote* G Th; Fr. *fait.*
7661 ye] Om. G; *we* Th.

7684   tyme] *tymes* Th Skt Rob Fsh.
7691–92   Th and eds. have this conclusion:

In diuynite for to rede
And to confessen out of drede
  If ye wol you nowe confesse
And leaue your synnes more and lesse
Without abode / knele downe anon
And you shal haue absolucion.
    FINIS.

See Expl. Notes for the corresponding French text and commentary on Th's spurious ending.

GLOSSARY

THE GLOSSARY includes entries for all words in the texts except for those used only a few times (and for which a page gloss has been provided for each appearance) and those that have the same meaning and the same or closely similar forms in modern English. A few words with obvious meanings have been included in order to provide the reader with a fuller understanding of Chaucer's vocabulary. The definitions are intended to illustrate some of the range of meanings and usages of

Chaucer's words, but they are necessarily brief and, in entries for words that have survived in modern English, they emphasize those meanings and usages peculiar to Middle English. Where necessary, the definitions are divided into numbered subsections; these are intended for clarity and not as a record of the semantic development of the words. The abbreviations for Chaucer's works are those listed on p. 779, with the exception of the Tales, which are identified by fragment number.

Variant spellings of the words cited are fully recorded, with the exception of variations of *i* and vocalic *y* (such as *him* and *hym*) and most occurrences of *u* and *w* (such as *dwelle* and *duelle*) and of *i* and *e* in inflectional endings (such as *-is* and *-es*). Parentheses are used to indicate forms that appear both with and without final *-n* and *-e* (ordinarily no attempt is made to distinguish nominative

and oblique cases in nouns or plurals and strong and weak declensions in adjectives). The spelling chosen for the entry form is ordinarily that which is most common in the texts or, in some cases, that most likely to present difficulties to the modern reader. Cross-references are provided for all but the most obvious variants.

Since this glossary is intended for readers unfamiliar with Middle English, inflected forms are fully recorded: genitives and plurals for nouns as well as those datives with a stem differing from that of the nominative and accusative (such as *lyve,* dative of *lyf*); comparatives and superlatives for adverbs and adjectives as well as plural and weak adjectives with forms differing from the singular or strong declension, (such as *deve,* plural of *deef*). (As noted above, no attempt is made to account for the presence or absence of final *e* in nouns and adjectives.) The infinitive (if it appears in the texts) is the entry form for verbs, and all other inflected forms are ordinarily listed, with the exception of the first person singular indicative in those cases where its form is the same as the infinitive that heads the entry. For reasons of space and clarity, verbal nouns (or gerunds) are ordinarily listed with the verb from which they derive.

Abbreviations

absol.	absolute		*intens.*	intensifier
acc.	accusative		*interr.*	interrogative
adj.	adjective		*intr.*	intransitive
adv.	adverb		*intro.*	introducing
art.	article		*masc.*	masculine
astro.	astronomical, astrological		*n.*	noun
aux.	auxiliary		*neg.*	negative
comb.	combining form		*nom.*	nominative
comp.	comparative		*Nth.*	Northern
conj.	conjunction		*num.*	numeral
contr.	contraction		*obj.*	object
dat.	dative		*pass.*	passive
def.	definite		*phr.*	phrase
demons.	demonstrative		*pl.*	plural
esp.	especially		*poss.*	possessive
fem.	feminine		*pp.*	past participle
fig.	figurative sense		*pr.*	present
gen.	genitive		*prec.*	preceded
imp.	imperative		*pred.*	predicate
impers.	impersonal		*prep.*	preposition
indef.	indefinite		*pro.*	pronoun
inf.	infinitive		*prp.*	present participle
interj.	interjection		*pt.*	preterite
			reflx.	reflexive
			rel.	relative
			sg.	singular
			subj.	subjunctive

The Glossary was prepared by Larry D. Benson, with the assistance of Patricia J. Eberle.

super.	superlative
tr.	transitive
usu.	usually
v.	verb
var.	variant form
vbl. n.	verbal noun
wk.	weak
1, 2, 3	first, second, third person

Alphabetical Organization

Note that *y* (vocalic) is alphabetized as *i*; e.g., *dy-* follows *de-* rather than *dw-*. Doubled vowels are alphabetized as if single; e.g., **beem** follows **bely** rather than **beden**. Past participles with *y-* and *i-* are alphabetized by the root; e.g., **ybete** is listed under **bete(n)**. Infinitives, adverbs, and adjectives with *y-* and *i-* (e.g., **ysee, ywis**) are alphabetized under *I*. Final *-e* in parentheses, indicating a variant form, is ignored in alphabetizing. Words that have forms both with and without final *-n*, indicated by parentheses, are alphabetized immediately following forms without such spellings (e.g., **be(n)** follows **be**; **clere(n)** follows **clere**).

A

a, a-, an *prep.* (1) on Rom A 163; **a-londe** on land LGW 2166; **an heigh** on high I.1065, I.3571; (2) (in expressions of time) on VII.180; **a day** during the day, by day I.2623; (3) **a pas** at a walk VI.866; **a-gree** in good part Rom B 349; (4) (in oaths) by, in I.854, I.3134 (see note), III.50; (5) (with *participle*, often untranslated **a-caterwawed** caterwauling III.354; **a-begged** a-begging V.1580; **a-blakeberyed** blackberry-picking VI.406; **an huntyng** a-hunting LGW 1191. Cf. **on**, *prep.*

a, an *indef. art.* (1) a, an I.43, BD 425; (2) (before plurals modified by **certayn, fewe**) a, an, or untranslated VII.2177, Tr 4.1280; (3) (before numerical units) untranslated **a twenty** III.600, **an thritty** VII.26; (4) (after qualifying *adj.*) untranslated **everich a word** I.733, **many a myrthe** III.399.

a *num.* one I.4181, Wom Unc 5; **on, upon a day** on one, certain day III.2047, LGW 631. Cf. **on**, *num.*

abaissen, abasshen *v.* to be abashed, embarrassed Rom A 1552, afraid Bo 4.pr7.77; *pt.* **abayst** IV.1011, **abasht** PF 447, **abayssched** Bo 1.pr1.79, **abasshed** Rom A 1519, **abaysshed** Rom B 3370, *prp.* **abaysschinge** Bo 4.pr1.38; *pp.* **abaysed** Tr 3.1233, **abasschid** perplexed Bo 3.m12.32.

abate *v.* reduce, decrease Rom A 286; subtract Bo 2.pr7.35; *3 pr. sg.* **abateth** X.730; *pr. subj. sg.* **abate** Astr 2.10.12; *imp. sg.* **abate** Astr 2.25.18; *pp.* **abated** Bo 3.pr5.46.

abaundoune *v.* devote (oneself), yield X.713, 874; *3 pr. sg.* **abaundoneth** VII.1577.

abedde *adv.* (1) in bed III.407, VII.177; (2) to bed III.1084, IV.1818.

abegge *see* **abye(n)**.

abeye *see* **abye(n)**.

abhomynable *adj.* (1) (physically) disgusting VI.471, X.122; (2) (morally) detestable VI.631, VII.3053, X.910.

abhomynacioun *n.* (1) **haven a. of** be disgusted by III.2179, X.687; (2) *pl.* **abhomynaciouns** disgusting practices II.88.

abyde(n) *v. intr.* (1) wait, be patient VII.1054, Tr 1.956, Tr 4.823, Tr 4.1327; (2) delay Tr 5.1202; linger over, dwell on Rom B 3720; (3) remain, stay (in a place) Tr 3.1810; (in a condition) III.255; *v. tr.* (1) wait for, await IV.119, Tr 4.156; (2) experience, endure, enjoy BD 247, Rom B 4125; (3) refrain V.1522; *2 pr. sg.* **abidest** Tr 5.1175; *3 pr. sg. (contr.)* **abit** Tr 1.1091; *3 pr. sg.* **abideth** Tr 2.987; *pr. pl.* **abiden** Rom C 7155; *pr. subj. pl.* **abyde** VI.747; *imp. sg.* **abyd(e)** III.169, Rom C 6294; *imp. pl.* **abideth** Tr 2.1715; *pt. sg.* **abod** Tr 4.156; **abood** BD 247; *prp.* **abidyng** I.3595; *pp.* **abiden** I.2982; *vbl. n.* **abydynge** duration Bo 2.pr7.98, expectation Bo 2.pr3.59.

abye(n), abegge, abeye *v.* (1) pay for I.3938, VI.756, Bo 4.pr4.80; **a. dere** pay a high price for I.3100, Ven 26; (2) pay the penalty for, suffer Rom A 272, Rom B 5888; *2 pr. sg.* **abyest** Bo 2.4.10; *3 pr. sg.* **abieth** Rom A 272; *pt. sg.* **aboughte** I.2303, **aboghte** X.267; *pt. pl.* **aboughte** Tr 5.1756; *pp.* **aboght** redeemed VI.503, **abought** LGW 1387.

abit *3 pr. sg. (contr.)* of **abyden** remains.

able *adj.* (1) competent, qualified I.1241; **a. to been** capable of being I.167, BD 786; (2) deserving, worthy LGW F 320, ABC 184; (3) (of things) suitable III.1472, Rom A 986.

abod, abood *see* **abyde(n)** waited.

abode, abood *n.* delay Rom B 3159, Rom C 7695; *pl.* **abodes** Tr 3.853.

aboght, abought(e) *see* **abye(n)**.

aboundance, abounde *see* **habundance** and **habounde**.

about(e) *adv.* (1) all around I.621, I.3239, HF 2132; (2) in a circular course II.15, BD 645; (3) on every side I.2133; (4) in the vicinity I.2579; (as *adj.*) nearby I.488, LGW 720; (5) here and there BD 300; from place to place III.653; (6) in turn I.890; (7) (as *adj.*) **ben a.** be diligent or eager I.1142; be ready, about (to do something) III.166; be engaged or busy in III.1449, Tr 5.1645; **bringen a.** cause to happen VI.821, Tr 4.1275; **comen a.** come to pass VII.2174; **goon a.** attend to, be busy with III.1530, VI.158.

aboute(n) *prep.* (1) around I.158, Tr 2.215; (2) in attendance on IV.1495, Tr 2.215; (3) here and there VIII.914; (4) approximately I.2198, I.3645; (5) concerning IV.2019, Tr 5.653.

above(n) *adv.* (1) overhead, in heaven I.2663, LGW 1527; (as *adj.*) overhead I.2479, III.207; at a higher level I.2204; (2) earlier (in discussion) VII.1470, VII.1785; (3) on top of I.1903, III.1065; (4) in the upper part VII.2953; (5) on the surface V.518; (6) in a higher rank or position V.795, Tr 1.230; **ben al a.** be successful, prosperous V.772; (7) in addition V.1155, Rom C 7515.

above(n) *prep.* (1) higher up than, at a higher level, above I.1962; (2) higher in rank V.1048, PF 394; (3) to a greater extent than, more than I.2769, III.1715; superior to IV.1376; (4) in addition to, besides VII.372.

abrayde, abreyde *v.* wake up, regain consciousness Tr 3.1113, Tr 5.520; start up Tr 1.724; speak Rom B 5156; *pr. subj. sg.* **abreyde** I.4190; *pt. sg.* **abreyd(e)** IV.1061, HF 110; **abrayd** BD 192.

abregge *v.* abridge, alleviate Tr 3.262, Tr 3.295; limit, curtail X.243; *vbl. n.* abregginge reduction X.568, short cut Bo 5.pr1.81 (see note).

absolut *adj.* (1) unrestricted Bo 5.pr4.55; free Bo 5.pr6.203; complete Bo 3.pr10.31; (2) absolved Bo 5.pr4.105.

absolut(ly) *adv.* unconditionally Bo 3.m9.17, Bo 4.pr2.200.

accident *n.* (1) occurrence Tr 3.918; (2) inessential attribute, outward appearance VI.539.

accidie *n.* sloth (the sin) X.388, 677.

accompl- *see* acomplice.

accompte *see* acounte.

accord, acord *n.* (1) good will V.791; (2) decision, agreement I.3082; **fallen of a.** come to an agreement V.741; **of, on a.** in agreement VI.25; (3) reconciliation X.992; (4) harmony VII.2879, PF 197; *pl.* acordes HF 695.

accordaunce *n.* agreement, concord Bo 2.m8.13.

accordaunt, accordant, acordaunt, acordant *adj.* (1) (with to) consonant with, in accord with I.37, V.103; harmonious with I.3363, PF 203; (2) (with in) in agreement with Bo 1.pr4.228.

accorde, acorde(n) *v.* (1) come to an agreement IV.2130; **fille accorded** came to an agreement III.812; (2) be in agreement I.818; *(reflx.)* Bo 3.pr12.76; (3) agree mutually, conspire I.3301, Tr 4.1109; consent VII.1205, VII.1204; (4) be consonant with LGW 1739; (5) *(impers.)* to be fitting Bo 4.pr3.48; *2 pr. sg.* accordest Bo 4.pr4.143; *3 pr. sg.* acordeth V.798, accordeth Bo 4.pr4.233; *pr. pl.* acorde(n) VII.947, LGW 1729; *pr. subj. sg.* accorde VIII.638; *pt. sg.* accorded I.244, acorded VI.314; *pt. pl.* acordeden LGW 168; *prp.* accordynge III.924, acordynge Bo 3.pr11.132; *pp.* acorded I.818, accorded in agreement III.812, agreed upon Tr 4.808, reconciled X.623.

accuse(n) *v.* (1) charge (with an offense), blame, reproach IV.2270, X.512, Tr 2.1081; **a. gilt** make a formal charge I.1765; (2) reveal Rom A 1591; *2 pr. sg.* accusest X.796; *pr. pl.* accusith Rom A 1591; *pt. sg.* acused I.1765, *pp.* accused LGW F 350, acused Tr 2.1081; *vbl. n.* accusynge accusation X.512.

acomplice, acomplisse(n), accomplice, accomplishe *v.* accomplish I.2864, X.734, Bo 4.pr2.149, Bo 4.pr2.267; fulfill, satisfy X.944, Rom B 5190; *3 pt. sg.* acomplisseth Bo 4.pr2.90; *pr. pl.* acomplissen Bo 4.pr4.23; *pr. subj. sg.* acomplise Bo. 3.pr10.64; *pt. sg.* accomplisshid Rom B 4537; *pp.* acompliced X.281, acomplissid Bo 4.pr4.23, accompliced VII.1132; *vbl. n.* acomplissynge X.473.

acounte *v.* (1) reckon, evaluate, value VII.1315; (2) recount (?) VII.2401 (see note); *pr. subj. sg.* accompte VII.1315; *2 pt. sg.* acountedest for reckoned as Bo 2.pr5.99; *3 pt. sg.* acounted BD 1237; *vbl. n.* acontynge Bo 1.m2.15.

acquite(n) *v.* (1) give in return Rom C 6742; make good II.37; (2) relieve (of an obligation) III.1599; fulfill (an obligation), acquit X.179; (3) *(reflx.)* act, behave IV.936; *imp. sg.* acquite requite Tr 2.1200; *imp. pl.* acquiteth II.37.

adoun, a-doun *adv.* (1) downwards, down I.393, I.990, BD 13; (as *prep.*) Tr 2.813; (2) below I.2023, III.2177, HF 889.

advocat *n.* lawyer VII.1020, VIII.68; *pl.* advocatz VI.29; advocattes Bo 4.pr4.255; advocattz Bo 4.pr4.254; advocates Rom B 5721.

afer *adv.* afar HF 1215, Tr 1.313, Tr 2.516.

afer(e), afyre, a-fere, a-fyr(e) *adv.* and *adj.* on fire III.726, III.971, Tr 1.229, Tr 3.24, ABC 94.

aferd, afered *adj.* afraid I.628, I.1518, Tr 1.974; leery I.4095.

affeccioun *n.* (1) emotion, feeling X.728, Tr 4.153, LGW 1522; **of a. with passion** II.586; (2) desire VIII.74, LGW 793; love LGW G 511; *pl.* affeccions V.55.

afferme(n) *v.* (1) ratify LGW 790; confirm VII.1050; (2) declare I.2349; declare as valid VII.3125, Bo 2.pr2.32; *3 pr. sg.* affermeth fixes in place Bo 4.m6.46; *pt. sg.* affermed VII.1050, *prp.* affermyng Rom B 3816; *pp.* affermed I.2349.

affray *n.* (1) assault VII.2083; (2) outcry, uproar, disturbance Rom B 2549; (3) fear, dismay II.1137, Rom B 3221, Rom B 3961; **in a.** frightened Mars 214.

affraye *v.* (1) arouse, startle IV.455, BD 296, Rom A 91; (2) frighten, disturb VII.400; *3 pr. sg.* affraieth Rom A 91; *pp.* affrayed II.563, afraied (as *adj.*) Rom A 154.

after *adv.* (1) behind I.2571; back Tr 4.1003; (2) afterwards, after I.162, I.989; **right a.** just as Tr 3.175.

after *prep.* (1) (in space) after, behind, following VII.3381; for I.136, II.467; (2) (in time) after, following I.989, I.1467, I.2059; (3) in order to get, for I.1266, I.2699, I.2762; (4) according to, in keeping with, as I.176, V.389; **a. oon** alike I.1781; in imitation of, according to, like I.731, I.3329, LGW 1072; (5) in proportion to VII.657; (6) in *comb.* forms after-dyner (-mete, -soper) the period after dinner, supper VII.255, IV.1921, V.302.

after *conj.* (1) (in time) after I.3357, V.364, Tr 4.935; **a. that** after the time when I.2522, V.477, X.99; (2) in the manner which Tr 2.1347, LGW F 575; (3) to the degree that, insofar as IV.203.

agayn *see* ageyn.

agayn(s) *see* ageyns.

agaynward, ayenward, ayeinward *adv.* back again II.441, Tr 3.750; Bo 4.pr5.34; again, on the other hand Tr 4.1027, Bo 2.pr4.114.

a-game *adv.* in jest Tr 3.636, Tr 3.648, Mars 277.

agaste *v.* (1) frighten VII.2205, VII.3088, Tr 2.901; (2) *(reflx.)* be frightened I.2424; *3 pr. sg.* agasteth LGW 1171; *pr. pl.* agasten Bo 3.m12.35; *pt. sg.* agaste VII.2205, LGW 1221; *pp.* agast I.4267, II.677, III.798.

ageyn, agayn, agen, ayeyn, ayen *adv.* (1) back (away from a place) Rom C 6295; (2) back (to a place) I.1488, PF 100; (3) back (to a former state) again Purse 21; (4) a second time Astr 2.12.27; (5) against, upon V.164; (6) in opposition, against Rom B 1940; (7) in return, in exchange I.4274; in reply I.1092.

ageyns, agen(s), ageynes, agayn(s), ayen(s), ayein, ayeyns, against, ageynst *prep.* (1) in front of, opposite Astr 2.2.2; facing toward, in response to V.53; (with *v.* of motion) toward II.391, III.1000; (2) in contact with, against, upon HF 1035; (3) in the presence of, before I.1509, VIII.1279, Tr 2.920; (4) in opposition to, against VII.2320; X.738, Lady 57; (5) with regard to, about X.1060; (6) in return for LGW

2193; (7) in comparison with LGW G 277, Rom A 1011; (8) in anticipation of, shortly before IX.301, X.685, Astr 2.23.12.

agilten *v. (intr.)* do wrong, sin Tr 5.1684, LGW F 436, Rom C 5833; *(tr.)* wrong, injure Tr 3.840; *2 pr. sg.* **agyltest** Rom C 7570; *pr. subj. sg.* **agilte** X.150; *pt. sg.* **agilt(e)** HF 329, Tr 3.1457; *pt. pl.* **agilte(n)** III.392, X.1043; *pp.* **agilt** offended Tr 3.1457.

ago(n), agoo(n) *pp.* departed, gone I.1276, I.2802, Tr 2.410; (of time) ago I.1813, I.3537, PF 18, Rom A 612.

agreggeth *3 pr. sg.* aggravates, makes worse VII.1287; *pr. pl.* **agreggen** X.892; *pt. pl.* **agreggeden** VII.1019; *pp.* **agregged** X.1017.

agreveth *3 pr. sg.* harms Tr 5.783; *pp.* **agreved** injured I.4181; angered I.2057, IV.500, LGW F 345.

agrief, agref, a-grief, a-gref *adv.* in *phr.* take it not a. do not be annoyed III. 191, Tr 3.1621, Tr 4.613, Rom C 7571; do not take it amiss VII.2893.

agryse(n) *v.* (1) tremble, shudder, be fearful, fear Bo 1.pr3.20, Tr 2.1435; cause to tremble III.1649; (2) loathe, dread Bo 2.pr1.64; *2 pr. sg.* **agrisest** Bo 2.pr1.64; *3 pr. sg.* **agryseth** Bo 1.m6.10; *pr. pl.* **agrysen** Bo 1.pr3.20; *pt. sg.* **agroos** Tr 2.930, **agros** LGW 2314; *pp.* **agrisen** Bo 3.pr1.16.

ay *adv.* (1) (of continuous action) always, forever IX.174, Tr 4.1645; (2) (of recurring actions) every time I.63, Tr 2.483; (3) (of a changing action or state) progressively; **ay neer and neer** nearer and nearer I.4304; **ay newe** always IV.2204, Tr 1.440; **ay the ner . . . the hotter** the nearer, the hotter Tr 1.449; (4) (in *phr.*) **ay wher** wherever Tr 2.200.

aylen, ailleth *see* **eyle(n)**.

ake *v.* ache Tr 2.549, Tr 3.1561; *pr. pl.* **aken** VII.923; *vbl. n.* **akyngge** aching Tr 1.1088.

al *adv.* (1) completely, all I.682, I.1377; (2) (as *intens.*) **al** only solely VII.1472.

al *conj.* (with verb-subject word order) although, even though, even if I.744, I.2264, Tr 2.325; **al be (it, that, so)** even if, whether I.297, LGW 1363.

al(le) *n.* all, everything I.319, VIII.773, BD 116; **al and al** everything BD 1003; **and al** and everything else BD 116; **al and som** the entire matter PF 650; **alle and (or) some** one and all I.3136, Tr 1.240; **at al** (with *neg.*) in any way VII.170; **at al** *(intens.)* in every way IV.1222; **in al** completely III.46; *gen.* **aller** I.586; **alder** (q.v.), **alther-** (q.v.).

al(le) *adj.* all, the whole of I.584, I.3636, BD 99; **alle thyng** every thing III.1475, BD 141; **al tyme** high time I.3908; *gen.* **oure aller** of us all I.799.

alday, al day *adv.* all day, all the time I.1380, I.3902; daily I.1168, VII.21; continually Tr 2.457.

alder (1) *gen.* of **al**, of us all LGW F 298, ABC 84; (2) (prefix) of all; **alderbeste** best of all BD 906, BD 1278, Tr 1.1008; **alderfayreste** fairest of all BD 1050; **alderfirst** VIII.423, Tr 3.97; **aldirfirst** Tr 1.1069; **alderferst** Bo 1.pr3.22; **alderlast** last of all Rom A 449; **alderlest** leat of all Tr 1.604; **alderlevest** dearest of all Tr 3.239; **aldermost(e)** most of all Tr 1.152, LGW 2117; **aldirmost** Tr 1.52; **aldernext** nearest of all PF 244; **alderwisest** wisest of all Tr 1.247; (see **alther-** for variants). Cf. **alther-**.

aleye *n.* alley, garden path VII.568, *pl.* **aleyes** IV.2324, V.1013.

algate(s), algatis *adv.* (1) in all ways, entirely V.246,

VIII.318; surely III.1514; (2) all the while, at all times VII.374; continuously III.588; (3) in any event, at any rate VIII.1096; especially Tr 3.24; (4) nevertheless III.1431, Bo 5.m4.46

alighte *v.* (1) descend from a position, dismount IV.981, Tr 5.189; (2) descend to a position, arrive VII.470; *pt.* **alighte** I.983 *(sg.)*, Tr 5.513 *(pl.)*; *pp.* **alyght** I.722.

allegge, alegge *v.*[1] cite, adduce as proof I.3000, IV.1658; *1 pr. sg.* **alegge** HF 314.

allege *v.*[2] alleviate, relieve Rom C 6626; *3 pr. sg.* **aleggith** Rom B 2588; *pt. sg.* **alegged** relieved Rom B 3764; *pp.* **alleged** mitigated Bo 4.pr4.17.

allye(n) *v.* (1) form an alliance VI.616, VII.2530; (2) join in marriage I.3945, IV.1414; *pp.* **allyed** Tr 1.87.

allone, alone, aloon, alloon *adj.* alone I.1633, I.2725, Tr 1.97.

allow(e), alowe *v.* admit the validity of Rom B 5175, Rom B 5186; allow praise V.676, Bo 5.pr3.27.

almes(se), almus *n.* (1) alms VII.1567, Rom C 6637; (2) benevolent or charitable action II.168, X.1029; (3) satisfaction made for sin X.814; (4) the will to relieve suffering, pity X.1029.

along(e) *adj.* (1) along Rom A 1329; (2) **a. on** because of Tr 2.1001.

als *adv.* and *conj.* (1) also I.4317, III.373; moreover Tr 2.726; (2) as I.3870, VII.1661; (as *conj. intro. subj.*) as I.4177. Cf. **also, as.**

also, alswa *adv.* and *conj.* (1) also I.64, I.4085, Tr 2.1563; (2) as I.3870, Tr 3.1633; (3) *(intro. subj. clause)* as (or untranslated IV.1226, VII.922; (4) (as correlative) **also . . . also** as . . . as HF 1943. Cf. **als, as.**

alther- *gen.* of **al** *(comb.)* in **alther-fairest** fairest of all Rom A 625; **alther-fastest** as fast as possible HF 2131; **altherferste** first of all BD 1173; **alther-most** Bo 5.pr3.163; **alther-worst** worst of all Bo 5.pr3.160. Cf. **alder.**

altogidre *adv.* altogether Bo 2.pr4.77, Bo 5.pr6.36.

alwey(s), alweyes, always *adv.* (1) always, continually I.185, I.275; (with *comp. adv.* or *adj.*) progressively I.4222, Tr 3.242; (2) **for a.** forever IV.1529; (3) anyway, in any event Tr 5.298.

amende(n) *v.* (1) remedy, correct IV.441, VIII.84; (2) relieve (suffering, grief) BD 551; (3) make amends Tr 2.245; (4) get better, improve Rom B 2154; (5) make better, improve BD 1102, Tr 2.854, Tr 3.1287; (6) excel, surpass VII.2858; (7) change I.3066; (8) *(usu. reflx.,* with **of**) mend one's ways, turn away from sin X.305; *3 pr. sg.* **amendeth** VII.1710; *pr. subj. sg.* **amende** III.1810; *pt. sg.* **amended** BD 1102; *pp.* **amended** I.910.

amendement *n.* (1) correction, rectification X.683; (2) redress, compensation I.4185; **doon a.** make amends X.443; (3) **comen to a.** be converted to Christian living X.443, X.606, X.903.

amenuse(n) *v.* (1) *(intr.)* grow less Astr 1.21.65; (2) *(tr.)* reduce, impair X.377, Bo 2.pr4.41; belittle X.481; I.65; *3 pr. sg.* **amenuseth** X.1044; *pt. sg.* **amenused** X.809; *pp.* **amenused** Bo 2.pr4.41; **amenuced** Bo 1.pr4.69; *vbl. n.* **amenusynge** diminution Bo 2.pr5.27, Bo 3.pr10.18.

amyd(de) *prep.* in the middle of I.3810, III.2149, LGW 2163.

amyddes *adv.* amidst, in the middle of I.2009, VII.2729, PF 277.

amys *adj.* wrong, amiss I.3736, III.2172; badly V.1298.

amys *adv.* amiss, wrongly I.3181, V.7, V.780.

amoeved, ameved *pt. sg.* changed IV.498; *pp.* moved (emotionally) X.670, Bo 1.pr5.3.

amonesteth *3 pr. sg.* (1) reminds, exhorts, warns X.76, Bo 5.m5.21; (2) recommends VII.1294; *pp.* amonested admonished X.583; *vbl. n.* amonestynge admonishment X.518, admonishing, advice Bo 5.pr1.4.

among(e), amonges *adv.* (1) together BD 298, Rom A 906; (2) continually, always Rom B 2842; (3) from time to time Rom B 2325; (as *adj.*) intermingled, variable Bo 2.pr1.106; mixed in Tr 3.1816.

among(e) *prep.* (1) among, in the presence of I.2349, BD 60; between Tr 2.88; (2) a. hemself with each other Bo 4.pr6.148; within HF 1687; (3) a. (al) this meanwhile IV.785, Anel 71.

amonges *prep.* among, amongst I.759, VII.228.

amorwe, a-morwe, a morwe *adv.* in the morning III.593, BD 1103; the next morning Tr 2.1521.

amounteth *3 pr. sg.* (1) amounts to, means I.2362, I.3901; (2) adds up to Astr 1.16.6.

an *see* a *prep.*

an *var.* of a *art. usu.* before vowels and *h-*.

and *conj.* (1) and I.24; (2) and yet, but BD 395; (3) if VII.1950, Tr 1.695, LGW 1790; and but unless IV.174.

angle *n.* (1) recess or corner of a building HF 1959; (2) angle V.230, Astr 2.26.33; (3) *(astro.)* a section of the zodiac II.304 (see note), V.263 (see note), Astr 2.4.17, Astr 2.4.46, Astr 2.37.2; *pl.* anglis V.230.

angwyssche, angwissh, anguyssch, angwyse *n.* (1) anxiety, worry, anguish I.1030, Bo 3.pr7.22, Bo 3.pr3.31 Tr 4.155; (2) hardship Bo 2.pr4.82; *pl.* anguysshes Bo 3.pr9.111.

angwisschous, angwissous, angwishus, anguyssous, angwysous, anguisshous *adj.* anxious, disturbed X.304, Bo 3.pr3.26 Rom A 520; Rom B 1813, Rom B 4671; painful Tr 3.816.

anhange *v.* hang VI.259; *pp.* anhanged VI.275, anhonged Tr 2.1620.

any, ony *adj.* (1) any I.198, I.3269, Tr 1.23; (2) (as *n.*) any I.4120; (3) (as *adv.* modifying *adj.*) any I.1611; withouten a. moore (mo) without anything further, unhesitatingly I.1541, I.3970.

anyght, a-nyght(es) *adv.* at night, by night I.2007, I.3214, HF 42.

anker, ancre *n.* anchor LGW 2501, For 38; *pl.* ancres Bo 2.pr4.54.

anoy *n.* (1) annoyance, discomfort Tr 4.845; affliction, vexation X.678, Rom B 1919; (2) source of trouble, cause of annoyance VII.130, Bo 3.m12.35; do a. cause trouble VII.1489; *pl.* anoyes X.518.

anoye(n) *v.* (1) disturb II.492, VIII.1036, X.512; (2) damage, injure V.875; (3) ben anoyed be reluctant X.687; *3 pr. sg.* anoyeth V.875; *pr. pl.* annoyen V.884; *pr. subj. sg.* anoye feel uneasy Bo 2.pr4.65; *imp. pl.* annoyeth II.494; *prp.* anoyinge Bo 1.m5.39; *pp.* anoyed III.1848.

anoyous(e), anoyos *adj.* (1) troublesome, disturbing VII.1243; (2) harmful X.365; grievous Bo 1.m2.4.

anon, anoon *adv.* at once, straightway LGW 1242; right

a. immediately I.2334; (right) a. as (that) as soon as V.615.

anonright(es), anoon-right *adv.* (also two words) immediately VIII.169, BD 354, PF 218, Tr 2.813.

answere(n), answer *v.* (1) answer I.3418, III.1077, Tr 2.985; (2) correspond Astr 2.10.9; *3 pr. sg.* answereth IV.1190; *pt. sg.* answerd(e) VII. 3029, Rom C 7498; answered(e) X.30, Tr 3.1656; *pt. pl.* answerde(n) LGW 1847, LGW 2193; *prp.* answeryng corresponding Tr 1.283, Astr 2.10.9, aunswering Astr 1.16.7; *pp.* answerd Bo 5.pr4.22 answered Tr 3.541; *vbl. n.* answeryng answer IV.512.

apayd, apayed, appayed *pp.* pleased, satisfied V.1548, X.1054; yvele a. displeased Tr 1.649; holde (oneself) a. be satisfied Tr 3.421; holde (oneself) yvele a. consider (oneself) badly treated, ill-used VII.390, VIII.921.

apaisen, apaysed(e) *see* apese.

apalled *see* appalled.

aparaunce *see* apparence.

ape *n.* (1) ape, monkey I.3935; (2) fool, dupe I.3389, I.4202; *pl.* apes I.706.

apeyren *v. (tr.)* injure, damage I.3147, X.1078; slander Tr 1.38; *pr. subj. pl.* appaire should perish Tr 2.329; *pt. sg.* apayred Rom C 7520; *pp.* apayred Bo 1.pr5.61.

aperceyve(n) *v.* (1) perceive IV.600, Tr 4.656; (2) conceive, comprehend Bo 5.pr4.85; *2 pr. sg.* aperceyvest Bo 4.pr6.30; *3 pr. sg.* aperveyveth IV.1018; *pr. pl.* aperceyven Bo 4.pr2.130; *pt. sg.* aperceyved(e) Bo 3.pr12.77, Rom C 6312; *pp.* aperceyved made known Bo 1.pr4.123; *vbl. n. pl.* aperceyvynges V.286.

apere *see* appere(n).

apert, appert *adj.* (1) plain, clear X.649, Rom C 6621; (2) open, not secret Rom C 6150; pryvee and a. in private and public, in all circumstances III.1114, IV.531.

apert *adv.* openly, publicly III.1136.

aperteneth *3 pr. sg.* (with to, unto) befits, is suitable to VII.1012; concerns Bo 3.m12.60; belongs Bo 2.pr5.63; *pr. pl.* apertenen X.85, appertenen X.1050, aperteignen pertain Bo 3.pr4.37; *prp.* apertenyng pertaining VIII.785.

apertly, apertely *adv.* clearly, manifestly X.1064, Bo 1.pr4.173.

apese, appesen *v.* (1) pacify, appease Tr 3.110, Rom B 2453; (2) placate VII.1100; alleviate, remedy IV.433, IX.98; soothe Tr 1.250, Rom B 2453; *3 pr. sg.* appeseth hym grows calm VII.1860; *pr. pl.* apaisen Tr 3.22; *imp. pl.* apeseth Mars 10; *pt. sg.* apaysed(e) Bo 4.m7.52, 54; *pp.* apesed Tr 1.250.

apoynte *v.* decide (often *reflx.*) Tr 2.691; specify 5.1620; *pt. sg.* apoynted IV.1595; *pt. pl.* apointeden Tr 4.454; *pp.* apoynted IV.1616.

apothecarie, pothecarie *n.* druggist VI.852, VI.859; *pl.* apothecaries I.425.

appalled, apalled *adj.* grown pale V.365; enfeebled I.3053.

apparail(l)e *n.* (1) furnishings, trappings X.432; (2) clothing Rom A 575; (3) personal characteristics IV.1208; behavior ABC 153.

apparaille(n), apparaylen, aparayle *v.* (1) prepare X.829, LGW 2473; (2) dress, provide with clothing III.343; deck out, ornament Bo 1.m2.23, Bo 2.pr2.40; *(fig.)* furnish with honors Bo 2.m2.11;

(reflx.) equip oneself, get ready VII.1344; *3 pr. sg.* **apparailleth** X.462; *pr. pl.* **apparailen** Bo 1.pr4.189; *imp. sg.* **apparaille thee** prepare yourself VII.1344; *pt. sg.* **apparayled** Bo 3.m4.2; *pp.* **apparailled** X.933; **aparayled** Bo 2.pr5.164; *vbl. n.* **apparaillynge** preparation I.2913.

apparence, aparaunce *n.* (1) visible form, figure LGW 1372; (2) (mere) appearance or show HF 265, Rom B 5550, Rom C 7465; (3) apparition or illusion raised by magic V.218, V.1157; *pl.* **apparences** V.1140.

appere(n), appeere, apere, apiere, appieren *v.* appear I.2346, III.1030, VII.837, VII.1874, Bo 5.pr6.237, Tr 2.909, LGW F 273; *3 pr. sg.* **appeereth** X.444, **apiereth** Bo 5.pr6.237; *pr. pl.* **apeeren** Bo 1.m3.9; *pt. sg.* **appeered** VII.1075; *pp.* **appered** LGW 934.

appetit *n.* (1) natural inclination, inherent drive IX.182, X.207, Bo 3.pr11.78; (2) desire or inclination I.1670, I.1680, Tr 5.1851; (3) appetite (for food or drink) VI.546, X.818; sexual appetite III.623, IX.189; *pl.* **appetites** I.1670.

applien *v.* (1) join or combine with Bo 5 pr4.12; (2) *imp. sg.* **applye** use Rom 2223.

appose *v.* question, consult Rom C 6555; *pt. sg.* **apposed** VIII.363.

approche(n), aproche(n) *v.* (1) go or come near III.178, HF 1115, Tr 5.1; come into (a person's) presence X.579; (2) be concerned, involved V.556; (3) come to resemble Bo 4.pr4.210, Bo 4.pr7.29; *3 pr. sg.* **approcheth** I.2095; *pr. pl.* **aprochen** Bo 1.pr1.45; *pt. sg.* **approched** II.903; *pr. subj. sg.* **approche** III.178; *imp. sg.* **approche** VII.698; *pp.* **approched** II.903, **aprochid** Bo 5.pr3.204; *vbl. n.* **approchynge** X.874.

approve *1 pr. sg.* approve Bo 3.pr7.24; test, examine VII.1155; prove true LGW G 21; *pr. 2 sg.* **approvest** Bo 2.pr1.61; *pp.* **approved** tested, proven by experience VII.1163, **approved** IV.1349, (as *adj.*) LGW F 21.

appul, appil *n.* apple I.4406, VIII.964, Rom A 819; *pl.* **apples** I.3262.

aqueyntaunce, aqueyntance, aquayntaunce, acqueyntance *n.* (1) intimate acquaintance or familiarity I.245, III.1342, Tr 5.122; (2) persons of one's acquaintance, companions III.1991, VIII.610, Rom C 6176; *pl.* **aqueyntaunces** friends III.1991, **aqueyntaunces** friendships HF 694.

aqueynte *v.* acquaint BD 532; *pt. pl.* **aqueynteden** HF 250; *pp.* **aqueynted** VII.29, **aqueynt** Rom B 5200.

arace, arrace *v.* uproot, tear away Bo 1.pr3.42, Bo 1.pr6.54, Tr 5.954; *pp.* **arased** Bo 1.pr3.42, **araced** Bo 5.m1.12, **arraced** Bo 3.pr11.151.

aray *see* **array**.

arbitre, arbitrie *n.* free will, the ability to choose for oneself Bo 5.pr3.81, Bo 5.pr6.209.

arch *see* **ark**.

arede *v.* (1) form an opinion, guess Tr 4.1112; (2) explain, interpret BD 289, Tr 4.1112, Tr 4.1570.

areyse *v.* (1) lift up Bo 4.m1.9, Bo 5.m5.22; elevate (oneself) in rank or fortune Rom B 4361; (2) incite, arouse Rom C 7159, Rom C 7539; (3) impose or collect (tax, fine) X.567; *3 pr. sg.* **areyseth** Bo 4.m2.11; *pr. pl.* **areysen** exalt, praise Bo 2.pr6.4; *imp. sg.* **areise** Bo 5.pr6.303; *pp.* **areised** Bo 5.m5.22.

areste(n), arresten *v.* (1) stop I.827, VII.3020; (2) restrain Bo 2.pr1.111, 4.m6.45; (3) seize V.1370; *3 pr.*

sg. **aresteth** Bo 4.m6.45; *pt. sg.* **arestide** captured Rom B 3316; *pp.* **areestid** Bo 1.m7.11.

arette *see* **arrete(n)**.

argument *n.* (1) process of reasoning Rom B 5414; **maken a.** reason, dispute II.1040, VII.2982; philosophical disputation I.4123, I.4329; (2) assertion II.228, IV.1619, V.886; **maken a.** make an assertion Tr 4.477; (3) piece of evidence, sign Tr 4.1179; (4) an angle or arc used in calculating the position or motion of a planet V.1277; *pl.* **argumentes** VI.1619, **argumentz** V.886.

arguwe *v.* debate, dispute Tr 4.497; *2 pr. sq.* **arguist** Bo 5.pr5.80; *3 pr. sq.* **argueth** Bo 5.m4.20; *pr. pl.* **argumenten** II.212; *pt. sg.* **argumented** Tr 1.377; *pr. p.* **arguynge** Tr 5.772; *vbl. n.* **arguynge** LGW F 475.

aright *adv.* (1) correctly, truly VIII.259, LGW G 59; **it stondeth not a.** all is not well I.3426; **gon (faren) a.** go well I.3115; be successful Tr 1.878, Tr 2.999; (2) straight I.4254; straightaway, directly Tr 3.462; (3) exactly, precisely I.267; certainly I.189.

arise(n) *v.* (1) stand up, get up VI.744, Tr 2.1462; rise from sleep I.1041; return from the grave III.1507; (2) (of a siege) be raised Tr 4.1480; (3) stand on end LGW F 831; (4) arise, move upwards Bo 4.m6.27; (5) *(fig.)* arise (from sin) X.683; (6) advance, thrive Rom A 474; (7) (of things) appear, occur Rom B 2774; spring up, arise I.249, VIII.703; blow up HF 209; *3 pr. sg.* **ariseth** III.1802, *(contr.)* **arist** II.265; *pr. pl.* **aryse(n)** III.1507, Tr 2.1598; *pr. subj. pl.* **arise** Tr 3.1190; *imp. sg.* **arys** I.1045; *imp. pl.* **ariseth** Tr 2.221; *pt. sg.* **aros** PF 575; *pt. pl.* **arisen** Tr 2.1598; *pp.* **arise(n)** I.1041, Tr 2.1462; *vbl. n.* **arisyng** V.1287, *pl.* **arysynges** Bo 1.m5.13.

aryved *see* **arryve(n)**.

ark, arch *n.* arc *(astro.)* II.2 (see note), IV.1795; *pl.* **arches** Astr 2.7.13.

armes *n. pl.* (1) weapons or armor Tr 1.470; **in a. dyght** armed I.874, Tr 3.1773; (2) fighting, warfare V.811, Tr 5.1556; heroic acts I.2238, Tr 5.1718; **man (hem) of a.** armed soldier I.1092, Tr 4.1363; **moeven a.** make war Bo 2.m5.27; (3) heraldic devices I.1012, I.2891, HF 1331.

arn *see* **be(n)**.

arowe *see* **arwe**.

arowe, a-rewe *adv.* (1) in a row LGW F 554; (2) successively Rom C 7604.

arrace *see* **arace**.

array, aray *n.* (1) preparation V.63; (2) arrangement II.299; order IV.262; (3) condition, state I.934, III.902; treatment IV.670; position I.3447; appearance II.775; behavior Tr 3.1798; (4) a crowd of people IV.273; (5) equipment, furnishings I.73, IV.2026; clothing I.1408, IV.965; **greet (riche) a.** splendid furnishings, magnificence I.2199, VII.2082.

arraye *v.* (1) arrange IV.961, IV.980, VII.3037; treat I.1801; (2) plan, plot II.1098; **it was arayed** it was destined Tr 2.200; (3) equip I.2046; (4) decorate V.910; (5) provide, construct I.2090; *3 pr. sg.* **arraieth hym** dresses I.3689; *pt. sg.* **arrayed** I.2090; *pp.* **arrayed** I.1389, **arayed** Tr 1.167.

arreest, areest, arest *n.* (1) delay LGW 806; (2) seizure; **maken a.** seize, take into custody VII.2900; **in, under a.** under restraint, in custody I.1310, IV.1282; moral restraint LGW F 397; (3) lance-rest Rom C 7559.

arresten *see* **areste(n)** *v.*

arette(n) *v.* ascribe, attribute (to) I.726; blame Bo 2.pr4.12, Rom B 3327; *3 pr. sg.* **arretteth upon** blames X.580; *pr. subj. pl.* **arrette** X.1082; *pp.* **aretted** I.2729.

arryve(n) *v.* (1) come into port II.386, II.469, Tr 1.526, LGW 1472; disembark LGW 1049; (2) reach one's destination III.922, HF 1047; (3) *(tr.)* drive a ship ashore Bo 4.m3.1; *3 pr. sg.* **aryveth** LGW 2309; *pt. sg.* **aryved** Bo 4.m3.1; *pp.* **arryved** II.386, **aryved** Tr 1.526.

art(e) *n.* (1) the arts curriculum of the university I.3191; academic learning I.4056; (2) craft, principles and practice of any field I.2791, IV.35, BD 788; art (of love) I.476, IV.1241; treatise on a craft V.1120, (3) skill Bo 3.pr2.39; knowledge, technique Tr 2.11; human skill (in contrast to nature) V.197; (4) trickery LGW 2546; clever scheme, plan I.2445, Rom A 511; *pl.* **artes** V.1120, **artz** Bo 3.pr2.39.

arte, artow *see* **be(n)**.

arwe, arowe *n.* arrow III.2068, IV.1673, Anel 185; *pl.* **arwes** I.104, **arowis** Rom A 939, **arwis** Rom B 1916, **arowes** Rom A 1337.

as *adv.* and *conj.* (1) as, in the way that, like I.152, I.187; **be as be may** be that as it may II.1012; (2) (with *subj.*) **as if**, as though I.2340, Tr 3.64; as, or untranslated (*intro. subj.* and *imp.* clauses) untranslated (e.g., **as beth**, be IV.7); (in oaths) so, as IV.136; (3) (as intensifier, with *adv.*) **as faste** very quickly VIII.1235, Tr 2.898; **as nowe** (**nowthe**) right now, at present I.462, I.2264; **as paramours** passionately Tr 5.158; **as swithe** immediately, quickly II.637, PF 623; (with comparisons) as I.263; (4) (with clauses describing contrasting circumstance) although, in spite of the fact that III.1949; (5) (with clauses giving a reason for an action) since, because, as for as much as X.387; (6) (of reference) as (or untranslated) **as by** I.244, **so as** I.39; **ther as** I.34; **as of** according to PF 26; **as who seith** as some say, one says VII.1084; (7) (of time) while, when, as IV.234, LGW 813; (8) (correlative) **as . . . as** PF 34, Tr 1.123, **also . . . as** III.2134; **moo . . . as** more than BD 408. Cf. **als**, **also**.

ascende *v.* *(astro.)* rise above the horizon X.11; *3 pr. sg.* **ascendith** Astr 2.4.25; *pr. subj. sg.* **ascende** Astr 2.4.10; *pt. sg.* **ascendid** Astr 2.40.42; *prp.* **ascendyng** V.264; *pp.* **ascended** VII.2857; *vbl. n.* **ascendyng** Astr 2.27.2.

ascendent *n.* *(astro.)* ascendant (see Astr 2.4 and notes for explanation) I.417, II.302, III.613; *pl.* **ascendentes** HF 1268.

ascensioun, ascencioun *n.* (1) *(astro.)* the rising of a zodiacal sign (see Astr 2.26–28 and notes for explanation) Astr 2.27.11; (2) distillation VIII.778; *pl.* **ascensions** Astr 2.26.24.

aschamed, asschamed, ashamed *pp.* (1) humiliated X.152, Bo 2.m7.6, disgraced Bo 1.pr4.135; **for pure a.** for very shame Tr 2.656; (2) embarrassed X.1061, Tr 2.656; diffident, fearful Tr 2.1047.

aske *see* **axe(n)**.

asonder, asondre, asondir *adv.* (1) apart I.491, Tr 3.660; (2) to pieces Bo 3.m1.2, Rom B 5392; (3) different, distinguishable III.1674.

aspye, aspied *see* **espye(n)**.

aspre, aspere *adj.* (1) bitter Tr 4.847; (2) fierce, harsh Bo 4.pr7.104.

assay *n.* (1) trial III.290, IV.621; **putten in a.** put to the test Tr 4.1508; character (as demonstrated by trial)

Rom B 4350; (2) investigation, experiment BD 552, LGW F 9; evidence LGW G 28; (3) attempt, effort VIII.1249, PF 2, LGW 1594; (4) **for noon a.** under no circumstances Rom B 3449; *pl.* **assayes** IV.697.

assaye(n), asay *v.* (1) test IV.454, Tr 5.783; tempt VII.1446; (2) investigate, experience IV.1740, Tr 1.646; try out VII.1959; (3) try, attempt V.1567, VIII.1252, Tr 5.788; *3 pr. sg.* **assaieth** Bo 3.m2.19, **asaieth** Tr 5.784; *pr. pl.* **assayen** LGW 487; *pr. subj. sg.* **assaye** IV.1229; *imp. sg.* **assay** VII.1216; *imp. pl.* **assayeth** IV.1740; *prp.* **assayinge** Tr 5.1760; *pp.* **assayed** III.286, **assayd** Rom B 2417.

assaut *n.* attack, assault I.989; *pl.* **assautes** VII.1423, **assawtes** Bo 1.pr4.56.

assege, asege *n.* siege Tr 2.123, Tr 5.857 LGW 2410.

assemble(e) *n.* (1) assembly, gathering II.403, Rom A 505, Rom A 635; (2) sexual congress X.907.

assemble(n) *v.* (1) *(intr.)* come together II.328; **a. flessly** have sexual intercourse X.939; combine VIII.50; (2) *(tr.)* bring together, combine I.1286; *pp.* **assembled** I.717; *vbl. n.* **assemblynge** assembly VII.1241, sexual congress X.904.

assent *n.* (1) consent I.852, II.35, Tr 4.165; **by noon a.** not at all I.945; **by oon a.** unanimously I.777, I.852, PF 557; (2) opinion I.3075; will, intent I.852, Tr 4.554, LGW 1547; **oon of (someone's)** in league (with someone) VI.758.

assente(n) *v.* (1) assent, agree to I.374, LGW 1983; consent to IV.129, IV.150, Tr 2.356; (2) come to an agreement X.61; approve VI.146; **ben a.** be agreed IV.1575; (3) submit IV.494; *3 pr. sg.* **assenteth** LGW 1596; *pr. pl.* **assenten** II.344; *pr. subj. sg.* **assente** IV.494; *2 pt. sg.* **assentedest** VIII.233; *pt. pl.* **assenteden** IV.1570; *prp.* **assentynge** II.342; *pp.* **assented** VI.146.

assise *n.* (1) county court, court of assizes I.314; (2) **gret a.** Last Judgment ABC 36; (3) proper place, position Rom A 900, Rom A 1237.

assoille, assoile(n) *v.* (1) absolve VI.933, VI.939, Rom C 6364; (2) loosen, release Bo 5.pr1.13; (3) resolve, explain Bo 5.pr3.29, Tr 5.1453; *pr. pl.* **assoilen** Bo 5.pr4.25; *imp. pl.* **assoilleth** resolve IV.1654; *pp.* **assoiled** absolved Rom C 6392; *vbl. n.* **assoillyng** I.661.

assure, asure *v.* (1) promise, pledge IV.1983, LGW 2119; (2) assure, guarantee I.926, PF 448; reassure Anel 331; (3) grow confident Tr 5.870; **ben assured** be confident Tr 3.1395; (4) *(reflx.)* be overconfident, take a chance LGW 908; (5) **in (someone) a.** trust, rely on Tr 1.680; *3 pr. sg.* **assureth** guarantees I.926, **asseureth** makes confident IV.93; *pr. pl.* **assuren** bind I.1924; *pr. subj. pl.* **assure** pledge IV.165; *imp. sg.* **assure** Tr 1.680; *pt. sg.* **assured** made confident VII.2188, **asseured** Bo 1.pr4.104; *pp.* **assured** entrusted IV.2191, (as *adj.*) confident HF 581.

asterte(n) *v.* escape VI.414, LGW 1615; slip out Tr 3.97; escape one's grasp III.1314; *pr. subj. sg.* **asterte** Tr 5.1343; *pt. sg.* **asterted** II.437, **asterte** Tr 1.1050; *pp.* **astert** I.1592.

astonyeth *3 pr. sg.* (1) dazes, stupifies PF 5; (2) takes by surprise, bewilders HF 1174; *pt. sg.* **astonyed** took by surprise IV.316; *pp.* **astoned** bewildered I.2361, surprised Bo 4.m5.32, benumbed Bo 4.pr3.11, paralyzed X.233, **astonyed** upset VI.316, bewildered HF 549; *vbl. n.* **astonynge** bewilderment Bo 1.pr2.13; **astonyenge** amazement Bo 4.pr5.31.

astralabie, astrelabie, astrolabie *n.* astrolabe (see introduction to Expl. Notes to Astr for explanation) I.3209, Astr Pro 5, Astr Pro 8.

astrologien *n.* astronomer III.324, Astr Pro 74.

asure *n.* azure VII.2862, Anel 330.

aswage, asswagen *v.* (1) mitigate, relieve Bo 1.pr1.51; be relieved V.835; (2) appease VII.2644; placate Bo 3.m12.16; (3) lessen, diminish IV.2082, V.835, Tr 4.255.

aswowne, a-swowe *adv.* in a faint I.3828, Anel 354.

at *prep.* (1) (of location) at, in I.20, I.51, I.2226; at (a certain point in a series) I.42; **at rest** to rest IV.1489; (2) (of persons) in company with III.1355; in the presence of III.2095; **axe at** seek advice of Tr 3.1682; (3) (of the goal of an activity) after I.2150; (4) (of time) at, during I.23; **atte ende** finally III.404; **at erst** for the first time Tr 1.842; **atte laste** at last I.707; (5) (of states, situations) in a state of I.3230, IV.1195; into a state of Tr 3.925; (6) (of activities) engaged in, at III.648, X.996; (7) (the object of an attitude) I.3840; (8) (of manner) in I.663; **atte beste** in the best way I.29, I.4147; by II.14; (9) (of means) I.551; (10) (of extent) **atte evene** exactly at Astr 2.23.44; **atte fulle** completely I.3936, II.203, IV.749; **atte leeste wey(e)** at least I.1121, V.1164, X.1027; **at al** completely IV.1222; (of value) at I.815; (11) **seen at ye** see clearly I.3016; **at ye** to the eye IV.1168, Rom B 5663; **at . . . cost** at (someone's) expense I.213, I.799; **at . . . large** free I.1327.

atayne *see* **atteyne.**

atake *v.* (1) overtake VIII.585; (2) overcome LGW 2182; (3) **wel a.** well met III.1384; *pp.* **atake** Mars 55.

atempraunce, attempraunce *n.* (1) moderation VII.1535; temperance VI.46; (2) temperament Bo 4.pr6.197; *pl.* **atempraunces** Bo 4.pr6.198.

atempreth, attemprith *3 pr. sg.* moderates, regulates Bo 4.m1.30, Bo 1.m5.20; *vbl. n.* **atemprynge** controlling Bo 5.pr4.89.

atyr *n.* clothing, attire X.430, Tr 1.181; adornment PF 228.

atones, at-ones, attones, atonys *adv.* at once, immediately II.670, IV.1178, IX.10; at the same time I.1836, Tr 4.841, LGW 1840.

atte *contr.* of **at the** I.29, I.125. *See* **at.**

atteyne, atayne, attayne, ateyne(n), atteigne *v.* (1) attain, achieve IV.447, Bo 4.pr2.269, Bo 4.pr2.270; (2) come or get (to a place) Bo 1.pr3.80; extend, reach to Rom B 5537; *3 pr. sg.* **atteyneth** Bo 2.pr7.143; *pp.* **ateynt** Bo 2.pr1.58, **ataynt** Bo 3.pr3.22.

attempre(e), atempre *adj.* moderate BD 1008, PF 204, Tr 1.953.

attemprely *adv.* moderately, in due measure VII.1380, VII.1538, X.861.

atwynne *adv.* apart Bo 3.pr11.146, Tr 4.1614.

atwixe(n) *prep.* between Tr 4.821, Tr 5.472.

atwo(o), a-two *adv.* in two I.3820, Anel 94, Rom B 4107; asunder X.887.

auctorite(e), autorite *n.* (1) legal power VIII.471, authority IV.1597; power to inspire or convince VII.1165, VII.2975; (2) written authority, an authoritative passage or statement I.3000, IV.1658, LGW 2394; an authoritative work III.1; *pl.* **auctoritees** III.1276, **autoritees** LGW G 83.

auctour, autor *n.* (1) creator, originator X.882; (2) author, authority HF 314; writer III.1212, Tr 5.1088; *pl.* **auctours** III.1212, **autours** LGW G 88.

audience *n.* (1) hearing, ability to hear IV.329; (2) **in a.** in the presence of an audience, aloud III.1032, VIII.466; **in open, general a.** publicly II.673; (3) opportunity to be heard IV.104, X.39, Tr 4.70.

aught, oght, ought *pro.* anything I.1571, II.738, HF 993; **for a. I woot, se** for all I know, see I.389, Tr 3.447, LGW 1611; any bit, part Rom B 2488.

aught, oght, ought *adv.* in any way, at all II.1034, Tr 1.123.

aughte(n) *see* **owe(n).**

aungelik *adj.* angel-like Tr 1.102.

aungelyke, aungellych *adv.* in the manner of an angel LGW F 236, LGW G 168.

auter *n.* altar I.2252, I.2292, PF 249, Tr 5.1466.

aut- *see* **auct-.**

availle(n), avayle(n) *v.* (1) *(tr.)* help, benefit III.1366, X.241; Tr 1.756; *(reflx.)* help oneself, succeed Tr 1.604; *(impers.)* help, be of use to I.3040, III.1324; (2) do good, be helpful, be of use IV.1194; (3) *(intr.)* be successful, prosper I.2401, Tr 2.1430; **a. agayn** prevail against X.1047; *3 pr. sg.* **availleth** I.3040, **availeth** Anel 216; *pr. pl.* **availlen** X.241, **avayle** PF 538; *pr. subj. sg.* **availle** Tr 1.20, **ayayle** Bo 1.pr4.278; *pp.* **avayled** Form Age 25.

avaunce(n) *v.* (1) prosper, succeed Rom B 2324; (2) help, cause to prosper I.246, Tr 1.47, Tr 5.1435; promote X.786, LGW 2022; (3) benefit *(intr.)* be profitable I.246; *3 pr. sg.* **avaunceth** Rom B 2780; *pp.* **avaunced** VI.410.

avaunt, avant *n.* boast Tr 2.727; *pl.* **avauntes** Tr 3.289.

avaunt *adv.* forward Rom B 3958, Rom B 4790.

avauntage, avantage *n.* (1) supremacy, superiority I.1293, I.2447; advantage II.216; (as *pred.*) advantageous II.146; **at his a.** in the best position V.772; (2) benefit X.609; **don a.** benefit Rom B 5575; (3) monetary gain X.851, Rom B 5808.

avaunte, avante(n) *v. (reflx.)* boast VII.1551, X.320, Anel 296; *pr. pl.* **avaunte** Tr 3.318; *pt. sg.* **avawntede** Bo 1.pr4.220; *pt. pl. (tr.)* **avaunted** encouraged Bo 1.m1.30; *vbl. n.* **avauntyng(e)** boasting I.3884, X.391.

avauntour *n.* boaster X.393, Tr 3.308, Tr 3.309, Tr 3.314.

avenaunt *adj.* pleasing Rom B 3679, Rom B 4622.

aventure *n.* (1) fortune, chance I.1465, I.1506, I.1516; **taken a.** take one's chances I.1186, III.1224, Mars 21; **god a.** good fortune Anel 324, PF 131; **by (of) a.** by chance, accidentally I.1516, V.1508, Rom B 2455; opportunity Tr 2.1519; (2) event, experience VII.3186, LGW 1177, Mars 199; mishap I.2722, VI.934, LGW 657; (3) danger, risk IV.1877; **in a.** uncertain X.1068, Tr 1.784; **putten in a.** wager VIII.946, LGW 909; (4) exploit, adventure V.659, LGW 1515; knightly undertaking HF 463; *pl.* **aventures** events I.795.

avys *n.* (1) thinking, deliberation; **taken a.** ponder, think over; judgment, advice I.1868, X.54, Tr 1.620; (2) discussion, consultation I.786.

avyse *v.* (1) look at Tr 5.1814; (2) consider Tr 2.1701; *(reflx.)* bethink oneself, consider IV.350, VIII.572, PF 648; (3) decide Tr 4.1262, Rom B 1807; (4) instruct, advise Tr 2.1695; *3 pr. sg.* **avyseth** III.1228; *pr. pl.* **avyse** Tr 2.276; *imp. sg.* **avyse thee** be forewarned I.4188; *imp. pl.* **avyseth yow** be forewarned I.3185, IV.1555; take thought Tr 2.1124, Tr 2.1730; *prp.* **avysyng(e)** deliberating VI.124, Tr 3.157, (with of) considering Tr 5.1657; *pp.* **avysed** considered VIII.572; contrived Rom A 475; **be well avysed** be forewarned, take heed I.3584; **yvele avysed** ill-considered IX.335; **sodeinly avysed** suddenly resolved Tr 3.1186.

avysely *adv.* carefully VII.1298, Astr 2.29.25; discreetly IX.327.

avysement *n.* (1) **with ful a.** with a clear view Tr 5.1811; (2) deliberation PF 555, Tr 2.343; **of ful a.** after careful consideration II.86; **taken a.** take thought VII.1751; (3) **tok a.** decided LGW 1417.

avysioun, avision *n.* dream, vision III.1858, VII.3114, HF 7 (see note); literary account of a dream VII.3123, HF 513; *pl.* **avisiouns** Tr 5.374.

avow *n.* vow I.2237, I.2414, BD 91.

avowtier *n.* adulterer III.1372; *pl.* **avowtiers** X.841.

avowtrye, avouterie *n.* adultery X.840, Rom B 4954.

awake(n) *n.* wake up, awake V.476, Tr 1.564; *3 pr. sg.* **awaketh** Tr 2.810; *imp. sg.* **awak** I.3478; *imp. pl.* **awaketh** I.3700, **awake** Tr 2.545; *pt. sg.* **awaked(e)** I.2523, Rom B 3820, **awake** Tr 5.254, **awook** I.3364.

awayt *n.* (1) ambush Rom B 4497; (2) watchfulness, caution Tr 3.457; **in a.** under surveillance VII.2725, IX.149; (3) delay Tr 3.579; *pl.* **awaytes** plots Bo 3.pr8.15.

awayteth *3 pr. sg.* (1) lies in ambush for Rom C 6205; (2) wait, wait for V.1299, VII.586; *imp. sg.* **awayte** pay attention Astr 2.35.8; *pt. sg.* **awayted** waited for Rom C 7521; *prp.* **awaityng on** observing III.2052; *pp.* **awayted** ambushed Rom A 1611, watched Rom B 3066; *vbl. n.* **awayting** solicitude, attentive service Anel 250.

awey(e), away *adv.* away I.1180, I.2318, HF 169; (as *adj.*) gone I.4071, V.1064, Tr 2.123; (as *interj.*) go away Tr 3.1321, 5.1525.

a-werke *adv.* to work I.4337, III.215.

awhaped *pp.* amazed, confounded LGW 814, LGW 2321; (as *adj.*) stunned Anel 215.

awreke *v.* avenge Pity 11; *3 pr. sg.* **awrekith** wreaks vengeance Rom A 278; *pp.* **awreke** IX.298, **awroken** I.3752.

axe(n), aske(n) *v.* (1) ask (a question), inquire IV.696; make a request I.2239, II.101; **a. conseil** seek advice VII.1156; (2) demand, order IV.348, VI.24; (3) (of things) require VII.1443; (4) seek VII.1162, Bo 4.pr6.134; *2 pr. sg.* **axest** seek Bo 5.m5.21, (with *pro.*) **axestow** Bo 1.pr6.60; *3 pr. sg.* **asketh** I.2777; *pr. pl.* **axen** VII.1029, **asken** VII.1091; *pr. subj. sg.* **aske** II.102; *imp. pl.* **axe** X.705; *pt. sg.* **axed(e)** I.3661, PF 50, **axide** Rom A 588, **askide** Rom B 2043; *pt. pl.* **axed** VIII.430, **asked** I.3195; *prp.* **axinge** VII.1774; *pp.* **axed** HF 1766; **asked** Rom B 3586; *vbl. n.* **axyng** request I.1826, **askyng** HF 1700.

ay- *see* **ag-**.

ayen, ayeyn *see* **ageyn**.

ayeynward *see* **agaynward**.

ayeyn(s), ayen(s) *see* **ageyns**.

B

bacheler, bachiler *n.* (1) young man I.80, IX.107; unmarried man Rom A 918; (2) young knight in the service of another knight I.3085; (3) **b. of lawe** holder of a first university degree in law V.1126; *pl.* **bacheleris** unmarried men IV.1274.

bacoun, bacon *n.* cured pork III.1753, VII.2845.

bad(e) *see* **bidde**.

badde *adj.* (1) wicked, evil I.3155, IV.1542; dishonorable IV.1593; (2) inferior, poor VII.2422, Rom A 238; debased IV.1167; (3) inadequate, worthless IV.1608; (4) unfortunate V.224; unfavorable Tr 3.716, LGW 2597; as *n.* evil, wickedness Tr 4.1676; *comp.* **badder** V.224.

bagge *n.* money-bag II.124, VII.82, Form Age 38, Rom C 6834; *pl.* **bagges** Rom B 5575.

bay(e) *adj.* reddish-brown (of horses) Tr 2.6124, Tr 5.1038.

bailly, bayly, baillif *n.* (1) sheriff's assistant, bailiff Rom C 6331; (2) steward, manager of a farm or manor Rom C 6218; *pl.* **baillyves** Rom C 6863.

bayte(n) *v.* (1) *tr.* torment (see *pp.*); bait (a hook) Mars 238; (2) *intr.* feed II.466, Tr 1.192; *3 pr. sg.* **baiteth** VII.913; *pp.* **baited** tormented Rom A 1612.

bak *n.* back I.1050, I.2143, Tr 2.639.

bake *v.* bake I.384; *3 pr. sg.* **baketh** Bo 2.m6.25; *pp.* **(y)bake** baked I.4312, LGW 709.

bal *n.* ball I.2614, Truth 9; *pl.* **balles** LGW 2003.

balaunce, balance *n.* (1) **in b.** in a scale VII.2586; (2) **in b.** at risk Tr 4.1560; **leye in b.** wager VIII.611; (3) **in b.** in suspense BD 1021, Wom Nobl 18, Rom B 5321; (4) **casten out of b.** cast down Rom B 5546.

bale *n.* suffering, misery VIII.1481, BD 535, Tr 4.738; *pl.* **baalis** Rom B 4441.

bane *n.* killer I.1681, HF 408; destruction (of life) VII.2960, Tr 2.320, LGW 2180; death Tr 5.602.

baner(e) *n.* personal banner I.966, I.976, I.2410.

bar(e), baar, baren *see* **bere(n)**.

bare *adj.* (1) not covered I.683, I.1758, I.2877; unsheathed Tr 4.1225; (2) unadorned, simple V.720; (3) deprived (of possessions), impoverished Tr 4.1168, Rom B 5457; (4) lacking in Anel 213; (5) empty, vacant I.4390; (6) inadequate, useless III.1480, Tr 1.662; (as *intens.*) bare, very Rom A 1059.

bareyne *adj.* (1) sterile, childless IV.448, X.576; (2) fruitless, leafless I.1977; (3) bare, desolate II.68, III.372; (4) devoid I.1244.

bargayn, bargeyn *n.* (1) business transaction, buying and selling V.1230; (2) enterprise Rom B 2551, Rom B 4929; *pl.* **bargaynes** buying and selling I.282.

barge *n.* (1) medium-sized sea-going sailing vessel LGW 621; (2) barge, river boat I.3550, V.1144.

baronage *n.* nobility I.3096, II.239.

baroun *n.* (1) baron Rom A 1204; (2) nobleman Tr 4.33, Tr 4.190; *pl.* **barouns** Rom A 1204.

barre *n.* bar I.1075; *pl.* **barres** bars Rom A 1103; strips of precious metal or silk X.433, LGW 1200; stripes I.329.

bataylle, batayle, bateil(l) *n.* (1) battle I.879, I.988, HF 1447; war Tr 2.630; trial by battle, judicial duel PF 539; **bere batayle** have hostility Bo 2.pr8.4; (2) body of warriors, battalion Bo 5.m1.3; *pl.* **batailles** I.61, **batayles** Bo 4.m4.4, **batels** Rom C 7346.

batayllen, bataylen *v.* give battle Bo 1.pr4.207, Bo 4.pr7.43.

bathe *v.* bask VII.3267, Tr 4.208; bathe Tr 1.22; *pr. pl.* **bathen** Tr 1.22; *pt. sg.* **bathed** III.1253; *pp.* **(y)bathed** Tr 4.815.

bathe *adj. Nth. var.* of **both** both I.4087, I.4112.

baude *n.* bawd, pimp III.1354, Tr 2.353; *pl.* **bawdes** III.1339.

be- *see* bi-.

be *see* by.

be(n), bee(n), bien *v.* to be I.813, I.2235, VIII.228, Bo 3.pr8.17, Tr 2.1056; *1 pr. sg.* am I.767, *(Nth.)* is I.4031; *2 pr. sg.* art I.1154, (with *pro.*) artow I.1141, (with *pro.* unstressed) arte Tr 5.1161, *(Nth.)* is I.4089; *3 pr. sg.* is II.260; *pr. pl.* ar VII.350, arn IV.342, been I.887, ben Tr 1.29, be Tr 2.113; *pr. subj. sg.* be I.733; be as be may be as it may, however it may be VII.2129, VIII.935; *pr. subj. pl.* be Tr 2.584; *imp. sg.* lat be IV.1052; lat be leave off, let alone I.840; *imp. pl.* beeth VII.207, beth PF 660; *1 & 3 pt. sg.* was I.116; *2 pt. sg.* were II.366, weere VII.2660; *pt. pl.* were(n) I.18, I.28, wern BD 1289; *pt. subj. sg.* were I.737, weere Bo 3.m3.1, wer LGW F 107; *pp.* ybe(e) LGW F 6, LGW F 289, be(n) I.929, BD 530, ben Bo 5.pr6.88, ybeen VII.3297; *vbl. n.* beynge VIII.340; *pl.* beynges Bo 3.pr11.160.

beaut(e), beute *n.* beauty II.162, V.34, BD 826 Bo 3.pr4.90; *pl.* beautes LGW F 254.

bede, beede *v.* (1) offer Anel 304, Tr 5.185; (2) present Tr 4.1105, Rom B 1710; (3) proclaim ABC 110; (4) command, order III.1030, LGW G 346; (5) request, wish Rom A 791; *3 pr. sg.* bedeth IV.1784; *pr. pl.* beede IV.360; *pp.* bode(n) III.1030, LGW G 346.

bede(n) *see* bidde.

befil, befel *pt. sg.* of bifalle happened BD 66, BD 1258.

beforn *see* biforn *adv.*

begyle, begylde, begiled *see* bigyle(n).

beh- *see* bih-.

beye, beyeth *see* bye(n).

beyng(e) *vbl. n.* being VIII.340, Bo 4.m6.59; *pl.* beynges Bo 3.pr11.160.

bek, beek *n.* beak PF 378; *pl.* bekes LGW F 148.

bele, beele *adj.* good, beautiful HF 1796, Tr 2.288.

beleve *see* bileve *n.*

beleve *see* bileve *v.* ²

bely *n.* (1) belly III.2267, VI.534; b.-naked stark naked IV.1326; (2) a bellows X.352.

beem *n.* (1) beam, timber crosspiece VII.3172; (2) horn HF 1240; (3) ray of light BD 337; *pl.* bemes VII.2942; beemys Rom B 2637; beemes Bo 1.m3.16; bemys Rom A 1574.

ben, been *pl.* of bee bees V.204, HF 1522.

ben, been, (y)been *see* be(n).

bende *v.* (1) bend (a bow) Anel 186; (2) bend, curve, twist Bo 3.m2.34; be arched I.3246, Rom A 861; (3) turn, go Tr 2.1250; *pr. subj. sg.* bende Tr 2.1378; *pt. sg.* bente IX.264; *pt. pl.* benten Tr 2.861; *vbl. n.* bendynge X.417.

bene *n.* bean I.3772, II.94.

benedicite(e), bendiste *interj.* (the Lord) bless you I.2115, I.3768, Tr 1.780.

benethen *see* bynethe(n).

benygne, benyngne *adj.* (1) (of persons) gracious, kind I.518, I.2215, IV.1097; (2) (of face, expression, *etc.*) showing kindness IV.554, IV.1742, BD 918; (3) (of the weather) mild V.52.

benignely, benyngnely *adv.* graciously IV.2093, IV.2186, PF 370.

benignyte(e), benyngnytee *n.* (1) good will, kindness IV.929, X.455, LGW G 361; goodness II.446; (2) (as form of address) youre b. your grace, you Tr 5.1859; *pl.* benignites Tr 5.1859.

ber *see* bere(n).

berafte, bereft *see* bireve(n).

berd *n.* (1) beard I.270, 332; in the b. face to face Tr 4.41; (2) trick I.3742; make a b. delude, trick I.4096, III.361; *pl.* berdys HF 689.

bere *n.* ¹ bear I.1640, I.2058; *pl.* beres I.2018.

bere, beere *n.* ² bier I.2871, I.2877.

bere(n) *v.* (1) bear, carry I.1422, II.457, Tr 1.650; spread abroad X.814; b. a burdoun carry the accompaniment (in music) I.673, I.4165; (2) wear I.158, I.3265, V.433; (3) hold up I.1387, IV.1358; (4) b. doun put down, overthrow I.3831; pierce I.2256; (5) have, keep IV.2044, Tr 5.460; b. charge be of some consequence BD 894; (6) get, obtain I.237; b. the bell take the prize, be the best Tr 3.198; (7) bear, endure IV.625, VII.1464, b. lif live IV.1552, Tr 2.835; b. sikly take ill, resent IV.625; (8) bear, give birth to IV.612; (9) *(reflx.)* conduct oneself, behave I.1405, I.1523, III.1108, PF 459; b. (oneself) hie act proud Tr 2.401; (10) b. companie accompany VIII.315, X.967; (11) b. on hand accuse III.393, deceive, convince of a falsehood III.232; b. witnesse support, testify VIII.336, Tr 4.1550; *2 pr. sg.* berest X.796; *3 pr. sg.* bereth I.796, berth II.620; *pr. pl.* bere(n) V.1367, BD 894; *pr. subj. sg.* bere I.2547; *imp. sg.* ber(e) I.2760, I.3397; *imp. pl.* bereth Tr 3.885; *pt. sg.* bar(e) I.105, IV.1068, baar I.108, beer LGW F 216; *pt. pl.* baren I.721, beren HF 1332; *prp.* berynge Bo 3.m9.12; *pp.* (y)bore I.378, V.178; bore(n) BD 1301, Bo 1.pr1.40; yborn I.1019; born(e) I.1073, IV.1790; born I.1073; *vbl. n.* beryng(e) conduct, bearing IV.1604, VI.47.

berye *n.* berry I.207, I.4368; *pl.* beryis VII.2965.

berie, burye(n) *v.* bury III.500, VI.884, VII.638; *3 pr. sg.* burieth IV.571; *pr. subj. pl.* bury BD 207; *pp.* beryed buried VI.405, LGW 787, (y)buryed I.946, IV.1178; *vbl. n.* buryinge LGW 698.

berne *n.* barn I.3258, VI.397; *pl.* bernes III.871.

beseche, beseke *see* biseche(n).

besegeth *3 pr. pl.* besieges LGW 1902; *pt. pl.* bysegeden Tr 5.1496; *pp.* beseged LGW 1694, biseged Tr. 1.802, bysegid Bo 4.m3.19.

besette *v.* (1) employ, use BD 772, LGW 1069; use up I.1952; (2) bestow X.365; set I.3012, BD 1043; *3 pr. sg.* bisett *(contr.)* Rom B 5262; *3 pt. sg.* besette LGW 2558, bisette Tr 3.1552; *pt. pl.* bisette passed, used up VII.375; *pp.* biset I.3299; beset BD 863; yvel biset ill used I.3715; wel beset proper, well employed PF 598.

besy- *see* bisy-.

besy *see* bisy.

best, beest *n.* beast III.1034, V.264; *pl.* beestes I.2929, HF 930.

best(e) *adj.* (1) best I.252, I.3056; (2) (as *n.*) best person, thing, idea, etc. I.1614; best course of action LGW 2439; oon the b. one of the best Tr 1.1081; don the b. do what is best Tr 3.927; oure b. (my, *etc.*) what is best for us (me, *etc.*) IV.1161, Tr 1.597; atte beste in the best way, most excellently I.29; with the b. ranking with the highest, among the finest II.76, Tr 5.839.

best(e) *adv.* most I.533, Tr 5.1473; most excellently I.2201, V.932, PF 116.

bet *adj. comp.* (1) better IV.2214, PF 166; more I.242; b. is it is better IV.1419, V.1422; me, yow was bet I, you should PF 152; (2) (as *n.*) him fil no bet he had no better luck I.3733; **hadde the bet** had the advantage III.404. Cf. **beter**.

bet *adv. comp.* better I.242, I.3711; **the b.** the better III.1951, Tr 2.1718; **hym liste the b.** he prefers Tr 4.1358; **b. and b.** better and better Tr 3.714; **what wol ye b. than wel?** why not leave well enough alone? I.3370, VIII.1283. Cf. **bettre**.

bete, beete *v.*¹ (1) mend I.3927; relieve X.421; improve, assuage Tr 1.665; (2) kindle, feed (a fire) I.2253; *pr. subj. sg.* **beete** Rom B 4441; *imp. sg.* **bete** assuage Tr 4.928; *pt. pl.* **betten** kindled VIII.518.

bete(n) *v.*² (1) beat, flog VIII.405, X.838, Tr 3.1416; (2) strike LGW 863; hammer (metal) I.2162, VI.17, LGW 1122; (3) embroider or paint, adorn I.979, Rom A 837; (4) throb Tr 4.910; (5) touch, border on Rom A 129; *3 pr. sg.* **beteth** Tr 4.910; *pr. pl.* **betyn** Bo 4.m5.22; *pr. subj. sg.* **bete** VI.14; *imp. sg.* **bet** Tr 1.932; *pt. sg.* **bet** Tr 4.752; *pt. pl.* **beete** I.4308, **bette** I.4316; *prp.* **betynge** LGW 863; *pp.* **bete(n)** III.511, VII.542, **ybet(e)** I.3759, III.1285, **ybeten** V.414; *vbl. n.* **betynge** HF 1034; *pl.* **betynges** Bo 3.m2.12.

beter, bettre, better *adj.* better, more I.256, I.1254, LGW 1665; **bettre arm** right arm Tr 2.1650. Cf. **bet** *adj.*

beth, beeth *see* **be(n)**.

betten *see* **bete**.

bettre, better *adv.* I.342, I.608, BD 787; **b. worthy** more worthy LGW F 317. Cf. **bet** *adv.*

by, be *prep.* (1) (location) near, by I.112, I.4036; in, in the direction of I.388, Tr 5.1193; (direction of movement) close to I.4250, BD 388; (2) (of association) among, between III.812; (3) (of time) at, in, on I.334, III.755, VIII.913; during I.97, Tr 1.452; (4) (agency) by, by means of I.25, I.1064, III.1596; (5) in accord with VI.183, IV.1967; (6) **by that weye** in that way VIII.460; **be no way** in no way HF 1258; **by al weyes** in every way BD 1271; (7) (of reference) **as by his facultee** in view of his profession I.244; **spak (sey) by** said (say) this about III.229, III.1922; **sette nat a straw by** do not consider worth a straw VII.3090; (in oaths) I.120, BD 6, PF 589; (8) in comparison with Tr 1.889; (9) (of number) by, in groups of V.354; (of amount, degree) by HF 1495; (10) by and by, side by side I.1011; (11) **lay by** had sexual intercourse with VI.486; **stonden by** stand by, defend II.345; (12) **do wel by** treat wel Tr 2.957; **feren by** happen to Tr 1.225, Mars 263.

by *see* **bye(n)**.

bycause *adv.* (with *of*) because of VII.407, Tr 4.1341. Also as two words. Cf. **cause**.

bycause *conj.* because Tr 3.991, Tr 4.223; (with *that*) Tr 4.717. Also as two words. Cf. **cause**.

bycome(n), become *v.* (1) become III.1644, VI.698, BD 115; **wher b. it** (me, him) what happens to it (me, him) Tr 2.795, Tr 2.1151, LGW 2214; (2) suit, befit III.603; *3 pr. sg.* **bycometh** Rom A 63; *pr. subj. sg.* **bycome** Tr 2.1151; *pt. sg.* **becam(e)** HF 243, LGW 1238; **bicom(e)** Tr 1.1079, Rom B 2035, **bicomen** Rom A 407, *pp.* **bicome** IV.1724.

bidde *v.* (1) ask, request, beg Tr 2.118, Tr 3.467, Tr 4.68; pray, say a prayer I.3641, VIII.140; (2) demand, order BD 187, HF 1569; (3) advise, urge I.3228, LGW 1134; (4) wish, desire Tr 3.1249; **b. farwel** say goodbye VII.320; *2 pr. sg.* **biddest** Tr 4.456; *3 pr. sg.* **biddeth** I.3641, *(contr.)* **bit** IV.1377; *pr. pl.* **bidden**

X.506; *imp. sg.* **bid** Tr 3.342; *imp. pl.* **bidde** V.321, **biddeth** Tr 1.36; *pt. sg.* **bad** V.1212, **bed** Rom C 7372; *pt. pl.* **beden** VII.1043; **bade** X.65; *prp.* **biddynge** VIII.140; *pp.* **bode(n), bede, bidde** II.440, III.1030, BD 194, Tr 3.691; *vbl. n.* **biddyng(e)** LGW 837.

byde *v.* (1) stay, remain, linger I.4237, Tr 4.162; (2) wait I.1576, Tr 1.1067; *pr. subj. sg.* **bide** Tr 2.1651; *imp. sg.* **byd** *(tr.)* wait for Tr 2.1519; *pt. sg.* **bood** Tr 5.29. Cf. **abyde(n)**.

bye(n), beye *v.* (1) buy, purchase III.167, VII.56, VII.272; **b. dere** pay a high price for II.420, Tr 1.136; (2) earn Bo 2.pr8.43; **dere bought** hard-won HF 1752; (3) pay the penalty for III.167; *3 pr. sg.* **byeth** VII.303; **beyeth** X.784; *pr. pl.* **bye(n)** X.772, Ven 26; *pr. subj. sg.* **by** Rom B 2737; *pt. sg.* **boghte** I.2088, **boughte** VI.293; *pt. pl.* **boghte** II.420; **boughten** Tr 1.136; *pp.* **(y)boght** I.3836, **bought** ABC 36; *vbl. n.* **byynge** I.569; **beyinge** Bo 1.pr4.89.

bifalle, befalle *v.* (1) befall, happen, occur I.1805; (2) **faire yow b.** good luck to you X.68; *3 pr. sg.* **bifalleth** IV.449; *pr. subj. sg.* **befalle** HF 101; *pt. sg.* **bifil** (with omission of subject) it happened I.19, **befil** BD 66, **befel** BD 1258; *pt. subj. sg.* **bifille** Bo 1.pr4.30; *pp.* **bifalle(n)** I.795, Bo 1.pr3.21; *vbl. n.* **bifalling(e)** happening, event Tr 4.1018, Tr 4.1076.

biforn, byfore(n), bifoore, beforn, before *adv.* (1) (time) before, previously I.1376, II.1184, VI.393, VI.789, HF 839, PF 486, Tr 2.966; **heer b.** herebefore VII.1716; **next b.** immediately preceding BD 225; (2) (space) in front I.337; **al b.** first IV.446.

biforn, bifor(e), before *prep.* (1) (space) before, in front of I.100; ahead of II.848, For 55; (2) (time) before BD 198, Tr 5.1122.

byg *adj.* strong, sturdy I.1424, VII.1921; *pl.* **bigge** Tr 4.40.

bigyle(n), begyle *v.* (1) deceive, delude I.3300, I.3404, LGW 1570, Rom A 1055; defraud I.4048; betray VI.274; (2) lead into error or sin II.582; (3) *2 pr. sg.* (with *pro.*) **bigilestow** X.1022; *3 pr. sg.* **bigilith** Rom B 5416; *pr. pl.* **begile** LGW 2550; *pr. subj. sg.* **bigyle** VII.3428; *pt. sg.* **begyld(e)** LGW 2199, **begiled** LGW 2545; *pt. pl.* **bigiled** II.549; *pp.* **bigyled** I.3914, **begiled** Bo 1.m6.6, **biguyled** Rom B 2043; *vbl. n.* **bigilyng** Rom C 6206.

bigynne(n) *v.* (1) begin I.42, I.428, Bo 1.m1.1; (2) **b. a question** put a question VIII.428; (3) (as *aux.*; cf. **ginnen**) does, did VII.1043, VII.2682, Tr 4.239; *2 pr. sg.* **begynnest** LGW G 261; *3 pr. sg.* **bigynneth** I.3641, **begynneth** Astr 1.17.53; *pr. pl.* **begynnen** VIII.1096; *pr. subj. sg.* **begynne** LGW F 566; *imp. sg.* **bigynne** VIII.1121; *1 & 3 pt. sg.* **bigan(ne)** I.44; **began** LGW 1354; *2 pt. sg.* **bigonne** VIII.442; *pt. pl.* **bigonne** V.1015, **begunne** HF 1220; *pp.* **bigonne(n)** I.52, **bygunne** Bo 1.pr4.60, **begonne(n)** LGW G 80, Rom A 43 (see also next entry); *vbl. n.* **bigynnyng** I.3007, **begynnyng(e)** Anel 7, Bo 2.pr6.23; **bygynnyng(e)** Tr 2.791, Bo 1.pr6.47; *pl.* **bynynnynges** Bo 4.pr6.157.

bygon, bygoon, bigoo, begoon *pp.* (1) covered, ornamented Rom A 943; (2) (of states) *impers.* **wel (wo,** *etc.*) be in such a happy (sad, *etc.*) situation II.918, III.606 PF 171, Rom A 693.

biheste, biheeste *n.* promise II.41, V.1163, Rom B 4446; *pl.* **bihestes** Tr 5.1431.

biheete(n), behette *see* byhote.

bihyght, bihighte(n) *see* byhote.

biholde(n), beholde, behelde *v.* (1) look at, gaze on I.1301, BD 325, Anel 80; (2) observe, notice, consider VII.1878; *2 pr. sg.* byholdest Bo 5.pr6.128; *3 pr. sg.* byholdeth Bo 5.m3.38; *imp. sg.* bihold Rom C 6211, bihoold VI.639; *pt. sg.* biheeld IX.241, biheld Tr 2.275, beheld HF 481, biheelde Rom B 2485; *pt. pl.* behelden Tr 1.177; *pt. subj. sg.* byhelde Tr 2.378; *prp.* byholding(e) Tr 1.186, Bo 5.pr6.150; *pp.* biholde(n) VIII.179, Bo 4.pr6.217, byhoolden Bo 3.pr1.48; *vbl. n.* biholdyng Rom B 2895.

byhote *v.* promise Rom B 4447; *1 pr. sg.* bihote promise I.1854, biheete assure VIII.707; *2 pr. sg.* byhetist Bo 4.pr2.2; *3 pr. sg.* biheteth X.379, bihooteth X.291, behoteth BD 621; *pr. pl.* byheten Bo 3.pr3.19, byheeten Bo 3.pr9.129; *pr. subj. pl.* bihete Tr 1.539; *pt. sg.* bihighte V.1559, Tr 5.510, behyght Bo 3.pr9.143; behette PF 436; *pt. pl.* bihighte(n) V.1327, Tr 3.319; *prp.* byhetynge Bo 2.pr8.14; *pp.* bihight X.251.

bihove *v.* (1) be appropriate to, befit Truth 5; (with *dat.*) is necessary V.602; **b. him (hire, etc.)** it behooves him (her, *etc.*), he (she, *etc.*) needs to, must IV.1359, Tr 1.858; *3 pr. sg.* byhoveth Tr 4.1007, behoveth Bo 2.pr3.6, boes *(Nth.)* I.4027; *pr. pl.* bihoven X.83; *pt. sg.* bihoved(e) Rom A 1479, Rom B 1792, bihovide Bo 5.pr6.225.

byjaped *pp.* tricked, deceived I.1585, VIII.1385; mocked Tr 1.531.

biknowe(n) *v.* make known, confess X.170, LGW 1058; admit Bo 3.pr3.60; reveal II.886; *3 pr. sg.* biknoweth X.481; *pt.* biknew(e) VII.3061 (pl.), LGW 1058 *(sg.)*; *pp.* byknowen Bo 5.pr4.39, beknowe Bo 3.pr10.80.

bilde(n), buylden *v.* (1) settle, live Bo 2.m4.6, Rom C 7006; (2) construct, build III.1977, HF 1133; *3 pr. sg.* buyldeth III.655; *pr. pl.* buylde IV.1279, bylden Rom C 6571; *pt. sg.* bilt HF 1135, bulte I.1548; *pp.* bilt ABC 183; *vbl. n.* buyldynge III.1979.

bileve, bileeve, beleve *n.* belief I.3456, VIII.63, Tr 5.593.

bileve, bleve(n) *v.*¹ (1) leave off, stop Tr 4.539; (2) remain, stay V.583; *pp.* bilefte (am) left Rom B 3360.

bileve, bileeven, beleve *v.*² believe I.3162, HF 990, Bo 2.pr7.148; *2 pr. sg.* bylevest Bo 1.pr6.89; *pr. pl.* bileeve(n) III.1178, X.605; *imp. sg.* bileve Tr 2.1502; *imp. pl.* bileveth VII.1511, VIII.1047.

bylyve *see* blyve.

bille *n.* (1) formal document IV.1937; (2) formal plea or charge VI.166; **writen the b.** pass judgment ABC 59; (3) formal petition; **putten the b.** submit a petition IV.1971; (4) **b. of somonce** a summons III.1586; (5) personal letter or message Tr 2.1130.

bilongeth *3 pr. sg.* belongs, pertains IV.1459, VII.2630; *pr. pl.* bilongen X.319.

bynde *v.* (1) tie, bind I.4070, I.4082; fetter (a prisoner) IX.8; (2) bind (a book) III.681; (3) ensnare Rom B 3648; (4) assume an obligation I.2414, Tr 2.359; **ben bounde(n)** be under obligation I.1149, X.1008; (5) prescribe rules, impose a duty Rom C 6900; condemn Tr 1.859; (6) join, combine, unite Bo 3.m9.18; join in marriage IV.1262, IV.1285, IV.2192; (7) **bounde in balaunce** kept in suspense;

Rom B 4667; *2 pr. sg.* byndest Bo 3.m9.18; *3 pr. sg.* bindeth Bo 2.pr8.20, bynt *(contr.)* Mars 47; *pr. pl.* bynden VII.1747; *pr. subj. sg.* bynde IV.1205; *imp. sg.* bynd Tr 3.1750; *pt. sg.* bond I.2991, boond I.4082 (cf. **bonde** *adj.*); *pt. pl.* bounde VII.2070; *prp.* byndynge Bo 3.m2.6; *pp.* bonde Buk 32, bounde(n) I.1316, Tr 1.859, ybounde(n) I.1149, I.2151, bownde(d) Bo 1.m7.20, Astr 2.39.16; *vbl. n.* byndyng(e) I.1304, Bo 5.m3.2.

bynethe(n) *prep.* and *adv.* below, beneath I.4041, III.2142; less worthy, inferior Bo 2.pr5.154.

bynyme(n), benymen *v.* take away, remove X.566, Bo 2.pr4.138, Bo 4.pr3.32; *3 pr. sg.* bynymeth X.335, X.560, bynemeth Bo 4.pr3.25; *pr. pl.* bynymen Bo 3.pr3.62; *pr. subj. pl.* benymen Bo 4.pr3.32; *pp.* bynomen Bo 3.pr3.65, bynomyn Bo 4.pr4.14.

bynt *see* bynde.

biquethe, bequethe *v.* bequeath I.2768, III.1121, Tr 4.786, Gent 17; *pp.* biquethe III.1164.

bireve(n), bereve *v.* take away, deprive, remove III.2113, Bo 3.pr8.7, Tr 1.685, Lady 12; *3 pr. sg.* bireveth III.2059, bereveth Rom B 5492; *pr. pl.* bireven X.902; *pr. subj. pl.* byreeve Tr 2.1722; *pt. sg.* birafte II.83; *pt. pl.* byrefte Bo 3.pr2.81; *pp.* biraft I.1361, bireved III.2071, berafte PF 87, byreft Bo 2.pr2.6, bereft Ven 78.

birthen *see* burden(e).

biseche(n), beseche, biseke, beseke, byseche(n) *v.* beseech, beg, pray BD 1132, Bo 3.pr8.10 Tr 3.77, LGW 2285; *3 pr. sg.* bisecheth V.1574; *pr. pl.* besechen HF 1554, biseke(n) I.918, Tr 2.1674; *pr. subj. pl.* biseche VIII.55; *2 pt. sg.* bisoughtest Tr 5.1734; *3 pt. sg.* bisoght(e) II.516, bisoughte II.1094; *pt. pl.* bisoght I.4118, besoughte(n) HF 1706, Tr 4.725; *pt. subj. sg.* bysoughte Tr 1.769; *prp.* bisechyng(e) II.379, Tr 3.162, bisekynge IV.178, besekyng PF 421.

bysegeden, biseged, bysegid *see* besegeth.

biseye, biseyn, beseye *pp.* (with *adv.*) richely (evyl, wel, *etc.*) **b.** rich (evil, good, *etc.*) in appearance, rich (good, *etc.*) looking IV.965, IV.984, BD 829.

biset, bisett(e) *see* besette.

bishrewe *1 pr. sg.* curse III.845; *pp.* (as *adj.*) beshrewede Rom C 7392.

bisy, besy, busy *adj.* (1) active, busy I.321; occupied IV.1029; diligent, industrious I.1491, IV.2422; (2) eager BD 1265, Rom B 4275; attentive, solicitous IV.603; anxious Tr 3.1042; (3) intense, continual I.2320, IV.134, PF 89; **b. cure** diligence I.2853, Tr 3.1042; **dide his b. cure** worked diligently; *comp.* bisier I.322.

biside(s), besyde *adv.* (1) at the side Rom A 1290; (2) **ther b.** nearby I.1478, II.398, Tr 2.76; (3) **gon b.** escape Tr 3.1781, go astray VIII.1416; (4) in addition, moreover IV.416, V.1241.

biside(s), beside *prep.* (1) next to, by the side of V.649, X.702, PF 211; alongside of I.874, IV.777; (2) near, close to I.445, I.620, HF 73; **hym bisides** near at hand I.402; (3) **b. leve** without permission HF 2105, Tr 2.734, Tr 3.622.

bisye *v.* (1) *(reflx.)* concern oneself, be busy about VIII.758, VIII.1258, VIII.1442; (2) agitate Bo 1.m2.17, Bo 4.m4.2; *3 pr. sg.* bisieth VIII.1258; *pr. pl.* bysien Bo 1.m2.17; *imp. sg.* bisye VII.1487; *pt. sg.* bisyed VIII.1146; *pt. pl.* beseyde PF 192.

bisili, besili, besely *adv.* (1) diligently, carefully I.3763, Astr 2.14.1; intently II.1095; (2) zealously, eagerly I.1883, V.88, Pity 33, Rom A 143; earnestly, anxiously I.301, Tr 2.1357.

bysynesse, besynesse, bysynes *n.* (1) work, activity I.3654, VI.399, Bo 1.m2.5; **diden b.** were occupied in, worked at I.1007; (2) task, undertaking IV.1015, VIII.1212; **doon b.** accomplish a task IV.1904; (3) diligence, effort I.520; (4) solicitude, attentiveness I.1928, III.933; *pl.* **besynesses** Tr 2.174.

bisoght, bisoughte *see* **biseche**.

bistad(de) *pp.* hard-pressed, in trouble Rom B 3370, Rom B 5796.

bistowe *v.* bestow, give I.3981, III.113; *pp.* **bistowed** VII.419, Tr 1.967, **bestowed** Lady 33, **bystowyd** Bo 3.pr12.203.

bit *see* **bidde**.

bitake, betake *v.* (1) give, grant, hand over VIII.541; (2) entrust IV.559, X.1043; *2 pr. sg.* **betakest** Bo 2.pr1.102; *pt. sg.* **bitook** VIII.541; *pp.* **bytaken** Bo 2.pr1.108.

byte(n) *v.* (1) pierce, cut I.2634, I.2640, V.153; (2) bite, sting I.3745, III.386, LGW 2318; (3) burn, corrode I.631; consume Anel 12; (4) irritate Rom C 6097; gnaw inwardly Tr 3.1651; *3 pr. sg.* **biteth** Tr 3.1651; *pr. subj. sg.* **byte** Anel 270, **bite** Tr 3.737; *pt. sg.* **boot** VII.2601; *prp.* (as *adj.*) **bitynge** piercing, sharp I.2546; *pp.* **biten** LGW 2318; *vbl. n.* **bytynge** Bo 2.pr6.41; *pl.* **bytynges** Bo 3.pr5.29.

bithynke(n), bethynke *v.* (often *reflx.*) (1) think, reflect Tr 1.545; consider, realize Tr 1.982; (2) think of, imagine III.772, Pity 107; (3) remember I.4403, X.700, Rom B 3343; (4) plan, devise LGW 1439; *1 pr. sg.* **bethenke** BD 698; *2 pr. sg.* **bithenkist** Rom B 2391; *3 pr. sg.* **bithynketh** X.352; *pr. subj. sg.* **bithenke** Rom B 2535; *imp. sg.* **bethenke** BD 1304; *pt. sg.* **bithought(e)** I.4403, Tr 1.545, **bethoghte** BD 1183, **bethoughte** LGW 1439; *pp.* **bithought** Tr 2.225; **am bythoght** have in mind I.767; **wel bithought** well-conceived Tr 2.225.

bityde(n), betyde(n) *v.* happen I.3450, II.714, PF 654, Bo 5.pr4.84, Tr 2.623; *3 pr. sg.* **bitydeth** VII.1224, **betideth** Bo 5.pr4.68, *(contr.)* **bitit** Tr 2.48, Tr 5.345; *pr. pl.* **bityden** VII.1225, **betyden** Bo 5.pr3.11; *pr. subj. sg.* **bytyde** Tr 4.1390; *pt. sg.* **bitidde** Tr 2.55; *pt. pl.* **bytiden** Bo 5.pr4.115; *pp.* **bityd** III.2191, **betyd** HF 384, **bytydde** Bo 3.pr3.28; *vbl. n.* **betydynge** Bo 5.pr3.85, **bytydynge** occurrence, event Bo 5.pr1.73; *pl.* **bytydinges** Bo 5.pr4.62, **bytydyngis** Bo 5.pr5.104.

bytyme(s), betyme *adv.* soon, quickly VIII.1008, Rom B 5624; **al b.** soon enough Tr 4.1105; **b. a-morwe** early in the morning Tr 2.1093.

bitit *see* **bityde(n)**.

bitokeneth, bitokneth *v.* betokens, is a sign of III.581, VII.2752, Tr 5.1513.

bitray(e) *v.* betray, deceive Rom B 2690, Rom B 4551; *pr. pl.* **bitrayen** VIII.897, **bytraien** LGW F 486; *pt. sg.* **betrayed(e)** HF 294, 407, **bytrayed** Tr 5.1247; *pp.* **bitrayed** VIII.1092, **betrayed** LGW 1390.

bitrayseth *3 pr. sg.* VI.92; *pr. pl.* **bytrayse(n)** betray X.616, Tr 5.1783; *pp.* **bitraysed** VII.2380, Tr 5.1780, **betraysed** BD 1120, **bitrasshed** Rom A 1520.

bitwene, bytwene *adv.* in between Tr 2.823; in the meanwhile Tr 5.1086.

bitwene, bytweene, between(e) *prep.* between I.2859, I.3105, HF 2028 Tr 2.1706, LGW 713, Astr 2.42.12.

bitwix, bitwixe(n), betwixe(n), betwex, bitwixt *prep.* between I.277, I.880, BD 156, HF 1476, PF 148, Rom B 4187; among II.1115.

biwaille(n), biwayle(n), bewayle *v.* bewail, lament II.26, IV.1381, X.87, X.88, X.179, Buk 16; *3 pr. sg.* **bywayleth** Bo 2.pr4.30, **bewayleth** Bo 2.pr4.85; *2 pt. sg.* **bewayledest** Bo 1.pr6.18; *3 pt. sg.* **bewayled** BD 1247; *prp.* **bywayling(e)** Tr 1.547, Tr 4.1251; *pp.* **biwailled** IV.530.

biwepe *v.* weep over, mourn X.178, Tr 1.762; *2 pt. sg.* **byweptest** Bo 1.pr6.19; *3 pt. sg.* **bywepte** Bo 4.m7.18; *pp.* (as *adj.*) **bywopen** tear-stained Tr 4.916.

biwreye(n), biwrye(n), bewreye, bewrye *v.* (1) betray (someone's confidence) III.974, VIII.150, PF 348, Rom B 3879; (2) reveal VII.1145, VIII.147, Tr 2.1370; *2 pr. sg.* **biwreyest** II.773; *imp. sg.* **biwreye** III.974; *pt. sg.* **biwreyed** III.533; *pp.* **biwreyed** IX.352; *vbl. n.* **biwreyyng** VII.1148.

blame *n.* (1) censure, criticism, reproach VII.3261, Bo 2.pr4.12; an accusation Bo 1.pr3.12, Bo 1.pr4.146; **in b.** in a state to be reproached Anel 275; **putten out of b.** relieve (someone) of a charge I.3185; (2) guilt Tr 2.210; **ben to b.** be at fault, be guilty I.375, I.3710, Anel 275; blameworthy VIII.1327; **for b.** for fear of doing wrong II.860; **rennen in a b.** make a mistake VIII.905; (3) disgrace Tr 3.265, Rom B 3329; *pl.* **blames** accusations Bo 1.pr3.12.

blame(n) *v.* (1) rebuke, blame, reproach II.372, IV.78, Tr 4.527; *2 pr. sg.* **blamest** II.106, (with *pro.*) **blamestow** Tr 1.841; *3 pr. sg.* **blameth** Tr 3.1374; *pr. pl.* **blamen** VII.1095; *imp. pl.* **blameth** I.3181; *pt.* **blamed** I.3863 (*sg.*), IV.1471 (*pl.*); *pp.* (y)blamed VII.1092, Bo 1.pr1.74.

blaundyssching(e) *adj.* (1) flattering Bo 2.pr1.29; (2) pleasant, gentle Bo 3.m12.20.

blede *v.* bleed VII.2509, Tr 1.502; *pr. pl.* **blede** I.1801; *pt. sg.* **blede** V.1194, **bledde** I.145; *prp.* **bledynge** VI.581; *vbl. n.* **bledyng** LGW 849.

blende(n) *v.* blind, deceive Tr 4.648, Bo 1.m7.19; *3 pr. sg.* **blendith** Bo 4.pr4.187, *(contr.)* **blent** VIII.1391; *pt. sg.* **blente** Tr 5.1195; *pp.* (y)blent I.3808, IV.2113.

blere *v.* (with *obj.* **eye**) blear, deceive I.4049; *pp.* **blered** VIII.730; *vbl. n.* **bleryng** I.3865.

blesse(n), blisse *v.* (1) bless IV.552, VII.1118; (2) *(reflx.)* cross oneself I.3448; *3 pr. sg.* **blesseth** II.449, **blisseth** II.868; *pr. subj. sg.* **blesse** I.3484; *pt. sg.* **blessed** IV.1916; *prp.* **blessynge** III.869; *pp.* (y)blessed I.3218, IV.1819; *vbl. n.* **blessyng(e)** VIII.1243, X.386.

bleve(n) *see* **bileve** *v.*[1]

blew(e) *adj.* (1) blue I.564, IV.2219; (2) livid, pale Mars 8 (see note).

blind(e), blynd(e) *adj.* (1) blind, unable to see II.561, For 50; (2) unable to understand, heedless VII.1997, Tr 5.1824, LGW 1756; (3) blind, closed at one end VIII.658; (4) makith b. hides Rom C 7170.

blis(se) *n.* (1) happiness, I.1230; (2) rejoicing I.3097; (3) source of joy VII.3166, BD 209, Tr 5.607; (4)

heavenly bliss III.830; **in b.** in heaven Tr 3.342; **so have I (ye) b.** as I (you) may have salvation II.33, III.830, LGW F 505; *pl.* **blisses** IV.1638.

blisful *adj.* (1) glad, happy II.726, III.220; (2) heavenly, glorious, blessed I.17, X.1077, Tr 3.705; (3) fortunate VII.1198; fair, beautiful I.3247, Tr 3.1.

blisfully *adv.* happily I.1236, Tr 5.1808.

blisfulnesse *n.* happiness, supreme happiness Bo 2.pr4.103, Bo 3.pr2.18; *pl.* **blisfulnesses** blessings Bo 4.pr1.54.

blisse *see* **blesse(n).**

blithe *adj.* (1) happy I.846, I.1878; (2) (as *adv.*) happily Rom A 79.

blythely *adv.* gladly, happily BD 749, BD 755.

blyve, byleve *adv.* (1) actively, energetically Tr 4.174, Tr 4.1355; (2) quickly III.1520, BD 152, Tr 1.595; **as (so) blyve** very quickly BD 248.

blod, blood *n.* (1) blood I.635; one of the four bodily humors V.352 (see note); (2) lineage, descent I.1018; kin I.1583, Tr 2.594.

blody *adj.* (1) bloody I.1010, I.1755; (2) war-like I.2512.

blosme *n.* blossom I.3324; *pl.* **blosmes** LGW F 143, **blossoms** Rom B 4749.

blosmeth *v. 3 pr. sg.* blooms, IV.1462; *pp.* **blosmed** covered with blossoms Rom A 108.

blosmy *adj.* filled with blossoms IV.1463, PF 183.

blowe *v.* (1) blow I.565; (2) spread abroad, make widely known I.2241, HF 1139; **thyn horn is blowe** your crimes are known LGW 1383 (see note); *3 pr. sg.* **bloweth** II.705; *pr. pl.* **blowen** I.2512; *pr. subj. sg.* **blowe** Bo 2.m3.12; *imp. sg.* **blow** HF 1626; *pt. sg.* **blew** VIII.1146; *prp.* **blowynge** Bo 1.pr3.65; *pp.* **(y)blowe** inflated VIII.440, spread abroad Tr 1.3841, **blowen** I.2241, **blown** LGW 1365; *vbl. n.* **blowyng(e)** VIII.923, HF 230.

bood *see* **byde.**

bode(n) *see* **bidde.**

body *n.* (1) body, object I.2283; **b. erect** upright object II.9; **celestiall b.** planet Astr Pro 89; (2) substance VIII.854; (3) person II.1185, VI.338; *pl.* **bodies** metals, planets VIII.820, VIII.825.

(y)boght, boghte *see* **bye(n).**

boy(e) *n.* (1) servant VI.670; (2) rascal, knave III.1322, Rom B 3849.

bokeler, bokeleer *n.* buckler, small shield I.112, I.3266.

bold, boold *adj.* (1) brave Tr 4.33, Tr 4.190; (2) confident VIII.1413, IX.258; (3) **ben (so) b.** dare, presume I.4271, VI.339, Mars 35; (4) (of persons) overconfident, brazen, rash VIII.1415; (of actions) shameless IV.2269; (5) strong, powerful I.458, Rom A 115; (6) **b. of speche** well-spoken I.755.

boldely, booldely *adv.* (1) bravely I.3433; (2) confidently IV.1358, V.581; (3) recklessly III.227, Rom B 3849; (4) vigorously III.1303.

boldnesse, booldnesse *n.* courage, self-assurance VI.71, BD 617; arrogance VIII.487.

bole *n.* bull VII.1325, X.898, Tr 3.723, Tr 4.239; **the white B.** the zodiacal sign, Taurus Tr 2.55; *gen. sg.* **boles** VIII.797; *pl.* **boles** I.2139.

bon, boon *n.* bone I.1177, III.511, Tr 2.926; **to the bare b.** completely Rom A 1059; *pl.* **bones** I.546, **banes** *(Nth.)* I.4073.

bond, boond, boonde *see* **bynde.**

bonde, boond, band *n.* (1) bond, something that binds Tr 3.1358; strap Rom A 240; fetter, shackle VII.2072; (2) promise, pledge V.1534, VII.368; (3) force that controls or dominates V.131 (see note), X.132, PF 438; force that binds Bo 1.m5.57; **his (youre) b.** his (your) control Tr 3.1768, LGW F 89, Rom B 1956; *pl.* **bondes** Tr 2.976, **boondes** VII.1828.

bonde *adj.* enslaved, bound to serve another III.378, III.1660, Tr 1.255; **boonde-folk, boonde-men** serfs X.754, X.753.

bone, boone *n.* request, prayer I.2669, VIII.356, BD 129, Tr 4.68.

bonte(e) *see* **bounte(e).**

boor *n.* boar I.2070, III.1829; *gen.* **bores** VII.870; *pl.* **bores** I.1658.

bord(e) *n.* (1) board, plank I.3440, BD 74; (2) dining table III.2167, III.2243; **the heigh b.** the head table V.85; **to b.** as boarder(s) III.528; (3) **into shippes b.** aboard ship I.3585; **over b.** overboard II.922, HF 438.

bordure *n.* (1) border Bo 1.pr1.28; (2) rim Astr 1.4.3; *pl.* **bordurs** ornamental borders on clothing Rom C 6911.

borel *see* **burel(l).**

(y)born, (y)bore, boren *see* **bere(n).**

borneth *3 pr. sg.* polishes, Tr 1.327. Cf. **burned.**

borwe, borowe, borugh *n.* (1) something given as security Rom C 7329; **to b.** as a pledge I.1622, V.1234; (2) one legally responsible for another's fulfilling a pledge VII.1807, Rom C 7307; **(Seint John, Venus,** *etc.*) **to b.** (with St. John, *etc.*) as a guarantor V.596, Tr 2.1524; *pl.* **borwes** VII.1807, **borowes** Rom C 7307, **borwis** Rom B 2064.

borwe *v.* borrow I.4417, II.105, Tr 1.488; *pt.* **borwed** VI.871; *pp.* **borwed** VIII.735; *vbl. n.* **borwynge** X.800.

bost(e), boost *n.* (1) boastful speech VI.764, Tr 3.298; **maken a b.** brag about II.401, III.98; (2) arrogance VII.2609, Tr 3.248; **leyen down (low) the b.** humble the pride VII.2099, VIII.441; (3) loud talk LGW 887; (4) threat Mars 37.

bosteth *3 pr. sg.* boast III.1672, X.393; *pr. pl.* **bosten** Bo 3.m6.9; *pt. sg.* **bosted** LGW 1262.

boot *n.* boat IV.1424, V.994, Tr 1.416.

boot *see* **byte(n).**

bote, boote *n.* (1) advantage, help, good III.472; **for b. ne bale** for good or bad BD 227; **don b.** do good, help Tr 2.345, Tr 5.672; (2) relief, remedy I.424, Tr 4.1259; **b. of bale** deliverance from trouble VIII.1481, Tr 4.739; **don b.** benefit, bring relief PF 276; **soules b.** salvation of souls, savior VII.456.

botel *n.* bottle III.1931, VI.886; *pl.* **botelles** VI.871, **botels** VI.877.

boterflye *n.* butterfly IV.2304, VII.2790, VII.3274.

both(e), booth, bothen *adj.* (1) (as *n.*) two together, both I.1839, VI.523, Tr 2.329, Rom B 3502; *gen.* **bother** Tr 4.168, **bothes** ABC 83; (2) (as *adj.*) I.990, VII.1024, LGW 834; **bathe** *(Nth.)* I.4087, I.4112; (3) (as *adv.*) both Anel 157.

botme, botom *n.* bottom VII.3101, VIII.1321, Tr 1.297, LGW 1961.

botoun *n.* bud Rom B 1761, Rom B 1770; *pl.* **botouns** Rom B 3045.

bounde, (y)bounde(n) *see* **bynde.**

boundes *n. pl.* (1) boundary markers VII.2118; (2) limits I.2993, IV.46; restraints, moral rules V.571, LGW F 546.

bounte(e), bonte(e), bownte(e) *n.* (1) goodness, virtue VIII.38; **sovereyn b.** perfect goodness IV.2289, VII.1079; prowess VII.2114; excellence Bo 2.pr5.40; (2) kindness, benevolence IV.159, X.466, Tr 3.882; generosity X.284, Pity 72, For 39; *pl.* **bountes** good deeds Bo 1.pr4.244; goodness Bo 2.pr4.35; **bountees** good qualities X.396.

bour *n.* inner room, bedchamber III.869, HF 1186; lady's chamber III.300; *gen.* **boures** I.3677; *pl.* **boures** III.869.

bow(e), bowgh, bough *n.* branch, bough I.1980, BD 423; PF 190; *pl.* **bowes** I.1642.

bowe(n), bow *v.* (1) bow or kneel X.598; (2) submit III.440, Rom B 1939; (3) bend IV.113; *3 pr. sg.* **boweth** Tr 2.1387; *imp. pl.* **boweth** IV.113; *pt. sg.* **bowide** Rom A 1703; *prp.* **bowynge** BD 1216; *pp.* **ibowed** diverted, turned away Bo 4.pr6.163.

box *n.* box tree, boxwood I.2922, VII.3398; **pale as b.** pale as box wood, very white LGW 866.

brayde *see* **breyde.**

brak *see* **breke(n).**

bras *n.* brass I.366, I.3944, HF 142.

brast *see* **breste(n).**

braunche, branche *n.* (1) branch IV.1641, PF 612; (2) line of descent III.1128; (3) species X.114, X.388, Tr 3.132; *pl.* **braunches** I.1067, **branches** X.728.

brawen, brawn *n.* (1) muscle I.546; (2) meat III.1750; *pl.* **brawnes** VII.1941; **braunes** LGW 1071.

bred(e), breed *n.*[1] (1) bread I.341, I.3628; (2) food BD 92, Tr 2.444, Rom C 6618.

brede, breede *n.*[2] (1) breadth I.1970; **hande-brede** the breadth of a hand I.3811; (2) area, space Tr 1.179; **on b.** abroad, widely Tr 1.530.

brede(n) *v.* breed, grow Tr 3.1546, Tr 5.1027, LGW 1156; *3 pr. sg.* **bredeth** IV.1783; *pt. sg.* bred, caused to grow **bredde** Tr 1.465; *pp.* **bred** II.364.

breyde, brayde *v.* (1) *(intr.)* move suddenly, start out (of sleep, swoon, *etc.*) V.477, Tr 5.1262; **b. out of wit** go out of one's mind V.1027, Tr 5.1262; (2) *(tr.)* snatch II.837; *pt. sg.* **breyde** moved suddenly I.4285, **brayde** snatched up HF 1678; *pp.* **breyd** gone Anel 124.

breke(n) *v.* (1) *(tr.)* break I.551, I.954; (2) break into, force an entry X.879; (3) violate a commandment X.883; **b. forward (biheste, trouthe)** fail to keep one's word II.40, V.1519, Tr 3.315; **b. (one's) day** fail (to pay) on the appointed day VIII.1040; (4) break off, interrupt VII.1043, Tr 5.1032; (5) *(intr.)* break I.954, Mars 233; *3 pr. sg.* **breketh** Tr 2.791, **brekith** Rom A 277; *pr. pl.* **breken** X.882; *pr. subj.* **breke** IV.2306 *(sg.)*, Tr 5.1032 *(pl.)*; *imp. sg.* **brek** VII.1900; *pt. sg.* **brak** I.1468; *pt. pl.* **broke** Rom B 3121; *pt. subj. pl.* **breeke** VII.3388; *pp.* **broke(n)** VIII.920, Tr 1.89, **ybroke(n)** HF 765, PF 282, (as *adj.*) **brokene** Bo 1.m4.9; *vbl. n.* **brekynge** X.884.

brenne(n), brynne *v.* burn III.52, III.1731, Tr 1.91; *3 pr. sg.* **brenneth** I.2404, **brennyth** Rom B 5706; *pr. pl.* **brenne(n)** X.196, LGW 2610; *pr. subj. sg.* **brenne** VIII.1423; *imp. pl.* **brenne** VIII.515; *pt. sg.* **brente** I.2403, **brende** I.3812, **brenned** Rom A 297; *pt.*

pl. **brende(n)** I.2425; *prp.* **brennynge** I.2000, *pp.* **(y)brent** I.946, I.2017, **(y)brend** VII.3365, Tr 5.309; **brend gold** refined (pure) gold I.2162, I.2896; *vbl. n.* **brennyng(e)** X.220, Mars 133.

brere *n.* briar, thorn IV.1825, Rom A 858; *pl.* **breres** I.1532.

brest(e), breest *n.* breast I.115, I.131, BD 174; *pl.* **brestes** I.3975, **breestis** Bo 5.m1.4.

breste(n) *v.* break, burst I.1980, IV.1169, Tr 2.408; *3 pr. sg.* **brest** I.2610; *pr. pl.* **breste** Tr 4.257; *pr. subj. sg.* **breste** V.759; *pt. sg.* **brast** IV.1480; *pt. pl.* **braste** Tr 2.326, **bruste** VI.234, **broste** II.671; *pt. subj. sg.* **brast(e)** II.697, BD 1193, **brest** Tr 2.1108; *pp.* **brosten** I.3829; *vbl. n.* **brestyng** V.973.

breth, breeth *n.* breath I.5, I.2806, Tr 1.801.

brethehed(e) *n.* (1) sworn brotherhood III.1399, VII.42; (2) guild, fraternity I.511.

bryd(e), bridd, byrde *n.* (1) bird IV.1281, V.460, Tr 3.10, Rom A 655, Rom A 1014; *(fig.)* sweetheart I.3726; *gen. sg.* **briddes** Tr 2.921; *pl.* **briddes** I.2929, **brydes** Rom A 71, **briddis** Rom A 618.

brydel, bridil *n.* bridle or reins I.169; **holden . . . by the b.** control Anel 184; **have the b.** have control I.2376, III.813; **bownde with b.** subject to restraint Bo 1.m7.20; *pl.* **bridles** X.433, **bridelis** Bo 1.m7.20.

brydeleth *3 pr. sg.* bridles, controls Mars 41; *imp. sg.* **bridle** control Tr 3.1635; *pt. sg.* **bridlede** controlled Tr 4.1678; *pp.* **ybrydeled** LGW 1114.

brymston, brymstoon *n.* brimstone, sulphur I.629, VIII.798, X.841.

brynge(n) *v.* (1) bring I.1613; **b. of (from) live** kill Tr 2.1608, Tr 5.1561, Rom C 7162; **b. (a word)** utter (a word) Tr 3.99, Tr 3.107; **b. to preve** put to the test Tr 3.307; *2 pr. sg.* **bringest** ABC 70, **bringes** I.4130, HF 1908; *3 pr. sg.* **bryngeth** II.974; *pr. pl.* **brynge(n)** II.964, Tr 3.1204; *pr. subj. sg.* **brynge** Tr 3.49; *2 pt. sg.* **broghtest** VII.3229; *3 pt. sg.* **broghte** I.566, **broughte** Tr 3.586; *pt. pl.* **broghte** I.1442, **broughte** Tr 2.914, **broghten** VII.1400; *prp.* **bryngynge** Bo 3.m11.28; *pp.* **(y)broght** I.1111, I.1490, **(y)brought** I.2697, PF 666.

brynke *n.* (1) shore, coast V.858, V.1160; river bank Bo 3.m10.15; (2) edge, brink IV.1401; *pl.* **brynkes** banks HF 803, Rom A 1417.

brynne *see* **brenne(n).**

broche, brooch *n.* brooch, pin I.160, I.3265, HF 1740; *pl.* **brooches** IV.255, **broches** VI.908.

brode, brood *adj.* (1) wide, broad I.3266, I.4124, V.191; (2) large, spacious LGW 782; (3) having a wide blade LGW 1190; *comp.* **brodder** III.1688.

brode *adv.* (1) widely HF 1683, LGW 851; (2) with wide-open eyes VIII.1420; (3) plainly Bo 2.pr5.158; frankly I.739.

(y)broght, (y)brought *see* **brynge(n).**

(y)broke, (y)broken *see* **breken** broken I.1168.

brond(e) *n.* burning piece of wood, firebrand, torch LGW 2252, Rom B 3706; *pl.* **brondes** I.2338.

broste(n) *see* **breste(n).**

brotel, brotil *adj.* fragile IV.1279; uncertain Tr 3.820; unreliable LGW 1885.

brotelnesse, brotilnesse *n.* instability, undependability IV.1279, Tr 5.1832, Wom Unc 15; fickleness IV.2241.

broun *adj.* (1) brown, dark or dull I.207, I.4368; **b.**

breed coarse bread made of bran VII.2844; (2) (of persons) dark complexioned, tanned I.109, I.394, Rom A 1009.

bruste *see* **breste(n)**.

buk(ke) *n.* adult male deer VII.756, PF 195; *gen. sg.* **bukkes** I.3387; *pl.* **bukkes** BD 429.

bulle *n.* bull, i.e., papal decree IV.748, VI.388, Rom C 6847; *pl.* **bulles** IV.739.

bulte *see* **bilde(n)**.

burden(e), burdon, burdoun, birthen, burthen *n.* (1) load, weight Rom B 4711, Rom B 5676; (2) burden Bo 3.pr12.7; (3) bass part in a song I.673, I.4165; *pl.* **burdons** Rom C 6902.

burel(l), borel *n.* coarse woolen cloth III.356; (as *adj.*) **b. man (men, folk)** layman, laymen, unlearned people III.1872, III.1874, V.716.

burgeys *n.* (1) prosperous businessman, citizen with full rights and privileges (*usu.* accorded only to merchants, master craftsmen) I.369, I.754, Tr 4.345; *gen. pl.* **burgeis** Rom C 6864.

burned *pp.* (as *adj.*) burnished, polished I.1983, V.1247, HF 1387; glowing VI.38. Cf. **borneth**.

burthe, byrthe, birthe *n.* birth II.192, II.314, Tr 3.717.

busk, bussch, bush *n.* (1) woods, thicket I.1517, I.2013; (2) a shrub, bush VII.468, HF 485; *pl.* **buskes** I.1579, **busschches** Bo 3.m1.3, **busshes** Form Age 34.

but *adv.* and *conj.* (1) but, except I.1226, I.1754, II.431, Tr 3.232; unless IV.174, LGW 506; **b. if** unless I.656, Purse 4; (2) only V.638; nothing but, no more than BD 39, Tr 1.223; *(prec. by neg.)* only, nothing more than I.2847, III.1728; **I nam (nere) b.** I am (would be) almost, as good as I.1122, VII.185, Tr 5.1246; (3) (after statement of impossibility or *subj.*) that IV.1665, X.339, LGW F 10; (4) **b. (if) it were** unless, if . . . not II.431, Tr 4.221; (5) (as *n.*) an exception X.494.

buttok *n.* buttock I.3803, III.2142; *pl.* **buttokes** I.3975.

buxom *adj.* submissive, obedient Lady 119, Rom B 4419.

C

(See also K and S)

cache, cacche(n), kacchen, kecche *v.* (1) grasp, seize I.1399, I.4273, Tr 2.448; **c. forth** draw (a weapon) suddenly LGW 1854, LGW 2654; hunt down Tr 3.1375; (2) catch, capture I.1214, Tr 5.703, Bo 3.m8.6; entrap I.145, I.2389, VIII.11; **c. with drynke** drunk X.823; (3) **c. a sleep** go to sleep I.4277; **c. countenance** regain composure IV.1110; **c. ayen his firste . . . chere** recovered his former expression Tr 1.280; get I.498, III.306; (4) receive, be given IV.2357, BD 780; have II.186, III.2003, PF 170; catch (a disease) Tr 5.602; **c. an hete** become hot Tr 2.942; **c. his deth (lyves ende)** HF 404, Tr 5.1554; (5) spot, catch sight of Astr 2.17.9, Astr 2.17.11; **caccheth** *3 pr. sg.* Rom B 2775; *pr. subj. sg.* **cacche** III.76; *imp. sg.* **cache** Tr 2.291; *pt. sg.* **caughte(e)** I.498, Tr 1.280, **kaughte** LGW 1854; *pt. pl.* **caughte** Tr 5.602, **kaught** BD 124; *pp.* **(i)caught** I.1214, (as *adj.*) Tr 1.534; **(y)kaught** I.145, BD 838.

caytyf, kaytyf *n.* (1) captive, prisoner VII.2079; (2) wretched or unfortunate person I.1717, VI.728;

scoundrel Rom A 1155; *pl.* **caytyves** I.924, I.1717, **kaytifs** Bo 4.pr4.52.

caytyf, kaytyf *adj.* captive, enslaved I.1552; wretched Rom A 211.

cake *n.* cake or loaf of bread I.4311, VI.322.

calcule *v.* calculate, *esp.* in astrology or astronomy Astr 1.21.87; *pt. sg.* **kalkuled** V.1284; *pp.* **calculed** Astr Pro 76; *vbl. n.* **calkulynge** Tr 1.71, **calkullynge** Tr 4.1398.

calle(n) *v.* call I.2085; *2 pr. sg* **callest** LGW 1380; *3 pr. sg* **calleth** IV.1081; *pr. pl.* **calle(n)** II.723, Tr 3.814, **call** Rom B 3269; *imp. sg.* **calle** Tr 3.401; *pt. sg.* **called(e)** V.1209, LGW 2569; *pt. pl.* **calden** Anel 251; *prp.* **(y)called** I.4264, III.1123; *pp.* **callyng** Tr 3.1700.

cam(e) *see* **comen**.

can *see* **kunne**.

capoun, capon *n.* capon, chicken III.1839, LGW 1389, LGW 1392; *pl.* **capouns** VI.856.

capul *n.* horse I.4105, IX.65; *pl.* **caples** III.1554.

carbuncle *see* **charboncle**.

care *n.* grief, trouble, sorrow I.1321, I.1489, PF 363; *pl.* **cares** V.1305.

careful *adj.* sorrowful Lady 127.

careyne, carayne *n.* carrion, corpse VII.2624, X.441, PF 177.

carf *see* **kerve(n)**.

carie(n), cary *v.* carry I.130, I.3410, HF 574; *3 pr. sg.* **carieth** I.1634; *pr. pl.* **carie(n)** VII.624, IX.96; *pt. sg.* **caried** VIII.567; *pt. pl.* **caryeden** I.2900; *prp.* **caryinge** HF 545; *pp.* **(y)caried** I.1021, VI.791; *vbl. n.* **cariyinge** VI.875.

carole, karole, karoll *n.* a dance performed in a circle and accompanied with singing Rom A 744, Rom A 793; song used in a carol LGW 687; *pl.* **caroles** I.1931.

carole *v.* perform a circular dance BD 849; sing to accompany a dance Rom A 745; *pt. sg.* **karolede** Rom A 745; *pp.* **karoled** Rom A 810; *vbl. n.* **carolynge** singing for a carol dance VIII.1345, **karolyng** Rom A 754.

cart(e) *n.* (1) cart, wagon I.2022; (2) chariot, war-chariot I.2041, HF 943; *pl.* **cartes** Bo 3.m9.34.

carter(e) *n.* cart-driver I.2022, III.1540, PF 102.

cas, caas *n.*[1] (1) situation, circumstance I.1411, Tr 2.422; **as in this (that) c.** in this (that) situation I.2357, I.3297, Tr 3.172, Tr 4.668, LGW 2217; **for no c., in no (maner) c.** under no circumstances III.665, III.1851, VIII.149, Tr 4.635; (2) event, occurrence IV.316, HF 254, Tr 4.420; (3) chance, fate I.844, Tr 2.285; **by, par, upon c.** by chance, by accident I.3661, Tr 1.271; **in c.** in the event that, if Tr 2.758, Tr 4.1509; (4) action, deed LGW 1838; (5) cause, reason, purpose V.1430, IX.308; (6) manner, concern I.2971, Tr 4.416; (7) case, type of situation X.105, Rom C 6715; **setten c.** suppose Tr 2.729; (8) a case at law II.36; *pl.* **caas** legal cases I.323, **cas** VI.163.

cas *n.*[2] quiver (for arrows) I.2080, I.2896, LGW 982.

cast *n.* (1) throwing (some object) Tr 2.868; trick, plot I.2468, I.3605; (2) form or design, shape HF 1178, PF 305; (3) **at thilke c.** under those circumstances VII.2287; *pl.* **castes** I.2468.

caste(n) *v.* (1) throw, cast I.2429, I.3712, Rom C 6183; **c. aweie** get rid of, throw away VI.542, VIII.384; **c.**

out drive out Tr 4.10; (2) cast down VII.3047, Tr 2.1389; *(intr.)* throw about, move quickly I.3330; (3) emit, shed VIII.244, Rom A 1574; **c. of** take off III.723; (4) utter Tr 2.1167; (5) place, put I.4017, VII.2714, VIII.939; **c. up** lift III.1249, Tr 1.204; put (forcibly) VI.268; (6) cast, direct (eyes) I.896, I.2081, HF 495; notice VIII.1414; (7) give, bestow Tr 5.1825, LGW 1878; (8) reckon, calculate I.2172; deliberate, think I.2854, X.692, HF 1148, Tr 1.749; (9) *(reflx.)* apply oneself to, devote oneself to VII.1591; practice VIII.738; set oneself to do VII.1858, Rom B 1860; (10) foreordain, arrange VI.880, VII.2701; *2 pr. sg.* **castest** Bo 2.pr1.104; plan, plot II.584, X.543, Pity 26; decide LGW 2605; *3 pr. sg.* **casteth** VIII.1414, *(contr.)* **cast** II.805; *pr. pl.* **caste(n)** II.212, VI.268, **kaste** LGW 1878; *imp. sg.* **cast** VIII.384; *imp. pl.* **casteth** Tr 5.1838; *pt. sg.* **cast(e)** I.1077, I.2081; **kaste** LGW 1856; *pt. pl.* **caste(n)** Tr 2.1485, Rom A 773; *pp.* **(y)cast** VI.880, VIII.939, **casten** VII.606; *vbl. n.* **castyng(e)** Bo 5.pr4.146, Rom C 7286.

castel(l) *n.* castle I.1057, BD 1332; *pl.* **castelles** VII.1333, **castels** III.870.

catel(l) *n.* property, possessions II.27, IV.1525, Rom B 5540.

cause *n.* (1) cause, source I.419, V.260, V.451; **ben in the c.** be the cause Tr 3.986; **bi (the) c. of** because of I.174, Tr 5.1352; **bi the (that) c. (that)** because I.2488, Tr 4.99, Tr 5.127; **for (the) c. of** for the sake of Bo 3.pr1.44; by reason of Bo 2.pr6.27; as one of the four causes described by Aristotle: **c. material** material from which something is produced VII.1359, **c. efficient** the means by which something is produced Bo 5.m4.42, **c. formal** disposition of the parts of the thing produced VII.1400 (here apparently used in the sense of "efficient cause"), **final c.** purpose for which a thing is produced VII.1401, X.939; **fer c.** remote cause VII.1395; **ny c.** immediate cause VII.1395; **first c.** original cause VI.499; **c. causyng** primary cause Tr 4.829; **c. accidental** incidental cause VII.1398; (2) occasion I.1256, VII.152, VI.296, Anel 257; (3) the reason why I.716, I.2977, I.4144; (4) motive X.142; justification IV.1185, X.707, Tr 1.854; pretext III.1378, Tr 3.1162; (5) aim, purpose III.123, IV.387, VIII.1307; **maken c.** further one's purpose Tr 5.80; (6) an affair or undertaking VII.1741, Tr 1.20; (7) legal action or case HF 1543; charge III.1398; (8) situation Tr 2.832, Tr 4.1227; (9) **bi (the) c. of** because of Tr 1.174, Tr 5.1352; **bi (the, that) c. (that)** because I.2488, Tr 4.99, Tr 5.127, Rom B 4518; **for (the) c. of** for the sake of Bo 3.pr1.44; by reason of Bo 2.pr6.27; **c. why** why V.185; *pl.* **causes** V.451.

cause(n) *v.* cause VIII.1009, HF 794; *3 pr. sg.* **causeth** I.2476; *pr. pl.* **causen** V.452; *pt. sg.* **caused** II.9; *prp.* **causynge** HF 796, (as *adj.*) **causyng** Tr 4.829.

cercle, cerkle, sercle *n.* (1) circle HF 791; **proeves in c.** circular arguments Bo 3.pr12.182; (2) magic circle drawn by a conjurer X.603; (3) circlet, diadem Rom A 1108, Rom A 1113; (4) orbit Bo 4.m6.7; sphere Bo 4.m1.17; *pl.* **cercles** I.2131, **cerklis** Bo 4.pr6.116, **circles** Astr 2.16.2.

cerclen *v.* (1) extend in a circle Ros 2; (2) encompass, surround Tr 3.1767, Rom A 1619; *3 pr. sg.* **cerclith** Rom A 1619; *pp.* **cercled** Ros 2.

certeyn(e), certayn, certein *n.* (1) a fixed amount VIII.1024; a definite but unspecified number I.3193,

VII.2177, Tr 3.596; (2) certainty, assurance X.1000; something certain Bo 5.pr4.126 Bo 5.pr5.102.

certeyn(e), certayn *adj.* (1) specified, fixed I.252a, I.815, Tr 3.1431; binding Bo 1.m6.22; (2) a definite but unspecified extent (of time) II.149, II.2167, (amount) II.242; (number) I.2967; (3) particular, specific I.1471, I.3494, II.481; (4) true, significant BD 119; **for c.** for sure, certainly HF 1336, Tr 4.120; **in c. for a fact** VII.728; (5) inevitable, predetermined Bo 4.pr4.57, Bo 5.pr5.83, Bo 5.pr5.103; fixed, invariable V.866, Tr 4.1012, Tr 2.1015; (6) reliable Bo 2.pr8.37; dependable Rom B 4443; (7) confident VII.1664; *pl.* **certeins** Bo 5.pr5.102.

certeyn, certayn *adv.* certainly, indeed I.3495, II.884, IV.646, Tr 1.492.

certeinly, certeinliche, certaynly *adv.* certainly I.204, I.235, HF 340, Tr 5.100.

certes, certis *adv.* certainly, indeed I.875, I.1237, BD 84; (as *n.*) **for c.** certainly III.609.

cese(n), cesse(n), ceessen *v.* (1) *(intr.)* cease, stop II.1066, Bo 4.m5.36, Mars 11, Rom B 3307; (2) *(tr.)* cause to stop Tr 1.445; *3 pr. sg.* **cesseth** V.257, **ceseth** Bo 4.pr6.129; *pr. pl.* **cesen** Bo 5.pr6.204; *pr. subj. sg.* **cese** Bo 5.pr6.29, **cesse** Tr 2.483; *pt. sg.* **cessed** VIII.538; *pt. subj. sg.* **cessed(e)** Bo 2.pr1.114, Tr 1.849; *pp.* **cessed** Tr 2.787.

chaast, chast(e) *adj.* chaste I.2015, I.2297, LGW 1577.

chace(n), chase(n) *v.* (1) pursue V.457, ABC 15, Rom B 3162; drive out, banish VII.566, Bo 1.pr4.125; **c. out** expel III.2157; **c. from (out) of** deprive II.366; (2) harass, afflict X.526, Rom C 5999, ABC 48; **c. at** rail at Tr 1.908, Tr 3.1801; (3) pursue, go on with IV.341, IV.393; *3 pr. sg.* **chaceth** X.544, **chaseth** Bo 2.pr6.103; *pr. pl.* **chasen** ABC 15, **chacen** X.526; *2 pt. sg.* **chacedest** Bo 1.pr4.255; *3 pt. sg.* **chaced** III.2157; *pp.* **chaced** II.366, **chased** Rom B 3619; *prp.* **chasynge** Bo 1.m4.6.

chaffare *n.* (1) trade, business I.4389, VII.340; (2) merchandise, wares II.138, III.521, IV.2438.

chayer(e), chaire *n.* (1) chair Rom C 6915; sedan chair VII.2613; (2) throne Bo 3.pr4.15; position of authority Bo 2.pr3.55, Rom C 6889; professorial chair III.1518; *pl.* **chayeres** Bo 1.m5.38, **chaieris** Rom C 6915.

chalenge *v.* challenge III.1200; *1 pr. sg.* **chalange** V.1324; *pt. sg.* **chalanged** Bo 2.pr6.32; *vbl. n.* **chalangyng** IV.264.

champioun, champion *n.* (1) athlete (*esp.* wrestler) VII.2023; courageous fighter Fort 17; (2) defender (of one of the parties) in a judicial duel II.631, III.1662, Tr 2.1427.

chanoun, chanon *n.* canon (cleric) VIII.578, VIII.1022; **c. reguler** a canon living under a quasimonastic rule Rom C 6694; *gen. sg.* **chanons** VIII.1101, **chanounes** VIII.1196; *pl.* **chanons** VIII.992, **chanouns** Rom C 6694.

chapeleyn(e) *n.* chaplain I.164 (see note), Rom C 6328; *pl.* **chapelleyns** X.617.

chapelet, chapelett *n.* (1) garland of flowers Rom A 908; (2) headband, diadem Rom A 563.

chapitre *n.* (1) division of a written work VII.3065, X.238; (2) meeting of members of a religious house III.1945; session of the archdeacon's court III.1361; *pl.* **chapitres** X.389, PF 32 (see note).

chapman *n.* merchant VII.254, VII.256, Rom B 5591; *pl.* **chapmen** VII.288.

char, chaar *n.* carriage or chariot Anel 24, Tr 3.1704.

charboncle, charbocle, carbuncle *n.* red gemstone HF 1363, VII.871, Rom A 1120.

charge *n.* (1) load Anel 32; something carried, burden HF 1439; (2) burden, hardship X.92, LGW 2514; (3) duty, responsibility IV.163, PF 507; order, command IV.193; **yeven in c.** order VII.432; (4) **taketh c.** be concerned III.321; **yeve litel c.** be little concerned, care little I.1284; (5) weight, significance V.359; matter to be discussed PF 507; importance I.1284, V.359, BD 894; **no c.** it does not matter VIII.749.

charge(n) *v.* (1) load III.1539, X.361, LGW 2151; (2) burden, weigh down IV.2211, VII.2366; (3) order, request II.802, III.2026, LGW F 493, Rom B 2695; (4) be important Tr 3.1576; *3 pr. sg.* **chargeth** LGW 1189; *pr. subj. sg.* **charge** X.360; *pt. sg.* **charged** II.209, **chargide** Rom B 2145; *pp.* **charged** IV.2211.

charite(e) *n.* (1) Christian virtue of love I.532, IV.221, Tr 1.49; such love, deeply upset I.452, X.1043; (2) benevolence Rom B 5744, Rom C 6681; an act of charity, good deed I.1433, X.374; **for (par seinte) c.** out of kindness, for goodness' sake I.1721, VII.3320; (3) fondness, affection Bo 3.pr11.175.

chasteleyn *n.* keeper of a castle Rom B 3740 (*fem.*); Rom C 6327 (*masc.*).

chaunce n. (1) event, happening I.1752, II.1045; lot, fate VIII.593, BD 1113; luck II.125; **par c.** by chance VI.606; (2) a winning throw in dice VI.653; *pl.* **chaunces** Tr 2.1347.

chaunge(n), changen *v.* (1) *(intr.)* change, vary V.1035, Tr 5.122, Tr 4.485, Rom B 4030; (2) *(tr.)* change (one's mind, feelings, attitude) IV.709, Tr 5.1683; **c. colour** grow pale (or red) I.1400, I.1637; shift, move IV.511, Bo 2.pr2.53; (3) exchange VI.724; *3 pr. sg.* **chaungeth** I.1538, **changeth** II.1134; *pr. pl.* **chaungen** Astr 2.39.22, **change** Astr 2.39.21; *pr. subj. sg.* **chaunge** Bo 3.m2.45; *imp. sg.* **chaunge** VII.1226; *imp. pl.* **chaungeth** Tr 2.303; *pt. sg.* **chaunged** I.348, **changed** V.320; *prp.* **chaungynge** (as *adj.*) IV.996; *pp.* **(y)chaunged** I.1370, Tr 4.865, **changed** V.709; (as *adj.*) **changed** Tr 3.92; *vbl. n.* **chaungyng(e)** I.1647, exchange Tr 4.231; *pl.* **chaungynges** Bo 2.m8.2.

chef, cheef, chief *adj.* chief, principal I.1057, I.1730, V.1046; **c. synnes** the capital (deadly) sins X.389.

cheyne *n.* (1) chain I.1343, VII.2364; (2) tie, bond I.2988, V.1356; *pl.* **cheynes** I.1343, **chaynes** Bo 3.m2.9.

cheke *n.* (1) cheek III.433, V.1078, Tr 4.130; (2) jawbone VII.2038; *pl.* **chekes** I.633.

chere, cheer(e), chiere *n.* (1) face IV.238, IV.599; (2) facial expression I.913, V.103, BD 545, Rom B 3372; **a c. make** assume the expression IV.535; (3) outward appearance HF 154, HF 277, Rom B 5486; manner, bearing I.139, IV.241, Tr 2.1507; manners I.139; attention, solicitude VII.6; (4) mood II.396, IV.7, IV.1211, Tr 1.879; good humor IV.1112, Rom B 3805; (5) kindness Anel 253; **maken c.** treat kindly, entertain VII.327; source of pleasure I.2683; (6) *(astro.)* aspect Mars 42; *pl.* **cheeres** Bo 2.m3.4, **cheres** Tr 2.1507.

cherete *see* **chiertee.**

cherice(n), cherisse, cherish *v.* (1) hold dear IV.1388, Tr 1.986, Tr 3.175; (2) take good care of, respect V.353, Rom B 5417; treat V.1554; (3) further, favor VII.2520; *3 pr. sg.* **cherisseth** V.1554; *imp. sg.* **cherisse** IV.1388, **cherish** Lak Sted 23; *imp. pl.* **cherisseth** V.353; *vbl. n.* **cherisynge** Tr 4.1534.

cherl *n.* (1) common man (of non-gentle birth or station) X.761, Rom A 880; fellow, chap VI.750, Tr 1.1024; peasant I.2459; slave X.763; (2) ill-mannered boor, ruffian I.3169, I.3917, III.2206; villain III.460; *gen.* **cherles** I.3169; *pl.* **cherles** Rom B 2333.

cherlyssh *adj.* churlish, villainous V.1523, Rom A 177.

cherlishly *adv.* viciously Rom B 3164.

ches *n.* chess V.900, BD 51, BD 619.

chese *n.* cheese III.1739, III.1747, VI.448; *pl.* **cheses** Rom C 7041.

chese(n), cheese *v.* (1) choose, select III.1232, III.1748, X.482, Tr 4.189; elect X.468; chosen of God, elected to Heaven, blessed X.1054; (2) decide III.1179; **c. amys** make the wrong choice I.3181; **may nat c.** have no choice III.1748; **c. rather** prefer V.1384; *3 pr. sg.* **chesith** Bo 5.m4.35; *(contr.)* **cheest** PF 623; *pr. pl.* **chese(n)** X.468, Tr 4.189; *pr. subj.* **chese** I.3177 *(sg.)*, I.3181 *(pl.)*; *imp. sg.* **ches(e)** III.1219, Tr 2.955, **chees** I.1595; *imp. pl.* **cheseth** III.1232, **chese** III.1227; *pt. sg.* **ches** LGW 965, **chees** IV.1597; *pt. pl.* **chose** LGW G 290; *pp.* **chose(n)** I.2109, BD 1004; *vbl. n.* **chesynge** choice, choosing IV.162.

cheste, chiste *n.* (1) strongbox, chest III.317; (2) coffin III.502, IV.29; (3) receptacle Tr 5.1368.

chevalrie, chivalrie *n.* (1) knights, body of knights I.878, VII.2681; the nobility II.235; **flour of c.** best of knights I.982, I.3059; (2) knighthood, knightly prowess I.2184, IX.126; (3) the ideal of knightly conduct I.45, I.2106.

chevalrous, chivalrous *adj.* brave, chivalric Tr 5.802, LGW 1905.

chevyssaunce, chevysaunce *n.* (1) expedient, remedy Rom B 3337; (2) financial arrangement *(esp. loan)* I.282, VII.329, VII.347; purchase LGW 2434.

chiche *see* **chynche.**

chide(n) *v.* (1) *(tr.)* criticize, scold III.419, X.632, Tr 5.1093; (2) *(intr.)* complain III.281, VII.428; *2 pr. sg.* **chidest** III.244; *3 pr. sg.* **chideth** VII.1707; *(contr.)* **chit** VIII.921; *pr. pl.* **chiden** III.1983; *pr. subj. sg.* **chide** X.632; *pt. sg.* **chidde** I.3999, III.223; *prp.* **chidyng** III.279; *vbl. n.* **chidyng(e)** X.525, X.633; *pl.* **chidynges** X.206.

chideresse *n.* scold Rom A 150, Rom B 4266.

chiere *see* **chere.**

chiertee, cherete *n.* fondness, love III.396; Rom B 3516.

chymenee, chymeneye *n.* hearth I.3776; fireplace Tr 3.1141; *pl.* **chemeneyes** chimneys Bo 1.m4.10.

chyn(ne) *n.* chin I.195, BD 174, Rom A 550.

chynche, chinchy, chiche *adj.* miserly Rom B 5588, Rom B 5998, Rom C 6002; (as *n.*) miser VII.1619.

chirche, cherche *n.* (1) church (building) I.460, I.708, VIII.546; (2) the church (as institution) I.3986, II.235; *gen.* **chirches** I.3983; *pl.* **chirches** III.1979.

chirketh *3 pr. sg.* chirps, twitters III.1804; *prp.* **chirkynge** groaning, roaring Bo 1.m6.10; *vbl. n.* **chirkyng(e)** creaking, squeaking I.2004, X.605; *pl.* **chirkynges** creakings HF 1943.

choys *n.* choice, decision IV.154, IV.170, PF 406; **fre(e)** c. free will VII.3246, Tr 4.971, Tr 4.980.

cipres(se), ciprees *n.* cypress VII.881, PF 179, Rom A 1381.

circumstaunce, circumstance *n.* (1) attendant condition X.964, X.967; relevant aspect I.1932, II.152; detail, feature VI.419; **with every (alle) c.** with (attention to) all the details X.610, X.976; with due propriety, with all ceremony I.2263, II.317; with great care IV.584; (2) general condition X.692; *pl.* **circumstaunces** I.2788, **circumstances** X.86.

cite(e) *n.* city I.939, I.989, Tr 1.59; *pl.* **citees** III.870, **cites** Bo 1.pr4.36.

cladde, (y)clad *see* **clothe(n)**.

clamb, clamben *see* **clymbe(n)**.

clappeth *3 pr. pl.* knocks III.1584; *pr. pl.* **clappen** talk noisily, chatter X.406; *pr. subj. sg.* **clappe** nay say VIII.965; *imp. pl.* **clappeth** IV.1200 wag your tongue, chatter; *pt. sg.* **clapte** clapped V.1203; clapped shut III.1699; **c. to** slammed shut I.3740, IV.2159; *vbl. n.* **clappyng** IV.999.

clarre(e) *n.* spiced and sweetened wine IV.1843, Rom C 5967, Rom C 6026.

clause *n.* sentence, brief passage Tr 5.1301; **in a c.** briefly I.715, I.1763, IV.1431; legal stipulation Tr 2.728.

cled, cledde *see* **clothe(n)**.

clefte *see* **cleve**.

cleyme(n), clayme *v.* (1) claim, demand X.926; (2) claim, call, name VII.36; declare oneself (to be) III.1120; *3 pr. sg.* **claymeth** VII.36; *pr. pl.* **clayme** III.1120.

clen(e), cleene *adj.* (1) clean I.504; pure, unpolluted II.1183, VI.873, Tr 3.257; (2) chaste, morally pure I.2326, III.93, Tr 2.580; (3) clear, unobstructed V.995, BD 423; (4) elegant, shapely III.598; (5) whole Rom B 2127.

clene *adv.* (1) cleanly I.133; (2) brightly, splendidly I.367, Rom A 1380; (3) fully, entirely V.626, Tr 4.10; **ful (al) c.** completely, entirely II.1106, VIII.625, Tr 5.1198.

clennesse *n.* purity, chastity III.1910, LGW G 297, LGW 1860.

clense *v.* cleanse I.631; *3 pr. sg.* **clenseth** X.312.

clepe(n) *v.* (1) speak, say, call out I.3577, V.374, BD 185; (2) call (a name) I.2730, I.3956, BD 810; **ben cleped** be called I.269, I.376, Tr 1.66; (3) ask X.289; (4) summon V.1487, VII.1157; (5) **c. ayein** recall, restore IX.354, Tr 5.914; recall, remember Tr 2.521; (6) **c. forth** induce (an effect) Bo 5.m4.55; produce PF 352; (7) **ben clepid togidre** be joined together Bo 5.m1.8; *2 pr. sg.* **clepest** X.760; *3 pr. sg.* **clepeth** III.102; *pr. pl.* **clepe(n)** I.620, II.191, **clepyn** Bo 2.pr6.11; *imp. sg.* **clepe** I.3432; *pt. sg.* **cleped** V.374, **clepid** Bo 3.pr4.11, **clepte** Rom A 1331; *pt. subj. sg.* **clepide** Bo 4.m6.47; *prp.* **clepyng** Tr 4.1157; *pp.* **(y)cleped** I.376, VIII.129; **(y)clept** VIII.272, VIII.863.

cler(e), cleer(e) *adv.* (1) brightly I.2331, II.11, LGW 2224; (2) loudly I.170, IV.1845, Tr 2.825.

clere *adj.* (1) bright, shining V.48, X.1078, Tr 3.1; (2) clear, free from impurity VI.914, (of sounds) IX.115, BD 347, Rom A 681, (of skies) I.1062, PF 210; (3) beautiful, splendid VII.858; (4) keen, perspicacious Bo 5.pr2.24, Tr 4.991; *comp.* **clerer** II.194.

clere(n) *v.* grow clear Tr 2.2, Tr 2.806; shine LGW 773.

clerk *n.* (1) member of the clergy VI.391, X.961; minor cleric I.3312; (2) student, scholar I.480, III.673, HF 1487; university student III.527; learned person IV.1293, V.1105; author, writer I.1163, I.4028; *gen.* **clerkes** I.4060; *pl.* **clerkes** I.3275.

clernesse, cleernesse, clerenesse *n.* (1) brightness VIII.403, X.222, Bo 4.m1.28, Rom B 2927; (2) splendor VIII.111, Bo 3.pr1.50; (3) fame Bo 3.pr2.53.

cleve *v.* (1) split Rom A 859; (2) crack LGW 758; (3) pierce Tr 3.375; *pr. sg. subj.* **cleve** Tr 3.375; *pt. sg.* **clefte** BD 72; *pp.* **clove(n)** I.2934, cleft, dimpled Rom A 550.

cleven *v.* cleave, adhere to Bo 2.pr6.90; *3 pr. sg.* **clyveth** Bo 3.m11.32; *pr. pl.* **cleven** Bo 3.pr11.103, **clyven** Bo 2.pr4.54; *prp.* **clyvynge** Bo 4.pr6.65.

clyf *n.* cliff LGW 1497; *pl.* **clyves** BD 161.

clifte *n.* chink, cleft LGW 744, LGW 746, LGW 776; cleft of the buttocks III.2145.

clyket *n.* latch-key IV.2117.

clymat *n.* region of the earth defined by latitude Astr 2.39.25; *pl.* **clymates** terrestrial latitudes Astr 1.3.4.

clymbe(n) *v.* climb I.3625, IV.2210, HF 2151; *3 pr. sg.* **clymbeth** VII.2776; *pt. sg.* **clamb** VII.797, **clomb** HF 1118; *pt. pl.* **clamben** HF 2512, **clomben** I.3636, **cloumben** VII.1400; *prp.* **climbing** Truth 3; *pp.* **clombe(n)** II.12, VII.3198, **cloumbe** VII.2402.

clyveth, clyven, clyvyng *see* **cleven**.

cloysterer *n.* monastic I.259, I.3661.

cloke *n.* cloak I.157, I.1999, Tr 3.738.

clokke *n.* clock II.14, VII.2854, X.5.

clomb(e), clombe(n) *see* **clymbe(n)**.

clos(e), cloos *pp.* (as *adj.*) of **close(n)** (1) closed VII.3332, IX.37; (2) concealed Rom B 3637; **kepen c.** keep secret, concealed VII.1146.

close(n) *v.* (1) obstruct Rom B 3936; shut BD 873, Rom B 5390; fill (a hole) Rom B 4097; (2) fold up Tr 2.968; (3) enclose Rom B 2968; summarize Bo 2.pr4.25; (4) confine Rom B 4372; **closed day** light engulfed in darkness Bo 1.m3.15; (5) contain Rom B 2834; *3 pr. sg.* **closeth** LGW G 52; *pt. sg.* **closide** Rom B 1842; *pp.* **(i)closed** Tr 2.968, LGW G 94; **clos** Rom A 1675; *vbl. n.* **closing** enclosure Rom A 527.

cloth, clooth *n.* (1) cloth I.447, I.2158, BD 255; (2) drapery I.2281; bedclothes Tr 2.1544; (3) garment, clothing III.1881, VII.2473; *pl.* **clothes** I.899, **clothis** Rom A 325.

clothe(n) *v.* clothe, dress VIII.42, X.933; *pr. pl.* **clothen** Bo 1.pr6.97; *pr. subj. sg.* **clothe** ABC 46; *imp. pl.* **clothe** X.1054; *pt. sg.* **cladde** I.1409; **cledde** Tr 3.1521; *pp.* **(y)clothed** I.911, I.1048, **(y)clad** I.103, Rom A 890, **cled** BD 252; *vbl. n.* **clothing(e)** VII.2304, VII.2366.

cloumb- *see* **clymbe(n)**.

clout *n.* rag Rom A 458; *pl.* **cloutes** tatters Bo 1.pr3.41.

clove(n) *see* **cleve**.

cofre *n.* (1) money-chest I.298, II.26; (2) coffin PF 177.

coghe, coughen *v.* cough IV.2208, Tr 2.254; *3 pr. sg.* **cougheth** I.3697, **cogheth** I.3788.

cok, kok *n.* cock, rooster I.823, I.3687, PF 350; cock-crow I.4233; *gen.* **cokkes** I.3675; *pl.* **cokkes** I.3357.

cokewold *n.* cuckold I.3226, IV.2256, VI.382.

col(e) *n.* coal I.2692, I.3731, Tr 2.1332; *pl.* **coles** VIII.1114.

col-blak *adj.* coal-black I.2142, I.3240.

cold(e), coold *adj.* (1) cold I.2778, I.2957; (2) cooled off V.402; chilling, painful I.1920, I.2467, Tr 3.1202; fatal VII.3256; (3) dominated by cold I.2443, Astr 1.21.65; (as *n.*) one of the four elementary qualities I.420, PF 380.

colde(n) *v.* grow cold, chill II.879, V.1023, PF 145.

coler *n.* collar I.3239, Tr 5.811, Rom A 1190.

colour *n.* (1) color I.1038; (2) complexion I.1400, V.370; (3) pigment, paint BD 332; (4) rhetorical device IV.16, V.723; (5) pretext, trick Bo 2.pr1.14; pretence III.399, Pity 66; *pl.* **colours** VI.36, **coloures** Rom A 898.

come(n) *v.* (1) come I.23, I.671; become, befit Tr 3.1721; (2) **c. to the effect** realize VIII.1261; **c. bi** understand (something) III.984, VIII.1395; *2 pr. sg.* **comest** III.246, (with *pro.*) **comestow** LGW 1887; *3 pr. sg.* **cometh** I.1643, **comth** I.3818, **comyth** Bo 2.pr7.77; *pr. pl.* **come(n)** I.2575, VI.477; *pr. subj. sg.* **coome** II.802; *pr. subj. pl.* **come** X.443; *pt. sg.* **cam(e)** I.547, II.414; **com(e)** BD 134, LGW F 314; *imp. sg.* **com** I.3709, **com of** come on, hurry up I.3728, PF 494; *imp. pl.* **cometh** I.839; *pt. sg.* **cam(e)** I.547, BD 388; **com(e)** BD 134, LGW F 314; *pt. pl.* **come(n)** II.145, Anel 30; **coome(n)** III.1571, V.1012; **came** BD 372; *prp.* **comyng(e)** I.2128, (as *adj.*) Tr 4.1075; *pp.* **come(n)** I.23, I.671, **ycome(n)** I.77, I.3942; *vbl. n.* **comynge(e)** IV.912, Rom B 2518, **commyng** Tr 3.1675.

commende *v.* praise, commend IV.1024; *3 pr. sg.* **commendeth** Bo 1.pr4.288; *pr. pl.* **comende(n)** Tr 5.761, LGW 1688; *pt. pl.* **commendeden** X.669; *pp.* **commended** Bo 2.pr5.165.

commoeve *v.* move, influence Bo 4.pr4.256; *3 pr. sg.* **commoeveth** Bo 5.m4.53, **commeveth** Tr 5.1783; *pr. subj. sg.* **commeve** Tr 5.1386; *pt. sg.* **commoevde** Bo 3.m12.278; *pt. pl.* **comeveden** Tr 3.17; *vbl. n.* **commoevynge** Bo 1.m4.6.

commune, comun(e) *adj.* (1) common, shared Tr 1.843; **in c.** generally I.1251, I.2681; (2) unanimous II.155, VI.601; (3) public IV.1583, Bo 1.pr4.41, Bo 1.pr4.70; **c. profit** common good, welfare of all IV.431, IV.1194, PF 47; **c. thynges** republics Bo 1.pr4.27; (as *n.*) land held in common IV.1313; (4) common, ordinary Bo 1.pr1.15, Rom C 6237; (5) familiar VII.1481, VII.2246; notorious VI.596; accustomed BD 812; (6) general, widespread V.107; (7) secular Rom C 6237.

compaignye, companye *n.* (1) group I.24, BD 807; professional group II.134; (2) fellowship, companionship I.2779, I.3204, VI.63; **holden (maken, beere) c.** keep III.1521, VII.1330, Tr 4.1202; **par c.** for fellowship's sake, companionship I.4167; **c. (of man)** sexual intimacy I.461, I.2311; (3) sociability Tr 3.396, Rom B 1862; *pl.* **compaignyes** I.2589.

compas, compace *n.* (1) cunning HF 462; figure Rom B 3208; (2) circle I.1889, LGW G 199, Rom B 4183; (3) circumference HF 798; realm Bo 2.m7.8, Bo 3.pr12.202; extent Mars 137; (4) **in c.** round about Rom A 526; (5) *(pl.)* a compass Astr 2.5.10; *pl.* **compasses** images HF 1302.

compasse *v.* (1) plot LGW 1414; (2) figure out Rom C 6932; (3) enclose, surround Bo 4.pr6.122; *3 pr. sg.* **compasseth** Bo 3.m11.8; *pt. sg.* **compassed** LGW 1414; *pp.* **compassed** LGW 1543, drawn with compasses Astr 1.18.1; *vbl. n.* **compassyng** plotting I.1996, dimension Rom A 1350; *pl.* **compassinges** devices HF 1188; schemes HF 1188.

compleyne, compleignen, complayne *v.* (1) lament IV.530, Tr 5.723, LGW 1980; (2) mourn Tr 4.786, Rom B 3498; (3) complain Bo 1.pr5.63; appeal LGW 1799; *3 pr. sg.* **compleyneth** Mars 294; *pr. subj. pl.* **compleyne** Mars 280; *imp. pl.* **compleyneth** Mars 290; *1 & 3 pt. sg.* **compleyned(e)** LGW 1968, Bo 1.pr1.87, Rom B 1869; *2 pt. sg.* **compleynedest** VII.3349; *prp.* **compleynynge** I.1072; *pp.* **compleyned** IV.530; *vbl. n.* **compleynynge** II.929.

compleint(e), complaynt(e) *n.* (1) lament V.920, Tr 4.784; (2) complaint Rom B 4563; (3) poetic lament IV.1881, BD 464 (4) statement of grievances Bo 3.pr3.64, LGW G 363; *pl.* **compleintes** V.948, **complayntes** Rom B 2326.

complexioun, compleccioun *n.* constitution, temperament determined by the humors I.333 (see note), X.585, Bo 4.pr6.199; *pl.* **complexions** Bo 4.pr6.198; **complexiouns** Tr 5.369, **complecciouns** VII.2924.

compoune *v.* (1) compound, combine in a whole Bo 3.m9.8; (2) compose, construct Astr Pro 9; *pr. pl.* **compounen** Bo 3.pr10.196; *pr. pl.* **comprehenden** Bo 5.pr6.4; *pp.* **compouned** composed HF 1029, tempered LGW 2585.

comprende, comprehende *v.* (1) contain, include VII.957, X.1042, Tr 3.1687; (2) understand V.223, Anel 83, Tr 4.891; *3 pr. sg.* **comprehendeth** X.1042; *pr. pl.* **comprehenden** Bo 5.pr6.4; *pp.* **comprehended** VII.957, **comprehendid** Bo 1.m2.14.

comune *n.* (1) commonwealth, republic Bo 2.pr7.10, Bo 2.pr7.20; (2) citizenry IV.70; (3) right to use land held in common IV.1313; *pl.* **communes** common soldiers I.2509.

comun(e) *see* **commune.**

comunly, communely, communly, comonly, comounly *adv.* ordinarily, commonly III.2257, IV.726, V.221, VII.1978, VIII.505, Astr 2.19.10.

conceit(e), conseyt(e), conseit *n.* (1) mind VIII.1078; (2) concept VIII.1214, LGW 1764; opinion Tr 1.692; **comune c.** consensus Bo 3.pr10.40; **wrong c.** misconception Tr 1.692; *pl.* **conceytes** ideas Tr 3.804.

conceyve *v.* (1) conceive (offspring) VII.472, X.577; engender, give rise to VII.1209, Rom B 3090; (2) feel (an emotion) X.552; (3) observe LGW 1746; (4) comprehend, understand V.336, Tr 5.1598; *3 pr. sg.* **conceyveth** Rom B 3040; *pp.* **conceyved** V.336.

conclude *v.* (1) include VIII.429; (2) summarize, conclude (a speech, argument) I.1895; end VIII.849, VIII.957; (3) succeed VIII.773; (3) deduce I.3067 III.1171, Bo 3.pr10.98; (4) decide IV.1607; *pr. pl.* **concluden** VIII.957; *pp.* **concluded** IV.1607.

conclusioun, conclusion *n.* (1) end II.683, Tr 2.259; purpose, goal III.115, Tr 1.480; **for (plat) c.** definitely I.1845, Tr 5.765; (2) result VIII.394; fate I.1869, I.4328; success VIII.672; (3) inference VII.3057, Bo 4.pr2.245; judgment, decision I.1743, I.3402, PF 526; *pl.* **conclusiouns** mathematical propositions I.3193.

condicioun, condicion *n.* (1) state, circumstances, situation II.99, II.2758, Tr 3.817, Tr 5.831; social position II.313, X.755; (2) nature Bo 1.pr4.231, Bo 4.pr3.125; quality X.1012; circumstance X.319; (3)

character, disposition I.1431; character trait VI.41, Tr 2.166; (4) stipulation V.529, PF 407; *pl.* **condiciouns** Tr 2.166.

conferme *see* **conforme.**

conferme(n), confirme *v.* (1) confirm, approve, ratify X.842; (2) strengthen Bo 4.pr6.268, Bo 4.pr7.85; (3) corroborate I.2350, IV.1508, HF 761; assert Bo 5.pr1.35; pursue (a course of action) VII.1222; (4) *(pp.)* established VI.136; make secure Tr 2.1526; promote VII.1222; (5) *(reflx.)* resolve VII.1777; *2 pt. sg.* **confermedest** Bo 1.pr4.26; *imp. pl.* **confermeth** Mars 20; *pp.* **confermed** I.2350.

conforme *v.* (1) conform Wom Nobl 16; (2) *(reflx.)* obey, consent IV.546, VII.1872; *pr. subj. sg.* **conferme** Bo 4.pr4.194; *pt. sg.* **conformed** VII.1872; *prp.* **conformynge** IV.546.

confort, counfort, comfort *n.* (1) assurance Rom B 2760; consolation V.826, X.740, X.1030, Rom B 1959; c. caughte was comforted PF 170; (2) pleasure, delight I.773, Tr 5.1168, Rom B 2802; god c. good cheer Tr 1.890; (3) alleviation Tr 4.74, Tr 4.318, Rom C 6506.

conforte(n), comforte(n) *v.* (1) encourage X.652; (2) console IV.1918, Tr 3.1134; (3) relieve Tr 5.234; (4) *(astro.)* enhance the influence of (a planet) Astr 2.4.47; *3 pr. sg.* **conforteth** I.958; *pr. pl.* **conforten** V.823; *prp.* **confortynge** IV.1935; *pp.* **conforted** V.832, **comforted** Bo 2.pr4.67.

confounde(n) *v.* (1) harass, distress II.100, X.774, Bo 4.pr5.23; harm, destroy II.362, X.529; encumber, overcome II.100, X.740; (2) perplex Bo 2.pr4.130, Bo 5.m3.12, Bo 5.pr6.140; *3 pr. sg.* **confowndeth** Bo 1.pr6.100; *pr. pl.* **confounden** Bo 4.pr5.23; *pr. subj. sg.* **confownde** Bo 4.pr7.95; *pp.* **confoundid(e)** VII.137, **confunded** Bo 1.pr6.74.

confus *adj.* (1) confused I.2230, VIII.463; (2) obscure Bo 4.m5.13.

confusioun *n.* (1) destruction, ruin I.1545; cause of pain III.1958, VII.1106; damnation VII.1943; (2) humiliation X.187, LGW 2652; cause of humiliation LGW 1369; (3) uneasiness Rom B 4460, Rom B 4480; (4) mixing Bo 5.pr3.172; disorder, chaos V.869, Bo 4.pr6.237.

conjecten, congecte *v.* (1) suppose, conjecture Bo 1.pr6.25, Bo 3.pr10.214; (2) plan, conspire Rom C 6928; *2 pr. sg.* **conjectest** Tr 4.1026; *3 pr. sg.* **conjecteth** Bo 5.pr3.56; *pr. subj. sg.* **conjecte** Bo 4.pr2.94; *vbl. n.* **conjectynge** VII.1402; *pl.* **conjectynges** VII.1408.

conjoyneth *3 pr. sg.* unites, joins together Bo 5.pr4.148; *pr. pl.* **conjoynen** Bo 3.pr10.161; *pp.* **conjoynt** X.924, **conjoigned** Bo 3.pr4.40, **conjoyned** composed Bo 3.pr10.203; *vbl. n.* **conjoynynge** VIII.95.

conjunccioun, conjunccion *n.* (1) joining together Bo 3.pr11.64; (2) *(astro.)* the apparent proximity of two or more heavenly bodies Astr 2.32.1; *pl.* **conjunccions** Bo 5.m3.3.

conscience, concience *n.* (1) conscience, sense of right and wrong IV.1635, VIII.434, X.979; (2) sense of fairness III.1438; scrupulousness I.398, I.526; (3) feelings, sensibility I.150, LGW 1255; *pl.* **consciences** Bo 4.pr6.324.

conseil, councel, counceil, counseyl, counsel(l) *n.* (1) a meeting, council I.3096; (2) discussing an issue VII.1042, Rom C 5812; (3) body of advisors to a ruler II.204; (4) an advisor I.1147; **ben of c.** be my advisor, confidante I.1141; (5) counsel, advice VIII.192, PF 631; **taken c.** deliberate VII.1121; **werken bi (with) c.** act after deliberation I.3530, IV.1485; scriptural counsel (as distinct from commandment) III.82; (6) plan, decision I.784, VII.1065; (7) secret I.665, I.3503, VIII.145, Rom B 5260; **kepen (hyden) c.** keep a secret III.980, VII.1143, Rom B 2358; **in c.** secretly III.1437, IV.2431; *pl.* **conseils** VII.3256.

conseille(n), counseillen, counceilen *v.* (1) teach, instruct III.66, PF 633, Tr 1.648, Rom C 6845; (2) persuade Bo 3.pr5.65; *1 pr. sg.* **consaille** IV.1200; *2 pr. sg.* **conseilest** Tr 2.1528; *3 pr. sg.* **conseileth** VII.1703; *pr. pl.* **conseille** VII.1026; **counseyle** Rom B 3315; *imp. sg.* **counsaile** ABC 155; *pt. sg.* **conseilled** VII.1049, **counseyled** Mars 67, **conseiled** X.125; *pt. pl.* **conseilled** VII.1350, **conseilleden** VII.1351; *pp.* **conseilled** VII.1082, **consyled** Bo 3.pr5.65; *vbl. n.* **conseillyng** III.67, VII.1002, **conseilynge** X.1033; *pl.* **conseillynges** VII.1163.

conseyt(e) *see* **conceit(e).**

consente(n) *v.* (1) consent, agree Tr 1.413, IV.803; **c. with** be consonant or consistent with VII.1386; **c. to** submit to, acquiesce in IV.537, VII.1382, X.498, Tr 2.1444; *(reflx.)* submit Tr 1.936; *3 pr. sg.* **consenteth** consents X.543; *pr. pl.* **consente(n)** X.902, LGW 2645; *pt. sg.* **consented** VII.1050; *pt. pl.* **consenteden** VII.1362; *vbl. n.* **consentynge** X.293; *pl.* **consentynges** X.293.

considere(n), considre *v.* (1) observe Astr 2.44.23; (2) think (about) VII.1154, Tr 4.1696; (3) take into account V.675, VIII.1388, Astr 2.31.1; realize VII.1508; **considered** *(pp.)* considering, taking into account VII.1849, Tr 2.1290; (4) take an interest I.2233, IV.78; *2 pr. sg.* **considerest** Bo 4.pr1.23; *3 pr. sg.* **considereth** VII.1497; *pr. pl.* **consideren** VII.1496; *imp. sg.* **consider(e)** I.2233, Astr 2.32.1; *imp. pl.* **considereth** VIII.1388; *pt. sg.* **considered** IV.78; *prp.* **considerynge** V.675, **considrynge** Wom Nobl 18; *pp.* **considered** (with **hath**) considered I.1763; (with **is**) observed V.1283, Astr 1.6.11, **considred** Astr 1.17.32.

constable *n.* (1) chief steward II.716; (2) warden of a royal castle II.512, II.575.

constellacioun, constellacion *n.* configuration of the heavenly bodies I.1088, IV.1969, Tr 4.745.

constreyne *v.* (1) (of persons) compel, force III.1071, IV.800; (of circumstances) constrain, impel VII.1570, Bo 3.pr11.84; (2) control, govern Bo 1.m5.4; Tr 3.1759; dominate, control V.764; *2 pr. sg.* **constreynest** Bo 1.m5.4; *3 pr. sg.* **constreyneth** restrains Tr 3.1759; *pr. pl.* **constreyne** Tr 2.1232; *pt. sg.* **constreyned(e)** LGW F 105, Bo 4.m6.48; *pt. subj. sg.* **constreynede** Bo 4.pr6.22; *prp.* (as *adj.*) **constreynynge** Bo 3.pr11.163; *pp.* **constreyned** III.1071, **constrayned** Rom C 7437; *vbl. n.* **constreynynge** Bo 5.pr4.98.

contenance, contenaunce, countenaunce, countynaunce *n.* (1) behavior, conduct IV.671, X.614, Rom B 4299, Rom C 7353; (2) self-control IV.1110; self-possession BD 613; (3) outward appearance L1916, I.4421; **maken god c.** appear composed II.320; **holden (for) c.** keep up appearances I.4421; **for c.** for show VIII.1264, For 34; (4) gesture, expression V.284, VII.8, Tr 2.1017; attitude, appearance Tr 3.979; *pl.* **contenaunces** expressions V.284, courtesies VII.8, **countenaunces** Rom A 1001.

contene, conteyne *v.* (1) have inside, contain Bo 2.pr7.37; comprise Bo 4.pr2.190; (2) consist of Astr 1.16.17; (3) take up, fill Tr 3.502; (4) bear, endure Rom B 2641, Rom B 4923; (5) *(reflx.)* behave Rom B 2248, Rom C 6805; *3 pr. sg.* **contienith** Bo 5.pr4.169, **contenith** Bo 5.pr4.169, **conteynith** Astr 1.16.17, **conteyneth** Astr 2.44.38; *pr. pl.* **contene** Bo 2.pr7.36, **contenen** Astr 1.9.2; *pt. sg.* **contenyde** held together Bo 3.pr12.37; *prp.* **contenyng** Astr 1.21.49; *pp.* **contened** Astr 2.39.16.

contrarie, contrary(e), contraire *n.* (1) opposite I.1667, I.3057, Bo 3.pr11.169, Pity 64; **in c. (of)** in opposition (to) Tr 1.418, VIII.1477; (2) hostile act VII.1280; difficulty X.720; **doon a c.** produce a conflict Rom B 4478; opponent I.1859, VII.3280; *pl.* **contraries** opposites VII.1017.

contrarie, contraire *adj.* (1) opposite, opposed Bo 4.pr3.60; (2) discordant X.342; (3) averse Rom B 4794, Rom B 5306; (4) harmful Rom B 2246; unfavorable VII.3069; (5) hostile LGW 1360.

contrarie(n) *v.* (1) oppose, resist IV.2319; (2) antagonize, offend V.705; (3) contradict III.1044, IV.1497, Bo 5.pr3.6; *pt. sg.* **contraried** III.1044, IV.1497.

contrarious(e), contrarius *adj.* (1) opposing Bo 2.m8.2; (2) different, contrary III.698; (3) unfavorable Bo 2.pr8.11; (4) hostile, rebellious III.780.

contre(e), cuntre(y), contrey *n.* (1) region I.216, III.1397; (2) nation, country I.2973, Rom B 5659, Rom C 5936; (3) countryside VI.933; *pl.* **contrees** I.2973, **cuntrees** Bo 1.pr5.19.

contrefete *see* countrefete.

conveyen, convoye, convay *v.* (1) escort, accompany I.2737, LGW 2305; (2) guide Rom B 2428; (3) communicate IV.55; *3 pr. sg.* **conveyeth** LGW 2305; *pr. pl.* **convoye** Rom B 2916; *pt. sg.* **conveyed** I.2737.

convenyent *adj.* (1) suitable, convenient Astr 2.4.4; (2) adapted Bo 3.pr11.107; (3) socially proper X.421; (4) morally proper Bo 1.pr4.262; (5) *pl.* **in proporcioneles convenientz** in planetary tables V.1278 (see note).

converte *v.* (1) (with **from**) turn aside VI.212; Tr 1.1004; change, convert Tr 1.308, Tr 1.999, Tr 2.903; (2) convert to a religious faith II.574, VIII.414; *3 pr. sg.* **converteth** II.574; *pr. pl.* **converten** Bo 3.pr12.93; *pt. sg.* **converted** Tr 1.999; *prp.* **convertynge unto** turning to I.3037; *pp.* **converted** VIII.414.

convoye *see* conveyen.

cope *n.* (1) cloak I.260, Tr 3.724, Rom A 408; (2) canopy, covering LGW 1527.

coper *n.* copper VIII.829, VIII.1292, HF 1487.

coppe, coupe, cuppe *n.* cup I.134, V.942, LGW 1122; *pl.* **coppes** I.2949.

corage, courage *n.* (1) heart (as the source of emotions), feelings I.22, IV.787, V.22, Tr 1.564; (2) inclination, desire IV.1254; sexual desire IV.907; determination, mood Tr 5.825; spiritual state X.585; (3) courage, valor II.939, X.689; bold act IV.1513; *pl.* **corages** I.11.

corageus, corageous, corajous *adj.* (1) brave VII.2337, Tr 5.800; (2) eager Rom B 4416; ardent X.585.

corde *n.* (1) rope, cord I.3569, LGW 2485; instrument

of torture I.1746; (2) string (on a musical instrument) Tr 5.443; *pl.* **cordes** ropes VIII.8.

corn, coorn *n.* (1) kernel VI.863, VII.3175; (2) best part, heart (of a story) LGW G 312, 529; *pl.* **cornes** grain crops VII.2035; seeds of grain HF 698; (3) (collective *n.*) grain I.562, I.3939, Bo 1.pr4.75.

(y)coroned, (y)corouned, crouned *pp.* (1) crowned VII.2365, LGW F 230; garlanded LGW F 219; (2) (as *adj.*) crowned I.161; sovereign, consummate V.526.

coroun(e), corone, croun(e) *n.* (1) crown IV.1118, BD 980; garland I.2290, IV.381, VIII.221; (2) top of the head I.4099, VII.309; (3) reward Bo 4.pr3.11, VIII.388; finest example Tr 5.547; *pl.* **corones** VIII.221, **corounes** HF 1317, **crounes** LGW 2614.

corps *n.* corpse I.2819, III.768, LGW 676.

correccioun *n.* (1) correction X.60; **under c.** subject to correction X.56, Tr 3.1332; (2) punishment VI.404; **doon c.** punish III.1320; fine III.1617; (3) jurisdiction III.1329.

correct(e) *v.* (1) correct V.1274, Adam 6; rectify, remedy VIII.999; (3) set right by rebuke or punishment III.661, X.673, Rom C 7230; direct, admonish VIII.162; *3 pr. sg.* **correcteth** VII.1473; *pp.* **corrected** III.181.

corrumpen *v.* (1) destroy, ruin Bo 3.pr11.141; corrupt (morally) X.819, (2) decay Bo 3.pr11.54; *3 pr. sg.* **corrumpeth** becomes corrupt LGW 2237; *pr. subj. sg.* **corrumpe** Bo 4.pr7.96; *pt. sg.* **corrumped** X.819; *pp.* **icorrumped** Bo 5.pr2.25; *vbl. n.* **corrumpynge** decay Bo 3.pr12.75.

corrupteth *3 pr. sg.* decays I.2746; *pp.* **corrupt(e)** corrupted II.519, VI.504; infectious IV.2252; decayed X.333.

cors *n.* (1) body I.3429, IX.67; corpse VI.665; (2) (as a semi-pronoun in asseverations) **his (thy) c.** him VII.908, you V.304.

corsednesse, cursednesse, cursednesse *n.* (1) sinfulness, wickedness VII.631, VIII.1301, Bo 3.pr10.95, Tr 4.994; (2) perversity, malice IV.1239.

corsen, curse(n) *v.* curse III.1624, X.621, Rom B 2719; excommunicate I.486; *3 pr. sg.* **curseth** IV.902, **corseth** Tr 5.207; *pr. pl.* **curse(n)** IV.898, **corse** Tr 3.1701; *pr. subj. sg.* **corse** IV.1308; *pt. pl.* **cursed** VII.1504; *pp.* **cursed** I.933, (as *adj.*) **cursed(e)** II.80, X.580, **corsed** Tr 5.1849; *vbl. n.* **cursyng(e)** I.660, III.1587; *pl.* **cursynges** X.206.

corteisly *see* curteisly.

corupcioun, corrupcioun, corrupcion *n.* (1) decayed matter X.535, X.942, PF 614, Bo 3.pr4.14; dissolution Bo 3.pr11.79; (2) cause of corruption X.899.

(y)corve(n) *see* kerve(n).

cosyn *n.* blood relative, kinsman I.1093, I.1131, Rom B 3968; closely related I.742, IX.210; *pl.* **cosyns** X.836, **cosynes** Bo 3.pr12.206.

cosynage *n.* kinship VII.139, VII.409.

costage *n.* expense, expenditure III.249, IV.1126; **doon c.** spend money VII.45; *pl.* **costages** VII.1336.

coste, coost *n.* (1) region, coast III.922; (2) a division or quarter of the heavens Astr 2.46.27; *pl.* **costes** Astr 1.19.8.

cost(e) *n.* cost, expense I.192, Tr 3.522; expenditures V.1557.

cote, coote *n.* (1) tunic, coat I.103, I.328, IV.913 Rom A 459; *pl.* **cotes** HF 1332.

couche(n), kouche *v.* (1) *(intr.)* lie down IV.1206; (2)

(tr.) lay something down, put down I.2933, I.3211, Rom C 6903; arrange VIII.1182; embroider I.2161; *pt. sg.* **couched(e)** arranged VIII.1179, PF 216; *pp.* **couched** arranged VIII.1182; *vbl. n.* **kouching** setting down Astr 2.29.26.

coude, koude, (y)koud *see* **kunne.**

counceilein *see* **conseille(n).**

counsaile *see* **conseille(n).**

counsel(l) *see* **conseil.**

counte *v.* (1) count Rom B 2746; (2) value at, consider I.4056, I.4192, Tr 5.363; *pt. sg.* **counted** BD 718.

countenance *see* **contenance.**

countour, contour *n.* (1) accountant I.359, BD 435; (2) counting house VII.213; **c.-hous** counting house VII.77; *pl.* **countours** auditors Rom C 6812.

countrefete, contrefete *v.* (1) imitate I.139, VI.13, BD 1241; (2) pretend, pass oneself off as Tr 5.1578; simulate, make a pretense VI.51, Tr 2.1532, LGW 1376; forge (a document) II.746, IV.743; *3 pr. sg.* **countrefeteth** HF 1213; *pt. sg.* **countrefeted** IV.2121; *pp.* **countrefeted** copied II.746; (as *adj.*) false, affected VI.51, BD 869.

coupe *see* **coppe.**

courser *n.* war horse, charger I.1513, I.1704, Tr 5.85; *pl.* **courseres** I.2501, **coursers** LGW 1195.

couthe, kouthe, kowthe *see* **kunne.**

coveite(n) *v.* (1) covet, desire III.1187; crave III.1189, X.459, Bo 2.pr6.14; lust for sexually III.266, X.844, LGW 1755; *2 pr. sg.* **coveytest** Bo 3.pr8.11; *3 pr. sg.* **coveyteth** Tr 4.1339; *pt. pl.* **coveyteden** Bo 2.pr6.14; *pp.* **coveyted** Bo 4.pr2.146; *vbl. n.* **coveytynge** desire LGW 1756.

coveitise, covetise *n.* (1) covetousness, greed VIII.1977, X.336, X.744; (2) strong desire or craving X.853.

coveitous *adj.* covetous, greedy VII.1131, VII.1838; (as *n.*) a covetous person Tr 3.1373.

covenable *adj.* suitable, appropriate VII.1592, X.80, Tr 2.1137.

covenably *adv.* suitably, fittingly VII.1233, Bo 4.pr6.339.

covenaunt, covenant *n.* (1) agreement LGW 2139; contract I.600; promise V.1587, Rom B 3476; (2) conditional provision Bo 3.m12.49; *pl.* **covenantz** I.1924.

covent *n.* organized group of friars or monks III.1863, VII.677, VIII.1007, Rom B 4904.

coverchief, coverchef, converechief *n.* (1) kerchief, headscarf III.510, Rom C 7367; (2) piece of cloth PF 272; *pl.* **coverchiefs** I.453.

covere(n), kevere *v.* cover I.1957, X.551, Anel 156, Tr 1.917; conceal Tr 3.31; recover LGW 762; *3 pr. sg.* **covereth** Bo 2.pr1.60; *pr. pl.* **covere** X.422; *pt. sg.* **covered** VII.2782; *pp.* **(y)covered** I.354, I.3212, **coverid** Bo 4.m3.10, **covred** Bo 1.m7.1, **kevered** HF 275, **kovered** Rom B 3020.

coverture *n.* (1) bedclothes X.198; (2) covering Bo 4.m2.1; concealment Rom A 1588, Rom B 2172; *pl.* **covertures** X.198.

craft *n.* (1) cleverness VIII.619, HF 1100; skill, art I.401, HF 1213, PF 1, Tr 3.1634; **don c.** try one's skill Rom B 1781; (2) cunning, guile III.1468, VI.84, LGW 2528; trick Tr 1.747; (3) trade, occupation I.692, VII.1270; trade guild I.4366; *pl.* **craftes** I.2409.

crafty *adj.* (1) skillful, ingenious VIII.1290, BD 662; artful BD 319; subtle VIII.1253; (2) deceitful VIII.655; (3) skilled in a craft I.1897; *comp.* **craftier** BD 662.

craftyly, craftely *adv.* skillfully II.48, VIII.903; artfully Tr 2.1026.

creaunce *v.* borrow money, obtain credit VII.289; *3 pr. sg.* **creaunceth** VII.303; *pp.* **creanced** VII.366.

creat *pp.* created VII.1103, X.218.

crepe *v.* (1) creep, move slowly HF 2086, Tr 5.1214; (2) have one's flesh crawl Rom B 2558; *3 pr. sg.* **crepeth** VI.565; *pr. pl.* **crepyn** Bo 5.m5.3; *pt. sg.* **creep** I.4226, **crepte** I.4193; *pt. pl.* **crepte(n)** III.1698, VII.2616; *prp.* **crepynge** Bo 2.pr6.42; *pp.* **cropen** I.4259, **crept** Bo 1.pr6.35.

crie(n) *v.* (1) shout, cry out I.636, 646, IX.301; announce I.2731, V.46, LGW 2332; (2) **c. on, upon** complain about, blame V.650, 1496, Tr 2.436; (3) **c. after** beg for I.2699, III.518, Tr 4.753; **c. upon (to)** implore I.4006, II.850, Anel 7; **c. out on** complain to VII.3043; (4) *(tr.)* beg for I.3288, II.1111, Tr 2.1076; (5) lament I.1221, II.919; weep VII.979, Tr 1.806; *3 pr. sg.* **crieth** I.1221; *pr. pl.* **crye(n)** I.2835, HF 1313; *imp. sg.* **crye** Tr 1.753; *1 & 3 pt. sg.* **cride** I.1078, **cried(e)** VII.2531, Tr 5.205; *2 pt. sg.* (with *pro.*) **cridestow** I.1083; *pt. pl.* **cride(n)** I.949, I.2562; **criede(n)** I.1756, Bo 4.m12.45; *prp.* **criyng(e)** I.2699, HF 170; **criand** Rom B 3138; *pp.* **cryd** IV.563, **cried** I.2344; *vbl. n.* **criyng(e)** I.906, I.1100; *pl.* **cryinges** Bo 2.pr2.67.

croys, croce, cros(se) *n.* cross I.699, III.484, Astr 1.5.4, Astr 1.16.12.

croked, crokid, crooked *pp.* (1) crooked, not straight VI.761, Rom A 987; (2) crippled II.560, Rom A 202; (3) wrong, evil ABC 70, Truth 8.

crop(e) *n.* (1) bud or shoot I.7, Bo 3.m2.33; foliage, top I.1532, BD 424, Rom A 1396; (2) **c. and more (roote)** the totality, perfection Tr 2.348, Tr 5.25, Tr 5.1245; *pl.* **croppes** BD 424.

cropen *see* **crepe.**

crosselet *n.* crucible VIII.1147, VIII.1153; *pl.* **crosletz** VIII.793.

croude, crowde *v.* (1) push, shove HF 2095; (2) push, drive II.801; *2 pr. sg.* **crowdest** II.296; *vbl. n.* **crowdyng** shoving HF 1359; driving, impelling II.299.

croun(e) *see* **coroun(e).**

crouned *see* **(y)coroned.**

crueel, cruel(e), cruell, crewel, crwel, cruwel *adj.* harsh, cruel, savage I.1303, HF 323, Bo 4.m7.39, Tr 1.9, Tr 1.839, Tr 4.1697, Rom B 2212.

cruelich, cruelly, crwely *adv.* cruelly VII.2329, Tr 4.1304, Tr 5.1756.

cuntre(y) *see* **contre(e).**

cuppe *see* **coppe.**

curacioun, curacion *n.* cure VII.1273, Tr 1.791.

curat, curaat *n.* curate I.219, III.2095; *pl.* **curates** X.791, **curatz** III.1816.

cure *n.* (1) attention VI.557; **do (take) (no) c.** pay (no) attention to I.303, Tr 2.284, Rom B 4770; **honest c.** regard for decency VI.557; (2) effort, diligence Tr 5.1539; **do (no) c.** take (no) pains I.1007, III.1074; **bisy c.** active diligence I.2853; (3) duty, responsibility IV.82; **have in c.** have in one's power II.230, VI.22, LGW 1176; jurisdiction III.1333; care, charge HF 464; (4) spiritual keeping Rom C 6562; (5) medicinal treatment V.1114, VII.1270; cure PF 128, Tr 1.469; *(fig.)* remedy, cure VIII.37, Tr 5.49; **out of all c.** beyond remedy Tr 5.713.

curious(e), curius *adj.* (1) (persons) skillful, expert I.577; diligent VII.243, Rom A 1052, Rom C 6578; (2) (things) skillfully made, intricate I.196; elaborate II.402; (3) (writing) arcane, difficult Astr Pro 45; occult arts V.1120; (4) painstaking IV.1577, VII.225.

curs *n.* curse, excommunication I.655, I.661, VI.946; **Cristes c.** damnation III.1347; *pl.* **curses** VIII.1405.

cursednesse, cursydnesse *see* **corsednes.**

curteis *adj.* (1) courtly, refined, courteous I.250, IV.1815; (2) generous, merciful X.246, Rom B 4036; (3) deferential I.99.

curteisie, curtesye *n.* courtliness, good manners, courtesy as a moral ideal I.46, I.132, II.166, Tr 2.1486, Rom A 957; act of good manners VI.739; **of (for) (your) c.** if you please I.725, III.1669.

curteisly, curtaysly, corteisly *adv.* politely III.1771, Ros 13; discreetly I.3997.

custume, custom(e) *n.* (1) custom III.682; (2) duty, tax X.567, X.752; *pl.* **customes** Bo 1.pr6.49.

cut *n.* lot I.845, VI.795; **draw c.** draw lots I.835, VI.793.

D

day(e) *n.* (1) day I.91, Mars 139; the light part of the day I.1040, I.1481, I.3438; **artificial d.** sunrise to sunset Astr 2.9.3; **by d.** in daylight V.297; **d. natureel** twenty-four-hour day V.116; **d. vulgar** from daybreak to dark Astr 2.9 Rubric; (2) period of time, term I.2998; lifetime IV.1136, V.1447; (3) time agreed for a meeting I.2095, IV.1998; (4) **al d.** every day, always IV.1155; **by d.** in daylight V.297; **d. by (be) d.** daily I.1407, LGW 2268; **fro d. to d.** daily I.3371, Tr 3.291; **on, upon a d.** on a certain day I.19, I.1414, VI.117; **upon a d.** in one day I.703; **ofte a d.** often Tr 5.689; **never a d.** never BD 1255; **tomorwe d.** tomorrow morning I.3784; *gen.* **dayes** I.1629; *pl.* **dayes** I.2736, **dawes** V.1180.

dayesye, daysey(e) *n.* daisy I.332, LGW F 224, LGW G 55; *pl.* **daysyes** LGW F 43.

dalf *see* **delve.**

daliaunce, daliance *n.* (1) sociable conversation, sociability III.565, III.1406, Rom B 2850; **do d.** be friendly, sociable VII.704, Ros 8; **have d.** converse LGW F 356; (2) flirting III.565, VI.66; *pl.* **daliaunces** flirtations VI.66.

damage *n.* (1) injury, harm VII.1012, X.419; (2) loss LGW 598; *pl.* **damages** VII.1389.

dame *n.* (1) (as a form of address) a woman of rank, lady I.3956, III.296; mistress of the household III.311, III.1797, VII.356; (2) dam I.3260; mother III.576, IX.317; *gen.* **dames** mother's III.583.

damysell, damoysele *n.* (1) young, usually unmarried gentlewoman VII.2870, Rom A 1240; (2) handmaiden Bo 2.pr1.45; *pl.* **damoysels** Rom A 1622.

dampnable *adj.* damnable, worthy of damnation VI.472, VII.2605, X.679.

dampnably, dampnablely *adv.* damnably VII.1826, X.604.

dampnacioun *n.* damnation III.1067, VI.500, ABC 23.

dampne *v.* damn, condemn LGW F 401, For 49; *3 pr. sg.* **dampneth** X.571; *pt. sg.* **dampned** III.2037; *pp.* **(y)dampned** I.1175, LGW 2030, **damned** II.843; *vbl. n.* **dampnyng** damnation Rom C 6643.

dan *see* **daun.**

dar, darest, darst, darstou *see* **durre.**

dar *var.* of *v.* **thar** need Bo 2.pr3.90, Rom B 3604.

dart(e) *n.* (1) spear Tr 4.771, LGW 2245; (2) (Love's) arrow I.1564, Tr 4.472; *pl.* **dartes** Tr 2.313.

daun, dan *n.* sir, master (as a title of respect) I.1379, I.2673, Tr 1.70.

daunce *n.* (1) dance III.993, V.277; dancing Anel 214; procession of dancers Tr 1.517; (2) *(pl.)* songs Rom A 508; (3) **the old d.** tricks of the trade, game of love I.476, VI.79, Tr 3.695; *pl.* **daunces** I.1931.

daunce(n) *v.* dance I.96, I.2202, BD 848; *3 pr. sg.* **daunceth** IV.1728; *pr. pl.* **daunce(n)** I.2486, V.272; *pt. sg.* **daunced** I.4380; *pt. pl.* **daunsedyn** PF 232; *prp.* **daunsynge** I.2201.

daunger(e), danger *n.* (1) domination, power Anel 186, Rom A 1470; (2) opposition, resistance Rom B 2034, Rom B 2318; **with d.** reluctantly III.521; **withouten d.** without objection, with no holding back, freely I.1849; disdain, standoffishness (of a lady to a lover) Tr 2.384, Tr 3.1321; (personified) Tr 2.1376, Rom B 3130 (see note), Rom B 3509; (3) *pl.* **daungers** perils, dangers I.402.

daungerous, dangerous *adj.* (1) domineering, disdainful I.517, Rom A 1482; (2) disdainful, standoffish III.514; unaccommodating, aloof Rom A 591, Rom B 2312; fastidious, hard to please VII.939, Rom B 2824; (3) niggardly, grudging III.151, III.1427.

daunte(n) *v.* (1) defeat Bo 4.m7.29; dominate Tr 4.1589, Rom A 880; (2) subdue, restrain VII.2609, X.270, Tr 2.399, Rom B 3300; *2 pr. sg.* **dauntest** PF 114; *3 pr. sg.* **daunteth** Tr 2.399; *imp. sg.* **daunte** control Truth 13; *pt. sg.* **daunted** VII.2609, **dawntide** Bo 4.m7.29; *prp.* **dauntyng** taming (by threats) Rom B 4032; *pp.* **daunted** frightened III.463.

dawe *v.* dawn IV.1842; *3 pr. sg.* **daweth** I.1676; *pr. subj. sg.* **dawe** I.4249; *pt. subj. sg.* **dawed** Rom B 2633; *pp.* **dawed** III.353; *vbl. n.* **dawyng** Tr 3.1466.

dawenyng(e) *n.* dawn LGW 1188; **in the d.** at dawn I.4234, BD 292.

de- *see also* **di-.**

debat, debaat *n.* (1) quarrel, dispute III.822, III.1288; **at d.** in conflict I.3230; mental conflict BD 1192, Rom B 4902; (2) conflict, warfare I.1754, II.130.

debate *v.* dispute, argue VI.412, Form Age 51; fight VII.868; *prp.* **debatyng** disputing Bo 1.pr3.38.

debonaire, debonere *adj.* (1) gracious, of good disposition BD 860; courteous LGW F 276; meek, submissive I.2282, Tr 1.214; gentle Bo 1.m5.22; (2) (as *n.*) gracious person BD 624, ABC 6.

debonairely, debonairly, debonerly *adv.* courteously, modestly BD 518, graciously VII.1064, X.315; meekly X.660, Anel 127, Tr 2.1259; tamely Bo 4.m3.15.

debonairete(e), debonairte(e) *n.* graciousness VII.1621, VII.1820, Lady 102; meekness X.1054.

deceite *n.* deceit, trickery III.401, VI.592; *pl.* **deceites** X.440, **desceytes** illusions Bo 2.pr1.15.

deceyvable, desceyvable, dissevable *adj.* deceitful, deceptive IV.2058, PF 65; false, unfaithful Bo 3.pr6.1, Bo 3.m10.3.

deceyve(n), desceyve, disceyve(n) *v.* deceive III.1467, IV.2423, X.608, Tr 2.285; *2 pr. sg.* deceyvest IV.2064; (with *pro.*) disseyvistow Bo 3.pr12.155; *3 pr. sg.* deceyveth VII.1705, desceyveth Bo 2.pr8.18; *pr. pl.* decyve(n) LGW 753, Tr 2.285; *pr. subj. sg.* desceyve Bo 3.pr10.12; *pt. sg.* desseyved Bo 2.pr1.56; *2 pt. sg.* desceyvedest Bo 2.pr3.65; *pt. pl.* desseyvede Bo 2.m5.4; *prp.* desceyvynge Bo 4.m2.14; *pp.* deceyved IV.1356, desceyved Bo 1.pr2.21, desseyved Bo 1.pr6.33, disseyvid Bo 3.m11.2; disceyved Rom B 2046; *vbl. n.* disseyvyng deceit Rom A 1590.

declaracioun *n.* (1) explanation Astr 2.2.12; (2) manifestation, evidence X.595; *pl.* declaracions corollaries Bo 3.pr10.135.

declare(n) *v.* (1) tell, declare I.2536, VII.482; **d. his confessioun** confess X.1018; (2) explain, make clear I.3002, II.572, Tr 2.1680; elucidate X.391; (3) reveal, show, make known I.2356, VIII.719; **oure wittes to d.** reveal our thoughts; *3 pr. sg.* declarith Astr 1.21.82; *pp.* declared II.206; *vbl. n.* declarynge explanation VII.1982; *pl.* declarynges corollaries Bo 3.pr10.153.

declinacioun, declinacion *n.* angular distance of a heavenly body from the celestial equator Astr 1.17.6; *pl.* declinaciouns Astr Pro 80.

declineth *3 pr. sg.* turns aside (from), declines Bo 4.pr6.177, Astr 2.19.11; *pr. pl.* declynen Bo 4.pr7.45, Astr 2.17.43.

decree *n.* (1) decretal, ecclesiastical law I.640, I.1167; judgment X.17; **in his d.** in his judgment VII.2477; (2) laws collectively, the body of canon law X.931; *pl.* decretz Bo 1.pr4.155.

ded(e), deed *adj.* dead I.145, I.942; deadly, deathlike I.1578, I.3643, VI.209; (of sleep) deep Tr 2.924; **I nam but d.** I'm as good as dead III.1006.

dede, deede *n.* (1) action, deed I.742, I.1775, ABC 45; military action I.2636, Tr 4.624; the sexual act LGW 2324; (2) effect, result VII.1668; **in d.** in truth, indeed I.659; in actuality VII.2321, BD 132, PF 8; **with the d.** immediately VIII.157, Tr 3.1301; simultaneously III.70; *pl.* dedes I.1438, dedis III.1155.

dedest *see* don.

deedly, dedly *adj.* (1) mortal, deadly PF 128, LGW 869; (2) destructive of the soul X.956; (3) like death, deathly I.1082, LGW 869; lifeless BD 162; dying, about to die V.1040; (4) grievous Anel 258, Tr 4.871.

deedly, dedlich *adv.* (1) intensely VIII.476, BD 462, Tr 4.898; (2) deathlike, deadly II.822, Tr 5.536.

deef *adj.* deaf I.446, III.636, Tr 1.753; *pl.* deve VIII.286.

deface *v.* (1) deface, spoil Tr 4.804; (2) obliterate IV.510, HF 1164; *pr. pl.* deface Tr 5.915; *pp.* defaced Tr 5.1335.

defame, diffame *n.* (bad) reputation, shame IV.730, VI.612; **for his d.** to cause him dishonor VII.2548.

defame, diffame *v.* (1) disgrace, bring dishonor on (someone) X.645, Tr 4.565; (2) accuse, slander I.3147, VI.415, HF 1581; *pr. pl.* defamen Tr 2.860; *pp.* defamed VI.415.

defaute *n.* (1) lack, absence BD 5; **d. agayn** lack of X.186; (2) fault, defect VIII.954; error Tr 5.1796; loss (of scent in hunting) BD 384 (see note); (3) misdeed, sin VI.370, X.1030; wickedness VII.2528; (4) fault, responsibility for failure Bo 2.pr7.55; *pl.* defautes faults III.1810; sins X.165.

defenced *pp.* protected, hedged around Rom B 4310.

defende(n), deffende(n) *v.* (1) prohibit, forbid VI.590, Tr 2.1733; (2) restrain VIII.1470; (3) avoid Rom B 4086; (4) defend II.933, Tr 1.511; beat off VII.1532; (5) protect VII.1441; (6) speak in support of X.584, Bo 1.pr4.218, Bo 2.pr3.5; *3 pr. sg.* deffendeth forbids X.651, defendeth defends Tr 1.603; *pr. pl.* defenden forbid VII.1221; *pr. subj.* defende forbid Tr 4.1647 *(sg.)*, defend Rom C 7038 *(pl.)*; *imp. sg.* defende ABC 95; *pt. sg.* defended forbad III.60; *pt. pl.* defendeden Bo 1.pr4.118; *prp.* defendyng protecting Rom B 5800; *pp.* deffended VII.988, defended protected VII.1336.

defense, deffense, defence, diffence, diffense *n.* (1) prohibition Tr 3.138; hindrance Rom A 1142; (2) defense VII.1533, LGW 606; means of defense III.467, VII.1161; **at d.** on guard, ready for battle IV.1195; **of no d.** offering no protection PF 273; (3) legal redress Bo 1.pr4.242; remedy Tr 4.287; **withouten any d.** without remedy, surely LGW F 279.

defye, diffye *1 pr. sg.* (1) repudiate, renounce I.1604, IV.1310; despise, scorn III.1928; *pr. pl.* defye LGW F 138, deffye LGW G 126; (2) defy (the power of) VII.3171, For 8; *imp. sg.* deffie reject IV.1310.

defoule(n) *v.* (1) trample on X.191; (2) injure, torment X.273; oppress Rom C 6000; disfigure Bo 4.m7.43; (3) pollute, defile V.1418, X.878; *3 pr. sg.* defouleth Bo 3.m2.28; *pr. pl.* defoulen X.882; *pp.* defouled defiled Bo 1.pr4.252, defowled Bo 4.m7.43.

degre(e) *n.* (1) step, stairway Rom A 485; (2) status, social rank I.1434, LGW 1506, Rom A 883; **after (at, in) (one's) d.** according to one's rank I.2192, I.2856; (3) situation, condition I.3040, IV.1494, IX.146; **ech in his d.** each in turn IV.263; **in my d.** insofar as I can IV.969; (4) manner, way PF 646; **in som (swich) d.** in some way, to some extent I.2844, III.1124; **at alle d.** in every way I.3724; **in ech d.** in all respects III.404; **in no d.** in no way, not at all V.198, VII.171, Tr 1.437; (5) *(astro.)* degree Astr 1.7.10; *pl.* degrees tiers, rows of seats I.1890, degres Astr 1.16.7.

deye(n), dye(n) *v.* die I.1109, I.2761, I.573, Tr 4.1081; *3 pr. sg.* deyth III.2039; *pr. pl.* deie Bo 3.pr11.108; *2 pt. sg.* deidest Tr 3.263; *3 pt. sg.* deyde X.642, dyed I.2843; *pt. pl.* deyde(n) III.1901, V.1429; *pt. subj. sg.* deyede PF 587, deyde I.3427, dyde III.965; *pt. subj. pl.* deyden III.1901; *prp.* deynge BD 588; *pp.* deyd LGW 1677 deied Rom C 6237; *vbl. n.* deyinge death Tr 1.572, diyng VII.2716.

deyne, deigne *v.* (1) condescend Anel 231, Tr 3.1811; grant, permit Tr 3.139, Tr 3.1435; (2) *(impers.)* **hym d. (nat) (did not)** seem proper to him, he deigned (disdained) VII.2134, LGW G 381; *2 pr. sg.* deynest Tr 3.1435; *3 pr. sg.* deyneth Anel 181; *pt. sg.* deigned VII.2134, deyned Mars 39; *pp.* deyned Tr 3.1811.

deynte(e) *n.* (1) pleasure, delight Anel 143, LGW F 206; **have d.** to take pleasure in, be eager II.139, V.681; (2) esteem Rom B 2677; **holde d. (of)** esteem V.70, X.477, consider it an honor Tr 2.164; **tolde no d.** did not value III.208; (3) fine food or drink, delicacy I.346, II.419; *pl.* deyntees delicacies II.419.

deynte(e) *adj.* (1) excellent I.168; pleasing LGW 920; (2) delicious Rom C 7042.

deys, dees *n.* dais, platform I.370, I.2200, HF 1360.

deite(e) *n.* deity, godhead VIII.1469, IX.101, Tr 3.1017; godly dominion V.1047.

del, deel(l), dell *n.* (1) bit, part, share BD 1001, Tr 2.1214; **ech a d.** every bit Tr 3.694; **every d.** all I.2091; completely I.1825; **never a (no) d.** not a bit III.561, Tr 1.1089; (fraction) **an hondred thousand d.** one hundred thousandth IX.137; (in comparisons) times HF 1495, Rom A 1074; (2) share, portion BD 1001; (3) **a (full) greet d.** (very) many I.415, Rom A 1356.

dele, deele(n) *v.* (1) (with **with**) deal with, have to do with I.247, Tr 2.706, Rom C 6979; (2) have sexual intercourse with X.908; *2 pr. sg.* **delest** Rom B 3265; *3 pr. sg.* **deles** portions out Rom B 5419; *pr. subj. sg.* **dele** Rom B 2537; *pt. sg.* **delte** VIII.1074; *pt. pl.* **deled** LGW 1517; *pp.* **deled** portioned out, divided III.2249.

deliberacioun, deliberacion *n.* deliberation, consideration, discussion VI.139, VII.1029, Tr 3.519.

delicaat, delicat *adj.* (1) delightful, pleasing IV.682; splendid X.432; choice X.828; (2) fond of luxury, self-indulgent VII.2471, X.835; (3) fastidious X.688.

delices *n. pl.* (1) self-indulgence Bo 2.pr4.70; (2) pleasures, luxuries X.633; delights VII.1411; (as *sg.*) beloved person Bo 2.pr3.67.

deliciously *adv.* delightfully V.79; voluptuously Rom C 6729; sumptuously X.377.

delit *n.* (1) pleasure, delight I.335, III.418, HF 309; **d. of foles** a senseless pleasure Tr 1.762; sexual intercourse VI.159; **foul d.** sexual intercourse V.1396; (2) **bi, with d.** delightfully VI.545, Rom A 874; *pl.* **delites** pleasures X.298.

delitable *adj.* delightful, sensuously pleasing IV.62, IV.199, LGW F 321; *pl.* **delitables** V.899.

delite(n) *v.* (1) *(intr.)* be delighted, enjoy (often *reflx.* with **in**) VII.2470, X.601; (2) *(tr.)* please, give pleasure PF 27, Bo 2.pr5.56; *3 pr. sg.* **deliteth** Tr 3.1652; *pr. pl.* **delite(n)** Tr 4.1433, Tr 2.256; *pt.* **delited** III.2044 *(sg.)*, Tr 4.1435 *(pl.)*; *prp.* **delitynge** IV.997.

delivere(n), delyvren *v.* (1) save X.586; **d. of (fro)** save from II.518, III.1724; (2) release, set free I.1769, II.941, Bo 3.m1.2; **d. of** be rid of, freed from Tr 3.223, Tr 3.1012, Rom C 6674; (3) **was d. of** gave birth to II.750; *3 pr. sg.* **delivereth** X.308; *pr. pl.* **delivere(n)** III.1724, Bo 1.pr1.59; *pr. subj. sg.* **delyvere** Tr 5.958; *imp. sg.* **delyvere** Tr 4.515; *imp. pl.* **delivereth** III.1729; *pt.* **delivered** VII.1100; *pp.* **delivered** II.750, **delivred** Bo 4.pr4.130.

delyverly, deliverliche *adv.* nimbly VII.3416; deftly Tr 2.1088; quickly Rom B 4022.

dell *see* **del.**

delte *see* **dele.**

delve *v.* dig I.536, V.638; *pt. sg.* **dalf** Bo 2.m5.33; *pt. subj. sg.* **dulve** Bo 5.pr1.77; *pp.* **dolven** buried Rom B 4070.

demande, demaunde *n.* (1) question VIII.430, VIII.1451; **that is no d.** there is no question about it Tr 4.1295; (2) request, demand Rom B 2062; *pl.* **demandes** requests, stipulations IV.348, **demaundes** Bo 1.pr6.2.

deme(n), deeme(n) *v.* (1) make a judgment, render a verdict VI.199, VII.1855; (2) condemn, sentence III.2024, VI.271; (3) judge PF 166; (4) suggest VII.449; (5) form a judgment or opinion V.1498, VII.1125, VII.1402; determine I.3194; (6) think V.44; suppose V.1486, X.1071, Tr 1.799, Tr 2.461; expect VII.1188; consider I.1881, I.3161, Tr 1.347; (7) express an opinion, argue V.221, V.261; (8) perceive V.563; *2 pr. sg.* **demest** HF 596, (with *pro.*) **demestow** Bo 1.pr6.77; *3 pr. sg.* **demeth** Rom C 7543; *pr. pl.* **demeth** V.221, **demen** V.224; *pr. subj. sg.* **deme** IV.1976; *imp. pl.* **demeth** I.1353; *pt. sg.* **demed** V.563; *pt. pl.* **demed(e)** V.502, LGW 1244; *pp.* **demed** VI.271, **demyd** Bo 3.pr10.211, **deemed** VII.1138; *vbl. n.* **demynge** judging Bo 5.pr4.208.

demonstracioun, demonstracion *n.* logical proof HF 727; **make a d.** prove III.2224; *pl.* **demonstracyons** Bo 2.pr4.169.

dep(e), deep *adj.* (1) deep I.3031, V.155, Rom B 4152; (as *n.*) depth Bo 3.m11.37; (2) profound VII.1406, Tr 2.151; *comp.* **deppere** Bo 2.pr3.12.

departe(n) *v.* (1) *(tr.)* separate, part I.1134, II.1158, Anel 285; (2) divide VI.812, X.356, X.426; share III.2133; (3) break up III.1049; differentiate Bo 2.pr8.39; (4) *(intr.)* depart, leave I.3060, III.1049, Tr 1.78; be removed from Bo 4.pr6.131; *3 pr. sg.* **departeth** X.3561; *pr. pl.* **departe(n)** I.3070, Tr 5.1073; *pr. subj. sg.* **departe** III.2133; *imp. sg.* **departe** differentiate Tr 3.404; *pt. sg.* **departed** Tr. 1.323; *pp.* **departed** I.1621; *vbl. n.* **departyng(e)** II.260; (5) *(intr.)* depart, leave I.3970, III.1049, Tr 2.531; be removed from Bo 4.pr6.130.

depe *n.* sea II.455; depth Bo 3.m7.37.

depe, deepe *adv.* (1) deep, deeply I.129, IV.1940, Tr 1.272, Rom A 4070; (2) deeply, thoroughly (of color) V.511; (3) profoundly Tr 4.589; (4) passionately, fervently I.1132; **ful d.** sincerely I.1132; *comp.* **depper** more deeply II.630, further Tr 2.485.

depeint, depeynted *pp.* (1) portrayed I.2027, I.2034, Rom A 478; (2) decorated Mars 86; (3) painted, stained VI.950, Tr 5.1599.

depnesse *n.* depth Bo 1.m2.2, Bo 3.m11.42.

depper *see* **depe** *adv.*

deppere *see* **dep(e)** *adj.*

der, deer *n. sg. and pl.* deer or animal(s) (the two meanings are not easily distinguishable) I.2150, Rom A 1453.

dere *n.* harm, injure Rom B 4336; *pp.* **dered** Rom B 2100.

dere, deere *adj.* (1) honored, dear I.1234, III.1823, VIII.272; **have (holde) d.** hold in high esteem I.1448, VII.2278; *comp.* **derre** I.1448; (2) (of things) excellent, fine V.341, Rom B 4178; (of abstractions) noble, excellent I.3588, II.237, III.827; (3) (of things) expensive III.522, VI.148; **deer ynough a leek (rysshe,** *etc.*) expensive enough at the cost of a leek, rush, *etc.* (worthless) Tr 4.684, Tr 3.1161; (4) beloved LGW 701; (5) pleasing Rom A 728, Rom C 6916.

dere, deere *adv.* (1) dearly, expensively VIII.1133, Mars 176; **(a)bye so (to, full) dere** gain at a (too) high price, pay for (too) dearly II.420, VI.100, Anel 255; (2) fervently LGW 1871; *comp.* **derre** more dearly, with greater loss Tr 1.136, at a higher price Tr 1.174.

dereworthe, derworth *adj.* precious Bo 2.pr1.75, Bo 2.pr6.28.

derk(e), dirke *adj.* (1) dark I.2082, I.3731, BD 155; (as *n.*) darkness BD 609; (2) not bright (in color), dull, dark Rom A 1009; (3) (morally) unclean X.1078, Bo 3.m5.9; (4) obscure, mysterious II.481, Bo 1.m7.19; (5) deceptive, malicious I.1995; (6) gloomy V.844, Tr

2.1307; *(astro.)* inauspicious Astr 2.6.18; *super.* **derk-est** III.1139.

derken, derkne, dirken *v.* (1) darken Bo 1.m3.8; (2) tarnish Bo 1.pr1.27; *(fig.)* Bo 1.pr4.250, Bo 4.pr3.52; *3 pr. sg.* **darketh** hides in the dark LGW 816; *pr. pl.* **derken** are dimmed Bo 5.pr2.37; *pp.* **derked** Bo 5.m3.14, (as *adj.*) **derked lookynge** blurred (mental) vision Bo 5.m3.14, **dirked** Bo 1.pr1.27, (as *adj.*) Bo 3.pr2.85.

derknes(se), dirknesse *n.* (1) darkness I.1451, Form Age 29, Rom B 2638; *(fig.)* obscurity Bo 1.pr1.25, Bo 1.m5.42; (2) blindness, ignorance Tr 3.826; (3) sinfulness, evil VIII.384, X.896; *pl.* **derknesses** Bo 1.m5.42, **dirknesses** Bo 1.m2.4.

dees *see* **deys**.

dees *see* **dys**.

desceytes *see* **deceite**.

desceyvedest, desceyveth, desceyvynge *see* **deceyve(n)**.

descende(n), discende *v.* (1) descend, come down IV.392, Tr 1.216, Rom A 1399; (2) decline, deteriorate I.3010, Bo 2.pr4.175; (3) derive, be descended from I.3984, Tr 5.1511; (4) proceed Tr 5.859, Tr 5.1511; **d. doun** to come to (in a speech) Tr 5.859; **d.** to come down to (specifics) VII.1355; *3 pr. sg.* **descendeth** Tr 2.1386, **descendith** Bo 3.pr10.28, **desscendeth** Bo 4.pr2.207; *pr. pl.* **descenden** Bo 2.pr5.2; *pt. sg.* **descended** Tr 5.1480, **descendede** Bo 2.pr2.62; *prp.* **descendynge** I.3010; *pp.* **descended** I.3984, **descendid** Rom A 1575.

descerne *var.* of **discerne**, discern Tr 3.9.

descharge(n) *v. (reflx.)* unburden oneself X.360, X.362; grant absolution (for sin) Rom C 6388.

desclaundred, desclandered *see* **disclaundre**.

descripsioun, descripcioun, discripsioun *n.* (1) account HF 987, Rom B 4702; interpretation X.741; (2) design I.2053; representation Astr 1.21.3.

descryve(n) *see* **discryve(n)**.

desdeyn, desdayn, disdeyn, disdayn *n.* (1) scorn, disdain VIII.41, Bo 3.pr4.9, Rom A 296; (as personification) PF 136, Tr 2.1217; **take (have) in d.** scorn, despise VIII.41, X.150; (2) indignation, anger Tr 4.1191; **have (take) in d.** be indignant, take offense I.789, V.700.

desdeyne, disdaignen, disdeyne, disdayn *v.* (1) disdain, scorn IV.98, Bo 3.pr4.9; (2) be offended or angered Bo 4.pr7.77; *3 pr. sg.* **disdeynith** Rom B 5686.

desert(e), dissert(e) *n.*[1] (1) what is deserved X.757; **after his d.** according to what he deserves V.532, Bo 4.pr4.125; (2) worthiness, merit X.396, Bo 4.pr6.45, Tr 3.1267, LGW 608; *pl.* **desertes** Tr 3.1267, **desertes** Bo 3.pr6.13; **disertes** Bo 4.m4.17.

desert *n.*[2] wasteland, wilderness, desert II.501, VII.1087, HF 488; *pl.* **desertes** Bo 2.pr7.40.

deserve, desserve, disserve *v.* (1) deserve, merit I.1232, I.2379, Tr 1.819; (2) earn, incur Rom B 3093; (3) **d. it unto you** repay you VIII.1352; *3 pr. sg.* **deserveth** X.972, **desserveth** Bo 2.pr8.4, **disserveth** X.756; *pr. pl.* **deserven** Rom A 1054, **disserven** Bo 5.pr3.196; *1 & 3 pt. sg.* **deserved** X.273, **desserved** Bo 1.pr3.27, **disservide** Bo 4.m7.60; *2 pt. sg.* **deservedest** VI.216, **desservedst** Bo 2.pr3.56; *pp.* **disserved** I.1716, **deserved** I.1726, **desservyd** Bo 1.pr4.301.

desespaired *see* **dispaire**.

desevere *see* **dissevere(n)**.

desgise *see* **disgise(n)**.

desherite *v.* disinherit VII.1835; *pp.* **desherited** VII.1751, **disherited** I.2926.

deshonest *see* **dishonest(e)**.

desolaat, desolat *adj.* (1) deserted Tr 5.540; (2) alone, lonely IV.321, LGW 1279; (3) **d.** of lacking II.131; destitute, powerless III.703; *(astro.)* in an unfortunate position Mars 286; (4) wretched VI.598.

desordeynee, disordene *adj.* excessive X.818, X.915, Bo 2.m2.18.

desordinat *see* **disordinat**.

despeir, disespeyr, dispayr, dispeir *n.* despair I.1245, X.693, Tr 1.605, Tr 1.813; **in d.** in a depression I.3474.

despeire(th), despeyred *see* **dispeire**.

despen- *see* **dispen-**.

despise(n), dispise *v.* (1) despise, look down on II.115, X.201, Mars 25; treat with contempt VIII.298, Tr 2.720; scorn, refuse (to do something) Bo 3.pr11.85, Bo 3.m12.40; (2) speak ill of VII.1019, X.663, Tr 3.1699, Rom B 2232, Rom C 6155; blaspheme X.599; *2 pr. sg.* **dispisest** HF 638; *3 pr. sg.* **despiseth** VII.1070; *pr. pl.* **despise(n)** X.189, Tr 3.1387; *pt. pl.* **despised** X.663; *pp.* **despised** Bo 1.pr1.26, **dispised** Rom A 467; *vbl. n.* **dispisynge** VII.1019.

despit(e), dispit *n.* (1) disdain, scorn III.1876, Tr 2.1246; **han d. of, han in d.** scorn III.1876, V.1395, X.395, Tr 3.1374, Tr 3.1787; **in youre d.** in scorn of you VII.563; aversion V.1395; (2) defiance, spite III.2061, X.392, X.429; **in his d.** in defiance of him LGW F 134; affront, insult III.2176, Tr 1.909; **in (for) d.** as an insult I.947, V.1371, Tr 5.1693; (3) malice, spite I.941; anger, resentment III.481, Tr 2.1037.

despitous, despitus, dispitous(e) *adj.* (1) scornful, disdainful X.395, Rom B 2212, Rom B 3457; (2) disobedient, spiteful III.761; (3) hateful, malicious I.516, I.1777, Tr 3.1458.

despitously, dispitously *adv.* angrily VII.2595; cruelly IV.535, Tr 5.1806.

despo- *see* **dispo-**.

desputen, desputestow *see* **dispute**.

desseyvede *see* **deceyve(n)**.

dessertes *see* **desert(e)** *n.*[1]

desteyned *see* **disteyne**.

destynal *adj.* predestined Bo 4.pr6.81, Bo 4.pr6.100, Bo 4.pr6.114.

destyne(e) *n.* destiny, fate I.1108, I.2323, Bo 4.pr6.64, Tr 1.520; Destiny (personified) I.1663.

destourbe(n), desturbe *v.* hinder, prevent VI.340, Tr 4.563, Tr 4.1103; *3 pr. sg.* **destourbeth** VII.977; **distourbeth** Bo 3.pr11.170, **distorbeth** Bo 4.m6.7, *pr. pl.* **destourben** X.83; *pr. subj. sg.* **destourbe** X.991; *pp.* **destourbed** Tr 2.622, **distorbed** Bo 5.pr4.30, **disturbed** Bo 1.pr4.142; *vbl. n.* **desturbyng** hindrance Ven 44.

destrayned, destreyn- *see* **distreyne**.

destresse *see* **distresse**.

destroye(n), destruye *v.* (1) destroy III.2080, V.883, Tr 4.1059; kill I.1330, LGW 1318; (2) harass III.377, VI.858; (3) damage, injure V.1251, X.220; ruin VII.1751; *3 pr. sg.* **destroyeth** III.377; *pr. pl.* **destroyen** X.790; *pt. sg.* **destroyed** IV.630; *pt. pl.* **destroyeden** Bo 2.m5.3, **destroyed** VI.858; *pp.* **destroyed** I.1330, **distroyed** LGW F 133.

destruccioun, destruccion, destruction, distruccioun

n. destruction, ruin I.2538, III.2007, HF 151, Tr 1.141, Mars 212; *pl.* **destrucciouns** Bo 2.m6.2.

determinat *adj.* definite III.1459; placed Astr 2.18 Rubric; fixed (of stars) Astr 1.21.6.

determine(n) *v.* (1) state, assert Rom B 4882; **d. of** discuss Bo 4.pr4.153, Rom C 6631; (2) come to an end, conclude Tr 3.379; *pr. pl.* **determynen** come to the end, end up HF 343; *pp.* **determined** brought to an end, decided Bo 4.pr6.17.

deth(e), deeth *n.* (1) death I.964, I.1134, I.1320; (2) **the d.** the plague I.605, Tr 1.483; *gen.* **dethis** Tr 3.1697, **dethes** Tr 4.1692.

dette *n.* (1) debt V.1578; indebtedness I.280, VII.376; (2) obligation X.252; **biheste is d.** a promise is a binding obligation II.41; **in (someone's) d.** be obligated, obliged to (someone) LGW F 541; (3) the marital debt (spouse's right to sexual intercourse) III.130, X.940; *pl.* **dettes.**

dettour *n.* debtor III.155, VII.397; *pl.* **dettours** VII.413.

devel, devyl *n.* (1) Satan, the Devil VI.1436, X.733, Rom C 6116; (2) any malignant spirit, demon VII.2936; (3) (in curses) III.476, III.1547, Tr 1.805; **a d. (twenty) weye** in the devil's (twenty devils') name I.3134, VIII.782; *gen.* **develes** X.351; *pl.* **develes** VII.2936, **develles** Rom C 7590.

dever, devoir *n.* duty X.764, Rom B 5299.

devyn, dyvyn *n.* soothsayer Tr 1.66; *pl.* theologians: **dyvynys** I.1323, **divines** X.957.

devyne, dyvyn(e) *adj.* divine I.122, III.1719, Bo 5.m1.22; *pl.* **devynes** Bo 5.pr2.23.

devyne(n), divyne *v.* (1) practice divination PF 182; foresee Tr 4.389; (2) guess, conjecture I.2515, III.26, VII.3266; **d. (upon, of)** suspect, be suspicious about Tr 2.1745, Tr 3.458, Tr 3.765; (3) speculate, ponder Tr 4.589; imagine Ros 19; *3 pr. sg.* **devyneth** suspects Tr 2.1741; *pr. pl.* **devyne** Tr 2.1745; *pr. subj. sg.* **devyne** HF 14; *prp.* **dyvynynge** I.2515; *vbl. n.* **divynynge** speculation I.2521, divination Bo 5.pr3.133.

devys *n.* (1) **at (one's) d.** according to (one's) desire I.816, Rom B 3621; (2) opinion; **as at my d.** as I suppose Rom A 651; (3) contrivance, scheme LGW 1102; (4) **at (point) d.** exactly, completely I.3689, HF 917; *pl.* **devyses** heraldic devices LGW 1272.

devyse(n), divyse *v.* (1) inspect, look upon Tr 1.277 LGW 1206; think about IV.1586; imagine I.1790, IV.108; (2) design, plan IV.2000; contrive Tr 3.612; arrange LGW 1453; (3) construct I.1901; compose IV.739, Tr 2.1063; (4) tell, narrate, set forth VIII.266; describe Rom A 888; explain I.1425; converse V.261, Tr 2.1599; (5) command I.1416; advise Tr 2.388; *2 pr. sg.* **devysest** think of Tr 4.543; *3 pr. sg.* **devyseth** III.1904; *pr. pl.* **devyse** PF 333; *pr. subj. sg.* **devyse** Bo 4.pr6.5; *pt. pl.* **devysed** Rom C 7360; *pp.* **devysed** Rom A 476; *vbl. n.* **devisynge** arranging, preparation I.2496.

devisioun *see* **divisioun.**

devocioun *n.* (1) reverence, piety I.2371, II.257; (2) worship, prayers I.3640, LGW 1017; meditation HF 33, Tr 1.555; (3) earnestness III.739, IV.1447, VIII.283; serious attention (to something) HF 666, LGW F 39; affection, interest Tr 1.187.

devoir *see* **dever.**

dewe *see* **due(we).**

dewete *see* **duete(e).**

di- *see also* **de-.**

did(e), didest, dide(n) *see* **don.**

diffame *see* **defame.**

diffence, diffense *see* **defense.**

diffyne, defyne *v.* (1) define, describe Tr 5.271, Rom B 4805; state exactly, specify PF 529, Bo 3.pr2.70, Tr 3.834; determine, conclude Tr 4.390; (2) come to an end, turn out HF 344; *pr. pl.* **diffynen** HF 344; *imp. pl.* **defyneth** Rom B 4805; *pp.* **diffyned** Bo 3.pr2.70.

diffinysshen *v.* define, explain Bo 5.pr1.89; *3 pr. sg.* **diffynysseth** Bo 5.pr1.64, **diffynyscheth** Bo 5.pr4.197; *pr. subj. pl.* **diffynisse** Bo 5.pr1.32; *pp.* **diffinysched** Bo 4.pr2.220, **dyffinysshed** Bo 3.pr10.8.

dighte *v.* (1) prepare, arrange IV.974, LGW 1288; dispose Tr 4.1188; get dressed I.1041; (2) decide Tr 4.1188; (3) furnish I.3205; (4) *(reflx.)* go, depart VII.1914, Tr 2.948; hasten LGW 2371; (5) have sexual relations, copulate with IX.312; *pr. pl.* **dyghte** LGW 1712; *3 pt. sg.* **dighte** III.398; *pp.* **dight** equipped Tr 3.1773, **ydight** adorned I.3205.

digne *adj.* (1) suitable, fitting II. 778, LGW 1738; worthy IV.411; (2) honorable II.1175, VI.695, LGW F 321; deserving X.494; (3) proud, haughty I.3964.

digneliche, dignely *adv.* (1) suitably Bo 2.pr6.92, Bo 3.pr10.81; (2) haughtily Tr 2.1024.

dignite(e), dignete *n.* (1) worthiness VII.456; **for Goddes d.** for God's sake I.4270, VI.782; excellence X.1040; gravity, dignity Bo 4.pr1.3; (2) esteem Bo 3.pr4.38, Gent 5; (3) high rank or office IV.470, VII.2170; honor Bo 1.pr4.249; (4) *(astro.)* position of heightened influence Astr 2.4.47; *pl.* **dignytes** honors Bo 1.pr4.303, **dignytees** Bo 2.pr2.9.

diligence *n.* (1) persistent effort, diligence III.1818, IV.230; **don (one's) d.** exert (one's) fullest effort I.2470, IV.1185, VII.44; (2) eagerness IV.1185, VII.44; **have d.** pay attention VII.1637.

dyner *n.* the first full meal of the day (usually between 9 A.M. and noon) II.1094, II.1118, VII.253.

dynt, dent *n.* loud clap (of thunder) I.3807, III.276, HF 534, Tr 5.1505.

direct *adj.* (1) addressed, dedicated II.748, Ven 75; (2) *(astro.)* from west to east (as the sun moves through the zodiac) Astr 2.35.16; (as *n.*) **in d. of** aligned with Astr 2.44.14; (as *adv.*) directly Astr 2.39.30.

dirk- *see* **derk-.**

dirryveth *3 pr. sg.* derives I.3006; *pp.* **dirryved** derived I.3038.

dys, dees *n. pl.* dice I.1238, Tr 2.1347; **the game of dice** I.4420.

disaventure *n.* misadventure, misfortune Tr 2.415, Tr 4.755.

discende *see* **descende(n).**

dischevelle(e), dischevele, dishevele *adj.* with hair unbound, hanging loose LGW 1315, LGW 1720, LGW 1829.

disclaundre *v.* defame, denounce III. 2212; *pp.* **desclaundred** II.674, **desclandered** disgraced LGW 1031.

disconfite *v.* overcome, defeat VII.1339, X.661; *3 pr. sg.* **disconfiteth** X.661; *pp.* **disconfited** X.530, **discounfited** Bo 2.m1.10, **discomfyt** Rom B 4067; *vbl. n.* **disconfitynge** defeat, dishonor I.2719.

disconfiture, discomfiture *n.* (1) defeat I.1008, dishonor I.2721; (2) thwarting Rom A 254; dejection Anel 326.

discomfort, discomfort *n.* (1) loss of courage, dismay I.2010; distress, sorrow VII.984, Tr 4.848; (2) misfortune V.896.

discordable *adj.* opposing, antagonistic Bo 4.m6.20, inclined to discord Tr 3.1753.

discordaunt, discordant *adj.* conflicting Bo 4.m4.12, dissonant Tr 2.1037.

discorde(n) *v.* (1) disagree Bo 3.pr10.244, Rom C 4716; (2) differ Bo 5.m5.14; *pr. pl.* discorden Bo 3.pr12.35; *prp.* discordynge disagreeing Bo 3.pr2.123.

discordes *n. pl.* disagreements HF 685, Bo 1.pr4.50.

discounfited *see* disconfite.

discovere(n), discure *v.* (1) reveal, disclose VII.1141, VIII.1465, BD 549; uncover Bo 2.pr8.6; betray (a secret) VIII.696; (2) betray, expose (someone by betraying his secrets) IV.1942, Tr 1.675, Rom B 5220; *2 pr. sg.* discoverest VIII.696; *3 pr. sg.* discovereth X.505; *pr. subj. sg.* discovere IV.1942; *imp. sg.* discovere VII.1141; *pt. sg.* discovered VII.1713; *pp.* discovered VIII.1468, discovred Rom B 4402; *vbl. n.* discovering betraying Rom B 5526.

discrecioun, discrecion *n.* (1) sound judgment I.1779, VIII.613, IX.282; moral discernment X.824, Sted 18; rational perception VII.2632; moderation, prudence III.622; by (no) d. (im)moderately III.622, X.861; (2) solution (of a question) Bo 3.pr10.191; power to decide Tr 3.1334; (3) distinction, differentiation Bo 5.pr3.173.

discrete, discreet *adj.* (1) judicious, prudent IV.1909, Tr 3.943; morally discerning VI.48; (2) courteous, respectful of decorum I.518, VII.2871.

discretly, discreetly *adv.* (1) judiciously, prudently VII.1268, X.1045; (2) courteously PF 241.

discripsioun, discripcioun *see* descripsioun.

discryve(n), descryve(n) *v.* (1) describe V.40, Tr 2.889; d. of tell about IV.1737, Rom A 865; (2) descry, discover BD 916; (3) inscribe Astr 1.17.1; *3 pr. sg.* discryveth describes IV.43; *pr. pl.* discreven Rom B 4803; *pp.* discrived Astr 1.17.1; *vbl. n.* discryvyng account X.535.

discure *see* discovere(n).

disd- *see* desd-.

disese *n.* distress, discomfort VIII.747, Anel 226, Mars 216.

disese(n) *v.* cause pain, distress Tr 2.1650, Tr 3.1468; *pp.* disesed distressed Tr 3.443.

disespeyr *see* despeir.

disfigure *v.* (1) deform, disfigure I.1403, VI.551, Tr 2.223; (2) disguise LGW 2046; *pp.* disfigured I.1403.

disgise(n), desgise *n.* *(reflx.)* dress, clothe oneself Rom B 2250; (2) disguise Tr 5.1577, Rom C 6358; *pp.* disgised dressed I.1412, disguised Rom C 7359; *vbl. n.* disgysynge style of clothing X.425.

disherited *see* desherite.

dishevele *see* dischevele(e).

dishonest(e), deshonest *adj.* dishonorable, unjust VII.1228, X.777, Rom B 3442; shameful IV.876; unchaste, immodest IV.876, IX.214, Rom B 4262.

disjoynt(e) *n.* difficulty, awkward situation I.2962, Tr 3.496, LGW 1631; predicament Tr 5.1618.

disobeysaunt *adj.* disobedient X.338, PF 429.

disordinat, desordinat *adj.* excessive X.415, X.431.

disordinaunce, disordenaunce *n.* rebelliousness, disorderly behavior X.277, Bo 5.pr1.40; disordering HF 27; *pl.* disordinaunces X.275.

dispayr *see* despeir.

dispaire *v.* (1) despair, lose hope (often *reflx.*) Tr 5.1569; (2) ben despeired out of (from) be deprived of, lack Tr 5.713, Lady 7; *3 pr. sg.* dispeireth X.698; *imp. pl.* dispeire IV.1669; *prp.* dispeiring Rom B 4707; *pp.* despeyred V.943, desespaired Lady 7, dispeyred in despair, discouraged V.1084, Tr 1.36.

dispende, despende *v.* (1) spend X.849, waste, squander (money) V.690; (2) distribute, give out VII.1370, X.812; (3) spend, waste (one's time, *etc.*) IV.1123, VII.931, VII.2310; *2 pr. sg.* despendest VII.931; *pr. pl.* dispendith Rom B 5681, despenden VII.1605, dispenden X.849; *pp.* despended VII.80, dispended VII.1370.

dispense, dispence, despence, despense *n.* (1) outlay of money, expenditure VII.16; expense VII.5; extravagant expenditures I.1928, III.700; fre of d. generous in spending IV.1209; esy of d. careful about spending I.441; (2) living expenses II.105, III.1432, Rom A 1144; *pl.* despenses VII.1652.

dispenseth *3 pr. sg.* metes out, administers Bo 4.pr6.298; *prp.* dispensynge Bo 5.pr6.296.

dispi- *see* despi-.

displesant *adj.* offensive X.544, X.697.

displesaunce *n.* (1) dissatisfaction, displeasure Tr 3.1295; take d. take offense VI.74; (2) source of displeasure, annoyance Tr 3.480; *pl.* doon us displesances injure us VI.420.

displese(n) *v.* offend, annoy VII.1438, IX.26, Tr 4.275; displease III.1222, IV.506; be displeasing Bo 1.pr3.67; *3 pr. sg.* displeseth III.293, displesith Rom C 6096; *pr. pl.* displese III.128; *pr. subj. sg.* displese IV.1982; *pt. subj. sg.* displeased Rom B 3661; *pp.* displesed VIII.1010; *vbl. n.* displesinge displeasure Compl d'Am.

dispoillen, despoile *v.* (1) undress, strip IV.374; (2) rob X.665, Rom B 5066; d. of deprived of, lacking Bo 1.pr4.303; *pp.* despoyled robbed X.665; *vbl. n.* dispoilynge spoil, booty Bo 4.m7.30.

disponyth *3 pr. sg.* regulate, dispose Tr 4.964; *pr. subj. sg.* dispone Tr 5.300; *pt. sg.* disponyde Bo 3.pr12.44; *pp.* disponyd Bo 4.pr6.93.

disport, desport *n.* (1) amusement, fun I.4043, I.4420; don (maken) d. amuse, give pleasure to I.775, IV.1924, HF 664; in d. amusing herself, at play PF 260; (2) pleasure VII.2791, Rom B 2894; comfort, source of comfort IV.1332; (3) greet d. excellent deportment I.137.

disporte(n), desporte *v.* (1) *(reflx.)* amuse oneself IV.2040, LGW 1441, Rom B 2014; *(intr.)* take comfort, cheer up Tr 5.1398; (2) *(tr.)* entertain, cheer up HF 571, Tr 4.724; *pr. pl.* disporten IV.2040.

disposeth *imp. pl.* arrange, prepare III.1659; *pt. sg.* disposide arranged Bo 3.pr12.135; *pp.* disposid arranged Astr 1.21.58; controlled, regulated X.336; decided IV.244; prepared IV.755; in a state to, inclined to Tr 4.230; wel d. favorably inclined Tr 2.682, in good health IX.33; nat wel d. unwell IX.33.

disposicioun, disposicion *n.* (1) preparation, arrangement Bo 4.m4.3, Tr 5.1543; (2) regulation, ordering Bo 4.pr5.44; (3) power to control, rule I.2364, Tr 2.526, Tr 5.2; (4) mental attitude I.1378, Bo 5.pr6.258; (5) *(astro.)* aspect, disposition (of a planet) I.1087, III.701; *pl.* disposiciounis Bo 4.pr6.355.

dispreyse(n) *v.* disparage, criticize VII.1071, Rom A

1053; *prp.* **dispreisynge** VII.1551; *vbl. n.* **dis-preisynge** VII.1686.

dispute, desputen *v.* engage in philosophic disputation Bo 5.m4.3, Rom C 6764; argue Tr 3.858; discuss (a topic) Rom C 6764; *2 pr. sg.* (with *pro.*) **disputestow** Bo 5.pr6.121; *1 pt. sg.* **disputed** BD 505; *2 pt. sg.* **disputedest** Bo 1.pr4.16; *prp.* **disputing** arguing Tr 4.1084; *vbl. n.* **disputynge** Bo 3.pr12.175.

disputisoun, disputison, disputesoun *n.* discussion IV.1474; scholarly, logical disputation V.890, VII.3238; logical argument Bo 5.pr1.27.

disseyvistow, disseyvid, disseyvyng *see* **deceyve.**

dissensioun, dissencion *n.* disagreement, dispute IV.747, VII.1691, Lak of Sted 9.

disser- *see* **desser-.**

dissevere(n) *v.* separate VII.1615, Pity 115; part, get away from Buk 15; *pr. subj. sg.* **desevere** Mars 49; *pp.* **disseovered** VII.1431.

dissimulen, dissimilen *v. (intr.)* dissemble, pretend Tr 3.434, Bo 5.pr6.307; *(tr.)* conceal Tr 1.322; *3 pr. sg.* **dissymuleth** VIII.466; *imp. sg.* **dissimule** IX.347; *vbl. n.* **dissymulynge** VIII.1073; *pl.* **dissymulynges** V.285.

distaf *n.* distaff, staff for holding unspun fiber during spinning I.3774 (see note), VII.1907, VII.2374.

disteyne *v.* make dim, pale LGW F 262, LGW F 269, LGW F 274; *pp.* **disteyned** stained Tr 2.840.

distourbeth, distorbed *see* **destourbe(n).**

distreyne, destreyne *v.* (1) restrain, confine X.269; keep Prov 8; (2) constrain, compel IX.161, Tr 5.596; (3) torment, afflict I.1816, Tr 3.1528; *3 pr. sg.* **distrayneth** grasps PF 337, **destrayneth** afflicts I.1455; *imp. sg.* **distreyne** Tr 5.596; *pp.* **distreyned** oppressed X.752, **destrayned** constrained Tr 1.355.

distresse, destresse *n.* (1) misfortune, hardship Tr 2.1372, LGW 1055; want Rom C 6181; suffering, grief V.916, VIII.76, Tr 1.439, LGW 664; (2) **in d.** under constraint, in control HF 1587.

disturbed *see* **destourbe(n).**

dite(e) *n.* literary work (poem) HF 622, Bo 3.m12.48, (drama) Bo 2.pr2.71, (tract) Rom B 5286; **d. of musyk** verse Bo 4.pr6.36; *pl.* **dytees** HF 622.

divers(e) *adj.* (1) differing III.701; divergent Bo 5.pr1.18; different HF 1574; (2) various, sundry I.3857, II.211, Tr 1.61; variegated Pity 17, Rom A 68; (3) separate, distinct X.489, Astr 2.14.10; **by d. tymes** in turn Bo 4.pr4.202; (4) contrary, hostile BD 653, Rom B 4102; adverse Tr 4.1195.

diversely, diversly *adv.* (1) differently, in differing ways III.1877, HF 1546; (2) with differing opinions I.3857, IV.1469, Rom A 1629.

diversite(e) *n.* (1) difference II.220; (2) distinction Tr 3.405; (3) variety Tr 5.1793; *pl.* **diversites** varieties Bo 3.pr12.44.

divynynge *see* **devyne(n).**

dyvynytee *n.* (1) divine nature VIII.340; the Divine Being VIII.316; (2) theology III.1512.

divyse *see* **devyse(n).**

divisioun, division, devysioun *n.* (1) dividing up X.1009, X.1011; (2) subdivision Astr 2.31.13, Bo 3.pr9.18; clan, division I.2024, Mars 273; (3) dividing line Astr 1.19.5; (4) distinction, difference I.1780, Fort 33; (5) dissension I.2476; *pl.* **divisiouns** Astr 1.19.5.

do(o) *see* **don.**

dogge *n.* dog III.1369; **d. for the bowe** dog trained to hunt with an archer III.1369; *pl.* **dogges** Tr 4.626.

doghter, doughter, dowhter *n.* daughter I.2064, I.2222, Bo 4.m3.4; *gen. sg.* **doghter** IV.608; *pl.* **doghtren** V.1429, **doughtren** Tr 4.22, **doghtres** V.1370, VI.73.

doke *n.* duck I.3576, PF 498; *pl.* **dokes** VII.3390.

dool *n.* grief, pain Rom B 2956, Rom B 4317.

dolven *see* **delve.**

dom, doom *n.* (1) judgment IV.1000; **sitten in d.** sit in judgment VI.257; **sweren in d.** take an oath in court X.592; **day of d.** the Last Judgment X.118; (2) judicial decision, sentence VI.163, Tr 4.1188; case at law X.594; (3) destiny LGW 2630; (4) opinion, judgment Bo 4.pr6.188; **(as) to my d.** in my opinion VII.1937; *gen.* **domes day** the Last Judgment HF 1284; *pl.* **doomes** VI.163, **domes** Bo 4.pr6.188.

dominacioun *n.* power, control I.2758, VI.560, Sted 16; **in his d.** dominant V.352 (see note).

don, don(e), do, doo(n) *v.* (1) do, perform I.78, I.268, BD 29; **d. bisynesse (cure, diligence)** take pains, work hard, be diligent I.1007, III.1074, IV.1298, IX.141, IX.172; **d. peyne** undergo hardship Tr 2.475; **d. law (right)** enforce the law VII.1439, Sted 27; **d. nedes** conduct business II.174; **d. profit** be useful, beneficial VII.1269, X.1003, Rom B 5376; **d. (one's own) profit (avantage)** derive benefit (for oneself) II.729, VII.1588; **d. reed** follow (someone's) advice Tr 4.1413; **is to d.** is to be done, is necessary III.2194, Tr 5.70; (2) cause, give (pleasure, ease, etc.) I.766, I.1248; (with *inf.*) cause (something) to be done III.1364, IV.253, V.46, BD 149; **dide (leet) doon sleen hem (cryen the feeste)** had them slain, had the feast announced III.2042, V.46; (3) place, put VIII.899; **d. wey** take away I.3287, Tr 2.111; **d. wey enough of this!** Tr 2.893, be done with VIII.487; **d. up** raise I.3801; **d. of** put off BD 516; (4) act, proceed, behave VII.1648, VIII.903, Tr 3.928; (5) as auxiliary forming periphrastic (*pr.*) I.3410, Tr 2.54, Tr 4.880, (emphatic) III.853, (*prt.*) Rom B 1803, Rom B 1912; *2 pr. sg.* **dost** Tr 2.1510, **doost** Tr 3.1436, **doist** Rom B 4016, (with *pro.*) **dostow** III.239; *3 pr. sg.* **dooth** I.98, **doth** III.1034, **doith** Rom B 4273; *pr. pl.* **doon** VI.100, **do(n)** III.1433, Bo 5.pr4.102; *pr. subj. pl.* **do** VII.1012; *imp. sg.* **do** I.3287; *imp. pl.* **dooth** VI.745, **do** I.2598; *1 & 3 pt. sg.* **did(e)** I.451, I.1004; *2 pt. sg.* **didest** HF 1846, **dedest** Tr 3.363; *pt. pl.* **dide(n)** I.1007, I.1177; *pt. subj. sg.* **did(e)** I.451 VI.746, **dede** Tr 1.369; *pt. subj. pl.* **diden** LGW 723; *prp.* **wel doand** well doing, acting well Rom B 2708; *pp.* **have do** finish up I.3728; **ydon** I.1025; **ydo(o)** VIII.899, BD 1236; **(y)doon** I.1083, VIII.386; *vbl. n.* **doyng(e)** VIII.421, BD 995; *pl.* **doynges** LGW 1681.

dong(e) *n.* dung, manure I.530, VI.535, VIII.807.

dore *n.* door I.460, III.6; *pl.* **dores** I.1987.

dorste, dorstestow *see* **durre.**

dote(n) *v.* (1) act foolishly IV.1441, VIII.983; (2) become feeble-minded LGW G 261; *pp.* (as *adj.*) **doted** (as *adj.*) foolish, feeble-minded Buk 13, Rom A 407.

double *adj.* (1) double I.262; (2) duplicitous, treacherous X.644, Tr 5.898.

doublenesse *n.* duplicity, treachery V.566, Rom B 2885, Rom B 5566.

doughter *see* **doghter.**

doumb, domb(e), domm *adj.* mute, speechless, dumb I.774, II.1055, VIII.286, HF 656, Rom B 2220.

doun *adv.* down, downward I.952, I.1103, BD 106; **beren d.** overcome I.3831, IV.2270; **up and d.** all over, in every way I.977, I.2054, BD 348; **up so d.** upside down I.1377, (as one word) VIII.625; *comp.* **downer** lower Astr 2.12.19.

doute *n.* (1) uncertainty, doubt VIII.833, X.91, Tr 4.1277; **withoute(n) (out of) d.** certainly I.487, I.1322, BD 820; **putte thee out of d.** resolve your uncertainty HF 598; (2) anxiety, fear Tr 5.1453; reverence X.1023; (3) danger IV.1721, LGW 1613; *pl.* **doutes** opinions, conjectures V.220.

douteles, doutelees *adv.* doubtless I.1831, I.2667, Tr 2.414.

doute(n) *v.* (1) *(tr.)* doubt Bo 3.pr12.23, Bo 4.pr3.56; *(intr.* with **of, hereof)** doubt, be in doubt about Bo 3.pr11.89, Bo 4.pr3.56; (2) fear, be afraid VII.1327, X.648, X.880, X.953, Rom B 2023; *inf.* **to doute** to be doubted Bo 3.pr12.27; **to douten** to be feared Bo 5.pr1.19; *2 pr. sg.* **doutest** Bo 1.pr6.27, (with *pro.*) **dowtestow** Bo 4.pr4.230; *3 pr. sg.* **douteth** X.953; *pr. subj.* **doute** VII.1327 (*sg.*), Rom B 2079 (*pl.*); *imp. sg.* **doute** Bo 4.pr5.47; *imp. pl.* **douteth** Tr 1.683; *2 pt. sg.* **doutedest** Bo 1.pr6.21; *3 pt. sg.* **douted** X.880; *pp.* **idouted** Bo 5.pr4.117; *vbl. n.* **doutyng** uncertainty Rom C 6074.

douve, dowve *n.* dove IV.2139, VI.397, PF 341; *pl.* **dowves** I.1962.

dowere, dowaire *n.* dowry IV.807, IV.848.

drad, dradde(n), (y)drad(d), drat *see* **drede(n).**

draught(e) *n.* (1) drink I.135, I.382, VI.315; (2) a move in chess BD 682, 685; *pl.* **draughtes** VI.568.

drawe(n) *v.* (1) draw, pull, drag I.842, Tr 3.1704; draw water I.1416; draw (a sword, *etc.*) LGW 1785, Rom B 1725; (breath) Tr 3.1119; **d. cut** draw lots I.842; **d. along** protract Bo 1.m1.28; pull, tear apart VII.633, Tr 1.833; (2) bring carry, drag I.3663, II.339; attract Bo 2.pr5.48; **d. draught** make a move (in chess) BD 682; lead, entice I.519, X.121; **d. in** lead to, cause X.1000, Tr 3.853; **d. (in)to memorie** remember I.2074, X.239; **d. to record** call to witness Scog 22; **d. to warraunt** offer as a pledge Rom A 6; get, obtain X.549, Rom B 2087; derive VIII.1440, Bo 3.m9.14; (3) go, move, come III.1549, LGW F 563; go toward, approach I.3633; **d. unto** agree with, come to agree IV.314; (4) draw (a line) Astr 2.38.27; *2 pr. sg.* **drawest** Bo 3.m9.14, (with *pro.*) **drawestow** Bo 5.pr4.31; *3 pr. sg.* **draweth** LGW G 52; *pr. pl.* **drawe(n)** IV.1817, V.252; *imp. sg.* **draw** Truth 26; *imp. pl.* **draweth** I.835; *1 & 3 pt. sg.* **drow** I.3633, **drough** I.3892, **drogh** LGW 1459, **drowh** Bo 4.m7.36, **drew** BD 864; *2 pt. sg.* **drowe** Scog 22; *pt. pl.* **drowe** Rom A 1678; *pr. pl.* **drawyng** Rom B 3885; *pp.* **(y)drawe** II.339, LGW 1788, **drawen** X.549.

drecche *v.* delay Tr 2.1264; trouble Tr 4.1471; *pr. pl.* **drecche** Tr 4.1446; *pp.* **drecched** troubled VII.2887; *vbl. n.* **drecchynge** delaying Tr 3.853, continuance X.1000.

drede, dreede *n.* (1) fear I.1396, II.657, BD 24; (2) anxiety, worry IV.134, VII.123, Tr 1.463; (3) awe, reverence Rom B 3843; **have in d.** hold in awe VII.2162; (4) doubt, uncertainty Tr 1.529, Tr 3.1315; **no d.** no doubt, without question II.869, III.1169; **withouten, out of d.** doubtless, certainly II.29,

V.1544; (5) danger, peril II.657, VII.1327; **putten in d.** to put (someone's life) in danger Buk 28; *pl.* **dredes** worries Tr 1.463.

drede(n) *v.* (1) (sometimes *reflx.*) be afraid, be fearful I.660, VII.2929, HF 38, Tr 2.455; (2) fear (something) IV.636, VIII.320, Tr 2.367; (3) hold in awe, reverence IV.1312, VIII.125, Sted 27; (4) avoid, abhor VII.1176, Tr 1.252; (5) doubt, be in doubt I.1593, IV.1316; *inf.* **to drede** to be feared Tr 1.84; *2 pr. sg.* **dredest** Bo 2.pr5.178; *3 pr. sg.* **dredeth** Tr 4.574, *(contr.)* **drat** Tr 3.328; *pr. pl.* **drede(n)** Bo 1.m4.13, Tr 3.25; *pr. subj. sg.* **drede** VIII.477; *imp. sg.* **dred** Sted 27; *imp. pl.* **dredeth** VII.2969, Tr 4.1520, **dreed** IV.1201; *1 & 3 pt. sg.* **dredde** Tr 2.874, **dradde** IV.523; *2 pt. sg.* **dreddest** For 19; *pt. pl.* **dredde(n)** Tr 4.56; *pt. subj. pl.* **dradden** VIII.15; *pp.* **drad** IV.69, **ydradd** Bo 2.m1.8, **(y)dred** Tr 3.1775, Bo 4.pr3.116; *vbl. n.* **dredyng** fearing Rom B 5219.

dredeful(l), dredful *adj.* (1) timid I.1479; fearful, apprehensive LGW F 109; (2) frightening II.937, VII.2368; *super.* **dredefullesle** Tr 5.248.

dredeles, dredelees, dredles, dreedles *adv.* (1) without fear Bo 3.m12.9; (2) doubtless Tr 1.1048, Tr 5.882, BD 1272.

dredfully *adv.* fearfully Tr 2.1128, LGW 2680.

dreye, drye *adj.* dry I.420, I.3024, I.3730; (as *n.*) one of the elemental qualities I.420 (see note).

dryen *v.* dry VII.2746; *3 pr. sg.* **dryeth** I.1495, **dreyeth** X.848; **dryede** Bo 1.pr2.28, **dreyed** LGW 775.

dreynt(e) *see* **drenche(n).**

drem(e), dreem *n.* dream II.804, PF 31, Tr 5.378; *pl.* **dremes** V.357.

dreme(n) *v.* dream VII.3092, Tr 5.248; imagine, dream up (things) Tr 2.800; *(impers.)* **me dremed** I dreamed VII.787; *2 pr. sg.* **dremest** Tr 5.1282; *3 pr. sg.* **dremeth** PF 101; *pr. pl.* **dreme(n)** Tr 5.377, Rom A 18; *pr. subj. sg.* **dreme** HF 98; *pt. sg.* **dremed** III.582; *vbl. n.* **dremyng** dream Rom B 2173; *pl.* **dremynges** VII.3090.

drenche(n) *v.* (1) drown, be drowned I.3521, II.455, HF 205, HF 923, LGW G 293; be engulfed (in tears, sorrow) Tr 4.510, LGW 1919, (2) sink X.363, BD 148, HF 233; (3) flood, inundate X.839, Tr 3.1761; *3 pr. sg.* **drencheth** X.363; *pt.* II.923 (*sg.*), **dreynte** V.1378 (*pl.*); *pp.* **dreynt(e)** I.3520, (as *adj.*) II.69, **drenched** LGW 2178; *vbl. n.* **drenchyng** I.2456.

drery *adj.* (1) sad IV.514, Tr 1.13; (2) frightened HF 179, LGW 810.

dresse *v.* (1) place, put IV.381; *(reflx.)* **d. hym up(ward)** get up, raise himself Tr 3.71; **doun hire d.** sit down LGW 804; (2) arrange, put in order I.3635, Tr 4.1182; (3) dress, arm Tr 2.635; (4) repair LGW 1190; (5) prepare IV.1049; *(reflx.)* get ready II.265; (6) address one's attention to V.290, VIII.77; care for, tend to I.106; (7) guide, direct VII.1118; (8) go, move II.416, V.290; (9) treat IV.2361; *3 pr. sg.* **dresseth** I.3635; *pr. pl.* **dresse(n)** I.2594, II.263; *pt. sg.* **dressed** I.3358; *prp.* **dressynge** Bo 4.pr6.170; *pp.* **(y)dressed** IV.381, PF 665.

drye(n) *v.* (1) bear up under, endure Tr 2.866; (2) suffer, experience Anel 333; (3) feel HF 1879; (4) perform Rom C 7482; *3 pr. sg.* **drieth** Tr 1.1092; *pr. pl.* **dryen** Tr 1.303.

drif *see* **dryve.**

drynke(n) *v.* (1) drink I.635, I.750, Tr 1.406, Tr

3.1214; *3 pr. sg.* **drynketh** IV.1807; *imp. sg.* **drynk** III.2053; *pt. sg.* **drank** II.743, **dronk** Tr 5.1440; *pt. pl.* **dronke(n)** I.820, *pp.* **dronke(n)** I.135, Tr 3.674, (as *adj.*) **drunk** X.822, **ydronke** VII.1411; *vbl. n.* **drynkynge** X.576.

dryve *v.* (1) drive, chase I.1859, I.2727; compel X.527, Tr 2.576, LGW 2430; (2) drive (a cart) III.1540, Tr 5.665; (3) drive (a nail) I.2007, III.769; (4) go rapidly II.505, III.1694; (5) pass, spend (time) PF 682, Tr 5.394; (6) conclude (a bargain) V.1230; (7) (with **forth**) bear up under, endure VII.231; *3 pr. sg.* **dryveth** II.505, *(contr.)* **drifth** Tr 5.1332; *pr. pl.* **dryve(n)** VII.1086, LGW 2620; *imp. sg.* **drif** Tr 4.1615; *pt. sg.* **droof** III.1540, **drof** Tr 3.994; *prp.* **dryvynge** II.947; *pp.* **(y)drive(n)** I.2007, I.4110.

drogh *see* **drawe(n)**.

droghte *n.* dryness, lack of rain I.2, I.595, V.118.

dronk, dronke(n), (y)dronke(n) *see* **drynke(n)**.

dronkelewe *adj.* addicted to drink X.626.

droppe *v.* (1) fall in drops, drip I.3895; (2) run with moisture VIII.580; (3) bespatter I.2004; *3 pr. sg.* **droppeth** X.632; *2 pt. sg.* **droppidest** drop, let fall Bo 1.pr4.258; *3 pt. sg.* **dropped** VIII.580; *prp.* **droppyng(e)** leaking X.631, (as *adj.*) leaky III.278; *pp.* **ydropped** I.2884; *vbl. n.* **droppyng** VII.1086.

drow, drowh *see* **drawe(n)**.

duc, duk *n.* duke I.860, I.873, I.893; *pl.* **dukes** I.2182.

due(we), duwe, dewe *adj.* (1) legal, customary X.561; **by d. manere** according to rule Bo 1.m5.33; (2) obligatory required X.867, LGW 603; payable IV.1452, Rom C 6638; (3) **in d. manere** properly VII.1254; **in d. tyme** at the proper time LGW G 324; (4) predestined I.3044.

duete(e), dewete *n.* (1) tax, fee owed to an authority III.1352, III.1391; (2) **of d.** as a matter of obligation or courtesy Tr 3.970, LGW G 360.

dul(le) *adj.* dull II.202, V.279, BD 900.

dulle(n) *v.* (1) become dull or dazed Rom B 4792; weaken Ven 76; (2) become bored Tr 4.1489; **to d.** to be bored, satiated Tr 2.1035; *(tr.)* depress VIII.1172; *3 pr. sg.* **dulleth** depresses VIII.1093; *pp.* **dulled** weakened X.233, **dullid** Bo 1.pr4.186.

dulve *see* **delve**.

duracioun *n.* duration, set period of time I.2996, HF 2114.

dure(n) *v.* (1) endure, IV.166, HF 353; remain Rom B 1961; (2) extend Rom C 7679; *3 pr. sg.* **dureth** Bo 2.pr4.125; *pr. pl.* **duren** Bo 3.pr4.80; *prp.* (as *adj.*) **durynge** enduring Tr 3.1754; *vbl. n.* **durynge** duration Bo 4.pr4.166.

durre *v.* dare Tr 5.840; *1 & 3 pr. sg.* **dar** II.273, X.692; *2 pr. sg.* **darest** Tr 1.768; **darst** I.1140; (with *pro.*) **darstou** VII.1147; *pr. pl.* **dar** X.507; *pr. subj.* **dar** LGW 1995 *(sg.)*, 2024 *(pl.)*; *1 & 3 pt. sg.* **dorste** I.227, **durst(e)** BD 929, Rom B 1324; *pt. pl.* **durst(e)** Rom C 7142, Rom C 7144; *1 pt. subj. sg.* **durste** BD 929; *2 pt. subj. sg.* **dorstestow** Tr 1.767; *3 pt. subj. sg.* **dorste** Tr 1.27; *vbl. n.* **durryng don** daring to do Tr 5.837.

dusked *pt. pl.* grew dark I.2806, Bo 1.pr1.26.

dust *pt. sg. (reflx.)* needed Rom A 1089, Rom A 1324. Cf. **thar**.

dwelle(n) *v.* (1) delay LGW 670; take time (to tell) BD 217, Tr 5.1484; (2) detain Tr 1.144; (3) remain, stay I.512, I.973, X.223, Tr 2.314; (4) reside, dwell I.4003, Tr 3.590; inhere in I.2804; (5) continue III.947, Tr 1.789; *2 pr. sg.* **duellest** Bo 3.m9.5; *3 pr. sg.* **dwelleth** I.1310; *pr. pl.* **dwelle(n)** VII.1373, VIII.656; *pr. subj.* **dwelle** Tr 1.789 *(sg.)*, Tr 2.1595 *(pl.)*; *imp. pl.* **dwelle** Tr 4.1449; *2 pt. sg.* **dweltest** VIII.48; *3 pt. sg.* **dwelte** I.512, **dwelled** I.2804; *pt. pl.* **dwelten** II.550; *pt. subj. sg.* **dwelte** Tr 5.910; *prp.* **dwelling(e)** I.702, abiding Bo 5.pr6.85; *pp.* **dwelled** I.1228, **dwelt** VIII.720; *vbl. n.* **dwellynge** abode I.1937; *pl.* **duellynges** delays Bo 1.m1.29.

E

ech, ecch, ich *pro.* each (one) I.427, I.791, I.1132, Tr 1.1078; **ech a** every III.256; **ech a deel** every part, entirely Tr 3.694.

ech, ecch *adj.* every III.404, III.1968, Tr 2.42.

eche, eke *v.* increase, add Tr 5.110, HF 2065, Rom B 1994, Rom B 2126; *3 pr. pl.* **eche** Tr 1.705; *pp.* **echid** Bo 3.pr6.14, **eched** Tr 3.1329.

echon(e), echoon *pro.* each one, everyone IV.124, VI.113, VI.349.

effect *n.* (1) result, realization HF 5, Bo 4.pr2.23; consequence I.2989; **in e.** in fact, actually IV.721, Tr 1.748; **take e.** have an effect X.607; (2) substance I.2207, III.1451; the point I.1189; significance Tr 5.1629; purpose I.1487; **to the e.** for this purpose, so that VII.1883; **to this e.** for this purpose VII.1883; *pl.* **effectes** I.2228, **effectz** Bo 2.pr6.102.

eft *adv.* (1) again, another time II.792, II.802, IV.1227; (2) immediately V.631; (3) likewise I.3647.

eftsone(s), eftsonys, eft-sonys, eftsoone(s), eftsoone(s) (also as two words) *adv.* (1) again III.1992, Tr 2.1468; another time VII.2286, VIII.933, Tr 2.1651; (2) immediately I.3489, Astr 2.23.16, Rom C 6649; (3) in return III.808, III.1992, Bo 4.m7.61, Tr 4.181.

egle *n.* eagle V.123, PF 373; *gen.* **egles** VII.2175; *pl.* **egles** PF 332.

egre *adj.* (1) bitter Bo 2.m5.24; (2) sharp Rom B 4179; (3) fierce Bo 4.pr7.93; (as *adv.*) painfully Rom B 5475.

eye, ye *n.* eye I.10, I.896; **at e.** plainly LGW F 100; *pl.* **eyen** I.152, **eyghen** Bo 3.pr8.41, **yen** VII.2070.

ey, I *interj.* oh, ah I.3892, Tr 2.113.

eighte, eighthe *adj.* eighth V.1280, Tr 5.1809.

eyle(n), aylen *v.* ail, afflict, cause trouble for I.3424, LGW 1833; *3 pr. sg.* **What eyleth (thee, yow,** *etc.*) What's the trouble with (you, *etc.*) I.1081, I.3769; **ailleth** Tr 1.766; *pt. sg.* **eyled** V.501.

ek(e), eek *adv.* also II.716, II.829, III.30, Tr 2.290.

eke *see* **eche**.

elde, eelde *n.* (1) age Anel 78; (2) old age I.2448, III.1207; (3) aging, passing years Anel 12, Tr 2.393.

elden *v. (intr.)* grow old, age Bo 2.pr7.7; *3 pr. sg.* **eldith** *(tr.)* makes old, ages Rom A 391.

elder(e) *comp.* of **old** older VII.2260, VII.2412; *super.* **eldest(e)** I.912, V.30.

eldres *n. pl.* elders, ancestors IV.65, VI.364.

eleccioun, eleccion *n.* choice PF 409, Purse 23; choice of (an astrologically) favorable time II.312; *pl.* **eleccions** Astr 2.4.2.

elf *n.* supernatural being, spirit (often evil) III.873; *pl.* **elves** I.3479.

elf-queene *n.* fairy queen VII.790.

elles *adj.* else, other III.1866, III.2203, BD 74.

elles, ellis *adv.* otherwise, else I.375, I.1151, Tr 1.345.

em, eem *n.* uncle Tr 2.355; *gen.* **emes** Tr 2.466.

embelif *adj. (astro.)* oblique, not at a right angle to the horizon Astr 2.19.15; (as *adv.*) obliquely Astr 2.26.9.

emeraude *n.* emerald PF 175; *pl.* **emeraudes** Rom A 1118.

empoysone *v.* poison X.514; *pt. pl.* **empoysoned** VII.2660; *pp.* **empoysoned** III.751; *vbl. n.* **empoisonyng(e)** VI.891, Bo 1.pr3.54.

emprise, enprise *n.* (1) enterprise VII.1067; (2) chivalric exploit V.732; knightly courage VII.2667; (3) difficult task X.691; (4) will, rule Rom B 1972, Rom B 4905.

enbrasen, enbrace, embrace *v.* embrace, comprehend, contain Bo 5.pr6.21, Bo 5.pr6.61, Prov 7; *2 pr. sg.* **enbracest** Bo 2.pr5.69; *3 pr. sg.* **enbraceth** Bo 5.pr6.67, Mars 90; **enbraseth** Bo 5.pr4.169; **embraseth** Bo 6.pr6.282, **embraceth** Bo 5.pr6.105; *pr. subj.* **embrase** Bo 5.pr6.35; *pt. pl.* **embraceden** X.193; *vbl. n.* **embracynge** embrace X.944; *pl.* **embracynges** X.944.

enbroude *v.* embroider LGW 2351, adorn LGW F 227; *pp.* **enbrowded** HF 1327, **enbrouded** (as *adj.*) LGW F 119, **embrouded** dressed in embroidered clothes I.89; *vbl. n.* **embroudynge** X.417.

enchesoun *n.* cause V.456; reason, occasion Tr 1.681.

enclyne *v.* (1) bow Rom C 6814; condescend II.1082; (2) be inclined (to do something) X.361, PF 325, Tr 2.674; *(tr.)* dispose PF 325; *3 pr. sg.* **enclyneth** turns Bo 4.m6.9; *imp. sg.* **enclyne** VII.1180; *imp. pl.* **enclyneth** VII.1594; *pt. sg.* **enclynede** Bo 1.pr4.233; *prp.* **enclynynge** bowing, acceding VII.1250, gathering together Bo 3.m11.5, (as *adj.*) bowing, humble Bo 5.m1.16; *pp.* **enclyned** VII.1250, (as *adj.*) PF 414; *vbl. n.* **enclynyng** inclination HF 734.

encombre, encumbre *v.* (1) hinder, prevent from operating (by being stuck) LGW 2006; (2) burden Rom B 4482; confuse Rom A 889; trouble, bother Rom C 7626; *3 pr. sg.* **encombrith** burdens, troubles Rom C 6675; *pp.* **encombred** hindered X.687, stuck I.508.

encres, encrees *n.* increase, growth I.2184, II.237; income Rom B 5727; assistance LGW 1087.

encrese(n), encrese(n), encreesen, encrescen *v.* increase II.1068, IV.1808, Pity 10, Tr 2.1337, Rom B 1995, *3 pr. sg.* **encresseth** I.1315, **encreeseth** X.350, **encreseth** Pity 29, **encrescith** Astr 2.1.64; *pr. pl.* **encressen** I.1338, **encreesen** X.321; **encrecen** Bo 5.pr2.40, **encreescen** VII.1740; *pr. subj. sg.* **encresse** Tr 5.1359; *pt. sg.* **encresede** PF 143, **encreside** Rom B 1785; *pt. pl.* **encreesceden** VII.1276; *prp.* **encresing** HF 2077; *pp.* **encressed** IV.408, **encreced** Bo 3.pr6.18, **encresed** Bo 3.pr6.14.

endelong *adv.* lengthwise HF 1458; from end to end Astr 2.40.33.

endelong *prep.* (1) from end to end, along V.992; down the length of V.416; across LGW G 144.

endite(n) *v.* (1) write, compose I.95, II.781, LGW F 371; describe (in writing) I.1872, Tr 2.886; draft (a legal document) I.325; (2) impose law, rules Tr 3.1748, Bo 2.m8.24; *2 pr. sg.* **enditest** HF 634; *3 pr. sg.* **enditeth** IV.41; *pr. pl.* **enditen** dictate Bo 1.m1.4; *pr. subj. pl.* **endite** IV.17; *prp.* **enditynge** Bo 1.pr1.45; *pp.* **endited** VII.1980; *vbl. n.* **endytyng(e)** Ven 77, Astr Pro 43; *pl.* **enditynges** X.1085.

enforce(n) *v.* (1) force III.340; (2) *(reflx.)* try, make an effort Bo 3.pr1.45; (3) strengthen, reinforce VII.958, grow stronger VII.1043, Bo 4.pr7.87; *2 pr. sg.* **enforcest** Bo 3.pr8.6, (with *pro.*) **enforcestow** Bo 2.pr1.110; *3 pr. sg.* **enforceth** X.730; *pr. pl.* **enforcen** VII.1151; *imp. sg.* **enforce thee** try VII.1047; *2 pt. sg.* **enforcedest** Bo 3.pr9.147; *3 pt. sg.* **enforcede** Bo 3.pr12.106; *pt. pl.* **enforceden** Bo 1.pr3.33; *pp.* **enforced** X.832.

engendrure *n.* (1) the act of procreation VII.1947; (2) offspring X.621; *pl.* **engendrures** offspring X.562.

engyn *n.* (1) intelligence, skill VIII.339; trickery Tr 2.565; (2) contrivance V.184; siege engine, catapult HF 1934; *pl.* **engynes** siege engines, catapults Rom B 4194, Rom C 7068, **engynnes** contrivances Rom C 7068, **engynnes** tricks Rom B 4549.

enhabyten *v.* dwell Bo 1.pr5.35, Rom C 6355; *3 pr. sg.* **enhabiteth** Bo 3.pr10.39; *pr. pl.* **enhabiten** Bo 2.pr4.109; *prp.* **enhabitynge** Bo 3.m10.3; *pp.* **enhabited** inhabited Bo 2.pr7.32, **enhabit to** settled on, devoted to Tr 4.443.

enhaunce(n), enhawnsen *v.* advance I.1434; increase (pride, *etc.*) X.614, Bo 4.pr3.97; *2 pr. sg.* **enhauncest** Bo 3.m9.32; *3 pr. sg.* **enhaunceth** strengthens X.730; *pr. pl.* **enhaunsen hemself** raise themselves, aspire to Bo 5.pr5.64; *pr. subj. pl.* **enhaunse us** aspire Bo 5.pr5.97; *pt. sg.* **enhaunced** exalted, advanced IV.1374; raised Astr 2.26.34; *vbl. n.* **enhaunsyng** Astr 2.39.23.

ensample, ensaumple, ensampul, exemple *v.* (1) example I.568, III.1580, Tr 3.872; **e. as thus** for example Astr 2.45.8; **e. why** for example Tr 1.1002; (2) **in e.** as a sign, symbolizing Astr 1.21.34; (3) illustrative story, exemplum VII.1998; (4) model, pattern I.505, I.520, Tr 1.232; *pl.* **ensamples** exempla, illustrative anecdotes VII.1998, **ensawmples** Tr 1.760; models LGW 1258.

ensure(n) *v.* assure VI.143, HF 2098; *pp.* **ensured** Rom C 7210.

entencioun, entencion *n.* intention, purpose VI.408, VIII.1443, Bo 3.pr11.85 Tr 1.211; will, disposition Tr 1.52, Tr 1.345; *pl.* **entenciouns** Rom C 7170.

entende *v.* (1) intend, plan III.1479; strive VII.2308; to be inclined Tr 2.853; hope for, wish Tr 3.27; Tr 4.1649; (2) pay attention to V.689; take care of V.1097; attend, wait upon IV.1900; (3) listen Tr 3.27, Tr 4.893; perceive Bo 1.pr2.3; *2 pr. sg.* (with *pro.*) **intendestow** Tr 5.478; *3 pr. sg.* **entendeth unto** strives toward III.275; *pr. pl.* **entenden** Rom A 82; *pt. sg.* **entendede** Bo 4.pr1.7; *pt. pl.* **entendeden** LGW 1155; *prp.* **entendynge** looking Bo 1.pr2.3.

entent(e) *n.* (1) purpose, intention II.40; plan II.206; attention LGW G 139, take care VIII.6; **fil in his e.** he decided Rom B 3437; **in hool e.** wholeheartedly IV.861; **in (ful) good e.** willingly I.958, in good faith II.824; (2) mind, heart V.1178; **seyde (al) his e.** spoke his (whole) mind III.1733; (3) meaning, view VII.1078; **as to commune e.** in plain language V.107; (4) legal claim Bo 1.pr4.150; *pl.* **ententes** HF 1267.

ententyf *adj.* (1) eager X.781; having a tendency to Rom A 339; (2) attentive Bo 3.pr1.20; devoted Rom A 436; (3) diligent VII.1015, Tr 2.838.

ententifly, ententiflich(e) *adv.* diligently HF 616, Tr 1.332; attentively Bo 3.pr12.81.

entrechaunge(n) *v.* (1) exchange, transpose Bo 5.pr6.260; (2) alternate Bo 5.pr6.262; *3 pr. sg.* **entre-**

chaungith Bo 5.pr6.262; *pr. pl.* **entrechaungen** Bo 3.pr2.44; *pt. pl.* **entrechaungeden** Tr 3.1368; *prp.* (as *adj.*) **entrechaungynge** Bo 5.m1.12; *pp.* **entrechaunged** mutual Tr 4.1043; varying Bo 5.m4.35; *vbl. n.* **entrechaungynge** mingling Bo 4.m4.14; *pl.* **entrechaungynges** Bo 2.m3.18.

entremette, entermete *v.* (usu. *reflx.*) concern oneself, intercede Rom B 2966; interfere, meddle III.834, Rom C 6498; *3 pr. sg.* **entremetteth** VII.1541, **entremetith** Rom C 5921; *imp. sg.* **entreme te** Tr 1.1026.

envenyme *v.* poison III.474, BD 641, Rom C 7470; *3 pr. sg.* **envenymeth** Bo 4.pr3.76; *pp.* **envenymed** infused with poison VII.2124, (as *adj.*) Rom A 979; *vbl. n.* **envenymynge** X.854.

envye *n.* (1) ill-will, spite VIII.1372; (2) envy I.907; (3) eagerness, desire Rom A 1653.

envie(n) *v.* contend, vie with BD 173, HF 1231; *imp. sg.* **envie** Tr 5.1789.

environ(e) *v.* (1) encircle, surround Rom C 7017; (2) move in a circle Rom A 526; (3) comprehend Bo 3.m9.40; *3 pr. sg.* **envyrouneth** encircles Bo 3.m9.36, comprehends Bo 5.pr4.208; *pt. sg.* **envyrounde** Bo 2.pr2.21; *pp.* **envyrouned** Bo 3.pr5.36; *prp.* **envyronyng** encircling Rom A 526; *vbl. n.* **envyrounynge** circumference Bo 2.pr7.25.

envyroun, envyron, enveroun *adv.* around LGW 227; **round (al) e.** all around LGW F 300, Rom B 3618, Rom B 3203.

equacions, equaciouns *n. pl.* calculations V.1279; (*astro.*) divisions of the sphere into equal parts Astr 2.37.12; *pl.* **e. of houses** division of the sphere into twelve parts Astr 2.36 Rubric.

equinoxial(l) *n.* celestial equator Astr 1.17.30.

er *adv.* before, formerly I.3789, VIII.1273, Tr 3.763; *super.* Cf. **erst(e)**, *adv.*, and **or** *adv.*

er *prep.* before III.1619, VII.2797. Cf. **or** *prep.*

er *conj.* before I.255, I.1040, Anel 115; **er that** before I.36, I.835, Anel 100. Cf. **or** *conj.*

ere, eere *n.* ear III.636, I.1021, Tr 1.106; ear of grain LGW F 76; *pl.* **erys** I.556, **eres** IV.498, **eeris** VII.1418.

ernest *n.* (1) seriousness Tr 2.452; **in e.** seriously I.1125; (2) serious matter VIII.710; **make e. of game** take a joke seriously I.3186; (3) sincere passion LGW 1287; (4) pledge Rom B 3680.

erre(n) *v.* (1) wander, deviate Astr 2.3.72; (2) blunder, err VII.1025; sin, do wrong Tr 1.1003; break the law Tr 4.549; *2 pr. sg.* **errest** wander Tr 4.302; *pr. pl.* **erren** VIII.449; *pr. subj. pl.* **erre** Tr 3.1774; *pp.* **erred** VII.1241.

errour *n.* (1) error Tr 4.933; heresy Tr 1.1008; sin ABC 5; (2) confusion PF 146, Tr 4.200; fickleness For 4; *pl.* **errours** Bo 3.pr3.8.

erst(e) *adj. super.* (as *n.*) **at e.** at first, for the first time VIII.151, VIII.264, Tr 1.842.

erst(e) *adv. super.* before, earlier IV.144, IV.336, Tr 1.299; **e. er** before III.2220, VI.662; **e. than** before I.1566.

erthe *n.* earth I.1246, PF 33; *pl.* **erthes** lands Bo 1.m5.52.

erthely, erthly, erthliche *adj.* earthly, mortal I.1166, VI.21, BD 19, Bo 2.pr6.29.

eschaufen *v.* (1) heat, make warm Bo 1.m5.28; grow warm Bo 1.m6.2; (2) inflame (with passion) Bo

4.pr6.324; *3 pr. sg.* **eschawfeth** grow hot, become angry X.657; *pt. sg.* **eschaufede** was angry Bo 1.pr5.62; *pp.* **eschawfed with** heated by X.546; *vbl. n.* **eschawfynge** heat X.537; *pl.* **eschawfynges** heat, excitement X.916.

eschue(n), eschuwe(n), eschewe(n) *v.* forego, eschew IV.1451, VIII.4; escape, flee from I.3043, Tr 4.1517; *3 pr. sg.* **escheweth** VII.1320, **eschueth** X.833; *pr. pl.* **eschuen** Bo 4.pr7.44; *pr. subj. sg.* **eschewe** X.632; *imp. sg.* **eschue** VII.1181; *pp.* **eschued** VII.1839, **eschewed** VII.3338; *vbl. n.* **eschewyng(e)** X.64, PF 140, **eschuynge** Bo 3.pr11.186.

ese, eyse, ease *n.* (1) ease, comfort IV.217; **at e.** comfortable III.2101; **with to gret an e.** too easily Tr 1.28; **take (one's) e.** rest I.969; (2) relief Tr 4.726; refreshment I.29; **don** (someone) **e.** please I.728; (3) pleasure IV.1643; (4) benefit Tr 4.86; (5) **lith in youre e.** is convenient for you VII.291.

ese(n), ease *v.* (1) entertain I.2194; (2) confort, relieve Tr 2.1400, Rom A 316; **e.** (someone's) **herte** please BD 556; (3) soothe (pain) Tr 3.950; *3 pr. sg.* **esith** comforts Rom B 5272; *imp. pl.* **eseth** Tr 3.197; *pp.* **esed** accommodated I.29, relieved I.2670, **eased** Rom B 2438; *vbl. n.* **esyng** comforting Tr 2.1287.

esy *adj.* (1) comfortable IV.1264; (2) lenient, gentle Tr 3.1363; **e. fir** moderate blaze VIII.768; **e. pas** slow pace Tr 2.620; (3) tractable Tr 1.1090; (4) not difficult X.1042; (5) moderate I.441; (6) suitable LGW 1116; *comp.* **esier(e)** more tolerable VII.1500, more gentle Bo 1.pr5.78.

esily, esely, esilich *adv.* (1) comfortably IV.423; (2) slowly HF 1675, Tr 1.317; **e. a pas** at an unhurried pace V.388; (3) easily V.115; (4) gently LGW F 394.

espace *var.* of **space** space of time VII.1029.

especes *var.* of **speces** kinds X.448.

especial *adj.* special, intimate VII.1166; special, particular X.893; **in e.** particularly Truth 25, to particulars VII.1234. Cf. **special.**

espye(n), aspye *v.* (1) waylay BD 836; (2) search out, discover I.1420; look about LGW 858, PF 194; (3) find out II.324; **tyme (leyser) e.** find an opportunity I.3293, Tr 5.556; reveal LGW F 265; (4) notice, see I.1112, HF 1689; take notice, take the measure of I.1420; *pt. sg.* **espide** VIII.1230, **aspied** LGW 1471; *pt. subj.* **espide** Tr 4.1388 (*sg.*), LGW 771 (*pl.*); *prp.* **espiyng** Rom B 3804; *pp.* **espied** VIII.895; *vbl. n.* **espying** Ven 34.

espiritueel, espirituel(l) *adj.* spiritual X.516, Rom A 650, Rom B 6758; *pl.* **espirituels** X.79.

estat, estaat *n.* (1) state, condition IV.610; quality Bo 5.pr6.69; (2) rank, social standing IV.1322, LGW F 305; status, power Tr 4.584; class IV.123; (3) term of office III.2018; (4) state, display LGW 1036; *pl.* **estatz** Bo 4.pr5.25, **estatis** Rom B 5468. Cf. **stat.**

estatlich, estatly, estaatly, statly *adj.* dignified I.140, I.281, VII.2712, LGW 1372.

estatutz *see* **statut.**

estraunge *see* **straunge.**

ete(n) *v.* eat I.947, IV.1812, BD 92; *3 pr. sg.* **eteth** PF 604; *pr. pl.* **eten** VI.468; *imp. sg.* **ete** VII.1416; *pr. subj. sg.* **ete** VII.1417; *pt. sg.* **eet** I.2048; *pt. pl.* **ete(n)** BD 432, Tr 2.1184; *prp.* **etyng** III.2167; *pp.* **eten** I.4351; *vbl. n.* **etynge** X.332.

even(e) *adj.* (1) flat, level Astr 2.38.5; (2) equal I.2588, PF 149; **evene-Cristen(e)** fellow Christian X.608,

X.808; (3) impartial I.1864; moderate I.83; tranquil IV.811.

even(e) *adv.* (1) straight BD 451, Astr 2.29.21; (2) exactly II.1143, HF 714; **e. atte fulle** exactly full V.1069; **in myn hond full e.** right in my hand BD 1329; **therwith e.** exactly then BD 275; directly I.1060; (3) equally, evenly I.2593; (4) correctly VIII.1200; (5) calmly I.1523; (6) indeed BD 120.

ever, evere *adv.* (1) ever, always I.50, I.335; (2) **e. (the) lenger (the moore)** increasingly IV.687, V.404, VII.975, Anel 129; **e. the gretter** proportionately greater X.916; **e. the hyer** greater and greater VI.597, X.891; (3) (as *intens.*) **e. among** continually Rom B 3771; **as, als e. as** I.1475, I.4177; **e. ylyche** always, invariably BD 1288; **e. in oon** continually Tr 5.451, always VII.27; **e. sithe** ever after I.3893; **e. yet** always before this III.545.

everemo, everemore, evermo(o), evermor(e), evermoore *adv.* always I.67; continually III.1086, BD 81, BD 604, BD 853, HF 2074, Lady 45; perpetually I.1229; eternally PF 1185; **e. in oon** always, continually IV.2086; **e. . . . the more (hatter, *etc.*) the more . . . the more (hotter, *etc.*)** Rom B 1787, Rom B 2472.

every, everich(e) *pro.* (1) each one I.1848; (2) every one Tr 5.170, Bo 4.pr4.28.

every, everich(e) *adj.* every, each I.15; **e. a** every single I.733; **e. maner wight** every sort of person I.1875; **in e. maner (wyse)** in all ways VII.245.

everichon(e), everichoon *pro.* everyone I.747, VII.1899, Tr 3.412; **alderlast of e.** last of all Rom A 449.

everydel, everydeel (also two words) *n.* everything V.1288, HF 65, Rom A 1076.

everydel(e), everydeel (also two words) *adv.* wholly, completely I.368, IV.1508, Rom A 126.

execucioun, execucion *n.* performance, action For 65; **putten in (to) e.** carry out (a plan) VII.1853; **doon e.** carry out (an intended act) IX.287, carry out (orders) IV.522, punish III.1303.

expounen, expounden, expowne *v.* explain, expound VII.535, VII.2208, VIII.86, Tr 5.1288; *pr. pl.* **expounden** Tr 5.1278; *pt. sg.* **expowned** VII.2156.

expres *adj.* explicit HF 2021.

expres, expresse *adv.* clearly, explicitly III.27, VI.586; **e. agayn** explicitly opposed to X.587.

F

fable *n.* (1) story X.31, BD 52; (2) fiction VI.155, LGW 702; (3) falsehood Sted 15; **holde you in f.** detain you in idle talk Rom A 1439; *pl.* **fables** fictions, falsehoods Rom A 2.

face *n.* (1) face I.199; **shrewe his f.** curse him III.2227; **in my f.** right at me VII.1904; (2) expression IV.1599, Tr 4.68; (3) appearance Tr 2.765, Bo 1.pr4.13; (4) (*astro.*) one-third (10 degrees) of a zodiacal sign Astr 2.4.63; *pl.* **faces** II.650.

faculte(e) *n.* (1) ability, faculty Bo 5.pr4.140; field of learning HF 248; official position I.244.

fader, fadir *n.* (1) father I.100, VIII.208, Rom A 271; (2) forefather VI.505; *gen. sg.* **fader** I.4038, **faderes** ABC 130, **fadres** II.861; *pl.* **fadres** II.129, **faderes** senators of Rome Bo 1.pr4.207.

fadme, fademe, fadome *n.* (as *pl.*) fathoms I.2916, V.1060, BD 422, Rom A 1393.

fay *see* **fey.**

fayerye, fairye *n.* (1) the realm of the supernatural IV.2227, V.96; (as collective) supernatural beings, the supernatural III.859, IV.2039; (2) something magic or enchanting IV.1743; *pl.* **fayeryes** III.872.

faile(n), faille(n), faylen *v.* (1) fail, disappoint I.1610, VIII.388, PF 85; (2) fail to do, accomplish (with *to*) IV.1632, Tr 2.1440; (with *of*) III.430, VIII.671; **f. of my day** fail to pay on the set day VII.275; (3) lack, be lacking VII.248, VII.2462; **f. you my thankes** be lacking in gratitude VII.188; (3) grow weak I.2798, I.3887; grow dim PF 85; *2 pr. sg.* **failest** ABC 112; *3 pr. sg.* **faileth** Tr 1.217; *pr. pl.* **faille(n)** VIII.671, VIII.851, **faylen** Bo 2.pr4.57; *pr. subj. sg.* **faile** IV.1632, **faille** Tr 4.273; *pt. sg.* **failled** V.1577; *pt. pl.* **failide** Rom A 775; *pt. subj. sg.* **faylede** Bo 4.pr4.214; *pp.* **fayled** Bo 1.pr5.10; *vbl. n.* **faylyng(e)** failure Tr 1.928, Bo 5.pr6.54.

faille, faile, fayle *n.* **sanz (sans) f.** doubtless, for certain HF 429; **withoute(n) f.** doubtless, for certain I.1644, I.1854, Tr 2.629.

fayn, feyn, fawe *adj.* happy, pleased II.787, Tr 4.1321; eager III.220.

fayn, feyn, fawe *adv.* gladly, eagerly II.41, BD 1101, Tr 1.691, Tr 4.887; *comp.* **fayner** Lady 71; *super.* **faynest** PF 480.

fayned *see* **feyne(n).**

faynte *v.* (1) (*intr.*) grow faint, weak VIII.753, BD 488; *1 pr. sg.* **feynte** Tr 1.410; *pr. subj. sg.* **feynte** VIII.753; *pt. sg.* **feynted** grew weak Rom B 1735; *vbl. n.* **feyntyng** weakening IV.970; (2) *2 pr. sg. (tr.)* **feyntest** enfeeble II.927.

fair(e) *n.* beauty V.518; fine thing I.165, Tr 3.850; **foule or (ne) f.** all circumstances II.525, V.121, Tr 4.1022.

fair(e) *adv.* (1) well I.94, I.124, III.1142; handsomely I.273; neatly I.3210; (2) courteously, pleasantly I.3289, II.1051, III.803; gently I.2697, VIII.536, V.347; (3) fully, completely VII.830, PF 503; **f. and wel** very well, completely I.539, I.1826, PF 594; (4) (with *prep.*) directly, squarely I.606, I.984, HF 1050.

fayre, fair(e), feir *adj.* (1) pleasing, attractive I.154, I.211, HF 833, Mars 256; **f. at (to) eye(n)** pleasant to see IV.1168, VIII.964; (2) shining I.3976; (3) favorable I.1861; I.1874, Tr 1.907; (4) convincing VII.1711, X.1022; (5) just LGW 2548; (6) gracious, benevolent I.1861; morally good X.1061; (7) (as form of address) dear II.245, II.319, Tr 2.1670; *comp.* **fairer** I.754; *super.* **fairest** I.2201.

falle(n) *v.* (1) fall, descend I.128, I.921; fall out or away from VII.2126, Tr 5.549; **f. away** turn aside Tr 3.1306; (2) decrease Tr 1.563, Tr 4.430; lose color BD 564; (3) fall into, come (to a condition) I.25, I.1418, X.1025; **f. forth** engage in Tr 5.107; **f. in grace** win (her) favor Tr 1.370; **f. in speche** speak Tr 5.855; **f. acorded** agree III.812; (4) **f. to (unto)** belong to, be appropriate to I.149, IV.259, Tr 1.142; **as fer as reson f.** insofar as was appropriate to reason V.570; (5) befall, happen I.585, I.1668, V.134; **f. faire (foule)** have good (bad) fortune, turn out well (badly) Tr 4.1022, LGW F 186, Rom A 798; **f. of** result from VII.1328; *2 pr. sg.* **fallest** VI.556; *3 pr. sg.*

falleth I.1669, **falles** I.4042, BD 257; *pr. pl.* **falle(n)** I.2327, X.100; *pr. subj. sg.* **falle** I.2555; *pt. sg.* **fil** I.845, **fel** I.1462; *pt. pl.* **fille(n)** I.949, I.2666, **felle(n)** Tr 1.3, Tr 1.145; *pt. subj. sg.* **fille** I.131; *pp.* **(y)falle** I.25, I.1240, **fallen** II.909; *prp.* **fallyng(e)** Bo 4.pr6.151, (as *adj.*) Tr 2.1382; *vbl. n.* **fallyng(e)** I.2464, I.2722.

fals *n.* falsehood, deceit HF 2108, Tr 3.298.

fals(e) *adj.* (1) deceitful, treacherous I.925, III.1670; counterfeit Form Age 20; (2) wicked I.4268, VI.154; (3) untrue I.640, III.382, Tr 1.593; wrong IV.2380; *comp.* **falser** LGW 2399.

fals *adv.* untruly III.1057, VII.1204.

false(n) *v.* (1) betray BD 1234, Tr 3.784; (2) misrepresent I.3175; *2 pr. sg.* **falsest** LGW 1377; *3 pr. sg.* **falsith** Rom B 5416; *pr. pl.* **falsen** LGW 1377; *pt. sg.* **falsed** Tr 5.1053; *pp.* **falsed** misrepresented V.627, betrayed Anel 147.

falshed(e), **falsheed(e)** *n.* falsehood VIII.979, VIII.1051, Rom B 2049, Rom B 3493, Rom B 5454.

falsly *adv.* (1) disloyally I.1142, I.1586, Tr 1.89; deceitfully VI.654, HF 389, LGW 665; (2) evilly III.738, VI.228; (3) untruly VI.415; (4) wrongfully, unjustly Tr 1.38.

falsnes(se) *n.* (1) deceitfulness, dishonesty VIII.976, VIII.1086, Anel 160; (2) illusoriness Bo 1.pr5.49; (3) misconception Bo 5.pr3.107.

fame *n.* (1) reputation, good or bad I.3055, IV.418, VI.111, HF 305; notoriety I.3148; (2) news II.995, IV.940; fame, rumor Tr 4.659; *gen.* **Fames** HF 786; *pl.* **fames** HF 1154.

familier, familer(e) *n.* (1) member of the household Bo 3.pr5.27; (2) close acquaintance Bo 1.pr3.47; *pl.* **familiers** Bo 1.pr3.47, **famylieres** Bo 3.pr5.44.

famulier, familier *adj.* (1) belonging to the household IV.1784; (2) intimate I.215, Rom B 4013; (3) courteous, friendly LGW 1606.

fantasye *n.* (1) imagination IV.1577, Tr 2.482; (2) an imagined notion V.844, BD 28; delusion I.3835, HF 593, Tr 3.1032; (3) fancy, desire I.3191; inclination III.516; **after** (one's) **f.** according to (one's) desire(s) III.190, V.205; **doon his f.** fulfill his amorous desire VII.2285; *pl.* **fantasies** VII.2275.

fare *n.* (1) behavior, conduct Tr 5.507; **nice f.** foolishness Tr 1.1025, Tr 2.1144; **frendes f.** friendly ceremonial, friendliness Tr 3.605; **strange f.** elaborate courtesy, formality VII.263; (2) commotion, fuss Tr 3.1106, HF 1065; **made f.** caused a fuss I.3999; (3) action Tr 5.335; business, ado Tr 3.1566, Tr 4.920, Tr 5.53; (4) condition, state Tr 2.1001, Pity 62; (5) happiness HF 682.

fare(n) *v.* (1) go II.512, Tr 5.359; (2) act, behave Tr 4.1087; **f. by** deal with, treat X.899, Tr 4.463; (3) fare, get along, do I.1265, I.4350, Tr 1.666; **how f. ye** how are you III.1801; **f. aright** do well Tr 1.878; (4) to be (well) provided for III.1773; (5) (*impers.*) happen I.4408, VIII.966, HF 271; *2 pr. sg.* **farest** HF 887, **farst** PF 599; *3 pr. sg.* **fareth** III.1088, **fares** (*Nth.*) I.4023; *pr. pl.* **fare(n)** I.1261, III.1094; *pr. subj. sg.* **fare** V.1579; *imp. sg.* **far** Tr 1.878; **far(e) wel** good luck, good-bye I.2740, I.4236, LGW F 551; *imp. pl.* **fareth wel** farewell Tr 5.1412; *pt. sg.* **ferd(e)** I.1372, Tr 4.1094; *pt. pl.* **ferde(n)** I.1647, Tr 4.918; *pt. subj.* **ferde** Rom A 271 (*sg.*), Tr 2.39 (*pl.*); *prp.* (as *adj.*) **well (beste) farynge** good (best) looking

V.932, handsome VII.1942, attractive BD 452; *pp.* **(y)fare** I.2436, Tr 4.1169, **faren** III.1773, **ferd** Tr 5.1358.

fasoun, fassoun *n.* appearance, fashion Rom A 885, Rom A 932; fabric, structure Bo 2.m8.19.

fast(e) *adj.* thick, dense Tr 5.1235, V.1068; *comp.* **faster(e)** firmer, stronger Bo 1.pr6.95, quicker V.1066.

fast(e) *adv.* (1) tightly, closely I.2151, III.520, IV.1821; firmly Tr 1.534, Tr 1.969; strictly III.652; (2) quickly I.1469, IV.1927, BD 140; **as f.** very quickly Tr 2.898, Tr 3.1094; **f. anon** immediately BD 1027; (3) close I.1478; **f. by** close to I.719, I.1476, III.970; (4) eagerly, heartily I.1266, III.672; (as *intens.*) **f. gapeth** opens wide LGW 2004; *comp.* **fastere** more tightly VII.2532.

fastne *see* **festne**.

faucon, faucoun *n.* falcon V.411, V.424, Tr 3.1784.

faught *see* **fighte(n)**.

fawe *see* **fayn** *adj., adv.*

fee *n.* (1) property III.630; **f. symple** unrestricted possession I.319; (2) payment BD 266; *pl.* **fees** I.1803.

feble, fieble *adj.* feeble, weak I.1369, III.306, IV.1198; *comp.* **feblere** Bo 3.pr9.28, (as *n.*) Bo 3.pr3.62.

fecche(n), feche(n) *v.* fetch, bring II.662, IV.276, Anel 338, LGW 1347; fetch, take away II.1064; *imp. sg.* **fecche** bring I.3492; *pr. subj. sg.* **fecche** take away III.1554; *pt.* **fette** III.2159 (*sg.*), VII.851 (*pl.*); *pp.* **(y)fet** I.819, V.174; *pp.* **to fette** to be fetched Tr 3.609; *vbl. n.* **fecchynge** abduction Tr 5.890.

feffe *v.* enfeoff, endow with Tr 3.901; *2 pt. sg.* (with *pro.*) **feffedstow** Bo 2.pr3.64; *pp.* **feffed** IV.1698.

fey, fay *n.* faith I.1126, III.203, Rom C 7578; trustworthiness Bo 4.pr2.17; **by (upon) (one's) f.** on one's good word I.1126, I.3284, III.203, Tr 2.1103.

feyne(n) *v.* (1) make up, invent, devise I.736, III.1377, Bo 3.pr10.86 (see note); (2) imitate, counterfeit III.1507, V.524; (3) dissemble, make false pretences V.510, Tr 2.1558; disguise Rom C 6342; (4) pretend IV.513, Tr 1.326; (*reflx.*) II.351, IV.1950, Bo 5.pr6.71; **f. thy wey** pretend to go another way VII.1311; (5) avoid (obeying a command) IV.529; evade (a duty), hold back (from doing something) Tr 2.997, Tr 3.167; *2 pr. sg.* **feynest** Tr 5.413; *3 pr. sg.* **feyneth** LGW 1266; *pr. pl.* **feyne** III.1507; *imp. sg.* **feyne** VII.1301; *pt. sg.* **feyned** IV.513, **fayned** Tr 1.354; *prp.* **feynynge** HF 1478; *pp.* **yfeyned** LGW G 327, **feyned(e)** VI.62, (as *adj.*) I.705, **feynt(e)** Rom A 433, Rom B 5563, **faynt** Rom C 7403; *vbl. n.* **feynyng(e)** V.556, LGW 1556; **withoute f.** wholeheartedly Rom B 1971.

feyntise *n.* (1) deceit, guile Rom B 1971, Rom B 2998; (2) faint-heartedness Rom B 2947.

feir *see* **fayre** *adj.*

feirs, feers *see* **fiers(e)**.

feith, faith *n.* (1) religious belief I.62, VIII.644, VIII.110; (2) confidence LGW F 31; (3) loyalty IV.1053, Tr 2.1503; (4) pledged word III.2139, **f. to borwe** my word as a pledge V.1234; (5) **in (good) f.** truly V.673, Tr 2.169; **by (on, upon) my f.** on my word, certainly III.841, III.1403.

feithful *adj.* (1) devout VIII.24; (2) loyal IV.310, IV.343; (3) true III.1425.

feithfully *adv.* (1) faithfully, devotedly II.461, IV.1111, Tr 3.1672; sincerely Tr 2.1577; (2) loyally Tr 2.263,

Tr 5.1076; (3) truly III.1420, HF 853, Tr 4.114; indeed, assuredly III.1433, IV.1066.

fel *see* **falle(n).**

fel, fell(e) *adj.* fierce, cruel I.1559, I.2630, Tr 4.44; terrible, dreadful Tr 1.470; *comp.* **feller** Rom B 4103.

felawe, felow(e) *n.* (1) companion, comrade I.890, BD 366, Rom B 3344; friend, associate I.1031, Tr 1.696, Rom B 5275; **good f.** agreeable fellow I.395 (see note), I.618; (2) equal partner I.1624, X.400; (3) fellow fighter I.2548; *pl.* **felawes** associates VII.2985, fellows of a college I.4112; **felowes** Rom C 6087.

felawshipe, felawship(e), felawsshyppe *n.* (1) company, fellowship I.26, I.32, VI.938, BD 978; household I.3539, LGW 965; (2) companionship, friendliness I.474, Tr 3.403; (3) equal partnership I.1626.

felawschipeth, felawschipith *3 pr. sg.* accompanies Bo 4.m1.12; *(reflx.)* joins Bo 4.pr6.126; *pp.* **ifelaschiped** joined Bo 2.pr6.84.

feld, feeld *n.* field I.886, I.984, Tr 1.1074; *pl.* **feeldes** I.977, **feldes** HF 897.

feld *see* **felle.**

felden *see* **falle(n).**

fele *adj.* many PF 329, Tr 4.512.

fele(n), feele(n), fel, feel(l) *v.* (1) feel VII.155, Tr 3.960, Rom A 565, Rom B 1824, Rom B 1844, Rom B 4357; **f. other weyes** think otherwise; (2) feel out, inquire indirectly Tr 2.387; (3) perceive VIII.155, VIII.711; realize Tr 2.1283; experience HF 826; *2 pr. sg.* **feelist** Bo 3.pr12.48; (with *pro.*) **felistow** Bo 1.pr4.1; *3 pr. sg.* **feeleth** I.1220, **feleth** Tr 3.1658; *pr. pl.* **feelen** X.581; *pr. subj. sg.* **feele** Tr 2.856 **fele** HF 826; *pr. subj. pl.* **fele** Rom B 5041; *1 & 3 pt. sg.* **felt(e)** I.1575, Tr 2.58, **feeled(e)** VIII.521, Bo 3.pr1.19; **feled** BD 492; *2 pt. sg.* **feltist** LGW 1379; *pt. pl.* **felte(n)** Tr 3.1222, Tr 3.1316; *prp.* **felynge** suffering Tr 4.840; *pp.* **felt** V.586, **feled** Tr 4.984.

felicite(e) *n.* happiness I.338, I.1266, Tr 5.763.

felyng(e), feelyng *vbl. n.* (1) sense of touch X.959; (2) consciousness Rom B 1738; (3) feeling, emotion III.610, BD 11, Tr 3.1090; (4) understanding Tr 3.1333.

fell(e) *see* **fel** *adj.*

felle *v.* fell, cause to fall I.1702; *pt. pl.* **felden** Rom A 911; *pp.* **feld** I.2924.

felle(n) *see* **falle(n).**

felly, felliche *adv.* fiercely Bo 2.m3.12, Rom B 3251.

felonye *n.* (1) crime, wickedness II.643, Rom A 165; (2) ill will, malice X.543; *pl.* **felonies** X.281.

felonous, felonows, felenous *adj.* (1) criminal, wicked X.438, Bo 1.m4.14; (2) hostile Bo 4.pr3.107.

felowe *see* **felawe.**

felthe *see* **filthe.**

fend, feend *n.* (1) demon VIII.984, Tr 4.437, LGW 1996; (2) **the f.** Satan, the Devil I.4288, II.454; *gen. sg.* **feendes** II.571; *pl.* **feendes** II.460, **fendes** Tr 2.896.

fendly, feendly, feendlych *adj.* devilish, demoniac II.751, II.783, V.868, BD 593.

fer(e), feer(e) *n.* fear VII.2906, Tr 2.770, Rom B 3163; (2) danger Tr 3.583, Tr 3.1144.

fer, far *adj.* far, remote VII.718, Tr 4.1426, LGW 1418; **f. cause** remote cause VII.1395; *comp.* **ferre** I.3393; *super.* (as *n.*) **ferreste** those farthest away I.494.

fer, far *adv.* far I.491, I.1648, Tr 1.1421; at a distance VII.2997; **f. ne ner** more or less I.1850 (see note);

comp. **ferre** I.48, I.2060, **ferrer** I.835; *super.* **ferrest** Bo 4.pr6.131.

ferd(e), fered *n.* in *phr.* **for f.** because of fear Tr 1.557, Tr 4.607.

ferd(e) *see* **fare(n).**

ferde(n) *see* **fare(n).**

fere, feere *n.*[1] (1) companion Tr 1.13, LGW 969; **in f.** together III.924, HF 250; (2) equal PF 416; (3) mate, spouse PF 416, Tr 4.791; *pl.* **feres** Tr 1.224.

fere, feere *n.*[2] (1) fear I.1333, I.2686; (2) cause of fear, danger Tr 3.583, Tr 3.1144.

fere *v.* frighten Tr 1.1333; *pp.* **fered** frightened, afraid VII.3386, VIII.924, Tr 2.124.

fereful *adj.* fearful, frightened VIII.660; *super.* **ferfulleste** Tr 2.450.

ferrest(e) *see* **fer** *adj., adv.*

forforth *adv.* far Tr 2.960, Tr 2.1106; **as f.** as in so far as, to the extent that II.1099, III.56, as much as Tr 1.121; **so f.** to such an extent V.567.

fery *see* **firy.**

ferme *adj.* steadfast, firm Bo 3.pr10.129, Bo 3.pr11.185.

ferme *adv.* firmly, steadfastly Rom A 1500; **holde f.** keep resolutely Tr 2.1525; **f. and stable** unswervingly, unshakably IV.663, IV.1499.

fermely, feermely *adv.* firmly, steadfastly X.309, Bo 3.m1.3, Tr 5.495.

ferre, ferreste *see* **fer** *adj.*

ferre, ferre(r) *see* **fer** *adv.*

fers *n.* queen (in chess) BD 654, BD 669; *pl.* **ferses** chess pieces BD 723 (see note).

fers(e) *see* **fiers(e).**

ferthe, fourthe *adj.* fourth II.17, X.943.

ferther *adj.* farther, far IV.2226, VII.496.

ferther *adv.* farther I.36, V.1177; *super.* **ferthest** Bo 4.pr6.124. Cf. **forther(e).**

fest, fist *n.* fist I.4275, III.792; *pl.* **fistes** Tr 4.243.

feste, feeste *n.* (1) religious festival Tr 1.168, Mars 22; (2) festival I.2736; feast I.2197, I.3684; festivity I.2483; (3) rejoicing Tr 2.421; **make f.** make merry VII.327; (4) welcoming attention Tr 2.361; **make(n) (swich) f.** pay (such) attention to Tr 3.1228, Tr 5.1429; treat respectfully IV.1109; show favor, pay court BD 638; *pl.* **festes** I.1931, **feestes** VI.65.

feste, feeste *v.* feast, dine II.1007, VI.1892; *3 pr. sg.* **festeth** entertains I.2139; *pr. pl.* **feste** LGW 2157; *prp.* **festeiynge** entertaining V.345; *vbl. n.* **festeiynge** festivity Tr 5.455; *pl.* **festeynges** Tr 3.1718.

festne, fastne *v.* fasten I.195; *pr. subj.* **fastne** Bo 1.m5.56; *1 pt. sg.* **festned** fixed (the gaze) Bo 2.pr2.1; *3 pt. sg.* **festened(e)** Bo 1.pr3.5, Bo 2.pr2.1; *pp.* **festnyd** Bo 1.m5.2.

fet(e), feet(e) *see* **fote.**

(y)fet *see* **fecche(n).**

fethere *n.* feather I.2144; *pl.* **fetheres** IX.304, **fetheris** wings Bo 1.m4.1; **fethres** HF 507, **fetheres** HF 530.

fethered, fethred *pt. sg.* clasped with (his) wings, copulated VII.3177; *pp.* covered, provided with feathers Tr 2.926, Rom A 742.

fetys *adj.* well-made, elegant VI.478, Rom A 532.

festisly *adv.* elegantly, neatly I.273, I.3319, III.1742.

fette *see* **fecche(n).**

fetures *n. pl.* features, appearance IX.121, Wom Nobl 6, Rom B 2813.

fycchen *v.* fix Bo 4.pr1.66; *3 pr. sg.* **ficcheth** Bo 5.m1.4;

pr. subj. sg. **ficche** Bo 3.m12.64; *pp.* **(i)fycched** Bo 3.pr11.218, Bo 4.pr6.114.

fiers(e), fers(e), feirs, feers *adj.* fierce, dangerous I.1598, I.1945, Tr 1.225.

fighte(n) *v.* fight I.984, I.1711; *3 pr. sg.* **fighteth** I.2559; fight PF 103; *pr. pl.* **fighte** I.4291; *pr. subj. pl.* **fighten** I.1836; *pt. sg.* **faught** I.989; *pt. pl.* **foughte(n)** I.1178, I.1699; *prp.* **fightyng** I.1661; *vbl. n.* **fightyng** I.1656.

figure *n.* (1) form, appearance III.1459; (human) form VII.2222; shape Scog 27; (2) image, likeness V.831; configuration I.2043 (see note); illustration Astr 2.26.36; (sense) impressions Bo 5.m4.13; impressed image Bo 5.m4.19; (3) parable I.499; **in f.** as a symbol, symbolically Tr 5.1449, ABC 94; rhetorical ornament, figure of speech IV.16, HF 858; composition Buk 25; *pl.* **figures** images HF 126; arabic numerals BD 37; markings, scale Astr Pro 66.

fil, fille(n) *see* **falle(n)**.

fille *n.* (al) (one's) **f.** as much as one wants I.1528, I.2559, LGW 817.

filthe, felthe *n.* (1) filth III.1215, Tr 3.381; (2) moral foulness, infamy III.1393, X.258, Bo 2pr.5.167; sinfulness X.606, X.882; *pl.* **filthes** foul things X.196.

fyn *n.* (1) end, conclusion VII.2694; **for f.** to this conclusion Tr 4.477; (2) outcome VII.2158; (3) object, purpose IV.2106, Tr 2.794, Mars 218; main point Rom A 1558.

fyn(e) *adj.* (1) fine, excellent IV.1863; refined LGW F 544; (2) sheer Tr 5.421; *comp.* **fyner** I.1039; *super.* **fynest(e)** I.194, HF 1351.

final *adj.* final, ultimate V.987; **f. cause** ultimate cause or purpose VII.1401, X.939, Tr 1.682.

fynde(n) *v.* (1) find, discover I.648, I.736, BD 102; (2) provide VI.169; provide for VI.537, VII.2829; (3) arrange, devise Tr 5.356; (4) fabricate, invent I.736, Tr 5.1580; **fond his countenaunce** assumed an expression Tr 3.979; *2 pr. sg.* **fyndest** Rom C 6857; *3 pr. sg.* **fyndeth** II.1150, **fynt** *(contr.)* I.4071, **fyndes** *(Nth.)* I.4130; *pr. pl.* **fynde(n)** III.1753, Bo 2.m5.14; *pr. subj. sg.* **fynde** PF 456; *imp. sg.* **fynd** I.2244; *1 & 3 pt. sg.* **foond** I.2445, **fond** I.701, **found** Anel 154, **fand** Rom B 2707; *2 pt. sg.* **fownde** Tr 3.362; *pt. pl.* **founde(n)** VI.769, Tr 1.137, **fonde** HF 1810, **foond** VII.2069; *pt. subj. sg.* **fond** VII.2331; *pp.* **(y)founde** I.1211, I.4059, **founden** be provided II.243, **fownde(n)** discovered Bo. 1.pr6.71, Bo 2.pr7.20; *vbl. n.* **fyndyng** I.3220.

fyne *adv.* fully, well Tr 1.661; **wel and f.** completely LGW 1715.

fynder *n.* founder BD 1168, originator Tr 2.844.

fyne, feyne *v.* finish, cease, stop Tr 4.26, Tr 5.776, Rom B 1797.

fyngres, fyngeres *pl.* of **fynger** fingers I.129, IV.380, Tr 4.737.

fynt *see* **fynde(n)**.

fyr(e), fyer, feere *n.* fire I.1246, Bo 3.m9.38, Tr 3.978, LGW 2612; passion LGW F 106; one of the four elements I.1246; **wilde f.** Greek fire III.373 (see note); erysipelas I.4172 (see note), IV.2252; **f. of seint Antony** erysipelas X.427 (see note); *pl.* **fyres** I.2292.

fyrbrond *n.* firebrand, torch IV.1727, PF 114.

firy, fery *adj.* fiery I.1493, I.1564, III.276.

firmament *n.* (1) the sky, the heavens IV.2219, BD 692; (2) celestial sphere II.295, BD 693.

first and forward, foreward *adv. phr.* first of all IV.2187, Bo 3.pr3.23.

fisshe(n) *v.* (1) fish I.3927; (2) lure, hunt III.1820; **f. a cause** invent a reason Tr 3.1162; *pp.* **fisshed fayre** made a fine catch Tr 2.328.

fist *see* **fest**.

fit *n.* (1) episode, experience I.4230, III.42; (2) canto, division of a poetic narrative VII.888.

flambe, flaumbe, flaume *n.* flame X.353, PF 250, Tr 4.118; *pl.* **flambes** VIII.515, **flawmes** ABC 89.

flater(e) *v.* (1) flatter X.617, Rom C 5938; (2) lie, deceive Mars 188; *2 pr. sg.* **flaterest** IV.2059; *pr. subj. sg.* **flatere** X.376; *pt. sg.* **flateryd** Bo 2.pr1.55; *prp.* **flaterynge** III.1294, (as *adj.*) Bo 637; *pp.* **yflatered** III.930; *vbl. n.* **flaterynge** flattery, X.612, deception II.405; *pl.* **flaterynges** Bo 2.pr1.90.

flatery(e) *n.* (1) flattery I.1927, III.932, Rom C 6040; (2) deception Anel 125; *pl.* **flateries** Bo 1.pr1.61.

flatour *n.* flatterer, deceiver VII.3325; *pl.* **flatereres** X.613.

flaugh *see* **fle** *v.*[2]

flawmes *see* **flambe**.

fle(n), flee(n) *v.*[1] (1) flee, run away II.121, III.279, HF 186, PF 147; (2) escape I.2993, VIII.1081; (3) go away, depart I.1469, IV.119; (4) avoid, shun VII.1484; *2 pr. sg.* **fleest** Tr 3.1435; *3 pr. sg.* **fleeth** I.1469; *pr. pl.* **fleen** II.121, **fle(e)** III.520, Bo 4.m7.67; *pr. subj.* **fle** X.1005 (*sg.*), Tr 2.1554 (*pl.*); *imp. sg.* **fle** Tr 2.1254; *imp. pl.* **fleeth** Mars 6; *pt. sg.* **fledde** II.544, **fleigh** VII.2689; *pt. pl.* **fledde(n)** I.2930, Tr 5.1198; *prp.* **fleeinge** ABC 41, **fleinge** (as *adj.*) Bo 5.m1.3; *pp.* **(y)fled** II.541, Tr 4.661, **fledde** Tr 1.463; *vbl. n.* **fleyng(e)** Bo 5.m5.8, Rom C 5864.

fle, flee(n) *v.*[2] fly V.122, HF 973, PF 388, Rom B 4772; *2 pr. sg.* **fleest** Tr 3.1435; *3 pr. sg.* **fleeth** Bo 3.m7.5; *pr. pl.* **fleen** HF 2118, **flyen** Rom A 910; *pt. 1 & 3 sg.* **fley** VII.3172, **fleigh** VII.3339; *2 pt. sg.* **flaugh** VII.3231; *pt. pl.* **flowen** VII.3391; *prp.* **fleynge** BD 178, (as *adj.*) **flyenge** Bo 3.m7.3; *pp.* **flowen** HF 905.

fledde(n) *see* **fle** *v.*[1]

fley, fleigh *see* **fle** *v.*[2]

fleigh *pt. sg.* of **fle** *v.*[1] fled VII.2689.

flemen *v.* drive away, expel Tr 2.852; *3 pr. sg.* **fleemeth** IX.182; *imp. sg.* **fleme** Bo 1.m7.16; *pt. sg.* **flemed** Rom C 6781; *pp.* **flemed** Rom B 3052; (as *adj.*) banished VIII.58; *vbl. n.* **flemyng** banishment Tr 3.933.

fleen *see* **flye**.

fles, flees *n.* fleece VII.997, LGW 1428, Form Age 18; *pl.* **fleezes** Bo 2.m5.12.

flessh *n.* (1) human flesh I.2640, VI.732; (2) body III.157, IV.1335; (3) physical or sensual nature VII.1421, X.336; meat I.147, I.344.

flesshly, fleshly *adj.* (1) well-fleshed, shapely Rom B 2506; (2) bodily, physical X.205; (3) sensual, carnal X.204.

flesshly *adv.* (1) physically X.333; (2) in a worldly manner X.202; (3) carnally, sensually X.939.

fleten, fleetyn *v.* (1) swim, float Bo 1.pr6.165, Bo 2.pr4.60, LGW 2552; **synke or f., or f. or synke** sink or swim Anel 182, Pity 110; (2) drift Bo 1.pr6.79; (3) **f. in (with)** overflow with, abound in Bo 1.m2.25, luxuriate in Tr 3.1671; *3 pr. sg.* **fleteth** II.901, **fleet** *(contr.)* drifts II.463; *pr. pl.* **flete(n)** Tr 3.1221, Bo 1.pr6.79; *pr. subj. sg.* **fleete** I.2397; *prp.* **fletyng(e)**

floating I.1956, overflowing Tr 2.53, (as *adj.*) fluid Bo 3.pr11.147, **fleetynge** drifting, insubstantial Bo 1.pr3.71.

flye *n.* (1) any flying insect LGW F 392; (2) housefly I.4352; (3) **nat worth a f.** worthless V.1132, VII.172, VIII.1150, PF 501; *pl.* **flyes** X.441, **fleen** Tr 4.1356.

flit(te), flette *v.* escape Rom B 1812; pass away X.368, Rom B 2732; *3 pr. sg.* **flytteth** Bo 3.m2.3; *imp. sg.* **flytte** move Bo 3.pr9.140; *prp.* **flyttynge** (as *adj.*) impermanent BD 801, Bo 2.pr1.82; *pp.* **iflyt** Bo 1.m2.13; **flitted** moved, transferred Tr 5.1544.

flod, flood *n.* (1) river HF 22, Bo 4.m7.43; (2) flood Tr 3.640; (3) high tide Astr 2.46.19; *pl.* **flodes** Tr 3.1760; **floodes** VII.2587.

flok *n.* flock, group I.824; *pl.* **flokkes** Rom A 661.

floryn *n.* gold coin I.2088, X.749; *pl.* **floryns** VI.770 (see note), **floreyns** LGW 1122.

flour *n.*¹ (1) flower I.4, I.2937; (2) ornament of one's reputation, virtue BD 630; virginity IV.2190; (3) prime of life I.3048, III.113; (4) best part I.4174; **bereth the f.** VII.901, takes first place; (5) (with **of**) the model, the best I.982, IV.919, VII.2497; *pl.* **floures** I.90, **flourys** LGW G 517.

flour *n.*² flour, meal I.4053, I.4093, III.477.

flouren *v.* flourish, thrive Bo 4.m5.8; *3 pr. sg.* **floureth** flourishes Tr 4.1577, blossoms Anel 306; *pr. subj. sg.* **floure** IV.120; *3 pt. sg.* **floured** VI.44; *prp.* **flowryng** flourishing Rom C 6256.

floury *adj.* flowery BD 398, Bo 4.m6.29, LGW F 174.

flourons *n. pl.* flowers LGW F 220.

flowen *v.* (1) flow, overflow Bo 1.pr5.75, Bo 2.m8.9, Tr 3.1758; (2) be at high tide For 61; *3 pr. sg.* **floweth** Bo 2.m1.5; *prp.* **flowynge** Bo 1.pr5.75, (as *adj.*) fluid, unstable Bo 5.m1.17.

flowen *see* **fle** *v.*²

fo(o) *n.* foe, enemy I.63, I.1590, Tr 1.837; *pl.* **foes** VII.970, **foos** Tr 1.1001, **fon** PF 103, **foon** VII.2706.

foghten *see* **fighte(n).**

fol, fool *n.* (1) fool I.1606, I.1799, BD 734; **f. of fantasye** victim of delusion Tr 5.1553; **f. of kynde** born fool Tr 2.370 (see note); (2) sinner, rascal IV.2278; **f. of hire body** promiscuous X.156; (3) jester, court fool VII.2081, Tr 2.400; *gen.* **foles** Tr 3.298; *pl.* **foles** Tr 1.1705, **fooles** Tr 1.202.

fol, fool *adj.* (1) foolish PF 505, Rom A 1253; senseless Bo 1.m2.32; (2) lecherous X.853.

fold(e), foolde *n.*¹ times (indicating multiplication); **hundred (thousand) f.** hundred (thousand) times II.1120, VI.40, Tr 3.1540; **many f.** in many ways, completely BD 260, Tr 2.697.

folde *n.*² (1) sheepfold I.1308; (2) (*fig.*) parish I.512.

folde *v.* (1) fold Tr 2.1085; (2) **in armes f.** embrace Tr 3.1201, Tr 4.1230; (3) *2 pr. sg.* **fooldiste togidre** join Bo 3.pr12.160; *pp.* **folden** folded Tr 4.359, **folde** clasped Tr 4.1689.

foly(e) *n.* (1) foolishness, folly I.1798, I.3146, BD 637; **doon f.** act foolishly I.3045, VII.1704, Tr 2.1510; idle tale, nonsense V.1131; (2) sin, wrong-doing VI.464, X.315, Tr 3.394; lechery, fornication I.3880; **doon f.** fornicate LGW 723; (3) insanity Tr 4.1257; *pl.* **folies** V.1002 foolish thoughts, VII.1801 foolish deeds.

foleyen *pr. pl.* act foolishly, mistakenly Bo 3.pr2.89, Bo 3.pr2.95.

folily *adv.* foolishly IV.1403, VIII.428, Mars 158.

fool-large *adj.* improvident, prodigal VII.1599, X.814; (as *n.*) spendthrift VII.1620, Bo 2.m2.11.

folwe(n), folowe(n) *v.* follow III.1124, IV.873, Tr 1.259, Gent 3; *2 pr. sg.* **folwest** LGW 2549; *3 pr. sg.* **folweth** II.865, **foloweth** Mars 131; *pr. pl.* **folwe(n)** I.2682, IV.897, **folowe(n)** Tr 3.1061, Rom C 7249; *pr. subj. sg.* **folowe** Rom B 5367; *imp. sg.* **folwe** VII.1692, **folowe** Tr 1.899; *imp. pl.* **folweth** IV.1189; *pt. sg.* **folwed** III.583, **folowed** Rom A 1450; *pt. pl.* **folwed** BD 397, **folowede** Tr 2.819, **folwyden** Bo 1.m1.8; *prp.* **folowynge** I.2367; *pp.* **yfolowed** BD 390.

foomen *n. pl.* foes, enemies VII.2068, VII.2080.

fomy *adj.* frothing I.2506; frothy (with spittle) LGW 1208.

fon, foon *see* **fo(o).**

fond(e), foond, founde(n) *see* **fynde(n).**

fonde *v.* try IV.283, IV.1410; strive BD 1020; test Tr 5.352.

for *prep.* (1) because of I.264, I.2144 (see note); **f. which (that)** therefore, on account of which I.2482, III.1541, Tr 2.1113; **f. why** therefore BD 461, because Tr 4.1496; **what f.** because of V.54, VII.2114; (2) for the sake of LGW 1986; (in prayers) I.4073; (in oaths) I.3526, VII.886; (3) on behalf of I.62, I.301; (4) by means of V.184, HF 2136; (5) for, for the purpose of II.283, VII.737, Tr 4.413; (with *inf.*) in order to I.17, I.73; **f. to** (with *inf.* untranslated *intens.*) I.3667, II.1067; (6) in order to (get something) I.191, I.1177, III.961; (7) in exchange for I.649, IV.1567, Tr 4.149; BD 1150; (8) to prevent, avoid VII.862, PF 657; as a protection against X.607; for fear of VII.2560; (9) **f. al** despite, notwithstanding I.2020, II.982, Tr 4.1164; **f. heigh and lough** regardless of anything Tr 3.418; **f. my deth** though I were to die LGW 1628, Mars 186; **f. to dyen** though (we) were to die I.1133; (10) instead of, in place of LGW F 513; as representative of I.1833, PF 505; (11) **point f. point** in detail IV.577; **word f. word** literally LGW 1002; (12) appropriate to, suitable for I.165, V.39; (13) as, as being III.320, VIII.457, Tr 1.987; as though, as if VII.972, Tr 4.733; **f. wod** madly HF 1747; (14) concerning, as regards I.387, I.3858, BD 1313, **as f.** concerning, as regards PF 631; (**as**) **f. me** so far as I am concerned I.1619; **f. aught (ought)** so far as I.389, Tr 4.1164, LGW 1611; (15) during Astr 2.17.23; **f. the nones (nonys)** for the time, for the purpose I.379, I.523, Tr 1.561; (16) **f. certes (certein)** certainly X.98, Tr 4.120; **f. fin** to the effect Tr 4.477; **f. conclusioun** in conclusion LGW 2723; **f. sothe** truly III.46, VIII.386.

for *conj.* (1) because I.4225; (2) since I.3667; as HF 2109; so that I.2879.

for as much(e) (muchel) as *adv. phr.* inasmuch as VII.33, VII.1267.

forage *n.* (1) feed for animals VII.783 (see note); (2) dried hay, straw I.3868, IV.1422.

forbar *see* **forbere(n).**

forbeede *v.* forbid I.3508, Tr 3.467; *1 pr. sg.* **forbede** LGW G 10; *3 pr. sg.* **forbedeth** III.652, *(contr.)* **forbet** Tr 2.717; *pr. subj. sg.* **forbed(e)** I.3508, PF 582, **forbeede** X.881; *pt. sg.* **forbad** IV.570, **forbed** Rom B 3399; *pp.* **forbode(n)** IV.2296; X.845.

forbere(n) *v.* (1) endure, forebear Bo 4.pr6.37; (2) forgo, refrain from Tr 3.173; *pt. sg.* **forbar** spared Tr

1.437, refrained from Tr 3.365; *imp. pl.* **forbereth** put up with LGW F 80; *vbl. n.* **forberynge** of abstinence from X.1049.

forby *adv.* by, past VI.125, VI.668, Tr 2.658.

force *see* **fors.**

fordo(n), fordoon *v.* (1) destroy, ruin Bo 2.m8.19, Tr 4.1091; (2) break, violate Tr 1.238; *pr. subj. pl.* **fordo** VII.127; *3 pt. sg.* **fordide** LGW 2557; *pp.* **fordo(n)** Tr 1.74, Tr 5.1687; **fordoon** IX.290.

fordryve(n) *pp.* wildly tossed about Bo 1.pr3.65, Rom B 3782.

foreyne *adj.* (1) foreign Bo 1.pr4.113; (2) outside, external Bo 2.pr5.126; alien to oneself, others Bo 2.pr5.96; (3) (as *n.*) privy LGW 1962.

foreknowynge *vbl. n.* foreknowledge Bo 5.pr6.272.

foreward *see* **forward** *n.*

foreward *see* **first** and **forward.**

forgat *see* **foryete(n).**

forgo(n), forgoon *v.* (1) give up III.315, VIII.610, X.812; refrain from, avoid IV.2085; (2) forfeit, lose IX.295; (3) lack, be without Tr 3.1384; *3 pr. sg.* **forgoth** Tr 4.713, **forgeth** X.556; *pr. pl.* **forgoon** Bo 2.pr5.32; *3 pt. sg.* **foryede** Tr 2.1330; *pp.* **forgo(on)** VII.993, X.945, exhausted HF 115.

forlete(n), foreleeten *v.* (1) leave, forsake X.583, Bo 3.pr5.63; (2) cease X.250; (3) lose VI.864; *3 pr. sg.* **forleteth** X.119; *pr. pl.* **forlete** X.93; *pr. subj. sg.* **forlete** renounce X.93, **forleete** Bo 2.pr3.90; *pt. pl.* **forleten** departed, left Bo 1.m3.2; *pp.* **forleten** neglected HF 694.

forlong *see* **furlong.**

forlore, forlorn *pp.* lost V.1557, LGW 2663.

forme, fourme, foorme *n.* (1) shape, form V.337, Tr 5.300; appearance V.1161, Tr 2.1243 (see note); (2) manner Tr 3.160, Tr 4.1579; literary style Tr 2.22, Tr 5.1854; (3) proper manner I.305; **holden the f.** preserve the proper usage Tr 2.1040, Tr 3.1674; **in f.** formally Tr 2.41; (5) pattern V.283, Bo 4.pr6.179; (6) lair of a hare VII.104; *pl.* **formes** I.2313 (see note), **foormes** Bo 5.m4.59.

forme(n) *v.* form, create VI.12, Bo 5.pr4.205; *1 & 3 pt. sg.* **formed(e)** Tr 2.1053, LGW 1792; *2 pt. sg.* **formedest** Bo 3.m9.12; *pp.* **(y)formed** VI.10, LGW F 256, **(i)fourmed** Tr 4.315, Rom A 1189.

formel *adj.* female bird PF 373, PF 418, PF 445.

forneys, fourneys *n.* (1) cauldron I.202, X.554; (2) furnace VII.2163.

fors, force *n.* (1) physical strength, power I.1927, I.2015, PF 221; **by (of) (fyne) f.** by (sheer) compulsion, force I.2554, Tr 4.1475; **by f.** by necessity VI.205; (2) (*usu.* **fors**) importance BD 522; **(is) no f.** does not matter VI.303; **(do) make no f.** pay no attention to, care nothing for III.1512, BD 542; **what f.** what does it matter IV.1295, Tr 2.378.

forsake(n) *v.* (1) repudiate, disavow LGW 2036; deny Bo 2.pr3.74; (2) refuse, reject VII.794, VII.1557; (3) abandon, desert IV.1290, VII.669, VII.2241; escape Rom B 1876; *3 pr. sg.* **forsaketh** X.562; *pr. pl.* **forsaken** Bo 2.pr7.117; *imp. pl.* **forsaketh** VI.286; *pr. subj. sg.* **forsake** III.1522; *pt. sg.* **forsook** III.644, **forsok** LGW G 265; *pp.* **forsake(n)** VI.80, X.994.

forseyde *pp.* aforesaid VII.1254, X.410, PF 120.

forsothe, forsouthe *adv.* (also two words) truly, indeed X.358, BD 341, Tr 2.883, Astr 2.39.38; in fact Bo 2.pr8.15.

forswere *1 pr. sg. (reflx.)* commit perjury Rom C 5973; *3 pr. sg.* **forswereth** Rom C 5970; *pt. sg.* **forswor** perjured HF 389; *pp.* **forswore** LGW 2235, (as *adj.*) **ben forsworn** false, traitorous LGW 1259; *vbl. n.* **forsweryng(e)** perjury VI.657, HF 153; *pl.* **forswerynges** VI.592.

forth(e), foorth, furth *adv.* (1) forth, onwards I.825, III.1540, Tr 2.1020; (2) away Anel 161; *(absol.)* set forth! Truth 18; **mot f.** must leave II.294, Tr 5.59; **driven (tarien) f. a day** pass a day, kill time I.2820, Tr 5.628; **dryven f. the world** pass the time VII.231; (3) **out,** out of LGW 2320, VII.293, VIII.312, PF 352; **strecche f.** stretch out VI.395, VII.3308; **bring f.** beget, give birth to Bo 2.pr7.79; (4) **heer f.** ahead, beyond III.1001; **fro this (thennes) f.** from then on, thenceforth VII.565, Tr 4.314; **and so f.** and so on III.1924, Astr 1.8.12; **doth f.** carry on IV.1015; **tell (speken) f.** tell on I.2816, VI.660, Tr 5.196; (5) afterwards V.1081, Tr 5.6; (6) (as *intens.* adding sense of continuation) III.1540, V.1552, PF 27, Tr 1.1092.

forther(e), further *adv.* (1) farther, onward I.4117, I.4222, Bo 2.pr2.163; **f. in age** older IV.712; (2) more than Tr 5.1094; **f. over** moreover X.437, Tr 4.1027. Cf. **ferther** *adv.*

fortheren, fortheryng *see* **forthre(n).**

forthermo, forthermoor(e), furthermore *adv.* (also two words) furthermore III.783, IV.169, VI.594, VII.3153, Astr 2.46.23.

forthy *adv.* therefore, for this reason I.1841, I.4031, Tr 1.232; **nat f.** nevertheless VII.975.

forthynke, forthenke *v. (tr.)* cause grief Tr 2.1414; *(intr.)* regret Rom B 3957; *3 pr. sg.* **(it) me forthynketh** that grieves me, I'm sorry IV.1906; *pr. subj. sg.* be displeased, resent Bo 2.pr4.66; *pt. subj. sg.* **forthoughte** Rom A 1671.

forthre(n), forthere(n), forther, further *v.* advance, aid I.1137, I.1148, HF 2023, Tr 5.1707, LGW G 462, Rom B 2881; *3 pr. sg.* **forthereth** Tr 2.1368; *pp.* **furthered** Anel 273, **forthred** Bo 2.pr4.64, **forthered** LGW G 399; *vbl. n.* **fortheryng** of aiding, providing for PF 384; *pl.* **furtherynges** HF 636.

forthward *adv.* forward II.263, V.1169; **henes f.** henceforth Astr 1.1.74.

fortunat, fortunaat *adj.* (1) fortunate, favored by fortune IV.1910, V.25, VII.2776, Tr 2.280; happy, successful IV.422; (2) (*astro.*) auspicious IV.1970, Astr 2.4.33.

fortune *n.* (1) (personified) Fortune I.915, VI.295, Tr 1.138; (2) chance, accident VII.238; destiny I.2659, V.1497; (3) state, condition VII.1559; *gen.* **fortunes** Tr 3.1625; *pl.* **fortunes** chances Bo 2.m3.19, property, possessions Bo 1.pr4.56.

fortunen *v.* calculate (the ascendant), make astrological calculations I.417 (see note); *2 pr. sg.* **fortunest** control destiny, grant fortune I.2377; *pp.* **fortuned** happened BD 288; (as *adj.*) **wel f.** favored by Fortune, successful Mars 180.

fortunows, fortunous *adj.* governed by fortune, accidental Bo 1.pr6.9, Bo 2.pr3.86; **f. hap** mere chance Bo 4.pr5.29.

forward, foreward *n.* agreement, promise I.829; **as f. is (was)** as is (was) agreed I.2619, II.34; **holde f.** keep one's promise LGW 2500; *pl.* **forwardis** Rom C 7301.

forward *adv.* onwards, forward Astr 2.12.4, Astr 2.35.7;

hennes forwardis Rom C 7302. *See* **first** and **forward**.

for-why, forwhi *adv.* and *conj.* (1) why Tr 3.1009; (2) because VI.847, BD 461, Tr 1.714; (3) wherefore Tr 2.12, Tr 2.1238; therefore Bo 5.pr4.103.

foryaf *see* **foryeve(n)**.

foryede *see* **forgo(n)**.

foryete(n), forgete(n) *n.* forget BD 1125, Bo 2.pr3.48, Tr 3.55, LGW G 312; **f. mynde (wit)** lose one's mind, wits II.527, LGW 1752; *3 pr. sg.* **foryeteth** Tr 2.375, *(contr.)* **forget** Rom A 61; *pr. pl.* **foryeten** Rom B 4838; *pr. subj. sg.* **foryete** I.1822, **forgete** Astr Pro 49; *imp. sg.* **foryet** I.2797, **forget** Astr 2.22.14; *imp. pl.* **forget** I.2797; *pt. sg.* **forgat(e)** I.4076, LGW F 540, **foryat** Tr 5.1535; *pp.* **forgete(n)** I.3054, BD 410, **foryeten** I.1914; *vbl. n.* **foryetynge** forgetfulness Bo 3.m11.29.

foryeve(n), foryive *v.* forgive I.743, X.810, LGW F 458; *2 pr. sg.* **foryevest** X.1043; *3 pr. sg.* **foryeveth** IX.206, **foryiveth** ABC 139; *pr. subj. sg.* **foryeve** IX.904, **foryive** Tr 1.937; *pr. subj. pl.* **forgyve** Rom C 6054; *imp. sg.* **foryeve** Tr 3.1183; *imp. pl.* **foryiveth** Compl d'Am 77; *pt. sg.* **foryaf** Tr 3.1129; *pp.* **foryeve(n)** Tr 2.595, Tr 3.1106, **foryive** BD 877; *vbl. n.* **forgyvyng** LGW 1852.

fostre *v.* (1) raise VI.219; educate IV.593; nourish, feed IX.165, IX.175, Bo 1.pr2.6; (2) support Rom A 389; *3 pr. sg.* **fostreth** pampers IV.1387; *imp. sg.* **fostre** IX.175; *pt. sg.* **fostred** IV.222; *pp.* **(y)fostred** I.3946, II.275; *vbl. n.* **fostryng** nourishment III.1845.

fote, foot(e) *n.* (1) foot I.2509; step I.1479, V.1177; **a f. on** foot Rom A 368; (2) foot (as measurement) Rom A 350; (3) poetic foot VII.1979; *pl.* **fete** Rom B 1829, **feet** X.8, (following *num.*) **foot** I.2607, I.4124.

foughte(n) *see* **fighte(n)**.

foul, fowel, foughel *n.* bird, foul PF 320, Tr 5.425, Compl d'Am 86; *gen.* **foules** PF 203; *pl.* **foules** PF 323, **foweles** I.9.

foul(e), fowle *adj.* (1) ugly II.764, III.265, IV.1209, V.869; frightening III.776; miserable, wretched I.3061, Tr 2.896; dirty, disgusting IV.1095, VI.536, Bo 4.pr3.122; **f. or fair(e)** any circumstances V.121, HF 767; painful LGW 2240; (2) shameful III.963, III.2049; defiled, evil II.586, Tr 5.383; *comp.* **fouler** III.999, VI.525; *super.* **fouleste** X.147.

foule *adv.* miserably I.4220, III.1312; dishonestly Rom A. 1061.

founde, fownden *v.* build, erect Tr 1.1065, Rom C 6828; establish Bo 2.m4.2; *pp.* **(y)founded** IV.61, BD 922.

founde(n) *see* **fynde(n)**.

fownde *see* **fynde(n)**.

fourmed *see* **forme(n)**.

foundement, fundament, fundement *n.* (1) foundation HF 1132; (2) anus VI.950, Bo 3.pr11.125; *pl.* **foundementz** bases (of reasoning) Bo 4.pr4.220.

fownde *see* **fynde(n)**.

frankeleyn *n.* landowner I.331 (see note); *pl.* **frankeleyns** I.216.

fraunchise, franchise *n.* (1) social status of a freeman X.452; (2) nobility of character, generosity of spirit Ven 59, (personified) Rom A 955.

fre(e) *adj.* (1) free (not servile), having the social status of a noble or freeman IV.2069, (as *n.*) Tr 1.840; noble VI.35, VII.1567, BD 484, (as *n.*) Tr 3.128; generous of spirit V.1622, VII.467; (2) unrestrained, free I.1292, III.49, IV.147; unconstrained (assent, choice, will) I.852, I.1606, IV.150; without obstruction VII.494; generous, liberal (in spending) I.4387, IV.1209, VII.43.

fre(e) *adv.* freely, without restrictions V.541, PF 649, Rom B 2379.

fredom, fredam *n.* (1) liberty Tr 1.235, Buk 32; national sovereignty or independence Bo 1.pr4.173; (2) free will Bo 5.pr3.7; (3) nobility of character, generosity II.168, IX.126, Anel 106, LGW 1010.

frely *adv.* (1) freely, without restraint I.1207, I.1849, III.150; without reservations, completely LGW 683; (2) nobly, generously VIII.55, Tr 3.1719; liberally V.1604, LGW 1550; willingly, gladly VIII.55.

fresh(e), fresh(e) *adj.* (1) new, unfaded, young I.90, I.365, PF 174; (2) blooming, lovely I.1068, I.2386, BD 484, Tr 1.166; (3) vigorous IV.1173, V.23; sexually vigorous III.508, III.1259, VII.177; (4) joyous V.284, Tr 2.552, Tr 3.611, LGW F 79; *comp.* **fressher** V.927; *super.* **fresshest** Tr 3.1722.

fressh(e), fresh(e) *adv.* (1) **al f.** newly, recently I.2832, VII.1309; (2) gaily I.1048, IV.781, LGW 1207.

fresshly, freshly *adv.* (1) **f. newe** afresh, with continuing vigor BD 1228, Tr 3.143, Tr 4.457; anew Tr 5.1010; (2) joyously Tr 5.390.

frete(n), freeten *v.* devour, eat (of or like an animal) I.2019, Anel 12; *3 pr. sg. (contr.)* **fret** Rom A 387; *pr. pl.* **freten** Bo 3.m2.20; *pt. pl.* **freeten** I.2068; *pp.* **frete(n)** II.475, LGW 1951.

fro, fra *adv.* **in phr. to (til) and f.** back and forth I.1700, I.4039, Tr 4.485.

fro, fra *prep.* (1) from I.44, I.397, I.671; away from VIII.22; (2) of II.453; **ware (thee) f.** beware of VI.905; **f. me ded** dead to me Tr 2.845.

from, fram *prep.* from I.15, I.77, PF 23.

fruyt *n.* (1) fruit I.3872, VI.510, Tr 1.385; (2) product, result III.114, VI.656, LGW 1160; fruition, happy outcome HF 2017; offspring IV.990; (3) profit, best part I.1282, IV.1270, V.74; essential part II.411, VI.3443; *pl.* **fruites** Form Age 3.

ful, full(e) *adj.* (1) (with **of**) filled to capacity, full I.233, I.2279; **f. yeris (yere)** years of plenty Bo 1.m2.25; **f. a strete (tyne)** a streetful Tr 4.929, a barrelful Ros 9; (2) full, sated Tr 2.1036, Tr 3.1661; complete, full, entire I.3075, II.86, VII.2938; **f. frend** true friend Tr 1.610; **ten days f.** a full ten days Tr 5.239; **took purpos f.** made a firm decision Tr 1.79; (3) (as *n.*) **atte (at the) f.** fully, completely BD 899; **unto the f.** fully, unreservedly Tr 3.213.

ful *adv.* (1) completely, fully HF 102, Mars 18; (2) (as *intens.* with *adj.* or *adv.*) very I.132, BD 103; completely I.4230, II.1106, Anel 243.

fulfille(n), fulfelle *v.* (1) fill (something) full III.859, X.947; (2) satisfy (lust, appetite, *etc.*) I.1318, III.1218, V.1372; (3) carry out, accomplish, execute II.284, VII.1744; (4) complete Tr 3.510; *3 pr. sg.* **fulfilleth** X.947; *2 pt. sg.* **fulfildest** Bo 2.pr3.59; *pt. pl.* **fulfilleden** VII.1523; *pp.* **fulfild** I.940, **fulfilled** VI.535; *vbl. n.* **fulfillynge** Bo 2.pr5.81; *pl.* **fulfillynges** Bo 3.pr7.3.

fully, fulliche *adv.* fully, completely I.876, I.969, Tr 1.316.

fundement *see* **foundement**.

furyus, furious *adj.* (1) raging Mars 123; (2) like that of the Furies in Hell V.1101.

furlong, forlong(e) *n.* (1) one-eighth of a mile I.4166, V.1172; (2) **f. wey** time needed to walk a furlong (about 2½ min.), a short time IV.516, II.557 (see note), HF 2064; stadium, race track Bo 4.pr3.10.

furthe *see* **forth(e)**.

G

ga *see* **go(n)**.

gabbe *1 pr. sg.* lie, chatter foolishly VII.5066, Bo 2.pr5.170; *2 pr. sg.* (with *pro.*) **gabbestow** Tr 4.481; *3 pr. sg.* **gabbith** Rom C 6700; *pr. pl.* **gabbe** Tr 3.301; *vbl. n.* **gabbyng** idle gossip Rom C 7610.

gadre(n), gadere, gaderyn *v.* (1) assemble Rom C 5831, Rom C 6175; (2) gather I.1053, IV.2231; (3) collect Bo 1.pr4.7; (4) conclude Bo 2.pr4.141; *3 pr. sg.* **gadereth** I.1053, **gadreth** Bo 4.m5.5; *imp. sg.* **gadere** Bo 2.pr4.141; *pt. sg.* **gadred(e)** I.824, I.4381, **gadered** IV.2231; *pp.* **gadered** I.2183, **gadrid** Bo 5.pr2.30; *vbl. n.* **gaderyng** VII.1575, **gadring** Rom B 5782.

gay(e) *adj.* (1) joyous, merry I.3254, III.1727, Tr 2.922; attractive, good-looking I.3769, III.355; (2) bright, ornamented I.111, III.355; fine, elegant I.3323, III.221; gaily dressed, richly attired I.74; (3) pleasant sounding I.296; *comp.* **gayer** more splendid BD 407.

gaye *adv.* handsomely I.3689, VIII.1017.

gayler *n.* jailer I.1474, VII.2433, LGW 1988.

gayneth *3 pr. sg. (impers.)* helps, avails (him, us, etc.) I.2755; *pt. sg.* **gayned** Tr 1.352.

galle *n.* (1) bile, secretion of the liver X.195, VIII.797, For 35; (2) bitterness VII.2347, Tr 4.1137, Tr 5.732; *pl.* **galles** feelings of envy Form Age 47.

galwes *n. pl.* gallows III.658, VII.2734.

game(n) *n.* (1) joy, happiness PF 226; (2) amusement, sport, revelry, I.853, I.2286, I.3117; amorous play PF 266; **no g.** no laughing matter BD 1220; (3) joke, jest I.4354, III.1279; **maken ernest of g.** take a joke seriously I.3186; **in (for) ernest or in (for) g.** in jest or earnest, in any case IV.609; **in (one's) g.** playfully, in jest VI.829, BD 238; (4) scheme, trick I.3408, Tr 3.250; *pl.* **games** Bo 4.pr2.152.

gan *see* **gynne**.

garlond(es) *see* **gerland**.

garner *see* **gerner**.

garnysoun *n.* body of armed men VII.1027; garrison Rom B 4204; protection VII.1337.

garnment, garnement *n.* garment Rom A 896, Rom B 2260.

gat *see* **gete(n)**.

gaure(n) *v.* (with **on**) stare at V.190, Tr 5.1153; *3 pr. sg.* **gaureth** VII.2369.

geant, geaunt *n.* giant VII.807, VII.828, Tr 5.838; *pl.* **geauntis** Bo 3.pr12.133, **geauntes** Bo 3.pr12.137.

general(l), generale *adj.* (1) all-inclusive, universal I.1663, I.2969, X.388; (as *n.*) **in g.** without exception II.417, Tr 3.1802; (2) of wide application X.464; as a rule For 56; not specifically I.2285, Tr 1.900; couched in general terms V.945, Astr 2.3.8; (3) (in titles) **ministre (vicaire) g.** chief servant, chief repre-

sentative I.1663, VI.20; (4) (as *n.*) genus, class of things Bo 3.pr10.22.

gentil(e) *adj.* (1) noble, well-born I.2539, III.1153, VII.2658; (2) noble in character I.1761, IV.1919, Tr 3.5; (3) superior, refined, excellent (sometimes ironically) I.567, I.647, I.718; *super.* **gentilleste** most noble IV.72, **gentilest** Tr 1.1080.

gentillesse, gentilesse *n.* (1) nobility of birth or rank III.1117, VII.2251, X.585; (2) nobility of character I.920, I.3382, II.853.

gentilly, gentily *adv.* nobly, courteously, honorably, I.3104, II.1093, Tr 2.187.

gentils *n. pl.* nobles VI.323, Anel 67.

gentrie, genterye *n.* noble birth X.461; nobility of character LGW F 364.

gerdone, gwerdone, guerdon *v.* reward, requite VII.1275, Tr 2.1295, LGW 2052; *pp.* **gerdoned** VII.1272, Bo 5.pr3.163; *vbl. n.* **guerdonynge** reward PF 455, granting of reward Tr 2.392.

gerdoun, gerdon, guerdon(e), guerdoun *n.* reward, requital V.973, V.1220, VII.2630, Tr 5.594; *pl.* **gerdons** VII.1052, **guerdouns** Bo 1.pr5.63.

gere, geere *n.* ¹ (1) apparel, clothing IV.372, Tr 2.1012; (2) armor, fighting equipment I.2180; (3) equipment, gear I.352, I.4016, II.800; possessions Tr 4.1523; *pl.* **geeris** apparatus V.1276.

gere, geere *n.* ² behavior, conduct I.1531; *pl.* **geres** ways of behaving I.1531.

gerland, gerlond, garlond *n.* wreath, garland I.1507, I.1931, HF 135; *pl.* **gerlandes** I.2937, **garlondes** LGW 2614.

gerner, garner *n.* granary Rom A 1148, Rom C 5988; *pl.* **gerneeris** Bo 1.pr4.75, **gerners** Rom B 5702.

gees *see* **gos**.

gesse(n) *v.* (1) perceive V.1486; suspect Tr 3.984; conclude X.175; judge Bo 1.pr4.165, Bo 3.pr2.40; (2) evaluate, estimate Rom A 1115; **for to g.** as an estimate (3) suppose, imagine II.622, HF 1814; **(as) I g.** as I believe, I suppose (often merely a tag; e.g., I.117); II.1143, V.1412; *3 pt. sg.* **gessed** *subj.* Rom C 7647; *prp.* **gessyng** intending LGW F 363; *vbl. n.* **gessynge** opinion Bo 1.pr4.293.

gest *n.* guest, visitor IV.338, Rom B 5106; *pl.* **gestes** IV.1016.

geste, geeste *n.* story, history (either true or fictitious), Tr 3.450; V.211, Tr 2.83; *pl.* **geestes** histories II.1126; **gestes** deeds, noteworthy actions HF 1737.

gete(n), gette, getin *v.* (1) get I.1512, III.230, HF 1857, Bo 4.pr2.18; save, preserve I.2755; (2) beget IV.1437; *2 pr. sg.* **getest** X.31; *3 pr. sg.* **geteth** I.3620; *pr. pl.* **gete(n)** I.4099, VII.1574; *pr. subj. sg.* **gett** Rom B 2856; *pr. subj. pl.* **gete** VII.1632; *imp. sg.* **get** I.3465; *3 pt. sg.* **gat** I.703; *pt. pl.* **gatt** Rom B 2692; *pp.* **(y)geten** I.291, I.3564, **gete** LGW 1123; *vbl. n.* **getyng(e)** acquiring VII.1597, Bo 4.pr2.158.

geth *see* **go(n)**.

gyde *n.* guide I.804, I.4020, II.164.

gyde *v.* lead, direct IV.776, VII.300, Tr 1.569; counsel, advise Tr 1.630; *3 pr. sg.* **gydeth** VII.300; *pr. subj.* **gyde** VII.259 *(sg.)*, II.245 *(pl.)*; *imp. pl.* **gydeth** VII.487; *pp.* **gided** Tr 1.569; *vbl. n.* **gydyng** Tr 5.643.

gye *v.* (1) lead, guide VII.2397, Anel 6; (2) advise, direct X.13, Anel 340; *(reflx.)* conduct oneself, act LGW 2045; (3) rule, control, govern I.3046, IV.75;

(4) protect, preserve VIII.136; *pr. subj.* **gye** I.2786, **guye** Anel 6.

gif, yif *conj.* if I.4190, BD 987, HF 143.

gyle, gile *n.* guile, deception VIII.195, BD 620, Rom A 151.

gilt *n.* (1) sin, offense, crime VII.1825, X.84; (2) culpability, fault Tr 2.1257; **in the g.** at fault III.244; **withouten g.** guiltless, innocent V.1039; *pl.* **giltes** sins X.1043.

gilte *adj.* (1) golden PF 267, LGW F 230, LGW F 249; (2) gilded VII.2364.

giltelees, giltles, giltlees, giltles *adj.* innocent I.1312, II.643, Tr 5.1084, MercB 17.

gilty *adj.* guilty I.660, II.668, VI.429.

giltif *adj.* guilty Tr 3.1019, Tr 3.1049.

giltle(e)s, giltele(e)s *adj.* guildless, blameless, innocent II.643, Tr 2.328.

gyn, gynne *n.* (1) device, contrivance V.322, LGW 1784; (2) trap, snare Bo 3.m8.5; (3) war engine, catapult Rom B 4176; *pl.* **gynnes** Rom A 1620.

gynne *v.* (1) begin HF 2004; (with **for, for to**) begin to I.3863, IV.2329, Tr 1.189; (2) as *aux.* with *inf.* forms the periphrastic present (e.g., **gynneth wepe** does weep, weeps Tr 5.1286) and past (e.g., *sg.* **gan ryde** did ride, rode, I.2659; *pl.* **gonne crye** did cry, cried I.2955); 2 *pr. sg.* **gynnest** Rom B 2445; *3 pr. sg.* **gynneth** I.4064; *pr. pl.* **gynne(n)** Tr 5.657, LGW F 38; *pt. sg.* **gan** I.1540; *pt. pl.* **gonne(n)** I.1658, Tr 2.99, **gunne** HF 1608; *vbl. n.* **gynnyng(e)** beginning Tr 1.377, Tr 2.671.

girdell, girdill, gurdel *n.* belt VII.731, Astr 1.17.41, Rom A 1085, Rom B 3719; *pl.* **girdles** I.368.

gyse *n.* manner, custom I.993, I.1255; fashion I.2125; way Tr 4.1370; **at his owene g.** after his own fashion, as he pleased I.1789; **in his g.** in his usual manner II.790; *pl.* **gises** Bo 4.pr6.50.

gyterne *n.* a cithern, guitar-like instrument I.3353; *pl.* **gyternes** VI.466.

glad(e), gladde *adj.* joyful, happy I.811, I.846, Tr 2.1351, Tr 3.229; *comp.* **gladder** I.3051; *super.* **gladdest** BD 1280.

glade(n) *v.* (1) gladden, comfort Tr 2.979, BD 563; (2) entertain, please VII.2811, VIII.598, Tr 5.455; (3) *(reflx.)* rejoice, take pleasure in, comfort oneself Tr 5.1184; *3 pr. sg.* **gladeth** IV.1107; *pr. subj. sg.* **glade** Tr 4.1655, **glaade** IV.822; *pr. pl.* **gladen** Bo 5.m5.9; *imp. sg.* **glade** Tr 1.897; *imp. pl.* **gladeth** rejoice Mars 1; *pt. sg.* **gladed(e)** Tr 1.116, 173, **gladded** HF 962; *pp.* **gladed** Tr 1.994.

gladly *adv.* (1) joyfully, with pleasure I.308, III.669; (2) willingly IV.665, VII.451; (3) habitually, commonly, usually, customarily X.887, Rom C 6966; fittingly X.887; *comp.* **gladlier** Tr 5.1777.

glede, gleede *n.* (1) ember, glowing coal Tr 5.303, LGW 735; (2) fire II.1111; *pl.* **gledes** Tr 2.538, **gleedes** I.3883.

glyde *v.* glide, move, pass I.1575, V.373, Tr 4.1215; *pt. sg.* **glood** wafted up, rose V.393; *pp.* **glyden** IV.1887.

glyteren *v.* glitter I.977; *pt. sg.* **glytered** I.2166; *prp.* **gliterynge** I.2890.

glorifie(n) *v. (usu. reflx.)* exult, be proud X.405, X.757, Tr 3.186; *pr. pl.* **glorifien** Bo 3.pr5.32.

glose *n.* (1) gloss, interpretation III.1920, BD 333, LGW F 328; (2) deception V.166.

glose(n) *v.* (1) interpret, explain (a text) LGW G 254; (2) use circumlocution IV.2351; (3) flatter, cajole III.509, Tr 4.1471; deceive VII.2140; *pr. subj. sg.* **glose** III.119; *prp.* **glosynge** (as *adj.*) deceitful Bo 2.pr3.64; *pp.* **(y)glosed** deceived, flattered IX.34, interpreted Rom C 6890; *vbl. n.* **glosynge** interpretation III.1793, flattery Bo 3.pr3.64.

glotonye, glotenye *n.* gluttony III.1916, III.1927; the sin of Gluttony X.831; *pl.* **glotonyes** greedy desires VI.514.

glotoun *n.* glutton VI.520, PF 610, PF 613; *pl.* **glotouns** gluttons (used as a general term of abuse) Rom B 4307.

go(n), goo(n) *v.* (1) walk I.2510, VII.1907; **ryde ne (or) go** ride nor (or) walk I.1351; (2) go I.12, HF 430, Tr 1.53; *(reflx.)* go, get oneself I.3434; **go (thy) wey** go away I.3712, Tr 1.574; (3) **g. on (the) grounde** be alive Tr 4.304, LGW 1669; *2 pr. sg.* **goost** III.273, **gost** LGW 926; *3 pr. sg.* **goth** II.1097, **gooth** I.3355, **geth** LGW 2145; **gas** *(Nth.)* I.4037; *pr. pl.* **goon** I.769, **gon** Tr 4.1099; *pr. subj.* **go** LGW 2069 (*sg.*) Tr 2.615 (*pl.*); *imp. sg.* **go** I.2760; *imp. pl.* **gooth** I.2558, **goth** II.1045; *2 pt. sg.* **yedest** Rom B 3227; *3 pt. sg.* **yede** VIII.1141; *pt. pl.* **yeden** Tr 2.936; *prp.* **goynge** BD 348; *pp.* **yede** VIII.1281, **(y)go** I.286, VIII.907, **goon** II.17, **(y)goon** I.1413, V.293; *vbl. n.* **going(e)** Tr 4.934; *pl.* **goinges** Bo 5.m5.11.

good(e) *n.* (1) abstract goodness, virtue VII.1289, X.328; (2) good person Tr 1.1017, Tr 4.1660; (3) good words III.1281, IV.2017; (4) useful knowledge HF 1, Tr 2.97; **connen g.** have useful knowledge II.1169, BD 800, Tr 2.1178, LGW 1175; **connen no g.** be ignorant, not know what to do BD 390, BD 998; **connen (one's) g.** know what is good for (one's) self III.231, Tr 5.106, LGW 1182; (5) good thing, benefit III.1195, X.312; **don g.** be beneficial to III.580, V.875, LGW F 134; (6) possessions, goods, wealth I.3983, III.1796, III.1952; *pl.* **goodes** VII.998.

good(e), god(e) *adj.* good I.74, I.183, BD 9, Astr 2.19.13; *comp. see* **bet** *adj.*; *super. see* **best(e)**.

goodlich(e), goodly *adj.* excellent, beautiful, pleasing, gracious V.623, VII.1731, Tr 1.173; (as *n.*) excellent, splendid, noble being Tr 1.450, Tr 3.1473; *super.* **goodlieste** PF 375.

goodlich, goodly *adv.* (1) excellently VII.1780; intently Tr 3.1345; beautifully Tr 5.578; (2) graciously VII.1875; gladly, willingly I.803; (3) (as *intens.*) **not g.** not easily, not at all VII.1670; **mai nat g.** can hardly Tr 1.253, VII.1230; **as g. as** as well as IV.1935.

godlyhed, goodlyheed(e), goodlyhede *n.* excellence, virtue, beauty, graciousness BD 829, Tr 5.1590, Rom B 4604; righteousness HF 274.

godsib(bes) *see* **gossip**.

gon, goon *see* **go(n)**.

gonne, gunne *n.* cannon LGW 637, Rom B 4176; *pl.* **gunnes** Rom B 4191.

gonne(n) *see* **gynne**.

gos, goos *n.* goose I.3317, I.4137, PF 594; *gen. sg.* **goses** PF 586; *pl.* **gees** IV.2275.

gost, goost *n.* (1) spirit, mind VI.43, HF 981, Tr 3.464; (2) the (**hooly**) **g.** the Holy Spirit VIII.328, X.250; evil spirit, demon II.404; (3) soul of a dead person, ghost I.2768, HF 185; *pl.* **goostes** Tr 4.1142.

goostly *adj.* spiritual X.392, X.962.

gostly, goostly *adv.* spiritually VIII.109; devoutly, figuratively Tr 5.1030 (see note).

gossip, godsib *n.* (1) god-parent or parent of one's god-child X.909; (2) close friend III.529; *pl.* **godsibbes** X.908.

goot *n.* goat I.688, VIII.886.

governaunce, governance *n.* (1) rule, control, government II.987, III.814, Tr 2.467; (2) behavior, manner IV.1603, BD 1008, Tr 2.219; self-control Pity 41; (3) control (of a machine) V.311.

governe(n) *v.* (1) govern, rule, control III.1237, Bo 3.pr12.58, Tr 3.373; (2) *(reflx.)* conduct oneself VII.994, Tr 2.375; *2 pr. sg.* **governest** Bo 1.m5.58; *3 pr. sg.* **governeth** VII.3000; *pr. pl.* **governe** I.303; *pr. subj. sg.* **governe** II.1161; *imp. pl.* **governeth** IV.322; *pt. sg.* **governed** III.219, **governyde** Bo 2.m6.19; *prp.* **governynge** Bo 1.m5.31; *pp.* **governed** Tr 1.746; *vbl. n.* **governyng(e)** I.599; *pl.* **governynges** VI.75.

governour *n.* ruler, master I.813, I.861, V.1031; *pl.* **governours** VII.1754, **gouvernours** Bo 4.pr5.13.

grace, gras *n.* (1) divine favor, grace I.573, PF 84, Tr 1.933, Rom B 4430; providence I.3595, V.1508, Tr 1.896; **fair (harde, sory) g.** good (bad) fortune III.746; Tr 1.713, Tr 1.907; **with sory (harde) g.** bad luck to (him, you, *etc.*) III.2228, VI.717; (2) good will, favor, kindness, love I.1120, I.1232, BD 1006; **harde g.** ill-will HF 1586; **stonden in** (someone's) **g.** find favor with (someone) IV.1590, LGW 1014; **do g.** be favorable to I.2322, do a favor to VI.737; **do me g.** allow me Tr 5.694; **dooth yourselven g.** spare yourself V.458; (3) graciousness VIII.67; **of your (thy) g.** by your (thy) kindness I.3080, V.161, Tr 3.719; **doon so fair a g.** behaved so graciously I.1874; (4) **g. of** sake of Bo 5.pr1.8; (5) power Rom A 1099; *pl.* **graces** thanks VII.1804.

grame *n.* (1) anger Tr 3.1028; (2) grief, sorrow VIII.1403, Tr 4.529; suffering Anel 276.

gramercy, grant mercy, graunt mercy *interj.* thank you III.1403, IV.1088, VII.2970, VIII.1156, BD 560, Tr 4.632.

gras *see* **grace.**

gras, gres *n.* grass I.3868, III.774; *pl.* **grasses** HF 1353.

graspe *v.* grope, feel around I.4293, Tr 5.223; *2 pr. sg.* **graspeth** I.4293.

graunt *n.* (1) command, decree I.1306, Tr 4.552; (2) privilege (of an exclusive territory for begging) I.252a; (3) **g. hym made** granted him Rom A 851.

graunte(n), grante(n) *v.* (1) grant, allow III.1174, IV.179, Tr 1.41; (2) agree, consent VI.327, Bo 3.pr9.63, Tr 1.785; **g. it thee (you)** agree with you PF 645; **g. it wel** admit, agree III.95; (3) ordain, appoint IV.179; *2 pr. sg. (with pro.)* **grauntestow** do you agree Bo 3.pr11.41; *3 pr. sg.* **graunteth** I.1828; *pr. subj. sg.* **graunteth** I.842 *(sg.)*, HF 2039 *(pl.)*; *imp. pl.* **graunte** HF 1609, **graunteth** PF 643, **granteth** ABC 137; *pt.* **graunted** I.3290 *(sg.)*, I.786 *(pl.)*; *pp.* **graunted** agreed I.810; *vbl. n.* **grauntyng(e)** I.2439, Bo 3.pr11.12.

grave(n) *v.* (1) bury IV.681; (2) dig LGW 677; (3) carve, engrave V.830, Tr 2.1241; *pr. pl.* **grave** engrave Tr 3.1462; *pr. subj. sg.* **grave** carve VI.15; *pp.* **(y)grave** engraved I.3796, buried III.1065, dug, cut BD 164; **graven** engraved HF 193, HF 433.

gre(e) *n.*[1] (1) degree IV.1375, Rom B 5743; (2) victory in battle I.2733.

gre(e) *n.*[2] in *phr.* **in g.** graciously, favorably Tr 4.321,

Ven 73; without complaint IV.1151; **at (atte) g.** graciously Rom B 1969, without complaint Rom B 4574.

greef *see* **grief.**

greyn *n.* (1) grain crop I.596, VI.374; edible part of a plant Bo 3.m1.5; (2) seed VII.662; cardamom seed I.3690; bit, quantity of a seed Tr 3.1016; (3) **g. of Portyngale** a red dyestuff VII.3459; **depe in g.** deeply dyed V.511; *pl.* **greynes** grains (of sand) HF 691.

greesse, grece *n.* grease I.135, VI.60.

gret(e), greet(e), great *adj.* (1) big, large in size or quantity I.559, VI. 1946, BD 295, Rom A 357; **g. and smal (lyte)** of every sort IV.382, VII.2932; coarse IV.1422; (2) great (in degree) I.84, I.137; much I.385, I.870; (3) great (in quality), excellent I.203, Tr 1.66; high (in status), important IV.1494, Tr 5.1025; chief, most important III.2005, Tr 3.505; (4) diligent, active I.318, IV.1001; frequent, energetic VI.164, IX.63; great, very much I.312, I.437; consummate III.1196, IV.1501; (as *n.*) the chief part, substance PF 35, LGW F 574, Tr 5.1036; *comp.* **gretter** I.197, **greatter** Rom B 3628; *super.* **grettest(e)** I.120, III.1116, **grettist** Rom A 610, **greatest** Rom C 7506.

grete, greete *v.* greet IV.1014, Tr 5.1569; *3 pr. sg.* **greteth** Rom C 7624; *imp. sg.* **grete** VII.363; *pt. sg.* **grette** II.1051; *pp.* **ygret** BD 517.

gretly, greetly *adv.* greatly IV.1829, BD 931; completely Bo 3.pr12.76.

grevaunce, grevance *n.* annoyance, pain, sorrow V.941, VII.1486, PF 205; affliction For 47; *pl.* **grevances** Tr 1.647, **grevaunces** Bo 3.pr12.112.

greve, grove *n.* grove VIII. 2823, Tr 5.1144; *pl.* **greves** groves I.1495, branches I.1507, BD 417.

greve(n) *v.* (1) cause pain, distress II.352, III.1490, Tr 3.1642; injure Tr 1.1001; insult Tr 5.590; (2) *(reflx.)* be annoyed, take offense I.3910, Tr 3.1004; be angry I.3859, Tr 1.343; *3 pr. sg.* **greveth** I.917; *pr. subj. sg.* **greeve** VI.186; *pr. subj. pl.* **greve** I.3910; *pt. sg.* **grevede** Rom B 2958; *pp.* **greved** VII.1490.

grevous(e), greevous *adj.* (1) grievous, painful I.1010, X.732, Tr 4.1492, ABC 20; (2) hostile, malicious X.641.

grevously, grevousliche *adv.* painfully VII.1001, X.667; gravely LGW F 369; strenuously X.667.

grief, greef *n.* (1) trouble III.2174, VII.127, Rom B 3997; (2) pain VIII.712, Tr 2.1632.

grym(me) *adj.* fierce, angry I.2042, I.2519, HF 541.

gripe(n) *v.* seize Rom A 204, Rom A 1156; *3 pr. sg.* **gripeth** X.863.

grone(n), groone *v.* groan, complain III.443, VII.2886, Tr 1.549; *3 pr. sg.* **groneth** I.3646; *pt. sg.* **gronte** VII.2709; *vbl. n.* **gronyng** VII.2907.

grope *v.* (1) *(intr.)* grope, feel about III.2148; (2) *(tr.)* test, examine I.644; *3 pr. sg.* **gropeth** I.4222; *pr. pl.* **grope** VIII.679; *imp. sg.* **grope** I.2141; *pt. sg.* **groped** I.4217.

grot(e) *n.* groat, a silver coin worth fourpence III.1292, VI.945, Tr 4.586; *pl.* **grotes** III.1964.

grove *see* **greve.**

grucche *v.* complain, bear a grudge against III.443, IV.1170; *3 pr. sg.* **gruccheth** I.3045; *pr. pl.* **grucche(n)** I.3058, X.507; *pt. sg.* **gruched** X.502, **gruchched** X.504; *vbl. n.* **grucchyng** III.406, **gruchchyng** X.499.

guerdon *see* gerdone *v.*

guerdoun(s), guerdon(e) *n. see* gerdoun *n.*

guye *see* gye.

gunne *see* gonne *n.*

gunne *see* gynne.

H

habit(e) *n.* (1) clothing III.342, VII.2343, Tr 1.109; (2) condition, nature Bo 2.pr1.9; physical condition I.1378.

habiten *v.* live, frequent Rom A 660, Rom C 7618.

habounde, abounde *v.* be full of (*usu.* with in) IV.1286; be plentiful Tr 2.159; *3 pr. sg.* haboundeth Bo 3.m8.14; *pr. pl.* habounden Bo 1.pr4.307; *prp.* haboundinge plentiful ABC 135.

habundaunce, habundance, haboundance, aboundaunce *n.* plenty, abundance III.1723, Tr 3.1042, For 29, Rom C 6528; fullness X.627; *pl.* habundances Bo 2.pr4.14, haboundances Bo 3.pr3.24.

habundaunt, haboundant, haboundaunt *n.* abundant VII.2925, X.913, Bo 4.pr2.18.

had(e), hadde(n), haddes(tow) *see* have.

haf, haaf *see* heve(n).

hay(e) *n.* hedge Rom A 54, Rom B 3175; *pl.* hayis Tr 3.351.

hayl *interj.* (greeting) good health, good fortune (to you) I.3579, III.1384; al h. (greeting) good day I.4022, Rom B 3219.

hayl(e) *n.* hail III.465, LGW 1220; *pl.* hayles hail storms HF 967.

halde *see* holde(n).

half, halve *adj.* half I.8, Tr 4.1545.

half *adv.* half I.1429.

halfe, halve *n.* (1) half Tr 3.344; (2) side HF 1136, Bo 2.pr4.72; a Goddes h. by God's side BD 370; (3) behalf BD 139, Tr 4.945; *pl.* halves sides I.3481.

haliday, holyday *n.* holy day I.3309, I.3340, LGW F 35; *pl.* halydayes LGW F 422.

hals *n.* neck HF 394, PF 458.

halt *see* holde(n).

halve(s) *see* half *n.*

halve *see* half *adj.*

halwen *v.* consecrate, hallow X.919; *pt. sg.* halwed VIII.551; *pp.* (y)halwed revered Tr 3.268, worshiped LGW 1871.

halwes *n. pl.* (1) saints VIII.1244; apostles BD 831; (2) shrines LGW 1310.

han *see* have(n).

hande(e) *see* hond(e).

hange(n) *see* honge.

hap *n.* (1) chance, fortune VII.2738, BD 810; luck, good fortune VIII.1209, BD 1039; (2) chance happening Bo 5.pr1.90; as h. was as it happened Tr 2.1696; *in h.* by chance Rom B 3284; *pl.* happes good fortunes BD 1279.

happe(n) *v.* occur by chance, happen I.585, Tr 5.991; (*impers.* with hit) (he, she, *etc.*) happens to, chances to VI.606, VI.885, PF 18; *3 pr. sg.* happeth V.592, happith Rom A 264; *pr. subj. sg.* happe III.1401; *pt. sg.* happed(e) I.1189, LGW 1910.

happy *adj.* lucky, fortunate VII.1680, HF 1758.

hard(e) *adj.* (1) hard, firm I.2135, I.3021; (2) cruel,

unyielding I.229, II.857, Tr 2.1241; (3) difficult III.271, III.1791, PF 2; of h. with difficulty Tr 2.1236; *comp.* harder Tr 4.905; *super.* hardest Tr 2.729.

harde *adv.* hard, strenuously I.3279, I.3476; intensely LGW G 260, LGW 1902.

yharded, ihardid *pp.* hardened V.245, Bo 4.m5.27.

hardily, hardely *adv.* certainly, surely III.2285, IV.25, Tr 2.1012; boldly IV.2273.

hardyment, hardement *n.* boldness, daring Rom B 2487, Rom B 3392.

hardynesse *n.* boldness, bravery II.939, Tr 1.566, Tr 2.634.

hardnesse *n.* (1) obstinacy X.486; resistance Tr 2.1245; cruelty Mars 232; (2) rigor, self-denial X.688; *pl.* hardnesses hardships Bo 4.pr5.35.

harlot *n.* (1) idle rogue, rascal I.4268, X.626, Rom A 191; (2) buffoon, jester I.647; (3) servant III.1754; *pl.* harlotes lechers X.885.

harm *n.* (1) injury, misfortune, evil II.836, VI.745, Tr 3.861; disease I.423; h. of peyne physical impairment X.624; slander IV.2310, X.498; (2) pain, grief, suffering II.479, BD 492; (3) pity I.385, IV.1908; *pl.* harmes evils VII.1840, X.390, sorrows I.2232.

harneys, harnays *n.* (1) arms, armor I.1613, I.1634; (2) equipment III.136; (3) trappings, circumstances X.974; *pl.* harneys sets of armor I.1630.

harrow *interj.* help! I.3286, I.3825; alas VI.238.

hasard *n.* gambling, dicing VI.591, VI.608.

hasardour *n.* gambler VI.596; *pl.* hasardours VI.613.

hasardrye *n.* gambling VI.599, X.793.

hast, hastou, hath *see* have(n).

haste(n) *v. (reflx.)* hasten, hurry I.2052, LGW 2456; (with *obj.*) VI.159; *3 pr. sg.* hasteth VII.1054, hastith Rom A 232; *pr. subj. pl.* haste VII.1052; *imp. pl.* hasteth VII.157; *pp.* hasted Bo 1.m1.14.

hastif *adj.* hasty, hurried I.3545, IV.349, Tr 4.1567.

hastifly, hastifliche *adv.* hastily II.388, II.1047.

hastifnesse *n.* hastiness, rashness VII.1122, VII.1133.

hat *see* hot(e).

hauberk, hawberk *n.* coat of mail I.2431; plate armor VII.863; *pl.* hauberkes I.2500.

hauk *n.* hawk III.1340, III.1938; *pl.* haukes I.2204.

haunte *v.* (1) frequent a place X.885; (2) busy oneself, practice X.780; make a practice of, do habitually VI.547; continue an activity, keep doing Bo 4.pr2.264; *3 pr. sg.* haunteth Tr 5.1556; *pr. pl.* haunte(n) X.847, X.794; *pt. pl.* haunteden VI.464; *pp.* hauntyd Bo 1.pr3.7; *vbl. n.* hauntyng dwelling place Rom C 6081.

hauteyn, hautayn *adj.* (1) haughty, proud X.614; (2) dignified PF 262; noble, excellent LGW 1120, Rom B 3739; impressive, loud VI.330.

have(n), han *v.* (1) (*aux.*) have III.1038, X.243, Bo 3.pr2.113; h. do(n) be done, finish up PF 492; (2) have, possess I.224, I.245; h. on hond be engaged in, have in hand IV.1686, Buk 30; (3) (*reflx.*) behave VII.1575; *var. inf.* ha Rom B 5569; *2 pr. sg.* hast I.1094, hastou (with *pro.*) II.676; *3 pr. sg.* hath I.688, has (*Nth.*) I.4026; *pr. pl.* have IV.633, han I.1807; *pr. subj. sg.* have I.2792; *imp. sg.* have III.445; *imp. pl.* haveth II.654; *1 & 3 pt. sg.* hadde I.691, had(e) I.554, Pity 9; *2 pt. sg.* haddest IV.2066, haddestow (with *pro.*) Tr 4.276; *pt. pl.* hadde(n) I.2859, Tr 4.719, had BD 383; *pt. subj. sg.* hadde PF 455; *pt. subj. pl.* hadde(n) VIII.681, LGW 1849; *prp.* havynge PF

426; *pp.* **had** I.4184; *vbl. n.* possessing, owning **hav-ynge** VII.1549.

he *1 sg. pro.* he I.45; as emphatic modifier (with proper *n.*) e.g., **he Moyses** this Moses V.250 VII.2673, HF 1468; (as *n.*) male person IV.2290; that fellow I.2519; **he and he** this one and that one Tr 2.1748, LGW 642.

hed(e), heed, heved *n.*[1] (1) head I.198, I.1054, Bo 1.m1.16; (2) source Tr 2.844, Scog 43; *pl.* **heddes** I.2180, **hedes** PF 554, **heedes** Rom C 7386, **hevedes** VII.842.

hed(e), heede *n.*[2] heed, attention I.303, Tr 3.639, PF 383; **mawgree (his, her) h.** despite (his, her) care, despite all (he, she) could do I.1169, III.887.

(y)hed *see* **hyde(n).**

hef *see* **heve(n).**

hegge *n.* hedge X.870, Tr 5.1144, Rom A 481; *pl.* **hegges** VII.3218.

heghte *see* **highte.**

hey *n.* hay I.3262, III.1539, III.1547.

heigh(e), hey(e), hy(e), high *adj.* (1) high, lofty I.2463, Bo 5.pr6.120; (2) exalted X.153, Truth 24; **an on h.** above I.1065, HF 215; divine Bo 4.m6.2; holy V.773, VI.913; noble, admirable I.2537, Tr 2.632; high in rank or power VII.2698, PF 683, LGW 1141; (3) strong, vigorous, powerful III.2291, IV.1513; prominent, well-formed I.2167, I.3975; (4) lofty, elevated in thought or language I.2989, IV.18, IV.41, X.957; (5) arrogant, haughty VII.2520, Tr 1.1084; dire, severe II.795, II.963; (6) much, great I.2913, IV.1577; (7) loud Tr 4.248; (8) (as *n.*) **an (on) h.** above, aloft HF 851, Bo 5.m2.8; **h. and lowe** all respects, all things I.817, II.993; all classes, everyone II.1142, Tr 3.27; *comp.* **heyere** Bo 4.pr6.376, **hyer** I.399; *super.* **heieste** Bo 1.pr1.31, **heygheste** Bo 2.m7.17.

heighe, hye, high(e) *adv.* (1) high I.271, I.4322, HF 921; (2) honorably, in a high social position I.3981; (3) loudly BD 183; *comp.* **heyer** Bo 1.pr1.18, **hier** HF 1117; **heygher** Astr 2.23.39; *super.* **hyest** Rom B 4363, **heyest** Bo 5.m5.17.

heighly *adv.* richly VII.1272; solemnly X.600; strictly Tr 2.1733.

held(e), helde(n), heeld(en) *see* **holde(n).**

hele, heel(e) *n.*[1] (1) health, well-being VII.2950, X.153; (2) prosperity, happiness I.3102, LGW F 296; (as salutation) Tr 5.1415; (3) salvation ABC 80.

hele, heele, *n.*[2] heel Tr 2.1750, Tr 4.728; *pl.* **heles** HF 2153, **helys** Rom A 1022.

hele(n), heel(e), heelen *v.*[1] heal IV.2372, V.641, V.471, BD 571, Tr 2.1315; *3 pr. sg.* **heeleth** VI.366; *pp.* **heeled** I.2706, **heled** Tr 3.1212; *vbl. n.* **helyng** Tr 1.857.

hele *v.*[2] hide, keep secret VII.1089, Rom B 2858; *pr. pl.* **hele** Rom C 6882; *pp.* **heled** VII.3055.

helm *n.* helmet I.2676, VII.877, Tr 2.638; *pl.* **helmes** I.2500.

helpe(n), help *v.* help I.584, Tr 4.429, Tr 4.983; *2 pr. sg.* **helpest** VIII.53; *3 pr. sg.* **helpeth** I.2820; *pr. pl.* **helpen** X.241; *pr. subj.* **helpe** I.1127 *(sg.)*, X.778 *(pl.)*; *imp. sg.* **help** I.2086; *imp. pl.* **helpeth** Tr 3.735; *pt. sg.* **heelp** I.1651; *pt. subj. sg.* **holpe** Rom A 1230, **halp** Rom B 1911; *pp.* **holpe(n)** Tr 2.1441, LGW F 461, **yholpe** Rom B 5505; *vbl. n.* **helpyng(e)** I.1468; *pl.* **helpynges** Bo 2.pr5.118.

hem *3 pl. pro. dat.* and *acc.* them I.11, I.18, Tr 2.256.

hemself, hemselve(n) *3 pl. pro. dat.* and *acc.* (emphatic) themselves I.1254, V.1378, HF 1215, Tr 1.922.

hende *adj.* courteous, gracious, pleasant III.1286, Rom A 285; as an epithet I.3199 (see note).

heng(e), heeng *see* **honge.**

henne, hennes, henes *adv.* hence HF 1284, Tr 1.572, Astr 1.1.3; **hennes forth** (also one word) henceforth V.658, Tr 3.167.

hente(n) *v.* (1) seize, grasp I.904, I.957; take Bo 1.pr4.98; (2) fetch, strike I.2638; **for to hente** to be seized LGW 2715; *3 pr. sg.* **hent** Tr 4.5; *pr. subj. sg.* **hente** VIII.7; *imp. sg.* **hent** III.1553; *pt. sg.* **hent(e)** I.698; *pt. pl.* **henten** I.904; *pp.* **(y)hent** III.1311, VI.868.

hep(e), heep *n.* (1) crowd, multitude I.575, BD 295; (2) heap, pile I.944, VIII.938; **on an h.** together HF 2149; (3) great quantity Tr 4.1281; *pl.* **on hepis** in piles Rom B 5598.

hepith *3 pr. sg.* heaps up, increases Bo 4.pr5.30; *pr. pl.* **hepe** Rom B 5771; *pp.* **heped** heaped up Tr 4.236.

her, heer, hyre *n.* hair I.589, BD 456, LGW G 147; *pl.* **heeris** I.2134, **heeres** I.2883, *pl.* **heres** LGW 1829, **herys** I.555.

her(e) *see* **hir(e)** *3 pl. poss. pro.*

her(e), heere *see* **hir(e)** *3 fem. sg. pro.*

her(e), heer(e) *adv.* here I.1610, I.1612, Anel 55, Tr 2.1751; in compounds (with or without hyphen): **heer-aboute** concerning this matter I.3562; **heerafter** after this VIII.706, Tr 1.945, **herafter** Tr 5.990, **here-after** Tr 4.604; **herafterward** after this III.1515; **heer-agayns** against this I.3039, **herayeins** on the contrary Tr 2.1380; **heerby** by this IV.1330; **herby** HF 263, about this III.2204; **heerbiforn** before this VII.1262, **herebefore** BD 1136, **here-beforn** BD 1304, **her-biforn** LGW F 73, **hirbyfore** Bo 3.pr9.51; **herebyforn(e)** Bo 5.pr.6.2, Tr 2.296; **herinne** in this place VIII.1292; **herof** about this Tr 2.108; **hereon** upon this HF 1135; **heerupon** at this, then IV.190, concerning this Tr 3.535; **hereupon** Tr 5.778; **heerto** for this purpose II.243, **hereto** to this BD 754; **heretofore** before now Tr 5.778; **her-withal** with this, at that HF 1606.

heraud *n.* herald I.2533; *pl.* **heraudes** I.2599.

herberger *n.* harbinger (servant who travels ahead to arrange lodging) Rom C 7583; *pl.* **herbejours** Rom B 5000, **herbergeours** II.997.

herberwe, herborwe *n.* (1) dwelling place I.4145, X.1031, Rom C 6201; *(astro.)* house, position in the zodiac V.1035; (2) harbor, anchorage I.403.

herberwe *v.* house, provide lodging Rom A 491; *imp. sg.* **herber** Rom C 7584; *pt. sg.* **herberedest** Rom B 5107; *pt. pl.* **herberweden** Bo 2.pr6.68; *vbl. n.* **herberwynge** I.4332.

here(n), heere(n) *v.* hear I.169, II.349, VII.2773, HF 180; *2 pr. sg.* **herist** HF 651, **herestow** (with *pro.*) I.3366; *3 pr. sg.* **heereth** X.599, **hereth** I.1641; *pr. pl.* **heere** VI.326, **here** HF 83; *pr. subj. sg.* **heere** I.3642; *imp. sg.* **heer** I.4263; *1 & 3 pt. sg.* **herde** I.221; *2 pt. sg.* (with *pro.*) **herdestow** I.4170; *pt. pl.* **herde(n)** III.2156, VII.1135; *prp.* **heryng** Tr 3.58; *pp.* **herd** I.849; *vbl. n.* **heryng(e)** X.207, Rom C 6120.

heremyte, hermyte *n.* hermit, recluse Rom B 3278, Rom C 6481.

heres *see* **hires** *3 fem. poss.* and *3 fem. sg. poss. pro.* **hers** PF 482.

herye(n) *v.* praise VIII.47, Tr 3.951, Tr 3.1672; worship Rom C 6241; *2 pr. sg.* **heryest** VII.2229; *3 pr. sg.* **heryeth** II.1155; *pr. pl.* **herye(n)** IV.616, VIII.47; *pt.*

pl. **heryed** LGW 786; *prp.* **herying(e)** VII.459, VIL678; *pp.* **(y)heried** II.872, Tr 2.973; *vbl. n.* **heriynge** praise Tr 3.48.

herken *v.* listen to, hear Tr 2.95, LGW F 343; *imp. sg.* **herke** II.425; *imp. pl.* **herketh** III.1656.

herkne(n), herkene *v.* listen, hear I.1526, I.2532, BD 752; *pr. sg.* **herkneth** Tr 2.31; *pr. pl.* **herkne** X.1081; *imp. sg.* **herkne** VIII.927, **herkene** HF 725; *imp. pl.* **herkneth** I.788, **herkeneth** Rom C 7513; *pt. sg.* **herkned** I.4173; *prp.* **herknyng(e)** V.78, **herkenyng** Tr 5.1812, **harknyng** Rom A 106; *pp.* **herkned** Rom A 630; *vbl. n.* **herknynge** Bo 3.pr1.3.

hert *n.* stag, full-grown red deer I.1689, BD 352; *gen.* **hertes** I.1681; *pl.* **hertes** V.1191.

herte *n.* heart I.229, I.150, BD 80; h. roote the bottom of one's heart III.471; sweetheart, love Tr 3.69, Tr 3.176; *gen.* **hertes** IV.112; **hertes line** imaginary line Tr 1.1068; *pl.* **hertes** I.1537.

hertely *adv.* heartily, sincerely I.762, III.1801, BD 85.

hertly, hertely *adj.* hearty, cordial IV.176, V.5, LGW 2124, Rom B 5433.

heste, heest(e) *n.* (1) command I.2532, II.1013, Anel 119; (2) commandment VI.647, X.798; (3) vow, promise Rom B 3181, Rom B 4477; *pl.* **heestes** commands II.284, **hestes** promises Tr 5.1208.

het(e), heet(e), hote *see* **hote(n).**

hete, heet(e), hote *n.* heat VI.38, VII.1593, Rom A 1508; heat of passion Tr 1.420.

heeth *n.* heath, field I.6, I.606, I.3262.

hethen *n.* heathen I.66, VII.2393.

hethen(e) *adj.* heathen II.378, II.549, LGW G 299.

hethenesse *n.* the non-Christian world I.49, II.1112.

hette *see* **hote(n).**

heve(n) *v.* (1) raise, lift, heave I.550, X.858; (2) to heve to be done, to exert oneself Tr 2.1289; *2 pr. sg.* **hevest** I.3466; *3 pr. sg.* **hevyth** Bo 5.m4.36; *imp. sg.* **heve** Tr 5.1159; *pt. sg.* **haf** I.2428, **haaf** I.3470, **hef** Bo 1.pr1.17.

heved(es) *see* **hed(e)** *n.* [1]

heven(e) *n.* heaven I.519, I.1090, I.2249; (as *adj.*) **hevene kyng (queene, bliss,** *etc.*) heavenly king (queen, bliss, *etc.*) I.3464, PF 72, ABC 24; *gen. sg.* **hevenes** of heaven VIII.87; *pl.* **hevenes** VIII.508.

hevenely, hevenlich(e) *adj.* heavenly X.598, Bo 1.m2.9, Truth 27.

hevenyssh(e) *adj.* heavenly HF 1395, Tr 1.104, Astr. 1.21.50.

hevy(e) *adj.* (1) heavy, III.1436, VIII.1404, IX.67, HF 738; grievous, burdensome Lady 52, Mars 12; (as *n.*) one of the elemental qualities PF 380; (2) sad VII.1702, Mars 12; gloomy V.822, BD 509; (of stars) dire in influence Bo 1.m6.1; (3) weighty, important, serious VII.1022, VII.1499, HF 1473, Rom B 2390; grave Purse 4; (4) sluggish, slow X.677, X.706, LGW 885; *comp.* **hevyere** heavier Bo 2.pr1.47.

hevyeth *pr. pl.* grow heavy or sluggish Bo 5.m5.15; *pp.* **ihevyed** Bo 5.m5.24.

hevynesse *n.* (1) weight Bo 3.m9.23, LGW F 231; (2) sadness I.2348; (3) drowsiness, sluggishness X.686.

hew(e) *n.* (1) color, complexion I.394, I.458, BD 497; (2) appearance IV.377, PF 354; guise, pretense V.508; **chaunge h.** change one's color, grow pale or red Tr 2.1470, Tr 3.1698; **cladde him in her h.** adopted her colors, became her servant Anel 145; *pl.* **hewes** colors I.2088, complexions Tr 3.94, **hewis** colors Tr 2.21.

hewe(n) *v.* hew, chop I.1422, I.2865.

hewed *pp.* hued, colored VII.2869, BD 905.

hy(e), high, hyer *see* **heigh(e)** *adj.*

hyde(n) *v.* hide I.1477, I.1481, HF 1707; **hideth to shew** refrains from showing X.394; *2 pr. sg.* (with *pro.*) **hydestow** III.308; *3 pr. sg.* **hideth** X.113, (*contr.*) **hit** V.512; *pr. pl.* **hiden** Bo 3.m8.5; *imp. sg.* **hyd** LGW 2655; *pt. sg.* **hidde** III.745, **hyd** IV.1944; *imp. sg.* **hid** Tr 1.595; *imp. pl.* **hyde** LGW F 254; *pp.* **hid** III.2143, (as *adj.*) II.777, **hydd** Bo 1.m3.4, **yhidd(e)** Bo 3.m8.11; **yhad** Bo 3.m8.21, **(y)hed** BD 175, LGW F 208; (as *adj.*) **hidde** Tr 1.530; *vbl. n.* **hidyng** Rom C 6147; *pl.* **hidyngis** II.777, Rom C 6712.

hyder, hidre *adv.* hither, here I.682, II.1041, Tr 4.932.

hiderto *adv.* hitherto, previously Bo 3.pr9.1, Rom B 3412.

hyderward *adv.* hitherward in this direction VII.426, VII.1969.

hidous(e) *adj.* hideous, terrible I.1978, I.3520, VII.3393.

hidously *adv.* fiercely, violently I.1701, vigorously HF 1599.

hye *n.* haste Tr 2.1712, Rom B 2393.

hye *v.* hasten, hurry (often *reflx.*) VII.210, VIII.1084, VIII.1151; *2 pr. sg.* **hiest** Tr 3.1441; *3 pr. sg.* **hieth** Tr 4.320; *pr. pl.* **hye(n)** Bo 3.pr11.214, Tr 5.489; *imp. sg.* **hy(e)** BD 152, VIII.1295; *pt. sg.* **hied** Tr 3.157; *pt. pl.* **hyed** BD 363; *pp.* **hyed** Tr 3.655.

hye, high(e), hier, hey(gh)er *see* **heighe** *adv.*

hierde, herde *n.* shepherd, herdsman LGW 1212; **herde-gromes** shepherd boys HF 1225; *pl.* **hierdes** Tr 3.619.

(i)hight, highte(n) *see* **hote(n).**

highte, height(e), heghte *n.* height I.1890, Bo 1.pr1.4, Astr 2.1.41; **(up)on h.** on high I.2607, I.2919; aloud I.1784; *pl.* **heightes** Bo 4.m6.4.

hild *see* **holde(n).**

hym *3 masc. sg. pro. acc.* and *dat.* him I.284, I.293; (*reflx.*) himself I.87, I.703; (as emphatic modifier with proper *n.*), *e.g.,* **hym Arcite** this Arcite I.1210, **hym Daryus** that Darius III.498; (as *n.*) **hym and here** man and woman II.460.

hym-ward *adv.* (with to) toward him Bo 5.pr6.138, Bo 5.pr6.153.

hyndre(n) *v.* hinder, impede I.1135, VII.1196, Rom B 5297; *2 pr. sg.* **hynderest** LGW F 324; *pr. subj. sg.* **hyndre** Rom B 5297.

hynesse, heighnesse *n.* high rank X.190, X.336, Lady 70.

hir(e), here *3 fem. sg. pro.* (1) *dat.* and *acc.* her I.163, I.1421; (as *n.*) him or h. man or woman HF 1003; (2) *poss.* her, hers I.3407, III.901.

hir(e), her(e) *3 pl. poss. pro.* their I.368, I.586, HF 1505.

hyre *see* **her** *n.*

hyre *n.* (1) payment, wages III.1973, Tr 4.125; **quit(e) (someone's) h.** repay (someone) III.1008, PF 9; (2) reward HF 1857; (3) ransom Tr 4.506.

hires, hyrs, heres *3 fem. sg. poss. pro.* hers II.227, BD 1041, PF 482, Tr 1.889.

hirs *3 pl. poss. pro.* theirs III.1926, HF 1505, Mars 52, Bo 3.pr11.132.

hyt, it *3 sg. neuter pro. nom., dat.,* and *acc.* it BD 186; *gen.* **his** its I.1036.

hitte *pt. sg.* hit I.2647, III.808, Tr 1.209; *pp.* **hit** I.4305.

ho(o) *interj.* stop! I.1706, I.2656, Tr 3.190; (as *n.*) ceasing Tr 2.1083.

hod, hood(e) *n.* hood I.103, I.195; **putte in the mannes h. an ape** make a monkey of the man VII.440; **find game in** (one's) **h.** be amused with someone HF 1810, Tr 2.1110; **don thyn h.** put on your hat, get going Tr 2.954; **by myn h.** by my hat, on my head (I swear) Tr 5.1151, LGW F 507; *pl.* **hodes** Rom C 7254.

hokede *pp.* (as *adj.*) hooked, provided with hooks Rom B 1712, Rom B 1749.

hol(e), hool(e) *adj.* (1) whole, entire I.533, I.961; **alle hole** complete Bo 3.pr10.28; **trewe and h.** completely true Tr 3.1001; (as *n.*) the whole I.3006; (2) sound, unhurt, healthy III.977, IV.1289, BD 553, Tr 2.976.

hol, hool *adv.* wholly, completely III.2033, IV.1438, Tr 1.1053; **al h.** completely Tr 4.1641; **h. in al** perfectly IV.1538.

holde, hoold *n.* (1) possession, keeping III.599, III.1607; **in, to** (one's) **h.** in (one's) possession VII.2874; (2) stronghold, castle II.507.

holde(n) *v.* (1) hold, grasp IV.1100, Tr 5.574, Rom A 431; hold up (an object) VI.697, IX.19, Tr 3.184; keep, retain Tr 4.1628; restrain VII.1326; (2) maintain, continue I.2236, III.1144; hold, continue (on one's way) I.1506, IV.287; hold to (one's word, *etc.*) II.41, BD 754; keep, observe (a religious festival) Tr 1.161; **h. in honde** cajole, encourage with false promises BD 1019, HF 692, Tr 2.477; (3) manage (household, business, *etc.*) I.4421, X.440; (4) consider, think III.572, III.1186, BD 36; **h. hym (her) ypayd (apayd)** consider himself (herself) rewarded, satisfied III.1185, IV.1512, BD 269; (5) *(pp.)* beholden, obligated, obliged III.135, Tr 3.1259, Tr 4.417; *var. inf.* **helde** keep, possess III.272; *2 pr. sg.* **holdest** consider LGW F 326, **holdestow** (with *pro.*) do you consider Bo 2.pr1.73; *3 pr. sg.* **holdeth** IV.1189, **haldeth** Bo 3.m11.31, *(contr.)* **halt** II.721; *pr. pl.* **holden** X.440, **halden** Bo 2.pr4.59; *pr. subj.* **holde** IV.287 *(sg.)*, VII.1598 *(pl.)*; *imp. sg.* **hoold** I.2668, **hold(e)** Tr 4.1120, Rom B 2486; *imp. pl.* **hoold** I.783, **hold(e)** VII.891, PF 521, **holdeth** consider I.1868; *pt. sg.* **heeld(e)** I.176, Bo 2.pr7.30, **held** Tr 1.126, **hild** Rom A 939; *pt. pl.* **helde(n)** I.2517, VII.2, **heelde(n)** Bo 2.m5.2, Rom C 7356; *pt. subj. sg.* **helde** V.916; *prp.* **holdyng(e)** I.2514; *pp.* **holde(n)** considered I.141, I.1307; kept I.1690, Rom A 922; **hoolden** X.432, **yholde(n)** I.2374, IV.1932 VI.598, **halde** *(Nth)* I.4208; *vbl. n.* **holdynge** X.437, Bo 3.m7.6.

holy, hooly *adj.* holy, sacred I.17, I.178, HF 57; *comp.* **hoolier** X.955.

holy, hoolly *adv.* wholly, completely I.599, III.211, Tr 2.1121; **al h.** completely I.1818, BD 746.

holily, hoolily *adv.* in a holy manner III.2286, IV.1455, IV.1507.

holynesse, hoolynesse *n.* holiness I.1158, I.3180, Tr 1.560; religion LGW F 424.

holpe(n), yholpe *see* **helpe(n)**.

holsom(e), hoolsome *adj.* wholesome, healthful VII.1090, PF 206, Tr 1.947.

holwe, holowe *adj.* hollow HF 1035, LGW 2193.

hom, hoom, ham *n.* home I.512, I.4032, Tr 1.126.

homycide *n.* (1) murder III.2009, VI.644, X.564; (2) murderer VII.2628; *pl.* **homycides** murderers VI.893.

homly, hoomly *adj.* (1) of the household, domestic IV.1794; familiar Rom C 6320; common Rom A 1373; (2) plain, unpretentious III.1843, IV.1785.

homly, hoomly, homliche *adv.* (1) familiarly Tr 2.1559; (2) plainly, without pretension I.328, VIII.608; clearly Bo 3.pr12.182.

hond(e), hand(e) *n.* (1) hand I.193, PF 169, LGW 972; **of** (someone's) **h.** feats of arms, deeds in battle I.2103, II.579; (2) handwriting Pity 43; (3) **bere(n)** (someone) **on h.** falsely accuse III.393, X.505, Anel 158; persuade (someone of a falsehood) III.575, Tr 4.1404; **holden** (someone) **in h.** encourage, cajole, with false promises Tr 2.477; (4) **have in h.** have under control III.211, III.327, PF 545; **have on h.** be involved or concerned with III.451, IV.1686, HF 1009; with verb (*e.g.,* **come, put, fall) in (on)** (one's) **h.** (come, put, *etc.*) into possession, into the power of V.684, Tr 3.1185, ABC 80; **redy to (in) his h.** at hand, III.1321, IV.66, VII.367; (5) **biforen-h.** beforehand, earlier VIII.1317; *pl.* **hondes** I.2874, **handes** I.186, **hondis** Rom A 96; **honden** Rom C 6665.

honest(e) *adj.* honorable, respectable, decent III.1183, VI.328, LGW 2133; honest IX.75.

honeste(e) *n.* (1) honor, honorable condition LGW 1673; honor, reputation Tr 4.1576; **in h.** honorably Tr 2.706, Gent 11; (2) propriety of behavior, decorum VII.2712, X.932; (3) chastity, moral purity VI.77, VIII.89.

honestete(e), honestitee *n.* (1) honor, virtue IV.422; (2) decency, decorum X.429; good appearance X.431; (3) honesty, truth Bo 1.pr5.49.

honestly *adv.* (1) honorably, decently VII.244, VIII.549, X.1046; (2) properly, modestly I.1444; suitably IV.2026.

honge, hange(n) *v.* hang I.2410, I.3565, PF 458; *3 pr. sg.* **hongeth** I.2415, **hangeth** IV.1516; *pr. subj. pl.* **honge** Tr 2.1242; *pt. sg.* **heng(e)** I.160, Rom A 224; **heeng** I.358; *pt. pl.* **honge** *(intr.)* I.2422, **henge** *(intr.)* I.677, **hongyng** *(tr.)* III.761; *prp.* **hangynge** I.392, II.73, **hongyng** Astr 2.23.39; *pp.* **hanged** I.2568; *vbl. n.* **hangyng** I.2458.

hor(e), hoor(e) *adj.* white III.2182, Bo 1.m1.15; white-haired or gray with age IV.1400, IV.1461, IV.1464, Tr 5.1284; (as *n.*) old age Rom A 356.

hord, hoord *n.* hoard, store I.3262, I.4406; storehouse VII.84, X.821; hoarding Truth 3.

hors *n.* horse I.94; *gen.* **horses** Tr 1.223; *pl.* **hors** I.74, **horses** X.432.

hors, hoors *adj.* hoarse, BD 347, Tr 4.1147.

host *see* **ost**.

hostage *see* **ostage**.

hostelrye *n.* inn I.23, I.718; *pl.* **hostelryes** I.2493.

hostileer, hostiler, hostiller *n.* innkeeper I.4360, VII.3029, VII.3060; *pl.* **hostilers** servants at an inn X.440.

hot(e), hoot(e), hat *adj.* hot I.394, VII.1036, PF 266, Rom B 2398; intense I.2319, I.3754; eager PF 362; **h. fare** rash conduct I.1809, passionate affair Tr 5.507; (as *n.*) one of the elemental qualities PF 380; *comp.* **hotter** Tr 1.449, **hatter** Rom B 2475.

hote, hoot(e) *adv.* hotly, passionately I.1737, II.586, Tr 3.1390; *comp.* **hotter** LGW F 59.

hote(n) *v.* (1) be named, be called; (2) promise, assure; (3) command; *inf.* **hoten** be called III.144, **hote promise** Rom B 3385, **hatte** be called Rom A 38, **hete(n)** promise, assure BD 1226, Rom C 6299; *1 pr. sg.* **hote** command HF 1719, **heete** promise, assure II.1132; *3 pr. sg.* **het** is called HF 1604, **hette** Tr 5.319, **hight(e)** I.719, HF 663, **highteth** Bo 1.m2.22, **hoteth** promises Rom B 5422; *pr. pl.* **hatte** are called HF 1303, **highte(n)** HF 1519, LGW F 423, **hightyn** Tr 1.788, **highten** promise Tr 2.1623; *pr. subj. sg.* **heete** promise I.2398; *pt. sg.* **hight(e)** was called I.4336, Rom A 1474, **highte** promised Tr 5.1636, **het** was called BD 948; *pt. pl.* **highte** were called I.2920, **highte(n)** promised Tr 2.1623, IV.496; *pp.* **hoote** called I.3941, **hatte** Tr 3.797, **heet** V.1388, **hight(e)** I.616, VII.2849, **ihight** Tr 5.541, **hight** promised I.2472, III.1024; (as *inf.*) **to highte** to be called I.1557.

hour(e) *n.* hour I.3519, II.3; planetary hour (*see* Astr 2.12) I.416, I.2217, I.2367 (see note), Astr 2.12.15; **h. equal** sixty-minute hour Astr 1.17.35; **h. inequal** one-twelfth of the time between sunrise and sunset I.2217 (see note), Astr 2.12.22; *pl.* **houres** I.2211.

hous(e) *n.* (1) house I.343, I.345, Tr 1.127; **in h.** indoors III.352; household V.24, VII.20, LGW 2619; family III.1153, VI.649; **come to h. upon** become acquainted, familiar with LGW 1546; (2) religious establishment I.252, VII.1931, VIII.993; (3) *(astro.)* division of the celestial sphere Astr 2.4.16; astrological house, sign of the zodiac II.304, V.672, Tr 2.681; *gen.* **houses** HF 1959; *pl.* **houses** I.491; **houses of office** IV.264.

housbondrye *n.* careful management I.4077, VII.2828; economy IV.1296; household goods III.288, IV.1380.

how *interj.* (to attract attention) ho! hey! I.3437, I.3577.

how *adv.* how I.187, I.284, I.1219; however I.1394, Tr 3.146; **h. that** although X.710; **h. that** how I.642, I.1385; **h. now?** what's going on? I.4025; **h. so that** no matter how Bo 3.pr2.122; **h. so** although Tr 2.1271; (with *adj.*) what, what a IV.333.

humblesse *n.* humility I.1781, I.2790, HF 630.

humour *n.* bodily fluid I.421 (see note to I.420), I.1375, VII.2933; *pl.* **humours** VII.2925.

hunte *n.* hunter BD 385; *pl.* **huntes** BD 361.

hurtlen, hurtelen *v.* attack Bo 2.pr1.27, LGW 638; *3 pr. sg.* **hurtleth adoun** knocks down I.2616, **hurteleth** strike Bo 5.m4.52; *3 pr. pl.* **hurtelen** LGW 638.

hust *adj.* hushed, quiet Tr 2.915, Tr 3.1094, LGW 2682; as *imp.* be quiet I.3722.

I

(See also Y)

i- prefix of past participles; *see under* the root syllable (*e.g.,* **ymaked** is alphabetized as **maked**).

I *see* **ey** *(interj.)*.

ich, I, y *1st sg. pro. nom.* I.20, II.39, Tr 4.1337.

ich *see* **ech** *pro.*

ydel(e) *adj.* (1) futile, worthless X.740; **y. swer-yng** profanity X.378, X.638; empty, useless Bo 5.m4.26, LGW 767; (as *n.*) **in (on) y.** in vain VI.642, Tr 5.272; (2) inactive I.2505, IV.217, HF 1733.

ydolastre *n.* idolator IV.2298, VII.2187.

ye(n) *see* **eye.**

if, yif *conj.* if I.145, I.503, BD 551; **if that** if I.144; **but if** unless I.1799.

yfere, yfeere *adv.* (1) together IV.1113, Tr 2.168, Tr 2.910; **met(te) y.** met one another II.394, Tr 2.152; (2) at the same time Tr 3.273. Cf. **in-fere.**

yfynde *inf.* find V.470, V.1153. Cf. **fynde(n).**

yheere *inf.* hear I.3176, IV.2154, Tr 4.1313. Cf. **here(n).**

yle *n.* isle, island II.68, II.545, HF 416.

ylyk(e), ylyche *adj.* alike, equal I.2734; like I.592; the same I.1539, HF 1328, LGW F 389. Cf. **lyk(e)** *adj.*

ylyk(e), yliche *adv.* alike, equally I.2526, III.2225; constantly, invariably IV.602, V.20. Cf. **lyk(e)** *adv.*

ilk(e) *adj.* (as *intens.* with **that, this, thise**) same, very I.175, I.3447, Tr 2.1706.

ill(e), il (1) *adj.* poor, bad (*Nth.*) I.4174; (2) (as *n.*) evil Rom B 2074.

ill(e) *adv.* poorly, evilly Rom B 2161, Rom B 2486.

ymaginable *adj.* endowed with imagination Bo 5.pr 4.199; capable of being imagined, conceivable Bo 5.pr4.194.

ymaginacioun, ymaginacion *n.* (1) the image-making faculty of the mind Bo 3.pr3.3, Bo 5.pr4.203; imagination, fancy, fantasy BD 14, LGW F 355; (2) ingenuity III.2218, HF 728; *pl.* **imaginaciouns** Bo 5.m4.8.

imaginen *v.* (1) form a mental picture, imagine Tr 2.836; (2) suppose mistakenly, fancy X.693, Bo 3.m11.23, Tr 5.617; deduce, believe II.889, Tr I.372, Tr 5.1441, LGW 1410; posit, assume Astr 1.21.40, Astr 2.39.2; (3) plan, devise Tr 4.1626; (4) worry about, consider Tr 5.454; *3 pr. sg.* **ymagineth** Bo 3.m11.23; *3 pt. sg.* **ymagined** Tr 5.617; *prp.* **ymaginyng(e)** considering IV.598, X.693, Tr 5.154; *pp.* **imagined** X.448, (as *adj.*) Astr 2.39.2; *vbl. n.* **ymaginyng** plotting I.1995, imagination, fancy LGW G 331, **ymagenyng** Ven 36.

in, inn *n.* inn, lodging, I.2436, I.3547, Rom B 5107; dwelling-place III.350.

in, inne *adv.* in, within I.3907, VIII.1164, Tr 1.387; therein Tr 2.875; (of clothing) I.41, VIII.881; (direction) in, into VIII.1240; to Tr 5.1545; in (favor) Tr 5.1519.

in *prep.* (1) inside, in I.298, I.4158; (2) enveloped in, wearing I.41, I.3954, LGW G 391; (3) in (a text) VII.2579, VII.3312; (4) (of feelings, ideas) in (the body, the mind) II.165, VIII.135, Tr 2.6; (5) (held) in I.4204, III.327; (6) into I.4094, Tr 4.467; (7) on IV.2137, Tr 4.1086.

in-fere, in-feere *adv.* together III.924 Rom B 4827. Cf. **yfere.**

infortune *n.* misfortune, bad luck VII.2401, Tr 3.1626, Tr 4.185.

ynly *adv.* inwardly, entirely BD 276, HF 31.

ynogh(e), ynough, ynow(e), inoghe *n.* (1) enough, a sufficiency I.3149, Bo 1.pr4.16, Bo 3.pr3.86, Rom A 753; **this (it) is y.** no more of this IV.1051; (2) plenty, an abundance III.1681, Tr 1.881.

ynogh, ynough, ynow(e), inowh(e) *adj.* (1) sufficient, enough I.373, V.708, Bo 4.pr6.13, Bo 4.m4.15, Tr 4.1266; (2) plenty of, abundant I.2836, III.332, Tr 4.107; great IV.792.

ynogh(e), ynough, ynow(e), ynowgh(e) *adv.* (1) very much, extremely, a great deal IV.1781, Bo 4.pr1.33, Tr 4.134, Rom B 2088; (2) enough, sufficiently I.888, Bo 1.pr4.102, Bo 4.pr4.131, LGW 2356; (3) **wel y.** perfectly, very well VI.79; (4) fully, completely, VII.2458.

inpacience *n.* impatience VII.1540, X.276.

inparfit *adj.* imperfect Bo 3.pr9.22, Bo 3.pr10.17, Astr 1.18.4

instrument *n.* instrument I.1367, BD 314; tool, device III.132, VIII.1119; *pl.* **instrumentz** I.1931.

intendestow *see* **entende(n).**

into, in to *prep.* (1) into I.23, I.1514; (2) onto, on I.3471, I.3585, Tr 2.1915; (3) to, unto I.692, VI.722; towards V.863; (4) until VII.1233, VIII.552.

inward *adj.* inner Bo 3.m11.4; interior Bo 5.m2.5.

inward *adv.* in, inwards I.1079, Tr 2.1725; inwardly, within VII.1645, Rom B 4411; on the way in, or privately Tr 2.1732.

inwardly *adv.* deeply Tr 2.264, Rom B 3922; intently Rom B 4968.

inwith, in-with *prep.* within, in II.797, IV.870.

ypocrisye *n.* hypocrisy VI.410, X.391, X.1023.

ypocryte *n.* hypocrite V.520, X.394; *pl.* **ypocrites** X.1060.

ire *n.* anger, irritability I.940, I.1560, Tr 1.793; **caught an i.** became angry III.2003; one of the Deadly Sins III.1834, X.388; *pl.* **ires** anger, rages Bo 2.m4.19.

iren *n.* iron I.500, I.1076, HF 1431.

irous *adj.* angry III.2016, III.2043, VII.1125, X.619.

is *see* **be(n).**

yse(e) *v. inf.* see IV.2402, BD 205, Tr 2.354; *imp. pl.* **ysee** look at, see Tr 2.1253; *pp.* **yseyn** IV.2404. Cf. **se(n).**

isse(n) *v.* issue, go out Tr 4.37; come forth Rom B 1992; *3 pr. sg.* **issist** Bo 3.pr12.158.

it *see* **hyt.**

yvel(e), evel *n.* evil I.4320, Bo 2.pr2.234; **for, on y. take** take (something) amiss Tr 4.606, Tr 5.1625; *pl.* **yveles** VII.1428, **eveles** Bo 4.pr1.20.

yvel(e), evel(e), evell, evyl *adj.* evil, malicious I.3173, LGW 1523, Rom B 4559, Rom B 5764; **y. wille** ill will, reluctance Tr 5.1637; **y. fare** misfortune Tr 2.1001; **(with) y. preef, thedam,** *etc.* bad luck (to someone) VII.405, HF 1786.

yvel(e), evel(e), evell *adv.* badly I.3715, IV.460, VIII.1225, BD 1204, Rom B 4730; **me list ful y.** I have no desire I.1127; **y. apayd** displeased, angry IV.2392, Anel 123, LGW G 68; **holden him y. apayed** consider oneself ill-used VII.390, VIII.921; **fare(n) y.** endure suffering, get on badly BD 501, Tr 1.626, Tr 5.238; **y. biseye** ill-looking IV.965; **y. avysed** ill-advised IX.335.

yvoyre, yvory *n.* ivory III.1741, VII.876, BD 946.

ywis *adv.* indeed, surely I.3277, I.3705, BD 657.

J

jalous(e), jelous, jelos *adj.* (1) jealous I.1329, I.1840, LGW 900, Anel 120; (as *n.*) jealous person Tr 3.1168, Ven 62; fervent, vigorous I.2634.

jalousie, jelousie, jelosye *n.* (1) jealousy I.1299, I.1333, LGW 722; zeal X.539; (2) solicitude, watchfulness LGW 722; *pl.* **jelousies** HF 685.

jangle *v.* chatter, gossip Tr 2.666; *2 pr. sg.* **janglest** II.774; *3 pr. sg.* **jangleth** VII.3435; *pr. pl.* **jangle** Tr 2.800; *prp.* (as *adj.*) **janglynge** PF 345; *vbl. n.* **jangelyng(e)** V.257, **jangelyngis** Rom C 6711.

jangler(e) *n.* gossip, chatterer IX.348, PF 457.

jangleresse *n.* female gossip, chatterbox III.638; *pl.* **jangleresses** IV.2307.

jape *n.* (1) trick, deceit I.4338, HF 96; (2) joke I.3799; *pl.* **japes** tricks I.705, jokes VI.319.

jape(n) *v.* (1) joke, jest VII.693; mock Tr 1.929, Tr 1.508; (2) deceive, trick Tr 2.140, Tr 5.1134; *pr. subj. sg.* **jape** IV.1389; *2 pt. sg.* **japedest** mocked Tr 1.508, joked Tr 1.924; *3 pt. sg.* **japed** deceived, tricked I.1729, joked Tr 5.509; *pp.* **(i)japed** tricked I.1729, mocked Tr 1.318.

japer(e) *n.* jester, trickster X.89, Tr 2.340; *pl.* **japeres** X.651, **japeris** X.652.

jaspre, jasper *n.* jasper (a gem) VII.1107, PF 230, Tr 2.1229.

joyne(n), joygnen *v.* join, unite Bo 2.pr6.90, Bo 5.pr4.13, Rom B 5075; *3 pr. sg.* **joyneth** VII.1614; *pr. pl.* **joygnen** Bo 2.pr6.125; *pt. sg.* **joyned** put close together BD 393; *pt. pl.* **joyneden** Tr 5.813; *prp.* **joynynge** adjoining LGW 1962, **joynant** I.1062; *pp.* **(i)joyned** VIII.95, Bo 4.pr1.25, **ijoygned** Bo 2.pr6.85; *vbl. n. pl.* **joynynges** joints HF 1187.

joly, jolyf *adj.* (1) merry, cheerful I.3355, V.48, Tr 2.1031; (2) spirited, playful I.3263; lusty, amorous I.3339, I.4232, VI.453; (3) pretty, attractive I.3316, III.860, LGW G 36; *comp.* **jolyer** finer V.927.

jolily *adv.* (1) merrily, gracefully I.4370; happily Rom C 7031; (2) prettily Rom B 2284.

jolite(e), joliftee *n.* (1) merriment, cheerfulness V.278, VI.780, Tr 1.559; pleasure X.1049; (2) passion, sexual desire I.1807; (3) attractiveness IX.197.

juge, jugge *n.* judge I.814, I.1719, Rom C 6419; *gen.* **juges** VI.175; *pl.* **juges** VI. 291.

jugement, juggement *n.* judgment I.778, I.805, Tr 4.1299; decree X.337; justice Bo 4.pr4.193; *pl.* **juggementz** IV.439.

jugen, juggen *v.* judge Bo 1.pr4.285, Tr 5.1203, Tr 2.21; give judgment PF 524, PF 629; think Tr 5.1203; *1 pr. sg.* **juge** PF 629; *2 pr. sg.* (with *pro.*) **juggestow** Bo 3.pr9.192; *3 pr. sg.* **juggeth** gives judgment VII.1031; *pr. pl.* **juggen** Bo 2.pr7.75; *pr. subj. sg.* **juge** Bo 4.pr6.5; *imp. pl.* **juggeth** Tr 3.1312; *pp.* **jugged** given judgment VI.228, **juged** HF 357.

jupartie, jupertie, jupardye *n.* (1) danger, risk Tr 5.916; **in j.** in jeopardy, at risk Tr 2.772, Tr 3.877, Rom B 4950; (2) taking risks, gambling VIII.743; *pl.* **jeupardyes** chess problems BD 666.

just(e) *adj.* (1) just, fair V.20, Tr 2.527; (2) true, exact III.2090, HF 719.

juste(n) *v.* joust I.2604, LGW 1274; *3 pr. sg.* **justeth** V.1098, **jousteth** Tr 3.1718; *pr. pl.* **justen** I.2486; *prp.* **justyng** V.1198.

K

kan, kanstow *see* **kunne.**

karf *see* **kerve(n).**

kembe *v.* comb HF 136, Rom A 599; *3 pr. sg.* **kembeth** I.3374; *pt. sg.* **kembde** V.560, *pp.* **(y)kembd** I.2143, **kempt** Rom A 577.

kene, keene *adj.* (1) bold, fierce VII.2249; cruel For 27; eager IV.1759, VII.2249; (2) keen, sharp I.104, I.1966.

kene *adv.* painfully Merc B 3; sharply Lady 57, Rom B 1885, Rom C 6197.

kep(e), keep *n.* in **take(n) k.** (1) take heed, pay attention to VI.90, BD 128; take notice, see IV.2398; (2) take care, be concerned for BD 6, Buk 26; (3) be alert, on guard Rom B 3475.

kepe(n), kepyn *v.* (1) keep I.4102, VI.798, Tr 1.627, Bo 2.pr5.118; **k. (thy) tonge** hold (your) tongue IX.319, Tr 3.294; (2) take care of, look after I.593, Tr 5.1048; protect, preserve I.2329, II.454, Tr 5.1077; sustain IV.229; (3) observe, hold to I.852, V.1479; (with *inf.* and *neg.*) care nothing about, be unconcerned about I.2960; **I k. han no los** I don't care to have fame VIII.1368; *2 pr. sg.* **kepest** VII.1144; *3 pr. sg.* **kepeth** IV.1133; *pr. pl.* **kepe(n)** V.956, Rom C 6817; *pr. subj.* **kepe** I.4247 *(sg.)*, VII.1139 *(pl.)*; *pt. sg.* **kepte** I.512; *pt. pl.* **kepte** II.269, **keped** LGW G 294; *imp. sg.* **kep** Tr 3.332, **keep** VII.432; *imp. pl.* **kepeth** II.764, **keepe** I.4101; *prp.* **kepyng(e)** V.571; *pp.* **ykept** protected I.276, LGW 722; *vbl. n.* **kepyng** guarding I.3851, preservation X.571.

kertels *see* **kirtel.**

kerve(n) *v.* carve, cut V.158, Tr 2.325, Rom A 945; *3 pr. sg.* **kerveth** X.888; *pt. sg.* **karf** III.2244, **carf** I.100; *pt. pl.* **korven** Bo 1.pr3.39; *prp.* (as *adj.*) **kerving** Tr 1.631; *pp.* **(y)corve(n)** I.2013, VIII.533, **(y)korve(n)** I.2696, VII.611, LGW 2695; *vbl. n.* **kervyng** sculpture I.1915; *pl.* **kervynges** sculptures HF 1302.

kesse, keste *see* **kisse(n).**

kevere, kevered *see* **covere(n).**

kyd, kidde *see* **kythe(n).**

kyn *n.* kin, family I.3942, IV.2197, Tr 1.90; **k. to** related to LGW 2244; **by my (youre) fader k.** on the honor of my (your) family IV.1515, VIII.829, IX.37; on your father's side VII.1931; *gen.* **som kynnes** some kind of II.1137.

kynde *n.* (1) nature III.1149, III.1706, BD 16; humankind VIII.41; natural form I.1401, Tr 4.865; natural disposition V.608, BD 494; manner VIII.981; **by k.** by instinct VII.3196; **by wey of k.** in the natural course of things VII.1783, Mars 282; **of (propre) k.** by nature, naturally V.619, Tr 2.1443; (2) sort, species I.1401, VIII.252, PF 174; family, descent III.1101, VIII.121; **sette in k.** classify VIII.789; (3) semen X.965; *gen.* **kyndes** Rom B 4854; *pl.* **kyndes** species HF 968; **of alle kyndes** in every way HF 204.

kynde *adj.* (1) natural HF 836, Tr 4.768; (2) kind I.647, III.823; *super.* **kindest** most kind Tr 5.1529.

kyndely, kyndeliche *adj.* natural X.491, BD 761, HF 829.

kyndely, kyndeliche *adv.* (1) naturally BD 778, Bo 3.m11.22; (2) kindly, benevolently VII.353.

kynrede *n.* kindred, family, lineage V.735, V.1565; *pl.* **kynredes** X.206.

kirtel, kirtle *n.* tunic I.3321; unadorned gown V.1580; *pl.* **kirtles** simple frocks, outer petticoats Rom A 778, **kertels** PF 235.

kisse(n), kesse *v.* kiss I.3284, IV.1057, Rom B 4817; *3 pr. sg.* **kisseth** IV.1823; *pr. pl.* **kissen** X.857; *pr. subj. sg.* **kisse** I.3797 *(sg.)*, VI.965 *(pl.)*; *imp. sg.* **kys(se)** II.861, HF 1108; *imp. pl.* **kysse** I.3716; *pt. sg.* **kiste**

I.3305, **keste** V.350, Tr 3.1129, **kyssid(e)** LGW 2208, Rom B 3760; *pt. pl.* **kiste** VI.968; *prp.* **kissyng(e)** IV.1083, Tr 5.1241, (as *adj.*) X.856; *pp.* **(y)kist** I.1759, Tr 4.1689, **kissed** Rom B 2040; *vbl. n.* **kyssyng(e)** I.3683, Rom B 3677.

kyte *n.* kite, vulture I.1179, V.624, PF 349.

kythe(n) *v.* make known, reveal, show Anel 228, For 63; *3 pr. sg.* **kitheth** V.483; *pt. sg.* **kidde** Tr 1.208; *pr. subj. sg.* **kithe** II.636; *imp. sg.* **kith(e)** III.1609, Tr 4.538; *imp. pl.* **kytheth** Mars 298; *pp.* **kyd** IV.1943, **kydde** Tr 1.208, **kithed** VIII.1054.

kitte *see* **kutte(n).**

knave *n.* (1) boy VII.310; **k. child** male baby IV.612; (2) servant I.3434, I.3469, LGW 1807, LGW 2366; (3) peasant X.188; churl, villain III.253, X.433, LGW 2390; *pl.* **knaves** servants I.2728.

knede *v.* knead I.4094; *pt. pl.* **gnodded** Form Age 11; *prp.* (as *adj.*) **knedyng** kneading (trough, tub) I.3548, I.3564; *pp.* **kneden** mixed together Rom A 217.

knele *v.* kneel Tr 1.806, Tr 3.892; *2 pr. sg.* **knelest** Scog 43; *3 pr. sg.* **kneleth** I.1819; *pr. pl.* **knele** III.2262; *pt. sg.* **khelide** Rom B 2037; *pt. pl.* **kneled(e)** I.897, LGW G 198; *imp. pl.* **kneleth** VI.925, **knele** Rom C 7695; *prp.* **knelyng(e)** II.383, LGW F 117; *pp.* **ykneled** LGW 1232; *vbl. n. pl.* **knelynges** X.1055.

knytte, knette *v.* join, fasten, draw together I.1128, PF 381, Mars 183; **k. up** conclude X.28 *(see note)*, X.47; *2 pr. sg.* **knyttest** II.307; *3 pr. sg.* **knytteth** VII.1614, **knetteth** Tr 3.1748; *imp. sg.* **knyt forth** sum up, go on with (your argument) Bo 4.pr2.111; *pt. sg.* **in knette** restrained, contracted Tr 3.1088; *pp.* **(y)knyt** IV.1391, fastened, tied I.4083; **(y)knet** PF 628, Tr 3.1734; *vbl. n.* **knyttynge** X.843; *pl.* **knyttynges** Bo 5.m3.17.

knokke *v.* knock I.3676; *1 pr. sg.* **knokke** VI.730; *3 pr. sg.* **knokketh** I.3764; *pr. pl.* **knokke** VI.541; *imp. sg.* **knokke** I.3432; *pt. sg.* **knokked(e)** I.3436, Rom A 534; *pt. pl.* **knokkeden** Mars 84; *vbl. n.* **knokkynge** beating X.1055.

knoppe *n.* bud Rom A 1683, Rom A 1685; *pl.* **knoppis** ornamental buttons, studs Rom A 1080; buds Rom A 1685.

knotte *n.* (1) knot I.197, Tr 3.1732; (2) gist, main point (of a tale) V.407; nub (of a question) Bo 5.pr3.30; conclusion (of a speech) X.494.

know(e), knowen *v.* (1) know I.730, BD 120, Tr 5.1295; (2) recognize I.382, II.649; (3) acknowledge VIII.2622, VIII.259; *2 pr. sg.* **knowest** I.1723, (with *pro.*) **knowestow** I.3156; *3 pr. sg.* **knoweth** II.50; *pr. pl.* **knowe(n)** I.642, HF 1257; *pr. subj. sg.* **knowe** Tr 3.407; *1 & 3 pr. sg.* **knew** I.240; *2 pt. sg.* **knewe** For 21; *pt. pl.* **knewe(n)** I.1017, LGW 2441; *pt. subj. sg.* **knewe** IV.1078; *pt. subj. pl.* **knewen** VIII.1371; *imp. sg.* **know(e)** Truth 19, Astr 2.40.4; *prp.* **knowynge** VIII.989; *pp.* **(y)knowe** I.423, I.1203, **knowe(n)** VI.156, Tr 1.638, **yknowen** Tr 2.792; *vbl. n.* **knowyng(e)** knowledge V.301, X.1079; *pl.* **knowynges** Bo 5.pr5.24.

knowe, kne(e) *n.* knee X.598, Tr 2.1202, LGW 2028; *pl.* **knowes** Tr 3.1592, **knees** I.1103, **knes** LGW F 115.

knoweleche, knowleche, knoweliche *n.* (1) knowledge X.75, Bo 4.m1.16; (2) acquaintance VII.30.

knowelecheth *3 pr. sg.* acknowledges VII.1774; *pr. pl.* **knowelichen** VII.1745; *prp.* **knowelechynge**

VII.1771; *vbl. n.* **knowlechyng(e)** knowledge BD 796, help VIII.1432, Bo 5.pr5.2.

kokkow, cokkow, cukkow *n.* (1) cuckoo I.1930, PF 358, PF 505; (2) the cry of the cuckoo PF 499.

konne(n) *see* **kunne.**

konnyng(e), kunnyng *see* **kunnyng(e).**

konnyng(e), kunnyng *adj.* skillful VII.2500, Pity 97; cunning Rom A 1111; knowledgeable Tr 1.302, Tr 5.970; *super.* **konnyngeste** most skillful Tr 1.331.

korven, (y)korve(n) *see* **kerve(n).**

koude *see* **kunne.**

kouthe, kowth(e) *see* **kunne.**

kunne, cunne *v.* (1) know I.210, I371; know, be informed about I.3193, Tr 1.757; know by heart VI.332, VII.543, Rom B 4796; **k. good** know what is right, have good sense BD 800, BD 1012; **k. maugre** be resentful Rom B 4399, Rom B 4559; **k. no bettre red** be helpless VII.2549; **k. red** have a plan BD 105; **k. wit** be wise IV.2245; **k. (one's) good** know what is good for one III.231; **k. (someone's) thank** be grateful to someone I.I808; (2) be in a position to do, be justified in III.1826, IV.1287, V.803, Tr 1.798; (3) have mastery of a skill I.110 I.210, I.476, I.3200; **c. lettrure** know how to read VIII.846; (4) (with *inf.*) be able to, know how to I.94, I.652, III.386; *inf.* **kunne** HF 2004, **cunne** Rom B 4559; *1 & 3 pr. sg.* **kan** I.643, **can** BD 34; *2 pr. sg.* **kanst** III.904, **canst** PF 163, (with *pro.*) **kanstow** II.632; *pr. pl.* **can** II.1165, **kan** III.980, **kunne(n)** Rom C 5889, Rom C 6174; **konne** I.4123, **konnen** IV.2438, **conne** Tr 1.776, **cunne** Rom B 2541; *pr. subj. sg.* **konne** I.4396, Tr 2.49, **kunne** Rom C 5992; *pr. subj. pl.* **konne** Astr Pro 55; *1 & 3 pt. sg.* **koud(e)** I.94, Tr 2.1582, **coude** Anel 63, **kowde** Tr 5.1729, **couthe** BD 800, **kouthe** I.390, **kowthe** Tr 1.984; *2 pt. sg.* **koudest** Tr 1.622, **coudest** LGW G 271; *pt. pl.* **koude** I.4104; *pt. subj. sg.* **koude** III.1008, X.946; *prp.* (as *adj.*) *see* **konnyng(e)** *above;* *pp.* **(y)koud** BD 666, BD 998, **couth** Tr 4.61, **kowth** IV.942, (as *adv.*) **kouthe** well-known I.14, (as *adj.*) **kouth** well-known HF 757.

kunnyng(e), cunning, konnyng(e), connyng(e) *vbl. n.* (1) ability, skill V. 251, Tr 3.999, Tr 5.866; (2) knowledge, understanding Tr 1.662, Rom B 4717; (3) intelligence wisdom Tr 2.1079; (4) cleverness, cunning Anel 89.

kutte(n) *v.* cut VI.954, Bo 4.m7.14; *3 pr. sg.* **kutteth** IX.342; *pt. sg.* **kitte** III.722, **kut** Rom C 6198; *imp. sg.* **kut** Rom C 6198; *pp.* **kut** Bo 4.pr6.17, **cut** LGW G 292, (as *adj.*) **kutted** X.422, **cutted** LGW 973; *vbl. n.* **kuttynge** Bo 4.m7.13.

L

label(l) *n.* moveable brass rule (on an astrolabe) Astr 1.21.87, Astr 2.3.13.

labour *n.* effort, work I.2913, I.3388; **do (one's) l.** make an effort, take pains III.381, VII.463; trouble, hardship II.423, LGW G 306; *pl.* **labours** Bo 3.m10.5.

laboure(n) *v.* labor, work I.186, I.2408; make an effort, take pains Tr 1.458; *3 pr. sg.* **laboureth** IV.1842; *pr. pl.* **labouren** X.251; *pt. sg. (reflx.)* **laboured me** took pains Tr 4.1009; *pp.* **laboured** put to work VII.108; *vbl. n.* **laboring** Rom C 6575.

(y)lad, ladde *see* **lede(n).**

lady *n.* lady, gentlewoman I.839, I.912; woman IV.2367; mistress, ruler I.2231, III.1048; beloved I.1143, I.1289; **(oure) l.** Virgin Mary VI.308, VII.474, ABC 16; *gen. sg.* **lady** I.88, **ladys** Tr 5.675; *pl.* **ladyes** I.898, **ladys** I.2579.

lafte(n), (y)laft *see* **leve(n)** *v.*²

lay *n.*¹ religious law, doctrine, or belief I.1001, II.572, LGW F 336.

lay *n.*² song BD 471; *pl.* **layes** Rom A 715.

lay(e), layde *see* **leye.**

lay, laye(n), y-layne *see* **lye(n)** *v.*¹

layser *see* **leyser.**

lak, lakke *n.* (1) lack, want III.1308, IV.2271; (2) flaw, fault Tr 2.1178; offense IV.2199; blame LGW G 298.

lakke(n) *v.* (1) find fault with, disparage Tr 1.189, Rom A 284; (2) *(intr.)* be lacking Tr 4.945; *(impers.)* **him (me, *etc.*) l.** (something) is lacking to him (me, *etc.*), he lacks X.16; *(tr.)* miss, lack Bo 4.pr3.5; *3 pr. sg.* **lakketh** IV.1998; *pr. pl.* **lakken** VIII.672; *pr. subj. sg.* VIII.1419; *pt. sg.* **lakked(e)** I.756, VI.41; **lakkide** Rom A 901; *pt. subj. sg.* **lakked** Tr 1.522; *prp.* **lakkynge** Bo 3.pr11.20; *pp.* **lakid** Bo 3.pr3.35; *vbl. n.* **lakking** stint Rom A 1146.

lamb(es), lambren *see* **lomb.**

land *see* **lond(e).**

langage *n.* (1) language I.4330, II.516, V.1000; (2) speech, words I.211, I.2227, Tr 3.1336; *pl.* **langages** Bo 2.pr7.55.

lange *see* **long(e)** *adj.*¹

langour *n.* sickness, suffering X.723, Tr 5.42, Tr 5.268; weakness ABC 7.

langwisse *v.* languish, suffer, grow weak HF 2018; *2 pr. sg.* **languyssest** Bo 2.pr1.10; *3 pr. sg.* **langwissheth** IV.1867, V.950; *pr. pl.* **languisshe** Ven 46; *pt. sg.* **langwisshed** Rom B 3486; *prp.* **languyssshyng** PF 472; *vbl. n.* **langwissynge** weakness X.913, **languisshynge** suffering Tr 1.529.

lappe *n.* (1) loose part of a garment, hem VIII.12, Tr 3.59; (2) fold in a garment or sleeve used as a large pocket I.686, IV.585, V.635; (3) lap VII.2454.

large *n.* (in *phr.*) **at (one's) l.** at (one's) liberty, free I.1292, I.1327; (as *adv. phr.*) freely I.1283; uncommitted Rom B 4388.

large *adj.* (1) generous, open-handed X.465, Rom A 1168; bountiful VII.3159; free-spending VII.431; lavish Tr 5.804; (2) large, ample I.472; big I.753; large, extensive I.2678; **l. quart** full quart I.3497; **pryme l.** fully prime, nine A.M. V.360; *comp.* **larger(e)** Bo 4.pr6.122, Rom C 6911; *super.* **largest** Astr 2.4.7.

large *adv.* generously ABC 174; freely I.734.

largely *adv.* fully I.1908, I.2738, Tr 2.1707; generally X.804.

larges(se) *n.* generosity VII.22, VII.1275, Tr 3.1724; generous gift HF 1309.

las, laas *n.* (1) lace, tie Rom A 843; (2) belt, cord VIII.574; (3) snare I.1951, I.2329, LGW 600.

lasse, lesse *n.* less VII.949; **l. and moore, moore and l.** everyone, everything I.1756, III.934, III.1562.

lasse, lesse *adj.* less I.3519, I.4409, BD 675; (as *comp.*) lesser Tr 2.470, smaller Tr 5.618; lower in rank VII.1072.

lasse, lesse *adv.* less X.358, BD 927, BD 933.

last(e) *super. adj.* (1) last I.2808, I.3430; farthest, most distant IV.266, Bo 3.m5.6; most extreme, greatest VI.221; lowest, most base Bo 2.pr5.49; (2) (as *n.*) **atte (at the) l.** finally, at last I.707, IV.547, BD 364; **to the l.** in the end Tr 2.255; last day Tr 1.537, Tr 2.870.

last *adv.* last I.2200, VII.2825.

laste(n) *v.* last, continue I.2557, X.551, Tr 1.1048; *3 pr. sg.* **lasteth** II.499, *(contr.)* **last** PF 49; *pr. subj. sg.* **laste** LGW 1239; *pt. sg.* **laste** V.574, **lasted** V.806; *prp.* **lastynge** enduring I.3072, (as *adj.*) VIII.98; *vbl. n.* **lastynge** Bo 2.pr7.98.

lat(e), laten *see* **lete(n).**

late *adj.* recent Bo 4.m5.6; *comp.* **latter(e)** more recent, later III.765, Bo 1.m.6.16; **lattre** Bo 1.pr5.65; **latter end** final outcome VII.3205.

late *adv.* **l. or yerne** at any time Tr 3.376; (1) late I.4196, III.750, Tr 2.398; (2) recently, lately I.77, I.690; **erly and l.** always I.4401, VI.730; **l. or now** just recently HF 2048; **til now l.** until recently BD 45, Rom C 6650; *comp.* **latter** slower X.971.

latoun, laton *n.* latten (a brass-like alloy) I.699 (see note), VI.350.

laude *n.* praise III.1353, VII.455, Tr 3.1273; *pl.* **laudes** early morning church service I.3655; praises HF 1322.

laughe(n), laugh *v.* laugh I.474, I.3722, Tr 5.569; *3 pr. sg.* **laugheth** I.1494; *pr. sg. subj.* **laughe** X.664; *pt. sg.* **lough** I.3114; *pt. pl.* **laugheden** Rom A 863; *prp.* **laughyng(e)** I.2011, (as *adj.*) Rom B 2809; *pp.* **lawghed** HF 409, **laughen** I.3855; *vbl. n.* **laughing** Rom B 2819.

launde *n.* clearing, glade I.1696, PF 302.

laurer, lorer *n.* (1) laurel tree I.2922, PF 182, Rom A 1379; (2) laurel leaves I.1027, I.2175; *pl.* **loreres** Rom A 1313.

laus(e) *see* **loos** *adj.*

law(e) *n.* (1) law I.309, I.577; justice Sted 27; (2) religion II.237, II.336; *gen. sg.* **lawes** VII.564; *pl.* **lawes** Tr 2.42.

laxatyf *n.* laxative, purgative I.2756, VII.2943; *pl.* **laxatyves** VII.2962.

leche *n.* physician, healer III.1956, VI.916, BD 920; *pl.* **leches** III.1957.

lechour, lecchour *n.* lecher III.242, III.767, IV.2257; *pl.* **lecchours** III.468.

led, leed *n.* (1) lead VIII.406, VIII.828 (see note), HF 1431; (2) leaden vessel, cauldron I.202.

lede(n), leede *v.* (1) lead, bring, take Bo 2.m5.22, Tr 4.1514, Rom B 4932; lead (a life, an age) Anel 302, Bo 2.m4.17, Tr 4.1342; (2) govern, control II.434, Tr 2.527; *2 pr. sg.* **ledest** V.866; *3 pr. sg.* **ledeth** PF 138, *(contr.)* **let** Tr 2.882; *pr. pl.* **lede(n)** II.1158, HF 37; *pr. subj. sg.* **lede** II.357; *pt. sg.* **ladde** I.1446, **ledde** Tr 3.59; *pt. pl.* **leden** V.898, **ledde(n)** VIII.392, Bo 4.pr4.264, **ladde(n)** IV.390, Rom A 1310; *pp.* **(y)lad** carried I.530, I.2620; **iladde** Bo 2.pr3.51; **(i)led** Bo 1.pr4.36, Tr 2.553; *vbl. n.* **ledyng** retinue Rom B 5863.

ledere *n.* leader Bo 1.pr3.70, Tr 4.1454.

leef *n.* (1) leaf I.1838, III.1667, Tr 3.1200; (2) page I.3177, III.635, III.667; *pl.* **leves** I.1496, **leeves** Rom A 911.

lef, leef *see* **leve(n)** *v.* ²

leef, lief, lef *adj.* (1) dear, beloved HF 1827, Tr 2.1693; (as *n.*) dear one, sweetheart I.3393, III.431; **ha(n) l.** love, hold dear V.572, Tr 3.869; (2) **ben l.** (with *indir.*

obj.) be pleasing, desirable (to someone), (someone) likes VII.159, VIII.1467, BD 8, Tr 3.1619; (3) desirous I.3510, VI.760; **han l.** be willing III.1574; **l. or looth** whether one likes it or not I.1837, IV.1961, for any reason LGW 1639; *wk. sg.* **leeve** I.1136, **leve** HF 816; *wk. pl.* **leeve** V.341; *comp.* **levere** dearer V.572; **were (hadde) lever(e)** (with indirect *obj.*) (one) would prefer II.1027, III.168, Tr 2.352; *super.* **levest** most preferable Bo 4.pr7.103.

left *see* **leve(n)** *v.* ²

left *see* **lift.**

leeful, leful *see* **leveful.**

legende *n.* saint's life I.3141; tale of martyrdom I.3141, III.742, VII.145; collection of saints' lives II.61, LGW F 483; *pl.* **legendes** III.686.

leye, leggen, laye *v.* (1) lay, place I.3269, Tr 2.1671, Tr 3.459; (2) wager, bet I.4009, Tr 2.1505; (3) *(reflx.)* lie down I.1384; *3 pr. sg.* **layth** I.4021, **leith** on works on I.4229, **leieth** Rom B 4143; *pr. pl.* **leyn** IX.222, **laye** VIII.783; *imp. sg.* **ley(e)** I.841, Tr 2.1517, **lay** I.4085; *pt. sg.* **leyde** Tr 2.1548, **layde** VI.232; *pt. pl.* **leyde(n)** II.213, LGW 2501, **laye** VIII.783; *pp.* **(y)leyd** I.81, LGW 2141, **layd** Purse 5.

(y)leyn *see* **lye(n)** *v.* ¹

leyser, layser *n.* (1) opportunity I.3293, PF 487, Tr 2.1369; (2) time, leisure I.1188, III.683, BD 172, Tr 2.1369; **bettre l.** more time III.551.

lemaille *n.* metal filings VIII.1164, VIII.1197, VIII.1267.

lemes *see* **lym** *n.* ¹

lemman, leman *n.* loved one, sweetheart, mistress I.3280, VII.788; paramour, lover II.917, III.722, LGW 1772; *pl.* **lemmans** III.1998, **lemmanes** X.903.

lene *v.* ¹ lean, incline VII.1448; *prp.* **lenynge** LGW F 179, LGW G 234.

lene *v.* ² lend I.611, VIII.1024; *3 pr. sg.* **leneth** Rom A 186; *pr. subj. sg.* **lene** may (God) grant LGW 2083; *imp. sg.* **lene** I.3777 **leene** VIII.1026; *imp. pl.* **lene** I.3082; *pt. sg.* **lente** VII.354; *prp.* **lenyng** Rom B 2373; *pp.* **(y)lent** VIII.1406, For 30; *vbl. n.* **in lenyng** as a loan Rom B 2373.

lene, leene *adj.* thin, lean I.287, I.591, Tr 5.709.

lenger, lengest *see* **long(e)** *adj.* ¹ and **long(e)** *adv.*

lengthe *n.* (1) length I.1970, I.2646; (2) height I.83, II.934; **by, on l.** at length, fully Tr 2.262, Tr 5.1491; **upon l.** at length, finally BD 352.

leonesse, lyonesse *n.* lioness III.637, LGW 805.

leoun, leon, lyoun *n.* lion I.1598, Tr 1.1074, Tr 5.830; *pl.* **leouns** VII.2261, **lyouns** Rom A 894.

lepe *v.* (1) leap, jump III.267; (2) rush, run I.4079, I.4378, HF 1823, Tr 2.512; *pr. pl.* **lepe** VIII.915; *pt. sg.* **leep** I.2687, **lep** LGW 2709, **lepte** Tr 2.1637; *prp.* **lepyng** I.4079, **lepande** Rom B 1928.

ler(e), leere *v.* (1) learn III.982, III.1516, HF 511, Rom B 4808; (2) teach Anel 98, Tr 2.1580; *inf.* **to lere** to be taught Tr 5.161; *pr. pl.* **leere** teach V.104, **ler** Rom B 4795; **lere** learn PF 25; *pr. subj. pl.* **leere** VIII.607; *imp. pl.* **leere** Tr 2.97; *pp.* **lered** learned Tr 3.406; (as *n.*) learned person(s) PF 46 *(sg.),* Tr 1.976 *(pl.);* (as *adj.*) learned VI.283.

lerne(n) *v.* (1) learn I.308, I.3192, III.1978; (2) teach VIII.844; *3 pr. sg.* **leerneth** Bo 3.m11.45; *pr. pl.* **lerne** IX.334; *imp. sg.* **lerne** IX.349; *imp. pl.* **lerneth** V.777; *1 pt. sg.* **lerned** V.719; *2 pt. sg.* **lernedest** Bo 2.pr2.72; *pt. pl.* **lerned** VII.498; *prp.* **lernynge** VII.516; *pp.*

lerned VIII.748, (as *adj.*) I.480; *vbl. n.* **lernyng(e)** learning, education I.300, Astr 2.5.5.

les, lees *n.* deception, falsehood LGW 1545; **with-oute(n) l.** without falsehood, truly LGW 1128, LGW 1518.

les, lees *see* **lye** *n.*

lese(n), leese(n) *v.* lose I.1215, III.2054, Bo 2.pr4.137, Rom C 6936; *3 pr. sg.* **leseth** BD 33, **leeseth** Bo 2.m3.7; *pr. pl.* **lesen** Rom A 448; *pr. subj. sg.* **lese** II.225; *pr. subj. pl.* **leese** VIII.1410, **leesen** Bo 3.pr4.96; *imp. pl.* **leseth** II.19; *pt. sg.* **les** HF 1414; **loste** III.721; *pt. pl.* **losten** I.936; *pp.* **lorn(e)** I.3536, Rom A 366, **(y)loren** LGW F 26, LGW 1048, **lore** BD 748, **(y)lost** I.2257, I.4314; *vbl. n.* **lesynge** loss I.1707.

lesyng(e) *vbl. n.* lie, lying VIII.479, HF 154; *pl.* **lesinges** lies HF 676, (personified) deceit I.1927.

lest(es) *see* **lust.**

lest(e) *see* **list(e)** *v.*

lest(e), leest(e) *super. adj.* least, smallest I.1701, IX.185, BD 283, Tr 3.1320; **atte (at the) l. weye** in any event, at least I.1121, I.3680, VIII.676; (as *n.*) **atte (at the) l.** at least I.3683, II.38, Rom B 5827; **meeste and l.** great and small, everyone I.2198, V.300.

lest, leest *adv.* least Anel 316, Tr 2.840, Lady 67.

lete(n), leeten, late(n) *v.* (1) grant, give Tr 4.599, Tr 5.1688, Rom A 1690; (2) surrender, give up Bo 2.pr5.156, Tr 4.1585, LGW G 397; **l. life** die VIII.406, ABC 72; (3) leave I.508, III.1276, V.290, Anel 45, Bo 1.pr3.17; (4) abandon PF 391; (5) (as *aux.* with *inf.*) cause, have, get (something done) VII.2159; **l. don** cause (something) to be done VI.173, VII.2152; (6) allow, permit I.128, III.767, Tr 5.351, Rom B 5574; (7) **l. blood** draw blood (as medical treatment) I.3326; (8) in exhortations, sometimes with imperative force I.855, II.170; in suppositions **l. men shette** say that men were to shut III.1141; (9) cease, stop (doing something) I.3311, I.4214; refrain (from doing something) Tr 2.1500; **l. be** give up Rom C 6283; leave alone III.1289, LGW G 529; desist from I.3145, III.242, Tr 2.248; stop I.3285, VI.947; (10) disregard, Rom C 6556; (11) consider Bo 2.pr3.25; (12) pretend Tr 2.543; *1 pr. sg.* **let(e)** IV.1781, PF 279, **lat(e)** Tr 1.133, LGW 628; *3 pr. sg.* **leteth** ceases Bo 3.m1.8, *(contr.)* **let** Tr 4.200, **lat** Rom B 5492; *pr. pl.* **lete(n)** let VII.2708, X.721; **leete(n)** V.1379, Bo 2.pr5.126; *pr. subj. sg.* **let(e)** III.504, HF 1556, **lat(e)** I.188, Rom B 3292; *pr. subj. pl.* **leete** VIII.1409, **lat(e)** PF 492, Tr 2.323; *imp. sg.* **let** Bo 3.m11.18, **leet** VI.731, **lat** Tr 2.1401; *imp. pl.* **leteth** cease LGW F 411, **lete** give up, abandon VI.659; *pt. sg.* **leet** I.128, I.175, **let(e)** Tr 5.226, Rom B 5108; *pt. pl.* **lete** I.4308, **leete(n)** V.1379, Tr 4.1135; *pt. subj. sg.* **lete** Tr 3.1762; *pp.* **lete(n)** III.767, HF 1934, **yleten** Bo 4.pr4.287, **laten** I.4346; *prp.* **letyng** leaving behind Tr 5.1810.

lette *n.* delay, stopping Tr 3.699, Tr 4.41.

lette(n), let *v.* (1) *(tr.)* hinder, delay, prevent II.1117, HF 1954, Rom B 1982, disturb VII.86; (2) *(intr.)* refrain from, desist from I.1317, Tr 1.150; stop, leave off PF 439, Tr 2.1089; *2 pr. sg.* **lettest** III.839; *3 pr. sg.* **letteth** hinders IV.1573, *(contr.)* **let** repels PF 151, **lette** desists X.995; *pr. subj.* **lette** *(sg.),* Tr 3.545 V.994 *(pl.);* *imp. sg.* **lette** Tr 3.725; *imp. pl.* **letteth** Tr 2.1136; *pt. sg.* **lette** VII.2840, **letted** I.1892; *pt. pl.* **lette** V.994; *pp.* **let** VII.2598, **lett** Rom B 5335, **ylet**

Bo 4.pr4.31, **yleten** Bo 4.pr4.287; *vbl. n.* **lettyng** Rom C 5931.

leve, leeve *n.* permission, leave I.1064, IV.888, BD 153; **by your l.** if you please, with your permission I.3916, III.112, Tr 2.1634; **(al) beside his, hir l.** without his, their permission HF 2105, Tr 2.734.

leve *v.* [1] allow LGW 2280; *pr. subj. sg.* **leve** may (God) grant VII.683, Tr 1.597, Tr 2.1212.

leve(n) *v.* [2] (1) leave, depart I.4414; (2) give up, quit V.828, VIII.287; stop, desist from Tr 4.1335; (3) remain BD 701; be left (after subtraction) Astr 2.10.14; *3 pr. sg.* **leveth** Astr 2.25.50; *pr. pl.* **leve** Rom B 5786; *imp. sg.* **leef** I.1614, **lef** III.2089, **leve** Truth 22; *imp. pl.* **leveth** LGW G 88; *pt. sg.* **left(e)** I.492, HF 403; **lafte** LGW 1666; *pt. pl.* **lefte(n)** I.2599, VII.972, **lafte(n)** VII.2198, LGW F 168; *pp.* **left** HF 2038, **(y)laft** I.2016, I.2746.

leve, leeve *v.* [3] believe, trust IV.2205, VIII.218, Tr 4.967, LGW F 10; *2 pr. sg.* (with *pro.*) **leevestow** do you believe VIII.212; *3 pr. sg.* **leeveth** IV.1001; *pr. pl.* **leve(n)** II.1181, Tr 2.1141; *imp. sg.* **leve** BD 1047, Tr 5.378; *imp. pl.* **leveth** Lady 82, **leeveth** I.3088; *pt. sg.* **leeved** Rom B 4535.

leve, leeve *see* **leef** *adj.*

levede *see* **live(n).**

leveful, leefful, leful *adj.* permitted, lawful VIII.5, X.41, Tr 3.1020.

levere, levest *see* **leef** *adj.*

leves, leeves *see* **leef** *n.*

lewed, lewd(e) *adj.* (1) ignorant, uneducated I.3455, V.221, VIII.497, Astr Pro 61, Rom C 6217; lay, non-cleric X.791; **l. man** layman, non-professional V.1494; (2) stupid, foolish IV.2275, VIII.925; uncouth, boorish I.3145, IV.2149; unsophisticated HF 1096; *super.* **lewedest(e)** lowest, most uncouth IX.194, most unlearned Rom B 4802.

lewedly *adv.* unskillfully, ignorantly VIII.430, IX.59; **kan but l. on** knows little about II.47.

lewednesse *n.* ignorance III.1928, V.223; boorish conduct PF 520.

lyche *see* **lyk(e)** *adj., adv.*

lycorys, lycorice *n.* licorice I.3207, I.3690, VII.761.

licour *n.* moisture, juice, sap I.3, VI.452; liquor, distilled juice Tr 4.520.

lye *n.* lie I.3015, I.3391; *pl.* **lyes** III.302, **lees** Rom A 8, **les** LGW 1022.

lye(n), ligge(n) *v.* [1] lie, recline, remain I.3651, Tr 3.660, Tr 3.1537, Rom B 2631; *2 pr. sg.* **lyest** Tr 1.797, *(contr.)* **list** Tr 1.797, (with *pro.*) **listow** IX.276; *3 pr. sg.* **lith** I.1218, **lyeth** BD 143; *pr. pl.* **lye(n)** Mars 5, VIII.779, **liggen** Tr 3.685; *pr. subj. sg.* **lye** IV.1292, **ligge** Tr 5.411; *imp. sg.* **ly** Tr 2.1519; *imp. pl.* **liggeth** Bo 2.m7.24; *pt. sg.* **lay(e)** was staying I.20, Bo 4.pr2.63; **by his suster lay** had sexual relations with his sister VII.2482; *pt. pl.* **laye(n)** I.3210, Tr 3.749; *pt. subj. sg.* **lay** I.1150; *prp.* **liggyng(e)** lying I.1011, I.2390, Tr 1.915; *pp.* **leyn** II.887, **yleyn** LGW 2410.

lye(n) *v.* [2] lie, deceive I.763, I.3513, BD 631; *2 pr. sg.* **lixt** III.1618, **lyest** VIII.486; *3 pr. sg.* **lyeth** V.217; *pr. subj.* **lye** IV.1741 *(sg.),* VII.2498 *(pl.);* *pt. sg.* **leigh** Tr 2.1077, **lyed** I.659; *pt. pl.* **lieden** Bo 1.pr4.251.

lief *see* **leef** *adj.*

lyer(e) *n.* liar VII.1066, Tr 3.309, Rom C 6542; *pl.* **lyeres** VII.1308.

lyf *n.* life I.71, I.1172, BD 64; *dat.* **lyve** BD 1278; **on**

lyve alive I.3039, Tr 2.138; **hys (here,** *etc.* **) lyve** during his (their, *etc.*) lifetime III.392, BD 247; **eterne on l.** eternally living III.5, IV.1652; **bring . . . of l.** kill Tr 2.1608, Tr 5.1561; *gen.* **lyves** IV.833 *(sg.),* I.2395 *(pl.);* (as modifier) **lyves body (creature)** living being I.2395, HF 1063, Tr 4.252; *pl.* **lyves** I.1718.

lifly, lyvely *adv.* in a life-like manner I.2087; bright, lively BD 905.

liflode *n.* sustenance X.685, Rom B 5602, Rom C 6663.

lift, left *adj.* left I.2953, VII.1312.

lige *adj.* liege III.1037, IV.310, V.111; *pl.* (as *n.*) **liges** subjects II.240.

ligge(n) *see* **lye(n)** *v.*[1]

light *adj.*[1] bright I.1783, VIII.381.

light(e) *adj.*[2] (1) light in weight I.2120, HF 743, PF 380, Tr 2.1238; (2) mild, easy to bear Rom B 4711; (3) easy (to do) VII.1040, BD 526, Tr 4.484; (4) active, quick, nimble LGW 1699, LGW 2711; (5) cheerful, happy I.4154, IV.1211, VIII.351; (6) foolish, fickle HF 1625; (7) inconsequential Bo 1.m1.24; *comp.* **lighter(e)** easier VII.1500, milder Bo 1.pr5.73; (as *adv.*) more easily LGW F 410.

lighte(n) *v.*[1] (1) *(tr.)* illuminate I.2426, Tr 4.313; brighten Tr 1.293; (2) ignite III.334; (3) *(intr.)* shine X.1037, Bo 3.m11.11; *pr. pl.* **lighte** X.1036; *pt. sg.* **lighte** VII.471, LGW 2506; *imp. sg.* **lighte** VIII.71; *pp.* **lighted** V.1050, (as *adj.*) ignited HF 769.

lighte *v.*[2] (1) lighten, relieve Tr 3.1082; cheer, gladden Tr 5.634; (2) become light V.396; (3) alight, descend HF 508; *3 pr. sg. (contr.)* **lighte** alights, dismounts II.786, V.169, V.1183; *pr. pl.* **lyghte** alight LGW 1713; *pr. subj. sg.* **lyghte** relieve HF 467; *pt. sg.* (possibly *pr.*) II.1104.

lyghte *adv.* (1) lightly Mars 84; brightly Rom A 1109; *comp.* **lyghter** more brightly HF 1289.

lightly *adv.* (1) with light clothing V.390; gently, easily VII.1863, Bo 2.pr7.131; (2) with little effort, easily III.517, X.1041; (3) quickly I.4099, VI.752, VII.1579, Tr 2.1388; (4) readily, eagerly VII.1174; by naturally inclined VII.1284, X.534; (5) cheerfully, happily Bo 2.pr4.92; (6) indifferently, not seriously X.1024, Bo 1.pr3.72; without good reason Tr 3.804.

lightne *v.* illuminate, light X.244; *3 pr. sg.* **lightneth** Bo 4.pr4.187; *vbl. n. pl.* **lightnynges** X.174.

lightnesse *n.*[1] brightness PF 263, Bo 1.m2.9.

lightnesse *n.*[2] (1) lightness in weight Bo 3.pr11.135, Bo 5.m5.6; (2) agility, nimbleness I.3383; (3) frivolity X.379, Bo 2.pr7.121.

ligne, lyne *var.* of **lynage** Tr 5.1481.

lyk(e), lyche *adj.* like I.259, V.62, BD 819; **l. to, unto** similar to, like II.361, II.1030, BD 963; similar X.631, Rom A 1073; (as *n.*) the same Tr 2.44; *comp.* **likker(e)** more like III.1925, Tr 3.1028. Cf. **ylyk(e)** *adj.*

lyk(e), lyche *adv.* like I.590, Rom C 7259; **l. even** the same HF 10; **l. to be(n)** likely to be HF 873, LGW 1068, Rom A 679; **l. as** as if VIII.576, HF 1508. Cf. **ylyk(e)** *adv.*

lyke, liken *v.* (1) please, give pleasure (to someone) IV.506, Tr 1.289, Tr 1.431; **ben to l.** are pleasing Tr 3.1363; *(impers.)* **hym (hire,** *etc.***) lyketh** it pleases (him, her, *etc.*), he (she, *etc.*) likes III.914, PF 401; (2) like, take pleasure in Tr 3.354; *3 pr. sg.* **liketh(e)** I.1847, Bo 3.m2.1; **likith** Rom A 256; *pr. subj. sg.*

lyke III.1278; *pt. sg.* **lyked(e)** I.2092, LGW 1672; *prp.* (as *adj.*) **lyking(e)** pleasing Tr 1.309, Rom A 1564; *pp.* **liked** Rom A 486; *vbl. n.* **lykyng(e)** pleasure, desire II.767, Rom A 76; *pl.* **lykynges** Bo 2.pr1.57.

likerous *adj.* (1) sensual, lecherous III.752, VI.549, IX.189; (2) eager V.1119; greedy, gluttonous IV.214, VI.540; self-indulgent Form Age 56; (3) delicious, delightful I.3345.

likerousnesse *n.* (1) lustfulness III.611; lecherous act X.859; self-indulgence X.430; greedy appetite VI.84, X.741.

likly *adj.* probable, likely I.1172, VI.64, Tr 3.1270; suitable Scog 32.

liklihede *n.* in *phr.* **by l.** probably IV.448, VII.596.

lyklynesse *n.* probability Rom C 7542; **by l.** probable IV.396, Compl d'Am 15.

likne *v.* liken, compare III.369, BD 636; *2 pr. sg.* **liknest** III.371; *imp. pl.* **likneth** X.156; *pp.* **likned** II.91.

lym *n.*[1] limb BD 499; *pl.* **lymes** I.2135, **lymmes** BD 959, **lemes** I.3886.

lym(e) *n.*[2] (1) quicklime (the first product of heating limestone) VIII.806, LGW 649; (2) mortar V.1149, VIII.910, LGW 765.

lymytour *n.* friar licensed to beg in a given district I.269, III.874; *pl.* **lymytours** III.866.

lynage *n.* lineage, family I.1550, I.1829, LGW 1820; noble birth VII.2251; *pl.* **lynages** Rom B 2190.

lynde *n.* lime or linden tree I.2922, IV.1211; *pl.* **lyndes** Rom 1385.

lisse *n.* (1) joy Tr 5.550; (2) respite, relief HF 220.

lisse(n) *v.* (1) relieve, alleviate Tr 1.702; (2) recover Rom B 3758; *pr. subj. sg.* **lysse** BD 210; *pp.* **(y)lissed** V.1170, Tr 1.1089.

list *see* **lust** *n.*

list(e), lest(e), lust(e) *3 pr. sg. (contr.)* (1) *(impers.* with indirect *obj.)* it pleases (him, her, *etc.*), he (she) pleases, likes I.1183, I.1201, I.1207, III.820, VII.1233, Rom A 344; **me l. ful (ryght) yvele** I have very little desire to I.1127, BD 239; **whil yow good l.** as long as you please Tr 1.119; (2) (personal uses) wish, want, be pleased I.3176, III.78, VII.2140, VIII.30, Tr 1.518; *1 pr. sg.* **leste** Tr 1.580; *3 pr. sg.* (full form) **listeth** chooses V.689, **lustith** Rom B 2075; *pr. pl.* **liste(n)** choose VII.1044, LGW F 575; are pleased Tr 3.1810; *pr. subj. sg.* **lyste** may choose Rom A 14, **leste** it please I.828, **luste** Rom B 2154; *pt. sg.* **lyste** I.102, **leste** I.750.

lystes *n. pl.* enclosed grounds for a tournament I.1859; **in l.** in formal combat I.63, I.1713; **for l.** for battle I.1852.

listeth *imp. pl.* listen VII.712, VII.833.

lite *n.* little, a small amount I.1334, I.1450, BD 249.

lite *adj.* little I.2627, PF 64; modest, humble VII.963, X.295; **much(e) and (or) l.** great and small, all I.494, Anel 107.

lite *adv.* little I.1520, I.1723, BD 884.

litel, litil *n.* I.1779, Ven 39; **into l.** nearly Tr 4.884.

litel, litil *adj.* little I.87, I.298, Mars 117.

litel *adv.* I.1489, BD 401; **l. and l.** little by little III.2235; **a l. for a while,** somewhat Bo 1.pr2.22.

lyve(s) *see* **lyf.**

live(n) *v.* live I.335, I.506, BD 17; *2 pr. sg.* **lyvest** LGW F 481, (with *pro.*) **lyvestow** VI.719; *3 pr. sg.* **lyveth;** *pr. pl.* **lyve(n)** II.1157, III.1257; *imp. sg.* **lyve** Tr 3.1513; *pt. sg.* **lyved(e)** I.2844, **levede** Tr 4.493; *pt. pl.* **lyved(en)** III.141, III.1877; *prp.* **lyvyng(e)** I.532,

Lady 76; (as *adj.*) LGW 2118; *pp.* **(i)lyved** I.1793, Tr 5.933; *vbl. n.* **lyvyng(e)** III.1122, X.596; *pl.* **ly-vynges** lives Bo 3.pr11.160.

lixt *see* **lye(n)** *v.* ²

lode-sterre, loode-stere *n.* lodestar, star (*usu.* pole star) used as a point of reference I.2059; *(fig.)* guiding star Tr 5.232, Tr 5.1392.

(y)logged *pp.* lodged VII.2991, VII.2996.

logh *see* **low(e)** *adj.*

lok, look *n.* look BD 840, Tr 1.599.

loke(n), looke(n) *v.* (1) look (at something) I.1783, I.3344, BD 537; (2) look, appear, seem I.289, III.1082. Tr 1.206; (3) look to, consider Bo 5.pr2.27; (3) consider, see, find out I.3433, IV.1371, Tr 3.316; (4) *(imp.)* **l. (that)** see to it, take care I.4345, VIII.1419; *2 pr. sg.* **lookest** VII.696; *3 pr. sg.* **looketh** I.1499; *pr. pl.* **looken** VIII.1420, **loken** Bo 3.pr8.49; *pr. subj. sg.* **loke** Bo 5.pr6.239; *imp. sg.* **looke** consider III.1113, take care **loke** Ven 61; *imp. pl.* **looketh** consider I.1798, **loketh** Tr 2.1648, **looke** VI.87, **loke** Tr 2.1109; *pt. sg.* **looked(e)** I.289, Bo 2.m6.9, **loked(e)** BD 294, Bo 3.m12.58, **lokide** Rom A 291; *pt. pl.* **lokeden** LGW 1972; *pt. subj. sg.* **lokide** Bo 3.pr8.43; *prp.* **lookynge** II.1015, **lokynge** I.2679; *pp.* **loked** Tr 3.1160, **looked** I.3515; *vbl. n.* **lookyng(e)** gaze, look I.2171, appearance IV.514, X.936; astrological aspect I.2469, Mars 51; **lokyng** Tr 1.173.

lokkes *n. pl.* locks (of hair) I.81, I.677.

lomb, lamb *n.* lamb I.3704, II.617, ABC 172; *gen. sg.* **Lambes** (*i.e.,* Christ's) II.452; *pl.* **lambes** X.792, **lambren** Rom C 7013.

lond(e), land *n.* (1) country, kingdom I.400, II.522, LGW 1403; (2) landed property I.579; farmland HF 485; (3) land, the earth III.372; **upon l.** in the country I.702; *pl.* **londes** I.14, **landes** VI.443.

long(e) *adj.* ¹ (1) long I.93, I.354, BD 20; **lange** (*Nth.*) I.4175; (2) distant in time VIII.1411, Tr 2.722; (3) long-lasting Tr 5.1671; *comp.* **lenger** I.3596; *super.* **longest** Tr 1.474.

long *adj.* ² (with **on**) dependent on, on account of VIII.922, VIII.930.

long(e) *adv.* long I.2415; for a long time I.286, Tr 3.1536; *comp.* **longer** Bo 2.m7.27, **lenger(e)** I.330, PF 657; *super.* **lengest** PF 549.

longe(n) *v.* ¹ (1) long, desire Tr 2.546, Tr 5.597, LGW 2260; **l. after** long for BD 83; (2) *(impers. with indirect obj.)* long IV.2332, Tr 2.312, Rom A 1222; *3 pr. sg.* **longeth** Tr 2.312; *pr. pl.* **longen** I.12; *pt. sg.* **longed** after for BD 83.

longen *v.* ² (1) be suitable, fitting I.2278; (2) be the business, concern of IV.285, Rom B 2321; **l. to (unto)** pertain to someone (as a right) VII.1468, X.802; be associated with HF 1200; be causally connected with V.1131; **l. to** be inherent in X.873; *3 pr. sg.* **longeth** IV.2024; *pr. pl.* **longen** I.3885; *pt. sg.* **longed** Rom A 1222; *prp.* **longynge for** pertaining to I.3209, V.39; **longynge to** belonging to LGW 1963.

lo(o) *interj.* look! take notice! I.1791, I.1844, BD 290.

lordynges *n. pl.* gentlemen, my lords (term of address) I.761, I.788, I.828.

lordship(e) *n.* (1) *(pl.)* masters, those having rule X.442, X.568; (2) sovereignty, power I.1625, IV.797, Tr 3.1756; (3) patronage, protection Tr 3.76, Tr 3.79; (4) **of (your) l.** by virtue of (your) office Tr 2.1420; *pl.* **lordshipes** official positions VII.1476.

lore, loore *n.* (1) teaching I.527, I.3527, Tr 1.645; advice Tr 1.1090; (2) learning IV.87; knowledge Anel 345.

lorn(e), (y)loren, lore *see* **lese(n).**

los, loss(e) *n.* ¹ loss I.2543, I.4186, BD 1139, Tr 4.27, Rom B 4975; perdition III.720.

los, loos *n.* ² (1) reputation VII.1644, HF 1621, HF 1626; (2) praise VIII.1368, HF 1722, HF 1817; renown LGW 1514; (3) infamy VIII.1009, Rom C 7081; (4) rumor LGW 1424; *pl.* **loses** reputations HF 1688.

loos, laus(e), lous *adj.* loose I.4138, I.4352, PF 570; free HF 1286.

losengeour, losenger *n.* flatterer VII.3326, Rom A 1030; *pl.* **losengeris** Rom A 1056, **losengers** Rom A 1064.

loth, looth *adj.* (1) displeasing, hateful I.3393, IV.491 (in *impers.* constructions) **be(n) l.** (**hym, hire,** *etc.*) (he, she, *etc.*) does not wish; (**hym, me,** *etc.*) **were** *(subj.)* **l.** (he, I, *etc.*) would not wish, would hate I.486, II.91, IV.364; (2) reluctant, unwilling Tr 3.154, Tr 3.369; (3) **l. or lef, dere** pleasant or not, whether one likes it or not I.1837, IV.1961, BD 8; (as *n.*) **for lef nor l.** for any reason LGW 1639; *comp.* **lother** more hateful LGW F 191; *super.* **lothest** most reluctant V.1313, Tr 2.237.

lough *see* **low(e)** *adj.*

lough(e) *see* **laughe(n).**

lous *see* **loos** *adj.*

loute *v.*. bow down, bend Tr 3.683, Rom B 4384; *3 pr. sg.* **lowteth** VII.1187; *pr. subj. pl.* **loute** Rom C 6917; *pt. sg.* **loutede** Rom A 1554.

love *n.* love I.475, I.672; (in compounds) **love-dayes** days of reconciliation I.258 *(see note)* HF 695; **love-drynke** aphrodisiac III.754; **love-drury** passionate love VII.895; **love-knotte** elaborate knot I.197; **love-likynge** love VII.850; **love-longynge** passionate, romantic love (only in comic contexts) I.3679, I.3705, VII.772; *gen. sg.* **loves** I.1815; *pl.* **loves** HF 86.

love(n) *v.* love II.586, VIII.160, BD 1078; *2 pr. sg.* **lovest** I.1581; *3 pr. sg.* **loveth** I.1731; *pr. pl.* **love(n)** III.321, III.921; *pr. subj.* **love** I.1799 *(sg.),* III.446 *(pl.);* *imp. sg.* **love** I.3280; *imp. pl.* **loveth** X.526; *pt. sg.* **loved(e)** I.3222, I.4376; *pt. pl.* **lovede(n)** I.1198, X.202; *prp.* **lovynge** II.625; X.202; *pp.* **loved** I.2794; *vbl. n.* **lovyng(e)** Tr 1.1010, LGW G 534.

lovyere, lover(e) *n.* lover I.80, I.1164, LGW F 466; *gen. sg.* **loveris** I.1373; *pl.* **loveres** I.1347, **loveris** II.53, **lovers** Tr 1.376.

low(e), logh, lough *adj.* (1) low I.107, I.522, Tr 2.968; short Rom B 3197; (2) quiet, soft I.2433; (3) low in rank, humble Tr 1.439, Tr 2.528; ignoble, churlish Anel 249, PF 601; **in heigh and l.** in all respects, in every way I.817, II.993; **heigh and (or) l.** all classes, everyone II.1142, Tr 3.418; *comp.* **lower** more ignoble IX.190; *super.* **lowest(e)** X.482, Astr 2.16.6.

lowe *adv.* (1) low I.1111, I.2023, Tr 2.689; (2) low (in pitch of singing) BD 304, Rom A 717; quietly V.216, Tr 1.178; (3) humbly I.1405, Anel 95; **held him l.** kept him in a humbled state Anel 192; *super.* **lowest** PF 327.

lowely, lowly *adj.* humble, modest I.99, I.250, Anel 142.

lowely, lowly *adv.* humbly IV.421, VII.1771, Tr 2.1072, LGW 2062.

lucre *n.* money, profit VIII.1402, Rom B 5323; **l. of vileyne** wicked profit VII.491.

lulleth *3 pr. sg.* soothes, caresses II.839, IV.1823; *pt. sg.* **lulled** IV.553.

lure *n.* bait (for luring hawks) III.1340 (see note), IX.72; *pl.* **lures** LGW 1371.

lust, lest, list *n.* (1) desire, wish II.762, II.763, IV.619, BD 908; sexual desire II.925, III.633, Tr 4.1573; (2) pleasure, delight IV.1643, V.812, Tr 3.1303; sexual pleasure III.927, X.845; (3) object of desire IV.660, Tr 2.998; beloved person HF 258; *pl.* **lustes** desires I.3066, pleasures IV.1679, BD 581, **leestes** HF 1738.

lust(e) *see* **list.**

lusty *adj.* (1) pleasing I.2176, PF 130; (2) full of vigor, lively I.80, (as *n.*) vigorous person Tr 3.354; eager I.4004, VIII.1345; cheerful I.1513, Tr 2.1099; admirable, fine III.553, Tr 1.958; (3) (of land) fruitful IV.59; *comp.* **lustier** more eager VIII.1345; *super.* **lustyeste** most attractive LGW 716.

lustihede, lustiheed *n.* pleasure V.288; delight IX.274; vigor BD 27, LGW 1530.

lustynesse *n.* pleasure Tr 3.177, Rom B 5118; vigor LGW 1405, Rom A 1282.

M

m' *contr.* of me before vowels Tr 1.1050, Tr 2.1401.

(y)mad, (y)maad *see* **make(n).**

mad, madde *adj.* (1) mad, crazy I.2342, I.4231, Tr 5.206; (2) overcome with emotion, distraught Tr 4.393.

madde *v.* go mad Tr 1.479, Mars 253; rave, speak foolishly Rom A 1052; *pr. subj. sg.* **madde** I.3156, I.3559.

made(n) *see* **make(n).**

mageste, majeste(e) *n.* majesty I.4322, II.1082, Bo 1.pr4.145, Fort 65.

may, mayst, maistow *see* **mowe(n).**

maydenhed(e), maydenhod *n.* virginity I.2329, II.888, VII.2269.

maister *n.* (1) master I.837, I.3446; teacher VII.2518; master tradesman I.4389; (2) as a title of respectful address I.3437, Buk 1; (3) Master of Arts I.261, III.2184; (4) (as *adj.*) main, chief I.2902, LGW 1016; *gen.* **maistres** V.1220; *pl.* **maistres** I.576.

maistresse, mistresse *n.* mistress IV.823, BD 797; governess V.374, VI.106; *pl.* **maistresses** governesses, VI.72.

maistry(e) *n.* (1) mastery, dominion III.818, III.1040; (2) skill I.3383, Rom B 3294; (3) admirable achievement VIII.1060, HF 1094, LGW F 400; **for the m.** extremely I.165.

make *n.* (1) mate III.270, IV.2080, PF 310; spouse IV.840, IV.1289; (2) opposite, opponent I.2556; equal HF 1172; *pl.* **makes** PF 389.

make(n) *v.* (1) make I.384, build I.1901, IV.2295; (2) compose, write (song, poems, *etc.*) I.95, I.325, HF 622; (3) make a formal promise (with **assurance, vow,** *etc.*) II.341, V.1535, VII.1807; (4) cause, bring about a condition III.1899, HF 155; **m. the coste** pay the expenses LGW 1448; **m. an ende** finish, conclude V.408, X.47; **m. it thus** take it this way Tr 2.1148; cause (with *obj.* and *inf.*) I.581, I.3092, BD 245; cause to be (with *obj.* and *adj.*) I.184, I.265, BD 491; **m. it**

hool perform their all Rom B 5443; *2 pr. sg.* **makest** LGW F 331, (with *pro.*) **makestow** II.371; *3 pr. sg.* **maketh** I.947; *pr. pl.* **make(n)** I.4051, VII.1974; *pr. subj. sg.* **make** Rom B 2326; *pr. subj. pl.* **make** X.1053; *imp. sg.* **make** Tr 3.703; *imp. pl.* **maketh** IV.2173, **mak** LGW G 221; *1 & 3 pt. sg.* **maked** I.526, **made** I.387, **maade** IV.678; *2 pt. sg.* **madest** II.368, **makedest** Bo 1.pr4.265; *pt. pl.* **makeden** Tr 4.121, **made(n)** I.33, III.594; *prp.* **makyng(e)** I.1366, Tr 4.1289; *pp.* **(y)maked** I.1247, VI.545, **(y)maad** I.3094, II.693, **mad** BD 404; *vbl. n.* **makyng(e)** making VIII.922, composition Tr 5.1789, composing LGW 473.

male *n.* pouch, traveling bag VI.920, Rom B 3263.

malencholi(e) *n.* (1) the humor of melancholy (black bile) VII.2933, Tr 5.360; (2) suffering from an excess of black bile, the condition of being melancholy BD 23, Tr 5.1646; (3) anger, rage III.252, (personified) Rom B 4998.

malgre *see* **maugre(e).**

malisoun *n.* curse VIII.1245, X.443; cursing X.619.

malt *see* **melte.**

man *n.* man I.228, I.477, BD 159; *gen. sg.* **mannes** IV.1331; *gen. pl.* **mennes** II.202; *pl.* **men** II.246; men, people in general V.209.

man *indef. pro.* one, anyone III.2002, V.553, BD 892. Cf. **men** *indef. pro.*

manace *n.* menace, threat I.2003, VII.2599; *pl.* **manaces** Bo 1.m4.5.

manace *v.* menace, threaten IV.1752; *3 pr. sg.* **manaceth** VII.122; *pt. sg.* **manaced** VII.1504; *prp.* **manasynge** Bo 2.m4.5; *vbl. n.* **manasynge** I.2035.

maner(e), maneere *n.* (1) manner, form V.337, Tr 2.916; **in m. of** in the shape of I.1889; **in no m.** in no way IV.818, IV.1237, Tr 3.1412; (2) way, manner I.876, Anel 106, ABC 29; means, method V.187, VIII.1057; **by m. of** by reason of VI.264; (3) manner, behavior I.140, V.546, BD 453; custom VII.142, Tr 1.1021, Tr 5.809; **al the m.** the whole affair II.880, LGW 1909; (4) due measure Bo 5.pr6.283; (5) (as *adj.*) sort of, kind of I.71, X.103, BD 499; *pl.* **maners** manners BD 1014, **maneres** ways, sorts X.358, **manners** Rom A 814.

manhede, manhod *n.* (1) manliness, qualities proper to a man I.1285, VII.2671, Tr 2.676; (2) gentility, courteous behavior I.756, IX.158.

many(e) *adj.* many I.1521, II.577, BD 59; (as *n.*) many II.999, VI.530; **m. a many** I.60, I.168, BD 254; **m. oon** many a one I.317, I.2118, HF 760.

mannes *see* **man** *n.*

mannyssh, mannysh *adj.* (1) human VII.1264; (2) mannish, unwomanly II.782, Tr 1.284; (3) (as *adv.*) **m. wod** IV.1536 (see note).

manly *adj.* manly, virile I.2130, V.99; proper to a man X.601; generous VII.43.

mansioun, mansyon *v.* (1) dwelling place I.1974, HF 754, HF 831; (2) (astro.) the "domicile" of a planet V.50 (see note); position of the moon V.1285, V.1289; *pl.* **mansiouns** V.1130, **mansiounes** Rom C 7001, **mansions** V.1154.

marbul, marble *n.* marble I.1893, V.500, Tr 1.700.

marchant, marchaunt *n.* merchant I.270, X.777; *gen.* **marchauntes** IV.2425; *pl.* **marchantz** X.779, **marchauntz** II.122, **merchantz** II.148.

mark, merk *n.* [1] (1) mark, birthmark III.619; (2) image V.880; **m. of Adam** image of Adam (*i.e.,* male sex)

III.696; **sette mark** agree, confirm (as by affixing seals) LGW 784.

mark, marc *n.*² mark, a monetary unit, two-thirds of a pound (13 shillings, 4 pence) VI.390, VIII.1026, VIII.1030; *pl.* **markis** Rom C 5986.

mased *see* **maze.**

masse *see* **messe.**

mat(e), maat *adj.* checkmated BD 660; defeated Anel 176, Rom B 3167; downcast, dejected I.955, Tr 4.342, Rom B 4671.

mater(e), mateere, matiere *n.* (1) physical matter VIII.811, X.333; material VIII.1232; (2) matter, business I.727, I.1259, II.205; subject matter II.322, Mars 173; (3) cause, ground VII.1536, X.491; *pl.* **materes** LGW G 279, **matires** VIII.770.

maugre(e), malgre *prep.* despite, in spite of I.2618, BD 1201, Tr 4.51, Mars 220.

maze *2 pr. pl.* you are bewildered, dazed IV.2387; *pp.* **mazed** II.526, (as *adj.*) II.628, **mased** (as *adj.*) BD 12, (as *adj.*) Anel 322.

me *see* **men** *indef. pro.*

mede, meeth *n.*¹ mead (alcoholic beverage made of fermented honey) I.3378, VII.852.

mede, meede *n.*² mead, meadow I.89, III.861, PF 184.

mede, meede *n.*³ payment, reward I.770, IV.885, Anel 305; bribe I.3380, VI.133; fulfillment Tr 2.423; *pl.* **meedes** Bo 4.pr1.28, **medes** Bo 4.pr3.37; **to medes** in return Tr 2.1201.

medewe *n.* meadow LGW G 91, Rom A 128.

medle *v.* (1) mix, mingle HF 2102, Bo 5.pr3.107; confuse, stir up Bo 1.m7.4; (2) be concerned with, take a hand in VIII.1184; *(reflx.)* concern oneself Rom C 6050; *3 pr. sg.* **medleth** intermingles Bo 3.m10.16, **medeleth** LGW 874; *pr. pl.* **medle** Rom C 6036; *pr. subj. pl.* **medle** Rom C 6036; *imp. pl.* **medleth** meddle, concern yourself with VIII.1424; *pp.* **(i)medled** mixed Bo 1.m6.21, Tr 4.339, **imeddled** Bo 4.pr6.263, **medlyd** Bo 4.pr4.108; *vbl. n.* **medling(e)** meddling Tr 4.167, mixture Rom A 898, confusion Bo 1.pr4.250.

meygned *pp.* maimed Rom B 3356.

meyne(e), meignee *n.* (1) household, household attendants I.1258, III.2156, Tr 1.127; (2) troop of followers, company IV.4381, V.391, VII.2342, HF 194.

meke, meeke *adj.* meek, gentle I.69, I.3202, HF 1402; *comp.* **meker** LGW 2198; *super.* **mekeste** IV.1552.

meke(n) *v.* subdue, humble Rom B 2244, Rom B 3541; *pr. subj. sg.* **meke me** humble myself VII.1684; *pt. sg.* **mekede** Rom C 3584.

mekely *adv.* meekly, humbly II.1079, III.432, Tr 2.16.

mekenesse, meknesse *n.* meekness, humility X.476, LGW F 250.

mele, meel (1) meal, ground grain I.3939, III.1739; (2) meal, repast III.1774, VII.2833; *pl.* **meles** meals BD 612.

melte *v.* melt Tr 4.367; *3 pr. sg.* **meltith** dissolves into tears Rom A 276; *pr. pl.* **melte** HF 1648, (of tears) Tr 3.1445; *pt. sg.* **malt** Tr 1.582; *pt. pl.* **malt** HF 922, **molte** Tr 5.10; *pp.* **molte** HF 1145.

membre *n.* (1) organ BD 495; bodily part, limb Rom A 1028; (2) part, division Bo 3.m9.27, Astr Pro 66; *pl.* **membres** sexual organs, genitals X.330; **membris** members, supporters Rom B 5441.

memorie, memoyre *n.* memory, consciousness I.1906, Anel 14; **have (in) m.** remember IV.1669, BD 945, Tr 3.829; **in m.** conscious I.2698; **maken m.** remind

VII.1974; **drawen (in)to m.** call to mind I.2074, X.239.

men *see* **man** *n.*

men *indef. pro. sg.* one, someone, anyone I.149, I.2777, Tr 4.866; **me** Rom B 4096, Rom C 7634. Cf. **man** *indef. pro.*

mene, meene *n.* (1) method, means Tr 3.254; agent, instrument IV.1671, ABC 125; means, device Tr 5.104; intermediary Tr 3.254; (2) moderation, mean (between extremes) X.833, Tr 1.689, Tr 3.254; *pl.* **meenes** II.480.

mene, meene *adj.* (1) moderate, average Tr 5.806 (2) middle Anel 286, Bo 3.m9.25; **m. while(s)** meanwhile II.546, II.668, Tr 3.50; **m. time** meantime VII.87.

mene(n), meene *v.* (1) mean, intend Tr 3.164; signify I.793, VII.2751, HF 1104, Tr 2.171; (2) say, speak VIII.1424, HF 1895; *2 pr. sg.* **menest** BD 743, (with *pro.*) **menestow** VIII.309; *3 pr. sg.* **meneth** I.2287; *pr. pl.* **mene** Tr 5.364, **meene** Tr 2.226; *pt. sg.* **mente** I.2990, said Tr 4.333, meant Tr 1.320, thought IV.89; *pt. pl.* **mente** V.399, **meneden** Bo 5.pr1.46; *pp.* **(y)ment** HF 1742, PF 158; *vbl. n.* **menyng(e)** meaning V.151, LGW F 474.

mennes *see* **man** *n.*

merciable *adj.* merciful V.1036, VII.688, LGW F 347.

mery(e), mury(e), myrie *adj.* merry, cheerful, pleasant I.235, I.802, III.1774, Tr 3.925, Ros 5; *comp.* **murier** VII.834.

merye, murye *adv.* merrily, cheerfully I.3575, VI.843, PF 592; *comp.* **murier** IV.2322, **myrier** Rom A 876.

meryly, murily, myrily *adv.* merrily, cheerfully III.330, VII.110, Rom A 1329; *comp.* **murierly** I.714.

merit(e) *n.* (1) character (deserving reward or punishment) Bo 1.pr4.159, Bo 4.pr6.290; reward VI.277, X.916; (2) spiritual credit, merit VIII.33, X.529, HF 669; *pl.* **merites** rewards Tr 4.965.

merk *see* **mark** *n.*¹

mervayle, mervaille, merveyle, merveille, marveyle *n.* marvel, wonder I.3423, II.502, Bo 4.pr6.201, Tr 1.476, Rom B 3646; *pl.* **mervaylles** V.660, **mervayles** HF 1442, **merveyles** LGW 1431, **marvayles** BD 288.

merveylen, merveillen *v.* marvel, wonder Bo 2.pr5.54, Bo 4.pr1.32; *(reflx.)* Bo 4.pr5.20; *3 pr. sg.* **merveilith** Rom B 4967; *pr. pl.* **merveylen** Bo 2.pr5.61; *imp. pl.* **merveyleth** Bo 4.pr6.210; *prp.* (as *adj.*) **merveylynge** Bo 1.m3.17.

merveillous, mervelous *adj.* astonishing, marvelous IV.454, HF 459.

meschaunce, meschance, myschaunce, myschance *n.* (1) misfortune, bad luck I.2009, II.602, III.1334, IV.1333; **with m.** bad luck (to him) I.4412; (2) misconduct VI.80; *pl.* **meschaunces** evil practices V.1292, **meschances** misadventures III.367.

meschief, mescheef, myscheef *n.* (1) trouble, misfortune I.493, I.1326, Tr 1.755; deprivation, need VIII.1072; **at m.** in distress, at a disadvantage I.2551; (2) wrong, mischief I.1326, III.2190, LGW 1261; *pl.* **myscheves** Rom B 5781.

message *n.* (1) message V.99, Tr 4.812; **don a m.** deliver a message II.1087, VIII.188; (2) errand Tr 3.401, LGW 1486; (3) emissary, diplomatic courier IV.738; *pl.* **messages** messengers Tr 2.936.

messager, messageer, messanger, messangeer *n.* messenger I.1491, II.6, BD 133, LGW 1479, Rom B 2919; *pl.* **messagers** X.967.

messe, masse *n.* mass III.1728, IV.1894, BD 928; **m. penny** offering for a mass III.1749.

meeste *see* **most(e)** *adj. super.*

mester *see* **myster.**

mesurable *adj.* moderate I.435, V.362; modest X.936.

mesure *n.* (1) measurement IV.256, X.776, Bo 1.pr1.15; **over m.** immeasurably PF 300; (2) moderation, restraint VII.991, BD 632; **by m.** in due proportion, moderately X.465, Rom A 543; **out of m.** immoderately VII.1417; very greatly VII.1745; cruel, without mercy VII.1848, Rom B 3279.

mesuren *v.* measure, reckon Bo 5.pr1.21; *3 pr. sg.* **mesureth** Bo 2.pr1.86; *pr. pl.* **mesuren** Bo 3.pr2.40; *imp. sg.* **mesure** Astr 2.38.22; *pt. sg.* **mesured** meted out, distributed ABC 174; *pp.* **mesured** X.776; *vbl. n.* **mesuryng** measurement Rom A 1349.

mete *n.* (1) food I.136, I.345, Anel 135; (2) meal V.173, Tr 2.1462, LGW 1108; **at m.** at dinner I.127, II.119; **after-mete** after dinner II.104, IV.1913; *gen.* **metes** space dinner time II.1014; *pl.* **metes** X.445.

mete, meete *adj.* suitable, fitting I.2291, BD 316, LGW 1043; (as *n.*) equal BD 486.

mete(n) *v.*¹ dream BD 118, PF 108; *1 pr. sg.* **meete** Tr 3.1344; *3 pr. sg. (contr.)* **met** PF 104; *pt. sg.* **mette** III.577; *(impers.)* **me (him,** *etc.*) **mette** I **(he,** *etc.*) dreamed I.3684, VII.2894, BD 276; *pp.* **met** VII.2926, VII.3255; *vbl. n.* **metynge** dream BD 282.

mete(n), meete *v.*² meet I.4374, PF 698, Tr 4.1685; *3 pr. sg.* **meeteth** I.1524; *pt. sg.* **mette** V.1508; *pt. pl.* **mette(n)** II.559, HF 2092; *prp.* **metynge** Bo 1.m5.6; *pp.* **(y)met** I.1636, I.2624; *vbl. n.* **metyng** Tr 3.1712.

meeth *see* **mede** *n.*¹

meve(d), mevynge(es) *see* **moeve(n).**

mewe, muwe *n.* cage, pen for birds I.349, V.643; **in m.** in hiding, in secret Tr 1.381; in hiding, withdrawn from society Tr 4.496.

mychel *see* **muchel** *adv.*

myght *n.* power, strength I.960, I.1607; **doon his (her,** *etc.*) **m.** exerts his (her, *etc.*) efforts IV.1123, Anel 116, Pity 73; ability, capacity I.538, III.1188; **over your (hir) m.** beyond your (her) capacity III.1661, VI.468; *pl.* **myghtes** Tr 3.1757.

myght(e), myghte(n), myghtest(ow) *see* **mowe(n).**

myghty, mighti *n.* (1) great, mighty I.1673, I.2536, HF 1504; strong, big, powerful I.108, I.1423, I.2611, Tr 5.801; (2) capable X.547.

myghtily *adv.* strongly I.3475, II.921, by strength VII.2592; greatly Tr 5.262.

mikel *see* **muchel** *adj.*

myle *n.* mile I.1504, Tr 5.403; **m. wey** twenty minutes, the time taken to walk a mile Astr 1.7.10; by a long way VII.276; *gen.* **miles** VI.928; *pl.* (with preceding *num.*) **myle** VIII.555, (with *num.* following) **miles** VIII.173.

myn(e) *1 sg. poss.* (1) *(adj.)* my, mine (*usu.* before vowels and **h-**) I.782, I.804, VII.1548; (following *n.*) I.2221, BD 1039; (2) *(pro.)* mine I.1159, I.2406, PF 437; (as *n.*) **my good m.** my own good one Tr 3.1009.

mynde *n.* (1) mind I.1402, BD 15; thought, consideration II.908; **have m. upon** be mindful of Purse 26; (2) reason, wits VI.494, BD 511, VII.594, Tr 3.930; (3) memory I.4077, IV.849, PF 679; **in m.** recorded, remembered Tr 4.18; **forgat hir m.** lost her memory

II.527; **out of m.** forgotten IV.2390, PF 69; (4) awareness, senses Bo 1.pr3.3, Tr 2.602.

myne *v.* undermine (as in a siege) Tr 4.471; *pr. pl.* **mynen** Rom C 6291.

mynstralcye, mynstralsye *n.* (1) music I.2197, I.2524, LGW 2615; (2) musical instrument IX.113, IX.267; (3) entertainment I.4394; *pl.* **mynstralcies** musical sounds HF 1217.

myrie *see* **mery(e)** *adj.*

myrie, myrier *see* **merye** *adv.*

myrily, myriely *see* **meryly.**

mirour, mirrour *n.* (1) mirror I.1399, IV.1582, Rom A 1601; (2) model, exemplar II.166, V.1454, BD 974; *pl.* **mirours** lens, magnifying glasses V.234.

myrth(e), murthe *n.* gaiety, mirth I.759, I.3554, Rom A 86; pleasure, cause of mirth I.766, II.410, III.399; *pl.* **myrthes** pleasures Bo 4.pr5.33.

mys *adj.* amiss Anel 279, Tr 5.1426; (as *n.*) **con m. do** wrong LGW G 266.

mysaventure, mysaunter *n.* misfortune I.616, Tr 1.766, Rom A 253; **with m.** bad luck (to him) III.1334.

myschaunce, myschance *see* **meschaunce.**

myscheef, myschef *see* **meschief.**

mysdo *v.* wrong, do wrong Rom B 3671; *3 pr. sg.* **mysdooth** VII.1922; *pp.* **mysdoon** X.85; *vbl. n.* **mysdoynge** VII.1708.

misericorde *n.* mercy, pity VII.1418, X.804; *pl.* **misericordes** feelings of pity Bo 3.m12.45.

mysese, myseyse *n.* distress, suffering X.177, X.194, Rom C 6807; *pl.* **myseses** Bo 1.pr4.66.

mysgo(n), mysgoon *pp.* gone astray I.4218, I.4252, I.4255, X.80.

myshappe *v.* suffer misfortune VII.1696; *pr. subj. sg. (impers.)* **me myshappe** I should suffer misfortune I.1646; *prp.* **myshappyng** causing misfortune Rom B 5543; *pp.* **myshapped** turned out badly VII.944.

mysledeth *3 pr. sg.* misleads Bo 3.pr2.24, Bo 3.m8.1; *pt. pl. (reflx.)* **mysledden** misconducted (themselves) Tr 4.48; *vbl. n. pl.* **mysledynges** misdirections Bo 3.pr8.2.

mysse *v.* (1) miss, fail to find I.4216, III.1416; lack VII.352, Rom B 5646; (2) fail I.3679, PF 40, Tr 3.1624; *1 pr. sg.* **mis** Lady 43; *pt. sg.* **missed** (with *dat. pro.*) was lacking Tr 3.445; *pp.* **missed** missed Tr 3.537.

myssey *v.* slander Rom B 2205; *2 pr. sg.* **mysseyest** slander LGW F 323; *3 pr. sg.* **mysseyeth** X.379; *pr. subj. sg.* **mysseye** speak wrongly Anel 317; *pt. sg.* **misseyde** spoke wrongly LGW F 430; *pp.* **mysseyd, myssayd** spoken out of turn IV.2391, IX.353, BD 528, slandered Rom A 1260; *vbl. n.* **misseiyng** speaking evil Rom B 2207.

mistakith *3 pr. pl.* do wrong Rom A 1540; *pp.* **mystake** done wrong BD 525; *(reflx.)* **mystaken** done wrong, made a mistake VII.1690, VII.1818.

myster, mester *n.* (1) craft, occupation I.613; (as *adj.*) kind of I.1710, Rom C 6332; (2) difficult situation I.1340; (3) necessity, need Rom A 1426, Rom B 2787, Rom B 5614.

mystorneth *3 pr. sg.* misleads Bo 3.pr3.8, Bo 4.pr6.175; *pp.* (as *adj.*) **mystorned** (those who are) misdirected Bo 4.pr2.177; *vbl. n.* **misturnyng** a turn for the worse Rom B 5545.

mystriste, mystruste(n) *v.* distrust VI.369, VII.1759,

Tr 1.688; *pr. pl.* **mystruste(n)** IV.2343, Tr 4.1606; *pr. subj. pl.* **mystruste** VII.1759; *imp. pl.* **mistrust** Tr 4.1609; *pp.* **mystrusted** Tr 2.431.

myswent *pp.* went astray Tr 1.633, Rom C 7182.

myte *n.* a small Flemish coin worth a farthing or half a farthing (used in expressing worthlessness) VIII.633, VIII.698, Anel 269; **dere ynough a m.** of no value Tr 4.684, to the slightest extent LGW 741.

mo *n.* more, others I.3183, Tr 1.613; **other(e) mo** many others IV.1215, IV.2263; **withouten mo** without any others, alone I.2725, VIII.207, Tr 4.1125. Cf. **more** *n.*

mo *adj.* more I.808, I.849, BD 266; **tymes mo** often IV.449; **other(e) ladyes** *(etc.)* **mo** many other ladies *(etc.)* III.894, Tr 2.1481, LGW 1923. Cf. **more** *adj.*

mo *adv.* more Tr 5.158, Tr 5.229; **never(e) m.** never again I.1346, III.1099, BD 1125; **never the mo** in any way III.691. Cf. **more** *adv.*

moch(e) *see* **much(e)** *adv.*

moche *see* **muche** *n., adj.*

mochel *see* **muchel** *n., adj., adv.*

moder, mooder *n.* (1) mother II.276, PF 292; (2) plate on an astrolabe Astr 1.3.1; *gen.* **moodres** II.786; *pl.* **moodres** VI.93.

moeble *n.* personal property, moveable possessions Tr 4.1380, Tr 5.300; *pl.* **moebles** IV.1314, VIII.540.

moeve(n), meve *v.* move X.133, PF 150, Bo 2.m5.26; **m. werre** begin or provoke war VII.1028, VII.1649; *3 pr. sg.* **moeveth** Bo 1.pr4.12, **moveth** HF 735; *pr. pl.* **moeven** X.128; *pr. subj. sg.* **moeve** Astr 2.35.7; *pt. sg.* **moeved(e)** II.1136, Bo 3.m9.10; *pp.* **moeved** X.293, **ymoeved** Bo 5.pr4.23, **meved** HF 813; *vbl. n.* **moeving** mover II.295, motion Bo 3.pr10.232; **movynge** motion HF 812, **mevynge** movements Tr 1.285; *pl.* **moevynges** movements X.655.

moyst(e) *adj.* (1) moist, damp VII.992; liquid Bo 5.m5.9 (see note); (as *n.*) moisture Rom A 1564; one of the elemental qualities I.420; (2) fresh, new VI.315, VII.764; supple (or new) I.457.

molte *see* **melte.**

mone, moone *n.*[1] moon I.2077, I.3352, LGW 825; position of the moon I.403; *gen.* **mones** Astr 2.34.5, **moones** V.1154.

mone, moone *n.*[2] lament, moan HF 362, Tr 1.696; complaint V.920; (with **make**) I.1366, II.656, Tr 4.950.

mony *see* **many(e).**

montaigne, montayne, monteyne, mowntaigne *n.* mountain II.24, VII.2586, VII.2627, Bo 1.m4.8; *pl.* **montaignes** VII.2264, **montaynes** HF 898, **mountaignes** Bo 3.m8.6.

montance *see* **mountaunce.**

moralite(e) *n.* (1) morality I.3180, III.2046, X.38; (2) discourse on morals VII.2497, X.1088; moral significance (of a tale) VII.3440; *pl.* **moralitees** moral qualities X.462.

mordre, moordre *n.* murder I.1256, VII.576, Rom A 1136.

mordre *v.* murder VII.3225, Anel 291, LGW 1556; *pr. pl.* **mordren** X.578; *pt. subj. pl.* **mordred** BD 724; *pp.* **mordred** III.801; *vbl. n.* **mordrynge** murder I.2001.

mordrour, morderour, mordrere, mortherere *n.* murderer IV.732, VII.3226, PF 353, LGW 2390.

more, moore *n.* (1) more (in quantity) III.1871; **m. and less(e), lasse and m.** the high (in rank) and the low, everyone I.1756, II.959, VI.53; (2) **withoute(n)** **(any) m.** without anything else I.1541, I.2316, without further ado Tr 3.973, Tr 4.133. Cf. **mo** *n.*

more, moore *adj.* more, greater in quantity, size, or extent I.2429, VII.5, VII.1259 BD 822; longer in duration Tr 5.659; **for the m. part** the greater part, the majority VII.1257, Tr 1.925. Cf. **mo** *adj.*

more, moore *adv.* more I.1307, VI.369, BD 190; (with *adj.* forming the *comp.* I.802, III.441, Tr 2.1328; **ever(e) lenger the m.** the longer (an activity continues) the more (intense the activity becomes) IV.687, V.404, LGW 1517. Cf. **mo** *adv.*

morne, mourne *v.* (1) mourn, complain III.848, Rom B 2445, Rom B 5007; (2) long for, yearn I.3704; *3 pr. sg.* **moorneth** mourns V. 819, **morneth** longs for Tr 5.793; *pr. pl.* **moorne** long for VII.743; *prp.* (as *adj.*) **mornynge** Bo 3.m2.30; *vbl. n.* **mournyng** mourning garments Rom B 4756; **moornyng(e)** mourning II.621, longing I.3706.

mortal, mortel *adj.* (1) mortal IV.1150, VIII.438, Tr 3.376; earthly Bo 1.pr2.26; (2) deadly I.61, I.1553, PF 135.

mortherere *see* **mordrour.**

mortifye *v.* (in alchemy) transmute VIII.1126, VIII.1431; *pp.* **mortefied** destroyed, killed X.233.

morwe(n), morowe *n.* morning I.334, BD 22, Tr 2.65, Mars 1; dawn Tr 3.1469; **morwe-tyde** morning time IV.2225, V.901; **erly by the m.** early in the morning LGW F 49; *pl.* **morwes** BD 411.

morwenynge *n.* morning, dawn I.1062, V.397, LGW 1483; *pl.* **morwenynges** III.875.

most(e), mostow *see* **mot.**

most(e), moost(e), meeste *adj. super.* most I.303, I.798, Rom B 5759; greatest, chief I.895, III.505, Bo 1.pr3.66; (as *n.*) **m. and leeste** one and all I.2198, Tr 1.167.

most(e), moost(e) *adv. super.* most I.2325, I.2394, PF 403; (forming *super.* of *adj.* or *adv.*) most I.2203, IV.979, BD 302.

mot, moot *1 & 3 pr. sg.* (1) (as *aux.,* with *inf.*) must I.732, BD 42; may I.738, I.1838; (2) (without *inf.*) must go II.294, HF 2139; **m. nedes** must necessarily I.1169, BD 42; *2 pr. sg.* **most** II.104, **must** Astr 2.23.38, (with *pro.*) **mostow** Bo 4.pr2.164, **mustow** Bo 3.pr11.44; *pr. pl.* **moote(n)** I.232, III.589, **mote(n)** PF 546, Tr 2.1669; **must** Rom B 1796; *pr. subj. sg.* **mote** may I.832, I.3918, Tr 1.341, **moot(e)** I.4177, VII.3330; *1 & 3 pt. sg.* (often *pr.* in meaning) **most(e), must** (1) (as *aux.,* with *inf.*) must I.847, BD 1202, Bo 1.pr4.83, Astr 2.23.41; (*impers.*) **us** (him, *etc.*) **m.,** we (he, *etc.*) must VIII.946, Rom A 1473; (2) (without *inf.*) must go II.282, HF 448; *pt. pl.* **moste(n)** IV.1334, VII.2992; **must(e)** Bo 3.pr11.214, Rom B 1796; *pt. subj. sg.* **most(e)** may, might II.380, VI.550, Adam 3.

moun *see* **mowe(n).**

mountaunce, mountance, montance *n.* amount, value IX.255; amount, length (of time, height, *etc.*) Tr 2.1707, LGW F 307, Rom A 1562; extent Tr 2.1707.

mowe(n) *v.* be able Bo 4.pr1.69, Rom B 2644; enable Tr 2.1594; *1 & 3 pr. sg.* **may** can I.230, may IV.2337; *2 pr. sg.* **mayst** I.1285, (with *pro.*) **maistow** I.2128; *pr. pl.* **mowe(n)** I.3550, VIII.681; **may** I.1268, HF 1759; *pr. subj.* **mowe** may I.3886 *(sg.),* VI.932 *(pl.);* *1 & 3 pt. sg.* **myght(e)** I.299, BD 44; *2 pt. sg.* **myghtest** I.1655, (with *pro.*) **myghtestow** Tr 4.262; *pt. pl.* **myghte(n)** I.568, II.470; *pt. subj. sg.* **myghte** IV.638;

vbl. n. **mowynge** power, ability (to do something) Bo 2.pr4.257.

mowntaigne *see* **montaigne.**

much(e), moch(e), myche *adv.* much, greatly I.1116, Bo 1.pr3.45, Bo 3.pr4.51, Tr 2.228, Rom A 252.

muche, moche, mych *n.* much IV.2292, III.2134, III.1747, Rom B 1768; **m. and (or) lite** great and small, everyone I.494, Anel 107.

muche, moche, myche *adj.* much I.1359, V.586, BD 713, Rom B 5783; **many** III.1273, VII.2770.

muchel, mochel *n.* much I.211, I.467; size, stature BD 454.

muchel, mochel, mikel *adj.* much I.2352, BD 796, LGW 1677; **many** VIII.673.

muchel, mochel, mychel *adv.* much, greatly I.132, BD 1102, Bo 3.pr11.4.

multiplie(n) *v.* multiply III.28, VII.1740, Tr 1.486; (2) transmute base metals into gold VIII.669, VIII.731; *3 pr. sg.* **multiplieth** VII.1580; *pr. pl.* **multiplie** VIII.1417; *pr. subj. sg.* **multiplie** VIII.1479; *prp.* **multipliynge** HF 801; *pp.* **(y)multiplied** Bo 2.pr7.104, (as *adj.*) Bo 3.pr11.125; *vbl. n.* **multiplying** increase VI.374, transmutation of base metals VIII.1391.

mury(e), murier *see* **mery(e)** *adj.*

murye, murier *see* **merye** *adv.*

murily, murierly *see* **meryly.**

murmur(e) *n.* murmuring, grumbling I.2459, III.406, IV.635, PF 520; *pl.* **murmures** murmurs, grumblings HF 686.

murmur(e) *pr. pl.* murmur, grumble X.507; *pt. pl.* **murmureden** V.204; *vbl. n.* **murmurynge** murmur I.2432.

murthe *see* **myrth(e).**

muse *v.* ponder, reflect Tr 3.563; *3 pr. sg.* **musith** Rom A 1592; *pt. sg.* **mused(e)** IV.1033, Rom A 1527; *pp.* **mused** HF 1827.

must *see* **mot.**

muwe *see* **mewe.**

N

n' *var.* of **ne** not (before vowels) VII.2841, Tr 1.884.

na *see* **no.**

nacioun, nacion *n.* nation II.268, HF 207; family III.1068; *pl.* **nacions** I.53.

nad, nadde *contr.* of **ne had(de)** *(sg.)* had not IX.51, Tr 3.1319.

nadde *contr.* of **ne hadde** *(pl.)*, had not VIII.879.

nay *adv.* no I.1126, *etc.*; (as *n.*) **it is no (na) n.** it cannot be denied I.4183, BD 147. Cf. **no** *interj.*

nayl *n.* (1) nail I.2007; (2) fingernail X.269; *pl.* **nayles** nails III.769, hooves I.2141, claws HF 542; **by nayles** by (God's) nails VI.288, VI.651.

naille *v.* nail, fasten IV.1184; *prp.* **nailynge** I.2503; *pp.* **nayled** IV.29.

naked, nakid *adj.* naked I.1956, I.2066, BD 125; bare, unadorned X.345, BD 577, LGW G 86; **n. text** literal text Rom C 6556; unsheathed (sword) V.84; **bely-naked** stark naked IV.1326; **n. or clad** in all circumstances Rom C 6867.

nam *1 pr. sg. contr.* of **ne am**, am not I.2811; **I n. but I** am as good as (dead, lost, *etc.*) I.1122, I.1274, BD 1188.

nam *3 pt. sg.* took VIII.1297. Cf. **nomen.**

name *n.* (1) name I.854, I.1556, BD 201; (2) reputation I.1437, I.2107, BD 1263; (3) condition, status X.766; *pl.* **names** I.2595.

namely, namelich(e) *adv.* namely, especially I.1437, I.3989, Tr 1.743.

namo *n.* no others I.544, III.957.

namo *adj.* no more, no other I.101.

namo *adv.* no more, never again V.573.

namore, namoore *n.* no more I.974, I.2741

namoore *adj.* no more IV.2318, X.188.

namoore, namore *adv.* no more I.98, I.2470, Tr 1.753; no longer I.4138, VII.160; never again VII.395.

nart *2 pr. sg. contr.* of **ne art**, (you) are not Bo 2.pr3.74, Bo 3.pr5.62.

narw(e) *adj.* narrow I.625, II.946, LGW 740; small VII.2822; *super.* **narwest** Astr 1.18.5.

narwe, narowe *adv.* (1) closely, tightly I.3224, III.1803, Anel 183; (2) carefully IV.1988; precisely Astr Pro 72.

nas *1 & 3 pr. sg. contr.* of **ne was** was not, was no I.251, I.288, BD 342; **nas but** was as good as (lost, dead, *etc.*) II.209, Tr 4.957.

nat, not *adv.* not I.246, I.3687, BD 996; **nat but** nothing but I.2722, VI.403, only III.1728, LGW 1899; **n. but ynough** more than enough VIII.601.

nath *1 & 3 pr. sg. contr.* of **ne hath** has not III.100, Tr 5.1199.

natheles, nathelees *adv.* none the less, nevertheless I.35, I.1832, BD 32.

nativite(e) *n.* (1) birth V.45, VII.2016; (2) position of planets at one's birth, horoscope Tr 2.685, LGW 2576; *pl.* **nativites** Astr 2.4.1.

nature *n.* (1) nature (as the controlling force of life) I.2758, BD 18; (2) nature, character (of a person or thing) X.658, BD 631; natural instinct VII.2855; (2) sperm, seed X.577; *gen.* **natures** V.353; *pl.* **natures** Bo 3.pr12.35.

naturel, natureel, natural(l) *adj.* natural I.2750, III.1144; normal HF 28; **magyk n.** science I.416, V.1125, HF 1266; **day n.** twenty-four hours V.116, Mars 122, Astr 2.7.18; *pl.* **naturales** Astr 2.15.8.

naturelly, natureelly, naturely *adv.* naturally, by nature II.298, III.1134, Bo 1.m5.41.

naught, nought, noght, noht *n.* nothing I.756, III.1549, Tr 1.444, Tr 1.894.

naught, nought, noght *adv.* (emphatic) not, in no way, not at all I.2068, I.3298, Tr 3.584; **right n.** not at all, III.582, HF 994.

navye, naveye *n.* navy, fleet HF 216, Bo 4.m7.10.

ne, n' *adv.* not (*usu.* with another negative) I.70, I.449.

ne *conj.* nor I.179, IV.304; **ne (nat) . . . ne** neither . . . nor VI.339, VII.1681, BD 22.

nece *n.* (1) niece III.383, III.537, Tr 1.957; (2) kinswoman, female relative (of any degree of relation) VII.100, VII.106; *gen.* **neces** Tr 2.76; *pl.* **neces** Tr 2.814.

necessarie, necessaire *adj.* necessary Tr 4.1020, Tr 4.1021; *pl.* **necessaries** Bo 5.pr4.118; (as *n.*) **necessaries** necessities II.711.

necessite(e) *n.* necessity I.3042, IV.94, Tr 4.1002; need VII.235; *pl.* **necessites** Bo 3.pr9.110.

necligence, negligence *n.* negligence I.1881, II.22, LGW F 537, Adam 7.

necligent, negligent *adj.* negligent III.1816, VI.101, PF 429, Rom B 3900.

ned(e), need(e) *n.* (1) need, necessity I.2505, I.4026, BD 1253, Tr 2.714; **be(n) n.** be necessary I.304, IV.461, BD 190; (with *dat.*) **yow (thee,** *etc.*) **ben n.** you (thou, *etc.*) need VII.109, VII.3453, Tr 5.336; (2) moment of need, crisis II.112, VII.2386, ABC 44; **cometh to the n.** becomes necessary Tr 3.1225; **at the n.** when it becomes necessary Tr 4.1106; (3) business I.3632, VII.303; affair, business IV.1631, Tr 1.772; *pl.* **nedes** affairs VIII.1199, Tr 1.355; duties VII.76.

nede(s), nedis *adv.* by necessity, necessarily I.1169, BD 42, Rom B 1939; **for n.** necessarily BD 1201; **n. cost** necessarily I.1477, (as one word) LGW 2697.

nede(n) *v.* (1) be necessary II.871, Rom C 5990; (2) need, require X.700; (3) *(impers.)* **him** *(etc.)* **n.** is needed by (him, *etc.*), he *(etc.)* needs III.1275, III.1955, BD 256; **what n.** what is the need of I.849, II.232, Tr 2.497; *3 pr. sg.* **nedeth** I.462, **needeth** I.3599; *pr. pl.* **neden** X.927; *pt. sg.* **neded(e)** I.4020, VI.106; *pt. pl.* **neded** Rom A 560; *pt. subj. sg.* **us neded** we should need Tr 4.1344.

nedeful(le), needfulle *adj.* (1) needy X.805; necessary VII.1643; (as *n.*) the needy II.112, X.1032; (2) needed VII.1643.

nedelees, nedeles *adv.* needlessly IV.621, X.698.

nedely, nedly *adv.* of necessity, necessarily III.968, VII.3244, Tr 4.940.

nedy *adj.* needy, poor VII.1417, X.778, Bo 2.m2.23; **ben n.** of be in need, Bo 4.pr9.29.

negh, neigh *see* **ny** *prep.*

neigh *see* **ny(e)** *adj., adv.*

nekke, necke *n.* neck I.238, BD 939, Rom A 1515; *pl.* **nekkes** PF 671.

nel(l) *see* **nyl(l).**

nempne(n) *v.* name II.507, V.318; *pt. sg.* **nempned** IV.609; *pp.* **(y)nempned** X.598, Rom C 6224.

ner, neer *adj.* nearer VII.1397, Tr 1.451.

ner, neer *adv.* near, nearby I.1439, Rom B 1786; **come n.** draw near I.839, III.433; *comp.* **neer** nearer I.968, **ner** Tr 1.448, **nerre** Rom B 5101; **never the n.** no nearer BD 38, no closer to one's goal, no better off VIII.721, PF 619.

ner, neer *prep.* near, next to, Pity 19, LGW F 318.

nere, neere *2 pt. sg. contr.* of **ne were** were not Bo 2.pr3.37, Mars 112; *pt. pl.* **nere** II.547; *pt. subj. sg.* **nere** were it not I.875; it would not be I.1129; *pt. subj. pl.* **nere** II.548, **neere** Bo 3.pr4.19.

net, nett *n.* net Astr 1.3.5; snare VII.1179; *pl.* **nettes** nets I.3927; snares Tr 3.1355, LGW 1190.

nether(e), nethir *adj. comp.* lower I.3852, Astr 1.12.8, Astr 2.45.54; *super.* **netherest(e)** Bo 1.pr1.28, **netherist** Astr 1.4.3.

neven(e) *v.* name HF 562, Rom C 5962; *pr. pl.* **nevene** LGW 2237; *pr. subj. sg.* **nevene** VIII.1473.

never(e) *adv.* never I.70; **n. a deel** not a bit, not at all I.3064, VII.403; **n. erst** never before IV.144, X.776; **n. mo** (more) never again I.1346, Anel 366, (as one word) X.129, Bo 2.m2.23; **n. the mo** in no way, not at all II.982, III.691, (as one word) IV.2089.

nevew, neveu *n.* nephew VII.2404, LGW 2659; grandson HF 617, LGW 1440.

new(e) *adj.* (1) new, fresh I.457, II.138; modern I.176, X.721; (2) (as *n.*) new one HF 302; **of n.** recent Tr 2.20, recently IV.938; for the first time VIII.1043; *comp.* **newer** VI.546.

new(e) *adv.* (1) newly, recently I.365, I.2162; **al n.** just now VII.3049; (2) anew Tr 5.650, Tr 5.1333; **ay (alwey) n.** always, continually BD 1228, Tr 5.1572; **n. and n.** again and again VI.929, Tr 3.116.

newe *v.* (*tr.*) renew Tr 3.305; *3 pr. sg.* **neweth** Bo 4.pr6.150; *pt. sg.* **newed** (*intr.*) renewed, made itself new BD 906; *pp.* **newed** VII.1846.

newefangelnesse, newfangelnesse, newfanglenesse *n.* novelty V.610; instability, desire for novelty Anel 141, LGW F 154.

newliche, newely *adv.* recently VII.1225, Rom A 1205; newly Bo 4.m3.13.

next(e) *adj.* nearest VI.870, LGW 2481; **n. way** II.807 most direct route; next I.2367; **next** VII.180.

next *adv.* the next time V.443, Tr 2.982; next Tr 3.1256; **n. befor** immediately preceding BD 225.

next *prep.* next to IV.694, HF 1486, Tr 1.948.

ny(e) *adj.* near, close X.836; **n. cause** immediate cause VII.1395; (as *n.*) the one who is near I.3392.

ny(e), nygh(e), neigh, negh *adv.* (1) near III.178; (2) nearly I.4400, Bo 5.pr1.64, Tr 1.60, Mars 289; close, closely I.588, Purse 19; **wel n.** very nearly, almost I.1330, I.1407, BD 3; (3) precisely I.732, Astr 2.17.2.

ny, neigh, negh *prep.* close to, near II.550, BD 907, Tr 5.148.

nyce *adj.* (1) foolish II.1088, III.938, HF 276; (2) scrupulous I.398, IV.2434.

nycete(e) *n.* (1) foolishness I.4046, VIII.463, PF 572; folly IX.152; lust III.412; (2) scrupulosity Tr 2.1288; shyness BD 613.

nygard, nygart *n.* miser III.333, VII.2915, Rom A 1175; *pl.* **nygardes** III.1263.

nyghte *v.* grow dark, become night PF 209, Tr 5.515.

nyl(l) *1 & 3 pr. sg. contr.* of **ne wyl** will not, do not wish to II.972, III.98, BD 92, Rom B 4813; *1 pr. sg.* **nele** LGW 2563, **nell** Rom B 3716; *2 pr. sg.* **nylt** Tr 2.1000; (with *pro.*) **nyltow** Tr 3.1427; *pr. pl.* **nel** III.941; *vbl. n.* **nyllinge** refusal Bo 3.pr11.83. See **nolde.**

nys *3 pr. sg. contr.* of **ne ys** is not I.901, I.1274, Tr 1.203.

nyst(e) *1 & 3 pt. sg. contr.* of **ne wiste** did not know I.3414, I.4225; *2 pt. sg.* **nystist** Bo 3.pr12.13.

no, noo *interj.* no! no indeed! (more emphatic than **nay**; *usu.* in answer to a negative question) IV.819, V.1000, HF 1066.

no, na *adj.* no, not any I.70, I.4134; nothing II.273; **no man** anyone VII.1584, Tr 2.569. Cf. **non(e)** *adj.*

no *adv.* no VI.958, *etc;* not VIII.212. Cf. **non(e)** *adv.*

noble *n.* a gold coin (6 shillings, 8 pence) I.3256; *pl.* **nobles** HF 1315.

nobley(e) *n.* nobility VIII.449; magnificence HF 1416.

noblesse *n.* (1) nobility, high rank III.1167, IV.468; nobleness, nobility of character II.185, II.248, Tr 1.287; (2) splendor, magnificence IV.782, HF 471, Tr 5.439.

noght *see* **naught** *n., adv.*

noyous *adj.* annoying, troublesome Rom B 3230, Rom B 4449.

noyse *n.* (1) noise I.2492, I.2534, Tr 3.662; sound I.2524, BD 297; clamor I.2534; sound, song IX.300, X.605; voice Tr 4.374; (2) uproar, disturbance VII.1035, VII.3393; (3) rumor, report Rom B 3971; *pl.* **noyses** uproars, disturbances VII.1514.

nold(e) *1 & 3 pt. sg. contr.* of **ne wolde** would not, did not want to I.2704, I.3122, Tr 2.33; *2 pr. sg.* **noldest**

BD 482, (with *pro.*) **noldestow** Tr 3.1264; *pt. pl.*
nolde(n) Bo 1.pr4.118, Tr 2.418. *See* **nyl.**

nombre, nomber, noumbre *n.* number I.716, Astr
2.44.25; proportion Bo 1.m2.14; *pl.* **nombres** numbers Astr 1.10.11, **noumbres** proportions PF 381, **n.**
of augrym Arabic numerals Astr 1.7.6.

nombren, noumbre *v.* number, count BD 439, Bo
4.pr7.20; *pp.* **nombred** X.218, **noumbred** Tr 3.1269.

nomen *pt. pl.* took Rom B 5404, Rom C 7421; *pp.*
ynome PF 38, LGW 2343, captured Tr 1.242; **no-**
me(n) taken Tr 3.606, Tr 5.514. Cf. **nam.**

non(e), noon(e) *pro.* none I.524, II.87, BD 958.

non(e), noon *adj.* no I.1787, III.415, BD 169; (*Nth.*)
neen I.4185, I.4187. Cf. **no** *adj.*

noon *adv.* no V.387; not III.2069, V.778. Cf. **no** *adv.*

nones, nonys *n.* **for the n.** for the occasion I.3126, Rom
A 709; at that time, then I.879, Tr 4.185; purposefully, indeed Tr 2.1381; indeed I.545, I.1423; **with**
the n. on the condition LGW 1540.

nonne *n.* nun I.118, Rom C 6350; *gen.* **nonnes**
VII.2809; *pl.* **nonnes** Rom C 6864.

nory *n.* pupil Bo 1.pr3.13, Bo 3.pr9.159.

norice, norys, norysshe *n.* nursemaid, governess
VII.3115, Bo 2.pr4.1, LGW 1346, Rom B 5418;
nourisher V.347, VIII.1; *pl.* **norices** X.613.

norice *v.* nourish VII.1014, Bo 1.pr1.51; *3 pr. sg* **nor-**
isseth VII.1594, **norissheth** Bo 2.pr4.88, **noryss-**
cheth Bo 4.m6.34; *pr. pl.* **norissen** X.613; *pr. subj. sg.*
noryssche Bo 3.m6.13; *pt. sg.* **norissched** Bo
2.pr2.17, **norysside** Bo 2.pr3.66; *pp.* **(y)norissed**
brought up, nurtured IV.399; **ynorisshed** Tr 5.821,
norissched Bo 1.pr2.5; *vbl. n.* **norissyng(e)** nourishment I.437, X.348, **norisshynge** growth I.3017, up-
bringing IV.1040; *pl.* **norysschynges** nourishments
Bo 3.m11.36, **noryssynges** Bo 4.pr6.36.

nost *2 pr. sg.* (*contr.* of **ne wost**) you know not, do not
know BD 1137, Tr 4.642; (with *pro.*) **nostow** you do
not know HF 1010.

not, noot *1 & 3 pr. sg.* (*contr.* of **ne wot, woot**) I (he)
know(s) not, do(es) not know I.1101, I.1263, BD 29.

nota *imp. sg.* (Latin) take note Astr 2.26.30, 2.34.18.

note, noote *n.* (1) melody VII.521, VII.547, PF 677;
(2) musical note BD 472; voice I.235; **by n.** in unison
BD 303, HF 1720; (3) written record Bo 5.m4.19;
pl. **notes** melodies BD 319; impressions, written
marks Bo 5.m4.25; notifications, indications Bo
5.m3.19.

nother *see* **nouther.**

nothing, no thyng *n.* nothing I.3598, BD7; (as *adv.*) in
no way, not at all V.1094, Anel 87, PF 470.

notifie *v.* take note of Tr 2.1591; *pr. pl.* **notifie** indicate
X.430; *pp.* **notified** indicated X.437; made known,
proclaimed II.256.

nought *see* **noght** *n., adv.*

noumbre *see* **nombre.**

nouther, nother *conj.* neither BD 342, BD 531, Tr
4.1264; (as *n.*) **never n.** neither one LGW F 192.

O

o *var.* of **on** (*prep.*) on Tr 3.552; **o poynt to** about to Tr
5.1285.

o, oo *var.* of **on** *num.* one I.304, I.1891, BD 1293; same
I.2475, Tr 2.37.

obeye(n), obey, obay *v.* obey IV.194, IV.532, Tr
3.1690, Rom B 1996, Rom B 4986; (with **to**
unto) be obedient VII.1550, VII.1742, Tr 2 1490, be
subject to Astr 2.28.36; (*reflx.*) be obedient VII.1684;
3 pr. sg. **obeyeth** IV.1961; *pr. pl.* **obeye(n** IV.194,
VII.1550; *pt. sg.* **obeyed** III.1255, **obeyde** Anel 119.

obeisant, obeisaunt *adj.* obedient IV.66, X.264,
X.676.

obeisaunce, obeisance, obesaunce *n.* (1) homage, act
of obedience I.2974; **do o.** obey; IV.24; (2) at (in)
(one's) o. in (one's) control LGW 587, Pity 84; (3)
respectful submission, deference IV.794, Tr 3.478; *pl.*
obeisaunces acts of respect V.515.

oblige *v.* pledge Tr 4.1414; *3 pr. sg.* **obligeth** X.847;
pr. pl. **oblige** VII.1747; *pp.* **obliged** Tr 3.1612.

observance, observaunce *n.* (1) duty I.1316; attention,
respectful act IV.1564, V.516; (2) ceremony, rite
I.2224, Tr 1.160; **don o.** perform a customary rite,
fulfil a religious duty I.1045, X.747, Tr 2.112; *pl.*
observaunces ceremonies I.2264, attentions V.516;
customs V.956, Tr 1.337; practices V.1291.

observe *v.* respect, observe (a practice) VII.631; *3 pr. sg.*
observeth X.303; *pr. pl.* **observen** respect, practice
X.947, attend to Astr 2.4.3; *pr. subj. sg.* **hym observe**
(*reflx.*) guard himself from Rom B 2024; *pt. pl.* **obser-**
vede took care X.429.

occasioun, occasion *n.* (1) cause X.946, LGW 994;
opportunity X.512, Rom B 2508; *pl.* **occasiouns**
X.1005, **occasions** VI.66.

occupie *v.* occupy, take up V.64; take possession of
II.424, VII.2237, Tr 4.836; *3 pr. sg.* **occupieth** Tr
5.1322; *pr. pl.* **ocupien** take X.884; *imp. sg.* **occupye**
take possession of Bo 4.pr7.96; *pp.* (as *adj.*) **occupied**
busy with VII.1596, **ocupyed** preoccupied Bo
3.pr1.37.

of, off *adv.* off III.783, VI.226, Rom B 2220; **don of**
take off I.2676, BD 516; **com(e) of** come on, hurry
III.1602, PF 494.

of, off *prep.* (1) (location) of I.55, *etc;* away from, over
V.288; over I.2246, IX.128; (2) (agency) by III.661,
LGW 2318; from I.3612, I.4253, VII.2399; because
of, for V.718, VII.2992, LGW G 118; by reason of,
because of VII.478, Tr 4.368; with III.591, IV.2243,
Anel 42; for (in requests) I.175, IV.178, Tr 2.1007;
(3) (of respect) concerning I.177, I.2812, Tr 2.389; in
respect to (following *adj.*) I.250, I.479, LGW 1267; at
I.3524, I.4046, Tr 2.1391; **as of** in regard to PF 299,
considering I.87; (4) (partitive) some, some of I.146,
III.187, VI.910; (5) (time) since IV.834, IV.964, BD
793, Tr 2.722.

offende(n) *v.* (1) do wrong, injure IV.1829; (2) displease IV.2164, Tr 2.244, Lady 123; (3) assail, transgress upon IV.1756; *3 pr. sg.* **offendeth** injures LGW
F 392, assails Tr 1.605; *pr. pl.* **offende** injure I.3065;
pt. sg. **offended** injured Anel 262; *pp.* **offended** injured I.2394, displeased X.986.

offense, offence *n.* (1) offence, transgression VII.1748,
Tr 1.556; harm Form Age 19; **doon o.** do wrong,
injure I.1083, III.2058, IV.922; (2) sense of injury
II.1138; *pl.* **offenses** VII.1882.

office *n.* (1) employment I.292, III.1421; role, function
VII.2256; **fil in o.** obtained employment I.1418; (2)
duty III.1137, VIII.924, PF 236; (3) religious rite

I.2863, I.2912; (4) function III.127, III.1144, Bo
4.pr2.102; (5) place of employment III.1577; *pl.*
offices official positions X.438; **houses of o.** storehouses, larders IV.264.

officer(e) *n.* (1) a court official, servant in a great
household I.1712; officer of the law VIII.497; (2) an
ecclesiastical official VII.65, VII.1935; (3) an official in
charge of jousts I.1712; *pl.* **officers** servants V.177,
officeres servants VI.480.

offre(n) *v.* make an offering (religious) VI.384, VI.386;
3 pr. sg. **offreth** X.1030; *pr. subj. sg.* **offre** VI.376; *pr.
subj. pl.* **offre(n)** VI.907, VI.929; *imp. sg.* **offre** Tr
5.306; *imp. pl.* **offreth** VI.910; *pt. pl.* **offrid** offered
Rom B 5567; *pp.* **offered** LGW 932, **offred** X.900;
vbl. n. **offrynge** offering (at mass) I.450, X.407; gifts
given at the offering I.489, III.1315.

oft(e), often *adv.* often I.55, I.310, VII.649, BD 103;
o. a day many times a day I.1356, I.2623, Tr 5.689;
comp. **ofter** more often IV.215, Tr 2.496.

ofte, often *adj.* frequent, repeated X.233; **o. sithe(s),
tyme(s)** very often, many times I.52, I.485, I.1312,
I.1877, I.4390, III.641, IV.233.

oght *see* **aught** *pro., adv.*

oghte, ought(e) *see* **owen.**

ok, ook *n.* oak I.1702, BD 447, PF 176; *pl.* **ookes** Bo
2.m5.6, **okes** I.2866.

old(e), oold *adj.* (1) old I.174, I.429, V.1153; (2) (as
n.) the aged I.2499, II.417; age I.2142; **of o.** long
since III.1615, IV.964; *comp.* **elder** VII.530; *super.*
eldeste I.912.

o-lofte, on-lofte *adv.* on high, above II.277, IV.229, Tr
5.8.

oon *indef. pro.* one, someone I.148, I.3817, II.271.

on *adv.* on, onward I.2558, I.3134, Tr 2.1341.

on *prep.* (1) on, in (location) I.271, *etc.;* **on highte** on
high I.2607, aloud I.1784; **on alle thyng** above all
BD 141; (2) (time, occasion), I.19, *etc.;* (3) (state,
occasion, condition) I.919, *etc.;* in IV.2370; **on ydel**
idly, in vain, Tr 1.955, Tr 5.95; **on yvel** in an evil
manner; **on six and sevene** at sixes and sevens, confused Tr 4.622, Tr 5.1625; **on slepe** asleep HF 114,
LGW F 209; **on huntyng** (also one word) a-hunting
I.1687, BD 355; **on lyve** alive I.3039, III.5, Tr 2.138;
(3) (direction) at, upon IV.2150, V.348, Tr 2.1157;
(with verbs **trust, waitynge, wynne,** *etc.*) I.501,
I.594, I.3642; (4) on, concerning I.438, VIII.923, Tr
3.783; about I.3478, Tr 5.1527; of For 43. Cf. **a** *prep.*
and **o** *prep.*

on, oon, o(o) *num.* (1) (as *adj.*) one I.148, III.573, Bo
3.m6.2; same I.1012, PF 557; (2) (as *pro.*) I.1013,
I.2334, BD 39; **evere in o.** always alike, continually
I.1771, I.3880, Tr 1.816; **many o.** many a one, many
I.317, VI.435, HF 1207; (3) (as *intens.*) **o. the fair-
este(best,***etc.*) the fairest (best, *etc.*) IV.212, V.734,
Tr 1.1081. Cf. **a** *num.*

ones, onis, oones *adv.* (1) once I.1034, III.10,
VII.1106, BD 1217; **o. for evere** for once and all Astr
2.3.8, Astr 2.3.59; (2) **al o.** agreed VI.696; **at o.** at the
same time HF 2008, Tr 3.119, (as one word) I.765;
(3) immediately Tr 4.183.

on-lofte *see* **o-lofte.**

open(e), opyn *adj.* open I.10, BD 872; public, manifest
II.636, Bo 4.pr2.261, Tr 2.40.

opene(n) *v.* open X.328, Bo 5.pr1.14; *3 pr. sg.* **openeth**
X.289, **opneth** Bo 2.pr8.6; *pt. sg.* **openyde** Rom A

538; *pt. pl.* **opened(en)** VIII.1218, X.329; *pp.*
opened IV.2152, **opned** Tr 3.1239; *vbl. n.* **openyng**
Rom A 544.

operacion, operacioun *n.* scientific process V.130,
V.1290; **ne doon hir o.** do not behave as they should
III.1148; *pl.* **operaciouns** V.1129.

opned *see* **opene.**

oppresse *v.* oppress V.1411, VII.1216, Tr 3.1089; suppress, overcome VIII.4, Tr 3.1089; repress Tr 5.398;
rape V.1385, V.1406; *pp.* **oppressed** raped V.1385,
overcome Tr 3.1089, oppressed Tr 5.177.

oppression, oppressioun *n.* wrong, oppression III.889,
III.1990, Tr 2.1418; repression LGW 2592.

or *prep.* LGW 2010, Rom A 864. See **er** *prep.*

or *conj.* ere, before II.289, BD 228, HF 101. See **er** *conj.*

or *see* **other** *conj.*

ordeyne *v.* grant, concede Bo 5.pr2.20; order, dispose
Rom C 7019; equip VIII.1277; *3 pr. sg.* **ordeyneth**
Bo 3.pr12.118, **ordeigneth** Bo 3.pr12.70, **ordeineth**
Bo 4.pr6.358; *pt. sg.* **ordeyned** X.771, **ordeynide** Bo
3.pr12.43; *prp.* **ordeynynge** Bo 5.pr6.298; *pp.* **ordeyned** arranged I.2553, appointed V.177, **ordeigned** aranged Rom B 4185.

ordinaunce, ordinance, ordenaunce, ordenance *n.* (1)
decree, order I.2567, I.3012, Tr 4.964, Bo 5.pr3.189;
law VIII.445, VIII.529; **at, in** (someone's) **o.** under
(someone's) authority III.763, For 44; (2) preparation
II.250, IV.961, Tr 3.535; plan II.805, X.19,
Tr 2.510; (3) orderly arrangement X.260, PF 390;
by, in o. in good order, correctly IV.961, VII.1113,
Tr 3.688; *pl.* **ordenaunces** arrangements Bo
4.pr6.355.

ordre, order, ordir *n.* (1) order, arrangement I.3003,
V.66, Tr 4.1017; **by o.** in order, sequentially I.1934,
V.92, LGW 2514, Astr 2.12.34; the order of the uni-
verse Bo 4.pr2.202; (2) manner V.66, VII.1529; (3)
rank X.891; (4) religious order I.214, III.2191; sect
Tr 1.336, Tr 4.782; religiously sanctioned condi-
tion IV.1347; (5) rule X.177, Mars 155; *pl.* **ordres**
I.210.

ordred *adj.* in religious orders, ordained X.962.

ordure *n.* (1) filth X.157, X.851; mud Bo 1.m7.9; rubbish, nonsense X.715, Tr 5.385; (2) excrement
X.428, X.885.

orison, orisoun *n.* prayer I.2261, I.2372, Rom C 6604;
pl. **orisons** II.537, **orisouns** X.1038.

orisonte, orisounte, orizonte *n.* horizon IV.1797, Astr
Pro 9, Astr 1.19.6.

ost, oost, host *n.* army I.1026, Tr 1.80, Tr 4.599, LGW
625; **ligging in o.** besieging Tr 4.29; **makynge an o.**
raising an army Bo 1.pr3.72; *pl.* **oostes** Bo 4.m4.13.

ostage, hostage *n.* hostage Rom B 2081, Rom B 2713;
pl. **ostages** Rom B 2064, **hostages** Rom B 2043.

oth, ooth *n.* oath I.120, Tr 3.1046; *pl.* **othes** I.810.

other(e), oother, othir, othre *pro.* other I.427, PF 134,
PF 332, Bo 5.pr3.167, Astr 1.10.8; **o. noon** nothing
else, no other III.2132, VIII.929, no other way
I.1182; **noon o.** (weyes) not otherwise I.1085,
VI.412; **ech after o.** one after another I.899; *gen.*
others Tr 5.1764, **otheres** VI.698, **othres** HF 800;
pl. **other(e)** I.2885, Tr 2.818, Bo 5.pr5.38; **othre** Bo
3.pr11.103.

other(e), othre, oother *adj.* other I.759, I.113, HF 54,
Tr 2.81, Bo 2.pr5.19, Astr 2.35.25.

other, oother *adv.* otherwise IV.2083, Rom B 5168.

other, or *conj.* either VII.60, PF 46. *See* **outher** *conj.*

otherweys, ootherweyes, ootherweyes, otherwise *adv.* otherwise, differently IV.1072, PF 654, Bo 5.pr4.144; **o . . . . o.** in one way . . . in another Bo 5.pr4.153.

otherwhile *see* **outherwhile.**

ought *see* **aught** *pro., adv.*

ought, oughte(n), oughtestow *see* **owen.**

our(e) *1 pl. poss.* (1) *(adj.)* our I.34, I.62, BD 43; (2) *(pro.)* ours PF 545; (after *ben*) **oures** ours VI.786, VII.273.

out *interj.* help! I.3286, I.3825.

out(e) *adv.* (1) out I.45, *etc.*; (with *aux.* and omission of *v.* of motion) go out, come out VII.576, VII.3052, Tr 4.210; (2) fully Tr 3.417; **o. and o.** all in all Tr 2.739; **al o.** utterly, completely Rom B 2101.

outen *v.* (1) display, show publicly IV.2438; make public VIII.834; (2) come out Tr 5.1444; *pr. pl.* **oute** display, spread out III.521; *pr. subj. sg.* **oute** Tr 3.1498.

outer, outter *adj.* outer, external VIII.498, Tr 3.664, Rom B 2987; *super.* **outreste** outmost Bo 3.pr11.118, **owtreste** uttermost Bo 4.pr4.53.

outher *adj.* either I.2556.

outher *conj.* either III.1828, BD 1100; **o. . . . or (outher)** either . . . or VIII.1149, neither . . . nor II.1136. *See* **other** *conj.*

outherwhile, otherwhile *adv.* sometimes VII.1543, VII.1667, (as two words) Bo 2.pr12.158; **o. . . . o.** sometimes, now . . . sometimes, now Bo 2.pr1.106–7.

out(e) of *prep. phr.* (1) outside of, out from I.181, I.4077; from Tr 2.14; (2) without I.487, I.1141.

outrage *n.* (1) excess X.834, Form Age 5; (2) act of violence VII.1525, VII.1527; (3) violence, excessive cruelty I.2012, VII.1536; (4) excessive, presumptuous act Rom B 2086; *pl.* **outrages** acts of violence VII.1438.

outrageous(e), outragious *adj.* (1) excessive, inordinate IV.2087, VI.650, PF 336; (2) flagrantly evil VII.1825, X.412; (3) arrogant, presumptuous Rom A 174.

outrely, outreliche, outterly, utterly *adv.* utterly, completely, flatly I.237, HF 296, HF 1541, Tr 2.710.

out-take(n) *prep.* except II.277, Rom A 948, Rom B 4474.

outward *adj.* external, outer IV.424, X.298, X.662.

outward *adv.* outside Tr 2.1704; externally X.656, HF 281; outwardly VII.1645.

over *adv.* (1) over I.3177, *etc.*; (2) too, excessively (in compounds) **over-hard** too severe VII.1696; **over-haste** excessive haste Tr 1.972; **over-hastily** too hastily VII.1576; **over-heye** too high Bo 3.m9.22; **over-hoot** too hot VIII.955; **over-greet** excessive VII.1686, VIII.648; **over-large** excessive VII.1599; **over-largely** excessively VII.1601; **over-lyght** too feeble Bo 4.m3.31; **over-long** too long HF 252; **overlonge** Bo 3.m7.6; **over-lowe, overlowe** too low VII.1465, Bo 3.m9.23; **over-muche(l)** too much, excessively VII.1467, HF 38; **overtymeliche** prematurely Bo 1.m1.16; **over-swifte** exceedingly swift Bo 4.m5.8; *sup.* **overeste** I.290.

over *prep.* over I.2140, *etc.*; beyond I.2998, II.277, PF 300; **o. al this** furthermore, in addition I.2850, V.137, Tr 3.1796.

overal(l), over-al *adv.* everywhere IV.1048, BD 171,

Rom B 5804; all over PF 284; in every way IV.2129, HF 684; **o. where** wherever PF 172.

overcome(n) *v.* overcome, defeat VII.1427, Bo 1.m1.7; *3 pr. sg.* **overcomith** *(intr.)* conquers Tr 4.1584, **overcometh** VII.1092; *pt. sg.* **overcom** LGW 2147; *pp.* **overcome(n)** I.2800, Bo 3.m12.15, came to pass, happened Tr 4.1069, **overcomyn** defeated Bo 1.pr2.11.

overgo(n), overgoo, over-go *v.* pass away Tr 1.846, Tr 4.424, Rom B 3784; *3 pr. sg.* **overgoth** overcomes Rom C 6821; *pr. pl.* **overgoon** go over, spread over Bo 2.pr7.37.

oversprede *v.* spread over, cover IV.1799; *3 pr. sg. (contr.)* **oversprat** Tr 2.767; *pt. sg.* **overspradde** I.678.

overthrowe *v.* (1) *(tr.)* cast down, ruin VII.2141; (2) *(intr.)* collapse, be ruined HF 1640; *3 pr. sg.* **overthroweth** Bo 4.pr6.314; *prp.* (as *adj.*) **overthrowynge** overwhelming Bo 1.m2.2, precipitate, hasty Bo 1.m6.22, Bo 2.m7.1, revolving, turning over Bo 3.m12.38, inclined toward Bo 4.pr6.299; *pp.* **overthrowe(n)** cast down, ruined Tr 4.385, Bo 1.pr4.310; *vbl. n.* **overthrowynge** casting down VII.1565; *pl.* **overthrowynges** Bo 2.m4.15.

overthwart *prep.* across Astr 1.5.1.

overthwert, overthwart *adv.* crosswise I.1991; **right o.** directly opposite Tr 3.685; askance, sidewise BD 863, Rom A 292.

owen *v.* (1) *(tr.)* owe X.76; (2) *(tr.)* own VI.361; (3) *(intr.)* as *aux.* (with *inf.*) ought to, should VII.1501, Bo 2.pr5.74; *1 pr. sg.* **owe** III.425; *2 pr. sg.* **owest** III.1615; *3 pr. sg.* **oweth** X.252, *(reflx.)* **hym oweth** he ought to, should LGW G 360; *pr. pl.* **owe(n)** owe III.2106, ought Bo 3.pr10.57; *1 & 3 pt. sg.* **him oughte** owed to him LGW 589, (as *aux.*) **oghte** should I.505, *(impers.)* **him (us,** *etc.***) oghte** he (we, *etc.*) should II.1097, **ought(e)** LGW F 27, LGW 2531; **aughte** Tr 1.649; *2 pt. sg.* **oughtest** Tr 1.894, **oghtist** Tr 1.894, (with *pro.*) **oughtestow** Tr 5.545; *pt. pl.* **oughten** Rom C 6466, **oghte(n)** VIII.6, VIII.1340, **aughten** Bo 3.pr12.128; *pp.* **owed** proper for Bo 4.pr5.74.

owen(e), owne *adj.* (following *poss. n.* or *pro.*) own I.213, Tr 5.49, LGW Pro F 408.

owher(e) *adv.* anywhere I.653, VIII.858, HF 478.

P

pace *see* **passe(n).**

page *n.* (1) servant, serving boy I.1427, I.3030, LGW 2037; (2) boy I.3972; **p. of the chambre** personal servant I.1427.

pay *n.* pleasure, satisfaction PF 271, Ven 70; **to (one's) p.** to (one's) satisfaction, satisfactorily PF 474, Ven 70.

paye(n) *v.* pay I.806, IV.2048, IX.78; *pr. pl.* **payen** VII.1962; *imp. sg.* **pay** III.1598; *imp. pl.* **paye** VII.291; *pt. sg.* **payd(e)** I.539, VII.366; *pp.* **(y)payed** paid, rewarded I.1802, I.4315, **payd** (with **holde**) pleased, satisfied III.1185, BD 269, **payed** (as *adj.*) rendered favorable (by *astro.* position) Tr 2.682.

payens *n. gen. pl.* Tr 5.1849 pagans'; *pl.* **payens** II.534.

payne(s) *see* **peyne** *n.*

payne(th) *see* **peyne** *v.*

paynted *see* **peynte(n).**

paire *see* **peyre.**

paleys, palays *n.* palace I.2199, IV.2415, HF 713; *(astro.)* zodiacal sign Mars 54, Mars 79.

palfrey *n.* riding horse I.207, I.4075, LGW 1116; *pl.* **palfreys** I.2495.

palys, palis *n.* palisade Bo 1.pr3.78, Bo 1.pr5.32, Bo 1.pr6.36.

papejay, papyngay, popynjay *n.* parrot IV.2322, VII.369, PF 359, Rom A 81.

paramour(e) *n.* lady-love, concubine III.454, III.1372, Rom B 5060; sexual desire IV.1450; wenching I.4372, I.4392; *pl.* **paramours** concubines VII.2867; courtly love-making I.3354, I.3758.

paramour(s) *adv.* passionately I.1155, I.2112, Tr 5.158, Tr 5.332; **as p.** by way of passionate love Tr 5.332.

paraventure, per aventure, paraunter, peraventure, per aventure, peraunter, perauntre *adv.* perhaps II.190, III.893, BD 556, Rom B 5192; by chance IV.234, Tr 2.921.

parcel *n.* portion V.852, X.1006, Pity 106.

parde(e), pardieux *interj.* by God! indeed! I.563, BD 721, Tr 1.197.

pardoun *n.* forgiveness, pardon VI.917, VII.1773; indulgence VI.906; *pl.* **pardoun** indulgences I.687, VI.920.

parfay, parfey *interj.* by my faith! indeed! I.3681, II.110, HF 938.

parfit(e), perfit *adj.* perfect, complete I.72, VII.152, Tr 1.104.

parfitly, parfitely, perfitly *adv.* perfectly, completely III.111, IV.690, Rom A 771, Astr Pro 18.

parfourne(n), parformen, perfourne, perfourme, performe(n) *v.* perform, carry out VII.1066, X.782, Bo 3.pr3.18, Bo 4.pr3.33, Tr 3.417, LGW 2457, Astr Pro 22; **p. up** complete III.2261; *2 pr. sg.* **parfournest** express VII.607; *3 pr. sg.* **parfourneth** X.736, **performeth** Bo 4.pr2.86; *imp. sg.* **perfourme out** carry out Tr 3.417; *pt. sg.* **parfourned** IV.2052; *pp.* **parfourned** carried out VI.151, expressed VII.456, **performed** LGW 2138, **perfourmed** Rom A 1178; completed III.2104, IV.1795; *vbl. n.* **parfournynge** doing X.807.

parlement *n.* parliament, assembly I.3076, Tr 4.143; debate I.2970; decision I.1306.

part(e) *n.* (1) part, portion I.1178, I.3006, PF 397; **the moore p.** the majority VII.1206, HF 336; **for the moore p.** for the most part, mostly Tr 1.925, Tr 3.306; **an hondred (twenty) thousand p.** by a hundred (twenty) thousand times III.2062, V.553; (2) party, side I.2446, I.2582, Tr 2.1328; **on every p.** on every side I.2185; **on (for) my (thi) p.** so far as I am (you are) concerned Tr 4.181, Tr 4.425, LGW 912; (3) **have p. on (of)** take possession of I.2792, VII.218.

parte(n) *v.* (1) divide, share III.1534, IV.1630, Tr 1.589; (2) separate, leave (one another) I.4362; depart, leave VI.649, Tr 1.5; *2 pr. sg.* **partest** leave VI.752; *3 pr. sg.* **parteth** departs LGW F 359; *pr. pl.* **parte** I.4362; *pt. pl.* **parted** Rom C 7347; *prp. (as adj.)* **partyng felawes** partners X.637; *pp.* **parted** divided III.1967, X.8; departed, taken away LGW 1110; *vbl. n.* **partyng** departure Tr 3.1528.

party, parti(e) *n.* part I.3008, II.17, Tr 2.394; partisan I.2657; faction, party (in a dispute) PF 496, LGW G 325; *pl.* **parties** parts Bo 3.m9.17, factions VII.1014.

pas, paas *n.* (1) step Tr 3.281; (2) pace, speed I.2901; walk (of a horse) I.825, VIII.575; **a p. at** a walk, slowly I.2217, I.2897, Tr 2.627; apace, quickly HF 1051, Tr 4.465; **a ful esy p.** very slowly LGW F 284; **a (ful) good p.** rapidly Tr 5.604, LGW 802; **a softe p.** quietly I.3760, at a slow gait II.399; **a sturdy p.** briskly III.2162; **esily a p., an esy p.** at an easy pace V.388, Tr 2.620, LGW G 200; **a sory p., sorwfully a p.** sadly, at a sad (slow) pace I.3741, Tr 5.61; (3) course Tr 2.1349; passage, difficult situation VII.1445; (4) *(pl.)* pace (unit of measurement, about a yard) Mars 121; *pl.* **paas** steps II.306, paces (yards) Bo 1.pr4.241; **pas** paces (yards) I.1890.

passe(n), pace *v.* (1) go, proceed I.2574; **pass for** Tr 1.371; leave aside VII.443, Tr 2.1595; (2) depart, pass by I.3578; (3) surpass IV.1417, VIII.857; (4) surpass, excel I.3089, LGW F 162; *3 pr. sg.* **passeth** proceeds, goes on I.1033; **passith** passes over, crosses Astr 2.17.8; *pr. sg.* **passe(n)** IV.117, VII.9, **pace** Tr 5.1791; *pr. subj. sg.* **passe** Tr 4.1592; *pr. subj. pl.* **passe** BD 41, **pace** Rom B 4922; *imp. sg.* **passe over** let it be VI.303; *pt. sg.* **passed(e)** surpassed I.448, LGW 1530; went Tr 2.554; **paste** went by Tr 2.658; *pt. pl.* **passeden** Bo 1.pr1.77; *prp.* **passyng(e)** going I.2848, surpassing I.2885, (as *adj.*) exceeding IV.1225, outstanding VIII.614; *pp.* **(y)passed** I.464, IV.1892, **past** VII.2289.

passioun, passion *n.* (1) passion, suffering I.3478, I.4327, Tr 3.1040; martyrdom VIII.26; (2) feeling, sensation Bo 5.pr5.6, emotion II.1138, Tr 4.705; *pl.* **passiouns** Bo 1.m7.18, **passiones** Tr 4.468.

pasture *n.* feeding place VII.1933, VII.3185; pasture land IV.1313.

Pater-noster *n.* the Lord's Prayer I.3485, I.3638.

pece *n.* piece PF 149; particular part Bo 5.pr4.162; *pl.* **peces** HF 1187, **pieces** VII.136, Tr 1.833.

pecock, pekok *n.* peacock I.104, I.3926; Tr 1.210.

peyn(e), payn(e) *n.* (1) punishment, penalty III.1314, VII.1749, Bo 1.m5.36, Rom B 2411, Rom B 4930; **up p. of** on the penalty of I.1707, I.2543, Tr 1.674, Tr 3.1502; **the p.** torture I.1133; (2) pain I.1297, I.1382, BD 587; (3) effort V.509; **don (one's) p.** devote (one's) efforts, work diligently V.730, IX.330, Tr 2.475; **wroghten al hir p.** devoted all their efforts Tr 1.63; *pl.* **peynes** pains I.1338, punishments X.229; **paynes** Rom A 1505.

peyne(n), payne *v.* (1) punish, inflict pain X.213; harm, hurt VII.2604; (2) *(reflx.)* endeavor, make an effort X.944, Tr 1.989, Rom C 7510; *2 pr. sg.* **peynest** the HF 627; *3 pr. sg.* **peyneth** II.320, **payneth** PF 339; *pr. pl.* **peynen** LGW 636; *imp. sg.* **peyne** PF 662; *pt. sg.* **peyned** I.139; *pp.* **peyned** tortured, punished X.273.

peynte(n) *v.* (1) paint I.2087, VI.312, BD 259; (2) adorn X.610, Tr 2.262; **p. my wordes** use circumlocutions HF 246; (3) disguise IV.2062; *pr. pl.* **peynte** V.725; *pt. sg.* **peynted** V.560, **peyntede** III.692; *pp.* **peynted** I.1934, (as *adj.*) **paynted** Tr 2.424, **peynt** Rom A 1436; *vbl. n.* **peyntyng** portrait Rom A 210, Rom A 289.

peyre, pair(e) *n.* pair X.555; set I.159, III.1741; **many a p.** a great many Rom A 1386; **hundred p.** hundreds Rom A 66; as *pl.* **peyre** pairs PF 238.

peler *see* pyler.

penaunce, penance *n.* (1) penance (for sin) I.223, LGW F 491; (2) misery, suffering I.1315, II.286, Anel 347; **doon p.** inflict suffering VIII.530; *pl.* **penaunces** miseries Tr 1.201, penances X.1052.

peny *n.* penny (one-twelfth of a shilling) I.4119, III.1575; **masse p.** money offered for the singing of a Mass III.1749; *pl.* **pens** VI.376, **penyes** Rom A 189.

peple, puple, pepil, people *n.* people I.706, I.962, V.198, HF 1283, Rom A 278; nation II.489, IV.995; army Tr 1.73; *gen.* **peples** IV.412, **peoples** Tr 3.584; *pl.* **peples** people Bo 2.m6.20, **peoples** Tr 3.1747.

per(e), peer(e) *n.* peer, equal I.4026, Tr 5.1803, Purse 11, Rom A 1300.

peraventure, per aventure, peraunter, perauntre *see* **paraventure.**

perce(n) *v.* pierce IV.1204, V.237, Bo 4.m3.45; pierce with the eye, look straight into PF 331; *3 pr. sg.* **perseth** PF 331; *pr. pl.* **percen** VIII.911; *pt. sg.* **perced(e)** VII.555, Bo 1.pr1.18; *pp.* **perced** I.2; *vbl. n.* **percynge** VII.862.

perdurable *adj.* eternal VII.1509, X.124, Bo 2.m3.21; *pl.* **perdurables** X.811.

perdurably, perdurablely *adv.* eternally Bo 3.pr6.31, Bo 3.pr11.127, Bo 3.pr11.193, Bo 5.pr4.166.

perfit *see* **parfit(e).**

perfitly *see* **parfitly.**

perfourne, perfourme, performe *see* **parfourne(n).**

perisse, perise, perysshe *v.* perish X.75, Bo 2.pr7.9, Bo 4.m4.14; *3 pr. sg.* **peryssheth** Bo 3.pr11.73; *pr. subj. pl.* **perisse** VI.99; *pp.* **perissed** killed X.579.

perle *n.* pearl LGW F 221; *pl.* **perles** I.2161, **peerles** VII.2468, **peerlis** Bo 3.m8.13.

perry(e), perre(e) *n.* precious stones, jewels I.2936, III.344, HF 124, HF 1393.

perseth *see* **perce(n).**

persevere *v.* continue, persevere III.148, VII.1264; *3 pr. sg.* **persevereth** lasts VI.497; *imp. sg.* **persevere** Tr 1.958; *vbl. n.* **perseverynge** constancy VIII.117.

persone, persoun(e) *n.*[1] person I.521, III.1313, Rom B 3202; **propre p.** own self VII.985, VII.1026; body X.591; *pl.* **persones** VII.1165.

person, persoun *n.*[2] parson I.478, I.702.

pes, pees *n.* (1) peace I.532, I.1447, BD 615; (2) silence, quiet II.228; **hoold** (one's) **p.** be quiet I.2668, VI.462, PF 572; (as *imp.*) hush, be quiet II.836, III.850, Tr 1.753.

Peter *interj.* by Saint Peter! III.446, III.1332, HF 1034.

philosophie *n.* (1) learning I.645, I.4050; philosophy I.295, II.1188, HF 857; (2) alchemy VIII.1058, VIII.1373.

philosophre, philosofre *n.* (1) philosopher, learned writer II.25, VI.620; **the p.** Aristotle X.658, LGW F 381; (2) astrologer II.310; magician V.1561; alchemist VIII.1122; *gen.* **philosophres** VIII.862; *pl.* **philosophres** VIII.113.

phisik *n.* science of medicine X.913; medicine, remedy I.411, I.443, Tr 2.1038.

pye *n.* magpie I.3950, III.456, PF 345; gossip, chatterbox Tr 3.527; *pl.* **pyes** magpies V.650; gossips, chatterboxes HF 703.

pieces *see* **pece.**

piete(e) *n.* (1) tenderness, pity Tr 4.246, Tr 5.1598; (2) piety, regard for duty Tr 3.1033.

pietous, pitous *adj.* pitiful Tr 3.1444, Tr 5.451; compassionate LGW 2582.

pike *v.* pick out, pluck Tr 2.1274; *3 pr. sg.* **pyketh** makes (himself) neat IV.2011; *pp.* **(y)pyked** picked out III.44a, sorted out VIII.941, robbed LGW 2467.

pile *v.* rob, plunder III.1362; *pr. pl.* **pilen** X.767; *pt. sg.*

piled LGW 1262; *pp.* (as *adj.*) **piled** bald (deprived of hair) I.3935, I.4306; thin, scanty I.627.

pyler, pileer, peler *n.* pillar I.1993, I.2466, BD 739; (as *adj.*) supporting (a vine) PF 177 (*see note*); *pl.* **pilers** VII.2084.

pilours *n. pl.* scavengers I.1007; thieves X.769.

pilwe, pilowe *n.* pillow IV.2004, BD 254, Tr 5.224; *pl.* **pilwes** Tr 3.444.

pyne *n.* pain I.1324, I.2382, HF 147; harm PF 335; misery, suffering II.1080, Tr 2.676.

pyne(n) *v.* torture, inflict pain I.1746, Rom B 3511; *3 pr. sg.* **pyneth** grieves Anel 205; punishes X.85; *pp.* **pyned** VII.3059.

pype(n) *v.* pipe, play the pipe, whistle I.3876, I.3927, HF 1220; **p. in an ivy leef** go whistle (in vain) I.1838 (see note), Tr 5.1433; *pp.* **piped** squeaked HF 785; *prp.* (as *adj.*) **pipyng** whistling, hissing I.3379.

pit *see* **putte(n).**

pitaunce *n.* gift, alms I.224, Rom C 7084; *pl.* **pitaunces** Rom C 7075.

pite(e), pittee *n.* pity I.920, BD 97, Mars 135; grief I.2833, II.292.

pith(e) *n.* (1) vigor III.475, Rom A 401; (2) essential part, main point Rom C 7172.

pitous(e) *adj.* (1) merciful, compassionate I.143, I.953, Tr 4.949; (2) pitiful, sorrowful I.955, I.1919, BD 84; pious X.1039.

pitously, pitouslich *adv.* (1) mercifully, compassionately Tr 5.1424; (2) piteously, sorrowfully I.949, I.1117, BD 711; pitifully Tr 5.313.

play- *see* **pley-.**

planten *v.* plant Rom C 6292; *2 pr. sg.* **plawntest** Bo 4.pr7.93; *imp. sg.* **plaunte** Tr 1.964; *pp.* **planted** III.764, **plaunted** Bo 1.pr4.254, **iplauntyd** Bo 3.pr2.23.

plat, platte *adj.* flat, blunt I.1845; blunt side of a sword V.164, (as *n.*) V.162.

plat *adv.* flat VII.675; flatly, clearly II.886, VI.648, Tr 1.681.

plate *n.* plate armor I.2121, VII.865, Form Age 49; plate of metal X.433, Astr 1.3.2; *pl.* **paire plates** set of plate armor I.2121.

platly *adv.* flatly, directly X.485, X.1022; bluntly Tr 3.786.

plaunte, plante *n.* plant V.1032, Tr 4.767; cutting III.763.

plede, pledynge(s), pletynge *see* **plete(n).**

pley(e), play *n.* (1) amusement VI.627, BD 50, PF 193; **do yow p.** amuse you Tr 2.121; (2) game IV.10; funeral game I.2964, Tr 5.1499; (3) dramatic performance III.558; (4) jest, joke III.1548; **in p.** in jest, jokingly I.1125, I.4355, IV.1030; playfully LGW 1698; (5) (*pl.*) tricks Rom B 4290; (6) player, worker (of deceptions) BD 648; *pl.* **pleyes** games Tr 5.304, dramatic performances III.558, **playes** tricks BD 570.

pleye(n), playe(n), play *v.* (1) play, amuse oneself II.558, Scog 35, Rom A 344; (*reflx.*) I.1127, I.3660, BD 239; jest, be playful I.758, VII.1963; (2) play amorously, flirt I.3273; have sexual intercourse IV.1841, Rom B 4827; (3) play (musical instrument or game) I.236, Tr 4.460; (4) act (a part), perform I.3384, V.219; (5) act, deal with (someone) III.2074, VI.654, Tr 2.462; work (tricks) V.1141; *2 pr. sg.* **pleyestow** Bo 3.pr12.154; *3 pr. sg.* **pleyeth** I.3306; *pr. pl.* **pleye(n)** I.2959, V.219; *imp. sg.* **pley** I.4198;

pt. sg. **pleyde** I.4068, **pleyed** Rom B 3234; *pt. pl.* **pleyde** I.3858; *prp.* **pleyynge** VI.608 (as *adj.*) playful Tr 1.280; *pp.* **pleyd** BD 668, **played** Tr 2.1240; *vbl. n.* **pleyyng(e)** I.1061, IV.1854, **pleynge** BD 605, **plaiyng(e)** Rom A 105, Rom A 1404.

pleyn(e), playne *v.* (1) lament I.1320, II.1067, Rom A 1472; (2) complain III.387, V.776, Tr 1.409; *(reflx.)* III.336, Anel 237; **p. (up)on** make complaint, or bring an accusation, against V.1355, VI.167, Tr 3.1020; *2 pr. sg.* **pleynest** Bo 2.pr2.33, (with *pro.*) **pleynestow** Bo 2.pr2.27; *3 pr. sg.* **pleyneth** I.4114; *pr. pl.* **pleyne(n)** I.1251, IV.97; *pr. pl. subj.* **pleyne** IV.97; *imp.* **pleyne** Bo 2.pr8.45 *(sg.)*, LGW G 222 *(pl.)*; *1 & 3 pt. sg.* **pleyned** III.390; *2 pt. sg.* **pleynedest** Bo 4.pr4.158; *pp.* **(y)pleyned** Tr 4.1688; *vbl. n.* **pleynynge** lament X.84, BD 599; *pl.* **pleynynges** Bo 2.pr2.5.

pleyn *adj.* [1] full, complete I.337, I.2461, IV.926; open (battle) I.988.

pleyn(e), playn *adj.* [2] (1) clear I.315, I.1487, VIII.284; **p. sentence** clear meaning PF 126; (as *n.*) **short and p.** brief, simple account I.1091, IV.577; (2) unadorned, simple V.720, VII.2091; sincere VI.50, Anel 87, Anel 116; smooth PF 180, Rom A 860; (3) open PF 528, Tr 2.1560.

pleyn, playn *adv.* [1] (1) clearly I.790, Tr 4.890; entirely I.327; closely, tightly Rom B 2269.

pleyn *adv.* [2] fully I.327, I.1464.

pleynly, pleynliche *adv.* [1] plainly, simply I.727, I.1209, Tr 2.1623.

pleynly *adv.* [2] fully I.1733, II.894, Tr 2.272.

pleynt(e) *n.* complaint, lament II.66, V.1029, Tr 1.408; *pl.* **pleintes** II.1068.

plente(e) *n.* plenty, abundance II.443, IV.264, Rom A 1083; **ful greet p.** in great abundance VI.811, Rom A 1083.

plentevous, plentyvous *adj.* plentiful I.344, Bo 1.pr1.57, Bo 1.m2.24.

plentevously, plentyvously *adv.* abundantly Bo 1.pr5.56, Bo 2.pr2.78, Bo 4.pr6.174.

plesaunce, plesance, pleasaunce *n.* (1) pleasure, amusement, delight I.1925, I.2485, BD 704, Ven 1; cause of pleasure Anel 248, Mars 238; **doon** (someone's) **p.** give pleasure to, please (someone) I.1571, III.408, III.1256, PF 676; (2) desire IV.501, PF 389; will II.762; favor Tr 5.314; **throgh p.** willingly BD 767; **doon** (someone's) **p.** do as (someone) wishes IV.658, VII.2866; *pl.* **plesaunces** pleasures Tr 4.1099.

plesaunt, plesant(e), pleasant *adj.* pleasing, agreeable I.138, IV.991, VII.1152, Rom B 4745.

plese(n), please *v.* please I.610, HF 90, Rom A 315; *3 pr. sg.* **plesith** Rom B 5271; *pr. pl.* **plesen** VII.3327; *pr. subj. pl.* **plese** IV.1680; *imp. sg.* **please** Rom B 2704; *pt. sg.* **plesed(e)** II.788, Rom B 1816; *prp.* **plesyng** Rom C 6865; *pp.* **(y)plesed** I.2446, III.930; *vbl. n. pl.* **plesynges** pleasures II.711.

plete(n), plede *v.* plead, sue at law VII.1369, Tr 2.1468; dispute, reason Bo 2.pr2.1; *imp. sg.* **pleet** Bo 2.pr2.7; *vbl. n.* **pledynge** plea X.166, dispute, litigation BD 615, **pletynge** argument, disputation PF 495; *pl.* **pledynges** law suits Bo 3.pr3.64.

plighte *1 pr. sg.* (with **trouthe**) pledge (one's word) V.1537, VII.198; *imp. sg.* **plight** III.1009; *pt. sg.* **plighte** III.1051; *pt. pl.* **plighten** V.1328; *pp.* **(y)plight** VI.702, Tr 3.782.

plighte *1 & 3 pt. sg.* pulled II.15, Tr 2.1120, LGW 2466; pulled out Rom B 1745; *pp.* **plyght** pulled out, plucked III.790.

plit(e) *n.* plight, condition IV.2335, VIII.952; position Tr 2.74.

plogh, plough *n.* plow I.3159, VII.288; (as modifier) **p. harneys** ploughing equipment I.3762.

plowngen, ploungen *v.* plunge Bo 3.pr2.42, Bo 3.m8.22; *pp.* **(i)ploungid** Bo 1.pr1.78, Bo 4.m6.15, **yplounged** Bo 3.pr11.112.

poynaunt, poignaunt, pugnaunt *adj.* spicy I.352, VII.2834; piercing X.130, Rom B 1879, Rom B 3813.

poynt *n.* (1) punctuation mark, period VIII.1480; (2) bit, small amount Tr 3.1509; (3) Astr 2.16.6; (4) point in space or time I.114, BD 660; (5) main point, subject PF 372; (6) item, detail VIII.344; **at poynt-devys** in every detail, to perfection I.3689, V.560, HF 917; **every p.** in detail VII.3022; **from p. to p.** from beginning to end, in every particular IV.577, PF 461; (7) state, condition I.200, X.921, Bo 2.pr4.25, Rom A 373; **in (o) p. to** (with *inf.*) about to, on the point of II.331, II.910, Tr 4.1153; (8) point (of a spear, *etc.*) I.114; (9) *(pl.)* laces, ties I.3322, Rom B 2263; **pointz** I.2971, **pointes** VIII.344, **poynts** LGW G 320.

poynte *v.* punctuate Rom B 2157; describe, specify Tr 3.497; *pr. pl.* **poynten** stab Rom A 1058; *pp.* **poynted** provided with points Tr 2.1034, Rom A 944.

pool *n.* pole *(astro.)* Bo 4.m5.4, Astr 1.18.18; *pl.* **poles** Astr 1.17.44.

popynjay *see* **papejay.**

porcioun *n.* share, portion Bo 3.pr5.22; part Astr 2.4.62; amount, quantity VII.56.

port *n.* (1) bearing, manner I.69, I.138, BD 834.

portreye, purtreye *v.* draw I.96, BD 783; depict ABC 81; *pt. sg.* **purtreyed** IV.1600; *prp.* **purtraynge** depicting in the mind Tr 5.716; *pp.* **portraied** adorned with drawings Rom A 140, Rom A 1077; **yportreied** Rom A 897; *vbl. n.* **portreyynge** portraiture I.1918.

portreiture, portrayture *n.* painting I.1968, Rom A 172; *pl.* **portreitures** I.1915, **portraitures** Rom A 141.

pose *1 pr. sg.* posit, suppose for the sake of argument I.1162, Tr 3.310, Tr 3.571.

poure, powren *v.* pore, gaze intently I.185, III.295, HF 1121; peep III.1738, IV.2112; *pr. pl.* **pouren** VIII.670; *pp.* **poured** gazed steadily Tr 1.299.

poure, pover(e), povre, poore, pore *adj.* poor I.225, III.1923, VII.586, HF 1552, LGW F 388, Rom A 466; (as *n.*) the poor, poor people X.373, X.461; *super.* **povrest** IV.205, **povereste** VI.449.

pray- *see* **prey-.**

pray(e), prey(e) *n.* prey I.2015, III.1376, III.1455, Tr 1.201; *pl.* **preyes** III.1472.

preche(n) *v.* preach I.481, I.712, II.1177; *2 pr. sg.* **prechest** III.247; (with *pro.*) **prechestow** III.366; *3 pr. sg.* **precheth** VII.1044; *pr. pl.* **preche(n)** III.436, V.824; *imp. pl.* **precheth** IV.12; *pt. sg.* **preched** Rom C 6679; *pp.* **preched** III.1714; *vbl. n.* **prechyng** VI.401.

prechour *n.* preacher III.165; *pl.* **prechoures** Rom B 5769; **Freres Preachours** Dominican friars Rom C 7456.

precious(e), precius *adj.* (1) precious III.338, X.591; (2) fastidious, fussy III.148; prudish IV.1962.

predicacioun *n.* sermon, preaching III.2109, VI.345.

pref, preef *see* **preve** *n.*

preye(n), praye(n), prey, pray *v.* pray, beseech, plead I.301, II.258, II.1146, III.184, VII.270, Rom B 5244; *2 pr. sg.* **prayest** X.1043; *3 pr. sg.* **preyeth** II.866, **prayeth** Rom A 33; *pr. pl.* **preye(n)** I.1260, III.1902, **praye(n)** HF 215, HF 1663, **pray** Rom C 6053; *pr. subj.* **preye** III.358 *(sg.)*, X.1084 *(pl.)*; *imp. sg.* **preye** V.1066, **pray** Truth 26; *imp. pl.* **prey(e)** V.1066, VII. 687, **preyeth** X.526, **prayeth** III.1663; *1 & 3 pt. sg.* **preyde** II.391, **preyed(e)** IV.1612, VI.251, **prayed(e)** BD 131, BD 771; *2 pt. sg.* **preydest** Tr 1.917, **preyedest** Bo 4.pr4.163; *pt. pl.* **preyeden** III.895, **preyden** I.811, **prayed** HF 1815, **prayeden** Bo 3.pr12.188; *prp.* **preyynge** IV.977; *pp.* **preyed** I.2108, **(y)prayed** IV.269, LGW 2533; *vbl. n.* **preyinge** Tr 1.571, **praiyng** Rom A 1484.

preyer(e), preier(e), prayer(e) *n.* prayer I.1204, III.1489, X.894, HF 107, Tr 2.453, Tr 4.111; *pl.* **preyeres** III.1884, **preieris** Bo 5.pr3.260, **prayeres** III.865, **praiers** Astr Pro 7, **preiers** Bo 2.m2.10.

preyse(n) *v.* (1) praise III.294, HF 627, Tr 3.1662; (2) appraise, value Bo 3.pr11.6, Rom A 1115; *inf.* **to preyse(n)** to be praised VII.1516, Rom A 70; *1 pr. sg.* **prayse** Rom B 2430; *3 pr. sg.* **preyseth** IV.1854; *pr. pl.* **preyse(n)** IV.935, Tr 2.95; *pr. subj. sg.* **preyse** IV.1546; *pt. pl.* **preised** VI.113; *pp.* **(y)preised** Tr 2.189; *vbl. n.* **preysing(e)** praise X.494, glory X.949; *pl.* **preisynges** praises X.454.

pres, prees *n.* (1) crowd, throng II.393, II.646, HF 1358, Tr 1.173; (2) difficulties VII.2137; (3) **bring in p.** undertake Tr 2.1649; **putte hem in p.** make an effort Form Age 33; **put hir (him) forth in p.** put her (himself) forward PF 603, Scog 40.

prescience *n.* foreknowledge I.1313, IV.659, Tr 4.987.

presse *n.* (1) cupboard, linen press I.3212; **lye (leye) on p.** set aside Tr 1.559, Fort 52; (2) casting mold I.263; curler I.81.

presse(n), presen, preesen *v.* (1) push forward Tr 1.446, Tr 2.1341, Tr 5.1011, Pity 19, Rom B 3072; (2) press down Bo 1.m6.13, LGW 1787; oppress Bo 4.pr5.22; (3) exert pressure, urge Tr 2.693; entreat III.520; *3 pr. sg.* **preseth** LGW 642, **preesseth** I.2530, **presseth** Bo 3.pr11.136; *pr. pl.* **pressen** Bo 4.pr5.22; *imp. sg.* **prese** Rom B 2899; *imp. pl.* **preesse** entreat III.520; *pt. sg.* **pressed** HF 1590; *pp.* **pressyd** Bo 1.m2.29; *vbl. n.* **presyng on** entreating Rom B 6436.

prest, preest *n.* priest I.501, II.1166, Bo 4.m7.12; *gen.* **preestes** VIII.1023 *(sg.)*, II.377 *(pl.)*; *pl.* **prestes** Tr 5.365, **preestes** I.164, **preestis** Bo 1.pr4.236.

prest(e) *adj.* ready, prompt PF 307; swift, quick Tr 2.785, Tr 4.661.

preve, preeve, pref, preef, proeve *n.* proof III.2272, LGW G 528, Bo 5.pr4.73; test IV.787, VIII.968; **armes p.** deeds of combat Tr 1.470; experience LGW F 28; **with yvel p.** bad luck to you III.247; *pl.* **proeves** Bo 3.pr12.182.

preve, preeve, proeve(n), prove(n) *v.* (1) test IV.699, IV.1330, Bo 3.pr10.47, Bo 4.pr2.245, Rom B 5223; (2) prove, demonstrate I.485, VI.169, HF 808, HF 1347; (3) find out, experience LGW G 9; (4) succeed VIII.1212; turn out IV.1000, IV.2425, VIII.645; (5) reprove VII.1437; *3 pr. sg.* **preeveth** IV.1155, **preveth** IV.2238, **proeveth** Bo 3.pr10.47, **prooeveth** Bo 2.m1.15, **proveth** V.455; *pr. pl.* **preve** Tr 4.969; *pr. subj. sg.* **preeve** IV.1152; *imp. sg.* **preeve** III.2057; *1 & 3 pt. sg.* **proved** I.547; *2 pt. sg.* **proved-**

est Bo 3.pr12.175; *pt. pl.* **preved** IV.2283; *pp.* **(y)preved** I.485, VII.1114, **preeved** I.3001, **(i)pro-evid** Bo 3.pr10.17, Bo 5.pr6.45, **proved** Bo 2.pr4.168; *vbl. n.* **prevyng** proof Rom C 7541.

prevely *see* **pryvely.**

prye(n) *v.* peer, gaze I.3458, IV.2112, Tr 2.404.

priken, prikke *v.* (1) prick VII.1326, Rom B 1836; (2) trouble, harass Tr 4.633; cause pain, ache III.1594; (3) spur, ride rapidly I.2678, VII.754; stab, pierce I.4231; (4) incite, urge I.11, I.1043, PF 389; *1 pr. sg.* **prike** PF 389; *3 pr. sg.* **priketh** III.656, **prikketh** Bo 3.pr9.103, **prikkith** Rom B 1925; *pr. subj.* **prike** VII.811 *(sg.)*, IV.1038 *(pl.)*; *imp. sg.* **prik(e)** LGW 1213, Rom B 2314; *pt. sg.* **pryked** VII.774, **prighte** V.418; *prp.* **prikyng** VII.837; *pp.* **priked** VIII.561; *vbl. n.* **prikyng(e)** I.2599, VII.775; *pl.* **prikkynges** prickings Bo 1.pr1.54.

prikke, pricke *n.* (1) point of a weapon I.2606; stinger X.468; (2) goad, pricking Bo 3.pr5.30; (3) pinpoint, dot HF 907, Astr 2.5.18, Astr 2.7.4; (4) **to that p.** (come, bring) to that point II.119, II.1029; (5) bull's eye Bo 3.pr11.220 (see note); *pl.* **prykkes** Bo 3.m7.2; **prickes** Astr 2.5.22.

pryme *n.* (1) the canonical hour (6 A.M.) VI.662; (2) the hours from six to nine in the morning IV.1857, V.73, Tr 5.15; (3) the beginning of prime, about 6 A.M. Tr 5.15; first hour, beginning Tr 1.157; (4) about 9 A.M. I.2189, I.2576, Tr 2.992; **fully p., p. large** 9 A.M. I.2576, V.360, VII.825; **half-wey p.** about 7:30 A.M. I.3906.

principles *n. pl.* dominant qualities, natural disposition V.487, Bo 3.m11.41.

prys *n.* (1) price, value I.815, III.523, Bo 1.pr4.77; **of p.** valuable, excellent VII.897, Rom A 1134; (2) prize, reward Bo 4.m7.61, LGW 2534; **ought of p. and ryght** rightly deserves Rom A 47; **baar (bereth) the (our) p.** took (takes) the (our) prize I.237, LGW F 298; (3) praise III.1152, IV.1026, Tr 1.375; reputation, honor I.67, I.2241.

prise(n) *v.* appraise, estimate Bo 1.pr4.164; praise Rom B 4960; **to pryse** to be praised Rom A 887.

pryve(e), privy *adj.* (1) secret I.2460, III.620; hidden BD 382; (2) private, confidential II.204, IV.192; discreet, secretive I.3201, Tr 3.921; guiltily secretive HF 285; **p. membres** private parts, sexual members X.427.

pryvee, privy *adv.* **p. and (or) apert** secretly or publicly, in all circumstances III.1114, V.531, HF 717; **loud or p.** aloud or in secret, in all circumstances HF 767, HF 810.

pryvely, pryvyly, priveliche, prevely *adv.* secretly, discreetly I.609, I.1222, HF 223, Tr 4.1601, Anel 138, LGW 733; alone VII.92.

pryvete(e), privite *n.* (1) privacy, secrecy VII.1194, Tr 3.283; (2) secret I.3164, I.3454; **in p.** secretly I.3493, I.3623; secret counsel, private affairs I.1411, I.3603, Rom B 5526; (3) hidden part Tr 2.1397, Tr 4.1111; private parts, sexual members VII.2715; *pl.* **pryvetees** hidden parts Bo 2.pr6.43.

procede(n) *v.* proceed IV.2020, VII.1341, Tr 3.455; come forth, originate VIII.328, Scog 6; *3 pr. sg.* **procedeth** VII.1873; *pr. pl.* **procede(n)** Tr 4.147, Tr 5.370; *pr. subj. sg.* **procede** take legal action against Scog 30; *prp.* **procedinge** proceeding Bo 5.pr1.93; *pp.* **proceded** Bo 1.pr6.43.

proces, processe *n.* (1) course of events VII.2321; ordinary course V.1345; business, undertaking Tr 2.485; (2) story, discourse V.658, HF 251, Tr 2.424; argument, case Tr 2.1615; (3) passage (of time) VII.1475, BD 1331; **by (in) p.** in time, at length, eventually I.2967, V.829, PF 430.

proeve(s) *see* **preve** *n.*

proeve(n), prove(n) *see* **preve** *v.*

professioun *n.* religious vows, religious order III.1925, III.2135, VII.155, Rom B 4910.

profit(e) *n.* (1) profit, advantage III.214, VII.1247; **do (one's) p.** work for (one's) advantage VII.1588, VII.1592; good VII.1688; **commune p.** common good, welfare of the state IV.431, IV.1194, PF 47; **syngular p.** personal pleasure HF 310; (2) profit, income I.249, III.1344.

profre(n) *v.* offer VIII.1123, Anel 331; *2 pr. sg.* (with *pro.*) **profrestow** Tr 3.1461; *3 pr. sg.* **profreth** I.1415, **profereth** LGW F 405; *pr. pl.* **profre** VIII.489, **profer** Rom B 3002; *pr. subj. sg.* **profre** VIII.489; *pt. sg.* **profred** VIII.1288, *(reflx.)* pressed his suit I.3289; *prp.* **proferyng** Rom B 1981; *pp.* **profred** IV.152.

progressiouns, progressions *n. pl.* natural processes I.3013, Bo 4.pr6.43, Bo 4.pr6.152.

propre *adj.* (1) own I.540, I.581; **owene p.** very own VII.985, X.1021; individual, peculiar I.3037, III.103, Tr 4.1152; *(as n.)* **in p.** as one's own Bo 2.pr2.12; (2) correct VI.417; comely, well-formed I.3345, I.3972; excellent HF 726; complete LGW G 259; **of p. kynde** by nature, naturally V.610, V.619, HF 43.

proprely, properly *adv.* (1) particularly X.485; (2) correctly, appropriately I.729, I.1459, VII.1239; handsomely I.3320; naturally III.1191.

proprete(e), propertee, propirte *n.* (1) individual property, possessions Tr 4.392, Rom C 6594; (2) nature, essential quality VII.1174; property, characteristic X.640, Astr 1.21.56; *pl.* qualities **propretes** Bo 3.m11.17, **propirtees** Astr 1.10.7.

provost *n.* magistrate VII.616, VII.629; prefect Bo 1.pr4.89.

prow *n.* profit, benefit, advantage VI.300, VII.408, HF 579.

prowesse, pruesse *n.* (1) bravery, excellence as a warrior Rom B 4519; skill Rom A 261; (2) excellence of character III.1129, Bo 4.pr3.64.

publisschen *v.* publish, make known Bo 2.pr7.45; *pr. pl. (reflx.)* **publysschen hem** propagate themselves Bo 3.pr11.123; *pp.* **publysschid** Bo 2.pr7.82, **publysshed** Tr 5.1095; **publiced** IV.415.

pugnaunt *see* **poynaunt.**

pulle(n) *v.* (1) pluck IX.304, Tr 5.1546, Rom A 1667; skin Rom C 6820; rob, swindle I.652 (see note), Rom C 5984; (2) pull IV.2353, Tr 1.210; *pr. pl.* **pulle(n)** LGW 2308, Rom C 6820; *imp. sg.* **pulle** Tr 1.965; *pt. sg.* **pulled(e)** I.1598, Rom B 3076; *pp.* **(y)pulled** I.177, I.3245; *vbl. n.* **pullyng** pulling out Rom B 1746.

punysse, punyce, punyssche(n), punysche, punyshe, punysshe(n) *v.* punish VII.1441, Bo 1.pr4.99, Bo 1.m5.37, Bo 4.pr6.316, Bo 4.pr7.11, Tr 5.1707, Rom C 6445, Rom C 7233; *3 pr. sg.* **punyssheth** Bo 1.m5.37, **punysseth** Bo 4.pr7.106; *pp.* **(y)punysshed** I.657, VII. 1419, **punysched** Bo 4.pr4.90, **punyschid** Bo 4.pr4.117, **punysschid** Bo 4.pr4.159; *vbl. n.* **punyssynge** punishment VII.1432, **punysshynge** III.1304, **punysschynge** Bo 4.pr1.22.

puple *see* **peple.**

purchace(n), purchase(n) *v.* purchase, acquire I.608, VIII.1405, Rom B 3481, Rom C 6607; bring about, provide VII.1690; *pr. pl.* **purchasen** bring about, provide VII.1680; *pr. subj. sg.* **God purchace** may God provide II.873; *imp. pl.* **yow purchace** provide yourself Tr 2.1125; *pt. sg.* **purchased** brought about BD 1122; *pp.* **purchaced** brought about VII.1690; *vbl. n.* **purchasyng(e)** acquisition Bo 4.pr7.69, legal conveyance of property I.320, acquisition of profits III.1449.

purchas, purchace *n.* acquisition, gain III.1530; income I.256, Rom C 6838.

pure *adj.* (1) pure, chaste VIII.48, X.1046, BD 250; (2) very, sheer I.1279, BD 490, Tr 4.1620; **the p. deth** Death itself BD 583; *super.* **purest** Bo 3.m9.22.

pure *adv.* purely, perfectly BD 942, BD 959, BD 1010.

purely *adv.* simply, exclusively BD 5, HF 39; wholly, unreservedly BD 843, Rom B 5656.

purge *v.* discharge, cleanse of bodily wastes III.134, VII.573; cleanse VIII.181; *pr. pl.* **purgen** X.428; *pr. subj. pl.* **purge yow** take a laxative VII.2947; *prp.* **purgynge** cleansing Bo 4.pr4.152; *pp.* **purged** cleansed VIII.181, **purgide** Bo 4.m7.3.

purpos, purpoos *n.* (1) plan, purpose I.2542, I.3978, Bo 1.pr3.66; **in p.** was intended I.3978; **was in p. grete** fully intended Tr 5.1576; **it cam hym to p.** he decided V.606; **take (a) p.** decide Tr 1.79, Tr 5.770; (2) subject, point Tr 2.897, Tr 5.176; **to p.** pertinent, to the point Tr 5.1460; **fall to p.** be pertinent, suitable Tr 1.142, Tr 3.1367; **now to p.** now to the point II.170, III.711, Tr 3.330.

purposen *v.* (1) intend X.87; suppose Bo 3.pr2.75; decide IV.706; *(reflx.)* resolve VII.1834; (2) propose, set forth Bo 3.pr10.111; state, propound Bo 3.pr12.19; *1 pr. sg.* **purpose** VII.1055; *2 pr. sg.* **purposest** VII.1203; *3 pr. sg.* **purposeth** X.734; *pr. pl.* **purposen** Tr 4.1350; *pt. sg.* **purposed** X.309, **purposide** Bo 5.pr6.226; *prp.* **purposynge** decided upon, intending V.1458; *pp.* **purposed** IV.706, (as *adj.*) **purposede** set out, displayed Bo 3.pr2.75.

purpre, purpur *n.* rich purple cloth X.933, Rom A 1071; *pl.* **purpres** purple robes Bo 3.m4.3.

purpre *adj.* purple Bo 1.m6.9, Tr 4.869, LGW 654.

pursue(n) *v.* (1) pursue X.355, Rom B 1717; (2) seek (a goal) Rom B 2316; (with **to**) petition VII.1694; *3 pr. sg.* **pursuweth** carries out Bo 4.pr2.86; *pr. pl.* **pursewen** persecute X.526; *2 pt. sg.* **pursuydest** Bo 2.pr1.30 pursued, wooed; *pp.* **pursuyed** persecuted Bo 1.pr3.51.

purtreye *see* **portreye.**

purveiaunce, purveiance, purveaunce *n.* (1) foresight, providence I.1252, I.1665, Bo 4.pr6.230, Tr 2.527; (2) arrangement, preparations I.3566, II.247, Tr 3.533; (3) provision III.570.

purveye(n) *v.* (1) foresee, foreknow Bo 5.pr3.87, Tr 4.1008; (2) prepare IV.191, VII.1342, Tr 2.504; (3) provide III.917, Tr 2.1160; *3 pr. sg.* **purveyeth** Tr 4.1066; *imp. sg.* **purveye** Tr 2.426; *pp.* **(i)purveyed** Tr 4.1052, Bo 5.pr3.40, (with **of**) provided with III.591, **purveyd** Tr 4.1055; *vbl. n.* **purveyinge** foresight, providence Tr 4.986, Tr 4.1015.

putte(n) *v.* (1) put VII.763, X.1045, BD 1332; **p. on** impute to VIII.455; (2) suppose VII.1477, Tr 1.783; *1 pr. sg.* **put** III.1231, **putte** I.1841; *2 pr. sg.* **puttest** VII.2685; *3 pr. sg.* **putteth** I.3802, *(contr.)* **put** Tr 4.1021, **putt(e)** Rom B 4444, Rom C 5949; *pr. pl.* **putte(n)** I.1435, Anel 268; *pr. subj. sg.* **putte**

VII.1753; *imp. sg.* **put** III.2140; *imp. pl.* **put** I.3185, **putte** VIII.1329; *1 & 3 pt. sg.* **putte** I.3732, BD 769; *2 pt. sg.* **puttest** VII.2685; *pt. pl.* **putte(n)** VII.2070, VIII.1338; *pp.* **(y)put** III.1333, *(Nth.)* **pit** I.4088, **putt** Rom A 463.

Q

quake *v.* tremble I.3614, V.860, HF 604, Tr 1.8871; *3 pr. sg.* **quaketh** Tr 2.809; *pr. subj. sg.* **quake** HF 604; *imp. pl.* **quaketh** Tr 2.302; *pt. sg.* **quook** I.1576, **quok** LGW 2317; *prp.* **quakyng(e)** IV.317, Rom C 6495, (as *adj.*) Bo 4.m5.25; **qwakynge** Bo 1.m4.17; *pp.* **quaked** VII.2641; *vbl. n.* **quakyng** Anel 214.

queynt(e) *adj.* (1) ingenious, clever I.3275, I.4051, Tr 4.1629; learned, complex II.1189, VIII.752, BD 531; (2) elaborately contrived I.1531, I.3605, BD 874; elegant, pleasing Rom A 65; tricky VII.236; (3) curious I.2333, III.516, BD 1330; (3) strange V.239; (4) (as *adv.*) elaborately HF 245; (4) (as *n.*) elegant, pleasing thing I.3276, (sexual favors) III.332, III.444.

queynte, (y)queynt *see* **quenche(n)**.

queyntelych, queyntely *adv.* elaborately, elegantly HF 1923, Rom A 569, Rom A 783.

quelle *v.* kill VI.854, VII.3390; *pr. pl.* **quelle** Tr 4.46; *pr. subj. sg.* **quelle** VIII.705.

quenche(n) *v.* quench, extinguish X.628; put an end to Tr 3.1058; *(intr.)* go out X.210, X.341; *pr. subj. sg.* **quenche** Tr 3.1456; *imp. sg.* **quenche** quench Tr 4.511; *pt. sg.* **queynte** went out I.2334; *pp.* **(y)queynt** I.2336.

questioun, question *n.* (1) question I.1347, V.579; (2) problem IV.1654, Bo 5.pr4.25; logical problem III.2223, Bo 3.pr10.206; **holdynge hir q.** debating I.2514; *pl.* **questiouns** Bo 4.pr6.25, **questions** Bo 4.pr6.376.

quyk(e) *adj.* (1) living X.658, Tr 1.411, Tr 2.52; alive BD 121; (2) lively V.194, vivid I.306; (as *adv.*) readily Rom B 5056; *super.* **quykkest** busiest V.1502.

quyke(n), quykene *v.* revive X.235, X.243; give life to VIII.481; arise Tr 1.295; grow lively Tr 1.443; kindle Tr 3.484; *pt. sg.* **quyked** rekindled I.2335; *pp.* **(y)quyked** kindled V.1050, stirred, enlivened X.536.

quit(e) *adj.* free from blame or obligation VIII.66, PF 663, Tr 1.529.

quite(n) *v.* (1) pay III.1292, VII.2374; pay for I.3127; ransom I.1032; (2) reward HF 670, PF 112, Tr 1.808; recompense, requite I.3119, VII.1053; (3) pay back (revenge) I.3746, I.3916, VI.420; **q.** (someone's) **hir(e)**, while repay II.584, III.1008, LGW 2227, Rom A 1542; (4) *(reflx.)* do one's duty, conduct one's self V.673, Rom B 3069; *3 pr. sg.* **quiteth** X.689; *pr. pl.* **quiten** X.154; *pr. subj. sg.* **quite** I.770; *pt. sg.* **quitt(e)** III.422, Rom B 3069; *pt. pl.* **quytte** released Tr 4.205; *pp.* **quyt(e)** I.4324, III.425, **yquit** V.673.

quod *pt. sg.* said I.788, I.2453, BD 90.

R

rad(de) *see* **rede(n)**.

rafte, (y)raft *see* **reve(n)**.

rage *n.* (1) madness, violent insanity I.2011, III.2166, BD 731; (2) passionate anger Tr 3.899, Rom A 156; grief V.836, Tr 4.811; passionate desire BD 731;

LGW 599, Rom A 1657; (3) rush of wind I.1985; turmoil Bo 1.m4.5.

raysed *see* **reyse(n)**.

rakel, rakle, racle *adj.* rash, hasty IX.278, Tr 1.1067, Tr 3.429, Tr 3.1437.

ransoun, raunson *n.* ransom I.1024, I.1176; **maad his r.** paid his penalty III.411.

rasour *n.* razor I.2417, VII.2056, HF 690.

rathe *adv.* early I.3768, VII.99; **late or r.** early or late, some time or other HF 2139, Rom C 6650; quickly Tr 2.1088; readily Tr 4.205.

rather *adj.* earlier, former Bo 2.pr1.11, Tr 3.1337.

rather(e), rathir *adv.* (1) earlier VI.643; sooner II.335, Tr 1.835; (2) rather I.487, Bo 5.pr3.33, LGW G 458; **never (naught) the r.** nevertheless BD 562, BD 868.

ravyne *n.* (1) robbery, greed PF 336, Rom C 6813; (2) **foules of r.** birds of prey PF 323; *pl.* **ravynes** robberies Bo 1.pr4.70.

ravysshe(n), ravyssche *v.* (1) seize, steal Bo 1.pr3.34, Bo 4.pr3.111; take away Bo 5.pr6.91; carry away, abduct Tr 4.530, Tr 4.637, Bo 2.m7.28; (3) entrance, enrapture IV.1750, Tr 4.1474; **r. on** be enraptured by IV.1774; *3 pr. sg.* **ravyssheth thee** steals from you Rom B 5198; *pr. pl.* **ravysschen** Bo 4.pr5.23; *2 pt. sg.* **ravysshedest** VII.469, **ravysschedest** Bo 3.pr1.21; *3 pt. sg.* **ravysshed** IV.2230, **ravysschide** Bo 4.m7.34; *prp.* (as *adj.*) **ravishyng** entrancing PF 198, **ravysschynge** powerful, violent Bo 1.m5.4, **ravysshynge** Bo 2.m2.5; *pp.* **ravysshed** III.1676, **ravyssched** Bo 1.pr3.70; *vbl. n.* **ravisshyng** abduction Tr 1.62, Tr 4.548.

real *see* **roial**.

reaume, reawme, reame, realme, rewme *n.* realm II.797, HF 704, LGW 1281, LGW 2091, Rom A 495; *pl.* **remes** VII.3136, **realmes** Bo 2.pr2.70, **rewmes** Bo 3.pr5.43.

recche *v.* care, be concerned for PF 593; *1 pr. sg.* **recche** I.1398, **reche** PF 606, **rekke** IV.1090; *(impers.)* **r. me** (**yow**, *etc.*) I (you, *etc.*) care III.53, IV.2276, LGW 605; esteem V.71; *2 pr. sg.* **rekkest** III.1453; *3 pr. sg.* **reccheth** I.2397, **rekketh** III.327, **recketh** Rom C 7549; *pr. pl.* **recche** V.71, **rekke(n)** X.905, X.944; *pr. subj. sg.* **recche** Tr 4.630; *pt. sg.* **roghte** I.3772, **roughte** Rom A 341; *pt. subj. sg.* **roghte** IV.685.

recchelees, reccheles, recheles, rechcheles *adj.* careless, reckless IV.488, VII.3107, HF 397, HF 668, PF 593; heedless of rules I.179 (see note); negligent II.229.

reccheleesnesse *n.* recklessness, carelessness X.111, X.611; rashness Scog 16.

receyve(n), resceyve(n), resseyve *v.* (1) receive II.259, II.991, VII.1511, Bo 1.pr5.76, Astr 1.13.4, Rom B 2185; (2) *(astro.)* favorably situated, welcomed (by an auspicious planet) II.307, Astr 2.4.9; *3 pr. sg.* **receyveth** II.396, **resceyveth** Bo 1.pr4.222, **resseyveth** Rom C 6313; *pr. pl.* **receyve(n)** X.106, X.127, **resceyven** Bo 2.pr4.126; **resseyven** Bo 3.pr11.156; *pr. subj. sg.* **receyve** ABC 148; *imp. sg.* **receyve** Truth 15; *imp. pl.* **receyveth** Ven 73; *pt.* **receyved** III.1889, **resceyved** Bo 2.pr2.16; *pp.* **received** IV.955, **resseyved** Bo 3.pr10.77, **iresceyved** Bo 5.pr3.206; *vbl. n.* **receyvynge** X.385.

reche *v.* reach for, get BD 47; start out, go Tr 2.447; reach (to) I.3696; *pt. sg.* **raughte** I.136; **reighte** HF 1374; *pt. pl.* **raughten** Rom A 1022.

recomaunde, recomende *v.* (1) commend VIII.544;

submit (for correction) VII.2719; (2) *(reflx.)* submit Tr 2.1070; *1 pr. sg.* **recomande** Tr 5.1414; *3 pr. sg.* **recomandeth** II.278, **recomaundeth** Tr 2.1122; *pr. subj. sg.* **recomande** Tr 1.1056.

reconforte *v.* (1) comfort, encourage VII.978, Tr 2.1672; *(reflx.)* take heart I.2852; *pr. subj. pl.* **recomforte** Tr 5.1395; *pt. sg.* **reconforted** VII.1660.

record(e) *n.* (1) reputation III.2049; **of r.** on record, recorded III.2117; (2) testimony Rom C 6706; promise BD 934; **to r.** as a witness Scog 22, Rom C 7311.

recorde *v.* (1) recall, bring to mind Tr 4.1518, LGW 2484; remind I.829; remember Tr 5.445; repeat, in order to remember PF 609; (2) pronounce I.1745; *2 pr. sg.* **recordist** remember Bo 3.pr12.2; *3 pr. sg.* **recordeth** narrates VII.1079; *pr. pl.* **recorden** recall Bo 3.m11.46; *imp. pl.* **yow recorde** remember Tr 3.1179; *1 & 3 pt. sg.* **recorded(e)** remembered Bo pr1.1, recounted Rom C 5845; *2 pt. sg.* **recordidest** Bo 3.pr10.170; *prp.* **recordyng(e)** saying, repeating Tr 3.51, LGW 1760; remembering Tr 5.718.

recovere(n) *v.* (1) remedy, make right Rom B 3236; (2) regain, get back PF 688, Tr 3.1406; obtain, get Tr 4.406; get in return Tr 3.181; *1 pr. sg.* **rekever** HF 354; *pr. pl.* **recoveren** Rom A 57; *pp.* **recovered** II.27; *vbl. n.* **recoverynge** Bo 1.pr6.70.

recreaunt, recreant *adj.* cowardly, confessing oneself defeated X.698, Tr 1.814; (as *n.*) **for r.** as a coward Rom B 4090.

red, reed *n.* (1) advice, counsel I.3527, IV.1357; good advice, remedy Tr 1.661, BD 203; advisor I.665; (2) assent, permission IV.653, Compl d'Am 37; (3) course of action I.1216, VII.2549; plan III.2030, VI.146, BD 105; **best to r.** best as a course of action, best to do Tr 4.679.

red(e), reed(e) *adj.* red I.90, HF 135, LGW F 535; (as *n.*) red material I.294; red wine VI.526, Tr 3.1384; *comp.* **redder** VII.2859.

rede(n), reede *v.* (1) read I.709, II.84, BD 49, PF 10; interpret I.741, II.203, BD 279; understand Tr 2.129; (2) study V.1120; lecture (as a professor) III.1518; (3) tell, say Tr 4.980; speak, narrate HF 1354, HF 1935, Tr 3.1383, LGW 2139; (4) advise I.3068, I.3071, IV.811, HF 491, Tr 1.83; *2 pr. sg.* **redest** HF 1001; *3 pr. sg.* **redith** Astr Pro 42, *(contr.)* **ret** Tr 2.413; *pr. pl.* **rede(n)** VIII.78, Tr 2.100; *pr. subj. sg.* **rede** HF 1067; *pr. subj. pl.* **rede** IV.1154; *imp. sg.* **rede** III.183, **reed** IX.344; *imp. pl.* **redeth** III.982; *pt. sg.* **redde** III.714, **radde** III.791; *pt. pl.* **redden** Tr 2.1706; *pp.* **rad** I.2595, **red** III.765.

reder(e) *n.* reader PF 132, Tr 5.270, Rom B 2161.

redy *adj.* ready I.21, I.352, PF 213; **al r.** already, right IV.299; quick-witted, resourceful Tr 5.964; **r. token** clear evidence VII.390.

redily, redely *adv.* (1) readily I.2276, VII.414; quickly, soon VI.667; (2) truly HF 130, HF 313, Rom A 144; **ful r.** indeed Rom A 93.

redowte *v.* fear Bo 1.pr3.19; *pp.* **redouted of** feared by Bo 2.pr7.65; *vbl. n.* **redoutynge** reverence, awe I.2050.

redresse *v.* (1) redress, set right, amend III.696, IV.431, Tr 3.1008; *3 pr. sg. (reflx.)* **redresseth it in** turns toward, addresses itself to X.1039; *pr. pl. (reflx.)* **redressen hem** straighten themselves Tr 2.969; *imp. sg.* **redresse** ABC 129; *pt. sg.* **redressed** vindicated V.1436; *pp.* **redressed** restored Bo 4.pr2.131.

refere, referren *v.* attribute (to a cause) Bo 1.pr4.24, Bo 5.pr3.182; ascribe to (as a cause) Bo 3.pr2.60, Bo 4.pr2.253; return to (a subject) Tr 1.266; *1 pr. sg.* **referre** Bo 1.pr4.24; *3 pr. sg.* **refereth to** refers, applies to VIII.1083; *pr. subj. sg.* **referre** Bo 5.pr6.238; *pp.* **referred** Bo 3.pr6.35, **reffered** Bo 3.pr10.185.

refreyde(n) *v. (intr.)* grow cold Tr 2.1343, Tr 5.507, Ros 21; *pp.* **refreyded** *(tr.)* cooled X.341.

refreyne, refrayne *v.* bridle, restrain X.382, X.385, Rom C 7509; *3 pr. sg.* **refreyneth** X.294.

refresshe, refreshen *v.* (1) renew one's strength LGW 1482; provide with food, refreshment I.2622, III.1767; (2) relieve, comfort LGW 1081; *pt. sg.* **refresshed** III.146; *pp.* **refresshed** III.38, **reffressched** Bo 4.pr6.344; *vbl. n.* **refresshyng(e)** relief X.78, X.220.

reft(e) *see* **reve(n)**.

refuse(n) *v.* refuse VII.1557, Bo 4.pr2.283; *2 pr. sg.* (with *pro.*) **refusestow** Bo 1.m5.32; *3 pr. sg.* **refuseth** Bo 2.pr6.84; *pr. pl.* **refusen** Bo 1.m6.5; *imp. sg.* **refuse** Tr 2.1154; *imp. pl.* **refuseth** Tr 1.255; *pt. pl.* **refuseden** IV.128; *pp.* **refused** For 41, **refus** rejected Tr 1.570.

refut, refuyt *n.* refuge II.546, II.852; dwelling place Tr 3.1014.

regard *n.* in *phr.* **at (to, in) r.** of compared to X.180, X.399; with respect to Bo 2.pr7.27. Cf. **reward**.

regne, reigne, reyne *n.* dominion, rule VII.2184, Tr 5.1544; kingdom, country I.866, Bo 4.pr1.34, LGW 992; **holden r. and hous in unitee** hold the world together Tr 3.29; *pl.* **regnes** I.2373, **reignes** Bo 3.pr2.116.

regne, reignen *v.* reign, rule Bo 3.pr2.35, Form Age 59; flourish II.816; *2 pr. sg.* **regnest** Tr 5.1864; *3 pr. sg.* **regneth** II.776; *pr. pl.* **regne(n)** II.816, Mars 50, **reignen** Bo 1.m7.21; *pt. sg.* **regned** VII.2655.

reherce(n), reherse(n) *v.* narrate, tell, repeat I.732, BD 190, Anel 166, Tr 3.493; *3 pr. sg.* **reherceth** Bo 3.pr2.84; *pr. pl.* **reherce** Rom C 6018; *pr. subj. sg.* **reherce** LGW F 574; *imp. sg.* **reherce** repeat Tr 2.1029; *prp.* **rehersynge** V.206; *pp.* **reherced** X.910, **rehersed** LGW 1464; *vbl. n.* **rehersyng(e)** talk, conversation I.1650; repetition LGW 1185; *pl.* **rehersynges** narrations, descriptions LGW F 24.

reighte *see* **reche**.

reyn, rayn *n.* rain I.492, I.595, IX.301, Anel 309; *pl.* **reynes** IV.2140.

reyne *n.* rein, bridle I.4083, V.313; *pl.* **reynes** I.904.

reyne *v.* rain Tr 3.551, Tr 4.299; *3 pr. sg.* **reyneth** I.1535; *pr. pl.* **reyne** Tr 4.846; *pt. sg.* **reyned** Tr 3.1557, **ron** Tr 3.640; *pp.* **reyn** Tr 3.1560.

reyse(n) *v.* (1) raise, build III.2102; raise (a fiend) VIII.861; exalt III.705, Tr 2.1585, Rom B 3621; (2) raise, gather in III.1390; arouse Tr 5.1471; *pp.* **reysed** raised BD 1278, **raysed** Rom B 3621.

rek- *see* **rec-**.

rekene(n), reken, rekne *v.* (1) enumerate, count BD 436, BD 441; (2) recount, tell I.1933, I.1954, IV.2433, Rom C 6239; (3) reckon, calculate I.401, VII.78, LGW 2510; (4) consider III.367; take account of II.110; *imp. sg.* **rekene** Astr 2.17.17, **rekene** Astr 2.32.5; *pt. sg.* **rekned** Astr 2.3.29; *prp.* **reknyng** Astr 1.21.69; *pp.* **rekned** Bo 3.pr2.56, **(y)rekned** III.367, Rom A 1390; *vbl. n.* **rekenynge** account I.600; account-keeping ABC 132, **withouten r.** without calculation, without saying anything more Tr 2.1640, **leye a reknynge with** present an account to, demand payment Bo 2.pr3.70; *pl.* **rekenynges** accounts VII.218; **maad oure r.** paid our bills I.760.

relees *n.* relief Rom B 2612, Rom B 4440; forgiveness ABC 3; **out of r.** without pause, unceasing VIII.46.

relesse *v.* release, set free from IV.153, V.1533; forgive (a debt) X.810; *1 pr. sg.* **releese** V.1613; *1 & 3 pt. sg.* **relessed** VII.2177; *2 pt. sg.* **relessedest** X.309; *pp.* **releessed** X.582, **relessed** Bo 1.pr4.50, **relesed** Rom B 3440; *vbl. n.* **relessyng(e)** forgiveness X.1026, setting free Bo 3.m12.30.

releve, releeve *v.* (1) relieve Bo 4.pr4.17, For 77; provide for LGW F 128; (2) rescue X.945, Tr 5.1042; aid, help VII.1490; *imp. sg.* **releeve** ABC 6; *pp.* **relevid** Bo 4.pr4.113, **releeved** VIII.872; **releved** I.4182 compensated; *vbl. n.* **releevynge** remedy X.804, relief X.805.

religioun *n.* (1) religious order VII.1944, VIII.972; (2) religion, faith VIII.477; religious life I.427; (2) **religiouns** Rom C 6352.

religious(e) *adj.* monastic, in a religious order VII.1960, Rom C 6149; a nun Tr 2.759.

relik(e) *n.* religious relic VI.949, Tr 1.153; treasure LGW F 321; *pl.* **relikes** I.701.

remembraunce, remembrance *n.* memory II.187, X.1087, Anel 211; **have r.** remember I.1046, Rom A 146; **make r.** remind IV.2284.

remembre(n) *v.* (1) remember HF 64, Rom A 1027; (with **on, upon**) VII.513, VII.999, Tr 1.24; (with **of**) X.466, BD 717; *(impers.)* III.469, X.133, Tr 3.361; *(reflx.)* IV.1898, X.1063, Tr 5.746; (2) remind V.1243; *2 pr. sg.* **remembrest** Bo 1.pr4.210, (with *pro.*) **remembrestow** Bo 1.pr6.37; *3 pr. sg.* **remembreth** LGW 1105; *pr. pl.* **remembre** V.1243; *imp. pl.* **remembreth** V.1542, *(reflx.)* **remembre yow** IV.881; *pt. sg.* **remembred** II.1057; *prp.* **remembryng(e)** I.1501, *(reflx.)* Tr 1.384; *pp.* **remembred** LGW 2717.

remes *see* **reaume.**

remoeven, remeve, remove *v.* remove, move away V.1221, Tr 1.691, Rom B 2464; *pr. subj. pl.* **remoeve** V.993; *imp. sg.* **remeve** Astr 2.5.21, **remove** Rom B 2464; *imp. pl.* **remoeveth** VIII.1008; *pt. pl.* **remoeved** V.1205; *pp.* **remoeved** Bo 1.m4.20.

remuwen *v.* move, remove Bo 2.pr6.50; *imp. sg.* **remewe** Astr 2.2.3; *pt. sg.* **remued** Rom C 7430; *pp.* **remewed** V.181, **remuwed** Bo 1.pr4.240.

rende *v.* tear Tr 4.1493; *3 pr. sg. (contr.)* **rent** LGW 646; *pr. pl.* **reenden** tear down, criticize Bo 3.pr12.124; *pt. sg.* **rente** I.990, *(intr.)* split VII.3101; *prp.* **rendynge** (as *adj.*) torn Bo 1.m1.4; *pp.* **(y)rent** II.844, HF 776. Cf. **renten.**

reneye(n) *v.* renounce II.376, VII.2561; *pr. subj. sg.* **reneye** VIII.464; *imp. sg.* **reneye** VIII.459; *pt. sg.* **reneyed** II.340; *pt. subj. sg.* **reneyed** Rom C 6787; *vbl. n.* **reneiynge** X.793.

renne(n) *v.* run I.3890, III.356, HF 202, Anel 316; *2 pr. sg.* **rennest** Tr 4.1549; *3 pr. sg.* **renneth** I.1761; *pr. pl.* **renne(n)** I.2868, I.4100; *imp. sg.* **ren** Tr 5.656; *imp. pl.* **renneth** rush Tr 1.1066; *pt. sg.* **ran** I.509; *pt. pl.* **ronnen** I.2925; *prp.* **rennyng(e)** BD 161; *pp.* **yronnen** I.2639, **(y)ronne** I.8, I.2693, (as *adj.*) **ronne in age** advanced in age Rom B 4495; *vbl. n.* **rennyng** run I.551.

renomyd, renomed *pp.* as *adj.* renowned Bo 2.pr4.81, Bo 3.pr2.109.

renoun, renone *n.* fame, renown I.316, I.1432, LGW 1513.

renovelle *v.* (1) *(tr.)* renew VII.1845; *imp. pl.* **reno-**

veleth Mars 19; *pr. pl. (intr.)* **renovellen** are renewed X.1027, **renovelen** *(reflx.)* renew themselves Bo 3.pr11.123; *pp.* **renovelled** renewed VII.1846.

rent(e) *n.* income I.256, Rom B 2255; rent I.579, III.1390; salary Bo 3.pr4.83; tribute II.1142, VII.2211, BD 765; **to r.** as tribute Tr 2.830; *pl.* **rentes** IV.1313.

renten, rent *v.* tear LGW 843, Rom A 324; *prp.* **rentynge** I.2834. Cf. **rende.**

repaire, repeire *v.* return V.589, Tr 5.1571, Rom B 4071; go VII.326, Tr 3.5; *3 pr. sg.* **repaireth** II.967, **repeireth** V.339; *imp. pl.* **repeyreth** Tr 5.1837; *pt. sg.* **repayred** Rom C 7519; *prp.* **repeirynge** V.608; *pp.* **repeyred** LGW 1136, **repayred** Rom C 7519.

repente(n) *v.* repent (often *reflx.*) III.1629, VI.431, BD 1116; *3 pr. sg.* **repenteth** VII.1135; *pr. pl.* **repente(n)** X.298, Rom B 4949; *pr. subj. pl.* **repente** III.1663; *imp. pl.* **repenteth** V.1321; *pt. sg.* **repented** III.632; *prp.* **repentynge** II.378; *vbl. n.* **repentyng** LGW F 147.

replenysseth *3 pr. sg.* fills X.920; *pp.* **replenyssed** X.1079, **replenysshid** Bo 1.pr4.276.

repreve, repreeve, repref, repreet, reprove *n.* reproof III.16, IV.2263, Rom B 5525, Rom C 7238; reproach VI.595, Tr 2.419, Rom B 4974; **youre r.** reproach to you VII.1223; shame III.84; *pl.* **repreves** insults X.258.

repreve(n), reprove *v.* reprove, blame (often with **of, for**) V.1537, VII.1536, Rom C 6100; *inf.* **to repreve, reprove** to be blamed, blameworthy VII.1032, Rom C 7546; *3 pr. sg.* **repreveth** X.33, **reproveth** Bo 5.m4.40; *pr. pl.* **repreve** III.1177; *pr. subj. sg.* **repreve** III.937, **reprove** Rom C 6513; *imp.* **repreve** Tr 1.669 *(sg.),* III.1206 *(pl.)*; *pt. pl.* **repreved** X.663; *pp.* **repreved** X.623, **reproved** proven false Bo 2.pr6.116; *vbl. n.* **reprevynge** blaming X.628; *pl.* **reprevynges** quarrels X.556.

requere(n) *v.* (1) ask, request III.1010, III.1052, VII.1737; (2) require, need Bo 3.pr10.220, Tr 3.405; *inf.* **to requiren** to be sought after Bo 3.pr10.227; *1 pr. sg.* **require** Rom B 3419; *2 pr. sg.* **requerist** Bo 4.m1.36; *3 pr. sg.* **requireth** X.376; *pr. pl.* **requere(n)** VII.1683, Tr 2.473, **requiren** Bo 3.pr10.229; *imp. sg.* **requere** Tr 1.902; *pt. sg.* **required** IV.430; *prp.* **requirynge** asking VII.1772; *pp.* **requered** Tr 3.405, **required** Tr 3.405.

resceyve(n), resceyveth, (i)resceyved *see* **receyve(n).**

rescowe *v.* rescue Tr 3.857, Tr 5.231; save Bo 4.m5.22; *pt. sg.* **rescowed** LGW F 515, **rescowyde** Bo 2.pr2.63, **rescued** LGW G 503; *vbl. n.* **rescowynge** X.805.

rescus, rescous *n.* rescue I.2643, Tr 1.478.

resigne *1 pr. sg.* consign II.780, ABC 80; resign Tr 1.432; *pr. pl.* **resygne** reject Tr 3.25.

resolven *pr. pl.* flow out Bo 5.m1.1; *pp.* **resolved** dissolved Bo 2.pr7.145, held in solution Bo 1.m7.9; **resolvyd** melted Bo 4.m5.27.

resoun, reson, raisoun *n.* (1) reason, judgment I.37, I.1766, BD 922, Rom B 4685; (2) argument I.3844, II.213, PF 534; (3) reason, cause V.406, VII.979, Bo 3.pr9.16; **by r. of** because VII.1024, X.801; (3) **ben r.** is reasonable, right I.847, III.2277, V.296; **by r.** reasonably, justly VI.458; **of r.** reasonable Tr 2.366; *pl.* **resons** opinions I.274, speeches Tr 3.90, arguments Bo 3.pr9.115; **resouns** reasons, causes VII.1025.

respit *n.* respite, delay I.948, VIII.543, PF 648.

respite(n) *v.* grant a respite V.1582, Anel 259.

resseyven, resseyved *see* **receyve(n).**

rest(e) *n.* rest I.1003, BD 245, HF 1956; **(un)to** (one's) **r.** to bed I.30, I.820, Tr 2.911; peace, tranquillity IV.160, IV.741, Tr 1.188; resting place PF 376, Bo 3.m9.47; Bo 3.m10.5; **hertes r.** peace of mind Tr 3.1045; **sette at r.** settle Tr 2.760; **bringe herte(s) at r.** ease one's mind Tr 3.966, Tr 3.1518; *pl.* **restes** times of rest Tr 2.1722.

reste(n), reste *v.* (1) rest VII.109, PF 265, Rom C 7414; (2) stay, remain III.1736; *3 pr. sg.* **resteth** stays X.821; *pr. subj.* **reste** PF 514 *(sg.)*, V.126 *(pl.)*; *pt. sg.* **rested** IV.1926, *(reflx.)* Rom A 1455; *prp.* (as *adj.*) **restyng** BD 1005; *pp.* **rested** Bo 3.m2.15.

resteles, resteless *n.* without rest VI.728, Tr 3.1584; unceasing Fort 70; (as *adv.*) Rom A 370.

restore(n), restoore *v.* restore, give back IV.867, VII.1110, Tr 4.1347, Tr 4.1348; repair X.645; *3 pr. sg.* **restoreth** X.312; *pt. sg.* **restored** I.991; *pp.* **restoored** X.870.

restreyne, restrayne *v.* restrain, hold in check VII.1432, VII.2587, Tr 1.676; *(reflx.)* VII.2606, Tr 4.940; control IX.329, Anel 235; prevent VII.1492, (with **for, from**) Tr 4.708, Tr 4.872; *2 pr. sg.* **restreynest** control Bo 1.m5.16; *3 pr. sg.* **restreyneth** prevents VII.1092; *pp.* **restreyned** confined Bo 2.pr7.84.

reet *see* **riet**.

ret *see* **rede(n)**.

rethorik(e), rethorice *n.* rhetoric, learned eloquence IV.32, V.719, Bo 2.pr1.44; **colours of r.** figures of speech V.726, HF 859.

retourne, retorne, returne *v.* return II.986, Tr 5.596, Mars 211; *3 pr. sg.* **retourneth** VII.1183, **retorneth** X.620; *pr. pl.* **retourne** Tr 5.1351, **retornen** Bo 4.pr6.335; *pr. subj.* **returne** X.236, **retourne** Tr 3.1483 *(sg.)*; IV.597 *(pl.)*; *imp. sg.* **retourne** Tr 4.1553; *imp. pl.* **retourneth** IV.809; *pt. sg.* **retorned** Tr 3.1534, **retourned** VII.1770; *prp.* **retornyng** *(tr.)* turning over, considering Tr 5.1023, **returnyng** X.176; *pp.* **retourned** VII.973; *vbl. n.* **retournynge** return I.2095, **retornynge** Bo 3.m2.41.

reule, rule, rewle *n.* (1) rule VII.1166, X.217, Astr 1.1.5; code of behavior for monastics I.173; (2) alidade, sighting device on an astrolabe Astr 1.13.1; *pl.* **reules** Astr Pro 26, **rewles** Astr Pro 103.

reule(n) *v.* (1) rule, govern IV.327, VII.3044; (2) *(reflx.)* conduct one's self, behave IV.237, Tr 5.758; *3 pr. sg.* **reulith** Tr 2.1377; *imp. sg.* **reule** Truth 6; *imp. pl.* **rule yow** X.592; *2 pt. sg.* **reuledest** Bo 1.pr4.212; *3 pt. sg.* **ruled** LGW F 163; *pp.* **reuled** I.816, **ruled** Tr 1.336.

reuthe, rewthe *see* **routh(e)**.

reve(n) *v.* rob, steal I.4011; take away VIII.376; deprive (one) of Tr 1.188, Tr 2.1659; *3 pr. sg.* **reveth** PF 86; *pr. subj. sg.* **reve** Rom B 4579; *pt. sg.* **rafte** III.888, **refte** IX.305, **reved** seized Rom B 4351; *pp.* **(y)raft** I.2015, LGW 2590, **reft** LGW 2325.

revel *n.* revelry I.2717, I.3652; merrymaking I.4402; festival, entertainment II.353, Ros 6; *pl.* **revels** festivals, entertainments VI.65.

reverence *n.* reverence, respect I.141, I.305, I.312, II.116; honor VII.2251, V.93, HF 624; ceremony I.525; **at r. of** (someone) in honor of X.40, Tr 3.40, Tr 3.1328; **doon** (someone) **r.** pay honor, respect to II.1001, III.206, HF 259; **have (hold) in r.** respect, honor VII.3213, Tr 1.516, LGW F 32.

reverent *adj.* worthy of respect Bo 3.pr4.2, Astr Pro 85; *pl.* **reverentz** Bo 3.m4.7.

reward *n.* (1) regard, consideration LGW F 399, Rom B 3832; **in r.** of with regard to, compared to Rom B 3254; (2) reward, compensation Rom B 4640. Cf. **regard**.

rewe, rowe *n.* row I.2866, HF 1692; **by r.** in a row, one after another III.506; *pl.* **rowes** rays Mars 2.

rewe(n) *v.* (1) (with **on, upon**) have mercy on, feel pity for I.1863, Anel 104, Tr 1.460; (2) *(intr.)* repent, rue I.3530, Tr 2.455; feel sorry Tr 3.114; (3) *(impers.)* cause to repent Anel 217, Tr 2.789, Tr 4.1531; *2 pr. sg.* **rewest** II.854; *3 pr. sg.* **me reweth of** I feel sorry for I.3462; *pr. subj.* **rewe** I.1863 *(sg.)*, Tr 4.98 *(pl.)*; *imp. sg.* **rewe** I.2233; *imp. pl.* **reweth upon** V.974, **rueth on** Tr 4.1501; *pt. sg.* **rewede** LGW 1237; *prp.* **rewyng** Rom B 3697; *pp.* **rewed** Tr 4.1141.

rewme *see* **reaume**.

rial *see* **roial**.

ribaudie *n.* ribaldry, coarse jesting I.3866, VI.324, Rom B 4926; debauchery X.464.

ribaudrie *n.* ribaldry, coarseness Rom B 2224.

riche *adj.* rich I.311, I.479, Tr 5.43; splendid, magnificent I.296, I.979, BD 1319; (as *n.*) rich people I.248; rich man PF 103; *comp.* **richer** VII.1548, **riccher** Rom B 4184; *super.* **richest(e)** I.2872, IV.2242.

riche *adv.* richly I.609; splendidly I.2577, HF 1327.

rychesse *n.* riches, wealth I.1253, I.1829, BD 1060; abundance Tr 3.349; **parfit r.** finest example Ven 12; *pl.* **richesses** riches VII.1370, **richeses** Rom B 5421.

ryde(n) *v.* ride I.27, I.94, BD 371; **r. out** ride forth on an expedition I.45, VII.750; **r. or go** ride or walk I.1351, I.2252, Tr 1.838; *2 pr. sg.* **rydest** III.1452, (with *pro.*) **rydestow** III.1386; *3 pr. sg.* **rideth** I.1691, *(contr.)* **rit** I.974; *pr. pl.* **ryde(n)** I.2897; *pr. subj. pl.* **ryde** VII.260; *imp. sg.* **ryd** Tr 2.1013; *imp. pl.* **ryde** VII.1927; *pt. sg.* **rood** I.169; *pt. pl.* **riden** I.825; *prp.* **ridynge** I.2159; *pp.* **riden** I.48; *vbl. n.* **ridyng(e)** equestrian display, jousting I.4377, X.432.

riet, reet *n.* the rete of an astrolabe *(see* Astr 1.21) Astr 1.3.4, Astr 1.17.1.

right *n.* right justice I.3089, III.1049, Tr 4.515; jurisdiction Bo 2.pr2.22; **by r.** by law, justly II.44, VI.183, Tr 4.396; **of r.** as a right V.1324, Tr 3.1795; *pl.* **ryghtis** HF 456, **rightes** X.802; **at alle rightes** in all respects I.1852, I.2100.

right(e) *adj.* (1) proper, true V.1311, BD 949, Tr 3.1472; right (as opposed to left) I.1959, VII.1312, HF 322; (2) just I.2718, Anel 224; (3) direct I.1263, II.556, ABC 75; straight Tr 3.228, Rom A 1701.

right *adv.* (1) (as *intens.*) right, exactly PF 627 (with **as**) I.554, I.659, BD 163; (with *adj.*) very I.288, I.857, BD 847; indeed I.257, I.757; **r. after** just as Tr 3.175; **r. no maistrie** (suspecioun, *etc.*) no mastery (suspicion, *etc.*) at all VI.58, VII.322; **r. ynogh (ynowe)** plenty III.2, V.470; **r. naught** (noght, nowthe) not at all IV.1011, HF 994, Tr 1.985; not a thing I.756, IV.2303; (with *adv.*) very I.1140, BD 755; just a I.535, PF 316; just now I.767; exactly I.2619, VI.765; (2) directly V.1390, VII.313; **ful r.** directly I.1691; carefully IV.243; **right anoon, anon-right** immediately I.965, IV.1656, Tr 2.1551.

rightful, rightfulle *adj.* righteous, just I.1719, II.814, Astr Pro 7.

rightwisnesse *n.* righteousness, justice III.1909, VI.637, Bo 1.pr4.105, For 66.

rym(e) *n.* rhyme, verse III.1127, VII.925, BD 54; versified tale VII.709, VII.928; *pl.* **rymes** verses II.96.

ryme *v.* versify I.1459, VII.932, PF 119; *pr. pl.* **ryme** Scog 41; *vbl. n.* **rymyng** versifying II.48, VII.930.

rynde *n.* bark Tr 4.1139, Rom B 3121; skin Tr 2.642.

rynge *v.* ring, reverberate I.2431, BD 312, Tr 2.233; sound, proclaim VI.331; *pr. pl.* **rynge(n)** sound I.2600, I.2359; *imp. sg.* **ryng** proclaim HF 1720; *pt. sg.* **rong** I.3215; *pt. pl.* **ronge** BD 1164; *pp.* **(y)ronge** sounded out, proclaimed HF 1655, Tr 5.1062; **runge** rung Rom B 5266.

riot *n.* debauchery, wanton behavior I.4392, VI.465.

riotour *n.* debauchee, profligate VI.692, VI.876; *pl.* **riotoures** VI.661.

ryse(n) *v.* rise, arise I.33, L.1047, Tr 3.756; *(reflx. with* **up***)* stand up Tr 2.812, Tr 4.232, LGW 810; *3 pr. sg.* **riseth** I.1493, *(contr.)* **rist** I.3688; *pr. pl.* **ryse(n)** I.3768, IV.1574; *imp. sg.* **rys** IV.2138; *imp. pl.* **riseth** X.161, **ris** Tr 2.1716; *pt. sg.* **roos** I.823, **ros** Tr 3.1521; *pp.* **risen** I.1065; *vbl. n.* **rysyng(e)** Bo 1.m5.15.

rit *see* **ryde(n)**.

ryve *v.* stab, pierce IV.1236, VI.828, Tr 5.1560; *3 pr. sg. (intr.)* **ryveth** splits Rom B 5718; *pt. sg.* **rof** HF 373.

ryver(e) *n.* (1) river I.3024, III.2080, HF 748; (2) river-bank, hawking ground V.1196; river bank PF 184, III.884; **for r.** to hawk for waterfowl VII.737, Tr 4.413; *pl.* **ryveres** V.898, **ryverys** Bo 5.m1.6.

ro *n.* roe, female deer PF 195; **ro-venysoun** venison Rom B 5718; *pl.* **roos** Bo 3.m8.8, **roes** BD 430.

roche, rok(ke) *n.* rock V.500, Tr 3.1497; *pl.* **roches** HF 1035, **rokkes** V.868.

rochet *see* **rokket**.

rood *see* **ryde(n)**.

rode, roode *n.* cross BD 992, HF 57, Tr 5.1860; **r. beeme** beam supporting a cross III.496.

rody, roddy *adj.* ruddy, fresh looking V.385, BD 143, Rom B 3629; red V.394, Bo 2.m3.8.

rof *see* **ryve**.

roghte, roughte *see* **recche**.

roial, real, rial *adj.* royal I.1018, I.1497, Tr 3.1534, Pity 59; *pl.* **roiales** VII.848; *comp.* **roialler** II.402.

roialliche, roially *adv.* royally, splendidly I.378, I.1687, I.1713.

rok(ke), rokke(s) *see* **roche**.

rokket, rochet *n.* frock Rom A 1242; cloak Rom B 4754.

rolle(n), roule *v.* (1) roll, consider, turn over (in the mind) Bo 3.m11.16, Tr 2.659; (2) wander III.653; *3 pr. sg.* **rolleth** rolls I.2614; considers Tr 5.1313; *pt. sg.* **rolled** considered III.2217; *prp.* **rollynge** rolling I.201; *pp.* **rolled** (on tongue) discussed, spoken of Tr 5.1061.

rombled *see* **rumbelen**.

rome(n) *v.* roam I.1099, IV.2184; HF 1293; *3 pr. sg.* **rometh** I.1119; *pr. pl.* **rome** VII.297; *pt. sg.* **romed** I.1113, **romede** LGW G 105; *pt. pl.* **romeden** V.1013, **romed** BD 443; *prp.* **romyng(e)** I.1071; *pp.* **romed** I.1528.

ron *see* **reyne**.

rong, (y)ronge *see* **rynge**.

yronge *see* **wrynge**.

ronne(n), (y)ronne *see* **renne(n)**.

rore, roore *v.* cry out loudly, lament VII.2888, HF 1589, Tr 4.373; *3 pr. sg.* **roreth** echoes .2881, laments Tr 4.241; *pr. pl.* **roren** Bo 3.m2.16; *p. sg.* **rored** LGW 1219; *prp.* **rorynge** roaring X.568; *vbl. n.* **roryng** lamentation IV.2364.

ros, roos *see* **ryse(n)**.

rosene, rosyn *adj.* rosy Bo 1.m2.23, Bo 2.m3.2; made of roses Rom A 845.

roser *n.* rose bush X.858, Rom A 1651; *pl.* **rosers** Rom B 4188.

rote, roote *n.* (1) root I.2, I.3206, LGW 2613; essential part VIII.1461; **r. and crop** the whole thing, the totality Tr 2.348, Tr 5.1245; (2) root, origin I.423, II.358, Tr 2.844; cause LGW 1368; (3) radix, date from which astronomical calculations can be made II.314, V.1276, Astr 2.44.2; (4) foot of a mountain IV.58; *pl.* **rootes** Bo 3.pr11.111.

roten *adj.* rotten I.3873, I.4406, HF 1778, Anel 314.

route, rowte *n.* company, crowd I.622, I.3854, BD 360; retinue, train Bo 2.pr5.90; *pl.* **routes** Tr 2.620.

route *v.* (1) snore BD 172; (2) murmur II.540; rumble, roar HF 1038, Tr 3.743; *3 pr. sg.* **routeth** I.3647; *vbl. n.* **rowtyng(e)** snoring I.4166, rumbling HF 1933.

routh(e), rowthe, reuthe, rewthe *n.* (1) pity, compassion IV.893, VI.261, BD 97; **han r. of (on, upon)** pity I.2392, Tr 2.1270, Lady 49; **maketh r.** pities, feels sorry I.4200; (2) pitiful sight or occurrence I.914, IV.562, Tr 2.664; (3) grief, sorrow Tr 5.1637, LGW 1063; (4) lament LGW 669.

routhelees, routheles, rewthelees *adj.* without compassion, pitiless II.863, Anel 230, Lady 27.

rowe(s) *see* **rewe** *n.*

rowne(n) *v.* whisper III.1572, VIII.894, Tr 2.568; *pr. pl.* **rowne(n)** III.241; *pt. sg.* **rowned** III.1021; *prp.* **rownynge** IV.2130; *pp.* **(y)rouned** HF 722, HF 2107; *vbl. n.* **rounynges** whisperings HF 1960.

rude *adj.* (1) rough IV.916, IV.1012, IV.1798 rugged, wild IX.170; (2) humble III.1172; ignorant, unlearned I.3227, IV.2351, VIII.432; (3) boorish IV.750; crude, impolite VII.2808, Rom A 752; (as *n. pl.*) boors Rom B 2268.

rudenesse *n.* boorishness Tr 4.1489; humble, unsophisticated condition IV.397.

rule *see* **reule** *n.*

rule(d) *see* **reule(n)** *v.*

rumbelen *v.* rumble LGW 1218; *3 pr. sg.* **rumbleth** makes a rumbling sound HF 1026; *pt. sg.* **rombled** rumbled about, groped VIII.1322; *pt. pl.* **rombled** murmured, made a rumbling sound VII.2535; *vbl. n.* **rumblynge** rumbling noise III.2233.

rumour *n.* general talk Bo 3.pr6.16; uproar Tr 5.53; *pl.* **rumours** Bo 2.pr7.117.

S

(See also C)

sad, sadde *adj.* (1) serious, sober I.2985, IV.602, BD 860; (2) steadfast, firm IV.220, VIII.397, LGW 1521; solid Bo 5.pr6.168; trustworthy II.135, IX.258, HF 2089, PF 578; (as *adv.*) firmly IV.564; (3) **wexen s.** be satisfied VIII.877.

sadly *adv.* (1) soberly VII.76; steadily II.743; (2) firmly I.2602, III.2264; tightly IV.1100.

sadnesse *n.* steadfastness, constancy IV.452, Bo 4.pr1.59; seriousness IV.1591, IV.1604, Lady 25.

say(e), sayen, saigh *see* se(n).

saille, sayle(n) *v.* sail II.321, LGW 1328, LGW 1441; *3 pr. sg.* **sailleth** II.445, **sayleth** LGW 951; *pr. pl.* **saille** IV.2108; *pt. sg.* **saylede** LGW 958; *pt. pl.* **seyled;** VII.3104; *prp.* **saillynge** II.968, **seillynge** V.851, **saylynge** PF 179, **saylyge** (as *adj.*) PF 179; *pp.* **yseyled** VII.3099.

sayn *see* se(n).

sal *pt. sg. & pl.* (*Nth.*) shall I.4043, I.4174, must. Cf. **shal.**

salue, saluwe, salewe *v.* greet, salute VII.533, X.407, Tr 2.1016; *3 pr. sg.* **salueth** I.1492, **saleweth** V.91; *pr. subj. sg.* **salue** Rom B 2220; *imp. sg.* **salewe** Rom B 2525; *pt. pl.* **salwed** LGW F 315, **salued** Rom C 7429; *pp.* **salewed** V.1310; *vbl. n.* **saluyng** greeting I.1649; *pl.* **saluynges** Tr 2.1568.

sapience *n.* wisdom IV.1481, IV.2243, VII.472; good judgment Rom B 4718; *pl.* **sapiences** the mental faculties VIII.338.

sat(e) *see* sitte(n) *v.*

sauf, save *adj.* safe, secure II.343, III.1015, Mars 197; **myn hono(u)r s.** preserving (keeping intact) my honor Anel 267, Tr 2.480, Tr 3.159; **s. your grace** with all respect, VII.1070, VII.1082.

sauf, sauff, save *prep.* except, save for I.683, Tr 1.395, Pity 50, Rom B 2002.

saufly *adv.* (1) safely III.878, HF 291; (2) confidently, without fear of contradiction IV.870, V.761, VII.3208, Tr 4.1320.

saugh, sawe *see* se(n).

savacioun, savacion, salvacioun, salvacion *n.* (1) salvation (of one's soul) III.621, III.1498, VIII.848; (2) safety, security Mars 213, Tr 1.464; preservation, saving HF 208, Tr 2.486.

save *see* sauf *prep.*

save *conj.* except that III.998, IV.2085, BD 160.

save(n) *v.* save I.3533, II.860, Tr 1.122; preserve, keep, maintain I.3949, BD 1230, Tr 2.738; *3 pr. sg.* **savith** I.661; **saveth** II.907; *pr. subj. sg.* **God save** may God preserve I.2563, I.3108, Tr 2.163; *imp. pl.* **saveth** II.229; *2 pt. sg.* **savedest** II.639; *3 pt. sg.* **saved(e)** II.473, LGW 1955; *prp.* **savynge** except for I.2838; keeping safe, preserving IV.1766; *pp.* **saved** III.1092; *vbl. n.* **savynge** preservation Bo 3.pr12.100.

saverous *adj.* pleasing Rom A 84, Rom B 2812.

savynge *prep.* except for, save for I.2838, I.3971; preserving, with all respect to (one's honor, worship, *etc.*) IV.1766, BD 1271.

savour *n.* (1) taste VII.1158; flavor Bo 3.m1.6; delight III.2196, Tr 2.269, Fort 20; (2) smell, odor III.2226, V.404, Rom A 925; *pl.* **savours** odors PF 274, pleasures Bo 3.m1.6.

savoure *v.* taste III.171; *3 pr. sg.* **savoureth** X.122; *pr. pl.* **savouren** enjoy X.820; *imp. sg.* **savour** enjoy Truth 5; *pp.* **wel savoured** with a good odor Rom A 547; *vbl. n.* **savourynge** taste X.959, **savoryng(e)** X.207, X.209.

sawe *n.* saying I.1163, III.660; speech, what is said I.1526, VIII.691, Tr 5.38; report HF 2089; *pl.* **sawes** speeches Tr 2.41, reports HF 676.

scape(n) *v.* escape I.1107, I.3608, Tr 5.908; *2 pr. sg.*

scapest LGW 2643; *pr. subj. sg.* **scape** I.3800; *pp.* **scaped** II.1151; *pp.* **skaped** LGW G 119; *vbl. n.* **scapynge** Bo 4.pr4.191.

scars, skars, scarce *adj.* miserly, niggardly VII.1599, Rom B 2329; **scarse** Form Age 36.

scathe, skathe *n.* harm Tr 4.207, Tr 5.938; misfortune, pity I.446, IV.1172, Rom C 7565.

sch- *see* sh-.

sche, she *pro.* she VII.1051, Bo 2.pr8.16.

science *n.* (1) knowledge I.316, III.699, HF 1091; (2) art, branch of learning VIII.680, VIII.721; (3) learned composition VII.476; *pl.* **sciences** branches of learning V.1122.

sclaundre, sclaunder, sklaundre, slaunder *n.* disgrace, ill fame VII.183, LGW 814, LGW 1416; (personified) HF 1580; scandal X.137.

sclaundre *v.* slander VIII.993, VIII.998; *2 pr. sg.* **slaundrest** VIII.695.

sclendre *see* sklendre.

scole *n.* (1) school VII.495, VII.498, LGW 1896; "schools" of the universities III.1277, III.2186, VII.3237; a lesson Tr 1.634; (2) method I.125, I.3329; *pl.* **scoles** III.44c.

scorne(n) *v.* scorn, deride VII.1142, VIII.506, Tr 1.234; *2 pr. sg.* (with *pro.*) **scornestow** Bo 3.pr12.154; *3 pr. sg.* **skorneth** BD 625, **scorneth** X.379; *pr. pl.* **scorne** Bo 1.pr3.80, **skorne** HF 91; *imp. sg.* **scorne** Tr 1.576; *pt. sg.* **scorned(e)** VII.3087, mocked Bo 2.pr7.122; *pp.* **scorned** X.276; *prp.* **scornynge** Bo 2.m4.18, (as *adj.*) **skornynge** PF 346; *vbl. n.* **scornynge** scorn X.511, derision Tr 1.105.

scripture *n.* writing Bo 1.pr4.168; passage, text LGW 1144; inscription Tr 3.1369; *pl.* **scriptures** books I.2044.

se(e) *n.* [1] sea I.276, I.698, BD 67, Tr 1.1109; **Grete s.** Mediterranean I.59, BD 140.

see *n.* [2] chair, throne VII.2149, HF 1361; seat Tr 4.1023; *pl.* **sees** HF 210.

se(n), see(n) *v.* (1) see I.831, I.1349, I.1352, Ven 54; (2) **s. on (upon)** look upon I.1082, Tr 5.667; **s. of** look after VII.339; (3) understand I.947, II.938, LGW 688; *inf.* **to se, see(n), sene, seene** to be seen, to look upon I.914, I.1035, V.1349, PF 175, Tr 3.1093; *2 pr. sg.* **seest** I.2232, (with *pro.*) **sestow** Tr 3.46, **seestow** For 37; *3 pr. sg.* **seeth** II.266, **seith** Bo 3.m2.27, **seth** Bo 4.m1.6; *pr. pl.* **seen** I.3016, **se** I.3025, PF 600; *pr. subj. sg.* **god you see** may God watch over you (a greeting) III.2169, VI.715, Tr 2.85; *imp. sg.* **se(e)** I.4037, Tr 1.901; *imp. pl.* **see** IX.9, **seeth** X.77; *1 & 3 pt. sg.* **sey(e)** Bo 2.pr3.50, Tr 2.1355; **seigh** I.193, say III.645, **saigh** Tr 5.165, **saugh** IV.1033, say saw IV.667, saw BD 44; *2 pt. sg.* **sawe** II.848; *pt. pl.* **seyen** BD 842, **sye(n)** IV.1804, VII.3378, **sawe** II.218, **sayen** Bo 1.pr4.86, **sayn** II.172; *prp.* **seyng** Tr 4.363; *pp.* **seyen** Rom A 870, **(y)seye** III.552, HF 1367, **(y)sene** I.134, I.592, **seen(e)** I.924, BD 809, **(y)seyn** I.4379, BD 854, **sayn** II.172; *vbl. n.* **seyng** Tr 4.423.

seche-, seeche *see* seke(n).

secre(e) *n.* secret, confidential information III.1341, VII.1141, VII.2021; *pl.* **secrees** secrets VIII.1447 (see note).

secre(e) *adj.* (1) secret III.1871, IV.1937, Tr 1.744; (2) trusty, discreet III.946, PF 395; able to keep a secret IV.1909; (as *adv.*) secretly V.1109.

secreely, secrely *adv.* secretly IV.763, IV.2006.

sege, seege, siege *n.* (1) siege I.56, V.306, LGW 1696; (2) seat, throne Bo 1.pr4.15, Bo 1.pr4.255.

sey(e), seyen, (y)seye *see* **se(n).**

seyde- *see* **seyn.**

seigh *see* **se(n).**

seyn, seye(n), sayn, say(e) *v.* say I.181, I.468, VII.3046, Scog 34, Rom B 5712; **herd s.** heard tell, heard it said VII.531; **men sayth** it is said I.4210, PF 22, Tr 2.724; **sooth to s.** to tell the truth I.284; **as who seyth** as one may say Tr 5.883; **(was) for to s.** (was) to mean, meant I.3605, VII.523; *2 pr. sg.* **seist** I.1605, (with *pro.*) **seistow** I.1125, **seystou** IV.2125; *3 pr. sg.* **seith** LGW 1352, **saith** Astr 1.8.13; *pr. pl.* **seye(n)** III.935, III.1797; **seyn** III.945, **sayn** I.1198; **sygge** Tr 4.194; *pr. subj.* **seye** III.119 *(sg.)*, Tr 2.801 *(pl.)*; *imp. sg.* **sey** VII.705; *imp. pl.* **sey** VII.2805, **seyeth** I.1868, **seyth** V.1526; *1 & 2 pt. sg.* **seydest** III.348, **saydest** Rom C 7521, (with *pro.*) **seydestow** VIII.334; *3 pt. sg.* **seyd(e)** VII.1891, BD 1145, **sayde** I.70, **sayede** BD 215; *pt. pl.* **seyde(n)** Tr 1.90, Tr 5.1265; *prp.* **seiyng** Rom B 4042; *pp.* **seyd** I.305, **(y)sayd** V.1547, BD 270; *vbl. n.* **seiyng** Rom B 4031.

sek- *see* **sik-.**

sek, seeke *see* **sik(e).**

seke(n), seche(n) *v.* (1) *(tr.)* seek, look for I.13, I.17, III.1957, Tr 1.704; examine, investigate II.60, VII.3136; (2) *(intr.)* seek, search I.2587, II.521; (with *prep.*) I.1266; look about II.521; **s. upon** harass III.1494; (3) *(intr.)* beseech, petition (with **to**) Pity 91; (with **of**) Tr 5.940, LGW 2440; *inf.* **to seche, seken** to be looked for, sought I.784, VIII.874; *1 pr. sg.* **seeche** ABC 78; *2 pr. sg.* **sekestow** Tr 3.1455; *3 pr. sg.* **seketh** III.919, **secheth** Bo 3.m11.9; *pr. pl.* **seke(n)** HF 626, III.1002, **seche(n)** VIII.863, Tr 2.1068, **seeke(n)** Bo 2.pr4.114, Bo 2.pr4.128; *imp. sg.* **seke** VII.1693, **seche** Ven 69, **seek** Bo 1.m6.12; *pt. sg.* **sought(e)** I.1200, Rom A 624, **soghte** I.4404; *pt. pl.* **soughte(n)** VI.772, Tr 2.937; *pt. sg. subj.* **soghte** VI.488; *prp.* **sekyng** Rom C 6352; *pp.* **(i)sought** Tr 3.1317, **(y)soght** HF 626, Anel 290; *vbl. n.* **sekynge** Bo 4.m1.15.

seel, sel *n.* seal II.882, Rom B 5145; *pl.* **selys** Tr 3.1462.

selde, seeld(e), seelden, seldom *adv.* seldom I.1539, IV.427, VII.1153, VII.1404, LGW F 35; (as *adj.*) **s. tyme** seldom IV.146.

self *see* **selve.**

sely *adj.* (1) happy Tr 2.683; innocent, blessed II.682, III.132, HF 513; (2) hapless, wretched I.3404, I.3423, Tr 1.871; insignificant Tr 1.338; poor VII.11; (3) ignorant Tr 4.1490.

selle(n) *v.* sell I.278, I.140, Tr 3.1461; *inf.* **to selle** to be sold, for sale III.414; *3 pr. sg.* **selleth** X.784; *pr. pl.* **sellen** X.439; *pt. sg.* **solde** VII.2065; *pt. subj. sg.* **solde** Rom A 452; *pp.* **soold** I.4347, **sold** Rom B 5808; *vbl. n.* **sellyng** Rom C 5907.

selve *adj.* same I.2584, I.2860, HF 1157; **selfsame** Tr 3.355; very II.115, Bo 1.pr1.18; **it self** itself X.1042; **silf** same Rom B 2020; *pl.* **us selven** ourselves III.812, **us self** IV.108.

semblable *adj.* similar IV.1500, VII.1104, Bo 3.m6.2; equitable, fair Rom C 5911; (as *n.*) resemblance Rom B 4855; *pl.* **semblables** similar (cases) Rom C 6759.

semblaunce, semblance *n.* appearance Bo 3.pr10.218, Rom A 145, Rom B 425; likeness Bo 4.pr6.361.

semblaunt, semblant *n.* semblance, outward appear-

ance IV.928, V.516, LGW 1735; **maken s.** feign, pretend Rom A 152, Bo 1.pr1.5.

seme(n), seeme *v.* (1) seem II.1092, IV.132, HF 1291, Tr 1.703; (2) *(impers.)* it seems, seemed (to me, you, *etc.*) III.1463, V.201; **hem semed** they seemed V.56; *2 pr. sg.* **semest** Tr 2.1516; *3 pr. sg.* **semeth** IV.2409; *pr. pl.* **seme(n)** V.869, Rom C 7671; *pr. subj. sg.* **seme** III.1199; *pt. sg.* **semed(e)** I.39, Rom A 856; *pt. pl.* **semeden** VII.1018, Bo 2.pr5.110; *pp.* **semed** V.1146.

semely, semly *adj.* seemly, impressive I.751; comely I.1960, Rom A 563; *super.* **semelieste** IX.119.

semely, semyly *adv.* in a seemly, comely manner I.123, I.136, Rom A 748.

sen(e), (y)sene *see* **se(n).**

sende(n) *v.* send I.426, I.2317, LGW 1418; *3 pr. sg.* **sendeth** I.2762, *(contr.)* **sent** IV.1151; *pr. subj.* **sende** III.1258 *(sg.)*, VII.1796 *(pl.)*; *imp. sg.* **sende** I.3598; *imp. pl.* **sendeth** VI.614; *pt. subj. sg.* **sente** should send IV.1665; *pt. sg.* **sent(e)** I.400, Anel 194, **sende** I.4136, Rom A 1158; *pt. pl.* **sente(n)** II.136; *pp.* **(y)sent** II.960, II.1041.

sentement *n.* emotion, feeling Tr 2.13, Tr 3.43, LGW F 69; feeling, sensation Tr 4.1177.

sentence *n.* (1) meaning, significance VII.952, VII.3165, HF 710, Tr 1.393; substance, essential meaning VII.947, X.58, Mars 24; (2) contents, theme I.798, III.162; subject III.1126, III.1518, VII.3214; (3) opinion I.3002, IV.636, PF 383; decision, verdict I.2532, IV.791; **hy (heigh) s.** good judgment I.306, IV.1507; (4) authoritative saying, maxim II.117, II.1139, Tr 4.197; *pl.* **sentences** opinions, teachings X.77.

serchen *v.* search, analyze VII.1407; search out Rom B 4245; *pr. pl.* **serchen** visit, haunt III.867; *pp.* **serched** sought out Rom B 4809.

sergeant *n.* officer of the law IV.519, IV.524; **s. of the Lawe** high ranking lawyer I.309 (see note); *pl.* **sergeantz** VIII.361.

serkle *see* **cercle.**

sermone *v.* preach VI.879; *3 pr. sg.* **sermoneth** Rom C 6219; *vbl. n.* **sermonyng(e)** discourse, argument I.3091, Rom B 3333; **sermounynge** LGW 1184.

sermoun, sermon *n.* sermon, discourse III.1789, VII.1044, Mars 209; **make s.** discourse Tr 2.1299; *pl.* **sermons** II.87.

sert- *see* **cert-.**

servage *n.* bondage, servitude, captivity I.1946, II.368, BD 769; service V.794.

serve(n) *v.* (1) serve (someone) I.1143, BD 844, LGW G 252; (2) be of service, useful IX.339, PF 216, Tr 4.279; (3) treat, deal with IV.641, LGW 2365; *2 pr. sg.* **servest** Rom B 2131; *3 pr. sg.* **serveth** I.1421; *pr. pl.* **serve(n)** Tr 3.1265, Tr 5.174; *pr. subj. pl.* **serve** Rom C 6985; *imp. pl.* **serveth** PF 660; *pt. sg.* **served(e)** I.749, IV.640; *prp.* **servynge** Bo 3.pr11.92; *pp.* **(y)served** I.187, I.963.

servyse, service *n.* service I.250, BD 302; devotion V.224; religious service I.122, V.297.

seson, sesoun *n.* season I.19, I.1043, Tr 1.168; *pl.* **sesons** I.347, **sesouns** Bo 1.m5.21.

set, sete(n), seet *see* **sitte(n).**

sete, seete *n.* seat, throne VII.2525, X.162; residence Bo 1.pr5.29; place Bo 3.pr11.116; *pl.* **seetes** thrones, seats I.2580, **setes** Rom C 6913.

sete(n) *see* **sitte(n)**.

seth, seeth *see* **se(n)**.

sette(n) *v.* (1) set, put I.815, III.726, Tr 4.781; **s. on attack**, assail LGW 636; (2) *(reflx.)* sit down I.1541, VI.207; **s. hym (hire,** *etc.***) on knees** kneel I.3723, II.638; *(pass.)* be seated I.2528, VI.392; (3) arrange, set, assign I.4383, Mars 52; **s. a-werk** assign a job, put to work I.4337, III.215; (4) value I.1570, I.3756, Tr 3.900; **s. at nought** take no account of, reckon as worth nothing V.821, Tr 1.444; (5) assume Tr 2.367; **s. a cas** assume Tr 2.729; (6) **s. hir cappe, his howve** deceive them, him I.586, I.3911; *2 pr. sg.* **settest** Astr 2.42.14; *3 pr. sg.* **setteth** VII.1179, *(contr.)* **set** II.299, **sett** Rom B 4925; *pr. pl.* **sette(n)** X.606, care Tr 2.432; *pr. subj. sg.* **sette** Tr 3.832; *imp. sg.* **sette** Tr 2.729, **set** Astr 2.3.22, **sett** Astr 2.5.18; *pt. sg.* **sette(n)** I.4383, LGW 784; *pp.* **(y)set** I.132, IV.409, **sette** placed, set LGW F 534, Rom A 1620, **(y)sett** set Rom A 900; (as *adj.*) **tyme, day (y)set** the assigned time (day) I.1635, IV.774; *vbl. n.* **settyng** Astr 2.3.7.

seur, sure *adj.* sure VII.1452, VII.1763, Rom B 4221; *comp.* **seurere** Rom C 5958.

seur, sure *adv.* surely, sure Tr 4.421, Rom B 4221.

seurete(e), seurte(e), suretee, suerte *n.* (1) safety, security X.735, Tr 2.833, Tr 3.1678, Form Age 46; safeguard VI.937; assurance III.903; **in s.** confidently HF 723; (2) pledge I.1604, V.528; collateral II.243; surety, guarantee (to fulfill a pledge) V.1581.

sewe, suen, suwe *v.* follow VII.1429, VII.1502, Tr 1.379, Rom B 4953; *3 pr. sg.* **seweth** HF 840; *imp. pl.* **seweth** VII.1538; *pt. sg.* **sewed** pursued VII.3337; *prp. (as adj.)* **sewynge** conformable BD 959; *pp.* **sewid** Rom A 570.

shadde, (i)schad *see* **shedeth**.

yshadwed, shadewed, shadowid *pp.* shadowed I.607, Tr 2.821, Rom A 1511; *vbl. n.* **shadowing** shadow Rom A 1503.

shake *v.* shake I.1473, IV.978, Tr 1.869; *3 pr. sg.* **shaketh** IV.1849; *pr. pl.* **shaken** Tr 3.890; *pt. sg.* **shook** I.2265, **shoke** LGW 2344; *pt. pl.* **shoken** poured out, cast about HF 1315; *pp.* **shake** I.406, **ischaken** shaken, shimmering Bo 1.m3.15; *vbl. n.* **shakynge** shaking I.2466.

shal, shall, schal *1 & 3 pr. sg.* (1) *(tr.)* owe Tr 3.791, Tr 3.1649; (2) **s. be** is said to be HF 2053 (see note), LGW 1725; (3) *(aux.)* (obligation) must, ought to I.731, I.792, Anel 217; (with ellipsis of *inf.*) must do V.750, must go II.279, Tr 4.210; (4) *(aux.)* (denoting futurity) will, shall I.187, I.500, BD 114; (with ellipsis of *inf.*) I.1183, II.1078, Tr 2.134; (with *v.* of motion understood) I.3467, II.279, Tr 4.264; *2 pr. sg.* **shalt** I.1145, **schalt** Bo 2.pr3.25, (with *pro.*) **shaltou** I.1391, **schaltow** Bo 1.m4.16; *pr. pl.* **shul** I.1821, **shuln** X.141, **shulle(n)** X.162, X.191, **schullen** Bo 4.m1.44, **schollen** Bo 5.m2.13; *1 & 3 pt. sg.* **shold(e)** I.184, **shuld(e)** BD 772, Astr 2.3.60, **scholde** Bo 4.pr4.272, **schulde** Bo 1.pr3.13; *2 pt. sg.* **sholdest** I.1137, **scholdest** Bo 4.pr4.155, **schuldest** Bo 3.pr12.204; (with *pro.*) **sholdestou** III.1944, **scholdestow** Bo 2.pr5.102; *pt. pl.* **sholde(n)** X.213, Tr 1.73, **shulde(n)** HF 869, Pity 67, **schulde(n)** Bo 1.pr2.10, LGW G 298, **scholden** Bo 4.pr4.236.

shame, schame *n.* (1) shame, disgrace II.829, VI.214,

BD 617, Bo 4.m7.49; **don s.** disgrace, harm I.1555, I.3050, BD 1017; **it is s.** it is shameful, blameworthy I.503, VII.1604, Tr 3.249; **for s.** *(interj.)* you should be ashamed VII.2891, HF 557, Tr 3.1127; (2) modesty III.342, III.782, Tr 2.1286; fear of disgrace III.1393, V.752; embarrassment VIII.1095, PF 583, Tr 3.80; *gen.* **shames** Tr 1.180, **shames deeth** a shameful death II.819, IV.2377, LGW 2064.

shame(n) *v.* shame V.1164, V.1565; *3 pr. sg. (impers.)* **thee shameth** you are ashamed II.101; *pp.* **shamed** ashamed X.1061, Tr 5.1727, **(y)shamed** disgraced HF 356, HF 1634.

shamefast, schamefast *adj.* modest I.2055, VI.55; embarrassed VII.1046, LGW 1535; shamed Bo 4.m7.44; possessed of a sense of shame X.987.

shamefastnesse *n.* modesty I.840, VI.55; sense of shame X.986.

shape(n) *v.* (1) fashion, create, shape III.1463, Tr 3.411; (2) devise (a plan) II.210, PF 502; arrange matters I.2541, VI.813, Tr 2.1363; (3) appoint II.253; destine, ordain I.1108, I.1225, Anel 243; (4) *(reflx.)* prepare I.809, I.3403, Tr 4.1273, Tr 5.1211; intend I.4179, VI.874, LGW 1289; *3 pr. sg.* **shapeth** IV.1408, **schapeth** Bo 1.pr4.308; *pr. pl.* **shape(n)** II.966, Rom B 4418; *imp. pl.* **shapeth** Tr 4.925; *pt. sg.* **shoop** III.1538, **shop** Tr 1.207; *pt. pl.* **shopen** V.897; *prp.* **shapynge** directing IV.783; *pp.* **(y)shapen** I.4179, III.139, **shapyn** Tr 2.1092, **(y)shape** I.1225, IX.43.

shave *v.* shave I.3326; *pp.* **(y)shave** I.588, VII.2071, **shaven** Rom A 941; *vbl. n.* **shaving** shaving VIII.1239.

shedeth *3 pr. sg.* sheds, emits (a liquid) X.577; *pr. pl.* **sheden** put forth, build up (leaves) Bo 3.pr11.113; *pt. sg.* **shedde** shed VII.2257, **shadde** *(intr.)* poured down VII.2731; *pp.* **(i)schad** scattered Bo 1.m1.16, Bo 3.m2.29, **ischadde** Bo 4.pr.5.13; **sched** Bo 3.m7.4; *vbl. n.* **shedyng** Rom B 4975.

shef, sheef *n.* sheaf I.104, LGW F 190, LGW 2579; *pl.* **sheves** HF 2140.

sheld, sheeld, scheeld *n.* shield I.2122, Bo 1.m4.10, Tr 2.201; a unit of monetary exchange (as *pl.*) VII.331; *pl.* **sheeldes** coins I.278, shields I.2499.

shelde *see* **shilde**.

shen(e), sheene *adj.* bright I.115, I.1509, Rom B 3713.

shende(n), sheend *v.* (1) ruin, destroy II.927, PF 494, Tr 4.79, Rom B 3220; injure, harm HF 1016, Tr 5.893; defile X.854; (2) disgrace, shame Tr 5.1060; reproach Tr 5.1274; *3 pr. sg.* **shendeth** II.28, *(contr.)* **shent** X.848; *pr. pl.* **shende(n)** Tr 2.590, III.376; *pr. subj. sg.* **shende** should corrupt I.4410, ruin Tr 1.972; *pt. sg.* **shente** VII.2841; *pt. subj. sg.* **shente** should ruin Tr 2.357; *pp.* **shent(e)** I.2754, II.931, **(y)shent** punished, scolded, rebuked III.1312, VII.541; ruined IV.1320; **schent** defeated LGW 652.

shene, sheene *adv.* brightly Tr 4.1239, Mars 87.

shere, sheere *n.* pair of shears, scissors I.2417, VII.2056; *pl.* **sheres** III.722, X.418.

sherte *n.* shirt III.1186, IV.1985, HF 1414, Tr 3.738; nightshirt IV.1852; smock Tr 4.96, Tr 4.1522; *pl.* **shertes** X.197.

shete, sheete *n.* sheet Tr 3.1056, Form Age 45; *pl.* **shetes** X.197, **sheetes** I.4140.

shete(n), sheete *v.* shoot I.3928, X.714, LGW 635, Rom A 959; *3 pr. sg.* **shetith** Rom A 960; *pr. subj. sg.*

shete X.574; *pt. sg.* shette VII.85, shet Rom B 1727; *pp.* shette Rom A 1341.

shette(n) *v.* shut III.1141, VIII.517, Tr 3.1549; *3 pr. sg.* shitteth Rom B 4100; *imp. sg.* shette VIII.1137; *pt. sg.* shette I.3499, I.3634, Tr 2.1090; *pt. pl.* shette(n) VIII.1218, Tr 1.148; *pp.* shet I.2597, yshette II.560, shett Rom A 529, ischet Bo 5.pr5.106, shit Rom B 2767; *vbl. n.* shittyng shutting Rom A 1598.

shewe(n), schewe(n) *v.* (1) show, display HF 281, Bo 4.pr4.67, Bo 5.pr4.142; reveal, set forth III.2093, III.2219, BD 147; do me s. let me see Tr 3.44; (2) *(intr.)* is shown X.331, X.696; appear Rom A 1113; (with *inf.*) pretend, make a show of VII.1196; *inf.* to shewe to behold, be seen HF 1305; *3 pr. sg.* sheweth II.882, scheweth(e) Bo 4.pr4.251, Bo 5.pr6.15; *pr. pl.* shewe(n) VII.459, X.425; *pr. subj. sg.* shewe VIII.916, schew(e) Bo 4.pr4.64, Bo 3.pr10.190; *imp. sg.* shewe III.1690; *imp. pl.* sheweth VI.179, shew Sted 26, schewe Bo 3.pr1.40; *1 & 3 pt. sg.* shewed(e) I.2268, Tr 1.286; shewide Rom A 1637, schewyd Bo 4.pr4.168; *2 pt. sg.* schewedest Bo 3.pr12.180, (with *pro.*) schewedestow Bo 3.pr9.146; *prp.* shewynge VII.1428, (as *adj.*) brode schewynge wide open Bo 2.m7.4, shewing B 5755; *pp.* (y)shewed I.1938, Tr 5.1521, (y)schewid Bo 4.pr4.61, Bo 4.pr4.168; *vbl. n.* shewyng(e) showing, demonstrating Tr 4.1016, Rom B 4041.

shilde *v.* protect Tr 4.188; *pr. subj. sg.* God shilde (shelde) may God protect IV.1787, HF 88; God shilde (shelde) that may God protect against, forbid that I.3427, IV.839, LGW 2082.

shyne, schyne(n) *v.* shine Bo 2.pr5.85, Bo 3.pr8.9, Tr 4.299, For 62; *3 pr. sg.* shyneth I.976, schyneth Bo 3.m11.12; *pr. pl.* shynen I.2043, schynen Bo 2.m2.6; *pr. subj. sg.* shyne Tr 3.768; *imp. sg.* schyn Bo 3.m9.45; *pt. sg.* shyned(e) LGW 1119, LGW 2194, shoon(e) I.198, HF 507; shon(e) HF 1289, LGW 1428; *prp.* shynyng(e) III.304, VII.1450, schynynge Bo 1.m5.6; *vbl. n.* shynyng I.3255, schynynge radiance, splendor Bo 3.pr4.91.

shit- *see* shette(n).

sho(o) *n.* shoe I.253, III.492; *pl.* shoos I.3318, shoes I.457, shoon VII.732, Rom A 843.

shof *see* shouveth.

shook, shoke, shoken *see* shake.

shol-, schol- *see* shal.

shon, shoon *see* shyne.

shop, shoop, shopen *see* shape(n).

yshore, (y)shorn *pp.* shorn I.589, VII.1952, Tr 1.222, Tr 4.996.

shorte *v.* shorten I.791, III.1261, Tr 5.96; *3 pr. sg.* shorteth X.727; *pr. subj. sg.* shorte III.365.

shour *n.* shower I.3520, Tr 4.751; battle, assault Tr 4.47; *pl.* shoures I.1, shours hardships Rom B 4658.

shouveth *3 pr. sg.* shoves, pushes Bo 2.pr1.104; *pt. sg.* shof shoved PF 154, Tr 3.487; *pp.* shove(n) moved V.1281, placed Tr 3.1026, pushed Bo 2.pr1.103; (y)shove driven about, widely known LGW 726, LGW 1381; *vbl. n.* showvynge shoving IX.53.

shrewe, schrewe *n.* (1) scoundrel I.3907, HF 1843, Bo 3.pr4.28; (2) scold, shrew IV.1222, IV.1534; (3) malignant planet *(astro.)* Astr 2.4.52; moost s. greatest scoundrel III.505; *pl.* shrewes VI.835, schrewes Bo 3.pr4.49.

shrewe *1 pr. sg.* curse III.446, III.1062.

shrewed, schrewed, schrewide *pp.* (as *adj.*) cursed, wicked III.54, X.495, HF 275, Bo 1.pr4.187, Bo 2.pr6.110.

shrewednesse, schrewednesse, schrewycnesse *n.* wickedness VII.1531, HF 1627, Bo 1.pr4.191, Bo 4.pr4.52, Bo 4.pr7.72; malignancy III.734; *pl.* shrewednesses wicked deeds X.442, schrewednesses Bo 4.pr4.44.

shrift(e) *n.* confession III.1818, VIII.277, BD 1114, LGW 745.

shrighte *pt. sg.* shrieked, cried aloud I.2817, V.417; *pt. pl.* skriked VII.3400; *pp.* shright Tr 5.320.

shryve(n) *v.* (1) *(reflx.)* confess X.129, X.305, Tr 2.440; *2 pr. sg.* shryvest X.1014; *3 pr. sg.* shryveth X.371; *pr. pl.* shryve(n) X.298, confess X.106; *pp.* yshryve I.226, (y)shryven confessed VI.380, revealed Tr 2.579 *vbl. n.* shryvyng Rom C 6448.

shul-, schul- *see* shal.

sich *see* swiche *pro.* and swich(e) *adj.*

syd(e) *n.* (1) side, I.112, I.558, PF 98, Rom B 4159; on every s. from all sides, everywhere IV.81, IV.1801; upon eche s. from all sides III.256; on any maner s. in any way Tr 1.321; on no s. in any way Tr 4.1078; (2) behalf IV.1392, IV.1410, VIII.475; on every s. for all concerned V.1521; *pl.* sydes I.2635.

sygge *see* seyn.

syk, sigh *n.* sigh I.1117, V.498, PF 246; *pl.* sikes I.1920, sighes Rom B 2449.

sik(e), seeke, sek(e) *adj.* sick I.18, BD 557, Rom B 5733; (as *n.*) sick person PF 104, sickness III.394.

sik(e), siken, sighe(n) *v.* sigh I.1540, I.3488, X.228, Rom B 2414, Rom B 2580; *3 pr. sg.* siketh I.3619; *pt. sg.* siked I.2985, sighte II.1035; sighed(e) Rom B 1783, Rom B 1868; *pp.* siked Tr 5.738; *vbl. n.* sikynge Tr 1.724, sighing Rom B 2728.

siker *adj.* (1) safe Tr 1.927, Tr 2.1370; (2) sure, true I.3049, III.2069; assured, certain X.93, Tr 1.673; *comp.* sikerer truer, more accurate VII.2853, more assured Rom C 7308; *super.* sikerest most safe Rom C 6147.

siker *adv.* (1) with assurance Tr 3.1237; (2) truly, certainly III.465.

sikerly, sekirly, sikirly(e) *adv.* truly, certainly I.137, III.44e, Tr 2.520, Rom B 3816.

sikernesse, sikirnesse, sekernesse *n.* security, safety II.425, IV.1280, Bo 2.pr5.187, Tr 2.773, Rom B 3941; certainty BD 608.

sikly, siklich(e) *adv.* sickly Tr 2.1528, Tr 2.1543; s. bereth resent, dislike IV.625.

siknesse, sicknesse, seknesse *n.* sickness I.493, BD 36, BD 607, HF 1966; *pl.* seknesses Bo 3.pr7.4.

simylitude *n.* (1) equal, counterpart I.3228; (2) comparison VIII.431.

symonye *n.* selling or buying of ecclesiastical offices III.1309, X.781.

symple *adj.* simple, unaffected, modest I.119, III.1789, BD 861; made it s. behaved with simplicity Rom B 3863; ordinary VII.3245; unrestricted possession I.319.

symplesse *n.* simplicity Bo 4.pr6.119, Wom Nobl 15, Rom A 954.

syn *prep.* since I.1193, II.365, PF 484.

syn *conj.* since I.853, Tr 1.256; s. that since, since the time that I.601; since, because I.2328, V.457, Tr 3.646.

synge(n) *v.* sing I.236, Anel 347; *2 pr. sg.* **singest** Anel 18, (with *pro.*) **syngestow** IX.244; *3 pr. sg.* **syngeth** I.3360; *pr. pl.* **synge(n)** II.642, VII.2096; *pr. subj. sg.* **synge** II.294; *imp. pl.* **syngeth** VII.3320; *1 & 3 pt. sg.* **soong** I.122, **song** BD 1158, **sang** VII.771; *2 pt. sg.* **songe** IX.294; *pt. pl.* **songe(n)** III.216, IV.1735; **sungen** LGW G 131; *pt. subj. sg.* **songe** BD 929; *prp.* **syngynge** I.91; *pp.* **(y)songe** I.266, Tr 4.799, **(y)songen** I.1529, LGW F 270; *vbl. n.* **syngyng(e)** VII.557, Bo 3.pr1.10; *pl.* **singynges** Tr 3.1716.

singuleer, synguler *adj.* individual, private, personal VII.1435, VIII.997, HF 310; particular X.299; separate Bo 5.m3.8.

synke(n) *v.* (1) *(intr.)* sink I.2397, PF 7; sink down, recline LGW F 178; (with **in, into**) sink into, penetrate I.951, Tr 4.1494; (2) *(tr.)* cause to sink V.1073; *pr. pl.* **synken** VIII.912; *pr. subj. sg.* **synke** Anel 182; *pt. sg.* **sank** X.839; *pp.* **sonken** V.892.

synne *n.* sin I.561, Tr 1.566; *pl.* **synnes** IV.13.

synne(n) *v.* sin VI.138, X.914; *3 pr. sg.* **synneth** VII.1435; *pr. pl.* **synnen** VII.1530; *pt. pl.* **synned** X.136, **synneden** X.324; *pp.* **synned** X.96; *vbl. n.* **synnyng** X.235.

sir(e), ser *n.* (1) master I.355, VIII.918; master of the house, husband III.713; father I.4246, Tr 4.1455; (2) (polite form of address) sir I.1715, II.570, Rom A 800, (of a knight, only in Thop) VII.717, VII.2089, (of a priest) VII.282; *gen.* **sires** father's IV.2265; *pl.* **syres** Tr 4.179.

sit *see* **sitte(n)**.

sith(e), sithen, sitthe(n) *adv.* since, since that time I.3893, II.58, HF 59; **s. many yeres (a day, long while)** many years (days), a long time ago I.1521, V.536, Tr 1.718; next, then I.2617, VI.839, VII.2677; afterwards ABC 117.

sith, sithen *conj.* since I.930, I.1732, Tr 1.941; **s. that** since I.2102, I.3231, HF 218.

sithe *n.* times II.733, Rom A 80; **ofte(n) s.** many times I.1877, IV.233; *pl.* **sithes** I.485.

sitte(n), siten, sitt *v.* (1) sit I.94, III.838, Tr 4.1032, Rom B 3124; (2) suit, fit VIII.132; *(impers.)* suit, befit IV.1710, IV.2315; (3) pain Tr 3.240, Tr 4.231; *2 pr. sg.* **sittest** HF 657; *3 pr. sg.* **sitteth** I.1527, *(contr.)* **sit** I.1599; *pr. pl.* **sitten** I.2204; *pr. subj.* **sitte** VIII.841 *(sg.)*, VIII.1195 *(pl.)*; *imp. sg.* **sit** III.2174; *imp. pl.* **sitteth** Tr 2.213, **sit** III.714; *pt. sg.* **sat** I.271, **seet** I.2075, **set** BD 501, **satte** Tr 2.117, **saat** Astr 2.40.70; *pt. pl.* **sate** BD 298, **sete(n)** V.92, BD 431; *pt. subj. sg.* **sate** Tr 1.985, **satt** Astr 2.40.39, **sete** BD 436; *prp.* **sittyng(e)** I.633, HF 1394; (as *adj.*) *see below*; *pp.* **sete(n)** I.1452, LGW 1109; *vbl. n.* **sittynge** seating arrangement IV.958, act of sitting Bo 5.pr3.62.

sittyng(e), sittand *adj.* suitable, fitting Bo 1.pr3.17, Tr 4.437, Rom A 986, Rom B 2263; *super.* **sittingest** PF 551.

ska- *see* **sca-**.

skile, skyl, skylle *n.* grounds, reason VII.1810; **is s.** is reasonable II.708, IV.1152, Tr 2.365, Rom B 3606; **out of s.** unreasonable Rom B 5290; *pl.* **skiles** reasons, arguments V.205.

skilful(e) *adj.* (1) reasonable, suitable BD 894, Tr 3.287; (2) discerning II.1038, VIII.327, BD 534.

skilfully *adv.* reasonably, justly VIII.320, Tr 4.1265, Mars 155.

sklendre, sclendre, slendre *adj.* lean, slender I.587,

IV.1602, Rom A 858; weak, feeble IV.1198, VII.1957; meager VII.2833.

skriked *see* **shrighte**.

slake(n) *v.* (1) *(intr.)* (with **of**) omit, pass over LGW 619; slacken Bo 2.m5.5, Rom B 3108; diminish, fail Tr 2.291; desist IV.705 (2) *(tr.)* slake, put an end to V.802, satisfy LGW 2006; *3 pr. sg.* **slaketh** IV.1107; *pr. pl.* **slaken** loosen, set free Bo 3.m2.17; *pr. subj. pl.* **slake** VI.82; *pt. subj. sg.* **slakede** were to loosen Bo 2.m8.17; *pp.* (as *adj.*) **slakid** loosened Bo 5.m1.19.

slakke *adj.* slack, loose IV.1849, Bo 1.m1.17; slow I.2901; *comp.* **slakkere** slower (to repay) VII.413.

slaunder *see* **sclaundre**.

slawe(n), (y)slawe *see* **sle(n)**.

sle(n), slee(n) *v.* (1) slay, kill I.661, I.1222, III.1658, Tr 1.815; (2) extinguish VII.2732; mortify (in alchemy) VIII.1436; *2 pr. sg.* **sleest** Tr 4.455; *3 pr. sg.* **sleeth** I.1118; *pr. pl.* **sleen** II.964, **sle** V.462; *pr. subj. sg.* **sle** Tr 2.459; *imp. sg.* **slee** VII.1899; *pt. sg.* **slough(e)** I.980, Bo 2.m6.5, Tr 5.1477, **slow** II.627, **slowh** Bo 4.m7.40, **slouhe** Bo 4.m7.32; *pt. pl.* **slowe(n)** V.1430, Bo 4.m7.42; *pt. subj. sg.* **slowe** Tr 4.506, **slowh** Tr 5.1272; *pt. subj. pl.* **slowen** Bo 3.pr5.50; *pp.* **(y)slayn** I.63, I.2708, **slayne** BD 1069, **(y)slawe** slain I.943, II.484, **slawe(n)** IV.544, Tr 3.721; **sleyn** BD 26. Cf. **slo(o)**.

sleigh(e), sly(e) *adj.* sly, cunning I.3201, I.3940, Tr 4.972; ingenious V.230; artful, tricky VIII.981, Tr 5.898; (as *n.*) sly one I.3392.

sleighte, slyght(e), sleght(e) *n.* (1) trickery, cunning I.604, VI.131, Anel 125, Rom A 1286; (2) adroitness LGW 2084; skill, ingenuity I.1948, I.4050; (3) ingenious plan, trick IV.2131, Tr 2.1512; *pl.* **sleightes** IV.2421, **sleghtes** Tr 4.1451.

slep(e), sleep *n.* sleep I.1044, I.3643, IV.1060, BD 5, HF 114; *pl.* **slepes** I.1920.

slepe(n), sleep *v.* sleep I.3406, I.3685; *1 pr. sg.* **sleep(e)** V.721, VIII.153; *2 pr. sg.* **slepist** Rom B 4008, (with *pro.*) **slepestow** I.4169; *3 pr. sg.* **slepeth** II.597; *pr. pl.* **slepen** I.10; *pr. subj. sg.* **slepe** Tr 2.1636; *pr. subj. pl.* **slepe(n)** IV.118, VII.126; *pt. sg.* **sleep** I.98, II.745, **slep** Tr 2.925, **slept(e)** I.4194, Rom C 7130; *pt. pl.* **slepte(n)** III.770, Tr 3.746, **slepen** V.360; *prp.* **slepynge** II.21, (as *adj.*) sleepy BD 162; *vbl. n.* **slepyng(e)** sleep X.193, Rom A 25.

slewthe *see* **slouthe**.

slyde *v.* slip away IV.82, pass through Tr 5.769, slide by, pass Tr 5.351; *3 pr. sg.* **slideth** Bo 3.pr12.190, *(contr.)* **slit** VIII.682; *pr. pl.* **slyden** Bo 5.pr2.29; *prp.* (as *adj.*) **slydynge** wavering, changeable Tr 5.825, Bo 1.m5.34, Bo 4.m2.14; slippery VIII.732; flowing Bo 5.m1.17.

slo(o) *v.* slay (Rom B only) Rom B 1953, Rom B 5521; *pr. subj. sg.* **slo(o)** Rom B 4992, Rom B 5643. Cf. **sle(n)**.

slough, slow, slowh, slowe(n) *see* **sle(n)**.

slough, slow(e) *adj.* (1) slow (in wits) II.315, LGW 840, Rom A 322; (2) slow, sluggish III.1816, X.724; idle HF 1778.

slouthe, slewthe *n.* sloth, laziness II.530, V.1232; inaction Tr 2.286; one of the Deadly Sins X.388.

smal(e), small *adj.* (1) small I.146, I.2076, Rom A 1032; little V.71, VII.536; Tr 3.1462; (2) insignificant, minor VII.283, IX.73, Tr 2.1191; petty BD 1033, Rom A 191; humble IV.483; (as *n.*) small, minor things LGW F 550; **grete and s.** of all ranks, everyone I.4323, VII.24, of every variety I.3178, VII.105; (3) slim, slender I.3234, IV.1602, Tr 3.1247; delicate I.153, X.197, LGW F 118; elegant I.158; (4) high (of the voice) I.688, I.3360; *comp.* **smaller** Astr 2.38.8; *super.* **smallist** Astr Pro 74.

smal(e) *adv.* (1) finely VIII.760; **but s.** but little III.592, V.71; (2) delicately, elegantly I.3245, I.3320, Ros 11.

smert(e) *n.* pain I.3813, Tr 4.373, Rom B 2328.

smert(e), smart *adj.* painful I.2225, I.2392, BD 507; brisk VIII.768, nimble Rom A 831.

smerte(n) *v.* (1) *(tr.)* inflict pain V.564, Tr 2.1097; (2) *(impers.)* suffer I.230; (3) *(intr.)* feel pain, suffer, smart III.2092, VIII.871, Tr 1.1049, Rom C 7057; *3 pr. sg.* **smerteth** Tr 1.667, *(contr.)* **smert** ABC 152; *pr. subj.* **smerte** I.1394 *(sg.)*, VII.2713 *(pl.)*; *pt. sg.* **smerte** I.534; *pt. pl.* **smerte** VII.2713; *pt. subj. sg.* **smerte** Tr 4.1186.

smerte *adv.* sharply, painfully I.149, VI.413, Tr 4.243.

smyte(n) *v.* (1) strike I.1220, I.1658, LGW 1817; (2) cut I.3569, VI.226; *3 pr. sg.* **smyteth** I.1709, *(contr.)* **smyt** IV.122; *pr. pl.* **smyte** HF 777; *pr. subj. pl.* **smyte** V.157; *imp. pl.* **smyteth** Tr 3.1573, **smyt** IX.285; *pt. sg.* **smoot** I.1704, **smot** Tr 1.273; *prp.* **smyting** Tr 4.243; *pp.* **smyten** X.871, **ysmyte** Bo 3.m7.6, **smete** Rom B 3755, **smytted** Tr 5.1545 (? see note).

smok, smokke *n.* shift, simple garment (over which more elaborate clothing—sleeves, bodices, *etc.*—could be worn) I.3238, III.783, IV.890, Rom A 1195.

snybbe(n) *v.* rebuke I.523, Rom B 4533; *pp.* **snybbed** V.688.

so *adv.* so I.11, *etc.;* such III.215, IV.1167; (in *phr.*) **al so** as IX.167; (as *intens.*) **so as** as I.39, VI.393, **whether so** whether VII.2619, **who so** whoever Bo 5.m3.47, **what so** whoever I.522, whatever VII.2912, **why so** why BD 33, **if so be(n)** if it be, if V.564; (with *subj.* or *imp.*) as (or untranslated) I.2237, III.823, Tr 3.266.

so *conj.* so, provided that PF 605, LGW 1319; **so that** provided that III.125, III.625, HF 709.

sobre *adj.* (1) grave, serious II.97, IV.366, Tr 2.1592; sober, abstemious III.1902, IV.1533; (2) humble, demure Tr 5.820, LGW 2672.

sobrely, sobrelich(e) *adv.* gravely, seriously IV.296, V.1585, Tr 5.929; humbly Tr 2.648; sadly LGW 1759.

socour(e), sokour *n.* succor I.918, II.644, Tr 4.131, Rom B 2114; *pl.* **socours** Tr 2.1354.

sodeyn *adj.* sudden, unforeseen II.421, IV.316, Tr 2.667; impetuous Bo 2.pr3.80, Tr 5.1024.

sodeynly, sodenly, sodeynliche *adv.* suddenly I.1118, I.1575, Tr 1.209, Merc B 1.

soft(e) *adj.* (1) soft, tender I.153, III.1840; gentle V.907, Rom B 3762, **a s. pas** slowly I.3760, II.399; weak Tr 1.137; (as *n.*) **for s. ne for sore** for ease or hardship, for any reason Rom B 5519; (2) lax, negligent VI.101; (3) soft, quiet BD 917, Tr 5.636; *comp.* **softer** I.3249.

softe *adv.* (1) gently I.1021, I.2781, Tr 3.72; tenderly II.275; easily VI.543; **slepe(n) s.** sleep comfortably, deeply BD 255, Tr 1.195; humbly, without objection Tr 5.347; (2) quietly I.1773, I.3697, Tr 1.279.

softely, softly, softeliche *adv.* quietly I.4058, Tr 5.506;

gently V.636, VII.672, Bo 4.pr4.1; slowly VII.886, Tr 2.627; comfortably X.835.

soghte, (y)soght *see* **seke(n).**

sojourne, sojurne, sojorne *v.* remain, dwell III.987, IV.1796, Tr 5.598; stop, tarry Tr 1.850; *3 pr. sg.* **sojorneth** remains, continues Tr 1.326; *pp.* **sojourned** II.148.

solace *v.* comfort, give pleasure I.4146, HF 2008, PF 297.

solas, solaas *n.* (1) comfort, solace X.206; (for love pains) I.3200, Tr 1.31; (2) pleasure I.798, entertainment I.3335; comfort, refreshment VII.782.

sold(e), soold *see* **selle(n).**

soole, soul *adj.* solitary IV.2080, Rom B 2396, Rom B 2955.

solempne *adj.* (1) splendid, impressive II.387, IV.1125, BD 302; (2) dignified, important I.209, I.364.

solempnely *adv.* ceremoniously, solemnly II.317, V.179; with dignity I.274.

solempnytee *n.* splendor, ceremony I.870, III.629.

som(e) *pro.* some I.3175; one I.2119; **al and s.** one and all, everyone I.2761, everything, the sum of it III.91, PF 650 (also *pl.* I.2187); **som . . . som** one . . . another I.3031 (also *pl.* III.925–27); **his tenthe som,** one of ten, he with nine others Tr 2.1249; *pl.* **somme** HF 6, **some** Tr 4.995.

som(e) *adj.* some I.776, I.2844, BD 244; a certain I.640, I.1088, Tr 1.500; **s. certain** a certain BD 119; *pl.* **somme** VII.2127.

somdel, somdell, somdeel, sumdel *adv.* somewhat I.446, I.3337, Tr 1.290, Rom A 169; (as *pro.*) a part PF 112.

somer *n.* summer I.394, I.1337, Tr 3.1061; spring PF 680, Bo 1.m2.22, LGW F 142; **lattere ende of s.** autumn Bo 1.m6.17; (as *adj.*) IV.2049, PF 299, **first s. seson** spring Bo 1.m6.14; *gen.* **someres** II.554, **somers** LGW F 142; *pl.* **someres** Astr 2.26.20.

somme *n.* sum V.1220, V.1225, LGW 1559; *pl.* **sommes** VIII.675.

somne, sompne *v.* summon I.1577, III.1347; invite VII.1462; *2 pr. sg.* **sompnest** invite VII.1463; *pt. sg.* **somonede,** invited Rom B 1815; *pp.* **somoned** III.1620.

somonour, sumnour *n.* summoner I.543, III.332; *pl.* **somonours** III.1641.

somtyme *adv.* once, formerly I.65, I.85, (as two words) III.527; sometimes, at times I.1668, I.3383, HF 2088; sometime, at some future time I.1243.

somwhat, sumwhat *pro.* something I.3119, I.4203, HF 1998; **in s.** to some extent X.246.

somwhat, sumwhat *adv.* somewhat, a bit I.264, HF 1097, LGW F 411.

sond, soond *n.*[1] sand I.3748, II.509, VII.3267; *pl.* **sondes** HF 691, **soondes** Bo 3.pr11.104, **sandes** Bo 2.m2.4.

sonde, soonde *n.*[2] (1) dispensation (of God) decrees II.523, II.760; God's gifts VII.219; (2) message II.388, II.1049, Tr 3.492; (3) messenger, agent, servant VIII.525.

sondry(e), soundry, sundry *adj.* various, differing I.14, I.25, Tr 1.440, LGW G 276, Rom A 1406.

sone, soone *adv.* soon, quickly I.1420, I.1467, Bo 5.m1.5, Tr 5.104; **(ful) s.** immediately I.1022, I.2270, BD 130; *comp.* **sonner** VII.1450; *super.* **sonnest** VII.2526.

song, soong, songe(n), songyn *see* **synge(n).**

sonken *see* **synke(n).**

sonne, sunne *n.* sun I.7, I.30, Astr 2.5.19; *gen.* **sonnes** Tr 3.3.

soper, sopeer *n.* meal, supper I.348, V.1189, Tr 2.947.

soor(e) *n.* pain, misery I.1454, I.2233; **sore** VI.358, Tr 4.944; *pl.* **sores** Anel 242, **soris** Rom A 966.

sore, soore *v.* soar V.123, HF 499, Tr 1.670.

sore, soor(e) *adj.* sore, painful I.2220, I.2419, PF 13.

sore, soore *adv.* sorely, painfully, bitterly I.148, I.230; intensely I.2315, I.4229, Tr 1.95; extremely Rom B 4305; **hit sat me s.** it was painful BD 1220, Tr 3.240; *comp.* **sorer** LGW F 502; *super.* **sorest** PF 444.

sory(e), soory *adj.* (1) sad, miserable I.2004, IV.1244, Bo 3.pr7.12, Tr 2.1351; **s. countenaunce (cheere)** sad facial expression I.2010, I.3618; (2) sad, feeling compassion (for someone or something) BD 523, Tr 2.94; (3) wretched II.466, VIII.1349; unfortunate Rom A 1639; **s. grace** ill fortune, bad luck III.746, HF 1790; **with s. grace** with bad luck, unfortunately VI.876, (as imprecation) bad luck (to someone) VIII.1189; *comp.* **sorier** X.459.

sormounte *see* **surmounte(n).**

sort *n.*[1] kind, class I.4381, I.4419; type I.4044; company II.141.

sort *n.*[2] (1) lot, fate I.844, Tr 2.1754; (2) divination, sortilege, casting of lots X.605, Tr 1.76.

sorwe, sorow(e) *n.* sorrow I.951, Mars 124, (personified) Rom A 301; lamentation I.1277, III.594, VII.988; **with s.** to (his) sorrow VII.3253, (in imprecations) bad luck (to someone) I.4412, III.308; *pl.* **sorwes** I.2419, **sorowes** Rom A 334.

sorwe(n) *v.* grieve Tr 4.394, (with *for*) repent X.296; *2 pr. sg.* **sorwest** Tr 4.640, (with *pro.*) **sorwestow** Bo 1.pr6.75; *3 pr. sg.* **sorweth** I.2652; *pr. pl.* **sorwen** I.2824; *prp.* **sorwynge** Tr 1.9; *pp.* **sorwed** Tr 4.883, **sorwyd** Bo 1.pr5.59; *vbl. n.* **sorwynge** BD 606.

sorweful, sorwful(l), sorowful *adj.* (1) sorrowful I.1070, I.1106, BD 14; (2) sad, pitiful VII.3204, Anel 356, Tr 3.1361; sad, grim Bo 4.m2.5; *super.* **sorwefulleste** IV.2098.

sorwefully, sorwfully, sorwfullich *adv.* sorrowfully, sadly I.2978, Tr 1.114, Tr 5.1633; **s. a pas** at a sorrowful (slow) pace.

sote, soot(e) *adj.* sweet-smelling, fragrant I.1, PF 274, Tr 3.1194. Cf. **swete** *adj.* and **swoote.**

sote *adv.* sweetly LGW 2612.

soth(e), sooth(e) *n.* truth I.845, I.1521, ABC 137, Rom B 4059; **for s.** in truth, truly I.283; **in s.** truly Tr 5.143, Tr 5.371; **(the) s. to seyn (telle)** to tell the truth I.284, II.243, Tr 1.12, Tr 5.1028; **seyn (full, right) s.** to tell the truth, to speak truly I.4356, BD 514; *pl.* **sothes** VII.1177.

soth(e), sooth *adj.* true I.4357, HF 676, Tr 4.1597; *comp.* **sother(e)** VIII.214, Bo 3.pr9.137.

sooth, soth *adv.* in sooth, truly VI.636, Tr 3.1357.

sothfast(e) *adj.* true Bo 2.pr10.128, Tr 3.30, Tr 4.870.

soothfastnesse, sothfastnesse *n.* truth IV.796, IV.934, Tr 4.1080; certainty X.380, VII.1405.

sothly, soothly, sothely *adv.* truly I.117, I.468, Tr 3.1508, Astr 2.40.50.

soothnesse, sothnesse *n.* truth VIII.261, Bo 1.pr6.16.

sotil(e) *see* **subtil(le).**

sotilly *see* **subtilly.**

sought(e), soughte(n), (i)sought *see* **seke(n).**

soun *n.* sound 1.674, 1.2881, BD 162; talk, boasting LGW F 267; *pl.* **sounes** 1.2512.

sound(e) *adj.* healthy, safe Tr 3.1526, LGW 1619; **hoole and s.** completely healthy and well II.1150, VII.1015, Bo 4.pr1.70.

soune, soun- *see* **sowne(n).**

soupe(n) *v.* dine V.1217, Tr 3.560; *pr. pl.* **soupen** V.297.

sourdeth *3 pr. sg.* arises, originates X.450, X.475; *pr. pl.* **sourden** X.448, X.865.

sourmounte, sourmounteth *see* **surmounte(n).**

sours *n.* (1) upward flight III.1938, HF 544; (2) source IV.49, Tr 5.1591.

soutil *see* **subtil(le).**

soutiltee *see* **subtilte(e).**

soverayn, sovereyn, soveraigne *n.* lord, master VIII.590, ABC 69, Wom Nobl 28; *pl.* **sovereyns** VII.1438.

soveraynetee, sovereynetee, sovereignte *n.* sovereignty, mastery III.818, III.1038, Tr 3.171.

sovereyn(e), soverayn, sovereigne *adj.* best, most excellent I.67, I.2407, VI.136; supreme VI.91, Tr 4.316; *(astro.)* superior (*i.e.*, being in the western side of the zodiac) I.1974; ruling, sovereign II.276, III.1048, PF 422; *pl.* **sovereynes** Bo 5.pr2.22.

sowdan *n.* sultan II.177, II.436.

sowdanesse *n.* sultaness II.358, II.958.

sowne(n), soune(n) *v.* (1) *(tr.)* play (a musical instrument) I.565, V.270, Tr 2.1031; (2) mean, signify Astr 1.21.52; imitate, repeat V.105, Tr 2.573; (3) *(intr.)* resound, sound Bo 4.m5.16, LGW F 91; (4) (with **in, into**) tend toward, be consonant with V.517, Tr 1.1036; *3 pr. sg.* **sowneth** Tr 5.678, **souneth** Tr 3.1414; *pr. pl.* **sownen** X.1086; *pt.* **souned** Tr 4.1676 *(sg.)*, **sowned** VII.2158 *(pl.)*; *prp.* **sownynge** I.275; (as *adj.*) **sounyng(e)** resounding Bo 1.m2.16, Rom A 715; *pp.* (as *adj.*) **sowned** played Tr 2.1031.

space, espace *n.* (1) space of time IV.1029, V.1493; **a s. a while** I.2982, IV.918, Tr 2.767; opportunity, time I.35, V.493, Tr 1.1064; (2) space, area I.4124, HF 1238, Tr 1.714; room, spaciousness 1.176; *pl.* **spaces** Bo 5.m5.8. Cf. **espace.**

spak(e) *see* **speke(n).**

spare(n) *v.* (1) spare, leave unhurt III.421, Tr 1.435; economize IV.1297; (2) desist, refrain I.192, I.1396, III.1328; hold back I.737, III.1543; *(reflx.)* hold oneself back, be reserved I.3966; *3 pr. sg.* **spareth** X.558; *pr. pl.* **spare** III.1543; *pr. subj. pl.* **spare** VII.286; *imp. sg.* **spare** III.1763; *imp. pl.* **spareth** III.186; *pt.* **spared** X.996 *(sg.)*, BD 320 *(pl.)*; *prp.* (as *adj.*) **sparynge** frugal VII.1599, **sparand** miserly Rom B 5363; *pp.* **(y)spared** IV.2301, Tr 5.204; *vbl. n.* **sparynge** frugality X.835.

sparhauk, sperhauk *n.* sparrow hawk VII.767, VII.3457, Tr 3.1192.

spece *n.* species, kind X.407, X.486, Bo 5.pr4.161; *pl.* **speces** X.83. Cf. **especes.**

speche *n.* speech, talk I.307, I.517, BD 919; conversation V.238, V.964, Tr 3.1710; talk, gossip Tr 2.1291, Tr 3.584; manner of speech I.3338, IX.205, Tr 2.34; language II.519, VIII.1443; *pl.* **speches** Tr 3.510.

special(e) *adj.* special, particular X.488, X.738, Astr 2.4.6; (as *n.*) particular VII.1355; **in s.** in particular, particularly I.444, Tr 1.260. Cf. **especial.**

spede, speed *n.* success Tr 1.17, Tr 1.1043; cause of success, help Tr 2.9; **commun s.** the good of all PF 507.

spede(n), speede *v.* (1) *(intr.)* succeed, prosper VI.134,

Tr 1.865, Bo 5.pr5.22; (2) *(reflx.)* hasten, hurry I.3728, III.1732, PF 385; (3) *(tr.)* help, give success, cause to prosper I.769, I.2258, Tr 1.1041; dispatch Bo 5.pr4.21; **nedes** s. accomplish one's purpose I.4205, Tr 2.954, Rom C 6983; speed, hasten I.4033; *pr. subj. sg.* **speede** 1.729, **spede** I.2258; **the devel spede him may the devil hasten (take) him** Tr 4.630; *imp. sg.* **speed** I.3562, **sped** PF 133; *imp. pl.* **spede** III.1732; *pt. sg.* **spedde** I.1217; *pt. pl.* **spedde(n)** Tr 5.501, Tr 5.508; *pp.* **(y)sped** I.4205, I.4220.

speke(n), **spekyn** *v.* speak I.142, I.413, BD 76, Bo 5.pr3.201; *2 pr. sg.* **spekest** V.676, (with *pro.*) **spekestow** III.837; *3 pr. sg.* **speketh** I.2203; *pr. pl.* **speke(n)** I.4146, II.214; *pr. subj. sg.* **speeke** IX.324, **speke** X.911; *imp. sg.* **spek** IX.346; *imp. pl.* **speketh** IV.19; *pt. sg.* **spak** I.124; *pt. pl.* **speeke(n)** V.247, VII.1267, **speke(n)** V.232, V.244, **spake(n)** Tr 1.565, Tr 3.-463; *pt. subj. sg.* **spake** Bo 2.pr3.1; *prp.* (as *adj.*) **wel spekyng** well-spoken Rom A 1268; *pp.* **yspoke(n)** I.2972, Tr 4.1108, **spoke(n)** I.31, VI.707; *vbl. n.* **spekyng(e)** IX.335, LGW 1500.

spende(n) *v.* spend, expend I.4135, III.1796, Tr 4.1376; pass (time) IV.391, LGW 650; **tales** s. make conversation Tr 4.702; *3 pr. sg.* **spendeth** VIII.832; *pr. pl.* **spende(n)** I.806, VI.781; *imp. sg.* **spende** Rom B 2274; *pt. sg.* **spente** I.300; *prp.* (as *adj.*) **spendyng** VIII.1018; *pp.* **spent** I.645, **ispendid** Bo 5.pr4.22.

spere *n.*[1] spear I.114, I.975, Tr 2.1427; *gen.* **speres** LGW 645; *pl.* **speres** I.1653.

spere, speer(e) *n.*[2] sphere, orbit V.1280, V.1283, Tr 3.1495, Astr 1.17.19; *pl.* **speres** PF 59, **speeris** Bo 1.m2.13.

sperhauk(e) *see* **sparhauk**.

spice *n.* spice, herb PF 206, Rom A 1367; *pl.* **spices** IV.1770; spiced cakes, sweetmeats V.291, Tr 5.852, LGW 1110.

spicerye *n.* mixture of spices VI.544, LGW 675; delicacies, tidbits VII.853; oriental goods (spices, cloth, *etc.*) II.136.

spye(n) *v.* spy III.316, Rom B 1717; espy, discover VIII.314; *pt. sg.* **spyed** watched for V.1506. Cf. **espye(n)**.

spille *v.* (1) *(tr.)* put to death, kill III.898, III.1611; ruin III.388, spill (blood, tears) X.571, Tr 5.880; waste IX.153; (2) *(intr.)* die I.3278; *2 pr. sg.* (with *pro.*) **spillestow** Bo 1.pr4.4; *pr. subj. sg.* **spille** should die II.285; *pt. sg.* **spilte** spoiled, ruined Rom B 5136; *pp.* **spilt** IX.326.

(y)spoke(n) *see* **speke(n)**.

sprede(n) *v.* spread VII.577, Bo 2.m3.2; expand Tr 1.278; *3 pr. sg.* **spredeth** Tr 2.980; *pr. pl.* **spreden** Tr 2.970; *pt. sg.* **spradde** IV.722, **spredde** Rom B 3633; *pp.* **(y)spradde** Tr 4.1422, Bo 3.pr6.20, **(y)sprad** I.2903, Bo 2.m7.10, **yspred** I.4140, **sprede** Rom B 3635.

sprynge *v.*[1] spring, rise up I.822, I.2173, Tr 1.745; leap 1.1871; become widespread Anel 74; *3 pr. sg.* **springeth** III.1939; *pr. pl.* **sprynge(n)** I.2607, V.1147; *pt. sg.* **sproong** I.3282, **sprong** VI.111, **sprang** IV.940; *prp.* (as *adj.*) **spryngyng(e)** Bo 2.pr5.67, Rom A 762; *pp.* **(y)spronge** I.1437, HF 2081, **sprongen** VII.1210; *vbl. n.* **spryngyng** IV.49.

springen *v.*[2] sprinkle, mingle II.1183; *pp.* **(y)spreynd** I.2169, II.422, **spraynd** Bo 2.pr4.119.

squier *n.* (1) young knight (knight bachelor, the first degree of knighthood) I.79, V.926; (2) squire, servant to a knight I.1410, I.2502; *pl.* **squieres** I.2502, **squiers** V.293.

stak *see* **stiken**.

stande, stant *see* **stonde(n)**.

starf *see* **sterve(n)**.

stat(e), staat *n.* condition, rank, state I.572, Rom B 5229, Rom B 5423; *pl.* **states** Rom C 6548. Cf. **estat**.

statut *n.* law, statute 1.327, III.198, PF 387; *(pl.)* rules statutes Astr Pro 101, **statutz** Scog 1, **estatutz** Bo 2.pr1.43.

stede, steede, stide *n.*[1] place HF 731, HF 829, Rom B 4862; **in** s. **of** instead of I.231, VI.953, HF 654; **stant in no** s. has no value VII.1090.

stede, steede *n.*[2] steed, war-horse I.2157, I.2727, Tr 5.1038; *pl.* **steedes** Tr 3.1703.

stedefastnesse, stedfastnesse, stidefastnesse, stidfastnesse *n.* steadfastness IV.699, IV.1050, Anel 81, Ven 5, Sted 7; loyalty IV.2063.

stel, steel(l), stiel *n.* steel PF 395, Tr 2.593, Tr 3.480, Rom A 946.

stele(n) *v.* (1) *(tr.)* steal I.562, I.3940, Tr 5.48; (2) *(intr.)* steal away, go quietly I.3786, Tr 4.1503; *3 pr. sg.* **steleth** II.21; *pr. pl.* **stelen** X.790; *pt. sg.* **stal** I.3995, **staal** BD 381; *pp.* **stole(n)** I.2627, II.744, **stoln** I.4111; *vbl. n.* **stelyng** X.800.

stent, stent- *see* **stynte(n)**.

stere, steere, styere *n.* (1) rudder HF 437, LGW 2416, Bo 3.pr12.74; **in** s. astern Tr 5.641; (2) guide II.448, II.833, Tr 3.1291.

stere, stire(n) *v.* (1) *(intr.)* stir, move HF 567, Rom B 1805; (with **to**) move, incite VI.346, VII.1506; (2) *(tr.)* excite, provoke (emotions) Tr 1.228, Tr 3.910; stir, cause to move about VIII.1278, HF 817; set forth, propose Bo 3.pr12.200; discuss Tr 3.1643; *3 pr. sg.* **stereth** HF 817, **stireth** VII.1127; *pt. sg.* **stired** VIII.1278; *prp.* **steryng** moving Tr 3.692, **stiryng** Tr 3.1236, (as *adj.*) **stiryng** HF 478; *pp.* **stired** X.446; *vbl. n.* **steryng(e)** movement HF 800, Rom B 2409, **stiryng(e)** X.355; *pl.* **stirynges** X.655.

sterne *see* **stierne**.

sterre *n.* star I.2061, II.852, PF 68; planet BD 824, HF 1376; *pl.* **sterres** BD 409; *gen. pl.* **sterres** IV.1124.

sterte(n) *v.* (1) move suddenly or vigorously I.1044, II.335; (with **up** or **doun**) leap I.952, I.1080, Tr 2.447; *(reflx.)* move oneself, leap I.1579; tremble I.1762; rush III.573, Tr 2.1634; flow (blood, tears) LGW 851, LGW 1301; suddenly awake I.1393, IV.1060; go Tr 4.93, LGW 811; (2) *(tr.)* flush out (game) Tr 3.949; s. **up** uncover Bo 3.pr12.140; *3 pr. sg. (contr.)* **stert** rouse, flush out (a hare) HF 681; *pr. pl.* **sterte** LGW 1301; *pt. sg.* **sterte** I.952, **sterte** III.1046; *pt. pl.* **stirte(n)** VI.705, VII.3377; *prp.* **stertyng** rushing LGW 1741; *pp.* **ystert** gone into, immersed in II.4, **stirt** leaped V.1377, **stert** IV.1060.

sterve(n) *v.* die I.1249, III.1242, Tr 1.17; *pr. subj. sg.* **sterve** I.1144; *pt. sg.* **starf** I.933; *pt. pl.* **storven** VI.888; *pp.* **ystorve** I.2014.

steven(e) *n.* (1) voice I.2562, VII.3197, BD 307; sound of the voice HF 561; talk, report Tr 3.1723; (2) sound BD 307, LGW 1219.

stid- *see* **sted-**.

stierne, sterne *adj.* stern, grim IV.465, X.170, Tr 4.94; cruel I.2154, I.2441; strong, violent I.2610, Tr 3.743.

stif *adj.* strong I.673, Rom A 115; hardy Rom A 1270; hard III.2267.

stiken *v.* (1) *(tr.)* pierce, stab I.1565, II.430, Tr 1.297;

(2) affix, place VII.907; *(intr.)* stick II.509; *3 pr. sg.*
stiketh I.3877; *imp. sg.* styke Astr 2.38.7; *pt. sg.*
styked II.509, steked LGW 2202, stak Tr 3.1372;
prp. stykynge piercing VI.211; *pp.* (y)stiked II.433,
V.1476, (as *adj.*) VI.556; *vbl. n.* stikynge placing
X.954.

stikke *n.* stick, twig VIII.1265, ABC 90; *pl.* stikkes tree
trunks I.2934.

still(e) *adv.* still, motionless I.1003, I.1527; quietly
I.2985, I.3721, HF 2107; still, continually, yet I.1335,
I.3420, Rom B 3124.

stille *v.* quiet, make peaceful VII.1487; silence Tr 2.230;
3 pr. sg. stilleth makes peaceful VII.1514.

stille *adj.* still, silent I.2535, V.497, PF 511.

stynge *v.* sting IV.2059; pierce LGW 1729; *3 pr. sg.*
styngeth III.1995; *pp.* stongen I.1079, ystonge
VI.355.

stynketh *3 pr. sg.* stinks VIII.1067; *pr. pl.* stynken
VIII.886; *pt. sg.* stank VII.2617; *prp.* (as *adj.*) stynk-
yng(e) VI.534, X.157.

stynte(n), stente(n) *v.* (1) *(intr.)* stop, cease I.4339, HF
1926; stop talking I.2811, VIII.927; cease, stop an
activity I.903, IV.703, Tr 2.1361; stop speaking about
I.1334, I.2479, Tr 1.1086; refrain VII.2735; hesitate,
delay LGW 633, LGW 821; (2) *(tr.)* stop, bring to a
stop I.2450, I.2732, Tr 2.383; *3 pr. sg.* stynteth Tr
3.898; *pr. subj. sg.* stente Ven 61; *pr. subj. pl.* stynte
I.4339; *imp. sg.* stynt I.3144; *imp. pl.* stynteth I.2674,
stynte Tr 2.1242; *pt. sg.* stynt I.2421, stente
IV.1023; *pt. pl.* stynten Tr 2.103, stente IV.340; *pt.
subj. sg.* stynte were to stop Tr 1.848; *prp.* stynt-
yng(e) hesitating BD 1213; *pp.* ystynt III.390, stynted I.2968, stent I.1368; *vbl. n.* styntynge ceasing Bo
2.m7.32.

stire(n), stireth, stiryng(es) *see* stere.

stiropes *n. pl.* stirrups II.1163, III.1665.

stirt(e), stirte(n) *see* sterte(n).

stole(n), stoln *see* stele(n).

stomak *n.* stomach Bo 3.m12.41, Tr 1.787; appetite
III.1847; compassion III.1441.

ston, stoon *n.* (1) stone I.774, 1888, Tr 2.600; (as
adj.) Tr 2.47; rock Tr 2.843; (2) gem I.2146,
IV.1888, HF 1184; (3) testicle VII.3448; *pl.* stones
I.3210.

stonde(n), stande(n) *v.* (1) stand (upright) I.3830,
I.4101, Tr 1.292; stand (be placed) I.745, I.3923, BD
156; **s. at,** to stand ready I.788, X.60; withstand PF
164; **s. by, at** defend II.345, IV.1185, VII.1912; **s.
agayn** resist, deny III.1488; **s. at,** to abide by II.36, PF
546; (2) **s. in** be (in grace, dread, *etc.*) I.88, IV.1091,
VII.237, Tr 2.714; **s. in** be in a condition of Tr 2.752,
Tr 4.1662; be, exist Bo 2.pr4.140; **s. so** is thus I.1322,
IV.346; **it s. with** (someone) someone's condition is
I.3426, Tr 1.602; **s. on, in** consists of, depends on
X.107, X.743, Truth 10; endure IV.2314; *2 pr. sg.*
stondest I.657; *3 pr. sg.* stondeth I.1639, standeth
VII.257, *(contr.)* stant I.3677 stont Rom B 5581; *pr.
pl.* stonden Tr 1.428; *imp. sg.* stond Tr 1.969, stand
I.4101; *imp. pl.* stondeth IV.1195; *pt. sg.* stood I.354,
stod LGW 1014; *pt. pl.* stode(n) II.176, II.678, stood-
e(n) IV.1715, IV.1902; *pt. subj. sg.* stood Tr 1.1039;
pp. stonden IV.1494, ystonde Tr 5.1612; *prp.* stond-
yng(e) II.68, Tr 3.506; *pp.* stonden IV.1494,
ystonde Tr 5.1612.

stongen, ystonge *see* stynge.

store, stoor *n.* livestock I.598, VI.365; possessions
III.2159; **to his s.** as his possession LGW 2337; **in s.**
in stock, in reserve IV.17; **tell(en) of no s.** regard as
of no value III.203, VII.3154.

storie, story(e) *n.* (1) historical narrative 1.1201,
I.1464, HF 149, LGW F 421; ecclesiastical narrative
I.709; (2) story, tale IV.1186; *pl.* stories I.859,
storyes LGW 2484.

(y)storve, storven *see* sterve(n).

stounde *n.* time, space of time I.1212, I.3992, Tr
3.1695; **in a s.** once, at a certain time I.3992; moment,
brief space of time II.1021, Tr 1.1086; *pl.* stoundes
III.286; **by stoundes** in turn Bo 4.m6.25.

stoupe *v.* stoop VIII.1311, Rom B 2662; *3 pr. sg.*
stoupeth IV.2348; *pr. pl.* stoupen Tr 2.968; *imp. pl.*
stoupeth VIII.1327; *prp.* (as *adj.*) IV.1738.

stout(e) *adj.* strong, sturdy I.545, Tr 5.1454; bold
I.2154, Tr 5.1493; proud, arrogant Rom B 4015,
Rom C 6158.

strangle, straungle *v.* strangle, destroy X.769, Bo
1.pr4.236; *3 pr. sg.* strangleth X.792; *pr. pl.* stranglen X.768; *pp.* strangled destroyed I.2018; *vbl. n.*
stranglyng(e) throttling I.2458, destruction X.1006,
strangelynge killing LGW 807.

straught(en) *see* strecche(n).

straunge, strange, estraunge *adj.* (1) foreign I.13,
I.464, II.178; strange, unknown IV.138, V.89; different Astr 2.19.6; unusual, surprising Tr 5.120; exotic
V.67, Tr 2.24; external III.1161; not of the family Tr
2.1660; (2) distant, reserved VII.263, PF 584; un-
friendly Rom A 1065; (as *n.*) strangers Tr 2.411;
made it s. raised difficulties I.3980, V. 1223; *comp.*
straunger Tr 4.388.

straungenesse, strangenesse *n.* distance, aloofness Rom
B 3611, Rom B 4056; estrangement VII.386; exotic
style X.414.

straunger *n.* stranger LGW 1075; *pl.* straungiers foreigners Bo 1.pr3.56, Bo 5.pr4.65.

strawen, strowe *v.* strew LGW F 207, LGW G 101; *pr.
subj. sg.* strawe V.613; *pp.* (y)strawed X.198, BD
629.

stre, straw *n.* straw I.2918, I.3873, Tr 2.1745; chaff
Rom C 6354; (with sette, roghte, *etc.*) nothing at all,
not a bit VII.3090, BD 671, HF 363; (as *interj.*) **s.
(for)** an expression of contempt IV.1567, V.695; *pl.*
strees BD 718.

strecche(n) *v.* (1) *(tr.)* stretch out VI.395, VII.3308 (2)
(intr.) extend VIII.469, VIII.1087; **s. to** extend to, be
concerned with Tr 1.888, be capable of Bo 5.pr5.63;
3 pr. sg. streccheth Tr 1.903; *pr. pl.* strecchen
VII.1825; *pt. sg.* streighte HF 1373; *pt. pl.* straughte
I.2916; *prp.* strecchynge VII.3332; *pp.* streyght(e)
Bo 3.pr1.4, (as *adv.*) streght stretched out Tr 4.1163,
straught(en) Bo 5.m5.3, (as *adv.*) stretched out Rom
A 1021; strecchid Bo 5.pr6.31.

streyght(e) *see* strecche(n).

streight(e), streght(e) *adj.* direct I.1690; straight BD
942, Tr 3.1247, Astr 2.26.22; *comp.* strayghter Rom
A 119.

streight, streght *adv.* directly, straightly I.671, Tr 1.53;
immediately I.1650, Tr 1.324, Tr 3.552.

streyne, strayne *v.* (1) clasp tightly IV.1753, Tr 3.1482,
Rom A 1471; press, constrict Tr 3.1071; strain (a
substance) Bo 1.m6.13; (2) constrain IV.144; restrain,
confine Astr 1.14.6, Rom A 1471; *3 pr. sg.* streyneth

constrains VII.3244; *pr. pl.* **streyne** strain VI.538; *pr. subj. sg.* **streyne** would constrain Bo 5.pr6.167; *pt. sg.* **streyned** constricted, pained Rom C 7629.

streit(e) *adj.* (1) narrow I.1984, Bo 3.m2.27; tight-fitting Rom B 2271; strict 1.174; (2) small 1.4122; scanty III.1426, VII.2989; **s. swerd** drawn sword VII.3357.

streite *adv.* tightly Tr 4.1689; strictly, closely IV.2129, LGW 723.

strem, streem *n.* stream, current I.464, I.3895, PF 138; *gen.* **stremes** Scog 43; *pl.* **stremes** I.402.

streng, stryng *n.* string III.2067, Tr 2.1033; *pl.* **strenges** PF 197; *pl.* **strynges** Tr 1.732.

strenger(e), strengest *see* **strong(e)**.

strepe(n), streepe *v.* strip I.1006, IV.863, Bo 4.m2.2; *3 pr. sg.* **strepeth** IV.894; *pr. pl.* **strepen** IV.1116.

strete, streete *n.* street, road I.2902, I.4384, Tr 2.612; *pl.* **stretes** Tr 2.1248.

strif *n.* strife I.1187, I.1282, Tr 2.780; **s. of Thebes** siege of Thebes II.200; **maken s.** cause trouble III.2000; **took s. ayens** argued against, contended with Bo 1.pr4.88.

strike *n.* stroke, line Astr 2.12.17; *pl.* **strikes** Astr 1.9.4; marks, divisions Astr 1.7.8.

striken *v.* strike III.1364; *pt. sg.* **strok** Rom B 3763; *pp.* **(y)strike** Merc B 34, Merc B 35.

stryve(n) *v.* strive, quarrel, I.3040, IV.170, Tr 4.175; vie, contend Bo 2.m8.19; *3 pr. sg.* **stryveth** Tr 3.38; *pr. pl.* **stryve(n)** I.1177, X.664; *pr. subj.* **stryve** X.664 *(sg.)*, PF 606 *(pl.)*; *imp. sg.* **stryf** Bo 2.pr2.7, **stryve** III.1986; *pt. sg.* **stroof** I.1038, **strof** Tr 5.819; *prp.* **stryvynge** Bo 4.m6.24, (as *adj.*) quarrelsome Bo 2.pr7.124; *pp.* **stryven** Bo 1.pr3.24; *vbl. n.* **stryvyng(e)** VI.550, VII.1484.

strogelest *see* **strugle**.

strok, strook *n.* stroke, blow I.1701, Tr 2.1382, Rom C 6468; *pl.* **strokes** I.1922.

strok *see* **striken**.

stronde *n.* strand, shore II.825, II.864, LGW 1498; *pl.* **strondes** I.13.

strong(e), stroong *adj.* strong, powerful I.1056, I.2373, Tr 1.57; difficult, painful VII.1445, Tr 5.864, LGW F 569, Rom B 2639; arrant, downright IV.2367, VI.789; *comp.* **stronger** VII.1348, **strenger(e)** VI.825, Bo 3.m12.54; *super.* **strongest(e)** VII.1337, VII.2075, **strengest** Tr 1.243.

stronge *adv.* firmly PF 231, Rom A 241; stoutly Rom A 944.

strugle *v.* struggle IV.2374, IV.2376; *2 pr. sg.* **strogelest** VI.829; *vbl. n.* **struglyng** II.921.

sturdy, stordy, stourdy *adj.* strong, obstinate III.612; stout III.1754, Tr 2.1380; harsh, cruel IV.698, IV.1049, Bo 3.m2.11; **a s. pas** angrily III.2162.

subget, subgett, subgect, suget, subgit, subject *adj.* subject, subordinate X.264, Bo 5.pr4.157, Bo 5.pr5.17, Bo 5.pr6.101, Tr 1.231, Tr 2.188.

subgetz, subgetis, subgitz *n. pl.* subjects, subordinates III.1990, IV.482, X.467, X.634, Bo 4.pr5.14.

substaunce, substance *n.* (1) substance, essential quality VI.539; actuality Tr 4.1505; meaning VII.2803; majority Tr 4.217; (2) income I.489; possessions VII.999; provisions Tr 4.1513; *pl.* **substaunces** Bo 5.pr2.24.

subtil(e), subtille, subtyl, sutile, soutil, sotil(e) *adj.*

(1) ingenious, skillful I.2049, I.3275, IV 1427, Tr 2.257, Rom A 688; crafty V.285; carefully compiled Astr Pro 75; complex Bo 5.m3.17; (2) delicate I.1054, Tr 1.305; thin I.2030, PF 272.

subtilly, subtyly, sotilly *adv.* craftily, subtly I.610, IV.2003, LGW 797; skillfully V.222, V.1284, Rom A 772.

subtilte(e), subtilite(e), soutiltee *n.* craftiness VIII.620, VIII.1371, Rom C 6172; subtlety HF 855; trickery, guile III.576; trick III.1420; treachery IV.691; *pl.* **subtilitees** tricks IV.2421.

suen *see* **sewe**.

suerte *see* **seurete(e)**.

suffisaunce, suffisance *n.* sufficiency I.490, IV.759, Tr 3.1309.

suffisaunt, suffisant, sufficeant, sufficient *adj.* sufficient I.1631, II.243, Bo 5.pr4.26; capable VI.922, LGW 1067, LGW 2524; adequate VII.1027, Astr Pro 8.

suffise(n), suffice *v.* suffice, be sufficient I.4125, II.1099, Tr 5.994, Rom B 5625; be capable of, able VII.1650, BD 902; able to endure Tr 4.258; *(impers.)* it enough I.1953, I.2039; **s. me (hym)** is enough for me (him) IV.1626, HF 1876; *3 pr. sg.* **suffiseth** I.1953, **sufficeth** HF 1762; *pr. pl.* **suffisen** III.1882; *pr. subj. sg.* **suffise to the let** this be sufficient for you Astr Pro 28, **may suffise** IV.740; *imp. sg.* **suffyce unto** be satisfied with Truth 2; *prp.* **suffisynge** I.3629; *pp.* **suffised** I.1233.

suffraunce, suffrance *n.* patience, forbearance IV.1162, X.625, Bo 5.m4.47.

suffre(n), soffre *v.* (1) allow, permit I.649, I.945, BD 468; (2) endure, suffer III.252, V.537, Tr 3.1105; *2 pr. sg.* **suffrest** Tr 3.1021, (with *pro.*) **suffrestow** Bo 1.m5.34; *3 pr. sg.* **suffreth** I.1219; *pr. pl.* **suffren** Tr 3.1018; *pr. subj.* **suffre** Sted 24 *(sg.)*, Tr 3.881 *(pl.)*; *imp. sg.* **suffre** Rom B 3461; *imp. pl.* **suffreth** II.437; *pt. sg.* **suffred(e)** VII.979, X.663, **sufferec** LGW 2092; *pt. pl.* **suffred** BD 1292, **suffered(e** LGW 1510, LGW 1575; **suffriden** Bo 1.pr4.72; *pp.* **(y)suffred** VII.1505, BD 37; *vbl. n.* **suffrynge** VII.1466, **sufferyng** Ven 45.

sugitz *see* **subgetz**.

sumwhat *see* **somwhat**.

suppose *v.* believe, think III.786, III.1791, Tr 2.1254; *imp. pl.* **supposeth** Rom B 3106; *pt. sg.* **supposed** V.575; *prp.* **supposynge** VIII.871; *pp.* **supposed** VII.595; *vbl. n.* **supposyng(e)** supposition IV.1041, VIII.873.

sur- *see* **seur-**.

surmounte(n), sormounte *v.* surpass, surmount Bo 5.pr5.66, Rom A 667; *3 pr. sg.* **surmounteth** LGW F 123, **sourmounteth** Tr 3.1038; *pr. pl.* **surmounten** Bo 4.pr6.115; *pt. sg.* **surmountede** LGW G 131; *pp.* **surmounted** BD 826.

suspecioun, suspeccion, susspecioun, suspecion *n.* suspicion I.681, IX.281, Tr 2.561, Rom B 2507, Rom B 5222.

suspecious *adj.* suspicious IV.540, Rom C 6110.

suspect *n.* suspicion VI.263; **have (be) in s. (of)** suspect, be suspicious of IV.905, VII.1197.

susten(e), susteene, susteyne *v.* sustain, support, maintain I.1993, II.160, Tr 2.1686, Rom B 5636, Rom B 6783; *3 pr. sg.* **sustenith** Bo 4.pr7.87; *pr. pl.* **sustenen** X.439; *pt. sg.* **susteynede** Bo 4.m7.59; *pp.* **sustened** VII.490, **sustenyd** Bo 4.pr7.18, **susteynec** Bo

3.pr11.174; *vbl. n.* **susteyning** sustenance Rom C 6697, **susteynyng** Rom B 2765.

suster *n.* sister I.871; *pl.* **sustren** Tr 5.3, **sustres** VII.2867.

suwen *see* sewe.

swatte *see* swete *v.*

sweigh(e) *n.* motion II.296, Bo 1.m5.4; swaying, momentum Tr 2.1383.

swelle *v.* swell I.2752, IV.2306; *3 pr. sg.* **swelleth** I.2743; *pr. subj. sg.* **swelle** VI.354; *pt. sg.* **swal** III.967; *pp.* **swollen** IV.950; *vbl. n.* **swellynge** X.391.

swelte *v.* grow faint, *(fig.)* die Tr 3.347; faint Mars 216; *2 pr. sg.* **swelte** Rom B 2480; *pt. sg.* **swelte** I.1356, Mars 128.

swelwe, swolwe, swalowe *v.* swallow VII.1618, IX.36, HF 1036; *3 pr. sg.* **swelweth** VII.1618; *pr. pl.* **swolwen** Bo 3.pr11.156; *pr. subj. sg.* **swelwe** IV.1188, **swolwe** X.731.

swerd *n.* sword I.112, I.558, Tr 2.203; *gen.* **swerdes** I.2646; *pl.* **swerdes** I.1700.

swere(n) *v.* swear I.454, X.594, Tr 3.269; *3 pr. sg.* **swerith** Tr 2.654, **swerth** Tr 5.1430, **swereth** X.596; *pr. pl.* **sweren** X.599, **swern** Rom B 4834; *pr. subj. pl.* **swere** VIII.147; *imp. sg.* **swere** BD 753; *imp. pl.* **swere** IV.357, **swereth** X.591; *pt. sg.* **swoor** I.959, **swor(e)** Tr 3.556, LGW 1378; *pt. pl.* **swore(n)** I.1826, IV.496; *pp.* **(y)sworn** I.1089, I.1182, **yswore** HF 421, **swore(n)** IV.403; (as *adj.*) VI.808, **sworne** III.1405; *vbl. n.* **sweryng(e)** VI.631, X.602.

swet(e), sweete *adj.* sweet, pleasing, dear I.5, BD 108, Rom B 2652; *comp.* **swetter** Rom A 622. Cf. **sote** *adj.* and **swoote**.

swete, sweete *n.* sweetness PF 161; sweetheart V.978, BD 204, Tr 1.533.

swete, sweete *v.* sweat VIII.522, HF 1042; *pr. pl.* **swete** Tr 2.943; *pt. sg.* **swatte** VIII.563.

sweete *adv.* sweetly, pleasingly, gently I.3305, I.3691, Tr 5.191.

swetely *adv.* sweetly, gently I.221, I.3215, BD 849.

swetnesse *n.* sweetness VII.555, Tr 1.638, Tr 1.1043.

sweven(e) *n.* dream VII.2740, VII.2896, BD 119; *pl.* **swevenes** VII.3091, **swevenys** VII.2921, **swevnes** Tr 5.358.

swich, sich *pro.* such, such a one V.41, V.519, Rom B 5047.

swich(e), such(e), sich(e) *adj.* such I.3, X.894, PF 283, Tr 1.296, Bo 3.pr9.132, LGW 1257, Rom A 26; **s. oon** such a one V.231, Tr 1.369, Tr 1.521, Rom B 2193.

swymme *v.* float I.3550, I.3575; swim LGW 2450; laze about, luxuriate Rom C 7007; *pr. pl.* **swymmen** swim in, are surrounded by III.1926; swim with, abound in PF 188.

swynk *n.* work, labor I.188, I.540, I.4253.

swynke(n) *v.* (1) *(intr.)* work I.186, III.202, LGW 2041; (2) *(tr.)* earn by working VIII.21; labor, employ HF 16; *3 pr. sg.* **swinkith** Rom B 5675; *pr. pl.* **swynke** I.3491; *prp.* **swynke** Rom C 6757; *pp.* **swonken** I.4235, **yswonke** IX.18; *vbl. n.* **swynkyng** Rom C 6703.

swithe *adv.* quickly II.730, PF 503; **as s.** immediately, without delay II.637, VIII.936, PF 623; **as s. as** as soon as Tr 5.1384.

swyve *v.* *(tr.)* copulate with I.4178, IX.256; (2) *(intr.)* copulated, fornicated I.4266; *pt. sg.* **swyved** IV.2378; *pp.* **swyved** I.3850.

swolwe(n) *see* swelwe.

swoote, swote *adj.* sweet, sweet-smelling I.2860, I.3205, Tr 3.1231, LGW F 173; (as *adv.*) sweetly Tr 1.158. Cf. **sote** *adj.* and **swete** *adj.*

swough, swogh *n.* ¹ sound of wind I.1979, HF 1031, PF 247; groan I.3619.

swough, swogh, swow *n.* ² swoon, faint III.799, IV.1100, Tr 3.1120; anguish, grief BD 215.

swowne *v.* swoon, faint Tr 2.574, Mars 216; *3 pr. sg.* **swowneth** V.430; *imp. pl.* **swouneth** Tr 3.1190; *pt. sg.* **swowned** I.2923; *prp.* **swownynge** I.2819; *pp.* **(y)swowned** I.913, LGW 1342; *vbl. n.* **swownyng(e)** IV.1080, IV.1087, **swonyng** Rom B 1737.

T

t' *contr.* of **to** often used before vowels (*e.g.,* **t'abide** Tr 5.33).

table *n.* (1) tablet, surface for writing I.1305, HF 142, Bo 5.m4.18; **first t.** first set of Commandments VI.639; (2) table I.100, VI.490, BD 646; **t. dormant** permanently set-up table I.333; (3) table (of astronomical calculations) Astr Pro 91; (4) plate Astr 1.14.3, Astr 2.21.5; (5) *(pl.)* backgammon V.900, X.793, BD 51; *pl.* **tables** tablets III.1741.

tache *see* tecche.

take(n) *v.* (1) *(tr.)* take I.34, II.963, Tr 2.69; **t. kepe** take heed I.503, VI.352, BD 138; **t. on (upon) hym (me,** etc.) undertake I.3160, VI.612, VIII.605; consider III.1116, Tr 1.344; **t. in desdayn (agref,** etc.) take in disdain, be upset, etc. I.789, III.191, Tr 5.1625; (2) give, bring VII.294, BD 48; give, strike III.792; (3) *(reflx.)* betake oneself, go X.842; (4) *(intr.)* (with **to)** come III.31; take place, come about Tr 4.1562; *inf.* (Nth.) **taa** I.4129, *2 pr. sg.* **takist** Astr 2.29.13, (with *pro.*) **takestow** VIII.435; *3 pr. sg.* **taketh** I.1217; *pr. pl.* **take(n)** I.1879, II.147; *pr. subj.* **take** BD 142 *(sg.),* VII.2893 *(pl.);* *imp. sg.* **tak** BD 138, Astr 1.1.3, **taak** VII.1180; *imp. pl.* **taak** I.789, **take** X.598, **taketh** VI.74; *pt. sg.* **took** I.303, **tok(e)** LGW 814, Astr 1.10.16; *pt. pl.* **tooke** IV.202; *pt. subj. sg.* **tooke** would take IV.1582; *prp.* **takyng** Astr 2.25.4; *pp.* **take(n)** I.1439, I.2551, **ytake(n)** I.3353, Bo 3.pr12.181; *vbl. n.* **takyng(e)** VII.1032, VII.1435.

tale *n.* (1) tale, narrative I.36, I.330, BD 60; conversation, talk BD 1213, Tr 2.218, Tr 2.267; something to say BD 553; (2) esteem, regard VII.3118, PF 326; *gen.* **tales** Tr 2.260; *pl.* **tales** conversations, talking Tr 3.149, tales I.792; gossip III.319.

tale(n) *v.* (1) talk Tr 3.231, Tr 3.1235; (2) tell tales I.772; *pr. subj. sg.* **tale** X.378.

talent *n.* inclination, desire VI.540, VII.1249, Tr 3.145; *pl.* **talentes** X.915, **talentz** Bo 4.pr4.189.

talke(n) *v.* talk V.692, VIII.663, Tr 5.668; *vbl. n.* **talkyng** VIII.684; *pl.* **talkynges** Rom C 6042.

tare *n.* weed, something worthless I.1570, I.4000.

targe *n.* shield I.471, I.955, Anel 33.

tarie(n) *v.* (1) *(tr.)* delay, keep (someone) waiting IV.1696, V.73, VII.2947; tarry, waste (day, time, etc.) I.2820, I.3905; (2) *(intr.)* tarry, delay I.3409, II.374; *3 pr. sg.* **tarieth** Tr 5.862; *pr. subj.* **tarie** Tr 3.1195 *(sg.)* V.1233 *(pl.);* *imp. sg.* **tarie** I.3905; *pt. sg.* **taried(e)** X.998, PF 415; *pp.* **taried** V.402, (as *adj.*) Tr 2.1739; *vbl. n.* delay **tarynge** I.821; **tariyng(e)**

I.3546, II.262; **tareing** Astr 2.25.30; **taryinge** PF 657, Tr 5.1437.

tecche, tache *n.* quality Rom B 5166; defect Wom Unc 18; *pl.* **tecches** qualities HF 1778, faults Tr 3.935.

teche(n) *v.* teach I.308, I.654; *3 pr. sg.* **techeth** V.104; *pr. pl.* **teche(n)** IX.132, Tr 1.698; *imp. sg.* **teche** III.1418; *imp. pl.* **teche** III.187, **techeth** Tr 3.41; *pt. sg.* **taught(e)** I.497, LGW F 544, **teched** Rom C 6680; *pt. pl.* **taughte** VI.364; *pp.* **(y)taught** I.127, II.224; *vbl. n.* **techyng(e)** I.518, VIII.93; *pl.* **techynges** VII.1870.

teyne *n.* flat metal rod or plate VIII.1225, VIII.1229; *pl.* **teynes** VIII.1332.

telle(n) *v.* (1) tell I.38, I.73, BD 34; **herd t.** heard it told III.1675; (2) count X.390, BD 440, HF 1380; enumerate VIII.799; (3) **t.** of respect, account IX.236; **t. no deyntee (tale)** of have no regard for III.208, PF 326; **t. of no stoor** regard as worthless III.203, VII.3154; *inf.* **to telle** to be told V.447; *2 pr. sg.* **tellest** Rom C 6798; *3 pr. sg.* **telleth** I.797, **telles** BD 73, **tellis** HF 426; *pr. pl.* **telle(n)** I.859, V.824; *pr. subj.* **telle** Tr 1.830 *(sg.)*, VII.2092 *(pl.)*; *imp. sg.* **tel** III.2251, **telle** V.702; *imp. pl.* **tel** I.808, **telleth** I.910; *1 & 3 pt. sg.* **toolde** VII.2021, **told** I.1059, **tald** *(Nth.)* I.4207; *2 pt. sg.* **toldest** Bo 4.pr1.14; *pt. pl.* **tolde(n)** I.3184; *pt. subj. sg.* **tolde** VII.2653; *prp.* **tellyng(e)** Tr 1.743, Tr 4.127; *pp.* **told** PF 224, **ytold** VIII.627, **(y)toold** I.2924, I.3109; *vbl. n.* **tellyng** VII.948.

temporel, tempoeel, temporal *adj.* temporal, worldly II.107, III.1132, VII.999; *pl.* **temporele** X.1039, **temporels** VII.998, **temporeles** X.685.

tempreth *3 pr. sg.* mixes VIII.901; *pt. sg.* **temprede** tempered, hardened PF 214, **tempride** harmonized, Bo 3.m12.19; *pp.* **tempred** mixed VIII.926, Rom B 4180, Rom B 5476.

tempte *v.* try, test III.1661, IV.452; *3 pr. sg.* **tempteth** IV.1153; *pt. sg.* **tempted** X.322; *pp.* **tempted** IV.621.

tene, teene *n.* (1) harm, trouble Anel 140, Tr 2.61, ABC 3; (2) sorrow, grief Anel 179, Tr 2.61; (3) source of vexation, grief I.3106, Tr 3.1226.

tercel, tersel *adj.* male (eagle) PF 393, PF 463; *pl.* **tercels** PF 540; (as *n.*) PF 405, PF 415.

tercelet, terslet *n.* young male falcon V.504, PF 533; *pl.* **tercelettes** V. 648, **tercelets** PF 659.

terme *n.* (1) period of time BD 79; specified period of time Tr 5.1090; **t. of (one's) lyf** duration of (one's) life III.644, III.820; appointed time Tr 5.696, Tr 5.1209; **terme-day** appointed day BD 730; (2) end, goal Bo 3.m9.48; limit, boundary Bo 2.m8.11, Bo 3.m12.57; (3) word, expression I.3917; technical language VI.311; (4) *(astro.)* term, a division of a zodiacal sign V.1288; *pl.* **termes** Year Books I.323; technical words I.639, IV.16; expressions I.3917.

than(ne), thenne *adv.* then I.12, I.42, BD 288, Bo 5.pr5.18, Rom C 7138.

than(ne) *see* **then.**

thank, thonk *n.* thanks, gratitude I.612, IV.1801, Tr 1.803; **kan (someone) t.** owe thanks, be grateful I.1808, I.3064; good will, favor Tr 3.1777; *gen.* (as *adv.*) **his (hir,** *etc.*) **thankes** willingly, voluntarily I.1626, III.272; *pl.* **thankes** VII.188.

thanke(n), thonke *v.* thank I.3069, V.557, Tr 2.1415, Tr 3.76, Tr 3.1594, Tr 3.1664; *3 pr. sg.* **thanketh**

II.383, **thonketh** V.1545; *pr. pl.* **thanke(r)** IV.616, V.354, **thonken** IV.188; *pr. subj. sg.* **thanke** IV.1088; *pr. subj. pl.* **thanke** VII.2197, **thonken** Tr 2.1719; *pt. sg.* **thanked** V.753, **thonked** Tr 3.1130; *pt. pl.* **thonked** I.1876; *imp. sg.* **thanke** LGW F 454; *imp. pl.* **thonketh** II.1113; *prp.* **thankyng** III.1868; *pp.* **(y)thanked** I.925, III.2118, **(y)thonked** IV.2385, Tr 4.2; *vbl. n. pl.* **thankynges** VII.1804.

thar *3 pr. sg. impers.* (with *inf.*) **him t., t. thee,** *etc.* he, you must, need I.4320, III.329, Tr 2.1661; *pt. subj. sg.* **thurste** Tr 3.572. Cf. **dar, durst.**

that *rel. pro.* that, which, who I.43, I.344, BD 212; what I.1425, VIII.642, Tr 5.187.

that *conj.* that I.226, I.297, BD 107; so that II.262; as soon as II.1036; (after *conj.* and *rel.,* untranslated) **though that** though I.68, **if that** if I.399, **wherfore that** why I.1568, **which(e) that** which IV.1587, *etc.*; (introducing exclamations) III.614, IV.2338, VII.1999.

that, thatt *def. art.* that I.102, I.113, Astr 2.4.11.

the, thee *2 sg. pro. dat.* and *acc.* you I.3728, *etc.*

(y)the, thee(n) *v.* succeed Tr 1.341, Tr 4.439. prosper, thrive III.2232, VII.817; *1 pr. sg.* (with *pro.*) **theek** I.3864, **theech** VI.947.

thef, theef *n.* thief I.1325, I.3791, LGW 2330; *gen.* **theves** LGW F 465; *pl.* **theves** VI.789, **theeves** ABC 15.

theigh *see* **thogh.**

then, than(ne) *conj.* than I.219, I.1153, HF 13, Bo 4.pr4.130.

thenke(n), thenche, thynke(n) *v.* (1) *(intr.)* think BD 100, HF 387, Rom B 4806; (2) *(tr.)* think, consider Tr 1.818; imagine I.346, I.3253, Tr 2.1255; believe I.1606, Tr 4.1498; intend VII.1834, VII.1834, Merc B 28; understand Bo 5.pr4.15; *2 pr. sg.* **thynkest** Tr 2.1506; (with *pro.*) **thynkestow** Tr 2.1373, **thenkist** Rom B 2818; *3 pr. sg.* **thenketh** Tr 4.1453, **thynketh** Tr 1.221; *pr. pl.* **thynke(n)** I.3701, III.2204, **thenke(n)** V.537, X.671; *pr. subj. sg.* **thenke** HF 806; *pr. subj. pl.* **thynke** VII.954; *imp. sg.* **thynk** I.1606, **thenk** I.3478; *imp. pl.* **thenketh** VI.75; *pt. sg.* **thoughte** I.1574, **thoghte** I.1767; *pt. pl.* **thoughte(n)** III.2030, Tr 1.927; *prp.* **thynkyng(e)** X.689, Tr 3.1539, **thenkynge** Tr 1.1062; *pp.* **thought** Tr 4.554; *vbl. n.* **thynkynge** X.111.

thenne *see* **thynne.**

thenne(s), thens *adv.* thence, from that place or time II.308, III.1141, HF 1038.

ther(e), theere, thare *adv.* (1) there I.43, I.208, Bo 5.pr1.88, Tr 5.1358; (2) where I.892; (3) (as introductory expletive) I.118, I.1179, PF 595; (with optative clauses of blessing or cursing, untranslated) I.2815, III.1561, Tr 3.947.

ther(e) *rel.* and *conj.* where I.892, I.2984; wherever I.3702, III.237; **overal t.** wherever III.128; wherein III.128; once, at that time VIII.724; **t. as** where I.172, BD 197.

therto(o) *adv.* to there I.48; to that VIII.738; to it Tr 1.266; for that purpose V.1330; moreover, in addition I.153, I.289, BD 1250.

therwith *adv.* with that I.678; with it I.3777; with this, with which Tr 3.884, Tr 4.1212; whereupon, immediately I.1299; **anoon (right) t.** immediately BD 500, Tr 3.199.

therwithal, therwithall(e) *adv.* therewith I.566, I.1078, LGW F 148, Rom A 226; moreover I.3233,

Anel 86; with that, immediately I.1078, Tr 5.253; simultaneously I.3788.

(i)thewed *pp.* endowed with good characteristics PF 47, Rom A 1008.

thewes *n. pl.* personal qualities, morals IV.409, IV.1542, Tr 2.743; good qualities HF 1851.

thider *adv.* thither, there I.2275, I.2545, LGW 1475.

thiderward *adv.* thither, toward there Tr 2.1250, HF 2144, Rom B 3192.

thikke *adj.* thick I.1056; dense, set closely together I.1579, IV.1824; **t. of** thick with, thickly set with I.1075, BD 399, BD 418; stout, sturdy I.549, I.3973, LGW 1198; (as *n.*) thick I.4066; *comp.* **thikkere** PF 273; *super.* **thikkest(e)** I.2612, Astro 1.3.1.

thikke *adv.* thickly, densely I.2510, I.3322, Tr 4.1356; frequently Tr 2.456.

thilk(e) *dem. adj.* that, that same I.182, I.1193, Rom A 145.

thyn(e) *poss.* (1) (as *adj. usu.* before vowel and **h-**) thy, your I.951, VII.2077, Tr 2.1022; (2) (as *pro.*) thine, yours I.1235, VI.653.

thyng *n.* thing I.985; document I.325; possessions I.490; **any t.** at all Tr 1.848; **for any t.** at all costs I.276; **on alle t.** whatever the circumstances BD 141; *pl.* **thynges** I.175.

thynke(n) *see* thenke(n).

thynke *v. impers.* (with *dat.*) seem Tr 1.405; *3 pr. sg.* **me, (yow, etc.) thynketh** (it) seems to (me, you, etc.), (I, you, *etc.*) think I.37, I.1867, BD 545; **us thinketh hem** they seem to us Tr 2.25; **me thenketh** it seems to me Rom B 4117; *pr. subj. sg.* **thynke** LGW 2671; *pt. sg.* **thoughte** I.385, **thoghte** LGW F 232; *pt. pl.* **thoughten** LGW 1697.

thynne, thenne *adj.* thin Bo 2.m7.20; sparse IV.1682, Form Age 36; (as *n.*) thin I.4066; (as *adv.*) I.679.

thirleth *3 pr. sg.* pierces Anel 211; *pp.* **thirled** I.2710, **thrilled** Rom C 7634.

this *dem. pro.* IV.785, VI.224, Tr 1.621; *pl.* **these** Anel 71.

this *dem. adj.* this I.269, I.929, Tr 1.113; *pl.* **thise** I.1531, **these** BD 817.

this *contr.* of **this is** I.2761, VII.3057, Tr 5.151.

tho *dem. pro. pl.* those I.2351, III.370, Tr 1.931.

tho *dem. adj. pl.* those I.1123, Tr 4.631.

tho *adv.* then I.993, I.2696, Tr 1.300.

thogh, though, theigh *adv.* though, although I.253, Tr 1.221, Tr 3.1630; (with **that**) I.68, I.727, Tr 1.148; (with **all**) Rom A 452, Astr 1.10.16; (with **as**) I.553, I.1079, Tr 1.872.

thoght, thought *n.* (1) thought I.479, IV.2359, BD 4; (2) anxiety, care V.822, VII.589, Tr 1.579; *pl.* **thoghtes** IV.116, **thoughtes** Bo 3.m8.25.

thoghte *see* thenke(n) and thynke *v.*

thombe *n.* thumb I.563, V.83, Astr 1.1.2.

thonder, thondre *n.* thunder I.492, III.732, Tr 2.233.

thonk *see* thank.

thonke(n), thonketh, (y)thonked *see* thanke(n).

thorpes *see* throop.

thorugh, thorough *see* thurgh.

thought *see* thenke(n).

thoughte *see* thenke(n) and thynke *v.*

thoughte(n) *see* thenke(n).

thow, thou *2 sg. pro. nom.* thou, you I.1559, *etc.*

thral, thrall *n.* servant, slave III.155, V.769, Tr 1.439, Rom B 3359; *pl.* **thralles** X.152.

thral, thrall *adj.* enslaved, bound (as a serf) I.1552, III.1660, X.838, Rom B 5142; *pl.* **thralle** VII.1561.

thraldom *n.* slavery, servitude II.286, X.142, Tr 2.856.

thralle(n) *v.* enslave Tr 1.235, Tr 2.773; *pr. pl.* **thrall** Rom B 4877; *pp.* **thralled** Rom B 5807.

thraste *see* threste(n).

thred, threed *n.* thread I.2030, Tr 4.1546, Rom A 104; *pl.* **thredes** Bo 1.pr1.21.

thredbare, threedbare *adj.* threadbare I.260, I.290, VIII.890.

thresshfold, thressechefold *n.* threshold I.3482, IV.288, Bo 1.pr1.77.

threste(n), thriste *v.* (1) (*intr.*) thrust, push I.2612, Bo 2.pr5.83; (2) (*tr.*) press upon, oppress Tr 4.254; thrust up, support Bo 4.m7.58; *pr. pl.* **thresten** Bo 2.pr5.140; *pt. sg.* **threste** IV.2003, **thriste** Tr 3.1574, **thraste** Tr 2.1155; *pt. pl.* **thraste** VI.260; *pp.* **thrist** Bo 4.pr4.200.

threte *v.* threaten LGW 754, Rom B 3161; *3 pr. sg.* **threteth** X.646; *vbl. n.* **thretyng** VIII.698.

thries *adv.* thrice I.63, I.463, Tr 5.9.

thrift *n.* prosperity, welfare VIII.739, VIII.1425, Rom C 6806; **good (yvel) t.** good (bad) luck (to someone) HF 1786, Tr 2.582, Tr 2.847; **by my t.** by my welfare (I swear) I.4049, Tr 2.1483, Tr 4.1630.

thrifty *adj.* (1) useful, serviceable II.138, III.238; provident, well managed VII.246; suitable II.46; (2) worthy II.1165, IV.1912, Anel 197; proper, decorous Tr 1.275; *super.* **thriftiest(e)** most worthy, admirable Tr 1.1081, Tr 2.737.

thriftily *adv.* properly I.105, I.3131; suitably politely V.1174, Tr 3.211.

thrilled *see* thirleth.

thringe *v.* thrust, press Tr 4.66, Rom C 7417; *3 pt. sg.* **throng** IV.2353; *prp.* **thryngyng** thronging Rom A 656; *pp.* **ithrungen** pressed Bo 2.pr7.46.

thrist(e) *see* threste(n).

thryve(n) *v.* thrive, succeed VIII.1212, Tr 5.759; grow, flourish Tr 1.966; *3 pr. sg.* **thryveth** Bo 5.m4.28; *pr. subj. sg.* **thryve** III.1764; *pt. sg.* **throf** became Bo 3.m4.4; *prp.* (as *adj.*) **thryvynge** vigorous Bo 5.m4.22; *pp.* **thryven** Rom C 5841.

throng *see* thringe.

throop *n.* village IV.199, IV.208; *gen.* **thropes** X.12; *pl.* **thropes** III.871, **thorpes** PF 350.

throte *n.* throat I.2013, Tr 2.325; *pl.* **throtes** BD 320.

throwe *n.* (1) period of time, while III.1815, Tr 4.384; **any t.** at, for any time VII.2136, Anel 93; (2) short while II.953, Tr 2.687; (with)**in a t.** instantly, immediately Tr 2.1655, LGW 866, LGW 1286, Pity 86.

throwe(n) *v.* throw IV.453, X.863, Tr 2.971; *3 pr. sg.* **throweth** Mars 99; *pr. subj. sg.* **throwe** HF 789; *pt. sg.* **threw** II.85; *pt. pl.* **threwe** Rom A 786; *pp.* (y)**throwe** VIII.940, LGW 1960, **throwen** Tr 4.1159.

ithrungen *see* thringe.

thurgh, through, thorugh, thorough, thorogh, throgh, thurgh, thurw(e) *prep.* (1) through, throughout I.1565, I.4151, BD 336, Tr 2.105, Mars 181; (2) by means of II.25, V.1295, BD 129, Bo 1.pr3.48, Bo 2.pr2.18, Tr 3.357, Scog 16; because of I.920, I.1328.

thurghout, thoroughout *prep.* throughout I.1096; through Tr 3.601.

thurst *n.* thirst II.100, X.343, Rom A 1507.

thurst *1 pr. sg.* thirst Tr 1.406; *3 pr. sg.* **thursteth** Tr 5.1406; *pt. sg.* (*impers.*) **thursted hym** he thirsted VII.2039.

thurste *see* **thar.**

tyde *n.* (1) tide of the sea II.510, II.1134; (2) time IV.3335, V.142, Tr 1.954; hour Bo 1.m5.19; *pl.* **tydes** I.401.

tyden *v.* betide, happen to (with *dat.*) II.337; *3 pr. sg.* **tydeth** Mars 202, (*contr.*) **tit** Tr 1.333, **tydes** I.4175; *pp.* **tid** Tr 1.907; *vbl. n.* **tyding(e)** event II.726; report, news IV.901, HF 648, Tr 2.951; *pl.* **tydynges** II.129.

til, till *prep.* until III.2012, Tr 2.1521, Tr 4.1657; to, into I.180, I.1132, Tr 1.1057; (as *adv.*) in **t. and fro** I.4039.

til *conj.* until I.698, Astr 2.43.4; **t. that** until I.983.

tyme *n.* time I.35, I.44, BD 20; **by tyme(s)** quickly, soon VII.913, X.236, LGW F 452; **in good t.** timely BD 370; **oft tyme(s)** often I.44, I.52, I.1312; **of olde t.** long ago II.50, HF 1155, Tr 5.470; **som t.** at some time I.2474, I.2846, sometimes II.948; once, formerly III.527; *pl.* **tymes** I.534.

too *n.* toe I.2716; *pl.* **toos** VII.3180, **toon** VII.2862, HF 2028.

to(o) *adv.* too II.420, IV.2434, LGW F 572; also Tr 1.540.

to *prep.* (1) to I.17, I.30, BD 239; for ABC 184; (2) as I.1289, I.1622, IV.793, BD 716; **as to** according to IV.53, V.677, PF 480; (as *adv.*) **t. and fro** here and there I.2508.

to-breke *v.* break in pieces, shatter I.3918; *3 pr. sg.* **tobreketh** HF 779; *imp. sg.* **tobreke** Bo 3.m9.44; *pp.* **to-broke(n)** Scog 1, (as *adj.*) I.4277.

tobreste *v.* break in pieces, shatter Tr 2.608; *pr. pl.* **tobreste** I.2611; *pr. subj. sg.* **tobreste** ABC 16; *pp.* **tobrosten** I.2691.

toforn *adv.* before, ahead Bo 5.pr5.8; previously Rom B 2969, Rom B 4140.

toforn, tofore *prep.* before V.268; **God t.** before God (I swear) Tr 1.1049, Tr 2.431, Tr 2.1409.

togidre(s), togedre(s), togeder(e), togider(e), togideres, togyder *adv.* together I.824, VI.702, BD 809, PF 555, Bo 3.m9.25, Tr 4.1322, Astr 2.44.19, Rom A 338, Rom B 5079; **also t.** likewise Bo 3.pr11.7.

to-hepe *adv.* together LGW 2009, Astr 1.14.6.

tohewen *pr. pl.* hew in pieces I.2609; *pp.* **tohewe(n)** II.430, Tr 2.638.

tok, took(e), tooke(n) *see* **take(n).**

token *n.* evidence VII.390; *pl.* **tokenes** proofs, confirming details VII.359, IX.258; **tokens** tokens LGW 1275.

tokenyng(e) *vbl. n.* sign Rom B 2439; **in t.** as a sign (of, that) VIII.1153, IX.302, Tr 4.779.

told(e), toold(e), (y)told, (y)toold *see* **telle(n).**

tomorwe, to-morwe *adv.* tomorrow I.780, I.1610, Tr 1.861; (as *n.*) VII.1795; (as *adj.*) Tr 3.385.

ton *contr.* of **the on,** the one Bo 4.pr2.76.

tonge(e), tunge *n.* tongue I.265, I.712, Tr 2.1681; speech Tr 5.804; language Tr 5.1796, Astr 1.21.53; *gen.* **tonges** Tr 1.395; *pl.* **tonges** VII.2307.

tonne *n.* barrel, cask I.3894, III.177, PF 104; *pl.* **tonnes** Bo 2.pr2.75.

toreenden *pr. pl.* tear in pieces, wound Bo 4.pr6.324; *pr. subj. pl.* (*reflx.*) **torende** torture, afflict (themselves)

Tr 2.790; *pt. sg.* **torente** tore apart VII.2025, LGW 820; *pt. pl.* **torente** afflicted Tr 4.341, tore in pieces VI.709; *pp.* **torent** VI.102 torn, slain; (as *adj.*) **torent(e)** tattered IV.1012, torn in pieces VII.2261.

torment, turment *n.* torment, suffering I.1298, Tr 1.8, Rom A 274; torture VII.628, HF 445, Tr 4.1698; *pl.* **tormentz** I.2228, **turmentz** Bo 1.pr3.55, **turmentes** Bo 4.pr3.6.

tormente, turmente *v.* torment, torture Tr 4.634, LGW 871, LGW 1165, Bo 1.pr4.87; *3 pr. sg.* **tormenteth** I.1314; *pr. pl.* **tormenten** X.183; *pr. subj. sg.* **turmente** Ven 53; *pp.* (**y)tormented** II 885, Bo 3.m12.37, **turmented** Bo 1.m5.54, **tourmented** Rom B 3247; *vbl. n.* **tormentynge** IV.1038.

tormentour, turmentour *n.* tormentor, torturer II.818, VIII.527, Bo 1.pr4.312; *pl.* **tormentoures** VIII.373, **turmentours** Bo 1.pr4.37, **turmentours** Bo 3.pr7.20.

torn, tourn, turn *n.* turn Scog 42; turning Rom B 5470; **freendes (good) t.** favor VI.815, Rom C 6947.

torne(n), tourne, turne(n) *v.* (1) turn (*intr.*) I.1488, I.2318, Tr 2.688; go I.1327, III.988; return Anel 187, Tr 3.719, LGW 2200; become, turn into Tr 4.119; (2) turn (*tr.*) I.3928, VIII.625, BD 447; transform, change (with **into, to**) IX.100, BD 599, Tr 3.179; *2 pr. sg.* **turnest** Bo 1.m5.3; *3 pr. sg.* **turneth** I.3390, **torneth** Tr 1.324; *pr. pl.* **torne(n)** Bo 4.pr6.117, **turnen** VI.539; *pr. subj. sg.* **turne** HF 1; *pr. subj. pl.* **turne** Anel 204, **torne** Tr 2.1709; *imp. sg.* **turn(e)** HF 925, Astr 2.11.12; *imp. pl.* **turne** VI.761, **turneth** VII.3409; *pt. sg.* **turned** V.1011, **torned(e)** Tr 4.855, Tr 5.1146; *pt. pl.* **turned** I.3842, **torned** Tr 2.1347; *pp.* (**y)torned** Bo 4.m5.2, Tr 3.1074, (**y)turned** I.1238, I.1377; *prp.* **turnynge** Bo 1.m7.3; *vbl. n.* **torning(e)** Tr 1.856, Bo 5.pr4.88, **tournyng** Rom A 761, **turnyng(e)** HF 182, Rom B 4134.

totere *pr. pl.* tear in pieces VI.474; *pt. sg.* **totar** VII.2611; *pp.* **totore** VIII.635 tattered, **totorn** distraught Tr 4.358, tattered PF 110; scattered, in disarray Rom A 327.

tother *contr.* of **the other** the other Bo 4.m3.11, Tr 4.434.

touche(n) *v.* (1) (*tr.*) touch III.87, X.327, Tr 2.1033; (2) touch upon, treat (a subject) III.1271, Tr 5.996, LGW 1693; concern I.3179, I.3494, Tr 1.744; (3) (*intr.*) (with **to**) concern VII.1299, suit, befit Tr 2.1662; *3 pr. sg.* **toucheth** Tr 2.1407; *pr. pl.* **touche(n)** Bo 3.pr12.127, Rom C 6905; *pr. subj. sg.* **touche** VII.2094, *pr. subj. pl.* **touche(n)** VIII.156, Tr 5.996 *pt. sg.* **touched(e)** I.2561, Anel 114; *prp.* (as) **touchyng(e)** concerning III.1988, III.2290, Tr 1.265; *pp.* **touched** III.1271; *vbl. n.* **touchynge** touch, touching X.207; handling, treatment Bo 1.pr5.78.

tough *adj.* tough, strong I.1992, Rom B 1726; **make it t.** be self-assured, put on airs Tr 2.1025, Tr 3.87; be unrelenting VII.379; be bold Tr 5.101.

toun(e) *n.* town I.217, VI.570, BD 310; *gen.* **townes** III.1285; *pl.* **tounes** I.3025.

tour *n.* tower I.1030, I.1056, BD 946; (*astro.*) mansion Mars 113; *pl.* **toures** I.2464.

tourneiyng(e) *vbl. n.* tournament I.2557, Rom A 1206.

trace *v.* go, tread Rom C 6745; *pr. pl.* **trace** PF 54, Rom B 5753.

trad *see* **tret.**

traisoun *see* **tresoun.**

translate(n) *v.* translate LGW F 370, LGW G 341; *pp.*

translated LGW F 329, **transformed** IV.385; **transported** Bo 2.pr5.21.

traas, trace *n.* track, footstep, trail Bo 5.m5.4, Gent 3; procession LGW F 285; *pl.* **traces** Bo 1.pr3.45.

traunce *n.* trance I.1572, III.2216, Tr 2.1306.

travaille, travayle, travel *n.* (1) effort, work I.2406, IV.1210, BD 602; Tr 1.21, Rom B 4452; **swich t.** such great deeds Tr 1.475; (2) suffering I.3646, VIII.781; difficulty Tr 2.3; *pl.* **travailles** X.256, **travailes** Bo 4.m7.28.

travaille(n), travaile *v.* (1) work, exert efforts III.1365, X.667; *(reflx.)* exert oneself Bo 3.pr2.5; (2) suffer X.985, Rom B 2011; (3) travel Rom A 370; *3 pr. sg.* **travailleth** VII.1590, **travaileth** Bo 3.pr9.96; *pr. pl.* **travaillen** X.652, **travailen** Bo 2.pr7.68; *pt. pl.* **travaileden** Bo 5.pr3.43; *prp.* **travaillynge** in childbirth I.2083; *pp.* **travailed** X.823; *vbl. n.* **travaillyng** X.257, **traveylyng** Rom C 6788.

tre(e) *n.* (1) tree I.2062, PF 137; cross I.3767, II.456; (2) wood III.101, IV.558, Tr 2.47, Rom A 948; *pl.* **trees** I.607.

trechery(e) *n.* treachery, treason VII.3330, VIII.1069, Rom C 7318; *pl.* **trecheries** Bo 1.pr4.116.

trede(n) *see* **tret.**

treget *n.* trickery Rom C 6312, Rom C 6825.

tregetour *n.* illusionist, sleight-of-hand artist HF 1277; *pl.* **tregetoures** VII.1141, **tregetours** HF 1260.

tresor, tresour, tresoor *n.* treasure II.442, III.204, Anel 32; *pl.* **tresors** Bo 3.m11.8, **tresouris** Rom A 184.

tresoun, treson, traisoun *n.* treason, treachery I.2001, VII.3117, Tr 1.117; *pl.* **tresons** I.2468.

trespace, trespas, trespaas *n.* wrong, fault, sin I.1764, I.1818, VII.2180.

trespace, trespasse *v.* (1) *(intr.)* transgress, sin Tr 3.1175, Rom B 2144, Rom B 2178; (with **to**) do wrong to IV.1828, Rom B 3555; (with **agayns**) trespass VII.2564; (2) *(tr.)* commit (sins) VII.1885; *3 pr. sg.* **trespaseth** X.1012, **trespasseth** Rom B 5399; *pr. pl.* **trespassen** X.138; *pr. subj. sg.* **trespasse** VI.741; *pp.* **(y)trespassed** VII.1419, VII.1877, **trespased** VI.416, **trespaced** Rom B 3862; *vbl. n.* **trespassyng(e)** LGW F 155, Rom C 7566.

tresse *v.* *(reflx.)* arrange or braid the hair Rom A 599; *pp.* **(y)tressed** (as *adj.*) with hair arranged III.344, Tr 5.810, adorned with tresses Tr 5.8.

tret *3 pr. sg. (contr.)* treads, steps III.2002; *pr. pl.* **trede(n)** I.3022, Bo 1.m5.39; *pt. sg.* **trad** copulated with VII.3178; *pt. pl.* **troden** trod, stepped on HF 2153; *pp. (intr.)* **troden** stepped VI.712; *vbl. n.* **tredyng** copulation VII.1955.

tretable *adj.* amenable X.658, BD 923; affable BD 533; docile LGW F 411.

tretee *n.* (1) treaty, agreement I.1288, VI.619, VII.2675; (2) discussion, negotiation IV.1692, V.1219.

trete(n) *v.* (1) speak about, discuss VI.64, VI.521, Tr 1.975; tell, assert VI.630, Tr 1.742; relate PF 34; (2) negotiate VII.1798, Tr 4.58, Tr 4.1346; (3) treat X.582, Tr 4.813, Tr 5.134; *pr. pl.* **trete(n)** X.582, LGW G 275; *pp.* **(y)treted** exercised (an office) Bo 4.pr5.11, discussed Bo 5.pr1.2.

tretys, tretice *n.* (1) treatise VII.957, X.957; document Tr 2.1697; (2) treaty II.233, Tr 4.670; (3) negotiation (for a treaty or contract) IV.331, Tr 4.64, Tr 4.136; *pl.* **tretes** Astr 2.34.14.

tretys, treitys *adj.* graceful, well formed I.152, Rom A 932, Rom A 1016.

treuthe *see* **trouth(e).**

trew(e), true *adj.* (1) true, faithful I.959, I.2418, Mars 281, Rom B 5146; honest I.1326, IV.1298; truthful I.3529, X.982; real, authentic I.531, I.3781; (2) (as *n.*) true servant Tr 3.141, *(pl.)* the faithful II.456; *comp.* **trewer** Lady 111; *super.* **trewest(e)** V.1539, VIII.969, **truest** Mars 187.

trew(e) *adv.* truly Rom B 2686, Rom B 5539; accurately Adam 4; *comp.* **trewer** BD 927.

trewe *n.* truce Tr 3.1779, Tr 4.1314; *pl.* **trewes** Tr 5.401.

trewely, trewly, trewelich(e), truly *adv.* (1) truly, honestly I.481, I.707, Tr 1.246, Mars 186; (2) accurately Astr 2.18 Rubric (3) (as expletive) indeed I.761, I.1267, Tr 1.246.

trist, trust *n.* trust X.738, Tr 1.83, Tr 3.1305; faith, object of fidelity Tr 3.1422.

triste(n), truste(n) *v.* (1) trust II.832, Tr 1.690, Tr 2.491, Tr 5.188, LGW 1885; *2 pr. sg.* **trustest** Tr 1.720; *(contr.)* **trust** Rom B 2871; *3 pr. sg.* **trusteth** VII.1646, **tristeth** Rom B 4010; *pr. pl.* **trust(e)** I.501, Rom B 5435, **tristen** Rom B 3932, **trust** Tr 4.510; *pr. subj. sg.* **trust** Tr 4.391; *imp. pl.* **trusteth** Tr 4.1590; *pt. sg.* **trusted** III.598; *prp.* **trustyng** Tr 5.1208; *pp.* **trusted** Tr 2.414, **tristed** Rom B 3929; (2) *imp. pl.* (used for emphasis) **trusteth me** VIII.889, IV.1561, **trust(e) wel** X.204, VII.1150, **trusteth wel** I.2182, II.1048.

triumphe *n.* triumphal procession II.400, VII.2363, Anel 43.

troden *see* **tret.**

trompe, trumpe *n.* trumpet I.674, II.705, HF 1240; *gen. sg.* **trompes** PF 344, **trumpes** HF 1642; *pl.* **trompes** I.2511, **trumpes** HF 1718.

trone *n.* throne 1.2529, V.275, Tr 4.1079.

trouble *v.* trouble, disturb Rom C 6407; *3 pr. sg.* **troubleth** X.544; *pr. pl.* **troublen** III.363, Bo 4.m5.31; *prp.* **troublynge** Bo2.m4.15; *pp.* **troubled** VIII.72, (as *adj.*) Mars 161, **trubled** Bo 5.pr3.4; *vbl. n. pl.* **trowblynges** disturbances Bo 4.m2.11.

trouble, truble *adj.* (1) troubled IV.465; disturbed, confused IX.279, X.537; (2) murky, stirred up X.816; turbulent Bo 1.m7.2; (as *n.*) storm Rom B 3777.

trouth(e), treuthe *n.* (1) pledge, I.763, VII.1285, BD 6; loyalty to one's word, fidelity I.46, I.2789, Tr 3.1297; honesty I.4397; (2) truth, truthfulness II.630, VIII.259, Truth 7; *pl.* **trouthes** 6.702.

trowe(n) *v.* (1) believe HF 699, Tr 5.1298, Rom B 3206; trust (in) VIII.378, Tr 2.956, Tr 5.1263; (2) suppose, think Bo 5.pr3.24, Tr 5.902; *1 pr. sg.* (as a weak expletive) **I trowe**, indeed, I warrant, I.155, III.217, III.600, BD 544; *2 pr. sg.* **trowest** III.1557, (with *pro.*) **trowestow** Bo 3.pr9.164; *3 pr. sg.* **troweth** VIII.288; *pr. pl.* **trowe(n)** VIII.420, Tr 4.1338; *pr. subj. sg.* **trowe** Tr 5.331; *imp. sg.* **trowe** III.1985; *imp. pl.* **trowe(th)** VII.1511, IX.284; *pt. sg.* **trowed** I.3416 *(pt. pl.)* **trowed** IV.403, **troweden** Bo 5.pr4.79; *pt. subj. pl.* **trowede** Bo 4.pr5.28; *prp.* **trowynge** VII.1446; *pp.* **trowed** Tr 4.383.

tubbe *n.* tub, vat I.3621; *pl.* **tubbes** I.3836.

turment- *see* **torment-.**

turn(e), turne(n), (y)turned *see* **torne(n).**

turtil, turtel, turtle *n.* turtledove I.3706, PF 355, PF 510; *gen.* **turtles** IV.2139; *pl.* **turtles** Rom A 662.

tweye, tweyn(e), twaye *adj.* two I.704, I.792, Tr 5.1307, Mars 95, Wom Unc 19.

twies *adv.* twice I.4348, II.1058, Tr 2.1399.

twynne(n) *v.* (1) *(intr.)* go, depart V.577, Anel 102, Anel 285; get away, escape VII.2005; separate, become separate Tr 4.1270, Tr 5.339; (2) *(tr.)* separate Tr 4.1197, Tr 5.679, Rom B 5077; *pr. pl.* **twynne** Tr 3.1711; *pr. subj. pl.* **twynne** I.855; *pp.* **(y)twynned** separated Tr 4.476, Tr 4.788; *vbl. n.* **twinning** separation Tr 4.1303.

twiste *n.* branch IV.2349, V.442; vine, tendril Tr 3.1230.

twiste *v.* press upon V.566, Tr 4.1129; *pr. subj. sg.* **twiste** would press, constrain Tr 3.1769; *pt. sg.* **twiste** tortured III.494, squeezed IV.2005; *pp.* **twyst** compressed HF 775.

U

unavysed *pp.* as *adj.* unaware Tr 1.378; reckless, thoughtless IX.280, Rom B 4739; unpremeditated X.449.

unbynde(n) *v.* unbind, free, deliver from X.277, X.1072, PF 523, Tr 4.675; untie Tr 3.1732; *3 pr. sg.* **unbyndeth** unbinds, breaks up X.511; *imp. sg.* **unbynd** LGW 1339; *pt. sg.* **unbond** Rom C 6416; *pp.* **unbounde(n)** Rom B 2226, Rom C 6413, (as *adj.*) Bo 1.m5.29.

unconning *see* **unkonnyng(e)** *adj.*

uncouth *see* **unkouth(e)**.

under *adv.* below, beneath VIII.518, HF 805, Tr 1.139.

under *prep.* under I.105, etc.; close to, next to, by I.1981, IX.3, Tr 2.919; in the direction of I.1697; along with, in addition to IX.198; among Bo 2.pr3.52.

understonde(n), understande(n), undirstande *v.* understand I.746, X.211, X.1049, Bo 1.pr6.3, Rom B 2061; believe VII.168; *1 pr. sg.* **undirstonde** Bo 3.pr10.188, **understande** VII.1333; *2 pr. sg.* (with *pro.*) **undirstondistow** Bo 4.pr4.145, **undirstandestow** Bo 2.pr8.8; *3 pr. sg.* **understondeth** VI.646; *pr. pl.* **understonde** VII.1278, **undirstanden** Bo 2.pr5.137; *imp. sg.* **understond** HF 1073, **undirstand** Bo 4.pr7.7; *imp. pl.* **understondeth** believe Tr 5.887, **understonde** X.563, **understoond** VII.1091; *pt. sg.* **understood** V.434, **understod** BD 1261, **undirstod** Rom B 5140; *pt. pl.* **undirstoden** Bo 5.pr1.86; *pt. subj. sg.* **understode** would believe Tr 1.1035; *pp.* **understonde(n)** II.520, VII.1284; *vbl. n.* **understondyng(e)** understanding, comprehension X.388, BD 761.

undertake, undirtake *v.* (1) undertake, begin an enterprise I.405, V.36; (2) declare, affirm, assert I.288, I.3532, Tr 3.338, Rom B 5058; *3 pr. sg.* **undertaketh** Tr 2.807, **undirtaketh** Bo 4.pr2.28; *pt. sg.* **undertok** LGW 1452; *pp.* **undertake** LGW G 71.

undo(n) *v.* (1) untie, open Tr 3.741; release Tr 3.1735; (2) explain, disclose BD 899; show, reveal Bo 3.pr11.9; *3 pr. sg.* **undoth** opens I.3727, explains Rom A 9; *imp. sg.* **undo** open up I.3765; *pt. sg.* **undide** opened Tr 4.352; *pp.* **undo** disclosed Rom A 1633, **undon** explained Rom B 2173, **undoon** Bo 5.pr6.224.

uneth(e) *see* **unnethe(s)**.

unfeyned *pp.* as *adj.* unfeigned, sincere VIII.434, Anel 289, Tr 2.839.

unfolde(n), onfold *v.* unfold Tr 2.1702; explain Bo 4.pr6.334; *3 pr. sg.* **unfooldeth** displays Bo 4.m5.7; *pp.* **unfolden** expanded Bo 4.pr6.77; *vbl. n.* **unfoldynge** explanation Bo 4.pr6.73.

unhap *n.* mishap, misfortune HF 89, Tr 1.552, Scog 29; *pl.* **unhappes** Tr 2.456.

unjoynen *v.* separate Bo 3.pr12.36; *pr. pl.* **unjoignen** Bo 5.m1.6; *pp.* **unjoyned** Bo 5.m3.1.

unkynde *adj.* unnatural, cruel II.88, VI.903, Tr 3.1438; faithless PF 358, PF 457; unkind Tr 4.16.

unkyndely *adv.* unnaturally VI.485; cruelly X.154; HF 295, Tr 1.617.

unkonnyng(e), unconnyng, unkunnynge *adj.* ignorant, unskillful I.2393, Bo 5.m3.36, Tr 5.1139, Lady 69.

unkonnynge, unkunnynge *n.* ignorance, lack of skill VII.1876, X.1082.

unkouth(e), uncouth *adj.* unfamiliar Tr 2.151; exotic, strange HF 1279; marvelous I.2497, V.284, HF 2010; striking Tr 3.1797.

unmyghty *adj.* unable Tr 2.858; impotent Bo 1.m4.16, Bo 4.pr2.126.

unmoevable *adj.* immovable, stable Bo 4.pr6.103, Bo 4.pr6.158.

unnethe(s), unneth, unethe *adv.* hardly, scarcely I.3121, II.1050, BD 270, LGW G 33; with difficulty Tr 1.354, LGW F 233.

unreste *n.* distress, discomfort III.1104, IV.719, LGW 1339.

unsely, unseely *adj.* unfortunate, unhappy I.4210, VIII.468, Tr 1.35.

unselynesse *n.* unhappiness Bo 4.pr4.54, Bo 4.pr4.113; *pl.* **unselynesses** types of unhappiness Bo 4.pr4.32.

until, untill *prep.* to (direction) I.3761; until II.1070, BD 41.

unto *prep.* (1) (direction) to, into, unto I.71, *etc.*; (2) (respect) to I.214, Tr 2.1379; for VII.1581, PF 177; as I.1486; about VII.3046; of Tr 1.429, Tr 1.968; (3) (time) until I.2412, II.765; (as *conj.*) until PF 647.

untressed *pp.* as *adj.* loose, unarranged I.2289, IV.379, PF 268.

untrewe *adj.* unfaithful IV.995, IV.1786, Anel 274; untrustworthy VIII.1042; false Tr 3.306; (as *adv.*) inaccurately I.735.

untrouthe *n.* faithlessness IV.2241, Anel 118, Tr 3.984; perjury II.687.

unwar *adj.* (1) unexpected II.427, VII.2764, Bo 2.pr2.69; (2) unaware Tr 1.304, Tr 1.1559.

unwar *adv.* (1) unexpectedly V.1356, Tr 1.549; (2) unwarily, heedlessly X.885.

unwarly *adv.* unexpectedly Bo 1.m1.13.

unwemmed *pp.* as *adj.* spotless, undefiled II.924, VIII.225; unharmed, sound Bo 5.pr6.289.

unwist *pp.* as *adj.* (1) unknown I.2977, Tr 2.1509, Tr 3.603; undetected Tr 2.1294, Tr 3.770; (2) uninformed Tr 1.93; unaware Tr 2.1400.

unwot *pr. sg.* does not know Bo 5.pr6.157; *prp.* **unwityng** of not knowing, unaware V.936, VIII.1320.

up *adv.* up I.681, *etc.*; **up and doun** in all respects, in every way III.119; from one end to the other I.977; **up so doun** topsy turvy, upside down I.1377, (hyphenated) VIII.625, Bo 5.pr3.84; (as *imp.*) lift up HF 1021; *comp.* **upper** higher HF 884.

up *prep.* on, upon I.2543, II.795.

uppe *adj.* up, open V.615; *super.* (as *n.*) **uppereste** highest Bo 1.pr1.37.

upon *adv.* on I.617, III.559, III.1382.

upon, uppon *prep.* (1) (position) on, upon I.111, Bo 1.m1.13; next to, beside I.3923, LGW 750; **u. land** in the countryside I.702; (2) (direction) at, upon V.1496, Tr 3.277; to I.4006, LGW 1946, at (of sight) I.3951, VII.124; (3) (time) on I.3554, I.3659, LGW 1162; in I.703; at BD 352, Tr 3.549; (4) (respect) concerning, about I.3632, I.4329, BD 1023; on I.1757, I.1774, Anel 132; at III.1666, IV.1723; of LGW 1610; **wayte u.** wait for HF 342; on pain of (losing) I.1344, III.1016, LGW F 548; **u. my (thy) trouthe (feithe)** by my (thy) faith I.1855, I.3502; **u. lyve** alive Tr 2.1030; into, on (a roar, *etc.*) I.3770, Tr 5.45; **u. lengthe** at last BD 352; **u. cas** by chance I.3661, Tr 4.649.

upper *see* **up** *adv.*

upright(e) *adj.* straight I.3264, Rom B 3639; perpendicular Bo 5.m5.18, Astr 2.38.8.

upright(e) *adv.* (1) upwards I.3444, Bo 3.m2.35; upright I.1387, IV.1844, BD 46; erect BD 622; (2) on one's back, face up BD 175; **bolt u.** flat on one's back I.4144, I.4266, BD 175.

us *1st pl. pr. dat. and acc.* us I.411, etc.; **us self** ourselves IV.108.

usage *n.* custom II.998, III.589, PF 15; habit Rom A 293; **of (old, verray) u.** by (long) habit VI.899, X.601, PF 15; experience, skill I.110, I.2448; *pl.* **usages** customs Tr 2.28.

usaunce *n.* custom PF 674, LGW 586, LGW 1476; *pl.* **opinyoun of usaunces** current opinion Bo 3.pr4.93.

use(n) *v.* (1) use, employ II.44, III.137, Tr 2.1038; practice (an art, skill) VI.428, VIII.1409, Tr 2.11; (2) *(intr.)* be accustomed to VIII.666, Tr 3.1023, Tr 4.182; *2 pr. sg.* **usest** Bo 3.pr12.123; *3 pr. sg.* **useth** VI.599; *pr. pl.* **use(n)** VII.1574, HF 1263; *pr. subj. pl.* **use** IV.1678; *imp. sg.* **use** VII.1602; *1 & 3 pt. sg.* **used** III.132; *2 pt. sg.* **usedest** I.2385; *pt. pl.* **useden** V.1293, **used** VII.499; *pp.* **used** III.562, (as *adj.*) customary, regular Bo 1.m5.14; *prp.* **usynge** using VII.1609, (as *adj.*) accustomed to III.777; *vbl. n.* **usyng(e)** practicing X.465, use Ven 42.

usure *n.* usury III.1309, VII.491, X.568.

utterest(e), uttreste, outtreste *adj. super.* (1) utmost IV.787, Bo 4.pr3.72; (2) outermost Bo 1.pr 1.85, Bo 4.pr6.122; earliest Bo 2.m6.15.

utterly *see* **outrely.**

V

valey(e) *n.* valley BD 155, BD 165, Tr 1.950; *pl.* **valeyes** HF 899.

vanysshe *v.* vanish V.328; waste away VI.732; *pr. pl.* **vanysschen** Bo 3.pr4.77; *pt. sg.* **vanysshed** V.342, **vanyshide** Rom B 2954; *pt. sg.* **vanyshed** LGW 1001; *pp.* **vanysshed** III.996; *vbl. n.* **vanysshynge** disappearance I.2360.

variaunce, variance *n.* variation IV.710, X.427, Tr 4.985; changeability, fickleness Tr 5.1670; change, mutability For 45.

varie(n) *v.* vary Tr 2.1621, Rom B 2304; *3 pr. sg.* **varieth** Bo 2.m8.1; *pr. pl.* **varie** Rom B 4477; *pr. subj. sg.* **varie** VII.954; *prp.* **varyinge** BD 802.

veyn(e) *n.* vein Tr 1.866; (of plants) I.3; **every v.** every part VIII.1241, PF 425, Tr 4.943.

veyn(e), vayn(e) *adj.* idle, foolish I.1094, I.2240, Tr 3.817; (as *n.*) **in v.** idly, in vain, Tr 4.314, Rom B 2109; **v. glorie** vainglory, empty pride I.2240, VI.411, X.394.

venge(n) *v.* (1) *(reflx.)* revenge (oneself) VII.1281, VII.1352; (2) *(tr.)* avenge VII.1371, VII.1531; *3 pr. sg.* **vengeth** VII.1468; *pp.* **venged** VII.1281.

vengeaunce, vengeance *n.* revenge, punishment I.2066, I.2302, VII.2742; *pl.* **vengeaunces** VII.1429.

venym *n.* (1) venom, poison I.2751, II.891, Tr 3.1025; (2) dye Bo 2.m5.11; *pl.* **venymes** poisons VII.3255, pains Bo 4.m2.10.

venymous, venymus, venemows, venemouse *adj.* poisonous VII.2105, X.576, Bo 2.m6.31, ABC 149, Rom B 5528.

venquysse *v.* vanquish VII.1339, X.661; *3 pr. pl.* **venquysseth** V.774, **venquysseth** Rom B 3546; *pr. pl.* **venquisshe(n)** VII.1090, VII.1094; *pp.* **venquysshed** II.291.

vermyn *n.* animal pests IV.1095, VI.858; insects, vermin Tr 3.381.

verray(e), veray, verry(e), verrey *adj.* (1) true I.1551, III.423, Bo 1.pr6.105, Bo 5.m3.6, Tr 3.6, Rom C 6454; faithful I.3609, IV.2285, LGW 1686; genuine, real, arrant III.253, Tr 1.202; (2) pure, sheer I.1748, V.166, Tr 3.92; (as *intens.*) indeed I.4103; **the v. devel** (hogges, *etc.*) the devil himself, even the hogs, *etc.* VI.480, VII.3385; (3) exact Astr 1.18.16, Astr 2.1.3.

verray *adv.* truly X.87, X.113; exactly HF 1079; genuinely LGW 1686.

verraily, verily, verraylich(e), verreily, verrely *adv.* truly Anel 288, Tr 3.1545, Tr 4.1424, Rom A 1630; exactly Astr 2.25.2, Astr 2.26.28.

vers, verce *n.* verse, line HF 1098; stanza VII.522, PF 679; *pl.* **vers** verses VII.1107, VII.3313, Rom B 2344.

vertu(e) *n.* (1) power I.4, V.146, Tr 3.1766; **v. expulsif (retentif,** *etc.***)** power of the body to expel (retain) fluids, *etc.* I.2749 (see note), X.913; ability I.1436, X.453, HF 526; mental faculty HF 550; usefulness Tr 4.315; **by (through) v. of** by the power of X.340; because of Tr 3.1288; (2) moral excellence, virtue I.307, II.164, PF 376, Bo 1.pr4.227; **maken v. of necessity** make the best of a situation I.3042, V.593, Tr 4.1586; *pl.* **vertues** X.197 **vertus** Bo 3.pr4.4.

vertuous(e) *adj.* virtuous I.515, X.652, Tr 1.254; capable, able I.251, V.687; powerful Rom A 1096.

viage *n.* (1) journey I.723, II.259; travel II.312; expedition I.77, LGW 1450; (2) business, undertaking III.1569, VII.371, Tr 2.1061; **don v.** begin a project Tr 2.75; *pl.* **viages** HF 1962.

vicaire, viker, vicary(e) *n.* deputy, vicar III.2008, X.22, PF 379, Rom C 7682.

vilayneus *adj.* rude, churlish Rom A 178.

vileyn, vilayn *n.* churl, peasant Rom B 1990, Rom B 2181; *gen.* **vileyns** X.627; *pl.* **vilayns** Rom B 2183.

vileynye, vilany(e), vylenye, vylonie *n.* (1) rudeness, churlishness I.70, I.728, VI.740, HF 96; (personified) Rom A 169; (2) shame, dishonor Bo 3.pr4.56, Tr 2.438, Rom B 3889; **don thee (hym,** *etc.***) v.** bring disgrace, shame on you (him, etc.) IV.1791, IV.2261; **him to v.** a dishonor to him IX.260; **in v.** shamefully, lecherously VIII.156, X.857; (3) reproach, disgrace III.34, IV.2303, Tr 4.21; (4) evil X.852, HF 96; **lucre of v.** ill-gotten gains; (5) harm, injury I.4191, VII.1357; *pl.* **vileynyes** VII.1458.

vileyns *adj.* evil, churlish III 1158, X.556, X.854; rude, churlish III.1268.

vileynsly, vilaynesly, vilaynsly *adv.* shamefully, crudely X.154, X.279, Rom A 1498; cruelly X.154, Rom B 3994.

vitayle *v.* victual, supply with provisions LGW 1093; *3 pt. sg.* **vitailled** I.3627; *pp.* **vitailled** II.869.

vitaille, vitayle *n.* food, victuals I.248, I.569, LGW 1488; *pl.* **vitayles** Bo 3.pr4.85.

voyd(e) *adj.* solitary Bo 2.pr5.180, Mars 114; **v. of** devoid of Tr 2.173, LGW F 167 Form Age 50.

voyde(n) *v.* (1) *(tr.)* expel, remove I.2751; get rid of IV.910; empty IV.1815, LGW 2625; nullify Bo 5.pr6.243; avoid Anel 295; (2) *(tr. and intr.)* leave, depart Tr 2.912, Tr 3.232; move V.188; (3) *(reflx.)* rid oneself Rom B 2922; *3 pr. sg.* **voideth** Rom B 2833; *imp. sg.* **voide** leave IV.806; *imp. pl.* **voyde** send away VIII.1136; *pt. sg.* **voyded** caused to disappear V.1150; *pt. pl.* **voydide** left Bo 1.pr4.123; *pp.* **(y)voyded** removed V.1159, departed Tr 2.912.

voys *n.* (1) voice I.688, I.1371, Tr 1.725; tone of voice II.449, III.1036, PF 191; **in Pilates v.** ranting loudly I.3124; (2) opinion II.155; decision, judgment PF 545; Tr 4.195; **with o v.** unanimously VII.1765, VIII.420, LGW F 296; esteem IV.1592, Tr 3.1723; (3) report II.169; praise IV.1592.

vouche(n) sauf, vouche saaf, vouchesauf, vouche-sauf *v.* grant, agree, permit I.812, Tr 5.1341, Tr 5.1858, LGW 2273, Astr Pro 107; *pr. pl.* **vouche(n) s.** VII.1115, Anel 254; *pr. subj. sg.* **vouche s.** IV.306; *pr. subj. pl.* **vouchesauf** I.1430; *imp. pl.* **voucheth s.** IV.885; *pt. sg.* **vouched s.** ABC 27; *pt. subj. sg.* **vouched s.** Compl d'Am 46.

W

wade(n) *v.* go IV.1684; proceed Tr 2.150; wade, walk through III.2084, Rom B 5022; go into, penetrate VII.2494.

waf *see* **weve(n).**

wayk(e), weyk(e) *adj.* weak I.887, II.932, X.311, Anel 341; fragile Rom A 225; *compar.* **weyker** VII.1483.

wailaway *see* **weylaway.**

waille, wayle(n) *v.* (1) *(intr.)* wail, lament I.931, I.3398, Tr 4.399; (2) *(tr.)* bewail, bemoan X.178; *2 pr. sg.* **wailest** Tr 1.556; *3 pr. sg.* **wayleth** I.1221, **wailleth** V.1348; *pt. sg.* **wayled** V.1116; *prp.* **waillynge** I.1366; *pp.* **wailed** Rom C 6271; *vbl. n.* **waylyng(e)** wailing, lamentation IV.1213, X.864; **waillynge** Tr 1.408.

waymenten *v.* lament X.230; *vbl. n.* **waymentynge** lamentation I.902, **weymentynge** Rom A 510.

wayte(n) *v.* (1) watch, watch for I.3302, IV.1303, Tr 1.190; await, seek an occasion I.1222, II.582; observe Astr 2.34.8; **w. bisily** watch intently V.88, Astr 2.38.12; (2) expect II.246, Tr 3.491; **w. on (upon)** wait for HF 342, Tr 3.534; **w. after** look for, desire II.467, IV.1303; look for, expect I.525; (3) attend LGW 1269; *3 pr. sg.* **waiteth** IV.708; *pr. pl.* **waiten** X.403; *pr. subj. pl.* **wayte** I.3295; *imp. sg.* **wayte** watch Astr 2.5.16 *(sg.)*, take note of III.517 *(pl.)*; *pt. sg.* **wayted** I.571; *prp.* **waityng(e)** I.929, III.1376; *vbl. n.* **waityng** watching IX.252.

wake(n) *v.* (1) *(tr.)* be or remain awake I.3354, I.3672, BD 236; pray or meditate all night III.1847; (2) wake up IV.2397, LGW 1787; (3) *(tr.)* awaken II.1187, Scog 38; *2 pr. sg.* **wakest** Rom C 7561; *3 pr. sg.* **waketh** I.3373; *pr. pl.* **wake(n)** PF 689, Tr 1.921; *pr. subj.* **wake** Rom B 4313 *(sg.)*, Rom B 2730 *(pl.)*; *imp. pl.* **waketh** III.1654; *pt. sg.* **wok** PF 695; *prp.* **wakyng(e)** LGW 685, Rom B 2665; (as *adj.*) watchful Bo 4.m7.34; *pp.* **waked** I.4284; *vbl. n.* **wakynge** waking hours II.22, keeping vigil X.1048; *pl.* **wakynges** vigils X.257.

walke(n) *v.* walk, go, roam I.2309, III.245, Tr 5.666; *2 pr. sg.* **walkest** I.1283; *3 pr. sg.* **walketh** I.1052; *pr. pl.* **walken** VI.530; *pr. subj. sg.* **walke** II.784; *imp. sg.* **walke** III.2087; *imp. pl.* **walketh** VIII.1207; *pt. sg.* **walked** I.3458, **welk** Tr 2.517; *pt. pl.* **walked** III.564; *pt. subj. sg.* **walked** VI.722; *prp.* **walkyng(e)** III.886, LGW G 47; *pp.* **walked** I.2368, **was go walked** walked away, gone III.1778, BD 387; *vbl. n.* **walkyng(e)** roaming III.397, V.408.

walwe, walowe *v.* wallow Tr 1.699, Rom B 2562; writhe, twist III.1102; *3 pr. sg.* **walweth** III.1085; *pr. pl.* **walwe** I.4178; *prp.* **walwynge** surging, tossing about I.3616, causing to toss about Bo 1.m7.3; *pp.* **walwed** covered with, wallowing in Ros 17.

wan *see* **wynne(n).**

wan *adj.* (1) wan, sickly I.3828, etc., (2) dark I.2456.

wanhope *n.* despair I.1249, X.693, Rom A 981.

wante *v.* (1) lack PF 287, Tr 4.1568; (2) be lacking, absent X.514, LGW F 361; *3 pr. sg.* **wanteth** VII.1028, *(impers.)* **hym wanteth** he lacks VII.1080; *pr. pl.* **wanten** Pity 76; *pr. subj. sg.* **wante** VII.1026; *pt. sg.* *(impers.)* **hym wanted** he lacked VII.1046; *vbl. n.* **wantynge** lack I.2665, VII.100.

wantownesse, wantonesse *n.* lasciviousness II.31, Rom B 4265; affectation I.264.

war(e) *imp. sg.* and *pl.* beware, take notice of VII.2956; **w. that** take notice of what III.1903; **w. fro(m)** beware of III.1994, X.628; *(reflx.)* **w. him** let him beware of I.662, Tr 2.868; **w. you** look out VI.905, VII.699.

war(e) *adj.* (1) aware I.157, I.896, BD 445; (2) **(be) w.** beware, take care I.1218, VII.439, BD 1030; **be w. by** be warned by (the example of) III.180, VII.2185, Tr 1.203; (3) prudent, discreet I.309, I.3604, Rom A 1258.

warante, warente *v.* protect VI.338; swear, affirm I.3791, Rom A 930.

ward(e) *n.* (1) watchtower Rom B 3191; (2) custody, possession VI.201, X.880, Rom B 3255.

wardeyn, warden *n.* (1) master (of a college) I.3999, I.4006; (2) guardian Tr 3.665, Tr 5.1177; *pl.* **wardeyns** guardians III.1216.

ware *n.* goods, merchandise VII.56, Rom C 5926.

warisshe, warice *v.* (1) *(tr.)* cure, treat VI.906, VII.1017; (2) *(intr.)* recover VII.982; *pp.* **warisshed** V.856, **warished** BD 1104; *vbl. n.* **warisshynge** cure VII.1015.

warne(n) *v.* warn Rom C 7655; warn, command to take heed I.3583, Astr 2.3.65; announce, inform VII.1462; *3 pr. sg.* **warneth** forewarns, foretells HF 46; *pr. subj. sg.* **warne** HF 893; *pt. sg.* **warned(e)** PF 45, VII.3146; *prp.* **warnynge** foretelling VII.3126; *pp.* **(y)warned** warned VII.3232; foretold HF 51, LGW 2658; *vbl. n.* **warning(e)** information VIII.593; summons, command Tr 3.195.

warne(n) *see* **werne.**

warnestoore *v.* fortify, garrison VII.1297, VII.1333; *pp.*

(as *adj.*) **warnstoryd** Bo 1.pr3.77; *vbl. n.* **warn-estooryng** VII.1335.

wasshe *v.* wash, cleanse II.356, VII.2756, Tr 4.646; *imp. sg.* **wassh** Tr 4.646; *pt. sg.* **wessh** I.2283, II.453, **wissh** Rom A 125; *pt. pl.* **wesshen** Tr 2.1184; *pp.* **wasshe(n)** I.3311, VI.353; **wasschen** Bo 4.m6.12.

wast *n.* wastefulness III.500, X.813, Rom B 5118.

waste(n) *v.* (1) *(tr.)* waste I.4416, X.848, PF 283; (2) *(intr.)* waste away I.3023, II.20, Tr 3.348; *2 pr. sg.* **wastest** Rom B 2443; *3 pr. sg.* **wasteth** III.2235; *pr. pl.* **wasten** VIII.1422; *imp. pl.* **waste** Rom B 2276; *pp.* **wasted** decayed I.3020, **wasted** III.1720; (as *adj.*) **waste** devastated I.1331; *vbl. n.* **wastynge** waste VII.1392.

water, watir *n.* water I.400, HF 814; one of the four elements I.246; *gen.* **watres** VIII.805; *pl.* **watres** VIII.853.

wawe *n.* wave II.508, X.363, LGW 2416; *pl.* **wawes** I.1958.

wax, waxe(n), ywaxe *see* **wexe(n).**

wedde(n) *v.* wed I.1832, I.3228, Tr 5.863; *pr. pl.* **wedde** III.1260; *pr. subj. sg.* **wedde** IV.346; *imp. sg.* **wed** join together Sted 28; *pt. sg.* **weddede** I.868; *pp.* **(y)wedded** I.2351, II.712; *prp.* (as *adj.*) **weddyng** IV.868; *vbl. n.* **weddyng(e)** wedding I.883, VII.2026; **wedyng** LGW 2250.

wede, weede *n.* (1) clothing I.1006, IV.863, Tr 1.177; (2) *pl.* **wedis** Rom B 5352.

weder, wedir *n.* weather II.873, III.2253, Tr 2.2, Rom A 455; *pl.* **wedres** storms PF 681, PF 686.

wey(e), way *n.* (1) way, path, road I.34, I.467, BD 154; go (**ryden**, *etc.*) **oure** (**his**, *etc.*) **w.** go (ride, *etc.*) on our (his, *etc.*) way I.856, I.3601, I.3712; **stondest now in w.** are on your way to, likely to Tr 3.247; (2) way, manner, means I.1291, II.217, Anel 283; **atte leeste w.** at least I.1121, I.3680, V.1417; **by (be) no (any) w.** in no (any) way II.1084, VII.2280, HF 1258, LGW F 493; (3) **furlong (mile) w.** as much time as it takes to walk a furlong (mile) I.4199, VII.276; (4) **a (twenty) devel w.** in the name of (twenty) devil(s) I.3134, I.3713; *gen.* (as *adv.*) **any weyes** in any way HF 1122; **oother weyes** in other ways III.2211, otherwise Tr 3.1658; **by al weyes** in every way BD 1271; *pl.* **weyes** ways Tr 2.822, **weys** Bo 5.pr1.10.

wey *adv.* away Tr 1.574; **do w.** take away I.3287, put aside VIII.487, Tr 2.110; leave it be Tr 2.893.

weyen *v.* weigh VII.2586, consider LGW F 398; *2 pr. sg.* **weyest noght** count for nothing VII.2233; *3 pr. sg.* **weyeth** considers, weighs I.1781; *pt. sg.* **weyed** out measured VIII.1298; *pt. pl.* **weyeden** weighed I.454.

weyk(e), weyker *see* **wayk(e).**

weylaway, weylawey, wailaway, welaway, welawey, wel-away, wel-awey *interj.* alas! I.938, I.3714, I.4072, III.216, III.2485, HF 170, HF 345, HF 383, Anel 338, Tr 2.1695, Tr 3.1695.

weys *see* **wyse** *n.*

weyve(n) *v.* (1) *(tr.)* abandon, give up III.1176, VIII.276, Anel 246; refuse Tr 2.284; (2) *(intr.)* turn aside Tr 2.1050; (with **fro, from**) deviate IV.1483; *3 pr. sg.* **weyveth** refuses IX.178; turns aside Tr 4.602; *pr. pl.* **weyve** deviate IV.2424; *pr. subj.* **weyve** refuse X.353 *(sg.)*, neglect VII.1066 *(pl.)*; *imp. sg.* **weyve** abandon Bo 1.m7.16; *pp.* **weyved** banished, turned away II.308.

weke *see* **wyke.**

wel, weel *adj.* (with **ben, seem**) well I.2109, II.308, BD 643, Tr 3.528.

wel(e), weel, well *adv.* well I.29, X.711, Bo 2.pr4.123, Mars 180; (as *intens.* of *adj.*) very much I.256, I.614, Tr 1.578; (as *intens.* of *adv.*) very I.1254, I.1330, BD 511; (with *num.*) fully, a good I.29, BD 420.

welde, weelde *v.* wield LGW 2000; control, handle VII.2262; wield (limbs), move with ease III.1947; *pt. sg.* **weelded** VII.2665, **welte** VII.2010; *vbl. n.* **weeld-ynge** control VII.1610.

wele *n.* happiness, prosperity I.895, I.1272, BD 603.

weleful, welful *adj.* happy, prosperous VII.1317, Bo 1.m1.11; blessed II.451.

welefulnesse *n.* happiness Bo 1.pr3.32, *etc.*

welfare *n.* welfare I.3063, V.838; happiness BD 582; source of happiness Tr 4.228.

welk *see* **walke(n).**

welken, welkne, wolken *n.* sky IV.1124, VII.2731, BD 339, Tr 3.551.

welle *n.* (1) well, spring, source I.1533, *etc.*; (2) source I.3037.

welle *v.* well up, gush Tr 4.709, Tr 5.215; **welle-stremes** springs PF 187; *pl.* **welles** BD 166.

welte *see* **welde.**

wenche *n.* girl, young woman (of low birth) I.3254, I.3973, IX.220; servant girl I.3631, HF 206; mistress, concubine VI.453; *pl.* **wenches** III.393.

wend, wende(n) *see* **wene(n).**

wende(n) *v.* go, travel I.16, I.21, Tr 2.1251; leave, depart II.253, III.915, PF 492; pass away I.3025; turn HF 1868; *2 pr. sg.* **wendest** I.4242; *3 pr. sg.* **wendeth** III.918, **weendeth** Bo 2.pr7.154, *(contr.)* **went** Tr 2.36; *pr. pl.* **wende** VI.927; *pr. subj.* **wende** VII.3081 *(sg.)*, Tr 4.1495 *(pl.)*; *1 & 3 pt. sg.* **wente** I.78; *2 pt. sg.* **wentist** Rom B 3224; (with *pro.*) **wentestow** I.3486; *pt. pl.* **wente(n)** I.999, I.2148; *pp.* **went** I.3665; *vbl. n.* **wendyng(e)** departure Tr 4.1344, Bo 2.pr1.96.

wene *n.* doubt Tr 4.1593, Rom A 574, Rom A 732.

wene(n), weene *v.* suppose, think III.786, Tr 1.575; believe BD 867; expect I.4320; *2 pr. sg.* **wenest** BD 744, (with *pro.*) **wenestow** III.211; *3 pr. sg.* **weneth** IV.2408; *pr. pl.* **wene(n)** IV.1280, consider themselves I.1804; *pr. subj. sg.* **wene** VII.1148; *imp. pl.* **wene** LGW F 188; *1 & 3 pt. sg.* **wende** I.1269, **wened** Rom C 6790; *2 pt. sg.* **wendest** Bo 3.pr12.22; *pt. pl.* **wende(n)** I.3994, IV.440; *2 pt. subj. sg.* **wend-est** should suppose Tr 1.1031; *3 pt. subj. sg.* **wende** would have thought VI.782; *pt. subj. pl.* **wenden** should think I.3962; *prp.* **wenyng(e)** VII.2590, intending Tr 4.88; *pp.* **wend** IV.691, **ywent** Tr 5.444; *vbl. n.* **wenynge** understanding Tr 4.992, belief Bo 5.pr6.58.

went(te), wente(n) *see* **wende(n).**

ywent *see* **wene(n).**

wente *n.* (1) path, passage BD 398, Tr 3.787; (2) turn, turning Tr 2.63, Tr 2.815.

wepe(n) *v.* weep I.230, I.144, Anel 293; *2 pr. sg.* (with *pro.*) **wepistow** Bo 1.pr4.3; *3 pr. sg.* **wepeth** I.221; *pr. pl.* **wepen** II.529, **wepyn** Bo 3.m12.36; *pr. subj. sg.* **wepe** Tr 4.591; *imp. sg.* **weep** I.2470; *pt. sg.* **weep** I.2345, **wep** Tr 3.115, **wepte** I.148; *pt. pl.* **wepen** II.820, **wepten** VIII.415; *prp.* **wepyng(e)** II.768, Tr 4.575; *pp.* **wopen** V.523, **wepen** Tr 5.279, **wept** IV.1544; *vbl. n.* **weping(e)** weeping I.231, Mars 143; *pl.* **wepynges** Bo 1.pr1.46.

wepen(e), wepne *n.* weapon(s) I.1591, I.1601, LGW 1994.

were *n.* (1) state of doubt HF 979; **without(e) w.** without doubt BD 1295, Rom B 2568; (2) distress LGW 2886.

were *v.* wear IV.886; *2 pr. sg.* **werest** HF 1840, (with *pro.*) **werestow** VII.1949; *3 pr. sg.* **wereth** III.1018; *pr. pl.* **were(n)** I.2948, Rom C 7246; *pr. subj. sg.* **were** Gent 14; *pt. sg.* **wered(e)** I.75, I.1388; *prp.* **weryng** Rom B 3864; *pp.* **wered** I.4303; *vbl. n.* **werynge** wearing X.1052.

wereyed *see* **werreye(n).**

wery, weery *adj.* I.3643, I.4107, BD 127; (with *inf.*) tired of (doing something) II.1071, IV.1291, LGW 2258; (with *pp.*) tired out by (doing something) II.596, HF 115, Bo 5.pr1.19, Rom A 664.

werynesse *n.* weariness X.257, LGW 2182, LGW 2429.

werk(e) *n.* (1) work, task I.3311, II.928; deed I.479, IV.28; (2) work, creation V.879; literary work Tr 2.16; (3) suffering Tr 4.852; *pl.* **werkes** HF 54; *gen. pl.* **werkes** deeds', labors' VII.2096.

werke(n), werche(n), wirche, worke(n), worche(n) *v.* work I.3430, IV.1661, VIII.14, Tr 3.1638, Rom B 5737; do, act I.779, I.3528, IV.2216, VII.1447; cause I.2072, Tr 3.1354; be effective I.2759; employ, use Astr Pro 70, Astr 2.5.6, Astr 2.40.45; **do w. make** VIII.545, HF 474; *2 pr. sg.* **worchist** Rom B 3142; *3 pr. sg.* **werketh** VII.1197, **worcheth** BD 815; *pr. pl.* **werke(n)** VII.2938, VIII.1139, **worken** Bo 5.pr6.310, **worchen** Rom B 5737; **werkes** *(Nth.)* I.4030; *pr. subj. sg.* **werke** IV.1357, **werche** PF 74, **worke** Astr 2.29.25; *pr. subj. pl.* **worchen** Rom B 3553; *imp. sg.* **werk(e)** VII.1003, VII.1170, **wirk** IV.1485, **worch** Astr 2.34.19, **work** Astr 2.25.59; *imp. pl.* **werketh** IV.504, **wirketh** Rom C 6665; *1 & 3 pt. sg.* **wroghte** I.497, **wroughte** V.1202; *2 pt. sg.* **wroghtest** II.856, (with *pro.*) **wroughtestow** VII.2393; *pt. pl.* **wroghte** IV.1692, **wrought(e)** Rom C 6565; *pp.* **(y)wroght** I.196, I.367, **(y)wrought** PF 305; *vbl. n.* **wirkyng(e)** III.698, X.250, **werkyng(e)** work VIII.116; deed IX.210; **worchyng(e)** operation Astr 2.35 rubric; act Rom C 6255; **wurchyng** acts Rom C 6123; *pl.* **werkynges** acts X.82, movements HF 1944; **worchynges** activities Rom C 6585.

werne, warne(n) *v.* refuse, deny HF 1559, Tr 3.149, ABC 11, Rom B 3652; forbid III.333, Tr 3.12; *pr. subj. pl.* **werne** Rom B 3749; *pt. sg.* **werned** HF 1539, **warned** Rom C 5840; *pp.* **werned** Rom A 442, **wernd** Bo 2.pr3.44, **warned** Rom C 7500; *vbl. n.* **wernyng** refusal Rom A 1142.

werre *n.* war I.47, I.1287, Tr 1.134; *pl.* **werres** VII.1650.

werreye(n), werry *v.* wage war (on) I.1484, I.1544, Rom C 6926; *2 pr. sg.* **werryest** LGW F 322; *3 pr. sg.* **werreyeth** X.401; *pr. pl.* **werreyen** Rom C 7018; *pt. sg.* **werreyed** V.10; *pp.* **wereyed** Tr 5.584, Rom C 6926; **werreid** Rom B 2078.

wers(e), wors(e) *comp. adj.* worse I.3174, I.3733, III.171, BD 814; (as *n.*) Tr 3.1074, Tr 4.840.

werst(e), worst(e), wurst *super. adj.* worst IV.83, VII.161, X.488, Tr 2.304, Tr 3.278, Rom B 4493; (as *n.*) I.1614, BD 1174, Tr 1.341.

wessh, wesshen *see* **wasshe.**

weste *v.* go westward PF 266, LGW F 61, LGW F 197.

wete *v.* wet, dampen HF 1785, Tr 3.1115; *pr. pl.* **weten** Bo 1.m1.6; *pt. sg.* **wette** I.129; *pp.* **ywet** I.4155.

wete, weet(e), *adj.* wet I.1280, I.4107, LGW 775; (as *n.*) wetness, damp weather VIII.1187.

wete(n) *see* **wite(n)** *v.*[1]

weve(n) *v.* weave LGW 2352, LGW 2358; *pt. sg.* **waf** LGW 2364; *pp.* **(y)woven** LGW 2360, Bo 1.pr1.22.

wex *n.* wax VIII.1268.

wexe(n), waxe(n) *v.* grow, increase III.28, VI.23, BD 415; become VIII.837, PF 444, Tr 2.908; *2 pr. sg.* **waxest** Bo 5.m5.20; *3 pr. sg.* **wexeth** I.3024, **waxeth** Tr 1.949; *pr. pl.* **wexe(n)** IV.998, VIII.1095, **waxen** Bo 4.m5.11; *pr. subj. sg.* **wexe** VII.1559; *pt. sg.* **wex** PF 206, **weex** II.563, **wax** I.4234; *pt. pl.* **wax** III.636, **wexen** BD 489, **wax(e)** LGW 727, Rom A 1674, **woxen** Bo 3.m12.36; *pt. subj. sg.* **waxe** Bo 2.pr7.8; *prp.* **wexyng** growing I.2078; *pp.* **(y)woxen** IV.1462, Tr 5.827, **woxe** X.1021, **waxen** BD 414, **ywaxe** BD 1275.

whan(ne), when(ne) *adv. and conj.* (1) when I.135, BD 135, Tr 5.1428, LGW F 101; whenever Anel 134, Tr 5.1417, Ven 54; **w. that** when I.1, BD 1222; whenever BD 962; **w. so that** whensoever V.1005; **w. that evere** whenever III.45; (2) *(interr.)* when VI.733, PF 495.

what *interj.* what! indeed! I.854, I.3366, Tr 1.192.

what *pro.* (1) *(interr.)* what I.3370, Tr 1.419; **w. thogh** what (does it matter) if IV.2293, VII.2815; who Tr 1.765, I.862; why III.167, Tr 1.812; (2) *(indef.)* **w. so** whatever I.3843, IV.306; (as *n.*) a little what slightly Bo 4.pr6.9; (3) *(rel.)* what, that which III.1735, IV.1460, HF 2058, Tr 3.484.

what *adj.* (1) whatever IV.10, IV.165, Anel 165; (2) *(interr.)* what I.905, I.1029; (3) *(rel.)* **w. thyng** what IV.1059.

what *adv. and conj.* (1) *(interr.)* why I.184, I.1307, II.56, LGW 2218; (2) (as *intens.*) how HF 300, Tr 2.464; (3) (as *conj.*) to the extent that, as much as Tr 4.35; **w. for** because of I.1453, V.54; **w. for . . . w. for** partly because of . . . and partly because of PF 15, Tr 1.387; **w. so** however much IV.1389.

wheither, whether *pro.* which (of two) III.1227, III.1234, Astr 2.7.14; whichever I.1856.

wheither, whether, whethir, wheder, wher(e) *adv. and conj.* (1) whether I.570, I.1857, I.2252, I.3073, VI.748, BD 783, Rom B 1874; **w. that** whether I.570, Tr 1.132; **w. so, wher-so (that)** whether V.778, BD 977; (3) *(interr.* introducing a question with alternatives)* (tell me) whether I.1125, III.2069, Tr 5.735. Cf. **wher(e).**

whelome *see* **whilom(e).**

whelp *n.* pup I.257, BD 389; cub I.2627; *pl.* **whelpes** VIII.60.

whenne(s) *adv.* whence V.588, VIII.432, Tr 1.402.

wher(e), wheer *adv. and conj.* (1) *(interr.)* where, in what place I.3486, BD 1298; (introducing a question with alternatives) (tell me) whether BD 91, Tr 4.831; (2) *(conj.)* where I.421, I.1351; wherever III.218; whereas, once VIII.727; **w. as** where I.1113, II.647; **w. on** on what Tr 2.691; **w. that** where I.897, PF 298; wherever I.1207, VIII.733, PF 172; (3) *(rel.)* where II.611, BD 1129. Cf. **wheither.**

wherby *adv.* by which I.2266, Bo 3.pr11.28; why Tr 3.778.

wherfor(e) *adv.* why I.1568, Tr 1.311; for which reason II.1049, VII.121, Tr 1.988.

wherof, whereof *adv.* from what III.72, Tr 5.1224; for which VIII.1148, Tr 3.1647; with which Rom A 703; why Tr 4.641, Tr 4.1365; for what IX.339.

wheron *adv.* on which Tr 5.1199; **w. it was long** what accounted for it VIII.930.

wherso, whereso *adv.* wherever VII.2638, BD 112; whatever BD 10.

wherthourgh, wherthrough, wherthurgh, wherethurgh *adv.* by means of which BD 120, Rom B 2418, Rom B 3733, Rom B 4096, Rom B 4774.

wherto, whereto, wharto *adv.* why VII.1612, VIII.640, BD 670, Bo 1.m4.12; to which Rom B 2526.

wherwith, wherewith *adv.* with which III.1718, X.468, Tr 1.942, Rom B 2526; *(interr.)* with what III.131; (as *pro.*) the wherewithal I.302.

whete *n.* wheat I.3988, I.3991, Rom B 5590.

whette, whetted, ywhet *pp.* whetted, sharpened Anel 212, Tr 5.1760, Lady 57.

why *see* **wy** *interj.*

why *adv.* (1) why I.1083, etc.; **w. so** VII.926; **w. that** why I.717, I.911; **cause w.** the reason (for this) I.4144; (as *n.*) the reason Tr 2.777; **do nought w.** do nothing (to cause this) Lady 108; (2) *(interr.)* why I.1083, *etc.*

which(e) *rel.* (1) *(pro.)* which Tr 3.198; whichever I.796; who III.1092, III.2029; **w. that** which III.2245, VII.2006, Tr 2.1395; who III.537, IV.780, Tr 5.1284; **for w.** because Tr 4.211, therefore Tr 4.708, Tr 4.769; **for w. for to** in order to Tr 1.78; *(indef.)* whichever I.796; (2) *(adj.)* which I.2972, III.676; what I.40, VI.279, PF 564.

which(e) *interr.* (1) *(pro.)* which V.1622; (2) *(adj.)* which Tr 2.1189; (in exclamations) what IV.2421, BD 859, **w. a** what a Tr 2.675, I.3611, Tr 1.803.

whil(e) *n.* time I.3299, PF 214; **a w.** a short time I.1437, VIII.1184, LGW 2551; **alas (weylawey) the w.** alas the time (it happened) IV.251, BD 619, Tr 3.1078; **any w.** for any time II.753; in any way IX.195; **every w.** continually Tr 1.328; **gon is a grete w.** long ago LGW F 427; **longe w.** for a long time HF 1287; **the mene (meen) w.** the meantime II.546, III.1445, Tr 5.401; **not gon ful longe w.** not very long ago Tr 2.507; **outher w. . . . outher w.** sometimes . . . sometimes Bo 2.pr1.107, Bo 3.pr12.158; *pl.* **in the meene whiles** meantime II.668; (as *adv.*) **the whiles** while VI.439.

whil(e) *conj.* while I.35, I.1295, Anel 280; when BD 56; **w. that** while I.397, Tr 1.315.

whiles, whils *conj.* while VIII.1137, VIII.1188.

whilom(e), whelome *adv.* once, formerly I.795, Bo 3.pr12.188, Bo 3.m12.4, Tr 1.508.

whit(e) *adj.* (1) white I.976, I.238, BD 250; fair, blond Tr 2.887, Tr 2.1062; (as *n.*) white wine VI.526; (2) bare, unpainted BD 780; innocent, pure VIII.115; **never so w.** ever so purely II.355; (3) specious, misleading Tr 3.901, Tr 3.1567; *comp.* **whitter** VII.2863.

who *pro.* (1) *(interr.)* who I.831; (2) *(indef.)* he who, whoever I.3152, I.4271, BD 32; **w. that** who V.771, he who Tr 2.867, Tr 4.180; **as w. seith** as if to say VII.1084, Tr 4.180; as one might say Tr 1.1011, Tr 3.268; *gen.* **whos** whose II.642 etc., **whoos** Bo 1.pr3.6; *dat.* and *acc.* **whom** whom I.501 etc.; **whom that** whom I.4334, II.665, Tr 1.717.

whoso, whooso *pro. nom.* whoever, anyone I.644,

I.3045, BD 574, LGW F 361; **w. that** whoever I.741, IV.2016, Bo 3.m11.1; *dat.* **whomso** whomsoever Tr 5.145.

wy, why *interj.* why, indeed I.3285, III.445.

wyd(e) *adj.* wide, roomy I.28, I.93, BD 861; *comp.* **wydder** HF 797; *super.* **widest** Astr I.17.45.

wyde *adv.* widely III.1524, IV.722, HF 1139; **wyde-wher(e)** far and wide II.136, Tr 3.404.

wydwe, widewe *n.* widow I.253, I.1171, Tr 1.97; *gen.* **wydwes** III.1581, **widewes** Tr 1.109; *pl.* **wydwes** IV.1423.

wyf(e) *n.* woman Tr 3.106, Tr 3.1296; wife I.445, I.932, BD 63; *gen.* **wyves** IV.599; *pl.* **wyves** I.234.

wyfly *adj.* womanly, having the skills or qualities proper to a woman IV.429, IV.919, LGW 1737.

wyfhod *n.* womanliness IV.699, LGW F 253; marriage III.149; fidelity as a wife II.76.

wyflees *adj.* without a wife, unmarried IV.1236, IV.1248.

wight *n.*[1] (1) creature, person, being I.71, I.537, BD 244; **no w.** no one I.280, V.1393, BD 1016; (2) **a litel w.** a little (while or bit) I.4283; Tr 5.927; *gen.* **wyghtes** PF 514; *pl.* **wightes** I.3479.

wight(e), weighte *n.*[2] weight I.2145, VII.1226, Rom A 1106; *pl.* **weyghtes** Bo 2.m5.34.

wight *adj.* strong, active, agile I.4086, VII.2267, Rom B 4761.

wyke, wowke, weke *n.* week I.1539, V.1295, Tr 4.1278, Rom B 4655; *gen.* **wikes** Tr 5.499; *pl.* **wykes** I.1850.

wyket *n.* wicket gate, door IV.2152, Rom A 528; *pl.* **wikketis** Rom B 4244.

wykke *adj.* wicked, evil I.1087, I.1580, Tr 1.403; miserable II.118; noxious Tr 1.946; ill-tasting Rom A 925; (as *n.*) bad Tr 3.1074, Tr 4.840.

wikked(e), wicked *adj.* wicked, evil I.3484, Bo 3.m4.6, Rom C 7535.

wikkedly, wickedly *adv.* wickedly I.1735, IV.723, Rom C 7457.

wikkednesse *adj.* wickedness, evil III.695, III.715, Tr 1.999; crime, wicked deed II.623; *pl.* **wikkednesses** evil, evil deeds X.275.

wil(le) *n.* will, desire I.1104, I.1317, BD 116; *gen.* **willes** V.568; *pl.* **willes** Tr 4.107.

wyle *n.* stratagem, trick I.3403, I.4047, BD 673; trickery, guile PF 215, Tr 3.1077; *pl.* **wiles** LGW 2294.

wilful, wilfull, willeful *adj.* voluntary III.1179, Bo 3.pr11.153; obstinate, willful Tr 3.935; (as *adv.*) willfully PF 429.

wilfully *adv.* voluntarily VI.441, VII.1422; willfully VII.3096, Tr 2.284; obstinately X.586.

wilfulnesse *n.* obstinacy I.3057, Tr 1.793; desire VII.1382.

wille(n) *v.* (1) wish, desire I.889, I.1042, VIII.1473, Tr 2.396, Rom B 2482; (2) *(fut. aux.)* will I.42, I.4029, BD 226; *inf.* **wille** IV.721; *1 pr. sg.* **wil** I.4178, **will** Bo 1.pr2.25, **wol** I.42; *2 pr. sg.* **wilt** Tr 3.1459, (with *pro.*) **wiltow** I.1156, **wolt** I.1595, (with *pro.*) **woltow** VIII.307; *3 pr. sg.* **wil** BD 42, **will** Rom A 1623, **wol(e)** I.945, I.1042, **willeth** HF 447; *pr. pl.* **wil** I.4111, **will** Rom C 7343, Mars 203, **wol** I.816, **wollen** Tr 3.768, **wole(n)** Rom C 6164, Bo 3.m10.11; *pr. subj. sg.* **wole** I.805; *pr. subj. pl.* **wole** LGW 1319, **wile** Rom B 1952; *1 & 3 pt. sg.* **wolde** I.276; *2 pt. sg.* **woldest** I.1142; (with *pro.*) **woldestow** Bo 3.pr1.32;

pt. pl. **wolde(n)** I.27, I.2714; *pt. subj. sg.* **wolde** I.766, III.444, IV.1764, **wolde she were** would that she were II.161, **wolde God** would that God (would grant) III.37, III.1103, IV.1758, **wolde I hadde** I wish I had III.1633, VI.952; *pt. subj. pl.* **wolde** would like to VII.1234; *pp.* **wold** desired VII.1000, **woold** willed VII.1425; *vbl. n.* **willyng(e)** will, desire IV.319, Rom C 5952; *pl.* **willynges** Bo 5.pr6.292.

wilne(n) *v.* desire, wish I.2114, X.517; *2 pr. sg.* **wilnest** I.1609; *3 pr. sg.* **wilneth** I.2564; *pr. pl.* **wilne(n)** Tr 3.121, Bo 4.m4.14; **wiln** Bo 3.pr9.45; *pt. sg.* **wilned** BD 1262; *pp.* **wilned** Bo 1.pr4.204; *vbl. n. pl.* **wilnynges** desires Bo 3.pr11.161.

wympel, wympul, wymple *n.* woman's headdress, covering all but the face I.152, LGW 813, Rom B 3864.

wynde *v.* wind, twist about III.1102; turn Tr 2.601; bend Tr 1.257; clasp, wrap VIII.42, Tr 3.1232; *3 pr. sg.* **wynt** turns, directs LGW F 85; *pt. sg.* **wond** turned, went LGW 2253; *vbl. n.* **wyndynge** folding X.417.

wynke *v.* close (both) one's eyes Tr 3.1537; sleep PF 482, Rom B 2348; *3 pr. sg.* **wynketh** VII.3431.

wynne(n) *v.* (1) win I.891, I.1486; earn III.1453, profit I.427; conquer Tr 2.1376, LGW 1915; **w. on** get the better of I.594; (2) **w. to** get to Anel 20, LGW 2427; **w. from** get away from Tr 4.1125; *3 pr. sg.* **wynneth** X.637; *pr. subj.* **wynne** I.1617 *(sg.)*, Rom B 4814 *(pl.)*; *pt. sg.* **wan** V.664; *pt. pl.* **wan** V.1401, **wonnen** Rom C 6567; *pp.* **ywonne** III.2293, **wonne(n)** I.51, I.3381; *vbl. n.* **wynnyng(e)** profit I.275, winning HF 1972; *pl.* **wynnynges** II.127.

wirche *see* **werke(n)**.

wys(e) *adj.* wise, prudent I.68, I.309, BD 1072; (as *n.*) wise one Tr 1.79, wise ones LGW F 19; **make it w.** deliberate on it, raise difficulties I.785; *comp.* **wyser** IV.1569; (as *n.*) superior (in wisdom) LGW 2634; *super.* **wisest(e)** I.4054, VIII.967.

wys *adv.* certainly, indeed HF 1819, Tr 2.474; (in asseverations with **so, also, as**) surely, truly I.2786, V.1470.

wyse, weys *n.* manner, way I.1913, I.2370, Bo 5.pr1.10; **in every, alle (maner) w.** in every way, completely II.1098, IV.605, VII.245; **in no (manner) w.** by no means, not at all III.1898, VIII.714, ABC 131; (as *adv.*) **double w.** doubly I.1338; *pl.* **wises** Tr 1.159.

wissh *see* **washe.**

wisly, wisely *adv.* certainly, surely I.4162, V.789, Tr 3.1653; (in asseverations with **as, so, also**) surely, truly I.1863, IV.822, Tr 2.1230.

wisse *v.* inform, instruct III.1008, Tr 1.622; guide, direct HF 491; *pr. subj. sg.* **wisse** III.1858; *imp. sg.* **wisse** ABC 155.

wiste *see* **wite(n)** *v.*[1]

wit *n.* (1) mind II.609, X.453, BD 505; spirit Lady 100; intelligence, judgment III.2291, V.674; (2) understanding BD 1095; (**as**) **to my w.** as I understand III.41, V.875, PF 547; opinion Tr 5.758, V.203; idea Tr 4.1425; (3) knowledge I.3091, II.10, II.888; (4) physical sensation Bo 5.pr5.26; the senses Bo 5.pr4.155 (see note), VII.1424; *gen.* **wittes** Tr 3.931; *pl.* **wittes** VII.1615.

wite *n.* blame, reproach VIII.953, Anel 268, Tr 2.1648; **yow to w.** a reproach to you Rom A 1541.

wite(n), wete(n) *v.*[1] know I.3555, IV.1740, Mars 188, Astr 2.44.45; **w. at** learn from VIII.621; *1 & 3 pr. sg.* **woot** I.389, **wot** BD 1237; *2 pr. sg.* **woost** I.1156,

wost Anel 277, (with *pro.*) **wostow** I.1163; *1, 2, & 3 pr. pl.* **wite(n)** I.1260, I.1794, VIII.906; *2 pr. pl.* **woot** I.740, **wote** LGW 1998; *imp. pl.* **witeth** Lady 90, **witteth** Tr 1.687; *1 & 3 pt. sg.* **wiste** I.224, III.553; *2 pt. sg.* **wistest** Bo 3.pr11.222, (with *pro.*) **wistestow** Tr 3.1644; *pt. pl.* **wiste(n)** VI.266, Tr 5.20; *pt. subj. sg.* **wiste** if he knew VI.513; *pp.* **wist** II.1072; *vbl. n.* **wyttynge** knowledge Tr 2.236, **wityng(e)** I.1611, Tr 4.991.

wyte(n) *v.*[2] blame X.1016, Anel 110 blame on, impute to Tr 2.1000, Tr 5.1335; *inf.* **to wite** to be blamed Tr 2.385, Tr 3.63; *2 pr. sg.* **wytest** accuse II.108; *imp. sg.* **wit** Tr 2.1000; *imp. pl.* **wyte** I.3140.

with *prep.* (1) with I.10, etc.; **w. that word** thereupon, immediately I.856, I.1399; **w. that** thereupon Tr 2.253, Tr 2.428; (2) by (agency) I.76, I.511, VII.2284; because of I.107; (3) concerning, with respect to IV.1499, VII.114, Bo 1.pr4.46; **w. a ren** at a run I.4079.

withal(le), with alle *adv.* withal, indeed I.127, I.283, Tr 1.288; moreover, also III.156, V.687, HF 212.

withdrawe *v.* withdraw X.143; withhold III.617, X.802; *3 pr. sg.* **withdraweth** Bo 4.m6.45; *pr. pl.* **withdrawen** X.449; *pr. subj. sg.* **withdrawe** X.377; *imp. sg.* **withdraugh** Bo 1.m5.55; **withdraw** subtract Astr 2.44.40; *imp. pl.* **withdraweth** VIII.1423; *pt. sg.* **withdrowghe** Bo 3.pr2.2, **withdrow** Astr 2.45.11; *pp.* **withdrawe(n)** Bo 1.pr1.60, Tr 4.886; *vbl. n.* **withdrawynge** withholding X.568.

withholde(n), witholde(n) *v.* (1) restrain, resist, hold back VII.1996, Rom B 3550; *(reflx.)* restrain oneself Rom A 723; **him to w.** of refrain from Tr 5.76; (2) retain, keep X.744, X.1041, Tr 4.597; maintain Bo 4.pr6.201, Bo 4.pr6.359; employ, hire I.511; *3 pr. sg.* **witholdeth** Bo 5.m3.51; *pp.* **withholde(n)** held, detained VIII.345; retained, in the service of LGW F 192, **witholde** LGW G 76; *vbl. n.* **witholdynge** retention VII.1223.

withoute *adv.* outside I.1888, PF 244; outwardly, on the outside V.1111, Rom B 4732; (as *n.*) **of w.** from out of town Tr 1.270.

withoute-forth, withoute forth, withouteforth *adv.* outwardly, on the outside X.172, Bo 5.m4.21; (as *n.*) **fro w.** Bo 3.pr11.84.

withseye, withseyn *v.* deny, gainsay I.805, I.1140, LGW F 367; *pr. subj. sg.* **withseye** deny, renounce VIII.447; *3 pt. sg.* **withseyde** spoke against Tr 4.215; *pp.* **withseid(e)** Bo 3.pr10.64, Bo 5.pr1.45.

withstonde(n) *v.* (1) withstand, resist III.1659, X.733, Tr 1.839; oppose Tr 4.160; restrain Rom B 3807; (2) *(tr.)* obstruct, make dim Bo 5.m2.8; *(intr.)* become dimmed, obstructed Bo 1.m7.7; *3 pr. sg.* **withstandeth** III.1497, **withstondeth** Bo 5.m2.10; *pr. pl.* **withstonden** Bo 3.pr8.43, **withstande** Bo 1.m7.7; *pr. subj. sg.* **withstonde** X.353; *pt. sg.* **withstood** Bo 1.pr4.77, **withstod** LGW 1183; *pt. subj. sg.* **withstoode** were to oppose Tr 4.552; *pp.* **withstonde(n)** X.953, Tr 1.253; *vbl. n.* **withstondynge** resisting X.455; preventing Bo 3.pr11.145.

witnesse *n.* testimony, evidence II.629, VI.169; **beren w.** provide evidence Tr 4.741, LGW F 527; **take to w.** offer as evidence VI.483; (2) **bere w.** offer testimony, swear Rom C 7079, Rom C 7310; **take (to) w.** offer as guarantor, witness III.233, IV.821.

witnessen, witness(e) *v.* (1) *(tr.)* testify to, provide evidence of X.594, Rom C 6958; (2) *(intr.)* prove X.842, X.1036; *3 pr. sg.* **witnesseth** VII.1459; *pr. pl.* **witnessen** VIII.1067; *imp. pl.* **witnesse on** take the evidence of, consider as a witness III.951, III.1491, IV.2282; *pp.* **iwitnessed** proven Bo 5.pr6.44; *vbl. n.* **witnessyng** testimony VI.194, **witnessynge** proof LGW F 299.

wityng(e) *see* **wite(n)** *v.*[1]

wityngly *adv.* knowingly X.401, X.579.

wo(o) *n.* woe I.351, I.900, *etc.;* **me (hym,** *etc.*) **is wo** woe to me (him, *etc.*), I (*etc.*) regret VII.10, Tr 3.1423; sorrow V.1027, Tr 1.582; pain Rom B 1906.

wo(o) *adj.* woeful BD 1192, Tr 3.66, Pity 3; (as *adv.*) **wo begon** afflicted, in distress Tr 4.822, LGW 2497, Rom A 336.

wod(e), wood(e) *adj.* mad, crazy I.184, I.582, BD 104; foolish VIII.450, Lady 84; (as *n.*) **for w.** madly HF 1747; (2) angry III.1327, III.1666; passionate LGW 736.

wode, woode *n.* wood I.1522, I.1618, BD 414; *gen.* **wodes** VII.3411; *pl.* **wodes** I.2297.

wodly, woodly *adv.* **madly** I.1301, LGW 1752.

woodnesse, wodnesse *n.* madness I.2011, I.3452, Tr 3.794; *pl.* **woodnesses** fury Bo 2.m4.18.

woful *adj.* woeful I.1063, *etc.*; *comp.* **wofuller** I.1340; *super.* **wofulleste** Tr 4.303.

wok, wook *see* **wake(n).**

wol(e), wole(n) *see* **wille(n).**

wolken *see* **welken.**

woll(e) *n.* wool I.3249, VI.448, LGW 1721, Rom A 238.

wollen, wolde- *see* **wille(n).**

wombe *n.* belly I.4290, VI.522, Bo 4.m7.21; womb IV.877, VII.2484.

wommanhede, woomanheede, wommanhode, womanhede, womanheed, womanhod *n.* femininity, womanliness, having the qualities proper to a woman I.1748, II.851, IV.1075, Tr 1.283, LGW 1041, Compl d'Am 39, Compl d'Am 65.

won(e), woon *n.* (1) resource, course of action Tr 4.1181; (2) place, retreat VII.801; dwelling HF 1166; (3) abundance BD 475, LGW 1652; number LGW 2161; *pl.* **wones** dwelling place III.2105.

wonde *see* **wynde.**

wonder, wondir *n.* marvel, miracle, object or cause of wonder I.502, II.408, Anel 148, Rom B 5405; *pl.* **wondres** miracles II.182.

wonder *adj.* wonderful, amazing VII.3078, BD 233.

wonder, wonders *adv.* wonderfully, amazingly I.483, I.1654, BD 443, Rom A 27.

wonderly, wonderlich(e) *adv.* wondrously, amazingly I.84, Tr 1.729, Tr 3.678.

wondre(n), wondryn *v.* wonder, be amazed IV.335, V.1514, Bo 4.m5.9, Tr 2.141; *(reflx.)* IV.687, Rom A 738; *2 pr. sg.* **wondrist** Bo 3.pr8.53; *3 pr. sg.* **wondreth** IV.669; *pr. pl.* **wondren** V.258; *imp. pl.* **wondreth** Tr 3.753; *pt. sg.* **wondred** I.1445, *(reflx.)* HF 1988; *pt. pl.* **wondred** V.225, **wondreden** V.307; *prp.* **wonderynge upon** wondering about IV.358; *pp.* **wondred** V.236; *vbl. n.* **wondryng** wondering, amazement V.305; **wonderynge** wonder Tr 2.35.

wone *n.* custom, wont, habit I.335, I.1040, Tr 2.318, Tr 5.647.

wone(n) *v.* dwell VIII.38, VIII.332, Tr 4.474; *3 pr. sg.*

woneth III.1573; *pr. pl.* **wonen** LGW 1317; *pt. sg.* **woned** III.2163; *pt. pl.* **woneden** I.2927; *prp.* **wonynge** I.388; *pp.* **woned** VII.3216; *vbl. n.* **wonyng(e)** dwelling I.606, ABC 145.

wonne(n) *see* **wynne(n).**

wont, woned *pp.* accustomed I.1195, I.1557, BD 150.

wopen *see* **wepe(n).**

worche(n), worcheth, worchynge *see* **werke(n).**

word(e) *n.* word I.304, *etc.*; decree I.1109, I.2350; **at o(o), a w.** in a word, briefly VIII.1360, BD 306, HF 257; **with that w.** thereupon I.856, I.948, BD 122; *pl.* **wordes** I.313, **woordes** Bo 3.pr1.45, **wordis** Rom A 288; **at short w.** briefly Tr 2.956, Tr 4.636; **in w. fewe** briefly VIII.618, Pity 56; **withoute(n) wordes mo** immediately I.3408, I.3650, Tr 2.1405.

world(e), werld *n.* world I.187, Bo 2.pr5.58, Bo 5.m2.7; **many w.** many ages PF 81; **new w.** modern times I.176; **what maner w.** what sort of carrying on III.2171; *gen.* (descriptive) **worldes** worldly, of this world VII.3200, BD 1040, PF 53; **werldes** Tr 4.1580; *pl.* **worldes** Tr 5.889.

worship(e), worshipp, wurshipp *n.* worship I.1904, LGW G 129, LGW 659, Rom C 5296; honor V.571; renown V.811, BD 630; dignity Fort 22; *pl.* **worshipes** Rom B 5747.

worshipe(n) *v.* worship I.2251; honor IV.166, Rom C 7239.

worshipful, worshipfull *adj.* honorable I.1435, IV.401, Rom A 797.

worth(e) *adj.* worth, equivalent in value to I.182, *etc.*; worthy VII.1515, VII.1707, Tr 2.866; worthwhile I.785.

worthe(n) *v.* (1) be, remain Tr 5.329; (2) go Mars 248; ascend, mount Bo 2.pr2.54, Tr 2.1011; *3 pr. sg.* **worth** mounts, gets on VII.751; (as *pr. subj.*) **wo (wel) worth(e)** woe (well) may it be, good (bad) luck to HF 53, Tr 2.344, Tr 4.747; *imp. sg.* **worth** get on, mount Tr 2.1011; *pp.* **yworth(e)** become BD 579.

worthy, wurthi *adj.* (1) respectable, having worth or standing I.43, I.64, PF 392; distinguished, excellent VII.3243, Tr 1.233; **w. of his hond** brave in battle II.579; (2) deserving ABC 23; (with *inf.*) deserving I.2794, II.457, Tr 1.91; able I.579, I.2380; fitting, suitable Tr 2.1328, Tr 3.1169, HF 727, LGW F 317; *comp.* **worthier** Tr 1.251; *super.* **worthiest(e)** IV.1131, Tr 1.244.

worthily *adv.* honorably I.2737, Tr 2.186; deservedly IV.1022.

worthinesse *n.* worthiness, excellence, honor I.50, I.2592, BD 1059.

wost, woost, wostow *see* **wite(n).**

wot, woot *see* **wite(n)** *v.*[1]

wowke *see* **wyke.**

woxe(n), (y)woxen *see* **wexe(n).**

wrak *see* **wreke(n).**

wrappe *v.* wrap V.583, V.636; cover, conceal V.507, Rom B 6260; *(reflx.)* joins himself to Astr Pro 6; *3 pr. sg.* **wrappeth** enfolds Bo 5.m1.14; *pr. pl.* **wrappen** wrap, wallow in X.586; *pp.* **(I)wrapped** wrapped V.1356; wrapped, wallowed in Bo 4.pr3.2; *vbl. n.* **wrappynge** covering X.423.

wratthe, wreththe, wrath(e), wraththe *n.* wrath VII.1124, BD 605, Anel 51, Bo 1.pr4.52, Tr 3.110, Rom C 7225; *pl.* **wratthes** Bo 3.m2.20.

wratthe *v.* anger, make angry IX.80; be angry with Tr

3.174; *(reflx.)* become angry X.1013; *pr. pl.* **wratthe** X.110; *pp.* **wrathed** X 132, **wraththed** BD 1151, **wratthed** Rom B 3097.

wrecche *n.* (1) wretch, miserable person I.931, III.1609, BD 577; (2) exile VIII.58; *pl.* **wrecches** I.1717, **wrechches** HF 1777.

wrecche, wreche, wrechche *adj.* (1) wretched HF 919, LGW 2214; (2) exiled II.285.

wrecched, wrecchid(e), wreched(e) *adj.* wretched I.921, I.950, Anel 60, Bo 4.m1.43, LGW G 414, LGW 900, Rom B 5648.

wrecchedly *adv.* wretchedly, miserably III.2054, VII.1977.

wrecchednesse, wrecchidnesse *n.* wretchedness, misery I.3897, II.941, Tr 2.286, Rom C 7086.

wreche, wrecche *n.* vengeance II.679, Tr 5.890, LGW 1892; punishment VII.2603; misery Tr 2.784.

wreye, wrie *v.* reveal, betray I.3503, V.944, Tr 3.284, Mars 91; *pr. subj. sg.* **wreye** I.3507; *vbl. n.* **wreying** betrayal Rom B 5220.

wreigh *see* **wrye(n)** *v.* ²

wreke(n) *v.* avenge I.961, VII.1036, Tr 1.62; *(reflx.)* revenge oneself VI.857, VII.1020, LGW F 395; *pr. pl.* **wreke** V.454; *pr. subj. sg.* **wreke** LGW 2340; *imp. sg.* **wrek** VII.1905; *pt. sg.* **wrak** Tr 5.1468; *pp.* **(y)wroken** Tr 1.88, Scog 26, **wreke(n)** III.809, V.784; *vbl. n.* **wrekynge** vengeance Bo 4.m7.4.

wrie *see* **wreye.**

wrye(n), wren *v.* ¹ (1) cover III.1827, Tr 3.1569, Rom A 56, Rom C 6684; (2) conceal Tr 1.329; *pr. pl.* **wrien** Tr 2.539; *imp.* **wry** cover LGW 735 *(sg.)*, **wre** conceal Tr 2.380 *(pl.)*; *pt. sg.* **wreigh** covered Tr 3.1056; *pp.* **(y)wrye** covered I.2904, LGW 1201; concealed, hidden Tr 3.620, **(y)wryen** covered BD 628, Rom A 912.

wrye(n) *v.* ² turn IX.262, Tr 2.906; change BD 627; *pt. sg.* **wryed** turned I.3283; *pp.* **iwryen** turned away, departed Tr 3.1451.

wrynge *v. (tr.)* squeeze, wring (hands) HF 299; wring VII.776; pinch III.492; press on, wrench Tr 3.1531; *(intr.)* wring (one's hands) IV.1212, squeeze (out) HF 2110; *3 pr. sg.* **wryngeth** pinches IV.1553; *pt. sg.* **wrong** Tr 4.738; **wroong** II.606; *pp.* **yronge** wrung, squeezed out LGW 2527.

write(n) *v.* write I.96, *etc.*; reveal I.3869; *2 pr. sg.* **writest** IV.1733; *3 pr. sg.* **writeth** reveals I.3869, *(contr.)* **writ** III.709; *pt. pl.* **write(n)** IV.2304, V.551; *pr. subj. sg.* **write** should write Tr 5.1293; *pr. subj. pl.* may write **writen** I.2814; *imp. sg.* **write** Tr 2.1026; *imp. pl.* **writeth** Tr 5.1399; *pt. sg.* **wroot(e)** II.725, III.1743; **wrot** Tr 1.655; *pt. pl.* **writen** V.233; *pt. subj. sg.* **write** were to write VII.2653; *pp.* **(y)writen** I.2350, II.191; **(y)write** I.161, VII.3442, **written** Rom A 1446; *vbl. n.* **writyng(e)** X.1052, Tr 5.1794; *pl.* **writynges** Bo 2.pr7.90.

writhe(n) *v.* turn away Tr 4.9, Rom B 4359; wriggle (out from) Tr 4.986; be diverted Bo 5.pr3.20; *3 pr. sg.* **writhith** out casts out in wreathes of rings Bo 1.m4.9, *(contr.)* **writh** wreathes about, encircles Tr 3.1231; *pp.* **writhen** encircled Rom A 160; *vbl. n.* **writhyng** turning V.127.

wroght-, wrought- *see* **werke(n).**

(y)wroken, ywroke *see* **wreke(n).**

wrong, wroong *see* **wrynge.**

wroth(e), wrooth(e) *adj.* angry I.451, III.125, BD 582, Tr 1.349; grieving, sad BD 1294.

wurchyng(e) *see* **werke(n).**

wurthi *see* **worthy.**

Y

(See also I)

y- past participles with this prefix are ordinarily alphabetized under the root syllable; infinitives, adjectives, and adverbs with this prefix are alphabetized under i-.

yaf *see* **yeve(n).**

yald *see* **yelde(n).**

yard *see* **yerd(e).**

yate *n.* gate Tr 2.617; *pl.* **yates** Tr 5.1177.

yave(n) *see* **yeve(n).**

ye *see* **eye.**

ye *2 pl. pro. nom.* you I.780, *etc.*

ye *adv.* yes I.3455, *etc.*

yede(n), yedest *see* **go(n).**

yelde(n) *v.* pay III.130, III.1821; yield, render X.378; surrender, give up III.912, IV.843; Tr 4.212; **y. up (one's) breath (ghost)** die I.3052, Tr 1.801, LGW 886; *3 pr. sg.* **yeldeth** pays X.941, gives off Bo 4.m6.29, *(contr.)* **yelt** yields Tr 1.385, **yalt** Rom B 4904; *pr. subj. sg.* **God yeelde yow** may God reward you III.1772, III.2177, **G. yelde y.** Tr 1.1055; *imp. sg.* **yeld** give up, hand over VI.189, **yilde** render, utter Bo 5.pr6.304; *imp. pl.* **yeldeth** give back VII.1292; *pt. sg.* **yald** gave Bo 4.m7.23; *prp.* **yeldyng(e)** paying LGW F 149, VII.1804; *pp.* **yolde(n)** surrendered Tr 3.1211, given up I.3052, dedicated Rom A 429, **iyolden** (as *adj.*) submissive Tr 3.96; *vbl. n.* **yeldynge** yielding I.596.

yelwe, yelow(e), yelewe *adj.* yellow I.675, I.1929, PF 186, Rom A 1021.

yeman *n.* yeoman, free-born servant I.101, VIII.562; free-born man I.3270; official III.1380, III.1387; *pl.* **yemen** free-born servants I.2509.

yer(e), yeer(e) *n.* year I.1203, I.1458, IV.402, LGW 1958, LGW 2589; as *pl.* with *num.* I.82, I.601, IV.1248, LGW 2075; *pl.* **yeres** I.1521, **yeeres** I.2828.

yerd(e), yeerd, yard *n.* yard, garden III.1798, V.1251, VII.2997, Rom A 1461; enclosure Tr 2.154; pen VII.2847.

yerde *n.* (1) stick, switch (for punishment) I.149, X.670, Tr 1.740; staff (of authority) I.1387; **under the (yowre) y.** subject to (your) authority IV.22, VII.97, PF 640; rod (weapon) Tr 2.1427; (2) bough, sapling Tr 1.257; trunk Bo 3.m2.32; (3) yard (measure) I.1050; *pl.* **yerdes** switches X.1055.

yerne *adv.* quickly VI.396, PF 3; eagerly PF 21; **as y.** very quickly Tr 3.151, Tr 4.112; very eagerly HF 910; **late or y.** late or early, at any time Tr 3.376.

yeve(n), yive(n), give *v.* give I.223, I.225, I.234, III.78, LGW 1925; *2 pr. sg.* **yevest** I.1284; *3 pr. sg.* **yeveth** I.1253, **yyveth** Bo 2.m2.10; *pr. pl.* **yeve(n)** VII.1113, Tr 5.235, **yive** BD 695; *pr. subj. sg.* **yeve** I.4335, **yive** BD 683; *imp. sg.* **yif** I.2260, **yef** Tr 1.1042; *imp. pl.* **yeve** BD 111, **gyve** III.78; **yeveth**

VII.1754; *1 & 3 pt. sg.* **yaf** I.177, **gaf** Rom A 757; *2 pt. sg.* **yave** Bo 2.pr3.63; **yaf** VII.2451; *pt. pl.* **yeve** Tr 3.19, **yave(n)** VII.1789, Tr 2.1323, Tr 4.710; *pt. subj. sg.* **yave** would give Tr 2.977; *pp.* **yeve(n)** IV.758, VII.407, **yyeven** Tr 3.1376, **yive(n)** III.401, Bo 2.m7.23, **yyive** Tr 3.1611, **yove** Rom B 5569, **geven** Rom C 7374, **goven** Rom B 5050; *vbl. n.* **yevyng(e)** giving X.567, Anel 44; **yyvynge** Bo 2.pr5.22.

yif *see* **yeve(n)**.

yif *conj.* if BD 1189; **y. that** if BD 969.

yift(e), yefte *n.* gift III.39, IV.1311, BD 247, Rom B 3664; *pl.* **yiftes** I.2198, **yeftis** Rom B 5481.

yilde *see* **yelde(n)**.

yis *adv.* yes, yes indeed (more emphatic than **ye**) I.3369, I.3526, Tr 1.1054.

yit, yitt, yet *adv.* yet I.70, PF 10, Tr 1.239, Rom B 5139.

yive(n) *see* **yeve(n)**.

yolde(n), iyolden *see* **yelde(n)**.

yond *adv.* yonder I.1099, III.1798, Tr 2.1184.

yong(e), young, ying *adj.* young I.7, I.79, BD 454, Rom B 2208, Rom C 7519; *super.* **yongest(e)** IV.1559, V.33.

yore, yoore *adv.* long ago, formerly I.3897, Anel 243, LGW 2353; **(full) y. ago(n)** long ago I.1813, I.1941; long since PF 17; before, formerly II.174, II.984, Tr 4.1497; for a long time I.4230, II.272, PF 476; **of y.** for a long time, since long before Tr 4.719; before, previously Tr 5.1734; **of tyme y.** for a long time V.963.

INDEX OF
PROPER NAMES

This index contains only brief identifications; full particulars are in the notes, ordinarily the note to the first line in which the name appears. The index is selective; allegorical personages and very common proper names (months and days, for example) are excluded. When a name appears more than three or four times in a single work (the individual tales are considered separate works) ordinarily only the first two references are given, followed by "etc." Forms of the genitive and plural are ordinarily cited only when they may present difficulties for the reader.

The abbreviations used are the same as those in the Glossary, with the addition of *dim.* for "diminutive." As in the Glossary, vocalic *y* is alphabetized with *i,* and variations of *y* and *i* are not noted; doubled vowels are alphabetized as if single (e.g., *Deeth of Blaunche* follows *Dertemouthe*). The abbreviations for Chaucer's works are those listed on p. 779, with the exception of the *Tales,* which are identified by fragment number.

A

Abigayl wife of Nabal (1 Sam. 25); IV.1369, VII.1100.
Abraham the Biblical patriarch (Gen. 11.27ff.); III.55.
Absolon (1) son of King David (2 Sam. 13–19.8); LGW F 249, LGW F 539, LGW G 203. (2) the parish clerk in MilT; I.3313, I.3339, etc.
Achademycis the Academics, followers of Plato; Bo 1.pr1.68.
Achate(s) Aeneas's armor-bearer and companion; HF 226; LGW 964, LGW 976, etc.
Acheloys, Acheleous, Achaleous Achelous, a river god; VII.2106; Bo 4.m7.43, Bo 4.m7.45.
Achemenye the empire of the Achemenides in Persia; Bo 5.m1.3.
Achille(s) the Greek hero of the Trojan War; II.198; V.239; VII.3148; BD 329, BD 1066; HF 398, HF 1463; PF 290; Tr 2.416, Tr 3.374, Tr 5.1806, etc.
Achitofel David's evil counselor (2 Sam. 15.31ff.); X.639, BD 1118.
Adam (1) first man; III.696; IV.1325; VI.505; VI.508; VII.1103; VII.2007, VII.2012, VII.3258; X.323, X.325, etc.; HF 970; LGW F 286, LGW G 189; ABC 182. (2) Chaucer's scrivener; Adam 1.

The Index of Proper Names was prepared by Larry D. Benson.

Adoon, Adoun Adonis, loved by Venus; I.2224, Tr 3.721.
Adrastus King of Argos and leader of the Seven against Thebes; Anel 61.
Adriane Ariadne, daughter of King Minos (see LGW 1886–2227); II.67; HF 407, HF 411; LGW F 268 and LGW 1969, etc.
Affrikan, Affrican (1) Scipio Africanus Major (c. 265–183 B.C.); PF 41, PF 44, etc. (2) Scipio Africanus Minor (185–129 B.C.); BD 287; *see* **Scipio(n).**
Affrike, Auffrike Africa VII.3124; HF 431, HF 1339; PF 37; Bo 2.pr6.71.
Agamenoun, Agamenon Agamemnon, leader of the Greek army at Troy; Bo 4.m7.1, Bo 4.m7 6, etc.; Tr 3.382.
Agaton Agathon or Agatho LGW F 526 (identity uncertain, see note).
Agenores doghter Europa, daughter of Agenor, king of Tyre; LGW F 114.
Aglawros sister of Herse; Tr 3.730.
Alayn *see* **Aleyn².**
Albyn probably Decius Albinus, a contemporary of Boethius; Bo 1.pr4.99, Bo 1.pr4.217.
Albyon Britain; Purse 22.
Albon, daun a name the Host uses for the Monk; VII.1930.
Alcathoe the citadel at Megara; LGW 1902.
Alcebiades, Alcypiades Alicibiades the Greek general (d. 404 A.D.); V.1439, BD 1057, Bo 3.pr8.44.
Alceste Alcestis, wife of Admetus; heroine of the Prologue of LGW (see LGW F 511–15, Tr 5.1527–33); II.75; V.1442; Tr 5.1778; LGW F 432, LGW G 179, LGW G 209, etc.
Alcione Alcyone (Halcyon), wife of Ceyx (see BD 63–220); II.57, BD 65, BD 76, etc.
Aldeberan Aldebaran, a star; Astr 1.21.16.
Aldiran a star; V.265.
Aleyn Alanus de Insulis (1125/30–1203); PF 316. *See* **Pleynt of Kynd.**
Aleyn, Alayn one of the clerks in RvT; I.4013, I.4031, etc.
Alete Alecto, a Fury; Tr 4.24.
Alexander, Alixandre Macedo *see* **Alisaundre.**
Algarsyf son of Cambyuskan in SqT; V.30, V.663.
Algezir Algeciras in Spain; I.57.
Algomeysa a star; Astr 1.21.17.
Alhabor Sirius, the Dog Star; Astr 2.3.47. *See* **Syrius.**
Alys (1) the Wife of Bath; III.320 (see **Alisoun,** sense 2). (2) the Wife of Bath's "gossip"; III.548.
Alisaundre, Alisandre Alexandria, in Egypt; I.51, VII.2392, VIII.975, BD 1026.
Alisaundre, Alisandre, Alexander, Alixandre Mac-

1311

D

Ethiopeen Ethiopian; X.345.

Etik unidentified; LGW F 166.

Euclide Euclid, the Greek mathematician (fl. 300 B.C.); III.2289.

Eufrates the river Euphrates in Mesopotamia; Bo 5.m1.1, Bo 5.m1.6.

Euripidis Euripides (c. 408–406 B.C.); Bo 3.pr7.25.

Eurippe the strait Euripus; Bo 2.m1.3.

Europe (1) Europa, daughter of Agenor, wooed by Zeus in form of a bull; Tr 3.722. (2) the continent; II.161, HF 1339.

Eurus the southeast wind; Bo 2.m.4.4, Bo 4.m3.1.

Eva, Eve the first woman; II.368; III.715; IV.1329; VIII.62; X.325, X.331, etc.

Evander Arcadian settler of Italy; Bo 4.m7.53, Bo 4.m7.55.

Evaungiles the Gospels; II.666.

Exodi Exodus; X.750.

Ezechie, Ezechias Hezekiah (Isaiah 38.15); X.135, X.983.

Ezechiel the biblical prophet; X.140, X.143, etc.

F

Fabricius Gaius Luscinus Fabricius (3rd cent. B.C.); Bo 2.m7.18.

Fairye, Fayerye (1) the land of the fairies; V.96, VII.802, VII.814. (2) the classical Underworld; IV.2227, IV.2234, IV.2316.

Fame, the book of Chaucer's *House of Fame;* X.1086. *See* **Hous of Fame.**

Femenye land of the Amazon women; I.866, I.877.

Ferrare Ferrara, in Italy; IV.51.

Fynystere Cape Finisterre, in northwest Spain; I.408.

Fyssh Pisces; V.273. *See* **Pisces.**

Fysshstrete a street in London; VI.564.

Flaundres Flanders, part of present-day Belgium; I.86, VI.463, VII.719.

Flegitoun Phlegethon, a river in the classical Underworld; Tr 3.1600.

Flexippe Criseyde's niece in Tr; Tr 2.816.

Flymyng Fleming; I.4357, VII.3396.

Flora the goddess of flowers; BD 402, LGW F 171.

Florence Florence; III.1125.

France, Fraunce France; V.1118; VII.116, VII.151, VII.194; PF 677; Ven 82; Rom A 495, Rom A 684, Rom A 1457, Rom B 3494, Rom C 6492.

Frere Menour Franciscan friar; Rom C 6338.

Freres Preachours Dominicans; Rom C 7476.

Frydeswyde, Seinte St. Frideswide (8th cent. A.D.); I.3449.

Frise Frisia, in present-day Holland; Buk 23, Rom A 1093.

Furies, Furiis the Furies; Bo 3.m12.34, Tr 2.436, LGW 2252. *See* **Herenus.**

G

Gabrielles *gen.* of Gabriel, the archangel; ABC 115.

Gaius Cesar Caligula, son of Germanicus; Bo 1.pr4.181.

Galathee Galatea, heroine of the *Pamphilles de amore;* V.1110. *See* **Pamphilles.**

Galaxye the Milky Way; HF 936, PF 56. *See* **Milky Wey; Watlynge Strete.**

Galgopheye probably Gargaphia, in Greece; I.2626.

Galice Galicia, in Spain; I.466.

Galien (1) Galen (129–99 A.D.), the Greek physician; I.431, X.831, BD 572. (2) Galen, Gallienus (emperor 253–68 A.D.); VII.2336.

Galilee a province of Palestine; III.11.

Gallus *see* **Symplicius Gallus.**

Ganymede cup-bearer to Jove; HF 589.

Gatesden John of Gaddesden (b. 1280); I.434.

Gaudencius one of Boethius's accusers; Bo 1.pr4.114.

Gaufred Geoffrey of Vinsauf (early 13th cent.); VII.3347.

Gaufride Geoffrey of Monmouth (c. 1100–1155); HF 1470.

Gaunt Ghent, the city in Belgium; I.448, Rom A 574.

Gawayn, Gaweyn Gawain, the hero of Arthurian romance; V.95, Rom B 2209.

Gawle, folk of Galatians; V.1411.

Gazan the biblical Gaza; VII.2047.

Geffrey Geoffrey Chaucer; HF 729. *See* **Chaucer.**

Gemini(s) the third sign of the zodiac; IV.2222; Astr 1.8.3, Astr 1.21.74, etc.

Genelloun, Genylon Ganelon, betrayer of Roland; VII.194, VII.3227; BD 1121.

Genesis Genesis; X.755.

Genylon-Olyver a paid traitor; VII.2389.

Gerland a dog in NPT; VII.3383.

Germaynes *gen.* Germanicus's (15 B.C.–19 A.D.), the Roman emperor; Bo 1.pr.4.181.

Gernade Granada, in Spain; I.56.

Gerounde the river Geronde, in France; V.1222.

Gerveys a blacksmith in MilT; I.3761, I.3765, etc.

Gy hero of the romance of Guy of Warwick; VII.899.

Gibbe (*dim.* of Gilbert) a tomcat in Rom; Rom C 6204.

Gilbertyn Gilbertus Anglicus (13th cent.); I.434.

Gile, Seint St. Giles (St. Aegidius, 6th or 7th cent. A.D.); VIII.1185, HF 1183.

Gille a maid in MilT; I.3556.

Gysen the river Gyndes, tributary of the Tigris; III.2080.

Glascurion a British bard; HF 1208.

God the Deity; I.533, etc.

Goodelief Herry Bailly's (q.v.) wife; VII.1894.

Golden Verses, The a book attributed to Pythagoras; Rom B 5650. *See* **Pictagoras.**

Golias Goliath (1 Sam. 17); II.934.

Gothes the Ostrogoths; Bo 1.pr4.73.

Gootland probably Gotland, an island in the Baltic; I.408.

Gower John Gower (d. 1408), Chaucer's fellow poet; Tr 5.1856.

Graunson Oton de Grandson (d. 1397); Venus 82.

Grec, Grek, Greek, Grekyssh, Grekissch, Grykkyssche Greek; VII.3228; HF 152; Tr 2.112, Tr 5.125; Bo 1.pr1.30, Bo 2.pr2.73, Bo 4.m7.9, etc.

Grece, Grees Greece; I.962; II.464; V.1444; VII.2657; BD 1081; Anel 53; Bo 1.pr1.32, Bo 1.pr1.68, Bo 3.pr12.193, Bo 4.m7.9; Tr 1.88, Tr 1.609, etc.; LGW 2271, LGW 2562.

Grece, See of the Mediterranean; II.464.

VII.1154, etc.; X.334; in oaths, I.4264, III.312, III.1443, VII.355, HF 885. (2) the shrine of St. James (Santiago) at Compostela, in Spain; I.466. (3) author of the Epistle of James; IV.1154; VII.1119, VII.1517, etc.; X.348.

Janekyn, Jankyn the Wife of Bath's fifth husband; III.303, III.548, etc.

Janicula, Janicle father of Grisilde in ClkT; IV.208, IV.404, etc.

Jankin (1) derisive name for a priest (*dim.* of John, q.v.); II.1172. (2) the lord's squire in SumT; III.2288, III.2293.

Januarie (1) *See* **Janekyn**. The aged husband in MerT; IV.1393, IV.1478, etc. (2) the month; Astr 1.10.12.

Janus Roman god of entrances; V.1252, Tr 2.77.

Jason, Jasoun Jason, unfaithful lover of Medea and Hypsipyle (LGW 1368–1678); II.74; V.548, V.549; BD 330, BD 727; HF 400, HF 401; LGW F 266, LGW 1368, etc.

Jepte Jephtha (Judges 11.1–12.7); VI.240.

Jeremeye the biblical prophet Jeremiah; VI.635; X.76, X.189, X.592.

Jerome, Seint St. Jerome (c. 340–420 A.D.); III.674; VII.1595; X.159, X.174, etc.; LGW G 281.

Jerusalem Jerusalem; I.463; III.495; VII.2147, VII.2196, VII.2596; X.51, X.80, X.589; Rom A 554.

Jew Jew; IV.2277; VI.351, VI.354, etc.; VII.570, VII.601; HF 1434; Astr Pro 32; *pl.* **Jues** VII.565; *gen.* **Jues** VII.559.

Jewerye, Juerie the Jewish nation; HF 1436; Jewish quarter, ghetto; VII.489, VII.551, VII.592.

Jhesu(s), Jesu(s) (Christ) Jesus Christ; I.698; X.284, etc. *See* **Crist; Xristus**.

Jhesus (filius) Syrak Jesus, son of Sirach, the author of Ecclesiasticus; IV.2250, VII.995, VII.1045, etc.

Joab a general of David's army (2 Sam [=2 Kings Vulg.] 2.28, 18.16, 20.22); IV.1719, HF 1245.

Job the biblical Job; III.436, III.1491, IV.932, VII.999, X.134, X.176, etc.

Joce St. Judocus (d. 699 A.D.); III.483.

Johan, Seint *see* **John, Seint**.

John (1) the old carpenter in MilT; I.3369, I.3501, etc. (2) one of the clerks in RvT; I.4013, I.4018, etc. (3) the friar in SumT; III.2171. (4) the monk in ShipT; VII.43, VII.58, etc. (5) a cant name for a priest; VII.1929, VII.2810 (*see* **Jankin**, sense 1). (6) St. John (see next entry).

John, Seint St. John, the evangelist III.1647; VII.582; VII.951; X.216, X.349, etc.; HF 1385; Rom C 7167, Rom C 7178, etc.; in oaths, II.18, II.1019; III.164, III.1800; V.596; VI.752; BD 1319; PF 451; Mars 9.

John, the Baptist John the Baptist; VI.491, Rom C 6998.

John Crisostom, Seint St. John Chrysostom (345–407 A.D.); X.109.

Jonas Jonah, the biblical prophet; II.486.

Jonathas Jonathan, friend of David (1 Sam. 13ff.); LGW F 251.

Joseph (1) the biblical Joseph (Gen. 37–50); VII.3130; X.443, X.880; BD 280. (2) St. Joseph, husband of Mary; X.286.

Josephus, Ebrayk Flavius Josephus Ebraecus (37–c. 95 A.D.); HF 1433.

Jove(s) Jupiter, chief of the Roman gods; I.2222; HF

219, etc.; Tr 3.722, Tr 3.1015, etc.; LGW F 525; the planet Tr 3.625; *gen.* **Jovis** IV.2224. Cf. **Juppiter**.

Jovinyan Jovinianus, adversary of St. Jerome; III.1929.

Jovinian, agayn(s) St. Jerome's *Epistola adversus Jovinianum;* III.675, LGW G 281.

Jubaltre Gibraltar; II.947.

Judas Judas Iscariot, the betrayer of Christ; III.1350; VIII.1003, VIII.1007; X.502, X.616, etc. *See* **Scariot**.

Judas Machabeus, Machabee Judas Maccabeus (d. 160 B.C.); VII.1658, VII.1659.

Judicum Book of Judges; VII.2046.

Judith Judith, slayer of Holofernes (see MkT VII.2567–74); II.939, IV.1366, VII.1099, VII.2571.

Juerie *see* **Jewerye**.

Julian, Seint St. Julian (4th cent. A.D.); I.340, HF 1022.

Julius Gaius Julius Caesar (100–44 B.C.), the Roman emperor; I.2031; II.199, II.400; VII.2673, etc.; HF 1502; Astr 1.10.9.

Juno the Roman goddess of women, daughter of Saturn and wife of Jupiter; I.1329, I.1543, etc.; BD 109, BD 129, etc.; HF 198, HF 461; Anel 51; Tr 4.1116, Tr 4.1538, etc.; LGW 2249.

Juppiter, Jupiter Jove, chief of the Roman gods; I.2442, I.2786, etc.; VII.2744, VII.2752; VIII.364, VIII.413; HF 199, HF 215, etc.; Bo 2.pr2.74; Tr 2.233, Tr 4.699, Tr 4.1683; LGW 1338, LGW 1806, LGW 2585; Form Age 56; the planet, VIII.828, Astr 2.12.24. *See* **Jove(s)**.

Justin, Justinus January's brother in MerT; IV.1477, IV.1519, IV.1689, etc.

Justinian Justinian I (483–565 A.D.), Roman emperor of the East; Rom C 6615.

Juvenal Decimus Junius Juvenalis (c. 60–140 A.D.); III.1192, Tr 4.197.

K

Kacus *see* **Cacus**.

Kay, Key one of King Arthur's knights; Rom B 2206, Rom B 2211.

Kayrudd home of Averagus in FranT; V.808.

Karibdous *see* **Caribdis**.

Kaukasous *see* **Caucasus**.

Kenelm, Seint St. Cenelm, King of Mercia (crowned 821 A.D.); VII.3110, VII.3112.

Kent Kent; I.3291, HF 1131.

Kenulphus Cenwulf, king of Mercia (796–821 A.D.); VII.3111.

Kynges, Book of I Kings (I Sam. in A.V.); X.897.

Kynges, seconde Book of II Kings (II Sam. in A.V.); VII.1668.

L

Laban father of Rachel (Gen. 29–31); X.443.

Laboryntus the Labyrinth in Crete; HF 1921. *See* **Dedalus; Domus Dedaly**.

Lacedomye, Lacidomye Lacedaemon (Sparta); V.1380, VI.605.

Lachesis one of the Fates; Tr 5.7.

Ladies, the book of the xxv. *The Legend of Good Women;* X.1086.

Ladomya *see* **Laodomya.**

Layus, King Laertes, King of Thebes; Tr 2.101.

Lamedon, Lameadoun Laomedon, father of Priam; BD 329, Tr 4.124.

Lamek, Lameth Lamech (Gen. 4.19); III.54, V.550, BD 1162, Anel 150.

Lamuel Lemuel (Prov. 31.4); VI.584, VI.585.

Laodomya, Laudomia, Ladomya Laodamia, wife of Protesilaus; II.71, V.1445, LGW F 263, LGW G 217.

Lapidaire Lapidarius, a treatise on gems (11th cent.); HF 1352.

Latyne Latinus, king of Latium; HF 453.

Latona the moon (?); Tr 5.655. *See* **Dyane.**

Latumyas Latumeus; III.757.

Laude, Clere Laude a trumpet belonging to Aeolus; HF 1575, HF 1673.

Launcelot Lancelot du Lac, hero of Arthurian romance; V.287.

Launcelot du Lake, book of the story of Lancelot and Guinevere; VII.3212.

Lavyne, Lavina, Laveyne (1) Lavinia, Italian wife of Aeneas; BD 331; HF 458; LGW F 257, LGW 1331, LGW G 211. (2) Lavinium, a city of Latium; HF 148.

Lazar the poor man in the parable (Luke 16.20ff.); III.1877.

Lazarus Lazarus, brother of Mary and Martha (John 11.35); VII.987.

Leandre Leander of Abydos, lover of Hero; II.69.

Legende *The Legend of Good Women;* LGW F 5793, LGW G 545. *See* **Seintes Legende of Cupide.**

Lemnon Lemnos, an island in the Aegean; LGW 1463.

Lenne, Frere N. Nicholas of Lynn (fl. 1386), English astronomer; Astr Pro 86.

Lente season of Lent; III.543, III.550, IV.12, X.103.

Leo, Leoun, Leon (1) the fifth sign of the zodiac; I.2462; Tr 4.1592, Tr 5.1019, Tr 5.1190; Astr 1.8.3, Astr 2.6.17, etc. (2) the constellation Leo; V.265.

Leonard St. Leonard (6th cent. A.D.); HF 117.

Leoun, the book of the a lost work by Chaucer; X.1087.

Lepe wine-growing district in Spain; VI.563, VI.570.

Lete Lethe, a river in the Underworld; HF 71.

Lettow Lithuania; I.54.

Lybeux, sir Libeaus Desconus, hero of medieval romance; VII.890.

Lybye Libya; HF 488, Bo 4.m7.52, LGW 959, etc.

Libra the seventh sign of the zodiac; X.11; Astr 1.8.4, Astr 1.17.16, etc.

Lyde Lydia, ancient kingdom (in present-day Turkey); VII.2727, VII.3138, HF 105.

Lydyens people of Lydia; Bo 2.pr2.58.

Lyeys Ayas in Armenia; I.58.

Lygurge Lycurgus, legendary king of Thrace, one of Palamon's supporters in KnT; I.2129, I.2644; LGW 2425.

Limote probably Elmyas the sorcerer (Acts 13.8); HF 1274.

Lyncoln Lincoln; VII.648.

Lynyan Giovanni da Lignano (c. 1310–83); IV.34.

Lyno Lynceus, husband of Hypermnestra; LGW 2569, LGW 2604, etc.

Lyvia Livia Drusilla (d. 29 A.D.); III.747, III.750.

Loy, Seinte St. Eligius (588–659 A.D.); I.120, III.1564.

Lollere a heretic; II.1173, II.1177.

Lollius Chaucer's fictitious authority for *Troilus*; HF 1468, Tr 1.394, Tr 5.1653.

London, Londoun London; I.382, I.509, I.3632, I.4325; III.550; VIII.1012; IX.11.

Longius Longinus, the centurion; ABC 163.

Loreyn(e) Lorraine, in France; Rom A 776, Rom A 767.

Looth Lot (Gen. 19.30–38); VI.485.

Lowys Chaucer's son; Astr Pro 1, Astr Pro 50, etc.

Luc St. Luke, the evangelist; VII.951; X.700, X.702.

Lucan (1) Marcus Annaeus Lucanus (39–65 A.D.); II.401, VII.2719, HF 1499, Tr 5.1792. (2) a member of Boethius's household; Bo 4.pr6.231.

Lucye, Lucia Lucilia, wife of the Roman poet Lucretius; III.747, III.752.

Lucifer (1) Satan; VII.1999, VII.2004; X.788 (*see* **Sathan**). (2) the morning star; Bo 1.m5.16, Bo 3.m1.9, Bo 4.m6.17; Tr 3.1417.

Lucina a name of Diana, as goddess of childbirth, I.2085; as moon, V.1045; Tr 4.1591, Tr 5.565. *See* **Dyane.**

Lucrece, Lucresse Lucretia, wife of Lucius Tarquinus Collatinus (see LGW 1680–1885); II.63; V.1405; BD 1082; Anel 82; LGW F 257, LGW 1686, etc.

Lumbardes bankers from Lombardy; VII.367.

Lumbardye Lombardy, an area in northern Italy; IV.46, IV.72, etc.; V.193; VII.2400; LGW F 374.

Luna the moon; VIII.826, VIII.1440.

M

Mabely the old woman in FrT; III.1626.

Macchabee (1) Book of Macabees (aprocryphal in A.V.); VII.2579, VII.2655. (2) *See* **Judas Machabeus.**

Macedo the Macedonian; HF 915.

Macedoyne, Macidoyne Macedonia; V.1435, VII.2656, BD 1062.

Macrobes, Macrobeus, Macrobye Ambrosius Theodosius Macrobius (fl. 395–423 A.D.); VII.3123, BD 284, PF 111, Rom A 7.

Madrian identity unclear; VII.1892 (see note).

Magdelene, Magdeleyne St. Mary Magdelene; X.502, X.504, X.947, etc.

Mahoun, Makomete Mohammed (c. 570–632 A.D.); II.224, II.333, etc.

Maius, May (1) the young wife in MerT; IV.1693, IV.1782, etc. (2) the month of May; III.546, Astr 1.10.4.

Makomete *see* **Mahoun.**

Malyne a form of *Malkyn*; the Miller's daughter in RvT; I.4236.

Malkyn Molly (*dim.* of Matilda). (1) a servant girl in NPT; VII.3384. (2) a lower-class woman; II.30.

Malle a form of *Malkyn*; the name of a sheep; VII.2831.

Manes spirits of the dead, gods of the lower world; Tr 5.892.

Mantoan of Mantua; LGW 924.

Marcia Marsyas, a satyr defeated by Apollo; HF 1229.

Marcia Catoun a faithful Roman wife; LGW F 252, LGW G 206.

Marcian Martianus Capella (1st half 5th cent. A.D.); IV.1732, HF 985.

Marcus Tulyus, Marcus Tullius Scithero Cicero; V.722; Bo 2.pr7.60, Bo 5.pr4.3. *See* Tullius.

Mardochee Mordecai, in the Book of Esther; IV.1373.

Marie, Egipcien St. Mary the Egyptian (5th cent. A.D.); II.500.

Marie, Seinte the Virgin Mary, II.641, II.841, II.920; IV.2418; VI.308; VII.690; in oaths and exclamations, III.1604; IV.1337, IV.1899; VI.685; VII.402, VII.784, etc.; VIII.1062; HF 573.

Mark St. Mark, the evangelist; III.145, VII.951.

Marmoryke Marmarica, in eastern Libya; Bo 4.m3.12.

Marrok, Strayte of the straights of Gibraltar; II.465.

Mars, Marte (1) the Roman god of war; I.975, I.1559, etc.; HF 1446; Anel 1, Anel 31, etc.; Tr 2.593, Tr 2.630, etc.; LGW F 533, LGW 2063, etc. (2) the planet II.301, II.305; III.619; V.50; VIII.817; Tr 3.22; Astr 2.4.35, Astr 2.12.24, Astr 2.12.28. (3) the main character in The Complaint of Mars (as both mythological character and planet) Mars; Mars 25, Mars 45, etc.

Martin, Seint St. Martin of Tours (c. 316–400 A.D.); VII.148.

Massynisse Masinissa (c. 238–149 B.C.), king of Numidia; PF 37.

Mathew St. Matthew, the evangelist; VI.634; VII.951; X.588, X.842, etc.; Rom C 6887.

Maudelayne the Shipman's barge; I.410.

Maure St. Maurus (d. 565 A.D.); I.173.

Maurice, Mauricius son of Constance and Alle in MLT; II.723, II.1063, etc.

Maxime, Maximus prefect converted by Cecilie in SNT; VIII.368, VIII.377, etc.

Mecene Messenia in Greece; V.1379.

Medea daughter of Aeëtes, king of Colchis (see LGW 1580–1670); I.1944; II.72; BD 330, BD 726; HF 401, HF 1271; LGW 1395, LGW 1599, etc.

Medes people of Media, in present-day northwestern Iran; VII.2235.

Megera Megaera, one of the Furies; Tr 4.24.

Melan, Milayne Milan; VII.2399, Rom C 7023.

Meleagre Meleager (see Tr 5.1464–84); I.2071; Tr 5.1474, Tr 5.1482, etc.

Melibee, Melibeus hero of Mel; VII.967, VII.973, etc.

Menelaus brother of Agamemnon and husband of Helen of Troy; Bo 4.m7.7.

Mercenrike the Anglo-Saxon kingdom of Mercia; VII.3112.

Mercurye, Mercurius the Roman god; I.1385; IV.1734; HF 429; Bo 4.m3.17; Tr 3.729, Tr 5.321, Tr 5.1827; LGW 1297; the planet III.697, III.699, etc.; V.672; Astr 2.12.26, Astr 2.12.32. *See* Cilenios.

Messenus Misenus, trumpeter to Hector and Aeneas; HF 1243.

Metellius a character from Valerius Maximus; III.460.

Methamorphosios Ovid's *Metamorphoses*; II.93.

Michias Micah, the biblical prophet; X.201.

Myda Midas, legendary king of Phrygia; III.951, III.953; Tr 3.1389.

Middleburgh a Dutch port; I.277.

Milayn *see* Melan.

Milesie Miletus, a town in Asia Minor; V.1409.

Milky Wey the Galaxy; HF 937. See Galaxye; Watlynge Strete.

Mynerva, Mynerve Roman goddess of wisdom; BD 1072; Tr 2.232, Tr 2.1062; LGW 932. *See* Pallas.

Mynos (1) judge of the dead; Tr 4.1188. (2) king of Crete, father of Ariadne and Phaedra; LGW 1886, LGW 1894, etc.

Mynotaur monstrous offspring of Pasiphaë and a bull; I.980; LGW 2104, LGW 2142, LGW 2145.

Mirra Myrrah, mother of Adonis; Tr 4.1139.

Moyses the biblical Moses; III.1885; V.250; VII.468; X.195, X.355; ABC 89, ABC 93; Rom C 6889.

Monesteo Mnestheus, son of Priam and Hecuba; Tr 4.51.

Morpheus the god of sleep; BD 136, BD 167, etc.

N

Nabal husband of Abigail (1 Sam. 25); IV.1370, VII.1100.

Nabugodonosor Nebuchadnezzar (Dan. 1–5; see MkT VII.2143–82); VII.2145, X.125, HF 515.

Narcisus loved by the nymph Echo (see Rom A 1439–1638); I.1941; V.952; BD 735; Rom A 1468, Rom A 1469, etc.

Narice, cuntre of Ithaca; Bo 4.m3.2.

Naso Ovid; LGW 725, LGW 928, LGW 2220. *See* Ovide.

Nazarenus the Nazarene; X.288, X.289.

Nembrot Nimrod (Gen. 10.8–12); Form Age 58.

Neptune, Neptunus Roman god of the sea; V.1047; LGW 2421; Tr 2.443, Tr 4.120.

Nero, Neroun the Roman emperor (reigned 53–68 A.D.; see MkT VII.2519–50); I.2032; VII.2463, VII.2504, etc.; VII.2537, VII.3370, VII.3373; Bo 2.m6.3, Bo 2.m6.13, etc.; Bo 3.m4.1, etc.; Bo 3.pr5.47, Bo 3.pr.5.55.

Nessus a centaur slain by Hercules; VII.2128.

Newegate Newgate prison, in London; I.4402.

Newe Toun Villeneuve, in France; VIII.1428.

Nicerates wyf wife of the Athenian Niceratus (fl. 404 B.C.); V.1437.

Nichanore (1) Nicanor, defeated by Judas Maccabeus (1 Maccabees 3, 2 Maccabees 8); VIII.2591. (2) one of Alexander the Great's generals (336 B.C.); V.1432.

Nicholas, Nicholay the clerk in MilT; I.3199, I.3579, etc.

Nicholas, Seint bishop of Myra (4th cent. A.D.); VII.514.

Nynyve(e) Nineveh, capital of Assyria; II.487, VIII.974, BD 1063.

Nynus founder of Nineveh; LGW 785.

Nyobe Niobe, queen of Thebes; Tr 1.699, Tr 1.759.

Nysus Nisus, king of Megara; LGW 1904.

Nysus doghter Scylla; Tr 5.1110, LGW 1908. *See* Silla.

Noe (1) Noah (Gen. 5, 9); X.766. (2) Noah as a character in the popular mystery plays; I.3534, I.3539, etc.; *gen.* Noes I.3518, Noees I.3616.

Nonyus a consul of Rome; Bo 3.pr4.12, Bo 3.pr4.15.

Normandye Normandy; Rom B 4234.

Northfolk Norfolk; I.619.

Northhumberlond, Northhumbrelond scene of part of MLT; II.508, II.578.

Note, Seinte St. Neot (d. 877 A.D.); I.3771.

Nothus the south wind; Bo 2.m6.25, Bo 3.m1.8. *See* Auster.

Nowelis flood Noah's flood; I.3818, I.3834.

O

Occian the sea that encircles the known world; II.505, Bo 4.m6.14.

Octovyan, Octavyen Octavius (63 B.C.–14 A.D.), later the emperor Augustus; BD 368 (identity doubtful), LGW 624. *See* **Cesar** sense 2.

Odenake Odenathus, husband of Zenobia; MkT VII.2272, VII.2291, etc.

Oenone the nymph whom Paris deserted; HF 399, Tr 1.654.

Oetes Aeëtes, king of Colchis and father of Medea; LGW 1438, LGW 1593.

Oyse the river Oise, near Paris; HF 1928.

Olde Testament the Old Testament; VI.575, VII.3128, Rom C 6891.

Oliphaunt, sire a giant in Thop; VII.808.

Olyver friend of Roland in the *Chanson de Roland*; VII.2387, BD 1123.

Oloferne, Olofernus Holofernes (see MkT VII.2551–74); II.940; IV.1368; VII.1099, VII.2556, VII.2567.

Omer, Homer Homer (9th cent. B.C.); V.1443; HF 1466, HF 1477; Bo 5.m2.1, Bo 5.m2.2; Tr 1.146, Tr 5.1792.

Opilion Opilio, adversary of Boethius; Bo 1.pr4.114.

Oreb the biblical Mt. Horeb (Mt. Sinai); III.1891. *See* **Synay.**

Orewelle Orwell Haven, in Suffolk; I.277.

Origines upon the Maudelayn a lost translation by Chaucer; LGW F 428, LGW G 418.

Orion Arion, Greek poet and harper; HF 1205.

Orkades the Orkneys; Tr 5.971.

Orliens Orleans, in France; V.1118, V.1124, etc.

Orpheus the legendary poet and harper (see Bo 3.m12); IV.1716; BD 569; HF 1203; Bo 3.m12.4, Bo 3.m12.17, etc.; Tr 4.791.

Oseneye, Osenay Osney, near Oxford; I.3274, I.3659, I.3400.

Osewold the Reeve; I.3151, I.3680, I.3909.

Ovide Ovid, Publius Ovidius Naso (43 B.C.–17 A.D.); II.54; III.952, III.982; IV.2125; VII.976, VII.1325, VII.1414; BD 568; HF 379, HF 397, HF 1487; Tr 5.1792; LGW 1367, LGW 1465, etc. *See* **Epistele(s) (of Ovyde); Methamorphosios; Naso; Ovydes art; Remedie of Love.**

Ovydes art Ovid's *Ars amatoria;* III.680.

Oxenford(e) Oxford; I.285; I.3187, I.3329; III.527; IV.1; Astr Pro 10, Astr 2.22 rubric, etc.

P

Padowe Padua, in Italy; IV.27.

Palamon, Palamoun the knight who marries Emelye in KnT; I.1014, I.1031, I.2882, etc.

Palamon and Arcite, love of an early version of The Knight's Tale; LGW F 420, LGW G 408.

Palatye Palathia, in Anatolia; I.65.

Palymerie Palmyra, a city of Syria; VII.2247.

Palinurus Aeneas's steersman; HF 443.

Palladion Palladium, image of Pallas Athene (Minerva); Tr 1.153, Tr 1.161, Tr 1.164.

Pallas Pallas Athene, goddess of war and wisdom; VI.49; Anel 5; Tr 2.425, Tr 3.730, etc. *See* **Mynerva.**

Pamphilles, Pamphilus hero of the poem *Pamphilus de amore*; V.1110; VII.1556, VII.1558, VII.1561.

Pan Pan, god of nature; BD 512.

Pandare, Pandarus Criseyde's uncle in Tr; Tr 1.548, Tr 1.582, Tr 1.618, etc.

Pandyon father of Philomela and Procne; LGW 2247, LGW 2279, LGW 2295.

Panik Panico, near Bologna in Italy; IV.590, IV.764, IV.939.

Papynian Aemilius Papinianus, a Roman jurist; Bo 3.pr5.50.

Parables of Salomon, Parablis Prov. 10.1 to 22.16 (Vulgate); III.679, Rom C 6530.

Parcas the Parcae, i.e., the Fates; Tr 5.3. *See* **Wirdes.**

Paris (1) Paris, son of Priam and abductor of Helen of Troy; IV.1754; V.548; BD 331; HF 399; PF 290; Tr 1.63, Tr 1.653, etc.; (2) the city of Paris; I.126; III.678; VII.57, VII.332, VII.366; Rom A 1654, Rom C 6554, etc.

Parlement of Briddes (Foules) Chaucer's work; X.1086, LGW F 419, LGW G 407.

Parmanydes Parmenides of Elea (born c. 539 B.C.); Bo 3.pr12.193.

Parnaso, Pernaso Mt. Parnassus, sacred to the Muses; V.721, HF 521, Anel 16, Tr 3.1810.

Parthes Parthians; VI.662, Bo 2.pr7.65.

Parthonope Parthenopaeus, one of the Seven against Thebes; Anel 58, Tr 5.1503.

Parvys the porch of St. Paul's Cathedral, London (cf. Rom C 7108); I.310.

Pathmos the Mediterranean island of Patmos; VII.583.

Paul, Poul, Paulus (Seint) St. Paul the Apostle; III.73; III.1647; III.1819; VI.521, VI.523; VII.989, VII.1291, etc.; VII.3441; X.32, X.162, etc.; Rom C 6661, Rom C 6679, Rom C 6776.

Paulyn Decius Paulinus, consul in 498 A.D.; Bo 1.pr4.92, Bo 1.pr4.93.

Paulus (1) *see* **Paul.** (2) Lucius Aemilius Paulinus (c. 229–160 B.C.), consul of Rome; Bo 2.pr2.64.

Pavye Pavia, in Italy; IV.1246, Rom A 1654.

Pedmark Penmarch in Brittany; V.801.

Pegasee the Pegasean (horse), i.e., Pegasus; V.207.

Pelleus Peleus, father of Achilles; LGW 1397, LGW 1400, etc.

Pemond Piedmont, a province of northern Italy; IV.44.

Pene Carthage; Bo 3.m2.8.

Penelope(e), Penalopee wife of Achilles; II.75, V.1443, BD 1081, Anel 82, Tr 5.1778, LGW F 252, LGW G 206.

Penneus *gen.* of Peneus, river god and father of Daphne; I.2064.

Pepyn Pepin, king of the Franks (d. 768 A.D.); Rom A 1458.

Perce Persia; VII.2252.

Percyen(s), Persiens, Perses Persian(s); III.2079; VII.2235, VII.2248, VII.2346; Bo 2.pr2.65 (see note).

Percyvell hero of Arthurian romance; VII.916.

Perkyn (Revellour) the apprentice in CkT; I.4371, I.4387.

Pernaso *see* **Parnaso.**

Perotheus friend of Arcite in KnT; I.1191, I.1202, etc.

Perses, Persien *see* **Percyen(s).**

Verone Verona, in Italy; Bo 1.pr4.213.

Vesulus, Mount Monte Viso, in Northern Italy; IV.47, IV.58.

Via Appia the Appian Way; VIII.172.

Vincent Vincent of Beauvais, Vincentius Bellovacensis (c. 1184/85–c. 1264); LGW G 307. *See* **Estoryal Myrour.**

Virgil(e), Virgilius Publius Vergilius Maro (70–19 B.C.); III.1519; HF 378, HF 449, HF 1244, etc.; Tr 5.1792; LGW 924, LGW 1002.

Virginia heroine in PhysT; VI.213.

Virginius father of Virginia in PhysT; VI.2, VI.167, etc.

Virgo the sixth sign of the zodiac; Astr 1.8.3, Astr 2.6.17, etc.

Viscounte *see* **Barnabo Viscounte.**

Visevus Vesuvius, the volcano; Bo 1.m4.8.

Vitulon Witelo, thirteenth-century Polish physicist; V.232.

Vulcano, Vulcanus Vulcan, husband of Venus; I.2222, I.2389; HF 138.

W

Wade Wade, an obscure legendary figure; IV.1424, Tr 3.614.

Walakye Wallachia, in southern Romania; BD 1024.

Walys Wales; II.544.

Walter husband of Griselda in ClT; IV.77, IV.421, etc.

Ware possibly the town in Hertfordshire; I.692, I.4336.

Wateryng of Seint Thomas a spring or brook about two miles from London; I.826.

Watlynge Strete Watling Street, here the Milky Way; HF 939. *See* **Galaxye; Milky Wey.**

Watte *dim.* of Walter; I.643.

White Monkes Cistercians; Rom C 6695.

Wilkyn *dim.* of William, one of the Wife of Bath's husbands; III.432.

William, kyng William the Conqueror (reigned 1066–87); I.324.

William *see* **Seynt Amour, William.**

Wyndesore Windsor, about 21 miles west of London; Rom A 1250.

Wirdes the Fates; LGW 2580. *See* **Parcas.**

Wrecched Engendrynge of Mankynde, Of the one of Chaucer's lost translations; LGW G 414.

X

Xantippa Xantippe, wife of Socrates; III.729.

Xristus Christ; ABC 161. *See* **Crist; Jhesu(s).**

Y

(See also I)

Yorkshire the county in Northern England; III.1709.

Z

Zakarie, Zacharie Zechariah, the biblical prophet; X.434, ABC 177.

Zanzis (1) Zeuxis, an Athenian painter (5th cent. B.C.); VI.16. (2) unidentified; Tr 4.414.

Zeno Zeno of Elea (born c. 488 B.C.); Bo 1.pr3.55.

Zepherus, Zephirus Zephyrus, the west wind; I.5; BD 402; Bo 1.m5.22, Bo 2.m3.10; Tr 5.10; LGW F 171, LGW 2681.